SPORTS
MARKET PLACE

2025
SPORTS
MARKET PLACE

GREY HOUSE PUBLISHING

PUBLISHER:	Leslie Mackenzie
EDITORIAL DIRECTOR & COMPOSITION:	Stuart Paterson
PRODUCTION ASSISTANTS:	Kadie MacDougal & Olivia Parsonson
MARKETING DIRECTOR:	Jessica Moody

Grey House Publishing, Inc.
4919 Route 22
Amenia, NY 12501
518.789.8700
Fax: 518.789.0545
www.greyhouse.com
books@greyhouse.com

While every effort has been made to ensure the reliability of the information presented in this publication, Grey House Publishing neither guarantees the accuracy of the data contained herein nor assumes any responsibility for errors, omissions or discrepancies. Grey House accepts no payment for listing; inclusions in the publication of any organization, agency, institution, publication, service or individual does not imply endorsement of the editors or publisher.

Errors brought to the attention of the publisher and verified to the satisfaction of the publisher will be corrected in future editions.

2025 Edition
Printed in the United States

Sports market place. – 2025
  v. ; 27.5 cm.
  Annual
  Continues: Sports market place

1. Sporting goods industry –United States—Directories. 2. Sporting goods industry –Canada—Directories. 3. Athletics—United States –Societies, etc. –Directories. 4. Athletics –Canada –Societies, etc. -Directories. 5. Sports—United States—Directories. 6. Sports—Canada—Directories. 7. Sports administration—United States—Directories. 8. Sports administration—Canada—Directories.

HD9992.U5 S667
381/.456887/02573
ISBN: 979-8-89179-095-7

Table of Contents

Introduction

Grey House Publishing's *Sports Market Place* is the classic sports reference work that has served the sports industry for over 50 years. Over the years, this work has grown to include nearly 2,000 pages of valuable content, including professional, college and youth leagues and teams, sports media, events, facilities, sponsors, manufacturers, and professional services.

According to the article, Deloitte's "2025 Sports Industry Outlook," which is reprinted in its entirety following this introduction, here are some issues that rise to the top:

- With sports now actively on streaming services, there are new opportunities for sports marketers.

- A greater offering of new teams, leagues, and niche sports means greater opportunities for sponsors.

- Sports organizations are expected to put a greater emphasis on star power in the front office, not just on the field.

- A continued focus on collecting, managing, enriching, utilizing, and monetizing fan data will be crucial to sports organizations' successes.

- Technological leaps in "immersive sports" experiences are expected, giving fans new ways to virtually attend their favorite games.

In addition, the front matter of this edition includes the "18th Annual Canadian Sponsorship Landscape Study."

Sports Market Place is your key to this dynamic industry. It is invaluable for media professionals, agents, athletic directors, professional & student athletes, equipment & apparel manufacturers, service providers, trainers, teachers, and job seekers. It includes full coverage of 103 sports, from Air Sports to Yachting, with statistics on the fastest growing and most popular – cycling, exercise and fitness, gymnastics, martial arts, running, swimming, and weight lifting.

Praise for previous editions:

"If doubts persist that sports is a major industry, this exhaustive reference volume will erase any such premise. In 10 chapters, the business of sports is documented in detail . . . Grey House continues to improve on a useful, comprehensive sports directory. For the professional involved in any aspect of the sports business, this is . . .essential . . ."

American Reference Book Association

"This large reference work has served the sports industry for many years [and is] recommended [for] academic and public libraries; all levels."

CHOICE

Arrangement

Arranged in useful, business-minded chapters, *Sports Market Place* compiles sections such as Single Sports, College Sports, Media, Professional Services, Facilities, Manufacturers, Retailers and Events. Each chapter is indexed separately, in addition to the three all-volume indexes at the back of the book, for a total of 13 indexes. Listings are full of valuable information, including company name, address, phone, fax, web site, e-mail, description, key personnel and detailed corporate data.

This Year's Stats

Sports Market Place, 2025 has nearly 13,500 listings. You'll find 11,484 websites, 6,047 primary e-mail addresses, and nearly 40,000 key executives. Here's a play-by-play:

- **Single Sports** has 2,109 sport-specific organizations, leagues and teams that comprise 103 specific sports. It includes professional, major and minor leagues, coaches, managers, and an alphabetical index.

- **Multi Sports** includes 12 specific categories, including athletic foundations, Olympic teams, halls of fame and youth sports organizations. It includes a total of 835 listings, and an alphabetical index.

- **College Sports** has 1,697 listings, with associations, conferences, degree programs, and division I, II and III schools. You'll find a comprehensive list of coaches and sports management programs, and an alphabetical index.

- **Media** includes prominent newspapers and radio and television sports programming. Listings include editors, commentators, show hosts and an alphabetical index.

- **Sports Sponsors** includes 119 sponsors that support most major sports, including college bowl games, and an alphabetical index.

- **Professional Services** comprises 13 categories, from executive search services to ticket services, for a total of 1,684 listings, and an alphabetical index.

- **Facilities** has 1,365 listings, and includes seven categories from arenas to facility concession services. You'll find stadiums, race tracks, architects, management services, and an alphabetical index.

- **Manufacturers & Retailers** include 1,929 listings, with a separate section for Software Manufacturers. Listings include valuable contact information including key executives, plus products and brands. This chapter includes a combined sport and subject index.

- **Events, Meetings & Trade Shows** include 1,060 listings, of which 130 are trade shows. Events and trade shows are listed separately by both sport and date. This section also includes two alphabetical indexes, one for trade shows and one for events.

- **Three All-Volume Indexes** are conveniently grouped in the back of the book. Entry Index is a straight alphabetical listing. Executive Index is a complete alphabetical list of all key personnel, including each executive's title and affiliated organization. Geographic Index organizes all listings by country and state.

For quick, easy access to this amazing compilation of data, *Sports Market Place* is also available online at https://gold.greyhouse.com. Subscribers have access to all of this data, and can search by Organization Name, Sport, Executive Name and Geographic Area. Plus, subscribers can download contact sheets to create their own mailing list of sales leads. Call 800-562-2139 for more information.

2025 global sports industry outlook

The global sports industry is professionalizing, with heightened stakes and increasing investments in talent, analytics, and fan experiences

ARTICLE • 20-MIN READ   • 13 FEBRUARY 2025   • Deloitte Center for Technology, Media & Telecommunications

As investors flock to the sports industry, athletes gain more agency, and the competition for fan attention intensifies, global sports are becoming even more professionalized. This transformation is not limited to the top leagues but extends to lower-tier leagues and college athletics in the United States, too. The stakes are high, and sports organizations should adapt to meet increased financial expectations. They may need to build stronger back offices, compete for top talent, leverage data and analytics strategically, and develop new organizational competencies.

In 2025, this shift could revolutionize how sports organizations approach talent and operations, aiming to maximize return on investment. Amid this dynamic landscape, a growing number of sports and leagues are expected to vie for the global fan's time and attention. New sports experiences, beyond the venue, could redefine what it means to "be at the game."

TMT Outlooks

Read more from the Deloitte Center for Technology, Media & Telecommunications' Outlooks collection

---

Will there be room to thrive and grow, or will mounting legal issues and financial pressures keep the focus on the near term? This global outlook explores these questions and more, providing insights into the future of the sports industry.

What's next for sports and streaming?

The shift to streaming for live sports coverage is no longer in the future—it's here. Major streaming video-on-demand (SVOD) providers won some of the biggest sports media deals that were up for grabs in recent years.[1] So, what's next for sports and streaming? For SVOD providers who've done their reps, we expect maturation and innovation in their integrations, technology, and content. New sports-focused SVOD services are also coming online to shake up the status quo.[2] Where does that leave the industry and the fans?

For providers who've been in the sports broadcasting game for consecutive seasons, we expect to see a focus on delivering new experiences that further engage fans, monetize content, and improve viewing quality. Immersive, real-time integrations like in-gaming betting, seamless merchandising capabilities, and social experiences are likely to become a reality.[3] Improving the advertising experience will likely also be top of mind for live event streamers (who are in a unique position to grab large audiences concurrently) as they look to grow their ad revenues and secure lucrative partnerships.[4] Behind the scenes, providers will work with their technology partners to improve broadcast quality and reliability[5]—which remains a challenge for some.[6] Generative artificial intelligence (AI) technology could lend a hand in personalizing fan content feeds, serving up relevant advertising to fan groups, and providing direct (and instant) customer support.[7]

Tech upgrades aside, more ancillary sports content may be on the way, including alternative sports telecasts ("altcasts") and original content. Some sports broadcasters and streamers have already seen success with the altcast format, from ESPN's "ManningCast" on Monday Night Football, to Amazon Prime Video's Next Gen Stats feed on Thursday Night Football.[8] Paramount+ is teeing up its own altcast featuring David Beckham for the Union of European Football Associations (UEFA) Champions League coverage.[9] Additionally, more original (or "shoulder") content may be produced in an attempt to secure yearlong subscribers and to reach new fans. Developing docuseries, documentaries, live talk shows, or reality-style TV shows that feature sports teams, athletes, or their families—though often expensive and time-consuming to produce—may be a way to not only engage fans in the offseason but create a whole new generation of fans.[10] And consumers, especially younger ones, are interested in this behind-the-scenes view: Forty percent of Gen Zs and millennials surveyed say they'd like more documentary-style content about sports and players in the offseason, according to our latest Digital Media Trends data.[11]

Competition is also expected to heat up as new sports-focused streaming services—including ESPN Flagship and All Women's Sport Network (AWSN)—plan their moves into the market. Emerging leagues, teams, or mega-events will likely also be searching for media partners. And when new sports rights are up for grabs, instead of having those rights broken up across broadcast, cable, and streaming providers (as many are now), we expect that some deals could land exclusively with streaming services. It's also likely that providers will get creative about how to monetize, deliver, and market the live sports rights they have, like offering single-game pricing options.[12]

The continued expansion of the sports streaming market contributes to further fragmentation of the landscape for fans, and it can make discoverability difficult and increase fans' costs. Consumer frustration is already apparent: Thirty-five percent of consumers in our Digital Media

Trends (fall 2024) survey say they need to subscribe to *too many* services to watch all the events they want to watch.[13] There have been some efforts in the industry to address this growing fragmentation, including the launch of Eurovision Sport (which aims to bundle rights from 100 different member networks into one single registration and login) and an ESPN-backed "Where to Watch" feature that guides fans to live sports broadcasts.[14] But fragmentation is a persistent concern that should be addressed in order to lock in consumer attention.

Not to mention that streaming providers are also up against social media platforms, where content feeds are algorithmically tuned to a user's interests, access is free of charge, and near-instant sports highlights are everywhere. More than 90% of Gen Z and millennial fans surveyed say they use social media to consume sports-related content, including game clips and highlights, live sporting events, and sports news and commentary.[15] Convincing younger fans—and future generations of fans—to commit to a paid SVOD service that adds to their costs and makes discovering live sports difficult may pose a challenge for leagues, teams, and sports streamers to face head-on.

As leagues, teams, and mega-events partner with streaming providers for media rights, they should aim to strike a balance between reaching a wide and global base of new subscribers and maintaining accessibility and affordability for existing and next-gen fans.

Strategic questions to consider

- How can SVOD providers use sports content strategically to help build loyalty and boost retention among their subscribers and keep them from churning?

- Can sports leagues and teams find a balance among monetizing their business, maximizing sports rights payouts and the best interests of the fans they serve (and the fans of the future)?

- How can leagues and teams use streaming video and social media platforms—and the content on them—to pique the interest of new fans and fuel that budding fandom?

A more crowded playing field

In recent years, there has been a global surge of new sports leagues, teams, and events. There are expanded offerings from traditional leagues, more women's professional leagues, new formats in established sports, and niche sports looking to capture the public's attention. This growth is being driven by several trends. Ratings, attendance, investment, and team valuations have been generally strong over the last few years.[16] There are also more digital distribution channels, such as streaming services and social media, enabling direct access to fans. There is increasing private equity investment in some smaller and newer leagues.[17] These leagues can be attractive because they often have greater growth potential, with the pool of top teams and leagues being limited and expensive. In 2025, fans are expected to have access to more sports content than ever. A question is, what is the upper limit of sports fans' attention and spending?

Traditional leagues are looking to expand their offerings to capture more attention from existing fans, reach new fans, and provide more opportunity for revenue, such as with media rights and advertising. In the United States, the NFL is working to expand the number of international games it plays in 2025 to eight and add new host countries.[18] The NBA added a new tournament to the 2023 to 2024 season, and the NCAA expanded its college football playoffs to 12 teams for the 2024 to 2025 season.[19] FIFA has added the new 2025 FIFA Club World Cup, expanded its Men's World Cup field to 48 for 2026, and is exploring doing the same for the Women's World Cup.[20]

Women's leagues, especially in the United States, are working to capitalize on their momentum and looking to increase their number of franchises, providing access to more fans. The WNBA is adding three new teams by 2026 (Golden State, Toronto, Portland) and wants to have 16 total by 2028.[21] The NWSL, which currently has 14 teams, is adding new teams in Boston and Denver in 2026.[22] Even the new Professional Women's Hockey League (PWHL), which has six teams, is looking to add two more for their 2025 to 2026 season.[23] For women's football (soccer) in Europe there is a reformatted UEFA Women's Champions League and the addition of a second club competition for the 2025 to 2026 season.[24]

The list for recently established leagues could go on and on—across football, volleyball, golf, cricket, lacrosse, kabaddi, baseball, and others.[25] In 2025, some of these new leagues could find their audience and some will likely fade away. There is an opportunity for innovations from these leagues to influence one another and more established leagues in gameplay, the treatment of athletes, media, and fan experiences. However, there are challenges around potential audience fragmentation, "carrying capacity" for fans, long-term revenue potential, and physical limits for athletes.[26] Has society reached peak sports and, if not, what will it take to break through the noise?

Strategic questions to consider

- How can leagues ensure that they're creating new products and experiences to improve and deepen the fan experience, not just to "add more sports"?

- How can leagues and their media partners best address potential audience fragmentation that all these new options could cause?

- How can established leagues develop a robust scouting function to learn from and incorporate innovations from newer and smaller leagues around the world?

The future of talent for sports organizations

Workers with sports industry experience are being sought after by a growing number of leagues and federations, governing bodies, individual teams, mega-events, and other sports-adjacent organizations. To help with the attraction this skilled talent pool, sports organizations have a unique opportunity to rethink and enhance their overall approach to human capital. Moving forward, we expect to see sports organizations thinking more holistically about their workforce, and how they attract, reward, incentivize, and retain talent to successfully meet business objectives. In short, sports organizations should look to develop star players both on the field and in the front office.

As the global sports industry evolves and expands—in ways that are explored throughout this outlook—there are more opportunities for professionals to work in sports. Historically, there's been an imbalance in the sports talent supply and demand: a lot of people who want to work in sports and not enough available positions in the industry.[27] But recent (and ongoing) shifts in the global sports industry have multiplied opportunities for talent, which means leagues, teams, and mega-events alike may need to up their recruitment game if they hope to lure top talent away from startups, media organizations, technology companies, and competing sports organizations—and keep their own talent from pursuing these types of opportunities.

Competition for talent often begins with a thoughtful refresh of compensation strategies to align and compete with current market forces. In the coming year, these organizations may focus on staying in lockstep with other sports teams, leagues, and federations to help ensure their compensation structure, incentives, and rewards draw in the best employees in the industry—and that these efforts align with achieving business goals. Consistently reviewing and refreshing compensation could go a long way to grab the attention of technically skilled, well-educated, and highly sought-after talent. Though, for many jobseekers across industries, it's no longer just about the paycheck.[28]

Keeping this top talent is also a critical piece. While some turnover is good, business leaders should think critically about their workforce to identify exceptional employees to retain. Not only is retention an important consideration for current and prospective employees when deciding where to work—especially for younger generations of workers who show interest in opportunities to grow and advance in their careers[29]—but studies show that employee retention is a smart business decision, too. The cost of hiring new talent far surpasses the cost of retaining current employees. In fact, the monetary cost associated with replacing an employee is often multiple times their annual salary.[30]

Building a winning culture is an important aspect of retention and can involve everything from encouraging community and collaboration, to leaning into purpose-driven initiatives.[31] Additionally, as sports organizations expand their digital offerings by developing fan databases, integrating AI capabilities, and partnering with streaming video and social media platforms, they should focus on having the right mix of talent to support these tech-focused capabilities.[32] This means hiring people with the right skills while also investing in, and upskilling, current employees, so in-house specialties align with organizational priorities.[33] Sports organizations should work to ensure that employees have opportunities to push their careers forward in other ways, too: either in their day-to-day work, in another internal role that aligns with their expertise, or through short rotations or "fellowship" experiences within the organization that allow them to gain new experiences and perspectives. We expect to see leading global sports organizations—and mega-events hoping to staff up for primetime—lean on these strategies.

Sports organizations need strong leaders, skilled players, and team players to win—both on the field and off. Moving forward, business leaders and human resources departments may need to work closer together to have core business conversations about acquiring and retaining top recruits.

Strategic questions to consider

- How can sports organizations refresh their people strategies—including their approach to compensation—to attract and retain top talent?

- Beyond salary, what incentives and growth opportunities can sports organizations provide to build culture, find alignment with business priorities, and win the talent race?

- In what ways can sports organizations invest in, and upskill, existing talent so they remain excited and energized about their careers while advancing the key priorities of the organization?

Fan data drives monetization for sports organizations

In recent years, many sports organizations have expanded their capabilities in collecting, managing, enriching, utilizing, and monetizing fan data.[34] Fan databases allow leagues, teams, and other sports entities to tailor their business strategies to enhance fan engagement, improve live-event experiences, secure profitable media valuations, and forge lucrative sponsorship deals.[35] As the global sports industry becomes more data-savvy and data-rich, organizations that maintain comprehensive fan databases—and are able to use that fan data to demonstrate value and ROI[36]—could gain a competitive advantage in securing attractive sponsorships. Moving forward, we expect to see access to meaningful and actionable fan data become an important selling point in negotiating and structuring these partnerships.

Extensive and well-maintained fan databases can be a powerful asset for sports organizations when securing and enhancing partnerships with brand partners. With access to detailed first- and third-party fan insights—such as demographics, purchasing behaviors, and individuals' engagement with other brands and entities—sports organizations can offer their partners access to highly specific information about their fans.[37] Sports organizations can use these fan databases, which not only hold deep knowledge about their own fanbase but about brands' potential customers, as an asset when approaching brands for potential partnerships.

Data clean rooms are an important part of this data-sharing process and could, for example, allow a sports league to securely share aggregated and anonymized fan data with a sponsor to identify overlap between the league's fans and its customers. The clean rooms can allow for secure data-sharing and real-time analysis and collaboration without compromising individual fans' privacy—offering a scenario where leagues and teams can increase their sponsorship value and partners can gain detailed data and actionable insights.[38]

Some major sports leagues are already set up for these types of partnerships. The National Football League (NFL) has developed a data ecosystem that aggregates data from various sources and creates detailed fan profiles, with more than 250 attributes per fan.[39] Similarly, FC Bayern Munich has developed the "Golden Fan Record," which brings together data from more than 50 systems and platforms to create detailed fan files.[40] These fan databases can be useful not only to leagues and teams in terms of their own marketing and revenue growth, but also they can provide value to premium advertisers looking to partner with sports organizations. On the flip side, not having robust fan data could deter top sponsors and partners.[41]

This signals a new era in sports industry sponsorship deals, in which fan data is not only an integral part of the agreement, it may also be the primary thing brands want. For brands, the ability to tap into rich fan databases provides an unparalleled opportunity to understand their target audience. For sports organizations, fan databases and the ability to measure the value of partnerships could become a meaningful way to differentiate themselves from the other teams. In turn, this will likely increase the dollar amount they put on sponsorship deals and could open a whole new revenue stream.

We expect these data-driven sponsorship deals to be a major focus for sports organizations in the coming year, but there are other reasons for leagues and teams to take fan data seriously. Fan data can enhance current revenue streams, like ticketing and merchandising. Sports organizations can also use this data to enhance fan experiences by delivering personalized content and offers, both in-stadium and through digital platforms, during the season and every other day, too. Personalized interactions, whether through in-stadium experiences or digital touch points, can enhance fan loyalty and satisfaction.[42] Additionally, fan data can play a pivotal role in securing media rights. Networks and streaming platforms value understanding audience preferences and engagement levels, which detailed fan insights can provide. This can strengthen an organization's bargaining power in negotiations for broadcasting deals, ultimately driving higher revenues.

Still, despite the upsides of fan data, there are challenges: Developing a robust data strategy requires financial investment, a modern technology stack, access to up-to-date and complete data sources, and technically skilled personnel. Sports organizations that prioritize fan data programs now may have the opportunity to partner with top brands, build their bottom line, and lead the sports industry into a data-driven future.

Strategic questions to consider

- How can sports leagues and teams bring differentiated value to their partners by collecting bespoke fan attributes or hyper-segmenting fan groups?

- How can sports organizations build out more robust strategies for first-party data collection to know their fans even better?

- How can organizations balance the need for data privacy with the growing demand for data-sharing capabilities in sponsorship agreements?

- In what ways can sports organizations get creative with data-driven, or data-first, partnerships to create new revenue streams and draw in high-visibility brands and brands that share their values?

The evolution of immersive sports

With consumer interest in attending live sporting events and ticket prices climbing, there is an opportunity in the making.[43] In our *2023 sports fan insights* report, we explored how emerging technologies and ways to consume entertainment were creating new possibilities in the era of "immersive sports."[44] In this era, fans can craft their own unique, personalized, digital sports reality—both at home and in venue. That future is still under construction; however, immersive sports are expected to see significant progress in 2025, as novel ways to experience sports in person may become more accessible.

With advances in display technology, fresh investment, and new partnerships, innovative out-of-venue experiences are coming to life.[45] Providers are looking to engage sports fans in new ways and expand the concept of sports as entertainment. Instead of simply watching an event, fans can be fully wrapped in an experience that rivals being in the actual venue. There will likely be a lot of hype around these new concepts in 2025. If some take off, we may see a whole new category of sports experiences emerge.

Companies are experimenting with different ways to interact with fans. Cosm is using proprietary display technologies (through video domes and walls) to bring top-tier sporting events in a larger-than-life way to fans through "shared reality."[46] It currently has locations in Los Angeles and

Dallas and will be opening facilities in Atlanta and Detroit in the next few years—co-locating its buildings near stadiums and sports districts.[47] Cosm has been expanding the number of deals it has with broadcasters and leagues to show football, soccer, basketball, hockey, and combat sports.[48]

Others have experimented with immersive sporting events as well. In September 2024, the Sphere hosted UFC 306 ("Noche UFC"), taking its product to a new level of production. The UFC spent US$20 million to develop and produce the event, which included remarkable visual backdrops and animations.[49] In IMAX theaters, IMAX broadcast the Opening Ceremony of the Paris Summer Olympics as well as a Big Ten college football game in November 2024 in partnership with NBCUniversal.[50]

Finally, TGL, which played its first matches in January 2025, is blending the physical and digital to provide an all-new hybrid golf experience. In a specially designed venue, teams of golfers compete against each other across a set of custom-designed holes.[51] They start by hitting into a large-screen simulator from real terrain and then transition to a transformable turntable as the green. Broadcasting innovations, designed to bring the experiences of the golfers closer to home viewers, were seen as critical from the start.[52]

Ultimately, fans may want to feel like they are part of the action. In the near future, this could be made possible by more player point-of-view experiences, field and court-level views in VR, and venues with large-scale displays that surround an audience. Will these new types of experiences drive more interest and engagement? Are they truly a new alternative or just a supplement? Fans may be on the cusp of a completely new type of live-sports experience in 2025.

Strategic questions to consider

- Are these new experiences just novelty, or will they last? What is their repeatability? Will there be additional entrants to the market?

- Will these experiences create new fans and expand the market or just create new revenue streams from existing fans?

- How will these technologies and experiences influence stadiums and other venue construction? Will fans' expectations increase?

- Will these new experiences suppress the development of VR applications for sports, or will they influence them?

Signposts for the future

The financial and cultural success of the sports industry is encouraging organizations to increasingly take a more professional approach—one that is transforming both how the industry operates and how it brings its experiences to market. In 2025, sports organizations will likely build stronger back offices, powered by a deeper bench of talent and wider flows of data. Engaging new sports experiences are expected to emerge, and the professionalization of college athletics may continue to have extraordinary impacts. Can this create a better future for everyone—athletes, fans, owners, and investors?

The future isn't static. Sports teams, leagues, governing bodies, and other organizations as well as media and entertainment companies should look for possible signposts—events and actions that can change how the future unfolds. Signposts can confirm what could transpire or create entirely new paths with their own opportunities and challenges.

For 2025, consider the following signposts:

1. New sports media rights deals going solely to a SVOD service

2. In-game betting capabilities becoming fully integrated into SVOD broadcasts

3. Sports organizations offering more competitive salaries and benefits packages, and more high-profile talent coming to the industry from tech, finance, and media companies

4. Growth in retention rates for sports industry jobs

5. The number of brands partnering with sports organizations largely for access to their proprietary fan data

6. Sports organizations increasingly working with technology partners to establish data clean rooms

7. New discoverability features and aggregation capabilities added to streaming services

8. Ratings and attendance for newer and smaller leagues (especially in their second and third years) and new events

9. More experiments with innovative out-of-venue experiences showing premiere sporting events

10. Attendance, ratings, and overall interest in immersive sports experiences

Endnotes

1. Sana Noor Haq, "MLS and Apple announce 10-year streaming deal," CNN, June 15, 2022; Kevin Skiver, "NFL on Amazon, explained: What to know about new 'Thursday Night Football' broadcasts for 2022," *Sporting News*, May 11, 2022.

2. Morgan Murrell, "Whoopi Goldberg is looking to change the way we view women's sports with a newly launched channel that will focus on ladies, and ladies only," *Yahoo Sports*, November 7, 2024; Todd Spangler, "ESPN flagship streamer will include ESPN+," *Variety*, October 17, 2024.

3. Pete Giorgio et al., "2023 sports fan insights: The beginning of the immersive sports era," *Deloitte Insights*, June 26, 2023.

4. Dade Hayes, "'Thursday Night Football' on Prime Video rolling out new ad & streaming enhancements as third season kicks off," *Deadline*, September 11, 2024; PYMNTS, "Instacart expands shoppable TV partnership with Roku," October 9, 2024; Emma Roth, "Disney brings playable 'advergames' to Hulu and ESPN," *The Verge*, June 14, 2024.

5. YouTube TV Help, "Watch NFL Sunday Ticket in multiview," accessed February 2025; Fubo, "Fubo launches Multiview beta feature on select Roku devices," press release, September 26, 2024.

6. Olivia Coryell, "ESPN launches 'Where to Watch' on ESPN App, ESPN.com," press release, ESPN, August 28, 2024.

7. Neil Sahota, "Streaming into the future: How AI is reshaping entertainment," *Forbes*, March 18, 2024.

8. Brian Steinberg, "Inside the ManningCast: How ESPN and two football brothers are transforming sports TV," *Variety*, February 10, 2022; Jacob Feldman, "Amazon's 'Thursday Night Football' adds more AI features in 2024," *Sportico*, September 10, 2024.

9. Todd Spangler, "David Beckham inks Paramount+ deal to host alternative UEFA Champions League telecast," *Variety*, September 17, 2024.

10. Steven Cole Smith, "How 'Drive to Survive' helped Formula 1 win over America," *Car and Driver*, August 21, 2022.

11. This data was collected as part of Deloitte's Digital Media Trends study, which surveyed 3,595 US consumers ages 14 and older in October 2024.

12. Associated Press, "Diamond Sports Group will offer single-game pricing for NBA, NHL games," ESPN, November 12, 2024.

13. Jana Arbanas et al., "'Funflation'—and live event hype—goes up against more cost-conscious consumers," *Deloitte Insights*, October 8, 2024.

14. K.J. Yossman, "Eurovision takes on sports with free live streaming service," *Yahoo Entertainment*, February 5, 2024; ESPN, "Where to Watch," accessed January 2025.

15. Giorgio et al., "2023 sports fan insights: The beginning of the immersive sports era."

16. Brett Knight and Justin Teitelbaum, "The world's 50 most valuable sports teams 2024," *Forbes*, December 12, 2024; Timothy Bridge, Kunal Sajdeh, and Lizzie Tantam, "Deloitte Football Money League 2025," Deloitte, January 23, 2025.

17. Andrea Gaini, "From padel to volleyball, PE targets increasingly niche sports," PitchBook, November 4, 2024.

18. Eric Jackson, "NFL international games to increase in 2025, Goodell says," Sportico, November 10, 2024.

19. Maya Ellison, "How the 12-team College Football Playoff will work: Teams, schedules, bids," NCAA, November 27, 2024; NBA, "NBA In-Season Tournament to debut in 2023–24 season," news release, July 8, 2023.

20. The Athletic, "World Cup 2026: The biggest tournament yet and a New York final," February 4, 2024; Ed Dixon, "Fifa 'in talks' to expand Women's World Cup to 48 teams," SportsPro, September 11, 2024.

21. Dustin Schutte, "WNBA looking to add another expansion team before 2028 season," Sports Illustrated, October 17, 2024.

22. Brad Adgate, "Professional women's sports leagues are busy adding franchises," Forbes, November 4, 2024; Just Women's Sports, "Denver lands bid for 2026 NWSL expansion team," January 3, 2025.

23. Hailey Salvian, "As PWHL prepares to grow, which cities are top candidates for expansion teams?," The Athletic, October 31, 2024.

24. UEFA, "New UEFA women's club football system explained," news release, July 30, 2024.

25. Examples include Women's Premier League (India, cricket, 2023), Kings League (Spain, football, 2022), Major League Cricket (US, 2023), LIV Golf (2022), Pro Volleyball Federation (US, 2024), Women's Lacrosse League (US, 2025), Snow League (winter sports, 2024), Women's Pro Baseball League (US, 2026), and Women's Kabaddi League (India, 2023); The Economist, "Why the world is teeming with so many new sports leagues," August 23, 2024.

26. Mark Ogden, "Is soccer heading for burnout ahead of longest-ever season? ," ESPN, August 13, 2024.

27. Glenn M. Wong, "What is it really like to work in the sports industry?," in The Comprehensive Guide to Careers in Sports, 2nd ed. (Burlington, MA: Jones & Bartlett Learning, 2012).

28. Ben Wigert, "The top 6 things employees want in their next job," Gallup, February 21, 2022.

29. Deloitte, 2024 Gen Z and Millennial Survey: Living and working with purpose in a transforming world, Deloitte, 2024.

30. Peter Cappelli and Ranya Nehmeh, "HR's new role ," Harvard Business Review magazine, May–June 2024.

31. John Forsythe et al., "One size does not fit all: How microcultures help workers and organizations thrive," Deloitte Insights, February 5, 2024.

32. Nate Paynter et al., "Navigating the tech talent shortage," Deloitte Insights, June 11, 2024.

33. Sue Cantrell et al., "The skills-based organization: A new operating model for work and the workforce," *Deloitte Insights*, September 8, 2022.

34. Pete Giorgio et al., *2024 sports industry outlook*, Deloitte, 2024.

35. Pete Giorgio et al., "How data can help drive sports sponsorship and fan engagement," Deloitte, 2017.

36. Alfredo Troncoso, Tamara Ojeaga, and Sagar Ramsinghani, "Determining sponsorship ROI," Kantar, April 2, 2023.

37. Giorgio et al., "How data can help drive sports sponsorship and fan engagement."

38. Howie Stein, Goutham Belliappa, and Ben Coffey, "Is your organization ready for data clean rooms?," *Deloitte's CIO Journal for the Wall Street Journal*, May 15, 2023.

39. Ari Entin, "Inside the NFL's innovative fan data platform powered by AWS," AWS for *M&E Blog*, July 12, 2024.

40. Claudio Brecht, "FC Bayern Munich perfects the fan experience with digital solutions," news release, SAP News Center, July 22, 2020; Joseph Miller, "Fan engagement: Football clubs consider themselves content providers. They need to start acting like it," FT Strategies, accessed January 2025.

41. Miller, "Fan engagement: Football clubs consider themselves content providers. They need to start acting like it."

42. Deloitte Digital, "Personalizing growth: It's a value exchange between brands and customers," accessed January 2025; Brett Davis et. al., "Personalize fan experiences at scale with data and AI," Deloitte, accessed January 2025.

43. Arbanas et al., "'Funflation'—and live event hype—goes up against more cost-conscious consumers"; Associated Press, "Messi-mania helps drive record attendance, growth for MLS," ESPN, October 22, 2024; WNBA "WNBA delivers record-setting 2024 season," press release, September 27, 2024; Eric Fisher, "MLB enters 2024 postseason with attendance up, game times down," *Front Office Sports*, October 1, 2024; Alex Silverman and David Broughton, "Panthers, Blackhawks lead NHL in 2023–24 attendance gains," *Sports Business Journal*, April 25, 2024.

44. Giorgio et al., "2023 sports fan insights: The beginning of the immersive sports era."

45. Cosm, "Cosm raises over $250 million in funding to expand experiential entertainment venues globally," news release, July 31, 2024.

46. Cosm, "Shared reality – The 'reality technology' of the future, today," January 1, 2021.

47. Cosm, "Cosm announces Detroit as new home for its fourth immersive sports and entertainment venue," news release, November 1, 2024; Eric Fisher, "Inside Cosm's plans for a fourth location—and beyond," *Front Office Sports*, November 1, 2024.

48. Jacob Feldman, "NFL to air Sunday night football in 'shared reality' Cosm domes," Sportico, accessed February 2025.

49. Emmanuel Morgan, "The octagon inside the Sphere: Bloody fights and soaring films," *New York Times*, updated September 23, 2024.

50. IMAX, "NBC Television Network's live coverage of 2024 Paris Olympics Opening Ceremony to make IMAX debut," press release, March 22, 2024; Etan Vlessing, "Penn State football White Out game headed to Imax screens in NBC Sports deal," *Hollywood Reporter*, November 4, 2024.

51. TGL, TGL Explained webpage, accessed January 2025.

52. George Winslow, "ESPN to bring tech-heavy TGL golf to primetime in 2025," *TVtech*, October 21, 2024.

Acknowledgments

The authors would like to thank **Akash Rawat** from Deloitte's Center for Technology, Media & Telecommunications for his substantial contribution to the research and writing of this outlook.

In addition, a special thanks goes to **Jenny Haskel, Timothy Bridge, John Skowron, John Tweardy, Adam Deutsch, Danny Ledger, Todd Kovin Suarez, Charlie Wagner, Li-Shen Lee, Lee Teller, Caitlin Jacklin, Nick Eyer, Elizabeth Ellerhorst, Leah Richardson, Patrick Parfey,** and **Shubham Oza** for their partnership and support on this research.

Cover image by: **Jaime Austin**; Adobe Stock

18th ANNUAL

CSLS

Canadian sponsorship
landscape study

Lead Author: Dr. Norm O'Reilly
Co-Authors: Liz Rose & Mike Alcorn
Special Thanks: SMCC Education Committee

CSLS LANDMARKS & BREAKTHROUGHS

2007
Activation Ratio: 0.43

First ever validation that activation in Canadian sponsorship was significantly behind other major countries of the world.

2008–2010
Recession Proof

As the 'Great Recession' hit many countries, including Canada, CSLS results showed sponsorship kept growing.

2013
Festivalization

CSLS authors coined the term "festivalization" as the festival category took similar proportion of sponsorship investment in Canada from 2011 to 2013.

2014 & 2018
Pro Sport Renaissances

The proportion of sponsorship spend dedicated to pro sport spikes in 2014 and again in 2018.

2018
$3 Billion

Total sponsor spend (rights fees plus activation) exceeds $3 billion for the first time. More than double the first year of CSLS.

2021
Not Pandemic Proof

Although sponsorship may have been resilient during the economic recession, it was impacted heavily (50% reduction) during the pandemic.

2023
Activation Growth

Activation reaches an all-time high, matching rights fees investment.

RESULTS #1: STRATEGY
LARGEST SPONSORSHIP CATEGORY

64.3%
Pro Sport

PRO SPORT

2023 Data.

Return to pro sport being dominant, followed by amateur sport and festivals.

- *Due to low Sample Size in 2023, combined with 2022 data*

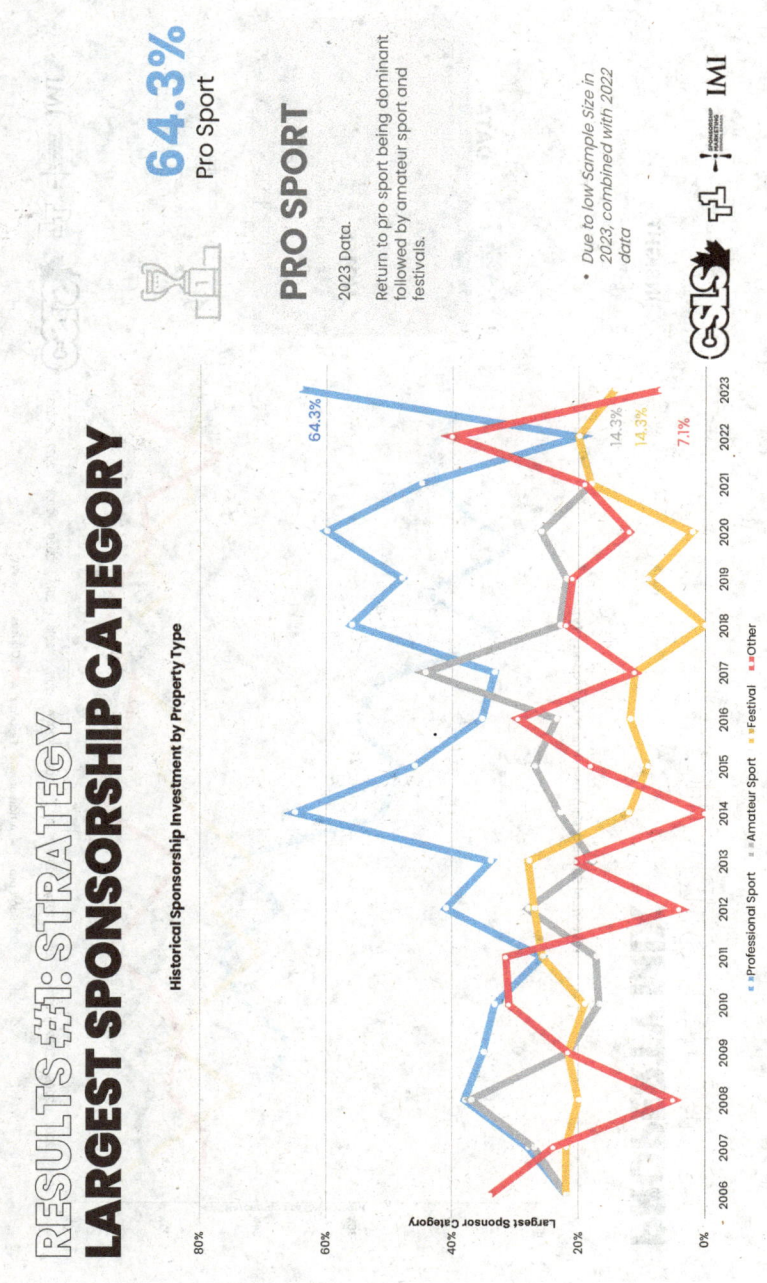

Historical Sponsorship Investment by Property Type

Largest Sponsor Category

80% — 60% — 40% — 20% — 0%

2006 2007 2008 2009 2010 2011 2012 2013 2014 2015 2016 2017 2018 2019 2020 2021 2022 2023

64.3%
14.3%
14.3%
7.1%

■ Professional Sport   ■ Amateur Sport   ■ Festival   ■ Other

RESULTS #1: STRATEGY
PROPERTY MIX

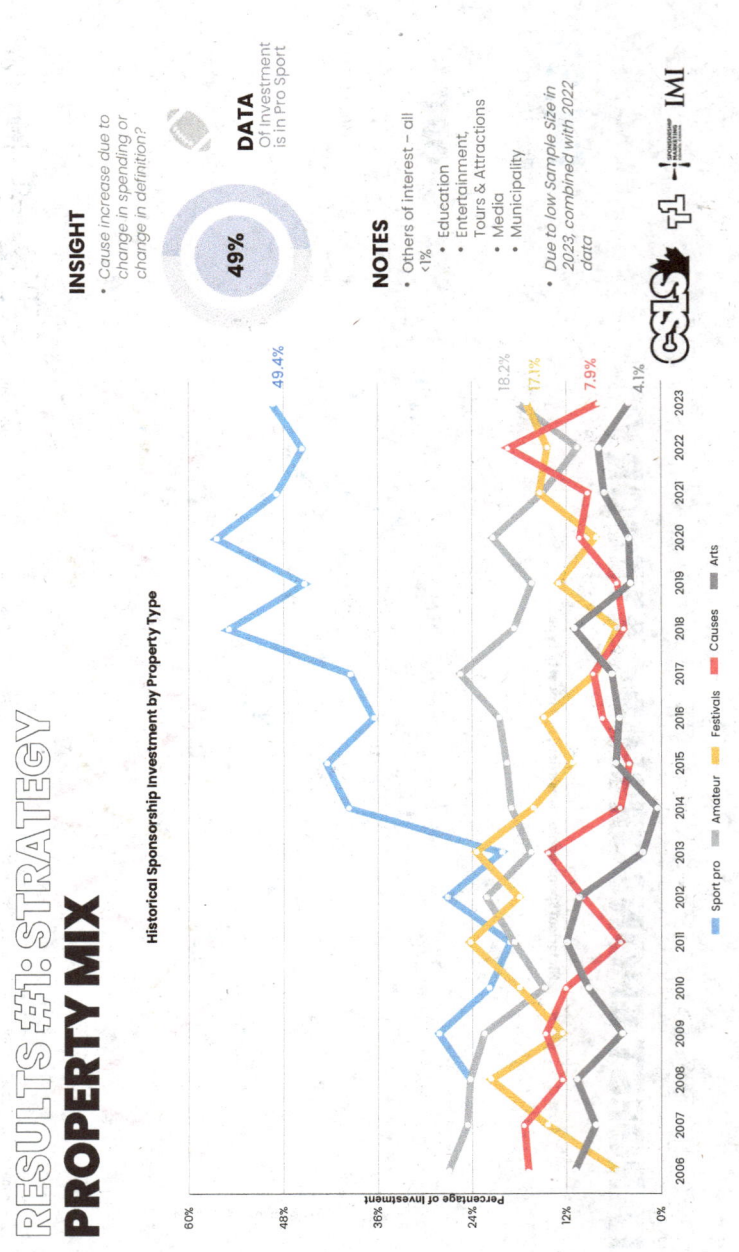

Historical Sponsorship Investment by Property Type

INSIGHT
- Cause increase due to change in spending or change in definition?

DATA
49%
Of Investment is in Pro Sport

NOTES
- Others of interest – all <1%
  - Education
  - Entertainment, Tours & Attractions
  - Media
  - Municipality
- Due to low Sample Size in 2023, combined with 2022 data

Sport pro · Amateur · Festivals · Causes · Arts

49.4%
18.2%
17.1%
7.9%
4.1%

Percentage of Investment
60% 48% 36% 24% 12% 0%

2006 2007 2008 2009 2010 2011 2012 2013 2014 2015 2016 2017 2018 2019 2020 2021 2022 2023

RESULTS #3: ACTIVATION

MIX OF INVESTMENT

Sponsor Reporting of Activation Spend in 2022/2023*
(2021 noted for each)

17.5% Advertising 23.0%

15.2% Branded Content 21.3%

19.9% Hosting & Hospitality 8.0%

17.1% Social Media 12.5%

3.6% Internal Marketing 3.5%

3.5% Athletes 3.8%

7.8% Ancillary Events 8.9%

6.8% Co-Promotions 9.0%

0.6% Product Sampling 0.3%

0.1% Packaging 0.0%

2.2% PR 4.1%

1.8% Sales & Consumer Promotions 5.4%

0.1% Trade Allowances 0.0%

0.0% Web3 0.0%

BIG CHANGE
Hosting & Hospitality is back
Web3 zero

*Low sample size for 2023

CSLS

IMI

xxv

RESULTS #3: ACTIVATION
MIX OF INVESTMENT

Agency List of Sponsor Client Activation spend in 2022/2023*
(2021 noted for each)

OBSERVATION (SAME AS LAST YEAR)

Drastic difference from sponsor mix; evidence that agency role changes activation.

INSIGHT Branded Content is Back

20.9% ↑ Branded Content (6.2%)

10.4% Social Media (11.5%)

8.0% PR (6.9%)

15.0% Advertising (16.7%)

11.4% Product Sampling (7.2%)

5.9% Athletes (7.7%)

3.7% Packaging (0.5%)

7.4% Other (18.1%)

6.4% Hosting & Hospitality (8.9%)

2.6% Internal Marketing (4.5%)

1.2% Ancillary Events (3.0%)

3.6% Co-Promotions (3.2%)

2.9% Sales & Consumer Promotions (5.5%)

0.4% Trade Allowances (0.0%)

0.1% Web3 (0.0%)

*Low sample size for 2023

Source: O'Reilly, Norm. "18th Annual Canadian Sponsorship Landscape Study." Reproduced with permission, 2025. https://the1agency.com/canadian-sponsorship-landscape-study.

1

single sports

single sports

Air Sports Organizations

AIR SHOW NETWORK
1110 EUGENIA PLACE
SUITE 300
CARPINTERIA, CA 93013
805-553-6637
jim@airshownetwork.com
www.airshownetwork.com
• Jim J. Breen, President
jim@airshownetwork.com
• Greg Smales, Vice President
judge@airshownetwork.com
Description:
Founded in 1983, the company has served over 1,000 air shows. The Air Show Network offers numerous services to air shows across American including food concessions, production services, chalet designs and marketing services.

BALLOON FEDERATION OF AMERICA
1601 NORTH JEFFERSON
PO BOX 400
INDIANOLA, IA 50125
515-961-8809
Fax: 515-961-3537
bfaoffice@bfa.net
www.bfa.net
• Dean Carlton, President
• Cheri White, Vice President
• Tim Cloyd, Secretary
• Glen Moyer, Ballooning Editor
• Mike Shrum, Youth Program Chair
Year Founded:
1960's
Number of Members:
3,500
Member Services:
Sanctions events; products; educational materials; film library.
Publications:
BALLOONING, bimonthly magazine
Membership Requirements:
Pay dues.
Nature of Sports Service:
A non-profit association dedicated to the advancement of the sport and science of lighter-than-air aviation, both hot air and gas balloons.

CANADIAN SPORT PARACHUTING ASSOCIATION
204 - 1468 LAURIER STREET
ROCKLAND, ON, CANADA K4K 1C7
613-419-0908
Fax: 613-916-6008
office@cspa.ca
www.cspa-acps.org
• Debbie Flanagan, President
debbie.flanagan@cspa.ca
• Michelle Matte-Stotyn, Executive Director
• Judy Renaud, Executive Secretary
• Ian Flanagan, Treasurer
• John Gustafson, Media Relations
Description:
A non-profit membership association dedicated to the continuance, improvement and promotion of safe skydiving in Canada.
Publications:
CanPara, bimonthly magazine
Membership Requirements:
Pay dues.
Year Founded:
1956

INTERNATIONAL AEROBATIC CLUB, INC.
3000 POBERENZY ROAD
OSHKOSH, WI 54902-8939
920-426-4800
Fax: 920-426-6579
iac@eaa.org
www.iac.org
• Doug Sowder, President
(920) 426-4800
Sport Organization:
Membership organization that sanctions all US based aerobatic competitions.

NATIONAL AERONAUTIC ASSOCIATION
REAGAN WASHINGTON NATIONAL AIRPORT
HANGAR 7
SUITE 202
WASHINGTON, DC 20001-6015
703-416-4888
Fax: 703-416-4877
www.naa.aero
• Jonathan Gaffney, President, CEO
• Jim Albaugh, Chairman
• Durwood W. Ringo, Vice Chairman
• Roy Kiefer, Treasurer
• Elizabeth Matarese, Secretary
Year Founded:
1905
Publications:
Air & Space Magazine; World and United States Aviation & Space Records
Member Benefits:
Air & Space Magazine, a yearly copy of World and United States Aviation & Space Records, and free sporting licenses
Description:
The primary mission of NAA is the advancememnt of the art, sport, and science of aviation and space flight by fostering opportunities to participate fully in aviation activities and by promoting public understanding of the importance of aviation and space flight to the United States.

PARACHUTE INDUSTRY ASSOCIATION
6499 SOUTH KINGS RANCH ROAD
SUITE 6
GOLD CANYON, AZ 85118
480-982-6125
hq@pia.com
www.pia.com
• Roberto Montanez, President
• Mark Procos, Vice President
• Elizabeth Johnson, Secretary
• Vinny Salatino, Treasurer
• George Galloway, Executive Advisor
Description:
Comprised of companies and individuals united by a common desire to improve business opportunities in this segment of aviation.

SOARING SOCIETY OF AMERICA
5425 WEST JACK GOMEZ BOULEVARD
HOBBS, NM 88241
575-392-1177
Fax: 575-392-8154
dlayton@ssa.org
www.ssa.org
• Layton Denise, CEO, COO
dlayton@ssa.org
• Ken Sorenson, Chairman
• Phil Umphres, Treasurer
Year Founded:
1932

Number of members:
12,000 plus
Membership Requirements:
Payment of dues.
Nature of Sports Service:
Promotes and fosters all phases of soaring, both nationally and internationally.
Member Benefits:
Monthly Soaring Magazine, participation in Badge Program, Contests, Scholarships, State/National/World Records, unlimited access to SSA website, eligibility to participate in SSA Group Hull and Liability insurance program.

SPORT CLASS AIR RACING
3000 POBERENZY ROAD
OSHKOSH, WI 54902-8939
920-426-4800
Fax: 920-426-6579
iac@eaa.org
www.iac.org
• Bob Mills, President
• Vicky Benzing, Vice President
• Rick Vandam, Treasurer
• Tom McNerney, Secretary
Description:
The Sport Class Air Racing Association highlights innovative work being done with aircrafts. They host training sessions to assist new pilots learn how to air race, and host numerous races throughout the year.

STAR CREST ASSOCIATION
4509 EVE STREET
BAKERSFIELD, CA 93307
661-831-7771
• Rachael Newell,
Year Founded:
1967
Number of members:
25,000
Member Services:
Permanent record of member's name and number kept in files of BBMSC; emblem; decal; certificate.
Publications:
STARCREST Magazine, bimonthly.
Membership Requirements:
Must be in a free-fall formation, complete membership form and pay one-time dues of $20. Must complete requirements for any of the SCR, SCS, NSCAR, SCSA, NSCSA or USA awards as described on the Star Crest Application sheet.
Nature of Sports Service:
Dedicated to the advancement of skydiving. Provides free-fall formation awards.

U.S. BASE ASSOCIATION/PHOTO SHOOTING
12619 MANOR DRIVE
HAWTHORNE, CA 90250
310-676-1935
Year Founded:
1981
Number of members:
5,000
Member Services:
Dissemination of information, technology, experiences, opinions; site and technique research; event organization; BASE jumper accreditation, award bestowal; video/film production and distribution. Annual plenum.
Publications:
The BASE Monitor, intermittent newsletter; USBA Curriculum and Coordination Guide;

BASEic Sport Parachuting, monograph; BASEics, preparatory guide for sky diver interested in BASE jumping.

Membership Requirements:
Extended to anyone interested in the concept of man jumping off of fixed objects. Acronym BASE is derived from the words: Building, Antenna tower (any tower or stack), Span (any bridge, arch, cable or dome), and Earth (any cliff or natural formation). Any individual making at least one jump from each category is awarded an officially recorded BASE number. Each jump must involve using parachute as life-saving device which cannot be inflated prior to jump.

Nature of Sports Service:
Dedicated to the safety, advancement and accurate positive public image of BASE jumpers and BASE jumping everywhere.

U.S. HANG GLIDING AND PARAGLIDING ASSOCIATION
1685 WEST UINTAH STREET
COLORADO SPRINGS, CO 80904
719-632-8300
800-616-6888
Fax: 719-632-6417
www.ushpa.aero
• Paul Murdoch, President
• Jamie Shelden, Vice President
• Mark Forbes, Treasurer
• Steve Rodrigues, Secretary
• Martin Palmaz, Executive Director
• Beth Van Eaton, Operations Manager
• Julie Spiegler, Program Manager

Year Founded:
1971

Member Services:
Pilot rating program, structured instructor certification program, training structure for tandem flight and aero towing, local club affiliation for the benefit of negotiated site insurance coverage, national magazine for flying, product and safety information, third party and participant liability insurance coverage for members.

Publications:
Hang Gliding & Paragliding magazine

Number of Members:
10,000

Nature of Sports Service:
A private, voluntary, membership, non-profit corporation, promotes the growth of sport flying in foot-launchable soaring aircraft.

UNITED STATES PARACHUTE ASSOCIATION
5401 SOUTHPOINT CENTRE BOULEVARD
FREDERICKSBURG, VA 22407
540-604-9740
Fax: 540-604-9741
uspa@uspa.org
www.uspa.org
• Sherry Butcher, President
• Jay Stokes, Chairman
• Randy Allison, Vice President
• Albert Berchtold, Treasurer
• Ray Lallo, Secretary
• Randy Connell, Competition and Records Coordinator

Description:
A voluntary membership organization of individuals who enjoy and support the sport of skydiving. Promotes safe skydiving through training, licensing and instructor

qualification programs; ensures skydiving's rightful place on airports and in the airspace system, and promotes competition and record-setting programs.

Number of Members:
32,000

Archery Organizations

FEDERATION OF CANADIAN ARCHERS
2255 ST. LAURENT
SUITE 108
OTTAWA, ON, CANADA K1G 4K3
613-260-2113
Fax: 613-260-2114
information@archerycanada.ca
www.archerycanada.ca
• Allan R. Wills, President/VP International
• William Currie, VP Committees & Projects
• Alec Denys, VP High Performance
• Robert Tataryn, VP Administration
• Tricia Oshiro, Athlete Representative

Nature of Service:
To promote and develop the timeless sport of archery in a safe and ethical manner by providing programs that empower all participants to enjoy themselves and achieve their personal goals.

Member Services:
Coaching clinic, award systems, insurance program, rules, standardization, interprovincial club program, equipment analysis; membership and tournament software applications; archery promo video.

Number of Members:
9,000

ARCHERY SHOOTERS ASSOCIATION
PO BOX 399
KENNESAW, GA 30156
770-795-0232
Fax: 770-795-0953
info@asaarchery.com
www.asaarchery.com
• Dee Falks, Federation Director
federationdirector@asaarchery.com

Description:
Promotes archery tournaments and professional level competitions.

Publications:
ASA TOUR GUIDE.

Member Services:
Sponsor contacts, tournament/event food and lodging discounts, club insurance policy, equipment discounts. Dues: $30/year.

Number of Members:
8,000

ARCHERY TRADE ASSOCIATION
101 NORTH GERMAN
SUITE 3
NEW ULM, MN 56073
507-233-8130
866-266-2776
Fax: 507-233-8140
info@archerytrade.org
www.archerytrade.org
• Jay McAninch, President and CEO
• Teresa Johnson, Director of Communications and Public Relations
• Amy Hatfield, Director of Content Marketing
• Emily Beach, Director of Partnership and Program Development

• Mitch King, Director of Government Relations

Year Founded:
1953

Number of members:
1,200

Description:
Provides the core funding and direction for two new foundations critical to the future of archery and bowhunting: ArrowSport and the Bowhunting Preservation Alliance. Also continues to direct the industry's annual archery and bowhunting trade show.

Publications:
Inside Archery, Archery Business and ArrowTrade magazines.

Membership Requirements:
Manufacturers, distributors, retailers, sales representatives, outfitters and others serving the archery and bowhunting industry.

INTERNATIONAL BOWHUNTING ORGANIZATION
PO BOX 398
VERMILION, OH 44089
440-967-2137
Fax: 440-967-2052
www.ibo.net
• Bryan J. Marcum, President
• Gene Bihler, Vice President
• Mike Stitt, Vice President

Description:
The International Bowhunting Organization's goal is to promote, encourage, and foster the sport of bowhunting and to provide education to bowhutners. They act as a regulatory body for bowhunters and aim to disperse essential bowhunter information to those who need it. The IBO prides itself in its ability to foster the conservation and preservation of wildlife, and to provide proactive support for wildlife management.

Year Founded:
1984

Member Benefits:
Subscription to Bowhunting World magazine, 2 window decals, official IBO rule book, accident insurance (US only) and a membership card.

NATIONAL FIELD ARCHERY ASSOCIATION
800 ARCHERY LANE
YANKTON, SD 57078
605-260-9279
Fax: 605-260-9280
www.nfaausa.com
• Bruce Cull, President
• Brian Sheffler, Vice President
• Natalie Vollmer, Executive Secretary
• Brennan Ewald, Membership Marketing Manager

Description:
A non-profit corporation dedicated to the practice of archery and is dedicated to the conservation and preservation of the game. It is resolved to foster, perpetuate and preserve the use of the bow in accordance with its ancient and honorable traditions.

Year Founded:
1939

Number of members:
50 chartered state associations and 1,100 affiliated clubs

Publications:
ARCHERY, official publication.

Membership Requirements:

Must join both state & national to be tournament member. Membership available through NFAA headquarters. Non-tournament member, join directly or through state organization.
Nature of Sports Services:
Hosts three National Championship tournaments, eight sectional indoor and eight sectional outdoor championships that draw more than 3,000.

UNITED FOUNDATION FOR DISABLED ARCHERS
20 NE 9TH AVENUE
PO BOX 251
GLENWOOD, MN 56334
320-634-3660
info@uffdaclub.com
www.uffdaclub.com
• Daniel Hendricks, President
Description:
Founded in 1994, the United Foundation for Disabled Archers aims to promote and provide a means to practice all forms of archery for the physically challenged.

USA ARCHERY
4065 SINTON ROAD
SUITE 110
COLORADO SPRINGS, CO 80907
719-866-4576
Fax: 719-632-4733
media@usarchery.org
www.teamusa.org/usa-archery
• Denise Parker, CEO
• Cindy Clark, Office/Finance Manager
cclark@usarchery.org
• Cindy Tobin, Membership Manager
Description:
USA Archery is the organization recognized by the U.S. Olympic Committee for the purpose of selecting and training men's and women's teams to represent the U.S. in Olympic Games. They also select teams for the World Championships and other international competitions.

WORLD ARCHERY FEDERATION
MAISON DU SPORT INTERNATIONAL
AVENUE DE RHODANIE 54
LAUSANNE, 1007
+41-(0) 21-614-3050
Fax: +41-(0) 21-614-3055
www.worldarchery.org
• Ugur Erdener, President
erdenerugur@gmail.com
• Mario Scarzella, First Vice President
presidente@fitarco-italia.org
• Philippe Bouclet, Vice President
p.bouclet@ffta.fr
• Tom Dielen, Secretary General/Executive Director
• Matteo Pisani, IT Manager
• Caroline Murat, Finance Manager
• Jenny Brugger, Officer Coordinator
• Chris Marsh, Events Director
Year Founded:
1931
Description:
Promotes and regulates archery world-wide in conformity with Olympic principles and organizes international competition.
Number of members:
140
Publications:
Target magazine, published two (three in Olympic years) times a year; monthly

newsletter called FITA INFO; FITA annual report.

Arm Wrestling Organizations

AMERICAN ARMSPORT ASSOCIATION
176 DEAN ROAD
MOORESBURG, TN 37811
423-272-6162
Fax: 423-272-6162
www.armsport.com
• Karen Bean, Executive Director
• Frank Bean, Executive Director
Year Founded:
1977
Number of Members:
56 U.S. armwrestling associations
Publications:
ARM BENDER, quarterly magazine.
Membership Requirements:
Payment of dues, $25 per year.
Description:
Represents the US in the WAF. Sponsors one national championship each year (Standing). Affiliate of World ArmSport Federation.

CANADIAN ARMWRESTLING FEDERATION
1635 8TH AVENUE
SASKATOON, SK, CANADA S7K 2X8
www.cawf.ca
• Rick Pinkney, President
• Ryan Espey, Vice President
• Tracey Arnold, Secretary/Treasurer
Description:
The Canadian Armwrestling Federation's purpose is to oversee organization, promotion and refereeing of the sport of armwrestling in Canada.

NEW YORK ARMWRESTLING ASSOCIATION, INC.
PO BOX 670952
FLUSHING, NY 11367-0952
718-544-4592
877-692-2767
nyawa@nycarms.com
www.nycarms.com
• Gene Camp, Founder, President
• Annette Camp, Vice President
• Bobby Buttafuoco, NY Regional Director
• Vivian Leber, NYAWA Executive Editor
nyawa@aol.com
Year Founded:
1977
Description:
The New York Arm Wresling Association is a unique property and is a NYS-registered not-for-profit organization that produces an exciting grass roots sporting event. It has drawn competition locally from the New York area and from 6 continents and 300 major cities in the USA.
Publications:
NYAWA (Call to Arms) Newsletter, quarterly.
Events:
Promotes arm wrestling events in the New York region including the Empire State Championship, N.Y.C. Junior Championships, Borough Championships, New York Golden Arms Series (9 events); the L.I. Pro Invitational and New York Golden Arms Series.

Number of Members
1595
Nature of Service:
Production of arm wrestling championships in NYC and each of the 5 NYC boroughs, Long Island and upstate New York. Event categories include mens, womens, amateur and pro categories, age groups, and weight classes.

WORLD ARMWRESTLING FEDERATION
SOFIA PARK TRADING ZONE
BUILDING 16B
FLOOR 1, OFFICE 1-2
SOFIA, 1766
359-888-96-8541
contact@waf-armwrestling.com
www.waf-armwrestling.com
• Fred Roy, President
(306) 763-0899
fred.roy@sasktel.net
• Dave Devoto, VP North America
(707) 537-7373
• Assen Hadgitorov, VP Europe
asenhdj@mail.com
• Agzamov Mukhamedolla, VP Asia
(+73) 72 33802
fgsakz_a@mail.ru
Year Founded:
1970
Description:
Founded in 1970. Sponsors world championships. Coordinates all activities of the W.A.F. members. Solicits new W.A.F. member countries.

Auto Sports Organizations

AMERICAN AUTO RACING WRITERS AND BROADCASTERS ASSOCIATION
922 NORTH PASS AVENUE
BURBANK, CA 91505-2703
818-842-7005
Fax: 818-842-7020
www.aarwba.org
• Norma Dusty Brandel, President & Executive Director
• Kathy Seymour, Vice President
kathyseu@hotmail.com
Year Founded:
1955
Number of members:
Over 400.
Member Services:
Breakfast meetings, monthly newsletter, membership directory.
Publications:
Monthly newsletter for members only, and annual directory.
Membership Requirements:
Media who cover motorsports, public relations and advertising personnel involved with racing teams, sponsors, sanctioning bodies.
Description:
Serves to upgrade coverage of auto racing, promote coverage and the stature of racing, and to secure the best possible conditions for auto racing media. All-American auto racing team selection committee.

AMERICAN RACING DRIVERS CLUB INC./ARDC
529 OLD MILL ROAD
MILLERSVILLE, MD 21108

570-275-0649
ardcmidget.com
• Wayne Lesher, President
wlesher@centurylink.net
• Tom Grumbine, Vice President
tgrumbine@hotmail.com
Year Founded:
1939
Publications:
Monthly newsletter.
Number of members:
Average of 30 registered drivers a year.
Membership Requirements:
There are four types of annual memberships available. Four are participatory and the other is for associate members.

AMERICAN THREE QUARTER MIDGET RACING ASSOCIATION
808 WOODLANE RD
MT. HOLLY, NJ 8060
610-217-2593
Fax: 609-267-3890
atqmra.com
• Buddy Sload, President
(484) 880-0907
• Paul Dodorico, Vice President
Year Founded:
1956
Member Services:
Scheduling and organization of racing events, provision of racing insurance, newsletter. Annual meeting held during October each year.
Publications:
ATQMRA NEWSLETTER, monthly.
Membership Requirements:
Open to all persons age 18 or over; Membership categories of Driver, Car Owner, Owner-Driver, Associate.
Description:
Organization and promotion of auto racing events, specifically single-seat, open-cockpit, T.Q. Midget, race cars, in Northeastern United States.

ARCA RACING SERIES
8117 LEWIS AVENUE
TEMPERANCE, MI 48182
734-847-6726
Fax: 734-847-3137
www.arcaracing.com
• Ron Drager, President & Chief Executive Officer
(734) 847-6726
• Mark Gundrum, VP, Business Development & Corporate Partners
(734) 847-6726
mgundrum@arcaracing.com
• Joe Wells, Dirextor, Race Operations & Administration
(734) 847-6726
jwells@arcaracing.com
Year Founded:
1953
Description:
Sanctioning body for various types of auto racing in U.S. sanctions national championship series for stocks (ARCA RE/MAX Series), Trucks (ARCA Lincoln Welders Truck Series). Also sanctions Toledo and Flat Rock Speedways.
Membership Requirements:
Applications open to drivers, mechanics and car owners.
Publications:

Full line of releases to accredited members of media; newsletter to members.

DIRTCAR RACING
1 SPEEDWAY DR
WEEDSPORT, NY 13166
315-834-6606
info@dirtcar.com
www.superdirtcarseries.com
• Joe Skotnicki, Director of Competition/Track Sanctioning
• Cory Reed, Director Series/Sanctioning
Year Founded:
1976
Description:
Sanctioning body for open wheel modified dirt track racing. Races organized and sanctioned by DIRT include the Rite-Aid 100 & 200, Eastern States Weekend and Advance Auto Parts modified Super Dirt Series.

DOVER MOTORSPORTS, INC.
1131 N DUPONT HIGHWAY
PO BOX 843
DOVER, DE 19903
302-883-6500
Fax: 302-672-0100
info@dovermotorsports.com
www.dovermotorsportsinc.com
Nature of Sports Service:
Owns and operates racetracks which include Dover International Speedway, Nashville Superspeedway, Gateway International Raceway.

FAST TRACK RACING
5540 MOREHEAD ROAD
HARRISBURG, NC 28075
704-455-1700
Fax: 704-455-6603
info@fasttrackracing.com
www.fasttrackracing.com
• Andy Hillenburg, Owner
• Bill McKee, General Manager
Year Founded:
1989
Description:
The school caters to the stock racing car enthusiast. It gives the student the opportunity to get behind the wheel of a ARCA style stock car. The enthusiast has an option of the 1 day or the 3 day course, 10, and 20 lap drives, and 3 lap rides. New for 2009 is the Short Track Driver Development School, ages 14 and older, conducted on the 1/2 mile track at Rockingham Speedway, with ARCA race cars.

FELD MOTOR SPORTS
4255 MERIDIAN PARKWAY
AURORA, IL 60504
630-566-6100
webmaster@monsterjam.com
monsterjam.com
• Magnus Danielsson, Intl VP
Nature of Sports Service:
Sanctioning body for Monster Jam and Thunder Nationals, as well as motocross and quad racing.

FORMULA RACE CAR CLUB OF AMERICA
570 WEST SADDLE RIVER ROAD
RIDGEWOOD, NJ 07450

570-669-9589
frcca2014@gmail.com
www.formularacecarclubofamerica.com
• Jeff Zeller, Treasurer
(914) 584-0132
• Andy Graham, President
(914) 584-0132
Year Founded:
1980
Member Services:
Driver's Points Fund; year-end championship; trophies.
Publications:
TRANSMISSIONS, newsletter, 12 times annually.
Membership Requirements:
$125 annual membership fee.
Description:
Sanctioning body for entry-level amateur Formula Ford(older models), Formula American car racing. Issues competition licenses based upon accomplishments in the previous class. Races are held in the Northeast and Southeast. The FRCCA endeavors to put emphasis on driving ability rather than the car, in racing.

FROST MOTORSPORTS, LLC
909 SENECA ROAD
WILMETTE, IL 60091
847-853-0294
Fax: 847-853-8763
twfrost@speedwaysonline.com
www.frostmotorsports.com
• Timothy W. Frost, President
twfrost@speedwaysonline.com
Nature of Service:
Feasibility studies, market demand studies, economic impact analysis, valuation and financial consulting of motorsports facilities and motorsports industry participants

GRAND PRIX ASSOCIATION OF LONG BEACH
GRAND PRIX ASSOC OF LONG BEACH
3000 PACIFIC AVENUE
LONG BEACH, CA 90806
562-981-2600
Fax: 562-981-2616
info@gpalb.com
www.gplb.com
• Jim Michaelian, President/CEO
(562) 490-4522
• Martin Bannon, Director, Marketing
(562) 490-4512
• Gemma Bannon, Exec. Asst. to the President & CEO, Offic
(562) 490-4521
• Allison Wilson, Exec. Asst. to President & CEO/Manager of Adv
(562) 490-4522
• Dwight Tanaka, Director, Operations
(562) 490-4526
• Chris Esslinger, Director, Communications
(532) 490-4514
• Tammy Johnson, Customer Service/Ticketing Manager
(562) 490-4562

IMCA
1800 WEST D STREET
VINTON, IA 52349
319-472-2201
Fax: 319-472-2218
www.imca.com
• Brett Root, President
(319) 472-2201

broot@imca.com
• Jim Stannard, VP, Operations
• Dave Brenn, Executive Director, Competition
Year Founded:
1915
Description:
The oldest active automobile racing sanctioning body in the United States.
Membership Requirements:
Pay dues.
Publications:
Newsletter, 12 issues yearly
Member Services:
Competitor insurance.

IMG
200 5TH AVENUE
7TH FLOOR
NEW YORK, NY 10010
212-489-8300
Fax: 646-558-8399
www.imgworld.com
• Chuck Bennett, President, IMG Golf, Tennis, Fashion & Events
Description:
Represents and manages leading events, associations, tracks, teams and talent.
Clients:
Danica Patrick, Formula D Drifting, Joe Gibbs Racing, John Force Racing, Gold Coast 300 (featuring the V8 Supercar Championship Series and A!GP World Cup of Motorsports), NASCAR, NHRA, Sir Jackie Stewart (legendary driver), World Speedway Grand Prix, World Speedway World Cup

Other locations:

IMG MOTORSPORTS (NC)
16810 KENTON DRIVE
SUITE 300
HUNTERSVILLE, NC 28078
704-987-4080
Fax: 704-568-4116
www.imgworld.com
• Chuck Bennett, President

IMPORT DRAG RACING CIRCUIT
11231 YOUNG RIVER AVE.
FOUNTAIN VALLEY, CA 92708
714-593-0280
Fax: 714-593-0281
www.importdrag.com
• Michael Ferrara, President
mferrara@hardmediainc.com
• Richard Tran, National Director
Description:
Founded in 1998, IDRc has established itself as the leader in the import and sport compact performance events arena
Membership:
DSport Magazine, Official IDRC Rulebook, permanent competition number, etc: $45/yr.

IMSA (INTERNATIONAL MOTOR SPORTS ASSOCIATION)
INTERNATIONAL MOTORSPORTS CENTER
ONE DAYTONA BOULEVARD
DAYTONA BEACH, FL 32114
386-310-6500
info@imsa.com
www.imsa.com
• Jim France, Chairman
• Ed Bennett, CEO
• Scott Atherton, President

Membership Benefits:
Subscription to AutoWeek, decal and patch, hat, t-shirt, lapel pin, and fan guide.
Description:
Sanctioning body for ALS, Star Mazda, Panoz Racing Series, IMSA GT3 Cup Challenge, and Formula BMW USA.

INTERNATIONAL COUNCIL OF MOTORSPORT SCIENCES
THE ICMS
9305 CRESTVIEW DRIVE
DENTON, TX 76207
940-262-3481
Fax: 940-262-3482
info@theicms.org
www.icmsmotorsportsafety.org
• Tom Weisenbach, Executive Director
Year Founded:
1988
Membership Requirements:
Includes physicians, psychologists, physiologists, race drivers and paramedic personnel.
Description:
An association of medical professionals, scientific, allied health and other interested persons with the improvement in performance and safety in motorsport.

INTERNATIONAL HOT ROD ASSOCIATION
300 CLEVELAND ROAD
NORWALK, OH 44857
419-663-6666
Fax: 419-663-4472
comments@ihra.com
www.ihra.com
• Scott Gardner, President
Description:
Promotes racing at all levels and a racing series in major cities in the United States and Canada.
Founded:
1971
Publications:
Drag Review magazine, 22 issues/yr.; IHRA Yearbook and Rulebook

INTERNATIONAL KART FEDERATION
1609 S GROVE AVE
SUITE 105
ONTARIO, CA 91761
909-923-4999
Fax: 909-923-6940
www.ikfkarting.com
• Roger Miller, President
Year Founded:
1957
Number of members:
3,000
Member Services:
Patch, decal, subscription to KARTER NEWS. Club and track insurance, regional point program, Grand national events.
Publications:
KARTER NEWS, monthly.
Membership Requirements:
$60.00 per year provides IKF membership plus sprint, 4-cycle and speedway, and road racing license. New members start at back of grid for three races.
Description:
Governing body for kart racing. It fosters fair and strong competition; provides reasonable rules for a variety of competition; administers the competition with impartiality;

and endeavors to reduce the hazards associated with karting.

MID-AMERICA OFF ROAD ASSOCIATION
PO BOX 664
GREENUP, IL 62428
• Spencer Rising-Moore, President
Description:
Sanctioning body for off-road racing in the United States.
Founded:
1972

NATIONAL ASSOCIATION FOR STOCK CAR AUTO RACING (NASCAR)
PO BOX 2875
DAYTONA BEACH, FL 32120
386-253-0611
Fax: 386-239-2811
fanfeedback@nascar.com
www.nascar.com
• Brian France, Chairman & CEO
• Mike Helton, Vice Chairman
Description:
The National Association for Stock Car Auto Racing oversees one of the most popular and fastest-growing spectator sports in the US. NASCAR runs more than 100 races each year in three racing circuits: the Nationwide Series, the Camping World Truck Series and the Sprint Cup Series

NATIONAL AUTO SPORT ASSOCIATION
PO BOX 2366
NAPA VALLEY, CA 94558
510-232-6272
Fax: 510-277-0657
www.nasaproracing.com
Description:
NASA's regional divisions host a variety of high-quality racing events for enthusiasts.
Founded:
1991

NATIONAL CHAMPIONSHIP RACING ASSOCIATION
7700 N BROADWAY
WICHITA, KS 67219
316-755-1781
Fax: 316-755-0665
www.racencra.com
• Mylissa Powers, Contact
Year Founded:
1971
Description:
Sanctioning group for dirt track late model and sprint car racing for the southwest. Organizes 60 races annually as well as the modifieds.
Publications:
Rule Book.

NATIONAL HOT ROD ASSOCIATION
2035 FINANCIAL WAY
GLENDORA, CA 91741
626-914-4761
Fax: 626-963-5360
nhra@nhra.com
www.nhra.com
• Peter Clifford, President
Year Founded:
1951
Description:
The largest and loudest auto racing organization. Dedicated to safety while providing millions of racing fans with The

Extreme Motorsport: the fastest and most spectacular form of entertainment on wheels.
Publications:
NATIONAL DRAGSTER, weekly
Membership:
80,000

NATIONAL STREET ROD ASSOCIATION
4030 PARK AVE
MEMPHIS, TN 38111
901-452-4030
www.nsra-usa.com
• Jim Rowlett, Marketing Director
(817) 581-9915
nsra1@aol.com
Year Founded:
1970
Description:
The organizing body that made the sport what it is today, and the reason the growth of enthusiast participation has continued at a steady pace. Provides leadership, guidance, and fun events for enthusiasts who favor driving their specialty vehicles wherever and whenever they want to.
Membership Requirements:
Annual fee: $30.00.
Publications:
Monthly subscription to StreetScene Magazine; Annual copy of Fellow Pages

NATIONAL TRACTOR PULLERS ASSOCIATION
6155-B HUNTLEY RD
COLUMBUS, OH 43229
614-436-1761
Fax: 614-436-0964
www.ntpapull.com
• Gregg Randall, Executive Director
• Michaela Kramer, Publications Editor
Year Founded:
1969
Publications:
THE PULLER magazine; PULL!, yearbook
Description:
Sets the standards in the pulling industry for safety and competition rules.

RAHAL LETTERMAN LANIGAN RACING
4601 LYMAN DRIVE
HILLIARD, OH 43026
614-529-7000
Fax: 614-529-7007
www.rahal.com
• David Letterman, Co-Owner
• Bobby Rahal, Co-Owner
Sports Service Founded:
1983
Athlete Management Services:
Media exposure, product endorsements, personal appearances, guest speakers.
Event Management Services:
Organize and direct Bobby Rahal Columbus Charities Pro-Am.

RHYS MILLEN RACING
17471 APEX CIRCLE
HUNTINGTON BEACH, CA 92647
714-847-2158
Fax: 714-848-6821
sales@rmrproducts.com
www.rhys-millen-racing.myshopify.com
• Rod Millen, President/Chief Executive Officer

Sports Service Founded:
1972.
Event Management Services:
Toyota North American Touring Car and Pikes Peak Hill Climb Racing. Private design and engineering work for rally and off-road race teams. Special event (off-road) race entries for short or long-term promotions. National and international marketing campaigns. Precision driving for television commercials.

RICHARD PETTY DRIVING EXPERIENCE
6022 VICTORY LANE
CONCORD, NC 28027
704-455-9443
800-237-3889
Fax: 704-455-5595
www.drivepetty.com
• Mike Bartelli, Chief Marketing Officer
Year Founded:
1990
Description:
Offering Drive and Ride-a-Long programs. Operating over 1168 track days at 27+ tracks nationwide. 60,000 driving experiences and 70,000 Ride-Alongs
Membership Requirements:
Drivers must be 16 years old and have a valid drivers license.
Entry Fee:
$109 and up.

SKIP BARBER RACING SCHOOL LLC
5290 WINDER HIGHWAY
BRASELTON, GA 30517
866-932-1949
800-221-1131
Fax: 860-435-1321
www.skipbarber.com

SOUTHERN UNITED PROFESSIONAL RACING
12561 SOUTH CHOCTAW
BATON ROUGE, LA 70815
225-275-5040
Fax: 225-273-3166
SUPRrace@aol.com
www.suprracing.com
Year Founded:
1990
Description:
A Lousiana-based touring group that ofers area racers an affordable alternative to high-cost traveling circuits. Organizes 25 races at 14 facilities in four states
Member Services:
A point fund established for those drivers with the most accumulated points for the year.

SPEEDWAY MOTORSPORTS, INC.
5555 CONCORD PKWY S.
CONCORD, NC 28027
704-455-3239
Fax: 704-455-1268
www.gospeedway.com
• Cary Tharrington, SVP & General Counsel
• Donald Hawk, Chief Racing Development Officer
• Jerry Caldwell, EVP & General Manager
Nature of Sports Services:
A marketer and producer of motorsports entertainment in the United States. The company owns and operates six motorsports facilities including Atlanta Motor Speedway, Bristol (TN), Motor Speedway,

Lowe's Motor Speedway, Las Vegas Motor Speedway, Infineon Raceway, and New Hampshire Speedway

SPORTS CAR CLUB OF AMERICA
6620 SE DWIGHT ST
TOPEKA, KS 66619-0400
785-357-7222
800-770-2055
Fax: 785-232-7228
membership@scca.com
www.scca.com
• Mike Cobb, President & CEO
Year Founded:
1944
Description:
To bring motorsports to the masses of American men and women who are passionate about automobiles, speed and competition. Exist to organize, support and develop auto racing at every level and provide an outlet for you to get out of the armchair and into the action.

SPORTSCAR VINTAGE RACING ASSOCIATION
1598 HART STREET
SUITE 100
SOUTHLAKE, TX 76092
603-640-6161
Fax: 817-953-3550
www.svra.com
• Alex Miller, National Competition Director
(610) 223-4834
• Kathy Swinford, Director, Services/Events Entry
• Kim Parella, Registrar
(850) 329-7485
Year Founded:
1976
Membership Requirements:
General Membership: $85.00 annually. SVRA/HSR Dual Membership: $105.00 annually.
Description:
Offers tightly regulated wheel-to-wheel racing for the men and women who own and maintain their vintage and historical cars, and the venues through which they can compete

UNITED MIDGET AUTO RACING ASSOCIATION/UMRA
530 W. LOCKPORT ST, STE 200
PLAINFIELD, IL 60544
815-439-9775
Fax: 815-439-9777
Year Founded:
1985
Publications:
UMARA Newsletter, monthly.
Membership Requirements:
Driver, owner or mechanic of midget cars ($165 dues for driver, $195 car owner/driver, $35 mechanic); spectators-associate members. Drivers required to take physicals. Drivers classified as rookies for first five races and must start at back of races.
Description:
Promotes midget cars, midget racing and the thrill of the short track race.

UNITED RACING COMPANY
2109 SOUTH DUPONT HIGHWAY
DOVER, DE 19901

302-697-3273
Fax: 302-697-6548
Year Founded:
1947
Member Services:
Stages approximately 35 races each year,
Season from early April to late October.
Annual Awards Banquet held in November
each year in Allentown, PA. Annual
meetings held in March and October every
year.
Publications:
Pictorial Yearbook, annual.
Membership Requirements:
83 drivers and owners. Must be a member
of the United Racing Club and run Goodyear
tires to participate, along with engine and
wing limitations.
Affiliations:
Sprint Car Racing organization
Number of Members:
200

US LEGEND CARS
5245 NC HWY 49 SOUTH
HARRISBURG, NC 28075
704-455-3896
Fax: 704-455-3820
www.uslegendcars.com
• GE Chapman, General Manager
(704) 455-3896
gechapman@uslegendcars.com
• Chad Honeycutt, Engine Shop Manager
(704) 455-3896
chadh@uslegendcars.com
Nature of Sports Service:
Founded in 1995, INEX was developed to
prmote, organize and sanction Legends Car,
Bandolero and Thunder Roadster racing
across the United State, Canada and
Europe.
Publications:
INEX Magazine and Rulebook for Legends
Cars, Bandolero and Thunder Roadster
Number of members:
3,500

WESTERN RACING ASSOCIATION
PO BOX 509
MONROVIA, CA 91017-0509
760-245-4023
www.westernracing.com
• John Wildharber, President
(626) 358-2284
• Seth Hammond, Vice President
(714) 389-9400
• Rick Turner, Race Director
(619) 449-1674
Year Founded:
1982
Member Services:
15 exhibition events are presented each
year at tracks like Calistoga, El Cajon,
Madera, Merced, Santa Maria, San
Bernardino and Tulare.
Members:
300+
Membership Requirements:
$45 yearly fee.
Description:
A non-profit corporation, dedicated to the
preservation of antique automobile racing
cars and fellowship.

WORLD KARTING ASSOCIATION
6051 VICTORY LANE
CONCORD, NC 28027

704-455-1606
Fax: 704-455-1609
info@worldkarting.com
www.worldkarting.com
• Marie Borsuk, Business Manager
(704) 455-1606
marie@worldkarting.com
• Jeanne Harrison, Membership Coordinator
(704) 455-1606
members@worldkarting.com
Year Founded:
1971
Description:
A membership-owned, non-profit corporation
formed to regulate and promote the sport of
competitive kart racing. Over 10,000
members and 120 sanctioned race tracks.
Publications:
WKA's Karting Scene. The official
publication of the World Karting Association
that provides its members and subscribers
schedules of events, race reports, official
event results, technical reports,
human-interest stories, and other related
information

WORLD RACING GROUP
7575-D WEST WINDS BLVD
CONCORD, NC 28027
704-795-7223
Fax: 704-795-7229
info@dirtcar.com
www.worldracinggroup.com;
www.dirtcar.com
• Brian Carter, CEO
Description:
World Racing Group (WRG) is the world
leader in the sanctioning and promotion of
dirt track auto racing. WRG owns the
premier national touring series for each of
the top three division in dirt track racing -
The Advance Auto Parts World of Outlaws
Sprint Car Series, World of Outlaws Late
Model Series and the Advance Auto Parts
Super DIRTcar Series. WRG also sanctions
weekly racing action at over 120 tracks
throughout the United States and Canada
under the DIRTcar Racing banner.
Year Founded:
2003

Auto Sports Racing Leagues/Teams

ARCA MENARDS SERIES EAST
www.arcaracing.com
Description:
One of two NASCAR regional
developmental divisions.

Teams:

BRAD SMITH MOTORSPORTS
586-206-8298
brad@bradsmithmotorsports.com
bradsmithmotorsports.com
• Brad Smith, CEO

CHAD BRYANT RACING
press@chadbryantracing.com
chadbryantracing.com

DGR-CROSLEY
111 BYERS CREEK ROAD
MOORESVILLE, NC 28117

dgrcrosley.com
• David Gilliland, Co-Owner
• Johnny Gray, Co-Owner

VENTURINI MOTORSPORTS
571 PITTS SCHOOL ROAD NW
CONCORD, NC 28027
704-784-2500
Fax: 704-784-2575
info@venturinimotorsports.com
www.venturinimotorsports.com

ARCA MENARDS SERIES WEST
www.arcaracing.com
Description:
A regional stock car racing division of
NASCAR.

Teams:

BILL MCANALLY RACING
916-676-0010
www.bmrnaparacing.com

GMS RACING
310 AVIATION DRIVE
STATESVILLE, NC 28677
info@gmsracing.net
gmsracing.net

JERRY PITTS RACING
• Jeff Jefferson, Co-Owner/Crew Chief
• Jerry Pitts, Co-Owner/Crew Chief

VENTURINI MOTORSPORTS
571 PITTS SCHOOL ROAD NW
CONCORD, NC 28027
704-784-2500
Fax: 704-784-2575
info@venturinimotorsports.com
www.venturinimotorsports.com

FERRARI CHALLENGE NORTH AMERICA
250 SYLVAN AVENUE
ENGLEWOOD CLIFFS, NJ 07632
877-933-7727
races.ferrari.com/en/corse-clienti/north-amer
ica
• Andrea Reggiani, Communications
Andrea.Reggiani@ferrari.com
Description:
The Ferrari Challenge North America is a
competition using the 458 racing model,
held at several circuit locations across
America.

FORMULA 1
www.formula1.com
• Stefani Domenicali, CEO

Teams:

ALFA ROMEO RACING
HINWIL,
• Frederic Vasseur, Team Chief
• Jan Monchaux, Technical Chief

ALPHATAURI
SCUDERIA ALPHATAURI
VIA BOARIA, 229
FAENZA, RAVENNA, ITALY 48018
info@scuderiaalphatauri.com
www.scuderiaalphatauri.com
• Franz Tost, Team Chief
• Jody Egginton, Technical Chief

ALPINE
ENSTONE,

- David Brivio, Team Chief
- Remi Taffin, Technical Chief
- Pat Fry, Technical Chief

ASTON MARTIN
SILVERSTONE,
- Otmar Szafnauer, Team Chief
- Andrew Green, Technical Chief

FERRARI
MARANELLO, MO, ITALY
formula1.ferrari.com
- Mattia Binotto, Team Chief
- Enrico Cardile, Technical Chief
- Enrico Gualtieri, Technical Chief
Sponsors:
Fiat, Santander, Shell, Etihad, Acer, Mubadala,
AMD and Bridgestone

HAAS
KANNAPOLIS, NC
www.haasf1team.com
- Gene Haas, Founder/Chairman
- Guenther Steiner, Team Chief
- Simone Resta, Technical Chief

MCLAREN
MCLAREN TECHNOLOGY CENTRE
CHERTSEY ROAD
WOKING, SURREY, ENGLAND GU21 4YH
www.mclaren.com/formula1
- Zak Brown, CEO
- Andreas Seidl, Team Chief
- James Key, Technical Chief

MERCEDES
MERCEDES-AMG PETRONAS FORMULA
ONE TEAM
OPERATIONS CENTRE
BRACKLEY, NORTHANTS NN13 7BD
enquiries@mercedesamgf1.com
www.mercedesamgf1.com
- Toto Wolff, Team Chief/CEO
- James Allison, Technical Chief

RED BULL RACING
ASTON MARTIN RED BULL RACING
BRADBOURNE DRIVE
TILBROOK
MILTON KEYNES, MK7 8BJ
feedback@redbullf1.com
redbullracing.redbull.com
- Christian Horner, OBE, Team Chief
- Pierre Wache, Technical Chief

WILLIAMS
GROVE
WANTAGE, OXFORDSHIRE, ENGLAND OX12
0DQ
www.williamsf1.com
- Simon Roberts, Team Chief
- Francois-Xavier Demaison, Technical Chief
Year Founded:
1977

HISTORIC SPORTSCAR RACING LLC
PO BOX 8110
CLEARWATER, FL 33758
727-573-1340
Fax: 727-573-1350
registrar@hsrrace.com
hsrrace.com
- David Hinton, Owner/President
(727) 573-1340
david@hsrrace.com
Races:
Race Series Classes; Race Series Points
System; Endurance Series; Dash Series;
BOSS Super Cup; Historic GTP/Group C &
WSC; Championship of Makes; Historic GT;
Historic Stock Car; Jo Bonnier Cup Series;
Klub Sport Porsche Challenge Series

Year Founded:
1966
Sponsors:
RaceWatches.com; Bob Woodman Tires;
Classic Motorsports Magazine; Gene Felton
Restorations; Hector Cademartori Motor
Racing Art; HSR West; Klub Sport Racing;
Lee Chapman Racing; Moorespeed Racing;
Phelon Motorsports; R Harrington
Photography; RM Motorsports; Traqmate;
Truechoice Motorsports; Sasco Sports, Inc;
Stand 21; Vintage Motorsport Magazine;
Vintage Racing Services Inc

IMSA MICHELIN PILOT CHALLENGE
INTERNATIONAL MOTORSPORTS
CENTER
ONE DAYTONA BOULEVARD
DAYTONA BEACH, FL 32114
386-310-6500
info@imsa.com
www.imsa.com

Teams:

ATLANTA SPEEDWERKS
470 WOODSMILL ROAD
SUITE E
GAINESVILLE, GA 30501
678-971-5300
atlspeedwerks.com
- Todd Lamb, Owner

AUTOMATIC RACING
6112 HANGING MOSS ROAD
ORLANDO, FL 32807
407-230-7575
drussell@automaticracing.com
automaticracing.com
- David Russell, Team Manager
- Danimal Paskan, Chief Mechanic

AWA INC.
7353 CASTLEDERG SIDEROAD
CALEDON EAST, ON, CANADA L7C 3E4
647-588-3044
andrew@awa.team
awa.team

BGB MOTORSPORTS
6C WEST TOWER CIRCLE
UNIT 102
ORMOND BEACH, FL 32174
386-265-1979
Fax: 386-492-7817
info@teambgb.com
www.teambgb.com

BIMMERWORLD RACING
4085 PEPPERELL WAY
DUBLIN, VA 24084
877-639-9648
info@bimmerworld.com
www.bimmerworldracing.com
- James Clay, President

BRYAN HERTA AUTOSPORT
www.bryanhertaautosport.com
- Nick Franzosi, Team Manager

CARBAHN MOTORSPORTS
2232 OLD MIDDLEFIELD WAY
MOUNTAIN VIEW, CA 94043

KMW MOTORSPORTS
1800 NW 1ST AVENUE
BOCA RATON, FL 33432
561-392-3020
kmwmotorsports@aol.com
kmwmotorsports.com

KohR MOTORSPORTS
5727 EXECUTIVE DRIVE E
WESTLAND, MI 48185
734-895-1543
www.kohrmotorsports.com

L.A. HONDA WORLD RACING
DOWNEY, CA
www.lahondaworldracing.com

MOTORSPORTS IN ACTION
1016 ARTHUR SAUVÂ☐ BLVD
LOCAL G
SAINT-EUSTACHE, QC, CANADA J7R 4K3
888-568-0069
info@motorsportsinaction.com
www.motorsportsinaction.com
- Carl Hermez, Team Manager

MURILLO RACING
5805 LABATH AVENUE
UNIT 4
ROHNERT PARK, CA 94928
707-280-6783
ken@murilloracing.com
www.murilloracing.com
- Ken Murillo, Team Owner

REBEL ROCK RACING
2001 INDUSTRIAL DR
DELAND, FL 32725

RILEY MOTORSPORTS
MOORESVILLE, NC

ROADSHAGGER RACING
roadshagger.com

STEPHEN CAMERON RACING
SONOMA RACEWAY
29121 ARNOLD DRIVE
BUILDING E5
SONOMA, CA 95476
707-996-1184
Fax: 707-938-1027
steve@cameronracingusa.com
www.cameronracingusa.com
- Cameron Steve, Team Manager
- Gary Rubio, Crew Chief

TEAM TGM
www.teamtgm.com
- Ted Giovanis, Owner

WINWARD RACING
HOUSTON, TX
winwardracing.com

IMSA PROTOTYPE CHALLENGE
INTERNATIONAL MOTORSPORTS
CENTER
ONE DAYTONA BOULEVARD
DAYTONA BEACH, FL 32114
386-310-6500
info@imsa.com
www.imsa.com/prototypechallenge

Teams:

ANDRETTI AUTOSPORT
7615 ZIONSVILLE RD
INDIANAPOLIS, IN 46268

CONQUEST RACING
3950 GUION LANE
INDIANAPOLIS, IN 46268
317-870-0007 EXT 34
ebachelart@conquestracing.com
conquestracing.com
- Eric Bachelart, President/CEO

FORTY 7 MOTORSPORTS
ONE MOTORSPORTS BLVD
MILLVILLE, NJ 08332
856-765-5858
info@race47.com
forty7motorsports.com

JDC MOTORSPORTS
12977 EAGLE CREEK PKWY
SAVAGE, MN 55378

ONE MOTORSPORTS
18400 STATE HIGHWAY 160
LAS VEGAS, NV 89161
702-496-2606
jeff@onemotorsports.com
www.onemotorsports.com

**PERFORMANCE TECH
MOTORSPORTS**
3000 SW 15 STREET
SUITE D
DEERFIELD BEACH, FL 33442
info@performancetechmotorsports.com
www.performancetechmotorsports.com
• Brent O'Neill, Team Owner

ROBILLARD RACING
5833 DEEP WATER DR
OXFORD, MD 21654

VOLT RACING
8800 WATSON RD
ST LOUIS, MO 63119

WIN AUTOSPORT
145 CATRON DR
RENO, NY 89512

WULVER RACING
1433 CORBETT RD
MONKTON, MD 21111

**IMSA WEATHERTECH SPORTSCAR
CHAMPIONSHIP**
INTERNATIONAL MOTORSPORTS
CENTER
ONE DAYTONA BOULEVARD
DAYTONA BEACH, FL 32114
386-310-6500
info@imsa.com
www.imsa.com/weathertech

Teams:

AF CORSE

ALEGRA MOTORSPORTS

ALLY CADILLAC RACING

BMW TEAM RLL
4601 LYMAN DRIVE
HILLIARD, OH 43026
614-529-7000
rahal.com
• Chris Mower, Team Manager
• Chris Danison, Crew Chief

CORE AUTOSPORT
283 LAKESHORE PARKWAY
ROCK HILL, SC 29730
803-325-9321
coreautosport.com
• Jon Bennett, Founder

CORVETTE RACING
www.corvetteracing.com

• Gary Pratt, Team Manager
• Dan Binks, Crew Chief

DRAGONSPEED RACING
JUPITER, FL

GRT GRASSER RACING TEAM
HAUPTSTRAÃ¡E 11
KNITTELFELD, 8720
management@grasser-racing.com
www.grasser-racing.com

JDC-MILLER MOTORSPORTS
8856 WOODHILL CIRCLE
SAVAGE, MN 55378
www.jdcmotorsport.com
• John Church, CEO
(952) 233-3075
jchurch@jdcmotorsports.com

MAGNUS RACING
4700 HIGHLAND DRIVE
SUITE B
SALT LAKE CITY, UT 84117
info@magnusracing.com
www.magnusracing.com
• John Potter, Owner

MAZDA MOTORSPORTS
1421 REYNOLDS AVENUE
IRVINE, CA 92614
800-435-2508
www.mazdamotorsports.com

**MEYER SHANK RACING W/
CURB-AGAJANIAN**
114 VENTURE DRIVE
PATASKALA, OH 43062
740-964-9998
www.michaelshankracing.com
• Mike Shank, Owner

PAUL MILLER RACING
pr@paulmillerracing.com
www.paulmillerracing.com
• Paul Miller, Principal

**PERFORMANCE TECH
MOTORSPORTS**
3000 SW 15TH STREET
SUITE D
DEERFIELD BEACH, FL 33442
info@performancetechmotorsports.com
www.performancetechmotorsports.com
• Brent O'Neill, Team Owner

PFAFF MOTORSPORTS
618 CHRISLEA ROAD
WOODBRIDGE, ON, CANADA L4L 8K9
289-596-4662
www.pfaffauto.com/motorsports
• Christopher Pfaff, CEO

PR1/MATHIASEN MOTORSPORTS
5801 E CLINTON AVENUE
FRESNO, CA 93727
559-277-1300
pr1motorsports@aol.com
pr1motorsports.com
• Bobby Oergel, Owner/Director

RISI COMPETIZIONE
6100 SOUTHWEST FREEWAY
HOUSTON, TX 77057
713-772-3868
www.risicompetizione.com
• Tony Nevotti, General Manager

SCUDERIA CORSA
7925 W ARBY AVENUE
SUITE 100
LAS VEGAS, NV 89113
888-644-0241
info@scuderiacorsa.com
www.scuderiacorsa.com

TURNER MOTORSPORT
800-280-6966
info@turnermotorsport.com
www.turnermotorsport.com/t-racing-home
• Will Turner, Owner

WHELEN ENGINEERING RACING
860-526-9504
www.whelen.com/motorsports/imsa
• Gary Nelson, Team Manager
• Bill Keuler, Crew Chief

INDY LIGHTS
10101 U.S. HIGHWAY 41 NORTH
PALMETTO, FL 34221
941-845-2500
info@roadtoindy.net
www.indylights.com
• Michelle Kish, COO
mkish@andersenpromotions.net
• Tamy Valkosky, Public Relations
pr@roadtoindy.net
Description:
The Indy Lights operates as a driver
development program for prospective
IndyCar drivers. It is the only driver
development program in the world to feature
a champion's scholarship at entry level to
advance to the next step on the ladder
system. They've produced some of the
IndyCar series biggest names.

Teams:

ANDRETTI AUTOSPORT
INDIANAPOLIS, IN
pr@andrettiautosport.com
www.andrettiautosport.com
• Michael Andretti, CEO/Chair
• J-F Thormann, President

ANDRETTI STEINBRENNER RACING
7615 ZIONSVILLE ROAD
INDIANAPOLIS, IN 46268
317-872-2700
amber.stevenson@andrettiautosport.com
www.andrettiautosport.com
• J.F. Thormann, President

CARLIN
7 COXBRIDGE BUSINESS PARK
ALTON ROAD
FARNHAM, SURREY, ENGLAND GU10 5EH
media@carlin.co.uk
www.carlin.co.uk
• Trevor Carlin, Founder
• Grahame Chilton, CEO
• Rupert Swallow, Managing Director

JUNCOS RACING
4401 GILMAN STREET
INDIANAPOLIS, IN 46224
317-552-2967
info@juncosracing.com
www.juncosracing.com/indy-lights
• Tom Vigne, Crew Chief

INDY PRO 2000
10101 U.S. HIGHWAY 41 N
PALMETTO, FL 34221
941-845-2500
info@roadtoindy.net
www.indypro2000.com

• Michelle Kish, COO
mkish@andersenpromotions.net
• Tamy Valkosky, Public Relations
pr@roadtoindy.net
Sponsors:
Mazda, Goodyear, Mazda Road To Indy, BBS,
Quarter Master, Performance Friction Brakes,
VP Racing

Teams:

ABEL MOTORSPORTS
3401 BASHFORD AVENUE COURT
LOUISVILLE, KY 40218
info@abelmotorsports.com
www.abelmotorsports.com
• Bill Abel, Contact

BN RACING
10031 VIRGINIA AVE
CHICAGO RIDGE, IL 60415
773-729-0296
• Bryn Nuttall, Contact

DEFORCE RACING
ONE PERFORMANCE DRIVE
ANGLETON, TX 77515
info@deforceracing.com
www.deforceracing.com
• Ernesto Martinez, Contact

EXCLUSIVE AUTOSPORT
PO BOX 32082
ERINDALE
SASKATOON, SK, CANADA S7S 1N8
www.exclusiveautosport.ca
• Michael Duncalfe, Contact

FATBOY RACING!
PO BOX 404
LOCUST VALLEY, NY 11560
brendan@fatboyracing.us
www.fatboyracing.us
• Brendan Puderbach, Contact

JAY HOWARD DRIVER DEVELOPMENT
305-915-7652
jay@jayhoward.com
www.jayhoward.com
• Jay Howard, Contact

JUNCOS RACING
4401 GILMAN STREET
INDIANAPOLIS, IN 46224
317-552-2967
info@juncosracing.com
www.juncosracing.com
• Ricardo Juncos, Contact

PABST RACING
35303 PABST ROAD
OCONOMOWOC, WI 53066
262-567-1771
information@pabstracing.com
www.pabstracing.com
• Augie Pabst, Contact

RP MOTORSPORT RACING
PIAZZA IV NOVEMBRE, 4
MILANO, ITALY, 20124
info@rpmotorsport.eu
rpmotorsportracing.com
• Fabio Pampado, Principal

INDYCAR
4551 W 16TH STREET
INDIANAPOLIS, IN 46222
317-492-6526
indycar@indycar.com
www.indycar.com

• Mark D. Miles, CEO
• Jay Frye, President
Description:
Founded 1994. Sanctions Indy 500 and
other races.

Teams:

A.J. FOYT RACING
19480 STOKES ROAD
WALLER, TX 77484
936-372-3698
info@ajfoytracing.com
www.foytracing.com
• A.J. Foyt, Owner
• Larry Foyt, President

ANDRETTI AUTOSPORT
INDIANAPOLIS, IN
pr@andrettiautosport.com
www.andrettiautosport.com
• Michael Andretti, CEO/Chair
• J-F Thormann, President
Sponsors:
DHL, Sun Drop, GoDaddy.com, Venom Energy
Drink, Window World, AirTran, Bryant Heating &
Cooling Systems, Dr. Pepper, ExactTarget,
Exel, OneAmerica, Palms, Peak Performance,
Conway, TLX, Inc., Snapple

ARROW MCLAREN SP
6803 COFFMAN ROAD
INDIANAPOLIS, IN 46268
317-209-0099
media@arrowmclarensp.com
arrowmclarensp.com
• Sam Schmidt, Co-Owner
• Ric Peterson, Co-Owner

CARLIN
7 COXBRIDGE BUSINESS PARK
ALTON ROAD
FARNHAM, SURREY, ENGLAND GU10 5EH
media@carlin.co.uk
www.carlin.co.uk
• Trevor Carlin, Founder
• Grahame Chilton, CEO

CHIP GANASSI RACING
7777 WOODLAND DRIVE
INDIANAPOLIS, IN 46278
317-802-0000
www.chipganassiracing.com
• Chip Ganassi, Owner/CEO
• Felix Sabates, Co-Owner
• Rob Kauffman, Co-Owner
• Mike Hull, Managing Director

DALE COYNE RACING
13400 S BUDLER ROAD
PLAINFIELD, IL 60544
dcrsupport@aol.com
dalecoyneracing.com
• Dale Coyne, Owner

**DALE COYNE RACING W/ VASSER
SULLIVAN**
13400 S BUDLER ROAD
PLAINFIELD, IL 60544
kdiamond@cvsindycar.com
dalecoyneracing.com
• Dale Coyne, Owner

ED CARPENTER RACING
7231 GEORGETOWN ROAD
INDIANAPOLIS, IN 46268
317-481-0195
Fax: 317-481-0322
www.edcarpenterracing.com
• Ed Carpenter, Owner
• Tim Broyles, General Manager

**MEYER SHANK RACING W/ ARROW
SPM**
114 VENTURE DRIVE
PATASKALA, OH 43062
740-964-9998
www.michaelshankracing.com
• Mike Shank, Owner
• Jim Meyer, Co-Owner

RAHAL LETTERMAN LANIGAN RACING
485 SOUTHPOINTE CIRCLE
SUITE 900
BROWNSBURG, IN 46112
317-858-3717
rahal.com
• David Letterman, Co-Owner
• Mike Lanigan, Co-Owner

TEAM PENSKE
200 PENSKE WAY
MOORESVILLE, NC 28115
www.teampenske.com
• Roger Penske, Founder/Chair

**LAMBORGHINI SUPER TROFEO NORTH
AMERICA**
VIA MODEN, 12
SANT'AGATA, BOLOGNESE, ITALY 40019
squadracorse.lamborghini.com/super-trofeo/
north-america
Description:
The Super Trofeo North America is a single
make racing series help at multiple circuits
across America.

**NASCAR (NATIONAL ASSOCIATION FOR
STOCK CAR AUTO RACING)**
DAYTONA BEACH, FL
www.nascar.com
• Jim France, Chairman/CEO
(305) 218-7839
Description:
Tracks include: Atlanta Motor Speedway,
Bristol Motor Speedway, Charlotte Motor
Speedway, Chicagoland Speedway,
Darlington Raceway, Daytona International
Speedway, Dover International Speedway,
Auto Club Speedway, Homestead-Miami
Speedway, O'Reilly Raceway Park, Iowa
Speedway, Kansas Speedwway, Kentucky
Speedway, Las Vegas Motor Speedway,
Gateway International Raceway, Michigan
International Speedway, Circuit Gilles
Villeneuve, Nashville Superspeedway, New
Hampshire Motor Speedway, Phoenix
International Raceway, Road America,
Richmond International Raceway, Talladega
Superspeedway, Texas Motor Speedway,
Watkins Glen International

NASCAR CUP SERIES
DAYTONA BEACH, FL
www.nascar.com/news/nascar-cup-series/se
ries
• Jim France, Chairman/CEO

Teams:

B.J. MCLEOD MOTORSPORTS
121 GOODWIN CIRCLE
MOORESVILLE, NC 28115
www.bjmcleodmotorsports.com

CHIP GANASSI RACING
8500 WESTMORELAND DRIVE NW
CONCORD, NC 28027
704-662-9642
www.chipganassiracing.com
• Chip Ganassi, Owner

FRONT ROW MOTORSPORTS
114 MEADOW HILL CIRCLE
MOORESVILLE, NC 28117
704-873-6445
Fax: 704-873-5120
www.teamfrm.com
• Bob Jenkins, Owner

GERMAIN RACING
299 AUSTIN LANE
LEXINGTON, NC 27295
336-731-8040
www.germainracing.com
• Bob Germain, Jr., Owner
• Matt Borland, Crew Chief

GO FAS RACING
www.gofasracing.com
• Archie St. Hilaire, Owner
• Ryan Sparkes, Crew Chief

HENDRICK MOTORSPORTS
4400 PAPA JOE HENDRICK BOULEVARD
CHARLOTTE, NC 28262
877-467-4890
www.hendrickmotorsports.com
• Rick Hendrick, Owner/Chair

JOE GIBBS RACING
13415 REESE BOULEVARD W
HUNTERSVILLE, NC 28078
joegibbsracing.com
• Joe Gibbs, Owner
• J.D. Gibbs, Co-Chairman
• Dave Alpern, President

JTG DAUGHERTY RACING
704-456-1221
jtgdaughertyracing.com
• Tad Geschickter, Owner
• Jodi Geschickter, Owner
• Brad Daugherty, Owner
• Gordon Smith, Owner

LEAVINE FAMILY RACING
6007 VICTORY LANE
CONCORD, NC 28027
medi@lfr95.com
www.lfr95.com
• Bob Leavine, Partner
• Matt Diliberto, Partner

MBM MOTORSPORTS
849 CONNOR STREET
STATESVILLE, NC 28677
www.mbmmotorsports.com
• Carl Long, Owner

PREMIUM MOTORSPORTS
222 RACEWAY DRIVE
MOORESVILLE, NC 28117
info@premiummotorsports.net
premiummotorsports.net
• Jay Robinson, Co-Owner
• Troy Stafford, Co-Owner
• Mark Bailey, Co-Owner
• Michael Sisk, Co-Owner

RICHARD CHILDRESS RACING
425 INDUSTRIAL DRIVE
WELCOME, NC 27374
info@rcrracing.com
www.rcrracing.com
• Richard Childress, Chairman/CEO
• Torrey Galida, President

RICHARD PETTY MOTORSPORTS
297 INDUSTRIAL DRIVE
LEXINGTON, NC 27265
richardpettymotorsports.com
• Richard Petty, Co-Owner
• Andrew Murstein, Co-Owner
• Brian Moffitt, CEO

RICK WARE RACING
111 SUNRISE CENTER
THOMASVILLE, NC 27360
wareracing.com
• Rick Ware, Owner

ROUSH FENWAY RACING
4600 ROUSH PLACE
CONCORD, NC 18027
social@roushfenway.com
www.roushfenway.com
• John Henry, Owner
• John W. Henry, Co-Owner

SPIRE MOTORSPORTS
19510 JETTON ROAD
SUITE 300
CORNELIUS, NC 28031
704-897-2880
spiresportsinc.com
• Jeff Dickerson, Co-Owner
• T.J. Puchyr, Co-Owner

STARCOM RACING
61 E WILLOW STREET
MILLBURN, NJ 07041
officeinfo@starcomracing.com
starcomracing.com
• Michael Kohler, CEO
• Matthew Kohler, President

STEWART-HAAS RACING
6001 HAAS WAY
KANNAPOLIS, NC 28081
704-652-4227
information@shracing.com
www.stewarthaasracing.com
• Tony Stewart, Co-Owner
• Gene Haas, Co-Owner

TEAM PENSKE
200 PENSKE WAY
MOORESVILLE, NC 28115
www.teampenske.com
• Roger Penske, Founder/Chairman

WOOD BROTHERS RACING
MOORESVILLE, NC
woodbrothersracing.com
• Eddie Wood, President/Co-Owner
• Glen Wood, Founder
• Len Wood, Executive VP/Co-Owner

Manufacturers:

CHEVROLET
www.chevrolet.com/motorsports/nascar

FORD
performance.ford.com/home.html

TOYOTA
www.trdusa.com/racing.html

**NASCAR GANDER OUTDOORS TRUCK
SERIES**
DAYTONA BEACH, FL
www.nascar.com/news/gander-outdoors-truck-series
• Jim France, Chairman/CEO

Teams:

AM RACING
2268 PEACHTREE ROAD
STATESVILLE, NC 28625
pr@amracing.racing
amracingteam.com
• Tim Self, Owner/President/CEO
• Eddie Troconis, Crew Chief

B.J. MCLEOD MOTORSPORTS
121 GOODWIN CIRCLE
MOORESVILLE, NC 28115
www.bjmcleodmotorsports.com

CHAD FINLEY RACING
11349 OLD US 27
DEWITT, MI 48820
www.chadfinley.com
• David Gilliland, Co-Owner
• Bo LeMastus, Co-Owner/CEO
• Bruce Cook, Crew Chief

DGR-CROSLEY
111 BYERS CREEK ROAD
MOORESVILLE, NC 28117
dgrcrosley.com
• David Gilliland, Co-Owner
• Bo LeMastus, Co-Owner

GMS RACING
310 AVIATION DRIVE
STATESVILLE, NC 28677
info@gmsracing.net
gmsracing.net
• Maury Gallagher, Co-Owner
• Spencer Gallagher, Co-Owner

HALMAR FRIESEN RACING
halmarracing.com
• Chris Larsen, Co-Owner
• Stewart Friesen, Co-Owner

HATTORI RACING ENTERPRISES
161 KNOB HILL ROAD
MOORESVILLE, NC 28117
704-663-0020
hre.us.com
• Shigeaki Hattori, Owner

JENNIFER JO COBB RACING
804A PERFORMANCE ROAD
MOORESVILLE, NC 28115
info@jenniferjocobb.com
www.cobbracingteam.com
• Jennifer Jo Cobb, Owner
• Steve Kuykendall, Crew Chief

JORDAN ANDERSON RACING
2668 PEACHTREE ROAD
STATESVILLE, NC 28625
jordanandersonracing.com
• Jordan Anderson, Owner

KYLE BUSCH MOTORSPORTS
351 MAZEPPA ROAD
MOORESVILLE, NC 28115
web@kylebusch.com
kylebuschmotorsports.com
• Kyle Busch, Owner
Other website:
www.kylebuschfoundation.org

NEMCO MOTORSPORTS
128 S IREDELL INDUSTRIAL PARK ROAD
MOORESVILLE, NC 28115
704-664-4287
nemcomotorsports.com
• Joe Nemechek, Owner

NIECE MOTORSPORTS
330 W AVIATION DRIVE
STATESVILLE, NC 28677
media@niecemotorsports.com
www.niecemotorsports.com
• Al Niece, Owner
• Phil Gould, Crew Chief

ON POINT MOTORSPORTS
3400 DENVER DRIVE
DENVER, NC 28037

704-966-0463
hjordan@onpmotorsports.com
onpmotorsports.com
• Steven Lane, Owner

REAUME BROTHERS RACING
1519 MECKLENBURG HIGHWAY
UNIT 221
MT. MOURNE, NC 28123-0331
www.reaumebrothersracing.com
• Josh Reaume, Owner

THORSPORT RACING
312 THORSPORT WAY
SANDUSKY, OH 44870
419-621-8800
info@thorsport.com
thorsport.com
• Duke Thorson, Co-Owner
• Rhonda Thorson, Co-Owner

YOUNG'S MOTORSPORTS
604 PERFORMANCE ROAD
MOORESVILLE, NC 28115
704-658-1019
info@youngsmotorsports.com
www.youngsmotorsports.com
• Randy Young, Owner

Manufacturers:

CHEVROLET
www.chevrolet.com/motorsports/nascar

FORD
performance.ford.com/home.html

TOYOTA
www.trdusa.com/racing.html

NASCAR PINTY'S SERIES
hometracks.nascar.com/international/pintys-series
Description:
NASCAR racing series in Canada, with one race in the United States.

NASCAR WHELEN ALL-AMERICAN SERIES
1-800-630-0535
hometracks.nascar.com/local/whelen-all-american-series
Description:
NASCAR-sanctioned local racetrack series operating in the United States and Canada.

NASCAR WHELEN MODIFIED TOUR
1-800-630-0535
hometracks.nascar.com/regional/whelen-modified-tour
Description:
Only open-wheeled division of NASCAR. Races are in the Northeast and Midwest.

NASCAR XFINITY SERIES
DAYTONA BEACH, FL
www.nascar.com/news/xfinity-series
• Jim France, Chairman/CEO

Teams:

B.J. MCLEOD MOTORSPORTS
121 GOODWIN CIRCLE
MOORESVILLE, NC 28115
www.bjmcleodmotorsports.com
• B.J. McLeod, Principal
• Kevyn Rebolledo, Crew Chief

BRANDONBILT MOTORSPORTS
FREDERICKSBURG, VA
• Jerry Brown,

DGM RACING
SAINT-MATHIEU-DE-BELOEIL, QC, CANADA
• Mario Gosselin, Owner

GMS RACING
310 AVIATION DRIVE
STATESVILLE, NC 28677
info@gmsracing.net
gmsracing.net
• Maury Gallagher, Co-Owner
• Spencer Gallagher, Co-Owner

JD MOTORSPORTS
1210 CHAMPION FERRY ROAD
GAFFNEY, SC 29341
864-488-1270
info@jdavismotorsports.com
www.teamjdmotorsports.com
• Johnny Davis, Co-Owner/General Manager
• Gary Keller, Co-Owner

JEREMY CLEMENTS RACING
71 COLDEN HILL ROAD
NEWBURGH, NY 12550
jeremyclements51.com
• Jeremy Clements, Co-Owner
• Tony Clements, Co-Owner

JIMMY MEANS RACING
FOREST CITY, NC
• Jimmy Means, Owner

JOE GIBBS RACING
13415 REESE BOULEVARD W
HUNTERSVILLE, NC 28078
joegibbsracing.com
• Joe Gibbs, Owner
• J.D. Gibbs, Co-Chairman
• Dave Alpern, President

JR MOTORSPORTS
349 CAYUGA DRIVE
MOORESVILLE, NC 28117
www.jrmracing.com
• Kelley Earnhardt Miller, Co-Owner/VP/Business Manager
• Dale Earnhardt, Jr., Co-Owner/President
• Rick Hendrick, Co-Owner

KAULIG RACING
PO BOX 1627
WELCOME, NC 27374
www.kauligracing.com
• Matt Kaulig, Owner
• Chris Rice, President

MBM MOTORSPORTS
849 CONNOR STREET
STATESVILLE, NC 28677
www.mbmmotorsports.com
• Carl Long, Owner

MIKE HARMON RACING
sites.google.com/view/mikeharmonracing74
• Mike Harmon, Owner

RICHARD CHILDRESS RACING
425 INDUSTRIAL DRIVE
WELCOME, NC 27374
336-731-3334 EXT 3101
info@rcrracing.com
www.rcrracing.com
• Richard Childress, Chairman/CEO
• Torrey Galida, President

RICK WARE RACING
111 SUNRISE CENTER DRIVE
THOMASVILLE, NC 27360
wareracing.com
• Rick Ware, Owner

RSS RACING
SUGAR HILL, GA
ryansiegracing.com
• Ryan Sieg, Principal

SS-GREEN LIGHT RACING
120 WILKINSON ROAD
MOORESVILLE, NC 28115
704-664-0808
www.ssgreenlight.com
• Bobby Dotter, Owner
• Ken Smith, Co-Owner
• Steve Urvan, Co-Owner

STEWART-HAAS RACING W/ BIAGI-DENBESTE
MOORESVILLE, NC
www.biagidenbesteracing.com
• Jon Hanson, Crew Chief
• Gene Haas, Co-Owner
• Fred Biagi, Co-Owner
• Greg Biagi, Co-Owner
• Bill DenBeste, Co-Owner
• Lori DenBeste, Co-Owner

TEAM PENSKE
200 PENSKE WAY
MOORESVILLE, NC 28115
www.teampenske.com
• Roger Penske, Founder/Chair

Manufacturers:

CHEVROLET
www.chevrolet.com/motorsports/nascar

FORD
performance.ford.com/home.html

TOYOTA
www.trdusa.com/racing.html

PORSCHE GT3 CUP CHALLENGE CANADA
INTERNATIONAL MOTORSPORTS CENTER
ONE DAYTONA BOULEVARD
DAYTONA BEACH, FL 32114
info@imsa.com
porschegt3cupcanada.imsa.com

PORSCHE GT3 CUP CHALLENGE USA
INTERNATIONAL MOTORSPORTS CENTER
ONE DAYTONA BOULEVARD
DAYTONA BEACH, FL 32114
info@imsa.com
porschegt3cupusa.imsa.com

Badminton Organizations

BADMINTON CANADA
700 INDUSTRIAL AVENUE
SUITE 401
OTTAWA, ON, CANADA K1G0Y9
613-569-2424
Fax: 613-748-5724
badminton@badminton.ca
www.badminton.ca

- Anil Kaul, President
- John Cowan, Vice President
- Martin Tam, Treasurer
- Mike Alexander, Director
- Jimena Gravelle, Events Manager

Membership Requirements:
Through provincial associations.

Description:
Responsible for developing world-class Canadian badminton players, coaches, officials and administrators; providing international and centralized support and/or leadership in furthering member association objectives; being the custodian, interpreter and adjudicator of the laws of Badminton in Canada.

BADMINTON PAN AM
AV. ANDRES REYES 437
OFICINA 601
LIMA, 27
51-99-422-5073
panambadminton@gmail.com
www.badmintonpanam.org
- Vishu Tolan, President
- Peter Golding, Deputy President
- Pilar Carrillo de la Fuente, Chief Operation Officer

Description:
Badminton Panam is the governing body of Badminton in the North, Central, and South Americas.

BADMINTON WORLD FEDERATION
AMODA BUILDING
22 JALAN IMBI
UNIT 17.05, LEVEL 17
KUALA LUMPUR, 55100
603-2141 7155
Fax: 603-2143 7155
bwf@bwfbadminton.org
www.bwfbadminton.org
- Thomas Lund, Chief Operating Officer
- Stuart Borrie, Director of Operations
- Darren Parks, Events Director
- Ian Wright, Development Manager
- Sharon Chan, Finance Manager

Description:
The Badminton World Federation acts as the international governing body for the sport badminton. The BWF serves to regulate, promote, develop and popularise the sport of badminton across the globe.

USA BADMINTON
ONE OLYMPIC PLAZA
COLORADO SPRINGS, CO 80909
719-866-4808
Fax: 719-866-4507
usab@usabadminton.org
www.teamusa.org/usa-badminton
- Fred Coleman, President
- Dan Cloppas, CEO/Secretary General
(719) 866-4808
dcloppas@aol.com
- Peggy Savosik, Director, Member & Financial Services
(719) 866-4808
- Mohan Subramaniam, Director, Coaching & High Performance
(719) 866-3642

Description:
USA Badminton is the organization recognized by the U.S. Olympic Committee for the purpose of selecting and training men's and women's teams to represent the U.S. in Olympic Games. They also select teams for the World Championships and other international competitions.

Bandy Organizations

USA BANDY
MINNEAPOLIS, MN 55425
952-883-0880
www.usabandy.com
- Chris Middlebrook, President
(612) 598-0966
- Andrew Knutson, Vice President
- Chris Halden, League Commissioner
- Kevin Bowen, Head Of Referees
- Scott Arundel, Rink Bandy League Commissioner
- Neal Logan, Referee Assessor

Description:
The governing body of the sport of bandy in the United States, and its representative in the International Bandy Federation.

Baseball Organizations

AMERICAN AMATEUR BASEBALL CONGRESS
555 E. MAIN ST.
FARMINGTON, NM 87401
505-327-3120
Fax: 505-327-3132
info@aabc.us
www.aabc.us
- Richard Neely, President
richardneely@aabc.us
- Mike Dimond, President Emeritus/Treasurer
mikedimond@aabc.us

Number of members:
240,000+

Member Services:
Composed of twelve different age divisions in the United States, Puerto Rico and Canada.

Publications:
Amateur Baseball News.

Membership Requirements:
Operates on a league concept. Each league must consist of at least 4 teams playing a minimum six game league schedule.

Description:
Founded in 1935. American Amateur Baseball Congress (AABC) is the largest amateur baseball organization in the United States for players above junior baseball age and the only amateur baseball program that provides progressive and continuous organized competition - sub teens through adults.

Divisions:
Roberto Clemente (8 and under); Willie Mays (10 and under); Pee Wee Reese (12 and under); Sandy Koufax (14 and under); Mickey Mantle (16 and under); Connie Mack (18 and under); and Stan Musial (unlimited age). Five national competitions are held in single age divisions.

AMERICAN BASEBALL COACHES ASSOCIATION
4101 PIEDMONT PARKWAY
GREENSBORO, NC 27410
336-821-3140
Fax: 336-886-0000
abca@abca.org
www.abca.org
- Craig Keilitz, Executive Director
(336) 821-3145
ckeilitz@abca.org
- Jon Litchfield, Deputy Executive Director
(336) 821-3142
jlitchfield@abca.org

Nature of Service:
ABCA assists in the promotion of baseball and acts as a sounding board and spokesperson on issues concerning the various levels of baseball. Further, the Association promotes camaraderie and rapport among all baseball coaches, including that between professional and amateur levels.

Membership Requirements:
High school, junior college, college or amateur baseball coaches.

Number of members:
15,000+

Membership Fees:
$75 a year for U.S. residents.

Publications:
Inside Pitch Magazine; Press Box weekly email; ABCA Instructional Coaching Books.

Year Founded:
1945

AMERICAN BASEBALL FOUNDATION
833 SAINT VINCENT'S DRIVE
SUITE 205A
BIRMINGHAM, AL 35205
205-558-4235
Fax: 205-918-0800
americanbaseballfoundation.com
- E.D. Osinski, Executive Director

Description:
The American Baseball Foundation Inc. delivers educational programs in two areas: a) injury prevention in youth baseball pitching; b) redressing summer learning loss among under-served children, ages 7 through 14, through its BASIC program which combines sport skill instruction with academics in reading and math all related to sports.

AMERICAN LEGION BASEBALL
700 N PENNSYLVANIA STREET
PO BOX 1055
INDIANAPOLIS, IN 46206
317-630-1200
800-433-3318
Fax: 317-630-1223
www.legion.org/baseball
- Paul E. Dillard, National Commander

Teams:
Over 3,400 teams across 50 states and Canada.

Members:
55,000 players and coaches.

Publications:
The Dugout E-Newsletter; The Dispatch; and Legion Magazine.

Year Founded:
1925

Membership Requirements:
Players must be under 19 years of age.

Description:
American Legion Baseball is an amateur league that hosts over 3,400 teams. Interestingly, most major league players played in the American Legion Baseball League. The purpose of American Legion

Baseball is to give young men an opportunity to develop their baseball skills.

ASSOCIATION OF PROFESSIONAL BALL PLAYERS OF AMERICA
23623 N SCOTTSDALE ROAD
SUITE 290
SCOTTSDALE, AZ 85255
602-730-4528
info@apbpa.org
apbpa.org
• Kameron Loe, President, Board of Directors
Nature of Service:
They provide financial assistance, educational and sobriety resources, mentors, networking, and support on multiple levels for life after baseball for professional baseball players, coaches, umpires, scouts and clubhouse men. No distinction is made between major league and minor league players. They have given out over $5 million in financial assistance since 1924.
Year Founded:
1924.
Clients Include:
Indy Ball, MiLB, MLB.
Membership Requirements:
Restricted to those who played or worked in professional baseball.
Membership Dues:
$150-currently on a Major League roster, $20-currently on a Minor League roster, $20-members no longer active in the game, $20-Scouts/Administrative personnel
Number of Members:
Over 101,500

BABE RUTH LEAGUE
670 WHITEHORSE-MERCERVILLE ROAD
HAMILTON, NJ 08619
609-695-1434
Fax: 609-695-2505
info@baberuthleague.org
www.baberuthleague.org
• Steven M. Tellefsen, President & CEO
Member Services:
Email Blasts & Bulletins; Media Guide, Rules and Regulations, Handbooks and miscellaneous materials.
Nature of Service:
Founded in 1951. Babe Ruth League, Inc., using regulation competitive baseball and softball rules, teaches skills, mental and physical development, a respect for the rules of the game, and basic ideals of sportsmanship and fair play. In all aspects, Babe Ruth League, Inc. is committed to providing its participants the very best educational sports experience possible. It is their fundamental belief that every child with a desire to play baseball or softball be afforded that opportunity. A baseball program for boys ages 13-15.
Sponsors:
BSN Sports; Rawlings.

BASEBALL ASSISTANCE TEAM
1271 AVENUE OF THE AMERICAS
NEW YORK, NY 10020
212-931-7822
Fax: 212-949-5433
bat@mlb.com
www.mlb.com/baseball-assistance-team
Description:
The primary objective of the Baseball

Assistance Team is to aid those members of the baseball family most in need. B.A.T. strives to provide a means of support to people who are unable to help themselves. Through charitable contributions from corporations, foundations and individuals, B.A.T. is there to assist those with financial, psychological or physical burdens.
Publications:
B.A.T. Newsletter, quarterly.
Year Founded:
1986

BASEBALL CANADA
2212 GLADWIN CRES
SUITE A7
OTTAWA, ON, CANADA K1B 5N1
613-748-5606
Fax: 613-748-5767
info@baseball.ca
www.baseball.ca
• Dickson Jason, CEO
• Greg Hamilton, Head Coach & Director, Men's National Teams
Incorporated
1964
Description:
Baseball Canada is the governing body for baseball in Canada. They are dedicated to developing and advancing baseball for all Canadians by promoting safety and ethics within the sport. Baseball Canada supports the achievement of excellence in baseball and prides itself on its focus on athletes. Baseball Canada strives to provide client programs that foster participation and involvement in baseball. Its programs allow participants to enjoy themselves and achieve their personal goals. They have also created 10 provincial associations which represent players, coaches and umpires.

BASEBALL FACTORY
7135 MINSTREL WAY
SUITE 102
COLUMBIA, MD 21045
410-715-5080
800-641-4487
Fax: 410-715-1975
www.baseballfactory.com
• Steve Sclafani, Founder & Chief Executive Officer
• Rob Naddelman, President
• Steve Bernhardt, Chief Baseball Officer
Major Sponsors:
Louisville Slugger; Diamond; FBR.com, Under Armour, Eyeblack.com.
Service Includes:
One day tryout at top facilities nationwide. They provide professional instruction, videotaping, pro-scout evaluations, placement counseling and targeted mail campaign to 50 colleges.
Description:
Offers a one-of-a-kind concept that provides baseball players nationwide with the very best in instruction, tournament competition, college planning and placement.
Programs:
Rookie program, B.A.T.S program, Player Development program, Exclusive program.
Member Services:
Timely recruiting information, program status information, account maintenance & transaction history and access to your pro scout evaluations.

Year Founded:
1994.

CONTINENTAL AMATEUR BASEBALL ASSOCIATION
PO BOX 1684
MT. PLEASANT, SC 29465
843-860-1568
info@cababaseball.com
www.cababaseball.org
• Larry Redwine, Chief Executive Officer
(513) 677-1580
cabaredwine@gmail.com
• John Rhodes, President & COO
(843) 860-1568
diamonddevils@aol.com
Nature of Sports Service:
The Continental Amateur Baseball Association was founded in 1984. The organizations objective is to promote a love of baseball and to provide a meeting place for tournament competitions at the state, regional and the World Series.
Membership Requirements:
CABA offers competition in individual age levels 8-16 and 18 and under. The high school division is established for players 17 and under regardless of class in school, along with players 18 years of age who will be returning to school in the fall following their tournament participation (as verified by the school's administrative authority). The Collegiate division CABA series teams are made up of players that were on some college level baseball team at any accredited college or university the previous season or are 22 years of age or under. However, a player must be at least 15 years of age on the day that they play in a CABA collegiate age
Publications:
Continental News, twice annually; Rule Books.
Member Services:
Computer statistical program package. World Series.
Membership Fee:
$35.00 (one time payment).

DIXIE BOYS BASEBALL
256 HONEYSUCKLE ROAD
SUITE 23
DOTHAN, AL 36305
334-793-3331
jjones29@sw.rr.com
baseball.dixie.org
• Sandy Jones, Commissioner & CEO
Description:
Founded in 1957. Primarily a youth baseball program for boys (ages 13-14 playing in a 80' diamond) and majors (ages 15-19 playing on a 90' diamond) to meet physical development of growing boys.

DIXIE YOUTH BASEBALL
256 HONEYSUCKLE ROAD
SUITE 23
DOTHAN, AL 36304
334-793-3331
youth.dixie.org
• William Wade, Commissioner
(334) 265-0294
• Kent Bruxvoort, President
(501) 279-8663
kent_bruxvoort@cargill.com
Description:
Promoting the development of strong

character, a positive attitude and a sense of responsibility and citizenship among youngsters since 1955.

DIZZY DEAN BASEBALL
2470 HWY 51 SOUTH
HERNANDO, MS 38632
dizzydeanbbinc.org
• Danny Phillips, Commissioner
(901) 262-2239
dannyphillips637@gmail.com
Description:
The organization is a non-profit youth group that promotes good sportsmanship and character to kids ages five through nineteen. The focus on local league play but do offer State and World series tournaments as well.
Founded:
1977.

LITTLE LEAGUE BASEBALL AND SOFTBALL
539 US ROUTE 15 HIGHWAY
PO BOX 3485
WILLIAMSPORT, PA 17701-0485
570-326-1921
Fax: 570-326-1074
www.littleleague.org
• Stephen D. Keener, President & CEO
• Hugh E. Tanner, Chairman
Description:
A non-profit organization whose mission is to promote, develop, supervise, and voluntarily assist in all lawful ways, the interest of those who will participate in Little League Baseball and Softball.
Membership Requirements:
Must be baseball or softball league players, ages 4 to 16.
Publications:
Little League Magazine, Little Leaguer Newsletter, World Series Programs (8 Divisions).
Member Services:
Official Playing and Tournament Rules. Safety Program. Annual meeting each November.
Number of Teams:
Over 180,000.
Founded:
1939 by Carl E. Stotz.

MAJOR LEAGUE BASEBALL PLAYERS ASSOCIATION
12 EAST 49TH STREET
24TH FLOOR
NEW YORK, NY 10017
212-826-0808
feedback@mlbpa.org
www.mlbplayers.com
• Tony Clark, Executive Director
Description:
Founded 1966. Serves as the labor organization representing all major league players with respect to terms and conditions of employment with major league clubs. (Also represents coaches, managers, and trainers for some purposes). In addition, the Players Association holds certain group licensing rights for all players and acts as a marketing representative for such rights.
Membership:
All players, managers, coaches and trainers who hold a signed contract with a Major League Club. Current membership includes players on the 40-person Major League rosters, as well as approximately 5,500

Minor League players employed by the 30 Major League baseball teams.

MAJOR LEAGUE BASEBALL UMPIRES ASSOCIATION
PO BOX 394
NEENAH, WI 54957
920-969-1580
Fax: 920-969-1892
• Bill Miller, President
• Ted Barrett, Vice President
Description:
Certified in 2000 by the National Labor Relations Board, the Major League Baseball Umpires Association (known as the World Umpires Association prior to 2018) is the bargaining agent for Major League Baseball's umpires.
Publications:
MLBUA; newsletter.

MAJOR LEAGUE BASEBALL/MLB
1271 AVENUE OF THE AMERICAS
NEW YORK, NY 10020
212-931-7800
866-800-1275
customerservice@website.mlb.com
www.mlb.com
• Rob Manfred, Jr., Commissioner of Baseball
• Dan Halem, Dep. Comm., Baseball Admin. & Chief Legal Officer
• Pat Courtney, Chief Communications Officer
Description:
Formed in 2000, Major League Baseball (MLB) focused on the worldwide growth of baseball through game development, broadcasting, special events, sponsorship and licensing.
Additional Offices:
China; Europe; India; Japan; Korea; and Mexico.
Newsletters:
MLB Ballpark; MLB Morning Lineup; MLB Insider.

MINOR LEAGUE BASEBALL
1271 AVENUE OF THE AMERICAS
NEW YORK, NY 10020
866-644-2687
customerservice@website.milb.com
www.milb.com
• Tim Brunswick, SVP, Baseball & Business Operations
• Brian Earle, Chief Operating Officer
Description:
Founded in 1901. Oversees operations of minor league professional baseball teams. Assists in increasing attendance for member clubs. Arbitrates disputes on rules and contracts. Promotes and protects the interests of players and umpires. MiLB consists of 120 teams across the United States, Canada and the Dominican Republic.
Membership Requirements:
Approved franchise in one of the member leagues.
Publications:
Minor League Baseball Information Guide; annual.
Number of members:
120 teams
Uniform Suppliers:
Diamond Sports, Jersey Express, Majestic Athletic, OT Sports, Rawlings, Russell

Athletic, Wilson Sporting Goods.
Sponsors:
AMI Graphics, LLC, Baseball America, Barton Malow Design/Construction Services.
Charity Partners:
ALS Association, Big Brothers Big Sisters, Special Olympics.
Nature of Service:
Professional baseball.
Clients Include:
Esurance, Crayola, John Deere, Bush's Beans, ServiceMaster, SunRun, Gallo Wines, FIS.

NATIONAL AMATEUR BASEBALL FEDERATION
5500 PLAZA DR
SUITE B
FLOWOOD, MS 39232
769-251-5158
www.nabf.com
• Derek J. Topik, Executive Director
(769) 251-5158
nabfexecdirector@gmail.com
• Paul Wolf, President
Number of members:
103,000
Member Services:
Eight Annual World Series and Tournaments and over 50 Regional Tournaments - Rookie Div (10 and under), Freshman Div (12 and under), Sophomore Div (14 and under), Junior Div (16 and under), High School Div, Senior (18 and under) Div, College Div (22 and under), Major (unlimited age) Div.
Publications:
Behind the Seams; 3 times annually. Tournament News; October annually.
Membership Requirements:
Leagues having four or more teams (amateur status); Associations that support amateur baseball and leagues.
Description:
Established in 1914, a nonprofit organization, hosts regional and national Championship tournaments held coast to coast.
Sponsors:
Baseball Warehouse, Baseball Factory, Rawlings, Louisville Slugger.

NATIONAL BASEBALL CONGRESS
300 N MEAD
SUITE 109
WICHITA, KS 67202
316-265-6236
nbcbaseball.com
• Sherii Farmer, Chair
Description:
Founded in 1935. Sanctions a series of state championships, semi-professional baseball tournaments leading to the national title tournament, the NBC World Series. Supplier of baseballs and equipment. One of the largest administering bodies for summer leagues and non-professional baseball.
Membership:
Sixteen member leagues in the U.S. and Canada.
Publications:
Official Baseball Rule Book.

NATIONAL HIGH SCHOOL BASEBALL COACHES ASSOCIATION
PO BOX 12843
TEMPE, AZ 85284
614-764-5800
contact_us@baseballcoaches.org
www.baseballcoaches.org
• Tim Saunders, Executive Director
tsaunders@baseballcoaches.org
Member Services:
Educational clinics; seminars; coach-of-the-year honors; hall of fame recognition; sponsor benefits; coaching enhancement exposure; annual meetings.
Membership Requirements:
Through state high school coaches' associations or directly by individual coaches.
Description:
Formed to provide services and recognition for baseball coaches and to help promote and represent high school baseball.
Sponsors:
Killebrew Rootbeer, BSN, Jostens, Baseball America, Turface, Smushballs, Phoenix Bats, GameSense Sports, Pitchkount, Baseball Rules in Black and White, Mindfulplayer, Ace Batting Tee, Relation Insurance.
Membership Publications:
Newsletter; a coaching instructional publication; BCA directory on the website. Officially formed in 1991.

NATIONAL JUNIOR COLLEGE ATHLETIC ASSOCIATION
8801 JM KEYNES DRIVE
SUITE 450
CHARLOTTE, NC 28262
719-590-9788
www.njcaa.org
• Christopher Parker, President & CEO
Description:
The program provides athletic participation in an environment that supports equitable opportunities consistent with the educational objectives of member colleges. The NCJAA is the leader in championing academic and athletic opportunities for student-athletes.

PEORIA DIAMOND CLUB
16101 N 83RD AVENUE
SUITE 2
PEORIA, AZ 85382
623-773-8710
info@peoriadiamondclub.org
peoriadiamondclub.org
• Roz Shanley, General Manager
Year Founded:
1993
Description:
Supplies operational support for the Spring Training of the Seattle Mainers and the San Diego Padres at the Peoria Sports Complex. Formed in response to the desire of the Seattle Mariners and the San Diego Padres to have a non-profit organization handle the operation of the Complex during their Spring Training.
Members:
500+ volunteer members

PONY BASEBALL AND SOFTBALL
1951 PONY PLACE
WASHINGTON, PA 15301
724-225-1060
Fax: 724-225-9852

info@pony.org
www.pony.org
• Abraham Key, President
a.key@pony.org
• Brent Liberatore, Chairman, Information Technology
b.liberatore@pony.org
Description:
Founded in 1951. Sponsors international amateur youth baseball and softball programs. PONY Baseball and Softball is designed to Protect Our Nation's Youth by providing experiences in youth baseball and softball that will help young people grow into healthier and happier adults.

PROFESSIONAL BASEBALL ATHLETIC TRAINERS SOCIETY
2970 CLAIRMONT RD.
SUITE 575
ATLANTA, GA 30329
404-875-4000 EXT 203
Fax: 404-892-8560
pbats.com
• Ron Porterfield, President
Number of Members:
63
Publications:
PBATS Newsletter; a semi-annual publication.
Member Services:
The mission of the Professional Baseball Athletic Trainers Society is to serve as an educational resource for the Major League and Minor League baseball athletic trainers. PBATS serves its members by providing for the continued education of the athletic trainer as it relates to the profession, helping improve his understanding of sports medicine so as to better promote the health of his constituency—professional baseball players. PBATS also serves as a resource to educate those outside the professional baseball athletic trainer community about the profession and about the athletic trainer's integral position within the sports medicine team.
Corporate Sponsorship:
EBI Sports Medicine.
Sponsors:
Major League Baseball, The James E. Olson Foundation, Cap CURE, Oral Health America's National Spit Tabacco Education Program, NATA, American Academy of Orthopaedic Surgeons.

PROFESSIONAL BASEBALL UMPIRE CORPORATION
9550 16TH STREET N
ST. PETERSBURG, FL 33716
877-799-8677
Fax: 727-456-1745
info@milbumpireacademy.com
www.milbumpireacademy.com
• Dusty Dellinger, Director
• Jess Schneider, Manager, Umpire Operations
Year Founded:
1999
Publications:
Manual for the Two-Umpire System, Professional Baseball Umpire Program Manual
Description:
Organization is responsible for training, evaluation, and recommendations for promotions, retentions or release of all

umpires in the minor league baseball system throughout the U.S. and Canada.

RANDY HUNDLEY'S FANTASY CAMPS, INC.
2118 PLUM GROVE ROAD
SUITE 285
ROLLING MEADOWS, IL 60008
847-991-9595
lori@cubsfantasycamp.com
www.cubsfantasycamp.com
• Randy Hundley, President
Requirements:
Any adult over 30 years old.
Nature of Services:
For years, Randy Hundley's Fantasy Baseball Camps have earned the highest form of praise. Our camp recreates an authentic major league experience. Randy Hundley's Fantasy Baseball Camp is the original fantasy camp.

SOCIETY FOR AMERICAN BASEBALL RESEARCH
555 N CENTRAL AVENUE
SUITE 416
PHOENIX, AZ 85004
602-496-1460
www.sabr.org
• Scott Bush, Chief Executive Officer
sbush@sabr.org
• Scott Carter, Executive Vice President
scarter@sabr.org
• Jacob Pomrenke, Director of Editorial Content
jpomrenke@sabr.org
Number of members:
6,000+
Member Services:
Numerous regional meetings; microfilm lending library; research exchange; research committees - Negro Leagues, Ball Parks, Biographical Research, Minor Leagues, Bibliography, Umpire and Rules, Oral History, Women in Baseball, Records, Statistical Analysis and Pictorial History. Latin America, Baseball Songs and Poems.
Publications:
The Baseball Research Journal; The National Pastime; Baltimore Baseball.
Membership Requirements:
Interest in professional baseball.
Description:
The purpose of SABR is to foster the research, preservation and dissemination of the history and records of baseball.
Year Founded:
1971

T-BALL USA ASSOCIATION
WEST PALM BEACH, FL 33401
teeballusa@aol.com
www.teeballusa.org
Description:
The national not-for-profit youth sports organization dedicated to the development of the game of tee ball. They offer a broad variety of programs and services and are the center for information on how to improve existing tee ball programs and establish new ones.
Ages for Playing Tee Ball:
Recommended ages are 3 1/2 through 7.

USA BASEBALL
2933 SOUTH MIAMI BLVD
SUITE 119
DURHAM, NC 27703
919-474-8721
Fax: 919-925-6108
info@usabaseball.com
www.usabaseball.com
• Paul Seiler, Executive Director & CEO
Description:
USA Baseball serves as the national governing body for the sport, and represents American baseball as a member of the United States Olympic Committee and the International Baseball Federation.
Publications:
USA Baseball National Team Yearbook, annual.
Member Services:
Selects official U.S.A. Baseball Teams, Sr. National Team, Jr (18-under), National Team, Youth National Team (16-under) for international competition.
Year Founded:
1978
Official Partners:
Gatorade, Greater Raleigh Sports Alliance, Next College Student Athlete (NCSA), Panini.

WORLD BASEBALL SOFTBALL CONFEDERATION
AVENUE GENERAL-GUISAN, 45
PULLY, SWITZERLAN CH-1009
+41-21 318 8240
Fax: +41-21 318 8241
office@wbsc.org
www.wbsc.org
• Riccardo Fraccari, President
• Beng Choo Low, Secretary General
Description:
World governing body for baseball and softball.

Baseball, Professional Leagues/Teams: Major

MAJOR LEAGUE BASEBALL/MLB
1271 AVENUE OF THE AMERICAS
NEW YORK, NY 10020
212-931-7800
866-800-1275
customerservice@website.mlb.com
www.mlb.com
• Rob Manfred, Commissioner of Baseball
• Dan Halem, Dep. Comm., Baseball Admin. & Chief Legal Officer
• Pat Courtney, Chief Communications Officer
Nature of Service:
Administrates professional baseball. Established and enforces rules regarding franchise operation. Supervises national radio and television contracts. Handles publicity and marketing of baseball and legal matters pertaining to baseball as an industry. Operates the World Series and All-Star games.
Membership Requirements:
Teams operating in the American or National Leagues.
Year Founded:
1903

AMERICAN LEAGUE OF PROFESSIONAL BASEBALL CLUBS, THE
1271 AVENUE OF THE AMERICAS
NEW YORK, NY 10020
866-800-1275
customerservice@website.mlb.com
www.mlb.com
• Robert D. Manfred, Baseball Commisioner
• Dan Halem, Deputy Commissioner, Baseball Admin.
Description:
The American League is the younger of two leagues comprising Major League Baseball (the other is the National League).
Teams:
15: United States (14) and Canada (1).
Year Founded:
1901.

Teams:

BALTIMORE ORIOLES
ORIOLE PARK AT CAMDEN YARDS
333 W CAMDEN STREET
BALTIMORE, MD 21201
410-685-9800
888-848-BIRD
Fax: 410-547-6277
birdmail@orioles.com
orioles.com
• John P. Angelos, Chair & Managing Partner
• Mike Elias, Executive VP & General Manager
• Eve Rosenbaum, Assistant General Manager
• Lindsay Henkel, Senior VP, Business Development
• Bob Ames, Senior Vice President, Chief Finanical Officer
• Scott Barringer, Head Athletic Trainer
• Koby Perez, VP, International Scouting & Operations
• Kent Qualls, Director, Minor League Operations
• Clay Plier, Assistant Head Groundskeeper
• Jennifer Grondahl, Senior VP, Development & Communications
• Troy Scott, VP, Ballpark Operations & Security
Stadium:
Oriole Park at Camden Yards became the official home of the Orioles on April 6, 1992. The construction of the park was completed in essentially 33 months. Seating capacity of 45,971.

BOSTON RED SOX
4 JERSEY STREET
BOSTON, MA 02215-3496
617-226-6000
www.mlb.com/redsox/
• John W. Henry, Principal Owner
• Thomas C. Werner, Chair
• Sam Kennedy, President & CEO
• Brian O'Halloran, EVP, Baseball Operations
• Tim Zue, EVP & Chief Financial Officer
• Jonathan Gilula, EVP & COO
• Ed Weiss, EVP, Corporate Strategy & General Counsel
• Raquel Ferreira, EVP & Assistant General Manager
• Pete Nesbit, SVP, Ballpark Operations
• Ben Crockett, SVP, Baseball Operations
• Gus Quattlebaum, VP, Scouting Development & Integration
• Jonathan Lister, VP, Facilities Management
Stadium:
Fenway Park - opened April 20, 1912. Seating capacity - 37,755. Fenway Park is actually the second home for the Sox. In 1901, the Boston Americans became one of the charter members of the fledgling American League. The Americans played ball at the Huntington Avenue Grounds, now a part of Northeastern University's campus.

CHICAGO WHITE SOX
US CELLULAR FIELD
333 W 35TH STREET
CHICAGO, IL 60616

312-674-1000
866-SOX-GAME
www.mlb.com/whitesox
• Chris Getz, SVP & General Manager
• Josh Barfield, Assistant General Manager
• Jin Wong, Assistant General Manager
• Dan Fabian, Senior Dir., Baseball Operations
• Tim Buzard, Senior VP, Administration
• Terry Savarise, Senior VP, Stadium Operations
• Scott Reifert, Senior VP, Communications
• Cris Quintana, Senior Director, Broadcasting
• Jo Simmons, Manager, Business Development
• Christine O'Reilly-Riordan, VP, Community Relations & ED, Charities
• John Corvino, VP, General Counsel
• Roger Bossard, Head Groundskeeper
• George McDoniel, Senior Dir., Corporate Partnerships Sales
• Kathy Potoski, Director, Minor League Administration
• Paul Janish, Director, Player Development
Stadium:
Guaranteed Rate Field. Opened on April 18, 1991. Seating capacity 40,615.

CLEVELAND GUARDIANS
PROGRESSIVE FIELD
2401 ONTARIO STREET
CLEVELAND, OH 44115
216-420-4487
www.mlb.com/guardians
• Chris Antonetti, President, Baseball Operations
• Brian Barren, President, Business Operations
• Mike Chernoff, General Manager
• Rich Dorffer, Senior VP, Finance & CFO
• Bob DiBiasio, Senior VP, Public Affairs
• Jim Folk, VP, Ballpark Improvements
• Max Kosman, VP, General Counsel
• Curtis Danburg, VP, Communications & Community Impact
• Richard Conway, Director, International Scouting
• Bart Swain, Director, Baseball Information & Player Relations
• Brandon Koehnke, Senior Director, Groundskeeping
• Ilana Mishkin, Assistant Director, Player Development
• Tony Amato, Home Clubhouse/Equipment Manager
• Mark Schickendantz, MD, Head Team Physician
Stadium:
Professional baseball in Cleveland is one of the city's oldest traditions, dating back to 1869. There is a passionate connection between the city of Cleveland and the Guardians (known as the Indians until 2021), as they are a study in revival. Both are working, living examples of the power of teamwork, conviction and dedication. Progressive Field is a Cleveland landmark that offers a fan-friendly facility within an intimate environment. Opened in 1994. Seating capacity 34,631.

DETROIT TIGERS
COMERICA PARK
2100 WOODWARD AVENUE
DETROIT, MI 48201-3470
313-471-7000
www.mlb.com/tigers/
• Christopher Ilitch, Chair & CEO
• Scott Harris, President, Baseball Operations
• Mike Singer, Senior VP, Corporate Partnerships
• Chris Lawrence, VP, Park Operations
• Zach Burek, Director, Business Development
• Mark Conner, Director, Amateur Scouting
• Taylor Olson, Director, Marketing
• Mike Bacallao, Associate Legal Counsel
• Scott Bream, Senior Advisor to the President & General Manager
Stadium:
Comerica Park which opened in 2000 was built around the configuration of the playing field. The design of the park was planned with the fan

sight lines as the highest priority. Seating capacity: 41,083.

HOUSTON ASTROS
DAIKIN PARK
501 CRAWFORD ST
HOUSTON, TX 77002
713-259-8000
www.mlb.com/astros/
• Jim Crane, Owner & Chair
• Dana Brown, General Manager
• Matt Hogan, Senior Director, Player Personnel
• Anita Sehgal, Senior VP, Marketing & Communications
• Marcel Braithwaite, Senior VP, Business Operations
• Michael Slaughter, Senior VP, Chief Financial Officer
• Matt Brand, Senior VP, Corporate Partnerships
• Doug Seckel, VP, Finance
• Gene Dias, VP, Communications
• Creighton Kahoalii, SVP, Affiliate Business Operations
• Giles Kibbe, Senior VP & General Counsel
Stadium:
Minute Maid Park. Seating capacity of 41,168.

KANSAS CITY ROYALS
KAUFFMAN STADIUM
ONE ROYAL WAY
KANSAS CITY, MO 64129
816-921-8000
Fax: 816-921-5775
fanfeedback@royals.com
www.mlb.com/royals
• John Sherman, Chair & CEO
• R. Brooks Sherman Jr., President, Business Operations
• J.J. Picollo, Executive Vice President & General Manager
• Scott Sharp, Sr. Vice President & Assistant GM
• Brian Himstedt, VP, Technology & Business Analytics
• George Brett, VP, Baseball Operations
• Bryan Ross, Senior Director, Ballpark Operations
• Sarah Feldkamp, Director, Finance
• Nick Kappel, Director, Media Relations
• Mike Arbuckle, Sr. Advisor To Gen. Mngr., Scouting & Player Devt.
• Vincent Key, Head Team Physician
Stadium:
Kauffman Stadium, opened on April 10, 1973, has a seating capacity of 37,903.

LOS ANGELES ANGELS OF ANAHEIM
ANGEL STADIUM OF ANAHEIM
2000 GENE AUTRY WAY
ANAHEIM, CA 92806
714-940-2000
888-796-4256
www.mlb.com/angels
• Arte Moreno, Owner
• Carole Moreno, Owner
• John Carpino, President
• Perry Minasian, General Manager
• Brian Sanders, Vice President, Ballpark Operations
• Molly Jolly, Senior VP, Finance & Administration
• Mike Fach, Vice President, Corporate Partnerships
Stadium:
Angel Stadium opened in April 9, 1966, and was renovated on April, 1998. Some unique features include terraced bullpens in the outfield, widened concourses, new restroom and concession areas, a large and updated press box and three full-service restaurants. Seating capacity: 45,517.

MINNESOTA TWINS
TARGET FIELD
1 TWINS WAY
MINNEAPOLIS, MN 55403

612-659-3400
800-33-TWINS
www.mlb.com/twins
• Dave St. Peter, President & CEO
• Jim Pohlad, Chair
• Jeremy Zoll, General Manager
• Derek Falvey, President, Baseball Operations
• Andy Weinstein, VP, Finance
• Paul Froehle, VP, Ticket Operations
• Victor Gonzalez, Assistant Director, Florida & Dominican Operations
• Mary Giesler, Special Counsel
Seating Capacity:
Target Field. Seating capacity: 38,544.
Stadium Opened:
2010
Publications:
Line Drives newsletter.

NEW YORK YANKEES
YANKEE STADIUM
ONE E 161ST STREET
BRONX, NY 10451
212-926-5337
www.mlb.com/yankees
• Randy Levine, Esq., President
• Lonn A. Trost, Esq., COO
• Brian Cashman, Senior VP & General Manager
• Deborah A. Tymon, Senior VP, Marketing
• Anthony Bruno, Senior VP & Yankee Global Enterprises CFO
• Brian Smith, Senior VP, Corporate/Community Relations
• Doug Behar, Senior VP, Stadium Operations
• Irfan Kirimca, Executive Director, Ticket Operations
Stadium:
The original Yankee Stadium opened in 1923, and in 2009 new Yankee Stadium opened just in time for opening day. Seating capacity: 46,537.
Publications:
The Final Season: The Official Retrospective, Official Opening Day Game Program, New York Yankees Official Yearbook, Yankees Magazine, Official New York Yankees Media Guides, and The Stadium Magazine Box Set
Yankee Foundation:
Founded in 1973, the New York Yankee Foundation donates funds for educational and recreational programs to youth organizations throughout New York.

OAKLAND ATHLETICS
400 BALLPARK DRIVE
WEST SACRAMENTO, CA 95691
510-638-4900
guestservices@athletics.com
www.mlb.com/athletics
• John Fisher, Owner
• Sandy Dean, Interim President
president@athletics.com
• David Forst, General Manager
• Dan Feinstein, Asst. General Manager, Major League
• Billy Owens, Asst. General Manager/Dir. of Player Personnel
• Catherine Aker, VP, Marketing & Communications
• David Rinetti, Vice President, Stadium Operations
• Kasey Jarcik, Senior Director, Finance
• Jeffrey Collins, Head Athletic Trainer
• Miguel Duarte, Chief of Staff
• Ellis D'Lonra, Chief Legal Officer
• Ed Sprague, Director, Player Development
• Steve Fanelli, VP, Sales & Business Operations
Stadium:
Oakland Coliseum opened on September 8, 1966 and was renovated in 1995, which added 22,000 seats, 90 luxury suites, two private clubs and two state-of-the-art scoreboards. Seating capacity: 46,847.

SEATTLE MARINERS
1250 1ST AVENUE SOUTH
SEATTLE, WA 98134

206-346-4001
www.mlb.com/mariners
• John Stanton, Chair & Managing Partner
• Kevin Martinez, President, Business Operations
• Tim Kornegay, Executive VP & CFO
• Justin Hollander, Executive VP & General Manager
• Trevor Gooby, Executive VP & COO
• Andy McKay, Vice President & Assistant General Manager
• Malcolm Rogel, Vice President, Fan Experience
• Kyle Torgerson, Head Athletic Trainer
Stadium:
T-Mobile Park (originally named Safeco Field). Seating capacity: 47,929.

TAMPA BAY RAYS
TROPICANA FIELD
ONE TROPICANA DRIVE
ST. PETERSBURG, FL 33705
888-326-7297
customerservice@raysbaseball.com
www.mlb.com/rays
• Stuart L. Sternberg, Principal Owner
• Matthew Silverman, Co-President
• Brian Auld, Co-President
• Erik Neander, President, Baseball Operations
• John Higgins, Senior VP, Administration/General Counsel
• Patrick Abts, VP, Marketing
• Melanie Lenz, Chief Planning & Development Officer
• Daveid Egles, Executive Director, Rays Baseball Foundation
• Rafaela Amador Fink, Chief Public Affairs & Communications Officer
• Jim Previtera, Senior Director, Team Security
• Ken Mallory, Administrator, Baseball Operations
• Rob Gagliardi, Chief Financial Officer
Stadium:
Tropicana Field, renovated in 1996, added 319,000 additional square feet of space and was again renovated in 2006. Various renovations included new bathrooms, lighting, fixtures, wall treatments, new premium seating club, changes to the press box and much more. Seating capacity: 25,000 (42,735 including tarp-covered seats). The fiberglass roof of Tropicana Field was mostly destroyed during Hurricane Milton in 2024, leaving the future of the stadium in question.

TEXAS RANGERS
GLOBE LIFE FIELD
734 STADIUM DRIVE
ARLINGTON, TX 76011
817-533-1972
guestservices@texasrangers.com
www.mlb.com/rangers
• Neil Leibman, CEO
• Ray C. Davis, Managing Partner & Majority Owner
• Bob R. Simpson, Chair, Executive Committee
• Chris Young, President, Baseball Operations
• Sean Decker, President, REV Entertainment
• Ross Fenstermaker, General Manager
• Travis Dillon, SVP, Marketing
• Rob Matwick, EVP, Business Operations
• Jim Cochrane, EVP & Chief Business Officer
• Kellie Fischer, EVP/Chief Financial Officer
• Chuck Morgan, EVP, Ballpark Entertainment & Productions
• Mike Healy, EVP, Venue Operations & Guest Experience
• Mike Lentz, Senior Director, Ticket Operations
• Keith Meister, Team Physician
Stadium:
Global Life Field. Seating capacity: 40,300.

TORONTO BLUE JAYS
ROGERS CENTRE
1 BLUE JAYS WAY
SUITE 3200
TORONTO, ON, CANADA M5V 1J1

416-341-1234
888-654-6529
bluejays.com
• Mark A. Shapiro, President & CEO
• Edward Rogers, Chair of the Board
• Ross Atkins, Exec. VP, Baseball Operations & General Manager
• Andrew Tinnish, VP, International Scouting & Baseball Operations
• Marnie Starkman, Executive VP, Business Operations
• Ben Sibley, Director, Marketing, Communications & Lotteries
Stadium:
Rogers Centre, a recently renovated stadium includes the TD Clubhouse, Batting Tunnel Club, Home Plate Club, and The Lounge. Also includes an Outfield District area with five distinct neighbourhoods and social spaces. Seating capacity 49,286.

NATIONAL LEAGUE OF PROFESSIONAL BASEBALL CLUBS, THE
MLB ADVANCED MEDIA, L.P.
1271 AVENUE OF THE AMERICAS
NEW YORK, NY 10020
212-931-7800
customerservice@website.mlb.com
www.mlb.com
• Rob Manfred, Commissioner
• Dan Halem, Chief Legal Officer & Deputy Commissioner
• Tony Reagins, Chief Baseball Development Officer
• Chris Marinak, Chief Operations & Strategy Officer
• Patrick Courtney, Chief Communications Officer
• Ed Weber, Chief Financial Officer
• Noah Garden, Deputy Commissioner, Business & Media
  Description:
  The National League of Professional Baseball Clubs is the older of the two leagues constituting Major League Baseball in the United States of America and Canada. (The other major league is the American League.) Beginning with the 1903 season, the regular season champions of the two leagues have met in the World Series. (The Series was not played in either 1904 or 1994.)
  Year Founded:
  1876

Teams:

ARIZONA DIAMONDBACKS
CHASE FIELD
401 E. JEFFERSON STREET
PHOENIX, AZ 85004
602-462-6500
www.mlb.com/dbacks
• Derrick Hall, President, CEO & General Partner
• Ken Kendrick, Managing General Partner
• Mike Chipman, General Partner
• Jeff Royer, General Partner
• Mike Hazen, Executive VP/General Manager
• Kenny Farrell, Senior VP, Marketing & Analytics
• Cullen Maxey, Executive VP, Business Ops/Chief Revenue Officer
• Mike Dellosa, VP, Ticket Sales & Service
• Josh Simon, VP, Ticket Operations
• Tom Harris, Executive VP/Chief Financial Officer
• Joe Walsh, Senior VP, People & Culture
• Bob Zweig, Senior VP & Chief Technology Officer
• Casey Wilcox, VP, Communications
• Kristyn Pierce, Director, Baseball Administration
• Jason Parks, Director, Professional Scouting
• Peter Wardell, Director, International Scouting
Stadium:
Chase Field. The most notable features of Chase Field are its signature swimming pool and its retractable roof. Since March 31, 1998, nearly 18 million fans have taken advantage of the opportunity to watch the Diamondbacks

without the fear of getting rained on or worrying about the Phoenix heat. Stadium capacity: 48,330.

ATLANTA BRAVES
TRUIST PARK
755 BATTERY AVENUE
ATLANTA, GA 30339
404-577-9100
www.mlb.com/braves
• Terry McGuirk, Chair
• Derek Schiller, President/CEO
• Alex Anthopoulos, President, Baseball Operations & General Manager
• Adam Zimmerman, Senior VP, Marketing & Content
• Anthony Esposito, Senior VP, Ticket Operations
• Jill Robinson, Executive VP/Chief Financial Officer
• Scott Waid, Senior VP, Head Of Technology Services
• Greg Heller, Executive VP/Chief Legal Officer
• DeRetta Rhodes, PhD, Executive VP & Chief Culture Officer
• George C. Poulis, Director, Player Health/Head Athletic Trainer
• Lee Kneer, Head Team Physician
Stadium:
Truist Park. Seating capacity: 41,084.
Publications:
Braves Beat; ChopTalk

CHICAGO CUBS
WRIGLEY FIELD
1060 W ADDISON STREET
CHICAGO, IL 60613-4397
773-404-2827
fanservices@cubs.com
www.mlb.com/cubs/
• Tom Ricketts, Chair
• Jed Hoyer, President, Baseball Operations
• Crane Kenney, President, Business Operations
• Carter Hawkins, General Manager
• Alex Sugarman, Executive VP, Business Ops./Chief Strategy Officer
• Dan Kantrovitz, VP, Scouting
• Colin Faulkner, Executive VP & Chief Commercial Officer
• Jon Greifenkamp, Executive VP, Chief Financial Officer
• Michael Lufrano, EVP, Community & Govt. Affairs/Chief Legal Officer
• Matt Dorey, VP, Player Personnel
• Louis Eljaua, VP, International Scouting
• Steve Inman, VP, Technology
• John Steinmillr, Senior Director, Media Relations
• Nick Frangella, Head Athletic Trainer
• Stephen Gryzlo, MD, Head Team Physician
Stadium:
Wrigley Field, built in 1914, is the second-oldest ballpark in the Major League behind Boston's Fenway Park (1912). In 2009, Wrigley Field will be playing host to Major League Baseball for the 96th season, and to the Cubs for the 94th year. Historic moments that have taken place in Wrigley Field include: Babe Ruth's 'called shot' during Game 3 of the 1932 World Series, Ernie Banks' 500th career home run on May 12, 1970, and Kerry Wood's 20-strikeout affair in 1998. Stadium capacity, 41,649.

CINCINNATI REDS
GREAT AMERICAN BALL PARK
100 JOE NUXHALL WAY
CINCINNATI, OH 45202
513-765-7000
ticketservices@reds.com
www.mlb.com/reds
• Robert H. Castellini, Principal Owner & Managing Partner
• Joseph W. Williams, Chair
• Phillip J. Castellini, President/CEO
• Nick Krall, President, Baseball Operations
• Mark Edwards, Director, Baseball Operations
• Karen Forgus, Chief Communications &

Community Officer
• Jacob Widerschein, VP, Ticket Operations
• Doug Healy, COO & CFO
• Larry Herms, Senior Director, Media Relations
• Jeff Graupe, VP & Asst. GM, Player Acquisition & Strategy
• Andrew Razzano, Team Physician
Stadium:
Located on the winding banks of the Ohio River in downtown Cincinnati, Great American Ball Park serves as the home of the Cincinnati Reds, baseball's first professional franchise. The stadium first opened in 2003 and seats 43,500.

COLORADO ROCKIES
COORS FIELD
2001 BLAKE STREET
DENVER, CO 80205-2000
303-292-0200
www.mlb.com/rockies
• Dick Monfort, Owner/Chairman/CEO
• Charlie K. Monfort, Owner/General Partner
• Gregory D. Feasel, President & COO
• Bill Schmidt, Senior Vice President & General Manager
• Brian Gaffney, VP, General Counsel
• Kevin H. Kahn, VP, Chief Customer Office, Ballpark Operations
• Douglas Mylowe, VP & Chief Financial Officer
• Rolando Fernandez, VP, International Scouting & Development
• Paul Egins, Senior Director, Major League Operations
• Cory Little, Senior Director, Communications
• Keith Dugger, Head Athletic Trainer
Stadium:
Coors Field. Seating capacity: 46,897 (50,144 with standing room).

LOS ANGELES DODGERS
DODGER STADIUM
1000 VIN SCULLY AVENUE
LOS ANGELES, CA 90012
866-363-4377
fanfeedback@ladodgers.com
www.mlb.com/dodgers/
• Mark Walter, Chair/Owner
• Stan Kasten, CEO/President
• Andrew Friedman, President, Baseball Operations
• Brandon Gomes, Executive Vice President & General Manager
• Lon Rosen, Executive VP/Chief Marketing Officer
• Erik Braverman, SVP, Marketing, Communications & Broadcasting
• Antonio Morici, SVP, Ticket Sales
• Seth Bluman, VP, Ticket Operations
• Eric Hernandez, VP, Finance
• Bob Wolfe, Executive VP/COO
• William Rhymes, VP, Player Development
• Ralph Esquibel, SVP, Information Technology
Stadium:
Since 1962, the beauty of Dodger Stadium has awed spectators with a breath-taking view of downtown Los Angeles to the south; green, tree-lined Elysian hills to the north and east; and the San Gabriel Mountains beyond. The stadium's seating capacity is 56,000 which extends across the 300 acres of beautiful landscaping.

MIAMI MARLINS
LOANDEPOT PARK
501 MARLINS WAY
MIAMI, FL 33125
305-480-1300
www.mlb.com/marlins
• Bruce Sherman, Chair & Principal Owner
• Caroline O'Connor, President, Business Operations
• Peter Bendix, President, Baseball Operations
• Sam Mondry-Cohen, VP, Player Development & Scouting
• Elliot Saks, Director, Events
• Yanelis Fundora, Director, Ticket Operations
• Mike Baraga, M.D., Medical Director

- Benjamin Lash, VP/General Counsel
- Nick Medrano, VP, Sales and Services
Stadium:
LoanDepot Park (formerly Marlins Park). Seating capacity: 36,742.

MILWAUKEE BREWERS
MILLER PARK
ONE BREWERS WAY
MILWAUKEE, WI 53214
414-902-4400
www.mlb.com/brewers/
- Rick Schlesinger, President, Business Operations
- Marti Wronski, Chief Operating Officer
- Pat Murphy, General Manager
- James Armstrong, VP, Domestic Scouting
- Sharon McNally, VP, Marketing
- Micheal Cosentino, VP, Ticket Sales
- Daniel Fumai, Chief Financial Officer
- Steve Ethier, Senior VP, Stadium Operations
- Mike Berger, Special Assistant
- Elizabeth Haas, Senior VP/General Counsel
- Lisa Brzeski, Executive Assistant, Revenue
- William Raasch, Head Team Physician
- Isaac Salazar, Director, Player Performance
Stadium:
American Family Field. Seating capacity: 41,900.

NEW YORK METS
CITI FIELD
41 SEAVER WAY
QUEENS, NY 11368
718-507-8499
www.mlb.com/mets/
- Steven A. Cohen, Owner, Chair & CEO
- David Stearns, President, Baseball Operations
- M. Scott Havens, President, Business Operations
- Katie Haas, VP, Ballpark Operations
- Andrew Goldberg, Director, Marketing
- Jake Bye, VP, Ticket Sales & Services
- Steve Canna, Chief Financial Officer
- Samantha Engelhardt, COO
- Jeff Deline, Executive VP/Chief Revenue Officer
- John McKay, Executive Director, Security
- Andrew Christie, Executive Director, Player Development
Stadium:
The Mets played their first game in Citi Field on April 13, 2009, and features natural grass. Seating capacity: 41,922.

PHILADELPHIA PHILLIES
CITIZENS BANK PARK
ONE CITIZENS BANK WAY
PHILADELPHIA, PA 19148
215-463-6000
www.mlb.com/phillies/
- David Dombrowski, President, Baseball Operations
- John Middleton, Managing Partner & CEO
- Preston Mattingly, Vice President, General Manager
- Anirudh Kilambi, Assistant General Manager
- Mike Ondo, Director, Professional Scouting
- Kurt Funk, VP, Marketing Programs & Events
- John Weber, Senior VP, Ticket Operations & Projects
- John Nickolas, Senior VP/Chief Financial Officer
- Kevin Greggs, VP, Communications
- Andy Mosiondz, Manager, Ballpark Operations
- Leslie Safran, Senior VP/General Counsel
- Sam Flud, Executive VP
- Luke Murton, Director, Player Development
- Steven Cohen, Director, Medical Services
Stadium:
The 42,901 seat, state-of-the-art Citizens Bank Park is the ultimate baseball and entertainment experience. Featuring natural grass and a dirt playing field, a scenic view of the Philadelphia skyline, an open-air atmosphere and more, the Ballpark is an exciting destination for all fans.

PITTSBURGH PIRATES
PNC PARK
115 FEDERAL STREET
PITTSBURGH, PA 15212
412-321-2827
800-BUY-BUCS
www.mlb.com/pirates
- Travis Williams, President
- Bob Nutting, Owner
- Derek Shelton, General Manager
- Trey Rose, Director, Baseball Operations & Pro Scouting
- Steve Williams, Senior Director, Player Personnel
- Justin Horowitz, Senior Director, Amateur Scouting
- John Baker, Senior VP, Baseball Development
- Dan Hart, Director, Media Relations
- Steve Williams, Senior Director, Player Personnel
- Todd Tomczyk, Director, Sports Medicine
- Jim Plake, Executive VP/Chief Financial Officer
- Patrick DeMeo, Medical Director
- Stephen Perkins, Executive VP, Marketing & Fan Engagement
Stadium:
PNC Park, which opened in spring 2001, is a classic-style ballpark, an intimate facility that embraces the progressiveness of Pittsburgh while saluting the spirit of early ballpark originals such as Forbes Field, Wrigley Field and Fenway Park. Seating capacity 38,747.

SAN DIEGO PADRES
PETCO PARK
100 PARK BOULEVARD
SAN DIEGO, CA 92101
619-795-5000
tickets@padres.com
www.mlb.com/padres/
- Erik Greupner, CEO
- A.J. Preller, President of Baseball Operations/General Manager
- Caroline Perry, Chief Operating Officer
- Allison Luneborg, Director, Baseball Operations
- Logan White, Director, Professional Scouting
- Mark Rogow, Head Athletic Trainer
- Mark Guglielmo, Senior VP, Ballpark Operations
- Anil Cannon, Senior Director, Ticket Operations
- Curt Waugh, VP, Ticket Sales & Services
- Sam Geaney, Senior Director, Player Development
- Ray Chan, VP, Information Technology
Stadium:
PETCO Park is spectacular in every way, combining the best sight lines in baseball with breathtaking views of San Diego. Architecturally magnificent, it celebrates the sea, the sky, the natural beauty, cultural diversity and unique spirit of our region. Innovative design features evoke the timeless traditions of baseball in an intimate setting, with state-of-the-art fan amenities to suit every taste and budget. Seating capacity 40,209.

SAN FRANCISCO GIANTS
ORACLE PARK
24 WILLIE MAYS PLAZA
SAN FRANCISCO, CA 94107
415-972-2000
customerservice@sfgiants.com
www.mlb.com/giants/
- Larry Baer, President/CEO
- Bill Schlough, Senior VP/Chief Information Officer
- Brian Melvin, General Manager
- Buster Posey, President, Baseball Operations
- Zack Minasian, Vice President, Pro Scouting
- Travis LoDolce, VP, Marketing & Advertising
- Mario Alioto, Executive VP, Business Operations
- Russ Stanley, Senior VP, Ticket Sales & Services
- Shana Daum, SVP, Community Relations & Public Affairs

- Leslie Gelb Lee, VP, Ballpark Operations
- Lisa Pantages, Senior VP/Chief Financial Officer
- Kyle Haines, Director, Player Development
- Amy Tovar, Senior VP & General Counsel
- Maria Jacinto, Senior Director, Broadcasting Services
- Matt Peterson, VP, Ticket Sales & Premium Seating
Stadium:
Opened in 2000, Oracle Park features a 9-foot statue of the legendary Willie Mays at the entrance, an 80-foot Coca-Cola bottle with playground slides and a mini AT&T Park that attracts children of all ages. Seating capacity 41,915.

ST. LOUIS CARDINALS
BUSCH STADIUM
700 CLARK STREET
ST. LOUIS, MO 63102
314-345-9600
guestservices@cardinals.mlb.com
www.mlb.com/cardinals/
- Chaim O. Bloom, President
- William O. DeWitt, Jr., Chair/CEO
- Mike Girsch, VP/General Manager
- John Mozeliak, President, Baseball Operations
- Dan Farrell, Senior VP, Sales/Marketing
- Brian Bartow, Director, Communications
- Matt Gifford, VP, Stadium Operations
- Mike Whittle, Senior VP/General Counsel
- Dan Good, VP, Business Development
- Adam Olson, Director, Medical Operations/Head Athletic Trainer
- Brad Wood, Senior VP/CFO
Stadium
Busch Stadium. Seating capacity: 44,383.

WASHINGTON NATIONALS
NATIONALS PARK
1500 SOUTH CAPITOL STREET SE
WASHINGTON, DC 20003
202-675-6287
Fax: 202-640-7999
ticketinfo@nationals.com
www.mlb.com/nationals/
- Mark D. Lerner, Principal Owner
- Mike Rizzo, General Manager/President, Baseball Operations
- Mike DeBartolo, Assistant General Manager/VP, Scouting Operations
- Wendy Bailey, SVP, Marketing, Broadcasting & Game Presentation
- Ryan Bringger, VP, Ticket Sales & Services
- Tyler Hubbard, Senior Director, Ticket Operations
- Ted Towne, Assistant General Manager/VP, Finance
- Jennifer Giglio, Senior VP, Chief Communications Officer
- Mike Carney, Executive VP, Business Operations
- Gregory McCarthy, Senior Vice President
- Alan Gottlieb, Chief Operating Officer, Lerner Sports
- Harvey Sharman, Executive Director, Medical Services
- Mark Scialabba, VP, Player Personnel/Assistant General Manager
- Ted Towne, Chief Financial Officer/Partner
Stadium:
Opened in 2008, the new Nationals Park achieved its goal to become the first major baseball stadium in the United States accredited as LEED Certified. The ballpark is equipped with state-of-the-art technology, and the exterior was designed to reflect the architecture of Washington, D.C. Seating capacity 41,339.

Baseball, Professional Leagues/Teams: Minor

AMERICAN ASSOCIATION OF INDEPENDENT PROFESSIONAL BASEBALL
1415 HWY 54 WEST
SUITE 210
DURHAM, NC 27707
919-401-8150
Fax: 919-401-8152
www.americanassociationbaseball.com
• Miles Wolff, Commissioner
• Dan Moushon, President
• Kevin Winn, Director of Umpires
Nature of Service:
Independent Professional Baseball League
Teams: 12
Fargo-Moorhead RedHawks, Sioux Falls Canaries, St. Paul Saints, Winnipeg Goldeyes, Gary SouthShore RailCats, Kansas City T-Bones, Lincoln Saltdogs, Sioux City Explorers, Laredo Lemurs, Joplin Blasters, Wichita Wingnuts, Texas Amarillo/Grand Prairie. Founded in 2005.

APPALACHIAN LEAGUE (ADVANCED ROOKIE)
759 182ND AVENUE EAST
REDINGTON SHORES, FL 33708
727-954-4876
www.milb.com/index.jsp?sid=l120
• Lee Landers, President/Treasurer
• Bobbi Landers, League Administrator
• David Lane, Corporate Secretary
Description:
The Appalachian League was founded in 1911 with teams in Asheville, NC; Bristol, VA; Cleveland, TN; Johnson City, TN; Knoxville, TN; and Morristown, TN. After four years, the league disbanded and reformed seven years later with only six teams. Again, that league managed to last midway through 1925 before disbanding. In 1937, the league re-formed with teams in Elizabethtown, TN; Johnson City, TN; Newport, TN; and Pennington Gap, VA. Twenty years later, in 1957, the modern Appalachian League began its first year as a short-season baseball league.
Teams: 10
Currently, the Appalachian League has 10 teams.

Teams:

BLUEFIELD BLUE JAYS
BOWEN FIELD
STADIUM DRIVE
PO BOX 365
BLUEFIELD, WV 24701
304-324-1326
Fax: 304-324-1318
www.milb.com/index.jsp?sid=t517
• George McGonagle, President
Ballpark:
Bowen Field. Seating capacity, 3,000.
MLB Affiliation:
Toronto Blue Jays
Years in League:
1946-55; 1957-Present

BRISTOL PIRATES
BOYCE COX FIELD
BOX 1434
BRISTOL, VA 24203
276-206-9946
Fax: 276-669-7686
www.milb.com/index.jsp?sid=t557
• Mark Young, Vice President of Community Relations
• Edgar Varela, Manager
Ballpark:
Boyce Cox Field at Devault Memorial Stadium, built in 1969, has a seating capacity of 2,000. It is in a city sports complex that also includes an immaculate football field.
Affiliate:
Chicago White Sox
Years in League:
1921-25; 1940-55; 1969-Present

BURLINGTON ROYALS
BURLINGTON ATHLETIC STADIUM
1450 GRAHAM STREET
BURLINGTON, NC 27217
336-222-0223
Fax: 336-226-2498
info@burlingtonroyals.com
www.milb.com/index.jsp?sid=t483
• Miles Wolff, President
• Ryan Keur, General Manager
• Mikie Morrison, Director of Operations
Ballpark:
Burlington Athletic Stadium first opened in 1958 and it has a seating capacity of 3,500.
Official Charities:
Stephen K. Gates Scholarship Fund.
Affiliate:
Kansas City Royals

DANVILLE BRAVES
AMERICAN LEGION POST 325 AT DANIEL MEMORIAL PARK
302 RIVER PARK DRIVE
DANVILLE, VA 24540
434-797-3792
Fax: 423-797-3799
danvillebraves@braves.com
www.milb.com/index.jsp?sid=t429
• David Cross, General Manager
• Bob Kitzmiller, Assistant General Manager
Ballpark:
Legion Field is the second largest in the Appalachian League. With a seating capacity of 2,588, it hosted 39,063 fans last season.
Affiliate:
Atlanta Braves
Years in League:
1993 - Present

ELIZABETHTON TWINS
208 NORTH HOLLY LANE
ELIZABETHTON, TN 37643
423-547-6441
Fax: 423-547-6442
www.milb.com/index.jsp?sid=t576
• Jim Rantz, Director
• Harold Mains, President
• Mike Mains, General Manager
• Ray Smith, Manager
Ballpark:
Joe O'Brien Stadium was built in 1974 and has a seating capacity of 1,500. The field was named after O'Brien, a longtime supporter of Elizabethton baseball and the E-Twins' first board chairman, in 1980. In 1996, significant upgrades were made to the ballpark, including new locker rooms and a new reserved seating section behind the plate.
Affiliate:
Minnesota Twins
Years in League:
1937-42; 1945-51; 1974-Present

GREENEVILLE ASTROS
PIONEER PARK
135 SHILOH ROAD
PO BOX 5192
GREENEVILLE, TN 37743
423-638-0411
Fax: 423-638-9450
greeneville@astros.com
www.mlb.com/index.jsp?sid=t413
• David Lane, General Manager
• Hunter Reed, Assistant General Manager
• Jim Crane, Owner and Chairman
• Reid Ryan, President, Business Operations
• Quinton McCracken, Director of Player Personnel
Ballpark:
Pioneer Park seats 2,572 fans and is owned by Tusculum College.
Affiliate:
Houston Astros
Years in League:
1988-Present

JOHNSON CITY CARDINALS
510 BERT STREET
JOHNSON CITY, TN 37601
423-461-4866
Fax: 423-461-4864
www.milb.com/index.jsp?sid=t438
• John Vuch, Director
• Tyler Parsons, General Manager
• Lee Sowers, President
• Chris Swauger, Manager
Ballpark:
Howard Johnson Field goes all the way back to 1923, although the current stadium structure went up in the 1950s. It's a city park which hosts both East Tennessee State University and the Johnson City Cardinals of the rookie-level Appalachian League. The field is a respectable size, with a right-field berm making balls to the wall very interesting (at least one fielder fell down playing the ball up the berm and off the wall).
Affiliate:
St. Louis Cardinals
Years in League:
1921-24; 1937-55; 1957-61; 1964-Present

KINGSPORT METS
HUNTER WRIGHT STADIUM
800 GRANBY ROAD
KINGSPORT, TN 37660
423-224-2626
Fax: 423-224-2625
info@kmets.com
www.milb.com/index.jsp?sid=t506
• Brian Paupeck, General Manager
• Josh Lawson, Tickets and Merchandise
Ballpark:
Hunter Wright Stadium opened in 1995 and has a 2,000 seating capacity.
Affiliate:
New York Mets
Years in League:
1921-25; 1938-52; 1957; 1960-63; 1969-82; 1984-Present

PRINCETON RAYS
H.P. HUNNICUTT FIELD
OLD BLUEFIELD RD
PRINCETON, WV 24740
304-487-2000
Fax: 304-487-8762
raysball@sunlitsurf.com
www.milb.com/index.jsp?sid=t455
• Mori Williams, President
• Jim Holland, General Manager
• Danny Scheaffer, Manager
Ballpark:
H.P. Hunnicutt Field. Seating capacity, 1,700.
Affiliate:
Tampa Bay Rays
Years in League:
1988-present

PULASKI YANKEES
CALFEE PARK
700 SOUTH WASHINGTON AVENUE
PULASKI, VA 24301
540-980-1070
Fax: 540-980-1850
info@pulaskiyankees.net
www.milb.com/index.jsp?sid=t425

- Randy Lavone, President/General Manager
- Jose Moreno, Manager

Ballpark:
Calfee Park, the ninth oldest professional minor-league Baseball Park in use in America, offers a nice, fan-friendly atmosphere for watching the game, and recent improvements are now complete. In addition to the new club house, Calfee Park features a new home team dugout, new grandstands, a new reserverd seating section with handicap accessibility, open air corporate box suite with patio tables and chairs, new lighting, underground watering and drainage system, concession area, parking lots and entrance.

Affiliate:
NY Yankees

ARIZONA FALL LEAGUE (ROOKIE LEVEL)
10201 S. 51ST ST, STE 230
PHOENIX, AZ 85044-3217
480-496-6700
Fax: 480-496-6384
mlb.com/mlb/events/afl/index.jsp
- Steve Cobb, Executive Vice President
- Joan McGrath, Office Administration

Description:
Owned and operated by the MLB and attracts many of the Minor League top prospects. The roots of the Arizona Fall League go back several years, when the Major Leagues wanted to create an easily accessible off-season league. There's a two-pronged mission to the AFL; one is for the players to accelerate, and hopefully jump a classification. The other is for the managers and umpires to develop.

Number of Teams:
6

Founded:
1992

Teams:

GLENDALE DESERT DOGS
CAMELBACK RANCH
10710 WEST CAMELBACK ROAD
PHOENIX, AZ 85037
623-302-5000
Fax: 623-877-8582
- Lance Parrish, Manager

Ballpark:
Camelback Ranch seats 10,500 fans and features a natural grass field.

MLB Affiliates:
Atlants Braves, Miami Marlins, Milwaukee Brewers, Oakland Athletics, Tampa Bay Rays.

MESA SOLAR SOX
SLOAN PARK
2330 WEST RIO SALADO PARKWAY
MESA, AZ 85201
480-668-0500
- Mark Johnson, Manager
- Steve Connelly, Pitching Coach
- Dan DeMent, Hitting Coach

Ballpark:
Sloan Park. Seating capacity, 15,000.

MLB Affiliations:
Baltimore Orioles, Chicago Cubs, Detroit Tigers, Houston Astros, Los Angeles Dodgers.

PEORIA JAVELINAS
PEORIA SPORTS COMPLEX
16101 NORTH 83RD AVENUE
PEORIA, AZ 85382
623-226-8000
Fax: 623-486-4366
- Rod Barajas, Manager

Ballpark:
Peoria Sports Complex seats 11,333 and is home to both the San Diego Padres and the Seattle Mariners.

MLB Affiliates:
San Diego Padres, Seattle Mariners, Minnesota Twins, Cincinnati Reds, Philadelphia Phillies.

SALT RIVER RAFTERS
SALT RIVER FIELDS AT TACKING STICK
7555 N. PRIMA RD
SCOTTSDALE, AZ 85258
480-270-5000
- Tripp Keister, Manager

Ballpark:
Salt River Field seats a capacity of 11,000 and features a natural grass field.

MLB Affiliates:
Arizona Diamondbacks, Chicago White Sox, Colorado Rockies, Toronto Blue Jays, Washington Nationals.

SCOTTSDALE SCORPIONS
SCOTTSDALE STADIUM
7408 EAST OSBORN ROAD
SCOTTSDALE, AZ 85251
480-941-1930
Fax: 480-941-3060
- Matt Quatraro, Manager

Ballpark:
Scottsdale Stadium is located in the middle of scenic downtown and a short walk from a wide selection of restaurants, clubs and galleries. Scottsdale Stadium is home to some of Scottsdale's most celebrated occasions including Cactus League Spring Training, Arizona Fall League, and a series of year-round meetings and events.

MLB Affiliates:
Cleveland Indians, Los Angeles Angels of Anaheim, New York Yankees, Pittsburgh Pirates, San Francisco Giants.

SURPRISE SAGUAROS
SURPRISE STADIUM
15930 NORTH BULLARD AVENUE
SURPRISE, AZ 85374
623-594-5600
- Carlos Subero, Manager

Ballpark:
Surprise Stadium seats 10,714 fans and has a natural grass field.

MLB Affiliates:
Boston Red Sox, Kansas City Royals, New York Mets, St. Louis Cardinals, Texas Rangers.

ARIZONA LEAGUE (ROOKIE)
9550 16TH STREET NORTH
ST. PETERSBURG, FL 33716
727-822-6937
Fax: 727-821-5819
www.milb.com/index.jsp?sid=l121
- Robert Richmond, President/Treasurer
- Bobby Evans, Vice President
- Ted Polakowski, Corporate Secretary

Number of Teams:
13

Publications:
Baseball AZ

Number of Games:
56

Player Eligibility:
No more than eight players 20 or older, and no more than two players 21 or older. At least 10 pitchers. No more than two years of prior service, excluding Rookie leagues outside the United States and Canada.

Teams:

ARIZONA ANGELS
TEMPE DIABLO STADIUM
2200 WEST ALAMEDA DRIVE
TEMPE, AZ 85282
480-858-7555
Fax: 480-858-7550
- Elio Sarmiento, Manager

Affiliate Team:
Los Angeles Angels of Anaheim.

ARIZONA ATHLETICS
FITCH PARK
ONE EAST 8TH STREET
MESA, AZ 85211
480-644-2711
- Webster Garrison, Manager

Affiliate Team:
Oakland Athletics

ARIZONA BREWERS
MARYVALE BASEBALL PARK
3600 NORTH 51ST AVENUE
PHOENIX, AZ 85031
623-245-5500
- Nestor Corredor, Manager
- Steve Cline, Pitching Coach

Affiliation:
MLB Milwaukee Brewers

ARIZONA CUBS
SLOAN PARK
2330 WEST RIO SOLADO PARKWAY
MESA, AZ 85201
480-668-0500
- Ricardo Medina, Manager

Affiliate Team:
Chicago Cubs

ARIZONA DIAMONDBACKS
SALT RIVER FIELDS AT TALKING STICK
7555 NORTH PIMA ROAD
SCOTTSDALE, AZ 85258
480-270-5000
- Hector de la Cruz, Manager

Ballpark:
Salt River Fields at Talking Stick.

ARIZONA DODGERS
CAMELBACK RANCH
10712 WEST CAMELBACK ROAD
PHOENIX, AZ 85037
623-302-5000
- Jack McDowell, Manager

Ballpark:
Camelback Ranch

Affiliate Team:
Los Angeles Dodgers

ARIZONA GIANTS
SCOTTSDALE STADIUM
7408 EAST OSBORN ROAD
SCOTTSDALE, AZ 85251
480-312-2586
Fax: 480-990-2349
- Mike Goff, Manager

Affiliates:
San Francisco Giants

ARIZONA INDIANS
PLAYER DEVELOPMENT COMPLEX
2601 SOUTH WOOD BOULEVARD
GOODYEAR, AZ 85338
623-302-5678
- Anthony Medrano, Manager

Affiliate:
Cleveland Indians.

ARIZONA MARINERS
PEORIA SPORTS COMPLEX
16101 NORTH 83RD AVENUE
PEORIA, AZ 85382
623-776-4818
- Darrin Garner, Manager

Affiliates:
Seattle Mariners.

ARIZONA PADRES
PEORIA SPORTS COMPLEX
16101 NORTH 83RD AVENUE
PEORIA, AZ 85382

623-412-4020
Fax: 623-487-1190
• Anthony Contreras, Manager
Affiliate Team:
San Diego Padres

ARIZONA RANGERS
SURPRISE STADIUM
15930 NORTH BULLARD AVENUE
SURPRISE, AZ 85374
623-222-2222
• Matt Siegel, Manager
Affiliate Team:
Texas Rangers

ARIZONA REDS
GOODYEAR BALLPARK
1933 SOUTH BALLPARK WAY
GOODYEAR, AZ 85338
623-882-3120
• Jose Nieves, Manager
Ballpark:
Goodyear Stadium
Affiliates:
Cincinnati Reds

ARIZONA ROYALS
SURPRISE STADIUM
15930 NORTH BULLARD AVENUE
SURPRISE, AZ 85374
623-222-2222
• Darryl Kennedy, Manager
Home Field:
Surprise Stadium

ARIZONA WHITE SOX
CAMELBACK RANCH
10712 WEST CAMELBACK ROAD
PHOENIX, AZ 85037
623-302-5000
Fax: 623-266-8032
• Tim Esmay, Manager
Affiliate Team:
Chicago White Sox

ATLANTIC LEAGUE OF PROFESSIONAL BASEBALL, THE
P.O. BOX 5190
LANCASTER, PA 17606
720-389-6992
suggestions@atlanticleague.com
www.atlanticleague.com
• Frank Boulton, Founder/Chairman
• Rick White, President
• Joe Klein, Vice President On-Field Operations
• Emily Merrill, League Administrator
Description:
The Atlantic League was created by seasoned professional baseball executives to bridge gaps in professional baseball palyer development. The atlantic League is funded by membership fees and dues. Founded in 1998, the Atlantic League has sent over 800 players to major league baseball organizations.
Number of Teams:
8
Year Founded:
1998

Teams:

BRIDGEPORT BLUEFISH
HARBOR YARD
500 MAIN STREET
BRIDGEPORT, CT 06604
203-345-4800 EXT 108
Fax: 203-345-4830
info@bridgeportbluefish.com
www.bridgeportbluefish.com

• Frank Boulton, Chief Executive Officer
• Jamie Toole, General Manager
• Drew LaBoy, Director of Ticket Sales/Operations
Ballpark:
The Bluefish are privileged to be playing baseball at The Ballpark at Harbor Yard. The $19 million ballpark was constructed in 1997-1998 and was funded though a combination of public and team contributions. It has a seating capacity of 5,500, with optional standing room admittance of 200 more for sold-out games.

LANCASTER BARNSTORMERS
CLIPPER MAGAZINE STADIUM
650 NORTH PRINCE STREET
LANCASTER, PA 17603
717-509-4487
Fax: 717-509-4486
info@lancasterbarnstormers.com
www.lancasterbarnstormers.com
• Jon Danos, President
• Kristen Simon, General Manager
• Don Pryer, Director, Stadium Operations
• Bob Ford, Director, Business Development
• Butch Hobson, Manager
Ballpark:
The stadium opened in May 2005 and is located in downtown Lancaster on a triangular plot of land bordered by North Prince Street and Harrisburg Pike.

LONG ISLAND DUCKS
BETHPAGE BALLPARK
3 COURT HOUSE DRIVE
CENTRAL ISLIP, NY 11722
631-940-3825
Fax: 631-940-3800
www.liducks.com
• Frank Boulton, Founder/CEO
• Seth Waugh, Owner
• Bud Harrelson, Owner
• Mike Pfaff, President and General Manager
Ballpark:
Opened in 2000, Bethpage Ballpark is a 6,002 seat state-of-the-art facility that is home to the Long Island Ducks. Among its many features are 20 luxury suites, spacious seating, and an indoor batting tunnel.

NEW BRITAIN BEES
NEW BRITAIN CITY HALL
27 WEST MAIN STREET
NEW BRITAIN, CT 06051
860-826-2337
info@nbbees.com
www.nbbees.com
• Frank Boulton, Principal Owner
• Katie Force, Promotions & Community Relations Coordinator
Ballpark:
The New Britain Stadium opened in 1996, and has a seating capacity of 6,146. The stadium contains skyboxes and split-level seating.

SOMERSET PATRIOTS
TD BANK BALLPARK
1 PATRIOTS PARK
BRIDGEWATER, NJ 08807
908-252-0700
Fax: 908-252-0776
patriots@somersetpatriots.com
www.somersetpatriots.com
• Steve Kalafer, Chairman Emeritus
• Patrick McVerry, President/General Manager
• Julio Mosquera, Manager
• Dave Marek, Senior Vice President, Marketing
• Bryan Iwicki, Vice President of Operations
• Marc Russinoff, Vice President of Public Relations
• Matt Kopas, Vice President of Ticketing
• Kevin Fleming, Director, Sales
• Brett Jodie, Manager
Ballpark:
TD Bank Park opened its gates on June 7, 1999 for the first ever Somerset Patriots home game.

The 6,100 seat ballpark is a multi-use facility that is the home of the Big East Baseball Championship Tournament and County Baseball Tournaments during the season. In the off-season, the ballpark is the site of the Big Apple Circus and the New Jersey State Fair.
Description:
Provides family affordable entertainment in a beautiful ballpark, with professional Minor League Baseball.

SOUTHERN MARYLAND BLUE CRABS
REGENCY FURNITURE STADIUM
11765 SAINT LINUS DRIVE
WALDORF, MD 20602
301-638-9788
Fax: 301-638-9877
info@somdbluecrabs.com
www.somdbluecrabs.com
• Patrick Day, General Manager
• Carlton Silverstro, Box Office Manager
• Alexandra Wohlenhaus, Office Manager
• Theresa Coffey, Finance Manager
• Candace Gick, Director of Sponsorship
• Samantha Slovik, Client Service Manager
• Stan Cliburn, Manager
Ballpark:
With a 6,000 seat capacity, Regency Furniture Stadium offers a full range of family-oriented features and attractions. A large, catered picnic area and amusement area for kids of all ages ensure a memorable experience for everyone. The ballpark also accomodates football, soccer, lacrosse and other sporting events.

SUGAR LAND SKEETERS
CONSTELLATION FIELD
101 STADIUM DRIVE
SUGARLAND, TX 77498
281-240-4487
Fax: 281-240-4550
www.sugarlandskeeters.com
• Gary Gaetti, Manager
• Miller Jay, President
Stadium:
Constellation Field seats 7,500 fans.

YORK REVOLUTION
SANTANDER STADIUM
5 BROOKS ROBINSON WAY
YORK, PA 17401
717-801-4487
Fax: 717-801-4499
ask@yorkrevolution.com
www.yorkrevolution.com
• Eric Menzer, President
(717) 801-4481
• John Gibson, General Manager
• Lori Brunson, Vice President of Finance
(717) 801-4483
lbrunson@yorkrevolution.com
• Cindy Brown, Director of Ticketing
• Mark Mason, Manager
Ballpark:
Owned by the York County Industrial Development Authority. Offers a full range of family friendly features and attractions, including a large catered picnic area overlooking the field and a fantastic amusement area for kids of all ages.
Seating Capacity:
7,312

CALIFORNIA LEAGUE (A-LEVEL)
3600 SOUTH HARBOR BOULEVARD
SUITE 122
OXNARD, CA 93035
805-985-8585
Fax: 805-985-8580
info@californialeague.com
www.californialeague.com
• Charlie Blaney, President
• Tom Volpe, Vice President
• Matt Blaney, Director of Operations and Marketing

Year Founded:
1941
League Description:
Founded by a group of Major and Pacific Coast League Clubs.
Player Eligibility:
No more than two players and one player-coach on the active list may have more than six years of experience.
Number of Teams:
10

Teams:

BAKERSFIELD BLAZE
SAM LYNN BALLPARK
4009 CHESTER AVENUE
BAKERSFIELD, CA 93301
661-716-4487
Fax: 661-322-6199
• Elizabeth Martin, General Manager
• Mike Candela, Assistant General Manager
Ballpark:
The 58-year old ballpark, Sam Lynn Ballpark, was named after Sam Lynn, the owner of the Coca-Cola bottling plant in Bakersfield during the 1930s.
Affiliate:
Cincinnati Reds

HIGH DESERT MAVERICKS
MAVERICKS STADIUM
12000 STADIUM WAY
ADELANTO, CA 92301
760-246-6287
Fax: 760-246-3197
info@hdmavs.com
• Ben Hemmen, General Manager
• Sarah Bosso, Assistant General Manager
• David Barry, Director of Tickets and Finance
• Ryan Cowan, Head Groundskeeper
Ballpark:
Stater Brothers Stadium has a seating capacity of 3,808, plus grass seating. Opened in 1991.
Affiliate:
Seattle Mariners

INLAND EMPIRE 66ERS
SAN MANUEL STADIUM
280 SOUTH EAST STREET
SAN BERNADINO, CA 92401
909-888-9922
Fax: 909-888-5251
info@ie66ers.com
www.66ers.com
• David Elmore, Co-Owner
• Donna F Tuttle, Co-Owner
• Ryan English, Assistant General Manager
• Joe Hudson, General Manager
• Ryan English, Assistant General Manager
Team History:
San Bernardino's single-A minor league baseball team in the California League, formerly known as the Stampede, has won league championships in 1995, 1999, 2000, 2003 and 2006. They became just the fourth team in California League history to win back-back titles when they won the crown in 2000
Ballpark:
San Manuel Stadium seats 5,000, with grass seating that can comfortably accomodate more fans. The ballpark boasts 12 skyboxes, each with its own private outdoor balcony, two large outdoor picnic areas and the only high-tech scoreboard featuring full-color video in the California League
Affiliate:
LA Angels

LAKE ELSINORE STORM
500 DIAMOND DRIVE
LAKE ELSINORE, CA 92531
951-245-4487
Fax: 951-245-0305

• Gary Jacobs, Owner
• Len Simon, Owner
• David Oster, Owner/President
(951) 245-4487
doster@stormbaseball.com
• Raj Narayanan, General Manager/Director of Sales
• Mark Beskid, Assistant General Manager
• Tim Arseneau, Director of Operations
Ballpark:
Lake Elsinore Diamond is a state of the art baseball park that is continually voted as one of the finest parks in all of Minor League Baseball. The park has 6,066 fixed seats, 11 luxury suites and a grass berm seating area on the right field line - allowing over 8,000 fans to take in a night or afternoon of Storm baseball.
Affiliate:
San Diego Padres

LANCASTER JETHAWKS
THE HANGAR
45116 VALLEY CENTRAL WAY
LANCASTER, CA 93536
661-726-5400
• Jake Kerr, Owner
• Jeff Mooney, Owner
• Andy Dunn, President
• Will Thornhill, General Manager
Ballpark:
Clear Channel Stadium has a seating capacity of 4,600 and was opened in April of 1996.
Affiliate:
Houston Astros

MODESTO NUTS
JOHN THURMAN FIELD
601 NEECE DRIVE
MODESTO, CA 95351
209-572-4487
Fax: 209-572-4490
fun@modestonuts.com
• Mike Gorrasi, Executive Vice President
• Fred Ocasio, Manager
• Ed Mack, Vice President - HWS Beverage
• Chris Ganoe, Operations Manager
Ballpark:
John Thurman Field has a seating capacity of 4,000 and opened in 1955. It was renovated in 1997.
Affiliate:
Colorado Rockies.

RANCHO CUCAMONGA QUAKES
LOANMART FIELD
8408 ROCHESTER AVENUE
RANCHO CUCAMONGA, CA 91730
909-481-5000
Fax: 909-481-5005
www.rcquakes.com
• Grant Riddle, Vice President/General Manager
• Brent Miles, President
• Monica Ortega, Vice President/Tickets
• Linda Rathfon, Assistant GM/Group Sales
(909) 481-5000
lrathfon@rcquakes.com
• Bill Haselman, Manager
Ballpark:
The Epicenter has recently undergone a seating renovation project that began in September of 2008. The renovations are complete, making the stadium look brand new.
Team History:
The Rancho Cucamonga Quakes have been playing top-notch Minor League ball since 1993 the franchise has been around for over 28 years, since 1966.
Affiliate:
Los Angeles Dodgers

SAN JOSE GIANTS
588 EAST ALMA AVENUE
SAN JOSE, CA 95112
408-297-1435
Fax: 408-297-1453
info@sjgiants.com

• Daniel Orum, President/Chief Executive Officer
• Mark Wilson, General Manager, Chief Operating Officer
• Juliana Paoli, Chief Marketing Officer
juliana@sjgiants.com
• Linda Pereira, Director of Player Personnel
lindapereira@sjgiants.com
• Lance Motch, Vice President of Ballpark Operations
• Jacquie Stuart, Ticket Operations Manager
• Russ Morman, Manager
Ballpark:
With a seating capacity of 2,900 it was built as part of Franklin Roosevelt's Works Progress Administration (WPA), Municipal Stadium was built for a total cost of $80,000 in 1942.
Affiliate:
San Francisco Giants

STOCKTON PORTS
BANNER ISLAND BALLPARK
404 WEST FREMONT STREET
STOCKTON, CA 95203
209-644-1900
Fax: 209-644-1931
info@stocktonports.com
www.stocktonports.com
• Pat Filippone, President
• Bryan Meadows, General Manager
• Tim Pollack, Director of Tickets
• Rick Magnante, Manager
Ballpark:
Banner Island Ballpark
Affiliate:
Oakland A's.
Team History:
The Stockton Ports didn't come into play until 1941 as the Ports were one of the founding members of the California League. Over the course of the Ports 55 years as a member of the California League, they have won 10 titles and have posted the highest winning percentage in Cal League history with a.527 mark.

VISALIA RAWHIDE
RECREATION PARK
300 NORTH GIDDINGS STREET
VISALIA, CA 93291
559-732-4433
Fax: 559-739-7732
info@rawhidebaseball.com
• Kevin O'Malley, Owner
• Tom Seidler, President
• Jennifer Pendergraft, General Manager
Ballpark:
A city park named Recreation Park, the stadium itself does not have its own name. An all-wood structure stood on the current site before the existing stadium was built in 1967.
Affiliate:
Arizona Diamondbacks

CAN-AM LEAGUE
610 YOUNT DR
DAYTON, OH 45433
862-283-5935
• Miles Wolff, Commissioner
Description:
The Can-Am league, also known as the Canadian-American Association of Professional Baseball, operates in cities where the major and minor leagues do not operate.

CAROLINA LEAGUE (A-LEVEL)
1806 PEMBROKE ROAD
SUITE 2B
GREENSBORO, NC 27408
336-691-9030
Fax: 336-464-2737
www.carolinaleague.com

- Steve Bryant, Executive Vice President
- Ken Young, Secretary
- Marnee Larkins, Office Assistant
Nature of Service:
Baseball Leagues.
League Description:
Over its first 59 years, the Carolina League has established itself as one of baseball's premier minor leagues, a circuit renowned for hot prospects, intense rivalries, memorable pennant races, and excellent play. Founded during World War II, the Carolina League's inaugural 1945 season featured two Southside Virginia cites. But throughout the 40s and 50s it was known as a predominately North Carolina League.
Number of Games:
140
Number of Teams:
8

Teams:

CAROLINA MUDCATS
1501 NC HIGHWAY 39
P.O DRAWER 1218
ZEBULON, NC 27597
919-269-2287
Fax: 919-269-4910
- Steve Bryant, President, Majority Owner
- Joe Kremer, Vice President, General Manager
- Eric Gardner, General Manager of Operations
- Yogi Brewington, Ticket & Corporate Sales Executive
- Janell Bullock, Director of Merchandise/Box Office Manager
- Patrick Ennis, Director of Stadium Operations
Stadium:
Five County Stadium.

FREDERICK KEYS
21 STADIUM DRIVE
FREDERICK, MD 21703
301-662-0013
Fax: 301-662-0018
info@frederickkeys.com
- Ken Young, President
- Dave Ziedelis, General Manager
- Bridget McCabe, Director of Marketing
- Christine Roy, Promotions Manager
- Matt Miller, Director of Group Sales
Team History:
Established in 1989, the Frederick Keys offer area families, business leaders, and civic groups a fun environment to be entertained. The fan base is wide spread averaging over 300,000 per season.
Ballpark:
Opened in 1990, Harry Grove Stadium is home to the Frederick Keys.
Affiliate:
Baltimore Orioles

LYNCHBURG HILLCATS
LYNCHBURG CITY STADIUM
3180 FORT AVENUE
LYNCHBURG, VA 24501
434-528-1144
Fax: 434-846-0768
info@lynchburg-hillcats.com
- Paul Sunwall, President/CEO
(434) 528-1144
- Ronnie Roberts, General Manager
- Darren Johnson, Director of Sales
- Ashley Stephenson, Director of Promotions
- Kyle West, Director of Broadcasting
- John Hutt, Director of Ticketing
Ballpark:
Founded in 1939 and a massive renovations project to Calvin Falwell Field was completed by Opening Day 2004, marking the dawn of a new era of baseball in Central Virginia. This grand, state of the art facility now places itself among the very elite venues in the Carolina League and in all of Class A Minor league baseball.

Affiliate:
Class A Advanced affiliate of The Atlanta Braves
Media Broadcast:
KD Country 105.5, WBRG Supertalk 1050-AM

MYRTLE BEACH PELICANS
TICKETRETURN.COM FIELD AT PELICANS BALLPARK
1251 21ST AVENUE NORTH
MYRTLE BEACH, SC 29577
843-918-6002
877-918-8499
Fax: 843-918-6001
info@myrtlebeachpelicans.com
- Chuck Greenberg, Chariman, Managing Partner
chuck@myrtlebeachpelicans.com
- Andy Milovich, President, General Manager
- Mike Snow, Assistant General Manager/Operations
- Dan Bailey, Merchandise Manager
Ballpark:
Ticketreturn.com Field at Pelicans Ballpark has 5200 fixed seats, but can accomodate 6000 with standing room.
Affiliate:
Texas Rangers

POTOMAC NATIONALS
PFITZNER STADIUM
7 COUNTY COMPLEX COURT
WOODBRIDGE, VA 22192
703-590-2311
Fax: 703-590-5716
info@potomacnationals.com
- Art Silber, Chairman/CEO
- Lani Silber Weiss, President/Chief Operating Officer
- Zach Prehn, General Manager, Vice President
- Aaron Johnson, Assistant General Manager, Dir. of Food/Beverage
- Shawna Hooke, Business Operations Manager
Years in League:
1978 - Present.
Ballpark:
G. Richard Pfitzner Stadium opened in 1984 and has a seating capacity of 6,000.
Media Sponsorships:
107.3, WMZQ 98.7-FM, Oldies 100.3
Affiliate:
Washington Nationals

SALEM RED SOX
LEWISGALE FIELD
1004 TEXAS STREET
SALEM, VA 24153
540-389-3333
Fax: 540-389-9710
- Ryan Shelton, General Manager
- Allen Lawrence, Vice President/Assistant GM
- Carlos Febles, Manager
- Steven Elovich, Director of Corporate Sponsorship
- Keegan Moody, Ticket Operations
- Samantha Barney, Marketing & Promotions Manager
Ballpark:
Lewisgale Field.
Affiliate:
Boston Red Sox
Broadcast Network:
WGMN 1240-AM, WVGM 1320-AM, WPIN 810-AM, WKEX ESPN 1430-AM, Broadcast Monsters (web streaming service), WDRL-TV UPN.

WILMINGTON BLUE ROCKS
FRAWLEY STADIUM
801 SHIPYARD DRIVE
WILMINGTON, DE 19801
302-888-2015
Fax: 302-888-2032
info@bluerocks.com
www.bluerocks.com
- Clark Minkler, Managing Partner and League Director
- Matt Minker, Honorary President

- Chris Kemple, General Manager
- Dave Heller, CEO
- Andrew Layman, Assistant General Manager
- Joe Valenti, Director of Marketing
- Steve Gold, Director of Field Operations
Ballpark:
Frawley Stadium was opened in 1993 and built by Minker Construction Company. It seats 6,532 guests.
Network Broadcast:
The Ticket 1290-AM, WDOV 1410-AM.
Affiliate:
KC Royals

WINSTON-SALEM DASH
BB&T BALLPARK
926 BROOKSTOWN AVENUE
WINSTON-SALEM, NC 27101
336-714-2287
Fax: 336-714-2288
info@wsdash.com
- Geoff Lassiter, President
- Ryan Manuel, VP - Baseball Operations
- Kurt Gehsmann, VP - Chief Financial Officer
- C.J. Johnson, VP - Ticket Sales
- Corey Bugno, VP - Corporate Partnerships
- Tim Esmay, Manager
Ballpark:
BB&T Ballpark
Affiliate:
Chicago White Sox
Network Broadcasting:
WSJS 600/1200

EASTERN LEAGUE (AA LEVEL)
30 DANFORTH STREET
SUITE 208
PORTLAND, ME 04101
207-761-2700
Fax: 207-761-7064
www.easternleague.com
- Joe McEacharn, President
- Bill Rosario, Assistant to the President
League Description:
The league was formed on March 23, 1923 at the Arlington Hotel in Binghamton, New York as a six-team circuit located entirely within the states of New York and Pennsylvania. The Eastern League (EL) is now composed of two six-team divisions with teams in eight different states. The first game in league history took place in Williamsport on May 9, 1923. Since then, more than 40,000 Eastern League games have been played in front of more than seventy-five million fans. The Eastern League set the current attendance record during the 2004 season, when a total of 3,914,027 fans passed through the gates at Eastern League ballparks.
Number of Teams:
12
Publications:
The League Leader newsletter.

Teams:

AKRON RUBBERDUCKS
CANAL PARK
300 SOUTH MAIN STREET
AKRON, OH 44308-1204
330-253-5151
800-972-3767
Fax: 330-253-3300
information@akronrubberducks.com
- Ken Babby, Owner/CEO
- Jill Popov, Executive Assistant to Ken Babby
- Jim Pfander, General Manager/COO
- Dave Wallace, Manager
- Tony Mansolino, Hitting Coach
Description:
The AA affiliate of the Cleveland Indians. The Aeros play at Canal Park in downtown, Akron

Ohio.
Ballpark:
Canal Park.
Ballpark Description:
The steel-framed beauty was built in 14 months, between January, 1996 and March, 1997 and has a seating capacity of 9,097
Major Team Affiliation:
Cleveland Indians.

ALTOONA CURVE
PEOPLES NATURAL GAS FIELD
1000 PARK AVENUE
ALTOONA, PA 16602
814-943-5400
877-99-CURVE
Fax: 814-943-9050
frontoffice@altoonacurve.com
• Bob Lozinak, President/Managing Director
• Joan Lozinak, President/Managing Director
• Steve Lozinak, Chief Administrative Officer
• Dave Lozinak, COO
• Rob Egan, General Manager
• Cory Homan, Director of Ticket Operations
• Mary Lamb, Director of Finance
• Doug Mattern, Ballpark Operations Manager
• Tom Prince, Manager
Ballpark:
Peoples Natural Gas Field
Ballpark Description:
The first game was on April 15, 1999 vs. Bowie. The stadium has a seating capacity of 7,210
Affiliate Team:
Pittsburg Pirates

BINGHAMTON METS
NYSEG STADIUM
211 HENRY STREET
BINGHAMTON, NY 13901
607-723-6387
Fax: 607-723-7779
bmets@bmets.com
www.bmets.com
• Bill Maines, Owner
• Michael Urda, President
• David Maines, Board of Directors
• Jim Weed, General Manager
• Richard Tylicki, Director of Stadium Operations
• Pedro Lopez, Manager
Ballpark:
NYSEG Stadium
Ballpark Description:
Originally known as Binghamton Municipal Stadium, the park was opened in 1992 and has a seating capacity of 6,000.
Media Broadcast:
WNBF-1290 AM.
Newspaper:
Binghamton Press & Sun Bulletin.
Major Team Affiliation:
New York Mets.

BOWIE BAYSOX
PRINCE GEORGES STADIUM
4101 CRAIN HIGHWAY
BOWIE, MD 20716
301-805-6000
Fax: 301-464-4911
info@baysox.com
www.baysox.com
• Brian Shallcross, General Manager
• Phil Wrye, Assistant General Manager
(301) 464-4852
• Charlene Fewer, Director of Ticket Operations
• Gary Kendall, Manager
Ballpark:
Prince George's Stadium.
Ballpark Description:
Opened in 1994. This minor league baseball stadium is the result of a cooperative venture between Maryland Baseball Limited Partnership and The Maryland-National Capital Park and Planning Commission. The stadium includes a lighted playing field, dugouts, locker rooms, 8,000 box and general admission seats, club seats, 9 skyboxes, a grass overflow area for 2,000 spectators, the concourse, concession stands, souvenir shops, ticket offices,

administrative offices, a restaurant, a carousel, group picnic areas, a children's play area, and parking lots.
Publications:
Cyber Club newsletter.
Major Team Affiliation:
Baltimore Orioles.

ERIE SEAWOLVES
JERRY UHT PARK
110 EAST 10TH STREET
ERIE, PA 16501
814-456-1300
Fax: 814-456-7520
seawolves@seawolves.com
• Greg Coleman, President
• Mike Pirrello, Assistant GM/Sales
• Justin Cartor, Ticket Operations Manager
• Greg Gania, Assistant GM/Communications
• Chris McDonald, Director of Operations
• Lance Parrish, Manager
Ballpark:
Jerry Uht Park.
Ballpark Description:
Historic Jerry Uht Park celebrated its 10th year anniversary following the 2004 season. The home of the SeaWolves since 1995
Major Team Affiliation:
Detroit Tigers.

HARRISBURG SENATORS
FNB FIELD
245 CHAMPIONSHIP WAY
HARRISBURG, PA 17101
717-231-4444
Fax: 717-231-4445
information@senatorsbaseball.com
• Mark Butler, Principal Owner
• Kevin Kulp, President
• Randy Whitaker, General Manager
rwhitaker@senatorsbaseball.com
• Tim Foreman, Facility Manager
tforeman@senatorsbaseball.com
Ballpark:
FNB Field
Team History:
Baseball in Harrisburg dates back to 1907, when the local team played in the class D Tri-State League. After the 1952 season, the then Harrisburg Senators and the class B league they played in at the time called it quits.
Years in League:
1924-35, 1987-present.
Affiliation:
Washington Nationals (2005).
Media Broadcast:
WKBO 1230-AM.

HARTFORD YARD GOATS
DUNKIN' DONUTS PARK
1214 MAIN STREET
HARTFORD, CT 06103
860-246-4628
Fax: 860-247-4628
info@yardgoatsbaseball.com
• Tim Restall, General Manager
• Mike Abramson, Assistant General Manager
• Josh Montinieri, Executive Director, Tickets
• Jeff Dooley, Director, Broadcasting & Media Relations
• Pat Kennedy, Director, Stadium Operations
• Darin Everson, Manager
Ballpark:
Dunkin' Donuts Park.
Ballpark Description:
Dunkin' Donuts Park is planned to open on April 2016, and will seat 6,000.
Major Team Affiliation:
Colorado Rockies.

NEW HAMPSHIRE FISHER CATS
NORTHEAST DELTA DENTAL STADIUM
ONE LINE DRIVE
MANCHESTER, NH 03101
603-641-2005
Fax: 603-641-2055
info@nhfishercats.com

• Art Solomon, Owner
• Steve Pratt, VP, Business Operations
• Rick Brenner, President/General Manager
rbrenner@nhfishercats.com
• Tom Gauthier, Executive Director, Broadcast & Media Relations
• Bobby Meacham, Manager
Ballpark:
Northeast Delta Dental Stadium

PORTLAND SEA DOGS
271 PARK AVENUE
PORTLAND, ME 04102
207-874-9300
Fax: 207-780-0317
seadogs@seadogs.com
• Charlie Eshbach, President
ceshbach@portlandseadogs.com
• Bill Burke, Chairman
• John Kameisha, Senior Vice President
john@portlandseadogs.com
• Geoff Iacuessa, General Manager/Executive VP
geoff@seadogs.com
• Chris Cameron, Assistant GM/Dir. of Media Relations
ccameron@portlandseadogs.com
• Dennis Meehan, Executive Director of Sales
• Dennis Carter, Ticket Office Manager
• Mike Antonellis, Director, Broadcasting
• Billy McMillon, Manager
Ballpark:
Hadlock Field.
Ballpark Description:
Hadlock Field was opened in 1994, the year the Portland Sea Dogs came to town. Hadlock Field seats 7,368 patrons and has all the amenities of the larger parks including luxury boxes, a full press box, a picnic area and a souvenir store.
Media Broadcast:
Journal Tribune, Portland Press Herald, Sun Journal, The Times Record, WCSH Channel 6, WGME Channel 13, WPXT Fox 51
Team Affiliate:
Boston Red Sox

READING FIGHTIN PHILS
1900 CENTRE AVENUE/RT 61 SOUTH
READING, PA 19605
610-375-8469
Fax: 610-373-5868
info@fightins.com
• Craig Stein, Managing Partner
• Scott Hunsicker, General Manager
• Todd Hunsicker, Director of Educational Programs, Music
• Mike Becker, Director of Tickets
• Mike Robinson, Director of Community & Fan Development
• Joe Bialek, Director of Sales
• Kevin Sklenarik, Director of Baseball Operations/Merchandise
• Dusty Wathan, Manager
Team History:
The Reading Phillies offer affordable family entertainment from early April through Labor Day weekend at FirstEnergy Stadium. The Phillies are well known for creating a festive, fan-friendly atmosphere from the time the gates open until the bottom of the ninth inning. Reading won the John H. Johnson President's Trophy in 2003. The Johnson Trophy is the top honor bestowed upon the complete franchise by Minor League Baseball. Twice in the last 15 years, Reading has been awarded the Larry MacPhail Trophy as the best promotional team in all of Minor League Baseball. In 2002 the city was dubbed Baseballtown.
Ballpark:
FirstEnergy Stadium.
Ballpark Description:
The stadium itself is one of Baseball's finest and is the oldest venue in the Eastern League. Completed in 1951, the original grandstand and exterior brick wall provide an old-time ballpark feel while the right field swimming pool and left field video board cater to the modern fan. The natural grass surface is immaculately maintained and provides the perfect accent to a

classic park.
Major Team Affiliation:
Philadelphia Phillies, currently the longest affiliation in baseball (since 1976).

RICHMOND FLYING SQUIRRELS
THE DIAMOND
3001 NORTH BOULEVARD
RICHMOND, VA 23230
804-359-3866
Fax: 804-359-1373
info@squirrelsbaseball.com
• Chuck Domino, Chief Executive Manager
• Bob Parney, Vice President, Chief Operations Officer
• Marty Steele, Director of Business Development
• Steve Pump, Director of Stadium Operations
• Patrick Flower, Director of Ticket Sales
• Steve Ruckman, Director of Field Operations
• Jose Alguacil, Manager
Ballpark:
The Diamond
Team Affiliate:
San Francisco Giants

TRENTON THUNDER
ARM & HAMMER PARK
ONE THUNDER ROAD
TRENTON, NJ 08611
609-394-3300
Fax: 609-394-9666
fun@trentonthunder.com
• Jeff Hurley, Chief Operations Officer/General Manager
• Eric Lipsman, Senior VP, Corporate Sales/Sponsorships
eric@trentonthunder.com
• Joe Pappalardo, Director of Merchandising
• Matt Pentima, Director of Ticket & Baseball Operations
• Steve Brokowsky, Director of Stadium Operations
• Adam Giardino, Broadcast & Media Relations Manager
• Al Pedrique, Manager
Ballpark:
Arm and Hammer Park.
Ballpark Description:
Built in 1994 along the banks of the Deleware River, Arm and Hammer Park has seating capacity for over 6000 fans. When Trenton joined the Eastern League in 1994, it was the first time since 1950, that this city has had a Minor League team.
Media Broadcast:
WBUD 1260-AM Radio, CN8 TV.
Team Affiliate:
New York Yankees

FLORIDA STATE LEAGUE
3000 GULF TO BAY
SUITE 219
CLEARWATER, FL 33759
727-724-6146
Fax: 727-724-6145
office@floridastateleague.com
• Ken Carson, President/Chairman/Treasurer
• John Timberlake, Executive Vice President
• Paul Taglieri, VP, South Division
• Ron Myers, VP, North Division
• Horace Smith, Secretary, General Counsel
League History:
1919-1927, 1936-1941, 1946-present

Teams:

BRADENTON MARAUDERS
MCKECHNIE FIELD
1611 9TH STREET WEST
BRADENTON, FL 34205
941-747-3031
Fax: 941-747-9442
maraudersinfo@pirates.com

• Trevor Gooby, Senior Director of Florida Operations
• Rachelle Madrigal, Director of Sales and General Manager
• AJ Grant, Director of Operations
• Michael Ryan, Manager
Team Affiliate:
Pittsburgh Pirates

BREVARD COUNTY MANATEES
5800 STADIUM PARKWAY
SUITE 101
VIERA, FL 32940
321-633-9200
Fax: 321-633-4418
• Kyle Smith, General Manager
• Tom Winters, Chairman
• Charlie Baumann, President
• Chad Lovitt, Assistant General Manager
• Kelley Wheeler, Director, Business Operations and Finance
• Joe Ayrault, Team Manager
Ballpark:
Space Coast Stadium.
Ballpark Description:
Constructed in 1993 with a capacity of 8,100, Space Coast Stadium was the first Spring Training home of the Florida Marlins. Opened in 1994.
Major Team Affiliation:
Milwaukee Brewers
Media Broadcast:
WMEL 920-AM.

CHARLOTTE STONE CRABS
CHARLOTTE SPORTS PARK
2300 EL JOBEAN ROAD
PORT CHARLOTTE, FL 33948
941-206-4487
Fax: 941-206-3599
• Jared Forma, General Manager
• Jeff Cook, Director of Ticket Operations
• Kelly Scott, Box Officer Manager
• Michael Johns, Manager
Ballpark:
Charlotte Sports Park
Team Affiliate:
Tampa Bay Rays

CLEARWATER THRESHERS
BRIGHT HOUSE FIELD
601 NORTH OLD COACHMAN ROAD
CLEARWATER, FL 33765
727-712-4300
Fax: 727-712-4498
info@threshersbaseball.com
www.threshersbaseball.com
• David Montgomery, General Partner
• John Timberlake, Director of Operations/General Manager
• Dan McDonough, Assistant GM/Sales
dmcdonough@threshersbaseball.com
• Jason Adams, Assistant General Manager/Ticketing
jason@threshersbaseball.com
• Jay Warren, Ballpark Operations Manager
jwarren@threshersbaseball.com
• Greg Legg, Manager
Ballpark:
Bright House Field.
Ballpark Description:
Opened in 2004, a fan-friendly ballpark with a capacity of 8,500 with 7,000 fixed seats. We are the Spring Training grounds for the Philadelphia Phillies.
Major Team Affiliation:
Philadelphia Phillies.

DAYTONA TORTUGAS
JACKIE ROBINSON PARK
105 EAST ORANGE AVENUE
DAYTONA BEACH, FL 32114
386-257-3172
Fax: 386-523-9490
• Tammy Devine, Director of Business Operations
• Josh Lawther, General Manager

• JR Laub, Assistant General Manager
• Paul Krenzer, Director of Ticket Operations
• Eli Marrero, Manager
Ballpark:
Jackie Robinson Ballpark. (The Jack)
Ballpark Description:
The historic ballpark opened on June 4, 1914 as Daytona City Island Ballpark. In memory of the first site hosting a racially integrated game in baseball history, the ballpark was renamed Jackie Robinson Ballpark in 1990.
Major Team Affiliation:
Cincinnati Reds.

DUNEDIN BLUE JAYS
FLORIDA AUTO EXCHANGE STADIUM
373 DOUGLAS AVENUE
DUNEDIN, FL 34698
727-733-9302
Fax: 727-734-7661
• Shelby Nelson, Director, Florida Operations/GM
(727) 738-7020
• Leon Harrell, Stadium Operations
• Jonathan Valdez, Manager of Ticket Operations/Community Relati
(727) 738-7036
• Bobby Meacham, Manager
Ballpark:
Florida Auto Exchange Stadium
Ballpark Description:
Knology Park, ranked by Sports Illustrated as one of the top 5 places to watch a Spring Training game, is a community ballpark in which Dunedin residents and visitors can enjoy Toronto Blue Jays Spring Training, Dunedin Blue Jays Minor League Baseball, Dunedin Falcons High School Baseball and various additional community events throughout the year. The park capacity is 5,491 individual seats and features include a press box level with air-conditioned skyboxes and a scoreboard with electronic message display, regulation-sized Major League playing field and lighting, half-field, batting tunnels, and full concession capabilities.
Major Team Affiliation:
Toronto Blue Jays.

FORT MYERS MIRACLE
14400 SIX MILE CYPRESS PARKWAY
FORT MYERS, FL 33912
239-768-4210
Fax: 239-768-4211
• Jason Hochberg, President
• Marv Goldklang, Principal Owner
• Steve Gliner, Chief Operating Officer
• Andrew Seymour, General Manager
• Bill Levy, Director of Ticket Operations
• John Kuhn, Director of Business Development
• Suzanne Reeves, Director of Business Operations
• Jeff Smith, Manager
Ballpark:
William Hammond Stadium.
Ballpark Description:
Opened in 1991 and spring home of the Minnesota Twins.
Major Team Affiliation:
Minnesota Twins.

JUPITER HAMMERHEADS
ROGER DEAN STADIUM
4751 MAIN STREET
JUPITER, FL 33458
561-775-1818
Fax: 561-691-6886
• Mike Bauer, General Manager
(561) 630-1840
m.bauer@rogerdeanstadium.com
• Alex Inman, Assistant General Manager
• Haile Urquhart, Director of Ticketing
Description:
The Jupiter Hammerheads are the Advanced-A affiliate for the Florida Marlins. We have been in existance since 1998 and were originally an affiliate of the Montreal Expos through 2001. Beginning in 2002, we became an affiliate of the

Florida Marlins organization.
Ballpark:
Roger Dean Stadium.
Ballpark Description:
The stadium was built in 1997 and opened in February 1998 for Spring Training. Roger Dean Stadium is currently the Spring Training home of the Florida Marlins and St. Louis Cardinals and the Florida State League home of the Jupiter Hammerheads and Palm Beach Cardinals. The facility is the only one in the country which serves as home for two Minor League Baseball teams.
Major Team Affiliation:
Miami Marlins

LAKELAND FLYING TIGERS
JOKER MARCHANT STADIUM
2125 NORTH LAKE AVENUE
#A
LAKELAND, FL 33805
863-686-8075
Fax: 863-688-9589
• Zack Burek, General Manager
• Ron Myers, Director of Florida Operations
• Shannon Follett, Administration and Operations Manager
• Ryan Eason, Ticket Operations
• Dave Huppert, Manager
Ballpark:
Joker Marchant Stadium.
Ballpark Description:
Marchant Stadium was named in honor of the late Joker Marchant, Lakeland's former parks and recreation director. The all-concrete grandstand of the stadium was built by the City of Lakeland at a cost of $500,000 and originally seated 4,900 spectators. Expansion projects beginning in the early 1970s brought the capacity to 7,100 and the recently completed renovation project upped the capacity to approximately 8,500. Previous renovations have included the addition of lights that allowed the first night game to be played in Lakeland in 1972 and a food and picnic court that was added in 1994 to increase the fan appeal of Joker Marchant Stadium.
Major Team Affiliation:
Detroit Tigers.

PALM BEACH CARDINALS
ROGER DEAN STADIUM
4751 MAIN STREET
JUPITER, FL 33458
561-775-1818
Fax: 561-691-6886
• Mike Bauer, General Manager, Jupiter Stadium
(561) 630-1848
• Alex Inman, General Manager, Palm Beach Cardinal's
• Liz Parent, Assistant to GM, Jupiter Stadium
(561) 630-1850
c.mcateer@rogerdeanstadium.com
• Dianne Detling, Office Manager
(561) 799-1376
• Haile Urquhart, Director of Ticketing
• Oliver Marmol, Manager
Description:
The Palm Beach Cardinals are the Advanced-A affiliate for the St. Louis Cardinals. They have been in existance since 2003 and are part of the East Division of the Florida State League.
Ballpark:
Roger Dean Stadium.
Ballpark Description:
The stadium was built in 1997 and opened in February 1998 for Spring Training. Roger Dean Stadium is currently the Spring Training home of the Florida Marlins and St. Louis Cardinals and the Florida State League home of the Jupiter Hammerheads and Palm Beach Cardinals. The facility is the only one in the country which serves as home to two Minor League Baseball teams.
Major Team Affiliation:
St. Louis Cardinals.

ST. LUCIE METS
TRADITION FIELD
525 NW PEACOCK BOULEVARD
PORT ST. LUCIE, FL 34986
772-871-2100
Fax: 772-878-9802
info@stluciemets.com
• Paul Taglieri, Executive Director
• Traer Van Allen, General Manager
• Clint Cure, Assistant General Manager
• Stephen Fox, Director, Ticketing and Merchandise
• Lauren Mahoney, Manager, Sales and Corporate Partnerships
• Kyle Gleockler, Manager, Ticketing and Merchandise
• John Gallagher, Manager, Food and Beverage Operations
Ballpark:
Tradition Field
Ballpark Description:
Tradition Field is home to the New York Mets Spring Training, the St. Lucie Mets Minor League Team and all the New York Mets Minor League operations. It has a seating capacity of 7,160 and is available for concerts, festivals, and much more.
Major Team Affiliation:
New York Mets.

TAMPA YANKEES
GEORGE M. STEINBRENNER FIELD
ONE STEINBRENNER DRIVE
TAMPA, FL 33614
813-673-3055
Fax: 813-673-3174
• C. Vance Smith, Director of Florida Operations/General Manager
• Matt Gess, Assistant General Manager, Marketing
• Jennifer Magliocchetti, Assistant Director of Ticket Operations
• Dave Bialas, Team Manager
Ballpark:
Steinbrenner Stadium
Ballpark Description:
Opened in 1996, Legends Field is a 31 acre complex and has a seating capacity of 10,000 seats. It was renamed to Steinbrenner Stadium in 2008.
Major Team Affiliation:
New York Yankees.

FREEDOM PRO BASEBALL LEAGUE
4301 NORTH 75TH STREET
SUITE 105
PO BOX 5403
SCOTTSDALE, AZ 85251
480-946-0211
Fax: 480-947-4099
• Tim Gross, Majority Owner
• Joe Perle, President & Minority Owner
Teams:
Goodyear Centennials; Peoria Explorers; Phoenix Prospectors; Prescott Montezuma Federals

FRONTIER LEAGUE OF PROFESSIONAL BASEBALL/INDEPENDENT LEAGUE
2041 GOOSE LAKE ROAD
SUITE 2A
SAUGET, IL 62206
618-215-4134
office@frontierleague.com
www.frontierleague.com
• Steve Tahsler, Commissioner
(812) 437-8709
stahsler@frontierleague.com
• Matt Shepardson, Deputy Commissioner
mshepardson@frontierleague.com
• John White, Umpire Supervisor
jwhite@umpcourse.com
League History:
In the winter of 1992-1993, several men got together and decided to start an independent professional baseball league to serve the West Virginia, eastern Kentucky and southeast Ohio areas. They believed they could bring professional baseball to areas that would never have a chance of affiliated professional baseball coming to their communities. The seed was planted and they named their project The Frontier League. In 2019, the Frontier League merged with the Canadian American Association of Professional Baseball (Can-Am League).

Teams:

EVANSVILLE OTTERS
BOSSE FIELD
23 DON MATTINGLY WAY
EVANSVILLE, IN 47711
812-435-8686
Fax: 812-435-8688
ottersbb@evansville.net
www.evansvilleotters.com
• Bix Branson, Vice President
• Jake Riffert, Director of Operations
• Joel Padfield, General Manager
• Celia Langford, Director of Community Relations
• Andy McCauley, Manager
Ballpark:
Bosse Field.
Ballpark Description:
Opening Day was on June 17 1915. Seating capacity listed is at 7,180.

FLORENCE FREEDOM
UC HEALTH STADIUM
7950 FREEDOM WAY
FLORENCE, KY 41042
859-594-4487
Fax: 859-594-3194
www.florencefreedom.com
• Clint Brown, President/Owner
(859) 594-4487
• Josh Anderson, General Manager
(859) 594-4487
• Kim Brown, Assistant General Manager of Operations
• Dennis Pelfrey, Field Manager
Description:
Champion Window Field in Northern Kentucky was recently renovated.

GATEWAY GRIZZLIES
GCS BALLPARK
2301 GRIZZLIE BEAR BOULEVARD
SAUGET, IL 62206
618-337-3000
Fax: 618-332-3625
grizzlies@accessus.net
www.gatewaygrizzlies.com
• Rich Sauget, Owner
• Steve Gomric, General Manager
• Chris Kellermannn, Director of Corporate Partnerships
• Phil Warren, Manager
pwarren@gatewaygrizzlies.com
Ballpark:
GCS Stadium.
Ballpark Description:
The Grizzlies' ballpark was built in 2002. The stadium can hold over 6,000 people and has reserved box seating, lawn seating, party suites and two hot tubs. The ballpark has been featured on digitalballparks.com as one of the best in the nation.
Corporate Sponsors:
Budweiser, GCS Federal Credit Union, GMC, Mrs. T's Pierogies, National City, Pepsi, US Bank, U.S. Cellular.

LAKE ERIE CRUSHERS
ALL PRO FREIGHT STADIUM
2009 BASEBALL BOULEVARD
AVON, OH 44011
440-934-3636
Fax: 440-934-2458
www.lakeeriecrushers.com
• Tom Kramig, President/CEO
• D.J. Saylor, Assistant Director of Stadium Operations
• Vicki Winkel, VP of Business Development
• Paul Siegwarth, VP Stadium Operations
• Kathleen Hudson, Controller

NEW JERSEY JACKALS
YOGI BERRA STADIUM
ONE HALL DRIVE
LITTLE FALLS, NJ 07424
973-746-7434
Fax: 973-655-8006
info@jackals.com
www.jackals.com
• Floyd Hall, Owner and Chairman
• Gregory L. Lockard, President
• Larry Hall, Executive Vice President
• Jennifer Fertig, VP of Finance & Operations
• Joe Calfapietra, Field Manager

NORMAL CORN BELTERS
THE CORN CRIB
1000 WEST RAAB ROAD
NORMAL, IL 61761
309-454-2255
Fax: 309-454-2287
www.normalbaseball.com
• Steve Malliet, President, General Manager
• Jeff Holtke, Assistant General Manager
• Mike Petrini, Assistant General Manager
• Deana Roberts, Business Manager

OTTAWA TITANS
OTTAWA TITANS BASEBALL CLUB
OTTAWA STADIUM
300 COVENTRY ROAD
OTTAWA, ON, CANADA K1K 4P5
343-633-2273
Fax: 343-633-2274
contact@ottawatitans.com
ottawatitans.com
• Sam Katz, President & CEO
• Martin Boyce, General Manager
mboyce@ottawatitans.com

QUEBEC CAPITALES
STADE CANAC
100 CARDINAL MAURICE-ROY ST
QUEBEC, QC, CANADA G1K 8Z1
418-521-2255
877-521-2244
Fax: 418-521-2266
info@capitalesdequebec.com
capitalesdequebec.com
• Jean Tremblay, Owner
• Philippe Tremblay, Owner
• Charles Demers, President
cdemers@capitalesdequebec.com

RIVER CITY RASCALS
T.R. HUGHES BALLPARK
900 T.R. HUGHES BOULEVARD
O'FALLON, MO 63366
636-240-2287
Fax: 636-240-7313
info@rivercityrascals.com
www.rivercityrascals.com
• Dan Dial, President/General Manager
• Lisa Fegley, Assistant General Manager
• Carrie Green, Business Manager
• Mo Stranz, Director of Food & Beverage
Ballpark:
T.R. Hughes Ballpark.
Ballpark Description:
The facility has 3,491 permanent seats and a grass berm and picnic area capable of holding an additional 1,700 fans. With clean, wholesome, family entertainment played in an intimate atmosphere, T.R. Hughes Ballpark has become the place to be every summer.
Media Broadcasting:
KSLQ 104.5-FM.

ROCKLAND BOULDERS
1 PALISADES CREDIT UNION PARK DRIVE
PALISADES CREDIT UNION PARK
POMONA, NY 10970
845-364-0009
Fax: 845-364-0001
info@rocklandboulders.com
www.rocklandboulders.com
• Ken Lehner, President
klehner@rocklandboulders.com
• Shawn Reilly, Executive Vice President/General Manager
sreilly@rocklandboulders.com
• Seth Cantor, Assistant General Manager/Voice of the Boulders
scantor@rocklandboulders.com
• Nick Barbalato, Assistant General Manager/Director of Operations
nbarbalato@rocklandboulders.com
Year Founded:
2011
Seating Capacity:
4,750

SCHAUMBURG BOOMERS
1999 SPRINGINSGUTH ROAD
SCHAUMBURG, IL 60193
847-461-3695
Fax: 630-439-3501
info@boomersbaseball.com
www.boomersbaseball.com
• Pete Laven, President/General Manager
• Mike Kline, Assistant General Manager/Director of Sales
• Rich Essegian, Director of Food and Beverage
• Mike Tlusty, Director of Facilities

SOUTHERN ILLINOIS MINERS
RENT ONE PARK
1000 MINERS DRIVE
MARION, IL 62959
618-998-8499
Fax: 618-969-8550
info@southernillinoisminers.com
www.southernillinoisminers.com
• Jayne Simmons, Owner
• Mike Pinto, Chief Operating Officer
• Casey Petermeyer, Director of Extra Events/Stadium Op.
• Jake Holtkamp, Director of Ticket Operations

SUSSEX COUNTY MINERS
SKYLANDS STADIUM
94 CHAMPIONSHIP PLACE
AUGUSTA, NJ 07822
973-383-7644
Fax: 973-383-7522
contact@scminers.com
www.sussexcountyminers.com
• Al Dorso, Sr., Owner, President
• Al Dorso, Jr., Vice President, Operations
• Mike Dorso, Vice President, Marketing
• Dave Chase, General Manager
• Tyler Borkowski, Assistant General Manager
• Dennis Mark, Director, Creative Services
• Andrew Luftglass, Director, Broadcasting & Media Relations

TRAVERSE CITY BEACH BUMS
333 STADIUM DRIVE
TRAVERSE CITY, MI 49685
231-943-0100
Fax: 231-943-0900
sales@traversecitybeachbums.com
www.traversecitybeachbums.com
• Jason Wuerfel, Vice President/Director of Baseball Operations
• John E. Wuerfel, President
• Leslye A. Wuerfel, Chief Financial Officer
• Tom Goethel, Assistant General Manager

TROIS-RIVIERES AIGLES
1760 GILLES-VILLENEUVE AVE
TROIS-RIVIERES, QC, CANADA G9A 5K8
819-379-0404
info@lesaiglestr.com
lesaiglestr.com
• Rene Martin, President
r.martin@lesaiglestr.com
• Jerome Duchesneau, General Manager
j.duchesneau@lesaiglestr.com

WASHINGTON WILD THINGS
CONSOL ENERGY PARK
ONE WASHINGTON FEDERAL WAY
WASHINGTON, PA 15301
724-250-9555
Fax: 724-250-2333
www.washingtonwildthings.com
• Bob Bozzuto, Field Manager
• Ben Moore, Pitching Coach

WINDY CITY THUNDERBOLTS
STANDARD BANK STADIUM
14011 SOUTH KENTON AVENUE
CRESTWOOD, IL 60445
708-489-2255
Fax: 708-489-2999
info@wcthunderbolts.com
www.wcthunderbolts.com
• Mike Lucas, General Manager
• Mike VerSchave, Assistant General Manager
• Marissa Miller, Director of Community Relations
Team History:
Founded in the winter of 1992-1993, the Windy City ThunderBolts are a minor league professional baseball club located in Crestwood, IL. They were formally known as the Cook County Cheetahs, but in 2004 they received a new ownership group, name, mascot, and a new look at minor league baseball. They are a member of the Frontier League, the premier independent professional baseball league in the country.
Ballpark:
Standard Bank Stadium
Ballpark Description:
This state of the art stadium has a capacity of over 3,000 fans and includes full-service concession areas, three picnic areas, a beer garden, and a kids' play area. Hawkinson Ford field is also one of the only minor league ballparks to have an upper deck.

GULF COAST LEAGUE
9550 16TH ST. N.
ST. PETERSBURG, FL 33716
727-456-1734
Fax: 727-821-5819
gcl@milb.com
www.milb.com
• Tim Brunswick, Vice President, Baseball & Business Operations
• Andy Shultz, Manager, Baseball & Business Operations
Teams:
Astros; Braves; Blue Jays; Cardinals; Marlins; Mets; Nationals; Orioles; Phillies; Pirates; Rays; Red Sox; Tigers; Twins; Yankees

INTERNATIONAL LEAGUE (AAA LEVEL)
55 SOUTH HIGH STREET
SUITE 202
DUBLIN, OH 43017
614-791-9300
Fax: 614-791-9009
www.ilbaseball.com
• Randy A. Mobley, President/Treasurer
• Dave Rosenfield, Vice President
• Chris Sprague, Assistant to the President
• Max Schumacher, Corporate Secretary

Years League Active:
1884-Present

Teams:

BUFFALO BISONS
COCA-COLA FIELD
ONE JAMES D. GRIFFIN PLAZA
BUFFALO, NY 14203
716-846-2000
Fax: 716-852-6530
info@bisons.com
• Robert E. Rich, Jr., Owner/President
• Michael Buczkowski, Vice President/General Manager
• Melinda R. Rich, President, Rich Entertainment Group
• William G. Gisel, Jr., Vice President/Secretary
• Joseph W. Segarra, Vice President, Chief Operating Officer
• Jonathan A. Dandes, President, Rich Baseball Operations
• Tom Sciarrino, Director of Stadium Operations
Ballpark:
Coca-Cola Park
Ballpark Description:
Praised as one of the finest ballparks in professional baseball. Dunn Tire Park opened on April 14, 1988 to a sellout crowd of 19,500. Since then, millions of fans have enjoyed great baseball action and exciting promotions.
Years in League:
1886-90, 1912-70, 1998-present.
Major Team Affiliation:
New York Mets

CHARLOTTE KNIGHTS
BB&T BALLPARK
324 SOUTH MINT STREET
CHARLOTTE, NC 28202
704-274-8300
Fax: 704-274-8330
knights@charlotteknights.com
• Dan Rajkowski, Vice President, Chief Operating Officer
• Scotty Brown, General Manager of Baseball Operations
• Julie Clark, Director of Special Programs & Events
• Chris Semmens, Vice President, Sales
• Matt Millward, Director of Ticket Operations
• Tommy Viola, Director of Public Relations
Ballpark:
BB&T Ballpark
Years in League:
1993-present.
Major Team Affiliation:
Chicago White Sox.

COLUMBUA CLIPPERS
330 HUNTINGTON PARK LANE
COLUMBUS, OH 43215
614-462-5250
Fax: 614-462-3271
info@clippersbaseball.com
• Ken Schnacke, President, General Manager
• Mark Warren, Assistant General Manager
• Bonnie Badgley, Director of Finance
• Steve Dalin, Director of Ballpark Operations
• Scott Ziegler, Director of Ticket Operations
• Mark Galuska, Director of Marketing and Sales
• Seth Rhodes, Director of Promotions & In-Game Entertainment
Team History:
When the Columbus Jets pulled up stakes and moved away after the 1970 season, it left Columbus without professional baseball for the first time in 75 years. For six years central Ohio fans did without baseball. In 1977, Cooper again pushed for a professional team and a major stadium renovation. The Columbus Clippers and Franklin County Stadium were born. The new home of the Clippers is Huntington Park in downtown Columbus.
Ballpark:
Huntington Park
Team Affiliate:
Cleveland Indians

DURHAM BULLS
DURHAM BULLS ATHLETIC PARK
409 BLACKWELL STREET
DURHAM, NC 27701
919-687-6500
Fax: 919-687-6560
info@durhambulls.com
www.durhambulls.com
• George Habel, Vice President
• Jared Sandberg, Manager
• Mike Birling, General Manager
Ballpark:
Durham Bulls Athletic Park.
Ballpark Description:
The $16-million brick ballpark opened in 1995 and was expanded to a 10,000-seat capacity for the 1998 season, the year the Bulls began playing in the Triple-A International League.
Media Broadcast:
WDNC 620-AM.
Major Team Affiliation:
Tampa Bay Rays.

GWINNETT BRAVES
2500 BUFORD DRIVE
LAWRENCEVILLE, GA 30043
678-277-0300
Fax: 678-277-0338
gwinnettinfo@braves.com
gwinnett.braves.milb.com
• North Johnson, General Manager
• Shari Massengill, Assistant General Manager
• Todd Pund, Director of Ticket Sales
• Ryan Stoltenberg, Manager of Stadium Operations
• Brian Snitker, Manager
Ballpark:
Coolray Field.
Major Team Affiliation:
Atlanta Braves.
Media Broadcast:
ESPN 950-AM.

INDIANAPOLIS INDIANS
VICTORY FIELD
501 WEST MARYLAND STREET
INDIANAPOLIS, IN 46225
317-269-3542
Fax: 317-269-3541
indians@indyindians.com
www.indyindians.com
• Max B. Schumacher, President/Chairman (317) 269-3542
• Cal Burleson, Vice President/Administration (317) 269-3542
burleson@indyindians.com
• Randy Lewandowski, General Manager (317) 269-3542
burleson@indyindians.com
• Brad Morris, Director, Business Operations (317) 269-3542
• Andrew Jackson, Operations Manager (317) 269-3542
• Matt Guay, Director of Tickets
Ballpark:
Victory Field.
Ballpark Description:
Victory Field draws its name from the Indianapolis Indians' former home. Originally opened as Perry Stadium in 1931, that ballpark held the name Victory Field from 1942 to 1967 celebrating the United States' victory in World War II.
Media Broadcast:
Indianapolis ESPN 950-AM.
Major League Affiliate:
Pittsburgh Pirates.

LEHIGH VALLEY IRON PIGS
COCA-COLA PARK
1050 IRONPIGS WAY
ALLENTOWN, PA 18109
610-841-7447
Fax: 610-841-1509
info@ironpigsbaseball.com
• Craig Stein, Owner
• Joe Finley, Owner
• Chuck Domino, Senior Advisor

• Kurt Landes, President & General Manager
• Howard Scharf, Assistant General Manager
• Michelle Perl, Finance Manager
• Scott Evans, Director of Ticket Sales
• Jason Kiesel, Director, Stadium Operations
• Dale Brundage, Manager
Team Affiliate:
Philadelphia Phillies

LOUISVILLE BATS
LOUISVILLE BATS BASEBALL CLUB
401 EAST MAIN STREET
LOUISVILLE, KY 40202
502-212-2287
Fax: 502-515-2255
info@batsbaseball.com
www.batsbaseball.com
• Gary Ulmer, President
gulmer@batsbaseball.com
• Dale Owens, Senior Vice President, Corporate Sales
dowens@batsbaseball.com
• Greg Galiette, Senior Vice President
ggaliette@batsbaseball.com
• Scott Shoemaker, Vice President, Operations and Technology
sshoemaker@batsbaseball.com
• Kyle Reh, Director, Business Operations
jbreeding@batsbaseball.com
• Jeff Hafling, General Manager
Ballpark:
Louisville Slugger Field.
Ballpark Description:
The stadium which opened in April of 2000 seats over 13,131 and was built on the banks of the Ohio River, within one block of the Waterfront Park.
Media Broadcast:
WGTK 970-AM.
Years in League:
1998-present.
Major Team Affiliation:
Cincinnati Reds.

NORFOLK TIDES
HARBOR PARK
150 PARK AVE
NORFOLK, VA 23510
757-622-2222
Fax: 757-624-9090
receptionist@norfolktides.com
www.norfolktides.com
• Ken Young, President (757) 622-2222
kyoung@norfolktides.com
• Joe Gregory, General Manager
• Ben Giancola, Assistant General Manager (757) 622-2222
bgiancola@norfolktides.com
• Gretchen Todd, Director, Ticket Operations (757) 622-2222
gtodd@norfolktides.com
• Mike Zeman, Director, Stadium Operations (757) 622-2222
mzeman@norfolktides.com
• Ron Johnson, Manager
Team History:
Norfolk had been without professional baseball since the Tars of the Piedmont League folded on July 13, 1955. The team operated in the South Atlantic League for two years, first as an independent, the second with a Cardinal working agreement. Granny Hamner, the former Phillie Whiz Kid, became the first manager.
Ballpark:
Harbor Park.
Ballpark Description:
Harbor Park, with its outstanding view and sound design, is one of the finest baseball facilities in existence. The ballpark is located in downtown Norfolk on the Elizabeth River, has a seating capacity of 12,067 and was opened in 1993.
Affiliation:
Baltimore Orioles

PAWTUCKET RED SOX
MCCOY STADIUM
ONE COLUMBUS AVENUE
PAWTUCKET, RI 02860
401-724-7300
Fax: 401-724-2140
info@pawsox.com
www.pawsox.com
• Larry Lucchino, Chairman of the Board
• Mike Tamburro, Vice Chairman
• Dan Rea, SVP/General Manager
• Matt White, Vice President/Chief Operating Officer
• Dave Johnson, Director of Warehouse Operations
• Bill Wanless, Vice President, Public Relations
• Michael Gwynn, Vice President of Sales & Marketing
• Kevin Boles, Manager
Ballpark:
McCoy Stadium.
Ballpark Information:
The stadium was erected in 1942 and was named in Honor of Thomas P. McCoy, mayor of Pawtucket from 1936-1945. The total seating capacity is 10,031.
Team Affiliate:
Boston Red Sox

ROCHESTER RED WINGS
FRONTIER FIELD
ONE MORRIE SILVER WAY
ROCHESTER, NY 14608
585-454-1001
Fax: 585-454-1056
info@redwingsbaseball.com
www.redwingsbaseball.com
• Naomi Silver, President, CEO/COO
• Gary Larder, Chairman of the Board
• Leonard Korn, Vice President
• Dan Mason, General Manager
• Will Rumbold, Assistant General Manager
• Matt Cipro, Senior Director of Sales
• Gene Buonomo, Director, Stadium Operations
• Mike Quade, Manager
• Tim Doherty, Hitting Coach
• Marty Mason, Pitching Coach
Ballpark:
Frontier Field.
Ballpark Description:
Frontier Field's official seating capacity is 10,840 with the possibility of an additional 2,500 to 3,000 more in bleacher and standing-room-only areas in the event of a sellout crowd.
Major League Affiliation:
Minnesota Twins

SCRANTON/WILKES-BARRE RAILRIDERS
PNC FIELD
235 MONTAGE MOUNTAIN ROAD
MOOSIC, PA 18507
570-969-2255
Fax: 570-963-6564
info@swbrailriders.com
www.swbrailriders.com
• Olerud Josh, President & General Manager
Ballpark:
PNC Field
Ballpark Description:
Opened in 1989.
Seating Capacity:
10,000
Team Affiliate:
New York Yankees

SYRACUSE CHIEFS
NBT BANK STADIUM
ONE TEX SIMONE DRIVE
SYRACUSE, NY 13208
315-474-7833
Fax: 315-474-2658
www.syracusechiefs.com
• Jason Smorol, General Manager
• Kathleen McCormick, Director of Sales and Marketing
• Billy Gardner, Manager
• Will Commisso, Director, Ticket Sales

Ballpark:
NBT Bank Stadium.
Ballpark Description:
Built on the former third base parking lot of MacArthur Stadium. Named on October 8 1996 and dedicated on April 2 1997. First game played on April 3 1997.
Media Broadcast:
WFBL 1390-AM.
Major Team Affiliation:
Washington Nationals

TOLEDO MUD HENS
FIFTH THIRD FIELD
406 WASHINGTON STREET
TOLEDO, OH 43604
419-725-4367
Fax: 419-725-4368
www.mudhens.com
• Joe Napoli, President, CEO
• Erik Ibsen, EVP, General Manager
• Kim McBroom, Chief Marketing Officer
• Lloyd McClendon, Manager
Ballpark:
Fifth Third Field.
Ballpark Description:
Toledo's new ballpark, Fifth Third Field opened in 2002 and has a seating capacity of 10,000
Media Broadcast:
WLQR 1470-AM, WFOB 1430-AM.
Camps:
Pepsi Baseball Camp.
Major Team Affiliation:
Detroit Tigers.

Teams:

JOLIET SLAMMERS
1 MAYOR ART SCHULTZ DRIVE
SLAMMERS STADIUM
JOLIET, IL 60432
815-722-2287
Fax: 815-726-4304
info@jolietslammers.com
www.jolietslammers.com
• Nick Semaca, President/Chief Executive Officer
• Heather Mills, General Manager
• Porscha Johnson, Manager Of Corporate Sale
• Lauren Rhodes, Account Executive
Year Founded:
2011
Seating Capacity:
6,500+

MEXICAN LEAGUE A.C. (AAA LEVEL)
INSURGENTES SUR 797
THIRD FLOOR
COL. NAPLES
BENITO JUAREZ, CP, MEXICO 03810
oficina@lmb.com.mx
LMB.com.mx
• Plinio Escalante Bolio, CEO
• Nestor Alba Brito, Director of Operations
• Patricio Perez Diego Ochoa, Player Registration and Control
• Oscarc Neri Rojas Salazar, Director of Administration
Description:
The Mexican League is a summer Triple AAA baseball league with teams based all along Mexico. The only Minor League baseball sanctioned outside of the US, and affiliated with Major League baseball.
Teams:
16

Teams:

AGUASCALIENTES RAILROADERS
LOPEZ MATEOS #101 TORRE A
PLAZA CRISTLA COLONIA
SAN LUIS, AGUASCALIENTES, MEXICO CP 20250

449-915 1596
www.rielerosags.com
• Marco Davalillo, Manager
Ballpark:
Parque Alberto Romo Chavez

BRONCOS DE REYNOSA
BRONCOS DE REYNOSA
ESTADIO ALDOLFO LOPEZ MATEOS
REYNOSA, TAMAULIPAS, MEXICO
• Jesus Sommers, Manager
Ballpark:
Estadio Aldolfo Lopez Mateos

CAMPECHE PIRATES
PIRATES DE CAMPECHE
ESTADIO NELSON BARRERA
CAMPECHE, MEXICO
• Dan Firova, Manager
Founded:
1980

DELFINES DEL CARMEN
www.delfinesbeisbol.com.mx
• Felix Fermin, Manager
Ballpark:
Estadio Resurgimiento

LAGUNA COWBOYS
VAQUEROS LAGUNA
ESTADIO REVOLUCION
TORREON, COAHUILA, MEXICO
• Luis Dovalina Flores, General Manager
• Jorge Luis Lechuga, Manager
Founded:
1940

MEXICO CITY RED DEVILS
MANUEL M. PONCE 87
FIRST FLOOR
COL. GUADALUPE INN
MEXICO CITY, MEXICO CP 01020
contacto@diablos-rojos.com
www.diablos.com.mx
• Roberto Mansure Galan, CEO
• Jorge Alum Kahwagi, General Manager
• Vania Ravelo, Media Manager
Founded:
1940

MONCOLVA STEELERS
ACEREROS DE MONCLOVA
ESTADIO DE BEISBOL MONCLOVA
MONCLOVA, COAHUILA, MEXICO C.P. 25750
52-866-636-2650
Fax: 52-866-636-2688
acererosdelnorte@prodigy.net.mx
• Donatian Garza Gutierrez, Managing Director
• Jorge Espinoza Lumbreras, Administrative Manager
• Oscar Romero Shot, Sports Manager
Founded:
1974

MONTERREY SULTANS
SULTANES DE MONTERREY
ESTADIO DE BEISBOL DE MONTERREY
AV. MANUEL BARRAGAN
MONTERREY, NUEVO LEON, MEXICO C.P. 64460
52-818-351-0209
Fax: 52-818-351-8022
www.sultanes.com.mx
• Jose Maiz Garcia, President
• Roberto Magdaleno Ramirez, Director General
Founded:
1939

OAXACA WARRIORS
GUERREROS DE OAXACA
ESTADIO EDUARDO VASCONCELOS
PRIVADA DEL CHOPO #115
OAXACA, MEXICO C.P. 68050

52-951-515-5522
Fax: 52-951-515-4966
www.guerreros.mx
• Vicente Perez Avella Villa, CEO
Founded:
1940

PUEBLA PARAKEETS
CALZADA IGNACIO ZARAGOZA
#666
COL. MARAVILLAS
PUEBLA, MEXICO CP 72220
11-52-222-222-2116
Fax: 11-52-222-222-2117
info@pericosdepuebla.com.mx
www.pericosdepuebla.com.mx
• Juan E. Villarreal, CEO
• Juan Emmanuel Bello Rustrian, COO
Ballpark:
Estadio de Beisbol Hermanos Serdan
Founded:
1924

QUINTANA ROO TIGERS
TIGRES DE QUINTANA ROO
ESTADIO DE BEISBOL BETO AVILA
CANCUN, QUINTANA ROO, MEXICO
• Francisco Minjarez, General Manager
Founded:
1955

SALTILLO SARAPE USERS
ESTADIO DE BEISBOL FRANSCISCO I
MADERO
BLVD NAZARIO S. ORTIZ GARZA
SALTILLO, COAHUILA, MEXICO C.P. 25280
52-844-416-9455
Fax: 52-844-439-0550
• Juan Rodriguez, Manager
Ballpark:
Estadio de Beisbol Francisco 1. Madero

TABASCO OLMECS
ESTADIO CENTENARIO 27 DE FEBRERO
COL. ATASTA DE SERRA
VILLAHERMOSA, TABASCO, MEXICO C.P.
86100
52-993-352-2787
Fax: 52-993-352-2788
olmecastab@prodigy.net.mx
• Raul Gonzalez Rodriguez, Executive President
• CP Luis Guzman Ramos, General Manager
• Lauro Jimenez Lopez, Media Chief/Public
Relations
Ballpark:
Estadio Centenario 27 de Febrero

TIJUANA BULLS
LA CASA DE NUESTROS TOROS DE
TIJUANA
BOULEVARD AGUA CALIENTE #11720
COL. HIPODROMO
TIJUNA, BC, MEXICO 22020
www.torosdetijuana.com
• Eddy Diaz, Manager
Ballpark:
Estadio Nacional de Tijuana

VERACRUZ RED EAGLES
ROJOS DEL AGUILA DE VERACRUZ
ESTADIO UNIVERSITARIO BETO AVILA
AV. JACARANDAS #244-B ESPANA
VERACRUZ, MEXICO CP 94294
52-229-935-5004
Fax: 52-229-935-5008
rojosdelaguila@prodigy.net.mx
• Jose Antonio Mansur Beltran, Executive
President
• Jean Paul Mansur Beltran, CEO
Ballpark:
Estadio Universitario Beto Avila

YUCATAN LIONS
LEONES DE YUCATAN
CALLE 50 #402-D

COL. JESUS CARRANZA
MERIDA, YUCATAN, MEXICO CP 97109
52-999-926-3022
Fax: 52-999-926-3631
www.leones.mx
• Propasa Dunosusa, Owner
• Jose Rivero, General Manager
• Edgar Tovar, Manager
Ballpark:
Estadio de Beisbol Kukulkan Alamo
Founded:
1954

___

MIDWEST LEAGUE (A LEVEL)
210 SOUTH MICHIGAN STREET
5TH FLOOR - PLAZA BUILDING
SOUTH BEND, IN 46601
574-532-1221
Fax: 574-234-4220
dickn@sni-law.com
www.midwestleague.com
• George H. Spelius, President Emeritus
• Richard A. Nussbaum, II,
President/Secretary
• Holly Voss, League Administrator
League History:
The Illinois State League began operation in
1947. Six cities in Southern Illinois formed
teams and banded together as a Class D
League, the lowest among the ranks of
organized Minor League Baseball. The
League was forced to change its name to
the Mississippi-Ohio Valley (MOV) League
in 1949. During the combined nine year
history of the leagues, membership was
unstable, wavering back and forth from six
to eight teams. In 1956, the Midwest League
(MWL) name became official as teams
moved out of Southern Illinois to larger
markets.
Years in League:
1947-present.

Teams:

BELOIT SNAPPERS
2301 SKYLINE DRIVE
BELOIT, WI 53511
608-362-2272
Fax: 608-362-0418
snappy@snappersbaseball.com
www.snappersbaseball.com
• Dennis Conerton, President
• Seth Flolid, General Manager
• Crystal Bowen, Director of Ticket Operations
• Robert T. Coon, Director of Media Relations &
Marketing
• Fran Riordan, Manager
Team History:
Before the Snappers arrived in town in 1982, the
only professional baseball team in Beloit was a
team affiliated with the old Class D Wisconsin
Association in 1905. The Beloit Snappers have
been a Class A affiliate of the Milwaukee
Brewers since the club joined the Midwest
League in 1982. The team was known as the
Beloit Brewers (named after the parent club)
through the 1994 season, when the club name
then changed to the Snappers.
Ballpark:
Pohlman Field.
Ballpark Description:
Built in 1981, the Harry C. Pohlman Field
(originally named Telfer Park) is the home of the
Beloit Snappers. It's seating capacity is 3,500.
Team Affiliate:
Oakland Athletics

BOWLING GREEN HOT RODS
BOWLING GREEN HOT RODS
300 8TH AVENUE
BOWLING GREEN, KY 42102

270-901-2121
Fax: 270-901-2165
fun@bghotrods.com
• Adam Nuse, General Manager/COO
• Eric Leach, Assistant General Manager
• Stephanie Morton, Director of Finance
• Jennifer Johnson, Director of Marketing and
Community Relations
• Matt Ingram, Director of Sales
• Jordan Gracey, Director of Creative Services
• Reinaldo Ruiz, Manager
Team Affiliate:
Tampa Bay Rays

BURLINGTON BEES
2712 MOUNT PLEASANT STREET
BURLINGTON, IA 52601
319-754-5705
Fax: 319-754-5882
staff@gobees.com
www.gobees.com
• Dave Walker, President
• Chuck Brockett, General Manager
chuck@gobees.com
• Bill Dowell, Vice President
• Kim Parker, Assistant GM, Director of Group
Outings
• Chad Tracy, Manager
Ballpark:
Community Field
Ballpark Description:
Built in 1947, burned in 1971 and rebuilt and
opened in 1973, then renovated in 2005. Seats
3,200.
Team Affiliate:
Los Angeles Angels of Anaheim

CEDAR RAPIDS KERNELS
PERFECT GAME FIELD
950 ROCKFORD ROAD SW
CEDAR RAPIDS, IA 52404
319-363-3887
800-860-3609
Fax: 319-363-5631
www.kernels.com
• Jake Mauer, Manager
• Brian Dinkelman, Hitting Coach
• J.P. Martinez, Pitching Coach
Ballpark:
Perfect Game Field.
Ballpark Description:
One of the two new ballparks in the Midwest
League in 2002. Veterans Memorial Stadium
has a seating capacity of 5,400.
Media Broadcast:
The Zone - ESPN 1600-AM.
Major League Affiliate:
Minnesota Twins

CLINTON LUMBERKINGS
ASHFORD UNIVERSITY FIELD
537 BALLPARK DRIVE
CLINTON, IA 52732
563-242-0727
Fax: 563-242-1433
lumberkings@lumberkings.com
www.lumberkings.com
• Ted Tornow, General Manager
• Tyler Oehmen, Director of Operations
• Shaun Thomas, Head Groundskeeper
• Greg Mroz, Director of Broadcasting & Media
Relations
• Alex Swartz, Director of Concessions
Ballpark:
Ashford University Field
Ballpark Description:
Built in 1937, Riverview Stadium was the orginal
name before changing to Alliant Field.
Media Broadcast:
KCLN 1390-AM.
Years in League:
1954-present.
Team Affiliate:
Seattle Mariners

DAYTON DRAGONS
FIFTH THIRD FIELD
220 NORTH PATTERSON BOULEVARD
DAYTON, OH 45402
937-228-2287
Fax: 937-228-2284
dragons@daytondragons.com
www.daytondragons.com
• Robert Murphy, President
teampresident@daytondragons.com
• Eric Deutsch, Executive Vice President
eric.deutsch@daytondragons.com
• Gary Mayse, Executive Vice President,
General Manager
gary.mayse@daytondragons.com
• Mark Schlein, Vice President of
Accounting/Finance
mark.schlein@daytondragons.com
• Jose Nieves, Manager
• Cody Oakes, Baseball Operations Manager
• Mike Vujea, Director of Group Sales
Ballpark:
Fifth Third Field.
Ballpark Description:
Opened in April 2000 with a seating capacity of
7,230.
Team Affiliate:
Cincinnati Reds

FORT WAYNE TINCAPS
PARKVIEW FIELD
1301 EWING STREET
FORT WAYNE, IN 46802
260-482-6400
Fax: 260-471-4678
info@tincaps.com
• Mike Nutter, Team President
• David Lorenz, VP, Corporate Partnerships
• Brian Schackow, VP, Finance
• Michael Limmer, VP, Marketing/Promotions
• Patrick Ventura, Director of Ticketing
• Francisco Morales, Manager
Major Team Affiliation:
San Diego Padres.
Media Broadcast:
ESPN Radio 1380-AM WONO.

GREAT LAKES LOONS
DOW DIAMOND
825 EAST MAIN STREET
MIDLAND, MI 48640
989-837-2255
888-678-2255
www.loons.com
• Paul Barbeau, President
• Scott Litle, VP, General Manager
• Jana Chotivkova, VP, Finance
• Kevin Schunk, Director of Corporate
Partnerships
• Jay Arons, Director of Sales
• Dan Straley, Director of Operations & Facilities
• Luis Matos, Manager
Stadium:
Dow Diamond
Team Affiliate:
LA Dodgers

KANE COUNTY COUGARS
NORTHWESTERN MEDICINE FIELD
34W002 CHERRY LANE
GENEVA, IL 60134
630-232-8811
Fax: 630-232-8815
info@kanecountycougars.com
www.kccougars.com
• Cheryl Froehlich, Owner & Board of Directors
• Bob Froehlich, Owner & Board of Directors
• Curtis Haug, VP, General Manager
Ballpark:
Fifth Third Bank Ballpark
Years in League:
1991-present.
Media Broadcast:
WBIG 1280-AM.
Major Team Affiliation:
Chicago Cubs

LAKE COUNTY CAPTAINS
CLASSIC PARK
35300 VINE STREET
EASTLAKE, OH 44095
440-975-8085
Fax: 440-975-8958
• Brad Seymour, General Manager
• Neil Stein, Assistant General Manager
• Rob Demko, Director of Finance
• John Klein, Director of Food & Beverage
• Drew LaFollette, Director of Promotions &
Marketing
• Wayne Loeblein, Director of Stadium
Operations
• Shaun Larkin, Manager
Team Affiliate:
Cleveland Indians

LANSING LUGNUTS
COOLEY LAW SCHOOL STADIUM
505 EAST MICHIGAN AVENUE
LANSING, MI 48912
517-485-4500
Fax: 517-485-4518
info@lansinglugnuts.com
www.lansinglugnuts.com
• Nick Grueser, General Manager
• Heather Viele, Director of Business Operations
• Dennis Busse, Stadium Operations Manager
• Ken Huckaby, Manager
Ballpark:
Cooley Law School Stadium
Ballpark Description:
Built in 1996, construction at the park was
completed in only one year by local craftspeople
and contractors. Oldsmobile Park is owned by
the City of Lansing and was financed by six local
banking institutions.
Major Team Affiliation:
Toronto Blue Jays.
Media Broadcast:
Lansing's Sports Radio 92.1/92.7-FM, WILX-TV
10.

PEORIA CHIEFS
DOZER PARK
730 SW JEFFERSON
PEORIA, IL 61605
309-680-4000
Fax: 309-680-4080
feedback@chiefsnet.com
www.peoriachiefs.com
• Rocky Vonachen, President
(309) 680-4001
rocky@chiefsnet.com
• Brendan Kelly, General Manager
(309) 680-4002
• Nathan Baliva, Director of Media & Baseball
Operations
(309) 680-4018
nathanb@chiefsnet.com
• Ryan Sivori, Box Office Manager
(309) 680-4006
ryans@chiefsnet.com
• Jason Mott, VP, Ticket Sales & Services
• Joe Kruzel, Manager
Team History:
Professional baseball in Peoria can be traced
back to 1878, with the formation of an
independent team named the Peoria Reds. In
the 1930s the team was called the Peoria
Tractors and though they played well,
attendance figures were disturbingly low. During
the time baseball was not present in Peoria, the
United States entered World War II, which led to
a shortage of professional baseball throughout
the entire country. In the fall of 1983, the team
was bought by a local businessman and
renamed the Chiefs, after the old Three-I
League team from the 1950s.
Ballpark:
Peoria Chiefs Stadium
Ballpark Description:
A $23 million multi-use facility built in 2002 with
a 7,000 seating capacity.
Sponsors:
O'Brien Automotive Team, WM Waste
Management, CEFCU, CAT, Pepsi, Bud Light,
Methodist Medical Center, Heart Technologies

Inc., Auto Owners Insurance.
Major Team Affiliation:
St. Louis Cardinals
Years in League:
1983-present.

QUAD CITIES RIVER BANDITS
MODERN WOODMEN PARK
209 SOUTH GAINES STREET
DAVENPORT, IA 52802
563-324-3000
Fax: 563-324-3109
bandit@riverbandits.com
www.riverbandits.com
• Andrew Chesser, General Manager
• Shawn Brown, Vice President of Sales
• Travis Painter, Assitant General Manager,
Baseball Operations
• Taylor Satterly, Assistant General Manager,
Special Events
• Mike Clark, Assistant General Manager of
Amusements
• Seth Reeve, Stadium Operations Manager
• Josh Bonifay, Manager
Team History:
On December 13 2007, a new era in Quad
Cities baseball began. The Midwest League
franchise that had been known as the Swing of
the Quad Cities for the previous four seasons
announced the overwhelming results of a recent
Name the Team contest, once again giving
baseball in the Quad Cities the name the
community has come to love: River Bandits.
Ballpark:
Modern Woodmen Park
Ballpark Description:
In the beginning Municipal Stadium (known then
as) was dedicated May 26 1931. A crowd of
2,791 watched the Davenport Blue Sox defeat
the Dubuque Tigers, 7-1. Municipal Stadium was
renamed in honor of former Davenport
Times-Democrat sports editor John O'Donnell
on May 27 1971, following O'Donnell's death.
Major Team Affiliation:
Houston Astros
Media Broadcast:
KBOB 104.9-FM.

SOUTH BEND CUBS
FOUR WINDS FIELD
501 WEST SOUTH STREET
SOUTH BEND, IN 46601
574-235-9988
Fax: 574-235-9950
cubs@southbendcubs.com
www.silverhawks.com
• Andrew Berlin, Owner & Chairman
• Joe Hart, President
• Peter Argueta, Assistant General Manager,
Operations
• Cheryl Carlson, Director of Finance and
Human Resources
• Nick Brown, Vice President/Business
Development
• Chris Hagstrom, Director of Creative Services
and Promotions
• Jimmy Gonzalez, Team Manager
Ballpark:
Coveleski Regional Stadium.
Ballpark Description:
Opened in 1988 and has 5,000 seating capacity.
Years in League:
1988-present.
Major Team Affiliation:
Chicago Cubs.

WEST MICHIGAN WHITECAPS
FIFTH THIRD BALLPARK
4500 WEST RIVER DRIVE
COMSTOCK PARK, MI 49326
616-784-4131
Fax: 616-784-4911
www.whitecaps-baseball.com
• Lew Chamberlain, CEO/Managing Partner
lchamberin@whitecapsbaseball.com
• Scott Lane, President
slane@whitecapsbaseball.com
• Denny Baxter, CFO/Director of Accounting

dbaxter@whitecapsbaseball.com
• Jim Jarecki, Vice President
jjarecki@whitecapsbaseball.com
• Steve McCarthy, VP of Sales
smccarthy@whitecapsbaseball.com
• Mickey Graham, Director of Marketing/Media Relations
• Chad Sayen, Director of Ticket Sales
• Andrew Graham, Manager
Team History:
When the West Michigan Whitecaps began play in the Grand Rapids area in 1994, it was the culmination of a 10-year labor of love for local businessmen Lew Chamberlin and Dennis Baxter. The two took on the challenge of bringing a minor league team to the area in 1984 and in February of 1993. Until the West Michigan Whitecaps began their inaugural season in 1994, Grand Rapids had been without a professional baseball team for 40 years, since the Grand Rapids Chicks disbanded in 1954.
Ballpark:
Fifth Third Ballpark.
Ballpark Description:
Fifth Third Ballpark is a $10 million state-of-the-art facility built in 1994 and expanded in 1995, 1996 and 1998. The stadium currently has a capacity of 11,000.
Major Team Affiliation:
Detroit Tigers.
Media Broadcast:
WBBL 1340-AM, WHTC 1450-AM, WSCG 1380-AM, WDEE 97.3-FM, WXSP-TV.

WISCONSIN TIMBER RATTLERS
FOX CITIES STADIUM
2400 NORTH CASALOMA DRIVE
APPLETON, WI 54912
920-733-4152
info@timberrattlers.com
www.timberrattlers.com
• Rob Zerjav, President
rzerjav@timberrattlers.com
• Aaron Hahn, Vice President, Assistant GM
rzerjav@timberrattlers.com
• Ron Kaiser, Director of Stadium Operations
• Chris Mehring, Media Relations
• Cathy Spanbauer, Controller
cspanbauer@timberrattlers.com
• Matt Erickson, Manager
Sponsors:
Sports Medicine Center, Pro/Net Consulting LLC, Virchow Krause & Company, Microtel.
Major Team Affiliation:
Midwest League affiliate of the Milwaukee Brewers

NEW YORK-PENNSYLVANIA LEAGUE (A LEVEL)
204 37TH AVENUE
N366
ST. PETERSBURG, FL 33704
727-289-7112
Fax: 727-683-9691
www.newyork-pennleague.com
• Ben J. Hayes, President
• Carl Gutelius, Corporate Secretary
• Jon Dandes, Treasurer
• Laurie Hayes, League Administrator
• Makenzie Burrows, Media
Nature of Service:
Baseball League.
Year Founded:
1939
League History:
The original New York-Pennsylvania League ran between 1923 and 1938 and was the immediate predecessor of the Eastern League. The current New York-Pennsylvania League was originally known as the PONY League in 1939-1956 before adopting the current New York-Pennsylvania League moniker in 1957.
Teams:
14

Teams:

ABERDEEN IRONBIRDS
RIPKEN STADIUM
873 LONG DRIVE
ABERDEEN, MD 21001
410-297-9292
Fax: 410-297-6653
www.ironbirdsbaseball.com
• Cal Ripken, Jr, Owner, Chair, Founder
• Joe Harrington, General Manager
• Chris Flannery, COO
• Bill Ripken, Co-Owner, Executive Vice President
• Luis Pujols, Manager
Ballpark:
Ripken Stadium
Major League Affiliation:
Baltimore Orioles

AUBURN DOUBLEDAYS
LEO PINCKNEY FIELD AT FALCON PARK
130 NORTH DIVISION STREET
AUBURN, NY 13021
315-255-2489
Fax: 315-255-2675
info@auburndoubledays.com
www.auburndoubledays.com
• Mike Voutsinas, General Manager
• Andrew Sagarin, Operations Manager
• Paul Mullin, Sponsorship Services Manager
• Derek Wohlfarth, Accounting Manager
• Jerad Head, Team Manager
Ballpark:
Falcon Park.
Ballpark Description:
Built in 1995 with a seating capacity of 2,800
Major Team Affiliation:
Washington Nationals
Media Broadcast:
WDWN 89.1-FM.
Years in League:
1958-80, 1982-present.

BATAVIA MUCKDOGS
DWYER STADIUM
299 BANK STREET
BATAVIA, NY 14020
585-343-5454
Fax: 585-343-5620
www.muckdogs.com
• Naomi Silver, Chair/COO
• Travis Sick, General Manager
• Don Rock, Director of Stadium Grounds
• Angel Espada, Team Manager
Years in League:
1939-53, 1957-59, 1961-present.
Team History:
In 1939 professional baseball came to Batavia and Genesee County. There had been talk of a professional baseball team for Batavia as early as 1936, but lack of a proper playing field including fences and lights which were the criteria, did not exist in the city. The Batavia franchise is unique in organized baseball because it is truly a community owned and operated in the strictest sense. There are no stockholders and no stock issue. The Genesee County Baseball Club Incorporated holds legal title to the franchise; its officers and directors are elected each year.
Ballpark:
Dwyer Stadium.
Ballpark Description:
The old Dwyer Stadium was demolished and replaced with a new three million dollar facility, which opened in time for the 1996 season.
Major Team Affiliation:
Miami Marlins
Media Broadcast:
WBSU 89.1-FM.

BROOKLYN CYCLONES
MCU PARK
1904 SURF AVENUE
BROOKLYN, NY 11224

718-449-8497
Fax: 718-449-6368
info@brooklyncyclones.com
www.brooklyncyclones.com
• Steve Cohen, Vice President
steve@brooklyncyclones.com
• Kevin Mahoney, General Manager
• Vladimir Lipsman, Operations Manager
vladimir@brooklyncyclones.com
• Gary J Perone, Assistant General Manager
• Tom Gamboa, Team Manager
Years in League:
2000-present.
Ballpark:
MCU Park.
Ballpark Description:
Opened in 2001
Media Broadcast:
WKRB 90.9
Major Team Affiliation:
New York Mets.

CONNECTICUT TIGERS
DODD STADIUM
14 STOTT AVENUE
NORWICH, CT 06360
860-887-7962
Fax: 860-886-5996
info@cttigers.com
• C.J. Knudsen, Senior Vice President
• Eric Knighton, General Manager
• Dave Schermerhorn, Assistant General Manager
• Heather Bartlett, Director of Concessions & Merchandise
• Brent Southworth, Director of Sales
• Jack Kasten, Director of Group Sales & Operations
Description:
The New York-Penn League and Minor League Baseball granted approval to the Oneonta Athletic Corporation to relocate their professional baseball franchise from Oneonta, New York to Norwich, Connecticut.
Affiliation:
Detroit Tigers, MLB

HUDSON VALLEY RENEGADES
DUTCHESS STADIUM
1500 ROUTE 9D
WAPPINGERS FALLS, NY 12590
845-838-0094
Fax: 845-838-0014
info@hvrenegades.com
www.hvrenegades.com
• Jeff Goldklang, President
• Eben Yager, Senior Vice President & General Manager
• Rick Zolzer, Vice President
• Kristen Huss, Assistant General Manager
• Vicky DeFreese, Director of Business Operations
vdefreese@hvrenegades.com
• Tim Parenton, Manager
Team History:
The Renegades officially arrived in the Hudson Valley on November 30, 1993 when team owner Marvin Goldklang and Club President Skip Weisman announced that the Erie Sailors franchise would be relocating to Dutchess County. Since that very memorable first season, the Renegades have become an integral part of the Hudson Valley community.
Ballpark:
Dutchess Stadium.
Ballpark Description:
The stadium opened it 1994 and seats 4,494
Media Broadcast:
WBNR 1260-AM, WLNA 1420-AM.
Years in League:
1994-present.
Affiliate:
Tampa Bay Rays

LOWELL SPINNERS
LELACHEUR PARK
450 AIKEN STREET
LOWELL, MA 01854

978-459-2255
Fax: 978-459-1674
www.lowellspinners.com
• Drew Weber, Owner/Chief Executive Officer
• Tim Bawmann, President, General Manager
• Jeff Cohen, Director of Merchandising
• Justin Williams, Director of Ticket Operations
• Joe Oliver, Manager
Ballpark:
Edward A. LeLacheur Park.
Ballpark Description:
Opened in 1998 and has a seating capacity of
5,000
Major Team Affiliation:
Boston Red Sox.

MAHONING VALLEY SCRAPPERS
EASTWOOD FIELD
111 EASTWOOD MALL BOULEVARD
NILES, OH 44446-1357
330-505-0000
Fax: 303-505-9696
info@mvscrappers.com
www.mvscrappers.com
• Alan Levin, Principal Owner
• Erik Haag, Executive Vice President
• Mike Rauch, Chief Financial Officer
• Jordan Taylor, General Manager/Vice
President
jtaylor@mvscrappers.com
• Brad Hooser, Assistant General Manager,
Operations
• Travis Fryman, Team Manager
Team History:
The Mahoning Valley Scrappers earned their
initial success during the 1999-opening season
and again in 2000. The team made its way to
the New York - Penn Minor League playoffs 2
years in a row, with spirit and support from the
Mahoning Valley.
Ballpark:
Eastwood Field.
Ballpark Description:
Completed in 1999, Eastwood Field's 6,300 seat
open-air stadium is an intimate entertainment
facility. This beautifully built stadium is located in
Niles, Ohio half way between Cleveland &
Pittsburgh. The new stadium was built in honor
of the late Cafaro Company Founder, William
Cafaro.
MLB Affiliate:
Cleveland Indians

STATE COLLEGE SPIKES
LUBRANO PARK
112 MEDLAR FIELD
UNIVERSITY PARK, PA 16802
814-272-1711
Fax: 814-272-1718
frontoffice@statecollegespikes.com
www.statecollegespikes.com
• Chuck Greenburg, Chairman and Managing
Partner
• Jason Dambach, President
• Scott Walker, General Manager
• Johnny Rodriguez, Manager
Team Affiliate:
St. Louis Cardinals
Ballpark:
Medlar Field at Lubrano Park

STATEN ISLAND YANKEES
75 RICHMOND TERRACE
RICHMOND COUNTY BANK BALLPARK
STATEN ISLAND, NY 10301
718-720-9265
Fax: 718-273-5763
www.siyanks.com
• Jane M. Rogers, President, General Manager
• Will Smith, Operating Partner
• Brian Levine, Vice President of Corporate
Relationships
• Jay Nazzaro, Chief Financial Officer
• T.J. Jahn, Vice President of Ticket Sales
• David Percarpio, Group Sales Manager
• Pat Osborn, Manager
Years in League:
1999-present.

Ballpark:
Richmond County Bank Ballpark.
Ballpark Description:
The Richmond County Bank Ballpark at St.
George is New York's premier waterfront
stadium and has become one of the standard
bearers in professional baseball parks across
the country. Opened on June 24 2001 the 7,171
seat home of the Staten Island Yankees was the
crown jewel of the borough and would soon
house not only baseball but concerts, picnics
and other special events.
Major Team Affiliation:
New York Yankees.
Media Broadcast:
WSIA 88.9-FM.

TRI-CITY VALLEYCATS
JOSEPH L. BRUNO STADIUM
80 VANDENBURG AVENUE
TROY, NY 12180
518-629-2287
Fax: 518-629-2299
info@tcvalleycats.com
www.tcvalleycats.com
• William L. Gladstone, President, Principal
Owner
• Matt Callahan, General Manager
• Michelle Skinner, General Manager
Ballpark:
Joseph L. Bruno Stadium.
Years in League:
1989-present.
Major Team Affiliation:
Houston Astros.
Media Broadcast:
WVKZ 1240-AM.

VERMONT LAKE MONSTERS
CENTENNIAL FIELD
ONE KING STREET FERRY DOCK
BURLINGTON, VT 05401
802-655-4200
Fax: 802-655-5660
www.vermontlakemonsters.com
• Ray C. Pecor, Principal Owner/President
• Kyle Bostwick, Vice President
• Nate Cloutier, Executive Director of Sales &
Marketing
• Joe Doud, General Manager
• Aaron Nieckula, Manager
Team History:
The Vermont Expos have been a member of the
Montreal Expos baseball system since 1994.
Over the past ten seasons, the Vermont Expos
have compiled a 372 win - 391 loss record,
including a 48 - 26 record and a NY-PENN
League Championship in 1996.
Ballpark:
Centennial Field.
Ballpark Description:
Located on the campus of the University of
Vermont in Burlington. Officially opened on April
17 1906. Since the Expos made Centennial
Field their home, they've completely rebuilt the
pitching mound and over 1,000 feet of warning
track, creating a field that compares favorably to
any in baseball.
Years in League:
1994-present.
MLB Affiliate:
Oakland A's

WEST VIRGINIA BLACK BEARS
MONONGALIA COUNTY BALLPARK
2040 GYORKO DRIVE
GRANVILLE, WV 26534
304-293-7910
wvblackbears@gmail.com
• Matthew Drayer, General Manager
• Wyatt Toregas, Manager
Team Affiliate:
Pittsburg Pirates.

WILLIAMSPORT CROSSCUTTERS
BB&T BALLPARK
1700 WEST FOURTH STREET
WILLIAMSPORT, PA 17701
570-326-3389
Fax: 570-326-3494
mail@crosscutters.com
www.crosscutters.com
• Doug Estes, VP, General Manager
• Gabe Sinicropi, VP, Marketing & Public
Relations
• Sarah Budd, Director, Ticket Operations &
Community Relations
• Bill Gehron, III, Director, Food & Beverage
• Pat Borders, Team Manager
Ballpark:
Bowman Field.
Ballpark Description:
One of baseball's oldest and most distinguished
ballparks is Williamsport's own Bowman Field.
Ground was broken for the ballpark in the fall of
1925. It was modeled after a ballpark in Johnson
City, New York. The first game played in the
new ballpark was an exhibition game between
the Williamsport Grays and the Bucknell
University baseball team on April 22 1926.
Years in League:
1923-37, 1968-72, 1994-present.
Major Team Affiliation:
Philadelphia Phillies

NORTHWEST BASEBALL LEAGUE
1271 AVENUE OF THE AMERICAS
NEW YORK, NY 10020
866-644-2687
customerservice@website.milb.com
www.milb.com

Teams:

BOISE HAWKS
MEMORIAL STADIUM
5600 GLENWOOD STREET
BOISE, ID 83714
208-322-5000
Fax: 208-322-6846
info@boisehawks.com
• Jeff Eiseman, President
• Bob Flannery, General Manager
• Britt Talbert, Corporate Sales Manager
• Jake Lusk, Director of Operations
• Frank Gonzales, Manager
Ballpark:
Memorial Stadium. Seating capacity, 3,452.

EUGENE EMERALDS
PK PARK
PO BOX 10911
EUGENE, OR 97440
541-342-5367
Fax: 541-342-6089
info@emeraldsbaseball.com
• Allan Benavides, General Manager
• Matt Dompe, Assistant General Manager
Ballpark:
PK Park. Seating capacity, 4,000.

EVERETT AQUASOX
EVERETT MEMORIAL STADIUM
3802 BROADWAY
EVERETT, WA 98201
425-258-3673
info@aquasox.com
www.aquasox.com
• Danny Tetzlaff, General Manager
Ballpark:
Everett Memorial Stadium. Seating capacity,
3,682.

HILLSBORO HOPS
RON TONKIN FIELD
4460 NW 229TH AVENUE
HILLSBORO, OR 97124
503-640-0887
info@hillsborohops.com

• Mike McMurray, President
• K.L. Wombacher, Executive Vice President &
General Manager
• Laura McMurray, Chief Financial Officer
• Shelley Duncan, Manager
Ballpark:
Ron Tonkin. Seating capacity, 3,534.

SALEM-KEIZER VOLCANOES
VOLCANOES STADIUM
6700 FIELD OF DREAMS NE
KEIZER, OR 97307
503-390-2225
Fax: 503-390-2227
info@volcanoesbaseball.com
• Jerry Walker, General Manager
• Tom Leip, Business Operations
• Rick Nelson, Stadium Operations
Ballpark:
Volcanoes Stadium. Seating capacity, 4,254.

SPOKANE INDIANS
AVISTA STADIUM
602 NORTH HAVANA STREET
SPOKANE, WA 99202
509-343-6886
mail@spokaneindians.com
• Bobby Brett, Managing Partner
• Andy Billig, Co-Owner & Senior Advisor
• Otto Klein, Senior Vice President
• Chris Duff, General Manager/Vice President
Ballpark:
Avista Stadium. Seating capacity, 6,803.

TRI-CITY DUST DEVILS
TRI-CITY STADIUM (GESA STADIUM)
602 BURDEN BOULEVARD
PASCO, WA 99301
509-544-8789
Fax: 509-547-9570
• Brent Miles, President
• Anthony Contreras, Manager
• Derrel Ebert, General Manager
Ballpark:
Gesa Stadium. Seating capacity, 3,654.

VANCOUVER CANADIANS
ROGERS FIELD AT NAT BAILEY STADIUM
4601 ONTARIO ST
VANCOUVER, BC, CANADA V5V 3H4
604-872-5232
Fax: 604-872-1714
www.milb.com/vancouver
• Allan Bailey, General Manager
(604) 872-5232
abailey@canadiansbaseball.com
• Walter Cosman, VP, Sales & Marketing
• Stephani Ellis, Assistant General Manager
Baseball:
Rogers Field at Nat Bailey Stadium. Seating
capacity, 6,500.

PACIFIC COAST LEAGUE OF
PROFESSIONAL BASEBALL CLUBS
(AAA LEVEL)
ONE CHISHOLM TRAIL
SUITE 4200
ROUND ROCK, TX 78681
512-310-2900
Fax: 512-310-8300
office@pclbaseball.com
www.pclbaseball.com
• Branch B. Rickey, President
• Melanie Fiore, Director of Business
• Dwight Hall, Director of Baseball
Operations
Nature of Service:
Baseball League.
Number of Members:
16 teams.

Teams:

ALBUQUERQUE ISOTOPES
1601 AVENIDA CESAR CHAVEZ SE
ISOTOPES PARK
SECOND FLOOR
ALBUQUERQUE, NM 87106
505-924-2255
Fax: 505-242-8899
info@abqisotopes.com
• Ken Young, President
• John Traub, General Manager/Vice President
• Emmett Hammond, Vice
President/Secretary/Treasurer
• Nick LoBue, Vice President, Corporate
Development
• Glenallen Hill, Manager
Years in League:
2003-present.
Ballpark:
Isotopes Park.
Ballpark Description:
Opened in 2003. Seating Capacity: 12,215
Media Broadcast:
KNML 610 The Sports Animal.
Major Team Affiliation:
Los Angeles Dodgers

COLORADO SPRINGS SKY SOX
4385 TUTT BOULEVARD
SECURITY SERVICE FIELD
COLORADO SPRINGS, CO 80922
719-597-1449
Fax: 719-597-2491
info@skysox.com
www.skysox.com
• Tony Ensor, President/General Manager
• Rick Sweet, Manager
• Whitney Shellem, Dir of New Media & Fan
Communication
Years in League:
1988-present.
Ballpark:
Security Service Field.
Ballpark Description:
Opened in 1988. Seating Capacity: 8500
Media Broadcast:
KRDO 1240-AM.
Major Team Affiliation:
Colorado Rockies.

EL PASO CHIHUAHUAS
SOUTHWEST UNIVERSITY PARK
1 BALLPARK PLAZA
EL PASO, TX 79901
915-242-2000
Fax: 915-242-2031
info@epchihuahuas.com
• Paul Foster, Owner/Chairman
• Brad Taylor, General Manager
• Pamela De La O, Director, Finance &
Administration
• Douglas Galeano, Director, Ballpark
Operations
Team Affiliate:
San Diego Padres
Ballpark:
Southwest University Park. Seating capacity,
7,500.

FRESNO GRIZZLIES
CHUKCHANSI PARK
1800 TULARE STREET
FRESNO, CA 93721
559-320-4487
Fax: 559-320-1216
ryoung@fresnogrizzlies.com
www.fresnogrizzlies.com
• Chris Cummings, President, Managing Partner
• Derek Franks, General Manager
• Tony DeFrancesco, Manager
Years in League:
1998-present.
Ballpark:
Chukchansi Park
Ballpark Description:
Opened in 2002. Seating capacity,

approximately 12,000.
Major Team Affiliation:
San Francisco Giants.
Media Broadcast:
KOOR 790-AM.

IOWA CUBS
PRINICIPAL PARK
ONE LINE DRIVE
DES MOINES, IA 50309
515-243-6111
Fax: 515-243-5152
www.iowacubs.com
• Michael Gartner, Chairman
mgartner@iowacubs.com
• Michael Giudicessi, Corporate Secretary
• Sam Bernabe, President/General Manager
sbernabe@iowacubs.com
• Marty Pevey, Manager
Years in League:
1998-present.
Ballpark:
Principal Park.
Ballpark Description:
Opened in 1992.
Major Team Affiliation:
Chicago Cubs.
Media Broadcast:
KXTK 940-AM.

LAS VEGAS 515
CASHMAN FIELD
850 LAS VEGAS BOULEVARD NORTH
LAS VEGAS, NV 89101
702-943-7200
Fax: 702-386-7214
info@lv51.com
www.lv51.com
• Don Logan, President/COO
• Chuck Johnson, General Manager
• Mike Rodriguez, VP, Ticket Operations
• Nick Fitzenreider, VP, Operations & Security
cjohnson@lv51.com
• Chip Vespe, Operations Manager
• Wally Backman, Manager
Years in League:
1983-present.
Ballpark:
Cashman Field.
Ballpark Description:
Opened in 1983. Seating Capacity, 9,334.
MLB Affiliate:
New York Mets

MEMPHIS REDBIRDS
198 UNION AVENUE
MEMPHIS, TN 38103
901-721-6050
Fax: 901-328-1102
www.memphisredbirds.com
• Craig Unger, General Manager
• Lisa Peterson, Manager, Group Sales
• Michael Whitty, Director of Media Relations
• Mike Shildt, Manager
Years in League:
1998-present.
Ballpark:
AutoZone Park.
Ballpark Description:
Opened in 2000.
MLB Affiliate:
St. Louis Cardinals.

NASHVILLE SOUNDS
FIRST TENNESSEE PARK
19 JUNIOR GILLIAM WAY
NASHVILLE, TN 37219
615-690-4487
Fax: 615-256-5684
info@nashvillesounds.com
www.nashvillesounds.com
• Garry Arthur, General Manager, COO
• Chris Sprunger, VP, Ticket Operations
• Paul Hemingway, VP, Corporate Sales &
Marketing
• Doug Scopel, VP, Operations
• Steve Scarsone, Manager

Years in League:
1998-present.
Ballpark:
Herschel Greer Stadium.
Ballpark Description:
Opened in 1978. Seating Capacity, 10,700.
Media Broadcast:
WAMB.
MLB Affiliate:
Milwaukee Brewers

NEW ORLEANS ZEPHYRS
6000 AIRLINE DRIVE
ZEPHYR FIELD
METAIRIE, LA 70003
504-734-5155
Fax: 504-734-5118
info@zephyrsbaseball.com
www.zephyrsbaseball.com
• Donald Beaver, Owner/President
• Mike Schline, General Manager
• Donna Light, Director of Finance and
Administration
• Dave Sachs, Director of Media Relations
• Andy Haines, Manager
Years in League:
1998-present.
Ballpark:
Zephyr Field.
Ballpark Description:
Opened in 1997. Seating capacity, 11,000.
Media Broadcast:
WTIX 690-AM.
MLB Affiliate:
Miami Marlins

OKLAHOMA CITY DODGERS
TWO SOUTH MICKEY MANTLE DRIVE
CHICKASAW BRICKTOWN BALLPARK
OKLAHOMA CITY, OK 73104
405-218-1000
Fax: 405-218-1011
• Michael Byrnes, President/General Manager
• Jenna Byrnes, Senior Vice President
• Armando Reyes, Director of Ticket Operations
• Kyle Daugherty, Director of Business
Development
• Damon Berryhill, Manager
Years in League:
1963-68, 1998-present.
Ballpark:
Red Hawks Ballpark.
Ballpark:
Opened in 1998. Seating Capacity, 12,000.
MLB Affiliate:
Houston Astros

OMAHA STORM CHASERS
WERNER PARK
12356 BALLPARK WAY
PAPILLION, NE 68046
402-734-2550
Fax: 402-734-7166
info@oroyals.com
www.oroyals.com
• Gary Green, Chief Executive Officer
• Martie Cordaro, General Manager/President
• Laurie Schlender, Assistant General Manager
• Andrea Stava, Assistant General Manager of
Operations
Years in League:
1998-present.
Ballpark:
Werner Park
Ballpark Description:
Opened in 1948. Seating Capacity, 22,000.
Major Team Affiliation:
Kansas City Royals.
Media Broadcast:
KOSR 1490-AM.

RENO ACES
ACES BALLPARK
250 EVANS AVENUE
RENO, NV 89501
775-334-4700
Fax: 775-334-4701

customerservice@renoaces.com
www.renoaces.com
• Eric Edelstein, President
• Andrew Daugherty, Executive Vice President
• Brian Moss, VP, Business Development
• Sarah Bliss, Ticket Operations Manager
• Audrey Hill, Director of Marketing
• Phil Nevin, Manager
Ballpark:
Aces Ballpark. Seating capacity, 9,013.
MLB Affiliate:
Arizona Diamondbacks

ROUND ROCK EXPRESS
DELL DIAMOND
3400 EAST PALM VALLEY BOULEVARD
ROUND ROCK, TX 78665
512-255-2255
Fax: 512-255-1558
info@rrexpress.com
www.roundrockexpress.com
• Don Sanders, Principal Owner
• Chris Almendarez, President
• Lynn Nolan Ryan, Principal Owner
• Bobby Jones, Manager
• Reid Ryan, Founder
• Reese Ryan, CEO
• Chris Almendarez, General Manager
• Ryan-Sanders Baseball, Owners
• Jason Wood, Manager
Ballpark:
Dell Diamond
Ballpark Description:
As the home of the Round Rock Express, the
Dell Diamond features numerous amenities
designed for the ultimate in fan comfort and
enjoyment.
MLB Affiliate:
Texas Rangers

SACRAMENTO RIVER CATS
400 BALLPARK DRIVE
RALEY FIELD
WEST SACRAMENTO, CA 95691
916-376-4722
Fax: 916-376-4710
info@rivercats.com
www.rivercats.com
• Susan Savage, Chief Executive Officer,
Majority Owner
• Jeff Savage, President
• Chip Maxson, General Manager
• John Krivacic, Director of Ticket Operations
• Jose Alguacil, Manager
Years in League:
2000-present.
Ballpark:
Raley Field.
Ballpark Description:
Opened in 2000. Seating Capacity, 11,093.
Media Broadcast:
KSTE 650-AM. KSQR 1240-AM (Spanish).
Major Team Affiliation:
Established in 2000, Raley Field is home of the
Oakland Athletics Triple-A affiliate and two-time
PCL champions, the Sacramento River Cats.

SALT LAKE BEES
SMITHS BALLPARK
77 WEST 1300 SOUTH
SALT LAKE CITY, UT 84115
801-350-6900
Fax: 801-485-6818
www.stingersbaseball.com
• Gail Miller, Owner
• Clark Whitworth, President
• Jim Olson, Chief Operations Officer
• Marc Amicone, General Manager
• Steve Klauke, Director of Broadcasting
• Dave Anderson, Manager
Years in League:
1915-25, 1958-65, 1970-84, 1994-present.
Ballpark:
Spring Mobile Park
Ballpark Description:
Opened in 1994. Seating Capacity, 15,500.
Media Broadcast:
KJQS ESPN 1230-AM.

Major Team Affiliation:
Los Angeles Anaheim Angels

TACOMA RAINIERS
CHENEY STADIUM
2502 SOUTH TYLER STREET
TACOMA, WA 98405
253-752-7707
Fax: 253-752-7135
www.tacomarainiers.com
• Aaron Artman, President
• Jim Flavin, VP, Business Development
• Pat Listach, Manager
Years in League:
1904-05, 1960-present.
Ballpark:
Cheney Stadium.
Ballpark Description:
Opened in 1960. Seating capacity, 9,600.
Media Broadcast:
KHHO 850-AM.
MLB Affiliate:
Seattle Mariners

PECOS LEAGUE (INDEPENDENT LEAGUE)
PO BOX 271489
HOUSTON, TX 77277
575-680-2212
info@pecosleague.com
www.pecosleague.com
• Andrew Dunn, Commissioner
• Wally Anderson, Vice President of
Baseball Operations

Teams:

ALPINE COWBOYS
KOKERNOT FIELD
400 LOOP ROAD
ALPINE, TX 79830
432-386-3402
• Andrew Dunn, Commissioner
• Ryan Stevens, Manager

GARDENCITY WIND
706 EAST MAPLE
GARDEN CITY, KS 67846
620-765-4129
www.gardencitywind.com
• Andrew Dunn, Commissioner
• Bill Moore, Manager

LAS CRUCES VAQUEROS
APODOCA PARK
801 EAST MADRID
LAS CRUCES, NM 88001
575-680-2212
www.lascrucesvaqueros.com
• Andrew Dunn, Commissioner
• J.D. Droddy, League Adjudicator

ROSWELL INVADERS
2500 SE MAIN STREET
ST. ROSWELL, NM 88203
575-680-2212
www.roswellinvaders.com
• Andrew Dunn, Commissioner
• Bryan Kloppe, Manager

SANTA FE FUEGO
FORT MARCY PARK
MURALES AND WASHINGTION AVENUE
SANTA FE, NM 87504
505-216-7870
www.santafefuego.com
• Andrew Dunn, Commissioner
• Consuelo Rios, Game Day Operations

TOPEKA ROBBERS
LAKE SHAWNEE
3421 SE LEISURE LANE
TOPEKA, KS 66605

575-680-2212
www.topekarobbers.com
• Andrew Dunn, Commissioner
• Bob Fritz, Manager

TRINIDAD TRIGGERS
TRINIDAD CENTRAL PARK
TRINIDAD, CO 81082
719-859-1008
www.trinidadtriggers.com
• Andrew Dunn, Commissioner
• Royce Holder, Manager

TUCSON SAGUAROS
KINO SPORTS COMPLEX
2500 EAST AJO WAY
TUCSON, AZ 85713
520-909-5600
www.saguarosbaseball.com
• Andrew Dunn, Commissioner
• J.D. Droddy, League Adjudicator

WHITE SAND PUPFISH
GRIGGS PARK
3000 NORTH FLORIDA AVENUE
ALAMOGORDO, NM 88310
575-680-2212
• Andrew Dunn, Commissioner
• Mickey Speaks, Manager

**PIONEER BASEBALL LEAGUE
(ADVANCED ROOKIE LEVEL)**
2607 S. SOUTHEAST BOULEVARD
BUILDING B
SUITE 115
SPOKANE, WA 99223
509-456-7615
Fax: 509-456-0136
fanmail@pioneerleague.com
www.pioneerleague.com
• Jim McCurdy, President,
Secretary-Treasurer
• Vinney Purpura, Vice President
• Mary Ann McCurdy, Executive Director
League History:
The Pioneer Baseball League, also known
as the Pioneer League, formed in 1939
under the auspices of founding president
Jack P. Halliwell. The Pioneer Baseball
League is a short-season, professional
minor league with teams in Idaho, Montana,
Utah, and Wyoming. The Billings Mustangs,
Great Falls Dodgers, Helena Brewers, and
Missoula Osprey comprise the Northern
Division. The Southern Division includes the
Casper Rockies, Idaho Falls Chukars,
Ogden Raptors, and Orem Owlz.
Requirements:
Each team is limited to 35 active players
with no more than 30 uniformed players at
each game.
Player Eligibility:
No more than 17 of the 35 active players
may be 21 and older, provided that no more
than two of the 17 are 23 or older. No active
player may have more than three years of
prior service.

Teams:

BILLINGS MUSTANGS
DEHLER PARK
2611 9TH AVENUE NORTH
BILLINGS, MT 59101
406-252-1241
Fax: 406-252-2968
mustangs@billingsmustangs.com
www.billingsmustangs.com
• Gary Roller, General Manager
(406) 252-1241
groller@billingsmustangs.com

• Chris Marshall, Director, Corporate Sales &
Partnerships
cmarshall@billingsmustangs.com
• Matt Schoonover, Director, Stadium
Operations
mschoonover@billingsmustangs.com
Ballpark:
In 2008, the Pioneer League's Billings Mustangs
moved into Dehler Park, a $12.5 million ballpark
built to replace Cobb Field. The playing field is
recessed 8 feet below street level, allowing the
seats in the ballpark to completely encircle the
playing field. The concourse features
concession stands and expanded restrooms that
are larger than those of Cobb Field.
Affiliate:
Cincinnati Reds
Years in League:
1948-63, 1969-present.

GRAND JUNCTION ROCKIES
SAM SUPLIZIO FIELD
1315 NORTH AVENUE
GRAND JUNCTION, CO 81501
970-255-7625
Fax: 970-241-2374
• Tim Ray, General Manager
• B.J. Miller, Assistant General Manager
Ballpark:
Sam Suplizio Field
Affiliate:
Colorado Rockies
Founded:
1978

GREAT FALLS VOYAGERS
CENTENE STADIUM
1015 25TH STREET NORTH
GREAT FALLS, MT 59405
406-452-5311
Fax: 406-454-0811
voyagers@gfvoyagers.com
• Scott Reasoner, General Manager
• Matt Coakley, Assistant General Manager
• Scott Lettre, Director of Sales
Ballpark:
Centene Stadium. Seating capacity, 4,000.
Affiliate:
Chicago White Sox

HELENA BREWERS
KINDRICK LEGION FIELD
1300 NORTH EWING STREET
HELENA, MT 59601
406-495-0500
Fax: 406-495-0900
info@helenabrewers.net
www.helenabrewers.net
• D.G. Elmore, Principal Owner
• Paul Fetz, President/General Manager
• Travis Hawks, Director of Ticketing & Stadium
Operations
• Tony Diggs, Manager
Ballpark:
Kindrick Field opened in 1939 and has a seating
capacity of 2,010.
Affiliate:
Milwaukee Brewers
Years in League:
1977-present.

IDAHO FALLS CHUKAR
MELALEUCA FIELD
900 JIM GARCHOW WAY
IDAHO FALLS, ID 83402
208-522-8363
Fax: 208-522-9858
chukars@ifchukars.com
www.ifchukars.com
• Kevin Greene, President, General Manager
• Paul Henderson, Assistant General Manager
• Alex Groh, Director of Operations
Ballpark:
Melaleuca Field opened in 2007 and has a
seating capacity of 3,400.
Years in League:
1940-42, 1946-present.

Affiliate:
Kansas City Royals.

MISSOULA OSPREY
OGREN PARK ALLEGIANCE FIELD
700 CREGG LANE
MISSOULA, MT 59801
406-543-3300
Fax: 406-543-9463
info@missoulaosprey.com
www.missoulaosprey.com
• Matt Ellis, Executive Vice President
mellis@missoulaosprey.com
• Jeff Griffin, General Manager, Vice President
• Joe Mather, Manager
Years in League:
1999-present.
Ballpark:
Ogren Park Allegiance Field has a seating
capacity of 3,500.
Affiliate:
Arizona Diamondbacks

OGDEN RAPTORS
LINDQUIST FIELD
2330 LINCOLN AVENUE
OGDEN, UT 84401
801-393-2400
Fax: 801-393-2473
www.ogden-raptors.com
• Dave Baggott, President
• Joey Stein, General Manager
• John Stein, Vice President
• John Shoemaker, Manager
Ballpark:
Lindquist Field was built in 1997 and has a
seating capacity of 5,001.
Years in League:
1939-42, 1946-55, 1966-74, 1994-present.
Affiliate:
Los Angeles Dodgers

OREM OWLZ
BRENT BROWN BALLPARK
970 WEST UNIVERSITY PARKWAY
OREM, UT 84058
801-377-2255
Fax: 801-377-2345
fan@oremowlz.com
www.oremowlz.com
• Rick Berry, General Manager
• Julie Hatch, Assistant General Manager
• Brett Stevens, Director of Marketing
• Dave Stapleton, Manager
Ballpark:
Brent Brown Ballpark. Seating capacity, 5,000.
Years in League:
1978-present.
Affiliate:
Los Angeles Anaheim Angels

SOUTH ATLANTIC LEAGUE (A LEVEL)
13575 58TH STREET NORTH
SUITE 141
CLEARWATER, FL 33760-3721
727-538-4270
Fax: 727-499-6853
office@saloffice.com
www.southatlanticleague.com
• Eric Krupa, President
Description:
Minor League Baseball League, consisting
of 14 teams.

Teams:

ASHEVILLE TOURISTS
MCCORMICK FIELD
30 BUCHANAN PLACE
ASHEVILLE, NC 28801
828-258-0428
Fax: 828-258-0320
info@theashevilletourists.com
www.theashevilletourists.com

- Brian DeWine, President
- Larry Hawkins, General Manager
- Warren Schaeffer, Manager
Years in League:
1976-present
Ballpark:
McCormick Field
Ballpark Description:
Opened in 1992; Seating Capacity: 4,000
Major Team Affiliation:
Colorado Rockies

AUGUSTA GREENJACKETS
SRP PARK
187 RAILROAD AVE
NORTH AUGUSTA, GA 29841
803-349-9467
Fax: 803-349-9434
info@greenjacketsbaseball.com
www.greenjacketsbaseball.com
- Tom Denlinger, Vice President
- Brandon Greene, General Manager
Years in League:
1988-present
Ballpark:
SRP Park
Ballpark Description:
Seating Capacity: 4,278
Major Team Affiliation:
San Francisco Giants.

CHARLESTON RIVERDOGS
360 FISHBURNE STREET
JOSPEH P. RILEY JR. PARK
CHARLESTON, SC 29403
843-723-7241
Fax: 843-723-2641
admin@riverdogs.com
www.riverdogs.com
- Marvin Goldklang, Chairman
- Mike Veeck, President
- Dave Echols, Executive Vice President, General Manager
- Luis Dorante, Manager
Years in League:
1973-78, 1980-present.
Ballpark:
Joseph P. Riley Jr. Park
Ballpark Description:
Opened in 1997. Seating Capacity: 5,094
Media Broadcast:
WQSC ESPN 1340-AM.
Major Team Affiliation:
New York Yankees.

COLUMBIA FIREFLIES
807 GERVAIS STREET
SUITE 100
COLUMBIA, SC 29201
803-726-4487
Fax: 803-726-3126
info@columbiafireflies.com
- John Katz, President
- Brad Shank, Executive Vice President
- Jose Leger, Manager
Ballpark:
Spirit Communications Park. Seating capacity, 8,500.

DELMARVA SHOREBIRDS
6400 HOBBS ROAD
PERDUE STADIUM
SALISBURY, MD 21804
410-219-3112
Fax: 410-219-9164
info@theshorebirds.com
www.theshorebirds.com
- Chris Bitters, General Manager
- Jimmy Sweet, Assistant General Manager
- Joel Chavez, Director of Stadium Operations
- Ryan Minor, Manager
Years in League:
1996-present.
Ballpark:
Arthur W. Perdue Stadium.
Ballpark Description:
Opened in 1996. Seating Capacity: 5,200

Media Broadcast:
WVES 99.3-FM.
Major Team Affiliation:
Baltimore Orioles.

GREENSBORO GRASSHOPPERS
408 BELLEMEADE STREET
FIRST NATIONAL BANK FIELD
GREENSBORO, NC 27401
336-268-2255
Fax: 336-273-7350
www.gsohoppers.com
- Donald Moore, President/General Manager
Years in League:
1979-present.
Prior Team Name:
Greensboro Bats.
Ballpark:
NewBridge Bank Park
Ballpark Description:
Opened in 2005. Seating Capacity: 6,000
Media Broadcast:
WPET 950-AM.
Major Team Affiliation:
Miami Marlins.

GREENVILLE DRIVE
945 SOUTH MAIN STREET
FLUOR FIELD
GREENVILLE, SC 29601
864-240-4500
Fax: 864-240-4501
info@greenvilledrive.com
www.greenvilledrive.com
- Craig Brown, Co-Owner/President
- Roy Bostock, Co-Owner
- Darren Fenster, Manager
- Mike DeMaine, General Manager
Ballpark:
Fluor Field, modeled after Fenway. Seating capacity, 5,700.
Major Team Affiliaton:
Boston Red Sox

HAGERSTOWN SUNS
274 EAST MEMORIAL BOULEVARD
MUNICIPAL STADIUM
HAGERSTOWN, MD 21740
301-791-6266
Fax: 301-791-6066
info@hagerstownsuns.com
www.hagerstownsuns.com
- Bruce Quinn, President
- Brian Saddler, Assistant General Manager
- Bob Bruchey, Director of Community Affairs
Years in League:
1993-present.
Ballpark:
Municipal Stadium.
Ballpark Information:
Opened in 1931. Seating Capacity: 4,600
Media Broadcast:
WHAG 1410-AM.
Major Team Affiliation:
Washington Nationals.

HICKORY CRAWDADS
CRAWDADS STADIUM
2500 CLEMENT BOULEVARD NW
HICKORY, NC 28601
828-322-3000
Fax: 828-322-6137
crawdad@hickorycrawdads.com
www.hickorycrawdads.com
- Don Beaver, President
- Mark Seaman, General Manager
- Charlie Downs, Assistant General Manager of Operations
- Peter Subsara, Director of Promotions
- Travis Gortman, Director of Group Sales
- Spike Owen, Manager
Years in League:
1952, 1960, 1993-present.
Ballpark:
L.P. Frans Stadium.
Ballpark Description:
Opened in 1993. Seating Capacity: 5,092

Media Broadcast:
WMNC 92.1-FM.
Major Team Affiliation:
Texas Rangers

KANNAPOLIS INTIMIDATORS
2888 MOOSE ROAD
INTIMIDATORS STADIUM
KANNAPOLIS, NC 28083
704-932-3267
Fax: 704-938-7040
www.milb.com
- Brad Smith, President
- Randy Long, General Manager
- Darren Cozart, Director of Operations
- Tommy Thompson, Manager
Years in League:
1995-present.
Ballpark:
Fieldcrest Cannon Stadium.
Ballpark Description:
Opened in 1995. Seating Capacity: 4,700
Major Team Affiliation:
Chicago White Sox.

LAKEWOOD BLUECLAWS
FIRSTENERGY PARK
TWO STADIUM WAY
LAKEWOOD, NJ 08701
732-901-7000
Fax: 732-901-3967
- Chris Tafrow, General Manager
- Steve Farago, VP of Baseball Operations & Special Events
Years in League:
2001-present.
Ballpark:
FirstEnergy Park.
Ballpark Description:
Opened in 2001. Seating Capacity: 6,588
Media Broadcast:
WADB 1310-AM.
Major Team Affiliation:
Philadelphia Phillies.

LEXINGTON LEGENDS
207 LEGENDS LANE
WHITAKER BANK BALLPARK
LEXINGTON, KY 40505
859-422-7867
Fax: 859-252-4487
webmaster@lexingtonlegends.com
www.lexingtonlegends.com
- Andy Shea, CEO/President
- Shannon Kidd, Director of Stadium Operations
- Keith Elkins, Director of Broadcasting & Media Relations
- Omar Ramirez, Manager
Years in League:
2001-present.
Ballpark:
Whitaker Bank Ballpark
Ballpark Description:
Opened in 2001. Seating Capacity: Approx. 6,000
Media Broadcast:
WLXG 1300-AM.
MLB Affiliate:
Houston Astros

ROME BRAVES
755 BRAVES BOULEVARD
STATE MUTUAL STADIUM
ROME, GA 30161
706-378-5100
706-378-5144
Fax: 706-368-6525
rome.braves@braves.com
www.romebraves.com
- Michael Dunn, General Manager
- Jim Jones, Assistant General Manager
- Brad Smith, Director of Operations
- Erin Elroo, Director of Special Projects
- Randy Ingle, Manager
Years in League:
1962-63, 1980-87, 1991-present.
Ballpark:

State Mutual Stadium.
Ballpark Description:
Opened in 2003. Seating Capacity: 5,000
Media Broadcast:
WLAQ 1410, WATG Oldies 95.7
Major Team Affiliation:
Atlanta Braves.

WEST VIRGINIA POWER
601 MORRIS STREET
SUITE 201
APPALACHIAN POWER PARK
CHARLESTON, WV 25301
304-344-2287
Fax: 304-344-0083
www.wvpower.com
• Tim Mueller, General Manager
• Jeremy Taylor, Assistant General Manager
• Brian Esposito, Manager
Years in League:
1987-present.
Prior Team Name:
Charleston Alley Cats.
Ballpark:
Appalachian Power Park. Seating capacity, 4,500.
Media Broadcast:
WBES 1240-AM.
Major Team Affiliation:
Pittsburg Pirates

SOUTHERN LEAGUE OF PROFESSIONAL BASEBALL CLUBS
2551 ROSWELL ROAD
SUITE 330
MARIETTA, GA 30062
770-321-0400
Fax: 770-321-0037
www.southernleague.com
• Lori Webb, President
• Steve Desalvo, Vice President
• Peter Webb, Media Relations
Nature of Service:
Headquarters for 10 teams in a Class Double-A Minor League Baseball league.
League History:
The Southern League originated during the outburst of athletic enthusiasm that surged across America late in the nineteenth century. In 1885, The Southern League of Professional Baseball Clubs was formed by civic leaders and baseball enthusiasts in eight southern cities.
Teams:
10
Publications:
Southern League Media Guide

Teams:

BILOXI SHUCKERS
105 CAILLAVET STREET
MGM PARK
BILOXI, MS 39530
228-233-3465
info@biloxishuckers.com
biloxishuckers.com
• Ken Young, President
• Hunter Reed, General Manager
• Garrett Greene, Media Relations Manager & Broadcaster
Description:
Franchise started in 2015 in Biloxi after relocating from Huntsville.

BIRMINGHAM BARONS
1401 FIRST AVENUE SOUTH
REGIONS FIELD
BIRMINGHAM, AL 35233
205-988-3200
Fax: 205-988-9698
barons@barons.com
www.barons.com

• Don Logan, Owner
• Stan Logan, Owner
• Jeff Logan, Owner
• Jonathan Nelson, General Manager
nelson@barons.com
• Julio Vinas, Manager
Years in League:
1964-65, 1967-75, 1981-present.
Ballpark:
Regions Park
Ballpark Description:
Opened in 1988. Seating Capacity: 10,800
Media Broadcast:
The Source 101.1-FM.
MLB Affiliate:
Chicago White Sox

CHATTANOOGA LOOKOUTS
201 POWER ALLEY
AT&T FIELD
CHATTANOOGA, TN 37402
423-267-2208
Fax: 423-267-4258
lookouts@lookouts.com
www.lookouts.com
• Rich Mozingo, President/General Manager
• Harold Craw, Assistant General Manager
• Doug Mientkiewicz, Manager
Years in League:
1964-65, 1976-present.
Ballpark:
AT&T Field
Ballpark Description:
Opened in 2000. Seating Capacity: 6,160
Media Broadcast:
WQMT 98.9-FM.
MLB Affiliate:
LA Dodgers

JACKSON GENERALS
FOUR FUN PLACE
THE BALLPARK AT JACKSON
JACKSON, TN 38305
731-988-5299
Fax: 731-988-5246
www.jacksongeneralsbaseball.com
• Jason Compton, General Manager
• Mike Peasley, VP of Sales and Marketing
• Nick Hall, Assistant General Manager of Game Operations
MLB Affiliate:
Seattle Mariners

JACKSONVILLE SUNS
301 A. PHILIP RANDOLPH BOULEVARD
BASEBALL GROUNDS OF JACKSONVILLE
JACKSONVILLE, FL 32202
904-358-2846
Fax: 904-358-2845
info@jaxsuns.com
www.jaxsuns.com
• Ken Babby, Owner/CEO
• Harold Craw, General Manager
• Dave Berg, Manager
Years in League:
1970-present.
Ballpark:
Baseball Grounds of Jacksonville.
Ballpark Description:
Opened in 2003. Seating Capacity: 11,000
Media Broadcast:
The Fox 930-AM.
MLB Affiliate:
Miami Marlins

MISSISSIPPI BRAVES
1 BRAVES WAY
TRUSTMARK PARK
PEARL, MS 39208
601-932-8788
Fax: 601-936-3567
mississippibraves@braves.com
www.mississippibraves.com
• Steve DeSalvo, General Manager
• Aaron Holbert, Manager
Years in League:
1984-present.

Stadium:
Trustmark Park
Ballpark Description:
Opened in 2005. Seating Capacity 7,416
MLB Affiliate:
Atlanta Braves

MOBILE BAYBEARS
755 BOLLING BROTHERS BOULEVARD
HANK AARON STADIUM
MOBILE, AL 36606
251-479-2327
Fax: 251-476-1147
info@mobilebaybears.com
www.mobilebaybears.com
• Mike Savit, Managing Partner
• Chris Morgan, General Manager
• Robby Hammock, Manager
Years in League:
1997-present.
Ballpark:
Hank Aaron Stadium.
Ballpark Description:
Opened in 1997. Seating Capacity: 6,000
Media Broadcast:
WABB 1480-AM.
MLB Affiliate:
Arizona Diamonbacks

MONTGOMERY BISCUITS
200 COOSA STREET
RIVERWALK STADIUM
MONTGOMERY, AL 36104
334-323-2255
Fax: 334-323-2225
www.biscuitsbaseball.com
• Greg Rauch, President
• Scott Trible, General Manager
• Staci Wilkenson, Marketing Director
• Steve Blackwell, Director of Stadium Operations
• Brady Williams, Manager
Years in League:
2004-present.
Ballpark:
Montgomery Riverwalk Stadium.
Ballpark Description:
Opened in 2004. Seating Capacity: 7,000
Media Broadcast:
WLWI 1440-AM.
Major Team Affiliation:
Tampa Bay Devil Rays.

PENSACOLA BLUE WAHOOS
351 WEST CEDAR STREET
PENSACOLA BAYFRONT STADIUM
PENSACOLA, FL 32502
850-934-8444
Fax: 850-791-6256
info@bluewahoos.com
• Quintan Struder, Owner, Director
• Bruce Balwin, President
• Delino Deshields, Manager
MLB Affiliate:
Cincinnati Reds
Ballpark:
Pensacola Bayfront Stadium. Seating capacity, 5,038.

TENNESSEE SMOKIES
3540 LINE DRIVE
SMOKIES STADIUM
KODAK, TN 37764
865-286-2300
Fax: 865-523-9913
info@smokiesbaseball.com
www.smokiesbaseball.com
• Doug Kirchhofer, Chief Executive Officer
• Chris Allen, President, COO
• Brian Cox, General Manager
• Buddy Bailey, Manager
Years in League:
1998-present.
Ballpark:
Smokies Park
Ballpark Description:
Opened in 1998. Seating Capacity: 6,412

Media Broadcast:
WTNE 97.7-FM.
MLB Affiliate:
Chicago Cubs

TEXAS BASEBALL LEAGUE (AA LEVEL)
2442 FACET OAK
SAN ANTONIO, TX 78232
210-545-5297
Fax: 210-545-5298
texasleague@sbcglobal.net
• Tom Kayser, President/Treasurer
• Scott Sonju, Vice President
• Matt Gifford, Corporate Secretary
• John Harris, Assistant to President
Nature of Service:
Baseball League.
Years League Active:
1888-1890, 1892, 1895-1899, 1902-1942, 1946-present.

Teams:

ARKANSAS TRAVELERS
400 WEST BROADWAY
DICKEY-STEPHENS PARK
NORTH LITTLE ROCK, AR 72114
501-664-1555
Fax: 501-664-1834
travs@travs.com
www.travs.com
• Paul Allen, General Manager
• Rusty Meeks, Assistant General Manager
• Patti Clark, Director of Finance
• Bill Richardson, Manager
Years in League:
1966-present.
Ballpark:
Dickey-Stephens Park. Seating capacity, 7,200.
Media Broadcast:
KASR 92.7-FM.
MLB Affiliate:
LAA Angels

CORPUS CHRISTI HOOKS
734 EAST PORT AVENUE
WHATABURGER FIELD
CORPUS CHRISTI, TX 78401
361-561-4665
Fax: 361-561-4666
• Jim Crane, Owner and Chairman
• Ken Schrom, President
• Michael Wood, Vice President, General Manager
• Jeremy Sturgeon, Stadium Operations
• Rodney Linares, Manager
Ballpark:
Whataburger Field
Ballpark Description:
Opened in 1990. Seating Capacity: 10,000.
Media Broadcast:
KHEY 1380-AM.
MLB Affiliate:
Houston Astros

FRISCO ROUGHRIDERS
7300 ROUGHRIDERS TRAIL
DR. PEPPER BALLPARK
FRISCO, TX 75034
972-731-9200
Fax: 972-731-5355
info@ridersbaseball.com
www.ridersbaseball.com
• Chuck Greenberg, CEO, General Partner
• Jason Dambach, Executive Vice President, General Manager
• Joe Mikulik, Manager
Years in League:
2003-present.
Ballpark:
Dr Pepper Ballpark
Ballpark Description:
Opened in 2003. Seating Capacity: 10,000
Media Broadcast:
The Ticket Sportsradio 1700-AM.

MLB Affiliate:
Texas Rangers

MIDLAND ROCKHOUNDS
5514 CHAMPIONS DRIVE
SECURITY BANK BALLPARK
MIDLAND, TX 79706
432-520-2255
Fax: 432-520-8326
rockhounds@nwol.net
www.midlandrockhounds.org
• Miles Prentice, President
• Bob Richmond, Executive Vice President
• Monty Hoppel, General Manager
• Jeff VonHolle, Assistant General Manager
Years in League:
1972-present.
Ballpark:
Security Bank Ballpark
Ballpark Description:
Opened in 2002. Seating Capacity: 6,670.
Media Broadcast:
KCRS 550-AM.
Description of Sport Organization:
We have a minor league Double A baseball team (Midland Rockhounds) and a Premier Development League soccer team (West Texas United Sockers).
Teams:
Midland Rockhounds- Double A affiliate of the Oakland A's; West Texas United Sockers- PDL Mid-South Division of Southern Conference.

NORTHWEST ARKANSAS NATURALS
3000 SOUTH 56TH STREET
ARVEST BALLPARK
SPRINGDALE, AR 72762
479-927-4900
Fax: 479-756-8088
• Justin Cole, General Manager
• Mark Zaiger, Sales Manager
• Jeff Windle, Director of Ballpark Operations
Stadium:
Arvest Ballpark
Seating Capacity:
6,500 (plus berm and picnic areas)
Field Surface:
Patriot bermuda overseeded with rye
Owned by:
City of Springdale
MLB Affiliate:
Kansas City Royals

SAN ANTONIO MISSIONS
5757 US HIGHWAY 90 WEST
WOLFF STADIUM
SAN ANTONIO, TX 78227
210-675-7275
Fax: 210-670-0001
sainfo@samissions.com
www.samissions.com
• Dave Elmore, Owner
• Burl Yarbrough, President
• Dave Gasaway, General Manager
• Mickey Holt, Assistant General Manager
• Rod Barajas, Manager
Years in League:
1888, 1892, 1895-99, 1907-42, 1946-64, 1968-present.
Ballpark:
Nelson W. Wolff Municipal Stadium.
Ballpark Description:
Opened in 1994. Seating Capacity: 6,200.
Media Broadcast:
KKYX 680-AM.
Major Team Affiliation:
San Diego Padres

SPRINGFIELD CARDINALS
955 EAST TRAFFICWAY
HAMMONS FIELD
SPRINGFIELD, MO 65802
417-863-0395
Fax: 417-863-2143
springfield@cardinals.com
www.springfieldcardinals.com

• Matt Gifford, VP/General Manager
• Scott Smulczenski, VP, Baseball & Business Operations
Stadium:
Hammons Field. Seating capacity, 10,486.
Affiliated Team:
St. Louis Cardinals

TULSA DRILLERS
201 NORTH ELGIN AVENUE
TULSA DRILLERS
TULSA, OK 74120
918-744-5998
Fax: 918-747-3267
mail@tulsadrillers.com
www.tulsadrillers.com
• Mike Melega, President/General Manager
• Jason George, Executive VP/Assistant GM
Years in League:
1933-42, 1946-65, 1977-present.
Ballpark:
Oneok Field
Ballpark Description:
Opened in 1981. Seating Capacity: 10,997.
Media Broadcast:
KTBZ 1430-AM, The Buzz.
Affiliates:
Double-A Affiliate of the Colorado Rockies

VENEZUELAN BASEBALL LEAGUE
www.lvbp.com
• Oscar Prieto Parraga, President
Founded:
1945
Teams:
Aguilas del Zulia; Bravos de Margarita; Cardenales de Lara; Caribes de Anzoategui; Leones del Caracas; Navegantes de Magallanes; Tiburones de la Guaira; Tigres de Aragua

Basketball Organizations

BIDDY BASKETBALL
2377 LEON C. SIMON DRIVE
NEW ORLEANS, LA 70122
985-630-3948
Fax: 504-283-8225
info@biddybb.com
www.biddybb.com
• Firmin Simms, President/National Director
• Laura Block, Vice President
• Jerry Simms, Assistant VP
• Carolyn Block, Assistant VP
Description:
The main focus of Biddy Basketball International is to provide the best tool for developing our youth, both boys and girls in the sport of basketball. To accomplish this goal the size of the balls, the height of the goals, and the distance of the free throws lines are modified to fit young athletes. Biddy Basketball International sponsors regional and national competitive basketball tournaments throughout the United States.

CANADA BASKETBALL
1 WESTSIDE DRIVE
SUITE 11
ETOBICOKE, ON, CANADA M9C 1B2
416-614-8037
Fax: 416-614-9570
info@basketball.ca
www.basketball.ca
• Michael Bartlett, President & CEO
mbartlett@basketball.ca
• Glen Grunwald, Executive Advisor, Basketball Operations

ggrunwald@basketball.ca
• Moyo Omole, Manager, Equity, Diversity & Inclusion
momole@basketball.ca
• Rowan Barrett, General Manager/Executive VP, Senior Men's Program
rbarrett@basketball.ca
• Andrea Driedger, Vice President, Finance & Admin.
adriedger@basketball.ca
Description:
Canada Basketball is the National Sporting Organization for the sport of Basketball in Canada. Canada Basketball is respected throughout the world and is recognized by the International Amateur Basketball Federation (FIBA) and the Government of Canada as the sole governing body of the sport of amateur basketball in Canada. Canada Basketball oversees programs at amateur and grassroots levels throughout Canada.
Member Services:
Selection, training, competitive programs of all Canadian Men's and Women's teams entering the Olympic Games, World Championships, Pan American Games, World University Games, World Junior Championships and World Under 22 Championships for Men. Provides programs for coaching development through the National Coaching Certification Program (NCCP); supports domestic competitive opportunities through the organization of the National Junior Championships and National Senior Club Championships for Men and Women.
Official Sports Partners:
FIBA, NBA, U SPORTS, Canadian Collegiate Athletic Association, Canadian Olympic Committee, CEBL.
Founded:
1923

FEDERATION INTERNATIONALE DE BASKETBALL (FIBA)
ROUTE SUISSE 5
MIES, 1295
+41-22-545-00-00
Fax: +41-22-545-00-99
info@fiba.com
www.fiba.com
• Hamane Niang, President
• Andreas Zagklis, Secretary General
Description:
FIBA acts as the international governing body for the sport of basktball, and is comprised of 213 National Basketball associations, including the US national team.

INDEPENDENT HOOPS
AUGUSTA, GA
www.independenthoops.com
Description:
Independant Hoops houses both the Lineage of Champions (LOCHoops) and the National Youth Basketball League. It is the premier middle school league in North America offering a platform for teams in the US and Canada. The League is designed to improve grassroots basketball at the middle school and junior high school levels. They encourage team development in an experience that cannot be duplicated anywhere else.

INTERNATIONAL ASSOCIATION OF APPROVED BASKETBALL OFFICIALS, INC.
PO BOX 355
CARLISLE, PA 17103-0355
717-713-8129
Fax: 717-718-6164
www.iaabo.org
• Felix Addeo, Executive Director
faddeo@iaabo.org
• Donnie Eppley, Director, Membership & Technology
deppley@iaabo.org
Description:
The IAABO aims to educate, train, develop and provide continuous instruction for basketball officials.
Membership Requirements:
Be a registered member of IAABO at the time of nomination whose status as an active officiating and/or active non-officiating member totals a minimum of 30 years. Be a minimum 55 years of age by December 31st of the nominating year. Have promoted and contributed to the growth, purpose and ideals of IAABO and to the welfare of the game of basketball in an outstanding way through service to their local area.

NATIONAL ASSOCIATION OF BASKETBALL COACHES
1111 MAIN STREET
SUITE 1000
KANSAS CITY, MO 64105
816-878-6222
Fax: 816-878-6223
www.nabc.com
• Craig Robinson, Executive Director
(816) 878-6222
• Nate Pomeday, Associate Executive Director
(816) 595-6153
• Stephanie Whitcher, Chief Finanancial Offier
(816) 595-6171
• Eric Wieberg, Director, Communications & Digital Media
(816) 595-6164
• Troy Hilton, Senior Director, Association Affairs
(816) 595-6155
History:
The National Association of Basketball Coaches (NABC), located in Kansas City, Missouri was founded in 1927 by Phog Allen, the legendary University of Kansas basketball coach. Since its beginning, the NABC has continually worked to further the best interests of the game of basketball as well as the players and coaches who participate in the sport. In doing so, the NABC works toward integrity, sportsmanship and teamwork among men's basketball coaches and the players whom they coach.
Membership Requirements:
Basketball coaches of high schools, junior colleges, colleges or universities.

NATIONAL BASKETBALL ASSOCIATION
645 FIFTH AVENUE
NEW YORK, NY 10022
nbaglobalfeedback@dazn.com
www.nba.com
• Adam Silver, Commissioner
• Mark A. Tatum, Deputy Commissioner/COO
Description:
The premier professional basketball league

in North America. Many of the world's best players play in the NBA, and the overall standard of the competition is considerably higher than any other professional competition. The NBA was founded in New York City on June 6th, 1946 as the Basketball Association of America (BAA). It adopted the name National Basketball Association in the fall of 1949 after adding several teams from the rival National Basketball League.
Founded:
1946

NATIONAL BASKETBALL PLAYERS ASSOCIATION/NBPA
1133 AVENUE OF THE AMERICAS
NEW YORK, NY 10036
212-655-0880
800-955-6272
Fax: 212-655-0881
info@nbpa.com
www.nbpa.com
• C.J. McCollum, President
• Grant Williams, First Vice President
• Harrison Barnes, Secretary-Treasurer
• Andre Iguodala, Executive Director
Description:
The NBPA is a unique labor institution. For over 40 years, the NBPA has fought to promote the best interests of NBA players both on and off the court.
Year Founded:
1954

NATIONAL INVITATIONAL TOURNAMENT
700 W WASHINGTON STREET
PO BOX 6222
INDIANAPOLIS, IN 46206-6222
317-917-6222
Fax: 317-917-6888
cfallon@ncaa.org
www.ncaa.org
• Mark Emmert, President (NCAA)
Description:
The National Invitational Tournament - held in Madison Square Garden - originated from the Basketball Writers Association in 1938. After two years, the association allowed local colleges to begin administering the tournament instead. The group became known as the Metropolitan Intercollegiate Basketball Committee and in 1948 became the Metropolitan Intercollegiate Basketball Association. Today, the association is comprised of representatives from the five New York City colleges, In 2005, the NIT was taken over by the NCAA.

NATIONAL JUNIOR BASKETBALL
180 E MAIN STREET
SUITE 105
TUSTIN, CA 92780
888-623-00124
Fax: 949-769-2557
info@njbl.org
www.njbl.org
• Dennis Murphy, President/Commissioner
damurphy@njbl.org
• Sean Murphy, President
smurphy@njbl.org
Description:
National Junior Basketball is a nonprofit organization that provides opportunities for youth to play in basketball leagues. The main focus of the organization is centered on the Divisional Play Program that is open

for all boys and girls, from grades 2 to 8. However, they also offer a Rookie League for those in 1st and 2nd grade.

NATIONAL WHEELCHAIR BASKETBALL ASSOCIATION
1130 ELKTON STREET
SUITE A
COLORADO SPRINGS, CO 80907
719-266-4082
Fax: 719-900-2282
info@nwba.org
www.nwba.org
• David Shaffer, Chief Executive Officer
• Brandon McBeain, Chief Operating Officer
• Tina Cain, Business Compliance Manager
Nature of Service:
Engages in the interpretation and standardization of competitive regulations for all teams playing organized wheelchair basketball. Assists in the development of teams and educates the public in the sport.
History:
Started in 1946 by the Veterans Administration Hospitals. It later spread across the nation to VA hospitals in Boston, Chicago, Memphis, Richmond and New York. Before long, the sport had spread across the border to Canada and across the ocean to England.
Membership Requirements:
Permanent physical disability of lower extremities. Players must have functional evaluations and physical classifications.

SPOKANE HOOPFEST
421 W REVERSIDE
SUITE 115
SPOKANE, WA 99201
509-624-2414
Fax: 509-624-0868
www.spokanehoopfest.net
• Riley Stockton, Executive Director
matt@spokanehoopfest.net
• Morgan Marum, Director, Corportate & Media Relations
morgan@spokanehoopfest.net
• Giff Marleau, Program Director
giff@spokanehoopfest.net
• Chad Smith, Director, Volunteers & Staffing
chad@spokanehoopfest.net
• Connor Walsh, Manager, Programs & Events
connor@spokanehoopfest.net
Description:
Spokane Hoopfest Association is committed to organizing and operating the best outdoor 3-on-3 basketball tournament in the country. With the effort and enthusiasm of thousands of volunteers, Hoopfest strives to create a dynamic downtown festival, transcending basketball through the celebration of athleticism, fair play and community involvement. Spokane Hoopfest Association also provides charitable support through distribution of profits to Special Olympics and basketball-related activities.

USA BASKETBALL
27 S TEJON STREET
SUITE 100
COLORADO SPRINGS, CO 80903
719-590-4800
Fax: 719-590-4811
FanMail@usabasketball.com
www.usabasketball.com

• Jim Tooley, CEO
• Renee Felton, Head, Communications
• Brent Baumberger, Chief Financial Officer
Description:
USA Basketball was organized in 1974 and known as the Amateur Basketball Association of the United States of America (ABAUSA). The name change from ABAUSA to USA Basketball occurred October 12, 1989, shortly after FIBA modified its rules to allow professional basketball players to participate in international competitions.
Membership Requirements:
This membership shall be open to all national sports organizations which actively conduct a national program in Basketball as a competitive sport. Active memberships may also be open to other organizations which actively conduct national programs in basketball as a competitive sport. In addition, national basketball coaches associations for men and women shall be included, as approved by the Board of Directors of USA Basketball. Such members shall have voting representation through their chosen officers, or other representatives, at meetings of the Congress membership.

WOMEN'S BASKETBALL COACHES ASSOCIATION
4646 LAWRENCEVILLE HIGHWAY
LILBURN, GA 30047
770-279-8027
Fax: 770-279-8473
www.wbca.org
• Danielle M. Donehew, Executive Director
(770) 279-8027
ddonehew@wbca.org
• Mary Ellen Gillespie, Deputy Director
(770) 279-8027
meg@wbca.org
• Latasha Lewis, Manager of Marketing Communications
(770) 279-8027
llewis@wbca.org
• Daniella Trujillo, Senior Manager, Events & Awards
(770) 279-8027
dtrujillo@wbca.org
• Jack Watford, Director, Communications
(770) 279-8027
jwatford@wbca.org
Nature of Service:
Professional organization that supports and provides educational opportunities for women's basketball coaches on all levels, and promotes the development of the game in all of its aspects as a sport for women and girls.
Member Services:
Select WBCA Coach of the Year, Player of the Year, All-America teams for colleges and universities. Provides annual coaching clinics, clinic manuals, camps. Announces coaching position opportunities/openings. National convention held in conjunction with Division I Women's Final Four.
Publications:
FAST BREAK ALERT, quarterly newsletter; COACHING WOMEN'S BASKETBALL, bi-monthly magazine, 8 times a year; AT THE BUZZER, newsletter, 8 times a year - for high school and AAU only, NET.NEWS, bi-monthly newsletter.
Number of Members:
3,000+

Founded:
1981

YOUTH BASKETBALL OF AMERICA
ADVENTHEALTH FIELDHOUSE & CONFERENCE CENTER
210 CYPRESS GARDENS BLVD
WINTER HAVEN, FL 33880
407-363-9262
membership@yboa.org
yboabasketball.com
Description:
Youth Basketball of America, the premier youth membership organization in the sport of basketball, strives to provide opportunities for personal growth and development of youth athletes while also reinforcing positive influences, self-confidence, self-esteem and the ability to excel on and off the court. Through participation, YBOA is dedicated to educate and motivate each member while encouraging teamwork, sportsmanship and fun through the spirit of basketball.
Membership Requirements:
Leagues, associations, departments, schools, coaches and officials, players.
Member Services:
Coaching clinics; rules; local, state, regional and national championship; tournaments and competition. International friendship tournament; now offers international tournament in various foreign countries.

Basketball, Leagues and Teams

HARLEM GLOBETROTTERS
157 TECHNOLOGY PARKWAY
SUITE 100
PEACHTREE CORNERS, GA 30092
678-497-1900
info@harlemglobetrotters.com
www.harlemglobetrotters.com
• Keith Dawkins, President
• Sunni Hickman, VP, Marketing
Description:
Competitive basketball team whose games are played primarily for entertainment.
First Game Played:
1926

NATIONAL BASKETBALL ASSOCIATION/NBA
645 FIFTH AVENUE
NEW YORK, NY 10022
844-622-8550
www.nba.com
• Adam Silver, Commissioner
• Mark A. Tatum, Deputy Commissioner/COO
Description:
The premier professional basketball league in North America. Many of the world's best players play in the NBA, and the overall standard of the competition is considerably higher than any other professional competition. The NBA was founded in New York City on June 6, 1946 as the Basketball Association of America (BAA). It adopted the name National Basketball Association in the fall of 1949 after adding several teams from the rival National Basketball League.

Teams:

ATLANTA HAWKS
101 MARIETTA STREET NW
SUITE 1900
ATLANTA, GA 30303
404-878-3800
866-715-1500
members@hawks.com
www.nba.com/hawks/
• Steven R. Koonin, CEO
• Tony Ressler, Principle Owner/Chair of the
Board of Directors
• Landry Fields, General Manager
• Quin Snyder, Head Coach
Team History:
The Hawks have played in Atlanta since 1968.
They play their home games at State Farm
Arena, in Atlanta, Georgia. Championships, 1;
Conference titles, 0; Division titles, 12.
Arena:
State Farm Arena (formerly Philips Arena).
Seating capacity: 16,600.

BOSTON CELTICS
100 CAUSEWAY STREET
SUITE 1210
BOSTON, MA 02114
866-423-5849
fanrelations@celtics.com
www.nba.com/celtics/
• Wyc Grousbeck, Managing Partner/CEO
• Rich Gotham, President, Basketball
Operations
• Joe Mazzulla, Head Coach
• Sam Cassell, Assistant Coach
• Louis Copolov, Director, Basketball
Administration
Team History:
The Celtics came into being on June 6, 1946.
They have won 17 NBA Championships, tied for
first along with the Los Angeles Lakers.
Championships, 18; Conference titles, 11;
Division titles, 34.
Arena:
TD Garden. Seating capacity: 19,156.

BROOKLYN NETS
168 39TH STREET
7TH FLOOR
BROOKLYN, NY 11232
718-933-3000
Fax: 718-942-9595
www.nba.com/nets
• Joe Tsai, Governor
• Sean Marks, Alternative Governor, General
Manager
• Jordie Fernandez, Head Coach
• Jeff Gewirtz, COO & General Counsel
• Peter Stern, EVP & Chief Financial Officer
History:
1967-76 known as New York Nets. 1976 joined
the NBA. 1977-2012 known as the New Jersey
Nets. 2012-Present, known as the Brooklyn
Nets. Championships, 2; Conference titles, 2;
Division titles, 5.
Arena:
Barclays Center. Seating capacity: 17,732.
Media Broadcast:
YES Network; WWOR-TV; WFAN

CHARLOTTE HORNETS
SPECTRUM CENTER
333 EAST TRADE STREET
CHARLOTTE, NC 28202
704-688-8600
Fax: 704-973-9411
info@hornets.com
www.nba.com/hornets/
• Rick Schnall, Co-Chair & Governor
• Gabe Plotkin, Co-Chair & Alternate Governor
• Jeff Peterson, General Manager/President,
Basketball Operations
• Dotun Akinwale, Asst. General Manager
• Michael Jordan, Alternate Governor
• Charles Lee, Head Coach

History:
The Charlotte Hornets was established in 1988.
Arena:
Spectrum Center. Seating capacity, 19,077.

CHICAGO BULLS
UNITED CENTER
1901 W MADISON STREET
CHICAGO, IL 60612-2459
312-455-4000
www.nba.com/bulls/
• Michael Andrew Reinsdorf, President/CEO
• Jerry Reinsdorf, Owner/Chair
• Marc Eversley, General Manager
• Billy Donovan, Head Coach
• Arturas Karnisovas, Executive VP, Basketball
Operations
Team History:
The Chicago Bulls joined the NBA for the
1966-67 season. Prior to the inception of the
Bulls organization, two pro-teams had failed in
Chicago.Championships, 6; Conference titles, 6;
Division titles, 9.
Arena:
United Center. Seating capacity: 20,917.
Media Broadcast:
WGN/WCIU-TV; Fox Sports Chicago, 1000-AM.

CLEVELAND CAVALIERS
ROCKET ARENA
ONE CENTER COURT
CLEVELAND, OH 44115
216-420-2000
800-807-2287
contactus@cavs.com
www.nba.com/cavaliers
• Dan Gilbert, Chair
• Koby Altman, President, Basketball Operations
• Kenny Atkinson, Head Coach
• Bernie Bickerstaff, Senior Advisor
• Len Komoroski, CEO
Team History:
Since the Cavaliers' inaugural 1970-71 NBA
season, for more than three decades the team
has been making memories for the fans of
northeast Ohio. Championship titles, 1;
Conference titles, 5; Division titles, 7.
Arena:
Rocket Arena. Seating capacity, 19,432.
Media Broadcast:
WTAM 1100-AM, WUAB-TV 43

DALLAS MAVERICKS
1333 N. STEMMONS FWY
SUITE 105
DALLAS, TX 75207
214-747-6287
www.mavs.com
• Adelson Miriam, Co-Owner
• Nico Harrison, General Manager/President,
Basketball Ops.
• Jason Kidd, Head Coach
• Rick Welts, COO
• Matt Wojciechowski, CFO
Team History:
The Dallas Mavericks joined the NBA in 1980-81
and quickly became a competitive franchise.
With premium draft selections the team steadily
improved through the 1980s. Championships, 1;
Conference titles, 3; Division titles, 5.
Arena:
American Airlines Center. Seating capacity:
19,200 (up to 21,146 with standing room).

DENVER NUGGETS
BALL ARENA
1000 CHOPPER CIRCLE
DENVER, CO 80204
303-405-1100
www.nba.com/nuggets/
• E. Stanley Kroenke, Owner & Governor
• Josh Kroenke, KSE Vice Chair
• Calvin Booth, General Manager
• Michael Malone, Head Coach
Team History:
The Denver Nuggets franchise traces its origins
to 1967-68 in the American Basketball

Association. A stable ABA franchise for nine
years, Denver carried its winning ways into the
NBA when the two leagues merged in 1976.
Championships 1; Conference titles 1; Division
titles, 12.
Arena:
Ball Arena. Seating capacity: 19,099.
Media Broadcast:
Fox Sports Rocky Mountain; KPXC/KTVD-TV;
KKFN Radio 950.

DETROIT PISTONS
313 PRESENTS
2525 WOODWARD AVENUE
DETROIT, MI 48201
www.nba.com/pistons
• Tom Gores, Owner & CEO
• Arn Tellem, Vice Chair
• Trajan Langdon, General Manager
• J.B. Bickerstaff, Head Coach
Team History:
Automobile-piston magnate Fred Zollner
launched the club in 1941 and christened it the
Fort Wayne Zollner Pistons. The Pistons joined
the National Basketball League, a circuit that
consisted primarily of teams fielded by Midwest
corporations. Championships, 5; Conference
titles, 5; Division titles, 15.
Arena:
Little Caesars Arena. Seating capacity: 19,515.

GOLDEN STATE WARRIORS
CHASE CENTER
1 WARRIORS WAY
SAN FRANCISCO, CA 94158
415-388-0100
ticketing@warriors.com
www.nba.com/warriors/
• Joe Lacob, Co-Executive Chairman/CEO
• Mike Dunleavy, Jr., General Manager
• Steve Kerr, Head Coach
Team History:
The franchise played as the Philadelphia
Warriors until 1962. Today the Warriors play in
the Arena in Oakland, California, and wear
jerseys of blue, white, and gold. The
Philadelphia Warriors won the first
championship of the Basketball Association of
America (BAA), the forerunner of the NBA, in
1947. In 1956 the Warriors won their first NBA
title, sparked by future Hall of Fame members
Paul Arizin and Neil Johnston. Championships,
7; Conference titles, 7; Division titles, 12.
Arena:
Oakland Arena. Seating capacity, 19,596.
Media Broadcast:
Fox Sports Bay Area; KICU Ch 36; KNBR Radio
680; KIQI Radio (Spanish) 1010

HOUSTON ROCKETS
TOYOTA CENTER
1510 POLK STREET
HOUSTON, TX 77002
713-758-7200
rocketscommunity@rocketball.com
www.nba.com/rockets/
• Tilman J. Fertitta, Owner
• Gretchen Sheirr, President, Business
Operations
• Rafael Stone, General Manager
• Ime Udoka, Head Coach
• Larry Kaiser, Chief Financial Officer
• Dawn Keen, VP, Corporate Partnerships
Team Description:
1969-71 as the San Diego Rockets.
1971-present as Houston Rockets.
Championships, 2; Conference Titles, 4; Division
Titles, 8.
Arena:
Toyota Center. Seating Capacity: 18,104.
Media Broadcast:
Fox Sports Southwest; KTRH Radio 740; KLAT
Radio 1010 (Spanish); KHWB-TV.

INDIANA PACERS
GAINBRIDGE FIELDHOUSE
125 S PENNSYLVANIA STREET
INDIANAPOLIS, IN 46204
317-917-2500
Fax: 317-917-2599
PacersInsider@Pacers.com
www.nba.com/pacers
• Herbert Simon, Owner & Chair
• Mel Raines, CEO
• Chad Buchanan, General Manager
• Kevin Pritchard, President, Basketball
Operations
• Rick Carlisle, Head Coach
Team History:
Founded in 1967 and joined the NBA in 1976.
Championships, 3; Conference titles, 1; Division
titles, 9.
Arena:
Gainbridge Fieldhouse. Seating capacity:
17,274.
Media Broadcast:
Fox Sports Midwest; WTTV WIBC Radio 1070

LOS ANGELES CLIPPERS
CRYPTO.COM ARENA
1111 S FIGUEROA STREET
LOS ANGELES, CA 90015
213-765-0520
www.nba.com/clippers
• Steve Ballmer, Chair
• Frank Lawrence, President, Basketball
Operations
• Trent Redden, General Manager
• Mark Hughes, Senior Vice President/Assistant
General Manager
• Tyronn Lue, Head Coach
History:
1970-78 known as Buffalo Braves. 1978-84
known as San Diego Clippers. 1984-present
presently known as the Los Angeles Clippers.
Division titles, 3.
Arena:
Crypto.com Arena. Seating Capacity: 19,079.

LOS ANGELES LAKERS
CRYPTO.COM ARENA
1111 S FIGUEROA STREET
LOS ANGELES, CA 90015
310-426-6000
feedback@la-lakers.com
www.nba.com/lakers
• Jeanie Marie Buss, Owner & President
• Tim Harris, President, Business Operations
• Rob Pelinka, VP, Basketball Operations &
General Manager
• Joe McCormack, Chief Financial Officer
• Darvin Ham, Head Coach
History:
1948-60 Known as The Minneapolis Lakers.
1960-present known now as The Los Angeles
Lakers. Championships, 18; Conference titles,
19; Division titles, 34; NBA Cup titles 1.
Arena:
Crypto.com Arena. Seating capacity: 19,079.
Media Broadcast:
Fox Sports; KCAL 9; KLAC Radio 570

MEMPHIS GRIZZLIES
FEDEX FORUM
191 BEALE STREET
MEMPHIS, TN 38103
901-205-1234
www.nba.com/grizzlies
• Robert J. Pera, Owner/Chair
• Zachary Kleiman, General Manager
• Taylor Jenkins, Head Coach
History:
Founded in 1995 in Vancouver; moved to
Memphis in 2001. Division titles 2.
Arena:
FedExForum. Seating capacity, 17,794.

MIAMI HEAT
KASEYA CENTER
601 BISCAYNE BOULEVARD
MIAMI, FL 33132

786-777-1000
Fax: 786-777-1600
guestservices@heat.com
www.nba.com/heat
• Micky Arison, Managing General Partner
• Nick Arison, CEO
• Pat Riley, President
• Andy Elisburg, General Manager
• Erik Spoelstra, Head Coach
History:
Founded in 1988 in Miami. Championships, 3;
Conference titles, 7; Division titles, 16.
Arena:
Kaseya Center (formerly known as FTX Arena
and American Airlines Arena). Seating capacity:
19,600.
Media Broadcast:
FanDuel Sports Network Sun; WAMI-TV; WINC
Radio 940; WIOD 610; WACC Radio 830.

MILWAUKEE BUCKS
FISERV FORUM
1111 VEL R PHILLIPS AVENUE
MILWAUKEE, WI 53203
414-227-0599
877-428-2825
tickets@bucks.com
www.nba.com/bucks
• Peter Feigin, President
• Jon Horst, General Manager
• Doc Rivers, Head Coach
• Patrick McDonough, Chief Financial Officer
History:
Founded in 1968 in Milwaukee. Championships,
2; Conference titles, 3; Division titles, 18.
Arena:
Fiserv Forum. Seating capacity, 17,385.

MINNESOTA TIMBERWOLVES
600 HENNEPIN AVE
SUITE 300
MINNEAPOLIS, MN 55403
612-673-1600
www.nba.com/timberwolves
• Glen Taylor, Co-Owner
• Ethan Casson, CEO
• Tim Connelly, President, Basketball
Operations
• Chris Finch, Head Coach
History:
Founded in 1989 in Minnesota. Division titles, 1.
Arena:
Target Center. Seating capacity: 18,798.

NEW ORLEANS PELICANS
OCHSNER SPORTS PERFORMANCE
CENTER
5800 AIRLINE DRIVE
METAIRIE, LA 70003
504-593-4971
fanexperience@pelicans.com
www.nba.com/pelicans
• Gayle Benson, Governor
• Dennis Lauscha, President
• Bryson Graham, General Manager
• Willie Green, Head Coach
History:
Founded in 1988 in Charlotte. Division titles, 1.
Arena:
Smoothie King Center. Seating capacity: 17,791.

NEW YORK KNICKS
MADISON SQUARE GARDEN
4 PENNSYLVANIA PLAZA
NEW YORK, NY 10001
www.nba.com/knicks
• Leon Rose, President
• James L. Dolan, Executive Chair
• Jamaal Lesane, COO, Madison Square
Garden Sports
• Tom Thibodeau, Head Coach
• Brock Aller, VP, Basketball Operations
History:
Founded in 1946 in New York. Championships,
2; Conference titles, 4; Division titles, 8.
Arena:
Madison Square Garden. Seating capacity:

19,812.
Media Broadcast:
ESPN Radio 1050-AM.

OKLAHOMA CITY THUNDER
CHESAPEAKE ENERGY CENTER
208 THUNDER DRIVE
OKLAHOMA CITY, OK 73102
405-208-4800
fans@okcthunder.com
www.nba.com/thunder/
• Clay Ike Bennett, Chair
• Sam Presti, EVP & General Manager
• Mark Daigneault, Head Coach
• Wynn Sullivan, VP, Basketball Operations
Team History:
Oklahoma City Thunder made their home debut
on October 14, 2008 against the LA Clippers.
Formerly the Seattle Supersonics.
Championships, 1; Conference titles, 4; Division
titles, 11.
Arena:
Paycom Center (formerly known as Chesapeake
Energy Arena). Seating capacity: 18,203.

ORLANDO MAGIC
KIA CENTER
400 W CHURCH STREET
SUITE 200
ORLANDO, FL 32801
407-916-2400
www.nba.com/magic
• Alex Martins, CEO
• Jeff Weltman, President
• Anthony Parker, General Manager
• Jamahl Mosley, Head Coach
History:
Founded in 1989 in Orlando, FL. Conference
titles, 2; Division titles, 7.
Arena:
Kia Center (formerly Amway Center), opened in
1989 with a current seating capacity of 18,846
(NBA).
Media Broadcast:
Magic Television Network (MTN); Sunshine
Network; WDBO Radio AM- 580; AM 1440
WPRD, AM 1400 WSDO or AM 1220 WOTS.

PHILADELPHIA 76ERS
55 HARBOUR BLVD
CAMDEN, NJ 08103
www.nba.com/sixers
• Josh Harris, Managing Partner
• Daryl Morey, President, Basketball Operations
• Elton Brand, General Manager
• Nick Nurse, Head Coach
• Peter Dinwiddie, Executive VP, Basketball
Operations
History:
1949-63 known as Syracuse Nationals.
1963-present known as Philadelphia 76ers.
Championships, 3; Conference titles, 5; Division
titles, 12.
Arena:
Wells Fargo Center. Seating capacity: 21,000.
Media Broadcast:
Comcast SportsNet, Channel 7 UPN, WIP Radio
610; WPSG-TV.

PHOENIX SUNS
FOOTPRINT CENTER
201 E JEFFERSON STREET
PHOENIX, AZ 85004
602-379-2000
www.nba.com/suns/
• Josh Bartelstein, CEO
• James Jones, General Manager & President
of Basketball Ops.
• Mike Budenholzer, Head Coach
• Morgan Cato, Assistant General Manager/VP,
Basketball Ops.
History:
Founded in 1968. Conference titles, 3; Division
titles, 8.
Arena:
Footprint Center (formerly known as Talking

Stick Resort Arena and Phoenix Suns Arena).
Seating capacity: 17,071.

PORTLAND TRAIL BLAZERS
MODA CENTER
ONE CENTER COURT
SUITE 200
PORTLAND, OR 97227
503-234-9291
ticketservices@trailblazers.com
www.nba.com/blazers
• Dewayne Hankins, President, Business
Operations
• Paul Allen, Chair
• Joe Cronin, General Manager
• Chauncey Billups, Head Coach
History:
Founded in 1970 in Portland. Championships, 1;
Conference titles, 3; Division titles, 6.
Arena:
Moda Center. Seating capacity: 19,393.
Media Broadcast:
Trail Blazers Flag Ship Station - KXL 750-AM.
MAGIA 1150-AM (Spanish).

SACRAMENTO KINGS
GOLDEN 1 CENTER
500 DAVID J STERN WALK
SACRAMENTO, CA 95814
916-928-0000
888-915-4647
www.nba.com/kings/
• Matina Kolokotronis, Chief Operating Officer
• Alex Rodrigo, SVP & General Manager
• Doug Christie, Head Coach
History:
Founded in 1923. 1923-44 Rochester
Seagrams, 1945-57 Rochester Royals, 1957-72
Cincinnati Royals, 1972-75 Kansas City Omaha
Kings, 1975-85 Kansas City Kings, 1985-present
Sacramento Kings. Championships, 2;
Conference titles, 0; Division titles, 6.
Arena:
Golden 1 Center. Seating capacity: 17,608.
Media Broadcast:
KHTK 1140-AM.

SAN ANTONIO SPURS
FROST BANK CENTER
ONE FROST BANK CENTER DRIVE
SAN ANTONIO, TX 78219
210-444-5000
www.nba.com/spurs/
• Gregg Popovich, Head Coach & President
• R.C. Buford, CEO
• Brian Wright, General Manager
History:
1967-70 as the Dallas Chaparrals, 1970-71
Texas Chapparrals, 1971-73 Dallas Chaparrals,
1973-present San Antonio Spurs. 1976 joined
the NBA. Championships, 5; Conference titles,
6; Division titles, 22.
Arena:
Frost Bank Center (formerly AT&T Center).
Seating capacity, 18,418.

TORONTO RAPTORS
SCOTIABANK ARENA
40 BAY STREET
SUITE 500
TORONTO, ON, CANADA M5J 2X2
416-815-5500
www.nba.com/raptors
• Masai Ujiri, Vice-Chairman, Team President,
Alternate NBA Gov.
• Bobby Webster, General Manager
• Darko Rajakovic, Head Coach
• Tyla Flexman, VP, Basketball Operations
History:
Founded in 1995 in Toronto. Championship
titles, 1. Conference titles, 1. Division Titles, 7.
Arena:
Scotiabank Arena. Seating capacity, 19,800
(20,511 with standing room).

UTAH JAZZ
DELTA CENTER
301 W SOUTH TEMPLE
SALT LAKE CITY, UT 84101
801-325-2500
www.nba.com/jazz
• Ryan Smith, Owner/Chair
• Justin Zanik, General Manager
• Will Hardy, Head Coach
History:
1974-79 New Orleans Jazz. 1979-present Utah
Jazz. Conference titles, 2; Division titles, 11.
Arena:
Delta Center (formerly Vivint Smart Home
Arena). Seating capacity: 18,306.

WASHINGTON WIZARDS
CAPITAL ONE ARENA
601 FRONT STREET NW
WASHINGTON, DC 20004
202-628-3200
www.nba.com/wizards
• Ted Leonsis, Founder/Chair/Chief Executive
Officer
• Will Dawkins, General Manager
• Brian Keefe, Head Coach
• Brett Greenberg, Assistant General Manager,
Strategy & Analytics
History:
Championships, 1; Conference titles, 4; Division
titles, 8.
Arena:
Capital One Arena (formerly known as Verizon
Center). Seating capacity: 20,356.

NATIONAL BASKETBALL LEAGUE OF CANADA
120 EGLINTON AVENUE EAST
8TH FLOOR
TORONTO, ON, CANADA M4P 1E2
info@nblcanada.ca
www.nblcanada.ca
• Audley Stephenson, VP, Basketball
Operations
audman@nblcanada.ca

Teams:

KW TITANS
901 VICTORIA STREET
NORTH UNIT 1
KITCHENER, ON, CANADA N2B 3C3
519-577-1212
info@kwtitans.com
www.kwtitans.com
• Mel Kobe, General Manager
• Cliff Clinkscales, Head Coach

LONDON LIGHTNING
75 BLACKFRIARS STREET
LONDON, ON, CANADA N6H 1K8
519-433-0634
www.lightningbasketball.ca
• Vito Frijia, Owner
• Mark Frijia, General Manager
mark@lightningbasketball.ca
• Doug Plumb, Head Coach
coachdoug@lightningbasketball.ca

SUDBURY FIVE
240 ELGIN STREET
SUDBURY, ON, CANADA P3E 3N6
705-815-5555
Fax: 705-675-3944
info@thefive.ca
thefive.ca
• Dario Zulich, Owner
• Logan Stutz, General Manager & Head Coach
• Michael Brovac, Player Deveopment

WINDSOR EXPRESS
405 VICTORIA AVENUE
WINDSOR, ON, CANADA N9A 4N1

519-800-3665
info@windsorexpress.ca
www.windsorexpress.ca
• Dartis Willis, Sr., President & CEO
dw@windsorexpress.ca
• Erin Basterfield, General Manager
gm@windsorexpress.ca
• Sinan Al Najjar, Coordinator, Sales And
Partnerships
sinan@windsorexpress.ca

NATIONAL BASKETBALL ASSOCIATION DEVELOPMENT LEAGUE
OLYMPIC TOWER
645 FIFTH AVENUE
NEW YORK, NY 10022
212-407-8000
Fax: 212-832-3861
gleague.nba.com
• Shareef Abdur-Rahim, President
Nature of Service:
Basketball League.
League Description:
Formerly the six-team National Basketball
Development League, the National
Basketball Association Development
League serves as the NBA's in-house minor
league. Founded in 2001, the league plays
almost 50 games a season and serves as a
place for aspiring hoops shooters to improve
their game and hopefully get called up to a
big league team. The NBA G-League is
currently comprised of 31 teams.

Teams:

AUSTIN SPURS
H-E-B CENTER AT CEDAR PARK
2100 AVENUE OF THE STARS
CEDAR PARK, TX 78613
512-236-8333
info@attcenter.com
austin.gleague.nba.com
• Brent Barry, General Manager
• Petar Bozic, Head Coach
Arena:
H-E-B Center at Cedar Park. Seating capacity:
8,700.
NBA Affiliate:
San Antonio Spurs

BIRMINGHAM SQUADRON
950 22ND AVE N
SUITE 925
BIRMINGHAM, AL 35203
205-719-0850
bhaminfo@pelicans.com
birmingham.gleague.nba.com
• Dennis Lauscha, President
• Trajan Langdon, General Manager
• T.J. Saint, Head Coach
NBA Affiliate:
New Orleans Pelicans
Arena:
Legacy Arena. Seating capacity: 19,000.

CLEVELAND CHARGE
WOLSTEIN CENTER
CLEVELAND STATE UNIVERSITY
2000 PROSPECT AVENUE, E.
CLEVELAND, OH 44145
216-420-2730
contactus@cavs.com
cleveland.gleague.nba.com
• Mike Gansey, General Manager
• Koby Altman, President, Basketball Operations
• Mike Gerrity, Head Coach
Arena:
Wolstein Center. Seating capacity: 15,00 with
floor seats.

DELAWARE BLUE COATS
401 GARASCHES LANE
WILMINGTON, DE 19801
302-504-7587
Fax: 302-351-5370
bluecoatsinfo@76ers.com
bluecoats.gleague.nba.com
• Larry Meli, President
• Jameer Nelson, General Manager
• Mike Longabardi, Head Coach
NBA Affiliate:
Philadelphia 76ers
Founded:
2007
Arena:
Chase Fieldhouse. Seating capacity: 2,500.

FORT WAYNE MAD ANTS
ALLEN COUNTY WAR MEMORIAL COLISEUM
4000 PARNELL AVENUE
FORT WAYNE, IN 46805
260-469-4667
fortwayne.gleague.nba.com
• Tim Bawmann, President
(260) 702-9561
tbawmann@ftwaynemadants.com
• Chris Taylor, General Manager
ctaylor@ftwaynemadants.com
• Tom Hankins, Head Coach
thankins@pacers.com
NBA Affiliate:
Indiana Pacers
Arena:
Allen County War Memorial Coliseum. Seating
capacity: 13,000.

GRAND RAPIDS GOLD
62 COMMERCE AVE SW
SUITE 201
GRAND RAPIDS, MI 49503
844-9GR-GOLD
info@nbagrandrapids.com
grandrapids.gleague.nba.com
• Steve Jbara, President
• Andre Miller, Head Coach
Affiliation:
Denver Nuggets
Arena:
Van Andel Arena. Seating capacity: 11,500.

GREENSBORO SWARM
2411 B WEST GATE CITY BLVD.
GREENSBORO, NC 27403
336-907-3600
swarm_tickets@gsoswarm.com
greensboro.gleague.nba.com
• Cole Teal, General Manager
• Jordan Surenkamp, Head Coach
NBA Affiliate:
Charlotte Hornets
Arena:
Greensboro Coliseum Complex. Seating
capacity: 35,000+.

IOWA WOLVES
WELLS FARGO ARENA
730 THIRD STREET
DES MOINES, IA 50309
515-564-8550
Fax: 515-564-8551
iowa.gleague.nba.com
• Drew Van Meeteren, President, Business
Operations
(515) 954-4487
drew.vanmeeteren@iawolves.com
• Jonathan Wallace, General Manager
• Ernest Scott, Head Coach
NBA Affiliate:
Minnesota Timberwolves
Arena:
Wells Fargo Arena. Seating capacity: 21,000.

LONG ISLAND NETS
NASSAU VETERANS MEMORIAL COLISEUM
1255 HEMPSTEAD TURNPIKE
UNIONDALE, NY 11553

934-948-2546
info@longislandnets.com
longisland.gleague.nba.com
• Morgan Taylor, VP, Business Operations
• Maggie Sheehan, Manager, Business
Operations
• Mfon Udofia, Head Coach
NBA Affiliate:
Brooklyn Nets
Arena:
Nassau Veterans Memorial Coliseum. Seating
capacity: 14,500.

MAINE CELTICS
PORTLAND EXPOSITION BUILDING
239 PARK AVENUE
PORTLAND, ME 04102
207-210-6655
Fax: 207-210-6659
maine.gleague.nba.com
• Dajuan Eubanks, President
(207) 210-6655
deubanks@maineceltics.com
• Louis Copolov, Manager, Basketball
Operations
• Blaine Mueller, Head Coach
Arena:
Portland Exposition Building (also known as The
Expo). Seating capacity: 3,000.
Established:
2009
NBA Affiliate:
Boston Celtics

MEMPHIS HUSTLE
LANDERS CENTER
4560 VENTURE DR
SOUTHAVEN, MS 38671
662-470-2131
memphis.gleague.nba.com
• Tommy Eames, General Manager
• Jason March, Head Coach
NBA Affiliate:
Memphis Grizzlies
Arena:
Landers Center. Seating capacity: 9,000.

MOTOR CITY CRUISE
6201 SECOND AVE
DETROIT, MI 48202
313-747-8667
info@cruisebasketball.com
detroit.gleague.nba.com
• Ben Carloni, General Manager
• Jamelle McMillan, Head Coach
Founded:
2003.
Arena:
Wayne State Fieldhouse. Seating capacity:
3,000.

OKLAHOMA CITY BLUE
208 THUNDER DR
OKLAHOMA CITY, OK 73102
405-208-4800
fans@okcthunder.com
oklahomacity.gleague.nba.com
• Nazr Mohammed, General Manager
• Kameron Woods, Head Coach
NBA Affiliate:
Oklahoma City Thunder
Arena:
Paycom Center. Seating capacity: 18,203.

ONTARIO CLIPPERS
TOYOTA ARENA
4000 E ONTARIO CENTER PARKWAY
ONTARIO, CA 91764
909-244-5500
ontarioclippers@clippers.com
ontario.gleague.nba.com
• Matt Morales, General Manager
mmorales@clippers.com
• Paul Hewitt, Head Coach
phewitt@clippers.com

Arena:
Toyota Arena. Seating capacity: 10,832.
NBA Affiliate:
LA Clippers

OSCEOLA MAGIC
SILVER SPURS ARENA
1875 SILVER SPUR LN
KISSIMMEE, FL 34744
407-447-2140
info@osceolamagic.com
osceola.gleague.nba.com
• Kevin Tiller II, General Manager
• Joe Barrer, Head Coach
NBA Affiliate:
Orlando Magic
Arena:
Silver Spurs Arena. Seating capacity: 8,000.

RAPTORS 905
PARAMOUNT FINE FOODS CENTRE
5500 ROSE CHERRY PLACE
MISSISSAUGA, ON, CANADA L4Z 4B6
905-306-6100
info@raptors905.com
raptors905.gleague.nba.com
• Luke Winn, General Manager
• Drew Jones, Head Coach
NBA Affiliate:
Toronto Raptors

RIO GRANDE VALLEY VIPERS
BERT OGDEN ARENA
4900 SI-69 C
EDINBURG, TX 78539
956-562-7362
Fax: 956-942-1150
riograndevalley.gleague.nba.com
• Rene Borrego, President/CEO
rene@rgvipers.com
• Travis Stockbridge, General Manager
• Kevin Burleson, Head Coach
NBA Affiliate:
Houston Rockets
Arena:
Bert Ogden Arena. Seating capacity: 7,688.

SALT LAKE CITY STARS
MAVERIK CENTER
3200 S. DECKER LAKE DRIVE
WEST VALLEY CITY, UT 84119
801-325-2500
saltlakecity.gleague.nba.com
• Jonathan Rinehart, President
• Steve Wojciechowski, Head Coach
NBA Affiliate:
Utah Jazz
Arena:
Maverik Center. Seating capacity: 12,500.

SANTA CRUZ WARRIORS
903 PACIFIC AVENUE
SUITE 101
SANTA CRUZ, CA 95060
831-713-4400
Fax: 831-466-3201
questions@santacruzbasketball.com
santacruz.gleague.nba.com
• Chris Murphy, President
cmurphy@warriors.com
• David Keo, Chief Operating Officer
dkao@warriors.com
• Nick Kerr, Head Coach
NBA Affiliate:
Golden State Warriors
Arena:
Kaiser Permanente Arena. Seating capacity:
2,505.

SIOUX FALLS SKYFORCE
SANFORD PENTAGON
2131 S MINNESOTA AVENUE
SIOUX FALLS, SD 57105
605-332-0605
info@skyforceonline.com
siouxfalls.gleague.nba.com

• Mike Heineman, Owner/President
mike@skyforceonline.com
• Jeremy DeCurtins, General Manager/Vice
President
jeremy@skyforceonline.com
• Kasib Powell, Head Coach
NBA Affiliate:
Miami Heat
Arena:
Sanford Pentagon. Seating capacity: 3,250.

SOUTH BAY LAKERS
2275 E MARIPOSA AVENUE
EL SEGUNDO, CA 90245
310-426-6000
feedback@sb-lakers.com
southbay.gleague.nba.com
• Dane Johnson, Head Coach
NBA Affiliate:
LA Lakers
Arena:
UCLA Health Training Center. Seating capacity:
750.

STOCKTON KINGS
ADVENTIST HEALTH ARENA
248 W FREMONT STREET
STOCKTON, CA 95203
888-KNGS-209
stockton.gleague.nba.com
• Gabriel Harris, General Manager
• Lindsey Harding, Head Coach
NBA Affiliate:
Sacramento Kings
Arena:
Adventist Health Arena. Seating capacity:
11,193.

TEXAS LEGENDS
COMERICA CENTER
2601 AVENUE OF THE STARS
SUITE 300
FRISCO, TX 75034
214-469-0822
texas.gleague.nba.com
• Terry Sullivan, General Manager
• Jordan Sears, Head Coach
NBA Affiliate:
Dallas Mavericks
Arena:
Comerica Center. Seating capacity:
4,000-4,500.

WESTCHESTER KNICKS
WESTCHESTER COUNTY CENTER
198 CENTRAL AVENUE
WHITE PLAINS, NY 10606
914-559-6889
westchesterknicks@msg.com
westchester.gleague.nba.com
• Allan Houston, General Manager
• DeSagana Diop, Head Coach
NBA Affiliate:
New York Knicks
Arena:
Westchester County Center. Seating capacity:
5,000.

WINDY CITY BULLS
NOW ARENA
5333 PRAIRIE STONE PKWY
HOFFMAN ESTATES, IL 60192
windycity.gleague.nba.com
• Chigozie Umeadi, General Manager
• Henry Domercant, Head Coach
NBA Affiliate:
Chicago Bulls
Arena:
Now Arena. Seating capacity: 10,543.

WISCONSIN HERD
549 HIGH AVE.
OSHKOSH, WI 54902
920-233-4373
wisconsin.gleague.nba.com

• Steve Brandes, President
sbrandes@wisconsinherd.com
• Arte Culver, General Manager
• Beno Udrih, Head Coach
NBA Affiliate:
Milwaukee Bucks
Arena:
Oshkosh Arena. Seating capacity: 3,500.

WOMEN'S NATIONAL BASKETBALL ASSOCIATION
OLYMPIC TOWER
645 FIFTH AVENUE
10TH FLOOR
NEW YORK, NY 10022
leaguepasssupport@wnba.com
www.wnba.com
• Cathy Engelbert, Commissioner
Marketing & Promotional Partners:
AT&T, CarMax, Continental Tire, Deloitte,
Discount Tire, Google, Meta, Mielle, Nike,
PlayStation, Scripps, State Farm, Skims,
U.S. Bank
Teams:
12
Founded:
1997

Teams:

ATLANTA DREAM
GATEWAY CENTER ARENA
2000 CONVENTION CENTER CONCOURSE
COLLEGE PARK, GA 30337
877-977-7729
dream.wnba.com
• Dan Padover, General Manager
• Tanisha Wright, Head Coach
History:
Founded in October of 2007
Arena:
Gateway Center Arena. Seating capacity 3,500.

CHICAGO SKY
2301 S. LAKE SHORE DR.
EAST BUILDING - LAKESIDE CENTER
CHICAGO, IL 60616
312-828-9550
tickets@chicagosky.net
sky.wnba.com
• Michael Alter, Principal Owner
• Margaret Stender, Minority Owner
• Adam Fox, President/CEO
• Jeff Pagliocca, General Manager
• Teresa Weatherspoon, Head Coach
History:
The Chicago Sky officially joined the Chicago
sports landscape on September 20, 2005.
Chicago Sky began play with the 2006 season
at the UIC Pavilion, located on the campus of
the University of Illinois at Chicago.
Arena:
Wintertrust Arena. Seating capacity: 10,387.

CONNECTICUT SUN
MOHEGAN SUN ARENA
ONE MOHEGAN SUN BOULEVARD
UNCASVILLE, CT 06382
877-SUN-TIXX
info@connecticutsun.com
sun.wnba.com
• Jennifer Rizzotti, Team President
jrizzotti@connecticutsun.com
• Darius Taylor, General Manager
• Stephanie White, Head Coach
History:
Founded in 1999
Arena:
Mohegan Sun Arena. Seating capacity: 9,323.

DALLAS WINGS
500 EAST BORDER STREET
SUITE 250
ARLINGTON, TX 76010

817-469-9464
wings.wnba.com
• Greg Bibb, President/CEO/Partner
• Latricia Trammell, Head Coach
History:
Founded in 1998; team has moved from
Michigan to Oklahoma to Texas.
Arena:
College Park Center. Seating capacity: 7,000.

INDIANA FEVER
125 S PENNSYLVANIA ST
INDIANAPOLIS, IN 46204
317-917-2500
pacersinsider@pacers.com
fever.wnba.com
• Allison Barber, President & COO
• Lin Dunn, General Manager
• Christie Sides, Head Coach
History:
Founded in 1999.
Arena:
Gainbridge Fieldhouse; Indiana Farmers
Coliseum (2021-2022).

LAS VEGAS ACES
MICHELOB ULTRA ARENA
3950 LAS VEGAS BOULEVARD S
LAS VEGAS, NV 89119
702-463-2252
info@lasvegasaces.com
aces.wnba.com
• Nikki Fargas, President
• Williams Natalie, General Manager
• Becky Hammon, Head Coach
Arena:
Michelob Ultra Arena (formerly Mandalay Bay
Events Center). Seating capacity: 12,000.

LOS ANGELES SPARKS
CRYPTO.COM ARENA
1111 S FIGUEROA ST
LOS ANGELES, CA 90015
sparks.wnba.com
• Vanessa Shay, President
• Karen Bryant, Chief Administrative Officer
kbryant@la-sparks.com
• Curt Miller, Head Coach
Arena:
Crypto.com Arena (formerly known as Staples
Center). Seating capacity: 19,079.
Media Broadcast:
FSN-TV West.

MINNESOTA LYNX
600 HENNEPIN AVE
SUITE 300
MINNEAPOLIS, MN 55403
612-673-8400
lynx.wnba.com
• Clare Duwelius, General Manager
• Cheryl Reeve, Head Coach & President,
Basketball Operations
History:
Founded in 1997. In April 1998, the WNBA
announced they would add two expansion
teams, to be managed by the Minnesota
Timberwolves and Orlando Magic, for the 1999
season. The Minnesota Lynx started their
inaugural season in 1999 with 12,000 fans in
attendance to watch the first regular-season
game, against Detroit at Target Center.
Arena:
Target Center. Seating capacity: 18,798.

NEW YORK LIBERTY
168 39TH STREET
7TH FLOOR
BROOKLYN, NY 11232
718-624-7000
info@nyliberty.com
liberty.wnba.com
• Keia Clarke, CEO
• Jonathan Kolb, General Manager
• Sandy Brondello, Head Coach

History:
1996-present.
Arena:
Barclays Center. Seating capacity: 17,732.

PHOENIX MERCURY
FOOTPRINT CENTER
201 E JEFFERSON STREET
PHOENIX, AZ 85004
602-514-8333
Fax: 602-379-7540
mercury.wnba.com
• Mat Ishbia, Owner
• Nick U'Ren, General Manager
• Nate Tibbetts, Head Coach
History:
1997-present.
Arena:
Footprint Center (formerly US Airways Center).
Seating capacity: 17,071.

SEATTLE STORM
16 WEST HARRISON ST.
SUITE 100
SEATTLE, WA 98119
206-217-9622
Fax: 206-281-5817
storm.wnba.com
• Alisha Valavanis, CEO/President
• Noelle Quinn, Head Coach
• Talisa Rhea, General Manager
History:
2000-present.
Arena:
Climate Pledge Arena. Seating capacity: 18,300.
Media Broadcast:
Sports Radio 950 KJR.

WASHINGTON MYSTICS
601 S ST NW
4TH FLOOR
WASHINGTON, DC 20001
mystics.wnba.com
• Mike Thibault, General Manager
• Eric Thibault, Head Coach
Arena:
Entertainment & Sports Arena. Seating capacity:
4,200.

Biathlon Organizations

BIATHLON CANADA
100-1995 OLYMPIC WAY
CANMORE, AB, CANADA T1W 2T6
403-678-4002
Fax: 403-678-3644
info@biathloncanada.ca
www.biathloncanada.ca
• Matthias Ahrens, National Team Head
Coach
(403) 678-4002
• Roddy Ward, National Team Coach
(403) 609-4744
rward@biathloncanada.ca
• Andy Holmwood, General Manager
(403) 609-4746
aholmwood@biathloncanada.ca
Nature of Service:
The combination of skiing and shooting
used in the sport today is founded on a
tradition of hunting, stemming back over four
thousand years. Petroglyphs found in
Norway depict hunters, with spears,
traveling on skis in pursuit of game. Written
descriptions of hunting on skis can be traced
back to 400 B.C. and the Roman poet,
Virgil. Biathlon's military uses have been
subsequently noted by generals, writers,
geographers, and historians such as
Xenophon, Strabol, Arrian, Theophanes,
Prokopius, and Acruni who described battles

of warriors equipped with skis.
Year Founded:
1985.

INTERNATIONAL BIATHLON UNION (IBU)

PEREGRINSTRASSE 14
SALZBURG, A-5020
biathlon@ibu.at
www.biathlonworld.com
• Anders Besseberg, President
• Olle Dahlin, Vice President, Development
olle.dahlin@ibu.at
• James E Carrabre, Vice President,
Medical Issues
jim.carrabre@ibu.at
• Nami Kim, Vice President, Special Issues
• Ivor Lehotan, Vice President, Information
• Klaus Leistner, Vice President, Finance
klaus.leistner@ibu.at
• Victor Maygurov, First Vice President
• Thomas Pfuller, Vice President, Marketing
• Nicole Resch, Secretary General
• Max Cobb, Vice President, Sport
max.cobb@ibu.at
Description:
The IBU serves as the international
governing body for the sport of biathlon,
sanctioning competitions and promoting the
sport.
Number of Members:
57
Publications:
Biathlon Calander (annual), BiathlonWorld
Magazine.

U.S. BIATHLON ASSOCIATION
49 PINELAND DRIVE
SUITE 301A
NEW GLOUCESTER HALL
NEW GLOUCESTER, ME 04260
207-688-6500
800-242-8456
Fax: 207-688-6505
info@usbiathlon.org
www.teamusa.org/US-Biathlon
• Max Cobb, President & CEO
(207) 688-6500
• Per Nilsson, National Team Head Coach
per.coach@gmail.com
Year Founded:
1980
Description:
The USBA promotes the development of
biathlon in the United States by organizing
training and competition around the country.
Membership Requirements:
Annual dues

Billiards Organizations

AMERICAN CUESPORTS ALLIANCE
101 SOUTH MILITARY AVENUE
SUITE P #131
GREEN BAY, WI 54303
920-662-1705
888-662-1705
Fax: 920-662-1706
jlewis@americancuesports.org
www.americancuesports.org
• Mike Wilson, President
• Sandra Chamberlain, Vice President
• John Lewis, Executive Director
• Thomas Fankhauser, Treasurer

• Annette Wood, Graphic Designer
• Janet Ybarra, Referee Administrator
Description:
Non-profit, member-governed USA-based
cue sports organization offering
league-sanction services and referee and
instructor certification.
Number of Members:
20,000
Year Founded:
2004

**AMERICAN POOLPLAYERS
ASSOCIATION, INC.**
1000 LAKE SAINT LOUIS BOULEVARD
SUITE 325
LAKE SAINT LOUIS, MO 63367
636-625-8611
Fax: 636-625-2975
pbellemi@aol.com
www.poolplayers.com
• Renee Lyle, President
(636) 625-8611
• Larry Hubbart, Co-Founder
• Terry Bell, Co-Founder
Nature of Service:
The APA, also known as the Canadian
Poolplayers Association in Canada, has
grown to more than 250,000 and boasts
more members than all other 'national'
leagues combined. The League is
administered locally by a network of
Franchise Operators. League play is
conducted weekly with both 8-Ball and
9-Ball team formats offered.
History:
The history of billiards is rich and interesting.
The game we know today has evolved over
centuries, morphing from games popular
during different periods of history. Billiards is
known to have evolved from a lawn game,
similar to croquet. Play was eventually
moved indoors to a wooden table with green
cloth, to simulate grass. The history of the
noble game of billiards is deep and vast, the
table, tools for play and rules have changed
century to century. Billiards enthusiasts
have included Kings, Queens, commoners,
Conquistadors, church officials, Presidents,
up to modern day players and professionals.
Member Services:
General information and APA member
services are available on our web site:
www.poolplayers.com.
Membership Requirements:
Must be 18 years of age to play in APA
Leagues. Membership request form
available on our web site.
Number of members:
Over 250,000
Publications:
The American Poolplayers (member
magazine); Billiards Buzz (member
e-newsletter).

**BILLIARD AND BOWLING INSTITUTE OF
AMERICA**
621 SIX FLAGS DRIVE
ARLINGTON, TX 76011
817-385-8441
Fax: 817-633-2940
answer@billiardandbowling.org
www.billiardandbowling.org
• Jeff Mraz, President
(800) 280-2695
jmraz@acemitchell.com
• Corey Dykstra, Vice President

(213) 725-3365
corey.dykstra@brunbowl.com
• Hank Boomershine, Secretary/Treasurer
(435) 723-9640
• Skip Nemececk, Director
(312) 733-7878
opiks@msn.com
• Joleen Lawson, Director
Nature of Service:
A not-for-profit association in Chicago to service the billiard and bowling industries. Comprised of leading bowling and billiard manufacturers, independent bowling distributors and major billiard retailers, BBIA aims to foster the growth of these two great sports throughout the world and advance of common interests of its members.
Year Founded:
1940
Membership Requirements:
Manufacturers or distributors of bowling, billiards, or related supplies as well as major billiard retailers and service firms may join.
Number of Members:
139
Publications:
Annual Directory; Newsletter BBIA NEWSLINE, quarterly; Bowling Participation Study; Billiards Participation Study. BOWLING FOR EVERYONE, instructional booklet.

BILLIARD CONGRESS OF AMERICA
10900 WEST 120 AVENUE
UNIT B7
BROOMFIELD, CO 80021
303-243-5070
866-852-0999
Fax: 719-264-0900
bca@netins.net
www.bca-pool.com
• Mike Serra, Chairman
• Chance Pack, Vice Chairman
• Jonathan Goudeau, Secretary
• Tony Stick, Treasurer
• Rob Johnson, Chief Executive Officer
Nature of Service:
Dedicated to promoting and growing cue sports worldwide throughindustry research and promotion. participating in the process of olympic recognition, hosting amateur, junior and professional tournaments, and supporting its business members by enhancing the image of billiards and broadening its appeal.
History:
The Billiard Congress of America was established in 1948, with early involvement by players like Willie Mosconi and Willie Hoppe. The objective was to organize the players and promote the sport through qualifying tournaments at the local, regional and national levels in Straight Pool and 3-Cushion billiards (the popular competitive disciplines of the era) and recognize those champions. Organizers were also determined to produce an official rulebook to standardize the sport and help fund the effort; and to involve billiard rooms, retailers and manufacturers in meeting these promotional goals.
Member Services:
Assists with rules, tournaments, leagues.
Number of members:
40,000
Publications:
OFFICIAL RULE BOOK, updated annually;

BREAK, bimonthly newsletter; other miscellaneous informational materials.

CANADIAN BILLIARDS & SNOOKER ASSOCIATION
24 WOODSTOCK AVENUE
UNIT 6
RIVERVIEW, NB, CANADA E1B 5H5
randall.morrison@cbsa.ca
www.cbsa.ca
• Randall Morrison, President
(403) 399-1972
randall.morrison@cbsa.ca
• John White, Vice President
john.white@cbsa.ca
• Frank Kakouros, Treasurer
frank.kakouros@cbsa.ca
• Candace Campbell, Secretary
candace.campbell@cbsa.ca
Description:
The CBSA is the governing body for cue sports in Canada. It is a registered non-profit organization and has been operating this way since opening in 1974. CBSA is also recognized by the Canadian Olympic Committee.
Nature of Service:
This association is responsible for arranging the national championships across all disciplines of cue sports and qualifying Canadian players to represent their country at international events staged by the world governing bodies.

CANADIAN CUE SPORTS ASSOCIATION
87 BRIGHTONSTONE GARDENS SE
CALGARY, AB, CANADA T2Z 0C6
403-271-9221
pplted@hotmail.com
www.cdnqsport.com
• Ted Harms, President
Description:
The Canadian Cue Sports Association contains a league system and a championship program that are managed by Canadians, for Canadians. They've partnered with the American CueSports Alliance to ensure that CCS members could compete in US National Championships. They are recognized as the official sanctioning organization for pool league play and related championships in Canada.

TAP, LLC
4315 MAGNUM STREET
SUITE D
LITTLE RIVER, SC 29566
800-984-7665
Fax: 888-870-0983
www.tapleague.com
• Loyd Schonter, Founder/CEO
• Celeste Schonter, Chief Administrative Officer
• Charlie Brocklehurt, Program Director
• Kelly Nace, Event Director
Description:
TAP aims to create an amateur pool league that brings respect to both the player and the game.

UNITED STATES BILLIARD ASSOCIATION
53 HAWTHORNE AVENUE
EAST ISLIP, NY 11730
516-238-6193
www.usba.net

• Jim Shovak, President
• Tom Paley, Secretary
tpaley@msn.com
• Merrill Hughes, Treasurer
hakey99@aol.com
Description:
The USBA acts as the governing body for all forms of carom billiards, including three-cushion billiards, in America.

VNEA
201 SOUTH HENRY STREET
BAY CITY, MI 48706
www.vnea.com
• Gregg Elliott, Executive Director
• Brian Elliott, Director of Marketing & Promotions
• James Powell, Floor Operations Manager
• Rhonda Reinarz, Administrative Assistant
Description:
Non-profit organization established to promote pool on coin operated equipment. Founded in 1979, the membership is over 100,000.

WOMEN'S PROFESSIONAL BILLIARD ASSOCIATION
416 CR 501
SUITE 108
BAYFIELD, CO 81122
855-367-9722
Fax: 704-344-8660
office1@wpba.com
www.wpba.com
• Kim White-Newsome, President
• Belinda Calhoun, Vice President
• John Newsome, Secretary
• Anne Craig, Treasurer
Nature of Service:
Originally formed under the name of the Women's Professional Billiard Alliance. The WPBA sanctions billiard events for female professionals in the sport of billiards.
Year Founded:
1976
Publications:
WPBA Newsletter

WORLD POOL BILLIARD ASSOCIATION
www.wpa-pool.com
• Ian Anderson, President/CEO
• Liwei Wang, Honorary Vice President
• Anamaria Matesic, Treasurer
• Victor Maduro, Board Member
Membership Requirements:
Recognizes the continental and national federations proven to be among the leading federations in its realm. Continental federation pays $12,500 annually to support WPA. Current continental federation members include: European Pocket Billiard Federation, Asian Pocket Billiard Union, Australasian Pool Association, Billiard Congress of America (North America), South African Pool Association, Aruban Billiard Federation, Dutch Caribbean Billiard Association.
Description:
Founded in 1987. It is the international governing body for pocket billiards. Services to promote all pocket billiard sports; to unite the continents and national pool federations and recognize and support them; delegates and supervises rules and tournament regulations for various games; approves and delegates international tournaments and players eligible to compete; acknowledges,

confirms and registers results achieved at official championships. Head quarters are located in Sydney, Australia.

Boating Organizations

AMERICAN BOAT & YACHT COUNCIL
613 THIRD STREET
SUITE 10
ANNAPOLIS, MD 21403
410-990-4460
Fax: 410-990-4466
www.abycinc.org
• John Adey, President
(410) 990-4460
jadey@abycinc.org
• Kevin Scullen, Membership Manager
(410) 990-4460
kscullen@abycinc.org
• Kenneth Weinbrecht, Chairman of the Board
• Brian Goodwin, Technical Director
(410) 990-4460
bgoodwin@abycinc.org
Nature of Service:
To develop quality technical practices and engineering standards for the design, construction, maintenance and repair of small crafts with refernce to their safety.

AMERICAN BOAT BUILDERS & REPAIRERS ASSOCIATION
NEWPORT SHIPYARD
1 WASHINGTON STREET
NEWPORT, RI 02840
401-236-2466
info@abbra.org
www.abbra.org
• Graham Wright, President
• Kirk Ritter, Vice President
• Peter Sabo, Treasurer
• Ron Helbig, Secretary
Nature of Service:
Serves to strengthen and to encourage the professionalism of the marine service industry through the sharing of knowledge and the search for solutions to common problems.
Year Founded:
1943
Publication:
Capstan Newsletter - Monthly.

AMERICAN BOATBUILDERS ASSOCIATION
THE BRUMBY BUILDING
MARIETTA STATION
127 CHURCH STREET, SUITE 210
MARIETTA, GA 30060
770-792-3070
Fax: 770-792-3073
glenna@aba.com
www.ababoats.com
• Jay Patton, President
• Ed Atchley, Senior Project Manager
Nature of Service:
Through the collective buying power of its members, the ABA strives to purchase high quality materials at the lowest cost of any boat building entity in the United States. They organize as necessary to bring the united voice of the independent builder to outside influences such as vendors, government, and industry associations.

Year Founded:
1992

AMERICAN POWER BOAT ASSOCIATION
17640 EAST NINE MILE ROAD
EASTPOINTE, MI 48021-0377
586-773-9700
Fax: 586-773-6490
apbahq@apba.org
www.apba.org
• Mark Wheeler, President
president@apba.org
• Dutch Squires, Vice President
• Ryan Berlin, Director of Operations
• Linda Likert, Bookeeper
Description:
The APBA is the US governing body for power boat racing.
Year Founded:
1903
Member Services:
Various.
Membership Requirements:
Complete application, pay fee.
Number of Members:
3,500+
Publications:
PROPELLER Magazine

AMERICAN WHITEWATER
629 WEST MAIN STREET
SYLVA, NC 28779
828-586-1931
Fax: 828-586-2840
membership@americanwhitewater.org
www.americanwhitewater.org
• Chris Bell, President
• Courtney Wilton, Vice President
• Trey Coleman, Treasurer
• Susan Hollingsworth-Elliott, Secretary
Nature of Service:
American Whitewater is a non-profit organization that aims to conserve and restore America's whitewater resources. It is a membership organization that aims to enhance opportunities for whitewater enthusiasts to enjoy the water safely.
Year Founded:
1954
Membership Benefits:
Six issues of the American Whitewater magazine, monthly online electronic newsletter, 10% discount on outdoor equipment from nantahalaoutdoor center store, catalog and online. 40% off the subscription of Kayak session magazine.

ASSOCIATION OF MARINA INDUSTRIES
50 WATER STREET
WARREN, RI 02885
866 367-6622
Fax: 401-247-0074
info@marinaassociation.org
www.marinaassociation.org
• Jeff Rose, Chairman
• Brad Gross, Vice Chairman
• Joe Riley, Treasurer
• Merritt Alves, Membership Coordinator
• Kate Stanley, Direcor of Events
Description:
The Association of Marina Industries is a nonprofit organization dedicated to the marine industry. The AMI is responsible for the International Marine Institute, including the Certified Marina Manager program and the annual International Marina & Boatyard Conference.

Membership:
Benefits include critical legislative and regulatory support; timely industry information, advice, and direction; money-saving programs including marina insurance program, fuel discount program, energy purchasing program, telecom savings program, penny wise office supplies program, personal insurance program; education, seminars and certifications; online discussion forum; and access to free internet classified postings.

BOAT OWNERS ASSOCIATION OF THE UNITED STATES (BOATUS)
880 SOUTH PICKETT STREET
ALEXANDRIA, VA 22304-4606
703-461-2878
800-283-2883
www.boatus.com
• Margaret Podlich, President
• Adam Wheeler, VP and Director of Towing
• John Condon, AVP, Towing Operations
• Heather Lougheed, VP, Membership
Nature of Service:
Provides savings, service and representation to millions of boat owners nationwide.
Year Founded:
1966
Number of Members
650,000

BOATING WRITERS INTERNATIONAL
108 NINTH STREET
WILMETTE, IL 60091
847-736-4142
www.bwi.org
• Alan Wendt, President
• Lenny Rudow, First Vice President
• Lindsey Johnson, Second Vice President
• Zuzana Prochazka, Board of Directors
• Greg Proteau, Executive Director, Secretary and Treasurer
Description:
Boating Writers International/BWI is a non-profit professional organization consisting of writers, broadcasters, editors, photographers, public relations specialists and others in the communications profession associated with the boating industry. Members include active marine journalists across the U.S., in Canada and Europe, supporting marine manufacturers and service entities, and associates in communication roles.

CANADIAN SAFE BOATING COUNCIL
400 CONSUMERS ROAD
TORONTO, ON, CANADA M2J 1P8
416-840-8938
www.csbc.ca
• John Gullick, Chair
• Vollmer Michael, Vice Chair
• Denis Vallee, Treasurer
• Susan Daly, Secretary
• Ted Fortuna, Officer
Description:
The Canadian Safe Boating Council aims to promote safe and responsible boating throughout Canada.

INDEPENDENT BOATBUILDERS INC.
215 NORTH LOGAN STREET
SUITE B
WEST FRANKFORT, IL 62896

618-932-4476
Fax: 618-932-8132
www.ibbi.com
• Tom Broy, President
• Lindsey Dillow, Accounting Assistant
• Jodi Sanders, Controller, Secretary, Treasurer
Nature of Service:
Independent Boat Builders, Inc. was formed as a marine purchasing cooperative by a group of independent, recreational boat builders. IBBI has maintained strict standards for membership, and today, we have 23, highly-regarded shareholders, each recognized in the industry for their top-quality boats, their integrity, and their financial stability.
Year Founded:
1989

INTERNATIONAL COUNCIL OF MARINE INDUSTRY ASSOCIATIONS
MARINE HOUSE
THORPE LEA ROAD
EGHAM, SURREY, ENGLAND TW20 8BF
+44-1784-22-3702
Fax: +44-1784-27-0428
info@icomia.com
www.icomia.com
• Udo Kleinitz, Secretary General
(+44) 1784 223 7
udo@icomia.com
• Patrick Hemp, Technical Manager
(+44) 1784 223 7
patrick@icomia.com
• Barbara Fountoukos, Communications Manager
(+44) 1784 223 7
• Trudie Bloomfield, Office Secretary
Nature of Sports Service:
Founded in 1966. Brings together in one global organization all the national boating federations and other bodies involved in the recreational marine industry, and to represent them at international level.

INTERNATIONAL JET SPORTS BOATING ASSOCIATION
330 PURISSIMA STREET
SUITE C
HALF MOON BAY, CA 94019
714-751-8695
Fax: 714-751-8609
info@ijsba.com
www.ijsba.com
• Scott Frazier, Executive Director
Nature of Service:
International membership association for personal watercraft owners with members in 35 countries. Sanctions personal watercraft boating races.
Year Founded:
1982
Number of members:
27,000
Publications:
JET SPORTS, 9 times a year.

NATIONAL MARINE MANUFACTURERS ASSOCIATION
231 SOUTH LASALLE STREET
SUITE 2050
CHICAGO, IL 60604
312-946-6200
webmaster@nmma.org
www.nmma.org

• Thomas Dammrich, President
(312) 946-6220
tdammrich@nmma.org
• Ben Wold, Executive Vice President
(312) 946-6234
bwold@nmma.org
• Carl Blackwell, Senior VP
(312) 946-6277
cblackwell@nmma.org
• Craig Boskey, Senior VP Finance
(312) 946-6232
cboskey@nmma.org
• Thomas Marhevko, Senior VP
(312) 946-6213
tmarhevko@nmma.org
Products & Services:
Dedicated to creating, promoting and protecting an environment where members can achieve financial success through excellence in manufacturing, in selling, and in servicing their customers.

RECREATIONAL BOATING & FISHING FOUNDATION
500 MONTGOMERY STREET
SUITE 300
ALEXANDRIA, VA 22314
703-519-0013
info@takemefishing.org
takemefishing.org
• Frank Peterson Jr., President & CEO
(703) 778-5157
fpeterson@rbff.org
Nature of Service:
The Recreational Boating & Fishing Foundation is a nonprofit organization whose mission is to increase participation in recreational angling and boating and thereby increase public awareness and appreciation of the need for protecting, conserving and restoring this nation's aquatic natural resources.
Year Founded:
1998
Publications:
NewsWaves, monthly e-newsletter

SAIL AMERICA
50 WATER STREET
WARREN, RI 02885
401-289-2540
Fax: 401-247-0074
www.sailamerica.com
• Katie Kelly, Association Manager
kkelly@sailamerica.com
Sports Service Founded:
1988
Event Management Services:
Nonprofit organization, promoting SAIL EXPO & Strictly Sail, sailboat shows.

SAIL CANADA
PORTSMOUTH OLYMPIC HARBOUR
53 YONGE STREET
KINGSTON, ON, CANADA K7M 6G4
613-545-3044
Fax: 613-545-3045
sailcanada@sailing.ca
www.sailing.ca
• Todd Irving, President
• Kai Bjorn, Board Member
Description:
Established in 1931, Sail Canada is the national governing body for the sport of sailing in Canada.

SUPER BOAT INTERNATIONAL
1323 20TH TERRACE
KEY WEST, FL 33040
305-296-6166
superboatracing@gmail.com
www.superboat.com
• John Carbonell, Founder
Description:
Involved in promoting Super Boat Racing events, leading to national and world championships.
Year Founded:
1992

THUNDERBOATS UNLIMITED INC.
1342 MAIN ST
SUITE B
RAMONA, CA 92065-2127
Nature of Service:
Thunderboats Unlimited, Inc. is a non-profit corporation established by a group of committed Southern California racing enthusiasts, to promote powerboat racing in San Diego, and increase tourism in the beach area. The group was initially brought together by the late legendary hydroplane racer Bill Muncey, for whom the 2Â« mile race course is named, but soon grew to include individuals from all aspects of the community.
Year Founded:
1964
Number of members:
1,450

UNITED MARINE MANUFACTURERS ASSOCIATION
714 SOUTH NATIONAL
SPRINGFIELD, MO 65804
417-869-9602
Fax: 417-869-9653
www.umma.com
• Kent Wooldridge, President
• Sherree Johnson, Accountant
• Jane Melton, Program Implementation
Description:
To empower the marine suppliers in a highly competitive and changing industry. We provide information to our members that improve their operational efforts and help build their market share, relative to the industry.
Year Founded:
1998

WOMEN'S OCEAN RACING SAILING ASSOCIATION
PO BOX 937
DANA POINT, CA 92629
949-722-7872
Fax: 949-846-1481
info@wsaoc.org
www.worsa.org
• Valerie Rhodes, Commodore
• Gabi Schwaiger, Vice Commodore
• Wayne Wallace, Treasurer
• Brenda Highley, Secretary
• Shannon Harshman, Membership Director
Nature of Service:
Provides opportunities for women to gain sailing knowledge on and off the water, to participate in all-female regattas, and to socialize with other women sailors. Membership includes both racers and cruisers - both males and females.
Year Founded:
1979

Member Services:
Sponsors annual women's regatta in October, racing clinics for women, annual cruise to the Isthmus at Catalina Island, and other services. Members of Southern California Yachting Association, sponsors of the annual SCYA women's sailing convention held in February of each year.
Description:
Founded in 1979. Provides opportunities for women to gain sailing knowledge on and off the water, to participate in all-female regattas, and to socialize with other women sailors. Membership includes both racers and cruisers - both males and females.
Publications:
THE WHISTLE, monthly newsletter.

Bobsledding Organizations

USA BOBSLED & SKELETON FEDERATION
1631 MESA AVENUE
COPPER BUILDING
SUITE A
COLORADO SPRINGS, CO 80906
Fax: 719-520-3212
www.teamusa.org/USA-Bobsled-Skeleton-Federation
• Darrin Steele, Chief Executive Officer
• Lisa Carlock, Finance & Operations Director
lisa.carlock@usabs.com
• Lenny Kasten, National Team Manager
Description:
This Federation was formed to advance, encourage, improve and promote amateur bobsledding and skeleton competition in the United States. It is also the National Governing Body of hte sports of bobsled and skeleton and recognized as such by the United States Olympic Committee and the Federation Internationale De Bob Sleigh De and Tobogganing Federation.
Member Services:
Passenger Rider / Sports / Supporting Memberships
Number of members:
525
Publications:
Quarterly newsletter

Bowling Organizations

AMERICAN BLIND BOWLING ASSOCIATION
7273 SOUTH RIDGELAND
CHICAGO, IL 60649
773-255-3121
www.abba1951.org
• Robert McDonald, President
(773) 255-3121
president@abba1951.org
• Joyce Spencer, 1st Vice President
(919) 796-5090
1stvicepresident@abba1951.org
• Charles Glaser, 2nd Vice President
(678) 521-2976
2ndvicepresident@abba1951.org
Description:
ABBA's goal is to allow blind and visually impaired individuals to bowl with the assistance of special guide rails. They host numerour tournaments throughout the year

in many different locations in North America.
Year Founded:
1940
Membership Requirements:
Any person 18 years of age or older, legally blind or sighted.
Publications:
INTRODUCING THE BLIND BOWLING ASSOCIATION. THE BLIND BOWLER, published three times annually with information about league and tournament activities and high score awards.

AMERICAN WHEELCHAIR BOWLING ASSOCIATION
713-849-9052
info@awba.org
www.awba.org
• Richard Carlson, Founder
• Wayne Webber, Chairman
• Eddy Hutchens, Vice Chairman
• Mark Shepherd, Treasurer
• Gary Ryan, Secretary
Description:
The American Wheelchair Bowling Association serves over 500 members throughout the United States. They've formed numeruos alliance with organizations, such as the Veterans Administration, Paralyzed Veterans of America, and some youth organizations.

BILLIARD AND BOWLING INSTITUTE OF AMERICA
615 SIX FLAGS DRIVE
ARLINGTON, TX 76011
817-385-8441
Fax: 817-633-2940
answer@billiardandbowling.org
www.billiardandbowling.org
• Jeff Mraz, President
(800) 280-2695
jmraz@acemitchell.com
• Corey Dykstra, Vice President
(213) 725-3365
corey.dykstra@brunbowl.com
• Hank Boomershine, Secretary/Treasurer
(435) 723-9640
• Skip Nemecek, Director
(312) 733-7878
opiks@msn.com
• Joleen Lawson, Director
Nature of Service:
A not-for-profit association in Chicago to service the billiard and bowling industries. Comprised of leading bowling and billiard manufacturers, independent bowling distributors and major billiard retailers, BBIA aims to foster the growth of these two great sports throughout the world and advance of common interests of its members.
Year Founded:
1940
Membership Requirements:
Manufacturers or distributors of bowling, billiards, or related supplies as well as major billiard retailers and service firms may join.
Number of Members:
139
Publications:
Annual Directory; Newsletter BBIA NEWSLINE, quarterly; Bowling Participation Study; Billiards Participation Study. BOWLING FOR EVERYONE, instructional booklet.

BOWL CANADA
250 SHIELDS COURT
UNIT 10A
MARKHAM, ON, CANADA L3R 9W7
905-479-1560
Fax: 905-479-8613
info@bowlcanada.ca
www.bowlcanada.ca
• Todd Britton, President
(204) 488-0000
todd@academylanes.ca
• Ray Brittain, Vice President
(250) 753-2341
brechinlanes@gmail.com
• Trevor Peters, Director
(204) 727-2695
• Rod Hennessey, Treasurer
(709) 744-2553
riverdalelanes@nl.rogers.com
• Paul Oliveira, Executive Director
paul@bowlcanada.ca
• Kevin Burns, Programs Coordinator
kevin@bowlcanada.ca
Description:
Bowl Canada is a not-for-profit association that works to support bowling centres, promote the benefits of the sport and recreation of bowling to the general public, and to create a better relationship between the many bowling establishments across Canada.

BOWLING PROPRIETORS' ASSOCIATION OF AMERICA
621 SIX FLAGS DRIVE
ARLINGTON, TX 76011
800-343-1329
bpaa.com
• Tom Martino, President
(732) 826-6800
ajjaguar@aol.com
• Nancy Schenk, President Elect
(910) 484-5178
nancy@bandblanes.com
• Randy Thompson, Secretary
(515) 255-1111
rt@plazalanesdm.com
• Jeff Boje, Treasurer
(813) 621-2363
jeffboje@aol.com
Nature of Service:
Perpetuates the best interest of its members, be it for business or bowling as a whole. Promotes better relationships among its members. Aids in formation of and recognizes qualified state, city, district and regional associations. Disseminates information to members beneficial to the conduct of their business. Cooperates and assists others in the furtherance of the best interests of bowling. Obtains beneficial publicity through all available media. Encourages clean and ideal conditions under which bowling shall be conducted by bowling proprietors. Discourages any practice contrary to the best interest of the game.
Year Founded:
1932
Number of members:
3,300
Publications:
Bowling Center Management magazine

CANADIAN 5 PIN BOWLERS' ASSOCIATION
#206 - 720 BELFAST ROAD
OTTAWA, ON, CANADA K1G 0Z5

613-744-5090
Fax: 613-744-2217
sheila.c5pba@gmail.com
www.c5pba.ca
• Dave Post, President
• Len Isleifson, 1st Vice President
• Dave Shepherd, 2nd Vice President
• Sheila Carr, Executive Director
• Chris Henderson, Corporate
Secretary/Treasurer
Description:
The Canadian 5 Pin Bowlers' Association
aims to promote 5 pin bowling and to instill a
sense of pride among it's members. The
association provides quality programs and
services to its members, given their
participation. The association regulates 5
pin bowling, resulting in standardization
within the sport.
Year Founded:
1978
Member Services:
Awards program, lane certification program,
logo merchandising, national
championships, range of technical/coaching
programs.
Membership Requirements:
Bowlers can purchase membership card
through the provincial territorial association
in the province which they reside.
Publications:
Coast to Coast Newsletter, Rule Book,
by-laws, annually; various manuals and
booklets concerning 5 pin bowling.

THE NATIONAL BOWLING ASSOCIATION, INC

9944 READING ROAD
EVENDALE, OH 45241-3106
513-769-1985
Fax: 513-769-3596
nationaloffice@tnbainc.org
www.tnbainc.org
• Gregory P. Green, President
• Dewann Clark, Vice President
(310) 846-4590
dewann.clark@tnbainc.org
• Annette R. Samuel, Executive Secretary,
Treasurer
(513) 769-1985
annette.samuel@tnbainc.org
• Luther Moses, National Director of
Tournaments
(303) 696-9410
Nature of Service:
The National Bowling Association, Inc. is a
non-profit corporation that fosters and
promotes the game of Ten Pins among both
men and women.
Year Founded:
1939
Member Services:
Awards to members according to their
achievements. Sponsor Annual
Scholarships.
Membership Requirements:
Interest in bowling.
Publications:
NBA BOWLER, five times annually; NBA
Souvenir Yearbook, annually.

NATIONAL DEAF WOMEN'S BOWLING ASSOCIATION

tazgayle@yahoo.com
• Gayle Willingham, President
tazgayle@yahoo.com
• Ali Martinez, Interim Vice President

geezam64@aol.com
• Jane Jacobson, Secretary Treasurer
ndwbast@gmail.com

PROFESSIONAL BOWLERS ASSOCIATION

55 EAST JACKSON BOULEVARD
SUITE 401
CHICAGO, IL 60604
206-332-9688
Fax: 312-341-1469
www.pba.com
• Tom Clark, Commissioner
• Kirk Von Krueger, Deputy Commissioner
Nature of Service:
Conducts tournaments on both national and
regional level with members competing for
an aggregate prize fund in excess of $6
million. National tour consists of 25
tournaments annually, with over 150
contested on a regional level.
Year Founded:
1958
Member Services:
Merchandise program. Free subscription to
Bowlers Journal International. A free
pba.com e-mail address and access to an
exclusive members only site.
Membership Requirements:
A 200 or better average in at least one
league for 66 or more games per season in
each of two years prior to applying.
Number of members:
4,300
Publications:
OFFICIAL TOUR PROGRAM; Regular
press releases to media.
Sponsors:
United States Bowling Congress, GEICO,
Pepsi-Cola, Brunswick, Bayer, Denny's
Motel 6, Ace Hardware, Etonic, Columbia
300, H&R, Discover Card.

UNITED STATES BOWLING CONGRESS

621 SIX FLAGS DRIVE
ARLINGTON, TX 76011
800-514-2695
bowlinfo@bowl.com
www.bowl.com
• Frank Wilkinson, President
• Cathy Desocio, Vice President
• Chad Murphy, Executive Director
• Neil Stremmel, Managing Director
Description:
Founded in 2005, the United States Bowling
Congress serves around two million
members in the United States. It serves as
the national governing body of bowling as
recognized by the United States Olympic
Committee.

WORLD BOWLING

2208 BROOKSIDE DRIVE
ARLINGTON, TX 76012
414-803-9188
www.worldbowling.org
• Kevin Dornberger, CEO World Bowling
• Sheikh Talal, World Bowling President
kbsclub@qualitynet.net
• Suwalai Satrulee, World Bowling 1st Vice
President
suwalaisatrulee@hotmail.com
• Addie Ophelders, ETBF President
ao@etbf.eu
Description:
World Bowling is responsible to promote
and administer bowling throughout the world

and to promote the Olympic movement.
Year Founded:
1952

YOUTH BOWL CANADA

250 SHIELDS COURT
UNIT 10A
MARKHAM, ON, CANADA L3R 9W7
905-479-1560
Fax: 905-479-8613
info@bowlcanada.ca
www.youthbowl.ca
• Todd Britton, President
(204) 488-0000
todd@academylanes.ca
• Ray Brittain, Vice President
(250) 753-2341
brechinlanes@gmail.com
• Trevor Peters, Director
(204) 727-2695
• Rod Hennessey, Treasurer
(709) 744-2553
riverdalelanes@nl.rogers.com
• Colleen Haider, Secretary
(306) 783-5183
c.haider@sasktel.net
• Kevin Burns, Program Coordinator
kevin@bowlcanada.ca

Boxing Organizations

BOXING CANADA

C/O CANADIAN OLYMPIC COMMITTEE
500, BOUL. RENE-LEVESQUE OUEST
MONTREAL, QC, CANADA H2Z 2A5
514-861-5513
1-800-861-1319
Fax: 514-819-9228
info@boxingcanada.org
boxingcanada.org
• Pat Fiacco, President
pfiacco@sasktel.net
• Ryan Savage, Vice President
• Marcel Toulouse, Treasurer
• Willie McNeil, Executive Committee
Member
• Val Ryan, Executive Committee Member
Description:
To promote, encourage & develop the
widest participation in amateur boxing in
Canada & the highest proficiency amoungst
its members in pursuit of excellence.
Nature of Services:
Development and maintenance of uniform
rules and regulations governing amateur
boxing competitions in Canada, coaching
and officials development, national and
international competitions, National Team
Programs (development, training and
competition) and international relations.

IBF/USBA

899 MOUNTAIN AVENUE
SUITE 2C
SPRINGFIELD, NJ 07081
973-564-8046
Fax: 973-564-8751
jsalazar@ibfboxing.com
www.ibfusbaregistration.com
• Daryl J. Peoples, President
• Lindsey E. Tucker, Championships
Chairman
• Randy Neurmann, Treasurer
• Louis Priluker, Secretary

Description:
Serves to rate boxers in different categories; approves championship bouts for titles; prepares and utilizes various safety mechanisms to provide for the overall safety of the industry; promulgates rules and regulations utilized worldwide for governing professional boxing events, and where there are no commissions, serves as a commission to oversee the activity in that area. Trains and licenses referees and judges and holds semi-annual and annual seminars for them to sharpen their skills.
Member Services:
Established retirement and trust plan for boxers worldwide; offers special assistance to retired boxers (SARB) fund.

INTERNATIONAL BOXING ASSOCIATION (AIBA)
MAISON DU SPORT INTERNATIONAL
AVENUE DU RHODANIE 54
LAUSANNE, 1007
info@aiba.org
www.aiba.org
• Ching-Kuo Wu, President
• Karim Bouzidi, Executive Director
Nature of Service:
AIBA is the international governing body for the sport of boxing, overseeing national federations across the globe, including USA Boxing.
Year Founded:
1946
Member Services:
Administrative services; Conduct of World Championships.
Membership Requirements:
National Federations on subscription basis.
Publications:
Boxing! The AIBA Magazine

INTERNATIONAL BOXING ORGANIZATION
340 MINORCA AVENUE
CORAL GABLES, FL 33134
305-446-0684
president@iboboxing.com
www.iboboxing.com
• Ed Levine, President
• John W. Daddono, Chairman
• Jeremy D. Levine, Vice President
• Robert Balogh, Vice President
Description:
The IBO aims to bring honesty, integrity and trust to the sport. They use the only independent objective computerized rankings in boxing today and place an emphasis on fairness and experience.

NORTH AMERICAN BOXING FEDERATION
911 KIMBARK STREET
LONGMONT, CO 80501
303-442-0258
Fax: 303-442-0380
www.nabfnews.com
• Duane B. Ford, President
• Craig Hubble, Vice President
• Joanna Aguilar, Executive Secretary
• David Sutherland, Membership Chairmen

USA BOXING
1 OLYMPIC PLAZA
COLORADO SPRINGS, CO 80909

719-866-2300
Fax: 719-866-2132
www.teamusa.org/USA-Boxing
• Mike McAtee, Interim Executive Director
mmcatee@usaboxing.org
Nature of Service:
A non-profit organization that is responsible for the administration, development and promotion of Olympic-style boxing in the United States.
Year Founded:
1888
Member Services:
Support and guidance in all facets of amateur boxing.
Membership Requirements:
Must register in the Local Boxing Committee that oversees their locality. Boxers must be eligible for competition in amateur boxing.
Number of members:
30,000
Publications:
USA Boxing Technical & Competition Rules

WORLD BOXING ASSOCIATION
47 OCEAN BUSINESS PLAZA
14TH FLOOR
OFFICE 14-05
MARBELLA, PANAMA
507-203-7680
Fax: 507-203-7681
info@wbanews.com
www.wbanews.com
• Gilberto Mendoza, Executive Vice President
• Julio Thyme, Operations
jthyme@wbanews.com
• Noryoli Gil, Operations
norygil@wbanews.com

WORLD BOXING ORGANIZATION
FIRST FEDERAL BUILDING
1056 MUNOZ RIVERA AVENUE
SUITE 711-714
SAN JUAN, 00927
787-765-4444
Fax: 787-758-9053
www.wboboxing.com
• Francisco Valcarcel, President
• Luis Batista-Salas, Founder/Chairman of the Championship Committee
• Ramon Acevedo, Past President
• John Duggan, First Vice President
• Jacinth Bryan-Labega, Second Vice President
• Adolfo Flores, Treasurer

Broomball Organizations

CANADIAN BROOMBALL FEDERATION
145 PACIFIC AVENUE
WINNIPEG, MB, CANADA R3B 2Z6
204-925-5656
Fax: 204-925-5792
www.broomball.ca
• George Brown, President
(613) 253-7787
president@broomball.ca
• Chris Pilon, VP Administration
• Gerry Wever, VP Technical
(613) 445-0904
• Greg Mastervick, Treasurer
(780) 459-7668
treasurer@broomball.ca

• Michelle Lechner, Secretary
secretary@broomball.ca
Description:
The role of the Canadian Broomball Federation is to provide leadership by promoting and developing broomball and by developing and coordinating programs and services designed to meet the needs of the broomball community.

INTERNATIONAL FEDERATION OF BROOMBALL ASSOCIATIONS
www.internationalbroomball.org
• Marc Desparois, VP Operations
• Conrad Morneau, VP Technical
• Alan Jabs, Secretary General
Description:
The program, beginning in 1988, was formed to promote international broomball championships.

USA BROOMBALL
PO BOX 20201
BLOOMINGTON, MN 55420
612-201-6088
www.usabroomball.com
• Kevin Denesen, President
• Perry, Director Of Operations
(763) 214-1789
• Perry Coonce, Director of Operations
(763) 241-1789
Nature of Service:
A non-profit organization whose purpose is to further the development of broomball in the United States. Broomball is played indoors on an ice hockey rink or outdoors on frozen ponds or lakes with rules very similar to Ice Hockey. Players wear special padded sponge rubber shoes, use a ball which is sized somewhere between a soccer ball and slow pitch softball, and use specially designed manufactured brooms which are made of wood or aluminum. The goal like hockey is to put the ball in the opposing net, a net which is larger than a hockey net but much smaller than an outdoor soccer goal.
Year Founded:
1995

Canoeing Organizations

AMERICAN CANOE ASSOCIATION
503 SOPHIA STREET
SUITE 100
FREDERICKSBURG, VA 22401
540-907-4460
Fax: 888-229-3792
aca@americancanoe.org
• Anne Maleady, President
• Peter Sloan, Treasurer
• Robin Pope, Secretary
Nature of Service:
Member-based, national nonprofit organization serving the broader paddling public by providing education related to all aspects of paddling, stewardship support to help paddling environmnents, and sanctioning of programs and events to promote paddlesport competition and recreation.

CANADIAN RECREATIONAL CANOE ASSOCIATION
446 MAIN STREET WEST
PO BOX 398
MERRICKVILLE, ON, CANADA K0G 1N0
613-269-2910
Fax: 613-269-2908
www.canoe.ca

CANOEKAYAK CANADA
2197 RIVERSIDE DRIVE
SUITE 700
OTTAWA, CANADA K1H 7X3
613-260-1818
Fax: 613-260-5137
admin@canoekayak.ca
www.canoekayak.ca
• Casey Wade, Chief Executive Officer
(613) 260-1818
cwade@canoekayak.ca
• John Edwards, Domestic Development Director
(613) 260-1818
jhedwards@canoekayak.ca
• Natalie Brett, National Team Manager
(613) 260-1818
nbrett@canoekayak.ca
• Peter Neidre, Director of Coach and Athlete Development
(613) 260-1818
• Sally Clare, Director of Finance
(613) 721-0504
sclare@canoekayak.ca
• James Cartwright, Slalom High Performance Manager
(613) 260-1818
jcartwright@canoekayak.ca
Nature of Service:
Recognized governing body responsible for promotion, growth and development of canoe racing in Canada. Represents Canada within the International Canoe Federation. Canoe disciplines include Olympic Sprint Racing, Marathon, Canoe Sailing, and White Water.
Year Founded:
1900
Number of members:
26,000
Publications:
PADDLES UP, 6 times a year - newsletter.

INTERNATIONAL CANOE FEDERATION (ICF)
AVENUE DE RHODANIE 54
LAUSANNE, SWITZERLAN CH 1007
info@canoeicf.com
www.canoeicf.com
• Jose Perurena, President
jose.perurena@canoeicf.com
• Farias Cecilia, Vice President
cecilia.farias@canoeicf.com
• Luciano Buonfiglio, Treasurer
• Simon Toulson, Secretary General
Nature of Service:
The ICF acts the international governing body for canoe sport, representing national canoe organizations like USA Canoe/Kayak, and sanctioning competition.

PADDLE CANADA
613-547-3196 EXT 10
888-252-6292
Fax: 613-547-4880
info@paddlecanada.com
www.paddlecanada.com

• Graham Ketcheson, Executive Director
• Dawn Callan, Events, National Paddling Week & PaddleSmart
• Adrian Camara, Media & Marketing Manager

PROFESSIONAL PADDLESPORTS ASSOCIATION
PO BOX 10847
KNOXVILLE, TN 37939
865-558-3595
office@americaoutdoors.com
www.propaddle.com

USA CANOE/KAYAK
503 SOPHIA STREET
SUITE 100
FREDERICKSBURG, VA 22401
540-907-4460 EXT 108
membership@usack.org
www.teamusa.org/usa-canoe-kayak
• Wade Blackwood, Chief Executive Officer
(804) 814-4077
wade@usack.org
• Amy Ellis, Membership Coordinator
(540) 907-4460
membership@usack.org
• Candy Patten, Insurance Coordinator
(540) 907-4460
insurance@usack.org
• Michele Eray, Sprint High Performance Director
(405) 552-4040
michele@usack.org
• Aaron Mann, Communications & Media
(301) 325-9504
aaron@usack.org
Description:
USA Canoe/Kayak is the national governing body for the Olympic sports of Canoe Sprint and Canoe Slalom, as well as the Paralympic sport of Paracanoe. The mission of USA Canoe/Kayak is to enable United States athletes to achieve competitive excellence in Olympic, Paralympic and Pan American competitions.

Climbing Organizations

AMERICAN ALPINE CLUB
710 TENTH STREET
SUITE 100
GOLDEN, CO 80401
303-384-0110
Fax: 303-384-0111
www.americanalpineclub.org
• Doug Walker, President
• Matt Culberson, Vice President
• Clark Gerhardt, Secretary
• Paul Gagner, Treasurer
Nature of Service:
Mountaineering and climbing organization. Represents U.S. in all matters relating to climbing domestically and internationally. Sponsors expeditions, and publishes climbing books.
Year Founded:
1902
Member Services:
Annual meeting held in February each year. World-wide rescue insurance. Discounts on AAC Press and Mountaineers books titles, access to European climbing huts, operates Grand Teton climbers ranch in Grand Teton National Park, public policy advocacy.

Membership Requirements:
Annual dues, climber for minimum of two years.
Number of members:
6,682
Publications:
AMERICAN ALPINE NEWS, quarterly, AMERICAN ALPINE JOURNAL, annual; ACCIDENTS IN NORTH AMERICAN MOUNTAINEERING, annual.

AMERICAN HIKING SOCIETY
8605 SECOND AVENUE
SILVER SPRING, MD 20910
301-565-6704
1-800-972-8608
info@americanhiking.org
www.americanhiking.org
• Gregory A. Miller, President
• Peter Olsen, VP for Programs and Government Relations
• Libby Wile, Senior Director of Volunteer Stewardship
• Kim Lyons, Director of Development and Marketing
Description:
American Hiking Society promotes and protects foot trails, their surrounding natural areas, and the hiking experience.

AMERICAN MOUNTAIN GUIDES ASSOCIATION
207 CANYON BOULEVARD
SUITE 201N
BOULDER, CO 80302-4932
303-271-0984
Fax: 303-271-1377
www.amga.com
• Rob Hess, President
(307) 733-4979
rob@jhmg.com
• Silas Rossi, Vice President
(207) 949-1736
silas@alpine-logic.com
• Annie Harrington, Secretary
(303) 894-6179
• Scott Soden, Treasurer
(303) 242-5758
scottsoden@alpinacapital.com
• Alex Kosseff, Executive Director
(303) 271-0984
alex@amga.com
• Jane Anderson, Logistics Coordinator
(303) 271-0984
jane@amga.com
Nature of Service:
AMGA's goal is to raise the standard of mountain guides in the United States to the international level through education and training.
Year Founded:
1979
Number of Members:
1,000
Sponsors:
Arc'teryx, Backcountry Access, Black Diamond, Gore-Tex/Windstopper, Malden Mills/Polartec, Mammut, Marmot, Mountain Headwear, Patagonia, Petzl, The North Face

ASSOCIATION OF CANADIAN MOUNTAIN GUIDES
900 MCGILL ROAD
KAMLOOPS, BC, CANADA V2C 5N3
403-678-2885
Fax: 250-371-5845

acmg@acmg.ca
www.acmg.ca
• Marc Ledwidge, President
(403) 762-4129
pres@acmg.ca
• Peter Tucker, Executive Director
(403) 949-3587
ed@acmg.ca
• Dwayne Congdon, Program Coordinator
(250) 371-5847
dcongdon@tru.ca

THE ACCESS FUND
207 CANYON BOULEVARD
SUITE 201S
BOULDER, CO 80302
303-545-6772
Fax: 303-545-6774
info@accessfund.org
www.accessfund.org
• Brady Robinson, Executive Director
(303) 545-6772
brady@accessfund.org
• Mark Baum, President
• Kenji Haroutunian, Vice President
• Ryan Gellert, Treasurer
• Alex Kutches, Secretary
• Jim Chase, Operations Director
(303) 545-6772
• Michael Allen, Development Director
(303) 545-6772
Description:
Dedicated to keeping climbing areas open &
to conserving the climbing environment.
Year Founded:
1989

Cricket Organizations

CRICKET CANADA
3 CONCORDE GATE
SUITE 301
TORONTO, ON, CANADA M3C 3N7
416-426-7209
www.gocricketgocanada.com
• Vimal Hardat, President
• Amit Joshi, Vice President
• Charles Pais, Treasurer
• Ingleton Liburd, General Manager
Description:
Cricket Canada aims to grow and develop
cricket across Canada in order to compete
successfully at the highest level of the
international game, while operating in a
professional, organized and fiscally
responsible manner.

INTERNATIONAL CRICKET COUNCIL
INTERNATIONAL CRICKET COUNCIL
STREET 69, DUBAI SPORTS CITY
SH MOHAMMED BIN ZAYED ROAD
DUBAI, UNITED ARA
971-4-382-8800
Fax: 971-4-382-8600
enquiry@icc-cricket.com
www.icc-cricket.com
• David Richardson, Chief Executive Officer
• N Srinivasan, Chairman
• Walter Edwards, Director (Australia)
• Nazmul Hassan, Director (Bangladesh)
Nature of Service:
As the international governing body for
cricket, the International Cricket Council
promotes the game as a global sport and
sacntions compeition.

Major events:
The International Cricket Council (ICC) is
the governing body for Test Match and
One-Day International (ODI) cricket. It is
also responsible for the global expansion of
the game through its Associate and Affiliate
Members and a major international
Development Program.
Publications:
Cricket Quarterly is the official newsletter of
the International Cricket Council. It is
published 4 times a year and is distributed
to all ICC member countries.

USA CRICKET ASSOCIATION
8461 LAKE WORTH ROAD
SUITE B-1-185
LAKE WORTH, FL 33467
561-839-1888
ibrulport@usaca.org
www.usaca.org
• Lisa Brulport, Executive Assistant
• Gladstone Dainty, President
• Antoni Grey, First Vice President
• Sankar Renganathan, Secretary
• Shakeel Yusuf, Treasurer

Croquet Organizations

CROQUET CANADA
24 DELORAINE AVENUE
TORONTO, ON, CANADA M5M 2A7
416-483-8229
Fax: 416-254-8256
chrisloat@bell.net
www.croquet.ca
• Ian MacGregor, President
(416) 868-3421
• Chris Loat, Treasurer
(905) 685-6939
• George Dej, Secretary
(416) 551-4548
• Bill Rowat, Director
(519) 565-5838

**UNITED STATES CROQUET
ASSOCIATION**
700 FLORIDA MANGO ROAD
WEST PALM BEACH, FL 33406
561-478-0760
Fax: 561-686-5507
usca@msn.com
www.croquetamerica.com
• Johnny Mitchell, Jr., President
(832) 725-8814
• Sara Low, 1st Vice President
(401) 447-6462
• Don Oakley, 2nd Vice President
(866) 364-8895
• Steve Mossbrook, Treasurer
(307) 851-6455
• Carla P. Rueck, Secretary
(516) 480-9930
Nature of Service:
Encourages the understanding and direct
involvement of individuals and clubs ranging
from school and college levels through
senior citizens and retirement organizations
as to the social and recreational rewards of
playing croquet. Principal source of income
is through tax-deductible contributions of
individuals and proceeds of the Annual Fall
U.S. Croquet Hall of Fame Awards Dinner,
and special Croquet Balls, parties and
events throughout the year by member clubs

and organizations.
Year Founded:
1977
Number of Members:
3,000
Publications:
USCA Croquet News, mailed quarterly;
USCA Croquet Directory; Official USCA
Rulebook

Curling Organizations

CANADIAN CURLING ASSOCIATION
1660 VIMONT COURT
ORLEANS, CANADA K4A 4J4
613-834-2076
800-550-2875
Fax: 613-834-0716
media@curling.ca
www.curling.ca
• Patricia Ray, Chief Operating Officer
(613) 834-2076
• Karen Ryan, Executive Assistant
(613) 834-2076
kryan@curling.ca
• JoAnne Viau, Coordinator, Financial
Services
(613) 834-2076
jviau@curling.ca
• Al Cameron, Director, Communications
and Media Relations
(403) 463-5500
acameron@curling.ca
• Karen Wan, Manager, Financial Services
(613) 834-2076
• Danny Lamoureux, Director,
Championship Services
(613) 834-2076
dlamoureux@curling.ca
• Glenn van Gulik, Director, Information
Services and Technology
(613) 834-2076
gvangulik@curling.ca
Nature of Service:
Ongoing organization and development of
all aspects of the sport of Curling in Canada.
Year Founded:
1990
Member Services:
Participation in all sanctioned events;
marketing and technical development
programs.
Membership Requirements:
Annual association dues.
Number of Members:
352,000 (17 provincial associations).
Publications:
EXTRA END magazine, annual.

U.S. CURLING ASSOCIATION
5525 CLEM'S WAY
STEVENS POINT, WI 54482
715-344-1199
1-888-287-5377
Fax: 715-344-2279
info@usacurl.org
www.teamusa.org/usa-curling
• Rich Lepping, Chairman of the Board
• Vic Huebner, Treasurer
vichuebner@optonline.net
• Gordon Maclean, Secretary
• Rick Patzke, Secretary General

WORLD CURLING FEDERATION
3 ATHOLL CRESCENT
PERTH, PH1 5NG
info@worldcurling.org
www.worldcurling.org
• Kate Caithness, President
• Bent Ramsfjell, Vice President (Europe)
• Colin Grahamslaw, Secretary General
Description:
WCF acts as the world governing body for Olympic and Paralympic curling.

Cycling Organizations

ADVENTURE CYCLING ASSOCIATION
150 EAST PINE STREET
MISSOULA, MT 59807
406-721-1776
800-755-2453
Fax: 406-721-8754
www.adventurecycling.org
• Wally Werner, President
• Donna O'Neal, Vice President
• Andrew Huppert, Treasurer
• Andy Baur, Secretary
• Jim Sayer, Executive Director
• Teri Maloughney, Director, Sales & Marketing
• Richard Darne, Database Administrator
Nature of Service:
Continues to expand network of bicycle touring routes - now totaling more than 26,000 miles of lightly traveled rural roads and off-pavement biking routes.
Member Services:
$35 per year dues.
Publications:
ADVENTURE CYCLIST, 9 time(s) a year; THE CYCLISTS' YELLOW PAGES, annually.
Member Services:
Tours programs-six to 90 day trips; sales catalog - books, maps, products - discounts on some maps, subscription to ADVENTURE CYCLIST Magazine, Advocacy program; annual meeting normally held in January each year, in Missoula

CYCLING CANADA
2197 RIVERSIDE DRIVE
SUITE 203
OTTAWA, ON, CANADA K1H 7X3
613-248-1353
Fax: 613-248-9311
general@cyclingcanada.ca
www.cyclingcanada.ca
• Greg Mathieu, CEO/Secretary General
 ext 2601
greg.mathieu@cyclingcanada.ca
• Jacques Landry, High Performance Director/Head Coach
 ext 2614
jacques.landry@cyclingcanada.ca
• Brett Stewart, Director, Finance & Administration
 ext 2605
brett.stewart@cyclingcanada.ca
• Mathieu Boucher, Director, Performance Development
 ext 2607
mathieu.boucher@cyclingcanada.ca
• Matthew Jeffries, Director, Marketing & Communications
 ext 2609
matthew.jeffries@cyclingcanada.ca
• Gleness Lapensee, Administrative

Assistant
 ext 2600
gleness.lapensee@cyclingcanada.ca
Nature of Service:
Encourages and promotes cycling in Canada while safeguarding the cyclists' right to the road.
Year Founded:
1882
Member Services:
Insurance benefits.
Membership Requirements:
Payment of membership fees to provincial associations.
Number of Members:
7,200
Publications:
LEARN-TO-RACE Manual and Video; Racing Rules

INTERNATIONAL POLICE MOUNTAIN BIKE ASSOCIATION (IPMBA)
583 FREDERICK ROAD
SUITE 5B
BALTIMORE, MD 21228
410-744-2400
Fax: 410-744-5504
info@ipmba.org
www.ipmba.org
• Bernie Hogancamp, President
president@ipmba.org
• Wren Nealy, Vice President
vp@ipmba.org
• Mike Harris, Treasurer
treasurer@ipmba.org
• Craig Lepkowski, Secretary
secretary@ipmba.org
• Maureen Becker, Executive Director
maureen@ipmba.org
• Michael A. Wear, Education Director
education@ipmba.org
• Tom Harris, Conference Coordinator
conferences@ipmba.org
• James Englert, Industry Liaison
industry@ipmba.org
• Brian Gillman, EMS Coordinator
emsc@ipmba.org
• Gary Strang, Membership Director
membership@ipmba.org
Nature of Service:
Governing body for organizing activities involving police mountain biking.
Year Founded:
1992
Membership Fee:
$55.00 yearly membership fee entitles the officer to discounted Police on Bikes® Conference registration, a subscription to IPMBA News, a subscription to Bicycling Magazine.
Number of Members:
3,000
Publications:
IPMBA News

NATIONAL BICYCLE DEALERS ASSOCIATION
3176 PULLMAN STREET
SUITE 117
COSTA MESA, CA 92626
949-722-6909
info@nbda.com
www.nbda.com
• Todd Grant, President/Executive Director
• Jeff Selzerr, Treasurer
• Mike Greehan, Secretary
• Mike Baker, Director, Marketing &

Communications
• John Francis, Newsletter Editor
Nature of Service:
Promotes general welfare of retail bicycle dealers and assists dealers in promoting the sport of cycling.
Year Founded:
1946
Member Services:
Representation of bicycle dealers to public, trade and government; credit card program; customer financing program; employee group insurance; publications; seminars.
Membership Requirements:
Be a legitimate bicycle dealership or member of bicycle industry.
Publications:
OUTSPOKIN', monthly.

NATIONAL CENTER FOR BICYCLING & WALKING (NCBW)
419 LAFAYETTE STREET
7TH FLOOR
NEW YORK, NY 10003
www.bikewalk.org
• Mark Plotz, Senior Associate/Program Manager
(212) 620-5660
mark@bikewalk.org
• John Williams, CenterLines Editor
news@bikewalk.org
• Jim Johnston, Web/Systems Administrator
jimmy@bikewalk.org
Nature of Service:
Promotes the increased, safe use of bicycles. Conducts research and planning projects for government agencies. Develops brochures, posters, and video materials to promote cycling and safety. Develops and implements public relations programs to encourage cycling.
Year Founded:
1977
Publications:
CenterLines, bi-weekly electronic news bulletin.

PERIMETER BICYCLING ASSOCIATION OF AMERICA, INC.
2609 EAST BROADWAY BOULEVARD
TUCSON, AZ 85716
520-745-2033
Fax: 520-745-1992
info@perimeterbicycling.com
www.perimeterbicycling.com
• Richard DeBernardis, President
• Sally Valenzuela, Advertising Sales
• Marilyn Hall, Media/Media Sales
• Elaine Mariolle, Public Affairs
Nature of Service:
Organizes the bicycling events El Tour de Tucson, El Tour de Mesa, Cochise County Cycling Classic, Indoor El Tour, Bicycle, Fitness & Health Expo, El Tour Adventure Walk/Run, and El Tour Fun Rides.
Membership Requirements:
Payment of dues ($35 for individual membership, $85 for family membership).
Publications:
TAIL WINDS, bimonthly; PERIMETER BICYCLING JOURNAL, annually.

ULTRAMARATHON CYCLING ASSOCIATION
PO BOX 18028
BOULDER, CO 80308-1028

303-545-9566
Fax: 303-545-9619
www.ultracycling.com
• Paul Carpenter, President
president@ultracycling.com
• Douglas Hoffman, Executive Director
executivedirector@ultracycling.com
• Drew Clark, Records Chairman
records@ultracycling.com
• Mark Newsome, Webmaster/Data
Manager
webmaster@ultracycling.com
Nature of Service:
Serves to organize Race Across America;
sanctions long distance cycling records;
organizes the National Points Challenge;
promotes ultra-marathon cycling. Divided
into two type of races: Solo or Four-Man
Relay.
Year Founded:
1980
Membership Requirements:
Payment of dues.
Publications:
ULTRA CYCLING MAGAZINE, quarterly;
UMCA Manual; Membership Directory;
Events Directory.

**UNION CYCLISTE INTERNATIONALE
(UCI)**
CH DE LA MELEE 12
1860 AIGLE
AIGLE, SWITZERLAN 1860
admin@uci.ch
www.uci.ch
• Brian Cookson, President
• Mohamed Wagih, Vice President
• Tracey Gaudry, Vice President
• David Lappartient, Vice President
• Sebastien Gillot, Head of Communications
• James Carr, Head of International
Relations
• Cyrille Jacobsen, Head of Marketing
Nature of Service:
Serves to foster worldwide competitive
cycling.
Year Founded:
1900
Publications:
Annual Reports.

USA CYCLING
210 USA CYCLING POINT
SUITE 100
COLORADO SPRINGS, CO 80919-2215
719-434-4200
Fax: 719-434-4300
help@usacycling.org
www.usacycling.org
• Derek Bouchard-Hall, President/CEO
• Bob Stapleton, Chairman
• Alex Nieroth, Vice Chairman
• Kevin Loughery, Communications
Manager
(719) 434-4277
• Steve Bitter, Digital & Social Media
Manager
(719) 434-4276
• Keri Kahn, Editorial & Internal
Communications Manager
(719) 434-4272
• Daniel Gillespie, Sponsorship & Member
Benefits Manager
(719) 434-4281

**USA/BMX, THE AMERICAN BICYCLE
ASSOCIATION**
1645 WEST SUNRISE BOULEVARD
GILBERT, AZ 85233
480-961-1903
Fax: 480-961-1842
www.usabmx.com
• B.A. Anderson, CEO
• John David, Chief Operating Officer
john@usabmx.com
• Craig Barrette, Chief Communications
Officer
gork@usabmx.com
• Nick Adams, Chief Marketing Officer
nick@usabmx.com
• Jon Schmieder, Executive Director
jons@usabmx.com
• Brad Hallin, Senior Track Director
brad@usabmx.com
• Maile Goldston, Receptionist
maile@usabmx.com
Nature of Service:
The ABA is the world's largest BMX
sanctioning body, with over 7,000 events,
54,000, 200 local facilities, 12 TV shows and
a monthly publication.
Year Founded:
1977
Sponsors:
Dan's Competition, Fly Racing, Tangent,
BOX Components, Promax, KMC,
FastSigns, Ciari, Staats, Answer,
Nationwide
Publications:
PULL Magazine.

Cycling, Leagues/Teams

LEAGUE OF AMERICAN BICYCLISTS
1612 K STREET NORTHWEST
SUITE 308
WASHINGTON, DC 20006
202-822-1333
bikeleague@bikeleague.org
www.bikeleague.org
• Alex Doty, Executive Director
• Bill Nesper, Vice President, Programs
• Caron Whitaker, Vice President, Policy
(202) 215-3908
• Lorna Green, Director, Operations
 ext 260
• Alison Dewey, National Bike Summit
Director
(202) 621-5443
• Ken McLeod, Legal & Policy Specialist
(202) 621-5447
Nature of Service:
Protects rights and promotes the interests of
bicyclists, provides information about
bicycling for its members and others, fosters
and serves a nationwide network of affiliated
cycling clubs and organizations. Sponsors
National Century Month; national bicycle
rallies; PEDAL FOR POWER cross country
rides for charity; serves as international
clearing house for Bike Month.
Year Founded:
1880
Membership Requirements:
Open to anyone upon payment of dues ($40
for individual membership, $60 for family
membership).
Number of Members:
300,000 cyclists including a membership of
40,000 individuals and over 600
organizations

Publications:
American Cyclist Magazine, quarterly

MAJOR LEAGUE CYCLING
PO BOX 10695
LANCASTER, PA 17605-0695
info@majorleaguecycling.com
www.majorleaguecycling.com
• David Butterworth, President
Description:
Features criterium and track racing between
city-based pro cycling teams, combined with
family destination weekend events featuring
other extreme sports, racing, and demos,
children's bicycle safety clinics, community
exhibits, etc.

PRIORITY HEALTH
1231 EAST BELTLINE NORTHEAST
GRAND RAPIDS, MI 49525
616-464-8571
www.teampriorityhealth.com
• Ann Vidro, Program Director
(616) 540-5115
avidro@creativestudiopromo.com
• Amy Miller, Corporate Press Contact
(616) 443-9800
amy.miller@priorityhealth.com
• Angie Scarlato, Calendar Of Events/Social
Media Captain
angiebarnes11@yahoo.com
Sponsors:
Priority Health, Advantage Benefits, First
Endurance, Giordana

USA CYCLING
210 USA CYCLING POINT
SUITE 100
COLORADO SPRINGS, CO 80919-2215
719-434-4200
Fax: 719-434-4300
help@usacycling.org
www.usacycling.org
• Derek Bouchard-Hall, President/CEO
• Bob Stapleton, Chairman
• Alex Nieroth, Vice Chairman
• Kevin Loughery, Communications
Manager
(719) 434-4277
• Steve Bitter, Digital & Social Media
Manager
(719) 434-4276
• Keri Kahn, Editorial & Internal
Communications Manager
(719) 434-4272
• Daniel Gillespie, Sponsorship & Member
Benefits Manager
(719) 434-4281
Nature of Service:
Serves as governing body for all forms of
bicycle racing, amateur cycling in America
and, as such, is responsible for selecting
Olympic, Pan-Am and World Championship
teams. Promotes events and programs,
television producer.
Year Founded:
1921
Sponsors:
Barbedo, Bike Thomson, Bonk Breaker,
Chase Bicycles, CLIF Bar, CUORE,
Development Foundation, Endurance
Conspiracy, Felt Bicycles, Kreitler,
NormaTec Recovery, Osmo Nutrition, Park
Tool USA, Shimano, Sierra Nevada,
Sportique, Thule, Tioga, Training Peaks,
USA Cycling, Vision, Vittoria, Voler,
Volkswagen

Teams:

JELLY BELLY CYCLING
1035 LAKE RIDE ROAD
SAN MARCOS, CA 92069
760-598-1138
www.jellybellycycling.com
• Dan Van Haute, Team Manager
Sponsors:
Jelly Belly, Maxxis, Fast Freddie Apparel, Argon 18

PRO CYCLING MIAMI
PO BOX 162555
MIAMI, FL 33116
786-973-5484
www.procyclingmiami.com
• Johan Ismail, President

REALITY BIKES
20 TRI COUNTY PLAZA
CUMMING, GA 30040
770-886-1175
todd@realitybikes.com
• Duncan McGuire, President
• Todd Muller, Club Coordinator
Year Founded:
1995
Sponsors:
FUJI, Atlanta Sports Medicine & Orthopaedic Center

TEAM COLAVITA
1 RUNYONS LANE
EDISON, NJ 08817
732-404-8300
www.teamcolavita.com
• Mary Zider, Sports Director
• Andrea Smith, Head Mechanic
• Amanda Rose Shission, Team Soigneur
Sponsors:
Colavita Olive Oil, Bianchi, Vittoria, Fine Cooking, Castelli, Rudy Project, Shimano, K3, Tetra Bike, Park Tool USA, Stages Cycling, Bar Fly, Osprey, CLIF Bar, Saris Cycling Group, CycleOps Power, HeadSweats

Dart Organizations

AMERICAN DARTS ORGANIZATION
230 NORTH CRESCENT WAY
SUITE K
ANAHEIM, CA 92801-6707
714-254-0212
Fax: 714-254-0214
office@adodarts.com
www.adodarts.com
• David Hascup, President
president@adodarts.com
• Joe Hogan, Vice President
joekat325@outlook.com
• Jeff Inman, Chief Financial Officer
jjinman23@oh.rr.com
• Carolyn Camp, General Secretary
Description:
Founded in 1976. Sanctioning, governing body for the sport of darts in the U.S. Regulates and selects U.S. teams for international competition, and selects the national champions (men's and women's).
Membership requirements:
Fee of $30.00 for one year of individual membership.
Publications:
Double Eagle, national, quarterly newsletter.
Member Services:
Travel agency, airline, hotel, and rental car discounts.

NATIONAL DART ASSOCIATION
9100 PURDUE ROAD
SUITE 200
INDIANAPOLIS, IN 46268
317-387-1299
800-808-9884
Fax: 317-387-0999
info@NDAdarts.com
www.ndadarts.com
• Leslie Murphy, Executive Director
(317) 387-1299
• Kim Paugh, Associate Executive Director
(734) 717-2855
kim@ndadarts.com
• Michelle Wells, Director of Communication
• Ashley Roy, Communication Coordinator
Member Services:
Annual team championships.
Publications:
THROWLINES.
Description:
Founded in 1985. Sanctions darts leagues, establishes rules for competition; promotes the sport of electronic darting.

NATIONAL DARTS FEDERATION OF CANADA
secretary@ndfc.ca
www.ndfc.ca
• Bill Hatter, President
(403) 548-2939
president@ndfc.ca
• Maggie LeBlanc, Vice President
(514) 637-2858
maggieleblanc417@hotmail.com
• Tammy Pottie, General Secretary
(902) 401-9650
secretary@ndfc.ca

NORTH AMERICAN PROFESSIONAL DARTS ALLIANCE
2 QUEEN STREET
LANGTON, ON, CANADA N0E 1G0
www.napda.net
• Robert Sinnaeve, President & CEO
• David Holmes, Vice President, Webmaster & Membership
• John McClellan, Treasurer & CFO
• Jay Tomlinson, Publicity Director
Description:
NAPDA was officially established in 2011 and serves as the first ranking system and professional dart tour for the North American dart player.

Diving Organizations

DIVING EQUIPMENT & MARKETING ASSOCIATION
3750 CONVOY STREET
SUITE 310
SAN DIEGO, CA 92111
858-616-6108
800-862-3483
Fax: 858-616-6495
info@dema.org
www.demashow.com
• Tim Webb, President
• Dan Orr, Senior Vice President
• Darcy Kieran, Vice President
• Tom Leaird, Treasurer
• Werner Kurn, Secretary
Number of Members:
2,000
Membership Requirements:

Must be a professional in the scuba diving industry.
Description:
Founded in 1972. Promotes growth and advancement in the diving industry; to establish continuing business education programs to aid industry members, their officers and employees; to facilitate exchange of industry information; to support the diving industry with communication services, media relations and resources; to support the industry in monitoring and communicating on legislation impacting diving; to support the industry in monitoring and protection of the environment through education and activities; and monitors state and national legislation.
Publications:
Monthly Newsletter.
Member Services:
Promote scuba diving.

DIVING PLONGEON CANADA
700 INDUSTRIAL AVENUE
SUITE 312
OTTAWA, ON, CANADA K1G 0Y9
613-736-5238
Fax: 613-736-0409
cada@diving.ca
www.diving.ca
• Penny Joyce, Chief Operating Officer
(613) 736-5238
penny@diving.ca
• Mitch Geller, Chief Technical Officer
(613) 736-5238
mitch@diving.ca
• Nancy Brawley, Director, National Officials Program
(613) 736-5238
nancy@diving.ca
• Sally Clare, Finance Manager
sally@diving.ca
• Jordanna Ostrega, Administration & Communication Coordinator
(613) 736-5238
jordanna@diving.ca
Number of Members:
5,000
Member Services:
Newsletter; Entry level program (Learn To Dive); Counseling program; Athlete program, Coaching & Official program.
Publications:
Newsletter, BI-monthly.
Membership Requirements:
Pay annual fee.
Description:
Founded in 1967. Provides all divers from entry level participants to Olympic and World Champions with the opportunity to achieve personal goals through programs and services. Also organizes two senior National Championships each year, as well as one international competition, and one Junior Nationals each year.

FEDERATION INTERNATIONALE DE NATATION (FINA)
AVENUE DE L'AVANT-POSTE 4
LAUSANNE, 1005
www.fina.org
• Julio C Maglione, President
• Husain Al Musallam, Vice President
• Cornel Marculescu, Executive Director
Year Founded:
1908
Publications:

FINA newsletter, FINA Handbook, FINA Aquatics World Magazine
Description:
Comprised of 207 national member federations, FINA holds competitions in swimming, open water swimming, diving, water polo, synchronised swimming, high diving and masters.

Equestrian Organizations

AMERICAN ASSOCIATION OF EQUINE PRACTITIONERS
4033 IRON WORKS PARKWAY
LEXINGTON, KY 40511
859-233-0147
800-443-0177
Fax: 859-233-1968
aaepoffice@aaep.org
www.aaep.org
• David Foley, Executive Director
dfoley@aaep.org
• Sally Baker, Director of Marketing & Public Relations
sbaker@aaep.org
• Brad Mitchell, Director of Finance & Operations
• Keith Kleine, Director of Industry Relations
kkleine@aaep.org
Description:
Founded in 1954. Serves to improve the health and welfare of the horse, to further the professional development of its members, and to provide resource and leadership for the benefit of the equine industry.
Membership Requirements:
Must be veterinarian in connection with equine practice.
Publications:
AAEP REPORT, 12 times annually.
Number of members:
6,500

AMERICAN HANOVERIAN SOCIETY
4067 IRON WORKS PARKWAY
SUITE 1
LEXINGTON, KY 40511
859-255-4141
Fax: 859-255-8467
AHSoffice@aol.com
www.hanoverian.org
• Edgar Schutte, President
(916) 645-1471
• Hugh Bellis-Jones, Executive Director
(859) 255-4141
hbjahs@aol.com
• Barbara Schmidt, Executive VP & Director
(859) 485-6000
bschmidtdvm@fuse.net
• Rick Toering, Vice President
(703) 472-9954
rick.toering@gmail.com
Number of members:
1,750
Member Services:
Horse registration, inspection for breeding approval.
Publications:
AHS YEARBOOK; AHS MEMBERS GUIDE, quarterly newsletter.
Membership Requirements:
Payment of $55 dues for associate membership, $80 for active voting membership.
Description:

Founded in 1971. Horse registration office for breed of horse originating in Germany called the Hanoverian. Dedicated to developing superior riding horse.

AMERICAN HORSE COUNCIL
1616 H STREET NW
7TH FLOOR
WASHINGTON, DC 20006
202-296-4031
www.horsecouncil.org
• James J. Hickey, Jr., President
(202) 296-4031
• Ben Pendergrass, Vice President, Government Affairs
(202) 296-4031
• Cliff Williamson, Director of Health & Regulatory Affairs
• Kara Mongello, Office Administrator
(202) 296-4031
• Ashley Furst, Director of Communications
(202) 296-4031
Publications:
Horse Owners & Breeders Tax Handbook; Horse Owners & Breeders Tax Handbook; The Economic Impact of the Horse Industry State Breakout Reports; American Horsepower; Tax Tips for Horse Owners; Horse Industry Directory
Membership Requirements:
Payment of annual dues. In addition to organizational and commercial memberships ($1,000 per year), offers individual membership categories including: Legislative ($40 per year), Congressional ($100 per year). Senatorial ($500 per year), and Cabinet ($1,000 per year) and President's Circle ($5,000 per year).
Description:
Founded in 1969. Its goal is to create the most positive environment possible for participation and investment in the horse world. Pursuing that objective, AHC is involved in all aspects of federal legislation affecting the horse business; works with federal agencies to promote equitable and realistic regulations to govern the industry; forwards the national and international growth and popularity of horse activities; encourages intelligent and humane treatment of the horse through informational and educational efforts; and maintains open lines of communication among diverse segments of the horse industry.

AMERICAN MINIATURE HORSE ASSOCIATION
5601 SOUTH INTERSTATE 35 WEST
ALVARADO, TX 76009
817-783-5600
Fax: 817-783-6403
info@amha.org
www.amha.org
• Sid Hutchcraft, President
(407) 656-4818
president@amha.org
• Al Bulgawicz, Vice President
(713) 870-1293
mini@willowcrest.com
• Clair Severson, Treasurer
(651) 437-5092
toysminis@aol.com
• Julie Good, Secretary
(717) 725-7784
azariah@meadowindfarm.com
• Harry Elder, Director
harry.james.elder@gmail.com

Number of Members:
12,000
Member Services:
Public relations and promotion of the American Miniature Horse; Production and management of the National Show and three regional shows annually; Breeders' list mailed to members; Sponsorship of 250 shows; Publishes informational booklets and the American Horse Studbook.
Publications:
THE MINIATURE HORSE WORLD, six times annually.
Membership Requirements:
Pay dues.
Description:
Founded in 1978. National and international registry. Official registry of miniature horses.

AMERICAN MORGAN HORSE ASSOCIATION
4066 SHELBURNE ROAD
SUITE 5
SHELBURNE, VT 05482
802-985-4944
Fax: 802-985-8897
www.morganhorse.com
• Jeff Gove, President
(508) 341-2263
jeffreygove@yahoo.com
• Julie Broadway, Executive Director
(802) 985-4944
• Kris Breyer, Vice President, Central Region
(847) 526-3012
• Carol Fletcher, Vice President of Finance
(425) 788-9233
Number of Members:
Approximately 8,000
Member Services:
Promotional literature; member/horse recognition programs; youth program; Regional and World Championship Horse Shows; Discounts from companies with horse-related products; trail riding; breed registry.
Publications:
THE MORGAN HORSE, monthly; Newspaper, THE NETWORK, monthly.
Description:
Registry started in 1908. Purpose of organization is for the preservation, perpetuate and promotion of the Morgan breed.
Teams:
Equestrian team - Team Morgan

AMERICAN PAINT HORSE ASSOCIATION
PO BOX 961023
FORT WORTH, TX 76161-0023
817-834-2742
Fax: 817-834-3152
www.apha.com
• Ron Shelly, President
(512) 863-0325
• George Ready, Vice President
(662) 429-7088
gbready@georgebreadyattorneys.com
• Craig Wood, Senior Committee Member
(859) 608-1014
chorse.wood@gmail.com
• Billy L. Smith, Executive Director
(817) 222-6401
Publications:
APHA Connection; Paint Horse Journal.
Description:
Founded in 1962 as American Paint

Stockhorse Association. Registers paint horses; sponsors national and world events for paint horses.
Number of Members:
104,000
Member Services:
Free on-line services; free member quarterly newsletter; reduced fees on transactions.
Membership Requirements:
Annual $40 member dues.

AMERICAN QUARTER HORSE ASSOCIATION
1600 QUARTER HORSE DRIVE
AMARILLO, TX 79104
806-376-4811
Fax: 806-349-6411
www.aqha.com
• Glenn Blodgett, President
• Sandy Arledge, First Vice President
• Ralph Seekins, Second Vice President
Description:
Founded in 1940. Serves to collect, record and preserve the pedigrees of American Quarter Horses. Also serves as an information center for its members and the general public on matters pertaining to shows, racing, legislative issues, contests and projects designed to improve the breed and aid the industry.
Membership Requirements:
Membership dues: $30 per year.
Publications:
THE AMERICAN QUARTER HORSE JOURNAL, monthly; AMERICA'S HORSE, bimonthly
Number of members:
336,000

AMERICAN SADDLEBRED HORSE ASSOCIATION
4083 IRON WORKS PARKWAY
LEXINGTON, KY 40511
859-259-2742
Fax: 859-259-1628
saddlebred@asha.net
www.asha.net
• Bob Funkhouser, President
• David B. Rudder, Vice President
• Bill Whitley, Executive Director
(859) 259-3888
b.whitley@asha.net
• David Mount, Treasurer
Number of members:
7,120
Events:
Futurity competitions at the Kentucky State Fair; other prize programs at nationwide prominent horse shows.
Member Services:
Subscription to magazine; free annual directory; discount savings on registrations and transfers; free literature, visual aids.
Publications:
THE AMERICAN SADDLEBRED, bimonthly magazine; THE HAYSHAKER, quarterly youth newsletter; Membership Directory, annual.
Membership Requirements:
Seven classes of individual memberships, each one with different requirements and benefits.
Description:
Founded 1891. Serves to stimulate, promote interest in and regulate any and all matters as may pertain to the history, breeding,

exhibition, publicity, use and improvement of the American Saddlebred horse.

AMERICAN VAULTING ASSOCIATION
1443 EAST WASHINGTON BOULEVARD
SUITE 289
PASADENA, CA 91104
323-654-0800
Fax: 323-654-4306
info@americanvaulting.org
www.americanvaulting.org
• Connie Geisler, President
(951) 440-4589
connie_geisler@hotmail.com
• Kelley Holly, Executive Vice President
(707) 665-9281
tambourine-farm@att.net
• Kathy Rynning, VP Competitions
(360) 888-2476
• Kathy Smith, VP Membership
(303) 434-9975
rockymtnhorsepk@yahoo.com
• Carolyn Bland, VP Education
(818) 497-2947
Number of Members:
1,200
Member Services:
Tape rental, insurance, all information relating to the sport of vaulting. Tapes and books also available for purchase.
Publications:
VAULTING WORLD, bimonthly.
Membership Requirements:
Annual individual membership of $50
Description:
Founded in 1968. Provides information and rules for sport of vaulting, which combines the sport of gymnastics and the skill of horsemanship.

ARABIAN HORSE ASSOCIATION
10805 EAST BETHANY DRIVE
AURORA, CO 80014
303-696-4500
Fax: 303-696-4599
www.arabianhorses.org
• Cynthia M. Richardson, President
(720) 480-0496
• Nancy Harvey, Vice President
(626) 390-8918
nancy.harvey@arabianhorses.org
• Robert Nash, Treasurer
(713) 302-9072
• Jan Decker, Secretary
(317) 861-4814
jandecker1@sbcglobal.net
Member Services:
Breed registration for purchsaed Arabian, Half-Arabian, Anglo-Arabian; awards and prize money; show recognition; national show production; world's largest database of Arabian horses.
Publications:
Arabian Horse Magazine.
Membership Requirements:
$20 lowest fee for associate membership on up.
Description:
Founded 1950. Non-profit membership organization established in 1950 for the purpose of coordinating the activities of all Arabian horse associations, and encouraging the breeding, exhibiting and perpetuation of the Arabian, Half-Arabian and Anglo-Arabian breeds.

BLOODHORSE MAGAZINE
821 CORPORATE DRIVE
LEXINGTON, KY 40503
859-278-2361
800-582-5604
Fax: 859-276-4450
admin@bloodhorse.com
www.bloodhorse.com
• Evan Hammond, Editorial Director
(859) 278-2361
editorial@bloodhorse.com
• Scott Carling, General Manager
admin@bloodhorse.com
• Kristi Heasley, Advertising Account Executive
advertise@bloodhorse.com
• Beth Alexander, Manager, Data Management
(859) 224-2855
• Steve Gillespie, General Manager, Operations
Description:
The Jockey Club Information Systems, Inc. (TJCIS) is a unique and diversified organization that provides instant access to information and expertise to aid decision-making and improve thoroughbred management and promotion. TJCIS is a wholly owned subsidiary of The Jockey Club and reinvests all profits in the thoroughbred industry.

BREEDERS' CUP
2525 HARRODSBURG ROAD
SUITE 500
LEXINGTON, KY 40504-4230
859-223-5444
800-722-3287
Fax: 859-223-3945
www.breederscup.com
• Craig Fravel, President & Chief Executive Officer
• Robert Elliston, EVP and Chief Operating Officer
• Michael Newman, VP, Treasurer
• Tim Schram, VP, Finance & Human Resources
Description:
Founded in 1984. It's primary purpose is to promote the sport of thoroughbred racing, thus strengthening opportunities within the industry for horsemen worldwide. Objectives have been accomplished through Breeders' Cup Championship, and through a year-round stakes program of 85 races across the United States and Canada.

CALIFORNIA THOROUGHBRED BREEDERS ASSOCIATION
201 COLORADO PLACE
ARCADIA, CA 91007
626-445-7800
800-573-2822
Fax: 626-574-0852
www.ctba.com
• Donald Valpredo, Chair
donald@valpredofarms.com
• Harris Aurbach, Vice Chair
hdauerbach@sbcglobal.net
• Doug Burge, President
(626) 445-7800
dburge@ctba.com
• John Barr, Director
oakcrest99@aol.com
• Tim Cohen, Treasurer
tcohen@ranchotemescal.com
• Sue Green, Secretary
sueshorse@aol.com

- Loretta Veiga, Advertising Manager
(626) 445-7800
loretta@ctba.com
Member Services:
Offers breeder, owner, stallion incentive
awards. Sponsors numerous horse
symposiums throughout the year geared to
better educate the California horseman.
Publications:
THE THOROUGHBRED OF CALIFORNIA
MAGAZINE, monthly.
Membership Requirements:
California owner and breeder of
thoroughbreds.
Description:
Founded in 1937. Dedicated to the
advancement of thoroughbred racing and
breeding in California. Serves as the official
registry of all California bred thoroughbred
horses.

EQUINE CANADA
308 LEGGET DRIVE
SUITE 100
OTTAWA, ON, CANADA K2K 1Y6
613-287-1515
866-282-8395
Fax: 613-248-3484
www.equinecanada.ca
- Al Patterson, President
- Eva Havaris, Chief Executive Officer
- Kalie McKenna, Director, Technical
Programs
(866) 282-8395
Number of members:
10,000
Publications:
Equine Canada Magazine
Membership Requirements:
Individuals are required to be members of
the Canadian Equestrian Federation to
compete in recognized shows and programs
organized by the CEF.
Description:
Governing body of equestrian sport in
Canada. Recognized by the Federation
Equestre Internationale, the Canadian
Olympic Association and the Federal
Government. Responsible for development
of all aspects of equestrian activity
(excluding racing) and provides the
standards under which competitions are
conducted.
Year Founded:
1977

FEDERATION EQUESTRE
INTERNATIONALE
HM KING HUSSEIN I BUILDING
CHEMIN DE LA JOLIETTE 8
LAUSANNE, SWITZERLAN 1006
www.fei.org
- Ingmar De Vos, President
(+41) 21 310 47
ingmar.devos@fei.org
- John Madden, 1st Vice President
(+1) 315 952 65
jms@johnmaddensales.com
- Sheik Khalid Bin Abdulla Al Khalifa, 2nd
Vice President
(973) 178 361 99
feigroup7@gmail.com
Description:
The International Federation for Equestrian
Sports acts as the international governing
body for this group of sports, sanctioning

world competitions and the Olympic and
Paralympic games.

HAMBLETONIAN SOCIETY
CRANBURY GATES OFFICE PARK
109 SOUTH MAIN STREET
SUITE 18
CRANBURY, NJ 08512
609-371-2211
Fax: 609-371-8890
www.hambletonian.org
- Tom Charters, President & CEO
- Callie Davies-Gooch, Stakes Manager
- Moira Fanning, Director Of Publicity
mfanning@hambletonian.org
- Mary Lou Dondarski, Office Manager
MLD@hambletonian.org
Description:
The Hambletonian Society is a non-profit
organization formed in 1924 to sponsor the
race for which it was named, the
Hambletonian Stake. The society
encourages and supports the breeding of
Standardbred horses through the
development, administration and promotion
of harness racing stakes, early-closing races
and other special events. These include
harness racing's most preeminent race, the
Hambletonian for 3-year-old trotters, its filly
division the Hambletonian Oaks and the
sport's championship series, the Breeders
Crown.
Membership Requirements:
Executives nominate a board of 25
directors.
Publications:
HAMBLETONIAN SOCIETY Newsletter, two
times annually.
Member Services:
Hambletonian, annually, at Meadowlands,
East Rutherford, NJ first and second
Saturday in August and 11 Breeders Crown
races.

HAMPTON CLASSIC HORSE SHOW
240 SNAKE HOLLOW ROAD
BRIDGEHAMPTON, NY 11932-3013
631-537-3177
Fax: 631-537-5443
www.hamptonclassic.com
- Dennis Suskind, President
- Lisa Deslauriers, Chairman
- Rosanna Braccini, Director of Special
Projects and Publications
rosanna@hamptonclassic.com
- Reyna Stein, Marketing Manager
reyna@hamptonclassic.com
- Bryan Cohen, Special Projects Coordinator
bryan@hamptonclassic.com
Sports Service Founded:
1976
Services:
Implements horse shows and oversees all
phases of this event, featuring world-class
competition attracting approximately 3,200
riders and horses, featured on Outdoor Life
Network; MSG, cause tie-ins. Celebrity
participants, corporate VIP tent seats.

HARNESS HORSE YOUTH FOUNDATION
16575 CAREY ROAD
WESTFIELD, IN 46074
317-867-5877
Fax: 317-867-1886
ellen@hhyf.org
www.hhyf.org

- Marlys Pinske, President
- Nicola Abrams, Vice President
- Leah Cheverie, Secretary
- Lillie Brown, Treasurer
Member Services:
Annual bids for Kids Stallion Auction;
Student Scholarships; Youth Camps; Works
with local 4-H Clubs and Future Farmers
chapters.
Publications:
EQUINE SCHOOL AND COLLEGE
DIRECTORY; HARNESS HERO CARDS,
harness racing trading cards.
Description:
Founded in 1976. National, non-profit
organization dedicated to the advancement
of harness racing among young people.
Aims to educate youth so that they are
aware of the multitude of career
opportunities in the industry.

HARNESS HORSEMEN INTERNATIONAL
319 HIGH STREET
SUITE 2
BURLINGTON, NJ 08016
609-747-1000
Fax: 609-747-1012
www.harnesshorsemeninternational.com
- Tom Luchento, President
- Kim Hankins, First Vice President
- Tony Somone, Second Vice President
tsomone@harnessillinois.com
- Sal DiMario, Secretary
- Gabe Prewitt, Director at Large
- Jerry Knappenberger, Director at Large
Number of Members:
35,000
Member Services:
Includes insurance plan.
Publications:
Newsletter.
Membership Requirements:
Member of a horseman's association.
Description:
Founded in 1964. International trade
association for harness racing industry.

HARNESS TRACKS OF AMERICA
12025 EAST DRY GULCH PL.
TUCSON, AZ 85749
520-529-2525
www.harnesstracks.com
- Paul Fontaine, President
- Hugh Mitchell, Chairman of the Board
- Brock Milstein, Vice Chairman of the
Board
- Paul J. Estok, Executive Vice President
Number of Members:
38
Publications:
Newsletter, daily; WEEKLY TRACK
TOPICS, weekly; reports, monthly;
Directory, annually.
Membership Requirements:
Must be pari-mutuel harness track.
Description:
Founded in 1954. Helps promote the
industry of pari-mutuel harness racing.

HORSE SHOWS IN THE SUN
319 MAIN STREET
SAUGERTIES, NY 12477
845-246-8833
Fax: 845-246-6371
info@hitsshows.com
www.hitsshows.com

• Kristen Vale-Mosack, Office Manager
Kristen@HitsShows.com
Number of Members:
7,500
Publications:
Prize List, annual; Official Show Program, annual.
Description:
Founded in 1982. Six-week series of international show jumping events attracting 1,600 horses and riders from more than six countries including the USA, Canada, Mexico, Japan, Ireland, and England. More than $1,000,000 in prize money offered.

HORSEMEN'S BENEVOLENT AND PROTECTIVE ASSOCIATION
870 CORPORATE DRIVE
SUITE 300
LEXINGTON, KY 40503-5419
859-259-0451
866-245-1711
Fax: 859-259-0452
racing@hbpa.org
www.nationalhbpa.com
• Leroy Gessmann, President
(515) 989-4944
• Eric J. Hamelback, CEO
(859) 259-0451
• Tom Metzen, 1st Vice President
(952) 496-6442
Member Services:
Insurance coverage; third party liability; race track negotiations; other services.
Membership Requirements:
Must be licensed owner or trainer of a race horse.
Description:
Founded in 1940. Represents horsemen in the racing industry.

JOCKEY CLUB
40 EAST 52ND STREET
NEW YORK, NY 10022
212-371-5970
Fax: 212-371-6123
www.jockeyclub.com
• Stuart S. Janney, III, Chairman
• Ogden Phipps, Honorary Chairman
• William M. Lear, Vice Chairman
• Ian D. Highet, Secretary-Treasurer
• James L. Gagliano, President & CEO
jgagliano@jockeyclub.com
Description:
Founded in 1894. National, international registry for thoroughbred horses. The Jockey Club is the breed registry for all thoroughbred horses in North America. As such, it is responsible for maintaining The American Stud Book, which includes all thoroughbreds foaled in the United States, Canada and Puerto Rico as well as thoroughbreds imported into those countries from nations around the world that maintain similar thoroughbred registries. The Jockey Club was formed on Feb. 9, 1894 in New York City by several prominent thoroughbred owners and breeders determined to bring a sense of order and authority to an increasingly chaotic sport.

JOCKEYS' GUILD
448 LEWIS HARGETT CIRCLE
SUITE 220
LEXINGTON, KY 40503
859-523-5625
866-GO-JOCKS (866-465-6257)

Fax: 859-219-9892
info@jockeysguild.com
www.jockeysguild.com
• John Velazquez, Chairman
• G.R. Carter, Vice Chairman
• Rodney Prescott, Secretary
• Joel Campbell, Treasurer
Member Services:
Health and life insurance available for jockeys and families. Annual Board of Directors meeting - December, Las Vegas, NV.
Publications:
JOCKEY NEWS, bimonthly.
Membership Requirements:
Must be licensed jockey, have won at least one race. To maintain membership, jockey must have 1 mount in twelve months for throughbred & quarter horse racing.
Description:
Founded in 1940. To promote, protect & serve the welfare & prestige of the american professional jockey community with integrity, equity & justice.

MARYLAND MILLION
30 EAST PADONIA ROAD
SUITE 303
TIMONIUM, MD 21094
410-252-2100
Fax: 410-560-0503
info@marylandmillion.com
www.marylandmillion.com
• Cricket Goodall, Executive Director
• Jordyn Egan, Assistant Director & Sponsorship
• Barroe Reightler, Director of Publications
• Nicole Hart, Finance
Description:
Founded in 1985, Maryland Million Day is the premier thoroughbred racing event that has become one of the nation's best known single days of horse racing excitement. Envisioned as a local version of the Breeders Cup, Maryland Million was so popular with both fans and horsemen that it soon attracted imitators throughout the nation. There are now many such days in different states featuring either state-bred or state-sired horses in festival-like atmospheres.

MARYLAND THOROUGHBRED HORSEMEN'S ASSOCIATION
500 REDLAND COURT
SUITE 105
OWINGS MILLS, MD 21117
410-902-6842
Fax: 410-902-6841
info@mdhorsemen.com
www.mdhorsemen.com
• Karin M. De Francis, President
• Robert J. Lillis, Executive Director
• Harry M. Harris, M.D., Medical Director
• Rosemary Lishia, Director of Finance
• Dago Dupay, Chaplain
Description:
Founded in 1995. Promotes the establishment of a multi-state licensing program for horse racing organizations, designed to ease the burden of licensing for thoroughbred and standardbred owners and trainers involved in racing.

NATIONAL CUTTING HORSE ASSOCIATION
260 BAILEY AVENUE
FORT WORTH, TX 76107
817-244-6188
Fax: 817-244-2015
www.nchacutting.com
• Jim Bret Campbell, Executive Director
• Pam Robison, Administrative Assistant
• Carl Mullins, Director of Business Development
• Angie Highland, Treasurer
• Shana Veale, Controller
Number of Members:
11,800
Member Services:
Right to participate in NCHA events, award winning cutting horse, CHATTER subscription, annual yearbook, rules book, casebook, NCHA decal, voting privileges, NCHA merchandise discounts.
Publications:
THE CUTTING HORSE CHATTER, monthly; Media Guide; Award Yearbook; Media Guide; Six Event Programs.
Membership Requirements:
Application and membership dues of $50 per year. Youth membership available.
Description:
Founded in 1946. Governing body for sport of cutting, sanctioning some 1,400 events nationwide and running six major cuttings each year, featuring 4,000 horses, 12,000 participants and $13,000,000 in purses.

NATIONAL STEEPLECHASE ASSOCIATION
400 FAIR HILL DRIVE
ELKTON, MD 21921
410-392-0700
Fax: 410-392-0706
info@nationalsteeplechase.com
www.nationalsteeplechase.com
• Beverly R. Steinman, Chairman
• Guy J. Torsilieri, President
• P. Douglas Fout, Vice President
• W Patrick Butterfield, Secretary
• Charles W. Strittmatter, Treasurer
Description:
Founded in 1895. The National Steeplechase Association is the official sanctioning body of American steeplechase horse racing. The NSA licenses participants, approves race courses, trains officials, coordinates race entries, enforces rules, compiles an official database and oversees the national marketing and public relations efforts of the sport. Among the groups the NSA serves are owners, trainers, jockeys, members, race meetings and race tracks. The NSA headquarters is located in Fair Hill, Md., home to a world-class steeplechase course, a thoroughbred training center, and an international three-day event course.
Membership Requirements:
Payment of dues.
Publications:
AMERICAN STEEPLECHASING, annual yearbook.
Number of Members:
1,500

NATIONAL THOROUGHBRED RACING
2525 HARRODSBURG ROAD
SUITE 510
LEXINGTON, KY 40504

866-678-4289
equinebenefits@ntra.com
www.ntra.com
• Alexander M. Waldrop, President & CEO
alexwaldrop@ntra.com
• Keith Chamblin, Chief Operating Officer
(859) 422-2645
• Amber Florence, Chief Financial Officer
(859) 422-2659
• Steve Koch, Executive Director
(859) 422-2668
• Jeffrey Burch, Senior Vice President
(859) 422-1225
• Michele Ravencraft, Senior Director of
Events
(859) 422-2657
Publications:
TRC MEDIA UPDATE, 33 times annually;
EquineCareWatch Media Bulletin, monthly;
Newsroom Guide to Thoroughbred Racing;
Thoroughbred Athlete and the Racing
Industry; TRC Notebook, weekly via
Associated Press wire service.
Description:
Founded in 1987. National, non-profit media
relations organization for the sport of
Thoroughbred racing in North America. This
is the NTRA headquarters. This office
handles advertising, sponsorship, publicity,
television and finance.

STADIUM JUMPING, INC.
1301 SIXTH AVENUE WEST
SUITE 406
BRADENTON, FL 34205
941-744-5465
800-237-8924
Fax: 941-744-0874
www.stadiumjumping.com
• Michael Morrissey, President
• Matt Morrissey, Marketing & Vendor
Operations
• Mary Silcox, Advertising & Publications
Publications:
Media Guide.
Membership Requirements:
Automatic upon participation in an AGA
event. Membership includes owners, riders,
trainers, show organizers, course designers,
AHSA and USET officials.
Description:
Founded in 1978. Non-profit organization
which promotes the highest caliber of grand
prix show jumping in the United States.
Works closely with the American Horse
Show Association and the U.S. Equestrian
team to improve the status of the sport and
increase benefits to the various show
organizers at each event, horse owners,
riders and trainers.

STANDARDBRED CANADA
2150 MEADOWVALE BOULEVARD
MISSISSAUGA, ON, CANADA L5N 6R6
905-858-3060
Fax: 905-858-3111
www.standardbredcanada.ca
• Caren Stockwell, Corporate Secretary &
Executive Assistant
(905) 858-3060
• Rosenna So, Chief Financial Officer
(905) 858-3060
• Heather Reid, Sales & Stakes Manager
(905) 858-3060
Publications:
TROT MAGAZINE, monthly.
Description:

Standardbred Canada is a non-profit
organization that aims to promote harness
racing while maintaining and distributing
records on registered Standardbreds in
Canada. They formed in 1998 as a result of
the merging of The Canadian Trotting
Association and The Canadian
Standardbred Horse Society.

THOROUGHBRED CLUB OF AMERICA
3555 RICE ROAD
LEXINGTON, KY 40510
859-254-4282
Fax: 859-231-6131
lgardner@thethoroughbredclub.com
www.thethoroughbredclub.com
• Shannon Arvin, President
• Gray Lyster, Vice President
• Louis Prichard, Secretary-Treasurer
• Laura Gardener, General Manager
lgardner@thethoroughbredclub.com
• Betty Flynn, Executive Director
Description:
Founded in 1932. The purpose of the club is
to promote better business relations among
Thoroughbred horse riders and to provide a
venue for intelligent discussion on breeding,
racing and marketing of Throughbred
horses.
Member Services:
Monthly meetings; club house with full scale
library.
Membership Requirements:
Members must be associated with the
thoroughbred horse industry (owners,
breeders, track or organizational executives)
and approved by the Board of Directors.

THOROUGHBRED OWNERS AND
BREEDERS ASSOCIATION
3101 BEAUMONT CENTRE CIRCLE
SUITE 110
LEXINGTON, KY 40513
859-276-2291
888-606-TOBA
Fax: 859-276-2462
toba@toba.org
www.toba.org
• Dan Metzger, President
• Carl Gough, Controller
• Andrew Schweigardt, Director of Industry
Relations and Development
Number of Members:
3,300
Member Services:
International Committee. Health Committee.
Owners Committee. National Awards dinner
held annually to recognize top state
breeders.
Publications:
THE BLOOD-HORSE, weekly.
Membership Requirements:
Dues payment of $275.
Description:
Founded in 1961. National organization
devoted to improving the quality of the
thoroughbred racing and breeding industry.

THOROUGHBRED RACING
ASSOCIATIONS
420 FAIR HILL DRIVE
SUITE 1
ELKTON, MD 21921
410-392-9200
Fax: 410-398-1366
www.tra-online.com

• Christopher N. Scherf, Executive Vice
President
(410) 392-9200
• Jane E. Murray, Director of Services
(410) 392-9200
• Margie Pollard, Executive Assistant
(410) 392-9200
• Karen Darling, Administrative
Assistant/Webmaster
(410) 392-9200
Description:
Founded in 1942. Trade association which
serves to insure the integrity of
thoroughbred racing.
Membership Requirements:
Must be racetrack or racing association.
Publications:
TRA DIRECTORY AND RECORD BOOK,
annual.
Member Services:
Meetings; surveys; public and media
relations; data bank.

U.S. TROTTING ASSOCIATION
6130 SOUTH SUNBURY ROAD
WESTERVILLE, OH 43081-9309
614-224-2291
877-800-USTA
Fax: 614-228-1385
webmaster@ustrotting.com
www.ustrotting.com
• Mike Tanner, Executive Vice President
webmaster@ustrotting.com
• Dan Leary, Director of Marketing and
Commnications
dan.leary@ustrotting.com
Number of Members:
18,000
Publications:
HOOF BEATS, monthly magazine.
Membership Requirements:
Anyone who works and/or participates in
harness racing.
Description:
Founded in 1939, the U.S. Trotting
Association is a not-for-profit association of
Standardbred owners, breeders, drivers,
trainers, and officials, organized to provide
administrative, rulemaking, licensing and
breed registry services to its members and
promote the sport of harness racing.

UNITED STATES DRESSAGE
FOUNDATION
4051 IRON WORKS PARKWAY
LEXINGTON, KY 40511
859-971-2277
Fax: 859-971-7722
www.usdf.org
• George W. Williams, President
(937) 603-9134
• Margaret C. Freeman, Secretary
(914) 548-4242
• Steven M. Schubert, Treasurer
(978) 360-6441
treasurer@usdf.org
• Lisa J. Gorretta, Vice President
(236) 406-5475
Number of Members:
38,000
Publications:
Yearbook, annually USDF Regional
Newsletter, four times annually; Calendar of
Competitions, annually.
Membership Requirements:
Group membership is attained by joining
one of USDF's 125 Group member

organizations. Members are eligible for USDF Rider Awards. Participating membership is issued directly by USDF, not through a group. They receive a copy of all USDF publications, and upon registering their horses with USDF, they are eligible for the entire USDF awards program, and are also eligible to receive a half-price subscription to DRESSAGE & CT Magazine. Business membership is issued directly by USDF. They receive all USDF publications, and receive discounted advertising and other promotional opportunities.

Description:
Founded in 1973. Non-profit educational organization dedicated to the promotion of dressage as a basic training for all horses, as well as a competitive sport.

UNITED STATES EQUESTRIAN FEDERATION
4047 IRON WORKS PARKWAY
LEXINGTON, KY 40511
859-258-2472
Fax: 859-231-6662
customercare@usef.org
www.usef.org
• Chrystine Tauber, President
(859) 225-2046
• Chris Welton, CEO
(859) 225-6912
• Colby Connell, Chief Marketing Officer
(859) 225-2024
• Will Connell, Director, Sport
(908) 326-1154
wconnell@usef.org
• Sonja Keating, SVP, General Counsel
(859) 225-2045
skeating@usef.org
Number of Members:
80,000
Member Services:
Eligibility to compete for national awards, free member services; insurance coverage; corporate discounts; free amateur status and travel discounts.
Publications:
HORSE SHOW Magazine, monthly; Rule Book, bi-annually.
Membership Requirements:
Payment of annual fee.
Description:
Founded in 1917. National Equestrian Federation of the United States. Establishes rules and regulations for 26 different breeds and disciplines including the three Olympic disciplines: Show Jumping, Dressage and Three Day Eventing. Sanctions over 2,600 horse shows throughout the United States each year. Offers variety of sponsorship programs (national championship events, award programs, etc.) in virtually every market in the U.S. purpose is to govern equestrian sports in the United States and represent the United States internationally.

UNITED STATES EQUESTRIAN TEAM FOUNDATION
1040 POTTERSVILLE ROAD
BEDMINSTER TOWNSHIP, NJ 07934
908-234-1251
Fax: 908-234-0670
info@uset.org
www.uset.org
• Brownlee O. Currey, Jr., Chairman of the Board
• Tucker S. Johnson, President and CEO

• James McNerney, Vice President
• Philip Richter, Treasurer
Member Services:
Publication, social activities. Annual meeting held in January each year.
Publications:
USET NEWS, six times annually.
Membership Requirements:
Active team members are selected on a competitive basis. Contributing members donate to support teams.
Sports Services Founded:
1950
Description:
Established as a not-for-profit organization, the USET Foundation's role is to help provide funding for the High Performance competition, training, coaching, travel and educational needs of America's elite and developing athletes and horses in partnership with the United States Equestrian Federation.

UNITED STATES EVENTING ASSOCIATION
525 OLD WATERFORD ROAD NORTHWEST
LEESBURG, VA 20176
703-779-0440
Fax: 703-779-0550
info@useventing.com
www.useventing.com
• Rob Burk, Chief Executive Officer
(703) 779-9895
rburk@useventing.com
• Jo Whitehouse, Developmental Officer
(703) 669-9999
jo@useventing.com
• Sharon Gallagher, Senior Director of Competitions
(703) 669-9995
sharon@useventing.com
• Jennifer Hardwick, Director of Member Services
(703) 669-9993
jennifer@useventing.com
Description:
Founded in 1959. Concerned with education in the sport of Combined Training (also known as Eventing or Horse Trials) and development of competitions throughout the country so that horses and riders from novice through Olympic level may gain necessary experience, and, at the same time, may enjoy this equestrian sport.
Membership Requirements:
Payment of dues - Full Member ($85), Junior Member ($60), Life Member ($1,500).
Publications:
EVENTING USA, bimonthly magazine; USCTA OMNIBUS, four issues per year; RULES FOR Eventing, other books, booklets and pamphlets; mailing lists.
Number of Members:
12,000

UNITED STATES POLO ASSOCIATION
9011 LAKE WORTH ROAD
LAKE WORTH, FL 33467
800-232-8772
www.uspolo.org
• Duncan Huyler, Chief Executive Officer
dhuyler@uspolo.org
• Susan Present, Chief Financial Officer
spresent@uspolo.org
• Kris Bowman, Executive Director
kbowman@uspolo.org

• Justin Powers, Director of Club Development
jpowers@uspolo.org
Number of members:
3,488
Member Services:
USPA Yearbook with name listing and handicap, access to movies of techniques of polo and on various games; identification stickers and opportunity to play in all USPA tournaments within given handicap.
Publications:
Polo Players' Edition
Membership Requirements:
Club - must have regulation field; and accommodations for horses and tack. Must have three registered USPA-playing members as members of the club. $200 per year. Player - must belong to a registered USPA club and must follow rules and regulations stated by USPA. $135 per year.
Description:
Founded 1890. Serves as regulatory body of polo events played in the U.S. and Canada. Overseas tournaments, assigns handicaps, promotes intercollegiate and interscholastic polo. The Polo Training Foundation, conducts polo schools across the country.

WALKING HORSE TRAINER'S ASSOCIATION
1101 NORTH MAIN STREET
SHELBYVILLE, TN 37162
931-684-5866
Fax: 931-684-5895
whtrainers@gmail.com
• Billy Young, President
• Bill Cantrell, 1st Vice President
• Jamie Hankins, 2nd Vice President
Description:
Founded in 1968. Organization of professional walking horse trainers to promote and improve their interests.
Membership Requirements:
Must be classified as a professional trainer, and must spend 100% of their working time working with horses and earn 100% of their income from working with horses. Also have A and AA licensed trainers.
Publications:
FROM THE HORSES MOUTH, newsletter; THE UPDATER.
Member Services:
Receive license free; receive newsletters; annual meeting held in December of each year.

WOODBINE ENTERTAINMENT GROUP
555 REXDALE BOULEVARD
TORONTO, ON, CANADA M9W 5L2
416-675-7223
1-888-675-7223
info@woodbineentertainment.com
www.woodbineentertainment.com
• James J. Lawson, Chief Executive Officer
• H.B. Clay Horner, Chairman
• Michelle E. DiEmanuele, President & CEO, Trillium Health Partners
Description:
Parent company of Woodbine, Ft. Erie, and Mohawk racetracks.

Equestrian, Commissions/Pari-Mutuel

AGRICULTURE AND AGRI-FOOD CANADA
960 CARLING AVENUE
CEF BUILDING 74
OTTAWA, ON, CANADA K1A 0C6
613-759-6100
1-800-268-8835
Fax: 613-759-6230
cpmawebacpm@agr.gc.ca
www.agr.gc.ca/csb/cpma-acpm/index_e.php
• Gerry Ritz, Minister Of Agriculture & Agri-Food
• Andrea Lyon, Deputy Minister Of Agriculture & Agri-Food
• Chris Forbes, Associate Deputy Minister
• Ron Nichol, Director Program Coordination & National Stan
Description:
Founded 1972. Provides supervision over pari-mutuel betting on horse races in Canada under the Criminal Code. Services provided include auditing of the tote system and betting transactions, testing horses for the presence of prohibited drugs, providing video race patrol and photo finish services, and research.
Publications:
Annual Report; Schedule of Drugs, Q&A Equine Drug control Booklet.

ALCOHOL AND GAMING COMMISSION OF ONTARIO
90 SHEPPARD AVENUE EAST
SUITE 200-300
TORONTO, ON, CANADA M2N 0A4
416-326-8700
1-800-522-2876
Fax: 416-326-5555
customer.service@agco.ca
www.agco.on.ca
• Jean Major, Chief Executive Officer
• Tom Mungham, Chief Operating Officer
• Jasmina Milanovich, Corporate Secretary & Director
• Teresa Tedesco, Chief Administrative Officer
Description:
Regulates the sale, service, and consumption of beverage alcohol to promote moderation and responsible use; ensures that casino and charitable gaming is conducted in the public interest, by people with integrity, and in a manner that is socially and financially responsible.

ARIZONA DEPARTMENT OF RACING
1110 WEST WASHINGTON
SUITE 450
PHOENIX, AZ 85007
602-364-1700
Fax: 602-364-1703
racing.az.gov
• Victoria Rogen, Licensing
(602) 364-1716
• Dan Reinertson, Chief Greyhound Steward
(520) 884-7576
Description:
The Department of Racing regulates the Arizona pari-mutuel horse and greyhound racing industry. The Department oversees and supervises all commercial horse, greyhound, and county fair racing meetings; licenses participants; collects state revenues generated by race meetings; promotes and encourages the breeding of horses and greyhounds in the State; and enforces laws and rules related to racing and wagering to protect industry participants and the public. The Department also regulates and supervises all boxing, kickboxing, tough man, and mixed martial arts events in Arizona.

BIRMINGHAM RACING COMMISSION
1000 JOHN ROGERS DRIVE
SUITE 102
BIRMINGHAM, AL 35210
205-838-7470
Fax: 205-328-0632
• Kip W. Keefer, Executive Secretary
• Valerie Carpenter, Administrative Assistant
• Leda Dimperio, Systems Administrator
brcval@mindspring.com
• Peter McCann, Veterinarian
(205) 838-7478
Description:
The Birmingham Racing Commission was organized in 1984 pursuant to the John Rogers Act, now codified as Chapter 65 of Title 11, Code of Alabama 1975. The Commission is a unique public corporation authorized to license and regulate thoroughbred and greyhound racing pari-mutuel wagering in Birmingham.

CALIFORNIA HORSE RACING BOARD
1010 HURLEY WAY
SUITE 300
SACRAMENTO, CA 95825
916-263-6000
www.chrb.ca.gov
• Rick Baedeker, Executive Director
• Jackie Wagner, Assistant Executive Director
• Bill Westermann, Chief of Licensing and Enforcement
• Wendy Voss, Chief of Administration
Description:
Regulatory body for pari-mutuel wagering in the state of California.

COLORADO RACING COMMISSION
1881 PIERCE STREET
SUITE 108
LAKEWOOD, CO 80214
303-205-2990
Fax: 303-205-2950
www.colorado.gov/pacific/enforcement/racing-commission-0
• Sean Beirne, Chair
• Pam Inmann, Vice Chair - Business Member
• Lori Scott, Veterinarian Member
Description:
The mission of the Colorado Division of Racing is to promote and foster the public confidence in the pari-mutuel industry, protect the welfare of the participants through fair, consistent, proactive enforcement of appropriate policies, statutes and Colorado racing commission rules. The Commission is responsible for promulgating all the rules and regulations governing greyhound and horse racing in Colorado.
Number of Members:
5-member commission
Publications:
Annual Report; Rule Book

HORSE RACING ALBERTA
9707 110TH STREET NW
SUITE 720
EDMONTON, AB, CANADA T5K 2L9
780-415-5432
1-888-553-7223
reception@thehorses.com
www.thehorses.com
• Shirley McClellan, Chief Executive Officer
(780) 415-5432
• Sharon Stell, Chief Financial Officer
(780) 415-5427
• Doug Fenske, Manager, Racing
(780) 415-5432
• Jeff Robillard, Manager of Marketing and Communications
(780) 415-5432
Description:
Horse Racing Alberta (HRA), is a private not-for-profit corporation that was established with the Alberta Governments proclamation of the Racing Corporation Act in 1996. The HRA was established to lead a racing industry renewal and to manage industry self-regulation.

IDAHO STATE POLICE
DEPARTMENT OF LAW ENFORCEMENT
700 SOUTH STRATFORD DRIVE
MERIDIAN, ID 83642
208-884-7080
Fax: 208-884-7098
isp.idaho.gov/racing/
• Paul J. Schneider, Chairman of the Commission
• Ardie Noyes, Racing Executive Director
ardie.noyes@isp.idaho.gov
• Jeremy Beck, Management Assistant
jeremy.beck@isp.idaho.gov
• Brent Archibald, Investigator
Description:
Regulatory body for pari-mutuel wagering in the state of Idaho.

ILLINOIS RACING BOARD
100 WEST RANDOLPH STREET
SUITE 5-700
CHICAGO, IL 60601
312-814-2600
Fax: 312-814-5062
irb.info@illinois.gov
www.illinois.gov/irb
• Domenic Dicera, Executive Director
domenic.dicera@illinois.gov
• Vitto Ezeji-Okoye, Chief Financial Officer
vitto.okoye@illinois.gov
• Ed Mingey, Director of Security
ed.mingey@illinois.gov
• Jackie Clisham, Director of Operations
jackie.clisham@illinois.gov
• Bob Lang, Director of Mutuels
Description:
Regulatory body for pari-mutuel wagering in the state of Illinois.

IOWA RACING & GAMING COMMISSION
DMACC CAPITOL CENTER
1300 DES MOINES STREET
SUITE 100
DES MOINES, IA 50309
515-281-7352
www.iowa.gov/irgc
• Jeff Lamberti, Commissioner
(515) 964-8777
jeff.lamberti@ankenylaw.com
• Richard Arnold, Commissioner
(641) 203-0298

rcarnold@sirisonline.com
- Carl Heinrich, Commissioner
(712) 323-7253
- Kristine Kramer, Commissioner
(641) 394-3086
kandwmotors@iowatelecom.net
- Dolores Mertz, Commissioner
(515) 395-2952
Description:
They are a State of Iowa regulatory agency that regulates the excursion boat/gambling structures casinos and pari-mutual tracks in Iowa.

KANSAS RACING AND GAMING COMMISSION
700 SOUTHWEST HARRISON
SUITE 500
TOPEKA, KS 66603
785-296-5800
Fax: 785-296-0900
krgc@krgc.ks.gov
krgc.ks.gov
- Don Brownlee, Executive Director
- Rochel Towle, Human Resources Manager
- Larry Moreland, Director
- Joe Herridge, Regional Security Manager
- Dennis Bachman, Director
- Brandi White, Director Of Administration
Description:
Dedicated to protect the integrity of these industries through enforcement of Kansas laws and is committed to preserving and instilling public trust and confidence.

KENTUCKY HORSE RACING COMMISSION
4063 IRON WORKS PARKWAY
BUILDING B
LEXINGTON, KY 40511
859-246-2040
Fax: 859-246-2039
Marc.Guilfoil@ky.gov
www.khrc.ky.gov
- Marc A. Guilfoil, Executive Director
(859) 246-2040
Marc.Guilfoil@ky.gov
- John Forgy, General Counsel
(859) 246-2040
John.Forgy@ky.gov
- Jamie Eads, Deputy Executive Director
(859) 246-2040
Jamie.Eads@ky.gov
Member Services:
Licensing of owners, trainers, jockeys, and stable employees; fingerprinting of licensees; licensing reciprocity.
Publications:
Biennial Report; Kentucky Rules of Racing.
Year Founded and Description:
Established in 1906, the KHRC is an independent government agency responsible for regulation of horse racing, wagering, and related activities in the state of Kentucky.

LOUISIANA RACING COMMISSION
320 NORTH CARROLLTON AVENUE
SUITE 2-B
NEW ORLEANS, LA 70119-5100
504-483-4000
Fax: 504-483-4898
horseracing.la.gov
- Bob F. Wright, Chairman
- Judy W. Wagner, 1st Vice Chairman

- Dion Young, 2nd Vice Chairman
- Kevin S. Delahoussaye, Commissioner
Number of Members:
9.
Publications:
Rules of Racing, Racing Calendar.
Member Services:
Enforcement/Regulation of Horse Racing Licensing.
Tradition and Excellence:
Reviews, regulates, governs and supervises all forms of horse racing and pari-mutuel wagering.

MAINE GOVERNMENT, DEPARTMENT OF AGRICULTURE, CONSERVATION & FORESTRY
22 STATE HOUSE STATION
18 ELKINS LANE
AUGUSTA, ME 04333
207-287-3200
Fax: 207-287-2400
dacf@maine.gov
www.maine.gov/dacf/index.shtml
- Walter E. Whitcomb, Commissioner

MANITOBA HORSE RACING COMMISSION
PO BOX 46086
RPO WESTDALE
WINNIPEG, MB, CANADA R3R 3S3
204-885-7770
Fax: 204-831-0942
www.manitobahorsecomm.org
- Tom Goodman, Chairman
mhrc@manitobahorsecomm.org
- Brian Billeck, Vice Chairman
mhrc@manitobahorsecomm.org
- Larry Huber, Executive Director
lhuber@manitobahorsecomm.org
Description:
Provides horsemen and racing organizations with the information and forms needed to facilitate their participation in pari-mutuel horse racing in Manitoba.

MARYLAND RACING COMMISSION
300 EAST TOWSONTOWN BOULEVARD
TOWSON, MD 21286
410-296-9682
Fax: 410-296-9687
dloplmarylandracingcommission-dllr@maryland.gov
www.dllr.state.md.us/racing/comm.shtml
- Bruce Quade, Chairman
Description:
In charge of licensing all persons, associations, or corporations that hold any horse racing meet within the State where racing is permitted for any stake, purse, or reward, as well as Satellite Simulcast Betting and intertrack betting.
Year Founded:
1920

MASSACHUSETTS GAMING COMMISSION
101 FEDERAL STREET
12TH FLOOR
BOSTON, MA 02110
617-979-8400
Fax: 617-725-0258
massgaming.com
- Catherine Blue, General Counsel
- Paul Connelly, Director of Licensing
- Elaine Driscoll, Director of Communications

- John R. Glennon, Chief Information Officer
- Jill Griffin, Director of Workforce
- Alexandra Lightbown, Director of Racing
- Mark Vander Linden, Director of Research and Responsible Gaming
Description:
To ensure fair and honest pari-mutuel racing, the Commission promulgates and enforces rules and regulations, proposes legislation and develops policies to better regulate the Racing Industry (horse and greyhound).

MICHIGAN GAMING CONTROL BOARD
3062 WEST GRAND BOULEVARD
SUITE L-700
DETROIT, MI 48202-6062
313-456-4100
Fax: 313-456-4200
MGCBweb@michigan.gov
www.michigan.gov/mgcb
- Richard S. Kalm, Executive Director
Description:
The Michigan Office of the Racing Commissioner issues track, race meeting, occupational licenses, and simulcasting permits; allocates racing dates and simulcasting schedules; collects racing license and tax revenues; appoints stewards and veterinarians to represent the state; hears appeals from decisions of stewards and on other matters; approves track appointed officials; monitors the daily conduct of live and simulcast racing; conducts equine and human drug testing programs and investigates any irregularities in racing which may lead to formal hearings, administrative disciplinary actions and/or criminal prosecution.

MINNESOTA RACING COMMISSION
15201 ZURICH STREET NE
SUITE 212
COLUMBUS, MN 55025
952-496-7950
Fax: 952-496-7954
www.mrc.state.mn.us
- Thomas DiPasquale, Executive Director
(952) 496-7950
tom.dipasquale@state.mn.us
- John Flynn, Director of Security
(952) 496-7950
john.flynn@state.mn.us
- Lynn Hovda, Chief Veterinarian
(952) 496-6487
lynn.hovda@state.mn.us
- Joe Scurto, Executive Deputy Director
(952) 496-7950
joe.scurto@state.mn.us
Description:
To regulate horse racing and card playing in Minnesota; to ensure that it is conducted in the public interest, and to take all necessary steps in ensuring the integrity of racing and card playing in Minnesota thus promoting the breeding of race horses in order to stimulate agriculture and rural agribusiness.

NEBRASKA STATE RACING COMMISSION
5903 WALKER AVENUE
LINCOLN, NE 68507
402-471-4155
diane.vandeun@nebraska.gov
racingcommission.nebraska.gov
- Dennis Lee, Chairman
- Janell Beveridge, Commissioner

- Jeffrey Galyen, Commissioner
- Tom Sage, Director
tom.sage@nebraska.gov
- John Frederick, Director Of Investigations
Description:
To protect, preserve, and promote agriculture and horse racing through effective and efficient effort to prevent and eliminate corrupt practices; insure fairness in decisions affecting licenses and patrons; ensure due process in administrative proceedings; be attentive to the public and licensees and provide information concerning the industry and commission operations.

NEVADA GAMING CONTROL BOARD
1919 COLLEGE PARKWAY
CARSON CITY, NV 89706
775-684-7750
Fax: 775-687-5817
www.gaming.nv.gov
- A.G. Burnett, Chairman
- Shawn R. Reid, Member
- Terry Johnson, Member
Nature of Services:
The State Gaming Control Board governs Nevada's gaming industry through strict regulation of all persons, locations, practices, association, and related activities. Through investigations, licensure, and enforcement of laws and regulations the Board protects the integrity and the stability of the industry and ensures the collection of gaming taxes and fees that are an essential source of State revenue.

NEW MEXICO RACING COMMISSION
4900 ALAMEDA NE
ALBUQUERQUE, NM 87113
505-222-0700
Fax: 505-222-0713
rc.info@state.nm.us
www.nmrc.state.nm.us
- Laura M. Valencia, Manager/CFO
- Rosemary Garley, Manager
- Fabian C. Lopez, IT, Licensing Manager
- April Abeita, Licensing Administrator
- Ray Mitcham, Auditor
- Rosa M. Silva, Financial Specialist
Description:
To provide regulation in an equitable manner to New Mexico's pari-mutuel horseracing industry to protect the interest of wagering patrons and the State of New Mexico in a manner which promotes a climate of economic prosperity for horsemen, horse owners and racetrack management.

NEW YORK STATE GAMING COMMISSION
PO BOX 7500
SCHENECTADY, NY 12301-7500
518-388-3300
info@gaming.ny.gov
www.gaming.ny.gov
- John A. Crotty, Commissioner
- John J. Poklemba, Commissioner
- Barry Sample, Commissioner
- Todd R. Snyder, Commissioner
- Peter J. Moschetti, Jr., Commissioner
Description:
Regulatory body for pari-mutuel wagering in the state of New York.

NH RACING AND CHARITABLE GAMING COMMISSION
14 INTEGRA DRIVE
CONCORD, NH 03301
603-271-2158
Fax: 603-271-3381
rcgc@racing.nh.gov
www.racing.nh.gov
- Paul M. Kelley, Division Director
- Sudhir Naik, Division Administrator IV
Description:
The New Hampshire Pari-Mutuel Commission oversees the regulation of pari-mutuel wagering at racetracks in New Hampshire, including Thoroughbred Racing, Harness Racing, and Greyhound Racing under RSA 284.

NORTH DAKOTA RACING COMMISSION
500 NORTH 9TH STREET
BISMARCK, ND 58501-4509
701-328-4633
Fax: 701-328-4280
racingcommission.nd.gov
- Jim Ozbun, Chairman of the Commission
circlez@ndsupernet.com
- Ray Trottier, Commissioner
rjtrots@hotmail.com
- John Hanson, Commissioner
jhanson@loggingcampranch.com
- David Piepkorn, Commissioner
dpiepkorn@nd.gov
Description:
The regulatory body in charge of regulating live and simulcast racing in North Dakota and administers three special funds for the benefit of the horse racing industry in North Dakota.

OHIO STATE RACING COMMISSION
77 SOUTH HIGH STREET
18TH FLOOR
COLUMBUS, OH 43215-6108
614-466-2757
Fax: 614-466-1900
www.racing.ohio.gov
- Robert K. Schmitz, Chairman
- Todd Book, Commissioner
- Gary G. Koch, Commissioner
- Mark Munroe, Commissioner
- Thomas R. Winters, Commissioner
Description:
Regulatory body for pari-mutuel wagering in the state of Ohio.
Year Founded:
1933.

OKLAHOMA HORSE RACING COMMISSION
SHEPHERD MALL
2401 NW 23RD STREET
SUITE 78
OKLAHOMA CITY, OK 73107
405-943-6472
Fax: 405-943-6474
ohrc@socket.net
www.ohrc.org
- Ran Leonard, Chairman
- Keith Sanders, Vice Chair
- Mel Bollenbach, Secretary
- Mike Dixon, Director of Law Enforcement
- Kelly G. Cathey, Executive Director
Description:
Encourages agriculture, the breeding of horses, and generates public revenue through the forceful control of the highest quality Commission-sanctioned racing which

maintains the appearance as well as the fact of complete honesty and integrity of horse racing in this state.

OREGON RACING COMMISSION
800 NE OREGON STREET
SUITE 310
PORTLAND, OR 97232
971-673-0207
Fax: 971-673-0213
- Jack McGrail, Executive Director
(971) 673-0209
jack.mcgrail@state.or.us
- Karen Parkman, Program and Administrative Coordinator
(971) 673-0208
karen.parkman@state.or.us
- Mike Twiggs, State Steward
(503) 285-9144
mike.twiggs@state.or.us
- Stacy Katler, Senior State Veterinarian
(503) 285-9144
Description:
To regulate and to facilitate all aspects of the pari-mutuel industry in the state of Oregon for the benefit of the citizenry, the licensees and participants.

PENNSYLVANIA DEPARTMENT OF AGRICULTURE
2301 NORTH CAMERON STREET
HARRISBURG, PA 17110
717-787-4737
www.agriculture.pa.gov
- Kelly King, Horse Racing Executive Assistant
(717) 787-1942
kelking@pa.gov
Description:
Regulatory body for pari-mutuel wagering on harness racing in the state of Pennsylvania.

RACING COMMISSIONERS INTERNATIONAL (ARCI)
1510 NEWTOWN PIKE
SUITE 210
LEXINGTON, KY 40511
859-224-7070
www.arci.com
- Mark Lamberth, Chair
- Edward J. Martin, President
- Judy Wagner, Secretary/Chair-Elect
- Jeff Colliton, Treasurer
Description:
To protect and uphold the integrity of the pari-mutuel sports of horse racing, dog racing and jai-alai through an informed membership, by encouraging uniform regulation and by promoting the health and welfare of the industry through various programs and projects.
Membership Requirements:
Must be racing commissioner or executive director of a commission; associate members need not be commissioners, but must be connected to the industry.
Number of members:
500
Year Founded:
1934

STATE OF DELAWARE, DEPARTMENT OF AGRICULTURE
2320 SOUTH DUPONT HIGHWAY
DOVER, DE 19901
302-698-4500
800-282-8685

Fax: 302-697-4748
dda.delaware.gov
• Ed Kee, Cabinet Secretary of Agriculture
• Austin E. Short, Deputy Secretary
• Holly Porter, Executive Assistant
• Lisa Wildermuth, Executive Secretary
Description:
The Delaware Department of Agriculture Harness Racing Commission regulates and oversees the sport of Harness racing in the state. Its primary objectives and principles are to protect, preserve, and promote agriculture and horse racing through effective and efficient efforts to prevent and eliminate corrupt practices; ensure fairness in decisions affecting licensees and patrons; ensure due process in administrative proceedings; be attentive to the public and licensees and provide information concerning the industry and commission operations.
Delaware License Application:
Licensing Information During Live Racing:
Dover Downs (302) 674-4600, Ext 3242,
Harrington Raceway (302) 398-7223.

STATE OF INDIANA HORSE RACING COMMISSION
1302 NORTH MERIDIAN
SUITE 175
INDIANAPOLIS, IN 46202
317-233-3119
www.in.gov/hrc/
• Thomas Weatherwax, Chairman
• Greg Schenkel, Vice Chairman
• Deena Pitman, Assistant Executive Director
• Lea Ellingwood, General Counsel
• Wendi Samuelson-Dull, Controller
• Holly Newell, Deputy General Counsel
Description:
Supervises pari-mutuel horse race betting in Indiana.

STATE OF NEW JERSEY, DEPARTMENT OF LAW & PUBLIC SAFETY
140 EAST FRONT STREET
PO BOX 088
4TH FLOOR
TRENTON, NJ 8625
609-292-0613
Fax: 609-599-1785
www.nj.gov/oag/racing
• Pamela J. Clyne, Chair
• Francesco Zanzuccki, Executive Director
Description:
To ensure that racing is conducted in a fair and responsible manner in the state of New Jersey.

STATE OF RHODE ISLAND DEPARTMENT OF BUSINESS REGULATION
1511 PONTIAC AVENUE
CRANSTON, RI 02920
401-462-9500
Fax: 401-462-9532
www.dbr.state.ri.us
• Christina Tobiasz, Chief Licensing Examiner, Racing & Athletics
(401) 462-9525
christina.tobiasz@dbr.ri.gov
• Mary F. Bernard, Chair
• Macky McCleary, Director, Business Regulation
(401) 462-9551
• John Mancone, Chief Public Protection

Inspector
(401) 462-9646
john.mancone@dbr.ri.gov
Description:
Responsible for supervising the enforcement of laws related to licensing and regulation of racing and athletics activities, including dog racing, jai alai, boxing, wrestling, kickboxing and simulcast wagering.

TEXAS RACING COMMISSION
8505 CROSS PARK DRIVE
SUITE 110
AUSTIN, TX 78754
512-833-6699
Fax: 512-833-6907
info@txrc.state.tx.us
www.txrc.texas.gov
• Chuck Trout, Executive Director
• Joel Speight, Deputy Executive Director
• John Perryman, Director of Administration
• Cathy Cantrell, Director Of Licensing
cathy.cantrell@txrc.texas.gov
Description:
State regulatory agency for horse and greyhound racing in Texas.

VERMONT RACING COMMISSION
109 STATE STREET
MONTPELIER, VT 05609
802-828-3333
Fax: 802-828-3339
governor.vermont.gov/boards_and_commissions/racing
• Peter Shumlin, Governor
• Harlan Sylvester, Commission Chair
Description:
This commission is based upon the taxing power and the police power of the state and provides for the establishment, licensing, regulation and control of the pari-mutuel system of wagering on horse races, and is for the protection of the public welfare and good order of the people of the state, the support and encouragement of agricultural fairs and the improvement of the breed of horses in Vermont.

VIRGINIA RACING COMMISSION
5707 HUNTSMAN ROAD
SUITE 201-B
RICHMOND, VA 23250
804-966-7400
www.vrc.virginia.gov/
• Bernard J. Hettel, Executive Secretary
(804) 966-7415
• David Lermond, Deputy Executive Secretary
• Kimberly Mackey, Office Administrator
• Rich Harden, Equine Medical Director
Description:
To grow, sustain, and control a native horse racing industry with pari-mutuel wagering by prescribing regulations and conditions that command and promote excellence and complete honesty and integrity in racing and wagering.

WASHINGTON HORSE RACING COMMISSION
6326 MARTIN WAY EAST
SUITE 209
OLYMPIA, WA 98516
360-459-6462
Fax: 360-459-6461
www.whrc.wa.gov

• Doug Moore, Executive Secretary
• Patty Brown, Confidential Secretary
Number of Members:
3 Commissioners, 4 Legislative Non-voting Ex-officio members, 2 Senators, 2 Representatives.
Description:
To provide a regulatory foundation for all aspects of pari-mutuel horse racing in order to protect the public and assure the overall health of the industry.
Year Founded:
1933
Nature of Service:
State government, regulation

WV RACING COMMISSION
900 PENNSYLVANIA AVENUE
SUITE 533
CHARLESTON, WV 25302
304-558-2150
Fax: 304-558-6319
www.racing.wv.gov
• Jack Rossi, Chairman
• Greg McDermott, Commissioner
Description:
The Commission licenses all persons, associations, or corporations that hold any horse racing meet within the State where racing is permitted for any stake, purse, or reward, as well as Satellite Simulcast Betting and inter-track betting. The Commission makes all regulations governing the races and, through its stewards and judges, officiates the conduct of racing.

WYOMING PARI-MUTUEL COMMISSION
ENERGY II BUILDING
951 WERNER COURT
SUITE 335
CASPER, WY 82601
307-265-4015
Fax: 307-265-4279
parimutuel.state.wy.us
• Charles Moore, Executive Director
Description:
Regulatory body for pari-mutuel wagering in the state of Wyoming.

Exercise/Fitness Organizations

AEROBICS AND FITNESS ASSOCIATION OF AMERICA
1750 EAST NORTHROP BOULEVARD
SUITE 200
CHANDLER, AZ 85286-1744
800-446-2322
customerservice@afaa.com
www.afaa.com
Description:
Dedicated to teaching and promoting safety and excellence in the fields of aerobics and fitness. Establishes instructor certification standards and guidelines and disseminates consumer fitness information. They service over 180,000 instructors in 73 countries and have more than 2,500 workshops per year.
Membership Requirements:
Payment of dues.
Year Founded:
1983

AMERICAN ACADEMY OF PODIATRIC SPORTS MEDICINE
3121 NE 26TH STREET
OCALA, FL 34470
352-620-8562
info@aapsm.org
www.aapsm.org
• Alex Kor, President
(410) 550-1511
alexkor@aapsm.org
• Amol Saxena, Department of Sports Medicine
(650) 853-2943
• Maggie Fournier, Secretary-Treasurer
(608) 797-6010
mfournier75@gmail.com
Member Services:
Informational pamphlets, lectures.
Publications:
Newsletter, quarterly; Podiatric Sports Information.
Membership Requirements:
A degree from an accredited college or university in podiatric medicine, physical education or biology.
Description:
Serves to advance the understanding, prevention and management of lower extremity sports and fitness injuries.
Year Founded:
1976

AMERICAN COLLEGE OF SPORTS MEDICINE
401 WEST MICHIGAN STREET
INDIANAPOLIS, IN 46202-3233
317-637-9200
Fax: 317-634-7817
www.acsm.org
• Carol Ewing Garber, President
• Mark Hutchinson, First Vice President
• Carrie Jaworsk, Second Vice President
Description:
Promotes and integrates scientific research, education and practical applications of sports medicine and exercise science to maintain and enhance physical performance, fitness, health and general quality of life.
Membership Requirements:
Must possess minimum of bachelor's degree or be a student in a field related to health, physical education, exercise science or biology; or, a degree in another field and working in one of the above areas; or, the equivalent of one of the above degrees and currently working in a related field. Professional membership - $185. Student membership - $80.
Member Services:
Certifies in the following: program director, exercise specialist, exercise test technologist, health/fitness director, health/fitness instructor and exercise leader/aerobics. Grants both Continuing Medical Education (CME) and Continuing Education Credits (CEC). Twelve Regional Chapters.
Year Founded:
1954

AMERICAN COUNCIL ON EXERCISE
4851 PARAMOUNT DRIVE
SAN DIEGO, CA 92123
888-825-3636
Fax: 858-576-6564

support@acefitness.org
www.acefitness.org
• Scott Goudeseune, President & CEO
• Alex Mirnezam, Chief Financial Officer
• Cedric X. Bryant, Chief Science Officer
Year Founded:
1985
Description:
A nonprofit organization committed to enriching quality of life through safe and effective physical activity. As America's Authority on Fitness, ACE protects all segments of society against ineffective fitness products, programs and trends through its ongoing public education, outreach and research.

AMERICAN FITNESS PROFESSIONALS & ASSOCIATES
1601 LONG BEACH BOULEVARD
BOX 214
SHIP BOTTOM, NJ 08008
609-978-7583
1-800-494-7782
Fax: 609-978-7582
www.afpafitness.com
• Mark J. Occhipinti, President/Chief Executive Officer
Description:
Offers some of the most highly regarded health, fitness, nutrition and sports certifications, education programs and educational opportunities available in the world.
Year Founded:
1994

AMERICAN OSTEOPATHIC ACADEMY OF SPORTS MEDICINE
2424 AMERICAN LANE
MADISON, WI 53704
608-443-2477
Fax: 608-443-2474
www.aoasm.org
• Scott R. Cook, President
(610) 779-2663
• Jeff Bytomski, First Vice President
(919) 681-0868
• John J. Dougherty, Second Vice President
(816) 283-2365
• Shawn Kerger, Secretary/Treasurer
(614) 544-2092

AMERICAN PHYSICAL THERAPY ASSOCIATION
1111 NORTH FAIRFAX STREET
ALEXANDRIA, VA 23214-1488
703-684-2782
800-999-2782
Fax: 703-706-8536
www.apta.org
• Michael J. Bowers, Chief Executive Officer
• Rob Batarla, Executive Vice President
Description:
The principal membership organization representing and promoting the profession of physical therapy, is to further the profession's role in the prevention, diagnosis, and treatment of movement dysfunctions and the enhancement of the physical health and functional abilities of members of the public.

ASSOCIATION OF OLDTIME BARBELL & STRONGMEN (AOBS)
PO BOX 680
WHITESTONE, NY 11357

718-661-3195
Fax: 718-661-3195
lifttech@earthlink.net
www.weightlifting.org/aobs.htm
• Vic Boff, Founder
Membership Requirements:
Men and women who are old time barbell, fitness trainees and strength athletes. Younger devotees invited to join.
Description:
Founded in 1982.

CANADIAN PHYSIOTHERAPY ASSOCIATION
955 GREEN VALLEY CRESCENT
SUITE 270
OTTAWA, ON, CANADA K2C 3V4
613-564-5454
800-387-8679
Fax: 613-564-1577
information@physiotherapy.ca
www.physiotherapy.ca
• Linda Woodhouse, President
Member Services:
National and international event coverage; national symposia; education programs and publications.
Membership Requirements:
Member of Canadian Physiotherapy Association.
Description:
To provide leadership and direction to the physiotherapy profession, foster excellence in practice, education and research, and promote high standards of health in Canada.
Year Founded:
1972

CANADIAN SOCIETY FOR EXERCISE PHYSIOLOGY
18 LOUISA STREET
SUITE 370
OTTAWA, ON, CANADA K1R 6Y6
877-651-3755
Fax: 613-234-3565
info@csep.ca
www.csep.ca
• Mary Duggan, Manager
mduggan@csep.ca
Description:
A voluntary organization composed of professionals interested and involved in the scientific study of exercise physiology, exercise biochemistry, fitness and health.
Member Services:
Journal, professional liability insurance, newsletter.
Year Founded:
1967

COLORADO HILL CLIMB ASSOCIATION
PO BOX 687
GREEN MOUNTAIN FALLS, CO 80819
www.chcaracing.com
• Jay Stewart, President
(719) 641-5352
jbug0353@aol.com
• Erny Shucraft, Vice President
(719) 649-8197
• Debbie Queen, Secretary
(719) 393-5966
queendbie@live.com
• Ginger Bartley, Treasurer
Description:
Sponsors a series of Colorado hill climb racing (motorized) events annually.

Year Founded:
1971

ECA WORLD FITNESS ALLIANCE
414 EAST BEECH STREET
LONG BEACH, NY 11561
516-432-6877
www.ecaworldfitness.com
• Lilli Koppelman, Event Director
• Sydell Radner, Finance Director
• Michelle Mascari, Creative Director
• Susan Kasper, Public Relations Liaison
Description:
Dedicated to furthering the education of
health and fitness professionals and the
promotion of current information and trends
in the rapidly changing fitness industry.
Year Founded:
1991

IDEA HEALTH & FITNESS ASSOCIATION
10455 PACIFIC CENTER COURT
SAN DIEGO, CA 92121
858-535-8979 EXT 7
(800) 999-4332
Fax: 858-535-8234
contact@ideafit.com
www.ideafit.com
• Peter Davis, President and CEO
• Kathie Davis, Executive Director
Nature of Service:
Provided health and fitness professionals
with unbiased data, pertinent information,
educational resources, career development
and industry leadership.
Membership Categories:
Business, Program Director, Personal
Trainer, Group Fitness, Health Professional,
Associate and Student Dues: $45-$175.
Publications:
IDEA HEALTH & FITNESS SOURCE, 10
times annually, IDEA PERSONAL
TRAINER, 10 times annually, IDEA
FITNESS MANAGER, 5 times annually;
IDEA FITNESS EDGE, 5 times annually.
Member Services:
Publications, insurance programs including
liability, occupational accident and medical
discount, special member pricing on events
and educational products, discounted
business services, Fax-on-Demand system,
CEC opportunities and more.
Year Founded:
1982

INTERNATIONAL FEDERATION OF BODYBUILDING AND FITNESS
28232 EUROPOLIS
LAS ROZAS
MADRID, SPAIN
headquarters@ifbb.com
www.ifbb.com
• Rafael Santonja, President
Description:
Founded in 1946. Sanctions amateur and
professional bodybuilding contests. IFBB
has 173 nations as members. Organizes a
world championship each year with an
international congress in a different country.

INTERNATIONAL HEALTH, RACQUET & SPORTSCLUB ASSOCIATION (IHRSA)
70 FARGO STREET
BOSTON, MA 02210
617-951-0055
800-228-4772

Fax: 617-951-0056
www.ihrsa.org
• Joe Moore, President & CEO
• Anita Horne Lawlor, Chief Operating
Officer

INTERNATIONAL SPORTS SCIENCES ASSOCIATION
1015 MARK AVENUE
CARPINTERIA, CA 93013
805-745-8111
Fax: 805-745-8119
www.issaonline.edu
• Sal Arria, Co-Founder & CEO
Description:
Provides new and improved methods and
services to the sports and fitness industries
as science and technology advance, and
addresses the need for standardization in
the club industry.
Year Founded:
1988
Member Services:
Fitness training programs, certification
seminars and examinations, youth fitness
certification programs, product discounts.

LIFELONG FITNESS ALLIANCE
2682 MIDDLEFIELD ROAD
SUITE Z
REDWOOD CITY, CA 94063
650-361-8282
855-361-8282
Fax: 650-529-9776
www.lifelongfitnessalliance.org
• Malinda Kaplan, Program Director
Description:
Fifty-plus lifelong fitness (formerly fifty-plus
fitness association) is a twenty-six year old
nonprofit organization whose mission is to
promote an active lifestyle for older people.
The organization started at Stanford
University as an outgrowth of medical
research on the value of exercise for older
persons. It currently has approximately
2,000 members across the United States.
Fifty-Plus publishes a newsletter, distributes
books and videos, and sponsors physical
activity events for mid-life and older adults.
Membership Requirements:
Anyone over the age of 50 interested in
fitness.
Year Founded:
1980

NATIONAL ACADEMY OF SPORTS MEDICINE
1750 EAST NORTHROP BOULEVARD
SUITE 200
CHANDLER, AZ 85286-1744
800-460-6276
Fax: 460-656-3276
www.nasm.org
• Andrew Wyant, President/General
Manager
• Brad Tucker, Vice President, Sales
• Bill Toth, Vice President, Operations

NATIONAL ATHLETIC TRAINERS' ASSOCIATION
1620 VALWOOD PARKWAY
SUITE 115
CARROLLTON, TX 75006
214-637-6282
Fax: 214-637-2206
kimmelcw@apsu.edu
www.nata.org

• Scott Sailor, President
scott_sailor@csufresno.edu
• MaryBeth Horodyski, Vice President
marybethatc@gmail.com
• Kathy Dieringer, Secretary/Treasurer
Member Services:
Placement, continuing education, public
relations, government affairs.
Publications:
JOURNAL OF ATHLETIC TRAINING,
quarterly; NATA NEWS, monthly newsletter.
Membership Requirements:
Involvement in the athletic training
profession.
Description:
Promotes the advancement and
improvement of the athletic training
profession.
Year Founded:
1950

NATIONAL FITNESS TRADE SHOW
WALLY BOYKO PRODUCTIONS, INC.
PO BOX 2490
WHITE CITY, OR 97503
541-830-0400
meshelle@nationalfitnesstradejournal.com
www.nationalfitnesstradejournal.com
Description:
Established to sanction Ms Fitness contests
worldwide; promotes, governs and
coordinates Ms Fitness competitions;
regulates judging criteria and production
format for all Ms Fitness competitions.
Year Founded:
1991

NATIONAL INSTITUTE FOR FITNESS AND SPORT
250 UNIVERSITY BOULEVARD
INDIANAPOLIS, IN 46202
317-274-3432
Fax: 317-274-7408
www.nifs.org
• Jerry Taylor, CEO
(317) 274-3432
• Trudy Coler, Communications Director
(317) 274-3432
• Melanie Roberts, Fitness Center Director
(317) 274-3432
Description:
A nonprofit organization committed to
enhancing human health, physical fitness
and athletic performance through research,
education and service.
Year Founded:
1985

NATIONAL OPERATING COMMITTEE ON STANDARDS FOR ATHLETIC EQUIPMENT / NOCSAE
11020 KING STREET
SUITE 215
OVERLAND PARK, KS 66210
913-888-1340
Fax: 913-498-8817
mike.oliver@nocsae.org
www.nocsae.org/
• Kenneth Stephens, President
• Robert Cantu, Vice President
• Terry Schlatter, Treasurer
• Lars Fuchs, Secretary
• Mike Oliver, Executive Director/Legal
Counsel
mike.oliver@NOCSAE.org
Description:
Commissions research on, and where

feasible, establishes standards for protective athletic equipment.
Membership Requirements:
National associations or organizations involved with athletics and with an interest in protective athletic equipment.
Member Services:
NOCSAE football, baseball/softball, lacrosse, helmet standards; football helmet inspection checklist.
Year Founded:
1969

NATIONAL STRENGTH AND CONDITIONING ASSOCIATION
1885 BOB JOHNSON DRIVE
COLORADO SPRINGS, CO 80906
719-632-6722
800-815-6826
Fax: 719-632-6367
nsca@nsca.com
www.nsca.com
• Gregory Haff, President
• Colin Wilborn, Vice-President
Description:
A nonprofit, educational organization that provides resources and opportunities for professionals in strength and conditioning and related fields.
Year Founded:
1978

PRESIDENT'S COUNCIL ON SPORTS, FITNESS & NUTRITION
1101 WOOTTON PARKWAY
SUITE 560
ROCKVILLE, MD 20852
240-276-9567
fitness@hhs.gov
www.fitness.gov
• Holli Richmond, Executive Director
Description:
The mission of the President's Council on Sports, Fitness & Nutrition is to increase sports participation among youth of all backgrounds and abilities and to promote healthy and active lifestyles for all Americans. Since 1956, the Council has created and promoted programs and initiatives that motivate people of all ages, backgrounds, and abilities to be active and eat healthy.
Publications:
Pamphlets and booklets for personal use and institutional use.
Year Founded:
1956

SHAPE AMERICA SOCIETY OF HEALTH AND PHYSICAL EDUCATORS
1900 ASSOCIATION DRIVE
RESTON, VA 20191
800-213-7193
Fax: 703-476-9527
www.shapeamerica.org
• Steve Jefferies, President
• Paul Roetert, CEO
Description:
To promote and support creative and healthy lifestyles through high quality programs in health, physical education, recreation, dance and sport, and to provide members with professional development opportunities that increase knowledge, improve skils, and encourage sound professional practices.
Membership Requirements:

Members must be professionals in their fields.
Membership Services:
Conferences, workshops, standards, position statements, consulting, speaker's bureau related to health education, dance, sport, physical education, fitness for all ages and recreation.
Publications:
Newsletter, periodically.
Year Founded:
1942

WELLNESS INSTITUTE OF GREATER BUFFALO
65 NIAGARA SQUARE
ROOM 607
BUFFALO, NY 14202
716-851-4052
Fax: 716-851-4309
wellness@city-buffalo.org
www.healthycommunitynetwork.com
• Philip L. Haberstro, Executive Director
Nature of Service:
Non-profit national membership association and network of state governor's councils and community coalition.
Publications:
National Employee Health and Fitness Day planning tool kit
Year Founded:
1979

WORLD NATURAL BODYBUILDING FEDERATION
inbf@epix.net
www.worldnaturalbb.com
Publications:
NATURAL BODYBUILDING AND FITNESS, quarterly.
Membership Requirements:
Must be totally drug-free for minimum 7 years; have won a qualifying event, and be willing to undergo stringent drug-testing.
Description:
Serves to reward abstinence from drug use by staging bodybuilding competitions that are drug-tested and that offer cash prizes to the best natural athletes.
Year Founded:
1989

YMCA USA
101 NORTH WACKER DRIVE
CHICAGO, IL 60606
312-977-0031
800-872-9622
fulfillment@ymca.net
www.ymca.net
• Jennie Carlson, Executive Vice President
Description:
Founded in 1851. Serves to put Christian principles into practice through programs that build healthy spirit, mind and body for all.
Membership Requirements:
Pay membership fees, scholarship assistance may be available
Publications:
Youth Sports Director's Manual; Organizing Successful YMCA Tournament; YMCA Gymnastics Manual; Rookie coaches guides in baseball, basketball, football, gymnastics, soccer, softball, tennis, volleyball, and wrestling; Basketball Players Manuals; Flag Football Players Manual; Soccer Players Manual.

YWCA USA
2025 M STREET NW
SUITE 550
WASHINGTON, DC 20036
202-467-0801
Fax: 202-467-0802
info@ywca.org
www.ywca.org
• Dara Richardson-Heron, CEO
• Casey Harden, Senior Vice President
• Jackie Sam, COO
• Paula Green Johnson, Secretary
• Dara Richardson-Heron, M.D., Chief Executive Officer
Description:
Serves women and girls and works to eliminate racism and sexism. Offers health, physical education and recreation programming and other programs which stress advocacy for social change.
Publications:
HPER programming info, Interchange, biannually. Student publications. ENCORE, YWCA Post Mastectomy Program Newsletter.
Membership Requirements:
Membership through local Associations.
Year Founded:
1858

Fencing Organizations

CANADIAN FENCING FEDERATION
44-1554 CARLING AVE
OTTAWA, ON, CANADA K1Z 7M4
647-476-2401
Fax: 647-476-2402
cff@fencing.ca
fencing.ca
• Caroline Sharp, Executive Director
(613) 323-5605
ed@fencing.ca
• Tim Stang, Technical Director
(647) 476-2401
• Monica Peterson, High Performance Manager
(250) 661-3542
hppc@fencing.ca
Member Services:
Governing body for fencing in Canada.
Membership Requirements:
Must join through provincial affiliates.
Description:
Promotion and development of fencing in Canada. Manages International High Performance Program; national ranking of registered fencers; elite ranking of fencers who travel abroad, facilitating elite travel arrangements, information about national and international events, funding elite athletes.
Year Founded:
1971

FEDERATION INTERNATIONALE D'ESCRIME (FIE)
MAISON DU SPORT INTERNATIONAL
AVENUE DE RHODANIE 54
LAUSANNE, 1007
+41-21 320 31 15
Fax: +41-21 320 31 16
info@fie.ch
fie.org
• Nathalie Rodriguez, Chief Executive Officer
nr@fie.ch

• Evgeni Tsoukhlo, Deputy Chief Executive Officer
tsoukhlo@mail.ru

NATIONAL INTERCOLLEGIATE WOMEN'S FENCING ASSOCIATION
www.niwfa.com
• Sharon Everson, President
sje112@frontiernet.net
• Jennette Starks-Faulkner, Vice President
jsfaulk1@sbcglobal.net
• Linda Vollkommer-Lynch, Vice President
lvollkom@stevens-tech.edu
Member Services:
Minutes, Directory, Newsletter, information on all events. Annual meetings held second weekend in December, second weekend in March.
Publications:
Newsletter. Minutes of annual meeting. Committee reports. Bylaws, rules and regulations governing competitions.
Membership Requirements:
Colleges and universities granting Bachelors Degrees. $15 annual dues.
Description:
Encourages, promotes and assists in the growth and establishment of women's fencing clubs and teams in the colleges in the U.S. It has conducted an annual team and individual championship since 1929.
Year Founded:
1929

UNITED STATES FENCING COACHES ASSOCIATION
www.usfca.org
• Peter Burchard, President
president@usfca.org
Publications:
SWORDMASTER MAGAZINE, four issues a year.
Membership Requirements:
Teaching of fencing.
Description:
Concerned with teaching and promulgation of the sport of fencing, professional development of fencing masters.
Year Founded:
1941

USA FENCING
4065 SINTON RD
SUITE 140
COLORADO SPRINGS, CO 80907
719-866-4511
Fax: 719-632-5737
information@usfencing.org
www.usfencing.org
• Kris Ekeren, Executive Director
(719) 866-3604
k.ekeren@usfencing.org

Figure Skating Organizations

ICE SKATING INSTITUTE
6000 CUSTER RD
BUILDING 9
PLANO, TX 75023
972-735-8800
Fax: 972-735-8815
www.skateisi.com

• Liz Manglesdorf, Managing Director
(972) 735-8800
liz@skateisi.org
• Elizabeth Kibat, Controller
(972) 735-8800
• Kim Hansen, ISI National Skating Program & Events Coordinator
(972) 735-8800
khansen@skateisi.org
• Liz Manglesdorf, ISI National Skating Programs Coordinator
(972) 735-8800
liz@skateisi.org
• Mary Ann Mangano, Membership Coordinator
(972) 735-8800
maryann@skateisi.org
• Jeff Anderson, Administrative Service Manager
(972) 735-8800
Jeff@skateisi.org
Description:
A not-for-profit association that represents all aspects of the ice arena industry and is dedicated to providing leadership, education and other services. They offer a Recreational Figure Skating Program and an educational instruction program for hockey and figure skating instructors.
Year Founded:
1959
Membership:
Categories for membership are individual, professional, administrative, and related services.

INTERNATIONAL SKATING UNION
AVENUE JUSTE-OLIVIER 17
LAUSANNE, 1006
www.isu.org
• Jan Dijkema, President
• Tron Espeli, 1st Vice President - Speed Skating
• Alexander Lakernik, 2nd Vice President - Figure Skating

PROFESSIONAL SKATERS ASSOCIATION
3006 ALLEGRO PARK LANE SW
ROCHESTER, MN 55902
507-281-5122
Fax: 507-281-5491
www.skatepsa.com
• Jimmie Santee, Executive Director
jsantee@skatepsa.com
Description:
An international organization that supports ice skating professionals and skating coaches through education and accreditation. Over 100 educational programs are provided each year to the more than 6,000 members. It is also the official coaches education, training and certification program of US Figure Skating to the US Olympic Committee.
Publications:
Professional Skater Magazine: Official bi-monthly newsletter.
Year Founded:
1938

SKATE CANADA
261-1200 ST LAURENT BLVD
PO BOX 15
OTTAWA, ON, CANADA K1K 3B8
613-747-1007
Fax: 613-748-5718

info@skatecanada.ca
skatecanada.ca
• Debra Armstrong, Chief Executive Officer
• Patricia Chafe, Chief Sport Development Officer
pchafe@skatecanada.ca
Description:
As the largest figure skating governing body it is committed to the development of personal excellence through participation in skating. The organization's structure relies heavily on volunteers and is divided into 13 sections. Each year an Annual Convention and General Meeting is held.
Publications:
Newsletter: Above the Crowd

U.S. FIGURE SKATING
20 FIRST ST
COLORADO SPRINGS, CO 80906
719-635-5200
Fax: 719-635-9548
info@usfigureskating.org
www.usfsa.org
• Sam Auxier, President
sauxier@usfigureskating.org
• David Raith, Executive Director
draith@usfigureskating.org
Description:
National governing body for the sport of figure skating in the U.S. Membership organization for all Olympic eligible, competitive athletes.
Membership Requirements:
Individual, or through sanctioned clubs.
Publications:
SKATING, 10 times annually. Rulebook, annual; Directory, annual; Media Guide, annual.
Member Services:
Competitions, seminars, test programs, camps, funding and training assistance.
Year Founded:
1921

USA ROLLER SPORTS
4730 SOUTH STREET
LINCOLN, NE 68506
402-483-7551
Fax: 402-483-1465
www.teamusa.org/USA-Roller-Sports

WORLD FIGURE SKATING MUSEUM AND HALL OF FAME
20 FIRST ST
COLORADO SPRINGS, CO 80906
719-635-5200
Fax: 719-635-9548
info@worldskatingmuseum.org
www.worldskatingmuseum.org
Description:
The international repository for the sport of figure skating. The Museum is dedicated to the preservation and interpretation of figure skating's history. The U.S. and World Halls of Fame honors the greatest names in figure skating.

Fishing Organizations

AMERICAN SPORTFISHING ASSOCIATION
1001 NORTH FAIRFAX ST
SUITE 501
ALEXANDRIA, VA 22314

703-519-9691
Fax: 703-519-1872
info@asafishing.org
asafishing.org
• Mike Nussman, President & CEO
(703) 519-9691
mnussman@asafishing.org
• Diane Carpenter, Vice President,
Operations & CFO
(703) 519-9691
dcarpenter@asafishing.org
Nature of Service:
The American Sportfishing Association
(ASA) is the sportfishing industry's trade
association, committed to looking out for the
interests of the entire sportfishing
community. It provides the industry with a
unified voice, speaking out out behalf of
sportfishing and boating industries, state
and federal natural resource agencies,
conservation organizations, angler advocacy
groups and outdoor journalists when
emerging laws and policies could
significantly affect sportfising business or
sportfishing itself.
Year Founded:
1921
Member Services:
Annual trade show, annual business
meeting, member discounts, advocacy,
consumer shows.
Membership Requirements:
Varies

B.A.S.S. LLC
bassmaster@emailcustomerservice.com
www.bassmaster.com
Description:
Sports marketing media firm providing an
integrated multi-media program in fishing for
marketers.
Year Founded:
1967

**CATSKILL FLY FISHING CENTER &
MUSEUM**
1031 OLD ROUTE 17
LIVINGSTON MANOR, NY 12758
845-439-4810
office@cffcm.com
www.cffcm.com
• Glenn Pontier, Executive Director
Description:
Fly fishing center and museum, founded in
1981.

**INTERNATIONAL CASTING SPORT
FEDERATION**
NOVOSUCHDOLSKA 37
PRAGUE, 16500
info@icsf-castingsport.com
www.icsf-castingsport.com
• Kurt Klamet, President
(+49) 1733910939
• Helmut Hochwartner, Vice President
(+43) 676 611397
helmut.hochwartner@icsf-castingsport.com
• Josef Dolezal, Secretary General
(420) 6034180490
dr.josef.dolezal@icsf-castingsport.com
year founded
1954

**INTERNATIONAL FEDERATION OF FLY
FISHERS**
5237 U.S. HIGHWAY 89 SOUTH
Suite 11
LIVINGSTON, MT 59047
406-222-9369
Fax: 406-222-5823
www.fedflyfishers.org
• Len Zickler, President & CEO
(406) 222-9369
Description:
Educating and conserving through Fly
Fishing
Year Founded:
1965
Number of Members:
12,000
Membership Requirements:
Various types of memberships available
including club, foreign association,
individual, family, junior, contributing, retail
shop, life and sustaining.

**INTERNATIONAL GAME FISH
ASSOCIATION**
300 GULF STREAM WAY
DANIA BEACH, FL 33004
954-927-2628
Fax: 954-924-4299
www.igfa.org
• Rob Kramer, President
• Michael J. Myatt, Director of Corporate
Relations
mmyatt@igfa.org
Publications:
World Record Game Fishes book,
International Angler, Junior Angler, Offshore
Tournament Program, Inshore Tournament
Program.
Membership Requirements:
Open to all interested individuals, fishing
clubs and organizations.
Description:
Is a nonprofit organization committed to the
conservation of game fish and the promotion
of responsible, ethical, angling practices
through science, education, rule making and
record keeping.

IZAAK WALTON LEAGUE OF AMERICA
707 CONSERVATION LANE
GAITHERSBURG, MD 20878
301-548-0150
info@iwla.org
www.iwla.org
• Jeff Deschamps, President
• Kelly Kistner, Vice President
• Jim Storer, Secretary
• Walter Lynn Jr., Treasurer
Publications:
OUTDOOR AMERICA, quarterly magazine;
OUTDOOR ETHICS, quarterly newsletter;
SPLASH!, quarterly newsletter of Save Our
Streams program.
Description:
To conserve, maintain, protect and restore
the soil, forest, water and other natural
resources of the United States and other
lands; to promote means and opportunities
for the education of the public with respect
to such resources and their enjoyment and
wholesome utilization.
Year Founded:
1922

**RECREATIONAL BOATING & FISHING
FOUNDATION**
500 MONTGOMERY ST
SUITE 300
ALEXANDRIA, VA 22314
www.takemefishing.org
• Frank Peterson Jr., President & CEO
(703) 778-5157
fpeterson@rbff.org
Nature of Service:
The Recreational Boating & Fishing
Foundation is a nonprofit organization
whose mission is to increase participation in
recreational angling and boating and
thereby increase public awareness and
appreciation of the need for protecting,
conserving and restoring this nation's
aquatic natural resources.
Year Founded:
1998
Publications:
NewsWaves, monthly e-newsletter

TROUT UNLIMITED
1777 N KENT STREET
SUITE 100
ARLINGTON, VA 22209
703-522-0200
800-834-2419
Fax: 703-284-9400
www.tu.org
• Chris Wood, President & CEO
• Elizabeth Maclin, Executive Vice President
• Matt Renaud, Chief Financial Officer
Publications:
TROUT, quarterly magazine.
Description:
Serves to conserve, protect and restore
North America's cold water fisheries and
their watersheds.
Year Founded:
1959

Football Organizations

AMERICAN FOOTBALL ASSOCIATION
115 HENRY STREET
SUITE 2041
BINGHAMTON, NY 13902
877-624-4485
Fax: 801-838-0175
www.americanfootballassn.com
• Roger Goodell, Comissioner
admin@americanfootballassn.com
Description:
The AFA is dedicated to the advancement of
semi-pro/minor league football throughout
the United States and serves as the
National Organization for non-professional
leagues and teams from coast-to-coast.
Year Founded:
1980

**AMERICAN FOOTBALL COACHES
ASSOCIATION**
100 LEGENDS LANE
WACO, TX 76706
254-754-9900
Fax: 254-754-7373
info@afca.com
www.afca.com
• Craig Bohl, Executive Director
• Bobby Staub, Deputy Director
• Adam Guess, CFO
• Mario Price, Director of Media Relations

Publications:
Extra Point (quarterly newsletter),
Convention Proceedings Manual, Summer
Manual, AFCA Directory
Member Services:
Free registration for Annual Convention and
publications. Members are eligible to attend
the AFCA Kickoff Luncheon and Awards
Luncheon. Members can attend the Coach
of the Year Banquet. AFCA members have
access to AFCA On-Line, the Association's
World Wide Web site.
Membership Requirements:
Levels of membership: active; not currently
coaching this season; international
Founded:
1998

AMERICAN YOUTH FOOTBALL
admin@myayf.com
www.americanyouthfootball.com
• Joe Galat, President/CEO
• Dee Grayer, Football Commissioner
• Craig Karahuta, VP, Operations
Description:
An international youth football organization
established to promote the wholesome
development of youth through their
association with adult leaders in the sport of
American football. Rules and regulations are
established to ensure that players play in an
atmosphere of safety with a competitive
balance between teams.
Year Founded:
1996

FOOTBALL CANADA
825 EXHIBITION WAY
SUITE 205
OTTAWA, ON, CANADA K1S 5J3
613-564-0003
Fax: 613-564-6309
admin@footballcanada.com
www.footballcanada.com
• Peter Baxter, Chair
• Kevin McDonald, Executive Director
kmcdonald@footballcanada.com
• Warren Craney, Coaching & Athlete
Development Director
wcraney@footballcanada.com
• Tracy Sturgeon, Senior Manager,
Administration
admin@footballcanada.com
Description:
National sports governing body whose
purpose is to initiate, regulate and manage
the programs, services and events that
promote participation and excellence in
Canadian Amateur Football. Membership
represents Flag, Touch, and Tackle football
as well as players, coaches, officials, and
administrators.
Governing Bodies:
British Columbia, Football Alberta, Football
Saskatchewan, Football Manitoba, Ontario
Football Alliance, Football Quebec, Football
Nova Scotia, Football PEI, Football QJFL,
CJFL, CFOA.
Year Founded:
1884

FOOTBALL WRITERS ASSOCIATION OF AMERICA
214-870-6516
tiger@fwaa.com
www.sportswriters.net/fwaa

• Ross Dellenger, President
• Steve Richardson, Executive Director
(214) 870-6516
tiger@fwaa.com
Description:
Consists of writers across America who
cover college football. Membership
organization that is open to accredited
members of the media and other
organizations affiliated with college football.
With over 1,000 members, the FWAA works
to improve communication among those
involved with the game of college football;
sponsors scholarships for aspiring writers;
and offers many membership benefits.
Year Founded:
1941

INTERNATIONAL FEDERATION OF AMERICAN FOOTBALL
16 BOULEVARD SAINT GERMAIN
PARIS, CS 70514-75237
info@americanfootball.sport
americanfootball.sport
• Pierre Trochet, President
• Andy Fuller, Managing Director
• Jim Mullin, Vice President
• Eric Mayes, Secretary
• Roope Noronen, Director, Competitions
Description:
Currently the IFAF is composed of 74
member nations on 6 continents. Works
closely with major US American Football
Oragnizations (USA Football, the NFL,
NCAA, etc.) with the goal of being part of
the international sporting community and
developing membership.
Membership:
Members are granted a membership status
that is suitable for them depending on their
level of development. Four levels of
membership: full, associated, temporary,
and IFAF Country Administrator.
Founded:
1998

MISSOURI VALLEY FOOTBALL CONFERENCE
1818 CHOTEAU AVENUE
ST. LOUIS, MO 63103
314-444-4360
Fax: 314-444-4361
pattyv@mvc.org
www.valley-football.org
• Patty Viverito, Commissioner
• Mike Kern, Associate Commissioner
kern@mvc.org
• Greg Walter, Associate Commissioner
• William Carollo, Coordinator of Officials
carollo@bigten.org
Description:
In 2008, the nine-member Gateway Football
Conference and the 10-member Missouri
Valley Conference approved changing the
Gateway Football Conference name to
Missouri Valley Football Conference.
Year Founded:
1985
Number of Members:
11
Members:
Illinois State, Indiana State, Missouri State,
North Dakota State, South Dakota State,
University of Northern Iowa, University of
South Dakota, Southern Illinois-
Carbondale, Western Illinois, Youngstown
State, University of North Dakota.

NATIONAL FOOTBALL SCOUTING
317-687-8100
800-331-9135
info@nfs-nic.com
www.nfs-nic.com
Founded:
In 1982

NFL ALUMNI ASSOCIATION
8000 MIDATLANTIC DRIVE
SUITE 120 S
MOUNT LAUREL, NJ 08054
877-258-6635
Fax: 862-772-0277
memberservice@nflalumni.org
www.nflalumni.org
• Brad Edwards, CEO
brad.edwards@nflalumni.org
• Ken Coffey, SVP & COO
Ken.Coffey@NFLAlumni.org
Description:
A charitable organization primarily
composed of former pro-football players
dedicated to volunteer efforts with the motto
Caring for Kids. The organization also offers
support to former pro-players experiencing
financial or medical hardships. The Alumni
Association is covered by a 14-member
Board of Directors comprised of retired
players. The organization is comprised of 40
regional chapters.
Year Founded:
1967
Membership:
Open to former major league professional
team members. Associate membership is
availble to those that would like to support
the charitable and educational goals of the
organization.

NFL INTERNATIONAL/NEW YORK
345 PARK AVENUE
NEW YORK, NY 10154
www.nfl.com
• Roger Goodell, Commissioner
Nature of Sports Service:
Designed to assist the league with its
ongoing international agenda. Responds to
the growing worldwide interest in the NFL.
Includes licensing, sponsorship,
merchandising, television distribution,
American Bowls and the World League. The
NFL International League has divisions in
Canada, China, Japan, Mexico, UK and
Latin America.

NFL PLAYERS ASSOCIATION
1133 20TH STREET NW
WASHINGTON, DC 20036
800-372-2000
800-372-5535
www.nflpa.com
• Lloyd Howell, Jr., Executive Director
• Jalen Reeves-Maybin, President
Description:
Professional association which represents
professional football players. It assures that
the rights of players are protected;
represents players in matters concerning
wages, hours and working conditions;
provides assistance to charitable and
community organizations; and provides
other member services and activities.
Year Founded:
1956
Membership Requirements:
Active and retired members of NFL clubs.

Member Services:
Career counseling, investment assistance, advice on licensing, compensation information, legal assistance.

POP WARNER LITTLE SCHOLARS
P.O. BOX 307
LANGHORNE, PA 19047
www.popwarner.com
• Jon Butler, Executive Director
• Tim Glase, Director, Operations & Development
• Beth Dietz, National Events Manager
Description:
The largest youth football, cheer, and dance program in the US providing programs for participants aged 5 to 16, in 42 states and several countries.
Year Founded:
1959 on national basis, 1929 on local basis.
Membership Requirements:
Teams must belong to a league that is committed to national standards and rules.
Number of Youth Participants:
325,000

PRO FOOTBALL WRITERS OF AMERICA
www.pfwa.org
• Lindsay Jones, President
• Jenny Vrentas, 1st Vice President
Description:
Founded 1962. Promotes the simplification and uniformity of rules in the scoring of games. Works for the improvement of facilities for reporting on professional football and the guarantee of facilities and opportunities on par with other media.
Membership Requirements:
Active Membership - individuals who cover football for a daily newspaper or press association. Statisticians who provide professional records to daily newspapers. Sports editors, assistant sports editors and columnists. Honorary Membership - former active members for ten years before their retirement.
Annual Meetings:
Prior to Super Bowl and NFL owners meeting in March.
Number of Members:
400

PROFESSIONAL FOOTBALL ATHLETIC TRAINERS SOCIETY
1620 VALWOOD PARKWAY
CARROLLTON, TX 75006
www.pfats.com
• Reggie Scott, President
• Sal Lopez, Secretary
Description:
A professional association whose members are the athletic trainers of the NFL. The members of PFATS provide, lead and manage health care for NFL athletes, club employees and members of the NFL community. PFATS is dedicated to ensuring that the highest quality health care is practiced in the NFL. PFATS is guided by the professional integrity and ethical standards of its members and by the unity they share.
Year Founded:
1982

PROFESSIONAL FOOTBALL RESEARCHERS ASSOCIATION
257 JOSLYN ROAD
GUILFORD, NY 13780
pfra@profootballresearchers.org
www.profootballresearchers.org
• Lee Elder, Executive Director
• George Bozeka, President
• Roy Sye, Vice President
• Dave Burch, Secretary
• Adam Connelly, Treasurer
Description:
Fosters the study of professional football as a significant social and athletic institution. Hopes to establish an accurate historical account of professional football and to disseminate research information. Founded in 1979.
Publications:
COFFIN CORNER, 6 issues per year; ANNUAL; Special publications throughout the year.
Membership Requirements:
Open to anyone with a serious interest in the history of professional football or related subjects. Membership dues are $35 a year.

UNITED STATES FLAG & TOUCH FOOTBALL LEAGUE
125 WOLF ROAD
ALBANY, NY 12204
833-558-7385
general@usftl.com
usftl.sportngin.com
Description:
Governing body of flag football. Hosts the National Flag Football Championships every year on MLK Day weekend in Kissimmee, FL. Partners with the NFL Flag Program for youth participants. Non-profit organization.
Members:
20,000+
Year Founded:
1988

USA FOOTBALL
45 N PENNSYLVANIA STREET
SUITE 800
INDIANAPOLIS, IN 46204
317-614-7750
877-536-6822
support@usafootball.com
www.usafootball.com
• Scott Hallenbeck, Executive Director
Description:
An independent non-profit organization that serves as the governing body of football on youth and amateur levels. It does not operate leagues or teams but serves and strengthens existing leagues through a variety of programs including hosting more than 100 annual training events and offering educational programs for coaches, game officials, youth commissioners, and young players.

Football, College Bowl/Classics

ALAMO BOWL
100 MONTANA STREET
SAN ANTONIO, TX 78203
210-226-2695
info@alamobowl.com
www.alamobowl.com

• Derrick Fox, President/CEO
• Rick Hill, VP Marketing/Communications
Description:
Founded 1991. NCAA college football bowl game in which BIG 12 Conference #4 team will play BIG 10 Conference #4 team. Held at the Alamodome in San Antonio. Previous sponsors have included Sylvania, Mastercard, and Valero.

ARMED FORCES BOWL
505 MAIN STREET
SUITE 270
FORT WORTH, TX 76102
817-810-0012
Fax: 817-810-0252
www.armedforcesbowl.com
• Brant Ringler, Executive Director
(817) 810-0506
Brant.B.Ringler@espn.com
• Monty Clegg, Associate Manager of Events
(817) 810-0016
Monty.Clegg@espn.com
• Trisha Branch, Ticket Manager
(817) 810-0012
Trisha.M.Branch@espn.com
Description:
NCAA post season bowl game in Fort Worth, Texas. Game pays tribute to the men and women of the armed forces.
Year Founded:
2003

BELK BOWL, CHARLOTTE SPORTS FOUNDATION
BANK OF AMERICA STADIUM
800 SOUTH MINT STREET
CHARLOTTE, NC 28202-1518
704-644-4047
Info@CharlotteSports.org
charlottesports.org/event/belk-bowl/
• Jerry Richardson, Owner
• Vacant, President
• Marty Hurney, General Manager
Year Founded:
2002

BIRMINGHAM BOWL
ESPN EVENTS
2 RIVERCHASE OFFICE PLAZA
SUITE 110
BIRMINGHAM, AL 35244
205-733-3776
birminghambowl.com
• Mark Meadows, Executive Director
Mark.R.Meadows@espn.com
• Missy Betres, Senior Manager, ESPN Events
missy.h.betres@espn.com
• Matt Wildt, Director of Ticketing
(205) 329-4121
• Ted Feeley, Media Relations Director
(205) 704-4147
Description:
Started in 2006, the Birmingham Bowl is one of fourteen bowl games owned and operated by ESPN Events.

BOCA RATON BOWL
FAU STADIUM
777 GLADES ROAD
BOCA RATON, FL 33431
561-362-3661
jena.lamendola@espn.com
www.cheribundibocaratonbowl.com

• Anthony Barbar, Executive Committee Chairman
Description:
Division I bowl game

CACTUS BOWL
CHASE FIELD
401 E JEFFERSON STREET
PHOENIX, AZ 85251
480-350-0900
Fax: 480-350-0915
fiestabowl.org/cactus-bowl/
• Stephen Leach, Chairman
• Randy Norton, Treasurer
• Gary Hanson, Secretary
Description:
Subdivison bowl competiion.

CAMELLIA BOWL
CRAMTON BOWL
220 HALL STREET
MONTGOMERY, AL 36104
404-862-4730
www.camelliabowl.com
• Will Pope, Sponsorship Director
wpope@camelliabowl.com
• Rusty Reed, National Sponsorship Director
Rusty.w.reed@espn.com
Description:
Division I bowl competition.

CHICK-FIL-A PEACH BOWL
3284 NORTHSIDE PARKWAY
SUITE 550
ATLANTA, GA 30327
404-586-8500
www.chick-fil-apeachbowl.com
• Matt Garvey, Vice President, Communications
mgarvey@cfabowl.com
• Dillon Faulkner, Communications Manager
Year Founded:
1968

CITRUS BOWL
FLORIDA CITRUS BOWL
1 CITRUS BOWL PLACE
ORLANDO, FL 32805
407-423-2476
www.buffalowildwingscitrusbowl.com
Description:
The Citrus Bowl presented by Overtons began as the Tangerine Bowl in 1947. The bowl hosts top teams from the Big Ten and Southeastern conferences.

COTTON BOWL CLASSIC
COWBOYS STADIUM
ONE LEGENDS WAY
FAIRPARK
ARLINGTON, TX 76011
817-892-4800
Fax: 817-892-4810
coach@attcottonbowl.com
www.attcottonbowl.com
• Rick Baker, President
• Marty MacInnis, Executive VP/CFO
• Charlie Fiss, VP Communications
charlie@attcottonbowl.com
• Michael Konradi, VP External Affairs
michael@attcottonbowl.com
• Amy Scott, Director Ticket Operations
Description:
Founded January 1, 1937. Collge bowl game between Big 12 Conference # 2 vs.

Southeastern Conference. Television: FOX Network.

DETROIT BOWL (QUICK LANE BOWL)
FORD FIELD EXECUTIVE OFFICES
2000 BRUSH STREET
SUITE 200
DETROIT, MI 48226
313-262-2010
Fax: 313-262-2009
www.motorcitybowl.com
• George Perles, Chief Executive Officer
• Lloyd Carr, President
• Ken Hoffman, Executive Director
• John Perles, Director of Operations
• Gary Van Dam, Director of Corporate Relations
• Tim Moore, Director of Media Relations
Nature of Sports Service:
NCAA college football bowl game in which Mid-American Conference team will play a BIG 10 Conference team. Formerly the Motor City Bowl. Played at Ford Field.
Year Founded:
1997

EAST-WEST SHRINE GAME
TROPICANA FIELD
ONE TROPICANA DR
ST. PETERSBURG, FL 33705
813-281-8686
Fax: 813-281-8687
www.shrinegame.com
• Nick Themas, Chairman
• Harold Richardson, Executive Director
• Tom Reeves, Director of Game Operations
Description:
The East-west Shrine Game is the oldest of the post-season collegiate bowl games. Since 1925, this annual event raises money for Shriners Hospitals for Children, an international heatlh care system of 22 hospitals dedicated to providing pediatric specialty care at no charge, regardless of need.

FAMOUS POTATO IDAHO BOWL
1109 MAIN STREET
SUITE 299B
BOISE, ID 83702
208-424-1011
Fax: 208-424-1121
• Kevin McDonald, Excevtive Director
• Danielle Brazil, Director Marketing
• Ron Dibelius, Director Sales
Description:
Founded in 1997. ACC v WAC. Held at Bronco Stadium in Boise. Television: ESPN

FIESTA BOWL
UNIVERSITY OF PHOENIX STADIUM
7135 EAST CAMELBACK RD
SUITE 190
TEMPE, AZ 85251
480-350-0900
www.fiestabowl.org
• Duane Woods, Chairman
• John Zidich, Secretary
• Dan Lewis, Chair-Elect
• John Junker, President/CEO
Description:
NCAA college football bowl game in which a PAC 10 Conference team will play a BIG East Conference team or Notre Dame. Sun Devil Stadium. Television: NFL Network
Year Founded:
1989

FOSTERS FARM BOWL
LEVIS STADIUM
4900 MARIE P. DEBARTOLO WAY
SANTA CLARA, CA 95054
415-972-1812
Fax: 415-947-2925
• Gary Cavalli, Executive Director
• Ryan Oppelt, Assistant Executive Director
• Doug Kelly, Media Services
• Sara M Hunt, Game Operations
Description:
A post-season college football bowl game certified by the NCAA that has been played annually in San Francisco, California, since 2002. The game matches teams from the Pac-10 and ACC conferences.

GATOR BOWL
EVERBANK FIELD
1 GATOR BOWL BLVD
JACKSONVILLE, FL 32202
904-798-1700
Fax: 904-632-2080
gba@gatorbowl.com
www.gatorbowl.com
• Daniel Kennedy Murphy, Chairman
• Stephen Tremel, Chairman-Elect/Marketing
• Heather Duncan, Secretary
Description:
The Gator Bowl Association was founded in 1945. In 1955, the Gator Bowl Classic was the first-ever coast-to-coast telecast of a Bowl game and it has been nationally televised ever since. Today, the Gator Bowl is held at Alltel Stadium in Jacksonville.
Sponsor:
Tax Slayer.com at Ever Bank Field

GODADDY BOWL
PO BOX 850909
LADD-PEEBLES STADIUM
MOBILE, AL 36685
251-635-0011
www.gmacbowl.com
• Jerry Silverstein, President
• Frank Modarelli, Executive Director
• Sherrie Dyal, General Manager
• Julie Jeter, Director Marketing/Media Relations
Nature of Sports Service:
NCAA college football bowl game in which a Mid-American Conference team plays a Conference USA team, originally known as the Alabama Bowl. Played in Ladd-Peebles Stadium in Mobile. (1999)

HAWAII BOWL
SHERATON HAWAII BOWL
841 BISHOP STREET
SUITE 2100
HONOLULU, HI 96813
808-523-3688
Fax: 808-523-3712
info@hawaiibowlfoundation.org
www.sheratonhawaiibowl.com
• David Matlin, Executive Director
• Daryl Garvin, Associate Executive Director
• Derek Inouchi, Media Relations
• Brad Motooka, Game Operations
Year Founded:
2002
Nature of Sports Service:
NCAA college football bowl game in which a Conference USA team will play Western Athletic Conference team.

HEART OF DALLAS BOWL
COTTON BOWL STADIUM
5201 N. O'CONNOR BLVD
SUITE 300
IRVING, TX 75039
214-774-1300
214-389-4299
• George Ellis, Chief Financial Officer
• Jon Heidtke, General Manager
• Andrew Hunt, Chief Executive Officer

HOLIDAY BOWL
QUALCOMM STADIUM
PO BOX 601400
SAN DIEGO, CA 92160
619-285-5061
Fax: 619-281-7947
info@holidaybowl.com
www.holidaybowl.com
• Bruce Binkowski, Executive Director
(619) 283-5808
bink@holidaybowl.com
• Mark Neville, Director Communications
(619) 283-5808
mneville@holidaybowl.com
• Cheryl Tishue, Game Operations
Description:
Post-season collegiate football game,
involving the third selection from the Big 12
Conference vs. the runner-up from the
PAC-10 Conference. Game played at
Qualcomm Stadium, San Diego, CA.
Television: ESPN. In 1978 at Qualcom
Stadium

INDEPENDENCE BOWL
401 MARKET STREET
SUITE 120
SHREVEPORT, LA 71101
318-221-0712
888-414-2695
Fax: 318-221-7366
www.independencebowl.org
• John Hubbard, Chairman
• Troy J. Broussard, Vice Chairman
• Kyle McInnis, First Vice Chairman
• Paul Pratt, Second Vice Chairman
Description
Founded in 1976. Currently called the
PetroSun Independence Bowl, this game is
held at Independence Stadium in
Shreveport.

LAS VEGAS BOWL
SAM BOYD STADIUM
2140 PEBBLE RD
SUITE 200
LAS VEGAS, NV 89123
702-732-3912
Fax: 702-732-4481
www.lvbowl.com
• Dan Hanneke, Executive Director
• Mark Wallington, Media Relations
• Melissa Meacham-Grossman, Game
Operations
Description:
NCAA college football bowl game in which
Mountain West Conference first pick team
will play PAC 12 Conference #4 or #5 team.
Year Founded:
1992
Stadium:
Sam Boyd Stadium

LIBERTY BOWL
LIBERTY BOWL MEMORIAL STADIUM
335 S HOLLYWOOD STREET
MEMPHIS, TN 38104-5923
901-729-4344
general@libertybowl.org
www.libertybowl.org
• Harold Graeter, Associate Executive
Director
hgraeter@libertybowl.org
• Ron Higgins, Media Liaison
Description:
Founded in 1959. Champion of Conference
USA vs. Champion of Southeastern
Conference. Television: ESPN.

MIAMI BEACH BOWL
MARLINS PARK
501 MARLINS WAY
MIAMI, FL 33125
305-480-1342
miamibeachbowl.com
• Blake Guthrie, VP Operations
• Maureen Licursi, Director,
Marekting/Ticket Sales
Description:
Division I bowl competition.

MILITARY BOWL
NAVY-MARINE CORPS MEMORIAL
STADIUM
1742 NORTH ST. NW
ANNAPOLIS, MD 20036
202-776-2509
• Steve Beck, President/CEO
• Maureen Licursi, Marketing & Media
Director
• Bob Treseler, Director Corporate
Development & Sales
• Lauren Schweiter, Game Operations
• Josh Barr, Media
Description:
Post-season college football game.
Founded 2008. Television: ESPN
Sponsor:
Northrop; Grumman

MUSIC CITY BOWL
414 UNION STREET
SUITE 800
NASHVILLE, TN 37219
615-743-3130
Fax: 615-244-3540
generalinfo@nashvillesports.com
www.musiccitybowl.com
• Scott Ramsey, President/CEO
(615) 743-3122
• Dave Herrell, VP Marketing/Development
(615) 743-3124
• Gary Karl Alexander, Senior VP/COO
(165) 743-3132
Description:
Founded 1998. Southeastern Conference
team vs. Big Ten team. Location Coliseum
in Nashville Tennessee. Television: ESPN.

NEW ERA PINSTRIPE BOWL
YANKEE STADIUM
ONE EAST 161ST STREET
BRONX, NY 10451
646-977-8400
pinstripebowl@yankees.com
web.pinstripebowl.com
• Mark Holtzman, Executive Director
• Emily Hamel, Director
• Sarah Schuler, Senior Manager, Marketing

Founded:
2010

NEW MEXICO BOWL
UNIVERSITY STADIUM
801 UNIVERSITY SE
SUITE 104
ALBUQUERQUE, NM 87106
505-925-5999
Fax: 505-272-7131
www.gildannewmexicobowl.com
• Jeff Siembieda, Executive Director
jeffrey.c.siembieda@espn.com
• RaeAnn McKernan, Media Information
• Cary Colbert, Sup. Of Ops & Sales
Fulfillment
cary.l.colbert@espn.com
Description:
The New Mexico Bowl was first held in
2006. It takes place on the Saturday after
Christmas at University Stadium on the
University of New Mexico campus, and pits
the Mountain West Conference against the
Western Athletic Conference in the state's
only annual nationally televised sporting
event.

NEW ORLEANS BOWL
MERCEDES-BENZ SUPERDOME
2020 ST. CHARLES AVE
NEW ORLEANS, LA 70130
504-525-5678
Fax: 504-529-1622
www.neworleansbowl.org
• Alison Comeaux, Game Operations
• Allison Hjortsberg, Media Relations
• Tricia Lowe, Marketing/Sales
Stadium:
Superdome
Description:
Certified by NCAA in April 2001

DISCOVER ORANGE BOWL
14360 NW 77TH COURT
MIAMI LAKES, FL 33016
305-341-4700
Fax: 305-341-4771
www.orangebowl.org
• Eric L. Poms, CEO
• Kim Garcia, Director of Events
• Larry Wahl, VP Media & Public Relations
• Jose Braojos, Director Ticket Sales
Description:
NCAA postseason football bowl game
played at Pro Player Stadium. Game is part
of the Bowl Championship Series.
Television: ABC.
Publications:
ORANGE BOWL TODAY, four times
annually; Game Program; Media Guide;
Corporate Report, four times annually.
Stadium:
Sun Life

OUTBACK BOWL
4211 WEST BOY SCOUT BOULEVARD
SUITE 560
TAMPA, FL 33607
813-874-2695
Fax: 813-873-1959
info@outbackbowl.com
www.outbackbowl.com
• Jim McVay, President/CEO
• Mike Schulze, Director Communications
• Becky Weightman, Coordinator of Events
Description:
New Years Day football bowl game. Big 10

single sports

91

Conference vs. Southeastern Conference. Held at Raymond James Stadium in Tampa.
Founded:
In 1986.

POINSETTIA BOWL
QUALCOMM STADIUM
9449 FRIARS ROAD, L-55
SAN DIEGO, CA 92108
619-285-5061
info@holidaybowl.com
• Bruce Binkowski, Executive Director
(619) 283-5808
bink@holidaybowl.com
• Mark Neville, Director Communications
(619) 283-5808
mneville@holidaybowl.com
• Callye Cannheim, Marketing Services
Description
The Poinsettia Bowl features a Mountain West Conference team against one of several naval bases in the San Diego area. It is presented by the San Diego Credit Union.

POPEYES BAHAMAS BOWL
11001 RUSHMORE DRIVE
CHARLOTTE, NC 28277
704-973-5077
www.popeyesbahamasbowl.com
• Richard Giannini, Executive Director
• Lea Miller, Director Of Sales/Marketing
• T.R. Hollis, Event Coordinator
Description:
DI bowl game hosted in Nassau, Bahamas annually.

ROSE BOWL
391 SOUTH ORANGE GROVE BOULEVARD
PASADENA, CA 91184
626-449-4100
rosepr@rosemail.org
www.tournamentofroses.com
• P. Scott McKibben, Executive Director
(626) 449-4100
• Sheri Wish, Chief Revenue Officer
(626) 449-4100
• Kevin R. Ash, Chief Administrative Officer, Rose Bowl Game
(626) 449-4100
• Gina Chappin, Director of Media, Rose Bowl Game
(626) 449-4100
Description:
Known as 'The Granddaddy of Them All', the Rose Bowl Game kicked off a myriad of college football legacies in 1902. Since then, the game has showcased 17 Heisman Trophy winners, produced 29 national champions, featured 193 consesnsus All-Americans and honored 101 college legends by inducting them into the Rose Bowl Hall of Fame.
Publications:
Rose Parade Program, Rose Bowl Program, Rose Bowl Media Guide.
Teams:
Big Ten Champion vs. Pac-12 Champion
Stadium:
Rose Bowl

RUSSELL ATHLETIC BOWL
1610 W CHURCH ST.
ORLANDO, FL 32805-2451
407-423-2476
800-297-2695

Fax: 407-425-8451
www.fcsports.com
• Steve Hogan, Chief Executive Officer
• Carol Herbster, Executive Assistant
• Greg Creese, Director Communications

SENIOR BOWL
151 DAUPHIN STREET
MOBILE, AL 36602
251-438-2276
888-736-2695
Fax: 251-432-0409
srbowl@seniorbowl.com
www.seniorbowl.com
• Steve Hale, President/CEO
• Chris Morgan, Director of Sales & Marketing
chris@seniorbowl.com
• Kevin McDermond, Public Relations Director
• Sonya Rayburn, Sales & Community Affairs Director
sonya@seniorbowl.com
Description:
College All-Star game featuring the best college seniors coached by NFL coaching staffs.

ST. PETERSBERG BOWL
TROPICANA FIELD
ONE TROPICANA DRIVE
ST. PETERSBURG, FL 33705
727-825-3137
888-326-7297
• Brett Dulaney, Executive Director
• Carlos Padilla II, Manages Event Sponsorship and Marketing
• Jeff Famis, Media Contact
Description:
The St. Pete Bowl is a new bowl game first played in 2008. Held at Tropicana Field in St. Petersburg, it is sponsored by magicJack.

SUGAR BOWL
MERCEDES-BENZ SUPERDOME
2020 ST. CHARLES AVE
NEW ORLEANS, LA 70130
504-525-5678
www.allstatesugarbowl.org
• Bill Ferrantie, Executive Director
• Tricia Lowe, Marketing & Sales
• Allison Hjortsberg, Media
• Alison Comeaux, Game Operations
Sponsors:
Greater New Orleans Sports Hall of Fame, The Manning Award, The College Football Hall of Fame, the local chapter of the National Football Foundation.
Description:
Known for its oustanding tradition of providing the best action that college football has to offer.

SUN BOWL
4150 PINNACLE STREET
SUITE 100
EL PASO, TX 79902-3116
915-533-4416
800-915-BOWL
Fax: 915-533-0661
kristie@sunbowl.org
www.sunbowl.org
• Bernie Olivas, Executive Director
• Joe Daubach, Special Events Director
• Ellen Hughes, Ticket Manager
• Trenten Hillburn, Director Media Relations

• Pam Carter, Financial Manager
• Jay Pritchard, Marketing Director
Description:
Founded 1934. Year-round community organization for city of El Paso, organized to achieve (1) year-round activities which draw national recognition and publicity for El Paso, and (2) put on nationally prominent college football bowl game. Games played at Sun Bowl Stadium. PAC 10 #3 vs. Big 10 #5. Television: CBS. Other events include: Sierra Sun Classic Basketball Tournament; Savane College All America Golf Classic. Hosts the 2nd oldest collegiate bowl game.
Stadium:
Sun Bowl Stadium

TEXAS BOWL
RELIANT STADIUM
2 RELIANT PARK
HOUSTON, TX 77054-1373
832-667-2000
www.thetexasbowl.com
• Jamey Rootes, Executive Director
• Davey Fletcher, Marketing/Sales
• Amy Palcic, Media
• Callye Dannheim, Game Operations

Football, Professional Leagues/Teams

CANADIAN FOOTBALL LEAGUE/CFL
50 WELLINGTON STREET E
3RD FLOOR
TORONTO, ON, CANADA M5E 1C8
416-322-9650
Fax: 416-322-9651
www.cfl.ca
• Randy Ambrosie, Commissioner
History:
The Canadian Football League was founded in 1958, in Montreal, Quebec, after the Canadian Football Council (CFC) left the Canadian Rugby Union (CRU). Since 2010 the league has expanded stadiums and added the Ottawa Redblacks to its rosters.
Teams:
9
Founded:
1958

Teams:

BC LIONS
800 WEST PENDER
UNIT 215
VANCOUVER, Bc, CANADA V6C 1J8
604-930-5466
fanservices@bclions.com
www.bclions.com
• Amar S. Doman, Owner
• Duane Vienneau, President
• Neil McEvoy, Vice President, Football Operations
• Buck Pierce, Head Coach
Home Field:
BC Place. Seating capacity 54,500.

CALGARY STAMPEDERS
MCMAHON STADIUM
1817 CROWCHILD TRAIL NW
CALGARY, AB, CANADA T2M 4R6
403-289-0205
www.stampeders.com
• Jay McNeil, President
• Dave Dickenson, General Manager & Head Coach

Home Field:
McMahon Stadium. Seating capacity 46,020.

EDMONTON ELKS
THE BRICK FIELD AT COMMONWEALTH
STADIUM
11000 STADIUM ROAD
EDMONTON, AB, CANADA T5H 4E2
780-448-3557
Fax: 780-448-2531
service@goelks.com
www.goelks.com
• Rick LeLacheur, Interim President & CEO
• Chris Jones, General Manager & Head Coach
Home Field:
Commonwealth Stadium. Seating capacity
60,081.

HAMILTON TIGER-CATS
TIM HORTONS FIELD
64 MELROSE AVE N
HAMILTON, ON, CANADA L8L 8C1
905-547-2287
Fax: 905-547-8423
customerservice@ticats.ca
ticats.ca
• Scott Mitchell, CEO
• Matt Afinec, President & COO, Business
Operations
mafinec@ticats.ca
• Orlondo Steinauer, President, Football
Operations
• Scott Milanovich, Head Coach & Offensive
Coordinator
Home Field:
Tim Hortons Field. Seating capacity 23,218.

MONTREAL ALOUETTES
4545 PIERRE-DE-COUBERTIN
MONTREAL, QC, CANADA H1V 0B2
S14-787-2500
Fax: 514-787-2565
info@montrealalouettes.com
www.montrealalouettes.com
• Pierre Karl Peladeau, Owner
• Mark Weightman, President & CEO
• Danny Maciocia, General Manager
• Jason Maas, Head Coach
Home Field:
Percival Molson Memorial Stadium. Seating
capacity 25,012.

OTTAWA REDBLACKS
TD PLACE
1015 BANK STREET
OTTAWA, ON, CANADA K1S 3W7
613-232-6767 EXT 1
Fax: 613-232-5586
info@ottawaredblacks.com
www.ottawaredblacks.com
• Mark Goudie, President & Chief Executive
Officer
• Bob Dyce, Head Coach
Home Field:
TD Place. Seating Capacity 24,000.

SASKATCHEWAN ROUGHRIDERS
1734 ELPHINSTONE STREET
TICKET OFFICE
REGINA, SK, CANADA S4P 1K1
888-474-3377
www.riderville.com
• Craig Reynolds, President & CEO
• Jeremy O'Day, VP, Football Operations &
General Manager
• Corey Mace, Head Coach & Defensive
Coordinator
Home Field:
Mosaic Stadium at Taylor Field. Seating
capacity 33,350.

TORONTO ARGONAUTS
45 MANITOBA DRIVE
TORONTO, ON, CANADA M6K 3C3

416-341-2746
ticketsales@argonauts.ca
www.argonauts.ca
• Michael (Pinball) Clemons, General Manager
• Ryan Dinwiddie, Head Coach & Offensive
Coordinator
Home Field:
BMO Field. Seating capacity 30,991.

WINNIPEG BLUE BOMBERS
INVESTORS GROUP FIELD
315 CHANCELLOR MATHESON ROAD
WINNIPEG, MB, CANADA R3T 1Z2
204-784-7448
bbombers@bluebombers.com
www.bluebombers.com
• Kyle Walters, General Manager
• Mike O'Shea, Head Coach
Home Field:
Investors Group Field. Seating capacity 32,343.

INDOOR FOOTBALL LEAGUE
1607 S LOCUST STREET
SUITE A
GRAND ISLAND, NE 68802
804-643-7277
info@goifl.com
www.goifl.com
• Todd Tryon, Commissioner
• Robert Loving, Chief Financial Officer
Description:
The Indoor Football League is a
professional football league serving the
purpose of entertaining communities and
promoting players to the NFL.
Teams:
14

Teams:

ARIZONA RATTLERS
FOOTPRINT CENTER
201 E JEFFERSON ST
PHOENIX, AZ 85004
602-379-2000
info@azrattlers.com
www.azrattlers.com
• Ron Shurts, Owner
• Jeff Jarnigan, General Manager
• Kevin Guy, Team President/Head Coach

BAY AREA PANTHERS
SAP CENTER
525 W SANTA CLARA ST
SAN JOSE, CA 95113
408-287-7070
www.bayareapanthers.com
• David Eisenberg, President
deisenberg@bayareapanthers.com
• Rob Keefe, Head Coach/President, Football
Operations
rkeefe@bayareapanthers.com

COLUMBUS WILD DOGS
225 E SPRING ST
COLUMBUS, OH 43215
614-826-7120
info@columbuswilddogs.com
www.columbuswilddogs.com
• Dave Whinham, President, CEO & General
Manager
• Titus Donnell, VP, Finance & Administration
• Bobby Olive, Head Coach

DAKOTA BUCKS
315 S 5TH ST
BISMARCK, ND 58504
701-595-0771
dakotabucks.com
• Gregory Schuh, General Manager
(701) 475-1307
gregs@bismarckbucks.com

DUKE CITY GLADIATORS
7802 MENAUL BOULEVARD NE
ALBUQUERQUE, NM 87110
505-226-8006 EXT 0
www.dukecitygladiators.com
• Gina Prieskorn-Thomas, Owner
(505) 261-1558
thomasginam@yahoo.com
• Fred Griggs, General Manager & Head Coach

FRISCO FIGHTERS
COMERICA CENTER
2601 AVENUE OF THE STARS
FRISCO, TX 75035
214-387-5600 EXT 0
info@friscofighters.com
www.friscofighters.com
• Joey Barnard, Director, Football Operations
• Andre Coles, Head Coach

GREEN BAY BLIZZARD
RESCH CENTER
820 ARMED FORCES DR
GREEN BAY, WI 54304
800-895-0071
office@greenbayblizzard.com
www.greenbayblizzard.com
• Kathy Treankler, Owner
• Larry Treankler, Owner
• Corey Roberson, General Manager & Head
Coach

IOWA BARNSTORMERS
WELLS FARGO ARENA
233 CENTER ST
DES MOINES, IA 50309
515-633-2255
www.theiowabarnstormers.com
• Juli Pettit, General Manager
julipettit@theiowabarnstormers.com
• Dave Mogensen, Head Coach
coachmogensen@theiowabarnstormers.com

MASSACHUSETTS PIRATES
2 MOUNT ROYAL AVENUE
SUITE 400
MARLBOROUGH, MA 01752
508-452-6277
contact@masspiratesfootball.com
masspiratesfootball.com
• Jawad Yatim, Co-Owner/President/General
Manager
• Ameer Ismail, Head Coach

NORTHERN ARIZONA WRANGLERS
FINDLAY TOYOTA CENTER
3201 MAIN ST
PRESCOTT VALLEY, AZ 86314
928-772-1819
www.nazwranglers.com
• Fred DePalma, Owner & President
• Ron James, Head Coach
ronjames@nazwranglers.com

SAN DIEGO STRIKE FORCE
3636 CAMINO DEL RIO N
SUITE 120
SAN DIEGO, CA 92108
619-340-1300
info@sdstrikeforce.com
www.sdstrikeforce.com
• Geno Gerbo, General Manager
• Taylor Genuser, Head Coach

SIOUX FALLS STORM
DENNY SANFORD PREMIER CENTER
1201 N W AVE
SIOUX FALLS, SD 57104
605-367-7288
800-338-3177
Fax: 605-338-1463
admin@siouxfallsstorm.com
www.siouxfallsstorm.com
• Andre Fields, Head Coach
• Peyton Riggs, Offensive Coordinator

SPOKANE SHOCK
157 S HOWARD STREET
SUITE 100
SPOKANE, WA 99201
509-934-2255
thespokaneshock.com
• Sam Adams, Owner & Chief Executive Officer
• Cedric Walker, Head Coach

TUCSON SUGAR SKULLS
KINO SPORTS COMPLEX
2500 E AJO WAY
TUCSON, AZ 85713
520-573-3000
info@tucsonsugarskulls.com
www.tucsonsugarskulls.com
• Cathy Guy, Owner
• Billy Back, Head Coach

NATIONAL FOOTBALL LEAGUE/NFL
345 PARK AVENUE
NEW YORK, NY 10154
www.nfl.com
• Roger Goodell, Commissioner
• Troy Vincent, Executive VP, Football Operations
• Dawn Aponte, Chief Football Administration Officer
• Kimberly Fields, Senior VP, Football Business Strategy
• Tracy Perlman, Senior VP, Player Operations
• Perry Fewell, Senior VP, Officiating Communications
• Akil Coad, VP, Football Operations & Compliance
Description:
Founded 1920. Promotes, regulates and governs 32 professional football franchises in the U.S.
Publications:
NFL RECORD & FACT BOOK, annual; GAMEDAY Magazine, for each game; NFL REPORT, quarterly.

Teams:

ARIZONA CARDINALS
STATE FARM STADIUM
1 CARDINALS DRIVE
GLENDALE, AZ 85305
602-379-0101
800-999-1402
askquestions@cardinals.nfl.net
www.azcardinals.com
• Michael J. Bidwill, Owner
• Monti Ossenfort, General Manager
• Jonathan Gannon, Head Coach
• Jeremy Walls, Chief Operating Officer
• Melissa Gaspard, VP, Executive Operations
• Steve Bomar, VP, Ticket Operations
• Lisa Manning, Senior VP, Marketing
• David Koeninger, Chief Legal Officer
• Rob Kisiel, VP, Player Personnel
• Shaun Mayo, Chief People Officer
• Drew Krueger, Head Athletic Trainer
• Matt Harriss, Director, Football Administration
Description:
State Farm Stadium. Seating capacity: 63,400.
Founded:
1920

ATLANTA FALCONS
4400 FALCON PARKWAY M
FLOWERY BRANCH, GA 30542
770-965-3115
fans@falcons.nfl.com
www.atlantafalcons.com
• Arthur Blank, Owner/Chair
• Rich McKay, Chief Executive Officer
• Greg Beadles, President
• Terry Fontenot, General Manager
• Raheem Morris, Head Coach

Founded:
1966
Description:
Mercedes-Benz Stadium. Seating capacity: 71,000.

BALTIMORE RAVENS
M&T BANK STADIUM
1101 RUSSELL STREET
BALTIMORE, MD 21230
410-261-7283
contact.us@ravens.nfl.net
www.baltimoreravens.com
• Stephen J. Bisciotti, Owner
• Eric DeCosta, Executive VP/General Manager
• John Harbaugh, Head Coach
• Simon Gelan, Senior VP, Operations
• Joey Cleary, Professional Scout
• Baker Koppelman, Senior VP, Ticket Sales & Operations
• Brad Downs, Senior VP, Marketing
• Jeff Goering, Chief Financial Officer
• Kevin Rochlitz, Chief Sales Officer
Founded:
1996
Description:
M&T Bank Stadium. Seating capacity: 70,745.

BUFFALO BILLS
HIGHMARK STADIUM
ONE BILLS DRIVE
ORCHARD PARK, NY 14127
www.buffalobills.com
• Terry Pegula, Owner/CEO/President
• Kim Pegula, Owner
• Brandon Beane, General Manager
• Sean McDermott, Head Coach
• Malik Boyd, Director, Pro Personnel
• Matt Bazirgan, Director, College Scouting
• Kevin Meganck, Senior VP, Football Administration
• John Polka, Executive Director, Stadium Operations
Description:
Highmark Stadium. Seating capacity: 71,608.

CAROLINA PANTHERS
BANK OF AMERICA STADIUM
800 SOUTH MINT STREET
CHARLOTTE, NC 28202
704-358-7000
feedback@panthers.nfl.com
www.panthers.com
• David A. Tepper, Owner
• Dan Morgan, President, Football Operations & General Manager
• Dave Canales, Head Coach
• Cole Spencer, Executive Director, Player Personnel
• Dave Dickerson, VP/Chief Financial Officer
• Bryan Lodigiani, VP, Ticket Sales & Services
Description:
Bank of America Stadium. Seating capacity: 74,867.
Founded:
In 1993.

CHICAGO BEARS
SOLDIER FIELD
1410 MUSEUM CAMPUS DRIVE
CHICAGO, IL 60605
312-235-7205
www.chicagobears.com
• George H. McCaskey, Chair
• Kevin Warren, President & CEO
• Ben Johnson, Head Coach
• Brek Ackley, Director, College Scouting
• Brendan Pierce, Director, Ticket Sales & Service
• Scott Hagel, Senior VP, Marketing & Communications
• Trey Koziol, Director, Player Personnel
• Karen Murphy, Chief Financial Officer
Description:
Soldier Field. Seating capacity: 61,500.

CINCINNATI BENGALS
1 PAYCOR STADIUM
CINCINNATI, OH 45202
513-455-8484
866-774-4776
webmaster@bengals.nfl.net
www.bengals.com
• Mike Brown, Owner & President
• Zac Taylor, Head Coach
• Duke Tobin, Director, Player Personnel
• Steven Radicevic, Director, Professional Scouting
• Bob Bedinghaus, Director, Business Development
• John Helmler, Chief Financial Officer
• Duane Haring, Director, Ticket Sales & Service
Founded:
In 1967.
Stadium:
Paycor Stadium. Seating capacity: 65,515.

CLEVELAND BROWNS
76 LOU GROZA BOULEVARD
BEREA, OH 44017
440-891-5000
fansquad@clevelandbrowns.com
www.clevelandbrowns.com
• J.W. Johnson, Executive VP & Partner
• Andrew Berry, General Manager/Executive VP, Football Ops
• Kevin Stefanski, Head Coach
• Glenn Cook, VP, Player Personnel
• Mike Cetta, Director, Scouting Research
• Jason Decker, Director, Ticket Operations
• Laurie Rice, Director, Finance
Description:
Huntington Bank Field. Seating capacity: 67,431.
Founded:
In 1945.

DALLAS COWBOYS
AT&T STADIUM
ONE AT&T WAY
ARLINGTON, TX 76011
817-892-8000
www.dallascowboys.com
• Jerry W. Jones, Owner/President/General Manager
• Stephen Jones, COO/Director, Player Personnel
• Charlotte Jones, Executive VP/Chief Brand Officer
• Brian Schottenheimer, Head Coach
• Jerry Jones, Jr., Executive VP, Sales & Marketing
Description:
AT&T Stadium. Seating capacity: 80,000.
Founded:
In 1960.

DENVER BRONCOS
13655 BRONCOS PARKWAY
ENGLEWOOD, CO 80112
303-649-9000
suggestions@broncos.nfl.net
www.denverbroncos.com
• Greg Penner, Owner & CEO
• George Paton, General Manager
• Damani Leech, President
• Kelly Kleine Van Calligan, Executive Director, Football Operations
• Sean Payton, Head Coach
• Chip Conway, Senior VP, Operations
• A.J. Durso, Director, Pro Personnel
• Abby Miller, Senior Director, Ticket Operations
• Bjorn Westlund, Senior Director, Events & Marketing
Description:
Empower Field at Mile High. Seating capacity: 76,125.
Founded:
In 1960.

DETROIT LIONS
FORD FIELD
2000 BRUSH STREET
DETROIT, MI 48226
313-262-2000
www.detroitlions.com
- Sheila Ford Hamp, Principal Owner/Chair
- Rod Wood, President/CEO
- Brad Holmes, Executive VP/General Manager
- Dan Campbell, Head Coach
- Rob Lohman, Director, Pro Scouting
- Brian Hudspeth, Director, College Scouting
- Kelly Kozole, Senior VP, Business Development
- Emily Griffin, VP, Marketing
- Brad Holmes, General Manager
Description:
Ford Field. Seating capacity: 65,000.
Founded:
In 1934.

GREEN BAY PACKERS
LAMBEAU FIELD ATRIUM
1265 LOMBARDI AVENUE
GREEN BAY, WI 54304
920-569-7500
Fax: 920-569-7301
www.packers.com
- Mark Murphy, President/CEO
- Brian Gutekunst, General Manager
- Matt LaFleur, Head Coach
- Russ Ball, Executive VP/Director, Football Operations
- Jason McDonough, Director, Ticketing & Premium Seating
- Gabrielle Valdez Dow, VP, Marketing & Fan Engagement
- Ed Policy, COO & General Counsel
- Maureen Smith, Chief Financial Officer
Founded:
In 1919.
Description:
Lambeau Field. Seating capacity: 81,441.

HOUSTON TEXANS
NRG STADIUM
TWO NRG PARK
HOUSTON, TX 77054-1573
888-849-4839
Fax: 832-832-667-2191
fanfeedback@houstontexans.com
www.houstontexans.com
- Cal McNair, Chair/CEO
- Janice McNair, Co-Founder/Senior Chair
- Nick Caserio, EVP & General Manager
- Mike Tomon, President, Business Operations
- Gary Garcia, SVP, Business Development, Tickets
- Brandyn White, Senior Director, Marketing
- Marilan Logan, Senior VP/Chief Financial Officer/Treasurer
Description:
NRG Stadium. Seating capacity: 72,220.
Founded:
In 2002.

INDIANAPOLIS COLTS
7001 W 56TH STREET
INDIANAPOLIS, IN 46254
317-297-2658
800-805-2658
Fax: 317-297-8971
webmaster@colts.com
www.colts.com
- Jim Irsay, Owner/CEO
- Chris Ballard, General Manager
- Shane Steichen, Head Coach
- Kevin Rogers, Director, Player Personnel
- Jon Shaw, Director, Pro Scouting
- Matt Terpening, Director, College Scouting
- Jim Van Dam, VP, Ticket Sales & Service
- Mike Bluem, Director, Football Administration
- Pete Ward, COO
- EJ Tolentino, Chief Financial Officer
- Matt Conti, VP, Communications
- Roger VanDerSnick, Chief Sales & Marketing Officer

Description:
Lucas Oil Stadium. Seating capacity: 63,000.
Founded:
In 1953, Baltimore Maryland. Relocated to Indianapolis in 1984.

JACKSONVILLE JAGUARS
EVERBANK STADIUM
1 EVERBANK STADIUM DRIVE
JACKSONVILLE, FL 32202
904-633-2000
myexperience@jaguars.com
www.jaguars.com
- Shad Khan, Owner
- Mark Lamping, President
- James Gladstone, General Manager
- Liam Coen, Head Coach
- Hamza Ahmad, Director, Football Operations
- Dejuan Polk, Director, Pro Scouting
- Michael Davis, Director, College Scouting
- Tim Bishko, Director, Ticket Operations
- Stephanie Lynn, Chief Marketing Officer
- Dylan Morton, VP, Football Communications
Description:
EverBank Stadium (formerly TIAA Bank Field). Seating capacity: 67,814 (expandable to 82,000).
Founded:
In 1995.

KANSAS CITY CHIEFS
ONE ARROWHEAD DRIVE
KANSAS CITY, MO 64129
816-920-9300
fanexperience@chiefs.com
www.chiefs.com
- Clark Hunt, Chair/CEO
- Mark Donovan, President
- Brett Veach, General Manager
- Andy Reid, Head Coach
- Tim Terry, Director, Player Personnel & Pro Scouting
- Ryne Nutt, Director, College Scouting
- Kirsten Krug, EVP, Business Development
- Dave Higdon, EVP, Communications
- Dan Crumb, Chief Financial Officer
Description:
GEHA Field at Arrowhead Stadium. Seating capacity: 76,416.
Founded:
In 1963.

LAS VEGAS RAIDERS
ALLEGIANT STADIUM
3333 AL DAVIS WAY
LAS VEGAS, NV 89118
510-864-5000
feedback@raiders.com
www.raiders.com
- Mark Davis, Owner
- Sandra Douglass Morgan, President
- John Spytek, General Manager
- Antonio Pierce, Head Coach
- Dwayne Joseph, Director, Pro Personnel
- Brandon Yeargan, Director, College Scouting
- Will Kiss, Public Affairs
Description:
Allegiant Stadium. Seating capacity: 65,000.
Founded:
In 1960.

LOS ANGELES CHARGERS
TRAINING FACILITY, BUSINESS OFFICE
(HOAG PERFORMANCE CENTER)
3333 SUSAN ST. BOULEVARD
CARSON, CA 92626
714-540-7100
877-242-7437
www.chargers.com
- Dean A. Spanos, Owner/Chair
- Jeanne M. Bonk, Executive VP & COO
- Joe Hortiz, General Manager
- Jim Harbaugh, Head Coach
- Dennis Abraham, Director, Pro Scouting
- Kevin Kelly, Director, College Scouting
- John Spanos, President, Football Operations

Description:
SoFi Stadium. Seating capacity: 70,240.
Founded:
In 1959.

LOS ANGELES RAMS
SOFI STADIUM
1001 STADIUM DR
INGLEWOOD, CA 90301
www.therams.com
- Stan Kroenke, Owner/Chair
- Kevin Demoff, President
- Les Snead, General Manager
- Sean McVay, Head Coach
- Sophie Harlan, Director, Football Operations
- James Gladstone, Director, Scouting Strategy
Description:
SoFi Stadium. Seating capacity: 70,240.
Founded:
In 1936.

MIAMI DOLPHINS
HARD ROCK STADIUM
347 DON SHULA DRIVE
MIAMI, FL 33056
305-943-8000
GuestExperience@HardRockStadium.com
www.miamidolphins.com
- Stephen M. Ross, Chair & Managing General Partner
- Tom Garfinkel, Vice Chair/President/CEO
- Chris Grier, General Manager
- Mike McDaniel, Head Coach
- Matt Winston, Assistant Director, College Scouting
- Wess Serrato, Senior Director, Ticket Operations
- Pri Shumate, SVP, Chief Marketing Officer
- Chris Clements, Chief Financial Officer
Description:
Hard Rock Stadium. Seating capacity: 64,767.
Founded:
In 1966.

MINNESOTA VIKINGS
2600 VIKINGS CIRCLE
EAGAN, MN 55121
952-828-6500
customerservice@vikings.nfl.net
www.vikings.com
- Zygi Wilf, Co-Chair/Owner
- Mark Wilf, Co-Chair/Owner
- Kewsi Adofo-Mensah, General Manager
- Kevin O'Connell, Head Coach
- Rob Brzezinski, Executive VP, Football Operations
- Ryan Grigson, SVP, Player Personnel
- Rich Wang, Director, Sales Analytics & Engagement
- Martin Nance, Executive VP/Chief Marketing Officer
- Kate Shibilski, Executive VP/Chief Financial Officer
Description:
US Bank Stadium. Seating capacity: 66,860 (expandable to 73,000).
Founded:
In 1960.

NEW ENGLAND PATRIOTS
GILLETTE STADIUM
1 PATRIOT PLACE
FOXBOROUGH, MA 02035
508-543-8200
800-543-1776
www.patriots.com
- Robert Kraft, Chair & CEO
- Jonathan A. Kraft, President
- Mike Vrabel, Head Coach
- Matt Groh, Director, Player Personnel
Description:
Gillette Stadium. Seating capacity: 64,628.
Founded:
In 1960.

NEW ORLEANS SAINTS
CAESARS SUPERDOME
1500 SUGAR BOWL DR
NEW ORLEANS, LA 70112
www.neworleanssaints.com
• Gayle Benson, Owner & CEO
• Dennis Lauscha, President
• Mickey Loomis, General Manager/EVP
• Kellen Moore, Head Coach
• Will Martinez, Pro Scouting Coordinator
• Ziad Qubti, College Scouting Coordinator
• Mike Stanfield, Senior VP, Sales
• Ben Hales, Senior VP/Chief Operating Officer
• Khai Harley, Executive VP, Football
Administration
• Greg Bensel, Senior VP, Communications
Description:
Caesars Superdome. Seating capacity: 73,208
(expandable to 76,468).
Founded:
In 1967.

NEW YORK GIANTS
METLIFE STADIUM
ONE METLIFE STADIUM DRIVE
EAST RUTHERFORD, NJ 07073
www.giants.com
• John K. Mara, Esq., President/CEO
• Steve Tisch, Chair/Executive VP
• Joe Schoen, SVP/General Manager
• Brian Daboll, Head Coach
• Kevin Abrams, SVP, Football Operations
• Chris Mara, Senior VP, Player Personnel
• Amy Matlins, Director, Ticketing
• Christine Procops, Senior VP/Chief Financial
Officer
• Pat Hanlon, Senior VP, Communications
Description:
Metlife Stadium. Seating capacity: 82,500.
Founded:
In 1925.

NEW YORK JETS
METLIFE STADIUM
ONE METLIFE STADIUM DRIVE
EAST RUTHERFORD, NJ 07073
973-549-4800
800-469-5387
www.newyorkjets.com
• Robert Wood Johnson, Chair
• Hymie Elhai, President
• Darren Mougey, General Manager
• Aaron Glenn, Head Coach
• Brian Friedman, EVP & COO
• Ray Agnew, Pro Scout
• Jeff Hecker, VP, Ticket Operations
• Timothy Kemp, VP, Marketing
• David Szott, Director, Player Development
Description:
Metlife Stadium. Seating capacity: 82,500.
Founded:
In 1960.

PHILADELPHIA EAGLES
LINCOLN FINANCIAL FIELD
ONE LINCOLN FINANCIAL FIELD WAY
PHILADELPHIA, PA 19148
215-463-2500
www.philadelphiaeagles.com
• Jeffrey Lurie, Chair/CEO
• Don Smolenski, President
• Howie Roseman, Executive VP/General
Manager
• Nick Sirianni, Head Coach
• Jen Kavanagh, Senior VP, Media & Marketing
• Frank Gumienny, Senior VP & COO
• Norman Vossschulte, VP, Fan Experience &
Sustainability
• Brandon Hunt, Senior Director, Scouting
• Anthony Patch, Senior Director, College
Scouting
Description:
Lincoln Financial Field. Seating capacity:
67,594.
Founded:
In 1933.

PITTSBURGH STEELERS
ACRISURE STADIUM
100 ART ROONEY AVENUE
PITTSBURGH, PA 15212
412-432-6018
Fax: 412-432-7878
www.steelers.com
• Arthur J. Rooney, II, President
• Omar Khan, General Manager
• Mike Tomlin, Head Coach
• Ryan Huzjak, VP, Sales & Marketing
• Doug Stuver, VP, Finance
• Dan Colbert, Director, College Scouting
• Ben Lentz, Director, Ticket Operations
• Sheldon White, Director, Pro Scouting
Description:
Acrisure Stadium. Seating capacity: 68,400.
Founded:
In 1933.

SAN FRANCISCO 49ERS
LEVI'S STADIUM
4900 MARIE P DEBARTOLO WAY
SANTA CLARA, CA 95054
www.49ers.com
• Denise DeBartolo York, Co-Chair
• John York, Co-Chair
• Jed York, CEO
• Al Guido, President, Business Operations
• John Lynch, President, Football Operations &
General Manager
• Kyle Shanahan, Head Coach
• Francine Melendez Hughes, EVP & General
Manager, Stadium Operations
• Brent Schoeb, Chief Revenue/Marketing
Officer
• Fred Gammage III, Director, Pro Scouting
• Dominic DeCicco, Director, College Scouting
• Brad Dugan, Senior Director, Ticketing &
Public Events
Description:
Levi's Stadium. Seating capacity: 68,500.
Founded:
In 1946.

SEATTLE SEAHAWKS
LUMEN FIELD
800 OCCIDENTAL AVENUE S
SEATTLE, WA 98134
888-635-4295
CustomerService@seahawks.com
www.seahawks.com
• Jody Allen, Chair
• Chuck Arnold, President
• John Schneider, President, Football
Operations & General Manager
• Mike MacDonald, Head Coach
• Nolan Teasley, Assistant General Manager
• Matt Berry, VP, Player Acquisition
• Chris Lawrence, VP, Tickets & Premium
• Tyson Flandreau, VP, Brand & Marketing
• Pete Fonfara, VP, Finance
Description:
Lumen Field. Seating capacity: 68,740.
Founded:
In 1976.

TAMPA BAY BUCCANEERS
ADVENTHEALTH TRAINING CENTER
ONE BUCCANEER PLACE
TAMPA, FL 33607
813-870-2700
800-795-2827
www.buccaneers.com
• Bryan Glazer, Owner/Co-Chair
• Jason Licht, General Manager
• Todd Bowles, Head Coach
• Mike Biehl, Director, Player Personnel
• Rob McCartney, Director, Player Personnel
• Shane Scannell, Director, Pro Scouting
• Shelton Quarles, Director, Football Operations
• Brian Ford, Chief Operating Officer
Description:
Raymond James Stadium. Seating capcity:
69,218.
Founded:
In 1976.

TENNESSEE TITANS
NISSAN STADIUM
ONE TITANS WAY
NASHVILLE, TN 37213
615-565-4000
www.titansonline.com
• Amy Adams Strunk, Owner & Co-Chair
• Kenneth S. Adams, IV, Co-Chair
• Burke Nihill, President/CEO
• Mike Borgonzi, General Manager
• Brian Callahan, Head Coach
• Adam Nuse, SVP/Chief Revenue Officer
• Reggie McKenzie, VP, Player Personnel
• Chris Sprunger, VP, Ticket Operations &
Strategy
• Brian Gardner, Director, Pro Scouting
• Jon Salge, Director, College Scouting
Description:
Nissan Stadium. Seating capacity: 69,143.
Founded:
1960 as the Houston Oilers, Tennessee Oilers
in 1997, and the Tennessee Titans in 1999.

WASHINGTON COMMANDERS
1600 FEDEX WAY
NORTH ENGLEWOOD, MD 20785
www.commanders.com
• Josh Harris, Managing Partner
• Mark Clouse, President, Business Operations
• Adam Peters, General Manager
• Dan Quinn, Head Coach
• Craig Fischer, Chief Financial Officer
Arena:
Northwest Stadium (formerly Commanders Field
and FedEx Field). Seating capacity: 62,000.
Founded:
In 1932.

UNITED STATES WOMEN'S FOOTBALL LEAGUE
ERIE, PA
814-897-5880
WSFLContact@gmail.com
www.facebook.com/wsflfrontoffice

Teams:

CINCINNATI SIZZLE
CINCINNATI, OH
cincinnatisizzle@gmail.com
cincysizzle.wixsite.com/cincinnatisizzle
• Charles Pankey, Jr., Head Coach

DETROIT PROWL
DETROIT, MI
info@detroitprowl.com
www.detroitprowl.com

MICHIGAN QUEENS
26150 5 MILE
SUITE 15
REDFORD, MI 48240
313-909-4666
keith@getlife.biz
leagues.bluesombrero.com/michiganqueenswo
mensfootballclub

RVA LADY TOMAHAWKS
RICHMOND, VA
rvaladytomahawks.com
• Shebeney Jackson, Owner
• Jason Niles, General Manager/Line Coach
• Mike Hickam, Head Coach

SOUTH CAROLINA SCORPIONS
IRMO, SC
803-983-8246
carolinascorpions.com

TENNESSEE THUNDER FOOTBALL
423-707-8007
tnthunderwomensfootball@gmail.com
www.facebook.com/TriCitiesThunder

WOMEN'S FOOTBALL ALLIANCE / WFA
30909 PALM DR
EXTER, CA 93221
info@wfaprofootball.com
wfaprofootball.com
• Lisa King, Commissioner
(559) 328-4321
lisa.king@wfaprofootball.com
• Wyndy Flato, Director, Operations
(303) 993-9945
wyn.dominy@wfaprofootball.com
• Chris Miller, Director, Officials
officials@wfaprofootball.com
Description:
Women's football league and partner with
Minor League Foorball Allinace (MLFA).
Year Founded:
2009
Teams:
60 active for 2025 season
WFA Pro:
Alabama Fire; Arlington Impact; Boston
Renegades; Cali War; Dallas Elite
Mustangs; D.C. Divas; Houston Energy;
Mile High Blaze; Minnesota Vixen; Nevada
Storm; New York Wolves; Pittsburgh
Passion; St. Louis Slam; Tampa Bay Inferno
Division 2:
Atlanta Rage; Austin Outlaws; Baltimore
Nighthawks; Capital City Savages; Carolina
Phoenix; Columbus Chaos; Derby City
Dynamite; Detroit Venom; Grand Rapids
Tidal Waves; Jacksonville Dixie Blues;
Miami Fury; Nebraska Pride; Oklahoma City
Lady Force; Portland Fighting Shockwave;
Sun City Stealth; Tri-State Warriors; Vegas
NVaders; West Palm Beach Coyotes
Division 3:
Arizona Outkast; Capital Pioneers; Cedar
Raptors; Central Valley Chaos; Cincinnati
Cougars; Connecticut Nightmare; East
Tennessee Valkyrie; Harrisburg Havoc; Iowa
Phoenix; Maine Mayhem; Midwest Mountain
Lions; Minnesota Minx; Music City Mizfits;
New Hampshire Rebellion; New Mexico
Banitas; New York Knockout; Oklahoma
Rage; Oregon Cougars; Orlando Anarchy;
Raleigh Express; Richmond Black Widows;
Rocky Mountain Thunderkatz; Sioux Falls
Snow Leopards; Upstate Lady Predators;
Virginia Panthers; Wasatch Warriors;
Zydeco Spice

Teams:

ALABAMA FIRE
BIRMINGHAM, AL
alabamafirefootball@gmail.com
www.facebook.com/alabamafire
• Cedric Lane, Head Coach
Founded:
2015

ARIZONA OUTKAST
4201 E KNOX ROAD
PHOENIX, AR 85044
officialazoutkast@gmail.com
www.azoutkastfootball.com
• Joe Griffin, Head Coach
Founded:
2011

ARLINGTON IMPACT
1015 E BROAD
MANSFIELD, TX 76063
817-226-6359
• Jeanette Fuller, Owner
• Brandon Lacy, Head Coach
Founded:
2011

ATLANTA RAGE
ATLANTA, GA 85044
404-993-2023
infoatlantarage@gmail.com
atlrage.com
• Blair Clark, Head Coach
Founded:
2022

AUSTIN OUTLAWS
HOUSE PARK
1301 SHOAL CREEK BLVD
AUSTIN, TX 78701
512-796-0108
austinoutlawsinfo@yahoo.com
www.austinoutlaws.com
• Jason Barlow, Head Coach
Founded:
2001

BALTIMORE NIGHTHAWKS
P.O. BOX 2151
BALTIMORE, MD 21203
info@BaltimoreNighthawks.com
baltimorenighthawks.com
• Tanya A. Bryan, CEO & Founder
• Mike Lynn, Head Coach
Founded:
2007

BOSTON RENEGADES
HARRY DELLA RUSSO STADIUM
75 PARK AVE
REVERE, MA 02151
info@bostonrenegadesfootball.org
www.bostonrenegadesfootball.org
• John Johnson, Head Coach
Founded:
2015

CALI WAR
LOS ANGELES, CA
caliwarteam@gmail.com
caliwar.com
• Jason Grant, Head Coach
Founded:
2018

CAPITAL CITY SAVAGES
LANSING, MI
thecapitalcitysavages@gmail.com
www.facebook.com/CapitalCitySavages
• Andre Broach, Head Coach
Founded:
2017

CAPITAL PIONEERS
SALEM, OR
president@salemwomensfootball.org
www.salemwomensfootball.org/pioneers
Founded:
2019

CAROLINA PHOENIX
GREENSBORO, NC
carolinaphoenix@gmail.com
thecarolinaphoenix.com
• Marilyn Williams, Founder
• Carla Hauser, Owner
• Maria Ormond, Head Coach & Co-Owner
Founded:
2006

CEDAR RAPTORS
CEDAR RAPIDS, IA 52405
cedarraptors@gmail.com
www.cedarraptors.com
• Quinton Ray, Head Coach
Founded:
2023

CENTRAL VALLEY CHAOS
BAKERSFIELD, CA
661-472-7254
centralvalleychaos@gmail.com
centralvalleychaos.com
• Keith Powell, Owner
• Dave Gambill, General Manager
• Tracy Terry, Head Coach
Founded:
2021

CINCINNATI COUGARS
CINCINNATI, OH
hello@cincinnaticougars.org
cincinnaticougars.org
• Angela Mason, President
• Travis Connor, Head Coach
Founded:
2022

COLUMBUS CHAOS
COLUMBUS, OH
614-354-6968
columbuswft@gmail.com
columbuschaos.com
• C.J. Johnson, Co-Owner
• Staci Alkula, Co-Owner
Founded:
2021

D.C. DIVAS
12240 BOND ST.
WHEATON, MD 20902
divasgm@gmail.com
www.dcdivas.com
• Rich Daniel, Owner/President
• Allysea Marful, Head Coach
• Ron Primm, General Manager/Director,
Football Operations
Founded:
2000

DALLAS ELITE MUSTANGS
817-691-5568
dallaselitewomensfootball@gmail.com
dallaselitewomensfootball.com
Founded:
2014

DERBY CITY DYNAMITE
LOUISVILLE, KY
270-268-6746
info@derbycitydynamite.com
derbycitydynamite.com
• Thelma Banks, President & Owner
• Marquita Board, General Manager
• Quanterrial Parmes, Head Coach
Founded:
2011

DETROIT VENOM
DETROIT, MI
586-255-7460
detroitvenomfootball@gmail.com
www.facebook.com/DetroitVenomFootball
• Andre Harlon, Head Coach
Founded:
2011

EAST TENNESSEE VALKYRIE
ELIZABETHTON, TN
etnvrecruiting@gmail.com
www.facebook.com/EastTNValkyrie
• Shannon Simpson, Head Coach
Founded:
2021

GRAND RAPIDS TIDAL WAVES
GRAND RAPIDS, MI
tidalwavesfootball@gmail.com
tidalwavesfootball.com
• Stacey Davis, Head Coach
Founded:
2017

HARRISBURG HAVOC
HARRISBURG, PA
717-693-4137
harrisburghavoc@gmail.com
wfaprofootball.com/team/harrisburg-havoc
• Jeff Thomas, Head Coach
Founded:
2021

HOUSTON ENERGY
HOUSTON, TX
281-799-9198
info@houstonenergyfootball.com
houstonenergyfootball.com
• Brian Wiggins, Owner & Head Coach
Founded:
2000

IOWA PHOENIX
DES MOINES, IA
515-519-5604
info@iowaphoenixfootball.com
iowaphoenixfootball.com
• DeMareo Darrah, Head Coach
Founded:
2018

JACKSONVILLE DIXIE BLUES
JACKSONVILLE, FL
dixiebluesfootball@outlook.com
dixiebluesfootball.net
• Michelle Robinson, Head Coach
Founded:
2001

MAINE MAYHEM
PORTLAND, ME
207-615-7213
info@mainemayhemfootball.com
mainemayhemfootball.com
• Bryant Oja, Head Coach
Founded:
2015

MIAMI FURY
P.O. BOX 771134
CORAL SPRINGS, FL
786-229-7487
info@miamifuryfootball.com
miamifuryfootball.com
• Gayla Harrington, Administration
• Raul Camaliche, Head Coach
Founded:
2000

MIDWEST MOUNTAIN LIONS
WAUKEGAN, IL
www.mwmountainlions.com
• Jahamal Hardy, Head Coach
Founded:
2019

MILE HIGH BLAZE
DENVER, CO
303-619-7758
contact@gymfitx.com
www.milehighblaze.com
• Rob Sandlin, Head Coach
Founded:
2013

MINNESOTA MINX
MINNEAPOLIS, MN
info@mnminx.com
www.mnminx.com
• Claire Romey, Interim President/Secretary
• Jim Jarvis, Director, Sports Performance
• Jodi Rehlander, Head Coach & Defensive
Coordinator
Founded:
2021

MINNESOTA VIXEN
P.O. BOX 2591
INVER GROVE HEIGHTS, MN 55076
385-999-8936
info@mnvixen.com
www.mnvixen.com
• Connor Jo Lewis, Head Coach
Founded:
1999

MUSIC CITY MIZFITS
NASHVILLE, TN
musiccitymizfits@gmail.com
musiccitymizfits.com
• Donald Ragsdale, Head Coach
Founded:
2016

NEBRASKA PRIDE
OMAHA, NE
nebraskapridesports@gmail.com
wfaprofootball.com/team/nebraska-pride
• Nancy Javaux-Major, Head Coach
Founded:
2023

NEVADA STORM
RENO, NV
775-525-0508
womensfootballnevadastorm@gmail.com
nevadastormfootball.com
• Chris Garza, Head Coach
Founded:
2011

NEW HAMPSHIRE REBELLION
MANCHESTER, NH
admin@newhampshirerebellion.com
newhampshirerebellion.com
• Arasi Chau, Head Coach
Founded:
2021

NEW MEXICO BANITAS
LAS CRUCES, NM
575-405-3140
wfaprofootball.com/team/new-mexico-banitas
• Brian Bartlett, Head Coach
Founded:
2022

NEW YORK KNOCKOUT
TROY, NY
518-857-1131
thenyknockout@gmail.com
www.nyknockoutfootball.com
• Theresa Petrone Butts, Owner
(914) 466-4067
• Melissa Messemer, General Manager
(518) 729-6952
• Lou Butts, Head Coach
Founded:
2012

NEW YORK WOLVES
P.O. BOX 664
LEVITTOWN, NY 11756
nywolvesfootball@gmail.com
www.newyorkwolves.com
• Thomas Farrell, Owner
• Shayna Ramos, General Manager
• Fabian Alesandro, Head Coach & Offensive
Coordinator
Founded:
2018

OKLAHOMA CITY LADY FORCE
OKLAHOMA CITY, OK
405-923-2292
okcforcefootball@gmail.com
okcladyforce.com
• Leonard Bulock, Head Coach
Founded:
2014

OKLAHOMA RAGE
TULSA, OK
oklahomaragefb@gmail.com
www.oklahomaragefb.com
• Brandon Webb, Owner, Head Coach &
Offensive Coordinator
Founded:
2022

OREGON COUGARS
EUGENE, OR
britt.pionke@gmail.com
www.oregonwomensfootball.com
• Chuck Hoffman, Head Coach
Founded:
2021

ORLANDO ANARCHY
ORLANDO, FL
contact@cfanarchy.com
cfanarchy.com
• Sherman Harlow, Head Coach
Founded:
2009

PITTSBURGH PASSION
1 RACQUET LANE
MONROEVILLE, PA 15146
724-452-9395
pittsburghpassion@gmail.com
www.pittsburghpassion.com
• Teresa Conn, Owner & Co-Head Coach
• Lisa Horton, Co-Head Coach
• Kim Zubovic, General Manager
kim.zubovic@pittsburghpassion.com
Founded:
2002

PORTLAND FIGHTING SHOCKWAVE
PORTLAND, OR
portlandfightingshockwave@gmail.com
www.facebook.com/PortlandFightingShockwave
Founded:
2002

RALEIGH EXPRESS
RALEIGH, NC
443-332-5421
raleighexpress@icloud.com
www.raleighexpress.net
• Earnest Thomas, Co-Owner
(336) 813-9518
• Star Walker, Co-Owner
• Lynn Phillips, Chief Administrative Officer &
General Manager
• Brent Fisher, Head Coach
Founded:
2022

RICHMOND BLACK WIDOWS
RICHMOND, VA
804-781-4419
info@richmondblackwidows.com
www.richmondblackwidows.com
• Steve Baxter, Head Coach
Founded:
2015

ROCKY MOUNTAIN THUNDERKATZ
COLORADO SPRINGS, CO
rockymountainthunderkatz@gmail.com
wfaprofootball.com/team/rocky-mountain-thunderkatz
• Demareo Pruitt, Head Coach
Founded:
2012

SIOUX FALLS SNOW LEOPARDS
SIOUX FALLS, SD 57106
308-672-4408
officialsfsl@gmail.com
officialsfsl.com
• Riley Key, Head Coach

Founded:
2021

ST. LOUIS SLAM
4701 SOUTH GRAND BLVD.
ST. LOUIS, MO 63111
314-884-0403
info@stlslamfootball.com
stlslamfootball.com
• Quincy Davis, Head Coach
Founded:
2003

SUN CITY STEALTH
EL PASO, TX
info@suncitystealth.com
wfaprofootball.com/team/sun-city-stealth
• Marcus Riley, Head Coach
Founded:
2019

TAMPA BAY INFERNO
SICKLES HIGH SCHOOL
7950 GUNN HWY
TAMPA, FL 33626
tampabayinferno@gmail.com
www.tbinferno.com
• Jen Moody, Owner
• Lori Johnson, General Manager
• Candi Thompson, Head Coach
Founded:
2009

TRI-STATE WARRIORS
NEW BRUNSWICK, NJ
347-867-4855
warriors@googlegroups.com
tristatewarriors.com
• Rich Harrigan, Co-Owner & Head Coach
• Lybrant Robinson, Co-Owner
• Rashidi Hendrix, General Manager
Founded:
2021

UPSTATE LADY PREDATORS
ROCHESTER, NY 14612
upstateladypredators@gmail.com
wfaprofootball.com/team/upstate-predators
• Jessica Coluzzi, Head Coach
Founded:
2023

VIRGINIA PANTHERS
NEWPORT NEWS, VA 23601
jelj8@aol.com
virginia-panthers.com
• James Lancaster, Owner & Head Coach
Founded:
2022

WASATCH WARRIORS
SALT LAKE CITY, UT
858-877-0073
wasatchwarriorsfootball@gmail.com
www.wasatchwarriorsfootball.com
• Abel Tenorio, Head Coach
Founded:
2019

WEST PALM BEACH COYOTES
WEST PALM BEACH, FL
561-294-0485
wpbcoyotes@gmail.com
wpbcoyotes.com
• Paul Gonsalves, Head Coach
Founded:
2019

ZYDECO SPICE
LAFAYETTE, LA
www.thezydecospice.com
• Josh Edison, Head Coach

Founded:
2009

Frisbee Organizations

USA ULTIMATE
5825 DELMONICO DR
SUITE 350
COLORADO SPRINGS, CO 80919
719-219-8322
800-872-4384
info@hq.usaultimate.org
www.usaultimate.org
• Tom Crawford, Chief Executive Officer
(719) 219-8322
Year Founded:
1979
Description:
To promote and support the sport of
Ultimate in the US. Our mission is to
increase participation in the sport of Ultimate
at all levels; to uphold the Spirit of the
Game, including personal responsibility and
integrity; and to provide a framework for
players to organize and conduct competition
and other activities
Membership Requirements:
$40 regular, $20 youth, and more
membership levels.
Members:
23,700
Publications:
UPA magazine: USA Ultimate, quarterly

WORLD FLYING DISC FEDERATION
5825 DELMONICO DRIVE
SUITE 350
COLORADO SPRINGS, CO 80919
+41-(0) 6138 9020 868
Volker.Bernardi@wfdf.org
www.wfdf.org
• Robert Rauch, President
(203) 570-9221
nob.rauch@wfdf.org
• Thomas Griesbaum, Secretary
(49) 162 214 526
thomas.griesbaum@wfdf.org
• Tomas Burvall, Overall Committee Chair
tomas.burvall@wfdf.org
• Kate Begeron, Treasurer
kate.bergeron@wfdf.org
• Brian Gisel, Ultimate Committee Chair
(517) 862-3182
brian.gisel@wfdf.org
Year Founded:
1985
Description:
Responsible for hosting World
Championships and developing the Rules of
the Game for the following flying disc sports:
Ultimate, Disc Golf, Freestyle, Guts, DDC,
Field Events
Number of members:
20,000+ in 46 member countries
Membership Requirements:
$1.25 US multiplied by the number of active
players belonging to the member
organization. The minimum dues for a
Regular Member is $250 US and the
maximum is $3000 US. Associate
Membership is $250 US annually.
Publications:
Annual rule book

Golf Organizations

AMERICAN GOLF CORPORATION
6080 CENTER DRIVE
SUITE 500
LOS ANGELES, CA 90045
310-664-4000
www.americangolf.com
• Jim Hinckley, President/CEO
• Rick Rosen, Chief Financial Officer
Description:
Manages more than 110 premier private,
resort and daily fee courses in the United
States. In addition to outstanding facilities
and world-class service, we are dedicated to
helping people of all ages and backgrouns
learn and enjoy the game of golf.
Notes:
Goldman Sachs and Starwood Capital
completed acquistion of National Golf
Properties and American Golf in 2003

AMERICAN JUNIOR GOLF ASSOCIATION
1980 SPORTS CLUB DRIVE
BRASELTON, GA 30517
770-868-4200
877-373-2542
Fax: 770-868-4211
www.ajga.org
• James E Nugent, III, President
• Gayle Champagne, Past President
• J.R. Smith, Chairman
• Joseph E. Quirk, III, Vice President
• Lewis C. Horne, Jr., Secretary
• Jason Miller, Chief Financial Officer
(770) 868-4200
Year Founded:
1977
Description:
A nonprofit organization dedicated to the
overall growth and development of young
men and women who aspire to earn college
golf scholarships through competitive junior
golf.
Membership Requirements:
For ages 12-18. Junior Membership $215;
College Bound Student Membership(CBS)
$270; Future Player Membership $95; Junior
Plus Membership $285
Number of Members:
More than 5,500
Publications:
The AJGA Link (electronic newsletter)

AMERICAN SINGLES GOLF
ASSOCIATION
710 MAIN STREET
PINEVILLE, NC 28134
704-889-4600
1-888-GOLFMATE
1-888-465-3628
Fax: 888-465-3295
asganational@aol.com
www.singlesgolf.com
• Tom Alsop, Founder/Chief Executive
Officer
GolfASGA@aol.com
Year Founded
1996
Description:
To serve its members and chapter leaders
so they can fully realize the benefits of
membership. The secondary goal is to
create new chapters and spread the concept
of SinglesGolf.

Number of members:
2,200

AMERICAN SOCIETY OF GOLF COURSE ARCHITECTS
125 N EXECUTIVE DRIVE
SUITE 302
BROOKFIELD, WI 53005
262-786-5960
Fax: 262-786-5919
www.asgca.org
• Lee Schmidt, President
(480) 483-1994
lslap@schmidt-curley.com
• Steve Smyers, Vice President
(863) 683-6100
ssgca@aol.com
• Greg Martin, Treasurer
(630) 482-2532
g-martin@mdpltd.com
• Rick Robbins, Immediate Past President
(919) 319-1004
rock@robbinsgolf.com
• John Sanford, Secretary
(561) 691-8601
john@sanfordgolfdesign.com
Year Founded:
1946
Description:
The first professional organization of golf course designers in America. Its members have designed some of the world's greatest courses.
Membership Requirements:
Must be at least 28 years of age and been practicing golf couse architecture for a minimum of eight years; have designed at least 18-hole equivalents, three of which must have opened i the past six years; and adhere to strict professional Code of Ethics.
Number of members:
177
Publications:
The Golf Course Development Process: Questions & Answers; Master Planning for Golf Courses: Questions & Answers; The Golf Course Remodeling Process: Questions & Answers; Selecting Your Golf Course Architect: Questions & Answers; Sample Request for Proposal for Golf Course Architectural Services; Life Cycle Chart; An Environmental Approach to Golf Course Development; BUilding a Practical Golf Facility

ASSOCIATION OF GOLF MERCHANDISERS
PO BOX 7247
PHOENIX, AZ 85011-7247
602-604-8250
Fax: 602-604-8251
info@agmgolf.org
www.agmgolf.org
• Darcy Lyberger, President
(301) 469-2003
darcy@ccclub.org
• Tracy Moffatt, Vice President
(239) 597-8383
tracymoffatt@aol.com
Year Founded:
1989
Description:
A professional association of golf-related vendors and professional merchandisers located all over the world.
Membership Requirements:
Must be buyer/merchandiser at a

recognized golf shop (merchandiser member) or a golf-related business (Affiliate member)
Members:
750
Member Services:
Educational seminars on successful golf merchandising (held throughout the country), membership rosters, job bulletins and referrals, and a reference/referral center for golf buyers and merchandisers
Publications:
The Merchandiser, bimonthly newsletter; AGM Merchandise Manual, issued to members only; Viewpoints, monthly color card w/visual display ideas

CADDIE ASSOCIATION
23 MALACOMPRA ROAD
PALM COAST, FL 32137
386-446-8721
dennis@pcahq.com
www.thecaddieassociation.com
• Dennis Cone, Founder/CEO
Description:
A membership driven organization that is open to all Caddies, independent Contractors, and those who want to support the game.

CANADIAN PROFESSIONAL GOLFERS' ASSOCIATION
13450 DUBLIN LINE
ACTON, ON, CANADA L7J 2W7
519-853-5450
800-782-5764
Fax: 519-853-5449
info@pgaofcanada.com
www.pgaofcanada.com
• Heather Bodden, Operations Manager
(519) 853-5450
• Eilon Milman, Chief Financial Officer
(519) 853-5450
eilon@pgaofcanada.com
• Chris Fry, Managing Director of Corporate
(519) 853-5450
• Jeff Dykeman, Chief Business Officer
(519) 853-5450
jeff@pgaofcanada.com
• Darcy Kral, Managing Director of Membership & Support Services
(549) 853-5450
darcy@pgaofcanada.com
• Adam LeBrun, Managing Director, Championships & Events
(519) 853-5450
• Gary Bernard, Chief Executive Officer
(519) 853-5450
Year Founded:
1911
Description:
A member based non-profit organization representing over 3,500 golf professionals across Canada.
Publications:
The Exchange - Official Publication of the CPGA produced by Score Golf

CEC BALALIS CORPORATION
1500 WEST BALBOA BOULEVARD
SUITE 201
NEWPORT BEACH, CA 92663
949-673-2282
Fax: 949-673-4286
• Paul Balalis, Chairman/President/CEO
Year Founded:
1999

Description:
Organization is engaged in the development, program and construction management, maintenance, and ownership of golf course facilities

CLINTWOOD PRODUCTIONS
www.celebritygolf.com
Year Founded:
1990
Description:
To support, promote, and help raise awareness for worthwhile charities. We provide a wide range of services to celebrity and charity events that maximize event visability year round

CLUBCORP
3030 LBJ FREEWAY
SUITE 600
DALLAS, TX 75234
972-243-6191
www.clubcorp.com
• Robert H. Dedman, Sr, Founder
• Jamie K. Walters, Executive Vice President, Sales
• Eric L. Affeldt, President & CEO, Director
• Mark Burnett, Chief Operating Officer
• Daniel Tilley, Executive Vice President & CIO
• Curt McClellan, Chief Financial Officer
• Ingrid J. Keiser, General Counsel, Secretary, & Executive VP
Year Founded:
1957
Description:
ClubCorp owns or operates nearly 200 golf courses, country clubs, private business and sports clubs, and resorts. Instrumental in the renaming of the Stonebridge Ranch to Dallas Stars Country Club
Members:
200,000

Other locations:

COLORADO SECTION PGA
6630 BEAR DANCE DRIVE
SUITE 200
LARKSPUR, CO 80118
303-681-0742
www.coloradopga.com
• Leslie Core-Drevecky, President, PGA
mcreekgolf@aol.com
• Ty Thomspon, Vice President, PGA
ty.thompson@pga.com
• Patrick Salva, Marketing & Communications Director
psalva@pgahq.com
• Eddie Ainsworth, Executive Director, PGA

ENGLAND & WALES BLIND GOLF
STATION HOUSE
NORTH STREET
HAVANT, PO9 1QU
www.blindgolf.co.uk
• Neil Baxter, Chairman
• Barry Ritchie, Secretary
Enquiries.blindgolf@gmail.com
• Ron Tomlinson, Financial Director
FD.blindgolf@gmail.com
• Derek Field, New Members Secretary
dgfield@ntlworld.com
Year Founded:
1982
Description:
To provide visually handicapped people with the facility to train and compete in the game

of golf. Training is provided by giving new members support to receive lessons from professional golfers. In addition each year the organization invites all members to attend a training weekend at which PGA professional teach the various aspects of the game. Assistance is also given to schools for the blind where pupils want to start to play golf

Fundraising/Sponsorship:
The Financial Director, 12 Nutbourne Road, Hayling Island Hampshire PO11 9RT; Tel: 023 92 460 120 Fax: 023 92 460 120

Press and Public Relations:
55a Queen Mary Rd, Upper Norwood London SE 19 3NN, Tel: 020 8761 1904 Fax: 020 8761 1904

EXECUTIVE WOMEN'S GOLF ASSOCIATION
300 AVE OF THE CHAMPIONS
SUITE 140
PALM BEACH GARDENS, FL 33418-3615
561-691-0096
www.ewga.com
• Pam Swensen, CEO, EWGA
• Sheryl Wilkerson, President
• Diana Gats, Secretary-Treasurer
• Hilary Tuohy, President-Elect
• Nona Footz, Board Member

Year Founded:
1991

Description:
To provide opportunities for women to learn, play, and enjoy the game of golf for business and for life

Number of Members:
20,000 members in over 120 Chapters across US and Canada.

Membership Requirements:
Interest in learning how to play a game of golf or desire to improve one's skills to use golf for business and career advancement, Local and Association dues apply annually (average $100.00 per year) Classic membership $155; Executive Distinction Membership $400; Seniors (65+) $125; Young Professionals (ages 18-30) $75; and Corporate Membership (10 or more) $125

Member Services:
EWGA provides opportunities for professional women to learn, play, and enjoy the game of golf for business and for life throughout 100+ local Chapters in the US and Canada

Publications:
Annual EWGA Member Handbook, Annual EWGA Yearbook Per Excellence, Golf for Women

FERRIS STATE UNIVERSITY/PROFESSIONAL GOLF MANAGEMENT PROGRAM
119 SOUTH STREET
BIG RAPIDS, MI 49307
231-591-2480
Fax: 231-591-2839
cob@ferris.edu
www.ferris.edu
• Mark Wilson, PGA Golf Management Player Development Coordinator
MarkWilson@ferris.edu
• Aaron Waltz, PGA Golf Management Director
AaronWaltz@ferris.edu
• Annette Keyt, PGA Golf Management Secretary

AnnetteKeyt@ferris.edu
• Diane Maguire, PGA Golf Management Assistant
DianeMaguire@ferris.edu

Year Founded:
1975

Undergrad Degree:
B.S. in Business; Major in Professional Golf Management; Class A PGA Membership eligible upon graduation.

Other locations:

GEORGIA STATE GOLF ASSOCIATION
121 VILLAGE PARKWAY
BUILDING 3
MARIETTA, GA 30067
770-955-4272
800-949-4742
Fax: 770-955-1156
info@gsga.org
www.gsga.org
• Dave Ballard, President
president@gsga.org
• David Burke, President-Elect
presidentelect@gsga.org
• Matt Williams, Executive Director
(678) 324-5960
• Olivia Flanagan, Secretary/Treasurer
• Jerri Smith, Senior Director
(678) 324-5973

Description:
Non-profit organization dedicated solely to serving the game of golf and its membership

Year Founded:
1916

Number of Members:
360 golf clubs, 85,000 individuals

GOLF CANADA
1333 DORVAL DRIVE
SUITE 1
OAKVILLE, ON, CANADA L6M 4X7
905-849-9700
800-263-0009
Fax: 905-845-7040
www.golfcanada.ca
• Paul McLean, President
• Doug Alexander, Past President
• Charlie Beaulieu, Secretary
• Roland Deveau, 1st Vice President
• Leslie Dunning, 2nd Vice President
• Liz Hoffman, Director At Large
• Dale Jackson, Director At Large

Year Founded:
1895

Description:
The mission, as the governing body of golf in Canada, is to promote participation in and a passion for the game while protecting its traditions and integrity.

Number of members:
1,650 golf clubs; 380,000 individual members

Member Services:
Rules of Golf; Greens Consulting; Conducting National Championships; Handicaps; Hall of Fame; Museum; Library; Amateur Status; Junior Development. Conducts Canadian Open Golf Championship, Senior Open Championships; Amateur Championships, Women's Open Championship, Handicap and Course Rating, Junior Development and International Teams. Publishes GOLF CANADA MAGAZINE

Membership Requirements:
Golf Clubs in Canada or public player programs

GOLF CLEARING HOUSE/NATIONAL GOLF SALES REPRESENTATIVES ASSOCIATION (NGSA)
PO BOX 6134
SCOTTSDALE, AZ 85261-6134
480-860-6348
Fax: 480-860-6919
• Tom Moynihan, President
• Bud Brown, Vice President
• Debbie Savona, Executive Director
• Jon Schwartz, Website Administrator

Description:
NGSA representing over 3,400 independent and Company Golf Sales Representatives. The NGSA Benefits are fully encompassing. The Sales Leader Reps Wanted a service for all Golf Manufacturers to list their need for qualified Sales Reps or to find qualified Management Personnel. The NGSA Register of 3,400 Sales Reps is available to all Company Members of the Golf Clearing House, Divsion of NSGA

Number of members:
450 Member Companies

GOLF COACHES ASSOCIATION OF AMERICA
1225 WEST MAIN STREET
SUITE 110
NORMAN, OK 73069
866-422-2669
Fax: 405-573-7888
info@collegiategolf.com
www.collegiategolf.com
• Ray Conrad, President
• Andrew Sapp, First Vice President
• Greg Sands, Second Vice President
• Mark Crabtree, Third Vice President

Year Founded:
1958

Description:
This non-profit organization is dedicated to educating, promotion and recognizing its members who participate in men's golf at all levels

Membership Requirements:
College golf coach

GOLF COURSE BUILDERS ASSOCIATION OF AMERICA
6040 S 58TH STREET
SUITE D
LINCOLN, NE 68516
402-476-4444
Fax: 402-476-4489
www.gcbaa.org
• Justin Apel, Executive Director
justin_apel@gcbaa.org
• Dennis Wagner, Vice President
• Samantha Huff, Program & Planning Manager
samantha_huff@gcbaa.org
• Lori Romano, Information & Education Coordinator
lori_romano@gcbaa.org
• Rick Boylan, President
• Scott Veazey, President-Elect
• Ellen Davis, Secretary
• Patrick Karnick, Treasurer

Year Founded:
1971

Description:
A nonprofit trade association of the world's foremost golf course builders and leading suppliers to the golf course construction insdustry.

Number of members:

19,000 (70 countries), 66 Chapters
Membership Requirements:
Builder must have constructed a minimum of three courses in the past five years. Associate: suppliers, specialty contractors, and international companies
Member Services:
Two annual meetings per year, one in conjunction with the annual PGA tournament, and one timed with the annual GCSAA Membership Directory., Newsline
Publications:
Earthshaping News, Membership Directory, Guide To Estimating Cost For Golf Course Construction

GOLFCOURSEHOME NETWORK
10 UNION STREET
PO BOX 821
VINEYARD HAVEN, MA 02568
203-270-9357
Fax: 866-424-5225
dlott@golfcoursehome.net
www.golfcoursehome.com
• David Lott, Founder & Publisher
(203) 270-9357
• Alan T. Pearce, Vice President Sales
(800) 673-0321
• Paul Stanton, Western Regional Sales Director
(916) 641-8255
• Elise Jeffress Ryan, Eastern Regional Sales Manager
(410) 433-0889
Year Founded:
1999
Description:
Provide executives who are looking for a golf or waterview home or homesite. Key information about world-class, amenity and country club communities in the U.S. and the world.

GOLF COURSE SUPERINTENDENTS ASSOCIATION OF AMERICA/GCSAA
1421 RESEARCH PARK DRIVE
LAWRENCE, KS 66049
785-841-2240
800-472-7878
Fax: 785-832-3643
www.gcsaa.org
• John J O'Keefe, President
• Peter J Grass, Vice President
• William H Maynard, Secretary/Treasurer
• J. Rhett Evans, Chief Executive Officer
• Cameron Oury, Chief Financial Officer
Year Founded:
1926
Description:
Dedicated to serving its members, advancing their profession and enhancing the enjoyment, growth and vitality of the game of golf.
Number of members:
21,000 in 75 countries
Membership Requirements:
Those persons directly participating in the production and management of fine golf turf
Publications:
GOLF COURSE MANAGEMENT MAGAZINE; GREENS & GRASS ROOTS, newsletter; GCSAA Membership Directory; EADERBOARD GOLF EXECUTIVE NEWSLETTER. Also produces Par For The Course, a 30-minute TV show

GOLF WRITERS ASSOCIATION OF AMERICA
golfwritersinc@aol.com
www.gwaa.com
• Ron Sirak, President
• Jack Berry, Secretary/Treasurer
Year Founded:
1947
Description:
Insures professional working conditions
Membership Requirements:
Must be actively writing golf
Publications:
Monthly newsletter, Membership Directory

INTERNATIONAL JUNIOR GOLF ACADEMY
55 HOSPITAL CENTER COMMON
HILTON HEAD ISLAND, SC 29926
843-686-1500
888-452-6642
www.ijga.com
• Kevin Smeltz, Director Of Instruction
• DaWayne Penberthy, Assistant Director Of Golf
• Karen Harrison, Director Of Health & Athletic Development
Year Founded:
1995
Description:
Dedicated to preparing junior golfers for success in tournament golf, academics, and life. We succeed when we instill in student athletes a sense of purpose and perspective.
Sponsors:
Nike Golf, Fitness for Golf, Promax, Champion's Golf Environments, Saegertown Beverages

INTERNATIONAL ASSOCIATION OF GOLF TOUR OPERATORS
CONCORDE HOUSE
GRENVILLE PL
LONDON, ENGLAND NW7 3SA
44-(0) 20 8906 3377
Fax: 44-(0) 20 8906 8181
info@iagto.com
www.iagto.com
• Corinne Korn, Office Manager
• Daniella Leao, Events Manager
• Peter Walton, President/Chief Executive Officer
• Carlton Carugati, General Manager
• Giles Greenwood, Golf Tourism Development Director
• Susannah Wilson, Marketing Executive & Special Projects
• Amila Udayanga, Programmer
• Peter Ellegard, Editor in Chief & Media Advisor
Year Founded:
1997
Description:
The global trade association of the golf tourism industry and its membership includes over 500 accredited golf tour operators, golf resorts, hotels, golf courses, receptive operators, airlines and tourism boards in more than 50 countries worldwide
Membership Requirements:
Annual Dues
Number of Members:
800 members, 63 countries

INTERNATIONAL BLIND GOLF ASSOCIATION
• Derrick Sheridan, Director
• Yoshinori Ikezawa, Director
• Alistair Reid, Director
• John White, Director
• Brian MacLeod, Director
Year Founded:
1998
Description:
The governing and sanctioning body of blind golf events world wide: dedicated to promoting the sport and assisting blind golfers enjoy golf.

INTERNATIONAL GOLF FEDERATION
MAISON DU SPORT INTERNATIONAL
AVENUE DE RHADANIE 54
1007 LAU SANNE, SWITZERLAN
41-216-23-12 12
Fax: 41-41 216 01 64 77
info@igfmail.org
www.igfgolf.org
• Antony Scanlon, Executive Director
• Wilson Sibbett, Joint Chairman of the Board
• Thomas O'Toole, Joint Chairman of the Board
• Peter Dawson, President
• Patsy Hankins, Women's Chairman
Year Founded:
1958
Description:
To encourage the International development of golf and to foster friendship and sportsmanship among the peoples of the world through the conduct biennially of Amateur Team Championships for the Eisenhower Trophy and the Espirito Santo Trophy
Number of Members:
65 member organizations, the women's division includes 44 countries
Membership Requirements:
Open to any organization which constitutes the sole central authority for amateur golf in its country and has adopted and administers the Rules of Amateur Status of either the Royal and Ancient Golf Club of St. Andrews, or the United States Golf Association.
Publications:
Record book of the WAG Team Championships

INTERNATIONAL JUNIOR GOLF TOUR/IJGT
55 HOSPITAL CENTER COMMONS
HILTON HEAD ISLAND, SC 29926
843-785-2444
888-358-1267
www.ijgt.com
• Brandon Nettles, Assistant Tournament Director
• Leigh Blake, Tournament Operations Associate
• Ben Jaklin, Tournament Operations Associate
• Chris Schramm, Northeast Tournament Director
(843) 785-2444
• Matt Molloy, Tournament Operations Associate
• Kira Jones, Marketing and Communications Associate
• Patrick Hauer, Tournament Operations Associate

Year Founded:
1995
Number of Members:
2000
Description:
Provides exceptional junior golfers the opportunity to develop and showcase their golf skills through competitive junior tournament golf. This is provided for junior golfers ages 19 and under

INTERNATIONAL NETWORK OF GOLF
556 TETON ST
LAKE MARY, FL 32746
407-328-0500
Fax: 407-878-4928
www.inggolf.com
• John Glozek, President
• Mandy Bumgarner, Events Coordinator
• Mike Jamison, Executive Director
Year Founded:
1990
Description:
A media-based, non-profit association that has been networking the golf industry. Mission is to enhance and promote communication and education in the golf industry.

JAPANESE BLIND GOLF ASSOCIATION
YUBINBANGO 167-0053 SUGINAMI-KU
NISHIOGI-MINAMI
2-18-9 HISHI-KEN BUILDING SECOND
FLOOR
TOKYO, JAPAN 167-0053
info@jbga.org
www.jbga.org
• Toshu Fukami, Chairman
• Masao Matsuda, President

KEMPERLESNIK
500 SKOKIE BOULEVARD
SUITE 444
NORTHBROOK, IL 60062
847-850-1818
Fax: 847-559-0406
info@kemperlesnik.com
www.kemperlesnik.com
• Gary Binder, Executive Vice President
• Steven K. Skinner, Chief Executive Officer
• Josh W. Lesnik, President
• Brian Milligan, Chief Financial Officer
• Steve Kelley, Vice President, General Counsel
Year Founded:
1967
Clients/Events:
KitchenAid, EA Sports, McDonalds Hich School All-American Games, PGA of America, Wilson Golf, EA Sports Maui Invitational
Description:
KemperLesnik is a sports/ event marketing and public relations agency based in Chicago. KemperLesnik specializes in owning, managing, creating selling and marketing events. The agency also consults with clients on sports marketing, activates sponsorships and develops strategic marketing and communication plans for events and clients. Events include the EA SPORTS Maui Invitational, The McDonald's All American High School Basketball games and PowerAde JamFest, the Senior PGA Championship presented by KitchenAid and the Champions For Change at Harbor Shores.

LADIES PROFESSIONAL GOLF ASSOCIATION/LPGA
100 INTERNATIONAL GOLF DRIVE
DAYTONA BEACH, FL 32124-1092
386-274-6200
Fax: 386-274-1099
www.lpga.com
• Michael Whan, Commissioner
• Vicki Goetze-Ackerman, President
• Karrie Webb, Vice President
• Laura Diaz, LPGA Player Director
• Katherine Kirk, LPGA Player Director
• Paige Mackenzie, LPGA Player Director
• Karen Stupples, LPGA Player Director
Year Founded:
1950
Description:
Professional women's golf tour of events; a membership organization for women teaching and club professionals
Membership Requirements:
Must successfully complete LPGA Qualifying School, for the LPGA Tour, meet membership requirements for T&CP Division
Number of members:
43 LPGA members, 40+ LPGA Teaching and Club Professional T&CP Division members
Publications:
MEDIA GUIDE; news releases, player profiles, tournament schedule, golf statistics, LPGA GOLF, distributed at LPGA tournaments, in the February Issue of GOLF MAGAZINE

LONG DRIVERS OF AMERICA
600 HENRIETTA CREEK ROAD
SUITE 200
ROANOKE, TX 76262
682-549-2105
888-233-4654
Fax: 682-549-2112
www.longdrivers.com
• Art Sellinger, Owner/Chief Executive Officer
• Rene Towell, Office Manager
• Thomas Kemp, General Counsel
tkemp@kemp-law.com
• Steve Wiley, VP Sales and Marketing
• Rod Moruss, Director of Events
• Mike Ambriz, Executive Vice President
Year Founded:
1993
Description:
Creates and implements Long Drive Tournaments
Membership Requirements:
Pay dues of $150 per year
Publications:
LDA Newsletter, approximately 6 times per year. Offers at least one long drive competition with a purse of $250,000

Other locations:

LOUISIANA GOLF ASSOCIATION
1003 HUGH WALLIS ROAD S.
SUITE A-2
LAFAYETTE, LA 70508
337-265-3938
www.lgagolf.org
• Lew Ward, President
• John Luffey, Vice President
• Richard Hunter, Secretary/Treasurer
• Carr McCalla, Executive Director
cmccalla@lgagolf.org
• Logan Ray, Director Of Championship Operations

loganr@lgagolf.org
• Tuyen Nguyen, Director Of Member Services
Nature of Service:
Exists to foster the enhancement and expansion of amateur golf through the development of member and information services, the promotion of oppportunities for all who want to play, and the protection of the game's integrity and valued traditions.
Year Founded:
1920
Number of Members:
20,000

METHODIST COLLEGE PROFESSIONAL GOLF MANAGEMENT PROGRAM
5400 RAMSEY STREET
FAYETTEVILLE, NC 28311
910-630-7000
800-488-7110
webmaster@methodist.edu
www.methodist.edu/pgm
• Jerry Hogge, Director PGA Golf Management
(910) 630-7144
jhogge@methodist.edu
• Bob Bruns, Associate Director
(910) 630-7180
rbruns@methodist.edu
• Steve Conley, Assistant Director
(910) 630-7146
sconley@methodist.edu
• Steve Dockery, Golf Course Superintendent
(910) 630-7604
sdockery@methodist.edu
• Tom Inczauskis, Assistant Director PGA Golf Management
(910) 630-7608
tinczauskis@methodist.edu
• Robbie Fritz, Director of Instruction, PGA Certified
(910) 630-7689
rfritz@methodist.edu
• Krista Lee, Office of Management, Admissions
(910) 630-7148
klee@methodist.edu
• Charles Koonce, Associate Director/Internship Director
(910) 630-7145
ckoonce@methodist.edu
Description:
Prepares students for a career as a PGA professional through an understanding of the business of golf, by encouraging integrity and ethical behavior in their service to their customers. The mission is to be achieved by providing students with an accredited business program, a competent and thorough PGM curriculum, access to a golf facility for skill improvemetn, and assistance in obtaining an entry level position upon graduation.

MISSISSIPPI STATE UNIVERSITY/GOLF MANAGEMENT PROGRAM
PO BOX 6217
309 McCOOL HALL
MISSISSIPPI STATE, MS 39762
662-325-3161
Fax: 662-325-1779
jadkerson@cobilan.msstate.edu
www.msupgm.com
• Jeff Adkerson, Director, PGA Golf Management
(662) 325-3161
jadkerson@business.msstate.edu
• Adam M. Scott, Assistant Director

(662) 325-3161
ascott@business.msstate.edu
• Daniel Soehren, Program Assistant
(662) 325-3161
• Angie Chrestman, Associate Director,
Career Center
(662) 325-3823
achrestman@career.msstate.edu
• Tony Luczak, Director of golf
(662) 325-3028
tluczak@golfcourse.msstate.edu
Description:
Undergrad Degree: B.A. in Mktg plus
Certification for 24 of 36 credits for the Class
A PGA Membership

MULTICULTURAL GOLF ASSOCIATION OF AMERICA
P.O. BOX 1081
WESTHAMPTON BEACH, NY 11978-7081
mgaagolf@aol.com
www.mgaagolf.org
• John David, Founder/President
• Paul David, Co-Founder/Executive Vice
President
• Richard Friedson, Treasurer
Year Founded:
1991
Description:
Mission is to make golf available and
accessible to all people, with the belief that
learning the game of gold leads to positive
character development, self-discipline,
academic achievement, self-reliance,
creativity, imagination, principle, values, and
a balanced approach for the youth of
America.

NATIONAL GOLF COURSE OWNERS ASSOCIATION
291 SEVEN FARMS DRIVE
SECOND FLOOR
CHARLESTON, SC 29492
843-881-9956
800-933-4262
Fax: 843-881-9958
www.ngcoa.org
• Matt Galvin, President
• Rock Lucas, Vice President
• Walter Lankau, Jr., Secretary
• Frank Romano, Treasurer
• Michael K Hughes, Chief Executive Officer
Year Founded:
1979
Description:
Mission is to enhance the lives of golf
course owners by making their business
more profitable, more efficient, better
managed and more stable.
Number of members:
6,000
Membership Requirements:
Open to existing privately owned and profit
oriented golf courses that are open to the
general public on a daily fee and/or annual
membership basis
Member Services:
Smart Buy Purchasing Program, involving
the negotiation of supplier agreements;
annual convention and seminars;
knowledgeline; annual trade show; tracks
pertinent legislative issues; insurance
program
Publications:
GOLF BUSINESS, monthly; Operations
Manual; Accounting for Public and Resort
Golf Courses; Marketing Plan Manual,

annual; GOLF BUSINESS, monthly
magazine

NATIONAL GOLF FOUNDATION
1150 SOUTH US HIGHWAY ONE
STE 401
JUPITER, FL 33477
561-744-6006
888-275-4643
Fax: 561-744-6107
www.ngf.org
• Chip Brewer, Chairman
• Joe Louis Barrow, Jr., Vice Chairman
• Dick Raskopf, Secretary/Treasurer
• Joseph F. Beditz, PhD, President & Chief
Executive Officer
• Greg Nathan, Senior Vice President
Year Founded:
1936
Description:
Provides the most timely and relevant
information on the golf industry with original
research on every aspect of the business.
Number of members:
6,000
Membership Requirements:
Charter membership: available to major golf
industry companies. Sponsor membership:
for all golf industry companies. Facility
membership: open to all golf facilities.
Association membership: available to
regional, national, and international golf
associations
Member Services:
Seminars, insurance plans and discounts on
all research reports
Publications:
Instructional guides for playing and teaching
golf; books on all phases of building and
operation of golf facilities; annual research
reports on all aspects of the game

NATIONAL HOLE-IN-ONE ASSOCIATION
1840 NORTH GREENVILLE AVENUE
SUITE 178
RICHARDSON, TX 75081
972-808-9001
1 (800) 527-6944
www.hio.com
• Douglas J. Burkert, President
• Sam Schachter, Marketing Director
Special Events
sschachter@hio.com
Year Founded:
1981
Description:
Offers Hole-in-One prize programs, with
limits up to $1,000,000 to corporate
sponsors wishing to advertise at golf events.
Also offers prize programs for sporting
events and promotional contests
Member Services:
National Hole-In-One Association and
National Media are the world's leading
provider of prize insurance coverage.
National Hole-In-One Association handles
prize coverage for golf tournament holes in
one in the USA, Europe, South America,
Africa and Australia. national Media handles
prize coverage on all other sports challenge
contests, as well as games of luck in the
same regions
London Address:
150 Fenchurch St, London, England
EC3M6BL, Phone 0800 833 863, Fax 0800
387 748, Email: nhio@btconnect.com

NATIONAL SENIOR GOLF ASSOCIATION
200 PERRINE ROAD
SUITE 201
OLD BRIDGE, NJ 08857
908-208-8691
Fax: 732-525-9590
mark@nationalseniorgolf.com
• Mark Gartenfeld,
• Roger Bakos,
Year Founded:
2003
Description:
Conducts regional and national golf
tournaments for members and other
interested persons, using group purchasing
power and off-season scheduling to obtain
economical rates
Number of Members:
500+
Membership Requirements:
Annual fee of $35
Publications:
Fore Seniors, semi-monthly

NGA HOOTERS PRO GOLF TOUR
550 HIGHWAY 9 EAST
UNIT B
LONGS, SC 29568
800-992-8748
Fax: 843-399-5125
www.swingthought.com
• Robin L. Waters, President
joy@swingthought.com
• Ryan Waters, Vice President, Tour
• Jeff Harlow, Tour Director
• Todd Barbee, Senior Tournament Director
Year Founded:
1988
Description:
We are proud to say that we are the only
developmental tour in the country to offer a
full week of activities that include free
practice rounds, free range balls, 72 hole
tournament, pro-ams, junior clinics, and
shootouts

Other locations:

NORTHERN OHIO GOLF ASSOCIATION
ONE GOLFVIEW LANE
NORTH OLMSTED, OH 44070
440-686-1070
www.noga.org
• Matt Konyesni, Communications and
Tournament Manager
(440) 686-1070
mkonyesni@noga.org
• Scotte Rorabaugh, Executive Director
(440) 686-1070
scotte@noga.org
• Frank Rihtar, Charities and Foundation
Director
(440) 686-1070
frank@noga.org
• Matt Duffy, Handicap Services Manager
(440) 686-1070
mduffy@noga.org
Nature of Service:
Founded as the Cleveland District Golf
Association to establish interclub competition for
the original eight clubs, the Northern Ohio Golf
Association has grown greatly to serve both its
member clubs and the remainder of the golf
industry in northern Ohio.
Year Founded:
1917
Number of Members:
28,000
Publications:
NOGA Fairways, e-Newsletter distributed 4-6
time(s) per year.

PGA 20/20
100 PGA TOUR BOULEVARD
PONTE VEDRA BEACH, FL 32082
904-285-3700
www.pgatour.com
• Timothy W. Fichem, Commissioner
• David Desmond, National Sales Director
(904) 273-2379
daviddesmond@pgatourhq.com
• Edward Moorhouse, Executive
VP/Co-COO
Year Founded:
1995
Services:
Exclusive domestic licensing agent for the
PGA Tour.
Marketing & Consulting Services:
Exclusive domestic licensing agent for the
PGA Tour

**PGA OF AMERICA/PROFESSIONAL
GOLFERS' ASSOCIATION OF AMERICA**
100 AVE OF THE CHAMPIONS
PALM BEACH GARDENS, FL 33418
561-624-8400
www.pga.com/pga-america
• Derek Sprague, President
• Allen Wronowski, Honorary President
• Peter Bevacqua, Chief Executive Officer
• Paul Levy, Vice President
• Suzy Whaley, Secretary
Year Founded:
1916
Description:
Elevates standards of the golf professional's
vocation. Promotes interest in golf. Protects
mutual interests of members. Holds
meetings & tournaments. Assists
unemployed members in obtaining a new
position. Improves economic opportunities
of members. Institutes a benevolent fund for
relief of members. And effects any other
objective determined by the Association
Number of members:
27,000
Membership Requirements:
Must successfully complete the Professional
Golf Training Program (average 2 1/2 years)
and Pass Playing Ability Test
Member Services:
Golf Professional Training Program,
Educational seminars, employment
conferences for members in various areas
of the country. Film library. Books and
pamphlets. 41 Sections throughout the U.S
Publications:
PGA MAGAZINE, monthly

Other locations:

ALOHA PGA SECTIONAL OFFICE
615 PIIKOI STREET
SUITE 1812
HONOLULU, HI 96814
808-593-2230
Fax: 808-593-2234
aloha411@pgahq.com
www.aspga.com
• Steve Murphy, President
• Wesley Wailehua, Executive Director
• Kyra Chun, Executive Secretary
• Charlee Kapiioho, Communications Manager
Year Founded:
1966
Number of Members:
260

CAROLINAS PGA SECTION
6271 BRYAN PARK RD
BROWNS SUMMIT, NC 27214
336-398-2742
Fax: 336-398-2743
carolinas@pgahq.com
www.carolinas.pga.com
• Ron Schmid, Executive Director
• Kurt Battenberg, Director of Operations and
Finance
kbattenberg@pgahq.com
• Cory Armstrong, Tournament Director
CArmstrong@pgahq.com
• Mike Whitenack, Senior Tournament Official
MWhitenack@pgahq.com
• David Kullenberg, Tournmant Official, PGA
• Liz Muroski, Director of Media and Promotions
• Nazmieh Kheir, Tournament Coordinator
Number of Members:
2,000
Membership Requirements:
Must be a member or apprentice with the PGA
of America
Publications:
CAROLINAS PGA MAGAZINE

**CENTRAL NEW YORK PGA
SECTIONAL OFFICE**
5011 JAMESVILLE ROAD
JAMESVILLE, NY 13078
315-446-5610
Fax: 315-446-5870
www.cny.pga.com
• Alan Seamens, Executive Director
• Steve Nacewicz, President
snaz@pga.com
• Richard Winstead, Vice President
richardwinsteadpga@gmail.com
• Bob Fuller, Secretary
rfgolfpro@gmail.com
• Stan Gorman, Honorary President
• Rich Chapman, Director
richsquid1@hotmail.com
• Ben Mastronardi, Tournament Director
• Trish Wheeler, Membership Director/Office
Manager
Description:
Represents the finest avenue for reaching golf
enthusiasts of all ages. The CNY PGA extends
from the Thousand Islands in the north to
Binghamton in the southern tier. From Utica to
Seneca Falls, golfers are in contact with CNY
PGA professionals on a regular basis.
Number of Members:
200

**CONNECTICUT PGA SECTIONAL
OFFICE**
931 MAIN STREET
CARRIAGE HOUSE
SOUTH GLASTONBURY, CT 06073
860-257-4653
www.ctpga.com
• Bill Flood, President
• Ian Marshall, Vice President
• John Steffen, Secretary
• Andrew Campbell, Director
• Ciaran Carr, Director
• Bob Clark, Director
• Don Malen, Director
• Peter Pulaski, Director
• Tom Hantke, Executive Director
• Sue Bell, Business Manager & Membership
Director
• Joe Mentz, Operations & Tournament Director
Description:
The Connecticut Section PGA is one of 41
sections chartered that together comprise the
Professional Golfer's Association of America
(PGA of America)
Number of Members:
364

DIXIE PGA SECTIONAL OFFICE
1300 BALLANTRAE CLUB DRIVE
PELHAM, AL 35124

205-621-6401
Fax: 205-664-3202
www.dixie.pga.com
• Bart Rottier, Executive Director
brottier@pgahq.com
• Wade Dockery, Tournament Director
wdockery@pgahq.com
• Lauren Webster, Operations Manager
• Steve Schepker, Tournament Assistant
• Steve Cutler, President, Dixie Section PGA
stevec@wynlakes.com
• Eric Eshleman, Vice President, Dixie Section
PGA
eeshleman@ccbham.com
• Steve Bobe, Secretary, Dixie Section PGA
sbobe1@pga.com
Number of Members:
313

GATEWAY PGA SECTIONAL OFFICE
17269 WILD HORSE CREEK ROAD
SUITE 110
CHESTERFIELD, MO 63005
636-532-3355
Fax: 636-532-0435
sbender@pgahq.com
www.gatewaypga.org
• Nathan Charmes, President
ncharnes@winghavencc.com
• Benjamin Kent, Vice President
bckent@pga.com
• Michael Suhre, Secretary
aceon4@yahoo.com
• Josh Riley, Executive Director
jriley@pgahq.com
• Steve Finn, Assistant Executive Director
• Ali Wells, Foundation Operations Director
awells@pgahq.com
• Bob Shogren, Rules Official
shogie@prodigy.net
• Susan Bender, Membership
sbender@pgahq.com
• Michael Brown, Junior Golf Director
mbrown@pgahq.com

GEORGIA PGA SECTIONAL OFFICE
590 WEST CROSSVILLE ROAD
SUITE 204
ROSWELL, GA 30075
678-461-8600
Fax: 678-461-0500
www.georgiapga.com
• Mike Paull, Executive Director
• Scott Gordon, Assistant Executive Director/Jr.
Golf Director
sgordon@pgahq.com
• Scott Gordon, Assistant Executive Director
sgordon@pgahq.com
• Pat Day, Tournament Director
pday@pgahq.com
• Eric Wagner, Operations Manager
• Mike Mongell, President
mmongell@cherokeetcc.org
• Brian Albertson, Vice President
BAMULLIGAN@bellsouth.net

**GULF STATES PGA SECTIONAL
OFFICE**
3115 6TH STREET
SUITE 110
METAIRIE, LA 70002
504-799-2444
Fax: 888-721-4037
www.gspga.com
• Todd Roberston, President
ttrr@msn.com
• Jeff Adkerson, Vice President
jwa4@msstate.edu
• Bryant Himes, Secretary
bhimes1839@aol.com
• Robert Brown, Executive Director/Chief
Executive Officer
rbrown@pgahq.com
• Brandon Roll, Tournament Director
• Patrick Murphy, Director of Player
Development and Communications
Year Founded:
1969

Number of Members:
380
Description:
An association of golf professionals whose mission is to promote interest, participation, and enjoyment in the game of golf; establish and maintain professional standards of practice; and enhance the well being of golf professionals.

ILLINOIS PGA SECTIONAL OFFICE
2901 WEST LAKE AVENUE
SUITE A
GLENVIEW, IL 60025
847-729-5700
Fax: 847-729-5599
illinois@pgahq.com
www.illinoispga.com
• Michael Miller, Executive Director
(847) 729-5700
mmiller@pgahq.com
• Jim Opp, President
• Mark Labiak, Vice President
• Jim Miller, Secretary
• Chris Gumbach, Honorary President
• Bill Ibrahim, Senior Director of Operations
(847) 729-5700
bibrahim@pgahq.com
• Mike Schoaf, Director Media & Communications
(847) 729-5700
mschoaf@pgahq.com
Description:
Conducts playing opportunities for PGA members, apprentices, and amateur golfers as well as support for the local golf professionals.
Number of Members:
555

INDIANA PGA
2625 HURRICANE ROAD
FRANKLIN, IN 46131
317-738-9696
800-779-7271
Fax: 317-738-9436
www.indianagolf.org
• Keith Clark, President
• Kelly Gaughan, Communications Director
(317) 739-3015
• Mike David, Executive Director
(317) 739-3016
mdavid@indianagolf.org
• Ryan Lambert, Assistant Executive Director
(317) 739-3019
• Todd Dehaven, Tournament Director
(317) 739-3013
tdehaven@indianagolf.org
• Judy Deiwert, Director of Accounting
(317) 739-3011
• Roger Lundy, Director of Junior Golf Development
(317) 739-3020
rlundy@indianagolf.org
Year Founded:
1972

IOWA PGA SECTIONAL OFFICE
3184 HIGHWAY 22
RIVERSIDE, IA 52327
319-648-0026
Fax: 319-648-0008
www.iowapga.com
• Troy Christensen, Executive Director
• David Schneider, President
• John Valliere, Vice President
• Aaron Krueger, Secretary
Description:
Non-profit association, consisting of qualified golf professionals dedicated to promoting the game of golf; elevating the image of the PGA and its members, providing educational and playing opportunities, as well ad perpetuating employment opportunities for its members

KENTUCKY PGA SECTIONAL OFFICE
1116 ELMORE JUST DRIVE
LOUISVILLE, KY 40245

502-243-8295
800-254-2742
Fax: 502-243-9266
kentucky@kygolf.org
www.kygolf.org
• Steve McMillen, Executive Director
smcmillen@kygolf.org
• Barbara Peak, Director of Finance
bpeak@kygolf.org
• Chris Osborne, President
• Tom Cooksey, Vice Pesident
• James Wagoner, Legal Counsel
• Steve McMillen, Executive Director
(800) 254-2742
• Barbara Peak, Director,
Finance-Administration
(800) 254-2742
bpeak@kygolf.org
Description:
An organization comprised of over 200 member clubs and courses throughout Kentucky, and is governed by a Board of Directors made up of representatives from facilities from across Kentucky.

METROPOLITAN PROFESSIONAL GOLFERS ASSOCIATION
49 KNOLLWOOD ROAD
SUITE 200
ELMSFORD, NY 10523
914-347-2325
Fax: 914-347-2014
www.met.pga.com
• Charlie Robson, Executive Director
(914) 347-2325
crobson@pgahq.com
• Kelli Clayton, Director of Operations
(914) 347-2325
kclayton@pgahq.com
• Jeff Voorheis, Tournament Director
(914) 347-2325
jvoorheis@pgahq.com
• Paul Giordano, Communications Manager
(914) 347-2325
pgiordano@pgahq.com
• Tony Murrell, Controller
(914) 347-2325

MICHIGAN PGA SECTIONAL OFFICE
15600 CHANDLER ROAD
BATH, MI 48808
517-641-7421
Fax: 517-641-7830
michigan@pgahq.com
www.michiganpgagolf.com
• Kevin Helm, Executive Director
khelm@michiganpga.com
• Justin Phillips, Director of Tournaments/Operations
jphillips@michiganpga.com
• Doug White, President
• Ron Osborne, Vice President
rjosborne@ci.battle-creek.mi.us
• Kevin McKinley, Secretary
kmckinley@treetops.com
• Gary Koenes, Honorary President
GaryK@pga.com
Description:
To promote the enjoyment and involvement in the game of golf and to contribute to its growth by providing services to golf professionals and the golf industry.

MIDDLE ATLANTIC PGA
1 PGA DRIVE
STAFFORD, VA 22554
540-720-7420
Fax: 540-720-7076
midatl@pgahq.com
www.mapga.com
• John Madden, President
(703) 759-2640
jmrbgcc@aol.com
• Matthew Schulze, Vice President
(757) 253-3906
mdspga@verizon.net
• J.P. Lunn, Secretary
(301) 524-3213

jplunn@comcast.net
• John Lyberger, Director at Large
(301) 469-2032
• Brian Dix, A-8 Director
(410) 409-5941
bdix1008@gmail.com
• Butch Butler, Tournament Chair
(301) 342-3597
butchbutler@pga.com
• John Malinowski, Honorary President
(410) 641-6057
jmalinowski@pga.com
• Jon Guhl, Executive Director
(540) 720-7420
jguhl@pgahq.com
• Jeremy Greiner, Tournament Director
(540) 720-7420
Number of Members:
750 members; 350 apprentices
Member Services:
Education Seminars; Employment Services; Grow the Game Initiatives; Tournaments; Jr Golf Foundation; Scholarship Foundation
Publications:
MAPGA Member Handbook; Middle Atlantic PGA Annual; MAPGA Golf Pass

MIDWEST PGA SECTIONAL OFFICE
1960 NW COPPER OAKS CIRCLE
BLUE SPRINGS, MO 64015
816-229-6565
877-625-6565
Fax: 816-220-9644
midwest@pgahq.com
midwest.pga.com
• Jay Kennedy, President
(816) 318-0004
eagles4jay@aol.com
• Chad Myers, Vice President/Treasurer
(785) 456-2649
• Julie Roberts, Secretary
(816) 942-4033
jroberts@orion-mgmt.com
• Brad Demo, Executive Director
(816) 229-6493

MINNESOTA PGA SECTIONAL OFFICE
BUNKER HILLS GOLF COURSE
12800 BUNKER PRAIRIE ROAD
COON RAPIDS, MN 55448
763-754-0820
Fax: 763-754-6682
info@minnesotapga.com
www.minnesotapga.com
• Steve Fessler, President
(763) 271-5000
• Peter Kurvers, Honorary President
(320) 587-3070
• Joel Burger, Vice President
(312) 436-7990
• Mark Foley, Secretary
(651) 766-4170
• Jon Tollette, Executive Director
jtollette@pgahq.com
• Darren DeYoung, Tournament Director
• Kathy Swanson, Director Of Member Services & Player Development

NEBRASKA PGA SECTIONAL OFFICE
601 J STREET
SUITE 10
LINCOLN, NE 68508
402-489-7760
Fax: 402-489-1785
nebraska@pgahq.com
www.nebraskapga.com
• Mike Antonio, President
mikea@happyhollowclub.com
• Tony Pesavento, Vice Pesident
• Nathan Kalin, Secretary
• Greg Neujahr, Honorary President/Special Awards Chair
gneujahr@championsomaha.com
• David Honnens, Executive Director/CEO
dhonnens@pgahq.com
• Sean O'Neill, Tournament Director
Number of Members:
220

NEW ENGLAND PGA SECTIONAL OFFICE
67A SHREWSBURY STREET
PO BOX 743
BOYLSTON, MA 01505
508-869-0000
Fax: 508-869-0009
www.nepga.com
• Mike Higgins, Executive Director
(508) 869-0000
mhiggins@pgahq.com
• Larry Kelley, President
(802) 558-0756
• Susan Bond, Vice President
(401) 322-7870
cslcbond@aol.com
• Ron Bibeau, Secretary
(207) 809-9030
rbibeau@thefirstteemaine.org
Description:
A non-profit association dedicated to promoting the game of golf, and is one of the 41 sections that comprise the PGA of America

NEW JERSEY PGA SECTION
255 OLD NEW BRUNSWICK ROAD
SUITE 100 SOUTH
PISCATAWAY, NJ 08854
732-465-1212
Fax: 732-465-9524
www.newjersey.pga.com
• Chris Bauer, Executive Director
(732) 465-1212
cbauer@pgahq.com
• Steve Bartowski, Director of Tournaments
(732) 465-1212
sbartkowski@pgahq.com
• Scott Paris, President
(908) 769-3666
• David Reasoner, Vice President
(201) 225-6521
dreasoner@rcc1890.com
• Joe Kelly, Secretary, Treasurer & Grievance Chairman
(973) 543-7297
jpkpga@yahoo.com

NORTH FLORIDA PGA SECTIONAL OFFICE
7593 GATHERING DRIVE
KISSIMMEE, FL 34747
386-256-1221
Fax: 386-765-1478
nflorida@pgahq.com
www.nfpga.com
• Greg Lecker, President
glecker@sawgrasscountryclub.com
• Jim Lohbauer, Vice President
jimlohbauer@gmail.com
• Anthony Vaughn, Secretary
anthony.vaughn@honoursgolf.com
• Pamela Shelley, Tournament Chair
pshelley@sawgrasscountryclub.com
• Rich Smith, Executive Director/CEO
rsmith@pgahq.com
• Jane Olier, Bookeeping and Finances
Year Founded:
1999
Number of Members:
1,500

NORTHEASTERN NEW YORK PGA SECTIONAL OFFICE
TOWN OF COLONIE GOLF COURSE
418 CONSAUL RD
SCHENECTADY, NY 12304
518-438-8645
Fax: 518-438-8670
neny@pgahq.com
www.neny.pga.com
• Tracie Warner, Executive Director
(518) 438-8645
twarner@pgahq.com
• Doug Evans, Tournament Director
(518) 438-8645
• Kevin Hughes, President
kevinhughes@pga.com

• Ron Ireland, Vice President
ron@saratogagolfpoloclub.org
• Mike Behan, Secretary
pgagolfcar@aol.com
Description:
The Northeastern New York PGA is one of the smallest sections in the country.
Number of Members:
178

NORTHERN CALIFORNIA SECTIONAL OFFICE
411 DAVIS STREET
SUITE 103
VACAVILLE, CA 95688
707-449-4742
Fax: 707-449-4755
ncal@pgahq.com
www.ncpgalinks.com
• Chris Thomas, Executive Director/Chief Operating Officer
• Jennifer Noel, Operations Director
• Cameron MacGregor, Tournament Director
• Suzy Schneider, Administrative Assistant
sschneider@pgahq.com
• Carol Pence, Employment Service Consultant
(510) 706-1583
• Nancy Maul, Assistant Executive Director
nmaul@pgahq.com
Description:
An organization committed to helping others through the game of golf. The association provides support to its golf professionals in the following areas: Education, Employment, Professional Tournaments, and Marketing/PR Services
Number of Members:
1,150

NORTHERN OHIO PGA SECTIONAL OFFICE
4735 RICHMOND ROAD
WARRENSVILLE HEIGHTS, OH 44128
216-765-1214
Fax: 216-765-0639
nohio@pgahq.com
thenorthernohiopga.com
• Scott Pollack, President
• Scott Sunderstrom, Vice President
• Ron Dejacimo, Secretary
• Mike Heisterkamp, Honorary President
• David Griffith, Tournament Director
dgriffith@pgahq.com
• Dominic Antenucci, Executive Director
• Eileen Antenucci, Junior Golf Director
Description:
Promote the enjoyment and involvement in the game of golf within the Section, and to contribute to its growth by providing services to golf professionals and the golf industry within our Section
Number of Members:
359 members, 212 golf facilities

NORTHERN TEXAS PGA SECTIONAL OFFICE
15150 PRESTON ROAD
SUITE 250
DALLAS, TX 75248
214-420-7421
Fax: 214-420-7424
mharrison@ntpga.com
www.ntpga.com
• Mark Harrison, Executive Director
(214) 420-7421
mharrison@ntpga.com
• Philip Bleakney, Honorary President
• Paul Earnest, President
• Tony Martinez, Vice Pesident
• Jason Hase, Secretary
• Courtney Connell, At-Large Director
Description:
In addition to managing the day-to-day affairs of the Section, the headquarters operates the Northern Texas PGA Junior Golf Foundation, a tax exempt organization
Number of Members:
750

PACIFIC NORTHWEST PGA SECTIONAL OFFICE
TUMWATER, WA
360-456-6496
800-688-4653
Fax: 360-456-6745
pacnw@pgahq.com
www.pnwpga.com
• Bryan Tunstill, President
(503) 285-8354
Bryan.Tunstill@cecc.com
• Greg Manley, Vice President
(253) 613-3133
greg@meridianvalleycc.com
• Greg Morris, Secretary
(406) 863-3106
• Marcus King, Honorary President
(425) 454-7971
mking@overlakegcc.com
• Jeff Ellison, Chief Executive Officer
JEllison@pgahq.com
• Molly Cooper, Director Of Tournament & Member Programs
MCooper@pgahq.com
Description:
Promote the enjoyment and involvement in the game of golf and to contribute to its growth by providing services to golf professionals and the golf industry
Number of Members:
1,100

PHILADELPHIA PGA SECTIONAL OFFICE
1009 PENLLYN PIKE
LOWER GWYNEDD, PA 19002
215-886-7742
Fax: 215-646-3961
www.philadelphia.pga.com
• Geoffrey Surrette, Executive Director
(215) 481-9083
gsurrette@pgahq.com
• Barbara Creveling, Assistant Executive Director
(215) 481-9081
bcreveling@pgahq.com
• Ellen Berlinger, Tournament Coordinator
(215) 481-9089
eberlinger@pgahq.com
• Leila Mackie, Comm & Player Development
(215) 481-9080
• John Pillar, President
(570) 685-8102
john.pillar@woodloch.com
• Ian Dalzell, Vice President
(215) 659-1584
idalzell@hvccpa.org
• John Rogers, Secretary
(717) 816-6110
jrpga@comcast.net
• Jeff Kiddie, Director Of Section Affairs
(215) 247-6001
jkiddie@aronimink.org
Number of Members:
860

ROCKY MOUNTAIN PGA SECTIONAL OFFICE
1303 SOUTH FIVE MILE ROAD
BOISE, ID 83709
208-939-6028
Fax: 208-939-6058
www.rockymountainpga.com
• Vaughn Jenkins, Executive Director
vjenkins@pgahq.com
• Laurie Draper, Member Services & Program Director
ldraper@pgahq.com
• David Snyder, President
dsnyder@wyoming.com
• Jim Brown, Vice President
jsb.brown@yahoo.com
Year Founded:
1986
Description:
The Rocky Mountain Section PGA and its member professionals are dedicated to nurturing and improving the quality of the game of golf for

single sports

the thousands of golfers using our member facilities.

SOUTH CENTRAL PGA SECTIONAL OFFICE
951 NORTH FOREST RIDGE BOULEVARD
BROKEN ARROW, OK 74014
918-357-3332
Fax: 918-357-3328
scentral@pgahq.com
www.southcentral.pga.com
• Peter Vitali, President
(405) 302-2810
• Michael Henderson, Vice President
(405) 372-3399
mhenderson@stillwater.org
• Barry Howard, Secretary
(501) 624-2661
barry@hotspringscc.com
• Brian Soerensen, Honorary President
(405) 341-5350
• Brian Davis, Executive Director
bdavis@pgahq.com
• Joyce Cherblanc, Operations Manager
jcherblanc@pgahq.com
• Cimarron Grubb, Tournament Director
(405) 388-2577
Description:
The local delivery system for PGA of America programs and activities to promote golf in this region and to enhance the skills of its members
Number of Members:
480

SOUTHERN CALIFORNIA PGA SECTIONAL OFFICE
3333 CONCOURS ST
BLDG 2, SUITE 2100
ONTARIO, CA 91764
951-845-4653
Fax: 951-769-6733
www.scpga.com
• Tom Addis, Executive Director/CEO
taddis@pgahq.com
• Jeff Johnson, Director of Operations/COO
• Max De Spain, Tournament Director
• John McNair, President
jmcnair@jcresorts.com
• Todd Keefer, Vice President
todd@wilshirecountryclub.com
Number of Members:
1,600

SOUTHERN OHIO PGA SECTIONAL OFFICE
66 SOUTH CENTRAL AVENUE
FAIRBORN, OH 45324
937-754-4263
Fax: 937-754-4663
www.thesouthernohiopga.com
• Pat Delaney, President
• Brett Slater, Vice President
• Jimmy Logue, Secretary
• Amanda Fisher, Executive Director
• Kevin Stanton, Tournament Director
Year Founded:
1921
Number of Members:
500

SOUTHERN TEXAS PGA SECTIONAL
21604 CYPRESSWOOD DRIVE
SPRING, TX 77373
832-442-2404
stexas@pgahq.com
www.stpga.com
• Mike Ray, Executive Director
mray@pgahq.com
• Jeff Giedd, Tournament Manager
• Clayton Hromadka, Director of Business Development & Tournaments
chromadka@pgahq.com
• Jeff Strong, President
• Brad Lardon, Vice President
• Doug DeSive, Secretary
• David Altemus, Honorary President

Description:
Offers an extensive tournament program within which professionals, amateurs and junior golfers can compete
Number of Members:
800

SOUTHWEST PGA SECTIONAL OFFICE
10685 NORTH 69TH STREET
SCOTTSDALE, AZ 85254
480-443-9002
Fax: 480-443-9006
swest@pgahq.com
www.southwest.pga.com
• Greg Leicht, President
• Michael Miller, Executive Director
• Mike Martino, Tournament Director
mmartino@pgahq.com
• Joe Hobby, Junior Golf Director
• Frank Calvin, Marketing Director
• Mike Burhans, Administration/Membership Services
Description:
Promote the game of golf in this region and to enhance the skills of its members
Number of Members:
1,400

SUN COUNTRY PGA SECTIONAL OFFICE
2316 SOUTHER BLVD SE
SUITE C
RIO RANCHO, NM 87124
505-897-0864
800-346-5319
Fax: 505-897-3494
INFO@SUNCOUNTRYGOLFHOUSE.COM
www.suncountry.pga.com
• Matt Molloy, President
• Pat Gavin, Vice President
• Jason White, Secretary
• Derek Gutierrez, Past President
• Dana Lehner, Executive Director
• Teresa Hitchcock, Director Of PGA Member Services
Year Founded:
1974
Description:
Promote participation and enjoyment in the game of golf for all levels of golfers
Number of Members:
136

TENNESSEE PGA SECTIONAL OFFICE
400 FRANKLIN ROAD
FRANKLIN, TN 37069
615-790-7600
Fax: 615-790-8600
tenn@pgahq.com
www.tennpga.com
• Jeff Abbot, Executive Director
(615) 465-6311
• Ken Crowder, President
(276) 523-0739
kcrowder1@yahoo.com
• Johnny Bridgemann, Vice President
(615) 373-9922
johnny@bccgolf.org
• Jim Vernon, Secretary
(615) 847-4001
• David Olinger, Tournament Director
(615) 465-6312
Year Founded:
1995
Number of Members:
400

TRI-STATE PGA SECTIONAL OFFICE
993 BROADHEAD RD
SUITE 204
MOON TOWNSHIP, PA 15108
724-774-2224
Fax: 412-375-7395
tristate@pgahq.com
www.tristate.pga.com
• Ed Habjan, President
(412) 793-2200

ehabjan@greenoakscc.com
• John Klinchock, Vice President
(724) 238-5438
ligolf@verizon.net
• Dennis J. Darak, Sr., Executive Director/CEO
• David Wright, Assistant Executive Director/Tournament Director
dwright@pgahq.com

UTAH PGA SECTIONAL OFFICE
580 WEST 3300 SOUTH
SALT LAKE CITY, UT 84115
801-566-1005
Fax: 801-326-8098
utah@pgahq.com
www.utahpga.com
• Chriss Stover, President
• Ryan Kartchner, Vice President
ryan@hiddenvalley.cc
• Dustin Volk, Secretary
dvolk@co.davis.ut.us
• Colby Cowan, Honorary president
• Scott Whittaker, Executive Director
• Annie Fisher, Programs Director
afisher@pgahq.com
Description:
Promotes involvment in and enjoyment of the game of golf for the golfers of Utah by providing services to its members, the golf industry, and to amateurs of all ages and skill levels.

WESTERN NEW YORK PGA SECTION OFFICE
8265 SHERIDAN DRIVE
WILLIAMSVILLE, NY 14221
716-626-7095
Fax: 716-626-5308
wnewyork@pgahq.com
www.westernnewyork.pga.com
• Jeff Mietus, President
jeffmietuspga@hotmail.com
• Michael O'Connor, Vice President
mjokah@aol.com
• Rob Horak, Secretary
bhhpro@rochester.rr.com
• Kirk Stauffer, Honorary President
paccpro1@verizon.net
• Joe Bertino, Executive Director
(716) 626-7095
• Alex Wright, Tournament Director
• Amanda Gingerich, Junior Golf Director
Year Founded:
1925
Description:
Mission is to establish the Section as a viable, valuable and visible organization in promoting the growth of golf and the advancement of the golfing professional.
Number of Members:
195

WISCONSIN PGA SECTIONAL OFFICE
11350 W THEO TRECKER WAY
WEST ALLIS, WI 53214
414-443-3570
Fax: 414-443-0817
wisc@pgahq.com
www.wisconsin.pga.com
• Rob Elliott, President
• Joe Stadler, Executive Director
jstadler@pgahq.com
• Chris Hoel, Director of Operations
choel@pgahq.com

PGA TOUR
100 PGA TOUR BOULEVARD
PONTE VEDRA BEACH, FL 32082
904-285-3700
www.pgatour.com
• Tim Finchem, Commissioner
• Charlie Zink, Executive VP/Co-Chief Operating Officer
• Lee Bushkil, Vice President Media Sales
• Luis Goicouria, Vice President, Digital Media Business Develo

• David Desmond, Sales Director, Digital Media & Entertainment
• Raef Godwin, Director, Sales & Marketing Operations
• Chris Wandell, Director, Business Development
• Cynthia Howard, Director, Digital Sales
• Paul Johnson, Senior Vice President, Strategic Development
Year Founded:
1974
Description:
A tax-exempt membership organization of professional golfers. Mission is to expand domestically and internationally to substantially increase player financial benefits while maintaining its commitment to the integrity of the game.
Membership Requirements:
Must complete qualifying requirements
Publications:
Tour Book, player bibliographies, statistics, etc

PRAIRIE GOLF
10708 SOUTH 149TH STREET
OMAHA, NE 68138
402-896-5079
800-528-5079
Fax: 402-881-8755
www.prairiegolf.com
• Scott Kasl, New Owner
Year Founded:
1995
Description:
Eight-event tour open to professionals and amateurs ages 16 and over. Operates in states of Iowa, Kansas, Missouri, and Nebraska
Membership Requirements:
$300 membership fee
Member Services:
Discounted entry fees for packages of event; free practice rounds; $7,200 Skins bonus pool at end of the schedule

PROFESSIONAL CADDIES ASSOCIATION WORLDWIDE, PCA
23 MALACOMPRA ROAD
PALM COAST, FL 32137
386-446-8721
Fax: 386-446-8721
pca@pcahq.com
www.pcahq.com
• Dennis Cone, Founder/CEO
Year Founded:
1997
Description:
Open to everyone worldwide who wants to help the mission. Over 11,000 walking billboards to advertise and promote the your company or products. World recognized Association for over 20 years and certification programs used at many top clubs worlwide. Helps train over 11,000 caddies/members who play golf daily with the decision maker of the world.
Number of Members:
5,500
Membership Requirements:
Dues is $50.00
Member Services:
Health, disability, retirement and marketing benefits and opportunities for caddies and their families. Worldwide travel company - health card. Available to all caddies working

or retired. Caddie certification programs and free insurance and benefits for members.

PROFESSIONAL PUTTERS ASSOCIATION
FORT BRAGG ROAD
PO BOX 35237
FAYETTEVILLE, NC 28303
910-485-7131
Fax: 910-485-1122
www.proputters.com
• Joe Aboid, PPA Commissioner
• Bill Baus, Players Committee Chairman
• Rick Rybaczek, Website Developer
• Joe Abode, PPA Commisioner
• Bill Baus,
Description:
Founded 1959.
Membership Requirements:
Two membership classifications: amateur and pro. Amateur and pro applications must be signed by local Putt-Putt Golf Course managing pro or forwarded to the executive offices for review by the Board of Advisors.

SYMETRA TOUR
100 INTERNATIONAL GOLF DRIVE
DAYTONA BEACH, FL 32124
386-274-6200
Fax: 386-274-1099
futuresfeedback@lpga.com
www.symetratour.com
• Vicki Goetze-Ackerman, Player Director-President (LGPA)
• Karrie Webb, Player Director- Vice President (LGPA)
• Laura Diaz, Player Director (LGPA)
• Michael Whan, Commissioner
• Mike L Nichols, Chief Business Officer of the Symetra Tour
Year Founded:
1981, Duramed Futures Golf Tour signed an agreement with sponsor Symetra in 2011 and became the Symetra Tour.
Description:
The Future's Golf Tour's mission has three primary objectives: to provide an opportunity for women professional golfers to develop their skills and pursue their competitive goals; for tournament host communities to meet and embrace future LPGA stars; and for business communities and corporate leaders at host sites to link with local charities to develop a proven fund raising vehicle by which to support local projects.
Membership Requirements:
We are the developmental tour of the LPGA. Our membership is over 300 players representing 26 different countries
Media Notes:
1999 - Signed a 5 year deal with the LPGA making it the official developmental tour
Sponsors:
Aruba Sport, Champ®, Eco Golf, Penske Truck Leasing, Sun Mountain® Sports, Yes! Golf

U.S. GOLF ASSOCIATION/USGA
77 LIBERTY CORNER ROAD
FAR HILLS, NJ 07931-0708
908-234-2300
www.usga.org
• Thomas J O'Toole, President
• Diana M Murphy, Vice President
• William Gist, IV, Vice President
• Sheila C Johnson, Secretary
• Mark E Newell, Treasurer

• Ernest J Getto, General Counsel
• Mike Davis, Executive Director
Year Founded:
1894
Description:
Governing body for the sport of amateur golf in the United States
Number of members:
700,000 members; 9,000 courses and clubs

Other locations:

ALASKA STATE GOLF ASSOCIATION
9360 OLD SEWARD HIGHWAY
ANCHORAGE, AK 99508
907-349-4653
golfalaska@gmail.com
www.agagolf.org
• Paul Blanche, President
• Jason Kimmel, Vice President
• Stacy Pettit, Treasurer
• Marcia Petros, Secretary
• Greg Sanders, Rules/Men's USGA Rep
• Bengie Sumulong, Trophies/Awards
• Rich Teders, Competitions

ANCHORAGE WOMEN'S GOLF ASSOCIATION
9360 OLD SEWARD HWY
ANCHORAGE, AK 99515
907-555-5555
Fax: 907-563-7552
awgaak@gmail.com
ghin.com/eClubhouse/eClubHome.aspx?cid=1068
• Nicole Harris, President
• Jamie Berge, Treasurer
• Leslie Fleming, Secretary
• Pam Chesla, Membership Chair
golf2201@aol.com
Year Founded:
1968
Description:
Promote and maintain the best interests and true spirit of the game of golf among women in the state of Alaska

ARIZONA GOLF ASSOCIATION
7600 E REDFIELD RD
SUITE 130
SCOTTSDALE, AZ 85260
602-944-3035
800-458-8484
Fax: 602-944-3228
aga1923@azgolf.org
www.azgolf.org
• Edward Gowan, Executive Director
edgowan@azgolf.org
• Michelle Evens, Club Program Manager
michelle@azgolf.org
• Lorraine Thies, Assistant Executive Director
lorraine@azgolf.org
• Brian Foster, Director of Marketing & Communications
bfoster@azgolf.org
• Derek McKenzie, Director of Handicapping and Course Rating
dmckenzie@azgolf.org
Year Founded:
1923
Description:
To foster the enhancement and expansion of the game of golf by leading in the development of member and information services, the promotion of opportunities for all who want to play, and the protection of the game's integrity and valued traditions

ARIZONA WOMEN'S GOLF ASSOCIATION
141 EAST PALM LANE
SUITE 210
PHOENIX, AZ 85004-1555
602-253-5655
800-442-2942
Fax: 602-253-6210

awga@awga.org
www.awga.org
• Mary Pomroy, Executive Director
mpomroy@awga.org
• Erin Groeneveld, Programs Manager
erin@awga.org
• Melanie R. Bridges, Secretary
• Robin Cook, Officer at Large
• Ginny Zak, President
• Sally Larson, Vice President
• Mary Byrd, Treasurer
Description:
Promote and maintain the best interests and true spirit of the game of golf among women in Arizona

ARKANSAS STATE GOLF ASSOCIATION
3 EAGLE HILL COURT
SUITE B
LITTLE ROCK, AR 72210
501-455-2742
800-984-2742
Fax: 501-455-8111
info@asga.org
www.asga.org
• Cippy Smith, President
• Chris Jenkins, Vice President
• Rob McSpadden, Treasurer
• Stan Lee, Secretary
• Jay Fox, Executive Director
Jay@asga.org
• Bryant Fortin, Director of Junior Golf
• Terri Green, Director Of Membership
Terri@asga.org

ARKANSAS WOMEN'S GOLF ASSOCIATION
PO BOX 280
CAVE SPRINGS, AR 72718
479-619-6082
dorherren@cox.net
www.awga.us
• Norma Hartney, President
n-hartney@sbcglobal.net
• Esther Tompkins, Vice President
tompkinsestherh@uams.edu
• Rosetta Parks, Secretary
rosieparks@cox.net
• Marilyn Lenggenhager, Treasurer
(501) 580-2171
Year Founded:
1924
Description:
To serve women golfers in Arkansas, which includes conducting championship tournaments, sponsoring Junior Girls championship tournaments, promote USGA Women's State Team competitions, participate in the prestigious Fore-State Cup matches, and provide handicap (GHIN) and course rating service

BUFFALO DISTRICT GOLF ASSOCIATION
8265 SHERIDAN DRIVE
WILLIAMSVILLE, NY 14231
716-632-0151
www.buffdga.org
• Robert Rosen, President
• Nick Amigone, III, First Vice President
• Nick Morreale, Secretary/Treasurer
• Thomas Sprague, Executive Director
• Whitey Nichols, Rules Chairman
Number of Members:
78
Member Services:
Organization/Administration of 13 District Golf Tournaments, Junior Scholarship Program, Course Measurement/Rating, Handicapping Service
Membership Requirements:
Annual Dues

CAROLINAS GOLF ASSOCIATION
140 RIDGE ROAD
SOUTHERN PINES, NC 28387

910-673-1000
Fax: 910-673-1001
www.carolinasgolf.org
• G. Jackson Hughes, President
• Jack Nance, Executive Director
• Andy Priest, Assistant Executive Director
• Jason Cox, Director of Junior Golf
• Tiffany Priest, Director of Women's Golf and Membership Services
Year Founded:
1909
Description:
Conduct championships and tournaments for amateur golfers in North and South Carolina, administer the USGA handicap system in the Carolinas
Number of Members:
720
Membership Requirements:
CGA member clubs pay annual dues of $50.00

CHICAGO DISTRICT GOLF ASSOCIATION
MIDWEST GOLF HOUSE
11855 ARCHER AVENUE
LEMONT, IL 60439
630-257-2005
Fax: 630-257-2088
www.cdga.org
• David R. Haverick, President
• Michael J Grandinetti, First Vice President
• Sheldon L. Solow, Second Vice President
• Robert Markionni, Executive Director
(630) 685-2303
rmarkionni@cdga.org
• C. Daniel Cochran, Treasurer
• Mike Nass, Secretary
• Matt Baylor, Senior Director of Communications
(630) 685-2302
mbaylor@cdga.org
• Lynn Boyd, Director of Handicapping
(630) 685-2304
lboyd@cdga.org
• Margie Lawlor, Controller
(630) 685-2320
mlawlor@cdga.org
• Denny Davenport, Foundation Consultant
(630) 272-7872
ddavenport@cdga.org
Year Founded:
1914
Description:
Promote amateur golf in the Midwest
Number of Members:
100,000

COLORADO GOLF ASSOCIATION
5990 GREENWOOD PLAZA BOULEVARD
SUITE 102
GREENWOOD VILLAGE, CO 80111
303-366-4653
800-228-4675
Fax: 303-344-8229
cga@coloradogolf.org
www.coloradogolf.org
• Edward Mate, Executive Director
• Ann Bley, Director of Finance
• Dustin Jensen, Managing Director of Operations
• Aaron Kellough, Director of Communications
• Ashley Barnhart, Junior Tournament Coordinator
Year Founded:
1915
Description:
Purpose is to represent, promote, and serve the best interests of golf in the state of Colorado, and has been throughout its history
Publications:
Colorado Golf Newsletter, the official membership publication of the CGA, 4 times year to all active members; Colorado Golf, the official guide to the Golf Courses of Colorado, mailed in April to all active members; Golf in Colorado, an independent Study of the Economic Impact and Environmental Aspects of Golf in Colorado

COLORADO WOMEN'S GOLF ASSOCIATION
6 INVERNESS CT E
ENGLEWOOD, CO 80112
303-366-7888
800-392-2942
Fax: 303-474-3007
cwga@coloradowomensgolf.org
www.coloradowomensgolf.org
• Joanie Ott, President
• Juliet Miner, Vice President
• Phyllis Jensen, Secretary
• Jeanne Surbrugg, Treasurer
• Ann Guiberson, Executive Director
• Alex Westman, Manager-Tournament Administration/Member Programs
Year Founded:
1916
Number of Members:
Approximately 18,000 individual members.
Description:
The CWGA's mission is to promote women's golf in the state of Colorado and preserve the integrity of the game.
Publications:
Colorado Golf Newsletter, the official membership publication of the CGA, four times a year to all active members; Colorado Golf, official guide to the Golf Courses of Colorado, mailed in April to all active members; Golf in Colorado, an Independent Study of the Economic Impact and Environmental Aspects of Golf in Colorado

COLUMBUS DISTRICT GOLF ASSOCIATION
1570 WEST FIRST AVENUE
COLUMBUS, OH 43212
614-487-1207
golfmaster@ohiogolf.org
www.ohiogolf.org
• Gary Price, President
• James M. Popa, Executive Director
Description:
The prime moving force behind the promotion and betterment of golf in Central Ohio is the Columbus District Golf Association

CONNECTICUT STATE GOLF ASSOCIATION
35 COLD SPRING ROAD
SUITE 212
ROCKY HILL, CT 06067
860-257-4171
Fax: 860-257-8355
info@csgalinks.org
www.csgalinks.org
• Stan McFarland, President
• Mike Moraghan, Executive Director
(860) 257-4171
mmoraghan@csgalinks.org
• Ben Briggs, Vice President Club Relations
• Shelly Guyer, Vice President Competitions
• Bill Cremins, Secretary
• Jim Healy, Jr., Treasurer
• Ryan Hoffman, Director, Operations
(860) 257-4171
rhoffman@csgalinks.org
• Brent Paladino, Director, Competitions & Communications
(860) 257-4171
bpaladino@csgalinks.org
Year Founded:
1899
Description:
Functions as an extension of the USGA and provides stewardship for amateur golf in Connecticut
Number of Members:
170

DELAWARE STATE GOLF ASSOCIATION
7234 OLD LANCASTER PIKE
SUITE 302-B
HOCKESSIN, DE 19707

302-234-3365
Fax: 302-234-3359
www.dsga.org
• Gary Mahoney, President
• Dick Matthias, Vice President
• Wayne Carey, Vice President
• Tim Freeh, Treasurer
• Bill Barrow, Executive Director
• Laura Heien, Tournament Operations & Communications Manager
• Cameron McDonald, Board Member
• Jeff Allen, Board Member

FLORIDA STATE GOLF ASSOCIATION

12630 TELECOM DR
TAMPA, FL 33637
813-632-3742
Fax: 813-910-2129
www.fsga.org
• Randy Briggs, President
• Chuck Phillips, Vice President
• Steve Carter, Secretary/Treasurer
• Jim Applegate, Immediate Past President
• Jim Demick, Executive Director
(813) 868-5801
• Kevin Kasubinski, Manager Of Club Services & IT
(813) 868-5803
kevin@fsga.org
• Debby Lamontagne, Controller
(813) 868-5811
debby@fsga.org
• Wally Les, GHIN Regional Manager-SE Florida
(561) 704-8355
Year Founded:
1913
Description:
Provides a variety of services to its member clubs, their members and the general golfing community of Florida.
Number of Members:
800

GOLF ASSOCIATION OF MICHIGAN

24116 RESEARCH DRIVE
FARMINGTON HILLS, MI 48335
248-478-9242
Fax: 248-478-5536
www.gam.org
• David Graham, Executive Director
(248) 478-9242
dgraham@gam.org
• Kelly Serr, Event Coordinator/Executive Administrator
(248) 478-9242
kserr@gam.org
• Susan Smiley, Manager Of Member Services & Communications
(248) 478-9242
ssmiley@gam.org
• Ken Hartmann, Senior Director Of Rules & Competition
(248) 478-9242
khartmann@gam.org
• Thomas Bollinger, President
• Steve Braun, Vice President
• James Koepke, Treasurer
• Chris Angott, Secretary
Year Founded:
1919
Description:
Our purpose is to represent, promote, and serve the best interests in the game of golf
Membership Requirements:
Blue Card Member, annual dues $30.00 with discount golf benefits and a free subscription to Michigan Links Magazine; Gold Card Member, annual dues $35.00 with full benefits, including official gam/usga handicap index and tournament eligibility
Publications:
Michigan Links Magazine free to all active members

GOLF ASSOCIATION OF PHILADELPHIA

1974 SPROUL ROAD
SUITE 400
BROOMALL, PA 19008
610-687-2340
Fax: 610-687-2082
email@gapgolf.org
www.gapgolf.org
• Robert M. Morey, President
• Kirby V. Martin, Director Of Competitions
(610) 687-2340
kmartin@gapgolf.org
• Christopher A. Roselle, Tournament Director
(610) 687-2340
croselle@gapgolf.org
• Mark E. Peterson, Executive Director
(610) 687-2340
mpeterson@gapgolf.org
• Martin D. Emeno, Jr., Director Operations
(610) 687-2340
• Mario Machi, Director of Handicapping
(610) 687-2340
mmachi@gapgolf.org
• Justin A Reasy, Tournament Assistant
(610) 687-2340
• Jan Garber, Programs Manager
(610) 687-2340
Year Founded:
1897
Description:
The purpose of the association is simple: to preserve, protect and promote the game of golf. Every GAP activity is designed to do just that
Number of Members:
132

GREATER CINCINNATI GOLF ASSOCIATION

9200 MOUNTGOMERY ROAD
SUITE 24B
CINCINNATI, OH 45242
513-522-4444
Fax: 513-521-4242
www.gcga.org
• Art Plate, President
• Todd Johnson, Executive Director
tjohnson@gcga.org
• James E. Stahl, Jr., Executive Vice President
• Matt Eilers, Treasurer
• Robert Gerwin, II, Secretary
• Teresa Silvers, Handicapping & Course Rating Director
tsilvers@gcga.org
Description:
Promote interest in, enthusiasm for and support for the game of golf among all golfers in the Greater Cincinnati area

HAWAII STATE GOLF ASSOCIATION

98-025 HEKAHA ST
UNIT 204A
AIEA, HI 96701
808-589-2909
Fax: 808-589-2915
info@hawaiistategolf.org
www.hawaiistategolf.org
• Paul Ogawa, Executive Director
paul@hawaiistategolf.org
• Jay Hinazumi, President
• Gary Wild, Vice President
• Darrell Yamagata, Treasurer
• Gordon Cho, Secretary
Year Founded:
1984
Description:
Non-profit organization dedicated to the goals and traditions of golf in Hawaii. Our main objective is to unite every golfer in Hawaii under one reliable and accurate handicapping system

HAWAII STATE WOMEN'S GOLF ASSOCIATION

HONOLULU, HI 96815
www.hswga.net
• Gwen Omori, President
gcomori@hawaiiantel.net

• Barbara Schroeder, Vice President
barbara.schroeder@outlook.com
• Marcia Lee, Treasurer
• Susan Church, Corresponding Secretary
wchurch1@hawaiiantel.net
Year Founded:
1976
Description:
Promote women's golf as a competitive sport and recreational activity in the State of Hawaii. We believe the game contributes to the overall self-betterment of girls and women by enhancing physical, emotional, social and mental development, and promoting lifelong values of personal motivation, discipline, integrity, patience and teamwork

IDAHO GOLF ASSOCIATION

4696 OVERLAND RD
SUITE 120
BOISE, ID 83705
208-342-4442
Fax: 208-345-5959
www.theiga.org
• Jennifer Swindell, President
(208) 473-8811
swindelljen@gmail.com
• Kelly Park, Vice President
rpark4@silverstar.com
• Brenda Sanford, Treasurer
bsanford@dlevans.com
• Genger Fahleson, Executive Director
Year Founded:
1969
Description:
Its purpose is to represent, promote and serve the best interests of golf in our state
Number of Members:
18,200
Membership Requirements:
$20 annual fee
What IGA Membership Supports:
IGA Clubs; IGA & Member Club Tournament Calendar; Handicapping; Current USGA Course Ratings for IGA Clubs; Member Education: Rules/Course Rating; Gold Course Superintendent's Association; USGA; PGA Snake River Chapter; Pacific Northwest Golf Association; Northwest Turfgrass Research; Junior Golf Activities for Girls and Boys; Publications for IGA Members; National Exposure for Idaho & Idaho Players; IGA Championships
Publications:
Intermountain Golf Magazine; Pacific NW Golfer; Idaho Gold Journal

INDIANA GOLF ASSOCIATION

2526 HURRICANE RD
PO BOX 516
FRANKLIN, IN 46131
317-738-9696
800-779-7271
Fax: 317-738-9436
www.indianagolf.org
• Mike David, Executive Director
(317) 739-3016
mdavid@indianagolf.org
• Todd Dehaven, Tournament Director
(317) 739-3013
tdehaven@indianagolf.org
• Matt Shepherd, President
• John Watts, First Vice President
• Steve Paquin, Second Vice President
• Mark Inman, Past President
• Steve Sterrett, Secretary
ext 240
• Brad Hardin, Treasurer
ext 235
• Ryan Lambert, Assistant Executive Director
(317) 739-3019
• Kristtini Hunt, Director of Womens Golf
(317) 739-3017
• Roger Lundy, Junior Golf Development
(317) 739-3020
rlundy@indianagolf.org
Year Founded:
1972

IOWA GOLF ASSOCIATION
1605 N ANKENY BLVD
SUITE 210
ANKENY, IA 50023
515-207-1062
888-388-4442
Fax: 515-207-1065
www.iowagolf.org
• Tom Christensen, President
• Joe Kehoe, Past President
• Andy Burton, Vice President
• Mike Pape, Secretary
• John Matovina, Treasurer
• Bill Dickens, Executive Director
• Clint Brown, Director Of Communications &
Marketing
clint@iowagolf.org
• Katelynn Hogenson, Director Of Membership
Services & Women's Golf
katelynn@iowagolf.org
Description:
Non-profit organization that works to preserve
and promote the best interests and spirit of the
game of golf and to encourage harmony and
cooperation among golf clubs and other related
associations

KANSAS CITY GOLF ASSOCIATION
8330 MELROSE DR.
LENEXA, KS 66214
913-649-5242
doug@kcgolf.org
www.kansascitygolfer.org
• Dick Sauer, Past President
• Doug Habel, Executive Director
ext 1
doug@kcgolf.org
• Taylor McCann, President
• Carol Gillard, Vice President
• Dick Swetala, Treasurer
• Gary Hruby, Secretary
• Jacque Madison, Director of Club Services
• Todd Stice, Director Of Rules & Competitions
ext 3
todd@kcgolf.org
Year Founded:
1912
Description:
Is a full service regional golf association
dedicated to the betterment of the amateur golf
community of greater Kansas City

KANSAS GOLF ASSOCIATION
1201 WAKARUSA DRIVE
SUITE B5
LAWRENCE, KS 66049
785-842-4833
Fax: 785-842-3831
kga@kansasgolf.org
www.kansasgolf.org
• Gary Lucas, President
• Rusty Hilst, Tournament Administrator
rhilst@cox.net
• Brian Burris, General Counsel
• John Alefs, Director
ext 202
• Sean Thayer, Secretary/Treasurer
• Mike Grosdidier, Vice President
• Jack Simpson, Past President
• Kim Richey, Executive Director
• Casey Old, Director Of Rules & Competitions
• Tyler Cummins, Director Of Member Services
& Junior Golf
Description:
Non-profit organization dedicated to promoting
and preserving the game of golf in the State of
Kansas
Year Founded:
1908
Number of Members:
24,000 members, 175 golf clubs
Publications:
Kansas Golfer Magazine

KANSAS WOMEN'S GOLF ASSOCIATION
TOPEKA, KS

KWGAPres@gmail.com
www.kwga.org
• Karen Hunt-Exon, President
(785) 266-0931
KWGAPres@gmail.com
• Jayne E. Clarke, Vice President
(785) 650-9610
KWGAVP@gmail.com
• Alice Kaul, Treasurer
(316) 207-4827
KWGATreasurer@gmail.com
• Kay Watts, Secretary
(316) 733-8692
KWGASecretary@gmail.com
• Debbie Slater, Tournament Director
(316) 208-9672
KWGATD@gmail.com
Year Founded:
1915
Description:
Promote the game of golf for female golfers, to
encourage sportsmanship and skill, and to
provide chamionships and events for women
golfers, and to engage in charitable efforts
related to the game of golf.
Number of Members:
4,789

KENTUCKY GOLF ASSOCIATION
GOLF HOUSE KENTUCKY
1116 ELMORE JUST DRIVE
LOUISVILLE, KY 40245
502-243-8295
800-254-2742
Fax: 502-243-9266
kentucky@kygolf.org
www.kygolf.org
• Chris Osborne, President
• Tom Cooksey, Vice President
• Barbara Peak, Director,
Finance-Administration
(800) 254-2742
bpeak@kygolf.org
• Steve McMillen, Executive Director
(800) 254-2742
• James Wagoner, Legal Counsel
• Erin Horn, Director
Communications-Membership
(800) 254-2742
Year Founded:
1911
Description:
Recognized as the governing body for amateur
golf in the Commonwealth
Number of Members:
200

LADIES BIRMINGHAM GOLF ASSOCIATION
lbgaemail@gmail.com
www.lbga.org
• Sharon Kellum, President
• Lynn Glover, 1st Vice President
• Jody Atchison, 2nd Vice President
• Missy Bibb, Secretary
• Pat Heilala, Treasurer
• Debbie Atchley, Past President
Year Founded:
1971

LOUISIANA WOMEN'S GOLF ASSOCIATION
JONESVILLE, LA 71343
• Mary Edwards, President
(318) 403-0111
contrarymary_@bellsouth.net
• Paula Karam, Treasurer
(318) 623-4339
pekdent211@aol.com
• Pam Washington, Secretary
(504) 452-7044
buzznrnd@hotmail.com
• Sandra Smith, Juniors
(318) 341-0575
ssmith2454@hotmail.com

MAINE STATE GOLF ASSOCIATION
58 VAL HALLA ROAD
CUMBERLAND, ME 04021
207-829-3549
Fax: 207-829-3584
msga@mesga.org
www.mesga.org
• Lowell Watson, President
• Nancy Storey, Executive Director
(207) 829-3549
• Brian Bickford, Treasurer
• Marty Crowe, Vice President
• Mike Doran, Director Of Tournament
Administration
(207) 829-3549
mike@mesga.org
Description:
Promote and serve the best interests of amateur
golf in Maine, and to sponsor a scholarship fund

MARYLAND STATE GOLF ASSOCIATION
EMICH HOUSE, COMMERCENTRE EAST
1777 REISTERSTOWN ROAD, SUITE 145
BALTIMORE, MD 21208
410-653-5300
Fax: 410-653-8810
www.msga.org
• Thomas Whelan, President
• William K Smith, Executive Director
• Stanard T. Klinefelter, Vice President
• Kimberly M. Ferguson, Director of Operations
• John J. Pauliny, Treasurer
• J. Robert Sherwood, Secretary
Year Founded:
1921
Description:
Promote the best interests of golf in the State of
Maryland

MARYLAND STATE GOLF ASSOCIATION - WOMEN'S DIVISION
1777 REISTERSTOWN ROAD
SUITE 145, COMMERCENTRE EAST
BALTIMORE, MD 21208
410-653-5300
Fax: 410-653-8810
• Deb Watkins, Treasurer
• Patsy DiMuzio, Corresponding Secretary
• William Smith, Executive Director
• Melly Tucker, President
• Joan Heiss, Vice President
• Carolyn Hudson, Recording Secretary
Year Founded:
1995
Description:
Promote the best interests of golf in the State of
Maryland

MASSACHUSETTS GOLF ASSOCIATION
300 ARNOLD PALMER BOULEVARD
NORTON, MA 02766
774-430-9100
800-356-2201
Fax: 774-430-9101
www.mgalinks.org
• Clarence J. Bennett, Esq., President
• Thomas Bagley, III, First Vice President
• Stephen R Dooley, Treasurer
• Jerry R. Green, Secretary
• Jesse Menachem, Executive Director
(774) 430-9102
jmenachem@mgalinks.org
• Becky Blaeser, Director Communications
(774) 430-9104
bblaeser@mgalinks.org
• Scott B. Whitcomb, Director- Field Operations
(774) 430-9108
swhitcomb@mgalinks.org
• Peter A. Caro, General Counsel
Year Founded:
1903
Description:
Dedicated to promoting and preserving amateur
golf in the Commonwealth

Number of Members:
100,000

METROPOLITAN AMATEUR GOLF ASSOCIATION
11777 CLAYTON ROAD
ST.LOUIS, MO 63131
314-576-6242
Fax: 314-261-9250
info@metga.org
www.metga.org
• Stanford S. Grossman, President Emeritus
• Curt Rohe, Executive Director
curt@metga.org
• Thomas O. Sobbe, Jr., Vice President
• Thomas J. O'Toole, Jr., Vice President
• G. Scott Engelbrecht, Treasurer
• M. Ray McCraine, Secretary
• Bill Burton, Director Communications
• Carole Waugh, Director Finance
• Francis Byron, General Counsel
Year Founded:
1992
Description:
Provide a variety of amateur golf services to its member clubs
Number of Members:
130

MIAMI VALLEY GOLF ASSOCIATION
263 REGENCY RIDGE DR
DAYTON, OH 45459
937-294-6842
Fax: 866-301-2974
www.miamivalleygolf.org
• Charles Rinehart, Jr., President
charlie_rinehart@yahoo.com
• Doug Miller, Vice President
• Steve Jurick, Executive Director
(937) 609-3387
• Dan Sutherly, Treasurer
drscoinc@gmail.com
• Jeff Scohy, Secretary
scohy@woh.rr.com
• Matt Wendelken, Assistant Director
(330) 618-3023

MIDDLE ATLANTIC GOLF ASSOCIATION
PO BOX 3040
GAITHERSBURG, MD 20885
301-869-6020
Fax: 301-869-6020
magainfo1902@yahoo.com
www.middleatlanticga.org
• Timothy G. Vigotsky, President
• Tim Merry, Vice President
• Randal P. Reed, Executive Director
rreed@middleatlanticga.org
• Joseph S. Burns, Treasurer
• Edward A. Johnston, General Counsel
Year Founded:
1902
Description:
Promote and serve golf in the Middle Atlantic
Number of Members:
125

MINNESOTA GOLF ASSOCIATION
6550 YORK AVENUE SOUTH
SUITE 211
EDINA, MN 55435
952-927-4643
800-642-4405
info@mngolf.org
www.mngolf.org
• Kip Colwell, President
• Ken Gerzsenyi, Past President
• Doug Hoffman, Tournament Director
(952) 345-3963
doug@mngolf.org
• Nancy LeRoy, Accounting Manager
(952) 345-3976
nleroy@mngolf.org
• Tom Ryan, Executive Director & COO
(952) 345-3971
tom@mngolf.org

• Barb Hanson, 1st Vice President
• Tom H. Smith, Secretary/Treasurer
Year Founded:
1901
Description:
Our mission is to uphold and promote the game of golf and its values for all golfers in Minnesota
Number of Members:
93,000
Publications:
Minnesota Golfer magazine published bi-monthly

MISSISSIPPI GOLF ASSOCIATION
400 CLUBHOUSE DRIVE
PEARL, MS 39208
601-939-1131
Fax: 601-939-0773
missgolf@missgolf.org
www.missgolf.org
• Richard Reed, President
• Brother Sandifer, Vice President
• Margo Coleman, Executive Director
• Ben Snow, Secretary/Treasurer
• Don Hershfelt, Tournament Director
donhershfelt@gmail.com
• Emily Sullivan, Director Of Membership & Club Services
emily@missgolf.org
Year Founded:
1925
Description:
Promote and conserve throughout the state of Mississippi the best interests and true spirit of the game of golf as embodied in its ancient and honorable traditions, and thereby promoting the common good and general welfare of the people of the state of Mississippi

MISSISSIPPI WOMEN'S GOLF ASSOCIATION
1515 SOUTH 40TH AVENUE
HATTIESBURG, MS 39402
601-268-6680
www.misswomensgolf.org/
• Sheila Haynes, President
shelagger@gmail.com
• Lynn Harmount, Treasurer
lharmount@comcast.net
• Dinah Kennedy, Secretary
Dsk080892@aol.com
Year Founded:
2006

MISSOURI GOLF ASSOCIATION
1616 OIL WELL DRIVE
JEFFERSON CITY, MO 65101
573-636-8994
Fax: 573-636-4225
www.mogolf.org
• Denny Payne, President
• Scott Hovis, Executive Director
• Cord Dombrowski, First Vice President
• Charlie Digges, Secretary/Treasurer
• Kent Lowry, Legal Counsel
• Karen Raithel, Director Of Membership & GHIN Services
Year Founded:
1905
Description:
Non-profit organization whose purpose is to promote the best interests and true spirit of the game of golf throughout the State of Missouri

MISSOURI WOMEN'S GOLF ASSOCIATION
1616 OILWELL DRIVE
JEFFERSON CITY, MO 65109
573-636-8994
Fax: 573-636-4225
• Nancy Sebastian, President
• Harriette Myers, Treasurer
• June Halsor, Secretary
• Karen Shippy, Vice President
• Dee Johnson, Membership Director
Year Founded:
1935

Description:
Our mission is the pursuit of amateur women's golf in the state of Missouri and Johnson County, Kansas. It takes and active interest in all phases of women's golf
Number of Members:
750

MONTANA STATE GOLF ASSOCIATION
HELENA, MT 59602
406-458-3359
www.msgagolf.com
• Steve Sherburne, President
(406) 226-4540
• Gerard Poore, Treasurer
(406) 442-8125
poore@bresnan.net
• Jim Opitz, Executive Director
(406) 458-3359
• Roger Amundson, Vice President
(406) 654-1130
rkamts@yahoo.com
• Emily Hulsey, Handicap/Website Coordinator
(800) 628-3752
emily@montana.net
• Nick Dietzen, MSGA Commmunications Director
(406) 459-3459
ndietzen@gmail.com
Year Founded:
1917
Description:
Non-profit organization of member clubs, governed by amateur golfers, and dedicated to serving the game of golf in Montana
Number of Members:
21,000

NEBRASKA GOLF ASSOCIATION
6618 SOUTH 118TH STREET
OMAHA, NE 68137
402-505-4653
Fax: 402-505-4695
www.nebgolf.org
• Greg Stine, President
• Craig W. Ames, Executive Director
cames@nebgolf.org
• Justin Ahrens, Assistant Executive Director
jahrens@nebgolf.org
• Ben Vigil, Manager, Association Services
bvigil@nebgolf.org
• Mike Jenkins, Vice President
Year Founded:
1966
Description:
Provides its member clubs with the latest in technological equipment, including the GHIN handicapping system and tournament pairing program and instructs the clubs on how to use the programs
Number of Members:
27,000

NEBRASKA WOMEN'S AMATEUR GOLF ASSOCIATION
6618 SOUTH 118TH STREET
OMAHA, NE 68137
402-505-4653
Fax: 402-505-4695
nwaga@nebgolf.org
www.nwaga.org
• Michele Gill, President
(308) 340-5864
nebgal1@gmail.com
• Teresa Snoozy, Vice President
tjsnoozy@gmail.com
• Maddy Toepfer, NWAGA Executive Director
(402) 505-4653
nwaga@nebgolf.org
• Barb Muldoon, Treasurer
(402) 691-8701
• Debbie Wilbeck, Secretary
(402) 305-6237
dwilbeck@cox.net
• Maggie Peters, Executive Secretary
(402) 727-6823
malcolm5136@aol.com
• Judy Duffy, Tee Off Time Editor

(402) 397-0742
judyduffy@aol.com
Year Founded:
1973
Description:
Is an organization of golf clubs and individuals governed by amateur women golfers and formed for the purpose of promotion and conserving the best interests and true spirit of the game of golf for all women in the State of Nebraska
Number of Members:
84

NEW HAMPSHIRE GOLF ASSOCIATION
56 S. STATE STREET
CONCORD, NH 03301
603-219-0371
Fax: 603-219-0565
membership@nhgolf.com
www.nhgolf.com
• Greg Howell, Director Of Member Services & Junior Golf
• Bill Krueger, Past President
• Matt Schmidt, Executive Director
mschmidt@nhgolf.com
• Pat Spooner, Secretary
• Joseph Kane, President
• Glenn Walton, Vice President
• Don DeNovellis, Treasurer
• John Jelley, Tournament Director

NEW HAMPSHIRE WOMEN'S GOLF ASSOCIATION
603-356-9051
info@nhwga.org
www.nhwga.org
• Dana Harrity, President
president@nhwga.org
• Chris Downall, Secretary
secretary@nhwga.org
• Rowena Wilks, Past President
pastpres@nhwga.org
• Mary Jane Cormier, 1st Vice President
1vp@nhwga.org
• Donna Harvey, 2nd Vice President
2vp@nhwga.org
• Dorene Bergeron, Treasurer
treasurer@nhwga.org
Description:
Promote, stimulate, organize, and maintain interest and activity in golf among women in the state of New Hampshire

NEW JERSEY STATE GOLF ASSOCIATION
3 GOLF DRIVE
SUITE 206
KENILWORTH, NJ 07033
908-241-4653
Fax: 908-245-4696
info@njsga.org
www.njsga.org
• H. Frank O-Brien, President
• William E. Frese, Secretary
• Michael F. McFadden, Treasurer
• Daniel Meehan, Vice President
• Mike McAneny, Director of Tournaments & Media Relations
mikem@njsga.org
• Rich Kennedy, Director of Handicapping & Membership Service
richk@njsga.org
• Mike Moretti, Director Of Communications
mmoretti@njsga.org
• Kevin Purcell, Executive Director
kevinp@njsga.org
Year Founded:
1900
Description:
Promotes, supports and ensures the quality, traditions and development of the game of golf for everyone throughout the State of New Jersey
Number of Members:
100,000

NEW YORK STATE GOLF ASSOCIATION
4933 JAMESVILLE ROAD
JAMESVILLE, NY 13078
315-471-6979
Fax: 315-471-1372
www.nysga.org
• Richard Galvin, President
• Bill Moore, Executive Director
bmoore@nysga.org
• Joseph Strykowski, First Vice President
• Warren Winslow, Second Vice President
• Andrew Hickey, Director, Rules & Competitions
andrew@nysga.org
• Henry Fust, Treasurer
Year Founded:
1923
Description:
Promotes and conserve the traditions of golf throughout New York State

NORTH DAKOTA GOLF ASSOCIATION
725 RIVERWOOD DRIVE
BISMARCK, ND 58504
701-226-5641
www.ndgolf.org
• Randy Westby, President
• Rick Kuhn, Vice President
• Tim Doppler, Executive Director
ndga2020@gmail.com
• Perry Bohl, Secretary/Treasurer
• Gary Lahr, Tournament and Course Rating Director
gplahr@hotmail.com
Description:
Formed and exists for the general purpose of promoting and conserving throughout the state of North Dakota the best interests and the true spirit of the game of golf

NORTHERN CALIFORNIA GOLF ASSOCIATION
3200 LOPEZ ROAD
PEBBLE BEACH, CA 93953
831-625-4653
Fax: 831-625-0150
www.ncga.org
• Lee Gidney, President
• Vaughn Kezirian, Executive Director
vkezirian@ncga.org
• Malinda Oliver, Executive Assistant
moliver@ncga.org
• John Ronca, Vice President
• Pat Quinn, Secretary/Treasurer
• Brian Morse, Immediate Past President
Year Founded:
1901
Description:
Provide an enjoyable and fulfilling golf experience to all involved
Number of Members:
180

NORTHERN NEVADA GOLF ASSOCIATION
PO BOX 5607
RENO, NV 89513
775-673-4653
Fax: 775-673-1144
www.nnga.org
• Larry Greenman, President
• Rich Brashear, Vice President
• Steve Rydel, Executive Director
(775) 846-8263
• Len Caley, Treasurer
• Joe Webster, Secretary
• Jack Gilbert, Past President
Description:
Promote and serve amateur golf and protect its traditions

NORTHERN NEVADA WOMEN'S GOLF ASSOCIATION
18124 WEDGE PARKWAY
SUITE 182
RENO, NV 89511

775-851-8102
www.nnwga.org
• Lori Elliott, President
(775) 857-1812
• Annette Ramirez, Vice President
(775) 882-2951
• Darla Smyth, Webmaster
(775) 851-8102
• Gretchen Legarza, Treasurer
(775) 828-4924
• Pat Hiatt, Secretary
(775) 742-4999
Year Founded:
1961
Description:
Promote interest in the game of golf for the women of Northern Nevada and the surrounding areas
Number of Members:
2,200
Publications:
NNWGA Newsletter: On and Off the Course is published 3 times a year and sent to each member via email

OKLAHOMA GOLF ASSOCIATION
2800 COLTRANE PL
SUITE 2
EDMOND, OK 73034
405-848-0042
Fax: 405-216-5795
www.okgolf.org
• Mark Felder, Executive Director
mfelder@okgolf.org
• Joby Wood, Director
• Morri Rose, Director Of Junior Golf
mrose@okgolf.org
• Jay Doudican, Director Of Ghin Services
jdoudican@okgolf.org
• Justin Limon, Tournament Director
Description:
Promotes the game of golf within the state of Oklahoma and monitors the playing thereof as an extension of the US Golf Association

OREGON GOLF ASSOCIATION
2840 HAZELNUT DRIVE
WOODBURN, OR 97071
503-981-4653
www.oga.org
• Barb Trammell, Chief Executive Officer
• Tom Gaffney, Vice President
• Eric Schoenstein, President
• Brent Whittaker, Director Of Tournament Operations
• Ryan Wyckoff, Senior Director Of Golf Course Operations
• Katie Norquist, Director of Finance, OGA & OGA Golf Course
• Henry Childs, Communications & Membership Coordinator
• Robyn Lorain, Director of Junior Golf
• Kelly Neely, Senior Director of Handicapping & Course Rating
• Gretchen Yoder, Manager of Handicapping & Course Rating
• Aaron Breniman, Director of Marketing & Communications
Year Founded:
1924
Description:
Our goal is to foster the enhancement and expansion of the game of golf by leading in the development of member and information services, the promotion of opportunities for all that want to play, and protection of the game's integrity and valued traditions. The governing body for the sport in Oregon & SW Washington.
Number of Members:
56,000
Membership Requirements:
Must be a member of a regular or associate golf club in Oregon or SW Washington
Member Services:
Handicapping, Course and Slope Rating, Tournaments, Rules of Golf
Publications:
Calendar of Events, Newsletter, Annual Report

PUERTO RICO GOLF ASSOCIATION
PARADISE COMMERCIAL CENTER
264 AVE. MATADERO
SUITE 11
SAN JUAN, PUERTO RIC 00920
787-793-3444
Fax: 787-273-3138
info@prga.org
www.prga.org
• Sidney Wolf, President
• James J Teale, Founder
• Ginelys Dahl, Communications & Web
Development
info@prga.org
• Pete Birmingham, Board Director
Handicapping & Club Relationship
• Julio Soto, Executive Director & USGA/GHIN
Affairs
• Fransico Rivera, Tournament Director
• Sajo Ruiz, Vice President, Marketing & Public
Relations
Year Founded:
1954
Description:
Governing body for the game of golf in Puerto
Rico at the amateur level, host of the 2004
World Amateur Team Championship and proud
host organization of the PGA Tour at the Puerto
Rico Open, presented by seepuertorico.com.
Number of Members:
Over 5,100

RHODE ISLAND GOLF ASSOCIATION
ONE BUTTON HOLE DRIVE
PROVIDENCE, RI 02909
401-272-1350
rward@rigalinks.org
www.rigalinks.org
• Luke T Hyder, President
• Jim McKenna, Director Of Rules &
Competitions
jmckenna@rigalinks.org
• Michael A. Montigny, Treasurer
• Kate McCurry, Office Manager
kmccurry@rigalinks.org
• Vincent J. Cavallaro, First Vice President
• Kevin W. Clary, Second Vice President
• Robert Ward, Executive Director
(401) 272-1350
rward@rigalinks.org
• Kevin S. McLoughlin, Secretary
• Katie DeCosta, Director of Women's Golf &
Member Services
kdecosta@rigalinks.org
Number of Members:
13,000
Membership Requirements:
Member of a member club
Member Services:
Handicapping; course rating, championships,
rules of golf seminars; club officers seminar
Publications:
RIGA News: quarterly newsletter

ROCHESTER DISTRICT GOLF ASSOCIATION
2024 WEST HENRIETTA ROAD
SUITE 5-H
ROCHESTER, NY 14623
585-292-5950
info@rdga.org
www.rdga.org
• Dan Overbeck, President, Assistant Rules
Official
danoverbeck@rdga.org
• Tim Vangellow, Executive Director
timvangellow@rdga.org
• Fredrick Lapple, Corporate Relationship&
Office Operations Chairman
fredlapple@rdga.org
• Mark Battle, Vice President, Women's
Committee
markbattle@rdga.org
• Mark Little, Jr. Tournament Committee
marklittle@rdga.org
• Dave Eaton, Communications Director
daveeaton@rdga.org
Year Founded:
1929

Description:
Promotes closer relationships among member
clubs, conducts tournaments for members of
clubs belonging to the association, promotes
and supports a USGA - approved handicap
system, provides course ratings and advances
the best interests of amateur golf

SAN DIEGO COUNTY WOMEN'S GOLF ASSOCIATION
SAN DIEGO, CA
858-673-1128
sdcwga@aol.com
www.sdcwga.net
• Elaine Michaels, President
emichaels760@yahoo.com
• Carolyn Hogan, Secretary
cfhogan7@cox.net
• Karen Miller, Major Tournaments
kpmiller748@roadrunner.com
• Cheryl Wohlgemuth, Executive Director
sdcwga@aol.com
Year Founded:
1934
Description:
Is a non-profit organization, chartered to
promote, supervise, and conduct competitive
golf for SDCWGA members

SOUTH CAROLINA GOLF ASSOCIATION
7451 CAROLINA IRMO DRIVE
COLUMBIA, SC 29212
803-732-9311
Fax: 803-732-7406
info@scgolf.org
www.scgolf.org
• John Lopez, President
• James Park, Director of Member Services
jpark@scgolf.org
• Steve Fuller, Vice President
• Happ Lathrop, Executive Director
• Ron Swinson, Treasurer
• Vic Hannon, Secretary
• Kirk Page, SCJGA Director of Competitions
• Chris Miller, Senior Director Of SCJGA
• Kent Hungerpiller, Immediate Past President

SOUTH DAKOTA GOLF ASSOCIATION
4809 WEST 41ST STREET
SUITE 202
SIOUX FALLS, SD 57106
605-338-7499
1-800-577-7342
sdga@sdga.org
www.sdga.org
• Bill Scholten, President
• Wade Merry, Executive Director
• Coralee Jorgensen, Executive Director, First
Tee of South Dakota
• Kelli Sinksen, First Tee of SD Program
Director
Description:
Provides USGA/GHIN handicaps, conducts ten
state championships, conducts junior clinics and
junior tournaments

SOUTH FLORIDA PGA
186 ATLANTIS BLVD
ATLANTIS, FL 33462
561-729-0544
Fax: 561-729-0914
sflorida@pgahq.com
www.sflorida.pga.com
• Warren Bottke, President
walkbot@aol.com
• Mark VanDyck, Vice President
markvandyck@hotmail.com
• Don Meadows, Secretary
dmeadows@quailvalleygolfclub.com
• Brian Peaper, Honorary Past President
bdppga@aol.com
• Geoff Lofstead, Executive Director
glofstead@pgahq.com
• Christopher Gilkey, Tournament Director
• Meredith Schuler, Director of Operations
mschuler@pgahq.com

Description:
Promote interest, participation and enjoyment in
the game of golf; establish and maintain
professional standards or practice; and enhance
the well-being of golf professionals
Year Founded:
1979
Number of Members:
1,600

SOUTH JERSEY GOLF ASSOCIATION
PO BOX 884
NORTH CAPE MAY, NJ 08204
609-760-7779
sjga1946@gmail.com
• Gail Reilly, President
(609) 760-7779
sjga1946@gmail.com
• Ralph Gonzalez, Vice President
• Jeanne Leisner, Treasurer
(609) 760-4113
jleisnersjga@gmail.com
• Joan Boyle, Secretary
• John Petronis, Tournament Director
(609) 760-4580
• Paul Wiegand, Webmaster
Description:
Provides services to member golfers, fifty-nine
public, semi-private and private clubs in the
eight county southern New Jersey area
Number of Members:
700

SOUTHERN CALIFORNIA GOLF ASSOCIATION
3740 CAHUENGA BOULEVARD
STUDIO CITY, CA 91604
818-980-3630
Fax: 818-980-2709
info@scga.org
www.scga.org
• Al Frank, President
• John Morello, Vice President
• Keenan Barber, Secretary
• Jon Bilger, Treasurer
• Ken Bien, Immediate Past President
• Kevin Heaney, Executive Director
Description:
Provides tournament results, golf expo
information, membership, courses, affiliate
clubs, and rules of golf

SOUTHERN GOLF ASSOCIATION
1025 MONTGOMERY HIGHWAY
SUITE 210
BIRMINGHAM, AL 35216
205-979-4653
Fax: 205-979-1602
www.sgagolf.com
• Clarke Rheney, President
• W. Cabell Moore, Jr., 1st Vice President
• James E Brown, 2nd Vice President
• Al Reynolds, Treasurer
• Buford R McCarty, Executive Secretary
• Adam Powell, Assistant Executive Secretary
• Donna Stephens, Office Manager
Year Founded:
1902
Number of Members:
500

SOUTHERN ILLINOIS GOLF ASSOCIATION
122 South Division ST
CARTERVILLE, IL 62918
618-985-9595
Fax: 618-985-9595
www.sigagolf.org
• Ralph Chapman, President
• Sarah Haas, Vice President
• Ryan Farley, Secretary
• Robin Lester, Treasurer
• Steward Gilmore, Director
Year Founded:
1924

SOUTHERN NEVADA GOLF ASSOCIATION
8010 W. SAHARA AVE.
SUITE 160
LAS VEGAS, NV 89117
702-458-4653
www.snga.org
• Tim Quinn, President
• Geno Withelder, Vice President
• Ann Sunstrum, Executive Director
(702) 458-4653
asunstrum@snga.org
• Tanner Bown, Director Of Competition
(702) 830-7972
• Tom Khamis, Secretary
• Tom Fitzgerald, Treasurer
Year Founded:
1967
Description:
Non-profit organization founded to represent, promote and serve the best interests of golf in the state of Nevada
Number of Members:
12,000

ST. LOUIS DISTRICT GOLF ASSOCIATION
560 MALINMOR DRIVE
WELDON SPRING, MO 63304
636-928-5056
Fax: 636-244-5056
www.stldga.com
• Mel Rector, President
• Andy Frost, Vice President
• Larry Etzkorn, Secretary Emeritus
• Roy Wilson, Executive Director
• Todd Burchyett, Assistant Executive Director/ Rules Chairman
Year Founded:
1916
Description:
Provide an association of private golf clubs throughout the St. Louis Metropolitan area

SUN COUNTRY AMATEUR GOLF ASSOCIATION
2316 SOUTHERN BLVD
SUITE D
RIO RANCHO, NM 87124
505-897-0864
800-346-5319
Fax: 505-897-3494
info@suncountrygolfhouse.com
• Mike Quinlan, President
• Dick Thorpe, 1st Vice President
• Dana Lehner, Executive Director
• Jan Schermerhorn, 2nd Vice President
• Bruce Buchman, Treasurer
• Cindy Smith, Secretary
Description:
Promote and serve amateur golf and protect its traditions
Number of Members:
22,000

TENNESSEE GOLF ASSOCIATION/TGA
400 FRANKLIN ROAD
FRANKLIN, TN 37069
615-790-7600
Fax: 615-790-8600
www.tngolf.org
• Matt Vanderpool, Executive Director
• Lynne Howd, Director, Handicapping
lhowd@tngolf.org
• Allison Brown, Director Of Women's Golf
abrown@tngolf.org
• Aon Miller, President
• Nathaniel Hantle, Manager, Course Rating & Member Services
nhantle@tngolf.org
Year Founded:
1914
Description:
Provides numerous services to its member clubs - the most important being the handicap service
Number of Members:
40,000

TEXAS GOLF ASSOCIATION
2909 COLE AVENUE
SUITE 305
DALLAS, TX 75204
214-468-8942
Fax: 214-468-8032
info@txga.org
www.txga.org
• Bill Hanley, President
• Jim Brown, First Vice President
• Carey Schulten, Second Vice President
• Rob Addington, Executive Director
raddington@txga.org
• Jonathan Shipley, Secretary/Treasurer
• Jim Spagnolo, Communications Manager
jim@txga.org
• Mary Harrison, Senior Director, Handicapping
mary@txga.org
• Cameron Crawford, Tournament Director
ccrawford@txga.org
• Ryan Finn, Managing Director Championships
rfinn@txga.org
Year Founded:
1906
Description:
Non-profit organization licensed through the USGA that represents, promotes and serves the best interest of golf in Texas
Number of Members:
Over 70,000
Membership Reqirements:
Must belong to a member club that pays annual dues
Member Services:
Conducts 11 statewide and seven regional golf championships, course rating, handicapping and educational seminars

TOLEDO DISTRICT GOLF ASSOCIATION
5533 SOUTHWYCK BOULEVARD
SUITE 204
TOLEDO, OH 43614
419-866-4771
www.tdgagolf.org
• John Byerly, President
• Doug Dantuono, Vice President
• Cliff Siehl, Executive Director, Tournament Chairman
• Bruce DeBoer, Treasurer
• Mickey Scott, Secretary

TRANS-MISSISSIPPI GOLF ASSOCIATION
2909 COLE
SUITE 305
DALLAS, TX 75204
214-468-8942
• Billy McBee, President
• Phil Patterson, Vice President
• Rob Addington, Executive Director
• Amanda Kolb, Tournament Administration
akolb@txga.org
• Hunter Nelson, Secretary
• Leo Corrigan, IV, Treasurer
• Cameron Crawford, Tournament Director
ccrawford@txga.org
Year Founded:
1900

UTAH GOLF ASSOCIATION
4444 S. 700 E.
SUITE 105
SALT LAKE CITY, UT 84107
801-563-0400
Fax: 801-563-0632
info@usga.org
www.uga.org
• Jim Harland, President
• Reese Nielsen, Vice President
• Bill Walker, Executive Director
bill@uga.org
• Steve Brinton, Treasurer
• Denise Vilven, Secretary
• Jacob Miller, Director Of Rules & Competition
jacob@uga.org
• Kelsey Chugg, Membership Director
kelsey@uga.org

Description:
Promote and protect the interest of golf and golfers within the state
Number of Members:
30,000

VALERO TEXAS OPEN
4330 MARRIOTT PKWY
SAN ANTONIO, TX 78261
210-345-3818
Fax: 210-345-3853
www.valerotexasopen.com
• Joe Gorder, President/Chief Executive Officer
• Stephanie Sage, Director of Marketing & Community Relations
• Larson Segerdahl, Executive Director
• Dawn Wood, Finance Coordinator
• Craig Smith, Director of Business Development
• Monica Villarreal, Director of Tournament Administration
Description:
Cowboy hats, golf caps and everything in between. PGA Tournament hosted at TPC San Antonio AT&T oaks Course, designed by Greg Norman and Sergio Garcia.

VERMONT GOLF ASSOCIATION
PO BOX 1612
STATION A
RUTLAND, VT 05701-1612
802-773-7180
800-924-0418
info@vtga.org
www.vtga.org
• Herb Eddy, Secretary
• Rick Simpson, President
• Roger Schoenbeck, Vice President/Treasurer
• Dave Pfannenstein, Executive Director
• Shari Pfannenstein, Website/Communications
Description:
The purpose of the VGA is to act as the authoritative body for golf in the state of Vermont; to hold such tournaments as may be arranged; to adopt, enforce and interpret the rules of golf in accordance with the rules adopted by the USGA; to promote and regulate competitions for all ages and abilities throughout Vermont; to establish, maintain, control and regulate a handicap system and course ratings for member clubs
Year Founded
1902
Number of Members:
67 Clubs, 11,000 Individuals

VERMONT STATE WOMEN'S GOLF ASSOCIATION
PO BOX 8235
ESSEX, VT 05451
802-662-4947
www.vswga.org
• Kathy Allbright, President, Director at Large
(603) 469-3487
puttquilt@aol.com
• Chris Johnson, Vice President, Director at Large, Liason-NE
(802) 626-5624
cjjohnson02@yahoo.com
• Phyllis Simon, Treasurer
(802) 244-7420
simonop@aol.com
• Kathy Sikora, Secretary
(802) 434-2583
g1946olf@gmavt.net
• Nancy Murphy, Past President
(802) 773-8702
nlmgolfer@yahoo.com
Description:
Serves women golfers of all ages and abilities in Vermont

VIRGINIA STATE GOLF ASSOCIATION
2400 DOVERCOURT DRIVE
MIDLOTHIAN, VA 23113

804-378-2300
Fax: 804-378-2369
www.vsga.org
• Matt Smiley, Director of Rules And Competitions
(804) 378-2300
• Andrew Blair, Director of Communications
(804) 378-2300
• Jamie Conkling, Executive Director
(804) 378-2300
• Natasha Triplett, Director Of Finance & Administration
(804) 378-2300
• Gary Beck, Treasurer
(757) 625-8181
• Michael Millen, Secretary
(434) 295-9616
• Gib Palmer, President
(804) 354-3794
• Bruce H. Matson, Vice President
(804) 783-2003
Year Founded:
1904
Description:
Promote the game of golf and serve the needs of golf in Virginia
Publications:
Virginia Golf, published bi-monthly; VSGA Yearbook and Media Guide; VIP Member Guide; Just Fore Juniors newsletter

WASHINGTON STATE GOLF ASSOCIATION
1010 SOUTH 336TH STREET
SUITE 310
FEDERAL WAY, WA 98003
206-526-8605
800-643-6410
Fax: 206-522-0281
www.thewsga.org
• Barbara Tracy, President
• Gary Rees, Vice President (District 1)
• Cathy Kay, Vice President (District 2)
• Doug Rohner, Vice President (District 3)
• Mike Welling, Vice President (District 4)
• Robert Black, Vice President (District 5)
• Troy Andrew, Executive Director/CEO
(206) 526-8605
• Steve Kay, Treasurer
• Frank Horton, Past President
• Tom Cade, Senior Director of Communications & Marketing
(253) 214-2918
• John Saegner, Jr., Senior Director Of Handicapping & Course Rating
 (253) 214-2914
• Scotty Crouthamel, Senior Director Rules & Competition
(253) 214-2924
• Shari Jacobson, Director Of Membership & Club Relations
(253) 214-2925
• Abell Smith, Web Developer & Content Manager
(253) 214-2911
• Kacie Bray, Director of Marketing
(253) 214-2916
Year Founded:
1922
Description:
Non-profit amateur golf association governed by volunteer, amateur golfers
Number of Members:
85,000

WEST VIRGINIA GOLF ASSOCIATION
2115 CHARLESTON TOWN CENTER
CHARLESTON, WV 25389
304-391-5000
Fax: 304-391-5050
www.wvga.org
• Amber Hooper, Managing Director of Membership & Finance
(304) 391-5000
ahooper@wvga.org
• Colton Dean, Tournament Coordinator
(304) 391-5000
cdean@wvga.org
• Jonathan Bartlett, Senior Director of The First

Tee of WV
(304) 391-5000
jbartlett@wvga.org
• Carter Page, Senior Director Of Rules & Competitions
(304) 391-5000
cpage@wvga.org
• Chris Slack, Director of Course Rating & Competitions
(304) 391-5000
cslack@wvga.org
• Zihui (Bella) Xu, Event & Public Relations Coordinator
(304) 391-5000
zxu@wvga.org
• Brad Ullman, Executive Director
(304) 391-5000
bullman@wvga.org
• Steve Fox, Vice President
Year Founded:
1913

WESTCHESTER GOLF ASSOCIATION
49 KNOLLWOOD ROAD
SUITE 220
ELMSFORD, NY 10523
914-347-2340
Fax: 914-347-2418
info@westchestergolf.org
www.westchestergolf.org
• Michael F. McCarthy, President
• Mike Zalmalkany, Tournament Director
• Bob Thomas, Executive Director
bthomas@westchestergolf.org
• George N. Tompkins, General Counsel
• Benjamin C. Kirschenbaum, Vice President
• Robert M. Miller, Secretary/Treasurer
• Robert H.M. Ferguson, Tournament Chairman
Year Founded:
1916
Number of Members:
30,000

WESTERN GOLF ASSOCIATION/EVANS SCHOLARS FOUNDATION
1 BRIAR ROAD
GOLF, IL 60029-0301
847-724-4600
Fax: 847-724-7133
www.wgaesf.org
• John Kaczkowski, President & CEO
kaczkowski@wgaesf.org
• Dennis O'Keefe, Chairman
• David Robinson, Vice Chairman
• John Mendesh, Secretary
• James M. O'Keane, Treasurer
• Daniel Coyne, General Counsel
• Amy Fuller, Director, Communications
fuller@wgaesf.org
• Steve Prioletti, Tournament Manager
prioletti@wgaesf.org
• Patrick Timson, Director, Tournament Operations
timson@wgaesf.org
Year Founded:
1899

WESTERN PENNSYLVANIA GOLF ASSOCIATION
324 FOURTH STREET
PITTSBURGH, PA 15238
412-826-2180
Fax: 412-826-2183
info@wpga.org
www.wpga.org
• Tim Fitzgerald, President
• Ron Moehler, Vice President
• Jeff Rivard, Executive Director
jrivard@wpga.org
• Claudette Graham, Treasurer
• Mark Caliendo, Secretary
• Terry Teasdale, Handicap Director
tteasdale@wpga.org
• Matt Rusinko, Championship Director
mrusinko@wpga.org
Year Founded:
1899

Description:
To foster, promote and advance the interests and the true spirit of the game of golf throughout Western Pennsylvania

WISCONSIN STATE GOLF ASSOCIATION
11350 WEST THEO TRECKER WAY
WEST ALLIS, WI 53214
414-443-3560
Fax: 414-443-0817
support@wsga.org
www.wsga.org
• Doug Fry, President
• Chuck Heath, First Vice President
• Mark Kannenberg, Vice President
• Phil Poletti, Vice President
• Mark Reinemann, Vice President
• John Knuteson, Secretary
• Rob Jansen, Executive Director
(414) 443-3561
rob@wsga.org
• David Cohn, Director Of Member Services & Communications
(414) 443-3569
• Aimee Linneman, Director Of Women's Golf & Operations
(414) 443-3577
• Bill Linneman, Director Rules & Competitions
(414) 443-3565
Year Founded:
1901
Description:
Promote and conserve throughout the State of Wisconsin, the best interests and the true spirit of the game of golf
Number of Members:
65,000
Publications:
Wisconsin Golfer Magazine available to all members with a current WSGA Number

WOMEN'S GOLF ASSOCIATION OF WESTERN PENNSYLVANIA
DELMONT, PA
412-551-8549
www.wgawp.com
• Mary Beth Morrissey, President
• Corrinne Lacich, Vice President & Tournament Chairman
• Kathy Campbell, Treasurer
• Lisa Popovich, Recording Secretary
Year Founded:
1922
Description:
Promote among women of Western Pennsylvania the best interests and true spirit of the game of golf and to regulate and govern all contests in which members participate
Number of Members:
700

WOMEN'S METROPOLITAN GOLF ASSOCIATION
49 KNOLLWOOD RD
2nd Floor
ELMSFORD, NY 10523
914-592-7888
Fax: 914-462-3229
www.wmga.com
• Valerie DePiro, President
• Nancy Early, Executive director
• Phyllis Gusick, Vice President Of Competitions
• Michele Greenfield, Vice President Of Outreach, Marketing& Initiatives
• Allison Kucinski, Treasurer
• Leanne Leonard, Secretary
Year Founded:
1899
Description:
Fosters good sportsmanship, and good fellowship and friendly rivalry while encouraging and developing skilled amateur women golfers through individual competition and team play. It is also the USGA-sanctioned course rating authority for women players throughout the metropolitan region

Number of Members:
2,500 members, 192 member clubs

WOMEN'S SOUTHERN CALIFORNIA GOLF ASSOCIATION
402 WEST ARROW HIGHWAY
SUITE 10
SAN DIMAS, CA 91773
909-592-1281
Fax: 909-592-7542
• Judy Altschuler, President
(909) 592-1281
• Sheri Hauck, First Vice President
(909) 592-1281
• Debra Moats, Second Vice President
(909) 592-1281
• Judy Anderson, Secretary
(909) 592-1281
• Mary Ann Kneist, Treasurer
(909) 592-1281
• Joanne Farmer, Rules Director
(909) 592-1281
• Pat Blalock, Executive Director
(909) 592-1281
• Louise Wright, Advisor
(909) 592-1281
Description:
Promote and foster interest in women's amateur golf through friendly organized competition
Membership Requirements:
Membership in the Association may only be obtained through the Member Club's women's organization. Each member of a Regular Member Club's Women's Organization shall also be required to be a member of this Association. Payment of Association dues: $27.00 membership fee for an 18-hole index and/or a 9-hole index. Minimum age: 18 years; however; WSCGA will provide a courtesy handicap index for any junior playing from a WSCGA Club

WYOMING STATE GOLF ASSOCIATION
1779 EAGLECREST CT.
LARAMIE, WY 82072
307-250-3044
dsnyder@wyoming.com
www.wygolf.org
• Rolf Peterson, President
• Karen Holcombe, Secretary
• Rachelle Pearson, Treasurer
• Jim Marshall, Vice President
• Dave Snyder, Executive Director
(307) 250-3044
dsnyder@wyoming.com
• Jim Marshall, Vice President
• Curtis Starkey, PGA Professional
• Roger Sheaffer, Vice President
• Kyle Wuss, Executive Director
Year Founded:
1922
Description:
The WSGA is the governing body of amateur golf in the state of Wyoming. Since its formation in 1922, the objective of the WSGA has been to promote and maintain the game of amateur golf throughout Wyoming.
Number of Members:
9,000
Publications:
Scorecard Magazine

UNITED STATES GOLF TEACHERS FEDERATION
1295 SE PORT ST. LUCIE BOULEVARD
PORT SAINT LUCIE, FL 34952
772-335-3216
888-346-3290
Fax: 772-335-3822
info@usgtf.com
www.usgtf.com
• Geoff Bryant, President
president@usgtf.com
• Suzy Johnson, Membership Services
• Bob Wyatt, Jr., National Coordinator
info@usgtf.com
• Mark Harman, Director Of Education

mark@usgtf.com
• Sam Bryant, Vice President
• Jennifer Russakis, Membership Services Director
info@usgtf.com
Year Founded
1989
Description:
Largest organization of golf teaching professionals in the nation. Offer seven day certification courses in all parts of the country. The USGTF establish a national and international standard in training and certification for golf teaching professionals. In addition provides services for its members and promotes the golf teaching profession
Number of members:
17,000
Member Services:
National standard of professional training & certification, Continuous educational development, International recognition, Employment referrals, Regional member tournaments, logoed USGTF merchandise, availability of self-help books on marketing & management skills, Liaison with other golf and sport associations, Opportunity to participate in the Biennial World Golf Teachers Cup & Conference, Commissionable income opportunity and discounts on golf equipment & training aids, USGTF ownership of National Training Center, Membership retirement fund, Membership liability insurance.
Publications:
Golf Teaching Pro Magazine

USBGA GOLF ASSOCIATION
NASHVILLE, TN
info@usblindgolf.com
www.blindgolf.com
• Jim Baker, President
(615) 679-9629
president@usblindgolf.com
• Diane Wilson, Vice President
(360) 437-4025
vicepresident@usblindgolf.com
Description:
The United States Blind Golf Association is organized and operated for the purposes of benefiting blind and vision impaired persons and promoting the public good through programs that advance, and increase public awareness of, golf among the blind and vision impaired throughout the United States
Membership Requirements:
Totally blind with no light perception up to 20/200 with Ophthalmologist statement, Support members also welcomed, Yearly dues totally blind $25.00, Vision impaired (B2-B3) $15.00, Support $10.00
Member Services:
Blind and vision impaired golf tournaments, Junior Blind Golf Programs.
Publications:
The Midnight Golfer, newsletter

WESTERN AUSTRALIA BLIND GOLF ASSOCIATION
www.blindgolf.com.au; www.wabga.org.au
• Ross Thompson, President
• Wendy Davidson, Secretary
• Gerry Brown, Vice President
• Cathy French, Treasurer
• Rod Mills, Director
• Geoff Walsh, Handicapper

Year Founded:
1987
Description:
To promote the game of golf amongst Blind and Vision Impaired Persons, and to co-ordinate blind golf between the States of Australia. We aid to represent Australian blind golf internationally and to create and maintain a register of blind golf events within Australia, players, sight classifications and handicaps.

WESTERN GOLF ASSOCIATION, EVANS SCHOLARS FOUNDATION
1 BRIAR ROAD
GOLF, IL 60029-0301
847-724-4600
Fax: 847-724-7133
www.westerngolfassociation.com
• Daniel W. Coyne, General Counsel
• Dennis M. O'Keefe, Chairman
• David M. Robinson, Vice Chairman
• John S. Mendesh, Secretary
• James M. O'Keane, Treasurer
• John Kaczkowski, President & CEO
• Steve Brueggeman, Chief Financial Officer
Year Founded:
1899
Description:
Conducts three major golf championships: the Western Open and the Western Amateur (both since 1899), the Western Junior (since 1914).Administers the Evans Scholars Foundation which sends more than 810 students to college annually on full tuition and housing scholarships
Membership Requirements:
Payment of membership fees by recognized golf clubs or course
Publications:
BMW Championship Souvenir Program

WOMEN'S GOLF ASSOCIATION OF BALTIMORE
WGA OF BALTIMORE
MCDONOGH SCHOOL
PO BOX 380
OWINGS MILLS, MD 21117
410-592-2500
Fax: 410-592-2577
www.wgabaltimore.org
• Maddy Blumberg, President
• Ann Dixon, Secretary
• Eileen Witte, Vice President
• Debbie Lane, Treasurer
• Susan Wolven, Corresponding Secretary
Year Founded:
1930
Description:
The object of the Association is to encourage better golf and friendly competition among local women players by conducting Open Day events and other tournaments. We are a non-profit organization made up of 19 affiliated gofl clubs and approximately 230 individual members.
Number of Members:
230

WOMEN'S GOLF COACHES ASSOCIATION
5905 NW 54th CIRCLE
CORAL SPRINGS, FL 33067
800-381-0769
Fax: 800-381-0769
community.wgcagolf.com
• Roger M Yaffe, Executive Director
roger@wgcagolf.com
• Amy Bond, President
abond@admin.fsu.edu
• Lisa Strom, Assistant Coach

Representative
strom.3@osu.edu
• Ginger Brown-Lemm, Communications Director
gbrownlemm@athletics.msstate.edu
• Kristi Knight, Vice President
ksugolf@kstatesports.com
• Kevin Williams, Treasurer
williamsk@ecu.edu
• Trelle McCombs, Secretary
Year Founded:
1983
Description:
Promotes participation women's collegiate golf. The vision is to encourage the playing of intercollegiate golf for women in correlation with a general objective of education and in accordance with the highest tradition o fintercollegiate competition.
Number of members:
400+ member coaches
Membership Requirements:
Division I, II, III, NAIA women's head golf coaches
Member Services:
Presents All-American, Coach Of The Year awards; Hall of Fame internship program for students
Publications:
Newsletter, quarterly

WORLD GOLF VILLAGE
TWO WORLD GOLF PLACE
ST. AUGUSTINE, FL 32092
904-940-6088
www.golfwgv.com
• Jack Peter, Chief Operating Officer
(904) 940-4029
• Angela Ivey, Director of Marketing
(904) 940-4031
• Dave Cordero, Director of Communications
(904) 940-4009
• Brodie Walters, Senior Director of Museum Operations
(904) 940-4010
• Elizabeth Hall, Manager of Sales & Events
(904) 940-4021
Golf Sponsor:
PGA Tour - Spa at Laterra.
Description:
Home to the World Golf Hall of Fame

Greyhound Racing Organizations

ARIZONA DEPARTMENT OF RACING
1110 W WASHINGTON
SUITE 260
PHOENIX, AZ 85007
602-364-1700
Fax: 602-364-1703
www.azracing.gov/
• Rudy Casillas, Director
• Dan Reinertson, Chief Greyhound Steward
(520) 884-7576
• Victoria Rogen, Licensing
(602) 364-1716
• Joyce Cozby, Deputy Director
(602) 364-1726

ASSOCIATION OF RACING COMMISSIONERS INTERNATIONAL
1510 NEWTOWN PIKE
SUITE 210
LEXINGTON, KY 40511
859-224-7070
arcicom.businesscatalyst.com/
• Mark Lamberth, Chair
• Edward J. Martin, President
• Jeff Colliton, Treasurer
• Judy Wagner, Chair Elect/ Secretary
• John Ward, Immediate Past-Chair
Description:
To protect and uphold the integrity of the pari-mutuel sports of horse racing, dog racing and jai-alai through an informed membership, by encouraging forcefull and uniform regulation, by promoting the health and welfare of the industry through various programs and projects.
Membership Requirements:
Must be racing commissioner or executive director of a commission; associate members need not be commissioners, but must be connected to the industry.
Number of members:
500
Year Founded:
1934

BIRMINGHAM RACING COMMISSION
1000 JOHN ROGERS DRIVE
SUITE 102
BIRMINGHAM, AL 35210
• Charles Chrockrom, Sr., Chairman
• Jarvis Patton, Vice Chairman
• Richard Arrington, Jr., Commissioner
• Joe Knight, Commissioner
• Thomas P. Dawkins, DVM, Commissioner
• Kip W. Keefer, Executive Secretary
(205) 838-7470
• Valerie Carpenter, Administrative Assistant
(205) 838-7470
brcval@mindspring.com
Description:
The Birmingham Racing Commission was organized in 1984 pursuant to the John Rogers Act, now codified as Chapter 65 of Title 11, Code of Alabama 1975. The Commission is a unique public corporation authorized to license and regulate thoroughbred and greyhound racing pari-mutuel wagering in Birmingham.

COLORADO RACING COMMISSION
1881 PIERCE STREET
SUITE 108
LAKEWOOD, CO 80214
303-205-2990
Fax: 303-205-2950
www.colorado.gov/pacific/enforcement/node/37806
• Mary Sharon Wells, Chair
• Sean Beirne, Vice Chair
• Charles D. Vail, Veterinarian Member
• Pam Inmann, Business Member
• Cynthia Jane Day, Racing Industry Member
Description:
The mission of the Colorado Division of Racing is to promote and foster the public confidence in the pari-mutuel industry, protect the welfare of the participants through fair, consistent, proactive enforcement of appropriate policies, statutes and Colorado racing commission rules. The Commission is responsible for promulgating

all the rules and regulations governing greyhound and horse racing in Colorado.

MASSACHUSETTS STATE RACING COMMISSION
101 FEDERAL ST.
23RD FLOOR
BOSTON, MA 02110
617-979-8400
Fax: 617-725-0258
www.mass.gov/src
• Stephen Crosby, Chairman
• Bruce Stebbins, Commissioner
• Enrique Zuniga, Commissioner
• Rick Day, Executive Director
• Catherine Blue, General Counsel
• John R. Glennon, Chief Information Officer
• Alexandra Lightbown, Interim Director of Racing
Description:
To ensure fair and honest pari-mutuel racing, the Commission promulgates and enforces rules and regulations, proposes legislation and develops policies to better regulate the Racing Industry (horse and greyhound).

NATIONAL GREYHOUND ASSOCIATION
PO BOX 543
ABILENE, KS 67410
785-263-4660
nga@ngagreyhounds.com
• Julia Ward, President
(785) 263-7272
julie@waynewardinc.com
• Frederick A. Fulchino, Vice President
(860) 963-7844
• Gary Guccione, Secretary/Treasurer
(785) 263-4660
garyg@ngagreyhounds.com
Number of members:
2,950
Publications:
GREYHOUND REVIEW—Monthly on Greyhound-racing and breeding-related activities.
Description:
The National Greyhound Association (NGA), a voluntary non-profit association operated in accordance with the laws of Kansas, is officially recognized by the entire Greyhound racing industry including, all Greyhound racetracks and individual racing jurisdictions, as well as foreign Greyhound registries and governing bodies as the sole registry for racing Greyhounds on the North American continent. Organized in 1906, it has functioned in this capacity ever since the inception of Greyhound track racing in this country of more than 4,600 Greyhound owners and breeders whose Greyhounds compete at tracks throughout the continent.
Member Services:
All registration services for Greyhounds in North America.
Membership Requirements:
Completion of two-page application, submittal of $100 initiation fee & $70 dues.

NEW HAMPSHIRE RACING AND CHARITABLE GAMING COMMISSION
21 SOUTH FRUIT STREET
CONCORD, NH 03301-2428
603-271-2158
Fax: 603-271-3381
www.racing.nh.gov/

• Paul M. Kelley, Director
RCG-director@racing.nh.gov
• Timothy J. Connors, Chairman
• Anthony B. Urban, Secretary
• Sudhir Naik, Deputy Director
RCG-director@racing.nh.gov
Description:
The New Hampshire Pari-Mutuel
Commission oversees the regulation of
pari-mutuel wagering at racetracks in New
Hampshire, including Thoroughbred Racing,
Harness Racing, and Greyhound Racing
under RSA 284.
Year Founded:
1933

Gymnastics Organizations

**BRITISH COLUMBIA RHYTHMIC
SPORTIVE GYMNASTICS FEDERATION**
828 W. 8TH AVENUE
VANCOUVER, BC, CANADA V5Z 1E3
604-333-3485
Fax: 604-909-1749
bcrsgf@rhythmicsBC.com
www.rhythmicsBC.com
• Kamena Petkova, Competitive
Development Committee Chair
kamenapetkova@gmail.com
• Helena Higgs, Secretary
(250) 339-4301
hilkka.higgs@telus.net
• Sashka Gitcheva, Program Coordinator
(604) 333-3485
• Mari Mitri, Director At Large
mmitri@shaw.ca
• Adrienne Arnold, President
(604) 261-2752
adriennearnold@shaw.ca
• Monika Alde, RG Development Chair
(250) 658-8341
• Adrianna Donaldson, Treasurer
adriannabd@yahoo.com
• Diana Nerman, VP Finance
(604) 671-7577
dianazoecoop@shaw.ca
Description:
Administers and delivers a variety of
programs for encouraging participation in
and developing excellence in rhythmic
gymnastics.

CANADIAN GYMNASTICS FEDERATION
1900 Promenade City Park Drive
SUITE 120
OTTAWA, ON, CANADA K1J 1A3
613-748-5637
Fax: 613-748-5691
www.gymcan.org/site/home.php
• Richard Crepin, Chair/President
• Jim Roycroft, Secretary
• Claude Aubertin, Director
• Richard Ikeda, Athlete Representative
• Peter Nicol, President & CEO
(613) 748-5637
pnicol@gymcan.org
• Dean Giesbrecht, Vice Chair
• Sue Ashton, Program Coordinator AG
(613) 748-5637
• Chantal Clermont, Director Of Finance
(613) 748-5637
chantal@gymcan.org
• Tony Smith, National Team Director MAG
tsmith@gymcan.org
Description:
Founded 1969. Serves to lead, promote,

facilitate and guide gymnastics in Canada
as a sport for the pursuit of excellence and
world prominence, and as an activity for
lifelong participation.
Membership Requirements:
Regular members are duly constituted
Provincial and Territorial Associations and
Federations. Annual meeting held each
June in Ottawa, Ontario.
Number of members:
160,000

**INTERNATIONAL GYMNASTICS
FEDERATION (FIG)**
AVENUE DE LA GARE 12
CASE POSTALE 630
LAUSANNE, SWITZERLAN 1001
info@fig-gymnastics.org
www.fig-gymnastics.com
• Nicolas Cuperus, President
Description:
International governing body for the sport of
trampoline.

**NATIONAL ASSOCIATION OF WOMEN'S
GYMNASTICS JUDGES**
EDEN PRAIRIE, MN 55346
513-829-5671
nawgjsec@gmail.com
www.nawgj.org
• Evelyn Chandler, President
presnawgj@aol.com
• Mary Lee Martin, Vice President
mlmartin77@gmail.com
• Patty Shipman, Director Of Finance
pship@aol.com
• Judy Hoefarlin, National Web Director
webmaster@nawgj.org
• Barbara Tebben, Secretary
nawgjsec@gmail.com
Number of members:
1801
Member Services:
Contracts judges; educates them through
symposiums and represents judges on
gymnastics boards.
Publications:
Newsletter, four times annually; State and
Regional Newsletters.
Description:
Founded 1974.

**NATIONAL ASSOCIATION OF
COLLEGIATE GYMNASTICS COACHES -
WOMEN**
1627 SLEEPY HOLLOW LANE
DEKALB, IL 60115-1749
815-970-0465
• Bobbie Cesarek, President
• Mike Jacki, President
(317) 823-1097
mikej@iquest.net
• Carl Leland, Vice President
(303) 871-3395
cleland@du.edu
• Cari DuBoi, Secretary
(510) 643-0282
• Gail Goodspeed, Treasurer
(603) 862-3834
gailg@cisunix.unh.edu
Number of members:
150
Member Services:
Statistical service; All-American awards;
Scholar Athletic Award; Training congress
once each year, Coach of the Year.
Publications:

Newsletter, four times annually; Coaches
Directory.
Membership Requirements:
Membership fees of $100 per year, Must
represent a university or college or
Associate member $50.00.
Description:
Founded 1973. Serves to help set direction
of the sport of women's gymnastics within
the NCAA.

**NATIONAL GYMNASTICS JUDGES
ASSOCIATION, INC.**
75-25 E 210 ST
BAYSIDE, NY 11364
718-545-6368
kenach@ngja.org
www.ngja.org
• Dan Bachman, President
• Jerry Donahue, General Technical Vice
President
• Mike Juszczyk, National Technical Vice
President
• Dean Schott, Jr. Olympic Vice President
• Greg Kester, National Technical Secretary
• Brian Richmond, National Treasurer
Member Services:
Meetings held annually, held in conjunction
with USA Gymnastics Congress and USA
Championships.
Publications:
National Gymnastic Rules Interpretation
Book, annually; NGJA Newsletter,
biannually.
Membership Requirements:
Association dues. Must take Junior Olympic,
national and international practical and
written certification exams, depending on
the level of certification sought. All NGJA
officials are evaluated every two years. Must
also hold USAG professional membership
and safety certification.
Description:
Founded 1969. Certifies and trains
gymnastic judges for men's artistic
gymnastics. Assigns men's gymnastics
officials for national, international and junior
competitions, interprets rules. President of
the NGJA serves on the USA Gymnastics
Board of Directors and on the USA
Gymnastics Independent Selection
Committee.

**U.S. ASSOCIATION OF INDEPENDENT
GYMNASTICS CLUBS/USAIGC**
450 North End Aveenue
SUITE 20 F
NEW YORK, NY 10282
Fax: 212-227-9793
www.usaigc.com
• Paul Spadaro, President
paul.spadaro@usaigc.com
Member Services:
Seminars annually held in August.
Publications:
IT'S YOUR BUSINESS, quarterly
newsletter.
Description:
Founded 1972. Gymnastics association
sponsoring tournaments, competitions.

U.S. SPORTS ACROBATICS/USSA
132 E. WASHINGTON ST
SUITE 700
INDIANAPOLIS, IN 46204
317-237-5050
Fax: 317-237-5069

membership@usagym.org
www.usagym.org
• Luan Peszek, Vice President Of Program
Development
(317) 829-5646
lpeszek@usagym.org
• Steve Penny, President/CEO
(317) 829-5050
spenny@usagym.org
• Ron Galimore, Chief Operation Officer
(317) 829-5631
rgalimore@usagym.org
• Renee Jamison, Director Of Administration
& Olympic Relations
(317) 829-5635
rjamison@usagym.org
• Katelyn Dapper, Executive Office
Coordinator
(317) 237-5914
• Lee Johnson, Vice President of Marketing
(317) 829-5647
ljohnson@usagym.org
• Justin Hirnisey, Director of marketing
(317) 829-5666
jhirnisey@usagym.org
• Jackie Magnuson, Event Marketing
Manager
(317) 829-5623
jmagnuson@usagym.org
Number of members:
1,300
Member Services:
Publication and interpretation of rules;
makes competition videotapes available for
purchase; conducts international and
regional competitions as well as local meets;
training seminars and clinics during the off
season; efforts to raise dollars to support
athlete travel to international competitions;
judges' training. Annual meeting of Board of
Directors - President's Day weekend in
February.
Publications:
ACROSPORTS, newsletter six times
annually.
Membership Requirements:
Interest in sports acrobatics, payment of
membership dues.
Description:
Founded 1974. Promotion of sports
acrobatics; conducts competitions;
publishes rules and educational materials.

Handball Organizations

**CANADIAN TEAM HANDBALL
FEDERATION**
453, RUE JACOB-NICOL
SHERBROOKE, QC, CANADA J1J 4E5
819-563-7937
Fax: 819-563-5352
www.handballcanada.ca
• Raquel Marinho, President
(647) 700-4919
raquelpedercini@hotmail.com
• Ward Hrabi, Vice President of Officials
(204) 668-9442
whrabi@shaw.ca
• Brian Hayes, Treasurer
• Francois LeBeau, Chief Operating Officer
Description:
Founded 1966. Amateur sports
organization.

**HANDBALL, INTERNATIONAL
FEDERATION**
PETER-MERIAN STRASSE 23
PO BOX 4002
BASLE, SWITZERLAN CH-4002
ihf.office@ihf.info
www.ihf.info/
• Hassan Moustafa, President
• Sandi Sola, Treasurer
• Miguel Roca Mas, 1st Vice President
Description:
International governing body for the sport of
handball.

U.S. HANDBALL ASSOCIATION
2333 N. TUCSON BLVD
TUCSON, AZ 85716
520-795-0434
Fax: 520-795-0465
handball@ushandball.org
www.ushandball.org
• Tom Sove, Vice President
(209) 575-2758
• Matt Krueger, Development Coordinator
(520) 795-0434
• Gary Cruz, Youth Development Director
• Mike Steele, President
(503) 352-2806
• LeaAnn Martin, Vice President
(360) 650-3054
• Steve Dykes, Secretary
• Mike Driscoll, Treasurer-South West
Region
(972) 235-9547
• Vern Roberts, Executive Director
(520) 795-0434
Nature of Service:
Promotes handball.
Year Founded:
1951
Membership Requirements:
Dues $40 annually.
Number of members:
8,500
Publications:
HANDBALL, bimonthly.

USA TEAM HANDBALL
2330 W CALIFORNIA AVENUE
SALT LAKE CITY, UT 84104
801-463-2000
info@usateamhandball.org
www.usateamhandball.org

Hockey, Field Hockey Organizations

FIELD HOCKEY CANADA
311 WEST 1ST STREET
NORTH VANCOUVER, BC, CANADA V7M
1B5
jsauve@fieldhockey.ca
www.fieldhockey.ca
• Jeff Sauve, Chief Executive Officer
jsauve@fieldhockey.ca
• Iann Baggott, Chair
• Robin Richardson, Treasurer
• Shaheed Devji, Creative & Communication
Manager
sdevji@fieldhockey.ca
• Anthony Farry, Head Coach, Men's
National Program
afarry@fieldhockey.ca
• Ian Rutledge, Head Coach,Women's
National Program

irutledge@fieldhockey.ca
• Lisa Northrup, High Performance Manager
Year Founded:
1991
Description:
Amalgamation of Canadian Field Hockey
Association (1961) and the Canadian
Women's Field Hockey Association (1962).
Objectives include the development and
promotion of field hockey across the
country, as well as the provision of services
and programs to assist individuals to
achieve their potential as athletes
Number of members:
10,271
Membership Requirements:
Member Teams (Senior), Junior Teams
(under 18 or high school), Associate
Members (Individuals) pay annual
membership fees. Other affiliate Junior
categories for nominal fee and few services
Member Services:
Insurance, group accident and liability,
access to national championship, national
team programs, magazine subscription, high
performance program access (national
teams); Certification Program for Coaches
and Umpires.

**FIELD HOCKEY, FEDERATION
INTERNATIONALE DE HOCKEY (FIH)**
RUE DU VALENTIN 61
LAUSANNE, SWITZERLAN CH-1004
info@fih.ch
• Leandro Negre, President
• Kelly Fairweather, Chief Executive Officer
• Diana Capsa, Head Of Finance
• David Luckes, Sport & Development
Director
• Sarah Massey, Marketing & Events
Director
Description:
International governing body for the sport of
field hockey.
Publication:
BDO WorldHockey Monthly, the 26 minute
programme is distributed free-of-charge
director from FIH to a wide selection of
global broadcasters every four weeks. The
programme showcases hockey with a range
of topics including highlights of major
tournaments; the Sahara WorldHockey
Team Rankings, news from hockey
competitions around the globe, and profiles
of some of hockey's international stars

U.S. FIELD HOCKEY ASSOCIATION
5540 NORTH ACADEMY
SUITE 100
COLORADO SPRINGS, CO 80918
719-866-4567
Fax: 719-632-0979
information@usafieldhockey.com
www.usfieldhockey.com
• Steve Locke, Executive Director
(719) 866-4361
• Simon Hoskins, Chief Operating Officer
(719) 866-4370
• Janet Paden, Chief Financial & Human
Resources Officer
(719) 866-4368
• Kait Mitchell, Communications Manager
(719) 866-4363
• Karen Collins, Director Of Events
(719) 866-4366
• Shawn Hindy, Chair of the Board

Hockey, Ice Hockey Organizations

AMERICAN HOCKEY COACHES ASSOCIATION/AHCA
7 CONCORD STREET
GLOUCESTER, MA 01930
978-376-5494
j2b2hockey@gmail.com
www.ahcahockey.com
• Grant Potulny, President
• Joe Bertagna, Executive Director
(978) 376-5494
j2b2hockey@gmail.com
• Brett Petersen, Treasurer
Year Founded:
1947
Description:
Promotes Ice Hockey
Membership:
Dues is as follows: Active, College, Division I Men: $315.00, Division II Women $315.00, Division II-III Men $185.00, Division II-III Women $185.00; Active, Non-College: $75.00; Allied $75.00; Amateur High School $25.00
Membership Requirements:
Active - college coaches from NCAA schools. Allied - anyone interested. Honorary - people in ice hockey who made contribution to game
Publications:
Meeting minutes, fall newsletter

CANADIAN ADULT RECREATIONAL HOCKEY ASSOCIATION
1420 BLAIR PLACE
SUITE 610
OTTAWA, ON, CANADA K1J 9L8
613-244-1989
800-267-1854
Fax: 613-244-0451
info@carhahockey.ca
www.carhahockey.ca
• Michael S. Peski, President
mpeski@carhahockey.ca
• Scott Wilson, Manager, Hockey Operations
swilson@carhahockey.ca
• Shannon Killeen, Senior Lead, Membership
Year Founded:
1975
Description:
Serves to promote and foster recreational hockey throughout Canada, increased recreational activity and physical fitness among Canadians through participation in recreational hockey; competitions for members in various tournaments
Membership Requirements:
Adult recreational and oldtimer hockey leagues, teams and players (19 years of age and older); Adult recreational hockey tournaments; Arenas (within Canada); Referees for adult recreation and oldtimer hockey
Member Services:
Membership program which includes benefits such as team welcome gifts, special promotions and offerings plus a comprehensive sport protection program (insurance). Tournament programs well organized, top quality adult recreational hockey tournaments from coast to coast

HOCKEY CANADA
151 CANADA OLYMPIC ROAD SW
SUITE 201
CALGARY, AB, CANADA T3B 5R5
888-777-2192
Fax: 403-777-3635
www.hockeycanada.ca
• Jonathan F. Goldbloom, Chair
• Katherine Henderson, CEO
Year Founded:
1914
Description:
Their mission statement reflects the commitment and dedication of Hockey Canada and the hundreds of thousands of volunteers in Canada, ensuring that hockey provides quality opportunities that both positive and fun for all participants
Number of members:
500,000+
Membership Requirements:
Any amateur hockey player who registers with one of the thirteen regional CHA branch offices across Canada. Must not have signed a professional contract in the same year as he/she signs an amateur card
Publications:
HOCKEY CANADA INSIDER, newsletter; CHA OFFICIAL HOCKEY RULES, every second year; NATIONAL JUNIOR TEAM MEDIA GUIDE, annually

HOCKEY EAST ASSOCIATION
591 NORTH AVE
#2
WAKEFIELD, MA 01880
781-245-2122
Fax: 781-245-2492
info@hockeyeastonline.com
www.hockeyeastonline.com
• Brian Smith, Associate Commissioner
• Kate McAfee, Associate Commissioner
• Brian Murphy, Supervisor, Men's Officials
• Dave Lezenski, Supervisor, Women's Officials
Year Founded:
1983
Teams:
Boston College, Boston University, University of Connecticut, Holy Cross (women only), University of Maine, University of Massachusetts (men only) University of Mass-Lowell (men only), Merrimack College, University of New Hampshire, Northeastern University, Providence College and University of Vermont.
Description:
Sponsors intercollegiate hockey play between member schools, including: Boston Col., Boston U., U. of Maine, U. of Mass. at Amherst, U. of Mass. at Lowell, Merrimack Col., U. of New Hampshire, Northeastern U., Providence Col
Publications:
HOCKEY EAST YEARBOOK, annual; Championship Souvenir Program, annual

HOCKEY NORTH AMERICA/NATIONAL NOVICE HOCKEY ASSOCIATION
45570 SHEPARD DR
SUITE 3
STERLING, VA 20164
800-446-2539
Fax: 703-421-9205
HockeyNorthAmerica@gmail.com
www.hna.com

Year Founded:
1980
Description:
Amateur adult hockey league operating in 24 cities in the United States, Europe, and Canada offering professional style competition for players of beginning, intermediate and advanced skill. NNHA offers instruction and competition for adult beginners
Number of members:
10,000
Membership Requirements:
Must pay registration fee of $25. Also must pay league fees in addition on a regular basis.
Member Services:
National championships held in June each year. Sponsor regional tournaments leading to national championship. Also sponsor invitational tournaments. Provides web site, comprehensive statistics reporting, newsletters, FAX on demand information services.

INTERNATIONAL ICE HOCKEY FEDERATION (IIHF)
BRANDSCHENKESTRASSE 50
POSTFACH 1817
8027
ZURICH, SWITZERLAN 8027
office@iihf.com
www.iihf.com
• Luc Tardif, President
• Bob Nicholson, Vice President (CAN)

NATIONAL HOCKEY LEAGUE ENTERPRISES
1185 AVENUE OF THE AMERICAS
15TH FLOOR
NEW YORK, NY 10036-2601
212-789-2000
Fax: 212-789-2020
• Dave McCarthy, Vice President, Consumer Products Marketing
Description:
The NHL's use of technology combined with existing client base demonstrate the breadth of applicability and growing stature as the standard for presenting numeric data online.

NATIONAL HOCKEY LEAGUE PLAYERS' ASSOCIATION/NHLPA
10 BAY STREET
SUITE 1200
TORONTO, ON, CANADA M5J 2N8
416-313-2300
Fax: 416-313-2301
www.nhlpa.com
• Marty Walsh, Executive Director
Description:
The National Hockey League Player's Association/NHLPA is a labor union whose members are the players in the National Hockey League (NHL). The NHLPA works on behalf of the players in varied disciplines.

NORTHERN COLLEGIATE HOCKEY ASSOCIATION
110 S MADISON STREET
ADRIAN, MN 49221
507-429-7229
www.nchahockey.org
• Jim Olson, Commissioner
(414) 305-5738
olsonjimncha@gmail.com

• Steve Schauer, Director, Communications
NCHAcommunications@gmail.com
Nature of Service:
Member schools: Adrian College, Aurora
University, Concordia University Wisconsin,
Lake Forest College, Lawrence University,
Marian University, Milwaukee School of
Engineering, St. Norbert College, Trine
University, University of Dubuque
Teams:
Men's Hockey: 10 teams; Women's Hockey:
8 teams.
Numbers of Members:
12

USA HOCKEY
1775 BOB JOHNSON DRIVE
COLORADO SPRINGS, CO 80906-4090
719-576-8724
Fax: 719-538-1160
usah@usahockey.org
www.usahockey.com
• Pat Kelleher, Executive Director
• Kim Folsom, Director, Member Services
kimf@usahockey.org
• Casey Jorgensen, General Counsel
cjorgensen@usahockey.org
• Kelly Mahncke, Assistant Executive
Director, Finance
kelly.mahncke@usahockey.org
Founded:
1937

WESTERN COLLEGIATE HOCKEY ASSOCIATION
2950 METRO DRIVE
SUITE 102
BLOOMINGTON, MN 55425
952-681-7947
pr@wcha.com
www.wcha.com
• Tracy Dill, Interim WCHA Commissioner
tdill@wcha.com
• Dean Thibodeau, Associate
Commissioner, Hockey Administration
(952) 426-4393
Year Founded:
1951
Description:
Sponsors intercollegiate ice hockey.
Member schools include: Bemidji State
University, University of Minnesota,
University of Minnesota Duluth, Minnesota
State University Mankato, Ohio State
University, St. Cloud State University,
University of St. Thomas, University of
Wisconsin-Madison

Hockey, Professional Hockey (NHL)

NATIONAL HOCKEY LEAGUE/NHL
1 MANHATTAN WEST
395 NINTH AVE.
NEW YORK, NY 10001
212-789-2000
Fax: 212-789-2020
nhltvsupport@nhl.com
www.nhl.com
• Gary B. Bettman, Commissioner
• William Daly, Deputy Commissioner
• Colin Campbell, Senior Executive Vice
President, Hockey Operations
Year Founded:
1917

Description:
League of professional hockey teams
Membership Requirements:
Approval by NHL Board of Governors
Publications:
NHL Rule Book, annual; NHL Schedule,
annual; NHL Media Directory, annual; NHL
Official Guide and Record Book, annual
Additional Offices:
Toronto: 50 Bay St., 11th Floor, Toronto,
ON, Canada M5J 2X8; 416-359-7900; Fax:
416-981-2779. Montreal: 1800 McGill
College Ave., Montreal, QC, Canada H3A
3J6; 514-841-9220.

Teams:

ANAHEIM DUCKS
HONDA CENTER
2695 E KATELLA AVENUE
ANAHEIM, CA 92806
714-940-2900
www.nhl.com/ducks
• Michael Schulman, Chair
• Bill Foltz, CEO
• Aaron Teats, Club President
• Pat Verbeek, General Manager
• Tim Ryan, EVP/Chief Commercial Officer
• Lisa Monson, Chief Human Resources Officer
• Greg Cronin, Head Coach
• Richard Clune, Assistant Coach
• Army Tim, Assistant Coach
• Sudarshan Maharaj, Goaltending Coach
• Jeremy Bettle, Director of High Performance
Year Founded:
1993
Description:
The Anaheim Ducks are a National Hockey
League team based in Anaheim, California
Home Arena:
Honda Center. Seating capacity 17,174.

ARIZONA COYOTES
UTAH HOCKEY CLUB
301 WEST SOUTH TEMPLE
SALT LAKE CITY, UT 84101
623-772-3200
Fax: 623-872-2000
fanservices@arizonacoyotes.com
www.nhl.com/coyotes
• Alex Meruelo, Majority Owner, Chair &
Governor
• Patrick Murphy, President, Business
Operations
Year Founded:
1972
Description:
The Arizona Coyotes are a National Hockey
League team based in Tempe, Arizona. In 2024,
the franchise was rendered inactive by the
Board of Governors, pending the construction of
an NHL-appropriate facility. The Coyotes' assets
were transferred to a Utah-based franchise in
the meantime.
Home Arena:
Mullett Arena. Seating capacity 4,600.

BOSTON BRUINS
TD GARDEN
100 LEGENDS WAY
BOSTON, MA 02114
617-624-1900
fanrelations@bostonbruins.com
www.nhl.com/bruins
• Jeremy M. Jacobs, Owner & Governor; Chair,
NHL Board of Governors
• Charlie Jacobs, Chief Executive Officer &
Alternate Governor
• Cam Neely, President & Alternate Governor
• Don Sweeney, General Manager
• Scott Bradley, Senior Advisor to the General
Manager
• Evan Gold, Assistant General Manager & Dir.,
Legal Affairs
• Jamie Langenbrunner, Assistant General
Manager, Player Personnel

• Jim Montgomery, Head Coach
• Chris Kelly, Assistant Coach
• Joe Sacco, Assistant Coach
• Glen Thornborough, Chief Revenue Officer
Year Founded:
1924.
Description:
The Boston Bruins are a National Hockey
League team based in Boston, Massachusetts.
Home Arena:
TD Garden. Seating capacity: 17,850.

BUFFALO SABRES
KEYBANK CENTER
ONE SEYMOUR H. KNOX III PLAZA
BUFFALO, NY 14203-4122
716-855-4100
Fax: 716-855-4122
www.nhl.com/sabres
• Terry Pegula, Owner & Chief Executive Officer
• Kim Pegula, Owner & President
• Kevyn Adams, General Manager
• Pete Guelli, COO
• Sam Ventura, VP, Hockey Strategy &
Research
• Adam Mair, Director, Player Development
• Lidy Ruff, Head Coach
• Seth Appert, Assistant Coach
Year Founded:
1970
Description:
The Buffalo Sabres are a National Hockey
League team based in Buffalo, New York
Home Arena:
KeyBank Center. Seating capacity 19,070.

CALGARY FLAMES
PO BOX 1540
STN M
CALGARY, AB, CANADA T2P 3B9
403-777-4646
customerservice@calgaryflames.com
www.nhl.com/flames
• N. Murray Edwards, Chairman & Owner
• Robert Hayes, President & CEO
• Don Maloney, President, Hockey Operations
• Lorenzo DeCicco, COO
• Paul Kong, CFO
• Mike Franco, VP, Sales, Customer Services &
Ticketing
• Craig Conroy, General Manager
• Ryan Huska, Head Coach
• Dan Lambert, Assistant Coach
• Cail MacLean, Assistant Coach
Year Founded:
1972
Description:
The Calgary Flames are a National Hockey
League team based in Calgary, Alberta
Home Arena:
Scotiabank Saddledome. Seating capacity
19,289.

CAROLINA HURRICANES
LENOVO CENTER
1400 EDWARDS MILL ROAD
RALEIGH, NC 27607
919-467-7825
Fax: 919-462-7030
pncarenaguestservices@pncarena.com
www.nhl.com/hurricanes
• Tom Dundon, Owner & Governor
• Eric Tulsky, President & General Manager
• Shaun Nicholson, Chief Financial Officer
• Tom Embrey, Vice President & General
Manager, Lenovo Center
• Nigel Wheeler, General Counsel
• Rod Brind'Amour, Head Coach
• Jeff Daniels, Assistant Coach
Year Founded:
1972
Description:
The Carolina Hurricanes Hockey Club is a
National Hockey League team based in Raleigh,
North Carolina
Home Arena:
Lenovo Center. Seating capacity 18,680.

CHICAGO BLACKHAWKS
1901 WEST MADISON STREET
CHICAGO, IL 60612
312-455-7000
Fax: 312-455-7070
www.nhl.com/blackhawks
• Danny Wirtz, Chair & CEO
• Jaime Faulkner, President, Business Operations
• Kyle Davidson, General Manager
• Meghan Hunter, Asst. General Manager, Hockey Operations
• Adam Rogowin, Vice President, Communications
• T.J. Skattum, Vice President, Finance
• Anders Sorensen, Head Coach
• Derek King, Assistant Coach
• Kevin Dean, Assistant Coach
• Derek Plante, Assistant Coach
Year Founded:
1926.
Description:
The Chicago Blackhawks are a National Hockey Legue team based in Chicago, Illinois.
Home Arena:
United Center. Seating capacity: 19,717.

COLORADO AVALANCHE
COLORADO AVALANCHE HOCKEY CLUB
BALL ARENA
1000 CHOPPER CIRCLE
DENVER, CO 80204
303-405-1100
www.nhl.com/avalanche
• E. Stanley Kroenke, Owner & Chair
• Josh Kroenke, President & Governor
• Joe Sakic, President, Hockey Operations
• Chris MacFarland, General Manager
• Jared Bednar, Head Coach
• Kevin Mathis, Assistant Coach
• Phil Loadholt, Assistant Coach
• Matthew Sokolowski, Head Athletic Trainer
Year Founded:
1972
Description:
The Colorado Avalanche are a National Hockey League team based in Denver, Colorado
Home Arena:
Ball Arena. Seating capacity: 18,000.

COLUMBUS BLUE JACKETS
NATIONWIDE ARENA
200 WEST NATIONWIDE BOULEVARD
SUITE LEVEL
COLUMBUS, OH 43215
614-246-3200
www.nhl.com/bluejackets
• John P. McConnell, Governor & Majority Owner
• Mike Priest, President & Alternate Governor
• Don Waddell, President, Hockey Operations
• Peter Lovins, General Counsel
• Cameron Scholvin, Senior VP & Chief Operating Officer
• T.J. LaMendola, Senior VP & Chief Financial Officer
• Kathryn Dobbs, Senior VP & Chief Marketing Officer
• Josh Flynn, Assistant General Manager
• Dean Evason, Head Coach
• Niklas Backstrom, Goaltending Coach
Year Founded:
2000.
Description:
The Columbus Blue Jackets are a National Hockey League team based in Columbus, Ohio.
Home Arena:
Nationwide Arena. Seating capacity: 18,500.

DALLAS STARS
2601 AVENUE OF THE STARS
FRISCO, TX 75034
214-387-5500
www.nhl.com/stars
• Tom Gaglardi, Owner & Governor
• Brad Alberts, President & CEO
• James R. Lites, Alternate Chair
• Jim Nill, General Manager
• Matt Bowman, Executive VP & Chief Revenue Officer
• Dan Stuchal, Chief Communications Officer
• Joe Calvillo, Director, Communications & Broadcasting
• Pete DeBoer, Head Coach
• Steve Spott, Assistant Coach
Year Founded:
1967
Description:
The Dallas Stars are a National Hockey League team based in Frisco, Texas
Home Arena:
American Airlines Center. Seating capacity: 18,532 (up tp 19,323 with standing room).

DETROIT RED WINGS
2645 WOODWARD AVE
DETROIT, MI 48201
313-471-6606
www.nhl.com/redwings
• Marian Ilitch, Owner & Secretary-Treasurer
• Chris Ilitch, Governor, President & CEO
• Steve Yzerman, EVP & General Manager
• Aaron Kahn, Assistant General Manager
• Paul MacDonald, Vice President, Finance
• Todd McLellan, Head Coach
• Trent Yawney, Associate Coach
• Alexa Tanguay, Assistant Coach
• Alex Westlund, Goaltending Coach
• Kyle Mackinnon, Director, Pro Scouting
• Kris Draper, Director, Amateur Scouting
Year Founded:
1926
Description:
The Detroit Red Wings are a National Hockey League team based in Detroit, Michigan.
Home Arena:
Little Caesars Arena. Seating capacity: 19,515.
Publications:
Inside Hockeytown; 48 Hours with the Detroit Red Wings; Detroit Red Wings History Book; Heroes of Hockeytown

EDMONTON OILERS
OILERS ENTERTAINMENT GROUP
300, 10214 104 AVE NW
EDMONTON, AB, CANADA T5J 0H6
780-414-4625
www.nhl.com/oilers
• Daryl A. Katz, Owner, Chair & Governor
• Jeff Jackson, Chief Executive Officer
• Stew MacDonald, President & Chief Revenue Officer
• Jason Quilley, Executive VP, Finance & CFO
• Stuart Ballantyne, President & COO
• Tim Shipton, EVP, Communications & Gaming
• Jeff Jackson, CEO, Hockey Operations
• Stan Bowman, General Manager & President, Hockey Operations
• Keith Gretzky, Assistant General Manager
• Paul Coffey, Special Advisor, Hockey Operations
• Kris Knoblauch, Head Coach
• Glen Gulutzan, Assistant Coach
Year Founded:
1972
Description:
The Edmonton Oilers are a National Hockey League team based in Edmonton, Alberta
Home Arena:
Rogers Place. Seating capacity 18,347.

FLORIDA PANTHERS
ONE PANTHER PARKWAY
2555 NW 136TH AVENUE
SUNRISE, FL 33323
954-835-7825
www.nhl.com/panthers
• Vincent J. Viola, Owner & Governor
• Douglas A. Cifu, Vice Chair, Partner & Alternate Governor
• Matthew Caldwell, President & CEO
• Bill Zito, General Manager
• Bryce Hollweg, Chief Operating Officer
• Shawn Thornton, Chief Revenue Officer
• James Suh, Chief Financial Officer
• Paul Maurice, Head Coach
• Jamie Kompon, Assistant Coach
• Robb Tallas, Goaltending Coach
Year Founded:
1993
Home Arena:
Amerant Bank Arena. Seating capacity: 19,250.

LOS ANGELES KINGS
CRYPTO.COM ARENA
1111 SOUTH FIGUEROA STREET
LOS ANGELES, CA 90015
213-742-7100
888-546-4752
feedback@lakings.com
www.nhl.com/kings
• Philip F. Anschutz, Owner
• Edward P. Roski, Jr., Owner
• Dan Beckerman, President & CEO, AEG & Alternate Governor
• Rob Blake, Vice President & General Manager
• Michael Altieri, Senior VP, Marketing, Communications & Content
• Jim Hiller, Head Coach
• Newell Brown, Assistant Coach
• D.J. Smith, Assistant Coach
• Mike Buckley, Goaltending Coach
Year Founded:
1967
Description:
The Los Angeles Kings are a National Hockey League team based in Los Angeles, California.
Home Arena:
Crypto.com Arena. Seating capacity: 18,230.

MINNESOTA WILD
317 WASHINGTON STREET
ST. PAUL, MN 55102
651-602-6000
Fax: 651-222-1055
info@wild.com
www.nhl.com/wild
• Craig Leipold, Owner & Governor
• Matt Majka, Chief Executive Officer
• Bill Guerin, General Manager & President, Hockey Operations
• Jeff Pellegrom, Chief Financial Officer & Executive VP
• Jamie Spencer, Executive VP, Business Development
• Carin Anderson, Senior VP, Corporate & Retail Management
• Mitch Helgerson, Senior VP, Marketing & Ticket Sales
• Tom Kurvers, Assistant General Manager
• John Hynes, Head Coach
• Jack Capuano, Assistant Coach
• Jason King, Assistant Coach
• Patrick Dwyer, Assistant Coach
• Frederic Chabot, Goaltending Coach
Year Founded:
2000
Description:
The Minnesota Wild are a National Hockey League team based in St. Paul, Minnesota.
Home Arena:
Xcel Energy Center. Seating capacity 17,954.

MONTREAL CANADIENS
1275, RUE SAINT-ANTOINE OUEST
MONTREAL, QC, CANADA H3C 5L2
514-932-2582
877-463-2674
www.nhl.com/canadiens
• Geoff Molson, Owner, President & CEO
• Jeff Gorton, Executive VP, Hockey Operations
• Kent Hughes, General Manager
• Sedgwick John, Assistant General Manager
• Martin Lapointe, Director, Player Personnel & Amateur Scouting
• Martin St. Louis, Head Coach
• Eric Raymond, Assistant Coach
Year Founded:
1909
Description:
The Montreal Canadiens are one of the oldest teams in the National Hockey League. They are based in Montreal, Quebec.

Home Arena:
Centre Bell. Seating capacity 21,105.

NASHVILLE PREDATORS
BRIDGESTONE ARENA
501 BROADWAY
NASHVILLE, TN 37203
615-770-2355
Fax: 615-770-2309
predators@nashvillepredators.com
www.nhl.com/predators
• Bill Haslam, Chair, Governor & Owner
• Sean Henry, Chief Executive Officer
• Barry Trotz, General Manager
• Michelle Kennedy, President, COO, &
Alternate Governor
• Keith Hegger, Chief Financial Officer
• Dionna Widder, Chief Revenue Officer
• Dave Urso, Senior VP, Operations
• Jeff Kealty, Assistant GM & Director, Scouting
• Brian Poile, Assisant GM & Director, Hockey
Operations
• Andrew Brunette, Head Coach
• Darby Hendrickson, Assistant Coach
• Mitch Korn, Goaltending Coach
Year Founded:
1998
Description:
The Nashville Predators are a National Hockey
League team basedin Nashville, Tennessee.
Home Arena:
Bridgestone Arena. Seating capacity 17,159.

NEW JERSEY DEVILS
PRUDENTIAL CENTER
25 LAFAYETTE STREET
NEWARK, NJ 07102
973-757-6200
mgmt@newjerseydevils.com
www.nhl.com/devils
• David Blitzer, Managing Partner, Chair &
Governor
• Josh Harris, Co-Managing Partner, Vice Chair
& Alt. Governor
• Jake Reynolds, President
• Brown Tad, CEO
• Tom Fitzgerald, President, Hockey Operations
& General Manager
• Martin Brodeur, Executive VP & Advisor,
Hockey Operations
• Stephen Rosebrook, Executive VP &
Prudential Center GM
• David Collins, Chief Financial Officer
• Adam Davis, Chief Commercial Officer
• Dan MacKinnon, Senior VP & Assistant
General Manager
• Sheldon Keefe, Head Coach
• Jeremy Colliton, Assistant Coach
• Chris Taylor, Assistant Coach
• Sergei Brylin, Assistant Coach
• Dave Rogalski, Goaltending Coach
Year Founded:
1974
Description:
The New Jersey Devils are a National Hockey
League team based in Newark, New Jersey.
Home Arena:
Prudential Center. Seating capacity 16,514.

NEW YORK ISLANDERS
ISLANDERS BUSINESS OFFICES
15 VERBENA AVE
FLORAL PARK, NY 11001
516-501-6700
Fax: 516-501-6762
customerservice@newyorkislanders.com
www.nhl.com/islanders
• Scott Malkin, Owner & Governor
• Lou Lamoriello, President, General Manager &
Alternate Governor
• Mike Cosentino, Senior VP, Sales, Service &
Business Intelligence
• Ryan Halkett, Senior VP, Game Presentation
• Lea del Rosario, Senior VP, Human
Resources
• Patrick Roy, Head Coach
• John Maclean, Associate Coach
• Piero Greco, Goaltending Coach

Year Founded:
1972
Description:
The New York Islanders are a National Hockey
League team based in Uniondale, New York.
Home Arena:
UBS Arena. Seating capacity: 17,255.

NEW YORK RANGERS
2 PENNSYLVANIA PLAZA
NEW YORK, NY 10121
212-465-6000
Fax: 212-465-6000
newyorkrangers@thegarden.com
www.nhl.com/rangers
• James L. Dolan, Executive Chair
• Chris Drury, President, General Manager &
Alternate Gov.
• Chris Drury, President & General Manager
• John Cudmore, Senior VP, Sports Strategy &
Administration
• Jeanine McGrory, Senior VP, Finance
• Mark Piazza, Senior VP, Sports Team
Operations
• Peter Laviolette, Head Coach
• Phil Housley, Assistant Head Coach
Year Founded:
1926
Description:
The New York Rangers are a National Hockey
League team based in New York City, New
York.
Home Arena:
Madison Square Garden. Seating capacity
18,006.

OTTAWA SENATORS
CANADIAN TIRE CENTRE
1000 PALLADIUM DR
OTTAWA, ON, CANADA K2V 1A5
613-599-0250
www.nhl.com/senators
• Cyril Leeder, President & CEO
• Crowe Erin, EVP & COO
• Steve Staios, President, Hockey Operations &
General Manager
• Dave Poulin, SVP, Hockey Operations
• Ryan Bowness, Assistant General Manager
• Tim Pattyson, Director, Hockey Operations
• Jordan Silmser, Director, Team Services
• Travis Green, Head Coach
• Jack Capuano, Associate Coach
Year Founded:
1990
Description:
The Ottawa Senators are a National Hockey
League team based in Ottawa, Ontario.
Home Arena:
Canadian Tire Centre. Seating capacity 19,153.

PHILADELPHIA FLYERS
WELLS FARGO CENTER
3601 S. BROAD ST.
PHILADELPHIA, PA 19148
215-336-3600
www.nhl.com/flyers
• Dan Hilferty, Chair, CEO & Governor
• Keith Jones, President, Hockey Operations &
Alternate Governor
• Daniel Briere, General Manager
• John Master, EVP, Chief Legal & Strategy
Officer/Alt. Gov.
• Blair Listino, Chief Financial & Administration
Officer/Alt. Gov.
• Cynthia Punsalan, SVP, Business
Administration
• John Tortorella, Head Coach
• Kim Dillabaugh, Goaltending Coach
Year Founded:
1967
Description:
The Philadelphia Flyers are a National Hockey
League team basedin Philadelphia,
Pennsylvania. They are owned by Comcast
Spectacor.
Home Arena:
Wells Fargo Center. Seating capacity 20,306.

PITTSBURGH PENGUINS
PPG PAINTS ARENA
1001 FIFTH AVENUE
PITTSBURGH, PA 15219
412-642-1800
Fax: 412-255-1980
www.nhl.com/penguins
• Mario Lemieux, Minority Owner
• Kevin Acklin, President, Business Operations
• Mike Dillon, Chief Financial Officer
• Chris Zaber, Chief Revenue Officer
• Tracey MacCants Lewis, Chief People Officer
& General Counsel
• Kyle Dubas, President, Hockey Operations &
General Manager
• Mike Sullivan, Head Coach
• Ty Hennes, Assistant Coach
• Mike Vellucci, Assistant Coach
• Andy Chiodo, Goaltending Coach
Year Founded:
1967
Description:
The Pittsburgh Penguins are a National Hockey
League team basedin Pittsburgh, Pennsylvania.
Home Arena:
PPG Paints Arena. Seating capacity 18,187.

SAN JOSE SHARKS
SAP CENTER
525 WEST SANTA CLARA STREET
SAN JOSE, CA 95113
408-287-7070
Fax: 408-999-5797
www.nhl.com/sharks
• Hasso Plattner, Owner
• Jonathan Becher, President
• Greg Matthews, Senior VP/CFO
• Scott Emmert, Vice President,
Communications
• Mike Grier, General Manager
• Joe Will, Assistant General Manager
• Tom Holy, Assistant General Manager
• Ryan Warsofsky, Head Coach
Year Founded:
1991
Description:
The San Jose Sharks are a National Hockey
League team based in San Jose, California.
Home Arena:
SAP Center. Seating capacity 17,435.

SEATTLE KRAKEN
CLIMATE PLEDGE ARENA
334 1ST AVE N
SEATTLE, WASHINGTON 98109
844-645-7825
info@seattlekrakenhockey.com
www.nhl.com/kraken
• Ron Francis, Executive VP/General Manager
• Jeff Tambellini, Director, Player Development
• Brennan Baxandall, Director, Team Services
• Dave Hakstol, Head Coach
Year Founded:
2021
Description:
The Seattle Kraken is a National Hockey League
team based in Seattle, Washington. It is the first
professional hockey team to play in Seattle
since the Seattle Totems who played their last
game in 1975.
Home Arena:
Climate Pledge Arena. Seating capacity: 17,151.

ST. LOUIS BLUES
ST. LOUIS BLUES HOCKEY CLUB
ENTERPRISE CENTER
1401 CLARK AVENUE AT BRETT HULL WAY
SAINT LOUIS, MO 63103
314-622-2500
customerservice@stlblues.com
www.nhl.com/blues
• Tom Stillman, Chairman/Governor
• Doug Armstrong, President, Hockey
Operations/GM/Alternate Governor
• Chris Zimmerman, President/CEO, Business
Operations/Alt. Governor
• Steve Chapman, Executive VP/Chief Revenue
& Marketing Officer

- Phil Siddle, Executive VP/Chief Operating & Financial Officer
- Keira Emerson, Vice President/Chief Strategy Officer
- Dave Taylor, Consultant to Hockey Operations
- Ryan Miller, Assistant GM, Hockey Operations
- Jim Montgomery, Head Coach
- David Alexander, Goaltending Coach

Year Founded:
1967
Description:
The St. Louis Blues are a National Hockey League team based in St. Louis, Missouri.
Home Arena:
Enterprise Center. Seating capacity 18,724.

TAMPA BAY LIGHTNING
AMALIE ARENA
401 CHANNELSIDE DRIVE
TAMPA, FL 33602
813-301-6500
membershipservices@amaliearena.com
www.nhl.com/lightning
- Jeff Vinik, Chair & Governor
- Steve Griggs, Chief Executive Officer & Vice Chair
- Casey Rodgers, Chief Financial Officer
- James Ruth, Chief Marketing Officer
- Rhett Blewett, VP, Facility Operations/Asst. GM, Amalie Arena
- Derrick Brooks, Executive VP, Corporate & Community Development
- Brian Breseman, Senior Director, Broadcasting, Programs & Comms.
- Julien BriseBois, VP/General Manager/Alternate Governor
- Mathieu Darche, Asst. General Manager/Director, Hockey Operations
- Jon Cooper, Head Coach
- Frantz Jean, Goaltending Coach

Year Founded:
1992
Description:
The Tampa Bay Lightning is a National Hockey League team based in Tampa, Florida.
Home Arena:
Amalie Arena. Seating capacity 19,092.

TORONTO MAPLE LEAFS
SCOTIABANK ARENA
40 BAY STREET
SUITE 400
TORONTO, ON, CANADA M5J 2X2
416-815-5500
www.nhl.com/mapleleafs
- Brendan Shanahan, President & Alternate Governor
- Brad Treliving, General Manager
- Ryan Hardy, Assistant General Manager
- Danielle Goyette, Director, Player Development
- Curtis McElhinney, Director, Goaltending Development & Scouting
- Reid Mitchell, Director, Hockey & Scouting Operations
- Mark Leach, Director, Player Personnel & Amateur Scouting
- Craig Barube, Head Coach
- Curtis Sanford, Goaltending Coach

Year Founded:
1917
Description:
The Toronto Maple Leafs are a National Hockey League team based in Toronto, Ontario.
Home Arena:
Scotiabank Arena. Seating capacity 18,800.

VANCOUVER CANUCKS
89 WEST GEORGIA STREET
VANCOUVER, BC, CANADA V6B 0N8
604-899-4625
Fax: 604-899-4625
fanservices@canucks.com
www.nhl.com/canucks
- Francesco Aquilini, Chair & Governor
- Michael Doyle, President, Business Operations
- Todd Kobus, COO & CFO

- Terry Kalna, Chief Revenue Officer
- Ed McLaughlin, Executive VP & General Manager, Rogers Arena
- Jim Rutherford, President, Hockey Operations
- Patrik Allvin, General Manager
- Ryan Johnson, Assistant General Manager
- Rick Tocchet, Head Coach
- Marko Torenius, Director, Goaltending
- Ryan Johnson, Assistant Director, Player Development

Year Founded:
1970
Description:
The Vancouver Canucks are a National Hockey League team based in Vancouver, British Columbia
Home Arena:
Rogers Arena. Seating capacity 18,910.

VEGAS GOLDEN KNIGHTS
T-MOBILE ARENA
3780 LAS VEGAS BOULEVARD SOUTH
LAS VEGAS, NV 89158
702-790-2663
www.nhl.com/goldenknights
- Bill Foley, Chair, CEO & Governor
- George McPhee, President, Hockey Operations & Alternate Governor
- Kelly McCrimmon, General Manager
- Heather Clayton, Chief Financial Officer
- Robert Foley, Chief Business Officer
- Peter Sadowski, Executive VP & Chief Legal Officer
- Eric Tosi, Senior VP & Chief Marketing Officer
- Jim Frevola, Senior VP & Chief Sales Officer
- Darren Eliot, Vice President, Hockey Programming & Operations
- Gerard Gallant, Head Coach
- Sean Burke, Goaltending Coach

Year Founded:
2017
Description:
The Vegas Golden Knights are a National Hockey League team based in Las Vegas, NV.
Home Arena:
T-Mobile Arena. Seating capacity 17,500.

WASHINGTON CAPITALS
CAPITAL ONE ARENA
601 F ST NW
WASHINGTON, DC 20004
202-628-3200
membershipservices@washcaps.com
www.nhl.com/capitals
- Ted Leonsis, Founder, Chair, Principal Partner & CEO
- Dick Patrick, Vice Chair, Partner, Monumental Sports
- Brian MacLellan, President, Hockey Operations & General Manager
- Tim McDermott, Chief Marketing Officer
- Anu Rangappa, Vice President, Communications
- Spencer Carbery, Head Coach
- Scott Murray, Goaltending Coach

Year Founded:
1974
Description:
The Washington Capitals are a National Hockey League team based in Washington, DC.
Home Arena:
Capital One Arena. Seating capacity 18,573.

WINNIPEG JETS
600-223 CARLTON STREET
WINNIPEG, MB, CANADA R3C 0V4
204-987-7825
www.nhl.com/jets
- Mark Chipman, Executive Chair
- Kevin Cheveldayoff, Executive VP & General Manager
- John Olfert, President & COO
- Kelly Shouldice, VP, Content & Communications
- Scott Arniel, Head Coach
- Davis Payne, Associate Coach

Year Founded:
2011

Description:
The Winnipeg Jets are a National Hockey League team based in Winnipeg, Manitoba. The franchise was formerly known as the Atlanta Thrashers until their purchase in 2011.
Home Arena:
Canada Life Centre. Seating capacity 15,321.

Hockey, Professional, Minor Leagues

AMERICAN HOCKEY LEAGUE/AHL
ONE MONARCH PLACE
SUITE 2400
SPRINGFIELD, MA 01144
413-495-1035
ahltv@theahl.com
theahl.com
- David A. Andrews, Chairman, Board of Governors
- D. Scott Howson, President & CEO
- Chris Nikolis, Executive VP, Business Development
cnikolis@theahl.com
- Hayley Moore, VP, Hockey Operations
- Alison Izzi, VP, Hockey Operations & Governance
- Jason Chaimovitch, VP, Communications

Year Founded:
1936
Description:
Professional ice hockey league that serves as the primary developmental circuit for the National Hockey League.
Membership Requirements:
Purchase of a franchise
Publications:
Official guide and record book; Rule book; Schedule; Year End Statistical Package

Teams:

BAKERSFIELD CONDORS
MECHANICS BANK CONVENTION CENTER
1001 TRUXTUN AVENUE
BAKERSFIELD, CA 93301-4799
661-324-7825
Fax: 661-324-6929
condors@bakersfieldcondors.com
www.bakersfieldcondors.com
- Daryl Katz, Owner
- Justin Fahsbender, SVP, Business Operations
- Jose Rivera, VP, Member Services & Ticket Operations
- Keith Gretzky, General Manager
- Colin Chaulk, Head Coach
- J-F Houle, Assistant Coach
- Dave Manson, Assistant Coach
- Sylvain Rodrigue, Goaltending Coach
Home Ice:
Mechanics Bank Arena. Seating capacity, 8,751.
NHL Affiliate:
Edmonton Oilers (NHL)

BELLEVILLE SENATORS
265 CANNIFTON RD
BELLEVILLE, ON, CANADA K8N 4V8
613-967-8067
info@bellevillesens.com
bellevillesens.com
- John Mathers, Senior VP, Business Operations
- Ryan Bowness, General Manager
- Ryan Bowness, Manager, Hockey Operations
- David Bell, Head Coach
- Andrew Campbell, Assistant Coach
Home Ice:
CAA Arena. Seating capacity 4,365.
NHL Affiliation:
Ottawa Senators.

BRIDGEPORT ISLANDERS
600 MAIN STREET
BRIDGEPORT, CT 06604
203-345-2400
info@bridgeportislanders.com
www.bridgeportislanders.com
• Scott Malkin, Co-Owner & Governor
• Jon Ledecky, Co-Owner & Alt. Governor
• Alan Fuehring, Director, Broadcasting & Communications
• Chris Lamoriello, General Manager
• Rick Kowalsky, Head Coach
• Eric Boguniecki, Assistant Coach
• Matt Carkner, Assistant Coach
• Chis Terreri, Goaltending Coach
Home Ice:
Total Mortgage Arena. Seating capacity, 8,412.
NHL Affiliation:
New York Islanders.

CALGARY WRANGLERS
SCOTIABANK SADDLEDOM
555 SADDLEDOME RISE SE
CALGARY, AB, CANADA T2G 2W1
403-777-4646
customerservice@calgaryflames.com
calgarywranglers.com
• Robert Hayes, President & CEO
• Mike Moore, Vice President
• Brad Pascall, General Manager
• Nathan MacDonald, Manager, Business Operations
mblades@CalgaryFlames.com
• Ryan Popowich, Director, Marketing & Promotions
rpopowich@CalgaryFlames.com
• Trent Cull, Head Coach
• Mackenzie Skapski, Goalie Development Coach
Home Arena:
Scotiabank Saddledome. Seating capacity 19,289.
NHL Affiliation:
Calgary Flames.

CHARLOTTE CHECKERS
2700 E. INDEPENDENCE BLVD.
CHARLOTTE, NC 28205
704-342-4423
Fax: 704-377-4595
tickets@charlottecheckers.com
charlottecheckers.com
• Michael A. Kahn, Owner, CEO & Governor
• Derek Wilkinson, Senior VP, Hockey Operations
• Paul Branecky, Vice President, Marketing & Communications
• Jamie Black, Director, Finance & Controller
• Geordie Kinnear, Head Coach
• Bobby Sanguinetti, Assistant Coach
Home Ice:
Bojangles Coliseum. Seating capacity, 8,600.
NHL Affiliation:
Florida Panthers.

CHICAGO WOLVES
2301 RAVINE WAY
GLENVIEW, IL 60025
847-724-4625
800-843-9658
Fax: 847-724-1652
info@chicagowolves.com
www.chicagowolves.com
• Don Levin, Chair & Governor
• Buddy Meyers, Vice Chair
• Wayne Messmer, Senior EVP
• Wendell Young, General Manager
• Courtney Mahoney, President, Operations
• Bob Nardella, Head Coach
• Bob Nardella, Assistant Coach
• Patrick Dwyer, Assistant Coach
• Stan Dubicki, Goaltending Coach
Home Ice:
Allstate Arena. Seating capacity, 16,692.
NHL Affiliation:
Carolina Hurricanes.

CLEVELAND MONSTERS
ONE CENTER ICE
CLEVELAND, OH 44115
216-420-0000
service@clevelandmonsters.com
www.clevelandmonsters.com
• Dan Gilbert, Chair
• Nic Barlage, CEO, Rock Entertainment Group
• Mike Ostrowski, President, Franchise Properties
• Chris Clark, General Manager
• Trent Vogelhuber, Head Coach
• Mike Haviland, Associate Coach
• Brad Thiessen, Goaltending Development Coach
Home Ice:
Rocket Mortgage FieldHouse. Seating capacity: 9,447 (expandable to 18,926).

COLORADO EAGLES
1601 PELICAN LAKES POINT
SUITE 201
WINDSOR, CO 80550
970-686-7468
info@coloradoeagles.com
www.coloradoeagles.com
• Martin Lind, Owner/CEO
• Ryan Bach, President/Alternate Governor
• Gavin Riches, EVP
• Kevin McDonald, Assistant General Manager
• Chris Augusto, Executive VP, Ticketing & Marketing
• Aaron Schneekloth, Head Coach
• Ryan Bach, Goaltending Coach
Home Ice:
Blue Arena. Seating capacity: 7,500.

GRAND RAPIDS GRIFFINS
130 WEST FULTON
SUITE 111
GRAND RAPIDS, MI 49503
616-774-4585
Fax: 616-336-5464
griff@griffinshockey.com
www.griffinshockey.com
• Dan DeVos, Co-Owner, CEO & Governor
• David Van Andel, Co-Owner & Chair
• Tim Gortsema, President
(616) 774-4585
tgortsema@griffinshockey.com
• Randy Cleves, Vice President, Communications
(616) 988-0246
rcleves@griffinshockey.com
• Shawn Horcoff, General Manager
• Dan Watson, Head Coach
Home Ice:
Van Andel Arena. Seating capacity: 10,834.

HARTFORD WOLF PACK
XL CENTER
ONE CIVIC CENTER PLAZA
HARTFORD, CT 06103
860-249-6333
WolfPack-Service@SpectraXP.com
www.hartfordwolfpack.com
• Ben Weiss, General Manager
• Ryan Martin, General Manager, Hockey Operations
• Matt Harlow, Director, Hockey Operations
• Bryan Dooley, Vice President, Corporate Sales
bdooley@global-spectrum.com
• Yasmeen Badich, Director, Marketing
• Bob Crawford, Director, Public Relations & Broadcasting
bcrawford@global-spectrum.com
• Frank Berrian, Community Relations & Game Presentation Manager
fberrian@global-spectrum.com
• Steve Smith, Interim Head Coach
• Gord Murphy, Associate Head Coach
• Eric Raymond, Goaltending Coach
Home Ice:
XL Center. Seating capacity: 14,750.
NHL Affiliation:
New York Rangers.

HENDERSON SILVER KNIGHTS
DOLLAR LOAN CENTER
200 S GREEN VALLEY PKWY
HENDERSON, NV 89012
information@hendersonsilverknights.com
www.hendersonsilverknights.com
• Tim Speltz, General Manager
• Ryan Craig, Head Coach
Home Ice:
Dollar Loan Center. Seating capacity: 5,567.
NHL Affiliation:
Vegas Golden Knights (NHL); Savannah Ghost Pirates (ECHL).

HERSHEY BEARS
550 WEST HERSHEYPARK DRIVE
HERSHEY, PA 17033
717-508-2327
Fax: 717-534-8996
www.hersheybears.com
• John Lawn, President & CEO
• Bryan Helmer, Vice President, Hockey Operations
• Dan Stuck, Manager, Wellness & Team Affairs
• Zack Fisch, Manager, Media Relations & Broadcasting
zasfisch@hersheypa.com
• Todd Nelson, Head Coach
• Patrick Wellar, Assistant Coach
• Steve Bergin, Assistant Coach
Home Ice:
Giant Center. Seating capacity: 10,500.
NHL Affiliation:
Washington Capitals.

IOWA WILD
WELLS FARGO ARENA
DES MOINES, IA 50309
515-564-8000
www.iowawild.com
• Todd Frederickson, President & Governor
todd.frederickson@iowawild.com
• Mike Murray, General Manager
• Eric Grundfast, Vice President, Sales
eric.grundfast@iowawild.com
• Brent Arnold, Senior Director, Sales
• Brett McLean, Head Coach
• Nate Dicasmirro, Assistant Coach
• Richard Bachman, Goaltending Coach
Home Ice:
Wells Fargo Arena. Seating capacity: 15,181.
NHL Affiliation:
Minnesota Wild.

LAVAL ROCKET
1950 CLAUDE-GAGNE STREET
SUITE 103
MONTREAL, QC, CANADA H7N 0E4
855-595-2200
info@rocketlaval.com
www.rocketlaval.com
• John Sedgwick, Governor & Vice President, Hockey Operations
• Pascal Vincent, Head Coach
• Marco Marciano, Goaltending Coach
• Daniel Jacob, Assistant Coach
• Martin Laperriere, Assistant Coach
Home Arena:
Place Bell. Seating capacity 10,062.
NHL Affiliation:
Montreal Canadiens.

LEHIGH VALLEY PHANTOMS
701 HAMILTON STREET
ALLENTOWN, PA 18101
610-224-4625
www.phantomshockey.com
• Jim Brooks, Co-Owner & Governor
• Rob Brooks, Co-Owner & Governor
• Dennis Begley, VP, Partnerships & Premium Seating
(484) 273-4560
• Jordan Cannon, VP, Ticketing & Marketing
• Ian Laperriere, Head Coach
• Bill Downey, Assistant Coach & Dir., Hockey Operations
• Dan Meinz, Strength & Conditioning Coach

Home Arena:
PPL Center. Seating capacity: 8,420 (9,046 with standing room).
NHL Affiliation:
Philadelphia Flyers

MANITOBA MOOSE
MANITOBA MOOSE HOCKEY CLUB
600-223 CARLTON STREET
WINNIPEG, MB, CANADA R3C 0V4
204-987-7825
info@tnse.com
moosehockey.com
• Craig Heisinger, General Manager
• Brad Andrews, Senior Director, Hockey & Business Operations
• Mark Morrison, Head Coach
• Morgan Klimchuck, Assistant Coach
• Drew MacIntyre, Developmental Goaltending Coach
Home Ice:
Canada Life Centre. Seating capacity 15,321.
NHL Affiliation:
Winnipeg Jets.

MILWAUKEE ADMIRALS
510 WEST KILBOURN AVENUE
MILWAUKEE, WI 53203
414-227-0550
Fax: 414-227-0568
ticketinfo@milwaukeeadmirals.com
www.milwaukeeadmirals.com
• Harris Turer, Owner & CEO
• Jon Greenberg, President
• Scott Nichol, General Manager
• Mike Wojciechowski, Vice President, Business Development
wojo@milwaukeeadmirals.com
• Charlie Larson, Vice President, Communications
clarson@milwaukeeadmirals.com
• Karl Taylor, Head Coach
• Scott Ford, Assistant Coach
• Greg Rallo, Assistant Coach
• Ryan Costello, Manager, Hockey Operations
Home Ice:
UW-Milwaukee Panther Arena. Seating capacity: 9,652.
NHL Affiliation:
Nashville Predators.

ONTARIO REIGN
TOYOTA ARENA
4000 ONTARIO CENTER
ONTARIO, CA 91764
909-244-5500
tickets@ontarioreign.com
www.ontarioreign.com
• Darren Abbott, President
• Richard Seeley, General Manager
• Steve Fraser, Senior Director, Business Operations
• Jasmyn Wilson, Senior Director, Ticket Operations
jwilson@ontarioreign.com
• Zach Dooley, Manager, Communications & Content
zdooley@ontarioreign.com
• Marco Sturm, Head Coach
• Chris Hajt, Assistant Coach
• Brad Schuler, Assistant Coach
• Matt Millar, Goaltending Development Coach
Home Ice:
Toyota Arena. Seating capacity: 9,736.
NHL Affiliation:
Los Angeles Kings (NHL); Greenville Swamp Rabbits (ECHL).

PROVIDENCE BRUINS
1 LA SALLE SQUARE
PROVIDENCE, RI 02903
401-273-5000
www.providencebruins.com
• H. Larue Renfroe, Owner
• Jeff Hagan, President
• David DeNitto, Chief Ticketing Officer
• Nathan Roberts, Chief Marketing Officer

• Don Sweeney, General Manager (de facto)
• Ryan Mougenel, Head Coach
• Trent Whitfield, Assistant Coach
• Ryan Mougenel, Assistant Coach
Home Ice:
Amica Mutual Pavilion. Seating capacity, 11,273.
NHL Affiliation:
Boston Bruins (NHL); Maine Mariners (ECHL).

ROCHESTER AMERICANS
ROCHESTER AMERICANS HOCKEY CLUB
ONE WAR MEMORIAL SQUARE
ROCHESTER, NY 14614
585-454-5335
Fax: 585-454-3954
ContactUs@Amerks.com
www.amerks.com
• Terrence M. Pegula, Owner & President
• Kim Pegula, Co-Owner
• Chad Buck, Interim Vice President, Business Operations
chad.buck@amerks.com
• Jody Gage, Director, Strategic Planning
• Warren Kosel, Senior Director, Public Relations
(585) 545-5335
wkosel@amerks.com
• Jason Karmanos, General Manager
• Seth Appert, Head Coach
• Gord Dineen, Assistant Coach
• Toby Petersen, Assistant Coach
Home Ice:
Blue Cross Arena. Seating capacity: 10,662.
NHL Affiliation:
Boston Sabres (NHL); Cincinnati Cyclones (ECHL)

ROCKFORD ICEHOGS
401 E. STATE STREET
ROCKFORD, IL 61104
815-986-6465
icehogs@icehogs.com
www.icehogs.com
• Mark Bernard, President, Hockey Operations/General Manager
• Nick Anderson, Assistant General Manager
• Ryan Snider, President, Business Operations
• Cris Carrico, VP, Business, Development & Revenue
• Mike Peck, VP, Marketing, Content & Operations
• Anders Sorensen, Head Coach
• Matt Smith, Developmental Goaltending Coach
Year Founded:
1995
Home Ice:
BMO Harris Bank Center. Seating capacity: 6,200.
NHL Affiliation:
Chicago Blackhawks.

SAN DIEGO GULLS
SAN DIEGO GULLS HOCKEY CLUB
7676 HAZARD CENTER DRIVE
SUITE 1075
SAN DIEGO, CA 92108
619-359-4700
www.sandiegogulls.com
• Matt Savant, President, Business Operations
• Michael Schulman, Chief Executive Officer
• Rob Dimaio, General Manager
• Matt McIlvane, Head Coach
• Jeff Glass, Goaltending Coach
Home Ice:
Pechanga Arena. Seating capacity, 12,920.
NHL Affiliation:
Anaheim Ducks.

SAN JOSE BARRACUDA
1500 S 10TH ST
SAN JOSE, CA 95112
www.sjbarracuda.com
• Jon Gustafson, President/SVP/Governor
• Joe Will, General Manager
• Daniel Bell, Game Presentation Manager

• Nick Nollenberger, Public Relations & Broadcasting Manager
• John McCarthy, Head Coach
• Nick Gialdini, Manager, Hockey Operations
Home Ice:
Tech CU Arena. Seating capacity: 4,200.
NHL Affiliation:
San Jose Sharks.

SPRINGFIELD THUNDERBIRDS
1277 MAIN ST
SPRINGFIELD, MA 01103
413-787-6610
info@springfieldthunderbirds.com
www.springfieldthunderbirds.com
• Nathan Costa, President
• Todd McDonald, Vice President, Sales & Strategy
• Matthew McRobbie, Director, Business Development
• Kevin Maxwell, General Manager
• Drew Bannister, Head Coach
• Daniel Tkaczuk, Associate Head Coach
Description:
Formed after the sale of the Springfield Falcons, and the relocation of the Portland Pirates.
Home Ice:
MassMutual Center. Seating capacity, 6,800.
NHL Affiliation:
St. Louis Blues.

SYRACUSE CRUNCH
800 SOUTH STATE STREET
SYRACUSE, NY 13202
315-473-4444
info@syracusecrunch.com
www.syracusecrunch.com
• Howard Dolgon, President, CEO & Governor
• Vance Lederman, SVP, Business Operations, CFO & Alt. Governor
(315) 473-4444
vlederman@syracusecrunch.com
• Jim Sarosy, Chief Operating Officer & Alt. Governor
(315) 474-4444
jsarosy@syracusecrunch.com
• Todd Cross, Vice President, Ticket Operations
(315) 473-4444
• Megan Cahill, Director, Public Relations & Digital Media
(315) 473-4444
mcahill@syracusecrunch.com
• Stacy Roest, General Manager
• Joel Bouchard, Head Coach
• Daniel Jacob, Assistant Coach
• A.J. Maclean, Assistant Coach
• Maxime Vaillancourt, Goaltending Coach
Home Ice:
Upstate Medical University Arena at Onondaga County War Memorial. Seating capacity: 7,000.
NHL Affiliation:
Tampa Bay Lightning.

TEXAS STARS
2100 AVENUE OF THE STARS
CEDAR PARK, TX 78613
512-600-5000
tickets@texasstars.com
www.texasstars.com
• R. Thomas Gaglardi, Owner
• Brad Alberts, President & Alternate Governor
• Michael Delay, COO & General Manager, H-E-B Center
• Scott White, General Manager
• Rebecca Miller, Senior Director, Corporate Sales & Sponsorship
• John Schloffman, Director, Ticket Operations
JSchloffman@texasstars.com
• Neil Graham, Head Coach
• Travis Morin, Assistant Coach
Home Ice:
H-E-B Center at Cedar Park. Seating capacity: 6,778.
NHL Affiliation:
Dallas Stars.

TORONTO MARLIES
45 MANITOBA DR
TORONTO, ON, CANADA M6K 3C3
416-597-7825
marlies.ca
• Laurence Gilman, Sr. VP & Governor
• Ryan Hardy, General Manager
• Mike Dixon, Assistant General Manager & Alt. Governor
• Marc Lira, Director, Business Operations & Alt. Governor
• John Gruden, Head Coach
• Hannu Toivonen, Goaltending Coach
Home Arena:
Coca-Cola Coliseum. Seating capacity 7,779.
NHL Affiliation:
Toronto Maple Leafs.

TUCSON ROADRUNNERS
44 E BROADWAY
SUITE 350
TUCSON, AZ 85701
866-774-6253
www.tucsonroadrunners.com
• Bob Hoffman, President
Bob.Hoffman@TucsonRoadrunners.com
• Denny Adrian, Sr. Director, Communications & Broadcasting
adrian.denny@tucsonroadrunners.com
• John Ferguson, Jr., General Manager
• Steve Potvin, Head Coach
• John Slaney, Assistant Coach
• John Slaney, Assistant Coach
Home Ice:
Tucson Convention Center. Seating capacity, 8,962.
NHL Affiliation:
Arizona Coyotes.

UTICA COMETS
400 ORISKANY STREET WEST
UTICA, NY 13502
315-790-9070
info@uticacomets.com
www.uticacomets.com
• Robert Esche, President
• Michael Potrzeba, Chief Financial Officer
• Adam Pawlick, Vice President
• Pierson McCallum, Ticket Operations Manager
• Michael Lehr, Director, Marketing
• Dan Mackinnon, General Manager
• Kevin Dineen, Head Coach
• Brian Eklund, Goaltending Coach
Home Ice:
Adirondack Bank Center at the Utica Memorial Auditorium. Seating capacity, 3,860.
NHL Affiliation:
New Jersey Devils (NHL).

WILKES-BARRE/SCRANTON PENGUINS
MOHEGAN SUN ARENA
40 COAL STREET
WILKES-BARRE, PA 18702
570-208-7367
Fax: 570-208-5432
webinquiry@wbspenguins.com
www.wbspenguins.com
• Jeff Barrett, Chief Executive Officer
• Greg Petorak, EVP, Special Projects
• Rob Belza, Vice President, Corporate Partnerships
• Brian Coe, Vice President, Operations
• Erik Heasley, General Manager
• J.D. Forrest, Head Coach
Home Ice:
Mohegan Sun Arena at Casey Plaza. Seating capacity: 8,300.
NHL Affiliation:
Pittsburgh Penguins

EAST COAST HOCKEY LEAGUE/ECHL
830 BROAD ST.
SUITE 3
SHREWSBURY, NJ 07702

609-452-0770
echl@echl.com
www.echl.com
• Ryan Crelin, Commissioner
• Dan Petrino, VP, Hockey Operations
Description:
The ECHL has teams across the United States and Canada, acting as a farm system for the American Hockey League (AHL) and National Hockey League (NHL).

Teams:

ADIRONDACK THUNDER
COOL INSURING ARENA
1 CIVIC CENTER PLAZA
GLENS FALLS, NY 12801
518-480-3355
Fax: 518-480-3356
info@echlthunder.com
www.echlthunder.com
• Jeff Mead, President
jmead@echlthunder.com
• Tadd Sipowicz, Chief Revenue Officer
tsipowicz@echlthunder.com
• Sean Driscoll, Director, Ticket Sales & Services
sdriscoll@echlthunder.com
• Rob Lippolis, Director, Communications
rlippolis@echlthunder.com
• Victoria Beagle, Director, Finance
vbeagle@coolinsuringarena.com
• Pete MacArthur, Head Coach & Director, Hockey Operations
• Mike Bergin, Assistant Coach
Home Ice:
Cool Insuring Arena. Seating capacity: 4,794.

ALLEN AMERICANS
CREDIT UNION OF TEXAS EVENT CENTER
200 EAST STACY ROAD
SUITE 1350
ALLEN, TX 75002
972-912-1000
info@allenamericans.com
www.allenamericans.com
• Myles Jack, Owner
• LaSonjia Jack, Owner
• Jonny Mydra, President
• Tommy Daniels, President, Hockey Operations
• Kevin Sikes-Gilbert, Chief Operating Officer
• Robert Fatta, Director, Ticket Operations
robert@allenamericans.com
• Chad Costello, Head Coach/General Manager
• Tony Curtale, Assistant Coach
• Thomas Speer, Goalie Coach
• Jaime Garcia, Athletic Trainer
Home Ice:
Credit Union of Texas Event Center. Seating capacity: 6,275.

ATLANTA GLADIATORS
2675 BRECKINRIDGE BLVD.
DULUTH, GA 30096
770-813-7500
www.atlantagladiators.com
• Steve Brown, Chief Revenue Officer
• Carder Berry, VP, Corporate Partnerships
• Jeff Pyle, Director, Hockey Operations
• Kari Reed, Business Operations Manager
• Derek Nesbitt, Head Coach
Home Ice:
Gas South Arena. Seating capacity: 13,100.

CINCINNATI CYCLONES
100 BROADWAY STREET
CINCINNATI, OH 45202
513-421-4111
Fax: 513-333-3040
www.cycloneshockey.com
• Ray Harris, President
• Kristin Ropp, Vice President & General Manager
• Jason Payne, Head Coach
Home Ice:
Heritage Bank Center. Seating capacity: 14,453.

FLORIDA EVERBLADES
11000 EVERBLADES PARKWAY
ESTERO, FL 33928
239-948-7825
Fax: 239-948-2248
info@floridaeverblades.com
www.floridaeverblades.com
• Craig Brush, President & Arena CEO
• Chris Palin, EVP & Chief Revenue Officer
• Adam Winslow, EVP & Chief Marketing Officer
• Trent Ferguson, Director, Sales
• Brad Ralph, General Manager & Head Coach
• Jesse Kallechy, Assistant Coach
• Chris Emrick, Athletic Trainer
Home Ice:
Hertz Arena. Seating capacity: 7,181.

FORT WAYNE KOMETS
1010 MEMORIAL WAY
SUITE 100
FORT WAYNE, IN 46805
260-483-0011
Fax: 260-483-3899
info@komets.com
www.komets.com
• David Franke, President, Hockey Operations/Co-Owner
• Scott Sproat, President, Business Operations/Co-Owner
scott@komets.com
• Gene Evans, Chief Financial Officer
• Chuck Bailey, Director, Communications
• Jesse Kallechy, Head Coach/Director, Player Personnel
• Olivier Legault, Assistant Coach
Home Ice:
Allen County War Memorial Coliseum. Seating capacity: 10,480.

GREENVILLE SWAMP RABBITS
BON SECOURS WELLNESS ARENA
650 NORTH ACADEMY STREET
GREENVILLE, SC 29601
864-250-4868
Fax: 864-250-4793
info@swamprabbits.com
www.swamprabbits.com
• Todd Mackin, President, Spire Hockey
tmackin@swamprabbits.com
• Tim Vieira, President
tvieira@swamprabbits.com
• Andrew DePuy, Vice President, Sales
adepuy@swamprabbits.com
• Andrew Lord, Head Coach/General Manager
• Alan Fuehring, Broadcaster/Media Relations Manager
(864) 250-4851
• Philip Barski, Assistant Coach
• Blair LaMarche, Athletic Trainer
Home Ice:
Bon Secours Wellness Arena. Seating capacity: 13,951.

IDAHO STEELHEADS
233 S CAPITOL BLVD
BOISE, ID 83702
208-331-8497
Fax: 208-383-0194
info@idahosteelheads.com
www.idahosteelheads.com
• Eric Trapp, President, Idaho Sports Properties
• Michael DiPalma, Vice President, Idaho Sports Properties
• Everett Sheen, Head Coach
• Dirk Manley, Director, New Business Development
• Ben Cottier, Director, Ticketing
Home Ice:
Idaho Central Arena. Seating capacity: 5,002.

INDY FUEL
INDIANA FARMERS COLISEUM
1202 EAST 38TH STREET
INDIANAPOLIS, IN 46205
317-927-7623
www.indyfuelhockey.com

- Larry McQueary, President & COO
(317) 522-5462
lmcqueary@indyfuelhockey.com
- Bill Stackhouse, Chief Financial Officer
(217) 522-5445
bstackhouse@indyfuelhockey.com
- Matthew Louck, VP, Operations
mlouck@indyfuelhockey.com
- Duncan Dalmao, Head Coach
- Tom Callahan, Director, Communications
- Steve Kuepper, Director, Ticket Sales
- Duncan Dalmao, Assistant Coach
Home Ice:
Indiana Farmers Coliseum. Seating capacity:
6,200.

JACKSONVILLE ICEMEN
JACKSONVILLE ICEMEN
3605 PHILIPS HIGHWAY
JACKSONVILLE, FL 32207
904-630-3900
info@jacksonvilleicemen.com
www.jacksonvilleicemen.com
- Andy Kaufmann, Owner
- Bob Ohrablo, President
- Scott Einhorn, Chief Operating Officer
- Phil Reitz, Chief Financial Officer
- Nick Luukko, Head Coach & Director, Hockey
Operations
Affiliates:
New York Rangers (NHL)
Home Arena:
VyStar Veterans Memorial Arena. Seating
capacity: 13,141.

KALAMAZOO WINGS
3600 VANRICK DRIVE
KALAMAZOO, MI 49001
269-345-1125
Fax: 269-345-6584
wingsinfo@kwings.com
www.kwings.com
- Toni Will, Governor/General Manager
- Joel Martin, Head Coach & Director, Hockey
Operations
- Derek Arnold, Corporate Sales Manager
DArnold@kwings.com
- Joe Roberts, Public Relations/Broadcaster
- Joel Martin, Assistant Coach/Goalie Coach
Home Ice:
Wings Event Center. Seating capacity: 5,113.

KANSAS CITY MAVERICKS
19100 EAST VALLEY VIEW PARKWAY
INDEPENDENCE, MO 64055
816-252-7825
info@kcmavericks.com
www.kcmavericks.com
- Lamar Hunt, Jr., Owner
- James Arkell, Owner
- Mike Cukyne, Team President
- Tad O'Had, Head Coach & General Manager
Home Ice:
Cable Dahmer Arena. Seating capacity: 5,800.
Founded:
2009
Description:
The Kansas City Mavericks are members of the
ECHL. The Mavericks currently are the ECHL
affiliate of the NHL's Calgary Flames and AHL's
Stockton Heat and are in their ninth season as a
franchise, fourth in the ECHL.

MAINE MARINERS
94 FREE STREET
PORTLAND, ME 04101
833-GO-MAINE
mariners-info@comcastspectacor.com
www.marinersofmaine.com
- Adam Goldberg, President & Governor
Adam_Goldberg@comcastspectacor.com
- Terrence Wallin, Head Coach & General
Manager
Affiliates:
Boston Bruins (NHL)
Home Arena:
Cross Insurance Arena. Seating capacity: 6,206.

NORFOLK ADMIRALS
201 EAST BRAMBLETON AVENUE
NORFOLK, VA 23510
757-640-1212
Fax: 757-622-0552
admiralsinfo@norfolkadmirals.com
www.norfolkadmirals.com
- Patrick Cavanagh, Owner & CEO
- Billy Johnson, President
- Weston Dewitt, Director, Broadcasting &
Communications
wdewitt@norfolkadmirals.com
- Casey Christensen, VP, Ticket Sales
cchristensen@norfolkadmirals.com
- Jeff Carr, General Manager & Head Coach
- Joel Rumpel, Assistant Coach
Home Ice:
Norfolk Scope Arena. Seating capacity: 8,701.

ORLANDO SOLAR BEARS
AMWAY CENTER
400 W CHURCH ST
SUITE 200
ORLANDO, FL 32801
407-951-8200
orlandoprohockey@gmail.com
www.orlandosolarbearshockey.com
- Chris Heller, President
cheller@orlandosolarbearshockey.com
- Dan Devos, Chair/Governor
- Alex Martins, CEO/Alternate Governor
- Matt Carkner, Head Coach & General
Manager
- Ben Holmstrom, Assistant Coach
- John Finley, Athletic Trainer
Home Ice:
Kia Center (formerly Amway Center). Seating
capacity: 17,353.

RAPID CITY RUSH
444 MOUNT RUSHMORE ROAD NORTH
RAPID CITY, SD 57701
605-716-7825
Fax: 605-716-6100
www.rapidcityrush.com
- Jared Reid, President
- Todd Mackin, President, Spire Holdings
- Scott Burt, Head Coach/General Manager
- Mark Binetti, Director, Media Relations
- Brandon Schumacher, Chief Business Officer
- Ashley Grable, Director, Marketing & Design
- Jennifer Durham, Director, Merchandise
- Jenna Zanter, Director, Corporate
Partnerships
- Peter Drikos, Assistant Coach
- Cody Lindhorst, Head Athletic Trainer
Home Ice:
The Monument. Seating capacity: 7,500.

READING ROYALS
SANTANDER ARENA
700 PENN STREET
READING, PA 19602
610-898-7825
info@royalshockey.com
www.royalshockey.com
- David Farrar, General Manager
(610) 898-7268
dfarrar@santander-arena.com
- Tammy Dahms, VP, Corporate Partnerships
(610) 898-7204
tdahms@santander-arena.com
- Dakota Procyk, VP, Operations
dprocyk@royalshockey.com
- Jason Binkley, Assistant Coach
Home Ice:
Santander Arena. Seating capacity: 6,500.
Major League Affiliate:
Philadelphia Flyers (NHL)

SOUTH CAROLINA STINGRAYS
NORTH CHARLESTON COLISEUM
5001 COLISEUM DR
NORTH CHARLESTON, SC 29418
843-529-5000
www.stingrayshockey.com

- Todd Halloran, President Owner & Governor
- Rob Concannon, President & Alt. Governor
- Zack Fisch, Director, Communications &
Broadcasting
- Ryan Blair, Director, Hockey Operations &
Head Coach
- Brenden Kotyk, Head Coach & Director,
Hockey Operations
- Scott Davidson, Assistant Coach
Home Ice:
North Charleston Coliseum. Seating capacity:
13,000.

TOLEDO WALLEYE
406 WASHINGTON STREET
TOLEDO, OH 43604
419-725-9255
Fax: 419-725-4368
info@toledowalleye.com
www.toledowalleye.com
- Joe Napoli, President/CEO
- Neil Neukam, Executive Vice
President/General Manager
- Erik Ibsen, Executive Vice President/General
Manager
- Kate Langenderfer, Director, Storytelling,
Production, & Omnichannel
- Pat Mikesch, Head Coach
- Brad Fredrick, Athletic Trainer
Home Ice:
Huntington Center. Seating capacity: 7,389
(8,300 with standing room).

TULSA OILERS
BOK CENTER
200 S DENVER AVE
TULSA, OK 74103
918-632-7825
Fax: 918-632-0006
www.tulsaoilers.com
- Taylor Hall, General Manager
taylor@tulsaoilers.com
- Amy Henderson, Vice President Brand &
Marketing
- Jessica Adams, Vice President, Operations
jessica@tulsaoilers.com
- Shawn Watring, Vice President, Ticket Sales
shawn@tulsaoilers.com
- Nick Barr, Vice President, Corporate
Partnerships
- Rob Loeber, Broadcaster & Director, Media
Relations
- Alan Parrent, Manager, Game Day Operations
- Rob Murray, Head Coach/Director, Hockey
Operations
- Sean Garner, Strength & Conditioning Coach
Home Ice:
BOK Center. Seating capacity: 17,096.

UTAH GRIZZLIES
3200 DECKER LAKE DRIVE
WEST VALLEY CITY, UT 84119
801-988-8888
www.utahgrizzlies.com
- Kevin Bruder, Chief Executive Officer
kbruder@maverikcenter.com
- Jill Roberts, CFO
jroberts@maverikcenter.com
- Jared Youngman, Vice President
- Brian Prutch, Vice President, Corporate
Partnerships/CMO
bprutch@utahgrizz.com
- Derek Stell, Community Relations Manager
(801) 988-8010
- Ryan Kinasewich, Head Coach
- Christian Horn, Assistant Coach
- Collin Lee, Athletic Trainer
Home Ice:
Maverik Center. Seating capacity: 10,100.

WHEELING NAILERS
1100 MAIN STREET
3RD FLOOR
WHEELING, WV 26003
304-234-4625
Fax: 304-233-4846

pr@wheelingnailers.com
www.wheelingnailers.com
• Brian Komorowski, President/Governor
kski@redp.org
• John Davis, Chief Operating Officer
jdavis@wheelingnailers.com
• Adam Bonenberger, Finance Manager
adam@redp.org
• John Parish, Director, Corporate Sales &
Service
jparrish@wheelingnailers.com
• Derek Army, Head Coach & Director, Hockey
Operations
• Lauren Rittle, Athletic Trainer
Home Ice:
WesBanco Arena. Seating capacity: 5,406.

WICHITA THUNDER
INTRUST BANK ARENA
500 E. WATERMAN
WICHITA, KS 67202
316-264-4625
www.wichitathunder.com
• Joel T. Lomurno, General Manager
jlomurno@wichitathunder.com
• Matt Brokaw, Vice President
mbrokaw@wichitathunder.com
• Jason Mals, Director, Communications
jmals@wichitathunder.com
• Bruce Ramsay, Head Coach
• John Gurskis, Assistant Coach
• Frank Jury, Equipment Manager
Home Ice:
Intrust Bank Arena. Seating capacity: 13,450.
Affiliates:
San Jose Sharks (NHL)

WORCESTER RAILERS
DCU CENTER - DOOR 22
105 COMMERCIAL ST
WORCESTER, MA 01608
508-365-1750
Info@RailersHC.com
www.railershc.com
• Susan Rucker, Owner
• Cliff Rucker, Owner
• Stephanie Ramey, President
stephanie@railershc.com
• Jordan Lavallee-Smotherman, General
Manager/Head Coach
Home Ice:
DCU Center. Seating capacity: 12,135.
Affiliates:
New York Islanders (NHL)

FEDERAL PROSPECTS HOCKEY
LEAGUE (FPHL)
5679 THOMPSON RD
SYRACUSE, NY 13214
267-261-0887
thefederalhockeyleague@yahoo.com
www.federalhockey.com
• Don Kirnan, Commissioner
(315) 254-5229
dlkirnan@aol.com
• Andy Richards, Vice-Commissioner
• Dave Smolnycki, Director, Game Day
Operations
• Ryan Harrison, Director, Marketing &
Corporate Sales
• Paul Jene, Director, Officiating
pjene@federalhockey.com
• Charles Apap, Manager, Social Media
No. of teams:
11

Teams:

BATON ROUGE ZYDECO
5235 FLORIDA BOULEVARD
SUITE G, 2ND FLOOR
BATON ROUGE, LA 70806

225-515-7825
info@brzydeco.com
www.brprohockey.com
• Barry Soskin, Governor, CEO & CFO
• Don Lewis, President & General Manager
• Everett Thompson, Head Coach
Home Arena:
Raising Cane's River Center Arena. Seating
capacity: 8,900.

BINGHAMTON BLACK BEARS
1 STUART STREET
BINGHAMTON, NY 13901
607-722-7367
info@binghamtonblackbears.com
www.binghamtonblackbears.com
• Andreas Johansson, Owner
• Brant Sherwood, Head Coach
Home Arena:
Visions Veterans Memorial Arena. Seating
capacity: 4,710.

BLUE RIDGE BOBCATS
200 APEX DRIVE
WYTHEVILLE, VA 24382
276-335-2100
www.blueridgebobcats.com
• Barry Soskin, Governor CEO, CFO, President
& General Manager
• Vojtech Zemlicka, Head Coach & General
Manager, Hocky Operations
Home Arena:
Appalachian Regional Exposition Center (APEX
Center)

CAROLINA THUNDERBIRDS
WINSTON-SALEM FAIRGROUNDS ARENA
414 DEACON BLVD
WINSTON-SALEM, NC 27105
336-774-8882
info@carolinathunderbirds.com
www.carolinathunderbirds.com
• Barry Soskin,
Governor/CEO/CFO/President/General Manager
• Steve Harrison, Head Coach
Home Arena:
Winston-Salem Fairgrounds Annex. Capacity:
4,000.

COLUMBUS RIVER DRAGONS
COLUMBUS CIVIC CENTRE
400 4TH ST
COLUMBUS, GA 31901
706-507-4625
dragonsden@rdragons.com
www.rdragons.com
• Jeff Croop, COO, Governor & Interim General
Manager
• Jerome Bechard, Head Coach & Alternate
Governor
Home Arena:
Columbus Civic Center. Seating capacity: 7,459.

DANBURY HAT TRICKS
1 INDEPENDENCE WAY
DANBURY, CT 06810
203-794-1704
www.danburyhattricks.com
• Chris Buonanno, Managing Partner
(203) 794-1704
chris.buonanno1@gmail.com
• Herm Sorcher, Managing Partner
(973) 713-7547
herm@danburyhattricks.com
• Billy McCreary, General Manager/Head
Coach/President, Hockey Ops.
billy@danburyhattricks.com
• Mat Voity, Director, Goaltending & Head
Coach
Home Ice:
Danbury Ice Arena. Seating capacity: 2,000.

DELAWARE THUNDER
CENTRE ICE ARENA
644 RD 316
HARRINGTON, DE 19952

302-398-7825
cpensdelawarethunder@gmail.com
delawarethunder.com
• Charles F. Pens, Sr., CEO/President/General
Manager
• Jeff Heacock, Director, Hockey Operations
• Lou Santini, Head Coach/General Manager
santini.l3080@gmail.com
Home arena:
Centre Ice Rink. Seating capacity: 700.

MISSISSIPPI SEA WOLVES
4063 GINGER DRIVE
SUITE D
D'IBERVILLE, MS 39540
228-999-8333
www.mississippiseawolves.com
• Barry Soskin, Owner
• Joe Pace, CEO & Director, Hockey Operations
• Dustin Skinner, Head Coach
Home Arena:
Mississippi Coast Coliseum. Seating capacity:
9,150.

MOTOR CITY ROCKERS
34400 UTICA ROAD
FRASER, MI 48026
info@mcrockershockey.com
www.mcrockershockey.com
• Scott Brand, President
• Nick Field, General Manager
nick.field@mcrockershockey.com
• Gordie Brown, Head Coach
gordie.brown@mcrockershockey.com
Home Arena:
Big Boy Arena. Seating capacity: 8,000.

PORT HURON PROWLERS
MCMORRAN PLACE
701 MCMORRAN BLVD
PORT HURON, MI 48060
810-966-0396
info@phprowlers.com
www.phprowlers.com
• Barry Soskin, Owner/Governor
• Will Wielgelman, Director, Media &
Communications/Group Sales
will@phprowlers.com
• Matt Graham, General Manager/Head Coach
Home Ice:
McMorran Place. Seating capacity: 3,400.

RIVER SHARKS
155 N MAIN STREET
ELMIRA, NY 14901
607-734-7825
info@elmirariversharks.com
www.elmirariversharks.com
• Donald Kirnan, President & CEO
• Tyler Gjurich, Head Coach
Home Arena:
First Arena. Seating capacity: 3,784.

WATERTOWN WOLVES
WATERTOWN MUNICIPAL ARENA
5675 THOMPSON RD
SYRACUSE, NY 13214
443-502-1798
www.watertownwolves.net
• Tyler Weese, Owner
• Charlie Pens, Jr., General Manager
• Stephen Esau, Head Coach
Home Arena:
Watertown Municipal Arena. Seating capacity:
1,523.

NORTH AMERICAN HOCKEY LEAGUE
5151 BELT LINE RD
SUITE 877
DALLAS, TX 75254
469-252-3800
Fax: 214-975-2250
www.nahl.com
• Mark Frankenfeld, President &
Commissioner

- Denny Scanlon, Deputy Commissioner
- Alex Kyrias, Director, Communications & Sales
- Shannon Smith, Director, Finance & Administration
- Fraser Ritchie, Director, Hockey Administration

No. of teams:
32

Teams:

ABERDEEN WINGS
12101 386TH AVE
WESTPORT, SD 57481
605-380-5852
www.aberdeenwings.com
- Aaron Smith, President
asmith@aberdeenwings.com
- Chris Odde, Vice President
- Pete Sauer, Director, Business Operations
- Aaron Smith, Director, Marketing & Media
asmith@aberdeenwings.com
- Scott Langer, Head Coach & General Manager
scottdlanger@gmail.com
- Mike Grattan, Director, Scouting/Assistant Coach

Home Ice:
Odde Ice Arena. Seating capacity: 1,600.

AMARILLO WRANGLERS
301 S. GRANT ST.
AMARILLO, TX 79101
806-378-4297
www.amarillowranglers.com
- Austin Sutter, President
sutter@amarillohockey.com
- Harry Mahood, Head Coach/General Manager
hmahood@amarillohockey.com
- Conor Yawney, Assistant Coach

Home Ice:
Amarillo Civic Center. Seating capacity: 4,912.

ANCHORAGE WOLVERINES
8123 HARTZELL RD.
ANCHORAGE, AK 99507
907-917-7119
info@anchoragewolverines.com
anchoragewolverines.com
- Keith Morris, General Manager
- Nick Walters, Head Coach

Home Ice:
Ben Boeke Ice Rink. Seating capacity: 688.

AUSTIN BRUINS
501 - 2ND AVE NE
P.O. BOX 451
AUSTIN, MN 55912
507-434-4978
austinbruins.com
- Brian Raduenz, Owner
- Brian Schulz, President
brian@austinbruins.com
- Jarred Becker, Director, Operations/Media Relations
JBecker@AustinBruins.com
- Michael Keeley, Broadcasting & Media Relations
keeley@austinbruins.com
- Becky Earl, Office Manager
- Steve Howard, Head Coach/General Manager
steve@austinbruins.com
- Keenan Kelly, Assistant Coach

Home Ice:
Riverside Arena. Seating capacity: 2,500.

BISMARCK BOBCATS
1200 NORTH WASHINGTON STREET
BISMARCK, ND 58501
701-222-3300
Fax: 701-222-3335
gobobcathockey@aol.com
www.bismarckbobcats.com
- Thom Brigl, Owner/Chief Executive Officer
gobobcathockey@aol.com

- Patrick Geshan, Director, Media & Broadcasting
psgeshan@gmail.com
- Trina Gilhooly, Housing Director
- Layne Sedevie, Head Coach/General Manager
- Brendon Ehlrich, Athletic Trainer
- Hunter Laslo, Assistant Coach

Home Ice:
V.F.W. Sports Center. Seating capacity: 1,289.

CHIPPEWA STEEL
839 1ST AVE
CHIPPEWA FALLS, WI 54729
715-861-2131
joey@chippewasteelho
chippewasteelhockey.com
- Kelly Kasik, President
- Chris Ratzloff, Head Coach & General Manager
chris@chippewasteelhockey.com

Home Ice:
Chippewa Area Ice Arena. Seating capacity: 1,280.

CORPUS CHRISTI ICERAYS
1901 NORTH SHORELINE BOULEVARD
SUITE 300
CORPUS CHRISTI, TX 78401
361-814-7825
Fax: 361-980-0003
www.goicerays.com
- Cassidy Lange, President
- Sylvain Cloutier, General Manager/Head Coach
- Tanya Perez, Vice President
- Amanda Marines, Front Office Manager
- Michael Benedict, Assistant Coach

Home Ice:
American Bank Center. Seating capacity: 10,000.

EL PASO RHINOS
4100 E PAISANOS
BUILDING B
EL PASO, TX 79905
915-479-7825
info@elpasorhinos.com
www.elpasorhinos.com
- Cory Herman, CEO
- Corey Heon, President
cheon@elpasorhinos.com
- Mike McCreary, General Manager
- Joe Coombs, Head Coach
- Josh Brown, Assistant Coach

Home Ice:
El Paso County Coliseum. Seating capacity, 6,500.

FAIRBANKS ICE DOGS
139 32ND AVENUE
FAIRBANKS, AK 99707
907-452-2111
Fax: 907-452-1643
info@fairbanksicedogs.com
www.fairbanksicedogs.com
- Rob Proffitt, General Manager
coachproffitt@fairbanksicedogs.com
- Ryan Theros, Head Coach
ryan@fairbanksicedogs.com
- Wendy Plavan, Office Manager/Billet Coordinator
(907) 632-0244
wendy@fairbanksicedogs.com
- Scott Deur, Assistant Coach
- Howard Beito, Assistant Coach
- Jim Kimbal, Certified Athletic Trainer

Home Ice:
Big Dipper Ice Arena. Seating capacity: 1,857.

JANESVILLE JETS
20 EAST MILWAUKEE STREET
SUITE 304
JANESVILLE, WI 53545
608-752-5387
www.janesvillejets.com
- Bill McCoshen, President, Founder & Managing Partner

- Brad Stepan, VP, Business Development & Operations
(608) 352-7488
brad@janesvillejets.com
- Joe Dibble, General Manager & Head Coach
(612) 978-0519
joe.dibble@janesvillejets.com
- Jon Jonasson, Assistant Coach
(952) 457.0525
Jon@JanesvilleJets.com

Home Ice:
Janesville Ice Arena. Seating capacity: 1,000.

JOHNSTOWN TOMAHAWKS
326 NAPOLEON STREET
SUITE 115
JOHNSTOWN, PA 15901
814-536-4625
info@johnstowntomahawks.com
www.johnstowntomahawks.com
- John Koufis, Owner, CEO & Governor
- John Saylor, Owner, President & Alternate Governor
csaylor@johnstowntomahawks.com
- Derek Partsch, Director, Business Operations
derek@johnstowntomahawks.com
- Brandon Shaffer, Director, Ticketing
brandon@johnstowntomahawks.com
- Melissa Kauffman, Director, Community Relations
melissa@johnstowntomahawks.com
- Mike Letizia, Head Coach
mletizia@johnstowntomahawks.com
- Nick Mish, Assistant Coach & Goaltending Coach
nmish@johnstowntomahawks.com

Home Ice:
Cambria County War Memorial Arena. Seating capacity: 4,001.

KENAI RIVER BROWN BEARS
538 ARENA AVE
SOLDOTNA, AK 99669
907-262-7825
Fax: 910-920-9050
www.kenairiverbrownbears.com
- Nate Kiel, General Manager
natekiel@krbbears.com
- Taylor Shaw, Head Coach
tshaw@krbbears.com
- Josh Romano, Director, Player Personnel
- Lori Karvonen, Trainer

Home Ice:
Soldotna Sports Complex. Seating capacity: 2,000.

LONE STAR BRAHMAS
8851 ICE HOUSE DRIVE
NORTH RICHLAND HILLS, TX 76180
817-336-4423
Fax: 817-336-3334
www.lonestarbrahmas.com
- Salvatore Trazzera, Owner/Chief Executive Officer
- Frank Trazzera, Owner/President
- Chad Siewert, Vice President
- Samuel Sequenzia, Director, Communications
- Dan Wildfong, Director, Hockey Ops & Head Coach
dwildfong10@gmail.com
- Logan Murphy, Assistant Coach
LoganHky21@gmail.com

Home Ice:
NYTEX Sports Centre. Seating capacity 2,400.

MAINE NORDIQUES
190 BIRCH ST
LEWISTON, ME 04240
207-783-2009 EXT 1
mainenordiques.com
- Nick Skerlick, Head Coach
- Ryan Shelley, Associate Head Coach

Home Ice:
Androscoggin Bank Colisee. Seating capacity: 2,634.

MARYLAND BLACK BEARS
PINEY ORCHARD ICE ARENA
8781 PINEY ORCHARD PKWY
ODENTON, MD 21113
410-874-7194
info@marylandblackbears.com
marylandblackbears.com
• Chris Rogers, President
crogers@marylandblackbears.com
• Clint Mylymok, Head Coach/General Manager
clint@marylandblackbears.com
Home Ice:
Piney Orchard Ice Arena

MINNESOTA WILDERNESS
1102 OLYMPIC DRIVE
CLOQUET, MN 55720
218-879-0910
www.wildernesshockey.com
• Barry Bohman, Board of Governor/Owner
• Brenda Bohman, Board of Governor/Owner
• David Boitz, General Manager
(612) 360-8405
dboitz@wildernesshockey.com
• Colten St. Clair, Head Coach
• Ryan Peltoma, Assistant General Manager
• Joshua Petrich, Assistant Coach
• Brandon Grecinger, Athletic Trainer
Home Ice:
Northwoods Credit Union Arena

MINOT MINOTAUROS
2501 WEST BURDICK EXPRESSWAY
MINOT, ND 58703
701-852-0101
contact@minotauroshockey.com
www.minotauroshockey.com
• Ken Oda, Director, Operations
Koda@GoTauros.com
• Anthony Vecchio, Operations Manager
• Cody Campbell, Head Coach & General Manager
• Tyler Ebner, Assistant Coach
• Wyatt Waselenchuk, Goaltending Coach
• Kevin Melby, Athletic Trainer
• Dawn Mattern, Team Doctor
Home Ice:
Maysa Arena. Seating capacity: 1,800.

NEW JERSEY TITANS
214 HARMONY ROAD
MIDDLETOWN, NJ 07748
732-856-9700
www.njtitansnahl.com
• Craig Doremus, General Manager/Head Coach
• Patrick Dooley, Equipment Manager
• Oktay Armagan, Assistant Coach
(732) 995-0254
frihockey@aol.com
• Nick Perri, Assistant Coach/Video Coach
(845) 709-2883
Home Ice:
Middletown Sports Complex. Seating capacity: 1,500.

NEW MEXICO ICE WOLVES
9530 TRAMWAY BLVD NE
ALBUQUERQUE, NM 87122
505-856-7595
www.nmicewolves.com
• Stan Hubbard, Chair & CEO
• Phil Fox, General Manager/Head Coach
Home Ice:
Outpost Ice Arenas

NORTH IOWA BULLS
100 S. FEDERAL AVE
SUITE 118
MASON CITY, IA 50401
641-423-4625
northiowabulls.com
• Alberto Fernandez, Majority Owner
• Tyler Shaffar, President
• Nick Bruneteau, Head Coach
nbruneteau@northiowabulls.com

Home Ice:
Mason City Arena

NORTHEAST GENERALS
1395 COMMERCE WAY
ATTLEBORO, MA 02703
844-623-5483
www.northeastgenerals.com
• Matt Dibble, General Manager
• Bryan Erikson, Head Coach
Home Ice:
New England Sports Village

ODESSA JACKALOPES
4201 ANDREWS HIGHWAY
ODESSA, TX 79762
432-552-7825
CarlinM@odessajackalopes.org
www.odessajackalopes.org
• Rick Matchett, President
rickm@odessajackalopes.org
• Tania Hall, Director, Office Operations
taniah@odessajackalopes.org
• Nick Nollenberger, Director, Media Relations & Broadcasting
• Tom Snoddy, Sales
• Scott Deur, Head Coach/General Manager
• Cody Campbell, Assistant Coach
• Ryan Traut, Assistant Director, Operations
• Eric Pike, Athletic Trainer
Home Ice:
Ector County Coliseum. Seating capacity: 5,131.

OKLAHOMA WARRIORS
BLAZERS ICE CENTRE
8000 S I-35 SERVICE RD.
OKLAHOMA CITY, OK 73149
405-601-4632
okwarriorssocial@gmail.com
www.oklahomawarriors.com
• Wade Chiodo, President, Head Scout & Dir., Player Personnel
wchiodo.okwarriors@gmail.com
• Garrett Roth, Head Coach & General Manager
groth.okwarriors@gmail.com
• Nate Weossner, Asst. General Manager & Assoc. Head Coach
nweossner.okwarriors@gmail.com
• Cory Berberian, Director, Broadcasting & Communications
cberberian.okwarriors@gmail.com
Home Ice:
Blazers Ice Centre

PHILADELPHIA REBELS
601 HOLLYDELL DRIVE
SEWELL, NJ 08080
856-589-5599
phillyrebels.com
• Justin Hale, Head Coach/General Manager
justinhale89@gmail.com
Home Ice:
Hollydell Ice Arena.

SHREVEPORT MUDBUGS
3207 PERSHING BLVD
SHREVEPORT, LA 71101
318-636-7094
www.mudbugshockey.com
• Tommy Scott, President/Managing Partner
tommy@mudbugshockey.com
• Scott Muscutt, General Manager
musky@mudbugshockey.com
Home Ice:
Hirsch Memorial Coliseum. Seating capacity: 10,300.

SPRINGFIELD JR. BLUES
FRANKLIN P. NELSON CENTER
1601 NORTH FIFTH STREET
SPRINGFIELD, IL 62702
217-525-2589
Fax: 217-525-6528
info@jrblues.com
www.jrblues.com

• Todd Pococke, Head Coach/General Manager
tpococke@jrblues.com
• Patrick Schafer, Assistant Coach
• Devin Spears, Head Athletic Trainer
• Amanda Wilson, Athletic Trainer
Home Ice:
Franklin P. Nelson Center. Seating capacity, 2,100.

ST CLOUD NORSEMEN
MUNICIPAL ATHLETIC COMPLEX (MAC)
5001 VETERANS DRIVE
ST CLOUD, MN 56303
info@stcloudnorsemen.com
www.stcloudnorsemen.com
• Kate Memkeen, Director, Operations
kate@stcloudnorsemen.com
• Corey Millen, Head Coach
coaches@stcloudnorsemen.com
Home Ice:
St. Cloud Municipal Athletic Complex

WISCONSIN WINDIGO
4149 WI-70
EAGLE RIVER, WI 54521
info@wisconsinjuniorhockey.com
www.wisconsinjuniorhockey.com
• David Rowe, Co-Owner & Managing Partner
david@wisconsinjuniorhockey.com
• Chris Hedlund, General Manager
chris@wisconsinjuniorhockey.com
• Blake Hietala, Head Coach
blake@wisconsinjuniorhockey.com
• Casey Kirley, Associate Head Coach
caseykirley@gmail.com
Home Ice:
Eagle River Stadium. Seating capacity: 2,000.

ONTARIO HOCKEY LEAGUE
305 MILNER AVE
SUITE 200
SCARBOROUGH, ON, CANADA M1B 3V4
416-299-8700
chl.ca/ohl
• Bryan Crawford, Commissioner
bcrawford@chl.ca
• Barclay Branch, Vice President, Hockey Operations
bbranch@chl.ca
• Cole Butterworth, SVP, Business Operations
cbutterworth@chl.ca
Year Founded:
1933

Teams:

BARRIE COLTS
SADLON ARENA
555 BAYVIEW DR
BARRIE, ON, CANADA L4N 8Y2
705-722-6587
operations@barriecolts.com
chl.ca/ohl-colts
• Howie Campbell, President & Owner
hcampbell@barriecolts.com
• Jim Payetta, VP, Business Development & Marketing
jpayetta@barriecolts.com
• Marty Williamson, General Manager/Head Coach
Home Arena:
Sadlon Arena. Seating capacity 4,195.

BRAMPTON STEELHEADS
CAA CENTRE
7575 KENNEDY RD. SOUTH
BRAMPTON, ON, CANADA L6W 4T2
905-502-7788
Fax: 905-502-0169
info@bramptonsteelheads.com
chl.ca/ohl-steelheads
• Kevin Borg, Owner
• Elliott Kerr, President & Owner

• Michael Hastings, VP, Team Services &
Business Operations
mhastings@mississaugasteelheads.com
• James Richmond, Head Coach & General
Manager
jrichmond@mississaugasteelheads.com
Home Ice:
CAA Centre. Seating capacity 5,000.

BRANTFORD BULLDOGS
BRANTFORD & DISTRICT CIVIC CENTRE
79 MARKET STREET SOUTH
BRANTFORD, ON, CANADA N3S 2E4
519-759-4150 EXT 5222
chl.ca/ohl-bulldogs
• Zach Hyman, President & Governor
• Stuart Hyman, CEO & Alternate Governor
• Matt Turek, General Manager
• Jay McKee, Head Coach
Home Arena:
Brantford & District Civic Centre. Seating
capacity 2,952.

ERIE OTTERS
833 FRENCH ST
ERIE, PA 16501
814-455-7779
Fax: 814-455-0911
office@ottershockey.com
www.ottershockey.com
• Jim Waters, Chair, Owner, President &
Governor
• Chad Westerburg, SVP, Business Operations
Chad@OttersHockey.com
• David Brown, General Manager & EVP
• Stan Butler, Head Coach
• Scott Grieve, Asst. General Manager & Dir.,
Hockey Operations
• Adrian Voipe, Goaltending Consultant
Home Ice:
Erie Insurance Arena. Seating capacity 6,716.

FLINT FIREBIRDS
3501 LAPEER ROAD
FLINT, MI 48503
810-744-0580
Fax: 810-744-2906
info@flintfirebirds.com
www.flintfirebirds.com
• Rolf Nilsen, Governor
• Jeremy Torrey, President
(810) 744-2906
• Monika Kronenberger, Director, Finance
(810) 742-0580
monika@flintfirebirds.com
• Dominic Gutierrez, Director, Marketing
(810) 744-0580
domg@flintfirebirds.com
• Kyle Warzybok, Director, Broadcasting
(810) 744-0580
kyle@flintfirebirds.com
• Dave McParlan, General Manager
dave@flintfirebirds.com
• Paul Flache, Head Coach
pflache@flintfirebirds.com
• Reijo Ruotsalainen, Assistant Coach
reijo@flintfirebirds.com
Home Ice:
Dort Financial Center. Seating capacity 4,365.

GUELPH STORM
55 WYNDHAM ST N
2ND FLOOR
GUELPH, ON, CANADA N1H 7T8
519-837-9690
Fax: 519-837-9692
info@guelphstorm.com
chl.ca/ohl-storm
• Scott Walker, President, Hockey Operations
• George Burnett, General Manager
(519) 837-9690
• Cory Stillman, Head Choach
(519) 837-9690
Home Arena:
Sleeman Centre. Seating capacity 5,100.

KINGSTON FRONTENACS
1 THE TRAGICALLY HIP WAY
KINGSTON, ON, CANADA K7K 0B4
613-542-4042
Fax: 613-542-2834
info@kingstonfrontenacs.com
chl.ca/ohl-frontenacs
• Doug Springer, President & Governor
• Kory Cooper, General Manager
• Troy Mann, Head Coach
Home Ice:
Slush Puppie Place. Seating capacity 5,614.

KITCHENER RANGERS
KITCHENER MEMORIAL AUDITORIUM
COMPLEX
1963 EUGENE GEORGE WAY
KITCHENER, ON, CANADA N2H 0B8
519-576-3700
info@kitchenerrangers.com
chl.ca/ohl-rangers
• Joe Birch, Chief Operating Officer & Governor
• Mike McKenzie, General Manager
• Jussi Ahokas, Head Coach
Home Arena:
Kitchener Memorial Auditorium. Seating capacity
7,131.

LONDON KNIGHTS
CANADA LIFE PLACE
99 DUNDAS ST
LONDON, ON, CANADA N6A 6K1
519-681-0800
Fax: 519-668-7291
info@londonknights.com
chl.ca/ohl-knights
• Basil McRae, Owner
• Dale Hunter, President & Head Coach
• Mark Hunter, Vice President & General
Manager
Home Arena:
Canada Life Place. Seating capacity 9,036.

NIAGARA ICEDOGS
ONE DAVID S HOWES WAY
ST. CATHARINES, ON, CANADA L2R 0B3
905-687-3641
Fax: 905-682-9129
info@niagaraicedogs.net
chl.ca/ohl-icedogs
• Darren DeDobbelaer, Owner
• Michele DeDobbelaer, Owner
• Wes Consorti, General Manager
• Ben Boudreau, Head Coach
Home Ice:
Meridian Centre. Seating capacity 5,300.

NORTH BAY BATTALION
BOART LONGYEAR MEMORIAL GARDENS
100 CHIPPEWA ST W
2ND FLOOR
NORTH BAY, ON, CANADA P1B 6G2
705-495-8603
Fax: 705-475-1673
info@battalionhockey.com
battalionhockey.com
• C. Scott Abbott, Owner & Governor
• Adam Dennis, President & Director, Hockey
Operations
• John Winstanley, General Manager
• Ryan Oulahen, Head Coach
Home Arena:
Boart Longyear Memorial Gardens. Seating
capacity 4,262.

OSHAWA GENERALS
99 ATHOL ST E
OSHAWA, ON, CANADA L1H IJ8
905-433-0900
admin@oshawagenerals.com
chl.ca/ohl-generals
• Rocco Tullio, President & Governor
• Roger Hunt, Vice President & General
Manager
rhunt@oshawagenerals.com

• Mike Kelly, Director, Hockey Operations
• Brad Malone, Interim Head Coach
Home Ice:
Tribute Communities Centre. Seating capacity
6,125.

OTTAWA 67'S
TD PLACE
1015 BANK STREET
OTTAWA, ON, CANADA K1S 3W7
613-232-6767
chl.ca/ohl-67s
• James Boyd, General Manager
• Dave Cameron, Head Coach
dcameron@ottawa67s.com
Home Ice:
TD Place Arena. Seating capacity 8,585.

OWEN SOUND ATTACK
1900 3RD AVENUE E
OWEN SOUND, ON, CANADA N4K 2M6
519-371-7452
loleary@attackhockey.com
chl.ca/ohl-attack
• Severs Bob, President
• Dale DeGray, General Manager
ddegray@attackhockey.com
• Scott Wray, Head Coach
Home Ice:
J.D. McArthur Arena, Harry Lumley Bayshore
Community Centre. Seating capacity 4,300.

PETERBOROUGH PETES
PETERBOROUGH MEMORIAL CENTRE
151 LANSDOWNE ST WEST
PETERBOROUGH, ON, CANADA K9J 1Y4
705-743-3681
Fax: 705-743-5497
info@gopetesgo.com
chl.ca/ohl-petes
• Dave Lorentz, President
• Michael Oke, General Manager & VP,
Operations
• Rob Wilson, Head Coach
Home Ice:
Peterborough Memorial Centre. Seating
capacity 4,329.

SAGINAW SPIRIT
6321 STATE STREET
SAGINAW, MI 48603
989-497-7747
Fax: 989-799-9261
info@saginawspirit.com
chl.ca/ohl-spirit
• Richard J. Garber, Owner
• Craig Goslin, President & Managing Partner
• Dave Drinkill, General Manager
• Chris Lazary, Head Coach
• Jake Grimes, Assistant Coach
• Garrett Rutledge, Assistant Coach
Home Ice:
Dow Event Center. Seating capacity 7,647.

SARNIA STING
1455 LONDON RD
SARNIA, ON, CANADA N7S 6K4
519-541-1717
info@sarniasting.com
chl.ca/ohl-sting
• David Legwand, President, Hockey Operations
• Dylan Seca, General Manager
• Mark Glavin, Director, Hockey Administration
mglavin@sarniasting.com
• Alan Letang, Head Coach
Home Ice:
Progressive Auto Sales Arena. Seating capacity,
5,500.

SAULT STE. MARIE GREYHOUNDS
269 QUEEN STREET EAST
SAULT STE. MARIE, ON, CANADA P6A 1Y9
705-253-5976
Fax: 705-945-9458
info@soogreyhounds.com
chl.ca/ohl-greyhounds

- Tim Lukenda, President/Governor
- Kyle Raftis, General Manager
- John Dean, Head Coach
- Daniel Nikandrov, Assistant Coach
Home Ice:
GFL Memorial Gardens. Seating capacity 4,928.

SUDBURY WOLVES
240 ELGIN STREET
SUDBURY, ON, CANADA P3E 3N6
705-675-3941
Fax: 705-675-3944
office@sudburywolves.com
chl.ca/ohl-wolves
- Dario Zulich, Owner, Governor & CEO
- Rob Papineau, Vice President & General Manager
- Ken MacKenzie, Head Coach & Assistant General Manager
Home Ice:
Sudbury Community Arena. Seating capacity 4,640.

WINDSOR SPITFIRES
8787 MCHUGH STREET
WINDSOR, ON, CANADA N8S 0A1
519-255-6400
frontoffice@windsorspitfires.com
chl.ca/ohl-spitfires
- John Savage, Owner & President
- Bill Bowler, GM & VP, Hockey Operations
bbowler@windsorspitfires.com
- Greg Walters, Head Coach
Home Ice:
WFCU Centre. Seating capacity 6,450.

QUEBEC MARITIMES MAJOR JUNIOR HOCKEY LEAGUE
1205 AMPERE STREET
OFFICE #101
BOUCHERVILLE, QC, CANADA J4B 7M6
450-650-0500
hockey@lhjmq.qc.ca
chl.ca/lhjmq
- Mario Cecchini, Commissioner
- Kevin Mitchell, Director, Hockey Operations
pleduc@lhjmq.qc.ca
- Raphael Doucet, Director, Communications
rdoucet@lhjmq.qc.ca
- Richard Trottier, Director, Officiating
rtrottier@lhjmq.qc.ca
Description:
Member of Canadian Hockey League. Formerly known as Quebec Major Junior Hockey League until 2023.

Teams:

ACADIE-BATHURST TITAN
14 SEAN COUTURIER AVE
BATHURST, NB, CANADA E2A 6X2
506-549-3300
1-877-549-3200
Fax: 506-549-3311
chl.ca/lhjmq-titan
- Gilles Cormier, Executive Director & Corporate Sales
gilles.cormier@letitan.com
- Gordie Dwyer, Head Coach & General Manager
- Matthew Smith, Director of Hockey Operations & Video Coach
Home Ice:
K.C. Irving Regional Centre. Seating capacity 3,524.

BAIE-COMEAU DRAKKAR
70, AVENUE MICHEL-HEMON
BAIE-COMEAU, QC, CANADA G4Z 2A5
418-296-8484

- Mario Durocher, Deputy General Director
- Gregoire Jean-Francois, General Manager & Head Coach
Home Ice:
Henry Leonard Center. Seating capacity 3,042.

BLAINVILLE-BOISBRIAND ARMADA
3600, BOUL. GRANDE-ALLEE
CP 9
BOISBRIAND, QC, CANADA J7H 1M9
450-276-2328
855-276-2328
info@armadahockey.ca
chl.ca/lhjmq-armada
- Pierre Cloutier, Vice President, Hockey Operations
- Olivier Picard, Managing Director
- Mathieu Turcotte, Head Coach
Home Ice:
Centre d'Excellence Sports Rousseau. Seating capacity 3,100.

CAPE BRETON SCREAMING EAGLES
PO BOX 8
481 GEORGE ST
SYDNEY, NS, CANADA B1P 1K5
902-567-6378
Fax: 902-567-6303
info@capebretoneagles.com
chl.ca/lhjmq-eagles
- Gerard Shaw, President
- Sylvain Couturier, General Manager
- Louis Robitaille, Head Coach
Home Ice:
Centre 200. Seating capacity 5,000-6,500.

CHARLOTTETOWN ISLANDERS
46 KENSINGTON RD
2ND FLOOR
CHARLOTTETOWN, PE, CANADA C1A 5H7
902-892-7351
admin@charlottetownislanders.com
chl.ca/lhjmq-islanders
- Craig Foster, President, Operations
- Jim Hulton, General Manager & Head Coach
Home Arena:
Eastlink Centre. Seating capacity 3,718.

CHICOUTIMI SAGUENEENS
643 RUE BEGIN
CHICOUTIMI, QC, CANADA G7H 4N7
418-549-9489
Fax: 418-698-3853
administration@sagueneens.com
chl.ca/lhjmq-sagueneens
- Richard Letourneau, President & Governor
- Serge Proulx, Director, Operations
serge.proulx@sagueneens.com
Home Ice:
George-Vezina Centre. Seating capacity 4,724.

DRUMMONDVILLE VOLTIGEURS
300 RUE COCKBURN
DRUMMONDVILLE, QC, CANADA J2C 4L6
819-477-9400
Fax: 819-477-0561
info@voltigeurs.ca
chl.ca/lhjmq-voltigeurs
- Eric Verrier, President
- David Boies, Director, Operations
dboies@voltigeurs.ca
- Lemay Yanick, General Manager
Home Ice:
Centre Marcel Dionne. Seating capacity 4,000.

GATINEAU OLYMPIQUES
125 RUE DE CARILLON
GATINEAU, QC, CANADA J8X 2P8
819-777-0661
hockey@olympiquesdegatineau.ca
chl.ca/lhjmq-olympiques
- Serge Beausoleil, President
- Serge Beausoleil, General Manager
- Alexis Loiseaur, Head Coach
Home Ice:
Robert Guertin Centre. Seating capacity 3,196.

HALIFAX MOOSEHEADS
1741 BRUNSWICK ST
SUITE 120
HALIFAX, NS, CANADA B3J 3X8
902-317-9860
Fax: 902-423-6413
mooseheads@halifaxmooseheads.ca
chl.ca/lhjmq-mooseheads
- Sam Simon, Chair & Owner
- Brian Urquhart, VP, Operations
- Cam Russell, General Manager
- Jim Midgley, Head Coach
Home Ice:
Scotiabank Centre. Seating capacity 11,093.

MONCTON WILDCATS
AVENIR CENTRE
150 CANADA ST
MONCTON, NB, CANADA E1C 0V2
506-382-5555
Fax: 506-858-2222
info@moncton-wildcats.com
chl.ca/lhjmq-wildcats
- Jean Brousseau, Governor
- Taylor MacDougall, General Manager, Hockey Operations
- Hugo Bernier, General Manager, Business Operations
- Gardiner MacDougall, Head Coach
Home Ice:
Avenir Centre. Seating capacity 8,500.

QUEBEC REMPARTS
CENTRE VIDEOTRON
250G, BOUL. WILFRID-HAMEL
QUEBEC, QC, CANADA G1L 5A7
418-525-1212
888-299-9595
Fax: 418-525-2242
info@remparts.ca
chl.ca/lhjmq-remparts
- Tommy Castonguay, Vice President, Operations
- Simon Gagne, General Manager
- Eric Veilleux, Head Coach
Home Ice:
Centre Videotron. Seating capacity 18,259.

RIMOUSKI OCEANIC
111, 2E RUE OUEST
CP 816
RIMOUSKI, QC, CANADA G5L 7C9
418-723-4444
800-463-4450
Fax: 418-725-0944
hockey@oceanic.qc.ca
chl.ca/lhjmq-oceanic
- Alexandre Tanguay, Co-Owner & Governor
- Danny Dupont, General Manager
- Joel Perrault, Head Coach
Home Ice:
Colisee Financiere Sun Life. Seating capacity 5,062.

ROUYN-NORANDA HUSKIES
ARENA GLENCORE
218 AVE MURDOCH
ROUYN-NORANDA, QC, CANADA J9X 1E6
819-797-3022
Fax: 819-797-4311
admin@huskies.qc.ca
chl.ca/lhjmq-huskies
- Gilles Berube, Operational Director
(819) 797-3022
gberube@huskies.qc.ca
- Yannick Gaucher, General Manager
Home Ice:
Arena Glencore. Seating capacity 3,500.

SAINT JOHN SEA DOGS
99 STATION STREET
SUITE 200
SAINT JOHN, NB, CANADA E2L 4X4
506-657-3647
Fax: 506-696-0611

info@saintjohnseadogs.com
chl.ca/lhjmq-seadogs
• Trevor Georgie, President
• Anthony Stella, General Manager
• Travis Crickard, Head Coach
Home Ice:
TD Station. Seating capacity 6,603.

SHAWINIGAN CATARACTES
CENTRE GERVAIS AUTO
1, RUE JACQUES-PLANTE
SHAWINIGAN, QC, CANADA G9N 0B7
819-537-6327
cats@cataractes.qc.ca
chl.ca/lhjmq-cataractes
• Martin Mondou, General Manager
• Daniel Renaud, Head Coach
Home Ice:
Centre Gervais Auto. Seating capacity 4,195.

SHERBROOKE PHOENIX
360 CEGEP STREET
2ND FLOOR
SHERBROOKE, QC, CANADA J1E 2J9
819-560-8842
info@hockeyphoenix.ca
chl.ca/lhjmq-phoenix
• Philippe Sauve, General Manager
• Gilles Bouchard, Head Coach
Home Ice:
Palais des Sports Leopold-Drolet. Seating
capacity 3,646.

VAL D'OR FOREURS
810, 6TH AVENUE
VAL-D'OR, QC, CANADA J9P 1B4
819-824-0093
Fax: 819-824-7602
reception@foreurs.qc.ca
chl.ca/lhjmq-foreurs
• Maxime Desruisseaux, General Manager &
Head Coach
• Sebastien Charpentier, Assistant General
Manager & Head Scout
Home Ice:
Centre Agnico Eagle. Seating capacity 3,504.

VICTORIAVILLE TIGERS
COLISEE DESJARDINS
400 BOULEVARD JUTRAS EST
VICTORIAVILLE, QC, CANADA G6P 7W7
819-752-6353
Fax: 819-758-2846
info@tigresvictoriaville.com
chl.ca/lhjmq-tigres
• Charles Pellerin, President
• Kevin Cloutier, General Manager
• Carl Mallette, Head Coach
Home Ice:
Desjardins Coliseum. Seating capacity 3,420.

**SOUTHERN PROFESSIONAL HOCKEY
LEAGUE**
11330 VANSTORY DRIVE
HUNTERSVILLE, NC 28078
704-897-0545
www.thesphl.com
• Doug Price, Commissioner
dprice@thesphl.com
• Allan Westerholt, Director,
Communications
No. of teams:
10

Teams:

BIRMINGHAM BULLS
500 AMPHITHEATER RD
PELHAM, AL 35124
205-620-6870
info@bullshockey.net
www.bullshockey.net
• Joe Stroud, President
• Craig Simchuk, Head Coach

Home Ice:
Pelham Civic Center

EVANSVILLE THUNDERBOLTS
FORD CENTER
1 SE MARTIN LUTHER KING JR BLVD
EVANSVILLE, IN 47708
812-422-2658
info@evansvillethunderbolts.com
evansvillethunderbolts.com
• Scott Schoenike, President
• Jeff Bes, Head Coach/Director, Hockey
Operations
(812) 435-7145
Home Ice:
Ford Center. Seating capacity: 9,000.

FAYETTEVILLE MARKSMEN
1960 COLISEUM DRIVE
FAYETTEVILLE, NC 28306
910-321-0123
Fax: 910-321-0200
info@marksmenhockey.com
www.marksmenhockey.com
• Chuck Norris, Owner & CEO
• Alex Wall, President
• Ryan Cruthers, Head Coach/Director, Hockey
Operations
RCruthers@MarksmenHockey.com
Home Ice:
Crown Coliseum. Seating capacity: 10,000.

HUNTSVILLE HAVOC
700 MONROE STREET
HUNTSVILLE, AL 35801
256-518-6160
Fax: 256-518-6164
info@huntsvillehavoc.com
www.huntsvillehavoc.com
• Glenn Detulleo, Executive General Manager
gdetulleo@huntsvillehavoc.com
• Justin Strickland, President
jstrickland@huntsvillehavoc.com
• Jared Johnson, Vice President, Ticket Sales
jjohnson@huntsvillehavoc.com
• Clay Gully, Vice President, Marketing
cgully@huntsvillehavoc.com
• Stuart Stefan, Head Coach
sstefan@huntsvillehavoc.com
• Tyler Piacentini, Assistant Coach
tpiacentini@huntsvillehavoc.com
Home Ice:
Von Braun Center. Seating capacity: 9,000.

KNOXVILLE ICE BEARS
500 HOWARD BAKER JR. DRIVE
KNOXVILLE, TN 37915
865-525-7825
Fax: 865-521-9725
info@knoxvilleicebears.com
www.knoxvilleicebears.com
• Mike Murray, President/General Manager
mmurray@knoxvilleicebears.com
• Dave Feather, Executive VP
• Andrew Harrison, Head Coach
• Jimmy Woodward, Controller
jwoodward@knoxvilleicebears.com
• Dave Feather, Assistant General Manager
dfeather@knoxvilleicebears.com
• Jamie Ronayne, Assistant Coach
• Andy Clark, Head Athletic Trainer
Home Ice:
Knoxville Civic Auditorium and Coliseum.
Seating capacity: 6,500.

MACON MAYHEM
200 COLISEUM DRIVE
MACON, GA 31217
478-803-1592
info@maconmayhem.com
www.maconmayhem.com
• Scott Gooch, Primary Owner
• Anna Marie Summers, General Manager
• Nick Niedert, Head Coach
nick@maconmayhem.com
Home Ice:
Macon Coliseum. Seating capacity: 9,000.

PENSACOLA ICE FLYERS
201 EAST GREGORY STREET
PENSACOLA, FL 35202
850-466-3111
Fax: 850-886-5641
info@iceflyers.com
iceflyers.com
• Greg Harris, Owner
• Brenden Arney, Director, Marketing &
Operations
Brenden@iceflyers.com
• Eric Kagdis, Account & Operations Executive
Eric@iceflyers.com
• Julia Demola, Merchandise & Community
Relations Coordinator
Julia@iceflyers.com
• Gary Graham, Head Coach
Gary@IceFlyers.com
Home Ice:
Pensacola Bay Center. Seating capacity: 8,049.

PEORIA RIVERMEN
201 SOUTHWEST JEFFERSON STREET
PEORIA, IL 61602
309-676-1040
info@rivermen.net
www.rivermen.net
• Bill Yuill, Chair/Chief Executive Officer
• Bart Rogers, Chief Operating Officer/Owner
• Jean-Guy Trudel, General Manager
• Mickey Gray, Assistant General Manager -
Corporate Partnerships
(309) 680-3721
• Katie Pogeman, Assistant General Manager -
Tickets
(309) 680-3791
kpogeman@rivermen.net
• Michelle Novak, Athletic Trainer
Home Ice:
Peoria Civic Center. Seating capacity (Carver
Arena) : 12,000.

ROANOKE RAIL YARD DAWGS
710 WILLIAMSON ROAD
ROANOKE, VA 24016
540-266-7343
marketing@railyarddawgs.com
www.railyarddawgs.com
• Mickey Gray, President
(540) 266-7343
• Dan Bremner, Head Coach/General Manager,
Hockey Operations
(540) 266-7343
Home Ice:
Berglund Center. Seating capacity: 8,672.

VERMILION COUNTY BOBCATS
100 WEST MAIN SREET
SUITE 143
DANVILLE, IL 61832
630-503-0651
info@vcbobcats.com
www.vcbobcats.com
• Ellen J. Tully, Owner/CEO
Home Ice:
David S. Palmer Arena. Seating capacity: 2,350.

UNITED STATES HOCKEY LEAGUE
P.O. BOX 307
TINLEY PARK, IL 60477
312-546-7300
Fax: 312-546-7330
web@ushl.com
www.ushl.com
• Glenn Heffernan, President &
Commissioner
• Stephanie Morgan, Executive Vice
President
• Ian Gentile, Vice President, Hockey
Operations
• Frank Butler, Director, Player Personnel
• Shaun Morgan, Director, Hockey
Operations
• Dennis LaRue, Director, Player Safety

• John Grandt, Director, Officials
• Paul Allan, Director, Communications
Member Teams:
Cedar Rapids Roughriders, Chicago Steel, Dubuque Fighting Saints, Green Bay Gamblers, Madison Capitols, Muskegon Lumberjacks, USA Hockey National Team Development Program, Youngstown Phantoms, Des Moines Buccaneers, Fargo Force, Lincoln Stars, Omaha Lancers, Sioux City Musketeers, Sioux Falls Stampede, Tri-City Storm, Waterloo Black Hawks
Member Requirements:
Tier 1 USA Hockey Jr. Hockey League
Publications:
USHL Media Guide

Teams:

CEDAR RAPIDS ROUGHRIDERS
1100 ROCKFORD ROAD SOUTHWEST
CEDAR RAPIDS, IA 52404
319-247-0340
www.roughridershockey.com
• Tammy Carlson, Director, Sales & Operations
tcarlson@roughridershockey.com
• Mark Carlson, Head Coach
• Chris Ipson, Director, Special Operations
• Mike Lysyj, Assistant Coach
• Hampus Sjdahl, Assistant Coach
• Levi Wade, Athletic Trainer
Home Ice:
ImOn Ice Arena. Seating capacity: 3,850.

CHICAGO STEEL
FOX VALLEY ICE ARENA
1996 S KIRK RD
GENEVA, IL 60134
855-51-STEEL
info@chicagosteelhockeyteam.com
www.chicagosteelhockeyteam.com
• Dan Lehv, President
dlehv@chicagosteelhockeyteam.com
• Mike Garman, Head Coach & General Manager
• Mike Fazio, Asst. General Manager & Dir., Player Development
• Tyler Haskins, Associate Head Coach
• Karel Popper, Assistant Coach
• Jim Schroeder, Athletic Trainer
Home Ice:
Fox Valley Ice Arena

DES MOINES BUCCANEERS
7201 HICKMAN ROAD
URBANDALE, IA 50322
515-278-2827
info@bucshockey.com
www.bucshockey.com
• Nate Teut, President
(515) 278-2827
nteut@bucshockey.com
• Matt Curley, Head Coach & General Manager
• Sarah Rivera, Senior Director, Sales & Ticketing
sarah@bucshockey.com
• Nicole Clark, Director, Communications & Social Media
Nicole@bucshockey.com
• Jake Toporowski, Assistant Coach & Director, Hockey Operations
• Hank Johnson, Assistant & Goalie Coach
• Nick Peyton, Athletic Trainer
Home Ice:
Buccaneer Arena. Seating capacity: 3,461.

DUBUQUE FIGHTING SAINTS
1800 ADMIRAL SHEEHY DRIVE
MYSTIQUE COMMUNITY ICE CENTER
DUBUQUE, IA 52001
563-583-6880
Fax: 563-583-6257
info@dubuquefightingsaints.com
www.dubuquefightingsaints.com

• Robert Miller, President of Business Operations
• Kalle Larsson, General Manager & President, Hockey Ops.
• Kirk MacDonald, Head Coach
kmacdonald@dubuquefightingsaints.com
Home Ice:
Mystique Community Ice Center. Seating capacity: 3,079.

FARGO FORCE
5225 31ST AVENUE SOUTH
FARGO, ND 58104
701-356-7656
Fax: 701-356-7655
fans@fargoforce.com
www.fargoforce.com
• Cary Eades, President, Hockey Operations/General Manager
CaryE@FargoForce.com
• Nick Oliver, Head Coach
• Corey Leivermann, Associate Head Coach
• Eli Rosendahl, Goaltender Coach
• Steve Baumgartner, Equipment Manager
• Phil Faught, FAKTR, ATC, Athletic Trainer/Strength Coach
Home Ice:
Scheels Arena. Capacity: 5,000.

GREEN BAY GAMBLERS
820 ARMED FORCES DR
GREEN BAY, WI 54304
920-494-3401
fans@gamblershockey.com
www.gamblershockey.com
• Jeff Mitchell, President
• Greg Lynch, Director, Business
• Mike Leone, Head Coach & General Manager
• Terry Charles, Manager, Public Relations
• Paula Testin, Manager, Marketing
• Cody Chupp, Assistant Coach
Home Ice:
The Resch Center. Seating capacity: 8,709.

LINCOLN STARS
1880 TRANSFORMATION DRIVE
LINCOLN, NE 68508
402-474-7827
admin@lincolnstars.com
www.lincolnstars.com
• Sal Miliotto, Vice President, Sales
ext 20
• Nick Fabrizio, General Manager
• Rocky Russo, Head Coach
• Artt Brey, Goaltending & Assistant Coach
abrey@lincolnstars.com
Home Ice:
The Ice Box. Seating capacity: 4,212.

MADISON CAPITOLS
2616 N. PLEASANT VIEW RD.
MIDDLETON, WI 53562
608-257-2277
info@madcapshockey.com
www.madcapshockey.com
• Andrew Joudrey, President & CEO, Legacy20
andrew@legacy20.com
• Juliette Makara, President
juliette@madcapshockey.com
• Diane Suter Hyames, Director, Hockey Operations
(608) 712-8687
diane@madcapshockey.com
• Andy Brandt, Head Coach/General Manager
andybrandt@madcapshockey.com
• Ryan Petersen, Assistant Coach
• Brent DuBois, Athletic Trainer
Home Ice:
Bob Suter's Capitol Ice Arena

MUSKEGON LUMBERJACKS
470 WEST WESTERN AVENUE
MUSKEGON, MI 49440
231-799-7000
info@muskegonlumberjacks.com
www.muskegonlumberjacks.com

• Steve Lowe, President, Hockey Operations
• Andrea Rose, President
arose@muskegonlumberjacks.com
• Jim McGroarty, General Manager
• Cara Mendelson, Sales & Marketing Coordinator
ext 224
• Katie Murphy, Sales & Event Coordinator
ext 255
• Parker Burgess, Head Coach
• Todd Robinson, Assistant Coach
ext 291
• Josh Shields, Assistant Coach
ext 233
Home Ice:
Mercy Health Arena. Seating capacity: 4,000.

OMAHA LANCERS
7300 Q STREET
RALSTON, NE 68127
402-344-7825
Fax: 402-934-4613
tickets@lancers.com
www.lancers.com
• Rich Zaber, President, Business Operations
rzaber@lancers.com
• Terri Phillips, VP, Business Operations/Dir., Game Night
tphillips@lancers.com
• Nick Blaesser, Director, Broadcasting & Media Relations
nblaesser@lancers.com
• Andrew Popelka, Director, Ticketing & Audio Specialist
• David Wilkie, General Manager & Head Coach
• Matt Bruneteau, Associate Head Coach
• Nick Hart, Head Athletic Trainer
Home Ice:
Liberty First Credit Union Arena. Seating capacity, 4,000.

SIOUX CITY MUSKETEERS
401 GORDON DRIVE
SIOUX CITY, IA 51101
712-252-2116
Fax: 712-252-2117
info@musketeershockey.com
www.musketeershockey.com
• Lloyd Ney, Owner/Managing Partner
• Travis Morgan, Chief Executive Officer
ext 12
• Sean Clark, General Manager
• Jason Kersner, Head Coach
• Rachael Long, Director, Sales
ext 11
• Connor Ryan, Digital Media & Public Relations
ext 18
• Michael Gershon, Associate Head Coach
• Jacob Pritchard, Assistant Coach
• Shane Clifford, Goalie Coach
• Zach Camins, Hockey Analyst
Home Ice:
Tyson Events Center. Seating capacity: 6,731, with standing room for at least 9,500.

SIOUX FALLS STAMPEDE
1111 N. LAKE AVE
SIOUX FALLS, SD 57104
605-336-4625
Fax: 605-333-0139
info@sfstampede.com
www.sfstampede.com
• Jim Olander, President & CEO
• Korey McDonald, Executive Vice President
korey@sfstampede.com
• Anthony Hegstrom, Sr. Director, Game Night Operations & Merchandise
• Brian Olthoff, Director, Sales
• Tony Gasparini, General Manager
• Eric Rud, Head Coach
• Brandon Wildung, Assistant Coach
• Ryan Cruthers, Assistant Coach
• Zach Sikich, Goalie Coach
• Matt Hunter, Athletic Trainer
Home Ice:
Denny Sanford Premier Center

TRI-CITY STORM
609 PLATTE ROAD
KEARNEY, NE 68847
308-338-8144
www.stormhockey.com
• Dave Vennetti, Majority Owner
• Mark Jalcovik, President, Business Operations/Owner
mjalcovik@stormhockey.com
• Anthony Noreen, President, Hockey Operations & Head Coach
• Andy Ogdahl, Vice President of Sales
• David Fine, Director, Media Relations & Broadcasting
• Jason Koehler, General Manager
• Leland Skeen, Corporate Sales Representative
• Ben Gordon, Assistant Coach
• Dan Bouska, Equipment Manager
• Colt Graf, Athletic Trainer
Home Ice:
Viaero Center

US NATIONAL TEAM DEVELOPMENT PROGRAM (USNTDP)
14900 BECK ROAD
PLYMOUTH, MI 48170
734-453-6400
Fax: 734-327-9256
www.usahockeyntdp.com
• Scott Monaghan, Assistant Executive Director
ScottM@USAHockey.org
• Nick Fahr, Under-18 Team Head Coach
NickF@usahockey.org
• Greg Moore, Under-17 Team Head Coach
Greg.Moore@usahockey.org
• Brock Bradley, Head Equipment Manager
brockb@usahockey.org
• Rebecca Northway, Team Physician
rnorthwa@med.umich.edu
• Dennis MacDonald, Athletic Trainer
dcmacdon@med.umich.edu
• Ryan Hardy, Director, Player Personnel
ryanh@usahockey.org

WATERLOO BLACKHAWKS
PO BOX 2222
WATERLOO, IA 50704
319-232-3444
www.waterlooblackhawks.com
• Joe Greene, President & COO
• Tim Harwood, VP, Communications
• Allison Longnecker, Manager, Retail Merchandising
allison@waterlooblackhawks.com
• Bryn Chyzyk, General Manager
• Matt Smaby, Head Coach
• Chad Kolarik, Assistant Coach
• Spenser Popinga, Strength & Conditioning Coach
Home Ice:
Young Arena

YOUNGSTOWN PHANTOMS
229 EAST FRONT STREET
YOUNGSTOWN, OH 44503
330-747-7825
Fax: 330-746-5175
info@youngstownphantoms.com
www.youngstownphantoms.com
• Bruce J. Zoldan, Co-Owner
• Murry Gunty, Co-Owner/Governor
• Keith Primeau, President, Hockey Operations
kprimeau@youngstownphantoms.com
• Ryan Kosecki, Co-General Manager/VP, Hockey Operations
kprimeau@youngstownphantoms.com
• Jason Deskins, Co-General Manager/VP, Hockey Operations
• Ryan Ward, Head Coach
• Brandon Gotkin, Assistant Coach
• Karl Linden, Player Development Director
• Amber Martinelli, Athletic Trainer
• Steven Smith, Equipment Manager
Home Ice:
Covelli Center

WESTERN HOCKEY LEAGUE
FATHER DAVID BAUER ARENA
2424 UNIVERSITY DRIVE NW
CALGARY, AB, CANADA T2N 3Y9
403-693-3030
Fax: 403-693-3031
info@whl.ca
chl.ca/whl
• Dan Near, Commissioner
• Yvonne Bergmann, VP, Commercial Strategy & Brand
• Richard Doerksen, VP, Hockey
Description:
Member of the Canadian Hockey League.

Teams:

BRANDON WHEAT KINGS
#2-1175-18TH ST
BRANDON, MB, CANADA R7A 7C5
204-726-3535
Fax: 204-726-3540
office@wheatkings.com
chl.ca/whl-wheatkings
• Jared Jacobson, Owner/Governor
• Marty Murray, General Manager/Head Coach
• Mark Derlago, Assistant Coach
Home Ice:
Westman Communications Group Place at Keystone Centre. Seating capacity 5,102.

CALGARY HITMEN
SCOTIABANK SADDLEDOME
555 SADDLEDOME RISE SE
CALGARY, AB, CANADA T2G 2W1
403-777-4646
Fax: 403-571-2211
info@hitmenhockey.com
chl.ca/whl-hitmen
• Robert Hayes, President & CEO
• Gary Davidson, General Manager
• Paul McFarland, Head Coach
Home Ice:
Scotiabank Saddledome. Seating capacity 19,289.

EDMONTON OIL KINGS
FORD HALL, ROGERS PLACE
10214 104 AVENUE NW
SUITE 300
EDMONTON, AB, CANADA T5J 0H6
chl.ca/whl-oilkings
• Kirt Hill, President, Hockey Operations/General Manager
• Luke Pierce, Head Coach
Home Arena:
Rogers Place. Seating capacity 18,347.

EVERETT SILVERTIPS
2000 HEWITT AVENUE
SUITE 100
EVERETT, WA 98201
425-252-5100
Fax: 425-257-0700
info@everettsilvertips.com
chl.ca/whl-silvertips
• Bill Yuill, President
• Zoran Rajcic, Chief Operating Officer
• Dennis Williams, General Manager/Head Coach
• Mike Field, Assistant Coach
• Dean DeSilva, Assistant Coach
• James Jensen, Goaltending Coach
Home Ice:
Angel of the Winds Arena. Seating capacity: 8,149.

KAMLOOPS BLAZERS
300 LORNE STREET
KAMLOOPS, BC, CANADA V2C 1W3
250-828-1144
Fax: 250-828-7822
info@blazerhockey.com
chl.ca/whl-blazers

• Shaun Clouston, General Manager & Head Coach
• Tim O'Donovan, Assistant General Manager
• Robbie Sandland, Director, Player Personnel
Home Ice:
Sandman Centre. Seating capacity 5,464.

KELOWNA ROCKETS
101-1223 WATER STREET
KELOWNA, BC, CANADA V1Y 9V1
250-860-7825
Fax: 250-860-7880
info@kelownarockets.com
chl.ca/whl-rockets
• Bruce Hamilton, Owner/President/General Manager
• Derrick Martin, Interim Head Coach
Home Ice:
Prospera Place. Seating capacity 6,886.

LETHBRIDGE HURRICANES
LETHBRIDGE HURRICANES HOCKEY CLUB
CITY OF LETHBRIDGE ENMAX CENTRE
#2-2510 SCENIC DRIVE SOTUH
LETHBRIDGE, AB, CANADA T1K 7V7
403-328-1986
Fax: 403-329-1622
admin@lethbridgehurricanes.com
chl.ca/whl-hurricanes
• Doug Paisley, President/Governor
• Peter Anholt, General Manager
• Terry Huisman, General Manager, Business Operations
terryhuisman@lethbridgehurricanes.com
• Bill Peters, Head Coach
Home Ice:
ENMAX Centre. Seating capacity 5,479.

MEDICINE HAT TIGERS
2802 BOX SPRINGS WAY NW
MEDICINE HAT, AB, CANADA T1C 0H3
403-526-2666
Fax: 403-526-3072
admin@tigershockey.com
chl.ca/whl-tigers
• Willie Desjardins, General Manager & Head Coach
Home Ice:
Co-op Place. Seating capacity 7,000.

MOOSE JAW WARRIORS
110 1ST AVENUE NW
MOOSE JAW, SK, CANADA S6H 3L9
306-694-5711
Fax: 306-692-7833
chl.ca/whl-warriors
• Bob Dougall, President & Governor
• Jason Ripplinger, General Manager
• Mark O'Leary, Head Coach
Home Ice:
Mosaic Place. Seating capacity 4,500.

PORTLAND WINTERHAWKS
300 NORTH WINNING WAY
PORTLAND, OR 97227
503-236-4295
Fax: 503-238-7629
hockey@winterhawks.com
chl.ca/whl-winterhawks
• Michael Kramer, Owner, Managing Partner
• Kerry Preete, Owner, Managing Partner
• Mike Johnston, President, General Manager & Head Coach
• Jeff McGillis, Chief Operating Officer
• Lisa Hollenbeck, Vice President, Operations
• James Blair, Director, Finance & Administration
• Graham Kendrick, Director, Media & Public Relations
• Kyle Gustafson, Assistant Coach
• Matt Bardsley, Assistant General Manager
Home Ice:
Veterans Memorial Coliseum. Seating capacity: 12,888.

PRINCE ALBERT RAIDERS
690 32ND STREET E
PRINCE ALBERT, SK, CANADA S6V 2W8
306-764-5348
info@raiderhockey.com
chl.ca/whl-raiders
• Michael Scissons, Business Manager
scissons@raiderhockey.com
• Cliff Mapes, Executive Director, Business
Operations
mapes@raiderhockey.com
• Curtis Hunt, General Manager
hunt@raiderhockey.com
• Jeff Truitt, Head Coach
truitt@raiderhockey.com
Home Ice:
Art Hauser Centre. Seating capacity 2,560.

PRINCE GEORGE COUGARS
102-2187 OSPIKA BOULEVARD S
PRINCE GEORGE, BC, CANADA V2N 6Z1
250-561-0783
Fax: 250-561-0743
info@pgcougars.com
chl.ca/whl-cougars
• John Pateman, President
• Mark Lamb, General Manager & Head Coach
Home Ice:
CN Centre. Seating capacity 5,971.

RED DEER REBELS
4847C 19TH STREET
RED DEER, AB, CANADA T4R 2N7
403-341-6001
info@reddeerrebels.com
chl.ca/whl-rebels
• Brent Sutter, Owner/General
Manager/President
• Dave Struch, Head Coach
Home Ice:
Peavey Mart Centrium. Seating capacity 7,819.

REGINA PATS
1463 ALBERT STREET
REGINA, SK, CANADA S4R 2R8
306-522-7287
pats@reginapats.com
chl.ca/whl-pats
• Alan Millar, VP, Hockey Operations & General
Manager
• Brad Herauf, Head Coach
Home Ice:
Brandt Centre. Seating capacity 6,000.

SASKATOON BLADES
THE FAN EXPERIENCE ZONE
105-2803 FAITHFUL AVE
SASKATOON, SK, CANADA S7K 8E8
306-975-8844
info@saskatoonblades.com
chl.ca/whl-blades
• Colin Priestner, President & General Manager
(306) 975-8844
• Steve Hildebrand, Associate General Manager
(306) 975-8844
• Dan DaSilva, Head Coach
Home Ice:
SaskTel Centre. Seating capacity 15,195.

SEATTLE THUNDERBIRDS
625 WEST JAMES STREET
KENT, WA 98032
253-239-7825
Fax: 253-856-6848
chl.ca/whl-thunderbirds
• Dan Leckelt, Owner & Governor
• Lindsey Leckelt, Owner & Alternate Governor
• Colin Campbell, President
• Russ Farwell, Vice President, Hockey
Operations
• Rick Ronish, Vice President, Business
Operations
(253) 856-6832
• Ian Henry, Director, Public & Media Relations
• Jason Thomsen, Director, Corporate
Partnerships

• Bil La Forge, General Manager
• Matt O'Dette, Head Coach
• Carter Cochrane, Assistant Coach
• Matt Marquardt, Assistant Coach
• Brad Guzda, Goaltender Coach
• Phil Varney, Athletic Trainer
Home Ice:
accesso ShoWare Center. Seating capacity:
7,141.

SPOKANE CHIEFS
700 WEST MALLON AVENUE
SPOKANE, WA 99201
509-328-0450
Fax: 509-328-7608
fanmail@spokanechiefs.com
chl.ca/whl-chiefs
• Bobby Brett, Owner/Majority Partner
bbrett@spokanechiefs.com
• Mark Miles, President
ext 320
mmiles@spokanechiefs.com
• Dave Pier, Chief Marketing Officer
ext 313
dpier@spokanechiefs.com
• Greg Sloan, Chief Financial Officer
ext 327
gsloan@spokanechiefs.com
• Matt Bardsley, General Manager
ext 341
mbardsley@spokanechiefs.com
• Ryan Smith, Head Coach
• Dustin Donaghy, Assistant Coach
Home Ice:
Spokane Veterans Memorial Arena. Seating
capacity: 10,366.

SWIFT CURRENT BRONCOS
PO BOX 2345
2001 CHAPLIN STREET E
SWIFT CURRENT, SK, CANADA S9H 4X6
306-773-1509
Fax: 306-773-5406
communications@scbroncos.com
chl.ca/whl-broncos
• Chad Leslie, General Manager
• Taras McEwan, Head Coach
Home Ice:
Innovation Credit Union iPlex. Seating capacity
2,879.

TRI-CITY AMERICANS
TOYOTA CENTER
7000 WEST GRANDRIDGE BOULEVARD
KENNEWICK, WA 99336
509-736-0606
Fax: 509-783-4591
info@amshockey.com
chl.ca/whl-americans
• Olaf Kolzig, Ownership Partner
• Stu Barnes, Ownership Partner/Head Coach
• Bob Tory, Governor/General
Manager/Ownership Partner
• Dennis Loman, Ownership Partner/Alternate
Governor
• Dan Mulhausen, VP, Business Operations &
Marketing Communications
(509) 737-3769
dmulhausen@amshockey.com
• Craig West, VP, Sponsorship Sales &
Broadcasting
(509) 737-3762
cwest@amshockey.com
• Jody Hull, Associate Coach
• T.J. Millar, Associate Coach
• Midge Peterson, Athletic Therapist
Home Ice:
Toyota Center. Seating capacity 5,694.

VANCOUVER GIANTS
220-7888 200TH STREET
LANGLEY, BC, CANADA V2Y 3J4
604-444-2687
info@vancouvergiants.com
chl.ca/whl-giants

• Ron Toigo, Majority Owner & President
• Barclay Parneta, General Manager
• Manny Viveiros, Head Coach
Home Ice:
Langley Events Centre. Seating capacity 5,276.

VICTORIA ROYALS
SAVE-ON-FOODS MEMORIAL CENTRE
1925 BLANSHARD STREET
VICTORIA, BC, CANADA V8T 4J2
250-220-2600
info@victoriaroyals.com
chl.ca/whl-royals
• Graham Lee, Owner & Governor
• Joey Poljanowski, VP, Hockey Operations
• Jake Heisinger, General Manager
• James Patrick, Head Coach
Home Ice:
Save-On-Foods Memorial Centre. Seating
capacity 7,006.

WENATCHEE WILD
TOWN TOYOTA CENTER
1300 WALLA WALLA AVENUE
WENATCHEE, WA 98801
509-888-7825
chl.ca/whl-wild
• David White, Owner
• Lisa White, Owner
• Bliss Littler, General Manager
blittler@wenatcheewildhockey.com
• Don Nachbaur, Head Coach
Home Ice:
Town Toyota Center. Seating capacity 4,300.

Hockey, Roller Hockey Organizations

USA ROLLER SPORTS
4730 SOUTH STREET
LINCOLN, NE 68506
402-483-7551
Fax: 402-483-1465
www.teamusa.org/USA-Roller-Sports

Horse Shoe Organizations

**NATIONAL HORSESHOE PITCHERS
ASSOCIATION**
100 BLUESTERN WAY
WENTZVILLE, MO 63385
262-835-9108
info@horseshoepitching.com
www.horseshoepitching.com
• Casey Sluys, President
• Joe Faron, Vice President
• Phyllis Quist, Secretary
• Gary Buehler, Treasurer
Member Services:
Rules available free on request.
Publications:
NEWSLINE, six times annually.
Membership Requirements:
Pay dues of $12.00 annually.
Description:
Founded 1909. The NHPA is a federation of
60 charters in the United States and
Canada, each with numerous clubs and
affiliates. The association strives to promote
and organize the sport of horseshoes, and
to standardize the rules, equipment and
playing procedures.

Inline Skating Organizations

AGGRESSIVE SKATERS ASSOCIATION
201 N RIVERSIDE DR
SUITE C
INDIALANTIC, FL 32903
321-722-9300
Fax: 321-722-9391
media@asaent.com
www.asaentertainment.com
• Rick Bratman, CEO
(321) 722-9300
• Todd Shays, Senior Vice President
• Mark Shays, Senior Vice President
• Valerie Belardinelli, Media/Public Relations
Member Services:
Hat, T-shirt, card, newsletter, insurance at all ASA-sanctioned events, discounted events.
Publications:
Newsletter.
Membership Requirements:
Professional members: $195 annual dues. Amateur members: Pay dues of $40 per year.
Description:
Founded 1994. Governing body of aggressive in-line skating. ASA Events is the largest action sports event and television production company in the US.

INTERNATIONAL INLINE SKATING ASSOCIATION & INLINE SKATING RESOURCE CENTER
C/O ZEPHYR ADVENTURES
P O BOX 16
RED LODGE, MT 59068
406-445-0802
1-888-758-8687
www.iisa.org
Description:
The Inline Skating Resource Center (ISRC) is the website originally operated by the International Inline Skating Association. The International Inline Skating Association (IISA) was founded in 1991 by a group of manufacturers, retailers, and skaters who chose to be proactive about enhancing the future of the sport of inline skating. For 14 years the IISA developed educational programs, promoted safe skating, and protected and expanded access to public skate ways across the country. Areas of emphasis of the IISA included the Instructor Certification Program, the National Skate Patrol, the Gear Up! Program, and the Government Relations Program.

USA ROLLER SPORTS
4730 SOUTH STREET
LINCOLN, NE 68506
402-483-7551
Fax: 402-483-1465
www.teamusa.org/USA-Roller-Sports

Jai-Lai Organizations

NATIONAL JAI-ALAI ASSOCIATION
5701 LESS STREET NE
ST PETERSBURG, FL 33073
www.national-jai-alai.com
• Paul Kubala, President
• Tom DeMint, Vice President
TJD1@aol.com

Description:
To introduce the game of Jai-alai to a new generation of all ages and assist in getting amateur courts built in the USA for them to play on. Through a structured format like Little League baseball, we wil focus on getting members to understand the true integrity and sport of the game.

Kayaking Organizations

PADDLE ASSOCIATION OF CANADA
PO BOX 126
STATION MAIN
KINGSTON, ON, CANADA K7L 4V6
613-547-3196
Fax: 613-547-4880
info@paddlecanada.com
www.paddlingcanada.com
• Graham Ketcheson, Executive Director
• Dawn Callan, Events, National Paddling Week & PaddleSmart
• Adrian Camara, Media & Marketing Manager

PADDLE CANADA
613-547-3196 EXT 10
888-252-6292
Fax: 613-547-4880
info@paddlecanada.com
www.paddlecanada.com
• Graham Ketcheson, Executive Director
(613) 547-3196

PROFESSIONAL PADDLESPORTS ASSOCIATION
7432 ALBAN STATION BLVD
P O Box 10847
Knoxville, TN 37939
865-558-3595
office@americaoutdoors.com
www.propaddle.com
• Don Roberts, Chairman
• David Brown, Executive Director
• David Brown, Executive Director
• Cheryl Saam, Treasurer/Director at Large
Nature of Service:
Provides the public with the safest, best quality, on-water outdoor recreational experience available commercially, protecting our nation's waterways and the right of the people to use them.
Year Founded:
1977
Number of Members:
450 Organizations.
Publications:
Paddler. Paddlesports Pro Online: Bi-weekly newsletter.

TRADE ASSOCIATION OF PADDLESPORTS
PO BOX 243
MILNER, BRITISH COLUMBIA, CANADA
V0X 1T0
604-514-5011
800-755-5228
Fax: 604-530-5901
www.gopaddle.org
• Michael Pardy, Executive Director
• Nikki Rekman, Events & Administration Director
Notes:
Formerly Trade Association of Sea Kayaking/TASK. Merged with North

American Paddle Sports Association.
Number of members:
400
Member Services:
Risk management programs, North America wide promotions for paddle sports, liability insurance benefits, special credit card rates. Trade shows; sponsors a national symposium, and co-sponsors two other symposia.
Publications:
TAPS Journal, bimonthly newsletter for members.
Membership Requirements:
Business involved in paddle sports. Membership fee based upon total gross income of the business derived from paddle sport ($100 and up). Adherence to T.A.S.K. bylaws; payment of dues.
Description:
Established in 1998 (merger). Promotes the sport of sea kayaking in a safe and environmentally sound manner.

USA CANOE/KAYAK
503 SOPHIA ST
SUITE 100
FREDERICKSBURG, VA 22401
540-907-4460
membership@usack.org
www.teamusa.org/USA-Canoe-Kayak

Kiting Organizations

AMERICAN KITEFLIERS ASSOCIATION
PO BOX 22365
PORTLAND, OR 97269
609-755-5483
800-252-2550
Fax: 800-252-2550
www.aka.kite.org
• John Lutter, President
(321) 412-1368
• Maria Miller, First VP
(253) 752-7051
Description:
The American Kitefliers Association was founded in 1964 by the late Robert M. Ingraham of New Mexico. Now, with over 4,000 members, in 35 countries, we are the largest association of kiters in the world. Our purpose is to educate the public in the art, history, technology, and practice of building and flying kites - to advance the joys and values of kiting in all nations.
Publications:
KITING quarterly magazine.
Member Services:
Liability Insurance, Discounts at Member Merchants, Website, publications, Kite Event Assistance, National Kite Month.
Number of Members:
3,000

KITE TRADE ASSOCIATION INTERNATIONAL
PO Box 6898
Bend, OR 97708
541-994-9647
800-243-8548
Fax: 503-419-4369
www.kitetrade.org
• Elaine Leitner, President
• Billy Jones, Vice President

• Lolly Hadszicki-Ryno, Secretary/Treasurer
• James Daniel, Director
Number of members:
300
Date Founded and Purpose:
Founded 1983. Serves to advance the cause of kiting and sport kiting in the U.S. and internationally.
Membership Requirements:
Please see www.kitetrade.org.
Publications:
Tradewinds: quarterly newsletter.
Member Services:
Please convention and trade show held every January. Please see www.kitetrader.com.

Lacrosse Organizations

CANADIAN LACROSSE ASSOCIATION
18 LOUISA ST
OTTAWA, CANADA K1R 6Y6
613-260-2028
Fax: 613-260-2029
info1@lacrosse.ca
www.lacrosse.ca
• Joey Harris, President
• Britany Gordon, Events and communications coordinator britany@lacrosse.ca
• Jane Clapham, Office Administrator jane@lacrosse.ca
• Joanne Thomson, Executive Director joanne@lacrosse.ca
Number of members:
150,000
Member Services:
Seven national championships hosted in various Canadian cities each year.
Publications:
CANADIAN LACROSSE NEWS, semi-annually; various technical manuals and programs.
Membership Requirements:
Limited to the governing organizations in the ten provinces and two territories and to the Can Am and Iroquois League. All lacrosse players in Canada (150,000) are members by affiliation.
Description:
Founded 1867. Promotes and develops all forms of lacrosse, the National Summer Sport of Canada - Box (Indoor), Men's Field, Women's Field and Inter-Lacrosse.

INTERCOLLEGIATE WOMEN'S LACROSSE COACHES ASSOCIATION
PO BOX 1124
GRAND LAKE, CO 80447
443-951-9611
Fax: 970-432-7058
www.iwlca.org
• Elizabeth Robertshaw, President earobert@bu.edu
• Liz Grote, Vice President egrote@bowdoin.edu
• Julie Young, Treasurer j.young@villanova.edu
Member Services:
Job openings reported, newsletter, Coach of the Year, All-American selections, team ranking, coaches clinics; Academic Squad, North-South Senior All-Star Games.
Publications:
Membership booklet; newsletter.
Description:

Founded 1982. Develops a deep sense of responsibility in teaching, promoting and maintaining the growth of women's lacrosse in accordance with the highest of ideals of fair play.

US LACROSSE
113 W. UNIVERSITY PKWY
BALTIMORE, MD 21210-3300
410-235-6882
Fax: 410-366-6735
info@uslacrosse.org
www.uslacrosse.org
• Rich Morgan, Chair
  ext 101
• Kristen Murray, Incoming Vice Chair
  ext 178
• George Graffy, Treasurer
  ext 120
• Geroge Hugdahl, Secretary
  ext 128
• Carter Abbott, WG Committee Chair
  ext 111
• Jim Carboneau, MG Committee Chair
• Larry Quinnon, Co-Counsel
  ext 149
Number of Members:
345,000.
Publications:
Lacrosse Magazine; Lacrosse Magazine Online(www.laxmagazine.com)
Description:
US Lacrosse is the national governing body of lacrosse. Through responsive and effective leadership, we provide programs and services to inspire participation while protecting the integrity of the sport.
Teams:
U.S. Men's and Women's National Teams

Lacrosse, Leagues/Teams

MAJOR LEAGUE LACROSSE
20 GUEST STREET
SUITE 125
BOSTON, MA 02135
617-746-2233
Fax: 617-746-9988
info@majorleaguelacrosse.com
www.majorleaguelacrosse.com
• David Gross, Commissioner
• Christopher Day, Broadcasting and Digital Media Manager
• Colin Keane, Lacrosse Operations Manager
• Kevin Murphy, Marketing and Brand Manager
• Keith Burkinshaw, Special Events Manager
Description:
A national league made up of over 350 players; season consists of 60 regular season games.

Teams:

ATLANTA BLAZE
3200 GEORGE BUSBEE PARKWAY NORTHWEST
KENNESAW, GA 30144
• Peter Trematerra, Team Owner
• John Tucker, Head Coach & General Manager
• Christopher Meegan, Director of Marketing & Communications
Stadium:
Fifth Third Bank Stadium. Seating capacity, 8,318.

BOSTON CANNONS
214 LINCOLN STREET
SUITE 320
ALLSTON, MA 02134
617-746-9933
info@bostoncannons.com
www.bostoncannons.com
• Kevin Barney, Vice President & General Manager
• Sara Berry, Director of Partnerships and Marketing
• Joe Shannon, Director of Ticket Sales
• Matthew Ryan, Marketing Operations Manager
• Sean Quirk, Head Coach
Stadium:
Harvard Stadium. Seating capacity, 30,323.

CHARLOTTE HOUNDS
210 EAST TRADE STREET
E-482
CHARLOTTE, NC 28202
704-206-1515
charlottehounds@gmail.com
• Jim McPhilliamy, President
• Wade Leaphart, Vice President
• Kristy Boyles, Operations and Community Relations
• Corbin Nyeste, Ticket Operations
• Jillian Fay, Communications Manager
• Patrick O'Leary, Ticket Sales Manager
Stadium:
American Legion Memorial Stadium. Seating capacity, 21,000.

CHESAPEAKE BAYHAWKS
1997 ANNAPOLIS EXCHANGE PARKWAY
SUITE 470
ANNAPOLIS, MD 21401
443-482-6094 EXT 1812
www.thebayhawks.com
• Brendan Kelly, Owner
• Dave Cottle, President
• Jon Kemezis, Vice President of Finance
Stadium:
Navy-Marine Corps Memorial Stadium. Seating capacity, 34,000.

DENVER OUTLAWS
INVESCO FIELD AT MILE HIGH
1701 BRYANT STREET
SUITE 700
DENVER, CO 80204
303-688-5297
Fax: 702-258-3050
www.denveroutlaws.com
• Mac Freeman, President
• Chuck Olney, Director of Business Development
• Tid Tseng, Director of Sales and Marketing
• Elizabeth Goodman, Ticket Sales Manager
• Tony Seaman, General Manager
Stadium:
Sports Authority Field at Mile High. Seating capacity, 76,125.

FLORIDA LAUNCH
777 GLADES ROAD
BOCA RATON, FL 33431
www.floridalaunchlacrosse.com
• Brian Clinton, President
• Michael Zeff, Director of Sales and Sponsorship
Stadium:
FAU Stadium. Seating capacity, 29,419.

NEW YORK LIZARDS
900 FULTON AVENUE
HEMPSTEAD, NY 11549
516-463-8499
www.NYlizards.com
• Jeffrey Rudnick, CEO
• Tom Dissette, VP, Corporate Sales and Services
• Jason Velez, VP, Ticket Sales and Operations
Description:
Shuart Stadium. Seating capacity, 11,929.

OHIO MACHINE
3811 ATTUCKS DRIVE
POWELL, OH 43065
614-754-1973
www.theohiomachine.com
• Gregg Klein, VP, Business Operations
• Bear Davis, VP, Head Coach
• Dave Brewer, Manager, Operations
Stadium:
Selby Field. Seating capacity, 9,100.

ROCHESTER RATTLERS
EMPIRE PROFESSIONAL LACROSSE
1100 UNIVERSITY AVE
SUITE 120
ROCHESTER, NY 14607
585-454-5425
Fax: 585-454-5453
www.rochesterrattlers.com
• Soudan Tim, General Manager
Stadium:
Eunice Kennedy Shriver Stadium. Seating
capacity, 10,000.

NATIONAL LACROSSE LEAGUE
1635 MARKET STREET
SUITE 1600
PHILADELPHIA, PA 19106
267-417-7951
www.nll.com
• Brett Frood, Commissioner
• Brian Lemon, VP, Lacrosse Operations
• Justin Rubino, Executive Vice President,
Business Operations
Description:
Founded 1986. Professional Indoor
Lacrosse League.

Teams:

BUFFALO BANDITS
First Niagara Centre
ONE SEYMOUR H. KNOX, III PLAZA
BUFFALO, NY 14203-3096
716-855-4100
888-223-6000
Fax: 716-855-4122
www.bandits.com
• Terry Pegula, Owner
• Steve Dietrich, General Manager
• Troy Cordingley, Head Coach
Home Arena:
First Niagara Center.

CALGARY ROUGHNECKS
SCOTIABANK SADDLEDOME
555 SADDLEDOME RIDE SE
CALGARY, AB, CANADA T2G 2W1
403-777-4646
Fax: 403-777-3695
info@calgaryroughnecks.com
calgaryroughnecks.com
• Robert Hayes, President/CEO
• Mike Moore, Vice President & Governor
• Mike Board, General Manager
• Josh Sanderson, Assistant General Manager
& Head Coach
Home Arena:
Scotiabank Saddledome. Seating capacity
19,289.

COLORADO MAMMOTH
1000 CHOPPER CIRCLE
DENVER, CO 80204
303-405-1100
Fax: 303-893-8022
mammoth@pepsicenter.com
www.coloradomammoth.com
• Steve Govett, President/General Manager
• Josh Gross, VP, Business Operations and
Alternate Governor
• Pat Coyle, Coach
• Chris Gill, Coach

• Ken Szarka, Performance Coach
• Joel Raether, Head of Sports Performance
Home Arena:
Pepsi Center

GEORGIA SWARM
6340 SUGARLOAF PARKWAY
SUITE 140
DULUTH, GA 30097
844-427-9276
info@georgiaswarm.com
www.georgiaswarm.com
• John J. Arlotta, Owner & Governor
• Andy Arlotta, Co-Owner & President
• Ed Comeau, Head Coach
Home Arena:
Infinite Energy Arena. Seating capacity 11,355.

HALIFAX
SCOTIABANK CENTRE
1800 ARGYLE ST
HALIFAX, NS, CANADA B3J 2V9
902-451-1221
halifaxnll.com

NEW ENGLAND BLACK WOLVES
MOHEGAN SUN ARENA
ONE MOHEGAN SUN BOULEVARD
UNCASVILLE, CT 06382-1355
860-862-4073
info@blackwolves.com
www.blackwolves.com
• Bill Tavares, Media Relations Manager
• Jen Hildebrand, Publicist
Home Arena:
Mohegan Sun Arena. Seating capacity, 7,700.

ROCHESTER KNIGHTHAWKS
BLUE CROSS ARENA
144 EXCHANGE BLVD
SUITE 102
ROCHESTER, NY 14614
585-454-4295
Fax: 585-454-6614
www.knighthawks.com
• Lewis Staats, President
• Curt Styres, Owner/General Manager
• Mike Hasen, Head Coach
• Ted Nolan, Special Advisor to President
• Bob Hathway, Director of Strategic
Development
• Jody Gage, VP of Player Personnel
• John Catalano, VP of Sales
Home Arena:
Blue Cross Arena.

SASKATCHEWAN RUSH
THE FAN EXPERIENCE ZONE
105-2803 FAITHFUL AVE
SASKATOON, SK, CANADA S7K 8E8
306-978-7874
sales@saskrush.com
www.saskrush.com
• Mike Priestner, Owner
• Geoff Sarjeant, President
Geoff@saskent.com
• Steve Hildebrand, Director, Operations &
Alternate Governor
• Derek Keenan, General Manager & Co-Head
Coach
• Jimmy Quinlan, Associate General Manager &
Co-Head Coach
Home Arena:
SaskTel Centre. Seating capacity 15,195.

TORONTO ROCK
1132 INVICTA DRIVE
2ND FLOOR
OAKVILLE, ON, CANADA L6H 6G1
416-596-3075
Fax: 905-339-3473
torontorock.com
• Jamie Dawick, Owner, President & General
Manager
• Matt Sawyer, Head Coach

Home Arena:
Scotiabank Arena. Seating capacity 18,800.

VANCOUVER WARRIORS
ROGERS ARENA
800 GRIFFITHS WAY
VANCOUVER, BC, CANADA V6B 6G1
604-899-4625
ticket.info@vancouverwarriors.com
vancouverwarriors.com
• Curt Malawsky, General Manager & Head
Coach
• Bob McMahon, Assistant General Manager &
Assistant Coach
Home Arena:
Langley Events Centre. Seating capacity 5,276.

Luge Organizations

U.S. LUGE ASSOCIATION
57 CHURCH STREET
LAKE PLACID, NY 12946-1805
518-523-2071
Fax: 518-523-4106
info@usaluge.org
www.usaluge.org
• Dwight Bell, President

Martial Arts Organizations

**AMATEUR ATHLETIC UNION KARATE
PROGRAM**
THE WALT DISNEY WORLD RESORT
PO BOX 10,000
LAKE BUENA VISTA, FL 32830
407-934-7200
Fax: 407-934-7242
WWW.AAUKARATE.ORG
• Bobby Dodd, President
• William Tooke, 1st Vice President
• Louis Stout, 2nd Vice President
• Roger Goudy, Secretary
• Ron Crawford, Treasurer
Year Founded:
1988
Description:
To provide amateur programs through a
volunteer base for all people to have the
physical, mental, and moral development of
amateur athletes and to promote good
sportsmanship and good citizenship in
Traditional and freestyle karate programs.
Membership Requirements:
Open to all.

**AMERICAN AMATEUR KARATE
FEDERATION**
1801 Century Park
24th Floor
LOS ANGELES, CA 90067
888-939-8882
Fax: 888-939-8555
office@aakf.org
www.aakf.org
• Alex Tong, President
• Robert Fusaro, VP
• Albert Chea, Secretary
• Mahmoud Tabassi, Treasurer
• Richard Kageyama, Executive Director
Member Services:
Ranking and examination guide; Ranking
recognition system; visiting instructorships;
annual national summer training camp;
Regional seminars; Regional Instructor
Training and Certification Program; Regional

and national karate championships.
Publications:
AAKF TIMES, quarterly; AAKF
DIRECTORY, annually; COMPETITION
RULES, Spanish and English editions.
Membership Requirements:
Open to all. Athletes, instructors, coaches, judges and administrators must satisfy AAKF amateur karate qualifications.
Description:
Founded 1961. Serves as national traditional karate governing body in the U.S. Organized as a public benefit, non-profit corporation whose purpose is to improve the physical and mental health of the U. S. public through traditional karate. Serves as U.S. representative within Pan American Karate Confederation and International Traditional Karate Federation.

AMERICAN TAEKWONDO ASSOCIATION
6210 BASELINE RD
P O Box 193010
LITTLE ROCK, AR 72209
501-568-2821
Fax: 501-568-2497
welcome@ataonline.com
www.ataonline.com
• In Ho Lee, Grand Master
Membership Requirements:
Must be student of ATA certified instructor.
Description:
Largest centrally administered martial arts organization in the world. Administers teaching of taekwondo. International division is Songahm Taekwondo Federation, founded in 1985, under same administration for ATA instructors residing in other countries.
Number of Members:
350,000
Publications:
THE WAY Magazine.

GEORGIA TAEKWONDO FOUNDATION
PO BOX 2043
KENNESAW, GA 30156
770-528-3580
Fax: 770-528-3590
gtf@georgiagames.org
www.georgiagames.org
• David Wilch, President
david.wilch@gmail.com
• Jenny Matsuoka, Vice President
jenmat123@aol.com
• Eric Pfeifer, Agent
(770) 528-3580
exdirector@georgiagames.org
Year Founded:
2011
Nature of Services:
The governing body for the sport of Taekwondo in State of Georgia.

INTERNATIONAL SPORT KARATE ASSOCIATION
333 SW 140TH TERRACE
JONESVILLE, FL 32669
352-331-0260
Fax: 352-331-2119
steve.repsold@iskaworldhq.com
www.iskaworldhq.com
• Cory Schafer, President
• Robert Mason, Commissioner
Description:
Maintains a continued commitment to training and certifying officials and updating

rules and regulations while recognizing both worthy champions and world rated contenders in more than twenty different types of martial arts and combat sports.

JUDO CANADA
212-1725 STREET LAURENT
OTTAWA, ONTARIO, CANADA K1G 3V4
613-738-1200
Fax: 613-738-1299
info@judocanada.org
www.judocanada.org
• Mike Tamura, President
• Roger Deschamps, Vice President
• Daniel Deangelis, General Secretary
• Allan Sattin, General Treasurer
Number of members:
22,000
Member Services:
Conducts official seminars and examinations; conducts grading; provides coaching seminars. Responsible for National Team Programs, including competitions and training camps. Hosts Senior National, Junior National, Juvenile National Tournaments annually.
Publications:
YUDANSHA JOURNAL, three times annually.
Membership Requirements:
Must be a minimum black belt. Associate members through provincial associations.
Description:
Founded 1956. Serves to produce world-caliber athletes while developing the sport of Judo in Canada.

U.S. JUDO, INC/USA JUDO
3625 NW 82 AV
SUITE 100-D
DORAL, FL 33166
786-332-4338
Fax: 719-866-4733
usjiadmin@aol.com
www.usjudo.org
• Lance Nading, President

U.S. TAEKWONDO UNION
ONE OLYMPIC PLAZA
SUITE 104C
COLORADO SPRINGS, CO 80909
719-632-5551
Fax: 719-866-4642
communications@usoc.org
www.usa-taekwondo.us
• Harris Bruce, CEO
• Patrick Wentland, Director of High Performance
• Steve McNally, Director of Marketing and Communications
• Gary Urie, Director of Finance
• Stacy Miller-Andrews, High Performance Manager
• Casey Miller, Membership Manager
tickets@usataekwondo.uservoice.com
• Jeanna Mendoza, Director of Events
• Michelle George, Dan Certification Manager
Number of members:
40,000
Member Services:
Insurance, school relocation listings, certification Black Belt), developmental camps, merchandising, information dissemination, Junior Olympic Taekwondo program.
Publications:

U.S. TAEKWONDO JOURNAL, quarterly.
Membership Requirements:
$35.00 dues for competitors, $12.00 non-competitors, $75.00 for Club, $500.00 for life and $1,000.00 for corporation.
Description:
Founded 1974. Objectives are the development of Taekwondo in the United States; to include grass roots, Pan Am and Olympic as well as public relations and media.

ULTIMATE FIGHTING CHAMPIONSHIP (UFC)
2960 WEST SAHARA AVENUE
LAS VEGAS, NV 89102
702-221-4780
www.ufc.com
• Lorenzo Fertitta, Chairman & CEO
• Dana White, President
• Marc Ratner, VP Regulatory Affairs
• Joe Silva, VP Talent Relations
Description:
The UFC is the world's largest Mixed Martial Arts (MMA) sports association, formed in 2001 by Zuffa LLC. MMA is a combat sports using interdisciplinary forms of fighting, including jiu-jitsu, judo, karate, boxing, and more.

UNITED STATES OF AMERICA NATIONAL KARATE-DO FEDERATION
1631 MESA AVE
SUITE A1
COLORADO SPRINGS, CO 80906
719-477-6925
Fax: 206-839-4148
natoffice@usankf.org
www.usankf.org
• John DiPasquale, President
• Phil Hampel, CEO
• Jessica Luna, Program Manager
• Brody Burns, Director of Operations and Events
Member Services:
National governing body for karate in the United States.
Membership Requirements:
$50 dues for athletes, $75 for coaches, $100 for club, $1,000 for life.

UNITED STATES SOO BAHK DO FEDERATION
20 MILLBURN AVENUE
SUITE 2
SPRINGFIELD TOWNSHIP, NJ 07081
973-467-3971
888-766-2245
Fax: 973-467-5716
headquarters@soobahkdo.com
www.soobahkdo.com
• Kwan Jang Nim HC Hwang, President
• Phil Hampel, Independent Director
• Tokey Hill, Coach Director
• Alex Miladi, Refree Director
• Clay Morton, Athlete Director
• Keith Wildonger, Board Chairman
Description:
Founded 1945. Sponsors competition and training in a special martial arts program, characterized by strict discipline, high kicks and traditional demonstrations.

USA KARATE FEDERATION
1300 KENMORE BOULEVARD
AKRON, OH 44314

330-753-3114
Fax: 330-753-6888
www.usakarate.us
• Patrick M. Hickey, President
• John Linebarger, Vice President
• Roger Jarrett, General Secretary
• Robert Burns, Esq., Treasurer
• Carol Hofer, Assistant Treasurer
• Brian Pendleton, Executive Director
• David G. Lang, CPA
Publications:
KARATE PROFILES, bimonthly magazine.
Description:
Founded 1981.

WORLD KARATE FEDERATION
GALERIA DE VALLEHERMOSO 4
3RD FLOOR
MADRID, SPAIN 28003
34-91-5359632
Fax: 34-91-5359633
www.wkf.net
• Antonio Espinos, President
• William Millerson, 1st Vice President
• Mike Dinsdale, Treasurer
• George Yerolimpos, General Secretary
secretariat@wkf.net

WORLD TAEKWONDO FEDERATION (WTF)
5TH FL, KOLON BLDG
15 HYOJA-RO, JONGNO-GU
SEOUL, KOREA 110-040
www.worldtaekwondofederation.net
• Chungwon Choue, President
• Jean-Marie Ayer, Secretary General
• Tae Eun Lee, Treasurer
• Phillip Walter Coles, Vice President
Description:
International governing body for the sport of taekwondo.

Motorcycle Organizations

AMERICAN MOTORCYCLIST ASSOCIATION
13515 YARMOUTH DRIVE
PICKERINGTON, OH 43147
614-856-1900
800-262-5646
Fax: 614-856-1920
ama@ama-cycle.org
www.americanmotorcyclist.com
• Maggie McNally, Chair
• Perry King, Vice Chair
• Ken Ford, Assistant Treasurer
• Paul Puma, Executive Committee
• Jeff Skeen, Executive Committee Member
Description:
Founded 1924. Member/service organization providing recreational and competition activities for motorcyclists at the amateur and professional levels. Maintains government relations staff to track state, federal and local legislation pertaining to motorcycling enjoyment. AMA Professional Racing Events are run ten months of the year and include events from coast to coast in three major championship series.
Membership Requirements:
Annual dues of $39, $750 for life membership.
Publications:
AMERICAN MOTORCYCLIST, monthly.
Member Services:

Sanctioning of amateur and professional racing and social events. Tracking legislation, monthly magazine, discounts on insurance, car rentals, etc.
Number of members:
265,000

INTERNATIONAL COUNCIL OF MOTORSPORT SCIENCES
9305 CRESTVIEW DRIVE
DENTON, TX 76207
940-262-3481
Fax: 940-262-3482
www.icmsmotorsportsafety.org
• Tom Weisenbach, Executive Director
Year Founded:
1988
Membership Requirements:
Includes physicians, psychologists, physiologists, race drivers and paramedic personnel.
Description:
An association of medical professionals, scientific, allied health and other interested persons with the improvement in performance and safety in motorsport.

MOTORCYCLE SAFETY FOUNDATION
2 JENNER STREET
SUITE 150
IRVINE, CA 92618-3806
949-727-3227
800-446-9227
Fax: 949-727-4217
msf@msf-usa.org
www.msf-usa.org
• Time Buche, President and CEO
• Robert Gladden, Vice President
Publications:
Catalog of publications available.
Membership Requirements:
Must be motorcycle manufacturer.
Description:
Founded 1973. The Motorcycle Safety Foundation is the internationally recognized developer of the comprehensive, research-based, Rider Education and Training System (MSF RETS). RETS curricula promotes lifelong-learning for motorcyclists and continuous professional development for certified RiderCoaches and other trainers. MSF also actively participates in government relations, safety research, public awareness campaigns and the provision of technical assistance to state training and licensing programs.

MOTORCYCLISTE, FEDERATION INTERNATIONALE
11, ROUTE DE SUISSE
MIES, SWITZERLAN CH-1295
41-0-22-950-95-00
Fax: 41-0-22-950-95-01
www.fim-live.com
• Vito Ippolito, President
• Nasser Khalilfa, Deputy President
• Juan Moreta, First Vice President
Description:
International governing body for the sport of motorcycling.

RACING ENTERPRISES MOTOCROSS
13223 BLACK MOUNTAIN ROAD
SUITE 1-176
SAN DIEGO, CA 92129
951-200-0699
Fax: 858-484-7056

remsatmx@gmail.com
www.remsatmx.com

WERA MOTORCYCLE ROADRACING
2555 MARIETTA HWY #104
Suite 104
CANTON, GA 30114
770-720-5010
Fax: 770-720-5015
wera@wera.com
www.wera.com
• Evelyne Clarke, President
Member Services:
Sanctions, promotes and oversees motorcycle; road racing in Amateur and Pro Levels across the U.S.
Membership Requirements:
Must have race school or previous raodracing experience. $100 race license good for one year.
Number of members:
2,850
Publications:
FASTLINE NEWSLETTER and yearly rulebook.

WOMEN ON WHEELS MOTORCYCLE ASSOCIATION
PO BOX 83076
LINCOLN, NE 68501
402-477-1280
800-322-1969
Fax: 360-653-1855
WowOffice@womenonwheels.org
www.womenonwheels.org
• Deana Foster, President
Member Services:
Sponsors annual international rally.
Publications:
WOMEN ON WHEELS, bimonthly magazine.
Membership Requirements:
$30 for one year membership.
Description:
Organization for female motorcycle enthusiasts.

Mountainboard Organizations

MBS MOUNTAINBOARDS
212 Sutton Lane
COLORADO SPRINGS, CO 80907
719-884-1000
877-627-4100
Fax: 719-884-1003
customerservice@mbs.com
www.mbs.com
• Jason Lee, Founder
• Patrick McConnell, Founder
Year Founded:
1992

Netball Organizations

NETBALL ASSOCIATIONS, INTERNATIONAL FEDERATION OF
19 Albion Street
ALBION WHARF
MANCHESTER, ENGLAND M1 5LN
441-(0) 161-234-6515
www.netball.org

• Sue Taylor, VP
• Ann Tod, Finance Director
• Realene Castle, Director
• Sarah Pickford, Global Development Manager
• Maggie Ross, Administration Manager
• Molly Rhone, President
• Urvasi Naidoo, CEO
Description:
International governing body for the sport of netball.

Orienteering Organizations

CANADIAN ORIENTEERING FEDERATION
1239 COLGROVE AVENUE NE
CALGARY, ALBERTA, CANADA T2E 5C3
403-283-0807
Fax: 403-451-1681
info@orienteering.ca
www.orienteering.ca
• Anne Teutsch, President

ORIENTEERING FEDERATION, INTERNATIONAL
DROTTNINGGATAN 47 31 1/2 TR
KARLSTAD, SWEDEN SE-65225
840-558-1817
Fax: 893-481-3113
iof@orienteering.org
www.orienteering.org
• Tom Hollowell, Secretary General/CEO
tomhollowell@orienteering.org

ORIENTEERING USA
824 SCOTIA ROAD
PHILADELPHIA, PA 19128
215-482-9479
contact@orienteeringusa.org
orienteeringusa.org
• Clare Durand, President
(215) 482-9479
contact@orienteeringusa.org

Pentathlon Organizations

UNION INTERNATIONALE DE PENTATHLON MODERNE (UIPM)
STADE LOUIS II, ENTREE E
13 AV. DES CASTELANS
MONTE CARLO, 98000
377-9777 8555
Fax: 377-9777 8550
uipm@pentathlon.org
www.uipmworld.org
• Shiny Fang, Secretary-General

USA PENTATHLON
1 OLYMPIC PLAZA
COLORADO SPRINGS, CO 80909
www.teamusa.org/USA-Modern-Pentathlon
• Rob Stull, Managing Director
robstull@aol.com

Petanque Organizations

FEDERATION OF PETANQUE USA
PO BOX 34
COPALIS BEACH, WA 98535

253-237-4735
secretary@usapetanque.org
usapetanque.org
• Frank Pipal, President
(707) 833-2020
president@usapetanque.org
• Christine Cragg, Vice President
(415) 302-5069
vicepresident@usapetanque.org
• Joe Martin, Treasurer
treasurer@usapetanque.org
• Dan Feaster, Secretary
(253) 237-4735
secretary@usapetanque.org
• Gilles Canesse, National Sport Director
(941) 724-1845
nsd@usapetanque.org
Member Services:
Communications, participation in international, national and FPUSA-sanctioned competitions.
Publications:
Newsletter, quarterly.
Membership Requirements:
Club membership - active operation as local petanque club with minimum of 10 members; Individual - subscribe to purposes and objectives of FPUSA, payment of dues, member of club or independent (if too distant).
Description:
Founded 1974. Purpose is to build a body of federation-affiliated clubs and individuals dedicated to spreading, practicing and enjoying Petanque, a world wide outdoor bowling game of modern French derivation via ancient Greece and Rome. Primary objective is to foster local, regional and national competitions, as well as U.S. participation in international tournaments and championships.

Platform Tennis Organizations

AMERICAN PLATFORM TENNIS ASSOCIATION
109 WESPORT DRIVE
PITTSBURGH, PA 15238
888-744-9490
apta@platformtennis.org
www.platformtennis.org
• Ann Sheedy, Executive Director
ann.sheedy@platformtennis.org
• Scott Bondurant, President
bondo59@gmail.com
• Bill O'Brien, Vice-President
bill.obrien@att.net
Member Services:
Information bureau, providing information/assistance to the media.
Publications:
PLATFORM TENNIS NEWS, Newsletter; PTN UPDATE, three times annually; Rules Book; Sportsmanship Pamphlet; HOW TO CONDUCT A TOURNAMENT DRAW.
Membership Requirements:
Annual dues - eight categories of membership.
Description:
Founded 1934. Provides information and publications about the game. Coordinates the scheduling of tournaments and assures uniformity in specifications of courts and equipment and establishes official rules.

Serves as non-profit organization chartered to promote the orderly growth of the game.

Polo Organizations

U.S. POLO ASSOCIATION
9011 LAKE WORTH ROAD
LAKE WORTH, FL 33467
800-232-8772
uspa@uspolo.org
www.uspolo.org
• Duncan Huyler, Chief Executive Officer
dhuyler@uspolo.org
• Susan Present, Chief Financial Officer
spresent@uspolo.org
• Kris Bowman, Executive Director
kbowman@uspolo.org
• Justin Powers, Director of Club Development
jpowers@uspolo.org
Number of members:
3,488
Member Services:
USPA Yearbook with name listing and handicap, access to movies of techniques of polo and on various games; identification stickers and opportunity to play in all USPA tournaments within given handicap.
Publications:
Polo Players' Edition
Membership Requirements:
Club - must have regulation field; and accommodations for horses and tack. Must have three registered USPA-playing members as members of the club. $200 per year. Player - must belong to a registered USPA club and must follow rules and regulations stated by USPA. $135 per year.
Description:
Founded 1890. Serves as regulatory body of polo events played in the U.S. and Canada. Overseas tournaments, assigns handicaps, promotes intercollegiate and interscholastic polo. The Polo Training Foundation, conducts polo schools across the country.

Racquetball Organizations

INTERNATIONAL RACQUETBALL FEDERATION (IRF)
1631 MESA AVENUE
COLORADO SPRINGS, CO 80906
719-433-2017
lstonge@internationalracquetball.com
www.internationalracquetball.com
• Osvaldo Maggi, President
• Marcelo Gomez, Executive Vice President
• Carlos Ruiz, Treasurer
• Cheryl Kirk, Secretary
Description:
Founded 1979 as the International Amateur Racquetball Federation. International governing body for the sport of racquetball, recognized by the IOC.

LADIES PROFESSIONAL RACQUETBALL TOUR
GEARBOX SPORTS
9375 CUSTOMHOUSE PLAZA
SUITE J
SAN DIEGO, CA 92154
877-443-2726
Fax: 619-474-8523
www.lprtour.com

• TJ Baumbaugh, President
tj@lprtour.com
Description:
The LPRT is a governing body representing top-tier professional women from the Americas and elsewhere.

USA RACQUETBALL
2812 W COLORADO AVENUE
Suite 200
COLORADO SPRINGS, CO 80904-2906
719-635-5396
Fax: 719-635-0685
www.teamusa.org/usa-racquetball
• Jason Thoerner, Executive Director
(719) 635-5396
jthoerner@usaracquetball.com
• Nick Irvine, Programming Manager
(209) 817-9984
nirvine@usaracquetball.com
• Reneâ€š Gundolff, Membership Manager
(719) 635-5396
rgundolff@usaracquetball.com
Member Services:
Sanctions 1,300 events annually, hosts 30+ regional and five national championships annually, supports adult and junior U.S. National Racquetball teams.
Publications:
RACQUETBALL, bimonthly; USRA Rulebook, Media Guide/Tournament Program, Program Brochures, released annually.
Membership Requirements:
$30 annual fee for competitive license, plus club recreational program membership available.
Description:
Founded 1968 as International Racquetball Association. National governing body for the sport of racquetball. Promotes sport of racquetball for the amateur, grass roots player.
Online Magazine:
www.racqmag.com

Ringette Organizations

RINGETTE CANADA
5510 CANOTEK ROAD
SUITE 201
OTTAWA, ON, CANADA K1J 9J4
613-748-5655
Fax: 613-748-5860
ringette@ringette.ca
www.ringette.ca
• Daniel Dussault, President
• Natasha Johnston, Executive Director
(613) 748-5655
natasha@ringette.ca
Description:
Founded 1975. Non-profit, volunteer-based organization. Promotes, develops and administrates the sport of Ringette in Canada. Team sport played on ice, using straight stick and rubber ring, and using ice skates. Develops and operates annual Canadian Ringette Championships
Membership Requirements:
Members are provincial or territorial Ringette associations.
Publications:
Official rules (English/French), National Officials Certification Program, Managers Certification Program, National Coaching Certification Program, brochures, posters,

gym ringette and various others.
Member Services:
Bilingual publications; audio-visuals: equipment; promotional videos; goaltending video.
Number of members:
27,000

Rodeo Organizations

INTERNATIONAL PROFESSIONAL RODEO ASSOCIATION (IPRA)
405-235-6540
Fax: 405-235-6577
www.ipra-rodeo.com
• Dale Yerigan, General Manager
(405) 235-6540
dale@iprarodeo.com
Number of members:
4,000
Description:
1999 International Rodeo Finals Jan 14-16.
Membership Requirements:
Must purchase membership and uphold rules and regulations of association. Publications: PRO RODEO WORLD, monthly.
Description:
Founded 1957. Promotes rodeo as a sport and profession.
Publications:
Pro Rodeo World monthly magazine

NATIONAL HIGH SCHOOL RODEO ASSOCIATION (NHSRA)
12011 TEJON STREET
SUITE 900
DENVER, CO 80234
303-452-0820
Fax: 303-452-0912
www.nhsra.org
• James Higginbotham, Executive Director
Nature of Service:
Annually holds worlds largest rodeo, competitions for national championships, team championships and scholarships.
Year Founded:
1949
Member Services:
College scholarship assistance, crisis fund, knowledge bowl, talent and art contests, safety clinics and training, sports medicine program, insurance.
Membership Requirements:
Grades 9 through 12. Meet minimum grade point average and meet conduct requirements.
Number of members:
13,038
Publications:
NHSRA TIMES, monthly magazine. NHSFR Souviner Program -annual rodeo program.

NATIONAL INTERCOLLEGIATE RODEO ASSOCIATION (NIRA)
2033 WALLA WALLA AVE
WALLA WALLA, WA 99362
509-529-4402
Fax: 509-525-1090
info@collegerodeo.com
www.collegerodeo.com
• Roger Walters, Commissioner
rogerwalters@collegerodeo.com
• Sarah Neely, Director of Public Relations & Administration

sarah@collegerodeo.com
• Claudia Kelly, Membership Director
claudia@collegerodeo.com
• Samantha Vandenberg, National Rodeo Secretary
samantha@collegerodeo.com
Description:
Founded 1949. Preserves the western heritage through the sport of college rodeo. Education is primary goal.
Membership Requirements:
Eligible according to educational standards.
Number of members:
3,500

NATIONAL LITTLE BRITCHES RODEO ASSOCIATION
5050 EDISON AVE
SUITE 105
COLORADO SPRINGS, CO 80915
719-389-0333
800-763-3694
Fax: 719-578-1367
info@nlbra.com
www.nlbra.com
• Jodi Stoddard, President
(605) 685-8003
jodistoddard7@gmail.com
• Scott Honeycutt, Vice President
(719) 588-7911
slhtophand@gmail.com
Nature of Service:
Promotes and organizes youth rodeo in the U.S.
Year Founded:
1952
Membership Requirements:
Pay dues of $75 per year - open to all ages 5-18.
Number of members:
5,000
Publications:
Monthly newspaper, NLBRA NEWS, distributed to membership and associates.

PROFESSIONAL BULL RIDERS (PBR)
101 W Riverwalk
Pueblo, CO 81003
719-242-2800
Fax: 719-242-2855
admin@pbr.com
www.pbr.com
• Jim Haworth, Chairman
• Sean Gleason, Chief Executive Officer
Sports Service Founded:
1992
Nature of Sports Service:
Organization was founded by 20 accomplished bull riders who joined together to make bull riding the most popular event in traditional rodeo. Since that time, the PBR, unlike any other rodeo or bull riding organization in North America, has been owned and operated by its athletes. Today more than 700 bull riders from the U. S., Canada, Brazil and Australia hold PBR memberships.

PROFESSIONAL RODEO COWBOYS ASSOCIATION (PRCA)
101 PRO RODEO DR
COLORADO SPRINGS, CO 80919
719-593-8840
Fax: 719-548-4876
prorodeo@prorodeo.com
www.prorodeo.org
• Karl Stressman, Commissioner

Publications:
ProRodeo Sports News; bi-weekly, PRCA Media Guide; annually, PRORODEO Souvenir Program distributed at more than 350 rodeo annually.
Membership Requirements:
Must win 1,000 on a PRCA permit allowing individual to gain full membership status. Annual dues: $350.
Description:
Founded 1975. Previously Cowboy Turtle Assn, (1936-1944); Rodeo Cowboys Assn (1945-1974). Serves the professional rodeo industry of the USA for their mutual protection and benefit. Approves and sanctions over 700 rodeos annually. Solicits and services sponsorships in rodeo.

Roller Skating Organizations

FEDERATION INTERNATIONALE ROLLER SPORTS (FIRS)
AV DE RHODANIE, 54
LAUSANNE, 1007
info@rollersports.org
www.rollersports.org
• Sabatino Aracu, President

ROLLER SKATING ASSOCIATION INTERNATIONAL
6905 CORPORATE DR
INDIANAPOLIS, IN 46278
317-347-2626
Fax: 317-347-2636
rsa@rollerskating.com
www.rollerskating.com
• Jim McMahon, Executive Director
Description:
Founded 1937. Non-Profit Trade association for rink operators and coaches.
Membership Requirements:
Must be roller skating rink operator.
Publications:
RSA TODAY COACHES' EDITION monthly newsletter, RSA TODAY biweekly newsletter, ROLLER SKATING BUSINESS bimonthly magazine, RSM NEWS, bimonthly newsletter.
Number of members:
1,000 rinks; 1,000 coaches; 1,000 judges.
Publications:
Roller Skating Business Magazine; RSA Today Newsletter

USA ROLLER SPORTS
4730 SOUTH STREET
LINCOLN, NE 68506
402-483-7551
Fax: 402-483-1465
www.teamusa.org/USA-Roller-Sports
• Richard Hawkins, Executive Director

Rowing/Crew Organizations

DAD VAIL REGATTA
SCHUYLKILL RIVER
2200 KELLY DRIVE
PHILADELPHIA, PA 19130
610-246-5902
levins51@verizon.net
dadvail.org

• Ed Levin, Publicity Director
(610) 246-5902
• John R Galloway, Chairman
Description:
Largest collegiate regatta in the United States.

EASTERN ASSOCIATION OF ROWING COLLEGES
www.ecac.org
• Phil Buttafuoco, Commissioner
• Mark Corino, President elect, 1st VP
• Mark Griffin, 2nd VP
• Mike Hardisky, Treasurer
• Gene Doris, President
Description:
Eighteen colleges and universities with men's rowing crews, mostly in the Northeast and Mid-Atlantic states, affiliated with the Eastern College Athletic Conference.

NATIONAL ROWING FOUNDATION
67 MYSTIC RD
N STONINGTON, CT 06359
860-535-0634
Fax: 860-535-0637
info@natrowing.org
natrowing.org
• Charles B Hamlin, Executive Director
(203) 434-5180
charlie@natrowing.org
Description:
Supports athletes who pursue excellence in the sport of rowing with the primary goal of promoting the United States' participation in international rowing competition, provide for the preservation of rowing history and manage the Rowing Hall of Fame.

PITTSBURGH THREE RIVERS REGATTA
PITTSBURGH, PA
Description:
Founded 1977. Major inland regatta in the U.S. Event includes powerboat races, drag boat races, national concert series, children's village, hot air balloon races, air shows, laser shows, fireworks show, champion lumberjack shows, 5 mile run and walk, rubber ducky race, senior citizen's day, night-lighted boat parade and many other events.

SCHOLASTIC ROWING ASSOCIATION OF AMERICA
contact@sraa.net
www.sraa.net
Member Services:
Annual regatta for boys' and girls' crews from throughout the world.
Membership Requirements:
Payment of dues.
Description:
Founded 1935. Promotes the advancement of rowing.

USROWING
2 Wall Street
PRINCETON, NJ 08540
609-751-0700
800-314-4769
Fax: 609-924-1578
members@usrowing.org
www.usrowing.org
• Glenn Merry, Chief Executive Officer
(609) 751-0701
glenn@usrowing.org

• Brian Klausner, Chief Financial Officer
(609) 751-0702
brian@usrowing.org
• Beth Kohl, Chief Marketing Officer
(203) 761-8643
beth@usrowing.org
• Brett Johnson, Director of Operations
(609) 751-0707
brett@usrowing.org
Nature of Service:
USRowing is a nonprofit membership organization recognized by the United States Olympic Committee as the national governing body for the sport of rowing in the United States. USRowing selects, trains and manages the teams that represent the U.S. in international competition including the world championships, Pam American Games and Olympics. USRowing serves and promotes the sport on all levels of competition. USRowing membership reflects the spectrum of American rowers - juniors, collegians, masters and those who row for recreation, competition of fitness.
Year Founded:
Founded in 1872 as the National Association of Amateur Oarsmen.
Membership:
$65/year (27 and over); $45/year (26 and under); $75/year (international)
Number of members:
1,050 organizations; 14,000 individuals

WORLD ROWING FEDERATION
MAISON DU SPORT INTERNATIONAL
AV. DE RHODANIE 54
LAUSANNE, 1007
info@fisa.org
www.worldrowing.com
• Matt Smith, Executive Director

Rugby Organizations

CAPE FEAR RUGBY FOOTBALL CLUB
fearrugby.com
• Nate Nemec, President
nrnemec@gmail.com
• Drew Gonzalez, Vice President
drew.gonzalez10@yahoo.com
• Harrison Hargett, Treasurer
hargetth@ymail.com
Publications:
PROGRAM, annual; Newsletter, quarterly.
Membership Requirements:
Entry fee; past successful participation; member in good standing of U.S. Rugby Football Union and its affiliates.
Description:
Founded 1975. Fosters growth of amateur Rugby Union Football by hosting a major seven-a-side international tournament.

MIDWEST RUGBY FOOTBALL UNION
www.midwestrugbyunion.org
• Jeremiah Johnson, President
jeremiahkjohnson@yahoo.com
• Adrian Gannon, Vice President - Competitions
rugbyteacher@sbcglobal.net
• Tom Rooney, Vice President - Collegiate & Youth
tomrooney@aol.com
• Stefan Palches, Secretary
spalches@gmail.com

• Tim Harn, Treasurer
tharn71@yahoo.com
Member Services:
Films, coaching clinics.
Publications:
IN TOUCH, eight times annually.
Membership Requirements:
Clubs that have full playing schedules and
have been in existence for at least one year.
Description:
Founded 1964. Organizes and coordinates
the activities of its member clubs.

USA RUGBY
2655 CRESCENT DR
UNIT A
LAFAYETTE, CO 80026
303-539-0300
Fax: 303-539-0311
www.usarugby.org
• Dan Payne, Chief Executive Officer
• Jen Gray, Director of Operations
Description:
Founded 1975. Promotes the development
and expansion of Rugby Union football in
the U.S. Improves standards of play,
coaching and refereeing. Encourages
international competition.
Membership Requirements:
Regional associations within the continental
U.S. that have local associations as
members.
Publications:
Magazine - to full membership
Member Services:
Address lists; coaching and refereeing
clinics; annual meeting - held 2nd weekend
in November; International Games, World
Cup Competition; local, regional, national
sponsorships. Car rental discounts and
Master Card discounts.
Number of Members:
50,000

WESTERN RUGBY FOOTBALL UNION
1409 E. MEADOW LANE
KIRKSVILLE, MO 63501
660-665-6505
www.wrfu.org
• William Sexton, President
(660) 665-6505
• Alan Sharpley, Vice President
(512) 288-3384
• David McPhail, Treasurer
Number of members:
5,500
Member Services:
Coordinates business of WRFU; oversees
operation of championships and all-star
teams; provides communications link with
USARFU and other Unions; represents
WRFU constituency to USARFU.
Publications:
Announcements; periodic newsletters.
Membership Requirements:
Composed of rugby organizations. Limited
to those local area rugby football unions
within jurisdiction of the Union.
Description:
Founded 1975. Coordinates the activities of
seven local area rugby unions throughout
the south central U.S.

**WESTERN SUBURBS RUGBY FOOTBALL
CLUB**
P.O BOX 441
FAIRFAX, VA 22038

www.rugbyfootball.com
• Patrick Robinson, President
• Ben Allen, Vice President
• Danta Moore, Match Secretary
• Mark Bevilacqua, Director of Youth Rugby
• Jeff Carrington, Head Coach
• Erich Weiss, Treasurer
• Jorge Arias, Secretary
Description:
Div II team in the PRU.

WORLD RUGBY
WORLD RUGBY HOUSE
8-10 PEMBROKE STREET LOWER
Dublin, D2
info@worldrugby.org
www.worldrugby.org
• Brett Gosper, Chief Executive Officer
Description:
International governing body of rugby union.
Formerly International Rugby Board (IRB).
Year Founded:
1886

Running Organizations

AMERICAN RUNNING ASSOCIATION
4405 EAST-WEST HWY
SUITE 405
BETHESDA, MD 20814
800-776-2732
Fax: 301-913-9520
• Dave Watt, Executive Director
• Barbara Baldwin, Projects Consultant
Year Founded:
1968
Description:
The American Running Association (ARA) is
a nonprofit membership and advocacy
organization committed to increasing the
physical activity levels of all Americans from
youths to adults through vigorous walking
and running. ARA has a division or sister
association, the American Medical Athletic
Association (AMAA) that is comprised of
physicians and other health professionals
who provide information and overnight a for
endurance sports events and the public.
Number of Members:
10,000
Publications:
AMAA Journal; e-Running & Fitness and the
American Medical Athletic Association
Journal.

**AMERICAN TRAIL RUNNING
ASSOCIATION**
PO BOX 9454
COLORADO SPRINGS, CO 80932
719-573-4133
Fax: 719-573-4408
nancyhobbs@trailrunner.com
www.trailrunner.com
• Adam Chase, President
• Nancy Hobbs, Executive Director
Description:
Founded in 1996, ATRA's mission is to
promote trail running, mountain running,
ultrarunning on trails, and to provide
resources for race directors and participants
in the sport.
Publications:
TRAIL TIMES (quarterly); monthly
e-newsletter; monthly race director
e-newsletter

Membership Requirements:
$25 annual dues for individual membership;
$50 for race/club membership.

**ASSOCIATION OF INTERNATIONAL
MARATHONS AND DISTANCE RACES**
OLYMPIC ATHLETIC CENTER OF
ATHENS
SPYROS LOUIS AVE
MAROUSI
ATHENS, 15123
aimshq@aims-worldrunning.org
www.aims-worldrunning.org
• Paco Borao, President
borao@correcaminos.org
• Morales Martha, Vice President
maratontangamanga@gmail.com
• Dave Cundy, Vice President
cundysm@ozemail.com.au
Year Founded:
1982

BIG SUR INTERNATIONAL MARATHON
3618 THE BARNYARD
CARMEL, CA 93923
831-625-6226
Fax: 831-625-2119
info@bsim.org
www.bsim.org

BOSTON ATHLETIC ASSOCIATION
185 DARTMOUTH STREET
6TH FLOOR
BOSTON, MA 02116
617-236-1652
Fax: 617-236-4505
info@baa.org
www.baa.org
• Joann E Flaminio, President
• Thomas S Grilk, Chief Executive Officer
• David McGillivray, Race Director
Description:
Founded 1887. Owns and organizes Boston
Marathon.

COLUMBUS MARATHON
c/o THE ATHLETIC CLUB OF COLUMBUS
136 E BROAD STREET
COLUMBUS, OH 43215
614-421-7866
Fax: 614-263-3518
info@columbusmarathon.com
www.columbusmarathon.com
• Darris Blackford, Race Director
Description:
Founded 1980. Organizes the tenth largest
marathon in the U.S., in Columbus Ohio,
with 5,000 runners.

GASPARILLA DISTANCE CLASSIC
215 Verne St
Suite C
TAMPA, FL 33606
813-254-7866
Fax: 813-254-9307
information@tampabayrun.com
www.tampabayrun.com
Description:
Founded 1978. Not-for-profit association
sponsoring the annual I5K and 5K races
with a wheelchair division. Purpose is to
raise funds for local youth charities.

LOS ANGELES MARATHON
871 FIGUEROA TERRACE
LOS ANGELES, CA 90012

213-542-3000
Fax: 213-542-3020
info@goconqur.com
www.lamarathon.com
Description:
6-month training program of the Honda LA Marathon.

NEW YORK ROAD RUNNERS
156 W 56TH STREET
3RD FLOOR
NEW YORK, NY 10019
www.nyrr.org
• Michael Capiraso, President & CEO
• Peter Ciaccia, Race Director
Description:
NYRR is dedicated to promoting the sport of distance running, enhancing health and fitness for all, and responding to community needs. The road races and other fitness programs draw upwards of 300,000 runners annually, and together with the magazine and web site, support and promote professional and recreational running.

ROAD RUNNERS CLUB OF AMERICA
1501 LEE HWY
SUITE 140
ARLINGTON, VA 22209
703-525-3890
office@rrca.org
www.rrca.org
• Mitchell Garner, President
president@rrca.org
• Jean Arthur, Vice President
vicepresident@rrca.org
• Jean Knaack, Executive Director
execdir@rrca.org
Description:
The RRCA is dedicated to supporting the growth of grassroots running clubs, training programs, and running events while promoting the common interests of runners throughout the United States.
Services:
The RRCA oofers a variety of service designed to support and promote the efforts of local running clubs and events. Through their services, RRCA provides a proven national infrastructure for the development of running clubs, training programs, and events.
Programs:
The RRCA strives to provide quality programming that can be replicated throughout the country by member clubs from small towns to large cities. The programs promote and support running and runners at all stages in life.
Membership:
The RRCA is the oldest and largest organization in the US dedicated to distance running. With over 1000 member clubs and events representing over 200,000 running club members, why run with anyone else?

SACRAMENTO RUNNING ASSOCIATION
4181 POWER INN RD
SUITE A
Saramento, CA 95826
916-737-2627
Fax: 916-737-7684
info@runsra.org
runsra.org
• Scott Abbott, Executive Director
Mission:
Since the SRA Board believes strongly in

the myriad of health benefits gained from running, the SRA's expanded mission is to find ways to encourage people of all ages and abilities to run.
Events:
California International Marathon; Super Bowl Sunday 10K Run; Sactown 10-Miler; Lake Natoma Four Bridges Half Marathon; Youth Fitness Programs

Sailing Organizations

SAIL AMERICA
50 WATER ST
WARREN, RI 02885
401-289-2540
Fax: 401-247-0074
www.sailamerica.com
• Katie Kelly, Association Manager
kkelly@sailamerica.com
Sports Service Founded:
1988
Event Management Services:
Nonprofit organization, promoting SAIL EXPO & Strictly Sail, sailboat shows.

US SAILING
15 MARITIME DRIVE
PORTSMOUTH, RI 02871
401-683-0800
800-877-2451
Fax: 401-683-0840
info@ussailing.org
www.ussailing.org
• Jack Gierhart, Chief Executive Officer
 ext 631
Number of members:
30,000+
Publications:
AMERICAN SAILOR, monthly.
Membership Requirements:
Open to interested individuals, clubs, sailing associations, corporations.
Description:
Founded in 1897 as the North American Yacht Racing Union. The National Governing Body for the sport of sailing, the mission is to provide leadership for the sport of sailing in the United States and works to achieve this mission through a wide range of programs and events, geared towards providing an equal level playing field for all sailors.

Scuba Organizations

PROFESSIONAL ASSOCIATION OF DIVING INSTRUCTORS (PADI)
30151 TOMAS
RANCHO SANTA MARGARITA, CA 92688
949-858-7234
800-729-7234
Fax: 949-267-1267
customerservice@padi.com
www.padi.com
• Drew Richardson, President & CEO
Number of members:
35,000
Member Services:
PAD - Professional Association of Diving Instructors - as the largest diver certification organization in the world, with offices in seven countries, accommodates scuba diving needs world-wide. Visit

www.padi.com/english/common/courses/pro/ for professional membership. Individual member and professional member levels available. Dive Centers are members of the International Retailers and Resort Association which provides product, training, and business support through all facets of the dive industry business.
Publications:
THE UNDERSEA JOURNAL, quarterly.
DIVE TRAVELER; Dive Travel Directory, semi-annually.
Membership Requirements:
Retail stores, diving resorts; Individuals - must become a PADI Divemaster or PADI instructor at a sanctioned training course. Individual, professional, retail and resort memberships.
Description:
Founded 1966. Serves to promote safe scuba diving as a recreational activity worldwide.

SCUBA SCHOOLS INTERNATIONAL (SSI)
902 CLINT MOORE RD
SUITE 210
BOCA RATON, FL 33487
800-821-4319
usa@divessi.com
www.divessi.com
Member Services:
Education and business support for SSI dealers and instructors.
Publications:
DIVE BUSINESS INTERNATIONAL, bimonthly.
Description:
Founded 1970. Professional SCUBA diving certification agency.

Shooting/Hunting Organizations

AMATEUR TRAPSHOOTING ASSOCIATION
1105 EAST BROADWAY
SPARTA, IL 62286
618-449-2224
Fax: 866-454-5198
info@shootata.com
www.shootata.com
• John Burke, President
jtburke@bbcwb.net
• Lynn Gipson, Executive Director
lgipson@shootata.com
Number of members:
102,686
Member Services:
Retains shooting records, classifies and handicaps shooters according to their ability, hosts regional national championships, governs the rules promotes National Trapshooting Day, conducts youth programs, consults shooting facilities and gun clubs.
Publications:
TRAP & FIELD Magazine, monthly.
Membership Requirements:
$18 for annual and $500 for life memberships.
Description:
Founded: 1900. Serves as the governing body for the sport of American-style trapshooting. The ATA's mission is to

promote and govern the sport throughout the world. The ATA provides trophies, financial Assistance and event management support to the state and provincial associations. The ATA hosts the Grand American World Trap Championships in Vandalia, OH with nearly 6,000 competitors annually.

INTERNATIONAL HANDGUN METALLIC SILHOUETTE ASSOCIATION
3061 SAND HILL RD
BISMARCK, ND 58503
801-733-8423
Fax: 801-733-8424
ihmsaheadquarters@gmail.com
www.ihmsa.org
• Steve Martens, President
smartensj@charter.net
• Bruce Barrett, Vice-President
bruce0162@att.net
Nature of Service:
Sanctioning body for all handgun silhouette matches held throughout the America and the rest of the world. IHMSA rules provide for four categories of competition: production single-shot guns, production revolvers and Unlimited guns, all shot freestyle. The fourth category is for production guns in the standing position. Targets include metallic chickens, pigs, turkeys and rams.
Year Founded:
1975
Member Services:
Rule book, patch, set of scale templates for making full size official silhouette targets.
Number of members:
2,500
Publications:
THE IHMSA NEWS, 10/year

INTERNATIONAL SHOOTING SPORT FEDERATION (ISSF)
BAVARIARING 21
MUNICH, 80336
munich@issf-sports.org
www.issf-sports.org
• Olegario Vazquez Rana, President

NATIONAL RIFLE ASSOCIATION OF AMERICA
11250 WAPLES MILL RD
FAIRFAX, VA 22030
800-672-3888
www.nra.org
• Wayne LaPierre Jr, Executive Vice President
Number of members:
2.6 million.
Member Services:
Hunter safety courses, gun safety and training courses for home and self-defense, law enforcement training, lobbying activities on behalf of its membership regarding gun and gun-related issues, clubs and association activities and range development services. Also serves as governing body for all sanctioned competition in the United States. Endowment, Patron and Benefactor members are also recognized at NRA events, able to vote in NRA elections, and receive certified credentials fit for framing.
Membership Requirements:
$35 for 1 year, $60 for 2 years, $85 for 3 years, $125 for 5 years, $1000 for life

membership, $1000 EPL (easy pay for life = 40 $25 payments); JUNIOR MEMBERSHIPS, Dues and Requirements-Age 15+: $15 1 year Junior, $550 Junior Life, $550 EPL Junior Life (22 payments of $25); DISTINGUISHED MEMBERSHIPS, Dues and Requirements-Age 65+ or Disabled Veteran: $30 1 year Distinguished, $375 Distinguished life, $375 EPL Ditinguished life (15 payments of $25); $10 1 year Magazine subscription. CONTRIBUTORY LIFE MEMBERSHIPS (Available to Fully Paid Life Members) Endowment Member $2000, Patron Member $3500, Benefactor $5000
Publications:
AMERICAN HUNTER, monthly; AMERICAN RIFLEMAN, monthly; SHOOTING SPORTS USA and SHOOTING ILLUSTRATED; INSIGHTS, written for junior members; AMERICA's 1st FREEDOM, monthly.
Description:
Founded 1871. Primary purpose is to protect and defend the Second Amendment rights of all law-abiding citizens, to promote proper gun safety and training, to foster and promote the shooting sports, to promote hunter safety and to promote and defend hunting as a shooting sport and as a viable and necessary method of fostering the conservation of our wildlife resources.

NATIONAL SHOOTING SPORTS FOUNDATION
FLINTLOCK RIDGE OFFICE CENTER
11 MILE HILL RD
NEWTOWN, CT 06470
203-426-1320
Fax: 203-426-1087
info@nssf.org
www.nssf.org
• Robert L Scott, Chairman
Description:
Founded 1961. NSSF is the trade association for firearms and ammunition industries, chartered to promote a better understanding of and a more active participation in the shooting sports. Conducts shooting-sport related special events and programs; SHOT Show.
Number of members:
5,600
Publicatios:
Range Report

NATIONAL SKEET SHOOTING ASSOCIATION (NSSA)
5931 ROFT RD
SAN ANTONIO, TX 78253
210-688-3371
800-877-5338
Fax: 210-688-3014
nssa-nsca.org
• Michael Hampton, Jr, Executive Director
(210) 688-3371
mhampton@nssa-nsca.com
• Gary Burley, NSSA Director
(210) 688-3371
gburley@nssa-nsca.com
Member Services:
Reports tournament winners in Skeet Shooting Review and records all scores shot by members for permanent record.
Number of Members:
20,000
Membership Requirements:

Interest in Skeet Shooting and payment of dues.
Description:
Founded 1946. Promotes and advances the interest, welfare and development of skeet shooting and related sports.
Publications:
NSSA SKEET SHOOTING REVIEW MAGAZINE, monthly. NSSA RECORDS ANNUAL.

NATIONAL SPORTING CLAYS ASSOCIATION (NSCA)
5931 ROFT RD
SAN ANTONIO, TX 78253
210-688-3371
800-877-5338
Fax: 210-688-3014
nssa-nsca.org
• Michael Hampton, Jr, Executive Director
(210) 688-3371
mhampton@nssa-nsca.com
• Brett Moyes, NSCA Director
(210) 688-3371
bmoyes@nssa-nsca.com
Member Services:
Subscription to SPORTING CLAYS magazine; national championships, tournaments, state and zone shoots; records of registered shoots; instructor certification courses; NSCA 5-stand sporting demonstration units; All American Teams selected for the Open, and the Ladies, Senior, Veteran, Junior and Sub Junior competitions; official rule book; fun shoots; discounts on rental cars.
Publications:
SPORTING CLAYS MAGAZINE, monthly.
Membership Requirements:
Shooting must be at registered tournaments. Memberships include monthly magazine. Life Membership: $350; One Year Regular Membership: $30; One Year Associate Membership: $20; Canadian and Foreign Membership: $20.
Description:
Founded 1989. Dedicated to the development of the sport of clay shooting at all levels of participation, and to the creation of an atmosphere of safe, healthy competition within the membership. NSCA is operated, directed, and advised by clay target shooters, range owners, and shooting industry representatives.

SHOOTING FEDERATION OF CANADA
45 SHIRLEY BLVD
NEPEAN, ON, CANADA K2K 2W6
613-727-7483
Fax: 613-727-7487
sfc-ftc.ca
• Pat Boulay, President
president@sfc-ftc.ca
Description:
Founded 1932, under the name of the Canadian Small Bore Rifle Association. Responsible for promotion, development and governing of organized recreational and competitive target shooting in and for Canada. Maintains communication with members and affiliates and other organizations with mutual interests; develops information programs for recreational shooters and for clubs, as well as training programs for competitive shooters, coaches and officials; promotes organized recreational and competitive

target shooting as a lifelong sporting activity; conducts international competitions, selecting teams, developing and sanctioning competitions at all

Membership Requirements:
General member $30/year.

Publications:
AIM Magazine, two times per year.

Member Services:
AIM, RTS Program, Insurance, Classifications participation in Registered Tournaments and National Championships/Team Trials to make National Team.

Number of members:
20,000

US PRACTICAL SHOOTING ASSOCIATION (USPSA)
1639 LINDAMOOD LN
BURLINGTON, WA 98233
800-995-5646
office@uspsa.org
www.uspsa.org
• Mike Foley, President

Description:
Non-profit amateur sports association dedicated to the promotion of practical shooting.

Sports Service Founded:
1984

Number of Members:
15,000

Publications:
Front Sight Magazine.

Member Services:
May visit web site (www.uspsa.org) or call the office (360) -855-2245 for more information.

USA SHOOTING
1 OLYMPIC PLAZA
COLORADO SPRINGS, CO 80909
719-866-4670
Fax: 719-866-4884
www.usashooting.org
• David Johnson, Interim CEO

Shuffleboard Organizations

INTERNATIONAL SHUFFLEBOARD ASSOCIATION
info@world-shuffleboard.org
world-shuffleboard.org

Number of members/players:
90,000 participating players; six member countries.

Member Services:
Organizes and promotes an International Tournament each year. Singles World Tournament 2017 to be held in Niteroi, Rio de Janeiro, Brazil.

Publications:
ISA Program Preview, annually with tournament

Membership Requirements:
Must be National Shuffleboard Association for the Country they represent. Fee of $500 to join.

Description:
Founded 1979. Organizes and promotes shuffleboard throughout the world. At present six countries are involved - USA, Brazil, Canada, Japan, Australia, Zimbabwe.

Skateboard Organizations

FEDERATION INTERNATIONALE ROLLER SPORTS (FIRS)
AV DE RHODANIE, 54
LAUSANNE, 1007
www.rollersports.org

INTERNATIONAL ASSOCIATION OF SKATEBOARD COMPANIES
315 S COAST HWY 101
SUITE U-253
ENCINITAS, CA 92024
949-455-1112
Fax: 949-455-1712
theiasc.org
• Don Brown, Chairman
• Glenn Brumage, Vice President

Nature of Sports Service:
Founded 1995. Dedicated to promoting the sport of skateboarding. Acts as a central voice and information center for media, legislators and others, IASC represents the skateboard industry as it fosters sound business practices and promotes high standards of conduct within the industry. Works with municipalities in the development of designated skateboarding venues, and with sanctioning guidelines for professional and amateur competitions.

Publications:
THE FIVE FIFTEEN, weekly newsletter, THE GRAPEVINE, quarterly report.

Member Services:
Communications resource, reference resource, collections, insurance product liability, sanctions and guidelines, public skate park development, legislative lobbying.

Membership Requirements:
Yearly dues vary based on company's annual revenue.

Skiing Organizations

ALPINE CANADA
CANADA OLYMPIC PARK
151 CANADA OLYMPIC ROAD SW
SUITE 302
CALGARY, AB, CANADA T3B 6B7
403-777-3200
Fax: 403-777-3213
info@alpinecanada.org
alpinecanada.org
• Mark Rubinstein, President & CEO
(403) 777-4246
mrubinstein@alpinecanada.org
• Nicholas Bass, Chief Operating Officer
(403) 777-3218
nbass@alpinecanada.org

Nature of Service:
Develops programs, events, and sponsorship for the Canadian Alpine Ski Team and National Junior team for elite male and female skiers. Membership includes competitive skiers and recreational coaches, medical staff.

Number of members:
45,000+.

Publications:
Newsletter, biweekly, Magazine, quarterly

AMERICAN BIRKEBEINER SKI FOUNDATION (ABSF)
10527 MAIN ST
HAYWARD, WI 54843
715-634-5025
Fax: 715-634-5663
birkie@birkie.com
www.birkie.com
• Ben Popp, Executive Director
• Paul Eckerline, President - 2018

Description:
Membership organization dedicated to hosting cross country ski events, maintaining trails and promoting healthy lifestyles.

AMERICAN SKI RACING ALLIANCE
570-344-2772
Fax: 570-348-2055
asra@skiracer.com
www.skiracer.com

Membership Requirements:
$35 annual dues for individual, $55 for family.

CANADIAN SKI PATROL
4531 SOUTHCLARK PLACE
OTTAWA, ON, CANADA K1T 3V2
613-822-2245
Fax: 613-822-1088
info@skipatrol.ca
www.skipatrol.ca
• Colin Saravanamuttoo, President & CEo

Number of members:
5,000

Member Services:
Central purchasing, training content and materials, communications.

Membership Requirements:
Must be 18 years of age, intermediate skier, complete CSPS training program.

Description:
Founded 1941. Charitable organization promoting skiing safety and offering first-aid services to injured skiers.

CANADIAN SNOWSPORTS ASSOCIATION
1451 WEST BROADWAY
SUITE 202
VANCOUVER, BC, CANADA V6H 1H6
604-734-6800
Fax: 604-669-7954
www.canadiansnowsports.com
• David Pym, Managing Director
dpym@isrm.com
• Lillian Alderton, Administrator
lillianalderton@hotmail.com

Number of members:
Over 85,000

Publications:
ALPINE GUIDE annually, FREESTYLE GUIDE annually, CROSS COUNTRY Annual Media Guide and Competition Guide, JUMPING/NORDIC COMBINED GUIDE annually, CROSS COUNTRY GUIDE annually, brochures, newsletters.

Membership Requirements:
Pay general fee.

Snowsports Represented:
Alpine Canadian Alpin, Canadian Association for Disabled Skiing, Canadian Freestyle Association, Canadian Speed Skating Association, Cross Country Canada, Nordic Combined Ski Canada, Ski Jumping Canada, Telemark Ski Canada Telemark,

Canadian Snowboard Federation, Canadian Ski Coaches Federation.

CROSS COUNTRY CANADA
BILL WARREN TRAINING CENTRE
1995 OLYMPIC WAY
SUITE 100
CANMORE, AB, CANADA T1W 2T6
403-678-6791
877-609-3215
Fax: 403-678-3885
info@cccski.com
www.cccski.com
• Shane Pearsall, Chief Executive Officer
(403) 678-6791
spearsall@cccski.com
• Jamie Coatsworth, Chair
(416) 486-0825
jamie.coatsworth@gmail.com
• Chris Dornan, Media Relations
(403) 620-8731
hpprchris@shaw.ca
• Thomas Holland, Director of High
Performance
(403) 678-6791
tholland@cccski.com
Description:
Serves as national sport governing body for
Cross Country Skiing in Canada.
Publications:
Monthly Cross Connections Newsletter
Membership Requirements:
Must belong to club affiliated with provincial
cross country association.
Member Services:
Jackrabbit program - for youth instruction;
School/Ski program - physical activity
program at elementary school level;
Coaching program - in conjunction with
Coaching Association of Canada,
Information Service - provides information
on any CCC program, National Ski Team
results, and other cross country news.
Number of members:
Over 50,000

CROSS COUNTRY SKI AREAS ASSOCIATION
603-239-4341
ccsaa@xcski.org
xcski.org
Number of members:
300
Membership Requirements:
Regular - must own or operate a cross
country ski facility in North America.
Associate - companies selling goods to the
cross country industry. Supporting - guides
and outfitters, ski school.
Description:
Founded 1977. Deals with and represents
interests of cross country ski operators in
North America including promotion and
support activities.

EASTERN WINTER SPORTS REPS ASSOCIATION
570-443-7180
Fax: 570-300-2715
info@ewsra.org
www.ewsra.org
• Kerry O'Flaherty, President
ofie@maine.rr.com
• Dave Kleeschulte, Vice President
dkleeschulte@nordicausa.com
Description:
Promotes general welfare of and improves

business conditions for persons engaged in
the business related to snow-skiing industry.
Membership Requirements:
Open to anyone who gains his livelihood
primarily as a sales rep for firms
substantially engaged in manufacturing of
goods associated with snow-ski industry and
located in ESRA territory (NY, NJ, PA). $750
initiation fee, $300 annual dues.
Publications:
Buyer's Guide, Retail List.
Number of members:
253

FEDERATION INTERNATIONALE DE SKI (FIS)
MARC HODLER HOUSE
BLOCHSTRASSE 2
OBERHOFEN/THUNERSEE, CH-3653
mail@fisski.ch
www.fis-ski.com
• Sarah Lewis, Secretary General

NATIONAL SKI & SNOWBOARD RETAILERS ASSOCIATION
1601 FEEHANVILLE DRIVE
SUITE 300
MOUNT PROSPECT, IL 60056
888-257-1168
Fax: 847-391-9827
info@nssra.com
www.nssra.com
• Teddy Schiavoni, Chairman
• Larry Weindruch, President
Nature of Service:
Develops, improves and promotes the
business of retailers, shops, areas and other
members of the ski and snowboard industry;
furthers the business interests of and
promotes friendly relationships with its
members; promotes the sports of skiing and
snowboarding.
Year Founded:
1987
Number of Members:
250
Publications:
NSSRA NEWSLETTER, 6 time(s) per year

NATIONAL SKI AREAS ASSOCIATION
133 S VAN GORDON ST
SUITE 300
LAKEWOOD, CO 80228
303-987-1111
Fax: 303-986-2345
nsaa@nsaa.org
www.nsaa.org
• Michael Berry, President
(303) 987-1111
Description:
Founded 1962. National trade association
for ski resorts and areas in North America.
Purpose is to stimulate and promote skiing,
snowboarding and safety and to meet the
needs of the ski area industry.
Membership Requirements:
Must be a ski area in operation or a supplier
of services to the ski and snowboard
industry.
Member Services:
Holds two regional winter shows and an
annual convention and trade show
exclusively for members.
Number of members:
The association represents 313 alpine
resorts and has 414 supplier members.

NATIONAL SKI PATROL
133 S VAN GORDON ST
SUITE 100
LAKEWOOD, CO 80228
303-988-1111
Fax: 303-988-3005
nsp@nsp.org
www.nsp.org
• John McMahon, Executive Director
• Bill Finley, Director of Finance
Number of members:
29,000
Publications:
SKI PATROL MAGAZINE, quarterly.
Membership Requirements:
An individual or unit (composed of one or
more individuals) who, whether volunteering
or receiving pay for services, has met or
exceeded the National Qualification
Requirements for Ski Patrollers established
by the National Ski Patrol System, Inc. and
who has registered with the National Ski
Patrol System, Inc. as a member of one of
its Ski Patrols, and who has remitted the
required registration fee. Must be a Winter
Emergency Care Technician, and tested
(after training) in patroller skills.
Description:
Founded 1938. Promotes the safety of those
engaged in winter sports and gives
emergency care to those who have suffered
injuries.

NEW ENGLAND SPORTS REPRESENTATIVES
21 SOUTH STREET
UNIT 3
WESTBOROUGH, MA 01581
508-898-9559
Fax: 508-772-0013
• Maureen Bliss, Executive Director
• Will Masson, President
(802) 985-4089
will.masson@rossignol.com
Nature of Service:
Organizes two trade shows for retailers in
the spring of each year, as well as an
On-Snow Demo during winter.
Year Founded:
1968
Membership Requirements:
Must represent a company or companies
that sell snow ski equipment, clothing or
accessories. $750 initiation fee, $450 annual
dues.
Number of members:
325
Publications:
BUYER'S GUIDE, sent to ski shops that
have attended previous shows.

PACIFIC NORTHWEST SKI ASSOCIATION
2671 FLOWERY TAIL ROAD
Usk, WA 99180
509-445-4454
Fax: 866-542-8664
pnsa@pnsa.org
www.pnsa.org
• Bill Brooks, President
• Curt Hammond, Vice President
cjhammond@msn.com
Nature of Service:
Division of the U.S. Skiing. Provides skiers
with an organized voice. Administers
competition ski programs.
Year Founded:
1931

Member Services:
Administration of competition programs.
Membership Requirements:
Interest in skiing. Dues.
Number of members:
2,200

PROFESSIONAL SNOWSPORTS INSTRUCTORS OF AMERICA - EASTERN
1-A LINCOLN AVE
ALBANY, NY 12205-4907
518-452-6095
Fax: 518-452-6099
psia-e@psia-e.org
www.psia-e.org
• Michael Mendrick, Executive Director
mmendrick@psia-e.org
Number of Members:
Over 11,000
Member Services:
Committee functions involving marketing, certification, education, equipment trends, sports research and information.
Membership Requirements:
Successfully complete an instructor registration clinic and certification exam. Pay annual dues and upgrade every two years.
Description:
Founded 1973. Serves as a non-profit organization whose purpose is the education and certification of Nordic ski instructors.

PROFESSIONAL SNOWSPORTS INSTRUCTORS OF AMERICA - NORTHWEST
338 N WENATCHEE AVENUE
WENATCHEE, WA 98801
206-244-8541
Fax: 206-241-2885
info@psia-nw.org
www.psia-nw.org
• Kirsten Huotte, Executive Director
kirsten@psia-nw.org
Number of members:
27,500
Publications:
Educational manuals; Ski school surveys; Member surveys; THE PROFESSIONAL SKIER, quarterly educational journal.
Membership Requirements:
Must be certified, associate or registered member of one of nine PSIA divisions. Division requirements vary, but basically all require a certain number of hours teaching experience, a classroom test knowledge, and an on-snow test of skill. $30 annual dues for division certified registered member, $70 for non-certified member.
Description:
Founded 1961. Promotes professional ski instruction to both the general public and the ski industry through its education foundation and PSIA marketing programs for its divisions, its member ski schools and its member instructors.

SKI FOR LIGHT
1455 W LAKE ST
MINNEAPOLIS, MN 55408
612-827-3232
www.sfl.org
• Scott McCall, President
• Robert Civiak, Vice President
Member Services:
Sponsors one international x-country ski event annually for visually and mobility

impaired persons. Regional programs. Summer programs entitled Sports For Health, for visually and mobility impaired individuals.
Publications:
Ski for Light bulletin, three times a year.
Membership Requirements:
Interest in working with disabled and able-bodied persons on one-on-one basis. Dues are $15 annual, $25 sustaining, $100 Corporate, $250 individual life.
Description:
Founded 1975. Advances and promotes athletic education and participation of blind and other disabled persons in outdoor activities and exposes blind and other disabled persons to the outdoors under supervised physical training.

SNOWSPORTS INDUSTRIES AMERICA
1918 PROSPECTOR AVE
PARK CITY, UT 84060
435-657-5140
Fax: 435-659-3434
info@snowsports.org
www.snowsports.org
• Nick Sargent, President
nick.sargent@snowsports.org
• Maria McNulty, Chief Operating Officer
mmcnulty@snowsports.org
• Mike Adams, Treasurer
• David Currier, Secretary
• Julie Garry, First Vice Chair
• David Ingemie, President
• Leslie L. Groves, Director Marketing/Communications
lgroves@snowsports.org
Nature of Service:
National non-profit trade association of ski, snowboard, on-snow, and outdoor action sports product manufacturers and distributors.
Year Founded:
1954
Membership Requirements:
Provided on written request.
Number of members:
Over 750
Publications:
SIA NEWSLETTERS, SIA SNOWSPORTS DIRECTORY, SIA INDUSTRY PLANNER, variety of research, public relations and educational information and materials.

U.S. DEAF SKI & SNOWBOARD ASSOCIATION
76 KINGS GATE NORTH
ROCHESTER, NY 14617
585-286-2780
info@usdssa.org
usdssa.org
• Ellen Roth, President
• Sean Esson, Vice President
Publications:
Newsletter, three times per year.
Membership Requirements:
Deaf with 55 db loss in hearing eligible to be competitors. Membership dues for individuals are $20 for two years, $30 for families.
Description:
Founded 1968. Promotes skiing for deaf people. Training for Olympics.

U.S. SKI AND SNOWBOARD ASSOCIATION (USSA)
1 VICTORY LANE
PARK CITY, UT 84060
435-649-9090
Fax: 435-649-3613
ussa.org
• Tiger Shaw, President & CEO
• Brooke McAffee, Vice President & Chief Financial Officer
• Trisha Worthington, EVP & Chief Development Officer
Description:
Provides opportunities for athletes in the most exciting Olympic action sports. USSA's programs provide education, development and competition opportunities for young athletes, with from grassroots USSA club programs up through national teams and the Olympic Winter Games.
Membership Requirements:
Anyone can join on an individual, family or club basis.
Publications:
Discipline competition guides (alpine, cross-country, freestyle, jumping/Nordic combined, Snowboard), American Ski Coach, periodically.
Year Founded:
1905

Sled Dog Organizations

IDITAROD
2100 S KNIK GOOSE BAY RD
WASILLA, AK 99654
907-376-5155
Fax: 907-373-6998
iditarod@iditarod.com
www.iditarod.com
• Stan Hooley, Chief Executive Officer
• Mark Nordman, Race Director
Description:
Founded 1973. Known as The Last Great Race On Earth, covers 1,049 miles. Begins first Saturday in March and ends approximately 10 days later.

INTERNATIONAL SLED DOG RACING ASSOCIATION
22702 REBEL RD
MERRIFIELD, MN 56465
218-765-4297
dsteele@brainerd.net
www.isdra.org
Number of members:
1,000+.
Membership Requirements:
$35 membership fee.
Publications:
Dog and Driver Magazine, six times a year.
Description:
Founded 1966.

JOHN BEARGREASE SLED DOG MARATHON
218-722-7631
info@beargrease.com
www.beargrease.com
• Jean Vincent, President
Description:
Founded 1980. Longest sled dog race in the lower 48 states.
Membership Requirements:
$30 trail membership, $100 mile marker

membership, $250 mid-distance membership, $500 marathon membership, $1,000 VIP membership.

Snowboarding Organizations

AMERICAN ASSOCIATION OF SNOWBOARD INSTRUCTORS
133 S VAN GORDON ST
SUITE 200
LAKEWOOD, CO 80228
844-340-7669
www.thesnowpros.org
• Nick Herrin, Chief Executive Officer
nherrin@thesnowpros.org
• Tom Spiess, Chief Financial Officer
tspiess@thesnowpros.org
Description:
World's largest organization dedicated to skiing and snowboarding instruction.
Founded:
1961
Members:
32,000
Member Services:
Professional Development Education Programs, Subaru Incentive Purchase Program, Certification, and Special Purchase Opportunities.
Publications:
THE PRO RIDER magazine, THE PROFESSIONAL SKIER magazine.

U.S. SKI AND SNOWBOARD ASSOCIATION (USSA)
1 VICTORY LANE
PARK CITY, UT 84060
435-649-9090
Fax: 435-649-3613
www.ussa.org
• Tiger Shaw, President & CEO
• Brooke McAffee, Vice President & Chief Financial Officer
• Trisha Worthington, EVP & Chief Development Officer

Snowmobile Organizations

AMERICAN COUNCIL OF SNOWMOBILE ASSOCIATIONS
271 WOODLAND PASS
SUITE 216
EAST LANSING, MI 48823
517-351-4362
Fax: 517-351-1363
info@snowmobilers.org
www.snowmobilers.org
• Bob Kirchner, President
whynotbobk@yahoo.com
Sports Service Founded:
1995
Membership Requirements:
$10 fee for individual, $15 for family, $25 for club.
Publication:
ACSA Newsletter 27 Trails.
Description:
American Council of Snowmobile Associations (ACSA) is a non-profit national association dedicated to providing leadership and advancing the efforts of all snowmobile-affiliated organizations to

promote the expansion and education of responsible snowmobiling in the United States. Acts as national coordinator and spokesperson for state volunteer snowmobile associations and snowmobile clubs.

CANADIAN COUNCIL OF SNOWMOBILE ORGANIZATIONS
807-345-5299
ccso.ccom@tbaytel.net
www.ccso-ccom.ca
• Dale Hickox, President
• Dennis Burns, Executive Director
Year Founded:
1974
Description:
Not-for-profit organization dedicated to providing leadership and support to organized snowmobiling in Canada.

INTERNATIONAL SNOWMOBILE MANUFACTURERS ASSOCIATION
1640 HASLETT ROAD
SUITE 170
HASLETT, MI 48840
517-339-7788
Fax: 517-339-7798
ismasue@aol.com
www.snowmobile.org
Nature of Service:
Organization representing the four snowmobile manufacturers. Coordinates committees within the industry to handle concerns such as snowmobile safety, the promotion of the life-style activity of snowmobiling, keeping accurate statistics, reporting the growth of the industry and the positive economic impact the life-style activity has throughout the world.
Member Services:
Communications, Good Relations.
Membership Requirements:
Manufacturer of Snowmobiles.
Number of Members:
4.

NEW HAMPSHIRE SNOWMOBILE ASSOCIATION
614 LACONIA ROAD
UNIT 4
TILTON, NH 03276
603-273-0220
Fax: 603-273-0218
nhsaoffice@nhsa.com
www.nhsa.com
• Roger Wright, President
(543) 3669
rogr.wright@comcast.net
• Bob Dohetry, Vice President
(899) 9878
• Marie Hixson, Treasurer
(968) 9038
doo-n@metrocast.net
Description:
An association made up of clubs, distributors and dealers working together to promote the sport of snowmobiling.
Year Founded:
1969

ONTARIO FEDERATION OF SNOWMOBILE CLUBS
501 WELHAM ROAD
UNIT 9
BARRIE, ON, CANADA L4N 8Z6

705-739-7669
Fax: 705-739-5005
info@ofsc.on.ca
www.ofsc.on.ca
Sports Service Founded:
1967
Description:
Dedicated to providing strong leadership and support to member clubs, establishing and maintaining quality snowmobile trails, and furthering the enjoyment of organized snowmobiling.

Soccer (Futsal) Organizations

U.S. FUTSAL
510-836-8733
Fax: 650-242-1036
info@futsal.com
www.futsal.com
• Alexander J C Para, President & CEO
Nature of Sports Service:
The national governing body for the sport of Futsal, in the United States. A rapidly growing derivative of soccer played with five-man teams on a basketball style court, with no walls and a low bouncing ball. The term FUTSAL is the international term used for the game. It is derived from the Spanish or Portuguese word for soccer, FUTbol or FUTebol, and the French or Spanish word for indoor, SALon or SALa.
Sports Service Founded:
1981

Soccer Organizations

AMERICAN YOUTH SOCCER ORGANIZATION
19700 S VERMONT AVENUE
SUITE 103
TORRANCE, CA 90502
800-872-2976
Fax: 310-525-1155
www.ayso.org
• Michael Karon, National President
MKreferee@gmail.com
Number of members:
400,000 children, 250,000, 800 leagues.
Publications:
Whistle Stop, weekly newsletter for referees and referee related positions. Hey Coach!, weekly newsletter for coaches and other coaching positions
Description:
A nationwide non-profit organization that develops and delivers quality youth soccer programs in a fun, family environment.
Year Founded:
1964

CANADA SOCCER
237 MECALFE STREET
OTTAWA, ON, CANADA K2P 1R2
613-237-7678
Fax: 613-237-1516
canadasoccer.com
• Alyson Walker, General Secretary
• Mathieu Chamberland, Chief Operating Officer
• Sean Heffernan, Chief Financial Officer
• Paulo Serna, Chief Communications &

Content Officer
• Jessie Daly, Director, Competitions &
Events
Number of members:
Nearly 1,000,000
Publications:
Canada Soccer Yearbook
Description:
Founded 1912. Strives to lead Canada to
victory and encourages Canadians towards
a life-long passion for soccer.

GEORGIA SOCCER
2323 PERIMETER PARK DRIVE
SUITE 200
ATLANTA, GA 30341-0505
770-452-0505
www.georgiasoccer.org
• Laura Halfpenny, Executive Director
(770) 452-0505
laura@georgiasoccer.org
Year Founded:
1967
Description:
GSSA is the operational governing body
authorized and recognized by US Soccer,
US Youth Soccer and US Amateur Soccer.
Promotes the sport of soccer statewide and
provides educational programs for coaches,
referees and administrators. Helps
coordinate the development of soccer
programs for all levels of play from
recreational up through Olympic
Development and fosters statewide, national
and international competitions and
tournaments. Membership is projected to be
75,000 soccer athletes, 5,000 coaches and
2,500 referees.

MY SOCCER LEAGUE.COM
www.mysoccerleague.com
Nature of Sports Service:
Organization provides youth leagues -
soccer, baseball, football, etc. - with
state-of-the-art, web-based league
scheduling, game results, standings, referee
and field assignments, plus league-wide
communications capabilities in an
easy-to-use and affordable online service.

**NATIONAL INTERCOLLEGIATE SOCCER
OFFICIALS ASSOCIATION**
communications@nisoa.com
nisoa.com
• Ben Trevino, President
btrevino@nisoa.com
• Jude Carr, Vice President
judecarr@gmail.com
Description:
Founded 1964. Promotes the improvement
of intercollegiate and high school soccer
refereeing in the U.S.
Membership Requirements:
All applicants must apply through a local
chapter.
Publications:
Newsletters, Camp Brochure, Be Informed
Brochure, Diagonal System of Control,
Dualsystem of Control, Double Dualsystem
of Control, Pre-game Guide for Each
System, Alternate Official Manual, Assistant
Referee Manual, Information National
Referee Program Directory, Lesson Plans
on all Topics, Critical Incident Tape, Rules
Change Tape
Member Services:
Referee Training Camps, National Referee

Clinics, Regional Clinics, Local Clinics.
Number of Members:
5,000+

NATIONAL SOCCER HALL OF FAME
9200 WORLD CUP WAY
SUITE 600
FRISCO, TX 75033
469-365-0043
info@nationalsoccerhof.com
www.nationalsoccerhof.com
Description:
Celebrates the history, honors the heroes
and preserves the legacy of the sport of
soccer in the United States.
Year Founded:
1950

**OHIO SOUTH YOUTH SOCCER
ASSOCIATION**
7228 COLUMBIA ROAD
SUITE 900
MAINEVILLE, OH 45039
513-576-9555
800-267-9721
Fax: 513-576-1666
office@ohio-soccer.org
www.ohio-soccer.org
• Gordon Henderson, Chief Executive
Director
Publications:
Newsletter

PRO-AM BEACH SOCCER
3032 FULTON STREET
SUITE 2
SAN FRANCISCO, CA 94118
415-308-0603
info@proambeachsoccer.net
proambeachsoccer.net
• Tighe O'Sullivan, CEO
Founded:
2009
Nature of Service:
Beach soccer tournaments

QUICKFOOT
16330 SCENIC CIRCLE
FORNEY, TX 75126
469-728-7700
sandra@quickfoot.com
www.quickfoot.com
Description:
Premier small-sided soccer tournament
organizers.

**SOCCER ASSOCIATION FOR YOUTH
USA**
9220 WORLD CUP WAY
FRISCO, TX 75033
972-334-9300
800-476-2237
www.usyouthsoccer.org
• Skip Gilbert, Chief Executive Officer
Number of Members:
150,000
Member Services:
Organization of Recreational Soccer
Administration on a National level.
Publications:
Ref News, The Tunnel, SAY Coaching
Manual, SAY Rulebook, SAY Coaches Club,
The Touchline
Membership Requirements:
Youth Recreational Soccer Player between
the ages of 4-18

Description:
Founded 1967; provides guidance and
instruction for new participants, an
organization structure to form soccer
leagues and schedule games, andrules and
regulations which will ensure safe, enjoyable
and fair competition forchildren 4-18 years
of age.

**SOCCER, FEDERATION
INTERNATIONALE DE FOOTBALL
ASSOCIATION (FIFA)**
FIFA-STRASSE 20
PO BOX 8044
ZURICH, 8044
contact@fifa.org
www.fifa.com
• Gianni Infantino, President
Description:
International association for the
development of football.
Year Founded:
1904
Member Associations:
211
Publications:
The FIFA Weekly

**TENNESSEE STATE SOCCER
ASSOCIATION**
237 CASTLEWOOD DRIVE
SUITE H
MURFREESBORO, TN 37129
615-590-2200
Fax: 615-590-2205
www.tnsoccer.org
• John Snyder, President
president@tnsoccer.org
• Rene Bustamante, Executive Vice
President
executivevp@tnsoccer.org
Year Founded:
1978
Nature of Sports Service:
Advances and promotes soccer at all levels
in a state well known for football and
baseball.
Number of Members:
41,000 registered players; 5,000 active
coaches, referees, and administrators; 105
local member organizations.

U.S. SOCCER FEDERATION
303 E WACKER DR.
SUITE 207
CHICAGO, IL 60601
312-808-1300
Fax: 312-808-1301
communications@ussoccer.org
www.ussoccer.com
• Cindy Parlow Cone, President
• J.T. Batson, Chief Executive Officer
Description:
Affiliated with International Soccer Body,
FIFA. Governing body for soccer in the U.S.
under the 1978 Sports Amateur Act.
Promotes soccer in U.S. including national
and international games and tournaments.
Administers all U.S. national teams.
Responsible for marketing the U.S. National
Teams' programs as well as marketing
programs for the Youth and Amateur
Divisions. Resolves questions and
controversies not adjustable under rules of
state associations concerned. Manages
U.S. Cup Tournament, National Challenge
Cup, National Amateur Challenge Cup,

National Women's Amateur Cup, National Youth Cup competitions, promotes goodwill through physical

Year Founded:
1913

Number of members:
3,000,000

Membership Requirements:
Must be association, league, approved by National Council.

Notes:
1998 - Awarded 12-year marketing, licensing and television rights to a partnership between International Management Group and Nike, expected to generate $500 million for U.S. Soccer. In 1997, Nike and U.S. Soccer agreed on a 10 year $120 million apparel agreement.

Sponsorships:
Allstate, Anheuser-Busch, AT&T, Chipotle, Coca-Cola, Deloitte, Nike, TRULY Hard Seltzer, Visa, Volkswagen

UNITED SOCCER COACHES
30 W PERSHING ROAD
SUITE 350
KANSAS CITY, MO 64108-2463
816-471-1941
Fax: 816-474-7408
membership@unitedsoccercoaches.org
unitedsoccercoaches.org
• Geoff VanDeusen, Chief Executive Officer
• Beth Sullivan, Chief Financial Officer
• Angie Eliason, Chief Operating Officer

Description:
Since its founding in 1941, United Soccer Coaches (formerly known as the National Soccer Coaches Association of America) has grown to include more than 30,000 members who coach both genders at all levels of the sport. In addition to a national rankings program for colleges and high schools, NSCAA offers an extensive recognition program that presents nearly 10,000 individual awards every year. The NSCAA fulfills its mission of coaching education through a nationwide program of clinics and week-long courses, teaching more than 6,000 soccer coaches each year.

Year Founded:
1941

Publications:
SOCCER JOURNAL, bi-monthly

Membership Requirements:
Individual meeting the requirements and qualifications provided by the by-laws.

Member Services:
Publications, awards, clinics, soccer academy, liability insurance, All America and Coach of the Year selection, national rankings for colleges and high schools, conventions, and discounts.

Number of members:
32,000+

UNITED STATES ADULT SOCCER ASSOCIATION
7000 S HARLEM AVENUE
BRIDGEVIEW, IL 60455
708-529-1175
www.usadultsoccer.com
• Bruce Bode, Executive Director
• John Motta, President
(603) 365-0415

Description:
A member if the United States Soccer Federation, and is currently the only adult soccer member organization of USSF. Promotes the game of soccer for men and women, in an atmosphere of fun, fair play and friendship.

Membership Requirements:
Must be a member of a state soccer association.

Member Services:
Supervises inter-state All-Star games and interstate cup competitions.

Number of Members:
250,000+

US SOCCER FOUNDATION
1140 CONNECTICUT AVENUE NW
SUITE 1200
WASHINGTON, DC 20036
202-872-9277
Fax: 202-872-6655
info@ussoccerfoundation.org
ussoccerfoundation.org
• Ed Foster-Simeon, President/CEO

Description:
National soccer-based youth development program.

US YOUTH SOCCER
9220 WORLD CUP WAY
FRISCO, TX 75033
972-334-9300
800-476-2237
www.usyouthsoccer.org
• Skip Gilbert, CEO

Number of members:
54 State Associations, 10,000 clubs, 2.5 million players.

Member Services:
Coaching program; young player development program; referee program; codes of conduct; Olympic Development Program; American Cup; Soccer Start program; Coach of the Year; Snickers U.S. Youth Soccer National Championship, Youth Referee of the Year. TOP Soccer (Outreach program for players with disabilities.

Publications:
FUEL SOCCER MAGAZINE, young player coaching video; U.S. YOUTH SOCCER NEWS, state soccer publications; U.S. Youth Soccer National Workshop; various fee and low cost brochures and books.

Description:
A non-profit and educational organization whose mission is to foster the physical, mental and emotional growth and development of America's youth through the sport of soccer at al levels of age and competition.

Soccer, Leagues/Teams

CANADIAN PREMIER LEAGUE
204 KING STREET E.
TORONTO, ONTARIO, CANADA M5A 4L4
416-219-2328
canpl.ca
• Mark Noonan, Commissioner
• Scott Mitchell, Chair
• Costa Smyrniotis, EVP, Soccer

Teams:

ATLETICO OTTAWA
1015 BANK STREET
OTTAWA, ON, CANADA K1S 3W7
info@atleticoottawa.club
atleticoottawa.canpl.ca
• Manuel Vega, Chief Executive Officer
• J.D. Ulanowski, Director, Soccer Operations
• Diego Mejia, Head Coach

CAVALRY FC
18011 SPRUCE MEADOWS WAY SW
CALGARY, AB, CANADA T2X 4B7
403-974-4567
info@cavalryfc.ca
cavalryfc.canpl.ca
• Linda A. Southern-Heathcott, Owner, Chair & CEO
• Ian Alisson, President & COO
• Tommy Wheeldon, Jr., General Manager & Head Coach

FC EDMONTON
FC EDMONTON HEAD OFFICE
9725 62 AVE NW
EDMONTON, AB, CANADA T5H 4E2
780-700-2600
info@fcedmonton.com
fcedmonton.canpl.ca
• Jeff Harrop, President
• Lori Clark, Business Operations & Administrative Coordinator
lclark@fcedmonton.com
• Alan Koch, Head Coach

FORGE FC
1 JARVIS ST
HAMILTON, ON, CANADA L8R 3J2
905-527-3674
info@forgefootball.club
forgefc.canpl.ca
• Bobby Smyrniotis, Head Coach & Sporting Director

HFX WANDERERS
301-5562 SACKVILLE STREET
HALIFAX, NS, CANADA B3J 1L1
902-444-3773
info@hfxwanderersfc.ca
hfxwanderersfc.canpl.ca
• Derek Martin, Founder & President
• Patrice Gheisar, Head Coach

PACIFIC FC
3024 GLEN LAKE ROAD
VICTORIA, BC, CANADA V9B 4B4
778-584-6732
memberservices@pacificfc.ca
pacificfc.canpl.ca
• Josh Simpson, President
• Rob Friend, CEO
• Dean Shillington, Chair
• James Merriman, Head Coach

VALOUR FC
INVESTORS GROUP FIELD
315 CHANCELLOR MATHESON ROAD
WINNIPEG, MB, CANADA R3T 1Z2
204-784-7660
memberships@valourfootball.club
valourfc.canpl.ca
• Wade Miller, President & CEO
• Phillip Dos Santos, Head Coach & General Manager

YORK UNITED FC
9929 KEELE ST
104
MAPLE, ON, CANADA L6A 1Y5
905-597-8877
main@yorkunitedfc.ca
yorkunitedfc.ca
• Eduardo Pasquel, Chief Executive Officer
• Ricardo Pasquel, President & General Manager
• Mateus Lima, Head Coach

CANADIAN SOCCER LEAGUE
75 INTERNATIONAL BOULEVARD
SUITE 203
TORONTO, ON, CANADA M9W 6L9
416-675-5256
info@canadiansoccerleague.ca
canadiansoccerleague.ca
• Kevin Blue, CEO & General Secretary
Description:
Semi-professional soccer league in
Southern Ontario.

Teams:

FC CONTINENTALS
505-1000 FINCH AVENUE W
TORONTO, ON, CANADA M3J 2V5
416-650-0019
fc.continentalstoronto@gmail.com
continentalsfc.com
• Igor Demitchev, Founder & Chair
• Denys Yanchuk, Manager
• Andrei Malynchenkov, Head Coach
Home Field:
Centennial Stadium. Seating capacity 2,200.

FC UKRAINE UNITED
CENTENNIAL STADIUM
56 CENTENNIAL PARK ROAD
TORONTO, ON, CANADA M9C 3T3
416-394-8766
admin@fcukraineunited.com
www.fcukraineunited.com
• Mykhailo Gurka, General Manager
• Andrei Malychenkov, Head Coach

SC WATERLOO
RIM PARK
2001 UNIVERSITY AVE E
WATERLOO, ON, CANADA N2K 4K4
519-884-5363
info@scwaterloo.ca
www.scwaterloo.ca
• Tony Kocis, President
• Lazo Dzepina, Manager
Home Stadium:
RIM Park.

SCARBOROUGH SC
75 INTERNATIONAL BLVD
SUITE 203
TORONTO, ON, CANADA M9W 6L9
416-675-6256
info@canadiansoccerleague.ca
• Kiril Dimitrov, General Manager
• Zoran Knezevic, Head Coach
Home Field:
Birchmount Stadium. Seating capacity 2,000.

SERBIAN WHITE EAGLES FC
30 TITAN ROAD
UNIT 15
TORONTO, ON, CANADA M8Z 5Y2
416-252-4762
info@serbianwhiteeagles.ca
serbianwhiteeagles.ca
• Dragan Bakoc, Club President
dragan@serbianwhiteeagles.ca
• Bojan Zoranovic, Head Coach
Home Field:
Centennial Park Stadium. Seating capacity
2,200.

CAPITAL AREA SOCCER LEAGUE
6025 CURRY LN.
LANSING, MI 48911
517-245-7150
forms@caslsoccer.org
caslsoccer.org
• Geoff Heyd, President
President@CASLSoccer.org

Description:
Provides instructional and competitive youth
soccer opportunities that enhance character,
community and loveof the game of soccer.
Also home toover 40,000 players, coaches,
officials, parents, volunteers and supporters.
Year Founded:
1974

MAJOR LEAGUE SOCCER
420 FIFTH AVENUE
7TH FLOOR
NEW YORK, NY 10018
212-450-1200
feedback@mlssoccer.com
www.mlssoccer.com
• Don Garber, Commissioner
• Mark Abbott, President & Deputy
Commissioner
• JoAnn Neale, President & Chief
Administrative Officer

Teams:

ATLANTA UNITED FC
MERCEDES-BENZ STADIUM
1 AMB DR NW
ATLANTA, GA 30313
470-341-1500
info@atlutd.com
www.atlutd.com
• Arthur Blank, Owner/Chair
• Garth Lagerway, President/CEO
• Ronny Deila, Head Coach
Stadium:
Mercedes-Benz Stadium

AUSTIN FC
Q2 STADIUM
10414 MC KALLA PL
AUSTIN, TX 78758
austinfc.com
• Anthony Precourt, Founder/Majority
Owner/CEO
• Andy Loughnane, President
• Nico Estâ€šVez, Head Coach
Stadium:
Q2 Stadium

CF MONTREAL
STADE SAPUTO
4750, RUE SHERBROOKE EST
MONTREAL, QC, CANADA H1V 3S8
514-328-3668
Fax: 514-328-1287
info@cfmontreal.com
cfmontreal.com
• Joey Saputo, Chair
• Laurent Courtois, Head Coach
Home Field:
Saputo Stadium. Seating capacity 19,619.

CHICAGO FIRE FC
1 NORTH DEARBORN ST
SUITE 1300
CHICAGO, IL 60602
888-657-3473
www.chicagofirefc.com
• Joe Mansueto, Owner/Chairman
• Dave Baldwin, President, Business Operations
• Gregg Berhalter, Head Coach
Stadium:
Soldier Field

COLORADO RAPIDS
DICK'S SPORTING GOODS PARK
6000 VICTORY WAY
COMMERCE CITY, CO 80022
303-727-3500
Fax: 303-727-3536
customerservice@dsgpark.com
www.coloradorapids.com

• E. Stanley Kroenke, Owner
• PÂ draig Smith, President
• Chris Armas, Head Coach
Stadium:
Dick's Sporting Goods Park

COLUMBUS CREW SC
96 COLUMBUS CREW WAY
COLUMBUS, OH 43215
www.columbuscrewsc.com
• Tim Bezbatchenko, President/General
Manager
• Wilfried Nancy, Head Coach
Description:
Lower.com Field

D.C. UNITED
AUDI FIELD
100 PTOMAC AVENUE SW
WASHINGTON, DC 20024
202-600-9098
ticketing@dcunited.com
www.dcunited.com
• Jason M. Levien, Co-Chair & Chief Executive
Officer
• Danita Johnson, President, Business
Operations
• Ally Mackay, General Manager & Chief Soccer
Officer
• Troy Lesene, Head Coach
Stadium:
Audi Field

FC CINCINNATI
TQL STADIUM
1501 CENTRAL PKWY
CINCINNATI, OH 45214
513-977-5435
www.fccincinnati.com
• Carl H. Linder, III, CEO/Owner
• Jeff Berding, Co-CEO
• Chris Albright, General Manager
• Pat Noonan, Head Coach
Stadium:
TQL Stadium

FC DALLAS
9200 WORLD CUP WAY
SUITE 202
FRISCO, TX 75033
214-705-6700
Fax: 214-705-0099
customerservice@fcdallas.com
www.fcdallas.com
• Clark Hunt, Chairman/CEO
• Dan Hunt, President
• Eric Quill, Head Coach
Stadium:
Toyota Stadium

HOUSTON DYNAMO
413 BASTROP ST.
HOUSTON, TX 77003
713-276-7500
info@houstondynamo.com
www.houstondynamofc.com
• Ted Segal, Majority Owner & Chair
• Jessica O'Neill, President, Business
Operations
• Pat Onstad, President, Soccer
• Ben Olsen, Head Coach
Stadium:
Shell Energy Stadium

INTER MIAMI CF
1350 NW 55TH ST
FORT LAUDERDALE, FL 33309
communications@intermiamicf.com
www.intermiamicf.com
• Jorge Mas, Managing Owner
• Raul Sanllehi, President, Football Operations
• Xavier Asensi, President, Business Operations
• Javier Mascherano, Head Coach
Stadium:
Chase Stadium (formerly Inter Miami CF
Stadium and DRV PNK Stadium)

LA GALAXY
DIGNITY HEALTH SPORTS PARK
18400 AVALON BOULEVARD
SUITE 200
CARSON, CA 90746
310-630-2200
877-342-5299
Fax: 310-630-2250
customerservice@lagalaxy.com
www.lagalaxy.com
• Will Kuntz, General Manager
• Greg Vanney, Head Coach
Stadium:
Dignity Health Sports Park

LAFC
818 W 7TH STREET
SUITE 1200
LOS ANGELES, CA 90017
213-334-4239
club@lafc.com
www.lafc.com
• John Thorrington, Co-President/General Manager
• Steve Cherundolo, Head Coach
Stadium:
BMO Stadium

MINNESOTA UNITED FC
4150 OLSON MEMORIAL HIGHWAY
SUITE 300
GOLDEN VALLEY, MN 55422
763-476-2237
Fax: 763-331-8788
info@mnufc.com
www.mnufc.com
• Shari Ballard, CEO
• Bill McGuire, Managing Partner
• Khaled El-Ahmad, Chief Soccer Officer & Sporting Director
• Eric Ramsay, Head Coach
Stadium:
Allianz Field

NASHVILLE SC
GEODIS PARK
501 BENTON AVE
NASHVILLE, TN 37203
615-750-8800
info@nashvillesc.com
www.nashvillesc.com
• Lindsey Paola, Chief Business Officer
• Mike Jacobs, General Manager
• B.J. Callaghan, Head Coach
Stadium:
Geodis Park

NEW ENGLAND REVOLUTION
GILLETTE STADIUM
ONE PATRIOT PLACE
FOXBOROUGH, MA 02035
508-543-8200
customerservice@revolutionsoccer.net
www.revolutionsoccer.net
• Brian Bilello, President
• Curt Onalfo, Sporting Director
• Caleb Porter, Head Coach
Stadium:
Gillette Stadium

NEW YORK CITY FC
600 THIRD AVENUE
30TH FLOOR
NEW YORK, NY 10016
212-738-5900
nycfc@nycfc.com
www.nycfc.com
• Brad Sims, CEO
• Jennifer O'Sullivan, COO
• Pascal Jansen, Head Coach
Stadium:
Yankee Stadium. Seating capacity: 28,743 (expandable to 47,309).

NEW YORK RED BULLS
SPORTS ILLUSTRATED STADIUM
600 CAPE MAY STREET
HARRISON, NJ 07029
888-370-7287
training@newyorkredbulls.com
www.newyorkredbulls.com
• Jochen Schneider, Head of Sport
• Julian De Guzman, Sporting Director
• Sandro Schwarz, Head Coach
Stadium:
Sports Illustrated Stadium (formerly Red Bull Arena)

ORLANDO CITY
655 W CHURCH STREET
ORLANDO, FL 32805
855-675-2489
Fax: 407-745-5376
www.orlandocitysc.com
• Jarrod Dillon, President, Business Operations
• Luiz Muzzi, EVP, Soccer Operations/GM
• Oscar Pareja, Head Coach
Stadium:
Inter&Co Stadium (formerly Exploria Stadium)

PHILADELPHIA UNION
2501 SEAPORT DRIVE
BH SUITE 100
CHESTER, PA 19013
610-497-1657
Fax: 610-497-3309
fanservices@philadelphiaunion.com
www.philadelphiaunion.com
• Jay Sugarman, Chair/Principal Owner
• Tim McDermott, President
• Ernst Tanner, Sporting Director
• Bradley Carnell, Head Coach
Stadium:
Subaru Park

PORTLAND TIMBERS
1844 SW MORRISON
PORTLAND, OR 97205
503-553-5400
Fax: 503-553-5405
www.timbers.com
• Merritt Paulson, Owner
• Heather Davis, CEO
• Ned Grabavoy, General Manager
• Phil Neville, Head Coach
Stadium:
Providence Park

REAL SALT LAKE
9256 SOUTH STATE STREET
SANDY, UT 84070
801-727-2700
Fax: 801-727-1469
FanRelations@RSL.com
www.rsl.com
• Ryan Smith, Co-Owner
• David S. Blitzer, Co-Owner
• John Kimball, President
• Kurt Schmid, Sporting Director
• Pablo Mastroeni, Head Coach
Stadium:
America First Field

SAN JOSE EARTHQUAKES
PAYPAL PARK
1123 COLEMAN AVENUE
SAN JOSE, CA 95110
408-556-7700
Fax: 408-796-5242
www.sjearthquakes.com
• John Fisher, Managing Partner/Board Member
• Chris Leitch, General Manager
• Luchi Gonzalez, Head Coach
Stadium:
PayPal Pal

SEATTLE SOUNDERS FC
800 OCCIDENTAL AVE S
SEATTLE, WA 98056

877-657-4625
customerservice@soundersfc.com
www.soundersfc.com
• Craig Waibel, General Manager/Chief Soccer Officer
• Brian Schmetzer, Head Coach
Stadium:
Lumen Field

SPORTING KANSAS CITY
2020 BALTIMORE AVENUE
KANSAS CITY, MO 64108
913-387-3400
888-452-4625
clientservices@sportingkc.com
www.sportingkc.com
• Peter Vermes, Head Coach
Stadium:
Children's Mercy Park

TORONTO FC
BMO FIELD
170 PRINCES' BOULEVARD
TORONTO, ON, CANADA M6K 3C3
416-360-4625
www.torontofc.ca
• Gabriel Gervais, President & CEO
• Laurent Courtois, Head Coach
• Vincenzo Benvenuto, Goalkeeper Coach
Home Field:
BMO Field. Seating capacity 30,991.

VANCOUVER WHITECAPS FC
201 - 788 BEATTY ST
VANCOUVER, BC, CANADA V6B 2M1
604-669-9283
Fax: 604-684-5173
info@whitecapsfc.com
www.whitecapsfc.com
• Axel Schuster, CEO & Sporting Director
• Manav Deol, General Counsel
• Jesper Sorensen, Head Coach
Home Field:
BC Place. Seating capacity 54,500.

NATIONAL WOMEN'S SOCCER LEAGUE
1556 S MICHIGAN AVENUE
FLOOR 2
CHICAGO, IL 60605
312-549-8900
info@nwslsoccer.com
www.nwslsoccer.com
• Jessica Berman, Commissioner
• Bill Ordower, Chief Legal Officer
Year Founded:
2012
Decsription:
The highest level of women's professional soccer league in North America. The mission is to be the premier women's soccer league in the world, and the global standard by which women's professional sports are measured.

Teams:

CHICAGO RED STARS
SEATGEEK STADIUM
7000 SOUTH HARLEM AVENUE
BRIDGEVIEW, IL 60455
312-241-2069
info@chicagoredstars.com
chicagoredstars.com
• Richard Fuez, General Manager
Stadium:
SeatGeek Stadium

HOUSTON DASH
2200 TEXAS AVE.
HOUSTON, TX 77003
info@houstondynamo.com
www.houstondynamo.com/houstondash

- Clarke Ricky, General Manager
- Emma Wright-Cates, Assistant Coach

Stadium:
Shell Energy Stadium

NJ/NY GOTHAM FC
24 MELANIE LANE
WHIPPANY, NJ 07981
888-723-2849
contact@gothamfc.com
gothamfc.com
- Yael Averbuch West, General Manager
- Juan Carlos Amoros, Head Coach

Stadium:
Sports Illustrated Stadium

NORTH CAROLINA COURAGE
WAKEMED SOCCER PARK
101 SOCCER PARK DRIVE
CARY, NC 27511
919-459-8144
www.nccourage.com
- Francie Gottsegen, Club President
- Sean Nahas, Head Coach

Stadium:
First Horizon Stadium at WakeMed Soccer Park.
Seating capacity: 10,000.

OL REIGN
800 OCCIDENTAL AVE S
SEATTLE, WA 98134
206-281-7555
info@olreign.com
www.olreign.com
- Laura Harvey, Head Coach

Stadium:
Lumen Field

ORLANDO PRIDE
655 W CHURCH ST
ORLANDO, FL 32805
1-855-ORL-CITY
Fax: 407-745-5376
orlandocitysc.com/pride
- Haley Carter, VP, Soccer Operations &
General Manager
- Seb Hines, Head Coach

Stadium:
Inter&Co Stadium (formerly Exploria Stadium)

PORTLAND THORNS FC
1844 SW MORRISON
PORTLAND, OR 97205
503-553-5400
Fax: 503-553-5405
www.timbers.com/thornsfc
- Jeff Agoos, General Manager & President,
Operations
- Rob Gale, Head Coach

Stadium:
Providence Park

RACING LOUISVILLE FC
801 EDITH ROAD
LOUISVILLE, KY 40206
502-568-2489
info@loucity.com
racingloufc.com
- John Neace, Chair & CEO
- James O'Connor, President
- Caitlyn Milby, General Manager
- Beverly Yanez, Head Coach

Stadium:
Lynn Family Stadium

USL CHAMPIONSHIP
1715 N WESTSHORE BOULEVARD
SUITE 825
TAMPA, FL 33607
www.uslchampionship.com
- Jeremy Alumbaugh, Chair
- Alec Papadakis, CEO & Managing Partner
- Justin Papdakis, Chief Operating Officer

Founded:
2011

Teams:

ATLANTA UNITED 2
FIFTH THIRD BANK STADIUM
3200 GEORGE BUSBEE PKWY NW
ATLANTA, GA 30144
470-578-4849
www.atlutd.com/2
- Steve Cooke, Head Coach

Stadium:
Fifth Third Bank Stadium. Seating capacity:
8,318.

BIRMINGHAM LEGION FC
2226 1ST AVE. S
SUITE 101
BIRMINGHAM, AL 35233
205-600-0496
info@bhmlegion.com
www.bhmlegion.com
- Jay Heaps, President/General Manager
- Tom Soehn, Head Coach & Technical Director

Stadium:
Protective Stadium

CHARLESTON BATTERY
75 PORT CITY LANDING
SUITE 320
MT. PLEASANT, SC 29464
843-971-4625
contact@charlestonbattery.com
charlestonbattery.com
- Ben Pirmann, Head Coach

Stadium:
Patriots Point Soccer Complex. Seating
capacity: 5,000.

CHARLOTTE INDEPENDENCE
AMERICAN LEGION MEMORIAL STADIUM
1218-1238 ARMORY DR
CHARLOTTE, NC 28204
704-206-1515
charlotteindependence@gmail.com
www.charlotteindependence.com
- Jim McPhilliamy, CEO & Managing Partner
- Tim Schuldt, COO & President
- Mike Jeffries, Head Coach

Stadium:
American Legion Memorial Stadium. Seating
capacity: 10,500.

COLORADO SPRINGS SWITCHBACKS
FC
234 N TEJON STREET
COLORADO SPRINGS, CO 80903
719-368-8480
info@switchbacksfc.com
switchbacksfc.com
- Dan Crandall, Business Development Director
- Anthony Mirabal, Director, Ticket Operations
- Stephen Hogan, Sporting Director
- James Chambers, Head Coach

Stadium:
Weidner Field. Seating capacity: 8,000.

EL PASO LOCOMOTIVE FC
SOUTHWEST UNIVERSITY PARK
1 BALLPARK PLAZA
EL PASO, TX 79901
915-235-4625
info@eplocomotivefc.com
www.eplocomotivefc.com
- Alan Ledford, President
- Andrew Forrest, General Manager/Business &
Technical Ops.
- Ray Saari, Head Coach & Technical Director

Stadium:
Southwest University Park. Seating capacity:
7,500.

FC TULSA
ONEOK FIELD
TULSA, OK 74120
918-744-5998
info@fctulsa.com
www.fctulsa.com
- Ryan Craft, President
- Caleb Sewell, Sporting Director & General
Manager
- Luke Spencer, Head Coach

Stadium:
ONEOK Field. Seating capacity: 7,833.

HARTFORD ATHLETIC
TRINITY HEALTH STADIUM
250 HUYSHOPE AVENUE
HARTFORD, CT 06106
860-298-9233
info@hartfordathletic.com
www.hartfordathletic.com
- Bruce Mandell, Chair
- Nick Sakiewicz, Chief Executive Officer
- Brendan Burke, Head Coach & General
Manager

Stadium:
Trinity Health Stadium

INDY ELEVEN
47 S PENNSYLVANIA STREET
SUITE 611
INDIANAPOLIS, IN 46204
317-685-1100
Fax: 317-635-1100
www.indyeleven.com
- Bruce Mandell, Owner/Chair
- Nick Sakiewicz, President/CEO
- Brendan Burke, Head Coach

Stadium:
Michael A. Carroll Stadium. Seating capacity:
10,524 (expanded to 12,111).

LAS VEGAS LIGHTS FC
CASHMAN FIELD
850 N LAS VEGAS BOULEVARD
LAS VEGAS, NV 89101
702-728-4625
www.lasvegaslightsfc.com
- Jose Bautista, Owner
- Gianleonardo Neglia, Sporting Director
- Antonio Nocerino, Head Coach

Stadium:
Cashman Field. Seating capacity: 9,334.

LOUDOUN UNITED FC
42095 LOUDOUN UNITED DRIVE
LEESBURG, VA 20175
202-655-2842
info@loudoununitedfc.com
www.loudoununitedfc.com
- Angela Baroni Berzonsky, Executive Business
Officer
- Ryan Martin, Head Coach

Stadium:
Segra Field. Seating capacity: 5,000.

LOUISVILLE CITY FC
LYNN FAMILY SPORTS VISION & TRAINING
CENTER
801 EDITH ROAD
LOUISVILLE, KY 40206
502-384-8799
info@loucity.com
www.loucity.com
- John Neace, Chair & CEO
- James O'Connor, President
- Danny Cruz, Head Coach

Stadium:
Lynn Family Stadium. Seating capacity: 15,304.

MIAMI FC
PITBULL STADIUM
11200 SOUTHWEST 8TH STREET
WESTCHESTER, FL 33199
www.miamifc.com

- Ricardo Silva, Owner
- Mario Roitman, President
- Gaston Maddoni, Head Coach
Stadium:
Pitbull Stadium (formerly FIU Stadium and Riccardo Silva Stadium). Seating capacity: 20,000.

MONTEREY BAY FC
CARDINALE STADIUM
4441 2ND AVENUE
SEASIDE, CA 93955
831-324-2560
www.montereybayfc.com
- Ray Beshoff, Owner/Chair
- Mike DiGiulio, President
- Jordan Stewart, Head Coach
Stadium:
Cardinale Stadium. Seating capacity: 6,000.

NEW MEXICO UNITED
1601 AVENIDA CESAR CHAVEZ SE
ALBUQUERQUE, NM 87106
505-209-7529
info@newmexicoutd.com
www.newmexicoutd.com
- Peter Trevisani, Owner & CEO
- Ron Patel, President
  ron@newmexicoutd.com
- Dennis Sanchez, Head Coach
Stadium:
Rio Grande Credit Union Field at Isotopes Park. Seating capacity: 13,500.

NEW YORK RED BULLS II
MSU SOCCER PARK
1 NORMAL AVE
MONTCLAIR, NJ 07043
877-727-6223
www.newyorkredbulls.com/2
- Julian De Guzman, Sporting Director
Stadium:
MSU Soccer Park at Pittser Field. Seating capacity: 5,000.

OAKLAND ROOTS SC
8TH STREET AND 5TH AVENUE
OAKLAND, CA 94607
510-488-1144
info@rootssc.com
oaklandrootssc.com
- Gavin Glinton, Head Coach
Stadium:
Laney College Football Stadium. Seating capacity: 5,500.

OKC ENERGY FC
120 ROBERT S KERR AVE
SUITE 701
OKLAHOMA CITY, OK 73102
405-235-5425
Info@EnergyFC.com
www.energyfc.com
- Court Jeske, President
- Leigh Veidman, Head Coach
Stadium:
Taft Stadium. Seating capacity: 7,500.

ORANGE COUNTY SC
ORANGE COUNTY SOCCER CLUB
20 FAIRBANKS
SUITE 181
IRVINE, CA 92618
949-647-4625
www.orangecountysoccer.com
- James Keston, Owner & CEO
- Peter Nugent, General Manager/President, Soccer Operations
- Danny Stone, Head Coach
Stadium:
Championship Soccer Stadium. Seating capacity: 5,500.

PHOENIX RISING FC
3801 EAST WASHINGTON
PHOENIX, AZ 85034
623-594-9606
info@phxrisingfc.com
www.phxrisingfc.com
- Pablo Prichard, Chief Executive Officer
- Brandon McCarthy, Sporting Director
- Pa-Modou Kah, Head Coach
Stadium:
Phoenix Rising Soccer Stadium. Seating capacity: 10,000.

PITTSBURGH RIVERHOUNDS SC
HIGHMARK STADIUM
510 W STATION SQUARE DRIVE
PITTSBURGH, PA 15219
412-224-4900
www.riverhounds.com
- Tuffy Shallenberger, Owner
- Jeff Garner, President
- Bob Lilley, Head Coach
Stadium:
Highmark Stadium. Seating capacity: 5,000.

REAL MONARCHS SLC
ZIONS BANK STADIUM
HERRIMAN, UT 84096
801-727-2700
Fax: 801-727-1469
www.rsl.com/monarchs
- Jacob Haueter, President
- Tony Beltran, General Manager
- Mark Lowry, Head Coach
Stadium:
Zions Bank Stadium. Seating capacity: 5,000.

SACRAMENTO REPUBLIC FC
428 J STREET
SUITE 700
SACRAMENTO, CA 95814
916-307-6100
goal@sacrepublicfc.com
www.sacrepublicfc.com
- Wilton Rancheria, Majority Owner
- Kevin Nagle, Managing Partner
- Todd Dunivant, President & General Manager
- Neill Collins, Head Coach
Stadium:
Heart Health Park. Seating capacity: 11,569.

SAN ANTONIO FC
TOYOTA FIELD
5106 DAVID EDWARDS DRIVE
SAN ANTONIO, TX 78233
www.sanantoniofc.com
- Marco Ferruzzi, Sporting Director
- Carlos Llamosa, Head Coach
Stadium:
Toyota Field. Seating capacity: 8,296.

SANTA BARBARA SKY FX
SANTA BARBARA, CA 93109
info@santabarbaraskyfc.com
www.santabarbaraskyfc.com
- Peter Moore, Founding Owner
- Sheralyn Baltes, Chief Operating Officer
Formerly Known As:
Memphis 901 FC; rights transferred November 13, 2024.

SPORTING KC CITY II
2020 BALTIMORE AVENUE
KANSAS CITY, MO 64108
913-387-3400
888-452-4625
youth@sportingkc.com
www.sportingkc.com/skcii
- Istvan Urbanyi, Head Coach
Stadium:
Rock Chalk Park.

TACOMA DEFIANCE
159 S. JACKSON STREET
SUITE 200
SEATTLE, WA 98104
253-752-7707
www.soundersfc.com/tacoma-defiance/
- Herve Diese, Head Coach
Stadium:
Cheney Stadium. Seating capacity: 6,500.

TAMPA BAY ROWDIES
230 1ST STREET SE
ST. PETERSBURG, FL 33701
727-222-2000
Fax: 813-282-3800
info@rowdiessoccer.com
www.rowdiessoccer.com
- Ryan Helfrick, President
- Robbie Neilson, Head Coach
Stadium:
Al Lang Stadium. Seating capacity: 7,227.

VENTURA COUNTY FC
DIGNITY HEALTH SPORTS PARK
18400 AVALON BOULEVARD
SUITE 200
CARSON, CA 90746
310-630-2000
Fax: 310-630-2250
vcfcpro.com
- Matt Taylor, Head Coach
Formerly Known As:
LA Galaxy II (2014-2024).
Stadium:
Dignity Health Sports Park. Seating capacity: 27,000.

USL LEAGUE ONE
1715 N WESTSHORE BOULEVARD
SUITE 825
TAMPA, FL 33607
www.uslleagueone.com
- Lee O'Neill, President
- Valerie Panou, Sr. Vice President, Communications & P.R.
Will.Kuhns@uslsoccer.com

Teams:

CHATTANOOGA RED WOLVES SC
6739 RINGGOLD RD
CHATTANOOGA, TN 37412
423-443-5516
www.chattanoogaredwolves-sc.com
- Bob Martino, Chair & Owner
- Sean McDaniel, President & General Manager
- Scott Mackenzie, Head Coach & Technical Director
Stadium:
CHI Memorial Stadium. Seating capacity: 5,500.

FORWARD MADISON FC
917 E MIFFLIN STREET
MADISON, WI 53703
608-204-0855
info@forwardmadisonfc.com
forwardmadisonfc.com
- Conor Caloia, Owner & COO
  conor@bigtopbaseball.com
- Vern Stenman, President
- Matt Glaesar, Technical Director/Head Coach
Stadium:
Breese Stevens Field. Seating capacity: 5,000.

GREENVILLE TRIUMPH
22 S. MAIN STREET
GREENVILLE, SC 29601
864-203-0565
customerservice@greenvilletriumph.com
greenvilletriumph.com
- Chris Lewis, President
- Rick Wright, Head Coach & Technical Director
Stadium:
Paladin Stadium. Seating capacity: 16,000.

INTER MIAMI CF II
CHASE STADIUM
1350 NW 55TH STREET
FORT LAUDERDALE, FL 33309
www.intermiamicf.com/intermiamicfii
• Ledesma Cristiano, Head Coach
• Javier Morales, Assistant Coach
Stadium:
Chase Stadium. Seating capacity: 21,550.

NEW ENGLAND REVOLUTION II
GILLETTE STADIUM
ONE PATRIOT PLACE
FOXBOROUGH, MA 02035
508-543-8200
revolutionsoccer.net/revolutionii
• Richie Williams, Head Coach
Stadium:
Gillette Stadium. Seating capacity: 20,000.

NORTH CAROLINA FC
801 CORPORATE CENTER DRIVE
SUITE 320
RALEIGH, NC 27607
919-459-8144
www.northcarolinafc.com
• Steve Malik, Owner & Chair
• Francie Gottsegen, President
• John Bradford, Head Coach & Sporting Director
Stadium:
First Horizon Stadium at WakeMed Soccer Park. Seating capacity: 10,000.

NORTH TEXAS FC
1000 BALLPARK WAY
ARLINGTON, TX 76011
469-365-0000
fcdallas.com/northtexassc
• Matt Denny, General Manager
• John Gall, Head Coach
Stadium:
Choctaw Stadium. Seating capacity: 48,114.

RICHMOND KICKERS
2001 MAYWILL STREET
SUITE 205
RICHMOND, VA 23230
804-644-5425
richmondkickers.com
• Rob Ukrop, Chair & CEO
• Camp Peery, President & COO
• Darren Sawatzky, Chief Sporting Officer/Head Coach
Stadium:
City Stadium. Seating capacity: 6,000.

SOUTH GEORGIA TORMENTA FC
100 TORMENTA WAY
STATESBORO, GA 30458
news@tormentafc.com
www.tormentafc.com
• Darin Van Tassell, President/Owner
• Ian Cameron, Head Coach/Technical Director
Stadium:
Optim Sports Medicine Field at Tormenta Stadium. Seating capacity: 5,300.

TORONTO FC II
BMO FIELD
170 PRINCES' BOULEVARD
TORONTO, ON, CANADA M6K 3C3
416-360-4625
www.torontofc.ca/tfc2/
• Gianni Cimini, Head Coach
Home Stadium:
BMO Field. Seating capacity 30,991.

TUCSON FC
3600 S COUNTRY CLUB RD
TUCSON, AZ 85713
520-600-3095
info@fctucson.com
www.fctucson.com

• Jon Pearlman, Founder & President
• Kyle Cornell, Chief Operating Officer
Stadium:
Kino North Stadium. Seating capacity of 3,200.

UNION OMAHA
12356 BALLPARK WAY
PAPILLION, NE 68046
402-884-8040
goal@unionomaha.com
unionomaha.com
• Martie Cordaro, President
• Dominic Casciato, Head Coach
Stadium:
Werner Park. Seating capacity: 9,023.

USL LEAGUE TWO
1715 N WESTSHORE BOULEVARD
SUITE 825
TAMPA, FL 33607
www.uslleaguetwo.com
• Chris Inman, Sr. Director, Operations
• Jason Collister, Director, Sporting Development
• Kike Molina, Manager, Operations
Description:
A development league in the U.S. soccer league system.
Founded:
1995
Number of Teams:
113

Teams:

AC CONNECTICUT
153 S MAIN STREET
NEWTOWN, CT 06470
203-270-3316
www.acconnecticut.com
• Peter D'Amico, Owner & President
• Robin Schuppert, Managing Director
• Antony Howard, Director of Coaching, Boys U15-19
Stadium:
Trinity Health Stadium (formerly Dillon Stadium)

ACADEMIA SOCCER CLUB
PO BOX 2619
TURLOCK, CA 95381
916-904-0036
info@academicasc.com
www.academicasc.com
• Simon Bettencourt, President
• Trisha Gonzales, Head Coach
Stadium:
Academica Field

AFC ANN ARBOR
3676 S STATE STREET
ANN ARBOR, MI 48108
734-408-1627
info@afcannarbor.com
www.afcannarbor.com
• Kevin Taylor, Head Coach
Stadium:
Hollway Field, Pioneer HS.

AHFC ROYALS
3601 CAMPBELL ROAD
HOUSTON, TX 77080
713-939-7473
sgreen@albionhurricanes.org
www.ahfcroyals.com
• James Clarkson, Head Coach

ASHEVILLE CITY SC
ASHEVILLE, NC
management@ashevillecitysc.com
ashevillecitysc.com
• Scott Wells, Head Coach

Stadium:
Greenwood Field, UNCA campus.

BLACK ROCK FC
APPLEJACK STADIUM
340 REC PARK RD
MANCHESTER CENTER, VT 05255
802-362-1439
www.blackrockfc.org
• Brad Agoos, Head Coach

BOSTON BOLTS
UMASS MOUNT IDA CAMPUS
100 CARLSON AVE
NEWTON, MA 02459
www.bostonbolts.com/programs/usl2
• Aidan Byrne, Head Coach
Stadium:
Alumni Field, capacity of 2,000.

BRAVE SC
H.G. MORSE RANGE STADIUM
251 BUFFALO TRAIL
THE VILLAGES, FL 32162
352-561-8239
info@bravesc.com
www.bravesc.com
• Anderson DaSilva, Sporting Director
Formerly:
The Villages SC
Stadium:
H.G. Morse Range Stadium

BRAZOS VALLEY CAVALRY FC
525 W CARSON STREET
BRYAN, TX 77801
979-779-7529
www.bvcavalryfc.com
• Uri Geva, Founder/Co-Owner
uri@bvcavalry.com
• Sam Bytheway, General Manager
• Gareth Glick, Head Coach
Soccer.Coach@bvcavalry.com
Stadium:
Edible Field

CALGARY FOOTHILLS FC
111 EXPLORATION AVE SE
CALGARY, AB, CANADA T3S 0B6
403-225-9388
admin@gofoothills.ca
gofoothills.ca
• Jay Wheeldon, Technical Director
jay@gofoothills.ca

CAPITAL FC ATLETICO
1678 LIBERTY STREET SE
SALEM, OR 97302
503-673-6708
www.cfcsalem.com
• Matthew Holstege, President
• Collin Box, Executive Director
• Joe Wentworth, Technical Director
Stadium:
John Chambers Field at CFC Complex

CEDAR STARS RUSH
3 EMPIRE BOULEVARD
CARLSTADT, NJ 27429
201-939-0651
info@cedarstarsrush.com
www.cedarstarsrush.com
• Justin Miller, Chief Executive Officer
jmiller@rushsoccer.com
• Anthony Nixon, Sporting Director/Head Coach

CHARLOTTE EAGLES
8510 MCALPINE PARK DRIVE
SUITE 109
CHARLOTTE, NC 28211
704-841-8644
contact@charlotteeagles.com
www.charlotteeagles.com

- Michael Kovach, Head Coach
mkovach@charlotteeagles.com

CHARLOTTE INDEPENDENCE 2
MANCHESTER MEADOWS SOCCER
COMPLEX
337 E MT GALLANT RD
ROCK HILL, SC 29730
704-206-1519
info@independencesoccer.club
www.independencesoccer.club
- Jim McPhilliamy, CEO & Managing Partner
- Tim Schuldt, COO & President

CHICAGO FC UNITED
3090 N LAKE TERRACE
GLENVIEW, IL 60026
847-386-6579
Fax: 847-410-3926
www.chicagofcunited.com
- David Roth, Executive Director

CINCINNATI DUTCH LIONS
7450 INDUSTRIAL ROAD
FLORENCE, KY 41042-2916
859-525-0887
www.uslleaguetwo.com/page/show/4731431-cin
cinnati-dutch-lions
- Sid Van Druenen, Director, Sporting
Development
- Kevin Minkovitz, Manager, Operations - USL
League Two

COLORADO RUSH
9665 ROXBOROUGH PARK RD
LITTLETON, CO 80125
720-624-9000
info@coloradorush.com
www.coloradorush.com/coloradorushsc
- Carroll John, President
jcarroll@coloradorush.com

CORPUS CHRISTI FC
10201 S PADRE ISLAND DRIVE
SUITE 205
CORPUS CHRISTI, TX 78418
361-214-3236
corpuscfc.com
- Kingsley Okonkwo, President
- Ignacio Dicun, Head Coach
- Manuel Iwabuchi, Co-Head Coach
Stadium:
Cabaniss Field

DALTON RED WOLVES SC
6739 RINGGOLD ROAD
SUITE B, C, D
CHATTANOOGA, TN 37412
423-443-5516
www.chattanoogaredwolves-sc.com
- Saif Alsafeer, Head Coach
Stadium:
Lakeshore Park

DAYTON DUTCH LIONS
5995 STUDENT STREET
WEST CARROLLTON CITY, OH 45449
937-331-8444
ddlfc.com
- Suresh Gupta, Owner
- Erik Tammer, Owner
- Mike Mossel, Owner
- Hans Pascoal, Head Coach
Stadium:
Dayton Outpatient Center Stadium

DES MOINES MENACE
1459 GRAND AVENUE
DES MOINES, IA 50309
515-457-6367
www.menacesoccer.com
- Charlie Bales, General Manager
(515) 457-6285
- Sydney Tatam, Soccer Operations Manager

(515) 457-6367
sydney.tatam@menacesoccer.com
Stadium:
Valley Stadium

EAST ATLANTA FC
admin@eastatlantafc.com
www.eastatlantafc.com
- Kelly Shirah, Executive Director
kshirah@eastatlantafc.com
- Sam Walker, Head Coach
swalker@eastatlantafc.com
Stadium:
Friends Field

FA EURO NEW YORK
7707 17TH AVENUE
BROOKLYN, NY 11214
718-331-6308
management@faeuro.com
faeuro.com
- Joe Balsamo, Owner & Head Coach
- Marco Balsamo, Owner
Stadium:
Poly Prep Country Day School

FC BASCOME BERMUDA
www.fcbascomebermuda.com
- Andrew Bascome, President & Director,
Football
- Karl Roberts, Operations Manager

FC FLORIDA U23
PORT ST. LUCIE, FL
info@fcflorida.com
www.fcflorida.com
- Cam Omsberg, Academy Director & Coach
- Cesar Montes, Director, Coaching

FC MANITOBA
WINNIPEG, MB, CANADA
www.footballclubmanitoba.ca
- Walter Obregon, Head Coach
Home Stadium:
Ralph Cantafio Soccer Complex. Seating
capacity 2,000.

FC MIAMI CITY
CENTRAL BROWARD REGIONAL PARK
3700 NW 11TH PLACE
LAUDERHILL, FL 33311
contact@fcmiamicity.com
www.fcmiamicity.com
- Ravy Truchot, President
- Jon Colino, Head Coach
Stadium:
Central Broward Park. Seating capacity: 20,000.

FLINT CITY BUCKS
ATWOOD STADIUM AT KETTERING
UNIVERSITY
701 UNIVERSITY AVENUE
FLINT, MI 48503
810-666-2515
www.flintcitybucks.com
- Dan Duggan, Chair & CEO
- Costa Papista, President
- Paul Doroh, Head Coach
Stadium:
Atwood Stadium at Kettering University

FLORIDA ELITE SA
FLORIDA ELITE SOCCER ACADEMY
P.O. BOX 57065
JACKSONVILLE, FL 32241
info@floridaelitesa.com
www.floridaelitesa.com
- Rodney Perry, Director, Coaching
Stadium:
Mandarin High School

GOLDEN STATE FORCE FC
fcgoldenstateforce.com

- Alex Lujan, Director, Football
- Robert Friedland, Head Coach
Rio Hondo College

HOUSTON FC
3038 N FRY RD
SUITE 18
KATY, TX 77449
512-784-2977
CTalbot@houstonfc-tx.com
www.houstonfctx.com
- Bruce Talbot, Head Coach/General Manager,
Youth Dir. of Coaching
(512) 709-8243
Stadium:
Westbury Christian Athletic Complex

KAW VALLEY FC
3120 MESA WAY
SUITE C
LAWRENCE, KANSAS 66049
785-749-0401
sportingkawvalley@gmail.com
www.uslleaguetwo.com/page/show/7332184-ka
w-valley-fc
- Alex Nichols, Head Coach
Stadium:
Rock Chalk Park

LANE UNITED FC
EUGENE, OR 97401
www.laneutd.com
- John Galas, Sporting Director & Head Coach
- Dave Galas, Managing Director
Stadium:
Civic Park

LEHIGH VALLEY UNITED
1344 N SHERMAN STREET
ALLENTOWN, PA 18109
610-841-0080
info@lehighvalleyunited.com
www.lehighvalleyunited.com
- Andrew Adlard, Head Coach
Stadium:
Rocco Calvo Field at Moravian College

LIONSBRIDGE FC
TOWNEBANK STADIUM
NEWPORT NEWS, VA 23606
lionsbridgefc@gmail.com
www.lionsbridgefc.com
- Chris Whalley, Head Coach
Stadium:
TowneBank Stadium

LONG ISLAND ROUGH RIDERS
1 CHARLES LINDBERGH AVENUE
UNIONDALE, NY 11553
516-622-8499
info@liroughriders.com
liroughriders.com
- Peter Zaratin, President
(516) 622-3900
pzaratin@globalconcepts.com
- Tanner Sands, General Manager
Tanner.Sands@globalconcepts.com
- Tom Bowen, Head Coach
Stadium:
Hofstra University Soccer Stadium

LOUISVILLE CITY FC U23
801 EDITH ROAD
LOUISVILLE, KY 40206
502-384-8799
info@loucity.com
www.loucity.com
- Mario Sanchez, Head Coach
Stadium:
Lynn Family Stadium

MANHATTAN SC
NEW YORK, NY

877-423-4672
soccer@manhattansc.org
www.manhattansc.org
• Rich Corvino, Executive Director
rcorvino@manhattansc.org
• Ray Selvadurai, Head Coach
Stadium:
Gaelic Park

MICHIANA FUTBOL CLUB
GRANGER, IN 46530
MichianaLionsFC@gmail.com
www.michianalionsfc.com
• Ritchie Jeune, Owner
• Shek Borkowski, Head Coach
Stadium:
Leighton Stadium

MISSISSIPPI BRILLA FC
PO BOX 281
CLINTON, MS 39060
601-924-3475
Fax: 601-488-0226
info@msbrillafc.org
brillasoccer.org
• Rusty Bryant, Executive Director & General Manager
rusty.bryant@brillasoccer.org
• Scott Taylor, VP, Operations
scott.taylor@brillasoccer.org
Stadium:
Clinton Arrow Stadium

NEW MEXICO UNITED U23
1601 AVENIDA CESAR CHAVEZ SE
ALBUQUERQUE, NM 87106
505-209-7529
info@newmexicoutd.com
www.newmexicoutd.com
• Peter Trevisani, Owner/President
• Ron Patel, President
ron@newmexicoutd.com
• Dennis Sanchez, Head Coach

NEW YORK RED BULLS U23
RED BULL ARENA
600 CAPE MAY STREET
HARRISON, NJ 07029
888-370-7287
training@newyorkredbulls.com
www.redbullsacademy.com
• Rob Elliott, Head Coach
Stadium:
Red Bull Training Facility

NORTH CAROLINA FC U23
801 CORPORATE CENTER DRIVE
SUITE 320
RALEIGH, NC 27607
919-459-8144
www.northcarolinafc.com
• Steve Malik, Chair & Owner
• John Bradford, Head Coach & Sporting Director
Stadium:
WakeMed Soccer Park

NORTHERN VIRGINIA FC
LEESBURG, VA
703-828-8149
info@novafc.org
www.novafcalliance.club
• Kareem Sheta, Head Coach & Director, Soccer
Stadium:
VAR Sportsplex

OAKLAND COUNTY FC
ROYAL OAK HIGH SCHOOL STADIUM
1500 LEXINGTON BLVD
ROYAL OAK, MI 48073
248-629-0251
info@oaklandcountyfc.com
www.oaklandcountyfc.com
• Steve Walker, Head Coach

Stadium:
Royal Oak High School

OCEAN CITY NOR'EASTERS
200 6TH STREET
OCEAN CITY, NJ 08226
609-432-8271
Fax: 609-399-4784
info@oceancityfc.com
www.oceancityfc.com
• Giancarlo Granese, Sr., President
• Giancarlo Granese, Jr., General Manager
• Kevin Nuss, Sporting Director

PEACHTREE CITY MOBA
1000 MOBA DRIVE
PEACHTREE CITY, GA 30269
678-817-1374
www.mobasoccer.com
• Brian Wilson, Boys Director, USL Academy Head Coach
bwilson@mobasoccer.com
• Joshua Villalobos, Girls Director & Sports Science Director
jvillalobos@mobasoccer.com
Stadium:
MOBA Soccer Stadium

PEORIA CITY
SHEA STADIUM
1523 W. NEBRASKA AVENUE
PEORIA, IL 61604
peoriacitysoccer.com
• Matt Sheehan, Vice President
mattsheehannews@gmail.com
• Mike Paye, Head Coach
Stadium:
Shea Stadium

PHILADELPHIA LONE STAR FC
6537 GUYER AVENUE
PHILADELPHIA, PA 19142
215-989-0501
info@philadelphialonestarfc.com
www.philadelphialonestarfc.com
• Paul A. Konneh, III, President & CEO
pkonneh@philadelphialonestarfc.com
• Fatoma Turay, Head Coach
fturay@philadelphialonestarfc.com
Stadium:
John Bartram HS Football Stadium

READING UNITED AC
PO BOX 6132
WYOMISING, PA 19610
610-376-2100
info@readingunitedac.com
www.readingunitedac.com
• Christian Bauer, President & Co-Owner
• Casey Moore, Head Coach
Stadium:
Alvernia University

SALEM CITY FC
TRUIST SPORTS PARK
428 TWINS WAY
BERMUDA RUN, NC 27006
info@salemcityfc.com
salemcityfc.com
• Chris Williams, Head Coach
Stadium:
Truist Sports Park

SALT CITY SC
9159 S STATE STREET
SANDY, UT 84070
801-307-5150
Fax: 801-998-8421
www.utahyouthsoccer.net/salt-city-sc
• Bryan Attridge, Chief Executive Officer
battridge@uysa.org
• Eric Landon, Head Coach

SAN FRANCISCO CITY FC
SAN FRANCISCO, CA
415-373-0543
cityfootball@sfcityfc.com
sfcityfc.com
• Berdi Merdanov, Coach
Stadium:
Kezar Stadium. Seating capacity: 10,000.

SAN FRANCISCO GLENS SC
2521 JUDAH STREET
SAN FRANCISCO, CA 94122
415-349-8333
info@sfglens.com
www.sfglens.com
• Mike McNeill, General Manager
• Liam Guest, General Manager
Stadium:
Skyline College Ground; Treasure Island Stadium under construction

SANTA CRUZ BREAKERS FC
P.O. BOX 2549
SANTA CRUZ, CA 95063
info@scunited.org
www.santacruzbreakers.org
• Harendra Goonetilleke, Operations Director

SARASOTA METROPOLIS FC
1620 MAIN STREET
SUITE 5
SARASOTA, FL 34236
941-330-8978
• Bill Unzicker, Head Coach

SC UNITED BANTAMS
455 ST. ANDREWS RD.
BUILDING B
SUITE 3
COLUMBIA, SC 29210
877-457-2832
Fax: 888-675-2704
www.southcarolinaunitedfc.com
• Rob Strickland, Executive Director
rob@scufc.com
• Lee Morris, Director, Player Development
lee@scufc.com
Stadium:
Southeastern Freight Lines Soccer Center

SEACOAST UNITED PHANTOMS
PO BOX 779
HAMPTON, NH 03843
www.seacoastunited.com
• Paul Willis, Founder & President
paul.willis@threestep.com
• Alex Ryan, Head Coach
aryan@seacoastunited.com
Stadium:
New England Sports Park

SOUND FC
12810 NE 178TH ST
SUITE 202
WOODINVILLE, WA 98072
425-899-7873
info@soundfc.org
www.soundfc.org
• Lane Smith, Owner/CEO
• Brandon Mitalas, Premier Director, Coaching
Stadium:
Sunset Chevrolet Stadium

SOUTHERN CALIFORNIA EAGLES
15911 EAST WHITTIER BOULEVARD
WHITTIER, CA 90603
714-739-8375
info@thesocaleagles.com
www.thesocaleagles.com
• Cody Snouffer, Executive Director
cody@thesocaleagles.com
• Todd Elkins, Head Coach
Stadium:
Al Barbour Field

SOUTHERN SOCCER ACADEMY
40 WHITLOCK PLACE
SUITE 200
MARIETTA, GA 30064
678-594-5041
admin@ssaelite.com
www.ssaelite.com
• Simon Davey, Executive Director
(678) 876-9261
sdavey@ssaelite.com
• Jordan Davis, Head Coach
jdavis@ssaelite.com
Stadium:
Marathon Park

ST. CHARLES FC
LUTHERAN HIGH SCHOOL
5100 MEXICO ROAD
ST. PETERS, MO 63376
stc2020fc.com
• Sean Hart, Boys Director
sean.hart@stc2020fc.com
• Shaun Edgar, Girls Director
shaun.edgar@stc2020fc.com

TAMPA BAY UNITED
PO BOX 272051
TAMPA, FL 33688
813-792-7757
info@tbusc.com
tbusc.com
• Tricia Taliaferro, Executive Director
ttaliaferro@tbusc.com
• Brian Johnson, Sporting Director
bjohnson@tbusc.com
Stadium:
Jesuit High School

TEXAS UNITED
JOHN CLARK STADIUM
6600 STADIUM DRIVE
PLANO, TX 75023
info@txunitedfc.com
• Kiran Devaprasad, Owner
Stadium:
John Clark Stadium

THUNDER BAY CHILL
CHAPPLES SOCCER PARK
535 CHAPPLES PARK DRIVE
THUNDER BAY, ON, CANADA P7E 2P2
807-623-5911
tbchill@tbaytel.net
www.thunderbaychill.com
• John Marrello, General Manager
• Tony Colistro, Executive Director

TOBACCO ROAD FC
750 STADIUM DRIVE
DURHAM, NC 27707
info@tobaccoroadfc.com
www.tobaccoroadfc.com
• Cedric Burke, Sporting Director & Head Coach
Stadium:
Durham County Memorial Stadium. Seating capacity: 8,500.

TORMENTA FC 2
2704 OLD REGISTER ROAD
STATESBORO, GA 30458
news@tormentafc.com
www.tormentafc.com/usl-league-two
• Darin Van Tassell, Owner/President
• Tom Morris, Head Coach
Stadium:
Optim Sports Medicine Field

TRI-CITIES OTTERS
LEGION STREET
JOHNSON CITY, TN 37601
360-632-3832
ottersoccer@gmail.com
ottersoccer.com
• David Strickland, President & Head Coach
• Lucas Christiansen, General Manager

Stadium:
TVA Credit Union Ballpark

TSS ROVERS
6111 RIVER ROAD
RICHMOND, BC, CANADA V7C 0A2
604-816-9611
info@tss.ca
www.tssfc.ca
• Will Cromack, General Manager
Home Stadium:
Swangard Stadium. Seating capacity: 5,288.

UTAH RED WOLVES SC
PO BOX 681410
PARK CITY, UT 84068
385-297-1296
kauget@redwolves-sc.com
www.redwolvesacademyutah.com
• Scott Mackenzie, Academy Director
smackenzie@redwolves-sc.com
• Caleb Wight, Academy Coach & Head of Recruitment
cwight@redwolves-sc.com
Stadium:
Judge Field

VENTURA COUNTY FUSION
701 E SANTA CLARA STREET
SUITE 21
VENTURA, CA 93001
805-830-8027
info@vcfusion.com
www.vcfusion.com
• Keith Costigan, Head Coach
Stadium:
Ventura College Sportsplex

VICTORIA HIGHLANDERS FC
468 BURNSIDE RD E
VICTORIA, BC, CANADA
www.highlandersfc.ca
• Thomas Niendorf, Managing Director & Head Coach
• George Konstantinov, Goalkeeper Coach

VIRGINIA BEACH UNITED
2044 LANDSTOWN CENTRE WAY
VIRGINIA BEACH, VA 23456
757-427-2990
nick@vbunited.com
www.vbunited.com
• Matt Mittelstaedt, General Manager
• Chris Mills, Head Coach
Stadium:
Viriginia Beach Sportsplex

WAKE FC
PO BOX 1211
HOLLY SPRINGS, NC 27540
919-249-5119
info@wakefc.com
www.wakefcusl.com
• David Allred, Executive Director
David.Allred@WakeFC.com
• Caleb Norkus, Director, Coaching
Caleb.Norkus@WakeFC.com
Stadium:
Ting Stadium. Seating capacity: 1,800

WEST CHESTER UNITED SC
901 S BOLMAR STREET
SUITE P
WEST CHESTER, PA 19382
610-399-5277
www.pennfusion.org
• Mark Thomas, Executive Director
mthomas@pennfusion.org
• Tino Mueller, Technical Director
tmueller@pennfusion.org
Stadium:
Kildare's Field

WEST VIRGINIA UNITED
www.wvutd.com
• Dan Gribben, Head Coach

WESTCHESTER FLAMES
FLOWERS PARK
491 5TH AVENUE
NEW ROCHELLE, NY 10801
845-269-1780
troy@westchesterflames.com
www.westchesterflames.com
• Jose Dos Santos, Head Coach
Stadium:
City Park Stadium

WESTERN MASS PIONEERS
PO BOX 457
LUDLOW, MA 01056
413-583-4814
info@wmpioneers.com
www.wmpioneers.com
• Carlos Chaves, President
• Joe Ferrara, Director, Soccer Operations
• Federico Molinari, Director, Coaching
Stadium:
Lusitano Stadium

WESTON FC
4181 WESTON ROAD
SUITE 264
WESTON, FL 33331
954-349-7261
information@westonfc.org
westonfc.org
• Luis Mendoza, Head Coach
luis.mendoza@westonfc.org
Stadium:
Cypress Bay High School

WOMEN'S PREMIER SOCCER LEAGUE
1907 N. BROADWAY AVE
SUITE C
OKLAHOMA CITY, OK 73103
405-601-0025
www.wpslsoccer.com
• Sean Jones, President
sjones@wpslsoccer.com
• Kendra Halterman, Commissioner
khalterman@wpslsoccer.com
Description:
Second tier of women's soccer in the U.S. with teams in the United States, Canada and Mexico.
Founded:
1998
Number of teams:
142

Teams:

865 ALLIANCE
2809 BALL CAMP BYINGTON ROAD
KNOXVILLE, TN 37931
865-659-6074
info@865alliance.com
www.wpslsoccer.com/teams/865-alliance
• Josh Gray, General Manager
joshgrayfca@gmail.com

AHFC ROYALS WPSL
3601 CAMPBELL ROAD
HOUSTON, TX 77080
713-939-7473
www.ahfcroyals.com
• Susan Green, Executive
sgreen@albionhurricanes.org

ALBION SAN DIEGO
3555 ROSECRANS STREET
SUITE 114, #556
SAN DIEGO, CA 92110

858-200-7992
info@albionsoccer.org
www.albionsoccer.org
• Noah Gins, CEO
• Wayne Crowe, Director, Soccer

ALBION SAN DIEGO
Fax: 619-272-6014
info@asc-sandiego.com
albionsandiego.com
• Daniel Cavar, Girls Academy Director

AMBASSADORS CLEVELAND
3819 E. AURORA ROAD
TWINSBURG, OH 44087
330-963-6599
Fax: 330-963-6570
wpsl@ambassadorsfootball.org
ac.ambassadorsfootball.org
• Caleb Fortune, Head Coach
cfortune@ambassadorsfootball.org

ARIZONA ARSENAL SOCCER CLUB
480-295-6707
arsenaltryouts@gmail.com
azarsenalsc.org
• Tanna Finnvik, President
tannafinnvik@azarsenalsc.org
• David Belfort, Technical Director
(470) 295-6707
davidbelfort@ymail.com

AUSTIN RISE FC
AUSTIN, TX
info@austinrisefc.com
www.austinrisefc.com
• Bethany Cyrtmus, Manager

BC UNITED
1301 UNION CENTER MAINE HIGHWAY
ENDICOTT, NY 13760
BCUnitedInfo@gmail.com
www.bcunitedsoccer.com
• Steve Ambrozik, President
ambrozik@verizon.net
• Paul Marco, Director, Coaching

BEADLING SOCCER CLUB
BEADLING SOCCER CLUB
PO BOX 435
BRIDGEVILLE, PA 15017
www.beadling.com
• Brian Shrum, Director of Girls Academy
Teams
Shrum@beadling.com
• Rob Fabean, Director of Club Administration
robert.fabean@comcast.net

BLUFFTON RUSH SC
25 SORRELWOOD DRIVE
BLUFFTON, SC 29910
843-384-6509
info@blufftonrush.com
blufftonrush.com
• Tucker Reynolds, Executive Director
• Mike Haughton, Technical Director

BROOKLYN CITY FC
14B 53RD STREET
BROOKLYN, NY 11232
917-548-9690
info@brooklyncityfc.org
www.wpslsoccer.com/teams/brooklyn-city-fc
• Jesse DeLorenzo, Contact

BROOMFIELD BURN
2150 W. 6TH AVE.
SUITE F
BROOMFIELD, CO 80020
303-466-0096
info@broomfieldsoccerclub.com
www.broomfieldburn.com
• Mike Schrad, Executive Director
• Craig Alston, Head Coach

CALIFORNIA STORM
4041 AMERICAN RIVER DRIVE
SACRAMENTO, CA 95864
530-401-1004
www.calstormsoccer.com
• Jamie Levoy, Executive Director
jamie@calstormsoccer.com

CAPE CORAL CYCLONES
PELICAN SOCCER COMPLEX
4020 SW 2ND COURT
CAPE CORAL, FL 33910
239-541-2272
admin1@capecoralsoccer.com
cyclones.capecoralsoccer.com
• Josh Bevington, President
joshb@capecoralsoccer.com
• Bajro Dizdarevic, Technical Trainer & Director,
Goalkeeping Dev.
coachbajro@gmail.com

CENTURY SOCCER
PO BOX 18527
PITTSBURGH, PA 15236
programs@centurysoccer.org
www.centurysoccer.org
• Pat Vereb, President
pat.vereb@centurysoccer.org
• Dave Gray, Director, Coaching
david.gray@centurysoccer.org

CHALLENGE RED DEVILS
9738 HUFSMITH ROAD
TOMBALL, TX 77375
832-563-0685
ashley.fendley@challengesoccer.com
www.wpslsoccer.com/teams/challenge-red-devil
s
• Patrick O'Toole, Contact
patotoole@challengesoccer.com

CHARLOTTE EAGLES
9305 MONROE ROAD
SUITE L
CHARLOTTE, NC 28270
info@charlotteeagles.com
www.charlotteeagles.com
• Spencer Lewis, Executive Director
slewis@charlotteeagles.com
• Jonathan Ramos, Club Director
jramos@charlotteeagles.com

CHATTANOOGA FC
436 MARKET STREET
UNIT 204
CHATTANOOGA, TN 37402
423-708-4625
info@chattanoogafc.com
www.mlsnextpro.com/chattanoogafc
• Rachel Hanson, General Manager
• Juan Hernandez, Head Coach

CHICAGO DUTCH LIONS FC
1000 S EDGELAWN DRIVE
AURORA, IL 60506
info@chicagodlfc.com
www.chicagodlfc.com
• Nikhil Erlebach, CEO
n.erlebach@chicagodlfc.com
• Bryan Sutherland, Director, Operations
b.sutherland@chicagodlfc.com

CHICAGO KICS
1245 S. MICHIGAN AVE.
#152
CHICAGO, IL 60605
info@kicsfc.com
kicsfc.com
• Matt Miller, Founder & CEO
• Paddy Hoepp, Head, Coach Development
paddy@kicsfc.com

CHICAGO STARS FC
CHICAGO, IL

chicagostars.com
• Karen Leetzow, President
• Richard Feuz, General Manager
• Lorne Donaldson, Head Coach

CINCINNATI SIRENS FC
CHRISTY ROSE DENNIS SOCCER STADIUM
1579 STADIUM DRIVE
FAIRFIELD, OH 45014
cincinnatisirens@gmail.com
cincinnatisirens.com
• John Vogt, Owner
• Craig Rhodis, Technical Director

CLARKSTOWN SOCCER CLUB
PO BOX 1961
NEW CITY, NY 10956
info@clarkstownsc.org
clarkstownsc.org
• Daniel Samimi, President & Head Coach
daniel.samimi@clarkstownsc.org
• John Moran, Director, Operations
John.Moran@clarkstownsc.org

COLORADO PRIDE
5955 LEHMAN DR
STE 100
CO SPRINGS, COLORADO 80918
719-597-6700
Fax: 719-597-4040
information@pridesoccer.com
pridesoccer.com
• Candy Brooks, Executive Director
cbrooks@pridesoccer.com
• Jay Rayner, Technical Director
jrayner@pridesoccer.com
• Andrew Kummer, Senior Director, Coaching -
Girls
akummer@pridesoccer.com

COLORADO RAPIDS WOMEN
DICK'S SPORTING GOODS PARK
6000 VICTORY WAY
COMMERCE CITY, CO 80022
303-727-3500
www.coloradorapids.com
• E. Stanley Kroenke, Owner
• Padraig Smith, President
• Chris Armas, Head Coach

COLORADO RUSH
3443 S GALENA STREET
SUITE 130
DENVER, CO 80231
720-624-9000
info@coloradorush.com
www.coloradorush.com
• John Carroll, President
• Mark Hiemenz, Executive Director
• Michael Haas, Girls Sporting Director

COLUMBUS EAGLES FC
850 TWIN RIVERS DR
SUITE 1192
COLUMBUS, OH 43216
614-868-5033
mark@columbuseaglesfc.com
www.columbuseaglesfc.com
• Mark Wise, CEO
• Matt Ogden, Head Coach

CORINTHIANS FC
210-773-4591
fernandaguirre.fa@gmail.com
www.wpslsoccer.com/teams/corinthians-fc-of-sa
n-antonio
• Joe Shafer, Director, Operations & General
Manager
jshafer.cfcacademy@gmail.com

DAKOTA FUSION FC
825 25TH ST SOUTH
UNIT D
FARGO, ND 58103

701-235-5772
operations@dakotafusionfc.com
dakotafusionfc.com
• Sajid Ghauri, Owner/General Manager
• Beth Garten, Director, Operations
• Alex Trent, Head Coach

DAYTON DUTCH LIONS FC
5995 STUDENT STREET
WEST CARROLLTON, OH 45449
info@ddlfc.com
www.ddlfc.com
• Ryan Gallagher, General Manager
r.gallagher@ddlfc.com

DELAWARE OSPREYS
740 EVANSON ROAD
HOCKESSIN, DE 19707
302-275-5947
defc@delawarefc.org
delawarefc.org
• Tom Antonelli, Executive Director
• Scott Mosier, Sporting Director

DIABLO VALLEY FC
330 FERRY STREET
MARTINEZ, CA 94553
info@diablovalleyfc.com
www.diablovalleyfc.com
• Jon Scoles, Executive Director
jonscoles@ymail.com
• Richard Weiszmann, Director, Coaching
bratisla@yahoo.com

DKSC BADTOP
2241 VALWOOD PARKWAY
SUITE 100
FARMERS BRANCH, TX 75234
info@dksclub.com
dksclub.com
• Juan Martinez, President & Executive Director
(214) 926-6370
• Hugh Bradford, Director, Coaching
(214) 675-5564

DOWNTOWN UNITED SOCCER CLUB
527 HUDSTON STREET
PO BOX 20211
NEW YORK, NY 10014
info@dusc.net
dusc.net
• Kevin McCarthy, Executive Director
• Paul O'Donnell, Director, Coaching

EL PASO SURF
13019 PELLICANO
EL PASO, TX 79938
info@elpasosurf.org
elpasosurf.org
• David Lopez, Executive Director
• Heather Borrego, Director, Operations
• Ramon Martinez, Sporting Director

ELITE DEVELOPMENT ACADEMY
1038 E BASTANCHURY RD
STE 280
FULLERTON, CA 92835
714-510-2888
info@socaleda.com
• Chris Hackett, President
chris@socaleda.com
• Michael Orozco, Head Coach

ERIE FC
4504 W RIDGE RD
ERIE, PA 16506
814-833-0950
pedro@eriepremiersports.com
eriefc.com
• Pedro Argaez, Co-Owner/President
pedro@eriepremiersports.com
• Dale White, Technical Director
• Andy Bennett, Head Coach

FC ARIZONA
5780 W OAKLAND ST
CHANDLER, AZ 85248
844-526-3229
info@fcarizona.com
www.fcarizona.com
• Jamie Landreman, Club Owner & Head Coach
jamie@fcarizona.com
• Brandy Taylor, Director, Club Operations
brandy.taylor@fcarizona.com
• Ryan Purtell, Director, Coaching
ryan@fcarizona.com

FC BERLIN
477 BANKSIDE DR
KITCHENER, ON, CANADA N2N 3J3
519-505-2922
www.berlinfa.com
• Gabriel Almada, President
(226) 338-2167

FC DALLAS
TOYOTA STADIUM
9200 WORLD CUP WAY
SUITE 202
FRISCO, TX 75033
214-705-6700
888-323-4625
customerservice@FCDallas.com
fcdallas.com
• Clark Hunt, Chair & CEO
• Dan Hunt, President
• Andre Zanotta, Chief Soccer Officer & Sporting Director

FC DAVIS
info@footballclubdavis.com
www.footballclubdavis.com
• Zachary Sullivan, Head Coach

FC DAYTON
PO BOX 750651
DAYTON, OH 45745
info@FCDayton.org
www.fcdayton.org
• Jeff Monbeck, Executive Director
Jeff.Monbeck@FCDayton.org
• Bradley Schluter, Technical Director
bradley.schluter@fcdayton.org

FC MILWAUKEE TORRENT
7300 CHESTNUT STREET
WAUWATOSA, WI 53213
414-335-7126
info@milwaukeetorrent.com
milwaukeetorrent.com
• Andreas Davi, Owner & CEO

FC PREMIER WOMEN
714-822-3963
info@fcpremier97.com
www.fcpremier97.com
• Dave Sabet, Executive Director
• Paola Aragon, General Manager
• Adrian Ruelas, Director, Soccer Operations

FC PRIDE
11960 EAST 62ND ST
INDIANAPOLIS, IN 46235
317-809-0036
admin@fcpride.org
www.fcpride.org
• Jamie Gilbert, Executive Director, Coaching
• Dean Slaughter, Club Administrator & Events Director

FC PRIME
4577 N NOB HILL ROAD
SUITE 101
SUNRISE, FL 33351
admin@fc-prime.com
www.fc-prime.com
• Russ Morgan, Coach
socceraccelerated@gmail.com

FC SPIRIT
EVANSVILLE, IN
www.wpslsoccer.com/teams/fc-spirit
• K.C. Bennett, Director of Operations
kcbesc@gmail.com

FC SURGE
8501 SW 68TH STREET ROAD
MIAMI, FL 33143
954-649-5521
info@fcsurgesoccer.com
www.fcsurgesoccer.com
• Marge Perry, General Manager
mperry@fcsurgesoccer.com
• Ramiro Vengoechea, Head Coach

FC TUCSON
3600 S COUNTRY CLUB RD
TUCSON, AZ 85713
520-600-3095
info@fctucson.com
www.fctucson.com
• Jon Pearlman, Founder & President
• Kyle Cornell, Chief Operating Officer
• Roberto Garcia, WPSL Head Coach

FEVER SC
4668 E BRISTOL ROAD
TREVOSE, PA 19053
feversc.com
• Brian Fregia, President
feversc@yahoo.com
• Renny Papendick, General Manager
rennyphillyfever@gmail.com
• Bobby Wilkinson, WPSL Head Coach

FLORIDA ELITE SOCCER ACADEMY
P.O. BOX 57065
JACKSONVILLE, FL 32241
info@floridaelitesa.com
www.floridaelitesa.com
• Steven Mail, President
steven@floridaelitesa.com
• Sean Bubb, Executive Director
sean@floridaelitesa.com

FLORIDA GULF COAST DUTCH LIONS FC
239-222-0261
info@fgcdlfc.com
www.fgcdlfc.com
• Mike Mossel, CEO
m.mossel@dutchlionsfc.com
• Chris Palumbo, Head Coach
c.palumbo@fgcdlfc.com
• Stephanie Al-Arnasi, Team Manager
s.al-arnasi@fgcdlfc.com

FLORIDA KRAZE KRUSH
1073 WILLA SPRINGS DRIVE
SUITE 1049
WINTER SPRINGS, FL 32708
407-542-4939
Fax: 850-254-7227
info@floridakrazekrush.com
www.floridakrazekrush.com
• Hue Menzies, Executive Director
hmenzies@floridakrazekrush.com
• Kristi Oettl, Office Manager & Club Registrar
koettl@floridakrazekrush.com
• Joe Avallone, Director, Coaching
javallone@floridakrazekrush.com

FLORIDA PREMIER FC
13553 STATE ROAD 54
#247
ODESSA, FL 33556
727-364-3477
info@floridapremierfc.com
www.floridapremierfc.com
• Novi Maric, CEO
n.maric@floridapremierfc.com
• Nathan Bender, Director, Soccer
n.bender@floridapremierfc.com

• Ljubo Korda, Girls Director, Coaching
l.korda@floridapremierfc.com

FLORIDA ROOTS
TOMMY OLIVER STADIUM
PANAMA CITY, FL 32401
850-276-1540
www.floridarootsfc.com
• Jonathan Hammond, Chief Executive Officer &
Head Coach
jona@floridaroots.org
• Kim Cooley, Chief Operations Officer
kim@floridaroots.org
• Larry Cecchini, Director, Soccer

FOX SOCCER ACADEMY
122 STATE SCHOOL ROAD
WARWICK, NY 10990
646-217-1111
info@foxsocceracademy.org
www.foxsoccer.academy
• Christian Fuchs, Co-Founder
• Raluca Fuchs, Co-Founder
• Mark Smith, International Program Director

FRESNO FREEZE FC
1486 TOLLHOUSE ROAD
SUITE 103
CLOVIS, CA 93611
559-322-1797
FresnoFreeze@cencalcosmos.com
www.fresnofreeze.com
• Kevin Botterill, Executive Director
executivedirector@fresnofreeze.com
• Ivan Janssens, Head Coach

GEORGIA IMPACT
150 NORTH STREET
SUITE B
CANTON, GA 30114
770-704-0187
info@gaimpact.com
www.gaimpact.com
• Shane Moore, Executive Director
s.moore@csaimpact.com
• Robert Roddie, Girls Director, Coaching &
Director, Operations
rroddie@gaimpact.com

GREEN BAY GLORY
stepup@greenbayglory.com
www.greenbayglory.com
• Kerry Geocaris, Co-Founder & Executive
Director
• Melissa Cruz-Cuene, Co-Founder & Director,
Operations
• Bree Rezachek, Director, Team Operations

HERSHEY FC
550 HOMESTEAD ROAD
HERSHEY, PA 17033
director@hersheysoccer.org
www.hersheysoccer.com
• Tony Potter, President
apotter@offitkurman.com
• Ben Shirk, General Manager
fcmanager@hersheysoccer.org
• Mark Brown, WSPL Head Coach
wpsl@hersheysoccer.org

HEX FC TEMPEST
admin@HEXFC.org
www.hexfc.com/hex-fc-tempest
• Marc Meoli, General Manager
marcmeoli@hexfc.org
• Tim Raub, Head Coach
tempestcoachraub@gmail.com

HOUSTON ACES
HOUSTON, TX
www.facebook.com/TheHoustonAces
• Jonathan Giraldo, Head Coach

INDIOS DENVER FC
indiosdenverfc.org
• Oscar Gonzalez, Founder
• Brittany Frysinger, Director, Operations
brittany.frysinger@gmail.com
• Marvin Gallegos, Head Coach

IOWA RAPTORS FC
319-720-5518
info@iowaraptorsfc.com
www.facebook.com/iaraptorsfc
• Patricia Hurwitz, Owner
(847) 209-3202

JOY ATHLETIC
3221 DAKOTA AVENUE
SAINT LOUIS PARK, MN 55416
952-215-1861
admin@joyofthepeople.org
www.joyathleticclub.com
• Ted Kroeten,
ted@joyofthepeople.org

KINGSTON CAPITALS
KINGSTON, NY
capitalswpslinfo@gmail.com
kingstoncapitals.net
• Dimitri Giatrakis, Head Coach

LA ROCA FC
LA ROCA PARK
128 E. SOUTH WEBER DRIVE
SOUTH WEBER, UT 84405
801-825-6040
larocafc.com
• Heidi Wheelwright, Executive Director
heidi.wheelwright@larocafc.com
• Adolfo Ovalle, Technical Director, Coach &
Founder
adolfo.ovalle@larocafc.com

LA SURF SOCCER CLUB
325 N ALTADENA DR
PASADENA, CA 91107
626-685-9503
www.wearelasurf.com
• Mike Davis, Head Coach

LAMORINDA UNITED
452 CENTER ST
#A
MORAGA, CA 94556
925-284-1559
admin@lamorindasc.com
www.lamorindasc.com
• Marie Yu, President
lmsc-president@lamorindasc.com
• Mohamed Mohamed, Technical Director
doc@lamorindasc.com

LONESTAR SC
12325 HYMEADOW DR
#1-200
AUSTIN, TX 78757
512-336-5425
info@lonestar-sc.com
www.lonestar-sc.com
• Dave Smith, Director, National Girls

LOU FUSZ ATHLETIC
social@loufuszathletic.com
www.loufuszathletic.com
• Daniel Gargan, Managing Director
• Matt Mueller, Director, Coaching &
Competition
• Caitlin Carr, Club Administrator

MANITOU FC
4525 WHITE BEAR PARKWAY
SUITE 214
WHITE BEAR LAKE, MN 55110
612-986-2320
www.manitoufc.org

• Steve Gaustad, President
• Edi Buro, Sporting Director

MANKATO UNITED SOCCER CLUB
PO BOX 991
MANKATO, MN 56002
www.mankatounited.org
• Rob Pipal, VP, Competitive League
• Hisham Sourour, Director of Coaching
(612) 800-2844

MAPLEBROOK FURY
MAPLEBROOK SOCCER ASSOCIATION
13570 GROVE DR
#109
MAPLE GROVE, MN 55311
www.maplebrooksoccer.com
• Jean-Yves Viardin, Executive Director
jviardin@maplebrooksoccer.com
• Aimee MacPherson, Director, Soccer
Operations
amacpherson@maplebrooksoccer.com

MIDWEST SELECT SA MUSKRATS
252-301-7405
muskrats@midwestselectsa.com
wpslsoccer.com/teams/midwest-select-sa-muskr
ats
• Jamie McNicholas, Head Coach
muskrats@midwestselectsa.com

MILWAUKEE TORRENT
7300 CHESTNUT STREET
WAUWATOSA, WI 53213
414-335-7126
info@milwaukeetorrent.com
www.milwaukeetorrent.com
• Andreas Davi, Owner & CEO

MINNESOTA DUTCH LIONS FC
ROCHESTER, MN 55901
dutchlionsfc.com/minnesota
• Bassem Fadlia, Head Coach

MINNESOTA THUNDER
6600 NICOLLET AVE S
RICHFIELD, MN 55423
763-334-0210
admin@mnthunderacademy.org
mnthunderacademy.org
• Adam Pribyl, Executive Director
• Tara Blastick, Operations Director
• Daniel Storlien, Girls Director

MISSOURI REIGN
573-301-2754
habitperform@gmail.com
www.missourireign.com
• Dakota Acock, Head Coach

NAPA VALLEY 1839
info@napavalley1839.com
www.napavalley1839.com
• Arik Housley, Owner & General Manager
arik@napavalley1839.com
• Josh Goss, Owner & Goalkeeper Coach
coachjosh1839@gmail.com

NASHVILLE RHYTHM
NASHVILLE, TN
615-713-7569
nashvillerhythmfc@gmail.com
www.nashvillerhythmfc.com
• Obed Compean, Owner & General Manager
• Scott Davidson, Head Coach

NEW YORK ATHLETIC CLUB
180 CENTRAL PARK S
NEW YORK, NY 10019
212-767-7000
www.nyac.org/soccer
• Bill Saporito, Acting Coach, Women's Team

NEW YORK DUTCH LIONS FC
1 UNIVERSITY PLAZA
BROOKLYN, NY 11201
dutchlionsfc.com/newyork
• Danny Dekker, CEO
d.dekker@nydlfc.com

NEW YORK SHOCKERS
969 WATERVLIET SHAKER RD
ALBANY, NY 12205
518-438-3131
NewYorkShockers@gmail.com
www.newyorkshockers.com
• PJ Motsiff, Women's Sporting Director
• Laurie Darling Gutheil, Women's Head Coach

NORTH PORT FUSION FC
PO BOX 7747
NORTH PORT, FL 34920
northportfusionfc.com
• Jeannie Brooks, President
president@northportsoccer.com
• Sergiy Opryshko, Head Coach
thisisserhio@gmail.com

OKLAHOMA CITY FC
OKLAHOMA CITY, OK
info@oklahomacityfc.com
www.oklahomacityfc.com
• Lexi Hardzog, Administrative Director
• Danny Gibson, Co-Head Coach
• Niall Crick, Co-Head Coach

PA CLASSICS
P.O. BOX 201
EAST PETERSBURG, PA 17520
717-215-8281
www.paclassics.org
• Doug Harris, President
(717) 572-4167
dharris@paclassics.org
• Steve Klein, Director, Coaching
steve@paclassics.org

PENN FUSION SA
901 S. BOLMAR ST
SUITE P
WEST CHESTER, PA 19382
610-399-5277
www.pennfusion.org
• Mark Thomas, Executive Director
mthomas@pennfusion.org
• Tino Mueller, Technical Director
tmueller@pennfusion.org
• James Le, Administrator
jle@pennfusion.org

QUAD CITIES RUSH
MOLINE, IL
webmaster@quadcitiesrush.com
www.quadcitiesrush.com
• Andy Shrake, President
ashrake@quadcitiesrush.com
• Chris Ellis, Director, Coaching
cellis@quadcitiesrush.com
• Jason White, Technical Director
jwhite@quadcitiesrush.com

READING UNITED A.C.
610-376-2100
info@readingunitedac.com
www.readingunitedac.com
• Christian Bauer, President & Co-Owner
• Jeff Blankenbiller, Director, Gameday
Operations
• Casey Moore, Head Coach

REAL CENTRAL NJ
12 W DELAWARE AVE
PENNINGTON, NJ 08534
609-429-4622
info@realcentralnj.soccer
www.realcentralnj.soccer

• Ben Chrnelich, Coach & Sporting Director
• Brian Thomsen, Head Coach
brian@realcentralnj.soccer

RHODE ISLAND ROGUES
riroguesfc@gmail.com
www.riroguesfc.com
• Brandon Iannelli, Head Coach

SALVO SC
612-503-4738
salvosc@salvosoccer.org
www.salvosoccer.org
• Matt Cross, General Manager
mcross@salvosoccer.org
• Delaney Marier, Technical Director
dmarier@salvosoccer.org

SAN ANTONIO BLOSSOMS
1501 LAVACA STREET
SUITE 720
AUSTIN, TX 78704
512-731-4024
metzgersoccer@gmail.com

SAN DIEGO PARCEIRO LADIES
619-501-7953
Fax: 619-450-6963
info@yeslinternational.com
www.sandiegoparceiroladies.com
• Stephanie Beall, Head Coach
stephanie@warnerathletics.com

SAN DIEGO STRIKERS
www.sdstrikers.com
• Ray Taila, Head Coach
(619) 549-4414

SAN FRANCISCO NIGHTHAWKS
85 CARL STREET
SUITE 7
SAN FRANCISCO, CA 94117
www.sfnighthawks.com
• Jill Lounsbury, General Manager
jillprod@yahoo.com
• Ash Watson, Head Coach

SAN RAMON FC
P.O. BOX 1135
SAN RAMON, CA 94583
info@sanramonfc.com
www.sanramonfc.com
• Dawn McQuiston, General Manager
dmcquiston@sanramonfc.com
• Zlatko Tomic, Executive Director
ztomic@sanramonfc.com

SC DEL SOL
1831 W ROSE GARDEN LANE
SUITE 8
PHOENIX, AZ 85027
480-310-3554
andyward@scdelsol.com
www.scdelsol.com
• Les Armstrong, Girls Coach
(612) 725-1851

SEMINOLE ICE
1900 SEMINOLE SOCCER LOOP
SANFORD, FL 32771
407-321-5264
Fax: 407-321-5280
admin@ocyouthsoccer.com
www.ocss-seminole.com
• Corey Bowles, Executive Director
Corey.Bowles@ocyouthsoccer.com
• Tanya Neidert, Assistant Executive Director
Tanya.Neidert@ocyouthsoccer.com

SF ELITE
4308 GEARY BLVD
SUITE 302
SAN FRANCISCO, CA 94118

415-750-5430
operations@sfea.org
www.sfelitesc.com
• Ihor Dotsenko, Sporting Director
idotsenko@sfea.org

SIOUX FALLS CITY FC
900 E QUAIL CIRCLE
SIOUX FALLS, SD 57108
605-351-4500
info@siouxfallscityfc.com
www.siouxfallscityfc.com
• Dale Weiler, Coach
daleweiler@siouxfallscityfc.com

SJEB FC
856-534-8853
www.sjebfc.com
• Stan Simmons, General Manager
stan@sjebfc.com
• John Thompson, Technical Director
john@sjebfc.com

SO CAL UNION FC
951-970-9221
socalunionfc@gmail.com
www.wpslsoccer.com/teams/so-cal-union-fc
• Josh Fredrickson, General Manager
josh@socalunionfc.com

SOCAL DUTCH LIONS FC
dutchlionsfc.com/socal
• Gino Verbeek, Director, Recruitment
g.verbeek@socaldlfc.com
• Chelly Velasquez, Assistant Coach
c.velasquez@socaldlfc.com

SODA CITY FC
SALUDA SHOALS SPORTS COMPLEX
6071 ST. ANDREWS ROAD
COLUMBIA, SC 29212
843-708-8928
info@sodacityfc.com
sodacitysoccer.com
• Tony Baker, President
• Joseph Bacino, Women's Technical Director

SOUTHSTAR FC
southstarfc.com
• Robert Olivieri, General Manager
• Aaron McGough, Head Coach

SPOKANE SC SHADOW
PO BOX 4786
SPOKANE, WA 99220
bookkeeper@spokanesc.org
spokanesounders.org
• Abbas Faridnia, Coach
abbas@spokanesc.org

ST. CROIX SOCCER CLUB
5525 MEMORIAL AVE N
SUITE 6
OAK PARK HEIGHTS, MN 55082
651-300-2114
admin@stcroixsoccer.org
www.stcroixsoccer.org
• Nathan Klonecki, Executive Director
• Donna Luttinen, Administration Director

STA
www.stasoccer.org
• Shane Bullock, Executive Director
• Tom Shields, Technical Director

SUNFLOWER STATE FC
913-638-8869
sunflowerstatefc@gmail.com
www.sunflowerstatefc.com
• Joseph Lipoff, President
jlipoffsunflowerstatefc@gmail.com
• Edgar Quezada, General Manager
edgarsunflowerstatefc@gmail.com

• Jose Ramos, Head Coach
josesunflowerstatefc@gmail.com

SUSA FC
271 CARLETON AVE
CENTRAL ISLIP, NY 11722
631-623-6535
info@susaacademy.com
www.susaacademy.com
• Moussa Sy, President
• J.R. Balzarini, Girls Technical Director

TAMPA BAY ROWDIES
230 1ST ST. SE
ST. PETERSBURG, FL 33701
727-222-2000
Fax: 813-282-3800
info@rowdiessoccer.com
www.rowdiessoccer.com
• Robbie Neilson, Head Coach
• Steve Coleman, Assistant Coach

TEAM BOCA BLAST
PO BOX 812650
BOCA RATON, FL 33481
www.teamboca.com
• Petro Andreadis, Club Director
pandreadis@sabrsoccer.net
• Mario Rincon, Girls Director of Coaching
MarioTeamBoca@gmail.com

TORCH FC
123 N. MAIN STREET
DUBLIN, PA 18917
215-869-5224
torch@torchsportsministry.org
www.torchsportsministry.org
• Rich Sparling, President
• Andy Schlosser, General Manager
• Maira Abreu De Campos, Head Coach

UNION KC SOCCER CLUB
8101 COLLEGE BOULEVARD
UNIT 100
OVERLAND PARK, KS 66210
816-955-0934
info@kcsgsoccer.org
www.unionkcsoccer.com/wpsl
• Chris Travalent, President
• Chuck Mathis, VP, Business Operations
• Dan Naidu, Director of Coaching, Girls
dnaidu@kcsgsoccer.org

UNITED SOCCER ALLIANCE
4387 LAKESHORE DRIVE
FLEMING ISLAND, FL 32003
904-278-1182
admin@unitedsocceralliance.org
www.unitedsocceralliance.org
• Matt Hollyoak, Executive Director
matt@unitedsocceralliance.org
• Edson Abreu, Girls Academy Director
• Kylie Harris, Girls Director & Goalkeeping
Director
kylie@unitedsocceralliance.org

UTAH AVALANCHE
7980 STATE ST
SUITE 700
MIDVALE, UT 84047
801-913-4155
www.utahavalanche.com
• Jo Barney, Executive Director
• David Newman, Executive Director
• Jimmie Powell, Director, Coaching

UTAH RED DEVILS
jg2fly@gmail.com
www.facebook.com/RedDevilsRDFCSaltLake
• Dennis Burrows, Coach
dennisburrows5876@hotmail.com

UTAH SURF
pipeline@utahsurfsoccer.com
www.utahsurfsoccer.com
• Brad Silvey, General Manager & Co-Head
Coach
• Izzy Gines, Co-Head Coach
• Kiona Silvey, Assistant Coach & Director,
Soccer Operations

VT FUSION
P.O. BOX 1693
MANCHESTER CENTER, VT 05255
802-558-9595
ccfusionsoccer@gmail.com
vtfusionsoccer.com
• Brandon Smith, President
• Chris Chapdelaine, Director, Operations
• Ray Nichols, Girls Director of Coaching

WASHINGTON DUTCH LIONS FC
dutchlionsfc.com/washington
• Martin de Groot, CEO
m.degroot@washingtondlfc.com
• Michel Vanderhart, Head Coach
m.vanderhart@washingtondlfc.com

WESTSIDE METROS FC
8231 SW CIRRUS DR.
BUILDING 16
BEAVERTON, OR 97008
503-626-2975
Fax: 503-924-4249
media@wsmetros.org
www.westsidemetros.org
• John Bain, Director, Soccer Operations
john.bain@wsmetros.org
• Cory Hand, Girls Director of Coaching
cory.hand@wsmetros.org
• Constantine Konstin, Technical Director
cony.konstin@wsmetros.org

**WOMEN'S FOOTBALL CLUB OF
CHARLOTTE**
615-618-2170
womensfootballclubcharlotte@gmail.com
www.wpslsoccer.com/teams/womens-football-cl
ub-of-charlotte
• Scott Ginn, Coach

Softball Organizations

**AMATEUR SOFTBALL ASSOCIATION OF
AMERICA (ASA)**
2801 NE 50TH STREET
OKLAHOMA CITY, OK 73111
405-424-5266
www.teamusa.org
• Craig Cress, Executive Director
• Mark Loehrs, Chief Financial Officer
• Steve Walker, Director of Operations
• Kevin Ryan, Director of Umpires
Description:
Established in 1933, the ASA is the national
governing body of softball in the U.S. and
oversees aspects of the grassroots
programs and national team programs. ASA
has more than 100 championships ranging
from 10-under fast pitch to 75-over slow
pitch, with more than 40,000 players every
year. There is a local association for each
state. USA Softball is a brand of the ASA
related specifically to the USA National
Teams that compete internationally for the
United States.
Publications:
Official publication, BALLS & STRIKES
SOFTBALL MAGAZINE, published five
times annually; OFFICIAL RULE BOOK and
SCOREBOOK, both annual.

DIXIE SOFTBALL INC
1101 SKELTON DRIVE
BIRMINGHAM, AL 35224
205-785-2255
obeidsi@aol.com
• James E. Evans, President
• Leonard Preston, Vice President
• Sharon Lafitte, Secretary
Description:
A primarily youth centered softball program
for girls 18 years of age and younger,
playing on a scaled-down diamond to meet
the physical development of the growing
child. The main purpose is to provide a
recreation outlet for as many as possible
with emphasis on local league play rather
than tournament play.

INTERNATIONAL SOFTBALL CONGRESS
PO BOX 1083
FINDLAY, OH 45839
801-447-8807
iscken@comcast.net
www.iscfastpitch.com
• Larry Fisher, Executive Director
(419) 722-7448
lfisher838@ameritech.net
• Dean Oscar, President
• Blair Setford, VP, Operations
(416) 625-1757
Publications:
ISC WORLD CHAMPIONSHIP GUIDE,
annually.
Membership Requirements:
Application to commissioners and
participation in area tournaments and/or
affiliated travel leagues.
Description:
A non-profit association for the promotion
and administration of mens and boys
fastpitch softball throughout North America
with athletes coming from literally all over
the world.

**INTERNATIONAL SOFTBALL
FEDERATION**
1900 SOUTH PARK ROAD
PLANT CITY, FL 33563
813-864-0100
Fax: 813-864-0105
info@ISFsoftball.org
www.isfsoftball.org
• Dale McMann, President
• Ron Radigonda, Executive Director
• Laurie Gouthro, Assistant Executive
Director
Description:
The International Softball Federation is a
member of the World Baseball Softball
Confederation. The ISF is in charge of
managing the world championship
competition in various softball events.

**NATIONAL FASTPITCH COACHES
ASSOCIATION/NFCA**
4641 GRINSTEAD DRIVE
LOUISVILLE, KY 40206
502-409-4600
Fax: 502-409-4622
nfca@nfca.org
nfca.org
• Rhonda Revelle, President
rrevelle@huskers.com
• Pat Conlan, 1st VP
pjc72@georgetown.edu
• Kate Drohan, 2nd VP
k-drohan@northwestern.edu

• Lacy Lee Baker, Executive Director
llb@nfca.org
Nature of Sports Service:
Professional organization for all levels of
softball coaches, including two & four year
colleges and universities, highschools and
travel teams.
Membership Requirements:
Annual fees for softball coaches, umpires
and affiliate members.
Member Services:
Subscription to membership newsletter,
annual directory, access to member only
content on web site, discounts on
convention and merchandise.
Publications:
FASTPITCH DELIVERY (monthly);
FASTPITCH CONNECTED (weekly); TOP
RECRUIT-ANNUAL; Directory of Information
(Membership directory)
Number of members:
4,700

**NATIONAL SLO-PITCH ATHLETICS
ENTERPRISES OF CANADA**
BAY 9
1925 - 39TH AVENUE NE
CALGARY, AB, CANADA T2E 6W7
403-250-9655
Fax: 403-769-9055
info@nsacanada.ca
nsacanada.ca
• Terry Sibbick, CEO/President
• Ewan Webster, Executive Vice President
• Wanda Sibbick, Vice President
• Jeremy Thiemann, National Director

NATIONAL SOFTBALL ASSOCIATION
PO BOX 7
NICHOLASVILLE, KY 40340
859-887-4114
Fax: 859-887-4874
nsahdqtrs@playnsa.com
www.playnsa.com
• Hugh Cantrell, CEO
hcantrell@playnsa.com
• Ray Cantrell, President
ecantrell@playnsa.com
• Faye Cantrell, National Office Manager
fcantrell@playnsa.com
Year Founded:
1982
Nature of Sport Services:
A full service organization that offers a
division of play and a level of competition
that youth and adults can enjoy.

**NATIONAL WHEELCHAIR SOFTBALL
ASSOCIATION**
13414 PAUL STREET
OMAHA, NE 68154
402-305-5020
bfroendt@cox.net
www.wheelchairsoftball.org
• Brian Chavez, President
(612) 388-0874
brianchavez1972@msn.com
• Bruce Froendt, Commissioner
(402) 305-5020
bfroendt@cox.net
• Juan Ortiz, 1st Vice President
juor3rd@gmail.com
• John Hamre, 2nd Vice President
jthamre@gmail.com
Publications:
National Wheelchair Softball Association
Newsletter, periodically.

Membership Requirements:
Membership made up of competing teams
of the Association and of the Associate
members.
Description:
Founded in 1976 and serves as the
governing body for wheelchair softball in the
United States. Played under the official rules
of the 16-inch slow pitch softball as
approved by the Amateur Softball
Association of America with some
expectations geared toward the wheelchair
user.

**OVER-THE-LINE PLAYERS
ASSOCIATION**
3890 CARSON STREET
SAN DIEGO, CA 92117
otlpanews@aol.com
• Faustino Medina, President
• Brian McGiveron, Vice President
• Fred Elliott, Secretary
• Gregg Williams, Treasurer
Description:
Founded in 1976. Promotes the sport of
over-the-line by sponsoring tournaments,
overseeing others' tournaments, putting on
clinics and publishing a monthly newsletter
that gives tournament results and supplies
tournament applications.

SENIOR SOFTBALL-USA
2701 K STREET
SUITE 101A
SACRAMENTO, CA 95816
916-326-5303
Fax: 916-326-5304
info@seniorsoftball.com
www.seniorsoftball.com
• Terry Hennessy, CEO
terryh@seniorsoftball.com
• Fran Dowell, Executive Director
• Ross McCulligan, Executives Assistant,
Umpires and Bookkeeping
Number of Members:
1.5 million men and women over 40
Member Services:
Softball tournaments, national and
international; softball newspapers; and
softball ID cards.
Publications:
Senior Softball-USA News
Membership Requirements:
Over 50 years old
Description:
Dedicated to informing and uniting the
Senior Softball Players of America and the
World. Sanctions tournaments and
championships, registers players, writes the
rulebook, hosts International Softball Tours
and promotes Senior Softball throughout the
world.

SOFTBALL CANADA
223 COLONNADE ROAD
SUITE 212
OTTAWA, ON, CANADA K2E 7K3
613-523-3386
Fax: 613-523-5761
info@softball.ca
www.softball.ca
• Kevin Quinn, President
• Hugh Mitchener, Chief Executive Officer
(613) 523-3386
• Mike Branchaud, Manager - National
Teams/Canadian Championships
(613) 523-3386

Member Services:
Publications, clinics, program development.
Publications:
RULES, COACHING, UMPIRING,
CASEBOOK, DRILLS.
Membership Requirements:
Ten provinces, two territories; each
provincial or territorial member has its own
membership structure.
Description:
Founded in 1965. Fosters, develops, and
regulates playing of amateur softball in
Canada.

SOFTBALL FACTORY
9212 BERGER ROAD
SUITE 200
COLUMBIA, MD 21046
855-822-5115
Fax: 410-715-1975
info@softballfactory.com
www.softballfactory.com
Description:
Provides nationwide instruction, college
planning and guidance to softball players.

**UNITED STATES SPECIALTY SPORTS
ASSOCATION**
611 LINE DRIVE
KISSIMMEE, FL 34744
321-697-3636
Fax: 321-697-3647
don.dedonatis@usssa.com
www.usssa.com
• Don DeDonatis, Chairman, Executive
Directionr & CEO
• Jim Swint, Assistant Executive Director
• Robert Boudreaux, Executive Vice
President
Description:
The USSSA is a non-profit, sports governing
body residing in Kissimmee, Florida.

**WORLD BASEBALL SOFTBALL
CONFEDERATION**
MAISON DU SPORT INTERNATIONAL
54, AVE DE RHODAINE
LAUSANNE, SWITZERLAN 1007
+41-2131-88240
Fax: +41-2131-88241
office@wbsc.org
Description:
Comprised of the International Softball
Federation (ISF) and the International
Baseball Federation (IBAF), the WBSC
serves as the global authority for baseball
and softball.

Softball, Leagues/Teams

MAJOR LEAGUE SOFTBALL
621 EAST WALNUT AVENUE
BURBANK, CA 91501
818-559-8787 EXT 3
www.mlsoftball.com

NATIONAL PRO FASTPITCH
3350 HOBSON PIKE
HERMITAGE, TN 37076
615-324-7861
info@profastpitch.com
www.profastpitch.com
• Cheri Kempf, President/Commissioner
• Gaye Lynn Wilson, Vice President

- Mike Raynor, Supervisor of Officials
- Erin Collins, Play By Play
- Barbara Jordan, Color Analyst
Nature of Sports Service:
Formerly the Women's Pro Softball League.
NPF is intended to provide family
entertainment for people of all ages and to
showcase the top talent in softball today. It
is the goal of the league to entertain and
provide positive role models for young
people. NPF demonstrates that a good work
ethic, dedication, and love for what one
does, will allow everyone to achieve their
life's goals. NPF athletes demonstrate this
by their actions, both on-and-off the field.
They are prominent people within their
communities and avail themselves to their
fans, particularly the young ones.
Sports Service Founded:
1989

Teams:

AKRON RACERS
1575 FIRESTONE PARKWAY
AKRON, OH 44301
330-376-8188
Fax: 330-376-8348
www.akronracers.org
- Stout Craig, Owner/CFO
- Joey Arrietta, Co-Owner/GM
(330) 376-8188
joeyarrietta@akronracers.us
- Brian Levin, Field Manager
Stadium:
Firestone Stadium. Seating capacity, 4,576.

CHICAGO BANDITS
27 JENNIE FINCH WAY
ROSEMONT, IL 60018
877-722-6348
Fax: 630-396-3095
banditsinfo@chicagobandits.com
www.chicagobandits.com
- Bill Sokolis, President/CEO
- Aaron M. M Moore, General Manager
- Jacquie Boatman, Director of Community &
Media Relations
- Johnny Sole, Director of Ticket Sales
Stadium:
Rosemont Stadium.

DALLAS CHARGE
6151 ALMA ROAD
MCKINNEY, TX 75070
724-242-7431
- Kevin Shelton, General Manager
- Laura Villa, Assistant General Manager
- Caitlin Hall, Athletic Trainer
- Richard Levy, Team Doctor
Stadium:
Gate Nesbitt Stadium. Seating capacity, 1,000.

PENNSYLVANIA REBELLION
ONE WASHINGTON FEDERAL WAY
WASHINGTON, PA 15301
724-250-9555
Fax: 724-250-2333
- Francine Williams, Managing Partner
- Steve Zavacky, General Manager
- Christine Blaine, Director of Marketing &
Communications
- Tony Buccilli, Director of Team Operations
- Elana D. Williams, Director of Operations
Stadium:
Consol Energy Park. Seating capacity, 3,200.

SCRAPYARD DAWGS
29607 ROBINSON ROAD
CONROE, TX 77385
855-793-2947
- Kevin Shelton, General Manager
- Whitney Cloer, Assistant General Manager

Stadium:
Scrapyard Softball Complex.

USSSA FLORIDA PRIDE
611 LINE DRIVE
KISSIMMEE, FL 34744
321-697-3635
info@usssapride.com
- Don DeDonatis, General Manager
- Gordon Glennie, Assistant General Manager
- Wendi Brockwell, Director of Accounting Ticket
Operations
- Bernie Guenther, Director of Broadcast
Operations
- Mike Davenport, Head Coach
Stadium:
Champion Stadium. Seating capacity, 9,500.

SLO-PITCH NATIONAL SOFTBALL
63 GALAXY BOULEVARD
UNIT 4
ETOBICOKE, ON, CANADA M9W5R7
416-674-1802
Fax: 416-674-8233
www.slo-pitch.com

Speedskating Organizations

**FEDERATION INTERNATIONALE
ROLLER SPORTS (FIRS)**
AV DE RHODANIE, 54
LAUSANNE, 1007
www.rollersports.org

**INTERNATIONAL SKATING UNION (ISU)
(ICE SKATING)**
AVENUE JUSTE-OLIVIER 17
LAUSANNE, SWITZERLAN 1006
info@isu.ch
isu.org
- Fredi Schmid, Director General
Description:
Founded in 1892, the ISU is the
International Governing Body for ice skating
athletics.

U.S. SPEEDSKATING
5662 S. COUGAR LANE
KEARNS, UT 84118
801-417-5360
Fax: 801-417-5361
media@usspeedskating.org
www.usspeedskating.org
- Ted Morris, Executive Director
tmorris@usspeedskating.org

USA ROLLER SPORTS
4730 SOUTH STREET
LINCOLN, NE 68506
402-483-7551
Fax: 402-483-1465
www.teamusa.org/USA-Roller-Sports

Squash Organizations

**COLLEGE SQUASH ASSOCIATION/MENS
& WOMEN'S INTERCOLLEGIATE
COMPETITION**
HATFIELD, MA
csa@collegesquashassociation.com
collegesquashassociation.com
- Wendy Lawrence, President/Women's
- Hansi Wiens, Vice President/Women's

- Martin Heath, President/Treasurer/Men's
- Tomas Fortson, Vice President/Men's
Membership Requirements:
Membership dues. Intercollegiate schedule
pursued. Competition in the National
Intercollegiate athletics.

PROFESSIONAL SQUASH ASSOCIATION
46 THE CALLS
LEEDS, ENGLAND LS2 7EY
office@psaworldtour.com
psaworldtour.com
- Alex Gough, CEO
alex@psaworldtour.com
- Lee Beachill, COO
lee@psaworldtour.com
- Hannah Ridgard-Mason, Tour Director
Number of members:
750+ Members
Membership Requirements:
Be a squash professional or squash
manufacturer.
Description:
The official sanctioning and membership
body for men's and women's squash World
Rankings.

SQUASH CANADA
20 JAMIE AVENUE
2ND FLOOR
NEPEAN, ON, CANADA K2E 6T6
613-228-7724
Fax: 613-228-7232
info@squash.ca
www.squash.ca
- Lolly Gillen, President
lollygillen@rogers.com
- Shaun Thorson, Vice President, Finance
shaunthor@me.com
- Steve Wren, Vice President Technical
swrenkiwi@gmail.com
- Dan Wolfenden, Executive Director
(613) 228-7724
dan.wolfenden@squash.ca
- Cheryl McEvoy, Operations Manager
(613) 228-7724
cheryl.mcevoy@squash.ca
Member Services:
Coaching and officiating instruction,
promotion, junior development, national
rankings, national championships, education
resource materials.
Description:
Provides a high performance system for
athletes, coaches and officials, and sets
standards for squash in Canada.

U.S. SQUASH
555 EIGHTH AVENUE
SUITE 1102
NEW YORK, NY 10018-4311
212-268-4090
Fax: 212-268-4091
office@ussquash.com
www.ussquash.com
- Marshall W. Pagon, Chairman of the
Board
- Kevin Klipstein, President/Chief Executive
Officer
(212) 268-4090
kevin.klipstein@ussquash.com
- Dent Wilkens, Senior Vice President
Operations
(212) 269-4090
dent.wilkens@ussquash.com
- Graham Bassett, Director of Doubles and
Professional Squash

(212) 268-4090
graham.bassett@ussquash.com
• Bill Buckingham, Director Of Member
Services
bill.buckingham@ussquash.com
• Kim Clearkin, Director of National
Championships
(212) 268-4090
kim.clearkin@ussquash.com
Number of members:
17,000+
Publications:
Squash Magazine.
Description:
Founded 1904. The national governing body
of squash in the United States. Manages 14
national championships and sanctions over
400 tournaments across the USA each year.
Pan American member of the United States
Olympic Committee. Promotes and governs
the game of squash.
Membership Services:
Provides tournaments, leagues and other
member services to promote the game of
squash for adults and juniors. It Supports
singles and doubles as well as softball and
hardball. The USSRA selects the teams to
represent the United States in Pan
American and World Competitions.

WORLD SQUASH FEDERATION/WSF
25 RUSSELL STREET
HASTINGS
EAST SUSSEX, ENGLAND TN34 1QU
www.worldsquash.org
• Jahangir Khan, Emeritus President
tunku_imran@antah.com.my
• Jacques Fontaine, President
• Sarah Fitz-Gerald, Vice President
• Andrew Shelley, Chief Executive
• Lorraine Harding, Operations Manager
• Jasmine Pascoe, Operations Assistant
Description:
International governing body for the sport of
squash.
Membership Requirements:
National Federation for Squash

Surfing Organizations

EASTERN SURFING ASSOCIATION
PO BOX 4736
OCEAN CITY, MD 21843
302-988-1953
Fax: 302-258-0735
info@surfesa.org
www.surfesa.org
• Michelle B. Sommers, Executive Director
Year Founded:
1967
Description:
The world's largest amateur surfing
association. The ESA is made up of districts
from Maine to Alabama. The organization
holds competitions and advocates for the
preservation of shoreline environments.
Membership Requirements:
Open to all — visit www.surfesa.org to join.

**INTERNATIONAL SURFING
ASSOCIATION**
5580 LA JOLLA BLVD
#145
LA JOLLA, CA 92037

858-551-8580
Fax: 858-551-8563
surf@isasurf.org
www.isasurf.org
• Karin Sierralta, Vice President
• Marcos Bukao, Contest Director
marcosbukao@isasurf.org
• Harrison Robbs, Manager of Event
Operations
• Fernando Aguerre, President
president@isasurf.org
• Barbara Kendall, Vice President
• Casper Steinfath, Vice President
• Kirsty Coventry, Vice President
Publications:
Monthly ISA Newsletter(members only),
Monthly ISA Press Release (goes to
International Media). All sent by email.
Description:
Dedicated to the development of these
sports worldwide. Provides guidance and
advice to its members around the world on
matters such as competition, judging, surf
education, adapted surfing, anti doping and
other areas of development of the sport.

**NATIONAL SCHOLASTIC SURFING
ASSOCIATION**
PO BOX 495
HUNTINGTON BEACH, CA 92648
714-906-7423
jaragon@nssa.org
www.nssa.org
• Janice Aragon, Executive Director
Member Services:
Provides organized surfing competition and
Scholarships for student surfers nationwide.
Membership Requirements:
Must be full time student in either
elementary, high school or college or a
non-student surfer.
Description:
Founded in 1978, the National Scholastic
Surfing Foundation develops fundamental
surfing skills and competition skills for young
people through participation in events.

**SURF INDUSTRY MANUFACTURERS
ASSOCIATION/SIMA**
27831 LA PAZ ROAD
LAGUNA NIGUEL, CA 92677
949-366-1164
Fax: 949-454-1406
info1@sima.com
www.sima.com
• Kelly Gibson, President
• John Wilson, Vice President
• Johnny Gehris, Treasurer
• Shannon Park Zseleczky, Managing
Director
• Sean Smith, Executive Director
Membership Requirements:
Primarily active sportswear and equipment
manufacturers serving beach/lifestyle
specialty stores.
Description:
An association representing the interests of
surfing industry product suppliers.
Year Founded:
1989

SURFLINE.COM
300 PACIFIC COAST HWY
SUITE 300
HUNTINGTON BEACH, CA 92648
714-374-0556
Fax: 714-374-0562

support@surfline.com
www.surfline.com
• Sean Collins, Founder/President
• Jeff Berg, Chariman and Chief Executive
Officer
• Mark Willis, Chief Meteorologist
Sports Service Founded:
1985
Nature of Sports Service:
Provider of surf report, forecast and editorial
content to consumers, businesses and
government agencies worldwide.

WORLD SURF LEAGUE
147 BAY ST
SANTA MONICA, CA 90405
310-450-1212
www.worldsurfleague.com
• Dirk Ziff, Chief Executive Officer
• Meg Bernardo, ASP North America
General Manager
(714) 322-6149
mbernardo@worldsurfleague.com
Description:
Governing body of professional surfing.
Established 1976.
Members:
1000+
Member Services:
World rankings/surfers; event promotion;
judging ranking; coordination of the World
Tour.

Swimming Organizations

**AMERICAN SWIMMING COACHES
ASSOCIATION**
5101 NW 21ST AVENUE, SUITE# 200
FORT LAUDERDALE, FL 33309
954-563-4930
800-356-2722
Fax: 954-563-9813
asca@swimmingcoach.org
www.swimmingcoach.org
• John Leonard, Executive Director
jleonard@swimmingcoach.org
• Guy Edson, Technology Director
gedson@swimmingcoach.org
• Kimberly Aranalde, Certification and
Marketing Coordinator
certification@swimmingcoach.org
Publications:
AMERICAN SWIMMING Magazine; ASCA
Newsletter; ASCA E-news; JOURNAL OF
SWIMMING RESEARCH.
Membership Requirements:
Open to all swimming coaches and
swimming enthusiasts.

**COLLEGE SWIMMING COACHES
ASSOCIATION OF AMERICA**
5101 NW 21ST AVENUE
SUITE 530
FORT LAUDERDALE, FL 33309
954-563-4930
cscaa@swimmingcoach.org
www.cscaa.org
• Susan Teeter, President
• Joel Shinofield, Executive Director
(540) 460-6563
Number of members:
2,000 member coaches.
Member Services:
Support for intercollegiate athletic issues;
All-American and All-Academic awards;

distinguished service awards.
Description:
The oldest organization of college coaches in America - is a professional organization of college swimming and diving coaches dedicated to serving and providing leadership for the advancement of the sport of swimming at the collegiate level.
Year Founded:
1922

LIFE SAVING/UTILITARIAN SPORTS, FEDERATION INTERNATIONALE DE
GEMEENTEPLEIN 26
LEUVEN, Belgium 3010
32-16-89-60-60
Fax: 32-16-89-70-70
info@ilsf.org
www.ilsf.org
• Graham Ford, President
• Dr. Harald Vervaecke PhD, Secretary General
Description:
The world authority for drowning prevention and lifesaving sport. ILS leads, supports and collaborates with national and international organisations engaged in drowning prevention, water safety, water rescue, lifesaving, lifeguarding and lifesaving sport.

SWIMMING/NATATION CANADA
307 GILMOUR STREET
OTTAWA, ON, CANADA K2P 0P7
613-260-1348
Fax: 613-260-0804
natloffice@swimming.ca
www.swimming.ca
• Ahmed El-Awadi, Chief Executive Officer
(613) 260-1348
aelawadi@swimming.ca
• John Atkinson, Director, High Performance
(613) 260-1348
jatkinson@swimming.ca
• Chris Wilson, Director, Marketing
(905) 691-2975
cwilson@swimming.ca
Sports Service Founded:
1909
Member Services:
Canadian non-profit sport organization provides services to registered amateur Competitive swimmers through programs and activities that range across a broad spectrum including coaching, officiating, swimming education, sport science, event coordination, promotion and communications. The organization's focus is on the development of world class competitive swimmers.
Membership Requirements:
Registration as required by the international governing body, LA Federation Internationale de Natation, The Aquatic Federation of Canada and Swimming/Natation Canada.

SYNCHRO CANADA
700 INDUSTRIAL AVE
SUITE 401
OTTAWA, CANADA K1G 0Y9
613-748-5674
Fax: 613-748-5724
info@synchro.ca
www.synchro.ca
• Jackie Buckingham, Chief Executive Officer
(613) 748-5674

jackie@synchro.ca
• Jadine Cleary, Domestic Technical Director
jadine@synchro.ca
• Stephane Cote, Events and Communications Director
(418) 420-2125
stephane@synchro.ca
• Audrey Frey, Finance & Administration Manager
(613) 748-5674
audrey@synchro.ca
• Isabelle Lecompte, High performance Manager
isabelle@synchro.ca
Nature of Service:
Fosters the pursuit of excellence while developing athletes, citizens and ambassadors of the sport of synchronized swimming at all levels.
Year Founded:
1969
Member Services:
Membership card; merchandise discounts. Annual meetings always in October. Events: National championships for senior and junior held once a year, Divisional Championships, Master National Championships, National Team Training.
Number of members:
7,000 +

U.S. LIFESAVING ASSOCIATION
www.usla.org
• Peter Davis, President
president@usla.org
• Rob Williams, Vice President
vicepresident@usla.org
• Nikki Bowie, Secretary
secretary@usla.org
• Michael Bradley, Treasurer
treasurer@usla.org
Publications:
American Lifeguard Magazine published three times a year, Lifeguard News
Membership Requirements:
Five membership categories. Professional, Alumnus Member, Associate Member, Associate Junior Lifeguard Member, Junior Lifeguard Member, Corporate Membership

U.S. SYNCHRONIZED SWIMMING, INC.
1 OLYMPIC PLAZA
COLORADO SPRINGS, CO 80909
719-866-2219
www.usasynchro.org
• Myriam Glez, Chief Executive Officer/High Performance Director
myriam@usasynchro.org
Description:
USSS acts as the National Governing Body for synchronized swimming competition.

USA SWIMMING
1 OLYMPIC PLAZA
COLORADO SPRINGS, CO 80909
719-866-4578
Fax: 719-866-4669
info@usaswimming.org
www.usaswimming.org
• Chuck Wielgus, President/Chief Executive Officer
• Jim Sheehan, Chair of the Board
Description:
USA Swimming acts as the National Governing Body for the sport, organizaing competitions and promoting participation.

ITTF NORTH AMERICA
18 LOUISA STREET
OTTAWA, ON, CANADA K1R 6Y6
613-733-6272 EXT 223
ittfnorthamerica.com
• Mireille Tallon, Program Coordinator

TABLE TENNIS CANADA
18 LOUISA STREET
OTTAWA, ON, CANADA K1R 6Y6
613-733-6272
Fax: 613-733-7279
ttcan@ttcan.ca
www.ttcan.ca
• Tony Kiesenhofer, Chief Executive Officer
(613) 733-6272
tonyk@ttcan.ca
• David Jackson, President
davidj@ttcan.ca
Nature of Sports Service:
Founded 1929. Incorporated in 1974. Develops and promotes table tennis at the highest level across Canada.
Membership Requirements:
Through each provincial organization.
Publications:
20/20, newsletter four times annually.
Member Services:
Support system for provinces; certification of coaches, officials; trains national team; promotes the sport; opportunity for members to obtain videos, manuals.

USA TABLE TENNIS
4065 SINTON RD
SUITE 120
COLORADO SPRINGS, CO 80907
719-866-4583
Fax: 719-632-6071
admin@usatt.org
www.teamusa.org/usa-table-tennis
• Gordon Kaye, CEO
(719) 866-4583
Gordon.Kaye@usatt.org
• Andy Horn, Director of Operations
(719) 866-4583
Andrew.Horn@usatt.org
Description:
National governing body for table tennis in the United States. It oversees a wide variety of membership services, the national teams, and other areas such as the rules of the game, the Hall of Fame, and numerous online instructional and historical articles.
Sports Service Founded:
1933
Description:
Oversees a wide variety of membership services, the national teams, and other areas such as the rules of the game, and numerous online instructional and historical articles.

AMERICAN MEDICAL TENNIS ASSOCIATION
2414 43RD AVENUE E
SUITE B-1
SEATTLE, WA 98112
800-326-2682
www.mdtennis.org

• Bruce Dalkin, MD, President
• Dr. John & Cori Kirkpatrick, Executive Directors

Description:
Founded 1967, a non-profit educational organization whose purpose is to provide Continuing Medical Education programs for physicians.

Membership Requirements:
Doctor of Medicine degree.

Publications:
Newsletter, quarterly. Membership Directory, biannually.

ATP WORLD TOUR
201 ATP TOUR BLVD
PONTE VEDRA BEACH, FL 32082
904-285-8000
Fax: 904-285-5966
www.atptour.com
• Chris Kermode, Executive Chairman/President
• Mark Young, Vice Chairman and Chief Legal and Media Officer
• Flip Galloway, Chief Operating Officer
• Gayle David Bradshaw, Executive Vice President, Rules & Competition
• Ross Hutchins, Chief Player Officer
• Alison Lee, Executive Vice President, International Group
• Gavin Forbes, Tournament Representative
• Mark Webster, Tournament Representative
• Charles Humphrey Smith, Tournament Representative
• David Egdes, Player Representative
• Justin Gimelstob, Player Representative
• Giorgio di Palermo, Player Representative

Additional Offices:
ATP Tour Europe, Monte Carlo Sun, 74 Blvd D'Italie, 98000 Monaco. +377-97-97-04-04; FAX: +377-97-97-04-00. ATP International Group, PO Box N662, Sydney, NSW 1220 Australia. +61-2-92502300; FAX: 61-2-92502333. ATP Executive Offices, IG House Palliser Road, London W14 9EB, United Kingdom, +44-20-7381-7890; FAX: +44-20-7381-7895.

Description:
Founded 1972. Partnership between men's professional tennis players and member tournaments which promote and protect the mutual interests of all men playing professional tennis with over 70 international tennis tournaments in 34 countries on six continents.

Membership Requirements:
Division I player: positioned in top 200 in South African Airways ATP Rankings (singles), or top 100 in ATP Doubles Rankings, and pay ATP dues. Division II player: any player who does not qualify for Division I membership and will be positioned among the top 500 players in the South African Airways ATP Rankings (singles), or top 250 in ATP Doubles Rankings, at the time of application.

Publications:
INTERNATIONAL TENNIS, official magazine; ATP Tour singles and doubles computer rankings.

Member Services:
ATP Tour University - provides information and training for players; ATP Tour Tennis, is seen in more than 180 countries.

INTERCOLLEGIATE TENNIS ASSOCIATION
1130 E UNIVERSITY DRIVE
SUITE 115
TEMPE, AZ 85281
609-497-6920
www.itatennis.com
• Jon Vegosen, Chairman Of The Board
• Timothy Russell, Chief Executive Director
(602) 687-6375
• Cory Brooks, Director Of Events & Championships
(602) 687-6383
cbrooks@itatennis.com
• Laura Schuessler, New Media & Marketing Coordinator
(602) 687-6378

Description:
The governing body of college tennis at all division levels.

Membership Options:
Corporate and Auxiliary Memberships incl. member categories: alumni, associate, association, collegiate parents, corporation, federation, junior players.

Member Services: (Dependent on Membership type)
Online Membership Directory access; news and ITA ranking updates; ITA Convention membership rates; discounted subscription to the ITA Online Tradeshow; discounted fee for booth at annual ITA Coaches Convention; potential to post video clips online; Junior Players may participate in summer circuit; exposure opportunities; travel dscounts when participating in ITA National & Regional Championship Events; ability to purchase mailing labels & lists of member Coaches; invitation to ITA General Membership Meeting at the ITA Convention.

INTERNATIONAL TENNIS FEDERATION
BANK LANE
ROEHAMPTON
LONDON, ENGLAND SW15 5XZ
communications@itftennis.com
www.itftennis.com
• David Haggerty, President
• Katrina Adams, Vice President
• Luca Santilli, Executive Director Tennis Development
• Mat Pemble, Head of Information And Communications Technology

Description:
The international governing body of tennis.

PETER BURWASH INTERNATIONAL
8909 WEST LANE
MAGNOLIA, TX 77354
281-764-8626
800-324-5494
pbihq@pbitennis.com
www.pbitennis.com
• Peter Burwash, Chief Executive Officer
• Rene Zondag, President

Description:
Founded 1975 by Canadian Davis Cup player, Peter Burwash. Contracts with tennis clubs, resorts and hotels worldwide to direct tennis operations, including instruction, marketing, promotion and management expertise. Provides coaching services and junior development programs to national tennis teams in different countries, as well as on an individual basis to tournament players. Also manages and designs tennis facilities.

Clients include:
Four Seasons, Jumeirah International, Rosewood Hotels & Resorts, Marriott, Hyatt, The American Club

Nature of service:
Tennis program operations, management and direction.

Publications:
PBI Magazine

PROFESSIONAL TENNIS REGISTRY
4 OFFICE WAY
SUITE 200
HILTON HEAD ISLAND, SC 29928
843-785-7244
800-421-6289
Fax: 843-686-2033
ptr@ptrtennis.org
• Dennis Van Der Meer, Chairman / President Emritus
• Dan Santorum, Chief Executive Officer
dan@ptrtennis.org
• Julie Jilly, Vice President of Marketing and Special Event
julie@ptrtennis.org
• Inaki Balzola, International Director
• Peggy Edwards, Director of Communications & Editor TennisPro
• Brian Parkkonen, Director of Development

Nature of Service:
Educates and certifies tennis teachers and coaches internationally.

Year Founded:
1976

Member Services:
Benefits to all aspects of tennis teaching profession.

Publications:
TennisPro Magazine

TENNIS CANADA
AVIVA CENTRE
1 SHOREHAM DRIVE
SUITE 100
TORONTO, ON, CANADA M3N 3A6
416-665-9777
877-283-6647
Fax: 416-665-9017
info@tenniscanada.com
www.tenniscanada.com
• John LeBoutillier, Chair
• Kelly D Murumets, President & Chief Executive Officer

Description:
Shall lead the growth, promotion and showcasing of the sport of tennis in Canada, build a system that helps produce world class players, and foster the pursuit of excellence for all. Owns and operates the men's and women's Rogers Cup events.

Founded:
1890

TENNIS INDUSTRY ASSOCIATION
5 NEW ORLEANS ROAD
SUITE 200
HILTON HEAD ISLAND, SC 29928
843-686-3036
866-686-3036
Fax: 843-686-3078
info@tennisindustry.org
www.tennisindustry.org
• Jolyn DeBoer, Executive Director

Year Founded:
1974

Description:
A not-for-profit trade association

representing the interest of its member cmopanies by keeping a pulse on the industry and its needs. Dedicated to maintaining the integrity of the sport and pursuing the growth and vitality of tennis.
Membership Levels:
Industry, Associate, TennisConnect, Supporting, Affiliate, Participating Partners
Publications:
USTA/TIA Participations Study, State of the Industry, market research and consumer reports.
Member Services:
Monthly racquet census, credit interchange, product liability and counterfeiting information, Washington lobbyist, trade show assistance. Participation research project. Meetings held during Sporting Goods Industry Association/SGMA meetings.

U.S. PROFESSIONAL TENNIS ASSOCIATION
3535 BRIARPARK DRIVE
SUITE 202
HOUSTON, TX 77042
713-978-7782
800-877-8248
Fax: 713-978-7780
uspta@uspta.org
www.uspta.com
• Chuck Gill, President
• John Embree, Chief Executive Officer
(713) 358-7782
john.embree@uspta.org
• Fred Viancos, Director Of Professional Development
(713) 358-7782
fred.viancos@uspta.org
• Kathy Buchanan, Director Of Computer Services
(713) 978-7780
kathy.buchanan@uspta.org
• Julie Myers, Director of Communications
(713) 978-7782
julie.myers@uspta.org
• Kimberly Forrester, Publications Manager/Managing Editor
(713) 978-7782
kim.forrester@uspta.org
Nature of Service:
The oldest and largest professional association of tennis-teaching professionals. Offers more than 60 professional benefits to its members, including certification and extensive educational opportunities.
Year Founded:
1927
Membership Requirements:
To be eligible for active membership status, a person must derive or intend to derive a major part of their income from teaching tennis. Persons who derive or intend to derive a major part of their income from prize money in professional tennis tournaments and exhibitions are also eligible. Corporate membership status is available to those persons who have some full-time connection with tennis, either in an executive, administrative or commercial capacity but who are not teachers. All certified members are offered a free, personalized site on the Internet.
Number of members:
15,000
Publications:
Annual Membership Directory; ADDvantage,

monthly magazine; World Conference Program, annual.

U.S. RACQUET STRINGERS ASSOCIATION
310 RICHARD ARRINGTON JR/ BLVD N #400
BIRMINGHAM, AL 35203
760-536-1177
Fax: 760-536-1171
usrsa@racquettech.com
www.racquettech.com
• Bob Patterson, MRT, Exective Director
(760) 536-1177
bob@racquettech.com
• Greg Raven, Technical Support &Webmaster
(760) 536-1177
greg@usrsa.com
• John Hanna, Ad Sales
(770) 650-1102
hanna@knowatlanta.com
• Dianne Pray, Membership Director/Office Manager
(760) 536-1177
dianne@racquettech.com
Number of members:
Over 7,000 worldwide.
Publications:
The Stringers Digest; RacquetTECH.com; Racquet Sports Industry Magazine; Racquet TECH Magazine; Racquet Service Video (4 volume set); Racquet Service Interactive CD-ROM workshops, certification, education and testing.
Description:
An organization of racquet technicians, teaching professionals, racquet sports retailers, manufacturers and sales organizations, and tennis, racquetball, squash and badminton players focusing on the servicing of racquets, strings, balls, courts, shoes, and stringing machines.
Year Founded:
1975

UNITED STATES TENNIS ASSOCIATION (USTA)
70 WEST RED OAK LANE
WHITE PLAINS, NY 10604
914-696-7000
www.usta.com
• Gordon Smith, Executive Director & Chief Operating Officer
• Andrea Hirsch, Chief Administrative Officer & General Counsel

Other locations:

USTA CARIBBEAN
PO BOX 190740
SAN JUAN, PUERTO RIC 00919-0740
787-726-8782
Fax: 787-982-7783
www.caribbean.usta.com
• Lydia de la Rosa, Executive Director
Description:
Embraces the concept that growth in tennis is best achieved by strategic alliances with other organizations, both inside and outside of tennis.

USTA EASTERN
70 WEST RED OAK LANE
WHITE PLAINS, NY 10604
914-697-2300
Fax: 914-694-2402
www.eastern.usta.com
• Jenny Schnitzer, Executive Director & Chief Operating Officer

Description:
One of the 17 geographic sections of the United States Tennis Association which is also the governing body of tennis in the United States. The Eastern Section has over 48,000 members throughout New York, Northern New Jersey and Greenwich, Connecticut. This section promotes and develops the growth of tennis as well as establishes and maintains rules of fair play, high standards of sportsmanship and represents in it jurisdiction, the programs and policies of the USTA.

USTA FLORIDA
1 DEUCE COURT
SUITE 100
DAYTONA BEACH, FL 32124
386-671-8949
www.ustaflorida.com
• Nancy Horowitz, President -Elect
• Bob Pfaender, President
• Barbara Manzo, Vice president
• Terri Florio, Secretary
• Karen McFarland, Treasurer
• Sherry Beckman, Volunteer Committee,Chair
• Donn Davis, Director At Large
• Robert Hollis, Vice President
Year Founded:
1949
Description:
A not-for-profit tennis association that relies on membership, sponsorships and fundraising to reach its mission-to promote and develop tennis in Florida. Offers tennis programs for all ages and ability levels, including League, Competitive, Recreational and Adaptive services, plus more
Members:
1,000+ member organizations; 50,000 individual members

USTA HAWAII PACIFIC
932 WARD AVENUE
SUITE 490
HONOLULU, HI 96814
808-585-9503
Fax: 808-585-9512
www.hawaii.usta.com
• Ron Romano, Executive Director
(808) 585-9526
romano@hawaii.usta.com
Description:
The USTA/Hawaii Pacific Section is one of 17 sections of the United States Tennis Association. The Hawaii Pacific Section is a not-for-profit volunteer organization. Our mission statement is to promote and develop the growth of tennis. The Hawaii Pacific Section has over 7,000 members and 100 organizations in Hawaii, American Samoa and Guam.

USTA INTERMOUNTAIN
9145 E KENYON AVENUE
SUITE 201
DENVER, CO 80237
303-695-4117
866-695-4117
Fax: 303-695-6518
wanderson@ita.usta.com
www.intermountain.usta.com
• Rob Scott, Executive Director
rscott@ita.usta.com
Description:
Committed to growing the game of tennis by offering quality recreational and competitive programs for people of all ages and abilities. Intermountain has more than 34,000 individual and over 230 organizational members in its six districts: Colorado, Idaho, Montana, Nevada, Utah and Wyoming.

USTA MID-ATLANTIC
11410 ISAAC NEWTON SQUARE NORTH
SUITE 270
RESTON, VA 20190
703-556-6120
Fax: 571-291-4432
www.midatlantic.usta.com

- Lynn Coddington, President
- Tara Fitzpatrick-Navarro, Executive Director

Sports Services Founded:
1923

Description:
The USTA/MAS, one of 17 sections of the United States Tennis Association, is a not-for-profit organization committed to promoting tennis by offering quality recreational and competitive programs for people of all ages and abilities. We serve 39,000 members in the District of Columbia, Virginia and eastern and southern West Virginia.

Number of Members:
39,000

USTA MIDDLE STATES
1288 VALLEY FORGE ROAD
SUITE 74
PO BOX 987
VALLEY FORGE, PA 19482-0987
610-935-5000
Fax: 610-935-5484
www.middlestates.usta.com
- Christian Sockel, President
- Marlynn Orlando, Executive Director
(484) 302-4404

Description:
The USTA/Middle States section encompasses Pennsylvania, Delaware, New Jersey (exclusive of a 35-mile radius around New york City) and northwestern West Virginia. Also dedicated to carrying out the goals of the national association within its region, particularly with respect to promoting tennis oppotunities for juniors and adults of all abilities and cultural backgrounds.

USTA MIDWEST
1310 EAST 96TH STREET
SUITE 100
INDIANAPOLIS, IN 46240
317-577-5130
Fax: 317-577-5131
feedback@midwest.usta.com
www.midwest.usta.com
- Mark Saunders, Executive Director
(317) 669-0441
- Chad Docktor, Director, Junior Tennis
(317) 669-0445
- Diane Ansay, Director, Adult Tennis
(317) 669-0451

Description:
The mission of the USTA/Midwest section is to promote, develop and service the game of tennis, focusing on the establishment of competitive, developmental, educationl and recreational programs for individuals of all ages and skill levels without regard to race, cree, color or national origin. Also promotes health, character, fair play, sportsmanship and social responsibility through tennis.

USTA MISSOURI VALLEY
6400 WEST 95TH STREET
SUITE 102
OVERLAND PARK, KS 66212
913-322-4800
888-368-8612
Fax: 913-322-4801
www.missourivalley.usta.com
- Stuart Dusenberry, President
sddins62@yahoo.com
- Mary Buschmann, Executive Director
(913) 322-4824
mbuschmann@movalley.usta.com

Description:
Not for profit organization covering a five state region of Iowa, Missouri, Nebraska, Oklahoma and parts of Illinois. This section has more than 22,500 individual members and more than 450 organization members. Also offers recreational and competitive tennis for all ages and abilities.

USTA NEW ENGLAND
110 TURNPIKE ROAD
WESTBOROUGH, MA 01581

508-366-3450
Fax: 508-366-5805
info@newengland.usta.com
www.newengland.usta.com
- Scott Steinberg, President
- Matt Olson, Executive Director & Chief Operating Officer
ext 29

Sports Services Founded:
1927

Description:
A non-profit organization, USTA New England uses its funds to promote and develop the growth of tennis at all levels, offering grants and resources to foster the implementation of programming for players from beginner to veteran; from recreational to competitive and from all ages and backgrounds.

USTA NORTHERN
1001 WEST 98TH STREET
SUITE 101
BLOOMINGTON, MN 55431
952-887-5001
800-536-6982
Fax: 952-887-5061
www.northern.usta.com
- Kathleen Lundberg, President
kathylundberg@comcast.net
- Mike Goldammer, Executive Director
(952) 358-3284

Sports Services Founded:
1953

Description:
A not-for-profit volunteer-based organization with approximately 35,000 adult members, 9,000 junior members and almost 700 organization members.

USTA NORTHERN CALIFORNIA
1920 NORTH LOOP ROAD
ALAMEDA, CA 94502-8018
510-748-7373
Fax: 510-748-7377
www.norcal.usta.com
- Margie Campbell, President
- Steve Leube, Executive Director
(510) 748-7362

Description:
Non profit volunteer based organization with 34,626 adult members, 7,816 junior members and 503 organization members. THe 8th largest geographic section, USTA Northern California Section has been promoting, servicing, and administering USTA programs for over 49 years. USTA NorCal is devoted to promoting and developing the growth of tennis in Northern California.

USTA PACIFIC NORTHWEST
9746 SW NIMBUS AVENUE
BEAVERTON, OR 97008
503-520-1877
info@pnw.usta.com
www.pnw.usta.com
- Allen Clendaniel, President
- Matthew Warren, Executive Director
ext 19

Description:
A not-for-profit organization comprised of over 24,000 individual and organizational members committed to promoting and developing recreational and competitive tennis. Over 200 volunteers and 300 tournaments make up the backbone for grassroots tennis in the Pacific Northwest.

USTA SOUTHERN
5685 SPALDING DRIVE
NORCROSS, GA 30092
770-368-8200
Fax: 770-368-9091
info@sta.usta.com
www.southern.usta.com
- Paula Hale, President & CEO
- John Callen, Executive Director & Chief

Operating Officer
(770) 368-8200

Description:
The 181,000+ members living in Alabama, Arkansas, Georgia, Kentucky, Louisianna, Mississippi, North Carolina, South Carolina, and Tennessee comprise the USTA Southern Section, and account for approximately 25% of the total USAT membership.

Year Founded:
1881

USTA SOUTHERN CALIFORNIA
420 CHARLES E. YOUNG DRIVE WEST
LOS ANGELES, CA 90024
310-208-3838
Fax: 310-824-7691
www.scta.usta.com
- William Kellogg, President
- Bruce Hunt, Executive Director
(310) 208-3838
bhunt@scta.usta.com

Sports Services Founded:
1887

Description:
Committed to promoting the game of tennis by offering quality recreational and competitive programs for people of all ages and abilities. Comprising Imperial, Kern, Los Angeles, Orange, Riverside, San Bernardino, San Luis Obispo, Santa barbara and Ventura Counties.

USTA SOUTHWEST
7010 E ACOMA DRIVE
SUITE 201
SCOTTSDALE, AZ 85254
480-289-2351
Fax: 480-289-2701
info@southwest.usta.com
www.southwest.usta.com
- Paul Burns, President
- Eric Mitchell, Executive Director
(480) 289-2351
mitchell@southwest.usta.com

Description:
To promote and develop tennis in the Southwest, the USTA Southwest Section services the needs of the playing public and encourages the growth of tennis by administering tennis programming, providing overall support and guidance to its eight Chatered USTA Community Tennis Associations and serving as a source for comprehensive information on tennis.

USTA TEXAS
8105 EXCHANGE DRIVE
AUSTIN, TX 78754
512-443-1334
Fax: 512-443-4748
www.texas.usta.com
- Frank Kelly, President
- Van Barry, Executive Director
(512) 443-1334

Sports Services Founded:
1985.

Description:
Not for profit volunteer organization with 47,000 individual members and 421 organizational members. The USTA Texas Section is the fastest growing of the 17 sections and features a Pathway of tennis programs for beginning, recreational and competitive juniors, adults and seniors.

WOMEN'S TENNIS ASSOCIATION TOUR
100 SECOND AVENUE SOUTH
SUITE 1100-S
ST. PETERSBURG, FL 33701
727-895-5000
Fax: 727-894-1982
www.wtatour.com
- Micky Lawler, President
- Steve Simon, Chairman/CEO
- Matthew Cenedella, Chief Operating Officer

• Melissa Pine, Vice President, Tournament Director
• Joan Pennello, Senior Vice President, Operations
• Jean Nachand, Vice President, Competition
• Heather Bowler, Senior Vice President, Communications
• Wendy Jang, Commercial VP, Asia Pacific
Nature of Sport Service:
Leading professional sport for women with over 2,500 players from over 100 nations, the WTA holds competitions comprising of 55 events and 4 grand slams annually.
WTA Tour European Headquarters:
Palliser House, Palliser Road London W14 9EB United Kingdom Phone: +44 20 7386 4100, Fax: +44 20 7386 4102

Tennis, Leagues/Teams

MYLAN WORLD TEAM TENNIS
1776 BROADWAY
SUITE 600
NEW YORK, NY 10019
212-586-3444
Fax: 212-586-6277
www.wtt.com
• Billie Jean King, Co-Founder
• Ilana Kloss, Chief Executive Officer & Commissioner
Description:
Founded 1981. Nation's only professional co-ed team sport. Each team consists of four players; two men and two women. Nationwide recreational program following the same format as the professional league.
Publications:
SUPERTIEBREAKER, annual magazine.
Teams:
Boston Lobsters, Philadelphia Freedoms, Washington Kastles, Newport Beach Breakers, plus teams listed below.

Teams:

BOSTON LOBSTERS
BOSTON LOBSTERS TENNIS CENTER
8 ATWATER AVENUE
MANCHESTER BY THE SEA, MA 01944
877-617-5627
• Colleen Hopkins, General Manager

CALIFORNIA DREAM
SUNRISE MALL
5912 SUNRISE MALL ROAD
CITRUS HEIGHTS, CA 95610
916-967-6000
• Jeff Launius, General Manager

ORANGE CITY BREAKERS
2549 EASTBLUFF DRIVE
SUITE 810
NEWPORT BEACH, CA 92660
949-434-4560
www.breakerstennis.com
• Allen Hardison, General Manager

PHILADELPHIA FREEDOMS
PO BOX 268
GWYNEDD, PA 19436
215-667-8132
www.philadelphiafreedoms.com
• Barbara Perry, General Manager

SAN DIEGO AVIATORS
2658 DEL MAR HEIGHTS ROAD
SUITE 199
DEL MAR, CA 92014
888-774-0110
www.sandiegoaviators.com
• Fred Luddy, Owner

SPRINGFIELD LASERS
1923 NORTH WELLER
SPRINGFIELD, MO 65803
417-864-1339
www.springfieldlasers.com
• Paul Nahon, General Manager

WASHINGTON KASTLES
509 7TH STREET NW
WASHINGTON, DC 20004
202-483-6647
www.washingtonkastles.com

USTA LEAGUE
70 WEST RED OAK LANE
WHITE PLAINS, NY 10604
914-696-7000
tennislink.usta.com
Description:
Largest recreational tennis league in the United States with four divisions: Adult, Senior, Super Senior and Mixed Doubles.
Members:
330,000+
Publications:
TENNIS magazine; Tennis Tuesday, weekly digital magazine; Bounce magazine (i)

Track & Field Organizations

ATHLETICS CANADA
2445 ST LAURENT BOULEVARD
SUITE B1-110
OTTAWA, ON, CANADA K1G 6C3
613-260-5580
Fax: 613-260-0341
www.athletics.ca
• Gordon Orlikow, Chairman Board of Directors
gordon.orlikow@kornferry.com
• Rob Guy, CEO
(613) 260-5580
rguy@athletics.ca
• Andrew Cameron, IT, Membership & static Service
(613) 260-5580
acameron@athletics.ca
• Sylvie King, Chief Financial Officer
(613) 260-5580
• Judy McCallum, Assistant,Finance
• Andrew Page, Manager, Coach Development
(613) 260-5580
andrew.page@athletics.ca
Member Services:
Coaching Certification Program. Officials Grading Program. National Team, Annual General Meeting each spring, Run Canada Division, Awards program, National Technical Assembly, each fall. Wide range of grassroots and nationally televised sponsorship programs available.
Membership Requirements:
Open to all interested in track and field athletics who pay annual membership fee. Membership categories include affiliated, individual, athletic, associate sustaining, life.
Description:
The national sport governing body for track

and field, including cross-country running and road running, Athletics Canada supports high performance athletics excellence at the world level and provides leadership in developmental athletics.

INTERCOLLEGIATE ASSOCIATION OF AMATEUR ATHLETES OF AMERICA/IC4A
39 OLD RIDGEBURY ROAD
SUITE 22
DANBURY, CT 06810
203-745-0434
Fax: 203-745-0440
www.ecac.org
• Steve Bartold, IC4A Administrator
(203) 245-5862
Stevebartold@sbcglobal.net
• Dylan Clark, ECAC Assistant For Championships, Leagues
(203) 745-2786
DClark@ecac.org
Description:
The Intercollegiate Association of Amateur Athletes of America is a men's division I indoor and outdoor track and field competition under the responsibility of the Eastern College Athletic Conference.

INTERNATIONAL ASSOCIATION OF ATHLETICS FEDERATIONS (IAAF)
6-8 QUAI ANTOINE
BP 359
MONTE CARLO, MONACO 98007
info@iaaf.org
www.iaaf.org
• Sebastian Coe, President
Description:
The International Amateur Athletic Federation is the international governing body for track and field sport.

U.S. TRACK & FIELD AND CROSS COUNTRY COACHES ASSOCIATION
1100 POYDRAS STREET
SUITE 1750
NEW ORLEANS, LA 70163
504-599-8900
Fax: 504-599-8909
www.ustfccca.org
• Sam Seemes, CEO
sam@ustfccca.org
• Mike Corn, Assistant Director
(504) 599-8903
mike@ustfccca.org
• Curtis Akey, Communications Manager
(504) 599-8905
curtis@ustfccca.org
• Tyler Mayforth, Communications assistant
(504) 599-8904
tyler@ustfccca.org
• Kristina Taylor, Membership Services And Operations
(504) 599-8901
kristina@ustfccca.org
Membership Requirements:
Collegiate cross country coach.
Description:
A non-profit lobbying for the interests of track and field coaches at all three divisional levels; membership consists of over 6,000.

USA TRACK & FIELD
132 EAST WASHINGTON STREET
SUITE 800
INDIANAPOLIS, IN 46204

317-261-0500
Fax: 317-261-0481
www.usatf.org
• Max Siegel, Chief Executive Officer
ceo@usatf.org
• Terry Crawford, Director Of Coaching
(317) 713-4671
Terry.Crawford@usatf.org
Description:
USA Track & Field acts as the National
Governing Body for track and field athletics.

USA TRACK & FIELD - NEW YORK
1365 NORTH RAILROAD AVENUE
#116
STATEN ISLAND, NY 10306
609-915-3039
lauren.primerano@newyork.usatf.org
www.newyork.usatf.org
• Lauren Primerano, President
(609) 915-3039
• John Padula, First Vice President
(718) 809-4915
Year Founded:
1980
Description:
Formerly The Metropolitan Athletics
Congress, the regional association of the
USA Track and Field (USATF), and
sanctions track and field events throughout
New York City and the metropolitan area
year-round.

Triathlon Organizations

BRITISH TRIATHLON ASSOCIATION
SIR JOHN BECKWITH BUILDING
LOUGHBOROUGH
PO Box 25
LOUGHBOROUGH, ENGLAND LE11 3WX
info@britishtriathlon.org
www.britishtriathlon.org
• Ian Howard, TD, President
• Jack Buckner, CEO
• Bill James, Director Triathlon England
• Andy Salmon, Director Triathlon Scotland
• Nicky Dick, Director Age-Group Team
• Jon Ridgeon, Director major & National
Events
• Craig Stewart, Independent Non-Executive
Director Finance
• Mike Battersby, Director Welsh Trialthon
Organization activities:
The British Triathlon Federation is a
govering organization made up of English,
Scotish, and Welsh triathlon associations.

INTERNATIONAL TRIATHLON UNION
998 HARBOURSIDE DRIVE
#220
NORTH VANCOUVER, BC, CANADA V7P
3T2
604-904-9248
Fax: 604-904-3195
ituhdq@triathlon.org
www.triathlon.org
• Marisol Casado, President
• Loreen Barnett, First Vice President

IRONMAN PROPERTIES
2701 NORTH ROCKY POINT DRIVE
SUITE 1250
TAMPA, FL 33607
813-868-5940
Fax: 813-868-5930

• Steve Johnston, President
Sports Service Founded:
1989
Event Management Services:
Producer of the Ironman Triathlon World
Championship.
Triathlon Sponsor:
Title Sponsor: Ironman Triathlon World
Championship.

TRIATHLON CANADA
1925 BIANSHARD STREET
SUITE 121
VICTORIA, BC, CANADA V8T 4J2
250-412-1795
Fax: 250-412-1794
info@triathloncanada.com
www.triathloncanada.com
• Les Pereira, President
• Kim Van Bruggen, CEO
kim.vanbruggen@triathloncanada.com
• Eugene Liang, High Performance Director
eugene.liang@triathloncanada.com
• Chris Dornan, Communications Manager
(403) 620-8731
hpprchris@shaw.ca
• Tenille Hoogland, Age Group Teams
Manager
tenille.hoogland@triathloncanada.com
Description:
Triathlon Canada is a national sanctioning
orgnaization which selects national team
members, organizes competitions, and
advoactes for the promotion and growth of
the sport in Canada.

USA TRIATHLON
5825 DELMONICO DRIVE
SUITE 200
COLORADO SPRINGS, CO 80919
719-955-2807
info@usatriathlon.org
www.teamusa.org/usa-triathlon
• Rob Urbach, Chief Executive Officer
• Tim Yount, Chief Operating Officer
(719) 955-2831
tim.yount@usatriathlon.org
Nature of Service:
USA Triathlon is the National Governing
Body for triathlon, duathlon, aquathlon and
winter triathlon in the United States.
Year Founded:
1982
Member Services:
USAT offers annual memberships which, in
addition to many other benefits, cover
members at all USAT sanctioned events for
12 full months. One-day licenses which
cover one event and annual elite
memberships are also available.

Tug of War Organizations

TUG OF WAR FEDERATION
4742 STATE HIGHWAY 213
PO BOX 77
ORFORDVILLE, WI 53576-0077
608-879-2869
Fax: 608-879-2103
twif@t6b.com
www.tugofwar-twif.org
• Anton Rabe, President
anton@hortgro.co.za
• Glen Johnson, Secretary General
(608) 879-2869

twif@t6b.com
• Dariusz Bajkowski, Senior VP
• Peter Dyer, Treasurer
pete.dyer@talktalk.net

Volleyball Organizations

**AMERICAN VOLLEYBALL COACHES
ASSOCIATION**
2365 HARRODSBURG ROAD
SUITE A325
LEXINGTON, KY 40504
859-226-4315
866-544-2822
Fax: 859-226-4315
members@avca.org
www.avca.org
• Christy Johnson-Lynch, President
(515) 294-3395
christyj@iastate.edu
• Mark Rosen, President elect
(734) 647-3035
rosenma@umich.edu
• Kirsten Bernthal Booth, Division I rep
(402) 280-5794
kbooth@creighton.edu
• Chuck Waddington, Division II rep
(325) 486-6068
cwaddington@angelo.edu
• Tammy Swearingen, Division III rep
(724) 946-7320
swearitl@westminster.edu
• David Weitl, Club Representative
(360) 779-3802
dw@wvba.org
• William Ebel, III, Assistant Coaches
Representative
(615) 491-2560
Publications:
Coaching Volleyball Magazine, print and
digital editions.
Description:
To advance the sport of volleyball and its
coaches.
Member Services:
Annual Convention; Awards Program;
Weekly Polls; Educational Opportunities.
Number of members:
Over 7,000.

**ASSOCIATION OF VOLLEYBALL
PROFESSIONALS/AVP**
6100 CENTER DR
9TH FLOOR
LOS ANGELES, CA 90045
949-678-3599
contact@avp.com
www.avp.com
• Tony Giarla, Director
tonyg@avp.com
• Marty Suan, Director Of Programs
Member Services:
Opportunity to compete in Professional
Beach Volleyball tournaments; publicity;
health and accident insurance.

**FEDERATION INTERNATIONALE DE
VOLLEYBALL (FIVB)**
CHATEAU LES TOURELLAS
EDOUARD-SANDOZ 2-4
LAUSANNE, SWITZERLAN 1006
info@fivb.org
www.fivb.org
• Ary S. Filho, Dr.
president.office.sec@fivb.org

Purpose of organization:
Acts as international governing body for the sport of volleyball.

LONE STAR CLASSIC NATIONAL VOLLEYBALL QUALIFIER
425 WOODWARD STREET
AUSTIN, TX 78704
512-479-8776
Fax: 512-479-0080
www.austinsportscenter.com
• Glen Lietzke, Executive Director
(512) 433-5110
glen@austinsportscenter.com
• Jonathan Paris, Director of Events
(512) 433-5114
jparis@austinsportscenter.com
• Scott Clouse, Communications/video speacialist
(512) 433-5120
scott@austinsportscenter.com
• Lindsay Dunn, Controller
(512) 433-5104
LDunn@austinsportscenter.com
Event Management & Consulting Services:
Owns and operates the Lone Star Classic National Qualifier and 3rd Coast Volleyball Championships. Creates and manages sports events, focusing on volleyball.

UNITED STATES YOUTH VOLLEYBALL LEAGUE
2771 PLAZA DEL AMO
SUITE 808
TORRANCE, CA 90503
310-212-7008
888-988-7985
Fax: 310-212-7182
info@usyvl.org
www.usyvl.org
• Allen Adams, President
• Jon Bitler, Vice President
• Randy Sapoznik, Secretary
• Bill Martinez, Treasurer
Membership Requirements:
Open registration for boys and girls ages 7-15.
Description:
The United States Youth Volleyball League is a non-profit instructional volley ball organization for children between the ages of 7 and 15.

USA VOLLEYBALL
4065 SINTON ROAD
SUITE 200
COLORADO SPRINGS, CO 80907
719-228-6800
Fax: 719-228-6899
postmaster@usav.org
www.usavolleyball.org
• Lori Okimura, Board Chair
loriokimura@hotmail.com
Organization purpose:
Acting as the national governing body for volleyball in the United States, USA Volleyball promotes growth of the sport and increased success in competition.

VOLLEYBALL CANADA
1A-1084 KENASTON STREET
OTTAWA, ON, CANADA K1B 3P5
613-748-5681
Fax: 613-748-5727
info@volleyball.ca
www.volleyball.ca

• Mark Eckert, President & CEO
(613) 748-5681
meckert@volleyball.ca
• Ian Halliday, High Performance Director
(403) 880-9845
ihalliday@volleyball.ca
• Jackie Skender, Communication Director
(613) 748-5681
jskender@volleyball.ca
• Caitlin Devlin, Domestic Events Coordinator
(613) 748-5681
caitlin@volleyball.ca
• Linden Leung, Finance & Operations Director
(613) 748-5681
linden@volleyball.ca
Description:
Founded 1953. Promotes the sport of volleyball in Canada.
Membership Requirements:
Provincial affiliation.
Publications:
Many technical publications (books, manuals and VHS videos) as well as yearly Indoor and Outdoor Rulebooks.
Member Services:
Organization of national championships; Publications; Elite development programs for coaches and officials; National team programs and events, Labatt Pro Beach Volleyball Tour.

Water Polo Organizations

AMERICAN WATER POLO COACHES ASSOCIATION
2124 MAIN STREET
SUITE 240
HUNTINGTON BEACH, CA 92648
714-500-5445
Fax: 714-960-2431
www.usawaterpolo.com
• Christopher Ramsey, Chief Executive Officer
(714) 500-8506
• Greg Mescall, Director Of Communications
(714) 500-5455
gmescall@usawaterpolo.org
• John Adbou, Chief High Performance Director
(714) 500-5445
jabdou@usawaterpolo.org
Description:
Organized to serve as the national governing body for the sport of water polo in the United States under the auspices of the United States olympic Committe.

WATER POLO CANADA
1084 KENASTON STREET
UNIT 1A
OTTAWA, CANADA K1B 3P5
613-748-5682
Fax: 613-748-5777
database@waterpolo.ca
www.waterpolo.ca
• Conrad Hadubiak, President
chadubiak@gmail.com
• Josee Lanouette, Vice President
j.lanouette@johnabbott.qc.ca
• Martin Goulet, Executive Director
(613) 748-5777
mgoulet@waterpolo.ca
• Mylene Turcotte-Fitzgerald, Communication And Domestic Operations

Coodinator
(613) 748-5682
mfitzgerald@waterpolo.ca
Member Services:
Insurance-liability and accident; Discounts on publications and merchandise; newsletter; national championships; player development programs, coaching development and officials development. Annual meeting in the month of October
Publications:
Wide range of coaching and refereeing materials; International Rules of Water Polo.
Membership Requirements:
Should be fully registered with both the provincial association as well as the national association.

Water Skiing Organizations

INTERNATIONAL WATER SKI & WAKEBOARD FEDERATION
POST BOX 564
UNTERAEGERI, SWITZERLAN 6314
iwwf@iwwfed.com
www.iwsf.com
• Kuno Ritschard, President
president@iwwfed.com
• Gillian Hill, Secreaty General
gill@mywaterskiemail.com
• David Skillen, Treasurer
daskillen@yahoo.com
Membership Requirements:
International governing body for towed watersports.

USA WATER SKI
1251 HOLY COW ROAD
POLK CITY, FL 33868
863-324-4341
Fax: 863-325-8259
usawaterski@usawaterski.org
www.usawaterski.org
• Jim Grew, President
(971) 871-5500
jimhgrewjr@cs.com
• Dale R. Stevens, Vice President
(561) 596-8710
stevensdalel@gmail.com
• Bob Crowley, Executive Director
(406) 599-1570
• Doug Robbins, Chair
(724) 935-5333
drobbins@teleplexinc.com
• Robert R. Rhyne, III, Treasurer
(704) 906-7779
robrhyne@hotmail.com
Nature of Service:
The national governing body of organized water skiing in the United States. A member of the International Water Ski Federation (world governing body), the Pan American Sports Organization and the United States Olympic Committee.
Year Founded:
1939
Member Services:
Sanction competition. Skier's rating system; instructor certification; summer camp program.
Membership Requirements:
Open - dues of $25 for Supporting and $80 for Competitive.
Number of members:
15,000
Publications:

THE WATER SKIER, 6 time(s) annually; how-to booklet series.

WATER SKI & WAKEBOARD CANADA
2420 BANK STREET
OTTAWA, ON, CANADA K1V 8S1
613-526-0685
Fax: 613-701-0385
info@wswc.ca
• Glenn Bowie, Chair
• Jasmine Northcott, Chief Executive Officer
(613) 526-0685
jasmine@wswc.ca
• Steve Jarrett, Director
• Karen McClintock, Director
• Jo-Anne Moore, Director
• Kevin Neveu, Director
Nature of Service:
The sole national sport governing body and recognized water skiing/wakeboard authority in Canada. Mission is to develop and promote organized water skiing, wakeboarding and other towed water sports from beginner to pro.
Year Founded:
1971
Member Services:
Coaching development programs; athlete development programs; publications; officials development program.
Publications:
What's Up In Water Sports (monthly newsletter)

WORLD SPORTS & MARKETING
460 N. ORLANDO AVE
SUITE 200
WINTER PARK, FL 32789
www.bonniercorp.com/other-brands
• Ben Greenwood, Sponsorship Sales
(407) 571-4518
• Evily Giannopoulos, Associate Director Of Public Relations
(407) 571-4587
• Priscilla Scollin, Marketing Manager & Registration
(407) 405-0121
Priscilla.Scollin@bonniercorp.com
Sports Service Founded:
1988
Services:
Sports: Clearinghouse for the Pro Wakeboard Tour including the coordination of the scheduling, television, global sponsorships, public relations, venue evaluation and event selection.
Event Management Services:
Managed all aspects of the US Pro Water Ski Tour, US Pro Wakeboard Tour, VANS Triple Crown of Wakeboarding, Malibu Just Ride Series, Malibu Open, Water Ski Magazine's America's Cup.

Weightlifting Organizations

INTERNATIONAL POWERLIFTING FEDERATION
1 RUE PASTEUR
DIFFERDANGE, 4642
info@powerlifting-ipf.com
www.powerlifting-ipf.com
• Gaston Parage, President
Gaston.Parage@powerlifting-ipf.com
• Sigurjon Petursson, Vice-President
sigurjonp@gmail.com

• Robert Keller, Secretary General
rhk@verizon.net
• Dietmar Wolf, Treasurer
Dietmar.Wolf@powerlifting-ipf.com
Description:
International governing body for the sport of powerlifting.

INTERNATIONAL WEIGHTLIFTING FEDERATION (IWF)
H-1146
BUDAPEST, ISTVANMEZEI ut 1-3, HUNGARY
iwf@iwf.net
www.iwf.net
• Tamas Ajan, President
• Ma Wenguang, General Secretary
Description:
International governing body for the sport of weightlifting.

U.S. POWERLIFTING ASSOCIATION
3921 E LA PALMER AVE B
ANAHEIM, CA 92807
661-333-9800
steve@uspa.net
uspa.net
• Steve Denison, President
steve@uspa.net
• Shelley Denison, Secretary/Treasurer
shelsters10@yahoo.com
Member Services:
Sanction meets, register clubs, select U.S. teams for international (including world) powerlifting meets, supervise sanctioned events, provide liability insurance.
Membership Requirements:
Minimum age 14, payment of annual dues.
Description:
Founded 1964. Serves to promote powerlifting.

Windsurfing Organizations

U.S. WINDSURFING
8211 SUN SPRING CIR.
UNIT 73
ORLANDO, FL 32825
877-386-8708
info@uswindsurfing.org
www.uswindsurfing.org
• Jerome Samson, President
samson_jerome@yahoo.com
• Jim McGrath, Acting Secretary
(510) 848-8071
macmcgrath@comcast.net
• Bryan McDonald, National Director
(408) 425-3782
dude1@apple.com
• Bill Keitel, VP
(507) 372-7175
bill.keitel@gmail.com
Membership Requirements:
Payment of dues.
Description:
Dedicated to making the whole windsurfing experience more positive for windsurfers in the USA, and to encourage participation and promote excellence in recreational windsurfing and racing in the United States.

Wrestling Organizations

EASTERN INTERCOLLEGIATE WRESTLING ASSOCIATION
641 TAYLOR STREET
BETHLEHEM, PA 18015
eiwawrestling.org
• Dan Wirnsberger, President - EIWA Coaches Association
djw020@bucknell.edu
• Mark Letcher, President - EWIOA Officials Association
• Greg Strobel, Executive Director
gos2@lehigh.edu
Description:
Member schools include: Brown, Columbia, Cornell, Franklin & Marshall, Harvard, Lehigh, Pennsylvania, Princeton, Syracuse, U.S. Military Academy, U.S. Naval Academy.

NATIONAL WRESTLING COACHES ASSOCIATION
1976 AUCTION ROAD
PO BOX 254
MANHEIM, PA 17545
717-653-8009
Fax: 717-665-35737
www.nwcaonline.com
• Mike Moyer, Executive Director
(717) 653-8009
• Pat Tocci, Senior Director
(717) 653-8009
• Amy Dicato, Office Manager
(717) 653-8009
• Don Shelly, Finance Manager
(717) 653-8009
Member Services:
Selects Coach of the Year. Provides All-American certificates to top eight places in each weight class at nationals. Provides award for outstanding NCAA Division 1 Wrestler. Provides award for most falls. Provides 25 year service awards. Sponsors NWCA All Star Classic, NWCA National Dual Meet Tournament, National Wrestling Scholastic Showcase, NWCA Annual Convention. Serves as a clearing house for information to both scholastic and collegiate wrestling coaches and fans. Recognizes the National high school coach and assistant coach of the year and the outstanding high school wrestler of the year.
Description:
A professional organization dedicated to serve and provide leadership for the advancement of all levels of the sport of wrestling with primary emphasis on scholastic and collegiate wrestling programs.
Year Founded:
1928

UNITED WORLD WRESTLING
6 RUE DU CHATEAU
CORSIER-SUR-VEVEY, SWITZERLAN 1804
info@unitedworldwrestling.org
unitedworldwrestling.org
• Nenad Lalovic, President
lalovic@unitedworldwrestling.org
• Stan Dziedzic, Vice-President
Founded:
1921
Description:

International governing body for amateur olympic wrestling.

USA WRESTLING
6155 LEHMAN DR
COLORADO SPRINGS, CO 80918
719-598-8181
Fax: 719-598-9440
www.usawrestling.org
• Bruce Baumgartner, President
• Rich Bender, Executive Director
rbender@usawrestling.org
Membership:
226,000 members
Organization mission:
As part of the United States Olympic Committee, USA Wrestling oversees and promotes amateur wrestling competition at the national level.

WORLD WRESTLING ENTERTAINMENT
1241 E MAIN STREET
STAMFORD, CT 6902
203-352-8600
Fax: 203-359-5109
www.wwe.com
• Vincent K. McMahon, Chairman/CEO
• George Barrios, CFO
• Kevin Dunn, Executive VP, Television Production
• Paul Levesque, Executive VP, Talent, Live Events & Creative
• Michael Luisi, President, WWE Studios
• Stephanie McMahon, Chief Brand Officer
• Michelle D Wilson, Chief Marketing Officer
Description:
An integrated media organization and recognized leader in global entertainment. The company consists of a portfolio of businesses that create and deliver original content 52 weeks a year to a global audience. WWE is committed to family-friendly, PG content across all of its platforms including television programming, pay-per-view, digital media and publishing. WWE programming is broadcast in more than 180 countries.

WRESTLING CANADA
7-5370 CANOTEK RD
OTTAWA, ON, CANADA K1J 9E6
613-748-5686
Fax: 613-748-5756
info@wrestling.ca
• Don Ryan, President
• Tamara Medwidsky, Executive Director
tamara@wrestling.ca

• Leigh Vierling, High performance Director
• Tonya Verbeek, International Coach
• Eric Smith, Finance and administrative coordinator
• Patrick Kenny, Communications Officer
media@wrestling.ca
Description:
The national sport governing body for Olympic style wrestling in Canada. The association's role is to encourage and develop the widest participation and highest proficiency in Olympic wrestling in Canada.
Membership Requirements:
Membership through provincial associations, National Team, Board of Directors.

Yachting Organizations

AMERICAN BOAT & YACHT COUNCIL
613 THIRD STREET
SUITE 10
ANNAPOLIS, MD 21403
410-990-4460
Fax: 410-990-4466
www.abycinc.org
• John Adey, President
(410) 990-4460
jadey@abycinc.org
• Kevin Scullen, Membership Manager
(410) 990-4460
kscullen@abycinc.org
• Kenneth Weinbrecht, Chairman of the Board
• Brian Goodwin, Technical Director
(410) 990-4460
bgoodwin@abycinc.org
Nature of Service:
To develop quality technical practices and engineering standards for the design, construction, maintenance and repair of small crafts with refernce to their safety.

SAIL CANADA
PORTSMOUTH OLYMPIC HARBOUR
53 YONGE STREET
KINGSTON, ON, CANADA K7M 6G4
613-545-3044
Fax: 613-545-3045
sailcanada@sailing.ca
www.sailing.ca
• Todd Irving, President
president@sailing.ca
• Don Adams, Chief Executive Officer
(613) 545-3944
• Ken Dool, Canadian Sailing Team Head coach

(613) 545-3044
ken@sailing.ca
• Sarah Case, Business Development Manager
(613) 545-3044
• Colleen Coderre, High Performance Coordinator
(613) 545-3044
Newsletter:
Canadian Sailing Review
Year Founded:
1931
Description:
The national governing body for the sport of sailing. Promotes sailing and power boating through collaboration with partners, the Provincial Sailing Associations, member clubs, schools, and many individual stakeholders.

WORLD SAILING
ARIADNE HOUSE
TOWN QUAY
SOUTHAMPTON, HAMPSHIRE, ENGLAND
SO14 2AQ
secretariat@isaf.co.uk
www.sailing.org
• Kim Andersen, President
Organization Description:
World Sailing acts as the international governing body for the sport of sailing, a responsibility which includes the international promotion of sailing, training of judges and administrators, and the development of rules and regulations for sailing competitions.

YACHTWORLD.COM
150 GRANBY STREEET
NORFOLK, VA 23510
877-354-4069
www.yachtworld.com
• Sam Fulton, President/Chief Executive Officer
Sports Service Founded:
1995
Nature of Sports Service:
Site uses the Internet to establish relationships between yacht brokers and boat dealers, and prospective buyers from around the world. More than 2,402 participating brokers, more than 108,403 current boat listings valued over $41,075,849,605 billion, and the largest photo database of boats for sale on the Internet.

2
multi sports

multi sports

multi sports

multi sports

Athletic Foundations

A.C. GREEN YOUTH FOUNDATION
904 SILVER SPUR ROAD
SUITE 416
ROLLING HILLS, CA 90274
310-465-1470
800-229-6884
Fax: 310-465-1471
info@acgreen.com
www.acgreen.com
• A.C. Green, Jr, Founder/President
Nature of Sports Service:
Provides youth leadership program focused on basketball; promotes abstinence and education on social issues effecting youth.

ANDRE AGASSI FOUNDATION FOR EDUCATION
1120 NORTH TOWN CENTER DRIVE
SUITE 160
LAS VEGAS, NV 89144
702-227-5700
Fax: 702-866-2928
info@agassi.net
www.agassifoundation.org
• Andre Agassi, Chairman/Founder
• Steve Miller, CEO
• Evy Nickell, Executive Assistant
• Julie Pippenger, COO
• Shawn Cable, Chief Financial Officer
• Francisco Aguilar, General Counsel
Year Founded:
1994
Description:
Created to provide recreational and educational oppotunities for at-risk children in Southern Nevada. Athlete: Andre Agassi - Professional Tennis player.

ARTHUR ASHE LEARNING CENTER
67 WEST STREET
SUITE 401
BROOKLYN, NY 11222
646-352-1774
www.arthurashe.org
Description:
A non-profit organization devoted to using the life and legacy of tennis player Arthur Ashe for the promotion of education.

BOOMER ESIASON FOUNDATION
483 10TH AVENUE
SUITE 300
NEW YORK, NY 10018
646-292-7930
Fax: 646-292-7945
www.esiason.org
• Boomer Esiason, Co-Chairman
• David B. B Rimington, President
• Etsuko Murase, Chief Financial Officer/Chief Operations Officer
• Michaela Johnson, President, Team Boomer
• Natalie Stout, Program Director
• Tami Amaker, Special Program Director
• Rich Hahn, Operations Director
• Katie Dougherty, Program Coordinator
Sports Service Founded:
1993
Description:
A foundation comprised of medical and business professionals providing support, education, and financial contributions for research aimed at curing cystic fibrosis.

BRIAN MITCHELL FOUNDATION, THE
PO BOX 230055
CENTREVILLE, VA 20120
866-968-8426
Fax: 866-968-8426

DAN MARINO FOUNDATION
400 NORTH AMERICAN AVENUE
FORT LAUDEDALE, FL 33301
954-368-6000
info@danmarinofoundation.org
www.danmarinofoundation.org
• Dan Marino, Co-Founder/Chairman
• Claire Marino, Co-Founder/Treasurer
• Mary Partin, Chief Executive Officer
mpartin@danmarinofoundation.org
• Charinus Johnson, Chief Operating Officer
cjohnson@danmarinofoundation.org
• Alice Moore, Director of Human Resources
amoore@danmarinofoundation.org
• Tammy Bresnahan, Director Of Academic Programs
tbresnahan@danmarinofoundation.org
• Betsy Christy, Director Of Accounting
bchristy@danmarinofoundation.org
• Mark Pfefer, Director Of Business Development
mpfefer@danmarinofoundation.org
Nature of Sports Service:
Non-profit supports independence for children with special needs, teenagers transitioning from foster care and young adults with disabilities.
Sports Service Founded:
1992

DETLEF SCHREMPF FOUNDATION
1904 THIRD AVENUE
SUITE 339
SEATTLE, WA 98101
206-464-0826
Fax: 206-464-8020
info@detlef.com
www.detlef.com
• Detlef Schrempf, President
• Mari Schrempf, Vice President
• Chris Levitt, Vice President
• Nicole P Morrison, Executive Director
NicoleM@detlef.com
Nature of Sports Service:
Committed to supporting organizations that provide hope, care and assistance to Northwest children and their families. Also fosters relationships with corporate partners that share their vision of serving commuity as a walk of life.
Sports Service Founded:
1996

DOUG FLUTIE, JR. FOUNDATION FOR AUTISM
PO BOX 2157
FRAMINGHAM, MA 01703
www.flutiefoundation.org
• Douglas Flutie, Jr, President/Co-Founder
• Laurie Flutie, Vice President/Co-Founder
• Lisa Borges, Executive Director
• Nicole Guglielmucci, Director of Marketing/Events
• Keith D'Entremont, Director of Development
Sports Service Founded:
1998
Nature of Service:
To promote awareness and support families affected by autism spectrum disorders. Committed to funding organizations that provide direct services, family support grants, education, advocacy and recreational opportunities with the purpose of improvine the quality of life for individuals with autism and their families.

FOREVER YOUNG FOUNDATION
1424 S STAPLEY DRIVE
MESA, AZ 85204
480-507-0416
800-994-3837
www.foreveryoung.org
• Steve Young, Founder/Co-Chair
• Barb Young, Founder/Co-Chair
• Sterling Tanner, President/Executive Director
sterling@foreveryoung.org
• Michelle Knox, Public Relations/Media Director
• Tina Kempken, Events/Programs Director
tina@foreveryoung.org
Sports Service Founded:
1993
Description:
A non-profit organization that serves children facing significant physical, emotional and financial challenges.

HUNTER'S HOPE FOUNDATION
6368 W QUAKER STREET
PO BOX 643
ORCHARD PARK, NY 14127
716-667-1200
info@huntershope.org
www.huntershope.org
• Chris Billman, Treasurer/Board Member
• Jim Kelly, Co-Founder
• Jill Kelly, Co-Founder
• Jacque Waggoner, CEO
jacque@huntershope.org
Sports Service Founded:
1997
Description:
Established to address the need for information and research with respect to Krabb Disease and realted Leukodystrophies.

JACKIE ROBINSON FOUNDATION
ONE HUDSON SQUARE
75 VARICK STREET, 2ND FLOOR
NEW YORK, NY 10013-1917
212-290-8600
Fax: 212-290-8081
www.jackierobinson.org
• Rachel Robinson, Founder
• Gregg A Gonsalves, Chairman
• Martin Edelman, Secretary
• Jose Rivera, Treasurer
• Della Britton-Baeza, President/CEO
• Danielle F Cornwall, Assistant Director Of Educational Programs
• La'Tonya Johnson, Vice President/Chief Operations Officer
• Ruth Moseley, Events Manager
Sports Service Founded:
1973
Nature of Sports Service:
A not-for-profit, organization founded as a vehicle to continue the legacy of Jackie Robinson through the advancement of higher education among underserved populations.

JEFF GORDON FOUNDATION
1310 S. TYRON STREET
SUITE 105
CHARLOTTE, NC 28027
980-999-5145
info@jgcf.org
www.jeffgordonchildrensfoundation.org
• Jeff Gordon, Founder
• Trish Kriger, Executive Director
tkriger@jgcf.org
• Susan Johnston, Director Of Communications
sjohnston@jgcf.org
Sports Service Founded:
1999
Description:
Supports children battling cancer by funding programs that improve a patients' quality of life, treatment programs that increase survivorship and pediatric medical research dedicated to finding a cure.

JOHN LYNCH FOUNDATION
PO BOX 172247
TAMPA, FL 33672
866-553-4747
Fax: 813-831-4441
maggie@johnlynchfoundation.org
www.johnlynchfoundation.org
• John Lynch, President
• Lynda Lynch, VP
• Maggie Robinson, Executive Director
maggie@johnlynchfoundation.org
Sports Service Founded:
2000
Description:
Provides encouragement and support programs for young people todevelop values and leadership through education, sport, and community involvement.

JUNIOR SEAU FOUNDATION
5275 MARKET DRIVE
SAN DIEGO, CA 92114
619-264-5555
info@juniorseau.org
www.juniorseau.org
Sports Service Founded:
1992
Description:
Educates and empowers underprivileged young people in San Diegothrough the support of child abuse prevention efforts, drug and alcohol awareness, recreational opportunitues, anti-juvenile delinquency efforts and complimentary educational programs.

KURT WARNER FIRST THING'S FIRST FOUNDATION
ONE N FIRST ST.
SUITE 735
PHOENIX, AZ 85004
602-385-0840
www.kurtwarner.org
• Kurt Warner, President/Founder
• Brenda Warner, Co-Founder
Nature of Sports Service:
Founded in 1999 to promote Christian values by providing opportunities and encouragement with those in need.

LANCE ARMSTRONG FOUNDATION
2201 E SIXTH STREET
AUSTIN, TX 78072
877-236-8820
www.livestrong.org
• Lance Armstrong, Founde/Board Emeritus
• Greg Lee, CPA, President
• Kelly Corley, Vice President Finance
• Lori O'Brien, Vice President National Development
• Candice Aaron, Chair
• Blaine P. Rollins, Secretary
Sports Service Founded:
1997
Nature of Sports Service:
Empowers the cancer community to address the unmet needs of cancer survivors. Encourages collaborations, knowledge-sharing and partnership. advocates for action in fighting the disease.

MAGIC JOHNSON FOUNDATION
9100 WILSHIRE BOULEVARD
SUITE 700 EAST
BEVERLY HILLS, CA 90212
310-246-4400
888-624-4205
• Earvin Johnson, Chairman
• Shane Jenkins, Vice President
• Jeanella Blair, Director Of Community Empowerment Centers
Sports Service Founded:
1991

MALIVAI WASHINGTON KIDS FOUNDATION
1096 W 6TH STREET
JACKSONVILLE, FL 32209
904-359-5437
Fax: 904-301-3789
info@malwashington.com
www.malwashington.com
• MaliVi Washington, Founder
• Terri Florio, Executive Director
terri@malwashington.com
• Michael G. Gulley, Jr., Associate Director
michael@malwashington.com
• Marc Atkinson, Head Tennis Professional
marc@malwashington.com
• Tiffany Atkinson, Senior Program Coordinator
tiffany@malwashington.com
Sports Service Founded:
1994
Member Services:
Tennis and Tutoring (TnT); After school tennis and recreational program for elemnetary, middle school youth Homework assistance and life skills programs also provided.
Description:
Uses the sport of tennis to support the academic achievement and leadership skills of youth in the Jacksonville area.

MARIO LEMIEUX FOUNDATION
TWO CHATHAM CENTER
SUITE 1661
112 WASHINGTON PLACE
PITTSBURGH, PA 15219
412-281-3466
Fax: 412-281-3066
www.mariolemieux.org
• Mario Lemieux, Chairman
• Tom Grealish, President
• Chuck Greenberg, Secretary
• Robert Hofman, Treasurer
• Nancy Angus, Executive Director
nangus@mlf66.org
• Andrew Parish, Marketing Manager
dparish@mlf66.org

Sports Service Founded:
1993
Nature of Sports Service:
The foundation raises funds for cancer and neonatal research, in addition to supporting an endowment for pediatric oncology research and an initiative to create family playrooms for children in medical care.

MARSHALL FAULK FOUNDATION
7222 OPPORTUNITY ROAD
SAN DIEGO, CA 92111
858-277-2828
Fax: 585-277-2814
info@marshallfaulk.com
www.marshallfaulk.com
• Marshall Faulk, Founder
• Brandi Greenleaf, Executive Director
brandi@marshallfaulk.com
Nature of Sports Service:
Dedicated to improving the quality of life for San Diego youth by sport and education.
Sports Service Founded:
1994

MIA HAMM FOUNDATION
5315 HIGHGATE DRIVE
SUITE 204
DURHAM, NC 27713
919-544-9848
www.miafoundation.org
• Mia Hamm, Founder
Description:
A non-profit, national organizatio raising funds and awareness for families in need of a marrow or cord blood transplant and the development of more opportunities for young women to participate in sport.

NATIONAL FOOTBALL LEAGUE ALUMNI
8000 MIDATLANTIC DRIVE
SUITE 130 SOUTH
MOUNT LAUREL, NJ 08054
877-258-6635
Fax: 862-772-0277
memberservice@nflalumni.org
www.nflalumni.org
• Joe Pisarcik, President/CEO
Joe.pisarcik@nflalumni.org
Description:
A non-profit retired players organization for former National Football League athletes and associates.

NOBIS WORKS CENTER
1480 BELLS FERRY ROAD
MARIETTA, GA 30066-6014
770-427-9000
Fax: 770-499-9191
www.tommynobiscenter.org
• Dave Ward, President/CEO
• Alan Moak, Board Chairman
• Lisa Hughes, Vice President, Human Resources & Administration
• Mike Hancock, Vice President, Business Development
• Cole Chase, Vice President, Vocational Rehabilitation
• Greg Weigle, Chief Financial Officer
Sports Service Founded:
1975
Description:
To develop and provide job training, employment and vocational support for youth and adults with disabilities and other barriers to employment.

TIGER WOODS FOUNDATION
121 INNOVATION
SUITE 150
IRVINE, CA 92617
Fax: 949-725-3002
help@tigerwoodsfoundation.org
www.tigerwoodsfoundation.org
• Tiger Woods, Founder
• Rick T Singer, President/CEO
• Michelle Bemis, Vice President Events &
Business Development
• Katherine Bihr, Vice President,
Programs/Education
• Jin Thatcher, Vice President, Operations &
Administration
• Marci Gentzkow, Senior Director,
Communications & Marketing
• Kelly Cheng, Finance Director
Sports Service Founded:
1996
Nature of Sports Service:
Organization empowers young people by
initiating and supporting community-based
programs that promote the health, education
and welfare of American children. Athlete:
Tiger Woods - Professional Golfer

TONY HAWK FOUNDATION
1611-A SOUTH MELROSE DRIVE
#360
VISTA, CA 92081
www.tonyhawkfoundation.org
• Tony Hawk, President
• Miki Vuckovich, Executive Director
Description:
The foundation empowers youth through
recreational programs and the creation of
public skateparks.

**WALTER AND CONNIE PAYTON
FOUNDATION**
1905 MARKETVIEW DRIVE
SUITE 234
YORKVILLE, IL 60560
630-885-4980
Fax: 630-552-7618
information@payton34.com
www.payton34.com
• Kelly Woods, Director
(630) 699-2202
kwoods03@aol.com
• Nancy Hewlett, Office Manager/Events
Coordinator
(630) 885-4980
nancy@payton34.com

Disabled Sports

BLIND GOLF CANADA
451 HIGHWAY 336
UPPER MUSQUODOBIT, NS, CANADA
B0N 2M0
www.blindgolf.ca
• Gerry Nelson, President
• Doug Stoutley, Handicap Secretary
• Boyde Stewart, Vice President Finance

**CANADIAN BLIND SPORTS
ASSOCIATION**
#325-5055 RUE JOYCE STREET
VANCOUVER BC, CANADA V5R 6B2
604-419-0480
877-604-0480
Fax: 604-419-0481
www.canadianblindsports.ca

• Jane D Blaine, Executive Director
jane@canadianblindsports.ca
• Bob Fenton, President
• Terry Parsons, Vice President
• Donna Jodhan, Communications Director
Membership Requirements:
Provincial associations, pay dues.
Number of members:
9 Provinces, reaching 1,000 - 2,000
Individuals
Description:
The recognized national sport organization
for the Paralympic Sport of Golfball, and
advocates within the sport system for
Canadians who are visually impaired or
blind.
Year Founded:
1976

CANADIAN PARALYMPIC COMMITTEE
225 METCALFE STREET
SUITE 310
OTTAWA ON, CANADA K2P 1P9
613-569-4333
Fax: 604-569-2777
www.paralympic.ca
• Henry Storgaard, CEO/Secretary General
(613) 569-4333
hstorgaard@paralympic.ca
• Eric Paterson, Executive Assistant
epaterson@paralympic.ca
• Alison Korn, Manager, Media Relations &
Communications
(61) -569-433
akorn@paralympic.ca
• Kalie Sinclair, Coordinator, Digital & Social
Media
(613) 569-4333
ksinclair@paralympic.ca
• Laurie Cairns, Director of Finance
(613) 569-4333
lcairns@paralympic.ca
Sports Service Founded:
1981
Membership Requirements:
National sport governing bodies for
Paralympic sports.
Member Services:
Organization of Canada's involvement in the
Paralympic Games; fundraising to support
Canadian Winter and Summer Paralympic
teams.
Description:
The mission of the Foundation is to develop
and grow the Paralympic Movement in
Canada. Recognized by the International
Paralympic Committee (IPC) as the National
Paralympic Committe of Canada. CPC is
responsible for all aspects of Canada's
involvement including the country's
participation in the Summer and Winter
Paralympic Games.

DISABLED SPORTS USA
451 HUNGERFORD DRIVE
SUITE 100
ROCKVILLE, MD 20850
301-217-0960
Fax: 301-217-0968
information@dsusa.org
• Kirk Bauer, Executive Director
kbauer@dsusa.org
• Robert Meserve Meserve, President
• Steven D Goodwin, 2nd Vice President
• Todd Sajauskas, Treasurer and Secretary
Sports Services Founded:
1967

Membership Requirements:
Open membership offered through more
than 80 community-based chapters, as well
as through a national at-large membership
program, to all people and organizations
with an interest in sports and recreation for
the disabled; currently serving more than
60,000 people, ages 5 to 85, with
information and programs.
Publications:
CHALLENGE Magazine, FITNESS
PROGRAMMING & PHYSICAL
DISABILITIES book.
Member Services:
Travel discounts; access to information on
disabled sports and recreational activities;
more than 80 community-based chapters in
the U.S.; regional teaching clinics for several
sports; nationally sanctioned regional and
national competition for disabled athletes.
Description:
Established by disabled Vietnam veterans to
serve the war injured. DS/USA now offers
nationwide sports rehabilitation programs to
anyone with a permanent disability.
Activities include winter skiing, water sports,
summer and winter competitions, fitness
and special sports events. Participants
include those with visual impairments,
amputations, spinal cord injury, dwarfism,
multiple sclerosis, head injury, cerebral
palsy, and other neuromuscular and
orthopedic conditions.

**INTERNATIONAL COMMITTEE OF
SPORTS FOR THE DEAF**
54 AV. DE RHODANIE
LAUSANNE, SWITZERLAN CH-1007
Fax: +41-78-733-35-67
office@ciss.org
www.ciss.org
• Valery N. Rukhledev, President
Sports Service Founded:
1924
Desciption:
Governing body for the summer and winter
Deaflympics, which promotes the
development of athletics and international
competition.

SPECIAL OLYMPICS INTERNATIONAL
1133 19TH STREET NW
WASHINGTON, DC 2036-3604
202-628-3630
800-700-8585
Fax: 202-824-0200
media@specialolympics.org
www.specialolympics.org
• Timothy Shriver, Chairman of the Board
info@specialolympics.org
• Mary Davis, CEO
• Caroline Chevat, Manager, Brand Content
& Communications
(202) 824-0211
Number of members:
5.7 million athletes and more than a million
coaches and volunteers in 172 countries.
Membership Requirements:
People who have intellectual disabilities.
Sports Services Founded:
The first International Special Olympics
Games were held in Chicago, Illinois, USA
in July 1968.
Description:
The mission of Special Olympics is to
provide year-round sports training and
athletic competition in a variety of

multi sports

193

Olympic-type sports for children and adults with intellectual disabilities. This gives them continuing opportunities to develop physical fitness, demonstrate courage, experience joy and participate in a sharing of gifts, skills and friendship with their families, other Special Olympics athletes and the community.

Other locations:

SPECIAL OLYMPICS ALABAMA
880 SOUTH COURT STREET
MONTGOMERY, AL 36104
334-242-3383
800-239-3898
Fax: 334-262-9794
soaloffice@aol.com
specialolympicsalabama.com
• Robert Bushong, Executive Director
soaled@bellsouth.net
• Finlay Randolph, Training Manager
soaltraining@bellsouth.net
• Marilyn Tell, Office Manager
soaltell@bellsouth.net
• Jane Cameron, Staff Assistant

SPECIAL OLYMPICS ALASKA
3200 MOUNTAIN VIEW DRIVE
ANCHORAGE, AK 99501
907-222-7625
888-499-7625
Fax: 907-222-6200
info@specialolympicsalaska.org
www.specialolympicsalaska.org
• Carmela Warfield, Chairman
• James Balamaci, President/CEO
jim@specialolympicsalaska.com

SPECIAL OLYMPICS AMERICAN SAMOA
PO BOX 6172
PAGO PAGO, AMERICAN S 96799
684-733-2351
specialolympicas@gmail.com
www.specialolympics.org
• Tulafono Solaita, Board Chair
tafaimamao@gmail.com
• Nyrese Pato, National Coordinator
n.pato@amsamoa.edu

SPECIAL OLYMPICS ARIZONA
2100 S 75TH AVENUE
PHOENIX, AZ 85043
602-230-1200
800-289-4946
Fax: 602-230-1110
www.specialolympicsarizona.org
• Tim Martin, President/CEO
(602) 230-1200
tim@specialolympicsarizona.org
• Douglas Steele, Chairperson

SPECIAL OLYMPICS ARKANSAS
2115 MAIN STREET
NORTH LITTLE ROCk, AR 72114
501-771-0222
800-722-9063
Fax: 501-771-1020
www.specialolympicsarkansas.org
• Terri Weir, Executive Director
terri@specialolympicsarkansas.org
• Irvin Humphrey, Director of Sports, Training, And Competition
irvin@specialolympicsarkansas.org

SPECIAL OLYMPICS CANADA
21 ST. CLAIR AVENUE EAST
SUITE 600
TORONTO, ON, CANADA M4T 1L9
416-927-9050
888-888-0608
Fax: 416-927-8475

info@specialolympics.ca
www.specialolympics.ca
• Mike Lamontagne, President and Chair
• Sharon Bollenbach, Chief Executive Officer
(416) 927-9050
sbollenbach@specialolympics.ca
• Lisa Dunbar, Director, Marketing & Communications
(416) 927-9050
ldunbar@specialolympics.ca
Description:
As part of the international Special Olympic movement, the organization works to enrich the lives of people with intellectual disabilities through sport/

SPECIAL OLYMPICS COLORADO
384 IVERNESS PARKWAY
SUITE 100
ENGLEWOOD, CO 80112
720-359-3100
800-777-5767
Fax: 303-592-1364
www.specialolympicsco.org
• Mindy Watrous, President/CEO
(720) 359-3111
• Becky Kennedy, Chief Financial Officer
• Chaka Sutton, VP Programs

SPECIAL OLYMPICS CONNECTICUT
2666 STATE STREET
SUITE 1
HAMDEN, CT 06517
203-230-1201
800-443-6105
Fax: 203-230-1202
specialolympicsct@soct.org
www.soct.org
• Robert Doherty, President
• Kelli Bigelow, Executive Assistant, President
kellib@soct.org
• Mike Mason, Senior Vice President/Chief Financial Officer
Description:
SOCT is a non-profit, charitable organization, which contributes to the lifelong physical, social and personal development of people with intellectual disabilities in the state of Connecticut. The SOCT program is one of the most innovative and dynamic in the world, involving thousands of people throughout the state in exciting and rewarding competition, training and events.

SPECIAL OLYMPICS DC
900 2ND STREET NE
SUITE 6
WASHINGTON, DC 20002
202-408-2640
www.specialolympicsdc.org
• Nicole J Preston, President/Chief Operating Officer
npreston@specialolympicsdc.org
• Maria-Nelly Johnson, Director of Finance/Administration
mjohnson@specialolympicsdc.org
• Tom Kling, Senior Director of Sports and Programs
• Anthony Sokenu, Assosiate Director of Sports
asokenu@specialolympicsdc.org
• Rodney Williams, Assistant Director of Sports

SPECIAL OLYMPICS DELAWARE
619 S COLLEGE AVENUE
NEWARK, DE 19716
302-831-4653
Fax: 302-831-3483
info@sode.org
www.sode.org
• Michael T. Nash, President
• Dick Huber, Vice-President
• Jeffrey Mitchell, Treasurer
• Ann Grunert, Executive Director
(302) 831-3480
agrunert@udel.edu
• Jon Buzby, Media Relations and Program Innovations Director

(302) 831-3484
jbuzby@udel.edu
• Gary Cimaglia, Senior Director Sports
(302) 831-3481
gcimag@udel.edu

SPECIAL OLYMPICS FLORIDA
1915 DON WICKMAN DRIVE
CLERMONT, FL 34711
352-243-9536
Fax: 352-243-9568
specialolympicsflorida.org
• Sherry Wheelock, President/CEO
(352) 243-9536
sherrywheelock@sofl.org
• Micheal Petramalo, Vice Chair
• Rick Beddow, Chief Operating Officer
(352) 243-9536
• Pam Bondi, Secretary
• Joe Dzaluk, Treasurer

SPECIAL OLYMPICS GEORGIA
4000 DEKALB TECHNOLOGY PARKWAY
BUILDING 400, SUITE 400
ATLANTA, GA 30340
770-414-9390
www.specialolympicsga.org
• Georgia Milton-Sheats, CEO
(770) 414-9390
georgia.milton-sheats@specialolympicsga.org
• Mike Twiner, Chairperson
• Lee Nunnally, Vice Chair
• Michael Knight, Treasurer
• Chris Turner, Secretatry
Description:
Provides year-round training and competition for people with intellectual disabilities to enrich their lives through sport.

SPECIAL OLYMPICS HAWAII
1833 KALAKAUA AVENUE
SUITE 100
HONOLULU, HI 96815
808-943-8808
888-531-1888
Fax: 808-943-8814
www.specialolympicshawaii.org
• Nancy Bottelo, President/CEO
(808) 695-3522
ceo@sohawaii.org
• Tom Weber, Chairperson
• Tim Brauer, Vice-Chairperson
• Nina Nakaahiki, Secretary
• Dan Epstein, VP Sports & Sports Marketing
(808) 695-3523
sports@sohawaii.org
Description:
The organization missions is to provide year-round training and competition for people with intellectual disabilities to enrich their lives through sport.

SPECIAL OLYMPICS IDAHO
199 E 52ND STREET
GARDEN CITY, ID 83714
800-915-6510
Fax: 208-323-0486
idso@idso.org
www.idso.org
• Laurie La Follette, Chief Executive Officer
(208) 323-0482
llafollette@idso.org
• Shannon Reece, COMMUNITY STATE COORDINATOR
(800) 915-6510
• Bryan Jackson, Finance Director
(208) 629-6989
• Dallas Leatham, VP Operations
(208) 915-6510
operations@idso.org
Description:
A non-profit organization that provides training and athletic competition in 15 Olympic-type sports, year-round and free of charge to over 2,500 children and adults with intellectual disabilities throughout the state of Idaho.

SPECIAL OLYMPICS ILLINOIS
605 EAST WILLOW STREET
NORMAL, IL 61761
309-888-2551
800-394-0562
Fax: 309-888-2570
website@soill.org
www.soill.org
• Jenny Fortner, Chair
• Karen Atwood, Vice-Chair
• Dave Breen, President/CEO
• Jeremy Davidson, Manager
Marketing/Communications
jdavidson@soill.org
• Tracy S Hilliard, VP Sports
Training/Competition
thilliard@soill.org
Description:
Organization mission is to provide year-round
training and competition for people with
intellectual disabilities to enrich their lives
through sport.

SPECIAL OLYMPICS INDIANA
6200 TECHNOLOGY CENTER DRIVE
SUITE 105
INDIANAPOLIS, IN 46278
317-328-2000
800-742-6012
Fax: 317-328-2018
information@soindiana.org
www.soindiana.org
• Michael Furnish, President/CEO
mfurnish@soindiana.org
• Deb Easterday, Chairperson
• Ron Stiver, Vice-Chair
• Phil Bounsall, Treasurer
• Dana Teasley, Secretary
Description:
Organization mission is to provide year-round
training and competition for people with
intellectual disabilities to enrich their lives
through sport.

SPECIAL OLYMPICS IOWA
551 SE DOVETAIL ROAD
PO BOX 620
GRIMES, IA 50111-0620
515-986-5520
Fax: 515-986-5530
www.soiowa.org
• Rich Fellingham, President/CEO
(515) 986-5520
rfellingham@soiowa.org
• Steve Palmer, Chair
Description:
Organization mission is to provide year-round
training and competition for people with
intellectual disabilities to enrich their lives
through sport.

SPECIAL OLYMPICS KANSAS
5280 FOXRIDGE DRIVE
MISSION, KS 66202
913-236-9290
Fax: 913-236-9771
kso@ksso.org
www.ksso.org
• Chris Hahn, President/CEO
(913) 236-9290
• Mark Malick, Chairperson
• Dale Chaffin, Treasurer
• Tim Rehder, Senior VP Program Operations
(913) 236-9290
rehdert@ksso.org
• Michele Johnson, Program Operations
Manager
(913) 236-9290
johnsonm@ksso.org
Sports Services Founded:
1970

SPECIAL OLYMPICS KENTUCKY
105 LAKEVIEW COURT
FRANKFORT, KY 40601
502-695-8222
800-633-7403

Fax: 502-695-0496
soky@soky.org
www.soky.org
• Trish Mazzoni, President/CEO
tmazzoni@soky.org
• Teresa Capps-McGill, VP Finance
tacpps-mcgill@soky.org
• Taylor Ballinger, Special Events Director
• Mark Buerger, Communications Director
mbuerger@soky.org
Description:
Organization mission is to provide year-round
training and competition for people with
intellectual disabilities to enrich their lives
through sport.

SPECIAL OLYMPICS LOUISIANA
1000 EAST MORRIS AVENUE
HAMMOND, LA 70403
985-345-6644
800-345-6644
Fax: 985-345-6649
www.laso.org
• John Saye, Chairperson
• Emily Jeffcott, Vice-Chairperson
• Pat Carpenter Bourgeois, President/CEO
• Rhonda Blanford-Green, Secretary
• Sylvia Alaniz, Vice President of Finance
Sports Services Founded:
1968

SPECIAL OLYMPICS MAINE
125 JOHN ROBERTS ROAD
SUITE 5
SOUTH PORTLAND, ME 4106
207-879-0489
Fax: 888-490-0672
www.specialolympicsmaine.org
• Phil Geelhoed, President & CEO
(207) 879-0489
philg@somaine.org
• Lisa Bird, Public Relations & Torch Run
(207) 879-0489
lisab@somaine.org
• Ian Frank, Training/Camp Tall Pines
(207) 879-0489
ianf@somaine.org
Member Services:
Year round program of athletic training and
opportunity for competition in sixteen different
Olympic Style Sports.
Membership Requirements:
Program serves children and adults with
intellectual disabilities in the state of Maine.

SPECIAL OLYMPICS MARYLAND
3071 COMMERCE DRIVE
SUITE 103
BALTIMORE, MD 21227
410-242-1515
800-541-7544
Fax: 410-242-5162
info@somd.org
www.somd.org
• Frank Andracchi, Chairman
• Jennifer Rapacki, Treasurer
• Wayne Luoma, Secretary
• Donny Boyd, At-Large director
• Jim Schmutz, President/CEO
(410) 242-1515
jschmutz@somd.org

**SPECIAL OLYMPICS
MASSACHUSETTS**
THE YAWKEY SPORTS TRAINING CENTER
512 FOREST ST
MARLBOROUGH, MA 1752
508-485-0986
Fax: 508-481-0786
www.specialolympicsma.org
• Mary Beth McMahon, President & CEO
marybeth.mcmahon@specialolympicsma.org
• Gayle Fehlmann, CFO
gayle.fehlmann@specialolympicsma.org
• Matt Ruxton, VP of Sports
matt.ruxton@specialolympicsma.org
• Steve Huftalen, AVP of Corporate

Development & Special Events
steve.huftalen@specialolympicsma.org

SPECIAL OLYMPICS MICHIGAN
CENTRAL MICHIGAN UNIVERSITY
MOUNT PLEASANT, MI 48859
989-774-3911
800-644-6404
Fax: 989-774-3034
somi@somi.org
www.somi.org
• Lois Arnold, President/CEO
lois.arnold@cmich.edu
• Alison Miller, Chief Development Officer
mille1as@cmich.edu
• Ann Guzdzial, Chief Program Officer
anna.guzdzial@cmich.edu
• Rick Brady, Sports & Training Coordinator
brady1rp@cmich.edu
Year Founded:
1968 by Eunice Kennedy Shriver. State
incorporated in 1972 (Special Olympics
Michigan).
Membership Requirements:
Persons aged 8+,identified as a person with an
intellectual disability.

SPECIAL OLYMPICS MINNESOTA
900 2ND AVENUE S.
SUITE 300
MINNEAPOLIS, MN 55402
612-333-0999
800-783-7732
Fax: 612-333-8782
info@somn.org
www.specialolympicsminnesota.org
• David Dorn, President/CEO
(763) 270-7130
david.dorn@somn.org
• Chad Trench, Operations Director
(763) 270-7127
chad.trench@somn.org
• Melissa Holmes, Director of Finance
(763) 270-7129
melissa.holmes@somn.org

SPECIAL OLYMPICS MISSISSIPPI
15 OLYMPIC WAY
MADISON, MS 39110
601-856-7748
Fax: 601-856-8132
www.specialolympicsms.org
• Kenny Williamson, Chairman
• Rick Webster, Vice Chairman
• Paul Rogers, Treasurer
Description:
Organization mission is to provide year-round
training and competition for people with
intellectual disabilities to enrich their lives
through sport.

SPECIAL OLYMPICS MISSOURI
1001 DIAMOND RIDGE
SUITE 800
JEFFERSON CITY, MO 65109
573-635-1660
Fax: 573-635-8233
www.somo.org
• Mark Musso, President/CEO
• Trish Lutz, Senior Director of Programs
Description:
Organization mission is to provide year-round
training and competition for people with
intellectual disabilities to enrich their lives
through sport.

SPECIAL OLYMPICS MONTANA
710 1ST AVENUE NORTH
GREAT FALLS, MT 59401
800-242-6876
info@somt.org
www.somt.org
• Bob Norbie, President/CEO
bnorbie@somt.org
• Rhonda McCarty, Chief Operating Officer
rmccarty@somt.org

multi sports

Description:
Organization mission is to provide year-round training and competition for people with intellectual disabilities to enrich their lives through sport.

SPECIAL OLYMPICS NEBRASKA
9427 F STREET
OMAHA, NE 68127
402-331-5545
800-247-0105
Fax: 402-331-5964
www.sone.org
• Carolyn Chamberlin, President/CEO
(402) 331-5545
cchamberlin@sone.org
• David Demyan, Director of Sports & Competition
(402) 331-5545
ddemyan@sone.org
Description:
Organization mission is to provide year-round training and competition for people with intellectual disabilities to enrich their lives through sport.

SPECIAL OLYMPICS NEVADA
5670 WYNN ROAD
SUITE H
LAS VEGAS, NV 89118
877-417-2742
Fax: 702-474-0694
www.sonv.org
• Littler Mendelson, P.C, Chair
• Joyce Whitney-Silva, Vice Chair
• David Solo, President/CEO
(925) 944-8801
davids@sonc.org
• Kevin Reeds, Chief Dvelopment Officer
(925) 944-8801
• Harry Mong, Regional Sports Director
(702) 474-0690
harrym@sonv.org
Description:
Special Olympics Nevada offers free sports training and competition opportunities to people with intellectual disabilities in several different sports.

SPECIAL OLYMPICS NEW HAMPSHIRE
650 ELM STREET
MANCHESTER, NH 3101
603-624-1250
Fax: 603-624-4911
www.sonh.org
• Mike Dennehy, Chairperson
• Mary Conroy, President
(603) 624-1250
• Doug Basnett, Secretary
• Butch Beers, Program Coordinator
• Chelsea Gill, Director of Development
(603) 624-1250
Description:
Special Olympics of New Hampshire (SONH) is a non profit organization providing sports training and athletic competition for children and adults with intellectual disabilities. Currently 2,994 participants and thousands of volunteers, friends and family members take part in SONH activities.

SPECIAL OLYMPICS NEW JERSEY
1 EUNICE KENNEDY SHRIVER WAY
LAWRENCEVILLE, NJ 8648-2301
609-896-8000
Fax: 609-896-8040
info@sonj.org
www.sonj.org
• Heather B. Andersen, President/Chief Executive Officer
HBA@sonj.org
• Richard Gelfond, Director of Operations
RSG@sonj.org
• Jeff Baldino, Competition Director
JJB@sonj.org
Description:
Organization mission is to provide year-round

training and competition for people with intellectual disabilities to enrich their lives through sport.

SPECIAL OLYMPICS NEW MEXICO
6600 PALOMAS NE
SUITE 207
ALBUQUERQUE, NM 87109
505-856-0342
Fax: 505-856-0346
www.sonm.org
• Jack Eichorn, Chairman
• Karen Hudson, Vice Chairman
• Randy Mascorella, Executive Director
randymascorella@sonm.org
• Christine Hidalgo, Director Of Development & Special Event
christine@sonm.org
Year Founded:
1968
Description:
Organization mission is to provide year-round training and competition for people with intellectual disabilities to enrich their lives through sport.

SPECIAL OLYMPICS NEW YORK
504 BALLTOWN ROAD
SCHENECTADY, NY 12304
518-388-0790
800-836-6976
Fax: 518-388-0791
specialolympics-ny.org
• Shelly Nangle, Executive VP & COO
• Neal J. Johnson, President/CEO
• Steve Fuller, VP Program & Competition
sfuller@nyso.org
• Bill Collins, Director of Training
bcollins@nyso.org
• Lauren Maneri, Program Specialist
• Stacy Eder, Director of Volunteer Management
seder@nyso.org
Sports Services Founded:
1969
Description:
Organization mission is to provide year-round training and competition for people with intellectual disabilities to enrich their lives through sport.

SPECIAL OLYMPICS NORTH CAROLINA
2200 GATEWAY CENTRE BOULVEARD
SUITE 201
MORRISVILLE, NC 27560
919-719-7662
800-843-6276
Fax: 919-719-7663
www.sonc.net
• Keith L. Fishburne, President/CEO
(919) 719-7662
kfishburne@sonc.net
• Kelly Vaughn, Senior Vice President
(919) 719-7662
kvaughn@sonc.net
• Rachel McQuiston, VP Communications
• Andrea Stamm, Vice President of Sports
(919) 719-7662
astamm@sonc.net
Membership Requirements:
Special Olympics North Carolina is not a membership organization. Volunteers serve as coaches, event committee organizers, fund raisers, and other roles. Registration criteria exists for athletes and volunteers.
Description:
Organization mission is to provide year-round training and competition for people with intellectual disabilities to enrich their lives through sport.

SPECIAL OLYMPICS NORTH DAKOTA
21616 SOUTH 26TH STREET
GRAND FORKS, ND 58201
701-746-0331
Fax: 701-772-1265

info@specialolympicsnd.org
www.specialolympicsnorthdakota.org
• John Erickson, Chairman
• Dr. Julie Blehm, Vice Chair
• Jon Godfread, Secretary
• John Schumacher, Treasurer/Vice Secretary
• Kathy Meagher, President & CEO
president@specialolympicsnd.org
Description:
Organization mission is to provide year-round training and competition for people with intellectual disabilities to enrich their lives through sport.

SPECIAL OLYMPICS NORTHERN CALIFORNIA
3480 BUSKIRK AVENUE
SUITE 340
PLEASANT HILL, CA 94523
925-944-8801
Fax: 925-944-8803
info@sonc.org
www.sonc.org
• Richard Rahm, Chair
• Gretchen Pearson, Secretary
• David Solo, President/CEO
(925) 944-8801
DavidS@sonc.org
• Mike Mayo, CFO
(925) 944-8801
Mike@sonc.org
Description:
Special Olympics Northern California serves over 14,000 individuals with developmental disabilities. From the Oregon border to Monterey and Tulare counties, athletes have the opportunity to participate in a wide variety of sports trainings and competitions that take place throughout the year.

SPECIAL OLYMPICS OHIO
3303 WINCHESTER PIKE
COLUMBUS, OH 43232
614-239-7050
Fax: 614-239-1873
www.sooh.org
• Kraig Makohus, Chief Executive Officer
• Marty Allen, Program Director
• Tim Etienne, Field Director
Sports Services Founded:
Incorporated in 1975.
Description:
Provides year round training and competition opportunities for children and adults with intellectual disabilities.

SPECIAL OLYMPICS OKLAHOMA
6835 SOUTH CANTON AVENUE
TULSA, OK 74136
918-481-1234
800-722-9004
Fax: 918-496-1515
info@sook.org
www.sook.org
• Linda McKown, Chairman
• Adrian DeWendt, President/CEO
• Donna Ham, Marketing Director
• Teri Hockett, Vice President of Programs
• John Seals, Sports Director
Decription:
Organization mission is to provide year-round training and competition for people with intellectual disabilities to enrich their lives through sport.
Additional Information:
3701 SE 15th Street, #B-1, Del City, OK 73115; (P) 405-670-3456 (F) 405-670-5678

SPECIAL OLYMPICS OREGON
5901 SW MACADAM AVENUE
SUITE 200
PORTLAND, OR 97239
503-248-0600
Fax: 503-248-0603
info@soor.org
www.soor.org

- Margaret Hunt, CEO
(543) 248-0600
- Chad Carter, Senior Director of Marketing
- Jenelle Clinton, Director of Development
- Joann Stoller, Senior Director of Sports
Sports Services Founded:
1972
Description:
Organization mission is to provide year-round training and competition for people with intellectual disabilities to enrich their lives through sport.

SPECIAL OLYMPICS PENNSYLVANIA
2570 BOULEVARD OF THE GENERALS
SUITE 124
NORRISTOWN, PA 19403
610-630-9450
800-235-9058
www.specialolympicspa.org
- Matthew B Aaron, President & CEO
- Michelle Boone, Senior Sport Director
- Eric Cushing, VP Development/Marketing
- Susan Wyland, VP Finance/Administration
Description:
Organization provides year-round training and competition for 20,000 people with intellectual disabilites in Pennsylvania.

SPECIAL OLYMPICS RHODE ISLAND
370 GEORGE WASHINGTON HIGHWAY
UNIT 1
SMITHFIELD, RI 2917
401-349-4900
info@specialolympicsri.org
specialolympicsri.org
- Thoams Maggiacomo, Chairman
- Lawrence LaSala, Vice Chair
- Michael Sarli, Secretary
- Dennis DeJesus, CEO
dennis@specialolympicsri.org
- Chris Hopkins, Programs Director
chris@specialolympicsri.org
- Gerri Walter, Marketing & Communications Director
gerri@specialolympicsri.org
Description:
Provides over 1,600 year-round sports training and athletic competitions for more than 3,200 athletes with intellectual disabilities.

SPECIAL OLYMPICS SOUTH CAROLINA
109 OAK PARK DRIVE
IRMO, SC 29063
803-772-1555
www.so-sc.org
- Barry Coats, President/CEO
(803) 772-1555
bcoats@so-sc.org
- Edwena Lassiter, Director of Volunteer & Family Services
(803) 772-1555
elassiter@so-sc.org
- Sue Maner, Executive Vice President
(803) 772-1555
smaner@so-sc.org
- Kelly Garrick, Director of Sports and Competition
(803) 772-1555
kgarrick@so-sc.org
- Barbara Oswald, Senior Director of Programs
(803) 772-1555
boswald@so-sc.org
- Sandye Williams, Director of Marketing and Development
(843) 367-2358
swilliams@so-sc.org
Description:
Organization mission is to provide year-round training and competition for people with intellectual disabilities to enrich their lives through sport.

SPECIAL OLYMPICS SOUTH DAKOTA
800 E, I-90 LANE
SIOUX FALLS, SD 57104

605-331-4117
800-585-2114
Fax: 605-331-4328
www.sosd.org
- Darryl Nordquist, CEO/Executive Director
dnordquist@sosd.org
- Melanie Frosch, Vice President, Sports and Competition
mfrosch@sosd.org
- Johna Thum, Vice President, Field Services
jthum@sosd.org
- Twila Nicholson Hansen, Office Manager
thansen@sosd.org
- Todd Bradwisch, Torch Run Liaison
Description:
Organization mission is to provide year-round training and competition for people with intellectual disabilities to enrich their lives through sport.

SPECIAL OLYMPICS SOUTHERN CALIFORNIA
1600 FORBES WAY
SUITE 200
LONG BEACH, CA 90810
562-502-1100
Fax: 562-502-1119
info@sosc.org
www.sosc.org
- Bill Shumard, President/CEO
- Kelly Johnson, Vice Chair/Treasurer
- Mary Ann Powell, Secretary
Description:
Organization mission is to provide year-round training and competition for people with intellectual disabilities to enrich their lives through sport.
Teams:
Aquatics, Basketball, Bocce, Bowling, Floor Hockey, Golf, Gymnastics, Soccer, Softball, Tennis and Volleyball

SPECIAL OLYMPICS TENNESSEE
461 CRAIGHEAD STREET
NASHVILLE, TN 37204
615-329-1375
800-383-8502
Fax: 615-327-1465
www.specialolympicstn.org
- Alan L Bolick, President
(615) 329-1375
abolick@specialolympicstn.org
- Sean Stake, Vice President Sports
(615) 329-1375
sstake@specialolympicstn.org
- Stacey Blackmore, Director of Finance
(615) 329-1375
sblackmore@specialolympicstn.org
Description:
Organization mission is to provide year-round training and competition for people with intellectual disabilities to enrich their lives through sport.

SPECIAL OLYMPICS TEXAS
1804 RUTHERFORD LANE
AUSTIN, TX 78754
512-835-9873
800-876-5646
info@sotx.org
www.sotx.org
- Margaret M. Larsen, President/CEO
(512) 835-9873
mlarsen@sotx.org
- Tela Mange, Vice President Communications
(512) 835-9873
tmange@sotx.org
Description:
Organization mission is to provide year-round training and competition for people with intellectual disabilities to enrich their lives through sport.

SPECIAL OLYMPICS UTAH
1400 S. FOOTHILL DRIVE
SUITE 238
SALT LAKE CITY, UT 84108

801-363-1111
information@sout.org
www.sout.org
- D'Arcy Dixon Pignanelli, President/Chief Executive Officer
dixon@sout.org
- Jonathan Embler, Vice President, Sports Programs
embler@sout.org
- Wendy Kelly, Dircetor of Community Outreach and Partnerships
kelly@sout.org
Description:
Provides year round sports training and competition in a variety of Olympic type sports for children and adults with intellectual disabilities.

SPECIAL OLYMPICS VERMONT
16 GREGORY DRIVE
SUITE 2
SOUTH BURLINGTON, VT 05403
802-863-5222
800-639-1603
Fax: 802-863-3911
info@vtso.org
specialolympicsvermont.org
- Lisa DeNatale, President/CEO
(802) 861-0272
Description:
Organization mission is to provide year-round training and competition for people with intellectual disabilities to enrich their lives through sport.

SPECIAL OLYMPICS VIRGINIA
3212 SKIPWITH ROAD
SUITE 100
RICHMOND, VA 23294
804-346-5544
800-932-4653
Fax: 804-346-9633
info@specialolympicsva.org
www.specialolympicsva.org
- Rick Jeffrey, President
(804) 726-3028
- Roy Zeidman, Senior VP Marketing & Development
(804) 726-3022
rzeidman@specialolympicsva.org
Description:
Organization mission is to provide year-round training and competition for people with intellectual disabilities to enrich their lives through sport.

SPECIAL OLYMPICS WASHINGTON
1809 7TH AVENUE
SUITE 1509
SEATTLE, WA 98101
206-362-4949
800-752-7559
Fax: 206-362-8158
info@sowa.org
specialolympicswashington.org
- Dave Lennox, President/CEO
- Joe Hampson, VP Sports & Community Outreach
Description:
Organization mission is to provide year-round training and competition for people with intellectual disabilities to enrich their lives through sport.

SPECIAL OLYMPICS WEST VIRGINIA
1206 VIRGINIA STREET
SUITE 100
CHARLESTON, WV 25301
304-345-9310
800-926-1616
Fax: 304-345-9338
info@sowa.org
www.sowv.org
- John Corbett, Chief Executive Officer
john@sowv.org
- Kendra Wallace, Director of Sports and Training

Description:
Organization mission is to provide year-round training and competition for people with intellectual disabilities to enrich their lives through sport.

SPECIAL OLYMPICS WISCONSIN
2310 CROSSROADS DRIVE
SUITE 1000
MADISON, WI 53718
608-222-1324
www.specialolympicswisconsin.org
• Kathleen H Roach, President/CEO
(608) 442-5660
kroach@specialolympicswisconsin.org
Description:
A statewide organization providing persons with cognitive disabilities year-round sports training and competition. Individuals who are at least eight years old and are identified as having a cognitive disability are eligible for participation.

SPECIAL OLYMPICS WYOMING
239 W 1ST STREET
CASPER, WY 82601
307-235-3062
800-735-8345
Fax: 307-235-3063
www.sowy.org
• Priscilla Dowse, President/CEO
pdowse@specialolympicswy.org
• Debbie Huber, Chairperson
• Mark Holland, Vice Chairperson
• Brian Cetak, Treasurer
• Mike Burnett, Secretary
Description:
Organization mission is to provide year-round training and competition for people with intellectual disabilities to enrich their lives through sport.

U.S. ASSOCIATION OF BLIND ATHLETES
1 OLYMPIC PLAZA
COLORADO SPRINGS, CO 80909
719-866-3224
Fax: 719-866-34
• Mark Lucas, Executive Director
mlucas@usaba.org
• Ryan Ortiz, Assistant Executive Director
rortiz@usaba.org
• John Potts, Goalball High-Performance Director
jpotts@usaba.org
Member Services:
Special literature; clinics; seminars; panel discussions; group meetings; conventions.
Sports Services Founded:
 1976
Description:
Enhances the lives of blind and visually impaired people by providing the opportunity for participation in sports and physical activity.

U.S. PARALYMPICS
ONE OLYMPIC PLAZA
COLORADO SPRINGS, CO 80909
719-632-5551
usparalympics.org
• Scott Blackmun, Chief Executive Officer
• Lisa Baird, Chief Marketing Officer
Sports Services Founded:
2001
Description:
A division of the U.S. Olympic Committee, dedicated to becoming the world leader in the paralympic sports movement, and promoting excellence in the lives of persons with physical disabilities.

UNITED FOUNDATION FOR DISABLED ARCHERS
20 NE 9TH AVENUE
PO BOX 251
GLENWOOD, MN 56334
320-634-3660
info@uffdaclub.com
www.uffdaclub.com
Description:
Promotes archery for persons with physical disabilties.
Year Founded:
1994

USA DEAF SPORTS FEDERATION
PO BOX 22011
SANTA FE, NM 87502
support@usdeafsports.org
• Jack C Lamberton, President
lamberton@usdeafsports.org
• Jeffrey L. Salit, Vice President
salit@usdeafsports.org
• Brianne Burger, Secretary
burger@usdeafsports.org
• Mark Apodaca, Chief Financial Officer
apodaca@usdeafsports.org
Member Services:
Club sports on recreational level; international competition for elite athletes; CISS deaflympics; national tournaments for the deaf.
Membership Requirements:
All deaf and hard of hearing individuals with a hearing loss of 55 db or greater in the better ear are eligible.
Description:
Founded in 1945, USADSF acts as the national governing body for deaf sports organizations, producing annual competitions and serving as a social community for the deaf.

USBGA GOLF ASSOCIATION
125 GILBERTS HILL ROAD
LEHIGHTON, PA 18235
info@usblindgolf.com
usblindgolf.com
• Dick Pomo, President
(520) 648-1088
pomodick@Q.com

WHEELCHAIR & AMBULATORY SPORTS
PO BOX 621023
LITTLETON, CO 80162
720-412-7979
Fax: 866-204-8018
www.wasusa.org
• Gregg Baumgarten, Chairperson
• Denise Hutchins, Vice Chair
• Mike Burns, Treasurer
• Cory Grant, Secretary
Description:
Founded in 1956, Wheelchair And Ambulatory Sports USA acts as an outreach program and competition administrator, promoting participation in sport for people with disabilities.

High School Sports

GLOBAL SPORTS & ENTERTAINMENT
300 N CONTINENTAL BLVD
SUITE 140
EL SEGUNDO, CA 90245

310-414-2690
Fax: 310-414-2693
info@globalsports-ent.com
www.globalsports-ent.com
• Nick Zaccagnino, Founder/President
• Evan Levy, Senior Event Manager/Talent Producer
• Ben Weiss, Senior Talent Booker/Director Of Digital Marketing
Year Founded:
1996
Description:
Global Sports & Entertainment is a talent booking and event management firm specializing in securing celebrity athletes for mass media programming and events.

NATIONAL FEDERATION OF STATE HIGH SCHOOL ASSOCIATIONS
PO BOX 690
INDIANAPOLIS, IN 46206
317-972-6900
Fax: 317-822-5700
www.nfhs.org
• Gary Musselman, President
• Bob Gardner, Executive Director
• JoAnne Bennett, Chief Financial Officer
• Davis Whitfield, Chief Operating Officer
Member Services:
Scorebooks and rule books for interscholastic sports. Sports videos used in the training of coaches, athletes, officials and spectators. Selection of the National High School Debate Topic, and other services in the fields of debate, speech and music. Athletics Participation Surveys.
Publications:
National High School Rules Books and related publications in 17 sports. National High School Sports Record Book. NFHS Handbook. NHFS NEWS, INTERSCHOLASTIC ATHLETIC ADMINISTRATION MAGAZINE. NATIONAL FEDERATION COACHES' QUARTERLY. NATIONAL FEDERATION OFFICIALS' QUARTERLY.
Membership Requirements:
State associations responsible for administering interscholastic activities.
Description:
Founded 1920. Represents state high school associations with more than 18,500 high schools, coaches and sponsors and officials and judges throughout the U.S. Provides sanctioning services for interstate and international events. Writes the playing rules for high school athletics. Analyzes equipment for licensing purposes.

Other locations:

ALABAMA HIGH SCHOOL ATHLETIC ASSOCIATION
7325 HALCYON SUMMIT DRIVE
MONTGOMERY, AL 36117
334-263-6994
Fax: 334-387-0075
www.ahsaa.com
• Steve Savarese, Executive Director
ssavarese@ahsaa.com
• Tony Stallworth, Associate Executive Director
tstallworth@ahsaa.com
Sports Service Founded:
1921
Publications:
AHSAA Sports Books; AHSAA eligibility by-laws; Coaches Directory.
Description:
AHSAA is a priavet agency which regulates, coordinates and promotes interscholastic

athletic programs among its member public and private schools. Over 75,000 students involved.

ALASKA SCHOOL ACTIVITIES ASSOCIATION
4048 LAUREL STREET
#203
ANCHORAGE, AK 99508
907-563-3723
Fax: 907-563-3739
contactus@asaa.org
www.asaa.org
• Billy Strickland, Executive Director
billy@asaa.org
• Deanna Montagna, Director Of Office Operations & Students Services
deanna@asaa.org
• Doug Stewart, Director of Development & Marketing
Sports Services Founded:
1956
Description:
To advocate participation in cocurricular activities; to regulate sanctioned interscholastic activities, contests and programs; and to promote the academic and social development of students.

ALBERTA SCHOOLS' ATHLETIC ASSOCIATION
11759 GROAT ROAD
EDMONTON, AB, CANADA T5M 3K6
780-427-8182
Fax: 780-415-1833
info@asaa.ca
www.asaa.ca
• Tom Christensen, President
(403) 556-3391
• Rick Gilson, Vice-Presdient
(403) 653-4991
rick.gilson@westwind.ab.ca
• John Paton, Executive Director
(780) 427-8182
john@asaa.ca
• Tyler Callaghan, Assistant Director
(888) 618-4530
• Morgan Munroe, Compliance Officer
(780) 415-1833
morgan@asaa.ca
Description:
A voluntary, non profit organization established to coordinate athletic programs for young people in Alberta schools.

ARIZONA INTERSCHOLASTIC ASSOCIATION
7007 N 18TH STREET
PHOENIX, AZ 85020-5552
602-385-3810
Fax: 602-385-3779
www.aiaonline.org
• Jacob Holiday, President
(928) 697-2172
jacob.holiday@kayenta.k12.az.us
• Harold Slemmer Ed.D, Executive Director
(602) 385-3811
hslemmer@aiaonline.org
Year Founded:
1925

ARKANSAS ACTIVITIES ASSOCIATION
3920 RICHARDS ROAD
NORTH LITTLE ROCK, AR 72117
501-955-2500
Fax: 501-955-2600
www.ahsaa.org
• Lance Taylor, Executive Director
(501) 955-2500
lance@ahsaa.org
• Joey Walters, Deputy Executive Director
(501) 955-2500
joey@ahsaa.org

BC SCHOOL SPORTS
2003A - 3713 KENSINGTON AVENUE
BURNABY, BC, CANADA V5B 0A7

604-477-1488
info@bcschoolsports.ca
www.bcschoolsports.ca
• Mike Allina, President
(604) 713-8215
mallina@vsb.bc.ca
• Rob Colombo, 1st Vice President
(604) 941-6053
rcolombo@sd43.bc.ca
• Mykola Misiak, 2nd Vice President
(604) 531-8354
misiak_m@surreyschools.ca
• Jordan Abney, Executive Director
(604) 477-1488
jabney@bcschoolsports.ca
• Merirlla Thorp, Financial Officer
(604) 477-1488
mthorp@bcschoolsports.ca
Description:
BC School Sports is an assocation of public and private schools governing school sport in the province.
Description:
BC School Sports is an assocation of public and private schools governing school sport in the province.

CALIFORNIA INTERSCHOLASTIC FEDERATION
4658 DUCKHORN DRIVE
SACRAMENTO, CA 95834
916-239-4477
Fax: 916-239-4478
www.cifstate.org
• Roger Blake, Executive Director
rblake@cifstate.org
• Ron Nocetti, Associate Director
rnocetti@cifstate.org
• Brian Seymour, Senior Director
bseymour@cifstate.org
• Chris Fahey, Director Of Corporate Sponsorships
cfahey@cifstate.org

COLORADO HS ACTIVITIES ASSOCIATION
14855 E 2ND AVENUE
AURORA, CO 80011
303-344-5050
www2.chsaa.org
• Eddie Hartnett, President
• Paul Angelico, Secretary-Treasurer
Description:
The association works for the advancement of, and the student's participation in, interscholastic activities.

CONNECTICUT INTERSCHOLASTIC ATHLETIC CONFERENCE
30 REALTY DRIVE
CHESHIRE, CT 06410
203-250-1111
Fax: 203-250-1345
ciacsports.com/site
• Paul Newton, CSAC Chair
• Richard Dellinger, Middle Level Vice President
• Karissa Niehoff, PhD, Executive Director
(203) 250-1111
• Stephanie Ford, Marketing Director
(203) 250-1111
Sports Services Founded:
1921
Membership:
Any public, private or parochial elementary, middle or senior high school which is approved by the State Board of Education.
Description:
Works to develop, maintain and enforce rules of eligibility and conduct that insure equitable athletic competition among Connecticut's secondary schools. The CIAC serves as the sole governing body for inter-scholastic athletic activities in Connecticut.

DELAWARE INTERSCHOLASTIC ATHLETIC ASSOCIATION
35 COMMERCE WAY
SUITE 1
DOVER, DE 19904
302-857-3365
www.doe.k12.de.us
• Thomas Neubauer, Executive Director
thomas.neubauer@doe.k12.de.us
Description:
Advocates for and promotes and the value of interscholastic athletics, and ensures fair competitions during competition. Promotes healthy lifestyles for youth.

FLORIDA HIGH SCHOOL ATHLETIC ASSOCIATION
1801 NW 80TH BOULEVARD
GAINESVILLE, FL 32606
352-372-9551
800-461-7895
Fax: 352-373-1528
www.fhsaa.org
• Frank Beasley, Director of Athletics
(352) 372-9551
fbeasley@fhsaa.org
• Roger Dearing, Executive Director
(352) 372-9551
rdearing@fhsaa.org
Description:
To promote, direct, supervise and regulate interscholastic athletic programs in which member high schools compete.
Year Founded:
1920

GEORGIA HS ASSOCIATION
151 S BETHEL STREET
PO BOX 271
THOMASTON, GA 30286-0004
706-647-7473
Fax: 706-647-2638
ghsa@ghsa.net
www.ghsa.net
• Gary Phillips, Executive Director
(706) 647-7473
• Lisa Moore Williams, Vice President
• Steve Figueroa, Director Media Relations
(706) 647-7473
Sports Service Founded:
1904
Description:
Promotes sports education in Georgia. Standardizes and encourages participation in athletics, and to promote sportsmanship and an appreciation for and study of music, speech, and other fine arts through Region and State competitions.

HAWAII HS ATHLETIC ASSOCIATION
PO BOX 62029
HONOLULU, HI 96839
808-800-4092
info@hhsaa.org
www.sportshigh.com
• Christopher Chun, Executive Director
• Russell Aoki, Associate Director
• Natalie Iwamoto, Director Of Information And Marketing
Sports Services Founded:
1956
Description:
The HHSAA serves public and private high schools by promoting althetics in the context of educational programming. As part of this work, the organization holds state championships, and leadership training seminars for coaches, officials and athletic directors.

IDAHO HS ACTIVITIES ASSOCIATION
8011 USTICK ROAD
BOISE, ID 83704
208-375-7027
Fax: 208-322-5505
admin@idhsaa.org
www.idhsaa.org

• Ty Jones, Executive Director
jonest@idhsaa.org

ILLINOIS HS ASSOCIATION
2715 MCGRAW DRIVE
BLOOMINGTON, IL 61704-6011
309-663-6377
Fax: 309-663-7479
general@ihsa.org
www.ihsa.org
• Craig Anderson, Executive Director
canderson@ihsa.org
• Kurt Gibson, Assistant Executive Director
kgibson@ihsa.org
Sports Service Founded:
1900
Description:
The IHSA serves member schools by providing leadership for equitable participation in interscholastic athletics and activities that enrich the educational experience.

INDIANA HS ATHLETIC ASSOCIATION
9150 MERIDIAN STREET
PO BOX 40650
INDIANAPOLIS, IN 46240
317-846-6601
Fax: 317-575-4244
www.ihsaa.org
• Debb Stevens, Chairperson
• Jim Brown, Vice-Chairperson
• Bobby Cox, Commissioner
bcox@ihsaa.org
• Jason Wille, Sports Information Director
jwille@ihsaa.org
Sports Services Founded:
1903
Description:
A not-for-profit organization which encourages and directs amateur athletics in the high schools of Indiana.

IOWA HS ATHLETIC ASSOCIATION
1605 SOUTH STORY STREET
PO BOX 10
BOONE, IA 50036
515-432-2011
Fax: 515-432-2961
www.iahsaa.org
• Alan Beste, Executive Director
• Brett Nanninga, Associate Director
bnanninga@iahsaa.org
• Todd Tharp, Assistant Director
ttharp@iahsaa.org
• Sandra Anderson, Finance Director
sanderson@iahsaa.org
• Lewie Curtis, Officials Director
lcurtis@iahsaa.org
• Bud Legg, Information Director
blegg@iahsaa.org
• Kylie Swanson, Communications Director
kswanson@iahsaa.org
• Laura Brooker, Asst Director of Officials
officials@iahsaa.org
• Chelsea Clark, Administrative Assistant
cclark@iahsaa.org
• Elisa Kahler, Office Manager
ekahler@iahsaa.org
• Amy McNace, Administrative Assistant
amcnace@iahsaa.org
• Kim Mechura, Administrative Assistant
kmechura@iahsaa.org
Description:
Founded in 1903. the association is a non-for-profit organization which officates cross country, fall golf, football, basketball, bowling, swimming, wrestling, soccer, spring golf, tennis, track & field and baseball for itsmember schools.

KANSAS STATE HS ACTIVITIES ASSOCIATION
PO BOX 495
TOPEKA, KS 66601
785-273-5329
Fax: 785-271-0236
kshsaa@kshsaa.org
www.kshsaa.org

• Juan Perez, President
(620) 356-3025
• Rod Wittmer, Vice-President
(785) 364-2181
r.wittmer@holtonks.net
• Britton Hart, Secretary-Treasurer
(620) 341-2365
• Gary Musselman, Executive Director
• Cheryl Gleason, Assistant Executive Director
cegleason@kshsaa.org
Description:
Provides guidance for the administration education based sport and other interscholastic activites in the state of Kansas.

KENTUCKY HS ATHLETIC ASSOCIATION
2280 EXECUTIVE DRIVE
LEXINGTON, KY 40505
859-299-5472
Fax: 859-293-5999
general@khsaa.org
www.khsaa.org
• Julian Tackett, Commissioner
(859) 299-5472
• Mike Barren, Assistant Commissioner
(859) 299-5472

LOUISIANA HS ATHLETIC ASSOCIATION
12720 OLD HAMMOND HIGHWAY
BATON ROUGE, LA 70816
225-296-5882
Fax: 225-296-5919
www.lhsaa.org
• Eddie Bonine, Executive Director
ebonine@lhsaa.org
• Keith Alexander, Assistant Executive Director
kalexander@lhsaa.org
• Rhonda Blanford-Green, Assistant Executive Director
rblanfordgreen@lhsaa.org
• BJ Guzzardo, Assistant Executive Director
bguzzardo@lhsaa.org
• Mitch Small, Director of Maeketing
msmall@lhsaa.org

MAINE PRINCIPAL'S ASSOCIATION
50 INDUSTRIAL DRIVE
AUGUSTA, ME 04330
207-622-0217
Fax: 207-622-1513
mpa@mpa.cc
www.mpa.cc
• Dan Welch, President
• Maggie Allen, President Elect
• Richard A. A Durost, Executive Director
• Michael Burnham, Assistant Executive Director
mburnham@mpa.cc
• Holly D. Couturier, Assistant Executive Director
• Tammy McNear, Secretary
tmcnear@mpa.cc
Description:
This non-profit organization is conprised of the Division of Professional Activities and Division of Interscholastic Activities.

MANITOBA HS ATHLETIC ASSOCIATION
145 PACIFIC AVENUE
WINNIPEG, MB, CANADA R3B 2Z6
204-925-5640
Fax: 204-925-5624
info@mhsaa.ca
www.mhsaa.ca
• Chris Gudziunas, President
(204) 326-6471
• JJ Ross, Urban Representative
• Chad Falk, Executive Director
chad@mhsaa.ca
• Greg Jarvis, Assistant Executive Director
(204) 925-5642
greg@mhsaa.ca
• Jo-Ann Waskul, Admin. Assistant:
(204) 925-5640
jo-ann@mhsaa.ca

Sports Service Founded:
1962
Description:
Encourages particiaption in high school sport as an essential component of education and personal development.

MARYLAND PUBLIC SECONDARY SCHOOLS ATHLETIC ASSOCIATION
200 WEST BALTIMORE STREET
BALTIMORE, MD 21201
410-767-0555
Fax: 410-333-3111
www.mpssaa.org
• R. Andrew Warner, Executive Director
• Jason Bursick, Assistant Director
Sports Services Founded:
1946
Description:
Promotes and directs public high school interscholastic activities to assure their contribution in the entire educational program of the state of Maryland.

MASSACHUSETTS INTERSCHOLASTIC ATHLETIC ASSOCIATION
33 FORGE PARKWAY
FRANKLIN, MA 02038
508-541-7997
Fax: 508-541-9888
miaa@miaa.net
www.miaa.net
• David King, President
• Marilyn Slattery, Vice President
Description:
Organization sponsors athletic activities in high school sport.

MICHIGAN HS ATHLETIC ASSOCIATION
1661 RAMBLEWOOD DRIVE
EAST LANSING, MI 48823
517-332-5046
Fax: 517-332-4071
info@mhsaa.com
www.mhsaa.com
• John E Roberts, Executive Director
• Nate Hampton, Assistant Director
• Dan Hutcheson, Assistant Director
• Jordan Cobb, Director of Information Systems
• John R Johnson, Communications Director
• Jeremy Sampson, Ticketing, Promotions & Marketing Coordinator

MINNESOTA STATE HS LEAGUE
2100 FREEWAY BOULEVARD
BROOKLYN CENTER, MN 55430-1735
763-560-2262
www.mshsl.org
• David Stead, Executive Director
(763) 560-2262
dstead@mshsl.org
• Lynne Johnson, Executive Assistant
ljohnson@mshsl.org
• Jody Redman, Associate Director
jredman@mshsl.org
• Ellen Rajkowski, Information Specialist
erajkowski@mshsl.org
• Nancy Myers, Ticket Assistant
(763) 560-2262
nmeyers@mshsl.org
Description:
Founded in 1916, this voluntary non-profit association of public and private schools serves area high schools with athletic and fine arts competicion and programming.

MISSISSIPPI HS ACTIVITIES ASSOCIATION
1201 CLINTON/RAYMOND ROAD
CLINTON, MS 39056
601-924-6400
Fax: 601-924-1725
www.misshsaa.com
• Don Hinton, Executive Director
• Lonnie Tillman, Associate Director

- Diane Bruser, Assistant Director
- Joyce Franklin, Financial Officer
jfranklin@misshsaa.com

MISSOURI STATE HS ACTIVITIES ASSOCIATION
1 N KEENE STREET
COLUMBIA, MO 65201-6645
573-875-4880
Fax: 573-875-1450
email@mshsaa.org
www.mshsaa.org

MONTANA HS ASSOCIATION
1 SOUTH DAKOTA AVENUE
HELENA, MT 59601
406-442-6010
Fax: 406-442-8250
www.mhsa.org
- Mark Beckman, Executive Director
mbeckman@mhsa.org
- Joanne Austin, Associate Director
- Janie Holmes, Business Office Manger
- Brian Michelotti, Assistant Director
Sports Services Founded:
1921.

NEBRASKA SCHOOL ACTIVITIES ASSOCIATION
500 CHARLESTON STREET
SUITE 1
LINCOLN, NE 68508-1119
402-489-0386
Fax: 402-489-0934
www.nsaahome.org
- Jim Tenopir, Executive Director
- Debra Velder, Associate Director
- Jennifer Schwartz, Assistant Director
- Megan Huber, Business Manager
Description:
Developes and regulates policies of competition and sportsmanship for activities of member high schools in interscholastic programs.

NEVADA INTERSCHOLASTIC ACTIVITIES ASSOCIATION
549 COURT STREET
RENO, NV 89501
775-453-1012
Fax: 775-453-1016
www.niaa.com
- Bart Thompson, Executive Director
- Jay Bessemyer, Assistant Director
jayb@niaa.com
- Donnie Nelson, Assistant Director
donnien@niaa.com
Year founded:
1922

NEW BRUNSWICK INTERSCHOLASTIC ATHLETIC ASSOCIATION
20 MCGLOIN ST
FREDERICTON, NB, CANADA E3A 5T8
506-457-4843
www.nbiaa-asinb.org
- Allyson Ouellette, Executive Director
(506) 457-4843
Vision:
NBIAA will promote quality experiences by enriching education and enhancing personal development through high school sports.
Mission:
To be the governing body of high school sports, where we create, promote, and facilitate positive sporting experiences in an educational environment in the province of New Brunswick.
Founded:
1926
Members:
75 member schools
Publications:
NBIAA Handbook; NBIAA Coaches Course

NEW HAMPSHIRE INTERSCHOLASTIC ATHLETIC ASSOCIATION
251 CLINTON STREET
CONCORD, NH 3301
603-228-8671
Fax: 603-225-7978
info@nhiaa.org
www.nhiaa.org
Description:
A voluntary organization operated by a continually changing committee structure and an athletic council. Committee membership is voluntary.

NEW JERSEY STATE INTERSCHOLASTIC ATHLETIC ASSOCIATION
1161 ROUTE 130
PO BOX 487
ROBBINSVILLE, NJ 8691
609-259-2776
Fax: 609-259-3047
www.njsiaa.org
- Steven J Timko, Executive Director
- Kim DeGraw Cole, Assistant Director
- Michele Perez, Accounting
Sports Services Founded:
1918

NEW MEXICO ACTIVITIES ASSOCIATION
6600 PALOMAS AVENUE NE
ALBUQUERQUE, NM 87109
505-923-3110
888-820-6622
Fax: 505-923-3114
feedback@nmact.org
www.nmact.org
- Sally Marquez, Executive Director
(505) 923-3267
sally@nmact.org
- Dusty Young, Associate Director
(505) 923-3268
dusty@nmact.org
Sports Service Founded:
1921

NEW YORK STATE PUBLIC HS ATHLETIC ASSOCIATION
8 AIRPORT PARK BOULEVARD
LATHAM, NY 12110
518-690-0771
Fax: 518-690-0775
www.nysphsaa.org
- Robert Zayas, Executive Director
(518) 690-0771
rzayas@nysphsaa.org
- Todd Nelson, Assistant Director
(518) 690-0771
tnelson@nysphsaa.org
- Joe Altieri, Assistant Director
(518) 690-0771
altieri@nysphsaa.org
- Chris Joyce, Director of Sales & Marketing
cjoyce@nysphsaa.org
- Lisa Arnold, Treasurer
larnold@nysphsaa.org

NORTH CAROLINA HS ATHLETIC ASSOCIATION
222 FINLEY GOLF COURSE
CHAPEL HILL, NC 27517
919-240-7401
Fax: 919-240-7399
info@nchsaa.org
www.nchsaa.org
- Que Tucker, Commissioner
(919) 240-7375
que@nchsaa.org
- Whitney Frye, Associate Commissioner
(919) 240-7379
whitney@nchsaa.org
Description:
Voluntary, non profit corporation which administers the state's interscholastic athletic program. Any North Carolina or non boarding

parochial school is eligible for membership, provided it is accredited by the State Department of Public Instruction and that the school adopts and maintains a prescribed code to guarantee fair competition.

NORTH DAKOTA HS ACTIVITIES ASSOCIATION
350 2ND STREET NW
PO BOX 817
VALLEY CITY, ND 58072
701-845-3953
Fax: 701-845-4935
www.ndhsaa.com
- Matthew Fetsch, Executive Director
matt.fetsch@ndhsaa.org
- Brian Bubach, Associate Director
brian.bubach@ndhsaa.org
Description:
A non-profit organization, which exists to contribute to the education of North Dakota High school students by administering programs, promoting citizenship and good sportsmanship, and providing fine arts and athletic programs to supplement general education.

OHIO HS ATHLETIC ASSOCIATION
4080 ROSELEA PLACE
COLUMBUS, OH 43214
614-267-2502
Fax: 614-267-1677
webmaster@ohsaa.org
www.ohsaa.org
- Andy Bixler, Board President
- Jeffrey Snyder, Board Vice President
- Todd Boehm, Comptroller
- Molly Downard, Executive Administrative Assistant
- Jason Fleming, Assistant Comptroller
Description:
Regulates and administers interscholastic athletic competition in a fair and equitable manner while promoting the values of participation in interscholastic athletics.

OKLAHOMA SECONDARY SCHOOL ACTIVITIES ASSOCIATION
7300 NORTH BROADWAY EXTENSION
PO BOX 14590
OKLAHOMA CITY, OK 73113-0590
405-840-1116
Fax: 405-840-9559
www.ossaa.com
- Mark Hudson, President
- Rick Pool, Vice President
Sports Service Founded:
1911

ONTARIO FED OF SCHOOL ATHLETIC ASSOCIATIONS
3 CONCORDE GATE
SUITE 204
TORONTO, ON, CANADA M3C 3N7
416-426-7391
Fax: 416-426-7317
www.ofsaa.on.ca
Description:
A provincial federation of Associations encompassing volunteer coaschs, students, and administrators. Dedicated to the promotion and enhacnement of the educational value and leadership in advancing the educational benefits of participation through its services, resources and the conduct of secondary school sport Championships.

OREGON SCHOOL ACTIVITIES ASSOCIATION
25200 SW PARKWAY AVENUE
SUITE 1
WILSONVILLE, OR 97070
503-682-6722
Fax: 503-682-0960
info@osaa.org
www.osaa.org

• Tony Guevara, President
(503) 391-2639
tonyguevara@blanchetcatholicschool.com
• Peter Weber, Executive Director
(503) 682-6722
peterw@osaa.org
• Cindy Simmons, Assistant Executive Director
(503) 682-6722
cindys@osaa.org
• Brad Garrett, Assistant Executive Director
(503) 682-6722
bradg@osaa.org
• Steve Walker, Sports Information Director
(503) 682-6722
stevew@osaa.org
Sports Services Founded:
1918

PENNSYLVANIA INTERSCHOLASTIC ATHLETIC ASSOCIATION
550 GETTYSBURG ROAD
PO BOX 2008
MECHANICSBURG, PA 17055-0708
717-697-0374
800-382-1392
Fax: 717-697-7721
website@piaa.org
www.piaa.org
• Robert A. R Lombardi, Execuitve Director
• Mark E. A Byers, COO
• Melissa N. N Mertz, Associate Executive Director
• Patrick B. L Gebhart, Esq, Assistant Executive Director
Member Services:
Establishes eligibility, sets contest rules for specific sports, provides registration and training for officials and organizes competitions for member schools.

RHODE ISLAND INTERSCHOLASTIC LEAGUE, INC.
RHODE ISLAND COLLEGE
600 MOUNT PLEASANT AVENUE
BUILDING 6
PROVIDENCE, RI 02908-1991
401-272-9844
Fax: 401-272-9838
info@riil.org
www.riil.org
• Thomas Mezzanotte, Executive Director
• Michael P Lunney, Assistant Director
Description:
The association is conprised of high school principals representing 60 institutions. The league sets rules and regulations for competition and carries out athletic programs in Rhode Island.
Year Founded:
1932

SOUTH CAROLINA HIGH SCHOOL LEAGUE
121 WESTPARK BLVD.
COLUMBIA, SC 29210
803-798-0120
schsl@schsl.org
www.schsl.org
• Mickey Pringle, President
mpringle@bellsouth.net
• Dan Matthews, Vice President
daniel.matthews@kcsdschools.net
• Jerome P Singleton, Commissioner
jsingle@schsl.org
• Nessie Harris, Associate Commissioner
• Skip Lax, Assistant Commissioner

SOUTH DAKOTA HS ACTIVITIES ASSOCIATION
804 NORTH EUCLID AVENUE
SUITE 102
PO BOX 1217
PIERRE, SD 57501
605-224-9261
Fax: 605-224-9262
www.sdhsaa.com

• Wayne Carney, Executive Director
• Jo Auch, Assistant Executive Director
jo.auch@sdhsaa.com

TENNESSEE SECONDARY SCHOOL ATHLETIC ASSOCIATION
3333 LEBANON ROAD
PO BOX 319
HERMITAGE, TN 37076
615-889-6740
Fax: 615-889-0544
tssaa@tssaa.org
www.tssaa.org
• Bernard Childress, Executive Director
bchildress@tssaa.org
• Matthew Gillespie, Assistant Executive Director
mgillespie@tssaa.org
• Stephen Bargatze, Student Services Director
sbargatze@tssaa.org
• Courtney Brunetz, Marketing Director
cbrunetz@tssaa.org
Sports Services Founded:
1925

TEXAS UNIVERSITY INTERSCHOLASTIC LEAGUE
1701 MANOR ROAD
AUSTIN, TX 78722
512-471-5883
Fax: 512-471-5908
www.uiltexas.org
• Charles Breithaupt, Executive Director
director@uiltexas.org
• Jamey Harrison, Deputy Director/Marketing
• Kim Carmichael, Chief Of Staff
cos@uiltexas.org
• Susan Doherty, Executive Assistant
director@uiltexas.org
• Caroline Walls, Event Coordinator
info@uiltexas.org
Sports Services Founded:
1909
Description:
Organizes and supervises competition at the high school level. It promotes healthy lifestyles, character building, and educational activities.

UTAH HIGH SCHOOL ACTIVITIES ASSOCIATION
199 EAST 7200 SOUTH
MIDVALE, UT 84047
801-566-0681
Fax: 801-566-0633
Submit@uhsaa.org
www.uhsaa.org
• Rob Cuff, Executive Director
cuff@uhsaa.org
• Kim Monkres, Assistant Director
monkres@uhsaa.org
• Ryan Bishop, Assistant Director
bishop@uhsaa.org
Description:
The UHSAA leads athletic and fine arts programming for high schools in Utah, and promotes involvement in these activities as part of education and citizenship.
Number of Members:
150 member scools
Publications:
UHSAA HANDBOOK: Annually, UHSAA YEARBOOK: Annually.

VERMONT PRINCIPALS' ASSOCIATION
2 PROSPECT STREET
SUITE 3
MONTPELIER, VT 5602
802-229-0547
Fax: 802-229-4801
www.vpaonline.org
• Patrick Burke, VPA President
pburke@sbschools.net
• Linda Wheatley, Development Coordinator
• Ken Page, Executive Director
• Bob Johnson, Associate Executive Director
bjohnson@vpaonline.org

Description:
A nonprofit groupn of education leaders collaborating on mentoring, professional development and networking while overseeing Vermont's co-curricular activities.

VIRGINIA HS LEAGUE
1642 STATE FARM BOULEVARD
CHARLOTTESVILLE, VA 22911
434-977-8475
info@vhsl.org
www.vhsl.org
• Jim Stemple, Chair
(540) 658-6840
• John W. Haun, Ed.D., Executive Director
bhaun@vhsl.org
• Shawn Knight, Assistant Director For Athletics
sknight@vhsl.org
• Kelley Haney, Assistant Director Of Athletics
khaney@vhsl.org
• Lisa Giles, Assistant Director of Activities
lgiles@vhsl.org
• David Hopkins, Director of Finance
dhopkins@vhsl.org
Description:
Virginia's public high schools, through their alliance as the Virginia High School League, serve their youth by establishing and maintaining standards for student activities and competitions that promote education, personal growth, sportsmanship, leadership and citizenship.

WASHINGTON INTERSCHOLASTIC ACTIVITIES ASSOCIATION
435 MAIN AVENUE SOUTH
RENTON, WA 98057
425-687-8585
Fax: 425-687-9476
www.wiaa.com
• Eric McCurdy, President
• Mike Colbrese, Executive Director
colbrese@wiaa.com
• Cindy Adsit, Assistant Executive Director
(425) 282-5232
cadsit@wiaa.com
• Leah Francis, Finance/Operations Director
(425) 282-5238
lfrancis@wiaa.com
Sports Services Founded:
1905
Description:
Exists to assist member schools in operating student programs that foster achievement, respect, equity, enthusiasm and excellence in a safe and organized environment. This Association shall plan, supervise and administer the interscholastic activities approved and delegated by the school districts boards of directors.

WEST VIRGINIA SECONDARY SCHOOL ACTIVITIES COMMISSION
2875 STAUNTON TURNPIKE
PARKERSBURG, WV 26104-7219
304-485-5494
Fax: 304-428-5431
wvssac@wvssac.org
www.wvssac.org
• Bernie Dolan, Executive Director
• Kelly Geddis, Assistant Executive Director
• Wayne Ryan, Assistant Executive Director

WYOMING HS ACTIVITIES ASSOCIATION
6571 EAST 2ND STREET
CASPER, WY 82609
307-577-0614
Fax: 307-577-0637
www.whsaa.org
• Ron Laird, Commissioner
rlaird@whsaa.org
• Trevor Wilson, Associate Commissioner
twilson@whsaa.org
Sports Services Founded:
1920

NATIONAL HIGH SCHOOL ATHLETIC COACHES ASSOCIATION
PO BOX 10277
FARGO, ND 58106
701-570-1008
www.hscoaches.org
• Dave Dougherty, Executive Director
Sports Services Founded:
1965
Publications:
www.hscoaches.org source for all NHSACA information.
Description:
The NHSACA is the only high school coaches association created by and governed by coaches. Also provides high school coaches across America with a voice in current national issues. Also provides high school coaches with the first recognition program available in America.

NATIONAL INTERSCHOLASTIC ATHLETIC ADMINISTRATORS ASSOCIATION/NIAAA
9100 KEYSTONE CROSSING
SUITE 650
INDIANAPOLIS, IN 46240
317-587-1450
Fax: 317-587-1451
www.niaaa.org
• Richard Barton, President
• Michael Blackburn, CMAA,Executive Director
• Josh Scott, Secretary
jscott@waynesville.k12.mo.us
Description:
The National Interscholastic Athletic Administration Association preserves, enhances and promotes the educational values of interscholastic athletics through the professional development of its members in the areas of education, leadership and service. The NIAAA's commitment to leadership programs, resources and services support the athletic administration's efforts in providing quality athletic participation opportunities for students.
Year Founded:
1977
Publications:
Interscholastic Athletic Administration, Hazing Education, Risk Management.

Other locations:

RESEAU DU SPORTETUDIANT DU QUEBEC
4545, AVENUE PIERRE-DE COUBERTIN
CP 1000, BRANCH M
MONTREAL, QB, CANADA H1V 3R2
514-252-3300
Fax: 514-254-3292
info@rseq.ca
www.rseq.ca
• Gustave Roel, President/Executive Director
groel@rseq.ca
• Pierre Boulerice, Vice President
• Jacques Desrochers, Secretary-Treasurer

STUDENT SPORTS
23954 MADISON STREET
TORRANCE, CA 90505
310-791-1142
800-660-1334
Fax: 310-791-4809
info@studentsports.com
www.studentsports.com

• Andy Bark, CEO/Founder
andy@studentsports.com
• Patrick Bark, Director Of Media
patrick@studentsports.com
Sports Service Founded:
1979

U.S. ARMY ALL-AMERICAN BOWL
100 FORGE WAY
SUITE 1
ROCKAWAY, NJ 07866
973-366-8448
www.allamericangames.com
• Doug Berman, Chairman
• Ed D'Ambola, Manager, Creative Media Services
• Nate Seamon, Vice President, Operations
College Bowl Game:
US Army All-American Bowl.

Other locations:

WISCONSIN INTERSCHOLASTIC ATHLETIC ASSOCIATION
5516 VERN HOLMES DRIVE
STEVENS POINT, WI 54482
715-344-8580
info@wiaawi.org
www.wiaawi.org
• Dave Anderson, Executive Director
danderson@wiaawi.org
• Deb Hauser, Associate Director
• Todd Clark, Communicators Director
tclark@wiaawi.org

Military Sports

INTERNATIONAL MILITARY SPORTS COUNCIL
RUE JACQUES JORDAENS 26
1000 BRUXELLES, BELGIUM
www.milsport.one
• Dorah Mamby Koita, Secretary General
• Olivier Verhelle, Director Administration and Human Resources

U.S. ARMED FORCES SPORTS
2455 REYNOLDD ROAD
FORT SAM HOUSTON
SAN ANTONIO, TX 78234
210-466-1335
www.armedforcessports.com
• Steven Dinote, Armed Forces Sports Secretariat
• Kenneth Polk, Deputy Secretary
Description:
Founded 1947. Conducts championships for men and women in basketball, volleyball, marathon, cross country, slow-pitch softball, golf, bowling, triathlon, track, soccer, and for men rugby, wrestling, and boxing. Sponsors international World Military Championships in basketball, cross country, volleyball, parachuting, track and field, shooting, naval pentathlon, modern pentathlon, taekwondo, wrestling and boxing, skiing, fencing, soccer and cycling.

Olympic, International Federations

BADMINTON WORLD FEDERATION
UNIT 17.05, LEVEL 17
AMODA BUILDING

22 JALAN IMBI
KUALA LUMPUR, 55100
bwf@bwfbadminton.org
bwfbadminton.com
• Thomas Lund, Secretary General
t.lund@bwfbadminton.org
Description:
To deliver quality services, world class events and innovative development initiatives which showcase the sport at the highest levels and increase the active participation in badminton at all levels worldwide.

FEDERATION EQUESTRE INTERNATIONALE (FEI)
HM KING HUSSEIN I BUILDING
CHEMIN DE LA JOLIETTE 8
LAUSANNE, SWITZERLAN 1006
www.fei.org
• Ingmar De Vos, President
• Sabrina Ibanez, Secretary General
Nature of Service:
International governing body for equestrian sports.
Number of Members:
132 affiliated national federations.

FEDERATION INTERNATIONALE DE SKI (FIS)
MARC HODLER HOUSE
BLOCHSTRASSE 2
OBERHOFEN/THUNERSEE, CH-3653
www.fis-ski.com
• Jolanda Bruelisauer, Assistant To President
bruelisauer@fisski.com
• Riikka Rakic, Communications manager
• Marcel Looze, Marketing Manager
• Richard Bunn, TV Consultant
• Francesco Cattaneo, IT Manager
it@fisski.com
• Christian Pirzer, CEO Marketing AG
• Sarah Lewis, Secretary General
• Sibylle Gafner, Finance & HR Manager
gafner@fisski.com
Sports Services Founded:
February 2, 1924
Description:
The organisation was founded during the first Olympic Games in Chamoix, France with 14 member nations. Today 107 National Ski Associations compise the membership of the FIS.

FEDERATION INTERNATIONALE DE LUGE DE COURSE (FIL)
RATHAUSPLATZ 9
BERCHTESGADEN, 83471
office@fil-luge.org
www.fil-luge.org
Description:
Founded 1957. Responsible for worldwide organization of the sport of luge. Sanctions international luge competitions including the Winter Olympic Games, World Championships, an annual eight race World Cup tour plus other numerous international events.
Membership Requirements:
Limited to national luge federations recognized by their nation's National Olympic Committee.
Publications:
FIL NEWS, twice annually.
Member Services:
Schedules races, sanctions international

competitions, certifies international officials, oversees regulations.

FEDERATION INTERNATIONALE D'ESCRIME (FIE)
MAISON DU SPORT INTERNATIONAL
AVENUE DE RHODANIE 54
LAUSANNE, CH 1007
info@fie.ch
www.fie.org
• Nathalie Rodriguez, Chief Executive Officer
nr@fie.ch
Description:
The organization which governs all over the world the sport of fencing. Based in Lausanne, Olympic Capital.
Members:
121 Member Federations

FEDERATION INTERNATIONALE DE FOOTBALL ASSOCIATION (FIFA)
FIFA-STRASSE 20
PO BOX 8044
ZURICH, 8044
contact@fifa.org
www.fifa.com
• Gianni Infantino, President
Description:
International association for the development of football.
Year Founded:
1904
Member Associations:
211
Publications:
The FIFA Weekly

FEDERATION INTERNATIONALE DE NATATION (FINA)
CHEMIN DE BELLEVUE 24a/24b
LAUSANNE, 1005
www.fina.org
• Julio C Maglione, President
• Husain Al Musallam, Vice President
• Cornel Marculescu, Executive Director
Year Founded:
1908
Publications:
FINA newsletter, FINA Handbook, FINA Aquatics World Magazine
Description:
Comprised of 207 national member federations, FINA holds competitions in swimming, open water swimming, diving, water polo, synchronised swimming, high diving and masters.

FEDERATION INTERNATIONALE DE VOLLEYBALL (FIVB)
CHATEAU LES TOURELLES
CH. EDOUARD-SANDOZ 2-4
LAUSANNE, 1006
info@fivb.org
www.fivb.org
• Ari S Graca Filho, President
• Fernando Lima, Secretary General
Description:
The governing body responsible for all forms of Volleyball on a global level. Working closely with national federations and private enterprises the FIVB aims to develop Volleyball as a major world media and entertainment sport through world-class planning and organization of competitions, marketing and development activities.

Publications:
Volley World Magazine, X-Press

INTERNATIONAL ASSOCIATION OF ATHLETICS FEDERATIONS (IAAF)
6-8, QUAI ANTOINE 1ER
BP 359
MONTE CARLO, MONACO 98007
www.iaaf.org
• Sebastian Coe, President
Sports Service Founded:
1912
Publications:
See publication list on www.iaaf.org.
Member Services:
Worldwide governing body of track & field athletics. Assistance at competitions (finance).
Membership Requirements:
Constitution in accord with IAAF's, stage National Championships annually, participation in at least one IAAF competition annually, have an office with technical infrastructure, pay annual fee and complete annual report form.

INTERNATIONAL BASKETBALL FEDERATION (FIBA)
ROUTE SUISSE 5
PO BOX 29
MIES, 1295
info@fiba.com
www.fiba.com
• Andreas Zagklis, Secretary General
• Hamane Niang, President

INTERNATIONAL BIATHLON UNION (IBU)

PEREGRINSTRASSE 14
SALZBURG, A-5020
biathlon@ibu.at
www.biathlonworld.com
• Anders Besseberg, President
• Olle Dahlin, Vice President, Development
olle.dahlin@ibu.at
• James E Carrabre, Vice President, Medical Issues
jim.carrabre@ibu.at
• Nami Kim, Vice President, Special Issues
• Ivor Lehotan, Vice President, Information
• Klaus Leistner, Vice President, Finance
klaus.leistner@ibu.at
• Victor Maygurov, First Vice President
• Thomas Pfuller, Vice President, Marketing
• Nicole Resch, Secretary General
• Max Cobb, Vice President, Sport
max.cobb@ibu.at
Description:
The IBU serves as the international governing body for the sport of biathlon, sanctioning competitions and promoting the sport.
Number of Members:
57
Publications:
Biathlon Calander (annual), BiathlonWorld Magazine.

INTERNATIONAL BOBSLEIGH & SKELETON FEDERATION
MAISON DU SPORT
AVENUE DE RHODANIE 54
LAUSANNE, CH 1007
office@ibsf.org
www.ibsf.org
• Ivo Ferriani, President
ivo.ferriani@ibsf.com

• Heike Groesswang, Secretary General
heike.groesswang@ibsf.org
Nature of Service:
The IBSF is the international organization governing the sports of bobsledding and skeleton tobogganing.
Year Founded:
1923

INTERNATIONAL BOXING ASSOCIATION (AIBA)
MAISON DU SPORT INTERNATIONAL
AVENUE DE RHODANIE 54
LAUSANNE, 1007
www.aiba.org
• Ching-Kuo Wu, President
• William Louis-Marie, Executive Director

INTERNATIONAL CANOE FEDERATION (ICF)
AVENUE DE RHODANIE 54
LAUSANNE, CH 1007
info@canoeicf.com
www.canoeicf.com
• Josâ€š Perurena, President
• Simon Toulson, Secretary General
Nature of Service:
To promote & foster foreign touring through production of appropriate river guides, & through the provision of programs about the possibilities of finding accommodation and places of interest.
Publications:
E-Canoeing Express, Canoeing International

INTERNATIONAL HANDBALL FEDERATION
PETER MERIAN-STRASSE 23
BASEL, CH-4052
ihf.office@ihf.info
www.ihf.info
• Hassan Moustafa, President

INTERNATIONAL HOCKEY FEDERATION (FIH)
RUE DU VALENTIN 61
LAUSANNE, 1004
info@fih.ch
• Narinder D Batra, President
• Jason McCracken, Chief Executive Officer

INTERNATIONAL ICE HOCKEY FEDERATION (IIHF)
BRANDSCHENKESTRASSE 50
POSTFACH 1817
ZURICH, 8027
www.iihf.com
• Renâ€š Fasel, President
• Horst Lichtner, General Secretary
Year Founded:
1908
Description:
A federation of member national hockey associations governing the sport of ice hockey and in-line hockey for both men and women.

INTERNATIONAL JUDO FEDERATION
NO.24 RESIDENCES
OUCHY-NAVIGATION
AVENUE DE LA HARPE 49
LAUSANNE, 1007
admin@ijf.org
www.ijf.org

- Jean Luc Rouge, General Secretary
- Marius I Vizer, President

Description:
International governing body of the Olympic sport of Judo recognized by the International Olympic Committee and consisting of 187 member National Federations grouped into 5 Continental Unions (Africa, Asis, Europe, Oceania and Panamerica)

INTERNATIONAL ORIENTEERING FEDERATION
DROTTNINGGATAN 47, 3Â« tr.
KARLSTAD, SE-65225
iof@orienteering.org
orienteering.org
- Tom Hollowell, Secretary General & CEO
tom.hollowell@orienteering.org

Description:
International governing body for the sport of orienteering. 72 member countries.
Year Founded:
1977

INTERNATIONAL SHOOTING SPORT FEDERATION (ISSF)
BAVARIARING 21
MUNICH, 80336
www.issf-sports.org
- Olegario Vazquez Rana, President
- Franz Schreiber, Secretary General

Description:
International governing body for the sport of shooting.

INTERNATIONAL SKATING UNION (ISU)
AVENUE JUSTE-OLIVIER 17
LAUSANNE, 1006
www.isu.org
- Jan Dijkema, President
- Fredi Schmid, Director General
Sports Service Founded:
1892
Description:
The oldest governing international winter sport federation.

INTERNATIONAL TABLE TENNIS FEDERATION (ITTF)
CHEMIN DE LA ROCHE 11
RENENS, 1020
www.ittf.com
- Judit Farago, Chief Executive Officer
- Thomas Welkert, President
Publications:
Table Tennis Illustrated

INTERNATIONAL TENNIS FEDERATION
BANK LANE
ROEHAMPTON
LONDON, SW15 5XZ
communications@itftennis.com
www.itftennis.com
- David Haggerty, President

INTERNATIONAL TRIATHLON UNION
MAISON DU SPORT INTERNATIONAL
AV DE RHODANIE 54
LAUSANNE, CH 1007
www.triathlon.org
- Antonio Arimany, Secretary General
Description:
The ITU is the world governing body for the Olympic sport of Triathlon and all related MultiSport disciplines: Duathalon, Aquathon and Winter Triathalon. ITU was founded in 1989 at the first ITU Congress in Avignon, France and has maintained its headquarters in Vancouver, Canada since then. It now has over 120 affiliated National Federations around the world and is the youngest International Federation in the Olympics. Triathalon was awarded Olympic status in 1994. ITU is proudly committed to supporting the development of the sport worldwide through the strong relationships with contintenal and national federations, working with its partners

INTERNATIONAL WEIGHTLIFTING FEDERATION (IWF)
MAISON DU SPORT INTERNATIONAL
AV DE RHODANIE 54
LAUSANNE, CH 1007
iwf@iwf.net
www.iwf.net
- Tamas Ajan, President
- Ma Wenguang, General Secretary

UNION CYCLISTE INTERNATIONALE (UCI)
CH DE LA MELEE 12
AIGLE, 1860
admin@uci.ch
www.uci.ch
- Brian Cookson, President
- Mohamed Wagih Azzam, Vice President
- Tracey Gaudry, Vice President
- David Lappartient, Vice President
Nature of Service:
Founded with the means to develop and promote all aspects of cycling. This is because cycling is more than just a competitive sport. It is a also a leisure activity and environmentally friendly means of transport.
Year Founded:
1900

UNION INTERNATIONALE DE PENTATHLON MODERNE (UIPM)
STADE LOUIS II, ENTREE E
13 AVENUE DES CASTELANS
MONTE CARLO, 98000
uipm@pentathlon.org
www.pentathlon.org
- Shiny Fang, Secretary
- Juan Antonio, 1st Vice President
- John Helmick, Treasurer
Description:
International governing body for the sport of modern pentathlon.

UNITED WORLD WRESTLING
RUE DU CHATEAU 6
CORSIER-SUR-VEVEY, 1804
info@unitedworldwrestling.org
unitedworldwrestling.org
- Nenad Lalovic, President
- Michel Dusson, General Secretary
Description:
International governing body for the sport of wrestling.
Number of Members:
145

WORLD BASEBALL SOFTBALL CONFEDERATION
AVENUE GENERAL-GUISAN, 45
PULLY, SWITZERLAN CH-1009
+41-21 318 8240
Fax: +41-21 318 8241
office@wbsc.org
www.wbsc.org
- Riccardo Fraccari, President
- Beng Choo Low, Secretary General
Description:
World governing body for baseball and softball.

WORLD CURLING FEDERATION
3 ATHOLL CRESCENT
PERTH, PH1 5NG
info@worldcurling.org
www.worldcurling.org
- Kate Caithness, President
Description:
International governing body for the sport of curling.
Number of Members:
45

WORLD ROWING FEDERATION (FISA)
MAISON DU SPORT INTERNATIONAL
AVENUE DE RHODANIE 54
LAUSANNE, CH 1007
info@fisa.org
www.worldrowing.com
- Matt Smith, Executive Director
matt.smith@fisa.org
Year Founded:
1892
Publications:
FISA Guide, World Rowing Magazine, World Rowing E-Newsletter.
Description:
To make rowing a universally practised and globally relevant sport.

WORLD SAILING
ARIADNE HOUSE
TOWN QUAY
SOUTHAMPTON, HAMPSHIRE, ENGLAND SO14 2AQ
www.sailing.org
- Helen Fry, Business Operations Director
Description:
World governing body for sailing, responsible for promoting the sport internationally.

Olympic, Organizations

AUSTRALIAN OLYMPIC COMMITTEE
LEVEL 4, 140 GEORGE ST
MUSEUM OF CONTEMPORARY ART
SYDNEY, NSW, AUSTRALIA 2000
corporate.olympics.com.au
- John D Coates, President
Description:
Commited to Australia's athletes and encourages the development of high performance sport through athlete support and funding initiatives. Aims to spread the Olympic spirit and ideals throughout Australia, even in the years between Olympic Games.

CANADIAN OLYMPIC COMMITTEE
21 ST. CLAIR AVE E
SUITE 900
TORONTO, ON, CANADA M4T 1L9
416-962-0262
Fax: 416-967-4902
olympic.ca
- Tricia Smith, President

multi sports

Nature of Sports Service:
Founded 1904. Recognized by IOC as Canada's National Olympic Committee in 1907. Jurisdiction over all aspects of Canada's participation in the Olympic, Olympic Winter and Pan American Games, including selecting Canadian teams and providing an extensive range of support services before and during Games. Promotes and protects the Olympic Movement in Canada. Conducting and/or financing programs to assist in the development of amateur sport in Canada.
Membership Requirements:
Nine types of membership: (A) The 30 National Sport Federations with jurisdiction over Olympic and Pan Am Sports appoint five members each, (B) Members at large elected by other members from all segments of Canadian society, (C) IOC members in Canada, (D) Honorary members (no voting power), (E) NSF's with jurisdiction over sports recognized by the IOC but whose sports are not included in the Olympics or Pan Am Games appoint 1 member each, (F) Representatives of each NSF on the COA's Athletes' Council, (G) Representatives of other agencies related to sport, (H) Coaches representative.
Publications:
ANNUAL REPORT, yearly; PODIUM, online monthly newsletter
Member Services:
Extensive range of support services for Canadian Olympic, Olympic Winter & Pan Am teams (including selection, transporting, insuring, housing, feeding, providing administrative and medical services, clothing, security, publicity); financial grants to National Sport Federations; youth and education programs; Olympic Academy of Canada; Canadian participation in International Olympic Academy; Olympic Athlete Career Centers; Olympic Club Canada; Canadian Amateur Sports Hall of Fame; Information Centre.
Number of members:
300

INTERNATIONAL OLYMPIC COMMITTEE (IOC)
OLYMPIC HOUSE
LAUSANNE,
www.olympic.org
• Jacques Rogge, President
• Christophe De Kepper, Chief of Staff
• Gilbert Felli, Executive Director, Olympic Games
Description:
International non-governmental, non-profit organisation and the creator of the Olympic Movement. The IOC exists to serve as an umbrella organisation of the Olympic Movement. It owns all rights to the Olympic symbols, flag, motto, anthem and Olympic Games. Its primary responsibility is to supervise the organisation of the summer and winter Olympic Games.

ORIENTEERING CANADA
1239 COLGROVE AVE NE
CALGARY, AB, CANADA T2E 5C3
403-283-0807
Fax: 403-451-1681
www.orienteering.ca
• Anne Teutsch, President
• Tracy Bradley, Executive Director

Description:
Founded 1967.
Publications:
O-zine Newsletter published 3 times a year; Orienteering Today, magazine; Orienteering North America, magazine

ORIENTEERING USA
824 SCOTIA RD
PHILADELPHIA, PA 19128
215-482-9479
contact@orienteeringusa.org
orienteeringusa.org
• Clare Durand, President
(215) 482-9479
contact@orienteeringusa.org
Member Services:
Subscription to ONA; discount on class A meet fees; national rankings; promotional materials and other assistance; some financial assistance for mapping projects; educational materials; membership in IOF indirectly; voting privileges.
Publications:
ORIENTEERING NORTH AMERICA, 10 times per year (official publication).
Membership Requirements:
Must be U.S. citizen or permanent resident, pay annual membership fee. Most members are indirect members, through member clubs (about 55 nationwide).
Sports Services Founded:
1971.
Description:
Recognized by the International Orienteering Federation and the US Olympic Committee as the National Governing Body for Orienteering in the United States. USOF is a non profit organization with 55 current member clubs and approximately 1,400 family and individual memberships. The Federation's programs are suppported by membership dues and tax-deductible contributions.

U.S. BIATHLON ASSOCIATION
49 PINELAND DRIVE
301A NEW GLOUCESTER HALL
NEW GLOUCESTER, ME 04260
207-688-6500
800-242-8456
Fax: 207-688-6505
info@usbiathlon.org
www.teamusa.org/us-biathlon
• Max Cobb, President & CEO
(207) 688-6500
• Per Nilsson, National Team Head Coach
per.coach@gmail.com
Year Founded:
1980
Description:
The USBA promotes the development of biathlon in the United States by organizing training and competition around the country.
Membership Requirements:
Annual dues

U.S. OLYMPIC AND PARALYMPIC FOUNDATION
ATTN: USOC DEVELOPMENT
1 OLYMPIC PLAZA
COLORADO SPRINGS, CO 80909
800-775-8762
Fax: 719-866-4188
foundation@usoc.org
www.teamusa.org/us-olympic-and-paralympic-foundation

• Jon Denney, President & Chief Development Officer
• Scott Blackmun, CEO

U.S. OLYMPIC TRAINING SITE
1401 PRESQUE ISLE AVE
NORTHERN MICHIGAN UNIVERSITY
MARQUETTE, MI 49855
906-227-2105
Fax: 906-227-2492
usoec@nmu.edu
www.nmu.edu
• Forrest Karr, Athletic Director
fkarr@nmu.edu
• Mike Kaurala, Operations Manager
mkaurala@nmu.edu
• Cora Ohnstad, Head Athletic Trainer
cora.ohnstad@mghs.org
Description:
Founded 1985. Provides a training and education environment for aspiring Olympic athletes.

UNITED STATES OLYMPIC COMMITTEE
ONE OLYMPIC PLAZA
COLORADO SPRINGS, CO 80909
888-222-2313
www.teamusa.org
• Scott Blackmun, Chief Executive Officer
Description:
To support U.S. Olypmic and Paralympic athletes in acheiveing sustained competitive excellence and preserve the Olmpic ideals, and thereby inspore all Americans.
Publications:
Official U.S. Olympic Book every four years; press guides; U.S. Olympic Newsletter; Historical Booklets and Annual Report.
Membership Requirements:
National Amateur sports organizations affiliated with an international body. Multi-sport national organization and Disabled in Sport Organizations.

USA DIVING
1060 N CAPITOL AVE
SUITE E-310
INDIANAPOLIS, IN 46204
317-237-5252
Fax: 317-237-5257
www.teamusa.org/usa-diving
• Linda Paul, President & CEO
linda.paul@usadiving.org

USA FENCING
4065 SINTON RD
SUITE 140
COLORADO SPRINGS, CO 80907
719-866-4511
Fax: 719-632-5737
information@usfencing.org
www.usfencing.org
• Kris Ekeren, Executive Director
k.ekeren@usfencing.org
Publications:
AMERICAN FENCING, quarterly; rule book and supplements; USFA National Newsletter, quarterly.
Membership Requirements:
Pay dues.
Description:
To develop fencers to achieve international success and to administer and promote the sport in the USA.
Year Founded:
1891

USA PENTATHLON

1 OLYMPIC PLAZA
COLORADO SPRINGS, CO 80909
www.teamusa.org/USA-Modern-Pentathlon
• Rob Stull, Managing Director
robstull@aol.com
Number of members:
600
Publications:
THE PENTATHLETE, quarterly newsletter for athletes and members.
Membership Requirements:
Individual and organization memberships, annual dues.
Sports Services Founded:
1948
Description:
USA Pentathlon's mission is to prepare American athletes to win medals in the Olympic and Pan American Games and at the World Championships. With National Training Centers in San Antonio, Texas and Colorado Springs, CO, USAPentathlon and its coaches work with elite athletes as well as developing Olympians and juniors to prepare them for the 2004 Athens Olympic Games and beyond.

Olympic, United States Major Governing Bodies

U.S. SKI AND SNOWBOARD ASSOCIATION (USSA)

1 VICTORY LANE
PARK CITY, UT 84060
435-649-9090
Fax: 435-649-3613
ussa.org
• Tiger Shaw, President & CEO
• Brooke McAffee, Vice President & Chief Financial Officer
• Trisha Worthington, EVP & Chief Development Officer
Description:
Provides opportunities for athletes in the most exciting Olympic action sports. USSA's programs provide education, development and competition opportunities for young athletes, with from grassroots USSA club programs up through national teams and the Olympic Winter Games.
Membership Requirements:
Anyone can join on an individual, family or club basis.
Publications:
Discipline competition guides (alpine, cross-country, freestyle, jumping/Nordic combined, Snowboard), American Ski Coach, periodically.
Year Founded:
1905

U.S. SOCCER

1801 S PRAIRIE AVE
CHICAGO, IL 60616
312-808-1300
Fax: 312-808-1301
www.ussoccer.com
• Cindy Parlow Cone, President
• J.T. Batson, Chief Executive Officer
Description:
Affiliated with International Soccer Body, FIFA. Governing body for soccer in the U.S. under the 1978 Sports Amateur Act. Promotes soccer in U.S. including national and international games and tournaments. Administers all U.S. national teams. Responsible for marketing the U.S. National Teams' programs as well as marketing programs for the Youth and Amateur Divisions. Resolves questions and controversies not adjustable under rules of state associations concerned. Manages U.S. Cup Tournament, National Challenge Cup, National Amateur Challenge Cup, National Women's Amateur Cup, National Youth Cup competitions, promotes goodwill through physical
Year Founded:
1913
Number of members:
3,000,000
Membership Requirements:
Must be association, league, approved by National Council.
Notes:
1998 - Awarded 12-year marketing, licensing and television rights to a partnership between International Management Group and Nike, expected to generate $500 million for U.S. Soccer. In 1997, Nike and U.S. Soccer agreed on a 10 year $120 million apparel agreement.
Sponsorships:
Allstate, Anheuser-Busch, AT&T, Chipotle, Coca-Cola, Deloitte, Nike, TRULY Hard Seltzer, Visa, Volkswagen

US EQUESTRIAN FEDERATION

1040 POTTERSVILLE ROAD
GLADSTONE, NJ 07934-2053
908-234-0848
www.uset.org
• Murray S Kessler, President
mkessler@usef.org
• William J Moroney, Chief Executive Officer
bmoroney@usef.org
• Will Connell, Director of Sport
wconnell@usef.org

US FIGURE SKATING

20 FIRST STREET
COLORADO SPRINGS, CO 80906
719-635-5200
Fax: 719-635-9548
info@usfigureskating.org
www.usfsa.org
• Samuel Auxier, President
• David Raith, Executive Director

US SAILING

15 MARITIME DRIVE
PORTSMOUTH, RI 02871
401-683-0800
800-877-2451
Fax: 401-683-0840
info@ussailing.org
www.ussailing.org
• Jack Gierhart, Chief Executive Officer
• Lauren Cotta, Director of Operations

US SPEEDSKATING

5662 S COUGAR LANE
KEARNS, UT 84118
801-417-5360
Fax: 801-417-5361
www.teamusa.org/us-speedskating
• Ted Morris, Executive Director
Sports Services Founded:
1966
Membership Requirements:
Fee of $50.
Publications:
ICE CHIPS, 8-10 times a year. RACING BLADE, 4 issues per year.
Description:
Mission is to be the premier speedskating organization in the world through excellence in leadership, development and performance.

USA ARCHERY

4065 SINTON RD
SUITE 110
COLORADO SPRINGS, CO 80907
719-866-4576
Fax: 719-632-4733
info@usarchery.org
www.teamusa.org/usa-archery
• Rod Menzer, Chair
Number of members:
6,000
Membership Requirements:
Payment of dues based on various categories
Year Founded:
1879
Description:
National governing body for the olympic sport of archery. dedicated to selecting and training male/female archers for Olympic and Pan american games and world level competitions.

USA BADMINTON

2099 S STATE COLLEGE BLVD
SUITE 600
ANAHEIM, CA 92806
714-765-2952
www.teamusa.org/usa-badminton
• Jeff Dyrek, Chief Executive Officer
(714) 765-2951
Description:
USA Badminton oversees sanctioned tournaments nationwide, develops grassroots initiatives to foster increased participation in the sport, certifies and educates coaches and prepares the best players in the nation to excel in international competition, including the Olympic Games.
Membership:
Regular Dues/$30 a year.
Member Services:
Provides memberships cards allowing for play in USA Badminton events; subscription to CrossCourt newsletter; Exclusive member discounts on USA Badminton merchandise; Games locator; special offers; and voting rights on leadership of USA Badminton governing body.
Number of members:
4,000

USA BASEBALL

2933 SOUTH MIAMI BLVD
SUITE 119
DURHAM, NC 27703
919-474-8721
Fax: 919-925-6108
info@usabaseball.com
www.usabaseball.com
• Paul Seiler, Executive Director & CEO
Description:
USA Baseball serves as the national governing body for the sport, and represents American baseball as a member of the United States Olympic Committee and the International Baseball Federation.
Publications:

USA Baseball National Team Yearbook, annual.
Member Services:
Selects official U.S.A. Baseball Teams, Sr. National Team, Jr (18-under), National Team, Youth National Team (16-under) for international competition.
Year Founded:
1978
Official Partners:
Gatorade, Greater Raleigh Sports Alliance, Next College Student Athlete (NCSA), Panini.

USA BASKETBALL
5465 MARK DABLING BLVD
COLORADO SPRINGS, CO 80918-3842
719-590-4800
Fax: 719-590-4811
www.usab.com
• Jim Tooley, CEO
• Renee Felton, Head, Communications
• Brent Baumberger, Chief Financial Officer
Description:
USA Basketball was organized in 1974 and known as the Amateur Basketball Association of the United States of America (ABAUSA). The name change from ABAUSA to USA Basketball occurred October 12, 1989, shortly after FIBA modified its rules to allow professional basketball players to participate in international competitions.
Membership Requirements:
This membership shall be open to all national sports organizations which actively conduct a national program in Basketball as a competitive sport. Active memberships may also be open to other organizations which actively conduct national programs in basketball as a competitive sport. In addition, national basketball coaches associations for men and women shall be included, as approved by the Board of Directors of USA Basketball. Such members shall have voting representation through their chosen officers, or other representatives, at meetings of the Congress membership.

USA BOBSLED & SKELETON
1631 MESA AVE
COPPER BUILDING
SUITE A
COLORADO SPRINGS, CO 80906
Fax: 719-520-3212
www.teamusa.org/USA-Bobsled-Skeleton-Federation
• Darrin Steele, Chief Executive Officer
• Lisa Carlock, Finance & Operations Director
lisa.carlock@usabs.com
• Lenny Kasten, National Team Manager
Description:
This Federation was formed to advance, encourage, improve and promote amateur bobsledding and skeleton competition in the United States. It is also the National Governing Body of hte sports of bobsled and skeleton and recognized as such by the United States Olympic Committee and the Federation Internationale De Bob Sleigh De and Tobogganing Federation.
Member Services:
Passenger Rider / Sports / Supporting Memberships
Number of members:

525
Publications:
Quarterly newsletter

USA BOXING
1 OLYMPIC PLAZA
COLORADO SPRINGS, CO 80909
719-866-2300
Fax: 719-866-2132
www.teamusa.org/USA-Boxing
• Mike McAtee, Interim Executive Director
mmcatee@usaboxing.org
Nature of Service:
A non-profit organization that is responsible for the administration, development and promotion of Olympic-style boxing in the United States.
Year Founded:
1888
Member Services:
Support and guidance in all facets of amateur boxing.
Membership Requirements:
Must register in the Local Boxing Committee that oversees their locality. Boxers must be eligible for competition in amateur boxing.
Number of members:
30,000
Publications:
USA Boxing Technical & Competition Rules

USA CANOE/KAYAK
503 SOPHIA STREET
SUITE 100
FREDERICKSBURG, VA 22401
504-907-4460 EXT 108
info@usack.org
• Wade Blackwood, CEO
(504) 907-4460
wade@usack.org
• Chris Stec, Chief Operating Officer
(540) 907-4460
chris@usack.org
• Chris Barlow, Sprint High Performance Manager
cbarlow.usack@gmail.com
• Aaron Mann, Communications and Media
(540) 907-4460
aaron@usack.org
• Silvan Poberaj, Head Coach, Whitewater Slalom
(301) 706-2680
spoberaj@usack.org
• Rafal Smolen, Slalom National Team Coach
(828) 301-4805
rafal@usack.org
• Claudiu Ciur, Sprint Nationalteam Coach
claudiuciur.usack@gmail.com

USA CURLING
5525 CLEM'S WAY
STEVENS POINT, WI 54482
715-344-1199
888-287-5377
Fax: 715-344-2279
info@usacurl.org
www.teamusa.org/usa-curling
• Rick Patzke, Secretary General
Description:
As the national governing body for the sport of curling, the USA Curling strives to grow the sport and to win medals in world championships and Olympic Games.
Membership Requirements:
Membership is through membership in a USA Curling member club.

Number of members:
13,000
Publications:
U.S. Curling News

USA CYCLING
210 USA CYCLING POINT
SUITE 100
COLORADO SPRINGS, CO 80919-2215
719-434-4200
help@usacycling.org
www.usacycling.org
• Derek Bouchard-Hall, President/Chief Operating Officer
• Bob Stapleton, Chairman
• Chuck Hodge, Vice President of Operations
chodge@usacycling.org
• Kevin Dessart, Coaching Education/Athlete Development Director
coaches@usacycling.org
• Emily Palmer, Interscholastic/Club Development Director
• Kelly Feilke, Executive Director
Nature of Service:
Serves as governing body for bicycle racing and amateur cycling in America and, as such, is responsible for selecting Olympic, Pan-Am and World Championship teams. Promotes events and programs, television production.
Year Founded:
1921

USA DIVING
1060 N. CAPITAL AVENUE
SUITE E-310
INDIANAPOLIS, IN 46204
317-237-5252
Fax: 317-237-5257
usadiving@usadiving.org
www.usadiving.org
• Linda Paul, President/Chief Operating Officer
linda.paul@usadiving.org
• Terry Powers, Vice President
terry.powers@usadiving.org
• Joe Clarke, Communications Coordinator
joe.clarke@usadiving.org
• Sean McCarthy, Interim High Performance Director
sean.mccarthy@usadiving.org
• Aurelie Gibson, Director of Education
aurelie.gibson@usadiving.org
Member Services:
Official rule book; annual directory; free admission to national championships, liability insurance.
Sports Services Founded:
1981
Description:
National governing body for the olympic sport of diving in the United States.

USA FIELD HOCKEY
5540 NORTH ACADEMY BLVD
SUITE 100
COLORADO SPRINGS, CO 80918
719-866-4567
Fax: 719-632-0979
www.teamusa.org/usa-field-hockey
• Bree Gillespie, Chair
breegillespie1@gmail.com
Description:
USA Field Hockey is the national governing body for the sport of field hockey in the United States and is a member of the United

States Olympic Committee (USOC), the Federation Internationale de Hockey (FIH), and the Pan American Hockey Federation (PAFH)

Member Services:
Quarterly Newsletter, Insurance, Events, Camps, National and International Competitions, Olympic Team Pipeline

Number of Members:
16,000

Publications:
Field Hockey News

USA GYMNASTICS
132 E WASHINGTON ST
SUITE 700
INDIANAPOLIS, IN 46204
317-237-5050
Fax: 317-237-5069
www.usa-gymnastics.org
• Ron Gailmore, Chief Operating Officer
(317) 829-5631
rgailmore@usagym.org
• Paul Parilla, Chairman of the Board
• Leslie King, VP Communications
(317) 826-5656
lking@usagym.org
• Lee Johnson, VP Marketing
(317) 829-5647
ljohnson@usagym.org

Description:
Founded in 1963. The sole national governing body for the sport of gymnastics in the United States. USA Gymnastics is responsibile for selection and training of the Olympic and World Championship teams, and the promotion of gymnastics.

Membership Requirements:
National organization, associations and individual as involved in gymnastics.

Member Services:
Athlete registration; club membership; professional memberships; general memberships, subscriptions; merchandise.

USA HOCKEY
1775 BOB JOHNSON DRIVE
COLORADO SPRINGS, CO 80906-4090
719-576-8724
Fax: 719-538-1160
usah@usahockey.org
www.usahockey.com
• Dave Ogrean, Executive Director
daveo@usahockey.org
• Jim Smith, President
• Ron DeGregorio, Chair
• Bill Hall, Secretary
• Kim Folsom, Executive Assistant
• John Beadle, Vice President
• Donna Guarglia, Treasurer

Description:
The National Governing Body for the sport of ice hockey in the United States. Its mission is to promote the growth of hockey in America and provide the best possible experience for all participants by encouraging, developing, advancing and administering the sport.

Year Founded:
1937

USA JUDO
ONE OLYMPIC PLAZA
COLORADO SPRINGS, CO 80909
719-866-4730
Fax: 719-866-4733
www.teamusa.org/usa-judo

• Keith Bryant, Chief Executive Officer
keith.bryant@usajudo.us
• Ed Liddie, Director of Athlete Performance
eddie.liddie@usajudo.us

Member Services:
Meetings held in conjunction with international invitational championship.

Description:
A non profit organization which is governed by a Board of Directors with representation from all areas of the judo family, including athletes, coaches, and referees.

USA LUGE
57 CHURCH STREET
LAKE PLACID, NY 12946-1805
518-523-2071
Fax: 518-523-4106
info@usaluge.org
www.teamusa.org/usa-luge
• Dwight Bell, President
• Jim Leahy, CEO & Executive Director

Sports Services Founded:
1978

Member Services:
Provide coaching, equipment for luge athletes. Coordination, organization, and funding of summer and winter training programs for National teams. Train, test, certify officials for luge competitions. Organizes and promotes World Luge Cup Race and numerous national competitions yearly. Selects Olympic and National Teams.

Number of members:
1,000

Description:
An Olympic class member organization of the United States Olympic Committee (USOC) and is the National Governing Body (NGB) for the sport of luge in the United States. To provide for the achievement of athletic excellence in the sport of luge, with the highest degree of sportsmanship, honor, dedication and vicorty as the standard.

USA ROLLER SPORTS
4730 SOUTH STREET
PO BOX 6579
LINCOLN, NE 68506
402-483-7551
Fax: 402-483-1465
www.usarollersports.org
• Trace Hansen, Chairman
• Bill Spooner, President
• Renee Hildebrand, Vice President
• Peggy Young, Secretary
pyoung@usarollersports.org

Description:
USA Roller Sports is the national governing body of competitive roller sports in the United States and is recognized by the United States Olympic Committee.

Sports Services Founded:
1937

USA SHOOTING
1 OLYMPIC PLAZA
COLORADO SPRINGS, CO 80909
719-866-4670
media@usashooting.org
www.usashooting.com
• Jeff Prince, Chair
• David Johnson, Interim Chief Executive Officer
dave.johnson@usashooting.org

Description:
Founded in 1995, prepares American athletes to win Olympic and Paralympic medals, promote the shooting sports throughout the US, and govern the conduct of international shooting in the country.

Membership Requirements:
Open to non-competitive shooting enthusiasts as well as competing shooters. Annual, life, junior and club memberships available.

Publications:
USA SHOOTING NEWS, 5 times yearly.

Member Services:
Eligible to qualify to compete at USA Shooting-sanctioned events, discounts on U.S. Shooting Team merchandise, additional benefits for life members and clubs, and magazine subscription.

USA SOFTBALL
2801 NE 50TH ST
OKLAHOMA CITY, OK 73111
405-424-5266
Fax: 405-424-3855
info@usasoftball.com
www.teamusa.org/usa-softball
• Craig Cress, Executive Director

Number of Members:
4,500,000 - 5,000,000.

Membership Requirements:
Registration with an ASA commissioner in a state/metro association.

Description:
Founded in 1933, a volunteer driven, not-for-profit organization that has evolved into the strongest softball organization in the country, that is the National Governing Body of Softball.3

USA SWIMMING
ONE OLYMPIC PLAZA
COLORADO SPRINGS, CO 80909
719-866-4578
info@usaswimming.org
www.usaswimming.org
• Chuck Wielgus, President/Chief Operating Officer
• Kathy Parker, Executive Coordinator
• Matt Farrell, Chief Marketing Officer

Description:
The National Governing Body for the sport of swimming in the United States that promotes participation in swimming and the development of the sport.

Membership Requirements:
Offers various types of membership: athletes (400,000 current), coaches, officials, administrators, clubs etc.

Members:
400,000

USA SYNCHRO
1 OLYMPIC PLAZA
COLORADO SPRINGS, CO 80909
719-866-2219
www.teamusa.org/USA-Synchronized-Swimming
• Myriam Glez, High Performance Director & CEO
myriam@usasynchro.org

Number of members:
5,700 +

Publications:
Synchro Swimming USA Magazine, USA Synchro E-Newsletter

Membership Requirements:

Membership Fees, which vary based on membership category.
Description:
Serves as the National Governing Body for the sport of synchronized swimming, appointed as such by the United States Olympic Committee. Provides leadership and resources for the promotion and growth of synchronized swimming, to achieve competitive excellence at all levels and to develop broad based participation.
Year Founded:
1977

USA TABLE TENNIS
1 OLYMPIC PLAZA
COLORADO SPRINGS, CO 80909-5769
719-866-4583
Fax: 719-632-6071
www.usatt.org
• Gordon Kaye, CEO
(719) 866-4583
Gordon.Kaye@usatt.org
• Andy Horn, Director of Operations
(719) 866-4583
Andrew.Horn@usatt.org
Description:
National governing body for table tennis in the United States. It oversees a wide variety of membership services, the national teams, and other areas such as the rules of the game, the Hall of Fame, and numerous online instructional and historical articles.
Sports Service Founded:
1933
Description:
Oversees a wide variety of membership services, the national teams, and other areas such as the rules of the game, and numerous online instructional and historical articles.

USA TEAM HANDBALL
801-463-2000
info@usateamhandball.org
www.usateamhandball.org
• Harvey W. Schiller, President
• Michael D. Cavanaugh, CEO
• Javier Garcia Cuesta, Head Coach
jgarciacusta@yahoo.com
• Scott Cronk, Media Specialist/Webmaster
scott@usateamhandball.org
• Dave Gascon, Director of High Performance
Description:
The national governing body for handball in the United States, which works to promote and develop the sport at all levels of competition.
Membership Requirements:
Payment of annual dues. Membership categories include Regular, 3-Year Adult, Junior, Special Event, Associate, Life, Group B.
Year Founded:
2008

USA TRACK & FIELD
132 EAST WASHINGTON STREET
SUITE 800
INDIANAPOLIS, IN 46204
317-261-0500
Fax: 317-261-0481
www.usatf.org
• Max Siegel, Chief Executive Officer
(317) 261-0500
ceo@usatf.org

• Renee Chube Washington, Chief Operating Officer
(317) 713-4657
Renee.Washington@usatf.org
• Jill Geer, Chief Marketing Officer
(317) 713-4654
Jill.Geer@usatf.org
• Duffy Mahoney, Chief of Sport Performance
Description:
The National Governing Body for track and field, long-distance running and race walking in the United States.
Membership Requirements:
Classifications: Associations, Amateur Sports Organizations, National Organizations, Affiliate, Sustaining and Life; registers athletes, and accepts Club Members, through Associations.
Member Services:
Training, development and competition for men and women in five classifications — Junior Olympics (10-under to 18), Youth Athletics (10-under to 18), Junior (14-19), Senior (14-up), Masters (40-80+). Committees: Sports - Men's Track and Field, Women's Track and Field, Men's Long Distance Running, Women's Long Distance Running, Men's and Women's Race Walking, Masters Track and Field, Masters Long Distance Running, Youth Athletics. Administrative: Associations, Athletes Advisory, Athletics for the Disabled, Budget and Audit, Men's Development, Women's Development, Law and Legislation, Membership, Officials and Coaching Education.

USA TRIATHLON
5825 DELMONICO DRIVE
SUITE 200
COLORADO SPRINGS, CO 80919
719-597-9090
Fax: 719-597-2121
info@usatriathlon.org
www.usatriathlon.org
• Rob Urbach, Chief Executive Officer
• Tim Yount, Chief Operating Officer
(719) 955-2831
tim.yount@usatriathlon.org
Nature of Service:
USA Triathlon is the National Governing Body for triathlon, duathlon, aquathlon and winter triathlon in the United States.
Year Founded:
1982
Member Services:
USAT offers annual memberships which, in addition to many other benefits, cover members at all USAT sanctioned events for 12 full months. One-day licenses which cover one event and annual elite memberships are also available.

USA VOLLEYBALL
4065 SINTON ROAD
SUITE 200
COLORADO SPRINGS, CO 80907
719-228-6800
Fax: 719-228-6899
postmaster@usav.org
www.usavolleyball.org
• Jamie Davis, CEO
jamie.davis@usav.org
• Kerry Klostermann, Secretary General
kerry.klostermann@usav.org
• Sarah Young, Finance Manager
Sarah.Young@usav.org

• June Sander, Finance/Corprate Operations Manager
june.sander@usav.org
Nature of Service:
The National Governing Body for the sport of volleyball in the United States and is recognized as such by the Federation International de Volleyball (FIB) and the United States Olympic Committee (USOC).
Year Founded:
1928
Member Services:
Clinics conducted for coaches, players and officials, competition conducted through regions; conducts elite and international volleyball programs. Member of USOC& FIVB.
Membership Requirements:
Organizations affiliated with volleyball.

Other locations:

ALASKA JUNIOR VOLLEYBALL (MIDNIGHT SUN VOLLEYBALL)
9650 BIRCH ROAD
ANCHORAGE, AK 99507
www.midnightsunvolleyball.com
• Virgil Hooe, Director

ALOHA REGIONAL COMMISSIONER/USA VOLLEYBALL
45-795 PO'OKELA STREET
KANE'OHE, HI 96744
www.aloharegion.com
• Kent Ma, Commissioner

ARIZONA REGIONAL COMMISSIONER/USA VOLLEYBALL
9100 S MCKEMY STREET
TEMPE, AZ 85284
480-626-6740
Fax: 480-626-6743
www.azregionvolleyball.org
• Harold Cranswick, Commissioner
(480) 626-6740
office@azregionvolleyball.org
• Becky Hudson, Secretary/Treasurer
(480) 626-6740
office@azregionvolleyball.org
Sports Services Founded:
1989
Description:
Formerly known as Cactus Region, promotes, governs, oversees, plans and coordinates amateur indoor and outdoor volleyball in the Arizona Region, in order to provide a variety of opportunities for all interested parties to participate in a safe, positive and apporpriately competitive environment.

BADGER REGIONAL VOLLEYBALL ASSOCIATION/USA VOLLEYBALL
2831 NORTH GRANDVIEW BOULEVARD
PEWAUKEE, WI 53072
414-507-1124
Fax: 262-349-9971
badgervolleyball.org
• Terry Paulson, Region Tournament Director
(414) 588-2665
badgerregiontd@wi.rr.com
• BJ Bryant, Secretary
(920) 277-0706
wivbacademy@gmail.com
• Anne Slattery, Treasurer
(414) 659-2663
arslatts@gmail.com
• Jennifer Armson-Dyer, Director of Operations
jarmsondyer@badgervolleyball.org

CAROLINA REGIONAL VOLLEYBALL ASSOCIATION/USA VOLLEYBALL
3770 CLEMMONS ROAD
SUITE C

PO BOX 1757
CLEMMONS, NC 27012-1757
336-766-3581
Fax: 336-766-3501
office@carolinaregionvb.org
www.carolinaregionvb.org
• Mike Spillman, President
(336) 993-8292
• Dan Colleran, Treasurer
(704) 799-7448
• Jim Ross, Secretary
(910) 233-8580
• Kevin Wendelboe, CEO/Executive Director
(336) 766-3581
ceo@carolinaregionvb.org
• Marilyn Thompson, Officials Program Director
Publications:
Carolina Volleyball Review Newsletter
Description:
The Carolina Regional Volleyball Association
organizes competition and promotes the sport of
volleyball at the State level as one the regional
association within USA Volleyball.

CHESAPEAKE REGIONAL
COMMISSIONER/USA VOLLEYBALL
42893 APPALOOSA TRAIL COURT
CHANTILLY, VA 20152
703-754-6185
www.chrva.org
• Rebecca Ruis-Johannes, President
(202) 409-7006
• Lisa DiGiacinto, Commissioner
(410) 768-4746
• Tia Storey, Treasurer
(703) 957-4247
Description:
The Chesapeake Region Volleyball Association
(CHRVA) is one of 40 Regional Volleyball
Associations (RVAs) of USA Volleyball. The
Region encompasses the States of Delaware
and Maryland, the District of Columbia, and the
northern counties of the Commonwealth of
Virginia.

COLORADO REGIONAL
COMMISSIONER/USA VOLLEYBALL
4155 E. JEWELL AVENUE
SUITE 909
DENVER, CO 80005
303-584-0376
www.rmrvolleyball.org
• Glenn Sapp, Commissioner/Pres
(720) 289-5797
commissioner@rmrvolleyball.org
• Wendy Sapp, Office Manager
(303) 584-0376
wendy@rmrvolleyball.org

COLUMBIA EMPIRE REGIONAL
COMMISSIONER/USA VOLLEYBALL
4840 SW WESTERN AVENUE
SUITE 450
BEAVERTON, OR 97005
503-644-7468
region@columbiaempirevolleyball.com
www.columbiaempirevolleyball.com
• Jeff Mozzochi, Executive Director
• Cody March, Director of Operations
• Jen Bolger, Membership & Comm Manager
Description:
CEVA represents Oregon and SW Washington
for Junior Girls, Junior Boys, Adults and Outdoor
Volleyball.

EVERGREEN REGIONAL
COMMISSIONER/USA VOLLEYBALL
7 S. HOWARD STREET
SUITE 418
SPOKANE, WA 99201
509-290-5552
Fax: 509-290-5318
office@evergreenregion.org
www.evergreenregion.org
• Meredith Coupland, Commissioner
mc2coupland@gmail.com
• Kevin Twohig, Assistant Commissioner

(509) 939-4029
• Margie Ray, Treasurer
(509) 484-7467
margieray.ref@gmail.com

FLORIDA REGIONAL
COMMISSIONER/USA VOLLEYBALL
15014 US HIGHWAY 441
EUSTIS, FL 32726
352-742-0080
Fax: 352-414-5304
www.floridavolleyball.org
• Steve Bishop, Executive Director/President
(352) 742-0080
steve@floridavolleyball.org
• Mary Andrew, Chair/Commissioner
(904) 242-6935
mary@floridavolleyball.org
• Michele Moriarty, Registrar/Office Manager
Description:
As one of the regional associations within USA
Volleyball, the organization pormotes the sport
and organizes competition at the State level.

GARDEN EMPIRE VOLLEYBALL
ASSOCIATION
PO BOX 554
WESTFIELD, NJ 07091-0554
914-930-6368
Fax: 908-360-1033
www.geva.org
• Bob Baker, Commissioner
(908) 524-0064
• Marianne Lepore, Office Administrator

GATEWAY REGIONAL
COMMISSIONER/USA VOLLEYBALL
10075 BAUER ROAD
ST. LOUIS, MO 63128
314-849-1221
Fax: 314-849-7865
mayer@gatewayvb.org
www.gatewayvb.org
• Tim Neels, Commissioner
Description:
As one of the 40 regional associations within
USA Volleyball, Gateway represents eastern
Missouri and southern Illinois, organizing
competition and promoting the sport at the State
level for over 7000 members.
Year Founded:
1994

GREAT LAKES REGION/USA
VOLLEYBALL
745 MCCLINTOCK DRIVE
SUITE 314
BURR RIDGE, IL 60527-0857
630-986-9000
Fax: 630-828-2663
greatlakesvolleyball@glrvb.com
www.greatlakesvolleyball.org
• Sandy Abbinanti, Commissioner/CEO

GREAT PLAINS REGIONAL
VOLLEYBALL ASSOCIATION
7515 MAIN STREET
RALSTON, NE 68127
402-593-9670
866-953-9670
info@gpvb.org
www.gpvb.org
• Sue Mailhot, Regional Commissioner
(402) 598-4782
sue@gpvb.org
• Bill Hamilton, Office Administrator

GULF COAST REGIONAL
COMMISSIONER/USA VOLLEYBALL
PO BOX 1985
ORANGE BEACH, AL 36561
251-979-4287
www.gulfcoastvolleyball.org
• Philip Bryant, Commissioner

HEART OF AMERICA REGIONAL
COMMISSIONER/USA VOLLEYBALL
548 SOUTH COY STREET
KANSAS CITY, KS 66105
913-233-0445
Fax: 913-233-0085
info@hoavb.org
www.hoavb.org
• Lisa Madsen, Commissioner
ha-commish@hoavb.org

HOOSIER REGION
COMMISSIONER/USA VOLLEYBALL
52428 WINDING WATERS LANE
ELKHART, IN 46514
574-262-9211
www.hoosiervolleyball.org
• Mitchell Stemm,
President/Commissioner/Junior Program
Coordin
(574) 370-9627
dallict@aol.com
• Charles Stemm, Vice President/Treasurer
hoosiervba@comcast.net
• Joan L. Stemm, Registrar
hoosiervba@comcast.net

INTERMOUNTAIN VOLLEYBALL
ASSOCIATION
72 DORMAN AVENUE
SAN FRANCISCO, CA 94124
801-618-8380
info@imvolleyball.org
imvolleyball.org
• Jason Badell, CFO/Commissioner
jasonbadell@imvolleyball.org
• Mike Deaver, Executive Vice President

IOWA REGION USA VOLLEYBALL
8170 HICKMAN ROAD
SUITE 5
CLIVE, IA 50325
515-727-1860
Fax: 515-727-1861
www.iavbreg.org
• Lynne Updegraff, Commisioner
lynne@iavbreg.org
• Martin Miller, Vice President & Northwest
District
(515) 292-7113
mgmiller@iastate.edu
• Tina Carter, Secretary & Southwest District
(515) 210-4353
tinacarter22@hotmail.com
Description:
IRV is one of the 40 regional associations within
USA Volleyball, promoting and organzing
competition at the State level.

KEYSTONE REGIONAL
COMMISSIONER/USA VOLLEYBALL
1013 BROOKSIDE ROADAD
SUITE 203
WESCOSVILLE, PA 18106
610-401-3362
Fax: 888-391-5782
registration@krva.org
www.krva.org
• Michelle Carlton, Commissioner
commissioner@krva.org
• Deborah Fajerski, Secretary
secretary@krva.org
• Jeff Stubblefield, Treasurer
treasurer@krva.org
Description:
KRVA is one of the 40 regional associations
within the National Governing Body USA
Volleyball, promoting the sport at the State level.

LONE STAR REGIONAL
COMMISSIONER/USA VOLLEYBALL
1608 CANYON OAK
SCHERTZ, TX 78154
210-945-4365
Fax: 210-945-8630
www.lsvolleyball.org

multi sports

• Will Vick, Commissioner
willvick@satx.rr.com
• Karen Tarmon, Registrar
(830) 358-7714
Publications:
Newsletter-Quarterly

MOKU O KEAWE REGIONAL COMMISSIONER/USA VOLLEYBALL
178 POHAI STREET
HILO, HI 96720
808-292-5916
mokuregion@yahoo.com
www.leaguelineup.com/mokuokeawe
• Elroy Osorio, Vice President
• Angie Andrade-Morioka, President/Regional Commissioner
(808) 292-5916

NEW ENGLAND REGIONAL COMMISSIONER/USA VOLLEYBALL
38983 ACUSHNET AVENUE
NEW BEDFORD, MA 02745
508-922-0803
commissioner@nevolleyball.org
www.nevolleyball.org
• Dave Peixoto, Commissioner

NORTH COUNTRY REGION/USA VOLLEYBALL
4445 WEST 77TH STREET D
SUITE 109
EDINN, MN 55435
952-831-9150
800-657-6967
Fax: 952-942-5584
www.ncrusav.org
• Judy Praska, Executive Director
(952) 831-9150
• Brad Aaberg, Officials Coordinator
(952) 831-9150

NORTH TEXAS REGIONAL COMMISSIONER/USA VOLLEYBALL
PO BOX 941
PLANO, TX 75094
469-326-1873
Fax: 469-326-1875
ntrdonise@gmail.com
ntrvolleyball.net
• Andy Reitinger, Commissioner/President
andysummit@yahoo.com
• Donise King, Executive Director
ntrdonise@gmail.com
• Steve Hargrave, Junior Coordinator
Description:
As one of the 40 regional associations within USA Volleyball, NTR sactions events and promotes the sport at the State level.

NORTHERN CALIFORNIA REGIONAL COMMISSIONER/USA VOLLEYBALL
72 DORMAN AVENUE
SAN FRANCISCO, CA 94124
415-550-7582
Fax: 415-550-7762
vball@ncva.com
www.ncva.com
• Diane Mazzei, Board Chair
• Donna Donaghy, Chief Executive Officer
donna@ncva.com
• Shannon Christie, Region Services Administrator

NORTHWEST VOLLEYBALL INC.
15801 NE 8TH STREET
REDMOND, WA 98052
425-497-1051
Fax: 425-671-5020
info@volleyballnw.com
nwjuniors.org
• Tony Miranda, Executive Director
(206) 550
tony@volleyballnw.com

OHIO VALLEY REGIONAL COMMISSIONER/USA VOLLEYBALL
315 JOHNSON ROAD
KENT, OH 44240
330-354-5332
wyzynski@ovr.org
www.ovr.org
• Bob Price, Commissioner/President
(614) 882-2468
Rwprice23@att.net
• Ronald J. Wyzynski, Executive Director/CEO
(614) 402-9445
wyzynski@ovr.org
Description:
As one of the 40 regional associations within USA Volleyball, OVR promotes and organizes the sport at the State level. As of 2017, membership is at 22,557.

OKLAHOMA REGIONAL COMMISSIONER/USA VOLLEYBALL
18605 ALBERTO PLACE
EDMOND, OK 73013
405-285-6622
Fax: 405-285-0607
www.okrva.com
• Bill Hamiter, President
(405) 789-6939
• Shawn McCarty, Commissioner
(405) 285-6622

OLD DOMINION REGIONAL COMMISSIONER/USA VOLLEYBALL
PO BOX 6828
RICHMOND, VA 23230
804-400-9758
info@odrvb.org
www.odrvb.org
• Skipp Weston, Commissioner
(804) 400-9758
commissioner@odrvb.org

PALMETTO REGIONAL COMMISSIONER/USA VOLLEYBALL
137 GARDENIA DRIVE
NINETY SIX, SC 29666
864-809-8222
office@palmettovb.com
www.palmettovb.com
• Jimmy Peden, Commissioner
• Kirsten Boessneck, Coordinator
Description:
The Palmetto Volleyball Region is a member of the USA Volleyball Organization. The Palmetto Region is a grassroots organization which sanction events for Club volleyball teams in the state of South Carolina. Teams include Adult and Junior teams for boys, girls, men and women.

PIONEER REGIONAL COMMISSIONER/USA VOLLEYBALL
OHIO VALLEY VOLLEYBALL CENTER
1820 TAYLOR AVENUE
LOUISVILLE, KY 40213
502-473-1200 EXT 21
www.pioneervb.com
• Ron Kordes, President
(502) 473-1200
ronkordes@ovvc.com
• Nancy Funk, Assistant Commissioner
(502) 239-1818
nfunk@twc.com

PUGET SOUND REGIONAL COMMISSIONER/USA VOLLEYBALL
22617 76TH AVENUE
SUITE 201
EDMONDS, WA 98026
425-673-4103
Fax: 425-673-4293
www.psrvb.org
• Bil Caillier, Chairperson
• Jim Amsbary, Treasurer
• Elise Quinn, Board Secretary
• John Bryant, Commissioner

Description:
PSR is a not-for-profit organization serving a geographic area in Washington State bound to the north by the Canadian border, on the west by the Pacific Ocean, on the east by the crest of the Cascade Mountains, and on the south by Lewis County. The purpose of PSR is to develop and promote the sport of volleyball through adult, junior, and youth programs at a local, regional, and national level.

ROCKY MOUNTAIN REGIONAL COMMISSIONER/USA VOLLEYBALL
4155 JEWELL AVENUE
SUITE 909
DENVER, CO 80222
303-584-0376
800-503-0969
Fax: 303-782-5577
www.rmrvolleyball.org
• Glenn Sapp, Commissioner
(303) 422-4209
• Wendy Sapp, Office Manager
wendy@rmrvolleyball.org

SOUTHERN CALIFORNIA REGIONAL COMMISSIONER/USA VOLLEYBALL
1500 SOUTH ANAHEIM BOULEVARD
SUITE 280
ANAHEIM, CA 92805
714-917-3595
Fax: 714-917-3596
info@scvavolleyball.org
www.scvavolleyball.org
• Ann Davenport, Regional Commissioner
ann@scvavolleyball.org
• Shannon Davenport, Office Manager
shannon@scvavolleyball.org
• Ken Taylor, Official's Chair
Description:
SCVA is one of the 40 non-profit associations within USA Volleyball, promoting and organzing the sport at the State level.

SOUTHERN REGIONAL COMMISSIONER/USA VOLLEYBALL
105 ROUNSAVILLE COURT
ROSWELL, GA 30076
844-219-2976
Fax: 770-649-9117
kencain23@gmail.com
www.srva.org

SUN COUNTRY REGIONAL COMMISSIONER/USA VOLLEYBALL
4233 W FARMERS
AMARILLO, TX 79110
806-681-5458
commissioner@suncountryvb.org
www.suncountryvb.org
• Mark Noble, Commissioner
(806) 681-5458
mnoble1822@gmail.com
• Steve Franco, Secretary
(505) 220-8873
secretary@suncountryvb.org
• Jake Bordenave, Treasurer
(505) 823-1344
treasurer@suncountryvb.org
Description:
SURVA is one of the 40 independant associations within USa Volleyball, promoting and organiazing competition for the sport at the State level.

WESTERN EMPIRE
58 MEADOWLARK DRIVE
PENFIELD, NY 14526
585-259-6557
www.wevavolleyball.org
• John W Hughes, Commissioner/Executive Director
wevajohn@gmail.com
• Rocco W Lucci, Jr, President
rocolucci@gmail.com
• Cindy D Errico, Junior Coordinator /Junior

Program Director
(585) 548-2598
wevacindy@hotmail.com
Sports Services Founded:
1989
Description:
The purpose of WEVA is the promotion of volleyball and playing the game in all of its forms. In addition to developing players, WEVA has committed resources to train coaches, officials, scorekeepers, and parent volunteers. This is one of 40 USA Volleyball regions representing the sport of volleyball in the 15 western most counties of New York State.

USA WATER POLO, INC.
2124 MAIN STREET
SUITE 240
HUNTINGTON BEACH, CA 92648
714-500-5445
Fax: 714-960-2431
www.usawaterpolo.org
• Christopher Ramsey, CEO
• Jonie Walbring, Human Resources Director
(714) 500-5448
jwalbring@usawaterpolo.org
• Annalece Montgomery, Marketing Coordinator
(714) 500-5434
• Stephanie London Krogius, Director of Advancement
(714) 500-5427
skrogius@usawaterpolo.org
Sports Services Founded:
1978
Description:
A not-for-profit corporation that serves as the national governing body for the sport of water polo in the United States under authority of the United States Olympic Committee.

USA WEIGHTLIFTING
1 OLYMPIC PLAZA
COLORADO SPRINGS, CO 80909
719-866-4508
Fax: 719-866-4741
usaw@usaweightlifting.org
www.usaweightlifting.org
• Phil Andrews, Chief Executive Officer/General Secretary
(719) 866-3386
Phil.Andrews@usaweightlifting.org
• Brad Suchorski, Membership Manager
(719) 866-3227
Membership Requirements:
No requirements - there are memberships of all kinds and dues related to each membership type.
Description:
USA Weightlifing is the national governing body for olympic weightlifting in the United States. USAW is a member of the US Olympic Committee and of the International Weightlifting Federation.

USA WRESTLING
6155 LEHMAN DR
COLORADO SPRINGS, CO 80918
719-598-8181
Fax: 719-598-9440
www.teamusa.org/usa-wrestling
• Rich Bender, Executive Director
(719) 598-8181
rbender@usawrestling.org
• Bruce Baungartner, President
• Greg Strobel, 1st Vice president
• Mark Reiland, 2nd Vice President

• Duane Morgan, Treasurer
• Tony Black, State Services Manager
(719) 598-8181
tblack@usawrestling.org
• Dwaine Cooper, Assoc Executive Director Finance/Administration
dcooper@usawrestling.org
• Gary Abbott, Special Projects/Communications Director
(719) 598-8181
gabbott@usawrestling.org
• Meredith Wilson, Information Technology Director
(719) 598-8181
mwilson@usawrestling.org
Description:
The national governing body for the sport of wrestling in the United States and, as such, is its representative to the United States Olympic Committee. The central organization that coordinates amateur wrestling programs in the nation and works to create interest and participation in these programs.

Professional Organizations

AMATEUR ATHLETIC UNION OF THE UNITED STATES, INC./AAU
PO BOX 22409
1910 HOTEL PLAZA BOULEVARD
LAKE BUENA VISTA, FL 32830
407-934-7200
800-228-4872
Fax: 407-934-7242
www.aausports.org
• Roger Goudy, President
roger@aausports.org
• Cynthia Diaz, Finance Director
(407) 828-3740
cynthia@aausports.org
Sports Services Founded:
1888
Membership Requirements:
Athlete membership is for anyone involved in an activity. One membership card allows participation in any and all of the AAU sports. Volunteers may participate in annual, sustaining, and lifetime membership programs.
Programs Include:
AAU Junior Olympic Games - The largest national multi-sport event for the youth of America. Encompasses the US territories and American children on military bases.
Other Programs include:
Presidential Sports Award, Presidential Challenge National Youth Physical Fitness Program.
Publications:
Official AAU Handbook, for each sport.
Description:
One of the largest non profit, volunteer, sports organizations in the United States. A multi sport organization, the AAU is dedicated exclusively to the promotion and development of amateur sports and physical fitness programs.

Other locations:

ADIRONDACK AAU ASSOCIATION
7 WATERMAN COURT
UNIT 4
DELMAR, NY 12054

518-475-9480
jmallery@aol.com
www.adirondackaau.org
• Mike Friello, Governor
officialaautaekwondo@gmail.com
• Jerry Mallery, Registrar
Sports Services Founded:
Organized January 31, 1920
Description:
Organizes competitions and over 35 sports for youths. Serves New York State East and North of Broome, Cortland, Dutchess, Onondaga, Orange, Oswego and Sullivan Counties. Neighboring Districts include Connecticut, Middle Atlantic, New England, New York Metropolitan and Niagara.

ALASKA AAU ASSOCIATION
THE WALT DISNEY WORLD RESORT
PO BOX 10,000
LAKE BUENA VISTA, FL 32830-1000
407-943-7200
www.aausports.org
Description:
Covers the State of Alaska.

ARIZONA AAU ASSOCIATION
602-228-3209
• Thomas Rogers, Governor
corogers@cox.net
Sports Services Founded:
Organized March 10, 1956

ARKANSAS AAU ASSOCIATION
40 LILES ROAD
BEEBE, AR 72012
501-303-8389
terrie@aamsco.net
www.arkansasaau.org
• Larry Bryant, Governor
(501) 388-1937
bryantlarry5@aol.com
• Farrin Cain, 1ST Lt Governor
aquatics.hfc@gmail.com
• Charlie Wood, 2nd Lt. Governor
(501) 351-1314
wood_charlie@hotmail.com
• Jane Nichols, Secretary
(501) 525-0441
sportsj43@att.net
• Lottie Keaton, Treasurer
(501) 244-5404
lkeatonbrooks@sbcglobal.net
Sports Services Founded:
Organized February 16, 1936
Description:
State of Arkansas and Bowie County, Texas. Neighboring Districts include Southeastern, Southern, Southwestern, Oklahoma, Missouri Valley and Ozark.

CENTRAL AAU ASSOCIATION
7291 CLEM DRIVE
GURNEE, IL 60031
847-456-2617
www.aaucentral.org; www.centralillinoisaau.org
• JB Mirza, Governor
jbmtko@aol.com
Sports Services Founded:
Organized in 1890
Description:
Illinois, except Calhoun, Greene, Jersey, Madison, Monroe and St. Clair counties.

CENTRAL CALIFORNIA AAU ASSOCIATION
1255 NORTH CHERRY AVENUE
524
TULARE, CA 93274
209-845-9868
centralcalaau@aol.com
www.centralcalaau.org
• Guy Fowler, Governor
• Karen Fowler, Registrar
oakdalegal@yahoo.com
• Dave Schlick, LT.Governor

Sports Services Foudned:
Organized in 1952.
Description:
Counties of Fresno, Inyo, Kern, Kings, Madera, Mariposa, Merced, Mona and Tulare in the State of California. Territory re-aligned December 1963.

CONNECTICUT AAU ASSOCIATION
525 BURNSIDE AVENUE
EAST HARTFORD, CT 6108
860-291-8241
866-341-8241
www.connecticutaau.org/
• Dan Dembinski, District Registrar
• Jack Bethke, District Govenor
jackbethke@yahoo.com
• George Keurtyka, Lieutenant Governor
kurtyka@sbcglobal.net
• Cindy D Hetu, District Treasurer
clhetu@yahoo.com
Sports Services Founded:
Organized September 17, 1929
Description:
State of Connecticut. Neighboring Districts include Adirondack, New England and New York Metropolitan.

FLORIDA AAU ASSOCIATION
4400 N HIGHWAY 19A
UNIT 6
MOUNT DORA, FL 32757
352-357-0477
Fax: 352-357-0474
www.aauflorida.org;
www.eteamz.com/floridaaau
• Chet Lemon, Director
gigi@sunshinesports.net
Sports Services Founded:
Organized in January 1925.
Description:
Florida, execept Miami-Dade Broward, that part of Hendry County West of Route 833, and Palm Beach Counties. Territory re-aligned, December 1958, 1959, 1963, 1972, 1999.

FLORIDA GOLD COAST AAU ASSOCIATION
www.aausports.org
Description:
Counties of Broward, Miami Dade, that part of Hendry County East of Route 833, and Palm Beach counties. Neighboring District is Florida.

GEORGIA AAU ASSOCIATION
770-380-9749
gaaau@comcast.net
www.gaaau.net
• James Henry, Governor
(770) 846-2009
• Wendy Miller, Registrar
(404) 401-4996
wendmill227@yahoo.com
• Jane Williamson, Secretary and Hospitality
(770) 646-5157
mjanewill2@aol.com
• Peg Adams, Treasurer
(706) 517-7947
pegaau@msn.com
Description:
Territory realigned September 1989. State of Georgia. Neighboring Districts include Florida, North Carolina, Southeastern and South Carolina.

GULF AAU ASSOCIATION
PO BOX 38913
HOUSTON, TX 77238
877-872-7481
info@texasgulfaau.com
www.texasgulfaau.com
• Lola Wesley, Governor
ola.wesley@att.net
Sports Services Founded:
Organized on March 6, 1931
Description:

Texas bounded on the North, including counties of Angelina, Houston, Leon, Nacogdoches, Robertson and Shelby, and including the counties of Austin, Brazos, Colorado, Fort Bend, Grimes, Matagorda, Robertson, Waller, Washington and Wharton. Territory re-aligned September 1992.

HAWAIIAN AAU ASSOCIATION
808-395-2422
www.aausports.org
• Grant K. Kidani, Governor
Sports Services Founded:
Organized November 1910
Description:
State of Hawaii

INDIANA AAU ASSOCIATION
4150 KIDEER DR. SUITE 2A
INDIANAPOLIS, IN 46237
317-362-0615
Fax: 317-362-0763
www.aausports.org
• Lewis Owens, Governor
lewisfowens@hotmail.com
Sports Services Founded:
Organized August 22, 1919
Description:
The State of Indiana except Clark, Dearborn and Floyd Counties.

INLAND EMPIRE AAU ASSOCIATION
PO BOX 9603
YAKIMA, WA 98909
509-453-2696
Fax: 509-457-0931
aau@ieaau.org
www.ieaau.org
• Paul Campbell, Governor
paul@yvn.com
Sports Services Founded:
Organized April 25, 1937
Description:
State of Washington, counties of Adams, Asotin, Benton, Chelan, Columbia, Douglas, Ferry, Franklin, Garfield, Grant, Kittias, Lincoln, Okanogan, Spokane, Stevens, Walla Walla, Whitman and Yakima County. State of Idaho, counties of Benewah, Bonner, Boundary, Clearwater, Idaho, Kootenai, Latah, Lewis, Nez Perce, Pend Oreille and Shoshone.

IOWA AAU ASSOCIATION
3021 38TH STREET
DES MOINES, IA 50310-4616
515-255-4058
Fax: 515-279-4971
parmentert@gmail.com
www.aauiowa.org
• Teresa Parmenter, Governor
parmentert13@gmail.com
Sports Services Founded:
Organized January 15, 1939.
Description:
State of Iowa. Neighboring Districts include Minnesota, South Dakota, Wisconsin, Missouri Valley, Nebraska, Ozark and Central.

KENTUCKY AAU ASSOCIATION
5609 BRUNS DRIVE
LOUISVILLE, KY 40216
502-449-0101
Fax: 502-449-0101
www.aaukentucky.org
• Jared Prickett, Governor
Sports Services Founded:
Organized February 27, 1939.
Description:
The State of Kentucky and Clark and Floyd County in the State of Indiana (except for the sports of wrestling and boys and girls basketball). Neighboring Districts include Central, Indiana, Ohio, Ozark, Southeastern, Virginia and West Virginia.

LAKE ERIE AAU ASSOCIATION
4843 MAYFIELD ROAD
LYNDHURST, OH 44124-2506
www.aausports.org
• Joe Gura, Governor
(440) 452-4481
jegura@roadrunner.com
• Lewis Fellinger, Registrar
(216) 288-3483
Sports Services Founded:
Organized January 5, 1931
Description:
Counties of Ashland, Ashtabula, Belmont Columbiana, Crawford, Cuyahoga, Erie, Geagua, Huron, Jefferson, Lake, Lorain, Mahoning, Medina, Portage, Richland, Seneca, Stark, Summit, Trumball, Tuscarawus and Wayne. Neighboring Districts include Ohio and Western Pennsylvania.

MARYLAND AAU ASSOCIATION
1304 PENTRIDGE ROAD
BALTIMORE, MD 21239
443-794-8967
www.marylandaau.org
• Antoinette Dubose, 1st Lt. Governor/Office Manager
(443) 794-8967
ndubose1744@aol.com
Sports Service Founded:
Organized 1981.
Description:
State of Maryland (except the counties of Montgomery and Prince Georges).

MICHIGAN AAU ASSOCIATION
18516 SNOW
FRASER, MI 48026
586-273-7910
www.michiganaau.org
• Cynthia Trombly-Martin, Governor
cinditrombly@aol.com
Sports Services Founded:
Organized November 1923
Description:
State of Michigan. Neighboring Districts include Indiana and Ohio.

MIDDLE ATLANTIC AAU ASSOCIATION
PO BOX 631
ARDMORE, PA 19003
215-327-9181
www.aausports.org
• Alison Eachus, Director
coacheaby@aol.com
Sports Services Founded:
Organized 1906
Description:
New Jersey, South of Mercer and Monmouth County, all of the state of Delaware and the Commonwealth of Pennsylvania, East of and including Bedford, Centre, Clinton, and Potter Counties. Neighboring Districts include Adirondack, New Jersey, New York Metropolitan, Niagara, Western Pennsylvania and Maryland.

MINNESOTA AAU ASSOCIATION
3610 E. MINNEHAHA PARKWAY
MINNEAPOLIS, MN 55406
651-955-9725
www.minnesotaaau.org
• Willie Braziel, Governor
wbraziel@aol.com
Description:
State of Minnesota. Neighboring Districts Iowa, North Dakota, South Dakota and Wisconsin.

MISSOURI VALLEY AAU ASSOCIATION
1815 N YORK STREET
INDEPENDENCE, MO 64058
816-935-2106
www.aaumissourivalley.org
• Kim Lassley, Governor
mvaaugovernor@aol.com

Sports Services Founded:
Organized February 14, 1931
Description:
All of Kansas and that portion of the western part of the state of Missouri including and bounded by Adair, Audrain, Benton, Callaway, Christian, Cole, Greene, Hickory, Macon, Montineau, Morgan, Polk, Randolph, Schuyler and Taney. Neighboring Districts include Iowa, Nebraska, Colorado, Oklahoma, Arkansas and Ozark.

MONTANA AAU ASSOCIATION
SIDNEY, MT
406-488-7330
mtaau.reg@gmail.com
www.aausports.org
• Jim Scollard, Governor
j_scollard@aol.com
Sports Services Founded:
Organized Febrauary 15, 1936
Description:
State of Montana. Neighboring Districts include Inland Empire, North Dakota, South Dakota and Wyoming.

NEW ENGLAND AAU ASSOCIATION
37 THURBER BLVD
SUITE 106
SMITHFIELD, RI 2917
401-349-4304
800-228-4872
www.neaau.org
• Jackie White, Director
oldpro77@msn.com
Sports Services Founded:
Organized 1890.
Description:
New Hampshire, Maine, Massachusetts, Rhode Island and Vermont. Neighboring Districts include Adirondack and Connecticut.

NEW JERSEY AAU ASSOCIATION
29 BROOKSIDE ROAD
LEONARDO, NJ 7737
732-291-2120
njaau@verizon.net
www.aaunewjersey.org
• Diane McGowan, Director
njaau@verizon.net
Sports Services Founded:
Organized April 21, 1930
Description:
New Jersey North of and including Hudson, Mercer and Monmouth Counties. Neighboring Districts include Middle Atlantic and New York Metropolitan.

NEW MEXICO AAU ASSOCIATION
2409 MILLER
CLOVIS, NM 88101
575-763-4572
www.aausports.org
• Pat Miner, Governor
janepatminer@msn.com
• Cathy Mills, Lt. Governor
cmills@plateautel.net
Sports Services Founded:
Organized May 29, 1947.
Description:
State of New Mexico, (except that area en-compassed by the Four Corners District), and the counties of Brewster, Culberton, Crockett, El Paso, Hudspeth, Jeff Davis, Presidio and Terrell in the State of Texas. Neighboring Districts include, Colorado, Utah, Arizona, West Texas, South Texas and Oklahoma.

NIAGARA AAU ASSOCIATION
4000 HARLEM ROAD
SNYDER, NY 14226
315-759-9457
humphrey@guardian.com
www.aausports.org
• Richard Hill, Governor

Sports Services Founded:
Organized September 27, 1919.
Description:
State of New York West of and including Broome, Cortland, Onondaga and Oswego Counties. Neighboring Districts include Adirondack, Middle Atlantic, and Western Pennsylvania.

NORTH CAROLINA AAU ASSOCIATION
128-A NORTH MCDOWELL STREET
CHARLOTTE, NC 28204
704-786-4754
800-228-4872
Fax: 704-795-1392
www.ncaau.org
• Jane Kilmartin, Director
rmssek@aol.com
Sports Services Founded:
Organized December 5, 1965
Description:
State of North Caolina. Neighboring Districts include Georgia, South Carolina, Southeastern and Virginia.

NORTH DAKOTA AAU ASSOCIATION
AAU HEADQUARTERS
PO BOX 10,000
LAKE BUENA VISTA, ND 32830-1000
407-934-7200
www.aausports.org
Sports Service Founded:
Organized December 1, 1962.
Description:
Neighboring Districts include Minnesota, Montana, and South Dakota.

OHIO AAU ASSOCIATION
7429 KILKENNY DRIVE
WEST CHESTER, OH 45069
www.ohioaau.org
• Mark Hecquet, Governor
ohioaau@gmail.com
Sports Services Founded:
Organized May 1, 1923
Description:
State of Ohio except the counties of Ashland, Ashtabula, Belmont, Crawford, Cuyahoga, Erie, Geauga, Huron, Jefferson; Lake, Lawrence, Lorain, Mahoning, Medina, Portage, Richland, Seneca, Stark, Summitt, Trumbull, Tuscarawus, Washington and Wayne; and the Dearborn County in the State of Indiana. Neighboring Districts include Indiana, Lake Erie, Michigan, Kentucky, West Virginia, and Western Pennsylvania.

OKLAHOMA AAU ASSOCIATION
5000 NW 61ST STREET
OKLAHOMA CITY, OK 73122
www.aausports.org
• Bill Meek, Governor
bmeek2004@aol.com
Sports Services Founded:
Organized Febrauary 23, 1936
Description:
State of Oklahoma. Neighboring Districts include Missouri Valley, Colorado, New Mexico, West Texas, Southwestern and Arkansas.

OREGON AAU ASSOCIATION
1535 HARBECK ROAD
GRANTS PASS, OR 97527
541-485-5474
oregonaau@comcast.net
www.oregonaau.org; www.aauoregon.org
• Chuck Wenger, Governor
wenger3826@comcast.net
• Diane Wenger, Secretary
wenger3826@aol.com
• Rosemary Honl, Registrar
jrhonl@msn.com
Sports Services Founded:
Organized September 23, 1935
Description:
State of Oregon and the following counties of

Washington: Clark, Cowlitz and Skamania. Neighboring Districts include Inland Empire, Pacific and Pacific Northwest.

OZARK AAU ASSOCIATION
900 WEIDMANN ROAD
TOWN & COUNTRY, MO 63017
hwcrawf@sbcglobal.net
www.aausports.org
• Jack Crider, Governor
jcrider01@sbcglobal.net
Sports Services Founded:
Organized 1935.
Description:
Missouri East and including the following counties, Camden, Dallas, Douglas, Knox, Miller, Monroe, Montgomery, Osage, Ozark, Pike, Scotland, Shelby, including the city of St. Louis and Webster. Counties of Calhoun, Greene, Jersey, Madison, Monroe and St. Clair in Illinois with reservation that all judo therein be controlled by Central District. Neighboring Districts include Arkansas, Central, Kentucky, Iowa, Missouri Valley and Southeastern.

PACIFIC AAU ASSOCIATION
PO BOX 52049
SPARKS, NV 89435
775-530-5446
Fax: 775-358-5598
www.aaupacific.com
• Matt Wiliams, Director
Sports Services Founded:
Organized 1890
Description:
The State of California, North of but not including the counties of Fresno, Madera, Mariposa, Merced, Mono and San Luis Obispo and the Counites of Churchill, Douglas, Humboldt, Lander, Lyon, Mineral, Ormsby, Pershing, Storey and Washoe in the State of Nevada. Neighboring Districts Central California, Inland Empire, Oregon, Southern Nevada and Southern Pacific.

PACIFIC NORTHWEST AAU ASSOCIATION
PO BOX 33305
SHORLINE, WA 98133
206-546-9405
nwsports@gte.net
www.pnaau.org; www.aaupacificnorthwest.org
• Mike Connors, Director
nwsports@pnaau.org
Sports Services Founded:
Organized June 1905
Description:
Washington, West of but not including Chelan, Kittitas, Okanogan and Yakima Counties and North of but not including Cowlitz, Klickitat and Skamania Counties. Neighboring Districts include Inland Empire and Oregon.

PACIFIC SOUTHWEST ASSOCIATION
6731 TOWNVIEW TERRACE
SAN DIEGO, CA 92120-1742
619-265-7675
info@aaupacificsouthwest.org
• Michael Brunker, Governor
michael.brunker@aaupacificsouthwest.org
• Maria Brunker, Registrar/Treasurer
Sports Service Founded:
Organized December 10, 1949
Description:
Original name was Southwest Pacific Border District. Name changed at 1956 Convention. Imperial and San Diego Counties.

POTOMAC VALLEY AAU ASSOCIATION
11705 CAPSTAN DRIVE
UPPER MARLBORO, MD 20772
301-374-9189
Fax: 301-324-4123
pksportss@yahoo.com
• Preston Martin, Governor
pksports@yahoo.com

multi sports

215

• Jamie Bennett, Registrar
(240) 381-4557
braiyonna@yahoo.com
Sports Services Founded:
Organized October 15, 1929
Description:
All territory within the District of Columbia, counties of Montgomery and Prince Georges in the State of Maryland, and counties of Arlington anf Fairfax and cities of Alexandria and Falls Church in the Commonwealth of Virginia. Neighboring Districts Maryland and Virginia.

PUERTO RICO AAU ASSOCIATION
WALT DISNEY WORLD RESORT
PO BOX 10,000
LAKE BUENA VISTA, FL 32830-1000
407-934-7200
www.aaupuertorico.org
Sports Service Founded:
Organized September, 8, 1984.
Description:
Puerto Rico and U.S. Virgin Islands

SOUTH CAROLINA AAU ASSOCIATION
2428 DUNCAN STREET
COLUMBIA, SC 29205
803-799-6332
bettiq@bellsouth.net
www.scaau.org; www.aausouthcarolina.org
• Frank Pollock, Governor
(803) 957-8692
fspollock@gmail.com
• Betty Quave, Secretary
(803) 799-6332
bettiq@bellsouth.net
Sports Services Founded:
Organized December 5, 1965
Description:
State of Carolina. Neighboring Districts include Georgia and North Carolina.

SOUTH DAKOTA AAU ASSOCIATION
PO BOX 702
EAGLE BUTTE, SD 57625
wohlebera@hotmail.com
• Bob Johnson, Governor
Sports Services Founded:
Organized December 4, 1964
Description:
State of South Dakota. Neighboring Districts include Iowa, Minnesota, Montana, Nebraska, North Dakota and Wyoming.

SOUTH TEXAS AAU ASSOCIATION
7314 S TRIPLE ELM
CHINA GROVE, TX 78263
210-656-7670
Fax: 210-656-7670
yayadebra@gmail.com
www.southtexasaau.org
• Augustus Labruce Bray, Governor
braylabruce@yahoo.com
Sports Services Founded:
Organized Novemeber 12, 1945
Description:
That part of the State of Texas bounded on the East by and including the counties of Burleson, Fayette, Jackson, Lavaca, Milam and on the South by the Gulf of Mexico and the Republic of Mexico; on the West by and including the counties of Schleicher, Sutton and Val Verde, and on the North by and including the counties of Bell, Burnett, Coryell, Falls, Lampasas, Llano, Mason and Menard. Neighboring Districts include Gulf, Southwest, South Texas, New Mexico and West Texas.

SOUTHEASTERN AAU ASSOCIATION
3885 S. PERKINS RD
STE 9
MEMPHIS, TN 38118
901-362-9550
Fax: 901-362-9716
leora@aausports.org
www.seaausports.com

• Darrel Lauderdale, Governor
Sports Services Founded:
Organized August 13, 1951
Description:
The State of Alabama and the State of Tennessee. Neighboring Districts include Kentucky, Virginia, North Carolina, Georgia, Southern, Arkansas and Ozark.

SOUTHERN AAU ASSOCIATION
3244 MASSACHUSETTS STREET
KENNER, LA 70065
504-464-0306
normasaau@aol.com
www.aausports.org
• Charles Domino, Governor
dominosaau@aol.com
Sports Services Founded:
Organized 1892
Description:
The State of Louisiana and the State of Mississippi. Neighboring Districts include Southeastern, Arkansas, Gulf and Southwestern.

SOUTHERN NEVADA AAU ASSOCIATION
2730 S. RANCHO DRIVE
LAS VEGAS, NV 89102
702-807-5404
www.aaulasvegas.com
• Ennis Wesley, Director
Sports Services Founded:
Organized January 15, 1959
Description:
Counties of Clark, Esmeralda, Lincoln, Nyle, all within the State of Nevada. Neighboring Districts include Inland Empire, Utah, Arizona, Central California, Pacific and Southern Pacific.

SOUTHERN PACIFIC AAU ASSOCIATION
PO BOX 100
LAKE BUENA VISTA, FL 32830-1000
407-93407200
www.aausouthernpacific.org; www.spa-aau.org
• Eric Elizdale, Governor
eric@socalaaubaseball.com
Sports Services Founded:
Organized November 1909
Description:
Including the counties of Los Angeles, Orange, Riverside, San Bernardino, San Luis Obispo, Santa Barbara and Ventura all within the State of California. Neighboring Districts include Arizona, Central California, Pacific, Pacific Southwest and Southern Nevada.

SOUTHWESTERN AAU ASSOCIATION
3610 S COOPER ST.
SUITE 124
ARLINGTON, TX 76010
s-lewis-mccann@sbcglobal.net
www.aausports.org
• Ivan Lewis, Governor
bushokaiusa@sbcglobal.net
Sports Services Founded:
Organized May 8, 1936
Description:
That part of the State of Texas bounded on the South but not including the counteis of Angelina, Brown, Callahan, Coryell, Falls, Houston, Lampasas, Leon, Milam, Mills, Nacogdoches, Robertson and Shelby; on the East by the State of Louisiana, State of Arkansas and the county of Bowie, Texas; on the North by the State of Oklahoma and the county of Bowie, Texas and on the West by the counties of, but not including Foard, Hardeman, Haskell, Jones and Knox in the State of Texas. Neighboring Districts include Oklahoma, Arkansas, Southern, Gulf, South Texas and West Texas.

UTAH AAU ASSOCIATION
3731 W. SOUTH JORDAN PARKWAY #411
SOUTH JORDAN, UT 84095

801-381-0326
• Michael Killpack, Governor
killerpup@comcast.net
Sports Services Founded:
Organized November 1910
Description:
State of Utah. Neighboring Districts include Inland Empire, Wyomoing, Colorado, New Mexico, Arizona and Southern Nevada.

VIRGINIA AAU ASSOCIATION
405 LORRAINE AVENUE
FREDERICKSBURG, VA 22408
540-710-1228
Fax: 540-710-7007
aauvirginia.com
• Jeremy Bullock, Governor
(540) 408-3789
jeremy@aauvirginia.com
Sports Services Founded:
Organized December 9, 1934
Description:
State of Virginia except the Counties of Arlington and Fairfax and the cities of Alexandria and Falls Church. Neighboring Districts include Potomac Valley, West Virginia, Kentucky, Southeastern and North Carolina.

WEST TEXAS AAU ASSOCIATION
THE WALT DISNEY WORLD RESORT
PO BOX 10,000
LAKE BUENA VISTA, FL 32830-1000
407-937-7200
www.aauwesttexas.org
• Shanny Rios, Compliance Service Coordinator
(407) 828-3785
Sports Services Founded:
Organized 1952
Description:
All that part of the State of Texas bounded on the South side and including the counteis of Concho, Irion, McCulloch, Pecos, Reeves, Regan, San Saba, Tom Green and Upton; on the West by the State of New Mexico; on the North by the State of Oklahoma; on the East by the State of Oklahoma and by including the counties of Brown, Callahan, Foard, Hardeman, Haskell, Jones, Knox, Mills and San Saba in the State of Texas. Neighboring Districts include Oklahoma, New Mexico, South Texas and Southwestern.

WESTERN PENNSYLVANIA ASSOCIATION
jonroux@comcast.net
• Jon Roux, Director
jonroux@comcast.net
Sports Services Founded:
Organized November 16, 1917
Description:
All counties in Pennsylvania West of Bedford, Centre, Clinton, Huntingdon and Potter, and the Counties of Brooke, Hancock, Marshall and Ohio in West Virginia. Neighboring Districts include Middle Atlantic, Niagara, Maryland, West Virginia, Ohio and Lake Erie.

WISCONSIN AAU DISTRICT
2409 STOUT ROAD
SUITE ONE
MENOMONIE, WI 54751
715-231-4000
• Keith Noll, Governor
slapshot@wwt.net
• Chuck Morning, Registrar
sportsref@wwt.net
Sports Services Founded:
Organized June 6, 1935
Description:
Sanctions AAU Wisconsin sporting events.
Membership Requirements:
AAU Membership

WYOMING ASSOCIATION
THE WALT DISNEY WORLD RESORT
PO BOX 10,000
LAKE BUENA VISTA, FL 32830-1000
407-934-7200
www.aausports.org
Sports Services Founded:
Organized December 9, 1968
Description:
State of Wyoming. Neighboring Districts include Montana, South Dakota, Nebraska, Colorado, Utah and Inland Empire.

AMERICA OUTDOORS/AO
P.O. BOX 10847
KNOXVILLE, TN 37939
865-558-3595
800-524-4814
Fax: 865-558-3598
www.adventurevacation.com;
www.americaoutdoors.org
• Julie Kahlfeldt, Executive Director
• Robin Brown, Communications Director
Nature of Service:
A national association representing adventure travel outfitters, tour companies and outdoor educators, the mission of America Outdoors is supporting and developing outfitting businesses in the United States.

AMERICAN HIKING SOCIETY
8605 SECOND AVENUE
SILVER SPRING, MD 20910
301-565-6704
800-972-8608
info@americanhiking.org
www.americanhiking.org
• Jack Hess, Chair
• Peter Olsen, Interim Executive Director/VP Programs
• Kim Lyons, Director of Development/Marketing
• Libby Wile, Director of Volunteer Stewardship
• Eric Albitz, Finance & Office Manager
Description:
Founded 1976. Promotes hiking and establishes, protects and maintains Foot trails. Promote and enhances interest in hiking activities.
Membership Requirements:
Pay dues.

AMERICAN LIFEGUARD ASSOCIATION
8300 BOONE BOULEVARD
5TH FLOOR
Vienna, VA 22182
703-761-6750
www.americanlifeguard.com
Sports Service Founded:
1990
Description:
Association that is currently one of the largest sponsors of Health and Safety training programs in the United States. Since our establishment in 1990 we have issued over 100,000 certifications in health and safety areas.

AMERICAN RECREATION COALITION
1200 G STREET NW
SUITE 650
WASHINGTON, DC 20005-3832
202-682-9530
Fax: 202-682-9529
bnasta@funoutdoors.com
www.funoutdoors.com/arc

• Derrick Crandall, President
• Catherine Ahern, Vice President Member Services
Member Services:
Recreation Forums - Quarterly discussions on recreation policy. Recreation Exchange - monthly meetings with key government officials. Member Letter - Periodic updates on recreation related issues and activities.
Membership Requirements:
Interest in outdoor recreation (organizations only).
Description:
Founded 1979. Works to enhance and protect outdoor recreation opportunities and resources.

AMERICAN RED CROSS NATIONAL HEADQUARTERS
431 18TH STREET NW
WASHINGTON, DC 20006
202-303-4498
800-733-2767
www.redcross.org
• Bonnie McElveen-Hunter, Chairman
• Gail McGovern, President/CEO
Description:
Sport Safety training, developed with the United States Olympic Committee, designed to meet the needs of coaches and others who work with athletes for sports-specific injury prevention and first aid (including CPR) training. Other training, safety training for swim coaches, life guarding, swimming and diving, oxygen administration, automated external defibrillation and small craft safety and basic water rescue.
Description:
Provides health and safety training nationwide. Trains organizations, staffs, instructors in sport safety training, first aid and CPR. Also delivers courses on-site to employees, students or members.

AMERICAN SPORT EDUCATION PROGRAM/ASEP
1607 NORTH MARKET STREET
PO BOX 5076
CHAMPAIGN, IL 61825-5076
217-351-5076
800-747-5698
Fax: 217-351-2674
asep@hkusa.com
www.humankinetics.com
• Rainer Martens, President
(217) 351-5076
rainer@hkusa.com
• James Schmutz, Executive Director
Description:
Since 1981, ASEP has been committed to improving amateur sports by encouraging coaches, officials, administrators, parents, and athletes to embrace the 'Athletes first, winning second' philosophy and by providing the education to put the philosophy to work. ASEP coaching education courses and resources are used and recognized by hundreds of local, state, and national youth sport organizations; state high school associations; individual school districts; national governing bodies of Olympic sports; and colleges and universities in certifying coaches.

AMERICAN SPORTS INSTITUTE
PO BOX 1837
MILL VALLEY, CA 94942

415-383-5750
info@americansportsinstitute.org
americansportsinstitute.org
Sports Services Founded:
1985
Description:
The institute promotes the value of sport culture to society at the personal, social and international level.

AMERICAN SPORTSCASTERS ASSOCIATION, INC.
225 BROADWAY
SUITE 2030
NEW YORK, NY 10007
212-227-8080
Fax: 212-571-0556
inquiry@americansportscastersonline.com
www.americansportscastersonline.com
• Louis O. Schwartz, President/Founder
lschwa8918@aol.com
• Patrick Turturro, Associate Editor
patrickturturro@americansportscastersonline.com
Member Services:
Blog, Job Bank, Library.
Sports Services Founded:
1979
Description:
Dedicated to promoting, supporting and enhancing the work sportscasters. Acts as a resource of information and guidance for those interested in becoming sportscasters, and encourages the highest standards of ethics, integrity and professional conduct.

AMERICAN VOLKSSPORT ASSOCIATION/AVA
1001 PAT BOOKER ROAD
SUITE 101
UNIVERSAL CITY, TX 78148
210-659-2112
Fax: 210-659-1212
AVAWebmaster@ava.org
www.ava.org
• Dennis A. Michele, President
(828) 628-4343
president@ava.org
• Henry Rosales, Executive Director
execdir@ava.org
• Erin Grosso, Finance Manager
Erin@ava.org

ASSOCIATION FOR APPLIED SPORT PSYCHOLOGY/AAASP
8365 KEYSTONE CROSSING
SUITE 107
INDIANAPOLIS, IN 46240
317-205-9225
Fax: 317-205-9481
info@appliedsportpsych.org
www.appliedsportpsych.org
• Angus Mugford, President
angusmugford@gmail.com
• Amy Baltzell, President-Elect
baltzell@bu.edu
• Todd Gilson, Ph.D., Secretary/Treasurer
tgilson@niu.edu
• Natalie Durand-Bush, Publications/Information
Number of members:
2,400
Member Services:
Will certify consultants in applied sport psychology and conduct continuing education programs.
Publications:

AAASP Newsletter-3x ayear; Membership Directory Online and Directory of Graduate Programs; Journal of Applied Sport Psychology; Supervision Brochure
Sports Services Founded:
1986
Description:
Estblished to promote the science and practice of sport psychology, while providing an opportunity for individuals to share information related to theory development, research, and the provisions of psychological services to consumers.

ASSOCIATION FOR WOMEN IN SPORTS MEDIA/AWSM
7742 SPALDING DRIVE
SUITE 337
NORCROSS, GA 30092
717-703-3086
www.awsmonline.org
• Jenny Dial Creech, President
Description:
Founded 1987. Professional organization for women in sports media promoting and helping women pursue careers in sports related media.
Membership Requirements:
Annual dues.
Member Services:
Offers job bank for members; scholarship program for female journalism students. Annual convention, job fair. Also offers a mentoring program for media related occupations.

ASSOCIATION OF LUXURY SUITE DIRECTORS
10017 MCKELVEY ROAD
CINCINNATI, OH 45231
513-674-0555
Fax: 513-674-0577
feedback@alsd.com
www.alsd.com
• Bill Dorsey, Chairman
bill@alsd.com
• Greg C. Hanrahan, President
• Brain Bucciarelli, Vice President
Description:
Founded 1990. Represents more than 500 facilities and affiliates, covers the premium seat marketplace and all its facets. This includes suites, club seats, stadium clubs, stadium and arena financing, and all that comprises the corporate hospitality market.
Publications:
SEAT, quarterly. Targeted to members of the premium-seat industry.
Member Services:
Annual Conference, Quarterly Newsletter, Suite Reference Manuals, Reference Library, Proprietary Suiteholder Studies.

ATHLETES IN ACTION
651 TAYLOR DRIVE
XENIA, OH 45385
937-352-1000
1-888-278-7233
Fax: 937-352-1001
communications@athletesinaction.org
www.athletesinaction.org
• Mark Householder, President
Sports Services Founded:
1966
Description:
Athletes in Action is uses sport as a platform for spiritual activity and growth.

ATHLETIC EQUIPMENT MANAGERS ASSOCIATION
207 E. BODMAN
BREMENT, IL 61813
217-678-1004
Fax: 217-678-1005
equipmentmanagers.org
• Mike Royster, Executive Director
(423) 755-4567
mike-royster@utc.edu
• Dan Siermine, President
(719) 333-6762
Membership Requirements:
Persons need to be actively engaged in athletic equipment management and have to take a certification exam in order to become certified.
Description:
Founded 1974. Promotes improvements in the field of athletic equipment management, and the safety of athletic equipment.

AWARDS AND PERSONALIZATION ASSOCIATION
8735 W. HIGGINGS ROAD
SUITE 300
CHICAGO, IL 60631
847-375-4800
Fax: 847-375-6480
info@awardspersonalization.org
awardspersonalization.org
• Richard Korbyl, President
(780) 438-3266
rkorbyl@columbia-awards.com
• Cody Stewart, President Elect
sales@eternitycreations.com
• Louise Ristau, Executive Director
(847) 375-4875
lristau@AwardsPersonalization.org
Description:
The association is comprised of reatilers and suppliers of awards, personalized and customized items.

BLACK ENTERTAINMENT & SPORTS LAWYERS ASSOCIATION INC
PO BOX 230794
NEWYORK, NY 10003
301-248-1818
Fax: 301-248-0700
info@besla.org
www.besla.org
• Elke F. Suber, Esq., Chairperson
• Khadijah Sharif-Drinkard, Esq., Vice President
• Emily M Dickens, Esq., Secretary
• Lawrence C. Hinkle II, Esq., President
• Chiquita Woolfolk Banks, Esq.,
Description:
Founded in 1980, the organization fosters a diversity in the entertainment and sports legal profession. An annual conference held in October, up to 15 CLE credits each year.
Membership Requirements:
General lawyer (licensed), Associate member practicing in a professional capacity such as financial, producer, etc., law student interested in the area of sports and entertainment.

BLACK SPORTS AGENTS ASSOCIATION
6100 CENTER DR
SUITE 1200
LOS ANGELES, CA 90045
310-858-6565
Fax: 310-858-1520

info@sportsagentsassociation.com
www.blacksportsagents.com
• Andre Farr, Chairman/CEO
Sports Service Founded:
1996
Member Services:
Develops conferences and workshops to update members on trends in the industry with the objective of providing industry data members on trends in the industry. Organization pursues endorsement trends, careers in sports, economic development and business partnerships, and youth development.
Description:
Organization mission is to develop and strengthen the involvment, credibility the involvement, credibility, representation, image and cohesiveness of African Americans in the Sports Industry.

BLACK WOMEN IN SPORT FOUNDATION
4300 MONUMENT ROAD
PHILADELPHIA, PA 19131
215-877-1925 EXT 320
Fax: 215-877-1942
info@blackwomeninsport.org
www.blackwomeninsport.org
• Paulette Branson, Executive Director
Sports Service Founded:
1992
History
The Black Women in Sport Foundation was founded by Tina Sloan Green, Alpha Alexander, Nikki Franke, and Linda Greene as a nonprofit organization dedicated to increasing the involvement of black women and girls in all aspects of sport, including athletics, coaching and administration. The Foundation is resolute in facilitating the involvement of women of color in every aspect of sport in the United States and around the world, through the hands-on development and management of grass roots level outreach programs.
Description:
Dedicated to facilitating the involvement of Black women in sports in the United States through outreach and grassroots intitiatives.

CANADIAN SOCIETY FOR PSYCHOMOTOR LEARNING & SPORT PSYCHOLOGY
360-125 UNIVERISTY PRIVATE
OTTAWA, ON, CANADA K1N 6N5
gvangyn@uvic.ca
www.scapps.org
• Chris Shields, President
• Tony Carlsen, Secretary/Treasurer
• Melanie Gregg, Secretary Communications
• Kelly Arbour, Director Sports& Exercise Psycology
• Nicola Hodges, Director, Motor Learning & Motor Control
Member Services:
Young Scientist Awards.
Publications:
Journal of Exercise, Movement, and Sport (annual)
Membership Requirements:
Membership fee.
Description:
Founded 1969. Disseminates information in areas of sport psychology and psychomotor learning, primarily through annual conference.

CANADIAN SPORTING GOODS ASSOCIATION
10-225 EAST MALL
UNIT 1272
TORONTO, ON, CANADA M9B 0A9
866-496-6805
info@csga.ca
www.csga.ca
• Julian Savory, President/Chief Operating Officer
• Kelly Falls, Director of Sales & Marketing
• Eric Keeping, Social Media Coordinator
Sports Services Founded:
Incorporated in 1945.
Description:
A professional organization for the Canadian sporting goods industry. It was founded to support and promote the growth of the Canadian sporting goods industry and to serve the interests of its memebers. The objective is to conduct quality trade shows and to provide an Industry forum responsive to the professional needs of its members and to initiate programs designed to stimulate sports activity participation.

CENTER FOR THE STUDY OF SPORT IN SOCIETY
360 HUNTINGTON AVENUE
42 BELVIDERE
BOSTON, MA 2115
617-373-4025
Fax: 617-373-8574
www.sportinsociety.org
• Dan Lebowitz, Executive Director
da.lebowitz@northeastern.edu
• Deb Jencunas, Senior Associate Director
• Lisa Markland, Assistant Director of Training
l.markland@northeastern.edu
• Richard E. Lapchick, Founder/Director Emeritus
(407) 823-4887
Sports Services Founded:
1984
Description:
The Center for the Study of Sport in Society, utilizing the power and appeal of sport; works locally, nationally and globally to identify and address social problems in sport and in society. They conduct research, develop programs that offer solutions, and educate and advocate on the emerging issues.

CHALLENGE ASPEN
PO BOX 6639
SNOWMASS VILLAGE, CO 81615
970-923-0578
Fax: 970-923-7338
info@challengeaspen.org
www.challengeaspen.com
• Jeff Hauser, Chief Executive Officer
(970) 923-0578
Description:
Founded 1995. Challenge Aspen is dedicated to impacting lives by presenting meaningful recreational and cultural experiences to individuals faced with mental or physical challenges. Committed to creating a community of like-minded individuals, fostering confidence and self-esteem among their participants in an effort to advance the quality of life of those with physical and mental disabilities. Their aim is to carefully orchestrate life changing recreational adventures, giving participants the courage to learn something new, trust their own abilities and carry that ideal forward, reaching toward goals in other areas of their lives.

CLUB MANAGERS ASSOCIATION OF AMERICA
1733 KING STREET
ALEXANDRIA, VA 22314
703-739-9500
cmaa@cmaa.org
www.cmaa.org
• Jeff Morgan, Chief Executive Officer
jeff.morgan@cmaa.org
• Margaret Meleney, Chief Financial Officer
margaret.meleney@cmaa.org
Member Services:
Executive career services; managerial openings lists; mid-management job opportunities listing; interim management and consultant service; outplacement service; certification program; continuing education services; group insurance programs; governmental affairs, bookmart and publications.
Membership Requirements:
General Manager, Manager, Assistant Manager, executive of private membership club.
Sports Services Founded:
1927
Description:
CMAA is a professional association for managers of membership clubs, such as country, city, athletic, faculty, yacht, town and military clubs.

COACHING ASSOCIATION OF CANADA
1155 LOLA STREET
SUITE 201
OTTAWA, ON, CANADA K1K 4C1
613-235-5000
Fax: 613-235-9500
coach@coach.ca
www.coach.ca
• Lorraine Lafranià€šre, Chief Executive Officer
(613) 235-5000
llafreniere@coach.ca
Sports Services Founded:
1970
Description:
An amateur sport organization with the mandate to improve the effectiveness of coaching across all levels of the sport system. Also to enhance the experiences of all Canadian athletes through quality coaching.

DESTINATION MARKETING ASSOCIATION INTERNATIONAL
2025 M STREET NW
SUITE 500
WASHINGTON, DC 20036
202-296-7888
Fax: 202-296-7889
info@destinationmarketing.org
www.destinationmarketing.org
• Joseph Marinelli, Chair
mgehrisch@destinationmarketing.org
• Jack Johnson, Chief Advocacy Officer
(202) 835-4217
jjohnson@destinationmarketing.org
Number of members:
4,100 professionals
Member Services:
Data base of meetings, conventions and trade shows.

Description:
Founded 1914 as the International Association of Convention Bureaus. Seeks to foster professionalism and education, to serve as a forum for communication in the industry, advocate on matters of concern to the industry. and encourage recognition and growth of tourism destinations.

DWARF ATHLETIC ASSOCIATION OF AMERICA
300 CENTER DRIVE
SUITE G #150
SUPERIOR, CO 80027
415-915-9572
www.daaa.org
• Lucy Woika, President
(415) 244-9756
• Ted Hannes, Vice President/Fundraising Chair
• Megan Schimmel, Treasurer
• Jeremy Harrison, Sports technical director
jeremy.harrison@daaa.org
Sports Services Founded:
1985
Description:
Formed to develop, promote and provide quality amateur level athletic opportunities for athletes with dwarfism in the United States. The DAAA mission is to encourage people with dwarfism to participate in sports regardless of their level of skills.

EUROPEAN ASSOCIATION FOR SPORT MANAGEMENT, THE
INSTITUTE FOR SPORTS STUDIES
ZERNIKEPLEIN 17
AS GROUNINGEN, HOLLAND 9747
31-612-189505
www.easm.net
• Per-Gâ€ran Fahlstrâ€m, President
• Ruth Crabtree, Vice President
• Gerco Van Dalfsen, Secretary General
• Claas Christian Germelmann, Treasurer
• Bo Carlsson, Scientific Committee
Editors Note:
The phone number listed is from the Portugal office.
Description:
An independent association for individuals or members representing associations, involved or interested in sport management. The association aims to promote, stimulate and encourage studies, research, scholarly writing and professional developments in the field of sport management.

EVENT SERVICE PROFESSIONALS ASSOCIATION
191 CLARKSVILLE ROAD
PRINCETON JUNCTION, NJ 8550
609-799-3712
Fax: 609-799-7032
info@espaonline.org
www.espaonline.org
• Paul Ruby, CMP, President
paul.ruby@sheraton.com
• Lynn McCullough, Executive Director
lmccullough@espaonline.org
• Nicole Lauzon, Membership Coordinator
nlauzon@espaonline.org
• Vikki Hurley-Schubert, Public Relations Manager
Description:
Organization comprised of convention Managers and Directors of Convention Centers, Hotels and Convention Bureaus.

FELLOWSHIP OF CHRISTIAN ATHLETES
8701 LEEDS ROAD
KANSAS CITY, MO 64129
816-921-0909
800-289-0909
Fax: 816-921-8755
fca@fca.org
www.fca.org
• Shane Williams, President/Chief Executive Officer
• Ken Williams, Executive Director - National Support Center
• Dan Britton, Executive Vice President - International Ministry
• Jeff Martin, Executive VP Ministry Programs
Description:
Organization promotes Christian faith through platform of athletics. FCA Huddle groups meet regularly on junior high, senior high and college campuses for Bible study, prayer and other faith-based activities.
Year Founded:
1954
Publications:
FCA In Action magazine

INDUSTRIAL FABRICS ASSOCIATION INTERNATIONAL
1801 COUNTY ROAD B WEST
ROSEVILLE, MN 55113
651-222-2508
800-225-4324
Fax: 651-631-9334
generalinfo@ifai.com
www.ifai.com
• Mary C Hennesy, President and CEO
(651) 255-6986
mjhennessy@ifai.com
• Katie Bradford, MFC, IFM, Chairman
• Steve L. Ellington, 1st Vice President
Member Services:
Provides information for technical, promotional, governmental and marketing assistance to its members.
Publications:
Advanced Textiles Source, online; Marine Fabricator; In Tents; Geosynthetics; Fabric Architecture; InTents, bi-monthly; Specialty Fabrics Review.
Membership Requirements:
Members are firms who manufacture industrial fabric products and firms who supply these manufacturers.
Sports Services Founded:
1912
Description:
Trade association with more than 2,000 member companies that represent the international specialty fabrics marketplace.

INSTITUTE FOR INTERNATIONAL SPORT
UNIVERSITY OF RHODE ISLAND
3045 KINGSTOWN ROAD
PO BOX 1710
KINGSTON, RI 02881-1710
401-874-2375
800-447-9889
Fax: 401-874-2375
info@internationalsport.org
www.internationalsport.org
• Daniel E Doyle, Jr, Founder/Executive Director
Description:
Founded 1986. Administers programs in international sports such as Sportscorps, National Sportsmanship Day, the World Scholar-Athlete Games, and the International Scholar-Athlete Hall of Fame.

INTERNATIONAL ASSOCIATION FOR SPORTS AND LEISURE FACILITIES
EUPEWER STR 70
KOLN, GERMANY 50933
info@iaks.org
• Klaus Meinel, Secretary General
meinel@iaks.org
• Silke Bardenheuer, Director of Operations
bardenheuer@iaks.org
• Thomas Kick, Marketing and Event Management
kick@iaks.org
Sports Services Founded:
1965
Description:
A non profit organization operating in the field of sports and leisure activities. The IAKS's task is to collect, evaluate and disseminiate information on the design, construction, equipping and maintenance of facilities for sport, games and recreation.
Publications:
sb Magazine: architecture of sports and leisure facilites, bi-monthly.

INTERNATIONAL ASSOCIATION FOR SPORTS INFORMATION
UNIVERSITY OF CALGARY LAW LIBRARY
2500 UNIVERSITY DRIVE NW
CALGARY ALBERTA, CANADA T2N 1N4
403-220-6097
gghent@ucalgary.ca
www.iasi.org
• Gretchen Ghent, President
Publications:
Newsletter annually, providing list of information means. Also publishes directory of international sports governing bodies.
Membership Requirements:
Corporate: $75. Personal: $50.
Description:
Founded 1960. A unique international association that brings together a worldwide network of information experts, librarians, sports sceintsis and managers of sport libraries, information and documentation centres. THe primary purpose is to stimulate and support activities in the field of international documentation, and promote the dissemination of information to physical educators, sports scientists, documentalists and sport researchers.

INTERNATIONAL ASSOCIATION OF VENUE MANAGERS/IAVM
635 FRITZ DRIVE
COPPELL, TX 75019-4442
972-906-7441
Fax: 972-906-7418
www.iavm.org
• Brad Mayne, President and CEO
(972) 538-1021
brad.mayne@iavm.org
• Ronald Melton, Chief Financial Officer/Chief Operations Officer
(972) 538-1034
ronald.melton@iavm.org
• Doug Booher, CFE, 1st Vice Chair
Sports Services Founded:
1924
IAVM History Task Force:
The History Task Force is an IAVM committee whose objective is to emphasize the importance of collecting historical materials served in the IAVM archives at the University of Texas- Austin.
IAAM Foundation:
A non-profit educational organization devoted to providing education and information services to the public assembly facility management profession and to exploring issues relevant to the profession.
Description:
Comprises leaders who represent a diverse industry such as entertainment, sports, conventions, trade, hospitality and tourism. These leaders manage, or provide products and services to public assembly facilities like arenas, ampitheaters, auditoriums, convention centers/exhibit halls, performing arts venues, stadiums and university complexes.

INTERNATIONAL LIVE EVENTS ASSOCIATION
330 N. WABASH AVENUE
SUITE 2000
CHICAGO, IL 60611-4267
312-321-6853
800-688-4737
Fax: 317-673-6953
info@ileahub.com
www.ileahub.com
• Christie Pruyn, Executive Director
Member Services:
Awards program; professional accreditation; ISES, bulletin board service; annual Conference for Professional Development.
Membership Requirements:
Pay dues. Be involved directly or indirectly in the special events business.
Description:
Founded 1987. Serves to educate, advance, and promote the creative events industry and its network of professionals along with related industries. Strives to uphold the integrity of the creative events profession to the general public throughout Principles of Professional Conduct and Ethics; acquires and disseminates useful business information; fosters spirit of cooperation among members and other special events professionals; Cultivates high standards of business practices.

KROENKE SPORTS ENTERPRISES
1000 CHOPPER CIRCLE
DENVER, CO 80204
303-405-1100
GuestRelations@pepsicenter.com
www.pepsicenter.com
• E Stanley Kroenke, Owner/Govenor
• Mark Waggoner, Sr VP Finance
Nature of Sports Service:
Organization owns NHL's Colorado Avalanche, NBA'S Denver Nuggets, NLL's Colorado Mammoth, AFL's Colorado Rapids.

LA84 FOUNDATION
2141 WEST ADAMS BOULEVARD
LOS ANGELES, CA 90018
323-730-4600
Fax: 323-730-9637
info@la84.org
la84.org
• Renata Simril, President/CEO
• Frank M. Sanchez, Chairman
• Wayne Wilson, VP Education Services
• Anna-Marie Jones, VP Grants/Programs

Description:
The Foundation was established to manage Southern California's share of the surplus from the highly successful 1984 Olympic Games in Los Angeles. The Foundation received $93 million at its inception. Since it began operations in 1985, it has invested more than $200 million in sports programs serving more than two and a half million youth in the eight Southern California counties of Los Angeles, Imperial, Orange, Riverside, San Bernardino, San Diego, Santa Barbara and Ventura. Its headquarters is located in the historic Britt House near downtown Los Angeles where it houses the world's premier sports library and meeting facilities. The Foundati

LICENSING INDUSTRY MERCHANDISERS' ASSOCIATION/LIMA
350 FIFTH AVENUE
SUITE 4019
NEW YORK, NY 10118
212-244-1944 EXT 113
info@licensing.org
www.licensing.org
• Charles Riotto, President
(212) 244-1944
info@licensing.org
• Maura Regan, Executive Vice President
(212) 244-1944
mregan@licensing.org
Description:
Founded 1985. Devoted to promoting professionalism in licensing through seminars, exhibits, research, regional and International meetings and publishing.
Membership Requirements:
Four categories of membership: manufacturers, licensers, support groups, retailers. Annual dues for calendar year.
Member Services:
Reference library, seminars; insurance; discount programs; mail rosters, Directories, sample agreements, annual survey on the size of the Licensing Industry.

MACCABI USA/SPORTS FOR ISRAEL
1511 WALNUT STREET
SUITE 401
PHILADELPHIA, PA 19102
215-561-6900
Fax: 215-561-5470
maccabi@maccabiusa.com
www.maccabiusa.com
• Robert Spivak, Chairman
• Sara Feinstein, Marketing Director
sfeinstein@maccabiusa.com
• Julie Churylo, Office Manager
jchurylo@maccabiusa.com
Sports Services Founded:
1948
Description:
The volunteer organization seeks to enrich the lives of Jewish youth in the United States, Israel and the Dispora through athletic, cultural and educational programs. We develop, promote and support international, national and regional athletic based activities and facilities.

MACCABI WORLD UNION
KFAR HAMACCABIAH
RAMAT GAN, Israel 52105
www.maccabi.org
• Eyal Tiberger, Executive Director
eyalt@maccabi.org

• Tzachi Eshkenazi, Controller
tzachi@maccabi.org
• Ilana Ben Namer Kevehazi, Assistnat to the ED
ilana@maccabi.org
Description:
A global Jewish organization spanning five continents and more than 50 countries, with clubs serving as community centers, providing a diversity of educational, cultural, social and sports activities. The Maccabi World Union comprises of six confederations. They are: Maccabi Israel, European Maccabi confederation, confederation Maccabi North America, confederation Maccabi Latin America, Maccabi South Africa and Maccabi Australia.
Membership:
400,000

MIDWESTERN REPRESENTATIVES ASSOCIATION
9450 TREETOP DRIVE
GALESBURG, MI 49053
269-200-3322
MRA@midwestreps.org
www.midwestreps.org
• Bonnie Rathbun, Executive Director
• Tim Simonson, President
Number of members:
115+
Publications:
Newsletter, quarterly; Store Directory, annually; Buyers Guide, annually.
Membership Requirements:
Open to manufacturers representatives who have been in the region for at least one year and/or upon approval of application by membership committee. Initiation fee and annual dues required.
Sports Services Founded:
1965
Description:
A Snow/Outdoor Sports organization representing states from as far east as New York and as far west as Minnesota. The members of the MRA represent products such as ski/snowboard equipment and apparel, outdoor camping/climbing and water sports products. MRA members serve retailers from Illinois, Wisconsin, Indiana, lower/upper Michigan, Ohio and Kentucky

NATIONAL ALLIANCE OF AFRICAN AMERICAN ATHLETES
PO BOX 60743
HARRISBURG, PA 17106-0743
717-312-8162
Fax: 717-260-3877
info@naaaa.com
www.naaaa.com
• J. Everette Pearsall, Executive Director
everette@naaaa.com
• Kevin Clark, Chair
kevin@naaaa.com
Sports Services Founded:
1989
Description:
The goal is to empower young African American males through athletics, education and public programs.

NATIONAL ASSOCIATION FOR GIRLS AND WOMEN IN SPORT
1900 ASSOCIATION DRIVE
RESTON, VA 20191-1599

703-476-3453
800-213-7193
Fax: 703-476-4566
www.aahperd.org/nagwa
• Lynda Randsell, President
• Karen Appleby, VP Marketing
• Charity Bryan, VP Research
Number of members:
4,000
Member Services:
Annual convention; leadership clinics; newsletters; informationpackets, and educational programs.
Publications:
Catalog of publications.
Description:
Founded 1899. Nonprofit, educational organization designed to serve the needs of administrators, teachers, coaches, leaders, and participants of sports programs for girls and women. Its goals include: (1) recruiting, developing, and promoting women for leadership programs, (2) serving as an advocate and promoting women's full participation in physical activity and sport leadership, (3) serving as an advocate for the initiation and enhancement of quality programs of sport and physical activity designed to accommodate females of all ages, races, creeds, ethnic origins, economic levels, abilities, and interests, and (4) promulgating the professi

NATIONAL ASSOCIATION OF POLICE ATHLETIC/ACTIVITES LEAGUES (NATL PAL)
1662 N US HIGHWAY 1
SUITE C
JUPITER, FL 33469
561-745-5535
Fax: 561-745-3147
www.nationalpal.org
• Mike Dillhyon, Executive Director
mdillhyon@nationalpal.org
• Christopher Hill, President
Sports Services Founded:
1914
Description:
As a membership organization, National PAL provides Chapters with resources and opportunities to grow their own programs and enhance the quality of individual programming. These resources include funding opportunities through various grants, general liability protection programs, programming opportunities through affiliate organizations, and goods and services provided by corporate partners and supporting organizations. In addition, National PAL provides Chapter members opportunities to bring their young athletes together to compete in a championship environment in several sports.
Member Services:
Training seminars, produces public service announcements, accident and liability insurance, group purchasing programs, fund-raising programs. Sponsors competition on national level for many sports.
Number of members:
360 (chapters).

NATIONAL ASSOCIATION OF SPORTS OFFICIALS
2017 LATHROP AVENUE
RACINE, WI 53405

262-632-5448
Fax: 262-632-5460
www.naso.org
• Barry Mano, President
• Bill Carollo, Treasurer
Sports Services Founded:
1980
Membership Requirements:
Regular - sports officials; sponsorship - companies; associate - anyone with an interest in sports. Fees are: $94 United States citizens; $121 Canada/Mexico; and $153 for any other.
Description:
The only national organization solely dedicated to officiating with membership at all levels of sport. From the National Football League to Pop Warner, from Major League Baseball to Little League of America, from the National Basketball Association to youth and recreational programs across America, NASO is there.
Publications:
REFEREE Magazine, monthly; IT'S OFFICIAL, monthly newsletter. Manuals. Cyberspace - The NASO Locker room.
Member Services:
Cassettes, videos and books; travel; discounts; $3 million liability insurance protection. Public service ads.
Number of members:
16,000

NATIONAL ASSOCIATION OF UNDERWATER INSTRUCTORS
9030 CAMDEN FIELD PKWY
RIVERVIEW, FL 33578
813-628-6284
800-553-6284
Fax: 813-628-8253
nauihq@naui.org
www.naui.org
• Jim Bram, President
• Jed Livingstone, VP Training & Development
• James R Yaufman II, Chief Information Officer
• Kathy Brownlow, Manager of Operations
• Randy Shaw, Manager Training Department
Member Services:
Certification, educational support material, instructor/training courses, leadership training courses, international conference on underwater education, retail store support program.
Publications:
SOURCES, THE JOURNAL OF; UNDERWATER EDUCATION, quarterly.
Membership Requirements:
Must be certified NAUI scuba instructor, pass the applicable leadership exam by 75% score or better, meet all course administrative requirements, CPR and First Aid sertified, meet all course prerequisites, and complete all portions of the course.
Description:
Founded 1959. Works to promote certification of scuba diving instructors and provides certification credentials to qualified NAUI scuba divers.

NATIONAL CLUB ASSOCIATION
1201 15TH STREET NW
SUITE 450
WASHINGTON, DC 20005

202-822-9822
800-625-6221
Fax: 202-822-9808
info@nationalclub.org
www.nationalclub.org
• Susanne R. Wegrzyn, President & Chief Executive Officer
• Thomas Gaston, Vice Chairman
• Samuel P. Bell, Treasurer
• Kirk O. Reese, Secretary
• Thomas E Gaston Jr. CCM, Chairman
Description:
Since 1961, The National Club Association (NCA) has served as the primary advocate for private clubs, representing their business, legal and legislative interests, while providing a wealth of invaluable resources to address educational needs of clubs related to operations, model club practices and effective leadership.
Membership Requirements:
Regular membership limited to private social, athletic and recreational membership clubs or organizations.
Publications:
CLUB DIRECTOR, quarterly magazine; NCAConnect, monthly newsletter; The National Club Association Smartbrief, weekly news digest; Washington Weekly Update, weekly newsletter.
Number of members:
7,000

NATIONAL CONGRESS OF STATE GAMES
1631 MESA AVENUE
SUITE E
COLORADO SPRINGS, CO 80906
719-634-7333
Fax: 719-634-5198
www.stategames.org
• Marc Riker, Board President
• Kevin Cummings, Vice President
Sports Services Founded:
1986
Membership Requirements:
To conduct or develop a Summer or Winter state game in your state join the National Congress of State Games yearly. NCSG has a yearly symposium and 2 board meetings a year.
Publications:
State of the Games Newsletter, quarterly.
Description:
A membership organization that has 37 Summer State Games and 14 Winter State Games organization and a community based membership of the United States Olympic Committee.

NATIONAL FEDERATION OF PROFESSIONAL TRAINERS
PO BOX 4579
LAFAYETTE, IN 479053
800-729-6378
Fax: 765-471-7369
info@nfpt.com
www.nfpt.com
• Ron Clark, CEO and Founder
• Angie Pattengale, Director of Certification
• Ryan Farrell, Marketing Coordinator
• April Pattee, Director of Customer Service
• Jason Pattee, Distribution Manager
• Charles DeFrancesco, Director of Continuing Education
Description:
Personal fitness trainer certification,

credibility and support. Internationally recognized Personal Fitness Trainer Certification. Over 200 professional examination sites around the world. Professional support magazine
Publications:
OnFitness Magazine, quarterly publication that circulates to over 75,000 people.
Member Services:
Personal fitness trainer certification.
Membership Requirements:
No formal education pre-requisites.

NATIONAL GYM ASSOCIATION INC./NGA, THE
PO BOX 970579
COCONUT CREEK, FL 33097
954-344-8410
Fax: 954-344-8412
info@nationalgym.com
www.nationalgym.com
• Richard Yaldizian, Medical Director
• Caryn Nistico, Nutrician Director
Description:
Provides the public and Fitness Professionals with the most advanced update fitness training program and principals in the industry. These fitness principals are our guiding light, which provides you with the best in personal fitness training certification, heatlh, nutrition, continuing education programs, along with being one of the only natural bodybuilding organizations.

NATIONAL INTRAMURAL RECREATIONAL SPORTS ASSOCIATION/NIRSA
4185 SW RESEARCH WAY
CORVALLIS, OR 97333-1067
541-766-8211
Fax: 541-766-8284
nirsa@nirsa.org
www.nirsa.org
• Pat Watts, Interim Executive Director
(541) 766-8211
• Cheri Christenson, Director of Professional Development
(541) 766-8211
Description:
Founded 1950. Offers the recreational sports administrator a variety of resources through individuals and information resource centers to understand all aspects of recreational sports programming.
Membership Requirements:
Institutional - College/University, Military or park/recreation departments; Professional - must be associated with administration of recreational sports programming field. Student - graduate/undergraduate in sport management field. Associate business with an active interest and market segment applicable to recreational sports.
Publications:
Recreational Sports Directory, published annual; Recreational Sports Journal; NIRSA Know Newsletter

NATIONAL RECREATION & PARK ASSOCIATION
22377 BELMONT RIDGE ROAD
ASHBURN, VA 20148
703-858-0784
800-626-6772
Fax: 703-858-0794

info@nrpa.org
www.nrpa.org
• Barbara Tulipane, President and CEO
• M. Lauren Yost, VP Operations
• Ted Mattingly, Director of Facilities and Admin
Description:
Founded 1965. Promotes the value of recreation and parks in the lives of individuals. Advocates the development and improvement of parks and recreational areas. Advances and improves recreation and park leadership. Educates the public on recreation and park matters beneficial to the communities and to the nation, thereby improving social, moral and industrial conditions.
Membership Requirements:
Annual dues for agencies - based on population of each jurisdiction; annual dues for individuals, based on salary.
Publications:
P&R Magazine; NRPA Cybrary; Journal of Leisure Research; Journal of Park & Recreation Administration; Schole; Therapeutic Recreation Journal; LRS Abstracts
Number of members:
19,000

NATIONAL SENIOR GAMES ASSOCIATION
PO BOX 82059
BATON ROUGE, LA 70884
225-766-6800
nsga@nsga.com
www.nsga.com
• Marc T. Riker, CEO
• Becky Wesley, Vice President of Association Relations
• Collen Keith, Senior Director of Business Affairs
• Jay B. Hall, Senior Director of Business Affairs
• Stephen Rodriguez, Chairman
• Kate Amack, Vice Chair
• Monica Paul, Treasurer
Description:
The National Senior Games Association (NSGA) is a not-for-profit organization founded in 1987 that is dedicated to promoting health and wellness for adults 50 and over through education, fitness and sport. The Organization governs the National Senior Games, the largest multi-sport championship in the world for seniors, and other national senior athletic events. NSGA is an umbrella for 54 Member State Organizations across the United States, Canada, and Mexico that host Senior Games or Senior Olympics.

NATIONAL SPORTS FOUNDATION/NATIONAL SPORTS MUSEUM
415 BARLOW COURT
JOHNS CREEK, GA 30022-6636
678-417-0041
Fax: 678-417-0043
www.natlsportsfoundation.com
• Ed Harris, President/Executive Director (678) 417-0041
Description:
Founded 1993 with the mission of preserving America's sports heritage. Enhances and supports amateur and professional sports organizations in America, annually honors athletes and

sports journalists for lifetime achievement; maintains National Sports Library and produces educational programs and exhibitions.
Publications:
Legend - Quarterly magazine

NATIONAL SPORTS MARKETING NETWORK (NSMN)
212-227-1300
www.sportsmarketingnetwork.com
• Jennifer L Karpf, Executive Director jenkarpf@sportsmarketingnetwork.com
Description:
The National Sports Marketing Network (NSMN) is a sports business industry trade organization. Founded in 1998, NSMN includes more than 13,000 individual and corporate members with chapters in major markets and members in more than 50 U.S. cities. The national organization is dedicated to the advancement of the sports business industry through networking and the production of issue-oriented seminars created to raise the level of discourse on critical sports industry issues. NSMN offers customized, member-to-member introductions; industry-wide discounts on trade publications and conferences; and career development services. NSMN is board-gover
Services:
Career development assistance; industry job board; member-to-member introductions and networking; and more
Membership:
Individual Membership: $125 per person/year
Individual Plus Membership: $175 per person/year
Corporate Membership: $600 per company/year
Corporate Plus Membership: $1,700 per company/year
Patron Membership: $3,500 per company/year
Patron Plus Membership: $5,000 per company/year
Student Membership: $50 per full-time student/year
Number of Members:
13,000+

NORTH AMERICAN SOCIETY FOR SPORT MANAGEMENT
C/O DR. ROBIN AMMON JR.
NASSM BUSINESS OFFICE
135 WINTERWOOD DR
BUTLER, PA 16001
724-482-6277
businessoffice@nassm.com
www.nassm.com
• Robin Ammon, President (724) 482-6277
• Robert Ammon, NASSM Business Office Manager
Nature of Sports Service:
Serves to promote, stimulate and encourage study, research, scholarly writing and professional development in the area of sport management. Members are concerned about theoretical and applied aspects of management theory and practice specifically related to sport, exercise, dance and play throughout all sectors of the population.
Publications:

JOURNAL OF SPORT MANAGEMENT, four times annually.

NORTH AMERICAN SOCIETY FOR THE SOCIOLOGY OF SPORT
BOWLING GREEN UNIVERSITY
BOWLING GREEN, OH 43403
419-372-2217
Fax: 419-372-8306
lv3@umail.umd.edu
www.nasss.org
• Genevieve Rail, President
• Brenda Riemem, Treasurer
Publications:
NASSS NEWSLETTER, quarterly; SPORT SOCIOLOGY JOURNAL, quarterly.
Membership Requirements:
Pay membership dues.
Description:
Founded 1977. Provides forum for communication and exchange of ideas and research and generally promotes benefits of study of sociology as it relates to sport in the U.S., and throughout the world.

NORTH AMERICAN SPORTS FEDERATION
1081 PEBBLE COURT
MECHANICSBURG, PA 17050
717-737-5800
Fax: 717-737-5800
joanna@specialmarkets.com
www.nasf.net
• Andy Loechner, President aloechner@verizon.net
Description:
Governing body for amateur sports for adults and youth in the sports of softball, volleyball, flag and touch football, soccer, basketball and baseball, body building, and iron sports.

NORTH COUNTRY TRAIL ASSOCIATION
229 EAST MAIN STREET
LOWELL, MI 49331
616-897-5987
866-445-3628
HQ@northcountrytrail.org
www.northcountrytrail.org
Sports Services Founded:
1981
Description:
Develops, maintains, preserves and promotes the North Country National Scenic Trail through a national network of volunteers, chapters, partner organizations and governmental agencies.

ORCA BAY SPORTS & ENTERTAINMENT
800 GRIFFITH WAY
VANCOUVER, BC, CANADA V6B 6G1
604-899-7400
888-GO-CANUKS
Fax: 604-899-7401
www.canucks.com
• John E. McCaw, Jr., Chairman/Governor, NHL
• Victor De Bonis, COO
• Harvey Jones, VP/Genral Manager
• Mike P. Gills, President/General Manager Canucks
Nature of Sports Service:
Parent company of the Vancouver Canucks (NHL) and General Motors Place.

OUTDOOR INDUSTRY ASSOCIATION
4909 PEARL EAST CIRCLE
SUITE 300
BOULDER, CO 80301
303-444-3353
Fax: 303-444-3284
info@outdoorindustry.org
www.outdoorindustry.org
• Frank Hugelmeyer, President
(303) 327-3507
fhugelmeyer@outdoorindustry.org
• Lori Herrera, Executive Vice
President/COO
(303) 327-3521
lherrera@outdoorindustry.org
Number of Members:
1,200.
Sports Services Founded:
1989
Description:
Provides trade services for over 4,000
manufacturers, distributors, suppliers, sales
representatives and retailers in the Outdoor
Industry. Members include brands like Black
Diamond, Columbia Sportswear, Eagle
Creek, JanSport, Johnson Outdoors, Kelty,
Malden Mills, Merrell, Mountain Hardwear,
Patagonia, Timberland, The North Face,
Perception, Pearl Izumi, Salomon, Swiss
Army Brands, W.L. Gore, Yakima, and
numerous others.

PALACE SPORTS & ENTERTAINMENT, INC.
5 CHAMPIONSHIP DRIVE
AUBURN HILLS, MI 48326
248-377-0100
Fax: 248-377-2154
www.palacenet.com
• Tom Gore, Owner
• Dennis Mannion, President
• Jeffrey Ajluni, Vice President
Description:
Owns and operates the NBA's Detroit
Pistons, the WNBA's Detroit Shock, and the
NHL's Tampa Bay Lightning.

PRO ATHLETES OUTREACH
PO BOX 801
PALO ALTO, CA 94302
650-206-2962
Fax: 650-206-2959
office@pao.org
www.pao.org
• Norm Evans, CEO
• Steve Stenstrom, President
• Mike Outlaw, Managing Director
Member Services:
Four annual Christian leadership training
conferences, information available on
request.
Publications:
Changing Athletes & Coaches From The
Inside Out, quarterly
Sports Services Founded:
1971
Description:
A leadership and life skills development
organization committed solely to meeting
the unique needs of pro athletes, coaches
and their families. Also has helped
thousands of active and retired athletes and
their spouses find lasting solutions for hte
intense pressures of a career in professional
sports.

PROFESSIONAL PADDLESPORTS ASSOCIATION
7432 ALBAN STATION BLVD
STE B-232
SPRINGFIELD, VA 22150
703-451-3864
www.propaddle.com

SCHOOL SPORT FEDERATION, INTERNATIONAL
59 RUE ARCHIMEDE
BRUSSELS, BELGIUM 1000
www.isfsports.org
• Laurent Petrynka, President
• Hrvoje Custonja, CEO & Secretary
General
Description:
Founded: 1965. International governing
body for school sports.

SHAPE AMERICA SOCIETY OF HEALTH AND PHYSICAL EDUCATORS
1900 ASSOCIATION DRIVE
RESTON, VA 20191-1598
703-476-3400
800-213-7193
Fax: 703-476-9527
www.shapeamerica.org
• Dolly Lambdin, President
• Gale Wiedow, Past President
• E. Paul Roetert, CEO
Publications:
Journal of Physical education, Recreation &
Dance (JOPERD); Research Quarterly for
Exercise & Sport (RQES); STRATEGIES;
Women in Sport & Physical Activity Journal;
International Journal of Health Education;
The Pulse Online Newsletter; American
Journal of Health Education; UPDATE
Description:
Founded 1938. Promotes school,
community and national programs of leisure
services and recreation education.

SPORTING GOODS AGENTS ASSOCIATION
1601 FREEHANVILLE DRIVE
SUITE 300
MOUNT PROSPECT, IL 60056
800-815-5422
Fax: 847-391-9627
www.nsga.org
• Jeff Brusati, Director
• Matt Carlson, President & CEO
Number of members:
1,300
Member Services:
Procurement of product lines for members
through manufacturers using the Direct Mail
service. Placement service for people
seeking sales jobs with established rep
agencies. Brochures aimed at start-up
manufactures as well as the role of agents
within the industry.
Publications:
Membership Roster and diskette, at cost of
$275. Q&A Booklet for agents and
manufacturers ($10)
Membership Requirements:
One year as an agent in the sporting goods
field, with two or more established lines.
Description:
Founded 1934. Keeps members informed of
industry functions and pertinent legislation

SPORTING GOODS MANUFACTURERS ASSOCIATION
8505 FENTON STREET
SUITE 211
SILVER SPRINGS, MD 20910
301-495-6321
Fax: 307-495-6322
info@sgma.com
• Tom Cove, President/CEO
(301) 495-6321
• Chip Baldwin, CFO
• Ron Rosenbaum, SVP of Marketing &
Business Management
• Bill Sells, VP Of Government Relations
• Jan Ciambor, Office Manager
• V J Mayor, Director, Marketing &
Communications
• Mike May, Director of Communications &
DTMBA
(561) 784-7325
Sports Services Founded:
1906
Description:
Our purpose is to support our member
companies and promote healthy
environment for the sporting goods industry
by providing access to insight, information,
influence and industry connections. SGMA
also enhances industry vitality and fosters,
sports, fitness and active lifestyle
participation.

SPORTS LAW PROGRAM AND NATIONAL SPORTS LAW INSTITUTE
ECKSTEIN HALL, ROOM 138A
1215 WEST MICHIGAN STREET
MILWAUKEE, WI 53233
414-288-5815
Fax: 414-288-5818
munsli@mu.edu
law.marquette.edu/national-sports-law-instit
ute/welcome
• Paul Anderson, Professor & Director
(414) 288-5816
paul.anderson@mu.edu
• Matt Mitten, Professor & Executive
Director
(414) 288-7494
Description:
Supports Sports Law Program training law
students at Marquette University Law
School. Annual Conferences and Seminars;
Internships and Externships for Marquette
Law Students
Founded:
1989
Publications:
Marquette Sports Law Review; Sports
Facility Reports; Recent Developments in
Sports Law
Member Services:
Conferences, CLE Programs.
Membership Requirements:
Students $50 annual; Gold $120 annual;
Blue $50 annual

SPORTS LAWYERS ASSOCIATION
12100 SUNSET HILLS ROAD
SUITE 130
RESTON, VA 20190
703-437-4377
Fax: 703-435-4390
www.sportslaw.org
• Anthony J Agnone, President
• Peter Roisman, Secretary
• Ash Narayan, Treasurer

Number of members:
1100
Member Services:
Yearly national law conference, annual membership directory, annual journal and special offers from Sports Business Daily and Sports Business Journal.
Publications:
The Sports Lawyer, electronic newsletter; The Sports Lawyers Journal, annual law journal.
Membership Requirements:
Regular - licensed attorneys; Associates - professional with interest in sports law; law educator - full/part time at accredited college of law. Student - full-time law student enrolled at an accredited school of law.
Description:
Founded 1976. Provides educational opportunities in the areas of sports law; provides a forum for sports law professionals to exchange a variety of perspectives and positions; promotes and, where necessary, establishes rules of ethics for its members.

SPORTS TURF MANAGERS ASSOCIATION
805 NEW HAMPSHIRE
SUITE E
LAWRENCE, KS 66044-6875
800-323-3875
Fax: 785-843-2977
www.stma.org
• James Michael Goatley, PhD, President
• Kim Heck, CEO
(800) 323-3875
kheck@stma.org
Number of Members:
2,500 National, 30 Chapters
Publications:
SportsTurf Magazine is the official publication; STMA website; ATMA Membership Roster; STMA E-Digest
Member Services:
Members Only Website section, Job Openings Contact Turf Information Files, Networking Annual Conference & Exhibition, Discount on books & clothing.
Membership Requirements:
Be in the sports turf industry and pay dues.

SPORTSACCORD
4 BD.JU JARDIN EXOTIQUE
MONACO, MONACO 98000
www.agfisonline.com
• Hein Verbruggen, President
• Tamas Ajan, VP
Membership Requirements:
Must be an International Sports Federation. Includes 99 members.
Description:
Founded 1967. GAISF is an association of International Sports Federations and other international organizations which contributes to the development of sport on an educational, scientific and technical level, and whose aim is to serve as a working tool and a center of cooperation, coordination and exchange of information.
Member Services:
Online calandar and directory. Annual convention held as a forum for exchange of ideas and discussion of common problems in sport.
Publications:
AGFIS/GAISF Magazine.

SPORTSPLEX OPERATORS AND DEVELOPERS ASSOCIATION/SODA
NEW YORK REGIONAL OFFICE
PO BOX 24263
WESTGATE STATION
ROCHESTER, NY 14624-0263
525-426-2215
Fax: 525-247-3112
info@SportsplexOperators.com
www.sportsplexoperators.com
• Diane Aselin, EVP
• Kelly Tharp, Secretary
• Norm Rice, Treasurer
• Don Aselin, Executive Director
• John Fitzgerald, President
Description:
Founded 1981. Provides sports complex operators and developers with educational programs and benefits which will make them successful.
Membership Requirements:
Sustained Membership - $995; Professional Membership - $295; Associate Membership - $295; Social Member - $125; Affiliate Member - $100.
Publications:
SODA SITE, bimonthly newsletter.

SSLASPA DBA SPORT & RECREATION LAW ASSOCIATION
C/O MARY MYERS
1608 N REDBARN
1845 Fairmont
Wichita, KS 67212-5855
316-978-3340
Fax: 316-978-5451
lori.miller@wichita.edu
• Colleen McGlone, President
• Mary Myers, Assistant Executive Director
Number of members:
183
Publications:
JOURNAL OF LEGAL ASPECTS OF SPORT, tri-annually; SSLASPA Newsletter, 2-3 times a year.
Description:
Founded 1990. Serves to further the study and dissemination of information regarding legal aspects of sport and physical activity. Addresses legal aspects of sport and physical activity within both public and private sectors. Objectives: (1) to serve as a medium for academic growth, (2) to provide service functions for members, (3) to assist in the development of curricula content, and (4) to cooperate closely with allied national and international organizations in related areas.

STADIUM MANAGERS ASSOCIATION
525 SW 5TH STREET
SUITE A
DES MOINES, IA 50309-4501
515-282-8192
Fax: 515-282-9117
sma@assoc-mgmt.com
www.stadiummanagers.org
• David Scott, President
• Mark Burk, Vice President
• Mike Grindle, Corporate Director
Publications:
Membership Directory.
Sports Services Founded:
1974.
Description:
Promotes the professional, efficient and state of the art management of stadiums around the world. Our members are administrators, operators, and marketing personnel from teams, government entities, colleges and universities, and suppliers to the industry.

UNDERWATER SOCIETY OF AMERICA
53 C APPIAN WAY
SOUTH SAN FRANCISCO, CA 94080
650-583-8492
408-286-8840
Fax: 408-294-3496
usafin@aol.com
www.underwater-society.org
• Carol Rose, President
croseusoa@aol.com
• Michael Gower, Secretary
usafin@aol.com
Number of members:
1,500
Member Services:
Life insurance; educational services.
Publications:
VISIBILITY, quarterly newsletter; HOW-TO MANUAL ON HOW TO FORM A DIVE CLUB; Underwater Hockey Referee Manual and Rule Books-free
Membership Requirements:
Active skin or scuba diver, payment of $20 annual dues.
Description:
Founded 1959. Works to make diving safer; active in areas of underwater sports, marine ecology, legislation, catch records.

UNGERBOECK SYSTEMS, INC.
100 UNGERBOEK PARK
O'FALLON, MO 63368-8694
636-300-5606
800-400-4052
Fax: 636-300-5607
marketing@ungerboeck.com
www.ungerboeck.com
• Dieter K K Ungerboeck, President
dieteru@ungerboeck.com
• Doug Archibald, COO
• Ryan Ungerboeck, Treasurer & Lead Developer, Financials
• Chris Bell, Vice President, Software Engineering
• Bruce Higgins, Vice President, Sales - The Americas
• Matt Harris, Vice President - Global Marketing
• Krister D Ungerboeck, Executive Vice President
kristeru@ungerboeck.com
• Krister Underboeck, CEO
Description:
Organization's Event Business Management System (EBMS) is designed to serve the needs of all sectors of the events industries. Exhibition and conference organizers, venues, event contractors and destination managers. Indeed, many of the leading participants operate with EBMS and give us a wealth of ideas for ongoing advancements, particularly regarding the electronic data interchange among each other.

UNITED STATES CORPORATE ATHLETICS ASSOCIATION
PO BOX 208
WEST SIMSBURY, CT 06092-0208

860-651-9453
Fax: 860-226-5670
www.uscaa.org
• Kevin Holtzclaw, President
• Lou Putnam, Vice President
• Sandra Berkner, Treasurer
sandra.berkner@cigna.com
• Cindy Richardson, Secretary
Sports Service Founded:
1985
Description:
A nationwide non profit organization that promotes health and fitness among corporate employees by sponsoring corporate athletic events.

UNITED STATES OLYMPIC EDUCATION CENTER
C/O NORTHERN MICHIGAN UNIVERSITY
SUPERIOR DOME
MARQUETTE, MI 49855
906-227-2888
Fax: 906-227-2848
usoec@nmu.edu
nmu.edu
• Brian Gaudreau, Interim Director
(906) 227-2888
bgaudrea@nmu.edu
• Michael Fields, Assistant Director
(906) 227-2896
mfields@nmu.edu
• Michael Kaurala, Operations Manager
(906) 227-2888
mkaurala@nmu.edu
Description:
Founded 1985. Provides a training and education environment for aspiring Olympic athletes.

UNITED STATES SPECIALTY SPORTS ASSOCATION
611 LINE DRIVE
KISSIMMEE, FL 34744
321-697-3636
Fax: 321-697-3647
www.usssa.com
• Beth Torina, Head Coach

WATER SPORTS INDUSTRY ASSOCIATION
PO BOX 568512
ORLANDO, FL 32856-8512
407-251-9039
Fax: 407-251-9039
www.watersportsindustry.com
• Larry Meddock, Executive Director
Description:
Founded 1978. Purpose is to expand interest and participation in water sports.
Number of members:
200

WESTERN WINTER SPORTS REPRESENTATIVES ASSOCIATION
726 TENACITY DR.
UNIT B
LONGMONT, CO 80504
305-532-4002
Fax: 866-929-4572
info@wwsra.com
www.wwsra.com
• Carri Garrison, Association Director
ext 1
• Rachael Mahoney, Territory Manager
ext 3
Number of members:
1,000+

Membership Requirements:
Must reside in the western U.S. and actively travel a territory in a sales capacity in the winter sports business. Trade shows not open to the public.
Sports Services Founded:
1949
Description:
Trade association for the purpose of sponsoring regional trade events for winter sports sales reps. Also to produce timely, cost effective regional events that benefit the membership, and to encourage growth and stability in the Winter and Active Sports Industry through service to membership.

WOMEN'S SPORTS FOUNDATION
1899 HEMPSTEAD TURNPIKE
SUITE 400
EAST MEADOW, NY 11554
516-542-4700
800-227-3988
Fax: 516-542-0095
info@womenssportsfoundation.org
www.womenssportsfoundation.org
• Kathryn Olson, CEO
• Laila Ali, President
• Lisa Cregan, Vice President, Treasurer
Description:
Founded 1974, the Women's Sports FOundation is a national charitable education organization. Mission is to advance the lives of girls and women through sports and physical activity.
Membership Requirements:
Donor membership $30 or more.
Publications:
WOMEN'S SPORTS EXPERIENCE, newsletter 4 times annually; SPORTSTALK, newsletter 4 times annually.
Member Services:
Resource Center, a clearinghouse for information on women's sports; Toll-free (800 227-3988) for information on women's sports; speakers bureau; library; Sportswoman of the Year awards; media awards; internships; Women's Sports Hall of Fame; films; lists; travel and training grants; leadership development grants.
Number of members:
10,000

WORLD FEDERATION OF THE SPORTING GOODS INDUSTRY
OBERE ZOLLGASSE 75
PO BOX 1664
3072 OSTERMUNDIGEN/BERN
BERN,
info@wfsgi.org
www.wfsgi.org
• Motoi Oyama, President
• Tom Cove, Vice President, USA
Publications:
International Handbook for the Sporting Goods Industry, annual; WFSGI NEWS ALERT, weekly.
Membership Requirements:
Regular Members: Must be a national organization representing sports equipment manufacturers only. SGMA (North Palm Beach) is the official U.S. delegate and founding member. Member organizations include Argentina, Australia, Austria, Brazil, Canada, Finland, France, Germany, Great Britain, Greece, Italy, Japan, Korea, Malaysia, Netherlands, Pakistan, Spain, Sweden, Switzerland, Taiwan, USA. Also

has sustaining and associate memberships.
Description:
The World Federation of the Sporting Goods Industry (WFSGI) is the world authoritative body for the sports industry officially recognized by the IOC as the industry representative within the Olympic family. WFSGI is an independent association with no objective of economic character for its own gains and formed by sports brands, manufacturers, suppliers, retailers, national federations and all sporting goods industry related businesses.

WORLD T.E.A.M. SPORTS
4250 VETERANS MEMORIAL HIGHWAY
SUITE 420E
HOLBROOK, NY 11741-4020
855-987-8326
Fax: 855-288-3377
info@worldteamsports.org
www.worldteamsports.org
• Van Brinson, President & CEO
vanbrinson@worldteamsports.org
• Richard Rhinehart, Director of Communications
richardrhinehart@worldteamsports.org
Description:
Founded 1993. World T.E.A.M. Sports changes lives through sports. For more than 20 years, we have used athletics to challenge disabled men, women and children to accomplish goals they never thought possible. In all our events - whether mountain climbing, biking, white water rafting or many other sports - we include both disabled and able-bodied participants.
Publications:
Newsletter.

Sports Commissions/Convention Visitors Bureau

AKRON SUMMIT CONVENTION & VISITORS BUREAU
77 EAST MILL ST
AKRON, OH 44308-1401
330-374-7560
800-245-4254
Fax: 330-374-7626
www.visitakron-summit.org
• Gregg Mervis, VP/COO
• James E Mahon, II, Director Marketing/Communications

ALABAMA GULF COAST CONVENTION & VISITORS BUREAU
3150 GULF SHORES PARKWAY
GULF SHORES, AL 36542
251-968-7511
800-745-7263
info@gulfshores.com
www.gulfshores.com
• Beth Gendler, VP Sales
• Mary Statkewicz, Sales Manager
Description:
Founded in 1993 and the primary responsibility is to market the Alabama Gulf Coast as a premier year-round destination.

ALABAMA SPORTS FOUNDATION
100 GRANDVIEW PLACE
SUITE 110
BIRMINGHAM, AL 35243
205-967-4745
Fax: 205-967-9940
www.brunoeventteam.com
• Gene Hallman, President/CEO
(205) 967-4745
• John Bochnak, Senior VP, Finance & Administration
(205) 967-4745
• Doug Habgood, Senior VP Golf division
• Amanda Hammac, Director Of Finance
• Lauren Addie, Creative Manager
• Will Borland, Tickets & Ops Coordinator
• Will Coleman, senior Event Manager-Zoom Motorsports
• Anna Lacy McMains, Sales Director
Year Founded:
1996
Description:
Committed to providing patrons and participants with world-class sporting events, presented with the highest standards of professionalism, that offer a return on the investment of our sponsors and vendors while giving back to, and elevating the image of, the community that plays host to the events.

ALBUQUERQUE SPORTS COUNCIL
PO BOX 26866
ALBUQUERQUE, NM 87125-6866
505-842-9918
800-733-9918
Fax: 505-247-9101
www.abqcvb.org
• Dale Lockett, President/CEO
• Jim Walther, Chair
Description:
Stimulates economic growth by marketing Albuquerque as a convention and visitor destination

ALPHARETTA CONVENTION & VISITORS BUREAU
178 SOUTH MAIN STREET
SUITE 200
ALPHARETTA, GA 30009
678-297-2811
877-202-5961
Fax: 678-297-9197
www.awesomealpharetta.com
• Janet Rodgers, President/CEO
janet@awesomealpharetta.com
• Beth Brown, Vice President of Sales
beth@awesomealpharetta.com
• Adam Bernos, Sports Sales Manager
adam@awesomealpharetta.com
Description:
Offers complimentary planning services including, securing group rates for hotels, welcome bags, site visits, vendor information and maps.

AMARILLO CONVENTION & VISITOR COUNCIL
1000 SOUTH POLK STREET
AMARILLO, TX 79101
806-374-1497
800-692-1338
Fax: 806-373-3909
rick@visitamarillotx.com
www.visitamarillotx.com
• Jerry Holt, Vice President
• Dan Quandt, Executive Director

• Jutta Matalka, Director of Tourism & Amarillo Film Commissio
• Tina Brohlin, Director of Convention Sales Agriculture, Spo
• Emilea White, Convention Sales Manager SMERF Markets
• Lindsey Arbeiter, Convention Sales Manager Associations
• Mary Ramirez, Executive Assistant
• Eric Miller, Communications Director

AMES AREA SPORTS COMMISSION
1601 GOLDEN ASPEN DRIVE
SUITE 110
AMES, IA 50010
515-232-4032
800-288-7470
www.visitames.com
• Julie Weeks, Director
(515) 956-4600
juliew@amescvb.com
• Seann Demaris, Sports Sales & Services
(515) 956-4604
seannd@amescvb.com
• Sandy Larson, Administrative Services
(515) 956-4603
Sports Services Founded:
Founded 1995.
Facilities:
Hilton Coliseum: Basketball, Wrestling, Volleyball, Gymnastics, Iowa State Cross Country Course; Lied Recreation Center: Track and Field, Martial Arts, Volleyball, Racquet Ball; Ames/ISU Ice Arena: Hockey, Curling, Broomball, Figure Skating; Furman Aquatics Center: Swimming, Water Polo, Synchronized Swimming
Description:
works to build economic activity in the Ames area by promoting convention and visitors activities. The Bureau is a members-based organization supporting businesses and groups, and exists to support member business growth.

ANAHEIM/ORANGE COUNTY VISITOR & CONVENTION BUREAU
800 WEST KATELLA AVENUE
ANAHEIM, CA 92802
855-405-5020
Fax: 714-991-8963
• Charles Ahlers, President
(714) 765-8840
• Charles Ahlers, President
• Jay Burress CTA, President and CEO
(714) 765-8840
• Byna Sipos, Excutive Assistant
(714) 765-8898

ARIZONA DEPARTMENT OF RACING
1110 W WASHINGTON
SUITE 260
PHOENIX, AZ 85007
602-364-1700
Fax: 602-364-1703
ador@racing.state.az.us
www.azracing.gov
• Wlilliam J. Walsh, Director

ARKANSAS DEPARTMENT OF FINANCE & ADMINISTRATION
1509 W 7TH STREET
SUITE 505
LITTLE ROCK, AR 72201
501-682-1467
Fax: 501-682-5273
www.dfa.arkansas.gov

• Cecil Alexander, Chairman
• Thomas Akin, Commissioner

ARLINGTON CONVENTION & VISITORS BUREAU
1905 EAST RANDOL MILL ROAD
ARLINGTON, TX 76011
817-461-3888
800-433-5374
Fax: 817-461-6689
www.experiencearlington.org
• Jay Burress, President/CEO
• Joel McLelland, VP Finance/Administration
Description:
Founded in 1992. It is a private, non-profit, non-membership organization, and is the official destination marketing organization for the City of Arlington, Texas.

ASHEVILLE CHAMBER OF COMMERCE
36 MONTFORD AVENUE
ASHEVILLE, NC 28801
828-258-6114
Fax: 828-251-0926
contactus@ashevillechamber.org
www.ashevillechamber.org
• Kit Cramer, President/CEO
(828) 258-6123
• Rojeanous Rush, VP Finance/Operations
(828) 258-6119
Publications:
Relocation Packet; Employment Resource Package (in print and CD ROM); Asheville Area Phone Book; Asheville Area Map; Asheville Fact Book; Major Employers Directory (in prin and CD ROM); Western North Carolina Industrial Directory (in print and CD ROM)

ASHEVILLE CONVENTION & VISITORS BUREAU
36 MONTFORD AVENUE
ASHEVILLE, NC 28801
828-258-6101
Fax: 828-254-6054
www.exploreasheville.com
• Marla Tambellini, Interim Executive Director
(828) 258-6138
• Jonna Reiff, Executive Director

ATLANTA SPORTS COUNCIL
235 ANDREW YOUNG INTERNATIONAL BOULEVARD NW
ATLANTA, GA 30303
404-880-9000
www.atlantasportscouncil.com
• Richard A Anderson, Chairman
• Sam A Williams, President
• Eric Oberman, Vice President, Business Properties
(404) 586-8506
eoberman@macoc.com
• Bari Love, VP Marketing & Communications
• Ken Chin, Vice President, Events
(404) 586-8492
kchin@macoc.com
• Patti Young, Executive Assistant
(404) 586-8500
pyoung@macoc.com
• Courtenay Carruthers, Member Services Coordinator
(404) 586-8510
Number of Members:
500+.
Publications:

Quarterly Newsletter, Annual Report.
Member Services:
Volunteer opportunities for local sporting events, Committee involvement, Access to tickets to local sporting events. Access to all luncheon, events & complimentary access to power house. Access to all ASC Golf Tournament. Membership fees: Individual $250; Corporate $500; Advisor $2,500.
Description:
Promotes the value of sports growth in Atlanta and Georgia by acting as an authority on the economic impact, viasbility and quality of life issues associated with the goal of building Atlanta's reputation as the Sports Capital of the World.

ATLANTA'S DEKALB CONVENTION & VISITORS BUREAU
1957 LAKESIDE PARKWAY
SUITE 510
TUCKER, GA 30084
770-492-5017
800-999-6055
Fax: 770-492-5033
www.dcvb.org
• James Tsismanakis, Executive Director & CEO
(770) 492-5011
Publications:
Sports DeKalb Facilities Guide; SPORTS DEKALB LEADER, SPORTS DEKALB LATEST LINE, newsletters.
Description:
Founded 1989. Private, not-for-profit sports council for DeKalb County in Metro Atlanta, dedicated to economic development. Represents athletic facilities and the hospitality industry to attract sporting events/visitors.

AUBURN/OPELIKA CONVENTION & VISITORS BUREAU
714 EAST GLENN AVENUE
AUBURN, AL 36830
334-887-8747
866-880-8747
Fax: 334-821-5500
info@aotourism.com
www.auburn-opelika.com
• John C Wild, CHA, President
johnwild@aotourism.com
• Robyn L Bridges, CRDE, Communication Director
rlbridges@aotourism.com
Description:
Am economic enhancement tool for the communities of Auburn, Opelika and Lee County. We promote and develop our area through the travel and tourism industry and introduce the unique spirit of Auburn-Opelika to visitors from around the world.

AUGUSTA SPORTS COUNCIL, GREATER
1450 GREENE STREET
SUITE 110
PO BOX 1331
AUGUSTA, GA 30901
706-722-8326
Fax: 706-823-6609
www.augustasportscouncil.org
• Brinsley Thigpen, CEO
• Randy DuTeau, Event Manager
Description:
Founded 1991. Mission includes bidding for, supporting, and developing quality sports

activities in the Greater Augusta area as well as recognizing sports achievements of areas outstanding youth and coaches in sports. Home of Ray Guy Award which recognizes the nation's top college punter.

AURORA AREA CONVENTION & VISITORS BUREAU
43 WEST GALENA BLVD
AURORA, IL 60506-4129
630-256-3194
www.EnjoyAurora.com
• Cort Carlson, Executive Director
(630) 256-3191
cort@enjoyaurora.com
• Pete Garlock, Director, Sales
(630) 256-3194
pete@enjoyaurora.com
Description:
Aurora is the second-largest city in Illinois, and the largest suburb of Chicago. The Aurora Area is comprised of 10 communities located west of Chicago and was established to market and promote these ten communities as a visitor destination for tour groups, meetings and sport events. The organization offers complimentary planning services, including facility and hotel availability, welcome bags, site visits, vendor information and maps.

BAKERSFIELD CONVENTION & VISITORS BUREAU, GREATER
515 TRUXTUN AVENUE
BAKERSFIELD, CA 93301
661-852-7282
866-425-7353
• David Lyman, Manager
(661) 852-7282
• Misty Glasco, Marketing & Events Specialist
(661) 852-7237

BATON ROUGE AREA SPORTS FOUNDATION
359 3RD STREET
BATON ROUGE, LA 7801
225-382-3596
Fax: 225-346-1253
• Jerry Stovall, President
(225) 382-3588
• Eric Engemann, Indoor Sports Coordinator
(225) 382-3571
• Kristen Chighizola, Outdoor Sports Coordinator
(225) 382-3596
Sports Services Founded:
1994
Decription:
To assist in the identification and promotion of athletic activities (competitions and meetings) in the community.
Facilities:
More than 40

BATTLE CREEK SPORTS PROMOTION
KELLOGG ARENA
1 MCCAMLY SQUARE
BATTLE CREEK, MI 49017
269-963-4800
Fax: 269-968-8840
www.kelloggarena.com
• Kevin Scheibler, General Manager
• Ben Randels, Operations Manager
brandels@kelloggarena.com
• Bob Bengttson, Finance Director

(269) 963-4800
bbengtsson@kelloggarena.com
Description:
Serves to attract sports events and meetings to the greater Battle Creek area.

BEAUMONT CONVENTION & VISITORS BUREAU
505 WILLOW STREET
BEAUMONT, TX 77701
409-880-3749
800-392-4401
Fax: 409-880-3750
www.Beaumontcvb.com
• Dean Conwell, Executive Director
(409) 880-3165
• Rebecca Woodland, Convention Sales Manager
(409) 880-3169
• Samantha Moye, Tourism Specialist
(409) 880-3749
• Stephanie Dollar Molina, Director Marketing
(409) 880-3170
• Freddie Willard, Director of Sales
(409) 880-3160
Publications:
Beaumont Official Visitors Packet; Annual Calender of Events; Beaumont Visitor Map; School Project Information Packet; E-mail Updates

BELLINGHAM/WHATCOM CHAMBER OF COMMERCE
119 N COMMERCIAL STREET
SUITE 110
BELLINGHAM, WA 98225
360-734-1330
www.bellingham.com
• Ken Oplinger, President/CEO
• Troy Wills, Secretary
• Peter Cutbill, Treasurer
• Jim Darling, Chair

BIRMINGHAM, GREATER CONVENTION & VISITORS BUREAU
2200 9TH AVENUE NORTH
BIRMINGHAM, AL 35203-1100
205-458-8000
800-458-8085
Fax: 205-458-8086
info@birminghamal.org
www.birminghamal.org
• Karen Dobnikar, Human Resource Manager
(205) 214-9220
kdobnikar@birminghamal.org
• Dilcy Hilley, VP Marketing
(205) 214-9229
dhilley@birminghamal.org
• Michael Gunn, Vice President Sales
(205) 214-9213
mgunn@birminghamal.org
Description:
Established for the purpose of marketing and promoting the greater Birmingham area as a destination for conventions, meetings, and tour and travel. The mission is to broaden and expand promotional efforts on behalf of the city and its business constituency through advertising and marketing programs designed to sell guest rooms in area lodging facilities.

BISMARCK-MANDAN CONVENTION & VISITORS BUREAU
1600 BURNT BOAT DRIVE
BISMARCK, ND 58503
701-222-4308
800-767-3555
Fax: 701-222-0647
www.discoverbismarckmandan.com
• Terry Harzinski, Executive Director
• LaRae Nelson, Destination Sales Specialist
• Lori Yantzer, Destination Sales Specialist
• Camie Lies, Communications Manager
• Barb Balzer, Travel Counselor
• Sheri Grossman, Director Sales
Description:
The mission of the Bismarck-Mandan CVB, in collaboration with our partners is to entake visitors from around the world to eat, meet, sleep and play in Bismarck-Mandan.
Facilities:
Bismarck Aquatics Center, Bismarck Civic Center, Bismarck Community Bowl, All Seasons Arena, Nishu Archery Arena, 30 Softball fields, 26 outdoor soccer fields, 10 outdoor and 4 indoor tennis courts.

BLOOMINGTON CONVENTION & VISITORS BUREAU
2855 NORTH WALNUT STREET
BLOOMINGTON, IN 47404
812-334-8900
800-800-0037
Fax: 812-334-2344
cvb@visitbloomington.com
www.visitbloomington.com
• Mike McAfee, Executive Director
(812) 355-7720
• Ryan Irvin, Graphic Designer
• Laura Newton, Assistant Director, COO
(812) 355-7721

BLOOMINGTON CONVENTION & VISITORS BUREAU
7900 INTERNATIONAL DRIVE
SUITE 990
BLOOMINGTON, MN 55425
952-858-8500
866-435-7425
800-346-4289
Fax: 952-858-8854
info@bloomingtonmn.org
www.bloomingtonmn.org
• Jennifer Schak, Marketing/Special Events Coordinator
Publications:
Sports Venue Guide 2005.
Member Services:
Site Inspections, Bid Booklets, Welcome Packets, Meet & Greet, Intineraries.

BLOOMINGTON-NORMAL AREA SPORTS COMMISSION
3201 CIRA DRIVE
SUITE 201
BLOOMINGTON, IL 61704
309-665-0033
800-433-8226
Fax: 309-661-0743
matt@visitbn.org
www.bloomingtonnormalcvb.org
• Amanda Borden, Convention & Tourism Marketing Manager
• Danny Harms, Graphic Design & Web Manager
• Matt Hawkins, Sports Marketing Manager
matt@visitbn.org

• Alesha Stevenson, Convention & Tourism Marketing Manager
• Crystal Howard, Director
Description:
Mission is to enhance the econoy of McLean County through promotion, attraction and retention of events, conventions and tourism.

BOISE CONVENTION & VISITORS BUREAU
250 S 5th STREET
SUITE 300
BOISE, ID 83702
208-344-7777
800-635-5240
Fax: 208-344-6236
www.boise.org
• John Cohen, Executive Director
(208) 472-5209
jcohen@boisecvb.org
• Terry Kopp, Director of Sales
(208) 472-5208
tkopp@boisecvb.org
• Lisa Edens, Senior Sales Manager
(208) 472-5207
ledens@boisecvb.org
Description:
Soccer, baseball, softball, basketball, biking, bowling, boxing, climbing, cricket, curling, disc golf, equestrian, football, golf, hockey, ice skating and mountain biking

BOSTON CONVENTION & VISITORS BUREAU/SPORTS MARKETING DIVISION, GREATER
TWO COPLEY PLACE
SUITE 105
BOSTON, MA 02116-6501
617-536-4100
888-SEEBOSTON
Fax: 617-424-7664
www.bostonusa.com
• Patrick Moscaritolo, Presdient & CEO
• David Gilbin, Chair
Description:
Founded 1993. Draws upon community individuals and resources to attract sport-related meetings and conventions to Boston.
Publications:
Official Visitor Information Kit; Official Guidebook to Boston; Boston & Cambridge Dining, Shopping and Nightlife Guide; BostonUSA Specials! Card; Travel Planner; Kids Love Boston; City Pass; Go Boston Card; Get Ready for Boston; We're Here; CD Images of Boston; CD Boston History; CD Boston Festivals & Holidays; CD Boston Seasons; CD Boston Sports; The Complete Guide; Boston Flip Flops - Men's; Boston Flip Flop - Women's

BUFFALO NIAGARA SPORTS COMMISSION
617 MAIN STREET
SUITE 200
BUFFALO, NY 14203-1496
716-852-0511
800-283-3256
Fax: 716-852-0131
info@buffalocvb.org
www.buffaloniagarasports.com
• Pete Harvey, Director of Sport Development
(716) 218-2929
harvey@buffalocvb.org

• Jay Josker, Sport Services Manager
(716) 218-2932
josker@buffalocvb.org
• Charles Giglia, Director of Sport Sales
(716) 218-2928
giglia@buffalocvb.org
Description:
The Buffalo Niagara Sports Commission promotes Buffalo & Erie County as a premier amateur sports destination. From empire state games to NCAA frozen four buffalo has the experience & facilities to host the event.

CANTON/STARK COUNTY CONVENTION & VISITORS BUREAU
THE MILLENNIUM CENTRE
222 MARKET AVENUE NORTH
CANTON, OH 44702
330-454-1439
800-552-6051
Fax: 330-456-3600
www.cantonstarkcvb.com
• John Kiste, Executive Director
• Allyson Bussey, Tourism Marketing Manager
Description:
To attract, orient and serve visitors, to educated local residents, and initiate projects and programs, which promote and grow tourism.

CEDAR RAPIDS TOURISM OFFICE
370 FIRST AVENUE NE
CEDAR RAPIDS, IA 52401
319-398-5211
sales@tourismcedarrapids.com
www.tourismcedarrapids.com
• Mary Lee Malmberg, Director of Sports Tourism
• Mark Meyer, Director of Business Development
General Description:
Cedar Rapids offers a wide variety of sports venues, including large arenas, sports complexes and stadiums.
Publications:
Cedar Rapids Area Visitors Guide, Cedar Rapids Area Sports Facilities Guide, Cedar Rapids Area Meeting Planners Guide.
Member Services:
Listing on website and in area visitors guide, business leads and networking opportunities.
Membership Requirements:
Must be located within 100 mile radius of Cedar Rapids.
Facilities Available for Sporting Events:
30,000 sq. ft. arena with seating for 8,000 (wrestling, volleyball, basketball, & cheerleading); Ice arena with NHL ice sheet with 3850 seats and an Olympic rink with viewing for 400; State-of-the-art minor leage baseball stadium seats 5300; Soccer complex with 20 fields and parking for 1,000.

CENTRAL FLORIDA SPORTS COMMISSION
400 W. CHURCH STREET
SUITE 205
ORLANDO, FL 32801
407-648-4900
Fax: 407-649-2072
www.centralfloridasports.org
• Brent Nelson, Interim President/CEO
bnelson@centralfloridasports.org

- Jennifer Lastik, Events Director
- Eileen Babich, Operations Assistant
- John Bisignano, President/CEO
(407) 648-0033
jbisignano@centralfloridasports.org
Sports Services Founded:
1992
Description:
Supports activities, events and sports related businesses that stimulate the Central Florida economy, construct and utilize sports facilities, enhance the area's image worldwide, provide outstanding entertainment and participatory opportunities, and contribute to Central Florida's quality of life.

CENTRAL PENNSYLVANIA/PENN STATE COUNTRY CVB
800 E. PARK AVE
STATE COLLEGE, PA 16803
814-231-1400
800-358-5466
Fax: 814-231-8123
www.centralpacvb.org
- Shirley Smith, Director of Sales
(814) 231-1401
- Betsey Howell, Executive Director
Nature of Sports Service:
Organization offers Site Selection/RFP Assistance, Housing Bureau Services, Hospitality Ambassadors, Team of Volunteers and Community Leaders, Family Welcome packets/coupons and other transporation and support services.

CHAMPAIGN COUNTY CONVENTION & VISITORS BUREAU
108 SOUTH NEIL STREET
CHAMPAIGN, IL 61820-7269
217-351-4133
800-369-6151
Fax: 217-351-0906
www.visitchampaigncounty.org
- Sorita Wilson, Chair
- Dennis Robertson, Vice Chair
- Teri Legner, Treasurer
- Jay DeLuce, Secretary
General Description:
The Champaign County Convention and Visitors Bureau (CVB) and the CVB Board of Directors would like to welcome you to their community. Whatever the occasion, the staff at CVB are there to answer questions, provide materials and ensure that you feel welcome. Planning a sporting event? Champaign County and the University of Illinois feature state-of-the-art sports complexes, indoor and outdoor recreational facilities, and parks that will accommodate just about any kind of youth, amateur or adult sporting event.

CHARLESTON METRO SPORTS COUNCIL
423 KING STREET
CHARLESTON, SC 29403
843-805-3030
www.sportscouncil.org
- Kathleen Cartland, Executive Director
kcartland@charlestoncvb.com
Sports Services Founded:
1999
Description:
To lead and support the local sports and recreational community in collaborative efforts to maximize the potential of area sports and sporting events. In adittion, to promote the Charleston metropolitan area as a destination for amateur sports and sporting events.
Number of Members:
100+
Publications:
Sports Scene Magazine.
Member Services:
Sports Business Conference, Sports Celebration Dinner, Golf Classic, Monthly membership program.

CHARLOTTE REGIONAL SPORTS COMMISSION
6337 MORRISON BOULEVARD
CHARLOTTE, NC 28211
704-644-4047
www.charlottesports.org
- Will Web, Executive Dierctor
(704) 644-4048
- Will Pitts, Operations Director
(704) 644-4046
Sports Services Founded:
1994
Description:
To bring sporting events to Charlotte which benefit the region in two major areas, economic impact and quality of life. In addittion, we also help attract conferences, sports organizations and teamd to our market.

CHATTANOOGA SPORTS & EVENTS COMMITTEE, GREATER
736 MARKET STREET
18TH FLOOR
CHATTANOOGA, TN 37402
855-345-0127
Fax: 423-265-1630
www.chattanoogasports.org
- Scott Smith, Chair
- Jeff Sikes, Vice Chairman
Description:
Founded 1992. Serves as the city's representative in bidding for/recruiting regional, national and international sports teams, events and meetings for the Chattanooga area; creates and stages sporting events in Chattanooga that have the potential to lure participants and/or spectators to the area; acts as catalyst for improving recreational facilities in area.

CHICAGO SOUTHLAND CONVENTION & VISITORS BUREAU
2304 173RD STREET
LANSING, IL 60438-6006
708-895-8200
888-895-8233
Fax: 708-895-8288
sports@visitchicagosouthland.com
www.playchicagosouthland.com
- Jim Garrett, President
- Sally Schlesinger, Executive Vice President
Decription:
The Chicago Southland is compromised of 62 south and southwest suburbs of Chicago. Only 25 minutes from Chicago and easily accessible via two airports and several interstates, the Southland is Chicago's most affordable region.
Publications:
Chicago Southland Visitors Guide, annually; Meeting Planner's Guide, as needed; Group Tour Guide, as needed; Sports Venue Guide, as needed; Traveler's Guide, annually; Festivals & Events, annually; Chicago Southland Coupon Book, bi-annually.

CINCINNATI SPORTS CORPORATION, GREATER
9514 KENWOOD ROAD
CINCINNATI, OH 45242
513-686-7782
Fax: 513-322-0139
www.cincyusa.com
- Leslie Spencer, Executive Director
LSpencer@CincyUSA.com
Description:
Founded 1989. Serves to promote sports development and attract sports events to the greater Cincinnati, Ohio area.

CITY OF GREENVILLE - SPECIAL EVENTS
206 S MAIN STREET, 6TH FLOOR
GREENVILLE, SC 29602
864-232-2273
aprosser@greenvillesc.gov
www.greenvillesc.gov
- Angie Prosser, Director Special Events
aprosser@greenvillesc.gov
- Beth Rusch, Permits & Event Coordination
(864) 467-6667

CITY OF HUNTSVILLE SPORTS COMMISSION
PO BOX 19064
HUNTSVILLE, AL 35804
256-427-6749
www.huntsvillesports.org
- Ralph Stone, Executive Director
Description:
A not-for profit advocacy organization that promotes an enhanced quality of life in the Huntsville area by identifying, recruiting, and promoting amateur events and meetings.

CLARKSVILLE MONTGOMERY COUNTY CONVENTION & VISITORS BUREAU
25 JEFFERSON ST.
SUITE 300
CLARKSVILLE, TN 37040
931-647-2331
800-530-2487
Fax: 931-645-1574
www.clarksville.tn.us
- Theresa Harrington, Executive Director
- James Chavez, President & CEO
- Sahron Green, Vice President, Finance & Administration of t
(931) 245-4335
sgreen@clarksville.tn.us
- Robin Burton, Vice President of Marketing and Communication
(931) 245-4337
rburton@clarksville.tn.us
- Lisa Knight, Human Resources Manager of the Economic Devel
(931) 245-4336
lisak@clarksville.tn.us
- Wendy Welch, Media Design Specialist of the Economic Devel
(93) -245-433
graphics@clarksville.tn.us
- Cortney Willamson, Accounting & Development Assistant of the Eco
(931) 245-4331
cwilliamson@clarksville.tn.us
Description:
A private, non-profit economic development

umbrella that provides staffing and management.

CLEVELAND SPORTS COMMISSION, GREATER
50 PUBLIC SQUARE
SUITE 950
CLEVELAND, OH 44113
216-621-0600
Fax: 216-621-2773
www.clevelandsports.org
• David E. Gilbert, President & CEO
Description:
Founded 1993, the Great Cleveland Sports Commission is responsible for attracting sports events to Northeast Ohio. The GCSC supports the local economy and serves to bring major sports events to Northeast Ohio, creating various sporting opportunities for athletes of all ages.
Nature of Service:
Event attraction, management, marketing, communications, volunteer services and operations.

CLINTON CONVENTION & VISITORS BUREAU
721 SOUTH SECOND STREET
CLINTON, IA 52732
563-242-5702
cvb@clintonia.com
www.clintoniowatourism.com
• Marsha Smith, Director Convention and Visitiors Bureau
• Mary Jo Kinkaid, Administrative Assistant
• Marsha Smith, Director
• Sue Raaymakers, Chair

COBB TRAVEL & TOURISM
ONE GALLERIA PARKWAY
SUITE 1A2A
ATLANTA, GA 30339
678-303-2622
800-451-3480
Fax: 678-303-2625
www.travelcobb.org
• Holly Bass, Chief Executive Officer
• Holly A. Bass, CEO
(678) 303-2641
Sports Service Founded:
1984
Nature of Sports Service:
The bureau markets Cobb County as a sports tourism destination for right holders and meeting planners to host there next event in our community. Our services are free to assist with hotel guest room packaging, bid proposals, venue research, media support, and convention services.
Publications:
Visitor's Guide
Number of Members:
Nine (9)

COLORADO SPRINGS SPORTS CORPORATION
1631 MESA AVENUE
SUITE E
COLORADO SPRINGS, CO 80906
719-634-7333
Fax: 719-634-5198
info@thesportscorp.org
www.thesportscorp.org
• Tom Osborne, President/CEO
(719) 634-7333
tom@thesportscorp.org
• Stori Peterson, Sports Director

• Doug Martin, COO
(719) 634-7333
• Mike Moran, Senior Media Consultant
(719) 634-7333
Description:
Founded 1978. Provides support to the USOC and National governing bodies, active with economic development and youth sports development. Host of the 2005 & 2007 State Games of America.

COLUMBIA REGIONAL SPORTS COUNCIL
1010 LINCOLN STREET
COLUMBIA, SC 29201
803-545-0000
800-264-4884
Fax: 803-545-0013
info@columbiasportscouncil.com
www.columbiasportscouncil.com
• Rick Luber, Executive Director
hubers@columbiasportscouncil.com
• Katie Rankin, Sales Manager
(803) 545-0016
kwilmesherr@columbiasportscouncil.com
Description:
The mission of the Columbia Regional Sports Council is to strengthen the area's economy by marketing and selling the Columbia Riverbanks Region as a premier destination for sporting events, partnering with local sports organizations to grow and develop existing events, and by recruiting new events which provide an economic benefit to the region by generating room nights, food and beverage sales, and associated tax revenues.

COLUMBUS, GA SPORTS & EVENTS COUNCIL
400 4TH STREET
PO BOX 1519
COLUMBUS, GA 31901
706-660-1996
Fax: 706-225-4533
msherman@columbusga.org
www.columbusgasports.com
• Herbert Greene, Executive Director
• Scott Ressmeyer, President
• Scott Ressmeyer, President
• David Boyd, Event Manager
Sports Services Founded:
1995
Description:
Strives to promote tourism through sporting events, creating a positive economic impact on the greater Columbus region.

CORPUS CHRISTI CONVENTION & VISTORS BUREAU
101 N SHORELINE BLVD
SUITE 430
CORPUS CHRISTI, TX 78401
800-678-6232
Fax: 361-887-9023
www.corpuschristi.tx.org
• Keith Arnold, CEO
(361) 881-1888
• Timothy J Carpenter, VP of Technology & Interactive Marketing
(361) 881-1861
Description:
Provides the community with marketing support for the tourism and convention industries.

DALLAS CONVENTION & VISITORS BUREAU
325 NORTH ST. PAUL STREET
SUITE 700
DALLAS, TX 75201
214-571-1000
800-232-5527
Fax: 214-571-1008
• Philip Jones, President & CEO
• Monica Paul, VP, Sports Marketing
• Phyllis Hammond, VP Public Relations
(214) 571-1077
Description:
Promotes Dallas as the ideal business and pleasure destination to the regional, national, and international marketplace, and to favorably impact the Dallas economy through conventions and tourism.

DALLAS CONVENTION CENTER
650 SOUTH GRIFFIN STREET
DALLAS, TX 75202
214-939-2750
877-850-2100
Fax: 214-939-2795
www.dallasconventioncenter.com
• Ron King, Director
(214) 939-2794
• Al Rojas, Asst Finance/Admin Director
(214) 939-2755
alberto.rojas@dallascityhall.com
• Charlotte Allen, Marketing/Public Relations Man
(214) 939-2738
charlotte.allen@dallascityhall.com
Description:
Founded 1988, as a non-profit public charity. Serves as the focal point of sports support and development activities within the greater Dallas region. Project Management: Manage sports programs, events and projects.
Publications:
DISC NEWS, quarterly newsletter, VIP invitations.

DANVILLE AREA CONVENTION & VISITOR BUREAU
100 WEST MAIN STREET
#146
DANVILLE, IL 61832
217-442-2096
800-383-4386
Fax: 217-442-2137
info@danvilleareainfo.com
www.danvilleareainfo.com
• Jeanie Cooke, Executive Director
(217) 442-2096
• Barbara Bein, Finance Administrator
BarbaraBein@danvilleareainfo.com
Facilities:
Danville Stadium (Baseball), Winter Park (Soccer), YMCA (Swimming), Harrison Park (Golf), Turtle Run (Golf), Wolfe Creek (Golf), Palmer Arena (Ice Skating/Hockey).

DAYTON/MONTGOMERY COUNTY CONVENTION & VISITORS BUREAU
1 CHAMBER PLAZA
SUITE A
DAYTON, OH 45402
937-226-8211
800-221-8235
Fax: 937-226-8294
www.daytoncvb.com

multi sports

231

• Jacquelyn Powell, Chief Executive Officer
• Ron Eifert, Senior Sales Manager
(937) 226-8284
Nature of Services:
The Dayton/Montgomery County Convention & Visitors Bureau is a destination marketing organization which provides numerous complimentary services to sports groups and organizations looking to host an event in the Dayton and Montgomery County area.

DC SPORTS & ENTERTAINMENT COMMISSION
2400 E CAPITOL STREET SE
WASHINGTON, DC 20003
202-608-1100
Fax: 202-547-7460
www.dcsec.com
• Erik A Moses, Senior VP & Managing Director
• Troy Scott, Event Operations
• Teri Washington, Director, Communications
• Adelle Chenier, Event Manager
• Gregory A. O'Dell, President and Chief Executive Officer
• Samuel R. Thomas, Senior Vice President and General Manager Con
(202) 249-3000
sthomas@eventsdc.com
• Erik A. Moses, Senior Vice President and Managing Director S
(202) 608-1100
• Henry W. Mosley, Chief Financial Officer
(202) 249-3000
hmosley@eventsdc.com
• Chinyere Hubbard, Vice President, Communications and Marketing
(202) 249-3217
chubbard@eventsdc.com
Venues:
Washington Convention Center, RFK Stadium, DC Armory, Nationals Park, Carnegie Library
Summary of Services:
The suite of services is designed to accommodate events of all sizes and the commitment to superior service to clients and patrons is second to none. From start to finish, the dedicated team of sales, event management and communications staff work together to make the event execution process a homerun every time.

DECATUR AREA CONVENTION & VISITORS BUREAU
202 EAST NORTH STREET
DECATUR, IL 62523
800-331-1479
Fax: 217-423-7455
www.decaturcvb.com
• Mark Avery, Treasurer
• Jeff Hendricks, Executive Director DACVB
• Teri Hammel, Director of Sales & Finance
• Bryce Swanson, Sports and Competitive Events Manager
• Katrina Wilkerson, Office and Services Manager
• Sandy Denton, President
• Carol Barnes, Vice-President

DENVER METRO CONVENTION & VISITORS BUREAU
1555 CALIFORNIA STREET
SUITE 300
DENVER, CO 80202-4262

303-892-1112
800-223-6837
Fax: 303-892-1636
www.denver.org
• Richard Scharf, President/CEO
• Jeff Ruffe, VP Finanace/Adminstration
Description:
Promotes Denver and the surrounding areas as a sight for sporting and entertainment events.

DES MOINES AREA SPORTS COMMISSION
400 LOCUST STREET
SUITE 265
DES MOINES, IA 50309
515-699-4960
800-451-2625
Fax: 515-244-9757
info@desmoinescvb.com
www.seedesmoines.com
• Chris Coleman, Chair
• Paul Rottenberg, Chair
• Rick Messerschmidt, Secretary/Treasurer
Description:
The Des Moines Area Sports Commission (DMASC) became an official supporting organization of the Greater Des Moines CVB in 2008. The DMASC, previously known as the Greater Des Moines Sports Authority, was established as an organization in 1992 and was known as the Sports Authority until 2002 when it entered into a support agreement and came under the umbrella of the Greater Des Moines CVB. Today the DMASC's mission is to establish Greater Des Moines as the premier Midwest community for recreational and competitive sport participation and competition.
Facilities:
Iowa Events Center: HyVee Hall, Wells Fargo Arena, Veterans Memorial Auditorium (various sports), Drake Stadium (Track & Field), James W. Cownie Soccer Complex (soccer), Richard O. Jacobson Exhibit Center (various sports)

DES MOINES CONVENTION & VISITORS BUREAU, GREATER
400 LOCUST STREET
SUITE 265
DES MOINES, IA 50309
800-451-2625
Fax: 515-244-9757
info@desmoinescvb.com
www.seedesmoines.com
• Nancy Goode, Vice President ofFinance & Administration
(515) 699-3441
• Greg Edwards, President & Chief Executive Officer
(515) 699-3438
• Vicki Comegys, Vice President, Sales & Service
(515) 699-3435
• Tiffany Tauscheck, Vice President, Marketing
(515) 699-3433
Description:
Formed in 1908, the Greater Des Moines Convention and Visitors Bureau is one of the oldest bureaus in the United States. The mission of the Greater Des Moines Convention and Visitors Bureau is to promote Greater Des Moines as an attractive, vibrant and affordable destination statewide, nationally and internationally.

Their focus increases visitors to the community through meetings, conventions, events, sports, leisure, travel and group tours, thereby contributing to the local economy.

DETROIT METRO SPORTS COMMISSION
211 WEST FORT STREET
SUITE 1000
DETROIT, MI 48226
313-202-1979
Fax: 313-202-1964
info@detroitsports.org
www.detroitsports.org
• David Beachnau, Executive Director
(313) 202-1979
dbeachnau@visitdetroit.com
• Dave Beachnau, Executive Director
• Sean Krabach, Director of Event Operations
• Andrew Green, Manager, Event Services
• Marty Dobek, Marketing and Communication
• Kris Smith, Sales Manager, Event Development
• Dave Beachnau, Executive Director
(313) 202-1982
dbeachnau@detroitsports.org
Description:
Markets and sells metro Detriot as a premier destination for regional, national and international amateur sporting events.

DICKINSON CONVENTION & VISITORS BUREAU
72 EAST MUSEUM DRIVE
DICKINSON, ND 58601
701-483-4988
800-279-7391
Fax: 701-483-9261
info@visitdickinson.com
www.visitdickinson.com
• Terri Thiel, Executive Director
Description:
Serves to attract sports events and meetings to the greater North Dakota geographic area.

DISCOVER LYNCHBURG
2015 MEMORIAL AVENUE
LYNCHBURG, VA 24501
434-845-5966
800-732-5821
Fax: 434-522-9592
djackson@lynchburgchamber.org
• Denise Jackson, Sales Manager
djackson@lynchburgchamber.org
Description:
Mission is to bring major sports and special events to Lynchburg and surrounding areas.
Sporting Events Held at Facilities:
Soccer; Baseball; Basketball; Paintball; Wrestling; Lacrosse; Golf; Fishing; Canoeing; Boating; Field Hockey; Equestrian; Softball; Tennis; and Track & Field

DIVISION OF BUSINESS & COMMUNITY DEVELOPMENT/SOUTH CAROLINA
1205 PENDLETON ST, STE 110
COLUMBIA, SC 29201
803-734-1700
866-224-9393
Fax: 803-734-1163
www.discoversouthcarolina.com

• Marion Edmonds, Director of Communications
• Amy Duffy, Chief of Staff
Description:
Promotes South Carolina as a sight for sports, entertainment and film.

DOTHAN AREA CONVENTION & VISITORS BUREAU
3311 ROSS CLARK CIRCLE
DOTHAN, AL 36303
334-794-6622
888-449-0212
Fax: 334-712-2731
www.dothanalcvb.com
• Robert Hendrix, Executive Director
• Carmen Bishop, Communications Director
Description:
Serves to attract sports events and meetings to the Dothan geographic area.

DUBLIN CONVENTION & VISITOR BUREAU
9 SOUTH HIGH STREET
DUBLIN, OH 43017
614-792-7666
800-245-8387
info@irishisanattitude.com
www.irishisanattitude.com
• Scott Dring, Executive Director
• Mary Szymkoiwak, Communications/Group Tour Specialist
• Josh Bricker, Sports & Events Sales Manager
Sports Services Founded:
1988
Description:
Mission is to identify and pursue opportunities to attract, service and retain overnight visitors.

DUPAGE CONVENTION & VISITORS BUREAU
915 HARGER ROAD
SUITE 240
OAK BROOK, IL 60523-1476
630-575-8070
800-232-0502
Fax: 630-575-8070
www.dupagecvb.com
• Skip Strittmatter, Executive Director
ext 210
• Beth Marchetti, Director of Development

DURHAM CONVENTION & VISITORS BUREAU
101 EAST MORGAN STREET
DURHAM, NC 27701
919-687-0288
800-446-8604
Fax: 919-683-9555
www.durham-nc.com
• Reyn Bowman, President
• Corey Bizzell, Director of Sales
Description:
A local tourism development authority chartered by state and local government in cooperation with the private sector to attract and serve visitors to the City and County of Durham by reinvesting a portion of the visitor paid room occupancy and tourism development tax in promotion and marketing.

ELGIN AREA CONVENTION & VISITORS BUREAU
77 RIVERSIDE DRIVE
ELGIN, IL 60120
847-695-7540
800-217-5362
Fax: 847-695-7668
• Pete Garlock, Director Of Sales
Description:
Regional convention and visitors bureau representing Chicagolands northern Fox River Valley.
Facilities Available for Sporting Events:
Elgin Sports Complex: Softball, Soccer, Baseball, BMX, Football, Rugby, Volleyball; The Centre of Elgin: Basketball, Cheerleading, Dance, Gymnastics, Martial Arts, Swimming, Volleyball, Team Handball, Wrestling; Elgin Community College: Baseball, Basketball, Cheer/Dance, Football, Rugby, Gymnastics, Martial Arts, Soccer, Softball, Volleyball, Wrestling, Team Handball; Judson University: Baseball, Basketball, Cheer/Dance, Gymnastics, Martial Arts, Soccer, Softball, Volleyball, Wrestling, Team Handball

EXPLORE FAIRBANKS
101 DUNKEL STREET
SUITE 111
FAIRBANKS, AK 99701-4806
907-457-3282
800-327-5774
Fax: 907-459-3757
info@explorefairbanks.com
www.explorefairbanks.com
• Deb Hickok, President & Chief Executive Officer
• Deb Hickok, President And CEO
(907) 459-3770
dhickok@explorefairbanks.com
• Dawn Murphy, Finance and Administrative Director
(907) 459-3774
dmurphy@explorefairbanks.com
• Michelle Middleton, Administrative and Finance Coordinator
(907) 459-3772
mmiddleton@explorefairbanks.com
• Amy Geiger, Director of Communications
(907) 459-3775
ageiger@explorefairbanks.com
• Bill Wright, Public Relations Manager
(90-) 59-3776
bwright@explorefairbanks.com
• Deb Hickok, President and CEO
(907) 459-3770
dhickok@explorefairbanks.com
• Michelle Middleton, Administrative and Finance
(907) 459-3772
Description:
The Fairbanks Convention and Visitors Bureau has served as the regional visitor center for fairbanks and interior Alaska for the past 28 years. The mission of the organiation is to enhance and contribute to the economic well-being of the Fairbanks area by marketing to potential visitors. Departments include: Administration, Visitor Services, Membership, Meetings & Conventions, Tourism & Advertising, and Public Relations.
Membership:
Over 400 members (also including non-profits & rural outreach). Categories of membership include: activities, events, shopping, dining, accomodations,

convention facilities and services, transportation, visitor planning, services. Any membership questions call direct to: Karen Lane (907) 451-1734, or klane@explorefairbanks.com
Member Services:
Benefits of member services include: vacancy listings, membership, luncheons, evening exchanges, membership mailouts, educational seminars, members-only website, website listings, open houses, membership orientation, prospect seminars, Golden Heart Greeter Program.
Publications:
Visitor Guide, Winter Guide, Meeting Planner Guide, Group tour Manual, Self-Guided Downtown Walking Tour, Membership Directory

FAIRFIELD COUNTY SPORTS COMMISSION
1 UNIVERSITY PLACE
STAMFORD, CT 6901
203-251-8481
Fax: 203-251-8482
• Harry E Peden, IV, President
• Jon Lese, Treasurer
Description:
A non-profit organization dedicated to promoting fitness and personel development through sports and an active healthy lifestyle.

FARGO-MOORHEAD CONVENTION & VISITOR BUREAU
2001 44TH STREET SW
FARGO, ND 58103
701-282-3653
800-235-7654
Fax: 701-282-4366
info@fargomoorhead.org
www.fargomoorhead.org
• Cole Carley, President/CEO
cole@fargomoorhead.org
• Charley Johnson, President and CEO
• Renee M Sander, Director of Operations
Description:
Exists to promote Fargo, North Dakota and Moorehead, Minnesota as a destination for visitors, tour groups, business travel, conventions, sporting events and trade shows.

FARMINGTON CONVENTION & VISITORS BUREAU
3041 EAST MAIN STREET
FARMINGTON, NM 87402
505-326-7602
800-448-1240
www.farmingtonnm.org
• Debbie Dusenbery, Executive Director
• Tonya Stinson, Executive Director
• Shawna Graham, Administrative & Membership Coordinator
• Ingrid Gilbert, Online Marketing Coordinator

FLORIDA SPORTS FOUNDATION
2930 KERRY FOREST PARKWAY
TALLAHASSEE, FL 32309
850-488-8347
Fax: 850-922-0482
www.flasports.com
• Larry Pendleton, President
• Steven V. Rodriguez, Vice President
• Nick Gandy, Communications Director

• Charlotte Cowen, Finance & Human Resources
Description:
Founded 1992. Official sports office for the state of Florida. Promotion and development of the state's sports industry.

FLORIDA'S SPACE COAST OFFICE OF TOURISM
430 BREVARD AVENUE
SUITE 150
COCOA VILLAGE, FL 32922
321-433-4470
877-572-3224
Fax: 321-433-4476
kalina.person@visitspacecoast.com
www.visitspacecoast.com
• Kalina Person, Promotions/Sports Manager
ksubido@aol.com
• Rusty Buchanan,
(321) 783-9283
• Connie Alden,
(321) 783-9283

FORT SMITH CONVENTION & VISITORS BUREAU
2 NORTH B STREET
FORT SMITH, AR 72901
479-783-8888
800-637-1477
Fax: 479-784-2421
info@FortSmithSports.com
www.FortSmithSports.com
• Amy Jones, Convention & Event Sales Manager
(479) 783-8888
• Russ Jester, Marketing Communications & Events Services Manager
Description:
Fort Smith CVB (1990) is the official destination marketing organization of Fort Smith, Arkansas. Fort Smith CVB promotes Fort Smith's unique assets that make it ideal for business and leisure tourism, as well as for large conventions, meetings and events, assisting sporting event planners.

FORT WORTH CONVENTION & VISITORS BUREAU
111 WEST 4TH STREET
SUITE 200
FORT WORTH, TX 76102-3951
817-336-8791
800-433-5747
www.fortworth.com
• David DuBois, CMP, CAE, President/CEO
(817) 698-7822
• Linda G De Jesus, MBA, CPA, CFP, Vice President Finance & Administration
(817) 698-7839
• Merianne Roth, Vice President Marketing & Communications
(817) 698-7841
Description:
The mission is to improve the area economy by attracting visitors to Fort Worth.

FOX CITIES CONVENTION AND VISITORS BUREAU
3433 WEST COLLEGE AVENUE
APPLETON, WI 54914
920-734-3358
800-236-6673
Fax: 920-734-1080
mtenhaken@foxcities.org
www.foxcities.org

• Adam Schanke, Sports Marketing Manager
• Matt Ten Haken, Director of Sports Marketing
mtenhaken@foxcities.org
Description:
The Fox Cities Convention and Visitors Bureau helps attract and organize sporting events in the Fox Cities of Wisconsin. Some of the services provided include: touring, evaluating venues and hotels, securing proposals, managing hotel arrangements, coordinating media information, recruiting volunteers, and providing visitor information.
Founded:
1988

FRESNO CONVENTION & VISITORS BUREAU
848 M STREET
3RD FLOOR
FRESNO, CA 93721
559-445-8300
800-788-0836
Fax: 559-445-0122
www.fresnocvb.org
• Wayne Bennett, Executive Director
• Billie Kerstetter, Director Convention Sales/Marketing
Year Founded:
1966
Nature of Service:
We host Conventions, Religious, Athletic, Commerical events at our Fresno Convention Center.

GAINESVILLE SPORTS COMMISSION
300 EAST UNIVERSITY AVENUE
SUITE 100
GAINESVILLE, FL 32601
352-338-9300
Fax: 352-338-0600
www.gainesvillesportscommission.com
• Jack Hughes, Executive Director
• James Di Virgilio, VP
• Bruce Cribbs, Treasurer
• Esther Yoder, Secretary
• Frank Saier, Legal Counsel
• Lynda Reinhart, President
Sports Services Founded:
1988
Description:
Strives to promote tourism through sports while creating a positive economic impact on Gainesville and Alachula County

GRAND FORKS CONVENTION & VISITORS BUREAU, GREATER
4251 GATEWAY DRIVE
GRAND FORKS, ND 58203
701-746-0444
800-866-4566
info@visitgrandforks.com
www.visitgrandforks.com
• Julie Rygg, Executive Director
• Deb Stewart, Sales Manager
(Sal) s Manage

GREATER AUSTIN SPORTS ASSOCIATION
PO BOX 28222
AUSTIN, TX 78767
512-239-8830
• Doris Mueller, Chairman
Description:
Founded 1986. Promotes Austin as a site

for local, state, national, and international sports events and meetings.

GREATER CLEVELAND SPORTS COMMISSION
334 EUCLID AVENUE
CLEVELAND, OH 44114
216-621-0600
Fax: 216-621-2773
info@clevelandsports.org
www.clevelandsports.org
• David E. Gilbert, President & CEO
Description:
Founded 1993, the Great Cleveland Sports Commission is responsible for attracting sports events to Northeast Ohio. The GCSC supports the local economy and serves to bring major sports events to Northeast Ohio, creating various sporting opportunities for athletes of all ages.
Nature of Service:
Event attraction, management, marketing, communications, volunteer services and operations.

GREATER COLUMBUS SPORTS COMMISSION
45 VINE STREET
COLUMBUS, OH 43215
614-221-6060
800-331-0092
Fax: 614-224-7301
www.ColumbusSports.org
• Linda Logan, Executive Director
LLogan@ColumbusSports.org
• Brain Ellis, Chair
• Paul Astleford, Experience Columbus
• Gregg DiPaolo, Time Warner Cable
• Butch Moore, The Dispatch Printing Company
• Linda Shetina Logan, Executive Director
• Brenda Carter, Executive Assistant, Office Manager
Description:
Mission is to provide leadership, guidance and marketing expertise in attracting regional, national and international sporting events and activities to benefit Greater Columbus economically and socially.

GREATER DENTON SPORTS COMMISSION
2436 S I-35E
SUITE 376-256
DENTON, TX 76205
888-598-1508
www.dentonsports.com
• Jason Piter, Chair
• Frank Kudlac, Treasurer
Description:
To attract, stimulate, and promote sports entertainment events and activities in the greater denton area

GREATER FORT LAUDERDALE CONVENTION & VISITORS BUREAU
1850 ELLER DRIVE
SUITE 303
FORT LAUDERDALE, FL 33316
954-765-4466
800-22-SUNNY
Fax: 954-765-4467
gflcvb@broward.org
www.sunny.org
• Nicki E Grossman, President & CEO
ngrossman@broward.org
• Francine Mason, Vice President

Communciations
(954) 765-4466
fmason@broward.org
Sports Service Founded:
1987
Description:
Funded by a portion of the five percent tax on hotel rooms. Promotes the Greater Fort Lauderdale area as a premier year-round leisure and marketing destination.
College Bowl Game:
2004 FedEx Orange Bowl.

GREATER LANSING CONVENTION & VISITORS BUREAU
500 EAST MICHIGAN AVENUE
SUITE 180
LANSING, MI 48912
517-487-0077
888-252-6746
Fax: 517-487-5151
www.lansing.org
• Linda Sims, Sr. Advisor on Multi-Cultural Diversity & Com
(517) 372-6892
ssserve@usa.net
• Deborah Bough, Computer & Information Systems Manager
(517) 377-1426
dbough@lansing.org
• Jack Schripsema, President
(517) 377-1404
jschripsema@lansing.org
• Michael B Zumbaugh, CDME, Vice President Finance and Administration
(517) 377-1403
mzumbaugh@lansing.org

GREATER LOUISVILLE CONVENTION & VISITORS BUREAU
401 WEST MAIN STREET
SUITE 2300
LOUISVILLE, KY 40202
502-584-2121
888-568-4784
Fax: 502-584-6697
info@gotolouisville.com
www.gotolouisville.com
• James Wood, President/CEO
jwood@gotolouisville.com
• Karen Williams, Executive Vice President
• Stacy Yates, VP Marketing/Communications
syates@gotolouisville.com
Description:
Since 1968, the primary goal has been to enhance the city's economy through tourism development. The Bureau enhances Greater Louisville's economy through tourism by positioning and selling Greater Louisville worldwide, in partnership with the public and private sector, as a premier destination for convention, tradeshows, corporate meetings, group tours and individual leisure travel.

GREATER OMAHA SPORTS COMMITTEE
7015 SPRING STREET
OMAHA, NE 68106-3518
402-346-8003
800-475-SHOW
Fax: 402-346-5412
info@showofficeonline.com
www.showofficeonline.com
• Bob Mancuso, Chairman
(402) 346-8003
info@showofficeonline.com

Number of Members:
200
Member Services:
Be active in bringing sporting events to city and metro area by working on various committees.
Membership Requirements:
Attend monthly meeting and take part in helping various sporting events in metro Omaha.
Description:
Founded 1971

GREENSBORO SPORTS COMMISSION
2200 PINECROFT ROAD
SUITE 200
GREENSBORO, NC 27407
336-378-4499
Fax: 336-378-1998
admin@greensborosports.org
www.greensborosports.org
• Karah Jennings, Operations Manager
• Mo Milani, Treasurer
• Michael F. Bumpass, Secretary
• Kim Strable, President
• Demp Bradford, VP of Operations
Description:
Founded 1989. Established to recruit, promote and host all types of sports events, sports conferences, and sports meetings. 23,000 seat coliseum adjacent to special events center comprised of 120,000 square feet of exhibit space and a 5,000 seat mini-arena with meeting facilities. Also offers excellent golf, tennis, soccer, cross country and event facilities.

GREENVILLE CONVENTION & VISITORS BUREAU
631 SOUTH MAIN STREET
SUITE 301
GREENVILLE, SC 29601
864-421-0000
800-351-7180
Fax: 864-421-0005
www.greenvillecvb.com
• Chris Stone, President
(864) 421-0000
• Chris Stone, President
• Jennifer Stilwel, Chief Marketing Officer
• Michelle Stoudemire, Senior Sales Manager
• Todd Bertka, Vice President, Sales

GWINNETT SPORTS COMMISSION
6500 SUGARLOAF PARKWAY
SUITE 200
DULUTH, GA 30097
770-623-1667
888-494-6638
Fax: 770-623-1667
www.gwinnettsportscommission.org
• Preston Williams, CEO
• Lisa Anders, Executive Director
Publications:
Meeting Planners Guide; Gwinnett Magazine; Facilities Guide

GWINNETT SPORTS COUNCIL
6500 SUGARLOAF PARKWAY
SUITE 200
DULUTH, GA 30097
888-494-6638
Fax: 770-623-1667
www.gcvb.org
• Lee Baker, Executive Director

Membership:
Annual membership fee is $125 per member.
Description:
Mission is to promote sports in Gwinnett area; promote local events to have a greater impact; bring new events to the area; publish a magazine dedicated to the sports in the area.

HAGERSTOWN-WASHINGTON COUNTY CONVENTION & VISITORS BUREAU
16 PUBLIC SQUARE
HAGERSTOWN, MD 21740
301-791-3246
888-257-2600
Fax: 301-791-2601
www.marylandmemories.org
• Tom Riford, President/CEO

HAMPTON ROADS CHAMBER OF COMMERCE
PO BOX 327
NORFOLK, VA 23501
757-622-2312
Fax: 757-622-5563
www.hamptonroadschamber.com
• John A Hornbeck, Jr, CCE, President/CEO
• John A Hornbeck, President/CEO
(757) 664-2500
• Sarah Bernick, Administrative Coordinator
(757) 622-2312
• Joel Pearce, Communications Manager
• Sarah Martin, Vice President, Development/Marketing
Description:
To create economic opportunity and prosperity for all of Hampton Roads

HAMPTON ROADS SPORTS COMMISSION
500 E MAIN STREET
SUITE 700
NORFOLK, VA 23510
757-664-2573
Fax: 757-622-5563
info@hamptonroadssports.org
www.hamptonroadssports.org
• Morgan Lang, Hampton Roads Sports Commission
• John Wilson, Chair
• Jack Hornbeck, President
• Sylvia Haines, Secretary-Treasurer
Description:
Attract major amateur athletic events to the area and to emphasize regional collaboration.

HARTFORD SPORTS COMMISSION, GREATER (CONVENTION & VISITORS BUREAU)
31 PRATT STREET
4TH FLOOR
HARTFORD, CT 6103
860-728-6789
800 446-7811
Fax: 860-293-2365
www.enjoyhartford.com
• Michael Van Parys, President
ext 222
• Phyllis Anderson, National Sales Manager
• Keith Voets, Sales/Marketing Manager
(860) 728-6789
Description:
The mission is to enhance the economic fabric and quality of life of Hartford.

235

HAWAII PACIFIC SPORTS
1493 HALEKKOA DRIVE
HONOLULU, HI 96821
808-732-8805
www.alohastategames.com
• Mark E. Zeug, President/Chief Executive Officer
Description:
Founded 1988. Owns and organizes Aloha State Games; promotes the attraction and development of sports events in the state of Hawaii. Also owns and operates Hawaii Senior Olympics.

HERITAGE CORRIDOR CONVENTION & VISITORS BUREAU
15701 INDEPENDENCE BLVD
ROMEOVILLE, IL 60446
815-727-2323
800-926-2262
Fax: 815-727-2324
info@hccvbil.com
www.heritagecorridorcvb.com
• Robert L Navarro, PhD, President/CEO
(630) 226-1753
• Mary Beth DeGrush, Vice President
(815) 727-4635
maryde@hccvbil.com
Description:
HCCVB was established in 1985. We service communities along the Illinois and Michigan Canal. Mission is to ignite, influence and impact the visitor's experience through tourism partnership.
Publications:
Sun & Fun Spring & Summer Events Guide, Heritage Corridor CVB Visitors Guide, Will/Grundy Visitors Guide, LaSalle County Visitor's Guide

HOT SPRINGS CONVENTION & VISTORS BUREAU
134 CONVENTION BLVD
HOT SPRINGS, AR 71901
501-321-2277
800-543-2284
Fax: 501-321-2136
hscvb@hotsprings.org
www.hotsprings.org
• Steve Arrison, CEO
Description:
Tourists and Arkansas residents alike will find lots of fun things to do in Hot Springs Arkansas.

HOUSTON SPORTS DIVISION/GREATER HOUSTON CONVENTION & VISITORS BUREAU
1331 LAMAR STREET
SUITE 700
HOUSTON, TX 77002
713-437-5200
800-446-8786
Fax: 713-227-6336
www.visithoustontexas.com
• Sara McPhillips, Executive Director
• Ramona Crayton, Convention Services Manager
• Judi Taliaferro, Convention Services/National Accounts
Description:
Serves to attract sports events and sports teams to Greater Houston, TX.

HUNTSVILLE/MADISON COUNTY CONVENTION & VISITORS BUREAU
500 CHURCH STREET
SUITE 1
HUNTSVILLE, AL 35801
256-551-2230
800-843-0468
Fax: 256-551-2324
info@huntsville.org
www.huntsville.org
• Judy Ryals, President and CEO
(256) 551-2230
jryals@huntsville.org
Description:
Serves to attract sports events and sports teams to the Huntsville area.
Member Services:
Provides complimentary brochures and maps of the area as well as other services based on the number of overnight sleeping rooms used.

ILLINOIS BUREAU OF TOURISM & FILM
100 W. RANDOLPH, STE 3-400
CHICAGO, IL 60601
312-814-7179
Fax: 312-814-6175
www.enjoyillinois.com
• Cathy Ritter, Deputy Director, Bureau of Tourism
• Desi Harris, Marketing Director
• Lourdes Ortiz, Assistant Director

INDIANA SPORTS CORPORATION
PAN AMERICAN PLAZA
201 SOUTH CAPITOL AVE
SUITE 1200
INDIANAPOLIS, IN 46225-1069
317-237-5000
800-HI-FIVES
Fax: 317-237-5041
info@indianasportscorp.com
• Susan Williams, President
• Allison Melangton, President
Member Services:
Membership fees: MVP $50, All-Star $100, All-American $250, Champion $500, and Hall of Fame $1000. Included in membership when available: Event VIP Hospitality passes; member receptions, including functions with world-class athletes in attendance; priority seating at select national and international sports events; preferred volunteer opportunities at selected spoting events; thank you gift; advance ticket purchasing opportunities for many events; one year subscription to ISC's Play-by-Play e-newsletter and Events Calender; recognition on ISC's website; and invitation to attend ISC's Holiday Open House.
Publications:
PLAY BY PLAY, newsletter quarterly; President's Letter, quarterly.
Membership Requirements:
Available for tax-deductible donation.
Description:
Founded 1979. Represents Indianapolis in the national and international sports marketplace. Attracts sporting organizations and events to the city and assists in staging. Private, not-for-profit company relying on individual and corporate memberships, contributions and grants as chief funding sources.

IRVING CONVENTION & VISITORS BUREAU
500 WEST LAS COLINAS BOULEVARD
IRVING, TX 75039
972-252-7476
800-2-IRVING
Fax: 972-401-7729
info@irvingtexas.com
www.irvingtexas.com
• Maura Gast, Executive Director
(972) 252-7476
mgast@ci.irving.tx.us
• Maura Gast, Executive Director
• Lori Fojtasek, Assistant Executive Director/Sales
• Jane Kilburn, Assistant Executive Director/Administration
• Mark D Thompson, Assistant Executive Director/Marketing
• Monty White, Marketing Manager
• Karla Prine, Secretary, Marketing and Communications
• Maura Gast, Executive Director
Year Founded:
1972

JACKSON CONVENTION & VISITORS BUREAU
111 EAST CAPITOL STREET
SUITE 102
JACKSON, MS 39201
601-960-1891
800-354-7695
Fax: 601-960-1827
www.visitjackson.com
• Wanda Wilson, President/CEO
• Robert Gibbs, Chairman
• Juanita S Doty, Secretary
• Ken Crowtell, Treasurer
• Wanda Wilson, JCVB President/CEO
• Jennifer Chance, VP of Finance & Administration
• Robert Gibbs, Chairman
Sports Service Founded:
1983
Description:
The Bureau's three departments which are Administration, Marketing and Sales and Services, provides services to visitors, conventions, group tour operators, local hotels, resturants, shops, special events, and attractions, and help to bring millions of dollars to local economy annually.

JACKSONVILLE AND THE BEACHES CONVENTION AND VISITORS BUREAU
208 N LAURA STREET
SUITE 102
JACKSONVILLE, FL 32202
904-798-9111
800-733-2668
Fax: 904-798-9103
www.jaxcvb.com
• Janice Lowe, Chair
• Bill Prescott, ViceChair
• Shane Frisbee, Marketing Committee Chair
• Barry Sondern, Sales Committee Chair
• Scott Wellington, Treasurer
Nature of Service:
Promotes Jacksonville and its surroundings. Setup and organize presentations. Publishes literature and maps. Assists with all customer needs.
College Sports Sponsor:
Gator Bowl Association - Chairman's Club Member.

Football Sponsor:
River City Showdown.
Golf Sponsor:
The Players Championship.
Baseball Sponsor:
ACC Baseball Championship.

JACKSONVILLE-ONSLOW COUNTY SPORTS COMMISSION
1099 GUM BRANCH ROAD
PO BOX 207
JACKSONVILLE, NC 28540
910-347-3141
800-835-9496
Fax: 910-347-4705
www.jacksonvilleonslowsports.org
• Jesse Newsom, Executive Director
• Julie Keoho, Program Specialist
Description:
Focuses on events, activities, and facilitation that puts people in the motels of our community, people in our restaurants, and shoppers in the stores from out of town. Our target is to encourage activities that bring in teams and people from out of the area who would likely spend the night.

JEDC SPORTS AND ENTERTAINMENT DIVISION/JACKSONVILLE FLORIDA
1 WEST ADAMS STREET
SUITE 200
JACKSONVILLE, FL 32202
904-630-3600
Fax: 904-630-3606
• Michael Bouda, Manager
Nature of Sports Service:
JEDC Sports and Entertainment exists to attract sporting events and activities in Jacksonville that appeal to a large cross-section of citizens; to provide financial and promotional assistance to major events; to provide a full array of fee-paid marketing services to help promoters maximize attendance; and to help bring national and international publicity to the City of Jacksonville.
Facilities Available for Sporting Events:
The Baseball Grounds of Jacksonville (Baseball); Jacksonville Municipal Stadium (variety); Veterans Memorial Arena (variety); Equestrian Center (Equestrian); Prime Osborn Convention Center (Cheerleading); Times Union Center for Performing Arts (variety)

JOHNSON CITY CONVENTION & VISITORS BUREAU
603 EAST MARKET STREET
PO BOX 180
JOHNSON CITY, TN 37061
423-461-8000
800-852-3392
Fax: 423-461-8047
www.johnsoncitytnchamber.com
• Brenda Whitson, Executive Director
(423) 461-8010
• Gary Mabrey, President / CEO
(423) 461-8008
• Glenda Britt, Director of Finance
(423) 461-8005
• Barbara Mentgen, Director of Operations
(423) 461-8011
• Elisa Britt, Executive Secretary
(423) 461-8006
britt@johnsoncitytnchamber.com
• Cindy Foster, Executive Assistant CVB
(432) 461-8002

JOPLIN CONVENTION & VISITORS BUREAU AND SPORTS AUTHORITY
602 SOUTH MAIN STREET
JOPLIN, MO 64801
417-625-4789
800-657-2534
Fax: 417-624-7948
cvb@joplinmo.com
• Mike Greninger, Executive Director/Sports Authority
• Mike McAffe, Director Joplin Convention/Visotrs Bureau
Description:
Promotes Joplin and surrounding areas as a location for sporting events.

JUNEAU CONVENTION & VISITORS BUREAU
800 GLACIER AVENUE
SUITE 201
JUNEAU, AK 99801
907-586-2201
800-587-2201
Fax: 907-586-1449
info@traveljuneau.com
www.traveljuneau.com
• Lorene Palmer, President
Sports Services Founded:
1985.
Description:
Organization dedicated to economic developmetn in Juneau, Alaksa through promoting and marketing Juneau as a year round visitor destination. The primary goal is to increase the overnight stay of business and pleasure travelers who support local businesses through consumer spending, and the city through payment of bed tax.

KANKAKEE COUNTY CONVENTION & VISITORS BUREAU
1 DEARBORN SQUARE
SUITE 1
KANKAKEE, IL 60901
815-935-7390
800-747-4937
Fax: 815-935-5169
info@visitkankakeecounty.com
www.visitkankakeecounty.com
• Larry Williams, Executive Director
• Vicki Layhew, Sales/Marketing Manager
• Nancy Fregeau, Operations/Communications
• Larry Williams, Executive Director
• Vicki Layhew, Sales & Marketing Manager
• Marilyn McAdoo, General Office Support
General Description:
Kankakee County is home to the Chicago Bears summer training camp, eight golf courses, spacious parks, 57 miles of winding river waters and numerous sports complexes. Located just an hour south of Chicago along Interstate 57 the county offers convenience and accessibility. Sports facilities are conveniently located close to dining, shopping, attractions, and lodging accomodations. Founded in 1983.
Facilities Available for Sporting Events:
Hidden Cove Sportsplex: Basketball, Mini Golf, Gymnastics, Wrestling, Paintball, Soccer, Volleyball; Diamond Sports Complex: Baseball, Softball; National City's River Road Softball Complex - Softball, Youth Baseball; OAK Orthopedic Sports Arena: Hockey, Figure Skating, Curling; Kankakee County Speedway: Stock Car Racing; Kankakee River: Boat Racing, Canoeing, Kayaking; Manteno Lake:

Swimming, Triathlons
Publications:
Kankakee County Visitors Guide; Kankakee County Outdoor Guide; Sports Event Planner Kit

KANSAS CITY SPORTS COMMISSION AND FOUNDATION
2600 GRAND BLVD
SUITE 100
KANSAS CITY, MO 64108
816-474-4652
Fax: 816-474-7979
info@sportkc.org
www.sportkc.org
• Kathy Nelson, President/CEO
(816) 474-4652
knelson@sportkc.org
• Jacob Robertson, Executive Coordinator
(816) 389-4193
jrobertson@sportkc.org
• Dave Borchardt, Director, Corporate & Community Relationships
(816) 389-4191
dborchardt@sportkc.org
Member Services:
Sporting Events, volunteer opportunities, networking opportunities.
Publications:
THE SPORTS PAGE.
Membership Requirements:
Annual fees.
Sports Services Founded:
1969
Number of Members:
600
Description:
Goals A) Aims to enhance the quality of life and economic success of Greater Kansas City by taking the lead in maintaining and selectively acquiring a diversity of amateur and professional sporting events. B) To collaborate with area economic development agencies to attract and retain amateur and professional sports organizations. C) To promote the lifetime benefits of sports for the youth of Greater Kansas City.

KINGSPORT CONVENTION & VISITORS BUREAU
400 CLINCHFIELD STREET
SUITE 100
KINGSPORT, TN 37660
423-392-8820
800-743-5282
Fax: 423-392-8803
kcvb@kcvb.org
www.kcvb.org
• Jud Teague, Executive Director
(423) 392-8832
jteague@kcvb.org
• Jud Teague, Executive Director
• Frank Lett, Associate Executive Director/Sports
(423) 392-8831
flett@kcvb.org

KISSIMMEE-ST. CLOUD CONVENTION & VISITORS BUREAU
1925 EAST IRLO BRONSON MEMORIAL HIGHWAY
KISSIMMEE, FL 34744
407-742-8200
800-327-9159
www.experiencekissimmee.com
• Tim Hemphill, Executive Director

multi sports

Description:
Staff develops and impliments programs and activities that produce solid results through reliable relationships with marketing.

KNOXVILLE TOURISM & SPORTS CORPORATION
• Kim Bumpas, President
• Chad Culver, Senior Director, Sports Commission
• Kristen Combs, Director, Communications
• Parker Medley, Director, Sports Sales
• Kelli Ryman, Director, Event Services
• Erin Simcox, Housing Manager
Description:
The Visit Knoxville Sports Commission promotes the Knoxville/Knox County as a destination for sports-related events. This includes youth events, collegiate events and professional events. The Commission works with local organizers, as well as National Governing Bodies.

LACKAWANNA COUNTY CONVENTION & VISITORS BUREAU
99 GLENMAURA NATIONAL BLVD
MOOSIC, PA 18507
570-496-1701
800-229-3526
Fax: 570-963-6369
info@visitnepa.org
www.visitnepa.org
• Morgan Christopher, Director of Sales
• Carl Puscavage, Marketing Sales Manager

LAFAYETTE CONVENTION & VISITORS BUREAU
1400 NW EVANGELINE TRWY
LAFAYETTE, LA 70501-2829
337-232-3737
800-346-1958
Fax: 337-232-0161
www.lafayettetravel.com
• Gerald Breaux, Executive Director
gerald@lafayettetravel.com
• Felicia Duhon, Controller
• Kelly Strenge, PR/Special Projects Manager
Sports Services Founded:
1974
Description:
Created to serves as a tourism promotion and marketing coordinator for all of Lafayette Parish.

LAFAYETTE-WEST LAFAYETTE CONVENTION & VISITORS BUREAU
301 FRONTAGE RD
LAFAYETTE, IN 47905-4564
765-447-9999
800-872-6648
Fax: 765-447-5062
agordon@homeofpurdue.com
www.homeofpurdue.com
• Ashley Gregory, Group Tours & Meeting Manager
• Amanda Gordon, Sports Marketing & CommunicationsManager
• Judy Ryan, Customer Services Coordinator
• Sara Erickson, PR & Social Media Specialist
• Jo Wilson Wade, President/CEO
• Lisa Morrow, Vice President
Description:
Purdue University-Swimming &

Diving/Golf/Fencing/Rugby/Soccer etc. Golf-two 4 1/2 star rated courses equipt for tournaments of any size, indoor and outdoor softball and volleyball, outdoor soccer and more.

LAKE COUNTY, ILLINOIS - CONVENTION & VISITORS BUREAU
5465 WEST GRAND AVENUE
SUITE 100
GURNEE, IL 60031
847-662-2700
800-LAKE NOW
Fax: 847-662-2702
tourism@lakecounty.org
www.lakecounty.org
• Maureen Riedy, President
• Peggy Altman, Visitor & Partner Services Coordinator
• Kimberly Ghys, Senior Sales Manager
• Hassan El Neklawy, Chair, Lincolnshire Marriott Resort
• Mike Allison, Treasurer
• Anthony Haag, Marketing Manager
• Theresa Lewis, Sales Manager
Description:
Mission is to increase awareness of Lake County, IL as a premier tourism destination through a collective sales and marketing approach that stimulates overnight stays and enhances visitor spending and ultimately generates a substantial economic impact for Lake County communities.

LAKE LANIER CVB
2875 BROWNS BRIDGE ROAD
GAINESVILLE, GA 30507
678-696-2491
Fax: 770-503-1349
jennifer@lakelaniercvb.com
www.lakelaniercvb.com
• Stacey Dickson, President
• Jennifer Miller, Vice President
Description:
Founded 1992. Serves to increase sports tourism in the greater Gainesville/Hall County area, to work with existing sports facilities and groups, and to foster new facilities and groups where the community recognizes a need for them.
Number of Members:
100
Members Services:
Co-op advertising; market facility in the facilities guide; trade show representation; CVB member website link.

LAS CRUCES CONVENTION & VISITORS BUREAU
211 NORTH WATER STREET
LAS CRUCES, NM 88001
575-541-2444
Fax: 575-541-2164
www.lascrucescvb.org
• Jennifer Bales, Director Of Sales
(575) 541-2258
• Phillip San Filippo, Executive Director
(505) 541-2444
psfilippo@las-cruces.org
• Chris Faivre, Director of Marketing and Communications
(575) 541-2258
cfaivre@las-cruces.org
• Edward S Carnathan, Sports Sales
(505) 541-2216
ecarnathan@las-cruces.org

LAS VEGAS CONVENTION & VISITORS AUTHORITY
3150 PARADISE ROAD
LAS VEGAS, NV 89109
702-892-0711
877-847-4858
www.visitlasvegas.com
• Tom Collins, Chairman
• Tom Jenkins, Treasurer
• Nancy Murphy, Vice President Sales
Nature of Service:
Promotes sports and economic development in Las Vegas and surrounding areas.
Auto Sports Sponsor:
NASCAR Sprint Cup Series: UAW-Dodge 400.
Rodeo Sponsor:
Clark County Fair & Rodeo; Bill Pickett Invitational Rodeo; Wrangler National Finals Rodeo.
Equestrian Sponsor:
Arabian Breeders World Cup.
Supercross/Motocross Sponsor:
Amp'D Mobile Supercross Series.
Wrestling Sponsor:
USA Wrestling World Team Trials.
Martial Arts Sponsor:
Tuff N' Uff Amateur Mixed Martial Arts.

LAS VEGAS EVENTS
770 EAST WARM SPRINGS ROAD
SUITE 140
LAS VEGAS, NV 89119
702-260-8605
Fax: 702-260-8622
www.lasvegasevents.com
• Pat Christenson, President
• Dale Eeles, VP Event Development
Description:
We produce, present, and support premier events that drive tourism and increase awareness of the Las Vegas area as the Entertainment Capital of the World. Events held are: Monster Jam World Finals 2006; 2006 NHRA SummitRacing.co Nationals; LPGA Takefuji Classic; Laughlin River Run; THQ World Superscross GP/THQ AMA Supercross Series Finals; NIRA West Coast Regional Finals Rodeo; AFL Arena Bowl Championships; Vegas Summer League; Las Vegas Prep Basketball Showcase; SCORE Las Vegas Terrible's Cup II; Prim 300 Score; Las Vegas 350(NASCAR Craftsman Truck Series); ACDelco Las Vegas NHRA Nationals; Aviation Nation; Senior Softball Winter Worlds; NF

LAWRENCE SPORTS CORPORATION
734 VERMONT STREET
SUITE 101
LAWRENCE, KS 66044-0586
785-865-4499
888-529-5267
Fax: 785-865-4400
admin@visitlawrence.com
www.visitlawrence.com/sports
• Bob Sanner, Director Sports Conventions
• Judy Billings, Director
(785) 865-4494
Sports Services Founded:
1988
Description:
Markets and promotes Lawrence as the preferred destination for athletic events that benefit the community both economically and socially. The LSC supports these

events with assistance in hte areas of funding, management, marketing and organization to help make them as successful as possible.

LEE ISLAND COAST VISITOR & CONVENTION BUREAU
12800 UNIVERSITY DRIVE
SUITE 550
FT. MYERS, FL 33907
239-338-3550
800-237-6444
Fax: 239-334-1106
VCB@leegov.com
www.leeislandcoast.com
• Suya T. Davenport, Executive Director
• Pamela Johnson, CDME, Sales Director
• Lee Rose, APR, Communications Manager
Description:
To increase tourism in the off season and to increase awareness about Lee County as a vacation destination. Serves to promote sports development and attract events and sport related meetings to the Lee County area which includes Fort Myers Beach, Lehigh Acres, Bonita Springs, Pine Island, Boca Grande and Sanibel/Captiva Islands, Cape Coral in the off peak tourist season, May through December.

LEHIGH VALLEY SPORTS COMMISSION
840 HAMILTON STREET
SUITE 200
ALLENTOWN, PA 18101
610-882-9200
800-747-0561
Fax: 610-882-0343
• Michael Kusinuk, Sports Marketing Director
• Kim Lilly, VP
Description:
Goal is to promote Lehigh Valley as a sports destination by attracting and retaining sporting events and tournaments, thereby ersulting in economic benefits for the region. Also supports the efforts of local sporting events and facilities.
Facilities Available
10 colleges and universities for multiple sports county parks & fields, Raach Field House, soccer fields, IAX, bowling, golf, basketball, baseball, softball, disc golf.

LEXINGTON AREA SPORTS AUTHORITY
301 EAST VINE STREET
LEXINGTON, KY 40507
859-244-7710
800-848-1224
Fax: 859-389-7225
• Rick Hatcher, President/Executive Director
rhatcher@visitlex.com
Description:
The primary purpose of the Lexington Area Sports Authority (LASA) is to promote amateur sports in the Lexington area by bringing in, and supporting, quality amateur athletic events. These events, which utilize local public and private facilities and resources, have a tremendous social and economic impact on the community.

LINCOLN SPORTS COMMISSION
1135 M ST, STE 200
LINCOLN, NE 68501
402-434-5335
800-423-8212

Fax: 402-434-2360
www.lincoln.org
• Jeff Maul, Executive Director
• Derek Feyerheim, Director Of Sales
Description:
Founded 1988. Develops and implements programs to attract sports events and sports meetings to Lincoln and Lancaster County Nebraska.

LISLE CONVENTION & VISITOR BUREAU
925 BURLINGTON AVENUE
LISLE, IL 60532
630-769-1000
800-733-9811
Fax: 630-769-1006
lislevisitor@stayinlisle.com
www.lislecvb.com
• Hilton Lisle, General Manager
Description:
A full service CVB that will be a valuable resource in making any event, meeting, reunion, retreat or vacation as enjoyable and successful as possible.

LONG ISLAND CVB & SPORTS COMMISSION
330 MOTOR PKWY
SUITE 203
HAUPPAUGE, NY 11788
631-951-3900
877-FUN-ON-LI
jrothman@discoverlongisland.com
www.discoverlongisland.com/sports
• Jennifer Rothman, Sales Manager
(631) 951-3900
jrothman@discoverlongisland.com
• R Moke McGowan, President
(631) 951-3900
mmcgowan@discoverlongisland.com
Description:
Founded 1992. Dedicated to attracting professional and amateur sporting events, championships and related industry conferences to Long Island for the purpose of economic development. Also provides assistance to organizations interested in hosting sporting events or functions on Long Island. Works directly with national governing bodies and sport event planners.
Member Services:
A division of the Long Island Convention & Visitors Bureau. Represents Long Island in the national and international sports marketplace.

LOS ANGELES SPORTS & ENTERTAINMENT COMMISSION
333 SOUTH HOPE STREET
18TH FLOOR
LOS ANGELES, CA 90071
213-236-2381
Fax: 213-326-2368
www.lasec.net
• Kathryn S Schloessman, President
(213) 236-2381
• Cindy Hanson, Sports Manager
(213) 236-2361
Sports Services Founded:
1995
Description:
The official organization for the City of Los Angeles to seek, host, promote and retain major sporting and entertainment events that postively impact the local economy. These events attract visitors to the city, give them a reason to stay longerand return more

frequently and reinforce Los Angeles as an event destination for national and international visitors.

LOS ANGELES SPORTS COUNCIL
350 SOUTH BIXEL STREET
SUITE 250
LOS ANGELES, CA 90017
213-482-6333
Fax: 213-482-6340
www.lasports.org
• Karen Brodkin, Chair
• Richard W. Cook, Vice Chair
• Sheldon I Ausman, Treasurer
Description:
A non-profit civic organization which works to attract major events to the area.

LOUISVILLE CONVENTION & VISITORS BUREAU
401 WEST MAIN STREET
SUITE 2300
LOUISVILLE, KY 40202
502-584-2121
888-568-4784
Fax: 502-584-6697
info@gotolouisville.com
www.gotolouisville.com
• Cleo Battle, Executive Vice President
cbattle@gotolouisville.com
• Jennifer Barnett, Vice President of Convention Development
jbarnett@gotolouisville.com
• Stacey Yates, Vice President of Marketing Communications
syates@gotolouisville.com
• James Wood, President/CEO
jwood@gotolouisville.com
• Karen Wiliams, Executive VP
kwilliams@gotolouisville.com
• Stacey Yates, Vice President Communications/Marketing
syates@gotolouisville.com
• Doris Sims, Director of Bureau Services
dsims@gotolouisville.com
Description:
Promotes Louisville and Jefferson County as a potential host sight for sporting events and meetings.

LUBBOCK SPORTS AUTHORITY
1500 BROADWAY
6TH FLOOR
LUBBOCK, TX 79401
806-747-5232
800-692-4035
Fax: 806-747-1419
www.visitlubbock.org
• John Osborne, CEO
• Amy Zientec, Director of Sales
Description:
Serves to attract sports events and meetings to the Lubbock, Texas area.

MACOMB AREA CONVENTION AND VISITORS BUREAU
201 SOUTH LAFAYETTE STREET
MACOMB, IL 61455
309-833-1315
Fax: 309-833-3575
www.makeitmacomb.com
• Tamara Parker, Interim Executive Director
• Katy Vizdai, Special Projects Coordinator
Description:
A non-profit organization began in July of 1998. The CVB is responsible for bringing in and assisting with conferences and

conventions while also organizing local events.

MACON-BIBB COUNTY CONVENTION AND VISITORS BUREAU
450 MARTIN LUTHER KING JR BLVD
MACON, GA 31201
478-743-3401
800-768-3401
www.maconga.org
• Monica W Smith, President/CEO
(478) 743-1074
• Valerie Bradley, Communications Manager
(478) 743-1074
vbradley@maconga.org
• Monica Smith CMP CASE CDME, President and CEO
(478) 743-1074
Description:
Founded 1980. Serves to attract sports events and meetings to the greater Macon area.

MANHATTAN AREA SPORTS COMMISSION (CONVENTION AND VISITORS BUREAU)
501 POYNTZ AVENUE
MANHATTAN, KS 66502
785-776-8829
sports@manhattan.org
www.manhattancvb.org
• Marcia Rozell, Tourism Sales Manager
• Karen Hibbard, Director
• Christy Chase, Convention Sales Manager
• Kendra Dekat, Service Coordinator
• Autumn Shoemaker, Marketing Coordinator

MARICOPA COUNTY SPORTS COMMISSION
ARIZONA CENTER
400 EAST VAN BUREN STREET
SUITE 600
PHOENIX, AZ 85004
602-258-6272
• John Schmieder, President
• Ed Durkin, Sales/Marketing Manager
Sports Services Founded:
1988
Description:
Mission is to represent the citizens of Maricopa County in the quest to establish Maricopa County as a premier national and international sports destination; to assist in the promotion of local events and teams; to develop programs that positively affect our community's youth and to provide Maricopa County residents the widest variety of great sports experiences possible.

MARYLAND SPORTS
WAREHOUSE AT CAMDEN YARDS
333 W CAMDEN ST
4TH FLOOR
BALTIMORE, MD 21201
410-223-4158
Fax: 410-333-1888
info@marylandsports.us
www.marylandsports.us
• Ashley Harper Cottrell, Project Manager
(410) 767-1416
acottrell@marylandsports.us
• Terry Hasseltine, Executive Director
(410) 223-4158
thasseltine@marylandsports.us
• Kelli Gerding, Project Coordinator
(410) 223-4671

Description:
Founded in 2008. Mission: Enhance Maryland's economy, image and quality of life through attraction, promotion, retention and development of regional, national and international sporting events.
Teams:
TEAM Maryland - a statewide initiative designed to collectively market Maryland to the entire sports industry by creating a synergistic approach to the way Maryland is marketed as a sports destination. Currently, fourteen counties have joined the program.

MASHANTUCKET PEQUOT TRIBAL NATION'S ATHLETIC COMMISSION
PO BOX 3378
MASHANTUCKET, CT 06339-3378
860-396-6727
Fax: 860-396-6723
www.boxrec.com
• Joe Letellier, Executive Director
• Richard Butler, Vice Chairman

MASON CITY CONVENTION & VISITOR BUREAU
9 NORTH FEDERAL AVENUE
MASON CITY, IA 50401
641-423-5724
Fax: 641-423-5725
www.masoncityia.com
• Robin Anderson, Executive Director
• Kara Ruge, Program Director
• Debra Derr, President
• Bob Klocke, Treasurer
• David Laundner, Government Affairs DVP
• Troy Swanson, DVP Workforce

MASSACHUSETTS SPORTS & ENTERTAINMENT COMMISSION
PO BOX 170427
BOSTON, MA 2117
617-614-1203
Fax: 617-507-8491
• Sam Weisman, Chairman
• Jonathan H Paris, Executive Director
Description:
Founded in 1992. A private, non-for-profit corporation established to attract and stage major sporting events and sports related meetings throughout Massachusetts. Its principal purposes are to increase economic impact through events, travel and tourism; to enhance the quality of life for all residents by the presence of exciting sporting events; and to improve opportunities for youth in sports.
Publications:
SportsMatters, quarterly newsletter.

MEMPHIS & SHELBY COUNTY SPORTS AUTHORITY
160 N MAIN STREET
MEMPHIS, TN 38103
901-222-2300
www.shelbycountytn.gov
• Bill McGaughey, Chairman
Sports Services Founded:
1997
Description:
To promote the Mid-South region by supporting and developing economic impact and quality of life through sporting events. Our main focus is to attract sporting events to the area, as well as supporting our professional, college and high school athletics.

MESA CONVENTION & VISITORS BUREAU
120 NORTH CENTER
MESA, AZ 85201
480-827-4700
800-283-6372
Fax: 480-827-4704
www.visitmesa.com
• Josh Todd, Sports Sales Manager
• Rick Elder, Communcations Manager
• Milt Ford, Sales/Marketing Director
Description:
Mesa Convention & Visitors Bureau; Mesa Sports & Tourism Development

METRO DENVER SPORTS COMMISSION
444 SHERMAN STREET
SUITE 300
DENVER, CO 80203
303-744-6372
Fax: 303-648-4408
• Sue Baldwin, Interim President
• Debora Hurley, Director Coroprate Membership
(303) 534-5517
Sports Service Founded:
2001
Description:
Founded to attract economically beneficial sporting events to the Denver market. The purpose of the Metro Denver Sports Commission is to create a legacy of economic and social vitality through sports.

METROPOLITAN RICHMOND SPORTS BACKERS
100 AVENUE OF CHAMPIONS
SUITE 300
RICHMOND, VA 23230
804-285-9495
Fax: 804-285-3132
info@sportsbackers.org
www.sportsbackers.org
• Jon Lugbill, Executive Director
jon@sportsbackers.org
• Scott Schricker, Marketing Director
scott@sportsbackers.com
Sports Services Founded:
1991
Description:
A 501(c) (3) charitable non-profit organization whose vision is to transform greater Richmond into the most physically active community in the nation by leading the area in embracing and celebrating an active lifestyle.
Publications:
Sports Backers Quarterly; e-Newsletters

METROPOLITAN SPORTS FACILITIES COMMISSION
900 S. 5TH ST
MINNEAPOLIS, MN 55415
612-332-0386
Fax: 612-332-8334
www.msfc.com
• William Lester, Executive Director
(612) 332-0386
• Steve Maki, PE, Director of Facilities & Engineering
• Mary Fox-Stroman, CPA, Director of Finance
Description:
In addition to being the bome of the Minnesota Vikings, the Metrodome serves the state of Minnesota by hosting amateur

events, cultural events, and family-focused activities.

METROPOLITAN TUCSON CONVENTION & VISITORS BUREAU
100 SOUTH CHURCH AVENUE
TUCSON, AZ 85701
520-624-1817
800-638-8350
Fax: 520-884-7804
info@visittucson.org
www.visittucson.org
• Jonathan Walker, President/CEO
(800) 638-8350
• Vince Trinidad, Director Sports Development
(800) 638-8350
• Allison Cooper, Director of Marketing

MIDLAND CHAMBER CONVENTION & VISITORS BUREAU
109 NORTH MAIN
MIDLAND, TX 79701
432-683-3381
800-624-6435
Fax: 432-686-3556
www.visitmidlandtx.com
• Bobby Burns, President & CEO, Midland Chamber of Commerce
bobby@midlandtxchamber.com
• Gaylia Olivas, Vice President, Convention & Visitors Bureau
• Norma Chavez, Administrative Assistant to CVB
• Brenda Kissko, Tourism & Public Relations Manager
• Katie Sangl, Sports Sales Manager
• Gaylia Olivas, Director, Convention & Visitors Bureau
Description:
Promotes the Midland Texas and surrounding areas as an ideal location for sporting events.

MINNEAPOLIS CONVENTION & VISITORS ASSOCIATION, GREATER
1301 SECOND AVENUE SOUTH
MINNEAPOLIS, MN 55401
612-335-6000
Fax: 612-335-6757
www.minneapolis.org
• Jeff D. Johnson, Executive Director
• Mark Zirbel, Director of Events
• Christine Hunjas, Director Business Administration
Description:
Actively solicits amateur and professional sporting events that result in a direct dollar benefit to Minneapolis and the Twin Cities area. Capable of coordinating all aspects of the bidding process.

MINNEAPOLIS METRO NORTH CONVENTION & VISITORS BUREAU
7100 NORTHLAND CIRCLE NORTH
SUITE 102
MINNEAPOLIS, MN 55428
763-566-7722
800-541-4364
Fax: 763-566-6526
info@visitminneapolisnorth.com
www.minneapolisnorthwest.com
• Dave Looby, Executive Director
(763) 252-1415
• Danielle Moon, Sales & Marketing Coordinator
(763) 252-1410
• Lindsay Spiros, Sales & Marketing Manager
(763) 252-1413
• Tim Zunker, Senior Sports & Marketing Manager
(763) 252-1412
• Katie Blake, Creative Marketing & Project Coordinator
(763) 252-1416
• Brooke Stoeckel-Whaylen, Director/Meetings & Events
(763) 252-1420
Member Services:
Site visits, bid presentations, team discounts from area businesses, lodgingproperties, welcome packets, itinerary planning assistance, familiarization tours.
Description:
A destination marketing organization representing 11 cities in the north and west suburbs of Minneapolis and Saint Paul. These cities include Anoka, Arden Hills, Blaine, Brooklyn Center, Coon Rapids, Fridley, Ham Lake, maple Grove, Mounds View & Shoreview.

MOBILE BAY CONVENTION & VISITORS BUREAU
PO BOX 204
MOBILE, AL 36601-0204
251-208-2000
800-566-2453
Fax: 251-208-2060
visitmobile@mobile.org
www.mobile.org
• David Buzzard, President
• Jay Garraway, Finance/Administration Director
jay-garraway@mobile.org
• Stacy Hamilton, Vice President Marketing/Commmunications
Description:
Founded 1986. Serves to promote sports development and attract sports events and conventions to the Mobile, Alabama area.

MONROE COUNTY SPORTS COMMISSION
400 ANDRES STREET
SUITE 100
ROCHESTER, NY 14604
585-262-3832
Fax: 585-232-3453
www.monroecountysports.org
• Steve Hausmann, President
• Tim Elie, Vice President
• Gary Mervis, Secretary
• Dan Manson, Treasurer
• Jim Lebeau, Managing Director
(585) 262-2009
jimlebeau@hotmail.com
• Rich Mackey, Marketing/Sales
(585) 262-3832
scottb@monroecountysports.org
• Jacob Linderberry, Sales & Operations
(585) 262-3832
Description:
Serves to promote sports development and attract sports events and conventions to the Rochester, New York Sports Area.

MUNCIE SPORTS COMMISSION INC
3700 SOUTH MADISON STREET
MUNCIE, IN 47302
765-284-2700
800-369-0082
Fax: 765-284-3002
www.visitmuncie.org
• Jim Mansfield, Executive Director
jim@visitmuncie.org
• Julie Ashton, Business Manager
Year Founded:
1993
Description:
Founded to advance economic development and to enhance the quality of life in Delaware County through the development of sports and hobby acticities. 11 Soccer fields with restroom and small concession building. 5 ball diamonds with restroom and concession
Facilities:
Muncie Sportsplex-soccer, softball/fastpitch/little league baseball

NASHVILLE SPORTS COUNCIL
414 UNION STREET
SUITE 800
NASHVILLE, TN 37201
615-743-3120
Fax: 615-244-3540
generalinfo@nashvillesports.com
www.nashvillesports.com
• Scott Ramsey, President and CEO
(615) 743-3122
SRamsey@NashvilleSports.com
• Gary Karl Alexander, Sr. VP and COO
(615) 743-3123
GAlexander@NashvilleSports.com
Description:
Founded 1992. The mission is to postively impact the economy and quality of life of the Greater Nashville Area by attracting and promoting professional and amateur sports.

NASSAU COUNTY SPORTS COMMISSION
1055 STEWART AVENUE
BETHPAGE, NY 11714
516-918-3799
Fax: 516-365-3632
www.nassausports.org
• Gary I. Wadler, Chairman/President
• Bryan Revello, Executive Director
• Edward Mangano, Ex Officio
Description:
Founded 1992. Promotes the advancement of sports in Nassau County from every perspective - amateur, professional, youth and master sports, and activities for the differently-abled. Works cooperatively with the public and private sectors in identifying, coordinating, and developing sports programs, facilities, and events for the benefit of the economy and the enjoyment of the community.

NEBRASKA DIVISION OF TRAVEL AND TOURISM
1135 M STREET
SUITE 300
LINCOLN, NE 68501
402-434-5335
800-423-8212
Fax: 402-436-2360
www.lincoln.org
• Derek Feyerherm, Director of Sales & Operations
(402) 436-2354
• Melanie Maynard, Social, Military, Education, Religious, Frate
(402) 436-2310

multi sports

• Jeff Maul, Executive Director
• Tracie Simpson, Service Coordinator
Publications:
Nebraska Travel Guide

NEW ORLEANS METROPOLITAN CONVENTION & VISITORS BUREAU
2020 ST CHARLES AVENUE
NEW ORLEANS, LA 70130
504-566-5011
800-672-6124
Fax: 504-566-5046
internet@neworleanscvb.com
www.neworleanscvb.com
• Kelly Schulz, Vice President
(504) 566-5019
• Sarah Forman, Community Coordinator
(504) 566-5021
Description:
Serves to attract sports-related meetings, conventions and shows to the greater New Orleans area. Provides assistance with hotel, meeting facility and venue selection, convention services and visitor information.

NEW ORLEANS SPORTS FOUNDATION, GREATER
2020 ST CHARLES AVENUE
4TH FLOOR
NEW ORLEANS, LA 70130
504-525-5678
Fax: 504-529-1622
media@gnosports.com
www.gnosports.com
• Jay Cicero, President/Chief Executive Officer
jcicero@gnosf.org
• Billy Ferrante, Vice President/Marketing/Events
bferrante@gnosf.org
• Sam Joffray, Vice President/Communications
administration@gnosf.org
• Alison Comeaux, Events/Operations
acomeaux@gnosf.org
Description:
Founded 1988.The Greater New Orleans Sports Foundation (GNOSF) was formed with a vision to enhance the city's ability to attract, promote and manage major sporting events that have a positive economic impact on the Greater New Orleans area. The GNOSF has been involved in attracting or promoting nearly 75 events including Super Bowl XXX1 (1997) and Super Bowl XXXVI (2002), The NCAA Final Four (1993) and the Olympic Track & Field Trials (1992). The GNOSF was selected as the Sports Commission of the Year in 1996 by the International Sports Summit.

NORFOLK CONVENTION & VISITORS BUREAU
232 EAST MAIN STREET
NORFOLK, VA 23510
757-664-6620
800-368-3097
Fax: 757-622-3663
rsteven@norfolkcvb.com
www.norfolkcvb.com
• Anthony J. DiFilippo, President & CEO
• Erin Filarecki, Media Relations Manager
• Sarah Caroll, Executive Assistant
• Jennifer Mullin, Marketing & Public Relations Assistant
• Mary Garrett, Director Marketing/Communications
mgarrett@norfolkcvb.com
• Donna Allen, Vice President of Sales & Marketing
dallen@norfolkcvb.com

NORMAN CONVENTION & VISITORS BUREAU
2424 SPRINGER DRIVE
SUITE 107
NORMAN, OK 73069
405-366-8095
800-767-7260
www.visitnorman.com
• Stephen Koranda, Executive Director
• Susan Bash, Sales Manager
• Stefanie Brickman, Communications Manager
• Michelle Samp, Group Sales Manager
• Taylor Mauldin, Visitor Services Specialist

NORTH CAROLINA AMATEUR SPORTS
406 BLACKWELL STREET
SUITE 120
DURHAM, NC 27701
919-361-1133
Fax: 919-361-2559
ncas@ncsports.org
www.ncsports.org
• Chuck Hobgood, President
  ext 5
• Ragan Williams, Event Director/State Games
  ext 3
Description:
Founded 1983. Develops and promotes amateur athletics and the Olympic movement in North Carolina. Hosts such activities as State Games of North Carolina. Sponsorship packages available for all events and forming a bicycle tour across North Carolina.

NORTH CAROLINA SPORTS DEVELOPMENT OFFICE
301 NORTH WILMINGTON ST
RALEIGH, NC 27601-1058
919-733-4151
800-VISIT NC
Fax: 919-733-8582
mmcglohon@nccommerce.com
www.nccommerce.com/sports
• Kristi Driver, Sports Manager
  ext 5
kdriver@nccommerce.com
Nature of Sports Service:
Founded 1990. Promotes North Carolina as a premier sports destination for amateur, collegiate and professional sports teams and organizations.
Publications:
North Carolina Sports Events Directory, annually with mid-year update. North Carolina Sports Facility Guide, annually.

NORTH LITTLE ROCK VISITORS BUREAU
PO BOX 5511
NORTH LITTLE ROCK, AR 72119
501-758-1424
800-643-4690
Fax: 501-758-5752
www.northlittlerock.org
• Shannon Harris, Sports & Special Events Coordinator
• Summer Toyne, VIC Coordinator
stoyne@northlittlerock.org

Description:
Founded 1975. Serves to promote sports development and attract sports events to the North Little Rock, and the Central Arkansas area.

NYC & COMPANY
810 SEVENTH AVENUE
3RD FLOOR
NEW YORK, NY 10019
212-484-1200
www.nycgo.com/sports
• Jeff Mohl, Vice President, Sports Marketing
• Evan Ely, Manager, Sports Marketing
Description:
The Sports Marketing Department at NYC & Company is responsible for attracting, creating and promoting sporting events throughout New York City's five boroughs. The department facilitates the production of a diverse line-up of high-profile professional and amateur events that excite area sports fans, generates revenue for the region and garners positive exposure for New York City.

OKLAHOMA CITY ALL SPORTS ASSOCIATION
211 NORTH ROBINSON
SUITE 250
OKLAHOMA CITY, OK 73102
405-236-5000
800-434-5000
Fax: 405-236-5008
• Tim Brassfield, Executive Director
• David Forester, Director of Event Operations
• Sean Maguire, Director of communications and marketing
• Claire Oliver, Events manager
• Tris Thomas, Controller
• Tim Brassfield, Executive Director
(405) 236-5000
Other Events Sponsored/Co-Sponsored:
All Sports Pro/Am golf Invitational Sportsfest (winter games of our state games). Big XII Baseball Tournament, NCAA Women's College World Series, Sooner State Games (State Games of Oklahoma).
Member Services:
Priority on ticket purchasing for events, plus two reserved seats for the All-College tournament with many other benefits depending on amount of sponsor participation.
Publications:
Souvenir programs for events.
Membership Requirements:
$200 VIP membership; $350 ELITE membership.
Description:
Founded 1957 as a non-profit Corporation. Promotes sponsor and finances the All-College Basketball Tournament and other sporting events in the Oklahoma City area.

OREGON SPORTS AUTHORITY
1888 SW MADISON STREET
2ND FLOOR
PORTLAND, OR 97205-1717
503-234-4500
Fax: 503-234-3853
info@oregonsports.org
• Drew Mahalic, Chief Executive Officer

Description:
Local sponsorhip opportunities for major Oregon sports events

---

OVERLAND PARK CONVENTION & VISITORS BUREAU
CORPORATE WOODS BUILDING 29
9001 W. 110TH STREET
SUITE 100
OVERLAND PARK, KS 66210
913-491-0123
800-262-7275
Fax: 913-491-0015
info@opcvb.org
• Jerry Cook, President
jcook@opcvb.org
• Judy Shellhorn, Information Services
(913) 491-0123
jshell@visitoverlandpark.com
• Libby Shilpey, Director of Finance
(913) 491-0123
libbysply@visitoverlandpark.com
• Brad Plumb, Sales Manager
(913) 491-0123
bplumb@visitoverlandpark.com
• Justin Stine, Director
(913) 491-0123
• Liron BenDor, Vice President of Marketing
(913) 491-0123
lbendor@visitoverlandpark.com
• Kelly Peetoom, Vice President Sales
kpeetoom@opcvb.org
Description:
Serves to promote Overland Park and the surrounding areas as a location for sports events, conventions, meetings etc.

PALM BEACH COUNTY SPORTS COMMISSION, INC.
1555 PALM BEACH LAKES BOULEVARD
SUITE 930
WEST PALM BEACH, FL 33401
561-233-3180
Fax: 561-233-3125
info@palmbeachsports.com
www.palmbeachsports.com
• Stephanie Lanza, Secretary/Treasurer
• George Linely, Executive Director
(561) 233-3123
glinley@palmbeachsports.com
• Kris Pursell, Director or Event Operations
(561) 233-3124
Member Services:
Discounts to luncheons and special events; other discounts; lapel pin; certificate; membership card.
Publications:
Annual Report; SCOREBOARD, monthly newsletter; Membership Directory.
Membership Requirements:
Pay dues of $50, $100, $500
Description:
Founded 1985. Serves to promote Palm Beach County as a location for sports entertainment. Also develops programs to improve the quality of life for the youth of Palm Beach County through sports.

PANAMA CITY BEACH CHAMBER OF COMMERCE
309 RICHARD JACKSON BOULEVARD
SUITE 101
PANAMA CITY BEACH, FL 32407
850-235-1159
Fax: 850-235-2301
chamber@pcbeach.org
www.pcbeach.org

• Beth Oltman, CEO, President
• Marta Rose, Vice President of Communications
• Derrick Bennett, Chairman
(850) 588-8909
derrick@derrickbennett.com
• Mike Burke, Secretary
(850) 236-4444
mburke@Burkeblue.com
• Jayna Leach, Treasurer
(850) 230-6110
jleach@sterlingresorts.com
Description:
Founded 1987.

PANAMA CITY BEACH CONVENTION & VISITORS BUREAU, INC.
17001 PANAMA CITY BEACH PARKWAY
PANAMA CITY BEACH, FL 32413
850-233-5070
800-327-8352
Fax: 850-233-5072
www.playpanamacitybeach.com
• Richard Sanders, VP of Sports Marketing
(850) 233-5070
rsanders@visitpanamacitybeach.com
• Richard Sanders, VP of Sports Marketing & Special Events

PENSACOLA SPORTS ASSOCIATION
P.O. BOX 12463
PENSACOLA, FL 32591
850-434-2800
Fax: 850-432-4237
www.pensacolasports.com
• James Currie, Event Specialist
• Jason Libbert, Events
(850) 748-0197
• Liz Hamrick, Event Coordinator
(850) 291-1787
• Ray Palmer, Executive Director
• Sally Garst, Special Events
(850) 434-2800
Description:
Promotes Pensacola and the surrounding areas as a location for sports events, meetings, conventions etc.
Year Founded:
1955

PEORIA AREA CONVENTION & VISITORS BUREAU
456 FULTON STREET
SUITE 300
PEORIA, IL 61602
309-676-0303
800-747-0302
info@peoria.org
www.peoria.org
• Don Welch, President/CEO
(309) 282-3273
dwelch@peoria.org
• Sue Altherton, Vice President of Sales and Marketing
(309) 282-3281
satherton@peoria.org
• Gail Erti, Vice Presidentof Finance and Administration
(309) 282-3275
gertl@peoria.org
• Lelonie Luff, Partnership/Tourism Sales Manager
(309) 282-3282
Description:
Founded in 1980. Promotes Peoria and the surrounding areas as a location for sports events, meetings, conventions, and leisure

and group travel to increase overnight visitors to the Peoria area.
Number of Members:
480
Member Services:
Members are promoted by PACVB and its staff. Members are listed in visitors guide, area maps and on PACVB website. Members are on PACVB mailing list to receive notices, updates of information and PACVB sponsored events
Member Requirements:
Annual Dues.
Publications:
Peoria Area Visitor Guide, Calendar of Events, Peoria area ePromoter newsletter, Website, Facilities and Destination Guide CD-Rom, Driving Maps, Illinois River Country, Online Business Directory.

PHILADELPHIA SPORTS CONGRESS
1700 MARKET STREET
SUITE 3000
PHILADELPHIA, PA 19103
215-636-3300
Fax: 215-636-3327
sportscongress@pcvb.org
• Dan Miller, Executive Director, Hotel Sales
(215) 636-3479
danm@pcvb.org
• Pat Kraft, Executive Director, Citywide Sales
(215) 636-3305
pkraft@pcvb.org
Publications:
E-Newsletter: Quarterly
Description:
Founded 1987. Promotes the Philadelphia region as a major sports capital, both nationally and internationally, by attracting, developing and supporting professional and amateur athletic events, meetings, conventions and clinics which will contribute to the economic development and quality of life throughout the region.

PHOENIX CONVENTION & VISITORS BUREAU, GREATER
400 EAST VAN BURENT
SUITE 60
PHOENIX, AZ 85004
602-254-6500
877-CALLPHX
Fax: 602-253-4415
visitors@visitphoenix.com
www.phoenixcvb.com
• Maria Lane, National Sales Manager
Online:
BLOG:
www.thehotsheetblog.com/visitphoenix;
FACEBOOK: visit phoenix; TWITTER: visitphoenix

PLANO CONVENTION & VISITORS BUREAU
2000 EAST SPRING CREEK PARKWAY
PLANO, TX 75074
972-941-5843
800-81-PLANO
Fax: 972-424-0002
• Melanie Copeland, Administration Assistant
(972) 941-5843
• Anastasia Hoosman, Convention Service Coordinator
(972) 941-5842
• Milleran Jockel, Marketing Manager

(972) 941-5825
• Cissy Aberg, Sports Marketing Manager
(972) 941-5849
• Karen Fogle, Association & Corporate
Sales Manager
(972) 941-5848
• Mark Thompson, CVB Director
(972) 422-6805
markth@plano.gov
Description:
Serves to recruit and promote amateur and
professional sports events to the greater
Plano and surrounding areas.

POLK COUNTY SPORTS MARKETING
2701 LAKE MYRTLE PARK ROAD
AUBURNDALE, FL 33823
863-551-4750
Fax: 863-551-4740
zimm@centralfloridasports.com
www.centralfloridasports.com
• Marc Zimmerman, Sales & Event Manager
mzimmerman@centralfloridasports.com
• Mark Jackson, Director Tourism/Sports
Marketing
mark@centralfloridasports.com
• Kris Keprios, Marketing Manager
kris@centralfloridasports.com
• Neal Duncan, Sponsorship Sales Manager
neal@centralfloridasports.com
Description:
Serves to recruit and promote amateur and
professional sports events to Polk County
and the surrounding areas.

**PRINCE GEORGE'S COUNTY
CONFERENCE & VISITORS BUREAU,
INC.**
9200 BASIL COURT
SUITE 101
LARGO, MD 20774
301-925-8300
Fax: 301-925-2053
visitorinfo@co.pg.md.us
www.visitprincegeorges.com
• J. Matthew Neitzey, Executive Director
mneitzey@co.pg.md.us
• Danny M. Brown, Administration Manager
dmbrown@co.pg.md.us
• Carl Smith, Jr., Marketing Manager
csmith@co.pg.md.us

**PRINCE WILLIAM COUNTY/MANASSAS
CONVENTION & VISITORS BUREAU**
10611 BALLS FORD ROAD
SUITE 110
MANASSAS, VA 20109
703-396-7130
800-432-1792
Fax: 703-396-7160
info@visitpwc.com
www.visitpwc.com
• Tabatha Mullins, Executive Director
(703) 396-7130
tmullins@visitpwc.com
Description:
The destination marketing organization for
Prince William County and Manassas.
Through targeted marketing efforts the CVB
promotes the region to potential leisure
visitors, tour groups, and media
representatives for the purpose of
increasing tourism and economic growth.
The CVB is an independent, non-profit
organization funded by Prince William
County.

QUAD CITIES SPORTS COMMISSION
1601 RIVER DRIVE
SUITE 110
MOLINE, IL 61265
800-747-7800
Fax: 309-764-9443
lhunt@visitquadcities.com
www.quadcitiessports.com
• Joe Taylor, Chair/President/CEO
• Lynn Hunt, Vice President Tourism
(309) 277-0937
lhunt@visitquadcities.com
Sports Service Founded:
1996
Description:
Quad Cities Sports Commission is a
not-for-profit (non-profit) organization
dedicated to developing the quality of life in
the Quad Cities by attracting and hosting
sporting events that bring a economic
impact to our communities. The QCSC is a
full-service sports commission that takes a
turn-key approach to attracting and hosting
each event it bring to the Quad Cities.
Description:
Promotes Moline and the surrounding Illinois
area for sports competitions, games,
conventions and meetings. The Quad Cities
is a cluster of communities located on the
Mississippi River, connecting eastern Iowa
and western Illinois. The sports commission
promotes tournaments, competitions, meets,
meeting & convention.

**RALEIGH CONVENTION & VISITORS
BUREAU (GREATER)**
421 FAYETTEVILLE ST SUITE 1505
RALEIGH, NC 27601-2995
919-834-5900
800-849-8499
info@raleighsports.org
www.raleighsports.org
• Scott Dupree, VP Sports Marketing
(919) 645-2657
sdupree@raleighsports.org
• Tori Collins, Assistant Director of Sports
Marketing
(919) 645-2664
tori@raleighsports.org
• Jason Philbeck, Sports Marketing
Manager
(919) 645-2660
jphilbeck@raleighsports.org
Publications:
Maps, Visitors Guide.

**RENO-SPARKS CONVENTION
AUTHORITY**
PO BOX 837
RENO, NV 89504-0837
775-827-7600
800-367-7366
www.visitrenotahoe.com
• Christopher Baum, President/Chief
Executive Officer
(775) 827-7618
• Christopher Baum, President/CEO
• Joe Kelly, Vice President of Facilities
• John Leinen, Vice President of Convention
& Tour
• Jennifer Cinningham, Executive Director of
Marketing
• Brain Rivers, Director of Finance
• Charlotte Andreson, ASSISTANT TO THE
PRESIDENT AND CEO
• Brian River, Vice President
Sales/Marketing
(775) 827-7626

Description:
Promotes Reno-Sparks and the surrounding
area for sports competitions, games,
conventions and meetings.

**ROANOKE VALLEY CONVENTION &
VISITORS BUREAU**
101 SHENANDOAH AVENUE NE
ROANOKE, VA 24016
540-342-6025
1-800-635-5535
Fax: 540-342-7119
info@visitroanokeva.com
www.visitroanokeva.com
• Landon C Howard, Executive Director
dlkjolhede@aol.com
• Kelly Burd-Adams, Director Convention
Sales
kburdadams@visitroanokeva.com
Publications:
MEETING PLANNERS GUIDE
Member Services:
Site Inspection Arrangements, Facility, Rate
and Contact Information, Local Support
Contacts, Family Activity Coordination,
Slides and Digital Photography.

**ROCHESTER AMATEUR SPORTS
COMMISSION**
30 CIVIC CENTER DRIVE SE
ROCHESTER, MN 55904
507-280-4701
Fax: 507-280-4703
www.rochsports.com
• Zac Carlson, Operations Coordinator
• Jay Fanta, Operations Assistant
• Ed Hruska, Executive Director
ehruska@rochsports.com
• Ben Boldt, Event Operations Manager
• Shelley Boettcher, Operations Manager
Description:
The Rochester Sports Commission (RASC)
was formed by a group of business and
sports visionaries. The vision was to bring to
Rochester, major national and international
events, and along with them, the recognition
of Rochester as a hub for amateur sports.

**ROCK HILL/YORK COUNTY
CONVENTION & VISITORS BUREAU**
452 SOUTH ANDERSON RD
PO BOX 11377
ROCK HILL, SC 29730
803-329-5200
888-702-1320
Fax: 803-329-0145
www.visityorkcounty.com
• Bennish Brown, Executive Director
• Lisa Meadows, Executive Director
(803) 329-5200
lmeadows@visityorkcounty.com
• Mikki rentschler, Director of Finance &
Administration
(803) 329-5200
• Sonja R Burris, Communications Manager
(803) 329-5200
sburris@visityorkcounty.com

**ROCKFORD AREA CONVENTION &
VISITORS BUREAU**
102 NORTH MAIN STREET
ROCKFORD, IL 61101-1102
815-963-8111
800-521-0849
Fax: 815-963-4298
www.gorockford.com

• Lindsey Arellano, Sports Sales Manager
(815) 489-1653
• John Groh, CEO, President
• Linda Heckert, Chairman
(815) 847-5014
• Darrel Snorek, Vice-Chairman
(815) 282-3535
• Patrick okeefe, Secretary
(815) 637-7269
• Solomon Foley, Treasurer
(815) 397-3377
• Beverly Broyles, Executive Director
(815) 964-9713
• Robert Bob Burden, City of Loves Park
Liaison
(815) 654-5034
Description:
Serves to promote sports development and
attract sports events to the Rockford Illinois
area.

ROSEVILLE PARKS AND RECREATION
2660 CIVIC CENTER DRIVE
ROSEVILLE, MN 55113
651-792-7000
Fax: 651-792-7100
www.ci.roseville.mn.us
• Lonnie Brokke, Director
• Jill Anfang, Assistant Director

ROSEVILLE VISITORS ASSOCIATION
1700 WEST HIGHWAY 36
SUITE 600
ROSEVILLE, MN 55113
651-633-3002
877-980-3002
Fax: 651-636-0475
info@visitroseville.com
www.visitroseville.com
• Julie Wearn, Executive Director
• Shannon Hirstein, Sales Manager
(651) 633-3002
shirstein@visitroseville.com
Description:
Roseville is located outside of Minneapolis
and Saint Paul. Home to the Guidant John
Rose Oval, and minutes from the University
of Minnesota, Bethel University, Hamline
University, and the University of Saint
Thomas and National Sports Center.

SACRAMENTO SPORTS COMMISSION
1606 I STREET
SACRAMENTO, CA 95814
916-808-7777
Fax: 916-566-6566
fan@sacsports.com
www.sacsports.com
• Brad M. Hillard, Director of sports
development
Description:
Founded 1988. Formed to attract major
professional and amateur sports events to
the city and county of Sacramento.

SAINT JOHN DESTINATION MANAGEMENT INC
CITY HALL
15 MARKET SQUARE
11TH FLOOR
SAINT JOHN, NB, CANADA E2K 1E8
506-658-2990
1-866-GO FUNDY
Fax: 506-632-6118
visitsj@saintjohn.ca
www.tourismsaintjohn.com

• Kevin Carson, Manager
(506) 658-4731
• Marcy Loeman, Administrative coordinator
• Shawnna Garnhum, Sales
• Jen Tupper, Manager of visitors
• Ross Jefferson, Executive director
Nature of Sports Service::
Destination management organization to
increase visitation to Saint John NB.

SALT LAKE CONVENTION & VISITORS BUREAU
90 SOUTH WEST TEMPLE
SALT LAKE CITY, UT 84101
801-534-4900
800-541-4955
Fax: 801-534-4926
www.visitsaltlake.com
• Scott Beck, President/CEO
(801) 534-4911
• Eric Thompson, Director Marketing
(801) 534-4912
• Shawn Stinson, Director Communications
(801) 534-4913
Description:
A private non-profit community organization
promoting Salt Lake as a travel destination.
The SLCVB and its members provide
assistance to convention & meeting
planners, tourism professionals, media and
visitors.

SAN ANTONIO SPORTS
PO BOX 830386
SAN ANTONIO, TX 78283
210-820-2100
Fax: 210-820-2199
www.sanantoniosports.org
• Susan Blackwood, Executive Director
(210) 820-2110
• David Blank, Volunteer Coordinator
(210) 820-2191
dblank@sanantoniosports.org
• Russ Bookbinder, President/CEO
(210) 820-2120
rbookbinder@sanantoniosports.org
• Jenny Carnes, Associate Executive
Director, Business Develo
(210) 820-2104
jcarnes@sanantoniosports.org
• Gina Castro, Youth Program Director
(210) 820-2102
• Karl Chapman, Finance Manager
(210) 820-2107
• Bill Hanson, Associate Executive Director
Operations
(210) 820-2111
• Mary Ullmann Japhet, Associate Executive
Director/External Affairs
(210) 820-2123
mjaphet@sanantoniosports.org
Description:
Founded 1984. A not-for-profit organization
dedicated to creating sports opportunities for
our community and its youth. We hold major
athletic events to generate money. Our
DREAMS FOR YOUTH program provides
training in six Olympic sports, and our
DIAMOND SHAMROCK GO!KIDS
CHALLENGE is designed to combat
childhood obesity through routine activity
and education.

SAN BERNARDINO AREA CONVENTION & VISITORS BUREAU
1955 HUNTS LANE
SUITE 102
SAN BERNARDINO, CA 92401
909-889-3980
800-867-8366
Fax: 909-888-5998
• Wayne Austin, President/Chief Executive
Officer
• Barbara Daugherty, Director of Business
Operations
Description:
The San Bernardino Convention & Visitors
Bureau (SBCVB) shall attract conventions,
conferences, group tours and business
meetings while coordinationg attractions,
resterraunts and services to meet each
organization's specific needs. The SBCVB
shall also provide aggressive marketing
strategies; develop and impliment special
events to generate additional visitor days for
the city of San Bernardino.

SAN JOSE SPORTS AUTHORITY
345 PARK AVENUE
MS E6-500
SAN JOSE, CA 95110
408-288-2930
Fax: 408-278-1868
info@sjsa.org
www.sjsa.org
• Patricia Ernstrom, Executive Director
• Carrie Benjamin, Event Manager
carrie@sjsa.org
• Greg Jamison, Chair
Description:
Formed to attract major sports events to the
city of San Jose and surrounding areas.

SAN MATEO COUNTY/SILICON VALLEY CONVENTION & VISITORS BUREAU
111 ANZA BLVD, STE 410
BURLINGAME, CA 94010
650-348-7600
800-288-4748
Fax: 650-348-7687
www.sanmateocountycvb.com
• Anne LeClair, President/Chief Executive
Officer
• Michelle Adle, Sports Marketing Manager
• Gina Allhands, Vice President, Chief
Financial Officer

SAVANNAH SPORTS COUNCIL
101 E. BAY ST
SAVANNAH, GA 31401
912-644-6414
info@savcvb.com
• Benjamin Wilder, Director
Description:
Founded 1992.The Savannah Sports
Council markets Savannah as a site for
major sports events in pre-Olympic training,
as well as enhancing participation in area
athletic programs and serves as a catalyst
to develop sports infrastructure in the
community.

SIOUX FALLS CONVENTION & VISITORS BUREAU
200 N. PHILLIPS AVENUE
SUITE 102
SIOUX FALLS, SD 57104
605-336-1620
800-333-2072

multi sports

Fax: 605-336-6499
www.siouxfallscvb.com
• Teri Ellis Schmidt, CVB Executive Director
• Krista Orsack, Sales/Marketing Director

SIOUXLAND SPORTS & CULTURAL EVENTS CONGRESS
801 4TH STREET
SIOUX CITY, IA 51101
712-279-4800
800-593-2228
Fax: 712-279-4800
www.siouxcitytourism.com
• Dennis Gann, Executive Director
(800) 593-2228
• Angie Watson, Marketing Director
Description:
Founded 1992. Serves to attract sporting and cultural events to the greater Sioux City area.

SOUTH CAROLINA PARKS, RECREATION & TOURISM
1205 PENDLETON STREET
SUITE 110
COLUMBIA, SC 29201
803-734-1700
866-224-9339
Fax: 803-734-1741
tnance@scprt.com
www.discoversouthcarolina.com
• Amy Duffy, Chief of Staff
• Marion Edmunds, Director of Communications
Description:
Promotes South Carolina as a good location for professional and amateur sporting events. Assists local communities in their sports development initiatives.

SOUTH PADRE ISLAND CONVENTION & VISITORS BUREAU
7355 PADRE BLVD
SOUTH PADRE ISLAND, TX 78597
956-761-3000
800-657-2373
Fax: 956-761-3024
www.sopadre.com
• Lacey Ekberg, Director of CVB
(956) 761-8308
• Dinora Garcia, Administrative Assistant to CVB Director
(956) 761-8308
• Lori Moore, Accounting Coordinator
• Celia Sally Garza, Services Manager
(956) 761-3000
• Dinora Garcia, Executive Assistant

TEAM SPARTANBURG
111 IDLE WYLDE COURT
SPARTANBURG, SC 29301
864-597-4180
Fax: 864-316-1326
www.teamspartanburgsc.org
• Laura Corbin, Chairwoman, Publicity Manager
Member Services:
Team Spartanburg, The Sports Council of the Spartanburg Convention & Visitors Bureau, Assists event holders with their events to make them successful.

SPOKANE REGIONAL SPORTS COMMISSION
714 N IRON BRIDGE WAY
SUITE 202
SPOKANE, WA 99202
509-456-5812
800-900-5837
Fax: 509-456-5837
chrisf@spokanesports.org
www.spokanesports.org
• Eric Sawyer, President/CEO
(509) 742-9371
erics@spokanesports.org
• Jodi Kyler, Ph.D., VP of Marketing and Communications
(509) 742-9389
chrisf@spokanesports.org
• Paul Christiarnsen, Director of Event Services
(509) 363-2682
Description:
Since 1988, the Spokane Regional Sports Commission has provided leadership in economic and community development through sports to the Spokane Region.

SPORTS AND EVENTS COUNCIL OF SEATTLE/KING COUNTY
701 PIKE STREET
SUITE 800
SEATTLE, WA 98101-2611
206-461-5800
Fax: 206-461-5855
www.seattlesports.org
• Ralph R. Morton, Executive Director
• Kirk Nelson, Vice Chair
• Greg Root, Secretary/Treasurer
Description:
Founded 1989. Mission is to bring major sports and special events to the region; create sports and special events for the region; support the existing sports franchises; and ensure modern, state-of-the-art facilities.

SPORTS PROMOTION - BATTLE CREEK, MICHIGAN
KELLOGG ARENA
1 MCCAMLY SQUARE
BATTLE CREEK, MI 49017
269-963-4800
Fax: 269-968-8840
www.kelloggarena.com
• Kevin M. Scheibler, General Manager
• Kevin Scheibler, GM
(269) 963-4800
• Lindsay Lerette, Sales and Marketing Manager
(269) 963-4800
• Jimmy Biggs, Food and Beverage Manager
(269) 963-4800
• Bob Benqtsson, Interim Director of Finance
(269) 963-4800
• Ben Randels, Operations Manager, Treasurer
• Sylvester Trease, Director of Finance
Description:
Identify and bring existing major sporting events to Battle Creek Michigan and the surrounding area.

SPORTS VIRGINIA INC.
405 LORRAINE AVE
FREDERICKSBURG, VA 22408

540-710-1228
Fax: 540-710-7007
Member Services:
Liaison between national governing bodies and Virginia member clubs; processes registrations; sanctions athlete's cards; collects fees for clubs.
Publications:
Virginia State Games Annual Program; annual reports; individual newsletters for each sport.
Description:
Founded 1989. Serves and promotes amateur sports groups in Virginia including the Amateur Athletic Union (AAU), USA Track & Field, the U.S. Diving Federation, U.S. Weightlifting Federation, and produces the Virginia State Games.

SPRINGFIELD AREA SPORTS COMMISSION
815 E ST. LOUIS STREET
SPRINGFIELD, MO 65806
417-881-5300
800-678-8767
Fax: 417-881-7201
lkettering@springfieldmo.org
www.springfieldmosports.org
• Bill Hobbs, Chair
• Tracy Kimberlin, Secretary
• Mary Decker, Treasurer
• Lance Kettering, Executive Director
• Shiela Fish, Assistant Director
Description:
Mission is to enhance the quality of life and stimulate positive economic growth for the community by promoting and developing the greater Springfield area as a sports venue for quality amateur and professional sporting events.

SPRINGFIELD, MO CONVENTION & VISITORS BUREAU
815 E SAINT LOUIS STREET
SUITE 100
SPRINGFIELD, MO 65806
417-881-5300
800-678-8767
Fax: 417-881-2231
cvb@springfieldmo.org
www.springfieldmo.org
• Tracy Kimberlin, Executive Director

ST. AUGUSTINE, PONTE VEDRA & THE BEACHES VISITORS & CONVENTION BUREAU
29 OLD MISSION AVENUE
ST. AUGUSTINE, FL 32084
904-829-1711 EXT 310
800-653-2489
Fax: 904-829-6149
www.getaway4florida.com
• Ron Goldman, Executive Director
(904) 829-1711
• Rick Hensler, Promotions Director
• Eris Masters, Database manager
• Richard Goldman, Executive Director
 ext 311
RGoldman@FloridasHistoricCoast.com
• Carey Cramer, Office Manager
(904) 829-1711
CCramer@FloridasHistoricCoast.com
Year Founded:
1994
Description:
Serves to attract sports meetings and events to the St. John's county area.

ST. CHARLES CONVENTION & VISITORS BUREAU, GREATER
230 SOUTH MAIN STREET
ST. CHARLES, MO 63301
636-366-2427
800-366-2427
Fax: 636-949-3217
gsccvb@historicstcharles.com
www.historicstcharles.com
• David A Leezer, CEO, Director

ST. CLOUD AREA CONVENTION VISITORS BUREAU
525 HIGHWAY 10 SOUTH
SUITE 1
ST. CLOUD, MN 56304
320-251-4170
800-264-2940
Fax: 320-656-0401
info@visitstcloudmn.com
www.granitecountry.com
• Julie Lunning, Executive Director
(320) 202-6711
• Judy Okerstrom, Director of Sales & Marketing
(320) 202-6712

ST. JOSEPH CONVENTION & VISITORS BUREAU/ REGIONAL SPORTS COMMISSION
109 SOUTH 4TH STREET
ST. JOSEPH, MO 64501
816-233-6688
800-785-0360
Fax: 816-233-9120
cvb@stjomo.com
www.stjomo.com
• Marci Bennett, Executive Director
mbennett@stjomo.com
• Mary Supple, Director Sales
msupple@stjomo.com
Description:
Serves to attract sports meetings and events to the St. Joseph Missouri Area.

ST. LOUIS SPORTS COMMISSION
308 NORTH 21ST STREET
SUITE 500
ST. LOUIS, MO 63101
314-345-5100
Fax: 314-621-1391
ncohan@stlouissports.org
• Frank Viverito, President
fviverito@stlouissports.org
• Chris Roseman, Vice President of Events
croseman@stlouissports.org
Description:
Founded 1989. Generate economic benefit and enhanced quality of life in the St. Louis region through sports events, national promotion, local awareness, amateur sports development, and youth programs.
Membership Requirements:
$250 for individuals; $500 for companies/organizations.
Publications:
Newsletter, quarterly.
Member Services:
Meetings, board meetings and frequent special events and activities.

ST. PETERSBURG/CLEARWATER SPORTS COMMISSION
13805 58TH ST
STE 2-200
CLEARWATER, FL 33760-3733

727-464-7200
877-352-2473
info@floridasbeachsports.com
www.floridasbeachsports.com
• Kevin Smith, Director Of Sports Commission
• Angel Natal, Senior Sales Manager
• Kit Dunbar, Sales manager of sports commission
• Robin Gwaltney-Harris, Administrative Assistant
Description:
Founded 1999. Serves to attract professional, collegiate, amateur and youth sports training and tournaments to the St. Petersburg/Clearwater area.

STOCKTON CONVENTION & VISITORS BUREAU
125 BRIDGE PLACE
STOCKTON, CA 95202
209-938-1555
877-778-6258
Fax: 209-938-1554
www.visitstockton.org
• Tim Pasisz, Sports Development Director
(209) 938-1556
Description;
Full service visitors bureau to assist in recruiting sporting events to Stockton. Site selection, logistic support & sponsorships available.

SYRACUSE CONVENTION + VISITORS BUREAU
115 WEST FAYETTE STREET
SYRACUSE, NY 13202-3320
315-470-1910
800-234-4797
Fax: 315-471-8545
www.visitsyracuse.org
• David C. Holder, President
(315) 470-1911
• Carol M. Eaton, Director of Market Development
(315) 470-1904
ceaton@visitsyracuse.org
Description:
Founded 1985. Serves to attract, organize and stage amateur sports events in the Syracuse area as well as coordinate the resources and efforts within the community in working toward that end.

TACOMA/PIERCE COUNTY SPORTS COMMISSION
1119 PACIFIC AVENUE
SUITE 500
TACOMA, WA 98402
253-327-1866
800-272-2662
Fax: 253-627-8783
www.tacomasports.com
• Tim Waer, TPCSC, Executive Director
Description:
Founded 1992. A non-profit organization that promotes the region of Tacoma/Pierce County as a destination for state, regional, national and international amateur sports events.

TALLAHASSEE SPORTS COUNCIL
106 EAST JEFFERSON STREET
TALLAHASSEE, FL 32301
850-606-2305
800-628-2866
Fax: 850-487-4621

• Lee Daniel, Executive Director
• Colleen Dwyer, Visitor Services Director
Description:
Fosters, encourages and promotes athletic events in the Tallahassee area for the economic benefits, visibility and civic pride these activities may bring to the community. Events include international, national, regional and state events and span a wide spectrum of sports and performance levels.

TAMPA BAY SPORTS COMMISSION
401 EAST JACKSON STREET
SUITE 2100
TAMPA, FL 33602
813-218-3892
info@tampabaysports.org
www.tampabaysports.org
• Rob Higgins, Executive Director
rhiggins@visittampabay.com
• Jason Aughey, Senior Director
• Tony Diaz, Sales and Events Coordinator
• Claire Lessinger, Sales/Events Manager
• Rob Higgins, Executive Director
RHiggins@VisitTampaBay.com
Description:
The Tampa Bay Sports Commission works to unite all interests in the Bay Area under one full-service approach that provides leadership and guidance for the benefit of all parties involved with amateur and youth sports. The Sports Commission works with area convention and visitors bureaus to provide a wealth of services to potential events and their governing bodies.

TAMPA CONVENTION & VISITORS BUREAU
401 EAST JACKSON STREET
STE 2100
TAMPA, FL 33602
813-223-1111
800-44tampa
Fax: 813-229-6616
www.visittampabay.com
• JoLynn Lokey, VP of Administration
(813) 342-4089
JLokey@VisitTampaBay.com
• Lisa Urban, Human Resources Coordinator
(813) 342-4064
LUrban@VisitTampaBay.com
• Gregory Orchard, Chief Financial Officer
(813) 342-4082
• Jennifer Finnegan, Accounting Coordinator
(813) 342-4059
JFinnegan@VisitTampaBay.com
• Alex Kaptzan, Vice President of Convention Sales and Servic
(81) -218-383
• Santiago Corrada, President/Chief Executive Officer
(813) 223-1111
SCorrada@VisitTampaBay.com
• JoLynn Lokey SPHR, VP of Administration
(813) 342-4089
JLokey@VisitTampaBay.com

TAMPA SPORTS AUTHORITY
4201 NORTH DALE MABRY HIGHWAY
TAMPA, FL 33607
813-350-6500
Fax: 813-350-6565
www.tampasportsauthority.com
• Janice Hosey, Executive assistant
• Eric Hart, President, CEO
(813) 350-6516

multi sports

247

• Mickey Farrell, Director of Operations
(813) 350-6507
mfarrell@tampasportsauthority.com
• Jeanette Baker, VP of finance and
administration
• Sue Maciejewski, HRM
Description:
Created 1965. Owns and operates
Houlihan's Stadium, owns Yankees training
complex and NHL Lightning Ice Palace and
manages 3 city-owned golf courses.
Currently building a 65,000 seat open air,
natural turf stadium adjacent to Houlihan's
Stadium.

SPORTS CLUB OF TAMPA BAY
P.O. BOX 10753
TAMPA, FL 33609
813-282-3400
Fax: 813-287-8369
• Mitch Shriber, President
• Gill Swalls, First Vice President
Description:
Promotes various functions to raise funds
for charitable donations. Hosts annual
Sports Award Banquet, Golf Tournament,
etc.

**TEXAS DEPT. OF ECO. DEVELOPMENT,
TOURISM DIV.**
P.O. BOX 12428
AUSTIN, TX 78711
512-936-0101
www.traveltex.com
Description:
Looks to develop and attract events to the
Austin Texas region.

THUNDERBIRDS, THE
7226 NORTH 16TH STREET
SUITE 100
PHOENIX, AZ 85020
602-870-0163
Fax: 602-870-4162
www.phoenixopen.com
• John Bridger, Executive Director
Nature of Sports Service:
Special Events Committee of the Phoenix
Chamber of Commerce, whose sole
purpose is to promote Phoenix and its
neighboring communities through sporting
events, such as the FBR Open golf
tournament, formerly the Phoenix Open.

TOURISM BUREAU ILLINOISOUTH
4387 NORTH ILLINOIS STREET
SUITE 200
SWANSEA, IL 62226
618-257-1488
800-442-1488
Fax: 618-257-3403
www.thetourismbureau.org
• Jo Kathmann, President/CEO
Publications:
Annual Free Visitors Guide, Bi-Monthly
News from the Road Magazine.
Member Services:
Web Link, Hospitality Training, AD Credit in
Visitors Guide, Marketing Consultation, AD
Placement, Levereged Buying. Housing and
group services.
Membership Requirements:
Membership levels range form $225.00 up.

**TOURISM VANCOUVER, THE GREATER
VANCOUVER CONVENTION & VISITORS
BUREAU**
STE 210-200 BURRARD ST
VANCOUVER, BC, CANADA V6C 3L6
604-682-2222
Fax: 604-682-1717
www.tourismvancouver.com
• Ted Lee, Chief Financial Officer & VP
Visitor Services
(604) 631-2807
• Stephen Pearce, Vice President
(604) 631-2808
• Patti Smolen, Director
(640) 631-2801
• Rick Antonson, President/Chief Executive
Officer
(604) 631-2888
ricka@tourismvancouver.com
• Paul Vallee, Executive Vice President
(604) 631-2815
pvallee@tourismvancouver.com
• Walt Judas, Vice President
(604) 631-2882
wjudas@tourismvancouver.com
Description:
Tourism Vancouver's focus is on building
exceptional relationships. Our primary
customers are meeting planners, travel
influencers, travel media, and independent
tourists. Our efforts generate demand for the
destination, thereby creating value for
members and stakeholders innovation,
partnership, research and accountability
guide our approach.

TRI-CITIES SPORTS COUNCIL
7130 W GRANDRIDGE BLVD
KENNEWICK, WA 99336
509-735-8486
800-254-5824
hector@visittri-cities.com
www.VisitTri-Cities.com
• Kris Watkins, President/CEO
kris@VisitTri-Cities.com
• Kim Shugart, SeniorVice President
• Jordan Youngs, Marketing & Public
Relations Director
• Michelle Chunn, Community Relations
Director
• Holly Siler, Director ofConvention Sales
Publications:
Tri-Cities Sports Facilities Guide.
Member Services:
Acts as a liaison with our hotel properties to
gather rates and availability information. The
Council can assist in locating sports venues
and playing fields to meet the needs of the
tournament as well as providing contact
information for local tournament directors
and officials. We can also provide an
assortment of informational brochures and
maps featuring the Tri-Cities to assis
visitors.

TULSA SPORTS COMMISSION
1 WEST 3RD STREET
SUITE 100
TULSA, OK 74103
918-560-0215
Fax: 918-592-6244
www.tulsasports.org
• Vince Trinidad, Executive Director
• Ray Hoyt, Sr. VP
Member Services:
Newsletter; preferred invitations; tickets.
Membership Requirements:
Financial contribution.

Description:
Founded 1993. Serves as a catalyst for the
solicitation and development of major
regional and national amateur sporting
events in the Tulsa metro area, while
fostering the development of improved
facilities and growth of local associations,
teams, and organizing committees
necessary to accommodate these events.

**TUPELO CONVENTION & VISITORS
BUREAU**
399 EAST MAIN STREET
PO BOX 47
TUPELO, MS 38801
662-841-6521
800-533-0611
Fax: 662-841-6558
visittupelo@tupelo.net
www.tupelo.net
• Neal McCoy, Director Sports Development
• Linda Elliff, Director of Sales
• Linda Butler-Johnson, Executive Director

**TUSCALOOSA CONVENTION &
VISITORS BUREAU**
1900 JACK WARNER PARKWAY
TUSCALOOSA
TUSCALOOSA, AL 35401
205-391-9200
800-538-8696
Fax: 250-759-2002
www.visittuscaloosa.com
• Robert Ratliff, Executive Director
• Susan West, CEO
• Don Staley, Executive Director of Sports
• Tina Jones, Director of Corporate & Group
Tourism
• Shaunee Lynch, AssistantDirector of
Corporate & Group Touri
• Kelsey Colglazier, Director of Sports
Marketing and Public Relat
• Jessika White, Multimedia Communication
& Public Relations M

UTAH SPORTS COMMISSION
201 SOUTH MAIN
SUITE 2125
SALT LAKE CITY, UT 84111
801-328-2372
Fax: 801-328-2372
www.utahsportscommission.com
• Jeff Robbins, President/Chief Executive
Officer
jlrobbins@utah.gov
• Laura Shaw, Marketing Director
(801) 323-4254
• Steve Rich, VP Operations
(801) 328-2361
Description:
The mission of the Utah Sports Commission
is to enhance Utah's economy, image, and
quality of life through the attraction,
promotion, and development of regional,
national, and international sports.

**UTAH VALLEY CONVENTION &
VISITORS BUREAU**
220 WEST CENTER STREET
SUITE 100
PROVO, UT 84601
801-851-2100
Fax: 801-851-2109
www.utahvalley.org
• Joel Racker, President/CEO
(801) 851-2101
• Candace Winmill, Executive Administrative

Assistant
• Courtney Brown, Marketing Assistant
• Andrella Cross, Visitor Information Specialist
• Julia Currey, Senior Sales Manager
(801) 851-2106
• Charlene Christensen, Director of Services
(801) 851-2102
Description:
Utah Valley Convention & Visitors Bureau staff are ready to assist tourists, business travelers, meeting planners, event organizers, film companies, tour operators, reunion planners, and conferences. Our staff members are professional, friendly, and knowledgeable. Our desire is to make your planning easy and to make certain your time in Utah Valley is successful, memorable and hassel-free.

VALDOSTA-LOWNDES COUNTY CONFERENCE CENTER & TOURISM AUTHORITY/CVB
1 MEETING PLACE
VALDOSTA, GA 31601
229-245-0513
800-569-8687
Fax: 229-245-5240
www.valdostatourism.com
• Joel Racker, President, Chief Executive Officer
• Charlene Christensen, Director of Services
Description:
Founded 1996. The Sports Commission is an affiliate of the Valdosta-Lowndes County Convention & Visitors Bureau, whose mission is to market Valdosta and Lowndes County as a destination for athletic competition; To enhance and stimulate positive economic growth through youth and adult sporting events.
Publications:
Sports Facilities Guide.

VENTURA VISITORS & CONVENTION BUREAU
101 S CALIFORNIA STREET
VENTURA, CA 93001
800-333-2989
Fax: 805-648-2150
www.ventura-usa.com
• Jim Luttjohann, Executive Director
• Marlyss Auster, Executive Director
Description:
Serves to attract and promote sporting events to Ventura California. Sports include: auto racing, baseball, basketball, beach volleyball, boating, equestrian, golf, junior Olympics, roller hockey, senior Olympics, soccer, softball, track and field, tennis, water polo.
Publications:
Ventura Official Visitors Guide; Meeting Planner Guide

VERMONT SPORTS & EVENTS COUNCIL
60 MAIN STREET
SUITE 100
BURLINGTON, VT 5401
877-686-5253
877-264-3503
www.vermontmeetings.org
• Dave Hakins, Executive Director
(802) 863-3489
Description:
The Vermont State Sports Council serves to

attract and initiate local, national, and international sporting events in Vermont.

VIRGINIA AMATEUR SPORTS, INC.
711 C FIFTH STREET NE
ROANOKE, VA 24016
540-343-0987
Fax: 540-343-7407
www.commonwealthgames.org
• Peter R. Lampman, President
pete@commonwealthgames.org
• Diane Williams, Marketing Director
dwilliams@commonwealthgames.org
Description:
Founded 1989. Established to promote the development of amateur athletics in the state. Sports event planner and organizer of the Coventry Commonwealth Games of Virginia.

VIRGINIA BEACH CONVENTION AND VISITOR BUREAU/SPORTS MARKETING
2101 PARKS AVE
STE 500
VIRGINIA BEACH, VA 23451
757-385-4700
800-700-7702
Fax: 757-437-4747
bwheeler@vbgov.com
• James B. Ricketts, Director
jrickett@VisitVirginiaBeach.com
• Brande Rumpf, Executive Assistant
brumpf@VisitVirginiaBeach.com
• Tiffany Twine, Media and Communications Coordinator
ttwine@VisitVirginiaBeach.com
• Chuck Applebach, Marketing and Strategic Partnerships
cappleba@vbgov.com
• Teresa Diaz, InteractiveCommunications
tdiaz@VisitVirginiaBeach.com
• Buddy Wheeler, Sports Marketing Coordinator
(757) 437-4795
bwheeler@vbgov.com
• Nancy Helman, Sales Marketing Representative
Description:
Serves to increase sport tourism to Virginia Beach. Assists sports event planners in all phases of the event, including facility acquisition, lodging, transportation coordination, visitor relations, and volunteer recruitment.

VISIT ANCHORAGE
524 W FOURTH AVENUE
ANCHORAGE, AK 99501-2212
907-276-4118
Fax: 907-278-5559
info@anchorage.net
www.anchorage.net
• R.J. (Jim) Henderson, VP Convention Sales
• Julie Dodds, Director of Convention Sales
Description:
Promotes Anchorage Alaska as a destination for tourism, events and meetings.

VISIT BINGHAMTON
5 SOUTH COLLEGE DR.
SUITE 102
BINGHAMTON, NY 13905
607-772-8860
800-836-6740
www.visitbinghamton.org

• Cassie Green, Sales & Social Media Manager
(607) 296-2103
cassandra@visitbinghamton.org
• Judi Hess, Director
judi@visitbinghamton.org
Description:
Greater Binghamton - a sports friendly community waiting to welcome new groups. CVB offers free services to event planners. Offering first class venues, plentiful & affordable hotel rooms and over 250 restaurants... Come and be part of our story.
Publications:
Travel Guide, Summer Calendar of Events, Map Brochure, Sports Venue Guide, Meeting Planners Guide, Group Tour Planner, Treasures Brochure, Golf Brochure

VISIT EAU CLAIRE
4319 JEFFERS ROAD
SUITE 201
EAU CLAIRE, WI 54703
715-831-2345
888-523-3866
Fax: 715-831-2340
info@chippewavalley.net
www.visiteauclaire.com
• Linda John, Executive Director
• Michael Strubel, Sports Sales
Description:
Promotes Eau Claire WI and surrounding areas as a host site for sports meetings and events.

VISIT FORT WAYNE
927 SOUTH HARRISON ST
FORT WAYNE, IN 46802
260-424-3700
800-767-7752
Fax: 260-424-3914
josie@visitfortwayne.com
www.visitfortwayne.com
• Dan O'Connell, CAE, President/CEO
dan@visitfortwayne.com
• Josie O'Connell, Sports Sales Manager
josie@visitfortwayne.com
Description:
Founded 1949. Acts as an agent for the city of Fort Wayne in attracting conventions, tourists, trade shows, and sporting events for the economic and social benefits of a prosperous visitor industry.
Facilities:
Extensive facilities for groups including basketball, soccer, ice sports and field sports.
Fort Wayne Professional Teams:
Fort Wayne Komet Hockey, Fort Wayne TinCaps, Fort Wayne Mad Ants

VISIT KNOXVILLE SPORTS COMMISSION
301 SOUTH GAY STREET
KNOXVILLE, TN 37902
865-523-7263
800-727-8045
Fax: 865-522-3974
cculver@knoxville.org
sports.visitknoxville.com
• Kim Bumpas, President
• Chad Culver, Senior Director, Sports Commission
• Kristen Combs, Director, Communications
• Parker Medley, Director, Sports Sales
• Kelli Ryman, Director, Event Services
• Erin Simcox, Housing Manager

Description:
The Visit Knoxville Sports Commission promotes the Knoxville/Knox County as a destination for sports-related events. This includes youth events, collegiate events and professional events. The Commission works with local organizers, as well as National Governing Bodies.

VISIT NEW HAVEN
127 WASHINGTON AVENUE
NEW HAVEN, CT 6473
203-777-8550
800-332-STAY
www.visitnewhaven.com
• Sarah Washburn, Tourism Sales Representative
(203) 777-8550
sarahw@rexdevelopment.org
• Virginia Kozlowski, Director
• Ginny Kozlowski, Executive Director
(203) 777-8550
ginnyk@visitnewhaven.com
Description:
Serves to promote New Haven and the surrounding area to attract sporting events and attractions.
Member Services:
Bid, market and host sporting events that generate positive economic impact on the community.

VISIT WINSTON-SALEM
200 BROOKSTOWN AVENUE
WINSTON-SALEM, NC 27101
336-728-4200
866-728-4200
Fax: 336-721-2202
info@visitwinstonsalem.com
www.visitwinstonsalem.com
• Bonny Bernat, Sports/Event Sales Manager
(336) 728-4215
bonny@visitwinstonsalem.com
• Richard Geiger, President
richard@visitwinstonsalem.com

WATERLOO CONVENTION & VISITORS BUREAU
5 W JEFFERSON STREET
WATERLOO, IA 50703
319-233-8350
800-728-8431
Fax: 319-233-4580
www.waterloocvb.org
• Aaron Buzza, Executive Director
• Lornnie Elmore, Director of Group Sales
• Susan Lewis, Director of Visitor Services
• Beth Kenny, Marketing & Communications

WAYNE COUNTY CONVENTION & VISITORS BUREAU
5701 NATIONAL ROAD EAST
RICHMOND, IN 47374
765-935-8687
800-828-8414
Fax: 765-935-0440
grouprequest@visitrichmond.org
www.visitrichmond.org
• Mary Walker, General Manager
Facilities:
Basketball, bowling, golf, baseball, gymnastics, martial arts, skating, water sports, fishing, swimming.

WENATCHEE VALLEY SPORTS COUNCIL
5 SOUTH WENATCHEE AVENUE
SUITE C-100
WENATCHEE, WA 98801
509-663-3723
800-572-7753
Fax: 509-663-3983
www.wenatcheevalleysports.com
• Trina Elmes, Secreatry
• Caryl Morrell, President
• Sally Brawley, Vice President
Description:
Formed to promote, market and sell the Wenatchee Valley as a destination for businesses and leisure travel including conventions, trade shows, corporate meetings, and tourist travel to maximize additional overnight visitors. visotor expenditures, state and local tax revenues, and job opportunities.

WICHITA AREA SPORTS COMMISSION, GREATER
515 S MAIN STREET
SUITE 515
WICHITA, KS 67202
316-265-6236
800-526-9424
Fax: 316-265-0162
bob@wichitasports.com
www.wichitasports.com
• Byron Crawford, Director of Marketing & Promotions
(316) 518-0482
byron@wichitasports.com
• Jared Simon, Event Manager
jared@wichitasports.com
• Robert E Hanson, President/CEO
(316) 461-7767
bob@wichitasports.com
• Brian Hargrove, Events Director
(316) 990-7689
brian@wichitasports.com
• Tonya Atta, Director of Operations & Communications
tonya@wichitasports.com
Year Founded:
1997
Description:
Promotes Whicita and the surrounding area as a location for sporting events. Manages annual events such as Wichita Corporate Challenge and Prairie Fire Marathon.
Facilities:
INTRUST Bank Arena, Hartman Arena, Lawrence-Dumont Stadium, Charles Koch Arena, Cessna Stadium

WISCONSIN CONVENTION & VISITORS BUREAU
648 NORTH PLANKINTON AVENUE
SUITE 425
MILWAUKEE, WI 53203
414-273-3950
800-554-1448
Fax: 414-273-5596
www.visitmilwaukee.org
• Paul Upchurch, President/Chief Executive Officer
• Dana Jones, Director of finance and administration
• Margaret Casey, Executive Assistant
• Daron Fine, Technology Manager
• Paul Upchurch, President and CEO
Publications:
Visitors Guide

Description:
Founded 1990. Packages, promotes the entire sports product of Wisconsin. Includes attracting new events to the state and promoting the current organizations, events, teams, and facilities. Promotes value of sports in Wisconsin by acting as authority on economic impact, visibility and quality of life issues with sports.

WISCONSIN SPORTS DEVELOPMENT CORPORATION
313 WEST BELTLINE HIGHWAY
SUITE 161
MADISON, WI 53713
608-226-4780
www.sportsinwisconsin.com
• Darien Schaefer, Executive Director
• Richard Barrett, Director of Sales
• Tracy Baltz, Director Marketing

WOODFIELD CHICAGO NORTHWEST CONVENTION BUREAU
1375 E WOODFIELD RD
SUITE 120
SCHAUMBURG, IL 60173
847-490-1010
800-847-4849
Fax: 847-490-1212
info@chicagonorthwest.com
www.chicagonorthwest.com
• Dave Parulo, President
Description:
Woodfield Chicago Northwest is a dynamic destination for all types of sporting events. The area is centrally located at the crossroads of major interstate highways, is minutes from O'Hare Airport, offers plenty of free parking, and affords easy access to downtown Chicago. Facilities include the 10,000 sq. ft. Renaissance Schaumberg Hotel & Convention Center, soccer fields, baseball/softball fields, college facilities, and indoor complexes. We offer unique attractions, an unparalleled choice of restaurants, and lodging properties from world-class to economy. You will find warm Mid-Western hospitality and service throughout the area.
Attractions:
LEGOLAND Discovery Center, the only one in the U.S.; Medieval Times Dinner and Tournament; Arlington Park Racecourse; IKEA; Cabela's World Foremost Outfitters; Dave & Buster's; Gameworks; TopGolf
Publication:
Woodfield Chicago Northwest Visitor Guide

YAKIMA VALLEY VISITORS & CONVENTION BUREAU
10 NORTH 8TH STREET
YAKIMA, WA 98901-2515
509-575-3010
800-221-0751
Fax: 509-575-6252
www.visityakima.com
• John Cooper, CEO, President
• Wendi Bixler, Controller and HR Manager

YPSILANTI AREA CONVENTION AND VISITORS BUREAU
106 WEST MICHIGAN AVENUE
YPSILANTI, MI 48197
734-483-4444
• Debbie Locke-Daniel, Executive Director
dlocke@ypsilanti.org
• Mary Zucchero, Director of Sales

• Taryn Sulkes, Sales Coordinator
• Christine Laughren, Manager of Marketing & Communications
• Cory Hamlin, Marketing and Communications Assistant
• Mitzi McMahon, Office Manager
Mmcmahon@ypsilanti.org
Description:
Promotes sporting events and meetings to the local area which includes attracting new events to the state and promoting the current organizations, events, teams, and facilities.

YUMA CONVENTION & VISITORS BUREAU
201 NORTH FOURTH STREET
YUMA, AZ 85364
928-783-0071
800-293-0071
Fax: 928-783-1897
info@visityuma.com
www.visityuma.com
• Linda Jordan, Executive Director
• Linda Morgan, Executive Director
Publications:
GUIDE TO YUMA, NATIONAL HERITAGE AREA WALKING MAP, GERMAN BROCHURE.
Member Services:
We can help you book your group from 20-800 people.

Sports Halls of Fame, Libraries, Museums

AMERICAN SPORT ART MUSEUM AND ARCHIVES (ASAMA)
ONE ACADEMY DRIVE
DAPHNE, AL 36526
251-626-3303
800-223-2668
Fax: 251-626-3874
asama@ussa.edu
www.asama.org
• Robert Zemmit, Curator
• Thomas Rosandich, President United States Sports Academy
• Jack B. Scharr, Chairman International Advisory Board
Description:
Founded 1984. ASAMA contains a unique collection of classic and contemporary art featuring works of the Academy's Sports Artists of the Year. Over 1,000 pieces in all media.
Membership:
Gold $1,000; Silver $500; Bronze $250; Coach $100; Other anything under $100. With a membership you will receive invitations to the opening receptions of the exhibits and a 10% discount on all purchases in the gift shop.

AMERICAN WATER SKI EDUCATIONAL FOUNDATION/WATER SKI HALL OF FAME/MUSEUM
1251 HOLY COW ROAD
POLK CITY, FL 33868-8200
863-324-2472
Fax: 863-342-3996
info@waterskihalloffame.com
www.waterskihalloffame.com
• Paul Chaplin, President
• kim Laskoff, Secretary

• Mark Harvet, Treasurer
• Carole Lowe, Director
• J.D Morgan, Board Of Trustee
• Jim Grew, Chairman of the Board
• Robert Reich, Vice President
Description:
Founded 1968. Dedicated to the preservation of the traditions of water skiing, and to the encouragement of and education in the safe enjoyment of the challenges of water skiing. To these ends, the Foundation administers the Water Ski Museum/Hall of Fame, supervises scholarship programs to further the education of deserving water skiers, and provides financing for other activities which are consistent with the spirit in which the Foundation was formed.
Publications:
The Water Skier Magazine published nine times a year.
Membership:
Prices range from Free to $60. There are over 37,500 members.

BABE RUTH BIRTHPLACE AND SPORTS LEGENDS MUSEUM
216 EMORY ST
BALTIMORE, MD 21230
410-727-1539
Fax: 410-727-1652
info@baberuthmuseum.com
baberuthmuseum.org
• Shawn M. Herne, Executive Director ext 3040
• Michael L. Gibbons, Director Emeritus & Historian ext 3040
• Cathy Zaorski, Communications & Media Director ext 3040

BARCELONA MUSEUM AND SPORTS STUDY CENTER
BUENOS AIRES ST 56-58 (TORRE)
BARCELONA, SPAIN 8036

• Ricardo Sanchez, Coordinator
Description:
Founded 1986. Promotes cultural aspects of sport, preserve the history of sports in Catalonia - an autonomous community - and projects the values of the Olympic movement.

BRITISH COLUMBIA SPORTS HALL OF FAME MUSEUM
777 PACIFIC BOULEVARD
VANCOUVER, BC, CANADA V6B 4Y8
604-687-5520
Fax: 604-687-5510
www.bcsportshalloffame.com
• Sue Griffin, Executive Director
• Gareth Rees, Chairman
• Alan Tynan, Vice-Chair
• John Ormiston, Secretary/Treasurer
• Allison Mailer, Executive Director
Publications:
FOR THE RECORD, twice annually.
Description:
Founded 1966. Serves to honor British Columbia athletes, builders and coaches; provides research facilities for the media and the public. Also has 18,000 square feet of exhibit space, including hands-on participation gallery. Non-profit Organization.

BRYANT MUSEUM, PAUL W.
300 PAUL W. BRYANT DRIVE
UNIVERSITY OF ALABAMA
BOX 870385
TUSCALOOSA, AL 35487
205-348-4668
866-772-BEAR (2327)
Fax: 205-348-8883
bryant-info@ua.edu
bryantmuseum.com
• Kenneth Gaddy, Director
kgaddy@bama.ua.edu
Description:
Founded in 1988. Named in honor of the legendary coach Paul 'Bear' Bryant the Museum exhibit gallery displays over 100 years of Alabama football history using memorabilia, photographs, art, audio and visual material from its exstensive collection. The Museum collects, preserves and researches material relating to the sports history of the University of Alabama and is a Must See attraction for all fans of college sports. The media, public and researchers rely on the BRyant Museum as areliable source for images and information. The collection facility continually acquires historic artifacts, library and archival materials which are interprete
Membership Requirements:
Bryant Gold Club, $1,000 and over; William Little Club, $500-$999; Director's Club, $250-499; Press Box Club, $100-$249; Locker Room Club, $30 fam/$20 ind; Sideline Club (Students) $15.
Publications:
Newsletter, three times annually.
Member Services:
Membership meetings, Complimentary admission and discounts on museum merchandise.

CANADA'S SPORTS HALL OF FAME
169 CANADA OLYMPIC ROAD SW
CALGARY, ALBERTA, CANADA T3B 5R5
403-776-1040
Fax: 416-260-9347
info@cshof.ca
www.sportshall.ca
• Jake G. Gaudaur, Chairman of the Board
• Mario W. Sicilliano, President and CEO
• Marnie Krell, Marketing & Communications Coordinator
mkrell@cshof.ca
• Sam Shefsky, Governor
• Robert Bundy, Governor
• Emerson Mascoll, Governor
• Dennis Flynn, Governor
Member Services:
Collects and displays sports memorabilia. Disseminates sports information and photographs. Maintains theater, library and archives.
Publications:
CANADIAN SPORTS ACHIEVERS; newsletter, two times annually; brochures.
Membership Requirements:
Decision of National Selection Committee.
Description:
Founded 1955. Works to preserve and promote Canada's sporting heritage by recognizing through selections of Honored Members important achievements by Canadians in the sports field. Maintains large display facility open throughout the year.

CATSKILL FLY FISHING CENTER & MUSEUM
1031 OLD ROUTE 17
PO BOX 1295
LIVINGSTON MANOR, NY 12758-1295
845-439-4810
Fax: 845-439-3387
office@cffcm.com
www.cffcm.com
• Jim Krul, Executive Director
Publications:
Newsletter Catskill Angler, Monthly
Calendar of Events April and October.
Member Services:
Members receive free admission to the
Museum, 10% off in our Museum Gift Shop
and notices of all events held at the Center.
Membership Requirements:
Individual membership $35.00, Family
membership $50.00, Student membership
$15.00, Contributing membership $75.00,
Sustaining membership $100.00, Patron
membership $250.00, Sponsor membership
$500.00, Benefactor membership $1000.00.
Description:
Is a nonprofit, educational organization
dedicated to: preserving America's flyfishing
heritage; teaching its future generations of
flyfishers; and protecting its flyfishing
environment.

COLLEGE FOOTBALL HALL OF FAME
433 E LAS COLINAS BLVD
SUITE 1130
SOUTH BEND, IN 75039
972-556-1000
800-440-3263
Fax: 972-556-9032
www.collegefootball.org
• Lisa Malin Klunder, Executive Director
• Archie Manning, Chair
• Steven J. Hatchell, President and CEO
ext 5706
• Clayton I. Bennett, Vice Chair
ext 5715
• Richard Allen, Multimedia & IT Manager
• Bill Donoghue, Volunteer Coordinator

DELAWARE SPORTS MUSEUM AND HALL OF FAME
801 SHIPYARD DRIVE
WILMINGTON, DE 19801-5121
302-425-3263
Fax: 302-425-3713
www.desports.org
• Bob Tattersall, President
• Beth Brown, Secretary
• Bill Hayes, Treasurer
• Tom Fort, President
• Ben Sirman, 1st Vice President
• Jack A. Holloway, CPA, 2nd
Vice-President
Description:
Since 1976 the Delaware Hall of Fame has
honored and promoted Delaware's
outstanding athletic performers including
those who have brought recognition to the
First State through their coaching, officiating
administrative and journalism contributions.
Additionally, the museum shall preserve the
performances of Delaware inductees and
other athletes through the display of
memorabilia, artifacts and photos and
videos.

DON GARLITS MUSEUM OF DRAG RACING AND INTERNATIONAL DRAG RACING HALL OF FAME
13700 SW 16TH AVENUE
I-75, EXIT 341
OCALA, FL 34473
352-245-8661
877-271-3278
Fax: 352-245-6895
www.garlits.com
• Don Garlits, Chief Executive Officer
(352) 245-8661
• Charles "Chuck" Keppel, Controller and
General Manager
(352) 245-8661
• Lisa Crigar, Personal Assistant and PR
Manager
(352) 547-9160
lcrigar65@gmail.com
Description:
Founded in 1976. A drag racing and antique
car museum.

FIGURE SKATING HALL OF FAME AND MUSEUM, THE WORLD
20 FIRST ST
COLORADO SPRINGS, CO 80906-3697
719-635-5200
Fax: 719-635-9548
info@worldskatingmuseum.org
www.worldskatingmuseum.org
• Jim Fox, Assistant to the Executive
Director
jfox@usfsa.org
• Karen Cover, Museum Archivist
(719) 228-3450
kcover@worldskatingmuseum.org
Description:
Founded 1956. The Hall of Fame contains
two separate halls of fame - World and U.S.
There presently are 33 World inductees and
23 U.S. inductees, with induction taking
place yearly. All memorabilia relating to
figure skating over the past 100 years are
displayed in the museum, including
international and U.S. medals for the past
100 years. There is an extensive art
collection from the seventeenth century to
the present, costumes of skaters from the
World War I period to the present, and a
skaters gallery with ice skates from 1200
years ago to the present. The museum is
the official world repository of U.S., World
and Olympic records. It also

GEORGIA SPORTS HALL OF FAME
301 CHERRY STREET
PO BOX 4644
MACON, GA 31208
478-752-1585
Fax: 478-752-1587
www.gshf.org
• Benjamin Baughman, Curator
benjaminb@gshf.org
• Ben Sapp, Managing Director
(478) 752-1585
bens@gshf.org
• Eric Thomas, Rental Coordinator
ext 107
Description:
Founded 1989. Promotes the health and
physical fitness of the citizens of Georgia;
promotes participation in amateur sports by
citizens of all ages and skill levels; promotes
statewide program of amateur athletic
competition, culminating with the Georgia
Games Championships; promotes state,
national and international amateur sports

through the establishment of Olympic
training facilities within the state.

GREEN BAY PACKER HALL OF FAME
LAMBEAU FIELD ATRIUM
1265 LOMBARDI AVENUE
GREEN BAY, WI 54304
920-569-7512 EXT 1
888-442-7225
Fax: 920-569-7144
www.lambeaufield.com
• Krissy Zegers, Hall of Fame & Stadium
Tour Manager

GREYHOUND HALL OF FAME
407 SOUTH BUCKEYE
ABILENE, KS 67410
785-263-3000
800-932-7881
Fax: 785-263-2604
www.greyhoundhalloffame.com
• Edward Scheele, Director

HARNESS RACING MUSEUM & HALL OF FAME, THE
240 MAIN STREET
GOSHEN, NY 10924
845-294-6330
Fax: 845-294-3463
hrm@frontiernet.net
www.harnessmuseum.com
• Gail C. Cunard, Executive Director
• E. T. Gerry, Jr., President
Year Founded:
1951

HOCKEY HALL OF FAME AND MUSEUM
BCE PLACE
30 YONGE STREET
TORONTO, ON, CANADA M5E 1X8
416-360-7735
Fax: 416-360-1501
info@hhof.com
www.hhof.com
• Bill Hay, Chairman/Chief Executive Officer
• Darren Bouko, Manager Business
Development
• Jackie Schwartz, Manager marketing &
Promotions
• Wendy Cramer, Co-Ordinator, group
Booking
• Jeff Denomme, President/Chief Operating
Officer/Treasurer
jdenomme@hhof.com
• Craig Baines, Vice President, Operations
cbaines@hhof.com
• Peter Jagla, Vice President, Marketing
pjagla@hhof.com
• Phil Pritchard, Vice President, Resource
Centre and Curator
ppritchard@hhof.com
• Ron Ellis, Director, Public Affairs/Assistant
to Preside
rellis@hhof.com
Publications:
LEGENDS-The Official Program of the
Hockey Hall of Fame.
Description:
Founded 1943, the Hockey Hall of Fame
exists in order to honour and preserve the
history of the game of ice hockey, and in
particular, those who have made
outstanding contributions and achievements
in the development of the game. Home of
the Stanley Cup, the world's most
exstensive collection of hockey memorabilia,
and the state-of-the-art interactive games,

the Hockey Hall of Fame offers guests of all ages and levels of interest a vibrant and innovative look at the game of hockey. The Hockey Hall of Fam

INDIANA BASKETBALL HALL OF FAME
ONE HALL OF FAME COURT
NEW CASTLE, IN 47362
765-529-1891
Fax: 765-529-0273
www.hoopshall.com
• Marvin Tudor, President
• Jim Callane, Executive Vice President
Description:
Founded 1966. Devoted to the history of Indiana high school basketball. Honors contributors to the game; explores what basketball means to the state's culture and personality. Celebrates Indian's basketball history with videos and artifacts of the greatest basketball players to come out of Indiana, Also includes great moments and interactive exhibits.
Publications:
INDIANA BASKETBALL HISTORY, quarterly magazine $15 year subscription.
Member Services:
$100 Annual fee includes unlimited free admission, free subscription to magazine, invitation to all events and activities given to hall of famers.

INDIANA FOOTBALL HALL OF FAME
815 NORTH A STREET
BOX 1035
RICHMOND, IN 47375
765-966-2235
www.indiana-football.org
• Richard Bryant, President
• Ken Jorden, VP
• Fred Goss, Secretary
Description:
Establishes endowments and scholarships for excellence in football in Indiana. Candidates for induction include coaches, players, officials, sport media and Indiana citizens who have made prominent contributions in the advancement of football excellence.
Year Founded:
1973

INDIANAPOLIS MOTOR SPEEDWAY HALL OF FAME MUSEUM
4790 WEST 16TH STREET
INDIANAPOLIS, IN 46222
317-492-8500
www.indyracingmuseum.org
• Ellen Bireley, Director
Publications:
OFFICIAL 500 PROGRAM, annually; INDY REVIEW, after each year's race, usually by November 15.
Description:
Founded 1956. Located on the grounds of the Indianapolis Motor Speedway. Displayed are more than 75 racing cars, including Indianapolis winners as well as race cars from international renowned motorsports events world wide. Also displayed are several examples of early antique and classic passenger cars. Surrounding the restored cars are numerous displays of engines, trophies, helmets, historic photographs, and other priceless memorabilia.

INTERNATIONAL BOWLING MUSEUM AND HALL OF FAME
612 SIX FLAGS DRIVE
ARLINGTON, TX 76011
817-385-8215
Fax: 314-231-4054
hofm@bowlingmuseum.com
www.bowlingmuseum.com
• Keith Hamilton, Chairman, President
• John Walker, VP
• Terry Brenneman, Treasurer
• Bob Gudorf, Secretary
Description:
Opened in June, 1984. Visitors will enjoy computerized exhibits, movie, art and sculpture, museum shop, and bowling on computerized or hand-set lanes. The museum is also home to the St. Louis Cardinals Hall of Fame Museum. Receptions, catered events and meeting space available.
Publications:
Hall of Fame newsletter, three times annually.

INTERNATIONAL BOXING HALL OF FAME
1 HALL OF FAME DRIVE
CANASTOTA, NY 13032
315-697-7095
Fax: 315-697-5356
www.ibhof.com
• Edward P. Brophy, Executive Director
Description:
Mission is to honor and preserve boxing's rich heritage, chronicle the achievements of those who excelled and provide an educational for our many visitors.

INTERNATIONAL GYMNASTICS HALL OF FAME & MUSEUM
120 NORTH ROBINSON
EAST CONCOURSE
OKLAHOMA CITY, OK 73102
405-235-5600
Fax: 405-235-5678
contact@ighof.com
www.ighof.com
• Whitney Anson, President
• Paul Ziert, Chief Executive Officer
Description:
Founded 1987. Serves to recognize the sport of Gymnastics and the personalities involved in all aspects.
Membership Requirements:
Donations.
Publications:
International Gymnastics HALL OF FAME Newsletter, random; INTERNATIONAL GYMNAST Magazine, 10 times annually.

INTERNATIONAL INSTITUTE FOR SPORT HISTORY
PO BOX 175
STATE COLLEGE, PA 16804
814-321-4018
habrams@iisoh.org
www.sportlibrary.org
• Harvey Abrams, President
(814) 321-4018
habrams@iisoh.org
Year founded:
2001
Description:
Specialized research library and museum for the history of sport, physical education, recreation, dance, sport in art and the

Olympic Games.
Online resources:
National Olympic Committee Directory, Sport in Pennsylvania, Sport in Austria, Sport in Art Poster Series at www.sportlibrary.org
Nature of Service:
Comprehensive Library & Museum for the History of Sport, Physical Education, Recreation, Dance, Sport in Art and the Olympic Games.

INTERNATIONAL JEWISH SPORTS HALL OF FAME
7922 TURNCREST DR
POTOMAC, MD 20854-2773
jsportslegends@aol.com
www.jewishsports.net
• Efraim Yaacobi, Executive Secretary
• Alan Sherman, Chairman
• R. Stephen Rubin, Honorary Chairman
• Joseph Siegman, Chairman Selection Committee Member Services
Address in Israel:
Wingate Institute, Wingate Post Office, Netanya, Israel
Description:
Honors Jewish men and women worldwide, elected annually in December, who have accomplished extraordinary achievements in sports, and recognizes other Jewish men and women who have made significant contributions to society through sports. Actual location of Hall of Fame is Wingate Institute for Physical Education, Netanya 42902 Israel.
Publications:
International Jewish Sports Hall of Fame and Jewish Sports Legends vol. 4. June 2005
Member Services:
Lifetime Achievement Award, awarded annually for outstanding contributions to the State of Israel, and society through sports.
Number of Members:
Over 420 inductees as of 2018.

INTERNATIONAL MOTOR SPORTS HALL OF FAME
PO BOX 1018
TALLADEGA, AL 35160
256-362-5002
Fax: 256-315-4565
www.motorsportshalloffame.com
• Grant Lynch, Executive Director
• Cindy Bradford, Office Manager
• Bruce Ramey, Hall of Fame Manager
Description:
Founded 1983. Serves to preserve the history of motorsports on a worldwide basis, and to enshrine forever the people that have been responsible for it's growth. Home of the Official International Motorsports Hall of Fame where the Inductees are permanently enshrined. Also features a collection of racing cars, memorabilia, race car simulator, gift shop and research library.

INTERNATIONAL SNOWMOBILE HALL OF FAME & MUSEUM
8481 HIGHWAY 70 WEST
PO BOX 720
ST. GERMAIN, WI 54558
715-542-4463
Fax: 715-542-4260
info@snowmobilehalloffame.com
www.snowmobilehalloffame.com

multi sports

253

• Loren R. Anderson, President
Description:
Founded 1983. Honors snowmobile racing greats and club volunteers; serves as museum of historic sleds from both trail and track.
Publications:
THE FINISH LINE, Newsletter, periodic.
Number of members:
53 Inductees.

INTERNATIONAL SPORTS HALL OF FAME AND OLYMPIC MUSEUM
110 NE HIGHWAY 101
DEPOE BAY, OR 97341
541-765-2923
Fax: 541-765-3231
• Eric Nash, Executive Director
enash327@yahoo.com
Description:
Founded 1992. Museum will display international Olympic memorabilia from 1896 to the present. Specializes in the 1984 Olympics, with one of the largest collections in the U.S. The collection includes: medals, banners, flags, posters, pins, programs, books, and reports.

INTERNATIONAL SPORTS HERITAGE ASSOCIATION
PO BOX 2384
FLORENCE, OR 32004-3093
541-991-7315
Fax: 904-997-3871
info@sportsheritage.org
www.sportsheritage.org
• Michael Gibbons, President
• Rick Walls, Vice President
Publications:
Newsletter, bimonthly 'Honoring Our Heroes'
Description:
Founded 1971. Serves as a forum for directors/curators of halls of fame and museums to exchange ideas and information and generally strengthen and promote their respective organizations.

INTERNATIONAL SWIMMING HALL OF FAME
ONE HALL OF FAME DRIVE
FT. LAUDERDALE, FL 33316
954-462-6536
Fax: 954-
www.ishof.org
• Bruce Wigo, President/CEO
brucewigo@yahoo.com
• Bob Duenkel, Executive Director
• Meg Keller Marvin, Assistant to CEO
• Ivonne Schmid, Assistant to Executive Director
• Laurie Marchwinski, Director of Basketball Operations
• Marcia Meiners, Assistant To The President
• Jarret Streiner, Webmaster
• Bob Duenkel, Executive Director/Curator
Description:
Founded 1965. Swimming, diving, pools, synchronized swimming, and water polo, past and present. Olympic gold medals and uniforms, trophies, short movies and Henning Library. Memorabilia from Johnny (Tarzan) Weissmuller, Esther Williams, Mark Spitz, Greg Louganis and many more.
Publications:
Newsletter, quarterly.
Member Services:

Site of College Coaches Swim Forum and national and international events each year. Annual meetings held in conjunction with Honor Ceremonies.

INTERNATIONAL TENNIS HALL OF FAME AND MUSEUM
194 BELLEVUE AVE
NEWPORT, RI 2840
401-849-3990
800-457-1144
Fax: 401-849-8780
newport@tennisfame.com
www.tennisfame.com
• Mark Stenning, Chief Executive Officer
• Amelia Ahlborg, Assistant To CEO
• Nancy Cardoza, Vice president
• Baebara Klassner, Accounting Manager
• Sarah Rivard, Accountant
• Jane Sherman, Office manager
• Mary Health, Chief Marketing Officer
New York Office:
100 Park Ave, 10th Floor, New York, NY 10017. 212 880-4179.
Description:
Founded 1954. Non-profit organization dedicated to preserving the history of the game and maintaining a museum in Newport, Rhode Island. The organization also promotes junior tennis and professional tennis tournaments. The Hall of Fame inducts outstanding players, officials and administrators. Since 1954, 175 enshrinees have been elected.
Publications:
Tennis Hall of Fame Newsletter.

JAPANESE BASEBALL HALL OF FAME AND MUSEUM
1-3-61, KORAKU
BUNKYO-KU
TOKYO, JAPAN 112-0004

• Yasuchika Negoro, Chairman
• Ryozo Kato, Chairman of the Board of Directors
• Hideo Okabe, Director
• Hajime Toyokura, Executive Director
Description:
Founded 1959, its purpose is to contribute to the development of baseball in Japan through a dedication of baseball greats-players, executives, and umpires, as Hall of Famers and the exhibition and collection of as many memorable baseball materials as possible, including various kinds of baseball literature.

JOYCE SPORTS RESEARCH COLLECTION, UNIVERSITY OF NOTRE DAME
221 HESBURGH LIBRARY
UNIVERSITY OF NOTRE DAME
NOTRE DAME, IN 46556-5629
574-631-6258
Fax: 574-631-6772
rarebook@nd.edu
• George Rugg, Curator
george.k.rugg.1@nd.edu
Description:
Comprises all of the University Librarie's sports related materials. These include a circulating collection of close to 10,000 volumes, and a non circulating collection.

KENTUCKY DERBY MUSEUM
704 CENTRAL AVENUE
LOUISVILLE, KY 40208
502-637-7097
Fax: 502-637-1111
info@derbymuseum.org
www.derbymuseum.org
• Lynn Ashton, Executive Director
lashton@derbymuseum.org
• Sherry Crose, Chief Operating Officer
scrose@derbymuseum.org
• Wendy Treinen, Public Relations Manager
cmangeot@derbymuseum.org
Description:
Founded 1985. Promotes sport of Thoroughbred racing, preserves the history and heritage of the Kentucky Derby and Churchill Downs, and serves as a forum for the equine industry.
Membership Requirements:
Completion of membership application to be returned with membership fee. Corporate farm and individual memberships available.
Publications:
THE INSIDE TRACK, quarterly newsletter.
Official Sponsor:
2002 - American Airlines.

LA84 FOUNDATION
2141 WEST ADAMS BOULEVARD
LOS ANGELES, CA 90018
323-730-4600
Fax: 323-730-9637
info@la84foundation.org
www.la84foundation.org
• Anita L. Defrantz, President
• Wayne Wilson, Vice President Education Services
• Conrad Freund, Chief Operating Officer
Description:
The LA84 Foundation is endowed with surplus funds from the 1984 Los Angeles Olympic Games. Their mission is to serve youth through sport and to increase knowledge of sport and its impact on people's lives. The LA84 Foundation supports a wide array of youth sports programming. They award grants to youth sports organizations within the eight southernmost counties of California. They also conduct their own youth sports and coaching education programs, a number of which have become models for similar programs nationwide.
Publications:
Biennial publications
Member Services:
Open to students, athletes, coaches, journalists, researchers and public. Copy capabilities; meeting and conference rooms; video and audio-visual equipment; computerized catalog system; on-line database.

LACROSSE MUSEUM AND NATIONAL HALL OF FAME MUSEUM
113 WEST UNIVERSITY PARKWAY
BALTIMORE, MD 21210
410-235-6882
Fax: 410-366-6735
info@uslacrosse.org
www.uslacrosse.org
• Bill Schoonmaker, Chief Operating Officer
• Steven Stenersen, President and CEO
Description:
Founded 1959. Displays and chronicles the history of the sport of lacrosse, from its

native American origin to the present day. Museum includes photographs, lithographs, trophies, equipment, uniforms, statues, books, videos and rare memorabilia for men's and women's lacrosse.

LITTLE LEAGUE BASEBALL MUSEUM
525 ROUTE 15 HIGHWAY
PO BOX 3485
WILLIAMSPORT, PA 17701-0485
570-326-1921
Fax: 570-326-1074
museum@littleleague.org
www.littleleague.org
• John Littner, Director
Description:
Founded 1982. Purpose is to chart history and growth of Little League Baseball and Softball movement from founding in Williamsport to its worldwide growth by means of visual and audio displays, exhibits and memorabilia that are both educational and entertaining.

MANITOBA SPORTS HALL OF FAME & MUSEUM INC.
SPORTS FOR LIFE CENTRE
145 PACIFIC AVENUE
WINNIPEG, MB, CANADA R3B 2Z6
204-925-5736
Fax: 204-925-5916
halloffame@sport.mb.ca
• Rick D. Brownlee, Executive Director
• Don Pincock, President
• Lois Howard, Secretary
Description:
Founded 1980. Preserves Manitoba's sport heritage; honors athletes, builders, teams with induction to the Hall of Fame.
Publications:
Newsletter, quarterly; Annual Induction Program.

MISSOURI SPORTS HALL OF FAME
3861 E. STAN MUSIAL DR
SPRINGFIELD, MO 65809
417-889-3100
800-498-5678
Fax: 417-889-2761
www.mosportshalloffame.com
• Jerald Andrews, President/Executive Director
• Marty Willadsen, Vp/Operations And Administration
• Jerry Vickery, Historian
Description:
Founded 1993, by John Q. Hammons. Serves to preserve sports history of Missouri; honor individuals and teams that have made significant contributions to sports, and to promote sports throughout the state of Missouri.

MOTORSPORTS MUSEUM AND HALL OF FAME OF AMERICA
43700 EXPO CENTER DRIVE
NOVI, MI 48375
248-349-RACE
800-250-7223
Fax: 248-349-2113
info@mshf.com
www.mshf.com
• Ronald A. Watson, President
• Tom Gravalos, Vice-Chairman
• John Doonan, Chairman
• Denny Darnell, Secretary
• Ross Hotz, Treasurer

Member Services:
Hall of Fame Induction held in August during NASCAR at the Michigan International Speedway. Membership package includes yearbook, poster, decal, Novi Race Car Pin, free admission to museum, discounts on gift items and subscription to HORSEPOWER Newsletter.
Publications:
Annual Hall of Fame Souvenir Yearbook
Description:
Serves as the Hall of Fame of America for Motorsports and as a museum. Over 70 racing vehicles in the following seven categories are displayed: Open Wheel, Stock Car, Sports Car, Drag Racing, Motorcycle, Air Racing and Power Boat.
Museum Location:
Novi Expo Center, S.W. Corner of I-96 and Novi Road

MUSEUM OF POLO AND HALL OF FAME
9011 LAKE WORTH ROAD
LAKE WORTH, FL 33467
561-969-3210
Fax: 561-964-8299
polomuseum@att.net
www.polomuseum.com
• George J Dupont Sr, Jr., Executive Director, Vice President
• Brenda Lynn, Director of Development
Publications:
Newsletter, annually.
Description:
Founded 1984. Museum houses polo's records, art, memorabilia, honors heroes of polo through Polo Hall of Fame, offers education and knowledge about polo and provides history of the sport.

MUSEUM OF YACHTING
FORT ADAMS STATE PARK
NEWPORT, RI 2840
401-847-1018
Fax: 401-847-8320
museum@moy.org
www.museumofyachting.org
• Terry Nathan, President
• Rhonda Landers, Chief Financial Officer
Description:
Founded 1980. Promotes yachting history and hosts annual classic yacht regatta.
Membership Requirements:
Interest in Yachting, past and present.
Publications:
Newsletter, quarterly.
Member Services:
Free admission to Museum; use of library, discounts on Museum programs, and events and merchandise.

NAISMITH MEMORIAL BASKETBALL HALL OF FAME
1000 WEST COLUMBUS AVENUE
SPRINGFIELD, MA 1105
413-781-6500
877-446-6752
www.hoophall.com
• John Doleva, President/Chief Executive Officer
doleva@hoophall.com
• Donald R. Senecal, Vice President/Finance/Operations
senecal@hoophall.com
Member Services:
Hall of Fame induction, Hall of Fame Tip-Off Classic, Frances Pomeroy Naismith Award,

Ed Steitz Award, John W. Bunn Award, Bob Cousy Collegiate Point-Guard Award, Curt Gowdy Media Award, Chip Hilton Award, Clare Bee Award, High School Excellence Award, Museum.
Publications:
Magazine, Yearbook.
Membership Requirements:
To be eligible to be inducted, candidate must first be nominated; players must be retired five years, coaches with 25 years of serve are eligible. Candidate must have made significant contributions to the game in many distinct areas.
Description:
Founded 1949. Preserves and promotes basketball at all levels, including the professional, collegiate, scholastic, international game and pays tribute to both men and women, trainers, referees, contributors.

NATIONAL ART MUSEUM OF SPORT
UNIVERSITY PLACE - IUPUI
850 WEST MICHIGAN ST
INDIANAPOLIS, IN 46202-5198
317-274-3627
Fax: 317-274-3878
• Elizabeth C. Varner, President
• Ann M. Rein, Executive Director
(317) 274-3627
Description:
Founded 1959. Brings to the public a comprehensive collection of Sport Art (over 50 different sports). Educates the public on the close relationship over the ages between art and sport.
Publications:
SCORE BOARD NEWSLETTER 3 issues per year. Exhibit check list.

NATIONAL AUTOMOBILE MUSEUM
10 SOUTH LAKE STREET
RENO, NV 89501-1558
775-333-9300
Fax: 775-333-9309
info@automuseum.org
www.automuseum.org
• Jackie Frady, President and ED
• Barbara Bolenbaker, Retail manager
• Barbara Clark, Sr Support services manager
• Becky Contos, Sales and marketing manager
Description:
Founded 1989. General automobile museum with collection of racing and speed record autos. Automotive research library available through mail service.

NATIONAL BASEBALL HALL OF FAME AND MUSEUM
25 MAIN STREET
COOPERSTOWN, NY 13326
607-547-7200
888-425-5633
Fax: 607-547-2044
info@baseballhalloffame.org
www.baseballhall.org
• William E. Haase, Senior Vice President (607) 547-7200
• Joe Morgan, Vice Chairman
• Jeff Idelson, President
• Craig Muder, Directoro of Communications
Publications:
Annual Hall of Fame Yearbook, Memories and Dreams Quarterly Magazine.

Membership Requirements:
Must have played at least 10 years in Major Leagues or Negro Leagues or can have been executive, manager or umpire.
Description:
Museum/Educational Facility

NATIONAL FOOTBALL FOUNDATION AND COLLEGE HALL OF FAME, INC., THE
433 LAS COLINAS BLVD
SUITE 1130
IRVING, TX 75039
972-556-1000
Fax: 972-556-9032
membership@footballfoundation.com
www.footballfoundation.com
• Archie Manning, Chairman
• Steven J. Hatchell, President and CEO
• Clayton I. Bennett, Vice Chair
• Matthew Sigo, Chief Operating Officer
Description:
Established: 1947. Our mission is to promote and develop the power of amateur football in developing the qualities of leadership, sportsmanship, competitive zeal and the drive for academic excellence in America's young people.
Number of Members:
13,000.
Publications:
Footballletter 4 times per year.
Member Services:
120 Chapters, Footballletter Magazine, Free Admission to the Hall of Fame, Grants, Programs, Scholorships.
Membership Requirements:
$40.00 year.

NATIONAL FRESH WATER FISHING HALL OF FAME
10360 ONE HALL OF FAME DR
HAYWARD, WI 54843
715-634-4440
www.freshwater-fishing.org
• Emmett A Brown, Executive Director
Description:
Museum displaying fishing artifacts, including 300 antique outboard motors, thousands of lures, rods, reels, mounted fish, tackle boxes and all other memorabilia involved in the sport of fresh water fishing.
Number of members:
6,500
Publications:
Quarterly Newsletter with record updates; Fish Record Book, early April; Annual Calendar.
Member Services:
Unlimited admission pass to members and family members under 18 to museum. Receipt of all publications.
Membership Requirements:
$30.00 Annual membership, $250.00 Lifetime membership, $50.00 Club and Business memberships.

NATIONAL HIGH SCHOOL SPORTS HALL OF FAME
PO BOX 690
1802 ALONZO WATFORD SR. DRIVE
INDIANAPOLIS, IN 46206
317-972-6900
Fax: 317-822-5700
www.nfhs.org

• Bruce L. Howard, Director of Publications and Communications
(816) 464-5400
Description:
Founded 1982. Currently housed in an auditorium area of the National Federation of State High School Associations. Induction into the Hall of Fame is conducted annually on the basis of special achievement in four categories - athlete, coach, official and administrator.

NATIONAL ITALIAN-AMERICAN SPORTS HALL OF FAME
1431 W. TAYLOR ST
CHICAGO, IL 60607
312-226-5566
Fax: 312-226-5678
www.niashf.org
• George Randazzo, Founder/Chairman
george@niashf.org
• Wayne Randazzo, Editor Red White & Green Magazine
Publications:
NIASHF Newsletter; Red White and Green Magazine
Description:
Founded 1977. Preservation of achievements of professional and amateur Italian-American athletes who have contributed to international sports.

NATIONAL MISSISSIPPI RIVER MUSEUM & AQUARIUM
350 EAST 3RD STREET HARBOR
PORT OF DUBUQUE
DUBUQUE, IA 52001
563-557-9545
800-226-3369
Fax: 563-583-1241
info@rivermuseum.com
www.mississippirivermuseum.com
• Jerry Enzler, Executive Director
• Cristin Waterbury, Curator
Member Services:
Annual meeting held in May in Dubuque, IA.
Publications:
Newsletter, quarterly.
Membership Requirements:
Pay annual dues.
Description:
Founded 1985. Serves to preserve the history of men and women of the inland waters of America - explorers, builders, inventors, river people and artists, writers and musicians; part of the Mississippi River Museum.

NATIONAL MOTORSPORTS PRESS ASSOCIATION
PO BOX 500
DARLINGTON, SC 29540
843-395-8900
Fax: 843-393-3911
www.nmpaonline.com
• Rea White, President
• Kenny Bruce, President
• Brian Nelson, VP
• Bob Pockrass, Secretary/Treasurer
Description:
Comprised of individuals in news media and other individuals in the automotive/racing field. Promotes better news coverage of motorsports news events. Maintains Stock Car Hall of Fame and Joe Weatherly Museum at Darlington Raceway. Sponsors competitions; bestows awards.

Publications:
NMPA NEWSLETTER, twice a year.

NATIONAL MUSEUM OF RACING HALL OF FAME
191 UNION AVENUE
SARATOGA SPRINGS, NY 12866-3566
518-584-0400
800-JOCKEY4
Fax: 518-584-4574
nmrmedia@racingmuseum.net
www.racingmuseum.org
• Christopher Dragone, Director
(518) 584-0400
• Christopher Dragone, Director
• Victoria Tokarowski, Membership and business manager
• Brien Bouyea, Communications coordinator
• Allan Carter, Historian
Membership Requirements:
Contributor, Donor, Associate, Patron, Benefactor, Gold Cup
Description:
Founded 1950. Interprets the history and conveys the excitement of Thoroughbred racing in America. Fosters education and understanding of Thoroughbred racing by providing public access to equine art, artifacts, memorabilia, film, video, books and historical archives. Collects, preserves, researches, interprets and exhibits the entire spectrum of Thoroughbred racing enhanced by interactive displays.

NATIONAL SOCCER HALL OF FAME
18 STADIUM CIRCLE
ONEONTA, NY 13820
607-432-3351
Fax: 607-432-8429
www.soccerhall.org
Description:
Celebrates the history, honors the heroes and preserves the legacy of the sport of soccer in the United States.
Year Founded:
1950

NATIONAL SOFTBALL HALL OF FAME & MUSEUM & STADIUM COMPLEX
2801 NE 50TH STREET
OKLAHOMA CITY, OK 73111
405-424-5266
Fax: 405-424-3855
www.asasoftball.org
• Ron Radigonda, Executive Director
(405) 424-5266
• Bill Plummer, Museum Curator
(405) 425-3433
• Kelly McKeown, Director Marketing
(405) 424-5266
Number of members
180
Description:
Founded 1957. Honors former outstanding players and traces evolution and history of softball with various displays and exhibits. Holds induction ceremonies annually.

NATIONAL SPORTING LIBRARY, THE
102 THE PLAINS ROAD
MIDDLEBURG, VA 20118
540-687-6542
Fax: 540-687-8540
www.nsl.org
• Rick Stoutamyer, Executive Director
• Melanie Leigh Mathews, Executive

Director
• Diana Kingsbury Smith, Development Coordinator
• Judy Sheehan, Event & Office Manager
• Charles T Akre jr, Treasurer
• Manuel H Johnson, Chairman Of The Board
• Jacqueline B Mars, Vice Chairman
• Lisa Campbell, Secretary
Description:
Founded 1954. Contains more than 15,000 volumes on horse and field sports dating back to 1523, including horsemanship, racing, breeding, foxhunting, veterinary care and sporting art.
Publications:
Newsletter, quarterly.

NATIONAL SPRINT CAR HALL OF FAME AND MUSEUM FOUNDATION, INC.
ONE SPRINT CAPITAL PLACE
KNOXVILLE, IA 50138
641-842-6176
800-874-4488
Fax: 641-842-6177
sprintcarhof@sprintcarhof.com
www.sprintcarhof.com
• Bob Baker, Executive Director
bbaker@sprintcarhof.com
Description:
Founded 1986. Historical preservation of the sport of sprint car racing. Exhibition of sprint cars from 1900 to the present and memorabilia.
Publications:
National Sprint Car Hall of Fame induction Program; HALLMARKS, quarterly newsletter.

NEGRO LEAGUES BASEBALL MUSEUM
1616 EAST 18TH STREET
KANSAS CITY, MO 64108
816-221-1920
888-221-6526
Fax: 816-221-8424
www.nlbm.com
• Bob Kenrick, President
• Betty Brown, Chairman
• Margo Weatherby, Treasuerer
• Monte Irvin, NATIONAL ADVISORY BOARD
• Don B. Motley, Executive Director Emeritus
• Michael R. Kanaley, Vice Chairman/Secretary
Description:
Founded 1991. Dedicated to researching, preserving and disseminating the history of Negro Leagues Baseball.

NEW BRUNSWICK SPORTS HALL OF FAME
PO BOX 6000
503 RUE QUEEN STREET
FREDERICTON, CANADA E3B SH1
506-453-3747
www.nbsportshalloffame.nb.ca
• Jamie Wolverton, Executive Director
(506) 453-8930
Publications:
Newsletter twice a year.

NEWPORT SPORTS MUSEUM
100 NEWPORT CENTER DRIVE
SUITE 100
NEWPORT BEACH, CA 92660
949-721-9333
Fax: 949-721-9399
www.newportsportsmuseum.org
• John W. Hamilton, Founder
• Stephen H Andreson, President, S.H.A. Enterprises
• Pat Bolter, Vice President/ General Manager, Mercedes Ben
Member Services:
Educational programs involved professional athletes speaking with youth concerning drug abuse, gang involvement and the importance of an education.
Description:
Non-profit organization dedicated to mentoring children and preserving the history of sport. Using the collection as a vehicle to mentor at-risk children about the virtues of athletics and academics and the dangers of drugs and gangs.

OLYMPIC HALL OF FAME AND MUSEUM
88 CANADA OLYMPIC ROAD SW
CALGARY, AB, CANADA T3B 5R5
403-247-5452
Fax: 403-286-7213
• Bob Nicolay, President/CEO
Description:
Founded 1988. Preserves the material heritage of the XV Olympic Winter Games; provides a tribute to the achievements of Canada's Olympians.

OLYMPIC MUSEUM, LIBRARY AND STUDIES CENTRE
1 QUAI D'OUCHY
PO BOX CH-1001
LAUSANNE, SWITZERLAN 1001
www.olympic.org
• Jacques Rogge, President
Description:
The world's largest repository of information on the Olympic Movement. A living tribute to the association of sport, art and culture, it retraces the history of the Olympics from Ancient Greece to the modern day. It is a new type of museum based on high technology-computer and audiovisual technology have generated a new art of the image.

OREGON SPORTS HALL OF FAME
4840 SOUTH WEST WESTERN AVENUE
SUITE 600
BEAVERTON, OR 97005
503-227-7466
Fax: 503-227-6925
info@oregonsportshall.org
www.oregonsportshall.org
• Donna Smoot, Administrative Assistant & Collection Manager
• Jack Elder, Executive Director
Description:
Serves to recognize and appreciate Oregon's rich athletic history. Our goal is for this legacy to inspire participation in sport and foster awareness of the values and life-long rewards gained from this participation.

PENNSYLVANIA SPORTS HALL OF FAME
PO BOX 7152
LANCASTER, PA 17601
717-684-2714
Fax: 717-684-2714
www.pashof.org
• Dr. Stephen J. George, Jr., President
• Edward L Ludwig, Executive Vice President
• Jeffery Fortna, State Treasurer
Description:
Founded 1962. Serves to perpetuate the memory of individuals who have brought lasting fame and recognition to the Commonwealth of Pennsylvania and its people through their achievements in athletics and sports.

PGA WORLD GOLF HALL OF FAME
1 WORLD GOLF PLACE
ST. AUGUSTINE, FL 32092
904-940-4000
www.worldgolfhalloffame.org
• Bruce Laht, General Manager
Description:
Founded 1974. Museum and hall of fame dedicated to the game of golf.

PIKES PEAK INTERNATIONAL RACEWAY
1631 MESA AVENUE
SUITE B-1
COLORADO SPRINGS, CO 80906
719-685-4400
Fax: 719-634-5198
info@ppihc.com
www.ppihc.com
• Megan Leatham, Director Operations
• Lincoln Floyd, Director of development
• Tom Osborn, Chairman, Board of Directors
• Megan Leatham, Executive director of operations
laytonpc123@msn.com
Description:
Founded 1989. Houses a collection of race vehicles from the Chevrolet Pikes Peak International Hill Climb, racing apparel and memorabilia. Organizes and runs the annual July 4 Pikes Peak International Hill climb. The second oldest continually run motorsporting event in the United States.

PRO FOOTBALL HALL OF FAME
2121 GEORGE HALAS DRIVE NW
CANTON, OH 44708
330-456-8207
Fax: 330-456-9080
www.profootballhof.com
• Stephen A Perry, President/Executive Director
• Steve Strawbridge, Vice President Merchandise Sales/Licensing
• Joe Horrigan, Vice President and Chief Financial Officer
• Bill Allen, Vice President/CFO
• Dave Motts, Vice President/Marketing/Operations
Description:
The mission of the Pro Football Hall of Fame is to honor, preserve, educate and promote. To honor individuals who have made outstanding contributions to professtional football. To preserve professional football's historic documents and artifacts. To educate the public regarding the origin, development and growth of professional football as an important part of American culture. To promote the positive values of the sport.
Year Founded:
1963

PROFESSIONAL GOLFERS' ASSOCIATION HALL OF FAME
100 AVENUE OF THE CHAMPIONS
PALM BEACH GARDENS, FL 33410
561-624-8400
www.pga.com
• Allen Wrukowski, President
• Ted Bishop, Vice President
Description:
The ultimate destination for the celebration and recognition of golf's greatest players and contributors and serves as an inspiration to golfers and golf fans throughout the world.

ROME SPORTS HALL OF FAME & MUSEUM
5790 LONDON ROAD
ROME, NY 13440
315-339-9038
www.when-in-rome.com
• Ruth M. Demers, Executive Director
• Bill Fleet, Co-Chairman
Membership Requirements:
Open membership, annual dues.
Description:
Founded 1977. Offers recognition and display of Rome sports personalities. Continued excellence inductees, etc. for City of Rome residents.

ROSE BOWL HALL OF FAME
391 S. ORANGE GROVE BLVD
PASADENA, CA 91184
626-449-4100
Fax: 626-449-9066
rosepr@rosemail.org
www.tournamentofroses.com
• Jeffery J Allen, COO and CFO
• Richard L Chinen, President
Description:
Founded 1989. The Rose Bowl Hall of Fame honors outstanding individuals whose achievements have contributed to the success of the Rose Bowl Game.
Membership Requirements:
Idividuals inducted into the Rose Bowl Hall of Fame include players, coaches, school administrators, athletic directors, conference officials and others who have made special contributions to the Rose Bowl Game.
Number of Inductees:
87
Publications:
ROSE BOWL GAME PROGRAM

SAN DIEGO HALL OF CHAMPIONS SPORTS MUSEUM, THE
2131 PAN AMERICAN PLAZA - BALBOA PARK
SAN DIEGO, CA 92101
619-234-2544
Fax: 619-234-4543
info@sdhoc.com
www.sdhoc.com
• Angela LaChica, Vice President
• Denise Cooper, President
Description:
The nations largest multi-sport museum, boasting three levels of memorabilia and 68,000 square feet. The museum offers a state-of-the-art theatre, an interactive media center and fascinating displays on the nation's favorite sports.

SPORT INFORMATION RESOURCE CENTER/SIRC
180 ELGIN STREET
SUITE 1400
OTTAWA, ON, CANADA K2P 2K3
613-231-7472
800-665-6413
Fax: 613-231-3739
webmaster@sirc.ca
www.sirc.ca
• Debra Gassewitz, President/CEO
• David Roberts, CEO
• Kim Sparling, Communications Manager
• Nancy Rebel, Director of Content Development
Description:
Founded in 1973, SIRC identifies, collects and organizes information about sports, fitness and other related fields. Every month, SIRC scans over 1,200 magazines and journals from around the world as well as monographs and theses covering practical and research material. From this information, SIRC produces the online SPORT Database and its equivalent on CD-ROM, the SPORT Discus. Also provides Sport Information Service on World Wide Web, www.SPORTQuest.com, which provides links to a wide range of sports web sites for Olympic Sports, Winter Sports, Water Sports, Professional Sports, Coaching, Statistics and Results, Sports Medicine and Individ

SPORTS IMMORTALS
6830 NORTH FEDERAL HWY
BOCA RATON, FL 33487
561-997-2575
Fax: 561-997-6949
www.sportsimmortals.com
• Jim Platt, Vice President
(561) 997-2575
• Joel Platt, Chairman
• John Murpy, Manager/Curator
(561) 997-2575
football@sportsimmortals.com
Year Founded:
1992.
Nature of Service:
Sports Immortals Museum and Memorabilia Mart Museum features over one million mementos, the largest collection on all sports in the world. The Memorabilia Mart offers a selection of over 20,000 items to purchase.

SPORTS MUSEUM OF NEW ENGLAND, THE
100 LEGENDS WAY
BOSTON, MA 2134
617-624-1234
Fax: 617-787-8152
www.sportsmuseum.org
• Rusty Sullivan, Executive Director
(617) 624-1237
rsullivan@dncboston.com
• Brian Codangnone, Associate Curator
(617) 624-1235
bcodagnone@dncboston.com
Number of members:
1,207
Membership Requirements:
$50 for individuals; $100 for family; $1,500 for corporate membership.
Description:
Founded 1977. Preserves and showcases the unique sports heritage of New England

through creative and interactive exhibits. Amateur, professional, Olympic, scholastic. Provides educational and community outreach programs that encourage achievement, establish friendships, and build leadership skills, especially in our youth.

ST. LOUIS CARDINALS HALL OF FAME MUSEUM
ST. LOUIS CARDINALS L.P.
700 CLARK AVENUE
ST. LOUIS, MO 63102
314-345-9600
Fax: 314-231-4054
• Jeff Boje, Co-Owner
Notes:
The St. Louis Cardinals Hall of Fame and Museum and the International Bowling Museum and Hall of Fame became partners. Dedicated to exhibit, educate and preserve. The two Museums can now be found under one roof.

STATE OF KANSAS SPORTS HALL OF FAME
515 SOUTH WICHITA ST
Wichita, KS 67202
316-262-2038
Fax: 316-263-2539
info@kshof.org
www.kshof.org
• Ted Hayes, Chief Executive Officer, President
• Laura Hartley, BoatHouse Event Manager
• Jordan Poland, Marketing Manager
jpoland@kshof.org
• Tim Daniel, Chairman
Description:
Founded 1961. Serves to preserve the Kansas tradition of producing world class teams and athletes. 90 of Kansas' most famous sports figures are presently enshrined in the Hall of Fame, including Jim Ryun, Gale Sayers, Walter Johnson, Adolph Rupp, Dean Smith, Barry Sanders, John Riggins and Lynette Woodard.

TEXAS SPORTS HALL OF FAME & MUSEUM
1108 SOUTH UNIVERSITY PARKS DRIVE
WACO, TX 76706
254-756-1633
800-567-9561
Fax: 254-756-2384
info@tshof.org
• Steve Fallon, Executive Director
• Betsy Edwards, Marketing & Sales Director
(757) 393-8031
• Jay Black, Curator
• Paige Davis, Collections Manager
Description:
The official sports hall of fame for the Commonwealth of Virginia. From memorabilia to interactives, it's fun for the whole family.

TRAPSHOOTING HALL OF FAME AND MUSEUM
601 W. NATIONAL RD
VANDALIA, OH 45377
937-898-4638 EXT 528
Fax: 937-898-5541
hof@shootata.com
www.traphof.org

- Gene Anastasio, President
- Tami Daniel, Office Coordinator

Description:
Founded 1968. Devoted solely to the history of Trapshooting. Extensive exhibits, large research library. Annual induction to Hall of Fame ceremonies.

U.S. BICYCLING HALL OF FAME
303 3RD STREET
DAVIS, CA 95616
530-341-3263
www.usbhof.org
- Joe Herget, Executive Director
- Anthony Costello, President

Description:
Founded 1986. Honors competitors and contributors to the sport and recreational activity of cycling. Establishes a permanent institution devoted to the past, present and future of bicycling in America.

Membership Requirements:
Annual memberships from $25 (individual) to $500 (corporate).

Publications:
Newsletter

Member Services:
Membership - newsletter, discount on merchandise. Annual Hall of Fame Memorial Day Weekend includes Super Saturday - road race - criterium events - Sunday annual induction ceremonies. Other events during the year; 4th of July and Labor Day Cycling Classic.

U.S. HOCKEY HALL OF FAME
801 HAT TRICK AVE
PO BOX 679
EVELETH, MN 55734-0657
218-744-5167
800-443-7825
Fax: 218-744-2590
www.ushockeyhall.com
- Doug Palazzari, Executive Director
- Tom Sersha, Curator
- David Tomassoni, Chairman Of The board
- Calvin Cossalter, President
- Bob Pazzelli, Vice President
- Mitch Brunfelt, Secretary
- Mike Lenich, Treasurer
- Michelle Putzel, Administrative Assistant,Coordinator

Annual event:
Enshrinement ceremonies each October.

Publications:
ENSHRINEE BIOGRAPHIES 1973-1983, with updated enshrinee listings.

Membership Requirements:
Enshrinees must be retired from the sport for five years, American birth and training and have made a significant contribution to hockey.

Description:
The United States Hockey Hall of Fame was dedicated in 1973 as the 'National Shrine of American Hockey,' to be America's hockey showplace to honor the legends of the gamewith the Great Wall of Fame of Enshrinees, and to preserve the precious memories of ice hocky in the United States. To date the Hall has honored 130 outstanding coaches, players,builders, administrators and 2 Olympic teams who have contributed to the success and promotion of American hockey. In 2007, USA Hockey reached an agreement with the hall to continue being the exclusive enshrinement museum of American hockey.

U.S. NATIONAL SKI HALL OF FAME & MUSEUM
610 PALMS AVENUE
PO BOX 191
ISHPEMING, MI 49849
906-485-6323
Fax: 906-486-4570
www.skihall.com
- Thomas J West, President/CEO
- Bernard Wenchsel, Chairman
- Tom Anderson, Executive Committee
- David Brule, Executive Committee
- Phillip Camp, Executive committee
- Rudy Maki, Executive Committee

Description:
Founded 1954. Honors persons who have contributed much to the sport of skiing. Preserves and protects artifacts and historically valuable lore of skiing, conducts research and dispenses information to those requesting it related to the sport of skiing.

Hall of Fame Induction Requirements:
Must be nominated and elected according to the U.S. Skiing Rules of Governance. U.S. Skiing administers the nomination and election of honored individuals. Annual memberships.

Membership:
Individual $40; Family $50; Supporting $100; Corporate $500; Patron $1,000; Benefactor $ 5,000; Olympic Circle $ 10,000

USGA MUSEUM AND LIBRARY
77 LIBERTY CORNER ROAD
PO BOX 708
FAR HILLS, NJ 7931
908-234-2300
Fax: 908-234-0319
www.usga.org
- Robert M. Williams, Director
(908) 234-2300
- Susan Wasser, Coordinator of Special Projects
(908) 234-2300

Year Founded:
1936

Description:
The USGA Museum and Arnold Palmer Center for Golf History showcases the nation's largest and most significant collection of golf artifacts and documents. The interactive multimedia exhibits tell the story of the game;s development in the United States, highlighting the greatest moments in the game's hisotry, with a particular focus on USGA champions and championships.

Facilities Available for Sporting Events:
Pynes Putting Course

VIRGINIA SPORTS HALL OF FAME & MUSEUM
206 HIGH STREET
PO BOX 370
PORTSMOUTH, VA 23704
757-393-8031
Fax: 757-393-8288
www.vshof.com
- Eddie Webb, President
webbe@vshfm.com
- Betsy Edwards, Director of Marketing/Sales
(757) 393-8031
- Elizabeth Goodwin, Museum Services

Director
(757) 393-8031
goodwine@vshfm.com

Description:
The official sports hall of fame for the Commonwealth of Virginia. From memorabilia to interactive, it's fun for the whole family.

Membership Requirements:
Fans and visitors are invited to become members and then nominate virginians for the hall. Inductees must meet residential requirements and should have achieved a level at success or had a mjaor impact on his record, school or community.

Publications:
Newsletter, quarterly; annual program, website (www.vshfm.com)

VOLLEYBALL HALL OF FAME INC.
444 Dwight Street
HOLYOKE, MA 1040
413-536-0926
Fax: 413-539-6673
info@volleyhall.org
www.volleyhall.org
- Jerry Fitzsimons, Executive Director
jerry.fitzsimons@volleyhall.org

Description:
The Volleyball Hall of Fame opened to the public on June 6 1987. A two day volleyball tournament was hosted by the Volleyball hall of Fame to celebrate the grand opening.

WOMEN'S BASKETBALL HALL OF FAME
700 HALL OF FAME DRIVE
KNOXVILLE, TN 37915
865-633-9000
Fax: 865-633-9294
dhart@wbhof.com
www.wbhof.com
- Dana Hart, President
- Josh Sullivan, Director of Basketball Operations and Technology
jsullivan@wbhof.com

Description:
Founded 1999. National and international hall of fame dedicated to honoring the past, celebrating the present and promoting the future of women's basketball.

WRESTLING HALL OF FAME, NATIONAL
405 WEST HALL OF FAME AVENUE
STILLWATER, OK 74075
405-377-5243
Fax: 405-377-5244
www.wrestlinghalloffame.org
- Lee Roy Smith, Executive Director
- Jim keen, Chairman
- Stan Zeamer, Vice Chairman
- Terry Shockley, Secretary
- Rusty Shaw, Treasurer
- David Barry, Member

Description:
Founded 1976. Perpetuates the history of wrestling in the U.S. through national museum featuring displays of memorabilia, uniforms, awards, photographs along with a library, theater and Honors Court of Distinguished Members.

multi sports

State Games Organizations

ALABAMA SPORTS FESTIVAL
2530 E. SOUTH BOULEVARD
MONTGOMERY, AL 36120
334-280-0065
800-467-0422
Fax: 334-280-0988
info@alagames.com
www.alagames.com
• Ronald J. Creel, Founder, President, CEO
• Tommy Kennedy, Director of Administration
• Chris Wilkins, Communications Director
Description:
The Alabama Sports Festival was organized in 1982 at the request of the United States Olympic Committee to develop grassroots Olympic-style competitions and expose athletes, volunteers and spectators of all ages and abilities, especially our youth, to Olympic sports and the overall Olympic experience with all of its tradition and ceremony.
Publications:
Official Registration Book.
Member Services:
Assists in promoting leadership, academics, good citizenship, sportsmanship and competitive values through Alabama amateur athletics.

ALASKA STATE FAIR
2075 GLEN HWY
PALMER, AK 99645
907-745-4827
800-850-3247
Fax: 907-746-2699
info@alaskastatefair.org
www.alaskastatefair.org
• Ray Ritari, General Manager
ritari@alaskastatefair.org
• John Harkey, President
• John Tracy, Vice-Presdeint
• Caroline Kenley, Secretary
• Danny Consenstein, Treasurer
• Richard Stryken, Director
• Kristy Bernier, Director
• Dean Phipps, Dir. Marketing Development & Corp. Partnershi
(907) 746-7153
dean@alaskastatefair.org
Description:
The Alaska State Fair is the gathering place to showcase the best of our great state as we kick off a celebration of Alaska's 50th Anniversary of Statehood on August 21, 2008.

AUSTRALIAN SPORTS COMMISSION
61-02-6214-1111
Fax: 61-02-6214-1836
asc@ausport.gov.au
www.ausport.gov.au
• Matthew Favier, Director
• Simon Hollingsworth, Chief Executive Officer
Description:
The ASC is the Australian Government body that managers, develops and invests in sport at all levels. It works closely with a range of national sporting organizations, state and local governments, schools and community organizations to ensure sport is well run and accessible.

BADGER STATE GAMES
219 JEFFERSON STREET
WAUSAU, WI 54403
715-355-8788
badger@badgerstategames.org
www.badgerstategames.org
• Darien Schaefer, Executive Director
• Richard Barrett, Sales Director
• Tracy Baltz, Marketing Director
Description:
Founded 1984. Provides opportunity for Olympic-style amateur sports competition for the citizens of the State of Wisconsin. Winter games held each February in Wausau and North Central Wisconsin; summer games every June in Madison.

BAY STATE GAMES
55 SIXTH ROAD
SUITE 200
WOBURN, MA 1801
781-932-6555
Fax: 781-932-3441
info@baystategames.org
www.baystategames.org
• Jeff Baker, Assistant Director
• Kevin Cummings, Executive Director
Description:
Founded 1982. Statewide amateur sports festival involving 12,000 athletes in 25 sports of the Olympic family. Promotes the development of opportunity through participation and advancement in amateur sports. Member National Congress of State Games. U.S. Olympic Committee games recognition. Provides $12,000 in scholarships for recognition in academics, athletics and community involvement.
Member Services:
Produces Bay State Games and Bay State Winter Games, statewide multi-sports festivals.
Publications:
THE TORCH, newsletter; annual yearbook, coaches manual,
Membership Requirements:
Massachusetts amateur athlete.

BIG SKY STATE GAMES
490 NORTH 31ST STREET
SUITE 304
BILLINGS, MT 59101
406-254-7426
Fax: 406-254-7439
info@bigskygames.org
www.bigskygames.org
• Karen Sanford Gall, Executive Director
• Liana Susott, Sports Director
• Kelly Elletson, Operations Director
Description:
The Big Sky Games is a privately funded, not-for-profit organization founded in 1986, that has responsibility of organizing an Olympic-style festival for the citizens of Montana. Big Sky State Games stands as the largest State Games per capita in the nation. During the summer of 2007 the games hosted over 10,500 athletes from over 250 communities in 36 different sporting events. The Big Sky State Games organizes a variety of other healthy lifestyle events and programs.
Nature of Service:
Providing quality competitions and programs to promote healthy and active lifestyles.

BIRMINGHAM, GREATER CONVENTION & VISITORS BUREAU
2200 9TH AVENUE NORTH
BIRMINGHAM, AL 35203-1100
205-458-8000
800-458-8085
Fax: 205-458-8086
info@birminghamal.org
www.birminghamal.org
• Karen Dobnikar, Human Resource Manager
(205) 214-9220
kdobnikar@birminghamal.org
• Dilcy Hilley, VP Marketing
(205) 214-9229
dhilley@birminghamal.org
• Michael Gunn, Vice President Sales
(205) 214-9213
mgunn@birminghamal.org
Description:
Established for the purpose of marketing and promoting the greater Birmingham area as a destination for conventions, meetings, and tour and travel. The mission is to broaden and expand promotional efforts on behalf of the city and its business constituency through advertising and marketing programs designed to sell guest rooms in area lodging facilities.

BLUEGRASS STATE GAMES
200 EAST MAIN STREET
LEXINGTON, KY 40507
859-255-0336
800-722-2474
Fax: 859-258-3022
info@bgsg.org
www.bgsg.org
• Amy Ratcliff, Operations Manager
• Terry Johnson, Executive Director
(859) 258-3040
Membership (Participation)
Requirements:
Must be amateur Kentucky resident.
Description:
Founded 1985. Produces state games in state of Kentucky for amateur athletes. Various competitions for all ages and levels with many events for the handicapped. Based on festival concept. Also holds clinics, symposiums and state-wide tournament.

BRYAN-COLLEGE STATION CONVENTION & VISITORS BUREAU, SPORTS DEPT
715 UNIVERSITY DRIVE EAST
COLLEGE STATION, TX 77840
979-260-9898
800-777-8292
Fax: 979-260-9800
www.visitaggieland.com
• Kindra Fry, Director of Sales-Sports & Conventions
• Pattie Sears, Destination Sales & Servicing Executive
Description:
A Department of the Bryan-College Station Convention & Visitors Bureau, the Sports Department prides itself on attracting quality sports events to the community with state-of-the-art facilities and services.

CALIFORNIA STATE GAMES
3260 ROSECRANS STREET
SAN DIEGO, CA 92110

619-223-2033 EXT 2127
Fax: 619-233-2242
info@calstategames.org
www.calstategames.org
• Sandi Hill, Executive Director
• Joe Rubendall, Sport manager
Description:
Mission is to promote and nurture the health, education, and competitive spirit of residents of California by managing a quality amateur sports event that encourages participation and provides an Olympic experience.

CANTON/STARK COUNTY CONVENTION & VISITORS BUREAU
THE MILLENNIUM CENTRE
222 MARKET AVENUE NORTH
CANTON, OH 44702
330-454-1439
800-552-6051
Fax: 330-456-3600
www.visitcanton.com
• John Kiste, Executive Director
• Tonja Marshall, Sports Program Manager

CENTRAL FLORIDA SPORTS COMMISSION
400 W CHURCH STREET
SUITE 205
ORLANDO, FL 32801
407-648-4900
Fax: 407-649-2072
www.centralfloridasports.org
• Brent Nelson, President/CEO
• John Bisignano, President/CEO
jbisignano@centralfloridasports.org
• Jennifer Lastik, Director of Events
jlastik@centralfloridasports.org
• Dave Zsembik, Seminole County Marketing & EventsManager
• Miranda Smith, Volusia County Marketing & EventsManager
• Georgiana Brown, Marketing & Communications Manager
gbrown@centralfloridasports.org
• Kevin Coulthart, Vice President
(407) 648-0465
Description:
Created to attract international, national and regional events and sports-related business and activities to Central Florida.

COMMONWEALTH GAMES FEDERATION
138 PICADILLY
LONDON, ENGLAND W1J 7NR
info@commonwealthgames.ca
www.thecgf.com
• Michael Hooper, Chief Executive Officer
Publications:
Directory.
Membership Requirements:
Each sport has a member and there are members-at-large. Officers are elected for a four-year term.
Description:
Founded 1930. Organizes and finances Canada's participation in the Commonwealth Games every four years.

COMMONWEALTH GAMES OF VIRGINIA
711 C FIFTH STREET NE
ROANOKE, VA 24016
540-343-0987
800-333-8274
Fax: 540-343-7407
www.commonwealthgames.org

• Peter R. Lampman, President
pete@commonwealthgames.org
• Diane Williams, Marketing/Fundraising Director
dwilliams@commonwealthgames.org
• Owen Grogan, Games Director
Description:
Virginia's Olympics for the citizens of the Commonwealth. A multi sport festival including opening ceremonies and 45 sports.

COWBOY STATE GAMES
WYOMING FINANCIAL BUILDING
400 EAST FIRST STREET
SUITE 315
CASPER, WY 85602
307-577-1125
Fax: 307-577-8111
www.cowboystategames.com
• Eileen Ford, Executive Director
Description:
Founded 1986. Provides Olympic style amateur sports festivals for athletes of all ages and abilities, enables all citizens the opportunity to utilize quality sports facilities, and creates an amateur sports network throughout Wyoming.
Member Services:
Participants receive CSG Tee-shirts and participant packets including passes to the Opening Ceremony, coupons, and mementos.
Publications:
Registration Handbook for each event.
Membership Requirements:
Summer Games - must be a Wyoming resident; Winter Sports Festival - open to residents of any state that does not conduct Winter Games.

EMPIRE STATE GAMES
1 EMPIRE STATE PLAZA
ALBANY, NY 12238
518-474-8889
Fax: 518-474-7944
esgstaff@global2000.net
www.empirestategames.org
• Frederick Smith, Executive Director
Description:
Founded 1978. Yearly amateur sports festival consisting of 28 summer sports and 10 winter sports for New York state athletes. Scholastic, open and masters divisions. Also conducts senior games and games for the physically challenged.

ESPN X GAMES
6033 WEST CENTURY BOULEVARD
SUITE 601
LOS ANGELES, CA 90045
310-642-1500
Fax: 310-568-8577
www.expn.com
• Jack Wienert, Executive Director
• Chris Stiepock, Vice President
• Deane Swanson, Senior Director of Operations
Editors Note:
The Xgames frequently change locations. In order to completely keep up please contact ESPN, or go to the website espn.com and look for Xgames.
Description:
Creation and implementation of annual sporting events focusing on adventure-type sports.

FLAGSTAFF CONVENTION AND VISITORS BUREAU
ONE EAST ROUTE 66
FLAGSTAFF, AZ 86001
928-213-2951
800-379-0065
visitorcenter@flagstaffaz.gov
www.flagstaffarizona.org
• Heldi Hansen, CVB Director
(800) 213-2921
hhansen@flagstaffaz.gov
• Heather Ainardi, Marketing and Public Relations Manager/Film
(800) 217-2367
hainardi@flagstaffaz.gov
• Carrie Nelson, Administrative Specialist
(928) 213-2919
cnelson@flagstaffaz.gov
• Gail Jackson, Meeting and Events Specialist
(928) 213-2920
gjackson@flagstaffaz.gov
• Heather Ainardi, Director, Film Commissioner
(928) 779-7645
• Carrie Nelson, Administrative Specialist
(928) 779-7636
Description:
Founded 1983. Honors snowmobile racing greats and club volunteers, serves as museum of historic sleds from both trail and track.
Publications:
THE FINISH LINE, Newsletter, periodic.
Number of Members:
67 Inductees as of 2005.

GARDEN STATE GAMES
44 FARRINGTON STREET
PO BOX 271
CALDWELL, NJ 7006
973-618-1111
Fax: 973-618-1112
mjg129@aol.com
comp.entryeeze.com/Home.aspx?cid=299
• Michael Garamella, Executive Director
(973) 575-8817

GEORGETOWN COLLEGE SPORTS COUNCIL
400 E. COLLEGE STREET
GEORGETOWN, KY 40324
502-863-8115
Fax: 502-868-8892
www.georgetowncollegeathletics.com
• Brian Evans, Director of Athletics
(502) 863-8040
• Austin Sparks, Associate AD/Compliance Director
• Jenny Elder, SID/Senior Women's Administrator
(502) 863-7972
• Randy McGuire, Head Athletic Trainer
(502) 863-7032
• Mary Brooks, Assistant Athletic Trainer
• Ricker Adkins, Athletic Trainer
• Ray Valentine, Head JV Men's Basketball Coach
(502) 681-3529
Description:
Goal is to promote sporting events in the surrounding Kentucky area.

GEORGIA STATE GAMES COMMISSION
PO BOX 2043
KENNESAW, GA 30156-9100

multi sports

770-528-3580
Fax: 770-528-3590
www.georgiagames.org
• Eric Pfeifer, Executive Director
Description:
Founded 1989. Mission is to promote grassroots amateur sports and development of active lifestyles among Georgia residents. Offers 42 sports during Championships in Atlanta in mid July and 160 events during eight District Sports Festivals throughout the state in May and June. Other activities include statewide Torch Run, Opening Ceremonies, World of Sports Expo, Art Exhibition, Environmental Expo, sports clinics, spring sports and other events throughout the year.

GRAND CANYON STATE GAMES
2120 EAST 6TH STREET
SUITE 4
TEMPE, AZ 85281
480-517-9700
Fax: 480-517-9739
• Erik Widmark, Executive Director
• Alan Young, Executive Director
• Maark R. Keith, Senior Director of Development
Description:
The Grand Canyon State Games is a multi-sport Olympic Festival for Arizona amatur athletes of all ages and abllites. The Games is organized by the Arizona Sports Council and is affiliated with 47 other state games throughout the United States. It is sanctioned by the U.S. Olympic Committee through the National Congress of State Games. The Games seeks to provide Arizonans with an avenue for personal development through sports.

HERMES SPORTS & EVENTS, INC.
1624 ST. CLAIR AVENUE
CLEVELAND, OH 44114
216-623-9933
Fax: 216-363-0698
jneroni@hermescleveland.com
www.hermescleveland.com
• Joe Neroni, Director of Sales & Marketing
jneroni@hermescleveland.com
• Neal Neroni, President/Principal
(216) 623-9933
nneroni@hermescleveland.com
• Nick Swingos, Principal
(216) 623-9933
nswingos@hermescleveland.com
• Katherine Gessner, Director of Race Operations
(216) 623-9933
Description:
hermes was founded in 1981 and has built a reputation as Northeast Ohio's premier sport and race management company. Hermes Road Racing manages and operates over 140 local and national races during the year. From course set up and event logistics, to marketing and promotional opportunities, to database management and services, Hermes offers full service management tools. The Cleveland Corporate Challenge is a health and wellness, business networking, team building, and charitable initiative promoting camaraderie, pride and fitness among employees and organizations in Northeast Ohio. And Hermes Sport & Social provides the highest quality sport

HOT SPRINGS CONVENTION & VISTORS BUREAU
134 CONVENTION BLVD
HOT SPRINGS, AR 71901
501-321-2277
800-543-2284
Fax: 501-321-2136
hscvb@hotsprings.org
www.hotsprings.org
• Steve Arrison, CEO
Description:
Tourists and Arkansas residents alike will find lots of fun things to do in Hot Springs Arkansas.

ILLINOIS HEALTH & SPORTS FOUNDATION
RICHLAND EXECUTIVE PLAZA
525 WEST MAIN STREET
SUITE 110
BELLEVILLE, IL 62220
618-233-8665
Fax: 618-233-8690
• Maureen Moore, President
Description:
The Illinois Health and Sports Foundation, through the Prairie State Games, provides Illinois citizens a wholesome avenue for personal development through organized sports competition and physical activity. Additionally, the Foundation seeks to further amateur athletics at the grassroots level through regional competition, training and education in sport.

INTERNATIONAL MASTERS GAMES ASSOCIATION
MAISON DU SPORT INTERNATIONAL
AVENUE DE RHODAINE
1007
LAUSANNE, SWITZERLAN
41-216 018 171
Fax: 42-216 018 173
imga@dif.dk
www.imga.ch
• Borge Kaas-Andersen, Secretary General
• Kai Holm, President
Description:
Constituted 1995. Governing body for the World Masters Games (25 different sports), held every four years.

INTERNATIONAL WORLD GAMES ASSOCIATION/IWGA
10 LAKE CIRCLE
COLORADO SPRINGS, CO 80906
719-471-8096
Fax: 719-471-8105
www.theworldgames.org
• Ron Froehlich, President
• Joachim Gossow, Chief Executive Officer
Description:
Founded 1981. Oversees World Games, which have been set up as a sporting events for non-Olympic sports, and is regarded as complementary to the Olympics. Sports in the World Games include: bowling, casting, cycling, faustball, korfball, netball, roller-skating, softball, tug of war, body building, powerlifting, sombo, racquetball, lifesaving, sport acrobatic, taekwondo, karate, trampoline, tumbling, field archery, fin swimming, water ski, and sport boule.

IOWA GAMES
1421 SOUTH BELL AVENUE
104
AMES, IA 50010
515-292-3251
888-777-8881
Fax: 515-292-3254
info@iowagames.org
www.iowagames.org
• Clarence Hudson, Executive Director
• Kevin Bourke, Chief Creations Officer
kevin@iowagames.org
• Lori Judge, Assistant Director Of Sports & Operations
lori@iowagames.org
Member Services:
Iowa Games Summer Sports Festival is held annually in Ames in Mid-July, also sponsors Winter Sports Festival in Dubuque the first weekend in February.
Membership Requirements:
Entry fees vary by sport. $15 per individual per sport.
Description:
Founded 1987. Provides Iowa citizens with a wholesome avenue for positive personal development through sports and physical activity. Also, Iowa games give Iowans the Olympic experience on a grassroots level.

KEYSTONE STATE GAMES, INC.
31 S. HANCOCK ST
PO BOX 1166
WILKES-BARRE, PA 18702
570-823-3164
888-445-4559
Fax: 570-822-6558
• Owen Costello, President/Chief Executive Officer
• James Costello, Director of Events
• David H. Farrand, Executive Director
keystones@aol.com
Description:
Founded 1981. Serves to develop a state-wide amateur athletic program to promote physical fitness.
Membership Requirements:
Must be a resident of Pennsylvania.
Member Services:
Conducts annual Summer Games in August, annual Winter Sports Festival in February, annual Pennsylvania Senior Games in July.

KISSIMMEE-ST. CLOUD CONVENTION & VISITORS BUREAU
1925 EAST IRLO BRONSON MEMORIAL HIGHWAY
KISSIMMEE, FL 34744
407-742-8200
800-327-9159
www.floridakiss.com www.visitstcloud.com
• Tim Hemphill, Executive Director
Description:
Staff develops and impliments programs and activities that produce solid results through reliable relationships with marketing.

MASSACHUSETTS AMATEUR SPORTS FOUNDATION
55 SIXTH ROAD
WOBURN, MA 1801
781-932-6555
Fax: 781-932-3441
www.baystategames.org
• Arthur Pappas, Chairman

Description:
Founded 1982. Creates and develops events and programs for the development of opportunities through amateur sports in Massachusetts.
Member Services:
Bay State Games, Bay State Winter Games, Lead By Example Scholarship, Bay State Games Sports Medicine Clinic. Assists in the development and management of amateur sports events and fundraising activities for local and national sports associations.

MICHIGAN FITNESS FOUNDATION
1213 CENTER STREET
SUITE D
LANSING, MI 48864
517-347-7891
877-4MI-EPEC
Fax: 517-347-8145
www.michiganfitness.org
• Marilyn Lieber, Preisdent/Chief Executive Officer
mlieber@michiganfitness.org
Description:
Represents the Governor's Council on Physical Fitness, Health and Sports, the Regional Fitness Council promote healthy lifestyles and physical activity at the local level.

MISSISSIPPI, STATE GAMES OF
5201 14TH STREET
PO BOX 5866
MERIDIAN, MS 39307
601-482-0209
800-482-0205
Fax: 601-483-0650
info@stategamesofms.org
www.stategamesofms.org
• Missye Dozier, Sports Director
• Carolyn Smith, Executive Director
Description:
Created in 1992, the State Games of Mississippi offers an opportunity for athletes of all ages and skill levels to compete in a variety of competitions. Games consist of 29 different, olympic-style sports.

NEBRASKA SPORTS COUNCIL
4903 NORTH 57TH
LINCOLN, NE 68507
402-471-2544
800-304-2637
Fax: 402-471-9712
info@cornhuskerstategames.com
www.cornhuskerstategames.com
• Dave Mlnarik, Executive Director
dmlnarik@nebraskasportscouncil.com
• Jeff Maul, Secretary/Treasurer
• Dave Mlnarik, Executive director
• Brian Larrington, President
• Roger Lempke, VP
Description:
Founded 1985. Amateur multi-sport festival for Nebraskans of all ages and skill levels. Involves 57 competitive activities.

NEW MEXICO GAMES
1205 CONSTITUTION NE
PO BOX 30627
ALBUQUERQUE, NM 87110
505-764-1510
Fax: 505-764-1719
• Fred Hultberg, Executive Director

NUTMEG STATE GAMES
975 MIDDLE STREET
UNIT G
MIDDLETOWN, CT 06457
860-788-7041
Fax: 860-894-2654
nutmeg@csmg.org
www.nutmegstategames.org
• Patrick Fisher, Executive Director
Description:
Founded in 1989, the Nutmeg State Games is a multi-sport festival of Olympic-style competition offering 24 different sports for Connecticut's amateur athletes. The Games are endorsed by the Governor's Committee on Physical Fitness & Health, governed by the National Congress of State Games and recognized by the United States Olympic Committee as the Official State Games of Connecticut.

OREGON, STATE GAMES OF
4840 SW WESTERN AVENUE
SUITE 900
BEAVERTON, OR 97005-3430
503-520-1319
Fax: 503-520-9747
• Kerry Duffy, President/Chief Executive Officer
• Dan Duffy, Executive Director
Publications:
Athlete entry handbooks, quarterly newsletters, annual; souvenir programs. Also presents Winter Games of Oregon and Learn to shoot Hoop Clinics.
Membership Requirements:
Must be a 30-day resident of Oregon.
Description:
Founded 1986. Oregon's largest Olympic-style amateur sports festival. For all ages and abilities. 40 different summer sports. Includes Oregon Senior Games for age 50+.

OVERLAND PARK CONVENTION & VISITORS BUREAU
CORPORATE WOODS BUILDING 29
9001 W. 110TH STREET
SUITE 100
OVERLAND PARK, KS 66210
913-491-0123
800-262-7275
Fax: 913-491-0015
info@opcvb.org
• Jerry Cook, President
jcook@opcvb.org
• Judy Shellhorn, Information Services
(913) 491-0123
jshell@visitoverlandpark.com
• Libby Shilpey, Director of Finance
(913) 491-0123
libbysply@visitoverlandpark.com
• Brad Plumb, Sales Manager
(913) 491-0123
bplumb@visitoverlandpark.com
• Justin Stine, Director
(913) 491-0123
• Liron BenDor, Vice President of Marketing
(913) 491-0123
lbendor@visitoverlandpark.com
• Kelly Peetoom, Vice President Sales
kpeetoom@opcvb.org
Description:
Serves to promote Overland Park and the surrounding areas as a location for sports events, conventions, meetings etc.

PRAIRIE ROSE STATE GAMES
400 EAST FRONT AVENUE
BISMARCK, ND 58504
701-223-4263
bisparks@bisparks.org
• Robert King, President
• Melanie Carvell, VP
• Arik Spencer, Secretary/Treasurer
Description:
Founded 1987. Promotes physical fitness and an active lifestyle through offering an annual sports festival. The program is designed for maximum participation and involvement.

PRAIRIE STATE GAMES
RICHLAND EXECUTIVE PLAZA
525 WEST MAIN STREET
SUITE 110
BELLEVILLE, IL 62220
618-233-8665
Fax: 618-233-8690
• Maureen Moore, President
Description:
Founded 1984. Provides Illinois amateur athletes with Olympic-style competition in over 25 sporting events throughout various venues in Southwestern Illinois. Program of the Illinois Health & Sports Foundation. A member of the national congress of state games. Recognized as the official sports festival for the state of Illinois.

QUAD CITIES SPORTS COMMISSION
1601 RIVER DRIVE
SUITE 110
MOLINE, IL 61265
800-747-7800
Fax: 309-764-9443
lhunt@visitquadcities.com
• Joe Taylor, Chair/President/CEO
• Lynn Hunt, Vice President Tourism
(309) 277-0937
lhunt@visitquadcities.com
Sports Service Founded:
1996
Description:
Quad Cities Sports Commission is a not-for-profit (non-profit) organization dedicated to developing the quality of life in the Quad Cities by attracting and hosting sporting events that bring a economic impact to our communities. The QCSC is a full-service sports commission that takes a turn-key approach to attracting and hosting each event it bring to the Quad Cities.
Description:
Promotes Moline and the surrounding Illinois area for sports competitions, games, conventions and meetings. The Quad Cities is a cluster of communities located on the Mississippi River, connecting eastern Iowa and western Illinois. The sports commission promotes tournaments, competitions, meets, meeting & convention.

SHOW ME STATE GAMES
UNIVERSITY OF MISSOURI
1105 CARRIE FRANCKE DRIVE
ROOM 1
COLUMBIA, MO 65211
573-882-2101
Fax: 573-884-4004
smsg@missouri.edu
www.smsg.org
• Ken Ash, Executive Director
(573) 882-2102

multi sports

• Emily Lorenz, Marketing Coordinator
• Karen Harms, Mr., Administrative
Assistant
(573) 882-2101
Description:
The Show-Me State Games is an
olympic-style sports festival with more than
40 sports for all ages and ability levels. Now
the largest state games in the nation. The
SMSG is hosted by the University of
Missouri, and is a non-profit program of the
Governor's Council of Physical Fitness and
Health. The SMSG hosts events year-round
to promote health, fitness, family and fun.

SOONER STATE GAMES
211 NORTH ROBINSON
SUITE 250
OKLAHOMA CITY, OK 73102
405-236-5000
Fax: 405-236-5008
www.soonerstategames.org
• Tim L. Brassfield, Executive Director
Member Services:
The games are held the last two weekends
in June every year. The Games also hosts
Sportsfest, the winter version, which is held
the first weekend in February.
Description:
Founded 1983. The Sooner State Games is
Oklahoma's amateur sports festival and is
the largest multi -sport event in the state.
Based on the Olympic format and endorsed
by the USOC, The games are open to every
athlete in the state.

SOUTH BEND/MISHAWAKA
CONVENTION & VISITORS BUREAU
401 EAST COLFAX AVENUE
SUITE 310
SOUTH BEND, IN 46617
574-400-4009
800-519-0577
Fax: 574-289-0358
www.visitsouthbend.com
• Rob DeCleene, Executive Director
(574) 400-4022
rdecleene@visitsouthbend.com
• Ben Murray, Creative Specialist
(574) 400-4031
bmurray@visitsouthbend.com
• Megan Huff, Sports Sales Manager
(574) 400-4021
mhuff@visitsouthbend.com
• Lindsey Talboom, Communications &
Public Relations Coordinator
(574) 400-4025
ltalboom@visitsouthbend.com
• Nicole Lawler, Director of
TourismMarketing & Development
(574) 400-4020
nlawler@visitsouthbend.com
• Carolyne Wallace, Director Of Sales
(574) 400-4023
Description:
Promotes South Bend and Mishawaka as a
host site for sports events, meetings etc.

SOUTH CAROLINA PARKS,
RECREATION & TOURISM
1205 PENDLETON STREET
SUITE 110
COLUMBIA, SC 29201
803-734-1700
866-224-9339
Fax: 803-734-1741

tnance@scprt.com
www.discoversouthcarolina.com
• Amy Duffy, Chief of Staff
• Marion Edmunds, Director of
Communications
Description:
Promotes South Carolina as a good location
for professional and amateur sporting
events. Assists local communities in their
sports development initiatives.

STAR OF THE NORTH STATE GAMES
ROCHESTER UNIVERSITY CENTER
FIELDHOUSE
ROCHESTER COMMUNITY & TECHNICAL
COLLEGE
851-30TH AVENUE SE
ROCHESTER, MN 55904
763-785-5603
800-756-STAR
Fax: 763-785-5699
sgames@mnsports.org
www.starofthenorthgames.org
• Barclay Kruse, Executive Director
bkruse@citilink.com
Membership Requirements:
Must be Minnesota resident to participate,
with limited exceptions for some sports.
Description:
Founded 1987. Series of events (winter and
summer) providing all Minnesota citizens an
opportunity to experience amateur sports in
a friendly atmosphere of fun and open
participation that promotes health, fitness,
and good sportsmanship.

STATE GAMES OF AMERICA
COLORADO SPRINGS SPORT
CORPORATION
1631 MESA AVENUE
SUITE E (COPPER BUILDING)
COLORADO SPRINGS, CO 80906
719-634-7333 EXT 1000
Fax: 719-634-5198
info@thesportscorp.org
www.thesportscorp.org
• Tom Osborne, President/CEO
• Dave Palenchar, Chairman Emeritus
• Carolyn Kruse, Vice Chairman
• Walt Glower, Treasurer
• Stan Kensinger, Secretary
• Mike Moran, Director Of Communications
• Theo Gregory, Assistant to the CEO
(719) 577-7081
Description:
The State Games of America (SGA) is the
premier, national multi-sport event for
athletes of all ages and abilities held every
biennium. Medal winners from 49 State
Games nationwide earn the right to compete
against other winners and match their skills
and competitive desire in a national arena.

SUNFLOWER STATE GAMES
820 S KANSAS AVENUE
TOPEKA, KS 66612
785-235-2295
888-774-7721
Fax: 785-235-1308
www.sunflowergames.com
• Mitch Gross, Executive Director
• Susie Coleman, President
• Rick Bryant, VP
• Doug Vance, Secretary
• Brad Rhoden, Treasurer
Description:
The Sunflower State Games is an Olympic

style sports festival for Kansans of all ages
and skill levels. The event takes place over
three weekends each July in Topeka,
Kansas, through sports and physical activity,
to recognize their dedication and
achievement, and to provide an opportunity
to participate in an Olympic-style event.

SUNSHINE STATE GAMES
FLORIDA SPORTS FOUNDATION
2930 KERRY FOREST PARKWAY
SUITE 101
TALLAHASSEE, FL 32309
850-488-8347
Fax: 850-922-0482
www.flasports.com
• Larry Pendleton, President/CEO
• Nick Gandy, Director of Communications
• Stephen V. Rodriguez, Vice President
Participation Requirements:
Must reside in the state of Florida or attend
a university or college in Florida or military
branch in Florida, and must have resided in
Florida for at least 3 months.
Description:
Founded 1980. Serves as direct support
non-profit organization of Florida Governor's
Council on Physical Fitness & Sports, and
actively holds amateur events throughout
Florida to promote physical fitness and
sports to Floridians. Events are multi-sport
Olympic styled sports festivals for athletes of
all ages.

TEXAS AMATEUR ATHLETIC
FEDERATION
421 NORTH IH 35
GEORGETOWN, TX 78628
512-863-9400
Fax: 512-869-2393
www.taaf.com
• Michael Anne Lord, Executive Director
Description:
Founded 1925. State governing body for
Texas amateur athletic programs conducted
by local parks and recreation departments.
Organizes and conducts 61 state
championships and the Games of Texas
(State Games for Texas) every year.

UTAH SUMMER GAMES
351 WEST UNIVERSITY BOULEVARD
CEDAR CITY, UT 84720
435-865-8421
Fax: 435-865-8548
usg@suu.edu
www.utahsummergames.org
• Casey McClellan, Director
mcclellan@suu.edu
• Jeannine Davis, Office Manager
• Bob Tate, Sports Director
• Steve Ahlgreen, Marketing/Operations
Coordinator
(435) 865-8423
ahlgreen@suu.edu
Description:
Founded 1986. Games are comprised of
10,000 athletes competing in 50 sports
(from Olympic to Action sports) Archery,
Baseball, Basketball, Soccer, Track & Field.

UTAH WINTER GAMES
PO BOX 718
PARK CITY, UT 84060
435-513-0207
Fax: 801-406-0108
• Matthew Terwillegar, Director

Description:
Founded 1987. Organizes and promotes Winter Sports Festival and competition to develop physical fitness and lifetime winter sports participation and grass roots developmental sports programs. Competitive events in all winter sports, from ski jumping and telemark to figure and speed skating. Sponsors over 30 free instructional clinics in every winter sport.

WINTER GAMES OF IDAHO
PO BOX 9047
BOISE, ID 83707
208-342-2722
800-442-3794
Fax: 208-343-6725
• Heather Price, Executive Director
Number of Members:
Over 3,500 athletes, sponsors and volunteers.
Publications:
Four color brochure
Member Services:
The Winter Games of Idaho is a non-profit sports festival created for Idaho's amateur athletes and is recognized as the state's official winter sports competition. This 16 year tradition brings fun winter competitions all acros Idaho in January and February each year.

Youth Organizations

ALL-AMERICAN SOAP BOX DERBY
789 DERBY DOWNS DRIVE
PO BOX 7225
AKRON, OH 44306
330-733-8723
Fax: 330-733-1370
soapbox@aasbd.org
www.aasbd.org
• William Ginter, Chairman of the Board
(330) 733-8723
Year Founded:
1934
Description:
A youth racing organization that consists of three divisions: Stock Division, ages 8 through 13. Super Stock Division, ages 10 through 17, and Masters Division, ages 10 through 17.

AMERICAN YOUTH FOOTBALL
1000 SOUTH POINTE DRIVE
TH-A9
MIAMI, FL 33139
800-622-7370
jlaufer@americanyouthfootball.com
www.americanyouthfootball.com

AMERICAN YOUTH SOCCER ORGANIZATION
19700 S VERMONT AVENUE
SUITE 103
TORRANCE, CA 90502
800-872-2976
Fax: 310-525-1155
www.ayso.org
• Michael Karon, National President
MKreferee@gmail.com
• Eileen Tabert, National VP, Admin. & Management
• Doug Ryan, Treasurer
• Margie Close, Secretary

Description:
AYSO has been the leader in establishing groundbreaking youth soccer programs in the United States. The organization is proud to have paved the road for youth soccer and looks forward to meeting the challenges of the 21st centruy.

BOYS & GIRLS CLUBS OF AMERICA
1275 PEACHTREE STREET NE
ATLANTA, GA 30309-3506
404-487-5700
Fax: 404-487-5789
info@bgca.org
www.bgca.org
• Emil J Brouck, Chairman
• Ronald J. Gidwitz, Chairman of the Board
• Emil J. Brolick, Chairman Emeritus
• Robert J. Bach, Chairman Emeritus
• Thomas J. Falk, Vice Chairman
• Gary C. Wendt, Treasurer
• Jean C. Crystal, Secretary
• James Clark, President, CEO
Description:
The mission of the Boys & Girls Clubs of America is to enable all young people especially those who need us most, to reach their fullest potential as productive, caring, responsible citizens.

CALIFORNIA POLICE ACTIVITIES LEAGUE
2000 EAST 14TH STREET
SAN LEANDRO, CA 94577
510-544-4300
800-622-5725
Fax: 510-544-4350
info@calpal.org
www.californiapal.org
• Gregg Wilson, Executive Director
• Barbara Robertson, Director of Finance
Description:
(CAL PAL) provides directly and indirectly through its 110 local pals, educational, recreational and athletic programs to the youth of California with an emphasis on 'disadvantaged or at risk youth. Support comes from individuals, business leaders, corporations and foundations.

CATHOLIC YOUTH ORGANIZATION (CYO)
1011 FIRST AVENUE
FLOOR 17
NEW YORK, NY 10022
212-371-1011 EXT 2972
Fax: 212-319-8265
karl.adler@archny.org
www.ny-archdiocese.org
• Fran Davies, Director of Communications & Marketing
(212) 371-1000
Fran.Davies@archny.org
• Pierette Imbriano, Director of Communications and Marketing
(646) 794-2477
Description:
CYO promotes the total spiritual and personal development of youth and young adults through various ministry centers, community centers, scouting programs, summer camps, athletic leagues, art and essay contests, leadership training programs and other religous, social and education activities in parishes.

DIXIE BOYS & MAJORS BASEBALL
PO BOX 8263
DOTHAN, AL 36304
334-793-3331
Fax: 334-793-3331
dixieoffice@gmail.com
www.dixie.org/boys
• J Sandy Jones, Commissioner/CEO
jjones29@se.rr.com
Description:
Primarily a youth baseball program for YOUTH (ages 12 & under playing on a 60'-70' diamond) and BOYS (ages 13-14 playing on a 80' diamond) to meet the physical development of growing boys. The main purpose of these programs is to provide a recreational outlet for as many boys as possible, with emphasis being on local league play rather than tournament play.

DIXIE SOFTBALL INC
110 SKELTON DRIVE
BIRMINGHAM, AL 35224
205-785-2255
obeidsi@aol.com
softball.dixie.org
• James Obie E. Evans, President

DIXIE YOUTH BASEBALL
C/O WES SKELTON
PO BOX 877
MARSHALL, TX 75671
903-927-2255
Fax: 903-927-1846
youth.dixie.org
• Wes Skelton, Commissioner
Description:
Promoting the development of strong character, a right attitude and a sense of responsibility and citizenship among youngsters since 1955. Visit on Facebook and Twitter.

LITTLE LEAGUE BASEBALL
539 US ROUTE 15 HWY
PO BOX 3485
WILLIAMSPORT, PA 17701-0485
570-326-1921
Fax: 570-326-1074
eastregion@littleleague.org
www.littleleague.org
• Don B. Soucy, Eastern Region Director
• Corey D. Wright, Assistant Eastern Region Director
cwright@littleleague.org
• Patrick Holden, Assistant Eastern Region Director
Description:
A non-profit organization whose mission is to promote, develop, supervise, and voluntarily assist in all lawful ways, the interest of those who will participate in Little League Baseball and Softball.
Membership Requirements:
Must be baseball or softball league - players ages 5-18
Publications:
Little League Magazine, Little Leaguer Newsletter, World Series Programs (8 Divisions).
Member Services:
Official Playing and Tournament Rules. Safety Program. Annual meeting each November.
Number of Members:
3.7 million.

multi sports

Sponsors:
ACE Hardware®, Active Network®, Allstate, Bank of America®, Choice Hotels International™, Dick's Sporting Goods®, Easton, Honda, Kellogg's Frosted Flakes®, Musco Lighting®, New Era™, Pledgeplay®, Powerade®, Russell Athletic®, M&M/Mars® Snickers®, Subway®, Sunkist®

MY SOCCER LEAGUE.COM
6114 LASALLE AVENUE
SUITE 502
OAKLAND, CA 94619
510-836-8733
Fax: 510-654-2253
sales@mysoccerleague.com
www.mysoccerleague.com
Nature of Sports Service:
Organization provides youth leagues - soccer, baseball, football, etc. - with state-of-the-art, web-based league scheduling, game results, standings, referee and field assignments, plus league-wide communications capabilities in an easy-to-use and affordable online service.

NATIONAL ALLIANCE FOR YOUTH SPORTS
2050 VISTA PARKWAY
WEST PALM BEACH, FL 33411
561-684-1141
800-729-2057
Fax: 561-684-2546
nays@nays.org
www.nays.org
• Fred C. Engh, President/CEO
fengh@nays.org
• John Engh, COO
• Yolanda Williams, CFO
• Emmy Martinez, VP Memberhip Programs
The National Alliance for Youth Sports' Youth Deve
Hook a Kid on Golf, SMART START, Kids on Target.
Parents Association for Youth Sports:
Features innovative materials and information for youth leagues to utilize to help make parents aware of their roles and responsibilities in youth sports. The program includes the Youth Sport Parent video which is ideal for preseason parent meetings and outlines the importance of positive parent-volunteer coach relationships to a child's well-being.
National Clearinghouse for Youth Sports Informati
Provides the public with access to a wide variety of resource information and materials pertaining to youth sports. Materials include academic research, publications, instructional videos and other general information relative to youth sports.
National Youth Sports Officials Association:
Trains youth sports officials through a certification program that covers basic skills, fundamentals and common problem areas. The program, which enhances the abilities of both beginning and veteran officials, also covers the eight characteristics every good official must possess. NYSOA officials also receive a variety of member benefits.
National Institute for Youth Sports Administration
Provides training, education and resource materials to assist administrators of youth sports programming in public, private and military organizations. Its Child Abuse and Youth Sports: A Comprehensive Risk Management Program features important information on the screening, training and evaluation of volunteers; policies and procedures on responding to abuse; how to safeguard organizations and participants, parental education and more. The NIYSA also provides administrators with the opportunity to become a Certified Youth Sports Administrator through the Academy for Youth Sports Administrators program which is held at various sites nationwide
National Youth Sports Coaches Association:
More than 2 million volunteer coaches have been trained on how to work with children in all aspects of sports through NYSCA's certification clinics. The clinics provide information on the psychology of coaching children, maximizing athletic performance, first aid, safety, organizing fun and interesting practices, tips on teaching proper sports techniques, as well as many other important areas. NYSCA coaches receive a variety of benefits. There are 3,300 NYSCA chapters that exist nationwide.

Other locations:

HOOK A KID ON GOLF
2050 VISTA PARKWAY
WEST PALM BEACH, FL 33411
561-684-1141
800-729-2057
Fax: 561-684-2546
www.nays.org/hook_a_kid_on_golf
• John Engh, President
• Fred Engh, CEO, President
Number of members:
20,000+ have participated.
Membership Requirements:
Youngsters ages 8-14.
Description:
Founded 1990. Provides neighborhood youngsters the opportunity to be introduced to golf and to continue playing. Includes introductory clinics for first time golfers. Follow-up programs include skills challenge competitions and challenge leagues.

NATIONAL CLEARINGHOUSE FOR YOUTH SPORTS INFORMATION
2050 VISTA PARKWAY
WEST PALM BEACH, FL 33411
561-684-1141
800-729-2057
Fax: 561-684-2546
nays@nays.org
www.nays.org
• Fred Engh, Founder/CEO
fengh@nays.org
• John Engh, COO
• Yolanda Williams, CFO
• Greg Bach, VP Communications
Description:
Founded 1993. Provides the public with access to a wide variety of resource information and materials pertaining to youth sports. Materials include academic research, publications, instructional videos and other general information relative to youth sports.

NATIONAL YOUTH SPORTS COACHES ASSOCIATION
2050 VISTA PARKWAY
WEST PALM BEACH, FL 33411
561-684-1141
800-668-2546
Fax: 561-684-2546
nays@nays.org
www.nays.org
• Fred Engh, Founder/CEO
fengh@nays.org
• John Engh, COO
• Yolanda Williams, CFO
• Greg Bach, VP Communications
Member Services:
$500,000 liability insurance for coaches, membership card, membership patch, education materials and eligibility for National Youth Sport Coach of the Year program.
Publications:
Youth Fitness Guide; Head Injuries Fact Sheet, Eating Disorders Fact Sheet, Coaching Education Fact Sheet, Individual Risk Factors Fact Sheet, In-Line Skating Injuries Fact Sheet, Eye Injuries Fact Sheet, Youth Sports Injuries, Yearbook of Youth Sports Safety.
Membership Requirements:
Volunteer coaches must successfully complete the NYSCA three-level training program, sign a Coaches' Code of Ethics pledge and remit a $15 annual membership fee.
Description:
Founded 1981. Provides parent and coach education programs for volunteers working with children in out-of-school youth sports. NYSCA focuses on the implementation of the Coaches' Code of Ethics which stresses the importance of coaches providing for the physical, emotional and psychological needs of children as their primary objective.

NATIONAL YOUTH SPORTS OFFICIALS ASSOCIATION
2050 VISTA PARKWAY
WEST PALM BEACH, FL 33411
561-684-1141
800-729-2057
Fax: 561-684-2546
nays@nays.org
www.nays.org
• Fred C. Engh, President/Chief Executive Officer
fengh@nays.org
• John Engh, COO
• Yolanda Williams, CFO
• Greg Bach, VP Communications
Member Services:
Membership card, benefits, training course. Insurance; educational materials including books, videos, audiocassettes; officiating equipment, apparel and accessories.
Description:
Founded 1995. Provides youth leagues and programs in training quality sports officials.

YOUTH DEVELOPMENT/A DIVISION OF THE NATIONAL ALLIANCE FOR YOUTH SPORTS
2050 VISTA PARKWAY
WEST PALM BEACH, FL 33411
561-684-1141
800-688-5437
Fax: 561-684-2546
nays@nays.org
www.nays.org
• Fred Engh, Founder/CEO
fengh@nays.org
• John Engh, COO
• Yolanda Williams, CFO
• Greg Bach, VP Communications
Description:
Founded 1993. Develops programs that build the proficiency and confidence youngsters need to participate and remain active in sports. Involves youngsters in programs that teach the basic motor skills necessary for meaningful sports participation. Programs include the Start Smart sports development program and Hook A Kid on Golf, and the Kids on Target archery program.

NATIONAL CENTER FOR SPORTS SAFETY
2316 FIRST AVENUE SOUTH
BIRMINGHAM, AL 35203
205-329-7535
866-508-6277
Fax: 205-329-7526

info@SportsSafety.org
www.sportssafety.org
• Matthew Lemak, Chairman
• Kathryn Gwaltney, Executive Director, Operations
• Beth Kates, Athletic Trainer/Outreach Coordinator
• Jennifer Byrd, Director, Athletic Training
• Pat Lynch, Coach

NATIONAL COUNCIL OF YOUTH SPORTS
7185 SE SEAGATE LANE
STUART, FL 34997
772-781-1452
Fax: 772-781-7298
youthsports@ncys.org
www.ncys.org
• Sally S. Johnson, Executive Director
• Wanda Rutledge, President
• Jon Butler, Vice President
Publications:
WIN OR LOSE-A guide to Sports Parenting
Member Services:
Member organizations of the National Council of Youth Sports (NCYS) comprise the youth sport industry representing more than 52,000,000 boys and girls in organized youth sports programs across the United States. Some of its members are Little League Baseball, Pop Warner Football, American Youth Soccer Organization, Boys & Girls Clubs of America, AAU-Amateur Athletic Union, Parks & Recreation Departments.

NATIONAL HIGH SCHOOL BASEBALL COACHES ASSOCIATION
PO BOX 12843
TEMPE, AZ 85284
614-764-5800
contact_us@baseballcoaches.org
www.baseballcoaches.org

NATIONAL LITTLE BRITCHES RODEO ASSOCIATION
5050 EDISON AVENUE
SUITE 105
COLORADO SPRINGS, CO 80915
719-389-0333
800-763-3694
Fax: 719-578-1367
info@nlbra.com
www.nlbra.com
• John Freeman, Vice President
• Rob Lay, President
Description:
One of the oldest, continuing junior rodeo associations in the nation. The aims and purposes of the organization are directed towards the interests of the western-minded youth of the nation. It is a non-profit venture to build sound, health minds and bodies-to develop character, self-reliance and good sportsmanship through competition in the great sport of rodeo.

NATIONAL VENTURING DIVISION, BOY SCOUTS OF AMERICA
1325 WEST WALNUT HILL LANE
IRVING, TX 75038
972-580-2000
Fax: 972-580-2502
www.scouting.org
• Dustin M. Readenour, President
• Sarah Mittrucken, Vice President
Description:
Helps advance Venturing as well as promote the idea that the venturing program for YOUNG ADULTS who want a broader experience in leadership, vocations, and hobbies.

NAVY RUN JUMP N' THROW
5248 N VALENTINE AVENUE
FRESNO, CA 93711
559-841-8400
navyrjt@yahoo.com
• Jim Santos, President/Founder
Year Founded:
2000
Nature of Sports Service:
The Navy Run Jump n'Throw program is supported by the United States Navy to enhance physical fitness, health and physical development for students grades 1-12 in the United States. The Navy RJT program is an excellent opportunity for kids in school or recreation programs to enjoy sports activities that are designed to meet their needs in sports.

OHIO SOUTH YOUTH SOCCER ASSOCIATION, INC.
25 WHITNEY DRIVE
SUITE 104
MILFORD, OH 45150
513-576-9555
Fax: 513-576-1666
office@osysa.com
www.osysa.com
• Gordon Henderson, Chief Executive Director
Publications:
Newsletter

POSITIVE COACHING ALLIANCE
1001 N RENGSTORFF AVENUE
SUITE 100
MOUNTAIN VIEW, CA 94303
703-888-3983
866-725-0024
Fax: 650-969-1650
pca@positivecoach.org
www.positivecoach.org
• Jim Thompson, Chief Executive Officer, Founder
(650) 354-0909
jim@positivecoach.org
• Heana Simpson, Deputy Director
(650) 354-0908
• David Jacobson, Marketing Communications Manager
(650) 354-0903
• Tina Syer, Associate Director
(415) 202-0905
• Silvia Rivas, Partnership Administrator
(408) 846-9619
silvia@positivecoach.org
Nature of Sports Service:
A Stanford University-based non-profit organization, works with coaches, organizational leaders and parents to teach young athletes not only how to win, but also how to learn about teamwork, discipline, respect and goal-setting through their sports experience.

Other locations:

POSITIVE COACHING ALLIANCE (CHICAGO)
4611 N RAVENSWOOD AVENUE
SUITE 207
CHICAGO, IL 60640
866-725-0024
• Jason Sacks, Executive Director
Description:
A non-profit organization, works with coaches, organizational leaders and parents to teach young athletes not only how to win, but also how to learn about teamwork, discipline, respect and a goal-setting through their sports experience.

POSITIVE COACHING ALLIANCE (HAWAII)
C/O UNIVERSITY OF HAWAII
DEPARTMENT OF KINESIOLOGY
1337 LOWER CAMPUS DRIVE
HONOLULU, HI 96822
866-725-0024
www.positivecoach.org
• Stacy Matsuda, Local Coordinator
Description:
Non-profit organization, works with coaches, organizational leaders and parents to teach young athletes not only how to win, but also how to learn about teamwork, discipline, respect and goal-setting through their sports experience.

POSITIVE COACHING ALLIANCE (WASHINGTON, DC)
1001 N RENGSTORFF AVENUE
SUITE 100
MOUNTAIN VIEW, CA 94303
703-888-3983
866-725-0024
Fax: 650-969-1650
www.positivecoach.org
• Clint Sanchez, Senior Partner Development Association
• Scott Chapman, Founder/CEO
• Karen Francis, Chairman & CEO
• Doug Galen, Chief RevenueOfficer

SOCCER ASSOCIATION FOR YOUTH
2812 EAST KEMPER ROAD
CINCINNATI, OH 45241
513-769-3800
800-233-7291
Fax: 513-769-0500
sayusa@saysoccer.org
www.saysoccer.org
• Shiela Shay-Mole, National Executive Director
• Doug Wood, National Marketing/Business Operations Direct
dwood@saysoccer.org
• Neil Bradford, National Director of Coaching
• Jamie Blanton, National Administrative Coordinator
jblanton@saysoccer.org
• Amanda Weiss, National Media Specialist/Graphic Designer
• Brain Begly, National Resource Manager
bbegley@saysoccer.org
Description:
Formed to provide an organization within which children could learn and play soccer, the worlds most popular sport.

U.S. YOUTH SOCCER ASSOCIATION
9220 WORLD CUP WAY
FRISCO, TX 75034
972-235-4499
800-476-2237
Fax: 972-334-9960
www.youthsoccer.org
• Jim Cosgrove, Executive Director
• Rob Martella, Director of Operations
• John Sutter, President
jsutter@usyouthsoccer.org
• Evelyn Gill, Vice-President
• Alan Blinzler, Secretary
• Dennis Brumfield, Treasurer

multi sports

Description:
US youth soccer is a non-profit and educational organization whose misson is to foster the physical, mental and emotional growth and development of America's youth through the sport of soccer at all levels of age and competition.

UNITED STATES YOUTH VOLLEYBALL LEAGUE
2771 PLAZA DEL AMO
SUITE 808
TORRANCE, CA 90503
310-212-7008
888-988-7985

Fax: 310-212-7182
questions@usyvl.org
www.usyvl.org

3

college sports

college sports

college sports

N

College Sports Alphabetical Index

college sports

college sports

College Associations

CANADIAN COLLEGIATE ATHLETIC ASSOCIATION
ST LAWRENCE COLLEGE
2 ST LAWRENCE DRIVE
CORNWALL, ON, CANADA K6H 4Z1
613-937-1508
Fax: 613-937-1530
www.ccaa.ca
• Leigh Goldie, President
(416) 780-539-29
lgoldie@gprc.ab.ca
• Alan Rogan, VP Eligibiity
(780) 853-8711
alan.rogan@lakelandcollege.ca
• Rogan Alan, VP Finance and Administration
(250) 489-8201
alan.rogan@lakelandcollege.ca
• Michelle McConney, Governance
(902) 7057221577
Michelle.McConney@GeorgianCollege.ca
• Sandra Murray-MacDonell, Executive Director
sandra@ccaa.ca
Description:
Founded 1973 to provide leadership, programs and services for student-athletes involved in intercollegiate sport. Conducts 10 national championships annually.
Membership Requirements:
Post-secondary school institution.
Number of Members:
92 collegiate institutions across Canada.

CANADIAN INTERUNIVERSITY SPORT
801 KING EDWARD, STE N205
OTTAWA, ON, CANADA KIN 6N5
613-562-5670
Fax: 613-562-5669
cis-sic.ca/splash/index
• Debbie Villeneuve, Director Finance & Administration
ext 24
• Sheila Ann Newton, Manager Events & Programs
ext 23
• Tom Huisman, Director Operations & Development
Description:
Founded 1961. Coordinates and administers university sports in Canada. Membership includes 48 universities coast to coast. Conducts 17 national championships in 11 sports and holds the Canadian franchise in the World University Games.
Membership Requirements:
Canadian post-secondary degree-granting institution with concurrent membership in one of six recognized regional associations.
Publications:
Championship Programs, annually; Almanac, annually; Membership Directory; Drug Education Handbook, annually.
Member Services:
Coordinating television schedules, corporate sponsorship, national promotional and publicity programs.

COLLEGE ATHLETIC BUSINESS MANAGEMENT ASSOCIATION/CABMA
24651 DETROIT ROAD
WESTLAKE, OH 44145
440-892-4000
Fax: 440-892-4007
www.nacda.com

• Chris Lacoi, President
(303) 310-206-68
ciacoi@athletics.ucla.edu
• Pat Manak, Senior Associate Executive Director
pmanak@nacda.com
• Bubba Cunningham, Director of Athletics
(919) 962-8200
bubbac@unc.edu
• Andy Platt, 1st Vice President
(310) 7065421306
aplatt@sports.uga.edu
• Omar Banks, 2nd Vice President
(301) 513-556-06
• Michael Boele, 3rd Vice President
(573) 951-827-54
• Katie Newman, Secretary
(417) 440-788-74
knewman@nacda.com
Membership Requirements:
Must be college athletic business manager or assistant or ticket manager or associate director of athletics or assistant systems manager, fund raisers, facility managers, and individuals performing similar duties but under different titles connected with colleges or universities.
Description:
Founded 1949. Promotes, establishes and maintains highest standards of integrity and efficiency in scope, policy and procedures of the management and administration of business in the athletics department of colleges and universities.

COLLEGE SPORTS INFORMATION DIRECTORS OF AMERICA/COSIDA
TEMPLE UNIVERSITY
1700 N BROAD STREET, 4TH FLOOR
PHILADELPHIA, PA 19122-0842
Fax: 740-368-3332
www.cosida.com
• Doug Vance, Executive Director
(785) 691-7708
• Barb Kowel, Director Of Professional Development
(785) 739-2905
barbkowal@cosida.com
• Will Roleson, Director of Internal Operations / Treasurer
(317) 490-2905
willroleson@cosida.com
Nature of Sports Service:
Founded 1957. Provides for the exchange of ideas among members of sports information profession.
Membership Requirements:
Active in the sports information field in the U.S. or Canada.
Publications:
COSIDA DIGEST, monthly newsletter. DIRECTORY OF SPORTS INFORMATION DIRECTORS, annually.
Member Services:
Job opportunity and placement service. Annual workshops, contests for brochures and programs. Academic All-America teams in football, men's and women's basketball, women's volleyball, baseball, women's softball, and men's and women's at large. COSIDA Scholarship Program.

COLLEGIATE COMMISSIONER'S ASSOCIATION
C/O MID-CONTINENT CONFERENCE
340 BUTTERFIELD 3-D
ELMHURST, IL 60126

630-516-0661
Fax: 630-516-0673
• Val Ackerman, Commissioner
• Rick Gentile, Senior Associate Commissioner (Men's Basketball)
• Katie Willett, Associate Commissioner (Compliance & Governance)
• Tracy Ellis-Ward, Associate Commissioner (Women's Basketball)
• Stu Jackson, Associate Commissioner
Description:
Founded 1939. Encourages and promotes intercollegiate athletics and high standards of sportsmanship as desirable incidents of higher education. Develops and adopts policies beneficial to intercollegiate athletics. Sponsors and develops uniformly high standards for all sports in intercollegiate athletics. Encourages discussion, consideration and promotion of the views and policies of members in relation to intercollegiate and other amateur athletics.
Publications:
Officiating Mechanics Manuals.
Member Services:
Administers National Letter of Intent Program.

COLLEGIATE SPORTS OF AMERICA
22900 VENTURA BLVD, SUITE 100
WOODLAND HILLS, CA 91364
818-844-Prepstar 844-773-7782
Fax: 818-225-1098
info@csaprepstar.com
csaprepstar.com
• Jeff Duva, Founder/President
Year Founded: 1981
Provides services for high school athletes assisting them in locating colleges, receiving financial aid, and getting admitted.
CSA Publication:
PrepSTAR Magazine - college football recruiting publication. www.PrepStar.com

FLORIDA COLLEGE SYSTEM ACTIVITIES ASSOCIATION
113 E. COLLEGE AVENUE
TALLAHASSEE, FL 32301
850-222-2949
Fax: 850-222-2327
www.flccaa.org
• Kelly Warren, Executive Director
(850) 222-2949
KellyWarren@thefcsaa.com
• John Schultz, President
Description:
A statewide non-profit corporation regulating, coordinating and promoting intercollegiate activities in: Athletics, Brain Bowl, Forensics, Music, Student Government, Student Publications, and Theatre.

INTERCOLLEGIATE OFFICIATING ASSOCIATION
P.O. BOX 16679
CLEVELAND, OH 44116
440-871-8100
Fax: 440-871-4221
ioa@northcoast.org
• Amy Williams, President
• Keri Luchowski, Executive Director
(734) 913-6078
ioa@northcoast.org
• Roger Ingles, Director Of Athletics
(317) 254-0714

• Joe Haklin, Director Of Athletics
(216) 269-3538
Description:
Oversees all aspects of officiating in the sports of men's and women's basketball and football for the North Coast Athletic Conference and other subscribers.
Year Founded:
1992

INTERNATIONAL COLLEGIATE LICENSING ASSOCIATION/ICLA
24651 DETROIT RD
WESTLAKE, OH 44145
440-892-4000
Fax: 440-892-4007
www.nacda.com
• Brett Eden, President
(801) 581-8298
brett.eden@aux.utah.edu
• Robin Cooper, 1st Vice President
(812) 855-8830
cooperrL@iu.edu
• Rachael Bickerton, 2nd Vice President
(208) 426-1358
• Tami Breymeyer, 3rd Vice President and Secretary
(785) 532-6269
Tbreymeyer@Kstatesports.com
• Don Tencher, Secretary
(401) 456-8007
dtencher@ric.edu
Description:
The purpose of ICLA is to foster the highest possible professional and ethical standards, while providing collegiate licensing practitioners a broad range of professional advancement opportunities. Further, it is ICLA's mission to improve the overall understanding and effectiveness of institutional trademarks/tradenames and licensing, while upholding the ideals of higher education.
Membership Requirements:
Open to all individuals whose responsibilities include the regular implementation of campus policies regarding trademark and licensing administration. There are five levels of membership — College/University, Affiliate/Conference, Student, Bowl/Conference and Emeritus.
Year Founded:
2002
Publications:
Athletics Administration published bi-monthly.

MID-STATES FOOTBALL ASSOCIATION
UNIVERSITY OF FINDLAY
1000 N. MAIN STREET
FINDLAY, OH 45840
419-434-4551
Fax: 419-423-2895
houdeshell@findlay.edu
www.mid-statesfootball.org
• Dave Laketa, Chairman
(815) 740-3842
• Gary Newsome, Commissioner
(815) 939-5120
gnewsome@olivet.edu
• Larry Alter, Information Director
(419) 427-8407
Year Founded:
1993
Affiliations:
Collegiate NAIA Conference

Member Schools:
Concordia College, Grand View College, Iowa Wesleyan College, Malone College, Marain College, McKendree College, Olivet Nazarene University, Quincy University, Siena Hts. College, St. Xavier University, St. Ambrose University, Taylor University, Trinity Int. University, University of Saint Francis-Indiana, University of Saint Francis-Illinois, Waldorf College, Walsh University, William Penn University.

NATIONAL ASSOCIATION OF ACADEMIC ADVISORS FOR ATHLETICS/N4A
240 JETER DRIVE
300 CASE ACADEMIC CENTER, NC STATE UNIV.
RALEIGH, NC 27695
919-513-1007
Fax: 919-513-0541
N4A@athletics.tamu.edu
www.nacda.com
• Jim Phillips, PhD, President
(847) 491-8880
• Tim Selgo, 1st Vice President
(616) 331-8800
selgot@gvsu.edu
• Chris Plonsky, 2nd Vice President
(512) 471-4787
cp@utexas.edu
• Don Tencher, Secretary
(401) 456-8007
dtencher@ric.edu
Year Founded:
1975
Description:
A diverse educational, service and professional nonprofit organization. N4A members are academic support and student services personnel who are committed to enhancing the opportunities for academic, athletic, and personal success for collegiate student-athletes. These objectives are achieved primarily by providing informed, competent advising and by serving as a liaison between the academic and athletic communities on college campuses across the country.
Publications:
THE ACADEMIC-ATHLETIC JOURNAL, biannually; THE N4A NEWS, three times annually.
Membership Requirements:
Regular; Affiliate; Student; Alumni.

NATIONAL ASSOCIATION OF ATHLETIC DEVELOPMENT DIRECTORS/NAADD
24651 DETROIT RD
WESTLAKE, OH 44145
440-892-4000
Fax: 440-892-4007
www.nacda.com
• Bob Vecchione, Executive Director
(208) 426-3557
• Pat Manak, Sr. Associate Executive Director
• Julie Work, Assistant Executive Director
(440) 788-7468
• Jason Galaska, Assistant Executive Director
(440) 788-7470
jgalaska@nacda.com
• Virtue Ryan, Manager-Affiliate Associations
(440) 788-7473
Year Founded:
1993

Member Services:
Reduced rates for the annual workshop; complimentary subscription to the bi-monthly magazine ATHLETICS ADMINISTRATION.
Membership Requirements:
Individuals employed by the athletics department or the development arm for the department of a college or university that is responsible for the development activities of the department.
Number of members:
520
Description:
A professional organization created by intercollegiate athletic development directors for intercollegiate athletic development directors. This professional organization provides for the exchange of current trends in intercollegiate fund raising and development.

NATIONAL ASSOCIATION OF COLLEGIATE DIRECTORS OF ATHLETICS/NACDA
24561 DETROIT RD
WESTLAKE, OH 44145
440-892-4000
Fax: 440-892-4007
www.nacda.com
• Bob J. Vecchione, Executive Director
(440) 788-7466
• Pat J. Manak, Senior Associate Executive Director
(440) 788-7467
• Julie Work, Assistant Executive Director
(440) 788-7485
• Jason Galaska, Assistant Executive Director
(440) 788-7470
jgalaska@nacda.com
Description:
Establishes educational standards and objectives among individuals responsible for administering college athletic programs.
Year Founded:
1965
Membership Requirements:
Athletics directors of two or four-year colleges in the U.S., Mexico or Canada. Associate Membership open to associate and assistant athletics directors, conference commissioners and their assistants.
Publications:
ATHLETICS ADMINISTRATION, bimonthly magazine.
Member Services:
Reduced fee for the NACDA convention and all meetings; NACDA's bi-monthly publication of ATHLETICS ADMINISTRATION.
Number of Members:
6,100 individuals; 1,600 institutions

NATIONAL ASSOCIATION OF COLLEGIATE MARKETING ADMINISTRATORS/
24651 DETROIT RD
WESTLAKE, OH 44145
440-892-4000
Fax: 440-892-4007
www.nacma.com
• Bob Vecchione, Executive Director
(440) 788-788-74
• Pat Manak, Sr. Associate Executive Director
(440) 788-7467

• Chris Green, Ass. Executive Director-Communications
(440) 788-7485
Year Founded:
1990
Description:
Serves to foster the highest possible professional and ethical standards in collegiate marketing, while providing athletics marketing and promotions practitioners a broad range of professional advancement opportunities.
Membership Requirements:
Individuals employed by athletics departments and engaged in administering sports marketing, public relations or promotion activities.
Publications:
NACMA IDEAS, quarterly newsletter.
Number of members:
500
Member Services:
Reduced rates to the NACMA convention, free copies of ATHETICS ADMINISTRATION magazine, access to the Member Only section of the website and access to the membership directory.

NATIONAL ASSOCIATION OF INTERCOLLEGIATE ATHLETICS/NAIA
1200 GRAND BLVD.
KANSAS CITY, MO 64106
816-595-8000
Fax: 816-595-8200
thasseltine@naia.org
www.naia.org
• Jim Carr, Interim President/CEO
(816) 595-8105
jcarr@naia.org
• Dan Wood, Executive Director
(913) 791-0044
dwood@thenccaa.org
• John Leavens, COO
(816) 595-8111
jleavens@naia.org
Year Founded:
1937
Nature of Sports Service:
Organizes and administers all areas of intercollegiate athletics. Conducts 23 national championships.
Membership Requirements:
Fully accredited four year colleges and universities that subscribe to NAIA policies and tenets.
Publications:
NAIA OFFICIAL HANDBOOK. NAIA Daily. NAIA Coaches/Events Manual. NAIA Championship Host Manual. National championship events programs.
Number of Members:
300 colleges and universities.

NATIONAL CHRISTIAN COLLEGE ATHLETIC ASSOCIATION/NCCAA
302 W. WASHINGTON ST
GREENVILLE, SC 29601
864-250-1199
Fax: 864-250-1141
info@thenccaa.org
www.thenccaa.org
• Dan Wood, Executive Director
• Ben Belleman, Director Of Member Services & Compliance
• Brandon Gilmore, Media & Communications Coordinator

Year Founded:
1966
Description:
Non-profit intercollegiate athletic association management serving 100 Christian colleges/universities through championship competition, sports outreach and program governance.
Publications:
The Pursuit
Number of Members:
101

NATIONAL COLLEGIATE ATHLETIC ASSOCIATION/NCAA
700 W WASHINGTON ST
PO BOX 6222
INDIANAPOLIS, IN 46206-6222
317-917-6222
Fax: 317-917-6888
www.ncaa.org
• Joni Comstock, Sr. VP President For Championships
• Bernard Franklin, Executive VP Of Education & Community Engagement
• Dan Gavitt, Sr. VP Of Basketball
• Brian Hanline, Sr. VP Anf Chief Medical Officer
• David Berst, Chief of Staff Division I
• Mike L. Racy, Chief of Staff Division II
• David Price, Enforcement/Reinstatement VP
• James L. Isch, Senor VP Administration/CFO
• Judy Sweet, Championships Vice President
• Ronald J. Stratten, Education Services Vice President
• Daniel Boggan, Chief Operations Officer
• Thomas W. Jernstedt, Executive Vice President
• Mark Emmert, President
• Phillip Austin, Chairman/Board of Directors Div. I
Year Founded:
1906
Description:
Promotes the sound administration of intercollegiate athletics for men and women among its more than 1,000 voluntary member institutions, conferences and affiliated organizations.
Membership Requirements:
Accredited colleges or universities that maintain a minimum of four intercollegiate sports, with one sport in each of the traditional seasons of the academic year. Compliance with all NCAA legislation dealing with financial aid, recruiting, playing and practice sessions, post-season competition and other areas of athletic administration.
Publications:
NCAA NEWS, weekly; rule books; records books; and general publications.
Member Services:
Statistics forms. Guides and rule books.
Number of Members:
1,250

NATIONAL JUNIOR COLLEGE ATHLETIC ASSOCIATION/NJCAA
8801 JM KEYNES DRIVE
SUITE 450
CHARLOTTE, NC 28262
719-590-9788
www.njcaa.org

• Dr. Christopher Parker, President & CEO
• Judy Rose, Special Assistant to the President
• Michelle Meadows, Vice President, Operations & COO
Description:
Puropse is to promote and foster junior college athletics on intersectional and national levels to that results will be consistent with the total educational program of its members.
Membership Requirements:
Accredited two-year college and comparable institutions that have been approved by their respective NJCAA regions.
Number of Members:
530 institutions; 50 national championship tournaments hosted, and 9 football bowl games.
Publications:
JUCO REVIEW
Frequency:
1 time(s) per month
Member Services:
Weekly polls and statistical information.

NATIONAL SPORTING GOODS ASSOCIATION
1601 FEEHANVILLE DR, STE 300
MT. PROSPECT, IL 60056
800-815-5422
Fax: 847-391-9827
info@nsga.org
• Matt Carlson, President/Chief Executive Officer
(800) 815-5422
• Meghan Beach, Director Of Membership
ext 1280
• Dan Wiersma, CFO
ext 1040
• Marty Maciaszek, Communications Director
ext 1260
• Dustin Dorbin, Director of Research & Information
ext 1170
Description:
Our mission is to help its members profit in a competitive marketplace. It does so by providing cost-saving services, information and education. In addition, NSGA serves as the voice of the retailer/dealer, speaking out on issues that affect sporting goods retailers/dealers.
Year Founded:
1929
Publications:
NSGA RETAIL FOCUS magazine; SPORTING GOODS ALERT newsletter; NSGA BUYING GUIDE; INTERNATIONAL DIRECTORY OF RETAIL SPORTING GOODS ASSOCIATIONS & BUYING ORGANIZATIONS

NATIONAL SPORTING GOODS CORPORATION
376 HOLLYWOOD AVE
SUITE 202
FAIRFIELD, NJ 7004
973-779-2323
800-242-7476
Fax: 973-779-0084
skater@chicagoskates.com
www.chicagoskates.com
• Joel Aranson, VP
• Greg Adelsheimer, President

Manufacturer, Distributor:
Bowling - Shoes; Ice Skating - Skate Bags;
In-Line Skating - Accessories, Skates; Roller
Skating - Skates; Skateboards,
Snowboards.
Brands:
Chicago Skates

NEW ENGLAND INTERCOLLEGIATE AMATEUR ATHLETIC ASSOCIATION
C/O JACK MCDONALD, PRESIDENT
QUINNIPIAC UNIVERSITY
275 MOUNT CARMEL AVENUE
HADEN, CT 6518
203-582-8200
NEICAAA@aol.com
• Irwin Cohen, Commissioner
• John L Lahey, President
(203) 582-8700
• Patricia Nicol, 1st Vice President
• Branwen Smith-King, 2nd Vice President
Year Founded:
1886
Description:
This Association is the second oldest
collegiate group in the country; only the
IC4A is older, having been formed in 1876.
Its purpose was the promotion and
protection of intercollegiate competition in
track and field among the colleges which
were members of the Association.
Member Schools:
Amherst, Bates, Bentley, Boston Col.,
Boston U., Bowdoin, Brandeis U., Brown U.,
Bryant, Central Connecticut State U., U. of
Connecticut, Colby, Dartmouth, Holy Cross,
Lowell Tech, U. of Maine, U. of
Maine-Portland/Gorham, Massachusetts
Inst. of Tech., U. of Massachusetts, U. of
New Hampshire, Nichols, Northeastern U.,
Norwich U., Providence Col., U. of Rhode
Island, Southern Connecticut State U.,
Springfield Col., St. Anselm's, Trinity, Tufts,
U. of Vermont, U.S. Coast Guard Academy,
Wesleyan U., Westfield State, Worcester
Poly.
Membership Requirements:
Membership is open to any recognized
college in New England which sponsors
cross country and or track and field and it is
one of the last remaining championships
that offers competition across all three levels
of NCAA membership.

NJCAA 1ST VICE PRESIDENT
SINCLAIR COMMUNITY COLLEGE
444 W. THIRD ST
DAYTON, OH 45402
937-512-2353
800-315-3000
Fax: 937-512-3056
info@sinclair.edu
www.sinclair.edu
• Norma Dycus, Athletic Director
Enrollment:
12000
Mascot:
Tartans.
Description:
National governing body for 2 year collegiate
athletics.

NJCAA REGION I MEN'S
C/O GREG SILOX
PARADISE VALLEY COMMUNITY
COLLEGE

18401 N 32ND STREET
PHOENIX, AZ 85032
602-787-7173
Fax: 602-787-6715
www.njcaa.org
• Paul Dale, President
(602) 787-6610
• Mary Lou Mosley, VP Academic Affairs
(602) 787-6607
marylou.mosley@pvmail.maricopa.edu
• Anthony Asti, Interim VP Administrative
Services
(608) 787-6601
• Shirley Green, Interim VP Student Affairs
(608) 787-6604
shirley.green@pvmail.maricopa.edu
• Paul Golisch, Dean of Information
Technology
(608) 787-7789
paul.golisch@pvmail.maricopa.edu
• Denise Digianfilippo, Dean of Academic
Affairs
(608) 787-6602
denise.digianfilippo@pvmail.maricopa.edu
• Julia Devous, Director of Development &
Community Relations
(608) 787-6684
julia.devous@pvmail.maricopa.edu
Number of Championships:
9
Championship Years:
1982, 1983, 1988, 1989, 1993, 1994, 1998,
2001, 2002
Mascot:
The Fighting Artichokes.
Enrollment:
6450

NJCAA REGION I WOMEN'S
SOUTH MOUNTAIN COMMUNITY
COLLEGE
7050 S 24TH STREET
PHOENIX, AZ 85040
602-243-8236
Fax: 602-243-8116
chris.haines@smcmail.maricopa.edu
• Todd Eastin, Interim Athletic
Director/Baseball Coach
(602) 243-8245
todd.eastin@smcmail.maricopa.edu
• Shai Olsen, President
• Danelle Dykstra-Wade, Athletic Trainer
(602) 243-8232
danelle.dykstra@smcmail.maricopa.edu
• Sophie Rodriguez, Office Coordinator
(602) 243-8236
sophie.rodriguez@smcmail.maricopa.edu
• Christa Pfeninger, Women's Softball Head
Coach
(602) 243-8242
christa.pfeninger@southmountaincc.edu
• Andy Walker, Men's Golf Head Coach
andres.walker@smcmail.maricopa.edu
• Andy Walker, Women's Golf Head Coach
andres.walker@smcmail.maricopa.edu
• Pat Mooney, Volleyball Head Coach
(602) 243-8239
pat.mooney@smcmail.maricopa.edu
• Daven Vo, Men's Basketball Head Coach
• Justin Bogus, Men's & Women's Soccer
Head Coach
(602) 243-8247
justin.bogus@smcmail.maricopa.edu
• Terry Robinson, Women's Basketball
Head Coach
 (602) 243-8244
Number of Championships:
1

Championship Years:
1994
Enrollment:
11104
Mascot:
Gauchos

NJCAA REGION II MEN'S
CONNORS STATE COLLEGE
ROUTE 1, BOX 1000
700 COLLEGE RD.
WARNER, OK 74469
918-463-2931
Fax: 918-463-2233
• Cameron Hendreson, Mens Basketball
Assistant Coach
• Eddie Kite,
• Jamie Fisher, Womens Basketball
Assistant Coach
• Perry Keith, Baseball Head Coach
• Bobby Foreman, Baseball Assistant Coach
• Bill Muse, Athletic Director/Men's
Basketball Head Coach
(918) 463-6231
• Donnie Nero, President
(918) 463-6214
Number of Championships:
1
Championship Years:
1990
Enrollment:
1616

NJCAA REGION II WOMEN'S
CONNORS STATE COLLEGE
700 COLLEGE ROAD
WARNER, OK 74469
918-463-2931
Fax: 918-463-2233
• Cameron Hendreson, Mens Basketball
Assistant Coach
• Rusty Laverentz, Womens Basketball
Head Coach
• Jamie Fisher, Womens Basketball
Assistant Coach
• Perry Keith, Baseball Head Coach
• Bobby Foreman, Baseball Assistant Coach
• Bill Muse, Athletic Director
(918) 463-6231
wmuse@connorsstate.edu
• Donnie Nero, President
(918) 463-6214
Number of Championships:
1
Championship Years:
1985

NJCAA REGION III MEN'S
JAMESTOWN COMMUNITY COLLEGE
525 FALCONER ST
PO BOX 20
JAMESTOWN, NY 14702-0020
716-338-1000
800-388-8557
www.sunyjcc.edu
• Keith Martin, Athletic Director
• Barry Andreson, Maintenance Mechanic II
• Laura Anderson, Assistant Professor
Spanish
• Curt Anderson, Small Business Advisor
• Mary Augustine, Assistant Director,
Campus Store
• Dawn Babbage, Associate Professor
• Aimee Brunelle, Athletic Trainer
• Gregory DeCinque, President
Number of Championships:
1

Championship Years:
2000
Mascot:
Jayhawks.
Enrollment:
2600
Year Founded:
1950

NJCAA REGION III WOMEN'S
ALFRED STATE COLLEGE
10 UPPER COLLEGE DR
ALFRED, NY 14802
607-587-4361
800-425-3733
Fax: 607-587-4331
www.alfredstate.edu
• John M Anderson, President
• Kelly Higgins, Athletic Director
(607) 587-4361
• Sandy Kinnerney, Department Secretary
(607) 587-4361
kinnersa@alfredstate.edu
• Paul Welker, Sports Information Director
(607) 587-4563
welkerpm@alfredstate.edu
• Gerard Gingras, Athletic Trainer
(607) 587-4388
gingrag@alfredstate.edu
• Alexe Paske, Assistant Athletic Trainer
(607) 587-4568
paskak@alfredstate.edu
Number of Championships:
1
Championship Years:
2003
Mascot:
Pioneers.
Enrollment:
2900

NJCAA REGION IV MEN'S
OAKTON COMMUNITY COLLEGE
1600 E. GOLF RD
DES PLAINES, IL 60016
847-635-1600
Fax: 847-635-1606
mreuter@oakton.edu
www.oakton.edu
• Lisa Bolinder, Athletic Trainer/Women's
Golf Head Coach
(847) 635-1729
lbolinde@oakton.edu
• Peg Lee, President
(847) 635-1801
plee@oakton.edu
Enrollment:
5354
Mascot:
Raiders.

NJCAA REGION IV WOMEN'S
SOUTH SUBURBAN COLLEGE
15800 S STATE STREET
S HOLLAND, IL 60473
708-596-2000 EXT 5718
Fax: 708-210-5733
• Steve Ruzich, Athletic Director
(708) 596-2000
• Don Manhing, President
Enrollment:
8063
Mascot:
Bulldogs.

NJCAA REGION IX MEN'S
SHERIDAN COLLEGE
BOX 1500
SHERIDAN, WY 82801
307-674-4664
800-913-9139
Fax: 307-674-4293
www.sheridan.edu
• Matt Hammer, Athletic Director/Men's
Basketball Coach
• Annette Murray, Public Information
Director
• Kati Sherwood, Chair
• R.Scott Ludwig, Vice-Chair
• Norleen Healy, Secretary
Enrollment:
1867
Mascot:
Generals/Lady Generals.

NJCAA REGION IX WOMEN'S
EASTERN WYOMING COLLEGE
3200 W. C ST
TORRINGTON, WY 82240
307-532-8248
Fax: 307-532-8215
• Tom Anderson, Director Of Athletics
(307) 532-8321
• Jordan Rice, Athletic Trainer
(307) 532-8249
Enrollment:
985
Mascot:
Lancers.
Year Founded:
1948

NJCAA REGION V MEN'S
SOUTH PLAINS COLLEGE
1401 S. COLLEGE AVE
LEVELLAND, TX 79336
806-894-9611 EXT 220
Fax: 806-897-0139
www.spc.cc.tx.us
• Joe Tubb, Athletic Director
• Mike Box, Chairman
• Bobby Neal, Vice-Chairman
Number of Championships:
6
Championship Years:
1986, 1991, 1993, 1995, 1996, 1997
Enrollment:
4230
Mascot:
Texans.

NJCAA REGION V WOMEN'S
MCLENNAN COMMUNITY COLLEGE
1400 COLLEGE DR
WACO, TX 76708
254-299-8811
Fax: 254-299-8814
strochim@mclennan.edu
www.mclennan.edu
• Johnette McKown, President
• Shawn Trochim, Athletic Director
• Teresa Lopez, Athletic Secretary
• Candice Kelm, Sports Information
Specialist
(254) 299-8833
Number of Championships:
3
Championship Years:
1997, 1998, 2002
Enrollment:
9,500
Mascot:

Highlanders.
Year Founded:
1965

NJCAA REGION VI MEN'S
GARDEN CITY COMMUNITY COLLEGE
801 CAMPUS DR
GARDEN CITY, KS 67846
620-276-7611
800-658-1696
Fax: 620-276-9646
www.gcccks.edu
• Vi Trilli, Athletic Director
• Ryan Ruda, Athletic Director
• Dan Delgado, SID/Promotions
(620) 276-9620
• Jacob Ripple, Assistant Athletic Director
for Student Succe
(620) 276-9610
• Dennis Harp, Director Of Athletic
Advancement
(620) 276-9595
• Bob Larson, Coordinator of Athletic
Activities
(620) 276-0352
Number of Championships:
3
Championship Years:
1992, 1994, 1995
Enrollment:
1364
Mastcot:
Broncbusters.

NJCAA REGION VI WOMEN'S
HIGHLAND COMMUNITY COLLEGE -
KANAS
606 W MAIN
HIGHLAND, KS 66035
785-442-6000
Fax: 785-442-6104
Gdelzeit@highlandcc.edu
www.highlandcc.edu
• Greg Delzeit, Athletic Director
• Arnold Aaron, Assistant Football Coach
(784) 442-6014
• Kyle Montgomery, Head Athletic Trainer
(785) 442-6049
• David Reist, President
(785) 442-6010
• Eberly Rick, Baseball Head Coach
(785) 442-6043
Enrollment:
659
Mascot:
Scotties.

NJCAA REGION VII MEN'S
VOLUNTEER STATE COMMUNITY
COLLEGE
1480 NASHVILLE PK
GALLATIN, TN 37066
615-452-8600
Fax: 615-355-8722
Bobby.Hudson@volstate.edu
www.volstate.edu
• Tyler Nordman, Athletic Director
tnordman@highlandcc.edu
• Melissa Humphres, Athletic Trainer
• Warren Nichols, President
Enrollment:
4,568
Mascot:
Pioneers.

college sports

NJCAA REGION VII WOMEN'S
CHATTANOOGA STATE TECHNICAL
COMMUNITY COLLEGE
4501 AMNICOLA HWY
CHATTANOOGA, TN 37406
423-697-4400
866-547-3733
Fax: 423-697-2405
www.chattanoogastate.edu
• Steve Jaecks, Athletic Director
• James Catanzaro, President
Enrollment:
4909
Mascot:
Tiger.

NJCAA REGION VIII WOMEN'S
OKALOOSA-WALTON COLLEGE
100 COLLEGE BLVD
NICEVILLE, FL 32578
850-729-5379
Fax: 850-729-5200
• Mickey Englett, Athletic Director
• Mike Holmes, Athletic Trainer
• James Richburg, President
Enrollment:
3739
Mascot:
Raiders.

NJCAA REGION X MEN'S
SPARTANBURG METHODIST COLLEGE
1000 POWELL MILL RD
SPARTANBURG, SC 29301
864-587-4000
800-772-7286
Fax: 864-587-4355
perduem@smcsc.edu
www.smcsc.edu
• Mark Perdue, Athletic Director
(864) 587-4237
perduem@smcsc.edu
• John Gramling, Chairman
• Bill Painter, Vice-Chairman
Number of Championships:
1
Championship Years:
1994
Enrollment:
740
Mascot:
Pioneers.

NJCAA REGION X WOMEN'S
LOUISBURG COLLEGE
501 N. MAIN ST
LOUISBURG, NC 27549
919-497-3249
Fax: 919-496-7330
mholloman@louisburg.edu
www.louisburg.edu
• Mike Holloman, Athletic Director
(919) 497-3249
mholloman@louisburg.edu
• Mandy Kiger, Athletic Trainer
(919) 497-3435
• Alyssa Rabert, Assistant Athletic Trainer
(919) 497-3435
Number of Championships:
2
Championship Years:
1981, 1992
Enrollment:
764
Mascot:
Hurricanes.

NJCAA REGION XI MEN'S
IOWA CENTRAL COMMUNITY COLLEGE
330 AVENUE M
FORT DODGE, IA 50501
515-576-7201
Fax: 515-576-7724
www.iowacentral.com
• Rick Sandquist, Athletic Director
(515) 574-1354
sandquist@iowacentral.edu
• Andrew Newell, Athletic Trainer
(515) 574-1349
• Dan Kinney, President
(515) 574-1150
kinney@iowacentral.edu
Number of Championships:
3
Championship Years:
1978, 1981, 2002
Enrollment:
3392
Mascot:
Tritons.

NJCAA REGION XI WOMEN'S
SOUTHWESTERN COMMUNITY
COLLEGE
1501 W. TOWNLINE ST
CRESTON, IA 50801
641-782-7081 EXT 459
Fax: 641-782-3312
• Bill Krejci, Athletic Director
(641) 782-7081
krejci@swcciowa.edu
• Bill Kejci, Athletic Director
(641) 782-7081
• Barbara Crittenden, President
Enrollment:
891
Mascot:
Spartans.

NJCAA REGION XII MEN'S
LAKELAND COMMUNITY COLLEGE
7700 CLOCKTOWER DR
KIRTLAND, OH 44094
440-525-7000
800-589-8520
Fax: 440-525-7636
sbarlow@lakelandcc.edu
www.lakelandcc.edu
• Scott Barlow, Athletic Director
sbarlow@lakelandcc.edu
• Julie Phillips, Athletic Trainer
• Morris Beverage, President
(440) 525-7177
mbeverage@lakelandcc.edu
Number of Championships:
2
Championship Years:
1978, 1980
Enrollment:
4874
Mascot:
Lakers.

NJCAA REGION XIII MEN'S
NORTHLAND COMMUNITY & TECHNICAL
COLLEGE
1101 HIGHWAY 1 EAST
THIEF RIVER FALLS, MN 56701
218-683-8800
800-959-6282
Fax: 218-681-6604
www.northlandcollege.edu
• Paul Peterson, Athletic Coordinator
(218) 683-8556

• Anita Lizakowski, Athletic Trainer
• Anne Temte, President
Enrollment:
2600
Mascot:
Pioneers.

NJCAA REGION XIII WOMEN'S
ROCHESTER COMMUNITY & TECHNICAL
COLLEGE
851 30TH AVENUE SE
ROCHESTER, MN 55904
507-285-7210
800-247-1296
Fax: 507-280-5577
www.rctc.edu/athletics
• Jean Musgjerd, Women's Athletic Director
• Jim Williams, Athletic Trainer
• Don Supalla, President
Enrollment:
4250
Mascot:
Yellowjackets.

NJCAA REGION XIV MEN'S
BLINN COLLEGE
902 COLLEGE AVE
BRENHAM, TX 77833
979-830-4170
Fax: 979-830-4032
greg.hinze@blinn.edu
www.blinn.edu
• Greg Hinze, Athletic Director
• Rob Redding, Athletic Trainer
• Becky Krebs, President
(979) 830-4112
bkrebs@blinn.edu
• Dan Holt, President
(979) 830-4112
Number of Championships:
22
Championship Years:
1987-1996
Enrollment:
2470
Mascot:
Buccaneers.

NJCAA REGION XIV WOMEN'S
ALVIN COMMUNITY COLLEGE
3110 MUSTANG RD
ALVIN, TX 77511-4898
281-756-3500
Fax: 281-756-3878
jhightower@alvincollege.edu
www.alvincollege.edu
• Jennifer Hightower, Athletic Director
• Rooney Allbright, President
(281) 756-3598
Number of Championships:
1
Championship Years:
1974
Enrollment:
1358
Mascot:
Dolphins.

NJCAA REGION XIX MEN'S
MIDDLESEX COUNTY COLLEGE
2600 WOODBRIDGE AVE
EDISON, NJ 08818-3050
732-548-6000
Fax: 732-906-4179
www.middlesexcc.edu

- Robert Wisniewski, Athletic Director
- Robert Edmonds, Athletic Trainer
- Joann La Perla-Morales, President
(732) 906-2517
jlaperla@middlesexcc.edu
Enrollment:
9554
Mascot:
Colts.

NJCAA REGION XIX WOMEN'S
OCEAN COUNTY COLLEGE
1 COLLEGE DR
TOMS RIVER, NJ 08754-2001
732-255-0400
Fax: 732-255-0408
icohen@ocean.edu
www.ocean.edu
- Ilene Cohen, Athletic Director
- Michael Klecan, Athletic Trainer
- Jon Larson, President
Number of Championships:
2
Championship Years:
1985, 1989
Enrollment:
5700
Mascot:
Vikings.

NJCAA REGION XV MEN'S
NASSAU COMMUNITY COLLEGE
1 EDUCATION DR
GARDEN CITY, NY 11530-6793
516-572-7501
Fax: 516-228-3531
pellicm@sunynassau.edu
www.ncc.edu
- Michael Pelliccia, Athletics Physical
Education Director
(516) 572-7537
michael.pelliccia@ncc.edu
- Tim Prohinsie, Athletic Trainer
- Kenneth P Saunders, President
(516) 572-7205
Kenneth.Saunders@ncc.edu
Number of Championships:
33
Championship Years:
1966, 1970-1976, 1978, 1980, 1982-1986,
1990, 1991, 1994, 1995, 1997-2004
Enrollment:
14000
Mascot:
Lions.

NJCAA REGION XV WOMEN'S
ORANGE COUNTY COMMUNITY
COLLEGE
115 SOUTH ST
MIDDLETOWN, NY 10940
845-344-6222
Fax: 845-341-4216
wsmith@sunyorange.edu
www.orange.cc.ny.us
- Wayne Smith, Athletic Director
- William Richards, President
- Carol Murray, Executive Assistant to the
President
Enrollment:
2100
Mascot:
Colts.

NJCAA REGION XVI MEN'S
1000 VIKING DRIVE
HILLSBORO, MO 63050

636-789-3000 EXT 386
Fax: 636-789-2419
dmaples@jeffco.edu
www.jeffco.edu
- Jo Ellen Stringer, Athletic Director
- Bill McKenna, President
Enrollment:
2839
Mascot:
Vikings.
Year Founded:
1991

NJCAA REGION XVI WOMEN'S
ST. LOUIS COMMUNITY COLLEGE -
FLORISSANT VALLEY
3400 PERSHALL RD
ST. LOUIS, MO 63135-1408
314-513-4200
Fax: 314-513-4732
jkinney@stlcc.edu
www.stlcc.edu
- Johnna Kinney, Athletic Director
- Craig H. Larson, Chair
- Doris Graham, Vice Chair
Number of Championships:
3
Championship Years:
1976, 1988, 1990
Enrollment:
6242
Mascot:
Norsemen/Norsewomen.

NJCAA REGION XVII MEN'S
ANDREW COLLEGE
501 COLLEGE ST
CUTHBERT, GA 39840-5550
912-732-5953
Fax: 229-732-2176
www.andrewcollege.edu
- Mike Riffe, Athletic Director
- Andy Brubaker, Director of Development
(229) 732-5935
- Jonathan Lodge, Development
Communications and Alumni Coordin
(229) 732-5941
- Hilliari Flippo, Development & Public
Relations Assistant
(229) 732-5990
- Beth Saunders, Director of Athletic
Training
(229) 209-5380
- David Seyle, President
Enrollment:
400
Mascot:
Fighting Tigers.

NJCAA REGION XVII WOMEN'S
GEORGIA PERIMETER COLLEGE
3251 PANTHERSVILLE RD
DECATUR, GA 30034-3832
678-891-2300
Fax: 770-604-3798
- Alfred Barney, Athletic Director
(678) 891-2360
- Anthony Tricoli, President
(678) 891-2700
Number of Championships:
1
Championship Years:
2000
Enrollment:
18986
Mascot:
Jaguars.

NJCAA REGION XVIII MEN'S
UTAH VALLEY STATE COLLEGE
800 W. UNIVERSITY PKWY
OREM, UT 84058
801-222-8998
Fax: 801-222-8813
www.uvu.edu
- Nathan B Mathis, Athletic Director
nate.mathis@uvu.edu
- Clint T Burgi, Athletic Director-Sports
Information
clint.burgi@uvu.edu
- Matthew Holland, President

NJCAA REGION XVIII WOMEN'S
SALT LAKE COMMUNITY COLLEGE
4600 S. REDWOOD RD
SALT LAKE CITY, UT 84123
801-957-7522
Fax: 801-957-4957
www.slcc.edu
- Norma Carr, Athletic Director
- Steven Earl, Athletic Trainer
- Cynthia Bioteau, President
Enrollment:
12000
Mascot:
Bears.

NJCAA REGION XX MEN'S
PRINCE GEORGE'S COMMUNITY
COLLEGE
301 LARGO RD
UPPER MARLBORO, MD 20774-2199
301-322-0066
Fax: 301-350-7868
jtodaro@pgcc.edu
www.pgcc.edu
- Jo Ann Todaro, Athletic Director
- Charlene M Dukes, President
(301) 336-6000
Enrollment:
6914
Mascot:
Owls.

NJCAA REGION XX WOMEN'S
GARRETT COLLEGE
687 MOSSER RD
MCHENRY, MD 21541
301-387-3000
Fax: 301-387-3055
www.garrettcollege.edu
- Ann Welham, Athletic Director
- Eric Hallenbeck, Head Baseball Coach
(301) 387-3331
eric.hallenbeck@garrettcollege.edu
- Angela Sincell, Head Cross Country
Coach
(301) 387-3717
angela.sincell@garrettcollege.edu
- Dennis Gibson, Athletic Director
(301) 387-3051
dennis.gibson@garrettcollege.edu
Enrollment:
562
Mascot:
Lakers.

NJCAA REGION XXI MEN'S
C/O DOUGLAS YARNALL
MITCHELL COLLEGE 437 PEQUOT AVE
437 PEQUOT AVE
NEW LONDON, CT 6320
860-701-5047
Fax: 860-701-5085

- Mo White, Athletic Director
(860) 701-5049
white_m@mitchell.edu
- Jim muren, Chairman
- Lucy Leske, Vice-Chairman
- Paul Nunes, Secretary
- Scott Gibson, Treasurer
- Nick Van Vught, Athletic Trainer
(860) 629-6144
athletictrainer@mitchell.edu
- Mary Ellen Jukoski, EdD, President

NJCAA REGION XXI WOMEN'S
DEAN COLLEGE
99 MAIN ST
FRANKLIN, MA 2038
508-541-1814
Fax: 508-541-1817
www.dean.edu
- John Jackson, Athletic Director
- Sandra Cain, Executive Assistant to the President
- Cindy Kozil, Vice President
- J. Darrell Kulesza, Vice-President
- John F. Marcus, Vice President
- Peter Martel, Vice President
- Brian Stefanik, Athletic Trainer
- Paula Rooney, President
Enrollment:
925
Mascot:
Bulldogs.

NJCAA REGION XXII WOMEN'S
JEFFERSON DAVIS COMMUNITY COLLEGE
220 ALCO DR
BREWTON, AL 36426
251-867-4832
Fax: 334-867-7399
www.jdcc.edu
- Daniel Head, Athletic Director
- Susan McBride, President
Enrollment:
844
Mascot:
Warhawks.

NJCAA REGION XXIII MEN'S
MISSISSIPPI GULF COAST COMMUNITY COLLEGE
PO BOX 548
PERKINSTON, MS 39573
601-928-5211
Fax: 601-928-6299
chris.calcote@mgccc.edu
www.mgccc.edu
- Robin Jeffries, Athletic Director
- Don Hammack, Sports Information Director
Number of Championships:
2
Championship Years:
1971, 1984
Enrollment:
9510
Mascot:
Bulldogs.

NJCAA REGION XXIII WOMEN'S
JONES COUNTY JUNIOR COLLEGE
900 S. COURT ST
ELLISVILLE, MS 39437
601-477-4000
Fax: 601-477-4250
www.jcjc.edu

- Katie Herrington, Athletic Director
- David Garner, Chairman
- William Boone, Vice-President
- Danielle M. Ready, Secretary
Enrollment:
5002
Mascot:
Bobcats.

NJCAA REGION XXIV MEN'S
SOUTHWESTERN ILLINOIS COLLEGE
2500 CARLYLE RD
BELLEVILLE, IL 62221
618-235-2700
Fax: 618-235-1578
jay.harrington@swic.edu
www.swic.edu
- Mike Juenger, Athletic Director
- Kathy Bernal, Asst. Athletic Director
- Neil Fiala, Athletic Program Coordinator
- Vicki Channer, Administrative Assistant
Enrollment:
6860
Mascot:
Blue Storm.

NJCAA REGION XXIV WOMEN'S
JOHN A. LOGAN COLLEGE
700 LOGAN COLLEGE RD
CARTERVILLE, IL 62918
618-985-3741
Fax: 618-985-6610
- Jerry Halstead, Athletic Director
(618) 985-3741
jerryhalstead@jalc.edu
- Robert Mees, President
Enrollment:
5301
Mascot:
Volunteers.

SPORTING GOODS AGENTS ASSOCIATION (SGAA)
PO BOX 998
GROVE, IL 60053
847-296-3670
Fax: 847-827-0196
sgaa998@aol.com
- Lois Hamilton, Chief Operating Officer
- Skip Nipper, President
- Tracy Paoletti, Vice President
- James Riebandt, Legal Counsel
Manufacturers:
Associations
Year Founded:
1934
Membership Requirements:
An applicant must be the principal of his or her agency for at least one year and act as an independent agent or independent contractor, representing one or more lines in the sporting goods business.
Number of Members:
500

U.S. COLLEGIATE SPORTS COUNCIL
C/O NICHOLAS RODIS, EXECUTIVE DIRECTOR
BRANDEIS UNIVERSITY
415 SOUTH ST
WALTHAM, MA 2454-9110
781-736-3657
Fax: 781-736-3656
- Fred Lawrence, President
(781) 736-3001
- Michael Doonan, PhD, Executive Director

Description:
Founded 1967. Selects teams for the World University Games.
Membership Requirements:
National collegiate sports bodies. National Collegiate Coaches Associations. National governing bodies for those sports included on World University Games calendar.

UNITED STATES COLLEGIATE ATHLETIC ASSOCIATION/USCAA
739 THIMBLE SHOALS BLVD
SUITE 1011 E
NEWPORT NEWS, VA 23606
757-706-3756
Fax: 757-706-3758
info@theuscaa.com
www.theuscaa.com
- Bill Casto, Executive Director
billcasto@cox.net
- Matthew Simms, COO
(757) 534-9229
Description:
Provides a national organization to hold national championships, name all-americans, scholar-athletes and promote USCAA member schools. The USCAA was incorporated to provide an opportunity for smaller college members to compete on an equal level of competition with schools of like size and athletic programs.
Year Founded:
2001

College Athletic Conferences

AMERICA EAST CONFERENCE
215 FIRST STREET
SUITE 140
CAMBRIDGE, MA 02110-1605
617-695-6369
Fax: 617-695-6380
americaeast@americaeast.com
www.americaeast.com
- Patrick Nero, Commissioner
(617) 695-6369
nero@americaeast.com
- Frank Sullivan, Assoc Commissioner Men's Basketball
(617) 695-6369
sullivan@americaeast.com
- Chad Dwyer, Director of Championships/Sports Administrator
(617) 695-6369
dwyer@americaeast.com
Members:
University at Albany, Binghamton University, Boston University, University of Hartford, University of Maine, University of New Hampshire, Baltimore County (UMBC), Stony Brook University, University of Vermont.
Year Founded:
1979
Description:
America East has evolved into one of the most comprehensive NCAA Division I conferences with a commitment to broad-based, competitive athletics programs, complementing the academic integrity and missions of the member institutions.

AMERICAN SOUTHWEST CONFERENCE
1221 W CAMPBELL RD
SUITE 171
RICHARDSON, TX 75080
972-234-0033
Fax: 972-234-4110
info@americansouthwestconf.org
www.americansouthwestconf.org
• R Morgan, President
• Tom Cedel, Vice President
Year Founded:
1996
Description:
A group of institutions with similar educational and athletic philosophies. The ASC was founded to provide a structure for intercollegiate athletics among the member institutions.
Member Schools:
Austin College, Concordia University at Austin, East Texas Baptist University, Hardin-Simmons University, Howard Payne University, LeTourneau university, Louisiana College, Mississippi College, McMurry University, Sul Ross State University, Schreiner University, Texas Lutheran University, University of the Ozarks, University of Texas at Tyler

APPALACHIAN ATHLETIC CONFERENCE
PO BOX 19371
ASHEVILLE, NC 28815
828-669-8011
sid@aacsports.com
www.aacsports.com
• John Sullivan, Commissioner
(828) 298-8822
commissioner@aacsports.com
• Bill Popp, Vice President
(770) 720-5568
WCP@reinhardt.edu
• Jay Stancil, Sports Information Director
(606) 546-1292
sid@aacsports.com
• Barb Robinson, Assistant to the Commissioner
(828) 230-3150
robinson.barb13@gmail.com
• Larry Inkster, Faculty Athletic Representative
linkster@unionky.edu
• Bill Greer, NAIA COP Representative
bgreer@milligan.edu
Member Schools:
Bluefield College, Bryan College, Milligan College, Montreat College, Point University, St. Andrews University, SCAD Atlanta, Reinhardt University, Tennessee Wesleyan College, and Union College.
Description:
The mission of the Conference is to promote the education and development of students and to provide athletic competition among its member institutions for the purpose of designating champions in sponsored sports, to increase visibility of its members to their publics, and to promote the highest ethical standards of character, conduct, sportsmanship, and fair play.

ATLANTIC 10 CONFERENCE
11827 CANON BLVD.
SUITE 200
NEWPORT NEWS, VA 23606
757-706-3042
Fax: 757-706-3042
www.atlantic10.com/

• Bernadette V McGlade, Commissioner
BMcGlade@atlantic10.org
• Jay DeFruscio, Associate Commissioner
JDeFruscio@atlantic10.org
• Mitchell Kendall, Associate Commissioner/Finance
• Jill Redmond, Assistant Commissioner/Compliance & Governance
• Caitlin Bonner, Director of Advanced Media
CBonner@atlantic10.org
• Lucas Feller, Assistant Commissioner/Administration & Operations
lFeller@atlantic10.org
Year Founded:
1976
Publications:
Media press guides, post season tournament guides, annually. Weekly press releases throughout academic year. Men's Basketball Fan Guide.
Description:
The idea of what is now the Atlantic 10 Conference was conceived. What started as an eight-school, men's basketball-only affiliation has grown into a 14-university, 21-sport league that is universally hailed as one of the best conferences in the country.
Member Schools:
University of Delaware, University of North Carolina at Charlotte, University of Dayton, Hofstra University, Duquesne University, James Madison University, Fordham University, University of Maine, University of Massachusetts, George Washington University, University of New Hampshire, LaSalle University, Northeastern University, University of Rhode Island, University of Richmond, Towson University, St. Bonaventure University, Villanova University, Saint Joseph's University, Saint Louis University, College of William & Mary, Temple University, Xavier University.

ATLANTIC COAST CONFERENCE
4512 WEYBRIDGE LANE
GREENSBORO, NC 27407
336-854-8787
Fax: 336-854-8797
feedback@theacc.org
www.theacc.com
• John D Swofford, Commissioner
• Mike Finn, Associate Commissioner/Football Communications
• W. Scott McBurney, Assoc. Commissioner of Advanced Media
• Nora Lynn Finch, Assoc Commissioner Women's Basketball/SWA
• Mike Burgemeister, Assoc. Commissioner Compliance/Governance
• Amy Yakola, Assoc Commissioner Public Realtions/Marketing
• Heather Hirschman, Website Coordinator
Year Founded:
1953
Description:
Provides athletic competition for baseball, men's and women's basketball, men's and women's cross country, women's field hockey, football, men's and women's golf, men's and women's indoor track, men's and women's outdoor track, men's and women's Lacrosse, men's and women's rowing, men's and women's soccer, women's softball, men's and women's swimming, men's and women's tennis, women's volleyball and wrestling.
Membership Requirements:

Must be voted upon by existing members.
Number of Members:
12
Members:
Boston College, Clemson University, Duke University, Florida State University, Georgia Institute of Technology, University of Louisville, University of Miami, University of North Carolina at Chapel Hill, North Carolina State University, University of Notre Dame, University of Pittsburgh, Syracuse University, University of Virginia, Virginia Tech, Wake Forest University
Corporate Sponsors:
RBC Centura, Alltel, Pepsi, Aquafina, Geico, Progress Energy, Chick-fil-A, Jeep, Chrysler, Food Lion.

ATLANTIC SUN CONFERENCE
3370 VINEVILLE AVE, STE 108-B
MACON, GA 31204-0790
478-474-3394
Fax: 478-474-4272
www.atlanticsun.org
• Ted Gumbart, Commissioner
(478) 474-3394
• Meredith Eaker, Associate Commissioner/Sports Administration
(478) 474-3394
• Mike Hagen, Asst. Commissioner for Compliance
(478) 474-3394
• Patrick McCoy, Assistant Director of Media Relations
• Keith Hendrix, Director for Championships
(478) 474-3394
• Melody Battle, Executive Assistant/Office Manager
(478) 474-3394
• Olivia Walter, Director of Broadcast Services
(478) 474-3394
Year Founded:
1978
Publications:
Men's BASKETBALL MEDIA GUIDE, annual; Women's BASKETBALL MEDIA GUIDE, annual; Men's RECORD BOOK, annual; Women's RECORD BOOK, annual; Officials Directory, annual; Prospectus for each conference sport, annually; Phone Directory, annually.
Membership Requirements:
NCAA Div I.
Description:
Organizes and promotes conference championships in baseball, basketball, cross country, golf, soccer, softball, tennis, volleyball.
Members:
Belmont Bruins, Campbell Camels, East Tennessee State Bucs, Florida Atlantic Owls, Gardner-Webb Bulldogs, Jacksonville Dolphins, Kennesaw State Owls, Lipscomb Bisons, Mercer Bears, North Florida Ospreys, Stetson Hatters.

BIG 12 CONFERENCE
2201 STEMMONS FREEWAY
28TH FL
DALLAS, TX 75207-2805
214-742-1212
Fax: 214-753-0145
www.big12sports.com
• Bob Bowlsby, Commissioner
• Tim Weiser, Deputy Commissioner
• Tim Allen, Sr. Associate Commissioner

BIG EAST CONFERENCE
655 THIRD AVENUE
NEW YORK, NY 10017
646-663-3444
Fax: 646-838-8304
www.bigeast.com
• Val Ackerman, Commissioner
vackerman@bigeast.com
• Lisa Zanecchia, Assistant to
Commissioner
• Nicholas Carparelli, Senior Associate
Commissioner
• James Greene, Director of Championships
• Tom Odjakjian, Associate Commissioner
• Donna DeMarco, Associate Commissioner
• Sara Naggar, Communications Director
• John Paquette, Associate Commissioner,
Sports Media Relations
jpaquette@bigeast.com
• Susan Eaton, Business Affairs Director
• Briana Weiss, Director of Conference
Operations
bweiss@bigeast.com
• Jackie Finn, Manager, Social Media and
Marketing Operations
jfinn@bigeast.com
• Brad Zakn, Manager, Digital Media
bzak@bigeast.com
Description:
Conducts championships, oversees
activities of the member schools. Men's
sports include baseball, football, cross
country, indoor track, outdoor track, golf,
tennis, soccer, swimming, basketball.
Women's sports include basketball, cross
country, field hockey, lacrosse, indoor track,
outdoor track, softball, swimming, tennis,
volleyball.
Membership Requirements:
Must be voted and approved by existing
membership. Must be 4-year school.
Publications:
BIGEAST newsletter.
Year Founded:
1979
Member Schools:
Butler University, Creighton University,
DePaul University, Georgetown University,
Marquette University, Providence College,
St. John's University, Seton Hall University,
Villanova University, Xavier University.
Corporate Sponsors:
OppenheimerFunds, Turn Heads,
Aeropostale, Comcast, Amtrak, Gatorade,
7-UP, Cooper Tires, MBNA.

BIG SKY CONFERENCE
2491 WASHINGTON BLVD, STE 201
OGDEN, UT 84401
801-392-1978
Fax: 801-392-5568
jkasper@bigskyconf.com
www.bigskyconf.com
• Ron Loghry, Senior Associate, Deputy
Commissioner
(801) 392-1978
• Doug Toole, Football Officials Coordinator
• Marla Denham, Coordinator of Basketball,
Volleyball Officials
• Jaynee Nadolski, Asst.
Commissioner/Championships Info
• Jon Kasper, Asst. Commissioner of Media
Relations
(801) 392-1978
jkasper@bigskyconf.com
• Doug Fullerton, Commissioner
(801) 392-1978
• Janet Carpenter, Administrative Assistant

(801) 392-1978
• Natanee Spencer, Business Manager
(801) 392-1978
• Jason Ashcraft, Media Relations Director
(801) 392-1978
• Dave Champlin, Director of Corporate
Partnerships
(801) 660-7066
Description:
Conducts championships in cross country,
basketball, golf, women's soccer, tennis,
indoor and outdoor track and volleyball.
Number of Members:
8
Year Founded:
1963
Affiliation:
NCAA, Division I-AA in football, Division I in
all other sports.
Member Schools:
Eastern Washington University, Idaho State,
University of Montana, Montana State
University-Bozeman, Northern Arizona
University, Portland State University,
California State University-Sacramento,
Weber State University.
Sponsors:
Hampton Inn Spokane, Red Lion Hotels,
Holiday Inn Spokane Airport, Spokane
Airport Ramada Inn, Hilton Garden Inn
Missoula, Best Western Grain Tree Inn,
Holiday Inn Flagstaff, Ramada Limited,
Fairfield Inn-Marriot, Days Inn in Flagstaff,
Hilton Sacramento Arden West, Double
Tree Sacramento, Sacramento Marriot
Rancho Cordova, Hampton Inn Layton,
Hampton Inn & Suites-Ogden, Holiday Inn
Express-Layton, Ogden Marriot, BestRest
Inn, Fairfield Inn by Marriott, TownPlace
Suites by Marriott, Courtyard by
Marriott-Layton, Hilton Garden Inn-Layton,
Sterling Savings Bank, Baden Sports,
Wilson Sporting Goods.

BIG SOUTH CONFERENCE
7233 PINEVILLE-MATTHEWS ROAD
SUITE 100
CHARLOTTE, NC 28226
704-341-7990
Fax: 704-341-7991
bigsouth@bigsouth.org
www.bigsouthsports.com
• Kyle Kallander, Commissioner
(704) 341-7990
• Jeff Jackson, Deputy Commissioner
• Mark Simpson, Assistant Commissioner
Public Relations
(704) 341-7990
• Chad Cook, Associate Commissioner
Marketing
(704) 341-7990
• Mark Bryant, Director of Multimedia
Development
(704) 341-7990
• Matt VanSandt, Director of Championships
(704) 341-7990
• Stephanie Roe, Director of Administration
(704) 341-7990
Year Founded:
1983
Number of Members:
11
Description:
Developing leadership through athletics.
Member Schools:
Campbell, Charleston Southern, Coastal
Carolina, Gardner-Webb, High Point,
Liberty, Presbtierian College, Radford, UNC

Asheville, VMC, Winthrop.
Publications:
Football Media Guide, Fan Guide,
Basketball Media Guide.

BIG TEN ATHLETIC CONFERENCE
1500 W. HIGGINS RD
PARK RIDGE, IL 60068-6300
847-696-1010
Fax: 847-696-1150
www.bigten.org
• James E Delany, Commissioner
• Wendy Fallen, Associate Commissioner,
Championships
• Chad Hawley, Associate Commissioner,
Compliance
• Mark Rudner, Senior Associate
Commissioner, Television Admin.
• Wayne Baskerville, Associate
Commissioner
• Brad Traviolia, Deputy
Commissioner/COO/CFO
• Teri Lenth, Corporate Sponsorships
Director
• Josh Munk, Associate Director of Football
Operations
• Bill Carollo, Football Officials Coordinator
• Patty Broderick, Women's Basketball
Officials Coord.
• Rick Boyages, Associate Commissioner,
Men's Basketball
• Jade Burroughs, Director, Branding
• Jessica Palermo, Director, Championships
• Kerry Kenny, Director, Compliance
• Scott Bailey, General Manager
Description:
An association of 11 world-class universities
who member institutes share a common
mission of research, graduate, professional
and undergraduate teaching and public
service.
Corporate Sponsors:
Cooper Tires, U.S. Bank, Liberty Mutual,
Gatorade, Ramada Worldwide, Under
Armour, 7-UP, Xbox Live.
Publications:
GAMETRACKER newsletter, SCORE, Big
Ten Records Book.
Year Founded:
1896
Member Schools:
University of Illinois, Indiana University,
University of Iowa, University of Michigan,
Michigan State University, University of
Minnesota, Northwestern University, Ohio
State University, Penn State University,
Purdue University, University of Wisconsin.

BIG WEST CONFERENCE
2 CORPORATE PARK, STE 206
IRVINE, CA 92606
949-261-2525
Fax: 949-261-2528
dfarrell@bigwest.org
www.bigwest.org
• Dennis Farrell, Commissioner
dfarrell@bigwest.org
• Rob Halvaks, Deputy Associate
Commissioner
rhalvaks@bigwest.org
• Jody McRoberts, Sr. Associate
Commissioner
jmcroberts@bigwest.org
• Mike Daniels, Assistant Commissioner
Marketing
• Mike Villamor, Assistant Commissioner
• Erica Satterfield, Assistant Commissioner
Compliance

• Christopher Hargraves, Assistant Information Director
chargraves@bigwest.org
• Julie St. Cyr, Director of Communications
jstcyr@bigwest.org
• Steve Chen, Director of New Media
Year Founded:
1969
Membership Requirements:
Must be voted/approved by the existing membership. Must be a 4-year school.
Publications:
Big West Conference Baseball, Men's & Women's Basketball, Softball, Volleyball Media Guides, annual.
Number of Members:
8
Description:
Providing a competitive athletic conference for institutions in the great state of California. It is also the home to prestigious California institutions that are at the forefront of academic success.

CALIFORNIA COLLEGIATE ATHLETIC ASSOCIATION
1350 TREAT BOULEVARD
SUITE 285
WALNUT CREEK, CA 94597
925-472-8299
Fax: 925-472-8887
www.goccaa.org
• Nathan Salant, Esq., Commissioner
(205) 999-8375
• Rebecca Bennett, Director of Communications
(925) 472-8299
• Bill Fusco, President
• Al Barba, Asst. Commissioner/Media Relations
(925) 472-8299
• Bill White, Officiating Coordinator
• Christine Halsey, Sr. Woman Administrator Coordinator
• Carol Rivera, Assistant Commissioner/Compliance and Internal Ops
(925) 472-8299
• John McCasey, Director of Championships and Marketing
(925) 472-8299
Year Founded:
1938
Description:
CCAA has been one of the nation's most successful intercollegiate athletic conferences since its establishment. The institutions compete in seven women's and six men's CCAA-sponsored sports. Fall sports include men's and women's cross country, men's and women's soccer and women's volleyball. Men's and women's basketball are contested in the winter, and women's tennis, men's golf, men's and women's outdoor track & field, softball and baseball comprise spring competition.
Member Schools:
Cal Poly Pomona, Cal State Bakersfield, Cal State Dominguez Hills, Cal State L.A., Cal State San Bernardino, Cal State Stanislaus, Chico State, UC San Diego, San Francisco State and Sonoma State, California State University-Monterey Bay.
Number of Members:
12
Corporate Sponsors:
Apple Computer, Wilson Sporting Goods, Brine, Molten USA, Enterprise Rent-A-Car.

CAROLINAS-VIRGINIA ATHLETICS CONFERENCE
26 CUB DR
THOMASVILLE, NC 27360
336-884-0482
Fax: 336-884-0315
• Angela Tressel, Assistant Commissioner
(336) 884-0482
• Brook Patterson, Associate Commissioner
(336) 884-0482
Year Founded:
1938
Description:
Sponsors intercollegiate athletics in baseball, basketball, cross country, golf, soccer, softball, tennis, volleyball.
Member Schools:
Anderson University, Barton College, Belmont Abbey College, Coker College, Erskine College, Lees-McRae College, Limestone College, Mount Olive College, Pfeiffer University, Queens University of Charlotte, St. Andrews Presbyterian College, Converse College.
Number of Members:
12

CASCADE COLLEGIATE CONFERENCE
C/O SOUTHERN OREGON UNIVERSITY
1250 SISKIYOU BLVD
ASHLAND, OR 97520
541-552-7672
Fax: 541-552-6543
www.cascadeconference.org
• Robert Cashell, Commissioner
(541) 605-0137
ccccommish@gmail.com
• Mickie Bush, Eligibility Coordinator
(503) 494-1277
mickiebush@gmail.com
• Sam Ghrist, Conference Statistician
(541) 962-3929
sam.ghrist1@frontier.com
Description:
Intercollegiate athletics men's and women's conference Sports include baseball, men's and women's basketball, men's and women's cross country, softball, track & field, women's volleyball.
Member Schools:
Albertson College, Cascade College, Concordia University, Corban College (formerly Western Baptist College), Eastern Oregon University, Evergreen State College, Northwest University, Oregon Institute of Technology, Southern Oregon University, Warner Pacific College.
Affiliation:
National Association of Intercollegiate Athletics.

CENTENNIAL CONFERENCE
563 COLLEGE AVE, STE B-101
LANCASTER, PA 17603
717-358-4463
Fax: 717-358-4480
steve.ulrich@centennial.org
www.centennial.org
• Kimberly Wenger, Associate Director
(717) 358-4463
kimberly.wenger@centennial.org
Year Founded:
1981
Description:
The Centennial Conference encourages athletic competition among national liberal arts colleges and universities that share

similar academic aspirations and a commitment to the importance of the total educational experience of students engaged in sports. Intercollegiate athletics programs are an integral part of the life of the member institutions and flow from their educational objectives. Each institution provides a comprehensive, broad-based athletics program. All varsity sports are treated equitably, and every sport is important.
Member Schools:
Bryn Mawr College, Dickinson College, Franklin & Marshall College, Gettysburg College, Haverford College, Johns Hopkins University, McDaniel College, Muhlenberg College, Swarthmore College, Ursinus College, Washington College.
Publications:
THE CENTENNIAL CONFERENCE MANUAL.

CENTRAL ATLANTIC COLLEGIATE CONFERENCE
111 WATER ST
PO BOX 35751
NEW HAVEN, CT 06525
203-298-4806
Fax: 203-773-6450
www.caccathletics.org
• Dan Mara, Internal Operations
(203) 298-4809
• Ellen O'Brien, Associate Commissioner/SWA
(203) 298-4807
eobrien@caccathletics.org
• Doug DeBaise, Assistant Commissioner for Strategic Communic
(203) 298-4806
• Allison McDonald, Internal Operations
(203) 298-4809
Member Schools:
Bloomfield College, Caldwell College, Dominican College, Felician College, Georgian Court College, Goldey-Beacom College, Holy Family College, NJIT College, Nyack College, Philadelphia University, Teikyo Post College, University of the Sciences in Philadelphia, Wilmington College.
Description:
Intercollegiate athletics conference.

CENTRAL INTERCOLLEGIATE ATHLETIC ASSOCIATION
22 ENTERPRISE PARKWAY
SUITE 210
HAMPTON, VA 23666
757-865-0071
Fax: 757-865-8436
TheCIAA@aol.com
www.theciaa.com
• Jacqie McWilliams, Commisioner
(757) 865-0071
• Jessica Incorminias, Assistant To The Commissioner
(757) 865-0071
jincorminias@ciaa.com
• Eddie Weatherington, Associate Commissioner of Governance/Complian
(757) 865-0071
eweatherington@theciaa.com
• Sherry Shaw, Associate Commissioner of Business Operations
(757) 865-0071
sshaw@theciaa.com
• Suzette McQueen, Assistant Commissioner of External Operations

(757) 865-0071
smcqueen@theciaa.com
Year Founded:
1912
Description:
An athletic conference consisting of historically African-American institutions of higher education.
Number of Members:
13
Member Schools:
Bowie State University, Elizabeth City State University, Fayetteville State University, Johnson C. Smith University, Livingstone College, North Carolina Central University, St. Augustine's College, St. Paul's College, Shaw University, Virginia State University, Virginia Union University, Winston-Salem State University.
Membership Requirements:
Historically black colleges and universities.

CENTRAL STATES FOOTBALL LEAGUE
709 OKLAHOMA BLVD
ALVA, OK 73717
580-327-8653
Fax: 508-772-3159
rshintergardt@nwosu.edu
• Andy Carter, Director of Athletics
(580) 327-8632
• Ryan Kaiser, Associate Director of Athletics for Internal
(580) 327-8578
• Wendy McManus, Associate Director of Athletics for Complianc
(580) 327-8632
Description:
Intercollegiate football league which represents five schools within the National Association of Intercollegiate Athletics.
Member Schools:
Bacone College, Northwestern Oklahoma State University, Peru State College, Southern Nazarene University, Texas College.
Year Founded:
2000

CHICAGOLAND COLLEGIATE ATHLETIC CONFERENCE
500 WILCOX STREET
JOLIET, IL 60435
815-740-3842
Fax: 815-740-3841
dlaketa@stfrancis.edu
www.ccacsports.com
• Dave Laketa, Interim Commissioner
dlaketa@stfrancis.edu
• Peter Haring, Vice Commissioner/Treasurer
(219) 473-4327
• Jeff Schimmelpfenning, Commissioner
(815) 592-5303
ccacjeff@gmail.com
• Tony Grimm, FAR/Eligibility Chairperson
(815) 939-5108
tgrimm@olivet.edu
Description:
An affiliated conference of the National Association of Intercollegiate Athletics. The CCAC sanctions play in five mens sports which are soccer, cross country, basketball division I, basketball division II, and baseball. There are six sanctioned womens sports which are soccer, volleyball, cross country, basketball division I, basketball division II, and softball. In all sports, it

sanctions regular season league play as well as a post-season tourney. It is the only conference in the NAIA nationally to be affiliated in both divisions of mens and womens basketball.
Year Founded:
1949
Member Schools:
Calumet St. Joseph, Cardinal Stritch, Holy Cross, Illinois Tech, Indiana, South Bend, Judson, Olivet Nazarene, Purdue Calumet, Purdue North Central, Robert Morris, Roosevelt, Saint Xavier, St. Francis, Trinity Christian, Trinity International
Number of Members:
15 Schools

CITY UNIVERSITY OF NEW YORK/CUNY ATHLETIC CONFERENCE
LEHMAN COLLEGE
250 BEDFORD PARK BOULEVARD W
BRONX, NY 10468
718-960-8000
Fax: 718-960-7194
dgansell@yahoo.com
www.lehman.edu
• Martin Zwiren, Athletics Director
martin.zwiren@lehman.cuny.edu
• Andrew Pearson, Sports Information Director/Intramurals Coord
andrew.pearson@lehman.cuny.edu
• Nichole Kieltyka, Athletic Trainer
nichole.kieltyka@lehman.cuny.edu
Year Founded:
1987
Description:
Sponsored sports include baseball, basketball (M & W), cross-country (M & W), soccer, softball, tennis (M & W), swimming & diving (M&W), track & field (indoor and outdoor/M & W), volleyball (M & W), Member schools include Bernard M. Baruch Col., Bronx CC, Brooklyn Col., City Col. of NY, Herbert H. Lehman Col., Hostos CC, Hunter Col., John Jay Col., Kingsborough Com. Col., New York City Technical College, Borough of Manhattan Community Col., Medgar Evers Col., New York City Tech. Col., Queensborough Community Col., Col. of Staten Island, York Col. (NY).
Member Schools:
Baruch College, Brooklyn College, The City College of New York, Hunter College, John Jay College, Lehman College, Medgar Evers College, New York City College of Technology, The College of Staten Island, York College.
Publications:
CUNY SPORTS newsletter.

COLLEGE CONFERENCE OF ILLINOIS AND WISCONSIN
C/O CHRIS MARTIN, COMMISSIONER
30 N. BRAINARD ST #402
NAPERVILLE, IL 60540
630-637-56934
Fax: 630-637-5694
cmartin@cciw.org
www.cciw.org
• Chris Martin, Commissioner
(630) 637-5693
cmartin@cciw.org
• Bill Carollo, Coordinator of Football Officials
carollo@bigten.org
• Justin Basovsky, Coordinator of Volleyball Officials

(847) 553-5297
footin86@hotmail.com
• Steve Siomos, Coordinator of Men's & Women's Soccer Officia
(630) 258-0883
siomos@aol.com
• Al Raya, Coordinator of Women's Basketball Officials
(773) 539-7938
arref_bb@yahoo.com
• Mike Krizman, Asst. Commissioner/Sports Info Dir.
(630) 637-5719
mkrizman@cciw.org
Year Founded:
1969
Description:
The CCIW exists to serve a select group of private colleges and universities of similar size and heritage, which share a deep commitment to superior undergraduate education and a common perspective on the role of intercollegiate athletics in that education.
Number of Members:
8
Member Schools:
Augustana College, Carthage College, Elmhurst College, Illinois Wesleyan University, Millikin University, North Central College, North Park University, Wheaton College.
Corporate Sponsors:
Select Sport America, Wilson Sporting Goods, Molten USA, Diamond Sports, Choice Hotels, La Quinta Inns & Suites, National Car Rental.

COLONIAL ATHLETIC ASSOCIATION
8625 PATTERSON AVE
RICHMOND, VA 23229
804-754-1616
Fax: 804-754-1973
www.caasports.com
• Jerry Stone, Senior Associate Commissioner
• Kathleen Batterson, Sr Assoc Commissioner/Internal Operations/SWA
• Robert Goodman, Sr Associate Commissioner, Marketing/Developm
• Rob Washburn, Asst. Commissioner of Communications
• Melissa Conti, Asst. Commissioner of Championships
• Brad Gregg, Operations Director
• Pamela Stone, Officiating Administrator
Description:
The CAA conducts championships in 21 sports. Male athletes compete for championships in baseball, basketball, cross country, golf, lacrosse, soccer, swimming & diving, tennis, track & field and wrestling. Female athletes battle for conference titles in basketball, cross country, field hockey, golf, lacrosse, soccer, softball, swimming & diving, tennis, track & field and volleyball. The CAA will also begin sponsorship of a 12-team Division I-AA football league in the fall of 2007.
Member Schools:
University of Delaware, Drexel University, George Mason University, Hofstra University, James Madison University, Northeastern University, Old Dominion University, Towson University, University of North Carolina-Wilmington, Virginia Commonwealth University, College of William & Mary, Georgia State University.

Year Founded:
1986
Number of Members:
12

CONFERENCE USA
5201 N. O'CONNOR BLVD
STE 300
IRVING, TX 75039
214-774-1300
www.conferenceusa.com
• Judy MacLeod, Commissioner
• Catrina Gibson, Assistant Commissioner
for Business Affairs
• Courtney Morrison-Archer, Assistant
Commissioner of Media Relations
Year Founded:
1995
Description:
We embrace a new era with fresh faces and
a renewed commitment to excellence and
leadership in athletics, academics and
community involvement. All C-USA
institutions sponsor Division I-A football,
along with several other men's and women's
athletic programs, many of which compete
regularly for NCAA Championships. C-USA
sponsors competition in 19 sports - nine for
men (baseball, basketball, cross country,
football, golf, soccer, tennis and indoor and
outdoor track and field) and 10 for women
(basketball, cross country, golf, softball,
soccer, swimming and diving, tennis, indoor
and outdoor track and field and volleyball).
Member Schools:
East Carolina University, University of
Houston, Marshall University, University of
Memphis, Rice University, Southern
Methodist University, University of Southern
Mississippi, Tulane University, University of
Tulsa, University of Alabama at Birmingham.
Corporate Sponsors:
Aeropostale.

DAKOTA-10 ATHLETIC CONFERENCE
C/O LAVERN JESSEN, COMMISSIONER
DICKINSON STATE - MAIL BOX 9
DICKINSON, ND 58601
605-336-1095
Fax: 605-336-8976
jimdahl@pop.ctctel.com
• LaVern Jessen, Commissioner
• Thomas Flickema, President
• Jim Dahl, Sports Information Director
• Allen Dockter, Football Officials Supervisor
• Ben Franson, Basketball Officials
Supervisor
Year Founded:
1921
Description:
The DAC is a member of the NAIA and
promotes sportsmanship and well-rounded
athletic programs that contribute to the total
education process of each athlete.
Member Schools:
Black Hills State, Dakota State, Dickinson
State, Jamestown College, Mayville State,
Minot State, South Dakota Tech, Valley City
State.

EASTERN COLLEGE ATHLETIC
CONFERENCE/ECAC
1311 CRAIGVILLE BEACH RD
CENTERVILLE, MA 2632
508-771-5060
Fax: 508-771-9486

kroberts@ecac.org
www.ecac.org
• Dan Coonan, President/CEO
(508) 771-5060
dcoonan@ecac.org
• John Rollins, VP Administration/CFO
(508) 771-5060
jrollins@ecac.org
• Meghan O'Brien, Director Of Marketing
And Communications
(508) 771-5060
mobrien@ecac.org
Description:
The mission is to initiate, stimulate and
improve intercollegiate athletics programs
for student-athletes and to promote and
develop educational leadership, athletic
excellence and athletics participation.
Publications:
ECAC newsletter.

EASTERN INTERCOLLEGIATE ATHLETIC
CONFERENCE
1463 GRANTLAND PL
GREENSBORO, NC 27410
336-855-0391
Fax: 336-855-0391
• Kenneth Free, Commissioner
• Willie Jefferson, President
• Henry Smith, Vice President
• David Eikerenkotter, Secretary
• Dorothy Patterson, Treasurer/Staff
Secretary
• Rodney Johnson, Sports Information
Director
• John Russell, Basketball Officials
Supervisor
Year Founded:
1983
Description:
Originating from the Southeastern Athletic
Conference, the SEAC was founded by
Bethune-Cookman College, Claflin College,
Florida Memorial College, and Morris
College. In 1968, Voorhees College joined
the SEAC along with Edward Waters
College. Florida Memorial College relocated
its campus to Miami, Florida and dropped
out of the SEAC.
Member Schools:
Allen University, Barber-Scotia College,
Clafin University, Edward Waters College,
Morris College, Voorhees College.
Number of Members:
6

EMPIRE 8
104 YORKTOWN DR
ROCHESTER, NY 14616
585-581-0834
Fax: 585-581-1127
cmitrano@empire8.com
www.empire8.com
• Mark Zupan, President
zupan@elmira.edu
• Chuck Mitrano, Commissioner
cmitrano@empire8.com
• Janelle Zera, Associate Commissioner
jzera@empire8.com
• Timothy Farrell, Assistant Commissioner
(216) 751-8836
tfarrell@empire8.com
Year Founded:
1964
Description:
Intercollegiate conference holding
competition (men) in sports of baseball,

basketball, cross country, golf, indoor and
outdoor track, lacrosse, soccer, swimming,
tennis. Women's competition offered in
basketball, cross country, outdoor track,
soccer, swimming, tennis and volleyball.
Publications:
EMPIRE8 NEWS BULLETIN.
Member Schools:
Alfred University, Elmira College, Hartwick
College, Ithaca College, Nazareth College,
Rochester Institute of Technology, St. John
Fisher College, Utica College.
Membership Requirements:
Academic achievement as well athletic
prowess and sportsmanship on the playing
fields.

FLORIDA SUN CONFERENCE
FLAGLER COLLEGE
74 KING ST
ST. AUGUSTINE, FL 32084
904-829-6481
Fax: 904-810-2253
jamie.joss@erau.edu
www.thesunconference.com
• Mark Pope, Commissioner
(904) 819-6252
sinconference@aol.com
• Jennifer Rinnert, Athletic Trainer
(904) 819-6402
jrinnert@flagler.edu
• John Jordan, Sports Information Director
(904) 819-6465
jjordan@flagler.edu
Year Founded:
1990
Description:
The institutions in the conference believe in
strong educational commitment combined
with balanced athletic competition. Originally
formed in March 1990 as the Florida
Intercollegiate Athletic Conference (FIAC),
the FSC was established as a conference
for small independent institutions within the
NAIA. The name Florida Sun Conference
was adopted in 1992.
Member Schools:
Embry-Riddle University, Flagler College,
Florida Memorial College, Northwood
University, St. Thomas University,
Savannah College of Art and Design,
Warner Southern College, Webber
International University.
Number of Members:
8

FRONTIER CONFERENCE
966 COLORADO AVENUE
WHITEFISH, MT
fronconf@in-tch.com
www.frontierconference.com
• Charlie Gross, Athletic Director
(406) 447-5479
• Reagan Rossi, Athletic Director
(208) 459-5850
• Thomas Evans, President
(406) 657-1015
Year Founded:
1935
Description:
Sponsors athletic competition in men's and
women's basketball, men's football, golf and
women's volleyball. Montana State
University-Northern and University of Great
Falls are participants in wrestling.
Member Schools:
Carroll College, Eastern Oregon University,

Montana State University-Northern, Rocky Mountain College-Montana, Westminster College-Utah, University of Great Falls, University of Montana-Western, Montana Tech of the University of Montana, Lewis-Clark State College.

GOLDEN STATE ATHLETIC CONFERENCE
AZUSA PACIFIC UNIVERSITY
901 E. ALOSTA AVE
AZUSA, CA 91702
626-812-3097
Fax: 626-812-3068
chamlow@apu.edu
www.gsacsports.org
• Brian Gleason, Administrative Assistant
(626) 815-4538
• Sheri Pine, Sports Information Director
(909) 392-9225
Year Founded:
1986
Description:
The members are all church-related Christian colleges. They are purposely aligned to be similar in enrollment, academics, athletics and student life.
Number of Members:
11
Member Schools:
Azusa Pacific University, Biola University, California Baptist University, Concordia University, Fresno Pacific University, Hope International University, The Master's College, Point Loma Nazarene University, San Diego Christian College, Vanguard University, Westmont College.

GREAT LAKES INTERCOLLEGIATE ATHLETIC CONFERENCE
1110 WASHINGTON AVE
BAY CITY, MI 48708
989-894-2529
Fax: 989-894-2825
www.gliac.org
• Jeff Ligney, Commissioner
jligney@gliac.org
Year Founded:
1972
Description:
Championships in 21 sports, 11 for men and 10 for women.
Member Schools:
Ashland University, Ferris State University, University of Findlay, Gannon University, Grand Valley State University, Hillsdale College, Lake Superior State University, Mercyhurst College, Michigan Tech University, Northern Michigan University, Northwood University, Saginaw Valley State University, Wayne State University.
Corporate Sponsors:
Bastian Brothers & Co., HoopMatch.com, Enterprises Rent-A-Car, Rawlings, Molten USA, Schelde, Wilson.
Number of Members:
13

GREAT LAKES VALLEY CONFERENCE
PAN AM PLAZA
201 S. CAPITOL AVE, STE 560
INDIANAPOLIS, IN 46225
317-237-2105
Fax: 317-237-5632
Jim@glvc-sports.org
www.glvcsports.com
• Jim Naumovich, Commissioner
(317) 237-5633
jim@glvc-sports.org
• Tonya Charland, Assistant Commissioner, Compliance/Senior Wom
(317) 237-5636
tonya@glvc-sports.org
• Jeff Smith, Assistant Commissioner, Communications
(317) 237-2106
jeff@glvc-sports.org
• Jennifer DeMotte, Public Information Assistant
(317) 237-2106
glvcsports@gmail.com
• Wispeny Ellis, Assistant Commissioner
• John Meisel, President
• Erin Merz, Sports Information Director
Year Founded:
1972
Description:
Men's sports include baseball, basketball, cross country, golf, soccer and tennis; women's include basketball, cross country, softball, tennis, volleyball.
Member Schools:
Bellarmine College, Indiana Purdue/Fort Wayne, University of Indianapolis, Kentucky Wesleyan College, Lewis University, Quincy University, St. Joseph College, Southern Illinois University at Edwardsville, University of Southern Indiana, University of Wisconsin-Parkside.

GREAT PLAINS ATHLETIC CONFERENCE
4728 BIRCH WAY
SIOUX CITY, IA 51106
712-226-4722
Fax: 303-374-5868
corey.westra@gpacsports.com
www.gpacsports.com
• Corey Westra, Commissioner
• Lucas Mohrman, Assistant Commissioner
lucas.mohrman@gpacsports.com
Year Founded:
1969
Description:
An affiliated conference of the National Association of Intercollegiate Athletics (NAIA), consisting of 13 private, faith-based colleges and universities in Nebraska, Iowa and South Dakota.
Member Schools:
Briar Cliff University, Concordia University, Dakota Wesleyan University, Dana College, Doane College, Dordt College, Hastings College, Midland Lutheran College, Morningside College, Mount Marty College, Nebraska Wesleyan University, Northwestern College, University of Sioux Falls.

GULF COAST ATHLETIC CONFERENCE
LOUISIANA COLLEGE
1140 COLLEGE DR
PINEVILLE, LA 71360
318-487-7102
Fax: 318-487-7288
howell@lacollege.edu
www.gcaconf.com
• Steve Martin, Commissioner
(504) 382-7694
steveb22@msn.com
• Kiki Barnes, President
(504) 816-4752
kbarnes@dillard.edu
• Dennis Cousin, Vice President
(504) 520-7330
• Grace Flickinger, Faculty Athletic Representative
(504) 520-7526
gflickin@xula.edu
• Robin Bunting, Secretary/Treasurer
(318) 229-3791
albunting4@gmail.com
Number of Members:
10
Member Schools:
Belhaven College, Dillard University, Loyola University New Orleans, Louisiana State University-Shreveport, University of Mobile-Alabama, Spring Hill College, Southern University at New Orleans, Tougaloo College, William Carey College, Xavier University of Louisiana.
Membership Requirements:
NAIA Division I, a minimum of one men's and one women's sport in fall, winter, and spring seasons.
Member Services:
Provides championship comptetition in 12 men's and women's sports for member schools.

GULF SOUTH CONFERENCE
2101 PROVIDENCE PARK
STE 200
BIRMINGHAM, AL 35242
205-991-9880
Fax: 205-437-0505
gulfsout@ix.netcom.com
www.gscsports.org
• Jim Cavale, Director of Broadcasting
jimcavale@mac.com
• A.A. Moore, Assistant Sports Information Director
(205) 991-9880
aamoore@gscsports.org
• Michael Stagno, Assistant Sports Information Director
(205) 991-9880
gsccompliance@gmail.com
• Matt Wilson, Commissioner
• Michael Anderson, Assistant Commissioner
(205) 991-9880
mikeanderson@gscsports.org
• Andrea Anderson, Assistant Commissioner for Complaince
(205) 991-9880
gsccompliance@gmail.com
Year Founded:
1970
Description:
GSC members feature comprehensive athletic programs that compete for 14 official conference championships: football, men's and women's cross country, men's and women's soccer, women's volleyball, men's and women's basketball, baseball, softball, men's and women's tennis and men's and women's golf.
Number of Members:
17
Member Schools:
Alabama-Huntsville; Christian Brothers; Delta State; New Orleans; North Alabama; Valdosta State; West Alabama; West Florida; West Georgia
Publications:
Media Guides, Tournament, Championship Programs.

HEART OF AMERICA ATHLETIC CONFERENCE
15221 MIDLAND DR
SHAWNEE, KS 66217
913-631-5579
Fax: 913-631-5579
splack@comcast.net
• Larry Lady, Commissioner
(913) 631-5579
• Steven Minnis, President
(913) 360-7400
president@benedictine.edu
• Charlie Gertenmayer, Board of Governors Chair
(913) 360-7583
cgartenmayer@benedictine.edu
• Eric Montgomery, Director of Sports info. / Marketing
(520) 954-4098
Year Founded:
1970
Description:
A college athletic conference affiliated with the NAIA. Member institutions are located in Iowa, Kansas, and Missouri in the United States.
Member Schools:
Avila University, Baker University, Benedictine College, Central Methodist University, Culver-Stockton College, Evangel University, Graceland University, Lindenwood University, MidAmerica Nazarene University, Missouri Valley College, William Jewell College.

HORIZON LEAGUE
201 S. CAPITOL ST
STE 500
INDIANAPOLIS, IN 46225
317-237-5622
Fax: 317-237-5620
www.horizonleague.org
• Jonathan LeCrone, Commissioner
• Cindy French, Senior Executive Associate
• Alfreeda Goff, Sr. Assoc. Commissioner/Chief Staff
• Beth Opell, Finance Director
• Wayne Burrow, Asst Commissioner, Championships/Sports Admin
• Bill Potter, Communications Director
Year Founded:
1979
Description:
Originally founded as the Midwestern City Conference, the League was a men's-only sports conference until the 1986-87 academic year when it added women's athletics. The Horizon League offers 19 championships (nine men's sports and 10 women's sports). The League enjoys NCAA automatic qualification in baseball, men's basketball, women's basketball, men's golf, men's soccer, women's soccer, softball, men's tennis, women's tennis and women's volleyball.
Member Schools:
Butler University, Cleveland State University, University of Detroit Mercy, University of Illinois at Chicago, Loyola University Chicago, University of Wisconsin-Green Bay, University of Wisconsin-Milwaukee, Wright State University, Youngstown State University.
Corporate Sponsors:
American Family Insurance, Sprint, Bill Estes Chevrolet, Nike, Merrill Lynch, Sirius Satellite Radio, Wilson Sporting Goods.

Publications:
GAMETRACKER newsletter.

ILLINIBADGER FOOTBALL CONFERENCE
CONCORDIA UNIVERSITY
12800 N. LAKE SHORE DR
MEQUON, WI 53097
262-243-4544
Fax: 262-243-4475
james.saleska@cuw.edu
www.cuw.edu
• Robert Barnhill, Athletic Director
(262) 243-4404
• Rick Riehl, Sports Information Director
(262) 243-4544
Year Founded:
1881

IOWA INTERCOLLEGIATE ATHLETIC CONFERENCE
222 THIRD ST SE
STE 423
CEDAR RAPIDS, IA 52401
319-366-4845
Fax: 319-366-4911
www.iowaconference.com
• Chuck Yrigoyen, Commissioner
• Dan Hammes, Deputy Commissioner
• Paula Carlson, Chair, Presidents Council
Year Founded:
1922
Description:
The IIAC consists of independent, regionally accredited, residential four-year, liberal arts colleges that share common academic philosophies and goals and that place primary emphasis on the academic progress of students. To that end the athletic programs of IIAC member institutions facilitate the intellectual, spiritual and physical development of all students, whether as participants or spectators.
Member Schools:
Buena Vista University, Central College, Coe College, Cornell College, University of Dubuque, Loras College, Luther College, Simpson College, Wartburg College.
Publications:
IIAC Yearbook & Directory.

IVY LEAGUE GROUP
228 ALEXANDER ST
PRINCETON, NJ 8544
609-258-6426
Fax: 609-258-1690
info@ivyleaguesports.com
www.ivyleaguesports.com
• Robin Harris, Executive Director
robinharris@ivyleaguesports.com
• Carolyn Campbell-McGovern, Deputy Executive Director
carolyn@ivyleaguesports.com
Year Founded:
1954
Description:
Sponsoring conference championships in 33 men's and women's sports, and averaging more than 35 varsity teams at each school. The Ivy League provides intercollegiate athletic opportunities for more men and women than any other conference in the country.
Number of Members:
8
Member Schools:
Brown University, Columbia University,

Cornell University, Dartmouth University, Harvard University, Penn State University, Princeton University, Yale University.
Membership Requirements:
Must be voted on by existing members.

KANSAS COLLEGIATE ATHLETIC CONFERENCE
BETHANY COLLEGE
335 E SWENSSON STREET
LINDSBORG, KS 67456
785-227-3380 EXT 8456
Fax: 785-227-2021
www.kcacsports.com
• Scott Crawford, Commissioner
(316) 337-5999
scott.crawford@kcacsports.com
• Robert Brennecke, Assistant Commissioner
(316) 337-5999
• Heidi Hoskinson, Conference Registrar
(316) 295-5861
heidi_hoskinson@friends.edu
• Joyce Pigge, Eligibility Chairm
Year Founded:
1902
Description:
A prominent intercollegiate athletics conference comprised of outstanding independent or private institutions of higher education in the state.
Number of Members:
10
Member Schools:
Bethany Colllege, Bethel College, Friends University, Kansas Wesleyan University, McPherson College, Ottawa University, Southwestern College, Sterling College, Tabor College, University of Saint Mary.

KENTUCKY INTERCOLLEGIATE ATHLETIC CONFERENCE
C/O BILLY C. MELTON, COMMISSIONER
313 BOCOTE DRIVE
BEREA, KY 40403
859-200-3510
www.kiacsports.com
• Joe Glover, President Elect/Secretary
• Ken Pickerill, Eligibility Chair/FAR
• Bill Melton, Commissioner
Year Founded:
1918
Description:
An association organized to promote and enhance the competitive experience of intercollegiate athletics.
Member Schools:
Alice Lloyd College, Asbury College, Berea College, Bethel College, Brescia University, Indian University Southeast, Mid-Continent College, Midway College, Spalding University, St. Louis College of Pharmacy.

LITTLE EAST CONFERENCE
C/O JONATHAN G HARPER, COMMISSIONER
285 OLD WESTPORT ROAD
NORTH DARTMOUTH, MA 2747
860-677-1269
Fax: 860-674-8363
www.LittleEast.com
• Jack Holleran, Assistant Commissioner
(508) 910-6287
• Ian Day, Treasurer
(508) 999-8722
iday@umassd.edu
• John P. Clark, Executive Committee Chair

(603) 535-2770
• Jonathan Harper, Commissioner
(508) 910-6299
• Donald Tencher, Secretary/Treasurer
• Mike Christie, Communications Director
Year Founded:
1986
Description:
Sports sponsored include baseball, basketball, men's and women's cross country, men's and women's soccer, field hockey (women), lacrosse (men and women), softball, swimming (women) and tennis (men and women), track & field indoor/outdoor (men and women), volleyball (women).
Number of Members:
8
Member Schools:
Eastern Connecticut State University, Keene State College, Plymouth State College, Rhode Island College, University of Massachusetts-Boston, University of Massachusetts-Dartmouth, University of Southern Maine, Western Connecticut State University.

LONE STAR CONFERENCE
1221 W. CAMPBELL ROAD
SUITE 171
RICHARDSON, TX 75080
972-234-0033
Fax: 972-234-4110
lscinfo2003@yahoo.com
www.lonestarconference.org
• Jay Poerner, Commissioner
(972) 234-0033
jay@lonestarconference.org
• Melanie Robotham, Assistant Commissioner
(972) 234-0033
melanie@lonestarconference.org
• Danielle Anderson, Assistant Commissioner
(972) 234-0033
danielle@lonestarconference.org
• Cheryl Scott, Business Manager
(972) 234-0033
cheryl@lonestarconference.org
Year Founded:
1931
Description:
Conducts conference championships in 15 sports (seven men and eight women). Men's championships include football, cross country, basketball, baseball, track and field, tennis and golf. Women's titles are determined in volleyball, soccer, cross country, basketball, softball, track and field, tennis and golf.
Member Schools:
Abilene Christian University, Angelo State University, Cameron University, University of Central Oklahoma, East Central State University, Eastern New Mexico University, Midwest State University, Northeastern State University, Southeastern Oklahoma State University, Southwestern Oklahoma State University, Tarleton State, Texas A&M University-Commerce, Texas A&M University-Kingsville, Texas Woman's University, West Texas A&M University.
Membership Requirements:
Approval by faculty representatives of member universities.

MASSACHUSETTS STATE COLLEGE ATHLETIC CONFERENCE
BRIDGEWATER STATE COLLEGE
131 SUMMER STREET
TINSLEY CENTER
BRIDGEWATER, MA 02325
508-531-1000
Fax: 508-531-1356
www.bridgew.edu
• Michele Wakin, Executive Assistant to the President
(508) 531-1793
mwakin@bridgew.edu
• Sue Chapman, Assistant Commissioner
• Tim Shea, Vice President
• Carey Williams-Eggen, Media Relations/Web Site Director
Year Founded:
1971
Description:
Sponsors intercollegiate athletic competition in baseball, basketball, cross country, football, ice hockey, soccer, track (men) and basketball, cross country, field hockey, soccer, softball, track, volleyball (women).
Member Schools:
Bridgewater State, Fitchburg State, Framingham State, Massachusetts College, Massachusetts Maritime, Salem State, Westfield State, Worcester State.
Member Services:
Rules interpretation and establishment; conference championships; post-season tournaments.

METRO ATLANTIC ATHLETIC CONFERENCE
712 AMBOY AVENUE
EDISON, NJ 8837
732-738-5455
Fax: 732-738-8310
www.maacsports.com
• Richard J Ensor, Commissioner
(732) 738-5455
• Rob DeVita, Assistant Commissioner for New Media
(721) 738-5455
• Jessica Hegmann, Senior Associate Commissioner
• Jordan Confessore, Asst. Commissioner of Championships
Year Founded:
1980
Description:
Sports include men's basketball, women's basketball, baseball, men's and women's crew, men's and women's golf plus men's and women's cross country, men's and women's indoor & outdoor track, men's and women's lacrosse, men's and women's soccer, softball, men's and women's tennis, men's and women's swimming, women's volleyball.
Member Schools:
Canisius College, Fairfield University, Iona College, Loyola College, Manhattan College, Marist College, Niagara University, Rider University, Saint Peter's College, Siena College, Duquesne University, La Salle University, Le Moyne College, Mount St. Mary's University, Providence College, Saint Joseph's University, Virginia Military Institute, Wagner College, St. Francis College, Villanova University.
Membership Requirements:
NCAA Division I.
Corporate Sponsors:
Pepsi, Verizon Wireless, Fye, Fidelis Care, Anaconda Sports, I Love NY Tourism, New York State Lottery, JetBlue Airways, Verizon Yellow Pages, Aeropostale, Coach USA, Fox 40, Gatorade, Sirius Satellite Radio, Broadway Marketing Ltd.

MICHIGAN INTERCOLLEGIATE ATHLETIC ASSOCIATION
29488 WOODWARD AVE
SUITE 308
ROYAL OAK, MI 48073
248-336-1677
Fax: 248-547-3445
miaacommish@ameritech.net
www.miaa.org
• David Neilson, Commissioner
(248) 336-1677
• Greg Chandler, Publicist
(616) 392-8434
Year Founded:
1888
Description:
NCAA DIII Athletic Conference- The Nation's Oldest Collegiate Athletic Conference.
Member Schools:
Adrian College, Albion College, Alma College, Calvin College, Hope College, Kalamazoo College, Olivet College, Saint Mary's (IN) College, Trine University (IN)
Membership Requirements:
NCAA Division III affiliation, endorsement of the NCAA Division III mission statement and adherence to NCAA Division III rules and regulations.
Publications:
MIAA FACT FINDER.

MID-AMERICA INTERCOLLEGIATE ATHLETICS ASSOCIATION
114 W 11TH STREET
SUITE 105
KANSAS CITY, MO 64105
816-421-6422
www.themiaa.com/athletics
• Mike Racy, Commissioner
mracy@themiaa.com
• Larry House, Asst Commissioner Championships/Business Dev
(816) 421-6422
lhouse@themiaa.com
• Josh Slaughter, Communications Director
(816) 421-6422
Year Founded:
1912
Description:
Conducts conference championships in eight men's and eight women's sports. Men's championships include football, cross country, basketball, indoor and outdoor track and field, baseball, tennis, and golf. Women's champions are determined in volleyball, soccer, cross country, basketball, indoor and outdoor track and field, softball and tennis.
Member Schools:
Central Missouri State University, Emporia State University, Missouri Southern State University, Missouri Western State University, Northwest Missouri State University, Pittsburg State University, Southwest Baptist University, Truman State University, Washburn University.

MID-AMERICAN ATHLETIC CONFERENCE
24 PUBLIC SQUARE
15TH FLOOR
CLEVELAND, OH 44113-2213
216-566-4622
Fax: 216-696-2622
www.mac-sports.com
• Jon Steinbrecher, Commissioner
• Bob Gennarelli, Senior Associate Commissioner/COO
(216) 566-4622
• Korinth Patterson, Director of Compliance/Championships
(216) 566-4622
• Betty Sislak, Finance Director
(216) 566-4622
• Erin Dugan, Assoc Director Media Relations & External Aff
(216) 566-4622
• Jeremy Guy, Communications Director
(216) 566-4622
Year Founded:
1946
Nature of Sports Service:
For men, championships are sponsored in football, basketball, baseball, cross country, soccer, swimming and diving, indoor track and field, outdoor track and field, wrestling, golf and tennis. For women, championships are sponsored in basketball, softball, volleyball, cross country, field hockey, golf, soccer, swimming and diving, gymnastics, indoor track and field, outdoor track and tennis.
Member Schools:
University of Akron, Ball State University, Bowling Green State University, Central Michigan University, University at Buffalo, Kent State University, Miami University, Ohio University.
Membership Requirements:
Invitation only.
Publications:
Annual football, basketball, volleyball, baseball and softball media guides and annual records book for all other sports.

MID-CENTRAL COLLEGE CONFERENCE
INDIANA WESLEYAN UNIVERSITY
4201 S. WASHINGTON STREET
MARION, IN 46953
765-677-2318
Fax: 765-677-2328
mfratzke@indwes.edu
www.mid-centralconf.org
• Kyle Schmidt, Sports Information
(765) 677-1938
• J.D. Collins, Commissioner
(765) 748-1776
• Eric Smith, Sports Information Director
(765) 998-4569
• Karen Roorbach, Registar
• Gabriel Wallis, Sports Information Director/Webmaster
stats@thenccaa.org
Nature of Sports Service:
The purpose and function is to promote intercollegiate athletics in a well-rounded athletic program, maintain high ideas and promote sportsmanship. The members are encouraged to stress the supporting role of athletics in the total education process and keep athletics in proper prospective.
Member Schools:
Bethel College, Goshen College, Grace College, Huntington University, Indiana Wesleyan University, Marian College, Spring Arbor University, Taylor University, University of St. Francis.

MID-EASTERN ATHLETIC CONFERENCE
2730 ELLSMERE AVENUE
PO BOX 10247
NORFOLK, VA 23513
757-951-2055
Fax: 757-951-2076
www.meacsports.com
• Dennis Thomas, Commissioner
thomasd@themeac.com
• Raynoid Dedeaux, Assistant Commissioner of Championships
dedeauxr@themeac.com
• Sonja O. Stills, Associate Commissioner for Administration
stillss@themeac.com
• Ryan McGuinty, Assistant Commissioner for Media Relations
mcgintyr@themeac.com
Year Founded:
1970
Description:
Made up of 11 outstanding historically black institutions across Atlanta Coastline.
Member Schools:
Bethune-Cookman College, Coppin State University, Delaware State University, Florida A&M University, Hampton University, Howard University, University of Maryland-Eastern Shore, Morgan State University, Norfolk State University, North Carolina A&T State University, South Carolina State University.
Member Services:
Weekly statistics, results, standings and releases; newsletter.
Corporate Sponsors:
Coke, Delta, Nike, Russell Athletic, State Farm.

MID-SOUTH CONFERENCE
401 W. MAIN STREET
SUITE 2200
LOUISVILLE, KY 40202
502-587-7767
Fax: 502-587-6767
www.mid-southconference.org
• Steve Baker, Commissioner
(502) 587-7767
• Chris Wells, Sports Information Director
(270) 384-8071
wellsc@lindsey.edu
• Mark Mulloy, Sports Information/Media Relations
• Gene Lovel, Eligibility Chair
Year Founded:
1995
Description:
The conference is unique in its broad based athletic competition for men and women, offering championships in 15 sports. The presidents of each school serves on the Board of Directors which directly oversees the conference and the office of the commissioner. This administrative hands on role of each school's president is unique among athletic conferences and ensures a proper balance in the academic pursuits of student athletes.
Number of Members:
13
Member Schools:
Campbellsville University, University of the Cumberlands, Georgetown College, Lindsey Wilson College, Pikeville College, University of Rio Grande, St. Catharine College, Shawnee State University, University of Virginia at Wise, West Virginia University Institute of Technology. Affiliate Member Schools- Belhaven College, Bethel University, Cumberland University, Faulkner University, Kentucky Christian University, Shorter College, and Union College.

MIDDLE ATLANTIC STATES COLLEGIATE ATHLETIC CORPORATION
LEBANON VALLEY COLLEGE
101 N. COLLEGE AVENUE
ANNVILLE, PA 17003-0501
717-867-6395
Fax: 717-867-5008
andrews@lvc.edu
www.gomacsports.com
• Ken Andrews, Executive Director
(717) 645-9809
andrews@lvc.edu
• Marie Stroman, Coordinator of MAC 100
(717) 645-9786
stroman@lvc.edu
• Patrick Ross, Director of Media Relations
(570) 854-1137
ross@lvc.edu
• Tim Flynn, Sports Information Director
(717) 867-6033
• Erin Kolacek, Athletic Trainer
(717) 867-6269
kolacek@lvc.edu
Year Founded:
1912
Description:
Formerly called the Middle Atlantic States Collegiate Athletic Conference, it was originated 1912 as a loose confederation of colleges. It was unified into an actual all-sports playing conference in 1952, and is the largest Division III Conference holding NCAA associate membership.
Member Schools:
Albright College, Delaware Valley College, Drew University, Elizabethtown College, Fairleigh-Dickinson College at Fordham, Juniata College, King's College, Lebanon Valley College, Lycoming College, Messiah College, Moravian College, University of Scranton, Susquehanna University, Widener University, Wilkes University.
Publications:
FACT BOOK, annual.

MIDLANDS COLLEGIATE ATHLETIC CONFERENCE
C/O AL WALLER, COMMISSIONER
COLLEGE OF THE OZARKS
PO BOX 17
POINT LOOKOUT, MO 65726-0017
417-334-6411 EXT 4568
• Steve Eckman, President
• Al Waller, Commissioner/Secretary/Treasurer
(417) 690-2568
• Jerod Dahlgren, Information Director
(716) 775-6747
• Hal Hoxie, President
(620) 241-0723
• Joyce Pigge, Eligibility Chair
(785) 227-3380
Description:
The main objective is to promote the development of athletic programs as an integral part of the educational offerings of member institutions by means of democratic participation at the conference level.
Member Schools:

Bellevue University, Central Christian College of Saint Mary, College of the Ozarks, Haskell University, Newman University, Oklahoma Wesleyan University, Park University, Peru State College, York College.
Membership Requirements:
Colleges in the states of Kansas, Missouri, Nebraska and Oklahoma which offers a minimum of four years of academic work, awards the bachelor's degree, are active members of the National Association of Intercollegiate Athletics and are accredited by the North Central Association of Colleges and Secondary Schools. Members have compatible purposes and histories as private, liberal arts institution of high learning.

MIDWEST CONFERENCE
C/O CHRIS GRAHAM, COMMISSIONER
RIPON COLLEGE
300 SEWARD STREET
RIPON, WI 54971
920-748-8157
Fax: 920-748-8158
www.midwestconference.org
• Chris Graham, Commissioner
• Cory Weibel, Sports Information Director
Year Founded:
1921
Description:
Sponsors intercollegiate athletics in baseball, basketball, cross country, football, golf, soccer, swimming, tennis, indoor and outdoor track, wrestling for men; basketball, cross country, indoor and outdoor track, soccer, softball, swimming, tennis, volleyball for women.
Number of Members;
10
Member Schools:
Beloit College, Carroll College, Grinnell College, Illinois College, Knox College, Lake Forest College, Lawrence University, Monmouth College, Ripon College, St. Norbert College.

MINNESOTA INTERCOLLEGIATE ATHLETIC CONFERENCE
475 CLEVELAND AVENUE NORTH
SUITE 307
SAINT PAUL, MN 55104
651-644-3965
Fax: 651-647-6422
dpmckane@miacathletics.com
www.miacathletics.com
• Dan McKane, Executive Director
(651) 644-3964
dpmckane@miacathletics.com
• Matt Higgins, Assistant to the Executive Director
(651) 644-3965
Year Founded:
1920
Description:
Sponsors championships in 22 sports; 11 for men and 11 for women. Conference teams are all affiliated with the NCAA Division III and the MIAC is recognized as one of the toughest NCAA Division III intercollegiate athletic conferences in the country.
Number of Members:
13
Member Schools:
Augsburg College, Bethel University, Carleton College, Concordia Moorhead

College, Gustavus Adolphus College, Hamline University, Macalester College, College of St. Benedict, College of St. Catherine, St. John's University, St. Mary's University, St. Olaf College, University of St. Thomas.

MISSOURI VALLEY CONFERENCE
1818 CHOUTEAU AVENUE
ST. LOUIS, MO 63103
314-444-4300
Fax: 314-421-3505
kern@mvc.org
www.mvc.org
• Doug Elgin, Commissioner
(314) 444-4324
• Patty Viverito, Senior Associate Commissioner
(314) 444-4343
pattyv@mvc.org
• Jack R. Watkins, Associate Commissioner
• Greg Walter, Assistant Commissioner for Institutional Serv
• Mike Kern, Associate Commissioner Communications
(314) 444-4356
kern@mvc.org
Year Founded:
1907
Description:
Promotes the proper role of intercollegiate athletics in education. Encourages high standards of competitive performance and promotes good sportsmanship among individuals and institutions.
Member Schools:
Bradley University, Creighton University, Drake University, University of Evansville, Indiana State University, Illinois State University, Missouri State University, University of Northern Iowa, Southern Illinois University, Wichita State University.
Membership Requirements:
Division I in all sports. Institutions with complete faculty control of athletics.
Publications:
CENTENNIAL BOOK, SOFTBALL MEDIA GUIDE, BASEBALL MEDIA GUIDE, SOCCER MEDIA GUIDE, VOLLEYBALL MEDIA GUIDE, WOMEN'S BASKETBALL GUIDE, MEN'S BASKETBALL GUIDE, MVC TOURNAMENT PROGRAM.

MISSOURI VALLEY FOOTBALL CONFERENCE
1818 CHOUTEAU AVENUE
ST. LOUIS, MO 63103
314-444-4360
Fax: 314-444-4361
pattyV@mvc.org
www.valley-football.org

MOUNTAIN WEST CONFERENCE
15455 GLENEAGLE DRIVE
SUITE 200
COLORADO SPRINGS, CO 80921-2591
719-488—4040
Fax: 719-487-7240
www.themwc.com
• Craig Thompson, Commissioner
(719) 488-4047
• Bret Gilliland, Deputy Commissioner
(719) 488-4045
bgilliland@themwc.com
• Jaime Hixson, Assistant Commisioner
(719) 488-4049
jhixson@themwc.com

• Jim Andrus, Assoc. Commissioner Business/Finance
(719) 488-4020
jandrus@themwc.com
Year Founded:
1999
Description:
Committed to excellence in intercollegiate athletics, while promoting the academic missions of its member institutions. Progressive in its approach, the MWC continues to cultivate opportunities for student-athletes to compete at the highest level, while fostering academic achievement and sportsmanship. Now in its seventh year, the MWC has been assertive in its involvement with the NCAA governance structure and has taken a leadership role in the overall administration of intercollegiate athletics.
Member Schools:
U.S. Air Force Academy, Brigham Young University, Colorado State University, University of New Mexico, University of Nevada-Las Vegas, San Diego State University, University of Utah, University of Wyoming, Texas Christian University.

NEW ENGLAND FOOTBALL CONFERENCE
C/O SUE LAUDER, COMMISSIONER
FITCHBURG STATE COLLEGE
160 PEARL STREET
FITCHBURG, MA 01420
• John Harper, Commissioner
(508) 954-0621
thenefc8@gmail.com
• Roger Crosley, Publicity Director
(603) 606-1134
nefc_14@hotmail.com
Year Founded:
1965
Description:
Sponsors intercollegiate football competition.
Number of Members:
16
Member Schools:
Bridgewater State College, Curry College, Endicott College, Fitchburg State College, Framingham State College, Maine Maritime Academy, Massachusetts Maritime Academy, MIT, Nichols College, Plymouth State University, UMass Dartmouth, United States Coast Guard Academy, Salve Regina University, Western New England College, Westfield State College, Worcester State College.

NEW JERSEY ATHLETIC CONFERENCE
528 ALCYON BOULEVARD
PITMAN, NJ 08071
856-582-3679
Fax: 856-582-5877
www.njacsports.com
• Terry Small, Commissioner
(856) 582-3679
tsmall@njacsports.com
• Michelle Serabian, Assistant Commissioner
(609) 709-4291
mserabian@njacsports.com
Year Founded:
1985
Description:
Championships were originally offered in twelve sports: men's and women's

basketball, baseball, softball, women's volleyball, men's golf, men's and women's tennis, men's and women's swimming and diving, wrestling and football. Today, the NJAC hosts seventeen championships: nine for women (cross country, basketball, field hockey, soccer, softball, tennis, indoor track and field, outdoor track and field, volleyball) and seven for men (cross country, baseball, basketball, football, soccer, indoor track and field, outdoor track and field).

Member Schools:
Kean University, Montclair State University, New Jersey City University, Ramapo College, Richard Stockton College, Rowan University, Rutgers-Camden, Rutgers-Newark, College of New Jersey, William Patterson University, SUNY Cortland, Western Connecticut State University.

NEW YORK COLLEGIATE ATHLETIC CONFERENCE
733 THIRD AVENUE
SUITE 1910
NEW YORK, NY 10017
212-682-6318
Fax: 212-286-1243
gonycac@nycac.net
www.nycac.net
• Edward Manetta, Commissioner
• Billi Godsey, Assoc. Commissioner of Operations
• Bob Hartwell, President
• Jerry Milani, Assoc. Commissioner Media Relations
• Gerry Oswald, Treasurer
Description:
Commited to the highest standards of scholarship, sportsmanship, teamwork, and citizenship. Its mission is to promote the total person concept in its student-athletes which stresses the abilities to excel in academic achievement, athletic competition, and positive character traits.
Member Schools:
Adelphi University, Concordia College, Dowling College, Mercy College, Molloy College, L.I.U.-CW Post College, Queens College, University of Bridgeport, University of New Haven, St. Thomas Aquinas, New York Institute of Technology.

NORTH CENTRAL INTERCOLLEGIATE ATHLETIC CONFERENCE
RAMKOTA INN
3200 W. MAPLE
SIOUX FALLS, SD 57107
605-338-0907
Fax: 605-338-1889
• Roger Thomas, Commissioner
• Melanie Nelson, Interim Commissioner
• Jon Martin, Assistant Commissioner
• Colin Kapitan, Officials Coordinator
Year Founded:
1921
Description:
Promotes intercollegiate athletics and conducts men's championships in football, basketball, baseball, outdoor track, indoor track, cross country, wrestling, swimming, golf, tennis. Conducts women's championships in basketball, cross country, golf, indoor track, outdoor track, softball, swimming, tennis and volleyball.
Number of Members:
7

Member Schools:
Augustana College, University of Minnesota-Duluth, Minnesota State University-Mankato, University of Nebraska-Omaha, University of South Dakota, St. Cloud State University, University of North Dakota.

NORTH COAST ATHLETIC CONFERENCE
815 CROCKER ROAD
BUILDING B, SUITE 5
WESTLAKE, OH 44145
440-871-8100
Fax: 440-871-4221
www.northcoast.org
• Marvin Krislov, President
(330) 569-5120
marvin.krislov@hiram.edu
• Rock Jones, Vice President
(440) 871-8100
Year Founded:
1983
Description:
Dedicated to fostering a complementary relationship between intercollegiate athletics and the pursuit of academic excellence. Consisting of 10 academically selective colleges and universities in Ohio, Indiana and Pennsylvania.
Member Schools:
Allegheny College, Denison University, Earlham College, Hiram College, Kenyon College, Oberlin College, Ohio Wesleyan University, Wabash College, Wittenberg University, College of Wooster.

NORTHEAST CONFERENCE
399 CAMPUS DRIVE
SOMERSET, NJ 8873
732-469-0440
Fax: 732-469-0744
rbalut@northeastconference.org
www.northeastconference.org
• Noreen Morris, Commissioner
nmorris@northeastconference.org
• Ralph Ventre, Assistant Director of Communications
rventre@northeastconference.org
• Benjamin Shove, Sports Services Director
bshove@northeastconference.org
• Michelle Boone, Assistant Commissioner
mboone@northeastconference.org
• Rachelle Held, Assistant Commissioner of Compliance
rheld@northeastconference.org
Year Founded:
1981
Description:
A 21 sport conference committed to enhancing the experience of its student-athletes, while strengthening its competitive position both regionally and nationally.
Number of Members:
11
Member Schools:
Central Connecticut State Univ., Fairleigh Dickinson Univ., Long Island Univ., UMBC, Monmouth Univ., Mount St. Mary's College, Quinnipiac Univ., Robert Morris Univ., Sacred Heart Univ., St. Francis (NY) College, St. Francis (PA) Univ., Wagner College.

NORTHEAST-10 CONFERENCE
792 SOUTH MAIN STREET
SUITE 104
MANSFIELD, MA 02048
508-230-9845
www.northeast10.org
• Julie Ruppert, Commissioner
(508) 230-9844
jruppert@northeast10.org
• Kerri Fagan, Assoc. Commissioner For Sports Admin
(508) 230-9844
kfagan@northeast10.org
• Molly Belden, Associate Commissioner For Compliance
(508) 230-9844
mmyers@northeast10.org
Year Founded:
1979
Description:
Men's basketball & baseball, soccer, cross country, football, golf, lacrosse, tennis. Women's basketball, field hockey, volleyball, cross country, softball, tennis, soccer. Men's and Women's indoor & outdoor track & field.
Member Schools:
American International College, Assumption College, Bentley University, Bryant University, Franklin Pierce College, Le Moyne College, Merrimack College, Pace University, Saint Anselm College, College of Saint Rose, Saint Michaels's College, Southern Connecticut State University, Southern New Hampshire University, Stonehill College, UMass Lowell University,
Publications:
Basketball tournament program; conference record book and directory; weekly statistical release.

NORTHERN ILLINOIS-IOWA CONFERENCE
C/O CHRIS COOK
EUREKA COLLEGE
300 E. COLLEGE AVENUE
EUREKA, IL 61530
309-467-6377
www.eureka.edu/athletics/directory
• Steve Thompson, Director Of Athletics
• Cory McCain, Asst. To The Athletics Director
(309) 467-6456
Year Founded:
1969
Description:
Offers conference competition in soccer, cross country, basketball, baseball, golf, tennis for men, and volleyball, tennis, basketball and softball for women. Selects annual all-scholastic team for athletes who excel in the classroom and on the field.
Number of Members:
6
Member Schools:
Aurora University, Benedictine University, Clarke College, Concordia University, Eureka College, Rockford College.

NORTHERN SUN INTERCOLLEGIATE CONFERENCE
2999 COUNTY ROAD 42 W
SUITE 136
BURNSVILLE, MN 55306
952-500-8052
Fax: 952-378-1694
media@northernsun.org
www.northernsun.org

college sports

• Erin Lind, Commissioner
lind@northernsun.org
• Michelle Beck, Asst. Commissioner For External Relations
• Nick Kornder, Asst. Commissioner For Media Relations
kornder@northernsun.org
• Melissa Sewick, Asst. Commissioner For Compliance
sewick@northernsun.org

Year Founded:
1932

Description:
Sponsors intercollegiate competition in baseball, basketball, cross country, tennis, football, golf, indoor and outdoor track, wrestling.

Number of Members:
8

Member Schools:
Bemidji State University, Concordia University-St. Paul, University of Minnesota-Crookston, Minnesota State University-Moorhead, Northern State University, Southwest Minnesota State, Wayne State College, Winona State.

NORTHWEST CONFERENCE
9594 1ST AVENUE NE
SUITE 332
SEATTLE, WA 98115
206-432-9531
Fax: 541-388-1943
www.nwcsports.com
• Wendy Guthrie, Interim Commissioner
(206) 432-9531
• Kimberly Wenger, Commissioner
(503) 352-2173
• Christopher Brown, Assistant Commissioner
(208) 861-9465

Year Founded:
1926

Nature of Sports Service:
Organization is a collegiate athletic conference. Sports include baseball, basketball, cross country, golf, soccer, softball, swimming, tennis, track, volleyball.

Number of Members:
9

Member Schools:
George Fox University, Lewis & Clark College, Linfield College, Pacific University, Pacific Lutheran University, University of Puget Sound, Whitman College, Whitworth College, Willamette University.

Membership Requirements:
Private colleges in the Northwest with comprehensive athletic programs.

OHIO ATHLETIC CONFERENCE
4990 MAHONING AVE
SUITE C
PO BOX 4656
AUSTINTOWN, OH 44515
330-259-9090
Fax: 330-259-9091
www.oac.org
• Tim Gleason, Commissioner
• Larry Shank, President of OAC Athletic Council
• Tom Simmons, VP Of OAC Athletic Council

Year Founded:
1902

Description:
Regulates men's and women's

intercollegiate athletics, establishes and enforces rules and regulations to maintain the proper balance between athletics and academics, sponsors championship competitions.

Number of Members:
10

Member Schools:
Baldwin-Wallace College, Capital University, Heidelberg College, John Carroll University, Marietta College, Mount Union College, Muskingum College, Ohio Northern University, Otterbein College, Wilmington College.

Membership Requirements:
Invitation only. Must be approved by existing membership, two-thirds vote.

OHIO VALLEY CONFERENCE
215 CENTERVIEW DRIVE
SUITE 115
BRENTWOOD, TN 37027
615-371-1698
Fax: 615-371-1788
information@ovc.org
www.ovcsports.com
• DeBauche Beth, Commissioner
(Ext) 6682
• Kate Barnett, Asst. Commissioner For Championships
(Ext) 6692
kbarnett@ovc.org
• Kyle Schwartz, Assistant Commissioner for Strategic Communication
• Brian Pulley, Assistant Commissioner for External Affairs

Year Founded:
1948

Description:
Sponsors the following sports: baseball, basketball, cross country, football, golf, tennis and track for men, and basketball, cross country, golf, soccer, softball, tennis, track and volleyball for women. In addition, the OVC also sponsors the combined men's and women's sport of rifle.

Number of Members:
11

Member Schools:
Austin Peay State University, Eastern Illinois University, Eastern Kentucky University, Jacksonville State University, Morehead State University, Murray State University, Samford University, Southeast Missouri State University, University of Tennessee-Martin, Tennessee State University, Tennessee Technological University.

Publications:
OVC HANDBOOK; Football, Basketball and Volleyball Media Guides; Weekly press releases (Aug-May).

Corporate Sponsors:
O'Reilly Auto Parts, HCA's TriStar Family of Hospitals, Aeropostale, Sirius Radio, Tachikara, Brine, Holiday Inn Brentwood, Schutt Sports, Big Idea.

OLD DOMINION ATHLETIC CONFERENCE
402-B IDAHO STREET
SALEM, VA 24153
540-387-9073
Fax: 540-389-6196
brad@odaconline.com
www.odaconline.com

• JJ Nekoloff, Commissioner
(540) 389-7373
jnekoloff@odaconline.com
• Chris Kilcoyne, Sports Information Director
• R. Carey Harveycutter, Civic Facilities Director
• Curt Kendall, President
ckendall@bridgewater.edu
• Molly Robertson, Assistant to Commissioner/Championships Direc
(540) 389-7373

Year Founded:
1975

Description:
Entering its 30th year, the Old Dominion Athletic Conference (ODAC) is one of the nation's largest Division III conferences. The 14-member ODAC, including Catholic's associate status, stands as the second-largest multi-sport NCAA Division III conference in the country behind the 15-member American Southwest Conference in Texas.

Number of Members:
14

Member Schools:
Bridgewater College, Catholic University, Eastern Mennonite University, Emory & Henry College, Guilford College, Hampden-Sydney College, Hollins University, Lynchburg College, Randolph-Macon College, Randolph-Macon Woman's College, Roanoke College, Sweet Briar College, Virginia Wesleyan College, Washington and Lee University.

Membership Requirements:
NCAA Div III, Private institutions.

Publications:
Weekly statistical reports. Annual information guide and directory, sport media guide.

PACIFIC WEST CONFERENCE
1777 ALA MOANA BLVD
SUITE 223
HONOLULU, HI 96815
808-285-5537
Fax: 808-922-4225
www.thepacwest.com
• Bob Hogue, Commissioner
• Jane Teixeria, Assistant Commissioner, Compliance
janeteixeira@thepacwest.com
• Jimmy Knodel, Director Of Strategic Positioning
(480) 983-6605
jimmyknodel@thepacwest.com
• Wayne Coito, Multimedia Specialist
waynecoito@thepacwest.com

Description:
An intercollegiate college athletic conference affiliated with NCAA Division II. Formed in 1992 when the Great Northwest Conference (a men's conference) merged with the Continental Divide Conference (a women's conference containing some of the same members, in response to several member-departures and new NCA legislation requiring conferences to have at least six members.

Number of Members:
4

Member Schools:
Brigham Young University, Chaminade University, University of Hawaii, Hawaii Pacific University.

PACIFIC-10 CONFERENCE
800 S. BROADWAY
SUITE 400
WALNUT CREEK, CA 94596
925-932-4411
Fax: 925-932-4601
www.pac-10.org
• Thomas Hansen, Commissioner
• Christine Hoyles, Asst. Commissioner Championships/Admin.
• James Muldoon, Asst. Commissioner of Public Relations
• Duane Lindberg, Asst. Commissioner Electronic Commun.
• Mike Matthews, Asst. Commissioner Compliance
• Ben Jay, Asst. Commissioner Business/Finance
• Tammy Newman, Governance/Enforcement Asst. Director
• David Hirsh, Public Relations Assistant Director
• Kevin Anderson, Championships Assistant Director
Year Founded:
1916
Nature of Sports Service:
Sponsors 11 men's sports and 11 women's sports. Additionally, the Conference is a member of the Mountain Pacific Sports Federation (MPSF) in four other men's sports and two other women's sports.
Number of Members:
10
Member Schools:
Arizona State University, University of Arizona, University of Cal-Berkeley, UCLA, University of Oregon, Oregon State University, University of Southern California, Stanford University, University of Washington, Washington State University.
Corporate Sponsors:
Satellite Radio, Pontiac, Cooper Tires, 7-UP, US Bank, Pacific Life, Gatorade, State Farm Insurance.

PATRIOT LEAGUE
3773 CORPORATE PARKWAY
SUITE 190
CENTER VALLEY, PA 18034
610-289-1950
Fax: 610-289-1951
www.patriotleague.com
• Jennifer Heppel, Commissioner
(610) 289-1950
• Deb Herman, Executive Assistant And Business Manager
• Richard Wanniger, Sr. Assoc. Commissioner For External Relations
• Ginger Fulton, Sr. Assoc. Commissioner
Year Founded:
1986
Description:
A unique collection of highly selective colleges and universities linked by a number of common values. Our institutions are relatively small in size and are focused on providing the highest quality education to our undergraduate students.
Number of Members:
9
Member Schools:
American University, Bucknell University, Colgate University, Lafayette College, Lehigh College, U.S. Military Academy, U.S. Naval Academy, Fordham University, Georgetown University.

PEACH BELT ATHLETIC CONFERENCE
503 BLACKBURN DRIVE
MARTINEZ, GA 30907
706-860-8499
Fax: 706-650-8113
www.peachbelt.com
• David Brunk, Commissioner
• Diana Kling, Assistant Commissioner for Internal Operation
• Ken Gerlinger, Assistant Commissioner for Communications
• Carl Segura, Director of External Operations
Year Founded:
1991
Description:
Committed to providing through its dependent collegiate members, a forum for student participation in athletic, academic and co-curricular events under the auspices of the National Collegiate Athletic Association, Division II. Sponsors men's baseball, basketball, cross country, golf, soccer, tennis, women's basketball, cross country, soccer, tennis and volleyball.
Member Schools:
Armstrong Atlantic State University, Augusta State University, Clayton State University, Columbus State University, Francis Marion University, Georgia College & State University, University of North Carolina-Pembroke, North Georgia College & State University, University of South Carolina-Aiken, University of South Carolina-Upstate.

PENNSYLVANIA STATE ATHLETIC CONFERENCE
LOCK HAVEN UNIVERSITY
206 ANNEX BUILDING
LOCK HAVEN, PA 17745
570-893-2780
Fax: 570-893-2206
wadair@lhup.edu
www.psacsports.org
• Carley McCool, Director of Strategic Communication & New Med
(570) 484-2884
• Steve Murray, Commissioner
(570) 893-2512
• Will Adair, Associate Commissioner
(570) 484-2780
• Carlin Chesick, Associate Commissioner
(570) 484-2512
cchesick@psacsports.org
Year Founded:
1951
Description:
Sponsors intercollegiate competition in baseball, basketball, cross country, field hockey, football, men's golf, women's lacrosse, soccer, softball, swimming, tennis, track, women's volleyball, wrestling.
Number of Members:
14
Member Schools:
Bloomsburg University of Pennsylvania, California University of Pennsylvania, Cheyney University of Pennsylvania, Clarion University, East Stroudsburg University of Pennsylvania, Edinboro University of Pennsylvania, Indiana University of Pennsylvania, Kutztown University, Lock Haven University, Mansfield University, Millersville University, Shippensburg University, Slippery Rock University, West Chester University.

Publications:
PSAC Handbook.

PRESIDENTS' ATHLETIC CONFERENCE
8500 BROOKTREE ROAD
SUITE 130
WEXFORD, PA 15090
724-933-4630
Fax: 724-933-4635
www.pacathletics.org
• Joe Onderko, Commissioner
• Kevin Fenstermacher, Assistant Commissioner / Director of Communic
(724) 456-7897
fenstermacher@pacathletics.org
Year Founded:
1955
Description:
Schools are located in Western Pennsylvania, West Virginia and Kentucky. Members in scheduling outside the conference will seek schools which most nearly follow the principles of the Presidents' Athletic Conference.
Number of Members:
7
Member Schools:
Bethany College, Grove City College, Thiel College, Thomas More College, Washington & Jefferson College, Waynesburg College, Westminster College.

RED RIVER ATHLETIC CONFERENCE
100 N. 6TH STREET
SUITE 201
WACO, TX 76701
254-755-8170
www.redriverconference.com
• Tony Stigliano, Commissioner
(254) 744-8542
tonystig@aol.com
• Ann Stigliano, Secretary
(254) 755-8170
stigann@aol.com
• Larry Earvin, President
(512) 505-3001
llearvin@htu.edu
Description:
Sponsored sports include; Men's basketball, baseball, cross country, track & field, soccer, women's cross country, track & field, softball and volleyball.
Number of Members:
13
Member Schools:
Bacone College, College of the Southwest-New Mexico, Houston Baptist University, Houston-Tillotson University, Jarvis Christian College, Northwood University, Paul Quinn College, SW Assemblies of God University, Texas College, Texas A&M International University, Texas Wesleyan University, University of Texas of the Permian Basin, Wiley College.

ROCKY MOUNTAIN ATHLETIC CONFERENCE
1867 AUSTIN BLUFFS PARKWAY
SUITE 101
COLORADO SPRINGS, CO 80918
719-471-0066
Fax: 719-471-0088
www.rmacsports.org
• Chris Graham, Commissioner
• Kirsten Ford, Assistant Commissioner

Year Founded:
1909
Description:
A premier NCAA Division II conference located in the states of Colorado, Kansas, Nebraska and New Mexico. The RMAC currently competes in 19 NCAA Division II sports and has earned 30 NCAA Division II national championships and 19 national runner-ups since 1992
Number of Members:
15
Member Schools:
Adams State Col., Chadron State Col., Colorado Christian, Colorado School of Mines, UC-Colorado Springs, Fort Hays State U., Fort Lewis Col., Metropolitan State College of Denver, Mesa State Col., U. of Nebraska-Kearney, New Mexico Highlands U., U. of Southern Colorado, Regis U., Western State Col.

SOONER ATHLETIC CONFERENCE
16200 SONOMA PARK DRIVE
EDMOND, OK 73013
405-848-1581
Fax: 405-840-4671
jhud@ionet.net
www.soonerathletic.org
• Stan Wagnon, Commissioner
stan.wagnon@gmail.com
• Justin Tinder, Information Director
(405) 878-2109
sacsportsinfo@gmail.com
Nature of Sports Service:
Intercollegiate athletic conference.
Number of Members:
10
Member Schools:
John Brown University (Ark), Lubbock Christian University, Northwestern Oklahoma State University, Oklahoma Baptist University, Oklahoma Christian University, Oklahoma City University, University of Science & Arts of Oklahoma, Southern Nazarene University, St. Gregory's University, Wayland Baptist University.

SOUTH ATLANTIC CONFERENCE
226 N. PARK DRIVE
GATEWAY PLAZA, SUITE 130
ROCK HILL, SC 29730
803-981-5240
Fax: 803-981-9444
www.thesac.com
• James T. Burch, Coordinator of Men's Basketball Officials
(919) 661-2751
jimtburch@aol.com
• Betsy Kidd, Coordinator of Softball Officials
(404) 786-0361
betsykidd@att.net
• Patrick Britz, Commissioner
(803) 981-5240
• Amanda Osburne, Asst. to Commissioner Internal Ops.
(803) 981-5240
• Eric Wieberg, Assistant Commissioner For Strategic Communic
(803) 981-5240
Year Founded:
1975
Description:
NCAA Div II conference, administers programs for basketball, baseball, cross country, football, golf, soccer, softball,

tennis, volleyball.
Number of Members:
8
Member Schools:
Carson-Newman College, Catawba College, Lenoir-Rhyne College, Mars Hill College, Newberry College, Presbyterian College, Tusculum College, Wingate University.
Membership Requirements:
Must be approved by current members.
Publications:
Media Guides, Fall, Winter, Spring Annually.

SOUTHEASTERN CONFERENCE/SEC
2201 RICHARD ARRINGTON BOULEVARD N. BIRMINGHAM, AL 35203
205-458-3000
Fax: 205-458-3031
www.secsports.com
• Greg Sankey, Commissioner
• Mark Womack, Executive Associate Commissioner
• Charlie Hussey, Associate Commissioner Sports Admin.
• Leslie Claybrook, Assistant Commissioner Championships
Year Founded:
1933
Description:
Administers intercollegiate athletics and encompasses athletics within the academic system.
Number of Members:
12
Member Schools:
University of Alabama, University of Arkansas, Auburn University, University of Florida, University of Georgia, University of Kentucky, Louisiana State University, University of Mississippi, Mississippi State University, University of South Carolina, University of Tennessee, Vanderbilt University.
Membership Requirements:
Must be accepted by the presidents of 3/4 of membership.
Publications:
Annual data books on baseball, basketball, football, gymnastics, soccer, volleyball. Weekly news releases on each sport (during the season).

SOUTHERN COLLEGIATE ATHLETIC CONFERENCE
2935 HORIZON PARK DR
SUWANEE, GA 30024-7229
678-546-3470
Fax: 770-495-9363
www.scacsports.com
• Stephen Argo, Commissioner
• Dwayne Hanberry, Sports Information Director
Year Founded:
1962
Description:
Sponsors conference championships in 19 sports, including nine for men and 10 for women. The SCAC currently hosts conference championships in baseball, men's basketball, women's basketball, men's cross country, women's cross country, field hockey, football, men's golf, women's golf, men's soccer, women's soccer, softball, men's swimming and diving, women's swimming and diving, men's tennis, women's tennis, men's outdoor track, women's outdoor track, and women's

volleyball.
Number of Members:
10
Member Schools:
Centre College of Danville, DePauw University, Hendrix College of Conway, Millsaps College of Jackson, Oglethorpe University of Atlanta, Rhodes College of Memphis, Rose-Hulman Institute of Technology of Terre Haute, The University of the South of Sewanee, Southwestern University of Georgetown, Trinity University of San Antonio.

SOUTHERN CONFERENCE, THE
702 N. PINE STREET
SPARTANBURG, SC 29303
864-591-5100
Fax: 864-591-3448
www.soconsports.com
• John Iamarino, Commissioner
jiamarino@socon.org
• Jason Yaman, Assistant Commissioner for Media Relations
Year Founded:
1921
Description:
The Conference currently consists of members in four states throughout the Southeast and sponsors 19 varsity sports and championships that produce participants for NCAA Division I Championships.
Number of Members:
11
Member Schools:
Appalachian State University, College of Charleston, The Citadel, Davidson College, Elon University, Furman University, Georgia Southern University, University of North Carolina at Greensboro, University of Tennessee at Chattanooga, Western Carolina University, Wofford College.
Publications:
Football, basketball press guides; basketball tournament programs; women's basketball press guide.
Membership Requirements:
Must be active NCAA Division I member with acceptable admissions requirements and academic standards.

SOUTHERN INTERCOLLEGIATE ATHLETIC CONFERENCE
PEACHTREE CENTER-SOUTH TOWER
225 PEACHTREE STREET NE
SUITE 1975
ATLANTA, GA 30303
404-221-1041
Fax: 404-221-1042
www.thesiac.com
• Gregory Moore, Commissioner
(404) 221-1041
gmoore@thesiac.com
• Kelly Elliott, Asst. Commissioner For Compliance
(404) 221-1041
• Britney R Reddick, Asst. Commissioner For New Media
(404) 221-1041
Year Founded:
1913
Description:
The SIAC is a member of the National Collegiate Athletic Association (NCAA) and participates at the Division II level. On an annual basis, the SIAC sponsors six men's

championships (baseball, basketball, cross country, football, outdoor track & field and tennis) and six women's championships (basketball, cross country, outdoor track & field, softball, tennis and volleyball).

Number of Members:
11

Member Schools:
Albany State University, Benedict College, Clark Atlanta University, Fort Valley State University, Kentucky State University, Lane College, LeMoyne-Owen College, Miles College, Morehouse College, Paine College, Tuskegee University.

SOUTHERN STATES ATHLETIC CONFERENCE
1364 BIRCH RIVER DR
DAHLONEGA, GA 30533
706-864-7060
Fax: 706-864-9342
www.ssacsports.com
• Kurt Patberg, Conference Consultant
(404) 434-5146
• Jonathan Wojciechowski, Interim/Assistant Commissioner
(770) 880-7839
jwojo411@yahoo.com
• Mike Hall, Commissioner
(864) 266-3621
mhall.ssac@gmail.com
• Sally Shouppe, Treasurer
(251) 442-2278
sshouppe@umobile.edu
• Katie Bright, Assistant Commissioner
(334) 300-8520
kbright.ssac@gmail.com
• Ron Melton, Eligibility Chairman
(912) 583-3238
rmelton@bpc.edu
Description:
NAIA Division I conference with schools and universities in Georgia, Alabama, South Carolina and Tennessee.
Member Schools:
Auburn University-Montgomery, Berry College, Brenau University, Brewton-Parker College, Columbia College, Emmanuel College, Faulkner University, Georgia Southwestern State University, Lee University, Reinhardt College, Shorter College, Southern Polytechnic State University, Southern Wesleyan University.

SOUTHLAND CONFERENCE
2600 NETWORK BLVD
SUITE 150
FRISCO, TX 75034
972-422-9500
Fax: 972-422-9225
tburnett@southland.org
www.southland.org
• Tom Burnett, Commissioner
tburnett@southland.org
• Bruce Ludlow, Assoc. Commissioner, Operations
• Jenny McGhee, Assoc. Commissioner, External Relations
(214) 350-7522
Year Founded:
1963
Description:
NCAA Division I Athletics
Number of Members:
12
Member Schools:
University of Central Arkansas, Lamar

University, McNeese State University, Nicholls State University, Northwestern State University, Sam Houston State University, Southeastern Louisiana University, Stephen F. Austin State University, University of Texas at Arlington, University of Texas at San Antonio, Texas A&M University-Corpus Christi, Texas State University-San Marcos
Corporate Sponsors:
O'Reilly Auto Parts, State Farm Insurance, Hibernia Bank, Advantage Rent-a-Car, Aeropostale, BellSouth, American Airlines, Best Western, Sign-a-Rama, Jostens, Wilson Sporting Goods, Rawlings, Brine, Team Tachikara USA.
Publications:
ALL-SPORT RECORD BOOK.

SOUTHWESTERN ATHLETIC CONFERENCE
2101 6TH AVENUE N
SUITE 700
BIRMINGHAM, AL 35203
205-521-7573
Fax: 205-297-9820
www.swac.org
• Duer Sharp, Commissioner
• Edgar Gantt, Associate Commissioner
  ext 3466
Year Founded:
1920
Description:
Organized exclusively for the purpose of encouraging, promoting, advancing, and conducting intercollegiate sports activities and other recreational and not-for-profit activities among the members of the Conference.
Number of Members:
10
Member Schools:
Alabama A&M University, Alabama State University, Alcorn State University, Grambling State University, Jackson State University, Mississippi Valley State University, Prairie View A&M University, Southern University and A&M University, Texas Southern University, University of Arkansas at Pine Bluff.
Corporate Sponsors:
Aeropostale, Burger King, Russell Athletic, Jostens, Alabama Power, Golden Flake, ESPN, Coca-Cola, City of Birmingham, Alabama, State Farm Insurance.

STATE UNIVERSITY OF NEW YORK ATHLETIC CONFERENCE
SUNY CORTLAND
PO BOX 2000
CORTLAND, NY 13045
607-753-2278
Fax: 607-753-2280
sunyac@fredonia.edu
• Tom Di Camillo, Commissioner
(607) 753-2279
sunyacsports@gmail.com
• Megan Cross, Assistant Commissioner
(607) 753-2277
info@sunyac.com
Year Founded:
1958
Description:
The conference members compete in 20 sports: nine for men and eleven for women.
Number of Members:
10

Member Schools:
SUNY Brockport, Buffalo State, SUNY Cortland, SUNY Fredonia, Geneseo, New Paltz, Oneonta, Oswego, Plattsburgh, Potsdam.
Membership Requirements:
Four year colleges and universities in the State University of New York system.

SUN BELT CONFERENCE
1500 SUGAR BOWL DRIVE
NEW ORLEANS, LA 70122
504-299-9066
Fax: 504-299-9067
www.sunbeltsports.org
• Bert Carter, Associate Commissioner/CFO
(504) 299-9066
• Karl Benson, Commissioner
(504) 556-0888
benson@sunbeltsports.org
• Kathy Keene, Sr. Associate Commissioner / COO
(504) 556-0887
keene@sunbeltsports.org
• Keith Nunez, Assistant Director of Communicaions
(504) 299-9066
nunez@sunbeltsports.org
Year Founded:
1976
Description:
Sponsors 19 sports; 9 for men and 10 for women. The men's sports include baseball, basketball, cross country, football, golf, tennis, indoor track and field, outdoor track and field and swimming and diving. The women's sports include basketball, cross country, golf, soccer, softball, swimming and diving, tennis, indoor and outdoor track and field, and volleyball.
Number of Members:
13
Member Schools:
Arkansas State University, Florida Atlantic University, Florida International University, University of Louisiana-Monroe, Middle Tennessee State, New Mexico State, University of Arkansas at Little Rock, University of Denver, University of New Orleans, University of North Texas, University of South Alabama, University of Louisiana - Lafayette, Western Kentucky University, and University of Denver.
Publications:
MEDIA GUIDES.

SUNSHINE STATE CONFERENCE
400 PARK AVENUE SOUTH
WINTER PARK, FL 32789
321-972-1803
Fax: 321-972-1805
www.sunshinestateconference.com
• Ed Pasque, Commissioner
• Maryanne Simkulak, Assistant Commissioner
• Robert Brennecke, Assistant Commissioner
Year Founded:
1975
Description:
Offers league championships in 14 intercollegiate sports. SSC institutions have won 4 NCAA titles in 2004-2005 and a total of 61 national championships in baseball, men's basketball,
Number of Members:
9

Member Schools:
Barry University, Eckerd College, Florida Southern College, Florida Tech, Lynn University, Nova Southeastern University, Rollins College, Saint Leo University, University of Tampa.

THE MIDWEST COLLEGIATE CONFERENCE
C/O RAY SHOVLAIN
518 W. LOCUST STREET
DAVENPORT, IA 52803
563-333-6229
Fax: 563-333-6239
• Rick Sanders, Commissioner
(888) 430-7705
• Ray Shovlain, President
(563) 333-6229
shovlainraymondj@sau.edu
• Kent Henning, President
• Adam Glatczak, Sports Information Director
Year Founded:
1988
Description:
The MCC links eight private universities and colleges in an athletic affiliation featuring 13 varsity level sports for men and women. MCC sports compete in the National Association of Intercollegiate Athletics (NAIA), and routinely send qualifying teams and individuals to NAIA national tournaments.
Member Schools:
Ashford University, Grand View College, Iowa Wesleyan College, Mount Mercy College, St. Ambrose University, Viterbo University, Waldorf College, William Penn University.

TRANSOUTH ATHLETIC CONFERENCE
C/O E.L. HUTTON, COMMISSION
506 MELODY LANE
MEMPHIS, TN 38120
901-767-6194
gruff@trevecca.edu
• E.L. Hutton, Commissioner
• Tommy Sadler, President
(731) 661-5218
tsadler@uu.edu
• Mike McCutchen, Vice President
(731) 989-6901
mmccutchen@fhu.edu
• Nancy Bennett, Secretary
(731) 989-6913
nbennett@fhu.edu
• Gregory Ruff, Sports Information Director
(615) 248-1606
gruff@trevecca.edu
Year Founded:
1996
Nature of Sports Service:
The conference changed its name to TranSouth Athletic Conference prior to the 1996-97 school year. Conference members have fielded NAIA national champions in women's basketball, men's basketball, baseball, and wrestling.
Number of Members:
8
Member Schools:
Blue Mountain College, Crichton College, Cumberland University, Freed-Hardeman University, Lyon College, Martin Methodist College, Trevecca Nazarene University, Union University.

UNIVERSITY ATHLETIC ASSOCIATION
30 CORPORATE WOODS
SUITE 280
ROCHESTER, NY 14623
585-784-8442
Fax: 585-784-8309
www.uaasports.info
• Joel Seligman, President
• John Sexton, President
• Russ J Hamberger, Assistant Provost
Year Founded:
1986
Description:
Sponsors competition in 22 sports, twelve sports for men and ten sports for women - including football, soccer, cross country, volleyball, basketball, fencing, wrestling, swimming and diving, indoor track and field, baseball, softball, outdoor track and field, tennis, and golf.
Number of Members:
9
Member Schools:
Brandeis University, Carnegie Mellon University, Case Western Reserve University, Emory University, Johns Hopkins University, New York University, University of Chicago, University of Rochester, Washington University-St. Louis.

USA SOUTH CONFERENCE
C/O RITA WIGGS, COMMISSIONER
5400 RAMSEY STREET
FAYETTEVILLE, NC 28311
910-630-7326
Fax: 910-630-7622
admin@USASouth.net
www.usasouth.net
• Rita Wiggs, Commissioner
commish@usasouth.net
• Kendall Schram, President
• Mike Christie, Assistant Commissioner
(910) 630-7326
sid@usasouth.net
Year Founded:
1963
Nature of Sports Service:
The Conference is comprised of eight full member institutions located in the North Carolina and Virginia area. Sports include women's basketball, cross country, lacrosse, soccer, tennis, volleyball, men's baseball, basketball, cross country, football, golf, soccer and tennis.
Member Schools:
Averett University, Christopher Newport University, Ferrum College, Greensboro College, Maryville College, Methodist College, North Carolina Wesleyan College, Peace College, Shenandoah University.
Corporate Sponsors:
Bank of America, Wells Trophy Sportswear & Specialties, Molten USA, The Rock.

WEST COAST CONFERENCE
1111 BAYHILL DRIVE
SUITE 405
SAN BRUNO, CA 94066
650-873-8622
Fax: 650-873-7846
www.wccsports.com
• Lynn Holzman, Commiosner
lholzman@westcoast.org
• Connie Hurlbut, Senior Associate Commissioner,Governance & Ad
(650) 873-1960
churlbut@westcoast.org

• Aaron Woliczko, Assistant Commissioner,Championships & Admini
(650) 873-3053
awoliczko@westcoast.org
Year Founded:
1952
Description:
The current members of the WCC span the western coast of the United States from Canada to Mexico. The WCC crowns champions in 13 sports: baseball, men's and women's basketball, men's and women's cross country, men's and women's golf, women's rowing, men's and women's soccer, men's and women's tennis and women's volleyball.
Number of Members:
8
Member Schools:
Gonzaga University, Loyola Marymount, Pepperdine University, University of Portland, Saint Mary's College, University of San Diego, University of San Francisco, Santa Clara University.
Publications:
Weekly press releases on NCAA Division I athletics.
Membership Requirements:
Requires approval of WCC Executive Committee.

WEST VIRGINIA INTERCOLLEGIATE ATHLETIC CONFERENCE
1422 MAIN STREET
PRINCETON, WV 24740
304-487-6298
Fax: 304-487-6299
• Barry Blizzard, Commissioner
• Ben Bronlee, Associate Commissioner for Internal Affairs
brownlee.wviac@gmail.com
• Brent Hager, Associate Commissioner for External Operation
wviacsid@gmail.com
• John Holt, Supervisor of Basketball Officials
jholt4golf@aol.com
• Joe Merendino, Supervisor of Baseball Officials
• Will Prewitt, Associate Commissioner
• Karen Mandeville, Administrative Assistant
Year Founded:
1925
Description:
The Conference sponsors and conducts 18 championships for men and women in baseball, basketball, cross country, football, golf, soccer, swimming, tennis.
Number of Members:
15
Member Schools:
Alderson-Broaddus College, Bluefield State College, Concord University, University of Charleston, Davis & Elkins College, Fairmont State University, Glenville State College, Ohio Valley University, Salem International University, Shepherd University, West Liberty State College, West Virginia State University, West Virginia University-Tech, West Virginia Wesleyan College, Wheeling Jesuit University.
Corporate Sponsors:
First Community Bank, Charleston Town Center Marriott, Embassy Suites Charleston, Hampton Inn-Downtown Charleston, Holiday Inn Express Civic Center, Rotary Clubs International, City of Vienna, Lion Clubs International.

WESTERN ATHLETIC CONFERENCE
9250 E. COSTILLA AVENUE
SUITE 300
ENGLEWOOD, CO 80112
303-799-9221
Fax: 303-799-3888
wac@wac.org
www.wacsports.com
• Jeff Hurd, Commissioner
• Mollie Lehman, Senior Associate
Commissioner, CFO
(303) 962-4205
• Vicky Eggleston, Director of Graphic
Design & Publications
(303) 962-4207
• David Chaffin, Asst. Commissioner for
Technology & Conferenc
(303) 962-4212
dchaffin@wac.org
• Mollie Lehman, Sr. Associate
Commissioner and CFO
(303) 962-4215
• Marlon Edge, Asst. Commissioner
Compliance
(303) 962-4211
Year Founded:
1962
Description:
The WAC crowns team and individual
champions in 19 sports - eight men's and 11
women's. For the men there are
championships in baseball, basketball, cross
country, football, golf, tennis, indoor track
and field and outdoor track and field.
Championships for women are held in
basketball, cross country, golf, gymnastics,
soccer, softball, swimming and diving,
tennis, indoor track and field, outdoor track
and field and volleyball.
Number of Members:
8
Member Schools:
Fresno State University, University of
Hawaii, University of Idaho, Louisiana Tech
University, University of Nevada, New
Mexico State University, San Jose State
University, Utah State University.
Corporate Sponsors:
XBOX Live, Gatorade, Molten, Sirius
Satellite Radio, Wells Fargo.
Publications:
WAC MEDIA GUIDES, annual for football,
basketball, volleyball, winter and spring
sports. Weekly releases on conference
sports.

**WISCONSIN INTERCOLLEGIATE
ATHLETIC CONFERENCE**
780 REGENT ST
MADISON, WI 53715
608-263-4402
Fax: 608-265-3176
gkarner@uwsa.edu
www.wiacsports.com
• Gary Karner, Commissioner
(608) 263-7683
gkarner@uwsa.edu
• Matt Stanek, Assistant Commissioner For
Media Relations
(608) 225-8662
mstanek@uwsa.edu
• Becky Blank, Coordinator of Women's
Basketball Officials
(262) 375-3849
beckyblank@hotmail.com
• Jim Doden, Coordinator of Baseball
Umpires

(920) 731-1556
jdoden@sbcglobal.net
Publications:
WIAC Records Book, annual; news release,
weekly.
Number of Members:
9
Description:
Founded 1913. Sponsors intercollegiate
competition in cross country, gymnastics
(women's), soccer (women's), football,
basketball, hockey, swimming, wrestling,
baseball, tennis (women's), golf (women's),
volleyball (women's), softball, indoor/outdoor
track & field. Member schools include the
University of Wisconsin at the following
locations: Eau Claire, La Crosse, Oshkosh,
Platteville, River Falls, Stevens Point, Stout,
Superior, Whitewater.

**WOLVERINE-HOOSIER ATHLETIC
CONFERENCE**
43747 CRANFORD
CANTON, MI 48187
734-981-9509
www.whac.net
• Rob Miller, Commissioner
• Mike Dean, Statistician
(913) 449-3356
• Dawn Harmon, Media Director
(913) 991-0878

NAIA I Colleges

ALBERTA ATHLETICS, UNIVERSITY OF
116 STREET & 85 AVENUE
EDMONTON, AB, CANADA T6G 2R3
780-492-2327
Fax: 780-492-7307
uascores@ualberta.ca
athletics.ualberta.ca
• Ian Reade, Director of Athletics
(780) 492-3365
ian.reade@ualberta.ca
• Vang Ioannides, Associates Athletic
Director
(780) 492-5603
• Katie Spriggs, Associate Athletic Director
• Tawana McLeod, Associate Athletic
Director

**ALBERTSON COLLEGE OF IDAHO
ATHLETICS**
2112 CLEVELAND BOULEVARD
CALDWELL, ID 83605
208-459-5011
Fax: 208-459-5175
yoteathletics.com
• Reagan Rossi, Director of Athletics
• Marty Holly, Associate Athletic Director
• Mark Owen, Compliance Officer

ALICE LLOYD COLLEGE ATHLETICS
100 PURPOSE ROAD
PIPPA PASSES, KY 41844
606-368-6000
888-280-4252
www.alc.edu/athletics
• Joe Stepp, President
• Gary Stepp, Athletic Director

ALLEN UNIVERSITY ATHLETICS
1530 HARDEN STREET
COLUMBIA, SC 29204

803-376-5700
Fax: 803-376-5733
www.allenuniversity.edu/campus-life/athletic
s
• Lady June Cole, President
• Chad Washington, Athletic Director
cwashington@allenuniversity.edu

AQUINAS COLLEGE ATHLETICS
1607 ROBINSON ROAD SE
GRAND RAPIDS, MI 49506-1799
616-632-8900
Fax: 616-732-4548
athletics@aquinas.edu
www.aquinas.edu/athletics
• Nick Davidson, Athletic Director
(616) 632-2475
• Linda Nash, Assistant Athletic Director
(616) 632-2473
• Dave Wood, Associate Athletic Director
(616) 632-2474
• Mike Wojciakowski, Sports Information
Director
(616) 632-2482
wojcimic@aquinas.edu

ASBURY COLLEGE ATHLETICS
ONE MACKLEM DRIVE
WILMORE, KY 40390
859-858-3511
athletics@asbury.edu
www.asbury.edu/athletics
• Mark Perdue, Athletic Director
(859) 858-3511
• Ron Anderson, Director of Financial Aid
(859) 858-3511
• Josh Stewart, Sports Information Director
(859) 858-3511
• Andrew Bolt, Head Athletic Trainer
(859) 858-3511

ASHFORD UNIVERSITY
400 NORTH BLUFF BOULEVARD
CLINTON, IA 52732
800-242-4153
• Andy Eberhart, Director of Athletics
andy.eberhart@ashford.edu
• Michelle Burton, Administrative Assistant
michelle.burton@ashford.edu
• Kelsay McCausland, Sports Information
Director
(563) 242-4023
kelsay.mccausland@ashford.edu
Description:
Formerly The Franciscan University
Athletics.

ATHENS STATE COLLEGE ATHLETICS
300 NORTH BEATY STREET
ATHENS, AL 35611
256-233-8100
www.athens.edu
• Bob Glenn, President
• Mike McCoy, Vice President for Financial
Affairs

**AUBURN UNIVERSITY AT
MONTGOMERY ATHLETICS**
PO BOX 244023
MONTGOMERY, AL 36124-4023
334-244-3000
800-227-2649
www.aum.edu; www.aumathletics.com
• Jessie Rosa, Director of Athletics
(334) 244-3541
jrosa@aum.edu

• Andree Houston, Assistant AD For
Compliance
(334) 244-3712
ahousto4@aum.edu
• Michelle Crompton, Athletic Program
Specialist
(334) 244-3541
mcrompto@aum.edu
• Tim Lutz, Sports Information Director
(334) 244-3832
tlutz1@aum.edu

AVILA UNIVERSITY ATHLETICS
11901 WORNALL ROAD
KANSAS CITY, MO 64145
816-501-3634
Fax: 816-941-4503
athletics@avila.edu
www.avilaathletics.com
• Cristina Cowan, Director Of Athletics
(816) 501-3778
christina.cowan@avila.edu
• Brandon Droge, Sports Information
Director
(816) 501-2936
brandon.droge@avila.edu

AZUSA PACIFIC UNIVERSITY ATHLETICS
901 EAST ALOSTA AVENUE
PO BOX 7000
AZUSA, CA 91702-7000
626-815-5081
Fax: 626-815-5084
www.apu.edu/athletics
• Gary Pine, Director of Athletics
(626) 815-5081
gpine@apu.edu
• April Hoy, Associate Athletics Director
(626) 815-6000
areed@apu.edu
• Peter Bond, Director of Athletic
Development
(626) 815-6000
pbond@apu.edu
Teams:
Acrobatics & Tumbling, Baseball, Basketball
(M/W), Cross Country (M/W), Football,
Soccer (M/W), Softball, Tennis (M/W), Track
& Field (M/W), Volleyball, Water Polo (W).

BACONE COLLEGE ATHLETICS
2299 OLD BACONE ROAD
MUSKOGEE, OK 74403
918-683-4581
888-682-5514
info@bacone.edu
athletics.bacone.edu
• Alan Foster, Athletics Director
(918) 685-0450
• John Pickens, Assistant Athletic Director
(918) 685-0450

BAKER UNIVERSITY ATHLETICS
618 EIGHTH STREET
BALDWIN CITY, KS 66006
785-594-6451
www.bakeru.edu/athletics
• Theresa Yetmar, Director of Athletics
(785) 594-8316
theresa.yetmar@bakeru.edu
• Tyler Price, Assistant Director of Athletics,
Communications
(785) 594-8495

BARBER-SCOTIA COLLEGE
145 CABARRUS AVENUE WEST
CONCORD, NC 28025
704-789-2900
Fax: 704-789-2901
ecummings@b-sc.edu
www.b-sc.edu
• Brenda Simms, Executive Administrator
• Sophia Woodward, Vice President for
Academic Affairs
• Jonathan Sisk, Athletic Director
bsimms@b-sc.edu

BELHAVEN COLLEGE ATHLETICS
1500 PEACHTREE STREET
BOX 171
JACKSON, MS 39202
601-968-5956
800-960-5940
Fax: 601-510-2789
jbrower@belhaven.edu
blazers.belhaven.edu
• Scott Little, Director of Athletics
(601) 968-5956
slittle@belhaven.edu
• Candace Dailey, Associate Director of
Athletics
(601) 968-8952
cdailey@belhaven.edu
• Layton Jackson, Director of Athletics
Communication
(601) 968-8765

BELLEVUE UNIVERSITY ATHLETICS
1000 GALVIN ROAD SOUTH
BELLEVUE, NE 68005
402-557-7058
Fax: 402-557-5407
onestop@bellevue.edu
www.bubruins.com
• Ed Lehotak, Athletic Director
(402) 557-7050
ed.lehotak@bellevue.edu

BENEDICTINE COLLEGE ATHLETICS
1020 NORTH 2ND STREET
ATCHINSON, KS 66002
913-367-5340
800-467-5340
Fax: 913-367-2564
www.ravenathletics.com
• Charles Gartenmayer, Athletic Director
cgartenmayer@benedictine.edu
• Michael Faucett, Assistant Athletic Director
• Josh Pound, Sports Information Director

BEREA COLLEGE ATHLETICS
290 CAMPUS DRIVE
BEREA, KY 40404
859-985-3000
beverly_harkleroad@berea.edu
www.bereaathletics.com
• Mark Cartmill, Director of Athletics
(859) 985-3922
mark_cartmill@berea.edu
• Ryan Hess, Assistant Director of Athletics
(859) 985-3426
ryan_hess@berea.edu
• Shawn Jakubowski, Sports Information
Director
(859) 985-3406
shawn_jakubowski@berea.edu

BERRY COLLEGE ATHLETICS
2277 MARTHA BERRY HIGHWAY NW
MOUNT BERRY, GA 30149

706-290-2146
Fax: 706-236-5497
www.berry.edu/athletics
• Todd Brooks, Director of Athletics
(706) 236-1721
• David Beasley, Assistand Athletics
Director
(706) 290-2146
dbeasley@berry.edu

BETHANY COLLEGE ATHLETICS (KS)
335 EAST SWENSSON STREET
LINDSBORG, KS 67456
785-227-3380
Fax: 785-227-2021
www.bethanyswedes.com
• Dane Pavlovich, Dean of Athletics
(785) 227-3380
• Sara Blackburn, Sports Information
Director
(785) 227-3380
blackburnsk@bethanylb.edu
• M.J Cerenio, Assistant Sports Information
Director
(785) 227-3380

BETHEL COLLEGE (TN) ATHLETICS
325 CHERRY AVENUE
MCKENZIE, TN 38201
731-352-4231
Fax: 731-352-4238
www.bethelathletics.com
• Dale Kelley, Director of Athletics
(731) 352-6428
• Rick Vaughn, Associate Athletics Director
(731) 352-4201
• Kristy Dunn, Athletic Operations
Coordinator
(731) 352-6428
dunnk@bethelu.edu
• Dave McCulley, Sports Information
Director
(731) 352-4231
mcculleyd@bethelu.edu

BIOLA UNIVERSITY ATHLETICS
13800 BIOLA AVENUE
LA MIRADA, CA 90639
562-903-6000
www.biola.edu/undergrad/athletics
• Bethany Miller, Director of Athletics
(562) 777-4082
bethany.miller@biola.edu
• Dave Holmquist, Senior Associate Athletic
Director
(562) 906-4519
• Terri Pixler, Assistant to Athletic Director
• Karen Stare, Athlete Department Secretary
(562) 903-4887

BLACK HILLS UNIVERSITY ATHLETICS
1200 UNIVERSITY STREET
UNIT 9424
SPEARFISH, SD 57799-9424
605-642-6096
www.bhsuathletics.com
• Jhett Albers, Director of Athletics
(605) 642-6885
jhett.albers@bhsu.edu
• Jade Temple, Assistant Athletic
Director/Compliance
(606) 642-6630
Jade.temple@bhsu.edu
• Ryan Hilgemann, Sports Information
Director
(605) 642-6832
ryan.hilgemann@bhsu.edu

• Aaron Siekmann, Athletic Performance
Director
aaron.siekmann@bhsu.edu

BLUE MOUNTAIN COLLEGE ATHLETICS
PO BOX 160
BLUE MOUNTAIN, MS 38610
662-685-4771
Fax: 662-685-4776
webmaster@bmc.edu
www.bmcsports.com
• Lavon Driskell, Athletic Director
ldriskell@bmc.edu

BLUEFIELD COLLEGE ATHLETICS
3000 COLLEGE AVENUE
BLUEFIELD, VA 24605
276-326-4316
www.bcrams.com
• Mike White, Interim Athletic Director
(276) 326-4316
mwhite@bluefield.edu
• Tom Price, Assistant Athletic Director
• Chase Neidig, Director of Athletic
Broadcasting
• Dee Odom, Division Manager for Athletics
• Bob Redd, Sports Information Director
rredd@bluefield.edu

BRENAU UNIVERSITY ATHLETICS
500 WASHINGTON STREET SE
GAINESVILLE, GA 30501
770-534-6231
www.brenautigers.com
• Mike Lochstampfor, Director of Athletics
(770) 534-6231
mlochstampfor@brenau.edu
• Pat Felt, Financial Assistnat
(770) 538-4443
pfelt@brenau.edu
• Kris Stewart, Sports Information Director
(770) 531-2048
kstewart@brenau.edu

BRESCIA COLLEGE ATHLETICS
717 FREDERICA STREET
OWENSBORO, KY 42301
270-686-6416
www.bresciabearcats.com
• Brian Skortz, Athletic Director
(270) 686-6416
brian.skortz@brescia.edu
• Andrew Dickson, Assistant Athletic
Director
(270) 686-4292
andrew.dickson@brescia.edu
• Jerry Forbes, Sports Information Director
jerry.forbes@brescia.edu

BREVARD COLLEGE ATHLETICS
ONE BREVARD COLLEGE DRIVE
BREVARD, NC 28712
828-884-8276
Fax: 828-884-8274
bctornados.com
• Juan Mascaro, Athletic Director
(828) 884-8108
• Jamie Atkinson, Assistant Athletic Director
(828) 884-8365
• Joseph Swanson, Athletic Media Relations
Director
(828) 884-8288
• Raychel Diver, Director of Internal
Operations
(828) 884-8280

• Matt Bummer, Head Athletic Trainer
(828) 884-8316

**BREWTON PARKER COLLEGE
ATHLETICS**
201 DAVID ELIZA FOUNTAIN CIRCLE
MOUNT VERNON, GA 30445
912-583-2241
Fax: 912-583-4352
www.gobaronsgo.com
• Steven Echols, President
sechols@bpc.edu
• Ronald Melton, Faculty Athletics
Representative
• Nate Tompkins, Sports Information
Director
• Katelynn Staley, Athletic Trainer

BRIAR CLIFF UNIVERSITY ATHLETICS
3303 REBECCA STREET
SIOUX CITY, IA 51104
712-279-5200
Fax: 712-279-1632
admissions@briarcliff.edu
www.bcuchargers.com
• Stephen Gast, Director of Athletics
(712) 279-1707
• Jared Bodammer, Associate Athletic
Director
(712) 279-1653

**BRITISH COLUMBIA ATHLETICS,
UNIVERSITY OF**
272-6081 UNIVERSITY BOULEVARD
WAR MEMORIAL GYMNASIUM
VANCOUVER, BC, CANADA V6T 1Z1
604-827-0707
www.gothunderbirds.ca
• Gilles Lepine, Director, Performance and
Team Support
(604) 827-0707
gilles.lepine@ubc.ca
• Gord Hopper, Director, Performance And
Team Support
gord.hopper@ubc.ca
• James Brotherhood, Senior Manager,
Sports Science & Sport Medicine
(604) 822-4176

BRYAN COLLEGE ATHLETICS
721 BRYAN HILL
PO BOX 7000
DAYTON, TN 37321
423-775-7568
info@bryan.edu
www.bryanlions.com
• Taylor Hasty, Athletic Director
(423) 775-7568
• Will Tholken, Coordinator of Athletic
Operations
(423) 775-7193
• Wesley Sanders, Sports Information
Director
(423) 775-2041
• T.J. Zinke, Interim Head Athletic Trainer
(423) 775-7240
• David Jenkinson, Medical Director & Team
Physician
(423) 285-1691
dmj@polyclinics.net

CALGARY ATHLETICS, UNIVERSITY OF
FACULTY OF KINESIOLOGY
2500 UNIVERSITY DRIVE NW
CALGARY, AB, CANADA T2N 1N4

403-220-8143
Fax: 403-210-8187
christine.stapleton@ucalgary.ca
www.godinos.com
• Christine Stapleton, Director of Athletics
(403) 220-3409
christine.stapleton@ucalgary.ca
• Mike Boyles, Associate Director
(403) 220-4413
mboyles@ucalgary.ca
• Ben Matchett, Assistant Athletic Director
(403) 220-8143
ben.matchett@ucalgary.ca

**CALIFORNIA - SANTA CRUZ ATHLETICS,
UNIVERSITY OF**
1156 HIGH STREET
SANTA CRUZ, CA 95064
831-459-2531
Fax: 831-459-4070
www.goslugs.com
• Cliff Dochterman, Director of Athletics
(831) 459-4524
• Collin Pregliasco, Associate Athletics
Director
(831) 459-4964
• Marcus Wirth, Assistant Athletics Director
(831) 459-4159
Description of Sport Organization:
Division III, Part of the Independent
Conference.
Teams:
Men/Women's Tennis, Men/Women's
Soccer, Men/Women's Volleyball,
Men/Women's Basketball, Men/Women's
Swimming/Diving, Women's Golf, and
Women's Cross Country.

**CALIFORNIA BAPTIST UNIVERSITY
ATHLETICS**
8432 MAGNOLIA AVENUE
RIVERSIDE, CA 92504
951-343-4318
Fax: 951-689-4754
miparker@calbaptist.edu
www.cbulancers.com
• Micah Parker, Director of Athletics
(951) 343-4318
miparker@calbaptist.edu
• Michael Scarano, Associate Athletic
Director
(951) 343-4839
mscarano@calbaptist.edu
• Bryan Engle, Assistant Athletic Director
(951) 343-5021
bengle@calbaptist.edu
• Sammi Wellman, Director of Sports
Information
(951) 343-4297
ssheppard@calbaptist.edu
• Amy Leonard, Director of Development for
Athletics
(951) 343-4689
aleonard@calbaptist.edu

**CALIFORNIA MARITIME ACADEMY
ATHLETICS**
200 MARITIME ACADEMY DRIVE
VALLEJO, CA 94590
707-654-1050
Fax: 707-654-1051
www.cmakeelhaulers.com
• Marv Christopher, Athletic Director
mchristopher@csum.edu
• Patrick Hollister, Associate Athletic
Director
(707) 654-1052

college sports

phollister@csum.edu
• Tony Lewis, Faculty Representative to Athletics
tlewis@csum.edu
• Jeff Ward, Head Trainer
(707) 654-1055
jward@csum.edu

CALIFORNIA STATE UNIVERSITY - SAN MARCOS ATHLETICS
M. GORDON CLARKE FIELD HOUSE, SUITE 106
CALIFORNIA STATE UNIVERSITY SAN MARCOS
333 SOUTH TWIN OAKS VALLEY ROAD
SAN MARCOS, CA 92096-0001
760-750-7100
Fax: 760-750-3660
www.csusmcougars.com
• Jennifer Milo, Director of Athletics
(760) 750-7100
jmilo@csusm.edu
• Todd Snedden, Associate Director of Athletics
(760) 750-7109
tsnedden@csusm.edu
• Michelle Hamilton, Assistant Director of Athletics
(760) 750-7111
mhamilto@csusm.edu
• Sean Briner, Director of Athletic Development
(760) 750-4404
sbriner@csusm.edu
• Fernando Brown, Equipment Manager

CALUMET COLLEGE OF ST. JOSEPH ATHLETICS
2400 NEW YORK AVENUE
WHITING, IN 46394
219-473-4276
www.ccsjathletics.com
• Rick Torres, Athletic Director
(219) 473-4323
etorres6@ccsj.edu
• Ashley Lake, Asst. Athletic Director
(219) 473-43275
• Rebecca Leevey, Coordinator for Student-Athletes
(219) 644-7207

CAMPBELLSVILLE UNIVERSITY ATHLETICS
1 UNIVERSITY DRIVE
CAMPBELLSVILLE, KY 42718
270-789-5257
Fax: 270-789-5048
athletics@campbellsville.edu
www.campbellsvilletigers.com
• Rusty Hollingsworth, Director of Athletics
(270) 789-5257
rhollingsworth@campbellsville.edu
• Jim Hardy, Assistant Athletics Director
(270) 789-5528
jhardy@campbellsville.edu
• Karen Fawcett, Athletics Secretary
• Jordan Alves, Sports Information Director
(270) 789-5276
jtalves@campbellsville.edu
• Richard RoBards, Sports Information Assistant
(270) 403-3905
rbrobards@gmail.com

CARDINAL STRITCH UNIVERSITY ATHLETICS
6801 NORTH YATES ROAD
MILWAUKEE, WI 53217
800-347-8822
Fax: 414-410-4127
www.stritch.edu
• Tim Van Alstine, Director of Athletics
(414) 410-4839
• John Pfaffl, Assistant Director of Athletics
(414) 410-1423
jppfaffl@stritch.edu
• Dan Kuklinski, Director of Athletic Communications
(414) 410-4043
dpkuklinski@stritch.edu
• Melissa Wenig, Head Athletic Trainer
(414) 410-4129

CARLOW COLLEGE ATHLETICS
3333 FIFTH AVENUE
PITTSBURGH, PA 15213
412-578-8826
Fax: 412-578-8704
athletics@carlow.edu
www.carlow.edu/athletics
• George Sliman, Director of Athletics
(412) 578-8826
gssliman@carlow.edu
• Maria Yeater, Athletic Trainers
(412) 578-6332
masunday@carlow.edu

CARROLL UNIVERSITY ATHLETICS
1601 NORTH BENTON AVENUE
HELENA, MT 59625
406-447-4300
800-992-3648
Fax: 406-447-4955
www.carrollathletics.com
• Joe Baker, Director Of Athletics
(406) 447-5480
• Michael Schulist, Associate Athletic Director
(406) 447-4374

CEDARVILLE UNIVERSITY ATHLETICS
251 NORTH MAIN STREET
CEDARVILLE, OH 45314
937-766-7768
Fax: 937-766-7742
yellowjackets.cedarville.edu
• Alan Geist, Athletic Director
(937) 766-7768
geista@cedarville.edu
• Chris Reese, Associate Athletic Director
(937) 766-7790
chrisreese@cedarville.edu
• Christopher Cross, Assistant Athletic Director
(937) 766-6222
ccross@cedarville.edu
• Wes Stephens, Head Athletic Trainer
(937) 766-7622
wrstephens@cedarville.edu

CENTRAL CHRISTIAN COLLEGE
1200 SOUTH MAIN STREET
PO BOX 1403
MCPHERSON, KS 67460
620-241-0723
800-835-0078
Fax: 620-241-6032
athletics@centralchristian.edu
www.ccctigers.com
• Twiggs Reed, Athletic Director
(620) 241-0723

steve.reed@centralchristian.edu
• Jeremy Nelson, Sports Information Director
(620) 241-0723
jeremy.nelson@centralchristian.edu
• Maggie Burnette, Head Athletic Trainer
(620) 241-0723
maggie.burnette@centralchristian.edu

CENTRAL METHODIST COLLEGE ATHLETICS
411 CENTRAL METHODIST SQUARE
FAYETTE, MO 65248
660-248-6225
Fax: 660-248-6266
www.cmueagles.com
• Ken Oliver, Vice President for Institutional Growth
(660) 248-6225
• Brian Spielbauer, Athletics Director
(660) 248-6390
bspielba@centralmethodist.edu
• Sally Hackman, Faculty Athletics Representative
(660) 248-6633
shackman@centralmethodist.edu

CENTRAL STATE UNIVERSITY ATHLETICS
1400 BRUSH ROW ROAD
PO BOX 1004
WILBERFORCE, OH 45384
937-376-6011
1-800-388-2781
Fax: 937-376-6291
www.maraudersports.com
• Jahan Culbreath, Vice President of Institutional Advancement
(937) 376-6289
jculbreath@centralstate.edu
• Harry Stinson, III, Associate Athletic Director
(937) 376-6295
• Nick Novy, Sports Information Director
(937) 376-6345
nnovy@centralstate.edu
• LaShaunta Jones, Sports Information Director
(937) 376-6345
ljones@centralstate.edu

CLARKE UNIVERSITY ATHLETICS
1550 CLARKE DRIVE
DUBUQUE, IA 52001
563-588-6657
800-383-2345
Fax: 563-588-6666
• Curt Long, Director of Athletics
(563) 588-6462
curt.long@clarke.edu
• Casey Tauber, Assistant Athletic Director
(563) 588-6397
casey.tauber@clarke.edu
• Jerry Hanson, Sports Information Director
(563) 588-6360
jerry.hanson@clarke.edu
• Marissa Stewart, Athletic Trainer
marissa.stewart@clarke.edu

COLUMBIA COLLEGE OF MISSOURI ATHLETICS
1001 ROGERS STREET
COLUMBIA, MO 65216
573-875-7433
Fax: 573-875-7415
www.columbiacougars.com

• Bob Burchard, Director of Athletics
(573) 875-7410
rpburchard@ccis.edu
• Cindy Potter, Associate Director of Athletics
(573) 875-7454
cnpotter@ccis.edu
• Drew Grzella, Assistant Director of Athletics
(573) 875-7419
• Kim Kliegel, Coordinator of Athletic Services
(573) 875-7433
kakliegel1@ccis.edu
• Jon Barfknecht, Head Athletic Trainer
(573) 875-7407
jbarfknecht@ccis.edu

COLUMBIA COLLEGE OF S. CAROLINA ATHLETICS
1301 COLUMBIA COLLEGE DRIVE
COLUMBIA, SC 29203
803-786-3778
800-277-1301
Fax: 803-786-3868
www.columbiasc.edu
• Kellyann Stubblefield, Director of Athletics
(803) 786-3723
kstubblefield@columbiasc.edu
• Lindsey Hughes, Assistant Athletic Director
(803) 786-3802
lhughes@columbiasc.edu
• Greyson Deal, Head Athletic Trainer
(803) 786-3089
gdeal@columbiasc.edu

CONCORDIA UNIVERSITY (MI) ATHLETICS
4090 GEDDES ROAD
ANN ARBOR, MI 48105
734-995-7300
1-877-995-7520
Fax: 734-995-4883
lonnie.priest@cuaa.edu
www.concordiacardinals.com
• Lonnie Pries, Director of Athletics
(734) 904-4685
lonnie.pries@cuaa.edu
• Karen Graves, Assistant Athletic Director
(734) 995-7342
karen.graves@cuaa.edu
• Zachary Johnston, Sports Information Director
(616) 902-3563
zachary.johnston@cuaa.edu

CONCORDIA UNIVERSITY (NE) ATHLETICS
800 NORTH COLUMBIA AVENUE
SEWARD, NE 68434
402-643-7328
800-535-5494
info@cune.edu
www.cune.edu/athletics
• Devin Smith, Athletic Director
(402) 643-7424
Devin.Smith@cune.edu
• Angela Muller, Associate Director Of Athletics
(402) 643-7424
angela.muller@cune.edu

CORBAN UNIVERSITY ATHLETICS
5000 DEER PARK DRIVE SE
SALEM, OR 97317-9392

503-375-7021
800-845-3005
Fax: 503-315-2947
athletics@corban.edu
www.corbanwarriors.com
• Greg Eide, Director of Athletics
(503) 589-8119
geide@corban.edu
• Bryce Bernard, Faculty Athletics Representative
(503) 375-7034
bbernard@corban.edu
• Danny Day, Sports Information Director
(503) 589-8121
dday@corban.edu

CORNERSTONE COLLEGE ATHLETICS
1001 EAST BELTLINE AVENUE NE
GRAND RAPIDS, MI 49525
616-949-5300
info@cornerstone.edu
www.cugoldeneagles.com
• Chip Huber, Director of Athletics
(616) 222-1425
• Aaron Sagraves, Assistant Athletics Director
(616) 977-5415
aaron.sagraves@Cornerstone.edu
• Phil Keith, Athletic Trainer
(616) 222-1425
phil.keith@cornerstone.edu

CROWN COLLEGE ATHLETICS
8700 COLLEGE VIEW DRIVE
SAINT BONIFACIUS, MN 55375
952-446-4100
800-68-CROWN
athletics.crown.edu
• Jamie Ross, Interim Director of Athletics
(952) 446-4106
• Luke Herbert, Assistant Athletic Director for Communication
(952) 446-4146
herbertl@crown.edu
• Danielle Hall, Assistant Athletics Director for Operations
(952) 446-4243
• Patty Pitts, Faculty Athletics Representative
(952) 446-4211
• Karen Moberg, Haed Athletic Trainer
(952) 446-4429

CULVER-STOCKTON COLLEGE ATHLETICS
ONE COLLEGE HILL
CANTON, MO 63435
573-288-6000
www.cswildcats.com
• Pat Atwell, Director of Athletics
(573) 288-6424
patwell@culver.edu
• John Schild, Assistant Athletic Director
(573) 288-6532
jschild@culver.edu
• Dan Mahoney, Faculty Athletic Representative
(573) 288-6358
dmahoney@culver.edu
• Rob Carmichael, Head Athletic Trainer
(573) 288-6304
rcarmichael@culver.edu

CUMBERLAND COLLEGE ATHLETICS
7526 COLLEGE STATION DRIVE
WILLIAMSBURG, KY 40769

606-539-4389
Fax: 606-539-4467
www.cumberlandpatriots.com
• Chris Kraftick, Athletic Director
(606) 539-4540
• Lana West, Athletics Administrative Assistant
(606) 539-4389
lana.west@ucumberlands.edu
• Tommmy Chasanoff, Sports Information Director
(606) 539-4479
thomas.chasanoff@ucumberlands.edu

CUMBERLAND UNIVERSITY ATHLETICS
ONE CUMBERLAND SQUARE
LEBANON, TN 37087
615-547-1348
800-467-0562
Fax: 615-443-8422
www.gocumberlandathletics.com
• Ron Pavan, Director of Athletics
(615) 547-1348
rpavan@cumberland.edu
• Mitch Walters, Assistant Athletics Director
(615) 547-1288
• Jo Jo Freeman, Sports Information Director
(615) 547-1350
jfreeman@cumberland.edu

DAKOTA STATE UNIVERSITY ATHLETICS
820 NORTH WASHINGTON AVENUE
MADISON, SD 57042
605-256-5229
888-378-9988
Fax: 605-256-5138
www.dsu.edu
• Jeff Dittman, Athletic Director
(605) 256-5229
jeff.dittman@dsu.edu
• Jared Indahl, Assistant Athletic Director
(605) 256-5229
• Nick Huntimer, Sports Information Director
(605) 256-5229
nick.huntimer@dsu.edu
• Brad Gilbert, Athletic Trainer
(605) 480-2608
Teams:
Baseball, Basketball (M & W), Cross Country (M & W), Football, Indoor Track (M & W), Outdoor Track (M & W), Softball.

DAKOTA WESLEYAN UNIVERSITY ATHLETICS
1200 WEST UNIVERSITY AVENUE
MITCHELL, SD 57301
605-995-2112
800-333-8506
Fax: 605-995-2150
www.dwuathletics.com
• Curt Hart, Assistant Athletics Director
cuhart@dwu.edu
• Jon Hart, Athletic Director
(605) 995-2898
johart1@dwu.edu
• Marlene Warnke, Athletic Business Manager
(605) 995-2112
mawarnke@dwu.edu
• Nick McCutcheon, Sports Information Director
(605) 995-2854
nimccutc@dwu.edu
• Jarod Guthmiller, Head Athletic Trainer

(605) 995-2144
jaguthmi@dwu.edu

DAVENPORT UNIVERSITY ATHLETICS
415 FULTON STREET EAST
GRAND RAPIDS, MI 49503-5926
616-451-3511
800-686-1600
Fax: 616-233-3410
www.davenport.edu
• Paul Lowden, Director of Athletics
(616) 554-5050
plowden@davenport.edu
• Ronda Varnesdeel, Associate Director of
Athletics
(616) 871-6183
rvarnesdeel@davenport.edu
• Lauren Ferullo, Assistant Director of
Athletics
(616) 871-6197
• Nicole Chase, Manager of Athletic
Facilities
(616) 554-5126
nchase2@davenport.edu
• Ryan Thompson, Assistant Director of
Athletics
(616) 554-5045
rthompson62@davenport.edu
• Nicole Chase, Manager of Athletic
Facilities

DICKINSON STATE UNIVERSITY
ATHLETICS
291 CAMPUS DRIVE
DICKINSON, ND 58601
701-483-2507
800 279-HAWK
Fax: 701-483-0501
dsu.hawk@dickinsonstate.edu
www.dsubluehawks.com
• Tim Daniel, Director of Athletics
(701) 483-2100
tim.daniel@dickinsonstate.edu
• Kristen Fleury, Assistant Athletic Director
(701) 483-2567
kristen.fleury@dickinsonstate.edu
• Jason Watson, Sports Information Director
(701) 483-2716
jason.p.watson@dickinsonstate.edu
• Tim Kreidt, Head Athletic Trainer
(701) 483-2184
timothy.kreidt@dickinsonstate.edu

DILLARD UNIVERSITY ATHLETICS
2601 GENTILLY BOULEVARD
NEW ORLEANS, LA 70122
504-283-8822
Fax: 504-816-4365
www.dillardbleudevils.com
• Kiki Baker Barnes, Athletic Director
(504) 816-4752
kbarnes@dillard.edu
• Habtom Keleta, Sports Information
Director
(504) 816-4953
• Britt Vallot, Athletic Trainer
(504) 816-4070
bvallot@ochsner.org

DOANE COLLEGE ATHLETICS
1014 BOSWELL AVENUE
CRETE, NE 68333
800-333-6263
Fax: 402-826-8600
athletics@doane.edu
www.doaneathletics.com

• Jill McCartney, Athletic Director
(402) 826-8583
• Cody Vance, Assistant Athletic Director
(402) 826-8549
cody.vance@doane.edu
• Rick Schmuecker, Sports Information
Director
(402) 826-8248
rick.schmuecker@doane.edu
• Greg Seier, Athletic Trainer
(402) 826-8500
greg.seier@doane.edu

DORDT COLLEGE ATHLETICS
498 4TH AVENUE NE
SIOUX CENTER, IA 51250-1606
712-722-6000
800-343-6738
Fax: 712-722-6303
www.dordt.edu/athletics
• Glenn Bouma, Athletics Director
(712) 722-6305
• Mike Byker, Sports Information Director
(712) 722-6301
mike.byker@dordt.edu

EASTERN OREGON UNIVERSITY
ATHLETICS
ONE UNIVERSITY BLVD
LA GRANDE, OR 97850-2807
541-962-3497
Fax: 541-962-3577
www.eousports.com
• Anji Weissenfluh, Director of Athletics
(541) 962-3236
aweissen@eou.edu
• Stephanie Upshaw, Assistant Athletic
Director
(541) 962-3518
upshaws@eou.edu
• Seth Dahle, Sports Information Director
(541) 962-3946
sdahle@eou.edu
• Sam Ghrist, Business Coordinator
(541) 962-3929
sam.ghrist@eou.edu

EDWARD WATERS COLLEGE
ATHLETICS
1658 KINGS ROAD
JACKSONVILLE, FL 32209-6199
904-470-8000
888-898-3191
• Stanley Cromartie, Assistant Director of
Athletics
(904) 470-8278
• Henry Smith, Sports Information Director
(904) 470-8045
hsmith@ewc.edu

EMBRY-RIDDLE AERONAUTICAL
UNIVERSITY ATHLETICS - (AZ)
3700 WILLOW CREEK ROAD
PRESCOTT, AZ 86301
928-777-3728
blakeba3@erau.edu
erauathletics.com
• John Phillips, Director of Athletics
(928) 777-3791
john.phillips@erau.edu
• John Adkison, Associate Director of
Athletics
(928) 777-3737
john.adkison@erau.edu
• Sonja Taylor, Executive Director Of
Student Support

(928) 777-6930
taylorso@erau.edu

EVANGEL UNIVERSITY ATHLETICS
1111 NORTH GLENSTONE
SPRINGFIELD, MO 65802
417-865-2815
Fax: 417-865-9599
www.evangelathletics.com
• Dennis McDonald, Director of Athletics
(417) 865-2815
mcdonaldd@evangel.edu
• Sara Underwood, Athletics Administrative
Assistant
(417) 865-2815
• Marisa Foltz, Head Athletic Trainer

EVERGREEN STATE UNIVERSITY
ATHLETICS
2700 EVERGREEN PARKWAY NW
OLYMPIA, WA 98505
360-867-6000
Fax: 360-867-6783
www.gogeoducks.com
• Andrew Beattie, Director Of Recreation &
Athletics
(360) 867-6549
beattiea@evergreen.edu
• Monica Heuer, Interim Assistant Director
of Athletics
(360) 867-6858
heuerm@evergreen.edu
• Brian Meade, Business Operations
Manager
(360) 867-6607
meadeb@evergreen.edu
• Nick Dawson, Sports Information Director
(360) 867-6525
dawsonn@evergreen.edu

FAULKNER UNIVERSITY ATHLETICS
5345 ATLANTA HIGHWAY
MONTGOMERY, AL 36109
800-879-9816 EXT 7148
www.faulknereagles.com
• Hal Wynn, Acting Athletic Director
(334) 386-7285
• Ryan Bartels, Sports Information
(334) 386-7525
• Cindy Walker, Faculty Athletic
Representative
(334) 386-7402
cwalker@faulkner.edu

FISHER COLLEGE ATHLETICS
1 ARLINGTON STREET
LOWER LEVEL
BOSTON, MA 02116
617-236-8877
www.fisherfalcons.com
• Robert Melaragni, Director of Athletics
(617) 670-4524
rmelaragni@fisher.edu

FLORIDA MEMORIAL UNIVERSITY
ATHLETICS
15800 NW 42ND AVENUE
MIAMI GARDENS, FL 33054
305-626-3600
Fax: 305-626-3169
www.fmuathletics.com
• Robert Smith, Athletic Director
(305) 626-3168
• Artis Maddox, Assistant Athletic Director
(305) 626-3165
artis.maddox@fmuniv.edu

• Damian Alexander, Sports Information Director
(305) 626-3194
damian.alexander@fmuniv.edu

FREED-HARDEMAN UNIVERSITY ATHLETICS
158 EAST MAIN STREET
HENDERSON, TN 38340
731-989-6000
800-FHU-FHU-1
Fax: 731-989-6910
mbarker@fhu.edu
www.gofhulions.com
• Mike McCutchen, Athletic Director
(731) 989-6901
mmccutchen@fhu.edu
• Matt Barker, Sports Information Director
(731) 989-6356
mbarker@fhu.edu
Year founded:
1869.

FRIENDS UNIVERSITY ATHLETICS
2100 WEST UNIVERSITY AVENUE
WICHITA, KS 67213
316-295-5000
800-794-6945
Fax: 316-295-5030
www.friends.edu/athletics
• Carole Obermeyer, Athletic Director
(316) 295-5779
obermeyer@friends.edu
• Luke Dechant, Sports Information Director
(316) 295-5116
sports_information@friends.edu

GENEVA COLLEGE ATHLETICS
3200 COLLEGE AVENUE
BEAVER FALLS, PA 15010
724-847-6650
855-979-5563
• Van Zanic, Athletic Director
(724) 847-6886
vgzanic@geneva.edu
• Alan Summer, Assistant Athletic Director
• Christy Lear, Sports Information Director

GEORGETOWN COLLEGE ATHLETICS
400 EAST COLLEGE STREET
GEORGETOWN, KY 40324
502-863-8115
Fax: 502-863-8892
www.georgetowncollegeathletics.com
• Brian Evans, Director of Athletics
(502) 863-8223
brian_evans@georgetowncollege.edu
• Austin Sparks, Associate Director of Athletics
(502) 863-8222
• Jenny Elder, Sports Information Director
(502) 863-7972
• Randy McGuire, Head Athletic Trainer
(502) 863-7032

GOSHEN COLLEGE ATHLETICS
1700 SOUTH MAIN STREET
GOSHEN, IN 46526
574-535-7496
Fax: 574-535-7531
info@goshen.edu
www.goleafs.net
• Josh Gleason, Athletic Director
(574) 535-7491
• Josh Keister, Associate Athletic Director
(574) 535-7475

• Erica Albertin, Head Athletic Trainer
(574) 535-7417
ealbertin@goshen.edu

GRACE COLLEGE ATHLETICS
200 SEMINARY DRIVE
WINONA LAKE, IN 46580
574-372-5100 EXT 6266
Fax: 574-372-5137
www.gclancers.com
• Chad Briscoe, Director of Athletics
(574) 372-5100
chad.briscoe@grace.edu
• Kelly Sharp, Athletic Office Manager
(574) 372-5100
• Abby Sroufe, Head Athletic Trainer
(574) 372-5100

GRACELAND UNIVERSITY ATHLETICS
1 UNIVERSITY PLACE
LAMONI, IA 50140
641-784-5000
www.gujackets.com
• Joe Worlund, Athletic Director
(641) 784-5341
joew1@graceland.edu
• Stew McDole, Associate Athletic Director
(641) 784-5346
mcdole@graceland.edu
• Erin Lundy, Head Athletic Trainer
(641) 784-5037

GRAND VIEW COLLEGE ATHLETICS
1200 GRANDVIEW AVENUE
DES MOINES, IA 50316
515-263-2800
800-444-6083
Fax: 515-263-2882
www.gvvikings.com
• Troy Plummer, Director of Athletics
(515) 263-6050
tplummer@grandview.edu
• Britt Erps, Assistant to the Athletic Director
(515) 263-6050
• Michelle Prange, Athletic Success Coordinator
(515) 263-6196
mprange@grandview.edu
• Luke Steele, Director of Athletic Training Services
(515) 263-6045
lsteele@grandview.edu
• Travis Dibbet, Athletic Trainer
(515) 263-6045
tdibbet@grandview.edu

GREAT FALLS ATHLETICS, UNIVERSITY OF
1301 20TH STREET SOUTH
GREAT FALLS, MT 59405
406-791-5925
800-856-9544
Fax: 406-791-5994
www.ugfargos.com
• Brad Beffert, Head Athletic Trainer
(406) 791-5222
• Dave Gantt, Vice President Of Athletics
(406) 791-5922

HANNIBAL-LA GRANGE COLLEGE ATHLETICS
2800 PALMYRA ROAD
HANNIBAL, MO 63401
573-221-3675
www.hlgtrojans.com

• Jason Nichols, Athletic Director
(573) 629-3211
jnichols@hlg.edu
• Michelle Mundle, Athletic Department Secretary
(573) 629-3210
mmundle@hlg.edu
• Jason Farr, Director of Sports Information
(573) 629-3227
jason.farr@hlg.edu
• Josh Miley, Head Athletic Trainer
(573) 629-3219
josh.miley@hlg.edu

HARRIS-STOWE STATE COLLEGE ATHLETICS
3026 LACLEDE AVENUE
ST. LOUIS, MO 63103
314-340-3530
Fax: 314-340-3322
www.hornetsathletics.com
• Jamaal Mayo, Director of Athletics
(314) 340-3534
• Tim Fuller, Sports Advisor
(314) 340-5721

HASKELL INDIAN NATIONS UNIVERSITY ATHLETICS
155 INDIAN AVENUE
BOX 5011
LAWRENCE, KS 66046
785-749-8459
Fax: 785-832-6632
www.haskellathletics.com
• Venida Chenault, University President
(785) 749-8497
venida.chenault@bie.edu
• Todd Davis, Athletic Director
(785) 749-8459
• Denise Cesare, Program Assistant
(785) 749-8459
• Tim Kriley, Athletic Trainer
(785) 830-2759
tkriley@haskell.edu

HASTINGS COLLEGE ATHLETICS
710 NORTH TURNER AVENUE
HASTINGS, NE 68901
402-461-7395
www.hastingsbroncos.com
• Patty Sitorius, Athletic Director
(402) 461-7331
• Chris Kranjc, Assistant Athletic Director
(402) 461-7707
• Adam Maser, Sports Information Director
(402) 461-7798

HOPE INTERNATIONAL UNIVERSITY ATHLETICS
2500 EAST NUTWOOD AVENUE
FULLERTON, CA 92831
714-879-3901
Fax: 714-681-7224
www.hiuroyals.com
• John Turek, Athletic Director
(714) 879-3901
jgturek@hiu.edu
• Midge Madden, Administrative Assistant
• Joe Lurker, Assistant Athletic Director
(714) 879-3901
jdlurker@hiu.edu
• Seth Preuss, Sports Information Director
(714) 879-3901
swpreuss@hiu.edu
• Jon Clasen, Compliance Director
(714) 879-3901
jaclasen@hiu.edu

college sports

• Kim Jaramillo, Head Athletic Trainer
(714) 879-3901
kajaramillo@hiu.edu

HOUSTON BAPTIST UNIVERSITY ATHLETICS
7502 FONDREN ROAD
HOUSTON, TX 77074
281-649-3096
Fax: 281-649-3040
www.hbuhuskies.com
• Steve Moniaci, Director of Athletics
(281) 649-3096
smoniaci@hbu.edu
• Ron Cottrell, Associate Athletic Director
(281) 649-3250
rcottrell@hbu.edu
• Tom Payne, Director of Business and
Operations
(281) 649-3743
tpayne@hbu.edu
• Ted Seilheimer, Assistant Athletic Director
(281) 649-3046
tseilheimer@hbu.edu

HUNTINGTON UNIVERSITY ATHLETICS
2303 COLLEGE AVENUE
HUNTINGTON, IN 46750
260-359-4212
Fax: 260-359-4295
lculler@huntington.edu
www.indianatechwarriors.com
• Lori Culler, Director of Athletics
(260) 359-4213
lculler@huntington.edu
• Mike Frame, Assistant for Auxiliary Athletic
Services
(260) 359-4082
mframe@huntington.edu
• Joanne Green, Sports Information Director
(260) 359-4284
jgreen@huntington.edu
• Lori Ingle, Athletics Secretary
(260) 359-4212
lingle@huntington.edu

HUSTON-TILLOTSON COLLEGE ATHLETICS
900 CHICON STREET
AUSTIN, TX 78702-2795
512-505-3000
Fax: 512-505-3190
htu.edu/athletics
• Charles H. Dubra, Interim Director of
Athletics
(512) 505-3050

INDIANA INSTITUTE OF TECHNOLOGY ATHLETICS
1600 EAST WASHINGTON BOULEVARD
FORT WAYNE, IN 46803
260-422-5561
dpwarren@indianatech.edu
www.indianatechwarriors.com
• Debbie Warren, Director of Athletics
(260) 422-5561
• Jessie Biggs, Assistant Athletic Director
(260) 422-5561
• Tyler Stevenson, Sports Information
Director
(260) 422-5561
• Rich Riles, Head Athletic Trainer
(260) 422-5561
rlriles@indianatech.edu

INDIANA UNIVERSITY NORTHWEST ATHLETICS
3400 BROADWAY
GARY, IN 46408
219-980-6793
www.iunredhawkathletics.com
• Kristofer Schnatz, Athletic Director
(219) 980-6793
• Anne Villanueva, Director of Operations
(219) 980-6944
avillanu@iun.edu
• Scott Fulk, Director of Student Activities
(219) 980-6792
sfulk@iun.edu
• Stephanie Smith, Head Athletic Trainer
(219) 981-5636

INDIANA UNIVERSITY SOUTH BEND ATHLETICS
1700 MISHAWAKA AVENUE
SOUTH BEND, IN 46615
574-520-4100
Fax: 574-239-5041
stbruce@iusb.edu
www.iusbtitans.com
• Steve Bruce, Director of Athletics
(574) 520-5084
stbruce@iusb.edu
• Tom Norris, Assistant Director of Athletics
(574) 520-4827
• Scott Strittmatter, Director of Student Life
(574) 520-5533
sstrittm@iusb.edu
• Rachel Weitzel, Head Athletic Trainer
(574) 520-4283

INDIANA UNIVERSITY SOUTHEAST ATHLETICS
4201 GRANT LINE ROAD
NEW ALBANY, IN 47150-6405
812-941-2432
Fax: 812-941-2434
athletics@ius.edu
www.iusathletics.com
• Joe Glover, Director of Athletics
(812) 941-2433
joglover@indiana.edu
• Denny Williams, Deputy Director of
Athletics
(812) 941-2482
• Eric Brian, Athletic Academic Coordinator
(812) 941-2172
erbrian@ius.edu
• Stephen Utz, Sports Information Director
(812) 941-2001
sutz@ius.edu
• Tiffany Hammond, Head Athletic Trainer
(812) 941-2099
tsettle@ius.edu

INDIANA WESLEYAN UNIVERSITY ATHLETICS
4201 SOUTH WASHINGTON STREET
MARION, IN 46953
765-677-2318
mark.demichael@indwes.edu
www.iwuwildcats.com
• Mark DeMichael, Athletic Director
(765) 677-2317
mark.demichael@indwes.edu
• Kyle Schmidt, Sports Information Director
(765) 677-1938
kyle.schmidt@indwes.edu
• Adam Thompson, Director of Athletic
Training Education
(765) 677-3482
adam.thompson@indwes.edu

• Mary Jacobs, Head Athletic Trainer
(765) 677-3484
mary.jacobs@indwes.edu

JARVIS CHRISTIAN COLLEGE ATHLETICS
PO BOX 1470
HAWKINS, TX 75765
404-679-4500
Fax: 404-679-4558

JOHN BROWN UNIVERSITY ATHLETICS
2000 WEST UNIVERSITY STREET
SILOAM SPRINGS, AR 72761
479-524-9500
Fax: 501-524-7412
jbuinfo@jbu.edu
www.jbu.edu/athletics
• Colin Sullivan, Deputy Director of Athletics
(401) 863-2272
• Grace Calhoun, PhD, Vice President,
Athletics & Recreation
(401) 863-2972
athdir@brown.edu
• Jake Silverman, Deputy Director of
Athletics, Administration
jake_silverman@brown.edu

JUDSON UNIVERSITY
1151 NORTH STATE STREET
ELGIN, IL 60123
847-628-2500
www.judsoneagles.com
• Chad Gassman, Athletic Director
(847) 628-1579
chad.gassman@judsonu.edu
• Darrell Cosden, Academics/Athletics
Liaison
(847) 628-1055
dcosden@judsonu.edu
• Joel Cotton, Associate Athletic Director
(847) 628-1551
jcotton@judsonu.edu
• Brandon Fowkes, Sports Information
Director
(847) 628-1580
brandon.fowkes@judsonu.edu
• Andrew Carlson, Head Athletic Trainer
(847) 628-1592

KANSAS WESLEYAN UNIVERSITY ATHLETICS
100 EAST CHAFLIN AVENUE
SALINA, KS 67401-6196
785-833-4400
www.kwucoyotes.com
• Mike Hermann, Director of Athletics
(785) 833-4410
• Hannah Martin, Athletics Administrative
Assistant
(785) 833-4400
• David Toelle, Sports Information Director
(785) 833-4402
sports.info@kwu.edu
• Dan O'Connell, Head Athletic Trainer
(785) 833-4430

LA SIERRA UNIVERSITY ATHLETICS
4500 RIVERWALK PARKWAY
RIVERSIDE, CA 92515
951-785-2084
Fax: 951-785-2291
athletics@lasierra.edu
www.lsugoldeneagles.com
• Javier Krumm, Athletic Director
(951) 785-2295

jkrumm@lasierra.edu
• Robert Castillo, Sports Information
Director
(951) 785-2603
rcastill@lasierra.edu
• Brian Murphy, Head Athletic Trainer
(951) 785-2534
bmurphy@lasierra.edu
• Brianne Carroll, Clubs and Leagues
Director
(951) 785-2608
bcarroll@lasierra.edu

LANGSTON UNIVERSITY ATHLETICS
PO BOX 1500
LANGSTON, OK 73050
405-466-3262
Fax: 405-466-3461
www.langstonsports.com

**LEWIS-CLARK STATE COLLEGE
ATHLETICS**
500 8TH AVENUE
LEWISTON, ID 83501
208-792-5272
Fax: 208-792-2731
www.lcwarriors.com
• Gary Picone, Athletic Director
(208) 792-2863
gapicone@lcsc.edu
• Brooke Cushman, Associate Athletic
Director
(208) 792-2675
blcushman@lcsc.edu
• Zachary Shore, Sports Information Director
(208) 792-2289
zrshore@lcsc.edu
• Allie Canfield, Athletic Operations
(208) 792-2492
djshirley@lcsc.edu
• Michael Benke, Director of Facilities &
Operations
(208) 792-2366
mbbenke@lcsc.edu

LINDSEY WILSON COLLEGE ATHLETICS
210 LINDSEY WILSON STREET
COLUMBIA, KY 42728
270-384-8070
Fax: 270-384-8078
poolerw@lindsey.edu
www.lindseyathletics.com
• Willis Pooler, Athletic Director
(270) 384-8186
poolerw@lindsey.edu
• Chris Wells, Assistant Athletic Director
(270) 384-8071
wellsc@lindsey.edu
• Mike Talley, Facilities and Event
Management
(270) 384-8074
talleym@lindsey.edu
• Chris Miller, Head Athletic Trainer
(270) 384-8167

**LOUISIANA STATE UNIVERSITY
(SHREVEPORT) ATHLETICS**
ONE UNIVERSITY PLACE
SHREVEPORT, LA 71115
318-797-5000
chad.mcdowell@lsus.edu
www.lsusathletics.com
• Chad McDowell, Athletic Director
(318) 798-4107
chad.mcdowell@lsus.edu
• David Gustavson, Associate Athletic
Director

(318) 797-5030
david.gustavson@lsus.edu
• Mark Cantrell, Sports Information Director
(318) 795-2475
mark.cantrell@lsus.edu
• Lance Champagne, Head Athletic Trainer
(318) 795-2446
lance.champagne@lsus.edu

**LOYOLA UNIVERSITY (NEW ORLEANS)
ATHLETICS**
6363 ST. CHARLES AVENUE
CAMPUS BOX 21
NEW ORLEANS, LA 70118-6143
504-864-7539
Fax: 504-864-7380
www.loyolaramblers.com
• Steve Watson, Director Of Athletics
(504) 864-7539
• Jermaine Truax, Deputy Director Of
Athletics
(504) 864-7396
• Tom Sorboro, Senior Associate Athletics
Director
(504) 864-7577
tsorboro@luc.edu

**LUBBOCK CHRISTIAN UNIVERSITY
ATHLETICS**
5601 19TH STREET
LUBBOCK, TX 79407-2099
800-933-7601
www.lcuchaps.com
• Paul Hise, Director of Athletics
(806) 720-7279
• Scott Larson, Associate Athletics Director
(806) 720-7266
scott.larson@lcu.edu
• Chris Due, Director of Athletic
Communication
(806) 720-7283
chris.due@lcu.edu
• Zack Chavez, Sports Information
Coordinator
(806) 283-2502
chavez_zack11@yahoo.com
• Dustin Driskill, Director of Sports Medicine
(806) 720-7284
dustin.driskill@lcu.edu

LYON COLLEGE ATHLETICS
2300 HIGHLAND ROAD
BATESVILLE, AR 72501
870-793-1764
Fax: 870-793-1763
athletics@lyon.edu
www.lyonscots.com
• Kevin Jenkins, Director of Athletics
(870) 307-7220
kevin.jenkins@lyon.edu
• John Krueger, Director of Sports
Information
(870) 307-7516
• Shawn Tackett, Head Athletic Trainer
(870) 307-7330

MADONNA UNIVERSITY ATHLETICS
36600 SCHOOLCRAFT
LIVONIA, MI 48150-1176
734-432-5608
Fax: 734-432-5611
sportsinfo@madonna.edu
www.madonnacrusaders.com
• Scott Kennell, Athletic Director
(734) 432-5604
skennell@madonna.edu
• Noel Emenhiser, Assistant Athletic

Director
(734) 432-5610
nemenhiser@madonna.edu
• Zachary Shore, Director of Sports
Information
(734) 432-5834
zshore@madonna.edu
• Peter Benjamin, Athletic Trainer
(734) 432-5605
pbenjamin@madonna.edu

**MAINE AT FORT KENT ATHLETICS,
UNIVERSITY OF**
23 UNIVERSITY DRIVE
FORT KENT, ME 04743
207-834-7500
athletics.umfk.edu
• Kyle Fisher, Athletic Trainer
(207) 834-7572
kyle.fisher@maine.edu
• Bill Ashby, Athletics Director
(207) 834-7571
bill.ashby@maine.edu
• Lucas Levesque, Assistant Director of
Athletics
(207) 834-7876
lucas.levesque@maine.edu
• Tom Bird, Sports Information Director
(207) 834-7828
thomas.bird@maine.edu
• James Harvey, Team Manager
jamesd_harveyjr@yahoo.com

**MAINE AT MACHIAS ATHLETICS,
UNIVERSITY OF**
116 O'BRIEN AVENUE
MACHIAS, ME 04654
207-255-1200
www.ummclippers.com
• Nicholas Cowell, Athletic Director
(207) 255-1290
nicholas.cowell@maine.edu
• Travis Cargnan, Athletic Director
(207) 255-1290
travis.carignan@maine.edu

MALONE COLLEGE ATHLETICS
2600 CLEVELAND AVENUE NW
CANTON, OH 44709
330-471-8300
Fax: 330-471-8298
www.malonepioneers.com
• Charlie Grimes, Director of Athletics
(330) 471-8438
• John Russell, Associate Athletic Director
(330) 471-8389
jcrussell@malone.edu
• Caleb Norrick, Assistant Athletic Director
(330) 471-8412
• Mike Leggett, Sports Information Director
(330) 471-8253
• Chris Watson, Director of Sports Medicine
(330) 471-8297

MARTIN LUTHER COLLEGE ATHLETICS
1995 LUTHER COURT
NEW ULM, MN 56073
507-354-8221 EXT 232
Fax: 507-354-8225
www.mlcknights.com
• Jim Unke, Athletic Director
(507) 354-8221
unkejm@mlc-wels.edu
• Randy Cox, Assistant Athletic Director
(507) 354-8221
coxra@mlc-wels.edu
• Sheree Danell, Administrative Assistant to

college sports

Athletics
(608) 354-8221
danellsj@mlc-wels.edu

MARTIN METHODIST COLLEGE ATHLETICS
433 WEST MADISON STREET
PULASKI, TN 38478
931-363-9868
800-467-1273
Fax: 931-363-9873
www.goredhawks.com
• Robby Shelton, Interim President
(931) 363-9876
rshelton@martinmethodist.edu
• Jeff Bain, Executive Director of Athletics
(931) 363-9872
jbain@martinmethodist.edu
• Kelly Bratton, Associate Athletic Director
(931) 363-9827
kbratton@martinmethodist.edu
• Wade Neely, Assistant Athletic Director
(921) 363-9883
wneely@martinmethodist.edu
• Grant Fairchild, Director of Athletic Training
(921) 363-9874
gfairchild@martinmethodist.edu

MASTER'S COLLEGE ATHLETICS, THE
21726 PLACERITA CANYON ROAD
SANTA CLARITA, CA 91321
661-362-2761
800-568-6248
Fax: 661-362-2697
www.masters.edu/athletics
• Steve Waldeck, Director of Athletics
(661) 362-2767
swaldeck@masters.edu
• Mike Crawford, Sports Information Director
(661) 362-2775
mcrawford@masters.edu
• Holly Gnuse, Administrative Assistant
(661) 362-2761
hgnuse@masters.edu
• Don Gilmore, Assistant Director, Sports Information
(661) 362-2811
dgilmore@masters.edu

MAYVILLE STATE UNIVERSITY ATHLETICS
330 THIRD STREET NE
MAYVILLE, ND 58257
800-437-4104
Fax: 701-788-4748
www.msucomets.com
• Mike Moore, Athletic Director
(701) 788-4706
mike.moore@mayvillestate.edu
• Scott Berry, Assistant Athletic Director
(701) 788-4771
scott.berry.2@mayvillestate.edu
• John Murphy, Assistant Sports Information Director
j.thiessenmurphy@gmail.com
• Tim O'Brien, Head Athletic Trainer
(107) 788-4844
tim.obrien@mayvillestate.edu

MCPHERSON COLLEGE ATHLETICS
1600 EAST EUCLID
PO BOX 1402
MCPHERSON, KS 67460
646-737-2725
Fax: 620-245-9706

sportsinfo@mcpherson.edu
www.macbulldogs.com
• Andrew Ehling, Director of Athletics
(620) 242-0578
• Joshua Schroeder, Director Of Athletic Communications
(646) 737-2725
• Phil Schoenwetter, Head Athletic Trainer
(620) 242-0584
schoenwp@mcpherson.edu

MENLO COLLEGE ATHLETICS
1000 EL CAMINO REAL
ATHERTON, CA 94027
800-556-3656
Fax: 800-556-3769
www.menloathletics.com
• Keith Spataro, Director of Athletics
(650) 543-3853
kspataro@menlo.edu
• Mark Fowler, Assistant Athletic Director
(650) 543-3852
mfowler@menlo.edu
• Aaron Gillespie, Sports Information Director
(650) 543-3912
aaron.gillespie@menlo.edu
• Lucas Armstrong, Director of Events and Game Ops
(650) 543-3729
• Ashley Vogds, Head Athletic Trainer
(650) 543-3931
ashley.vogds@menlo.edu

MICHIGAN-DEARBORN ATHLETICS, UNIVERSITY OF
4901 EVERGREEN ROAD
DEARBORN, MI 48128
313-593-3534
umdearbornathletics@gmail.com
athletics.umdearborn.edu
• Matt Beaudry, Director of Athletics & Recreation
(313) 593-3534
• Byan Earl, Assistant Director of Athletics
(313) 593-5671
earlb@umich.edu

MIDAMERICA NAZARENE UNIVERSITY ATHLETICS
2030 EAST COLLEGE WAY
OLATHE, KS 66062-1899
913-973-3760
Fax: 913-971-3456
www.mnusports.com
• Todd Garrett, Director of Athletics
(913) 971-3760
tgarrett@mnu.edu
• Chad Jenkins, Sports Information Director
(913) 973-3457
cwjenkins@mnu.edu
• Kristine Farrell, Director of Sports Medicine
(913) 973-3388
brpowers@mnu.edu

MIDLAND UNIVERSITY
900 NORTH CLARKSON STREET
FREMONT, NE 68025
402-941-6360
800-642-8382
Fax: 401-721-9406
info@midlandu.edu
www.midlandathletics.com
• Dave Gillespie, Director of Athletics
(402) 941-6545
• Keith Kramme, Director of Retention

(402) 941-6059
kkramme@midlandu.edu
• Theo Bland, Assistant Athletic Director
(402) 941-6062

MIDWAY UNIVERSITY ATHLETICS
512 STEPHENS STREET
MIDWAY, KY 40347
859-354-8221
Fax: 859-354-5754
www.gomidwayeagles.com
• Rusty Kennedy, Athletic Director
(859) 846-5456
wkennedy@midway.edu
• John Kenger, Assistant Athletic Director
(859) 846-5726
jkenger@midway.edu
• Dylan Brown, Sports Information Director
(859) 846-5394
dpbrown@midway.edu

MILLIGAN COLLEGE ATHLETICS
1 BLOWERS BOULEVARD
MILLIGAN COLLEGE, TN 37682
423-461-8700
www.milliganbuffs.com
• Mark Fox, Vice President for Athletics
(423) 461-8784
mpfox@milligan.edu
• Ray Smith, Associate Athletic Director for Facilities
(426) 461-8990
resmith@milligan.edu
• Daniel Manget, Sports Information Director
(423) 461-8980
sportsinfo@milligan.edu
• Zach Allen, Head Athletic Trainer
(423) 461-8991
zlallen@milligan.edu

MISSOURI BAPTIST COLLEGE ATHLETICS
ONE COLLEGE PARK DRIVE
SAINT LOUIS, MO 63141-8698
314-434-1115
877-434-1115
Fax: 314-434-7596
www.mbuspartans.com
• Thomas Smith, Associate VP, Director of Athletics
(314) 392-2264
smitht@mobap.edu
• Pitzer Lowell, Faculty Athletics Representative
(314) 392-2279
• Meredith Dill, Head Athletic Trainer
(314) 392-2399
dillm@mobap.edu

MISSOURI VALLEY COLLEGE ATHLETICS
500 EAST COLLEGE
MARSHALL, MO 65340
660-831-4000
Fax: 831-831-4003
www.moval.edu/athletics
• Tom Fifer, Director of Athletics
(660) 831-4219
fifert@moval.edu
• Mike Maccholz, Associate Athletic Director
(660) 831-4158
machholzm@moval.edu
• Colin Smith, Assistant Athletic Director
(660) 831-4230
smithc@moval.edu

MOBILE ATHLETICS, UNIVERSITY OF
5735 COLLEGE PARKWAY
MOBILE, AL 36613
251-675-5990
www.umobilerams.com
• Joe Niland, Athletic Director
(251) 442-2288
jniland@umobile.edu
• Jacob Lewis, Head Athletic Trainer
(251) 442-2561
jlewis@umobile.edu

**MONTANA STATE
UNIVERSITY-NORTHERN ATHLETICS**
300 WEST 13TH STREET
HAVRE, MT 59501-7751
406-265-3761
Fax: 406-265-4129
www.msun.edu/athletics
• Christian Oberquell, Athletic Director
(406) 265-4109
coberquell@msun.edu
• Nichole Borst, Head Athletic Trainer
(406) 265-3593
• Nichole Yazzie, Sports Information
Director
(406) 265-3779

MONTANA TECH ATHLETICS
1300 WEST PARK STREET
BUTTE, MT 59701
406-496-4105
1-800-445-8324
Fax: 406-496-4711
www.godiggers.com
• Chuck Morrell, Head Coach/Athletic
Director
(406) 496-4325
CMorrell@mtech.edu
• Nick Bowsher, Associate Athletic Director
(406) 496-4737
NBowsher@mtech.edu
• Chris Heard, Head Athletic Trainer
(406) 496-4296
cheard@mtech.edu

**MONTANA WESTERN ATHLETICS, THE
UNIVERSITY OF**
710 SOUTH ATLANTIC STREET
DILLON, MT 59725
406-683-7220
www.umwbulldogs.com
• Russ Richardson, Director of Athletics
(409) 683-7220
ryan.nourse@umwestern.edu
• Megan Woolley, Administrative Assistant
(406) 683-7220
megan.woolley@umwestern.edu

MONTREAT COLLEGE ATHLETICS
310 GAITHER CIRCLE
PO BOX 1267
MONTREAT, NC 28757
828-669-8012
Fax: 828-669-8014
www.montreatcavaliers.com
• Jose Larios, Athletic Director
(828) 669-8011
jlarios14@montreat.edu
• Jason Lewkowicz, Sports Information
Director
(573) 795-5807
jlewkowicz@montreat.edu
• Mark Neely, Head Athletic Trainer
(216) 401-8850
mneely@montreat.edu

MORNINGSIDE COLLEGE ATHLETICS
1501 MORNINGSIDE AVENUE
SIOUX CITY, IA 51106
712-274-5000
800-831-0806
Fax: 712-274-5101
www.morningside.edu
• Tim Jager, Athletic Director
(712) 274-5313
• Dave Rebstock, Sports Information
Director
(712) 274-5127
• Katy Burford, Head Athletic Trainer
(712) 274-5314
burfordk@morningside.edu

MORRIS COLLEGE ATHLETICS
100 WEST COLLEGE STREET
SUMTER, SC 29150-3599
803-934-3200
Fax: 803-773-3687
chouck@morris.edu
www.morris.edu/athletics
• Clarence Houck, Athletic Director
(803) 934-3235
chouck@morris.edu

MOUNT MARTY COLLEGE ATHLETICS
1105 WEST 8TH STREET
YANKTON, SD 57078-3725
605-668-1545
Fax: 605-668-1508
www.mmclancers.com
• Chuck Iverson, Athletic Director
(605) 668-1529
• Andy Bernatow, Sports Information
Director
(605) 668-1601
• Sara Bortscheller, Athletic Trainer
(605) 668-1397

MOUNT MERCY COLLEGE ATHLETICS
1330 ELMHURST DRIVE
CEDAR RAPIDS, IA 52402-4797
319-363-1323 EXT 1376
Fax: 319-363-6341
pgavin@mtmercy.edu
www.mountmercymustangs.com
• Paul Gavin, Director of Athletics
(319) 363-1323
pgavin@mtmercy.edu
• Rhonda Martin, Athletics Office Manager
(319) 363-1323
rmartin@mtmercy.edu
• Jason Furler, Sports Information Director
(319) 363-1323
furler@mtmercy.edu
• Lydia LaMere, Associate Head Athletic
Trainer
(319) 363-1323
llamere@mtmercy.edu

**MOUNT VERNON NAZARENE
UNIVERSITY ATHLETICS**
800 MARTINSBURG ROAD
MOUNT VERNON, OH 43050
740-392-6868
keith.veale@mvnu.edu
www.mvnucougars.com
• Keith Veale, Director of Athletics
(740) 393-6868
keith.veale@mvnu.edu
• Jeana Howald, Assistant Director of
Athletics
(740) 393-6868
jeana.howald@mvnu.edu
• Hannah Miller, Sports Information Director

(740) 392-6868
kirk.mcdonnell@mvnu.edu
• Brian Humphrey, Athletic Trainer
(740) 392-6868
brian.humphrey@mvnu.edu

NORTHWEST COLLEGE ATHLETICS
231 WEST 6TH STREET
POWELL, WY 82435
800-560-4692
www.nwc.edu
• Lourra Barthuly, Athletic Director
(307) 754-6441
lourra.barthuly@nwc.edu
• Leslie Kenney, Head Athletic Trainer
(307) 754-6053
leslie.kenney@nwc.edu
• Janis Beal, Women's Basketball Coach
(307) 754-6026

**NORTHWESTERN COLLEGE (IA)
ATHLETICS**
101 7TH STREET SW
ORANGE CITY, IA 51041
712-707-7292
earl@nwciowa.edu
nwcraiders.com
• Earl Woudstra, Athletic Director
(712) 707-7292
earl@nwciowa.edu
• Alison Cahill, Athletic Facilities Director
(712) 707-7270
allison.fredin@nwciowa.edu
• Matt Bos, Sports Information Director
(712) 707-7289
matt.bos@nwciowa.edu

**NORTHWESTERN COLLEGE (MN)
ATHLETICS**
3003 SNELLING AVENUE NORTH
ST. PAUL, MN 55113-1598
651-631-5219
Fax: 651-628-3350
unweagles.com
• Matt Hill, Vice President for Student Life &
Athletics
(651) 631-5362
mbhill@unwsp.edu
• Tim Grosz, Associate Director of Athletics
(651) 631-5238
tsgrosz@unwsp.edu
• Bell Wilmeth, Assistant Director of
Athletics
(651) 286-7486
bkwilmeth@unwsp.edu
• Dave Hieb, Head Mens Athletic Trainer
(651) 631-5345
dhieb@unwsp.edu
• Melissa Vavra, Head Womens Athletic
Trainer
(651) 628-3499
mmvavra@unwsp.edu

**OHIO DOMINICAN UNIVERSITY
ATHLETICS**
1216 SUNBURY ROAD
COLUMBUS, OH 43219
614-251-4577
Fax: 614-252-2556
athleticsdepartment@ohiodominican.edu
www.ohiodominicanpanthers.com
• Jeff Blair, Athletic Director
(614) 251-4735
• Sandy Rowley, Assistant Athletic Director
(614) 251-4538
rowleys@ohiodominican.edu
• Cindy Hahn, Director of Compliance

(614) 251-4642
hahnc@ohiodominican.edu
• Jamison French, Head Athletic Trainer
(614) 253-4851
frenchj@ohiodominican.edu

OKLAHOMA ATHLETICS, UNIVERSITY OF SCIENCE & ARTS OF
1727 WEST ALABAMA AVENUE
CHICKASHA, OK 73018
405-224-3140
800-933-8726
facmcphersonb@usao.edu
www.usao.edu
• Brisco McPherson, Athletic Director
(405) 574-1249
• Leslie Beaty, Athletic Trainer
(405) 574-1398
lbeaty@usao.edu
• Justin Tinder, Sports Information Director
(405) 574-1210
jtinder@usao.edu

OKLAHOMA CITY UNIVERSITY ATHLETICS
2501 NORTH BLACKWELDER AVENUE
OKLAHOMA CITY, OK 73106
405-208-5000
800-633-7242
Fax: 405-208-5305
www.ocusports.com
• Jim Abbott, Director of Athletics
(405) 208-5301
jabbott@okcu.edu
• Greg Kersgieter, Associate Athletic Director
(405) 208-5317
gkersgieter@okcu.edu
• Kelly Perry, Assistant Athletic Director
(405) 208-5660
kperry@okcu.edu
• Joe Fidelie, Athletic Trainer
(405) 208-6500
jifidele@okcu.edu
• Rich Tortorelli, Assistant Athletic Director for Communications
(405) 208-5304
rtortorelli@okcu.edu

OKLAHOMA WESLEYAN UNIVERSITY ATHLETICS
2201 SILVER LAKE ROAD
BARTLESVILLE, OK 74006
918-335-6219
800 468-6292
info@okwu.edu
www.okwu.edu/athletics
• Mark Molder, Director of Athletics
mmolder@okwu.edu
• Matt Parker, Assistant Director of Athletics
mparker@okwu.edu
• Nick Morris, Sports Information Director
(918) 327-4373
nmorris@okwu.edu

OLIVET NAZARENE UNIVERSITY ATHLETICS
ONE UNIVERSITY AVE
BOURBONNAIS, IL 60914-2345
815-939-5011
800-648-1463
www.onutigers.com
• Gary Newsome, Director of Athletics
(815) 939-5372
gnewsome@olivet.edu
• Brian Hyma, Athletic Training Program Director

(819) 939-5115
bhyma@olivet.edu
• Scott Armstrong, Associate Director of Athletics
(815) 939-5372
sarmstr2@olivet.edu
• Wendy Reid, Sports Information Director
(815) 953-8908
wkreid@olivet.edu
• Nick Birkey, Assistant Sports Information
(815) 928-5565
nbirkey@olivet.edu

OREGON INSTITUTE OF TECHNOLOGY ATHLETICS
3201 CAMPUS DRIVE
KLAMATH FALLS, OR 97601
541-885-1000
800-422-2017
www.oit.edu
• Greg Stewart, Director of Athletics
(541) 885-1452
• Paul Poetsch, Associate Athletic Director
(541) 885-1632
• Michael Garrard, Sports Information
(541) 885-1851

OTTAWA UNIVERSITY ATHLETICS
1001 SOUTH CEDAR STREET
OTTAWA, KS 66067
785-242-5200 EXT 5420
Fax: 785-229-1015
www.ottawabraves.com
• Arabie Conner, Director of Athletics
(785) 248-2600
arabie.conner@ottawa.edu
• Bruce Tate, Associate Director of Athletics
(785) 248-2603
bruce.tate@ottawa.edu
• Kathy Hinderliter, Athletic Department Coordinator
(785) 248-2601
katherine.hinderliter@ottawa.edu
• Jennifer Raybern, Head Athletic Trainer
(785) 248-2627
jennifer.raybern@ottawa.edu

OZARKS ATHLETICS, COLLEGE OF THE
100 OPPORTUNITY AVENUE
POINT LOOKOUT, MO 65726
800-222-0525
bobcats.cofo.edu
• Steve Shepherd, Athletic Director
shepherd@cofo.edu
• Dori Rapinchuk, Sports Information Director
• Gary Turbak, Athletic Trainer
turbak@cofo.edu

PACIFIC UNION COLLEGE ATHLETICS
ONE ANGWIN AVENUE
ANGWIN, CA 94508
707-965-6346
Fax: 707-965-6780
www.puc.edu/pioneers
• Brittany Brown, Athletics Director
(707) 965-6349
bjbrown@puc.edu
• Brandon Lucas, Assistant Athletic Director
(707) 965-6652
blucas@puc.edu
• Michael Hellie, Faculty Athletic Representative
(707) 965-6346
mlhellie@puc.edu

PARK UNIVERSITY PIRATE ATHLETICS
8700 NORTHWEST RIVER PARK DRIVE
PMB 66
PARKVILLE, MO 64152
816-584-6425
Fax: 816-505-5448
www.parkathletics.com
• Claude English, Director of Athletics
(816) 584-6492
• Steve Wilson, Assistant Athletic Director
(816) 584-6490
• Nadine Leishman, Sports Communications Coordinator
(816) 584-6751
• Jamal James, Lead Athletic Trainer
(816) 584-6353

PATTEN UNIVERSITY ATHLETICS
2433 COOLIDGE AVENUE
OAKLAND, CA 94601
415-813-6147
Fax: 415-299-6339
patten.edu

PAUL QUINN COLLEGE ATHLETICS
3837 SIMPSON STUART
DALLAS, TX 75241
214-379-5551
Fax: 214-302-3559
www.pqc.edu/athletics
• Kelsel Thompson, Athletic Director
(214) 379-5551
kthompson@pqc.edu
• Archie Cooley, Football Coach
• Keith McKinnon, Men's Basketball Coach
• Tina Wagoner, Women's Basketball Coach

PERU STATE COLLEGE ATHLETICS
600 HOYT STREET
PERU, NE 68421
800-742-4412
www.pscbobcats.com
• Steve Schneider, Athletic Director
(402) 872-2393
sschneider@peru.edu
• Ted L. Harshbarger, Associate Athletic Director
(402) 872-2380
tharshbarger@peru.edu
• Brenda Lutz, Project Coordinator
(402) 872-2350
blutz@peru.edu

PHILANDER SMITH COLLEGE ATHLETICS
900 WEST DAISY L. GATSON BATES DRIVE
LITTLE ROCK, AR 72202
501-375-9845
Fax: 501-370-5260
www.philanderathletics.com
• Nathan Cochran, Athletic Director
(501) 370-5317
• Roderick Smothers, President
(501) 370-5224
• Daniel Egbe, Faculty Athletic Representative
(501) 370-5232
degbe@philander.edu

POINT PARK UNIVERSITY ATHLETICS
DEPARTMENT OF ATHLETICS
POINT PARK UNIVERSITY
201 WOOD STREET
PITTSBURGH, PA 15222-1984

412-392-3844
Fax: 412-392-4780
www.pointpark.edu/athletics
• Dan Swalga, Director of Athletics
(412) 392-3911
dswalga@pointpark.edu
• Kevin Taylor, Director of Athletic
Communications
(412) 392-3997
ktaylor@pointpark.edu

POINT UNIVERSITY ATHLETICS
507 WEST 10TH STREET
WEST POINT, GA 31833
706-385-1000
www.pointskyhawks.com
• Alan Wilson, Interim Athletic Director
(706) 385-1059
alan.wilson@point.edu
• Monroe Bell, Asst. Sports Information
Director
(706) 385-1414
monroe.bell@point.edu
• Steve Schwepker, Sports Information
Director
(706) 385-1093

PRESENTATION COLLEGE ATHLETICS
1500 NORTH MAIN STREET
ABERDEEN, SD 57401
605-229-8587
800-437-6060
Fax: 605-229-8548
www.pcsaints.com
• Greg Heier, Director of Athletics
(605) 229-8587
• Robb Garofalo, Sports Information Director
(605) 229-8310
• Blake Spindler, Director of Athletic
Training Services
(605) 229-8321

**PURDUE UNIVERSITY CALUMET
ATHLETICS**
2200 169TH STREET
HAMMOND, IN 46323
219-989-2400
Fax: 219-989-2766
www.purduecalsports.com
• Rick Costello, Director of Athletics
(219) 989-2540
• Jennifer Madgiak, Associate Athletic
Director
(219) 989-2728
• Nicole Watkins, Assistant Athletic Director
(219) 989-2506
• John Friend, Athletics Consultant
(219) 989-2540

**PURDUE UNIVERSITY NORTH CENTRAL
ATHLETICS**
1401 SOUTH U.S. 421
WESTVILLE, IN 46391
219-785-5200
www.pncathletics.com
• Tom Albano, Athletic Director
(219) 785-5273
• Shane Prance, Athletic Coordinator
(219) 785-5660
• Doug Cassell, Athletic Trainer
(219) 785-5562

REINHARDT UNIVERSITY ATHLETICS
7300 REINHARDT CIRCLE
WALESKA, GA 30183-2981

770-720-5600
Fax: 770-720-5622
www.reinhardteagles.com
• Bill Popp, Director of Athletics
(770) 720-5568
wcp@reinhardt.edu
• Devante Wynn, Coordinator of Athletic
Operations
(770) 720-5825
ddw1@reinhardt.edu
• Jason Hanes, Sports Information Director
(770) 720-9129
jah@reinhardt.edu
• Jeffrey Pourchier, Assistant Athletic
Director
(770) 720-5824
jmp@reinhardt.edu
• Ashley Wolary, Head Athletic Trainer
(770) 720-5821
alw@reinhardt.edu

**RIO GRANDE ATHLETICS, UNIVERSITY
OF**
218 NORTH COLLEGE AVENUE
RIO GRANDE, OH 45674
740-245-7295
800-282-7201
Fax: 740-245-7555
www.rioredstorm.com
• Jeff Lanham, Athletic Director
(740) 245-7485
jlanham@rio.edu
• Randy Payton, Sports Information Director
(740) 245-7213
rpayton@rio.edu
• Tara Gerlach, Head Athletic Trainer
(740) 245-7299
tgerlach@rio.edu

**ROBERT MORRIS COLLEGE (IL)
ATHLETICS**
401 SOUTH STATE STREET
CHICAGO, IL 60605
312-935-6801
www.rmueagles.com
• Megan Smith Eggert, Director of Athletics
(312) 935-4141
• Jared Williamson, Associate Athletic
Director - Chicago
(312) 935-4110
• Tom Czop, Director of Sports Information
(312) 935-4047

**ROBERTS WESLEYAN COLLEGE
ATHLETICS**
2301 WESTSIDE DRIVE
ROCHESTER, NY 14624
585-594-6100
800-777-4RWC
Fax: 585-594-6580
www.roberts.edu/athletics
• Micah Chapman, Sports Information
Director
(585) 594-6168

**ROCKY MOUNTAIN COLLEGE
ATHLETICS**
1511 POLY DRIVE
BILLINGS, MT 59102
406-657-1000
800-877-6259
Fax: 406-259-9751
www.rocky.edu/athletics
• Bruce Parker, Director of Athletics
(406) 657-1124
bruce.parker@rocky.edu
• Jeff Malby, Sports Information Director

SAINT MARY ATHLETICS, COLLEGE OF
7000 MERCY ROAD
OMAHA, NE 68106-2377
402-399-2400
800-926-5534
Fax: 402-399-2381
www.csmflames.com
• Peter Haze Haring, Athletic Director
(402) 399-2332
pharing@csm.edu
• Emilie Powell, Assistant Athletic Director
(402) 399-2607
• Carolyn Todd Bray, Sports Information
Director
(402) 399-6287
cbray@csm.edu

**SAINT MARY ATHLETICS, UNIVERSITY
OF**
4100 SOUTH 4TH STREET
LEAVENWORTH, KS 66048
913-682-5151
Fax: 913-758-6140
www.gospires.com
• Dale Lennon, Director of Athletics
(701) 355-8315
dclennon@umary.edu
• Daniel Huntley, Associate Director,
Athletics
(701) 355-8337
djhuntley@umary.edu
• Lucas Oerter, Associate Director of
Athletics, Compliance
(701) 355-8386
lmoerter@umary.edu
• Mike Offerdahl, Asst. Director of Athletics,
Operations
(701) 355-8373
mlofferdahl@umary.edu

**SAINT MARY'S UNIVERSITY (TX)
ATHLETICS**
ONE CAMINO SANTA MARIA
SAN ANTONIO, TX 78228
210-436-3528
Fax: 210-436-3040
www.rattlerathletics.com
• Elizabeth Dalton, Athletics Director
(210) 436-3605
• Brian Martinek, Associate Athletics
Director
(210) 436-3434
bmartinek@stmarytx.edu
• Chris Thompson, Assistant Athletics
Director
(210) 436-3528
• Nathan Byerley, Head Athletic Trainer
(210) 436-3342
• Brittany Davis, Assistant Athletic Trainer
(210) 436-5043

SAINT XAVIER UNIVERSITY ATHLETICS
3700 WEST 103RD STREET
CHICAGO, IL 60655
773-298-3001
Fax: 773-298-3111
www.sxucougars.com
• Ken Alston, Interim Athletics Director
kalston@sxu.edu

**SAN DIEGO CHRISTIAN COLLEGE
ATHLETICS**
200 RIVERVIEW PARKWAY
SANTEE, CA 92071
619-201-8700
Fax: 619-201-8797
www.sdcchawks.com

college sports

• Carolyn Peters, Director of Athletics
(619) 201-8746
cpeters@sdcc.edu
• Nick Fortini, Director of Sports Information
(619) 540-9185
nfortini@sdcc.edu
• Jon DePriest, Compliance and Eligibility
Officer
(619) 201-8746
jon.depriest@sdcc.edu
• Carolyn Peters, Head Athletic Trainer
(619) 201-8734
cpeters@sdcc.edu

SCHREINER UNIVERSITY ATHLETICS
2100 MEMORIAL BOULEVARD
KERRVILLE, TX 78028-5697
830-896-5411
800-343-4919
Fax: 800-436-5435
athletics.schreiner.edu
• Ron Masosko, Director of Athletics
(830) 792-7482
rpmacosko@schreiner.edu
• Ryan Brisbin, Sports Information Director
(830) 792-7292
rsbrisbin@schreiner.edu
• Carlile Janel, Head Athletic Trainer
(830) 792-7299
jacarlile@schreiner.edu

SCIENCE AND ARTS OF OKLAHOMA ATHLETICS, UNIVERSITY OF
1727 WEST ALABAMA AVENUE
CHICKASHA, OK 73018
405-224-3140
Fax: 405-574-1220
www.usao.edu/sports
• Brisco McPherson, Athletic Director
(405) 574-1249
facmcphersonb@usao.edu
• Leslie Beaty, Athletic Trainer
(405) 574-1398
lbeaty@usao.edu
• Justin Tinder, Sports Information Director
(405) 574-1210
jtinder@usao.edu

SEATTLE UNIVERSITY ATHLETICS
SEATTLE UNIVERSITY ATHLETICS
901 12TH AVENUE
PO BOX 222000
SEATTLE, WA 98122
206-296-2154
Fax: 206-296-2154
www.goseattleu.com
• Shaney Fink, Director of Athletics
(206) 296-5451
hoganw@seattleu.edu
• Eric Guerra, Associate Athletic Director
(206) 296-6027
guerrae@seattleu.edu
• Erin Engelhardt, Assistant Athletic Director
(206) 296-5603
engelhardte@seattleu.edu
• Suzy Barcomb, Women's Basketball Head
Coach
(206) 296-6406
• Sarah Finney, Athletics Communications
Director
(206) 296-5915
finneysa@seattleu.edu

SETON HILL UNIVERSITY ATHLETICS
ONE SETON HILL DRIVE
GREENSBURG, PA 15601

724-834-2200
800-826-6234
Fax: 724-830-1127
athletics.setonhill.edu
• Chris Snyder, Executive Director of
Athletics
(724) 830-1895
csnyder@setonhill.edu
• Bruce Ivory, Associate Athletic Director
(724) 552-1714
• Jason Greene, Director of Athletic
Communication
(724) 830-1132
greene@setonhill.edu

SHAWNEE STATE UNIVERSITY ATHLETICS
940 SECOND STREET
PORTSMOUTH, OH 45662-4344
740-351-3205
jhamilton@shawnee.edu
www.ssubears.com
• Jeff Hamilton, Athletic Director
(740) 351-3393
jhamilton@shawnee.edu
• Jonathon Loughridge, Sports Information
Director
(740) 351-3313
jloughridge@shawnee.edu
• Jeff Nickel, Women's Basketball Head
Coach
(740) 351-3271
jnickel@shawnee.edu

SIENA HEIGHTS UNIVERSITY ATHLETICS
1247 EAST SIENA HEIGHTS DRIVE
ADRIAN, MI 49221
517-264-7876
800-521-0009
Fax: 517-264-7737
shusaints.com
• Fred Smith, Athletic Director
(517) 264-7876
fsmith@sienaheights.edu
• Sue Syljebeck, Assistant Athletic Director
(517) 264-7871
ssyljebe@sienaheights.edu
• Crystal Wilcoxen, Sports Information
Director
(517) 264-7843

SOUTHERN OREGON UNIVERSITY ATHLETICS
1250 SISKIYOU BOULEVARD
ASHLAND, OR 97520
541-552-7672
Fax: 541-552-6543
souraiders.com
• Matt Sayre, Director of Athletics
(541) 552-6273
sayrem@sou.edu
• Bobby Heiken, Associate Athletic Director
(541) 552-6824
heikenb@sou.edu
• Josh McDermott, Sports Information
Director
(541) 552-6801
mcdermotj@sou.edu
• Kristy Johnson, Head Athletic Trainer
(541) 552-6830

SOUTHERN UNIVERSITY (NEW ORLEANS) ATHLETICS
6400 PRESS DRIVE
NEW ORLEANS, LA 70126

504-286-5000
Fax: 504-284-5520
www.suno.edu/athletics
• Yhann Plummer, Interim Athletic Director
(504) 286-5191
yplummer@suno.edu

SOUTHWEST ADVENTIST UNIVERSITY
100 WEST HILLCREST
KEENE, TX 76059
817-645-3921
800-433-2240
Fax: 817-556-4744
• James The, Vice President for Student
Services
(817) 202-6719
jthe@swau.edu

SOUTHWEST ATHLETICS, COLLEGE OF THE
6610 NORTH LOVINGTON HIGHWAY
HOBBS, NM 88240
505-392-6561
800-530-4400
Fax: 505-392-6006
• William J. Weidner, Director of Athletics
(575) 492-2187
wweidner@usw.edu
• Betty Casey, Student-Athlete Academic
Support Liaison
(575) 492-2143
bcasey@usw.edu
• Dana Lambert, Sports Information Liaison
(575) 492-2144
dlambert@usw.edu
• Steve Burback, Head Athletic Trainer
(575) 492-2150
sburback@usw.edu

SOUTHWESTERN ASSEMBLIES OF GOD UNIVERSITY ATHLETICS
1200 SYCAMORE STREET
WAXAHACHIE, TX 75165
972-937-4010
888-YES-SAGU
info@sagu.edu
www.sagu.edu/athletics/athletics-home
• Jesse Godding, Athletic Director
(975) 825-4811
jgodding@sagu.edu
• Stuart Dunn, Athletic Trainer
(972) 825-4671
sdunn@sagu.edu
• Natalie Tristan, Sports Information Director
ntristan@sagu.edu

SOUTHWESTERN COLLEGE ATHLETICS
100 COLLEGE STREET
WINFIELD, KS 67156-2499
620-229-6359
800-846-1543
Fax: 620-229-6124
www.buildersports.com
• Matt Shelton, Associate Athletic Director
(620) 229-6359
matt.shelton@sckans.edu
• Scott Nuss, Assistant Athletic Director
(620) 229-6299
• Jeanice Lowry, Athletic Administrative
Assistant
(620) 229-6218
• Lock Schnelle, Head Athletic Trainer
(620) 229-6375
lock.schnelle@sckans.edu

SPALDING UNIVERSITY ATHLETICS
845 SOUTH THIRD STREET
LOUISVILLE, KY 40203
502-585-9911
800-896-8941
Fax: 502-585-7117
www.spaldingathletics.com
• Roger Burkman, Director of Athletics
(502) 873-7141
• Brian Clinard, Sports Information Director
(502) 873-4206

SPRING ARBOR COLLEGE ATHLETICS
106 EAST MAIN STREET
SPRING ARBOR, MI 49283
517-750-6503
800-968-0011
Fax: 517-750-2745
www.saucougars.com
• Ryan Cottingham, Athletic Director
(517) 750-6505
ryan.cottingham@arbor.edu
• Ryan Frost, Assistant Athletic Director
(517) 750-6568
ryan.frost@arbor.edu
• Betsy Martinez, Assistant Athletic Director
(517) 750-6523
elizabeth.martinez2@arbor.edu
• Chris Bauman, Sports Information Director
(517) 750-6504
christopher.bauman@arbor.edu

SPRING HILL COLLEGE ATHLETICS
4000 DAUPHIN STREET
MOBILE, AL 36608
251-380-3485
800-742-6704
Fax: 251-460-2196
www.shcbadgers.com
• Jim Hall, Director of Athletics & Recreation
(251) 380-3491
• Chad LeBlanc, Assistant Athletic Director
(251) 380-4077
cleblanc@shc.edu
• Jim Stennett, Sports Information Director
(251) 380-4468

ST. ANDREWS PRESBYTERIAN ATHLETICS
1700 DOGWOOD MILE
LAURINBURG, NC 28352
910-277-5555
800-763-0198
Fax: 910-277-5020
battengt@sa.edu
www.sauknights.com
• Glenn Batten, Athletic Director
(910) 277-5556
battengt@sa.edu
• Elizabeth Burris, Director of Compliance
(910) 277-5480
burrises@sa.edu
• Troy Baranik, Sports Information Director
(910) 277-5751
baraniktn@sa.edu
• Brianne Morith, Head Athletic Trainer
(910) 277-3977

ST. FRANCIS ATHLETICS, UNIVERSITY OF
500 WILCOX STREET
JOLIET, IL 60435
815-740-3464
800-735-7500
Fax: 815-740-3841
dlaketa@stfrancis.edu
www.gofightingsaints.com

• Dave Laketa, Director of Athletics
(815) 740-3842
dlaketa@stfrancis.edu
• Cara Currier, Assistant Director of Athletics
(815) 740-3407
ccurrier@stfrancis.edu
• Art Campos, Head Certified Athletic Trainer
(815) 740-3845
acampos@stfrancis.edu
• Dave Hilbert, Sports Information Director
(815) 740-3614
dhilbert@stfrancis.edu

ST. JOSEPH ATHLETICS, COLLEGE OF
71 CLEMENT ROAD
RUTLAND, VT 05701
802-773-5900
802-773-5900
www.csj.edu/athletics
• Jeffrey Brown, Athletic Director
(802) 776-5278
• Jack Boymer, Sports Information Director
(802) 776-5278

ST. LOUIS COLLEGE OF PHARMACY ATHLETICS
4588 PARKVIEW PLACE
ST. LOUIS, MO 63110
314-367-8700
800-2STLCOP
www.eutecticsports.com
• Jill Harter, Director of Athletics
(314) 446-8346
• Katie Payne, Athletic Department Assistant
(314) 446-8343
• Briana Hepfinger, Sports Information Director
(314) 446-8348

STATE UNIVERSITY OF NEW YORK AT DELHI ATHLETICS
2 MAIN ST
DELHI, NY 13753
607-746-4675
Fax: 607-746-4119
delhibroncos.com
• Bob Backus, Director of Athletics
(607) 746-4677
• Lynn Oles, Athletics Department Secretary
(607) 746-4794

STERLING COLLEGE ATHLETICS
125 WEST COOPER
STERLING, KS 67579
620-278-4335
800-346-1017
Fax: 620-278-4319
www.scwarriors.com
• Gary Kempf, Athletic Director
(620) 278-4469
gkempf@sterling.edu
• Justin Morris, Assistant Athletic Director
(620) 278-4324
jmorris@sterling.edu
• Caden Ford, Sports Information Director
(858) 204-4762
caden.ford@sterling.edu
• Joe Streckfus, Certified Athletic Trainer
(620) 278-4338
jstreckfus@sterling.edu

TABOR COLLEGE ATHLETICS
400 SOUTH JEFFERSON
HILLSBORO, KS 67063
620-947-3121
Fax: 620-947-6276
www.taborbluejays.com
• Rusty Allen, Vice President of Athletics
(620) 947-3121
• Karol Hunt, Associate Athletic Director
(620) 947-3121
karolh@tabor.edu
• John Ruder, Assistant Athletic Director
(620) 947-3121
johnr@tabor.edu

TALLADEGA COLLEGE ATHLETICS
627 WEST BATTLE STREET
TALLADEGA, AL 35160
256-326-0206
www.talladegatornadoes.com
• Kevin Herod, Athletic Director
(256) 761-8757
• Demond Walker, Associate Athletic Director
(256) 589-2001
• Demond Walker, Sports Information Director
(256) 761-6411
dlwalker@talladega.edu

TAYLOR UNIVERSITY ATHLETICS
236 WEST READE AVENUE
UPLAND, IN 46989
765-998-5311
Fax: 765-998-4920
amstucky@taylor.edu
athletics.taylor.edu
• Kyle Gould, Athletics Director
(765) 998-5314
kygould@taylor.edu
• Amy Stucky, Associate Athletics Director
(765) 998-4635
amstucky@taylor.edu
• Seth Mikel, Assitant Athletics Director for Communications
(765) 998-4569
stmikel@taylor.edu

TENNESSEE WESLEYAN COLLEGE ATHLETICS
204 EAST COLLEGE STREET
ATHENS, TN 37303
423-745-7504
800-742-5892
Fax: 423-744-9968
www.twcbulldogs.com
• Donny Mayfield, Athletic Director
(423) 746-5253
dmayfield@twcnet.edu
• Jennifer Harrison, Director of Sports Information
(423) 252-1365
jharrison@twcnet.edu
• Kelley Seekins, Head Athletic Trainer
(423) 252-1104
mneffendorf@twcnet.edu

TEXAS AT TYLER ATHLETICS, UNIVERSITY OF
3900 UNIVERSITY BOULEVARD
TYLER, TX 75799
903-566-7105
Fax: 903-566-7078
www.uttylerpatriots.com

TEXAS COLLEGE ATHLETICS
2404 NORTH GRAND AVENUE
TYLER, TX 75702
903-593-8311 EXT 67
800-306-6299
Fax: 903-593-0588
www.texascollege.edu/pages/athletics
• Elissia Burwell, Athletic Director
(903) 593-8311
eburwell@texascollege.edu
• Angela Lawson, Athletic Coordinator
(903) 593-8311
alawson@texascollege.edu

**TEXAS WESLEYAN UNIVERSITY
ATHLETICS**
1201 WESLEYAN STREET
FORT WORTH, TX 76105
817-531-4857
Fax: 817-531-4208
www.ramsports.net
• Steven Trachier, Director of Athletics
(817) 531-4874
satrachier@txwes.edu
• Kevin Millikan, Associate Athletic Director
(817) 531-7518
kmillikan@txwes.edu

**TEXAS-PERMIAN BASIN ATHLETICS,
UNIVERSITY OF**
4901 EAST UNIVERSITY
ODESSA, TX 79762
432-552-2675
Fax: 432-552-3675
www.utpbfalcons.com
• Steve Aicinena, Athletics Director
(432) 552-2675
aicinena_s@utpb.edu
• Erin Brohn, Director of Compliance
(432) 552-3676
bohn_e@utpb.edu

THOMAS UNIVERSITY ATHLETICS
1501 MILLPOND ROAD
THOMASVILLE, GA 31792
229-226-1621
800-538-9784
Fax: 229-226-1653
www.tunighthawks.com
• Mike Lee, Athletic Director
(229) 584-2432
mlee@thomasu.edu
• Ricky Zambrano, Associate Athletic
Director
(229) 584-2437
rzambrano@thomasu.edu

TOUGALOO COLLEGE ATHLETICS
500 WEST COUNTY LINE ROAD
TOUGALOO, MS 39174
601-977-7700
Fax: 601-977-7866
www.tougaloo.edu/athletics
• Yolanda Brown, Assistant Athletic Director
(601) 977-6171
ybrown@tougaloo.edu

TRINE UNIVERSITY ATHLETICS
HERSHEY HALL
1 UNIVERSITY AVE
ANGOLA, IN 46703
260-665-4142
Fax: 260-665-4839
trinethunder.com
• Matt Land, Athletic Director
(260) 665-4142

landm@trine.edu
• Brooks Miller, Assistant Athletic Director
(260) 665-4843
millerb@trine.edu
• Matt Vader, Sports Information Director
(260) 665-4446

**TRINITY CHRISTIAN COLLEGE
ATHLETICS**
6601 WEST COLLEGE DRIVE
PALOS HEIGHTS, IL 60463
708-239-4779
Fax: 708-396-7460
athletics@trnty.edu
athletics.trnty.edu
• Bill Schepel, Athletics Director
(708) 239-4805
bill.schepel@trnty.edu
• Josh Lenarz, Assistant Athletics Director
(708) 239-4824
josh.lenarz@trnty.edu
• Melanie Monroe, Head Athletic Trainer
(708) 239-4774
melanie.monroe@trnty.edu

UNION COLLEGE (KY) ATHLETICS
310 COLLEGE STREET
BARBOURVILLE, KY 40906
606-546-1236
800-489-8646
Fax: 606-546-1286
www.ucbulldogs.com
• Tim Curry, Director of Athletics
(606) 546-1682
tcurry@unionky.edu
• Jay Stancil, Director of Strategic Sports
Communications
(606) 546-1292
jstancil@unionky.edu
• Jon North, Director of Sports Broadcasting
(606) 546-1546
jnorth@unionky.edu
• Clay Butler, Director of Sports Medicine
(606) 546-1303
cbutler@unionky.edu

UNITY COLLEGE ATHLETICS
90 QUAKER HILL ROAD
UNITY, ME 04988
207-509-7100
Fax: 207-948-5626
info@unity.edu
athletics.unity.edu
• Chris Kein, Athletic Director
(207) 509-7283
ckein@unity.edu

**UNIVERSITY OF JAMESTOWN
ATHLETICS**
6000 COLLEGE LANE
JAMESTOWN, ND 58405
701-252-3467
800-336-2554
Fax: 701-253-4318
www.jimmieathletics.com
• Sean Johnson, Director of Athletics
sean.johnson@uj.edu
• Tom Hager, Associate Athletics Director
thager@uj.edu
• Kelsey Titus, Assistant Athletics Director
ktitus@uj.edu
• Ryan Mikkelson, Sports Information
Director
rmikkels@uj.edu
• Mitch Lang, Head Athletic Trainer
lang@uj.edu

UNIVERSITY OF PIKEVILLE ATHLETICS
147 SYCAMORE STREET
PIKEVILLE, KY 41501
606-218-5250
Fax: 606-218-5269
athletics@pc.edu
upikebears.com
• Robert Staggs, Athletic Director
(606) 218-5357
• Dan White, Assistant Athletic Director
(606) 218-5350
• Meg Wright Sidle, Athletics Compliance
Officer
(606) 218-5290
• Erica Pitt, Head Athletic Trainer
(606) 218-5359

URBANA UNIVERSITY ATHLETICS
579 COLLEGE WAY
URBANA, OH 43078
937-484-1325
Fax: 937-772-9238
athletics@urbana.edu
www.uublueknights.com
• Larry Cox, Director of Athletics
(937) 772-9238
• Nikki Pluger, Associate Athletic Director of
Compliance
(937) 772-9305
nicole.pluger@urbana.edu
• Derrick Blyberg, Sports Information
Director
(937) 772-9211
• Jassen Dobyns, Head Athletic Trainer
(937) 772-9304

**VANGUARD UNIVERSITY OF SOUTHERN
CALIFORNIA ATHLETICS**
55 FAIR DRIVE
COSTA MESA, CA 92626
714-556-3610
athletics@vanguard.edu
www.vanguardlions.com
• Rhett Soliday, Athletic Director
(714) 619-6601
rhett.soliday@vanguard.edu
• Jeff Bussell, Associate Athletic Director
(714) 619-6602
jeffrey.bussell@vanguard.edu
• Mike Teague, Coordinator of Compliance
(714) 619-6605
michael.teague@vanguard.edu
• Darin Voigt, Head Athletic Trainer
(714) 619-6617
dvoigt@vanguard.edu

VITERBO ATHLETICS UNIVERSITY
400 VITERBO DRIVE
LA CROSSE, WI 54601
608-796-3811
Fax: 608-796-3818
athletics@viterbo.edu
www.viterboathletics.com
• Barry Fried, Director of Athletics
(608) 796-3812
bjfried@viterbo.edu
• Wayne Wagner, Assistant Athletics
Director
(608) 796-3814
wrwagner@viterbo.edu
• Jo Ann Marson, Faculty Athletics
Representative
(608) 796-3363
jmmarson@viterbo.edu
• Nicole Ross, Athletic Trainer
(608) 796-3815
nrross@gundersenhealth.org

VOORHEES COLLEGE ATHLETICS
213 WIGGINS DRIVE
PO BOX 678
DENMARK, SC 29042
803-780-1234
866-685-9904
Fax: 803-793-4584
www.voorhees.edu/athletics
• Willie Jefferson, Director of Athletics
(803) 780-1049

WALDORF COLLEGE ATHLETICS
106 SOUTH 6TH STREET
FOREST CITY, IA 50436
641-585-8182
Fax: 641-585-8184
www.waldorfwarriors.com
• Denny Jerome, Director of Athletics
(641) 585-8163
jeromed@waldorf.edu
• Kristi Osheim, Manager of Athletic
Operations
(641) 585-8782
osheimk@waldorf.edu
• Joe Squires, Director of Athletic Events
(641) 585-1655
joe.squires@waldorf.edu
• Heidi Laube, Head Athletic Trainer
(641) 585-8394
whiteh@waldorf.edu

WALSH UNIVERSITY ATHLETICS
2020 EAST MAPLE STREET
NORTH CANTON, OH 44720
330-490-7090
800-362-9846
Fax: 330-490-7038
athletics.walsh.edu
• Dale Howard, Director of Athletics
(330) 490-7303
dhoward@walsh.edu
• Jason Fautas, Assistant Athletic Director
(330) 490-7437
jfautas@walsh.edu
• Logan Smith, Sports Information Director
(330) 490-7254
lsmith@walsh.edu

WARNER PACIFIC COLLEGE ATHLETICS
2219 SE 68TH AVENUE
PORTLAND, OR 97215
503-517-1261
Fax: 503-517-1352
www.wpcknights.com
• Frank Johnson, Interim Athletic Director
(503) 734-6463
fjjohnson@warnerpacific.edu
• Matt Gregg, Assistant Athletic Director
(503) 517-1370
mgregg@warnerpacific.edu
• Amy Engilis, Head Athletic Trainer
(503) 517-1063
aengilis@warnerpacific.edu

WARNER UNIVERSITY ATHLETICS
13895 HIGHWAY 27
LAKE WALES, FL 33859
863-638-1426
800-309-9563
Fax: 863-638-3776
www.warnerroyals.com
• Kevin Jones, Athletic Director
(863) 638-7297
• John Dunlap, Assistant Athletic Director
(863) 638-7135

**WAYLAND BAPTIST UNIVERSITY
ATHLETICS**
1900 WEST 7TH STREET
PLAINVIEW, TX 79072
806-291-1000
800-588-1928
Fax: 806-291-1962
rick.cooper@wbu.edu
www.wbuathletics.com
• Rick Cooper, Athletics Director
(806) 291-3801
rick.cooper@wbu.edu
• Landon Schumacher, Head Athletic
Trainer
(806) 291-3803
schumacherl@wbu.edu

**WEBBER INTERNATIONAL UNIVERSITY
ATHLETICS**
1201 NORTH SCENIC HIGHWAY
BABSON PARK, FL 33827
863-638-2980
1-800-741-1844
Fax: 863-638-2979
www.webberathletics.com
• Richie Darren, Director of Athletics
(863) 638-2953
richieda@webber.edu
• Tim Desmarteau, Assistant Athletic
Director
(863) 638-2989
desmarteautj@webber.edu
• Kyle Blue, Sports Information Director
(863) 638-2980
bluekyler@webber.edu
• Jen Hamil, Game Day Operations
Coordinator
(863) 899-1431
hamilje@webber.edu

**WEST VIRGINIA UNIVERSITY INSTITUTE
OF TECHNOLOGY ATHLETICS**
405 FAYETTE PIKE
MONTGOMERY, WV 25136
304-442-3121
Fax: 304-442-3499
tech-athletics@mail.wvu.edu
goldenbearathletics.com
• Kenneth Howell, Director of Athletics
(304) 442-3380
kenneth.howell@mail.wvu.edu
• Jenna Everhart, Senior Woman
Administrator
(304) 981-6216
• Becky Brouse, Sports Information Director
(304) 981-6211
rsbrouse@mail.wvu.edu
• Carrie Williams, Athletic Trainer
(304) 442-3181
cwilliam@mail.wvu.edu

WESTMONT COLLEGE ATHLETICS
955 LA PAZ ROAD
SANTA BARBARA, CA 93108
805-565-6000
Fax: 805-565-6221
athletics.westmont.edu
• Dave Odell, Director of Athletics
(805) 565-6010
dodell@westmont.edu
• John Moore, Associate Athletic Director
(805) 565-6013
moore@westmont.edu
• Kirsten Moore, Associate Athletic Director
(805) 565-6836
kirstenmoore@westmont.edu

WILEY COLLEGE ATHLETICS
711 WILEY AVENUE
MARSHALL, TX 75670
903-927-3300
Fax: 903-938-8100
www.wileyathletics.com
• Joseph Morale, Acting Director of Athletics
(903) 927-3233
jmorale@wileyc.edu
• Andrew Glover, Sports Information
Director
(903) 927-3399
adglover@wileyc.edu
• Jameus Hartsfield, Assistant Sports
Information Director
(903) 927-2486
jlhartsfield@wileyc.edu
• LaKyva Bason, Assistant Athletic Director
(903) 927-3294
lwalton-bason@wileyc.edu

WILLIAM CAREY COLLEGE ATHLETICS
498 TUSCAN AVENUE
HATTIESBURG, MS 39401
601-318-6051
Fax: 601-318-6454
www.wmcarey.edu
• Steve Knight, Athletic Director
(601) 318-6415
sknight@wmcarey.edu
• Kevin Rosiere, Graduate Asst Sports
Informations Golf Head C
(601) 466-6380

WILLIAM PENN UNIVERSITY ATHLETICS
201 TRUEBLOOD AVENUE
OSKALOOSA, IA 52577
641-673-1018
Fax: 641-673-1373
www.statesmenathletics.com
• Greg Hafner, Athletics Director
(641) 673-2168
hafnerg@wmpenn.edu
• Mike Christner, Assistant Athletic Director
(641) 673-1707
• Wade Steinlage, Sports Information
Director
(641) 673-1025
steinlagew@wmpenn.edu

**WILLIAM WOODS UNIVERSITY
ATHLETICS**
ONE UNIVERSITY AVE
FULTON, MO 65251
573-642-2251
Fax: 573-592-1146
wwuowls.com
• Jason Vittone, Director of Intercollegiate
Athletics
(573) 592-1642
jason.vittone@williamwoods.edu
• Tracy Gastineau, Associate Director of
Intercollegiate Athletics
(573) 592-4326
tracy.gastineau@williamwoods.edu

**WILLIAMS BAPTIST COLLEGE
ATHLETICS**
60 WEST FULBRIGHT AVE
WALNUT RIDGE, AR 72476
870-886-6741
Fax: 870-886-3924
www.wbceagles.com
• Jeff Rider, Director of Athletics
(870) 759-4194
• Shane Stolz, Sports Information Director
(870) 759-4156

college sports

• Misty Colvey, Head Athletic Trainer
(870) 759-4196

WINDSOR ATHLETICS, UNIVERSITY OF
401 SUNSET AVENUE
WINDSOR, ON, CANADA N9B 3P4
519-253-3000 EXT 2437
lancers@uwindsor.ca
golancers.ca
• Mike Harvey, Athletic Director
havey@uwindsor.ca
• Eric Vandenbroucke, Associate Athletic
Director
evander@uwindsor.ca
• Elisa Mitton, Sports Information
Coordinator

**XAVIER UNIVERSITY OF LOUISIANA
ATHLETICS**
1 DREXEL DR
CAMPUS BOX 92
NEW ORLEANS, LA 70125
504-520-7329
www.xulagold.com
• Jason Horn, Director of Athletics and
Recreation
(504) 520-7329
jhorn1@xula.edu

YORK COLLEGE (NE) ATHLETICS
1125 EAST 8TH STREET
YORK, NE 68467
402-363-5635
800-950-9675
Fax: 402-363-5738
www.ycpanthers.com
• Jared Stark, Director of Athletics
(402) 363-5635
jastark@york.edu
• Trent Hinton, Sports Information Director
(402) 363-5698
thinton@york.edu
• Chad Karcher, Athletic Trainer
(402) 363-5734
cekarcher@york.edu

NCAA Division I Colleges

AKRON ATHLETICS, UNIVERSITY OF
DEPT. OF INTERCOLLEGIATE
ATHLETICS
INFOCISION STADIUM
375 E EXCHANGE ST
AKRON, OH 44304
330-972-6920
888-992-5766
Fax: 330-972-5473
gozips.com
• Matthew Juravich, Interim Director of
Intercollegiate Athletics
(330) 972-2308
mjuravich@uakron.edu
• Markus Jennings, Deputy Director,
Athletics/Chief Operating Officer
(330) 972-5517
mjennings1@uakron.edu
• Jackie Wallgren, Senior Associate
Athletics Director/SWA

ALABAMA ATHLETICS, UNIVERSITY OF
DEPT. OF INTERCOLLEGIATE
ATHLETICS
UNIV. OF ALABAMA
PO BOX 870323
TUSCALOOSA, AL 35487

205-348-3600
www.rolltide.com
• Greg Byrne, Director, Athletics
(205) 348-3600
• Shane Lyons, Executive Deputy Director of
Athletics/COO
slyons@ia.ua.edu

**ALABAMA BIRMINGHAM ATHLETICS,
UNIVERSITY OF**
617 13TH ST S
BIRMINGHAM, AL 35294
www.uabsports.com
• Mark Ingram, Associate Vice
President/Director of Athletics
(205) 934-0766
ingramad@uab.edu

**ALABAMA STATE UNIVERSITY
ATHLETICS**
ALABAMA STATE UNIVERSITY
915 S JACKSON STREET
MONTGOMERY, AL 36106
334-229-4800
Fax: 334-262-2971
asuathletics@alasu.edu
www.bamastatesports.com
• Jason Cable, Director of Athletics
HornetAD@alasu.edu
• Cyrus Russ, Deputy Director of
Athletics/External Operations
 ext 7612
cruss@alasu.edu

**ALCORN STATE UNIVERSITY
ATHLETICS**
1000 ASU DRIVE
SUITE 510
LORMAN, MS 39096
601-877-6500
Fax: 601-877-3821
www.alcornsports.com
• Garry Lewis, Assistant Athletic Director for
Compliance
(601) 877-6115
• Cyrus K. Russ, Assistant Vice President
for Athletic Compliance
(601) 877-6115
ckruss@alcorn.edu
• Jivana Smith, Coordinator of
Student-Athlete Services
(601) 877-6497
jivanna@alcorn.edu
• LaDonna Cook, Athletic Academic
Advisor/Learning Specialist
(601) 877-6386
lcook@alcorn.edu

AMERICAN UNIVERSITY ATHLETICS
AMERICAN UNIVERSITY ATHLETICS
BENDER ARENA
4400 MASSACHUSETTS AVENUE NW
WASHINGTON, DC 20016
202-885-3104
Fax: 202-885-3029
eaglesclub@american.edu
www.aueagles.com
• JM Caparro, Director of Athletics &
Recreation
(202) 885-3001
walker@american.edu
• Brian Chepulis, Assoc. AD, Facilities &
Operations
(202) 885-3074
chepulis@american.edu

**APPALACHIAN STATE UNIVERSITY
ATHLETICS**
ATHLETICS CENTER
ASU BOX 32025
BOONE, NC 28608
828-262-7825
Fax: 828-262-2556
www.appstatesports.com
• Doug Gillin, Director of Athletics
(828) 262-7825
gillindp@appstate.edu
• Jonathan Reeder, Exec. Assoc. Athletics
Director/CFO
(828) 406-5992
reederjb@appstate.edu
• Rene Salinas, Faculty Athletics
Representative
(828) 262-2866
salinasra@appstate.edu
• Erika Cheung, Sr. Associate Athletics
Director
(828) 262-8580
cheungee@appstate.edu

ARIZONA ATHLETICS, UNIVERSITY OF
MCKALE CENTER
1 NATIONAL CHAMPIONSHIP DRIVE
PO BOX 210096
TUCSON, AZ 85721
520-621-2200
arizonawildcats.com
• Dave Heeke, Vice President/Director of
Athletics
(520) 621-4622
uofaad@arizona.edu

**ARIZONA STATE UNIVERSITY
ATHLETICS**
CARSON CENTER
PO BOX 872505
TEMPE, AZ 85287-2505
480-965-3482
sparkycares@asu.edu
thesundevils.com
• Graham Rossini, Vice President for
University Athletics
(480) 965-0983
• Lisa Young, Deputy Athletics Director
(480) 965-8054

**ARKANSAS LITTLE ROCK ATHLETICS,
UNIVERSITY OF**
2801 S UNIVERSITY AVENUE
JACK STEPHENS CENTER
LITTLE ROCK, AR 72204
lrtrojans.com
• Frank Cuervo, Director of Athletics
(501) 916-3167
• Michael Gibbs, Deputy AD for Internal
Operations
(501) 914-9475
magibbs1@ualr.edu
• Maggie Bailey, Associate AD/Senior
Woman Administrator
(501) 569-3448
mestrange@ualr.edu

**ARKANSAS PINE BLUFF ATHLETICS,
UNIVERSITY OF**
1200 NORTH UNIVERSITY DRIVE
MAIL SLOT 4891
PINE BLUFF, AR 71601
www.uapblionsroar.com
• Chris Robinson, Director of Athletics
(870) 575-7950
robinsonec@uapb.edu
• Roger Totten, Deputy Athletics Director

(870) 575-8544
tottenr@uapb.edu

ARKANSAS STATE UNIVERSITY ATHLETICS
ARKANSAS STATE ATHLETIC DEPT.
217 OLYMPIC DRIVE
JONESBORO, AR 72401
870-972-3880
www.astateredwolves.com
• Jeff Purinton, Vice Chancellor for Intercollegiate Athletics
(870) 972-3983
athleticsdirector@astate.edu
• Rich Zvosec, Deputy Director of Athletics
(870) 972-3005
rzvosec@astate.edu
• Amy Holt, Executive Senior Associate AD/SWA
(870) 680-4163
aholt@astate.edu

AUBURN UNIVERSITY ATHLETICS
AUBURN ATHLETICS COMPLEX
392 S DONAHUE DRIVE
AUBURN, AL 36849
855-282-2010
athletics@auburn.edu
www.auburntigers.com
• John Cohen, Athletics Director
athletic_director@auburn.edu

AUSTIN PEAY STATE UNIVERSITY ATHLETICS
WINFIELD DUNN CENTER
CORNER OF MARION STREET & ROBB ABENUE
ROOM 227
CLARKSVILLE, TN 37040
931-221-7904
letsgopeay.com
• Gerald Harrison, Director of Athletics
(931) 221-7904
• Toni-Ann Derby, Sr. Associate Director, Athletics
(931) 221-7454
derbyt@apsu.edu
• Niesha Campbell, Deputy Director of Athletics
campbelln@apsu.edu

BALL STATE UNIVERSITY ATHLETICS
BALL STATE ATHLETICS
HP 260
MUNCIE, IN 47306-0929
www.ballstatesports.com
• Jeff Mitchell, Director of Athletics
(765) 285-5131
athletics@bsu.edu
• Alex Perry, Deputy Athletics Director
• Emma Kumar, Associate Director of Athletics
(765) 285-4988
emma.kumar@bsu.edu

BAYLOR UNIVERSITY ATHLETICS
1500 S UNIVERSITY PARKS DRIVE
WACO, TX 76706
254-710-1234
www.baylorbears.com
• Mack Rhoades, VP & Director of Intercollegiate Athletics
(254) 710-1222
lauren_phillips@baylor.edu

BELMONT UNIVERSITY ATHLETICS
1900 BELMONT BOULEVARD
NASHVILLE, TN 37212-3757
615-460-6420
Fax: 615-460-5584
www.belmontbruins.com
• Scott Corley, Director of Athletics
(615) 460-5547
scott.corley@belmont.edu
• Steve Barrick, Associate AD/Director of Facilities
(615) 460-6857
steve.barrick@belmont.edu
• Renee Schultz, Associate AD, Student Services/SWA
(615) 460-6015
renee.schultz@belmont.edu

BETHUNE-COOKMAN UNIVERSITY ATHLETICS
640 DR. MARY MCLEOD BETHUNE BOULEVARD
DAYTONA BEACH, FL 32114
386-481-2000
www.bcuathletics.com
• Reggie Theus, Athletic Director/Men's Head Basketball Coach
• George Bright, Deputy Director of Athletics
(386) 481-2202
brightg@cookman.edu
• Clarissa West-White, Faculty Athletics Representative
(386) 481-2198
whitec@cookman.edu
• Cassandra Abrams, Asst. Athletic Dir., Academic Support Services
(386) 481-2191
abramsc@cookman.edu

BINGHAMTON UNIVERSITY ATHLETICS
PO BOX 6000
BINGHAMTON, NY 13902-6000
607-777-2043
www.bubearcats.com
• Eugene Marshall, Jr., Director of Athletics
(607) 777-2043
athletics@binghamton.edu
• Leigh Ann Savidge-Morris, Sr. Assoc. Dir. of Athletics, Internal Ops./SWA
(607) 777-3323
lsavidge@binghamton.edu

BIRMINGHAM-SOUTHERN COLLEGE ATHLETICS
900 ARKADELPHIA ROAD
BIRMINGHAM, AL 35254
www.bscsports.net
• Kyndall Waters, Athletics Director
(205) 226-4935
kwaters@bsc.edu
• Kenneth Cox, Assistant AD/SWA
(205) 226-7780
kcox@bsc.edu
• Jan Weisberg, Associate AD, Internal Relations
(205) 226-4797
jweisber@bsc.edu

BOISE STATE UNIVERSITY ATHLETICS
1910 UNIVERSITY DRIVE
MAIL STOP 1020
BOISE, ID 83725-1020
www.broncosports.com
• Jeramiah Dickey, Director of Athletics
(208) 426-1826
athleticdirector@boisestate.edu
• Christina Van Tol, Sr. Associate Athletic

Director
(208) 426-1655
cvantol@boisestate.edu

BOSTON COLLEGE ATHLETICS
CONTE FORUM
140 COMMONWEALTH AVENUE
CHESTNUT HILL, MA 02467
617-552-3000
bceagles.com
• Blake James, Director of Athletics
(617) 552-4680
ad@bc.edu

BOSTON UNIVERSITY ATHLETICS
285 BABCOCK STREET
BOSTON, MA 02215
617-353-4630
Fax: 617-353-5286
gobu@bu.edu
goterriers.com
• Drew Marrochello, Director of Athletics
(617) 353-4631
bmkane@bu.edu
• Kate Bergstrom, Senior Associate Director of Athletics/SWA
(617) 353-4683
kbergs@bu.edu
• Brittany Kane, Senior Associate Director of Athletics
(617) 353-4630
bmkane@bu.edu

BOWLING GREEN STATE UNIVERSITY ATHLETICS
SEBO ATHLETIC CENTER
1610 STADIUM DRIVE
BOWLING GREEN, OH 43403
419-372-2401
bgsufalcons.com
• Derek van der Merwe, Director of Athletics & Recreation
athleticdirector@bgsu.edu
• Stacy Kosciak, Senior Associate AD/SWA, Deputy Title IX Coord.
(419) 372-7056
smkosci@bgsu.edu
• Jim Elsasser, Senior Associate AD, Internal Affairs
(419) 372-7054
jelsass@bgsu.edu
• Dan Meyer, Senior Associate AD, Resource Development
(419) 372-7057
dbmeyer@bgsu.edu

BRADLEY UNIVERSITY ATHLETICS
RENAISSANCE COLISEUM
1501 W BRADLEY AVENUE
PEORIA, IL 61625
309-677-2666
Fax: 309-677-3626
www.bradleybraves.com
• Chris Reynolds, Vice President, Intercollegiate Athletics
• Jennifer Jones, Sr. Associate AD, Academics & Student Dev./SWA
(309) 677-2846
jenjones@bradley.edu

BRIGHAM YOUNG UNIVERSITY ATHLETICS
331 STUDENT ATHLETE BUILDING
PROVO, UT 84602
801-422-2096
byucougars.com

- Tom Holmoe, Director of Athletics
(801) 422-7649
- Brian Santiago, Deputy Athletic Director
(801) 422-9059
- Liz Darger, Sr. Associate AD/SWA
(801) 422-7306
- Bob Schirmer, Associate Athletic Director, Finance
(801) 422-2098
bob_schirmer@byu.edu
- Chad Lewis, Associate AD, Development
(801) 422-4858

BROWN UNIVERSITY ATHLETICS
235 HOPE STREET
PO BOX 1932
PROVIDENCE, RI 02912
410-863-2773
www.brownbears.com
- Tim Fitzpatrick, Deputy Director of Athletics, COO

BRYANT UNIVERSITY ATHLETICS
1150 DOUGLAS PIKE
SMITHFIELD, RI 02917
401-232-6513
Fax: 401-232-6361
bryantbulldogs.com
- Bill Smith, Director of Athletics & Recreation
(401) 232-6071
bsmith8@bryant.edu
- John Ruppert, Deputy Director of Athletics
(401) 232-6737
jruppert@bryant.edu
- Nicole Lambert, Sr. Assoc. AD/SWA
(401) 232-6202
nlambert@bryant.edu

BUCKNELL UNIVERSITY ATHLETICS
KENNETH LANGONE ATHLETICS & RECREATION CENTER
ONE DENT DRIVE
LEWISBURG, PA 17837
www.bucknellbison.com
- Jermaine Truax, Director of Athletics
(570) 577-3054
jmt027@bucknell.edu
- Tim Pavlechko, Deputy Director of Athletics
(570) 577-3588
tpavlech@bucknell.edu

BUTLER UNIVERSITY ATHLETICS
510 W 49TH STREET
INDIANAPOLIS, IN 46208
317-940-9375
butlersports.com
- Grant Leiendecker, Director of Athletics
(317) 940-6803
athleticdirector@butler.edu
- Mike Freeman, Sr. Associate AD, External Operations
(317) 940-6452
msfreema@butler.edu
- Ralph Reiff, Sr. Associate AD, Student-Athlete Health
(317) 940-9379
rreiff@butler.edu

CAL STATE FULLERTON ATHLETICS
P.O. BOX 6810
FULLERTON, CA 92834
657-278-2777
www.fullertontitans.com

- Jim Donovan, Director of Athletics
(657) 278-2777
jdonovan@fullerton.edu
- Greg Paules, Senior Associate Athletics Director
(657) 278-7791
gpaules@fullerton.edu
- Greg Paules, Senior Associate Athletics Director
(657) 278-7791
gpaules@fullerton.edu

CAL STATE NORTHRIDGE ATHLETICS
18111 NORDHOFF STREET
NORTHRIDGE, CA 91330-8276
818-677-3208
Fax: 818-677-4762
www.gomatadors.com
- Shawn Chin-Farrell, Director of Athletics
shawn.chin-farrell@csun.edu
- Dr. Cedric Hackett, Faculty Athletic Representative
cedric.hackett@csun.edu
- James Covell, Administrative Analyst for Athletic Director
james.covell@csun.edu

CAMPBELL UNIVERSITY ATHLETICS
78 DR. MCKOY ROAD
BUIES CREEK, NC 27506
www.gocamels.com
- Hannah Bazemore, Director of Athletics
(910) 893-1325
campbellAD@campbell.edu
- Melissa Wendt, Senior Associate Athletics Dir./SWA
(910) 893-1334
mwendt@campbell.edu
- Chris Hemeyer, Senior Associate Athletics Dir., External Affairs
(910) 893-1822
hemeyerc@campbell.edu
- Jason Williams, Associate Athletic Dir., Comms. & Branding
(910) 814-4367
jwilliams@campbell.edu
- Nathan Rice, Associate Athletics Director, Advancement
(910) 814-4354
rice@campbell.edu
- Jared Fries, Assoc. AD, Student-Athlete High Performance & Dev.
(910) 814-4366

CANISIUS COLLEGE ATHLETICS
2001 MAIN STREET
BUFFALO, NY 14208
716-883-7000
Fax: 716-888-3174
gogriffs.com
- Bill Maher, Director of Athletics
(716) 888-2972
maherw@canisius.edu
- Lisa Liotta, Associate AD/SWA
(716) 888-2959
liottal@canisius.edu

CENTRAL CONNECTICUT STATE ATHLETICS
CCSU DEPT. OF ATHLETICS
1615 STANLEY STREET
NEW BRITAIN, CT 06050
860-832-2583
www.ccsubluedevils.com
- Thomas Pincince, Director of Athletics
(860) 832-3035
pincincet@ccsu.edu

- Amy Strickland, Associate AD, Compliance & Student Services/SWA
(860) 832-3019
StricklandA@ccsu.edu
- Mike Ericksen, Associate AD, External Services
(860) 832-3085
EricksenM@ccsu.edu
- Molly McCarthy, Assistant AD, Compliance & Student Services
(860) 832-3048
McCarthyM@ccsu.edu
- Michael Piper, Associate AD, Sports Performance
(860) 832-3082
piper@ccsu.edu

CENTRAL FLORIDA ATHLETICS
UCF ATHLETICS
ROTH ATHLETICS CENTER
4192 NORTH ORION BOULEVARD
ORLANDO, FL 32816
407-823-1000
ucfknights.com
- Terry J. Mohajir, VP & Director of Athletics
adoffice@athletics.ucf.edu
- Chris McFarlane, Deputy AD, External Relations & Business Dev.
cmcfarlane@athletics.ucf.edu
- Rich Zvosec, Deputy AD, Internal Operations
rzvosec@athletics.ucf.edu
- Mark Wright, Deputy AD, Associate Vice President, Chargeon Fund
mwright@athletics.ucf.edu

CENTRAL MICHIGAN UNIVERSITY ATHLETICS
100 ROSE CENTER
MOUNT PLEASANT, MI 48859
989-774-3041
www.cmuchippewas.com
- Amy Folan, Director of Athletics
(989) 774-3043
athleticdirector@cmich.edu
- Chris Walker, Deputy Athletic Director, External Operations
walke11c@cmich.edu

CHARLESTON SOUTHERN UNIVERSITY ATHLETICS
9200 UNIVERSITY BOULEVARD
CHARLESTON, SC 29406
www.csusports.com
- Jeff Barber, Director of Athletics
(843) 863-7678
jbarber@csuniv.edu
- Courtney Hall, Deputy Director of Athletics/Chief of Staff
(843) 863-7670
chall@csuniv.edu
- Michael Causey, Asst. AD, Communications/Public Relations
(843) 863-7433
mcausey@csuniv.edu
- Nathan Richards, Assoc. AD, Facilities/Events
nrichards@csuniv.edu
- Carrie Gomez, Assoc. AD, Academics/SWA
(843) 863-7629
cgomez@csuniv.edu

CHICAGO STATE UNIVERSITY ATHLETICS
JCC 1502
9501 S KING DRIVE
CHICAGO, IL 60628
773-995-2295
Fax: 773-995-3656
www.gocsucougars.com
• Dr. Monique Carroll, Director of Intercollegiate Athletics
(773) 995-2295
athleticdirector@csu.edu
• Julie Hall, Deputy Athletic Director/Chief Operating Officer
(773) 995-2230
jhall31@csu.edu
• Courtney Washington, Associate AD, Student Services & Compliance
cwashi54@csu.edu

CINCINNATI ATHLETICS, UNIVERSITY OF
RICHARD E. LINDNER CENTER
2751 O'VARSITY WAY
CINCINNATI, OH 45221-0021
513-556-4603
Fax: 513-556-0405
gobearcats.com
• John Cunningham, Director of Athletics
(513) 556-0626
bearcat.ad@uc.edu
• Karen Hatcher, Exec. Sr. Assoc. AD
(513) 556-2539
karen.hatcher@uc.edu
• Maggie McKinley, Deputy AD/SWA
(513) 556-3559
maggie.mckinley@uc.edu

CITADEL ATHLETICS, THE
MCALISTER FIELD HOUSE
7 JONES AVE.
CHARLESTON, SC 29403
843-953-5070
www.citadelsports.com
• Art Chase, Athletic Director
(843) 953-5070
citadelathletics@citadel.edu
• Joni Stevens, Associate Athletic Dir., Internal Ops./SWA
(843) 953-6604
jstephe9@citadel.edu.
• Lauren Pavlick, Sr. Assoc. AD, Finance/Operations
(843) 953-7161
lpavlick@citadel.edu

CLEMSON UNIVERSITY ATHLETICS
JERVEY ATHLETIC CENTER
300 PERIMETER ROAD
CLEMSON, SC 29634-0031
800-253-6766
www.clemsontigers.com
• Graham Neff, Director of Athletics
(864) 656-1935
neffg@clemson.edu
• Steve Duzan, Sr. Assoc. AD, Student-Athlete Services
(864) 656-0945
sduzan@clemson.edu
• Stephanie Ellison, Sr. Assoc. AD, Sports Administrator/SWA
(864) 656-7163
saellis@clemson.edu

CLEVELAND STATE UNIVERSITY ATHLETICS
PE BUILDING - WOODLING GYM
2451 EUCLID AVENUE
ROOM 337
CLEVELAND, OH 44115
216-687-4848
Fax: 216-687-9242
www.csuvikings.com
• Kelsie Gory Harkey, Director of Athletics
(216) 687-4539
CSUDirectorOfAthletics@csuohio.edu
• Chelsea Blakely, Deputy Athletic Director, External Operations
(216) 687-5235
c.blakely@csuohio.edu

COASTAL CAROLINA UNIVERSITY ATHLETICS
132 CHANTICLEER DRIVE WEST
CONWAY, SC 29526
843-349-2231
Fax: 843-349-2893
www.goccusports.com
• Chance Miller, Director of Intercollegiate Athletics
(843) 349-2231
cmiller5@coastal.edu
• Cari Rosiek, Associate AD, Student-Athlete Enhancement/SWA
(843) 349-4126
cari@coastal.edu
• Andy Humes, Deputy Athletic Director
(843) 349-6959
ahumes@coastal.edu
• Jess Dannelly, Associate AD, Community Outreach
(843) 349-6699
jess@coastal.edu

COLGATE UNIVERSITY ATHLETICS
13 OAK DRIVE
HAMILTON, NY 13346
gocolgateraiders.com
• Yariv Amir, Director of Athletics
(315) 228-7783
colgateAD@colgate.edu
• Juliana Smith, Deputy AD/SWA
(315) 228-7852
• Laura Sgrecci, Senior Associate AD, External Affairs
(315) 228-7996
lsgrecci@colgate.edu

COLLEGE OF CHARLESTON ATHLETICS
301 MEETING STREET
CHARLESTON, SC 29401
843-953-5556
www.cofcsports.com
• Matt Roberts, Director of Athletics
(843) 953-8254
robertsmj1@cofc.edu
• Kate Tiller, Senior Associate AD, Student-Athlete Success/SWA
(843) 953-3660
tillerk@cofc.edu

COLORADO ATHLETICS, UNIVERSITY OF
2150 STADIUM DRIVE
CHAMPIONS CENTER
FIFTH FLOOR
BOULDER, CO 80309
cubuffs.com
• Rick George, Athletic Director
(303) 492-6843
rick.george@colorado.edu

• Jason DePaepe, Deputy Athletic Director
(303) 735-5494
ryan.gottlieb@colorado.edu
• Ryan Gottlieb, Sr. Associate AD/Revenue Generating Officer
(303) 492-3806
ryan.gottlieb@colorado.edu

COLORADO STATE UNIVERSITY ATHLETICS
MCGRAW ATHLETIC CENTER
FORT COLLINS, CO 80523-0120
970-491-7217
Fax: 970-491-1348
csurams.com
• John Weber, Director of Athletics/Sports Admin.: Football
ath_athletic_director@mail.colostate.edu
• Scott Sidwell, Deputy Director of Athletics
scott.sidwell@colostate.edu
• Kyle Saunders, NCAA Faculty Athletics Representative
(970) 491-5751
kyle.saunders@colostate.edu
• Matt Klein, Senior Assoc. AD, Business Ops./CFO
(970) 491-2686
matthew.klein@colostate.edu
• Terry DeZeeuw, Sr. Assoc. AD, Health & Performance
(970) 491-6756
terry.dezeeuw@colostate.edu
• Chris Ferris, Executive Sr. Assoc. AD, External Affairs
(970) 491-0438
chris.ferris@colostate.edu
• Mark Paquette, Sr. Assoc. AD, Facilities & Stadium Manager
(970) 491-7414
mark.paquette@colostate.edu

COLUMBIA UNIVERSITY ATHLETICS
DODGE PHYSICAL FITNESS CENTER
3030 BROADWAY
MAIL CODE 1900
NEW YORK, NY 10027
www.gocolumbialions.com
• Peter Pilling, Director of Intercollegiate Athletics
(212) 854-4774
ppilling@columbia.edu
• Erich Ely, Director of Athletics Development
(212) 851-4278
ee2133@columbia.edu
• Jacqueline Blackett, Sr. Assoc. AD, Athletics/SWA
(212) 854-2544
jpb3@columbia.edu

CONNECTICUT ATHLETICS, UNIVERSITY OF
OFFICE OF ATHLETIC DIRECTOR
2095 HILLSIDE ROAD
UNIT 1173
STORRS, CT 06269
860-486-2725
Fax: 860-486-3300
www.uconnhuskies.com
• David Benedict, Director of Athletics
athleticdirector@uconn.edu
• Annie Fiorvanti, Deputy Director of Athletics/SWA
ann.fiorvanti@uconn.edu
• Jason Butikofer, Deputy Director of Athletics/COO
jason.butikofer@uconn.edu

COPPIN STATE UNIVERSITY ATHLETICS
COPPIN STATE DEPT. OF ATHLETICS
2523 GWYNNS FALLS PARKWAY
BALTIMORE, MD 21216-3698
410-951-3737
Fax: 410-951-3717
www.coppinstatesports.com
• Derek Carter, Director of Athletics
(410) 951-3743
decarter@coppin.edu
• Nichole Person, Associate AD/SWA
(410) 951-3732
nperson@coppin.edu

CORNELL UNIVERSITY ATHLETICS
TEAGLE HALL
512 CAMPUS ROAD
ITHACA, NY 14853
cornellbigred.com
• Nicki Moore, Director of Athletics &
Physical Education
(607) 255-8832
CornellAD@cornell.edu
• Anita Brenner, Deputy Director of
Intercollegiate Athletics/SWA
(607) 255-8283
amb42@cornell.edu
• Lisa Zehr, Deputy Director of Athletics,
Finance & Admin.
lrz8@cornell.edu

CREIGHTON UNIVERSITY ATHLETICS
CREIGHTON ATHLETIC DEVELOPMENT
OFFICE
RYAN ATHLETIC CENTER
2500 CALIFORNIA PLAZA
OMAHA, NE 68178
402-280-4483
gocreighton.com
• Marcus Blossom, Athletic Director
(402) 280-1795
marcusblossom@creighton.edu
• Mike Odum, Executive Associate AD,
External Operations
mikeodom@creighton.edu
• Lisa Chipps, Ed.D., Associate Athletic
Director/SWA
(402) 280-5832
lbchipps@creighton.edu

DARTMOUTH COLLEGE ATHLETICS
DARTMOUTH ATHLETICS
6083 ALUMNI GYM
HANOVER, NH 03755
sportspub@dartmouth.edu
www.dartmouthsports.com
• Mike Harrity, Director of Athletics &
Recreation
(603) 646-2465
athletics.director@dartmouth.edu
• Kristine Fowler, Sr. Deputy Athletics
Dir./COO/SWA
(603) 646-2871
kristine.r.fowler@dartmouth.edu

DAVIDSON COLLEGE ATHLETICS
PO BOX 7158
DAVIDSON, NC 28035
704-894-2373
www.davidsonwildcats.com
• Chris Clunie, Director of Athletics
(704) 894-2373
chclunie@davidson.edu
• Scott Applegate, Senior Associate Athletic
Director
(704) 894-2914
scapplegate@davidson.edu

• Katy McNay, Senior Associate Director of
Athletics/SWA
(704) 894-2637
kamcnay@davidson.edu
• Dick Cooke, Associate Director of Athletics
(704) 894-2368
dicooke@davidson.edu

DAYTON ATHLETICS, UNIVERSITY OF
300 COLLEGE PARK
DAYTON, OH 45469
Fax: 937-229-4969
daytonflyers.com
• Neil Sullivan, Director of Athletics
(937) 229-2165
ad@udayton.edu
• Mike Kelly, Assistant to the Athletic
Director
(937) 229-4404
mkelly1@udayton.edu
• Scott DeBolt, Senior Associate Athletics
Director
(937) 229-4613
sdebolt1@udayton.edu
• Joe Owens, Senior Associate AD,
Performance Enhancement
(937) 229-2663
jowens1@udayton.edu
• Angie Petrovic, Sr. Associate AD,
Compliance & Bus. Services/SWA
(937) 229-1285
apetrovic1@udayton.edu
• Susan Bertke, Senior Administrative
Assistant
(937) 229-4422
sbertke1@udayton.edu

**DELAWARE ATHLETICS, UNIVERSITY
OF**
631 S COLLEGE AVE
BOB CARPENTER CENTER
NEWARK, DE 19716
302-831-8600
www.bluehens.com
• Chrissi Rawak, Dir. of Intercollegiate
Athletics & Rec. Services
(302) 831-4006
athletics-dir@udel.edu
• Jordan Skolnick, Interim Director of
Athletics
(302) 831-1075
jsko@udel.edu
• Dan Watson, Senior Associate AD, Sport
Performance
(302) 831-7228
dwatson@udel.edu
• Jen Vining-Smith, Deputy Athletic Director,
Sport Administration
(302) 831-0883
jvining@udel.edu
• Chelsea Burk, Deputy Athletic Director,
Internal Operations/COO
cpburk@udel.edu

**DELAWARE STATE UNIVERSITY
ATHLETICS**
1200 N DUPONT HWY
DOVER, DE 19901
www.dsuhornets.com
• Alecia Sheifls-Gadson, Director of
Athletics
(302) 857-6030
• Christina Epps-Chiazor, Assistant Athletics
Director/SWA
(302) 857-7087

DENVER ATHLETICS, UNIVERSITY OF
ATHLETICS DEPARTMENT
2201 EAST ASBURY AVE
DENVER, CO 80210
www.denverpioneers.com
• Josh Berlo, Vice Chancellor for Athletics
(303) 871-3399
Josh.Berlo@du.edu
• Josh Boone, Deputy Athletic Director for
Strategy/CFO
(303) 871-4224
joshua.boone@du.edu
• Lynn Coutts, Deputy AD, Student-Athlete
Excellence
(303) 871-3892
lynn.coutts@du.edu
• Stu Halsall, Associate Vice Chancellor,
KMC, Wellness & Rec.
(303) 871-3058
shalsall@du.edu
• Brandon MacNeill, Deputy AD/Chief
Revenue Officer
(303) 871-2785
brandon.macneill@du.edu
• Bob Willis, Deputy AD, Community &
Diversity
(303) 871-4966
robert.willis@du.edu

DEPAUL UNIVERSITY ATHLETICS
SULLIVAN ATHLETICS CENTER
2323 N SHEFFIELD AVENUE
CHICAGO, IL 60614
773-325-7526
www.depaulbluedemons.com
• DeWayne Peevy, Director of Athletics
(773) 325-7504
athleticsdirector@depaul.edu
• Jill Hollembeak, Senior Associate AD/SWA
(773) 325-4034
jhollemb@depaul.edu
• Peter Tombasco, Senior Associate AD,
Athletic Performance
(773) 325-7245
ptombasc@depaul.edu

**DETROIT MERCY ATHLETICS,
UNIVERSITY OF**
4001 W MCNICHOLS ROAD
DETROIT, MI 48221
313-993-1700
Fax: 313-993-2449
www.detroittitans.com
• Robert C. Vowels, Jr., Director of Athletics
(313) 993-1700
vowelsrc@udmercy.edu
• Teri Kromrei, Associate AD/SWA
(313) 993-1700
teri.kromrei@udmercy.edu
• Mike Miller, Associate AD
(313) 585-4786
millerma@udmercy.edu

DRAKE UNIVERSITY ATHLETICS
2507 UNIVERSITY AVENUE
DES MOINES, IA 50311-4505
515-271-2889
Fax: 515-271-4189
www.godrakebulldogs.com
• Brian Hardin, Director of Athletics
(515) 271-2889
drakead@drake.edu
• Blake Boldon, Senior Associate AD
(515) 271-2114
blake.boldon@drake.edu
• Megan Franklin, Ph.D., Senior Associate
AD/SWA

(515) 271-2809
megan.franklin@drake.edu
• Tesar Tim, Ph.D., Senior Associate AD, External Affairs
(515) 271-2132
tim.tesar@drake.edu

DREXEL UNIVERSITY ATHLETICS
DASKALAKIS ATHLETIC CENTER
3141 CHESTNUT STREET
PHILADELPHIA, PA 19104
www.drexeldragons.com
• Maisha Kelly, Director of Athletics
(215) 895-1977
mk3883@drexel.edu
• Nick Gannon, Deputy AD/COO
(215) 895-1589
njg24@drexel.edu
• Mary Mulvenna, Chief of Staff/Senior Associate Athletics Director
(215) 895-1782
mm5557@drexel.edu
• Kathy O'Brien, Assoc. AD, Academic Services
(215) 895-2031
ko33@drexel.edu

DUKE UNIVERSITY ATHLETICS
SCOTT FAMILY ATHLETICS
PERFORMANCE CENTER
ROOM 364
110 WHITFORD DRIVE
DURHAM, NC 27708
919-681-2583
www.goduke.com
• Nina King, Vice President/Director of Athletics
• Chris Kennedy, Senior Deputy AD
(919) 668-5702
ckennedy@duke.edu
• Jon Jackson, Deputy AD, Men's Basketball & External Affairs
(919) 684-2624
jon.jackson@duke.edu
• Mitch Moser, Deputy AD/Resource Development & Management/CFO
(919) 668-5705
mmoser@duke.edu

DUQUESNE UNIVERSITY ATHLETICS
A.J. PALUMBO CENTER
600 FORBES AVENUE
PITTSBURGH, PA 15282
www.goduquesne.com
• Dave Harper, Director of Athletics
(412) 396-6565
harperd1@duq.edu
• Sherene Brantley, Associate AD, Academic & Student Services/SWA
(412) 396-5243
lemoniass@duq.edu
• Bryan Colonna, Associate AD, Development & Corporate Partnerships
(412) 396-5927
colonna770@duq.edu
• Rick Christensen, Associate AD, Admin. & Compliance
(412) 396-4917
christensen@duq.edu
• Megan Jahrling, Associate AD, External Relations
(412) 396-5333
jahrlingm@duq.edu
• Liam Halferty, Associate AD, Media Relations
(412) 396-5861
halfertyl@duq.edu

• Michael Scerbo, Associate AD, Sports & Facilities Operations
(412) 396-5244
scerbom@duq.edu
• Joseph Setting, Associate AD/CFO
(412) 396-1359
settingj@duq.edu

EAST CAROLINA UNIVERSITY ATHLETICS
WARD SPORTS MEDICINE BUILDING
1 FICKLEN DR
MAIL STOP 158
GREENVILLE, NC 27858-4353
252-737-4600
www.ecupirates.com
• Jon Gilbert, Director of Athletics
(252) 737-4502
athletic_director@ecu.edu
• Ryan Robinson, Executive Associate AD/Revenue Generation
(252) 737-4882
robinsonry18@ecu.edu
• Alex Keddie, Senior Associate AD/Compliance
(252) 737-4533
keddiea19@ecu.edu
• Caroline Bevillard, Senior Associate AD, Administration/SWA
(252) 737-4531
bevillardc18@ecu.edu

EAST TENNESSEE STATE UNIVERSITY ATHLETICS
PO BOX 70707
JOHNSON CITY, TN 37614
www.etsubucs.com
• Richard Sander, Athletic Director
• Lauren Aksionoff, Senior Associate AD for Academic Services/SWA
(423) 439-4809
aksionoff@mail.etsu.edu
• Steve Cunningham, Assistant Athletic Director of Business Operations
(423) 439-8215
cunninghamsf@etsu.edu
• Sheryll Hanks, Associate Director For Compliance
(423) 439-4204
hankssa@etsu.edu

EASTERN ILLINOIS UNIVERSITY ATHLETICS
EASTERN ILLINOIS ATHLETIC DEPT.
600 LINCOLN AVENUE
CHARLESTON, IL 61920
217-581-6014
www.eiupanthers.com
• Tom Michael, Athletic Director
(217) 581-6014
trmichael@eiu.edu
• Mark Bonnstetter, Deputy AD
(217) 581-7614
mdbonnstetter@eiu.edu
• Rich Moser, Associate AD, Media & Public Relations
(217) 581-7480
rlmoser@eiu.edu

EASTERN KENTUCKY UNIVERSITY ATHLETICS
521 LANCASTER AVENUE
RICHMOND, KY 40475
www.ekusports.com
• Matt Roan, Director of Athletics
matt.roan@eku.edu
• Mark Howard, Sr. Associate AD,

Operations
(859) 622-8422
mark.howard@eku.edu

EASTERN MICHIGAN UNIVERSITY ATHLETICS
GEORGE GERVIN GAMEABOVE CENTER
799 N HEWITT ROAD
YPSILANTI, MI 48197
734-487-1050
www.emueagles.com
• Scott Wetherbee, Director of Athletics/VP
(734) 487-1050
scott.wetherbee@emich.edu
• Erin Kido, Deputy AD, Internal Operations/SWA
(734) 487-8172
ekido@emich.edu
• Gretchen Fox, Assoc. AD, Sports Medicine (Volleyball)
(734) 487-5183
gbuskirk@emich.edu
• Dan McLean, Senior Associate AD, Development
(734) 487-1050
dmclean4@emich.edu
• Andy Rowdon, Deputy AD, External Operations
(734) 487-1050

EASTERN WASHINGTON UNIVERSITY ATHLETICS
EWU ATHLETICS DEPARTMENT
207 PHYSICAL EDUCATION BUILDING
CHENEY, WA 99004
509-359-2463
Fax: 509-359-2828
www.goeags.com
• Lynn Hickey, Director of Athletics/Associate Vice President
(509) 359-2347
lhickey@ewu.edu
• Todd McGann, Deputy Athletic Director
(509) 359-2079
tmcgann@ewu.edu

ELON UNIVERSITY ATHLETICS
2500 CAMPUS BOX
100 CAMPUS DRIVE
ELON, NC 27244
elonphoenix.com
• Dave Blank, Director of Athletics
(336) 278-6800
• Kyle Wills, Sr. Assoc. Dir. of Athletics for Business & Ops.
willsk@elon.edu

EVANSVILLE ATHLETICS, UNIVERSITY OF
UE ATHLETICS
1800 LINCOLN AVENUE
EVANSVILLE, IN 47722
812-488-2237
Fax: 812-488-2199
athletics@evansville.edu
gopurpleaces.com
• Kenneth "Ziggy" Siegfried, Director of Athletics
• Sarah Solinsky, Senior Associate AD, Internal Operations/SWA
(812) 488-2759
ss78@evansville.edu
• Bob Pristash, Associate AD, Media Relations
(812) 488-2285
rp113@evansville.edu
• Terry Collins, Associate AD, Sports

Medicine
(812) 488-2091
tc7@evansville.edu

FAIRFIELD UNIVERSITY ATHLETICS
WALSH ATHLETIC CENTER
1073 NORTH BENSON ROAD
FAIRFIELD, CT 06824
203-254-4130
fairfieldstags.com
• Paul Schlickmann, Director of Athletics
(203) 254-4000
kgeiling@fairfield.edu
• Zach Dayton, Deputy AD
(203) 254-4000
zdayton@fairfield.edu
• Alison Sexton, Senior Associate AD,
Internal Affairs/SWA
(203) 254-4000
asexton@fairfield.edu

FAIRLEIGH DICKINSON UNIVERSITY ATHLETICS
1000 RIVER ROAD
H-AT1-01
TEANECK, NJ 07666
201-692-2208
Fax: 201-692-9361
fduknights.com
• Bradford Hurlbut, Director of Athletics
• Cathy Liggett, Deputy Director of Athletics
(201) 692-2172
liggett@fdu.edu
• Jennifer Quirk, Senior Associatte Athletic
Director, Compliance
(201) 692-9892
quirk@fdu.edu
• Jason Young, Senior Associate Athletic
Dir., External Affairs
(201) 692-9552
jryoung@fdu.edu

FLORIDA A&M UNIVERSITY ATHLETICS
1835 WAHNISH WAY
TALLAHASSEE, FL 32310
850-599-3868
Fax: 850-599-3810
www.famuathletics.com
• Tiffani-Dawn Sykes, Director of
Intercollegiate Athletics
• Brittney Johnson, Senior Associate AD for
Compliance/SWA
brittney.johnson@famu.edu
• Carrie Hickey Tollison, Associate Athletic
Dir., Student-Athlete Success
(850) 412-7079
carrie.hickey@famu.edu

FLORIDA ATHLETICS, UNIVERSITY OF
UNIVERSITY ATHLETICS ASSN.
PO BOX 14485
GAINESVILLE, FL 32604
352-375-4683
floridagators.com
• Scott Stricklin, Director of Athletics
 ext 6000
administration@gators.ufl.edu
• Jay Jacobs, Executive Associate AD,
External Affairs
 ext 6047
JayJ@gators.ufl.edu
• Chip Howard, Executive Associate AD,
Internal Affairs
 ext 6047
chiph@gators.ufl.edu
• Lynda Tealer, Executive Associate AD,
Administration

ext 6055
lyndat@gators.ufl.edu

FLORIDA ATLANTIC UNIVERSITY ATHLETICS
DEPARTMENT OF ATHLETICS
777 GLADES ROAD
BOCA RATON, FL 33431
Fax: 561-297-3963
www.fausports.com
• Brian White, Director of Athletics
(561) 297-3199
• Mary Giardina, Sr. Assoc. AD,
Administration/SWA/Chief of Staff
(561) 297-3199
mgiardina@fau.edu
• Lisa Anne Higgins, Executive Assistant to
the VP/AD
(561) 297-3199
lhiggins2015@fau.edu

FLORIDA INTERNATIONAL UNIVERSITY ATHLETICS
FIU ATHLETICS
11200 SW 8TH STREET
MIAMI, FL 33199
305-348-8392
www.fiusports.com
• Scott Carr, Athletics Director
athleticsdirector@fiu.edu
• Heath Glick, Senior Associate Athletic
Director/COO
(305) 348-6711
glickh@fiu.edu
• Alex Kelley, Associate AD, Revenue
Generation & Engagement
(305) 348-2971
ajkelley@fiu.edu
• Kevin D. Kendrick, Senior Associate AD,
Compliance
(305) 348-2843
kkendric@fiu.edu

FLORIDA STATE UNIVERSITY ATHLETICS
FSU ATHLETICS DEPARTMENT
403 STADIUM DRIVE W
ROOM D0107
TALLAHASSEE, FL 32306
850-645-2527
Fax: 850-644-7293
seminoles.com
• Michael Alford, Director of Athletics
(850) 644-1079
AD@athletics.fsu.edu
• Cindy Hartmann, Deputy AD,
Administration
(850) 645-2368
cmhartmann@fsu.edu
• Ross Cobb, Senior Associate AD/CFO
(850) 644-8091
ross.cobb@fsu.edu
• Jim Curry, Senior Associate AD
(850) 644-7926
jmcurry@fsu.edu
• Lisa Varytimidis, Senior Associate
AD/SWA
(850) 645-9162
avarytimidis@fsu.edu
• Rob Wilson, Associate AD,
Communications
(850) 644-5678
rlwilson@fsu.edu

FORDHAM UNIVERSITY ATHLETICS
ROSE HILL CAMPUS
441 E FORDHAM ROAD
BRONX, NY 10458
www.fordhamsports.com
• Ed Kull, Director of Intercollegiate Athletics
(718) 817-4302
athleticdirector@fordham.edu
• Charlie Elwood, Deputy Athletic Director
(718) 817-4308
celwood@fordham.edu
• Steve Westerduin, Senior Associate AD,
Facilities & Event Management
(718) 817-4265
swesterduin@fordham.edu
• Michael Sainte, Senior Associate AD,
Compliance & Governance
(718) 817-4305
msainte1@fordham.edu

FRESNO STATE ATHLETICS
FRESNO STATE ATHLETICS DEPT.
1620 E BULLDOG LANE, OF 87
FRESNO, CA 93740
559-278-2643
www.gobulldogs.com
• Terry Tumey, Director of Athletics
• Carrie Coll, Senior Associate AD, Sport
Services/SWA
(559) 278-8262
ccoll@csufresno.edu
• Tim Collins, Senior Associate AD,
Development
(559) 278-8256
tcollins@csufresno.edu
• Frank Pucher, Senior Associate AD,
External Relations
(559) 278-8006
fpucher@csufresno.edu

FURMAN UNIVERSITY ATHLETICS
FURMAN UNIVERSITY
3300 POINSETT HIGHWAY
GREENVILLE, SC 29613-5684
864-294-3469
800-878-7535
Fax: 864-294-3530
www.furmanpaladins.com
• Jason Donnelly, Vice President for
Intercollegiate Athletics
athletics.director@furman.edu
• Erin Wissing, Sr. Assoc. AD/Director of
Athletics Development
(864) 294-3732
erin.wissing@furman.edu

GARDNER-WEBB UNIVERSITY ATHLETICS
110 S MAIN STREET
BOILING SPRINGS, NC 28017
www.gwusports.com
• Andrew Goodrich, Vice President &
Director of Athletics
(704) 406-2692
agoodrich1@gardner-webb.edu
• Pam Scruggs, Associate Athletic
Director/SWA
(704) 406-4341
pscruggs@gardner-webb.edu
• Tyler Rosenberger, Assistant AD,
Compliance
(704) 406-3329
trosenberger@gardner-webb.edu
• Kevin Jones, Assistant AD, Athletic
Training
(704) 406-3926
kjones@gardner-webb.edu

• Marc Rabb, Assistant AD, Media Relations
(704) 406-4355
mrabb@gardner-webb.edu

GEORGE MASON UNIVERSITY ATHLETICS
GEORGE MASON ATHLETICS
MS 3A5
4400 UNIVERSITY DRIVE
FAIRFAX, VA 22030
www.gomason.com
• Nena Rogers, Interim Director of Athletics
(703) 993-3594
nrogers1@gmu.edu
• Todd Bramble, Deputy AD, Intercollegiate Sports
(703) 993-3209
tbramble@gmu.edu
• Zack Bolno, Deputy AD, External Operations
(703) 993-3217
zbolno@gmu.edu
• Malcom Grace, Deputy AD, Compliance & NCAA Governance
(703) 993-5420
mgrace7@gmu.edu

GEORGE WASHINGTON UNIVERSITY ATHLETICS
GW DEPT. OF ATHLETICS AND REC.
CHARLES E. SMITH CENTER
600 22ND STREET NW
WASHINGTON, DC 20052
202-994-1000
www.gwsports.com
• Tanya Vogel, Director of Athletics
(202) 994-5558
gwad@gwu.edu
• Chandra Bierwirth, Associate AD, Compliance
(202) 994-6282
cbwirth@gwu.edu
• Brian Sereno, Associate AD, Communications
(202) 994-6654
bsereno@gwu.edu
• Chris Hennelly, Associate AD, Student-Athlete Health
(202) 994-3557
henz@gwu.edu
• Danya Ellman, Sr. Associate Athletics Dir., Internal Ops./SWA
(202) 994-2495
dellman@gwu.edu

GEORGETOWN UNIVERSITY ATHLETICS
ATHLETIC DEPARTMENT
MCDONOUGH ARENA
WASHINGTON, DC 20057
202-687-2435
www.guhoyas.com
• Lee Reed, Director of Athletics
(202) 687-6513
athleticdirector@georgetown.edu
• Dan O'Neil, Senior Associate AD, External Affairs
(202) 687-6708
djo23@georgetown.edu
• Ariel "AP" Pesante, Senior Associate AD, Internal Operations
(202) 687-6573
ap1923@georgetown.edu
• Sharon Brummell, Exec. Senior Associate Ad, Business & Finance/SWA
(202) 687-2669
sdb46@georgetown.edu

GEORGIA ATHLETICS, UNIVERSITY OF
1 SELIG CIRCLE
ATHENS, GA 30602
706-542-9036
georgiadogs.com
• Josh Brooks, Director of Athletics
(705) 542-9037
• Darrice Griffin, Senior Deputy AD
(706) 542-9103
dgriffin@sports.uga.edu
• Magdi El Shahawy, Deputy AD, Academics & Student Development
(706) 542-8388
magdi@sports.uga.edu
• Will Lawler, Deputy AD, Legal & Regulatory Affairs
(706) 542-9103
wlawler@sports.uga.edu
• Stephanie Ransom, Deputy AD, Finance
(706) 542-1306
sransom@sports.uga.edu

GEORGIA SOUTHERN UNIVERSITY ATHLETICS
DAN J. PARRISH SR. BUILDING
651 FAIR ROAD
STATESBORO, GA 30458
912-478-2845
Fax: 912-478-0095
gsathletics@georgiasouthern.edu
www.gseagles.com
• Jared Benko, Director of Athletics
(912) 478-2845
gsathletics@georgiasouthern.edu
• Brandy Clouse, Senior Associate AD, Administration/SWA
(912) 478-7581
bpetty@georgiasouthern.edu
• Tracy Ham, Senior Associate AD, Administration
(912) 478-5366
tham@georgiasouthern.edu
• Gleen Hart, Senior Associate AD, Student-Athlete Development
(912) 478-5817
ghart@georgiasouthern.edu
• Keith Roughton, Senior Associate AD, NCAA Compliance
(912) 478-0747
kroughton@georgiasouthern.edu
• Reggie Simpkins, Senior Associate AD, Student-Athlete Services
(912) 478-8467
rsimpkins@georgiasouthern.edu

GEORGIA STATE UNIVERSITY ATHLETICS
GEORGIA STATE STADIUM
755 HANK AARON DRIVE
ATLANTA, GA 30315
404-413-4000
www.georgiastatesports.com
• Charlie Cobb, Director of Athletics
(404) 413-4004
• Doug Justice, Senior Associate AD/Chief of Staff
(404) 413-4013
djustice@gsu.edu
• Kelcey Roegiers, Senior Associate AD/SWA
(404) 413-4005
kroegiers@gsu.edu
• Brad Horton, Senior Associate AD, Student-Athlete Development
(404) 413-4045
• Elisha Howell-Williams, Senior Associate AD, Business & Human Resources

(404) 413-4016
ehowell@gsu.edu

GEORGIA TECH ATHLETICS
GEORGIA TECH ATHLETIC ASSOCIATION
150 BOBBY DODD WAY NW
ATLANTA, GA 30332
404-894-5447
www.ramblinwreck.com
• J. Batt, Director of Athletics
(404) 894-5411
athleticdirector@athletics.gatech.edu
• Jon Palumbo, Executive Deputy AD/COO
jpalumbo@athletics.gatech.edu

GONZAGA UNIVERSITY ATHLETICS
502 E BOONE
SPOKANE, WA 99258-0066
509-313-4202
Fax: 509-313-5787
www.gozags.com
• Cris Standiford, Athletic Director
(509) 313-4202
standiford@gonzaga.edu
• Shannon Strahl, Deputy Athletic Director & COO/SWA
(509) 313-5700
strahl@gonzaga.edu
• Jared Hertz, Sr. Assoc. AD, Major Gifts
(509) 313-4203
hertzj@gonzaga.edu

GRAMBLING STATE UNIVERSITY ATHLETICS
HOBDY ASSEMBLY CENTER
100 NORTH STADIUM DRIVE
GRAMBLING, LA 71245
318-274-2374
www.gsutigers.com
• Trayvean Scott, Vice President, Intercollegiate Athletics
• Taylor Stewart, Associate AD, External Relations/Chief of Staff
(318) 274-2374
stewartta@gram.edu

GRAND CANYON UNIVERSITY ATHLETICS
GCU ATHLETICS
3300 W CAMELBACK ROAD
PHOENIX, AZ 85017
www.gculopes.com
• Jamie Boggs, Vice President of Athletics
• Nick Ojea, Assistant Vice President/Deputy Athletic Director
(602) 639-7455
nicholas.ojea@gcu.edu
• Nicole Alderson, Associate AD, Student-Athlete Dev./SWA
(602) 639-7285
nicole.alderson@gcu.edu

HAMPTON UNIVERSITY ATHLETICS
200 WILLIAM R. HARVEY WAY
121 HOLLAND HALL
HAMPTON, VA 23668
757-727-5641
Fax: 757-728-6995
hamptonpirates.com
• Paula Jackson, Chief of Staff/Interim Director of Athletics

HARTFORD ATHLETICS, UNIVERSITY OF
DEPT. OF ATHLETICS
SPORTS CENTER

college sports

331

200 BLOOMFIELD AVE
WEST HARTFORD, CT 06117
860-768-4653
Fax: 860-768-5047
www.hartfordhawks.com
• Sharon Beverly, Acting Vice President of
Athletics & Recreation
(860) 768-4145
sbeverly@hartford.edu
• Alicia Naylor, Assistant to the VP of
Athletics & Recreation
(860) 768-4145
naylor@hartford.edu
• Denise Marchese, Associate Director of
Athletics/SWA
dmarchese@hartford.edu

HARVARD UNIVERSITY ATHLETICS
MURR CENTER
65 N HARVARD STREET
BOSTON, MA 02163
617-495-3454
www.gocrimson.com
• Erin McDermott, Director of Athletics
(617) 495-3633
emcdermott@fas.harvard.edu
• Gerrie Mahoney, Senior Associate AD
(617) 495-2781
gamahon@fas.harvard.edu
• Tim Troville, Senior Associate AD
(617) 384-8426
ttroville@fas.harvard.edu

HAWAII ATHLETICS, UNIVERSITY OF
OFFICE OF INTERCOLLEGIATE
ATHLETICS
1337 LOWER CAMPUS RD
HONOLULU, HI 96822
Fax: 808-956-4637
hawaiiathletics.com
• David A.K. Matlin, Athletics Director
(808) 956-7301
athdir@hawaii.edu

HIGH POINT UNIVERSITY ATHLETICS
ONE UNIVERSITY PARKWAY
HIGH POINT, NC 27268
Fax: 336-841-9182
www.highpointpanthers.com
• Dan Hauser, Athletic Director
(336) 841-9281
dhauser@highpoint.edu
• Drew Sanchez, Deputy Athletic Director
(336) 841-4652
dsanchez@highpoint.edu
• April Wines, Associate AD/SWA
(336) 841-4645
awines@highpoint.edu
• Kim Grissett, Senior Associate AD,
Business & Tickets
(336) 841-9276
kgrisset@highpoint.edu

HOFSTRA UNIVERSITY ATHLETICS
JAMES C. METZGER HALL
147 HOFSTRA UNIVERSITY
HEMPSTEAD, NY 11549
516-463-5315
gohofstra.com
• Rick Cole, Jr., Director of Athletics
(516) 463-6750
rick.coleJr@hofstra.edu
• Jay Artinian, Assistant Vice President of
Athletics/COO
(516) 463-7931
jay.m.artinian@hofstra.edu
• Cindy Lewis, Senior Associate AD/SWA

(516) 463-6748
cindy.lewis@hofstra.edu

HOLY CROSS ATHLETICS, COLLEGE OF THE
DEPARTMENT OF ATHLETICS
ONE COLLEGE STREET
WORCESTER, MA 01610
508-793-2571
www.goholycross.com
• Kit Hughes, Associate VP, Intercollegiate
Athletics
athleticdirector@holycross.edu
• Rosemary Shea, Senior Associate
AD/SWA
(508) 793-2318
rshea@holycross.edu
• Nick Smith, Senior Associate AD, External
Operations
(508) 793-3583
nasmith@holycross.edu

HOUSTON ATHLETICS, UNIVERSITY OF
3204 CULLEN BOULEVARD
HOUSTON, TX 77204-6002
713-743-9969
www.uhcougars.com
• Chris Pezman, Vice President for Athletics
directorofathletics@uh.edu
• David Tagliarino, Deputy Athletics
Director, External
dtagliar@central.uh.edu
• Monty Porter, Deputy Athletics
Director/COO
mmporte2@central.uh.edu

HOWARD UNIVERSITY ATHLETICS
BURR GYMNASIUM
6TH & GIRARD STREETS NW
SUITE 1013
WASHINGTON, DC 20059
202-806-7141
Fax: 202-806-9090
www.hubison.com
• Kery Davis, Director of Athletics
(202) 806-7141
kery.davis@howard.edu
• Nicholas Latham, Associate AD,
Operations
(202) 806-7144
nicholas.latham@howard.edu
• Paul Bowden, Associate AD,
Student-Athlete Support Services
(202) 806-5165
hubison.compliance@howard.edu

IDAHO ATHLETICS, UNIVERSITY OF
KIBBIE-ASUI ACTIVITY CENTER
875 PERIMETER DRIVE
MS 2302
MOSCOW, ID 83844-2302
208-885-0200
Fax: 208-885-0254
govandals.com
• Terry Gawlik, Director of Athletics
(208) 885-0243
ath-director@uidaho.edu
• Tim Mooney, Deputy Athletic
Director/Internal Operations
(208) 885-0258
tmooney@uidaho.edu
• Matt Brewer, Associate AD, Compliance
mbrewer@uidaho.edu
• Mahmood Sheikh, Senior Associate
Athletic Director
(208) 885-4566
msheikh@uidaho.edu

IDAHO STATE UNIVERSITY ATHLETICS
IDAHO STATE ATHLETICS
921 S 8TH
STOP 8173
POCATELLO, ID 83209-8173
www.isubengals.com
• Pauline Thiros, Director of Athletics
thirpaul@isu.edu
• Steve Schaack, Senior Associate AD,
Internal Operations/SWA
(208) 282-5349
robynsharp@isu.edu

ILLINOIS AT CHICAGO ATHLETICS, UNIVERSITY OF
FLAMES ATHLETIC CENTER
839 W ROOSEVELT ROAD
CHICAGO, IL 60608
Fax: 312-996-8349
uicflames.com
• Michael Lipitz, Director of Intercollegiate
Athletics
(312) 996-4639
uicad@uic.edu
• Farrah Manthei, Deputy AD/SWA/COO
(312) 996-5633
fmanthei@uic.edu
• Frank Cuervo, Deputy Athletics Director,
External Operations
(312) 996-2042
fcuervo@uic.edu

ILLINOIS ATHLETICS, UNIVERSITY OF
BIELFELDT ATHLETIC ADMIN. BLDG.
1700 S FOURTH STREET
CHAMPAIGN, IL 61820
217-333-3631
fightingillini.com
• Josh Whitman, Director of Athletics
(217) 333-3631
illiniad@illinois.edu
• Roger Denny, Executive Senior Associate
Dir. of Athletics/COO
(217) 333-0745
rdenny@illinois.edu
• Sara Burton, Executive Senior Associate
AD/SWA
(217) 300-8112
sarab4@illinois.edu

ILLINOIS STATE UNIVERSITY ATHLETICS
CAMPUS BOX 2660
NORMAL, IL 61790-2660
309-438-2000
www.goredbirds.com
• Kyle Brennan, Director of Athletics
(309) 438-3636
ksbren1@ilstu.edu
• Leanna Bordner, Deputy Director of
Athletics/SWA
(309) 438-7143
lkbordn@ilstu.edu
• Mark Muhlhauser, COO/Deputy Director of
Athletics & External Ops.
(309) 438-5526
mamuhlh@ilstu.edu

INDIANA STATE UNIVERSITY ATHLETICS
401 NORTH 4TH STREET
ISU ARENA
SUITE 110
TERRE HAUTE, IN 47809
Fax: 812-237-4041
gosycamores.com
• Sherard Clinkscales, Director of Athletics
(812) 237-4092

• Angie Lansing, Senior Associate AD/SWA
(812) 237-4091
angie.lansing@indstate.edu
• John Sherman, Senior Assistant AD
(812) 237-3047
john.sherman@indstate.edu
• Joel McMullen, Associate Athletic Director, Compliance
(812) 237-8025
joel.mcmullen@indstate.edu
• Dennis Darke, Assistant AD, Facilities & Operations
(812) 237-4158
dennis.darke@indstate.edu

INDIANA UNIVERSITY ATHLETICS
SIMON SKJODT ASSEMBLY HALL
1001 E 17TH STREET
BLOOMINGTON, IN 47408-1590
812-855-2794
iuhoosiers.com
• Scott Dolson, Vice President & Dir., Intercollegiate Athletics
(812) 855-1966
athldir@indiana.edu

INDIANA UNIVERSITY-PURDUE UNIVERSITY FORT WAYNE
DEPT. OF INTERCOLLEGIATE ATHLETICS
2101 E COLISEUM BOULEVARD
FORT WAYNE, IN 46805-1499
www.gomastodons.com
• Kelley Hartley Hutton, Athletic Director
(260) 481-5445
• Christine Kuznar, Senior Associate AD, Academics/SWA
(260) 481-6192
kuznarc@pfw.edu
• Rachel Holycross, Associate AD, Compliance
(260) 481-0281
newstedr@pfw.edu

INDIANA UNIVERSITY-PURDUE UNIVERSITY INDIANAPOLIS
IUPUI ATHLETICS
250 UNIVERSITY BOULEVARD
INDIANAPOLIS, IN 46202
317-278-5247
Fax: 317-278-2683
iupuiad@iupui.edu
www.iupuijags.com
• Roderick Perry, Director of Athletics
(317) 278-5247
perryrd@iupui.edu
• Ed Holdaway, Senior Associate AD, External Affairs
(317) 274-2725
eholdawa@iupui.edu
• Laura Hue, Associate AD, Compliance
(317) 278-4281
lhue@iupui.edu
• Denise O'Grady, Associate AD, Academics
(317) 278-1648
dogrady@iupui.edu

IONA COLLEGE ATHLETICS
HYNES CENTER
715 NORTH AVENUE
NEW ROCHELLE, NY 10801
914-633-2654
athletics@iona.edu
www.icgaels.com
• Matt Glovaski, Director of Athletics
(914) 633-2311

mglovaski@iona.edu
• Jamie Fogarty, Senior Associate AD/SWA
(914) 633-2320
jfogarty@iona.edu
• Brian Beyrer, Senior Associate AD, Communications
(914) 637-2726
bbeyrer@iona.edu
• Sam De Rosa, Senior Associate AD, Sports Medicine
(914) 633-2333
sderosa@iona.edu
• Tom Moran, Deputy AD, Advancement & External Affairs
(914) 633-2627
tmoran@iona.edu

IOWA ATHLETICS, UNIVERSITY OF
N410 CARVER-HAWKEYE ARENA
IOWA CITY, IA 52242-1020
319-335-9323
800-424-2957
Fax: 319-335-9726
tickets@hawkeyesports.com
hawkeyesports.com
• Gary Barta, Director of Athletics Chair
(319) 335-9435
gary-barta@uiowa.edu
• Beth Goetz, Deputy AD/SWA/COO
beth-goetz@uiowa.edu
• Matt Henderson, Deputy Director of Athletics, External Relations
(319) 335-6487
matt-henderson@uiowa.edu
• Marcus Wilson, Senior Associate AD, Event Mngmnt. & Sport Admin.
(319) 335-9247
marcus-m-wilson@uiowa.edu

IOWA STATE UNIVERSITY ATHLETICS
JACOBSON ATHLETIC BUILDING
1800 S FOURTH STREET
AMES, IA 50011-1140
515-294-3662
Fax: 515-294-6006
cyclones.com
• Jamie Pollard, Director of Athletics
(515) 294-0123
jbp@iastate.edu
• Chris Jorgensen, Senior Associate AD, Operations
(515) 294-0307
cjorg@iastate.edu
• Nick Joos, Senior Associate AD, Communications
(515) 294-5095
njoos@iastate.edu
• Frank Nogel, Special Advisor, Athletics Director
fnogel@iastate.edu
• Calli Sanders, Senior Associate AD, Sports Administration
csanders@iastate.edu
• Shamaree Brown, Senior Associate AD, Student Services
shamaree@iastate.edu

JACKSON STATE UNIVERSITY ATHLETICS
1400 JOHN R. LYNCH STREET
P.O. BOX 17810
JACKSON, MS 39217
601-979-2291
Fax: 601-979-9291
www.gojsutigers.com
• Ashley Robinson, Vice President & Director of Athletics

• Derek Scott, Associate AD, Internal Operations
(601) 979-7821
derek.l.scott@jsums.edu
• Alyse Wells-Kilbert, Associate AD & SWA
(601) 979-0867
alyse.wells-kilbert@jsums.edu
• Duane Lewis, Associate AD, PR & Sports Media
(601) 979-0857
duane.c.lewis@jsums.edu

JACKSONVILLE STATE UNIVERSITY ATHLETICS
JSU ATHLETIC DEPT.
700 PELHAM ROAD N
JACKSONVILLE, AL 36265
jsugamecocksports.com
• Greg Seitz, Athletic Director
(256) 782-5368
gseitz@jsu.edu
• Greg Bonds, Senior Associate AD
(256) 782-5988
gbonds@jsu.edu

JACKSONVILLE UNIVERSITY ATHLETICS
2800 UNIVERSITY BOULEBARD N
JACKSONVILLE, FL 32211
904-256-7400
www.judolphins.com
• Alex Ricker-Gilbert, Athletic Director/Sr. Vice President
(904) 256-7400
• Hannah Gleichenhaus, Senior Associate AD, Administration/SWA
(904) 256-7425
hwilcox@ju.edu
• Justin Wilkins, Senior Associate AD, Internal Affairs
(904) 256-7357
jwilkin6@ju.edu

JAMES MADISON UNIVERSITY ATHLETICS
800 SOUTH MAIN STREET
HARRISONBURG, VA 22807
540-568-6164
jmusports.com
• Jeff Bourne, Director of Athletics
(540) 568-6164
fearcg@jmu.edu
• Geoff Polglase, Deputy Director of Athletics
(540) 568-6164
polglagh@jmu.edu
• Jennifer Phillips, Associate AD, Compliance/SWA
(540) 568-7834
phill2jr@jmu.edu
• Kevin White, Associate AD, Sports Programs
(540) 568-6104
whitekj@jmu.edu

KANSAS STATE UNIVERSITY ATHLETICS
BRAMLAGE COLISEUM
1800 COLLEGE AVENUE
MANHATTAN, KS 66502
800-221-2287
www.kstatesports.com
• Gene Taylor, Director of Athletics
(785) 532-6910
gtaylor@kstatesports.com
• Jill Shields, Deputy AD/SWA
(785) 532-6620

jshields@kstatesports.com
• Jim Bach, Associate AD, Business Operations
(785) 532-6020
jbach@kstatesports.com
• Casey Scott, Exec. Associate AD, Internal Ops. & Event Mngmt.
(785) 532-5263
cscott@kstatesports.com
• Kenny Lannou, Executive Associate AD, Communications/PR
(785) 532-7977
klannou@kstatesports.com
• Kristin Waller, Associate AD of Student-Athlete Services
(785) 532-5409
kwaller@kstatesports.com

KANSAS UNIVERSITY ATHLETICS
ALLEN FIELDHOUSE
1651 NAISMITH DRIVE
LAWRENCE, KS 66045
785-864-8200
kuathletics@ku.edu
kuathletics.com
• Travis Goff, Director of Athletics
(875) 864-3143
kuathletics@ku.edu
• Sean Lester, Deputy AD, Administration
(785) 864-3470
slester@ku.edu
• Nicole Corcoran, Deputy Athletics Dir. for Sports Admin./SWA
(785) 864-5999
ncorcoran@ku.edu

KENNESAW STATE UNIVERSITY ATHLETICS
3380 TOWN POINT DRIVE
SUITE 340
KENNESAW, GA 30144
470-578-6284
Fax: 470-578-9029
www.ksuowls.com
• Milton Overton, Director of Athletics
(470) 578-6284
moverton@kennesaw.edu
• Brad Ledford, Deputy AD
jledfo23@kennesaw.edu
• Travis Glasgow, Senior Associate AD
(470) 578-7793
tglasgo2@kennesaw.edu

KENT STATE UNIVERSITY ATHLETICS
MAC CENTER
PO BOX 5190
KENT, OH 44242
330-672-5974
kentstatesports.com
• Randale L. Richmond, Director of Athletics
(330) 672-3120
KSUAD@kent.edu
• Greg Glaus, Senior Deputy Athletics Director
(330) 672-7994
gglaus@kent.edu
• Amy Densevich, Associate AD, Academic Services
(330) 672-2961
adensevi@kent.edu
• Angie Hull, Senior Associate Athletics Director
(330) 672-4733
hull@kent.edu
• Trent Stratton, Senior Associate Athletics Director
(330) 672-8426

tstratto@kent.edu
• Suzette McQueen, Executive Senior Associate Athletics Dir./SWA
(330) 672-2256
smcquee1@kent.edu

KENTUCKY ATHLETICS, UNIVERSITY OF
UK ATHLETICS
JOE CRAFT CENTER
338 LEXINGTON AVENUE
LEXINGTON, KY 40506-0604
859-257-8000
ukathletics.com
• Mitch Barnhart, Athletics Director
(859) 257-8015
mbarn@uky.edu
• Marc Hill, Deputy Athletics Director
(859) 257-1423
mhill@uky.edu

LA SALLE UNIVERSITY ATHLETICS
TRUMARK FINANCIAL CENTER
1900 WEST OLNEY AVENUE
PHILADELPHIA, PA 19141
215-951-1999
Fax: 215-951-1694
www.goexplorers.com
• Brian Baptise, Vice President for Athletics & Recreation
athletics@lasalle.edu
• Donease Smith, Chief of Staff/SWA
(215) 951-1673
smithdm@lasalle.edu
• Christine Pereira, Assistant AD, Compliance
(215) 951-1390
pereira@lasalle.edu
• Phil Snead, Associate AD, Business Strategy & Analytics
(215) 951-1678
snead@lasalle.edu
• Dan Lobacz, Associate AD, External Relations
(215) 951-1932
lobacz@lasalle.edu

LAFAYETTE COLLEGE ATHLETICS
KIRBY SPORTS CENTER
700 W PIERCE STREET
EASTON, PA 18042
610-330-5470
Fax: 610-330-5702
www.goleopards.com
• Sherryta Freeman, Director of Athletics
(610) 330-5470
athleticdirector@lafayette.edu
• Andrew Foster, Associate AD, Operations & Facilities
(610) 330-5472
fostera@lafayette.edu
• Michael Chamberlain, Sr. Assoc. AD, Compliance & Student-Athlete Dev.
(610) 330-4421
chambemi@lafayette.edu

LAMAR UNIVERSITY ATHLETICS
211 REDBIRD LANE
BEAUMONT, TX 77710
Fax: 409-880-1814
luathletics@lamar.edu
www.lamarcardinals.com
• Jeff O'Malley, Director of Athletics
(409) 880-2248
• Moses Dupre, Assistant Athletic Director, Compliance
(409) 880-8323
moses.dupre@lamar.edu

• Helene Thill, Associate AD/SWA
(409) 880-8333
helene.thill@lamar.edu

LEHIGH UNIVERSITY ATHLETICS
641 TAYLOR STREET
BETHLEHEM, PA 18015
610-758-4300
Fax: 610-758-6629
www.lehighsports.com
• Joe Sterrett, Dean of Athletics
(610) 758-4320
jds7@lehigh.edu
• Taryn Gall, Associate AD, Compliance & Admin./SWA
(610) 758-4607
taf6@lehigh.edu
• Stacy Shiffert, Associate AD, Business & Budget
(610) 758-6332
stsa@lehigh.edu
• Chris Wakely, Associate AD, Recruitment
(610) 758-6553
cjw5@lehigh.edu

LIBERTY UNIVERSITY ATHLETICS
1971 UNIVERSITY BOULEVARD
LYNCHBURG, VA 24515
434-582-2100
Fax: 434-582-2205
www.liberty.edu/flames
• Ian McCaw, Director of Athletics
athletics@liberty.edu
• Mickey Guridy, Senior Associate AD, Internal Operations
maguridy@liberty.edu
• Tim East, Senior Associate AD, External Operations
tmeast@liberty.edu
• Todd Patulski, Senior Associate AD/CFO
tpatulski@liberty.edu
• Scott Lawrenson, Assistant AD, Sports Medicine
slawrenson@liberty.edu
• Erin Hagen, Sr. Associate AD, Admin./SWA
ehagen1@liberty.edu

LIPSCOMB UNIVERSITY ATHLETICS
ONE UNIVERSITY PARK DRIVE
NASHVILLE, TN 37204
615-966-5850
(800) 333-4358
Fax: 615-966-1806
www.lipscombsports.com
• Philip Hutcheson, Athletic Director
(615) 966-5850
• Brent McMillian, Associate AD, External Affairs
(615) 966-5166
brent.mcmillian@lipscomb.edu
• John Ezell, Associate AD, Compliance & Budgets
(615) 966-5911
john.ezell@lipscomb.edu
• Grace A Miller, Associate AD, Academics/SWA
(615) 966-5999
graceann.miller@lipscomb.edu

LONG BEACH STATE ATHLETICS
BARRETT ATHLETIC ADMIN. CENTER
1250 BELLFLOWER BOULEVARD
LONG BEACH, CA 90840
562-985-4655
Fax: 562-985-8197
www.longbeachstate.com

• Ted Kadowaki, Interim Executive Director of Athletics
(562) 985-7976
Ted.Kadowaki@csulb.edu
• Tiffany Edlin, Senior Associate AD/SWA
(562) 985-1626
Tiffany.Edlin@csulb.edu
• Mark Edrington, Sr. Associate AD, Capital Enhancements/Operations
(562) 985-5661
mark.edrington@csulb.edu

LONG ISLAND UNIVERSITY BROOKLYN ATHLETICS
1 UNIVERISITY PLAZA
BROOKLYN, NY 11201
718-780-4591
www.liuathletics.com
• William E. Martinov, Jr., Director of Athletics
(516) 299-2289
• Ryan Kelly, Deputy Athletic Director
ryan.kelly@liu.edu
• Craig Angelos, Senior Deputy Athletic Director
• Jamilah Ali-Shaffer, Associate Athletic Director/SWA
jamilah.ali@liu.edu

LONGWOOD UNIVERSITY ATHLETICS
201 HIGH STREET
TABB BUILDING
FARMVILLE, VA 23909
434-395-2057
Fax: 434-395-2568
www.longwoodlancers.com
• Tim Hall, Athletics Director
halltw@longwood.edu
• Tim Person, Vice President Emeritus & Athletic Dept. Liaison
piersontj@longwood.edu
• Iain Byers, Associate Athletics Director, Internal Operations
byersid@longwood.edu

LOUISIANA AT LAFAYETTE ATHLETICS, UNIVERSITY OF
COX COMMUNICATIONS BUILDING
201 REINHARDT DRIVE
LAFAYETTE, LA 70506
337-482-5393
Fax: 337-482-1041
ragincajuns.com
• Bryan Maggard, Ph.D., Vice President for Intercollegiate Athletics
(337) 482-5393
• Duane Bailey, Deputy Director of Athletics/CFO
(337) 482-1362
duane.bailey@louisiana.edu
• Jessica Leger, Ph.D., Deputy AD/SWA
(337) 482-5393
jessica@louisiana.edu
• Trey Frazier, Deputy AD
thomas.frazier@louisiana.edu

LOUISIANA AT MONROE ATHLETICS, UNIVERSITY OF
ULM ATHLETICS
308 WARHAWK WAY
MONROE, LA 71209
318-342-5360
www.ulmwarhawks.com
• Andrea Tepe, Chief of Staff
(225) 578-8001
• Clay Harris, Deputy Director of Athletics, Revenue Generation

• John Lewandowski, Senior Associate AD, Communications
(318) 342-5378
lewandowski@ulm.edu
• Lori Williams, Deputy Athletics Director, Leadership & Strategy

LOUISIANA STATE UNIVERSITY ATHLETICS
LSU ATHLETICS ADMIN. BLDG.
BATON ROUGE, LA 70803
225-578-8001
www.lsusports.net
• Scott Woodward, Director of Athletics
(225) 578-8001
• Verge Ausberry, Executive Deputy AD, External Relations
(225) 578-6603
vausbe1@lsu.edu
• Stephanie Rempe, Executive Deputy AD/COO
(225) 578-8001
srempe@lsu.edu
• Miriam Segar, Sr. Assoc. AD/SWA
(225) 578-5785
msegar@lsu.edu

LOUISIANA TECH UNIVERSITY ATHLETICS
THOMAS ASSEMBLY CENTER
1650 W ALABAMA
PO BOX 3046
RUSTON, LA 71270
www.latechsports.com
• Wood A Eric, Athletics Director/Vice President
athleticdirector@latech.edu
• Mary Kay Hungate, Deputy Athletics Director/SWA
(318) 257-5654
mhungate@latech.edu
• Reggie McIntyre, Associate AD, External Relations
(318) 257-5332
mcintyre@latech.edu

LOUISVILLE ATHLETICS, UNIVERSITY OF
ATHLETIC DEPT., SAC BUILDING
2100 S FLOYD STREET
LOUISVILLE, KY 40208
502-852-5735
gocards.com
• Josh Heird, Director of Athletics
ad@GoCards.com
• John Carns, Senior Associate AD, Compliance
(502) 852-7728
john@gocards.com
• Marvin Mitchell, Deputy AD/Student Services & Diversity
(502) 852-7100
marvin@gocards.com
• Amy Calabrese, Deputy AD/SWA
(502) 852-4939
amyc@GoCards.com

LOYOLA MARYMOUNT UNIVERSITY
1 LMU DRIVE
MS 8505
LOS ANGELES, CA 90045
310-338-2765
www.lmulions.com
• Craig Pintens, Athletic Director
(310) 338-3047
craig.pintens@lmu.edu
• Ashley Armstrong, Deputy AD/SWA

(310) 258-7246
ashley.armstrong@lmu.edu
• Maria Behm, Senior Associate AD, Business Affairs
(310) 338-7645
mbehm@lmu.edu
• James Batley, Senior Associate AD, Development
(310) 338-7880
james.batley@lmu.edu

LOYOLA UNIVERSITY CHICAGO ATHLETICS
THE NORVILLE CENTER
6526 N WINTHROP AVENUE
CHICAGO, IL 60626
773-508-2747
Fax: 773-508-3884
www.loyolaramblers.com
• Steve Watson, Director of Athletics
(773) 508-2747
swatson4@luc.edu
• Holly Strauss-O'Brien, Deputy Director of Athletics/SWA
(773) 508-2655
hstraussobrien@luc.edu
• Tom Sorboro, Senior Associate AD, External Operations
(773) 508-2731
tsorboro@luc.edu
• Tom Hitcho, Senior Associate AD, Operations
(773) 508-2567
thitch@luc.edu

LOYOLA UNIVERSITY MARYLAND ATHLETICS
4501 N CHARLES STREET
BALTIMORE, MD 21210
410-617-5013
Fax: 410-617-2008
www.loyolagreyhounds.com
• Donna M. Woodruff, Director of Athletics
(410) 617-5013
• Teddi Burns, Associate AD, Facils. & Ops./SWA
(410) 617-2643
tburns@loyola.edu
• Dave Gerrity, Associate AD
(410) 617-2547
dgerrity@loyola.edu
• Bill Wnek, Associate AD, Compliance
(410) 617-2172
bwnek@loyola.edu
• Chris Archacki, Associate AD, Business & Internal Operations
(410) 617-2718
carchacki@loyola.edu
• Ryan Eigenbrode, Associate AD, Communications & Strategic Marketing
(410) 617-2337
rceigenbrode@loyola.edu

MAINE ATHLETICS, UNIVERSITY OF
5747 MEMORIAL GYMNASIUM
ORONO, ME 04469-5747
207-581-1865
goblackbears.com
• Jude Killy, Director of Athletics
• Samantha Hegmann-Wary, Associate Athletic Director, Compliance/SWA
brian.faison@maine.edu
• Seth Woodcock, Senior Associate AD, Development
seth.woodcock@maine.edu
• Tyson McHatten, Senior Associate AD, External Ops./Communications

college sports

335

(207) 581-3596
tysone.mchatten@maine.edu
• Logan Desmond, Interim Associate AD,
Internal Operations
(207) 581-2358
logan.desmond@maine.edu

MANHATTAN COLLEGE ATHLETICS
4513 MANHATTAN COLLEGE PARKWAY
RIVERDALE, NY 10471
718-862-7777
Fax: 718-862-7219
www.gojaspers.com
• Marianne Reilly, Director of Intercollegiate
Athletics
(718) 862-7891
• Denise Thompson, Senior Associate AD,
External Relations/SWA
(718) 862-7936
dthompson04@manhattan.edu

MARIST COLLEGE ATHLETICS
MCCANN CENTER
3399 NORTH ROAD
POUGHKEEPSIE, NY 12601
845-575-3000
www.goredfoxes.com
• Tim Murray, Director of Athletics
(845) 575-3000
athletics@marist.edu
• Elizabeth Donohue, Associate AD,
Compliance/SWA
(845) 575-3000
elizabeth.donohue@marist.edu
• Darren McCormack, Associate AD,
Facilities & Operations
(845) 575-3000
darren.mccormack1@marist.edu
• Harrison Baker, Associate AD/Dir. of
External Affairs
(845) 575-3000
harrison.baker@marist.edu

MARQUETTE UNIVERSITY ATHLETICS
770 N 12TH STREET
MILWAUKEE, WI 53233
414-288-6303
www.gomarquette.com
• Bill Scholl, Director of Athletics
(414) 288-6303
athleticdirector@marquette.edu
• Mike Broeker, Deputy Athletic Director
(414) 288-5287
michael.broeker@marquette.edu
• Danielle Josetti, Exec. Associate AD,
Compliance, Marketing & Sales
(414) 288-3983
danielle.josetti@marquette.edu
• Adrienne Ridgeway, Exec. Assoc. AD,
Academic Srvcs. & Student Prgms.
(414) 288-0266
adrienne.ridgeway@marquette.edu
• Sarah Bobert, Executive Associate AD,
Internal Operations/SWA
(414) 288-5253
sarah.bobert@marquette.edu

MARSHALL UNIVERSITY ATHLETICS
MARSHALL ATHLETIC DEPT.
PO BOX 1360
HUNTINGTON, WV 25715
www.herdzone.com
• Christian Spears, Director of Athletics
(304) 696-5408
athleticdirector@marshall.edu
• Debra Boughton, Executive Associate
Athletic Director

boughton@marshall.edu
• Beatrice Crane Banford, Senior Associate
Athletic Dir., Olympic Sports/SWA
(304) 696-5225
craneb@marshall.edu
• John Sutherland, Associate AD,
Development
(304) 696-3402
sutherland@marshall.edu

MARY ATHLETICS, UNIVERSITY OF
UM ATHLETICS
7500 UNIVERSITY DRIVE
BISMARCK, ND 58504
701-335-8200
Fax: 701-335-8302
www.goumary.com
• Daniel Huntley, Interim Director of
Athletics
(701) 355-8337
djhuntley@umary.edu
• Daniel Huntley, Associate AD
(701) 355-8337
djhuntley@umary.edu

MARYGROVE COLLEGE ATHLETICS
8100 CURTIS STREET
DETROIT, MI 48221
313-928-1487
athletics@marygrove.edu
www.marygrovemustangs.com
• Jonathan T. Bradbury, Director of Athletics
(313) 928-1487
sbloomfi@marygrove.edu
• Andrew D. Thompson, Assistant AD
(313) 927-1484
wpugh@marygrove.edu

MARYLAND ATHLETICS, UNIVERSITY OF
DEPT. OF INTERCOLLEGIATE
ATHLETICS
XFINITY CENTER
8500 PAINT BRANCH DRIVE
COLLEGE PARK, MD 20742
301-314-7070
www.umterps.com
• Damon Evans, Director of Athletics
(301) 314-0013
devans16@umd.edu
• Colleen Sorem, Deputy AD
(301) 314-7046
csorem@umd.edu
• Brian Ullmann, Executive Associate
AD/CSO
(301) 314-1482
ullmann@umd.edu

**MARYLAND EASTERN SHORE
ATHLETICS, UNIVERSITY OF**
WILLIAM P. HYTCHE ATHLETIC CENTER
BACKBONE ROAD RM. 1133
PRINCESS ANNE, MD 21853
www.easternshorehawks.com
• Tara A. Ownens, Director of Athletics
(410) 651-6496
taowens@umes.edu
• Collene Dean, Assistant Athletic Director
for Academics
(410) 651-6539
cndean@umes.edu

**MARYLAND-BALTIMORE COUNTY
ATHLETICS, UNIVERSITY OF**
UMBC RETRIEVER ACTIVITIES CENTER
1000 HILLTOP CIRCLE
BALTIMORE, MD 21250

www.umbcretrievers.com
• Brian Barrio, Director of Athletics
(410) 455-2207
mctewey@umbc.edu
• Whitney Ames, Associate AD & SWA
(410) 455-3164
whitames@umbc.edu
• Gary Wohlstetter, Senior Associate AD,
P.E. & Recreation
(410) 455-2638
wohlstet@umbc.edu

**MCNEESE STATE UNIVERSITY
ATHLETICS**
700 E MCNEESE STREET
LAKE CHARLES, LA 70609
337-562-4678
Fax: 337-475-5220
tickets@mcneese.edu
www.mcneesesports.com
• Heath Schroyer, Director of Athletics
(337) 475-5480
hschroyer@mcneese.edu
• Bridget Martin, Senior Associate AD,
Compliance/SWA
(337) 475-5296
bmartin@mcneese.edu

MEMPHIS ATHLETICS, UNIVERSITY OF
570 NORMAL
MEMPHIS, TN 38152
901-678-2335
gotigersgo.com
• Laird Veatch, VP & Dir. of Intercollegiate
Athletics
(901) 678-5395
athleticdirector@memphis.edu
• Jeff Crane, Deputy Athletic Director
(901) 678-5395
jeff.c@memphis.edu
• Adam Walker, Executive Associate AD,
Admin.
(901) 678-1720
awalker9@memphis.edu
• Blair DeBord, Associate AD, External
Engagemet
(901) 678-1369
bdebord@memphis.edu
• Andrew Roberts, Senior Associate AD,
Finance
(901) 678-4142
andrew.roberts@memphis.edu

MERCER UNIVERSITY ATHLETICS
MERCER ATHLETICS
1501 MERCER UNIVERSITY DRIVE
MACON, GA 31207
478-301-2994
mercerbears.com
• Jim Cole, Director of Athletics
(478) 301-2737
cole_jm@mercer.edu
• Sybil Blalock, Deputy AD, Acad.
Affairs/SWA
(478) 301-2301
blalock_sa@mercer.edu
• Brian Gerrity, Deputy AD/Executive
Director, MAF
(478) 301-4003
gerrity_bt@mercer.edu

MIAMI ATHLETICS, UNIVERSITY OF
5821 SAN AMARO DRIVE
HECHT ATHLETIC CENTER
CORAL GABLES, FL 33146

305-284-3822
canestix@miami.edu
miamihurricanes.com
• Dan Radakovich, Vice President/Director of Athletics
• Jennifer Strawley, Senior Deputy Director of Athletics
j.strawley@miami.edu
• Jason Layton, Deputy Director of Athletics
jlayton@miami.edu

MIAMI UNIVERSITY ATHLETICS
230 MILLETT HALL
OXFORD, OH 45056
513-529-3113
Fax: 513-529-0407
wellspl@miamioh.edu
www.miamiredhawks.com
• David Sayler, Director of Athletics
(513) 529-7286
• Jennifer Gilbert, Associate Athletic Director/SWA
(513) 529-7285
gilberj2@miamioh.edu
• Lisa Miller, Associate AD, Internal Operations
(513) 529-3113
mille780@miamioh.edu

MICHIGAN ATHLETICS, UNIVERSITY OF
ATHLETIC DEPARTMENT
1000 S STATE STREET
ANN ARBOR, MI 48109-2201
734-647-2583
Fax: 734-764-3221
mgoblue.com
• Warde Manuel, Director of Athletics
(734) 764-9416
• Rob Rademacher, Executive Senior Associate AD/COO
(734) 647-9763
• Katie Fraumann, Executive Associate AD, Development
(734) 647-9895
• Doug Gnodtke, Executive Associate AD/Chief of Staff
(734) 936-1992

MICHIGAN STATE UNIVERSITY ATHLETICS
ATHLETICS ADMIN.
1855 PLACE
550 S HARRISON RD
EAST LANSING, MI 48823
517-355-1630
www.msuspartans.com
• Alan Haller, Vice President & Athletic Director
(507) 355-1630
ad@ath.msu.edu
• Jennifer Smith, Deputy Athletic Director/SWA
(517) 432-2606
smith170@ath.msu.edu

MIDDLE TENNESSEE ATHLETICS
MTSU BOX 77
MURFREESBORO, TN 37132
615-898-2450
Fax: 615-898-2777
goblueraiders.com
• Chris Massaro, Director of Athletics
(615) 898-2452
chris.massaro@mtsu.edu
• Lee De Leon, Deputy AD, External Operations
(615) 898-5563

lee.deleon@mtsu.edu
• Diane Turnham, Senior Associate AD/SWA
(615) 898-2938
diane.turnham@mtsu.edu

MINNESOTA ATHLETICS, UNIVERSITY OF
516 15TH AVENUE SE
MINNEAPOLIS, MN 55455
gophers@umn.edu
www.gophersports.com
• Mark Coyle, Director of Athletics
icaadmin@umn.edu
• Tim McCleary, Sr. Associate AD/Business Operations/CFO
• Julie Manning, Deputy Athletics Director/SWA
jmanning@umn.edu

MISSISSIPPI ATHLETICS, UNIVERSITY OF
SOUTH OXFORD CAMPUS
5TH FLOOR
P.O. BOX 1848
UNIVERSITY, MS 38677
662-915-7241
800-GO-REBEL
www.olemisssports.com
• Keith Carter, Vice Chancellor for Intercollegiate Athletics
(662) 915-7546
jkcarter@olemiss.edu
• Jennifer Saxon, EdD, Executive Associate AD/SWA
(662) 915-7546
jnsaxon@olemiss.edu
• Allen Greene, Senior Deputy AD, External Relations
(662) 915-7546
agreene@olemiss.edu

MISSISSIPPI STATE UNIVERSITY ATHLETICS
MISSISSIPPI STATE, MS 39762
hailstate.com
• Zac Selmon, Director of Athletics
(662) 325-0863
athleticdirector@athletics.msstate.edu
• Eric George, Deputy AD/CFO
(662) 325-8670
egeorge@athletics.msstate.edu
• Bo Hemphill, Deputy AD, Development
(662) 325-1533
bhemphill@athletics.msstate.edu

MISSISSIPPI VALLEY STATE UNIVERSITY ATHLETICS
DEPT. OF ATHLETICS
14000 HIGHWAY 82 WEST
BOX 7246
ITTA BENA, MS 38941
662-254-3550
Fax: 662-254-3639
www.mvsusports.com
• Hakim McClellan, Director of Athletics
(662) 254-3550
• Jarrad Ratliff, Sr. Associate Athletic Dir., Compliance
(662) 254-3552
jarrad.ratliff@mvsu.edu
• Lee Smith, Sr. Associate Athletic Dir., Internal Operations
(662) 254-3721
lcsmith@mvsu.edu

MISSOURI ATHLETICS, UNIVERSITY OF
MIZZOU ATHLETICS
1 CHAMPIONS DRIVE
SUITE 200
COLUMBIA, MO 65211
573-884-7297
Fax: 573-882-6501
mutigers.com
• Desiree Reed-Francois, Director of Athletics
(573) 882-2055
muathmizzouad@missouri.edu
• Desiree Reed-Francois, Director of Athletics
(573) 882-2055
mizzouad@missouri.edu

MISSOURI STATE ATHLETICS
901 S NATIONAL AVENUE
SPRINGFIELD, MO 65897
417-836-5402
www.missouristatebears.com
• Kyle Moats, Director of Athletics
(417) 836-5244
athletics@missouristate.edu
• Casey Hunt, Senior Associate AD/SWA
(417) 836-5244
caseyhunt@missouristate.edu
• Keith Boaz, Sr. Assoc. AD, Athletics & Entertainment
(417) 836-5240
keithboaz@missouristate.edu

MISSOURI-KANSAS CITY ATHLETICS, UNIVERSITY OF
5030 HOLMES
KANSAS CITY, MO 64110
816-325-2752
Fax: 816-235-1035
garciacr@umkc.edu
www.kcroos.com
• Brandon Martin, Director of Athletics
(816) 235-1020
martinbran@umkc.edu
• Ursula Gurney, Deputy Director of Athletics/SWA
(816) 235-5093
gurneyu@umkc.edu
• Curt Jacey, Deputy AD, External Relations
(816) 235-1039
jaceyc@umkc.edu

MONMOUTH UNIVERSITY ATHLETICS
400 CEDAR AVENUE
WEST LONG BRANCH, NJ 07764
732-571-3415
Fax: 732-571-3535
monmouthhawks.com
• Jeff Stapleton, Director of Athletics
(732) 263-5190
• Greg Viscomi, Senior Associate AD, External Affairs
(732) 571-4447
gviscomi@monmouth.edu
• Jennifer Sansevero, Senior Associate AD/SWA
(732) 571-3604
jsanseve@monmouth.edu

MONTANA ATHLETICS, UNIVERSITY OF
MONTANA ATHLETICS
ADAMS CENTER
32 CAMPUS DRIVE
MISSOULA, MT 59812
gogriz.com
• Kent Haslam, Director of Athletics
(406) 243-5348

college sports

kent.haslam@mso.umt.edu
• Jean Gee, Senior Associate AD/SWA
(406) 243-5370
jean.gee@mso.umt.edu
• Greg Sundberg, Senior Associate AD,
External Operations
(406) 243-6481
sundbergg@mso.umt.edu
• Chuck Maes, Senior Associate AD,
Facilities & Events
(406) 243-2213
maescf@mso.umt.edu
• Ryan Martin, Senior Associate AD/CFO
(406) 243-6926
ryan.martin@mso.umt.edu

**MONTANA STATE UNIVERSITY
ATHLETICS**
MONTANA STATE UNIVERSITY
1 BOBCAT CIRCLE
PO BOX 173380
BOZEMAN, MT 59717-3380
406-994-4221
Fax: 406-994-2278
info@msubobcats.com
msubobcats.com
• Leon Costello, Director of Athletics
(406) 994-3499
lcostello@msubobcats.com
• Thijs Goossens, Deputy AD, Internal
Operations/CFO
(406) 994-3742
thijs.goossens@msubobcats.com
• Casey Fox, Deputy AD, External
Operations
(406) 994-5707
casey.fox2@msubobcats.com
• Bethany Cordell, Associate AD, Annual
Giving & Fan Development
(406) 994-6267
bcordell@msubobcats.com

**MOREHEAD STATE UNIVERSITY
ATHLETICS**
195 ACADEMIC-ATHLETIC CENTER
MOREHEAD, KY 40351
606-783-2088
Fax: 606-783-5035
www.msueagles.com
• Jaime Gordon, Director of Athletics
(606) 783-2089
j.gordon@moreheadstate.edu
• Richard Fletcher, Deputy Director of
Athletic/Compliance
(606) 783-5136
r.fletcher@moreheadstate.edu
• Jamey Carver, Assistant AD for
Athletics/Compliance
(606) 783-2086
j.carver@moreheadstate.edu
• Kenna Gauche, Senior Associate Dir. of
Athletics/SWA
(606) 783-9018
k.gauche@moreheadstate.edu

**MORGAN STATE UNIVERSITY
ATHLETICS**
1700 E COLD SPRING LANE
BALTIMORE, MD 21251
443-885-3333
www.morganstatebears.com
• Dena Freeman-Patton, Director of
Athletics
 ext 3050

**MOUNT ST. MARY'S UNIVERSITY
ATHLETICS**
16300 OLD EMMITSBURG ROAD
EMMITSBURG, MD 21727
301-447-5384
www.mountathletics.com
• Lynne Robinson, Director of Athletics
(301) 447-3808
lrobinso@msmary.edu
• Doug White, Assistant AD, Operations
(301) 447-5385
dwhite@msmary.edu
• Mark Vandergrift, Associate AD, Athletic
Communications
(301) 447-5384
vandergrift@msmary.edu
• Justine Miller, Associate Dir. of Athletics
for Academics/SWA
(301) 447-6782
justine_miller@msmary.edu

**MURRAY STATE UNIVERSITY
ATHLETICS**
RACER ATHLETICS
217 STEWART STADIUM
MURRAY, KY 42071
270-809-6800
goracers.com
• Nico Yantko, Director of Athletics
(270) 809-3164
• Matt Kelly, Sr. Associate AD,
Student-Athlete Support Services
(270) 809-4424
mkelly@murraystate.edu
• Dave Winder, Associate AD,
Communication & Public Relations
(270) 809-4271
dwinder@murraystate.edu

NEBRASKA ATHLETICS, UNIVERSITY OF
ONE MEMORIAL STADIUM
800 STADIUM DRIVE
LINCOLN, NE 68588
402-472-4224
800-755-2565
www.huskers.com
• Trev Alberts, Vice Chancellor, Director of
Athletics
(402) 472-3011
ad@huskers.com
• Marquita Armstead, Executive Associate
AD/SWA
(402) 472-3011
marmstead@huskers.com
• Garrett Klassy, Senior Deputy AD
(402) 472-3011
gklassy@huskers.com
• Bob Burton, Executive Associate AD,
Facilities
(402) 472-3011
bburton@huskers.com

**NEVADA AT LAS VEGAS ATHLETICS,
UNIVERSITY OF**
UNLV ATHLETICS DEPARTMENT
4505 MARYLAND PARKWAY
LAS VEGAS, NV 89154
www.unlvrebels.com
• Erick Harper, Director of Athletics
(702) 895-4729
erick.harper@unlv.edu
• Jackie Perez, Director of Executive
Administration
(702) 895-4753
jackie.perez@unlv.edu
• Mike Ketcham, Deputy Athletics Director,
External

(702) 895-4486
michael.ketcham@unlv.edu
• Eric Nepomuceno, Deputy Athletics
Director/Chief Operating Officer
(702) 895-1314
eric.nepomuceno@unlv.edu

NEVADA ATHLETICS, UNIVERSITY OF
UNIV. OF NEVADA ATHLETICS
1664 N VIRGINIA STREET
LEGACY HALL/MS 232
RENO, NV 89557-0232
Fax: 775-784-4497
nevadawolfpack.com
• Stephanie Rempe, Director of Athletics
(775) 682-6969
• Joseph Flores, Senior Associate AD,
Compliance Services
(775) 682-6962
josephflores@unr.edu

**NEW HAMPSHIRE ATHLETICS,
UNIVERSITY OF**
UNH FIELD HOUSE
145 MAIN STREET
DURHAM, NH 03824
www.unhwildcats.com
• Allison Rich, Director of Athletics
(603) 862-2013
athletic.director@unh.edu
• Michelle Bronner, Deputy Director of
Athletics/SWA
(603) 319-7491
michelle.bronner@unh.edu
• Fumi Kimura, Deputy Director of Athletics,
External Operations
(603) 862-4677
fumi.kimura@unh.edu

**NEW MEXICO STATE UNIVERSITY
ATHLETICS**
NEW MEXICO STATE UNIVERSITY
FULTON CENTER
1815 WELLS STREET
LAS CRUCES, NM 88003-8001
575-646-1658
nmstatesports.com
• Mario Moccia, Director of Athletics
(575) 646-7630
moccia@nmsu.edu
• Braun Cartwright, Deputy AD/COO
(575) 646-5713
braunc@nmsu.edu
• Chet Savage, Deputy AD/AAC
(575) 646-2569
savagec@nmsu.edu

NEW MEXICO, UNIVERSITY OF
UNIVERSITY OF NEW MEXICO
ATHLETICS
1414 UNIVERSITY DRIVE
ALBUQUERQUE, NM 87106
golobos.com
• Eddie Nunez, Director of Athletics
(505) 925-5510
eddienunez@unm.edu
• David Williams, Deputy AD, External
Affairs
(505) 925-5500
davidwilliams@unm.edu

**NEW ORLEANS ATHLETICS,
UNIVERSITY OF**
THE HUMAN PERFORMANCE CENTER
2000 LAKESHORE DRIVE
NEW ORLEANS, LA 70148

504-280-6102
Fax: 504-280-3977
athletics@uno.edu
www.unoprivateers.com
• Tim Duncan, Vice President of Athletics & Recreation
(504) 280-6102
athleticdirector@uno.edu
• Steve Stroud, Deputy Athletic Dir./Chief Dev. & Revenue Officer
(504) 280-7403
sstroud1@uno.edu
• Kimberly Gallow, Associate Athletic Dir., Ops. & Capital Projects
(504) 280-3874
kgallow1@uno.edu

NEWMAN UNIVERSITY ATHLETICS
3100 MCCORMICK AVENUE
WICHITA, KS 67213
316-942-4291
Fax: 316-942-4483
www.newmanjets.com
• Joanna Pryor, Athletic Director
(316) 942-4291
pryorj@newmanu.edu
• Maureen Rohleder, Associate AD, Compliance/SWA
(316) 942-4291
rohlederm@newman.edu
• Zane Ehling, Assistant Athletic Director, Marketing & Comms.
(316) 942-4291
brakez@newmanu.edu

NIAGARA UNIVERSITY ATHLETICS
UPPER LEVEL GALLAGHER CENTER
PO BOX 2009
NIAGARA UNIVERSITY, NY 14109
716-286-8600
purpleeagles.com
• Simon Gray, Associate Vice President for Athletics
(716) 286-8600
sgray@niagara.edu
• Stephen Butler, Deputy DA/COO
(716) 286-8602
• Susan Petronsky, Associate AD/SWA
(716) 286-8781
sroarke@niagara.edu

NICHOLLS STATE UNIVERSITY ATHLETICS
PO BOX 2032
THIBODAUX, LA 70310
www.geauxcolonels.com
• Jonathan Terrell, Director of Athletics
jonathan.terrell@nicholls.edu

NORTH CAROLINA A&T STATE UNIVERSITY ATHLETICS
DEPT. OF ATHLETICS
1601 E MARKET STREET
GREENSBORO, NC 27411
www.ncataggies.com
• Earl Hilton, III, Director of Intercollegiate Athletics
(336) 334-7686
hiltone@ncat.edu
• Shamika Pyfrom, Associate AD, Athletics Development
(336) 285-3063
spyfrom@ncat.edu
• Cory Lima, Associate AD, Compliance
(336) 285-3620
cmlima@ncat.edu
• Brian Holloway, Associate AD,

Communications
(336) 285-3608
bmhollow@ncat.edu
• Billy Edrington, Associate AD, Facilities
(336) 398-8673
edringst@ncat.edu

NORTH CAROLINA ASHEVILLE ATHLETICS, UNIVERSITY OF
ATHLETICS DEPT.
JUSTICE CENTER, CPO#2600
ONE UNIVERSITY HEIGHTS
ASHEVILLE, NC 28804
828-251-6459
Fax: 828-251-6386
www.uncabulldogs.com
• Janet R. Cone, Sr. Administrator for University Enterprises & AD
(828) 251-6459
jcone@unca.edu

NORTH CAROLINA AT CHAPEL HILL ATHLETICS, UNIVERSITY OF
UNC ATHLETIC DEPT.
PO BOX 2126
CHAPEL HILL, NC 27515
919-962-6000
goheels.com
• Bubba Cunningham, Athletic Director
(919) 962-6000
bubba.cunningham@unc.edu
• Larry Gallo, Executive Associate AD
(919) 962-6000
athgallo@unc.edu
• Dwight Hollier, Senior Associate AD, Student-Athlete Health
(919) 962-6000
dhollier@unc.edu
• Vince Ille, Senior Associate AD
(919) 962-6000
ille@unc.edu

NORTH CAROLINA ATHLETICS, UNIVERSITY OF
UNC ATHLETIC DEPT.
PO BOX 2126
CHAPEL HILL, NC 27515
919-962-6000
goheels.com
• Bubba Cunningham, Athletic Director
(919) 962-6000
bubba.cunningham@unc.edu
• Larry Gallo, Exec. Assoc. AD
(919) 962-6000
athgallo@uncaa.unc.edu

NORTH CAROLINA CENTRAL UNIVERSITY ATHLETICS
DEPT. OF ATHLETICS
MCDOUGALD-MCLENDON ARENA
616 E LAWSON STREET
DURHAM, NC 27701
919-530-7057
athletics@nccu.edu
nccueaglepride.com
• Louis "Skip" Perkins, Director of Athletics
(919) 530-7057
athletics@nccu.edu
• Kendra Greene, Deputy AD, Internal Affairs/SWA
(919) 530-7295
kendra.greene@nccu.edu
• Kyle Serba, Deputy AD, External Affairs
(919) 530-7054
kserba@nccu.edu

NORTH CAROLINA CHARLOTTE ATHLETICS, UNIVERSITY OF
CHARLOTTE 49ERS ATHLETICS
9201 UNIVERSITY CITY BOULEVARD
CHARLOTTE, NC 28223
704-687-1054
www.charlotte49ers.com
• Mike Hill, Director of Athletics
(704) 687-1054
athleticdirector@uncc.edu
• Darin Spease, Deputy AD
(704) 687-0400
dspease@uncc.edu
• Chris Fuller, Deputy AD, External Affairs
(704) 687-1419
cfulle21@uncc.edu

NORTH CAROLINA GREENSBORO ATHLETICS, UNIVERSITY OF
UNIVERSITY OF NORTH CAROLINA AT GREENSBORO
DEPARTMENT OF INTERCOLLEGIATE ATHLETICS
1400 SPRING GARDEN STREET - COLEMAN BUILDING
GREENSBORO, NC 27412
www.uncgspartans.com
• Brian Mackin, Director of Athletics
(336) 334-5952
bwmackin@uncg.edu
• Chase Blake, Associate Athletic Director, Development
(910) 690-5466
cbblake@uncg.edu
• Jody Smith, Executive Associate AD/SWA
(336) 334-4076
jody.smith@uncg.edu

NORTH CAROLINA STATE UNIVERSITY ATHLETICS
WEISIGER BROWN BLDG.
2500 WARREN CARROLL DRIVE
CAMPUS BOX 8502
RALEIGH, NC 27695
919-515-2101
gopack.com
• Boo Corrigan, Director of Athletics
(919) 515-2109
wolfpackad@ncsu.edu
• Staphanie Menio, Deputy AD
(919) 515-4778
samenio@ncsu.edu

NORTH CAROLINA WILMINGTON ATHLETICS, UNIVERSITY OF
601 SOUTH COLLEGE ROAD
WILMINGTON, NC 28403
uncwsports.com
• Jimmy Bass, Director of Athletics
(910) 962-3571
• Tiffany Tucker, Deputy AD/SWA
(910) 962-3767
tuckert@uncw.edu
• Mark Wagner, Senior Associate AD, Internal Operations
(910) 962-3580
wagnerm@uncw.edu
• Joe Browning, Senior Associate AD, Communications
(910) 962-3236
browningj@uncw.edu

NORTH TEXAS ATHLETICS, UNIVERSITY OF
1301 S BONNIE BRAE STREET
DENTON, TX 76207

940-565-2789
www.meangreensports.com
• Jared Mosley, Director of Athletics/Vice President
• Ryan Peck, Deputy AD, External Operations
(940) 369-7630
ryan.peck@unt.edu

NORTHEASTERN STATE UNIVERSITY ATHLETICS
600 N GRAND AVENUE
TAHLEQUAH, OK 74464
www.goriverhawksgo.com
• John Sisemore, Director of Athletics
(918) 444-3901
sisemorj@nsuok.edu
• Scott Pettus, Assistant AD, Academic Services
(918) 444-3955
pettusr@nsuok.edu
• Don Vieth, Assistant AD, Strategic Communications
(918) 444-3930
vieth@nsuok.edu

NORTHEASTERN UNIVERSITY ATHLETICS
360 HUNTINGTON AVENUE
219 CABOT CENTER
BOSTON, MA 02115
617-373-2672
Fax: 617-373-8988
www.gonu.com
• Jim Madigan, Director of Athletics and Recreation
r.mitchell@northeastern.edu
• Regina Sullivan, Executive Senior Associate AD/SWA
re.sullivan@northeastern.edu
• Marshall Foley, Executive Sr. Associate AD, Operations
ma.foley@northeastern.edu
• Matthew Houde, Associate AD, Communications
m.houde@northeastern.edu

NORTHERN ARIZONA UNIVERSITY ATHLETICS
PO BOX 15400
1705 S SAN FRANCISCO STREET
FLAGSTAFF, AZ 86011
928-523-5353
Fax: 928-523-6035
www.nauathletics.com
• Mike Marlow, Vice President for Intercollegiate Athletics
(928) 523-5353
lumberjackad@nau.edu
• Uri Farkas, Deputy AD
(928) 523-3095
uri.farkas@nau.edu
• Beth Vechinski, Senior Associate AD, Internal Operations/SWA
(928) 523-3326
Beth.Vechinski@nau.edu
• Matt Howdeshell, Sr Associate AD, Administration & Capital Projects
(928) 523-0293
matt.howdshell@nau.edu
• Syed Moinuddin, Senior Associate AD, Compliance
(928) 523-6763
syed.moinuddin@nau.edu

NORTHERN ILLINOIS UNIVERSITY ATHLETICS
INTERCOLLEGIATE ATHLETICS
CONVOCATION CENTER
DEKALB, IL 60115
815-753-7225
Fax: 815-753-7700
www.niuhuskies.com
• Sean T. Frazier, Director of Athletics
(815) 753-9473
athleticdirector@niu.edu
• John Cheney, Deputy Athletic Director
(815) 753-1801
jcheney2@niu.edu

NORTHERN IOWA ATHLETICS, UNIVERSITY OF
203 MCLEOD CENTER
CEDAR FALLS, IA 50614-0312
unipanthers.com
• David Harris, Director of Athletics
(319) 273-2470
uniad@uni.edu
• Justin Schemmel, Deputy AD, Internal Operations
(319) 273-2410
justin.schemmel@uni.edu
• Beth West, Senior Associate AD, Business
(319) 273-7855
beth.west@uni.edu

NORTHERN KENTUCKY UNIVERSITY ATHLETICS
133 BB&T ARENA
500 NUNN DRIVE
HIGHLAND HEIGHTS, KY 41099
859-572-6639
www.nkunorse.com
• Christina Roybal, Director of Athletics
(859) 572-6539
• Dan McIver, Deputy AD
(859) 572-7744
mciverd1@nku.edu
• Chris Hafling, Associate AD, Operations & Event Management
(859) 572-7665
haflingc1@nku.edu
• Debbie Kirch, Associate AD, Compliance/SWA
(859) 572-5140
kirchd1@nku.edu

NORTHWESTERN OKLAHOMA STATE UNIVERSITY ATHLETICS
709 OKLAHOMA BOULEVARD
ALVA, OK 73717
580-327-8639
Fax: 580-327-8669
www.riderangersride.com
• Brad Franz, Director of Athletics
(580) 327-8632
bmfranz@nwosu.edu
• Tim Lauderdale, Associate AD, Internal Operations
(580) 327-8578
tjlauderdale@nwosu.edu
• Jeremy Jones, Associate AD, Compliance/Student Services
(580) 327-8635
jjjones@nwosu.edu

NORTHWESTERN STATE UNIVERSITY OF LOUISIANA ATHLETICS
ATHLETIC FIELDHOUSE
468 CASPARI DRIVE
NATCHITOCHES, LA 71497

athleticsinfo@nsula.edu
www.nsudemons.com
• Kevin Bostian, Director of Athletics
(318) 357-5251
bostiank@nsula.edu
• Patric DuBois, Deputy Athletic Director
(318) 357-5001
duboisp@nsula.edu
• Dustin Eubanks, Associate AD, Compliance & Special Services
(318) 357-4210
eubanksd@nsula.edu

NORTHWESTERN UNIVERSITY ATHLETICS
WALTER ATHLETICS CENTER
2255 CAMPUS DRIVE
EVANSTON, IL 60208
847-491-3205
nusports.com
• Denee Barracato, Deputy AD, Operations & Capital Projects
(847) 491-4646
denee.barracato@northwestern.edu
• Janna Blais, Deputy AD, Admin./SWA
(847) 491-7893
j-blais@northwestern.edu
• Jesse Marks, Deputy AD, Development
(847) 467-3575
jesse.marks@northwestern.edu

NOTRE DAME ATHLETICS, UNIVERSITY OF
C113 JOYCE CENTER
NOTRE DAME, IN 46556
www.und.com
• Jack Swarbrick, Director of Athletics
• Missy Conboy, Senior Deputy AD, Sports Operations
(574) 631-1602
• Jim Fraleigh, Deputy AD, Corporate Relations
(574) 631-8801
• Jody Sadler, Deputy AD, Competitive Excellence
(574) 631-8801

OHIO STATE UNIVERSITY ATHLETICS
2400 OLENTANGY RIVER ROAD
COLUMBUS, OH 43210
614-292-7572
www.ohiostatebuckeyes.com
• Gene Smith, Athletics Director
(614) 292-2477
athletic_director@osu.edu
• Dan Cloran, Executive Associate AD, Development
(614) 292-7744
cloran.10@osu.edu
• Joe Odoguardi, Executive Associate AD/CFO
(614) 292-5263
odoguardi.1@osu.edu
• Mike Penner, Executive Associate AD, Internal Operations
(614) 292-1848
penner.2@osu.edu

OHIO UNIVERSITY ATHLETICS
OHIO UNIVERSITY
INTERCOLLEGE ATHLETICS
CONVOCATION CENTER
ATHENS, OH 45701
740-593-1173
www.ohiobobcats.com
• Julie Cromer, Director of Athletics
(740) 593-0983

athleticsdir@ohio.edu
• Amy Dean, Deputy AD/SWA
(740) 593-1171
deana@ohio.edu
• Ken Winstead, Senior Associate AD,
Development
(740) 593-1197
winstead@ohio.edu
• Michael Stephens, Senior Associate AD,
External Operations
(740) 597-1375
stephem1@ohio.edu
• Randee Duffy, Senior Associate AD,
NCAA Eligibility
(740) 593-1172
duffyr1@ohio.edu
• Mary Ann Boyle, Senior Associae AD,
Internal Operations
(740) 593-2512
boylem1@ohio.edu

OKLAHOMA ATHLETICS, UNIVERSITY OF
MCCLENDON CENTER FOR
INTERCOLLEGIATE ATHLETICS
180 W BROOKS
NORMAN, OK 73019
405-325-8200
www.soonersports.com
• Joe Castiglione, Director for Athletics
(405) 325-8208
• Larry Naifeh, Executive Associate AD
(405) 325-8241
lnaifeh@ou.edu
• Macus Bowman, Depty AD, CFO &
Business Strategy
(405) 325-1844
mbowman@ou.edu
• Armani Dawkins, Deputy AD/Chief of Staff
& Administration
(405) 325-7321
adawkins@ou.edu

**OKLAHOMA STATE UNIVERSITY
ATHLETICS**
ATHLETICS CENTER
OKLAHOMA STATE UNIV.
STILLWATER, OK 74078
405-744-7714
Fax: 405-744-7754
admissions@okstate.edu
okstate.com
• Chad Wieberg, Director of Athletics
(405) 744-7714
athletic.director@okstate.edu
• Jason Lewis, Executive Senior Associate
AD
(405) 744-7132
jason.lewis@okstate.edu

OLD DOMINION UNIVERSITY ATHLETICS
INTERCOLLEGIATE ATHLETICS
JIM JARRETT ATHLETIC ADMIN. BLDG.
NORFOLK, VA 23529-0201
757-683-3369
www.odusports.com
• Camden Wood Selig, Athletic Director
(757) 683-3369
wselig@odu.edu
• Ken Brown, Deputy AD
(757) 683-5224
klbrown@odu.edu

OREGON ATHLETICS, UNIVERSITY OF
2727 LEO HARRIS PARKWAY
EUGENE, OR 97401

541-346-4481
Fax: 541-346-5031
goducks.com
• Rob Mullens, Athletic Director
(541) 346-5455
athleticdirector@uoregon.edu
• Eric Roedl, Deputy Athletic Director
(541) 346-5942
roedl@uoregon.edu
• Lisa Peterson, Deputy Athletic
Director/SWA
(541) 346-5329
lpete@uoregon.edu

**OREGON STATE UNIVERSITY
ATHLETICS**
104 GILL COLISEUM
CORVALLIS, OR 97331
541-737-3969
wecare@oregonstate.edu
osubeavers.com
• Scott Barnes, Director of Intercollegiate
Athletics
(541) 737-3969
k.bjornstad@oregonstate.edu

**PACIFIC ATHLETICS, UNIVERSITY OF
THE**
3601 PACIFIC AVE
STOCKTON, CA 95204
www.pacifictigers.com
• Janet Lucas, Director of Athletics
(209) 946-3208
athleticdirector@pacific.edu
• Tim Dickson, Executive Associate AD,
Development
(209) 946-3177
tdickson@pacific.edu
• Holly Trexler, Senior Associate AD,
Compliance/SWA
(209) 946-2307
htrexler@pacific.edu
• Wes Yourth, Deputy Director of
Athletics/COO
(209) 946-7408
wyourth@pacific.edu

PENN STATE UNIVERSITY ATHLETICS
201 OLD MAIN, UNIVERSITY PARK
UNIVERSITY PARK, PA 16802
www.gopsusports.com
• Sandy Barbour, Vice President for
Intercollegiate Athletics
(814) 865-1086
athletic_director@athletics.psu.edu
• Lynn Holleran, Deputy AD, Administration
(814) 867-6352
lkh5222@psu.edu
• Scott Sidwell, Deputy AD, External
(814) 867-6115
sas7431@psu.edu
• Joseph Foley, Senior Associate AD,
Advancement
(814) 867-1598
foley@psu.edu
• Lauren Rhodes, Senior Associate AD,
Student-Athlete Perf./SWA
(814) 865-1104
lrhodes@psu.edu
• Carl Heck, Senior Associate AD,
Capital/Events/Facilities
(814) 865-1104
ckh5446@psu.edu
• Rick Kaluza, Senior Associate AD,
Finance & Business Operations
(814) 865-7780
rck11@psu.edu

**PENNSYLVANIA ATHLETICS,
UNIVERSITY OF**
WEIGHTMAN HALL
235 S 33RD STREET
PHILADELPHIA, PA 19104
athletics@dria.upenn.edu
www.pennathletics.com
• Alanna W. Shanahan, Director of Athletics
& Recreation
(215) 898-1096
athdir@upenn.edu
• Joy De JesÂ£S, Senior Associate AD,
Finance & Internal Ops.
(215) 898-4430
joydejesus@upenn.edu
• Tim Folan, Senior Associate AD, Dev. &
Alumni Relations
(215) 573-0315
tfolan@upenn.edu
• Rudy Fuller, Senior Associate AD,
Intercollegiate Programs
(215) 746-7125
bfuller@upenn.edu
• Scott Ward, Senior Associate AD/COO
(215) 898-6153
sward2@upenn.edu
• Kevin Bonner, Senior Associate AD,
Governance & Admin.
(215) 898-9192
bonnerke@upenn.edu

PEPPERDINE UNIVERSITY ATHLETICS
24255 PACIFIC COAST HIGHWAY
MALIBU, CA 90263
310-506-4150
www.pepperdinewaves.com
• Steve Potts, Director of Athletics
(310) 506-4749
steven.potts@pepperdine.edu
• Amanda Kurtz, Senior Associate AD/SWA
(310) 506-6813
amanda.kurtz@pepperdine.edu

**PITTSBURGH ATHLETICS, UNIVERSITY
OF**
PETERSEN EVENTS CENTER
3719 TERRACE STREET
PITTSBURGH, PA 15261
412-648-8230
Fax: 412-648-8306
pittsburghpanthers.com
• Heather Lyke, Director of Athletics
(412) 648-8230
athleticdirector@athletics.pitt.edu
• Christian Spears, Deputy Athletic
Director/COO
(412) 648-8280
cspears@athletics.pitt.edu

PORTLAND ATHLETICS, UNIVERSITY OF
DEPT. OF ATHLETICS
5000 N WILLAMETTE BOULEVARD
PORTLAND, OR 97203-5798
www.portlandpilots.com
• Scott Leykam, Vice President for Athletics
(503) 943-8420
leykam@up.edu
• Karen Peters, Senior Associate AD/SWA
(503) 943-8110
peters@up.edu
• Jason Brough, Senior Associate AD
(503) 943-8439
brough@up.edu
• Karina Handerland, Senior Associate AD
(503) 943-7808
handelan@up.edu

college sports

PORTLAND STATE UNIVERSITY ATHLETICS
PETER W. STOTT CENTER
930 SW HALL STREET
PORTLAND, OR 97201
503-725-4000
goviks.com
• Linda Williams, Director of Athletics
(Interim)
law36@pdx.edu
• Mike Lund, Associate AD, Media &
Communication
(503) 725-5602
lundm@pdx.edu
• Dana Cappelucci, Associate AD,
Compliance/SWA
(503) 725-5621
dlc2@pdx.edu
• Josh Keller, Associate AD, Development
(503) 725-5607
kellerj@pdx.edu

PRAIRIE VIEW A&M UNIVERSITY ATHLETICS
PVAMU ATHLETICS DEPT.
PO BOX 519 - MAIL STOP 1500
PRAIRIE VIEW, TX 77446
936-261-9100
Fax: 936-261-9159
pvpanthers.com
• Donald Reed, Athletic Director
(936) 261-9100
• Alicia Pete, Assoc. AD, Internal
Operations/SWA
(936) 261-9100
alpete@pvamu.edu
• Brittney Johnson, Associate AD,
Compliance
(936) 261-9108
bnjohnson@pvamu.edu

PRINCETON UNIVERSITY ATHLETICS
PRINCETON UNIVERSITY
JADWIN GYM
PRINCETON, NJ 08544
609-258-3534
goprincetontigers.com
• John Mack, Ford Family Director of
Athletics
(609) 258-3535
athdirector@princeton.edu
• Anthony Archbald, Executive Associate
Director of Athletics
(609) 258-4948
archbald@princeton.edu
• Chris Brock, Executive Associate AD,
Finance & Admin.
(609) 258-5073
cbrock@princeton.edu

PROVIDENCE COLLEGE ATHLETICS
ONE CUNNINGHAM SQUARE
PROVIDENCE COLLEGE
PROVIDENCE, RI 02918
www.friars.com
• Robert G. Driscoll, Jr., Athletic
Director/Vice President
(401) 865-2265
rdriscol@providence.edu
• Jill LaPoint, Deputy Athletic
Director/SWA/Associate VP
(401) 865-2588
jlapoint@providence.edu
• Steve Napolillo, Senior Executive
Associate AD, External Relations
(401) 865-2677
snapolil@providence.edu

PURDUE UNIVERSITY ATHLETICS
MACKEY ARENA, ROOM 2315
900 JOHN R WOODEN DRIVE
WEST LAFAYETTE, IN 47907
765-494-3189
Fax: 765-494-1178
www.purduesports.com
• Mike Bobinski, Director of Intercollegiate
Athletics
(765) 494-3189
mbobinski@purdue.edu

QUINNIPIAC UNIVERSITY ATHLETICS
275 MOUNT CARMEL AVENUE
HAMDEN, CT 06518
203-582-8200
quinnipiacbobcats.com
• Greg Amodio, Director of Athletics
(203) 582-8621
greg.amodio@qu.edu
• Sarah Fraser, Deputy Director of Athletics
(203) 582-8090
sarah.fraser@qu.edu
• Bill Mecca, Senior Associate AD
(203) 582-8624
mecca@quinnipiac.edu
• Shanna Kornachuk, Senior Associate AD,
Compliance & Student Dev.
(203) 582-7332
shanna.kornachuk@qu.edu

RADFORD UNIVERSITY ATHLETICS
PO BOX 6913
RADFORD, VA 24142
540-831-5228
Fax: 540-831-6095
www.radfordathletics.com
• Robert Lineburg, Director of Athletics
(540) 831-6194
• Cory Durand, Deputy AD
(540) 831-6423
cdurand@radford.edu

RHODE ISLAND ATHLETICS, UNIVERSITY OF
THREE KEANEY ROAD
SUITE ONE
KINGSTON, RI 02881
Fax: 401-874-4935
www.gorhody.com
• Thorr Bjorn, Director of Athletics
(401) 874-5245
tbjorn@uri.edu

RICE UNIVERSITY ATHLETICS
MS 548
6100 MAIN STREET
HOUSTON, TX 77005
713-348-6957
www.riceowls.com
• Joe Karlgaard, Director of Athletics, Rec. &
Lifetime Fitness
(713) 348-4077
• Rick Mello, Deputy Athletics Director
(713) 348-8872
• Tanner Gardner, Senior Associate
AD/COO
(713) s48-8258
• Stacy Mosely, Senior Associate AD/SWA
(713) 348-5829
• Mike Melendez, Senior Associate
AD/Chief Development Officer
(713) 348-6970

RICHMOND ATHLETICS, UNIVERSITY OF
ROBINS CENTER
365 COLLEGE ROAD
RICHMOND, VA 23173
804-289-8363
Fax: 804-287-1919
richmondspiders.com
• Jasmonn Coleman, Associate Athletic
Director for Development
(804) 287-1283
jasmonn.coleman@richmond.edu
• Chris Schaefer, Assistant Athletic Director
for Annual Giving
(804) 287-6341
cschaefe@richmond.edu

RIDER UNIVERSITY ATHLETICS
2083 LAWRENCEVILLE ROAD
LAWRENCEVILLE, NJ 08648-3001
www.gobroncs.com
• Don Harnum, Athletic Director
(609) 896-5054
• Karin Torchia, Sr. Associate AD, External
Operations/SWA
(609) 896-5249
ktorchia@rider.edu
• Greg Busch, Senior Associate AD,
Compliance & Internal Ops.
(609) 895-5642
gbusch@rider.edu

ROBERT MORRIS UNIVERSITY ATHLETICS
DEPT. OF ATHLETICS
6001 UNIVERSITY BLVD
MOON TOWNSHIP, PA 15108-1189
412-397-4949
Fax: 412-397-4943
rmucolonials.com
• Chris King, Director of Athletics
(412) 397-4965
kingc@rmu.edu
• Marty Galosi, Senior Associate AD/Chief
of Staff
(412) 397-4920
galosi@rmu.edu
• Vacant, Deputy AD/SWA/Chief Marketing
Officer
• Kim Graham, Deputy AD/COO
(412) 397-4928
grahamk@rmu.edu

ROLLINS COLLEGE ATHLETICS
1000 HOLT AVENUE
WINTER PARK, FL 32789
407-646-2366
www.rollinssports.com
• Pennie Parker, Director of Athletics
(407) 646-2636
pparker@rollins.edu
• Margie Sullivan, Assistant AD,
Compliance/SWA
(407) 646-2531
msullivan@rollins.edu
• Paul Giannotti, Assistant AD, Sports
Medicine
(407) 646-2361
pgiannotti@rollins.edu

RUTGERS UNIVERSITY ATHLETICS
RUTGERS ATHLETIC CENTER
83 ROCKAFELLER ROAD
PISCATAWAY, NJ 08854
scarletknights.com
• Pat Hobbs, Director of Intercollegiate
Athletics

(732) 445-8610
ad@scarletknights.com

SACRED HEART UNIVERSITY ATHLETICS
DEPT. OF ATHLETICS
5151 PARK AVENUE
FAIRFIELD, CT 06825
203-371-7917
Fax: 203-365-7696
www.sacredheartpioneers.com
• Judy Ann Ricio, Director of Athletics
• Charlie Dowd, Deputy AD, External Operations
(203) 396-8181
dowdc@sacredheart.edu

SAINT FRANCIS UNIVERSITY ATHLETICS
DEPT. OF ATHLETICS
140 LAKEVIEW DRIVE
LORETTO, PA 15940
Fax: 814-472-3209
sfuathletics.com
• James Downer, Director of Athletics
(814) 472-3280
jdowner@francis.edu
• Lisa Swope, Sr. Associate AD, Admin./SWA
(814) 472-3294
lswope@francis.edu
• Jim Brazill, Senior Associate AD
(814) 472-2774
jbrazill@francis.edu

SAINT LOUIS UNIVERSITY ATHLETICS
DEPT. OF ATHLETICS
CHAIFETZ ARENA
3330 LACLEDE AVENUE
ST. LOUIS, MO 63103
314-977-3177
Fax: 314-977-3178
www.slubillikens.com
• Chris May, Director of Athletics
(314) 977-3167
sluadmay@slu.edu
• Janet Oberle, Senior Assocociate AD/SWA
(314) 977-3265
janet.oberle@slu.edu

SAINT PETER'S UNIVERSITY ATHLETICS
2641 JOHN F. KENNEDY BOULEVARD
JERSEY CITY, NJ 07306
Fax: 201-761-7301
saintpeterspeacocks.com
• Rachelle Paul, Director of Athletics
(201) 761-7302
• Debbie Gregory, Senior Associate AD, Business Affairs
(201) 761-7304
dgregory@saintpeters.edu

SAM HOUSTON STATE UNIVERSITY ATHLETICS
SAM HOUSTON ATHLETICS
PO BOX 2268
HUNTSVILLE, TX 77341
www.gobearkats.com
• Bobby Williams, Athletic Director
(936) 294-3286
bwilliams@shsu.edu
• Chris Thompson, Senior Associate AD, Student Services
(936) 294-3542
cthompson@shsu.edu

• Greg Hinze, Senior Associate AD, Operations
(936) 294-1725
ghinze@shsu.edu

SAMFORD UNIVERSITY ATHLETICS
800 LAKESHORE DRIVE
BIRMINGHAM, AL 35229
205-726-2966
samfordsports.com
• Martin Newton, Director of Athletics
(205) 726-2966
cnewton@samford.edu
• Michelle Durban, Deputy AD, Student-Athlete Well-Being/SWA
(205) 726-4562
mldurban@samford.edu
• Bo Kerr, Deputy AD, Development & Corp. Affairs
(205) 726-2139
jkerr@samford.edu

SAN DIEGO ATHLETICS, UNIVERSITY OF
5998 ALCALA PARK
SAN DIEGO, CA 92110
619-260-4803
www.usdtoreros.com
• Bill McGillis, Exec. Director of Athletics
(619) 260-2982
athleticdirector@sandiego.edu
• Marcy Lanoue, Senior Associate AD/SWA
(619) 260-4755
mlanoue@sandiego.edu
• Dan Yourg, Senior Associate AD, Administration
(619) 260-2845
yourg@sandiego.edu

SAN DIEGO STATE UNIVERSITY ATHLETICS
DEPT. OF ATHLETICS
5500 CAMPANILE DRIVE
SAN DIEGO, CA 92182-4313
619-594-3019
www.goaztecs.com
• John David Wicker, Director of Intercollegiate Athletics
(619) 594-6357
adsdsu@sdsu.edu
• Jenny Bramer, Executive Associate AD/SWA
(619) 594-0394
jbramer@sdsu.edu
• Derek Grice, Executive Associate AD, Mission Valley Development
dgrice@sdsu.edu

SAN FRANCISCO ATHLETICS, UNIVERSITY OF
2130 FULTON STREET
SAN FRANCISCO, CA 94117
415-422-2873
www.usfdons.com
• Joan McDermott, Director of Athletics
jmcdermott2@usfca.edu
• Frank Allocco, Executive Sr. Associate AD, External Relations
(415) 422-6561
fallocco@usfca.edu
• Linda Lappe, Senior Associate AD/SWA
llappe@usfca.edu

SAN JOSE STATE UNIVERSITY ATHLETICS
ONE WASHINGTON SQUARE
SAN JOSE, CA 95192-0062

408-924-1200
www.sjsuspartans.com
• Jeff Konya, Athletics Director
(408) 924-1596
jeff.konya@sjsu.edu
• Bob Clark, Senior Deputy AD
(408) 924-1175
gloria.jimenez@sjsu.edu

SANTA CLARA UNIVERSITY ATHLETICS
500 EL CAMINO REAL
SANTA CLARA, CA 95053
408-554-4063
Fax: 408-554-6969
www.santaclarabroncos.com
• Renee Baumgartner, Director of Athletics
(408) 554-5344
rbaumgartner@scu.edu
• Staci Gustafson, Deputy AD
(408) 554-6982
sgustafson@scu.edu
• Bob De Carolis, Deputy AD
(408) 551-1782
rdecarolis@scu.edu
• Vacant, Senior Associate AD, Development

SETON HALL UNIVERSITY ATHLETICS
400 SOUTH ORANGE AVENUE
RICHIE REGAN REC. & ATHLS. CENTER
SOUTH ORANGE, NJ 07079
shupirates.com
• Bryan Felt, Director of Athletics
(973) 761-9498
jaclyn.panepinto@shu.edu
• Tatum Colitz, Senior Associate AD, Compliance/SWA
(973) 761-9494
tatum.colitz@shu.edu
• Jay Judge, Sr. Assoc. AD, Development & External Operations
(973) 275-2202
jay.judge@shu.edu
• Kathy Matta, Senior Associate AD, Recreational Services
(973) 761-9723
kathleen.matta@shu.edu
• Jimmy O'Donnell, Senior Associate AD, Team Operations
(973) 761-9725
jimmy.odonnell@shu.edu
• Jim Semerad, Senior Associate AD, Internal Operations
(973) 761-9724
james.semerad@shu.edu
• Kevin Sponzo, Senior Associate AD, Facilities & Operations
(973) 761-2949
kevin.sponzo@shu.edu

SIENA COLLEGE ATHLETICS
515 LOUDON ROAD
LOUDONVILLE, NY 12211-1462
518-783-2551
Fax: 518-783-2449
www.sienasaints.com
• John D'Argenio, Director of Athletics/Vice President
(518) 783-2450
dargenio@siena.edu
• Andrew Santandera, Associate AD, Operations
(518) 782-6454
asantandera@siena.edu

SOUTH ALABAMA ATHLETICS, UNIVERSITY OF
ATHLETICS ADMINISTRATION BUILDING
300 JOSEPH E. GOTTFRIED DR.
MOBILE, AL 36688
Fax: 251-460-6505
www.usajaguars.com
• Joel Erdmann, Ph.D., Director of Athletics
(251) 460-7121
jerdmann@southalabama.edu
• Daniel McCarthy, Ed.D., Deputy AD
(251) 460-6057
dmccarthy@southalabama.edu
• Jinni Frisbey, Senior Associate AD/SWA
(251) 445-9551
jfrisbey@southalabama.edu
• Greg Keel, Assistant AD, External Relations
(251) 461-1431
gkeel@southalabama.edu

SOUTH CAROLINA ATHLETICS, UNIVERSITY OF
RICE ATHLETICS CENTER
1304 HEYWARD STREET
COLUMBIA, SC 29208
803-777-4202
Fax: 803-777-8226
www.gamecocksonline.com
• Ray Tanner, Athletics Director
addirect@mailbox.sc.edu
• Chance Miller, Senior Deputy AD
ccmiller@mailbox.sc.edu
• Judy Van Horn, Deputy AD, Internal Ops. & Risk Mangement
vanhorn@mailbox.sc.edu

SOUTH CAROLINA STATE UNIVERSITY ATHLETICS
300 COLLEGE STREET NE
ORANGEBURG, SC 29117
803-533-3743
Fax: 803-533-3634
www.scsuathletics.com
• Stacy Danley, Director of Athletics
(803) 533-3743
sdanley@scsu.edu
• Melissa Dwason, Executive Associate AD/SWA
(803) 533-3904
mdawson4@scsu.edu
• Kemberly Greene, Assistant AD, Community Relations & Dev.
(803) 516-4562
kgreen29@scsu.edu

SOUTH DAKOTA SCHOOL OF MINES & TECHNOLOGY ATHLETICS
501 EAST SAINT JOSEPH STREET
RAPID CITY, SD 57701
605-394-2511
800-544-8162
gorockers.com
• Joel Lueken, Athletic Director
(605) 394-2352
joel.lueken@sdsmt.edu
• Cassie Kosiba, Associate AD, Internal Ops./SWA
(605) 394-2643
cassie.kosiba@sdsmt.edu

SOUTH FLORIDA ATHLETICS, UNIVERSITY OF
USF ATHLETICS DEPT.
4202 E FOWLER AVENUE, ATH 100
TAMPA, FL 33620
813-974-2125
gousfbulls.com
• Michael Kelly, Vice President of Athletics
(813) 974-1442
michaelskelly@usf.edu
• Barry Clements, Deputy AD/Capital Projects
(813) 974-1442
clements@usf.edu
• Lelo Prado, Deputy AD, Development
(813) 974-5045
leloprado@usf.edu

SOUTHEAST MISSOURI STATE UNIVERSITY ATHLETICS
ONE UNIVERSITY PLAZA
MS0200
CAPE GIRARDEAU, MO 63701
semoredhawks.com
• Brady Barke, Director of Athletics
(573) 651-2227
bbarke@semo.edu
• Kim Schuette, Associate AD, Admin./SWA
(573) 651-2997
kschuette@semo.edu
• Nate Saverino, Associate AD, External Affairs
(573) 651-2962
nsaverino@semo.edu
• Betsy Wilcox, Director, Academics & Student-Athlete Dev.
(573) 986-6182
bwilcox@semo.edu

SOUTHEASTERN LOUISIANA UNIVERSITY ATHLETICS
500 W UNIVERSITY AVE
HAMMOND, LA 70402
985-549-2253
Fax: 985-549-3495
www.lionsports.net
• Jay Artigues, Director of Athletics
(985) 549-2395
jartigues@southeastern.edu
• Andrew Bechac, Deputy Director of Athletics
(985) 549-3419
andrew.bechac@southeastern.edu
• Lindsey C. Owens, Associate Athletic Dir. for External Ops./SWA
(985) 549-5226
lindsey.cramer@southeastern.edu

SOUTHERN CALIFORNIA ATHLETICS, UNIVERSITY OF
3501 WATT WAY
LOS ANGELES, CA 900089-0602
213-740-3843
usctrojans.com
• Mike Bohn, Director of Athletics
(213) 740-4154
uscad@usc.edu
• Joyce Bell Limbrick, Executive Senior Associate Athletic Director/SWA
(213) 740-3566
joyce.bell@usc.edu
• Nick Bowes, Exec. Sr. Associate Athletic Dir/COO
nbowes@usc.edu

SOUTHERN ILLINOIS UNIVERSITY ATHLETICS
SIU ATHLETICS
MAILCODE 6620, LINGLE HALL 118
1490 DOUGLAS DRIVE
CARBONDALE, IL 62901
618-453-5311
siusalukis.com
• Matt Kupec, Interim Athletic Director
(618) 453-5279
SIUAD@siu.edu
• Jeff Jones, Executive Senior Associate AD, Internal Ops.
(618) 453-5481
jeffrey.jones@siu.edu

SOUTHERN METHODIST UNIVERSITY ATHLETICS
PO BOX 750315
5800 OWNBY DRIVE
DALLAS, TX 75275
214-768-4301
smumustangs.com
• Rick Hart, Director of Athletics
(214) 768-4301
rlhart@smu.edu
• Kurt Pottkotter, Deputy Director of Athletics
(214) 768-3639
kpottkotter@smu.edu
• Lauren Adee, Senior Associate AD, Executive Affairs
(214) 768-1650
ladee@smu.edu
• Kyle Conder, Senior Associate AD, Compliance
(214) 768-4051
kconder@smu.edu
• Brad Sutton, Senior Associate AD, External Affairs
(214) 768-1651
bsutton@smu.edu
• Matt Peters, Senior Associate AD, Development
(214) 768-7009
mjpeters@smu.edu

SOUTHERN MISS ATHLETICS
118 COLLEGE DRIVE
#5017
HATTIESBURG, MS 39406-0001
601-266-5017
Fax: 601-266-6595
www.southernmiss.com
• Jeremy McClain, Director of Athletics
(601) 266-5017
athleticdirector@usm.edu
• Jeff Mitchell, Deputy AD
(601) 266-5017
jeff.mitchell@usm.edu
• E.K. Franks, Executive Senior Associate AD
(601) 266-5252
ek.franks@usm.edu

SOUTHERN NEW HAMPSHIRE UNIVERSITY
2500 N RIVER ROAD
MANCHESTER, NH 03106
603-645-9604
Fax: 603-645-9686
athletics@snhu.edu
www.snhupenmen.com
• Anthony Fallacaro, Director of Athletics & Recreation
(603) 645-9604
a.fallacaro@snhu.edu
• Tom Wilkins, Associate AD
(603) 645-9786
t.wilkins@snhu.edu
• Tricia Cote, Associate AD, Business Manager/SWA
(603) 645-9699
p.cote1@snhu.edu

• James Gassman, Associate AD, Operations
(603) 645-9788
j.gassman@snhu.edu
Year Founded:
1992
Description:
Offers B.S. Sport Managment, B.S. Business Studies with concentration in Sport Managment, M.B.A. with certificate in Sport Administration, M.S. Sport Managment.

SOUTHERN UNIVERSITY ATHLETICS
SU ATHLETICS DEPT.
A.W. MUMFORD FIELDHOUSE
P.O. BOX 9942
BATON ROUGE, LA 70813
225-771-3171
www.gojagsports.com
• Roman Banks, Director Of Athletics
(225) 771-5609
Roman_banks@subr.edu
• Rodney Kirschner, Sr. Associate AD/Dir. of Media Relations
(225) 771-5609
rodney_kirschner@subr.edu

SOUTHERN UTAH UNIVERSITY ATHLETICS
351 W UNIVERSITY BOULEVARD
CEDAR CITY, UT 84720
435-865-8355
Fax: 435-865-8078
www.suutbirds.com
• Debbie Corum, Athletic Director
ad@suu.edu
• Todd Brown, Deputy Director of Athletics, Success & Wellness
brownt@suu.edu
• Sonia Hahn, Deputy AD, Competitive Excellence/SWA
soniahahn@suu.edu
• Shon Spevak, Executive Senior Associate AD, Revenue Generation
(435) 586-7872
spevak@suu.edu

ST. BONAVENTURE UNIVERSITY ATHLETICS
DEPT. OF ATHLETICS
3261 W STATE ROAD
ST. BONAVENTURE, NY 14778
716-375-2282
Fax: 716-375-2280
gobonnies.sbu.edu
• Joe Manhertz, Director of Athletics
(716) 375-2282
• Barb Questa, Deputy Director of Athletics/SWA
(716) 375-2290
bquesta@sbu.edu

ST. JOHN'S UNIVERSITY ATHLETICS
DEPT. OF ATHLETICS
8000 UTOPIA PARKWAY
QUEENS, NY 11439
718-990-6138
www.redstormsports.com
• Mike Cragg, Director of Athletics
(718) 990-6138
craggm@stjohns.edu
• Kathleen Meehan, Senior Deputy AD/SWA
(718) 990-6173
meehank@stjohns.edu
• John Diffley, Deputy AD/COO
(718) 990-6836
diffleyj@stjohns.edu

ST. JOSEPH'S UNIVERSITY ATHLETICS
ATHLETIC DEPT.
5600 CITY AVENUE
PHILADELPHIA, PA 19131
610-660-1707
www.sjuhawks.com
• Jill Bodensteiner, Athletic Director
(610) 660-1707
athleticdirector@sju.edu
• Renie Shields, Senior Associate AD, Student Experience/SWA
(610) 660-2584
shields@sju.edu
• Rob Sullivan, Senior Associate AD, Basketball Admin.
(610) 660-1768
robert.sullivan@sju.edu
• Eric Laudano, Senior Associate AD, High Performance
(610) 660-1753
elaudano@sju.edu

ST. MARY'S COLLEGE ATHLETICS
DEPT. OF ATHLETICS
PMB 5100
MORAGA, CA 94575
www.smcgaels.com
• Mike Matoso, Vice President for Intercollegiate Athletics
(925) 631-4399
snittler@stmarys-ca.edu
• Kami Gray, Deputy AD, Internal Operations/SWA
(925) 631-4521
kgray@stmarys-ca.edu
• Ryan Reggiani, Deputy AD, External Operations
(925) 631-4402
rmr9@stmarys-ca.edu

STANFORD UNIVERSITY ATHLETICS
ARRILLAGA FAMILY SPORTS CENTER
641 EAST CAMPUS DRIVE
STANFORD, CA 94305-6201
650-723-4591
Fax: 650-725-8642
gostanford.com
• Bernard Muir, Director of Athletics
(650) 723-4596
athleticdirector@stanford.edu
• Ray Purpur, Deputy AD
(650) 723-1820
ray.purpur@stanford.edu

STEPHEN F. AUSTIN STATE UNIVERSITY ATHLETICS
SFA ATHLETICS
PO BOX 13010
SFA STATION
NACOGDOCHES, TX 75962
936-468-3501
sfajacks.com
• Ryan Ivey, Director of Athletics
(936) 468-4540
iveyrm@sfasu.edu
• Rob Meyers, Associate AD, Business
(936) 468-4080
rmeyers@sfasu.edu
• Brandi Bryant, Associate AD, Student-Athlete Services
(936) 468-5800
brandi.bryant@sfasu.edu
• Loree McCary, Associate AD, Administration/SWA
(936) 468-3751
lmccary@sfasu.edu

STETSON UNIVERSITY ATHLETICS
421 N WOODLAND BOULEVARD
UNIT 8359
DELAND, FL 32723
Fax: 386-822-7486
www.gohatters.com
• Jeff Altier, Director of Athletics
(386) 822-7157
ad@stetson.edu
• Alicia Queally, Deputy AD/SWA
(386) 738-6676
aqueally@stetson.edu

SUNY BUFFALO
102 ALUMNI ARENA
BUFFALO, NY 14260
716-645-3142
Fax: 716-645-3756
www.ubbulls.com
• Mark Alnutt, Athletic Director
(716) 645-3142
athleticdirector@buffalo.edu
• Eric Gross, Deputy AD, External Operations
(716) 645-6761
etgross@buffalo.edu
• Nate Wills, Deputy AD/COO
(716) 645-5548
ntwills@buffalo.edu
• D'Ann Keller, Senior Associate AD, Administration/SWA
(716) 645-6866
dannkell@buffalo.edu

SYRACUSE UNIVERSITY ATHLETICS
MANLEY FIELD HOUSE
1301 E COLVIN STREET
SYRACUSE, NY 13244
315-443-2385
cuse.com
• John Wildhack, Director of Athletics
(315) 443-8705
jwildhac@syr.edu
• Herman Frazier, Senior Deputy AD
(315) 443-8705
hrfrazie@syr.edu

TEMPLE UNIVERSITY ATHLETICS
TEMPLE ATHLETICS
STAR COMPLEX
1816 N 15TH STREET, 3RD FLOOR
PHILADELPHIA, PA 19121
215-204-7759
athletics@temple.edu
owlsports.com
• Arthur Johnson, Vice President/Director of Athletics
(215) 204-7759
athletics@temple.edu
• Craig Angelos, Deputy Director of Athletics
(215) 204-8555
cangelos@temple.edu
• Jessica Reo, Executive Senior Associate AD/SWA
(215) 204-7871
jessica.reo@temple.edu

TENNESSEE CHATTANOOGA ATHLETICS, UNIVERSITY OF
615 MCCALLIE AVENUE
DEPT. 3503
CHATTANOOGA, TN 37403
gomocs.com
• Mark Wharton, Director of Athletics
• Laura Herron, Executive Associate AD/SWA

(423) 425-4583
laura-herron@utc.edu

TENNESSEE KNOXVILLE ATHLETICS, UNIVERSITY OF
PO BOX 15016
KNOXVILLE, TN 37901-5016
865-974-1224
utsports.com
• Daniel J. White, Director of Athletics
athleticdirector@utk.edu
• Ryan Alpert, Deputy AD/COO
(865) 974-6570
ralpert@utk.edu

TENNESSEE MARTIN ATHLETICS, UNIVERSITY OF
554 UNIVERST ST.
MARTIN, TN 38238
731-881-7661
www.utmsports.com
• Kurt McGuffin, Athletic Director
(731) 881-7661
kmcguffi@utm.edu
• Danelle Fabianich, Senior Associate AD, Aministration/SWA
(731) 881-3688
danellef@utm.edu

TENNESSEE STATE UNIVERSITY ATHLETICS
CAMPUS BOX 9633
3500 JOHN A. MERRITT BOULEVARD
NASHVILLE, TN 37209
615-963-5000
Fax: 615-963-7589
www.tsutigers.com
• Mikki Allen, Director of Athletics
• Dusty Bennett, Executive AD, Admin. & Capital Projects
dbenne15@tnstate.edu
• Jennifer Bell, Associate AD, Compliance
(615) 963-5887
jbell@tnstate.edu

TENNESSEE TECH UNIVERSITY ATHLETICS
1100 MCGEE BOULEVARD
TTU BOX 5057
COOKEVILLE, TN 38505
931-372-3940
800-825-3948
www.ttusports.com
• Mark Wilson, Director of Athletics
(931) 372-6306
mwilson@tntech.edu
• Frank Harrell, Special Assistant to the Director of Athletics
(931) 372-3939
fharrell@tntech.edu
• Mandy Thatcher, Assistant AD, Compliance/SWA
(931) 372-3949
amiller@tntech.edu

TEXAS A&M UNIVERSITY ATHLETICS
TEXAS A&M ATHLETICS
1228 TAMU
COLLEGE STATION, TX 77843-1228
979-845-5129
12thman.com
• Ross Bjork, Director of Athletics
• Michael Thompson, Jr., Deputy AD, External Relations & Business Dev.
mtjr@athletics.tamu.edu

TEXAS AT ARLINGTON ATHLETICS, UNIVERSITY OF
1309 W MITCHELL STREET
ARLINGTON, TX 76019-0079
817-272-2261
Fax: 817-272-5037
www.utamavs.com
• Jim Baker, Director of Athletics
(817) 272-7170
jimbaker@uta.edu
• Russell Warren, Deputy Director of Athletics
(817) 272-5706
rwarren@uta.edu
• Debbie Garcia, Executive Senior Associate AD/SWA
(817) 272-2047
ranee@uta.edu

TEXAS AT AUSTIN ATHLETICS, UNIVERSITY OF
403 DELOSS DODDS WAY
AUSTIN, TX 78712
512-471-5757
texassports.com
• Chris Del Conte, Athletic Director
• Shawn Eichorst, Deputy AD/COO
(512) 232-2144
• Chris Plonsky, Executive Senior Associate AD
(512) 471-4787
• Drew Martin, Executive Senior Associate AD, External Affairs
(512) 471-8689

TEXAS AT EL PASO ATHLETICS, UNIVERSITY OF
500 W UNIVERSITY AVE
BRUMBELOW BUILDING
EL PASO, TX 79968-0579
915-747-5347
utepathletics.com
• Jim Senter, Director of Athletics
(915) 747-6822
jsenter@utep.edu
• Jeff Darby, Senior Associate AD, External Relations
(915) 747-6652
jdarby@utep.edu
• Julie Levesque, Senior Associate AD/SWA
(915) 747-6806
jmlevesque@utep.edu

TEXAS AT SAN ANTONIO ATHLETICS, UNIVERSITY OF
UTSA DEPT. OF INTERCOLLEGIATE ATHLETICS
ONE UTSA CIRCLE
SAN ANTONIO, TX 78249-0691
210-458-8820
Fax: 210-458-4813
www.goutsa.com
• Lisa Campos, Athletics Director
(210) 458-4444
roadrunnerad@utsa.edu
• Darren D'Attilio, Assistant VP, Revenue Gen. & External Operations
(210) 458-4078
darren.dattilio@utsa.edu
• Mike Bazemore, Depity AD, Finance & Strategic Initiatives
(210) 458-4666

TEXAS CHRISTIAN UNIVERSITY ATHLETICS
TCU ATHLETICS DEPT.
TCU BOX 297600
FORT WORTH, TX 76129
817-257-5658
Fax: 817-257-7656
www.gofrogs.com
• Jeremiah Donati, JD, Director of Intercollegiate Athletics
athleticsdirector@tcu.edu
• Mike Sinquefield, Deputy AD, Internal Affairs
m.sinquefield@tcu.edu

TEXAS RIO GRANDE VALLEY ATHLETICS, UNIVERSITY OF
UTRGV DEPT. OF INTERCOLLEGIATE ATHLETICS
1201 W UNIVERSITY DRIVE
EDINBURG, TX 78539
956-665-2221
Fax: 956-665-2261
goutrgv.com
• Chasse Conque, Director of Athletics
(956) 665-2221
chasse.conque@utrgv.edu
• Vince Volpe, Deputy Director of Athletics/Chief Revenue Officer
(956) 665-3897
vince.volpe@utrgv.edu
• Molly Castner, Deputy Director of Athletics/SWA
(956) 665-2205
molly.castner@utrgv.edu

TEXAS SOUTHERN UNIVERSITY ATHLETICS
3100 CLEBURNE STREET
HOUSTON, TX 77004
713-313-6830
www.tsusports.com
• Kevin Granger, Vice President of Intercollegiate Athletics
(713) 313-4378
kevin.granger@tsu.edu
• Michael Moleta, Senior Associate AD
(713) 313-7629
michael.moleta@tsu.edu

TEXAS STATE UNIVERSITY ATHLETICS
TSU DEPT. OF ATHLETICS
DARREN B. CASEY ATHLETIC ADMIN. COMPLEX
601 UNIVERSITY DRIVE
SAN MARCOS, TX 78666
Fax: 512-245-8387
athletics@txstate.edu
txstatebobcats.com
• Don Coryell, Director of Athletics
(512) 245-2114
dc32@txstate.edu
• Tracy Shoemake, Executive Senior Assoc. AD, Internal Ops./SWA
(512) 245-2114
ts23@txstate.edu
• Travis Comer, Executive Senior Associate AD, Dev. & Admin.
(512) 245-2247
tc26@txstate.edu

TEXAS TECH UNIVERSITY ATHLETICS
2508 6TH ST.
LUBBOCK, TX 79409
806-742-3355
texastech.com

- Kirby Hocutt, Director of Athletics
- Tony Hernandez, Deputy Director of Athletics
(806) 834-6167
tony.hernandez@ttu.edu
- Brandi Stuart, Executive Senior Associate AD/SWA

TOLEDO ATHLETICS, UNIVERSITY OF
UNIVERSITY OF TOLEDO - ATHLETIC
DEPARTMENT - MS302
SAVAGE ARENA
2801 W BANCROFT STREET
TOLEDO, OH 43606
Fax: 419-530-4428
utrockets.com
- Mike O'Brien, Director of Athletics
(419) 530-4987
michael.obrien6@utoledo.edu
- Dave Nottke, Deputy Director of Athletics
(419) 530-2510
david.nottke@utoledo.edu
- Kelly Andrews, Senior Associate AD/SWA
(419) 530-2810
kelly.andrews@utoledo.edu

TOWSON STATE UNIVERSITY ATHLETICS
DEPT. OF ATHLETICS
8000 YORK RD
TOWSON, MD 21252
410-704-2000
1-855-888-4437
towsontigers.com
- Dan Crowley, Director of Athletics (Interim)

(410) 704-4185
dcrowley@towson.edu
- Tricia Turley Brandenburg, Deputy Director of Athletics/SWA
(410) 704-4177
tbrandenburg@towson.edu

TROY UNIVERSITY ATHLETICS
TINE DAVIS FIELDHOUSE
5000 VETERANS STADIUM DRIVE
TROY, AL 36082
334-670-3482
Fax: 334-670-3278
www.troytrojans.com
- Brent Jones, Director of Athletics
(334) 670-3682
brentjones@troy.edu
- Sandy Atkins, Deputy AD, Administration/SWA
(334) 670-5745
satkins@troy.edu
- Kyle George, Executive Associate AD, External Ops.
(334) 670-5650
kylegeorge@troy.edu

TULANE UNIVERSITY ATHLETICS
JAMES W. WILSON JR.
INTERCOLLEGIATE ATHLETICS CENTER
333 BEN WEINER DRIVE
NEW ORLEANS, LA 70118
504-865-5017
Fax: 504-862-8569
tulanegreenwave.com
- Troy Dannen, Director of Athletics
(504) 865-5569
tdannen@tulane.edu
- Charvi Greer, Deputy AD/COO
(504) 862-8448
jgreer1@tulane.edu
- Chris Maitre, Deputy AD, Internal

Operations
(504) 314-2261
cmaitre@tulane.edu

TULSA ATHLETICS, UNIVERSITY OF
800 S TUCKER DRIVE
TULSA, OK 74104
918-631-3112
tulsahurricane.com
- Rick Dickson, Director of Athletics
(918) 631-3112
- Brian Scislo, Senior Associate AD, Administration
(918) 631-2703
brain-scislo@utulsa.edu

U.S. AIR FORCE ACADEMY ATHLETICS
ATHLETIC DEPT.
2168 FIELD HOUSE DRIVE
Colorado Springs, CO 80840-9500
719-333-4008
www.goairforcefalcons.com
- Nathan Pine, Director of Athletics
(719) 333-4008
ad@usafa.edu
- Jen Block, Executive AD
(719) 333-4008
ad@usafa.edu
- Nancy Hixon, Deputy AD, External Affairs
(719) 333-3501

U.S. MILITARY ACADEMY ATHLETICS
ARMY WEST POINT ATHLETICS
639 HOWARD ROAD
WEST POINT, NY 10996
Fax: 845-938-8707
goarmywestpoint.com
- Mike Buddie, Director of Athletics
(845) 938-3701
- Dan McCarthy, Ph.D., Deputy AD
(845) 938-9699
dan.mccarthy@westpoint.edu

U.S. NAVAL ACADEMY ATHLETICS
RICKETTS HALL
566 BROWNSON ROAD
ANNAPOLIS, MD 21402
Fax: 410-293-8954
www.navysports.com
- Chet Gladchuk, Director of Athletics
(410) 293-8910
gladchuk@usna.edu
- Eric Ruden, Deputy Director of Athletics
(410) 293-8748
ruden@usna.edu
- Robb Dunn, Deputy Director of Athletics, Administration
(410) 293-8776
rdunn@usna.edu

UC BERKELEY ATHLETICS
HAAS PAVILION #4422
BERKELEY, CA 94720-4422
510-642-0580
Fax: 510-642-3399
calbears.com
- Jim Knowlton, Director of Athletics
- Jennifer Simon-O'Neill, Executive Senior Associate AD/SWA
jenny.simon@berkeley.edu
- Ryan Cobb, Senior Assoc. AD, Performance, Health & Welfare
ryancobb@berkeley.edu
- Jay Larson, Senior Associate AD, Administration
jlarson@berkeley.edu

- Josh Hummel, Sr. Associate AD, Facilities & Events
johummel@berkeley.edu
- Tom Lowry, Senior Associate AD/CFO
thomaslowry@berkeley.edu

UC IRVINE ATHLETICS
INTERCOLLEGIATE ATHLETICS BUILDING
IRVINE, CA 92697-4500
949-824-6931
athleticsdirector@uci.edu
ucirvinesports.com
- Paula Smith, Director of Intercollegiate Athletics
(949) 824-6932
paula.smith@uci.edu
- Phil Wang, Senior Associate AD, External Affairs
(949) 824-7591
philw@uci.edu
- Paul Hope, Senior Associate AD, Facilites & Ops.
(949) 824-5941
phope@uci.edu
- John Hauscarriague, Senior Associate AD, Finance & Admin.
(949) 824-6979
jhauscar@uci.edu

UC LOS ANGELES ATHLETICS
J.D. MORGAN CENTER
325 WESTWOOD PLAZA
LOS ANGELES, CA 90095
310-825-8699
Fax: 310-206-7047
uclabruins.com
- Martin Jarmond, Director of Athletics
ad@athletics.ucla.edu
- Matt Elliott, Senior Associate AD, Internal Operations
melliott@athletics.ucla.edu
- Christopher Iacoi, Senior Associate AD, CFO
ciacoi@athletics.ucla.edu
- Josh Rebholz, Senior Associate AD, External Relations
jrebholz@athletics.ucla.edu
- Christina Rivera, Senior Associate AD/SWA
crivera@athletics.ucla.edu
- Scott Markley, Senior Associate AD, Communications
smarkley@athletics.ucla.edu

UC SANTA BARBARA ATHLETICS
INTERCOLLEGIATE ATHLETICS DEPARTMENT
ICA BUILDING
SANTA BARBARA, CA 93106-5200
805-893-8272
Fax: 802-893-8640
www.ucsbgauchos.com
- Kelly Barsky, Interim Athletics Director/SWA
(805) 893-2247
Kelly.Barsky@athletics.ucsb.edu
- Tom Hastings, Deputy Athletics Director
(805) 893-6019
tom.hastings@athletics.ucsb.edu

UMASS AMHERST ATHLETICS
MULLINS CENTER
200 COMMONWEALTH AVE.
3RD FLOOR
AMHERST, MA 01003

413-545-9652
www.umassathletics.com
• Ryan Bamford, Director of Athletics
(413) 545-9652
rbamford@umass.edu
• Kirsten Britton, Senior Associate AD,
Administration/SWA
(413) 545-1086
britton@umass.edu
• David Biancamano, Senior Associate AD,
Development
(413) 545-4290
dbiancamano@umass.edu
• Jeff Smith, Senior Associate AD, External
Operations
(413) 545-2866
jbsmith@umass.edu

UTAH ATHLETICS, UNIVERSITY OF
ATHLETICS DEPT.
1825 E SOUTH CAMPUS DRIVE
SALT LAKE CITY, UT 84112-0900
801-581-8171
utahutes.com
• Mark Harlan, Athletics Director
athleticsdirector@utah.edu
• Charmelle Green, Deputy AD, Internal
Operations & COO
(801) 646-6514
cgreen@huntsman.utah.edu
• Scott Kull, Deputy AD, External Operations
(801) 201-5724
skull@huntsman.utah.edu

UTAH STATE UNIVERSITY ATHLETICS
7400 OLD MAIN HILL
LOGAN, UT 84322
435-797-1850
www.utahstateaggies.com
• John Hartwell, Athletics Director
(435) 797-2060
john.hartwell@usu.edu
• Jerry Bovee, Deputy AD, External Affairs
(435) 797-1880
jerry.bovee@usu.edu
• Amy Crosbie, Executive Associate AD,
Internal Affairs/SWA
(435) 797-0612
amy.crosbie@usu.edu

VALPARAISO UNIVERSITY ATHLETICS
ATHLETICS-RECREATION CENTER
(ARC)
1009 UNION STREET
VALPARAISO, IN 46383
www.valpoathletics.com
• Mark LaBarbera, Director of Athletics
(219) 464-6894
valpoad@valpo.edu

VANDERBILT UNIVERSITY ATHLETICS
2601 JESS NEELY DRIVE
NASHVILLE, TN 37212
615-322-4653
Fax: 615-343-7064
www.vucommodores.com
• Candice Storey Lee, Athletics Director
• Trace Wilgus, Senior Associate AD,
Internal Affairs
(615) 322-2083
trace.wilgus@vanderbilt.edu
• Martin Salamone, Associate AD, Fan
Engagement & Hospitality
(615) 343-2580
martin.salamone@vanderbilt.edu

VERMONT ATHLETICS, UNIVERSITY OF
PATRICK GYMNASIUM
97 SPEAR STREET
BURLINGTON, VT 05405
802-656-3074
www.uvmathletics.com
• Jeff Schulman, Director of Athletics
(802) 656-7417
jeffrey.schulman@uvm.edu

VILLANOVA UNIVERSITY ATHLETICS
800 EAST LANCASTER AVENUE
JAKE NEVIN FIELD HOUSE
VILLANOVA, PA 19085
610-519-8334
www.villanova.com
• Mark Jackson, Director of Athletics
(610) 519-4110
athleticsdirector@villanova.edu
• Lynn Tighe, Senior Associate AD/SWA
(610) 519-4121
lynn.tighe@villanova.edu
• Ashwin Puri, Senior Associate AD/COO
(610) 519-6721
ashwin.puri@villanova.edu
• Rob Hagan, Senior Associate AD,
Student-Athlete Welfare
(610) 519-6485
robert.hagan@villanova.edu
• Dean Kenefick, Senior Associate AD,
Communications
(610) 519-6514
dean.kenefick@villanova.edu

VIRGINIA ATHLETICS, UNIVERSITY OF
MCCUE CENTER
PO BOX 400846
CHARLOTTESVILLE, VA 22904
434-982-5100
Fax: 434-982-5012
www.virginiasports.com
• Carla Williams, Director of Athletics
cgw4j@virginia.edu
• Jim Booz, Deputy AD, Administration
jwb8q@virginia.edu
• Edward Scott, Deputy AD

VIRGINIA COMMONWEALTH UNIVERSITY ATHLETICS
VCU ATHLETICS
SIEGEL CENTER, 1200 W BROAD ST
PO BOX 843013
RICHMOND, VA 23284-3013
Fax: 804-828-9428
www.vcuathletics.com
• Ed McLaughlin, Director of Athletics
(804) 828-6692
athleticsdir@vcu.edu
• Mak Afework, Deputy Director of Athletics
(804) 827-0805
mafework@vcu.edu

VIRGINIA MILITARY INSTITUTE ATHLETICS
LEXINGTON, VA 24450
540-464-7266
ticketoffice@vmi.edu
www.vmikeydets.com
• Lenny Brown, Deputy Director of
Intercollegiate Athletics
(540) 464-7035
brownhl@vmi.edu
• Wade Branner, Associate AD, Athletic
Communications
(540) 464-7515
brannerwh@vmi.edu
• Lance Fujiwara, Associate AD, Sports

Medicine
(540) 464-7310
fujiwaralm@vmi.edu
• Daniel Whitehead, Associate AD,
Communications
(540) 464-7514
whiteheaddk@vmi.edu

VIRGINIA TECH ATHLETICS
25 BEAMER WAY
BLACKSBURG, VA 24061
540-231-9984
Fax: 540-231-3060
www.hokiesports.com
• Whit Babcock, Director of Athletics
(540) 231-3977
hokiead@vt.edu
• John Ballein, Executive Associate AD
(540) 231-3357
jballein@vt.edu

WAGNER COLLEGE ATHLETICS
ONE CAMPUS ROAD
STATEN ISLAND, NY 10301-4495
718-390-3433
Fax: 718-390-3347
www.wagnerathletics.com
• Walt Hameline, Director of Athletics
(718) 390-3488
whamelin@wagner.edu
• Brendan Fahey, Deputy AD
(718) 390-3210
brendan.fahey@wagner.edu

WAKE FOREST UNIVERSITY ATHLETICS
519 DEACON BOULEVARD
WINSTON-SALEM, NC 27109
336-758-5616
www.wakeforestsports.com
• John Currie, Director of Athletics
(336) 758-3140
wfuad@wfu.edu
• Lindsey Babcock, Deputy AD, Internal
Operations/SWA
(336) 758-1028
lbabcock@wfu.edu

WASHINGTON ATHLETICS, UNIVERSITY OF
DEPT. OF INTERCOLLEGIATE
ATHLETICS
BOX 354070
GRAVES BUILDING
SEATTLE, WA 98195
206-543-2210`
gohuskies.com
• Jennifer Cohen, Director of Athletics
huskyad@uw.edu
• Jason Butikofer, Chief Operating Officer
jbuti@uw.edu
• Erin O'Connell, Deputy AD/SWA
oconnell@uw.edu
• Kim Durand, Senior Associate AD, Student
Development
durand@uw.edu
• Jay Hilbrands, Senior Associate AD,
External Relations
jayhil6@uw.edu

WASHINGTON STATE UNIVERSITY ATHLETICS
WSU ATHLETICS
BOHLER ATHLETIC COMPLEX
COUGAR WAY
PULLMAN, WA 99164-1602

509-335-0320
Fax: 509-335-0328
wsucougars.com
• Patrick Chun, Director of Athletics
(509) 335-0200
athleticdirector@wsu.edu
• Anne McCoy, Deputy AD/SWA
(509) 335-7149
amccoy@wsu.edu

WEBER STATE UNIVERSITY ATHLETICS
3870 STADIUM WAY
DEPT. 2701
OGDEN, UT 84408
801-626-6817
weberstatesports.com
• Tim Crompton, Director of Athletics
(801) 626-7738
tcrompton@weber.edu
• Will Pridemore, Associate AD, Student
Athlete Services
(801) 626-8552
williampridemore@weber.edu
• Jerry Graybeal, Assoc. AD, Development
(801) 626-8114
jgraybeal@weber.edu
• Ron Goch, Assoc. AD, External Ops.
(801) 626-6731
rongoch@weber.edu

WEST VIRGINIA UNIVERSITY ATHLETICS
PO BOX 0877
MORGANTOWN, WV 26507-0877
304-293-9873
Fax: 304-293-4904
wvusports.com
• Shane Lyons, Director of Athletics
(304) 293-5621
• Keli Zinn, Deputy Athletic Director
(304) 293-6758
keli.zinn@mail.wvu.edu
• Steve Uryasz, Deputy Athletics Director
(304) 293-5682
steven.uryasz@mail.wvu.edu

WESTERN CAROLINA UNIVERSITY ATHLETICS
92 CATAMOUNT ROAD
RAMSEY CENTER
CULLOWHEE, NC 28723
828-227-7338
Fax: 828-227-7688
www.catamountsports.com
• Alex Gary, Director of Athletics
(828) 227-7338
athleticsdirector@email.wcu.edu
• Stacey Miller, Associate AD, Student
Success/SWA
(828) 227-2541
srmiller@email.wcu.edu
• Kyle Pifer, Deputy Athletics Director/COO
(828) 227-2666
kpifer@email.wcu.edu
• Amanda Murchie, Assistant Athletics
Director, Business Ops.
(828) 227-7442
amagruder@email.wcu.edu
• Chad Gerrety, Associate AD, External
Affairs
(828) 227-2767
cgerrety@email.wcu.edu

WESTERN ILLINOIS UNIVERSITY ATHLETICS
1 UNIVERSITY CIRCLE
MACOMB, IL 61455
www.goleathernecks.com

• Danielle Surprenant, Director of Athletics
(309) 298-1190
DE-Surprenant@wiu.edu
• Mark Izquierdo, Assistant Athletic Director,
Compliance
(309) 298-2221
mm-izquierdo@wiu.edu

WESTERN KENTUCKY UNIVERSITY ATHLETICS
E.A. DIDDLE ARENA
1605 AVENUE OF CHAMPIONS
BOWLING GREEN, KY 42101-6412
270-745-3542
wkusports.com
• Todd Stewart, Director of Athletics
(270) 745-5276

WESTERN MICHIGAN UNIVERSITY ATHLETICS
WMU BRONCO ATHLETICS
READ FIELDHOUSE
1903 W MICHIGAN AVENUE
KALAMAZOO, MI 49008
269-387-3120
Fax: 269-387-3668
wmubroncos.com
• Dan Bartholomae, Director of Athletics
(269) 387-3061
amy.washington@wmich.edu
• Jeff Stone, Senior Associate AD,
Compliance Services
(269) 387-3082
jeffrey.stone@wmich.edu
• Keanah Smith, Senior Associate AD/SWA
(269) 387-3090
keanah.smith@wmich.edu

WICHITA STATE UNIVERSITY ATHLETICS
WSU DEPT. OF INTERCOLLEGIATE
ATHLETICS
1845 FAIRMOUNT STREET
WICHITA, KS 67260-0018
316-978-3251
goshockers.com
• Darron Boatright, Director of Athletics
(316) 978-5498
dboatright@goshockers.com
• Sarah Adams, Senior Associate AD/SWA
(316) 978-5534
sadams@goshockers.com
• Rege Klitzke, Senior Associate AD,
Business Ops.
(316) 978-3251
rklitzke@goshockers.com
• Brad Pittman, Senior Associate AD,
Facilities & Operations
(316) 978-5556
bpittman@goshockers.com

WILLIAM & MARY ATHLETICS, COLLEGE OF
PO BOX 399
WILLIAMSBURG, VA 23187
757-221-3400
Fax: 757-221-2048
www.tribeathletics.com
• Brian Mann, Athletics Director
(757) 221-3332
athleticdir@wm.edu
• Chelsey Burk, Deputy AD
(757) 221-3373
cpburk@wm.edu
• Peel Hawthorne, Senior Associate AD,
Student Services/SWA
(757) 221-3360

pshawt@wm.edu
• Ricky Ray, Senior Associate AD, External
Operations
(757) 221-7557
rray@wm.edu

WILLIAM JEWELL COLLEGE ATHLETICS
500 COLLEGE HILL STREET
BOX 1021
LIBERTY, MO 64068
816-781-7700
www.jewellcardinals.com
• Tom Eisenhauer, Director of Athletics
(816) 415-5292
eisenhauer@william.jewell.edu

WINTHROP UNIVERSITY ATHLETICS
WINTHROP COLISEUM
1162 EDEN TERRACE
ROCK HILL, SC 29733
803-323-2129
Fax: 803-323-2433
winthropeagles.com
• Chuck Rey, Interim Athletic Director
(803) 323-2129
reyc@winthrop.edu
• Kim Whitestone, Interim Deputy Athletic
Director/SWA
(803) 323-2129
whitestonek@winthrop.edu
• Shea Maple, Assistant Athletic Director,
External Affairs
(803) 323-2129
maples@winthrop.edu

WISCONSIN ATHLETICS, UNIVERSITY OF
INTERCOLLEGIATE ATHLETICS
KELLNER HALL
1440 MONROE STREET
MADISON, WI 53711
608-262-1866
Fax: 608-265-8051
contactus@uwbadgers.com
uwbadgers.com
• Chuck McIntosh, Director of Athletics
• Barnes Adam, Associate AD/CFO,
Business Operations
AB5@athletics.wisc.edu

WISCONSIN GREEN BAY ATHLETICS, UNIVERSITY OF
2420 NICOLET DRIVE
GREEN BAY, WI 54311-7001
920-465-2145
Fax: 920-465-2652
www.greenbayphoenix.com
• Josh Moon, Director of Athletics
moonj@uwgb.edu
• Jermaine Rolle, Deputy Director of
Athletics, Compliance
(920) 465-2837
rollej@uwgb.edu
• Alan Savage, Associate AD, Development

WISCONSIN MILWAUKEE ATHLETICS, UNIVERSITY OF
MILWAUKEE ATHLETICS
PO BOX 413
THE PAVILION - ROOM 150
MILWAUKEE, WI 53201
414-229-5151
Fax: 414-229-5749
mkepanthers.com
• Amanda Braun, Director of Athletics
(414) 229-5151

uwm-ad@uwm.edu
• Cathy Rossi, Deputy Athletics Director
(414) 229-2655
rossic@uwm.edu
• Kathy Litzau, Senior Associate AD/SWA
(414) 750-4510
kclitzau@uwm.edu
• Adam Schemm, Senior Associate AD,
External Relations
(414) 229-1105
schemm@uwm.edu

WRIGHT STATE UNIVERSITY ATHLETICS
ERVIN J. NUTTER CENTER
3640 COLONEL GLENN HIGHWAY
DAYTON, OH 45435
937-775-2771
Fax: 937-425-0736
www.wsuraiders.com
• Bob Grant, Director of Athletics
(937) 775-2771
bob.grant@wright.edu
• Joylynn Brown, Senior Associate AD/SWA
(937) 775-2721
joylynn.brown@wright.edu
Description:
NCAA, Division I Department, Horizon
League, 16 sports.

WYOMING ATHLETICS, UNIVERSITY OF
DEPT. OF INTERCOLLEGIATE
ATHLETICS
DEPT. 3414
1000 E UNIVERSITY AVENUE
LARAMIE, WY 82071
307-766-2929
gowyo.com
• Tom Burman, Director of Athletics
(307) 766-2292
uwad@uwyo.edu
• Matt Whisenant, Deputy Director of
Athletics
(307) 766-5551
mwhise@uwyo.edu

XAVIER UNIVERSITY ATHLETICS
ATHLETICS DEPT.
3800 VICTORY PARKWAY
CINCINNATI, OH 45207-7530
goxavier.com
• Greg Christopher, Director of Athletics
(513) 745-3417
athleticdirector@xavier.edu
• Susan Cross Lipnickey, Associate AD,
Student-Athlete Services/SWA
(513) 745-2855
lipnickeys@xavier.edu
• Brian Hicks, Associate AD, External
Relations
(513) 745-3604
hicksb@xavier.edu
• Tom Eiser, Associate AD,
Communications
(513) 745-3124
eiser@xavier.edu
• Mario Mercurio, Associate AD, Basketball
Admin.
(513) 745-3417
mercuriom@xavier.edu

YALE UNIVERSITY ATHLETICS
PO BOX 208216
NEW HAVEN, CT 06520-8216
203-432-4747
Fax: 203-432-7772
www.yalebulldogs.com

• Victoria M. Chun, Director of Athletics
(203) 432-1414
• Ann-Marie Guglieri, Deputy AD
ann-marie.guglieri@yale.edu
• Mary Berdo, Deputy AD
mary.berdo@yale.edu

YOUNGSTOWN STATE UNIVERSITY ATHLETICS
ATHLETIC DEPT.
ONE UNIVERSITY PLAZA
YOUNGSTOWN, OH 44555
330-941-1910
Fax: 330-941-2733
ysusports@gmail.com
ysusports.com
• Ron Strollo, Exec. Director of
Intercollegiate Athletics
(330) 941-1910
rastrollo@ysu.edu
• Rebecca Fink, Senior Associate AD/SWA
(330) 941-2283
rjfink01@ysu.edu
• Tim Stuart, Senior Associate AD
(330) 941-1910
testuart@ysu.edu
• Tory Lindley, Deputy AD, Performance
Excellence
tlindley@ysu.edu

NCAA Division II Colleges

ABILENE CHRISTIAN UNIVERSITY ATHLETICS
ACU BOX 27916
ABILENE, TX 79699-7916
325-674-2287
800-766-0228
Fax: 325-674-6798
athleticdirector@acu.edu
www.acusports.com
• Lee De Leon, Director of Athletics
(325) 674-2353
athleticdirector@acu.edu
• Dave Kinard, Senior Associate Director of
Athletics
(325) 674-6483

ADAMS STATE UNIVERSITY ATHLETICS
208 EDGEMONT BOULEVARD
ALAMOSA, CO 81101
719-587-7401
Fax: 719-587-7276
www.asugrizzlies.com
• Larry Mortensen, Athletic Director
(719) 587-7402
lsmorten@adams.edu
• Dianne Lee, Associate Athletic Director
(719) 587-7401
• Michael Skinner, Sports Information
Director
(719) 587-7825
• Josh Dreher, Head Athletic Trainer
(719) 587-8233

ADELPHI UNIVERSITY ATHLETICS
1 SOUTH AVENUE
GARDEN CITY, NY 11530
516-877-4179
Fax: 516-877-4237
www.aupanthers.com
• Danny McCabe, Director of Athletics
(516) 877-4231
dmccabe@adelphi.edu
• Kate Whalen, Senior Associate Athletic

Director
(516) 877-4235
• Emily Dorko, Associate Athletic Director
(516) 877-4293
edorko@adelphi.edu

ALABAMA A&M ATHLETICS
4900 MERIDIAN STREET
NORMAL, AL 35762
256-372-8057
Fax: 256-372-5372
www.aamusports.com
• Bryan Hicks, Director of Athletics
(256) 372-4001
bryan.hicks@aamu.edu
• Cara Wright, Assoc. Director Of
Athletics/SWA
(256) 372-4759
cara.wright@aamu.edu
• Bud McLaughlin, Director of Sports
Information
(256) 372-4005
aamusportsinfo@yahoo.com

UNVIERSITY OF ALASKA ANCHORAGE ATHLETICS
3550 PROVIDENCE DRIVE
ANCHORAGE, AK 99508
907-786-1250
Fax: 907-786-1142
athletics@uaa.alaska.edu
www.goseawolves.com
• Keith Hackett, Director of Athletics
(907) 786-7800
khackett2@uaa.alaska.edu
• Tim McDiffett, Senior Associate Director of
Athletics
(907) 786-1307
tim@uaa.alaska.edu

ALBANY STATE COLLEGE ATHLETICS
504 COLLEGE DRIVE
ALBANY, GA 31705
229-430-4754
Fax: 229-430-1774
www.asugoldenrams.com
• Arthur N. Dunning, University President
(229) 430-4605
art.dunning@asurams.edu
• Richard H. Williams, Director of Athletics
(229) 430-4763
richard.williams@asurams.edu
• Stephanie Harrison-Dyer, Assistant
Athletic Director
(229) 460-1394
stephanie.harrison@asurams.edu
• Stan McCormick, Sports Information
Director
(229) 420-7013
stanley.mccormick@asurams.edu

ALDERSON-BROADDUS UNIVERSITY ATHLETICS
101 COLLEGE HILL DRIVE
PHILIPPI, WV 26416
304-457-6262
Fax: 304-457-6291
www.gobattlers.com
• Dennis Creeham, Athletic Director
(304) 457-6404
creehandw@ab.edu
• Carrie Bodkins, Senior Associate Athletic
Director
(304) 457-6347
bodkinscl@ab.edu
• Luke Harrigan, Assistant Athletic Director
(304) 457-6265

harriganlw@ab.edu
• Craig Butler, Sports Information Director
(304) 457-6445
butlercj@ab.edu

AMERICAN INTERNATIONAL COLLEGE ATHLETICS
1000 STATE STREET
BOX 4B
SPRINGFIELD, MA 01109
413-205-3916
800 242-3142
Fax: 413-205-3916
richard.bedard@aic.edu
www.aicyellowjackets.com
• Matt Johnson, Director of Athletics
(413) 205-3539
matthew.johnson@aic.edu
• Benjamin Rosenfeld, Associate Athletic Director
(413) 654-1738
benjamin.rosenfeld@aic.edu
• Art Wilkins, Assistant Athletic Director
(413) 205-3545
art.wilkins@aic.edu
• John Culp, Head Athletic Trainer
(413) 205-3541
john.culp@aic.edu

ANDERSON UNIVERSITY ATHLETICS
316 BOULEVARD
ANDERSON, SC 29621
864-231-2029
Fax: 864-231-5601
autrojans.com
• Bill D'Andrea, Athletic Director
(864) 231-2023
• Jennifer Bell, Associate Athletic Director
(864) 231-5679
• Randy Jones, Sports Information Director
(864) 231-2097
rjones@andersonuniversity.edu
• Ed Duvall, Head Athletic Trainer
(864) 231-2144
wduvall@andersonuniversity.edu

ANGELO STATE UNIVERSITY ATHLETICS
2601 WEST AVENUE NORTH
SAN ANGELO, TX 76909
324-942-2091
800-946-8627
Fax: 325-942-2277
www.angelosports.com
• James Reid, Interim Director of Athletics
(325) 942-2267
james.reid@angelo.edu
• Christina Whetsel, Assistant Athletics Director
(325) 486-6072
christina.whetsel@angelo.edu
• Steve Mahaffey, Associate Athletics Director
(325) 486-6584
steven.mahaffey@angelo.edu
• Joe'l Sefcik, Director of Athletic Academic Services
(325) 486-6048

ARKANSAS TECH UNIVERSITY ATHLETICS
TUCKER COLISEUM
1604 COLISEUM DRIVE
RUSSELLVILLE, AR 72801
479-968-0245
Fax: 479-964-0829
arkansastechsports.com

• Steve Mullins, Director of Athletics
(479) 968-0345
smullins@atu.edu
• Paul Smith, Director of Athletic Communications
(479) 968-0645
psmith6@atu.edu
• Brett Waldon, Head Athletic Trainer
(479) 968-0642
bwaldon@atu.edu

ARKANSAS-MONTICELLO ATHLETICS, UNIVERSITY OF
663 UNIVERSITY DRIVE
MONTICELLO, AR 71656
870-460-1058
Fax: 870-460-1458
www.uamsports.com
• Chris Ratcliff, Director of Athletics
(870) 460-1058
• Matt Whiting, Associate Athletic Director
(870) 460-1758
• Seth Dutton, Assistant Athletic Director
(870) 460-1756
• Mike Newell, Men's Basketball Head Coach
(870) 460-1258
• Bob Boldon, Women's Basketball Head Coach
(870) 460-1357
• Kevin Downing, Baseball Head Coach
(870) 460-1257

ARMSTRONG ATLANTIC STATE UNIVERSITY ATHLETICS
11935 ABERCORN STREET
SAVANNAH, GA 31419-1997
912-344-2813
800-633-2349
Fax: 912-344-3422
armstrongpirates.com
• Lisa Sweany, Director of Athletics
(912) 344-2813
• Jennifer Rushton, Associate Director of Athletics
(912) 344-3368
• Chad Juckson, Director of Sports Communications
(912) 344-3114
• Ken Tessier, Head Athletic Trainer
(912) 344-2866

ASHLAND UNIVERSITY ATHLETICS
ATHLETIC DEPARTMENT
KATES GYMNASIUM
401 COLLEGE AVENUE
ASHLAND, OH 44805
419-289-4142
800-882-1548
Fax: 419-289-5468
goashlandeagles.com
• Al King, Director of Athletics
(419) 289-5959
aking@ashland.edu
• Adam Bracken, Assistant Athletic Director
(419) 289-5297
abracken@ashland.edu
• Dusty Sloan, Sports Information Director
(419) 289-5954
dsloan2@ashland.edu
• Jeremy Hancock, Head Athletic Trainer
(419) 207-6195
jhancock@ashland.edu

ASSUMPTION COLLEGE ATHLETICS
500 SALISBURY STREET
WORCESTER, MA 01609

508-767-7279
Fax: 508-798-2568
www.assumptiongreyhounds.com
• Nick Smith, Director of Athletics
(508) 767-7297
• Peter Gardula, Senior Associate Director of Athletics
(508) 767-7427
• Christine Lowthert, Associate Director of Athletics
(508) 767-7086
c.lowthert@assumption.edu
• Jim Mullen, Assistant Director of Athletics
(508) 767-7288

AUGUSTA STATE UNIVERSITY ATHLETICS
3109 WRIGHTSBORO ROAD
AUGUSTA, GA 30909
706-737-1626
Fax: 706-729-2445
www.jaguarsroar.com
• Clint Bryant, Director of Athletics
(706) 737-1626
cbryant1@gru.edu
• John Sullivan, Assistant Athletic Director
(706) 731-7908
jsullivan1@gru.edu
• Taylor Lamb, Director of Athletic Media Relations
(706) 731-7925
talamb@gru.edu
• Dip Metress, Men's Basketball Head Coach
(706) 731-4765
• Josh Gregory, Mens's Golf Head Coach
(706) 731-7992

BAPTIST BIBLE COLLEGE
628 EAST KEARNEY STREET
SPRINGFIELD, MO 65803
417-268-6000
Fax: 800-819-8330
gobbc.edu
• Daniel Blakeslee, President

BARCLAY COLLEGE ATHLETICS
607 NORTH KINGMAN
HAVILAND, KS 67059
620-862-5252
800-862-0226
Fax: 620-862-5403
www.barclaycollege.edu
• Royce Bryan, Athletic Director
• Ray Anderson, Assistant Athletic Director
ray.anderson@barclaycollege.edu

BARRY UNIVERSITY ATHLETICS
11300 NE SECOND AVENUE
MIAMI SHORES, FL 33161-6695
305-899-3000
800-756-6000 ext. 3550
dkluka@barry.edu
gobarrybucs.com
• Michael L. Covone, Director of Athletics
mcovone@barry.edu
• Jamie Carrig, Associate Director of Athletics
jcarrig@barry.edu
• Cesar Odio, Assistant Director of Athletics

BARTON COLLEGE ATHLETICS
PO BOX 5000
WILSON, NC 27893
252-399-6317
800-345-4973

Fax: 252-399-6572
www.barton.edu
• Todd Wilkinson, Director of Athletics
(259) 399-6552
twilkinson@barton.edu
• Matt Atkins, Assistant Athletic Director
(252) 399-6609
mgakins@barton.edu
• Benny Benton, Sports Information Director
(252) 399-6515
bbenton@barton.edu
• Ricardo Oliveira, Athletic Operations
Coordinator
(252) 399-6610
roliveira@barton.edu
• Nathan Pickel, Head Athletic Trainer
(252) 399-6568
nspickel@barton.edu
• Tim Dornemann, Director of Sports
Performance
(252) 399-6534
tdornemann@barton.edu

BELLARMINE UNIVERSITY ATHLETICS
2001 NEWBURG ROAD
LOUISVILLE, KY 40205
502-272-8380
800-274-4723
athletics.bellarmine.edu
• Scott Wiegandt, Director of Athletics
swiegandt@bellarmine.edu
• Pam Stackhouse, Associate Director of
Athletics
pstackhouse@bellarmine.edu
• John Spugnardi, Sports Information
Director
jspugnardi@bellarmine.edu
• Melanie Brunsdon, Assistant Director of
Athletics
mbrunsdon@bellarmine.edu

BEMIDJI STATE UNIVERSITY ATHLETICS
1500 BIRCHMONT DRIVE NE
BEMIDJI, MN 56601-2699
218-755-2001
800 475-2001
Fax: 218-755-4048
www.bsubeavers.com
• Tracy Dill, Director of Athletics
(218) 755-4022
tdill@bemidjistate.edu
• Sarah Levesque, Associate Athletic
Director
(218) 755-2142
slevesque@bemidjistate.edu
• Wayne Chadwick, Assistant Athletic
Director
(218) 755-3784
wchadwick@bemidjistate.edu
• Debbie Slough, Athletics Secretary
(218) 755-2941
dslough@bemidjistate.edu
• Bill Crews, Head Athletic Trainer
(218) 755-2769
wcrews@bemidjistate.edu

BENEDICT COLLEGE ATHLETICS
1600 HARDEN STREET
COLUMBIA, SC 29204
803-705-4910
Fax: 803-705-4840
washingtonw@benedict.edu
www.benedicttigers.com
• Willie Washington, Athletic Director
(803) 705-4734
washingtonw@benedict.edu
• Fred Watson, Associate Athletic Director

(803) 705-4735
watsonf@benedict.edu
• Margaret Jones, Athletics Compliance
Coordinator
(803) 705-4437
jonesm@benedict.edu
• Loraine Dunbar, Athletics Operations
Coordinator
(803) 705-4426
dunbarl@benedict.edu

BENTLEY UNIVERSITY ATHLETICS
175 FOREST STREET
WALTHAM, MA 02452-4705
781-891-2000
Fax: 781-891-2648
www.bentleyfalcons.com
• Bob DeFelice, Director of Athletics
(781) 891-2256
rdefelice@bentley.edu
• Kevin Loftus, Associate Athletics Director
(781) 891-2196
kloftus@bentley.edu
• Cindy Scott, Assistant Athletic Director
(781) 891-2218
cscott@bentley.edu
• Courtney Finn, Athletic Operations
Assistant
(781) 891-2368
cfinn1@bentley.edu

BLOOMFIELD COLLEGE ATHLETICS
467 FRANKLIN STREET
BLOOMFIELD, NJ 7003
973-748-9000 EXT 363
Fax: 973-259-1085
www.bcbearsathletics.com
• Sheila Wooten, Athletic Director
(973) 748-9000
• Gerald Holmes, Assistant Director of
Athletics
(973) 748-9000
• Gladstone Harris, Sports Information
Director
(973) 748-9000
• Lauren Mastrobuoni, Head Athletic Trainer
(973) 748-9000
• Jackie Cividanes, Associate Athletic
Trainer
(973) 748-9000

BLOOMSBURG UNIVERSITY ATHLETICS
400 EAST SECOND STREET
BLOOMSBURG, PA 17815-1301
570-389-4000
Fax: 570-389-4724
www.buhuskies.com
• Michael McFarland, Director of Athletics
(570) 389-4050
mcfarland@bloomu.edu
• Kathy Heitzman, Associate Director of
Athletics
(570) 389-4555
kheitzma@bloomu.edu
• James Updike, Director of Athletic
Operations
(570) 389-4371
• David Leisering, Interim Director of Sports
Information
(570) 389-4413
• Allen Larsen, Head Athletic Trainer
(570) 389-4369
alarsen@bloomu.edu

BLUEFIELD COLLEGE ATHLETICS
3000 COLLEGE DRIVE
BLUEFIELD, VA 24605

276-326-4253
800-872-0175
Fax: 276-326-4386
mwhite@bluefield.edu
www.bcrams.com
• Mike White, Interim Athletic Director
(276) 326-4316
mwhite@bluefield.edu
• Tom Price, Assistant Athletic Director
(276) 326-4254
• Chase Neidig, Director of Athletic
Broadcasting
• Bob Redd, Sports Information Director
(276) 326-4342
rredd@bluefield.edu

BOWIE STATE UNIVERSITY ATHLETICS
14000 JERICHO PARK ROAD
BOWIE, MD 20715-9465
301-860-3570
Fax: 301-860-3585
bsubulldogs.com
• Clyde Doughty, Jr., Athletic Director
(301) 860-3559
cdoughty@bowiestate.edu
• Arlene Creek, Associate Athletic Director
(301) 860-3588
acreek@bowiestate.edu
• Gregory Goings, Sports Information
Director
(301) 860-3574
ggoings@bowiestate.edu
• Teresa Gruchacz, Head Athletic Trainer
(301) 860-3581
tgruchacz@bowiestate.edu

**BRIGHAM YOUNG UNIVERSITY-HAWAII
ATHLETICS**
55-220 KULANUI STREET
LAIE, HI 96762
808-675-3211
Fax: 808-675-3763
byuhawaiisports.com
• Brad Jones, Athletic Director
(808) 675-3760
bjones@byuh.edu
• Dawn Akana, Assistant Athletic Director
(808) 675-3318
kuriharC@byuh.edu
• Spencer Shamo, Sports Information
Director
(808) 675-3397
spencer.shamo@byuh.edu

CALDWELL UNIVERSITY ATHLETICS
120 BLOOMFIELD AVENUE
CALDWELL, NJ 07006
973-618-3260
Fax: 973-618-3370
admissions@caldwell.edu
www.caldwellathletics.com
• Mark A. Corino, Director of Athletics
(973) 618-3260
mcorino@caldwell.edu
• Dean Johnson, Associate Director of
Athletics
(973) 618-3321
djohnson@caldwell.edu
• Megan Bratkovich, Assistant Director of
Athletics
(973) 618-3591
mbratkovich@caldwell.edu
• John Tagliaferri, Director of Athletic Media
Relations
(973) 618-3567
jtagliaferri@caldwell.edu
• Mike Molinaro, Athletic Trainer

(973) 618-3574
mmolinaro@caldwell.edu

CALIFORNIA POLY STATE UNIVERSITY ATHLETICS
MOTT ATHLETICS CENTER
1 GRAND AVENUE
SAN LUIS OBISPO, CA 93407-0388
805-756-2924
Fax: 805-756-2699
www.gopoly.com
• Don Oberhelman, Director of Athletics
(805) 756-2924
obe@calpoly.edu
• Nick Pettit, Deputy Director of Athletics
(805) 756-2882
ndpettit@calpoly.edu
• Chris Baker, Associate Athletic Director
(805) 756-7188
baker@calpoly.edu
• Ashley Offerman, Associate Athletic Director, Development
(805) 756-0280
aofferma@calpoly.edu

CALIFORNIA STATE POLY UNIVERSITY ATHLETICS
KELLOGG GYM, BUILDING 43 ROOM 116
3801 WEST TEMPLE AVENUE
POMONA, CA 91768
909-869-2810
Fax: 909-869-2814
www.broncoathletics.com
• Brian Swanson, Director of Intercollegiate Athletics
(909) 869-2810
bswanson@cpp.edu
• Stephanie Duke, Associate Athletic Director
(909) 869-3778
sduke@cpp.edu
• Ruem Malasarn, Assistant Athletics Director
(909) 869-2834
rmalasarn@cpp.edu

CALIFORNIA STATE UNIVERSITY-CHICO ATHLETICS
DEPARTMENT OF INTERCOLLEGIATE ATHLETICS
ACKER GYM 131
CHICO, CA 95929-0300
530-898-6470
Fax: 530-898-6582
abarker@csuchico.edu
www.chicowildcats.com
• Anita Barker, Athletic Director
(530) 898-6470
abarker@csuchico.edu
• Scott Barker, Head Athletic Trainer
(530) 898-5873
sbarker@csuchico.edu
• Mitch Cox, Associate Director of Athletics
(530) 898-6470
mscox@csuchico.edu

CALIFORNIA STATE UNIVERSITY-DOMINGUEZ HILLS ATHLETICS
DEPARTMENT OF ATHLETICS
1000 EAST VICTORIA STREET
CARSON, CA 90747
310-243-3893
Fax: 310-217-6975
www.gotoros.com
• Jeff Falkner, Athletics Director
(310) 243-3893

jfalkner@csudh.edu
• Jamie Purnell, Associate Director of Athletics/SWA
(310) 243-2224
jbouyer@csudh.edu
• Mel Miranda, Assistant Athletics Director
(310) 243-3135
mmiranda@csudh.edu
• Ashley Musick, Head Athletic Trainer
(310) 243-2492
amusick@csudh.edu

CALIFORNIA STATE UNIVERSITY-EAST BAY ATHLETICS
25800 CARLOS BEE BOULEVARD
HAYWARD, CA 94542
510-885-3038
Fax: 510-885-2282
www.eastbaypioneers.com
• Jason Carmichael, Director of Athletics
(510) 885-3039
• Darrell Bailey, Jr., Assistant Athletics Director
(510) 885-3585
• Steve Connolly, Director of Athletic Communications
(510) 885-4509
• Patrick Lazaro, Interim Head Athletic Trainer
(510) 885-3055

CALIFORNIA STATE UNIVERSITY-LOS ANGELES ATHLETICS
5151 STATE UNIVERSITY DRIVE
LOS ANGELES, CA 90032
323-343-3080
Fax: 323-343-6535
calstatelaathletics.com
• Daryl Gross, Executive Director of Intercollegiate Athletics
(323) 343-3080
daryl.gross@calstatela.edu
• Daniel Garrett, Assistant Director of Intercollegiate Athletics
(323) 343-5466
dgarret4@calstatela.edu
• Lori Rudd, Athletic Head Trainer
(323) 343-3097

CALIFORNIA STATE UNIVERSITY-SAN BERNARDINO ATHLETICS
5500 UNIVERSITY PARKWAY
SAN BERNARDINO, CA 92407-2318
909-537-5011
Fax: 909-537-5984
csusbathletics.com
• Morgan Walker, Interim Director Of Athletics
(909) 537-5011
mwalker@csusb.edu
• Morgan Walker, Senior Associate Athletics Director
(909) 537-5020
mwalker@csusb.edu

CALIFORNIA STATE UNIVERSITY-STANISLAUS ATHLETICS
ONE UNIVERSITY CIRCLE
TURLOCK, CA 95382
209-667-3016
Fax: 209-667-3084
mmatoso@csustan.edu
www.warriorathletics.com
• Michael Matoso, Director of Athletics
(209) 667-3016
mmatoso@csustan.edu
• Kim Duyst, Associate Athletics Director

(209) 667-3312
kduyst@csustan.edu
• Hung P. Tsai, Assistant Athletics Director
(209) 667-3168
htsai@csustan.edu
• Dake Walden, Head Athletic Trainer
(209) 664-6838
dwalden@csustan.edu

CALIFORNIA UNIVERSITY OF PENNSYLVANIA ATHLETICS
250 UNIVERSITY AVE
BOX 34
CALIFORNIA, PA 15419
724-938-4000
Fax: 724-938-5849
www.calvulcans.com
• Karen Hjerpe, Athletic Director
(724) 938-4167
hjerpe@calu.edu
• Ron McGrew, Director of Athletic Facilities
(724) 938-4524
sealy_r@calu.edu
• Jenni Morrison, Assistant to the Athletic Director
(724) 938-5790
morrison@calu.edu
• Jamie Weary, Head Athletic Trainer
(724) 938-4562
weary@calu.edu

CAMERON UNIVERSITY ATHLETICS
2800 WEST GORE BOULEVARD
LAWTON, OK 73505
580-581-2460
Fax: 580-581-5537
jjackson@cameron.edu
www.cameronaggies.com
• Jim Jackson, Athletic Director
(580) 581-2306
jjackson@cameron.edu
Affiliations:
Members of the Lone Star Conference - NCAA Division II
Teams:
Baseball, Basketball (M/W), Cheerleading, Cross Country (M), Golf (M/W), Softball, Tennis, Volleyball.
Description:
Athletics have played a large role in campus life since Cameron's inception in 1908. Over the years, the Aggies have won numerous conference (42), regional (44), and national (9) titles - including a women's tennis regional championship in 2011, baseball and men's tennis conference championships in 2009 and a men's tennis regional championship in 2008. To further celebrate these milestones, the CU Athletic Department, in 2007, established an Athletic Hall of Fame to highlight CU's athletic history and feature numerous Aggie greats. The CU Athletic Department offers 11 intercollegiate athletic programs and is a proud member of both the NCAA Di

CARSON-NEWMAN COLLEGE ATHLETICS
HOLT FIELDHOUSE
2130 SOUTH BRANNER AVENUE
JEFFERSON CITY, TN 37760
865-471-3360
Fax: 865-471-3514
amorgan@cn.edu
www.cneagles.com
• Allen Morgan, Athletics Director
(865) 471-3372

college sports

amorgan@cn.edu
• Eddie Carter, Assistant Athletic Director
(865) 471-3365
ecarter@cn.edu
• Mikeee Van Bruggen, Director of Sports
Medicine
(865) 471-3368
mvanbruggen@cn.edu

CATAWBA COLLEGE ATHLETICS
2300 WEST INNES STREET
SALISBURY, NC 28144
704-637-4474
Fax: 704-645-4887
www.gocatawbaindians.com
• Larry Leckonby, Athletic Director
(704) 637-4474
lleckonb14@catawba.edu
• Craig Turnbull, Associate Athletics Director
(704) 637-4475
• Peter Bourque, Assistant Athletic Director
(704) 637-4485
• Bob Casmus, Head Athletic Trianer
(704) 637-4350

UNIVERSITY OF CENTRAL ARKANSAS ATHLETICS
201 DONAGHEY AVENUE
CONWAY, AR 72035
501-450-3150
Fax: 501-450-3151
bteague@uca.edu
ucasports.com
• Brad Teague, Athletic Director
(501) 450-3150
bteague@uca.edu
• Darrell Walsh, Associate Athletic Director
(501) 450-3255
darrellw@uca.edu
• Natalie Shock, Assistant Athletic Director
(501) 450-3212
natalies@uca.edu
• Kai Caddy, Video Marketing Coordinator
(501) 450-3219
kcaddy@uca.edu

CENTRAL MISSOURI STATE UNIVERSITY ATHLETICS
203 MULTIPURPOSE BUILDING
500 SOUTH WASHINGTON STREET
WARRENSBURG, MO 64093
660-543-4250
Fax: 660-543-8034
ucmathletics.com
• Jerry Hughes, Athletics Director
(660) 543-4250
hughes@ucmo.edu
• Kathy Anderson, Senior Associate Athletic
Director
(660) 543-4310
klanderson@ucmo.edu
• Mike Knipper, Assistant Athletic Director
(660) 543-4312
• Bob Jackson, Marketing & Promotions
Director
(660) 543-8194
jackson@ucmo.edu

CENTRAL OKLAHOMA ATHLETICS, UNIVERSITY OF
100 NORTH UNIVERSITY DRIVE
EDMOND, OK 73034
405-974-2142
Fax: 405-974-3820
www.bronchosports.com
• Joe Muller, Athletic Director
(405) 974-2500

jmuller2@uco.edu
• Gunnar Poff, Assistant Athletic Director
(405) 974-2176
gpoff@uco.edu
• Britni Brannon, Assistant Athletic Director
(405) 974-2168
bbrannon@uco.edu
• Ed Kabrick, Head Athletic Trainer
(405) 974-2188
ekabrick@uco.edu

CENTRAL WASHINGTON UNIVERSITY ATHLETICS
NICHOLSON PAVILION
400 EAST UNIVERSITY WAY
ELLENSBURG, WA 98926-7570
509-963-1914
Fax: 509-963-2390
www.wildcatsports.com
• Dennis Francois, Director of Athletics
(509) 963-1945
francoisd@cwu.edu
• Gary Hyatt, Associate Athletic Director
(509) 963-1681
hyattg@cwu.edu
• Tyler Unsicker, Assistant Athletic Director
(509) 963-3290
unsickert@cwu.edu
• Chris Thew, Head Athletic Trainer
(509) 963-3238
christopher.thew@cwu.edu

CHADRON STATE COLLEGE ATHLETICS
ARMSTRONG BUILDING
1000 MAIN STREET
CHADRON, NE 69337
308-432-6345
Fax: 308-432-6493
rrhine@csc.edu
chadroneagles.com
• Randy Rhine, President
(308) 432-6201
rrhine@csc.edu
• Joel R. Smith, Athletic Director
(308) 432-6253
jsmith@csc.edu
• Kaleb Center, Interim Sports Information
Director
(308) 432-7082
kcenter@csc.edu
• Don Watt, Head Athletic Trainer
(308) 432-6340
dwatt@csc.edu
• Chris Green, Associate Athletic Director
(308) 432-6344
cgreen@csc.edu

CHAMINADE UNIVERSITY ATHLETICS
3140 WAIALAE AVENUE
HONOLULU, HI 96816
808-735-4790
Fax: 808-739-4695
www.goswords.com
• Bill Villa, Director of Athletics
(808) 739-8578
william.villa@chaminade.edu
• Bonnie Bedoya, Assistant to the Athletic
Director
(808) 735-4790
bonnie.bedoya@chaminade.edu
• Kevin Hashiro, Sports Information Director
(808) 739-8579
athletics-sid@chaminade.edu

CHARLESTON ATHLETICS, UNIVERSITY OF
2300 MACCORKLE AVENUE SE
CHARLESTON, WV 25304
304-357-4820
Fax: 304-357-4989
www.ucwv.edu
• Bren Stevens, Director of Athletics
(304) 357-4911
brenstevens@ucwv.edu
• Todd Diuguid, Associate Athletic Director
(304) 357-4827
todddiuguid@ucwv.edu
• Travis Chandler, Assistant Athletic Director
(304) 357-4751
travischandler@ucwv.edu
• Raymond Loeser, Sports Information
Director
(304) 357-4976
rayloeser@ucwv.edu
• Michael Nyquist, Head Athletic Trainer
(304) 357-4395
michaelnyquist@ucwv.edu

CHESTNUT HILL COLLEGE ATHLETICS
9601 GERMANTOWN AVENUE
PHILADELPHIA, PA 19118
215-248-7060
Fax: 215-248-7047
athletics@chc.edu
www.griffinathletics.com
• Lynn Tubman, Director of Athletics
(215) 248-7046
tubmanl@chc.edu
• Jesse Balcer, Associate Director of
Athletics
(215) 753-3790
balcerj@chc.edu
• Jessica Day, Assistant Director of Athletics
(215) 242-7729
dayj@chc.edu
• Gregory Gornick, Athletic Communications
Coordinator
(215) 248-7060
gornickg@chc.edu
• Erin Fidler, Head Athletic Trainer
(215) 248-7191
fidlere@chc.edu

CHEYNEY UNIVERSITY ATHLETICS
1837 UNIVERSITY CIRCLE
PO BOX 200
CHEYNEY, PA 19319
610-399-2441
Fax: 610-399-2291
www.cheyneywolves.com
• Suzanne Kilian, Interim Athletic Director
(610) 399-2110
skilian@cheyney.edu
• Conrad DeJoy, Interim Sports Information
Director
(305) 586-9530
• Andrew Dunn, Athletic Trainer
(610) 399-2310

CHOWAN COLLEGE ATHLETICS
HELMS CENTER
ONE UNIVERSITY PLACE
MURFREESBORO, NC 27855
252-398-6378
Fax: 252-398-6532
akolezynski0814@chowan.edu
gocuhawks.com
• Ozzie McFarland, Director of Athletics
(252) 398-6244
• Meredith Long, Deputy Athletics Director
(252) 398-6468

longm@chowan.edu
• Alexis Avery, Assistant Athletic Director, Compliance
(252) 398-6243
averya@chowan.edu
• Lisa Bland, Director of Sports Medicine
(252) 398-6458
blandl@chowan.edu
• Eric Gustafson, Head Athletic Trainer
(252) 398-6442
gustae@chowan.edu

CIRCLEVILLE BIBLE COLLEGE
1476 LANCASTER PIKE
CIRCLEVILLE, OH 43113
740-474-8896
877-762-8669
Fax: 740-477-7755
www.ocutrailblazers.com
• David Bireline, Athletic Director
(740) 477-7769
dbireline@ohiochristian.edu
• Ryan Wall, Sports Information Director
(740) 477-7769
sportsinformation@ohiochristian.edu

CLAFLIN UNIVERSITY ATHLETICS
400 MAGNOLIA STREET
ORANGEBURG, SC 29115-9970
803-535-5362
Fax: 803-535-5610
athletics.claflin.edu
• Jerome Fitch, Athletic Director
(803) 535-5549
jfitch@claflin.edu
• Marilynn Stacey-Suggs, Assistant Athletics Director
(803) 535-5365
mstacey-suggs@claflin.edu
• Romanda Noble-Watson, Sports Information Director
(803) 535-5548
rnoble-watson@claflin.edu
• Akeem Boneparte, Athletic Academic Advisor
(803) 535-5022
akeem.bonepart@claflin.edu
• Tiffany Davis, Head Athletic Trainer
(803) 535-5726

CLARION UNIVERSITY OF PENNSYLVANIA ATHLETICS
112 TIPPIN GYM
CLARION, PA 16214
814-393-1997
Fax: 814-393-2430
www.clariongoldeneagles.com
• Wendy Snodgrass, Interim Athletic Director
(814) 393-1997
wsnodgrass@clarion.edu
• D.J. Bevevino, Interim Associate Athletic Director
(814) 393-1989
dbevevino@clarion.edu
• Scott Courtney, Athletics Event/Promotions Coordinator
(814) 393-2057
scourtney@clarion.edu
• Jim Thornton, Head Athletic Trainer
(814) 393-2456
jthornton@clarion.edu

CLARK ATLANTA UNIVERSITY ATHLETICS
223 JAMES P. BRAWLEY DRIVE SW
ATLANTA, GA 30314

404-880-8123
Fax: 404-880-8397
clarkatlantasports.com
• Lin Dawson, Athletics Director
(404) 880-8123
jldawson@cau.edu
• Cliff Huff, Senior Associate Athletics Director
(404) 880-8798
chuff@cau.edu
• James Vallone, Sports Information
(404) 880-6685
jvallone@cau.edu
• Rick Flateau, Head Athletic Trainer
(404) 880-8943
rflateau@cau.edu

CLAYTON COLLEGE & STATE UNIVERSITY ATHLETICS
2000 CLAYTON STATE BOULEVARD
MORROW, GA 30260
678-466-4692
Fax: 678-466-4699
timothyduncan@clayton.edu
www.claytonstatesports.com
• Tim Duncan, Director of Athletics
(678) 466-4692
timothyduncan@clayton.edu
• Echols Sherry, Athletics Business Manager
(678) 466-4692
• Mike Mead, Assistant Athletic Director
(678) 466-4679
mikemead@clayton.edu
• Alicia M. Roane, Head Athletic Trainer
(678) 466-4685
• Joshua J. Darling, Sports Information Director
(678) 466-4681

COKER COLLEGE ATHLETICS
300 EAST COLLEGE AVENUE
HARTSVILLE, SC 29550
843-383-8073
Fax: 843-383-8167
www.cokercobras.com
• Lynn Griffin, Vice President of Athletics
(843) 383-8071
lgriffin@coker.edu
• Mary Buchner, Assistant To The VP For Athletics
(843) 383-8262
mbuchner@coker.edu
• Chris Jeppson, Head Athletic Trainer
(843) 383-8390
cjeppson@coker.edu

COLORADO ATHLETICS, UNIVERSITY OF (COLORADO SPRINGS)
1420 AUSTIN BLUFFS PARKWAY
UNIVERSITY CENTER
COLORADO SPRINGS, CO 80918
719-255-3029
Fax: 719-255-3131
gomountainlions.com
• Nathan Gibson, Executive Athletic Director
• Sandee Mott, Senior Associate Athletic Director/SWA
(719) 255-3601
smott@uccs.edu
• Heather Sanders, Assistant Athletic Director
(719) 255-3004
hsander2@uccs.edu

COLORADO CHRISTIAN UNIVERSITY ATHLETICS
8787 WEST ALAMEDA AVENUE
LAKEWOOD, CO 80226
303-963-3026
Fax: 303-963-3187
cougars@ccu.edu
www.ccucougars.com
• Brian Wall, Athletic Director
(303) 963-3187
bwall@ccu.edu
• Christy Hinch, Assistant Athletic Director/SWA
(303) 963-3185
chinch@ccu.edu
• Heidi Tebrink, Head Athletic Trainer
(303) 963-3199
htebrink@ccu.edu
• Brooke Carbajal, Director of Sports Information
(303) 963-3026
bcarbajal@ccu.edu

COLORADO SCHOOL OF MINES ATHLETICS
1500 ILLINOIS STREET
GOLDEN, CO 80401
303-273-3360
Fax: 303-273-3362
www.csmorediggers.com
• David Hansburg, Director of Athletics
(303) 273-3300
hansburg@mines.edu
• Dixie Cirillo, Associate Athletics Director
(303) 273-3206
dcirillo@mines.edu
• Tim Flynn, Assistant Athletics Director
(303) 273-3095
flynn@mines.edu

COLUMBUS STATE UNIVERSITY ATHLETICS
4225 UNIVERSITY AVENUE
COLUMBUS, GA 31907
706-507-8800
866-264-2035
Fax: 706-569-3435
www.csucougars.com
• Todd Reeser, Director of Athletics
(706) 565-3669
treeser@columbusstate.edu
• Jimbo Davis, Assistant Athletic Director
(706) 568-2317
davis_james@columbusstate.edu
• Julio Llanos, Associate Athletic Director
(706) 507-8297
llanos_julio@columbusstate.edu
• Stephen Williams, Sports Information Director
(706) 569-3434

CONCORD UNIVERSITY ATHLETICS
VERMILLION STREET
PO BOX 1000
ATHENS, WV 24712-1000
304-384-5340
Fax: 304-384-5117
www.cumountainlions.com
• Kevin Garrett, Director of Athletics
(304) 384-5340
coachgarrett@concord.edu
• Tracy Gill, Assistant Athletic Director
(304) 384-5954
tmccallister@concord.edu
• Kenny Osborne, Associate Athletic Director
(304) 384-5344

college sports

355

coachosborne@concord.edu
• Wes McKinney, Sports Information
Director
(304) 384-6259
sportsinformation@concord.edu

CONCORDIA COLLEGE (NY) ATHLETICS
171 WHITE PLAINS ROAD
BRONXVILLE, NY 10708
914-337-9300
Fax: 914-395-4515
www.concordiaclippers.com
• Kathy Laoutaris, Director of Athletics/SWA
(914) 337-9300
kathy.laoutaris@concordia-ny.edu
• Kathy Laoutaris, Associate Athletic
Director
(914) 337-9300
• Jillian Ayson, Head Athletic Trainer
(914) 337-9300

**CONCORDIA UNIVERSITY (OR)
ATHLETICS**
2811 NORTHEAST HOLMAN STREET
PORTLAND, OR 97211
503-280-8582
Fax: 503-280-8591
www.gocugo.com
• Brian Jamros, Director of Athletics
(503) 280-8554
• Lauren Eads, Associate Athletics
Director-Busines Mgmt
(503) 280-8516
• Amy Dames Smith, Assistant Athletics
Director
(503) 280-8581
• Cisco Reyes, Director of Athletic
Performance
• Kyle Nelson, Head Athletic Trainer
(503) 280-8695
• Joe Danahey, Assistant AD For Sports
Information
(503) 280-8506

**CONCORDIA UNIVERSITY IRVINE
ATHLETICS**
1530 CONCORDIA WEST
IRVINE, CA 92612-3203
949-854-8002 EXT 1423
Fax: 949-854-6771
www.cuieagles.com
• Mo Roberson, Interim Director of Athletics
(949) 214-3210
mo.roberson@cui.edu
• Brittany Brasington, Assistant Athletic
Director
(949) 514-3212
brittany.brasington@cui.edu
• Crystal Rosenthal, Senior Woman
Administrator
(949) 214-3223
crystal.rosenthal@cui.edu
• Brian Gaul, Director of Athletic
Communications
(949) 214-3211
brian.gaul@cui.edu
• Terilyn Jackson, Director of Equity and
Inclusion
(949) 214-3039
terilyn.jackson@cui.edu
• Glory Fung, Head Athletic Trainer
(949) 214-3245
glory.fung@cui.edu

DAEMEN COLLEGE ATHLETICS
4380 MAIN STREET
AMHERST, NY 14226

716-839-8346
800-462-7652
Fax: 716-566-7858
www.daemen.edu
• Bridget Niland, Director of Athletics
• Mike MacDonald, Associate Athletics
Director
• Tom McDermott, Sports Information
Consultant
• Stephen Beatty, Athletics Operations
Assistant
(716) 566-7698

**DALLAS BAPTIST UNIVERSITY
ATHLETICS**
3000 MOUNTAIN CREEK PARKWAY
DALLAS, TX 75211
214-333-5324
Fax: 214-333-5306
sports@dbu.edu
dbupatriots.com
• Connor Smith, Director of Athletics
(214) 333-5324
connors@dbu.edu
• Tyler Knox, Associate Director of Athletics
(214) 333-5349
tyler@dbu.edu
• Chris Weatherly, Director of Athletic
Operations
(214) 333-5436
chriswe@dbu.edu
• Josh Freeze, Director of Athletic Facilities
(214) 333-5350
joshf@dbu.edu

DELTA STATE UNIVERSITY ATHLETICS
C/O CHADWICK-DICKSON ATHLETIC
FIELD HOUSE
DSU BOX A3
CLEVELAND, MS 38733
662-846-4300
800.GO.TO.DSU
athletics@deltastate.edu
www.gostatesmen.com
• Ronnie Mayers, Director of Athletics
(662) 846-4730
rmayers@deltastate.edu
• David Pryor, Assistant Athletic Director,
Sports Medicine
(662) 846-4280
dpryor@deltastate.edu

**DISTRICT OF COLUMBIA ATHLETICS,
UNIVERSITY OF**
4200 CONNECTICUT AVENUE NW
BUILDING 47, ROOM A02
WASHINGTON, DC 20008
202-274-5024
Fax: 202-274-5065
www.udcfirebirds.com
• Patricia Thomas, Director of Intercollegiate
Athletics
(202) 274-7257
pthomas@udc.edu
• Joseph Lang, Senior Associate Director of
Athletics
(202) 274-6314
jlang@udc.edu
• Andre Myers, Aquatics Director
(202) 274-5343
andrew.myers@udc.edu
• Alison Hammer, Assistant Director of
Athletics, Sports Medicine
(202) 274-6269
alison.hammer@udc.edu

DOMINICAN COLLEGE ATHLETICS
470 WESTERN HIGHWAY
ORANGEBURG, NY 10962
845-848-7702
Fax: 845-398-3042
www.chargerathletics.com
• Joseph Clinton, Director of Athletics
(845) 848-7700
joe.clinton@dc.edu
• Kelly-Ann Di Giulio, Director of Sports
Information
(845) 848-7706
kellyann.digiulio@dc.edu
• Rick Giannetti, Assistant Director of
Athletics
(845) 848-7707
rick.giannetti@dc.edu
• Samantha James, Head Athletic Trainer
(845) 848-7709
samantha.james@dc.edu

**DOMINICAN UNIVERSITY OF
CALIFORNIA ATHLETICS**
1475 GRAND AVENUE
SAN RAFAEL, CA 94901
415-482-3500
Fax: 415-485-9746
amy.henkelman@dominican.edu
www.dominicanathletics.com
• Amy Henkelman, Acting Director of
Athletics
amy.henkelman@dominican.edu
• Cassandra Urroz, Associate Director of
Athletics and Compliance
(415) 482-3503
• Patrick Huser, Assistant Director of
Athletics
(415) 485-3219
patrick.huser@dominican.edu

DOWLING COLLEGE ATHLETICS
RUDOLPH-OAKDALE CAMPUS
150 IDLE HOUR BOULEVARD
OAKDALE, NY 11769
631-244-3030
800-369-5464
Fax: 631-244-3317
• Melody Cope, Vice President for Athletics
(631) 244-3023
• Jason Trufant, Senior Associate Athletic
Director
(631) 244-1113
• Kevin DesLauriers, Assistant Athletics
Director
(631) 244-1075
• Jackie Rogers, Director of Athletic
Communications
(631) 244-1095

DRURY UNIVERSITY ATHLETICS
900 NORTH BENTON AVENUE
SPRINGFIELD, MO 65802
417-873-7879
800-922-2274
Fax: 417-873-7510
drury@drury.edu
www.drury.edu
• Mark Fisher, Athletic Director
(417) 873-7294
• Eric Pannell, Assistant Director of Sports
Information
(417) 873-7374
• Barbara Cowherd, Associate Director of
Athletics
(417) 873-7363
• Bryan Beatty, Assistant Athletic Director,

Compliance
(417) 873-6382

EAST CENTRAL UNIVERSITY ATHLETICS
1100 EAST 14TH STREET
ADA, OK 74820
580-332-8000
jwillims@ecok.edu
ecutigers.com
• Jeff Williams, Director of Athletics
(580) 559-5261
jwillims@ecok.edu
• Justin Graham, Assistant Athletic Director
(580) 559-5653
juspgra@ecok.edu
• Teri LaJeunesse, Sports Information Director
(580) 559-5258
tlajeune@ecok.edu

EAST STROUDSBURG UNIVERSITY OF PENNSYLVANIA ATHLETICS
KOEHLER FIELDHOUSE
200 PROSPECT STREET
EAST STROUDSBURG, PA 18301
570-422-3211
Fax: 570-422-3306
www.esuwarriors.com
• Josh Looney, Director of Athletics
(570) 422-3642
• Carey Snyder, Associate Athletic Director
(570) 422-3034
csnyder@esu.edu
• Philip Miller, Assistant to the Athletic Director
(570) 422-3578
• Greg Knowlden, Sports Information Director
(570) 422-3312
gknowlden@esu.edu
• Wendy Dietrich, Athletic Trainer
(570) 422-3166
wwheeler@esu.edu

EASTERN NEW MEXICO UNIVERSITY ATHLETICS
ENMU STATION 17
1500 SOUTH AVENUE K
PORTALES, NM 88130
575-562-1011
Fax: 505-562-2822
athletics@enmu.edu
www.goeasternathletics.com
• Greg Waggoner, Athletic Director
(575) 562-2153
greg.waggoner@enmu.edu
• Lora Ferguson, Head Athletic Trainer
(575) 562-2273
lora.ferguson@enmu.edu
• Kimberley Sites, Athletic Office Coordinator
(575) 562-2153
• Adam Pitterman, Director of Athletic Communications
(575) 562-4309
adam.pitterman@enmu.edu

ECKERD COLLEGE ATHLETICS
4200 54TH AVENUE SOUTH
ST. PETERSBURG, FL 33711
727-867-1166
800-456-9009
Fax: 727-864-8968
www.eckerdtritons.com
• Bob Fortosis, Director of Athletics
(727) 864-8252

• Tom Ryan, Associate Director of Athletics
(727) 864-8305
ryantj@eckerd.edu
• Bill Matthews, Assistant Director of Athletics
(727) 864-8253
mathewwj@eckerd.edu
• Jeff Bromley, Director of Athletics Development
(727) 864-8403

EDINBORO UNIVERSITY OF PENNSYLVANIA ATHLETICS
MCCOMB FIELDHOUSE
455 SCOTLAND ROAD
EDINBORO, PA 16444-0001
814-732-1834
Fax: 814-732-2190
www.gofightingscots.com
• Bruce Baumgartner, Director of Athletics
(814) 732-1823
bbaumgartner@edinboro.edu
• Todd Jay, Associate Athletic Director
(814) 732-1835
jay@edinboro.edu
• Dave Higham, Athletic Administrative Coordinator
(814) 732-1825
dhigham@edinboro.edu
• Gary Hanna, Head Athletic Trainer
(814) 732-1860
ghanna@edinboro.edu
• Bob Shreve, Sports Information Director
(814) 732-1834
rshreve@edinboro.edu

ELIZABETH CITY STATE UNIVERSITY ATHLETICS
1704 WEEKSVILLE ROAD
CAMPUS BOX 900
ELIZABETH CITY, NC 27909
252-335-3388
Fax: 252-335-3627
www.ecsuvikings.com
• Derrick Johnson, Athletic Director
(252) 335-3396
dajohnson2@ecsu.edu
• Alico Dunk, Assistant Athletic Director - Academics
(252) 335-3461
ajdunk@ecsu.edu
• John Westbrook, Sports Information Director
(252) 335-3278
jwwestbrookjr@ecsu.edu

EMBRY-RIDDLE AERONAUTICAL UNIVERSITY ATHLETICS - (FL)
600 SOUTH CLYDE MORRIS BOULEVARD
DAYTONA BEACH, FL 32114
386-226-6100
erauathletics.com
• John Phillips, Director of Athletics
(386) 323-5020
john.phillips@erau.edu
• John Mark Adkison, Associate Director of Athletics
(386) 323-5033
john.adkison@erau.edu
• Maryellen Wynn, Director of Finance - Athletics
(386) 323-5004
maryellen.wynn@erau.edu
• Jenni Craig, Director of Sports Marketing and Promotions
(386) 323-5037
craig10@erau.edu

• Alison Smalling, Director of Sports Information
(386) 323-5001
alison.smalling@erau.edu

EMMANUEL COLLEGE (EC) ATHLETICS
181 SPRINGS STREET
PO BOX 129
FRANKLIN SPRINGS, GA 30639
706-245-2917
800-860-8800
Fax: 706-245-4424
www.goeclions.com
• Nate Moorman, Athletic Director
(706) 245-2884
nmoorman@ec.edu
• JaVonte Ashford, Assistant Athletic Director
(706) 988-0103
• Richard Reiselt, Faculty Athletics Representative
(706) 245-7226
rreiselt@ec.edu
• Sandy Campbell, Director for Sports Medicine
(706) 245-2889
scampbell@ec.edu
• Kethan Darbar, Sports Information Coordinator
(731) 444-4737
kdarbar@ec.edu

EMPORIA STATE UNIVERSITY ATHLETICS
1 KELLOGG CIRCLE
HPER 113
CAMPUS BOX 4020
EMPORIA, KS 66801
620-341-5354
Fax: 620-341-5603
www.esuhornets.com
• Kent Weiser, Athletic Director
(620) 341-5350
kweiser@emporia.edu
• Shane Shivley, Senior Associate Athletic Director
(620) 341-6988
sshivley@emporia.edu
• Don Weast, Assistant Athletic Director
(620) 341-5526
dweast@emporia.edu
• Tess Shepherd, Athletic Business Manager
(620) 341-5925
• Dustin Enslinger, Head Athletic Trainer
(620) 341-5021

ERSKINE COLLEGE ATHLETICS
PO BOX 338
2 WASHINGTON STREET
DUE WEST, SC 29639
864-379-8859
888-359-4358
Fax: 864-379-2197
erskinesports.com
• Mark Peeler, Vice President for Intercollegiate Athletics
(864) 379-8850
mlp@erskine.edu
• Kevin Nichols, Associate Director of Athletics
(864) 379-8890
nichols@erskine.edu
• Thomas Holland, Co-Sports Information Director
(864) 379-6782
tholland@erskine.edu

FAIRMONT STATE UNIVERSITY ATHLETICS
1201 LOCUST AVENUE
FAIRMONT, WV 26554
304-367-4220
Fax: 304-333-3597
www.fightingfalcons.com
• Tim McNeely, Director of Athletics
(304) 367-4220
tim.mcneely@fairmontstate.edu
• Bob Cable, Associate Athletic Director
(304) 367-4273
rcable@fairmontstate.edu
• Chad Fowler, Assistant Athletic Director for Development
(304) 333-3650
chad.fowler@fairmontstate.edu
• Chris Thomas, Sports Information Director
(304) 367-4264
christopher.thomas@fairmontstate.edu

FAYETTEVILLE STATE UNIVERSITY ATHLETICS
FELTON J. CAPEL ARENA
1200 MURCHISON ROAD
FAYETTEVILLE, NC 28301
910-672-1314
Fax: 910-672-1241
www.fsubroncos.com
• Anthony Todd Bennett, Director of Athletics
(910) 672-1314
abennett@uncfsu.edu
• LaWanda Miller, Assistant Athletics Director
(910) 672-1420
lmiller@uncfsu.edu
• Carlitta Moore, Director of Sports Medicine
(910) 672-1065
cmmoore02@uncfsu.edu

FELICIAN COLLEGE ATHLETICS
ONE FELICIAN WAY
RUTHERFORD, NJ 07070
201-559-3333
Fax: 201-559-3601
felicianathletics.com
• Ben DiNallo, Jr., Director of Athletics
(201) 559-3507
Dinallob@felician.edu
• Lori McGuinness, Assistant Director of Athletics, Compliance
(201) 559-3996
kwiatkowskil@felician.edu
• Mark Mentone, Sports Information Director
(201) 559-3257
mentonem@felician.edu
• Dan Trinh, Head Athletic Trainer
(201) 559-3502
trinhd@felician.edu

FERRIS STATE UNIVERSITY ATHLETICS
1201 SOUTH STATE STREET
BIG RAPIDS, MI 49307
231-591-2860
Fax: 231-591-2869
www.ferrisstatebulldogs.com
• Perk Weisenburger, Athletics Director
(231) 591-2862
weisenj1@ferris.edu
• Jon Coles, Associate Athletic Director
(231) 591-2864
coelsj@ferris.edu
• Rob Bentley, Assistant Athletic Director, Communications
(231) 591-3821
bentleyr@ferris.edu

• Dave Lucey, Head Athletic Trainer
(231) 250-7931
luceyd@ferris.edu

FINDLAY ATHLETICS, UNIVERSITY OF
1000 NORTH MAIN STREET
FINDLAY, OH 45840
419-434-4663
800-472-9502
Fax: 419-434-4618
athletics.findlay.edu
• Brandi Laurita, Director of Athletics
(419) 434-4663
laurita@findlay.edu
• Jim Givens, Associate Athletic Director
(419) 434-4793
givens@findlay.edu
• David Buck, Assistant Athletic Director
(419) 434-4727
buckd@findlay.edu
• Fiona Hanks, Head Athletic Trainer
(419) 434-6785
hanks@findlay.edu

FLAGLER COLLEGE ATHLETICS
74 KING STREET
ST. AUGUSTINE, FL 32084
904-829-6481
athletics.flagler.edu
• Jud Damon, Director of Athletics
(904) 819-6252
jdamon@flagler.edu
• Ryan Erlacher, Associate Director of Athletics
(904) 819-6488
rerlacher@flagler.edu
• John Jordan, Sports Information Director
(904) 819-6465
jjordan@flagler.edu
• Cade Smith, Athletics Operations Coordinator
(904) 826-8632
ksmith@flagler.edu
• Aerial Tirado, Head Athletic Trainer
(904) 819-6361
atirado@flagler.edu

FLORIDA GULF COAST UNIVERSITY ATHLETICS
10501 FGCU BOULEVARD SOUTH
FORT MYERS, FL 33965
239-590-7012
Fax: 239-590-7014
pblankenship@fgcu.edu
www.fgcuathletics.com
• Ken Kavanagh, Director of Athletics
kavanagh@fgcu.edu
• Trish Blankenship, Administrative Assistant
pblankenship@fgcu.edu
• Mike Estes, Senior Associate AD, Administration
(239) 590-7006
mestes@fgcu.edu
• Kathy Peterson, Assoc. AD, Student-Athlete Svcs./Snr. Woman Admin.
(239) 590-7018
kpeterson@fgcu.edu
Team Nickname:
Eagles
Conference:
NCAA Division I
Founded:
1997
Enrollment:
15,000

FLORIDA INSTITUTE OF TECHNOLOGY ATHLETICS
150 WEST UNIVERSITY BOULEVARD
MELBOURNE, FL 32901
321-674-8032
Fax: 321-984-8529
bjurgens@fit.edu
www.floridatechsports.com
• Bill Jurgens, Jr., Athletic Director
(321) 674-8032
bjurgens@fit.edu
• Frank M. Webbe, Faculty Athletics Representative
(321) 674-8104
• Michael Craig, Assistant Athletic Director, Communications
(321) 674-8250
• Jay Johnson, Head Athletic Trainer
(321) 674-8438

FLORIDA SOUTHERN COLLEGE ATHLETICS
111 LAKE HOLLINGSWORTH DRIVE
LAKELAND, FL 33801-5698
863-680-4246
Fax: 863-680-4122
fscmocs.com
• Pete Meyer, Director of Athletics
(863) 680-4264
pmeyer@flsouthern.edu
• Al Green, Head Athletic Trainer
(863) 680-4267
agreen@flsouthern.edu
• Drew Howard, Associate Athletic Director
(863) 680-4266
ahoward@flsouthern.edu
• Brink Schoonmaker, Manager of Athletic Facilities
(750) 919-3054
bschoonmaker@flsouthern.edu

FORT HAYS STATE UNIVERSITY ATHLETICS
600 PARK STREET
HAYS, KS 67601-4099
785-628-3478
Fax: 785-625-4881
fhsuathletics.com
• Curtis Hammeke, Athletic Director
(785) 628-4050
chammeke@fhsu.edu
• Brad Haynes, Assistant Athletic Director
(785) 628-5288
behaynes@fhsu.edu
• Ryan Prickett, Sports Information Director
(785) 628-5903
rpricket@fhsu.edu

FORT LEWIS COLLEGE ATHLETICS
1000 RIM DRIVE
DURANGO, CO 81301
970-247-7171
Fax: 970-247-7655
www.goskyhawks.com
• Gary Hunter, Director of Athletics
(970) 247-7224
• Steve Stovall, Faculty Athletics Representative
• Wayne Barger, Director of Sports Medicine
(970) 247-7576
• Adam Ruetschie, Athletic Operations Coordinator
(970) 247-7171

FORT VALLEY STATE UNIVERSITY ATHLETICS
1005 STATE UNIVERSITY DRIVE
FORT VALLEY, GA 31030
478-825-3054
Fax: 478-825-6889
www.fvsusports.com
• Darryl Pope, Director of Athletics
(478) 825-6238
• LuWanna Williams, Associate Director of Athletics
(478) 825-6179
williamsl@fvsu.edu
• Jerry Haywood, Faculty Athletic Representative
(478) 825-6710
• Willie K. Patterson, Jr., Director of Sports Information
(478) 825-6437

FRANCIS MARION UNIVERSITY ATHLETICS
PO BOX 100547
FLORENCE, SC 29502-0547
843-661-1240
Fax: 843-661-4645
www.fmupatriots.com
• Murray Hartzler, Athletics Director
(843) 661-1237
mhartzler@fmarion.edu
• Dean Blackburn, Director of Smith University Center
(843) 661-1189
dblackburn@fmarion.edu
• Reghan Boehmke, Head Athletic Trainer
(843) 661-1358
rboehmke@fmarion.edu

FRANKLIN PIERCE UNIVERSITY ATHLETICS
40 UNIVERSITY DRIVE
RINDGE, NH 03461
603-899-4087
Fax: 603-899-4328
• Bruce Kirsh, Director of Athletics
(603) 899-4080
kirshb@franklinpierce.edu
• Dan Blair, Associate Director of Athletics
(603) 899-4367
blaird@franklinpierce.edu
• Stephanie Dragan, Assistant Athletics Director
(603) 899-4084
dragans@franklinpierce.edu
• Matthew Janik, Director of Athletic Communication
(603) 899-4223
janikm@franklinpierce.edu
• Cynthia Arman, Head Athletic Trainer
(603) 899-4083
armanca@franklinpierce.edu

FRESNO PACIFIC UNIVERSITY ATHLETICS
DEPARTMENT OF ATHLETICS
1717 SOUTH CHESTNUT AVENUE
FRESNO, CA 93702
559-453-2009
Fax: 559-453-2005
fpuathletics.com
• Aaron Henderson, Director of Athletics
(559) 453-2009
aaron.henderson@fresno.edu
• Jeremiah Wood, Assistant Athletics Director for Communications
(559) 453-4646
jeremiah.wood@fresno.edu

• Jessi Wallace, Assistant Director for External Relations
(559) 453-5694
jessi.wallace@fresno.edu

GANNON UNIVERSITY ATHLETICS
109 UNIVERSITY SQUARE
ERIE, PA 16541
814-871-7000
Fax: 814-871-7794
www.gannonsports.com
• Lisa Goddard McGuirk, Director of Athletics
(814) 871-7664
mcguirk001@gannon.edu
• Don Sherman, Associate Director of Athletics
(814) 871-7763
sherman001@gannon.edu
• Dan Teliski, Assistant Director of Athletics, Media Relations
(814) 871-7418
teliski002@gannon.edu
• Todd Matlak, Head Athletic Trainer
(814) 871-7420

GEORGIA COLLEGE & STATE UNIVERSITY ATHLETICS
231 WEST HANCOCK STREET
MILLEDGEVILLE, GA 31061
478-445-1779
800-342-0471
Fax: 478-445-1790
gsu.sid@gcsu.edu
www.gcsu.edu/athletics
• Wendell Staton, Athletic Director
(478) 445-6341
wendell.staton@gcsu.edu
• Jimmy Wilson, Associate Athletic Director
(478) 445-2082
jimmy.wilson@gcsu.edu
• Steve Barsby, Assistant Athletic Director
(478) 445-1778
steve.barsby@gcsu.edu
• Paul Higgs, Head Athletic Trainer
(478) 445-1787
paul.higgs@gcsu.edu

GEORGIA SOUTHWESTERN STATE UNIVERSITY ATHLETICS
800 GSW UNIVERSITY DRIVE
AMERICUS, GA 31709
229-931-2222
800-388-0082
Fax: 229-931-2143
www.gswcanes.com
• Mike Leeder, Athletic Director
(229) 931-2225
mike.leeder@gsw.edu
• Christie Ward, Associate Athletic Director for Compliance
(229) 931-7012
christie.ward@gsw.edu
• Keith Michlig, Assistant Athletic Director for Sports Information
(229) 931-2217
keith.michlig@gsw.edu

GEORGIAN COURT COLLEGE ATHLETICS
900 LAKEWOOD AVENUE
LAKEWOOD, NJ 08701
732-987-2683
Fax: 732-987-2002
www.gculions.com
• Laura Liesman, Director of Athletics & Recreation

(732) 987-2683
liesmanl@georgian.edu
• Christopher McKibben, Associate Director of Athletics
(732) 987-2690
mckibbenc@georgian.edu
• Joe Friedrich, Coordinator of Sports Medicine
(732) 987-2676
friedrichj@georgian.edu

GLENVILLE STATE COLLEGE ATHLETICS
200 HIGH STREET
GLENVILLE, WV 26351
304-462-4102
Fax: 304-462-8619
www.glenville.edu
• Marcel Lazenby, Athletic Director/Compliance Coordinator
(304) 462-7361
• Jonathan Griffin, Sports Information Director
(304) 462-6238

GOLDEY BEACOM COLLEGE ATHLETICS
4701 LIMESTONE ROAD
WILMINGTON, DE 19808
302-225-6352
Fax: 302-998-6823
hammond@gbc.edu
www.gbcathletics.com
• Tom Brennan, Director of Athletics
(302) 225-6352
brennan@gbc.edu
• Bethann Burke, Assistant Director of Athletics
(302) 225-6334
burkeb@gbc.edu
• Derek Crudele, Sports Information & Communications Specialist
(302) 225-6330
crudele@gbc.edu
• Brandon Sonson, Certified Athletic Trainer
(302) 225-6217
atc@gbc.edu

GRAND VALLEY STATE UNIVERSITY ATHLETICS
92 FIELDHOUSE, 1 CAMPUS DRIVE
ALLENDALE, MI 49401
616-331-5000
www.gvsulakers.com
• Keri Becker, Athletic Director
(616) 331-8800
keri_becker@gvsu.edu

HARDING UNIVERSITY ATHLETICS
915 EAST MARKET AVENUE
SEARCY, AR 72149-5615
501-279-4305
Fax: 501-279-4138
gharnden@harding.edu
www.hardingsports.com
• Greg Harnden, Athletic Director
(501) 279-4305
gharnden@harding.edu
• Brenda Seawel, Assistant Athletic Director
(501) 279-4770
bseawel@harding.edu
• Scott Goode, Assistant Athletic Director, Sports Information
(501) 279-4760
sgoode@harding.edu
• Nathan Looney, Assistant Sports Information Director

(501) 279-4760
nclooney@harding.edu

HAWAII PACIFIC UNIVERSITY ATHLETICS
1060 BISHOP STREET
SUITE 400
HONOLULU, HI 96813
808-356-5214
Fax: 808-566-2405
athletics@hpu.edu
www.hpusharks.com
• Vince Baldemor, Executive Director of Athletics
(808) 544-0209
vbaldemor@hpu.edu
• Natasa Revere, Associate Athletics Director
(808) 356-5278
nsubotic@hpu.edu
• Bill Powers, Sports Information Director
(808) 544-0220
bpowers@hpu.edu
• Chelsea Patton, Athletics Business Manager
(808) 687-7046
cpatton@hpu.edu

HAWAII-HILO ATHLETICS, UNIVERSITY OF
200 WEST KAWILI STREET
HILO, HI 96720-4091
808-932-7170
Fax: 808-974-7711
hiloathletics.com
• Patrick Guillen, Director of Athletics
(808) 932-7170
pguillen@hawaii.edu
• Diane Wissing, Assistant Compliance Officer
(808) 932-7801
dwissing@hawaii.edu

HENDERSON STATE UNIVERSITY ATHLETICS
1100 HENDERSON STREET
BOX 7630
ARKADELPHIA, AR 71999
870-230-5161
Fax: 870-230-5408
jonessh@hsu.edu
www.hsusports.com
• Shawn Jones, Director of Athletics
(870) 230-5072
jonessh@hsu.edu
• Lenette Jones, Assistnat Athletic Director
(870) 230-5881
joneslc@hsu.edu
• Troy Mitchell, Sports Information Director
(870) 230-5197
mitchet@hsu.edu
• Rob Redding, Director for Sports Medicine
(870) 230-5069
reddinr@hsu.edu

HILLSDALE COLLEGE ATHLETICS
33 EAST COLLEGE STREET
HILLSDALE, MI 49242
517-437-7341
Fax: 517-437-3923
www.hillsdalechargers.com
• Don Brubacher, Director of Athletics
(517) 437-7364
dbrubacher@hillsdale.edu
• Jeff Lantis, Director of External Relations
(517) 607-3182
jlantis@hillsdale.edu

• Anita Gordon, Aid To Athletic Director
(517) 607-3140
agordon@hillsdale.edu
• Brad Monastiere, Assistant Athletic Director
(517) 607-3172
bmonastiere@hillsdale.edu
• Lynne Neukom, Head Athletic Trainer
(517) 607-3157
lneukom@hillsdale.edu

HOLY FAMILY COLLEGE ATHLETICS
9801 FRANKFORD AVENUE
PHILADELPHIA, PA 19114
215-637-6675
Fax: 215-827-0137
athletics@holyfamily.edu
athletics.holyfamily.edu
• Sandra Michael, Assistant Vice President of Athletics
(267) 341-3368
smichael@holyfamily.edu
• Robin Arnold, Associate Athletic Director
(267) 341-3675
rarnold1@holyfamily.edu
• Jermaine Rolle, Assistant Athletic Director
(267) 341-3663
jrolle@holyfamily.edu
• Jami Hughes, Assistant Athletic Director-Daily Operations
(267) 341-3514
jhughes2@holyfamily.edu

HOLY NAMES COLLEGE ATHLETICS
3500 MOUNTAIN BOULEVARD
OAKLAND, CA 94619
510-436-1047
Fax: 510-436-1553
www.hnuhawks.com
• Debbie Snell, Director of Athletics
(510) 436-1049
snell@hnu.edu
• Marcie Haduca, Associate Director of Athletics
(510) 436-1428
haduca@hnu.edu

HUMBOLDT STATE UNIVERSITY ATHLETICS
ATHLETIC DEPARTMENT
1 HARPST STREET
ARCATA, CA 95521-8299
707-826-3666
Fax: 707-826-5446
www.hsujacks.com
• Tom Trepiak, Interim Athletic Director
(707) 826-3666
trt2@humboldt.edu
• Kelly Kime, Interim Associate Athletic Director/SWA
(707) 826-5959
kjk42@humboldt.edu
• Laurie Sheppard, Assistant Athletic Director, Business Operations
(707) 826-4530
sheppard@humboldt.edu

ILLINOIS AT SPRINGFIELD ATHLETICS, UNIVERSITY OF
2171 UNIVERSITY DRIVE
SPRINGFIELD, IL 62703
217-206-6674
Fax: 217-206-7706
kpate80@uis.edu
www.uisprairiestars.com
• Jim Sarra, Director of Athletics
(217) 206-7592

kpate80@uis.edu
• Hayley Ross Treadway, Associate Athletic Director/SWA
(217) 206-8547
hross3@uis.edu
• Ashlyn Beasley, Director for Game Operations
(217) 206-7017
jdors2@uis.edu
• Katie Bowers, Head Athletic Trainer
(217) 206-7597
kbowe6@uis.edu

INCARNATE WORD ATHLETICS, UNIVERSITY OF THE
4301 BROADWAY
SAN ANTONIO, TX 78209
210-829-6052
Fax: 210-805-3574
witt@uiwtx.edu
www.cardinalathletics.com
• Mark Papichs, Director of Athletics
(210) 829-6053
papich@uiwtx.edu
• Dustin York, Deputy Athletic Director
(210) 283-6968
dyork@uiwtx.edu
• Lydia Andrade, Faculty Athletic Representative
(210) 829-3877
andrade@uiwtx.edu

INDIANA UNIVERSITY OF PENNSYLVANIA ATHLETICS
711 PRATT DRIVE
SUITE 204
INDIANA, PA 15705
724-357-4295
Fax: 724-357-2754
www.iupathletics.com
• Steve Roach, Athletic Director
(724) 357-4295
sroach@iup.edu
• Samantha Traver, Assistant Athletic Director
(724) 357-6948
traver@iup.edu
• Ryan Rebholz, Sports Information Director
(724) 357-2747
rrebholz@iup.edu

INDIANAPOLIS ATHLETICS, UNIVERSITY OF
1400 EAST HANNA AVENUE
INDIANAPOLIS, IN 46227
317-788-3412
Fax: 317-788-3472
athletics@uindy.edu
athletics.uindy.edu
• Sue Willey, Vice President for Intercollegiate Athletics
(317) 788-3412
swilley@uindy.edu
• Jackie Paquette, Associate Athletics Director
(317) 788-5008
• Matt Donovan, Sr. Associate AD For Development
(317) 788-6122
mdonovan@uindy.edu
• Kyle Piercy, Sports Information Director
(317) 788-3494
• Ned Shannon, Head Athletic Trainer
(317) 788-6112

JOHNSON C. SMITH UNIVERSITY ATHLETICS
100 BEATTIES FORD ROAD
CHARLOTTE, NC 28216
704-378-1205
Fax: 704-378-1170
www.goldenbullsports.com
• Stephen Joyner, Athletic Director
(704) 378-3522
• K.C. Culler, Sports Information Director
(704) 378-1118
• Katie Hanes-Romano, Head Athletic Trainer
(704) 378-1222

KENTUCKY STATE UNIVERSITY ATHLETICS
400 EAST MAIN STREET
FRANKFORT, KY 40601
502-597-6000
Fax: 502-597-6466
william.head@kysu.edu
www.ksuthorobreds.com
• William K. Graham, Director of Athletics
(502) 597-6922
william.graham@kysu.edu
• Kim Harriford, Assistant to the Athletic Director
(502) 597-6011
kim.harriford@kysu.edu
• Anthony Passarette, Head Athletic Trainer
(502) 597-5558
anthony.passarette@kysu.edu

KENTUCKY WESLEYAN COLLEGE ATHLETICS
3000 FREDERICA STREET
OWENSBORO, KY 42301
270-852-3330
Fax: 270-852-3356
rmallory@kwc.edu
www.kwcpanthers.com
• Rob Mallory, Director of Athletics
(270) 852-3331
rmallory@kwc.edu
• Tom DeVinney, Assistant Athletic Director
(270) 852-3349
• Roy Pickerill, Sports Information Director
(270) 852-3347
• Martin Daniel, Director of Athletic Training
(270) 852-3333
billhu@kwc.edu

KING UNIVERSITY ATHLETICS
1350 KING COLLEGE ROAD
BRISTOL, TN 37620
423-652-4779
jdhicks@king.edu
kingtornado.com
• David Hicks, Athletic Director
(423) 652-4779
jdhicks@king.edu
• Sheila Crockett, Head Athletic Trainer
(423) 652-4762
sccrocke@king.edu
• George Pitts, Head Coach
(423) 652-4781
gspitts@king.edu
• Nancye Rahn, Assistant Athletic Director
(423) 652-6469
nrahn@king.edu

KUTZTOWN UNIVERSITY ATHLETICS
15200 KUTZTOWN ROAD
KUTZTOWN, PA 19530

610-683-4094
Fax: 610-683-1379
www.kubears.com
• Greg Bamberger, Director of Athletics
(610) 683-4094
• Michelle Gober, Associate Director of Athletics
(610) 683-4096
gober@kutztown.edu
• Alta Hart, Assistant to the Director of Athletics
(610) 683-4681
• Jason Lanter, Faculty Athletics Representative
(610) 683-4458
lanter@kutztown.edu
• Bryan Salvadore, Sports Information Director
(610) 683-4182
salvadore@kutztown.edu
• Rennie Sacco, Director of Sports Medicine
(610) 683-4085
sacco@kutztown.edu

LAKE SUPERIOR STATE UNIVERSITY ATHLETICS
650 WEST EASTERDAY AVENUE
NORRIS CENTER
SAULT STE. MARIE, MI 49783
906-632-6841
Fax: 906-635-2753
foundation@lssu.edu
www.lssu.edu
• Kris Dunbar, Athletic Director
(906) 635-2625
kdunbar@lssu.edu
• Eddie Bishop, Sports Information Director
(906) 635-2807
ebishop@lssu.edu
• Jennifer Constantino, NCAA Compliance Officer
(906) 635-2809
jconstantino@lssu.edu

LANDER UNIVERSITY ATHLETICS
320 STANLEY AVENUE
GREENWOOD, SC 29649
864-388-8000
Fax: 864-388-8898
www.landerbearcats.com
• Jeff May, Director of Athletics
(864) 388-8314
• Kent Atkins, Sports Medicine Director
(864) 388-8818
katkins@lander.edu
• Sophia Bonadies, Athletic Trainer
(864) 388-8281
sbonadies@lander.edu
• Bob Stoner, Assistant Athletic Director, Media
(864) 388-8962

LE MOYNE COLLEGE ATHLETICS
1419 SALT SPRINGS ROAD
SYRACUSE, NY 13214
315-445-4450
Fax: 315-445-4678
www.lemoynedolphins.com
• Matthew Bassett, Director of Athletics
(315) 445-4450
bassetmd@lemoyne.edu
• Steve Evans, Associate Athletics Director
(315) 445-4416
evanssw@lemoyne.edu
• Scott Peterson, Head Athletic Trainer
(315) 445-4686
peterssm@lemoyne.edu

LE MOYNE-OWEN COLLEGE ATHLETICS (LOC)
807 WALKER AVENUE
MEMPHIS, TN 38126
901-435-1235
Fax: 901-435-1244
athletics.loc.edu
• Clint Jackson, Athletic Director
(901) 435-1238
• Angela Littlejohn, Sports Information Director
(901) 435-1226
• Kristal Coleman, Athletic Business Coordinator
(901) 435-1235

LEE UNIVERSITY ATHLETICS
1120 NORTH OCOEE STREET
PO BOX 3450
CLEVELAND, TN 37320-3450
423-614-8440
www.goleeflames.com
• Larry Carpenter, Athletic Director
(423) 614-8440
lcarpenter@leeuniversity.edu
• Andrea Hudson, Assistant Athletic Director
(423) 614-8453
ahudson@leeuniversity.edu
• Jessica McIntyre, Director of Internal Affairs
(423) 473-1191
jmcintyre@leeuniversity.edu
• Andrea Hudson, Volleyball Head Coach
(423) 614-8453
ahudson@leeuniversity.edu
• George Star, Sports Information Director
(423) 614-8442
gstarr@leeuniversity.edu

LEES-MCRAE COLLEGE ATHLETICS
191 MAIN STREET
PO BOX 128
BANNER ELK, NC 28604
828-898-5241
800-280-4562
Fax: 828-898-8742
lmcbobcats.com
• Craig McPhail, Vice President of Athletics
(828) 898-2483
mcphail@lmc.edu
• Chris Parker, Director of Sports Information
(828) 898-8725
parkerc@lmc.edu
• Jeff Merrill, Director of Compliance
(828) 898-8793
merrillj@lmc.edu
• Rita Smith, Director of Athletic Training
(828) 898-8768
smithr@lmc.edu
• Zsachlayne Roguska, Head Athletc Trainer
(828) 898-8868
roguskaz@lmc.edu

LENOIR-RHYNE UNIVERSITY ATHLETICS
625 7TH AVENUE NE
PO BOX 7356
HICKORY, NC 28603
828-328-7116
Fax: 828-267-3445
www.lrbears.com
• Kim Pate, Executive Director of Intercollegiate Athletics
(828) 328-7128
kim.pate@lr.edu
• Shena Hollar, Associate Athletics Director/SWA

(828) 328-7114
hollars@lr.edu
• John Karrs, Sports Information Director
(828) 328-7174
karrsjd@lr.edu
• Michael McGee, Athletic Training Program Director
(828) 328-7127
mcgee@lr.edu
• Michael Flicker, Director of Athletic Training
(828) 328-7054

LEWIS UNIVERSITY ATHLETICS
ONE UNIVERSITY PARKWAY
ROMEOVILLE, IL 60446-2200
815-838-0500
800-897-9000
Fax: 815-836-5002
www.lewisu.edu
• Jill Siegfried, Director of Student Recreation
(815) 836-5277
siegfrji@lewisu.edu
• Adam Burkhart, Assistant Director of Student Recreation
(815) 836-5835
burkhaad@lewisu.edu

LIFE PACIFIC COLLEGE ATHLETICS
1100 WEST COVINA BOULEVARD
SAN DIMAS, CA 91773
909-599-5433
877-886-5433
Fax: 909-706-3070
athletics@lifepacific.edu
www.lpcwarriors.org
• Tim Cook, Athletics Director
(909) 599-5433
tcook@lifepacific.edu
• Micah Mulock, Sports Information Director
(909) 599-5433
mmulock15@lifepacific.edu
• Dana Haines, Head Athletic Trainer
(909) 599-5433
dhaines@lifepacific.edu

LIMESTONE COLLEGE ATHLETICS
1115 COLLEGE DRIVE
GAFFNEY, SC 29340
864-488-8370
Fax: 864-488-8249
www.limestone.edu
• Michael H. Cerino, Vice President for Intercollegiate Athletics
(864) 488-4564
mcerino@limestone.edu
• Amber Anthony, Assistant Athletic Director
(864) 488-8289
aanthony@limestone.edu
• Curt Lamb, Assistant Athletic Director
(864) 488-8354
clamb@limestone.edu
• Adam Ranns, Head Athletic Trainer
(864) 488-8361
aranns@limestone.edu

LINCOLN MEMORIAL UNIVERSITY ATHLETICS
6965 CUMBERLAND GAP PARKWAY
HARROGATE, TN 37752
423-869-6285
800-325-0900
Fax: 423-869-6382
www.lmurailsplitters.com
• Matt Green, Athletic Director
(423) 869-6241

matthew.green@lmunet.edu
• Mike Smith, Associate Athletic Director
(423) 869-6239
mike.smith@lmunet.edu
• Cameron Whicker, Assistant Athletic Director
(423) 869-6346
cameron.whicker@lmunet.edu
• Bill Porter, Director of Athletic Statistics
(423) 869-6376
bill.porter@lmunet.edu
• Scott Erland, Director of Athletic Communications
(423) 869-6236
scott.erland@lmunet.edu

LINCOLN UNIVERSITY (MISSOURI) ATHLETICS
820 CHESTNUT STREET
JEFFERSON CITY, MO 65101
573-681-5342
Fax: 573-681-5998
athletics@lincolnu.edu
www.lubluetigers.com
• John Moseley, Interim Director of Athletics
(573) 681-5333
moseleyj@lincolnu.edu
• Betty Kemna, Assistant Athletic Director
(573) 681-5953
kemnab@lincolnu.edu
• Dan Carr, Assistant Athletic Director, Media
(573) 681-5343
carrd@lincolnu.edu
• Austin Matlock, Head Athletic Trainer
(573) 681-5331
matlocka@lincolnu.edu

LINCOLN UNIVERSITY ATHLETICS
1570 BALTIMORE PIKES
PO BOX 179
LINCOLN UNIVERSITY, PA 19532-0999
484-365-7391
Fax: 484-365-8120
www.lulions.com
• Anthony Pla, Interim Director of Athletics\Facilities Director
(484) 365-7391
apla@lincoln.edu
• Kisha Middleton, Athletic Business Manager
(484) 365-7632
kmiddleton@lincoln.edu
• Dana Flint, Faculty Athletics Representative
(484) 365-7299
flint@lincoln.edu
• Chris Vigneault, Director of Sports Medicine
(484) 365-7343

LINDENWOOD UNIVERSITY ATHLETICS
209 SOUTH KINGSHIGHWAY
ST. CHARLES, MO 63301
636-949-4600
Fax: 636-949-4636
www.lindenwoodlions.com
• Brad Wachler, Vice President For Intercollegiate Athletics
(636) 949-4777
• Tom Wagganer, Associate Athletics Director
(636) 949-4533
• Anna Girdwood, Director of Compliance
(636) 949-4654
• Carl Hutter, Assistant Athletics Director
(636) 949-4813

• Kathy Kinkeade, Athletics Business Manager
(636) 949-4339
• Randy Biggerstaff, Director of Athletic Training
(636) 949-4683

LIVINGSTONE COLLEGE ATHLETICS
701 WEST MONROE STREET
SALISBURY, NC 28144
704-216-6012
Fax: 704-216-6278
bluebearathletics.com
• Jimmy R. Jenkins, Sr., President
(704) 216-6098
jjenkins@livingstone.edu
• Andre Springs, Director of Athletics
(704) 216-6012
asprings@livingstone.edu
• Charles Pinckney, Faculty Athletic Representative
(704) 216-6053
cpinckney@livingstone.edu
• Jaime Kent, Head Certified Athletic Trainer
(704) 216-6011
jkent@livingstone.edu

LOCK HAVEN UNIVERSITY ATHLETICS (LHU)
THOMAS FIELDHOUSE
401 NORTH FAIRVIEW STREET
LOCK HAVEN, PA 17745
570-484-2102
Fax: 570-484-2414
www.golhu.com
• Tom Gioglio, Director of Athletics
(570) 484-2102
tmg252@lhup.edu
• Danielle Barney, Associate Director of Athletics
(570) 484-2871
dbarney@lhup.edu
• Cheryl Gardner, Athletic Department Secretary
(570) 484-2102
• Doug Spatafore, Director of Sports Information
(570) 484-2350
dspatafo@lhup.edu

LONG ISLAND UNIVERSITY, C.W. POST ATHLETICS
C.W. POST CAMPUS
720 NORTHERN BOULEVARD
BROOKVILLE, NY 11548
516-299-2000
Fax: 516-299-3829
www.liuathletics.com
• Brad Cohen, Director of Athletics
(718) 488-1030
brad.cohen@liu.edu
• Margaret Alaimo, Deputy Director of Athletics
(718) 488-1524
margaret.alaimo@liu.edu
• Casey Snedecor, Director of Media Relations
(718) 488-1420
catherine.snedecor@liu.edu

LYNN UNIVERSITY ATHLETICS
3601 NORTH MILITARY TRAIL
BOCA RATON, FL 33431
561-237-7279
800-888-5966
Fax: 561-237-7268
www.lynnfightingknights.com

- Devin Crosby, Director of Athletics
(561) 237-7213
dcrosby@lynn.edu
- Sara Quatrocky, Associate Athletics Director
(561) 237-7765
squatrocky@lynn.edu
- Jon Lobbe, Assistant Athletics Director
(561) 237-4403
jlobbe@lynn.edu
- Chad Beattie, Director of Athletic Communications
(561) 237-7341
cbeattie@lynn.edu
- Sarah Holton, Head Athletic Trainer
(561) 537-7058

MANSFIELD UNIVERSITY ATHLETICS
DECKER GYMNASIUM
70 SOUTH STADIUM DRIVE
MANSFIELD, PA 16933
570-662-4860
Fax: 570-662-4116
www.gomounties.com
- Ryan Ehrie, Director of Athletics
(570) 662-4636
- Diane Monkiewicz, Interim Assistant Director of Athletics
(570) 662-4632
dmonkiew@mansfield.edu
- Laurie Zaparzynski, Head Athletic Trainer
(570) 662-4467
lzaparzy@mansfield.edu

MARS HILL UNIVERSITY ATHLETICS
100 ATHLETIC STREET
MARS HILL, NC 28754
828-689-1373
866-642-4968
Fax: 828-689-1440
www.marshilllions.com
- David Riggins, Athletic Director
(828) 689-1215
- Rick Baker, Sports Information Director
(828) 689-1373
- Chelsea Lawing, Assistant Athletic Trainer
(828) 689-1108
- Allen Shelley, Head Athletic Trainer
(828) 689-1176

MARYVILLE UNIVERSITY ATHLETICS
650 MARYVILLE UNIVERSITY DRIVE
ST. LOUIS, MO 63141
314-529-9300
www.maryvillesaints.com
- Marcus Manning, Director of Athletics
(314) 529-9288
mmanning@maryville.edu
- Austin DeBoer, Assistant Athletic Director
(314) 529-6886
adeboer@maryville.edu
- Alden Craddock, Faculty Athletics Representative
(314) 529-6687
acraddock@maryville.edu
- Scott Harley, Head Athletic Trainer
(314) 529-9314
sharley@maryville.edu
- Chuck Yahng, Director for Communications
(314) 529-9312
cyahng@maryville.edu

UMASS-LOWELL ATHLETICS
1 UNIVERSITY AVENUE
LOWELL, MA 01854

978-934-2310
athletics@uml.edu
goriverhawks.com
- Dana Skinner, Director of Athletics
(978) 934-2301
Dana_Skinner@uml.edu
- Peter Casey, Deputy Director of Athletics
(978) 934-2310
peter_casey@uml.edu
- Artie Poitras, Head Certified Athletic Trainer
(978) 934-2321
j_poitras@uml.edu

MCKENDREE UNIVERSITY ATHLETICS
701 COLLEGE ROAD
LEBANON, IL 62254
618-537-6513
Fax: 618-537-8316
mckbearcats.com
- Chuck Brueggemann, Athletic Director
cebrueggemann@mckendree.edu
- Brad Oster, Athletics Equipment Manager
(618) 537-6918
bjoster@mckendree.edu
- Lance Ringhausen, Head Athletic Trainer
(618) 537-6929
llringhausen@mckendree.edu
- Danny Jackson, Head Baseball Coach
(618) 537-6906

MERCY COLLEGE ATHLETICS
555 BROADWAY
DOBBS FERRY, NY 10522
914-674-7220
Fax: 914-674-7561
athletics@mercy.edu
www.mercyathletics.com
- Matt Kilcullen, Jr., Director of Athletics
(914) 674-3065
mkilcullen@mercy.edu
- Bill Sullivan, Senior Associate Director of Athletics
(914) 674-7566
wsullivan@mercy.edu
- Jordan Levine, Associate Director of Athletics
(914) 674-7343
jlevine@mercy.edu
- Danielle Minerva, Head Athletic Trainer
(914) 674-7281
dminerva@mercy.edu

MERCYHURST UNIVERSITY ATHLETICS
501 EAST 38TH STREET
ERIE, PA 16546
814-824-2228
Fax: 814-824-2591
hurstathletics.com
- Joe Kimball, Director of Athletics
(814) 824-2559
- Lauren Packer, Associate Director of Athletics
(814) 824-3101
- Stacey Gaudette, Assistant Athletic Director
(814) 824-2079
- Josh Reilly, Director of Athletic Communications
(814) 824-2525
- Andy Simon-Wambach, Head Athletic Trainer
(814) 824-2259

MERRIMACK COLLEGE ATHLETICS
315 TURNPIKE STREET
NORTH ANDOVER, MA 01845

978-837-5341
Fax: 978-837-5032
www.merrimackathletics.com
- Jeremy Gibson, Director of Athletics
(978) 837-3555
gibsonj@merrimack.edu
- Brad Davis, Associate Athletic Director
(978) 837-5364
davisb@merrimack.edu
- Birgid Hopkins, Director of Sports Medicine
(978) 837-5332
hopkinsb@merrimack.edu
- Chris Aliano, Director of Athletic Communications
(978) 837-3472

MESA STATE COLLEGE ATHLETICS
1100 NORTH AVENUE
GRAND JUNCTION, CO 81501
970-248-1503
Fax: 970-248-1980
cmumavericks.com
- Tom Spicer, Director of Athletics
(970) 248-1669
tspicer@coloradomesa.edu
- Kristin Mort, Senior Assciate Director Of Athletics For Finance
(970) 248-1714
kmort@coloradomesa.edu
- Bryan Rooks, Associate Athletic Director
(970) 248-1252
brooks@coloradomesa.edu
- Ian Marks, Sports Information Director
(970) 248-1143
imarks@coloradomesa.edu

METROPOLITAN STATE UNIVERSITY OF DENVER ATHLETICS
CAMPUS BOX 9
PO BOX 173362
DENVER, CO 80217-3362
303-556-2158
Fax: 303-556-2720
roadrunnersathletics.com
- Anthony Grant, Director of Athletics
- Shawn Worthy, Faculty Athletics Representative
(303) 556-2158
worthys@msudenver.edu
- Jim Gillen, Associate Athletic Director
(303) 556-4062
- Stephanie Begley, Head Athletic Trainer
(303) 556-3871

MICHIGAN TECHNOLOGICAL UNIVERSITY ATHLETICS
1400 TOWNSEND DRIVE
HOUGHTON, MI 49931
906-487-3070
Fax: 906-487-3062
srsanreg@mtu.edu
www.michigantechhuskies.com
- Suzanne Sanregret, Athletic Director
(906) 487-3070
srsanreg@mtu.edu
- Joel Isaacson, Associate Athletic Director
(906) 487-1915
jdisaacs@mtu.edu
- Dave Nordstrom, Associate Athletic Director, Operations
(906) 487-2578
dpnordst@mtu.edu

college sports

MIDWESTERN STATE UNIVERSITY ATHLETICS
DEPARTMENT OF ATHLETICS
MIDWESTERN STATE UNIVERSITY
3410 TAFT BOULEVARD
WICHITA FALLS, TX 76308
904-397-4044
888-MSU-9977
Fax: 940-397-4892
msumustangs.com
• Suzanna Shipley, President
(940) 397-4211
• Charlie Carr, Athletic Director
• Kurt Portman, Executive Associate Athletic Director
• Blake Barington, Sports Information Director

MILES COLLEGE ATHLETICS
5500 MYRON MASSEY BOULEVARD
FAIRFIELD, AL 35064
205-929-1615
Fax: 205-929-1616
www.miles.edu
• Phillip Wallace, Jr., Athletic Director
(205) 929-1063
pwallace@miles.edu
• Deleon Fancher, Jr., Faculty Athletic Rep.
(205) 929-1816
• Deborah Jones, Assistant Athletic Director
(205) 929-1109

MILLERSVILLE UNIVERSITY ATHLETICS
ONE SOUTH GEORGE STREET
PO BOX 1002
MILLERSVILLE, PA 17551
717-872-3011
Fax: 717-871-2125
mgallagher@millersville.edu
www.millersvilleathletics.com
• Miles Gallagher, Director of Athletics
(718) 871-7694
mgallagher@millersville.edu
• Peg Kauffman, Associate Director of Athletics
(717) 871-7693
pkauffman@millersville.edu
• Ethan Hulsey, Director of Athletic Communications
(717) 871-4154
ehulsey@millersville.edu
• Donna Eshleman, Athletic Operations
(717) 871-4230

MINNESOTA STATE UNIVERSITY - MOORHEAD ATHLETICS
1104 7TH AVENUE SOUTH
MOORHEAD, MN 56563
218-477-2622
Fax: 218-477-2324
president@mnstate.edu
www.msumdragons.com
• Anne Blackhurst, President
(218) 477-2243
president@mnstate.edu
• Doug Peters, Director of Athletics
(218) 477-2306
petersd@mnstate.edu
• Chad Markuson, Deputy Athletic Director
(218) 477-2401
chad.markuson@mnstate.edu
• Andrea Scott, Head Athletic Trainer
(218) 477-2626
scotta@mnstate.edu

MINNESOTA STATE UNIVERSITY - MANKATO ATHLETICS
135 MYERS FIELD HOUSE
MANKATO, MN 56001
507-389-6111
Fax: 507-389-2904
www.msumavericks.com
• Kevin Buisman, Director of Athletics
(507) 389-6111
kevin.buisman@mnsu.edu
• Paul Allan, Associate Athletic Director
(507) 389-2625
paul.allan@mnsu.edu
• Jeffrey Chambers, Assistant Athletic Director
(507) 389-3229
jeffrey.chambers@mnsu.edu
• Jeffrey Pribyl, Faculty Athletic Representative
(507) 389-6024
jeffrey.pribyl@mnsu.edu

MINNESOTA-CROOKSTON ATHLETICS, UNIVERSITY OF
139 SPORTS CENTER
2900 UNIVERSITY AVE
CROOKSTON, MN 56716
218-281-8506
Fax: 218-281-8430
helgeson@umn.edu
www.goldeneaglesports.com
• Stephanie Helgeson, Director of Athletics
(218) 281-8422
helgeson@umn.edu
• Jason Tangquist, Assistant Athletic Director
(218) 281-8424
jtangqui@umn.edu
• Shawn Smith, Sports Information Director
(218) 281-8414
smithsd@umn.edu
• Don Stopa, Assistant Sports Information Director
(218) 281-8435
djstopa@umn.edu

MINNESOTA-DULUTH ATHLETICS, UNIVERSITY OF
170 SPORTS & HEALTH CENTER
1216 ORDEAN COURT
DULUTH, MN 55812
218-726-8168
Fax: 218-726-6529
www.umdbulldogs.com
• Josh Berlo, Athletic Director
(218) 726-8718
jpberlon@d.umn.edu
• Karen Stromme, Associate Athletic Director
(218) 726-7143
kstromme@d.umn.edu
• Bob Nygaard, Assistant Athletic Director
(218) 726-8191
bnygaard@d.umn.edu
• Bob Nygaard, Athletic Communications
(218) 726-8514
bnygaard@d.umn.edu

MINOT STATE UNIVERSITY ATHLETICS
500 UNIVERSITY AVENUE WEST
MINOT, ND 58701
701-858-3041
Fax: 701-858-3136
rick.hedberg@minotstateu.edu
www.msubeavers.com
• Andy Carter, Athletic Director
(701) 858-3042

andrew.carter@minotstateu.edu
• Wendy McManus, Associate Athletic Director/SWA
(701) 858-4451
wendy.mcmanus@minotstateu.edu
• Michael Linnell, Assistant Athletic Director
(701) 858-3681
michael.linnell@minotstateu.edu
• Josh Sandy, Director of Athletic Marketing & Promotions
(701) 858-4094

MISSISSIPPI COLLEGE ATHLETICS
200 SOUTH CAPITOL STREET
CLINTON, MS 39056
601-925-3000
Fax: 601-925-7294
www.gochoctaws.com
• Mike Jones, Athletic Director
(601) 925-3819
jones01@mc.edu
• Susan Musselwhite, Assistant Athletic Director
(601) 925-3362
musselwh@mc.edu
• Kyle Lewis, Sports Information Director
(601) 925-7890
klewis1@mc.edu

MISSOURI SOUTHERN STATE UNIVERSITY ATHLETICS
3950 EAST NEWMAN ROAD
JOPLIN, MO 64801
417-625-3075
800-606-6772
Fax: 417-625-9601
info@mssu.edu
mssulions.com
• Jared Bruggeman, Director of Athletics
(417) 625-9317
• Rachel Burleson, Associate Athletics Director
(417) 625-9712
• Darin Moore, Head Athletic Trainer
(417) 625-9337
• Randon Coffey, Director of Marketing
(417) 625-3075

MISSOURI WESTERN STATE COLLEGE ATHLETICS
4525 DOWNS DRIVE
ST. JOSEPH, MO 64507
816-271-4481
Fax: 816-271-5901
gogriffons.com
• Kurt McGuffin, Director of Athletics
(816) 271-5623
• Brett Esely, Associate Director of Athletics
(816) 271-5904
esely@missouriwestern.edu
• Mike Halloran, Director of Athletic Facilities
(816) 271-4556
mhalloran@missouriwestern.edu
• Nick McCutcheon, Director of Athletic Media Relations
(816) 271-4257
nmccutcheon@missouriwestern.edu

MISSOURI-ROLLA ATHLETICS, UNIVERSITY OF
705 WEST 10TH STREET
ROLLA, MO 65409
573-341-4175
Fax: 573-341-4880
minerathletics.com
• Mark Mullin, Director of Athletics
(573) 341-4175

memullin@mst.edu
• Ron Henderson, Assistant Director of Athletics
(573) 341-4673
hendersonro@mst.edu
• Josh Lind, Assistant Athletics Compliance Director
(573) 341-7598
lindja@mst.edu

MOLLOY COLLEGE ATHLETICS
1000 HEMPSTEAD AVENUE
ROCKVILLE CENTER, NY 11571
516-323-3608
Fax: 516-323-3622
www.molloylions.com
• Susan Cassidy-Lyke, Director of Athletics
(516) 323-3608
scassidy@molloy.edu
• Michael Grasso, Associate Director of Athletics
(516) 323-3602
mgrasso@molloy.edu
• Kevin DesLauriers, Assistant Director of Athletics, Operations
(516) 323-3603
kdleslauriers@molloy.edu
• Kelly Thompson, Director of Athletic Communications
(516) 323-3605
kthompson3@molloy.edu

MONTANA STATE UNIVERSITY BILLINGS ATHLETICS
1500 UNIVERSITY DRIVE
BILLINGS, MT 59101-0298
406-657-2369
Fax: 406-657-2919
sports@msubillings.edu
www.msubsports.com
• Krista L. Montague, Athletic Director
(406) 657-2061
kmontague@msubillings.edu
• Evan O'Kelly, Director of Communications
(406) 657-2130
evan.okelly@msubillings.edu
• Thomas Ebel, Head Athletic Trainer
(406) 657-2375
tebel@msubillings.edu

MONTEVALLO ATHLETICS, UNIVERSITY OF
75 COLLEGE DRIVE
MONTEVALLO, AL 35115
205-665-6600
Fax: 205-665-6587
www.montevallofalcons.com
• Mark Richard, Director of Athletics
(205) 665-6612
mrichard11@montevallo.edu
• Dawn Makofski, Assistant Athletic Director
(205) 665-6633
makofskidb@montevallo.edu
• Marcelo Takejame Galafassi, Head Athletic Trainer
(205) 665-6602
mgalafassi@montevallo.edu
• Wesley Hallman, Sports Information Director
(205) 665-6197
whallman@montevallo.edu

MOREHOUSE COLLEGE ATHLETICS
830 WESTVIEW DRIVE SW
ATLANTA, GA 30314

404-681-2800
Fax: 404-521-9073
athletics.morehouse.edu
• Andre Pattillo, Director of Athletics
(404) 215-2669
apattillo@morehouse.edu
• Yusuf Davis, Sports Information Director
(404) 222-2575
yusuf.davis@morehouse.edu
• Craig Boyd, Head Athletic Trainer
cboyd@morehouse.edu

MOUNT OLIVE COLLEGE ATHLETICS
586 HENDERSON STREET
MOUNT OLIVE, NC 28365
919-658-7759
Fax: 919-658-7180
www.umotrojans.com
• Jeff Eisen, Vice President of Athletics
(919) 658-7759
jeisen@umo.edu
• LaToya Greene, Associate Director of Athletics
(919) 658-4928
llindsey@umo.edu
• Kristen Gibson, Director of Sports Medicine
(919) 658-7810
kgibson@umo.edu
• Ryan Smith, Director of Athletics Communications
(919) 658-7802
rjsmith@umo.edu

NEBRASKA AT OMAHA ATHLETICS, UNIVERSITY OF
SAPP FIELDHOUSE
6001 DODGE STREET
OMAHA, NE 68182
Fax: 402-554-2555
• Trev Alberts, Vice Chancellor, Athletics
(402) 554-2305
trevalberts@unomaha.edu
• Ann Oatman, Senior Associate Athletic Director
(402) 554-3270
aoatman@unomaha.edu
• Connie Claussen, Athletic Director Emeritus
• Dave Ahlers, Assistant Athletic Director, Communications
(402) 554-3387
dahlers@unomaha.edu

NEBRASKA-KEARNEY ATHLETICS, UNIVERSITY OF
DEPT OF INTERCOLLEGIATE ATHLETICS
2501 15TH AVENUE
KEARNEY, NE 68849
308-865-8514
Fax: 308-865-8187
www.lopers.com
• Paul Plinske, Athletic Director
(308) 865-8514
plinksep@unk.edu
• Josh Jorgensen, Senior Associate Athletic Director
(308) 865-8069
jorgensenjm@unk.edu
• Peter Yazvac, Assistant Athletic Director, Media Relations
(308) 865-8334
yazvacpa@unk.edu

NEW HAVEN ATHLETICS, UNIVERSITY OF
CHARGER GYM
300 BOSTON POST ROAD
WEST HAVEN, CT 06516
203-932-7016
Fax: 203-932-7470
newhavenchargers@newhaven.edu
www.newhavenchargers.com
• Jim McCoy, Interim Director of Athletics
(203) 932-7020
jmccoy@newhaven.edu
• Robin Salters, Associate Director of Athletics, Facilities
(203) 932-7022
rsalters@newhaven.edu
• Janet Dinihanian, Athletics Administrative Specialist
(203) 932-7016
jdinihanian@newhaven.edu
• Dan Ruede, Director of Athletic Communications
(203) 932-7025
druede@newhaven.edu

NEW HOPE CHRISTIAN COLLEGE
2155 BAILEY HILL ROAD
EUGENE, OR 97405
541-485-1780
800-322-2638
Fax: 541-343-5801
www.godeacons.com
• Matt Binkerd, Athletic Director

NEW MEXICO HIGHLANDS UNIVERSITY ATHLETICS
PO BOX 9000
LAS VEGAS, NM 87701
877-850-9064
Fax: 505-426-2014
nmhucowboys.com
• Bob Clifford, Athletic Director
bclifford@nmhu.edu
• Jim Deisler, Assistant Athletic Director
(505) 426-2017
jedeisler@nmhu.edu
• Cwynnci Lobaugh, Sports Information Director
(505) 454-3361
cwynnci@nmhu.edu
• Yvette Pomponi, Head Athletic Trainer
(505) 454-3355
ypomponi@nmhu.edu

NEW YORK INSTITUTE OF TECHNOLOGY ATHLETICS
PO BOX 8000
NORTHERN BOULEVARD
OLD WESTBURY, NY 11568-8000
516-686-1216
Fax: 516-686-1168
athletics@nyit.edu
www.nyitbears.com
• Dan Velez, Director of Intercollegiate Athletics
(516) 686-1216

NEWBERRY COLLEGE ATHLETICS
2100 COLLEGE STREET
NEWBERRY, SC 29108
803-321-5127
Fax: 803-321-5632
www.newberrywolves.com
• Ralph Patterson, Director of Athletics
(803) 947-2064
ralph.patterson@newberry.edu
• Mike Hold, Director of External Operations

college sports

(803) 321-5247
mike.hold@newberry.edu
• Randall Stewart, Director of Athletic
Communications
(803) 321-5667
randall.stewart@newberry.edu
• John Lopez, Director of Sports Medicine
(803) 321-3327
john.lopez@newberry.edu

NORFOLK STATE UNIVERSITY ATHLETICS
700 PARK AVENUE
NORFOLK, VA 23504
757-823-8152
Fax: 757-823-2566
mlmiller@nsu.edu
www.nsuspartans.com
• Marty L. Miller, Athletics Director
(757) 823-8152
mlmiller@nsu.edu
• Carray Banks, Faculty Athletics
Representative
(757) 823-2421
cbanks@nsu.edu
• Alisha Tucker, Director of Student
Services
(757) 823-2337
amtucker@nsu.edu
• Matt Michalec, Director of Sports
Communications
(757) 823-2628
mmichalec@nsu.edu

NORTH ALABAMA ATHLETICS, UNIVERSITY OF
UNA BOX 5071
FLORENCE, AL 35632
256-765-4397
Fax: 256-765-4685
www.roarlions.com
• Mark Linder, Director of Athletics
(256) 765-4397
mdlinder@una.edu
• Todd Vardaman, Assistant Athletic
Director of Compliance
(256) 765-4618
tdvardaman@una.edu
• Jeff Dodges, Director of Communications
(256) 765-4595
sportsinformation@una.edu
• Josh Penny, Head Athletic Trainer
(256) 765-4563
jdpenny@una.edu

NORTH CAROLINA, PEMBROKE ATHLETICS, UNIVERSITY OF
ONE UNIVERSITY DRIVE
PO BOX 1510
PEMBROKE, NC 28372-1510
910-521-6227
Fax: 910-521-6540
athletics@uncp.edu
www.uncpbraves.com
• Andrea Branch, Executive Assistant
(910) 521-6227
andrea.branch@uncp.edu
• Dick Christy, Athletics Director
(910) 521-6227
dick.christy@uncp.edu
• Todd Anderson, Director of
Communications
(910) 521-6371
todd.anderson@uncp.edu
• Michael Blackburn, Director of Sports
Medicine

(910) 522-5727
michael.blackburn@uncp.edu

NORTH DAKOTA ATHLETICS, UNIVERSITY OF
UND ATHLETICS
HYSLOP SPORTS CENTER ROOM 120
2751 2ND AVENUE NORTH
GRAND FORKS, ND 58202
701-777-2234
Fax: 701-777-2285
www.undsports.com
• Brian Faison, Athletics Director
brian.faison@athletics.und.edu
• Daniella Irle, Deputy Director of Athletics
daniella.irle@athletics.und.edu
• Steve Brekke, Associate Athletic Director,
Development
• Jayson Hajdu, Director of Media Relations
jayson.hajdu@athletics.und.edu
• Amanda Hajdu, Director of Academic
Services
amanda.hajdu@athletics.und.edu

NORTH DAKOTA STATE UNIVERSITY ATHLETICS
1340 ADMINISTRATION AVENUE
FARGO, ND 58102
701-231-8981
Fax: 701-231-6246
www.gobison.com
• Matt Larsen, Director of Athletics
(701) 231-8985
matthew.larsen@ndsu.edu
• Todd Phelps, Deputy Director of Athletics
(701) 231-7807
todd.phelps@ndsu.edu
• Ryan Perreault, Director of Athletic
Communications
(701) 231-8331
ryan.perreault@ndsu.edu

NORTH GEORGIA COLLEGE & STATE UNIVERSITY ATHLETICS
130 GEORGIA CIRCLE
DAHLONEGA, GA 30597
706-864-1758
Fax: 706-897-2850
ungathletics.com
• Lindsay Reeves, Director of Athletics
(706) 867-3212
lindsay.reeves@ung.edu
• Derek Suraine, Associate Director of
Athletics
(706) 867-2770
derek.suranie@ung.edu
• Lee Glenn, Assistant Director of Athletics
(706) 867-3250
lee.glenn@ung.edu
• Matt Daniel, Head Athletic Trainer
(706) 864-1669
matt.daniel@ung.edu

NORTHERN COLORADO ATHLETICS, UNIVERSITY OF
270D BUTLER COLORADO ATHLETICS
GREELEY, CO 80639
970-351-1890
Fax: 970-351-2018
events@unco.edu
uncbears.com
• Darren Dunn, Director of Athletics
(970) 351-2362
• Kobee Stalder, Director of Athletic
Communications
(970) 351-1065
kobee.stalder@unco.edu

• Bob Heiny, Faculty Athletics
Representative
(970) 351-2049
robert.heiny@unco.edu

NORTHERN MICHIGAN UNIVERSITY ATHLETICS
1401 PRESQUE ISLE AVENUE
MARQUETTE, MI 49855
906-227-2105
Fax: 906-227-2492
www.nmuwildcats.com
• Forrest Karr, Director of Athletics
(906) 227-1826
fkarr@nmu.edu
• Carl Bammert, Assistant Athletic Director
(906) 227-2465
cbammert@nmu.edu
• Alex Tieso, Director of Compliance
(906) 227-1780
altieso@nmu.edu

NORTHERN STATE UNIVERSITY ATHLETICS
1200 SOUTH JAY STREET
ABERDEEN, SD 57401
605-626-7748
Fax: 605-626-2238
ashley.n.gabler@northern.edu
nsuwolves.com
• Josh Moon, Director of Athletics
(605) 626-3336
• Zach Flakus, Deputy Director of Athletics
(605) 626-7741
• Terri Holmes, Assistant Director of
Athletics
(605) 626-2578
terri.holmes@northern.edu
• Ashley Gauer, Director of Athletic
Communications
(605) 626-7748
ashley.gauer@northern.edu
• Sara Christensen Blair, Faculty Athletic
Representative
(605) 626-2515

NORTHWEST MISSOURI STATE UNIVERSITY ATHLETICS
800 UNIVERSITY DRIVE
MARYVILLE, MO 64468
660-562-1212
Fax: 660-562-1493
coacht@nwmissouri.edu
www.bearcatsports.com
• Mel Tjeerdsma, Director of Athletics
(660) 562-1306
coacht@nwmissouri.edu
• Lori Hopkins, Associate Athletic Director
(660) 562-1142
lorih@nwmissouri.edu
• Mark Clements, Director for Internal
Operations
(660) 532-1308
mclem@nwmissouri.edu
• Kelly Quinlin, Head Athletic Trainer
(660) 562-1313
kellyq@nwmissouri.edu

NORTHWOOD UNIVERSITY (MI) ATHLETICS
4000 WHITING DRIVE
MIDLAND, MI 48640
989-837-5244
800-622-9000
Fax: 989-837-4484
career@northwood.edu
www.northwood.edu

- Dave Marsh, Athletic Director
(989) 837-4389
dmarsh@northwood.edu
- Krista Plummer, Assistant Athletic Director
(989) 837-4817
plummek@northwood.edu
- Kate Dornbos, Head Athletic Trainer
(989) 837-4387
dornbosk@northwood.edu
- Travis McCurdy, Sports Information Director
(989) 837-4239
mccurdyt@northwood.edu

NOTRE DAME COLLEGE ATHLETICS
4545 COLLEGE ROAD
SOUTH EUCLID, OH 44121
216-373-5138
877-632-6446
Fax: 216-373-5400
www.notredamefalcons.com
- Scott Swain, Director of Athletics
(216) 373-6365
sswain@ndc.edu
- John Van Benschoten, Assistant Athletic Director
(216) 373-6362
jvanben@ndc.edu
- Isaac Hunt, Manager of Sports Information
(216) 373-6342
ihunt@ndc.edu
- Matt Murphy, Manager of Athletic Operations
(216) 373-5171
mmurphy@ndc.edu
- Jay Garfield, Head Athletic Trainer
(216) 373-5354
jgarfield@ndc.edu

NOTRE DAME DE NAMUR UNIVERSITY ATHLETICS
1500 RALSTON AVENUE
BELMONT, CA 94002
650-508-3500
Fax: 650-508-3691
www.ndnuargos.com
- Joshua Doody, Director of Athletics
(650) 508-3638
jdoody@ndnu.edu
- George Puou, Assistant Athletics Director
(650) 508-3655
- Scott Kimmelman, Sports Information Director
(650) 508-3690
- Christian Stamates, Athletic Trainer
(650) 508-3448

NYACK COLLEGE ATHLETICS
1 SOUTH BOULEVARD
NYACK, NY 10960
845-675-4776 EXT 181
Fax: 845-353-2147
athletics.nyack.edu
- Keith Davie, Athletic Director
(845) 675-4770
keith.davie@nyack.edu
- Amanda Aikens, Assistant Athletic Director
(845) 675-4772
mandy.aikens@nyack.edu
- Matt Cornacchione, Director of Athletic Facilities
(845) 675-4787
- Penny Foland, Head Athletic Trainer
(845) 675-4780
penny.foland@nyack.edu

OAKLAND UNIVERSITY ATHLETICS
ATHLETICS DEPARTMENT
201 ATHLETICS CENTER
ROCHESTER, MI 48309
248-370-3190
Fax: 248-370-4056
www.goldengrizzlies.com
- George W. Hynd, President
(248) 370-3500
- Jeff Konya, Director of Athletics
(248) 370-2669
- Marshall Foley, Associate Athletic Director
(248) 370-4004
- Evan Dermidoff, Athletics Academic Adviser
(248) 370-3224
dermido2@oakland.edu

OKLAHOMA BAPTIST UNIVERSITY ATHLETICS
500 WEST UNIVERSITY
SHAWNEE, OK 74804
405-275-2850
www.obubison.com
- Robert Davenport, Director of Athletics
(405) 585-5300
robert.davenport@okbu.edu
- Steve Fluke, Associate Athletics Director for Compliance
(405) 585-5305
robert.davenport@okbu.edu
- Anna Howle, Assistant Athletics Director
(405) 585-5355
anna.howle@okbu.edu
- Ray Fink, Director of Athletic Media Relations
(405) 585-5304

OKLAHOMA CHRISTIAN UNVERSITY ATHLETICS
2501 EAST MEMORIAL ROAD
EDMOND, OK 73013
405-425-5350
800-877-5010
Fax: 405-425-5351
athletics@oc.edu
www.oceagles.com
- David Lynn, Director of Athletics
(405) 425-5358
david.lynn@oc.edu
- Curtis McAuliff, Director of Athletic Training
(405) 425-1960
curtis.mcauliff@oc.edu
- Sydney Ringer, Head Athletic Trainer
(405) 425-1961
sydney.ringer@oc.edu

OUACHITA BAPTIST UNIVERSITY ATHLETICS
410 OUACHITA STREET
OBU BOX 378
ARKADELPHIA, AR 71998-0001
870-245-5181
Fax: 870-245-5598
www.obutigers.com
- David Sharp, Director of Athletics
(870) 245-5182
sharpd@obu.edu
- Margaret McGraw, Assistant Athletic Director
(870) 245-5397
- Kyle Parris, Sports Information Director
(870) 245-5186
- Terry DeWitt, Coordinator of Athletic Training

(870) 245-5264
dewitt@obu.edu

PACE UNIVERSITY ATHLETICS
ATHLETICS DEPARTMENT
861 BEDFORD ROAD
PLEASANTVILLE, NY 10570
914-773-3411
Fax: 914-773-3491
mbrown@pace.edu
www.paceuathletics.com
- Mark R. Brown, Director of Athletics
(914) 773-3285
mbrownn@pace.edu
- Mike Winn, Associate Athletics Director
(914) 773-3272
mwinn@pace.edu
- David Spiegel, Director of Athletic Communications
(914) 773-3888
dspiegel@pace.edu

PAINE COLLEGE
1235 FIFTEENTH STREET
AUGUSTA, GA 30901
706-821-8200
Fax: 706-396-8154
www.paineathletics.com
- Selina B. Kohn, Director of Athletics
(706) 821-8428
skohn@paine.edu
- J.C. Gafford, Sports Information Director
(706) 821-8438
jgafford@paine.edu
- Lisa Branon, Athletic Trianer
(706) 396-7567
lbranon@paine.edu

PALM BEACH ATLANTIC UNIVERSITY ATHLETICS
901 SOUTH FLAGLER DRIVE
WEST PALM BEACH, FL 33401
561-803-2333
Fax: 561-803-2532
pbasailfish.com
- Carolyn Stone, Director of Athletics
(561) 803-2333
carolyn_stone@pba.edu
- Michael Brown, Senior Associate Athletic Director
(561) 803-2529
michael_brown@pba.edu
- Goeun Lee, Assistant Athletic Director for Compliance
(561) 803-2399
goeun_lee@pba.edu
- Chi Ly, Student-Athlete Development Coordinator
(561) 803-2520
chi_ly@pba.edu
- TJ Budd, Sports Information Director
(561) 803-2525
tj_budd@pba.edu
- Sam Eisen, Head Athletic Trainer
(561) 803-2338
sam_eisen@pba.edu

PANHANDLE STATE UNIVERSITY ATHLETICS
PO BOX 430
GOODWELL, OK 73939
580-349-2611
800-664-6778
Fax: 580-349-2302
www.opsuaggies.com
- Wayne Stewart, Athletic Director
(580) 349-1408

college sports

rwstewart@opsu.edu
• Justine Gaskamp, Sports Information Director
(580) 349-1354
• Brian Lankford, Head Athletic Trainer
(580) 349-1338
brian@opsu.edu

PFEIFFER UNIVERSITY ATHLETICS
48380 US HIGHWAY 52
MISENHEIMER, NC 28109
704-521-9116
Fax: 704-463-5051
gofalconsports.com
• Bob Reasso, Vice President for Athletics
(704) 463-3203
• Tony Faticoni, Deputy Director of Athletics
(704) 463-3214
tony.faticoni@pfeiffer.edu
• Jeremy Zalacca, Director for Athletic Communications
(704) 463-3192
• Robyn Horner, Assistant Athletic Director
(704) 463-3227

PHILADELPHIA UNIVERSITY ATHLETICS
4201 HENRY AVENUE
PHILADELPHIA, PA 19144
215-951-2720
Fax: 215-951-2775
www.philaurams.com
• Tom Shirley, Director of Athletics
(215) 951-2720
shirleyt@philau.edu
• Rose Kelly, Assistant Director of Athletics
(215) 951-5638
kellyr@philau.edu
• Chris O'Brien, Assistant Director of Athletics
(215) 951-5943
obrienc@philau.edu

PITTSBURG STATE UNIVERSITY ATHLETICS
1701 BROADWAY STREET
PITTSBURG, KS 66762
620-231-7000
Fax: 620-235-4661
www.pittstategorillas.com
• Jim Johnson, Athletic Director
(620) 235-4389
jjohnson@pittstate.edu
• Russ Jewett, Senior Associate Athletic Director
(620) 235-4659
rjewett@pittstate.edu
• Phil Carr, Head Athletic Trainer
(620) 249-4401
pcarr@pittstate.edu
• Dan Wilkes, Associate Director Of Communications
(620) 235-4138
dwilkes@pittstate.edu

PITTSBURGH-JOHNSTOWN ATHLETICS, UNIVERSITY OF
450 SCHOOLHOUSE ROAD
JOHNSTOWN, PA 15904
814-269-7000
Fax: 814-269-2026
pittjohnstownathletics.com
• Pat Pecora, Athletic Director
(814) 269-2001
ppecora@pitt.edu
• Chris Caputo, Sports Information Director
(814) 269-2031
ccaputo@pitt.edu

• Elissa Till, Head Athletic Trainer
(814) 269-1935
till@pitt.edu

POINT LOMA NAZARENE UNIVERSITY ATHLETICS
3900 LOMALAND DRIVE
SAN DIEGO, CA 92106
619-849-2265
Fax: 619-849-2553
www.plnusealions.com
• Ethan Hamilton, Athletic Director
(619) 849-2265
ethanhamilton@pointloma.edu
• Brian Thornton, Senior Associate Athletic Director
(619) 849-2944
brianthornton@pointloma.edu
• Steven Riddle, Assistant Athletic Director
(619) 849-2268
steveriddle@pointloma.edu
• Shawna Baker, Head Athletic Trainer
(619) 849-2914
shawnabaker@pointloma.edu

PRESBYTERIAN COLLEGE ATHLETICS
PRESBYTERIAN COLLEGE ATHLETICS
105 ASHLAND AVENUE
CLINTON, SC 29325
864-833-8240
Fax: 864-833-8323
www.gobluehose.com
• Ed Steers, Interim Athletic Director
(864) 833-8242
• James Downer, Senior Associate Athletic Director
(864) 833-8253
jmdowner@presby.edu
• Simon Whitaker, Director of Sports Information
(864) 833-8252
swhitaker@presby.edu

QUEENS COLLEGE (NEW YORK) ATHLETICS
65-30 KISSENA BOULEVARD
QUEENS, NY 11367
718-997-2795
Fax: 718-997-5745
athleticsinfo@qc.cuny.edu
www.queensknights.com
• China Jude, Assistant Vice President, Athletics
(718) 997-2795
• Rob Twible, Associate Athletics Director, Facilities
(718) 997-2754
robert.twible@qc.cuny.edu

QUEENS UNIVERSITY OF CHARLOTTE
1900 SELWYN AVENUE
CHARLOTTE, NC 28274
704-337-2509
800-849-8400
Fax: 704-337-2237
www.queensathletics.com
• Cherie Swarthout, Interim Director of Athletics
(704) 688-2809
swarthoutc@queens.edu
• Robbie Garriett, Coordinator of Administrative Services
(704) 337-2509
garriettr@queens.edu
• Tim Burke, Assistant Athletic Director
(704) 688-2818
burket@queens.edu

QUINCY UNIVERSITY ATHLETICS
1800 COLLEGE AVENUE
QUINCY, IL 62301
217-222-8020
Fax: 217-228-5034
quhawks.com
• Marty Bell, Vice President of Intercollegiate Athletics
(217) 228-5432
bellma@quincy.edu
• Danielle Surprenant, Associate Athletic Director
(217) 228-5432
• Mike Davis, Assistant Athletic Director
(217) 228-5432
• Stephanie Killday, Athletic Trainer
(217) 228-5432

REGIS UNIVERSITY ATHLETICS
3333 REGIS BOULEVARD
DENVER, CO 80221-1099
303-458-4070
800-388-2366
Fax: 303-964-5499
dspafford@regis.edu
www.regisrangers.com
• David Spafford, Interim Director of Athletics
(303) 964-6648
dspafford@regis.edu
• Kelly McLaughlin, Associate Athletic Director
(303) 458-4071
kmclaughlin001@regis.edu
• Whitney Lawler, Sports Information Director
(303) 458-4052
wfranker@regis.edu

ROCKHURST UNIVERSITY ATHLETICS
1100 ROCKHURST ROAD
KANSAS CITY, MO 64110
816-501-4000
Fax: 816-501-4241
gary.burns@rockhurst.edu
www.rockhursthawks.com
• Gary Burns, Director of Athletics
(816) 501-4854
• Kathy Strecker, Assistant Director of Athletics
(816) 501-4857
kathleen.strecker@rockhurst.edu
• John Dodderidge, Sports Information Director
(816) 501-4850
john.dodderidge@rockhurst.edu
• Jaime Rojas, Head Athletic Trainer
(720) 778-6490
jaime.rojas@rockhurst.edu

ROLLINS COLLEGE ATHLETICS
1000 HOLT AVENUE
WINTER PARK, FL 32789
407-646-2000
Fax: 407-646-1562
pparker@rollins.edu
www.rollinssports.com
• Pennie Parker, Director of Athletics
(407) 646-2636
pparker@rollins.edu
• Margie Sullivan, Assistant Athletics Director
(407) 646-2531
msullivan@rollins.edu
• Paul Giannotti, Director of Sports Medicine
(407) 646-2361
pgiannotti@rollins.edu

• Clay Starrett, Director for Athletic
Communications
(407) 646-2661
cstarrett@rollins.edu

**SAGINAW VALLEY STATE UNIVERSITY
ATHLETICS**
7400 BAY ROAD
UNIVERSITY CENTER, MI 48710-0001
989-964-4000
Fax: 989-964-7389
sid@svsu.edu
www.svsucardinals.com
• Mike Watson, Athletic Director
(989) 964-7306
mewatson@svsu.edu
• Angela Pohl, Associate Athletic Director
(989) 964-7311
aspohl@svsu.edu
• Eric Brookhouse, Director of Athletic
Media Relations
(989) 964-4053
embrookh@svsu.edu

SAINT ANSELM COLLEGE ATHLETICS
100 SAINT ANSELM DRIVE
PO BOX 1727
MANCHESTER, NH 03102
603-641-7800
Fax: 603-641-7172
athletics@anselm.edu
www.saintanselmhawks.com
• Daron Montgomery, Director of Athletics
(603) 641-7800
dmontgomery@anselm.edu
• Neil Duval, Associate Director of Athletics
(603) 641-7802
nduval@anselm.edu
• Chris Barroso, Director of Athletic
Communications
(603) 641-7810
cbarroso@anselm.edu
• Michael Sirois, Head Athletic Trainer
(603) 641-7807
msirois@anselm.edu

SAINT JOSEPH'S COLLEGE ATHLETICS
PO BOX 870
RENSSELAER, IN 47978
219-866-6000
Fax: 219-866-6276
athletics.saintjoe.edu
• Bill Massoels, Athletic Director
• Linda Deno, Associate Director of Athletics
(219) 866-6275
• Ken Badylak, Sports Information Director
(219) 866-6141

SAINT LEO UNIVERSITY
33701 STATE ROAD 52
PO BOX 6665
SAINT LEO, FL 33574
800-334-5532
800-334-5532
Fax: 912-353-9937
fran.reidy@saintleo.edu
www.saintleolions.com
• William J. Lennox, University President
(352) 588-8242
• Francis X. Reidy, Director of Athletics
fran.reidy@saintleo.edu
• Michelle Edwards, Associate Athletic
Director
(352) 588-7314
michelle.edwards05@saintleo.edu
• Barbara Wilson, Director of Sports
Medicine

(352) 588-8222
barbara.wilson@saintleo.edu

SAINT MARTIN'S COLLEGE ATHLETICS
5300 PACIFIC AVENUE SE
LACEY, WA 98503
360-438-4305
Fax: 360-412-6191
bgrisham@stmartin.edu
www.smusaints.com
• Bob Grisham, Athletic Director
(360) 438-4368
bgrisham@stmartin.edu
• Chris Gregor, Associate Athletic Director
(360) 438-4510
cgregor@stmartin.edu
• Austin Byrnes, Sports Information Director
(360) 438-4328
aloebsack@stmartin.edu
• Ramzy Assaf, Assistant Athletic Trainer
(360) 438-4536
rassaf@stmartin.edu

SAINT ROSE ATHLETICS, COLLEGE OF
432 WESTERN AVENUE
ALBANY, NY 12203
518-454-5158
Fax: 518-458-5457
gogoldenknights.com
• Catherine Cummings Haker, Director of
Athletics
(518) 454-5282
• David Alexander, Director for
Communications
(518) 458-5491
alexandd@strose.edu
• Lisa Geiger, Director for Athletic Training
(518) 454-2009
geigerl@strose.edu

**SALEM INTERNATIONAL UNIVERSITY
ATHLETICS**
223 WEST MAIN STREET
SALEM, WV 26426
304-782-6143
800-283-4562
Fax: 304-782-5246
www.siutigerpride.com
• Florin Marton, Athletic Director
(304) 326-1540
fmarton@salemu.edu
• Steve Potts, Assistant Athletic Director
(304) 326-1394
spotts@salemu.edu
• Douglas Page, Sports Information Director
(304) 326-1299
• Tera Fetty, Head Athletic Trainer
(304) 326-1561
tfetty@salemu.edu

**SAN FRANCISCO STATE UNIVERSITY
ATHLETICS**
1600 HOLLOWAY AVENUE
SAN FRANCISCO, CA 94132
415-338-2218
Fax: 415-338-1967
charlesg@sfsu.edu
www.sfstategators.com
• Charles Guthrie, Director Of Athletics
(415) 338-1579
• Joey Logan, Associate Athletic Director
For Compliance
(415) 338-2485
• Cathy McDermott, Assistant Director of
Athletics for Developme
(415) 338-1193
• Trevor Getz, Faculty Athletic

Representative
(415) 338-2716
tgetz@sfsu.edu

**SCIENCES IN PHILADELPHIA
ATHLETICS, UNIVERSITY OF THE**
600 SOUTH 43RD STREET
PHILADELPHIA, PA 19104-4495
215-895-3133
athletics@usciences.edu
www.devilsathletics.com
• Marc Caserio, Athletic Director
(215) 596-7432
m.caseri@usciences.edu
• Scott Sisson, Associate Athletic Director
(215) 895-1109
s.sisson@usciences.edu
• Nicole Shipos, Head Athletic Trainer
(215) 596-7430

SHAW UNIVERSITY ATHLETICS
118 EAST SOUTH STREET
RALEIGH, NC 27601
919-546-8200
Fax: 919-546-8444
alcarter@shawu.edu
www.shawbears.com
• Alfonza Carter, Director of Athletics
(919) 546-8527
alcarter@shawu.edu
• Jacques Curtis, Associate Athletic Director
(919) 546-8597
jcurtis@shawu.edu
• Jolisa Williams, Sports Information
Director
(919) 546-8311
jamesm@shawu.edu
• David Mills, Director of Sports Medicine
(919) 546-8582
dmills@shawu.edu

**SHIPPENSBURG UNIVERSITY OF
PENNSYLVANIA ATHLETICS**
1871 OLD MAIN DRIVE
SHIPPENSBURG, PA 17257
717-477-1711
Fax: 717-477-4090
www.ship.edu
• Jeff Michaels, Director of Athletics
(717) 477-1711
• Carrie Michaels, Associate Director of
Athletics
(717) 477-1711
camichaels@ship.edu
• Ashley Grimm, Assistant Director of
Athletics
(717) 477-1711
ajgrimm@ship.edu
• Wes Mallicone, Director of Sports
Medicine
(717) 477-1749
wrmall@ship.edu
• Bill Morgal, Sports Information Director
(717) 477-1206
wjmorgal@ship.edu

SHORTER UNIVERSITY ATHLETICS
315 SHORTER AVENUE
ROME, GA 30165
706-233-7347
Fax: 706-233-7575
goshorterhawks.com
• Aaron Kelton, Interim Athletic Director
(706) 233-7469
• Amber Lee, Senior Woman Administrator
(706) 233-7348
• Karen Allen, Assistant Athletic Director

(706) 233-7966
kallen@shorter.edu
• Andre Roach, Associate Athletic Director
(706) 233-7468
aroach@shorter.edu

SIMON FRASER UNIVERSITY ATHLETICS
8888 UNIVERSITY DRIVE
BURNABY, BC, CANADA V5A 1S6
778-782-3111
athletics.sfu.ca
• Theresa Hanson, Senior Director of
Athletics
theresa_hanson@sfu.ca
• Shelley Howieson, Manager of Facilities
(778) 782-3931
howieson@sfu.ca
• Kelly Weber, Manager of Compliance
(778) 782-3314
weber@sfu.ca
• Steve Frost, Sports Information
Coordinator
(778) 782-4057
sfrost@sfu.ca

**SIOUX FALLS ATHLETICS, UNIVERSITY
OF**
1101 WEST 22ND STREET
SIOUX FALLS, SD 57105
605-331-6791
Fax: 605-331-6792
athletics.web@usiouxfalls.edu
www.usfcougars.com
• Josh Snyder, Athletic Director
(605) 331-6895
• Pam Gohl, Associate Athletic Director
(605) 331-6652
• Ben Krush, Assistant Athletic Director
(605) 575-2032
• Dan Genzler, Sports Information Director
(605) 331-6774
• Zach Mathers, Head Athletic Trainer
(605) 575-2035

**SLIPPERY ROCK UNIVERSITY
ATHLETICS**
1 MORROW WAY
SLIPPERY ROCK, PA 16057
724-738-2027
Fax: 724-738-4797
www.rockathletics.com
• Paul Lueken, Director of Athletics
(724) 738-2767
paul.lueken@sru.edu
• Torry Rollins, Associate Athletic Director
(724) 738-4491
torry.rollins@sru.edu
• Jon Holtz, Director of Athletic
Communication
(724) 738-4925
jonathan.holtz@sru.edu

**SOUTH CAROLINA-SPARTANBURG
ATHLETICS, UNIVERSITY OF**
800 UNIVERSITY WAY
SPARTANBURG, SC 29303
864-503-5141
Fax: 864-503-5130
info@uscupstate.edu
www.upstatespartans.com
• Julio Freire, Athletic Director
(864) 503-5140
• Michael Sandago, Director of Sports
Medicine
(864) 503-5104
ssandago@uscupstate.edu
• Kanett Haynes, Athletics Business

Manager
(864) 503-5173
khaynes@uscupstate.edu

**SOUTH DAKOTA STATE UNIVERSITY
ATHLETICS**
2820 STANLEY J. MARSHALL CENTER
BROOKINGS, SD 57007
605-688-5625
Fax: 605-688-5999
Justin.Sell@sdstate.edu
www.gojacks.com
• Justin Sell, Director of Athletics
(605) 688-6388
justin.sell@sdstate.edu
• Jennifer Sell, Director of Academics
(605) 688-4094
jennifer.sell@sdstate.edu
• Jonathan Treiber, Director of Athletic
Marketing
(605) 688-6747
jonathan.treiber@sdstate.edu

**SOUTHEASTERN OKLAHOMA STATE
UNIVERSITY ATHLETICS**
1405 NORTH 4TH
DURANT, OK 74701
580-745-2000
800-435-1327
Fax: 580-745-7493
www.se.edu
• Keith Baxter, Director of Athletics
(580) 745-2250
kbaxter@se.edu
• Cherrie Wilmoth, Associate Athletics
Director
(580) 745-2690
cwilmoth@se.edu
• Blake Allen, Assistant Athletics Director
(580) 745-3386
ballen@se.edu
• Matt Thomas, Sports Information Director
(580) 745-2646
mthomas@se.edu
• Scott Willman, Head Athletic Trainer
(580) 745-2026

**SOUTHERN COLORADO ATHLETICS,
UNIVERSITY OF**
MASSARI ARENA
2200 BONFORTE BOULEVARD
PUEBLO, CO 81001
719-549-2711
Fax: 719-549-2570
www.gothunderwolves.com
• Joe Folda, Director of Athletics
(719) 549-2730
joe.folda@csupueblo.edu
• Jackie Wallgren, Associate Athletic
Director
(719) 549-2021
jackie.wallgren@csupueblo.edu
• Racheal Morris, Associate Athletic Director
(719) 549-2013
racheal.morris@csupueblo.edu
• Dax Larson, Athletic Media Relations
Director
(719) 549-2022
dax.larson@csupueblo.edu
• Roger Clark, Director of Athletic Training
(719) 549-2530
roger.clark@csupueblo.edu

**SOUTHERN CONNECTICUT STATE
UNIVERSITY ATHLETICS**
MOORE FIELDHOUSE
125 WINTERGREEN AVENUE
NEW HAVEN, CT 06515
203-392-6045
Fax: 203-392-6006
www.southernctowls.com
• Jay Moran, Director of Athletics
(203) 392-6045
moranj15@southernct.edu
• Michael Kobylanski, Associate Director of
Athletics Communications
(203) 392-6005
• Joe Hines, Interim Coordinator of Athletic
Facilities
(203) 392-6016
hinesj1@southernct.edu
• Carol Nelson, Head Athletic Trainer
(203) 392-6007

**SOUTHERN INDIANA ATHLETICS,
UNIVERSITY OF**
8600 UNIVERSITY BOULEVARD
EVANSVILLE, IN 47712
812-464-1846
Fax: 812-465-1129
www.gousieagles.com
• Jon Mark Hall, Director of Athletics
(812) 464-1846
jmhall@usi.edu
• Alex Eaton, Associate Director of Athletics
(812) 464-1841
aceaton1@usi.edu
• Mandi Fulton, Assistant Director of
Athletics
(812) 465-1022
mfulton@usi.edu
• Scott Hooker, Head Athletic Trainer
(812) 465-1298
sjhooker@usi.edu
• Ray Simmons, Director of Athletic
Communications
(812) 465-1622
rsimmons@usi.edu

**SOUTHERN NAZARENE UNIVERSITY
ATHLETICS**
6729 NORTHWEST 39TH EXPRESSWAY
BETHANY, OK 73008
405-789-6400
Fax: 405-491-6387
www.snuathletics.com
• Bobby Martin, Director of Athletics
(405) 491-6339
bgmartin@snu.edu
• Paul McGrady, Associate Director of
Athletics
(405) 491-6338
pmcgrady@snu.edu
• Kathy League, Assistant Athletics Director
(405) 717-6280
kleague@snu.edu
• David Noblett, Director of Athletics
Communications
(405) 491-6619
• Mike Mathis, Head Athletic Trainer
(405) 717-6236
mmathis@snu.edu

**SOUTHERN NEW HAMPSHIRE
UNIVERSITY ATHLETICS**
2500 NORTH RIVER ROAD
MANCHESTER, NH 03106
603-645-9604
Fax: 603-645-9686

info@snhu.edu
www.snhupenmen.com
• Anthony Fallacaro, Director of Athletics
(603) 645-9604
a.fallacaro@snhu.edu
• Tom Wilkins, Associate Director of
Athletics
(603) 645-9786
t.wilkins@snhu.edu
• Shawn Green, Assistant Director of
Athletics
(603) 645-9783
s.green@snhu.edu
• Eric Coplin, Director of Athletics
Communications
(603) 645-9638
e.coplin@snhu.edu

SOUTHERN WESLEYAN UNIVERSITY ATHLETICS
907 WESLEYAN DRIVE
CENTRAL, SC 29630
864-644-5000
877-644-5556
swuathletics.com
• Chris Williams, Director of Athletics
(864) 644-5303
• Becky Bowman, Director of Compliance
(864) 644-5307
• Grace Eckert, Sports Information Director
(864) 644-5308
geckert@swu.edu

SOUTHWEST BAPTIST UNIVERSITY ATHLETICS
1600 UNIVERSITY AVENUE
BOLIVAR, MO 65613
417-328-1948
Fax: 417-328-2009
mpitts@sbuniv.edu
sbubearcats.com
• Mike Pitts, Director of Athletics
(417) 328-1412
mpitts@sbuniv.edu
• Chris Martin, Assistant Athletics Director
(417) 328-1784
ccmartin@sbuniv.edu
• Jeff Weseloh, Director of Athletics Media
Relations
(417) 328-1799
• Mike Wolhoy, Head Athletic Trainer
(417) 328-3296
mwolhoy@sbuniv.edu

SOUTHWEST STATE UNIVERSITY ATHLETICS
1501 STATE STREET
MARSHALL, MN 56258
507-537-7271
Fax: 507-537-6578
smsumustangs.com
• Rick Hart, Director of Athletics
(507) 537-7984
• Kelly Loft, Athletic Communications
Director
(507) 537-7177
kelly.loft@smsu.edu
• Tim Steinbach, Athletic Development
Director
(507) 537-7204
tim.steinbach@smsu.edu
• Jenn Graven, Director of Marketing and
Promotions
(507) 537-6233
jennifer.graven@smsu.edu
• Laura Crowell, Head Athletic Trainer

(507) 537-7165
laura.crowell@smsu.edu

SOUTHWESTERN OKLAHOMA STATE UNIVERSITY ATHLETICS
100 CAMPUS DRIVE
WEATHERFORD, OK 73096
580-774-3068
Fax: 580-774-7106
todd.thurman@swosu.edu
www.swosuathletics.com
• Todd Thurman, Director of Athletics
(580) 774-3701
todd.thurman@swosu.edu
• Doug Self, Sports Information Director
(580) 774-7162
doug.self@swosu.edu
• Edwin Detweiler, Head Athletic Trainer
(580) 774-3073
edwin.detweiler@swosu.edu

SPRINGFIELD COLLEGE ATHLETICS
263 ALDEN STREET
SPRINGFIELD, MA 01109
413-748-3692
Fax: 413-748-3022
athleticdirector@springfieldcollege.edu
www.springfieldcollegepride.com
• Craig Poisson, Director of Athletics
(413) 748-3333
athleticdirector@springfieldcollege.edu
• Kiki Jacobs, Associate Director of Athletics
(413) 748-3334
• Barclay Dugger, Coordinator of Athletic
Training Services
(413) 748-3650
rdugger@springfieldcollege.edu
• Brian Magoffin, Director of Sports
Communications
(413) 748-3341
bmagoffin@springfieldcollege.edu

ST. AUGUSTINE'S UNIVERSITY ATHLETICS
1315 OAKWOOD AVENUE
RALEIGH, NC 24610
919-516-4250
Fax: 919-516-4639
saintaugfalcons.com
• Everett B. Ward, President
(919) 516-4200
• George Williams, Athletic Director
(919) 516-4236
gdwilliams@st-aug.edu
• Anthony Jeffries, Sports Information
Director
(919) 516-4517
awjeffries@st-aug.edu
• LaKida Whetstone, Head Athletic Trainer
(919) 516-4219
lmwhetstone@st-aug.edu

ST. CLOUD STATE UNIVERSITY ATHLETICS
720 FOURTH AVENUE SOUTH
ST. CLOUD, MN 56301-4498
320-308-0121
Fax: 320-308-6164
hlweems@stcloudstate.edu
www.scsuhuskies.com
• Heather Weems, Director of Athletics
(320) 308-3102
hlweems@stcloudstate.edu
• Chad Sheetz, Associate Athletics Director
of Operations
(320) 308-4910
• Nate Swenson, Assistant AD Of Marketing

& Promotions
(320) 308-2137
nsswenson@stcloudstate.edu
• Thomas Nelson, Director of Athletic Media
Relations
(320) 308-5400
tcnelson@stcloudstate.edu

ST. EDWARDS UNIVERSITY ATHLETICS
3001 SOUTH CONGRESS AVENUE
AUSTIN, TX 78704
512-448-8448
Fax: 512-416-5834
athl@stedwards.edu
athletics.stedwards.edu
• Debbie Taylor, Athletic Director
(512) 448-8744
deboraw@stedwards.edu
• Melinda Terry, Associate Athletic Director
(512) 233-1637
• Jameson Adams, Associate Athletic
Director
(512) 233-1495
• Lisa Lowe, Assistant Athletic Director
(512) 448-8498

ST. FRANCIS COLLEGE ATHLETICS
180 REMSEN STREET
BROOKLYN HEIGHTS, NY 11201
718-489-5490
Fax: 718-797-2140
www.sfcathletics.com
• Irma Garcia, Director of Athletics
igarcia@sfc.edu
• Anthony Kurtin, Associate Director of
Athletics
akurtin@sfc.edu
• Carl Quigley, Assistant Athletic Director
cquigley@sfc.edu
• Jim Hoffman, Director of Compliance
jhoffman@sfc.edu
• Meghan O'Brien, Director of Athletic
Marketing/Senior Woman A
mobrien@sfc.edu

ST. MICHAEL'S COLLEGE ATHLETICS
ONE WINOOSKI PARK
COLCHESTER, VT 05439
802-654-2450
802-654-2000
Fax: 802-654-2497
www.smcathletics.com
• Chris Kenny, Director of Athletics
(802) 654-2200
ckenny@smcvt.edu
• Meggan Dulude, Associate Director of
Athletics
(802) 654-2506
mdulude@smcvt.edu
• Tacy Lincoln, Associate Director of
Athletics
(802) 654-2507
tlincoln@smcvt.edu
• Josh Kessler, Director of Athletic
Communications
(802) 654-2537
jkessler@smcvt.edu
• Renee Breault, Head Athletic Trainer
(802) 654-2496
rbreault2@smcvt.edu

ST. THOMAS AQUINAS COLLEGE ATHLETICS
125 ROUTE 340
SPARKILL, NY 10976

845-398-4000
Fax: 914-359-8136
www.stacathletics.com
• Gerry Oswald, Athletics Director
(845) 398-4186
goswald@stac.edu
• Nicole Ryan, Associate Athletic
Director/SWA
(845) 398-4163
goswald@stac.edu
• Kim Lusk, Assistant Athletic Director
(845) 398-4026
• Lori Rahaim, Head Athletic Trainer
(845) 398-4057
lrahaim@stac.edu

STATE UNIVERSITY OF WEST GEORGIA ATHLETICS
1601 MAPLE STREET
CARROLLTON, GA 30118
678-839-6533
Fax: 678-839-6538
www.uwgsports.com
• Daryl Dickey, Athletic Director
(678) 839-6539
• Laura Clayton, Assistant Athletic Director
(678) 839-3964
lclayton@westga.edu
• Skip Fite, Head Baseball Coach
(678) 839-3956
• Michael Cooney, Men's Basketball Coach
(678) 839-3974
mcooney@westga.edu
• Scott Groninger, Women's Basketball
Coach
(678) 839-3967
sgroning@westga.edu

STILLMAN COLLEGE ATHLETICS
BATCHELOR HALL
3601 STILLMAN BOULEVARD
TUSCALOOSA, AL 35403
205-366-8980
Fax: 205-366-8865
• Donte Jackson, Director of Athletics
(205) 366-8980
djackson@stillman.edu
• Daphne Hood, Assistant Athletic Director
(205) 247-8184
dhood@stillman.edu
• Joel Worthington, Sports Information
Director
(205) 247-8101
jworthington@stillman.edu
• Pam Phillips, Senior Women's
Administrator
(205) 247-8041

STONEHILL COLLEGE ATHLETICS
320 WASHINGTON STREET
NORTH EASTON, MA 02357
508-565-1384
Fax: 508-565-1460
www.stonehillskyhawks.com
• Dean O'Keefe, Director of Athletics
(508) 565-1384
dokeefe@stonehill.edu
• MacDonald Cindy, Sr. Associate Director
of Athletics
(508) 565-1064
cmacdonald@stonehill.edu
• Doug Monson, Director of Athletic
Communications
(508) 565-1352
dmonson@stonehill.edu
• Pete Krysko, Head Athletic Trainer

(508) 565-1514
pkrysko@stonehill.edu

TAMPA ATHLETICS, UNIVERSITY OF
401 WEST KENNEDY BOULEVARD
BOX 1
TAMPA, FL 33606
813-253-6240
Fax: 813-253-6288
tampaspartans.com
• Larry Marfise, Athletic Director
(813) 257-3100
lmarfise@ut.edu
• Tom Kolbe, Assistant Athletic Director,
Communications
(813) 257-3473
tkolbe@ut.edu
• Scott Brickett, Assistant Athletic Director,
Sports Medicine
(813) 257-3264
wbrickett@ut.edu

TARLETON STATE UNIVERSITY ATHLETICS
BOX T-0080
DEPARTMENT OF ATHLETICS
STEPHENVILLE, TX 76402
254-968-9178
Fax: 254-968-9674
www.tarletonsports.com
• Lonn Reisman, Athletics Director
reisman@tarleton.edu
• Troy Jones, Assistant Athletics Director,
Operations
(254) 968-9546
tjones01@tarleton.edu
• Nathan Bural, Director of Athletic
Communications
(254) 968-1802
bural@tarleton.edu
• Rod Cole, Director for Athletic
Performance
(254) 968-9671
rcole@tarleton.edu
• Adam Deimling, Head Athletic Trainer
(254) 968-1809

TEXAS A&M INTERNATIONAL UNIVERSITY ATHLETICS
5201 UNIVERSITY BOULEVARD
LAREDO, TX 78041-1900
956-326-3000
Fax: 956-326-2889
www.godustdevils.com
• Pablo Arenaz, President
(956) 326-2320
pablo.arenaz@tamiu.edu
• Griz Zimmermann, Director of Athletics
(956) 326-2890
griz@tamiu.edu
• Daniel Lathey, Associate Athletic Director
(956) 326-2892
• Amanda Ruthman, Sports Information
Director
(956) 326-3007

TEXAS A&M UNIVERSITY-COMMERCE ATHLETICS
PO BOX 3011
COMMERCE, TX 75429
903-886-5558
Fax: 903-468-3033
timm@tamuc.edu
www.lionathletics.com
• Tim McMurray, Director of Athletics
(903) 886-5568
timm@tamuc.edu

• Conner Moreno, Assistant AD For
International Operations
(903) 468-8760
conner.moreno@tamuc.edu
• Dustan Thrift, Director of Sports Medicine
(903) 468-3035
dustan.thrift@tamuc.edu
• Josh Manck, Assistant AD For
Communications
(903) 886-5131
josh.manck@tamuc.edu
• Chase Stoltenberg, Assistant Athletics
Trainer
(903) 468-3193
chase.stoltenberg@tamuc.edu

TEXAS A&M UNIVERSITY-KINGSVILLE ATHLETICS
700 UNIVERSITY BOULEVARD
MSC 202
KINGSVILLE, TX 78363
361-593-2800
Fax: 361-593-3587
www.javelinaathletics.com
• D. Scott Gines, Vice President of
Intercollegiate Athletics
(361) 593-2800
• Ruben Cantu, Head Athletic Trainer
(361) 593-2493
• Kelvin Queliz, Director of Sports
Information
(361) 593-2870

TIFFIN UNIVERSITY ATHLETICS
155 MIAMI STREET
TIFFIN, OH 44883
419-448-3359
www.gotiffindragons.com
• Lonny Allen, Athletic Director
(419) 448-3359
lallen@tiffin.edu
• Darby Roggow, Assistant Athletic Director
(419) 448-3425
• Shane O'Donnell, Sports Information
Director
(419) 448-3288
sodonnel@tiffin.edu

TOCCOA FALLS COLLEGE ATHLETICS
107 KINCAID DRIVE
TOCCOA FALLS, GA 30598
706-886-6831
athletic@tfc.edu
www.tfc.edu
• Kevin Hall, Athletic Director
khall@tfc.edu
• Jeff Mullikin, Assistant Athletic Director
jmullikin@tfc.edu
• Kaelyn Watson, Sports Information
Director
kwatson@tfc.edu

TREVECCA NAZARENE UNIVERSITY ATHLETICS
333 MURFREESBORO ROAD
NASHVILLE, TN 37210-2877
615-248-1606
Fax: 615-248-1565
www.tnutrojans.com
• Mark Elliott, Director of Athletics
(615) 248-1275
melliott@trevecca.edu
• Larry Knight, Compliance Coordinator
(615) 248-1639
• Gregory Ruff,
Communications/Broadcasting

(615) 248-1606
gruff@trevecca.edu

TRUMAN STATE UNIVERSITY ATHLETICS
PERSHING BUILDING #212
100 EAST NORMAL
KIRKSVILLE, MO 63501
660-785-4236
Fax: 660-785-4189
athletics@truman.edu
www.trumanbulldogs.com
• Jerry Wollmering, Director of Athletics
(660) 785-4236
jerryw@truman.edu
• Liz Jorn, Faculty Athletic Representative
(660) 785-7747
ljorn@truman.edu
• Kevin White, Director of Athletic Communications
(660) 785-4276
kwhite@truman.edu
• Michelle Boyd, Head Athletic Trainer
(660) 785-7364
mboyd@truman.edu

TUSKEGEE UNIVERSITY ATHLETICS
DEPARTMENT OF ATHLETICS
1200 WEST MONTGOMERY ROAD
TUSKEGEE, AL 36088
334-724-4545
Fax: 334-724-4233
www.goldentigersports.com
• Curtis Campbell, Director of Athletics
(334) 724-4545
• Joe Jimmeh, Faculty Athletic Representative
(334) 724-4495
• Deana Person, Director of Compliance
(334) 727-8926
• Travis Jarome, Director of Athletic Communications
(334) 727-8150

UC RIVERSIDE ATHLETICS
900 UNIVERSITY AVENUE
RIVERSIDE, CA 92521
951-827-5432
Fax: 951-827-3569
www.gohighlanders.com
• Tamica Smith Jones, Director of Intercollegiate Athletics
(951) 827-5432
athleticsdirector@ucr.edu
• Michael Boele, Senior Associate Athletics Director
(951) 827-5446
• Tony Ontiveros, Director of Sports Medicine
(951) 827-3813
tony.ontiveros@ucr.edu
• Walter Clark, Faculty Athletics Representative
(951) 827-2114
walter.clark@ucr.edu

UNION UNIVERSITY ATHLETICS
1050 UNION UNIVERSITY DRIVE
JACKSON, TN 38305
731-661-5130
Fax: 731-661-5182
tsadler@uu.edu
uuathletics.com
• Tommy Sadler, Director of Athletics
(731) 661-5218
tsadler@uu.edu
• Teresa Thomas, Athletics Secretary

(731) 661-5325
tthomas@uu.edu
• Rebekah McFarland, Head Athletic Trainer
(731) 661-5221
rmcfarland@uu.edu
• Steven Aldridge, Sports Information Director
(731) 661-5027
saldridge@uu.edu

UNIVERSITY OF ALABAMA IN HUNTSVILLE ATHLETICS
205 SPRAGINS HALL
HUNTSVILLE, AL 35899
256-824-6100
Fax: 256-824-7306
www.uah.edu/Athletics
• E. J. Brophy, Director of Athletics
(256) 824-2677
• Sam Baldwin, Sports Information Coordinator
(256) 824-2201
samuel.baldwin@uah.edu
• Taylor Flatt, Sports Information Director
(256) 824-6008

UNIVESRITY OF ALASKA FAIRBANKS ATHLETICS
ATHLETICS AND RECREATION DEPARTMENT
211 PATTY CENTER
PO BOX 757440
FAIRBANKS, AK 99775-7440
907-474-7205
Fax: 907-474-5162
• Gary Gray, Director of Athletics
(907) 474-6812
grgray@alaska.edu
• Kelly Wien, Assistant Athletic Director
(907) 474-6870
kelly.wien@alaska.edu
• Nona Letuligasenoa, Assistant Athletic Director, Communications
(907) 474-6805
nona.l@alaska.edu

UNIVERSITY OF BRIDGEPORT ATHLETICS
126 PARK AVENUE
BRIDGEPORT, CT 06604
203-576-4000
Fax: 203-576-4057
anthonyv@bridgeport.edu
www.ubknights.com
• Anthony Vitti, Director of Athletics
(203) 576-4733
anthonyv@bridgeport.edu
• Kate Smullen, Assistant Athletic Director
(203) 576-4725
kbackman@bridgeport.edu
• Chuck Sadowski, Sports Information Director
(203) 576-4726
csadowsk@bridgeport.edu
• Scott Baird, Associate Athletic Trainer
(203) 576-4798
sbaird@bridgeport.edu

UNIVERSITY OF CALIFORNIA, DAVIS - ATHLETICS
HICKEY GYM 264
ONE SHIELDS AVENUE
DAVIS, CA 95616
530-752-1111
Fax: 530-752-6681
www.ucdavisaggies.com

• Kevin Blue, Athletic Director
(530) 752-4557
athleticsdirector@ucdavis.edu
• Rocko DeLuca, Deputy Director Of Athletics
(530) 752-5096
• Scott Carrell, Faculty Athletics Representative
(530) 752-5858

UNIVERSITY OF MISSOURI-ST. LOUIS ATHLETICS
225 MARK TWAIN BUILDING
ONE UNIVERSITY BOULEVARD
ST. LOUIS, MO 63121
314-516-5661
Fax: 314-516-5503
www.umsltritons.com
• Lori Flanagan, Director of Athletics
(314) 516-5661
• Mary Ann Mitchell, Assistant Director of Athletics
(314) 516-5660
tierneym@umsl.edu
• Mike Berry, Director of Sports Medicine
(314) 516-5686
berrymp@umsl.edu
• Josh McMillian, Head of Sports Performance
(314) 516-5663
mcmillianj@umsl.edu

UPPER IOWA UNIVERSITY ATHLETICS(UIU)
ATHLETICS DEPARTMENT
605 WASHINGTON STREET
PO BOX 1857
FAYETTE, IA 52142
563-425-5700
Fax: 563-425-5334
info@uiu.edu
www.upperiowaathletics.com
• David Miller, Director of Athletics
(563) 425-5293
millerds@uiu.edu
• Kent McElvania, Associate Athletic Director
(563) 425-5285
mcelvaniak@uiu.edu
• Brock Wissmiller, Assistant Athletic Director
(563) 425-5700
wissmillerb@uiu.edu
• Angie Leete, Program Director
(563) 425-5782
leetea@uiu.edu
• Matt Rueckert, Head Athletic Trainer
(563) 425-5364
rueckertm@uiu.edu

URSULINE COLLEGE ATHLETICS
2550 LANDER ROAD
PEPPER PIKE, OH 44124
440-684-6102
Fax: 440-684-6097
info@ursuline.edu
www.ursulinearrows.com
• Cindy McKnight, Athletic Director
(440) 684-6102
cmcknight@ursuline.edu
• Cathy Rook, Athletic Trainer
(440) 684-6100
crook@ursuline.edu
• Brandon Stewart, Sports Information Director
(440) 684-6062
brandon.stewart@ursuline.edu

college sports

VALDOSTA STATE UNIVERSITY ATHLETICS
DEPARTMENT OF ATHLETICS
1500 NORTH PATTERSON STREET
VALDOSTA, GA 31698
229-333-5890
Fax: 229-333-5972
www.vstateblazers.com
• Herb Reinhard, Director of Athletics
(229) 333-5462
hreinhar@valdosta.edu
• Mason Barfield, Director of Internal Operations
(229) 293-6069
• Whit Chappell, Director of Athletic Development
(229) 249-2631
wchappel@valdosta.edu
• Matt Malone, Sports Information Director
(229) 333-5903
mwmalone@valdosta.edu

VIRGINIA STATE UNIVERSITY ATHLETICS
20720 FOURTH AVENUE
PETERSBURG, VA 23806
804-524-5030
Fax: 804-524-5763
govsutrojans.com
• Peggy Davis, Director of Athletics
(804) 524-5030
pdavis@vsu.edu
• Deborah C. Mallory, Associate Athletic Director, Compliance
(804) 524-5571
dmallory@vsu.edu
• John E. Wilson, Jr., Assistant Athletic Director, Logistics
(804) 524-5020
jwilson@vsu.edu
• Roland T. Lovelace, Head Athletic Trainer
(804) 524-6798
rlovelace@vsu.edu

VIRGINIA UNION UNIVERSITY ATHLETICS
1500 NORTH LOMBARDY STREET
RICHMOND, VA 23220
804-257-5600
800-368-3227
Fax: 804-342-3511
visitus@vuu.edu
vuusports.com
• Joe Taylor, Director of Athletics
(804) 342-1484
jdtaylor@vuu.edu
• Felicia Johnson, Associate Athletic Director
(804) 342-5933
fmjohnson@vuu.edu
• Jim Junot, Sports Information Director
(804) 342-1493
jjunot@vuu.edu
• Valerie Allen, Head Athletic Trainer
(804) 359-9408

WASHBURN UNIVERSITY OF TOPEKA ATHLETICS
1700 SW COLLEGE AVENUE
TOPEKA, KS 66621
785-670-1134
Fax: 785-670-1091
www.wusports.com
• Loren Ferre, Director of Athletics
(785) 670-1794
• Brittany Simmerman, Assistant Athletic Director

(785) 670-1790
• Gene Cassell, Sports Information Director
(785) 670-1791
gene.cassell@washburn.edu
• Brent Hogan, Marketing and Special Events Coordinator
(785) 670-1333
• Steve Ice, Head Athletic Trainer
(785) 670-1753
steve.ice@washburn.edu

WAYNE STATE COLLEGE
1111 MAIN STREET
WAYNE, NE 68787
402-375-7000
Fax: 402-375-7271
www.wscwildcats.com
• Mike Powicki, Athletic Director
(402) 375-7520
mipowic1@wsc.edu
• Mike Barry, Associate Director of Athletics
(402) 375-7521
mibarry1@wsc.edu
• Linda Anderson, Assistant Athletic Director, Internal Affairs
(402) 375-7308
liander1@wsc.edu
• Muffin Morris, Head Athletic Trainer
(402) 375-7700
mumorri1@wsc.edu

WAYNE STATE UNIVERSITY ATHLETICS
5101 JOHN C. LODGE
101 MATTHAEI BUILDING
DETROIT, MI 48202
313-577-4280
Fax: 313-577-5996
www.wsuathletics.com
• Rob Fournier, Director of Athletics
ai5611@wayne.edu
• Jason Clark, Executive Senior Associate Athletics Director
jason.clark@wayne.edu
• Theresa Arist, Chief of Staff
theresa.arist@wayne.edu
• Michael Chan, Head Athletic Trainer
michaelchan@wayne.edu

WEST ALABAMA ATHLETICS, UNIVERSITY OF
UWA STATION 5
LIVINGSTON, AL 35470
205-652-3784
Fax: 205-652-3600
www.uwaathletics.com
• Stan Williamson, Director of Athletics
(205) 652-3784
• Janet Montgomery, Associate Athletic Director
(205) 652-3630
jlm@uwa.edu
• R.T. Floyd, Director of Athletic Training & Sports Medicine
(205) 652-3714
rtf@uwa.edu
• Kent Partridge, Director for Athletic Communications
(205) 652-3719
kpartridge@uwa.edu

WEST CHESTER UNIVERSITY ATHLETICS
700 SOUTH HIGH STREET
WEST CHESTER, PA 19383
610-436-1000
Fax: 610-436-1020
www.wcupagoldenrams.com

• Edward Matejkovic, Director of Athletics
(610) 436-3555
ematejkovic@wcupa.edu
• Terry Beattie, Associate Athletic Director
(610) 436-3317
tbeattie@wcupa.edu
• James Zuhlke, Sports Information Director
(610) 436-3316
jzuhlke@wcupa.edu
• Craig Stevens, Faculty Athletic Representative
(610) 436-2386
cstevens@wcupa.edu

WEST FLORIDA ATHLETICS, UNIVERSITY OF
11000 UNIVERSITY PARKWAY
BUILDING 54
PENSACOLA, FL 32514
850-474-3003
Fax: 850-474-3342
dscott@uwf.edu
goargos.com
• Dave Scott, Director of Athletics
(850) 474-3003
dscott@uwf.edu
• Meghan Barter, Associate Athletic Director
(850) 474-3055
mbarter@uwf.edu
• Jake Marg, Assistant Athletic Director
(850) 474-3057
• Brian Henry, Director of Athletic Communications
(850) 474-2140
• Arnold Gamber, Head Athletic Trainer
(850) 474-2985

WEST LIBERTY UNIVERSITY ATHLETICS
101 FACULTY DRIVE
WEST LIBERTY, WV 26074-0295
304-336-5000
Fax: 304-336-8304
hilltoppersports.com
• Aaron Huffman, Athletic Director
(304) 336-8046
ahuffman@westliberty.edu
• Lynn Ullom, Associate Athletic Director
(304) 336-8320
ullomlyn@westliberty.edu
• Heather Gallagher, Assistant Director of Athletics
(304) 336-8225
• Herb Minch, Head Athletic Trainer
(304) 336-8476

WEST TEXAS A&M UNIVERSITY ATHLETICS
2403 RUSSELL LONG BOULEVARD
CANYON, TX 79015
806-651-0000
Fax: 806-651-2213
www.gobuffsgo.com
• Michael McBroom, Director of Intercollegiate Athletics
(806) 651-4400
mmcbroom@wtamu.edu
• David Rausch, Faculty Athletic Representative
(806) 651-2423
drausch@wtamu.edu
• Paul Sweetgall, Director for Compliance
(806) 651-4437
psweetgall@wtamu.edu
• Chris Dane, Head Athletic Trainer
(806) 651-3640
• Sarah Ramey, Head Strength & Conditioning Coach

(806) 651-4433
sramey@wtamu.edu

WEST VIRGINIA STATE COLLEGE ATHLETICS
PO BOX 1000
INSTITUTE, WV 25112-1000
304-766-3165
800-987-2112
Fax: 304-766-4126
www.wvsuyellowjackets.com
• Sandy Kessell, Athletic Department Secretary
(304) 766-3165
skessel1@wvstateu.edu
• Nate Burton, Interim Athletic Director
(304) 766-3165
nburton2@wvstateu.edu
• Shannon Gerencir, Assistant Athletic Director
(304) 766-5750
• John Simms, Sports Information Director
(304) 766-5760
simmsj@wvstateu.edu

WEST VIRGINIA WESLEYAN ATHLETICS
59 COLLEGE AVENUE
BUCKHANNON, WV 26201
304-473-8000
Fax: 304-472-2571
www.wesleyanbobcats.com
• Randy Tenney, Athletic Director
(304) 473-8098
tenney_r@wvwc.edu
• Rae Emrick, Head Athletic Trainer
(304) 473-8002
emrick_r@wvwc.edu
• Patrick Holguin, Assistant Athletic Director
(304) 473-8101
• Allison Hull, Faculty Athletic Representative
(304) 473-8061
• Duane Carpenter, Sports Information Director
(304) 473-8102

WESTERN OREGON UNIVERSITY ATHLETICS
345 MONMOUTH AVENUE NORTH
MONMOUTH, OR 97361
503-838-9030
Fax: 503-838-8370
www.wouwolves.com
• Barbara Dearing, Executive Director of Intercollegiate Athletics
(503) 838-8094
dearingb@wou.edu
• Randi Lydum, Director of Compliance
(503) 838-8121
lydumr@wou.edu
• John Bartlett, Director of Athletic Facilities
(503) 838-8531
bartlej@wou.edu
• John Potter, Director of Media Relations
(503) 838-8051
potterj@wou.edu
• Kurtis Kidd, Head Athletic Trainer
(503) 838-8343
kiddk@wou.edu

WESTERN STATE COLLEGE ATHLETICS (WSC)
210 PAUL WRIGHT GYM
600 NORTH ADAMS
GUNNISON, CO 81231

970-943-2079
Fax: 970-943-2754
www.gomountaineers.com
• Miles Van Hee, Director of Athletics
mvanhee@western.edu
• Kim Miller, Associate Athletic Director
(970) 943-2021
• Shaun Wicen, Assistant Sports Information Director
(970) 943-2223
• Don Mundell, Head Athletic Trainer
(970) 943-2080

WESTERN WASHINGTON UNIVERSITY ATHLETICS
516 HIGH STREET
BELLINGHAM, WA 98225
360-650-3000
Fax: 360-650-3495
www.vu.wwu.edu
• Steven Card, Director of Athletics
steven.card@wwu.edu
• Steve Brummel, Associate Athletic Director Facilities
steve.brummel@wwu.edu
• Jeff Evans, Director of Sports Info
jeff.evans@wwu.edu
• Lonnie Lyon, Head Athletic Trainer
lonnie.lyon@wwu.edu

WESTMINSTER COLLEGE (UT) ATHLETICS
1840 SOUTH 1300 EAST
SALT LAKE CITY, UT 84105
801-832-2344
Fax: 801-474-2511
www.westminstergriffins.com
• Shay Wyatt, Director of Athletics
(801) 832-2344
swyatt@westminstercollege.edu
• Susan Heath, Associate Athletic Director
(801) 832-2283
sheath@westminstercollege.edu
• Rick Hackford, Head Athletic Trainer
(801) 832-2355
rhackford@westminstercollege.edu

WHEELING JESUIT UNIVERSITY ATHLETICS
316 WASHINGTON AVENUE
WHEELING, WV 26003
304-243-2365
Fax: 304-243-2243
www.wju.edu/athletics
• Kevin Forde, Director of Athletics
(304) 243-2291
• Dan Sancomb, Director of Athletic Fundraising
(304) 243-2053
• Chris Myers, Sports Information Director
(304) 243-2012
mmcdonald@wju.edu

WILMINGTON UNIVERSITY ATHLETICS (DELAWARE)
320 NORTH DUPONT HIGHWAY
NEW CASTLE, DE 19720
877-967-5464
infocenter@wilmu.edu
athletics.wilmu.edu
• Linda Van Drie-Andrzjewski, Director of Athletics
linda.m.andrzjewski@wilmu.edu
• Brian August, Associate Athletic Director
(302) 356-6753
brian.m.august@wilmu.edu
• Erin Harvey, Assistant Athletic Director

(302) 356-2023
erin.t.harvey@wilmu.edu

WINGATE UNIVERSITY ATHLETICS
230 NORTH CAMDEN ROAD
WINGATE, NC 28174
704-233-8193
Fax: 704-233-8170
www.wingatebulldogs.com
• Steve Poston, Director of Athletics
(704) 233-8194
• Michelle Caddigan, Associate Athletic Director, Internal Operations
(704) 233-8174
• David Sherwood, Director for Sports Information
(704) 233-8186
dsherwood@wingate.edu
• Robby Wise, Director of Sports Medicine
(704) 233-6706

WINONA STATE UNIVERSITY ATHLETICS
PO BOX 5838
WINONA, MN 55987
507-457-5210
Fax: 507-457-5479
www.winonastatewarriors.com
• Eric Schoh, Director of Athletics
(507) 457-5212
eschoh@winona.edu
• Myranda Nash, Associate Athletics Director
(507) 457-2250
mnash@winona.edu
• Stacey Czaplewski, Head Athletic Trainer
(507) 457-2333
sczaplewski@winona.edu

WINSTON-SALEM STATE UNIVERSITY ATHLETICS
ATHLETICS DEPARTMENT
200 C.E. GAINES CENTER
WINSTON-SALEM, NC 27110
336-750-2141
Fax: 336-750-8880
www.wssurams.com
• Tonia Walker, Director of Athletics
(336) 750-2141
• George Knox, Associate Director for Compliance
(336) 750-2146
knoxge@wssu.edu
• Kevin Manns, Director of Athletics for Media Relations
(336) 750-2152
mannskj@wssu.edu
• Ian Mushinski, Head Athletic Trainer
(336) 750-2597
mushinskiia@wssu.edu

WISCONSIN-PARKSIDE ATHLETICS, UNIVERSITY OF
900 WOOD ROAD
PO BOX 2000
KENOSHA, WI 53141-2000
262-595-2345
Fax: 262-595-2225
www.parksiderangers.com
• Tamie Falk-Day, Director of Athletics
(262) 595-2485
tamie.falk-day@uwp.edu
• Roger McAfee, Director for Sports Media Relations
(262) 595-2045
• Kenny Wilka, Director of Sports Medicine
(262) 595-2164

wilka@uwp.edu
• Tyler Martin, Athletic Trainer
(262) 595-2164
tylerm@uwp.edu

WOFFORD COLLEGE ATHLETICS
429 NORTH CHURCH STREET
SPARTANBURG, SC 29303
864-597-4090
Fax: 864-597-4129
athletics@wofford.edu
athletics.wofford.edu
• Richard Johnson, Director of Athletics
(864) 597-4090
athletics@wofford.edu
• Jameica Hill, Faculty Athletic
Representative
(864) 597-4635
• Andy Kiah, Director of Athletic Facilities
(864) 597-4157
kiahal@wofford.edu
• Will Christman, Head Athletic Trainer
(864) 597-4114
christmanwl@wofford.edu

NCAA Division III Colleges

ADRIAN COLLEGE ATHLETICS
110 SOUTH MADISON STREET
ADRIAN, MI 49221
517-265-5161
800-877-2246
Fax: 517-264-3802
adrianbulldogs.com
• Michael Duffy, Athletic Director
(517) 264-3997
mduffy@adrian.edu
• Patrick Stewart, Sports Information
Director
(517) 264-3280
• Jamie Fetter, Head Athletic Trainer
(517) 264-3969
jfetter@adrian.edu

**ALBERTUS MAGNUS COLLEGE
ATHLETICS**
700 PROSPECT STREET
NEW HAVEN, CT 06511
203-773-8596
Fax: 203-776-7533
athletics.albertus.edu
• Jim Abromaitis, Director of Athletics
(203) 773-8578
jabromaitis@albertus.edu
• Nicholas Wajnowski, Associate Director of
Athletics
(203) 773-8579
nwajnowski@albertus.edu
• Samantha Masayda, Sports Information
Director
(203) 773-8586
smasayda@albertus.edu

ALBION COLLEGE ATHLETICS
611 EAST PORTER STREET
ALBION, MI 49224
517-629-1000
Fax: 517-629-0495
marend@albion.edu
gobrits.com
• Matt Arend, Athletic Director
(517) 629-0583
marend@albion.edu
• Greg Polnasek, Associate Athletic Director
(517) 629-0288

gpolnasek@albion.edu
• Andy Lawrence, Head Athletic Trainer
(517) 629-0522
alawrence@albion.edu
• Bobby Lee, Director of Sports Information
(517) 629-0434

ALBRIGHT COLLEGE ATHLETICS
13TH & BERN STREETS
PO BOX 15234
READING, PA 19612-5234
610-921-7535
Fax: 610-921-7566
athletics@alb.edu
www.albrightathletics.com
• Rick Ferry, Co-Director of Athletics
(610) 921-7825
rferry@albright.edu
• Janice Luck, Co-Director of Athletics
(610) 921-7824
jluck@albright.edu
• Jeff Feiler, Assistant Director of Athletics
(610) 921-7678
jfeiler@albright.edu
• Rick Partsch, Head Athletic Trainer
(610) 921-7827
rpartsch@albright.edu

ALFRED UNIVERSITY ATHLETICS
ONE SAXON DRIVE
ALFRED, NY 14802
607-871-2193
Fax: 607-871-2712
gosaxons.com
• Paul Vecchio, Athletic Director
(607) 871-2030
vecchio@alfred.edu
• Mark Whitehouse, Sport Information
Director
(607) 871-2904
whitehouse@alfred.edu
• Jessica Hurlbut, Head Athletic Trainer
(607) 871-2916
dunster@alfred.edu

ALLEGHENY COLLEGE ATHLETICS
520 NORTH MAIN STREET
MEADVILLE, PA 16335
814-332-3350
Fax: 814-337-1217
alleghenysports.com
• Portia Hoeg, Director of Athletics
(814) 332-3350
• Samantha Avery, Manager of Athletic
Operations
(814) 332-3350
• Jim Berger, Director of Athletic
Communications
(814) 332-5952
• Jamie Plunkett, Head Athletic Trainer
(814) 332-2817
james.plunkett@allegheny.edu

ALMA COLLEGE ATHLETICS
614 WEST SUPERIOR STREET
ALMA, MI 48801
989-463.7279
Fax: 989-463-7018
www.goalmascots.com
• Steven Rackley, Athletic Director
• Paul Thomas, Sports Information Director
(989) 463-7114
• Brett Knight, Head Athletic Trainer
(989) 463-7288
knightbd@alma.edu

ALVERNIA UNIVERSITY ATHLETICS
400 SAINT BERNARDINE STREET
READING, PA 19607
610-796-8276
Fax: 610-796-8349
bill.stiles@alvernia.edu
athletics.alvernia.edu
• Bill Stiles, Director of Athletics
(610) 796-3015
bill.stiles@alvernia.edu
• Laura Gingrich, Associate Athletic Director
(610) 796-8273
laura.gingrich@alvernia.edu
• Mike Miller, Assistant Athletic Director
(610) 796-8471
mike.miller@alvernia.edu
• Tom Porrazzo, Head Athletic Trainer
(484) 256-6194
tom.porrazzo@alvernia.edu

AMHERST COLLEGE ATHLETICS
ALUMNI GYMNASIUM
PO BOX 5000
AMHERST, MA 01002-5000
413-542-2000
Fax: 413-542-2026
athletics@amherst.edu
athletics.amherst.edu
• Don Faulstick, Director of Athletics
(413) 542-8266
drfaulstick@amherst.edu
• David Hixon, Senior Associate Athletics
Director
(413) 542-2069
• Gregg DiNardo, Assistant Athletic Director
(413) 542-5630
gdinardo@amherst.edu
• Chris Attwood, Director of Athletic
Communications
(413) 542-2390
cattwood@amherst.edu
• Stan Zieja, Director of Sports Medicine
(413) 542-8188
smzieja@amherst.edu

ANDERSON UNIVERSITY ATHLETICS
1100 EAST FIFTH STREET
ANDERSON, IN 46012
765-641-4479
800-428-6414
Fax: 765-641-3857
mjtaylor@anderson.edu
athletics.anderson.edu
• Marcie Taylor, Athletic Director
(765) 641-4495
mjtaylor@anderson.edu
• Steve Heath, Sports Information Director
(765) 641-4479
• Adam Crosby, Head Athletic Trainer
(765) 641-4491

ANNA MARIA COLLEGE ATHLETICS
50 SUNSET LANE
PAXTON, MA 01612
508-849-3447
800-344-4586
Fax: 508-849-3449
lhabacker@annamaria.edu
goamcats.com
• Serge DeBari, Interim Athletic Director
(508) 849-3447
sdebari@annamaria.edu
• Shawn Conrad, Assistant Athletic Director
(508) 849-3310
sconrad@annamaria.edu
• Ray LeBoeuf, Jr., Head Athletic Trainer
(508) 849-3448

rleboeuf@annamaria.edu
• Sammi Chickering, Sports Information Director
(508) 849-3252
schickering@annamaria.edu

ARCADIA UNIVERSITY ATHLETICS
450 SOUTH EASTON ROAD
GLENSIDE, PA 19038
215-572-2955
877-272-2342
Fax: 215-572-2159
granatab@arcadia.edu
athletics.arcadia.edu
• Brian Granata, Director of Athletics
(215) 572-2955
granatab@arcadia.edu
• Rick Brownell, Associate Director of Athletics
(215) 572-4066
brownelr@arcadia.edu
• Justin Scott, Assistant Athletic Director
(215) 572-2976
• Darryl Konicki, Sports Information Director
(215) 572-4048
• Danielle Duffy, Head Athletic Trainer .
(215) 572-2848
duffyd@arcadia.edu

AUGSBURG COLLEGE ATHLETICS
2211 RIVERSIDE AVENUE SOUTH
MINNEAPOLIS, MN 55454
612-330-1000
Fax: 612-330-1372
athletics.augsburg.edu
• Jeff Swenson, Athletic Director
(612) 330-1241
swensonj@augsburg.edu
• Kelly Anderson Diercks, Associate Athletic Director
(612) 330-1245
diercks@augsburg.edu
• Don Stoner, Sports Information Director
(612) 330-1677
stoner@augsburg.edu
• Missy Strauch, Head Athletic Trainer
(612) 330-1310
strauch@augsburg.edu

AUGUSTANA COLLEGE ATHLETICS
639 38TH STREET
ROCK ISLAND, IL 61201-2296
309-794-7000
athletics.augustana.edu
• Mike Zapolski, Director of Athletics
(309) 794-7223
mikezapolski@augustana.edu
• Dave Wrath, Associate Director of Athletics
(309) 794-7265
davewrath@augustana.edu

AURORA UNIVERSITY ATHLETICS
347 SOUTH GLADSTONE AVENUE
AURORA, IL 60506-4892
630-892-6431
Fax: 630-844-7809
athletics.aurora.edu
• Jim Hamad, Director of Athletics
(630) 844-6181
jhamad@aurora.edu
• Nicki Pieart, Assistant Director of Athletics
(630) 844-6174
npieart@aurora.edu
• Brian Kipley, Director of Sports Information
(630) 844-7575
bkipley@aurora.edu

AVERETT UNIVERSITY ATHLETICS
707 MOUNT CROSS ROAD
DANVILLE, VA 24540
434-791-5700
Fax: 434-791-5740
www.averettcougars.com
• Meg Stevens, Director of Athletics
(434) 791-5700
mstevens@averett.edu
• Danny Miller, Associate Director of Athletics
(434) 791-5737
dmiller@averett.edu
• Drew Wilson, Sports Information Director
(434) 791-5621
drew.wilson@averett.edu
• Thomas Underwood, Head Athletic Trainer
(434) 791-7270
tunderwood@averett.edu

BABSON COLLEGE ATHLETICS
231 FOREST STREET
BABSON PARK, MA 02457-0310
781-239-4250
Fax: 781-239-5218
www.babsonathletics.com
• Mike Lynch, Interim Director of Athletics
(781) 239-4250
mlynch4@babson.edu
• Judy Blinstrub, Associate Athletics Director
(781) 239-4418
blinstrub@babson.edu
• Andy Dutton, Assistant Athletics Director
(781) 239-5650
• Rick Burr, Director of Athletics Performance
(781) 239-5690
rburr@babson.edu

BALDWIN-WALLACE COLLEGE ATHLETICS
275 EASTLAND ROAD
BEREA, OH 44017
440-826-2900
Fax: 440-826-2192
info@bw.edu
www.bwyellowjackets.com
• Kris A. Diaz, Director of Athletics
(440) 826-2309
kdiaz@bw.edu
• Duane Smith, Stadium Operations Director
(440) 826-2195
djsmith@bw.edu
• Cindy Zilko, Interim Head Athletic Trainer
(440) 826-2186
czilko@bw.edu
• Garry Miller, Assistant Athletic Trainer
(440) 826-8570
gmiller@bw.edu

BARD COLLEGE ATHLETICS
PO BOX 5000
ANNANDALE-ON-HUDSON, NY 12504-5000
845-758-7531
Fax: 845-758-7647
athletics@bard.edu
www.bardathletics.com
• Kristen Hall, Director of Athletics
(845) 758-7528
• Jim Sheahan, Director of Athletic Communications
(845) 752-4929
• Sarah Cartmill, Assistant Director of Athletics
(845) 758-6822

• Sam McMullen, Head Athletic Trainer
(845) 758-7694

BARUCH COLLEGE ATHLETICS
ATHLETIC DEPARTMENT
BOX B1-110
55 LEXINGTON AVENUE
NEW YORK, NY 10010
646-312-5049
Fax: 646-312-5041
athletics.baruch.cuny.edu
• Carrie Thomas, Administrator in Chargector
(646) 312-5053
carrie.thomas@baruch.cuny.edu
• Machli Joseph, Deputy Director of Athletics
(646) 312-5044
• John Neves, Director of Sports Information
(646) 312-5048
john.neves@baruch.cuny.edu
• Naomi Chang, Athletic Trainer
(646) 312-5059
• John Alesi, Athletic Coordinator
(646) 312-5064
john.alesi@baruch.cuny.edu

BATES COLLEGE ATHLETICS
130 CENTRAL AVENUE
LEWISTON, ME 04240
207-786-6255
Fax: 207-786-8232
athletics.bates.edu
• Kevin McHugh, Director of Athletics
(207) 786-6341
kmchugh@bates.edu
• Sue Harriman, Assistant Athletic Director
(207) 786-6238
sharrima@bates.edu
• Mike Verville, Director of Sports Medicine
(207) 786-6359
mvervill@bates.edu

BECKER COLLEGE
964 MAIN STREET
LEICESTER, MA 01524
508-791-9241
Fax: 508-892-8131
info@becker.edu
www.beckerhawks.com
• Frank Millerick, Director of Athletics
(774) 354-0481
• Gene Alley, Associate Athletic Director
(774) 354-0484
• Steve Hoar, Assistant Athletic Director
(774) 354-0483
• Matt Tittle, Director of Sports Information
(774) 354-0485
• Brenda LaRow, Head Athletic Trainer
(774) 354-0490

BELOIT COLLEGE ATHLETICS
700 COLLEGE STREET
BELOIT, WI 53511-5509
608-363-2229
Fax: 608-363-2044
www.beloit.edu/athletics
• Tim Schmiechen, Director of Athletics
(608) 363-2259
schmiech@beloit.edu
• Dave DeGeorge, Assistant Director of Athletics
(608) 363-2039
degeorge@beloit.edu
• Terry Owens, Director of Sports Information
(608) 363-2229

college sports

• Peggy Steffen, Business Operations
Manager
(608) 363-2296

BENEDICTINE UNIVERSITY ATHLETICS
5700 COLLEGE ROAD
LISLE, IL 60532
630-829-6140
Fax: 630-960-0899
benueagles.com
• Mark McHorney, Director of Athletics
(630) 829-6150
mmchorney@ben.edu
• Paul Nelson, Associate Director of
Athletics
(603) 829-6144
pnelson@ben.edu
• Matthew Jones, Assistant Director of
Athletics
(630) 829-6135
mjones@ben.edu
• Jessica Steadman Jelinek, Director of
Athletic Marketing
(630) 829-6143
jjelinek@ben.edu
• Tarah Ellington Geve, Head Athletic
Trainer
(630) 829-6154
tgeye@ben.edu

BETHEL COLLEGE ATHLETICS
1001 BETHEL CIRCLE
MISHAWAKA, IN 46545
574-807-7000
Fax: 574-807-7426
www.bethelcollegepilots.com
• Tom Visker, Athletics Director
(574) 807-7259
• Christopher Hess, Assistant Athletics
Director
(574) 807-7236
• Natalie Young, Sports Information Director
(574) 807-7031

BLACKBURN COLLEGE ATHLETICS
700 COLLEGE AVE
CARLINVILLE, IL 62626
217-854-3231
800-233-3550
Fax: 217-854-5520
john.malin@blackburn.edu
www.blackburnbeavers.com
• John Malin, Athletic Director
(217) 854-5572
john.malin@blackburn.edu
• Michael Neal, Sports Information Director
(217) 854-5699
michael.neal@blackburn.edu
• Malia Murphy, Head Athletic Trainer
(217) 854-5610

BLUFFTON COLLEGE ATHLETICS
1 UNIVERSITY DRIVE
BLUFFTON, OH 45817-2104
419-358-3227
800-488-3257
Fax: 419-358-3070
sportsinfo@bluffton.edu
www.bluffton.edu/athletics
• Phil Talavinia, Athletics Director
(419) 358-3227
talaviniap@bluffton.edu
• Bill Hanefeld, Jr., Sports Information
Director
(419) 358-3241
sportsinfo@bluffton.edu
• Kim Schimmoeller, Associate Athletics

Director
(419) 358-3221
schimmoellerk@bluffton.edu

BOWDOIN COLLEGE ATHLETICS
9000 COLLEGE STATION
BRUNSWICK, ME 04011
207-725-3326
Fax: 207-725-3019
tryan@bowdoin.edu
athletics.bowdoin.edu
• Tim Ryan, Ashmead White Director of
Athletics
(207) 725-3247
tryan@bowdoin.edu
• Alice Wiercinski, Associate Director of
Athletics
(207) 798-4342
awiercin@bowdoin.edu
• James Caton, Director for
Communications
(207) 725-3254
jcaton@bowdoin.edu
• Dan Davis, Director of Athletic Training
(207) 725-3018
ddavies@bowdoin.edu
• Liz Grote, NCAA Compliance Coordinator
(207) 798-4148
egrote@bowdoin.edu

BRANDEIS UNIVERSITY ATHLETICS
GOSMAN SPORTS CENTER
MS 007
WALTHAM, MA 02254-9110
781-736-3668
Fax: 781-736-3656
www.brandeisjudges.com
• Lynne Dempsey, Acting Director of
Athletics
(781) 736-3635
dempsey@brandeis.edu
• Tom Rand, Associate Director of Athletics
(781) 736-3632
rand@brandeis.edu
• Jim Zotz, Assistant Director of Athletics
(781) 736-3649
zotz@brandeis.edu
• Adam Levin, Sports Information Director
(781) 736-3631
aslevin@brandeis.edu
• Lisa Denicola, Head Athletic Trainer
(781) 736-3666
denicola@brandeis.edu

BRIDGEWATER COLLEGE ATHLETICS
402 EAST COLLEGE STREET
BRIDGEWATER, VA 22812
540-828-8000
800-759-8328
Fax: 540-828-5484
bridgewatereagles.com
• Curt Kendall, Director of Athletics
(540) 828-5407
ckendall@bridgewater.edu
• Jean Willi, Associate Director of Athletics
(540) 828-5400
jwilli@bridgewater.edu
• Jimmy McCumber, Director of Athletic
Media Relations
(540) 828-5615
jmccumber@bridgewater.edu
• Heather Grant, Director of Clinical Athletic
Training
(540) 828-5368
hgrant@bridgewater.edu
• Brandon Beach, Director of Strength and
Conditioning

(540) 828-5783
bbeach@bridgewater.edu

**BRIDGEWATER STATE COLLEGE
ATHLETICS**
131 SUMMER STREET
335 PLYMOUTH STREET
BRIDGEWATER, MA 02325
508-531-1352
Fax: 508-531-1356
bsubears.com
• Marybeth Lamb, Director of Athletics
(508) 531-1353
marybeth.lamb@bridgew.edu
• Mike Storey, Associate Director of
Athletics
(508) 531-2350
mstorey@bridgew.edu
• Michael Holbrook, Director of Sports
Information
(508) 531-2656
mholbrook@bridgew.edu
• Dan Rezendes, Director of Fitness
(508) 531-2976
drezendes@bridgew.edu
• Jeanne O'Brien, Director for Sports
Medicine
(508) 531-1765
j5obrien@bridgew.edu

BUENA VISTA UNIVERSITY ATHLETICS
SIEBENS FIELDHOUSE
610 WEST FOURTH STREET
STORM LAKE, IA 50588
712-749-2253
Fax: 712-749-1460
phelpss@bvu.edu
bvuathletics.com
• Jack Denholm, Director of Athletics
(712) 749-2016
denholmj@bvu.edu
• Amy Santucci, Assistant Director of
Athletics
(712) 749-2254
santuccia@bvu.edu
• Dominic Worrell, Head Athletic Trainer
(712) 749-2258
worrelld@bvu.edu
• Steven Phelps, Director of Sports
Information
(712) 749-2633
phelpss@bvu.edu
• Ryder Weischedel, Director of Athletic
Performance
(712) 749-2291
weischedelr@bvu.edu

BUFFALO STATE COLLEGE ATHLETICS
1300 ELMWOOD AVENUE
HOUSTON GYM 248
BUFFALO, NY 14222
716-878-6533
Fax: 716-878-3401
www.buffalostateathletics.com
• Jerry Boyes, Director of Athletics
(716) 878-6534
boyesjs@buffalostate.edu
• Jeff Ventura, Sports Information Director
(716) 878-6030
venturjm@buffalostate.edu
• Jim Fowler, Athletics Budget Manager
(716) 878-6516
fowlerjc@buffalostate.edu
• Sean Roberts, Head Athletic Trainer
(716) 878-5328
robertsm@buffalostate.edu

CABRINI COLLEGE ATHLETICS
610 KING OF PRUSSIA ROAD
RADNOR, PA 19087
610-902-8387
Fax: 610-902-8385
brk39@cabrini.edu
www.cabriniathletics.com
• Brad Koch, Director of Athletics
(610) 902-8571
brk39@cabrini.edu
• Orlin Jespersen, Associate Director of
Athletics
(610) 225-3909
ojj722@cabrini.edu
• Jess Huda, Assistant Director of Athletics
(610) 902-8318
jess.huda@cabrini.edu
• David Howell, Sports Information Director
(610) 902-8529

**CALIFORNIA - SANTA CRUZ ATHLETICS,
UNIVERSITY OF**
1156 HIGH STREET
SANTA CRUZ, CA 95064
831-459-2531
Fax: 831-459-4070
admissions@ucsc.edu
www.goslugs.com
• Cliff Dochterman, Director of Athletics
(831) 459-4524
• Collin Pregliasco, Associate Athletics
Director
(831) 459-4964
• Marcus Wirth, Assistant Athletics Director
(831) 459-4159
Description of Sport Organization:
Division III, Part of the Independent
Conference.
Teams:
Men/Women's Tennis, Men/Women's
Soccer, Men/Women's Volleyball,
Men/Women's Basketball, Men/Women's
Swimming/Diving, Women's Golf, and
Women's Cross Country.

**CALIFORNIA INSTITUTE OF
TECHNOLOGY ATHLETICS**
1200 EAST CALIFORNIA BOULEVARD
MC 1-2
PASADENA, CA 91125
626-395-3253
Fax: 626-584-0589
wjack@caltech.edu
gocaltech.com
• Betsy Mitchell, Director of Athletics
(626) 395-6148
betsy.mitchell@caltech.edu
• John Carter, Associate Director of
Athletics
(626) 395-3252
john.carter@caltech.edu
• Heather Semelmacher, Assistant Director,
Intercollegiate Teams
(626) 395-4695
heather.semelmacher@caltech.edu
• Mark Becker, Director of Sports
Information
(626) 395-3262
mbecker@caltech.edu
• Sally Alway, Head Athletic Trainer
(626) 395-1205
salway@caltech.edu

**CALIFORNIA LUTHERAN UNIVERSITY
ATHLETICS**
60 WEST OLSEN ROAD
THOUSAND OAKS, CA 91360
805-493-3400
Fax: 805-493-3860
tmaple@callutheran.edu
www.clusports.com
• Daniel Kuntz, Athletic Director
(805) 493-3400
kuntz@callutheran.edu
• Debby Day, Assistant Athletic Director
(805) 493-3408
dday@callutheran.edu
• Kecia Davis, Head Athletic Trainer
(805) 493-3406
kgdavis@callutheran.edu
• Tracy L. Olson, Sports Information Director
(805) 493-3153
tmaple@callutheran.edu
• Thomas Dodd, Director of Aquatics
(805) 493-3530
dodd@callutheran.edu

CALVIN COLLEGE ATHLETICS
3201 BURTON STREET SE
GRAND RAPIDS, MI 49546
616-526-6000
Fax: 616-526-6060
meyn@calvin.edu
www.calvinknights.com
• Nancy Meyer, Director of Athletics, Internal
Operations
(616) 526-6224
meyn@calvin.edu
• James Timmer, Director of Athletics,
External Relations
(616) 526-6037
jrt3@calvin.edu
• Jeff Febus, Sports Information Coordinator
(616) 526-6169
jfebus@calvin.edu
• Joe Dykstra, Head Athletic Trainer
(616) 526-7630
jhd7@calvin.edu
• Justin TeBrake, Facilities Manager
(616) 526-7741
jtebra33@calvin.edu

CAPITAL UNIVERSITY ATHLETICS
1 COLLEGE AND MAIN
COLUMBUS, OH 43209
614-236-6209
Fax: 614-236-6178
sbruning@capital.edu
athletics.capital.edu
• Steve Bruning, Director of Athletics
(614) 236-6528
sbruning@capital.edu
• Dixie Jeffers, Associate Director of
Athletics
(614) 236-6551
djeffers@capital.edu
• Alex Borchers, Director of Intramurals
(614) 236-6979
aborchers2@capital.edu
• Ryan Gasser, Sports Information Director
(614) 236-6174
rgasser@capital.edu

CARLETON COLLEGE ATHLETICS
ONE NORTH COLLEGE STREET
NORTHFIELD, MN 55057
507-222-4057
Fax: 507-646-5550
llunder@carleton.edu
apps.carleton.edu/athletics
• Gerald Young, Athletic Director
(507) 222-4057
gyoung@carleton.edu
• Heidi Jaynes, Associate Athletic Director

(507) 222-4447
hjaynes@carleton.edu
• Jenny Bourne, Faculty Athletic
Representative
(507) 222-4007
jbourne@carleton.edu
• David Pape, Sports Information Director
(507) 222-4185
dpape@carleton.edu
• Chad Alladin, Head Athletic Trainer
(507) 222-7371
calladin@carleton.edu

**CARNEGIE MELLON UNIVERSITY
ATHLETICS**
SKIBO GYMNASIUM TECH AND FREW
STREETS
PITTSBURGH, PA 15213
412-268-8551
Fax: 412-268-3099
jcentor@andrew.cmu.edu
athletics.cmu.edu
• Josh Centor, Director of Athletics
(412) 268-8054
jcentor@andrew.cmu.edu
• Patrick Sterk, Associate Director of
Athletics
(412) 268-6042
• Sara Gauntner, Assistant Director of
Athletics
(412) 268-7030
sarap@andrew.cmu.edu
• Mark Fisher, Sports Information Director
(412) 268-3087
mwfisher@andrew.cmu.edu
• Adam Hindes, Head Athletic Trainer
(412) 268-2222
ahindes@andrew.cmu.edu

CARTHAGE COLLEGE ATHLETICS
2001 ALFORD PARK DRIVE
KENOSHA, WI 53140
262-551-5942
Fax: 262-551-5995
athletics.carthage.edu
• Robert Bonn, Director of Athletics
(262) 551-5931
rbonn@carthage.edu
• Chris Barker, Director of Athletic
Operations
(262) 551-6177
cbarker1@carthage.edu
• Phil Burwell, Director of Athletic
Communications
(262) 551-5740
pburwell@carthage.edu
• Jake Dinauer, Head Athletic Trainer
(262) 551-6107
jdinauer@carthage.edu

**CASE WESTERN RESERVE UNIVERSITY
ATHLETICS**
10900 EUCLID AVENUE
CLEVELAND, OH 44106
216-368-2420
Fax: 216-368-5475
athletics@case.edu
athletics.case.edu
• Amy Backus, Director of Athletics
(216) 368-0848
amy.backus@case.edu
• Pat Kennedy, Associate Athletic Director
(216) 368-3874
patrick.kennedy@case.edu
• Jon Schwartz, Sports Information Director
(216) 368-6517
jon.schwartz@case.edu

college sports

• Jessica White, Head Athletic Trainer
(216) 368-2863
jessica.m.white2@case.edu

CASTLETON STATE UNIVERSITY ATHLETICS
190 COLLEGE STREET
CASTLETON, VT 05735
802-468-6275
Fax: 802-468-2189
www.castletonsports.com
• Deanna Tyson, Associate Dean of Athletics and Recreation
(802) 468-1365
• Tim Barrett, Senior Associate Director of Athletics
(802) 468-1468
• Brittany Higgins, Assistant Director of Compliance
(802) 468-6422
• Steve Austin, Head Athletic Trainer
• Benjamin Stockwell, Director of Athletic Communications
(802) 468-6172

CATHOLIC UNIVERSITY OF AMERICA ATHLETICS
DUFOUR ATHLETIC CENTER
3606 JOHN MCCORMACK DRIVE NE
WASHINGTON, DC 20064
202-319-5286
Fax: 202-319-6199
www.cuacardinals.com
• Sean Sullivan, Director of Athletics
(202) 319-5286
• Dan Ambrose, Assistant Athletic Director
(202) 319-6043
• Mike Gambardella, Director for Communications
(202) 319-5610

CAZENOVIA COLLEGE ATHLETICS
22 SULLIVAN STREET
CAZENOVIA, NY 13035
315-655-7266
Fax: 315-655-1099
athletics@cazenovia.edu
www.cazenoviawildcats.com
• Michael Brooks, Director of Intercollegiate Athletics
(315) 655-7141
mdbrooks@cazenovia.edu
• Pete Way, Senior Associate Director of Athletics
(315) 655-7142
pmway@cazenovia.edu
• Bryon McAllister, Director for Sports Medicine
(315) 655-7321
mcallister@cazenovia.edu
• Chris Comino, Sports Information Contact
(315) 655-7184
ccomino@cazenovia.edu
• Bryon McAllister, Sports Information Contact
(315) 655-7321
bmcallister@cazenovia.edu

CENTRAL COLLEGE ATHLETICS
812 UNIVERSITY STREET
PELLA, IA 50219
641-628-5226
Fax: 641-628-5356
www.central.edu/athletics
• Eric Van Kley, Athletic Director
(641) 628-5422
vankleye@central.edu

• Alicia O'Brien, Associate Athletics Director
(641) 628-5434
obriena@central.edu
• Jeffy Schuring, Athletics Office Manager
(641) 628-5226
schuringj@central.edu
• Frank Neu, Head Athletic Trainer
(641) 628-5451
neuf@central.edu

CENTRE COLLEGE ATHLETICS
600 WEST WALNUT STREET
DANVILLE, KY 40422
859-238-5491
Fax: 859-236-6081
centrecolonels.com
• Brad Fields, Director of Athletics and Recreation
(859) 238-5485
brad.fields@centre.edu
• Gina Nicoletti, Associate Athletic Director
(859) 238-5493
gina.nicoletti@centre.edu
• Sonny Evans, Director of Athletic Facilities
(859) 238-8734
sonny.evans@centre.edu
• Jamey Gay, Head Athletic Trainer
(859) 238-5497
jamey.gay@centre.edu
• Liam Halferty, Director of Athletics Communications
(859) 238-6158

CHAPMAN UNIVERSITY ATHLETICS
ONE UNIVERSITY DRIVE
ORANGE, CA 92866
714-997-6691
Fax: 714-532-6010
www.chapman.edu
• Terry Boesel, Director of Athletics
(714) 997-6818
boesel@chapman.edu
• Doug Aiken, Associate Director of Athletics
(714) 997-6900
daiken@chapman.edu
• Mike Bokosky, Assistant Athletics Director
(714) 532-6083
bokosky@chapman.edu
• Steven Olveda, Sports Information Director
(714) 744-7889
olveda@chapman.edu
• Pam Gibbons, Director of Athletic Training
(303) 997-6640
gibbons@chapman.edu

CHICAGO ATHLETICS, UNIVERSITY OF
5530 SOUTH ELLIS AVENUE
CHICAGO, IL 60637
773-702-7684
Fax: 773-702-6517
athletics.uchicago.edu
• Erin McDermott, Director of Athletics
(773) 702-7684
• Rosalie Resch, Associate Athletic Director, Compliance
(773) 702-4659
rresch@uchicago.edu
• Nathan Lindquist, Director of Sports Information
(773) 702-4638
nlindquist@uchicago.edu
• Jennifer Coleman, Associate Athletic Director, Facilities
(773) 834-1664

CHRISTOPHER NEWPORT UNIVERSITY ATHLETICS
1 UNIVERSITY PLACE
NEWPORT NEWS, VA 23606
757-594-7025
Fax: 757-594-7839
cnusports.com
• Carrie Gardner, Associate Director of Athletics
(757) 594-7462
carrie.gardner@cnu.edu
• Francis Tommasino, Director of Athletic Communications
(757) 594-7884
ftommasi@cnu.edu
• Shanika Ellis, Athletics Finance Manager
(757) 594-7288
sellis@cnu.edu
• Rob Silsbee, Sports Information Director
(757) 594-7382
rob.silsbee@cnu.edu

CITY COLLEGE OF NEW YORK ATHLETICS
160 CONVENT AVENUE
NEW YORK, NY 10031
212-650-8228
Fax: 212-650-8230
www.ccnyathletics.com
• Kevin H. Abdur-Rahman, Director of Athletics
(212) 650-7556
krahman@ccny.cuny.edu
• Karina Jorge, Assistant Director of Athletics
(212) 650-7524
kjorge@ccny.cuny.edu
• Roberto Ignaccolo, Head Coach
(212) 650-5448
rignacocolo@ccny.cuny.edu
• Catherine Prince, Sports Information Director
(212) 650-6925
cprince@ccny.cuny.edu

CLAREMONT-MUDD-SCRIPPS COLLEGES ATHLETICS
500 EAST NINTH STREET
CLAREMONT, CA 91711
909-607-2904
Fax: 909-621-8848
www.cmsathletics.org
• Michael Sutton, Director of Athletics
(909) 607-3562
michael.sutton@cms.claremont.edu
• Adam Pruett, Director of Recreational Sports
(909) 607-8331
adam.pruett@cms.claremont.edu
• Emily Nordhoff, Sports Information Director
(909) 607-1123
emily.nordhoff@cms.claremont.edu
• Steve Graves, Head Athletic Trainer
(909) 607-3248
steve.graves@cms.claremont.edu

CLARK UNIVERSITY ATHLETICS
950 MAIN STREET
WORCESTER, MA 01610
508-793-7161
Fax: 508-793-7627
www.clarku.edu/athletics
• Patricia Cronin, Director of Athletics
(508) 793-7305
tcronin@clarku.edu
• Joe Brady, Associate Athletic Director
(508) 421-3796

jbrady@clarku.edu
• Paul E. Phillips, Assistant Athletic Director
(508) 793-7170
pephillips@clarku.edu
• Kevin D. Anderson, Sports Information
Director
(508) 793-7164
keanderson@clarku.edu

CLARKSON UNIVERSITY ATHLETICS
8 CLARKSON AVENUE
BOX 5830
POTSDAM, NY 13699
315-268-6622
Fax: 315-268-7613
www.clarksonathletics.com
• Steve Yianoukos, Athletic Director
(315) 268-7021
stevey@clarkson.edu
• Laurel Kane, Associate Athletic Director
(315) 268-6594
lkane@clarkson.edu
• Mick Maquire, Assistant Athletic Director
(315) 268-3745
• Kelly Norman, Fitness Center Director
(315) 268-3768
normankl@clarkson.edu
• Mike Pitts, Head Athletic Trainer
(315) 268-2123

COE COLLEGE ATHLETICS
1220 FIRST AVENUE NORTHEAST
CEDAR RAPIDS, IA 52402
319-399-8500
800-332-8404
Fax: 319-399-8816
www.coeathletics.com
• John Chandler, Athletic Director
(319) 399-8622
jchandle@coe.edu
• Ryan Workman, Sports Information
Director
(319) 399-8570
sid@coe.edu
• Steve Cook, Assistant Athletic Director
(319) 399-8849
scook@coe.edu
• Nick Bender, Director of Athletic Training
Services
(319) 399-8653

COLBY COLLEGE ATHLETICS
4900 MAYFLOWER HILL
WATERVILLE, ME 04901-8849
207-859-4900
athletics@colby.edu
www.colby-sawyerathletics.com
• Tim Wheaton, Director of Athletics
(207) 859-4904
tim.wheaton@colby.edu
• Tom Burton, Associate Director of
Athletics
(207) 859-4922
tom.burton@colby.edu
• Bill Sodoma, Sports Information Director
(207) 859-4940
wcsodoma@colby.edu
• Tim Weston, Head Athletic Trainer
(207) 859-4970
tsweston@colby.edu
• Dawn Strout, Strength & Conditioning
Coordinator
(207) 859-4944
dawn.strout@colby.edu

COLBY-SAWYER COLLEGE ATHLETICS
541 MAIN STREET
NEW LONDON, NH 03257
603-526-3610
Fax: 603-526-3435
www.colby-sawyerathletics.com
• Bill Foti, Director of Athletics
(603) 526-3613
• Ryan Emerson, Director of Athletics for
Sports Information
(603) 526-3783
remerson@colby-sawyer.edu
• Ruth Clark, Athletic Program Manager
(603) 526-3610
rclark@colby-sawyer.edu
• Scott Roy, Head Athletic Trainer
(603) 526-3607

COLLEGE OF NEW JERSEY ATHLETICS (TCNJ)
2000 PENNINGTON ROAD
PO BOX 7718
EWING, NJ 08628-0718
609-771-2230
Fax: 609-637-5133
www.tcnjathletics.com
• Sharon Beverly, Executive Director of
Athletics
(609) 771-2231
beverlys@tcnj.edu
• LaKitha Murray, Senior Associate Director
of Athletics
(609) 771-3037
murrayl@tcnj.edu
• Dawn Henderson, Associate Director of
Athletics
(609) 771-3030
dhenders@tcnj.edu
• Megan Guicheteau, Head Athletic Trainer
(609) 771-2387
quichete@tcnj.edu
• Aaron Becker, Athletics Facilities
Coordinator
(609) 771-2288
beckera@tcnj.edu

COLORADO COLLEGE ATHLETICS
14 EAST CACHE LA POUDRE
COLORADO SPRINGS, CO 80903
719-389-6476
Fax: 719-389-6873
cctigers.com
• Ken Ralph, Director of Athletics
(719) 389-6475
ken.ralph@coloradocollege.edu
• Greg Capell, Senior Associate Director of
Athletics
(719) 389-6493
greg.capell@coloradocollege.edu
• Andy Obringer, Assistant Athletics Director
(719) 389-6107
andy.obringer@coloradocollege.edu
• Jerry Cross, Director of Athletics
Communications
(719) 389-6755
jerry.cross@coloradocollege.edu
• Ian Wood, Coordinator of Sports Medicine
(719) 389-6813
ian.wood@coloradocollege.edu

CONCORDIA COLLEGE (MN) ATHLETICS
901 8TH STREET SOUTH
MOORHEAD, MN 56562
218-299-4000
Fax: 218-299-4189
concordiamn.prestosports.com

• Rich Glas, Athletic Director
(218) 299-4231
glas@cord.edu
• Rachel Bergeson, Associate Athletic
Director
(218) 299-4728
bergeson@cord.edu
• Jim Cella, Sports Information Director
(218) 299-3194
cella@cord.edu
• Don Bruenjes, Head Athletic Trainer
(218) 299-4208
bruenjes@cord.edu

CONCORDIA UNIVERSITY (WI) ATHLETICS
12800 NORTH LAKE SHORE DRIVE
MEQUON, WI 53097
262-243-4385
Fax: 262-243-4475
www.cuwfalcons.com
• Rob Barnhill, Director of Athletics
(262) 243-4404
rob.barnhill@cuw.edu
• Steve Crook, Associate Director of
Athletics
(262) 243-4419
steve.crook@cuw.edu
• Erik Halling, Director of Athletic Relations
(262) 243-4549
erik.halling@cuw.edu
• Steven Schauer, Director of Athletic
Communications
(262) 243-2664
steven.schauer@cuw.edu
• Angela Steffen, Director of Sports
Medicine
(262) 243-4537
angela.steffen@cuw.edu

CONCORDIA UNIVERSITY AT AUSTIN ATHLETICS
11400 CONCORDIA UNIVERSITY DRIVE
AUSTIN, TX 78726
512-313-4524
Fax: 512-313-4599
athletics.concordia.edu
• Ronda Seagraves, Director of Athletics
(512) 313-4501
ronda.seagraves@concordia.edu
• Stan Bonewitz, Assistant Athletics Director
(512) 313-4504
stan.bonewitz@concordia.edu
• Martha Baldwin, Head Athletic Trainer
(512) 313-4506

CONCORDIA UNIVERSITY CHICAGO ATHLETICS
7400 AUGUSTA STREET
RIVER FOREST, IL 60305-1402
708-209-3116
Fax: 708-209-3154
crfathletics@cuchicago.edu
www.cucougars.com
• Jeff Hynes, Vice President for Student
Services
(708) 209-3444
jeff.hynes@cuchicago.edu
• Pete Gnan, Director of Athletics
(708) 209-3192
pete.gnan@cuchicago.edu
• Mandy Semenik, Assistant Director of
Athletics
(708) 209-3735
• Jim Egan, Sports Information Director
(708) 209-3541
james.egan@cuchicago.edu

• Terri Woods, Head Athletic Trainer
(708) 209-3120

CONNECTICUT COLLEGE ATHLETICS
270 MOHEGAN AVENUE
NEW LONDON, CT 06320
860-439-2541
Fax: 860-439-2516
camelathletics.com
• Crocker Cooker, Director of Athletics
(860) 439-2570
bscro@conncoll.edu
• Eva Kovach, Athletic Department
Coordinator
(860) 439-2541
edkov@conncoll.edu
• John Heck, Interim Head Athletic Trainer
(860) 439-5155
jphec@conncoll.edu

CORNELL COLLEGE ATHLETICS
600 FIRST STREET SOUTHWEST
MOUNT VERNON, IA 52314
319-895-4483
Fax: 319-895-5682
www.cornellrams.com
• John Cochrane, Director of Athletics
(319) 895-4230
jcochrane@cornellcollege.edu
• Dick R. Simmons, Associate Director of
Athletics
(319) 895-4270
dsimmons@cornellcollege.edu
• Shanda Ness, Asssitant Director of
Athletics
(319) 895-4411
sness@cornellcollege.edu
• Kerry Kahl, Sports Information Director
(319) 895-4483
kkahl@cornellcollege.edu
• Eric Dybvig, Head Athletic Trainer
(319) 895-4009
edybvig@cornellcollege.edu

COVENANT COLLEGE ATHLETICS
14049 SCENIC HIGHWAY
LOOKOUT MOUNTAIN, GA 30750
706-419-1525
Fax: 706-419-1660
sid@covenant.edu
athletics.covenant.edu
• Derek Halvorson, President
(706) 419-1117
president@covenant.edu
• Brad Voyles, VP for Student Development
(706) 419-1107
brad.voyles@covenant.edu
• Kyle Taylor, Director of Athletics
(706) 419-1516
• Andrew Mindeman, Sports Information
Director
(706) 419-1514
• Meredith Atwood, Head Athletic Trainer
(706) 419-1523

CURRY COLLEGE ATHLETICS
1071 BLUE HILL AVENUE
MILTON, MA 02186
617-333-0500
Fax: 617-333-2027
www.curryathletics.com
• Vinnie Eruzione, Athletic Director
(617) 333-2202
veruzion@curry.edu
• Ken Golner, Director for Communications
(617) 333-2324
kgolner@curry.edu

• Caitlin Roberts, Sports Information
Director
(617) 333-2324
kgolner@curry.edu
• Kelly Melville, Head Athletic Trainer
(617) 333-2203

D'YOUVILLE COLLEGE ATHLETICS
320 PORTER AVENUE
BUFFALO, NY 14201
716-829-8000
800-777-3921
athletics.dyc.edu
• Brian Cavanaugh, Director of Athletics
(716) 829-7878
• Rob Kennuth, Head Athletic Trainer
(716) 829-8309
• Stephen McCarthy, Sports Information
Director
(716) 829-8131
• Earl Schunk, Assistant Athletic Director
(716) 829-8300

DALLAS ATHLETICS, UNIVERSITY OF
1845 EAST NORTHGATE DRIVE
IRVING, TX 75062-4376
972-721-5009
Fax: 972-721-5208
www.udallasathletics.com
• Dick Strockbine, Athletics Director
(972) 721-5207
dick@udallas.edu
• Robb Leibold, Lead Athletics Trainer
(972) 721-5010
• Nathan Yacovissi, Sports Information
Manager
(972) 721-5378

DANIEL WEBSTER COLLEGE ATHLETICS
20 UNIVERSITY DRIVE
NASHUA, NH 03063
603-577-6381
Fax: 603-577-6597
• Chris Gilmore, Director of Athletics
(603) 577-6381
• Ken Belbin, Sports Information Director
(603) 577-6648
• Andrea Woodbury, Assistant Athletic
Director
(603) 577-6495
• Charles Barfelz, Head Trainer
(603) 577-6492

DE PAUW UNIVERSITY ATHLETICS
702 SOUTH COLLEGE AVENUE
PO BOX 37
GREENCASTLE, IN 46135-0037
765-658-4800
800-446-5295
Fax: 765-658-4964
depauwtigers.com
• Stevie Baker-Watson, Director of Athletics
(765) 658-6075
steviebaker-watson@depauw.edu
• Kellen Wells-Mangold, Assistant Athletics
Director, Internal Operations
(765) 658-4934
kwells-mangold@depauw.edu
• Kris Huffman, Assistant Athletics Director
(765) 658-4960
khuffman@depauw.edu

DE SALES UNIVERSITY ATHLETICS
BILLERA HALL
2755 STATION AVENUE
CENTER VALLEY, PA 18034
610-282-1100
Fax: 610-282-2279
athletics.desales.edu
• Scott Coval, Director of Athletics
(610) 282-1100
scott.coval@desales.edu
• Gracia Perilli, Assistant Director of
Athletics
(610) 282-1100
gracia.perilli@desales.edu
• BJ Spigelmyer, Sports Information Director
(610) 282-1100
william.spigelmyer@desales.edu

DEFIANCE COLLEGE ATHLETICS
701 NORTH CLINTON STREET
DEFIANCE, OH 43512
419-783-2342
Fax: 419-783-2369
www.defianceathletics.com
• Jodie Holava, Interim Director of Athletics
(419) 783-2379
• Kathleen Westfall, Asst. Athletics
Director/SWA
(419) 783-2345
kwestfall@defiance.edu
• Derek Woodley, Interim Asst. Athletics
Director
(419) 783-2341
dwoodley@defiance.edu

DELAWARE VALLEY COLLEGE ATHLETICS
700 E. BUTLER AVENUE
DOYLESTOWN, PA 18901
215-489-2268
Fax: 215-230-2963
athletics.delval.edu
• Steve Cantrell, Director of Athletics
(215) 489-2268
• Matt Levy, Director of Sports Information
(215) 489-2937
• Carol Di Girolamo, Assistant Athletic
Director
(215) 489-2300
carol.digirolamo@delval.edu
• Valerie Rice-Smith, Head Athletic Trainer
(215) 489-2353

DENISON UNIVERSITY ATHLETICS
200 LIVINGSTON DRIVE
GRANVILLE, OH 43023
740-587-6580
Fax: 740-587-6362
carneydebord@denison.edu
denisonbigred.com
• Nan Carney-DeBoard, Director of Athletics
(740) 587-6428
carneydebord@denison.edu
• Lynn Schweizer, Senior Associate Director
of Athletics
(740) 587-6657
schweizer@denison.edu
• Larry Schneiderer, Director of Athletic
Operations
(740) 587-5560
schneiderer@denison.edu
• Craig Hicks, Sports Information Director
(740) 587-6546
hiscksc@denison.edu

DICKINSON COLLEGE ATHLETICS
20 SOUTH COLLEGE STREET
CARLISLE, PA 17013
717-245-1320
Fax: 717-245-1441
www.dickinsonathletics.com
• Joe Giunta, Director of Athletics
(717) 245-1320
• Joel Quattrone, Senior Associate Athletics
Director
(717) 245-1364
quattron@dickinson.edu
• Charlie McGuire, Director of Sports
Information
(717) 245-1652
mcguire@dickinson.edu
• Janelle Nolt, Head Athletic Trainer
(717) 245-1651
noltj@dickinson.edu
• Bob Penner, Equipment Manager
(717) 245-1265
penner@dickinson.edu

DOMINICAN UNIVERSITY ATHLETICS
7900 WEST DIVISION STREET
RIVER FOREST, IL 60305
708-524-6232
Fax: 708-488-5095
athletics@dom.edu
www.dustars.com
• Erick Baumann, Director of Athletics
(708) 488-5054
ebauman@dom.edu
• Mark White, Associate Director of Athletics
(708) 524-6518
mkwhite@dom.edu
• Jeff Halsema, Assistant Director of
Athletics
(708) 524-6552
jhalsema@dom.edu
• Ken Trendel, Director of Sports Information
(708) 524-6232
ktrendel@dom.edu
• Erica Albertin, Head Athletic Trainer
(708) 524-6226
ehedges@dom.edu

DREW UNIVERSITY ATHLETICS
36 MADISON AVENUE
MADISON, NJ 7940
973-408-3441
Fax: 973-408-3014
www.drewrangers.com
• Jason Fein, Director of Athletics
(973) 408-3441
jfein@drew.edu
• Vincent Masco, Associate Director of
Athletics
(973) 408-3443
vmasco@drew.edu
• Matt Choquette, Director of Athletic
Communications
(973) 408-3574

DUBUQUE ATHLETICS, UNIVERSITY OF
2000 UNIVERSITY AVENUE
DUBUQUE, IA 52001
563-589-3000
Fax: 563-589-3425
www.dbq.edu/athletics
• Dan Runkle, Director of Athletics
(563) 589-3599
drunkle@dbq.edu
• Jason Berna, Assistant Athletic Director
(563) 589-3786
jberna@dbq.edu
• Debra R. Runkle, Head Athletic Trainer

(563) 589-3244
drrunkle@dbq.edu

EARLHAM COLLEGE ATHLETICS
801 NATIONAL ROAD WEST
RICHMOND, IN 47374-4095
765-983-1414
Fax: 765-983-1446
www.goearlham.com
• Mike Bergum, Director of Athletics
(765) 983-1624
• Kaitlin Leach, Associate Director of
Athletics
(765) 983-1481
leachka@earlham.edu
• Mitch Blankespoor, Director of Sports
Marketing
(765) 983-1795
blankmi@earlham.edu
• Bill Kinsey, Head Athletic Trainer
(765) 983-1312
kinsebi@earlham.edu
• Catheryn Dickman, Director of Wellness
Programs
(765) 983-1899
cathrynd@earlham.edu

**EASTERN CONNECTICUT STATE
UNIVERSITY ATHLETICS**
ATHLETIC DEPARTMENT
83 WINDHAM STREET
WILLIMANTIC, CT 06226
860-465-5172
Fax: 860-465-4696
molta@easternct.edu
gowarriorathletics.com
• Lori Runksmeier, Director of Athletics
(860) 465-5091
runksmeierl@easternct.edu
• Cynthia Washburne, Associate Director of
Athletics
(860) 465-4347
washburnec@easternct.edu
• Bob Molta, Sports Information Director
(860) 465-5172
molta@easternct.edu
• Julie Alexander, Athletic Trainer
(860) 465-5506
alexanderju@easternct.edu

**EASTERN MENNONITE UNIVERSITY
ATHLETICS**
1200 PARK ROAD
HARRISONBURG, VA 22802-2462
540-432-4440
Fax: 540-432-4443
www.emuroyals.com
• Dave King, Director of Athletics
(540) 432-4646
david.king@emu.edu
• Mike Downey, Head Athletic Trainer
(540) 432-4336
mike.downey@emu.edu
• James De Boer, Sports Information
Director
(540) 432-4441
james.deboer@emu.edu

**EASTERN NAZARENE COLLEGE
ATHLETICS**
23 EAST ELM AVENUE
QUINCY, MA 02170
617-745-7000
Fax: 617-745-3938
athletics.enc.edu
• Brad Zarges, Director of Athletics
brad.zarges@enc.edu

• Jim Aller, Assistant Athletic Director
(617) 745-3637
james.aller@enc.edu
• Rob Rossi, Sports Information Director
(617) 745-3641
robert.rossi@enc.edu

EASTERN UNIVERSITY ATHLETICS
1300 EAGLE ROAD
ST. DAVIDS, PA 19087
610-341-1736
Fax: 610-341-1317
www.goeasterneagles.com
• Nate Stewart, Director of Athletics
(610) 225-5032
• Heidi Birtwistle, Associate Athletic Director
(610) 341-1738
hbirtwis@eastern.edu
• Dan Mouw, Assistant Athletic Director for
Promotions
(215) 888-4422
dmouw@eastern.edu
• Justin Farrell, Sports Information Director
(610) 608-0233
• John Post, Director for Sports Medicine
(610) 341-1316
jpost@eastern.edu

EDGEWOOD COLLEGE ATHLETICS
1000 EDGEWOOD COLLEGE DRIVE
MADISON, WI 53711
608-663-4861
Fax: 608-663-2391
www.edgewoodcollegeeagles.com
• Al Brisack, Director of Athletics
(608) 663-3289
abrisack@edgewood.edu
• Susann Saltzberry, Assistant Director of
Athletics
(608) 663-3249
ssaltzberry@edgewood.edu
• David Petroff, Director of Athletics
Communications
(608) 663-6734
deptroff@edgewood.edu
• Adam Krueger, Head Athletic Trainer
(608) 663-3326
adamkrueger@edgewood.edu

ELIZABETHTOWN COLLEGE ATHLETICS
ONE ALPHA DRIVE
ELIZABETHTOWN, PA 17022
717-361-1137
Fax: 717-361-1488
www.etownbluejays.com
• Chris Morgan, Director of Athletics
(717) 361-1407
morganc@etown.edu
• Cliff Smith, Assistant Director of Athletics
(717) 361-1463
• Bob Schlosser, Associate Director of
Athletics
(717) 361-1141
schlosra@etown.edu
• Yvonne Kauffman, Director of Atletic
Advancement
(717) 361-1138
• Bridget Spooner, Head Athletic Trainer
(717) 361-1591
• Matt Heffelfinger, Director of Athletic
Communications
(717) 361-1311

ELMHURST COLLEGE ATHLETICS
190 PROSPECT AVENUE
ELMHURST, IL 60126-3296

630-617-3140
Fax: 630-617-3726
athletic@elmhurst.edu
www.elmhurstbluejays.com
• Paul Krohn, Director of Athletics
(630) 617-3142
paulk@elmhurst.edu
• Julie Hall, Assistant Athletic Director
(630) 617-3145
julieh@elmhurst.edu
• Kevin Juday, Director of Sports Information
(630) 617-3380
kevinj@elmhurst.edu
• Anne Hutchins, Head Athletic Trainer
(630) 617-3174
anneh@elmhurst.edu

ELMIRA COLLEGE ATHLETICS
ONE PARK PLACE
ELMIRA, NY 14901
607-735-1730
Fax: 607-735-1717
athletics@elmira.edu
athletics.elmira.edu
• Pat Thompson, Vice President of Athletics
(607) 735-1730
pthompson@elmira.edu
• Jen Bozek, Senior Associate Director of
Athletics
(607) 735-1748
jbozek@elmira.edu
• Jerry Fisk, Assistant Athletic Director of
Event
(607) 735-1110
gfisk@elmira.edu
• Don Sherman, Director of Sports
Information
(607) 735-1131
dsherman@elmira.edu
• Dave Tomkalski, Head Athletics Trainer
(607) 735-1752
dtomkalski@elmira.edu

EMERSON COLLEGE ATHLETICS
120 BOYLSTON STREET
BOSTON, MA 02116-4624
617-824-8500
Fax: 617-824-8529
athletics@emerson.edu
www.emersonlions.com
• Patricia Nicol, Director of Athletics
(617) 824-8969
• Stanford Nance, Senior Associate Director
of Athletics
(617) 824-8930
stanford_nance@emerson.edu
• Matt Ulrich, Director of Media Relations
(617) 824-8458
• Mandy Nicoles, Head Athletic Trainer
(617) 824-3232

EMORY & HENRY COLLEGE ATHLETICS
12228 ITTA BENA ROAD
PO BOX 947
EMORY, VA 24327
276-944-6233
Fax: 276-944-6738
www.gowasps.com
• Myra Sims, Director of Athletics
(276) 944-6236
• Dave Griffore, Associate Director of
Athletics
(276) 944-6747
• Trey McCall, Assistant Director of Athletics
(276) 944-6860
tmccall@ehc.edu
• Melissa Davis, Head Athletic Trainer

(276) 944-6786
mdavis@ehc.edu
• Joe Matthews, Director of Sports
Information
(276) 944-6830
jmatthews@ehc.edu

EMORY UNIVERSITY ATHLETICS
26 EAGLE ROW
ATLANTA, GA 30322
404-727-6547
Fax: 404-727-4989
www.emoryathletics.com
• Michael Vienna, Director of Athletics
(404) 727-6532
mvienna@emory.edu
• Timber Hines, Director of Athletic Facilities
(404) 712-2435
• Blair Vickery, Athletics Business Manager
(404) 727-1771
bvicker@emory.edu
• John Farina, Sports Information Director
(404) 727-6553
jfarina@emory.edu

ENDICOTT COLLEGE ATHLETICS
376 HALE STREET
BEVERLY, MA 01915
978-232-2312
Fax: 978-232-2600
www.ecgulls.com
• Brian Wylie, Director of Athletics
(978) 232-2440
bwylie@endicott.edu
• Jodi Kenyon, Associate Athletic Director
(978) 232-2234
jkenyon@endicott.edu
• Jodi Cipolla, Marketing & Promotions
(978) 232-2303
jcipolla@endicott.edu
• Jay Lilly, Director of Arena Operations
(978) 998-7731
jlilly@endicott.edu

EUREKA COLLEGE ATHLETICS
300 EAST COLLEGE AVENUE
EUREKA, IL 61530
309-467-6370
Fax: 309-467-6402
www.eurekareddevils.com
• Steve Thompson, Director of Athletics
(309) 467-6370
• Kurt Barth, Assistant Athletic Director
(309) 467-6369
kbarth@eureka.edu
• Alex Hess, Sports Information Director
(309) 467-6456
• Chris Sharkey, Head Athletic Trainer
(309) 467-6370
csharkey@eureka.edu

**FAIRLEIGH DICKINSON
UNIVERSITY/FLORHAM**
285 MADISON AVENUE
MADISON, NJ 07940
973-443-8500
fdudevils.com
• Bill Klika, Director of Athletics
(973) 443-8972
klikaad@fdu.edu
• Roger Kindel, Associate Director of
Athletics
(973) 443-8964
kindel@fdu.edu
• Bryan Jackson, Director of Sports
Information
(973) 443-8965

bjackson@fdu.edu
• Jay Ashby, Equipment Manager
(973) 443-8966
• Tom Wilkinson, Head Athletic Trainer
(973) 443-8967
tgwsr@fdu.edu

**FARMINGDALE STATE UNIVERSITY
(FSU) ATHLETICS**
2350 BROADHOLLOW ROAD
FARMINGDALE, NY 11735
631-420-2482
Fax: 631-420-2994
www.farmingdalesports.com
• Michael Harrington, Director of Athletics
(631) 420-2482
harrinm@farmingdale.edu
• Tom Azzara, Associate Athletic Director
(631) 420-2599
azzaratf@farmingdale.edu
• Deana Ward, Assistant Athletic Director
(631) 420-2178
warddt@farmingdale.edu
• Don Haworth, Director of Sports Medicine
(631) 794-6282
hawortde@farmingdale.edu

FERRUM COLLEGE ATHLETICS
590 FERRUM MOUNTAIN ROAD
FERRUM, VA 24088
540-365-4493
Fax: 540-365-4540
anaff@ferrum.edu
ferrumpanthers.com
• Abe Naff, Director of Athletics
(540) 365-4488
anaff@ferrum.edu
• Gary Holden, Sports Information Director
(540) 365-4306
gholden@ferrum.edu
• Gail Holley, Athletics Office Manager
(540) 365-4493
gholley@ferrum.edu
• John Zubal, Head Athletic Trainer
(540) 365-4528
jzubal@ferrum.edu

FINLANDIA UNIVERSITY (FU) ATHLETICS
601 QUINCY STREET
HANCOCK, MI 49930
906-482-5300
800-682-7604
Fax: 906-487-7383
www.fulions.com
• Chris Salani, Director of Athletics
(906) 487-7378
• Curtis Wittenberg, Assistant Athletic
Director for Operations
(906) 487-7214
curtis.wittenberg@finlandia.edu
• Nate Larson, Certified Athletic Trainer
(906) 487-7532
nlarson@portagehealth.org

FISK UNIVERSITY ATHLETICS
1000 SEVENTEENTH AVENUE NORTH
NASHVILLE, TN 37208-3051
615-329-8826
Fax: 615-329-8686
www.fisk.edu
• Larry E. Glover, Athletics Director
lglover@fisk.edu
• Sarah Grams, Assistant Athletics Director
• Russell Acklin, Sport Information Director
racklin@fisk.edu
• Bradford Sims, Director of Operations

FITCHBURG STATE COLLEGE ATHLETICS
160 PEARL STREET
FITCHBURG, MA 01420-2697
978-665-3314
Fax: 978-665-3710
www.fitchburgfalcons.com
• Sue Lauder, Director of Athletics
(978) 665-3314
• Bettiann Michalik, Sports Information Director
(978) 665-3343
bmichali@fitchburgstate.edu
• Merry MacDonald, Assistant Director of Athletics
(978) 665-4681
• Todd Souliere, Head Athletic Trainer
(978) 665-3774

FONTBONNE UNIVERSITY ATHLETICS
6800 WYDOWN BOULEVARD
ST. LOUIS, MO 63105
314-889-1444
Fax: 314-889-4507
athletics@fontbonne.edu
fontbonnegriffins.com
• Maria Eftink, Director of Athletics
• Maureen Sias, Compliance Director
(314) 719-4356
msias@fontbonne.edu
• Ann Schmerbauch, Head Athletic Trainer
(314) 719-3510
aschmerbauch@fontbonne.edu
• Danielle Donze, Sports Information Director
(314) 719-8032
ddonze@fontbonne.edu

FRAMINGHAM STATE UNIVERSITY ATHLETICS
100 STATE STREET
PO BOX 9101
FRAMINGHAM, MA 01701-9101
508-626-4614
Fax: 508-626-4069
tkelley@framingham.edu
www.fsurams.com
• Thomas Kelley, Director of Athletics
(508) 626-4614
tkelley@framingham.edu
• Carey Eggen, Associate Director of Athletics
(508) 626-4565
ceggen@framingham.edu
• Kathy Lynch, Sports Information Director
(508) 626-4612
klynch@framingham.edu
• Laura Rusk, Head Athletic Trainer
(508) 626-4564
lrusk@framingham.edu

FRANKLIN & MARSHALL COLLEGE ATHLETICS
PO BOX 3003
LANCASTER, PA 17604-3003
717-358-4477
Fax: 717-358-4440
www.godiplomats.com
• Daniel R. Porterfield, President
(717) 358-3971
president@fandm.edu
• Patricia Epps, Director of Athletics
(717) 358-3819
patty.epps@fandm.edu
• Mickey Blymier, Director of Athletic Communications
(717) 358-4857

• Matt Keller, Director of Sports Medicine
(717) 358-4111
matthew.keller@fandm.edu

FRANKLIN COLLEGE ATHLETICS
101 BRANIGIN BOULEVARD
FRANKLIN, IN 46131
317-738-8123
Fax: 317-738-8175
kprather@franklincollege.edu
franklingrizzlies.com
• Kerry Prather, Director of Athletics
(317) 738-8121
kprather@franklincollege.edu
• Lance Marshall, Assistant Director of Athletics
(317) 738-8136
lmarshall@franklincollege.edu
• Mary Johnston, Assistant Director of Athletics
(317) 738-8130
• Dale Long, Sports Information Director
(317) 738-8184

FROSTBURG STATE UNIVERSITY ATHLETICS
HAROLD J CORDTS PHYSICAL EDUCATION CENTER
101 BRADDOCK ROAD
FROSTBURG, MD 21532
301-687-4371
Fax: 301-687-4780
www.frostburgsports.com
• Troy Dell, Director of Athletics
(301) 687-4455
tadell@frostburg.edu
• Rubin Stevenson, Associate Athletic Director
(301) 687-4086
rstevenson@frostburg.edu
• Crystal Satterfield, Assistant Athletic Director
(301) 687-4455
cgsatterfield@frostburg.edu
• Karla Schoenly, Head Athletic Trainer
(301) 687-3027
kschoenly@frostburg.edu
• Noah Becker, Director of Athletic Communications
(301) 687-4371
nzbecker@frostburg.edu

GALLAUDET UNIVERSITY ATHLETICS DEPARTMENT
800 FLORIDA AVENUE NE
WASHINGTON, DC 20002
202-651-5603
Fax: 202-651-5274
sam.atkinson@gallaudet.edu
www.gallaudetathletics.com
• Michael Weinstock, Athletic Director
(202) 250-2685
• Lynn Ray Boren, Assistant Athletic Director
(202) 250-2461
lynn.boren@gallaudet.edu
• Sam Atkinson, Sports Information Director
(202) 448-7081
sam.atkinson@gallaudet.edu
• Mariko Kobanawa, Head Athletic Trainer
(202) 651-5265
mariko.kobanawa@gallaudet.edu

GEORGE FOX UNIVERSITY ATHLETICS
414 NORTH MERIDIAN STREET
NEWBERG, OR 97132

503-538-8383
Fax: 503-554-3864
ctaylor@georgefox.edu
athletics.georgefox.edu
• Craig Taylor, Director of Athletics
(503) 554-2911
ctaylor@georgefox.edu
• Elise Trask, Associate Director of Athletics
(503) 554-2934
• Sarah Reid, Director of Sports Marketing
(503) 554-2105
• Danny Cross, Sports Information Director
(503) 554-2926

GETTYSBURG COLLEGE ATHLETICS
300 NORTH WASHINGTON STREET
BOX 400
GETTYSBURG, PA 17325
717-337-6300
Fax: 717-337-6528
www.gettysburgsports.com
• David Wright, Assistant Vice President for Athletics
(717) 337-6400
dwright@gettysburg.edu
• Susan Furmagalli, Associate Director of Athletics
(717) 337-6401
sfumagal@gettysburg.edu
• Carol Cantele, Assistant Director of Athletics
(717) 337-6404
ccantele@gettysburg.edu
• Mike Cantele, Head Athletic Trainer
(717) 337-6429
mcantele@gettysburg.edu

GORDON COLLEGE ATHLETICS
255 GRAPEVINE ROAD
WENHAM, MA 01984
978-927-2300
Fax: 978-867-4682
info@gordon.edu
athletics.gordon.edu
• Jonathan Tymann, Director of Athletics
(978) 867-4039
jon.tymann@gordon.edu
• Cory Ward, Assistant Athletic Director for Operations
(978) 867-4334
cory.ward@gordon.edu
• Bess Watson, Director of Athletic Communications
(978) 867-4330
bess.watson@gordon.edu
• Josh Cornwall, Sports Information Director
(978) 867-4516
joshua.cornwall@gordon.edu

GOUCHER COLLEGE ATHLETICS
1021 DULANEY VALLEY ROAD
TOWSON, MD 21204
410-337-6383
Fax: 410-337-6576
athletics.goucher.edu
• Geoffrey Miller, Director of Athletics
(410) 337-6385
gmiller@goucher.edu
• Sally Baum, Associate Athletic Director
(410) 337-6389
sbaum@goucher.edu
• Tati Korba, Assistant Athletic Director
(410) 337-6577
korba@goucher.edu
• Mike Sanders, Sports Information Director
(410) 337-6474
msanders@goucher.edu

• Jean Perez, Director of Sports Medicine
(410) 337-6286
jean.perez@goucher.edu

GREEN MOUNTAIN COLLEGE ATHLETICS
ONE BRENNAN CIRCLE
POULTNEY, VT 05764
802-287-8238
800-776-6675
Fax: 802-287-8099
• Kip Shipley, Athletic Director
(802) 287-8244
• James Thivierge, Associate Athletic Director
(802) 287-8244

GREENSBORO COLLEGE ATHLETICS
815 WEST MARKET STREET
GREENSBORO, NC 27401
336-272-7102 EXT 5250
Fax: 336-217-7237
greensboro.sidearmsports.com
• Bryan Galuski, Director of Athletics
(336) 272-7102
bgaluski@greensboro.edu
• Randy Tuggle, Assistant Director of Athletics
(336) 272-7102
randy.tuggle@greensboro.edu
• Wes Gullett, Director of Sports Information
(336) 272-7102
wgullett@greensboro.edu
• Ray Babnik, Head Athletic Trainer
(336) 272-7102
ray.babnik@greensboro.edu

GREENVILLE COLLEGE ATHLETICS
315 EAST COLLEGE AVENUE
GREENVILLE, IL 62246-1145
618-664-6622
800-345-4440
Fax: 618-664-1060
www.greenville.edu/athletics
• Kent Krober, Athletic Director
(618) 664-6622
kent.krober@greenville.edu
• Tracy Cromer, Senior Women's Administrator
(618) 664-6835
tracy.cromer@greenville.edu
• B.J. Schneck, Sports Information Director
(618) 664-6621
william.schneck@greenville.edu
• Mike Peppler, Head Athletic Trainer
(618) 664-6731
mike.peppler@greenville.edu

GRINNELL COLLEGE ATHLETICS
1201 10TH AVENUE
GRINNELL, IA 50112
641-269-4000
Fax: 641-269-3818
pioneers.grinnell.edu
• Greg Wallace, Director of Athletics
(641) 269-4219
wallaceg@grinnell.edu
• Erin Hurley, Senior Women's Administrator
(641) 269-4848
hurley@grinnell.edu
• Ted Schultz, Sports Information Director
(641) 269-3675
schultzt@grinnell.edu

GROVE CITY COLLEGE ATHLETICS
100 CAMPUS DRIVE
GROVE CITY, PA 16127
724-458-2000
Fax: 724-458-3855
www.gcc.edu/sports
• Todd Gibson, Director of Athletics
(724) 458-2147
tdgibson@gcc.edu
• Mike Dreves, Interim Department Chair
(724) 458-2151
mfdreves@gcc.edu
• Kay Mitchell Emigh, Head Athletic Trainer
(724) 458-2108
kmemigh@gcc.edu
• Ryan Briggs, Sports Information Director
(724) 458-3365
rabriggs@gcc.edu

GUILFORD COLLEGE ATHLETICS
5800 WEST FRIENDLY AVENUE
GREENSBORO, NC 27410
336-316-2107
Fax: 336-316-2953
athletics@guilford.edu
www.guilfordquakers.com
• Tom Palombo, Director of Athletics
(336) 316-2190
tpalombo@guilford.edu
• Stephanie Flamini, Assistant Athletics Director
(336) 316-2344
• Dave Walters, Sports Inforamtion Director
(336) 316-2107
• Gary Rizza, Head Athletic Trainer
(336) 316-2513
rizzagn@guilford.edu

GUSTAVUS ADOLPHUS COLLEGE ATHLETICS
800 WEST COLLEGE AVENUE
SAINT PETER, MN 56082
507-933-7617
Fax: 507-933-8412
web@gustavus.edu
www.gustavus.edu/athletics
• Tom Brown, Athletics Director
(507) 933-7005
brownie@gustavus.edu
• Jared Phillips, Assistant Athletic Director
(507) 933-8493
jphilli2@gustavus.edu
• Troy Banse, Head Athletic Trainer
(507) 933-6463
tbanse@gustavus.edu
• CJ Siewert, Sports Information Director
(507) 933-7647
siewert@gustavus.edu

GWYNEDD MERCY COLLEGE ATHLETICS
1325 SUMNEYTOWN PIKE
PO BOX 901
GWYNEDD VALLEY, PA 19437
215-646-7300 EXT 2152
Fax: 215-542-4683
gwyneddathletics.com
• Keith Mondillo, Director of Athletics
(215) 641-5574
mondillo.k@gmercyu.edu
• Paul Murphy, Associate Director of Athletics
(215) 641-5533
• Laura-Ann Lane, Senior Women's Administrator
(215) 646-7300
• Chris Panter, Sports Information Director

(215) 646-7300
panter.c@gmercyu.edu
• Jenna Allonardo, Head Athletic Trainer
(215) 646-7300
allonardo.j@gmercyu.edu

HAMILTON COLLEGE ATHLETICS
198 COLLEGE HILL ROAD
CLINTON, NY 13323
315-859-4751
Fax: 315-859-4117
jhind@hamilton.edu
athletics.hamilton.edu
• Joe Hind, Director of Athletics
(315) 859-4116
jhind@hamilton.edu
• Miriam Merrill, Associate Director of Athletics
(315) 859-4753
• Todd Rayne, Faculty Athletics Representative
(315) 859-4698
trayne@hamilton.edu
• Scott Siddon, Director of Sports Medicine
(315) 859-4766
ssiddon@hamilton.edu
• Jim Taylor, Sports Information Director
(315) 859-4685
jtaylor@hamilton.edu

HAMLINE UNIVERSITY ATHLETICS
1536 HEWITT AVENUE
SAINT PAUL, MN 55104
651-523-2800
Fax: 651-523-2390
www.hamlineathletics.com
• Jason Verdugo, Athletic Director
(651) 523-2035
• Beth Rittler, Associate Director for Athletics
(651) 523-2838
bbjork@hamline.edu
• Chris Hartman, Assistant Athletic Director
(651) 526-2716
chartman01@hamline.edu
• Dave Wright, Sports Information Director
(651) 523-2786
• Tara Dooley, Head Athletic Trainer
(651) 523-3094
tdooley01@hamline.edu

HAMPDEN-SYDNEY COLLEGE ATHLETICS
PO BOX 698
HAMPDEN-SYDNEY, VA 23943
434-223-6151
Fax: 434-223-6348
info@hsc.edu
hscathletics.com
• Richard Epperson, Athletic Director
(434) 223-6153
repperson@hsc.edu
• Davis Yake, Director for Media Relations
(434) 223-6156
dyake@hsc.edu
• Scott Harris, Assistant Sports Information Director
(434) 223-6168
sharris@hsc.edu
• Brandon Davis, Head Athletic Trainer
(434) 223-6237
bdavis@hsc.edu

HANOVER COLLEGE ATHLETICS
484 BALL DRIVE
PO BOX 108
HANOVER, IN 47243

812-866-6800
Fax: 812-866-6818
info@hanover.edu
www.hanover.edu/athletics
• Lynn Hall, Athletic Director
(812) 866-7385
hall@hanover.edu
• John Jones, Associate Athletic Directors
(812) 866-7382
jjones@hanover.edu
• M. Tony Carlton, Head Athletic Trainer
(812) 866-7378
carlton@hanover.edu

HARDIN-SIMMONS UNIVERSITY ATHLETICS
2200 HICKORY
ABILENE, TX 79698
325-670-1435
Fax: 325-670-1572
jneese@hsutx.edu
hsuathletics.com
• John Neese, Director of Athletics
(325) 670-1273
jneese@hsutx.edu
• Chad Grubbs, Director of Athletic Communication
(325) 670-1473
cgrubbs@hsutx.edu
• Bert De Ka Garza, Assistant Athletic Trainerach
(325) 670-1358
bgarza@hsutx.edu
• Wade Green, Head Athletic Trainer
(325) 670-1188

HARTWICK COLLEGE ATHLETICS
ONE HARTWICK DRIVE
PO BOX 4020
ONEONTA, NY 13820
607-431-4700
Fax: 607-431-4018
fierkek@hartwick.edu
www.hartwickhawks.com
• Kim Fierke, Director of Athletics
(607) 431-4702
fierkek@hartwick.edu
• Betty Powell, Associate Director of Athletics
(607) 431-4701
powellb@hartwick.edu
• Chris Gondek, Director of Athletic Communications
(607) 431-4703
gondekc@hartwick.edu
• Matt Pohren, Assistant Athletic Director
(607) 431-4711
• Heidi Hofbauer-Buzzy, Head Athletic Trainer
(607) 431-4694
hofbauerh@hartwick.edu

HAVERFORD COLLEGE ATHLETICS
370 LANCASTER AVENUE
HAVERFORD, PA 19041
610-896-1117
Fax: 610-896-4220
www.haverfordathletics.com
• Wendy Smith, Director of Smith
(610) 896-1120
w1smith@haverford.edu
• Casey Londergan, Faculty Athletic Representative
(610) 896-1217
clonderg@haverford.edu
• Jim Kenyon, Facilities Manager
(610) 896-1125

• Cory Walts, Fitness Center Director
(610) 795-7014
• Curt Mauger, Head Athletic Trainer
(610) 896-1425
cmauger@haverford.edu
• Justin Grube, Director of Sports Information
(610) 896-1042

HEIDELBERG UNIVERSITY ATHLETICS
310 EAST MARKET STREET
TIFFIN, OH 44883-2462
419-448-2019
1-800-434-3352
www.heidelberg.edu
• Matt Palm, Athletic Director
(419) 448-2009
• Jeff Garvin, Director of Athletic Marketing & Information
(413) 448-2140
jgarvin@heidelberg.edu

HENDRIX COLLEGE ATHLETICS
1600 WASHINGTON AVENUE
CONWAY, AR 72032
501-505-2966
Fax: 501-450-3805
www.hendrixwarriors.com
• Amy Weaver, Director of Athletics
(501) 450-3899
weaver@hendrix.edu
• Rebecca Beagley, Senior Woman Administrator
(501) 450-1382
begley@hendrix.edu

HILBERT COLLEGE ATHLETICS
5200 SOUTH PARK AVENUE
HAMBURG, NY 14075
716-926-8794
Fax: 716-649-6429
info@hilbert.edu
www.hilberthawks.com
• John Czarnecki, Director of Athletics
(716) 926-8800
jczarnecki@hilbert.edu
• Kara Rehbaum, Assistant Athletics Director
(716) 926-8805
krehbaum@hilbert.edu
• Matt Diegelman, Athletic Facilities Coordinator
(716) 926-8796
mdiegelman@hilbert.edu
• Greg Peri, Head Athletic Trainer
(716) 926-8806
gperi@hilbert.edu

HIRAM COLLEGE ATHLETICS
11715 GARFIELD ROAD
PO BOX 1777
HIRAM, OH 44234
330-569-5340
Fax: 330-569-5392
athletics@hiram.edu
www.hiramterriers.com
• Ellen Dempsey, Director of Athletics
(330) 569-5340
dempseyee@hiram.edu
• Jim Schweickert, Director of Facilities and Operations
(330) 569-5365
schweickertjm@hiram.edu
• Jim Johnston, Head Athletic Trainer
(330) 569-5351
johnstonjw@hiram.edu
• Andrew Korba, Director of Sports

Information
(330) 569-5495
korbaam@hiram.edu

STATESMEN
HOBART ATHLETICS
BRISTOL GYMNASIUM
300 PULTENEY STREET
GENEVA, NY 14456
315-781-3565
Fax: 315-781-3570
www.hwsathletics.com
• Mike Hanna, Director of Athletics
(315) 781-3574
hanna@hws.edu
• Ken DeBolt, Director of Athletic Communications
(315) 781-3146
debolt@hws.edu
• Brian Miller, Assistant Athletics Director for Compliance
(315) 781-3548
bmiller@hws.edu
• Nick Cooke, Coordinator of Sports Medicine
(315) 781-3568
cooke@hws.edu
Year Founded:
1822

HOOD COLLEGE ATHLETICS
401 ROSEMONT AVENUE
FREDERICK, MD 21701
301-696-3499
Fax: 301-696-3488
www.hoodathletics.com
• Tom Dickman, Director of Athletics
(301) 696-3494
dickman@hood.edu
• Staci Brennan, Associate Director of Athletics
(301) 696-3785
brennans@hood.edu
• Geoff Goyne, Sports Information Director
(301) 696-3978
goyne@hood.edu
• Jennie Bowker, Head Athletic Trainer
(301) 696-3836
bowker@hood.edu

HOPE COLLEGE ATHLETICS
DEVOS FIELDHOUSE
222 FAIRBANKS AVENUE
HOLLAND, MI 49423
616-395-7070
Fax: 616-395-7175
schoonveld@hope.edu
athletics.hope.edu
• Tim Schoonveld, Co-Athletic Director
(616) 395-7698
schoonveld@hope.edu
• Melinda Larson, Co-Athletic Director
(616) 395-7694
• Lindsey Engelsman, Athletics Brand Manager
(616) 395-7688
engelsman@hope.edu
• Alan Babbitt, Sports Information Director
(616) 395-7856
babbitt@hope.edu
• Tim Koberna, Head Athletic Trainer
(616) 395-7705
koberna@hope.edu
• Meg Frens, Athletic Training Program Director
(616) 395-7450

HOUGHTON COLLEGE ATHLETICS
1 WILLARD AVENUE
HOUGHTON, NY 14744
585-567-9645
Fax: 585-567-9365
harold.lord@houghton.edu
athletics.houghton.edu
• H. Skip Lord, Executive Director of
Athletics
(585) 567-9645
harold.lord@houghton.edu
• Deanna Hand, Associate Director of
Athletics
(585) 567-9563
deanna.hand@houghton.edu
• Jason Mucher, Director of Compliance and
Communications
(585) 567-9276
jason.mucher@houghton.edu
• Eden Palmer, Athletic Trainer
(585) 567-9563
eden.palmer@houghton.edu

HUNTER COLLEGE ATHLETICS
695 PARK AVENUE
NEW YORK, NY 10065
212-772-4783
Fax: 212-650-3161
athletic@hunter.cuny.edu
www.huntercollegeathletics.com
• Terry Wansart, Director of Athletics
(212) 722-4783
terry.wansart@hunter.cuny.edu
• Stephanie Thorburn, Associate Athletic
Director
(212) 650-3123
stephanie.thorburn@hunter.cuny.edu
• Kelsey Campbell, Sports Information
Director
(212) 396-6773

HUNTINGDON COLLEGE ATHLETICS
1500 EAST FAIRVIEW AVENUE
MONTGOMERY, AL 36106
334-833-4565
Fax: 334-833-4486
www.huntingdonhawks.com
• Mike Turk, Director of Athletics
(334) 833-4322
mturk@hawks.huntingdon.edu
• Buzz Phillips, Director of Athletics
Emeritus
(334) 833-4581
• Eric Levanda, Associate Athletic Director
(334) 833-4335
elevanda@hawks.huntingdon.edu
• Wesley Lyle, Sports Information Director
(334) 833-4579
sid@hawks.huntingdon.edu
• Kyle Huff, Head Athletic Trainer
(334) 833-4025

HUSSON UNIVERSITY ATHLETICS
ONE COLLEGE CIRCLE
BANGOR, ME 04401-2929
207-941-7026
Fax: 207-973-1015
athletics@husson.edu
• Frank Pergolizzi, Director of Athletics
(207) 973-1069
pergolizzif@husson.edu
• Janine Gmitter, Senior Woman
Administrator
(207) 941-7021
gmitterj@husson.edu
• Janine Gmitter, Head Athletic Trainer

(207) 941-7021
gmitterj@husson.edu

ILLINOIS COLLEGE ATHLETICS
1101 WEST COLLEGE AVENUE
JACKSONVILLE, IL 62650
217-245-3400
Fax: 217-245-3398
www.illinoiscollegeathletics.com
• Mike Snyder, Director of Athletics
(217) 245-3000
mike.snyder@mail.ic.edu
• Meghan Roman, Senior Woman
Administrator
(217) 245-3197
meghan.roman@mail.ic.edu
• Alex Keil, Sports Information Director
(217) 245-3894
• Terry Geirnaeirt, Head Athletic Trainer
(217) 245-3397
tlgeirna@mail.ic.edu

ILLINOIS WESLEYAN UNIVERSITY ATHLETICS
1312 PARK STREET
BLOOMINGTON, IL 61701
309-556-1000
Fax: 309-556-3484
iwusports.com
• Mike Wagner, Athletic Director
(309) 556-3341
mwagner@iwu.edu
• Norm Eash, Associate Athletic Director
(309) 556-3344
neash@iwu.edu
• Kim Nelson-Brown, Senior Women
Administrator
(309) 556-3349
knbrown@iwu.edu
• Tony Bankston, Assistant Athletic Director
bankston@iwu.edu
• Bill Kauth, Head Athletic Trainer
(309) 556-3601
bkauth@iwu.edu
• Stew Salowitz, Sports Information Director
(309) 556-3206
salowitz@iwu.edu

IOWA WESLEYAN COLLEGE ATHLETICS
601 NORTH MAIN STREET
MOUNT PLEASANT, IA 52641
319-385-6332
Fax: 319-385-6384
www.iwtigers.com
• Steve Williamson, Athletic Director
(319) 385-6332
• B.J. Wagy, Assistant Athletic Director
(319) 385-6305
• Derek Zander, NCAA Compliance Officer
(319) 385-6349
• Andy Niemann, Athletic Trainer
(319) 385-6417
• Dave Stecker, Assistant Athletic Trainer
(319) 385-6417

ITHACA COLLEGE ATHLETICS
953 DANBY ROAD
ITHACA, NY 14850-7198
607-274-3209
Fax: 607-274-1667
ithacan@ithaca.edu
athletics.ithaca.edu
• Susan Bassett, Director of Intercollegiate
Athletics
(607) 274-3209
• Will Rothermel, Associate Athletic Director
(607) 274-3199

jrothermel@ithaca.edu
• Michelle Manning, Senior Woman
Administrator
(607) 274-5708
mmanning@ithaca.edu
• Sean Fitzmaurice, Coordinator of Facilities
(607) 274-1972
sfitzmaurice@ithaca.edu

JOHN CARROLL UNIVERSITY ATHLETICS
ONE JOHN CARROLL BOULEVARD
UNIVERSITY HEIGHTS, OH 44118
216-397-1886
Fax: 216-397-3043
www.jcusports.com
• Laurie Massa, Director of Athletics
(216) 397-1525
• Gretchen Weitbrecht, Associate Athletic
Director
(216) 397-4194
• Christopher Wenzler, Sports Information
Director
(216) 397-4676

JOHN JAY COLLEGE OF CRIMINAL JUSTICE ATHLETICS
525 WEST 59TH STREET
NEW YORK, NY 10019
212-237-8371
Fax: 212-237-8474
ckashow@jjay.cuny.edu
www.johnjayathletics.com
• Carol Kashow, Director of Athletics
(212) 393-6329
ckashow@jjay.cuny.edu
• Catherine Alves, Senior Associate Athletic
Director
(212) 237-8395
calves@jjay.cuny.edu
• Corey Berg, Assistant Athletics Director
(212) 237-8396
cberg@jjay.cuny.edu
• Brandon Fieland, Sports Information
Director
(212) 237-8322
bfieland@jjay.cuny.edu
• Lindsay Roderick, Head Athletic Trainer
(212) 237-8324
lroderick@jjay.cuny.edu

JOHNS HOPKINS UNIVERSITY ATHLETICS
3400 NORTH CHARLES STREET
BALTIMORE, MD 21218
410-516-7490
Fax: 410-516-7482
tcalder@jhu.edu
www.hopkinssports.com
• Alanna Shanahan, Director of Athletics
(410) 516-7490
• Bill Harrington, Senior Associate Director
of Athletics
(410) 516-5279
aggie@jhu.edu
• Grant Kelly, Director of Development
(410) 516-4096
gkelly@jhu.edu
• Ernie Larossa, Director of Athletic
Communications
(410) 516-0552
elarossa@jhu.edu

JOHNSON STATE COLLEGE ATHLETICS
337 COLLEGE HILL
JOHNSON, VT 05656

802-635-1485
800-635-2356
Fax: 802-635-1497
athletics.jsc.edu
• Jamey Ventura, Director of Athletics and
Recreation
(802) 635-1285
• Miles Smith, Assistant Athletics Director
(802) 635-1470
• Elaine Harvey, Assistant Athletics Director
for Communications
(802) 635-1384
• James Nichols, Head Athletic Trainer
(802) 635-1487

JUNIATA COLLEGE ATHLETICS
1700 MOORE STREET
HUNTINGDON, PA 16652
814-641-3512
Fax: 814-641-3508
info@juniata.edu
www.juniatasports.net
• Greg Curley, Athletic Director
(814) 641-3521
curleyg@juniata.edu
• Danny Young-Uhrich, Senior Woman
Administrator
(814) 641-3518
youngd@juniata.edu
• Scott McKenzie, Director for Athletic
Communications
(814) 641-3503
mckenzs@juniata.edu
• David Heberger, Sports Information
Director
(814) 641-3134
• Jeff Leydig, Head Athletic Trainer
(814) 641-3516
leydigj@juniata.edu

KALAMAZOO COLLEGE ATHLETICS
1200 ACADEMY STREET
KALAMAZOO, MI 49006
269-337-7082
Fax: 269-337-7401
sports@kzoo.edu
hornets.kzoo.edu
• Kristen Smith, Director of Athletics
(269) 337-7090
• Kathy Milliken, Senior Woman
Administrator
(269) 337-7091
• Steve Wideen, Sports Information Director
(269) 337-7287
swideen@kzoo.edu
• Kathleen White, Interim Head Athletic
Trainer
(269) 337-7093
ofarrell@kzoo.edu

KEAN UNIVERSITY ATHLETICS
1000 MORRIS AVENUE
UNION, NJ 07083
908-737-0600
Fax: 908-737-0605
www.keanathletics.com
• Jack McKiernan, Director of Athletics
(908) 737-0604
• Denise Wujciak, Head Athletic Trainer
(908) 737-5454
wujciakd@kean.edu
• Kimberly DeRitter, Director of Sports
Information
(908) 737-0615
kderitte@kean.edu

KEENE STATE COLLEGE ATHLETICS
229 MAIN STREET
KEENE, NH 03435
603-358-2813
Fax: 603-358-2888
keeneowls.com
• Kemal Atkins, Director of Athletics
(603) 358-2108
• Abe Osheyack, Sports Information Director
(603) 358-2630
abe.osheyack@keene.edu
• Bob Merrow, Head Athletic Trainer
(603) 358-2824
rmerrow@keene.edu

KENYON COLLEGE ATHLETICS
221 DUFF STREET
KENYON ATHLETIC CENTER
GAMBIER, OH 43022
740-427-5456
Fax: 740-427-5402
athletics.kenyon.edu
• Peter Smith, Director of Athletics
(740) 427-5811
smithp@kenyon.edu
• Justin Newell, Assistant Athletic Director
(740) 427-5460
newellj@kenyon.edu
• Andy Wheeler, Head Athletic Trainer
(740) 427-5553
• Marty Fuller, Sports Information Director
(740) 427-5471
fullerm@kenyon.edu

KEUKA COLLEGE ATHLETICS
141 CENTRAL AVENUE
KEUKA PARK, NY 14478
315-279-5249
Fax: 315-279-5325
dsweet@keuka.edu
www.kcwolfpack.com
• David Sweet, Director of Athletics
(315) 279-5682
dsweet@keuka.edu
• Jeff Bray, Associate Athletics Director
(315) 279-5656
jbray@keuka.edu
• Jonathan Accardi, Assistant Athletics
Director
(315) 279-5690
jaccardi@keuka.edu
• Jimmy Habecker, Sports Information
Director
(315) 279-5241
jhabecker@keuka.edu

KING'S COLLEGE ATHLETICS
133 NORTH RIVER STREET
WILKES-BARRE, PA 18711
570-208-5934
Fax: 570-208-5937
www.kingscollegeathletics.com
• Cheryl Ish, Director of Intercollegiate
Athletics
(570) 208-5900
cherylish@kings.edu
• J.P. Andrejko, Assistant Director of
Intercollegiate Athletics
(570) 208-5900
johnandrejko@kings.edu
• Megan Mundy, Athletic Business and
Operations Coordinator
(570) 208-5855
meganmundy@kings.edu
• Bob Ziadie, Director of Sports Information
(570) 208-5934
robertziadie@kings.edu

KNOX COLLEGE ATHLETICS
2 EAST SOUTH STREET
GALESBURG, IL 61401-4999
309-341-7000
Fax: 309-341-7806
athletics@knox.edu
• Chad Eisele, Director of Athletics
(309) 341-7280
• Scott Sunderland, Assistant Athletic
Director
(309) 341-7378
ssunderl@knox.edu
• James Clark, Sports Information Director
(309) 341-7714
• Andy Gibbons, Fitness Center Director
(309) 341-7379
agibbons@knox.edu

KNOXVILLE COLLEGE ATHLETICS
901 KNOXVILLE COLLEGE DRIVE
KNOXVILLE, TN 37921
865-524-6511
Fax: 865-524-6603
www.knoxvillecollege.edu
• Geoffery Mallory, Men's Basketball Head
Coach
• Will Dorsey, Men's Basketball Assistant
Coach

LA GRANGE COLLEGE ATHLETICS
601 BROAD STREET
LA GRANGE, GA 30240
706-880-8330
Fax: 706-880-8350
www.lagrangepanthers.com
• Jennifer Claybrook, Athletic Director
(706) 880-8262
jclaybrook@lagrange.edu
• Kendal Wallace, Assistant Athletic Director
(706) 880-8328
kwallace@lagrange.edu
• Jenna Jones, Athletics Program
Coordinator
(706) 880-8330
jjones@lagrange.edu
• John Hughes, Sports Information Director
(706) 880-8318
jhughes@lagrange.edu
• Rob Dicks, Director of Athletic Training
(706) 880-8099
rdicks@lagrange.edu

LA ROCHE COLLEGE ATHLETICS
9000 BABCOCK BOULEVARD
PITTSBURGH, PA 15237
412-536-1041
Fax: 412-536-1012
www.larochesports.com
• Jim Tinkey, Director of Athletics
(412) 536-1011
jim.tinkey@laroche.edu
• Katherine Golebie, Assistant Director of
Athletics
(412) 536-1019
katherine.golebie@laroche.edu
• Chase Rowe, Manager of Athletic
Facilities
(412) 536-1046
chase.rowe@laroche.edu
• Jimmy Finley, Sports Information Director
(412) 536-1041

LA VERNE ATHLETICS, UNIVERSITY OF
1950 THIRD STREET
LA VERNE, CA 91750
909-593-3511 EXT 4261
Fax: 909-392-2760

jkline@laverne.edu
www.leopardathletics.com
• Julie Kline, Director of Athletics
(909) 448-4345
jkline@laverne.edu
• Julie Smith, Assistant Athletics Director
(909) 448-4343
jsmith2@laverne.edu
• Joanna Engel, Director of Athletic Training
Services
(909) 448-4986
jengel@laverne.edu
• Sean Lee, Athletics Communication
Director
(909) 448-4639
slee5@laverne.edu

LAKE FOREST COLLEGE ATHLETICS
555 NORTH SHERIDAN ROAD
LAKE FOREST, IL 60045
847-735-6054
Fax: 847-735-6299
wajerski@lakeforest.edu
www.goforesters.com
• Jackie Slaats, Director of Athletics
(847) 735-5290
slaats@lakeforest.edu
• Cheryl Brazil, Assistant Director of
Athletics
(847) 735-6134
cbrazil@lakeforest.edu
• Chris Pier, Operations Director for
Compliance
(847) 735-5288
cpier@lakeforest.edu
• Blake Theisen, Director of Athletic
Programming
(847) 735-6155
theisen@lakeforest.edu
• Mike Gilboe, Head Athletic Trainer
(847) 735-5296
gilboe@lakeforest.edu
• Brian Bruha, Director of Athletic Facilities
(847) 735-5293
bruha@lakeforest.edu

LAKELAND COLLEGE ATHLETICS
PO BOX 359
SHEBOYGAN, WI 53082-0359
920-565-1024
Fax: 920-565-1069
lakelandmuskies.com
• April Arvan, Director of Athletics
(920) 565-1024
arvanaa@lakeland.edu
• Aaron Aanonsen, Senior Associate
Director of Athletics
(920) 565-1024
aanonsenaa@lakeland.edu
• Dona Richardson, Head Athletic Trainer
(920) 565-1024
richardsonda@lakeland.edu
• Adam Glatczak, Sports Information
Director
(920) 565-1028
glatczakaj@lakeland.edu

LASELL COLLEGE ATHLETICS
1844 COMMONWEALTH AVENUE
NEWTON, MA 02466
617-243-2000
Fax: 617-243-2037
kwalter@lasell.edu
laserpride.lasell.edu
• Kristy Walter, Director of Athletics
(617) 243-2147
kwalter@lasell.edu

• Aaron Galletta, Facilities Coordinator
(617) 243-2188
agalletta@lasell.edu
• Todd Montana, Assistant Director of
Athletics
(617) 243-2232
tmontana@lasell.edu
• Emily Machado, Director of Sports
Information
(617) 243-2035
emachado@lasell.edu
• Christopher Noyes, Head Athletic Trainer
(617) 243-2297
cnoyes@lasell.edu

LAWRENCE UNIVERSITY ATHLETICS
711 EAST BOLDT WAY
APPLETON, WI 54911
920-832-7000
Fax: 920-832-7349
www.lawrence.edu
• Christyn Abaray, Director of Athletics
(920) 832-6888
christyn.abaray@lawrence.edu
• Kim Tatro, Associate Director of Athletics
(920) 832-6975
kimberly.n.tatro@lawrence.edu
• Joel DePagter, Assistant Director of
Athletics
(920) 993-6281
• Joe Vanden Acker, Director of Athletic
Media Relations
(920) 832-6878
joseph.m.vandenacker@lawrence.edu
• Jami Rogers, Head Athletic Trainer
(920) 832-6762

**LEBANON VALLEY COLLEGE
ATHLETICS**
101 NORTH COLLEGE AVENUE
ANNVILLE, PA 17003-1400
717-867-6260
Fax: 717-867-6990
godutchmen.com
• Rick Beard, Director of Athletics
(717) 867-6363
rbeard@lvc.edu
• Stacey Hollinger, Assistant Athletic
Director
(717) 867-6891
sholling@lvc.edu
• Thomas Klemick, Director of Athletic
Communications
(717) 867-6580
klemick@lvc.edu
• Erin Ulrich, Head Athletic Trainer
(717) 867-6269
ulrich@lvc.edu
• Kevin Yeiser, Director of Grounds
(717) 867-6342
yeiser@lvc.edu

LEHMAN COLLEGE ATHLETICS
250 BEDFORD PARK BOULEVARD WEST
BRONX, NY 10468
718-960-8101
Fax: 718-960-8815
lehmanathletics.com
• Martin L. Zwiren, Director of Athletics
(718) 960-1117
martin.zwiren@lehman.cuny.edu
• Robert Harris, Fitness Center Director
(718) 960-1133
robert.harris@lehman.cuny.edu
• Durval Morgan, Head Athletic Trainer
(718) 960-7175
eric.harrison@lehman.cuny.edu

• Lenn Margolis, Director of Sports
Information
(718) 960-1130
lenn.margolis@lehman.cuny.edu
• David Gonzalez, Director of Sports
Medicine
(718) 960-1171
dgonzale@montefiore.org

LEWIS & CLARK COLLEGE ATHLETICS
0615 SW PALATINE HILL ROAD
PORTLAND, OR 97219-7889
503-768-7545
Fax: 503-768-7058
www.lcpioneers.com
• Shana Levine, Director of Athletics
(503) 768-7548
• Sharon Sexton, Associate Director of
Physical Education
(503) 768-7073
sextons@lclark.edu
• Mark Pietrok, Head Athletic Trainer
(503) 768-7065
pietrok@lclark.edu
• Ryan Goff, Interim Sports Information
Director
(503) 768-7067

LINFIELD COLLEGE ATHLETICS
900 SE BAKER STREET
MCMINNVILLE, OR 97128
503-883-2200
Fax: 503-434-2453
www.linfield.edu/sports
• Scott Carnahan, Athletic Director
(503) 883-2229
scarnah@linfield.edu
• Lisa Macy-Baker, Compliance Officer
(503) 883-2710
lmacybak@linfield.edu
• Doug Hire, Assistant Athletic Director
(503) 883-2419
dhire@linfield.edu
• Kelly Bird, Sports Information Director
(503) 883-2439
kbird@linfield.edu
• Duane Duey, Certified Athletic Trainer
(503) 883-2415
dduey@linfield.edu

LOUISIANA COLLEGE ATHLETICS
1140 COLLEGE DRIVE
PINEVILLE, LA 71360
318-487-7559
Fax: 318-487-7174
athletics@lacollege.edu
www.lcwildcats.net
• Dennis Dunn, Athletics Director
(318) 487-7725
• Jonathan Small, Associate Athletics
Director
(318) 487-7965
• Paula Hunter, Assistant Athletics Director
(318) 487-7559
paula.hunter@lacollege.edu
• Jon Hay, Head Athletic Trainer
(318) 487-7792

LUTHER COLLEGE ATHLETICS
700 COLLEGE DRIVE
DECORAH, IA 52101
563-387-1575
Fax: 563-387-1228
www.sports.luther.edu
• Renae Hartl, Athletic Director
(563) 387-1575
hartre01@luther.edu

• Alex Smith, Associate Athletic Director for Operations
(563) 387-1382
• Bryan Nikkel, Director of Facilities
(563) 387-1590
nikkbr01@luther.edu
• Dave Blanchard, Sports Information Director
(563) 387-1586
blanchda@luther.edu

LYCOMING COLLEGE ATHLETICS
700 COLLEGE PLACE
WILLIAMSPORT, PA 17701
570-321-4110
Fax: 570-321-4158
clarkm@lycoming.edu
athletics.lycoming.edu
• Mike Clark, Director of Athletics
(570) 321-4110
clarkm@lycoming.edu
• Joe Guistina, Associate Athletic Director of Communications
(570) 321-4028
guistina@lycoming.edu
• Christen Ditzler, Assistant Athletic Director
(570) 321-4261
ditzler@lycoming.edu
• Andrea Lucas, Head Athletic Trainer
(570) 321-4271
• Christen Ditzler, SWA/Head Women's Basketball Coach
(570) 321-4261
ditzler@lycoming.edu
• Jamie Spencer, Head Golf Coach

LYNCHBURG COLLEGE ATHLETICS
TURNER GYM, 1501 LAKESIDE DRIVE
LYNCHBURG, VA 24501-3199
434-544-8100
Fax: 434-544-8365
www.lynchburg.edu
• Jon Waters, Athletic Director
(434) 544-8498
waters.j@lynchburg.edu
• Steve Koudelka, Assistant Athletic Director
(434) 544-8494
koudelka@lynchburg.edu
• Kelley Gunter, Coordinator of Athletic Operations
(434) 544-8286
gunter@lynchburg.edu
• Mike Carpenter, Sports Information Director
(434) 544-8495
• Chris Casola, Director of Athletic Training Services
(434) 544-8180

LYNDON STATE COLLEGE ATHLETICS
1001 COLLEGE ROAD
PO BOX 919
LYNDONVILLE, VT 05851
802-626-6200
800-225-1998
www.lyndonstate.edu/athletics
• Chris Ummer, Director of Athletics
(802) 626-6224
• Kate Roy, Associate Director of Athletics
(802) 626-6439
• Zac Harrison, Sports Information Coordinator
(802) 626-6341
• Evita Sandoval, Head Athletic Trainer
(802) 626-6477

MACALESTER COLLEGE ATHLETICS
1600 GRAND AVENUE
SAINT PAUL, MN 55105
651-696-6000
Fax: 651-696-6328
athletics.macalester.edu
• Kim Chandler, Director of Athletics
(651) 696-6366
kchandle@macalester.edu
• Vanessa Seljeskog, Associate Director of Athletics
(651) 696-6736
seljeskog@macalester.edu
• Ron Osterman, Assistant Athletic Director
(651) 696-6607
osterman@macalester.edu
• Matt McLagan, Director of Sports Information
(651) 696-6563
mmclagan@macalester.edu
• Paula Natvig, Head Athletic Trainer
(651) 696-6162
natvig@macalester.edu

MACMURRAY COLLEGE ATHLETICS
447 EAST COLLEGE AVENUE
JACKSONVILLE, IL 62650
217-479-7142
Fax: 217-479-7147
athletics@mac.edu
www.mac.edu/athletics
• Justin Fuhler, Athletic Director
(217) 479-7142
• Randi Armstrong, Sports Information Director
(217) 479-7157
• Bryan Langan, Athletic Trainer
(217) 479-7193

MAINE AT FARMINGTON ATHLETICS, UNIVERSITY OF
111 SOUTH STREET
FARMINGTON, ME 04938
207-778-7535
Fax: 207-778-8177
athletics.umf.maine.edu
• Julie Davis, Director of Athletics
(207) 778-7264
jadavis@maine.edu
• Jamie Beaudoin, Associate Athletics Director
(207) 778-8168
jbeaudoin@maine.edu
• Dustin Parker, Director of Athletics Communications
(207) 778-7535
dustin.parker@maine.edu

MAINE AT PRESQUE ISLE ATHLETICS, UNIVERSITY OF
181 MAIN STREET
PRESQUE ISLE, ME 04769
207-768-9400
Fax: 207-768-9777
owls.umpi.edu/athletics
• Mike Holmes, Athletic Director
michael.s.holmes@umpi.edu
• Doug Carter, Assistant Athletic Director
(207) 768-9523
douglas.carter@umpi.edu
• Mike Pankow, Sports Information Director
(207) 768-9792
michael.pankow@maine.edu
• Patrick Baker, Head Athletic Trainer
(207) 968-9474
lucas.bartlett@maine.edu

MAINE MARITIME ACADEMY ATHLETICS(MMA)
ONE PLEASANT STREET
CASTINE, ME 04420
207-326-0299
Fax: 207-326-2513
marinersports.org
• Steve Peed, Director of Athletics
(207) 326-2451
steve.peed@mma.edu
• Tricia Carver-Watson, Associate Athletic Director
(207) 326-0253
tricia.carverwatson@mma.edu
• Riana Sidelinger, Athletic Communications Coordinator
(207) 326-0113
• Richard Osheim, Certified Athletic Trainer
(207) 326-0238

MANCHESTER UNIVERSITY ATHLETICS
604 EAST COLLEGE AVENUE
NORTH MANCHESTER, IN 46962
260-982-5390
800-852-3648
Fax: 260-982-5032
sportsinfo@manchester.edu
www.muspartans.com
• Rick Espeset, Director of Athletics
(260) 982-5390
rbespeset@manchester.edu
• Josh Dzurick, Assistant Director of Athletics
(260) 982-5379
jndzurick@manchester.edu
• Tami Hoagland, Athletic Department Office Manager
(260) 982-5390
tlhoagland@manchester.edu
• Mark Adkins, Sports Information Director
(260) 982-5035
mtadkins@manchester.edu

MANHATTANVILLE COLLEGE ATHLETICS
2900 PURCHASE STREET
PURCHASE, NY 10577
914-323-5280
Fax: 914-323-5130
www.govaliants.com
• Keith Levinthal, Director of Athletics
(914) 323-7270
levinthal@govaliants.com
• Julene Fisher, Assistant Director of Athletics
(914) 323-7285
fisher@govaliants.com
• Steve Sheridan, Director of Athletics for Communications
(914) 323-7280
sheridan@govaliants.com
• Casey Schermick, Sports Information Director
(914) 323-7280
• Scott McIver, Head Athletic Trainer
(914) 323-7276
mciver@govaliants.com

MARANATHA BAPTIST UNIVERSITY
745 WEST MAIN STREET
WATERTOWN, WI 53094
920-206-2376
Fax: 920-261-9109
www.mbu.edu
• Rob Thompson, Athletic Director
(920) 206-2377
rob.thompson@mbu.edu

• Ann Bolton, Assistant Athletic Director
(920) 206-2379
ann.bolton@mbu.edu
• Taylor Pill, Sports Information Director
(920) 206-2379
taylor.pill@mbu.edu
• Zachary Sweatman, Certified Athletic
Trainer
(920) 206-3476
zachary.sweatman@mbu.edu

**MARIAN COLLEGE OF FOND DU LAC
ATHLETICS**
45 SOUTH NATIONAL AVENUE
FOND DU LAC, WI 54935-4699
920-923-8156
Fax: 920-923-8134
www.sabreathletics.com
• Jason Bartelt, Director of Athletics
(920) 923-8090
jbartelt@marianuniversity.edu
• Kerri Huebel, Assistant Athletic Director
(920) 923-8516
kahuebel@marianuniversity.edu
• Dennis Driscoll, Director of Athletic
Communications
(920) 923-8155
• Kim Sorensen, Head Athletic Trainer
(920) 923-8754
kasorensen61@marianuniversity.edu

MARIETTA COLLEGE ATHLETICS
215 FIFTH STREET
MARIETTA, OH 45750
740-376-4665
Fax: 740-376-4674
pioneers.marietta.edu
• Larry Hiser, Athletics Director
(740) 376-4667
larry.hiser@marietta.edu
• John Tynan, Faculty Athletic
Representative
(740) 376-4873
john.tynan@marietta.edu
• Jeanne Arbuckle, Associate Athletics
Director
(740) 376-4668
arbucklj@marietta.edu
• Sam Crowther, Director of Athletic Training
Program
(740) 376-4774
crowthes@marietta.edu
• Jaclyn Schwieterman, Head Athletic
Trainer
(740) 376-4773
sj004@marietta.edu

**MARY HARDIN-BAYLOR ATHLETICS,
UNIVERSITY OF**
900 COLLEGE STREET
UMHB BOX 8010
BELTON, TX 76513
254-295-8642
Fax: 254-295-4614
jwallin@umhb.edu
www.cruathletics.com
• Randy Mann, Vice President for Athletics
(254) 295-4618
rmann@umhb.edu
• Darla Kirby, Associate Athletic Director
(254) 295-5046
dkirby@umhb.edu
• Jon Wallin, Sports Information Director
(254) 295-4611
jwallin@umhb.edu
• Jake Fralicks, Office and Ticket
Coordinator

(254) 295-5593
jfralicks@umhb.edu

**MARY WASHINGTON UNIVERSITY
ATHLETICS**
1301 COLLEGE AVENUE
FREDERICKSBURG, VA 22401
540-654-1039
Fax: 540-654-1892
umweagles.com
• Ken Tyler, Director of Athletics
(540) 654-1876
ktyler2@umw.edu
• Dana Hall, Senior Associate Director of
Athletics
(540) 654-1890
dhall@umw.edu
• Clint Often, Director of Communications
(540) 654-1743
coften@umw.edu
• Philip Pierce, Director of Athletic
Development
(540) 654-1153
ppierce@umw.edu
• Ian Rogol, Head Athletic Trainer
(540) 654-1872
irogol@umw.edu

MARYMOUNT UNIVERSITY
2807 NORTH GLEBE ROAD
ARLINGTON, VA 22207
703-284-1619
Fax: 703-527-3684
www.marymount.edu/athletics
• Jamie Reynolds, Director of Athletics
(703) 908-7619
• Sarah Gustin, Associate Athletics Director
for Compliance
(703) 284-3334
• Kyle Gurganious, Director of Athletic
Communications
(703) 284-3332
• Ryan Wildenhain, Head of Sports
Medicine
(703) 284-1672
rwildeha@marymount.edu

MARYWOOD UNIVERSITY ATHLETICS
2300 ADAMS AVENUE
SCRANTON, PA 18509-1598
570-961-4724
Fax: 570-961-4730
marywoodpacers.com
• Mary Jo Gunning, Director of Athletics and
Recreation
(570) 961-4724
• Eric Grundman, Assistant Director of
Athletics
(570) 961-4724
• Andrew Smith, Director of Athletics for
Communications
(570) 961-4724
aesmith@marywood.edu
• Nicole Malloy, Director of Athletics for
Internal Operations
(570) 961-4724
malloy@marywood.edu
• Scott Summers, Head Athletic Trainer
(570) 961-4724

**MASSACHUSETTS BOSTON ATHLETICS,
UNIVERSITY OF**
100 MORRISSEY BOULEVARD
BOSTON, MA 02125-3393
617-287-7801
Fax: 617-287-7840
www.umb.edu

• Charlie Titus, Director of Athletics
(617) 287-7810
• Chris Collins, Interim Associate Director of
Athletics
(617) 287-7861
• Paula Ayers, Director of Finance
(617) 287-7808
paula.ayers@umb.edu
• Terry Condon, Senior Associate Director of
Athletics
(617) 287-7832
terry.condon@umb.edu

**MASSACHUSETTS COLLEGE OF
LIBERAL ARTS ATHLETICS**
375 CHURCH STREET
NORTH ADAMS, MA 01247
413-662-5411
Fax: 413-662-5357
athletics.mcla.edu
• Laura Mooney, Director of Athletics
(413) 662-5411
laura.mooney@mcla.edu
• Dot Houston, Associate Athletic Director
for Administration
(413) 662-5437
d.houston@mcla.edu
• Jeff Puleri, Assistant Athletic Director for
Communications
(413) 662-5403
j.puleri@mcla.edu
• Matthew Boillat, Head Athletic Trainer
(413) 662-5414
matthew.boillat@mcla.edu

**MASSACHUSETTS DARTMOUTH
ATHLETICS, UNIVERSITY OF**
TRIPP ATHLETIC CENTER
285 OLD WESTPORT ROAD
DARTMOUTH, MA 02747-2300
508-999-8720
Fax: 508-999-8867
www.corsairathletics.com
• Amanda Van Voorhis, Director of Athletics
(508) 999-9114
avanvoorhis@umassd.edu
• Jack Holleran, Associate Director of
Athletics
(508) 990-9651
jholleran@umassd.edu
• Jim Mullins, Assistant Director of Athletics
(508) 910-6930
jmullins@umassd.edu
• Megan Erbes, Sports Information Director
(508) 910-9528
merbes@umassd.edu

**MASSACHUSETTS INSTITUTE OF
TECHNOLOGY (MIT) ATHLETICS**
120 VASSAR STREET
CAMBRIDGE, MA 02139-7404
617-253-4498
Fax: 617-258-7343
athletics@mit.edu
mitathletics.com
• Julie Soriero, Director of Athletics
(617) 253-4499
jsoriero@mit.edu
• Dan Martin, Director of Facilities and
Operations
(617) 253-5003
djmartin@mit.edu
• John Benedick, Associate Director of
Athletics
(617) 253-9892
• Tom Cronan, Director of Sports Medicine
(617) 253-3473

cronan@mit.edu
• Carrie Sampson Moore, Director of Physical Education
(617) 253-5004
clsmoore@mit.edu
• Tim Mertz, Director of Recreational Sports
(617) 452-4364
tmertz@mit.edu

MASSACHUSETTS MARITIME ACADEMY ATHLETICS
101 ACADEMY DRIVE
BUZZARDS BAY, MA 02532
508-830-5054
Fax: 508-830-5224
mmabucs.com
• Garin Veris, Director of Athletics
(508) 830-5055
• Patricia O'Brien, Assistant Director of Athletics
(508) 830-5076
• Jim Seavey, Director of Sports Information
(508) 830-5054
• Chris Barry, Head Athletic Trainer
(508) 830-5000
cbarry@maritime.edu

MCDANIEL COLLEGE ATHLETICS
2 COLLEGE HILL
WESTMINSTER, MD 21157
410-857-2580
Fax: 410-857-2586
www.mcdanielathletics.com
• Paul Moyer, Director of Athletics
(410) 386-4043
pmoyer@mcdaniel.edu
• Becky Martin, Assistant Director of Athletics
(410) 857-2577
rmartin@mcdaniel.edu
• Luke Stillson, Director of Sports Information
(410) 857-2291
sid@mcdaniel.edu
• Phil Smith, Director of Athletics Facilities
(410) 857-2568
pdsmith@mcdaniel.edu
• Kim Easterday, Director of Athletics Operations
(410) 857-2717
keasterd@mcdaniel.edu
• Gregg Nibbelink, Head Athletic Trainer
(410) 857-2584
gnibbeli@mcdaniel.edu

MCMURRY UNIVERSITY ATHLETICS
1400 SAYLES BOULEVARD
MCM STATION BOX 188
ABILENE, TX 79697
325-793-4633
Fax: 915-793-4659
www.mcmurrysports.com
• Sam Ferguson, Director of Athletics
(325) 793-4647
ferguson.sam@mcm.edu
• Robert Wallace, Faculty Athletics Representative
(325) 793-3895
rwallace@mcm.edu
• Shusaku Hayashi, Head Athletic Trainer
(325) 793-4648
• Dave Beyer, Sports Information Director
(325) 793-4612

MEDGAR EVERS COLLEGE ATHLETICS
1150 CARROLL STREET
BROOKLYN, NY 11225

718-270-6072
Fax: 718-804-8204
rbostic@mec.cuny.edu
www.mecathletics.com
• Renee Bostic, Director of Athletics
(718) 270-6071
rbostic@mec.cuny.edu
• Chetara M. Murphy, Assistant Director of Athletics
(718) 270-6067
cmurphy@mec.cuny.edu
• Videl Price, Director of Compliance
(718) 270-6494
vprice@mec.cuny.edu
• Christopher Ryan, Sports Information Director
crryanchris@gmail.com

MESSIAH COLLEGE ATHLETICS
ONE COLLEGE AVENUE
SUITE 4501
MECHANICSBURG, PA 17055
717-691-6018
Fax: 717-691-2310
www.gomessiah.com
• Jack Cole, Director of Athletics
(717) 796-1800
jcole@messiah.edu
• Brad McCarty, Associate Athletics Director for Facilities
(717) 796-1800
bmccarty@messiah.edu
• Amy Weaver, Associate Athletics Director for Operations
(717) 796-1800
aweaver@messiah.edu
• Steve King, Associate Athletics Director for Communications
(717) 796-1800
sking@messiah.edu

METHODIST COLLEGE ATHLETICS
5400 RAMSEY STREET
FAYETTEVILLE, NC 28311
910-630-7175
Fax: 910-630-7676
www.mumonarchs.com
• Bob McEvoy, Director of Athletics
(910) 630-7182
mcevoy@methodist.edu
• DeeDee Jarman, Senior Associate Athletic Director
(910) 630-7283
djarman@methodist.edu
• Dave Eavenson, Assistant Director of Athletics
(910) 630-7396
deavenson@methodist.edu
• Nate Jervey, Sports Information Director
(910) 630-7172
sportsinfo@methodist.edu
• Brandon Reynolds, Head Athletic Trainer
(910) 630-7177
brandonr@methodist.edu

MIDDLEBURY COLLEGE ATHLETICS
219 SOUTH MAIN STREET
MIDDLEBURY, VT 05753
802-443-5250
Fax: 802-443-2124
athletics.middlebury.edu
• Erin Quinn, Director of Athletics
(802) 443-5253
quinn@middlebury.edu
• Katharine DeLorenzo, Assistant Athletic Director
(802) 443-5422

kdeloren@middlebury.edu
• Kelly Bevere, Director of Compliance
(802) 443-5386
kbevere@middlebury.edu
• Brad Nadeau, Director of Athletic Communications
(802) 443-5193
nadeau@middlebury.edu
• Kelly Cray, Acting Director of Sports Medicine
(802) 443-5259
cray@middlebury.edu

MILLIKIN UNIVERSITY ATHLETICS
1184 WEST MAIN STREET
DECATUR, IL 62522
217-362-6429
Fax: 217-362-6414
ccwhite@millikin.edu
athletics.millikin.edu
• Craig White, Director of Athletics
(217) 424-6344
ccwhite@millikin.edu
• Patrick Allgeier, Assistant Athletic Director
(217) 424-3605
pallgeier@millikin.edu
• Bryan Marshall, Director for Sports Information
(217) 362-6429
bmarshall@millikin.edu
• Travis Wilcoxen, Faculty Athletics Representative
(217) 424-6236
twilcoxen@millikin.edu

MILLS COLLEGE ATHLETICS
5000 MACARTHUR BOULEVARD
OAKLAND, CA 94613
510-430-2255
millscyclones.com
• Themy Adachi, Director of Athletics
(510) 430-3285
• Allie Fox, Communications and Compliance Coordinator
(510) 430-2232
afox@mills.edu
• Natalie Sprangler, Head Athletic Trainer
(510) 430-3323
nspangle@mills.edu
• Hilary Worthen, Assistant Athletic Trainer
(510) 430-3323

MILLSAPS COLLEGE ATHLETICS
1701 NORTH STATE STREET
JACKSON, MS 39210
601-974-1190
Fax: 601-974-1209
gomajors.com
• Tim Wise, Associate Athletic Director
(601) 974-1188
wiseta@millsaps.edu
• Will Purcell, Sports Information Director
(601) 974-1394
purcews@millsaps.edu

MILWAUKEE SCHOOL OF ENGINEERING ATHLETICS
1025 NORTH BROADWAY
MILWAUKEE, WI 53202-3109
414-277-6497
800-332-6763
millerbj@msoe.edu
go-raiders.com
• Brian Miller, Athletic Director
(414) 277-6947
millerbj@msoe.edu
• Jessica Ott, Assistant Athletic Director

(414) 277-2411
ott@msoe.edu
• Jimmy Banks, Director of Intramurals
(414) 277-7493
banks@msoe.edu
• Kevin Conway, Sports Information Director
(414) 277-2412
conway@msoe.edu
• Dave Bugalski, Head Athletic Trainer
(414) 277-2812
bugalski@msoe.edu

MINNESOTA-MORRIS ATHLETICS, UNIVERSITY OF
600 EAST FOURTH STREET
MORRIS, MN 56267
320-589-6035
Fax: 320-589-6428
ummcougars.org
• Jason Herbers, Director of Intercollegiate Athletics
(320) 589-6406
jherbers@morris.umn.edu
• Paul Grove, Assistant Athletic Director
(320) 589-6433
grovep@morris.umn.edu
• Stephen Batcher, Sports Information Director
(320) 589-6423
sabatche@morris.umn.edu
• Raymond Bowman, Head Athletic Trainer
(320) 589-6438
bowmanr@morris.umn.edu

MISERICORDIA UNIVERSITY ATHLETICS
301 LAKE STREET
DALLAS, PA 18612
570-674-6374
Fax: 570-674-3024
athletics.misericordia.edu
• Chuck Edkins, Athletic Director
(570) 674-6397
cedkins@misericordia.edu
• Scott Crispell, Sports Information Director
(570) 674-6398
scrispel@misericordia.edu

MITCHELL COLLEGE ATHLETICS
437 PEQUOT AVENUE
NEW LONDON, CT 06320
860-701-5049
Fax: 860-701-5085
athletics@mitchell.edu
mitchellathletics.com
• Dana Fulmer Garfield, Director of Athletics
(860) 701-5050
• David Longolucco, Sports Information Director
(860) 701-5078
longolucco_d@mitchell.edu
• Aimee Sevigny Krenicki, Head Athletic Trainer
(860) 629-6156

MONMOUTH COLLEGE ATHLETICS
700 EAST BROADWAY
MONMOUTH, IL 61462-1998
309-457-2311
Fax: 309-457-2168
rogerh@monmouthcollege.edu
www.monmouthscots.com
• Roger Haynes, Director of Athletics
(309) 457-2177
rogerh@monmouthcollege.edu
• Tom Burek, Director of Aquatics
(309) 457-2265
• Bob Foster, Head Athletic Trainer

(309) 457-2180
jfoster@monmouthcollege.edu
• Dan Nolan, Sports Information Director
(309) 457-2322

MONTCLAIR STATE UNIVERSITY ATHLETICS
MONTCLAIR, NJ 7043
973-655-5234
Fax: 973-655-5390
www.montclairathletics.com
• Holly Gera, Director of Athletics
(973) 655-5234
• Rob Chesney, Associate Director of Athletics
(973) 655-6804
chesneyr@mail.montclair.edu
• Anita Kubicka, Assistant Director of Athletics
(973) 655-6790
kubickaa@mail.montclair.edu
• Michael Scala, Director of Sports Publicity
(973) 655-6787

MORAVIAN COLLEGE ATHLETICS
1200 MAIN STREET
BETHLEHEM, PA 18018
610-861-1534
Fax: 610-625-7954
dapps@moravian.edu
moraviansports.com
• Scott Dapp, Interim Director of Athletics
dapps@moravian.edu
• John Byrne, Associate Athletics Director
(610) 861-1321
byrnej@moravian.edu
• Sara Steinman, Assistant Athletic Director
(610) 861-1531
steinmans@moravian.edu
• Bob Ward, Head Athletics Trainer
(610) 861-1537
bward@moravian.edu

MOUNT ST. JOSEPH ATHLETICS, COLLEGE OF
5701 DELHI ROAD
CINCINNATI, OH 45233-1670
513-244-4311
Fax: 513-244-4928
www.msjsports.com
• Steve Radcliffe, Director of Athletics
(513) 244-4381
steve.radcliffe@msj.edu
• Melanee Wagener, Associate Director of Athletics
(513) 244-8585
• Ryan Lengerich, Director of Sports Information
(513) 244-4319
ryan.lengerich@msj.edu
• Brian Lewton, Head Athletic Trainer
(513) 244-8588
brian.lewton@msj.edu

MOUNT ST. MARY COLLEGE ATHLETICS
330 POWELL AVENUE
NEWBURGH, NY 12550
845-569-3594
Fax: 845-569-3589
athletics@msmc.edu
www.msmcknights.com
• Dan Twomey, Director of Athletics
(845) 569-3591
dan.twomey@msmc.edu
• Jessica Mushel, Assistant Director of Athletics
(845) 569-3684

jessica.mushel@msmc.edu
• Michele Dreistadt, Director of Intramurals
(845) 569-3583
michele.dreistadt@msmc.edu
• Mike Doughty, Sports Information Director
(845) 569-3341
michael.doughty@msmc.edu
• Steven Iorio, Director of Sports Medicine
(845) 569-3342
steven.iorio@msmc.edu

MOUNT ST. VINCENT ATHLETICS, COLLEGE OF
6301 RIVERDALE AVENUE
RIVERDALE, NY 10471
718-405-3267
Fax: 718-405-3765
www.cmsvathletics.com
• Laura Pruitt, Director of Athletics
(718) 405-3789
laura.pruitt@mountsaintvincent.edu
• Brian Nigro, Associate Director of Athletics
(718) 405-3415
• Nathan Rauscher, Assistant Director of Athletics
(718) 405-3410
• Brendan Kennedy, Director of Sports Information
(718) 405-3413

MUHLENBERG COLLEGE ATHLETICS
ATHLETIC DEPARTMENT
2400 CHEW STREET
ALLENTOWN, PA 18104-5586
484-664-3100
Fax: 484-664-3035
muhlenbergsports.com
• Corey Goff, Director of Athletics
(484) 664-3380
• Megan Patruno, Assistant Athletic Director
(484) 664-3785
mpatruno@muhlenberg.edu
• Steve Nemes, Head Athletic Trainer
(484) 664-3391
snemes@muhlenberg.edu
• Dawud Abdur-Rahkman, Coordinator of Diversity
(484) 664-4085

MUSKINGUM UNIVERSITY ATHLETICS
163 STORMONT STREET
NEW CONCORD, OH 43762
740-826-8211
Fax: 740-826-8300
www.fightingmuskies.com
• Larry Shank, Athletic Director
(740) 826-6109
lshank@muskingum.edu
• Tom Caudill, Sports Information Director
(740) 826-8022
tcaudill@muskingum.edu
• Ken Blood, Head Athletic Trainer
(740) 826-8327
kblood@muskingum.edu

NEBRASKA WESLEYAN UNIVERSITY ATHLETICS
5000 SAINT PAUL AVENUE
LINCOLN, NE 68504-2794
402-465-2360
Fax: 402-465-2170
www.nwusports.com
• Ira Zeff, Director of Athletics
(402) 465-2360
izeff@nebrwesleyan.edu
• Jo Bunstock, Assistant Athletic Director
(402) 465-2355

jeb@nebrwesleyan.edu
• Alex Linden, Sports Information Director
(402) 465-2151
alinden@nebrwesleyan.edu
• Jason Ensrud, Head Athletic Trainer
(402) 465-7508
jensrud@nebrwesleyan.edu

NEUMANN UNIVERSITY ATHLETICS
ONE NEUMANN DRIVE
ASTON, PA 19014-1298
610-459-0905
Fax: 484-840-4798
neumann@neumann.edu
www.neumannathletics.com
• Chuck Sack, Director of Athletics
(484) 840-4711
sackc@neumann.edu
• Len Schuler, Associate Athletic Director
(484) 840-4712
lschuler@neumann.edu
• Jill Weigel, Director of Sports Information
(484) 840-4715
weigelj@neumann.edu
• Mike Cox, Head Athletic Trainer
(484) 840-4719
coxm@neumann.edu

NEW ENGLAND ATHLETICS, UNIVERSITY OF
11 HILLS BEACH ROAD
BIDDEFORD, ME 04005
207-602-2499
Fax: 207-602-5963
athletics.une.edu
• Jack McDonald, Director of Athletics
(207) 602-2499
jmcdonald10@une.edu
• Curt Smyth, Sports Information Director
(207) 602-2562
• Dennis Leighton, Faculty Athletics
Representative
(207) 221-4594
dleighton@une.edu
• Brian Razak, Head Athletic Trainer
(207) 602-2496
brazak@une.edu

NEW ENGLAND COLLEGE ATHLETICS
98 BRIDGE STREET
HENNIKER, NH 03242
603-428-2335
Fax: 603-428-6023
athletics.nec.edu
• Lou Izzi, Director of Athletics
(603) 428-2292
lizzi@nec.edu
• Renee Hellert, Associate Athletic Director
(603) 428-2335
• Heather Jones, Head Athletic Trainer
(603) 428-2260
hjones@nec.edu

NEW JERSEY CITY UNIVERSITY ATHLETICS
2039 KENNEDY BOULEVARD
JERSEY CITY, NJ 07305
201-200-3317
Fax: 201-200-2365
www.njcugothicknights.com
• Alice De Fazio, Director of Athletics
(201) 200-2243
adefazio@njcu.edu
• George Deaver, Assistant Director of
Athletics
(201) 200-2155
gdeaver@njcu.edu

• Juan E. Arroyo, Faculty Athletics
Representative
(201) 200-3570
jarroyo@njcu.edu
• Ira Thor, Director of Sports Information
(201) 200-3301
ithor@njcu.edu
• Ann Marie Stoebling, Head Athletic Trainer
(201) 200-3163
astoebling@njcu.edu

NEW JERSEY INSTITUTE OF TECHNOLOGY ATHLETICS
80 LOCK STREET
NEWARK, NJ 07103-
973-596-3623
Fax: 973-642-7333
kaplan@njit.edu
www.njithighlanders.com
• Lenny Kaplan, Director of Athletics
(973) 596-3638
kaplan@njit.edu
• Andrew Schwartz, Senior Associate
Director of Athletics
(973) 642-7224
aschwart@njit.edu
• Stephanie Pillari, Assistant Sports
Information Director
(973) 596-8324
pillari@njit.edu
• Tim Camp, Director for Sports Information
(973) 596-8461
• Matt Koscs, Head Athletic Trainer
(973) 596-3661
mkoscs@njit.edu

NEW YORK UNIVERSITY ATHLETICS
181 MERCER STREET
NEW YORK, NY 10012
212-998-2021
Fax: 212-995-4591
christopher.bledsoe@nyu.edu
www.gonyuathletics.com
• Christopher Bledsoe, Director of Athletics
(212) 998-2040
christopher.bledsoe@nyu.edu
• Janice Quinn, Senior Associate Director of
Athletics
(212) 998-2033
jq1@nyu.edu
• Jeffrey Bernstein, Athletic Director of
Sports Information
(212) 998-2031
jeffrey.bernstein@nyu.edu
• Nikki Webb, Coordinator of Athletic
Training
(212) 998-2083
nikki.webb@nyu.edu

NICHOLS COLLEGE ATHLETICS
129 CENTER ROAD
DUDLEY, MA 01571
508-213-1560
800-470-3379
Fax: 508-213-2490
reference@nichols.edu
www.nicholsathletics.com
• Chris Colvin, Director of Athletics
(508) 213-2281
• Eric Gobiel, Associate Director of Athletics
(508) 213-2351
eric.gobiel@nichols.edu
• Kristan Mallet, Assistant Director of
Athletics
(508) 213-2369
kristan.mallet@nichols.edu
• Pete DiVito, Sports Informatino Director

(508) 213-2352
pete.divito@nichols.edu
• Tim Bennett, Head Athletic Trainer
(508) 213-2183
timothy.bennett@nichols.edu

NORTH CAROLINA WESLEYAN COLLEGE ATHLETICS
3400 NORTH WESLEYAN BOULEVARD
ROCKY MOUNT, NC 27804
252-985-5213
Fax: 252-985-5252
jthompson@ncwc.edu
www.ncwcsports.com
• John Thompson, Director of Athletics
(252) 985-5218
jthompson@ncwc.edu
• Martha Proctor, Coordinator of Internal
Operations
(252) 985-5213
mproctor@ncwc.edu
• Rikki C. Rich, Assistant Athletic Director of
Communications
(252) 985-5271
rcrich@ncwc.edu
• Carol Carson, Head Athletic Trainer
(252) 985-5221
ccarson@ncwc.edu

NORTH CENTRAL COLLEGE ATHLETICS
30 NORTH BRAINARD STREET
NAPERVILLE, IL 60540
630-637-5500
Fax: 630-637-5521
northcentralcardinals.com
• Troy Hammond, President
• James Miller, Athletic Director
(630) 637-5513
jlmiller@noctrl.edu
• Susan Kane, Assistant Athletic Director
(630) 637-5501
smkane@noctrl.edu
• Sara Furlette-Koski, Head Athletic Trainer
(630) 637-5534
• Clark Teuscher, Sports Information
Director
(630) 637-5302
ccteuscher@noctrl.edu
• James Kluckhohn, Athletic Facilities and
Recreation Manager
(630) 637-5581
jckluckhohn@noctrl.edu

NORTH PARK UNIVERSITY ATHLETICS
3225 WEST FOSTER AVENUE
CHICAGO, IL 60625
773-244-5685
Fax: 773-244-4952
athletics.northpark.edu
• Jack Surridge, Director of Athletics
(773) 244-5685
jsurridge@northpark.edu
• Susan Zimmer, Associate Director of
Athletics
(773) 244-5673
szimmer@northpark.edu
• Kevin Shepke, Director of Sports
Information
(773) 244-5594
• Eric McQuaid, Head Athletic Trainer
(773) 244-5701
emcquaid@northpark.edu

NORTHLAND COLLEGE ATHLETICS
1411 ELLIS AVENUE
ASHLAND, WI 54806-3999

college sports

395

715-682-1699
kfalkenhagen@northland.edu
www.northlandcollegesports.com
• Kim Falkenhagen, Director of Athletics
(715) 682-1868
kfalkenhagen@northland.edu
• Seamus Gregory, Assistant Athletic
Director
(715) 682-1395
sgregory@northland.edu
• Chas Johnson, Sports Information Director
(715) 682-1985
cjohnson@northland.edu
• Abby Kaufman, Athletic Trainer
(715) 682-1245
akaufman@northland.edu

NORWICH UNIVERSITY ATHLETICS
158 HARMON DRIVE
NORTHFIELD, VT 05663
802-485-2230
Fax: 802-485-2234
www.norwichathletics.com
• Anthony Mariano, Director of Athletics
(802) 485-2232
tmariano@norwich.edu
• Derek Dunning, Director of Athletic
Communications
(802) 485-2902
ddunning@norwich.edu
• Jeff Dobbin, Assistant Director of Athletic
Communications
(802) 485-2241
jdobbin@norwich.edu
• Dave Botelho, Head Athletic Trainer
(802) 485-2236
dbotelho@norwich.edu

OBERLIN COLLEGE ATHLETICS
200 WOODLAND AVENUE
OBERLIN, OH 44074
440-775-8500
Fax: 440-775-8957
www.goyeo.com
• Natalie Winkelfoos, Director of Athletics
(440) 775-6463
natalie.winkelfoos@oberlin.edu
• Creg Jantz, Senior Associate Director of
Athletics
(440) 775-6401
creg.jantz@oberlin.edu
• Eric Lahetta, Director of Athletics for
Intercollegiate Sports
(440) 775-8534
• Mike Mancini, Director of Athletics for
Communications
(440) 775-8503
mike.mancini@oberlin.edu
• Tim Carver, Director of Sports Medicine
(440) 775-8589
tim.carver@oberlin.edu

OCCIDENTAL COLLEGE ATHLETICS
1600 CAMPUS RD
DEPARTMENT OF ATHLETICS M-19
LOS ANGELES, CA 90041
323-259-2608
800-765-8002
Fax: 323-341-4993
jhoffman@oxy.edu
www.oxyathletics.com
• Jaime Hoffman, Athletic Director
(323) 259-2699
dfarmer@oxy.edu
• Andy Holmes, Sports Information Director
(323) 259-2724
holmesa@oxy.edu

• Dale Widolff, Football Coach
(323) 259-2708
dwidolff@oxy.edu
• Brian Newhall, Men's Basketball Coach
(323) 259-2608
bnewhall@oxy.edu
• Kevin Hall, Women's Basketball Coach
(323) 259-2682
khall@oxy.edu

OGLETHORPE UNIVERSITY ATHLETICS
4484 PEACHTREE ROAD NE
ATLANTA, GA 30319
404-364-8419
Fax: 404-364-8445
athletics@oglethorpe.edu
gopetrels.com
• Becky Hall, Director of Athletics
• Iona Wynter Parks, Faculty Athletics
Representative
iwynterparks@oglethorpe.edu
• Mike Rulison, Faculty Athletics
Representative
mrulison@oglethorpe.edu

**OHIO NORTHERN UNIVERSITY
ATHLETICS**
KING HORN CENTER
525 SOUTH MAIN STREET
ADA, OH 45810
419-772-2440
Fax: 419-772-2470
www.onusports.com
• Tom Simmons, Athletic Director
(419) 772-2450
t-simmons@onu.edu
• Kate Witte, Senior Woman Administrator
(419) 772-2446
k-witte@onu.edu
• Brian Hofman, Assistant Athletic Director
(419) 772-1878
b-hofman@onu.edu
• Tim Glon, Sports Information Director
(419) 772-2046
t-glon@onu.edu
• Kurt Wilson, Head Athletic Trainer
(419) 772-2559
k-wilson.1@onu.edu

**OHIO WESLEYAN UNIVERSITY
ATHLETICS**
61 SOUTH SANDUSKY STREET
DELAWARE, OH 43015
740-368-3725
Fax: 740-368-3751
www.battlingbishops.com
• Roger Ingles, Athletics Director
(740) 368-3738
• Mike DeWitt, Associate Athletics Director
(740) 368-3744
mddewitt@owu.edu
• Kris Boey, Associate Athletics Director
(740) 368-3731
kwboey@owu.edu
• Todd Miller, Athletic Trainer
(740) 368-3747
tcmiller@owu.edu

OLIVET COLLEGE ATHLETICS
320 SOUTH MAIN STREET
OLIVET, MI 49076
269-749-7601
Fax: 269-749-7229
www.olivetcomets.com
• Ryan Shockey, Athletic Director
(269) 749-7189
rshockey@olivetcollege.edu

• Megan Merchant, Senior Woman
Administrator
(269) 749-6677
mjmiller@olivetcollege.edu
• Charlie Wilson, Coordinator of Eligibility
and Compliance
(269) 749-6649
chwilson@olivetcollege.edu
• Geoff Henson, Sports Information Director
(269) 749-7602
ghenson@olivetcollege.edu

OTTERBEIN UNIVERSITY ATHLETICS
ONE SOUTH GROVE STREET
WESTERVILLE, OH 43081
614-823-3546
Fax: 614-823-1966
dstewart@otterbein.edu
www.otterbeincardinals.com
• Dawn Stewart, Director of Athletics
(614) 823-3518
dstewart@otterbein.edu
• Connie Richardson, Associate Athletic
Director
(614) 823-3517
crichardson@otterbein.edu
• Tim Doup, Assistant Athletic Director
(614) 823-3527
tdoup@otterbein.edu
• Adam Prescott, Sports Information
Director
(614) 823-1951
aprescott@otterbein.edu
• Charles Goodwin, Head Athletic Trainer
(614) 823-1634
cgoodwin@otterbein.edu

**OZARKS ATHLETICS, UNIVERSITY OF
THE**
415 NORTH COLLEGE AVENUE
CLARKSVILLE, AR 72830
479-979-1465
Fax: 479-979-1330
• Jimmy Clark, Athletic Director
(479) 979-1484
jclark@ozarks.edu
• Matt Torok, Assistant Athletic Director
(479) 979-1210
• Josh Peppas, Sports Information Director
(479) 979-1483
jpeppas@ozarks.edu
• Chad Floyd, Head Athletic Trainer
(479) 979-1472
cfloyd@ozarks.edu

**PACIFIC LUTHERAN UNIVERSITY
ATHLETICS**
1010 122ND STREET SOUTH
TACOMA, WA 98447
253-535-7350
Fax: 253-535-7584
athletic@plu.edu
golutes.com
• Laurie Turner, Director of Athletics
(253) 535-7361
turnerll@plu.edu
• Jennifer Thomas, Associate Director of
Athletics
(253) 535-8109
thomasjl@plu.edu
• Jessica Roswell, Assistant Athletic
Director for Marketing
(253) 535-8504
roswellj@plu.edu
• Aaron Gunther, Head Athletic Trainer
(253) 535-7366
guntheam@plu.edu

• Tyler Scott, Director of Athletics
Communications
(253) 535-7356

PACIFIC UNIVERSITY ATHLETICS
2043 COLLEGE WAY
FOREST GROVE, OR 97116
503-352-2767
Fax: 503-352-2209
www.goboxers.com
• Ken Schumann, Director of Athletics
(503) 352-2180
schumank@pacificu.edu
• Lauren Esbensen, Associate Director of
Athletics
(503) 352-2186
• Scott Cowan, Assistant Facilities Manager
(503) 352-2284
• Angela Moberg, Director of Intramurals
(503) 352-2138
• Russ Blunck, Sports Information Director
(503) 352-2161
• Eric Pitkanen, Head Athletic Trainer
(503) 352-2896

PENN STATE BEHREND ATHLETICS
5103 STATION ROAD
ERIE, PA 16563-0400
814-898-6163
Fax: 814-898-6013
www.psblions.com
• Brian Streeter, Director of Athletics
(814) 898-6379
• Torie Craven, Assistant Athletic Director
(814) 898-6240
• Jill Yamma, Sports Information Director
(814) 898-6322
jey117@psu.edu
• Jeff Webster, Head Athletic Trainer
(814) 898-6340

PIEDMONT COLLEGE ATHLETICS
1021 CENTRAL AVENUE
DEMOREST, GA 30535
706-778-3000 EXT 1358
Fax: 706-776-0145
piedmontlions.com
• Jim Peeples, Director of Athletics
(706) 778-3000
jpeeples@piedmont.edu
• Liz Butikofer, Director of Daily Operations
(706) 778-3000
lbutikofer@piedmont.edu
• Jamie Purdy, Assistant Director of
Athletics
(706) 778-3000
jpurdy@piedmont.edu
• Debra Dooley, Faculty Athletic
Representative
(706) 778-3000
ddooley@piedmont.edu
• Timmy McCormack, Assistant Director of
Athletics
(706) 778-3000
tmccormack@piedmont.edu

PITTSBURGH AT BRADFORD
ATHLETICS, U. OF
300 CAMPUS DRIVE
BRADFORD, PA 16701
814-362-7521
800-872-1787
Fax: 814-362-7503
athletics.pittbradford.org
• Bret Butler, Athletic Director
(814) 362-5093
bab15@pitt.edu

• Tina Phillips, Assistant Athletic Director
(814) 362-5086
tmp14@pitt.edu
• Tim Sneeringer, Director of Recreation
(814) 362-7526
sneering@pitt.edu
• Josh Horton, Director of Sports Information
(814) 362-7564
jhorton@pitt.edu
• Jeff Timlin, Interim Athletic Trainer
(814) 362-7516
jtimlin@pitt.edu

PLYMOUTH STATE UNIVERSITY
ATHLETICS
P.E. CENTER
MSC #32
PLYMOUTH, NH 03264
603-535-2770
Fax: 603-535-2777
athletics.plymouth.edu
• Kim Bownes, Interim Athletic Director
(603) 535-2771
kbownes@plymouth.edu
• Courtney O'Clair, Associate Athletic
Director
(603) 535-2750
c_oclair@plymouth.edu
• Lauren Lavigne, Assistant Athletic Director
(603) 535-2763
l_lavign@plymouth.edu
• Mark Legacy, Head Athletic Trainer
(603) 535-2757
mdlegacy@plymouth.edu
• Kent Cherrington, Sports Information
Director
(603) 535-2477
kcherrington@plymouth.edu

POMONA-PITZER COLLEGES
ATHLETICS
333 NORTH COLLEGE WAY
CLAREMONT, CA 91711
909-621-8423
Fax: 909-621-8547
www.pe.pomona.edu
• Lesley Irvine, Director of Athletics
(909) 621-8016
lesley.irvine@pomona.edu
• Lisa Beckett, Associate Director of
Athletics
(909) 621-8428
lbeckett@pomona.edu
• Brandon Johnson, Director of Intramurals
(909) 621-8420
brandon.johnson@pomona.edu
• Kirk Jones, Head Athletic Trainer
(909) 607-2473
kjones@pomona.edu
• Sam Porter, Sports Information Director
(909) 607-3737
samuel.porter@pomona.edu

PRATT INSTITUTE ATHLETICS
200 WILLOUGHBY AVENUE
BROOKLYN, NY 11205
718-636-3600
Fax: 718-636-3772
www.goprattgo.com
• Walter Rickard, Director of Athletics
(718) 636-3771
wrickard@pratt.edu
• Ryan McCarthy, Associate Director for
Intercollegiate Athletics
(718) 399-4530

PRINCIPIA COLLEGE ATHLETICS
1 MAYBECK PLACE
ELSAH, IL 62028
618-374-5024
800-277-4648
Fax: 618-374-5221
www.principiaathletics.com
• Lee Ellis, Athletic Director
(618) 374-5030
lee.ellis@principia.edu
• Mary Ann Sprague, Associate Athletic
Director
(618) 374-5038
• Heather Fairbanks, Sports Information
Director
(618) 374-5456
heather.fairbanks@principia.edu

PUGET SOUND ATHLETICS, UNIVERSITY
OF
1500 NORTH WARNER STREET
CMB 1044
TACOMA, WA 98416-1044
253-879-3140
Fax: 253-879-3634
ahackett@pugetsound.edu
www.loggerathletics.com
• Amy Hackett, Director of Athletics
(253) 879-3426
ahackett@pugetsound.edu
• Robin Hamilton, Associate Athletic
Director
(253) 879-3141
rhamilton@pugetsound.edu
• Gregor Walz, Director of Athletic
Communications
(253) 879-3974
gwalz@pugetsound.edu
• Paige McFeeley, Assistant Director of
Athletic Communications
(253) 879-3458
pmcfeeley@pugetsound.edu
• Craig Bennett, Director of Sports Medicine
(253) 879-3441
cabennett@pugetsound.edu

RAMAPO COLLEGE OF NEW JERSEY
ATHLETICS
505 RAMAPO VALLEY ROAD
MAHWAH, NJ 07430
201-684-7674
Fax: 201-684-7958
www.ramapoathletics.com
• Harold Crocker, Director of Athletics
(201) 684-7091
• Kathleen Finnegan, Associate Director of
Athletics
(201) 684-7683
kfinnega@ramapo.edu
• Megan Bageorgos, Head Athletic Trainer
(201) 684-7913
• Rachel L. Pinton, Director of Sports
Information
(201) 684-7679
rpinton@ramapo.edu

RANDOLPH-MACON COLLEGE
ATHLETICS
103 EAST PATRICK STREET
ASHLAND, VA 23005
804-752-7223
jburns@rmc.edu
rmcathletics.com
• Jeff Burns, Director of Athletics
(804) 752-7367
jburns@rmc.edu
• MK Geratowski, Director of Compliance

(804) 752-7366
mkgeratowski@rmc.edu
• Phil Stanton, Sports Information Director
(804) 752-7387
philipstanton@rmc.edu
• Heather Bauby, Head Athletic Trainer
(804) 752-3215
hbauby@rmc.edu

REDLANDS ATHLETICS, UNIVERSITY OF
1200 EAST COLTON AVE
REDLANDS, CA 92373-0999
909-748-8400
866-946-3294
Fax: 909-335-4088
jill_joiner@redlands.edu
www.goredlands.com
• Jeff Martinez, Director of Athletics
(909) 748-8400
jeff_martinez@redlands.edu
• Rachel Roche, Sports Information Director
(909) 748-8418
rachel_roche@redlands.edu
• Janelle Kratz, Head Athletic Trainer
(909) 748-8399
janelle_kratz@redlands.edu

RENSSELAER POLYTECHNIC INSTITUTE ATHLETICS
110 8TH STREET
TROY, NY 12180
518-276-2187
Fax: 518-276-8997
www.rpiathletics.com
• Lee McElroy, Athletic Director
(518) 276-6685
• Karen Hansen, Associate Athletic Director for Business
(518) 276-6264
• Kevin Beattie, Associate Athletic Director for Communications
(518) 276-2187
• Sachi Vines, Director of Marketing
(518) 276-4855
enas@rpi.edu
• Chris Thompson, Head Athletic Trainer
(518) 276-6186
thompc@rpi.edu

RHODE ISLAND COLLEGE ATHLETICS
600 MOUNT PLEASANT AVENUE
PROVIDENCE, RI 2908
401-456-8007
Fax: 401-456-8514
dtencher@ric.edu
www.goanchormen.com
• Donald Tencher, Director of Athletics and Recreation
(401) 456-8007
dtencher@ric.edu
• Jo-Ann D'Alessandro, Associate Athletic Director
(401) 456-9882
jdalessandro@ric.edu
• Scott Roy, Assistant Athletic Director
(401) 465-8515
sroy@ric.edu
• Carlo Cantarella, Head Athletic Trainer
(401) 456-4686
ccantarella@ric.edu

RHODES COLLEGE ATHLETICS
2000 NORTH PARKWAY
MEMPHIS, TN 38112
901-843-3063
Fax: 901-843-3749
rhodeslynx.com

• Mike Clary, Director of Athletics
(901) 843-3939
clary@rhodes.edu
• Jeff Cleanthes, Assistant Athletic Director
(901) 843-3456
cleanthesj@rhodes.edu
• Janes Wells, Senior Womens Administrator
(901) 843-3013
• James Hill, Coordinator of Sports Information
(901) 843-3063
• Drew Gibson, Head Athletic Trainer
(901) 843-3465
gibsona@rhodes.edu

RICHARD STOCKTON COLLEGE OF NJ ATHLETICS
101 VERA KING FARRIS DRIVE
GALLOWAY, NJ 08205
609-652-4874
Fax: 609-748-5510
folksl@stockton.edu
www.stocktonathletics.com
• Lonnie Folks, Director of Athletics and Recreation
(609) 652-4877
folksl@stockton.edu
• Jon Heck, Director of Athletic Operations
(609) 652-4952
heckj@stockton.edu
• Linda Yost, Associate Director of Intercollegiate Athletics
(609) 652-4875
yostl@stockton.edu
• Brooke Rollman, Assistant Director of Athletics - Finance
(609) 652-4517
rollmanb@stockton.edu
• Chris Rollman, Sports Information Director
(609) 626-6011
rollmanc@stockton.edu

RIPON COLLEGE ATHLETICS
300 SEWARD STREET
PO BOX 248
RIPON, WI 54971-0248
800-947-4766
Fax: 920-748-7386
redhawks.ripon.edu
• Julie Johnson, Athletic Director
(920) 748-8772
• Ron Ernst, Assistant Athlteic Director
(920) 748-8708
ernstr@ripon.edu
• Brian Azinger, Head Athletic Trainer
(920) 748-8775
azingerb@ripon.edu

RIVIER UNIVERSITY ATHLETICS
420 SOUTH MAIN STREET
NASHUA, NH 03060
603-888-1311
Fax: 603-897-8616
jmerrill@rivier.edu
www.rivierathletics.com
• Joanne Merrill, Athletic Director
(603) 897-8257
jmerrill@rivier.edu
• Craig Kolek, Associate Athletic Director
(603) 897-8467
ckolek@rivier.edu
• Anthony Perry, Sports Informatino Director
(603) 897-8760
aperry@rivier.edu
• Laura Ray, Senior Women Administrator
(603) 897-8763

lray@rivier.edu
• Keith Rupp, Head Athletic Trainer
(603) 897-8616
krupp@rivier.edu

ROCHESTER ATHLETICS, UNIVERSITY OF
GOERGEN ATHLETIC CENTER
LIBRARY ROAD
BOX 270296
ROCHESTER, NY 14627
585-275-4301
Fax: 585-461-5081
uofrathletics.com
• George VanderZwaag, Executive Director of Athletics
(585) 275-4301
zwaag@sports.rochester.edu
• Jane Possee, Associate Director of Recreation
(585) 275-6914
jane@sports.rochester.edu
• Terry Gurnett, Associate Director of Advancement
(585) 275-6698
tgurnett@sports.rochester.edu
• Eric Rozen, Head Athletic Trainer
(585) 275-9540
erozen@sports.rochester.edu
• Dennis O'Donnell, Director of Athletic Communications
(585) 275-5955
dennis.odonnell@rochester.edu

ROCHESTER INSTITUTE OF TECHNOLOGY ATHLETICS
CLARK GYMNASIUM
51 LOMB MEMORIAL DRIVE
ROCHESTER, NY 14623-5603
585-475-2614
Fax: 716-475-2617
ammgla@rit.edu
www.ritathletics.com
• Lou Spiotti, Jr., Executive Director of Athletics
(585) 475-2615
lxs4798@rit.edu
• Scott McVean, Senior Associate Director of Athletics
(585) 475-7448
rsmatl@rit.edu
• Lex Sleeman, Associate Director of Intercollegiate Athletics
(585) 475-7372
atsped@rit.edu
• Joanne Bagley, Senior Staff Specialist
(585) 475-5814
jpbatl@rit.edu
• Ben Emke, Head Athletic Trainer
(585) 475-4513
bweatl@rit.edu

ROCKFORD COLLEGE ATHLETICS
5050 EAST STATE STREET
ROCKFORD, IL 61108
815-226-4000
Fax: 815-226-4166
kking@rockford.edu
www.goregents.com
• Kristyn King, Director of Athletics
(815) 394-5061
kking@rockford.edu
• Bob Koopmann, Assistant Athletic Director
(815) 394-5062
rkoopmann@rockford.edu
• Jessica Stanek, Senior Women Administrator

(815) 394-5065
jstanek@rockford.edu
• Brian Vanden Acker, Sports Information Director
(815) 394-5060
bvandenacker@rockford.edu
• Holli Newcomer, Head Athletic Trainer
(815) 394-5075
hnewcomer@rockford.edu

ROGER WILLIAMS UNIVERSITY ATHLETICS
ONE OLD FERRY ROAD
BRISTOL, RI 02809
401-254-3050
Fax: 401-254-3535
nwilliams@rwu.edu
rwuhawks.com
• Mark J. Andreozzi, Fitness Coordinator, Club Sports Director
(401) 254-3069
mandreozzi@rwu.edu
• Amanda Callahan, Assistant Athletic Director
(401) 254-5325
acallahan@rwu.edu
• Jon Egan, Athletic Operations Coordinator
(401) 286-2086
jegan@rwu.edu
• David Kemmy, Director of Athletics
(401) 254-3428
dkemmy@rwu.edu
• Joshua King, Head Athletic Trainer
(401) 254-3287
jnking@rwu.edu
• Nicholas Williams, Athletics Communications Director
(401) 254-3852
nwilliams@rwu.edu

ROSE-HULMAN INST. OF TECH ATHLETICS
5500 WABASH AVENUE
TERRE HAUTE, IN 47803
812-877-1511
Fax: 812-877-8407
athletics.rose-hulman.edu
• Jeff Jenkins, Athletic Director
(812) 877-8209
jenkins@rose-hulman.edu
• Jon Prevo, Associate Athletic Director
(812) 877-8932
prevo@rose-hulman.edu
• Kevin Lanke, Director for Sports Information
(812) 877-8180
lanke@rose-hulman.edu
• Scott Keller, Head Athletic Trainer
(812) 877-8270
scott.keller@rose-hulman.edu

ROWAN UNIVERSITY ATHLETICS
201 MULLICA HILL ROAD
GLASSBORO, NJ 08028
856-256-4000
Fax: 856-256-4916
www.rowanathletics.com
• Dan Gilmore, Athletic Director
(856) 256-4686
gilmore@rowan.edu
• Penny Kempf, Associate Athletic Director
(856) 256-4679
kempf@rowan.edu
• Gabby Lisella, Assistant Athletic Director
(856) 256-4681
lisella@rowan.edu
• Sheila Stevenson, Director of Athletic

Communications
(856) 256-4253
stevenson@rowan.edu
• Colleen Grugan, Head Athletic Trainer
(856) 256-4699
grugan@rowan.edu

RUST COLLEGE ATHLETICS
150 RUST AVENUE
HOLLY SPRINGS, MS 38635
662-252-8000
Fax: 662-252-8862
www.rustcollegesports.com
• Ishmell Edwards, Athletics Director
(662) 252-8000
iedwards@rustcollege.edu
• Aurby Burdine, Student Activities Coach
(662) 252-8000

RUTGERS UNIVERSITY-CAMDEN ATHLETICS
301 LINDEN STREET
CAMDEN, NJ 08102
856-225-6198
Fax: 856-225-6024
mballard@camden.rutgers.edu
scarletraptors.com
• Jeff Dean, Director of Athletics
(856) 225-2747
jldean@camden.rutgers.edu
• Tom Thomasson, Associate Director of Athletics
(856) 225-2746
tthomass@camden.rutgers.edu
• Karen Freed, Assistant Director of Athletics
(856) 225-6200
• Michael Ballard, Sports Information Director
(856) 225-6198
mballard@camden.rutgers.edu

RUTGERS UNIVERSITY-NEWARK ATHLETICS
GOLDEN DOME ATHLETIC CENTER
42 WARREN STREET
NEWARK, NJ 07102
973-353-5474
Fax: 973-353-1431
markg@newark.rutgers.edu
www.rutgersnewarkathletics.com
• Mark Griffin, Director of Athletics
(973) 353-1458
markg@newark.rutgers.edu
• Mary Stadelmann, Senior Woman Administrator
(973) 353-1460
mary.stad@rutgers.edu
• Mike Alvarez, Assistant Athletic Director
(973) 353-3716
• Rob Kulish, Director of Athletic Communications
(973) 353-1466
robert.kulish@rutgers.edu

SAINT MARY'S UNIVERSITY (MN) ATHLETICS
700 TERRACE HEIGHTS
WINONA, MN 55987
507-457-1579
Fax: 507-457-6640
www.saintmaryssports.com
• Nikki Fennern, Athletic Director
(507) 457-1638
• Mike Lester, Director of Compliance
(507) 457-6954
• Donny Nadeau, Sports Information

Director
(507) 457-1634
• Jill Collum, Head Athletic Trainer
(507) 457-1759

SAINT NORBERT COLLEGE ATHLETICS
100 GRANT STREET
DE PERE, WI 54115-2099
920-337-3181
Fax: 920-403-3128
www.snc.edu
• Tim Bald, Athletic Director
(920) 403-3986
tim.bald@snc.edu
• Jim Purtill, Football Coach
(920) 403-3172
• Paul DeNoble, Men's Basketball Coach
(920) 403-3137
• Connie Tilley, Women's Basketball Coach
(920) 403-3033
connie.tilley@snc.edu
• Joann Krueger, Softball Coach
(920) 403-4080
joann.krueger@snc.edu
• Thomas Winske, Baseball Coach
(920) 403-3545

SAINT SCHOLASTICA ATHLETICS, COLLEGE OF
1200 KENWOOD AVENUE
DULUTH, MN 55811
218-723-6000
Fax: 218-723-5958
www.csssaints.com
• Don Olson, Athletics Director
(218) 723-5934
• Merissa Edwards, Director of Compliance
(218) 723-6551
• Jesse Robinson, Director of Athletics Communications
(218) 723-6643
jrobinso@css.edu
• Tom Rheaume, Head Athletic Trainer
(218) 723-5918
trheaume@css.edu

SAINT VINCENT COLLEGE ATHLETICS
300 FRASER PURCHASE ROAD
LATROBE, PA 15650-2690
724-532-6600
sports@stvincent.edu
athletics.stvincent.edu
• Myron Kirsch, Athletic Director
(724) 805-2111
myron.kirsch@email.stvincent.edu
• Sue Hozak, Associate Athletic Director
(724) 805-2112
sue.hozak@stvincent.edu
• Jeff Zidek, Sports Information Director
(724) 805-2476
jeff.zidek@stvincent.edu
• Aaron Thompson, Assistant Sports Information Director
(724) 805-2741
aaron.thompson@stvincent.edu
• Becky Pizer, Head Athletic Trainer
(724) 805-2400
becky.pizer@stvincent.edu

SALEM STATE COLLEGE ATHLETICS
O'KEEFE SPORTS COMPLEX
225 CANAL STREET
SALEM, MA 1970
978-542-7260
Fax: 978-542-2926
www.salemstatevikings.com

college sports

• Peggy Carl, Director of Athletics &
Recreation
(978) 542-7260
pcarl@salemstate.edu
• Jason Doviak, Senior Associate Director of
Athletics
(978) 542-6569
jdoviak@salemstate.edu
• Kelly Janos, Associate Director of Athletics
(978) 542-4442
• Joseph Beitz, Sports Information Director
(978) 542-6544
jbeitz@salemstate.edu
• Carey MacDonald, Head Athletic Trainer
(978) 542-7195
cmacdonald@salemstate.edu

SALISBURY UNIVERSITY ATHLETICS
1101 CAMDEN AVENUE
SALISBURY, MD 21801
410-548-3503
Fax: 410-546-2639
www.suseagulls.com
• Gerry DiBartolo, Athletic Director
(410) 548-3503
grdibartolo@salisbury.edu
• Dawn Chamberlin, Associate Athletic
Director
(410) 548-2588
drchamberlin@salisbury.edu
• Tim Brennan, Sports Information Director
(410) 543-6016
tmbrennan@salisbury.edu
• Pat Lamboni, Head Athletic Trainer
(410) 543-6355
pmlamboni@salisbury.edu

SALVE REGINA UNIVERSITY ATHLETICS
100 OCHRE POINT AVENUE
NEWPORT, RI 02840-4192
401-341-2268
Fax: 401-341-2960
www.salveathletics.com
• Jody Mooradian, Director of Athletics
(401) 341-2268
jody.mooradian@salve.edu
• Kelly Scafariello, Associate Director of
Athletics
(401) 341-2247
• Ed Habershaw, Sports Information Director
(401) 341-2271
habershe@salve.edu
• David Cox, Head Athletic Trainer
(401) 341-3221
david.cox@salve.edu
• Tom Blaney, Fitness Center Manager
(401) 341-2606
tom.blaney@salve.edu

**SAVANNAH COLLEGE OF ART & DESIGN
ATHLETICS**
115 EAST YORK STREET
SAVANNAH, GA 31401
912-525-4800
Fax: 912-525-4814
savannah.scadathletics.com
• Doug Wollenburg, Athletics Director
(912) 525-4781
dwollenbu@scad.edu
• Darrell Naylor-Johnson, Faculty Athletics
Representative
(912) 525-5723
dnaylorj@scad.edu
• Tommy Chasanoff, Sports Information
Director
(912) 525-4815
tchasano@scad.edu

• Eddie Concepcion, Director of Intramurals
and Recreation
(912) 525-6958
egconcep@scad.edu

SCRANTON ATHLETICS, UNIVERSITY OF
THE UNIVERSITY OF SCRANTON
800 LINDEN STREET
SCRANTON, PA 18510
570-941-7440
Fax: 570-941-4223
athletics@scranton.edu
athletics.scranton.edu
• Dave Martin, Director of Athletics
(570) 941-7440
david.martin2@scranton.edu
• Toby Lovecchio, Associate Director of
Athletics
(570) 941-7441
francis.lovecchio@scranton.edu
• Colleen Pivirotto, Senior Woman
Administrator
(570) 941-6191
colleen.pivirotto@scranton.edu
• Erin Maguire, Athletics Operations
Manager
(570) 941-7440
erin.maguire@scranton.edu
• Randy Shemanski, Athletics
Communications Manager
(570) 941-7029
randall.shemanski@scranton.edu
• Kristin Littzi, Sports Medicine Manager
(570) 941-7473

**SEWANEE, UNIVERSITY OF THE SOUTH
ATHLETICS**
735 UNIVERSITY AVENUE
SEWANEE, TN 37383
931-598-1284
Fax: 931-598-1673
sewaneetigers.com
• Mark Webb, Director of Athletics
(931) 598-1388
mwebb@sewanee.edu
• Nancy Ladd, Assistant Director of Athletics
(931) 598-1320
nladd@sewanee.edu
• Dickie McCarthy, Director of Internal
Operations
(931) 598-1323
dmccarth@sewanee.edu
• Clayton Felts, Director of Athletic
Communication
(931) 598-1136
cafelts@sewanee.edu
• Ray Knight, Head Athletic Trainer
(931) 598-1293
rknight@sewanee.edu

SHENANDOAH UNIVERSITY ATHLETICS
1460 UNIVERSITY DRIVE
WINCHESTER, VA 22601
540-665-4566
Fax: 540-665-4934
www.suhornets.com
• Doug Zipp, Athletic Director
(540) 665-4566
dzipp@su.edu
• Sarah Pelster, Associate Athletic Director
(540) 545-7366
spelster@su.edu
• Kevin Anderson, Assistant Athletic Director
(540) 665-4531
kanders2@su.edu
• Scott Musa, Athletic Communications
Director

(540) 655-5417
smusa@su.edu

SIMPSON COLLEGE ATHLETICS
701 NORTH C. STREET
INDIANOLA, IA 50125
515-961-6251
simpsonathletics.com
• Brian Niemuth, Director of Athletics
(515) 961-1670
brian.niemuth@simpson.edu
• Lana Smith, Assistant Athletic Director
(515) 961-1641
lana.smith@simpson.edu
• Bryan Geelan, Athletics Communication
Director
(515) 961-1577
bryan.geelan@simpson.edu

SKIDMORE COLLEGE ATHLETICS
815 NORTH BROADWAY
SARATOGA SPRINGS, NY 12866
518-580-5370
Fax: 518-580-5395
info@skidmore.edu
skidmoreathletics.com
• Gail Cummings-Danson, Athletics Director
(518) 580-5370
gcumming@skidmore.edu
• Megan Buchanan, Associate Athletic
Director
(518) 580-5351
mbuchana@skidmore.edu
• Nekisha Quinney, Assistant Athletic
Director
(518) 580-5456
• Bill Jones, Athletic Marketing Manager
(518) 580-5364
bjones@skidmore.edu
• Meghan Nicchi, Head Athletic Trainer
(518) 580-5390
mnicchi@skidmore.edu

**SOUTHERN MAINE ATHLETICS,
UNIVERSITY OF**
37 COLLEGE AVENUE
GORHAM, ME 04038
207-780-5430
Fax: 207-780-5994
sid@usm.maine.edu
www.southernmainehuskies.com
• Al Bean, Director of Athletics
(207) 780-5588
albean@maine.edu
• Meredith Bickford, Associate Director of
Athletics
(207) 780-5997
meredith.bickford@maine.edu
• B. L. Elfring, Director of Athletics for
Compliance
(207) 780-5434
elfring@maine.edu
• Robert Kuech, Faculty Athletics
Representative
(207) 780-5089
robert.kuech@maine.edu
• Matthew Gerken, Head Athletic Trainer
(207) 780-5140
matthew.gerken@maine.edu

**SOUTHERN VERMONT COLLEGE
ATHLETICS**
982 MANSION DRIVE
BENNINGTON, VT 05201-6002
802-447-4000
Fax: 802-447-4652
www.svcathletics.com

• Sharief Hashim, Interim Director of Athletics
(802) 447-4606
• Ashley Hodges, Assistant Athletics Director/Senior Womens Admin
(802) 447-4670
• Michael Nosek, Sports Information Director
(802) 447-4672
• Bob Kurtzner, Strength & Conditioning Coordinator

SOUTHERN VIRGINIA UNIVERSITY ATHLETICS
ONE UNIVERSITY HILL DRIVE
BUENA VISTA, VA 24416
540-261-8507
800-229-8420
Fax: 540-266-3866
athletics@svu.edu
athletics.svu.edu
• Jason Lamb, Director of Athletics
(540) 261-8525
• Deidra Dryden, Associate Athletic Director
(540) 261-8516
deidra.dryden@svu.edu
• Tony Caputo, Assistant Athletic Director
(540) 261-8526
• Scott Winterton, Athletic Relations
(540) 261-8524

SOUTHWESTERN UNIVERSITY ATHLETICS
1001 EAST UNIVERSITY AVENUE
GEORGETOWN, TX 78626
512-863-1381
Fax: 512-863-1393
athletics@southwestern.edu
southwesternpirates.com
• Glada Munt, Director of Intercollegiate Athletics
(512) 863-1381
muntg@southwestern.edu
• Glenn Schwab, Director of Athletic Training Services
(512) 863-1697
schwabg@southwestern.edu
• Bill Raleigh, Chair of Exercise & Sports Science
(512) 863-1611
• Megan Hardin, Sports Information Director
(512) 863-1254

ST. JOHN FISHER COLLEGE ATHLETICS
3690 EAST AVENUE
ROCHESTER, NY 14618
585-385-8309
Fax: 585-385-7308
athletics.sjfc.edu
• Bob Ward, Athletics Director
(585) 385-8310
bward@sjfc.edu
• Jill McCabe, Associate Athletics Director
(585) 385-8312
• Norm Kieffer, Sports Information Director
(585) 385-8421
nkieffer@sjfc.edu
• Jennifer Granger, Assistant Athletics Director
(585) 385-8315
jgranger@sjfc.edu
• Jim Grant, Head Athletic Trainer
(585) 899-3744
jgrant@sjfc.edu

ST. JOSEPH'S COLLEGE (NY) ATHLETICS
212 VANDERBILT AVENUE
BROOKLYN, NY 11205
718-940-5833
Fax: 718-940-5328
www.sjcbears.com
• Alex Winnicker, Interim Director of Athletics
(718) 940-5348
• Hope Mitchell, Director for Sport Programs
(718) 940-5835
• Maciej Siekierski, Director of Recreational Sports
(718) 940-5325
• Anthony Macapugay, Manager of Athletic Communications
(718) 940-5834
• Oscar Melendez, Head Athletic Trainer
(718) 940-5806

ST. LAWRENCE UNIVERSITY ATHLETICS
23 ROMODA DRIVE
CANTON, NY 13617
315-229-5421
Fax: 315-229-5589
ckennedy@stlawu.edu
www.saintsathletics.com
• Bob Durocher, Director of Athletics
(315) 229-5870
ckennedy@stlawu.edu
• Randy LaBrake, Associate Director of Athletics
(315) 229-5466
rlabrake@stlawu.edu
• Fran Grembowicz, Assistant Director of Athletics
(315) 229-5780
fgrembowicz@stlawu.edu
• Wally Johnson, Director of Athletic Media Relations
(315) 229-5588
wjohnson@stlawu.edu
• Brian Atkins, Head Athletic Trainer
(315) 229-5835
batkins@stlawu.edu

ST. MARY'S COLLEGE OF MARYLAND ATHLETICS
18952 EAST FISHER ROAD
ST. MARY'S CITY, MD 20686-3001
240-895-4295
Fax: 240-895-4480
swdevine@smcm.edu
www.smcmathletics.com
• Scott Devine, Director of Athletics
(240) 895-4295
swdevine@smcm.edu
• Jim Cranmer, Athletic Director for Operations
(240) 895-2167
wjcranmer@smcm.edu
• Crystal Gibson, Senior Woman Administrator
(240) 895-4323
clgibson@smcm.edu
• Nairem Moran, Sports Information Director
(240) 895-4482
nmoran@smcm.edu
• Jen Robertson, Head Athletic Trainer
(240) 895-2102

ST. OLAF COLLEGE ATHLETICS
1520 ST. OLAF AVENUE
NORTHFIELD, MN 55057

507-646-3638
Fax: 507-646-3572
athletics.stolaf.edu
• Ryan Bowles, Athletic Director
(507) 786-3965
• Mike Ludwig, Sports Information Director
(507) 786-3834
• Natalie Walseth, Assistant Athletic Director for New Media
(507) 786-3834
• Dan Hagen, Head Athletic Trainer
(507) 786-3261

ST. THOMAS UNIVERSITY ATHLETICS
2115 SUMMIT AVENUE
ST. PAUL, MN 55105
651-962-5903
Fax: 651-962-5910
www.tommiesports.com
• Steve Fritz, Athletic Director
(651) 962-5901
• Michelle Morgan, Associate Athletic Director
(651) 962-6186
• Tyler Grey, Assistant Athletic Director
(651) 962-5976
grey0003@stthomas.edu
• Gene McGivern, Sports Information Director
(651) 962-5903
ejmcgivern@stthomas.edu
• Jim Rakow, Head Athletic Trainer
(651) 962-5973
rako0006@stthomas.edu

SUNY AT NEW PALTZ ATHLETICS
1 HAWK DRIVE
NEW PALTZ, NY 12561
845-257-3910
Fax: 845-257-3920
www.nphawks.com
• Stuart Robinson, Director of Athletics
(845) 257-3908
• Brian Williams, Associate Director of Athletics
(845) 257-3912
williamb@newpaltz.edu
• Keith Kenney, Director of Wellness & Recreation
(845) 257-6956
kenneyk@newpaltz.edu
• Shanna Vitale, Senior Woman Administrator
(845) 257-3929
vitales@newpaltz.edu
• Ryan Novitsky, Athletic Operations Manager
(845) 257-2341
• Bryan Lurie, Head Athletic Trainer
(845) 257-3913
lurieb@newpaltz.edu

STATE UNIVERSITY OF NEW YORK COLLEGE AT BROCKPORT ATHLETICS (SUNY)
350 NEW CAMPUS DRIVE
BROCKPORT, NY 14420
585-395-5328
Fax: 585-395-2160
athletics@brockport.edu
www.gobrockport.com
• Erick Hart, Director of Athletics
(585) 395-2579
ehart@brockport.edu
• Susan Hoffman, Associate Director of Athletics
(585) 395-5327

shoffman@brockport.edu
• Liam Welsh, Assistant Director of Athletics
(585) 395-5329
• Lynda Cochran, Faculty Athletics
Representative
(585) 395-5490
lcochran@brockport.edu
• Stacey Corry, Director of Athletic
Communications
(585) 395-2218

**SUNY COLLEGE AT GENESEO
ATHLETICS**
1 COLLEGE CIRCLE
GENESEO, NY 14454
585-245-5000
Fax: 585-245-5347
mooney@geneseo.edu
geneseoknights.com
• Mike Mooney, Director of Athletics
(585) 245-5343
mooney@geneseo.edu
• George Gagnier, Assistant Director of
Athletics
(585) 245-5208
gagnier@geneseo.edu
• Jim Lyons, Assistant Director of Athletics
(585) 245-5450
lyons@geneseo.edu
• Tim Volkmann, Director of Athletic
Communications
(585) 245-5346
volkmann@geneseo.edu
• Angelo Zegarelli, Head Athletic Trainer
(585) 245-5341
zegarelli@geneseo.edu

**SUNY COLLEGE AT OLD WESTBURY
ATHLETICS**
223 STORE HILL ROAD
PO BOX 210
OLD WESTBURY, NY 11568
516-876-3241
Fax: 516-876-3230
athletics@oldwestbury.edu
www.oldwestburypanthers.com
• Lenore Walsh, Director of Athletics
(516) 876-3241
walshle@oldwestbury.edu
• Harris Rappel, Sports Information Director
(516) 876-3032
harrisrappel@oldwestbury.edu
• Brittany Villalta, Athletics Facility Manager
(516) 876-3238
ranaldob@oldwestbury.edu
• Zsolt Hajdu, Head Athletics Trainer
(516) 876-3468
hajduz@oldwestbury.edu

**SUNY COLLEGE AT ONEONTA
ATHLETICS**
ALUMNI FIELD HOUSE
RAVINE PARKWAY
ONEONTA, NY 13820
607-436-3494
Fax: 607-436-3581
www.oneontaathletics.com
• Tracey Ranieri, Director of Athletics
(607) 436-2446
tracey.ranieri@oneonta.edu
• Ryan Hooper, Associate Director of
Athletics
(607) 436-2317
ryan.hooper@oneonta.edu
• Geoffrey Hassard, Sports Information
Director
(607) 436-2106

geoff.hassard@oneonta.edu
• Nate Jones, Associate Sports Information
Director
(607) 436-2106
geoff.hassard@oneonta.edu
• Alicia Simmonds, Head Athletic Trainer
(607) 436-3580
alicia.simmonds@oneonta.edu

**SUNY COLLEGE AT OSWEGO
ATHLETICS**
SUNY OSWEGO
LAKER HALL
OSWEGO, NY 13126
315-312-2488
Fax: 315-312-6397
oswegolakers.com
• Susan Viscomi, Director of Athletics
(315) 312-3056
susan.viscomi@oswego.edu
• Eric Summers, Associate Director of
Athletics
(315) 312-3303
• Malcolm Huggins, Assistant Director of
Athletics
(315) 312-3360
• Michael Bielak, Director of Athletic
Communications
(315) 312-2488

**SUNY COLLEGE AT PLATTSBURGH
ATHLETICS**
101 BROAD STREET
PLATTSBURGH, NY 12901-2681
518-564-3140
Fax: 518-564-4155
dutt1167@plattsburgh.edu
gocardinalsports.com
• Stephanie Dutton, Interim Athletic Director
(518) 564-4536
dutt1167@plattsburgh.edu
• Cheryl Cole, Senior Woman Administrator
(518) 564-4147
coleca@plattsburgh.edu
• Tom Curle, Assistant Athletic Director
(518) 564-4143
curleto@plattsburgh.edu
• Allan Leavy, Interim Sports Information
Director
(518) 564-4148
aleav001@plattsburgh.edu
• Merritt Spear, Director of Sports Medicine
(518) 564-3089
spearmf@plattsburgh.edu
• Jason Pachter, Head Athletic Trainer
(518) 564-3089
pachteja@plattsburgh.edu

**SUNY INSTITUTE OF TECHNOLOGY
ATHLETICS**
100 SEYMOUR ROAD
UTICA, NY 13502
315-792-7520
Fax: 315-792-7536
• Kevin Grimmer, Athletic Director
(315) 792-7520
kevin.grimmer@sunyit.edu
• Kevin Edick, Assistant Athletic Director
(315) 792-7520
kevin.edick@sunyit.edu
• Kelly Colbert, Assistant Athletic Director
(315) 792-7519
kelly.colbert@sunyit.edu
• Patrick Baker, Sports Information Director
(315) 792-7515
patrick.baker@sunyit.edu
• Matthew Madia, Head Athletic Trainer

(315) 792-7520
matthew.madia@sunyit.edu

**STATEN ISLAND ATHLETICS, COLLEGE
OF**
2800 VICTORY BOULEVARD
1R-204
STATEN ISLAND, NY 10314
718-982-3160
Fax: 718-982-3138
www.csidolphins.com
• Charles Gomes, Director of Athletics
(718) 982-3160
• David Pizzuto, Sports Information Director
(718) 982-3169
david.pizzuto@csi.cuny.edu
• Fran Mitilieri, Assistant Athletic Director
(718) 982-3167
• Joe Abruzzo, Head Athletic Trainer
(718) 982-3135

**STEVENS INSTITUTE OF TECHNOLOGY
ATHLETICS**
CASTLE POINT ON HUDSON
HOBOKEN, NJ 7030
201-216-5693
Fax: 201-216-8244
rrogers@stevens.edu
www.stevensducks.com
• Russell Rogers, Director of Athletics
(201) 216-5688
rrogers@stevens.edu
• Michael Lippencott, Senior Associate
Director of Athletics
(201) 216-8038
mlippenc@stevens.edu
• Celine Cunningham, Senior Woman
Administrator
(201) 216-8056
ccunning@stevens.edu
• Emily Kaczmarek, Assistant Athletic
Director for Administration
(201) 216-5078
ekaczmar@stevens.edu
• Danny Vohden, Athletic Director for
Communications and Events
(201) 216-8740

STEVENSON UNIVERSITY
11001 OWINGS MILLS BOULEVARD
OWINGS MILLS, MD 21117
443-394-9379
Fax: 443-352-4278
ffidler@stevenson.edu
gomustangsports.com
• Brett Adams, Director of Athletics
(443) 352-4250
bcadams@stevenson.edu
• Kathy Railey, Associate Athletics Director
(443) 352-4255
krailey@stevenson.edu
• Jackie Boswell, Assistant Athletics Director
(443) 352-4048
jboswell@stevenson.edu
• Scott Zema, Head Athletic Trainer
(443) 352-4263
• Matthew Grimm, Director of Campus
Recreation
(443) 352-4280
mgrimm@stevenson.edu

SUFFOLK UNIVERSITY ATHLETICS
73 TREMONT STREET
BOSTON, MA 02108
617-573-8379
Fax: 617-227-4935
www.gosuffolkrams.com

• Cary McConnell, Director of Athletics
(617) 573-8575
cmcconnell@suffolk.edu
• Anthony Del Prete, Associate Director of Athletics
(617) 994-6459
ajdelprete@suffolk.edu
• Jaclyn Davis, Senior Women's Administrator
(617) 994-6457
jmdavis@suffolk.edu
• Jeff Stone, Head Athletic Trainer
(617) 573-8772
jstone@suffolk.com
• Amy Barry, Sports Information Director
(617) 305-1756
abarry7@suffolk.edu

SUL ROSS STATE UNIVERSITY ATHLETICS
EAST HIGHWAY 90
ALPINE, TX 79832
432-837-8226
Fax: 432-837-8234
www.srlobos.com
• Bobby Mesker, Director of Athletics
(432) 837-8231
bmesker@sulross.edu
• Sandra Chambers, Assistant Athletic Director
(432) 837-8277
schambers@sulross.edu
• Sierra White, Head Athletics Trainer
(432) 837-8241
sierra.white@sulross.edu
• Travis Hendryx, Sports Information Coordinator
(432) 837-8673
travis.hendryx@sulross.edu

SUSQUEHANNA UNIVERSITY ATHLETICS
514 UNIVERSITY AVENUE
SELINSGROVE, PA 17870
570-372-4270
Fax: 570-372-2758
gallese@susqu.edu
www.gosusqu.com
• Pamela S. Samuelson, Director of Athletics
(570) 372-4273
• Frank Marcinek, Assistant Director of Athletics
(570) 372-4230
marcinek@susqu.edu
• Katie Meier, Director of Athletic Communications
(570) 372-4587
• Mike Keeney, Head Athletic Trainer
(570) 372-4278
keeney@susqu.edu

SWARTHMORE COLLEGE ATHLETICS
500 COLLEGE AVENUE
SWARTHMORE, PA 19081
610-328-8218
Fax: 610-328-7798
athletics@swarthmore.edu
www.swarthmoreathletics.com
• Adam Hertz, Director of Athletics
(610) 328-8325
• Nnenna Akotaobi, Associate Athletics Director
(610) 328-8222
nakotao2@swarthmore.edu
• Renee Clarke, Facilities Operations Coordinator

(610) 690-6883
• Brandon Hodnett, Director of Athletic Communications
(610) 328-8206
• Marie Mancini, Head Athletic Trainer
(610) 328-8223
mmancin1@swarthmore.edu

TEXAS AT DALLAS ATHLETICS, UNIVERSITY OF
800 WEST CAMPBELL ROAD
RICHARDSON, TX 75080-3021
972-883-4490
Fax: 972-883-4496
cometsports.utdallas.edu
• Bill Petitt, Director of Intercollegiate Athletics
(972) 883-2055
bpetitt@utdallas.edu
• Bruce Unrue, Associate Athletic Director
(972) 883-6308
bruceunrue@utdallas.edu
• Angela Marin, Assistant Athletic Director
(972) 883-4498
angela.marin@utdallas.edu
• Tom Monagan, Head Athletic Trainer
(972) 883-4066
tomm@utdallas.edu

TEXAS LUTHERAN UNIVERSITY ATHLETICS
1000 WEST COURT STREET
SEGUIN, TX 78155
830-372-8000
Fax: 830-372-8135
sports@tlu.edu
www.tlubulldogs.com
• Bill Miller, Director of Athletics
(830) 372-8124
bmiller@tlu.edu
• Tiffany Davis, Senior Woman Administrator
(830) 372-8130
• Tim Kent, Head Athletic Trainer
(830) 372-8133
tkent@tlu.edu

THIEL COLLEGE ATHLETICS
ATHLETICS DEPARTMENT
75 COLLEGE AVENUE
GREENVILLE, PA 16125
724-589-2138
Fax: 724-589-2880
aschafer@thiel.edu
thielathletics.com
• Amy Schafer, Director of Athletics
(724) 589-2212
aschafer@thiel.edu
• Joe Schaly, Assistant Director of Athletics
(724) 589-2138
jschaly@thiel.edu
• Lori Schimmel, Director of Compliance
(724) 589-2164
• Ed Topoleski, Director of Sports Information
(724) 589-2180
etopoleski@thiel.edu

THOMAS COLLEGE ATHLETICS
180 WEST RIVER ROAD
WATERVILLE, ME 04901
207-859-1111
Fax: 207-859-1114
info@thomas.edu
www.thomas.edu
• David Roussel, Director of Athletics
(207) 859-1404

• Deb Biche-Labbe, Associate Athletic Director
(207) 859-1406
biched@thomas.edu
• Andrea Thebarge, Senior Assistant Director of Athletics
(207) 859-1314
thebargea@thomas.edu
• Joshua Schroeder, Director of Athletic Communications
(207) 859-1408
athsi@thomas.edu

THOMAS MORE COLLEGE ATHLETICS
333 THOMAS MORE PARKWAY
CRESTVIEW HILLS, KY 41017
859-344-3536
Fax: 859-344-3536
athletics@thomasmore.edu
www.tmcsaints.com
• Terry Connor, Director of Athletics
(859) 344-3308
terry.connor@thomasmore.edu
• Jeff Hetzer, Associate Athletic Director
(859) 344-3532
jeff.hetzer@thomasmore.edu
• Cory Blackson, Director of Athletic Communications
(859) 344-3672
cory.blackson@thomasmore.edu
• Theresa Behan, Head Athletic Trainer
(859) 344-4060
theresa.behan@thomasmore.edu

TRANSYLVANIA UNIVERSITY ATHLETICS
300 NORTH BROADWAY
LEXINGTON, KY 40508
859-233-8300
Fax: 859-233-8797
www.transysports.com
• Holly Sheilley, Vice President of Athletics
(859) 233-8270
hsheilley@transy.edu
• Keith Cecil, Assistant Athletic Director
(859) 281-3690
• Justin Sweeney, Sports Information Director
(859) 233-8284
• Alaina White, Head Athletic Trainer
(859) 233-8850

TRINITY COLLEGE ATHLETICS
300 SUMMIT STREET
HARTFORD, CT 06106
860-297-2057
Fax: 860-297-2492
www.trincoll.edu
• Michael Renwick, Director of Athletics & Recreation
(860) 297-2055
michael.renwick@trincoll.edu
• JoAnn Acquarulo, Assistant Athletic Director for Operations
(860) 297-4262
• David Kingsley, Director of Sports Communications
(860) 297-2137
david.kingsley@trincoll.edu
• Justin LeDuc, Head Athletic Trainer
(860) 297-2575

TRINITY UNIVERSITY ATHLETICS
ONE TRINITY PLACE
SAN ANTONIO, TX 78212-7200
210-999-8237
Fax: 210-999-8292

athletics@trinity.edu
trinitytigers.com
• Bob King, Director of Athletics
(210) 999-8237
rking2@trinity.edu
• Julie Jenkins, Associate Director of
Athletics
(210) 999-8274
jjenkins@trinity.edu
• Sylvia Finch, Athletics Business Manager
(210) 999-8224
sfinch@trinity.edu
• Justin Parker, Sports Information Director
(210) 999-8447
jparker@trinity.edu
• Marc Powell, Head Athletic Trainer
(210) 999-8293
mpowell@trinity.edu

UNION COLLEGE (NY) ATHLETICS
807 UNION STREET
ALUMNI GYMNASIUM
SCHENECTADY, NY 12308
518-388-6284
Fax: 518-388-6695
www.unionathletics.com
• Jim McLaughlin, Director of Athletics
(518) 388-6284
mclaughj@union.edu
• Joanne Little, Senior Associate Director of
Athletics
(518) 388-6433
littlej@union.edu
• Beth Tiffany, Associate Athletics Director
(518) 388-6286
tiffanye@union.edu
• Eric McDowell, Sports Information Director
(518) 388-6170
mcdowele@union.edu
• Adam Brinker, Assistant Athletics Director,
Facilities
(518) 388-8365
brinkera@union.edu

UNITED STATES COAST GUARD
ACADEMY ATHLETICS
33 MOHEGAN AVENUE
NEW LONDON, CT 06320-8104
860-444-8600
Fax: 860-444-8607
www.uscgasports.com
• Tim Fitzpatrick, Director of Athletics
(860) 444-8600
timothy.m.fitzpatrick@uscga.edu
• Dan Rose, Director of Physical Education
(860) 701-6798
dan.c.rose@uscga.edu
• Tim Opstrup, Associate Athletic Director
for Finance
(860) 444-8602
timothy.j.opstrup@uscga.edu
• Jason Southard, Director of Media
Relations
(860) 701-6800
jason.s.southard@uscga.edu
• Ken Niedzwiecki, Head Athletic Trainer
(860) 444-8619
ken.j.niedzwiecki@uscga.edu

UNITED STATES MERCHANT MARINE
ACADEMY ATHLETICS
300 STEAMBOAT ROAD
KINGS POINT, NY 11024
516-726-5800
Fax: 516-773-5469
www.usmmasports.com

• Mo White, Director of Athletics
(516) 726-5632
• Mike Toop, Associate Athletic Director
(516) 726-5262
toopm@usmma.edu
• Michael Notebaert, Assistant Athletic
Director
(516) 726-5259
notebaertm@usmma.edu
• Joe Guster, Sports Information Director
(516) 726-5609
gusterj@usmma.edu

UNIVERSITY OF MOUNT UNION
ATHLETICS
1972 CLARK AVENUE
ALLIANCE, OH 44601
330-823-4880
athletics.mountunion.edu
• Larry Kehres, Director of Athletics
(330) 823-4880
kehreslt@mountunion.edu
• Leonard Reich, Assistant to the Athletic
Director
(330) 823-6093
reichl@mountunion.edu
• Melanie Patterson, Assistant Sports
Information Director
(330) 823-4780

URSINUS COLLEGE ATHLETICS
601 EAST MAIN STREET
PO BOX 1000
COLLEGEVILLE, PA 19426-1000
610-409-3000
Fax: 610-409-3620
www.ursinusathletics.com
• Laura Moliken, Director of Athletics
(610) 409-3606
lmoliken@ursinus.edu
• Erin Stroble, Associate Athletic Director
(610) 409-3761
estroble@ursinus.edu
• Kevin Small, Assistant Director of Athletics
(610) 409-3350
ksmall@ursinus.edu
• Pam Chlad, Head Athletic Trainer
(610) 409-3104
pchlad@ursinus.edu
• Andy Edwards, Director of Athletic
Communications
(610) 409-3612

UTICA COLLEGE ATHLETICS
1600 BURRSTONE ROAD
UTICA, NY 13502
315-792-3051
Fax: 315-792-3211
www.ucpioneers.com
• David Fontaine, Director of Athletics
(315) 792-3050
dsfontai@utica.edu
• Jim Murnane, Associate Athletic Director
(315) 792-3281
jmurnan@utica.edu
• Gil Burgmaster, Sports Information
Director
(315) 792-3772
• Chris Warner, Head Athletic Trainer
(315) 792-3461

VASSAR COLLEGE ATHLETICS
124 RAYMOND AVENUE
BOX 750
POUGHKEEPSIE, NY 12604
845-437-7450
Fax: 845-437-7033

athletics@vassar.edu
www.vassarathletics.com
• Michelle Walsh, Director of Athletics
(845) 437-7452
michwalsh@vassar.edu
• Kim Culligan, Associate Director of
Athletics
(845) 437-7453
kiculligan@vassar.edu
• Kathy Campbell, Director of Physical
Education
(845) 437-7460
kacampbell@vassar.edu
• Marc Graham, Director of Athletics
Operations
(845) 437-7456
magraham@vassar.edu
• Jamie Chagnon, Athletic Communications
Director
(845) 437-7469
jachagnon@vassar.edu

VIRGINIA WESLEYAN COLLEGE
ATHLETICS
1584 WESLEYAN DRIVE
NORFOLK, VA 23502
757-455-3303
Fax: 757-461-2262
vwcathletics.com
• Joanne Renn, Executive Director of
Athletics
(757) 455-5723
• Jeff Bowers, Associate Director of
Athletics
(757) 455-3285
• Stephany Dunmyer, Assistant Director of
Athletics
(757) 455-2122
• Cody Clifton, Sports Information Director
(757) 455-3393
• Corey Wingen, Head Athletic Trainer
(757) 455-3417

WABASH COLLEGE ATHLETICS
301 WEST WABASH AVENUE
CRAWFORDSVILLE, IN 47933
765-361-6220
Fax: 765-361-6447
webmaster@wabash.edu
sports.wabash.edu
• Joseph Haklin, Director of Athletics
(765) 361-6233
haklinj@wabash.edu
• Brent Harris, Director of Sports Information
(765) 361-6165
harrisb@wabash.edu
• Mark Elizondo, Head Athletics Trainer
(765) 361-6235
elizondm@wabash.edu

WARTBURG COLLEGE ATHLETICS
100 WARTBURG BOULEVARD
WAVERLY, IA 50677
319-352-8447
Fax: 319-352-8213
www.go-knights.net
• Rick Willis, Athletic Director
(319) 352-8470
rick.willis@wartburg.edu
• Marcus Newsom, Assistant Athletic
Director
(319) 352-8356
marcus.newsom@wartburg.edu
• Monica Severson, Senior Woman
Administrator
(319) 352-8469
monica.severson@wartburg.edu

• Katie Jo Kuhens, Sports Information Director
(319) 352-8208
katiejo.kuhens@wartburg.edu
• Ryan Callahan, Head Athletic Trainer
(319) 352-8534
ryan.callahan@wartburg.edu

WASHINGTON & JEFFERSON COLLEGE ATHLETICS
HENRY MEMORIAL CENTER
60 SOUTH LINCOLN STREET
WASHINGTON, PA 15301
724-223-6054
Fax: 724-250-3329
gopresidents.com
• Scott McGuinness, Director of Athletics
(724) 250-3308
smcguinness@washjeff.edu
• Mark Lesako, Head Athletic Trainer
(724) 503-1001
mlesako1@washjeff.edu
• Jeff Mountain, Assistant Director of Athletics
(724) 250-3306
jmountain@washjeff.edu
• Sean King, Sports Information Director
(724) 223-6080
sking@washjeff.edu

WASHINGTON AND LEE UNIVERSITY ATHLETICS
WARNER CENTER
204 WEST WASHINGTON STREET
LEXINGTON, VA 24450
540-458-8670
Fax: 540-458-8173
www.generalssports.com
• Jan Hathorn, Athletic Director
(540) 458-8671
hathornj@wlu.edu
• Elizabeth Igo LeRose, Associate Athletic Director
(540) 458-8687
lerosee@wlu.edu
• Neil Cunningham, Assistant Athletic Director
(540) 458-8056
cunninghamn@wlu.edu
• Brian Laubscher, Sports Information Director
(540) 458-8676
blaubsch@wlu.edu

WASHINGTON COLLEGE ATHLETICS
300 WASHINGTON AVENUE
CHESTERTOWN, MD 21620
410-778-2800
800-422-1782
Fax: 410-778-7741
washingtoncollegesports.com
• Bryan Matthews, Director of Athletics
(410) 778-7232
bmatthews2@washcoll.edu
• Thad Moore, Deputy Athletic Director
(410) 778-7243
tmoore2@washcoll.edu
• Jeff Shirk, Assistant Athletic Director
(410) 778-7248
jshirk2@washcoll.edu

WASHINGTON UNIVERSITY ATHLETICS
ONE BOOKINGS DRIVE
CAMPUS BOX 1067
ST. LOUIS, MO 63130-4899

314-935-5220
Fax: 314-935-5545
bearsports.wustl.edu
• Josh Whitman, Director of Athletics
(314) 935-5534
• Chris Peacock, Deputy Director of Athletics
(314) 935-7015
cpeacock@wustl.edu
• Chris Mitchell, Athletic Director for Communications
(314) 935-5077
• Kelcey Buck, Sports Information Director
(314) 935-4709
• Andrew Koch, Director of Facilities
(314) 935-4703
ajkoch@wustl.edu

WAYNESBURG COLLEGE ATHLETICS
51 WEST COLLEGE STREET
WAYNESBURG, PA 15370
724-852-3230
Fax: 724-852-4122
www.waynesburgsports.com
• Larry Marshall, Director of Athletics
(724) 852-3477
• Bobby Fox, Sports Information Director
(724) 852-3334
• Andy Palko, Head Athletic Trainer
(724) 852-3306

WEBSTER UNIVERSITY ATHLETICS
470 EAST LOCKWOOD AVENUE
ST. LOUIS, MO 63119-3914
314-968-6984
Fax: 314-963-6092
www.websterathletics.com
• Scott Kilgallon, Director of Athletics
(314) 246-7576
• Chris Bunch, Assistant Athletics Director
(314) 246-7529
bunch@webster.edu
• Niel DeVasto, Sports Information Director
(314) 246-6989
devastnd@webster.edu

WENTWORTH INSTITUTE OF TECHNOLOGY ATHLETICS
550 HUNTINGTON AVENUE
BOSTON, MA 02115
617-989-4590
Fax: 617-989-4150
athletics@wit.edu
www.wentworthathletics.com
• Cheryl Aaron, Director of Athletics
(617) 989-4159
aaronc@wit.edu
• Bill Gorman, Associate Director of Athletics
(617) 989-4147
gormanb@wit.edu
• Danielle Ferrara, Senior Woman Administrator
(617) 989-4432
ferrarad@wit.edu
• Ben Butterfield, Director of Sport Performance
(617) 989-4103
butterfieldb@wit.edu

WESLEY COLLEGE ATHLETICS
120 NORTH STATE STREET
DOVER, DE 19901
302-736-2435
Fax: 302-730-3894
www.gowesleyathletics.com

• Mike Drass, Executive Director of Athletics
(302) 736-2363
• Tracey Short, Associate Director for Compliance
(302) 736-2541
• Brett Ford, Sports Information Director
(302) 736-2450
• Brandon Sonson, Head Athletic Trainer
(302) 736-2553

WESLEYAN UNIVERSITY ATHLETICS
FREEMAN ATHLETIC CENTER
161 CROSS STREET
MIDDLETOWN, CT 6459
860-685-2690
Fax: 860-685-2691
www.wesleyan.edu/athletics
• Mike Whalen, Director of Athletics
(860) 685-2908
mwhalen@wesleyan.edu
• Rachel Ludwig, Associate Director of Athletics
(860) 685-3555
rludwig@wesleyan.edu
• Mike O'Brien, Director of Athletic Communication
(860) 685-2887
mobrien03@wesleyan.edu

WESTERN CONNECTICUT STATE UNIVERSITY ATHLETICS
181 WHITE STREET
DANBURY, CT 06810
203-837-9015
Fax: 203-837-9050
www.wcsuathletics.com
• Scott Ames, Interim Athletic Director
(203) 837-9014
amess@wcsu.edu
• Jill Cook, Senior Woman Administrator
(203) 837-8624
cookj@wcsu.edu
• Mark Allen, Head Athletic Trainer
(203) 837-9016
allenm@wcsu.edu

WESTERN NEW ENGLAND COLLEGE ATHLETICS
1215 WILBRAHAM ROAD
SPRINGFIELD, MA 01119
413-782-1202
Fax: 413-796-1508
www.wnegoldenbears.com
• Mike Theulen, Director of Athletics
(413) 782-1503
mtheulen@wne.edu
• Joe Sassi, Senior Associate Director of Athletics
(413) 782-1208
jsassi@wne.edu
• Lori Mayhew, Assistant Athletic Director
(413) 796-2230
lmayhew@wne.edu
• Wes Poplizio, Director of Athletic Communications
(413) 782-1227
wes.popolizio@wne.edu
• Mike Vallee, Head Athletic Trainer
(413) 782-1599
mvallee@wne.edu

WESTFIELD STATE COLLEGE ATHLETICS
577 WESTERN AVENUE
WESTFIELD, MA 01086-1630

413-572-5405
Fax: 413-572-5477
www.westfieldstateowls.com
• Richard Lenfest, Athletics Director
(413) 572-8229
rlenfest@westfield.ma.edu
• Nancy Bals, Associate Athletics Director
(413) 572-5515
nbals@westfield.ma.edu
• Nathan Bashaw, Sports Information
Director
(413) 572-8155
• Cheryl Lee, Head Athletic Trainer
(413) 572-5418
clee@westfield.ma.edu

**WESTMINSTER COLLEGE (MO)
ATHLETICS**
501 WESTMINSTER AVENUE
FULTON, MO 65251
573-592-5200
Fax: 800-475-3361
www.wcbluejays.com
• Matt Mitchell, Athletics Director
(573) 592-5301
matt.mitchell@westminster-mo.edu
• Julie Moses, Athletic Department Manager
(573) 592-5200
julie.moses@westminster-mo.edu
• Tracey Braden, Senior Women's
Administrator
(573) 592-5345
bradent@westminster-mo.edu
• Alysha Hodge, Sports Information Director
(573) 592-5302
alysha.hodge@westminster-mo.edu
• Josh Thompson, Head of Athletic Training
(573) 592-5332
josh.thompson@westminster-mo.edu

**WESTMINSTER COLLEGE (PA)
ATHLETICS**
319 SOUTH MARKET STREET
NEW WILMINGTON, PA 16172-0001
724-946-7307
Fax: 724-946-7187
athletics.westminster.edu
• Jim Dafler, Director of Athletics
(724) 946-7313
daflerje@westminster.edu
• Tammy Swearingen, Senior Women's
Administrator
(724) 946-7320
swearitl@westminster.edu
• Shaun Toomey, Head Athletic Trainer
(724) 946-7314
toomeysj@westminster.edu
• Nathan LaRiccia, Sports Information
Director
(724) 946-6357
lariccnj@westminster.edu

WHEATON COLLEGE (IL) ATHLETICS
501 COLLEGE AVENUE
WHEATON, IL 60187-5593
630-752-5000
Fax: 630-752-7007
webmaster@wheaton.edu
athletics.wheaton.edu
• Julie Davis, Director of Athletics
(630) 752-5079
julie.davis@wheaton.edu
• Bill Stukes, Associate Athletics Director
(630) 752-5734
william.stukes@wheaton.edu
• Kent Madsen, Assistant Athletic Director
(630) 752-7057

kent.madsen@wheaton.edu
• Brett Marhanka, Athletics Communications
Director
(630) 752-5747
brett.marhanka@wheaton.edu

WHEATON COLLEGE (MA) ATHLETICS
26 EAST MAIN STREET
NORTON, MA 2766
508-286-8200
Fax: 508-286-8249
info@wheatoncollege.edu
wheatoncollege.edu
• John Sutyak, Director of Athletics
(508) 286-8216
• Lisa Yenush, Associate Director of
Athletics
(508) 286-3982
yenush_lisa@wheatoncollege.edu
• Gregory J. Steele, Head Athletic Trainer
(508) 286-3986
gsteele@wheatoncollege.edu

WHEELOCK COLLEGE ATHLETICS
200 THE RIVERWAY
BOSTON, MA 02215
617-879-2022
Fax: 617-879-2277
• Dwight Datcher, Director of Athletics
(617) 879-2238
ddatcher@wheelock.edu
• Stephanie Smyrl, Senior Women's
Administrator
(617) 879-2189
ssmyrl@wheelock.edu
• Amanda Cuiffo, Associate Director of
Athletics
(617) 879-2171
acuiffo@wheelock.edu
• Meghan Griffin, Director of Sports
Information
(617) 879-2022
mgriffin@wheelock.edu
• Jayson Hill, Head Athletic Trainer
(617) 879-2305
jhill@wheelock.edu

WHITMAN COLLEGE ATHLETICS
345 BOYER AVENUE
WALLA WALLA, WA 99362
509-527-5111
Fax: 509-527-5960
athletics.whitman.edu
• Dean Snider, Athletics Director
(509) 527-5288
• Michelle Ferenz, Associate Athletic
Director
(509) 527-5261
ferenzmk@whitman.edu
• Gregg Petcoff, Sports Communications
Director
(509) 527-5902
• John Eckel, Head Athletic Trainer
(509) 527-5590
eckeljw@whitman.edu

WHITTIER COLLEGE ATHLETICS
GRAHAM ATHLETICS CENTER
13847 EARLHAM DRIVE
WHITTIER, CA 90602
562-907-4271
Fax: 562-945-8024
www.wcpoets.com
• Robert Coleman, Executive Director of
Athletics
(562) 907-4268
rcoleman@whittier.edu

• Rock Carter, Associate Director of
Athletics
(562) 907-4972
rcarter@whittier.edu
• Mike Rizzo, Assistant Director of Athletics
(562) 907-4967
mrizzo@whittier.edu
• Lance Franey, Director of Communications
(562) 907-4852
lfraney@whittier.edu
• Keith Candelaria, Head Athletic Trainer
(562) 907-4965

WHITWORTH COLLEGE ATHLETICS
300 WEST HAWTHORNE ROADD
SPOKANE, WA 99251
509-777-1000
Fax: 509-777-3720
sflegel@whitworth.edu
www.whitworthpirates.com
• Tim Demant, Director of Athletics
(509) 777-3600
tdemant@whitworth.edu
• Jo Ann Wagstaff, Senior Women's
Administrator
(509) 777-4311
jwagstaff@whitworth.edu
• Steve Flegel, Sports Information Director
(509) 777-3239
sflegel@whitworth.edu
• Jon Bosh, Head Athletics Trainer
(509) 777-3728
jbosh@whitworth.edu

WIDENER UNIVERSITY ATHLETICS
ONE UNIVERSITY PLACE
CHESTER, PA 19013
610-499-4442
Fax: 610-499-4481
widenerpride.com
• Jack Shafer, Director of Athletics
(610) 499-4437
jlshafer@widener.edu
• Larissa Gillespie, Associate Director of
Athletics
(610) 499-4434
lagillespie@widener.edu
• Chris Carideo, Assistant Athletic Director
(610) 499-4454
cjcarideo@widener.edu
• A.J. Duffy, III, Head Athletic Trainer
(610) 499-4445
aduffy@widener.edu
• Matt Chmura, Sports Information Director
(610) 499-4436
machmura@widener.edu

WILLAMETTE UNIVERSITY ATHLETICS
900 STATE STREET
SALEM, OR 97301
503-370-6420
Fax: 503-370-6379
athletics@willamette.edu
www.wubearcats.com
• Valerie Cleary, Athletics Director
(503) 370-6262
• Judy Gordon, Senior Woman Administrator
(503) 370-6506
• Ken Smith, Head Athletic Trainer
(503) 370-6672
kosmith@willamette.edu
• Robert McKinney, Athletics
Communications Director
(503) 370-6110

WILLIAM PATERSON UNIVERSITY OF NEW JERSEY ATHLETICS
300 POMPTON ROAD
WAYNE, NJ 07470
973-720-2356
Fax: 973-720-3017
wpupioneers.com
• Sabrina Grant, Director of Athletics
(973) 720-2754
grantsa@wpunj.edu
• Cindy Cohen, Associate Athletic Director
(973) 720-3861
cohenc@wpunj.edu
• Alison Moquin, Head Athletic Trainer
(973) 720-2358
moquina@wpunj.edu
• Heather Brocious, Sports Information Director
(973) 720-2705
brocioush@wpunj.edu

WILLIAMS COLLEGE ATHLETICS
22 SPRING STREET
WILLIAMSTOWN, MA 01267
413-597-2366
Fax: 413-597-4272
athletics.williams.edu
• Lisa Melendy, Director of Athletics
(413) 597-3511
lmelendy@williams.edu
• Gary Guerin, Associate Director for Operations
(413) 597-3321
gguerin@williams.edu
• Judy Fraser, Assistant Director of Athletics
(413) 597-3006
jfraser@williams.edu
• Dick Quinn, Sports Information Director
(413) 597-4982
dquinn@williams.edu

WILMINGTON COLLEGE ATHLETICS
1870 QUAKER WAY
WILMINGTON, OH 45177
937-382-6661
800-341-9318
Fax: 937-383-8557
wilmingtonquakers.com
• Terry Rupert, Director of Athletics
(937) 481-2255
terry_ruper:@wilmington.edu
• Stacey Conley, Athletics Business Manager
(937) 481-2467
stacey_conley@wilmington.edu
• Jayson Ameer Rasheed, Director of Athletic Communications
(937) 481-2347
• Brian Dykhuizen, Head Athletic Trainer
(937) 481-2252
brian_dykhuizen@wilmington.edu

WISCONSIN - EAU CLAIRE ATHLETICS, UNIVERSITY OF
131 GARFIELD AVENUE
EAU CLAIRE, WI 54701
715-836-3062
Fax: 715-836-4074
sportsinfo@uwec.edu
www.blugolds.com
• Dan Schumacher, Director of Athletics
(715) 836-5858
schumadj@uwec.edu
• Robin Baker, Associate Athletic Director
(715) 836-5529
bakerrk@uwec.edu
• Amanda Hopkins, Assistant Athletic

Director
(715) 836-3939
hopkinak@uwec.edu
• Jill Millis, Sports Information Director
(715) 836-4184
millisjl@uwec.edu
• Garry Grant, Head Athletic Trainer
(715) 836-3877
grantga@uwec.edu

WISCONSIN - OSHKOSH ATHLETICS, UNIVERSITY OF
785 HIGH AVENUE
OSHKOSH, WI 54901
920-424-1034
Fax: 920-424-1035
www.uwoshkoshtitans.com
• Darryl Sims, Director of Athletics
(920) 424-1034
sims@uwosh.edu
• Vicci Stimac, Senior Woman Administrator
(920) 424-1384
stimacv@uwosh.edu
• Kennan Timm, Sports Information Director
(920) 424-0365
timmk@uwosh.edu
• Wade Peitersen, Head Athletic Trainer
(920) 424-7138

WISCONSIN LUTHERAN COLLEGE ATHLETICS
8800 WEST BLUEMOUND ROAD
MILWAUKEE, WI 53226
414-443-8800
Fax: 414-443-8514
sports.info@wlc.edu
wlcsports.com
• Skip Noon, Director of Athletics
(414) 443-8871
skip.noon@wlc.edu
• Pam Tullberg, Senior Woman Administrator
(414) 443-8876
pamela.tullberg@wlc.edu
• Dave Reinemann, Assistant Athletics Director
(414) 443-8990
dave.reinemann@wlc.edu
• Bill Curtis, Director of Athletic Development
(414) 443-8546
william.curtis@wlc.edu
• Adam Heinzen, Director of Athletic Communications
(414) 443-8746
sports.info@wlc.edu

WISCONSIN - LA CROSSE ATHLETICS, UNIVERSITY OF
126 MITCHELL HALL
1725 STATE STREET
LA CROSSE, WI 54601
608-785-8616
Fax: 608-785-8674
athletics@uwlax.edu
www.uwlathletics.com
• Kim Blum, Director of Athletics
(608) 785-8194
• David Johnson, Assistant Athletic Director for Media Relations
(608) 785-8493
djohnson@uwlax.edu
• Jason Murphy, Facilities Director
(608) 785-5175
jmurphy@uwlax.edu
• Joel Luedke, Director of Athletic Training

Services
(608) 785-6542

WISCONSIN - PLATTEVILLE ATHLETICS, UNIVERSITY OF
1 UNIVERSITY PLAZA
PLATTEVILLE, WI 53818
608-342-1567
Fax: 608-342-1576
athletics@uwplatt.edu
• Mike Emendorfer, Interim Athletic Director
(608) 342-1801
emendorm@uwplatt.edu
• Deb Schulman, Associate Athletic Director
(608) 342-1255
schulman@uwplatt.edu
• Megan Wilson, Sports Information Coordinator
(608) 342-1488
wilsonmeg@uwplatt.edu
• Ryanne Breckenridge, Head Athletic Trainer
(608) 342-1575
breckenridgr@uwplatt.edu

WISCONSIN - RIVER FALLS ATHLETICS, UNIVERSITY OF
410 SOUTH THIRD STREET
RIVER FALLS, WI 54022
715-425-3911
Fax: 715-425-3257
sportsinformation@uwrf.edu
www.uwrfsports.com
• Roger Ternes, Director of Athletics
(715) 425-3246
• Amber Dohlman, Co-Sports Information Director
(715) 425-3846
amber.dohlman@uwrf.edu
• Jake Wissing, Co-Sports Information Director
(715) 425-3846
jacob.wissing@uwrf.edu
• Andrew Baker, Head Athletic Trainer
(715) 425-3130
andrew.baker@uwrf.edu

WISCONSIN - STEVENS POINT ATHLETICS, UNIVERSITY OF
2050 FOURTH AVENUE
STEVENS POINT, WI 54481
715-346-4494
Fax: 715-346-4655
athletics.uwsp.edu
• Frank O'Brien, Interim Director of Athletics
(715) 346-3888
fobrien@uwsp.edu
• Shirley Egner, Senior Woman Administrator
(715) 346-3397
segner@uwsp.edu
• Kris Ficken, Director of Sports Medicine
(715) 346-3931
• Holly Schmies, Director of Athletic Training Education
(715) 346-2922
hschmies@uwsp.edu

WISCONSIN - STOUT ATHLETICS, UNIVERSITY OF
712 SOUTH BROADWAY STREET
MENOMONIE, WI 54751
715-232-1122
Fax: 715-232-1684
naatzd@uwstout.edu
athletics.uwstout.edu

• Duey Naatz, Athletic Director
(715) 232-2758
naatzd@uwstout.edu
• Susan Lew, Head Athletic Trainer
(715) 232-2213
lews@uwstout.edu
• Layne Pitt, Sports Information Director
(715) 232-2275
pittl@uwstout.edu

WISCONSIN - WHITEWATER ATHLETICS, UNIVERSITY OF
800 WEST MAIN STREET
WHITEWATER, WI 53190-1790
262-472-4661
Fax: 262-472-2791
www.uwwsports.com
• Amy Edmonds, Director of Intercollegiate Athletics
(262) 472-4661
edmondsa@uww.edu
• Bob Lanza, Associate Athletic Director
(262) 472-3190
lanzar@uww.edu
• Keri Carollo, Senior Woman Administrator
(262) 472-5782
carollok@uww.edu
• Chris Lindeke, Director of Athletic Communications
(262) 472-1147
lindekec@uww.edu
• Steve Hillmer, Director of Athletic Training
(262) 472-1150
hillmers@uww.edu

WITTENBERG UNIVERSITY ATHLETICS
PO BOX 720
SPRINGFIELD, OH 45501
937-327-6415
Fax: 937-327-6428
www.wittenbergtigers.com
• Gary Williams, Director of Athletics & Recreation
(937) 327-6458
williamsg1@wittenberg.edu
• Sarah Jurewicz, Senior Woman Director
(937) 327-6457
sjurewicz@wittenberg.edu
• Joe Fincham, Associate Director of Athletics
(937) 327-6498
wfincham@wittenberg.edu
• Matt Croci, Assistant Director of Athletics
(937) 327-6469
crocim@wittenberg.edu
• Ryan Maurer, Director of Atheltics Communications
(937) 327-6114
rmaurer@wittenberg.edu

WOOSTER ATHLETICS, THE COLLEGE OF
1189 BEALL AVENUE
WOOSTER, OH 44691
330-263-2000
Fax: 330-263-2537
kbeckett@wooster.edu
www.woosterathletics.com
• Keith Beckett, Director of Athletics
(330) 263-2189
kbeckett@wooster.edu
• Russell Houser, Assistant Director of Athletics
(330) 263-2183
• Ashley Reid, Assistant Athletic Director for Inclusion
(330) 263-2181

• Tom Love, Head Athletic Trainer
(330) 263-2184
tlove@wooster.edu
• Hugh Howard, Director of Sports Information
(330) 263-2374

WORCESTER POLYTECHNIC INSTITUTE ATHLETICS
100 INSTITUTE ROAD
WORCESTER, MA 01609-2280
508-831-5243
Fax: 508-831-5775
athletics@wpi.edu
athletics.wpi.edu
• Dana L. Harmon, Director of Athletics
(508) 831-5243
dharmon@wpi.edu
• Cherie Galasso, Associate Athletic Director
(508) 831-5063
cgalasso@wpi.edu
• Wendy Walsh, Assistant Athletic Director
(508) 831-5327
wlwc@wpi.edu
• Rusty Eggen, Sports Information Director
(508) 831-5328
rusty@wpi.edu

WORCESTER STATE UNIVERSITY ATHLETICS
486 CHANDLER STREET
WORCESTER, MA 01602
508-929-8034
Fax: 508-929-8184
schapman@worcester.edu
www.wsulancers.com
• Michael Mudd, Director of Athletics
(508) 929-8034
mmudd@worcester.edu
• John Meany, Deputy Director of Athletics
(508) 929-8746
jmeany@worcester.edu
• Karen Tessmer, Associate Athletic Director
(508) 929-8769
ktessmer@worcester.edu
• Dave Lindberg, Assistant Athletic Director
(508) 929-8593
dlindberg@worcester.edu
• Jessica Meany, Head Athletic Trainer
(508) 929-8024
jessica.meany@worcester.edu

YESHIVA UNIVERSITY ATHLETICS
500 WEST 185TH STREET
NEW YORK, NY 10033
212-960-5211
Fax: 212-960-0088
jbednrsh@yu.edu
www.yumacs.com
• Joe Bednarsh, Athletic Director
(212) 960-0015
jbednrsh@yu.edu
• Shelley Whitaker, Associate Athletics Director
(212) 960-0042
• Erica Lemm, Senior Woman Administrator
(212) 340-7727
• A.J. O'Hagan, Sports Information Director
(212) 960-5291
anthony.ohagan@yu.edu
• Aaronn Baker, Women's Athletic Trainer
(347) 758-2266
• Xavier Alzate, Men's Athletic Trainer
(212) 960-5486
xavier.alzate@yu.edu

YORK COLLEGE (CUNY) ATHLETICS
94-20 GUY R. BREWER BOULEVARD
JAMAICA, NY 11451
718-262-5101
Fax: 718-262-5216
stjohn@york.cuny.edu
www.yorkathletics.com
• Ronald St. John, Director of Athletics
(718) 262-5114
stjohn@york.cuny.edu
• Jessica Cherry, Senior Women Administrator
(718) 262-5115
jcherry@york.cuny.edu
• John Scarinci, Sports Information Director
(718) 262-5104
jscarinci@york.cuny.edu
• Dan Matte, Head Athletic Trainer
(718) 262-5212
matte@york.cuny.edu

YORK COLLEGE (PENNSYLVANIA) ATHLETICS
441 COUNTRY CLUB ROAD
YORK, PA 17405-7199
717-846-7788
Fax: 717-849-1626
www.ycpspartans.com
• Paul Saikia, Assistant Dean for Athletics
(717) 815-1245
psaikia@ycp.edu
• Matt Day, Associate Director for Athletics
(717) 815-6604
gday@ycp.edu
• Jen Muston, Assistant Director of Athletics
(717) 815-1516
jmuston@ycp.edu
• Scott Guise, Director of Athletic Communications
(717) 815-1394
sguise@ycp.edu
• Nate Cooke, Head Athletic Trainer
(717) 815-1962
ncooke@ycp.edu

Sport Management Degree Programs

ADAMS STATE COLLEGE
208 EDGEMONT BLVD.
ALAMOSA, CO 81101
719-587-7011
800-824-6494
Fax: 719-587-7522
www.adams.edu/athletics
• Eric Carpio, Assistant Vice President for Enrollment Management
• Karie Velleses, Administrative Assistant
(719) 587-8152
• David Svaldi, President
• Larry Mortensen, Athletic Director
Description:
Founded in 1921 as a teachers' college, Adams State is now a comprehensive liberal arts college offering 16 undergraduate majors with 28 minors and emphases, as well as 8 master's degree programs- most offered online. Offering sport management programs in Bachelor's and Master's degree.
Mission:
Adams State College dedicates its resources to provide opportunity and access for all students. The College is an innovative leader that recognizes the inherent

408

educational value of diversity. It is a catalyst for the educational, cultural, and economic interests of rural Colorado, the surrounding region, and the global community.

About Sport Management Program:
The online MA in Sport Management at Adams College is a 36-credit program that offers a wide range of courses and practical experiences in order to prepare students for employment in sport management related careers. All courses are offered online which allows for greater flexibility and optimum convenience for students who hold full-time careers or cannot relocate. Students can complete the program in two years which includes all coursework and two short on-campus residencies. The MA in Sport Management at Adams State is the least expensive of any other fully online master's degree in the US. Applications are due May 1st and cohorts begin ea

ADELPHI UNIVERSITY - RUTH S. AMMON SCHOOL OF EDUCATION
ADELPHI UNIVERSITY
1 SOUTH AVE
P.O BOX 701
GARDEN CITY, NY 11530-0701
516-877-4100
800-233-5744
Fax: 516-877-4258
www.adelphi.edu
• Robert A. Scott, Adelphi University President
• Audrey Blumberg, Sr. Associate Provost Academic Affairs
(516) 877-3159
Description:
M.S. in Sport Management; The Sport Management program prepares students for management roles in academic or professional sports. With the assistance of an advisor, graduate students tailor the sport management and business electives to target their desirable career goals.

ALCORN STATE UNIVERSITY
DEPARTMENT OF HPER
1000 ASU DRIVE
ALCORN STATE, MS 39096
601-877-6100
Fax: 601-877-3821
www.alcorn.edu
• David Gomez, HPER Instructor
(601) 877-4083
dgomez@alcorn.edu
• Garry Lewis, HPER Assistant Professor
(601) 877-6278
glewis1@alcorn.edu
• Willie McGowan, Jr., HPER Instructor
(601) 877-6465
w_mcgowan@alcorn.edu
• Richard Myles, Sr., HPER Instructor
(601) 877-6505
rmyles@alcorn.edu
• Kevin Montgomery, HPER Instructor
(601) 877-6275
kevinm@alcorn.edu
Description:
Undergrad Degree: B.S. Recreation. Grad Degree: M.E.D. Areas of Specialization: Undergrad: Recreation. Grad: Athletic Administration and Coaching.

ALFRED STATE COLLEGE- SUNY COLLEGE OF TECHNOLOGY
10 UPPER COLLEGE DRIVE
ALFRED, NY 14802
607-587-4215
800-425-3733
www.alfredstate.edu/athletics
Description:
Alfred State College is a public, coeducational, two- and four- year, nonsectarian college of approximately 3,700 undergraduates. The College was founded in 1908 and joined the newly organized State University of New York (SUNY) system in 1948.
Information on Sport Management Program:
The goal of the sports management program is to provide students with a concentration of courses aimed at preparing them for a career in the management and administration of the sport and fitness industry. A laptop computer is recommended, but not required, for students entering the sports management program.
Entrance Requirements & Recommendations:
Required: Algebra, Geometry (Math A)
Recommended: Algebra 2/Trigonometry (Math B)

ALVERNIA COLLEGE
400 SAINT BERNARDINE STREET
2ND FLOOR STUDENT CENTER
READING, PA 19607
610-796-8269
888-253-7642
Fax: 610-790-2873
admissions@alvernia.edu
Description of Sport Management Program:
Alvernia College's interdiciplinary and comprehensive program provides students with specific competencies in management, marketing, communication, law, finance and accounting, economics, ethics, and computer literacy as they relate to sport. In addition, the program provides critical thinking, writing, and problem solving skills that are essential ingredients to success in today's workplaces. Internships are an integral part of the Alvernia Sport Management program.

AMERICAN MILITARY UNIVERSITY
10110 BATTLEVIEW PARKWAY
SUITE 114
MANASSAS, VA 20109
877-777-9081
info@apus.edu
• Wallace E Boston, President & Chief Executive Officer
• Harry T. Wilkins, CPA, Executive Vice President, Chief Financial Officer
• Sharon van Wyk, Executive Vice President, Chief Operations Officer
• Carol Gilbert, Executive Vice President, Programs & Marketing
• Karan Powell, Executive Vice President, Provost
• Peter W Gibbons, Senior Vice President, Chief Administrative Office
• Gwen Hall, Sr Vice President, Academic Operations Officer
• W. Dale Young, Sr Vice President, Chief Information Officer

Description of Sports Management Program:
This degree is designed for those who are interested in sports management, coaching, and administration. The core curriculum includes the social contexts of sport in historical and modern society, fundamentals of the sports industry, and specifically focuses on sports law, marketing, promotion, public relations, finance, and economics. Students are provided with and opportunity to concentrate in an area of specific interest, to include sports administration for the aspiring collegiate, community, or high school athletic official; coaching theory and strategy for those interested in leading and coaching teams; management for those interested i

APPALACHIAN STATE UNIVERSITY
DEPARTMENT OF HEALTH, LEISURE AND EXERCISE SCIENCE
PO BOX 32071
BOONE, NC 28608
828-262-2120 EXT 2120
Fax: 828-262-3138
admissions@appstate.edu
www.hles.appstate.edu
• Michael W. Kernodle, Professor
(828) 262-3138
kernodlemw@appstate.edu
• Magdalena Anoufriev, Staff
(036) 262-3141
anoufrievm@appstate.edu
• Gregory Anoufriev, Clinical Assistant Professor
(082) 262-7466
anoufrievg@appstate.edu
• Debbie Arnette, Women's Equipment Supervisor
arnetteda@appstate.edu
• Melanie Austin, Practitioner in Residence
(828) 262-3142
austinm@appstate.edu
• Rebecca A Battista, Associate Professor
(828) 262-3047
battistara@appstate.edu
• Mary Ann Bo Bolick, Lecturer
(828) 262-2935
bolickma@appstate.edu
• Jeffrey T. Soukup, Asst Professor
(828) 262-3138
soukupjt@appstate.edu
Description:
Grad Degree: M.A. in Sport Management; Exercise Science, Spec in Sports Management; M.S. in Exercise Science. Areas of Specialization: Athletic Administration and Sport Management; Exercise Science. The mission of the Department of Health, Leisure, and Exercise Science (HLES) is to deliver student-centered education that is accentuated by quality teachin, scholarly activity, and service.

AQUINAS COLLEGE SPORTS MANAGEMENT PROGRAM
1607 ROBINSON ROAD S.E.
GRAND RAPIDS, MI 49506-1799
616-632-8900
admissions@aquinas.edu
www.aquinas.edu/athletics
• Juan Olivarez, Ph.D, President
(616) 632-2881
• Charles D. Gunnoe, Jr., Ph.D., Provost & Dean of Faculty
(616) 632-2151

• Gregory W. McAleenan, J.D., VP for Institutional Advancement
(616) 632-2809
odonndeb@aquinas.edu
• Paula T. Meehan, B.A., VP For Enrollment Management
(616) 632-2852
• Nathalie Meyer, Secretary
• Michael Lown, Treasurer
Description of Sport Management Program:
Aquinas developed the Business Administration/Sport Management major in 1996 with Ernie Romine as the founder. This major provides students with the knowledge and background of a business degree and the field specific knowledge needed for success in the careers tracks of sport, athletics, and fitness. In addition, students can gain hands on experience through internships and the Sport Management Club. One of the top ten largest majors on campus, sport management is a growing field with great potential for any student interested in sports and business.

ARIZONA STATE UNIVERSITY
TEMPE CAMPUS
UNIVERSITY DRIVE & MILL AVENUE
TEMPE, AZ 85287
480-965-9011
www.thesundevils.com
• Ray Artigue, Executive Director Sports Business Program
Degree Offered
B.S. concentration in Tourism Development & Management, from College of Public Programs; B.S. concentration in Parks & Recreation Management, from college of public programs; B.A. concentration in Business (Tourism) from W.P. Carey School of Business

ARKANSAS STATE UNIVERSITY - DEPT OF HEALTH, PE & SPORT SCIENCES
State University, AR 72467
870-972-3066
Fax: 870-972-3096
www.astateredwolves.com
• David LaVetter, Director, Sport Management Program
Degree:
B.S. Sport Management, College of Education Department of Health, PE, and Sport Sciences. The BS degree in Sport Management is designed to provide students the needed background, knowledge, and experiences to be prepared for careers in intercollegiate and professional athletics organizations.

ARKANSAS, UNIVERSITY OF
232 SILAS H. HUNT HALL
1 UNIVERSITY OF ARKANSAS
FAYETTEVILLE, AR 72701
479-575-5346
800-377-8632
Fax: 479-575-7515
uofa@uark.edu
www.uark.edu
• David G. Gearhart, Chancellor
Degrees Offered:
Bachelor of Science in Education with major in recreation and sport management.

ASHLAND UNIVERSITY
401 COLLEGE AVENUE
ASHLAND, OH 44805
419-289-4142
800-882-1548
www.goashlandeagles.com
• Frederick J Finks, President
Description of Sport Management Program:
Majors in athletic training, exercise science, physical education and sport management train well-rounded students for professional careers in all areas of wellness and sport. Students are prepared in and out of the classroom with relevant course content, professional development days with people already working for major sport organizations, and plenty of field experience leading up to a full-time internship.

AUBURN UNIVERSITY SPORT MANAGEMENT PROGRAM
AUBURN, AL 36849
334-844-4000
www.education.auburn.edu/kinesiology
Description of Sport Management Program:
The Higher Education program with a minor in Sport Management is structured in conformity with the curriculum requirements of the North American Society for Sport management (NASSM). The 18 hours of sport courses are distributed among sport management, sociology of sport, sport finance and marketing, sport ethics and public relations, and practicum in athletic administration.

AVERETT COLLEGE SPORT MANAGEMENT PROGRAM
420 WEST MAIN ST
DANVILLE, VA 24541
434-791-5600
800-AVERETT (283-7388)
www.averettcougars.com
Sport Management Program:
Averett offers a bachelor's degree in physical education in a number of concentrations including: physical education (non-teaching), physical education: PK-12, sport management, wellness/ sports medicine, & coaching. Physical education majors are encouraged to develop in-depth competency in at least one performance area or one sport. Students have the opportunity to participate in a variety of internships.

BALDWIN-WALLACE COLLEGE
DEPT OF HEALTH AND PHYSICAL EDUCATION
275 EASTLAND ROAD
BEREA, OH 44017-2088
440-826-2900
Fax: 440-826-6980
www.bw.edu
• Gregory Flanik, CIO
(440) 826-2700
gflanik@bw.edu
• Donna Gutschmidt, Technical Writer
(440) 826-2705
dgutschm@bw.edu
• Verlyn Mol, Manager of Administrative Information Systems
(440) 826-2316
vmol@bw.edu
• Mardele Hawley, Administrative Support

Coordinator
(440) 826-2318
mhawley@bw.edu
• Randy Lingenfelter, ERP Systems Administrator
(440) 826-2701
rlingenf@bw.edu
• Lorrie Morehouse, Institutional ResearchAnalyst
(440) 826-2315
lmorehou@bw.edu
• Scott Armstrong, Dept. Chairperson
Description:
Undergrad Degree: B.A. in HPE, with concentration in sport management or fitness management combined with second major or minor in business administration. Areas of Specialization: General within guidelines of program.

BALL STATE UNIVERSITY
PHYSICAL EDUCATION, SPORT AND EXERCISE SCIENCE
2000 W. UNIVERSITY AVENUE
MUNCIE, IN 47306
765-289-1241
800-382-8540
mwhaley@bsu.edu
www.bsu.edu
• Mitchel Whaley, Dept. Chairperson
(765) 285-3206
mwhaley@bsu.edu
• Ronald Davis, Dept. Associate Chairperson
(765) 285-1462
rdavis@bsu.edu
• Gina Pauline, Sport Administration/Mgmt Instructor
(765) 285-4211
Description:
This area of specialization is designed to prepare individuals to administer intercollegiate athletic programs and professional sport organizations. This program is open to graduate physical education majors and to graduates with majors in fields other than physical education.
Requirements:
A minimum of twelve hours in this area of specialization must be taken in the College of Business. The capstone course is a sport management internship with a college/university or a professional sports organization.

BARRY UNIVERSITY
SCHOOL OF HUMAN PERFORMANCE & LEISURE SCIENCES PROGRAM
11300 NE 2ND AVENUE
MIAMI SHORES, FL 33161-6695
305-899-3490
800-756-6000, ext 3490
Fax: 305-899-3556
www.barry.edu
• Kathryn Ludwig, Associate Professor, Chair, Sport and Exercis
• Tal Amasay, Assistant Professor, Coordinator, Physical Ed
• Carl Cramer, Associate Dean HPLS
• Claire Egret, Assistant Professor, Coordinator, Biomechanic
• Annie Clement, Sport Management Coordinator/Professor
Description:
Barry University's program is designed to give students the skills and experience to excel in supervisory positions, and, at Barry,

students have the option of enhancing their sport management degree with an MBA. The sport management masters from Barry University can also prepare students for entry into a top-rated doctoral program.

BARTON COLLEGE
DEPARTMENT OF PHYSICAL
EDUCATION AND SPORT STUDIES
PO BOX 5000
WILSON, NC 27893
252-399-6300
800-345-4973
Fax: 252-399-6516
www.barton.edu/athletics
• Claudia Duncan, Dept. Chairperson
cduncan@barton.edu
Description:
B.S. sport management; The Sport Management curriculum provides for a variety of opportunities for students. They can focus only on sport management or very easily add another major or minor in the business area as most students do. Students complete internships in either a sport setting or a business setting, whichever will provide them with the best experience for their future employment.

BAYLOR UNIVERSITY
DEPARTMENT OF HEALTH, HUMAN
PERFORMANCE & RECREATION
ONE BEAR PLACE
#97313
WACO, TX 76798-7313
254-710-3505
Fax: 254-710-3527
www.baylor.edu
• Andy Pittman, Ph.D., Graduate Program
Coordinator
andy_pittman@baylor.edu
• Brain Leutholtz, Graduate Program
Director
• Andrew Gallucci, Undergraduate Program
Directors
• Ted Poers, Administrative Coordinators
• Andrew Gallucci, Laboratory Directors
• Eva Rhodes, Staff
• Janet Green, Administrative Associate
• John Faribault, Program Coordinator
Description:
Prepare students for careers as Health Educators, Exercise Physiologists, Sport Management Specialists, Physical Education Specialists, or Coaches. A six hour core curriculum is required for each major. Students then specialize in one of the following areas; Exercise Physiology, Health Education, Sport Management, Sport Pedagogy.
Degrees Offered:
M.S. Ed., Sport Management.

BELLEVUE UNIVERSITY
1000 GALVIN ROAD SOUTH
BELLEVUE, NE 68005
402-293-2000
www.bubruins.com
• Keith B. Edquist, Treasurer
• Robert S. Howard, Secretary
Sports Management Program:
The Sports Management major prepares students to enter sports management careers with the knowledge and skills, including critical thinking, communication, management, problem solving, and leadership, required to be successful in

today's sports industry. Students are encouraged to pursue a Business Administration minor, which enhances the knowledge and skills of the Sports Management major.

BELMONT UNIVERSITY SPORT MANAGEMENT PROGRAM
1900 BELMONT BLVD
NASHVILLE, TN 37212
615-460-6000
www.belmont.edu/athletics
Sport Administration:
The Master Sport Administration (MSA) is designed to prepare graduate students for work in the sport industry.

BEMIDJI STATE UNIVERSITY
DEPARTMENT OF HUMAN
PERFORMANCE, SPORT & HEALTH
SPORT MANAGEMENT PROGRAM
1500 BIRCHMONT DRIVE NE #29
BEMIDJI, MN 56601-2699
218-755-2940
Fax: 218-755-3898
www.bemidjistate.edu
• Donna Palivec, Department Chair
dpalivec@bemidjistate.edu
Description:
Sport Management offers specialized training and education for individuals seeking careers in the sport business industry. The Sport Management curriculum is designed to meet the NASPE/NASSM accreditation requirements: sociocultural dimensions, management and leadership, ethics, marketing, communications, budget and finance, legal aspects, economics, and governance.
Degrees Offered:
BA; Sport Management, Minor; Sport Management.

BOWLING GREEN STATE UNIVERSITY
SPORT MANAGEMENT DIVISION
112 EPPLER CENTER
BOWLING GREEN, OH 43403-0248
419-372-2876
Fax: 419-372-6015
mebobb@bgsu.edu
www.bgsu.edu/
• Jacquelyn Cuneen, Chair/Professor
(419) 372-7231
jcuneen@bgsu.edu
Description:
Undergrad Degree: B.S. Grad Degree: M.Ed. Areas of Specialization: Undergrad: Athletic Training and Clinic Management; Sport Marketing; Sports Information; Sport Enterprise. Grad: Sport Administration.

BROOKLYN COLLEGE OF THE CITY UNIVERSITY OF NEW YORK
2900 BEDFORD AVENUE
BROOKLYN, NY 11210
718-951-5000
Fax: 718-951-4882
www.brooklyncollegeathletics.com
• Bruce Filos, Director of Recreation, Intramurals and Inter
(718) 951-5366
bfilosa@brooklyn.edu
Degrees Offered:
M.S. Sports Management, Physical Education

BUCKS COUNTY COMMUNITY COLLEGE - DEPT OF HEALTH, PE & NURSING
275 SWAMP ROAD
GYMNASIUM 102
NEWTON, PA 18940
215-968-8451
admissions@bucks.edu
www.bucks.edu/athletics
• Priscilla Rice, Director
ricep@bucks.edu
Degrees/Majors Offered:
A.A.; The Sport Management major prepares the undergraduate student for a career in sport management, athletics, marketing, campus recreation, intramurals, student activities, as well as other related areas.

CAL STATE UNIVERSITY - BAKERSFIELD, SCHOOL OF BUSINESS AND PUBLIC ADMINISTRATION
9001 STOCKDALE HWY.
BAKERSFIELD, CA 93311-1022
661-654-CSUB (2782)
excellence@csub.edu
www.gorunners.com
• John Emery, Ph.D., Dean and Professor of Finance
(661) 654-2023
jemery@csub.edu
• Mark Evans, Associate Dean & Professor of Economics
(661) 654-2023
mevans@csub.edu
• Margaret Moorhead, Administrative Analyst/Specialist
(661) 654-2234
mmoorhead@csub.edu
• Isabel Gonzalez, Administrative Coordinator
(661) 654-2023
igonzalez4@csub.edu
Sport Management Program:
Courses include; Introduction to Sports Management, Sports Marketing, Sport in Court, Professional Sport Selling and Sport Sponsorship, Special Topics in Sports Management, & Internship in Sports Management.

CALIFORNIA BAPTIST UNIVERSITY
8432 MAGNOLIA AVENUE
RIVERSIDE, CA 92504
951-689-5771
800-782-3382
Fax: 951-351-1808
www.cbulancers.com
• Micah Parker, Director of Athletics
(951) 343-4318
miparker@calbaptist.edu
Degree Offered:
M.S. Kinesiology with a concentration in sport management.

CALIFORNIA POLYTECHNIC STATE UNIVERSITY - RECREATION, PARKS, &TOURISM DEPT.
SAN LUIS OBISPO, CA 93407
805-756-1111
www.gopoly.com

CALIFORNIA STATE UNIVERSITY-FRESNO- CRAIG SCHOOL OF BUSINESS
PETERS BUSINESS BUILDING, #388
5245 N. BACKER AVE, M/S PB 7
FRESNO, CA 93740-8001

559-278-7830
Fax: 559-278-8577
kathyu@csufresno.edu
www.craig.csufresno.edu
Sports Management Program offered:
Graduate master's in sports management

CALIFORNIA STATE UNIVERSITY- LONG BEACH- DEPARTMENT OF KINESIOLOGY
COLLEGE OF HEALTH AND HUMAN SERVICES
1250 BELLFLOWER BLVD
LONG BEACH, CA 90840-8306
562-985-2044
Fax: 562-985-7581
gpsm.ga@gmail.com
www.csulb.edu/athletics
Description:
The Master of Arts in Kinesiology, Option: Sport Management program is offered by the Department of Kinesiology in partnership with College of Continuing and Professional Education (CCPE), at California State University, Long Beach. This accelerated 36-unit program allows students to earn a master's degree in 18 months and is designed to prepare students for a career in the management and administration of sport.

CALIFORNIA STATE UNIVERSITY-FULLERTON
DEPARTMENT OF KINESIOLOGY
800 N. STATE COLLEGE BOULEVARD
ROOM KHS-121
FULLERTON, CA 92634
714-278-3316
Fax: 714-278-5317
• Kathy Koser, Department Chairperson
(714) 278-3316
kkoser@fullerton.edu
• Debra Rose, Kinesiology Graduate Coordinator
(714) 278-5846
drose@fullerton.edu
• Patti Laguna, Kinesiology Undergraduate Coordinator
(714) 278-3783
plaguna@fullerton.edu
Description:
Grad Degree: M.S. in Phys Ed, with emphasis on Sport and Exercise Management. Areas of Specialization: Grad: Corporate Fitness Management, Professional Sports Management, etc.

CALIFORNIA UNIVERSITY OF PENNSYLVANIA
DEPARTMENT OF HEALTH AND SPORT STUDIES
250 UNIVERSITY AVENUE
CALIFORNIA, PA 15419
724-938-4356
Fax: 724-938-4454
yarbrough@calu.edu
www.calvulcans.com
• Roy Yarbrough, Ed.D, Professor
(724) 938-4356
yarbrough@calu.edu
• Brian Wood, Assistant Professor
(724) 938-5033
wood_b@calu.edu
Description:
The sport management studies program is one of the largest programs at California University of Pennsylvania. In sports

business, the term 'player' takes on a new meaning. From the executive boardroom to the playing field, to creating the balance sheets, and even at the scoreboard, sport management majors are doing it all. Three distinct sport management tracks are offered: Sport Management; Professional Golf Management; and Wellness and Fitness (online).

CAMPBELL UNIVERSITY - COLLEGE OF ARTS & SCIENCES
DEPARTMENT OF EXERCISE SCIENCE
PO BOX 567
BUIES CREEK, NC 27506
910-893-1360
800-334-4111
Fax: 910-893-1424
www.campbell.edu
• William Freeman, Chairman/Professor
(910) 893-1362
• Brian Bergemann, Exercise Science Professor
(910) 893-1352
bergemannb@campbell.edu
Description:
B.S. athletic training, fitness wellness management, kinesiology, exercise and sport science, pysical education, sport management.

CANISIUS COLLEGE - SCHOOL OF EDUCATION & HUMAN SERVICES
SCHOOL OF EDUCATION & HUMAN SERVICES
BAGEN HALL 201
2001 MAIN STREET
BUFFALO, NY 14208-1098
716-888-3294
800-843-1517
Fax: 716-888-3164
www.canisius.edu
• Don Sheldon, Director of Athletic Communications
(716) 888-8265
reitnoum@canisius.edu
• Shawn O'Rourke, Associate Dean for Undergraduate & Graduate P
orourke1@canisius.edu
• Yann Abdourazakou, Assistant Professor
• Nicholas Lorgnier, Assistant Professor
lorgnien@canisius.edu
• Matt Reitnour, Director of Athletic Communications
reitnoum@canisius.edu
• Traci Murphy, Associate Athletic Director
• Bill Maher, Director of Athletics
maherw@canisius.edu
Description:
M.S. in Sports Administration. This bachelor's degree program provides students with the skills and training to effectively manage in a wide variety of sports related fields. Graduates of this program are prepared to work in fields such as intercollegiate athletics, amateur and professional sports, sport-marketing firms, special event management as well as facility management. Students gain practical experience through an internship opportunity in a wide variety of settings in the sport industry.

CAPITAL UNIVERSITY
DEPARTMENT OF HEALTH & SCIENCE
1 COLLEGE AND MAIN
COLUMBUS, OH 43209

614-236-6911
Fax: 614-236-6178
lreich@capital.edu
www.capital.edu
• Leonard Reich, Sports Information Director
(614) 236-6174
Description:
Undergrad Degree: B.A. Areas of Specialization: Sport Management.

CARDINAL STRITCH UNIVERSITY- SPORT MANAGEMENT PROGRAM
6801 N. YATES ROAD
MILWAUKEE, WI 53217
414-410-4000
800-347-8822
www.stritch.edu/mssm/
Master's program sport management- Program is designed for working adults seeking to become leaders in the sports industry in a variety of settings, including professional and collegiate sports, health and fitness clubs, recreation departments, sport organizations, and retail sporting goods stores.

CASTLETON STATE COLLEGE
86 Seminary Street
Castleton, VT 5735
802-468-5611
Fax: 802-468-5237
www.castleton.edu/athletics
• John Feenick, Director
Degrees/Majors Offered:
B.S. sports medicine, athletic training, exercise science, physical education, and teaching license. The sports administration concentration trains and develops students for employment in the sport industry. The goal is to prepare students for administrative positions in professional and amateur athletics, recreation, stadium, arena and convention facilities, college and university athletic departments, health and fitness centers, management companies, sports marketing and other programs that require a sports and business background.

CAZENOVIA COLLEGE
7 NICKERSON STREET
CAZENOVIA, NY 13035
315-655-7992
800-654-3210
Fax: 315-655-2157
mjbrimecombe@cazenovia.edu
www.cazenovia.edu
• Michelle Brimecombe, Assistant Professor & Program Director, Sport
(315) 655-7992
mjbrimecombe@cazenovia.edu
Bachelor of Professional Studies:
The Sport Management program at Cazenovia College prepares students for a number of interesting and exciting career opportunities in the sport industry - from youth to scholastic to collegiate to professional sport management and marketing, from event and facility management to sport sport agency. The Sport Management curriculum combines both classroom learning and internship experiences that help broaden the students' understanding as well as experiential and networking opportunities.

CEDARVILLE UNIVERSITY- DEPARTMENT OF KINESIOLOGY AND ALLIED HEALTH
251 N. MAIN STREET
CEDARVILLE, OH 45314
937-766-7755
www.cedarville.edu
Sport Management Program:
Students can major in; Allied Health, Athletic Training, Exercise Science- Bachelor of Arts, Exercise Science - Bachelor of Science, Multi-Age Physical Education, Sport and Exercise Studies, and Sport Management.

CENTENARY COLLEGE- SPORTS MANAGEMENT BUSINESS PROGRAM
400 JEFFERSON STREET
HACKETTSTOWN, NJ 7840
908-852-1400
800-236-8679
Description:
Major in business administration with a concentration in Sports Management.

CENTRAL FLORIDA, UNIVERSITY OF
COLLEGE OF BUSINESS ADMINISTRATION
4000 CENTRAL FLORIDA BLVD
PO BOX 161991
ORLANDO, FL 32816-1991
407-823-2766
Fax: 407-823-6442
business.ucf.edu
• Richard Lapchick, Director, DeVos Sport Business Management Pro
Degree Offered:
MSBM Sport Business Management

CENTRAL MICHIGAN UNIVERSITY
DEPARTMENT OF PHYSICAL EDUCATION AND SPORT
2240 HEALTH PROFESSIONS BUILDING
MT. PLEASANT, MI 48859
989-774-1040
Fax: 989-774-5391
globalsportleadership@cmich.edu
www.chp.cmich.edu
• James Hornak, Dept. Chairman
(517) 774-6659
horna1je@cmich.edu
• Scott Smith, Sport Management Division Co-Director
(517) 774-2859
Scott.J.Smith@cmich.edu
• Marcia Mackey, Sport Management Program Director
(989) 774-2377
Marcia.J.Mackey@cmich.edu
Description:
Undergrad Degree: B.A. with major in Sport Studies and Minor in Business Management. Grad Degree: M.A. in Sport Administration; M.A. in Phys Ed/Athletic Administration. Areas of Specialization: Grad: Sport Administration, Athletic Administration.

CENTRAL MISSOURI STATE UNIVERSITY
DEPARTMENT OF HEALTH & HUMAN PERFORMANCE
PO BOX 800
WARRENSBURG, MO 64093
660-543-4256
877-729-8266
Fax: 660-543-4167
admit@ucmo.edu

• Dan Gerdes, Health Human Performance Professor
(660) 543-4732
Description:
Undergrad Degree: B.S. Grad Degree: M.S. Areas of Specialization: Undergrad: Coaching. Grad: Exercise and Sport Science; Athletic Training; Athletic & Business Administration.

CENTRAL WASHINGTON UNIVERSITY
DEPARTMENT OF HEALTH, HUMAN PERFORMANCE & RECREATION
400 E. UNIVERSITY WAY
ELLENSBURG, WA 98926
509-963-1111
Fax: 509-963-1848
buschr@cwu.edu
www.cwu.edu
• Bob McGowan, Chairman/Professor
(509) 963-1051
mcgowanr@cwu.edu
• Kirk Mathias, Physical Education Director
(509) 963-1051
mathiask@cwu.edu
Description:
Undergrad Degree: B.S., Fitness and Sport Management. Grad Degree: M.S. in PEHLS. Areas of Specialization: Undergrad: Athletic Training, Coaching. Grad: Health Ed; Leisure Services; Athletic Adm; Exercise Science; Pedagogy/Coaching.

CHOWAN UNIVERSITY
SCHOOL OF ARTS & SCIENCES; SPORTS STUDIES & PE
200 JONES DRIVE
MURFREESBORO, NC 27855
252-398-6243
Fax: 252-398-1390
www.chowan.edu
Description:
B.S. in Sport Management; Sports Science Major - Directed for Personal Trainers, Fitness, Cardiac Evaluations; Physical Education Teacher Education; Athletic Training. Internships offered in a variety of areas.

CHRISTIAN BROTHERS UNIVERSITY
SCHOOL OF BUSINESS
650 EAST PARKWAY SOUTH
MEMPHIS, TN 38104
901-321-3000
877-321-4228
www.cbu.edu
Program Description:
Bachelor's in Sport Management from CBU School of Business.

CITADEL, THE
DEPT OF HEALTH, EXERCISE AND SPORT SCIENCE
DEAS HALL
171 MOULTRIE STREET
CHARLESTON, SC 29409
843-953-5060
Fax: 843-953-6798
garnerd1@citadel.edu
www.citadel.edu
• Harry Davakos, Director
harry.davakos@citadel.edu
• Terry Giguiere, Dept. Coordinator
terry.giguiere@citadel.edu
Description:
B.S. health, exercise and sport science, concentration in sport management.

CLAFLIN UNIVERSITY
400 MAGNOLIA STREET
ORANGEBURG, SC 29115
803-535-5000
800-922-1276
www.claflin.edu/athletics
• Marta N Mack, Chair/Director
Description:
B.A. sport management: Courses in the core program are interdisciplinary with the Sport Management program and the Business Administration program. The Sport Management program prepares students to become highly-trained managers who find success in complex and varied sport settings.

CLEVELAND STATE UNIVERSITY
HPERD BUILDING
2121 EUCLID AVENUE
CLEVELAND, OH 44115-2214
216-687-2000
Fax: 216-687-5410
www.csuohio.edu
• Nancy Carlucci Smith, Communication Account Representative
(216) 687-2290
pr@csuohio.edu
• Eddie Lam, Sport Management Program Coordinator
(216) 687-5051
t.lam@csuohio.edu
Description:
Undergrad Degree Major Sport Management; Minor Sport Management. Grad Degree M.Ed Sport Management; M.Ed Exercise Science.

COASTAL CAROLINA UNIVERSIY- COLLEGE OF SCIENCE
843-349-2026
800-277-7000
Fax: 843-349-6436
www.coastal.edu/rsm/
Sport Management Program:
The Department of Kinesiology, Recreation, and Sport Studies at Coastal Carolina University is a dynamic unit of high quality faculty and academic programs that study and promote human movement as applied to current and emerging physical activity, sport, therapeutic, and recreation settings.

COLBY-SAWYER COLLEGE
DEPARTMENT OF EXERCISE AND SPORT SCIENCES
541 MAIN STREET
NEW LONDON, NH 3257
603-526-3000
rmedbery@colby-sawyer.edu
www.colby-sawyerathletics.com
• Russell Medbery, Ph.D, Associate Professor and Chair
(603) 526-3870
rmedbery@colby-sawyer.edu
• Gregory R Austin, Ph.D., Associate Professor
(603) 526-3615
Degree Offered:
The Exercise and Sport Sciences Department offers B.S. degrees in Athletic Training, Exercise Science and Sport Management. All three majors integrate the liberal arts and sciences with professional preparation.
Description:
An expanding field that integrates the study

of sport and business to provide a thorough background in the sport industry. You will develop skills necessary to assume leadership in the implementation, development, management and marketing of sport programs. As opportunities and interest in sport continue to develop, career options have expanded. These include, but are not limited to, marketing directors, athletics administrators, sport facilities managers, youth sport and recreation directors, corporate sponsor coordinators, event managers and coaches.

Requirements:
In addition to requirements for all exercise and sport sciences majors, the following courses are required for the sport management program; Exercise and Sport Science, Business, Economics, Sociology.

COLLEGE OF IDAHO
2112 CLEVELAND BOULEVARD
CALDWELL, ID 83605
208-459-5011
Fax: 208-459-5175
• James R. Fennell, Director
Degree:
B.S. exercise science, B.A. physical education (teaching), B.A. physical education (non-teaching),B.A. sport and fitness center management.

COLLEGE OF MOUNT ST. JOSEPH- SPORT MANAGEMENT DEPARTMENT
5701 DELHI ROAD
CINCINNATI, OH 45233-1670
513-244-4200
800-654-9314
Fax: 513-244-4601
www.msj.edu
Bachelor's Program for Sport Management:
This degree is designed to develop skills related to planning, organizing, directing, controlling, budgeting, leading and evaluating an organization or department whose primary product or service is related to sport and/or recreation. Career possibilities related to this field include work in a variety of sport or sport-related settings such as: professional athletics/franchise management, college athletics, corporation fitness/health club management, facility operations, corporate sport marketing/public relations, event marketing and management, journalism/communications, media relations and sports equipment sales, specialized sports managem

COLLEGE OF SAINT ROSE, ALBANY- SCHOOL OF BUSINESS
432 WESTERN AVENUE
ALBANY, NY 12203
518-454-5158
800-637-8556
Fax: 518-458-5457
www.strose.edu
Concentration Sports Management:
Sport Management is a broad area of study that introduces students to the concepts and techniques needed to successfully work within a host of organizations in a sport-related context. Courses provide students with a firm foundation in the human relations, marketing and ethical and legal aspects that influence and shape the people and organizations in the business of sport.

COLORADO MESA UNIVERSITY - DEPARTMENT OF KINESIOLOGY
1100 NORTH AVENUE
GRAND JUNCTION, CO 81501-3122
970-248-1020
800-982-6372
www.coloradomesa.edu/kinesiology
Program Description:
Bachelor of Science in Sport Management: MBA Sport Management

COLUMBIA COLLEGE CHICAGO- ARTS, ENTERTAINMENT AND MEDIA MANAGEMENT
600 S. MICHIGAN AVENUE
CHICAGO, IL 60605
312-369-7652
mmaye@colum.edu
www.colum.edu/academics
Description:
The Sports Management Concentration leads to professions in the Sports Industry in the fields of audience building, box office management, special events, facilities management, career and talent development, broadcasting and media management, and merchandising. This unique to Chicago region concentration offers a comprehensive curriculum that emphasizes specifics of Sports Entertainment Management while providing knowledge and skills applicable to other areas of entertainment management.

COLUMBIA UNIVERSITY
SCHOOL OF CONTINUING EDUCATION
203 LEWISOHN HALL
2970 BROADWAY, MC 4119
NEW YORK, NY 10027
212-854-1754
www.ce.columbia.edu/Sports-Management
• Lucas Robin, Director of Sports Management Program
Degree Offered:
MS Sport Management

COLUMBUS STATE COMMUNITY COLLEGE
UNION HALL
550 E. SPRING STREET
PO BOX 1609
COLUMBUS, OH 43215
614-287-5353 EXT 5422
Fax: 614-287-5144
information@cscc.edu
www.cscc.edu/athletics
• Amy Hart, Associate Professor, Sports & Exercise Studies
(614) 287-2581
ahart@cscc.edu
• Antoinette Perkins, Associate Professor
(614) 287-5744
aperki01@cscc.edu
Degrees Offered:
Associate Degrees in Exercise Science; Physical Education; and Sport Management
Description:
The Sport and Exercise Studies program prepares students to work in sport, recreation, health and/or fitness centers. From private clubs to public facilities, trained managers, instructors, and programmers are needed to develop, train, staff, and implement programming to address the wellness needs of the general public or specific clients/populations, in compliance with local, state, and federal guidelines.

Exercise science, strength and resistance training, risk management, human nutrition, anatomy, physiology, sport business/marketing, and health and physical education courses blends with the college's General Education course work.

COLUMBUS STATE UNIVERSITY
DEPARTMENT OF COUNSELING EDUCATION & PROFESSIONAL STUDIES
103 JORDAN HALL
4225 UNIVERSITY AVENUE
COLUMBUS, GA 31907-5645
706-568-2301
Fax: 706-568-5088
• Tom Ford, Dept. Chairperson
• Patty Jamieson, Dept. Coordinator
Description:
Undergrad Degree: B.S. Areas of Specialization: Undergrad: Sport Fitness Management. Associate Degree - Exercise Science Major, Associate Degree- Physical Education Major, Associate Degree- Sport Management Major, Exercise Specialist Certificate.

CONCORDIA UNIVERSITY OF CHICAGO
7400 AUGUSTA STREET
RIVER FOREST, IL 60305
708-771-8300
• Lynn Lashbrook, Professor, Program Coordinator
Degrees:
Online Programs: Ed.D. Sports Leadership & Management; Ph.D. Sports Leadership & Management; MASL (M.A. in Sports Leadership); The bachelor of science in sports management includes an in-depth business curriculum covering classes focusing on business and sports.

CONNECTICUT, UNIVERSITY OF
NEAG SCHOOL OF EDUCATION, DEPARTMENT OF KINESIOLOGY
249 GLENBROOK ROAD
UNIT 1110
STORRS, CT 06269-1110
860-486-3623
Fax: 860-486-1123
• Carl Maresh, Department Head/Professor
(860) 486-5322
carl.maresh@uconn.edu
• Laura Burton, Sport Management Assistant Professor
(860) 486-3095
laura.burton@uconn.edu
Description:
The Sport Management program offers two undergraduate degrees and two graduate degrees. The Coaching and Administration Concentration prepares students to coach teams at amateur, collegiate, and professional levels. The undergraduate program in Sport Management is designed to prepare students to enter careers in the sport industry. The M.A. and Ph.D. degrees in Sport Management prepare students in the theoretical, research-oriented, and applied dimensions of the sport industry.

COPPIN STATE UNIVERSITY
DEPARTMENT OF HEALTH, PHYSICAL EDUCATION, RECREATION & DANCE
2500 W. NORTH AVENUE
BALTIMORE, MD 21216
410-951-3384
800-635-3674

Fax: 410-951-3376
health@coppin.edu
www.coppin.edu/athletics
• Edna Simmons, Ph.D, Dept.
Chairperson/Professor
(410) 951-3384
• Beahta Davis, Ph.D, Sports Management
Adjunct Instructor
(410) 951-3377

Description:
Sports Management program at Coppin State University prepares undergraduate students for professional careers in Sports Management, including both the private and public sectors. The program is designed to assist students in acquiring organizational and managerial expertise in the health, fitness and sports management fields as well as to assist students in gaining an understanding of personnel management and supervision.

Courses:
B.S. sports management, concentrations in sport business, sport marketing, sport journalism and sports medicine.

CORBAN UNIVERSITY- HUMAN PERFORMANCE, SPORT MANAGEMENT
5000 DEER PARK DRIVE SE
SALEM, OR 97317
503-581-8600
admissions@corban.edu
www.corban.edu

Program Description:
The foundational basis of the program lies in its focus on biblical principles through which individual understanding and development prepare one for a life of service to others. A primary function of the program is to provide the student with activity-oriented knowledge and problem solving skills to meet the demands of a life of ministry in the human performance fields. The Human Performance major may select one of three emphases: Exercise Science, Sports Management or Physical Education. The Exercise Science option has a research project requirement with an option for majors to add an internship experience. The Sports Management option has

DAEMEN COLLEGE- DIVISION OF HEALTH & HUMAN SERVICES
4380 MAIN STREET
AMHERST, NY 14226
800-462-7652
www.daemen.edu

Program Description:
Division of Health & Human Services: Undergraduate program of Bachelor of Science in Business Administration, Specialization; Sport Management.

DAKOTA WESLEYAN UNIVERSITY
1200 W. UNIVERSITY AVENUE
MITCHELL, SD 57301
605-995-2600
800-333-8506
www.dwu.edu/athletics
• Scott Gines, Director
scgines@dwu.edu

Degree:
DWU offers three emphases within the sports management program: Marketing and Sports Information, Human Resource Management, and Finance.

DALLAS BAPTIST UNIVERSITY
3000 MOUNTAIN CREEK PARKWAY
DALLAS, TX 75211
214-333-5329
800-460-1328
Fax: 214-333-5306
sports@dbu.edu
www.dbupatriots.com

Teams:
NCAA Sports: Men's Baseball, Men's Basketball, Women's Soccer, Women's Volleyball, Men and Women's Tennis, Men and Women's Golf, Men and Women's Cross Country, Men and Women's Indoor Track, Men and Women's Outdoor Track Club Sports: Bass Fishing, Ice Hockey, Drill Team, Cheerleading

DANIEL WEBSTER COLLEGE
20 UNIVERSITY DRIVE
NASHUA, NH 3063
603-577-6000
800325-6876
• Robin Seidman, Director of Athletics
(603) 577-6381

Description:
One of very few such programs offered by the business and management division at an American college. You'll be prepared for work in professional and recreational sports in areas such as public relations, marketing and sales; sports facilities management; athletic administration at secondary school, collegiate and professional levels; sports information; or recreational sport management in a private or public setting.

Degrees Offered:
BS; Sport Management.

DAVENPORT UNIVERSITY- BUSINESS ADMINISTRATION DEPARTMENT
45 OTTAWA NW
GRAND RAPIDS, MI 49503
616-698-7111 EXT 1361
800-686-1600
info@davenport.edu
www.davenport.edu

Program Description:
Bachelor of Business Administration, Sport Management. Students gain skills in business fundamentals and specific sport management disciplines in a learning environment that balances textbook theory with real-world business application. Through varied learning methodologies including an internship, students are exposed to the legal, regulatory, marketing and operational aspects of sport venue management. Graduates earn a Bachelor of Business Administration degree with a major in Sport Management.

DAVIS & ELKINS COLLEGE
DEPARTMENT OF HEALTH, SPORT & MOVEMENT SCIENCE
100 CAMPUS DRIVE
ELKINS, WV 26241-3996
304-637-1348
Fax: 304-637-1414
• Mary Ann DeLuca, Dept. Chairperson
• Jeffrey Goodman, Associate Professor

Description:
Undergrad Degree: B.S. Areas of Specialization: Physical Education, Exercise Science; Athletic Training, Sport Management, Health.

DAYTON, UNIVERSITY OF
DEPARTMENT OF HEALTH AND SPORT SCIENCE
300 COLLEGE PARK
DAYTON, OH 45469-2925
937-229-5600
Fax: 937-229-5601
• Paul Vanderburgh, Dept. Chairperson
(937) 229-4213
vanderburgh@udayton.edu
• George DeMarco, Associate Professor/Coordinator
(937) 229-4210
George.DeMarco@notes.udayton.edu

Description:
Undergrad Degree: B.S. in Education. Areas of Specialization: 2 core areas: Sports Business, Sports Marketing. Through studies in sport management, students gain an understanding of facilities, finance, human resource management, law, marketing, media and sales - and how they relate to sports.

DE SALES UNIVERSITY
2755 STATION AVE
CENTER VALLEY, PA 18034
610-282-1100 EXT 1894
Fax: 610-282-2279
www.desales.edu
• Brian Turner, Director
• Jay C Lacke, Chair/Director

Degree Offered:
Undergrad Degree: B.S. Sports Administration/Management. Areas of Specialization: Sport and Fitness Management; Athletic Administration. The Sport Management major at DeSales University provides a curriculum that combines theory and practice with the wide world of sport and business.

DEFIANCE COLLEGE- BUSINESS & ALLIED HEALTH DIVISION
701 N. CLINTON ST.
DEFIANCE, OH 43512
800-520-4632
www.defiance.edu/pages/bus_majors_sports_management.html

Sport Management Program:
The program is designed to prepare students to either obtain an entry-level position upon graduation or to continue studies in graduate school. Sport management lets students participate in the exciting world of sports from a business standpoint. In this major, students learn about various sports, the psychological principles at work behind them, and how sports fit into society. Also gain a strong knowledge foundation in business, examining how the worlds of business and sports interact and how they can make those interactions more profitable and beneficial for every person and interest involved. At Defiance College, sport management professo

DELAWARE STATE UNIVERSITY
DEPARTMENT OF SPORT SCIENCES
1200 N. DUPONT HIGHWAY
MEMORIAL HALL ROOM 163
DOVER, DE 19901
302-857-6600
Fax: 302-857-6601
www.desu.edu/student-life/athletics

• Li Chen, Dept. Chairperson
• Jan Blade, Sports Administration Director
(302) 857-6602
jblade@desu.edu
Degree/Majors Offered:
BS; Sport Management. Master of Science in Sport Administration offered by Department of Sport management within College of Health and Public Policy, Delaware State University that professionally prepares ethical leaders for advanced responsibilities within sport organizations and/or to design and implement new sport or sport-relatec to changing economic, legal, political, and social influences.

DELTA STATE UNIVERSITY
DEPARTMENT OF HEALTH, PHYSICAL EDUCATION AND RECREATION
HIGHWAY 8 WEST
CLEVELAND, MS 38733
662-846-4555
800-468-6378
Fax: 662-846-4680
www.deltastate.edu
• Darvin Barnes, Dept. Chairperson
(662) 846-4561
dbarnes@deltastate.edu
Description:
Undergrad Degree: B.S. in Phys Ed. Grad Degree: M.E.D. Areas of Specialization: Undergrad: Health, Recreation, Sport Management, Sports Information. Grad: Phys Ed.

DENVER, UNIVERSITY OF
DANIELS COLLEGE OF BUSINESS
2050 E. EVANS AVENUE, SUITE 30
DENVER, CO 80208
303-871-2150
800-622-4723
Fax: 303-871-4466
career@du.edu
www.daniels.du.edu
• Wayne Murdy, Chair
• Micheal John, Vice Chair
• Scott Lowery, Vice Chair
• Stewart Glendinning, CEO
• George Spentzos, Executive Advisory Board
• Peg Bradlet-Doppes, Vice Chancellor for Athletics and Recreation
(303) 871-3399
Description:
M.S., and M.B.A. in sport management concentration.

DESALES UNIVERSITY- DIVISION OF BUSINESS
2755 STATION AVENUE
CENTER VALLEY, PA 18034
610-282-1100
web1.desales.edu/default.aspx?pageid=304
Program Description:
The Bachelor of Science degree in Sport Management provides you with career and professional training in sport management within the context of a liberal arts education. The program is one of only 20 approved by the Sport Management Program Review Council (SMPRC) at the undergraduate level in the United States. The Sport Management program is also endorsed by The National Association for Sport and Physical Education (NASPE) and The North American Society for Sport Management

(NASSM). The major focuses on the conceptual, managerial, and practical skills that prepare you to become a visionary leader in various areas of the sport industry.

DEVOS SPORT BUSINESS MANAGEMENT
4000 CENTRAL FLORIDA BOULEVARD
COLLEGE OF BUSINESS ADMINISTRATION
ORLANDO, FL 32816
407-823-4887
Fax: 407-823-4771
rlapchick@bus.ucf.edu
www.bus.ucf.edu/athletics
• Richard Lapchick, Director Chair
rlapchick@bus.ucf.edu
• C. Keith Harrison, Associate Professor
• William A Sutton, Associate Director
Description:
The DeVos Program has been named one of the nation's top five programs by the Wall Street Journal, ESPN The Magazine and the New York Times. In 2009 it was named the number 1 MBA program in the nation for volunteer service.

DOWLING COLLEGE
150 IDLE HOUR BOULEVARD
Oakdale, NY 11769
631-244-3000
800-DOWLING
• Marilyn Mather, Director
• Christopher Celano, Sports Information Director
Degrees/Major Offered:
B.S. sport management. A combine degree that integrates the qualities and expertise of two of the most dynamic departments at Dowling College: The Department of Physical Education and the Department of Management.

DREXEL UNIVERSITY
3141 CHESTNUT STREET
Philadelphia, PA 19104
215-895-2000
• Dave O'Brian, Director of Sport Management
Degrees/Majors Offered:
M.S. in sport management through Goodwin College. Four areas of focus are sports marketing, sports business, sports media and sports law. Online program is also available.

DUQUESNE UNIVERSITY
600 FORBES AVENUE
PITTSBURGH, PA 15282
412-396-6000
admissions@duq.edu
www.duq.edu/athletics
• Keith M Gorse, EdD, ATC, Clinical Coordinator
(412) 396-5959
gorse@duq.edu
• Paula Sammarone Turocy, EdD, ATC, Department Chair
(412) 396-5695
turocyp@duq.edu
Degrees Offered:
B.S. in Athletic Training; B.S., M.H.M.S. in Health Management Systems; M.S. in Health Sciences Master of Science; M.S. in Occupational Therapy; D.P.T. in Physical Therapy; M.P.A.S. in Physician Assistant Studies; M.S. in Speech-Language

Pathology; Ph.D. in Rehabilitation Science; M.S. in Leadership, Concentration in Sports Leadership
Description:
Students in the Rangos School are challenged with contemporary curricula, clinically-skilled, nationally-known faculty, master their clinical skills in state-of-the-industry laboratories, and have varied and excellent internship/clinical placements.

EAST CAROLINA UNIVERSITY - DEPARTMENT OF KINESIOLOGY
A-20 MINGES COLISEUM
GREENVILLE, NC 27858
252-328-4643
sartorem@ecu.edu
www.ecu.edu/athletics
• Melanie Sartore-Baldwin, Assistant Professor
(252) 328-4643
sartorem@ecu.edu
Description:
M.A. exercise and sport science, concentration in sport management.

EAST CENTRAL UNIVERSITY- SCHOOL OF BUSINESS
1100 E. 14TH STREET
ADA, OK 74820
580-332-8000
www.ecok.edu/
Sports Administration:
Master of Education in Secondary Education - Sports Administration.

EAST STROUDSBURG UNIVERSITY OF
DEPARTMENT OF SPORTS STUDIES
SPORT MANAGEMENT PROGRAM
200 PROSPECT STREET
EAST STROUDSBURG, PA 18301-2999
570-422-3211
Fax: 570-422-3423
www.esu.edu
• Paula M Parker, Associate Professor
• Robert P. Fleischman, Professor/Sport Management Program Coordinator
(570) 422-3316
• Frank M Pullo, Chair/Director
(570) 422-3265
fpullo@po-box.esu.edu
Degrees Offered:
B.S. sport management, M.S. sport management, M.S. management and leadership studies, concentration in sport management.

EAST TENNESSEE STATE UNIVERSITY- KINESIOLOGY DEPT
DEPT OF KINESIOLOGY, LEISURE, & SPORT SCIENCES
BOX 70654
JOHNSON CITY, TN 37614-1701
423-439-4362
Fax: 423-439-5383
KLSS@etsu.edu
www.etsu.edu
Program Description:
The ETSU undergraduate Sport Management Concentration introduces students to the sport industry and provides them with the opportunity to study a wide variety of fulfilling sport-related careers. Program emphasizes a unique mix of academic preparation along with required real-world practical field experiences. The

curriculum examines three main segments of the sport industry (performance, production, promotion), and it encompasses all levels of sport: youth, high school, collegiate, professional, amateur, competitive, non-competitive, recreational, private, and nonprofit/profit organizations.

EASTERN STATE UNIVERSITY
DEPARTMENT OF HEALTH & PHYSICAL EDUCATION
SPORTS CENTER
83 WINDHAM STREET
Willimantic, CT 6226
860-465-5371
Fax: 860-465-0186
horrocks@easternct.edu
gowarriorathletics.com
• Neil Williams, Professor/Chair
(860) 465-5170
williamsn@easternct.edu
Degrees/Majors Offered:
B.S. sport leisure management.

EASTERN ILLINOIS UNIVERSITY
BUZZARD HALL, ROOM 1420
600 LINCOLN AVENUE
CHARLESTON, IL 61920
217-581-5000
Fax: 217-581-2518
ceps@eiu.edu
www.eiu.edu
• Nancy Crone, Academic Advisor
(217) 581-8582
• Phyllis Croisant, Professor
(217) 581-7596
ptcroisant@eiu.edu
• Larry Ankenbrand, Professor
(217) 581-2215
Description:
Undergrad Degree: B.S. Grad Degree: M.S. Areas of Specialization: Undergrad: Corporate Fitness and Club Management; Grad: Specialization: Sport Management in the Education Sector - designed to prepare athletic directors at the high school and college levels; Sport Management in the Private Sector - may include entrepreneurial approach or professional sports management approach depending on type of internship experience chosen by the student.

EASTERN KENTUCKY UNIVERSITY
521 LANCASTER AVENUE
MOBERLY 231
RICHMOND, KY 40475-3134
859-622-1887
Fax: 859-622-1254
www.ess.eku.edu
• Doug Whitlock, President
Description:
Undergrad Degree: B.S. Degree, M.S. Degree. Areas of Specialization; Undergrad; Athletic Training, Sports Administration; Wellness. K-12 Teaching, Adult fitness, Sports Administration, Generalist.

EASTERN MICHIGAN UNIVERSITY-COLLEGE OF HEALTH & HUMAN SERVICES
SCHOOL OF HEALTH PROMOTION AND HUMAN PERFORMANCE
318 PORTER BUILDING
YPSILANTI, MI 48197
734-487-0090
www.emich.edu

Program Description:
Graduate studies in Sport Management MS Degree. The Sport Management program at Eastern Michigan University is designed for students who are interested in athletic administration (high school sports) and sport management in elite level sports (such as collegiate sport). Although there is a program of study for students, it remains flexible so that they can receive the education that is best suited for their future careers.

ELMS COLLEGE- BUSINESS AND LAW DIVISION
291 SPRINGFIELD STREET
CHICOPEE, MA 01013-2839
413-594-2761
www.elms.edu
Program Description:
Bachelor of Arts Degree, Major in Sport Management.

ELON UNIVERSITY
DEPARTMENT OF LEISURE AND SPORT MANAGEMENT
100 CAMPUS DRIVE
ELON, NC 27244-2010
336-278-2000
Fax: 336-278-5918
drummond@elon.edu
www.elon.edu
Description:
The Sport and Event Management major prepares students to plan, manage and sustain effective, sport and recreation experiences in private, public and commercial settings. Through classroom and real world experiences students develop an understanding of service and skills applicable to the sport, event and recreation professions.

ENDICOTT COLLEGE
376 HALE ST
BEVERLY, MA 1915
978-927-0585
800-325-1114
Fax: 978-232-2600
dswanton@endicott.edu
www.endicott.edu
• Deborah Swanton, Dean of Sport Science & Fitness Studies
dswanton@endicott.edu
Description:
Within the School of Sport Science and Fitness Studies, students select innovative programs in Athletic Training, Sport Management, Physical Education Teacher Licensure, Physical Education Exercise Science, and Exercise Science minor.

ERSKINE COLLEGE- DEPT OF HEALTH, PE, SPORTS MANAGEMENT
2 WASHINGTON ST.
DUE WEST, SC 29639
864-379-8840
888-359-4358
Fax: 864-379-2197
alston@erskine.edu
www.erskine.edu
• Scott DeCiantis, Athletic Training Ed. Program Director
(864) 379-8899
deciantis@erskine.edu
• Adam Hayes Weyer, Head Athletic Trainer

(864) 379-8890
weyer@erskine.edu
Degrees Offered:
B.S. Sport Management. Physical education, Sports Management-Fitness Concentration; Athletic Training.

EVANSVILLE, UNIVERSITY OF
DEPARTMENT OF EXERCISE AND SPORT SCIENCE
1800 LINCOLN AVENUE
EVANSVILLE, IN 47722
812-479-2848
Fax: 812-479-2717
exss.evansville.edu
• Pam Young, EXSS Administrative Assistant
(812) 488-2848
• Terry Collins, Instructor
(812) 488-2091
• Gregg Wilson, Department Chair/Exercise & SportsScience
(812) 488-2847
• Kathy Liu, Assistant Professor/Exercise & Sports Science
(812) 488-2284
• Laura McDonald, Assistant Professor/Exercise & SportsScience
(812) 488-2358
• Michael Newhouse Bailey, Assistant Professor/Exercise & SportsScience
(812) 488-2288
• Payal Patel Dovlatabadi, Assistant Professor/Exercise & SportsScience
(812) 488-2210
• Donald Rodd, Professor Exercise SportScience/Physical The
(812) 488-1026
• Troy Coppus, Instructor
(812) 488-2202
Degrees Offered:
Undergrad Degree: B.S. Grad Degree: M.S. Areas of Specialization: Undergrad: Sports Administration; Athletic Training; Sports Communications; Sports Studies. Grad: Physical Therapy.

FINGER LAKES COMMUNITY COLLEGE
3325 MARVIN SANDS DRIVE
Canandaigua, NY 14424
585-394-FLCC
www.flccathletics.com
• Barbara Risser, President/ Chief Executive Officer
• Charles P. McCausland, Chair
Degrees/Majors Offered:
A.S. sports and tourism studies.

FLAGLER COLLEGE
74 KING STREET
ST. AUGUSTINE, FL 32084
904-819-6481
800-304-4208
admissions@flagler.edu
www.flagler.edu
• Bernadette Twardy, Professor, Department Chair
• Danielle Stanley, Adjunct Sports Management
• Allan Bohl, Adjunct Sports Management
• Anne DeMartini, Assistant Professor
• Calvin Hunter, Professor, Sport Management
Degree Offered:
B.A. Sport Management

FLORIDA A&M UNIVERSITY-DEPARTMENT OF HEALTH & PHYSICAL EDUCATION
1800 WAHNISH WAY
LAWSON MULTIPURPOSE
CTR/TEACHING
GYM SUITE 433
TALLAHASSEE, FL 32307
850-599-3135
Fax: 850-599-8365
www.famu.edu/athletics
• Janet M. Sermon, Chair & Assistant Professor
(850) 599-3135
janet.sermon@famu.edu
Degree/Majors Offered:
M.S. physical education.

FLORIDA ATLANTIC UNIVERSITY COLLEGE OF BUSINESS
777 GLADES ROAD
FLEMING HALL WEST 116
BOCA RATON, FL 33431
561-297-3000
Fax: 561-297-4054
jriordan@fau.edu
www.fau.edu/mbasport
• Dr Jim Riordan, MBA Sport Management Program Director
jriordan@fau.edu
• David Abrams, Executive Director/Sports Financing
Description:
Florida's Original AACSB-Accredited MBA in Sports Management Program. Admission to, and retention in program is highly competitive and rigorous. MBA Sports students may not work outside the sports industry while enrolled in the program. Transfer students are not accepted into the program. MBA Sport is not designed for those aspiring to be coaches, fitness trainers, athletic trainers, or other sport medicine professions.
Curriculum
The MBASport curriculum consists of the core courses required of all FAU MBA students, plus a 12 credit specialization in Sport Management. Full-time course load is considered to be nine hours for the fall and spring semesters and six hours in the summer semester. Part-time study or a certificate program is not offered.

FLORIDA INTERNATIONAL UNIVERSITY
DEPARTMENT OF LEADERSHIP & PROFESSIONAL SERVICES
BS & MS IN RECREATION AND SPORT MANAGEMENT
MIAMI, FL 33199
305-348-2114
Fax: 305-348-1515
robert.wolff@fiu.edu
• Robert Wolff, Professor/Program Director
(305) 348-2114
wolffr@fiu.edu
• Richard Lopez, Assoc. Professor/Program Coordinator
(305) 348-2075
lopezr@fiu.edu
• Charmaine DeFrancesco, Associate Professor
(305) 348-3163
defrance@fiu.edu
Description:
BS and MS degrees in Recreation and Sport Management.

FLORIDA SOUTHERN COLLEGE-BARNEY BARNETT SCHOOL OF BUSINESS & FREE ENTERPRISE
CARLISLE ROGERS BUILDING
MCDONALD STREET
111 LAKE HOLLINGSWORTH DRIVE
LAKELAND, FL 33801-5698
863-680-4280
Fax: 863-680-4355
www.flsouthern.edu//athletics
• Anne B. Kerr, President of Florida Southern College
Degree/Majors Offered:
Business degree, concentration in sport management.

FLORIDA STATE UNIVERSITY
THE COLLEGE OF EDUCATION,FLORIDA STATE UNIVERSITY
P.O BOX 3064450, 1114 W. CALL STREET
SUITE 1100 STB
TALLAHASSEE, FL 32306-4450
850-644-6885
Fax: 850-644-2725
www.coe.fsu.edu
• Jordan Bass, Coordinator, Lifetime Activities Program
(850) 644-7903
jbass@fsu.edu
• Karen L White, Executive Support Assistant
(850) 644-0371
klwhite@fsu.edu
• Janice Reed, Executive Support Assistant
(850) 644-1141
jreed@fsu.edu
• Shannon Barksdale, Departmental Accounting Associate
(850) 644-4854
sbarksdale@fsu.edu
• Kerry Behnke, Administrative Support Asstistant
(850) 645-8382
kbehnke@fsu.edu
• Michaela Densmore, Research and Information Coordinator
(850) 644-8823
mdensmore@admin.fsu.edu
• Derek Taylor, Human Resources Administrator
(850) 644-4944
det02@admin.fsu.edu
• Erika Bettilyon, Office Manager
(850) 644-7197
ebettilyon@fsu.edu
Description:
Undergrad Degree: B.S. Grad Degree: M.S., Ph.D., Ed.D. Areas of Specialization: Undergrad: Degree in Physical Education with Major in Sport Management. Grad: Degree in Physical Education with Major in Sport Administration. Non-Degree Specialization: Coaching.

FLORIDA, UNIVERSITY OF
PO BOX 118205
GAINESVILLE, FL 32611
352-392-3261
Fax: 352-392-5262
www.ufl.edu
• Charles E. Young, President of the University
• Bernie Macheen, President
• David R. Colburn, Provost & Vice President Academic Affairs
• Winfred M. Phillips, VP for Research & Dean of the Graduate School

• Ed Poppell, Vice President Academic Affairs
Description:
B.S. in Sport Management; M.S. in Sport Management, PH.D. with a majow in sport management.

FONTBONNE UNIVERSITY- ECKELKAMP COLLEGE OF GLOBAL BUSINESS & PROFESSIONAL STUDY
6800 WYDOWN BOULEVARD
ST. LOUIS, MO 63105
314-862-3456
800-205-5862
fbyou@fontbonne.edu
www.fontbonne.edu
Sports Management Major:
Fontbonne's sports management program is unique because of its emphasis on business, science, nutrition and health. Plus, with Fontbonne's student-centered approach to teaching and small student-to-teacher ratio, student's always receive individual attention.

FRANKLIN PIERCE UNIVERSITY
40 UNIVERSITY DRIVE
Rindge, NH 03461-0060
603-899-4000
800-437-0048
• Rodney Blackman, Assistant Professor, Business Administration
blackmanr@franklinpierce.edu
Degrees/Majors Offered:
B.S. within Division of Business Administration in sports and recreation management, marketing, arts management, accounting/finance.

FRESNO PACIFIC UNIVERSITY-
1717 S. CHESTNUT AVENUE
FRESNO, CA 93702-4709
559-453-2000
www.fresno.edu

GARDNER-WEBB UNIVERSITY
110 SOUTH MAIN STREET
PO BOX 997
BOILING SPRINGS, NC 28017
704-406-4000
800-253-6472
admissions@gardner-webb.edu
www.gardner-webb.edu/athletics
• A Frank Bonner, President
Description:
Sport management

GARRETT COLLEGE
ADVENTURESPORT INSTITUTE
687 MOSSER ROAD
MCHENRY, MD 21541
301-387-3000
Fax: 301-387-3325
adventuresports@garrettcollege.edu
www.garrettcollege.edu/athletics
• Michael Logsdon, Chair/Director
avs@garrettcollege.edu
Description:
A.A.S. adventure sports, certificate in adventure sports

GEORGE MASON UNIVERSITY- SCHOOL OF RECREATION, HEALTH, AND TOURISM
4400 UNIVERSITY DRIVE MS4F3
FAIRFAX, VA 22030

www.csm.gmu.edu
Sports Management Program Description:
Mission at the Center for Sport Management is to advance the study and practice of sport management in all of its dimensions. The Center will support substantive research initiatives and provide service to stakeholders in sport for the purpose of enhancing sport industry practice. The Center for Sport Management was founded in the Spring of 2008 under a George Mason University Charter prepared by Dr. Robert E. Baker. The Center is housed within the College of Education and Human Development.

GEORGE WASHINGTON UNIVERSITY - THE GW SCHOOL OF BUSINESS
2201 G STREET NW
DUQUES HALL
WASHINGTON, DC 20052
202-994-6380
Fax: 202-994-2286
delpy@gwu.edu
www.business.gwu.edu
• Edard Barrientos, President & CEO
• Mitchell Blaser, CFO & COO
• James T. Blumenthal, Executive Vice President & CFO
• Burlie Brunson, President and Chief Operating Officer Defense
• Doug Guthrie, Professor/ Dean GS School of Business
(202) 994-6623
delpy@gwu.edu
• Cassandra Howard, Administrative Director
(202) 994-4530
• Laura Ortiz-Calder, Associate Director
(202) 994-9326
Description:
Graduate degrees, fields of concentration: sport management, event and meeting management, individualized studes; M.B.A. and online programs.

GEORGETOWN UNIVERSITY
SCHOOL OF CONTINUING STUDIES
3307 M ST, NW
SUITE 202
WASHINGTON, DC 20007
202-687-8700
• Matt Winkler, Associate Dean of MPS Sports Industry Management
(202) 687-7149
mvw4@georgetown.edu
• Kristen Consolo, MPS Sports Industry Management Program Manage
(202) 687-0924
kac225@georgetown.edu
Degrees Offered:
MPS Sports Industry Management

GEORGIA SOUTHERN UNIVERSITY-DEPT OF HOSPITALITY, TOURISM, & FAMILY CONSUMER SCI
PO BOX 8034
STATESBORO, GA 30460
912-478-5345
Fax: 912-681-0386
www.georgiasouthern.edu
• Henry Eisenhart, Chair/Director
(912) 681-5462
henry_e@georgiasouthern.edu
• Tony Lachowetz, Professor

• Willie Burden, Associate Professor
(912) 681-5922
Description:
Undergrad Degree: B.S. Health Science, with Major in Sport Management. Grad Degree: M.S. in Sport Management. Areas of Specialization: Athletic Administration; Sport Promotion; Sport Communications.

GEORGIA STATE UNIVERSITY
125 DECATUR STREET
ATLANTA, GA 30303
404-651-2536
Fax: 404-651-4814
www.georgiastatesports.com
• Jeffrey Rupp, Exercise Science Associate Professor
(404) 651-3978
jrupp@gsu.edu
• Cheryl Levick, Director of Athletics
(404) 413-4005
• James Greenwell, Executive Senior Associate Athletics Director
(404) 413-4007
• Jamie Boggs, Senior Associate Athletics Director, Compliance
(404) 413-4008
• Tiffany Daniels, Senior Associate Athletics Director, External
(404) 413-4018
tdaniels8@gsu.edu
• John Portland, Senior Associate Athletics Director, Internal
(404) 413-4006
• Mark Nagel, Recreation Associate Professor
(404) 651-4680
• Sekeia Smith, Administrative Coordinator
(404) 651-2536
ssmith@gsu.edu
Description:
Grad Degree: M.S. Areas of Specialization: College and University; Sports Club Management; Facilities Management; Sports Information; Sports Marketing & Promotion; Coaching.

GEORGIA, UNIVERSITY OF
DEPARTMENT OF KINESIOLOGY
115 RAMSEY
ATHENS, GA 30602
706-542-4378
Fax: 706-542-3148
www.coe.uga.edu
• Priscilla Carter, Academic Advisor II
• David Avin, Senior Accounatant
(706) 542-4384
• Thomas Baker, Assistant Professor - Sport Management Progra
• Ted Baumgartner, Professor - Exercise Science Program
• Kevin Byon, Assistant Professor - Sport Management Progra
• Billy Hawkins, Sport Studies Program Coordinator
(706) 542-4427
bhawk@uga.edu
• Ted Baumgartner, Graduate Program Coordinator/Prof.
(706) 542-4424
Description:
Grad Degree: M.Ed. Areas of Specialization: Intercollegiate and Pofessional Sport Management; Facility and Event Management; Management of Sports Agencies and/or Organizations. M.Ed., M.S. and PhD. in sport studies

GLENVILLE STATE COLLEGE-
200 HIGH STREET
GLENVILLE, WV 26351
304-462-7361
800-924-2010
www.glenville.edu
Sport Management Program:
Offers bachelor's undergraduate studies in sport management.

GRACELAND UNIVERSITY-COLLEGE OF LIBERAL ARTS AND SCIENCES
DIVISION OF HEALTH & MOVEMENT SCIENCES
1 UNIVERSITY PLACE
LAMONI, IA 50140
641-784-5000
800-833-0524
www.graceland.edu
Programs:
B.A. in Sport Management

GRAMBLING STATE UNIVERSITY
SCHOOL OF GRADUATE STUDIES
GSU BOX 4244
ASSEMBLY CENTER ROOM 148
GRAMBLING, LA 71245
318-274-2294
Fax: 318-274-6053
www.gram.edu
• Willie Daniel, Director
(318) 274-2294
• Robert Lyons, Coordinator
• Darlene Kluka,
Description:
Grad Degree: M.S. Areas of Specialization: Sport Administration.

GREENSBORO COLLEGE
815 WEST MARKET STREET
GREENSBORO, NC 27401
800-346-8226
www.greensborocollegesports.com
• Randy Hunt, Chair/Director
Description:
B.S. athletic training, B.S. physical education, B.S. exercise and sport studies. Concentrations in exercise science, sport administration, sport behavior, sport coaching.

GREENVILLE COLLEGE
DEPARTMENT OF HEALTH, PHYSICAL EDUCATION & RECREATION
315 E. COLLEGE AVENUE
GREENVILLE, IL 62246-1145
618-664-2800
800-345-4440
Fax: 618-664-1060
www.greenville.edu
• Roy Molholland, Department Chair/Associate Professor
(618) 664-6625
roy.molholland@greenville.edu
• Eugene Dunkley, Biology Department Chair and Associate Profes
(618) 664-6543
eugene.dunkley@greenville.edu
• Doug Faulkner, Athletic Director; Associate Professor of Hea
(618) 664-6620
doug.faulkner@greenville.edu
• Norm Hall, Vice President and Dean of Student Developmen
(618) 664-7119
norm.hall@greenville.edu
• Steven Heilmer, Art Department Chair and

Associate Professor
(618) 664-6811
susan.hughey-rasler@greenville.edu
• Richard Huston, History and Political
Science Department Chai
(618) 664-6824
richard.huston@greenville.edu
• Darell Ller, Chemistry Department Chair,
Professor of Chem
(618) 664-6540
darrell.iler@greenville.edu
• Robert Johnson, Professor/Department
Head
(618) 664-6626
robert.johnnson@greenville.edu
Description:
Undergrad Degree: B.S. in Recreation.
Areas of Specialization: Adult Fitness,
Sports Administration, Recreation
Leadership.

GUILFORD COLLEGE
DEPARTMENT OF SPORT STUDIES
5800 W. FRIENDLY AVENUE
GREENSBORO, NC 27410
336-316-2000
Fax: 336-316-2956
www.guilford.edu
• Robert Malekoff, Sport Studies
Coordinator
(336) 316-2329
• Lavon Williams, Chairman/Associate
Professor
(336) 316-2495
Description:
Undergrad Degree: B.S., Sport
Management. Areas of Specialization: Sport
Management, Physical Education
Teaching/Coaching, Sports Medicine.

HAMPTON UNIVERSITY
130 HOLLAND HALL, ROOM 130
HAMPTON, VA 23668
757-727-5000
Fax: 757-727-5813
www.hamptonu.edu
• William R. Harvey, President of Hampton
University
Description:
B.S. in Sport Management.

HARDIN-SIMMONS UNIVERSITY
2200 HICKORY
ABILENE, TX 79698-6210
325-670-1000
877-GO-HSUTX
Fax: 325-670-1572
www.hsuathletics.com
• Bob Moore, Director for Kinesiology, Sport
And Recreatio
(325) 670-1265
bemoore@hsutx.edu
Degrees Offered:
M.Ed. Sports and Recreation Management;
M.Ed. Advanced Physical Education,
Physical Therapy.

HARDING UNIVERSITY
915 E. MARKET AVENUE
SEARCY, AR 72143
501-279-4761
Fax: 501-279-4138
Kinesiology@harding.edu
www.harding.edu
• Stephen Burks, Department Chairman
(501) 279-4761

Description:
College recreational setting.
Affiliations:
Member of NCAA Division II

HENDERSON STATE UNIVERSITY
1100 Henderson Street
ARKADELPHIA, AR 71999-0001
870-230-5000
hsusports.com
• Ron Dewlen, Director
Degree:
B.S.E. physical education, B.S. recreation,
B.S. athletics training, M.S. sport
administration, M.S.E. crriculum
instruction/physical education.

**HIGH POINT UNIVERSITY - EARL N.
PHILLIPS SCHOOL OF BUSINESS**
833 MONTIEU AVENUE
HIGH POINT, NC 27262
800-345-6993
www.highpoint.edu/sport-management
• Jim Wehrley, Dean of the School of
Business
(336) 841-4560
jwehrley@highpoint.edu
Description:
B.S. sport management, M.S. sports studies

HOLY FAMILY UNIVERSITY
9801 Frankford Avenue
Philadelphia, PA 19114
215-637-7700
Fax: 215-637-6675
• Tony DiPrimio, Director
• Sandra Michael, Athletics Director
(215) 637-7700
smichael@holyfamily.edu
Degree/majors offered:
B.A. sports marketing management.

HOUSTON, UNIVERSITY OF
104 GARRISON GYMNASIUM
HOUSTON, TX 77204-6321
713-743-9849
Fax: 713-743-9860
www.hhp.uh.edu
• Norma Olvera, Director
• James J. Zhang, Associate Professor
(713) 743-9869
• Demetrius Pearson, Associate Professor
and Program Coordinator
• Warren Whisenant, Director
wwhisenant@uh.edu
Description:
B.S. in Kinesiology with concentration in
Sports Administration/M.Ed, in Sports and
Fitness Administration.

HOWARD PAYNE UNIVERSITY
1000 Fisk Street
Brownwood, TX 76801
325-649-8020
800-880-4HPU
Fax: 325-649-8901
enroll@hputx.edu
www.hputx.edu
• Rick Beelby, Director
rbeelby@hputx.edu
Degree:
B.S. exercise and sport science with the
following specialization: physical education,
exercise and sport management, athletics
training.

**IDAHO STATE UNIVERSITY-
DEPARTMENT OF SPORT SCIENCE AND
PHYSICAL EDUCATION**
921 S 8TH AVE, STOP 8105
POCATELLO, ID 83209-8089
208-282-2783
www.ed.isu.edu
Sport Management Program:
Offering Sport Management as a minor
course of study in the undergraduate
program.

IDAHO, UNIVERSITY OF
RECREATION DEPARTMENT
875 PERIMETER DR.
MS 2302
MOSCOW, ID 83844-2302
208-885-7921
Fax: 208-885-2862
www.govandals.com
• Kathy Browder, Interim Dept. Chairperson
(208) 885-7921
hperd@uidaho.edu
• Rob Spear, Director of Athletics
(208) 885-0243
• Matt Kleffner, Associate AD for
Administration
(208) 885-0214
• Tim Mooney, Associate AD for External
Operations
(208) 885-0258
• John Wallace, Associate AD for
Compliance and Eligibility
(208) 885-0219
• Mario Reyes, Faculty Athletic
Representative
(208) 885-6478
• Emily Adams, Administrative Assistant Sr.
(208) 885-0259
Description:
Undergrad Degree: B. S. Recreation. Grad
Degree: M.S. Recreation. Areas of
Specialization: Sport & Recreation
Management; Sports Science; Athletic
Training.

ILLINOIS AT CHICAGO, UNIVERSITY OF
DEPT OF KINESIOLOGY
901 W. ROOSEVELT RD
CHICAGO, IL 60608
312-996-9685
Fax: 312-413-3699
www.uc.edu
Description:
Grad Degree: M.S. Areas of Specialization:
Sport Management, Adult Fitness, Exercise
Physiology, Curriculum and Instruction.

**ILLINOIS AT URBANA-CHAMPAIGN,
UNIVERSITY OF**
DEPARTMENT OF RECREATION, SPORT
AND TOURISM
104 HUFF HALL
1206 S. 4TH STREET
CHAMPAIGN, IL 61820
217-333-4410
Fax: 217-244-1935
www.rst.uiuc.edu
• Cary McDonald, Dept. Head
• Bill McKinney, Ph.D, Dept. Associate
Professor
• Jim Hefferman, Wrestling Head Coach
(217) 333-5853
Description:
B.S. in Leisure Studies with a concentration
in Sport Management/M.S., PhD in Sport
Management.

ILLINOIS STATE UNIVERSITY
SCHOOL OF KINESIOLOGY AND
RECREATION
CAMPUS BOX 5120
NORMAL, IL 61790-5120
309-438-8661
Fax: 309-438-5559
kinrec@ilstu.edu
www.kinrec.ilstu.edu
• Babara Arboqast, Office Support Specialist
(304) 438-5952
barbogas@ilstu.edu
• Terri Jordan, Chief Clerk
(309) 438-5782
tljorda@ilstu.edu
• Miranda D. Kinney, Academic Advisor
(309) 438-5782
mdkinn2@ilstu.edu
• Alan Lacy, Professor & Director
(309) 438-3054
aclacy@ilstu.edu
• Alan Lacy, Professor/Director
(309) 438-8661
aclacy@ilstu.edu
• Robert Rossman, Ph.D, Professor/Dean
(309) 438-7602
jrrossm@ilstu.edu
• Steve McCaw, Professor
Description:
Grad Degree: M.S. in Health & Physical
Education, with concentration in Sports
Administration. Areas of Specialization:
Sport Management, Recreational Sport
Management, Recreational Park
Administration.

INCARNATE WORD, UNIVERSITY OF THE
SPORT MANAGEMENT
4301 BROADWAY
SAN ANTONIO, TX 78209
210-829-6000
800-749-WORD
Fax: 210-805-3574
www.uiw.edu/athletics

INDIANA STATE UNIVERSITY
200 NORTH SEVENTH STREET
TERRE HAUTE, IN 47809-1902
812-237-2183
Fax: 812-237-2493
www.indstate.edu
• Dan McLean, Chairperson
• Linda Swift, Office Manager
(812) 237-2183
l-swift@indstate.edu
Description:
Grad Degree: M.S./M.A. Areas of
Specialization: Sports Management, On-line
Degree.

INDIANA UNIVERSITY
KELLEY SCHOOL OF BUSINESS
INDIANA UNIVERSITY
1309 E. 10TH STREET
BLOOMINGTON, IN 47405-1701
812-855-0221
Fax: 812-855-8679
kelleyse@indiana.edu
• Thomas Bowers, Co-Director
bowers@indiana.edu
• Timothy Baldwin, Co-Director
Degrees Offered:
M.B.A. with majors in marketing, strategic
management, consulting, finance,
e-business.

**INDIANA UNIVERSITY OF
PENNSYLVANIA**
1011 South Drive
Indiana, PA 15705
724-357-2100
iupathletics.com
• Elaine Blair, Director
bkostel@iup.edu
Degree/Majors Offered:
Bachelor's in physical education and sport,
sport administration track, master's in sport
science, sport management track.

**INDIANA UNIVERSITY, BOOMINGTON-
DEPARTMENT OF KINESIOLOGY**
1025 E.7TH STREET
HPER 112
BLOOMINGTON, IN 47405
812-855-5523
www.indiana.edu
Sport Management Program:
Graduate sport management program offers
course work providing an interdisciplinary
approach to the study of sport management
intended to provide a thorough foundation in
business and sport while allowing flexibility
for students to explore a wide variety of
opportunities within the field.

**INDIANA UNIVERSITY-PURDUE
UNIVERSITY INDIANAPOLIS**
SCHOOL OF PHYSICAL EDUCATION &
TOURISM MANAGEMENT
420 UNIVERSITY BLVD.
INDIANAPOLIS, IN 46202
317-274-5555
www.iupui.edu
Program Description:
The curriculum for Bachelor of Science in
Physical Education includes classes from a
variety of disciplines, a minor or certificate in
business, and culminates with an internship
program designed to give the student
hands-on experience in the field. Students
must pursue the business minor or business
certificate in conjunction with sport
management courses to earn their degree.

IOWA STATE UNIVERSITY
DEPARTMENT OF HEALTH AND HUMAN
PERFORMANCE
FORKER BUILDING
AMES, IA 50011
515-294-8009
Fax: 515-294-8740
hhp@iastate.edu
www.facsen.iastate.edu
• Rick Sharp, Professor/Graduate
Coordinator
(515) 294-8650
rlsharp@iastate.edu
• Suzzane Hendrich, President
• Jerry Thomas, Dept. Chairperson
Degrees Offered:
Undergrad Degree: B.S. Emphasis - Sports
Management. Grad Degree: Ph.D.
Emphasis - Sports Management, M.S.
Emphasis - Sports Management, M.Ed.
Emphasis - Sports Management.

IOWA, UNIVERSITY OF
DEPARTMENT OF HSS
E115 FIELD HOUSE
IOWA CITY, IA 52242-1111
319-335-9335
Fax: 319-335-6669

joyce-murphy@uiowa.edu
www.uiowa.edu
• Susan Birrell, Dept. Chairperson
(319) 335-9335
susan-birrell@uiowa.edu
• Katie Dougherty, Womens Tennis Head
Coach
(319) 335-9259
katherine-dougherty@uiowa.edu
• Christine Grant, Athletic Administration
(319) 335-9186
christine-grant@uiowa.edu
• Larry Wieczorek, Track And Field Head
Coach
(319) 335-3257
larry-wieczorek@uiowa.edu
• Sharon Dingman, Volleyball Head Coach
(319) 335-8181
sharon-dingman@uiowa.edu
Degrees Offered:
M.A. Sport and Leisure Management Ph.D.
Athletic Administration

ITHACA COLLEGE
DEPARTMENT OF SPORT MANAGEMENT
& MEDIA
12 HILL CENTER
ITHACA, NY 14850-7193
607-274-3192
Fax: 607-274-1943
jwocohan@ithaca.edu
www.ithaca.edu
• Annemarie Farrel, Associate Professor
and Chair
• Criag Paiement, Assistant Professor and
Chair Graduate Progra
• Wayne Blann, Professor
• Beth Cavalier, Lecturer
• Heather Dicter, Assistant Professor
• Lana Walsh, Administrative Assistant
• John Wolohan, Department Chair, Sports
Management/Media
Degrees Offered:
Offfers both undergraduate and graduate
sports management programs.
Undergraduate focus is on sports media and
sports studies; graduate focus is on sports
management.

**JACKSONVILLE UNIVERSITY- SCHOOL
OF EDUCATION**
2800 UNIVERSITY BLVD N
JACKSONVILLE, FL 32211
800-255-2027
www.ju.edu
Sport Management Program:
The School of Education offers a Masters of
Education with three concentrations:
Instructional Leadership and Organizational
Development, Sport Management and
Leadership, and Educational Leadership
(Aspiring Principals).

JERSEY CITY STATE COLLEGE
ATHL RECREATIONAL FITNESS CENTER
324-338 W. SIDE AVE
JERSEY CITY, NJ 7305
201-547-3315
www.njcu.edu
• Eugene E. Bacha, Chairman Sport &
Leisure Studies
Description:
Undergrad Degree: B.S. in Business, with
concentration in Sport Management. Also
offer minors in Fitness Specialist and
Movement Training.

college sports

JOHNSON & WALES UNIVERSITY
SPORTS ENT. / EVENT MANAGEMENT
THE HOSPITALITY COLLEGE
8 ABBOTT PARK PLACE
PROVIDENCE, RI 2903
401-598-1475
Fax: 401-598-1125
www.jwu.edu
• Richard Brush, Dean
(401) 598-4621
• Katie Davin, Dept. Chairperson/Associate
Professor
(401) 598-4623
kdavin@jwu.edu
• Jennifer Adams-Gailpeau, Associate
Professor
(401) 598-1813
jennifer.galipeau@jwu.edu
Description:
Undergrad Degree: B.S. Sports/Facilities.
Grad Degree: Hospitality Administration.
Areas of Specialization: Skills necessary to
manage sports/entertainment venues, public
assembly facilities and event operations.

JUDSON UNIVERSITY- COLLEGE OF
LIBERAL ARTS & SCIENCES
1151 N. STATE STREET
ELGIN, IL 60123
847-628-2500
www.judsonu.edu/
Sport Management Program:
Sport Administration is a cross-divisional
concentration (sport, physical education,
business administration and communication
arts).

KANSAS UNIVERSITY
DEPARTMENT OF HEALTH, SPORT AND
EXERCISE SCIENCES
ROBINSON CENTER, ROOM 161
1301 SUNNYSIDE DRIVE
LAWRENCE, KS 66045-7567
785-864-5552
Fax: 785-864-3343
hsesinfo@ku.edu
www.soe.ku.edu
• James LaPoint, Graduate Coordinator
• Keith Tennant, Dept. Chairman
• Leon Greene, Undergraduate Coordinator
(785) 864-0775
jlg@ku.edu
Description:
Undergrad Degree: B.S. in Ed. Grad
Degree: M.S., Ph.D., Ed.D. Areas of
Specialization: Undergrad: Sport Sciences;
Sport Administration (in Physical Education);
Grad: Sport Administration (Specialization in
Physical Education) at Master's, Doctorate
level.

KENNESAW STATE UNIVERSITY
DEPARTMENT OF EXERCISE SCIENCE
AND SPORT MANAGEMENT
1000 CHASTAIN ROAD
KENNESAW, GA 30144
470-578-6000
tdonovan@kennesaw.edu
www.kennesaw.edu
Description:
Undergrad Degree: B.S. in Sport
Management.

KENT STATE UNIVERSITY
SCHOOL OF FOUNDATION, LEADERSHIP
AND ADMIN. -SPORT ADM.

264 MEMORIAL ANNEX
KENT, OH 44242
330-672-2015
Fax: 330-672-4106
www.kent.edu
• Mark Lyberger, Sports
Coordinator/Professor
mlyberge@kent.edu

KENTUCKY, UNIVERSITY OF
UK ATHLETICS
JOE CRAFT CENTER
338 LEXINGTON AVE.
LEXINGTON, KY 40506-0219
859-257-8000
www.ukathletics.com
• Mitch Barnhart, Director of Athletics
(859) 257-8015
mbarn@uky.edu
• Gary Henderson, Baseball Head Coach
(859) 257-2880
Description:
M.S. in Sport Management; Ed.D with
emphasis in Sport Management.

KEUKA COLLEGE
141 CENTRAL AVENUE
KEUKA PARK, NY 14478
315-279-5000
800-33-KEUKA
keukaathletics.com
• Ann M Tuttle, Director
atuttle@mail.keuka.edu
• David Sweet, Athletics Director
(315) 279-5682
dsweet@mail.keuka.edu
• Seth Fikes, Sports Information Director
(315) 279-5241
Degrees/Majors Offered:
Management major, concentration in sports
management.

KEYSTONE COLLEGE- SPORT AND
RECREATION MANAGEMENT
ONE COLLEGE GREEN
PO BOX 50
LA PLUME, PA 18440-0200
570-945-8000
877-426-5549
www.keystone.edu/
Program:
Bachelor's Degree in Sport and Recreation
Management.

KUTZTOWN UNIVERSITY- DEPARTMENT
OF SPORT MANAGEMENT
15200 KUTZTOWN ROAD
KUTZTOWN, PA 19530
610-683-4499
www2.kutztown.edu
Description:
Leisure & sport studies, Kutztown
University's leisure & sport studies program
allows students to become prepared for a
variety of opportunities ranging from
community recreation program and health
club management to the world of
professional athletics operations.

LAKE ERIE COLLEGE-
391 WEST WASHINGTON STREET
PAINESVILLE, OH 44077
440-296-1856
800-533-4996
www.lec.edu

Description:
Offers undergraduate Bachelor's degree in
Sport Management.

LANCASTER BIBLE COLLEGE-
901 EDEN ROAD
LANCASTER, PA 17601
717-569-7071
800-544-7335
www.lbc.edu
Sports Management & Ministry:
The Sports Management & Ministry major
prepares men and women to serve Christ in
the fields of sports management, sports
ministry, and coaching. Students learn how
to use biblical principles as they work in
secular organizations, churches, or
parachurch ministries. Field internships are
key to the students' education because it is
where they put into practice what they have
learned in the classroom.

LASELL COLLEGE- SPORT
MANAGEMENT DEPARTMENT
1844 COMMONWEALTH AVENUE
NEWTON, MA 2466
617-243-2000
Fax: 617-243-2380
www.lasell.edu
Program Description:
B.S. in Sport Management

LAURENTIAN UNIVERSITY
SCHOOL OF SPORTS ADMINISTRATION
935 RAMSEY LAKE ROAD
SUDBURY, ON, CANADA P3E 2C6
705-675-1151 EXT 4834
705-675-4834
Fax: 705-675-4836
www.laurentian.ca
• Ann Pegoraro, Director and Associate
Professor
(705) 675-1151
• Lynn Levac, Administrative Assistant
(705) 675-4834
• Anthony Church, Associate Professor/
Internship Coordinator
(705) 675-1151
• Claude Vincent, Assistant Professor
(705) 675-1151
• Xiaoyan Xing, Assistant Professor
(705) 675-1151
Year Founded:
1972
Description:
Undergrad Degree: School of Sports
Administration - Hon. B. Comm. (Sports
Administration). Areas of Specialization:
Undergrad: Sport Business Management.
Number of Members:
5 (4 faculty and 1 staff)

LE TOURNEAU UNIVERSITY
2100 S. MOBBERLY
LONGVIEW, TX 75602
903-753-0231
800-759-8811
Fax: 903-233-3495
www.letu.edu
• Melba Burry, Director Physical Education
Description:
Undergrad Degree: B.S. w/option in Sport
Management.

LEES-MCRAE COLLEGE- WILLIAMS PHYSICAL EDUCATION CENTER
191 MAIN STREET
BANNER ELK, NC 28604
828-898-2484
Fax: 828-898-8742
www.lmc.edu
Sports Management Program:
The BS in Sport Management program is designed for those students with a career interest in athletic administration, coaching, recreational management, facilities management, and sport marketing.

LEHIGH CARBON COMMUNITY COLLEGE
4525 EDUCATION PARK DRIVE
SCHNECKSVILLE, PA 18078
610-799-2121
gocougarsports.com
• Joseph M Flaherty, Director
jflaherty@lccc.edu
Degree/Majors Offered:
A.S. sport management.

LENOIR-RHYNE COLLEGE
625 7TH AVENUE NE
HICKORY, NC 28601
828-328-7300
800-277-5721
Fax: 828-267-3445
• Michael McGee, Professor, Program Chair
(828) 328-7127
mcgee@lr.edu
• Katherine Pasour, Professor, Dean College of Health Sciences
(828) 328-7126
pasourk@lr.edu
Description:
Several quality programs are offered to students interested in athletic training, physical education, health and exercise science, and sports management. The programs are designed to provide optimum development of both physical and mental abilities in these areas.

LEWIS UNIVERSITY
ONE UNIVERSITY PARKWAY
ROMEOVILLE, IL 60446-2200
815-838-0500
800-897-9000
www.lewisu.edu/academics/sportsmanage/
Sport Management Program:
BA in Sport Management.

LIBERTY UNIVERSITY
SPORT MANAGEMENT DEPARTMENT
1971 UNIVERSITY BOULEVARD
LYNCHBURG, VA 24506
434-582-2445
Fax: 434-582-2468
www.liberty.edu/academics/education/sport
• Christoper Amos, Assistant Professor
• Philip Blosser, Associate Professor
• Andrew Coleman, Assistant Professor
• Jordan Davies, Adjunct Professor
• Scott Hawkins, Chairperson/Assistant Professor
(434) 582-2155
• Vicky Martin, Associate Professor,Chair
(434) 582-2445
Description:
The mission is to help students develop skills to organize, administer, and facilitate sport programs at the corporate, agency, professional, and amateur levels.

Opportunities are provided to develop knowledge and skills relevant to the performance of these functions.
Degrees:
Undergrad Degree: B.S. Sport Management.

LIMESTONE COLLEGE- SPORT MANAGEMENT
1115 COLLEGE DR.
GAFFNEY, SC 29340-3799
864-489-7151
www.limestone.edu
Sport Management Major:
The Sport Management major is designed to provide students with an introductory understanding and preparation necessary to become successful managers in academic institutions or the sports industry. The program combines cor courses from the business administration and physical education disciplines that emphasize management skills, human resource skills, sound accounting practices, facilities management and wellness.

LINCOLN COLLEGE- SPORT MANAGEMENT PROGRAM
715 W. RAAB ROAD
NORMAL, IL 61761
309-452-0500
800-569-0558
www.lincolncollege.edu
Sport Management Program:
offers a bachelors degree program in sports management.

LINDENWOOD UNIVERSITY- SCHOOL OF BUSINESS & ENTREPRENEURSHIP
209 S. KINGSHIGHWAY
ST. CHARLES, MO 63301
636-949-4840
www.lindenwood.edu/business/index.html
Sports Management Program:
The MA in Sport Management is designed to prepare students for a career within the expanding sport industry. The MA curriculum is a unique blend of formal coursework and opportunities designed for practical experience.

LIPSCOMB UNIVERSITY- GRADUATE SCHOOL OF BUSINESS
ONE UNIVERSITY PARK DRIVE
NASHVILLE, TN 37204-3951
615-966-1000
800-333-4358
www.lipscomb.edu/gsb
Sport Management Program:
Offers A masters in business administration with concentration in sport management.

LIVINGSTONE COLLEGE
701 W. MONROE STREET
SALISBURY, NC 28144
704-216-6012
Fax: 704-216-6278
www.bluebearathletics.com
• Jimmy R. Jenkins Sr., President
(704) 216-6098
jjenkins@livingstone.edu
• Andre Springs, Men's Golf Coach
(704) 216-6933
asprings@livingstone.edu
• Blanche Ford, Administrative Assisstant
(704) 216-6012
• Jamie Kent, Senior Womens Admin

(704) 216-6011
jkent@livingstone.edu
• Justin Davis, Track Head Coach
(704) 216-6317
jdavis@livingstone.edu
• James Stinson, Head Coach Men's Basketbal
(704) 216-6016
jstinson@livingstone.edu
• John Daniels, Athletic Photographer
(704) 216-6934
Description:
B.S. physical education, B.S. sport management

LOCK HAVEN UNIVERSITY OF PENNSYLVANIA
401 N. FAIRVIEW STREET
LOCK HAVEN, PA 17745
570-484-2011
www.lhup.edu/catalog/sport_administration/
Program Description:
B.S. Sport Administration. This well-reputed LHU degree is approved by the North American Society for Sport Management (NASSM). It emphasizes the administration of athletic programs and activities as well as sport business, marketing, media, and communications.

LONG BEACH STATE UNIVERSITY
DEPARTMENT OF KINSIOLOGY
HHS2 BUILDING, 1ST FLOOR
1250 BELLFLOWER BOULEVARD
LONG BEACH, CA 90840
562-985-4051
Fax: 562-985-8067
www.csulb.edu/programs/sportmanagement
• Sharon Guthrie, Ph.D, Dept. Chairperson
• Stephem Buchan, Associate Program Director / Adjunct Professo
• Diane Higgs, Manager of Student Affairs
• Ketra Armstrong, Ph.D, Graduate Program Director
• Chris Tsangaris, Managing Director/Internship Coord.
Description:
Undergrad Degree: B.A. Phys Ed. Grad Degree: M.A., Phys Ed, Sports Management specialization.

LORAS COLLEGE
1450 ALTA VISTA
PO BOX 178
CENTER GROVE, IA 52001
563-588-7053
Fax: 563-588-4975
www.loras.edu
• Susie Wehring, Physical Ed. Chair/Sports Program Dir.
• William Joensen, Dean of Campus Spiritual Life
(563) 588-7463
william.joensen@loras.edu
• Collen Kuhl, Director of Campus Ministry
(563) 588-7924
colleen.kuhl@loras.edu
• Robert Gross, Associate Chaplain
(563) 588-7108
• Heather Jungblut, Executive Assistant to the Dean of Campus Spi
(563) 588-7104
heather.jungblut@loras.edu
• Debbie Gross, Campus Minister
(563) 588-7934
debbie.gross@loras.edu
• Matt Garrett, Sport Management

Coordinator
(319) 588-7165
matthew.garrett@loras.edu
• Lori Behnke, Academic Secretary
Degrees Offered:
B.A. Sport Management, M.A. Sport Administration.

LOUISIANA STATE UNIVERSITY
DEPARTMENT OF KINESIOLOGY
112 LONG FIELDHOUSE
BATON ROUGE, LA 70803-2401
225-578-2036
Fax: 225-578-3680
www.lsu.edu/athletics
• Amelia Lee, Dept. Chairperson/Professor
(225) 578-3551
amlee@lsu.edu
• Roy Hill, Sport Studies Instructor
Coordinator
(225) 578-2926
rhill@lsu.edu

LOUISVILLE, UNIVERSITY OF
DEPARTMENT OF HEALTH AND SPORT SCIENCE
CRAWFORD GYM
ROOM 211
LOUISVILLE, KY 40292
502-852-6645
Fax: 502-852-4534
• Adelson Jill, Assistant Profesor
(502) 852-4877
• Meera Alagaraja, Assistant Professor
(502) 852-0617
m0alag01@louisville.edu
• Tammy Albers, Academic Advisor
(502) 852-3204
tammy.albers@louisville.edu
• Oscar A Aliaga, ProgramDirector
(502) 852-0585
oaalia01@louisville.edu
• Micheal ball, AdministrativeAssistant
(502) 852-6645
jmball01@louisville.edu
• Anita Moorman, Associate Professor/Asst. Dept. Chair
amm@louisville.edu
• Mary Hums, Sport Administration Professor
mhums@louisville.edu
Description:
Undergrad Degree: B.S. in Sport Administration, Graduate Degree: M.S. in Sport Administration. Minors in Business, Marketing, Communications, Exercise Science and Health Promotion.
Requirements:
Need 123 Hours in order to graduate with a degree in Health and Human Performance or Sport Administration, must apply for a degree check after completing 80-90 hours, apply for a degree during the first three weeks that you are going to graduate, must have 50 hours of 300 level or above courses in order to graduate, must have a 2.25 GPA in order to graduate, the normal load is 15 hours - maximum load is 17 hours; students wishing to take more than 17 hours must make application to seek permission.

LOYOLA UNIVERSITY CHICAGO
WATER TOWER CAMPUS
820 NORTH MICHIGAN AVENUE
CHICAGO, IL 60611
312-915-6000
www.luc.edu/athletics

• Keith Lambrecht, Director, Sport Management Program
(312) 915-6514
klambre@luc.edu

LUTHER COLLEGE
DEPARTMENT OF PHYSICAL EDUCATION AND HEALTH
700 COLLEGE DRIVE
DECORAH, IA 52101
563-387-2000
800-458-8437
Fax: 563-387-1458
thompsjo@luther.edu
www.luther.edu
• Joe Thompson, Dept. Chairperson/Associate Professor
(563) 387-1583
thompsjo@luther.edu
• Brian Solberg, Associate Prof. of HPE and Prog. Director Ath
(563) 387-1246
solberbr@luther.edu
• Gregory Lonning, Director of the Nena Amundson Lifetime Wellne
(563) 387-2075
• Ellen Stoen, Assistant Professor of Health and Physical Ed
(563) 387-1587
drewesel@luther.edu
• Joe Thompson, Director of Intercollegiate Athletics
(563) 387-1575
thompsjo@luther.edu
• Jeffery Wettach, Assistant Professor of Health and Physical Ed
(563) 387-1577
wettacje@luther.edu
• Jacquelyn Wright, Associate Professor of Health and Physical Ed
(563) 387-1581
wrightja@luther.edu
• Mary Moen, HPE Secretary
(563) 387-1245
Description:
Undergrad Degree: B.A. Areas of Specialization: Phys Ed and Management programs.

LYNCHBURG COLLEGE- SPORT MANAGEMENT
1501 LAKESIDE DRIVE
LYNCHBURG, VA 24501
434-544-8100
www.lynchburg.edu/academics/majors-and-minors/sport-management
Sport Management Program:
offers bachelor's programs in sports management.

LYNN UNIVERSITY
3601 N. MILITARY TRAIL
BOCA RATON, FL 33431
561-237-7279
Fax: 561-237-7268
www.lynnfightingknights.com
• Kristen Migliano, Director of Athletics
(561) 237-7765
gmalfitano@lynn.edu
• Rudy Garbalosa, Baseball Head Coach
(561) 237-7242
• Scott McMillin, Men's Basketball Head Coach
(561) 237-7053
• Niki Washington, Women's Basketball Head Coach
(561) 237-7282

nwashington@lynn.edu
• Niki Alvarez, Women's Swimming/Women's Cross Country Head C
nalvarez@lynn.edu
Description:
Undergraduate degree in sports management that includes The Final Four, taking students into the field from Baseball Winter Meetings to the PGA Golf Tour.

MACMURRAY COLLEGE- SPORT MANAGEMENT
447 EAST COLLEGE AVENUE
JACKSONVILLE, IL 62650
217-479-7000
800-252-7485
publicinformation@mac.edu
www.mac.edu/
Sports management:
Offers a bachelor's program in sport management.

MADONNA UNIVERSITY- SPORT MANAGEMENT
36600 SCHOOLCRAFT ROAD
LIVONIA, MI 48150
800-852-4951
Fax: 734-432-5393
www.madonna.edu
Program Description:
The Sport Management program offers several educational opportunities.

MARIAN COLLEGE
DEPARTMENT OF SPORT STUDIES
3200 COLD SPRING ROAD
INDIANAPOLIS, IN 46222
317-955-6124
800-772-7264
morrell@marian.edu
• Lynn Morrell, Dept. Chairperson
morrell@marian.edu
• Leigh Ann Bussell, Sport Studies Professor
Description:
The operation side of the sport industry. Sport management professionals, found both in amateur and professional realms, may be found performing a variety of tasks which include marketing, management, advertising, ticket sales, directing facilities and events, public relations, working in conjunction with sport agents, directing recreation programs, operating fitness systems, and working as a coach both in and outside school systems.
Requirements:
Major for Bachelor Degree (B.A. or B.S.) Sport Management: 37 to 40 hours, including HPE 128, 139, 230, 310, 354, 360, 410, ACC 210, BUS 101, 240, 250, ECN 200 or 201 or 202, MIS 102, 103, 104, PSY 101 or 220. Sport management majors desiring to minor in business must consult with the business department chair.

MARIAN UNIVERSITY-FOND DU LAC, SPORT MANAGEMENT PROGRAM
45 S. NATIONAL AVENUE
FOND DU LAC, WI 54935-4699
800-262-7426
Program:
Offering undergraduate programs in sports management.

MARQUETTE UNIVERSITY
1250 W. WISCONSIN AVENUE
MILWAUKEE, WI 53233
414-288-7250
800-222-6544
Fax: 414-288-5818
www.marquette.edu
• William E Cullinan, Ph.D., Dean, College of Health Science
(414) 288-5053
william.cullinan@marquette.edu
• Kim L Halula, R.D.H., Ph.D., Associate Dean
(414) 288-0656
kim.halula@marquette.edu
Description:
Departments within the College of Health Sciences include: Athletic Training; Biomedical Sciences; Clinical Laboratory Science; Exercise Science; Physical Therapy; Physician Assistant; and Speech Pathology and Audiology

MARSHALL UNIVERSITY
DIV OF ESSR
COLLEGE OF EDUCATION
ONE JOHN MARSHALL DR
HUNTINGTON, WV 25755
304-696-5408
800-642-3463
Fax: 304-696-6448
www.marshall.edu
• T. Jeff Chandler, Chairman
Description:
Undergrad Degree: B.S. Sport Management & Marketing. Grad Degree: M.S. in Phys Ed with concentration in Athletic Administration and Sport Management. Areas of Specialization: Undergrad: Interdisciplinary comprehensive program in Sport Management and Marketing. Arena Management, Athletic Administration. Grad: Athletic Administration.

MARTIN METHODIST COLLEGE
SPORT MANAGEMENT
433 W. MADISON STREET
PULASKI, TN 38478
931-363-9804
800-467-1273
Fax: 931-363-9868
info@martinmethodist.edu
www.martinmethodist.edu
• Tim Wilson, Assistant Professor of Sport Management
(931) 363-9847
twilson@martinmethodist.edu
• Jeff Bain, Director of Athletics
Degree Offered:
B.S. Sport Management

MARYLAND, UNIVERSITY OF
DEPARTMENT OF KINESIOLOGY
HHP BUILDING, ROOM 2351
COLLEGE PARK, MD 20742-2611
301-405-2450
Fax: 301-405-5578
www.hhp.umd.edu/KNES/
• Jane Clark, Ph.D, Dept. Chairperson
jeclark@umd.edu
• Steve McDaniel, Pro General Manager Coordinator
• Wallace D. Loh, President
• Yunjoo Koo, HHP Coordinator
(301) 405-2497
ykoo@umd.edu

Description:
Grad Degree: M.A. Areas of Specialization: Professional sport, educational sport, club management, executive fitness programs.

MARYMOUNT UNIVERSITY- SPORT MANAGEMENT
2807 NORTH GLEBE ROAD
ARLINGTON, VA 22207
703-522-5600
www.marymount.edu
Program Description:
The Sport Management specialty focuses on marketing, law, economics, and promotions within a sports context. In addition, the required internship provides students with an opportunity to gain a real-world experience with sports-related organizations and professional, semiprofessional, and collegiate teams in the DC area. Graduates with a Sport Management specialty are prepared for a variety of positions in the sports industry, including marketing specialist, consultant, agent, and more.

MARYVILLE UNIVERSITY - JOHN E. SIMON SCHOOL OF BUSINESS
650 MARYVILLE UNIVERSITY DRIVE
ST. LOUIS, MO 63141
314-529-9300
800-627-9855
www.maryville.edu/academics-bu-sportsmanagement.htm
Sport Business Management Program:
The Maryville Sport Business Management program focuses on the general business disciplines of management, finance, marketing, operations management and communications and teaches students how to apply them to the sports industry.

MASSACHUSETTS AMHERST, UNIVERSITY OF
104 SKINNER HALL
AMHERST, MA 1003
413-545-0441
Fax: 413-577-0642
umsmdb@sportstudy.umass.edu
www.umassathletics.com
• Tracy Schoenadel, Director, Center for Sports Research
• Lisa Pike Masteralexis, Chair/Director
swl@sportmgt.umass.edu
• Ed Matz, Women's Soccer Head Coach
(413) 545-4343
edmatz@admin.umass.edu
• Elaine Sortino, Softball Head Coach
(413) 545-4099
elaine@admin.umass.edu
• Russ Yarworth, Men's Swimming & Diving Head Coach
(413) 545-0093
yarworth@admin.umass.edu
• Bob Newcomb, Women's Swimming & Diving Head Coach
(413) 545-4342
rnewc@admin.umass.edu
Degree Offered:
Ranking as the second oldest sports management department in the country, UMASS Amherst offers a B.S., M.S.,P.M.B.A./M.S., & Ph.D. in Sport Management. It has one of the few programs with a stand alone department in the business school.

MASSACHUSETTS COLLEGE OF LIBERAL ARTS- SPORT MANAGEMENT PROGRAM
375 CHURCH STREET
NORTH ADAMS, MA 1247
413-662-5000
Description:
B.A. with concentration in sport management

MCDANIEL COLLEGE - EXERCISE SCIENCE & PHYSICAL EDUCATION DEPARTMENT
2 COLLEGE HILL
WESTMINSTER, MD 21157
410-848-7000
www.mcdaniel.edu
Description:
B.A. & M.S. in Sport Management

MEDAILLE COLLEGE
SPORT MANAGEMENT
18 AGASSIZ CIRCLE
BUFFALO, NY 14214
716-880-2000
Fax: 800-292-1582
www.medaille.edu
• Richard Jacob, Sport Management Program Coordinator
• Douglas Hoard, Vice-President
• Judith Horoitz, Associate Professor, Associate Vice President
• Norman Muir, Associate Professor, and Dean, Undergraduate
• Illana Lane, Dean, School of Education, Associate Professo
• Brad Hollingshead, Associate Professor and Associate Dean for Fo
Description:
Undergrad Degree: B.S. Areas of Specialization: Sport Management, Recreation, Sports Communication.

MEMPHIS, UNIVERSITY OF
UNIVERSITY OF MEMPHIS
101 ILDER TOWER
MEMPHIS, TN 38152-3520
901-678-3480
Fax: 901-678-3591
• Mike Hamrick, Dept. Chairperson
(901) 678-4165
mhamrick@memphis.edu
• Richard Irwin, Director
(901) 678-3476
rirwin@memphis.edu
• Ryan Luttrell, National Sports Forum (NSF) Competition
Description:
Grad Degree: M.S. in Sport and Leisure Commerce. Areas of Specialization: Professional and Commercial Sport and Leisure, With Emphasis in Marketing. B.S. Ed. in Sport and Leisure Studies.

MENLO COLLEGE - SPORTS MANAGEMENT PROGRAM
1000 EL CAMINO REAL
ATHERTON, CA 94027-4301
650-543-3936
Fax: 650-543-4003
academics@menlo.edu
www.menlo.edu/academics/degrees/sports-management-degree
Description:
Sports Management Option in Management Major, B.S. in Business; The Sports Management program exposes students to

college sports

all facets of the business of sports, including sports sponsorship relationships, team and league equity issues, labor and personnel management, and a wide variety of ethical and social issues facing business professionals in both professional and amateur athletics.

MERCY COLLEGE - SCHOOL OF HEALTH & NATURAL SCIENCES
555 BROADWAY
DOBBS FERRY, NY 10522
877-637-2946
www.mercy.edu
Sport Management Program Description:
B.S. in Exercise Science; The B.S. in Exercise Science is also valuable to help prepare students moving into graduate programs for careers in physical therapy, occupational therapy, sports psychology, and physicians assistants, and kinesiology.

MERCYHURST COLLEGE
501 E. 38TH STREET
ERIE, PA 16546-0001
814-824-2000
Fax: 814-824-2172
www.mercyhurst.edu
• David Rubino, Ph.D., Interim Dean of Walker School
(814) 824-3034
• Amy Doolan, MBA, DBA, Associate Professor & Associate Dean
(814) 824-3604
Degree Offered:
B.A. Sport Business Management
Description:
The business of sport is one of the largest industries in the United States. Today's sport business managers need to have skills in the areas of planning, budgeting, managing, marketing, and leading organizations whose focus is on the sport industry. The curriculum of the sport business management major will prepare students for leadership roles in professional and amateur sports, school and college sports programs, the sporting goods industry, the sports news media, resorts, military and social agency sports programs, health and fitness clubs, and sport marketing and consulting firms.

MEREDITH COLLEGE
DEPARTMENT OF HEALTH, EXERCISE & SPORTS SCIENCE
3800 HILLSBOROUGH STREET
101 WEATHERSPOON ANNEX
RALEIGH, NC 27607
919-760-8309
Fax: 919-760-2828
campbellm@meredith.edu
www.meredith.edu
• Melinda Campbell, Dept. Head/Professor
Description:
B.S. exercise and sports science; B.S. exercise and sports science, concentration in physical education; B.S. exercise and sports science, concentration in fitness and sports management.

MERRIMACK COLLEGE - SPORT MANAGEMENT PROGRAM
315 TURNPIKE STREET
NORTH ANDOVER, MA 1845
978-837-5000
www.merrimack.edu/academics/business/sport-management/
Program Description:
B.S. in Sport Management: The sport management concentration is ideal for anyone who desires a career in sport marketing, events management, athletic administration, or facilities management, but also seeks the general business preparation for other career opportunities.

MESSIAH COLLEGE
One College Avenue
Grantham, PA 17027
717-766-2511
800-233-4220
www.messiah.edu/athletics
• Jack Cole, Director
jcole@messiah.edu
Degree/Majors Offered:
B.A. sport and exercise science, sport management concentration.

METHODIST COLLEGE
5400 RAMSEY STREET
FAYETTEVILLE, NC 28311
910-630-7000
800-488-7110
webmaster@methodist.edu
www.mumonarchs.com
• Greg Combs, Sports Management Coordinator
gcombs@methodist.edu
Description:
Graduates with a concentration in Sports Management (SMA) will have the skills and knowledge necessary to become effective entry-level managers and administrators in the business of sport. Students who choose a concentration in Sports Management are qualified for entry level management positions within professional sports teams and businesses affiliated with sport, sporting goods manufacturers, recreation facilities, and health and fitness clubs.
Degrees Offered:
B.A. major in sports management, sports administration concentration; B.A. major in sports management, well/fitness concentration; B.S. major in sports management, sports administration concentration; B.S. major in sports management, wellness/fitness concentraton.
Requirements:
Writing-Enrichment Course: BUS 352, Computer Intensive Course: BUS 225, Ethics Course: BUS 315. Requirements for the concentration in Sports Management: 21 s.h. _ SMA 321, SMA 322, SMA 421, SMA 422, BUS 354, BUS 375, and a 3 s.h. internship.

METROPOLITAN STATE COLLEGE OF DENVER - SPORT MANAGEMENT PROGRAM
CAMPUS BOX 25
PO BOX 17336
DENVER, CO 80217-3362
Program Description:
Human Performance and Sports Major with the Sports Industry Operations concentration. Students can get up to 16 hours of real world experiences for credit with two field experiences and an optional 10-credit hour internships are vital to the development of skills for individuals seeking a career in Sport Industry Operations. From player relations and media to day-of-game operations or facility management, the courses are designed to inspire and equip students with the knowledge they need to get the ball rolling.

MIAMI, UNIVERSITY OF
DEPARTMENT OF EXERCISE & SPORTS SCIENCES
SCHOOL OF EDUCATION
PO BOX 248065
CORAL GABLES, FL 33124-2040
305-284-3024
Fax: 305-284-5168
www.cehd.umn.edu
• Arlette Perry, Phd., Chairman
aperry@miami.edu
• Andy Gillentine, Chair/Director
soe@miami.edu
Description:
Undergrad Degree: Fifteen (15) credit undergraduate minors in Sports Management, Exercise Physiology and Sports Medicine. B.S.C.D. Sports Administration and B.S. Biology/Exercise Physiology; Grad Degree: M.S. Ed., Sports Administration, Sports Medicine and Exercise Physiology. Areas of Specialization: Intercollegiate and Professional Sports Management, Exercise & Sports Sciences, Human Performance and Wellness, Sports Medicine.

MICHIGAN STATE UNIVERSITY - DEPARTMENT OF KINESIOLOGY
102 IM SPORTS CIRCLE
MICHIGAN STATE UNIVERISTY
EAST LANSING, MI 48824-1049
517-432-1514
Fax: 517-432-2426
McNeilR@msu.edu
www.msu.edu
Program Description:
M.S. Concentration in Sport Administration: The master's degree concentration in sports administration is designed for individuals who are preparing for careers in administration of intercollegiate and interscholastic sport and recreation programs. Internships are available at local high schools, college/university settings, and other sports-related organizations and agencies.

MIDAMERICA NAZARENE UNIVERSITY - HEALTH AND EXERCISE SCIENCE
2030 E. COLLEGE WAY
OLATHE, KS 66062-1899
913-782-3750
800-800-8887
www.mnu.edu
Description:
B.A. in Sports Management

MIDDLE TENNESSEE STATE UNIVERSITY - HPERS DEPARTMENT
1301 EAST MAIN STREET
MURFREESBORO, TN 37132-0001
615-898-2300
Program Description:
M.S. in Sport Management; The graduate sport management concentration offers a cross discipline curriculum, focusing on professional preparation for the sports industry. Students will complete a degree program that includes courses in

management, legal issues and facility design. Sport management courses will focus on the business aspects of sport in culture, interscholastic/intercollegiate and professional sports, facility management, sport ethics, sport marketing, sport law and sport finance.

MIDWAY COLLEGE - BUSINESS DEPARTMENT
512 E. STEPHENS ST.
MIDWAY, KY 40347
859-846-4421
800-755-0031
www.midway.edu/majors-programs/schools/business
Description:
B.A. in Sport Management

MILLERVILLE UNIVERSITY
OFFICE OF GRADUATE STUDIES
104 DILWORTH HALL
PO BOX 1002
MILLERVILLE, PA 17551-0302
717-872-3490
Fax: 717-871-2393
www.millersvilleathletics.com
• Stanley Kabacinski, Dept. Chairperson
• Rebecca Mowrey, Graduate Program Coordinator
• Esther Hernandez-Montano, Dept. Secretary
• Kyle Almoney, Women's Swimming Head Coach
(717) 872-3872
• Shari Bucklin-Webber, Men's and Women's Tennis Head Coach
(717) 872-3946
• Brian Smith, Women's Volleyball Head Coach
(717) 872-3946
bsmith1@millersville.edu
Degree Offered
M.Ed. Sport Management

MILLIKIN UNIVERSITY - COLLEGE OF PROFESSIONAL STUDIES
1184 WEST MAIN STREET
DECATUR, IL 62522
800-373-7733
www.millikin.edu/ess
Description:
B.S. in Sport Management; Students will learn the business of sports through a combination of coursework from the Department of Exercise Science & Sport and the Tabor School of Business. The business core provides a broad spectum of courses in specialized areas of the sport business community. The Sport Management curriculum follows the recommendations of the North American Society for Sport Management (NASSM).

MINNESOTA STATE UNIVERSITY-MANKATO
DEPARTMENT OF HUMAN PERFORMANCE
228 WIECKING CENTER
MANKATO, MN 56002-8400
507-389-6313
Fax: 507-389-5618
www.mnsu.edu
• Kent Kalm, Dept. Acting Chairperson
kent.kalm@mnsu.edu
• Jill Binstock, Dept. Secretary
(507) 389-6313

jilane.binstock@mnsu.edu
• Gary Rushing, Graduate Coordinator
Sports Administration
(507) 389-2217
Description:
Undergrad Degree: B. S. Grad Degree: M.A., M.S. Areas of Specialization: Sports Administration, Psycho-Social Aspects of Sports.

MINNESOTA, UNIVERSITY OF
DEPARTMENT OF KINESIOLOGY
111 COOKE HALL
1900 UNIVERSITY AVENUE SE
MINNEAPOLIS, MN 55455
612-625-5300
Fax: 612-626-7700
kin@umn.edu
• Mary Jo Kane, Director/Professor
maryjo@umn.edu
• Jo Ann Buysse, Sport Studies Program Coordinator
(612) 625-5331
buyss003@umn.edu
Description:
Grad Degree: M.A. and Ph.D. in Kinesiology or Recreation & Leisure Studies. Areas of Specialization: Multi-Disciplinary Program including Business, Communications, Education and Sociology, in addition to Kinesiology and Leisure Studies courses.

MISERICORDIA UNIVERSITY
301 Lake Street
Dallas, PA 18612
570-674-6400
info@misericordia.edu
www.misericordia.edu/athletics
• Deron G Grabel, Director
dgrabel@misericordia.edu
• David Martin, Athletics Director
(570) 674-6294
dmartin@misericordia.edu
Degrees/Majors Offered:
B.S. sport management.

MISSISSIPPI STATE UNIVERSITY
ATHLETIC DEPARTMENT
P.O. BOX 5327
MISSISSIPPI STATE, MS 39762
662-325-2066
Fax: 662-325-0589
www.hailstate.com
• Scott Stricklin, Director of Athletics
(662) 325-0863
Degree Offered:
M.S. Sport Administration

MISSISSIPPI, UNIVERSITY OF
DEPARTMENT OF HEALTH, EXERCISE SCIENCE & RECREATION MGMT
215 TURNER CENTER
PO BOX 1848
UNIVERSITY, MS 38677
662-915-5521
Fax: 662-915-5525
jlmcbrid@olemiss.edu
www.olemiss.edu
• David Scott Hargrove, Dept. Interim Chairperson
jlmcbrid@olemiss.edu
• Scott G Owens, Interim Chair of Health, Exercise Science and
(662) 915-5527
• Martha Bass, Associate Professor of Health and Exercise Sc
(662) 915-5563

mabass1@olemiss.edu
• Christi Brewer, Instructor in Exercise Science Health, Exerci
(662) 915-5528
• Christoper Black, Assistant Professor of Health, Exercise Scien
(662) 915-5521
vblackcd@olemiss.edu
• Kim Beason, Professor of Park & Recreation Management and
(662) 915-5555
hpbeason@olemiss.edu
• Dale Bramlett, HESRM Senior Secretary
(662) 915-5844
• Michael Dupper, HESRM Assistant Professor
(662) 915-5564
mad@olemiss.edu
Description:
Undergrad Degree: B.S. Areas of Specialization: Sports Management.

MISSOURI BAPTIST UNIVERSITY
One College Park Drive
St. Louis, MO 63141-8698
314-434-1115
877-434-1115
Fax: 314-434-7596
• P. Greg Comfort, Director
comfort@mobap.edu
Degrees/Majors Offered:
B.S., B.A. sport management, B.S. sport medicine, B.S.E., B.S., B.A. kinesiology, B.S.E., B.S., B.A. health; graduate certificate in sport management.

MISSOURI WESTERN STATE COLLEGE
DEPARTMENT OF HEALTH, PHYSICAL EDUCATION & RECREATION
214 LOONEY COMPLEX
ST. JOSEPH, MO 64507
816-271-4491
Fax: 816-271-5940
blessing@missouriwestern.edu
www.missouriwestern.edu/HPER
• Brenda Blessing, Professor of Recreation/Chairperson
(816) 271-4208
blessing@missouriwestern.edu
• Paul Choi, Assistant Professor of Recreation
(816) 271-4246
hchoi@missouriwestern.edu
• Regan Dodd, Assistant Professor of Health
(816) 271-4474
rdodd@missouriwestern.edu
• Rick Hardy, Assistant Professor of Recreation
(816) 271-5931
• Britton Johnson, Assistant Professor of Physical Education
• Justin Kraft, Assistant Professor of Physical Education
(816) 271-4290
jkraft@missouriwestern.edu
• Nannette Wolford, Physical Education Asst. Professor
(816) 271-4487
wolford@missouriwestern.edu
Description:
Undergrad Degree: B.S. Areas of Specialization: Sports Marketing/Management.

college sports

427

MISSOURI, UNIVERSITY OF
HEALTH AND EXERCISE SCIENCES
102 ROTHWELL GYMNASIUM
COLUMBIA, MO 65211
573-882-6501
Fax: 573-882-4720
www.missouri.edu
• Linda Schoonmaker, Coordinator
Description:
Grad Degree: M.Ed. Areas of Specialization:
Sport Management, Human Performance.

**MONTANA STATE
UNIVERSITY-BOZEMAN**
DEPARTMENT OF HEALTH & HUMAN
DEVELOPMENT
218 HERRICK HALL
PO BOX 173540
BOZEMAN, MT 59717-3360
406-994-3242
Fax: 406-994-6314
hhd@montana.edu
www.montana.edu
• Craig Stewart, Dept.
Chairperson/Professor
cstewart@montana.edu
• Lynn Owens, Dept. Coordinator
lowens@montana.edu

MOUNT SAINT MARY'S UNIVERSITY
16300 OLD EMMITSBURG ROAD
EMITTSBURG, MD 21727
301-447-6122
www.msmary.edu/athletics
• Karl W Einolf, Chair/Director
einolf@msmary.edu
Description:
B.S. busines, concentration in sports
management

NATIONAL-LOUIS UNIVERSITY
2840 SHERIDAN RD
EVANSTON, IL 60201
847-475-1100
Fax: 847-256-1057
www.nl.edu
• Curtis McCray, President
(847) 475-1100
Description:
Undergrad Degree: B.A. Grad Degree: M.S.
Areas of Specialization: Exercise
Physiology, specializing in preventive and
rehabilitative cardiovascular health.

NEBRASKA WESLEYAN UNIVERSITY
DEPARTMENT OF HEALTH AND HUMAN
PERFORMANCE
5000 ST. PAUL AVENUE
LINCOLN, NE 68504
402-465-2366
800-541-3818
Fax: 402-465-2179
bmj@nebrwesleyan.edu
nwusports.com
• Berniece Jones, Dept.
Chairperson/Associate Professor
(402) 465-2364
bmj@nebrwesleyan.edu
• Patricia Dotson, Dept. Professor
(402) 465-2361
pdp@nebrwesleyan.edu

NEUMANN COLLEGE
ONE NEUMANN DR
ASTON, PA 19014
610-459-0905
800-9-NEUMANN
Fax: 484-840-4798
slabiks@neumann.edu
www.neumann.edu/athletics
Degrees Offered:
B.S. Sport Management; M.S. Sport
Management.
Description:
The Sport and Entertainment Management
major offers career-minded students the
opportunity to gain a broad based
understanding of the major areas of Sport
and Entertainment Management. Graduates
move on to challenging and exciting careers
in academic settings, professional sports,
sports and recreation facilities, as well as
health, fitness, and sport clubs.

NEVADA, LAS VEGAS, UNIVERSITY OF
DEPARTMENT OF KINESILOGY
4505 S. MARYLAND PARKWAY
PO BOX 453034
LAS VEGAS, NV 89154-3035
702-895-0996
Fax: 702-895-1500
www.unlvrebels.com
• John Mercer, Ph.D, Dept. Chairperson
(702) 895-4672
jmercer@unlv.nevada.edu
• John Massengale, Sports Studies Director
(702) 895-4096
• Cindy Fredrick, Volleyball Head Coach
(702) 895-1898

NEW ENGLAND COLLEGE
24 Bridge Street
Henniker, NH 3242
603-428-2211
www.nec.edu/athletics
• John O'Connor, Director
joconnor@nec.edu
• Lori Runksmeier, Athletics Director
(603) 428-2292
lrunksmei@nec.edu
Degrees/Majors Offered:
B.A. sport and recreeation management.

NEW HAMPSHIRE, UNIVERSITY OF
HEIIT HALL
105 MAIN STREET
THE UNIVERSITY OF NE HAMPSHIRE
DURHAM, NH 3824
603-862-1234
800-735-2964
Fax: 603-862-0154
www.unh.edu/sport-studies
• Karen Collins, Option Coordinator
• Heather Barber, Associate Professor
• Tim Ashwell, Sr. Lecturer
Description:
B.S. Kinesiology: sport studies, M.S.
kinesiology: sport studies.

NEW HAVEN, UNIVERSITY OF
DEPT OF SPORT MANAGEMENT
300 Boston Post Road
W. HAVEN, CT 6516
203-932-7016
800-225-5864
Fax: 203-932-7470
asack@newhaven.edu
www.newhavenchargers.com
• Deborah Chin, Associate Vice President,
Director of Athleti
(203) 932-7020
dchin@newhaven.edu
• Sue Zawacki, Senior Associate Director of
Athletics
(203) 932-7357
• Robin Salters, Associate Director of
Athletics for Facilitie
(203) 932-7022
rsalters@newhaven.edu
• Bryan Graff, Associate Director of Athletics
for External
(203) 932-7017
bgraff@newhaven.edu
• lou Scala, Director of Sports Medicine
(203) 479-4890
• Allen L. Sack, Coordinator Sports
Management
asack@newhaven.edu
• Gil Fried, Professor/Chair
gfried@newhaven.edu
Description:
B.S. management of sports industries, B.S.
business administration with a concentration
in sports management, M.S. management of
sports industries, M.S. management of
sports industries with a concentration in
facility management, M.B.A. with a
concentration in sports management.
Number of Members:
Three full time faculty.

NEW YORK UNIVERSITY
PRESTON ROBERT TISCH CENTER
7 EAST 12TH STREET
NEW YORK, NY 10003
212-998-9104
Fax: 212-995-4676
tish.center@nyu.edu
www.scps.nyu.edu/tischcenter
• Jennifer Burns, Director of Industry
Relations and Administration
Degrees Offered:
B.S. in sport management and leisure
studies.

NEWBERRY COLLEGE
DEPARTMENT OF PHYSICAL
EDUCATION
2100 COLLEGE STREET
NEWBERRY, SC 29108
803-321-5161
800-845-4955
www.newberrywolves.com
• Peggy Barnes, Dept. Chair/PE Associate
Professor
pbarnes@newberry.edu
• Cody McMurtry, Physical Education Asst.
Professor
(803) 321-5163
• Jason Valek, Wrestling Head Coach
(803) 321-5659
jason.valek@newberry.edu
• Emily Bikowski, Women's Lacrosse Head
Coach
(803) 321-5199
emily.bikowski@newberry.edu
• Amber Morrell, Cheerleading Head Coach
amber.morrell@newberry.edu

NHTI, CONCORD COMMUNITY COLLEGE
31 COLLEGE DRIVE
CONCORD, NH 3301
603-271-6426
Fax: 603-271-6431
www.nhti.edu
• Paul Hogan, Director of Athletics/Men's
Basketball Head C
(603) 271-6426
nhtiathletics@ccsnh.edu

Teams:
Baseball, Basketball (M/W), Bowling, Cross Country (M/W), Dance, Golf, Soccer (M/W), Softball, Spirit.

NICHOLS COLLEGE
SPORT MANAGEMENT PROGRAM
124 CENTER ROAD
PO BOX 5000
DUDLEY, MA 1571
508-213-1560
800-470-3379
Fax: 508-213-2225
www.nichols.edu/athletics
• Timothy Liptrap, Sport Management Assistant Professor
• Colleen Colles, Chairperson/Assistant Professor
(508) 213-2254
Description:
The sport management program provides the academic and practical experiences needed to gain successful employment in the field. The specialization provides the skills necessary for success in a variety of areas including: sport facility management, event management, high school and collegiate athletics, sporting goods manufacturers, and amateur and professional sports organizations.
Requirements:
A Bachelors of Science in Business Administration requires the successful completion of 121 academic credit hours (approximately 40 courses). To specialize in Sport Management, students are required to complete 30 credit hours (7 classes and one-9 credit internship) in this area of expertise.
Degree Offered:
B.S. business administration with emphasis in sport management, M.B.A. with emphasis in sport management.

NORTH CAROLINA STATE UNIVERSITY
COLLEGE OF NATURAL RESOURCES
2820 FAUCETTE DRIVE
BILTMORE HALL
RALEIGH, NC 27695-8001
919-515-2883
Fax: 919-515-7231
naturalresources@ncsu.edu
www.cfr.ncsu.edu
• Michael A. Kanters, Chair/Director
mkanters@ncsu.edu
• Mary Atzin, Dean
(919) 513-5723
• Julia Brooks, Executive Assistant to the Dean
(919) 513.0152
• Robert Bardon, Associate Dean for Extension and Engagement
(919) 515-5575
Robert_Bardon@ncsu.edu
• David Ashcraft, Director of External Relations & Development
(919) 515.5723
• Jennifer Viets, Assistant Director of External Relations
(919) 513.7734
Jennifer_Viets@ncsu.edu
• Jennifer Piercy, Director of the Pulp and Paper Foundation
(919) 515.7709
Jennifer_Piercy@ncsu.edu
Description:
B.S. parks, recreation and tourism

management, concentration in sport management; B.S. sport management.

NORTH CAROLINA, UNIVERSITY OF
DEPARTMENT OF EXERCISE AND SPORT SCIENCE
FETZER GYM
CAMPUS BOX 8700
CHAPEL HILL, NC 27599-8700
919-962-0017
Fax: 919-962-0489
atkins@email.unc.edu
www.unc.edu/depts
• Cindy Atkins, Dept. Administrative Assistant
atkins@email.unc.edu
• Frederick Mueller, Sport Administration Professor
mueller@email.unc.edu
• Barbara Osborne, Sport Admin. Specialization Coordinator
(919) 962-5173
sportlaw@unc.edu
Description:
B.A. exercise and sport science, sport administration; M.S. sport administration, M.A./J.D. sport administration and law dual degree.

NORTH FLORIDA UNIVERSITY OF
4567 ST JOHN'S BLUFF ROAD
JACKSONVILLE,, FL 32224
904-628-1000
www.unfospreys.com
• Jennifer Kane, Chair/Director
Description:
B.A.E. sport leadership

NORTHEASTERN UNIVERSITY
360 HUNTINGTON AVE
BOSTON, MA 2115
617-373-2672
Fax: 617-373-8988
www.northeastern.edu
• Robert Curtin, Chairman Sport & Leisure Studies
• Richard Lapchick, Executive Director
Description:
Undergrad Degree: B.S. Grad Degree: M.S. Areas of Specialization: Undergrad: Cardiovascular Health and Exercise; Athletic Training; Physical Education; Health Education; Recreation Management. Grad: Clinical Exercise Physiology; Recreation/Sport/Fitness Management.

NORTHERN COLORADO, UNIVERSITY OF
SCHOOL OF SPORT AND EXERCISE SCIENCE
GUNTER 2590
PO BOX 39
GREELEY, CO 80639
970-351-2535
Fax: 970-351-1762
www.unco.edu/nhs/ses
• Shannon Courtney, Athletic Training
• Jim Turk, Athletic Training
• Gary Heise, Biomechanics
• Scott Douglas, Teacher Education
• Melissa Parker, Teacher Education
• David Stotlar, Director
david.stotlar@unco.edu
• Linda Sharp, Professor
linda.sharp@unco.edu
Description:
M.A., and Ph.D. in sport and exercise

science,with an emphasis in sport administration.

NORTHERN ILLINOIS UNIVERSITY
228 AN
DEKALB, IL 60115
815-753-3907
Fax: 815-753-1413
rcaughron@niu.edu
• Rod Caughron, Director of Graduate Studies in Sport Managem
Description:
MS in Sport Management: Program is a sport business program with an emphasis on leadership, communications (oral/written), and sound business and sales practices.

NORTHERN KENTUCKY UNIVERSITY
DEPARTMENT OF MANAGEMENT & MARKETING
BEP 475
NUNN DRIVE
HIGHLAND HEIGHTS, KY 41099-7500
859-572-6559
Fax: 859-572-5150
• Matthew Shank, Dept. Chairperson/Professor
(859) 572-6642
• Tom Gamble, Sports Business Program Inaugural Dir.
(859) 572-5906
Description:
Sports Business is the multidisciplinary study of business principles and processes applied to the sports industry. The sports business certificate is for individuals that seek a solid foundation in the principles and practices of the sports industry. Students enrolled in this certificate program must meet all course pre-requisites except class standing and certification.
Required Courses:
SPB 305 Sports Marketing, SPB 308 Sports Promotion Tools, SPB 330 Sports Legal Environment, SPB 480 Sports Business Strategies and Policies.

NORTHWESTERN STATE UNIVERSITY OF LOUISIANA
DEPARTMENT OF HEALTH & HUMAN PERFORMANCE
143 HEALTH AND HUMAN PERFORMANCE BUILDING
NATCHITOCHES, LA 71497
318-357-5126
Fax: 318-357-5904
health@nsula.edu
www.nsula.edu
• Vickie Gentry, Dept. Chairperson
gentryv@nsula.edu
• Susan Molstad, Professor
molstad@nsula.edu
• Newton C. Wilkes, Professor
wilkes@nsula.edu
Description:
Grad Degree: M.Ed. in Phys Ed. Areas of Specialization: Sport Administration, Health Promotion, Physical Education.

NORTHWESTERN UNIVERSITY
SPORTS ADMINISTRATION/MANAGEMENT
339 E. CHICAGO AVENUE
CHICAGO, IL 60611-3008
312-503-6951
Fax: 312-503-4942

scsadmissions@northwestern.edu
www.nusports.com
• Maureen Harty, Athletic Director
Description:
The School of Continuing Studies has developed a master's program to prepare students to take on leadership positions in all segments of the sports industry. Students who are serious about the business of sports will gain an understanding of theoretical concepts and the ability to apply those concepts in a 10-course curriculum encompassing the diverse aspects of the sports profession.
Degree Offered:
MSA in Sports Administration

NORTHWOOD UNIVERSITY FLORIDA CAMPUS
2600 MILITARY TRAIL
WEST PALM BEACH, FL 33409
561-478-5500
Fax: 561-697-9495
www.northwood.edu/athletics
• Dennis Bechtol, Chair/Director
Description:
Bachelor's in business administration, major in sport and entertainment management.

OHIO NORTHERN UNIVERSITY
SPORTS CENTER
525 S. MAIN ST
ADA, OH 45810
419-772-2000
Fax: 419-772-2470
r-beaschler@onu.edu
www.onu.edu
• Ron Beaschler, Coordinator
Description:
Undergrad Degree: B.S. Grad Degree: M.Ed. in Sports Management. Areas of Specialization: Sports Management.

OHIO STATE UNIVERSITY
395 DREESE LABORATIES
2015 NEIL AVE.
COLUMBUS, OH 43210-1277
614-292-5813
Fax: 614-292-2911
sportmanagement@osu.edu
www.cse.ohio-state.edu
• Catrena Collins, Human Resources Officer
• Tamera Cramer, Annual Report, Faculty Search Secretary, Depa
• Donald Havard, Fiscal Officer
• Janet Fink, Sport Management Program Coord/Prof.
(614) 292-0867
fink.26@osu.edu
• Packianathan Chelladurai, Professor
(614) 692-0816
chelladurai.1@osu.edu
• David Brown, Associate Athletic Director
• Justin Doyle, Director of Business Development
Description:
A specialization of the Sport and Exercise Sciences program in the School of Physical Activity and Educational Services, provides programs of study that will lead to Master's and doctoral degrees. Established in 1978, more than 500 alumni of the Sport Management program now hold prestigious positions in all segments of the industry and serve as athletic directors for universities, general managers of professional sport franchises, and executive directors of public

and private sport, leisure, and fitness organizations.
Degrees:
Grad Degree: M.A., Ph.D. Areas of Specialization: Collegiate Athletic Administration; Professional Sport Management; Recreation and Intramural Sport Management; Arena and Facility Management.

OHIO UNIVERSITY
DEPARTMENT OF RECREATION AND SPORT SCIENCES
GROVER CENTER E-160
ATHENS, OH 45701
740-593-4656
Fax: 740-593-0284
rsps@ohio.edu
www.hhs.ohiou.edu/
• James Kahler, Sports Administration Exec. Director
(740) 593-4666
kahler@ohio.edu
• Ming Li, Dept. Dir./Sports Admin. Assoc. Prof.
mingli@ohio.edu
• Andrew Kreutzer, Sports Administration Assoc. Professor
(740) 593-9495
kreutzer@ohio.edu
• Andrew Agro, National Sports Forum (NSF) Competition
• AJ Andrassy, National Sports Forum (NSF) Competition
• David Bamford, National Sports Forum (NSF) Competition
Description:
One of the few undergraduate programs in the United State that have received program approval from the Sport Management Program Review Council. The curriculum provides the student with academic preparation and practical training required for success in such career fields as professional sport, college athletics, youth sports, or corporate positions with a sport-related component. Related areas to the sport industry include facility management, sport promotion and marketing, sport media, customer or community relations, sport sponsorship, licensing, sport information and sport law.
Degrees:
Grad Degree: Master in Sports Administration. Areas of Specialization: Sports Administration, Facility Management. Dual Degree of M.B.A./M.S.A. Joint Degree with The Capital University Law Center; M.S.A/J.D.
Requirements:
See web site for list.

OKLAHOMA STATE UNIVERSITY
DEPARTMENT OF MANAGEMENT
320 SPEARS SCHOOL OF BUSINESS
STILLWATER, OK 74078-5070
405-744-5201
Fax: 405-744-5180
mgmt@okstate.edu
www.spears.okstate.edu/management
• Ken Eastman, Dept. Head/Associate Professor
(405) 744-5201
ken.eastman@okstate.edu
Description:
Undergrad Degree: B.S. Health, Phys Ed & Leisure. Grad Degree: M.S., Ed.D. Health, Phys Ed & Leisure. Areas of Specialization:

Undergrad: Sport Science. Grad: Sport Administration, Exercise Science, Adapted Phys Ed, Pedagogy.

OKLAHOMA, UNIVERSITY OF
DEPARTMENT OF HEALTH AND EXERCISE SCIENCE
633 ELM AVENUE
NORMAN, OK 73019-3118
405-325-2077
Fax: 405-325-7709
cas@ou.edu
• Laurette Taylor, Dept. Chairperson
etaylor@ou.edu
• Paul Bell, Dean and Vice Provost for Instruction
(405) 325-2077
pbell@ou.edu
• Sharron Oelke, Assistant to the Dean
(405) 325-4303
soelke@ou.edu
• Edward Sankowski, Associate Dean
(405) 325-0321
esankowski@ou.edu
• Kelly Damphousse, Associate Dean
(405) 325-2529
kdamp@ou.edu
• Gail Brown, Administrative Assistant
(405) 325-2077
gtbrown@ou.edu
• David Quirk, Director of Development
(405) 325-3724
dquirk@ou.edu
Description:
An interdisciplinary program integrating the study of legal aspects within sport, marketing, management and promotion of sport as a business, and the study of the behavioral aspects of management and leadership.
Degrees:
Undergrad Degree: (1) Sports Sciences, (2) Health Promotion. Grad Degree: M.S. Areas of Specialization: Sport Management; Sport Marketing; Sport Psychology; Exercise Physiology, Health Promotion.

OLD DOMINION UNIVERSITY
STUDENT RECREATION CENTER
ROOM 2025
NORFOLK, VA 23529
757-683-5962
Fax: 757-683-4270
rcase@odu.edu
www.odu.edu/sprtmgt
• Robert Case, Graduate Program Director
(757) 683-5962
rcase@odu.edu
• Lynn Ridinger, Undergraduate Program Coordinator
(757) 683-4353
lridinge@odu.edu
Degrees Offered:
Undergrad Degree: B.S. Grad Degree: M.S. in Physical Education with emphasis on Sport Management.

OREGON, UNIVERSITY OF/ WARSAW SPORTS MARKETING CENTER
LUNDQUIST COLLEGE OF BUSINESS
1208 UNIVERSITY OF OREGON
EUGENE, OR 97403-1208
541-346-3495
Fax: 541-346-3341
www.warsawcenter.com
• Paul Swangard, Director
• Dennis Howard, Professor

Degrees/Majors offered:
B.A., M.B.A., and Ph.D. business administration with a sports business concentration.

PACIFIC CHRISTIAN
PHYS ED DEPT
2500 E. NUTWOOD AVE
FULLERTON, CA 92631
909-879-3901
Fax: 909-526-0231

PACIFIC, UNIVERSITY OF THE
SPORT MANAGEMENT PROGRAM
C/O SPORT SCIENCES DEPT
3601 PACIFIC AVE
STOCKTON, CA 95211
209-946-2531
Fax: 209-946-3225
lkoehler@uop.edu
• Linda S. Koehler, Coordinator Sports Management
(209) 946-2531
lkoehler@uop.edu
• Linda Lyman, Director
(209) 946-2531
llyman@pacific.edu
Degrees/Majors offered:
B.A. sport sciences concentrations: sport management, pedagogy, athletics training, sports medicine.

PALM BEACH ATLANTIC UNIVERSITY
SPORT MANAGEMENT
901 S. FLAGER DRIVE
PO BOX 24708
WEST PALM BEACH, FL 33416
561-803-2450
Fax: 561-803-2455
www.pba.edu/athletics
• Robert Myers, Dept. Dean
Robert_Myers@pba.edu
• Ed Langlois, MBA Program Director
Ed_Langlois@pba.edu
• Susan Williams, Secretary
Susan_Williams@pba.edu
Description:
Sport Management involves applying the management principles of planning, organizing, leading, and directing to the unique industry of sport. Emphasis is placed on the production, facilitation, promotion, and organization of sport products.

PENN STATE UNIVERSITY/PGA SANCTIONED GOLF MANAGEMENT PROGRAM
201 MATEER BUILDING
UNIVERSITY PARK, PA 16802
814-863-7000
Fax: 814-863-4257
www.psu.edu
Year Founded:
1991
Description:
Prepares undergraduate students for a career in professional golf management. Entrance Requirements: Meet university requirements plus have golf handicap of eight (8) or lower

PFEIFFER UNIVERSITY
48380 US HIGHWAY 52 NORTH
MISENHEIMER, NC 28109
704-463-1360
800-338-2060

Fax: 704-463-1363
gofalconsports.com
• Jack Ingram, Chair/Director
Description:
B.A. sports management.

POINT PARK UNIVERSITY
201 Wood Street
Pittsburgh, PA 15222
412-391-4100
800-321-0129
www.pointpark.edu/athletics
• Robert D. Bunnell, Director
rbunnell@pointpark.edu
Degree/Majors Offered:
B.S. sport, arts and entertainment management.

PRINCIPIA COLLEGE
SPORT MANAGEMENT
1 MAYBECK PLACE
ELSAH, IL 62028
618-374-2131
Fax: 618-374-5221
www.principia.edu
• Lee Ellis, Atletic Director
(618) 374-5030
lee.ellis@principia.edu
Degree Offered:
BA in Sports Management.

QUINCY UNIVERSITY
1800 COLLEGE AVE
QUINCY, IL 62301-2699
217-228-8020
Fax: 217-228-5034
• Ivan Paul, Sport Management Program Director
Description:
This four-year undergraduate program leads to the Bachelor of Science degree in Sport Management. The sports management curriculum is designed to prepare students for a variety of exciting careers. Growth in professional sports, intercollegiate athletics, recreation, corporate fitness, private health clubs, sports broadcasting and writing, and a constant media exposure combine to make sports management a diverse and dynamic field.

RADFORD UNIVERSTIY
PHYSICAL AND HEALTH EDUCATION
PO BOX 6957
RADFORD, VA 24142
540-831-6650
Fax: 540-831-6650
www.ruhighlanders.com
• Bev Zeakes, Dept. Chairperson
(540) 831-5305
• April Hunt, Dept. Administrator
• Brent Chumbley, Men's & Women's Cross Country/Track & Field C
schumbley@radford.edu
• Marci Jenkins, Women's Volleyball Head Coach
(540) 831-5879
mtjenkins@radford.edu
Degrees Offered:
M.S. Research Areas: Sports Science Sports Administration Coaching Education Physical Education Pedagogy

RICE UNIVERSITY
DEPARTMENT OF HP & HS
6100 MAIN ST
HOUSTON, TX 77005-1892
713-527-4077
Fax: 713-527-6019
www.sport.rice.edu
• Harmon Gallant, Sport Management Director
• Clark Haptonstall, Director
Description:
B.A. in sport management.

ROBERT MORRIS UNIVERSITY
DEPARTMENT OF SPORT ADMINISTRATION
6001 UNIVERSITY BOULEVARD
MOON TOWNSHIP, PA 15108-1189
412-262-8416
800-762-0097
Fax: 412-262-8494
synowka@rmu.edu
www.rmu.edu
• David Synowka, Chairman/Program Head Sports Management
synowka@rmu.edu
Degrees Offered:
B.S. business administration; M.S. sport management; M.B.A., concentration in sport management.

RUTGERS
70 Lipman Drive
New Brunswick, NJ 08901-8525
848-932-9525
Fax: 732-932-9151
www.exsci.rutgers.edu
• Jan Houtman, Administrative Assistant
Degrees/Majors Offered:
B.S. exercise science and sports studies, sport management option.

SACRED HEART UNIVERSITY
JOHN F. WELCH COLLEGE OF BUSINESS
5151 PARK AVE
FAIRFIELD, CT 06825-1000
203-371-7999
Fax: 203-365-7538
santomierj@sacredheart.edu
www.sacredheart.edu
• Joshua Shuart, Ph.D., Chair, Department of Marketing & Sport Manage
(203) 416-3601
sportmanagement@sacredheart.edu
Degree Offered
B.S. Sport Management
Curriculum:
The Sport Management curriculum provides a theoretical and skill-based framework in core business disciplines, functional business skills and in specific sport management areas. Focus is on the financial, marketing, media, legal and ethical dimensions of sport management. The program provides students with dynamic internship opportunities.

SALEM STATE COLLEGE
352 Lafayette Street
Salem, MA 1970
978-542-6000
www.salemstate.edu/athletics
• Stuart G McMahon, Director
smcmahon@salemstate.edu
Degrees/Majors Offered:
B.S. sport, fitness and leisure studies with a concentration in sport management.

college sports

431

SAN FRANCISCO, UNIVERSITY OF
WAR MEMORIAL GYMNASIUM
2130 FULTON STREET
SAN FRANCISCO, CA 94117-1080
415-422-6891
Fax: 415-422-2510
sfm@usfca.edu
www.usfdons.com
• Scott Sidwell, Director of Athletics
(415) 422-6893
sasidwell@usfca.edu
• Nino Giarrantano, Baseball Head Coach
(415) 422-2934
giarrantano@usfca.edu
• Rex Walters, Men's Baskebtall Head
Coach
Degrees/Majors offered:
M.A. sport management.

SAN JOSE STATE UNIVERSITY
DEPARTMENT OF HUMAN
PERFORMANCE
1 WASHINGTON SQUARE
SAN JOSE, CA 95192-0054
408-924-3019
Fax: 408-924-3053
www2.sjsu.edu/depts/hup/SM/
• Mark Nagel, Chairman
(408) 924-3019
• Tracy Spencer, Athletic Ticket Manager
• Sonja Lilienthal, Director
Description:
B.S., and M.A. in kinesiology, and emphasis
in sport management.

SEATTLE PACIFIC UNIVERSITY
DEPARTMENT OF PHYSICAL
EDUCATION & EXERCISE SCIENCE
3307-3RD AVENUE W.
SEATTLE, WA 98119
206-281-2081
Fax: 206-281-2784
wndnh2o@spu.edu
www.spu.edu/depts/pe
• Dan Tripps, Dept. Chairperson
dtripps@spu.edu
Description:
Undergrad Degree: B.A. Physical Education,
B.S. Exercise Science; Grad Degree: M.A.
Sport and Exercise Leadership.

SETON HALL UNIVERSITY
SETON HALL ATHLETICS
400 SOUTH ORANGE AVENUE
REGAN ATHLETICS CENTER
SOUTH ORANGE, NJ 07079-2692
973-761-9498
Fax: 973-761-9675
www.shupirates.com
Degrees Offered:
B.S., B.A. with a concentration in sport
management; M.B.A. with a concentration in
sport management; joint M.B.A./J.D. sport
management/sport and entertainment law;
postgraduate certificate sport management.

SHAWNEE STATE UNIVERSITY
ATHLETICS DEPARTMENT
940 SECOND STREET
PORTSMOUTH, OH 45662
740-351-4778
srader@shawnee.edu
www.ssubears.com

SHEPHERD UNIVERSITY
PO BOX 3210
SHEPHERDSTOWN, WV 25443
304-876-5000
800-344-5231
Fax: 304-876-3101
www.shepherd.edu/athletics
• Matthew McIntosh, Chair/Director
mmcintos@shepherd.edu
Description:
Recreation and leisure studies, sport and
event management, commercial recreation
and tourism, sport communication,
therapeutic recreation, fitness/exercise
science, health and physical education
teacher education.

SIENA HEIGHTS UNIVERSITY
BUSINESS AND MANAGEMENT DIVISION
1247 E. SIENA HEIGHTS DRIVE
ADRIAN, MI 49221
517-264-7624
• Mary Beth Leibold, Sport Management
Program Coordinator
Description:
The field of sport has experienced
phenomenal growth; thus, this is an
excellent time for students to pursue an
academic degree that will allow them to
specialize in the area of sport management.
Through a curriculum that includes both
theoretical foundations of sport and practical
experience opportunities, Siena Heights
University's Sport Management Program is
designed to provide students with this
specialization which will provide them an
opportunity to compete for a highly
competitive and exciting careers in sport.

SLIPPERY ROCK UNIVERSITY
WEST GYM, #224
C/O SPORT MANAGEMENT
COORDINATOR
SLIPPERY ROCK, PA 16057
724-738-2967
Fax: 724-738-4858
www.rockathletics.com
• Robin Ammon, Jr., Director
(724) 738-2967
robert.ammon@sru.edu
• Robertha A. Abney, Associate Professor
robertha.abney@sru.edu
• Catriana Higgs, Professor
• Jeff Messer, Assistant Professor
jeffrey.messer@sru.edu
• Brian Crow, Assistant Professor
Degrees Offered:
Undergrad Degree: B.S. in Sport
Management; Grad Degree: M.S. in Sport
Management.

SOUTH CAROLINA, UNIVERSITY OF
DEPARTMENT OF SPORT &
ENTERTAINMENT MANAGEMENT
COLLEGE OF HOSPITALITY, RETAIL AND
SPORTS MANAGEMENT
CAROLINA COLISEUM, ROOM 2012
COLUMBIA, SC 29208
803-777-4690
Fax: 803-777-8788
www.hrsm.sc.edu
• Thomas Regan, Dept. Chairperson
(803) 777-4690
regan@gwm.sc.edu
• Matthew Bernthal, Dept. Associate
Professor
• Peter Graham, Dept. Professor

Description:
Master's in sport and entertainment
management, with an emphasis in public
assembly facility management and live
entertainment; B.S. sport and entertainment
management.

SOUTHEAST MISSOURI STATE
UNIVERSITY
DEPARTMENT OF HEALTH, HUMAN
PERFORMANCE & RECREATION
1 UNIVERSITY PLAZA
Cape Girardeau, MO 63701
573-651-2197
Fax: 573-651-5150
www.semo.edu/athletics
• Beth Easter, Sport Management Program
Director
(573) 986-6744
baeaster@semo.edu
• Joseph Pujol, Dept. Chairperson
(573) 651-2664
jpujol@semo.edu
Description:
The Sport Management program at
Southeast Missouri State University is the
only sport management of its kind in
Missouri. Sport Management is a field of
study preparing students to work in the sport
industry. Our program combines sport
specific courses with a business
administration minor. The curriculum is
designed to meet the curricular guidelines
for sport management established by
professional organizations
Degree/Majors Offered:
B.S. sport management with a minor in
business administration, M.A. higher
education with option in athletics
administration.

SOUTHEASTERN LOUISIANA
UNIVERSITY
DEPARTMENT OF KINESIOLOGY AND
HEALTH STUDIES
TENNESSEE AVENUE
SLU 10845
HAMMOND, LA 70402
985-549-2130
800-222-7358
Fax: 985-549-5119
www.selu.edu
• Eddie Hebert, Dept. Head/Associate
Professor
(985) 549-2130
ehebert@selu.edu
• Linda Synovitz, Graduate Coordinator
(985) 549-3867
Description:
Undergrad Degree: B.A. Grad Degree: M.A.
Areas of Specialization: Undergrad:
Non-teaching Phys Ed degree in which
students can choose alternate career
options in Sport Management,
Health/Fitness Promotion. Grad: Health
Promotion, Exercise Science.

SOUTHERN ILLINOIS UNIVERSITY AT
EDWARDSVILLE
KINESIOLOGY AND HEALTH EDUCATION
SPORT MANAGEMENT
VADALABENE CENTER 1126
EDWARDSVILLE, IL 62026-1126
618-650-3252
Fax: 618-650-3369
dbruegg@siue.edu
www.siusalukis.com

• Bill Vogler, Dept. Chairperson
(618) 650-2984
wvogler@siue.edu
• John Baker, Sport Management Program
Coordinator
(618) 650-3028
jobaker@siue.edu
• David Ray, Wrestling Head Coach
(618) 650-2949
daray@siue.edu
Description:
Prepares students with management skills
for careers as administrators in athletics
programs, physical education departments,
community recreation programs, and for
management positions in the burgeoning
sport industry.
Degrees Offered:
M.S.Ed. Kinesiology; Research Areas:
Exercise, Sport, Health and Rehabilitation
Psychology, Exercise Physiology, Sport
Administration/Management

SOUTHERN MISSISSIPPI, UNIVERSITY OF
DEPARTMENT HUMAN PERFORMANCE
AND RECREATION
118 COLLEGE DRIVE
HATTIESBURG, MS 39406-5142
601-266-6085
Fax: 601-266-4445
www.usm.edu/hpr
• Lou Marciani, Dept. School Director
lou.marciani@usm.edu
• Matthew Wilson, Sport Management
Assistant Professor
matthew.j.wilson@usm.edu
• Benito Velasquez, Dept. Assistant Director
benito.velasquez@usm.edu
Description:
Undergrad Degree: B.S. Grad Degree: M.S.
Areas of Specialization: Undergrad:
Coaching; Sports Administration; Fitness
Management; Strength Training &
Conditioning. Grad: Sports Administration,
Fitness Management; Strength Training and
Conditioning Coach, and Coaching
Education options.
Marketing Partner
International Sports Properties Inc.

SOUTHERN NEW HAMPSHIRE UNIVERSITY
SCHOOL OF BUSINESS
2500 N. RIVER RD
MANCHESTER, NH 03106-1045
603-644-3145
Fax: 603-629-4693
d.blais@snhu.edu
www.snhu.edu/athletics
• Doug Blais, Ph.d., Professor & Chair,
Sport Management Department
(603) 644-3145
d.blais@snhu.edu
• Deb Robitaille, Softball Head Coach
(603) 645-9776
d.robitaille@snhu.edu
• Greg Coache, Men's & Women's Tennis
Head Coach
(603) 645-9741
g.coache@snhu.edu
• Peter Viteritti, Volleyball Head Coach
(603) 645-9764
p.viteritti@snhu.edu
Degrees Offered:
B.S. Sport Management, B.S. Business
Studies with a concentration in Sport
Managament; M.B.A. with a certificate in

Sport Administration, M.S. Sport
Management.

SOUTHWEST MISSOURI STATE UNIVERSITY
901 South National
Springfield, MO 65804
417-836-5000
• Philip Rothschild, Director
pcr259f@smsu.edu
Degree/Majors Offered:
B.S. entertainment management.

SPRING ARBOR COLLEGE
DEPT OF EXER & SPORT SCIENCE
106 E. MAIN ST
SPRING ARBOR, MI 49283
517-750-6508
800-968-0011
Fax: 517-750-2745
www.arbor.edu
• Ted Comden, Chairman
Description:
Undergrad Degree: B.A. Areas of
Specialization: Sports Administration,
Fitness Management.

SPRINGFIELD COLLEGE
263 ALDEN ST
SPRINGFIELD, MA 01109-3797
413-748-3332
Fax: 413-748-3855
• Ronald Ziemba, Director Marketing
• Matthew J. Pantera, Chair/Director
• Dana M. Riefer, Assistant Director
Athletics
• Charles Redmond,
(413) 748-3231
• Susan Langlois,
(413) 748-3809
Description:
Undergrad Degree: B.S., concentration in
Phys Ed or Sport Management. Grad
Degree: M.Ed., M.P.E., or M.S. Areas of
Specialization: Sport Management/Athlete
Administration.

ST. CLOUD STATE UNIVERSITY
329 HALENBECK HALL
720 FOURTH AVENUE S.
ST. CLOUD, MN 56301-4498
320-308-3102
Fax: 320-308-6146
hperss@stcloudstate.edu
Degree Offered:
M.S. Sports Management

ST. EDWARDS UNIVERSITY
SCHOOL OF MANAGEMENT AND
BUSINESS
3001 S. CONGRESS AVENUE
TRUSTEE HALL 1049
AUSTIN, TX 78704
512-448-8400
Fax: 512-448-1975
www.stedwards.edu/athletics
• Marsha Kelliher, Dean of School
Management & Business
• Donna Goodner, Administrative
Coordinator
(512) 448-8593
Description:
The Sports Management Concentration
provides students who are interested in
sport related organizations with the
opportunity to learn the skills necessary to

manage in either the private or public sector.
This concentration is made up of four
courses that familiarize students with the
theoretical and practical implications of the
management, marketing, legal, and ethical
aspects of sports. The scope of sports
management in this context includes small
public schools' athletic departments, startup
entrepreneurial ventures, professional
sports, and the larger sports industry.

ST. JOHN FISHER COLLEGE
3690 EAST AVE
ROCHESTER, NY 14618
585-385-8441
Fax: 585-385-7311
tharrison@sjfc.edu
• Todd Harrison, Program Chair, Sport
Management Dept.
(585) 385-8441
tharrison@sjfc.edu
Degree Offered:
B.S. in Sport Management
Curriculum:
The Sport Studies Department seeks to
develop in students the knowledge, skills
and experience that will enable them to
obtain leadership positions in the sport
management field. Serving students directly
and the sport management industry
indirectly, the department provides a
broad-based curriculum that is grounded in
the liberal arts and encourages critical
analysis of the cultural and social
significance of sport, the need for ethical
and moral decision-making and the role of
sport as a business.

ST. JOHN'S UNIVERSITY
SPORT MANAGEMENT PROGRAM
201 BRENT HALL
8000 UTOPIA PARKWAY
JAMAICA, NY 11439
718-390-4449
misserea@stjohns.edu
www.stjohns.edu
• Anthony Missere, Chairperson/Sport
Mgmt. Program Dir.
(718) 990-7391
misserea@stjohns.edu
• Carol Fletcher, Sports Management
Assistant Professor
Description:
The program in sport management at St.
John's University leads to a Bachelor of
Science degree and is available on both the
Queens and Staten Island campuses. Sport
management also offers a certificate
program which is open to individuals who
have completed a bachelor's degree in an
unrelated area.
Degrees Offered:
B.S. sport management.

ST. LEO UNIVERSITY
DIV OF PROFESSIONAL STUDIES/MC
2067
33701 STATE ROAD 52
ST. LEO, FL 33574
352-588-8304
Fax: 352-588-8289
tphillip@saintleo.edu
www.saintleo.edu
• Stewart Gillman, Program Chair
stewart.gillman@saintleo.edu
• Susan Brown Foster, Chair/Director
susan.foster@saintleo.edu

Degrees Offered:
Undergrad Degree: B.A. Areas of Specialization: Sports Management, Physical Education-Teaching and B.S. sport management.

ST. THOMAS UNIVERSITY
16401 NW 37TH AVE
MIAMI GARDENS, FL 33054
305-628-6634
800-367-9010
800 367-9006
Fax: 305-628-6790
spo-ad@stu.edu
www.stu.edu
• Jan Bell, Director
(305) 628-6634
jbell@stu.edu
• Ted Abernethy, Undergraduate Program Coordinator
(305) 628-6630
tabernet@stu.edu
• Seok-Ho Song, Assistant Professor
(305) 474-6909
ssong@stu.edu
Description:
St. Thomas University offers an academic major in sports administration that prepares students to work in the business aspects of sports.

STETSON UNIVESITY
421 NORTH WOODLAND BOULEVARD
DELAND, FL 32723
386-822-7100
800-688-0101
admissions@stetson.edu
www.stetson.edu/athletics
• Michele Skelton, Chair/Director
Description:
B.A. sport management

SUNY, STATE UNIVERSITY OF NEW YORK-BROCKPORT
DEPARTMENT OF PHYSICAL EDUCATION & SPORT
TUTTLE N. 212
350 NEW CAMPUS DRIVE
BROCKPORT, NY 14420
585-395-5332
Fax: 585-395-2771
• William Stier, Director: Athletic Admin/Sport Mgmt & Coaching Edu
(585) 395-5331
• Susan Peterson, Department Chair
(585) 395-5332
Departments:
Kinesiology, Sports Studies, and Physical Education
Description:
Degrees in: Sports, Sports Management, Aports Health, Physical Education, Athletic Administration; BS in Sports Management, Ed.M. Physical Education/Athletic Administration; online degree options.

SUNY, STATE UNIVERSITY OF NEW YORK-CORTLAND
PO BOX 2000-PARK P.E.R. CENTER
CORTLAND, NY 13045
607-753-4953
Fax: 607-753-4929
www.cortland.edu
• Suzanne Wingate, Coordinator
• Ted Fay, Chair/Director
fayt@cortland.edu

Description:
B.S., B.A. sport management.

TAMPA, UNIVERSITY OF
DEPARTMENT OF EXERCISE SCIENCE AND SPORT STUDIES
401 W. KENNEDY BOULEVARD
TAMPA, FL 33606
813-253-3333
Fax: 813-253-6288
www.ut.edu
• Robert Birrenkott, Dept. Associate Professor
(813) 253-3333
rbirrenkott@ut.edu
• Eric Vlahov, Dept. Chairperson
(813) 253-3333
evlahov@ut.edu
• Jay Jisha, Sports Management Assistant Professor
(813) 253-3333
jjisha@ut.edu
Description:
Sport management trains new professionals in a variety of sport business fields. This is the choice for those who crave the excitement of front office positions with professional sports teams or the busy world of stadium and arena management.
Degrees Offered:
Undergrad Degree: B.A. sports management.

TEMPLE UNIVERSITY
SPORT AND RECREATION MANAGEMENT
1700 N. BROAD STREET
PHILADELPHIA, PA 19122
215-204-8701
Fax: 215-204-8705
jeffrey.montague@temple.edu
• Ira Shapiro, Dept. Chairperson
(215) 204-6295
• Jeff Montague, Undergraduate Coordinator/Asst. Dean
(215) 204-8701
jeffrey.montague@temple.edu
• Michael Jackson, Graduate Program Dir. in Sport Admin.
Degrees Offered:
BS, Sport and Recreation Management; M.Ed, Sport and Recreation Administration.

TENNESSEE STATE UNIVERSITY
DEPARTMENT OF HUMAN PERFORMANCE & SPORT SCIENCES
3500 JOHN A MERRITT BLVD
NASHVILLE, TN 37209-1561
615-963-5000
Fax: 615-963-5594
www.tnstate.edu
• Catana Starks, Dept. Acting Chairperson/Professor
cstarks@tnstate.edu
• James Bass, Assistant Professor
jbass@tnstate.edu

TENNESSEE, KNOXVILLE, UNIVERSITY OF
DEPARTMENT OF EXERCISE, SPORT AND LEISURE STUDIES
1914 ANDY HOLT AVENUE
KNOXVILLE, TN 37996-2700
865-974-1282
Fax: 865-974-8981
desensi@utk.edu
www.coe.utk.edu

• Joy DeSensi, Dept. Head/Professor
desensi@utk.edu
• David Bassett, Professor
(865) 974-8766
dbassett@utk.edu
• Frankie Stroud, Dept. Receptionist/Senior Secretary
fstroud@utk.edu

TENNESSEE-CHATTANOOGA, UNIVERSITY OF
CHATTANOOGA ATHLETICS
615 MCCALLIE AVE., DEPT3505
CHATTANOOGA, TN 37403-2598
423-425-4323
Fax: 423-425-4457
www.gomocs.com
• Rick Hart, Director of Intercollegiate Athletics
(423) 425-2270
Rick-Hart@utc.edu
Description:
B.S. Sport Management.

TEXAS A&M UNIVERSITY
DEPARTMENT OF HEALTH & KINESIOLOGY
TAMU 4243
COLLEGE STATION, TX 77845
979-845-3109
Fax: 979-847-8987
info@hlkn.tamu.edu
• Stephen Crouse, Dept. Head/Chairperson/Professor
s-crouse@tamu.edu
• Michael Sagas, Sports Management Assistant Professor
msagas@hlkn.tamu.edu
Description:
This specialization prepares students for teaching and research careers in sport management. Graduates are trained for post-doctoral appointments and positions in universities, industry, and research institutions. The program prepares students to conduct research in applied and basic areas of sport management.
Degrees Offered:
Undergrad Degree: B. S. in Kinesiolgy with specialization in Sport Management. Grad Degree: M.S., and Ph.D. in Kinesiology with specialization in Sport Management.

TEXAS AT AUSTIN, UNIVERSITY OF
DEPARTMENT OF KINESIOLOGY AND HEALTH EDUCATION
SPORT MANAGEMENT
BELLMONT 222
AUSTIN, TX 78712
512-471-1273
Fax: 512-471-8914
education.utexas.edu/departments/kinesiology-health-education
• John Ivy, Dept. Chairperson
(512) 471-1273
johnivy@mail.utexas.edu
• Laurence Chalip, Ph.D, Sport Management Program Coordinator
(512) 232-2373
• Phillip Salazar, Graduate Program Coordinator
(512) 232-6015
• Richard Hogeda, Graduate Program Coordinator
(512) 471-1273
rhogeda1@mail.utexas.edu

Description:
An outstanding faculty and curriculum prepare graduates for work in the growing sport industry. Many graduates from the Sport Management program at The University of Texas at Austin have enjoyed prosperous careers in all levels of sport, both in the United States and internationally. These alumni, along with several other experienced sport administrators connected to the program, serve as a valuable network for both graduate and undergraduate students studying Sport Management.

Degrees Offered:
BS, MA, M.Ed, Ph.D. in kinesiology with a major in sport management.

TEXAS WESLEYAN UNIVERSITY
DEPARTMENT OF EXERCISE AND
SPORTS STUDIES
1201 WESLEYAN STREET
FT. WORTH, TX 76105
817-531-4964
Fax: 817-531-4208
• Karen Denny Wallace, Dept. Assistant
Professor
kwallace@txwes.edu
• Albert Peters, Exercise Sports Studies
Professor
apeters@txwes.edu
Description:
Undergrad Degree: B.S. Areas of
Specialization: Sports Management
Teaching.

**THE COLLEGE AT BROCKPORT STATE
UNIVERSITY OF NEW YORK**
SCHOOL OF HEALTH AND HUMAN
PERFORMANCE
350 NEW CAMPUS DRIVE
BROCKPORT, NY 14420-2989
585-395-5332
Fax: 585-395-2771
www.brockport.edu/athletics
• Susan C Peterson, Ed.D., Associate
Professor & Chair
(585) 395-5341
speterse@brockport.edu
• Cathy Houston-Wilson, Associate
Department Chairperson
(585) 395-5352
chouston@brockport.edu
Degree Offered:
The Kinesiology, Sport Studies and Physical
Education Department supports five majors:
Athletic Training, Exercise Physiology,
Kinesiology, Physical Education Teacher
Education and Sport Management. Two
concentrations include: Adapted Physical
Education and Sport Management -
Coaching

TIFFIN UNIVERSITY
SCHOOL OF BUSINESS DEPARTMENT
155 MIAMI STREET
TIFFIN, OH 44883
419-448-3423
800-YOU-OHIO
Fax: 419-443-5007
www.tiffin.edu
• Debra Gatton, Dept. Chairperson
(419) 488-3307
• Paul Marion, President
• Lillian Drimmer, Associate Professor of
Management
(419) 488-5688
• Bonnie Tiell, Sports Management

Instructor
(419) 488-3261
btiell@tiffin.edu
Description:
Undergrad Degree: B.S. in Bus Adm. Grad
Degree: MBA. Areas of Specialization: Sport
Management.

**TOMPKINS CORTLAND COMMUNITY
COLLEGE**
SPORT MANAGEMENT PROGRAM
170 N. STREET
PO BOX 139
DRYDEN, NY 13053
607-844-8211
888-567-8211
Fax: 607-844-9665
• Kevin Haverlock, Business Dept.
Chairperson
• Larry Chase, Sport Management Program
Coordinator
Description:
The A.S. degree in Sport Management
provides an overview of the sports industry,
with emphasis on business and the liberal
arts, sports information, and media relations.
The program includes a two-credit practicum
involving supervised work experiences in
game and event administration. Course
work also includes a foundation in
accounting, finance, management,
marketing, and economics and general
education course work in the arts,
communication, computer applications,
history, humanities, mathematics, natural
sciences, and the social sciences.
Degrees/Majors Offered:
A.S. sport management.

TOWSON STATE UNIVERSITY
DEPARTMENT OF KINESIOLOGY
8000 YORK ROAD
TOWSON, MD 2000
410-704-2384
Fax: 410-830-4322
• Vince Angotti, Sports Management
Program Coordinator
(410) 704-2384
• Gaul Parr, Associate Professor
gparr@towson.edu
Description:
Undergrad Degree: B.S. Areas of
Specialization: Sport Studies; Sport
Management; Sports Communications.

TULANE LAW SCHOOL
SPORTS LAW PROGRAM
6329 FERET STREET
NEW ORLEANS, LA 70118-6231
504-862-8826
Fax: 504-865-6748
www.law.tulane.edu
• Gary Roberts, Law Program Director
Degree Offered
JD with a certificate in Sports Law

UNITED STATES SPORTS ACADEMY
ONE ACADEMY DRIVE
DAPHNE, AL 36526-7055
251-626-3303
800-223-2668
Fax: 251-625-1035
admissions@ussa.edu
www.ussa.edu
• Thomas Rosandich, President
(251) 626-3303
president@ussa.edu

• Andrea Jordan, Assistant Dean of
Administration and Finance
(261) 626-3303
ajordan@ussa.edu
• Annita Alldredge, Finance Director
(261) 626-3303
Description:
An independent, non-profit, special mission
school offering sport-specific residential and
online distance learning programs to
students, teachers and administrators
around the world.
Description:
Provides a wide range of services including:
facility consulting to marketing equipment
packages domestically and internationally;
fitness-related programs including cardio
risk assessment, nutritional analysis and
other types of health-related programs.
Year Founded:
1972

**UNIVERSITY OF ALABAMA - COLLEGE
OF EDUCATION/ HUMAN
ENVIRONMENTAL SCIENCES**
DEPARTMENT OF HUMAN STUDIES
901 13TH STREET SOUTH
BIRMINGHAM, AL 35294-1250
205-934-4642
Fax: 205-975-8040
act@uab.edu
www.uab.edu
• David Macrina, Human Studies Professor
dmacrina@uab.edu
• Retta Evens, Health Education
• larry Tyson, Counceler Education
• Loucrecia Collins, Educational Leadership
• Andre McKnight, Educational Foundations
• Maxie Kohler, Educational Psychology and
Research
• Donna Hester, Physical Education
Program Coordinator
(205) 934-8336
dhester@uab.edu
Description:
College of Education- Master of Arts in
Human Performance, emphasis in Sport
Management; College of Human
Environmental Sciences- Master of Science,
General Studies in HES, Sport Management

UNIVERSITY OF DALLAS
GRADUATE SCHOOL OF MANAGEMENT
1845 E. NORTHGATE DRIVE
IRVING, TX 75062
972-721-5007
www.udallas.edu/gsm
• Scott Wysong, Ph.D., Department Chair
(972) 721-5007
Description:
Our unique program combines the
managerial knowledge to work in both the
sports and entertainment industries by using
a combination of full-time faculty with
academic expertise and part-time faculty
with industry experience. Our program
liberates students from the idea that work is
never fun.
Degrees Offered:
MBA, MS-MBA, MM and a Graduate
Certificate Program in Sports and
Entertainment Management.

UNIVERSITY OF DELAWARE
Newark, DE 19716
302-831-2000
www.udel.edu/athletics

• Matthew J Robinson, Director
mjrobins@udel.edu
Degree/Majors Offered:
Undergraduates degree in health behavior
management, with a concentration in sport
management.

UNIVERSITY OF MOUNT UNION
ATHLETICS
1972 CLARK AVENUE
ALLIANCE, OH 44601
330-823-4880
www.mountunion.edu
• Ronald Mendel, Chair of Human
Performance/Sport Business Dept.
(330) 823-4765
mendelrw@mountunion.edu

UNIVERSITY OF NEBRASKA KEARNEY
DEPARTMENT OF HEALTH, PE,
RECREATION & LEISURE STUDIES
905 W. 25TH STREET
KEARNEY, NE 68849
308-865-8331
Fax: 308-865-8073
unruhnc@unk.edu
www.unk.edu/acad/hperls
• Nita Unruh, Department Chair
Description:
The Sports Administration major is a
business oriented program designed for
individuals who desires a career in the
business side of sports. Students complete
a set of comprehensive courses including
sport psychology and sociology, sport law,
sport marketing, organization and
administration of sport and financing sport,
as well as an array of business courses. We
strongly encourage the majors to complete
an additional six business courses which
would qualify them for a business
administration major to compliment their
Sports Administration Major.
Degree/Majors Offered:
B.S. sport administration, B.S. sports
administration comprehensive, master's in
general physical education.

UNIVERSITY OF NEW ENGLAND
DEPARTMENT OF EXERCISE AND
SPORT PERFORMANCE
11 HILLS BEACH ROAD
BIDDEFORD, ME 4005
207-283-0171
Fax: 207-602-5900
• Richard LaRue, Dept. Chairperson/Sport
Mgmt. Coord.
(207) 602-2605
• Wayne Lamarre, Assistant Professor
(207) 602-2412
Degrees/Majors Offered:
B.S. sport management, athletics training
education, and exercise and health
promotion.

UNIVERSITY OF WEST GEORGIA
DEPARTMENT OF PHYSICAL
EDUCATION & RECREATION
1600 MAPLE STREET
CARROLLTON, GA 30118
678-839-6530
Fax: 678-839-6195
• Frank Butts, Department Chair, Associate
Professor
• Leigh Ann Bussell, Assistant Professor
• Courtney Flowers, Assistant Professor

Description:
This course provides an overview of basic
knowledge areas for the successful sport
manager. Fundamental sports management
principles and key skills as well as
information on current issues are
emphasized.

VALPARAISO UNIVERSITY
DEPARTMENT OF PHYSICAL
EDUCATION
252 ATH-REC CENTER
VALPARAISO, IN 46383
219-464-5235
Fax: 219-464-5154
www.valpo.edu
• Jerry Stieger, Ph.D, Sports Management
Program Coordinator
(219) 464-5235
jerry.stieger@valpo.edu
• Mark LaBarbera, Director of Athletics
(219) 464-6894
Mark.LaBarbera@valpo.edu
• Stephen Anthony, Associate Director of
Athletics for Business
(219) 464-5242
Stephen.Anthony@valpo.edu
• Anne VanKeppel, Associate Director of
Athletics for Marketing
(219) 464-6130
Anne.VanKeppel@valpo.edu
• Homer Drew, Associate Director of
Athletics
(219) 464-5231
Homer.Drew@valpo.edu
• john kuka, Associate Director of Athletics
(219) 464-5967
• Adam Klos, Assistant Director of Athletics
for Event Man
(219) 464-6125
Adam.Klos@valpo.edu
• Marba Paskash, Department
Administrative Assistant
(219) 464-5235
Description:
Undergrad Degree: B.S. Sports
Management. Areas of Specialization:
Athletic Administration, Facilities
Management, Fitness Management, Sports
Information, Sports Promotion, Sports
Business Management.

VIRGINIA COMMONWEALTH
UNIVERSITY
SPORTS MEDICINE BUILDING
1300 W. BROAD STREET
RICHMOND, VA 23284-3013
804-827-7821
Fax: 804-828-4938
sportscenter@vcu.edu
www.vcu.edu/sportscenter
• Richard Sander, Asst. to President &
Athletics Dir.
• Gary Ness, Sport Management Adjunct
Professor
Degree Offered:
M.S. sport leadership.

WARNER SOUTHERN COLLEGE
13895 HIGHWAY 27
LAKE WALES, FL 33859
863-638-1426
800-949-7248
Fax: 863-638-1472
www.warnerroyals.com
• Dennis Obermeyer, Chair/Director

Description:
B.A. sports management, B.A. exercise
science

WASHBURN UNIVERSITY OF TOPEKA
DEPARTMENT OF HEALTH, PHYSICAL
EDUCATION, EXERCISE SCIENCE
PETRO 201
1700 SW COLLEGE AVENUE
TOPEKA, KS 66621
785-670-1010
Fax: 785-231-1059
www.washburn.edu
• Bill Sparks, Chairman/Professor
• Susan Miller, Associate Professor
Susan.miller@washburn.edu
• Nancy Province, Department Secretary
nancy.province@washburn.edu
Description:
Undergrad Degree: B.Ed., B.A. Areas of
Specialization: Physical Education K-12
Teaching, Athletic Training, Sports Facilities
Management, Exercise Physiology.

WASHINGTON STATE UNIVERSITY
SPORT MANAGEMENT PROGRAM
COLLEGE OF EDUCATION
PO BOX 642114
PULLMAN, WA 99164-2136
509-335-1738
Fax: 509-335-0328
mc@wsu.edu
www.wsu.edu
• Jo Washburn, Program Coordinator
(509) 335-6363
jwashbur@mail.wsu.edu
• Cathryn Claussen, Associate Professor
(509) 335-7232
claussen@wsu.edu
• Judy Schultz, Instructor & Advisor
(509) 335-5672
jaschultz@wsu.edu
Description:
A sport management education provides
students with the planning and
administrative skills needed for the success
of organizations that focus on sport
activities, sport products, or sport services.
Degrees:
Under Grad, BA in Sports Management.
Grad Degree: M.A.; Ed.M. Areas of Athletic
Administration. Areas of specialization:
Business, Communications, Leadership
Studies.

WAYNE STATE COLLEGE
1111 Main Street
Wayne, NE 68787
800-228-9972
www.wsc.edu/athletics
• Tammy Evetovich, Director
Degrees:
Sport management, M.S. education in sport
management.

WAYNE STATE UNIVERSITY
DEPARTMENT OF ATHLETICS
5101 JOHN C. LODGE 101 MATTHAEI
DETROIT, MI 48202
313-577-4280
Fax: 313-577-0208
www.wsuathletics.com
• Jason Clark, Senior Assoc. Athletics
Director
jason.clark@wayne.edu
• Mary Beth Buchan, Assoc. Athletics
Director/Fiscal Operations

ay3203@wayne.edu
• Lisa Seymour, Assistant Athletics Director
aw6975@wayne.edu
• Nicole Blaszczyk, Asst. Athletics Director
for Marketing & Prom
aw4970@wayne.edu
• Jim Campbell, Supervisor, Multipurpose
Indoor Facility
soupy@wayne.edu
• Robert M. Ackerman, Faculty Athletics
Representative
ackerman@wayne.edu
• Fournier Rob, Director of Athletics
(313) 577-5996
ai5611@wayne.edu
Degrees Offered:
Grad Degree: M.A. Sports Administration.
Areas of Specialization: Interscholastic
Athletic Administration; Intercollegiate
Athletic Administration; Professional Sports
Administration; Commercial Sports Program
Administration.

WEBBER INTERNATIONAL UNIVERSITY
1201 NORTH SCENIC HIGHWAY
BABSON, FL 33827
863-638-2929
800-741-1844
Fax: 863-638-1317
registrar@webber.edu
• Thomas C Aaron, Chair/Director
tomaaron@msn.com
Description:
B.S. busness administration, concentration
in sport management;M.B.A., concentration
in sport management.

WEST CHESTER UNIVERSITY
DEPARTMENT OF KINESIOLOGY
206 STURZEBECKER HEALTH SCIENCES
CENTER
WEST CHESTER, PA 19383
610-436-2610
Fax: 610-436-2860
rzetts@wcupa.edu
• Raymond Zetts, Chairperson
(610) 436-2610
rzetts@wcupa.edu
• Diane Riley, Department Secretary
• Kendall Walkes, Mens Soccer Head
Coach
(610) 436-2221
• Bett Ann Kempf Townsley, Womens
Soccer Head Coach
(610) 436-6903
ekempf@wcupa.edu
• Diane Lokey, Softball Head Coach
(610) 436-2170
dlokey@wcupa.edu
• Jamie Ruddisill, Swimming and Diving
Head Coach
(610) 436-2127
Description:
Grad Degree: M.S. Areas of Specialization:
Physical Education; Sport and Athletic
Administration; Exercise and Sport
Physiology.

WEST VIRGINIA UNIVERSITY
COLLEGE OF PHYSICAL ACTIVITY AND
SPORT SCIENCES
PO BOX 6116
MORGANTOWN, WV 26506-6116
304-293-0861 EXT 5265
Fax: 304-293-4641
dbranch@wvu.edu
www.wvu.edu

• Dallas Branch, Jr., Sport Management
Program Coordinator
(304) 293-0861
dbranch@mail.wvu.edu
• Floyd Jones, Sport Mgmt. Undergraduate
Coordinator
(304) 293-3295
Floyd.Jones@mail.wvu.edu
• Tina Samara, Women's Tennis Head
Coach
(304) 293-9882
tina.samara@mail.wvu.edu
• Sean Cleary, Women's Track and Cross
Country
(304) 293-9875
sean.cleary@mail.wvu.edu
• Jill Kramer, Women's Volleyball Head
Coach
(304) 293-4234
Description:
Undergrad Degree: B.S. Grad Degree: M.S.
Areas of Specialization: Undergrad: Sport
Management. Grad: Sport
Management/Administration.

WESTERN CAROLINA UNIVERSITY
WESTERN CAROLINA UNIVERSITY
RAMSEY CENTER-ATHLETICS
CULLOWHEE, NC 28723
828-227-7338
Fax: 828-227-7688
www.catamountsports.com
• Randy Eaton, Director of Athletics
(828) 227-7338
jreaton@email.wcu.edu
• Bobby Moranda, Baseball Head Coach
(828) 227-7338
• Larry Hunter, Men's Basketball Head
Coach
(828) 227-7338
hunter@email.wcu.edu
Description:
B.S. sport management. Concentrations:
athletic administration, exercise science and
fitness management, event and facility
management and marketing, professional
sports management sales, sports
information.

WESTERN ILLINOIS UNIVERSITY
DEPARTMENT OF KINESIOLOGY
BROPHY HALL 212
1 UNIVERSITY CIRCLE
MACOMB, IL 61455
309-298-1981
Fax: 309-298-2981
kinesiology@wiu.edu
www.wiu.edu/kinesiology
• Janet Wigglesworth, Professor/Department
Chairperson
(309) 298-1981
• Darlene Young, Sports Management
Coordinator
(309) 298-1225
DS-Young@wiu.edu
• April Hall, Volleyball Head Coach
(309) 298-1855
ak-hall2@wiu.edu
Degree Offered:
The Master of Science degree in Sport
Management was established in 1972 and is
one of the oldest Sport Management
programs in the United States. The mission
of the degree program is to develop
students' conceptual skills, theoretical
comprehension, and practical knowledge in
order that they are prepared to become the
next generation of leaders in the sports

industry. Students finish the program ready
to embark on careers as practioners,
managers, admnistrators and
researchers/scholars. In addition, the
program at WIU provides current students
with an active and comprehensive network
of alumni working in all aspects of the sports
industry.

WESTERN MICHIGAN UNIVERSITY
DEPARTMENT OF HEALTH, PHYSICAL
EDUCATION & RECREATION
1903 W. MICHIGAN AVENUE
4024 STUDENT RECREATION CENTER
KALAMAZOO, MI 49008
269-387-2710
Fax: 269-387-2704
• Debra Berkey, Dept. Chairperson
debra.berkey@wmich.edu
• Ronald Winter, Dept. Associate Professor
(269) 387-2694
ronald.winter@wmich.edu
• Jody Brylinsky, Ph.D, Dept. Professor
(269) 387-2677
jody.brylinsky@wmich.edu

WESTERN NEW ENGLAND COLLEGE
DEPARTMENT OF MANAGEMENT
1215 WILBRAHAM ROAD
SPRINGFIELD, MA 01119-2684
413-782-1389
Fax: 413-782-1746
www.wnegoldenbears.com
• Sharianne Walker, Dept. Chair/Sport Mgmt
Asst. Prof.
(413) 782-1389
• Daniel Covell, Associate Professor
(413) 782-1689
• Jennifer Kolins, Men's Tennis Head Coach
(413) 796-2230
jkolins@wne.edu
• Lori Mayhew, Softball Head Coach
(413) 796-2230
lmayhew@wne.edu
• Andrea Daley, Women's Swimming Head
Coach
(413) 796-2228
daleyandrea@hotmail.com
• Bret Stothart, Women's Volleyball Head
Coach
(413) 782-1550
bstothart@wne.edu
Description:
Unlike some colleges where sport
management is aligned with physical
education, the Sport Management Program
at Western New England College
emphasizes the business side of the field. In
our leading edge program, you'll take a
common core of business and liberal arts
classes including accounting, business law,
marketing and more. The sport
management curriculum includes such
courses as the Economic of Sports, Sport
Facility Planning and Management, and the
Structure of Sport Industry.
Degrees Offered:
B.S,.B.A. in Sport Management.

WICHITA STATE UNIVERSITY
DEPT. of SPORT MANAGEMENT
109 HESKETT CENTER
WICHITA, KS 67260-0127
316-978-5445
Fax: 316-978-5451
www.goshockers.com

college sports

• Eric Sexton, Director of Athletics
(316) 978-3250

WIDENER UNIVERSITY
1 UNIVERSITY PL
CHESTER, PA 19013
610-499-4300
www.widener.edu/athletics
• Joe DiAngelo,
• Brian Larson, Director
Degree Offered
Degree in Sports Management.

WILLIAM WOODS UNIVERSITY
One University Avenue
Fulton, MO 65257
800-995-3159
www.williamwoods.edu/athletics
• Marshall Robb, Director
smrobb@williamwoods.edu
Degree/Majors Offered:
Athletics training, exercise science, physical education, sport management.

WILMINGTON COLLEGE
SPORT MANAGEMENT
320 N. DUPONT HIGHWAY
NEW CASTLE, DE 19720-6491
877-967-5464
• Janice Wardle, Sports Management Program Coordinator
• Robert Edelson, Business Division Chairperson
Description:
Students receive a broad-based, personalized education in sports management. The program, which integrates theory with practical internship requirements, develops students for the opportunities available in sports management. In addition to the sports management curriculum, the program includes a strong business management component, providing students with the skills necessary to succeed in the corporate areas of this field.
Degree/Majors Offered:
B.S. sport management.

WINDSOR, UNIVERSITY OF
HUMAN KINETICS BUILDING
401 SUNSET AVENUE
WINDSOR, ON, CANADA
519-253-3000 EXT 2432
hk@uwindsor.ca
www.uwindsor.ca/athletics
• Robert Boucher, Dean of Human Kinetics
(519) 253-3000
bouche4@uwindsor.ca
• Wayne Marino, Head of Human Kinetics
(519) 253-3000
wmarino@uwindsor.ca
Degree Offered
Bachelor's and Master's of Human Kinetics
(Sport Management)

WINGATE UNIVERSITY
DEPARTMENT OF SPORT SCIENCES
220 N. CAMDEN ST.
PO BOX 159
WINGATE, NC 28174
704-233-8000
800-755-5550
Fax: 704-233-8170
wingatebulldogs.com

• Dennis Johnson, Sport Sciences Assoc. Prof./Asst. Dean
(704) 233-8182
• Lauren Merkle, Sport Sciences Assistant Professor
(704) 233-8297
Description:
Sport Management combines courses in Sport Sciences with courses in Business Administration to provide today's student with the skills necessary for success in the new millennium. In addition to the general education requirements (GER) of the university, the student will take courses in facility management, sport law, sport history, and sport leadership from the Department of Sport Sciences as well as courses in economics, accounting, marketing, and business management from the School of Business and Economics.
Description:
B.S. sport management.

WINSTON-SALEM STATE UNIVERSITY
WSSU DEPT. OF ATHLETICS
200 C.E. GAINES CENTER
WINSTON-SALEM, NC 27110
336-750-2141
Fax: 336-750-8880
www.wssurams.com
• William Hayes, Director of Athletics
(336) 750-2142
hayeswl@wssu.edu
Description:
B.S. sport management major.
Requirements:
Completion of the general studies program, a minimum of 2.5 grade point average prior to entry, volunteer experiences in sport management or related areas and a commitment toward full participation in the Major's Club.

WINTHROP UNIVERSITY
DEPARTMENT OF HEALTH & PHYSICAL EDUCATION
114 TILLMAN HALL
ROCK HILL, SC 29733
803-323-2225
Fax: 803-323-3001
www.winthrop.edu
• Linda Schoonmaker, Associate Professor
schoonmakerl@winthrop.edu
• Curt Laird, Assistant Professor
lairdc@winthrop.edu
Degree Offered
BS in Sport Management

WISCONSIN, LA CROSSE, UNIVERSITY OF
EXERCISE AND SPORT SCIENCE
147 MITCHELL HALL
1725 STATE STREET
LA CROSSE, WI 54601
608-785-8683
Fax: 608-785-8686
www.uwlax.edu
• Patrick DiRocco, Assoc. Professor/Dept. Chairman
(608) 785-8173
• John Porcari, Professor/Executive Director
(608) 785-8684
• Chris Heilixon, Softball Head Coach
(608) 785-6536
chelixon@uwlax.edu
• Sara Burton, Soccer Head Coach
(608) 785-6534

• Lily Hallock, Volleyball Head Coach
(608) 785-8191
Description:
Undergrad Degree: B.S. Grad Degree: M.S. Cardiac Rehab/Human Performance; M.S. Sport Administration. Areas of Specialization: Undergrad: Athletic Administration; Sport Management; Fitness Management. Grad: Exercise Physiology, Adult Fitness, Sport Administration.

WISCONSIN-PARKSIDE, UNIVERSITY OF
DEPARTMENT OF HEALTH, EXERCISE SCIENCE AND SPORT MANAGEMENT
900 WOOD ROAD
PO BOX 2000
KENOSHA, WI 53141-2000
262-595-2345
Fax: 262-595-2225
lyter@uwp.edu
• Penny Lyter, Dept. Chairperson
(262) 595-2494
lyter@uwp.edu
• William Miller, Sport Management Advisor
(262) 595-3359
Description:
The Sport and Fitness Industry has experienced dramatic growth over the past twenty years. The need for expertise in sport and fitness management has grown into a discipline where specialization exists in a multidimensional sense in the various areas of business, communications, and health-related areas. Professional positions in this exciting area require that persons are trained and qualified in many areas such as programming, marketing, management, communications, facility development, finance, economics, politics, and legal aspects.

WITTENBERG UNIVERSITY
DEPARTMENT OF HEALTH/SPORT SCIENCE
BOX 720
SPRINGFIELD, OH 45501
937-327-6452
Fax: 937-327-6340
www.wittenberg.edu
• Thomas Martin, Professor
(937) 327-6470
tmartin@wittenberg.edu
• Linda Arena, Professor/Chairperson
(937) 327-6452
• Steven Dawson, Associate Professor
(937) 327-6456
sdawson@wittenberg.edu
• Natalie Koukis, Men's and Women's Swimming/Diving Head Coach
(937) 327-6446
• Justin Stuckey, Men's and Women's Head Coach
(937) 327-6453
• Paco Labrador, Volleyball Head Coach
(937) 327-6492
Description:
Undergrad Degree: B.A. Areas of Specialization: Sports Medicine; Corporate Fitness; Sport Management; Sport Psychology; Exercise Physiology; Recreation.

XAVIER UNIVERSITY
3800 VICTORY PARKWAY
CINCINNATI, OH 45207-7530

513-745-3417
Fax: 513-745-4930
www.goxavier.com
• Mike Bobinski, Director of Athletics
(513) 745-3417
athleticdirector@xavier.edu
• Scott Googins, Baseball Head Coach
(513) 745-2891
googins@xavier.edu
Description:
Sport management includes any combination of skills related to planning, organizing, directing, controlling, budgeting, leading and evaluating in an organization or department whose primary product or service is related to sport and/or physical activity.
Degrees:
Undergrad Degree: B.S. in Sport Management or Sport Marketing. Grad Degree: M.S. in Sports Administration. Areas of Specialization: Undergrad: Sport Management or Sport Marketing. Grad:

Sports Administration.
Requirements:
Beyond the core curriculum, sport management students must successfully complete 71 semester hours of required courses.

YORK COLLEGE OF PENNSYLVANIA
SPORT MANAGEMENT
YORK, PA 17405-7199
717-815-1366
Fax: 717-849-1642
pmassa@ycp.edu
www.ycp.edu/athletics
• Patrick Massa, Dept. Chairperson/Professor
(717) 815-1366
pmassa@ycp.edu
• Tim Newman, Program Coordinator/Professor
(717) 815-1794
Description:
The mission of the Sport Management program encompasses the following: to provide an environment rich in academics and in the field experiences oriented toward developing broad-based leadership skills in the many areas of the sport industry, not limited to but including, management, sport media, and entrepreneurship.
Requirements:
Sport Management majors are required to complete an elective sequence in another academic discipline. An elective sequence consists of between 15 and 18 credits of coursework in one of the following areas: accounting, aquatic facility management, asset protection, athletic administration, entrepreneurial Studies human resource management, information Systems, management, marketing, Operations Management, organizational development, public relations, retailing, Speech Communication, Student Initiated
Degree Offered:
BS in Sport Management

college sports

4

media

media

DECATUR DAILY, 482
DECATUR DAILY DEMOCRAT, 482
DEGREES IN SPORTS, 594
DELAWARE COUNTY DAILY TIMES, 482
DELAWARE GAZETTE, 482
DELAWARE STATE NEWS, 482
DELTA DEMOCRAT-TIMES, 482
DEMOCRAT AND CHRONICLE, 482
DENTON RECORD-CHRONICLE, 482
DENVER POST, 482
DERRICK, 482
DES MOINES NEWS AND HIGHLINE TIMES, 483
DES MOINES REGISTER, 483
DESERET MORNING NEWS, 483
DESERT BOWLER, 556
DESERT DISPATCH, 483
DESERT SUN, 483
DETROIT FREE PRESS, 483
DETROIT NEWS, 483
DEVILS LAKE DAILY JOURNAL, 484
DIALGLOBAL, INC., 604
DIARIO LAS AMERICAS, 484
DICKINSON PRESS, 484
DIRECTV, INC., 686
DIRT RAG, 556
DISH NETWORK, 686
DISPATCH (CA), 484
DISPATCH (IL), 484
DODGE CITY DAILY GLOBE, 484
DOLPHIN DIGEST, 556
DOMINION-POST, 484
DOTHAN EAGLE, 484
DOUGLAS COUNTY SENTINEL, 484
DOWAGIAC DAILY NEWS, 484
DRAG RACER MAGAZINE, 557
DRAG REVIEW, 557
DRESSAGE TODAY, 557
DU QUOIN EVENING CALL, 484
DULUTH NEWS-TRIBUNE, 484
DUNCAN BANNER, 484
DUNDALK EAGLE, 485
DURANGO HERALD, 485
DURANT DAILY DEMOCRAT, 485
DUSTY TIMES, 557
DYNOCOMM SPORTS TV, 598

E

E-SPORTS MEDIA GROUP, INC., 713
EAGLE HERALD, 485
EAGLE-TIMES, 485
EAGLE-TRIBUNE, 485
EAGLES DIGEST, 557
EAST OREGONIAN, 485
EAST VALLEY TRIBUNE, 485
EASTERN BASKETBALL, 557
EASTSIDER, 485
EDWARDSVILLE INTELLIGENCER, 485
EFFINGHAM DAILY NEWS, 485
850 KOA RADIO, 611
EL BOHEMIO NEWS, 485
EL DIARIO LA PRENSA, 485
EL DORADO NEWS-TIMES, 485
EL DORADO TIMES, 485
EL HISPANO NEWS, 486
EL INFORMADOR HISPANO, 486
EL MUNDO, 486
EL NUEVO HERALD, 486
EL NUEVO HERALDO BROWNSVILLE, 486
EL NUEVO PATRIA, 486
EL PASO TIMES, 486
EL TIEMPO DE NUEVA YORK, 486
EL TIEMPO LATINO, 486
ELIZABETHTON STAR, 486
ELKHART TRUTH, 486
ELKO DAILY FREE PRESS, 486
ELLWOOD CITY LEDGER, 486
EMPIRE SPORTS REPORT, 683
EMPLOYEE SERVICES MANAGEMENT, 557
EMPORIA GAZETTE, 486
ENID NEWS AND EAGLE, 486
ENNIS DAILY NEWS, 486
ENQUIRER-JOURNAL, 487
ENSIGN, 487
ENTERPRISE, 487
ENTERPRISE LEDGER, 487
ENTERPRISE-JOURNAL, 487
ENTERTAINMENT LAW REPORTER, 557
EPM LICENSING LETTER SOURCEBOOK, 557

EPM LICENSING LETTER SOURCEBOOK, THE, 594
EQUESTRIAN, 557
EQUIERY, 557
EQUINE JOURNAL, 558
EQUINE TIMES, 558
EQUUS, 558
ERNIE SAXTON'S MOTORSPORTS
    SPONSORSHIP MARKETING, 558
ESPN, 683
ESPN 1490 THE FAN, 612
ESPN CLASSIC SPORTS NETWORK, 674
ESPN NETWORK, 604
ESPN ON ABC, 604
ESPN OUTDOORS/B.A.S.S., 558
ESPN RADIO - SUNDAY GAMENIGHT, 608
ESPN RADIO 1000, 612
ESPN RADIO 1250 PITTSBURGH, 612
ESPN RADIO 920, 612
ESPN REGIONAL TELEVISION, 599
ESPN TELEVISION, 674
ESPN THE MAGAZINE, 608
ESPN990 SPORTS RADIO, 612
ESTHERVILLE DAILY NEWS, 487
EVANSVILLE COURIER & PRESS, 487
EVENING NEWS, 487
EVENING SUN (NY), 487
EVENING SUN (PA), 487
EVENING TELEGRAM, 487
EVENING TIMES (NY), 487
EVENING TIMES (PA), 487
EVENT SPECIALIST OF NEW ORLEANS, 674
EXAMINER, 487
EXAMINER-ENTERPRISE, 487
EXCELSIOR, 487
EXECUTIVE GOLFER, 558
EXPONENT TELEGRAM, 487
EXPRESS-TIMES, 488
EXTRA POINTS, 679

F

FACILITIES & EVENT MANAGEMENT
    MAGAZINE, 558
FACTS, 488
FAIRBANKS DAILY NEWS-MINER, 488
FAIRBORN DAILY HERALD, 488
FAIRFAX JOURNAL, 488
FAIRWAYS, 559
THE FAN 590, 635
FANTASY SPORTS, 559
FAR POST, 559
FARIBAULT DAILY NEWS, 488
FARMINGTON PRESS, 488
FAYETTEVILLE OBSERVER, 488
FIELD & STREAM MAGAZINE, 559
FINE PRINT NEWS, 488
FINGER LAKES TIMES, 488
FIRST 4 SPORTS - SATURDAY, 679
FIRST 4 SPORTS - SUNDAY, 679
FISH MASTERS, 679
THE FISHING REPORT WITH BRIAN HOFFMAN,
    607
FITNESS BUSINESS CANADA
    MAGAZINE/FITNESS TRAINER CANADA
    MAGAZINE, 559
FITNESS INFORMATION TECHNOLOGY, 559
5 SPORTS LIVE, 678
FLINT JOURNAL, 488
FLORIDA GOLF NEWS, 559
FLORIDA GREEN, 559
FLORIDA HORSEMEN, 559
FLORIDA SPORTS & FITNESS MAGAZINE, 559
FLORIDA SPORTSMAN, 559
FLORIDA TENNIS, 560
FLORIDA TIMES-UNION, 488
FLORIDA TODAY, 488
FLY FISHING WITH GLEN BLACKWOOD, 679
FOOTBALL DIGEST, 560
FOOTBALL GREEN BOOK, 594
THE FOOTBALL GREEN BOOK, 597
FOOTBALL NEWS, 560
FOOTWEAR PLUS, 560
FORE, 560
FORT BEND HERALD & TEAXS COASTER, 488
FORT MORGAN TIMES, 489
FORT SCOTT TRIBUNE, 489
FORT WORTH STAR-TELEGRAM, 489
FORUM, 489
44 BLUE PRODUCTIONS, INC., 597

48 DEGREES NORTH, 548
FOURTH DOWN ON FOUR, 679
FOX 13 SPORTS PAGE, 679
FOX 59 OVERTIME, 679
THE FOX 8 10:00 PM WEEKEND NEWS, 682
FOX SPORTS ASIA, 674
FOX SPORTS DIRECT, 686
FOX SPORTS INTERNATIONAL, 674
FOX SPORTS NET ARIZONA, 674
FOX SPORTS NET CHICAGO, 674
FOX SPORTS NET DETROIT, 675
FOX SPORTS NET FLORIDA, 675
FOX SPORTS NET MIDWEST, 675
FOX SPORTS NET NORTH, 675
FOX SPORTS NET SOUTH, 675
FOX SPORTS NET SOUTHWEST, 599
FOX SPORTS NET WEST, 675
FOX SPORTS NETWORKS/FOX SPORTS NET,
    675
FOX SPORTS OHIO, 675
FOX SPORTS PRIME TICKET, 675
FOX SPORTS SUNDAY, 679
FOX SPORTS XTRA, 679
THE FRED HONSBERGER SHOW, 607
FREDERICK NEWS-POST, 489
FREE LANCE, 489
FREE LANCE-STAR, 489
FREE PRESS, 489
FREEDOM SPORTS NETWORK/DELCOM
    MARKETING GROUP, 599
FREEMAN, 489
FREESKIER, 560
FREMONT TRIBUNE, 489
FRESNO BEE, 489
FRONT ROW, 683
FULTON SUN, 490
FUTBOL TELEMUNDO, 683
FX NETWORKS, LLC, 675

G

GADSDEN TIMES, 490
GAINESVILLE DAILY REGISTER, 490
GAINESVILLE SUN, 490
GAISF CALENDAR OF INTERNATIONAL
    SPORTS COMPETITIONS, 594
GALAVISION, 676
GALION INQUIRER, 490
GALLUP INDEPENDENT, 490
GALVESTON COUNTY DAILY NEWS, 490
THE GAME 730 AM/WVFN, 635
GAMEDAY, 609
GAMENIGHT, 609
GARDEN ISLAND, 490
GARDNER NEWS, 490
THE GARY RADNICH SHOW, 607
GASTON GAZETTE, 490
GATER RACING PHOTO NEWS, 560
GATOR BAIT, 560
GATOR IMG SPORTS NETWORK, 605
GAZETTE, 490
GAZETTE COLORADO SPRINGS, 490
GETTYSBURG TIMES, 490
GLEANER, 490
GLENDALE NEWS-PRESS, 490
GLENWOOD SPRINGS POST INDEPENDENT,
    490
GLOBAL REACH SPORTS, 713
GLOBAL SPORTS PRODUCTIONS, 594
GLOBAL TELEVISION NETWORK, LTD., 676
GLOBE-GAZETTE, 490
GLOUCESTER COUNTY TIMES, 491
GOLD SHEET, 560
GOLF BUSINESS, 560
GOLF CHANNEL, THE, 687
GOLF CONNOISSEUR MAGAZINE, 560
GOLF COURSE MANAGEMENT, 561
GOLF COURSE NEWS, 561
GOLF DIGEST, 561
GOLF FOR WOMEN, 561
GOLF GEORGIA, 561
GOLF ILLUSTRATED, 561
GOLF MAGAZINE, 561
GOLF MARKETING BY BIGGS, 599
GOLF NEWS, 561
GOLF ON CAPE COD, 561
GOLF PRODUCT NEWS, 561
GOLF RANGE TIMES, 562
THE GOLF SHOW, 610
GOLF TIPS, 562

media

media

449

WCBG-AM, 640
WCBI-TV, 700
WCBL-FM, 640
WCBS-TV, 700
WCBT-AM, 640
WCCB-TV, 700
WCCO, 640
WCCO-TV, 700
WCCP, 640
WCCW-AM, 640
WCDK-FM, 640
WCDO-AM, 640
WCEM-AM, 641
WCFM-FM, 641
WCFN-TV, 700
WCFW-FM, 641
WCGQ-FM, 641
WCHC-FM, 641
WCHO-AM, 641
WCHO-FM, 641
WCHS-TV, 700
WCIA-TV, 700
WCIV-TV, 700
WCJB-TV, 700
WCJW-AM, 641
WCKY-AM, 641
WCLG-FM, 641
WCLH-FM, 641
WCLN-AM, 641
WCLO-AM, 641
WCLT-AM, 641
WCNC - NBC6, 701
WCNC-AM, 641
WCNC-AM / WZBO-AM, 641
WCNC-TV, 701
WCOS, 641
WCPO-TV, 701
WCSC-TV, 701
WCSH-TV, 701
WCSL, 641
WCSL-AM, 642
WCST-AM, 642
WCTA-AM, 642
WCTK-FM, 642
WCUM-AM, 642
WCVB-TV, 701
WCVM-FM, 642
WCWT-FM, 642
WCYJ-FM, 642
WDAE-AM 620, 642
WDAF-TV, 701
WDAM-TV, 701
WDAS-AM, 642
WDAZ-TV, 701
WDBJ-TV, 701
WDBO-AM, 642
WDBQ-AM, 642
WDDD-AM, 642
WDDD-FM, 642
WDDK-FM, 642
WDEF, 701
WDEF-TV, 701
WDEL-AM, 642
WDFN, 642
WDFN - 1130 AM THE FAN, 642
WDHC-FM, 643
WDIV-TV, 701
WDJT-TV, 701
WDKD-AM, 643
WDKX-FM, 643
WDLB, 643
WDLZ-FM, 643
WDNE-FM, 643
WDOE-AM/FM, 643
WDOG-FM, 643
WDOR-FM, 643
WDOW-AM, 643
WDPN-AM, 643
WDSL-AM, 643
WDSM SPORTS RADIO 710, 643
WDSM-AM, 643
WDUN-AM, 643
WDUX-AM/FM, 643
WDUX-FM, 644
WDZN-FM, 644
WE ARE THERE SATURDAY, 610
WEAI-FM, 644
WEAQ-AM, 644
WEAR-TV, 701
WEAS-FM, 644

WEATHERFORD DEMOCRAT, 546
WEAU-TV, 701
WEBB ELECTRONICS, 603
WECT-TV, 701
WEDM-FM, 644
WEDO-AM, 644
WEEB-AM, 644
WEEI SPORTS RADIO, 644
WEEK-TV, 702
WEEKDAY SPORTSBEAT, 608
WEEKEND, 546
WEEKEND GAMENIGHT, 610
WEEO-AM, 644
WEEU-AM, 644
WEEX-AM, 644
WEHT-TV, 702
WEIDER PUBLICATIONS, 592
WEIU-FM, 644
WEJL-AM, 644
WEKS-FM, 644
WEKT-AM, 644
WEKX-FM, 644
WELLINGTON DAILY NEWS, 546
WELLSVILLE DAILY REPORTER, 546
WELM-AM, 644
WELW-AM, 645
WEMJ-AM, 645
WENATCHEE WORLD, 546
WENE, 645
WENG, 645
WENK-AM, 645
WENY-TV, 702
WEPG-AM, 645
WERQ-FM, 645
WESH-TV, 702
WEST BEND DAILY NEWS, 546
WEST CENTRAL TRIBUNE, 546
WEST COUNTY TIMES, 546
WEST GLEN COMMUNICATIONS, INC., 603
WEST HAWAII TODAY, 546
WEST PLAINS DAILY QUILL, 546
WEST VALLEY VIEW, 546
WEST-AM, 645
WESTERN GUIDE TO SNOWMOBILING, 592
WESTERN HORSEMAN, 592
WESTERN OUTDOOR NEWS, 592
WESTERN OUTDOORS, 592
WESTERN SPORTS GUIDE, 597
WESTWOODONE, 604
WETM-TV, 702
WEVR-AM, 645
WEVR-FM, 645
WEWS-TV, 702
WFAA-TV, 702
WFAN SPORTS RADIO, 645
WFAT-FM, 645
WFDF 910AM RADIO, 645
WFEB, 645
WFEB-AM, 645
WFFC-FM, 645
WFFF-AM, 646
WFGN-AM, 646
WFHR, 646
WFIE-TV, 702
WFIN RADIO, 646
WFIS-AM, 646
WFLA-TV, 702
WFLD TV CHANNEL 32 CHICAGO/FOX, 702
WFLD-TV, 702
WFLF-AM, 646
WFMB-AM SPORTS RADIO 1450, 646
WFMJ-TV, 702
WFMQ-FM, 646
WFMY-TV, 702
WFMZ-TV, 702
WFNR, 646
WFNR-AM, 646
WFNZ-AM 610 SPORTS RADIO, 646
WFPR-AM, 646
WFRD-FM, 646
WFRM-AM, 646
WFRV-TV, 702
WFRX-AM, 646
WFSB-TV, 702
WFSE-FM, 646
WFTG-AM, 646
WFTS-TV, 702
WFTV-TV, 703
WFUV-FM, 647
WFXE-FM, 647

WFYY-FM, 647
WGAB, 647
WGAD, 647
WGAD-AM, 647
WGAI-AM, 647
WGAL-TV, 703
WGAN, 647
WGAN-AM, 647
WGAP-AM, 647
WGAW-AM, 647
WGBA-TV, 703
WGBK-FM, 647
WGCL-TV, 703
WGCM-AM, 647
WGCY-FM, 647
WGEM-TV, 703
WGET, 647
WGFR-FM, 647
WGGA-AM, 647
WGGB-TV, 703
WGH-AM THE SCORE, 647
WGHB-AM, 647
WGHT-AM, 648
WGL-AM, 648
WGLU-FM, 648
WGLV-FM, 648
WGMA-AM, 648
WGME-TV, 703
WGMN-AM, 648
WGN-9 CHICAGO'S CW, 703
WGN-AM, 648
WGNC, 648
WGOM-AM, 648
WGOW-AM, 648
WGR 55 SPORTS RADIO, 648
WGRE-FM, 648
WGRM-AM, 648
WGRM-FM, 648
WGXA-TV, 703
WHAI-FM/WPVQ, 648
WHAM-TV, 703
WHAN-AM, 648
WHB-AM, 648
WHBC-FM, 648
WHBG-AM, 649
WHBN-AM, 649
WHBQ SPORTS 56, 649
WHBQ-TV, 703
WHBU 1240, 649
WHBU-AM, 649
WHBY-AM, 649
WHCC-FM, 649
WHCY-FM, 649
WHDH-TV, 703
WHDL-AM, 649
WHEELIN' SPORTSMAN, 592
WHEELING NEWS-REGISTER, 546
WHEELSTV, 678
WHEN, 649
WHHB-FM, 649
WHHS-FM, 649
WHIO-TV, 703
WHIP-AM, 649
WHIT, 649
WHIZ-TV, 703
WHKS-AM, 649
WHKY-TV, 703
WHLA-TV, 704
WHMB-TV, 704
WHME-TV, 704
WHNT-TV, 704
WHO-TV, 704
WHOC-AM, 649
WHOI-TV, 704
WHOL-AM, 650
WHRM-TV, 704
WHTC-AM, 650
WHTG-AM, 650
WHTG-FM, 650
WHTK, 650
WHTK-AM, 650
WHTL-FM, 650
WHTM-TV, 704
WHTQ-FM, 650
WHWC-TV, 704
WHYN-AM, 650
WIAT - CBS 42, 704
WIBC, 650
WIBM-AM, 650
WIBN-FM, 650

WIBR, 650
WIBW AM 580 RADIO, 650
WICHITA EAGLE, 547
WICHITA FALLS TIMES RECORD NEWS, 547
WICK-AM, 650
WICO-AM, 650
WICU-TV, 704
WIFR-TV, 704
WIGG-AM, 650
WIKC-AM, 650
WILD-AM, 650
WILEN MEDIA CORPORATION, 678
WILLIAMSON DAILY NEWS, 547
WILLIAMSPORT SUN-GAZETTE, 547
WILLTIME MOTORSPORTS, 608
WILMINGTON NEWS JOURNAL, 547
WILMINGTON STAR NEWS, 547
WILQ-FM, 651
WILSON DAILY TIMES, 547
WILT-AM, 651
WILX-TV, 704
WIMA-AM, 651
WIMZ-FM, 651
WINCHESTER STAR, 547
WINCHESTER SUN, 547
WINDSURFING, 592
WINFIELD DAILY COURIER, 547
WINGFOOT, 592
WINK-TV, 704
WINNERCOMM, INC., 603
WINONA DAILY NEWS, 547
WINSTON-SALEM JOURNAL, 547
WINW-AM, 651
WIP SPORTSRADIO 610, 651
WIQB-AM, 651
WIRO, 651
WIRQ-FM, 651
WIRY-AM, 651
WIS-TV, 704
WISC-TV, 704
WISCONSIN GOLFER, 592
WISCONSIN SOCCER POST, 592
WISCONSIN STATE JOURNAL, 547
WISH-TV, 704
WISK-FM, 651
WITN-TV, 704
WIUS-AM, 651
WIVB-TV, 704
WIVQ-FM, 651
WIVV-AM, 651
WIXT-TV, 705
WIXX-FM, 651
WJAG-AM, 651
WJAW-FM, 651
WJBC, 651
WJBK-TV, 705
WJBO-AM, 651
WJCI-AM, 651
WJDB-AM, 652
WJDK-FM, 652
WJEL-FM, 652
WJFD-FM, INC., 652
WJFW-TV, 705
WJGA-FM, 652
WJHG-TV, 705
WJHL-TV, 705
WJJB-AM, 652
WJJC-AM, 652
WJJO-FM, 652
WJJQ-AM, 652
WJJT-AM, 652
WJLA-TV, 705
WJOX-AM SPORTS RADIO, 652
WJPF-AM, 652
WJPZ-FM, 652
WJR-AM, 652
WJRS-FM, 652
WJTN-AM, 652
WJTV-TV NEWS CHANNEL 12, 705
WJUN-AM, 652
WJVL-FM, 652
WJVS-FM, 653
WJW-TV, 705
WJXT-TV, 705
WJZ-TV, 705
WKAN AM 1320, 653
WKAN-AM, 653
WKAV-AM, 653
WKBF-AM, 653
WKBH-AM SPORTS RADIO, 653

WKBK-AM, 653
WKBN-TV, 705
WKBW-TV, 705
WKCL-FM, 653
WKDE-FM, 653
WKEE-FM, 653
WKEF-TV, 705
WKEQ, 653
WKGS-FM, 653
WKHS-FM, 653
WKIX-FM, 653
WKJQ-FM 97.3, 653
WKKJ-FM, 653
WKKS-FM, 654
WKLK-AM, 654
WKLK-FM, 654
WKLV-AM, 654
WKMG-TV, 705
WKNH-FM, 654
WKNR SPORTS RADIO, 654
WKNW-AM, 654
WKOW-TV, 705
WKRC-TV, 705
WKRK-AM, 654
WKRN-TV, 705
WKRV-AM, 654
WKTV-TV, 706
WKUB-FM, 654
WKVG-AM, 654
WKVM-AM, 654
WKVX-AM, 654
WKWF-AM, 654
WKWZ-FM, 654
WKXQ-FM, 654
WKXW-FM, 654
WKYC-TV, 706
WKYR-FM, 654
WKYT-TV, 706
WKZO-AM, 654
WKZS-FM, 655
WLAP-AM, 655
WLBR-AM, 655
WLBT-TV, 706
WLDY-AM, 655
WLEF-TV, 706
WLER-FM, 655
WLEY-AM, 655
WLFI-TV, 706
WLFN-AM, 655
WLGC, 655
WLHT-FM, 655
WLIO-TV, 706
WLKF-AM, 655
WLKL-FM, 655
WLKR-AM, 655
WLKR-FM, 655
WLLG-FM, 655
WLLL-AM, 655
WLLN-AM, 655
WLLY-AM, 655
WLMD-FM, 655
WLOB-AM, 656
WLOH-AM, 656
WLOW-FM, 656
WLQM-FM, 656
WLRT-AM, 656
WLS-TV, 706
WLS-TV CHANNEL 7 ABC (CHICAGO), 706
WLSC-AM, 656
WLTP-AM, 656
WLTV-TV, 706
WLUR-FM, 656
WLVI-TV, 706
WLW, 656
WLWT-TV, 706
WMAM-AM, 656
WMAQ TV CHICAGO, 706
WMAQ-TV, 706
WMAZ-TV, 706
WMBA 1460, 656
WMBB-TV, 706
WMBE-AM AND WCLB, 656
WMC-TV, 706
WMCE-FM, 656
WMCR-FM, 656
WMEB-FM, 656
WMEV-FM, 656
WMFD-AM, 656
WMFR-AM, 656
WMGM-TV, 707

WMHW-FM, 657
WMIK-AM, 657
WMJI-FM, 657
WMJK-FM, 657
WMJZ-FM, 657
WMKX-FM, 657
WMLM-AM, 657
WMLN-FM, 657
WMMC-FM, 657
WMML-AM, 657
WMMS-FM, 657
WMNA-AM, 657
WMOI-FM, 657
WMOP-AM, 657
WMPX-WMRX AM AND FM, 657
WMRC-AM, 657
WMRN-AM, 657
WMRX-FM, 657
WMSR-AM, 657
WMSS-FM, 657
WMTL-AM, 657
WMTR-FM, 658
WMTW-TV, 707
WMUF 1047FM/97.5AM 1000, WRQR AM/FM,
94.1 FM, 658
WMUH-FM, 658
WMUR-TV, 707
WMVX-FM, 658
WNBC-TV, 707
WNBH-AM, 658
WNCN-TV, 707
WNDE, 658
WNDH-FM, 658
WNEG-AM, 658
WNEM-TV, 707
WNER-AM, 658
WNES-AM, 658
WNFL 1140-AM, 658
WNJC-AM, 658
WNJU-TV, 707
WNKT-FM, 658
WNLS, 658
WNMH-FM, 658
WNML AM/FM, 658
WNML-AM, 658
WNNJ-FM, 658
WNNZ-AM, 659
WNOI-FM, 659
WNPL-FM, 659
WNPV-AM, 659
WNSR/WMGC RADIO, 659
WNSS-AM, 659
WNST-AM, 659
WNSV-FM, 659
WNTR, 659
WNUS-FM, 659
WNWO-TV, 707
WNYG-AM, 659
WNYW-TV, 707
WNYY, 659
WOAI, 659
WOAI-TV, 707
WOBN-FM, 659
WOBT-AM, 659
WOES-FM, 659
WOFL-TV, 707
WOFX-AM, 659
WOHS, 659
WOI-TV, 707
WOIC-AM, 660
WOIO-TV, 707
WOIZ-AM, 660
WOLFPACKER, 593
WOLO-TV, 707
WOLVERINE, 593
WOMEN'S PRO RODEO NEWS, 593
WONN-AM, 660
WONQ-AM, 660
WOODENBOAT, 593
WOODWARD NEWS, 547
WOON-AM, 660
WOPP-AM, 660
WORD, 660
WORD-AM, 660
WORG-FM, 660
WORLD, 548
WORLD OF RACING, 610
WORLD WIDE SKI CORPORATION, 604
WORLD WIDE SPORTS RADIO NETWORK, 593
WORW-FM, 660

WORX-FM, 660
WOSO-AM, 660
WOSQ-FM, 660
WOWO-AM, 660
WOWT-TV, 707
WOYL-AM, 660
WPAX-AM, 660
WPBN-TV, 707
WPCD-FM, 661
WPCH-AM, 661
WPCV-FM, 661
WPDE-TV, 707
WPDM-AM/WSNN-FM, 661
WPDR RADIO, 661
WPEN-AM, 661
WPEZ-FM, 661
WPHL-TV, 708
WPHM-AM, 661
WPIC-AM, 661
WPIG-FM, 661
WPIX-TV, 708
WPKY-AM, 661
WPLG-TV, 708
WPLO-AM, 661
WPMB-AM, 661
WPMI - NBC 15, 708
WPMZ-AM, 661
WPNE-TV, 708
WPOP-AM SPORTS RADIO, 661
WPPA-AM, 661
WPRI-TV, 708
WPRN-FM, 661
WPRO, 661
WPRO-AM, 662
WPRZ-AM, 662
WPTV-TV, 708
WPTY-TV, 708
WPVI-TV, 708
WPXI-TV, 708
WPXN-FM, 662
WQAD-TV, 708
WQAL-FM, 662
WQAM 560 SPORTS RADIO, 662
WQBB-AM, 662
WQBX-FM, 662
WQCM-FM, 662
WQDK-AM, 662
WQEL-FM, 662
WQIC-FM, 662
WQIO-FM, 662
WQKE-FM, 662
WQKR-AM, 662
WQKT-FM, 662
WQLA-FM, 662
WQPM-AM, 662
WQSE-AM, 662
WQSN AM 1660, 662
WQTM, 663
WQXI 790, 663
WQXI-AM, 663
WQXX-FM, 663
WRAC-FM, 663
WRAM-AM, 663
WRAY-AM, 663
WRAY-FM, 663
WRBL-TV, 708
WRC-TV, 708
WRCB-TV, 708
WRCC-FM, 663
WRCT-FM, 663
WRCU-FM, 663
WRDL-FM, 663
WRDU-FM, 663
WRDW-AM, 663
WREG-TV, 708
WREK-FM, 663
WREV-AM, 664
WRFW-FM, 664
WRGB-TV, 708
WRGM SPORTS RADIO 1440, 664
WRGS-AM, 664
WRHU-FM, 664
WRIC TV-8, 708
WRIC-TV, 709
WRIL-FM, 664
WRJW-AM, 664
WRKD-AM, 664
WRKR-FM, 664
WRLS-FM, 664
WRMS-FM, 664

WRNA-AM, 664
WRNL-AM, 664
WRNN-TV, 709
WRNX-FM, 664
WRRG-FM, 664
WRSC, 665
WRSE-FM, 665
WRSN-FM, 665
WRSW-AM, 665
WRTK, 665
WRUC-FM, 665
WRUF, 665
WRXL-FM, 665
WRXX-FM, 665
WSAL-AM, 665
WSAW-TV, 709
WSAZ-TV, 709
WSB-AM, 665
WSB-TV, 709
WSBK-TV, 709
WSBT-TV, 709
WSBU-FM, 665
WSCR THE SCORE SPORTSRADIO 670, 665
WSDM-FM/WBOW-AM ESPN SPORTS RADIO, 665
WSDP-FM, 665
WSEE-TV, 709
WSEW-FM, 666
WSFA-TV, 709
WSFN-AM, 666
WSFN-AM SPORTS RADIO, 666
WSHN-AM, 666
WSHR-FM, 666
WSHW-FM, 666
WSIF-FM, 666
WSIG-FM, 666
WSIL-TV, 709
WSJB-FM, 666
WSJM-AM, 666
WSKW, 666
WSLI-AM, 666
WSLJ-FM, 666
WSLL-FM, 666
WSLO-FM, 666
WSLS-TV, 709
WSMG-AM, 666
WSMI-AM, 666
WSMK-FM, 666
WSMV-TV, 709
WSNS-TV, 709
WSNV-FM, 667
WSOC-TV, 709
WSOU-FM, 667
WSPA-TV, 709
WSPD, 667
WSQR-AM, 667
WSRN-FM, 667
WSRW-AM, 667
WSRW-FM, 667
WSSO-AM, 667
WSTP-AM, 667
WSVN-TV, 709
WSYL-AM, 667
WSYY-AM, 667
WTAD-AM, 667
WTAP-TV, 710
WTAW, 667
WTBU-AM, 667
WTCC-FM, 667
WTCH-AM, 667
WTCO-AM, 667
WTCQ-FM, 667
WTCR-AM, 668
WTDK-FM, 668
WTDY AM 1670, 668
WTEM SPORTS RADIO, 668
WTEN NEWS 10/ABC, 710
WTEN-TV, 710
WTEV-TV, 710
WTGG-FM, 668
WTGZ-FM, 668
WTHI-TV, 710
WTHR-TV, 710
WTIC-TV, 710
WTIG-AM, 668
WTIV-AM, 668
WTKG-AM, 668
WTKR-TV, 710
WTKT-AM, 668
WTKY-FM, 668

WTLC-FM, 668
WTLX-FM, 668
WTMJ, 668
WTMJ-TV, 710
WTNH-TV, 710
WTNS-FM, 668
WTNY-AM, 668
WTOC-TV, 710
WTOD-AM, 668
WTOL-TV, 710
WTOM-TV, 710
WTON-AM, 669
WTOP-FM, 669
WTOU-AM, 669
WTOV-TV, 710
WTPA-FM, 669
WTPR-AM, 669
WTRF-TV, 710
WTRN-AM, 669
WTRP-AM, 669
WTRS-FM, 669
WTSP-TV, 710
WTSX-FM, 669
WTTF-AM, 669
WTTG-TV, 710
WTTR-AM, 669
WTVC-TV, 710
WTVD-TV, 711
WTVF-TV, 711
WTVH-TV, 711
WTVJ-TV, 711
WTVM-TV, 711
WTVO-TV, 711
WTVT-TV, 711
WTVW-TV, 711
WTVY-TV, 711
WTXF-TV, 711
WTXM-FM, 669
WTZN-AM, 669
WTZX-AM, 669
WUAB-TV, 711
WUCZ-FM, 669
WUMP 730, 669
WUNR-AM, 669
WUPR-AM, 669
WUSA-TV, 711
WUSB-FM, 670
WUSI-FM, 670
WUVA-FM, 670
WVAC-FM, 670
WVBU-FM, 670
WVCH-AM, 670
WVEC-TV, 711
WVEE-FM, 670
WVEI-AM, 670
WVGM-AM, 670
WVII-TV, 711
WVIT-TV, 711
WVLT-TV, 711
WVLZ-AM, 670
WVMJ-FM, 670
WVMW-FM, 670
WVRY-FM, 670
WVTM-TV, 712
WVUM-FM, 670
WVUT-TV, 712
WVXU-FM, 670
WWAG-FM, 670
WWAY-TV, 712
WWBF-AM, 670
WWBT-TV, 712
WWCD-FM, 670
WWDW-FM, 670
WWEL-FM, 671
WWFG-FM, 671
WWIS-AM, 671
WWIZ-FM, 671
WWKA-FM, 671
WWKC-FM, 671
WWKY-FM, 671
WWL, 671
WWLP-TV, 712
WWLU-FM, 671
WWMT-TV, 712
WWOR-TV, 712
WWSB-TV, 712
WWTM, 671
WWTN-FM, 671
WWTV-TV, 712
WWUP-TV, 712

media

Newspapers

ABERDEEN AMERICAN NEWS
124 SOUTH 2ND STREET
PO BOX 4430
ABERDEEN, SD 57402
605-229-5555
800-925-4100
news@aberdeennews.com
www.aberdeennews.com
• John Papendick, Sports Editor
• Ryan Deal, Sports Reporter
Frequency:
7 time(s) per week

ABILENE REPORTER NEWS
101 CYPRESS STREET
PO BOX 30
ABILENE, TX 79601-5816
325-673-4271
Fax: 325-670-5270
www.reporternews.com
• Trish Choate, Sports Editor
• Nellie Doneva, Sports Writer
• Rick Myers, Sports Columnist
Frequency:
7 time(s) per week

ADA EVENING NEWS
116 NORTH BROADWAY
ADA, OK 74820
580-332-4433
800-259-8489
Fax: 580-332-8734
www.adaevingnews.com
• Jeff Cali, Sports Editor
(580) 310-7526
• Maurisa Nelson, Advertising Director
(580) 310-7502
Frequency:
6 time(s) per week

ADIRONDACK DAILY ENTERPRISE
54 BROADWAY
SARANAC LAKE, NY 12983-1703
518-891-2600
Fax: 518-891-2756
adirondackguide.com
• Morgan Ryan, Sports Editor
Frequency:
6 time(s) per week

ADVERTISER-TRIBUNE
320 NELSON STREET
TIFFIN, OH 44883-9359
419-448-3200
800-448-3235
Fax: 419-447-3274
rweaver@advertiser-tribune.com
www.advertiser-tribune.com
• Zach Baker, Sports Reporter
(419) 448-3256
zbaker@advertiser-tribune.com
• Tony Maluso, Sports
(419) 448-3256
tmaluso@advertiser-tribune.com
Frequency:
7 time(s) per week

ADVOCATE
7290 BLUEBONNET BLVD.
BATON ROUGE, LA 70810
225-383-1111
Fax: 225-388-0371
www.2theadvocate.com/

• Joseph Schierfelbein, Executive Sports Editor
(225) 388-0321
jschiefelbein@theadvocate.com
• Les East, Sports Reporter
(225) 388-0325
Frequency:
7 time(s) per week

ADVOCATE-MESSENGER
330 SOUTH 4TH STREET
DANVILLE, KY 40422-2033
859-236-2551
800-428-0409
Fax: 859-236-9566
advocate@amnews.com
www.amnews.com
• Larry Vaught, Sports Editor
(859) 236-2551
• Mike Marsee, Sports Writer
(859) 236-2551
Frequency:
6 time(s) per week

AIKEN STANDARD
P.O. BOX 456
AIKEN, SC 29801-4083
803-648-2311
Fax: 803-648-6052
editorial@aikenstandard.com
www.aikenstandard.com
• Noah Feit, Sports Editor
(803) 644-2389
• Jeremy Timmerman, Sports Reporter
(803) 644-2339
Frequency:
7 time(s) per week

AKRON BEACON JOURNAL
44 EAST EXCHANGE STREET
AKRON, OH 44308
330-996-3000
800-777-7232
Fax: 330-376-9235
www.ohio.com
• Scott Fagerstrom, Sports Editor
(330) 996-3828
sfagerstrom@thebeaconjournal.com
• Marla Ridenour, Sports Columnist
mridenour@thebeaconjournal.com
Frequency:
7 time(s) per week

ALAMEDA JOURNAL
1516 OAK STREET
ALAMEDA, CA 94501
510-748-1666
888-978-2760
www.insidebayarea.com/alameda
• Dave Belli, Assistant Sports Editor
(925) 977-8592
• Joe Deloach, Sports Copy Editor
(925) 943-8122
• Jimmy Durkin, Sports Reporter
(510) 208-6457
• Ron Ellis, Sports Copy Editor
(925) 943-8244
• Ben Enos, Sports Reporter
(925) 943-8108
• Don Peterson, Sports Copy Editor
(925) 943-8194
Frequency:
7 time(s) per week

ALBANY DEMOCRAT-HERALD
600 LYON STREET, S.W.
PO BOX 130
ALBANY, OR 97321-0041
541-926-2211
Fax: 541-926-5298
news@dhonline.com
www.democratherald.com
• Les Gehrett, Sports Editor
(541) 812-6092
• Jesse Sowa, Assistant Sports Editor
(541) 812-6091
jesse.sowa@lee.net
Frequency:
7 time(s) per week

ALBANY HERALD
126 N WASHINGTON ST
ALBANY, GA 31701
229-888-9300
800-234-3725
Fax: 229-888-9312
news@albanyherald.com
www.albanyherald.com
• John Millikan, Sports Reporter
(229) 888-9307
• Tim Morse, Sports Reporter
(229) 888-9306
Frequency:
7 time(s) per week

ALBERT LEA TRIBUNE
808 WEST FRONT STREET
ALBERT LEA, MN 56007-1947
507-373-1411
800-657-4996
Fax: 507-373-0333
news@albertleatribune.com
www.albertleatribune.com
• Micah Bader, Sports Editor
(507) 379-3434
• Drew Claussen, Sports Reporter
(507) 402-6610
Frequency:
6 time(s) per week

ALBUQUERQUE JOURNAL
7777 JEFFERSON STREET, NE
ALBUQUERQUE, NM 87109-4343
505-823-3800
800-990-5765
Fax: 505-823-3994
journal@abqjournal.com
www.abqjournal.com/
• Ed Johnson, Assistant Sports Editor
(505) 823-3933
• Mark Smith, Assistant Sports Editor
(505) 823-3935
• Randy Harrison, Sports Editor
(505) 823-3907
rharrison@abqjournal.com
Frequency:
7 time(s) per week

ALEXANDRIA DAILY TOWN TALK
PO BOX 7558
ALEXANDRIA, LA 71306
318-487-6397
800-523-8391
Fax: 318-487-6488
sports@thetowntalk.com
www.thetowntalk.com
• Randy Benson, Sports Editor
(318) 487-6431
Frequency:
7 time(s) per week

459

ALICE ECHO NEWS
405 EAST MAIN STREET
PO BOX 1610
ALICE, TX 78333
361-664-6588
Fax: 361-668-1030
www.aliceechonews.com
• Stephen Garcia, Sports Reporter
(361) 664-6588
Frequency:
6 time(s) per week

ALLIANCE REVIEW
40 SOUTH LINDEN AVENUE
ALLIANCE, OH 44601-2447
330-821-1300
Fax: 330-821-8258
reviewedit@the-review.com
www.the-review.com
• Michael Brown, Sports Editor
mjbrown@the-review.com
• Jeffrey Zupanic, Sports Reporter
jzupanic@the-review.com
Frequency:
6 time(s) per week

ALLIANCE TIMES-HERALD
114 EAST FOURTH STREET
PO BOX G
ALLIANCE, NE 69301
308-762-3060
Fax: 308-762-3063
www.alliancetimes.com
• Kristi Hulsey, Sports Editor
(308) 762-3060
Frequency:
6 time(s) per week

ALPHARETTA NEIGHBOR
10930 CRABAPPLE ROAD
SUITE 9
ROSWELL, GA 30075
770-993-7400
Fax: 770-518-6062
www.neighbornewspapers.com
Frequency:
1 time(s) per week

ALTOONA MIRROR
P.O. BOX 2008
301 CAYUGA AVE.
ALTOONA, PA 16602-4323
814-946-7411
800-222-1962
Fax: 814-946-7547
news@altoonamirror.com
www.altoonamirror.com
• Buck Frank, Sports Editor
(814) 946-7461
bfrank@altoonamirror.com
• Philip Cmor, Assistant Sports Director
(814) 946-7440
pcmor@altoonamirror.com
Frequency:
7 time(s) per week

ALTUS TIMES
PO BOX 578
218 W. COMMERCE
ALTUS, OK 73521
580-482-1221
800-303-1221
Fax: 580-482-5709
editor@altustimes.com
www.altustimes.com

• Mark Glenn, Sports Editor
(580) 482-1221
Frequency:
6 time(s) per week

AM NEW YORK
240 W. 35TH STREET
9TH FLOOR
NEW YORK, NY 10001
646-293-9499
Fax: 212-239-2828
www.amny.com
• Scott Fontana, Sports Writer
Frequency:
5 time(s) per week

AMARILLO GLOBE-NEWS
P.O. BOX 2091
900 S. HARRISON
AMARILLO, TX 79101
806-376-4488
800-692-4052
Fax: 806-373-0810
www.amarillo.com
• Lance Lahnert, Sports Editor
(806) 345-3312
lance.lahnert@amarillo.com
• Terrence Hunley, Sports Reporter
(806) 345-3307
terrence.hunley@amarillo.com
• Lee Passmore, Sports Reporter
(806) 345-3313
lee.passmore@amarillo.com
Frequency:
7 time(s) per week

AMERICA OGGI
475 WALNUT STREET
NORWOOD, NJ 07648-1318
201-358-6692
Fax: 201-258-0250
americoggi@aol.com
www.americaoggi.info
• Antonio Cirino, Sports Editor
(201) 358-6692
americoggi@aol.com
Frequency:
7 time(s) per week

AMERICAN PRESS
PO BOX 2893
LAKE CHARLES, LA 70602
337-494-4080
800-531-4080
Fax: 337-494-4070
news@americanpress.com
www.americanpress.com
• Alex Hickey, Sports Writer
(337) 494-4071
• Scooter Hobbs, Sports Editor
(337) 494-4075
shobbs@americanpress.com
Frequency:
7 time(s) per week

AMERICUS TIMES-RECORDER
101 HIGHWAY 27 EAST
PO BOX 1247
AMERICUS, GA 31709
229-924-2751
Fax: 229-928-6344
www.AmericusTimesRecorder.com
• Scott Phillips, Sports Editor
(229) 924-2751
Frequency:
Daily

ANCHORAGE DAILY NEWS
P.O. BOX 149001
ANCHORAGE, AK 99514-9001
907-257-4200
800-478-4200
Fax: 907-258-2157
newsroom@adn.com
www.adn.com
• Beth Bragg, Sports Editor
(907) 257-4335
Frequency
Daily

ANDALUSIA STAR NEWS
207 DUNSON STREET
ANDALUSIA, AL 36420-3705
334-222-2402
Fax: 334-222-6597
www.andalusiastarnews.com
• Andrew Garner, Sports Editor
Frequency:
Daily

ANDERSON INDEPENDENT-MAIL
1000 WILLIAMSTON RD
ANDERSON, SC 29621-6508
864-224-4321
888-789-0820
Fax: 864-260-1276
www.independentmail.com
• Scott Adamson, Executive Sports Editor
(864) 260-12367
Frequency:
7 time(s) per week

ANN ARBOR NEWS
301 E LIBERTY STREET
SUITE 700
ANN ARBOR, MI 48104
734-623-2500
800-589-6397
Fax: 734-222-0298
sports@annarbor.com
www.annarbor.com
• Peter Cunningham, Sports Director
• Kyle Austin, Sports Reporter
kyleaustin2@mlive.com
Frequency:
Thursday and Sunday.

ANNISTON STAR
4305 MCCLELLAN BOULEVARD
PO BOX 189
ANNISTON, AL 36202
256-236-1551
866-814-9253
Fax: 256-241-1991
www.annistonstar.com
• Al Muskewitz, Golf and JSU Teams Writer
(256) 235-3577
• Joe Medley, Sports Columnist
(256) 235-3576
Frequency:
7 time(s) per week

ANTELOPE VALLEY PRESS
37404 SIEERA HIGHWAY
PO BOX 4050
PALMDALE, CA 93590-4050
661-273-2700
Fax: 661-947-4870
editor@avpress.com
www.avpress.com
• Brian Golden, Sports Writer
(661) 267-5344
• Alan Hendry, Sports Writer

(661) 267-4170
ahendry@avpress.com
• Merisa Jensen, Sports Writer
(661) 267-4158
mjensen@avpress.com
Frequency:
7 time(s) per week

ANTIGO DAILY JOURNAL
612 SUPERIOR STREET
ANTIGO, WI 54409-2049
715-623-4191
Fax: 715-623-4193
ADJ@dwave.net
antigodailyjournal.com
• Fred Berner, Publisher
(715) 623-4191
adj@dwave.net
Frequency:
7 time(s) per week
Teams:
Antigo High School, Elcho High School,
White Lake High School,
Wittenberg-Birnamwood High School.
Sports:
Football, volleyball, boys & girls soccer,
boys & girls tennis, boys & girls track, boys
& girls hockey, boys & girls crosscountry,
boys & girls basketball, softball, wrestling,
gymnastics, and boys golf.

APPEAL-DEMOCRAT
1530 ELLIS LAKE DRIVE
MARYSVILLE, CA 95901-4258
530-749-4700
800-831-2345
Fax: 530-741-1195
www.appeal-democrat.com
• Jimmy Graben, Sports Editor
(530) 749-4791
• Andy Arrenquin, Sports Reporter
(530) 749-4790
Frequency:
7 time(s) per week

ARGUS LEADER
200 S MINNESOTA AVENUE
PO BOX 5034
SIOUX FALLS, SD 57117
605-331-2200
800-952-0127
Fax: 605-331-2294
argusnews@argusleader.com
www.argusleader.com
• Matt Zimmer, Sports Editor
(605) 331-2213
• Michael Klinski, Assistant Sports Editor;
News Reporter
(605) 331-2213
Frequency:
7 time(s) per week

ARGUS-PRESS
201 EAST EXCHANGE STREET
OWOSSO, MI 48867
989-725-5136
Fax: 989-725-6376
www.argus-press.com
• Jason Barczy, Sports Editor
• Jerome Murphy, Sports Reporter
Frequency:
7 time(s) per week

ARIZONA DAILY STAR
4850 SOUTH PARK AVENUE
TUCSON, AZ 85714-1637

520-573-4220
800-695-4111
Fax: 520-573-4141
support@azstarnet.com
www.azstarnet.com
• Ryan Finley, Sports Editor
(520) 4312
rfinley@azstarnet.com
• Paul Brown, Sports News Assistant
(520) 573-4145
• Charles Constantino, Sports News
Assistant
(520) 573-4145
Frequency:
7 time(s) per week

ARIZONA DAILY SUN
1751 SOUTH THOMPSON
FLAGSTAFF, AZ 86001
928-774-4545
Fax: 928-773-1934
azdsnews@azdailysun.com
www.azdailysun.com
• Cody Bashore, Sports Editor
(928) 556-2251
cbashore@azdailysun.com
Frequency:
7 time(s) per week

ARIZONA REPUBLIC
200 EAST VAN BUREN STREET
PHOENIX, AZ 85004-2238
602-444-8000
800-331-9303
Fax: 602-444-8044
newstips@arizonarepublic.com
www.azcentral.com
• Dan Bickley, Sports Columnist
(602) 444-8253
dan.bickley@arizonarepublic.com
• Paul Coro, Sports/NBA Reporter
(602) 444-2470
paul.coro@arizonarepublic.com
• Mark Faller, Sports Editor/Director of
Sports Center
(602) 444-4937
Mark.Faller@arizonarepublic.com
• Richard Obert, High School Sports
Reporter
(602) 444-4894
richard.obert@arizonarepublic.com
• Kent Somers, Sports/Cardinals Reporter
(602) 444-8335
kent.somers@arizonarepublic.com
Frequency:
7 time(s) per week

ARKANSAS CITY TRAVELER
200 EAST 5TH AVENUE
PO BOX 988
ARKANSAS CITY, KS 67005-2606
620-442-4200
Fax: 620-442-7483
www.arkcity.com
• Joey Sprinkle, Sports Editor
Frequency:
6 time(s) per week

ARKANSAS DEMOCRAT-GAZETTE
121 EAST CAPITOL AVENUE
LITTLE ROCK, AR 72201-3819
501-378-3400
800-345-2395
Fax: 501-372-4765
news@ardemgaz.com
www.arkansasonline.com

• Jim Bailey, Contributing Sports Columnist
(501) 378-3539
jbailey@arkansasonline.com
• Tim Cooper, Sports Reporter
(501) 378-3576
tcooper@arkansasonline.com
• Bob Holt, Razorbacks Beat Reporter
(479) 770-8464
bholt@arkansasonline.com
• Jeff Krupsaw, Deputy Sports Editor
(501) 399-3637
jkrupsaw@arkansasonline.com
• Robert Yates, Horse Racing/High School
Football Sports Reporter
(501) 378-3579
ryates@arkansasonline.com
Frequency:
7 time(s) per week

ARTESIA DAILY PRESS
PO BOX 190
ARTESIA, NM 88211-0190
575-746-3524
Fax: 575-746-8795
sports@artesianews.com
www.artesianews.com
• Brienne Green, Sports Editor
Frequency:
5 time(s) per week

ASBURY PARK PRESS
3601 HIGHWAY 66
PO BOX 1550
NEPTUNE, NJ 07754
732-922-6000
800-822-9770
Fax: 732-922-4818
sports@app.com
www.app.com
• Steve Feitl, Sports Editor
Frequency:
7 time(s) per week

ASHEVILLE CITIZEN-TIMES
14 O. HENRY AVENUE
ASHEVILLE, NC 28801-2604
828-232-5866
800-800-4204
Fax: 828-251-0585
news@citizen-times.com
www.citizen-times.com
• Andrew Pearson, High School Sports
Reporter & Blogger
(828) 232-5863
apearson@citizen-times.com
Frequency:
7 time(s) per week

ASHLAND TIMES-GAZETTE
40 EAST SECOND STREET
ASHLAND, OH 44805-2304
419-281-0581
888-463-9711
Fax: 419-281-5591
newsroom@times-gazette.com
www.times-gazette.com
• Doug Haidet, Sports Editor
(419) 281-0581
dhaidet@times-gazette.com
• Becky Tener, Sports Writer
(419) 281-0581
btener@times-gazette.com
Frequency:
6 time(s) per week

media

ASPEN TIMES
310 EAST MAIN STREET
ASPEN, CO 81611
970-925-3414
Fax: 970-925-6240
mail@aspentimes.com
www.aspentimes.com
• Dale Strode, Sports Editor
(970) 925-3414
Frequency:
6 time(s) per week

ASSOCIATED PRESS
50 ROCKEFELLER PLAZA
NEW YORK, NY 10020
212-621-1500
Fax: 212-621-5447
info@ap.org
www.ap.org
• Rick Haas, SNTV North America Editor
(212) 621-7417
Frequency
All day, every day

ATCHISON DAILY GLOBE
308 COMMERCIAL STREET
PO BOX 247
ATCHISON, KS 66002
913-367-0583
800-748-7615
Fax: 913-367-7531
globe@npgco.com
www.atchisondailyglobe.com
• Logan Jackson, Sports Editor
• Christy McKibben, Advertising Manager
christym@npgco.com
Frequency:
7 time(s) per week

ATHENS BANNER-HERALD
1 PRESS PLACE
ATHENS, GA 30601-2605
706-208-2200
800-553-4252
Fax: 706-543-5234
news@onlineathens.com
www.onlineathens.com
• Marc Weiszer, UGA Beat Writer
(706) 208-2238
marc.weiszer@onlineathens.com
• Nicole Saavedra, Sports Reporter
nicole.saavedra@onlineathens.com
• Rachel G. Bowers, Sports Editor
(706) 208-2237
rachel.bowers@onlineathens.com
Frequency:
7 time(s) per week

ATHENS DAILY REVIEW
PO BOX 32
201 S. PRAIRIEVILLE ST.
ATHENS, TX 75751-2541
903-675-5626
Fax: 903-675-9450
editor@athensreview.com
www.athensreview.com
• Jayson Larson, Sports Editor
(903) 675-5626
Frequency:
6 time(s) per week

ATHENS MESSENGER
P.O. BOX 4210
9300 JOHNSON HOLLOW ROAD
ATHENS, OH 45701

740-592-6612
800-233-6611
Fax: 740-592-4647
info@athensmessenger.com
www.athensohiotoday.com
• Jason Arkley, Ohio University Sports
(740) 592-6612
• Kevin Wiseman, Sports Editor
(740) 592-6612
kwiseman@athensmessenger.com
Frequency:
6 time(s) per week

ATHENS NEWS COURIER
410 W. GREEN ST
ATHENS, AL 35611
256-232-2720
Fax: 256-233-7753
ann@athensnews-courier.com
enewscourier.com
• Jonathan Deal, Sports Writer
Frequency
6x weekly

ATHOL DAILY NEWS
225 EXCHANGE STREET
PO BOX 1000
ATHOL, MA 01331
978-249-3535
Fax: 978-249-9630
www.atholdailynews.com
• Josh Talbot, Sports Editor
(978) 249-3535
Frequency:
6 time(s) per week

ATLANTA JOURNAL-CONSTITUTION
223 PERIMETER CENTER PKWY
ATLANTA, GA 30346
404-526-5151
800-846-6672
Fax: 404-526-5746
listen@ajc.com
www.ajc.com
• Ray Cox, Sports Content Editor
Frequency:
7 time(s) per week

ATLANTIC NEWS-TELEGRAPH
PO BOX 230 STREET
ATLANTIC, IA 50022-1365
712-243-2624
800-926-6397
Fax: 712-243-4988
news@ant-news.com
www.swiowanewssource.com
• Drew Herron, Sports Editor
sports@ant-news.com
Frequency:
6 time(s) per week

AUBURN JOURNAL
1030 HIGH STREET
AUBURN, CA 95603-4707
530-885-5656
Fax: 530-885-7235
www.auburnjournal.com
• Matthew Kimel, Sports Editor
(530) 852-0240
Frequency:
6 time(s) per week

AUGUSTA CHRONICLE
725 BROAD STREET
AUGUSTA, GA 30901-1305

706-724-0851
866-249-0851
Fax: 706-823-3408
newsroom@augustachronicle.com
www.chronicle.augusta.com
• John Boyette, Sports Editor
• Chris Gay, Sports Reporter
• Wayne Staats, Sports Writer
• Scott Michaux, Sports Columnist
• David Lee, Sports Writer
Frequency:
7 time(s) per week

AUGUSTA DAILY GAZETTE
204 EAST 5TH STREET
PO BOX 9
AUGUSTA, KS 67010
316-775-2218
Fax: 316-775-3220
www.augustagazette.com
• Jeremy Costello, Sports Editor
jcostello@augustagazette.com
Frequency:
5 time(s) per week

AUSTIN AMERICAN-STATESMAN
PO BOX 670
AUSTIN, TX 78767-1200
512-445-3500
800-445-9898
Fax: 512-445-3679
news@statesman.com
www.statesman.com/
• James Wangemann, Assistant Sports Editor
(512) 445-3659
• Richard Tijerina, Deputy Sports Editor
(512) 445-3627
• Kevin Lyttle, Sports Writer
(512) 445-3615
• Danny Davis, H.S. Sports Reporter
(512) 445-3952
Frequency:
7 time(s) per week

AUSTIN DAILY HERALD
310 2ND STREET NE
AUSTIN, MN 55912-3436
507-433-8851
Fax: 507-437-8644
www.austindailyherald.com/
• Rocky Hulne, Sports Editor
(507) 434-2234
rocky.hulne@austindailyherald.com
Frequency:
6 time(s) per week

AZTECA NEWS
810 N BROADWAY
SANTA ANA, CA 92701-3424
714-972-9912
Fax: 714-973-8117
www.aztecanews.com
Frequency:
1 time(s) per week

BAKER CITY HERALD
1915 1ST STREET
PO BOX 807
BAKER CITY, OR 97814-3338
541-523-3673
888-318-7508
Fax: 541-523-6426
news@bakercityherald.com
www.bakercityherald.com

- Kathy Orr, Sports Photographer
- Gerry Steele, Sports Editor
Frequency:
5 time(s) per week

BAKERSFIELD CALIFORNIAN
P.O. BIN 440
1707 EYE STREET
BAKERSFIELD, CA 93302-0440
661-395-7500
800-540-0646
Fax: 661-395-7285
opinion@bakersfield.com
www.bakersfield.com
- Ron Stapp, Sports Copy Editor
(661) 395-7388
rstapp@bakersfield.com
- Zach Ewing, H.S. Sports Reporter
(661) 395-7324
- Tony Lacava, Sports Editor
(661) 395-7393
- Jeff Evans, College Sports Reporter
(661) 395-7389
jevans@bakerfield.com
- Mike Griffith, Condors/Racing Reporter
(661) 395-7390
Frequency:
7 time(s) per week

BALTIMORE SUN
501 N CALVERT STREET
BALTIMORE, MD 21278
410-332-6000
800-829-8000
Fax: 410-783-2518
customersatisfaction@baltsun.com
www.baltimoresun.com
- Andrew Knobel, Deputy Sports Editor
(410) 332-6659
andy.knobel@baltsun.com
- Dan Connolly, Orioles and National
Baseball Reporter
(410) 332-6200
- Ron Fritz, Head of Sports
(410) 332-6421
ron.fritz@baltsun.com
Frequency:
7 time(s) per week
Baseball Sponsor:
MLB Baltimore Orioles.

BANGOR DAILY NEWS
491 MAIN STREET
PO BOX 1329
BANGOR, ME 04402-1329
207-990-8000
800-432-7964
Fax: 207-941-9476
www.bangornews.com/
- Joseph McLaughlin, Sports Editor
(207) 990-8229
Frequency:
5 time(s) per week

BANNER-GRAPHIC
100 NORTH JACKSON STREET
PO BOX 509
GREENCASTLE, IN 46135
765-653-5151
800-778-8877
Fax: 765-653-2063
news@bannergraphic.com
www.bannergraphic.com
- Grant Wieman, Sports Editor
gwieman@bannergraphic.com
Frequency:
6 time(s) per week

BANNER-NEWS
130 SOUTH WASHINGTON
MAGNOLIA, AR 71753-3523
870-234-5130
Fax: 870-234-2551
www.bannernews.net
- William Korff, Sports Reporter
- Chris Gilliam, Sports Editor
cgilliam@bannernews.net
Frequency:
6 time(s) per week

BARABOO NEWS REPUBLIC
714 MATT'S FERRY ROAD
PO BOX 9
BARABOO, WI 53913
608-356-4808
Fax: 608-356-0344
bnr-sports@capitalnewspapers.com
www.wiscnews.com/baraboonewsrepublic/
- Pete Watson, Sports Editor
(608) 356-4808
Frequency:
6 time(s) per week

BASTROP DAILY ENTERPRISE
119 EAST HICKORY
PO BOX 311
BASTROP, LA 71220-
318-281-4421
Fax: 318-283-1699
news@bastropenterprise.com
www.bastropenterprise.com
- Marq Mitcham, Sports Editor
(318) 281-2691
Frequency:
5 time(s) per week

BATESVILLE GUARD
258 WEST MAIN STREET
PO BOX 236
BATESVILLE, AR 72503
870-793-2383
870-559-2383
Fax: 870-793-9268
news@guardonline.com
www.guardonline.com
- Paul Glover, Sports Editor
(870) 793-2383
- John David Sonnier, Sports Writer
(870) 793-2383
Frequency:
5 time(s) per week

BATTLE CREEK ENQUIRER
77 EAST MICHIGAN AVENUE
SUITE 101
BATTLE CREEK, MI 49017-3002
269-964-7161
Fax: 269-964-0299
amorin@battlecr.gannett.com
www.battlecreekenquirer.com
- Nick Buckley, General Sports
(269) 966-0679
- Bill Broderick, Sports Editor
(269) 966-0678
bbroderi@battlecr.gannett.com
- Will Kowalski, Golf, Bowling, General
Sports
(269) 966-0657
Frequency:
7 time(s) per week

BAXTER BULLETIN
16 W. 6TH STREET
PO BOX 1750
MOUNTAIN HOME, AR 72653-3508
870-508-8000
Fax: 870-508-8020
newsroom@baxterbulletin.com
www.baxterbulletin.com/
- Sonny Elliott, Sports Editor
(870) 508-8060
sonnye@baxterbulletin.com
- Scott McDonald, Sports Writer
- Neal Denton, Sports Reporter
(870) 508-8061
ndenton@baxterbulletin.com
Frequency:
6 time(s) per week

BAY CITY TIMES
311 5TH STREET
BAY CITY, MI 48708-5806
989-894-9641
800-219-9919
Fax: 989-893-0649
bcsports@mlive.com
www.mlivemediagroup.com
- Lee Thompson, Sports Reporter
(989) 895-3542
lthomps2@mlive.com
- Cory Butzin, Sports Reporter
Frequency:
7 time(s) per week

BAY CITY TRIBUNE
2901 CAREY SMITH BOULEVARD
BAY CITY, TX 77414
979-245-5555
Fax: 979-244-5908
support@baycitytribune.com
www.baycitytribune.com
- Barry Halvoson, Sports Editor
sports@baycitytribune.com
Frequency:
5 time(s) per week

BAYTOWN SUN
1301 MEMORIAL DRIVE
PO BOX 90
BAYTOWN, TX 77520-2401
281-422-8302
Fax: 281-427-6283
sunnews@baytownsun.com
www.baytownsun.com
- Todd Hveem, Assistant Editor/Sports
Editor
(281) 425-8031
Frequency:
5 time(s) per week. Tues-Sat
Circulation:
10,000

BEACH REPORTER
2615 PACIFIC COAST HIGHWAY
SUITE 329
HERMOSA BEACH, CA 90254
310-372-0388
Fax: 310-372-6113
www.tbrnews.com
- Erin Michael Stitt, Sports Editor
(310) 372-0388
estitt@tbrnews.com
Frequency:
1 time(s) per week

BEACON-NEWS
495 N COMMONS DRIVE
SUITE 200
AURORA, IL 60504
630-978-8880
800-244-5844
Fax: 630-978-8509
www.beaconnews.suntimes.com
• Jason Bauman, Assistant Sports Editor
(630) 978-8412
• R.J. Gerber, Sports Editor
(630) 978-8175
Frequency:
7 time(s) per week

BEATRICE DAILY SUN
200 NORTH 7TH STREET
BEATRICE, NE 68310
402-223-5233
800-666-5233
Fax: 402-228-3571
news@beatricedailysun.com
www.beatricedailysun.com
• Janet Harms, Advertising Manager
Frequency:
6 time(s) per week

BEAUMONT ENTERPRISE
380 MAIN STREET
BEAUMONT, TX 77701-2331
409-838-2815
Fax: 409-838-2869
localnews@beaumontenterprise.com
www.beaumontenterprise.com
• David Berry, Sports Reporter
(409) 880-0747
• Avi Zaleon, Sports Reporter
(409) 838-2839
• Jared Ainsworth, Sports Reporter
(409) 880-0723
• Christopher Dabe, Sports Editor
(409) 880-0746
Frequency:
7 time(s) per week

BEAVER COUNTY TIMES
400 FAIR AVENUE
BEAVER, PA 15009-1907
724-775-3200
800-899-6397
Fax: 724-775-4180
timesnews@timesonline.com
www.timesonline.com
• Mike Bires, Sports Reporter
(724) 775-3200
mbires@timesonline.com
• Ed Rose, Sports Editor
(724) 266-3330
Frequency:
6 time(s) per week

BEAVERCREEK NEWS CURRENT
1836 WEST PARK SQUARE
XENIA, OH 45385
937-372-4444
Fax: 937-372-1951
www.beavercreeknewscurrent.com
• Shawn Bauman, Sports
(937) 372-4444
• Wayne Baker, Sports
(937) 372-4444
Frequency:
6 time(s) per week

BELLEFONTAINE EXAMINER
127 EAST CHILLICOTHE AVENUE
PO BOX 40
BELLEFONTAINE, OH 43311-1957
937-592-3060
Fax: 937-592-4463
news@examiner.org
www.examiner.org/
• Matt Hammond, Sports Editor
(937) 592-3060
Frequency:
6 time(s) per week

BELLEVILLE NEWS-DEMOCRAT
120 SOUTH ILLINOIS
PO BOX 427
BELLEVILLE, IL 62222-2130
618-239-2552
800-642-3878
Fax: 618-345-4223
newsroom@bnd.com
www.belleville.com
• Dean Criddle, Sports Reporter
(618) 239-2665
• Steve Korte, Sports Reporter
(618) 239-2522
• Pat Kuhl, Sports Editor
(618) 239-2537
• Norm Sanders, Sports Writer
(618) 239-2454
• Dave Wilhelm, Sports Reporter
(618) 239-2661
Frequency:
7 time(s) per week

BELLEVUE GAZETTE
10990 WILSHIRE BLVD
LOS ANGELES, CA 90024
310-966-4101
Fax: 905-949-4984
admin@landmarksport.com
www.landmarksport.com
• Elliott Kerr, President
Founded:
1987
Frequency:
Daily newspaper (Tuesday - Saturday)
Teams Covered:
Bellevue, Ohio, Redman, & Lady Red

BELLINGHAM HERALD
1155 NORTH STATE STREET
SUITE 200
BELLINGHAM, WA 98225-5037
360-676-2660
Fax: 360-756-2826
www.bellinghamherald.com
• Colin Howser, Sports Copy Editor
(360) 715-2268
• David Rasbach, Sports Editor
(360) 715-2271
• Andrew Lang, Sports Reporter
(360) 715-2862
Frequency:
7 time(s) per week

BENICIA HERALD
820 1ST STREET
BENICIA, CA 94510
707-745-0733
Fax: 707-745-8583
beniciaherald@gmail.com
beniciaherald.wordpress.com
• Donna Beth Weilenman, Staff Reporter
• Steve Guertin, Sports Editor
Frequency:
5 time(s) per week

BENNINGTON BANNER
425 MAIN STREET
BENNINGTON, VT 05201-2141
802-447-7567
800-245-0254
Fax: 802-442-3413
news@benningtonbanner.com
www.benningtonbanner.com
• Austin Danforth, Sports Reporter
(802) 447-7567
• Adam Samrov, Sports Editor
(802) 447-7567
Frequency:
6 time(s) per week

BENTON COUNTY DAILY RECORD
104 SOUTHWEST A STREET
BENTONVILLE, AR 72712-5867
479-271-3700
Fax: 479-271-3744
www.nwanews.com
• Paul Gatling, Sports Editor
(479) 271-3792
sports@nwanews.com
• Carolyn Kirkland, Advertising Manager
(479) 770-8414
carolynk@nwanews.com
• Diane Williams, Classified Manager
(479) 571-6421
dwilliams@nwanews.com
Frequency:
7 time(s) per week

BENTON EVENING NEWS
111 EAST CHURCH STREET
BENTON, IL 62812
618-438-5611
Fax: 618-435-2413
www.bentoneveningnews.com
• Allen Parker, Sports Editor
sports@bentoneveningnews.com
Frequency:
6 time(s) per week

BERKELEY HEIGHTS/NEW PROVIDENCE INDEPENDENT PRESS
80 SOUTH STREET
NEW PROVIDENCE, NJ 07974-1941
908-464-1025
Fax: 908-464-9085
ipeditors@njnpublishing.com
www.nj.com/independentpress
• Art Polakowski, Sports Editor
Frequency:
1 time(s) per week

BERKSHIRE EAGLE
75 SOUTH CHURCH STREET
PO BOX 1171
PITTSFIELD, MA 01202-6132
413-447-7311
800-245-0254
Fax: 413-499-3419
news@berkshireeagle.com
www.berkshireeagle.com
• Matt Sprague, Sports Editor
(413) 496-6254
• Howard Herman, Sports Columnist
(413) 496-6253
hherman@berkshireeagle.com
Frequency:
7 time(s) per week

BERWYN-CICERO-STICKNEY-FOREST VIEW LIFE
1101 W. 31ST STREET
SUITE260
DOWNERS GROVE, IL 60515-5581
708-447-9810
Fax: 708-447-9871
www.mysuburbanlife.com
• David Good, Sports Editor
(630) 427-6270
dgood@shawmedia.com
Frequency:
3 time(s) per week

BILLINGS GAZETTE
P.O. BOX 36300
BILLINGS, MT 59101-1243
406-657-1200
800-543-2505
Fax: 406-657-1208
news@billingsgazette.com
www.billingsgazette.com
• Mike Zimmer, Sports Editor
(406) 657-1291
• Mike Scherting, Assistant Sports Editor
(406) 657-1302
mscherting@billingsgazette.com
Frequency:
7 time(s) per week

BIRMINGHAM NEWS
P.O. BOX 2553
BIRMINGHAM, AL 35203-3802
205-325-2444
800-283-4048
Fax: 205-325-2283
epage@bhamnews.com
www.bhamnews.com
• Tom Arenberg, Sports Editor
(205) 325-2433
• Charles Hollis, Assistant Editor
(205) 325-2161
Frequency:
7 time(s) per week

BISBEE DAILY REVIEW
12 MAIN STREET
BISBEE, AZ 85603
520-432-2231
Fax: 520-432-2356
www.svherald.com
• Matt Hickman, Sports Editor
(515) 520-4612
• Shar Porier, Bisbee Reporter
(520) 515-4692
Frequency:
6 time(s) per week

BISMARCK TRIBUNE
P.O. BOX 5516
BISMARCK, ND 58506
701-223-2500
800-472-2273
Fax: 701-223-2063
www.bismarcktribune.com/
• Lou Babiarz, Sports Editor
(701) 250-8243
• Steve Thomas, Sports Reporter
(701) 250-8244
steve.thomas@bismarcktribune.com
• Mike Weber, Sports Reporter
(701) 355-8839
mike.weber@bismarcktribune.com
• Eric Hammond, Sports Copy Editor
(701) 250-8246
• Cindy Peterson, Sports Reporter
(701) 250-8245

Frequency:
7 time(s) per week

BLACK HILLS PIONEER
315 SEATON CIRCLE
PO BOX 7
SPEARFISH, SD 57783-3212
605-642-2761
800-676-2761
Fax: 605-642-9060
news@bhpioneer.com
www.bhpioneer.com
• Dennis Knuckles, Sports Editor
sports@bhpioneer.com
Frequency:
6 time(s) per week

BLACKWELL JOURNAL-TRIBUNE
113 EAST BLACKWELL AVENUE
PO BOX 760
BLACKWELL, OK 74631-0760
580-363-3370
Fax: 580-363-4415
www.blackwelljournaltribune.net
• Belinda Ramsey, Publisher/Editor
(580) 363-3370
Frequency:
5 time(s) per week

BLADE
541 NORTH SUPERIOR STREET
TOLEDO, OH 43660-1000
419-724-6000
800-245-3317
Fax: 419-724-6391
letters@theblade.com
www.toledoblade.com
• Frank Corsoe, Sports Editor
(419) 724-6115
• Donald Emmons, Sports Writer
(419) 724-6110
• Dave Hackenberg, Sports Reporter
(419) 724-6110
• Dan Firestone, Assistant Sports Editor
(419) 724-6110
• Matt Markey, Outdoors Editor
(419) 724-6110
• Mark Monroe, Sports Writer
(419) 724-6110
mmonroe@theblade.com
Frequency:
7 time(s) per week

BLADE-EMPIRE
510 WASHINGTON STREET
CONCORDIA, KS 66901-2117
785-243-2424
Fax: 785-243-4407
www.bladeempire.com
• Jim Lowell, Sports Editor
Frequency:
5 time(s) per week

BLUEFIELD DAILY TELEGRAPH
P.O. BOX 1599
BLUEFIELD, WV 24701-2744
304-327-2800
800-763-2459
Fax: 304-327-6179
sports@bdtonline.com
www.bdtonline.com
• Terri Hale, Advertising Director
(304) 327-2816
thale@bdtonline.com
Frequency:
7 time(s) per week

BOLIVAR COMMERCIAL
821 NORTH CHRISMAN AVENUE
PO BOX 1050
CLEVELAND, MS 38732-1050
662-843-4241
Fax: 662-843-1830
news@bolivarcommercial.com
• Andy Collier, Sports Editor
(662) 843-4241
Frequency:
5 time(s) per week

BONNER COUNTY DAILY BEE
310 CHURCH STREET
PO BOX 159
SANDPOINT, ID 83864
208-263-9534
Fax: 208-263-9091
www.bonnercountydailybee.com
• Eric Plummer, Sports Editor
eplummer@bonnercountydailybee.com
Frequency:
6 time(s) per week

BOONVILLE DAILY NEWS
412 HIGH STREET
BOONVILLE, MO 65233-1242
660-882-5335
Fax: 660-882-2256
news@boonvilledailynews.com
www.boonvilledailynews.com
• Chris Bowie, Sports Editor
(660) 882-5335
cbowie@boonvilledailynews.com
Frequency:
5 time(s) per week

BORGER NEWS-HERALD
PO BOX 5130
BORGER, TX 79008
806-273-5611
Fax: 806-273-2552
editor@borgernewsherald.com
www.borgernewsherald.com
• Mikala Reiswig, Sports Editor
sports@borgernewsherald.com
Frequency:
6 time(s) per week

BOSTON GLOBE
135 WILLIAM MORRISSEY BOULEVARD
BOSTON, MA 02125-3310
617-929-2000
Fax: 617-929-3186
localnews@globe.com
www.boston.com
• Gregory Lang, Assistant Sports Editor
(617) 929-2531
glang@globe.com
• Pete Goodwin, Copy Editor
(617) 929-2847
p_goodwin@globe.com
• Nicholas Cafardo, Sports Reporter
(617) 929-2878
cafardo@globe.com
• Chad Finn, Sports Media Columnist
(617) 929-3080
finn@globe.com
• Bob Hohler, Sports Reporter
(617) 929-2860
hohler@globe.com
• Robert Holmes, Sports Assistant Editor
(617) 929-2876
r_holmes@globe.com
• Nancy Marrapese-Burrell, Sports Reporter
(617) 929-3014
marrapese@globe.com

• Shira Springer, Sports Reporter
(617) 929-2835
springer@globe.com
Frequency:
7 time(s) per week

BOSTON HERALD
ONE HERALD SQUARE
BOSTON, MA 02205
617-426-3000
800-882-2024
Fax: 617-619-6450
sports@bostonherald.com
www.bostonherald.com
• Steve Buckley, Sports Columnist
(617) 426-3000
• Steve Bulpett, Basketball Reporter
(617) 426-3000
sports@bostonherald.com
• Jim Clark, High School Sports Reporter
(617) 426-3000
sports@bostonherald.com
• John Connolly, Sports Reporter
(617) 426-3000
sports@bostonherald.com
• Mark Torpey, Sports Executive Editor
(617) 426-3000
sports@bostonherald.com
• Mark Murphy, Deputy Sports Editor
(617) 426-3000
• Michael Silverman, Sports Reporter
(617) 426-3000
sports@bostonherald.com
• Rich Thompson, Sports Reporter
(617) 426-3000
sports@bostonherald.com
Frequency:
7 time(s) per week

BOURNE ENTERPRISE
50 DEPOT AVENUE
FALMOUTH, MA 02540-2302
508-548-4700
800-286-7744
Fax: 508-540-8407
www.capenews.net
• Dan Crowley, Sports Editor
(508) 548-4700
Frequency:
1 time(s) per week

BOWIE BLADE-NEWS
2000 CAPITAL DRIVE
ANNAPOLIS, MD 21401
410-268-5000
Fax: 410-280-5953
tips@capgaznews.com
www.hometownbowie.com
• Gerry Jackson, Sports Editor
(410) 280-5926
• Dave Broughton, Sports Writer
(410) 280-5940
• John McNamara, Sports Writer/Maryland
(410) 280-5925
• Mike Peters, High School Sports Editor
(410) 280-5923
• Bill Wagner, Sports Writer/Navy
(410) 280-5952
Frequency:
1 time(s) per week

BOZEMAN DAILY CHRONICLE
2820 WEST COLLEGE
PO BOX 1190
BOZEMAN, MT 59718-3925
406-587-4491
800-275-0401

Fax: 406-587-7995
citydesk@dailychronicle.com
www.bozemandailychronicle.com
• Jon Maletz, Sports Editor
(406) 582-2690
jmaletz@dailychronicle.com
Frequency:
7 time(s) per week

BRADENTON HERALD
102 MANATEE AVENUE WEST
BRADENTON, FL 34205-8810
941-748-0411
Fax: 941-745-7097
www.bradenton.com
• Alan Dell, Sports Reporter
(941) 745-7080
• Tim Wolfrum, Sports Editor
(941) 748-0411
• Jason Dill, Sports Reporter
(941) 748-0411
jdill@bradenton.com
Frequency:
7 time(s) per week

BRADFORD ERA
43 MAIN STREET
BRADFORD, PA 16701-2019
814-368-3173
800-346-7353
Fax: 814-362-6510
www.bradfordera.com
• Joe Vinelli, Sports Editor
(814) 362-6531
joev@bradfordera.com
Frequency:
6 time(s) per week

BRAINERD DAILY DISPATCH
506 JAMES STREET
BRAINERD, MN 56401-2942
218-829-4705
800-432-3703
Fax: 218-829-7735
www.brainerddispatch.com
• Mike Bialka, Sports Editor
(218) 855-5861
mike.bialka@brainerddispatch.com
• Jeremy Millsop, Sports Writer
(218) 855-5856
jeremy.millsop@brainerddispatch.com
Frequency:
6 time(s) per week

BRANSON TRI-LAKES DAILY NEWS
200 INDUSTRIAL PARK DRIVE
PO BOX 1900
HOLLISTER, MO 65672-5327
417-334-3161
Fax: 417-334-1460
www.bransondailynews.com
• Pat Dailey, Sports Editor
Frequency:
2 time(s) per week

BRAZIL TIMES
100 NORTH MERIDIAN STREET
PO BOX 429
BRAZIL, IN 47834-2172
812-446-2216
800-489-5090
Fax: 812-446-0938
www.thebraziltimes.com
• Carey Fox, Sports Editor
(812) 446-2216
redwood17257@yahoo.com

Frequency:
6 time(s) per week

BRENHAM BANNER-PRESS
PO BOX 585
BRENHAM, TX 77834
979-836-7956
Fax: 979-830-8577
sports@brenhambanner.com
www.brenhambanner.com
• Matt Keyser, Sports Editor
(979) 836-7956
sports@brenhambanner.com
Frequency:
6 time(s) per week

BRIDGETON NEWS
100 EAST COMMERCE STREET
BRIDGETON, NJ 08302-2602
856-451-1000
Fax: 856-455-2633
www.nj.com/bridgeton
• Eric Goldstein, Sports Editor
(856) 451-1000
Frequency:
6 time(s) per week

BRISTOL HERALD COURIER
320 BOB MORRISON BOULEVARD
BRISTOL, VA 24201
276-669-2181
Fax: 276-669-3696
sports@bristolnews.com
www.tricities.com
• Jim Sacco, Sports Editor
(276) 645-2569
Frequency
7x/week

BRISTOL PRESS
188 MAIN STREET
BRISTOL, CT 06010
860-584-0501
800-220-6229
Fax: 860-584-2192
editor@bristolpress.com
www.bristolpress.com
• Brad Carroll, Executive Sports Editor
(860) 225-4601
bcarroll@newbritainherald.com
• Paul Angilly, Sports Editor
(860) 584-0501
Frequency:
7 time(s) per week

BROOKINGS REGISTER
312 5TH STREET
BROOKINGS, SD 57006
605-692-6271
Fax: 605-692-2979
register@brookings.net
www.brookingsregister.com/
• Troy Maroney, Sports Editor
(605) 692-6271
sports@brookingsregister.com
Frequency:
6 time(s) per week

BROWNSVILLE HERALD
1135 EAST VAN BUREN STREET
BROWNSVILLE, TX 78520
956-542-4301
800-488-4301
Fax: 956-542-0840
www.brownsvilleherald.com

• Bryan Read, Sports Director
(956) 542-4301
bread@brownsvilleherald.com
Frequency:
7 time(s) per week

BROWNWOOD BULLETIN
700 CARNEGIE STREET
BROWNWOOD, TX 76801-7040
325-646-2541
Fax: 325-646-6835
news@brownwoodbulletin.com
www.brownwoodbulletin.com/
• Derrick Stuckly, Sports Editor
(325) 646-2541
news@brownwoodbulletin.com
Frequency:
6 time(s) per week

BRUNSWICK NEWS
3011 ALTAMA AVENUE
BRUNSWICK, GA 31520-4608
912-265-8320
Fax: 912-264-4973
editor@thebrunswicknews.com
www.thebrunswicknews.com
• Dave Jordan, Sports Editor
(912) 265-8320
Frequency:
6 time(s) per week

BRYAN TIMES
127 SOUTH WALNUT STREET
BRYAN, OH 43506
419-636-1111
Fax: 419-636-8937
www.bryantimes.com
• Nate Parsons, Sports Editor
• Amy Thompson, Classified Manager
amy@bryantimes.com
• Tom Voigt, Advertising Manager
Frequency:
6 time(s) per week
Description:
Daily Newspaper

BRYAN-COLLEGE STATION EAGLE
1729 BRIARCREST
BRYAN, TX 77802-2712
979-776-4444
Fax: 979-774-0053
news@theeagle.com
www.theeagle.com
• Robert Cessna, Sports Editor
(979) 731-4638
robert.cessna@theeagle.com
• Tammye Mineo, Advertising Manager
(979) 776-4444
Frequency:
7 time(s) per week

BUCKS COUNTY COURIER TIMES
8400 NORTH BRISTOL PIKE
LEVITTOWN, PA 19057
215-949-4000
Fax: 215-949-4177
feedback@phillyburbs.com
www.phillyburbs.com
• Timothy J. Birch, Advertising Director
(215) 949-4120
tbirch@phillyburbs.com
• Kate Rochelle, Classified Manager
(215) 949-4107
krochelle@phillyburbs.com
• Gary Silvers, Sports Editor
(215) 949-4212

gsilvers@phillyburbs.com
• Kevin Cooney, Sports Writer
(215) 949-4209
kcooney@phillyBurbs.com
Frequency:
6 time(s) per week

BUFFALO NEWS
1 NEWS PLAZA
BUFFALO, NY 14240
800-777-8610
Fax: 716-856-5150
sports@buffnews.com
www.buffnews.com
• Steve Jones, Sports Editor
• Tom Borrelli, Sports Writer
• Greg Connors, Sports Reporter
gconnors@buffnews.com
• Greg Connors, Sports Writer
gconnors@buffnews.com
• Dennis Danheiser, Sports Assistant Editor
(716) 849-4461
• Bob Dicesare, Sports Columnist
(716) 849-4463
• Mark Gaughan, Sports Writer
(716) 849-4461
• Bucky Gleason, Sports Writer
(716) 849-4461
• Tim Graham, Sports Writer
(716) 849-4461
• Mike Harrington, Sports Writer
mharrington@buffnews.com
• Scott Johnston, Sports Assistant Editor
(716) 849-4461
• Steve Jones, Sports Deputy Editor
• Rodney McKissic, Sports Reporter
• Keith McShea, Sports Writer
• Mary Jo Monnin, Sports Writer
(716) 849-4461
• Amy Moritz, Sports Writer
(716) 849-4002
• Milt Northrop, Sports Writer
mnorthrop@buffnews.com
• Howard Smith, Sports Executive Editor
• Jerry Sullivan, Sports Columnist
(716) 849-4461
• Bob Summers, Sports Writer
(716) 849-4461
• John Vogl, Sports Writer
• Allen Wilson, Sports Writer
(716) 849-4461
Frequency:
7 time(s) per week

BULLETIN
P.O. BOX 6020
BEND, OR 97702
541-382-1811
Fax: 541-385-5804
news@bendbulletin.com
www.bendbulletin.com
• Bill Bigelow, Sports Editor
(541) 383-0359
• Zack Hall, Sports Reporter
(541) 617-7868
Frequency:
7 time(s) per week

BURBANK LEADER
221 N BRAND BLVD, 2ND FLOOR
GLENDALE, CA 91203
818-637-3200
Fax: 818-241-1975
burbankleader@latimes.com
www.burbankleader.com

• Jeff Tully, Sports Editor
(818) 637-3245
jeff.tully@latimes.com
Frequency:
2 time(s) per week

BURLINGTON COUNTY TIMES
4284 ROUTE 130
WILLINGBORO, NJ 08046-2027
609-871-8000
Fax: 609-871-0490
bct.letters@phillyburbs.com
www.phillyburbs.com
• Wayne Richardson, Sports Editor
(609) 871-8000
wrichardson@phillyburbs.com
• Reuben Frank, Sports Reporter
(609) 871-8054
rfrank@phillyburbs.com
Frequency:
6 time(s) per week

BURLINGTON FREE PRESS
191 COLLEGE STREET
BURLINGTON, VT 05402-0494
802-863-3441
Fax: 802-660-1802
metro@burlingtonfreepress.com
www.burlingtonfreepress.com
• John Fantino, Sports Editor
(802) 651-4851
jfantino@burlingtonfreepress.com
• Kevin Commo, Sports Reporter
(802) 660-1855
Frequency:
7 time(s) per week

BUTLER EAGLE
P.O. BOX 271
BUTLER, PA 16001
724-282-8000
Fax: 724-282-4180
news@butlereagle.com
www.butlereagle.com
• John Enrietto, Sports Editor
(724) 282-8000
jenrietto@butlereagle.com
• Mace Pavelek, Advertising Director
(724) 282-8000
macepavelek@hotmail.com
Frequency:
6 time(s) per week

CALEDONIAN RECORD
190 FEDERAL STREET
SAINT JOHNSBURY, VT 05819-2636
802-748-8121
800-523-6397
Fax: 802-748-1613
www.caledonianrecord.com
• Craig Beck, Sports Writer
• Michael Beniash, Sports Editor
beniashm@caledonian-record.com
Frequency:
6 time(s) per week

CALGARY HERALD
PO BOX 2400, STATION M
CALGARY, AB, CANADA T2P0W8
403-235-7100
800-372-9219
Fax: 403-235-7379
letters@calgaryherald.com
www.calgaryherald.com

media

• Keith Bradford, Sports Editor
(403) 235-7578
kbradford@calgaryherald.com

CALL
75 MAIN STREET
WOONSOCKET, RI 02895-4312
401-762-3000
800-934-3142
Fax: 401-765-0303
news@woonsocketcall.com
www.woonsocketcall.com
• Terry Nau, Sports Editor
(401) 727-9292
sports@woonsocketcall.com
Frequency:
7 time(s) per week

CALL-LEADER
317 SOUTH ANDERSON STREET
ELWOOD, IN 46036-2018
765-552-3355
Fax: 765-552-3358
www.elwoodpublishing.com
• Ed Hamilton, Sports Editor
Frequency:
6 time(s) per week

CAMDEN NEWS
113 MADISON AVENUE
CAMDEN, AR 71701
870-836-8192
Fax: 870-837-1414
www.camdenarknews.com
• Kelly Blair, Sports Editor
(870) 836-8192
Frequency:
5 time(s) per week

CANTON LIFE
106 SOUTH STREET
WEST HARTFORD, CT 06110
860-953-0444
Fax: 860-953-0455
www.ctlife.net
• Steve Frank, Sports Editor
(860) 953-0444
Frequency:
1 time(s) per month

CAPE COD TIMES
319 MAIN STREET
HYANNIS, MA 02601-4037
508-775-1200
800-451-7887
Fax: 508-771-3292
news@capecodonline.com
www.capecodonline.com
• Bill Higgins, Sports Editor/Columnist
(508) 862-1151
• Walter Bingham, Sports Writer
(508) 775-1200
Frequency:
7 time(s) per week

CAPE CORAL DAILY BREEZE
2510 DEL PRADO BOULEVARD
CAPE CORAL, FL 33904-5750
239-574-1110
Fax: 239-574-5693
news@breezenewspapers.com
www.flguide.com
• Jim Linette, Sports Editor
(941) 574-1110
jlinette@breezenewspapers.com

Frequency:
6 time(s) per week

CAPITAL
2000 CAPITAL DRIVE
ANNAPOLIS, MD 21401
410-268-5000
Fax: 410-268-4643
capstaff@capitalgazette.com
www.hometownannapolis.com
• Dave Broughton, Sports Writer
(410) 280-5940
• Gerry Jackson, Sports Editor
(410) 280-5926
gjackson@capitalgazette.com
• John McNamara, Sports Writer
(410) 280-5925
• Bill Wagner, Sports Writer
(410) 280-5952
bwagner@capitalgazette.com
• Mike Peters, Sports Reporter
(410) 280-5923
Frequency:
7 time(s) per week

CAPITAL JOURNAL
333 WEST DAKOTA AVENUE
PIERRE, SD 57501
605-224-7301
800-658-3063
Fax: 605-224-9210
news@capjournal.com
www.capjournal.com
• April Pullman, Advertising Manager
(605) 224-7301
• Chris Mangan, Sports Editor
Frequency:
5 time(s) per week

CAPITAL TIMES
P.O. BOX 8060
MADISON, WI 53713-1248
608-252-6400
800-362-8333
Fax: 608-252-6445
www.madison.com
• Brent Engh, Sports Reporter
(608) 252-6471
• Todd Finkelmeyer, Sports Reporter
(608) 252-6465
• Joe Hart, Sports Columnist
(608) 252-6479
• Mike Lucas, Sports Columnist
(608) 252-6470
• Adam Mertz, Sports Editor
(608) 252-6474
• Jim Polzin, Sports Reporter
(608) 252-6473
polzin@madison.com
• Rob Schultz, Sports Reporter
(608) 252-6487
rschultz@madison.com
• Dennis Semrau, Sports Reporter
(608) 252-6490
• Tamira Surprenant, Sports Reporter
(608) 252-6472
Frequency:
6 time(s) per week

CARMI TIMES
323 EAST MAIN STREET
CARMI, IL 62821-1810
618-382-4176
800-245-4488
Fax: 618-384-2163
www.carmitimes.com

• Toby Brown, Sports Editor
(618) 382-4176
• Linda Prince, Advertising Manager
Frequency:
5 time(s) per week

CARROLL COUNTY TIMES
201 RAILROAD AVENUE
WESTMINSTER, MD 21158
410-848-4400
Fax: 410-857-8749
cctnews@carrollcountytimes.com
www.carrollcounty.com
• Bob Blubaugh, Sports Editor
(410) 857-7895
bob.blubaugh@carrollcountytimes.com
• Pat Stoetzer, Sports Reporter
(410) 751-7894
• Aaron Wilson, Sports Writer
(410) 857-7896
Frequency:
7 time(s) per week

CASA GRANDE DISPATCH
200 WEST 2ND
CASA GRANDE, AZ 85230
520-836-7461
Fax: 520-836-0343
dkramerjr@trivalleycentral.com
www.trivalleycentral.com
• Ed Petruska, Sports Editor
Frequency:
6 time(s) per week

CECIL WHIG
601 BRIDGE STREET
ELKTON, MD 21921
410-398-3311
800-220-3311
Fax: 410-398-4044
www.cecilwhig.com
• Mike Curry, Sports Editor
• John Davis, Sports Reporter
• Robert DeAngelo, Sports Editor
(410) 398-3311
Frequency:
5 time(s) per week

CENTRAL KITSAP REPORTER
9989 SILVERDALE WAY, N.W. SUITE 109
SILVERDALE, WA 98383
360-308-9161
Fax: 360-308-9363
www.centralkitsapreporter.com
• Mike Baldwin, Sports Writer
Frequency:
2 time(s) per week

CENTRAL MICHIGAN LIFE
436 MOORE HALL
MT. PLEASANT, MI 48859
989-774-5433
Fax: 989-774-3040
www.cm-life.com
• Andrew Stover, Sports Reporter
stove1aj@cmich.edu
• Matt Thompson, Sports Writer
thomp3mj@cmich.edu

CENTRAL NEWS/JOURNAL/STAR WAVE
4201 WILSHIRE BOULEVARD SUITE 600
LOS ANGELES, CA 90010-3601
323-556-5720
800-404-9283
Fax: 323-556-5704
www.wavenewspapers.com

• Ron Guild, Sports Writer
(323) 556-5720
Frequency:
2 time(s) per week

CENTRALIA SENTINEL
232 EAST BROADWAY
CENTRALIA, IL 62801-3251
618-532-5604
800-371-9892
Fax: 618-532-1212
news@morningsentinel.com
www.morningsentinel.com
• Mike McManus, Sports Reporter
Frequency:
7 time(s) per week

CENTRE DAILY TIMES
3400 EAST COLLEGE AVENUE
STATE COLLEGE, PA 16801
814-238-5000
800-327-5500
Fax: 814-238-1811
www.centredaily.com
• Walt Moody, Sports Editor
(814) 231-4630
• Jeff Rice, Sports Reporter
(814) 231-4609
Frequency:
7 time(s) per week

CENTRE VIEW
1606 KING STREET
ALEXANDRIA, VA 22314
703-917-6444
Fax: 703-917-0991
centreview@connectionnewspapers.com
www.connectionnewspapers.com
• Jeff Graham, Sports Editor
(703) 917-6445
Frequency:
1 time(s) per week

CHANUTE TRIBUNE
15 NORTH EVERGREEN
CHANUTE, KS 66720-1831
620-431-4100
Fax: 620-431-2635
news@chanute.com
www.chanute.com
• Nancy Isaac, Advertising Manager
tribune@chanute.com
• Jason Peake, Sports Editor
sports@chanute.com
Frequency:
6 time(s) per week

CHAPEL HILL NEWS
505 WEST FRANKLIN STREET
CHAPEL HILL, NC 27516-2315
919-932-2003
Fax: 919-968-4953
www.chapelhillnews.com
• Elliott Warnock, Sports Editor
(919) 932-8743
Frequency:
3 time(s) per week

CHARLES CITY PRESS
801 RIVERSIDE DRIVE
CHARLES CITY, IA 50616-2248
641-228-3211
Fax: 641-228-2641
editor@charlescitypress.com
www.charlescitypress.com

• Ryan Kronberg, Sports Editor
sports@charlescitypress.com
• Joel Gray, Advertising Manager
Frequency:
5 time(s) per week

CHARLESTON GAZETTE
1001 VIRGINIA STREET, EAST
CHARLESTON, WV 25301-2835
304-348-5100
800-982-6397
Fax: 304-348-1233
gazette@wvgazette.com
www.wvgazette.com
• Larry Levak, Advertising Manager
(304) 348-4895
• Renae Roberts, Classified Manager
(304) 348-1221
• Mitch Vingle, Sports Editor
(304) 348-4827
Frequency:
7 time(s) per week

CHARLOTTE OBSERVER
600 S TRYON STREET
CHARLOTTE, NC 28202
704-358-5000
800-332-0686
Fax: 704-358-5036
www.charlotte.com
• Rick Bonnell, Sports Reporter
(704) 358-5129
• Scott Fowler, Sports Columnist
(704) 358-5140
sfowler@charlotteobserver.com
• Ron Green, Jr., Sports Writer
(704) 358-5118
• Harry Pickett, Sports Deputy Editor
(704) 358-5127
• David Scott, Sports Columnist
(704) 358-5889
• Tom Sorensen, Sports Columnist
(704) 358-5119
• Jim Utter, Sports Reporter
(704) 358-5113
• Langston Wertz, Reporter
(704) 358-5133
lwertz@charlotteobserver.com
• Gary Schwab,
(704) 358-5120
Frequency:
7 time(s) per week

CHARLOTTE SUN HERALD
23170 HARBORVIEW ROAD
PORT CHARLOTTE, FL 33980
941-206-1000
800-830-7861
Fax: 941-629-2085
www.sun-herald.com
• Gary Brown, Sports Writer
(941) 206-1140
• Debbie Dunn-Rankin, Advertising Manager
(941) 206-1500
• John Fineran, Sports Columnist
(941) 206-1122
• John Fineran, Sports Editor
(941) 206-1122
Frequency:
7 time(s) per week

CHATTANOOGA TIMES FREE PRESS
400 EAST 11TH STREET
CHATTANOOGA, TN 37402
423-757-6322
Fax: 423-668-5052

news@timesfreepress.com
www.timesfreepress.com
• Jay Greeson, Sports Editor
(423) 757-6273
jgreeson@timesfreepress.com
Frequency:
7 time(s) per week

CHEBOYGAN DAILY TRIBUNE
308 NORTH MAIN STREET
CHEBOYGAN, MI 49721-1545
231-627-7144
Fax: 231-627-5331
www.cheboygannews.com/
• Jared Greenleaf, Sports Editor
sports@cheboygantribune.com
Frequency:
5 time(s) per week

CHESTERTON TRIBUNE
193 SOUTH CALUMET ROAD
CHESTERTON, IN 46304-2433
219-926-1131
Fax: 219-926-6389
chestertontrib@earthlink.net
www.chestertontribune.com
• T.R Harlen, Sports Editor
• Harry Lewis, Advertising Manager
Frequency:
5 time(s) per week

CHICAGO CHINESE NEWS
424 FORT HILL, BLDG. 100
NAPERVILLE, IL 60540
630-717-4567
Fax: 630-717-7999
www.chicagochinesenews.com
• Judy Lee, Advertising Manager
• Danny Lee, Sports Editor
(312) 388-8011
Frequency:
6 time(s) per week

CHICAGO SUN-TIMES
350 NORTH ORLEANS STREET, 10TH FLOOR
CHICAGO, IL 60654
312-321-3000
Fax: 312-321-3027
metro@suntimes.com
www.suntimes.com
• Lacy Banks, Sports Reporter
(312) 321-2632
• Dale Bowman, Sports Writer (Outdoors)
dbowman@suntimes.com
• Greg Couch, Sports Columnist
(312) 321-2604
• Chris De Luca, Sports Editor
(312) 321-3000
• Brian Hanley, Sports Writer (Hockey)
(312) 321-2664
• Roman Modrowski, Assistant Sports Editor
(312) 321-2619
• Mike Mulligan, Sports Columnist
(312) 321-2651
• Jim O'Donnell, Sports Columnist/Reporter
(312) 321-2605
• Mark Potash, Sports Reporter
(312) 321-2634
mpotash@suntimes.com
• Ron Rapoport, Sports Columnist
(312) 321-2613
• Carol Slezak, Sports Columnist
(312) 321-2636
• Steve Tucker, High School Sports Editor
(312) 321-2247
• Len Ziehm, Sports Writer

(312) 321-2664
• Tina Akouris, High School Sports Reporter
(312) 321-2663
Frequency:
7 time(s) per week

CHICAGO TRIBUNE
435 NORTH MICHIGAN AVENUE
CHICAGO, IL 60611-4066
312-222-4440
Fax: 312-222-4674
www.chicagotribune.com
• Tim Bannon, Sports Editor
(312) 222-2434
• Mark Gonzales, Sports Reporter
• Lee Gordon, Associate Sports Editor
(312) 222-3478
• Teddy Greenstein, Sports Reporter
• Jim Harding, Assistant Editor
• Brian Hamilton, Sports Reporter
(312) 222-4204
• Steven Huang, Sports Copy Editor
• K.C. Johnson, Sports Writer
• Fred Mitchell, Sports Columnist
(312) 222-5428
kick3485@aol.com
• Avani Patel, Sports Reporter
(312) 222-4440
• Ken Paxson, Sports Associate Editor
 (312) 222-4171
• Phil Rogers, Sports Writer
• Steve Rosenbloom, Sports Columnist
(312) 222-3038
• Mike Sansone, Sports Associate Editor
(312) 222-5018
• Benjamin Trecroci, Sports Assistant Editor
Frequency:
7 time(s) per week

CHICO ENTERPRISE-RECORD
400 EAST PARK AVENUE
CHICO, CA 95928-7127
530-891-1234
Fax: 530-342-3617
localnews@chicoer.com
www.chicoer.com
• Fred Crosthwaite, Advertising Director
(530) 896-7751
fcrosthwaite@chicoer.com
• Dave Davies, Sports Editor
(530) 896-7779
ddavies@chicoer.com
Frequency:
7 time(s) per week

CHILLICOTHE CONSTITUTION-TRIBUNE
818 WASHINGTON STREET
CHILLICOTHE, MO 64601-2232
660-646-2411
800-373-0256
Fax: 660-646-2028
ctribune@greenhills.net
www.chillicothenews.com
• Andrea Graves, Advertising Manager
• Paul Sturm, Sports Editor
ctsports@chillicothenews.com
Frequency:
5 time(s) per week

CHRISTIAN SCIENCE MONITOR
210 MASSACHUSETTS
BOSTON, MA 02115-3195
617-450-2000
800-288-7090
Fax: 617-450-2031
www.csmonitor.com

• Mark Sappenfield, Editor
sappenfieldm@csps.com
Frequency:
5 time(s) per week

CHRONICLE (CT)
1 CHRONICLE ROAD
WILLIMANTIC, CT 06226
860-423-8466
Fax: 860-423-7641
chron@thechronicle.com
www.thechronicle.com
• Jean Beckley, Advertising Manager
(860) 423-8466
sales@thechronicle.com
• Mike Sypher, Sports Editor
(860) 423-8466
msypher@thechronicle.com
Frequency:
6 time(s) per week

CHRONICLE (WA)
321 NORTH PEARL STREET
CENTRALIA, WA 98531-0351
360-736-3311
800-562-6084
Fax: 360-736-4796
news@chronline.com
www.chronline.com
• Aaron Van Tuyl, Sports Editor
(360) 807-8229
• Tom May, Advertising Manager
(360) 736-3311
Frequency:
6 time(s) per week

CHRONICLE-TELEGRAM
225 EAST AVENUE
ELYRIA, OH 44035-5634
440-329-7000
800-848-6397
Fax: 440-329-7282
www.chronicletelegram.com
• Kevin Aprile, Sports Editor
(440) 329-7135
• Linda Cudlin, Sports Reporter
(440) 329-7130
lcudlin@chroniclet.com
• Scott Petrak, Sports Reporter
(440) 329-7254
spetrak@chroniclet.com
Frequency:
7 time(s) per week

CHRONICLE-TRIBUNE
610 SOUTH ADAMS STREET
MARION, IN 46953-2041
765-664-5111
800-955-7888
Fax: 765-668-4256
www.chronicle-tribune.com/
• Kristine Dowell, Advertising Manager
• Chuck Landis, Sports Reporter
(765) 664-5111
clandis@marion.gannett.com
• Adam Wire, Sports Editor
(765) 671-1264
Frequency:
7 time(s) per week

CINCINNATI ENQUIRER
312 ELM STREET
CINCINNATI, OH 45202-2724
513-721-2700
Fax: 513-768-8340

news@enquirer.com
www.enquirer.com
• Barry Forbis, Sports Editor
(513) 768-8301
• Paul Daugherty, Sports Columnist
(513) 768-8454
pdaugherty@enquirer.com
• Joe Reedy, Sports Reporter
(513) 768-8684
jreedy@enquirer.com
• John Fay, Sports Reporter
Frequency:
7 time(s) per week

CINCINNATI POST
125 EAST COURT STREET
CINCINNATI, OH 45202-1214
513-352-2000
Fax: 513-621-3962
www.cincypost.com
• Mike Gleason, Advertising Manager
(513) 768-6965
mgleason@enquirer.com
• Keith Herrell, Sports Editor
Frequency:
6 time(s) per week

CIRCLEVILLE HERALD
210 NORTH COURT STREET
CIRCLEVILLE, OH 43113-1608
740-474-3131
Fax: 740-474-9525
www.circlevilleherald.com/
• Brad Morris, Sports Editor
• Jerry Shasteen, Advertising Manager
news@circlevilleherald.com
Frequency:
6 time(s) per week

CITIZEN
25 DILL STREET
AUBURN, NY 13021-3632
315-253-5311
800-878-5311
Fax: 315-253-6031
www.auburnpub.com
• Tom Kirkwood, Advertising Manager
(315) 282-2224
• Ryan Day, Sports Editor
(315) 282-2258
Frequency:
7 time(s) per week

CITIZEN TRIBUNE
1609 WEST 1ST NORTH STREET
MORRISTOWN, TN 37814-3724
423-581-5630
Fax: 423-581-8863
www.citizentribune.com
• Lee Huguenard, Classified Manager
• Brian Trent, Sports Editor
(423) 581-5630
• Mike Walker, Advertising Manager
(423) 581-5630
• Chris Ayers, Sports Reporter
(423) 581-5630
Frequency:
6 time(s) per week

CITIZENS' VOICE
75 N. WASHINGTON ST
WILKES-BARRE, PA 18711-0502
570-821-2000
Fax: 570-821-2247
www.citizensvoice.com

• Neil Corbett, Sports Editor
sports@citizensvoice.com

CITRUS COUNTY CHRONICLE
1624 NORTH MEADOWCREST
BOULEVARD
CRYSTAL RIVER, FL 34429-5760
352-563-6363
Fax: 352-563-3280
newsdesk@chronicleonline.com
www.chronicleonline.com
• Andy Marks, Sports Editor
• Khuong Phan, Sports Writer
(352) 563-3261
Frequency:
7 time(s) per week

CLAREMORE DAILY PROGRESS
315 WEST WILL ROGERS BOULEVARD
CLAREMORE, OK 74017-7021
918-341-1101
Fax: 918-341-1131
maned@swbell.net
www.claremoreprogress.com
• Tom Ritter, Sports Editor
• Cindy Vaughan, Advertising Director
Frequency:
5 time(s) per week

CLARION HERALD
P.O. BOX 53247
NEW ORLEANS, LA 70153
504-596-3030
Fax: 504-596-3020
clarionherald@clarionherald.org
www.clarionherald.org
• Ron Brocato, Sports Editor
(504) 596-3030
rbrocato@clarionherald.org
Frequency:
2 time(s) per month

CLARION-LEDGER
P.O. BOX 40
JACKSON, MS 39201-4202
601-961-7000
800-367-3384
Fax: 601-961-7211
www.clarionledger.com
• Rick Cleveland, Sports Columnist
(601) 961-7210
rcleveland@clarionledger.com
• Rusty Hampton, Sports Editor
(601) 961-7293
rhampton@clarionledger.com
• Roland Weeks, Advertising Director
(601) 961-7143
rweeks@jackson.gannett.com
Frequency:
7 time(s) per week

CLARKSDALE PRESS REGISTER
128 EAST SECOND STREET
CLARKSDALE, MS 38614
662-627-2201
Fax: 662-624-5125
www.pressregister.com
• Josh Troy, Sports Writer
sports@pressregister.com
Frequency:
6 time(s) per week

CLAY CENTER DISPATCH
805 5TH STREET
CLAY CENTER, KS 67432-2502

785-632-2127
Fax: 785-632-6526
dispatch@claycenter.com
www.claycenter.com
• David Berggren, Sports Editor
• Kathy Pippenger, Advertising Manager
Frequency:
5 time(s) per week

CLEAR-RIDGE REPORTER
6225 SOUTH KEDZIE AVENUE
CHICAGO, IL 60629-3304
773-476-4800
Fax: 773-476-7811
www.swnewsherald.com
• Tom Danz, Sports Editor
(773) 476-4800
Frequency:
1 time(s) per week

CLEBURNE TIMES-REVIEW
P.O. BOX 1569
CLEBURNE, TX 76031-5602
817-645-2441
Fax: 817-645-4020
www.cleburnetimesreview.com
• Zack Cunningham, Sports Editor
(817) 645-2441
sports@trcle.com
• Kay Helms, Publisher
(817) 645-2441
kpace@trcle.com
Frequency:
6 time(s) per week

CLEVELAND DAILY BANNER
P.O. BOX 3600
CLEVELAND, TN 37320-3600
423-472-5041
Fax: 423-476-1046
lifestyles@clevelandbanner.com
www.clevelandbanner.com
• Jack Bennett, Advertising Manager
(423) 472-5041
advertising@clevelandbanner.com
• Richard Melvin, Sports Editor
(423) 472-5041
Frequency:
6 time(s) per week

CLINTON DAILY NEWS
522 AVANT AVENUE
CLINTON, OK 73601-3436
580-323-5151
Fax: 580-323-5154
cdnews@swbell.net
www.clintondailynews.com
• Reba Donley, Advertising Manager
cdnads@swbell.net
• Sean Stephens, Sports Editor
Frequency:
6 time(s) per week

CLINTON HERALD
221 6TH AVENUE SOUTH
CLINTON, IA 52733-2961
563-242-7101
800-729-7101
Fax: 563-242-3854
news@clintonherald.com
www.clintonherald.com
• Sherri Enwright, Classified Manager
(563) 242-7101
senwright@clintonherald.com
• Jon Gremmels, Sports Editor
(563) 242-7142

• Wayne Larkey, Advertising Manager
(563) 242-7101
• Kurt Ritzman, Assistant Sports Editor
(563) 242-7101
Frequency:
6 time(s) per week

CLINTON JOURNAL
11 S MONROE
PO BOX 615
CLINTON, IL 61727
217-935-3171
Fax: 217-935-6086
www.theclintonjournal.com
• Luke Smucker, Sports Editor
• Byron Painter, Sports Editor
(217) 935-3171
Frequency:
5 time(s) per week

COEUR D'ALENE PRESS
201 NORTH 2ND STREET
COEUR D ALENE, ID 83814
208-664-8176
Fax: 208-664-0212
www.cdapress.com
• Paul Burke, Advertising Director
pburke@cda.com
• Mark Nelke, Sports Editor
(208) 664-8176
mnelke@cdapress.com
Frequency:
7 time(s) per week

COFFEYVILLE JOURNAL
8TH & ELM STREETS
COFFEYVILLE, KS 67337
620-251-3300
Fax: 620-251-1905
• Tina Alvidrez, Advertising Director
• Kevin Krier, Sports Reporter
Frequency:
5 time(s) per week

COLORADOAN
1300 RIVERSIDE AVENUE
FORT COLLINS, CO 80524
970-493-6397
Fax: 970-224-7899
news@coloradoan.com
www.coloradoan.com
• Sean Duff, Sports Editor
(970) 224-7750
Frequency:
7 time(s) per week

COLUMBIA DAILY TRIBUNE
P.O. BOX 798
COLUMBIA, MO 65201-4416
573-815-1700
800-333-6799
Fax: 573-815-1701
editor@tribmail.com
www.columbiatribune.com
• Joe Walljasper, Sports Editor
(573) 815-1783
jwalljasper@tribmail.com
Frequency:
7 time(s) per week

COLUMBIA MISSOURIAN
221 S EIGHTH ST
COLUMBIA, MO 65201
573-882-5700
Fax: 573-882-5702

editor@columbiamissourian.com
www.columbiamissourian.com
• Michael Knisley, Sports Editor
Frequency:
6 time(s) per week

COLUMBIAN
P.O. BOX 180
VANCOUVER, WA 98660-0180
360-699-6006
800-743-3391
Fax: 360-699-6033
metrodesk@columbian.com
www.columbian.com
• Paul Danzer, Sports Writer
(360) 759-8020
• Nick Daschel, Sports Columnist
(360) 759-8056
• Greg Jayne, Sports Editor
(360) 759-8059
greg.jayne@columbian.com
• Tim Martinez, Assistant Sports Editor
(360) 759-8057
tim.martinez@columbian.com
• Tim Pyle, Sports Reporter
(360) 759-8070
• Andy Seligman, Sports Reporter
(360) 759-8051
• Al Thomas, Sports Reporter
(360) 759-8054
• Dan Trujillo, Sports Reporter
(360) 759-8051
• Paul Valencia, Sports Reporter
(360) 759-8055
Frequency:
7 time(s) per week

COLUMBUS DISPATCH
34 SOUTH 3RD STREET
COLUMBUS, OH 43215-4201
614-461-5200
Fax: 614-461-7580
letters@dispatch.com
www.dispatch.com
• Michael Arace, Sports Reporter
(614) 461-5000
marace@dispatch.com
• Bob Baptist, Sports Reporter
• Ray Stein, Sports Editor
rstein@dispatch.com
• Steve Blackledge, Sports Reporter
(614) 461-5000
sblackle@dispatch.com
• Scott Davis, Assistant Sports Editor
(614) 461-5000
sdavis@dispatch.com
• Ken Gordon, Sports Reporter
(614) 461-5000
kgordon@dispatch.com
• Brian Hofmann, Assistant Sports Editor
(614) 461-5200
bhofmann@dispatch.com
• Bob Hunter, Sports Columnist
(614) 461-5148
bhunter@dispatch.com
• Todd Jones, Sports Columnist
(614) 461-8756
tjones@dispatch.com
• Jim Massie, Sports Reporter
(614) 461-5000
jmassie@dispatch.com
• Tim May, Sports Reporter
(614) 461-5000
tmay@dispatch.com
• Gary Merrell, Advertising Vice President
• Rob Oller, Sports Reporter
(641) 461-5234
roller@dispatch.com

• Aaron Portzline, Sports Reporter
(614) 461-5000
aportzli@dispatch.com
• Bill Rabinowitz, Sports Reporter
(614) 461-5000
brabinow@dispatch.com
• Barnet D. Wolf, Advertising Reporter
• Mark Znidar, Sports Reporter
(614) 461-5000
mznidar@dispatch.com
Frequency:
7 time(s) per week

COLUMBUS LEDGER-ENQUIRER
17 WEST 12TH STREET
COLUMBUS, GA 31901-2413
706-324-5526
800-282-7859
Fax: 706-576-6290
hwilliams@ledger-enquirer.com
www.ledger-enquirer.com
• Kevin Price, Sports Editor
(706) 571-8590
• Chris White, Sports Writer
Frequency:
7 time(s) per week

COLUMBUS TELEGRAM
P.O. BOX 648
COLUMBUS, NE 68601-5656
402-564-2741
800-279-1123
Fax: 402-563-7500
telegram@megavision.com
www.columbustelegram.com
• Don Strecker, Sports Editor
(402) 564-2741
• Lincoln Arneal, Sports Editor
(402) 564-2741
Frequency:
6 time(s) per week

COMMERCIAL APPEAL
P.O. BOX 334
MEMPHIS, TN 38103-3217
901-529-2345
800-444-6397
Fax: 901-529-2787
appeal@gomemphis.com
www.commercialappeal.com
• Randy Bruce, Sports Assistant Editor
(901) 529-2822
bruce@commercialappeal.com
• Geoff Calkins, Sports Columnist
(901) 529-2364
calkins@commercialappeal.com
• Ron Higgins, Sports Writer
(901) 529-2525
higgins@commercialappeal.com
• Linda Moore, Business Columnist
(901) 529-2702
lmoore@commercialappeal.com
• Marlon Morgan, Sports Writer
(901) 529-2792
morgan@commercialappeal.com
• Gary Robinson, Executive Sports Editor
(901) 529-2352
robinson@commercialappeal.com
• Jason Smith, Sports Writer
(901) 529-5804
SmithJas@commercialappeal.com
• Mike Stanley, Classified Manager
(901) 529-2221
• Phil Stukenborg, Sports Writer
(901) 529-2543
stukenborg@commercialappeal.com
• Ronald Tillery, Sports Writer

(901) 529-2353
tillery@commercialappeal.com
• David Williams, Sports Content Editor
(901) 529-2310
williams@commercialappeal.com
Frequency:
7 time(s) per week

COMMERCIAL DISPATCH
516 MAIN STREET
COLUMBUS, MS 39701
662-328-2424
Fax: 662-796-9016
voice@cdispatch.com
www.cdispatch.com
• Beth Proffitt, Advertising Director
(662) 328-2427
• Adam Minichino, Sports Editor
Frequency:
6 time(s) per week

COMMERCIAL NEWS
17 WEST NORTH STREET
DANVILLE, IL 61832-5765
217-446-1000
800-729-2992
Fax: 217-446-9625
admin@dancomnews.com
www.dancomnews.com
• Marvin Hollman, Sports Reporter
(217) 477-5210
mholman@dancomnews.com
• Chad Dare, Sports Editor
(217) 477-5151
cdare@dancomnews.com
Frequency:
7 time(s) per week

COMMONWEALTH-JOURNAL
110-112 EAST MOUNT VERNON STREET
SOMERSET, KY 42501-1411
606-678-8191
Fax: 606-679-9225
jneal@somerset-kentucky.com
www.somerset-kentucky.com
• Steve Cornelius, Sports Editor
(606) 678-8191
scornelius@somerset-kentucky.com
Frequency:
6 time(s) per week

COMMUNICATOR NEWS
90 WEST CAMPUS VIEW BOULEVARD
COLUMBUS, OH 43235
614-781-1160
Fax: 614-781-1176
tcneditor@aol.com
www.communicatornews.com
• Ron Rall, Assistant Sports Editor
• Charlene Rall, Sports Editor
Frequency:
1 time(s) per week

COMMUNITY JOURNAL-CLERMONT
394 WARDS CORNER ROAD SUITE 170
LOVELAND, OH 45140-8300
513-248-8600
Fax: 513-248-1938
www.communitypress.com
• Anthony Amorini, Sports Reporter
(513) 248-7570
aamorini@communitypress.com
• Mark Chalifoux, Sports Reporter
(513) 576-8255
Frequency:
1 time(s) per week

COMMUNITY NEWS
5748 HELEN AVENUE
JENNINGS, MO 63136-3615
314-261-5555
Fax: 314-261-2776
• Jerry Baute, Sports Editor
Frequency:
1 time(s) per week

CONCORD CALL
9977 LIN FERRY DRIVE
SAINT LOUIS, MO 63123
314-843-0102
Fax: 314-843-0508
news@callnewspapers.com
www.callnewspapers.com
• Mike Anthony, Sports Editor
news1@callnewspapers.com
Frequency:
1 time(s) per week

CONCORD MONITOR
1 MONITOR DRIVE
CONCORD, NH 03301-1834
603-224-5301
800-464-3415
Fax: 603-224-5301
news@cmonitor.com
www.concordmonitor.com
• Ray Duckler, Sports Columnist
(603) 224-5301
• Jefferey Novotny, Sports Assistant Editor
(603) 224-5301
• Sandra Smith, Sports Editor
(603) 224-5301
Frequency:
7 time(s) per week

CONNECTICUT POST
410 STATE STREET
BRIDGEPORT, CT 06604-4501
203-333-0161
800-423-8058
Fax: 203-366-3373
grogo@ctpost.com
www.ctpost.com
• Chris Casavant, Sports Writer
(203) 330-6210
• Rich Elliott, Sports Reporter
• Chris Elsberry, Sports Columnist
celsberry@ctpost.com
• Michael Fornabaio, Sports Reporter
mfornabaio@ctpost.com
• Brenda MacDonald, Advertising Sales
Director
(203) 330-6460
• Neill Ostrout, Sports Reporter
(203) 330-6210
nostrout@ctpost.com
• Dirk Perrefort, Sports Writer
(203) 878-2130
dperrefort@ctpost.com
• Gary Rogo, Sports Editor
(203) 330-6223
grogo@ctpost.com
Frequency:
7 time(s) per week

CONNERSVILLE NEWS-EXAMINER
406 CENTRAL AVENUE
CONNERSVILLE, IN 47331-1926
765-825-0581
Fax: 765-825-4599
newsexaminer@newsexaminer.com
www.newsexaminer.com
• Grady Tate, Sports Editor

Frequency:
6 time(s) per week
Description:
Daily newspaper

CONROE COURIER
100 AVENUE A
CONROE, TX 77301-2946
936-756-6671
800-659-8313
Fax: 936-756-6676
www.thecourier-online.com
• Mike Jones, Sports Editor
(936) 756-6671
careersports@hcnonline.com
• Karen Mauermann, Advertising Director
(936) 442-3439
kmauermann@hcnonline.com
Frequency:
7 time(s) per week

CONTINENTAL
212 48TH STREET
UNION CITY, NJ 07087
201-864-9505
Fax: 201-864-9456
continews@aol.com
• Mario Ciria, Sports Editor
Frequency:
1 time(s) per week

CONTRA COSTA TIMES
2640 SHADELANDS DRIVE
WALNUT CREEK, CA 94598
925-935-2525
Fax: 925-943-8362
www.contracostatimes.com
• Mike Lefkow, Sports Editor
(925) 943-8149
mlefkow@bayareanewsgroup.com
• Steve Corkran, Sports Reporter (NFL)
(925) 943-8122
• Rick Hurd, Sports Reporter
(925) 977-8589
• Cam Inman, Sports Columnist
(925) 977-8493
• Phil Jensen, Sports Reporter
(925) 943-8243
pjensen@cctimes.com
• Jonathan Okanes, Sports Reporter
(925) 943-8194
• Gary Peterson, Sports Columnist
(925) 943-8338
• Joe Stiglich, Sports Staff Writer
(925) 943-8108
• Marcus Thompson, Sports Reporter
(925) 847-2196
• Mike Wood, Assistant Sports Editor
(925) 977-8493
Frequency:
7 time(s) per week

CORAL SPRINGS-PARKLAND FORUM
4611 JOHNSON ROAD SUITE 4
COCONUT CREEK, FL 33073
954-420-0955
Fax: 954-420-0415
• Rick Menning, Sports Editor
Frequency:
1 time(s) per week

CORPUS CHRISTI CALLER-TIMES
PO BOX 9136
CORPUS CHRISTI, TX 78401
361-884-2011
800-827-2011

Fax: 361-886-3732
metrodesk@caller.com
www.caller.com
• Gaylon Krizak, Sports Editor
(361) 886-3663
• Lee Goddard, Sports Reporter
(361) 886-3613

CORSICANA DAILY SUN
405 EAST COLLIN
CORSICANA, TX 75110-5325
903-872-3931
Fax: 903-872-6878
www.corsicanadailysun.com
• Joe Zigtema, Sports Editor
Frequency:
7 time(s) per week

CORTLAND STANDARD
PO BOX 5548
CORTLAND, NY 13045
607-756-5665
Fax: 607-756-5665
office@cortlandstandard.net
www.cortlandstandard.net
• Michael Anderson, Advertising Manager
(607) 756-5665
addesign@cortlandstandard.net
• Al Butler, Sports Editor
(607) 756-5665
sports@cortlandstandard.net
Frequency:
6 time(s) per week

CORVALLIS GAZETTE-TIMES
P.O. BOX 368
CORVALLIS, OR 97333
541-753-2641
800-653-3755
Fax: 541-758-9505
news@gtconnect.com
www.gazettetimes.com
• Steve Greff, Sports Editor
(541) 758-9544
• Gary Tackett, Advertising Director
(541) 812-6074
Frequency:
7 time(s) per week

COSHOCTON TRIBUNE
550 MAIN STREET
COSHOCTON, OH 43812-1612
740-622-1122
800-589-8689
Fax: 740-622-7341
www.coshoctontribune.com
• Jim Barstow, Sports Editor
(740) 622-1122
jbarstow@nncogannett.com
Frequency:
7 time(s) per week

COURIER
P.O. BOX 887
RUSSELLVILLE, AR 72811-0887
479-968-4037
800-369-5252
Fax: 479-968-4037
www.couriernews.com
• Kevin Hill, Assistant Sports Editor
sports@couriernews.com
• Michelle Harris, Advertising Director
michelle@couriernews.com
• Sean Ingram, Sports Editor
sportseditor@couriernews.com

media

Frequency:
7 time(s) per week

COURIER NEWS
92 EAST MAIN STREET, SUITE 202
SOMERVILLE, NJ 08876
908-707-3111
Fax: 732-565-7209
cnbusiness@c-n.com
www.c-n.com
• Steve Feiti, Sports Editor
(732) 643-4232
hntsports@mycentraljersey.com
Frequency:
7 time(s) per week

COURIER-EXPRESS
P.O. BOX 407
DU BOIS, PA 15801-2430
814-371-4200
800-442-4217
Fax: 814-371-3241
newsroom@thecourierexpress.com
www.thecourierexpress.com
• Scott Shindledecker, Sports Editor
(814) 371-4200
sports@thecourierexpress.com
• Don Harris, Sports Reporter
(814) 371-4200
Frequency:
6 time(s) per week

COURIER-JOURNAL
P.O. BOX 740031
LOUISVILLE, KY 40202-2206
502-582-4691
800-765-4011
Fax: 502-582-4200
neighborhoods@courier-journal.com
www.courier-journal.com
• C.L. Brown, Sports Reporter
(502) 582-4044
cbrown@courier-journal.com
• Richard Bozich, Sports Columnist
(502) 582-4650
• Glenn Brownstein, Sports Assistant Editor
(502) 582-4362
gbrownstein@courier-journal.com
• Harry Bryan, Sports Editor
(502) 582-4060
hbryan@courier-journal.com
• Eric Crawford, Sports Writer
(502) 582-4372
ecrawford@courier-journal.com
• Jody Demling, Sports Reporter
(502) 582-7176
jdemling@courier-journal.com
• Creig Ewing, Assistant Sports Editor
(502) 582-4043
cewing@courier-journal.com
• Nick Lazaroff, Advertising Director
(Display)
(502) 582-4011
• Jennie Rees, Sports Writer
(502) 582-4042
jrees@courier-journal.com
• Michael Smith, Sports Reporter
(859) 254-7888
mssmith@courier-journal.com
Frequency:
7 time(s) per week

COURIER-NEWS
495 COMMONS DRIVE
AURORA, IL 60504
630-978-8880
couriernews.suntimes.com

• R. J. Gerber, Sports Editor
(630) 978-8175
• Jason Bauman, Assistant Sports Editor
(630) 978-8412
Frequency:
7 time(s) per week

COURIER-OBSERVER
5 BEAL STREET
POTSDAM, NY 13676-1746
315-661-2512
Fax: 315-386-2855
www.mpcourier.com
• Al St. Pierre, Sports Editor
(315) 393-1000
Frequency:
5 time(s) per week

COURIER-POST
301 CUTHBERT BOULEVARD
CHERRY HILL, NJ 08002
856-486-2600
Fax: 856-663-2831
www.courierpostonline.com
• Gary Silvers, Sports Editor
(856) 486-2420
gsilvers@courierpostonline.com
• Don Benevento, Sports Reporter
(856) 486-2424
dbenevento@courierpostonline.com
• Kevin Callahan, Sports Reporter
(865) 486-2424
kcallahan@courierpostonline.com
• Chuck Gormley, Sports Reporter
(856) 486-2424
cgormley@courierpostonline.com
• Ray Ventura, Sports Reporter
• Bob Viggiano, Sports Reporter
bviggiano@courierpostonline.com
• Celeste Whittaker, Sports Reporter
(856) 486-2424
cwhittaker@courierpostonline.com
Frequency:
7 time(s) per week

COURIER-TIMES
201 SOUTH 14TH STREET
NEW CASTLE, IN 47362-3328
765-529-1111
800-489-2472
Fax: 765-529-1731
www.thecouriertimes.com
• Jeremy Hines, Sports Editor
(765) 529-1111
Frequency:
6 time(s) per week

CRAIG DAILY PRESS
466 YAMPA AVENUE
CRAIG, CO 81625
970-824-7031
Fax: 970-824-6810
www.craigdailypress.com
• David Pressgrove, Sports Writer
(970) 824-7031
Frequency:
5 time(s) per week

CRESCENT-NEWS
624 WEST 2ND STREET
DEFIANCE, OH 43512-2161
419-784-5441
Fax: 419-784-1492
crescent@crescent-news.com
www.crescent-news.com

• Bruce Hefflinger, Sports Editor
(419) 784-5441
• Mark Ryan, Advertising Manager
(419) 784-5441
Frequency:
6 time(s) per week

CRESTON NEWS-ADVERTISER
503 WEST ADAMS STREET
CRESTON, IA 50801-3112
641-782-2141
Fax: 641-782-6628
office@crestonnews.com
www.crestonnewsadvertiser.com
• Matt Pfiffner, Sports Editor
(641) 782-2141
mfiffner@crestonnews.com
• Craig Mittag, Advertising Manager
(641) 782-2141
cmittag@crestonnews.com
Frequency:
5 time(s) per week

CROOKSTON DAILY TIMES
124 SOUTH BROADWAY
CROOKSTON, MN 56716-1955
218-281-2730
Fax: 218-281-7234
editor@crookstontimes.com
www.crookstontimes.com
• Calvin Anderson, Advertising Manager
calvin@crookstontimes.com
• Derek Martin, Sports Editor
sports@crookstontimes.com
Frequency:
5 time(s) per week

CROWLEY POST-SIGNAL
602 NORTH PARKERSON AVENUE
CROWLEY, LA 70526-4354
337-783-3450
Fax: 337-788-0949
crowleyps@aol.com
www.crowleypostsignal.com
• Chris Quebedeaux, Sports Editor
chris.quebedeaux@crowleytoday.com
Frequency:
5 time(s) per week

CULLMAN TIMES
300 4TH AVENUE, S.E.
CULLMAN, AL 35055
256-734-2131
Fax: 256-737-1006
www.cullmantimes.com
• Justin Graves, Sports Editor
(256) 734-2131
• Stan Veitch, Sports Writer
(256) 734-2131
• Kathy McLeroy, Advertising Director
(256) 734-2131
Frequency:
6 time(s) per week

CULPEPER STAR-EXPONENT
471 JAMES MADISON HIGHWAY, SUITE
201
CULPEPER, VA 22701
540-825-0771
Fax: 540-825-0778
www.starexponent.com
• Ron Counts, Sports Reporter
(540) 825-0771
• Gloria Williams, Advertising Manager
(540) 825-0771

Frequency:
7 time(s) per week

CUMBERLAND TIMES-NEWS
19 BALTIMORE STREET
CUMBERLAND, MD 21502-3023
301-722-4600
Fax: 301-722-5270
ctn@times-news.com
www.times-news.com
• Mike Burke, Sports Editor
(301) 722-4600
Frequency:
7 time(s) per week

CUSHING DAILY CITIZEN
202 N HARRISON
CUSHING, OK 74023
918-285-5555
www.cushingcitizen.com
• Amy Grissom, Advertising Manager
(918) 225-3333
• Luke Boyd, Sports Reporter
Frequency:
5 time(s) per week

CUYAHOGA FALLS NEWS-PRESS
1619 COMMERCE DRIVE
STOW, OH 44224
330-688-0088
800-966-6565
Fax: 330-688-1588
www.recordpub.com
• Tom Nader, Sports Editor
(330) 296-9657
Frequency:
1 time(s) per week

DAILY ADVANCE
P.O. BOX 588
ELIZABETH CITY, NC 27909
252-335-8076
Fax: 252-335-4415
www.dailyadvance.com
• Chic Riebel, Sports Editor
(252) 335-8123
• Will Harris, Sports Writer
(252) 335-8124
Frequency:
7 time(s) per week

DAILY ADVOCATE
P.O. BOX 220
GREENVILLE, OH 45331-1926
937-548-3151
Fax: 937-548-3913
editor@dailyadvocate.com
www.dailyadvocate.com/
• Kyle Shaner, Sports Editor
(937) 548-3151
Frequency:
7 time(s) per week

DAILY AMERICAN
334 WEST MAIN STREET
SOMERSET, PA 15501-1508
814-445-5900
800-452-0823
Fax: 814-445-2935
news@dailyamerican.com
www.dailyamerican.com
• Ron Pritts, Sports Editor
(814) 444-5926
ronp@dailyamerican.com
Frequency:
6 time(s) per week

DAILY AMERICAN REPUBLIC
208 POPLAR STREET
POPLAR BLUFF, MO 63901-5842
573-785-1414
888-276-2242
Fax: 573-785-2706
info.darnews.com
• Christy Pierce, Advertising Manager
(573) 785-1414
• Brian Rosener, Sports Editor
(573) 785-1414
Frequency:
6 time(s) per week

DAILY ARDMOREITE
117 WEST BROADWAY
ARDMORE, OK 73401-6226
580-223-2200
800-873-0211
Fax: 580-226-0050
www.ardmoreite.com
• James Jordan, Sports Writer
(580) 221-6527
• Erik Horne, Sports Editor
(580) 221-6522
• Lisa Wilkinson, Advertising Manager
(580) 221-6513
Frequency:
6 time(s) per week

DAILY ASTORIAN
949 EXCHANGE STREET
ASTORIA, OR 97103-4605
503-325-3211
800-781-3211
Fax: 503-458-6000
daily.astorian@dailyastorian.com
www.dailyastorian.com
• Gary Henley, Sports Writer
ghenley@dailyastorian.com
Frequency:
5 time(s) per week

DAILY BREEZE
21250 HAWTHORNE BLVD
TORRANCE, CA 90503
310-540-5511
Fax: 310-540-6272
newsroom@dailybreeze.com
www.dailybreeze.com
• Todd Bailey, Sports Editor
(310) 540-5511
• Tony Ciniglio, Sports Columnist
(310) 540-5511
• Bill Cizek, Sports Reporter
(310) 540-5511
• Phil Collin, Sports Reporter
(310) 540-5511
phil.collin@dailybreeze.com
• Bob Holtzman, Sports Columnist
(310) 540-5511
• Eric Mandel, Sports Reporter
(310) 540-5511
• Jim Thomas, Sports Reporter
(310) 540-5511
• Mike Waldner, Sports Reporter
(310) 540-5511
• Woody Woodburn, Sports Columnist
Frequency:
7 time(s) per week

DAILY CAMERA
PO BOX 591
BOULDER, CO 80306
303-442-1202
Fax: 303-449-9358
www.dailycamera.com

• Jennifer Osieczanek, Sports Editor
(303) 473-1316
• Mark Kranjcec, Retail Advertising Director
• Kyle Ringo, Sports Reporter
(303) 442-1202
• Mike Sandrock, Sports Reporter
(303) 442-1202
• Chris Shelton, Sports Editor
(303) 442-1202
• Ryan Thorburn, Sports Reporter
thorburnr@thedailycamera.com
Frequency:
7 time(s) per week

DAILY CAPITAL NEWS
210 MONROE STREET
JEFFERSON CITY, MO 65101-3210
573-636-3131
Fax: 573-636-7035
news@newstribune.com
www.newstribune.com
• Debbie Kiser, Advertising Manager
(573) 761-0226
display@newstribune.com
• Tom Rackers, Sports Editor
sports@newstribune.com
Frequency:
7 time(s) per week

DAILY CHRONICLE
1586 BARBAR GREENE RD
DEKALB, IL 60115
815-756-4841
Fax: 815-758-5059
www.daily-chronicle.com
• John Sahly, Sports Editor
jsahly@shawsuburban.com
• Karen Pletsch, Advertising Director

DAILY CITIZEN
3000 EAST RACE
SEARCY, AR 72143
501-268-8621
800-400-3142
Fax: 501-268-6277
www.thedailycitizen.com
• Craig Woodson, Sports Editor
(513) 763-5500
• Terasa Harvey, Advertising Director
(800) 400-3142
tharvey@thedailycitizen.com
Frequency:
6 time(s) per week

DAILY CLAY COUNTY ADVOCATE-PRESS
105 WEST NORTH AVENUE
FLORA, IL 62839
618-662-2108
Fax: 618-662-2939
www.advocatepress.com
• Mike Linville, Sports Editor
Frequency:
5 time(s) per week

DAILY COMET
104 HICKORY STREET
THIBODAUX, LA 70301
985-448-7600
800-256-1305
Fax: 985-448-7606
www.dailycomet.com
• Marion Long, Advertising Director
• Brent St. Germain, Sports Editor
(985) 448-7616
brent.st.germain@dailycomet.com

Frequency:
5 time(s) per week

DAILY COMMERCIAL
212 EAST MAIN STREET
LEESBURG, FL 34748
352-365-8200
Fax: 352-365-1951
news@dailycommercial.com
www.dailycommercial.com
• Frank Jolley, Sports Editor
(352) 365-8283
frankjolley@dailycommercial.com
Frequency:
7 time(s) per week

DAILY CORINTHIAN
1607 SOUTH HARPER ROAD
CORINTH, MS 38834
662-287-6111
Fax: 662-287-3525
news@dailycorinthian.com
www.dailycorinthian.com
• Lee Smith, Sports Editor
(662) 287-6111
Frequency:
6 time(s) per week

DAILY COURIER (AZ)
1958 COMMERCE CENTER CIRCLE
PRESCOTT, AZ 86301
928-445-3333
Fax: 928-445-2062
www.prescottaz.com
• Keith Jiron, Sports Editor
• Dick Larson, Advertising Director
• Tom Regnier, Advertising Manager
Frequency:
6 time(s) per week

DAILY COURIER (PA)
127 WEST APPLE STREET
CONNELLSVILLE, PA 15425-3132
724-628-2000
800-801-9000
Fax: 724-626-3567
• Jason Black, Sports Editor
(724) 626-3534
Frequency:
6 time(s) per week

DAILY DEMOCRAT
711 MAIN STREET
WOODLAND, CA 95695-3406
530-662-5421
Fax: 530-406-6262
www.dailydemocrat.com
• Bruce Burton, Sports Editor
(530) 406-6236
Frequency:
7 time(s) per week

DAILY DISPATCH
530 E 11TH STREET
DOUGLAS, AZ 85607-2014
520-364-3424
Fax: 520-364-6750
editor@douglasdispatch.com
www.douglasdispatch.com
• Bruce Whetten, Sports Reporter
(520) 364-3424
Frequency:
5 time(s) per week

DAILY DUNKLIN DEMOCRAT
203 1ST STREET
KENNETT, MO 63857-2052
573-888-4505
Fax: 573-888-5114
www.dddnews.com
• Dustin Ward, Sports Editor
dward@dddnews.com
• Terri Coleman, Advertising Manager
tcoleman@dddnews.com
Frequency:
5 time(s) per week

DAILY FREEMAN
79 HURLEY AVENUE
KINGSTON, NY 12401
845-331-5000
Fax: 845-331-3557
news@freemanonline.com
www.midhudsoncentral.com
• Gregory Appel, Advertising Director
• Babara Norton, Retail Advertising
Manager
(845) 331-5000
• Ron Rosner, Sports Editor
(845) 331-5000
rrosner@freemanonline.com
Frequency:
7 time(s) per week

DAILY FREEMAN-JOURNAL
720 2ND STREET
WEBSTER CITY, IA 50595-1437
515-832-4350
Fax: 515-832-2314
editor@freemanjournal.net
www.freemanjournal.net
• Troy Banning, Sports Editor
(515) 832-4350
sports@freemanjournal.net
Frequency:
5 time(s) per week

DAILY GATE CITY
1016 MAIN STREET
KEOKUK, IA 52632
319-524-8300
800-779-8819
Fax: 319-524-4363
www.dailygate.com
• Brad Cameron, Editor
(319) 524-8300
sports@dailygate.com
• Doug Shipman, Advertising Manager
(319) 524-8300
advertising@dailygate.com
Frequency:
5 time(s) per week

DAILY GAZETTE (IL)
3200 EAST LINCOLN WAY
STERLING, IL 61081
815-625-3600
800-798-4085
Fax: 815-625-9390
news@svnmail.com
www.saukvalley.com
• Dan Goetz, Advertising Director
(815) 625-3600
jbaratta@svnmail.com
• Brian Weidman, Sports Editor
bweidman@svnmail.com
Frequency:
7 time(s) per week

DAILY GAZETTE (NY)
2345 MAXON RD (12308)
PO BOX 1090
SCHENECTADY, NY 12301-1090
518-374-4141
800-262-2211
Fax: 518-395-3072
www.dailygazette.com
• Butch Walker, Sports Editor
(518) 395-3160
• Tom Boggie, Assistant Sports Editor
(518) 395-3153

DAILY GLOBE (MI)
P.O. BOX 548
IRONWOOD, MI 49938-2120
906-932-2211
800-236-2887
Fax: 906-932-5358
www.ironwoodglobe.com/
• Jason Juno, Sports Editor
(906) 932-2211
• Cathy Syreini, Advertising Manager
(906) 932-2211
Frequency:
6 time(s) per week

DAILY GLOBE (OH)
37 WEST MAIN STREET
SHELBY, OH 44875-1238
419-342-4276
Fax: 419-342-4246
globe@sdgnewsgroup.com
www.sdgnewsgroup.com
• Chuck Ridenour, Sports Editor
(419) 342-3261
Frequency:
6 time(s) per week

DAILY GUIDE
108 HOLLY DRIVE
SAINT ROBERT, MO 65584
573-336-3711
Fax: 573-336-4640
www.waynesvilledailyguide.com
• Brent Foster, Sports Editor
sports@waynesvilledailyguide.com
Frequency:
5 time(s) per week

DAILY HAMPSHIRE GAZETTE
115 CONZ STREET
NORTHAMPTON, MA 01061
413-584-5000
Fax: 413-585-5299
newsroom@gazettenet.com
www.gazettenet.com
• Mark Elliott, Advertising Manager
(413) 584-5000
• Stanley Moulton, Sports Editor
(413) 584-5000
sports@gazettenet.com
Frequency:
6 time(s) per week

DAILY HERALD (IL)
155 EAST ALGONQUIN ROAD
ARLINGTON HEIGHTS, IL 60005-4617
847-427-4300
Fax: 847-427-4608
news@dailyherald.com
www.dailyherald.com
• Robert Frisk, Assistant Managing
Editor/Sports
(847) 427-4441
bfrisk@dailyherald.com

• Aaron Gabriel, Sports Editor
(847) 427-4439
agabriel@dailyherald.com
• Mike Imrem, Sports Columnist
(847) 427-4456
mimrem@dailyherald.com
• Tom Quinlan, Sports Editor
(847) 427-4455
tquinlan@dailyherald.com
Frequency:
7 time(s) per week

DAILY HERALD (UT)
P.O. BOX 717
PROVO, UT 84603-0717
801-373-5050
800-880-8075
Fax: 801-344-2985
www.heraldextra.com
• Darnell Dickson, Sports Editor
(801) 344-2555
ddickson@heraldextra.com
Frequency:
7 time(s) per week

DAILY IBERIAN
926 EAST MAIN STREET
NEW IBERIA, LA 70560-3866
337-365-6773
Fax: 337-367-9640
dailyiberian@bellsouth.net
www.iberianet.com
• Chris Landry, Sports Editor
(337) 365-6773
chris.landry@daily-iberian.com
• Alan Rini, Advertising Manager
(337) 365-6773
iberianadmgr@bellsouth.net
Frequency:
7 time(s) per week

DAILY INDEPENDENT
P.O. BOX 311
ASHLAND, KY 41101-7606
606-326-2600
800-955-5860
Fax: 606-326-2678
letters@dailyindependent.com
www.dailyindependent.com
• Nikki Clay, Advertising Director
(606) 326-2611
• Adam Vankirk, Sports Editor
(606) 326-2664
• Rocky Stanley, Sports Writer
(606) 326-2671
rstanley@dailyindependent.com
Frequency:
7 time(s) per week

DAILY INTER LAKE
P.O. BOX 7610
KALISPELL, MT 59901-3202
406-755-7000
Fax: 406-752-6114
edit@dailyinterlake.com
www.dailyinterlake.com
• Cindy Cece, Advertising Director
• David Lesnick, Sports Editor
(406) 758-4426
dlesnick@dailyinterlake.com
Frequency:
7 time(s) per week

DAILY IOWEGIAN
105 N MAIN ST
CENTERVILLE, IA 52544-1732

641-856-6336
Fax: 641-856-8118
www.dailyiowegian.com
• Becky Maxwell, Advertising Manager
• Jason McGrann, Sports Editor
(641) 856-6336
Frequency:
5 time(s) per week

DAILY ITEM (MA)
38 EXCHANGE STREET
LYNN, MA 01901
781-593-7700
Fax: 781-581-3178
www.itemlive.com
• B. J. Frazier, Advertising Director
(781) 593-7700
• Steve Krause, Sports Editor
(781) 593-7700
Frequency:
6 time(s) per week

DAILY ITEM (PA)
200 MARKET STREET
SUNBURY, PA 17801-3402
570-286-5671
Fax: 570-988-5348
news@dailyitem.com
www.dailyitem.com
• Will Strout, Advertising Manager
• Bill Bowman, Sports Editor
(570) 286-5671
bbowman@dailyitem.com
Frequency:
7 time(s) per week

DAILY JEFFERSON COUNTY UNION
28 MILWAUKEE AVENUE WEST
FORT ATKINSON, WI 53538-2018
920-563-5553
Fax: 920-563-2329
www.dailyunion.com
• Diane Niemeyer, Advertising Manager
(920) 563-5553
• Sam Rodriguez, Sports Editor
(920) 563-5553
• Jeff Seisser, Sports Editor
(920) 563-5553
Frequency:
5 time(s) per week

DAILY JEFFERSONIAN
P.O. BOX 10
CAMBRIDGE, OH 43725
740-439-3531
800-897-2262
Fax: 740-432-6219
newsroom@daily-jeff.com
www.daily-jeff.com
• Ed Archibald, Advertising Manager
(740) 439-3531
• Jeff Harrison, Sports Editor
(740) 439-3531
sports@daily-jeff.com
Frequency:
6 time(s) per week

DAILY JOURNAL (IL)
8 DEARBORN SQUARE
KANKAKEE, IL 60901
815-937-3300
800-892-1861
Fax: 815-937-3301
www.daily-journal.com
• Dave Surico, Sports Editor
(815) 937-3391

• Ken Munjoy, Advertising Director
(815) 937-3303
Frequency:
6 time(s) per week

DAILY JOURNAL (MO)
1513 SAINT JOE DRIVE
PARK HILLS, MO 63601-2402
573-431-2010
800-660-8166
Fax: 573-431-7640
mbelken@pulitzer.net
• Donn Adamson, Sports Editor
(573) 431-2010
Frequency:
7 time(s) per week

DAILY LEADER (IL)
318 NORTH MAIN STREET
PONTIAC, IL 61764-1930
815-842-1153
Fax: 815-842-4388
www.pontiacdailyleader.com
• Judy Sweitzer, Advertising Manager
(815) 842-1153
jsweitzer@pontiacdailyleader.com
• Erich Murphy, Sports Editor
(815) 842-1153
Frequency:
6 time(s) per week

DAILY LEADER (MS)
P.O. BOX 551
BROOKHAVEN, MS 39601
601-833-6961
800-833-6961
Fax: 601-833-6714
news@dailyleader.com
www.dailyleader.com
• Tom Goetz, Sports Editor
(601) 833-6961
sports@dailyleader.com
• David Culpepper, Advertising Director
Frequency:
6 time(s) per week

DAILY LEDGER
53 WEST ELM STREET
CANTON, IL 61520-2511
309-647-5100
Fax: 309-647-4665
editor@cantondailyledger.com
www.cantondailyledger.com
• Stephen Shank, Sports Editor
sports@cantondailyledger.com
Frequency:
6 time(s) per week

DAILY LOCAL NEWS
250 NORTH BRADFORD AVENUE
WEST CHESTER, PA 19382-2800
610-696-1775
800-456-6397
Fax: 610-430-1194
news@dailylocal.com
www.dailylocal.com
• Bryan Davis, Sports Editor
(610) 430-1179
news@dailylocal.com
Frequency:
7 time(s) per week

DAILY MAIL
100 SUMMIT AVENUE
HAGERSTOWN, MD 21740

301-733-5131
Fax: 301-714-0245
news@herald-mail.com
www.herald-mail.com
• Mark Keller, Sports Editor
(301) 733-5131
Frequency:
7 time(s) per week

DAILY MESSENGER
73 BUFFALO STREET
CANANDAIGUA, NY 14424-1001
585-394-0770
Fax: 585-394-1675
www.mpnnow.com/
• Paul Gangarossa, Sports Editor
(585) 394-0770
• Ron Wilson, Sports Reporter
(585) 394-0770
Frequency:
6 time(s) per week

DAILY MINING GAZETTE
P.O. BOX 368
HOUGHTON, MI 49931-2134
906-482-1500
800-682-7607
Fax: 906-482-2726
www.mininggazette.com
• Brandon Veale, Sports Editor
(906) 483-2216
• Yvonne Robillard, Advertising Manager
(906) 483-2220
yrobillard@mininggazette.com
Frequency:
6 time(s) per week

DAILY MOUNTAIN EAGLE
1301 VIKING DRIVE
JASPER, AL 35501-4983
205-221-2840
800-518-6397
Fax: 205-221-6203
jasper@mountaineagle.com
www.mountaineagle.com
• Jonathan Bentley, Sports Editor
(205) 221-2840
jonathan.bentley@mountaineagle.com
• Jerry Geddings, Advertising Director
ads@mountaineagle.com
Frequency:
7 time(s) per week

DAILY NEWS (CA)
21860 BURBANK BOULEVARD
SUITE 200
WOODLAND HILLS, CA 91367
818-713-3000
Fax: 818-713-0058
www.dailynews.com
• Jon Clifford, Sports Editor
(818) 713-3628
• Steve Dilbeck, Sports Columnist
• Rick Hazeltine, Sports Assistant Editor
(818) 713-3632
• Tom Hoffarth, Sports Columnist
(Television)
• Kevin Modesti, Sports Columnist
(818) 713-3617
kevin.modesti@dailynews.com
Frequency:
7 time(s) per week

DAILY NEWS (KY)
813 COLLEGE STREET
BOWLING GREEN, KY 42101

270-781-1700
800-599-NEWS
Fax: 270-783-3237
www.bgdailynews.com
• Malcolm Knox, Sports Editor
(270) 783-3271
• Michael Compton, Sports Reporter
(270) 783-3247
• Mark Mahagan, Advertising Director

DAILY NEWS (WA)
770 11TH AVENUE
LONGVIEW, WA 98632-2412
360-577-2500
Fax: 360-577-2536
www.tdn.com
• Zack Buchanan, Sports Editor
(360) 577-2527
• Rick McCorkle, Sports Reporter
(360) 577-2529
rmccorkle@tdn.com
• Steve Quaife, Advertising Manager
(360) 577-2559
squaife@tdn.com
• Ben Zimmerman, Sports Editor
(360) 577-2541
Frequency:
7 time(s) per week

DAILY NEWS JOURNAL
P.O. BOX 68
MURFREESBORO, TN 37130-3622
615-893-5860
Fax: 615-896-8702
online@dnj.com
www.dnj.com
• Jolene McKenzie, Advertising Director
(615) 893-5860
jmckenzie@dnj.com
• Greg Pogue, Executive Sports Editor
(615) 893-5860
Frequency:
7 time(s) per week

DAILY NEWS OF NEWBURYPORT
23 LIBERTY STREET
NEWBURYPORT, MA 01950
978-462-6666
Fax: 978-465-8505
www.newburyportnews.com
• Bill Trefethen, Advertising Manager
btrefethen@newburyportnews.com
• Dan Guttenplan, Sports Editor
(978) 462-6666
Frequency:
6 time(s) per week

DAILY NEWS SUN
10102 SANTE FE DRIVE
SUN CITY, AZ 85351
623-977-8351
Fax: 623-876-3698
www.northwestvalleynewspapers.com
• Rich Bolas, Sports Editor
(623) 876-2523
Frequency:
6 time(s) per week

DAILY NEWS TRANSCRIPT
254 2ND AVENUE
NEEDHAM, MA 02494
781-433-6700
Fax: 781-433-8375
neponset@cnc.com
www.townonline.com

• Tom Fargo, Sports Editor
tfargo@cnc.com
• Adam Kurkjian, Sports Writer
(781) 433-8371
akurkjin@cnc.com
Frequency:
5 time(s) per week

DAILY NEWS TRIBUNE
738A MAIN STREET
WALTHAM, MA 02451
781-647-7898
Fax: 781-398-8010
newstribune@cnc.com
www.dailynewstribune.com
• Cris Warren, Advertising Manager
(781) 433-8313
cwarren@cnc.com
• Scott Souza, Sports Editor
(781) 398-8006
ssouza@cnc.com
Frequency:
5 time(s) per week

DAILY NEWS-RECORD
231 SOUTH LIBERTY STREET
HARRISONBURG, VA 22803
540-574-6200
Fax: 540-433-9112
letters@dnronline.com
www.dnronline.com
• Chris Simmons, Sports Editor
(540) 574-6291
• Steve Turner, Advertising Director
(540) 574-6229
sturner@dnronline.com
Frequency:
6 time(s) per week

DAILY NONPAREIL
535 WEST BROADWAY SUITE 300
COUNCIL BLUFFS, IA 51503
712-328-1811
Fax: 712-325-5776
editorial@nonpareilonline.com
www.nonpareilonline.com
• Tony Boone, Sports Writer
(712) 325-5756
• Evan Bland, Sports Writer
(712) 325-5758
• Kevin White, Sports Editor
(712) 325-5718
Frequency:
7 time(s) per week

DAILY POST-ATHENIAN
320 SOUTH JACKSON STREET
ATHENS, TN 37303-4715
423-745-5664
Fax: 423-745-8295
www.dpa.xtn.net
• Sarah Jane Locke, Advertising Manager
• Sarah Jane Locke, Classified Manager
• Jack Slayton, Sports Editor
Frequency:
5 time(s) per week

DAILY PRESS (VA)
7505 WARWICK BOULEVARD
NEWPORT NEWS, VA 23607-1517
757-247-4730
800-543-8908
Fax: 757-245-8618
news@dailypress.com
www.dailypress.com

• Dave Fairbank, College Sports Reporter
(757) 247-4637
dfairbank@dailypress.com
• Warner Hessler, Sports Reporter
(757) 247-4648
whessler@dailypress.com
• Dave Johnson, College Sports Reporter
(757) 247-4649
djohnson@dailypress.com
• David Nicholson, Advertising Reporter
(757) 247-4794
dnicholson@dailypress.com
• Marty O'Brien, Sports Reporter
(757) 247-4963
mobrien@dailypress.com
• Ed Richards, Sports Reporter
(757) 247-4645
erichards@dailypress.com
• Doug Roberson, Sports Editor
(757) 247-4638
droberson@dailypress.com
• David Teel, Sports Columnist
(757) 247-4636
dteel@dailypress.com
• Jennifer Williams, College Sports Reporter
(757) 247-4644
jwilliams@dailypress.com
• Norm Wood, College Sports Reporter
(757) 247-4642
nwood@dailypress.com
Frequency:
7 time(s) per week

DAILY PRESS (WI)
122 WEST 3RD STREET
ASHLAND, WI 54806-1620
715-682-2313
Fax: 715-682-4699
ashpress@cheqnet.net
www.ashlandwi.com
• Larry Servinsky, Sports Editor
(715) 682-2313
• Jeff Swiston, Advertising Manager
Frequency:
6 time(s) per week

DAILY PROGRESS
P.O. BOX 9030
CHARLOTTESVILLE, VA 22901-1413
434-978-7200
Fax: 434-978-7223
www.dailyprogress.com
• John Kimbel, Advertising Manager
(434) 975-7112
• Jerry Ratcliffe, Sports Editor
(434) 978-7251
• Todd Merchant, Sports Writer
(434) 978-7250
Frequency:
7 time(s) per week

DAILY RACING FORM
708 THIRD AVENUE, 12TH FLOOR
NEW YORK, NY 10017
212-366-7600
800-306-3676
editor@drf.com
www.drf.com
• Steven Crist, Editor
(212) 366-7700
scrist@drf.com
• Steven Crist, Publisher
(212) 366-7700
• Duke Dosik, Managing Editor
(212) 366-7623
• Rich Rosenbush, Executive Editor
(212) 366-7651

Frequency:
7 time(s) per week

DAILY RECORD (OH)
P.O. BOX 918
WOOSTER, OH 44691-4348
330-264-1125
800-686-2958
Fax: 330-264-3756
news@the-daily-record.com
www.the-daily-record.com
• Aaron Dorksen, Sports Editor
(330) 264-1125
• Rhonda Geer, Advertising Director
(330) 287-1653
• Art Holden, Sports Writer
(330) 264-1125
aholden@the-daily-record.com
• Bruce Polen, Classified Manager
(330) 264-1125
• Kevin Lynch, Sports Writer
(330) 674-5676
klynch@the-daily-record.com
• Mike Plant, Sports Writer
(330) 264-1125
mplant@the-daily-record.com
Frequency:
7 time(s) per week

DAILY RECORD (WA)
401 NORTH MAIN STREET
ELLENSBURG, WA 98926-3107
509-925-1414
Fax: 509-925-5696
dailyrecord@kvnews.com
www.kvnews.com
• Tyler Miller, Advertising Director
• Colter Nuanez, Sports Writer
(509) 925-1414
Frequency:
6 time(s) per week

DAILY REFLECTOR
P.O. BOX 1967
GREENVILLE, NC 27834
252-752-6166
800-849-6166
Fax: 252-754-8140
www.reflector.com
• Jim Gentry, Sports Editor
(252) 329-9594
• Nate Summers, Sports Writer
(252) 329-9595
nsummers@reflector.com
• Betty Williams, Advertising Director
(252) 329-9511
• Tony Castleberry, Sports Writer
(252) 329-9591
Frequency:
7 time(s) per week

DAILY REGISTER
35 SOUTH VINE STREET
HARRISBURG, IL 62946
618-253-7146
800-283-8117
Fax: 618-252-0863
www.dailyregister.com
• Michael Dann, Sports Editor
(618) 253-7146
• Doris Wilson, Advertising Manager
(618) 253-7416
Frequency:
6 time(s) per week

DAILY REPUBLIC
1250 TEXAS STREET
FAIRFIELD, CA 94533
707-425-4646
Fax: 707-425-5924
www.dailyrepublic.com
• Mike Corpos, Sports Writer
(707) 427-6979
• Sharon Guy, Advertising Director
(707) 425-4646
• Paul Farmer, Sports Editor
(707) 425-4646
pfarmer@dailyrepublic.net
Frequency:
7 time(s) per week

DAILY REPUBLICAN REGISTER
115 EAST 4TH STREET
MOUNT CARMEL, IL 62863-0550
618-262-5144
Fax: 618-263-4437
www.tristate-media.com
• Robert Livingston, Sports Editor
(618) 262-5144
• Brenna Crooks, Advertising Manager
Frequency:
5 time(s) per week

DAILY REVIEW (CA)
22533 FOOT HILL BOULEVARD
HAYWARD, CA 94541-
510-783-6111
800-595-9595
Fax: 510-293-2490
www.dailyreviewonline.com
• Jon Becker, Sports Editor
(925) 416-4803
• Dave Newhouse, Sports Reporter
(510) 208-6466
• Monte Poole, Sports Columnist
• Mark Saxon, Sports Reporter
• Ken Silman, Sports Reporter
(510) 293-2455
• Art Spander, Sports Reporter
(510) 531-8068
typoes@aol.com
• Carl Steward, Sports Reporter
(510) 293-2451
• Josh Suchon, Sports Reporter
Frequency:
7 time(s) per week

DAILY REVIEW (PA)
116 MAIN STREET
TOWANDA, PA 18848-1832
570-265-2151
800-253-3662
Fax: 570-265-6130
rhosie@epix.net
www.thedailyreview.com
• Brian Fees, Sports Editor
(570) 265-1631
reviewsports@thedailyreview.com
• Beverly Kline, Advertising Director
(570) 265-1624
bkline@epix.net
Frequency:
7 time(s) per week

DAILY REVIEW ATLAS
400 SOUTH MAIN STREET
MONMOUTH, IL 61462
309-734-3176
Fax: 309-734-7649
www.reviewatlas.com
• Jeff Holt, Sports Editor
• Wendy Todd, Advertising Manager

Frequency:
5 time(s) per week

DAILY SENTINEL (CO)
P.O. BOX 668
GRAND JUNCTION, CO 81501-7737
970-242-5050
800-332-5832
Fax: 970-241-6860
www.gjsentinel.com
• Patti Arnold, Sports Editor
(970) 242-5050
patti.arnold@gjsentinel.com
Frequency:
7 time(s) per week

DAILY SENTINEL (NY)
333 WEST DOMINICK STREET
ROME, NY 13440-5701
315-337-4000
Fax: 315-337-4704
sentinel@rny.com
www.rny.com
• Linda Carlson, Classified Manager
• Joe Entelisano, Advertising Manager
(315) 337-4000
joesano@rny.com
• Joseph Silkowski, Sports Editor
(315) 337-4000
release@rny.com
Frequency:
7 time(s) per week

DAILY SENTINEL STAR
50 CORPORATE ROW
GRENADA, MS 38901
662-226-4321
Fax: 662-226-8310
editor@grenadastar.com
www.grenadastar.com
• Chuck Hathcock, Sports Editor
(662) 226-4321
sports@grenadastar.com
Frequency:
5 time(s) per week

DAILY SITKA SENTINEL
112 BARRACKS STREET
SITKA, AK 99835
907-747-3219
Fax: 907-747-8898
news@sitkasentinel.com
www.sitkasentinel.com
• Susan McFadden, Advertising Manager
(907) 747-3219
susan@sitkasentinel.com
• Cyndi Cassedy, Classified Manager
• Garland Kennedy, Sports Editor
(907) 747-3219
garland@sitkasentinel.com
• Craig Giammona, Sports Editor
(907) 747-3219
Frequency:
5 time(s) per week

Sports page- Daily newspaper

DAILY SOUTHERNER
504 WEST WILSON STREET
TARBORO, NC 27886-4239
252-823-3106
Fax: 252-823-4599
www.dailysoutherner.com
• Calvin Adkins, Sports Editor
(252) 823-3106
• Gene Hudson, Advertising Manager

(252) 823-3106
dailysoutherner@gmail.com
Frequency:
5 time(s) per week

DAILY SPARKS TRIBUNE
1002 C STREET
SPARKS, NV 89431
775-358-8061
800-669-1338
Fax: 775-359-3837
www.sparkstribune.net
• Dan Eckles, Sports Editor
(775) 358-8061
Frequency:
6 time(s) per week

DAILY STANDARD
123 EAST MARKET STREET
CELINA, OH 45822-1730
419-586-2371
Fax: 419-586-6271
sports@dailystandard.com
www.dailystandard.com
• Ryan Hines, Sports Editor
(419) 586-2371
sports@dailystandard.com
• John Lake, Advertising Manager
jlake@dailystandard.com
Frequency:
6 time(s) per week

DAILY STAR
725 SOUTH MORRISON BOULEVARD
HAMMOND, LA 70403-5401
985-254-7827
800-844-2333
Fax: 985-543-0006
www.hammondstar.com
• Fred Batiste, Sports Reporter
(985) 254-7822
• Al Guidry, Sports Reporter
• John Lenz, Sports Editor
(985) 254-7821
sports@hammondstar.com
Frequency:
6 time(s) per week

DAILY TIDINGS
1661 SISKIYOU BOULEVARD
ASHLAND, OR 97520
541-482-3456
Fax: 541-482-3688
www.dailytidings.com
• Joe Zavala, Sports Editor
(541) 482-3456
Frequency:
6 time(s) per week

DAILY TIMES (NM)
201 NORTH ALLEN AVENUE
FARMINGTON, NM 87499
505-325-4545
800-395-6397
Fax: 505-564-4630
www.daily-times.com
• John Livingston, Sports Reporter
• Renee Lucero, Sports Reporter
• Yvonne Gomez, Advertising Director
Frequency:
7 time(s) per week

DAILY TIMES (OK)
105 SOUTH ADAIR
PRYOR, OK 74361-3625

918-825-3292
Fax: 918-825-1965
prynews@swbell.net
www.pryordailytimes.com
• Kerrll Lester, Sports Editor
Frequency:
5 time(s) per week

DAILY TIMES CHRONICLE
1 ARROW DRIVE
WOBURN, MA 01801-2039
781-933-3700
Fax: 781-932-3321
news@woburnonline.com
www.woburnonline.com
• Steve Algeri, Sports Editor
(781) 933-3700
woburnnews@rcn.com
• Thomas R. Kirk, Advertising Director
(781) 933-3700
Frequency:
5 time(s) per week

DAILY TIMES LEADER
221 EAST MAIN STREET
WEST POINT, MS 39773
662-494-1422
Fax: 662-494-1414
www.dailytimesleader.com
• Brian Davis, Sports Editor
Frequency:
5 time(s) per week

DAILY TRIBUNE (IA)
317 5TH STREET
AMES, IA 50010-6101
515-232-2160
800-234-8742
Fax: 515-232-2364
news@amestrib.com
www.amestrib.com
• Mark Sharpe, Advertising Manager
(515) 663-6968
msharpe@amestrib.com
• Bobby LaGesse, Sports Editor
(515) 663-6929
Frequency:
6 time(s) per week

DAILY TRIBUNE (WI)
220 1ST AVENUE SOUTH
WISCONSIN RAPIDS, WI 54495-4154
715-423-7200
800-362-8315
Fax: 715-421-1545
editor@wisconsinrapidstribune.com
www.wisconsinrapidstribune.com
• Mark Massoglia, Sports Editor
(715) 422-6736
mark.massoglia@cwnews.net
Frequency:
6 time(s) per week

DAILY TRIBUNE NEWS
P.O. BOX 70
CARTERSVILLE, GA 30120
770-382-4545
Fax: 770-382-2711
news@daily-tribune.com
www.daily-tribune.com
• David Royal, Sports Writer
(770) 382-4545
• Chike Nwakamma, Associate Sports
Editor
(770) 382-4545

Frequency:
6 time(s) per week

DAILY WORLD
315 MICHIGAN STREET
ABERDEEN, WA 98520-6037
360-532-4000
Fax: 360-533-6039
press_releases@thedailyworld.com
www.thedailyworld.com
• Rob Burns, Sports Editor
(360) 537-3926
Frequency:
7 time(s) per week

DALLAS MORNING NEWS
508 YOUNG STREET
DALLAS, TX 75202
214-977-8222
800-431-0010
Fax: 214-977-8319
feedback@dallasnews.com
www.dallasnews.com
• Kevin B. Blackistone, Sports Columnist
(214) 977-8780
• Terry Blount, Sports Reporter
(214) 977-7661
• Chip Brown, Sports Writer
(214) 977-8444
• Chuck Carlton, Sports Reporter
(214) 977-8444
ccarlton@dallasnews.com
• Rachel Cohen, Sports Reporter
(214) 977-8444
• Tim Cowlishaw, Sports Columnist
(214) 977-8446
wtcowlishaw@dallasnews.com
• Sylvia Curiel, Sports Group Leader
(214) 977-8075
• Brian Davis, Sports Reporter
(214) 977-8869
• Jason Dugger, Sports Copy Editor
(214) 977-7665
• Gerry Fraley, Sports Columnist
(214) 977-8377
gfraley@dallasnews.com
• Brandon George, Sports Reporter
(817) 695-3319
bgeorge@dallasnews.com
• Rick Gosselin, Sports Columnist
(214) 977-8033
• Evan Grant, Sports Reporter (Baseball)
(214) 977-8184
egrant@dallasnews.com
• Kate Hairopoulos, Sports Reporter
(214) 977-8032
khairopoulos@dallasnews.com
• Dennis Hall, Sports Assistant Editor
(214) 977-8972
dhall@dallasnews.com
• Cathy Harasta, Sports Reporter
(214) 977-8759
• Mike Heika, Sports Reporter
(214) 977-8034
mheika@dallasnews.com
• Gary Jacobson, Sports Editor
(214) 977-2791
• Randy Jennings, Sports Reporter
(817) 695-3323
• Mark Konradi, Sports Assistant Editor
(214) 977-8983
Mkonradi@dallasnews.com
• Tim MacMahon, Sports Reporter
(214) 977-7632
• Jeff Miller, Sports Reporter
(214) 977-8174
• Bill Nichols, Sports Reporter
(214) 977-8455

• Dan Noxon, Sports Copy Editor
(214) 977-8444
dnoxon@dallasnews.com
• Roxanna Pellin-Scott, (214) 977-8961
Sports Assistant Editor
• Dave Renbarger, Sports Assistant Editor
(214) 977-8961
drenbarger@dallasnews.com
• Ray Sasser, Sports Writer (Outdoors)
(214) 977-8380
rsasser@dallasnews.com
• Damon L. Sayles, Sports Reporter
(817) 695-3321
• Shawna Seed, Sports Deputy Editor
(214) 977-8385
• Eddie Sefko, Sports Writer (NBA)
(214) 997-8451
esefko@dallasnews.com
Frequency:
7 time(s) per week

DALLES DAILY CHRONICLE
315 FEDERAL STREET
THE DALLES, OR 97058
541-296-2141
Fax: 541-298-1365
www.thedalleschronicle.com
• Jodi Nofziger, Sports Editor
(541) 506-4618
• Skip Tschanz, Advertising Manager
(541) 506-4609
Frequency:
6 time(s) per week

DANVILLE NEWS
14 EAST MAHONING STREET
DANVILLE, PA 17821-1934
570-275-3235
Fax: 570-275-7624
www.thedanvillenews.com
• William Bowman, Sports Editor
(570) 275-3235
Frequency:
6 time(s) per week

DANVILLE REGISTER AND BEE
700 MONUMENT STREET
DANVILLE, VA 24541-1512
434-791-7971
Fax: 434-797-2299
news@registerbee.com
www.registerbee.com
• Damien Sordelett, Sports Editor
(434) 791-7998
dsordelett@registerbee.com
Frequency:
7 time(s) per week

DAVIS COUNTY CLIPPER
P.O. BOX 267
BOUNTIFUL, UT 84011
801-295-2251
Fax: 801-295-3044
www.clippertoday.com
• Russ Riggs, Sports Editor
(801) 295-2251
• Ben De Voe, Sports Editor
(801) 295-2251
Frequency:
2 time(s) per week

DAVIS ENTERPRISE
315 G STREET
DAVIS, CA 95616-4119
530-756-0800
Fax: 530-756-6707

newsroom@davisenterprise.net
www.davisenterprise.com
• C. Colton, Sports Writer
(530) 747-8059
• Nancy Hannell, Advertising Director
ads@davisenterprise.net
• Matt O'Donnell, Sports Editor
(530) 747-8049
Frequency:
6 time(s) per week

DAY
P.O. BOX 1231
NEW LONDON, CT 06320
860-442-2200
800-542-3354
Fax: 860-442-5599
www.theday.com
• Chuck Banning, Sports Editor
(860) 701-4441
c.banning@theday.com
• Dave Davis, Sports Wire Editor
(860) 701-4443
d.davis@theday.com
Frequency:
7 time(s) per week

DAYTON DAILY NEWS
1611 SOUTH MAIN STREET
DAYTON, OH 45402
937-225-2275
800-686-6397
Fax: 937-225-2489
localnews@coxohio.com
www.daytondailynews.com/
• Bucky Albers, Sports Writer
(937) 225-2412
balbers@daytondailynews.com
• Tom Archdeacon, Sports Columnist
(937) 225-2156
tarchdeacon@daytondailynews.com
• Greg Billing, Motorsports Reporter
(937) 225-2250
gbilling@daytondailynews.com
• Doug Harris, College Sports Reporter
(937) 324-0376
dharris@DaytonDailyNews.com
• Marc Katz, Sports Reporter
(937) 225-2157
mkatz@daytondailynews.com
• Brian Kollars, Sports Section Editor
(937) 225-2163
bkollars@daytondailynews.com
• Dave Long, Sports Reporter
(937) 225-2251
dlong@daytondailynews.com
• Chick Ludwig, Sports Reporter
(937) 225-2253
cludwig@daytondailynews.com
• Sean McClelland, Sports Writer
(937) 225-2408
smcclelland@DaytonDailyNews.com
• Hal McCoy, Sports Columnist
(937) 225-2250
hmccoy@daytondailynews.com
Frequency:
7 time(s) per week

DAYTONA BEACH NEWS-JOURNAL
P.O. BOX 2831
DAYTONA BEACH, FL 32117
386-252-1511 EXT 2281
Fax: 386-258-8465
www.news-journalonline.com
• Burke Noel, Sports Columnist
(386) 681-2416
• Jordan Kahn, Outdoors Writer

(386) 681-2798
• Godwin Kelly, Sports Editor (Motor Sports)

godwin.kelly@news-jrnl.com
• Ken Willis, Sports Columnist
(386) 681-2549
ken.willis@news-jrnl.com
Frequency:
7 time(s) per week

DE SOTO TIMES TODAY
2445 HWY 51
HERNANDO, MS 38632
662-429-6397
Fax: 662-429-5229
editor@desototimes.com
www.desototimes.com
• Ron Caldwell, Sports Editor
sports@desototimes.com
Frequency:
5 time(s) per week

DECATUR DAILY
201 1ST AVENUE, S.E.
DECATUR, AL 35609
256-353-4612
888-353-4612
Fax: 256-340-2366
news@decaturdaily.com
www.decaturdaily.com
• Mark Edwards, Sports Editor
(256) 340-3461
• Scott Brown, Advertising Manager
(256) 340-2381
Frequency:
7 time(s) per week

DECATUR DAILY DEMOCRAT
141 SOUTH 2ND STREET
DECATUR, IN 46733-1664
260-724-2121
Fax: 260-724-7981
comp@decaturdailydemocrat.com
www.decaturdailydemocrat.com
• Ron Platt, Advertising Manager
(260) 724-2121
advertising@decaturdailydemocrat.com
• Joe Spaulding, Sports Editor
(260) 724-2121
Frequency:
6 time(s) per week

DELAWARE COUNTY DAILY TIMES
500 MILDRED AVENUE
PRIMOS, PA 19018-2914
610-622-8800
Fax: 610-622-8887
www.delcotimes.com
• Rob Parent, Sports Editor
(610) 622-8884
rparent@delcotimes.com
• Dennis Deitch, Sports Reporter
(610) 622-8800
sports@delcotimes.com
Frequency:
7 time(s) per week

DELAWARE GAZETTE
18 EAST WILLIAM STREET
DELAWARE, OH 43015-2332
740-363-1161
Fax: 740-363-6262
www.delgazette.com
• Ryan Oswald, Advertising Manager
(740) 363-1161
• Ben Stroup, Sports Editor

Frequency:
6 time(s) per week

DELAWARE STATE NEWS
WEBBS LANE & NEW BURTON ROAD
DOVER, DE 19901
302-674-3600
800-282-8586
Fax: 302-741-8252
newsroom@newszap.com
www.newszap.com
• Diane Cahall, Advertising Manager
• Andy Walter, Sports Editor
(302) 674-3600
Frequency:
7 time(s) per week

DELTA DEMOCRAT-TIMES
988 NORTH BROADWAY
GREENVILLE, MS 38701-2349
662-335-1155
800-844-1618
Fax: 662-335-2860
www.ddtonline.com
• Kenneth Mister, Sports Editor
(662) 378-0722
Frequency:
6 time(s) per week

DEMOCRAT AND CHRONICLE
55 EXCHANGE BOULEVARD
ROCHESTER, NY 14614-2001
585-232-7100
800-767-7539
Fax: 585-258-2237
editor@DemocratandChronicle.com
www.democratandchronicle.com/
• Thomas Batzold, Sports Editor
(585) 258-2262
sports@democratandchronicle.com
• Steve Bradley, Sports Assistant Editor
(585) 258-2569
sbradley@democratandchronicle.com
• James Castor, Assistant Sports Editor
(585) 258-2352
• James Johnson, Sports Reporter
(585) 258-2754
• James Mandelaro, Sports Writer
(585) 258-2761
jmand@democratandchronicle.com
• Robert Matthews, Sports Columnist
(585) 258-2325
matthews@democratandchronicle.com
• Kevin Oklobzija, Sports Writer
(585) 258-2277
kevino@democratandchronicle.com
• Scott Pitoniak, Sports Writer
(585) 258-2455
spitoniak@democratandchronicle.com
• Leo Roth, Sports Columnist
(585) 258-2764
lroth@democratandchronicle.com
Frequency:
7 time(s) per week

DENTON RECORD-CHRONICLE
P.O. BOX 369
DENTON, TX 76202
940-387-3811
800-275-1722
Fax: 940-566-6888
drc@dentonrc.com
www.dentonrc.com
• Todd Jorgenson, Sports Editor
(940) 566-6871
• Adam Boedeker, Sports Reporter
(940) 566-6872

Frequency:
7 time(s) per week

DENVER POST
101 WEST COLFAX AVENUE
DENVER, CO 80202
303-954-1201
800-336-7678
Fax: 303-954-1369
sports@denverpost.com
www.denverpost.com
• Jim Armstrong, Sports Writer
(303) 954-1294
• Jason Blevins, Sports Reporter
(303) 820-1374
• Patrick Saunders, Online Sports Editor
(303) 954-1720
psaunders@denverpost.com
• Bill Briggs, Sports Writer
(303) 820-1720
• Mike Chambers, Sports Writer
(303) 954-1357
mchambers@denverpost.com
• Anthony Cotton, Sports Writer
(303) 820-1292
• Kevin Dale, Assistant Managing Editor
(303) 954-1294
smonserud@denverpost.com
• Adrian Dater, Sports Writer
(303) 954-1201
• Neil Devlin, Sports Editor (High School)
(303) 820-1714
• Nick Groke, Sports Writer
(303) 954-1015
• Thomas George, Sports Columnist
(303) 820-1994
• Mark Kiszla, Sports Writer
(303) 954-1053
mkiszla@denverpost.com
• Nancy Lofholm, Skiing Reporter
(970) 256-1957
• John Meyer, Sports Writer
(303) 954-1010
jmeyer@denverpost.com
• Charlie Meyers, Outdoors Editor
(303) 954-1294
• Woody Paige, Sports Columnist
(303) 820-1398
• Joseph Sanchez, Sports Reporter
(303) 820-1294
• Patrick Saunders, Sports Writer
(303) 954-1201
psaunders@denverpost.com
• Adam Thompson, Sports Writer
(303) 820-5447
Frequency:
7 time(s) per week

DERRICK
1510 WEST 1ST STREET
OIL CITY, PA 16301-3211
814-676-7444
800-352-1002
Fax: 814-677-8351
newsroom@usachoice.net
www.thederrick.com
• Ed Brannon, Sports Editor
(814) 676-7444
sports.thederrick@gmail.com
• Ned Cowart, Advertising Director
(814) 676-7444
info@thederrick.com
• Ed Finck, Sports Writer
(814) 676-7056
• Carla Sheatz, Classified Manager
(814) 676-7444
info@thederrick.com

Frequency:
6 time(s) per week

DES MOINES NEWS AND HIGHLINE TIMES
133 SW 153RD STREET
BURIEN, WA 98166-2311
206-444-4873
Fax: 206-444-4877
hteditor@robinsonnews.com
www.robinsonnews.com
• Tim Clinton, Sports Editor
(253) 838-7622
sports@robinsonnews.com
Frequency:
1 time(s) per week

DES MOINES REGISTER
P.O. BOX 957
DES MOINES, IA 50306
515-284-8000
Fax: 515-286-2504
metroiowa@dmreg.com
www.dmregister.com/
• Nancy Clark, Sports Reporter
(515) 286-2517
nclark@dmreg.com
• Rob Gray, Sports Writer (High School)
(515) 284-8194
rgray@dmreg.com
• Marc Hansen, Media Columnist
(515) 284-8534
mhansen@dmreg.com
• Dan Johnson, Sports Reporter
(515) 284-8375
dansjohn@dmreg.com
• Gary Lake, Sports Assistant Editor
(515) 284-8573
• Andrew Logue, High School Sports Writer
(515) 284-8368
alogue@dmreg.com
• Bryce Miller, Executive Sports Editor
(515) 284-8130
brmiller@dmreg.com
• John Naughton, High School/Prep Sports Chief
(515) 284-8000
jnaughto@dmreg.com
• Randy Peterson, Sports Reporter
(515) 284-8000
rapeters@dmreg.com
• Brad Robertson, Advertising Vice President
(515) 284-8384
brobertson@dmreg.com
• Dave Stockdale, Sports Copy Editor
(515) 284-8284
dstockdale@dmreg.com
• Tom Witosky, Sports Writer (Football)
(515) 284-8522
twitosky@dmreg.com
Frequency:
7 time(s) per week

DESERET MORNING NEWS
55 NORTH 300 WEST
SALT LAKE CITY, UT 84101
801-236-6000
800-662-9076
Fax: 801-237-2121
www.deseretnews.com
• Tim Buckley, Sports Writer
(801) 237-2161
• Jeff Call, Sports Writer
(801) 437-7605
jeffc@desnews.com
• Kent Condon, Sports Editor

(801) 236-6075
kcondon@desnews.com
• Rich Evans, Sports Writer
(801) 236-6075
• Dirk Facer, Sports Writer
(801) 236-6073
• Linda A. Hamilton, Sports Writer
(801) 237-2161
• Jay Hinton, Sports Writer
(801) 237-2114
• Loren D. Jorgensen, Sports Writer
(801) 236-6056
• Jon Ringwood, Sports Writer
(801) 236-6035
• Brad Rock, Sports Columnist
(801) 333-7454
• David Schneider, Sports Editor
(801) 237-2158
daves@desnews.com
• Mike Sorensen, Sports Writer
(801) 236-6055
• Scott Taylor, Sports Editor
(801) 437-7601
taylor@desnews.com
Frequency:
7 time(s) per week

DESERT DISPATCH
130 COOLWATER LANE
BARSTOW, CA 92311-3222
760-256-2257
Fax: 760-256-0685
www.desertdispatch.com
• Bea Lint, Advertising Director
(760) 256-4140
• David Heldreth, Sports Editor
(760) 256-4124
Frequency:
7 time(s) per week

DESERT SUN
PO BOX 2734
PALM SPRINGS, CA 92263
760-322-8889
800-834-6052
Fax: 760-778-4659
www.mydesert.com
• Larry Bohannan, Sports Reporter
larry.bohannan@thedesertsun.com
• Jeff Hendrickson, Sports Editor
(760) 778-4632
jeff.hendrickson@thedesertsun.com
• Michelle Rico, Classified Manager
(760) 778-4517
michelle.rico@thedesertsun.com
• Matt Solinsky, Sports Editor
(760) 778-4629
matt.solinsky@thedesertsun.com
• Leighton Ginn, Sports Reporter
(760) 778-4631
Leighton.ginn@thedesertsun.com
Frequency:
7 time(s) per week

DETROIT FREE PRESS
600 WEST FORT STREET
DETROIT, MI 48226-3138
313-222-6400
Fax: 313-222-5981
letters@freepress.com
www.freep.com
• Mitch Albom, Sports Columnist
(313) 223-4581
malbom@freepress.com
• Joann Barnas-Taylor, Sports Reporter
(313) 222-2037
barnas@freepress.com

• Paul Barrett, Sports Editor
• Brad Betker, Sports Copy Editor
betker@freepress.com
• Mike Brudenell, Sports Staff Writer
(313) 222-2115
mbrudenell@freepress.com
• Bill Collison, Sports Copy Editor
bcollison@freepress.com
• Nicholas J. Cotsonika, Sports Reporter
• Bernie Czarniecki, Sports Editor
czarni@freepress.com
• David Darby, Sports Editor
darby@freepress.com
• Owen Davis, Sports Deputy Managing Editor
davis@freepress.com
• Jim Dwight, Sports Editor
dwight@freepress.com
• Bob Ellis, Sports Copy Editor
ellis@freepress.com
• Perry A. Farrell, Sports Reporter
(313) 222-2555
farrell@freepress.com
• Matt Fiorito, Sports Writer (Bowling)
(313) 222-6721
fiorit@freepress.com
• Maureen Ground, Sports Copy Editor
ground@freepress.com
• Gene Guidi, Sports Reporter
(313) 222-6665
guidi@freepress.com
• Krista Ann Latham, Sports Reporter
• John Lowe, Sports Reporter
(313) 223-4053
• Tim Marcinkoski, Sports Copy Editor
(313) 223-4427
marcinkoski@freepress.com
• Mick McCabe, Sports Reporter (Prep)
(313) 223-4744
mccabe@freepress.com
• Carlos Monarrez, Sports Copy Editor
(313) 222-6697
monarrez@freepress.com
• Carlos Monarrez, Sports Writer
(313) 222-6697
monarrez@freepress.com
• Gene Myers, Sports Editor
(313) 222-6400
gmyers@freepress.com
• Gene Myers, Sports Editor
(313) 222-6736
myers@freepress.com
• Tom Panzenhagen, (313) 222-6730
Sports Assistant Editor
• Dave Robinson, Sports Deputy Managing Editor
(313) 222-6736
• Michael Rosenberg, Sports Columnist
(313) 222-6052
mrosenberg@freepress.com
• Steve Schrader, Sports Assistant Editor
• Drew Sharp, Sports Columnist
(313) 223-4055
dsharp@freepress.com
• Shannon Shelton, Sports Reporter
(313) 222-6400
slshelton@freepress.com
Frequency:
7 time(s) per week

DETROIT NEWS
615 WEST LAFAYETTE BOULEVARD
DETROIT, MI 48226-3124
313-222-2300
800-678-4115
Fax: 313-222-2451
letters@detnews.com
www.detnews.com

- Robert Allstetter, Sports Deputy Editor
(313) 222-1486
rallstetter@detnews.com
- Rod Beard, Sports Producer
rbeard@detnews.com
- Dave Dye, Sports Reporter
(313) 222-2260
ddye@detnews.com
- Ron French, Sports Reporter
rfrench@detnews.com
- Tom Gage, Sports Reporter
(313) 222-1495
tgage@detnews.com
- Joanne Gerstner, Sports Reporter
(313) 223-4644
jgerstner@detnews.com
- Dave Goricki, Sports Reporter
dgoricki@detnews.com
- Brian Handley, Sports Assistant Editor
- Lynn Henning, Sports Reporter
lhenning@detnews.com
- Ted Kulfan, Sports Reporter
(313) 222-2260
tkulfan@detnews.com
- Phil Laciura, Sports Editor
placiura@detnews.com
- Ruben Luna, Sports Editor
(313) 222-4642
rluna@detnews.com
- Tom Markowski, Sports Reporter
(313) 222-4633
tmarkowski@detnews.com
- Chris McCosky, Sports Reporter
(313) 222-2300
cmccosky@detnews.com
- William McMillan, Sports Ass't Managing Editor
(313) 222-4643
wmcmillan@detnews.com
- Tenisha Mercer, Advertising Reporter
tmercer@detnews.com
- Michael O'Hara, Sports Writer (Pro Football)
(313) 222-1488
mohara@detnews.com
- Rob Parker, Sports Columnist
(313) 222-2260
rparker@detnews.com
- James Russ, Sports Assistant Editor
jruss@detnews.com
- Jim Spadafore, Sports Reporter
(313) 222-4638
jspadafore@detnews.com
Frequency:
7 time(s) per week

DEVILS LAKE DAILY JOURNAL
516 4TH STREET
DEVILS LAKE, ND 58301
701-662-2127
Fax: 701-662-3115
news@devilslakejournal.com
www.devilslakejournal.com
- Ray Maloney, Sports Editor
(701) 662-2127
- Paula Ramsey, Advertising Manager
(701) 662-2127
advertising@devilslakejournal.com
Frequency:
5 time(s) per week

DIARIO LAS AMERICAS
P.O. BOX 593177
MIAMI, FL 33142-5149
305-633-3341
Fax: 305-635-7668
cartas@diariolasamericas.com
www.diariolasamericas.com

- Marino Martinez, Sports Editor
- Jose A. Yuste, Classified Manager
(305) 633-3341
Frequency:
6 time(s) per week

DICKINSON PRESS
1815 1ST STREET WEST
DICKINSON, ND 58602
701-225-8111
Fax: 701-225-6653
newsroom@thedickinsonpress.com
www.thedickinsonpress.com/
- Dustin Monke, Sports Editor
- Justin Nutter, Sports Writer
Frequency:
6 time(s) per week

DISPATCH (CA)
6400 MONTEREY ROAD
GILROY, CA 95020-6628
408-842-6400
Fax: 408-842-7105
editor@gilroydispatch.com
www.gilroydispatch.com
- Anna Patejdl, Sports Reporter
(408) 842-6400
- Josh Weaver, Sports Editor
(408) 842-1694
Frequency:
5 time(s) per week

DISPATCH (IL)
1720 5TH AVE
MOLINE, IL 61265
309-764-4344
Fax: 309-797-0321
www.qconline.com
- Bill Allee, Sports Editor
- Tom Johnston, Sports Reporter
- Steve Tappa, Sports Reporter

DODGE CITY DAILY GLOBE
705 2ND AVENUE
DODGE CITY, KS 67801
620-225-4151
800-279-8795
Fax: 620-225-4154
dcnews@dodgeglobe.com
dodgeglobe.com
- Nicole Dirks, Advertising Director
(620) 408-9919
- Ryan Buchan, Sports Editor
(620) 408-9913
Frequency:
6 time(s) per week

DOMINION-POST
1251 EARL CORE ROAD
MORGANTOWN, WV 26505-5881
304-292-6301
800-654-4676
Fax: 304-291-2326
www.dominionpost.com
- Drew Rubenstein, Sports Editor
(304) 291-9431
drubenstein@dominionpost.com
Frequency:
7 time(s) per week

DOTHAN EAGLE
227 NORTH OATES STREET
DOTHAN, AL 36303-4555
334-792-3141
Fax: 334-712-7992
www.dothaneagle.com

- Jon Johnson, Sports Editor
(334) 712-7965
jjohnson@dothaneagle.com
Frequency:
7 time(s) per week

DOUGLAS COUNTY SENTINEL
8501 BOWDEN STREET
DOUGLASVILLE, GA 30134
770-942-6571
Fax: 770-949-7556
news@douglascountysentinel.com
www.douglascountysentinel.com
- Bill Evans, Sports Reporter
(770) 942-6571
evans@douglascountysentinel.com
Frequency:
6 time(s) per week

DOWAGIAC DAILY NEWS
205 SPAULDING STREET
DOWAGIAC, MI 49047-1451
269-782-2101
888-725-0108
Fax: 269-782-5290
www.leaderpub.com
- Diana Kingsley, Advertising Director
- Scott Novak, Sports Editor
scott.novak@leaderpub.com
- Hal Shue, Classified Manager
(269) 782-2101
Frequency:
5 time(s) per week

DU QUOIN EVENING CALL
9 NORTH DIVISION STREET
DU QUOIN, IL 62832
618-542-2133
800-455-2133
Fax: 618-542-2726
www.duquoin.com
- Terri Fisher, Advertising Manager
(618) 542-2133
admanager@frontier.com
- Doug Daniels, Sports Editor
(618) 542-2133
dqsports@frontier.com
- John Croessman, Publisher
(618) 542-2133
jcroessman@frontier.com
Frequency:
6 time(s) per week

DULUTH NEWS-TRIBUNE
424 WEST 1ST STREET
DULUTH, MN 55802-1516
218-723-5303
800-456-8181
Fax: 218-720-4120
sports@duluthnews.com
www.duluthnewstribune.com
- Rick Weegman, Sports Reporter
(218) 720-4138
rweegman@duluthnews.com
- Rick Lubbers, Sports Editor
(218) 723-5307
rlubbers@duluthnews.com
- Kevin Pates, Sports Reporter
- John Nowacki, Sports Reporter
jnowacki@duluthnews.com
Frequency:
7 time(s) per week

DUNCAN BANNER
1001 ELM STREET
DUNCAN, OK 73533-4746

580-255-5354
Fax: 580-255-8889
news@duncanbanner.com
www.duncanbanner.com
• Paula Blair, Classified Manager
(580) 255-5354
paula.blair@duncanbanner.com
• Ron Booth, Sports Editor
• Dana Boyles, Advertising Manager
(580) 255-5354
Frequency:
6 time(s) per week

DUNDALK EAGLE
4 NORTH CENTER PLACE
DUNDALK, MD 21222-4300
410-288-6060
Fax: 410-288-6963
info@dundalkeagle.com
www.dundalkeagle.com
• William Gates, Sports Editor
sports@dundalkeagle.com
Frequency:
1 time(s) per week

DURANGO HERALD
1275 MAIN AVENUE
DURANGO, CO 81301
970-247-3504
800-530-8318
Fax: 970-259-5011
herald@durangoherald.com
www.durangoherald.com
• Dominick McCullough, Advertising
Manager
(970) 375-4519
• Aaron Unterreiner, Sports Editor
(970) 375-4557
Frequency:
7 time(s) per week

DURANT DAILY DEMOCRAT
200 WEST BEECH STREET
DURANT, OK 74701
580-924-4388
800-729-4388
Fax: 580-924-0962
www.durantdemocrat.com
• Karl Oakley, Advertising Manager
• Beau Simmons, Sports Editor
Frequency:
6 time(s) per week

EAGLE HERALD
1809 DUNLAP AVENUE
MARINETTE, WI 54143-1706
715-735-6611
800-777-0345
Fax: 715-735-0229
news@eagleherald.com
www.eagleherald.com
• Jim Hofer, Advertising Manager
(715) 735-6611
• Jody Korch, Sports Editor
(715) 735-6611
• Tom Kaeser, Assistant Sports Editor
(715) 735-6611
Frequency:
7 time(s) per week

EAGLE-TIMES
401 RIVER ROAD
CLAREMONT, NH 03743
603-543-3100
Fax: 603-542-9705

news@eagletimes.com
www.eagletimes.com/
• Jeff Miller, Sports Editor
(603) 543-3100
• Clyde Pinson, Advertising Director
(603) 543-3100
Frequency:
6 time(s) per week

EAGLE-TRIBUNE
100 TURNPIKE STREET
NORTH ANDOVER, MA 01845
978-946-2000
Fax: 978-685-1588
news@eagletribune.com
www.eagletribune.com
• Bill Burt, Sports Executive Editor
(978) 946-2227
bburt@eagletribune.com
• Dave Dyer, Sports Writer
ddyer@eagletribune.com
• Hector Longo, Sports Reporter
• Mike Muldoon, Sports Writer
• Joe Murphy, Sports Writer
Frequency:
7 time(s) per week

EAST OREGONIAN
211 SOUTHEAST BYERS STREET
PENDLETON, OR 97801
541-276-2211
800-522-0255
Fax: 541-278-2688
www.eastoregonian.info
• Bill Marcum, Advertising Manager
(541) 278-2669
• Matt Entrup, Sports Editor
(541) 966-0838
Frequency:
7 time(s) per week

EAST VALLEY TRIBUNE
120 WEST FIRST AVENUE
MESA, AZ 85210-1312
480-898-6500
800-541-8016
Fax: 480-898-6362
newstips@aztrib.com
www.eastvalleytribune.com
• Scott Bordow, Sports Columnist
(480) 898-6598
• Bob Romantic, Sports Editor
(480) 898-6538
• Matt Simpson, Sports Reporter
(480) 898-6497
• Dan Zeiger, Sports Writer
(480) 898-6525
Frequency:
7 time(s) per week

LOUDOUN TIMES-MIRROR
9 EAST MARKET STREET
LEESBURG, VA 20176
703-771-0036
Fax: 703-771-0036
www.loudountimes.com
• Carl Lulat, Sports Editor
(703) 209-5148
Frequency:
1 time(s) per week

EASTSIDER
13650 11 MILE ROAD
WARREN, MI 48089-1422

586-756-8800
Fax: 586-498-9627
www.candgnews.com
• Susan Shanley, Sports Editor
(586) 498-1048
sshanley@candgnews.com

EDWARDSVILLE INTELLIGENCER
117 NORTH 2ND STREET
EDWARDSVILLE, IL 62025
618-656-4700
Fax: 618-656-7618
www.theintelligencer.com
• Christopher Templeton, Sports Reporter
(618) 656-4700
• Bill Yarbrough, Sports Editor
Frequency:
6 time(s) per week

EFFINGHAM DAILY NEWS
201 NORTH BANKER STREET
EFFINGHAM, IL 62401
217-347-7151
Fax: 217-342-9315
www.effinghamdailynews.com
• Seth Whitehead, Sports Editor
(217) 347-7151
• Scott Richey, Sports Reporter
(217) 347-7151
Frequency:
7 time(s) per week, Monday-Sunday

EL BOHEMIO NEWS
4178 MISSION STREET
SAN FRANCISCO, CA 94112
415-469-9579
Fax: 415-469-9481
bohemio@ix.netcom.com
www.bohemionews.com
• Santiago Hernandez, News Director
(415) 469-9579
bohemio@ix.netcom.com
Frequency:
1 time(s) per week

EL DIARIO LA PRENSA
345 HUDSON STREET 13TH FLOOR
NEW YORK, NY 10014
212-807-4600
Fax: 212-807-4705
editorial@eldiariony.com
www.eldiariony.com
• Mario Concha, Sports Editor
(212) 807-4779
• Ricardo Vasconcellos, Sports Editor
(212) 807-4789
Frequency:
7 time(s) per week

EL DORADO NEWS-TIMES
P.O. BOX 912
EL DORADO, AR 71730-6124
870-862-6611
Fax: 870-862-5226
editorial@eldoradonews.com
epaper.wehco.com/Daily/Skins/ElDorado/index.asp
• Tony Burns, Sports Editor
(870) 862-6611
sports@eldoradonews.com
Frequency:
7 time(s) per week

EL DORADO TIMES
114 NORTH VINE
EL DORADO, KS 67042-2028

316-321-1120
Fax: 316-321-7722
www.eldoradotimes.com
• Diane Lacy-Trostle, Advertising Manager
• John Curtis, Sports Editor
Frequency:
6 time(s) per week

EL HISPANO NEWS
2102 EMPIRE CENTRAL
DALLAS, TX 75235-4302
214-357-2186
Fax: 214-357-2195
www.elhispanonews.com
• Gustavo Burgadt, Sports Editor
(214) 357-2186
Frequency:
1 time(s) per week

EL INFORMADOR HISPANO
2235 NORTH MAIN STREET
FORT WORTH, TX 76106
817-626-8624
888-269-8353
Fax: 817-626-1855
www.elinformadorhispano.com
• Jose Tiscareno, Sports Editor
Frequency:
1 time(s) per week

EL MUNDO
750 N. EASTERN
LAS VEGAS, NV 89101
702-649-8553
Fax: 702-649-7429
editorial@elmundo.net
www.elmundo.net
• Francisco Alexander, Sports Editor
(702) 649-8553
• Antonio Carranza, Sports Writer
(702) 649-8553
editorial@elmundo.net
Frequency:
1 time(s) per week

EL NUEVO HERALD
ONE HERALD PLAZA
MIAMI, FL 33132-1609
305-376-3535
Fax: 305-376-2378
perspectiva@elnuevoherald.com
www.elherald.com
• Jorge Ebro, Deportero de Deportes
(305) 376-3535
jebro@elnuevoherald.com
• Manolo Hernandez, Sports Editor
(305) 376-2055
• Luis Sanchez, Sports Reporter (Soccer)
(305) 376-3535
perspectiva@elnuevoherald.com
• Luis Sanchez, Sports Editor
Frequency:
7 time(s) per week

EL NUEVO HERALDO BROWNSVILLE
1135 EAST VAN BUREN
BROWNSVILLE, TX 78520
956-542-4301
www.elnuevoheraldo.com
• Juan Sanchez, Sports Editor
(956) 982-6623
Frequency:
52 time(s) per week

EL NUEVO PATRIA
P.O. BOX 2
MIAMI, FL 33014
305-530-8787
Fax: 305-376-2378
patrianews@aol.com
www.miami.com/mld/elnuevo
• Sarvelio Delvalle, Sports Editor
(305) 530-8787
patrianews@aol.com
• Sarvelio DelValle, Sports Editor
(305) 530-8787
patrianews@aol.com
Frequency:
1 time(s) per week

EL PASO TIMES
300 NORTH CAMPBELL STREET
EL PASO, TX 79901-1402
915-546-6300
Fax: 915-546-6415
elpasonews@elpasotimes.com
www.elpasotimes.com
• Margaret Gallardo, Sports Editor
(915) 546-6166
mgallardo@elpasotimes.com
• Mike Price, Advertising Director
(915) 546-6250
mprice@elpasotimes.com
• Robert Rios, Advertising Manager
(915) 546-6231
rrios@elpasotimes.com
Frequency:
7 time(s) per week

EL TIEMPO DE NUEVA YORK
37 37 88TH STREET SUITE A 8
JACKSON HEIGHTS, NY 11372
718-507-0832
Fax: 718-507-2105
www.tiempo.com/nueva-york.htm
• Armando Dalebera, Sports Editor
Frequency:
1 time(s) per week

EL TIEMPO LATINO
1150 15TH STREET NW
WASHINGTON, DC 22201-2909
202-334-9100
Fax: 202-496-3599
ramon@eltiempolatino.com
www.eltiempolatino.com/
• Miguel Guilarte, Sports Editor
(202) 334-9142
miguel@eltiempolatino.com
Frequency:
1 time(s) per week

ELIZABETHTON STAR
P.O. BOX 1960
ELIZABETHTON, TN 37643
423-928-4151
Fax: 423-542-2004
www.starhq.com
• Ivan Sanders, Sports Editor
(423) 542-4141
• Tim Chambers, Sports Writer
(423) 297-9061
Frequency:
6 time(s) per week

ELKHART TRUTH
COMMUNICANA BLDG
PO BOX 487
ELKHART, IN 46515-0487

574-294-1661
Fax: 574-294-3895
• Mary Alexander, Advertising Director
• Ben Ford, Sports Writer
• Bill Beck, Sports Editor

ELKO DAILY FREE PRESS
3720 IDAHO STREET
ELKO, NV 89801
775-738-3118
Fax: 775-778-3131
editor@elkodaily.com
www.elkodaily.com/
• Mike Christianson, Sports Editor
(775) 738-3118
sports@elkodaily.com
• Ashley Wilson, Advertising Manager
(775) 748-2706
Frequency:
6 time(s) per week

ELLWOOD CITY LEDGER
P.O. BOX 471
ELLWOOD CITY, PA 16117-5908
724-568-7529
Fax: 724-758-2410
eclnews@ellwoodcityledger.com
www.ellwoodcityledger.com
• Randy Senior, Sports Editor
(724) 758-7529
• Don Vaccari, Advertising Manager
Frequency:
6 time(s) per week

EMPORIA GAZETTE
517 MERCHANT STREET
EMPORIA, KS 66801-7206
620-342-4800
Fax: 620-342-8108
newsroom@emporiagazette.com
www.emporiagazette.com
• Stuart Goldman, Sports Editor
(620) 342-4805
sports@emporiagazette.com
• Carolyn Hatting, Advertising Manager
(620) 342-4800
Frequency:
6 time(s) per week

ENID NEWS AND EAGLE
227 WEST BROADWAY
ENID, OK 73701-4017
580-233-6600
800-299-6397
Fax: 580-548-8147
www.enidnews.com
• Mark Rountree, Sports Editor
(580) 548-8153
• Bruce Campbell, Sports Columnist
(580) 548-8144
bcampbell@enidnews.com
Frequency:
7 time(s) per week

ENNIS DAILY NEWS
213 NORTH DALLAS STREET
ENNIS, TX 75119-4011
972-875-3801
Fax: 972-875-9747
www.ennisdailynews.com/
• Tye Chandler, Sports Editor
(972) 875-3801
Frequency:
6 time(s) per week

ENQUIRER-JOURNAL
500 WEST JEFFERSON STREET
MONROE, NC 28111
704-289-1541
Fax: 704-289-2929
news@theej.com
www.enquirerjournal.com
• Jerry Snow, Sports Editor
(704) 261-2225
jsnow@theej.com
• Justin Murdock, Sports Writer
(704) 261-2224
Frequency:
6 time(s) per week

ENTERPRISE
1324 BELMONT STREET
SUITE 10
BROCKTON, MA 02301
508-586-6200
Fax: 508-586-6506
newsroom@enterprisenews.com
enterprisenews.com
• Bill Abramson, Sports Editor
(508) 427-4049
newsroom@enterprisenews.com
• Win Bates, Sports Writer
(508) 427-4052
• Mark Ducharme, Sports Reporter
(508) 427-4051
• Ron Dziergowski, Sports Writer
(508) 427-4051
• Jim Fenton, Sports Writer
(508) 427-4048
jfenton@enterprisenews.com
• Michael Harwood, Advertising Director
(508) 427-4009
• Mark Mahoney, Advertising Services
Manager
(508) 427-4089
mmahoney@enterprisenews.com
• Linda Siemers, Classified Manager
(508) 427-4070
Frequency:
7 time(s) per week

ENTERPRISE LEDGER
106 NORTH EDWARDS STREET
ENTERPRISE, AL 36330-2524
334-347-9533
Fax: 334-347-0825
www.eprisenow.com/
• Brandon Patterson, Sports Editor
(334) 347-9533
Frequency:
5 time(s) per week

ENTERPRISE-JOURNAL
112 OLIVER EMMERICH DRIVE
MCCOMB, MS 39648-6330
601-684-2421
800-748-9845
Fax: 601-684-0836
news@enterprise-journal.com
www.enterprise-journal.com
• Lauren Devereaux, Advertising Manager
advertising@enterprise-journal.com
• Dale Constance, Sports Editor
(601) 684-2421
sports@enterprise-journal.com
Frequency:
6 time(s) per week

ESTHERVILLE DAILY NEWS
10 NORTH 7TH STREET
ESTHERVILLE, IA 51334

712-362-2622
Fax: 712-362-2624
esthervilledailynews.com/
• David Swartz, Sports Editor
(712) 362-2622
dswartz@esthervilledailynews.com
Frequency:
6 time(s) per week

EVANSVILLE COURIER & PRESS
300 EAST WALNUT STREET
EVANSVILLE, IN 47713-1945
812-424-7711
800-288-3200
Fax: 812-422-8196
courier@courierpress.com
www.courierpress.com
• Tim Etheridge, Sports Editor
(812) 464-7416
• Steve Ford, Sports Reporter
(812) 464-7511
Frequency:
7 time(s) per week

EVENING NEWS
109 ARLINGTON STREET
SAULT SAINTE MARIE, MI 49783-1901
906-632-2235
Fax: 906-632-1222
www.sooeveningnews.com
• Cathy Kaiser, Classified Manager
enclass@sooeveningnews.com
• Rob Roos, Sports Editor
(906) 632-2235
sports@sooeveningnews.com
Frequency:
6 time(s) per week

EVENING SUN (NY)
29 LACKAWANNA AVENUE
NORWICH, NY 13815-1404
607-334-3276
800-836-6780
Fax: 607-334-8273
news@evesun.com
www.evesun.com
• Russell Foote, Advertising Manager
• Patrick Newell, Sports Editor
Frequency:
6 time(s) per week

EVENING SUN (PA)
135 BALTIMORE STREET
HANOVER, PA 17331-3111
717-637-3736
800-877-3786
Fax: 717-637-7730
news@eveningsun.com
www.eveningsun.com
• Chuck Curley, Sports Editor
(717) 637-3736
ccurley@eveningsun.com
• Travis Johnson, Sports Reporter
(717) 637-3736
Frequency:
7 time(s) per week

EVENING TELEGRAM
111 GREEN STREET
HERKIMER, NY 13350
315-866-2220
Fax: 315-866-5913
trends@herkimertelegram.com
www.herkimertelegram.com
• Gary Urich, Sports Editor
sports@herkimertelegram.com

Frequency:
6 time(s) per week

EVENING TIMES (NY)
347 SOUTH 2ND STREET
LITTLE FALLS, NY 13365-1411
315-823-3680
Fax: 315-823-4086
news@littlefallstimes.com
www.littlefallstimes.com
• Jon Rathbun, Sports Editor
(315) 823-3682
• Peggy Vespi, Advertising Manager
(315) 823-3680
• Beth Brewer, Publisher
(315) 866-2222
Frequency:
6 time(s) per week

EVENING TIMES (PA)
201 NORTH LEHIGH AVENUE
SAYRE, PA 18840-2220
570-888-9643
800-459-6397
Fax: 570-888-6463
news@morning-times.com
www.morningtimes.com
• Vickee Mike, Advertising Manager
• Dave Post, Sports Editor
dpost@morning-times.com
Frequency:
6 time(s) per week

EXAMINER
410 S. LIBERTY
INDEPENDENCE, MO 64050
816-254-8600
Fax: 816-254-0211
examiner.net
• Bill Althaus, Sports Writer
(816) 350-6333
bill.althaus@examiner.net
• Charlie Slenker, Assistant Sports Editor

EXAMINER-ENTERPRISE
4125 NOWATA ROAD
BARTLESVILLE, OK 74006-5120
918-335-8200
Fax: 918-335-3111
• Tom Bradley, Advertising Director
• Mike Tupa, Sports Editor
(918) 335-8239
mtupa@examiner-enterprise.com
Frequency:
6 time(s) per week

EXCELSIOR
523 N GRAND AVE
SANTA ANA, CA 92701
714-796-4300
Fax: 714-796-4319
www.ocexcelsior.com
• Francisco Valverde, Sports Editor
(714) 796-4300
Frequency:
1 time(s) per week

EXPONENT TELEGRAM
324 HEWES AVENUE
CLARKSBURG, WV 26302
304-626-1400
Fax: 304-624-4188
www.cpubco.com
• Danny Carpenter, Sports Editor
(304) 626-1444

• Sara Shingleton, Classified Manager
(304) 626-1415
Frequency:
7 time(s) per week

EXPRESS-TIMES
P.O. BOX 391
EASTON, PA 18042-3528
610-258-7171
800-360-3601
Fax: 610-258-1434
news@express-times.com
www.lehighvalleylive.com
• Edward Laubach, Sports Editor
(610) 258-7171
sports@express-times.com
• David Yanoshik, Advertising Vice
President
Frequency:
7 time(s) per week

FACTS
720 SOUTH MAIN STREET
CLUTE, TX 77531-5411
979-265-7411
800-864-8340
Fax: 979-265-9052
news@thefacts.com
www.thefacts.com
• Chris Greene, Sports Editor
(979) 265-7411
news@thefacts.com
Frequency:
7 time(s) per week

FAIRBANKS DAILY NEWS-MINER
P.O. BOX 70710
FAIRBANKS, AK 99701
907-456-6661
Fax: 907-452-7917
newsroom@newsminer.com
www.newsminer.com
• Bob Eley, Sports Editor
(907) 459-7581
beley@newsminer.com
• Paula Kothe, Advertising Director
(907) 459-7525
pkothe@newsminer.com
Frequency:
7 time(s) per week

FAIRBORN DAILY HERALD
30 SOUTH DETROIT STREET
XENIA, OH 45385
937-372-4444
Fax: 937-372-1951
wbaker@xeniagazette.com
www.xeniagazette.com
• Wayne Baker, Sports Editor
(937) 372-4444
wbaker@xeniagazette.com
• Tammy Tootle, Classified Manager
(937) 372-9609
Frequency:
6 time(s) per week

FAIRFAX JOURNAL
6408 ESALL
ALEXANDRIA, VA 22312
703-560-4000
Fax: 703-846-8366
www.jrnl.com
• Michelle Gates, Marketing/Promotions
Manager
• Kevin Dunleavy, Sports Editor

FARIBAULT DAILY NEWS
P.O. BOX 249
FARIBAULT, MN 55021
507-333-3131
Fax: 507-333-3102
www.faribault.com
• Corey Voegele, Sports Editor
(507) 333-3129
• Sean Lafavor, Sports Writer
(507) 333-3131
Frequency:
6 time(s) per week

FARMINGTON PRESS
218 NORTH WASHINGTON STREET
FARMINGTON, MO 63640-3169
573-756-8927
Fax: 573-756-9160
dsmith@pulitzer.net
www.dailypress.com
• Matt King, Sports Editor
(573) 431-2010
Frequency:
7 time(s) per week

FAYETTEVILLE OBSERVER
458 WHITFIELD STREET
FAYETTEVILLE, NC 28306-1698
910-486-3500
800-682-3476
Fax: 910-486-3545
sports@fayobserver.com
www.fayobserver.com
• Michael Arnholt, Executive Editor
(910) 486-3558
arnholtm@fayobserver.com
• Larry Graham, Sports Editor
(910) 486-3530
• Thomas Pope, Assistnat Sports Editor
(910) 486-3520
Frequency:
7 time(s) per week

FINE PRINT NEWS
806 FILLMORE AVENUE
BUFFALO, NY 14212-1356
716-855-3810
Fax: 716-855-3810
• Vincent Cook, Sports Editor
(716) 855-3810
Frequency:
1 time(s) per week

FINGER LAKES TIMES
218 GENESESE STREET
GENEVA, NY 14456-2323
315-789-3333
800-388-4346
Fax: 315-789-4077
www.fltimes.com
• Alan Brignall, Sports Editor
(315) 789-3333
abrignall@fltimes.com
• Diane Lahr-Smith, Advertising Manager
(315) 789-3333
fltimes@fltimes.com
Frequency:
6 time(s) per week

FLINT JOURNAL
200 EAST FIRST STREET
FLINT, MI 48502-1925
810-766-6200
Fax: 810-767-7518
www.mlive.com/flintjournal

• Tom Eason, Advertising Director
(810) 766-6381
• Dave Graham, Sports Writer
(810) 766-6306
• Rickey Hampton, Sports Columnist
(810) 766-6396
• Dean Howe, Sports Columnist
(810) 766-6392
• Len Hoyes, Sports Reporter
(810) 766-6184
• Bill Khan, Assistant Sports Editor
(810) 766-6184
• Dan Nilsen, Sports Reporter
(810) 766-6394
• Jody O'Hara, Sports Reporter
(810) 766-6184
• Tammy Reaves, Classified Manager
(810) 766-6155
• Brendan Savage, Sports Reporter
(810) 766-6388
• Mark Csapo, Sports Writer
(810) 766-6184
Frequency:
7 time(s) per week

FLORIDA TIMES-UNION
1 RIVERSIDE AVENUE
JACKSONVILLE, FL 32202
904-359-4111
800-472-6397
Fax: 904-359-4478
www.jacksonville.com
• Michael Dirocco, Sports Writer
(904) 705-3878
michael.dirocco@jacksonville.com
• Jeffrey Elliott, Sports Writer
(904) 359-4292
jeff.elliott@jacksonville.com
• Chet Fussman, Sports Editor
(904) 359-4574
chet.fussman@jacksonville.com
• Scott Kendrick, Assistant Sports Editor
(904) 359-4646
scott.kendrick@jacksonville.com
• Francine King, Sports Writer
(904) 359-4372
francine.king@jacksonville.com
• Bobby Smith, Sports Copy Editor
(904) 359-4246
robert.smith@jacksonville.com
• Garry Smits, Sports Reporter
(904) 359-4362
garry.smits@jacksonville.com
• Kevin Upright, Sports Copy Editor
(904) 359-4354
kevin.upright@jacksonville.com
Frequency:
7 time(s) per week

FLORIDA TODAY
P. O. BOX 419000
MELBOURNE, FL 32940
321-242-3500
800-633-8449
Fax: 321-242-6620
communities@floridatoday.com
www.floridatoday.com
• Michael Parsons, Sports Editor
(321) 242-3576
Frequency:
7 time(s) per week

**FORT BEND HERALD & TEAXS
COASTER**
1902 SOUTH 4TH STREET
ROSENBERG, TX 77471

281-342-4474
Fax: 281-342-3219
www.fbherald.com
• Lee Hartman, Advertising Manager
• Gary Martin, Sports Editor
(281) 342-4474
Frequency:
6 time(s) per week

FORT MORGAN TIMES
329 MAIN STREET
FORT MORGAN, CO 80701
970-867-5651
Fax: 970-867-7448
www.fmtimes.com
• Veronica Ivey, Sports Reporter
(970) 867-5651
• John LaPorte, Sports Editor
(970) 867-5651
Frequency:
6 time(s) per week

FORT SCOTT TRIBUNE
12 E WALL STREET
FORT SCOTT, KS 66701
620-223-1460
Fax: 620-223-1469
snuzum@fstribune.com
• Scott Nuzum, Sports Editor
(620) 223-1462
snuzum@fstribune.com
Frequency:
6 time(s) per week
Publications:
Fort Scott Tribune (Tu-F); Weekend
Herald-Tribune (Sat.)

FORT WORTH STAR-TELEGRAM
P.O. BOX 1870
FORT WORTH, TX 76101
817-390-7761
800-776-7827
Fax: 817-390-7789
newsroom@star-telegram.com
www.star-telegram.com
• Joe Garza, Sports Managing Editor
(817) 390-7241
• Wendell Barnhouse, Senior Reporter
(817) 390-7760
• Don Bowman, Sports Reporter
(817) 390-7760
• Ray Buck, Sports Columnist
(817) 390-7760
• Jimmy Burch, Staff Writer
(817) 390-7475
• Andy Clay, Sports Copy Editor
(817) 390-7374
• Mac Engel, Sports Reporter (Rangers)
(817) 390-7400
tengel@star-telegram.com
• Jennifer Floyd Engel, Sports Reporter
(817) 390-7760
• Bryan French, Sports Copy Editor
(817) 390-7191
• Andy Friedlander, Sports Reporter
(817) 390-7760
• Randy Galloway, Sports Columnist
 (817) 390-7760
• Arthur Garcia, Sports Writer (College)
(817) 390-7400
• Clarence Hill, Sports Reporter (High
School)
(817) 390-7760
• Brett Hoffman, Sports Reporter
(817) 390-7707
• Bob Hood, Sports Reporter (Outdoors)
(817) 390-7735

• David Humphrey, Sports Deputy Editor
(817) 390-7162
• Tom Johanningmeier, Sports Deputy
Editor
(817) 390-7383
tjohanningmeier@star-telegram.com
• Mike Jones, Sports Writer (College)
(817) 390-7760
thejonz@email.com
• Vince Langford, Sports Copy Editor
• Gil LeBreton, Sports Columnist
(817) 390-7760
• Mercedes Mayer, Sports Reporter
(817) 390-7760
• Carlos Mendez, Sports Reporter
(817) 548-5413
• Randall Perry, Sports Copy Editor
• Troy Phillips, Sports Writer
• Roger Pinckney, (817) 390-7760
Sports Copy Editor
• Charles Polansky, Sports Writer
(817) 390-7760
• Tim Price, Sports Reporter (Horse Racing)

(972) 237-4845
• Dwain Price, Sports Reporter
(817) 390-7760
• Jim Reeves, Sports Columnist
(817) 390-7760
• John Sturbin, Auto Racing Staff Writer
(817) 390-7408
Frequency:
7 time(s) per week

FORUM
101 5TH STREET NORTH
FARGO, ND 58102
701-235-7311
Fax: 701-241-5406
news@forumcomm.com
www.inforum.com
• James Boberg, Advertising Manager
(701) 241-5410
• Kevin Schnepf, Sports Editor
(701) 241-5549
kschnepf@forumcomm.com
• Tom Mix, Sports Writer
Frequency:
7 time(s) per week

FREDERICK NEWS-POST
351 BALLENGER CENTER DRIVE
FREDERICK, MD 21703
301-662-1177
800-486-1177
Fax: 301-662-8299
www.fredericknewspost.com
• Stan Goldberg, Sports Editor
(301) 662-1177
sgoldberg@fredericknewspost.com
Frequency:
7 time(s) per week

FREE LANCE
350 6TH STREET
HOLLISTER, CA 95023
831-637-5566
Fax: 831-637-4104
www.freelancenews.com
• Cindy Courter, Advertising Manager
(408) 842-1922
• Andrew Matheson, Sports Editor
(831) 637-5566
sports@freelancenews.com
Frequency:
5 time(s) per week

FREE LANCE-STAR
616 AMELIA STREET
FREDERICKSBURG, VA 22401
540-374-5000
800-877-0500
Fax: 540-373-8455
newsroom@freelancestar.com
www.fredericksburg.com/
• Steve DeShazo, Sports Editor
(540) 374-5433
sdeshazo@freelancestar.com
Frequency:
7 time(s) per week

FREE PRESS
418 SOUTH 2ND STREET
MANKATO, MN 56001-3727
507-625-4451
800-657-4662
Fax: 507-388-4355
editor@mankatofreepress.com
mankatofreepress.com
• Chad Courrier, Sports Reporter
(507) 344-6353
ccourrier@mankatofreepress.com
• Brian Ojanpa, Sports Reporter
(507) 344-6316
Frequency:
6 time(s) per week

FREEMAN
801 NORTH BARSTOW STREET
WAUKESHA, WI 53186
262-542-2501
Fax: 262-542-6082
thaffemann@conleynet.com
www.gmtoday.com
• Jim Baumgart, Advertising Director
(262) 513-2621
jbaumgart@conleynet.com
• Lee Fensin, Sports Editor
(262) 513-2667
Frequency:
6 time(s) per week

FREMONT TRIBUNE
P.O. BOX 9
FREMONT, NE 68025-5673
402-721-5000
800-927-7598
Fax: 402-721-8047
newsroom@fremonttribune.com
www.fremontneb.com
• Brent Wasenius, Managing Editor
(402) 721-5000
bwasenius@hotmail.com
• Brent Wasenius, Sports Editor
(402) 941-1430
brent.wasenius@lee.net
Frequency:
6 time(s) per week

FRESNO BEE
1626 E-STREET
FRESNO, CA 93706-2006
559-441-6111
800-877-7300
Fax: 559-441-6436
www.fresnobee.com
• Matt Lloyd, Sports Reporter
(559) 441-6340
mlloyd@fresnobee.com
• Jeff Davis, Sports Reporter
(559) 441-6401
• David Cooper, Assistant Sports Editor
(559) 441-6623

Frequency:
7 time(s) per week

FULTON SUN
115 EAST 5TH STREET
FULTON, MO 65251-1714
573-642-7272
Fax: 573-642-0656
news@fultonsun.com
www.fultonsun.com
• Ryan Boland, Sports Editor
• Rachel Reed, Display Advertising
Manager
display@fultonsun.com
Frequency:
5 time(s) per week

GADSDEN TIMES
P.O. BOX 188
GADSDEN, AL 35901-3737
800-762-2464
Fax: 256-549-2105
www.gadsdentimes.com
• Glenn Porter, Advertising Director
(256) 549-2000
• Kim Craft, Sports Editor
(256) 549-2051
• Nick Johnston, Sports Writer
(256) 549-2052
Frequency:
7 time(s) per week

GAINESVILLE DAILY REGISTER
306 EAST CALIFORNIA STREET
GAINESVILLE, TX 76240
940-665-5511
Fax: 940-665-0920
www.gainesvilleregister.com
• Darin Allred, Sports Editor
(940) 665-5511
Frequency:
6 time(s) per week

GAINESVILLE SUN
P.O. BOX 147147
GAINESVILLE, FL 32608
352-374-5000
800-443-4245
Fax: 352-338-3128
sun@atlantic.net
www.gainesvillesun.com
• Arnold Feliciano, Sports Editor
(352) 374-5055
Frequency:
7 time(s) per week

GALION INQUIRER
378 NORTH MARKET STREET
GALION, OH 44833-1924
419-468-1117
Fax: 419-468-7255
www.galioninquirer.com
• Jon Kleinknecht, Sports Editor
Frequency:
6 time(s) per week

GALLUP INDEPENDENT
500 NORTH 9TH STREET
GALLUP, NM 87301-5379
505-863-6811
800-545-3817
Fax: 505-722-5750
www.gallupindependent.com
• Alan Arthur, Sports Editor
(505) 863-6811

• Mike Peretti, Sports Writer
(505) 863-6811
Frequency:
6 time(s) per week

GALVESTON COUNTY DAILY NEWS
8522 TEICHMAN ROAD
GALVESTON, TX 77554-9119
409-683-5200
800-561-3611
Fax: 409-744-7679
news@galvnews.com
www.galvnews.com
• Leonard Woolsey, Publisher
(409) 683-5207
leonard.woolsey@galvnews.com
• Michael Smith, Editor
(409) 683-5206
michael.smith@galvnews.com
Frequency:
7 time(s) per week

GARDEN ISLAND
P.O. BOX 231
LIHUE, HI 96766
808-245-3681
800-296-2880
Fax: 808-245-5286
www.thegardenisland.com
• David Simon, Sports Writer
(808) 245-3681
dsimon@thegardenisland.com
• Casey Quel, Advertising Director
Frequency:
7 time(s) per week

GARDNER NEWS
309 CENTRAL STREET
GARDNER, MA 01440
978-632-8000
Fax: 978-630-2231
www.thegardnernews.com
• Tom Trainque, Sports Editor
(978) 632-8000
sports@thegardnernews.com
• John Ballou, Sports Writer
(978) 632-8000
jballou@thegardnernews.com
Frequency:
6 time(s) per week

GASTON GAZETTE
1893 REMOUNT ROAD
GASTONIA, NC 28054
704-864-3291
Fax: 704-884-3031
www.gastongazette.com/
• Gabe Whisnant, Sports Editor
(704) 869-1841
gwhisnant@gastongazette.com
• Jamey Jenkins, Advertising Manager
(704) 869-1741
Frequency:
7 time(s) per week

GAZETTE
500 3RD AVE, SE
CEDAR RAPIDS, IA 52401
319-398-8211
800-397-8211
Fax: 319-398-5861
www.thegazette.com
• Steve Gravelle, Sports Editor
(319) 398-5819

GAZETTE COLORADO SPRINGS
30 S. PROSPECT STREET
COLORADO SPRINGS, CO 80903
719-636-0250
Fax: 719-636-0163
www.gazette.com
• Jim O'Connell, Sports Editor
(719) 636-0263
jim.oconnell@gazette.com
• Nathan Van Dyne, Deputy Sports Editor
(719) 636-0195
nathan.vandyne@gazette.com
Frequency:
7 time(s) per week

GETTYSBURG TIMES
1570 FAIRFIELD ROAD
GETTYSBURG, PA 17325
717-334-1131
Fax: 717-334-4243
info@gburgtimes.com
www.gettysburgtimes.com
• Josh Martin, Sports Editor
(717) 334-1131
sports@gburgtimes.com
Frequency:
6 time(s) per week

GLEANER
P.O. BOX 4
HENDERSON, KY 42419
270-827-2000
Fax: 270-827-2765
news@thegleaner.com
www.thegleaner.com
• Tim Ethridge, Sports Editor
(812) 464-7416
tethridge@thegleaner.com
Frequency:
6 time(s) per week

GLENDALE NEWS-PRESS
221 N BRAND BLVD
GLENDALE, CA 91203
818-637-3247
Fax: 818-241-1975
gnp@latimes.com
www.glendalenewspress.com
• Grant Gordon, Sports Editor
(818) 637-3225
grant.gordon@latimes.com
• Charles Rich, Sports Reporter
(818) 637-3225
charles.rich@latimes.com
Frequency:
6 time(s) per week

GLENWOOD SPRINGS POST INDEPENDENT
2014 GRAND AVENUE
GLENWOOD SPRINGS, CO 81601-4162
970-945-8515
Fax: 970-945-4487
news@postindependent.com
www.postindependent.com
• Jeff Caspersen, Sports Editor
(970) 384-9123
• Gunilla Asher, Advertising Manager
(970) 949-9170
Frequency:
6 time(s) per week

GLOBE-GAZETTE
300 NORTH WASHINGTON AVENUE
MASON CITY, IA 50401

641-421-0500
800-421-0546
Fax: 641-421-0516
news@globegazette.com
www.globegazette.com
• Jared Patterson, Sports Editor
Frequency:
7 time(s) per week

GLOUCESTER COUNTY TIMES
309 SOUTH BROAD STREET
WOODBURY, NJ 08096
856-845-3300
Fax: 856-845-5480
www.nj.com/gloucester/
• Shawn Leary, Sports Editor
(856) 686-3633
• Marie Vito, Classified Manager
(856) 686-3637
• Kevin Minnick, Sports Reporter
(856) 845-7484
Frequency:
6 time(s) per week

GRAND FORKS HERALD
P.O. BOX 6008
GRAND FORKS, ND 58206
701-780-1100
800-477-6572
Fax: 701-795-4604
www.gfherald.com
• Zack Ahrens, Advertising Manager
• Wayne Nelson, Sports Editor
wnelson@gfherald.com
• Jeff New, Assistant Sports Editor
Frequency:
7 time(s) per week

GRAND HAVEN TRIBUNE
101 N 3RD ST
GRAND HAVEN, MI 49417-1209
616-842-6400
800-874-7180
Fax: 616-842-9584
bvargo@grandhaventribune.com
www.grandhaventribune.com
• Matt DeYoung, Sports Editor
(616) 842-6400
mdeyoung@grandhaventribune.com
• Matt Tjapkes, Sports Writer
(616) 842-6400
• Mike Kohon, Sports Writer
(616) 842-6400
Frequency:
6 time(s) per week

GRAND RAPIDS PRESS
155 MICHIGAN STREET, N.W.
GRAND RAPIDS, MI 49503-2353
616-222-5400
800-878-1411
Fax: 616-222-5269
www.mlive.com/grpress/
• Robert Becker, Sports Editor
(616) 222-5674
• Dave Mayo, Sports Writer
(616) 222-5670
Frequency:
7 time(s) per week

GRANTS PASS DAILY COURIER
409 S.E. 7TH STREET
GRANTS PASS, OR 97526-3003
541-474-3700
800-228-0457
Fax: 541-474-3824

news@thedailycourier.com
www.thedailycourier.com/
• Lance Ogden, Sports Editor
(541) 474-3729
• Zack Urness, Sports Reporter
(541) 474-3825
Frequency:
6 time(s) per week

GREAT FALLS TRIBUNE
P.O. BOX 5468
GREAT FALLS, MT 59405-1854
406-791-1444
800-438-6600
Fax: 406-791-1431
tribcity@greatfallstribune.com
www.greatfallstribune.com
• George Geise, Sports Editor
(406) 791-1470
ggeise@greatfal.gannett.com
Frequency:
7 time(s) per week

GREELEY TRIBUNE
501 8TH AVENUE
GREELEY, CO 80631-3913
800-275-0321
800-275-0321
Fax: 970-356-5780
www.greeleytribune.com
• Mike Distelhorst, Advertising Director
(970) 392-4406
• Scott Rosenberg, Sports Editor
(970) 392-4441
Frequency:
7 time(s) per week

GREEN BAY PRESS-GAZETTE
435 EAST WALNUT STREET
GREEN BAY, WI 54301-5001
920-431-8400
800-444-0007
Fax: 920-431-8379
businessnews@greenbaypressgazette.com
www.greenbaypressgazette.com
• Mike Vandermause, Sports Editor
(920) 431-8413
mvandermause@greenbaypressgazette.com
• Jeff Ash, Assistant Sports Editor
(920) 431-8336
jash@greenbaypressgazette.com
Frequency:
7 time(s) per week

GREENEVILLE SUN
P.O. BOX 1630
GREENEVILLE, TN 37743-4923
423-638-4181
Fax: 423-638-3645
info@greenevillesun.com
www.greenevillesun.com
• Wayne Phillips, Sports Editor
(423) 359-3137
• Artie Wehenkel, Advertising Director
(423) 359-3160
artie.wehenkel@greenevillesun.com
• Joe Byrd, Assistant Sports Editor
(423) 359-3140
Frequency:
6 time(s) per week

GREENSBORO NEWS & RECORD
200 EAST MARKET STREET
GREENSBORO, NC 27401

336-373-7000
800-553-6880
Fax: 336-373-7067
www.news-record.com
• Jeff Carlton, Sports Reporter
• Rob Daniels, Sports Reporter
• Ed Hardin, Sports Columnist
• Charles Hardin, Sports Writer
• Bill Hass, Sports Writer
• Dustin Long, Sports Writer
(704) 987-0624
• John Newsom, Sports Assistant Editor
(336) 373-7312
jnewsom@news-record.com
• Joe Sirera, Sports Editor
jsirera@news-record.com
Frequency:
7 time(s) per week

GREENSBURG DAILY NEWS
135 SOUTH FRANKLIN STREET
GREENSBURG, IN 47240-2023
812-663-3111
Fax: 812-663-2985
www.greenburgdailynews.com
• Nick Gonnella, Sports Editor
(812) 663-3111
• Laura Welborn, Advertising Manager
(812) 663-3111
Frequency:
6 time(s) per week

GREENVILLE HERALD BANNER
2305 KING STREET
GREENVILLE, TX 75401-3257
903-455-4220
Fax: 903-455-6281
www.heraldbanner.com/
• David Claybourn, Sports Editor
(903) 455-4220
• Latarah Edmond, Advertising Manager
(903) 455-4220
Frequency:
7 time(s) per week

GREENVILLE NEWS
P.O. BOX 1688
GREENVILLE, SC 29601
864-298-4100
800-736-7136
Fax: 864-298-4395
www.greenvillenews.com
• Bart Wright, Sports Editor
(864) 298-4239
rbwright@greenvillenews.com
• Jim Rice, Sports News Editor
(864) 298-4268
jdrice@greenvillenews.com
• Willie Smith, III, Sports Reporter
(864) 298-4038
wtsmith@greenvillenews.com
Frequency:
7 time(s) per week
Number of Members:
13 full time
Teams:
Clemson University, Furman University,
Carolina Panthers, Atlanta Falcons, Univ. of
South Carolina, Greenville Drive (MILB),
Greenville Road Warriors (ECHL)
Publications:
The Greenville News, Greenvilleonline.com,
TigersNow.com, The Tribune-Times,
Greater GreenNews and Pickens County
News.

GREENWICH POST
10 CORBIN DRIVE, FLOOR 3
DARIEN, CT 06820
203-861-9191
Fax: 203-861-0023
www.greenwich-post.com
• Paul Silverfarb, Sports Editor
(203) 861-9191
Frequency:
1 time(s) per week

GREENWICH TIME
1455 EAST PUTNAM AVENUE
GREENWICH, CT 06870
203-625-4400
Fax: 203-964-2345
letters.greenwichtime@scni.com
www.greenwichtime.com
• Chris McNamee, Sports Editor
(203) 330-6324
chris.mcnamee@scni.com
Frequency:
7 time(s) per week

GREENWOOD COMMONWEALTH
PO BOX 8050
GREENWOOD, MS 38935
662-453-5312
Fax: 662-453-2908
commonwealth@gwcommonwealth.com
www.gwcommonwealth.com
• Larry Alderman, Advertising Manager
(662) 453-5312
lalderman@gwcommonwealth.com
• Bill Burrus, Sports Editor
(662) 453-5312
bburrus@gwcommonwealth.com
Frequency:
6 time(s) per week

GRIFFIN DAILY NEWS
323 EAST SOLOMON
GRIFFIN, GA 30224
770-227-3276
Fax: 770-412-1678
www.griffindailynews.com
• John Sullivan, Sports Editor
jsullivan@griffindailynews.com
Frequency:
7 time(s) per week

GWINNETT DAILY POST
P.O. BOX 603
LAWRENCEVILLE, GA 30046
770-963-9205
Fax: 770-339-8081
news@gwinnettdailypost.com
www.gwinnettdailypost.com/
• Will Hammock, Sports Editor
(770) 963-9205
will.hammock@gwinnettdailypost.com
• Ben Beitzel, Sports Reporter
(770) 963-9205
Frequency:
6 time(s) per week

HANFORD SENTINEL
300 WEST 6TH STREET
HANFORD, CA 93230-4518
559-582-0471
Fax: 559-582-8631
www.hanfordsentinel.com
• Rich De Give, Sports Editor
(559) 583-2430
Frequency:
7 time(s) per week

HARRISON DAILY TIMES
PO BOX 40
HARRISON, AR 72602
870-741-2325
Fax: 870-741-5632
www.harrisondailytimes.com
• Jason Overman, Advertising Manager
• Jeff Brasel, Sports Editor
(870) 741-2325
jeffb@harrisondaily.com
Frequency:
6 time(s) per week

HARTFORD COURANT
285 BROAD STREET
HARTFORD, CT 06115-2510
860-241-6200
800-524-4242
Fax: 860-241-3865
letters@courant.com
www.ctnow.com
• Dom Amore, Sports Reporter (Baseball)
(860) 241-3988
damore@courant.com
• Woody Anderson, Sports Reporter
(College)
(860) 241-6441
• William Armstrong, Sports Assistant Editor
(860) 241-3145
• Bruce Berlet, Sports Writer (Golf)
(860) 241-3732
• Desmond Conner, Sports
Reporter/Columnist
(860) 241-3871
• Shawn Courchesne, Sports Reporter
(860) 241-6200
• Paul Doyle, Sports Reporter (Baseball)
(860) 241-6699
• Jeff Goldberg, Sports Columnist/Reporter
(860) 241-6435
• David Heuschkel, Sports Reporter
(Baseball)
(860) 241-6707
• Jeff Jacobs, Sports Columnist
(860) 241-3983
• Jack O'Connell, Sports Reporter
(Baseball)
(860) 241-6435
• Jeffrey Otterbein, Sports Editor
(860) 241-6434
• Terry Price, Sports Reporter (Boxing)
(860) 241-6437
• Paul Rosano, Assistant Sports Editor
(860) 241-3978
• Jeff Smith, Sports Deputy Editor
(860) 241-3820
jsmith@courant.com
• Tom Yantz, Sports Reporter (College)
(860) 241-3985
Frequency:
7 time(s) per week

HASTINGS TRIBUNE
908 WEST 2ND STREET
HASTINGS, NE 68902
402-462-2131
800-742-6397
Fax: 402-461-4657
tribune@hastingstribune.com
www.hastingstribune.com
• Vince Kuppig, Sports Editor
(402) 461-1270
• Kathy Avis, Advertising Manager
(402) 461-1234
Frequency:
6 time(s) per week

HATTIESBURG AMERICAN
PO BOX 1111
HATTIESBURG, MS 39401
601-582-4321
800-844-2637
Fax: 601-584-3130
www.hattiesburgamerican.com
• Alan Hinton, Sports Editor
(601) 584-3136
Frequency:
7 time(s) per week

HAWAII TRIBUNE-HERALD
PO BOX 767
HILO, HI 96721
808-935-6621
Fax: 808-969-9100
www.hawaiitribune-herald.com
• Bill O'Rear, Sports Editor
(808) 935-6621
• Alice Sledge, Advertising Director
asledge@hawaiitribune-herald.com
Frequency:
6 time(s) per week

HAWK EYE
800 SOUTH MAIN STREET
BURLINGTON, IA 52601-5850
319-754-8461
Fax: 319-754-6824
news@thehawkeye.com
www.thehawkeye.com
• Susan Denk, Sports Reporter
(319) 758-8146
• Matt Levins, Sports Reporter
(319) 758-8147
mlevins@thehawkeye.com
• Laurie Trautner, Classified Manager
(319) 758-8128
• John Bohnenkamp, Sports Editor
(319) 758-8133
jbohnenkamp@thehawkeye.com
Frequency:
7 time(s) per week

HAYS DAILY NEWS
507 MAIN STREET
HAYS, KS 67601-4228
785-628-1081
800-657-6017
Fax: 785-628-8186
newsroom@dailynews.net
www.hdnews.net
• Nick McQueen, Sports Editor
nmcqueen@dailynews.net
Frequency:
6 time(s) per week

HELENA INDEPENDENT RECORD
317 CRUSE AVE
HELENA, MT 59601
406-447-4000
Fax: 406-447-4052
irads@helenair.com
www.helenair.com
• Jeff Windmueller, Sports Editor
(406) 447-4065
• Randy Rickman, Publisher
(406) 447-4002

HENDERSON DAILY DISPATCH
304 SOUTH CHESTNUT STREET
HENDERSON, NC 27536-4225
252-436-2700
800-326-3894
Fax: 252-430-0125

news@hendersondispatch.com
www.hendersondispatch.com
• Eric Robinson, Sports Editor
(252) 436-2840
• Deborah Tuck, Advertising Manager
(252) 436-2821
Frequency:
6 time(s) per week

HENDERSON DAILY NEWS
PO BOX 30
HENDERSON, TX 75653
903-657-2501
Fax: 903-657-0056
www.hendersondailynews.com
• J.D. Issac, Sports Editor
(903) 657-2501
Frequency:
6 time(s) per week

HERALD & REVIEW
601 EAST WILLIAM STREET
DECATUR, IL 62523-1142
217-429-5151
800-437-2533
Fax: 217-421-7965
www.herald-review.com
• Mike Albright, Sports Editor
(217) 421-7909
mike.albright@lee.net
• Mark Tupper, Executive Sports Editor
(217) 421-7983
mark.tupper@lee.net
Frequency:
7 time(s) per week

HERALD (CT)
ONE HERALD SQUARE
NEW BRITAIN, CT 06050
860-225-4601
800-327-3237
Fax: 860-223-8171
www.newbritainherald.com.
• Matt Straub, Sports Editor
(860) 225-4601
• Brad Carroll, Executive Sports Editor
(860) 225-4601
bcarroll@newbritainherald.com

HERALD (WA)
1213 CALIFORNIA AVENUE
EVERETT, WA 98201
425-339-3000
Fax: 425-339-3049
sports@heraldnet.com
www.heraldnet.com
• Kirby Arnold, Sports Reporter
(425) 339-3478
• Kevin Brown, Sports Editor
(425) 339-3474
• Aaron Coe, Sports Reporter
(425) 339-3471
• Steve Hawes, Advertising Manager
(425) 339-3051
• Sally Kortekaas, Classified Manager
(425) 339-3070
• Bob Mortenson, Sports Reporter
(425) 339-3489
• Rich Myhre, Sports Reporter
(425) 339-3478
• John Sleeper, Sports Reporter
(425) 339-3478
Frequency:
7 time(s) per week

HERALD AND NEWS
2703 FOOTHILLS BOULEVARD
KLAMATH FALLS, OR 97603
541-885-4411
800-275-0982
Fax: 541-885-4456
sports@heraldandnews.com
www.heraldandnews.com
• Steve Matthies, Sports Editor
(541) 885-4411
Frequency:
6 time(s) per week

HERALD DEMOCRAT
P.O. BOX 1128
SHERMAN, TX 75090-7258
903-893-8181
Fax: 903-868-2106
news@heralddemocrat.com
www.heralddemocrat.com
• Todd Hutchinson, Sports Editor
sports@heralddemocrat.com
• Jason Dellarosa, Sports Writer
(903) 893-8181
Frequency:
6 time(s) per week

HERALD JOURNAL
75 WEST 300 NORTH
LOGAN, UT 84321
435-752-2121
800-275-0423
Fax: 435-753-6642
www.hjnews.com
• Shawn Harrison, Sports Editor
(435) 752-2121
sharrison@hjnews.com
• Rick G. Wallace, Advertising Director
(435) 792-7275
Frequency:
7 time(s) per week

HERALD NEWS
1 GARRET MOUNTAIN PLAZA
WEST PATERSON, NJ 07424
973-569-7000
Fax: 973-569-7129
hncitydesk@northjersey.com
• Ives Galarcep, Sports Reporter
(973) 586-8180
galarcep@northjersey.com
• Kerry Rubin, Classified Manager
Frequency:
7 time(s) per week

HERALD TIMES-REPORTER
902 FRANKLIN STREET
MANITOWOC, WI 54221-4514
920-684-4433
800-783-7323
Fax: 920-684-4416
htrnews@htrnews.com
www.htrnews.com
• Pete Barth, Sports Editor
(920) 453-5156
pbarth@sheboyganpress.com
• James Maurer, Advertising Manager
(920) 686-2124
jmaurer2@htrnews.com
Frequency:
7 time(s) per week

HERALD-BULLETIN
1133 JACKSON STREET
ANDERSON, IN 46015

765-622-1212
800-750-5049
Fax: 765-640-4815
newsroom@heraldbulletin.com
www.theheraldbulletin.com
• Rick Teverbaugh, Sports Writer
(765) 622-1212
Frequency:
7 time(s) per week

HERALD-CITIZEN
P.O. BOX 2729
COOKEVILLE, TN 38502
931-526-9715
Fax: 931-526-1209
editor@herald-citizen.com
www.herald-citizen.com
• Buddy Pearson, Sports Editor
(931) 526-9715
sports@herald-citizen.com
• Albert Thompson, Advertising Manager
(931) 526-9715
ads@herald-citizen.com
• Thomas Corhern, Sports Writer
(931) 526-9715
sports@herald-citizen.com
Frequency:
6 time(s) per week

HERALD-DISPATCH
P.O. BOX 2017
HUNTINGTON, WV 25701
304-526-4000
800-955-6110
Fax: 304-526-2857
news@heralddispatch.com
www.hdonline.com
• Rick McCann, Sports Editor
(304) 526-2759
• Amy Howat, Advertising Director
(304) 526-2820

HERALD-JOURNAL
PO BOX 1657
SPARTANBURG, SC 29304
864-582-4511
800-922-4158
Fax: 864-594-6350
online@shj.com
www.goupstate.com
• Robert Dalton, Sports Editor
(864) 562-7293
bob.dalton@shj.com
• Mark Egan, Sports Copy Editor
(864) 562-7244

HERALD-NEWS
300 CATERPILLAR DRIVE
JOLIET, IL 60436
815-729-6031
800-397-9397
Fax: 815-729-6059
www.suburbanchicagonews.com
• Dick Goss, Sports Editor
(815) 729-6040
• Ron Kremer, Sports Writer
(815) 729-6040
• Bill Scheibe, Sports Writer
(815) 729-6040
• Steve Vanisko, Advertising Manager
(815) 729-6120
Frequency:
7 time(s) per week

HERALD-PALLADIUM
3450 HOLLYWOOD ROAD
SAINT JOSEPH, MI 49085-9581
269-429-2400
800-356-4262
Fax: 269-429-4398
www.heraldpalladium.com
• Jason Mitchell, Sports Editor
(269) 429-1294
jmitchell@heraldpalladium.com
Frequency:
7 time(s) per week

HERALD-STANDARD
8-18 CHURCH STREET
UNIONTOWN, PA 15401-3563
724-439-7565
800-342-8254
Fax: 724-439-7559
www.heraldstandard.com
• Rob Burchianti, Assistant Sports Editor
(724) 439-7565
• Mike Ciarochi, Sports Editor
(724) 439-7576
mciarochi@heraldstandard.com
• Maureen Zorichak, Advertising Manager
mzorichak@heraldstandard.com
Frequency:
6 time(s) per week

HERALD-STAR
401 HERALD SQUARE
STEUBENVILLE, OH 43952-2059
740-283-4711
800-526-7987
Fax: 740-284-7355
www.hsconnect.com
• Judy Gelestor, Advertising Manager
• Mike Mathison, Sports Editor
(740) 283-4711
mmathison@heraldstaronline.com
Frequency:
7 time(s) per week

HERALD-SUN
2828 PICKETT ROAD
DURHAM, NC 27705-5613
919-419-6500
800-672-0061
Fax: 919-419-6889
www.heraldsun.com
• Jimmy Dupree, Sports Editor
(919) 419-6674
• Brian Gorman, Sports Reporter
(919) 419-6664
• Bryan Strickland, Sports Reporter
(919) 419-6671
Frequency:
7 time(s) per week

HERALD-TIMES
P.O. BOX 909
BLOOMINGTON, IN 47401-7720
812-332-4401
800-422-0070
Fax: 812-331-4285
www.heraldtimesonline.com
• Pat Beane, Sports Editor
(812) 331-4340
pbeane@heraldt.com
Frequency:
7 time(s) per week

HERNANDO TODAY
15299 CORTEZ BLVD
BROOKSVILLE, FL 34613-6005

352-544-5280
Fax: 352-544-5246
jcason@hernandotoday.com
www.hernandotoday.com
• Antonio Castro, Sports Editor
(352) 544-5278
acastro@hernandotoday.com
Frequency:
7 time(s) per week

HIBBING DAILY TRIBUNE
2142 1ST AVENUE
HIBBING, MN 55746-1805
218-262-1011
Fax: 218-262-4318
www.hibbingmn.com
• Gary Giombetti, Sports Editor
(218) 262-1011
ggiombetti@hibbingdailytribune.net
• Brian Palokangas, Advertising Director
Frequency:
7 time(s) per week

HICKORY DAILY RECORD
1100 PARK PLACE 11TH BOULEVARD
S.E.
HICKORY, NC 28603
828-322-4510
800-849-8586
Fax: 828-328-9378
www.hickoryrecord.com
• Peter Cook, Advertising Director
• Chris Hobbs, Sports Editor
(828) 322-4510
Frequency:
7 time(s) per week

HIGH POINT ENTERPRISE
210 CHURCH AVENUE
HIGH POINT, NC 27262-4806
336-888-3500
800-933-5760
Fax: 336-841-5582
www.hpe.com
• Lynn Wagner, Advertising Director
(336) 888-3545
• Benny Phillips, Sports Editor
(336) 888-3520
• Tom Berry, Sports Columnist
(336) 888-3500
Frequency:
7 time(s) per week

HIGHLANDS TODAY
231 US 27 NORTH
SEBRING, FL 33870
863-382-4947
Fax: 863-382-2509
www.highlandstoday.com
• Mark Pinson, Sports Editor
(863) 382-4947
Frequency:
7 time(s) per week

HIGHLINE TIMES
133 SOUTHWEST 153RD STREET
BURIEN, WA 98166-2311
206-444-4873
Fax: 206-444-4877
hteditor@robinsonnews.com
www.robinsonnews.com
• Tim Clinton, Sports Editor
(253) 838-7622
Frequency:
1 time(s) per week

HOBBS DAILY NEWS-SUN
201 NORTH THORP
HOBBS, NM 88240-6058
575-393-2123
800-993-2123
Fax: 575-393-5724
www.hobbsnews.com
• Jason Watkins, Sports Editor
(505) 391-5430
Frequency:
6 time(s) per week

HOLDREGE DAILY CITIZEN
PO BOX 344
HOLDREGE, NE 68949-2219
308-995-4441
Fax: 308-995-5992
holdredgecitizen@aol.com
• Richard Headley, Sports Editor
• Barbara Penrod, Advertising Manager
• Jack Donoghue, Sports Editor
(308) 995-4441
Frequency:
5 time(s) per week

HOLLAND SENTINEL
54 WEST 8TH STREET
HOLLAND, MI 49423-3104
616-392-2311
800-968-3497
Fax: 616-392-3526
newsroom@hollandsentinel.com
www.hollandsentinel.com
• Alan Babbitt, Sports Editor
(616) 546-4271
alan.babbitt@hollandsentinel.com
• Janet Johnson, Advertising Manager
(616) 546-4227
Frequency:
7 time(s) per week

HOME NEWS TRIBUNE
35 KENNEDY BOULEVARD
EAST BRUNSWICK, NJ 08816
732-246-5500
800-627-4663
Fax: 732-565-7208
metro@thnt.com
www.thnt.com
• Brenda Cumomo, Advertising Manager
(732) 565-7420
apads@adtransit.injersey.com
• Jack Genung, Sports Editor
(732) 565-7231
jgenung@thnt.com
• Keith Sargeant, Sports Writer
(732) 246-5500
• Paul Franklin, Sports Writer
(732) 246-5500
Frequency:
7 time(s) per week

HONOLULU ADVERTISER
500 ALA MOANA BOULEVARD
#7-500
HONOLULU, HI 96813-4920
808-529-4700
877-233-1133
Fax: 808-529-4898
citydesk@staradvertiser.com
www.staradvertiser.com
• Stacy Kaneshiro, Sports Reporter
(808) 525-8042
• Ferd Lewis, Sports Reporter
(808) 525-8044
• Paul Arnett, Sports Editor
(808) 529-4786

• Wes Nakama, High School Sports Reporter
(808) 535-2456
• Kyle Sakamoto, High School Sports
(808) 525-8041
• Stephen Tsai, Sports Reporter
(808) 525-8051
Frequency:
7 time(s) per week

HOPE STAR
522 W THIRD STREET
HOPE, AR 71802
870-777-8841
Fax: 870-777-3311
www.hopestar.com
• Richard Haycox, Advertising Manager
(870) 777-8841
• Garren Smith, Sports Editor
(870) 777-8841
Frequency:
5 time(s) per week

HOUR
1 SELLECK STREET
NORWALK, CT 06855
203-846-3281
Fax: 203-840-1802
features@thehour.com
www.thehour.com
• Matthew Doran, Sports Editor
(203) 354-1058
• Steve Geoghegan, Sports Writer
(203) 354-1119
Frequency:
7 time(s) per week

HOUSTON CHRONICLE
P.O. BOX 4260
HOUSTON, TX 77210
713-362-7171
800-735-3820
Fax: 713-362-6677
news@chron.com
www.chron.com
• David Barron, Sports Reporter
(713) 362-6922
david.barron@chron.com
• Charlie Crixell, Assistant Sports Editor
(713) 362-7171
• Fred M. Faour, Sports Editor
(713) 362-6931
• Terrance Harris, Sports Writer
(713) 362-2167
• Neil Hohlfeld, Sports Writer
• Richard Justice, Sports Columnist
(713) 362-7171
• John Lopez, Columnist
(713) 362-6968
• Brian McTaggart, Sports Columnist
(713) 362-2950
• Jesus Ortiz, Sports Reporter
(713) 362-7891
jesus.ortiz@chron.com
• Doug Pike, Sports Writer
(713) 362-6095
• Dale Robertson, Sports Columnist
(713) 362-7891
dale.robertson@chron.com
• Jeff Rosen, Sports Sunday Editor
(713) 362-4293
• William H. Stickney, Sports Reporter
(713) 362-7891
• Carlton Thompson, Sports Editor
(713) 362-6926
• Shannon R. Tompkins, Sports Columnist
shannon.tompkins@chron.com

Frequency:
7 time(s) per week

HOUSTON DEFENDER
12401 SOUTH POST OAK #233
HOUSTON, TX 77288
713-663-6996
Fax: 713-663-7116
www.defendernetwork.com
• Darrel Ardison, Sports Editor
(713) 663-6996
Frequency:
1 time(s) per week

HOY-NEW YORK
330 WEST 34TH STREET
NEW YORK, NY 10001
917-339-0800
Fax: 212-971-4412
www.holahoy.com
• Juan Aya, Sports Reporter
(917) 339-0800
• Sadiel Lebron, Sports Reporter
(917) 339-0800
Frequency:
6 time(s) per week

HUGO DAILY NEWS
128 EAST JACKSON STREET
HUGO, OK 74743-4035
580-326-3311
800-900-3311
Fax: 580-326-6397
www.hugonews.com
• Maddie Kuhn, Sports Reporter
(580) 326-3311
hdnsports@sbcglobal.net
Frequency:
5 time(s) per week

HUNTINGTON HERALD-PRESS
7 NORTH JEFFERSON STREET
HUNTINGTON, IN 46750-2839
260-356-6700
Fax: 260-356-9026
hpnews@h-ponline.com
www.h-ponline.com
• Marty Alexander, Advertising Manager
(260) 356-6700
• Brenda Ross, Classified Manager
• Paul Siegfried, Sports Editor
(260) 356-6700
Frequency:
6 time(s) per week

HUNTSVILLE ITEM
1409 10TH STREET
HUNTSVILLE, TX 77320
936-295-5407
Fax: 936-435-0135
www.itemonline.com
• Tom Waddilld, Sports Editor
(936) 295-5407
• Cody Smith, Assistant Sports Editor
(936) 295-5407
• Gene Schullenberg, Sports Writer
(936) 295-5407
Frequency:
7 time(s) per week

HUNTSVILLE TIMES
P.O. BOX 1487
HUNTSVILLE, AL 35801
256-532-4000
800-239-5271

Fax: 256-532-4420
www.htimes.com
• Billy Bryant, Sports Executive Editor
(256) 532-4407
• Mark McCarter, Sports Columnist
(256) 532-4234
• Steve Wilson, Retail Advertising Manager
(256) 532-4269
Frequency:
7 time(s) per week

HURON DAILY TRIBUNE
211 NORTH HEISTERMAN STREET
BAD AXE, MI 48413
989-269-6461
800-322-1184
Fax: 989-269-9435
www.michigansthumb.com
• Mike Bogan, Sports Editor
(989) 269-6461
• Vicki Yaroch, Advertising Manager
vyaroch@hearstnp.com
Frequency:
6 time(s) per week

HUTCHINSON NEWS
300 WEST 2ND STREET
HUTCHINSON, KS 67501-5211
620-694-5700
800-766-3311
Fax: 620-662-4186
jgreen@hutchnews.com
www.hutchnews.com
• Pat Sangimino, Sports Editor
(620) 694-5742
Frequency:
7 time(s) per week

IDAHO PRESS-TRIBUNE
P.O. BOX 9399
NAMPA, ID 83652
208-467-9251
Fax: 208-467-9562
newsroom@idahopress.com
www.idahopress.com
• Matt Davidson, Advertising Manager
• Colin Howser, Sports Editor
(208) 465-8111
sports@idahopress.com
Frequency:
7 time(s) per week

IDAHO STATE JOURNAL
305 SOUTH ARTHUR AVENUE
POCATELLO, ID 83204-1510
208-232-4161
800-275-0774
Fax: 208-233-8007
newsclerk@journalnet.com
www.journalnet.com/
• Brady Slater, Sports Editor
(208) 232-4161
Frequency:
7 time(s) per week

IDAHO STATESMAN
P.O. BOX 40
BOISE, ID 83706-1239
208-377-6400
800-635-8934
Fax: 208-377-6449
newsroom@idahostatesman.com
www.idahostatesman.com
• Chadd Cripe, Sports Reporter
(208) 377-6398
ccripe@idahostatesman.com

• Johnna Espinoza, Sports Reporter
(208) 377-6430
• Nick Jezierny, Sports Reporter
(208) 377-6420
• Mike Prater, Sports Editor
(208) 377-6421
Frequency:
7 time(s) per week

IMPERIAL VALLEY PRESS
205 8TH STREET, N.
EL CENTRO, CA 92243-2902
760-337-3400
Fax: 760-353-3003
www.ivpressonline.com
• Mario Renteria, Sports Editor
(760) 337-3434
• John Yanni, Advertising Manager
(760) 337-3430
advertising@ivpressonline.com
• Chris Grant, Sports Editor
(760) 337-3400
Frequency:
6 time(s) per week

INDEPENDENCE DAILY REPORTER
320 NORTH 6TH STREET
INDEPENDENCE, KS 67301-3129
620-331-3550
Fax: 620-331-3550
• Steve McBride, Advertising Manager
• Brian Thomas, Sports Editor
(620) 331-3550
Frequency:
6 time(s) per week

INDEPENDENT (NE)
422 WEST 1ST STREET
GRAND ISLAND, NE 68801
308-382-1000
800-658-3160
Fax: 308-382-8129
editor@theindependent.com
www.theindependent.com
• Terry Douglass, Sports Editor
(308) 381-9414
Frequency:
7 time(s) per week

INDEPENDENT (OH)
50 NORTH AVENUE, N.W.
MASSILLON, OH 44647-5444
330-833-2633
Fax: 330-833-2635
www.indeonline.com
• Joe Shaheen, Managing Editor
• Chris Easterling, Sports Editor
(330) 775-1128
chris.easterling@indeonline.com
Frequency:
7 time(s) per week

INDEPENDENT RECORD
317 CRUSE AVENUE
HELENA, MT 59601-5003
406-447-4000
800-523-2272
Fax: 406-447-4052
irstaff@helenair.com
www.helenair.com
• Jeff Windmueller, Sports Editor
(406) 447-4065
• Tonda Meyer, Advertising Manager
(406) 447-4015
Frequency:
7 time(s) per week

INDEPENDENT TRIBUNE
363 CHURCH STREET N STE. 140
CONCORD, NC 28025
704-789-9147
Fax: 704-786-0645
news@independenttribune.com
www.independenttribune.com
• Steve Winzenread, Sports Editor
(704) 789-9147
• Lynn Wagner, Advertising Manager
(704) 786-9102
Frequency:
7 time(s) per week

INDEX-JOURNAL
610 PHOENIX STREET
GREENWOOD, SC 29646
864-223-1411
Fax: 864-223-7331
www.indexjournal.com
• Paul Still, Advertising Manager
(864) 943-2509
• Scott Chancey, Sports Editor
(864) 223-1813
Frequency:
7 time(s) per week

INDIANA GAZETTE
899 WATER STREET
INDIANA, PA 15701
724-465-5555
Fax: 724-465-0402
www.sportsindianagazette.net
• Tony Coccagna, Sports Editor
tonyc@indianagazette.net
• Bob Yaselonis, Advertising Manager
• Robert Yesilonis, Advertising Director
Frequency:
7 time(s) per week

INDIANA HERALD
2170 NORTH ILLINOIS STREET
INDIANAPOLIS, IN 46202
317-923-8291
Fax: 317-923-8292
www.indianaherald.com
• Leroy Bryant, Sports Editor
(317) 923-8291
Frequency:
1 time(s) per week

INDIANAPOLIS STAR
P.O. BOX 145
INDIANAPOLIS, IN 46204
317-444-6246
800-669-7827
Fax: 317-444-6200
indystarnewsroom@indystar.com
www.indystar.com
• Steve Ballard, Sports Reporter
(317) 444-6184
steve.ballard@indystar.com
• Curt Cavin, Sports Reporter
(317) 444-6409
curt.cavin@indystar.com
• Mike Chappell, Sports Reporter
(317) 444-6830
mike.chappell@indystar.com
• Howard Hewitt, Sports Reporter
(317) 444-2703
howard.hewitt@indystar.com
• Terry Hutchens, Sports Reporter
(317) 444-6469
terry.hutchens@indystar.com
• Bob Kravitz, Sports Columnist
(317) 444-6643
bob.kravitz@indystar.com

• Jim Lefko, Sports Editor
(317) 444-6352
jim.lefko@indystar.com
• Jim Lefko, Sports Desk Editor
(317) 444-6352
jim.lefko@indystar.com
• Jim Lefko, Sports Editor
(317) 444-6352
jim.lefko@indystar.com
• Nat Newell, Sports Reporter
(317) 444-6649
nat.newell@indystar.com
• Michael Pointer, Sports Reporter
(317) 444-2709
michael.pointer@indystar.com
• Jeff Rabjohns, Sports Reporter
(317) 444-6183
jeff.rabjohns@indystar.com
• Phil Richards, Sports Reporter
(317) 444-6408
phil.richards@indystar.com
• Phillip Wilson, Sports Reporter
(317) 444-6642
phillip.wilson@indystar.com
• David Woods, Sports Reporter
(317) 444-6195
david.woods@indystar.com
Frequency:
7 time(s) per week

INLAND VALLEY DAILY BULLETIN
P.O. BOX 4000
ONTARIO, CA 91764
909-987-6397
Fax: 909-948-9038
www.dailybulletin.com
• Louis Brewster, Sports Editor
(909) 483-9363
• Jim Gazzolo, Sports Editor
(909) 483-9374
Frequency:
7 time(s) per week

INTELLIGENCER
1500 MAIN STREET
WHEELING, WV 26003-2826
304-233-0100
800-852-5475
Fax: 304-232-1399
mccabe@thein.net
www.theintelligencer.net
• Shawn Rine, Sports Editor
(304) 233-0100
rine@theintelligencer.net
• Mike Myer, Executive Editor
(304) 233-0100
myer@news-register.net
Frequency:
6 time(s) per week

INTELLIGENCER JOURNAL
P.O. BOX 1328
LANCASTER, PA 17603-3824
717-291-8811
800-809-4666
Fax: 717-399-6507
intellnews@lnpnews.com
lancasteronline.com
• Russell C. Gillespie, Classified Director
(717) 291-8722
• Jeff Young, Sports Editor
jyoung@lnpnews.com
• Kevin Freeman, Sports Writer
(717) 291-8666
Frequency:
6 time(s) per week

INTERMOUNTAIN JEWISH NEWS
1177 GRANT STRET
DENVER, CO 80203
303-861-2234
Fax: 303-832-6942
email@ijn.com
www.ijn.com
• Gerald Mellman, Sports Editor
(303) 823-6625
carol@ijn.com
Frequency:
1 time(s) per week

INTERNATIONAL HERALD TRIBUNE
229 WEST 43RD STREET
NEW YORK, NY 10036
212-556-7714
800-882-2884
Fax: 212-556-7706
www.iht.com
• Peter Berlin, Sports Editor
• Rob Hughes, Sports Reporter
• Huw Richards, Sports Reporter
Frequency:
6 time(s) per week

IOLA REGISTER
302 SOUTH WASHINGTON STREET
IOLA, KS 66749-3255
620-365-2111
800-365-1901
Fax: 620-365-6289
editorial@iolaregister.com
www.iolaregister.com
• Mark Hastings, Advertising Manager
registerdisplay@gmail.com
• Jocelyn Sheets, Sports Editor
sports@iolaregister.com
Frequency:
6 time(s) per week

IOWA CITY GAZETTE
201 SOUTH CLINTON STREET SUITE 200
IOWA CITY, IA 52240
319-339-3155
Fax: 319-354-1266
www.gazetteonline.com
• Steve Gravelle, Sports Editor
(319) 338-5819
Frequency:
7 time(s) per week

IOWA CITY PRESS-CITIZEN
P.O. BOX 2480
IOWA CITY, IA 52245
319-337-3181
Fax: 319-834-1083
newsroom@press-citizen.com
www.press-citizen.com
• Susan Harman, Sports Reporter
(319) 337-3181
sharman@press-citizen.com
• Andy Hamilton, Sports Writer
(319) 337-3181
Frequency:
7 time(s) per week

IRONTON TRIBUNE
2903 SOUTH 5TH STREET
IRONTON, OH 45638-2866
740-532-1441
Fax: 740-532-1506
publisher@irontontribune.com
www.irontontribune.com
• Jim Walker, Sports Editor
jim.walker@irontontribune.com

Frequency:
6 time(s) per week

ISLAND PACKET
10 BUCK ISLAND ROAD
BLUFFTON, SC 29910
843-706-8100
877-706-8100
Fax: 843-706-3070
newsroom@islandpacket.com
www.islandpacket.com
• Sandra Gillis, Advertising Director
(843) 706-8160
• Justin Jarrett, Sports Editor
(843) 706-8120
Frequency:
7 time(s) per week

ITEM
P.O. BOX 1677
SUMTER, SC 29150
803-774-1226
Fax: 803-774-1210
www.theitem.com
• Dennis Brunson, Sports Editor
(803) 774-1241
• Jack Osteen, Advertising Director
(803) 774-1238
jack@theitem.com
• Bobby Touchberry, Classified Manager
(803) 774-1252
bobbyt@item.com
• Justin Driggers, Sports Writer
(803) 774-1235
Frequency:
7 time(s) per week

ITHACA JOURNAL
123 WEST STATE STREET
ITHACA, NY 14850-5427
607-272-2321
800-328-2860
Fax: 607-272-4335
ithjournal@clarityconnect.com
www.theithacajournal.com
• Carol Becker, Advertising Director
• Chris Feaver, Sports Editor
(607) 274-9214
cfeaver@ithaca.gannett.com
Frequency:
6 time(s) per week

JACKSON CITIZEN PATRIOT
214 SOUTH JACKSON STREET
JACKSON, MI 49201-2282
517-789-1250
800-878-6397
Fax: 517-787-9711
sports@citpat.com
www.mlive.com
• Jeff Bleiler, Night Editor
(517) 768-4984
• Mike Pryson, Sports Reporter
(517) 768-4963
• Gary Kalahar, Sports Reporter
(517) 768-4966
Description:
Newspaper

JACKSON COUNTY FLORIDAN
4403 CONSTITUTION LANE
MARIANNA, FL 32448
850-526-3614
Fax: 850-482-4478
www.jcfloridan.com

• Valeria Roberts, Advertising Manager
(850) 526-3614
• Amy Fuller, Sports Editor
(850) 526-3614
Frequency:
5 time(s) per week

JACKSON SUN
245 WEST LAFAYETTE AVENUE
JACKSON, TN 38301-6126
731-427-3333
800-372-3922
Fax: 731-425-9604
contactus@jacksonsun.com
www.jacksonsun.com
• Brandon Shields, Sports Editor
(731) 425-9751
bjshields@jacksntn.gannett.com
Frequency:
7 time(s) per week

JACKSONVILLE DAILY PROGRESS
525 EAST COMMERCE STREET
JACKSONVILLE, TX 75766-4909
903-586-2236
Fax: 903-586-0987
www.jacksonvilleprogress.com
• Jay Neal, Sports Editor
sports@jacksonvilleprogress.com
• Toni Johnson, Advertising Director
addirector@jacksonvilleprogress.com
Frequency:
6 time(s) per week

JACKSONVILLE FREE PRESS
903 EDGEWOOD AVENUE WEST
JACKSONVILLE, FL 32208-3279
904-634-1993
Fax: 904-765-8611
jfreepress@aol.com
www.jacksonvillefreepress.com
• Charles Griggs, Sports Editor
(904) 634-1993
jfreepress@aol.com
Frequency:
1 time(s) per week

JACKSONVILLE JOURNAL-COURIER
235 WEST STATE STREET
JACKSONVILLE, IL 62651-1048
217-245-6121
Fax: 217-245-1226
www.myjournalcourier.com
• Tom Linstromberg, Advertising Manager
• Dennis Mathes, Sports Editor
(217) 245-6121
• Jeanne Strubbe, Classified Manager
(217) 245-6121
Frequency:
7 time(s) per week

JACKSONVILLE PATRIOT
PO BOX 5329
CABOT, AR 72023-1058
501-982-6506
Fax: 501-370-8391
www.jacksonvillepatriot.com/
• Susie Magie, Advertising Manager
• Jeff Reed, Sports Editor
(501) 370-8317
Frequency:
4 time(s) per week

JANESVILLE GAZETTE
P.O. BOX 5001
JANESVILLE, WI 53545-3928

608-754-3311
Fax: 608-755-8349
www.gazetteextra.com
• Dave Wedeward, Sports Editor
(608) 755-8249
• Dan White, Advertising Vice President
(608) 755-8216
• John Barry, Sports Writer
(608) 755-8247
Frequency:
7 time(s) per week

JEFFERSON COUNTY JOURNAL
1405 NORTH TRUMAN
FESTUS, MO 63028
636-931-6636
800-931-6636
Fax: 636-931-2638
www.yourjournal.com
• Dennis Barnidge, Sports Editor
Frequency:
2 time(s) per week

JERSEY JOURNAL
30 JOURNAL SQUARE
JERSEY CITY, NJ 07306
201-653-1000
Fax: 201-653-2243
jjletters@jjournal.com
www.nj.com/jjournal/
• Ron Zeitlinger, Deputy Managing Editor
(201) 217-2429
rzeitlinger@jjournal.com
Frequency:
6 time(s) per week

JOHNSON CITY PRESS
P.O. BOX 1717
JOHNSON CITY, TN 37604-6212
423-929-3111
Fax: 423-929-7484
newsroom@johnsoncitypress.com
www.johnsoncitypress.com
• Robbie Carson, Classified Manager
• Tom Harris, Advertising Manager
(423) 929-3111
• Kelly Hodge, Managing Sports Editor
(423) 929-3111
• Joe Avento, Sports Reporter
(423) 929-3111
javento@johnsoncitypress.com
Frequency:
7 time(s) per week

JONESBORO SUN
PO BOX 1249
JONESBORO, AR 72401-3128
870-935-5525
800-237-5341
Fax: 870-935-5823
newsroom@jonesborosun.com
www.jonesborosun.com
• Kevin Turbeville, Sports Editor
(870) 935-5525
kturbeville@jonesborosun.com
Frequency:
7 time(s) per week

JOPLIN GLOBE
117 EAST 4TH STREET
JOPLIN, MO 64802
417-623-3480
800-444-8514
Fax: 417-623-8450
www.joplinglobe.com

• Jim Henry, Sports Editor
(417) 627-7268
Frequency:
7 time(s) per week

JOURNAL
13650 11 MILE ROAD
WARREN, MI 48089-1422
586-756-8800
Fax: 586-498-9627
www.candgnews.com
• Susan Shanley, Sports Editor
(586) 498-8000
sshanley@candgnews.com

JOURNAL AND COURIER
217 NORTH 6TH STREET
LAFAYETTE, IN 47901-1420
765-423-5511
800-407-5813
Fax: 765-742-5633
editor@journalandcourier.com
www.jconline.com
• Jim Holm, Advertising Manager
(765) 423-5511
• Jim Stafford, Sports Editor
(765) 420-5235
jstafford@journalandcourier.com
Frequency:
7 time(s) per week

JOURNAL GAZETTE
600 W MAIN STREET
FORT WAYNE, IN 46802
260-461-8333
Fax: 260-461-8648
jgnews@jg.net
www.journalgazette.net
• Justin Cohn, Sports Reporter
(260) 461-8333
jgnews@jg.net
• Mark Jaworski, Sports Editor
(260) 461-8260
mjaworski@jg.net
• Michael Rothstein, Sports Writer
(260) 461-8223
Frequency:
Daily - 7 time(s) per week

JOURNAL INQUIRER
P.O. BOX 510
MANCHESTER, CT 06040
860-646-0500
800-237-3606
Fax: 860-646-9867
cpowell@journalinquirer.com
www.journalinquirer.com
• Brian Coyne, Sports Editor
(860) 646-0500
bcoyne@journalinquirer.com
• Bill Cybert, Advertising Manager
• Phil Chardis, Sports Reporter
(860) 646-0500
Frequency:
6 time(s) per week

JOURNAL NEWS
1 GANNETT DRIVE
WHITE PLAINS, NY 10604-3402
914-694-9300
Fax: 914-696-8396
letters@lohud.com
www.lohud.com/
• Sean Mayer, Sports Editor
(914) 696-8527

Frequency:
7 time(s) per week

JOURNAL STAR
1 NEWS PLAZA
PEORIA, IL 61643
309-686-3000
800-225-5757
Fax: 309-686-3296
news@pjstar.com
www.pjstar.com
• Joe Bates, Sports Reporter
(309) 686-3000
• Scott Blicharz, Sports Editor
(309) 686-3211
• Dave Eminian, Sports Reporter
(309) 686-3206
deminian@pjstar.com
• Jeff Lampe, Sports Reporter
(309) 686-3212
• Andy Latora, Sports Copy Editor
(309) 686-3215
alatora@pjstar.com
• Bill Liesse, Sports Editor
(309) 686-3213
• Jane Miller, Sports Reporter
(309) 686-3207
• Ryan Ori, Sports Reporter
(309) 686-3208
• Dave Reynolds, Sports Reporter
(309) 686-3210
dreynolds@pjstar.com
• Nick Vlahos, Sports Copy Editor
(309) 686-3203
nvlahos@pjstar.com
• Kirk Wessler, Executive Sports Editor
(309) 686-3216
kwessler@pjstar.com
Frequency:
7 time(s) per week

JOURNAL TIMES
212 4TH STREET
RACINE, WI 53403
262-634-3322
Fax: 262-631-1702
www.journaltimesonline.com
• Steve Lovejoy, Editor
(262) 631-1722
• Susan Shemanske, Sports Editor
(262) 631-1708
susan.shemanske@lee.net
• Heidi Ward, Retail Advertising Manager
(262) 631-1742
heidi.ward@lee.net
Frequency:
7 time(s) per week

JOURNAL TRIBUNE
457 ALFRED STREET
BIDDEFORD, ME 04005-9447
207-282-1535
Fax: 207-282-3138
www.journaltribune.com
• Al Edwards, Sports Editor
(207) 282-1535
Frequency:
6 time(s) per week
Sports:
New England pro, minor league, York
County High School and York County
non-high school affiliated

JOURNAL-ADVOCATE
504 NORTH 3RD STREET
STERLING, CO 80751

970-522-1990
Fax: 970-522-2320
www.journal-advocate.com
• Brent Arnold, Advertising Manager
• Jonathan Seib, Sports Reporter
(970) 526-9285
Frequency:
6 time(s) per week

JOURNAL-REVIEW
119 NORTH GREEN STREET
CRAWFORDSVILLE, IN 47933-1708
765-362-1200
800-488-4414
Fax: 765-364-5424
www.journalreview.com
• Jeff Arenz, Sports Editor
(765) 362-1200
• Mark Deacon, Advertising Manager
Frequency:
6 time(s) per week

JOURNAL-WORLD
609 NEW HAMPSHIRE
LAWRENCE, KS 66044-2243
785-843-1000
800-578-8748
Fax: 785-843-4512
news@ljworld.com
www.ljworld.com
• Gary Bedore, Sports Assistant Editor
(785) 832-7186
• Chuck Woodling, Sports Editor
(785) 832-7148
Frequency:
7 time(s) per week

JUNEAU EMPIRE
3100 CHANNEL DRIVE
JUNEAU, AK 99801-7814
907-586-3740
888-458-6328
Fax: 907-586-3028
editor@juneauempire.com
www.juneauempire.com
• Paul Hay, Vice President of Advertising
(907) 523-2274
• Lee Leschper, Advertising Manager
(907) 523-2246
• Matthew Tynan, Sports Reporter
(907) 523-2267
Frequency:
6 time(s) per week

KALAMAZOO GAZETTE
401 SOUTH BURDICK STREET
KALAMAZOO, MI 49007-5217
269-345-3511
800-466-2472
Fax: 269-388-8447
news@kalamazoogazette.com
www.kalamazoogazette.com
• Linda Depta, Advertising Director
(269) 388-8460
• Howard Thomas, Sports Editor
(269) 345-3511
Frequency:
7 time(s) per week

KANE COUNTY CHRONICLE
333 N. RANDALL ROAD
SUITE 2
ST. CHARLES, IL 60174
630-232-9222
Fax: 630-444-1641

kcchronicle@aol.com
www.kcchronicle.com
• Terri Landa, Advertising Manager
(630) 845-5236
tlanda@kcchronicle.com
• Jay Schwab, Sports Editor
(630) 232-9222
jschwab@shawsuburban.com
Frequency:
6 time(s) per week

KANSAS CITY KANSAN
P.O. BOX 122800
KANSAS CITY, KS 66112
913-371-4300
Fax: 913-342-8620
www.kansascitykansan.com
• Jeremy Banks, Editor
(913) 371-4300
• Ken Yarnevich, Advertising Manager
(913) 371-4300
Frequency:
5 time(s) per week

KANSAS CITY STAR
1729 GRAND BOULEVARD
KANSAS CITY, MO 64108-1413
816-234-4141
Fax: 816-234-4926
www.kcstar.com
• David Boyce, Sports Reporter
(816) 234-4745
• Randy Covitz, Sports Reporter
(816) 234-4796
• Mike DeArmond, Sports Writer
(816) 234-4355
• Bob Dutton, Sports Reporter
(816) 234-4352
• Mike Fannin, Managing Editor/Sports and
Features
(816) 234-4355
• Jeffrey Flanagan, Sports Reporter
(816) 234-4355
• Tom Ibarra, Sports Assistant Editor
(816) 234-4882
• Blair Kerkhoff, Reporter
(816) 234-4730
bkerkhoff@kcstar.com
• Jason King, Sports Reporter
(816) 234-4141
• Holly Lawton, Deputy Sports Editor
(816) 234-4350
• Bob Luder, Sports Reporter
(816) 234-4877
• Jennifer Mann, Reporter -Advertising,
Marketing, Public
(816) 234-4453
• Sam Mellinger, Sports Writer
(816) 234-4389
• Jim Pedley, Sports Writer
(816) 234-4860
• Joe Posnanski, Sports Columnist
(816) 234-4355
• Howard Richman, Sports Reporter
(816) 234-4701
• Mechelle Voepel, Sports Reporter
(816) 234-4351
• Jason Whitlock, Sports Reporter
(816) 234-4869
• Mark Zeligman, Assistant Sports Editor
(816) 234-4339
Frequency:
7 time(s) per week

KEARNEY HUB
13 EAST 22ND STREET
KEARNEY, NE 68847

308-237-2152
800-950-6113
Fax: 308-233-9736
news@kearneyhub.com
www.kearneyhub.com
• Seth Blank, Sports Reporter
(308) 233-9729
• Buck Mahoney, Sports Editor
(308) 233-9750
buck.mahoney@kearneyhub.com
Frequency:
6 time(s) per week

KEENE SENTINEL
60 WEST STREET
KEENE, NH 03431-3373
603-352-1234
Fax: 603-352-0437
news@keenesentinel.com
www.sentinelsource.com
• Lorraine Ellis, Classified Manager
• David Lanier, Sports Editor
(603) 352-1234
Frequency:
7 time(s) per week

KENNEBEC JOURNAL
274 WESTERN AVENUE
AUGUSTA, ME 04330-4976
207-623-3811
800-537-5508
Fax: 207-623-2220
www.kjonline.com
• Scott Martin, Sports Editor
(207) 621-5618
• Gary Hawkins, Deputy Sports Editor &
Columnist
(207) 621-5638
ghawkins@centralmain.com
Frequency:
7 time(s) per week

KENOSHA NEWS
5800 7TH AVENUE
KENOSHA, WI 53140
262-657-1800
Fax: 262-657-8455
newsroom@kenoshanews.com
www.kenoshacounty.com
• Dave Marran, Sports Editor
(262) 656-6290
• Lani Renneau, Advertising Director
(262) 656-6243
Frequency:
7 time(s) per week

KENTON TIMES
201 EAST COLUMBUS STREET
KENTON, OH 43326-1544
419-674-4066
Fax: 419-673-1125
kteditor@kentontimes.com
www.kentontimes.com
• Lesa Heacock, Advertising Manager
(419) 674-4066
lheacock@kentontimes.com
• Kendrick Jesionowski, Sports Editor
(419) 674-4066
ktsports@kentontimes.com
Frequency:
6 time(s) per week

KENTUCKY NEW ERA
P.O. BOX 729
HOPKINSVILLE, KY 42240-4430

270-886-4444
877-463-9372
Fax: 270-887-3222
editor@kentuckynewera.com
www.kentuckynewera.com
• Joe Wilson, Sports Editor
(270) 887-3230
• Alex Byington, Sports Writer/Columnist
(270) 887-3230
Frequency:
6 time(s) per week

KERRVILLE DAILY TIMES
429 JEFFERSON STREET
KERRVILLE, TX 78028
830-896-7000
800-898-7000
Fax: 830-896-1150
www.dailytimes.com
• Joe Harrington, Sports Editor
(830) 257-0318
sports@dailytimes.com
Frequency:
6 time(s) per week

KETCHIKAN DAILY NEWS
501 DOCK STREET
KETCHIKAN, AK 99901
907-225-3157
Fax: 907-225-1096
news@ketchikandailynews.com
www.ketchikandailynews.com
• Lyle Goulding, Sports Editor
lyle@ketchikandailynews.com
Frequency:
6 time(s) per week

KING COUNTY JOURNAL
600 WASHINGTON AVENUE SOUTH
KENT, WA 98032-5708
253-872-6600
Fax: 253-854-1006
www.kingcountyjournal.com
• Jim Cnockaert, Sports Editor
(253) 872-6678
• Michael Stevens, Advertising Manager
(253) 872-6729
Frequency:
7 time(s) per week

KINGMAN DAILY MINER
3015 STOCKTON HILL ROAD
KINGMAN, AZ 86401 3909
928-753-6397
Fax: 928-753-5661
kingmannewspapers@mcimail.com
www.kingmandailyminer.com
• Brent Hinckley, Sports Editor
(928) 753-6397
• Colleen Machado, Advertising Manager
(928) 753-6397
Frequency:
6 time(s) per week

KINGSPORT TIMES-NEWS
701 LYNN GARDEN DRIVE
KINGSPORT, TN 37660
423-246-8121 EXT 323
800-251-0328
Fax: 423-392-1385
retail@timesnews.net
www.timesnews.net
• Andy Barnes, Creative Services Director
• Pat Kenney, Sports Editor
(423) 723-1434

Frequency:
7 time(s) per week

KIRKSVILLE DAILY EXPRESS & NEWS
110 EAST MCPHERSON STREET
KIRKSVILLE, MO 63501-3506
660-665-2808
Fax: 660-665-2608
• Bud Schrader, Sports Reporter
dailyexpress_sports@yahoo.com
• George Wriedt, Advertising Manager
kvdaily@sbcglobal.net
Frequency:
6 time(s) per week

KNOXVILLE NEWS-SENTINEL
2332 NEWS SENTINEL DR
KNOXVILLE, TN 37921-5766
865-523-3131
800-237-5821
Fax: 865-342-6400
gvpolitics@hotmail.com
www.knoxnews.com
• John Adams, Sports Editor
Frequency:
7 time(s) per week

KOKOMO TRIBUNE
300 NORTH UNION STREET
KOKOMO, IN 46901-4612
765-454-8584
800-382-0696
Fax: 765-456-3815
ktnews@kokomotribune.com
www.komotribune.com
• Bryan Gaskins, Sports Editor
(765) 459-3121
bryan.gaskins@kokomotribune.com
Frequency:
7 time(s) per week

KOREAN CENTRAL DAILY
690 WILSHIRE PLACE
LOS ANGELES, CA 90005-3980
213-368-2500
Fax: 213-389-6196
www.koreadaily.com
• Ja G Ku, Sports Editor
• Thomas Yang, Sports Editor
(213) 368-2696
Frequency:
6 time(s) per week

LA CROSSE TRIBUNE
401 3RD ST N
LA CROSSE, WI 54601-3281
608-782-9710
800-262-0420
Fax: 608-782-9723
news@lacrossetribune.com
www.lacrossetribune.com
• Joel Badzinski, Sports Reporter
(608) 791-8402
• Jeff Brown, Sports Editor
(608) 791-8202
jbrown@lacrossetribune.com
• Jared Heintz, Assistant Sports Editor
(608) 791-8877
Frequency:
7 time(s) per week

LA GRANGE DAILY NEWS
105 ASHTON STREET
LAGRANGE, GA 30241-3111

706-884-7311
Fax: 706-884-8712
www.lagrangenews.com
• Kevin Eckleberry, Sports Editor
(706) 884-7311
• Karen Brown, Advertising Director
(706) 884-7311
• Natalie Trout, Sports Writer
Frequency:
7 time(s) per week

LA OFERTA NEWSPAPER
1376 NORTH 4TH STREET
SAN JOSE, CA 95112-4713
408-436-7850
Fax: 408-436-7861
www.laoferta.com
• Patty Canz, Sports Writer
• Frank Andrade, Publisher
Frequency:
1 time(s) per week
Circulation:
20,000
Description:
Tab size newspaper whose primary audience is the spanish citizens.

LA OPINION
P.O. BOX 15093
LOS ANGELES, CA 90013-1000
213-622-8332
Fax: 213-896-2171
editorial@laopinion.com
www.laopinion.com
• Rafael Ramos, Sports Editor
(213) 622-8332
Frequency:
7 time(s) per week

LA PORTE HERALD-ARGUS
701 STATE STREET
LA PORTE, IN 46350-3328
219-362-2161
Fax: 219-362-2166
www.heraldargus.com
• Adam Parkhouse, Sports Editor
(219) 362-3869
sports@heraldargus.com
• Donna Maglio, Advertising Manager
(219) 326-3881
Frequency:
6 time(s) per week

LA PRENSA DE SAN ANTONIO
318 SOUTH FLORES STREET
SAN ANTONIO, TX 78204-1106
210-242-7900
Fax: 210-242-7901
www.laprensa.com
• Jose Franco, Sports Editor
(210) 242-7900
Frequency:
2 time(s) per week

LA PRENSA SAN DIEGO
651 3RD AVENUE, SUITE C
CHULA VISTA, CA 91910
619-425-7400
Fax: 619-336-0372
www.laprensa-sandiego.org
• Daniel Munoz, Editor
• Paco Zavala, Sports Writer
• Fred Sidhu, Sports Editor
Frequency:
1 time(s) per week

LA TRIBUNA DE NORTH JERSEY
300 36TH STREET
UNION CITY, NJ 07087-4724
201-617-1360
Fax: 201-617-0042
rumolenaar@aol.com
www.latribuna.com
• Pablo Laserna, Sports Editor
Frequency:
2 time(s) per month

LAKE CHARLES AMERICAN PRESS
4900 HWY 90 E.
LAKE CHARLES, LA 70615
337-433-3000
Fax: 337-494-4070
news@americanpress.com
www.americanpress.com
• Scooter Hobbs, Sports Editor
(337) 494-4069
shobbs@americanpress.com
• Brett Downer, Editor

LAKE CITY REPORTER
P.O. BOX 1709
LAKE CITY, FL 32056-1709
386-752-1297
Fax: 386-752-9400
news@lakecityreporter.com
www.lakecityreporter.com
• Tim Kirby, Sports Editor
(386) 754-0421
tkirby@lakecityreporter.com
Frequency:
6 time(s) per week

LAKE COUNTY RECORD-BEE
2150 SOUTH MAIN
LAKEPORT, CA 95453-5620
707-263-5636
Fax: 707-263-0600
www.record-bee.com
• Brian Sumpter, Sports Editor
(707) 263-5636
RBSports@aol.com
Frequency:
5 time(s) per week

LAMAR DAILY NEWS
310 SOUTH 5TH STREET
LAMAR, CO 81052-2712
719-336-2266
Fax: 719-336-2526
www.lamardaily.com
• John Contreras, Editor
Frequency:
2 time(s) per week
Circulation:
2,800
Sports:
Area High School, Some National - AP

LANCASTER EAGLE-GAZETTE
P.O. BOX 848
LANCASTER, OH 43130-4308
740-654-1321
Fax: 740-681-4456
lancaster@nncogannett.com
www.lancastereaglegazette.com/
• Joe Arnold, Sports Editor
(740) 681-4358
jarnold@nncogannett.com
Frequency:
7 time(s) per week

LANCASTER NEW ERA
8 WEST KING STREET
LANCASTER, PA 17608-3824
717-291-8733
800-809-4666
Fax: 717-399-6506
neweranews@lnpnews.com
www.lancasteronline.com
• Dennis Fisher, Sports Editor
(717) 291-8779
• Jeffrey Reinhart, Sports Writer
(717) 291-8778
jreinhart@lnpnews.com
• Keith Schweigert, Sports Writer
(717) 291-8777
• Harold Zeigler, Sports Writer
(717) 291-8778
Frequency:
6 time(s) per week

LANSING STATE JOURNAL
120 EAST LENAWEE STREET
LANSING, MI 48919
517-702-4257
Fax: 517-377-1298
www.lansingstatejournal.com
• Mark Meyer, Sports Editor
(517) 377-1073
• Barry Kiel, Sports Assistant Editor
(517) 267-1393
bkiel@lsj.com
• Neil Koepke, Sports Reporter
(517) 377-1070
Frequency:
7 time(s) per week

LARAMIE DAILY BOOMERANG
320 EAST GRAND AVENUE
LARAMIE, WY 82070-3712
307-742-2176
Fax: 307-742-2046
www.laramieboomerang.com
• Robert Hammond, Sports Editor
(307) 742-2176
• Matt Petrie, Advertising Manager
Frequency:
6 time(s) per week

LAREDO MORNING TIMES
111 ESPERANZA DRIVE
LAREDO, TX 78041
956-728-2500
Fax: 956-723-1227
www.lmtonline.com
• Dennis Silva, Sports Editor
(956) 728-2579
• Salo Otero, Assistant Sports Editor
(956) 728-2578
• Kenny Ryan, Sports Reporter
(956) 728-2576
Frequency:
7 time(s) per week

LAS CRUCES SUN-NEWS
256 WEST LAS CRUCES AVENUE
LAS CRUCES, NM 88005
505-541-5400
800-745-5851
Fax: 505-541-5499
www.lcsun-news.com
• Teddy Feinberg, Sports Editor
(505) 541-5455
tfeinberg@lcsun-news.com
• Heidi Melendrez, Advertising Director
Frequency:
7 time(s) per week

LAS VEGAS DAILY OPTIC
614 LINCOLN AVENUE
LAS VEGAS, NM 87701
505-425-6796
800-767-6796
Fax: 505-425-1005
composing@lasvegasoptic.com
www.lasvegasoptic.com
• Sherry An Clancy, Advertising Manager
• Dave Wesner, Sports Editor
Frequency:
5 time(s) per week

LAS VEGAS REVIEW-JOURNAL
1111 WEST BONANZA ROAD
LAS VEGAS, NV 89106
702-383-0211
Fax: 702-383-4676
letters@reviewjournal.com
www.reviewjournal.com
• Mark Anderson, Sports Reporter
(702) 387-2914
manderson@reviewjournal.com
• Steve Carp, Reporter
(702) 387-2913
• Jim Fossum, Sports Editor
(702) 383-4618
• Karen Grover, National Advertising Manager
• Joe Hawk, Sports Editor
(702) 387-2912
jhawk@reviewjournal.com
• Kevin Iole, Sports Reporter
(702) 387-2916
• Allen Leiker, Sports Assistant Editor
(702) 383-0297
ALeiker@reviewjournal.com
• Damon Seiters, Sports Editor (High School)
(702) 380-4587
DSeiters@reviewjournal.com
• Jeff Wolf, Sports Reporter & Columnist
(702) 383-0247
• Steve Addy, Sports Copy Editor
(702) 383-0442
Frequency:
7 time(s) per week

LAS VEGAS SUN
2275 CORPORATE CIRCLE DRIVE SUITE 300
HENDERSON, NV 89074
702-385-3111
Fax: 702-383-7264
www.lasvegassun.com
• Adam Candee, Sports Reporter
(702) 259-2312
candee@lasvegassun.com
• Steve Guiremand, Sports Reporter
steveg@lasvegassun.com
• Brian Hilderbrand, Motorsports Reporter
(702) 259-4089
bh@lasvegassun.com
• Ron Kantowski, Sports Columnist
(702) 259-4088
ron@lasvegassun.com
• Rob Miech, Sports Reporter
miech@lasvegassun.com
• Jeff Haney, Sports Columnist
(702) 259-4041
jeff.haney@lasvegassun.com
Frequency:
7 time(s) per week

LATINO INTERNATIONAL-ORLANDO
672 NORTH SEMORAN BOULEVARD
SUITE 304
ORLANDO, FL 32807
407-381-9119
Fax: 407-381-3197
latinointl@aol.com
www.latinointlnews.com
• Zulay Perez, Sports Editor
Frequency:
1 time(s) per week

LATROBE BULLETIN
P.O. BOX 111
LATROBE, PA 15650-1921
724-537-3351
Fax: 724-537-0489
lb.news@verizon.net
• Randy Skubek, Sports Editor
Frequency:
6 time(s) per week

LAUREL LEADER-CALL
130 BEACON STREET
LAUREL, MS 39440
601-428-0551
Fax: 601-426-3550
editor@laurelleadercall.com
www.leadercall.com
• Randy Hammons, Sports Editor
(601) 428-0551
sports@laurelleadercall.com
• John Blackledge, Sports Reporter
(601) 428-0551
llcsportswriter@gmail.com
Frequency:
7 time(s) per week

LAWTON CONSTITUTION
102 SOUTHWEST 3RD STREET
LAWTON, OK 73502-4031
580-353-0620
Fax: 580-585-5103
www.swoknews.com
• Jim Garrett, Advertising Manager
(580) 585-5107
• Joey Goodman, Sports Editor
(580) 585-5124
Frequency:
7 time(s) per week

LE MARS DAILY SENTINEL
41 1ST AVENUE, N.E.
LE MARS, IA 51031-0930
712-546-7031
Fax: 712-546-7035
www.lemarssentinel.com
• Jesse Geleynse, Sports Editor
(712) 546-7031
• Monte Jost, Advertising Manager
(712) 546-7031
Frequency:
5 time(s) per week

LEADER
34 WEST PULTENEY STREET
CORNING, NY 14830-2211
607-936-4651
Fax: 607-936-9939
www.the-leader.com
• Kurt Bartenstein, Advertising Manager
(607) 936-4651
• Shawn Vargo, Sports Editor
(607) 936-4651
svargo@the-leader.com

Frequency:
7 time(s) per week

LEADER-TELEGRAM
701 S. FARWELL ST
EAU CLAIRE, WI 54701
715-833-9200
800-236-8808
Fax: 715-833-9244
• Joe Ziemer, Sports Reporter
(715) 833-9212
• John Casper, Sports Editor
(715) 833-9212

LEADER-TIMES
115-121 NORTH GRANT AVENUE
KITTANNING, PA 16201-1401
724-543-1303
Fax: 724-545-6768
• Gavin Jenkins, Sports Editor
(724) 543-1303
• Kathy Master, Advertising Coordinator
(724) 543-1303
Frequency:
6 time(s) per week

LEAF-CHRONICLE
P.O. BOX 31029
CLARKSVILLE, TN 37040
931-552-1808
Fax: 931-648-8001
news@theleafchronicle.com
www.theleafchronicle.com
• Robb Scott, Advertising Manager
(931) 552-1808
• Jimmy Trodglen, Sports Editor
(931) 245-0261
jimmytrodglen@theleafchronicle.com
• George Robinson, Sports Reporter
(931) 245-6747
georgerobinson@theleafchronicle.com
Frequency:
7 time(s) per week

LEAVENWORTH TIMES
422 SENECA STREET
LEAVENWORTH, KS 66048-1910
913-682-0305
Fax: 913-682-1114
www.leavenworthtimes.com
• Sara Mettlen, Sports Editor
Frequency:
6 time(s) per week

LEBANON DEMOCRAT
402 NORTH CUMBERLAND STREET
LEBANON, TN 37087-2306
615-444-3952
Fax: 615-444-1358
www.lebanondemocrat.com
• Andy Reed, Sports Editor
(615) 444-3952
andy.reed@lebanondemocrat.com
Frequency:
5 time(s) per week

LEDGER
P.O. BOX 408
LAKELAND, FL 33802
863-802-7000
Fax: 863-802-7810
features@theledger.com
www.theledger.com
• Ray Beasock, Sports Copy Editor
(863) 802-7537
ray.beasock@theledger.com

• Lisa Coffey, Sports Reporter
(863) 401-6971
• Del Milligan, Outdoors Editor
(863) 802-7555
del.milligan@theledger.com
Frequency:
7 time(s) per week

LEDGER INDEPENDENT
P.O. BOX 518
MAYSVILLE, KY 41056-1101
606-564-9091
800-264-9091
Fax: 606-564-6893
www.maysville-online.com
• Patty Moore, Advertising Manager
• Chuck Hamilton, Sports Editor
(606) 564-9091
Frequency:
6 time(s) per week

LEWISTON MORNING TRIBUNE
505 CAPITAL STREET
LEWISTON, ID 83501-1843
208-743-9411
800-745-9411
Fax: 208-746-7341
city@lmtribune.com
www.lmtribune.com
• Matt Baney, Sports Editor
mbaney@lmtribune.com
• Dana Strong, Sports Writer
Frequency:
7 time(s) per week

LEXINGTON HERALD-LEADER
100 MIDLAND AVENUE
LEXINGTON, KY 40508-1943
859-231-3200
800-274-7355
Fax: (85- 231-3332
hleditorial@herald-leader.com
www.kentucky.com
• Gene Abell, Sports Editor
(859) 231-3237
• John Clay, Sports Columnist
(859) 231-3226
jclay@herald-leader.com
• Chip Cosby, Sports Reporter
(859) 231-3440
• Mike Fields, High School Sports Reporter
(859) 231-3337
• Mat Graf, Assistant Sports Editor
(859) 231-3529
mgraf@herald-leader.com
• Rob Kandt, News Editor
(859) 231-3513
• Mark Maloney, Sports Reporter
(859) 231-3229
• Mark Story, Sports Columnist
(859) 231-3230
mstory@herald-leader.com
• Jerry Tipton, Sports Reporter
(859) 231-3227
Frequency:
7 time(s) per week

LINCOLN COURIER
P.O. BOX 740
LINCOLN, IL 62656-2825
217-732-2101
800-747-5462
Fax: 217-732-7039
courier@lincolncourier.com
www.lincolncourier.com
• Dylan Polk, Sports Editor
(217) 732-2101

Frequency:
6 time(s) per week

LINCOLN JOURNAL STAR
926 P STREET
LINCOLN, NE 68508
402-475-4200
800-742-7315
Fax: 402-473-7291
newsroom@journalstar.com
www.journalstar.com
• Ken Hambleton, Sports Reporter
(402) 473-7331
• John Mabry, Sports Editor
(402) 473-7331
sports@journalstar.com
• Curt McKeever, Sports Columnist
(402) 473-7431
Frequency:
7 time(s) per week

LINTON DAILY CITIZEN
79 SOUTH MAIN STREET
LINTON, IN 47441-1818
812-847-4487
Fax: 812-847-9513
www.dailycitizen.com
• BJ Hargis, Sports Editor
(812) 847-4487
hargisbj@gmail.com
Frequency:
6 time(s) per week

LIVINGSTON COUNTY DAILY PRESS & ARGUS
323 EAST GRAND RIVER
HOWELL, MI 48843
517-548-2000
Fax: 517-548-3005
www.hometownlife.com
• Tim Robinson, Sports Editor
(517) 552-2863
Frequency:
7 time(s) per week

LOCKPORT UNION-SUN & JOURNAL
170 EAST AVENUE
LOCKPORT, NY 14094
716-439-9222
Fax: 716-439-9239
www.lockportjournal.com
• Diane Crowe, Advertising Manager
(716) 439-9222
• John D'Onofrio, Sports Editor
Frequency:
7 time(s) per week

LODI NEWS-SENTINEL
125 NORTH CHURCH STREET
LODI, CA 95240-2102
209-369-7035
Fax: 209-369-6706
news@lodinews.com
www.lodinews.com
• Kimberly Anger, Advertising Director
(209) 369-2761
• Scott Howell, Sports Editor
(209) 369-7035
scotth@lodinews.com
• Joelle Milholm, Sports Reporter
Frequency:
6 time(s) per week

LOG CABIN DEMOCRAT
1058 FRONT STREET
CONWAY, AR 72032-4356

501-327-6621
800-678-4523
Fax: 501-327-6787
www.thecabin.net
• Fran Plymale, Classified Manager
(501) 505-1242
• Mark Burke, Sports Editor
(501) 505-1237
• Rhonda Overbey, Advertising Manager
Frequency:
6 time(s) per week

LOGAN BANNER
PO BOX 720
LOGAN, WV 25601
304-752-6950
Fax: 304-752-1239
www.loganbanner.com
• Paul Adkins, Sports Editor
(304) 752-6950
• Kathy Chafin, Advertising Manager
(304) 752-6950
• Dottie Hatfield, Classified Manager
Frequency:
6 time(s) per week

LOGAN DAILY NEWS
72 EAST MAIN STREET
LOGAN, OH 43138-1221
740-385-2107
Fax: 740-385-4514
info@logandaily.com
www.logandaily.com
• Craig Dunn, Sports Editor
• James Shine, Publisher
(740) 385-2107
Frequency:
5 time(s) per week

LONGMONT DAILY TIMES-CALL
350 TERRY STREET
LONGMONT, CO 80501
303-776-2244
800-796-8201
Fax: 303-678-8615
opinion@times-call.com
www.longmontfyi.com
• Penny Dille, Advertising Director
(303) 776-2244
• Karen Lambert, Classified Manager
(303) 635-3603
• Brian Howell, Sports Editor
(303) 684-5298
Frequency:
7 time(s) per week

LONGVIEW NEWS-JOURNAL
P.O. BOX 1792
LONGVIEW, TX 75601-7323
903-757-3311
Fax: 903-757-3742
info@news-journal.com
www.news-journal.com
• Gabriel Brooks, Sports Reporter
(903) 237-7745
• Jack Stallard, Sports Editor
(903) 237-7760
jstallard@news-journal.com
Frequency:
7 time(s) per week

LOS ALAMOS MONITOR
256 D.P. ROAD
LOS ALAMOS, NM 87544

505-662-4185
Fax: 505-662-4334
www.lamonitor.com
• Matt Hietala, Sports Editor
(505) 662-4185
Frequency:
5 time(s) per week

LOS ANGELES SENTINEL
3800 CRENSHAW BOULEVARD
LOS ANGELES, CA 90008-1813
323-299-3800
Fax: 323-299-3896
sentinelrd@aol.com
www.losangelessentinel.com/index.html
• Frank Reneau, Sports Editor
(323) 299-3800
Frequency:
1 time(s) per week

LOS ANGELES TIMES
202 WEST 1ST STREET
LOS ANGELES, CA 90012-4105
213-237-5000
800-528-4637
Fax: 213-237-4712
www.latimes.com
• J.A. Adande, Sports Columnist
(213) 237-7145
j.a.adande@latimes.com
• Dan Arritt, High School Sports Staff Writer
(213) 237-6471
dan.arritt@latimes.com
• Athan Atsales, Assistant Sports Editor
(213) 237-3615
athan.atsales@latimes.com
• Ben Bolch, College Sports Staff Writer
(213) 237-6479
ben.bolch@latimes.com
• Thomas Bonk, Sports Reporter
(213) 237-7145
thomas.bonk@latimes.com
• Mike Bresnahan, Professional Basketball Staff Writer
(213) 237-6482
mike.bresnahan@latimes.com
• Tim Brown, Sports Reporter (Baseball)
tim.brown@latimes.com
• Todd Brownrout, Advertising Senior VP
• Bill Christine, Sports Writer (Horse Racing)

(310) 376-9989
bill.christine@latimes.com
• John Cherwa, Deputy Editor
(213) 237-7617
john.cherwa@latimes.com
• Jerry Crowe, Sports Reporter (Clippers)
(213) 237-3653
jerry.crowe@latimes.com
• Mike DiGiovanna, Sports Reporter (Baseball)
mike.digiovanna@latimes.com
• Lisa Dillman, Sports Reporter (Tennis)
(213) 237-7145
lisa.dillman@latimes.com
• Chris Dufresne, Sports Reporter
(213) 237-7145
chris.dufresne@latimes.com
• Bill Dwyre, Executive Sports Editor
(213) 237-3569
bill.dwyre@latimes.com
• Helene Elliott, Sports Columnist
(213) 237-2508
helene.elliott@latimes.com
• Sam Farmer, Sports Reporter (National)
(213) 237-7145
sam.farmer@latimes.com
• Chris Foster, Sports Reporter (Kings)

(213) 237-7145
chris.foster@latimes.com
• Shav Glick, Sports Writer (Motor Sports)
shav.glick@latimes.com
• Paul Gutierrez, Sports Writer (Soccer)
paul.gutierrez@latimes.com
• Mark Heisler, Sports Reporter (Basketball)

(213) 237-7145
mark.heisler@latimes.com
• Martin Henderson, Sports Writer
martin.henderson@latimes.com
• Steve Henson, Sports Writer
(213) 237-5000
stephen.hench@latimes.com
• Mike Hiserman, Sports Senior Assistant Editor
(213) 237-3633
mike.hiserman@latimes.com
• Greg Johnson, (213) 237-5000
Sports Writer
greg.johnson@latimes.com
• Grahame Jones, Sports Reporter (Soccer)
(213) 237-7145
grahame.jones@latimes.com
• Mike Kennedy, Sports Reporter (Local)
mike.kennedy@latimes.com
• Alex Kimball, Assistant Sports Editor
(213) 237-7145
alex.kimball@latimes.com
• Gary Klein, Sports Reporter (USC)
(213) 237-7145
gary.klein@latimes.com
• Mike Kupper, Senior Assistant Sports Editor
(213) 237-7145
mike.kupper@latimes.com
Frequency:
7 time(s) per week

LOVELAND DAILY REPORTER-HERALD
201 EAST 5TH STREET
LOVELAND, CO 80537-
970-669-5050
Fax: 970-667-1111
news@reporter-herald.com
www.lovelandfyi.com
• Mike Brohard, Sports Editor
(970) 635-3633
• Linda Story, Advertising Manager
(970) 635-3614
Frequency:
7 time(s) per week

LUBBOCK AVALANCHE-JOURNAL
710 AVENUE J
LUBBOCK, TX 79401
806-762-8844
800-692-4021
Fax: 806-744-9603
www.lubbockonline.com
• Courtney Linehan, Sports Editor
(806) 766-8735
courtney.linehan@lubbockonline.com
• George Watson, Assistant Sports Editor
(806) 766-2166
george.watson@lubbockonline.com

LUDINGTON DAILY NEWS
202 NORTH RATH AVENUE
LUDINGTON, MI 49431-1663
231-845-5181
800-748-0407
Fax: 231-843-4011
ldn@ludingtondailynews.com
www.ludingtondailynews.com

• John Walker, Advertising Manager
• Lloyd Wallace, Sports Editor
(231) 845-5182
Frequency:
6 time(s) per week

LUSO AMERICANO
66 UNION STREET
NEWARK, NJ 07105
973-344-3200
Fax: 973-344-4201
www.lusoamericano.com
• Ilidio Martins, Sports Editor
(973) 344-3200
imartins@lusoamericano.com
Frequency:
2 time(s) per week

MACOMB DAILY
100 MACOMB DAILY DRIVE
MOUNT CLEMENS, MI 48043-5802
586-469-4510
Fax: 586-469-2892
ken.kish@macombdaily.com
www.macombdaily.com
• Roger Hages, Retail Advertising Manager
(586) 783-0234
• Bruce MacLeod, Sports Columnist
(586) 783-0358
• George Pohly, Sports Editor
(586) 783-0270
george.pohly@macombdaily.com
Frequency:
7 time(s) per week

MACOMB JOURNAL
203 NORTH RANDOLPH STREET
MACOMB, IL 61455
309-833-2114
800-237-6858
Fax: 309-833-2346
www.macombjournal.com
• Shelby Burget, Sports Editor
(309) 833-2345
• Lynne Campbell, Advertising Manager
Frequency:
6 time(s) per week

MACON CHRONICLE-HERALD
204 WEST BOURKE STREET
MACON, MO 63552-1504
660-385-3121
Fax: 660-385-3082
www.maconch.com
• Chuck Kindle, Advertising Manager
• Jim Brown, Sports Editor
(660) 385-3121
Frequency:
4 time(s) per week

MACON TELEGRAPH
120 BROADWAY
MACON, GA 31201-3444
478-744-4411
800-342-5845
Fax: 478-744-4385
www.macontelegraph.com
• Rick Nolte, Sports Editor
(478) 744-4401
Frequency:
7 time(s) per week

MADERA TRIBUNE
100 EAST 7TH STREET
MADERA, CA 93638-3742

559-674-2424
Fax: 559-673-6526
cdoud@maderatribune.net
www.maderatribune.net
• Paul Stanford, Sports Writer
(559) 674-8134
• Corrie Valdez, Advertising Manager
Frequency:
6 time(s) per week

MADISON COURIER
310 COURIER SQUARE
MADISON, IN 47250
812-265-3641
800-333-2885
Fax: 812-273-6903
news@madisoncourier.com
www.madisoncourier.com
• Mark Campbell, Sports Editor
mcampbell@madisoncourier.com
• Curt Jacobs, Advertising Manager
(812) 265-3641
Frequency:
6 time(s) per week

MADISON DAILY LEADER
214 SOUTH EGAN AVENUE
MADISON, SD 57042
605-256-4555
Fax: 605-256-6190
news@madisondailyleader.com
www.madisondailyleader.com
• Dan Holsworth, Sports Editor
sports@madisondailyleader.com
• Karen Maxwell, Classified Manager
Frequency:
5 time(s) per week

MADISON INDEPENDENT PRESS
80 SOUTH STREET
NEW PROVIDENCE, NJ 07974
908-464-1025
Fax: 908-464-9085
ipeditors@njnpublishing.com
www.nj.com/independentpress/
• Art Polakowski, Sports Editor
Frequency:
1 time(s) per week

MADISON PRESS
55 WEST HIGH STREET
LONDON, OH 43140-1066
740-852-1616
800-282-3838
Fax: 740-852-1620
www.madison-press.com
• David Biddle, Sports Editor
• Linda Marx, Classified Manager
(740) 852-1616
Frequency:
5 time(s) per week

MALONE TELEGRAM
469 EAST MAIN STREET
MALONE, NY 12953
518-483-2000
Fax: 518-483-8579
news@mtelegram.com
• Karen Carre, Advertising Manager
(518) 483-2000
ads@mtelegram.com
• Eric Meachen, Sports Editor
(518) 483-2000
sports@mtelegram.com
Frequency:
6 time(s) per week

MALVERN DAILY RECORD
219 LOCUST STREET
MALVERN, AR 72104
501-337-7523
800-582-5794
Fax: 501-337-1226
www.malvern-online.com
• Sean Rock, Sports Writer
sports@malvern-online.com
Frequency:
6 time(s) per week

MANASSAS JOURNAL MESSENGER
P.O. BOX 431
MANASSAS, VA 20110
703-368-3101
Fax: 703-368-9017
www.manassasjm.com
• Dave Fawcett, Sports Editor
(703) 530-3911
dfawcett@insidenova.com
• Brent Morris, Advertising Director
(703) 530-3930
• Robert Daski, Sports Reporter
(703) 530-3913
Frequency:
7 time(s) per week

MANHATTAN MERCURY
318 NORTH 5TH STREET
MANHATTAN, KS 66502-5910
785-776-2200
Fax: 785-776-8807
news@themercury.com
www.themercury.com
• Mark Janssen, Sports Editor
(785) 776-2200
• Steve Stallwitz, Advertising Manager
(785) 776-2200
adv@themercury.com
Frequency:
6 time(s) per week

MANTECA BULLETIN
531 EAST YOSEMITE AVENUE
MANTECA, CA 95336-5806
209-249-3500
Fax: 209-249-3551
news@mantecabulletin.com
www.mantecabulletin.com/
• Jonamar Jacinto, Sports Editor
(209) 249-3538
jjacinto@mantecabulletin.com
Frequency:
7 time(s) per week

MARIETTA DAILY JOURNAL
P.O. BOX 449
MARIETTA, GA 30060
770-428-9411
Fax: 770-422-9533
lifestyle@mdjonline.com
www.mdjonline.com
• John Bednarowski, Sports Editor
(770) 428-9411
sportseditor@mdjonline.com
Frequency:
7 time(s) per week

MARIETTA TIMES
700 CHANNEL LANE
MARIETTA, OH 45750-2342
740-373-2121
800-531-1215
Fax: 740-376-5475
www.mariettatimes.com

• Ron Johnston, Sports Editor
(740) 376-5441
rjohnston@mariettatimes.com
Frequency:
6 time(s) per week

MARIN INDEPENDENT JOURNAL
P.O. BOX 6150
NOVATO, CA 94949-6665
415-883-8600
Fax: 415-382-7209
www.marinij.com
• Dave Allen, Sports Editor
(415) 382-7206
dallen@marinij.com
Frequency:
7 time(s) per week

MARSHALL INDEPENDENT
PO BOX 411
MARSHALL, MN 56258-1317
507-537-1551
Fax: 507-537-1557
news@marshallindependent.com
www.marshallindependent.com
• Joe Brown, Sports Editor
(507) 537-1551
• Tara Brandl, Advertising Manager
(507) 537-1551
tbrandl@marshallindependent.com
Frequency:
6 time(s) per week

MARSHALL NEWS MESSENGER
P.O. BOX 730
MARSHALL, TX 75670-3475
903-935-7914
Fax: 903-935-6242
www.marshallnewsmessenger.com
• Edward Carifo, Sports Editor
(903) 935-7914
• Deb Green, Advertising Manager
(903) 927-5984
Frequency:
7 time(s) per week

MARSHFIELD NEWS-HERALD
111 WEST 3RD STREET
MARSHFIELD, WI 54449-2811
715-384-3131
Fax: 715-387-4175
www.marshfieldnewsherald.com
• Chris Schulte, Sports Editor
cschulte@wdhprint.com
• Tara Marcoux, Advertising Manager
tmarcoux@marshfieldnewsherald.com
Frequency:
7 time(s) per week

MARYLAND GAZETTE
306 CRAIN HIGHWAY SOUTH WEST
GLEN BURNIE, MD 21061
410-766-3700
Fax: 410-280-5953
gazletters@mdgazette.com
www.hometownglenburnie.com
• Sean Burns, Sports Editor
(410) 766-3700
Frequency:
2 time(s) per week

MARYLAND INDEPENDENT
7 INDUSTRIAL PARK DRIVE
WALDORF, MD 20602-2700

301-645-9480
Fax: 301-645-2175
www.maryland-independent.com
• Jason Jay, Sports Editor
(301) 645-9480
Frequency:
2 time(s) per week

MARYSVILLE JOURNAL-TRIBUNE
207 NORTH MAIN STREET
MARYSVILLE, OH 43040-1161
937-644-9111
Fax: 937-644-9211
www.marysivllejt.com
• Tim Miller, Sports Editor
tim@marysvillejt.com
• Marie Woodford, Advertising Manager
(937) 644-9111
mariew@marysvillejt.com
Frequency:
6 time(s) per week

MARYVILLE DAILY FORUM
111 EAST JENKINS STREET
MARYVILLE, MO 64468-2318
660-562-2424
888-660-2424
Fax: 660-562-2823
newsroom@asde.net
www.maryvilledailyforum.com
• Charlie Slenker, Sports Editor
Frequency:
5 time(s) per week

MATTOON JOURNAL GAZETTE
100 BROADWAY
MATTOON, IL 61938-4512
217-235-5656
800-627-0151
Fax: 217-235-1925
editorial@jg-tc.com
www.jg-tc.com
• Brian Nielsen, Sports Editor
(217) 238-6856
Frequency:
6 time(s) per week

MAUI NEWS
100 MAHALANI STREET
WAILUKU, HI 96793-2529
808-244-3981
800-827-0347
Fax: 808-242-9087
www.mauinews.com
• Dana McBratney, Sports Editor
sports@mauinews.com
• Dawne Miguel-Minford, Advertising Manager
(808) 242-6319
advmgr@mauinews.com
Frequency:
7 time(s) per week

MCALESTER NEWS-CAPITAL
500 SOUTH 2ND STREET
MCALESTER, OK 74502-5812
918-423-1700
Fax: 918-426-3081
editor@mcalesternews.com
www.mcalesternewscapital.com
• Jay Knight, Sports Writer
(918) 421-2025
• Charlotte Klutts, Advertising Manager
(918) 421-2006
Frequency:
6 time(s) per week

MCCOOK DAILY GAZETTE
P.O. BOX 1268
MCCOOK, NE 69001
308-345-4500
Fax: 308-345-7881
regionalnews@mccookgazette.com
www.mccookgazette.com
• Karry Coburn, Advertising Manager
(308) 345-4500
• Steve Kodad, Sports Editor
(308) 345-4500
sports@mccookgazette.com
Frequency:
6 time(s) per week

MCCURTAIN DAILY GAZETTE
107 SOUTH CENTRAL AVENUE
IDABEL, OK 74745-4847
580-286-3321
Fax: 580-286-2208
paper@mccurtain.com
www.mccurtain.com
• Marge Jones, Advertising Manager
• Brad Reesing, Sports Editor
(580) 286-3321
paper@mccurtain.com
Frequency:
5 time(s) per week

MCDOWELL NEWS
26 NORTH LOGAN STREET
MARION, NC 28752-3944
828-652-3313
Fax: 828-652-4769
news@mcdowellnews.com
www.mcdowellnews.com
• Keith Austin, Advertising Manager
(828) 652-3313
• Marty Queen, Sports Editor
sports@mcdowellnews.com
Frequency:
5 time(s) per week

MCKINNEY COURIER-GAZETTE
624 KRONA DRIVE
SUITE 170
PLANO, TX 75074
972-398-4200
Fax: 972-398-4470
www.courier-gazette.com
• Andrew May, Sports Editor
(972) 398-4246
Frequency:
6 time(s) per week

MCPHERSON SENTINEL
301 SOUTH MAIN STREET
MCPHERSON, KS 67460-4831
620-241-2422
Fax: 620-241-2425
www.mcphersonsentinel.com
• Chris Swick, Sports Editor
Frequency:
6 time(s) per week

MEADVILLE TRIBUNE
947 FEDERAL COURT
MEADVILLE, PA 16335-3234
814-724-6370
800-879-0006
Fax: 814-724-8755
tribune@meadvilletribune.com
www.meadvilletribune.com
• Dominick Dinardo, Sports Editor
(814) 724-6370

• Lon Wilson, Advertising Director
(814) 724-6370
Frequency:
7 time(s) per week

MEDFORD MAIL TRIBUNE
111 NORTH FIR STREET
MEDFORD, OR 97501-2772
541-776-4411
Fax: 541-776-4376
news@mailtribune.com
www.mailtribune.com
• Tim Trower, Sports Editor
(541) 776-4479
• Dena DeRose, Advertising Manager
(541) 776-4425
Frequency:
7 time(s) per week

MERCED SUN-STAR
P.O. BOX 739
MERCED, CA 95340-2108
209-722-1511
800-310-8080
Fax: 209-385-2460
www.mercedsun-star.com
• Samantha Yniguez, Advertising Director
(209) 385-2498
• James Tennapel, Sports Editor
(209) 385-2417
sports@mercedsun-star.com
Frequency:
7 time(s) per week

MERCURY
24 NORTH HANOVER STREET
POTTSTOWN, PA 19464-5410
610-323-3000
Fax: 610-323-0682
mercury@pottsmerc.com
www.pottsmerc.com
• Maryann Edlemann, Classified Manager
• Don Seeley, Sports Editor
(610) 323-3000
Frequency:
7 time(s) per week

MERIDIAN STAR
P.O. BOX 1591
MERIDIAN, MS 39301
601-693-1551
800-232-2525
Fax: 601-485-1275
publisher@themeridianstar.com
www.meridianstar.com
• Ricky Higginbotham, Sports Editor
(601) 693-1551
Frequency:
7 time(s) per week

MESQUITE NEWS
303 NORTH GALLOWAY STREET
MESQUITE, TX 75149
972-285-6301
Fax: 972-288-9383
www.mesquitenews.com
• Devin Hasson, Sports Editor
(972) 285-6301
Frequency:
1 time(s) per week

MESSENGER
PO BOX 659
FORT DODGE, IA 50501
800-622-6613
800-622-6613

Fax: 515-574-4529
editor@frontiernet.net
www.messengernews.net
• Eric Pratt, Sports Editor
(515) 574-4435
sports@messengernews.net
Frequency:
6 time(s) per week

METRO
30 SOUTH 15TH STREET 9TH FLOOR
PHILADELPHIA, PA 19102
215-717-2600
Fax: 215-717-2626
www.metropoint.com
• Christopher Baud, Sports Editor
Frequency:
5 time(s) per week

METROWEST DAILY NEWS
33 NEW YORK AVENUE
FRAMINGHAM, MA 01701-8805
508-626-3800
800-397-5852
Fax: 508-626-3900
metrowest@cnc.com
www.metrowestdailynews.com
• Art Davidson, Sports Editor
(508) 626-4403
artd@wickedlocal.com
• Mark Olivieri, Advertising Director
(508) 626-3925
molivier@cnc.com
Frequency:
7 time(s) per week

MEXICO LEDGER
300 NORTH WASHINGTON
MEXICO, MO 65265-2756
573-581-1111
Fax: 573-581-2029
news@mexicoledger.com
www.mexicoledger.com
• Jim Stanley, Sports Editor
ledgersports@socket.net
Frequency:
5 time(s) per week
Circulation:
6,125

MIAMI HERALD
1 HERALD PLAZA
MIAMI, FL 33132-1693
305-350-2111
800-437-2535
Fax: 305-376-5287
heralded@miamiherald.com
www.herald.com
• Kevin Baxter, Sports Reporter
(305) 376-3655
• Jason Cole, Sports Writer
(305) 376-3675
• Greg Cote, Sports Columnist
(305) 376-3492
gcote@herald.com
• Andre Fernandez, High School Sports Writer
(305) 350-2111
• Dan Lebatard, Sports Columnist
(305) 376-3498
• Jorge Rojas, Sports Editor
• Manny Navarro, Sports Writer
(305) 350-2111
• David Neal, Sports Reporter (Hockey)
(305) 376-3559
dneal@herald.com
• Santos Perez, Sports Writer

(305) 350-2111
• Mike Phillips, Sports Reporter
(305) 350-2111
• Edwin Pope, Sports Columnist
(305) 376-3483
• Linda Robertson, Sports Columnist
lrobertson@herald.com
• Gorge Rojas, Sports Editor
• Armando Salguero, Sports Reporter
(305) 376-3675
• Jeff Shain, Sports Writer
(305) 376-3500
• Clark Spencer, Sports Reporter
(305) 376-3603
• Judy Stapleton, Sports News Assistant
Frequency:
7 time(s) per week

MICHIGAN CHRONICLE
479 LEDYARD STREET
DETROIT, MI 48201
313-963-5522
800-203-2229
Fax: 313-963-8788
chronicle4@aol.com
www.michronicleonline.com
• Terry Cabell, Sports Writer
(313) 963-5522
Frequency:
1 time(s) per week

MIDDLEBORO GAZETTE
148 WEST GROVE STREET
MIDDLEBORO, MA 02346-1457
508-947-1760
Fax: 508-947-9426
editor@gazettenewsonline.com
• Jon Haglof, Sports Editor
(508) 947-1760
sports@gazettenewsonline.com
Frequency:
1 time(s) per week

MIDDLESBORO DAILY NEWS
P.O. BOX 579
MIDDLESBORO, KY 40965-1024
606-248-1010
Fax: 606-248-7614
www.middlesborodailynews.com
• Patricia Cheek, Advertising Manager
• Jay Compton, Sports Editor
(606) 248-1010
Frequency:
6 time(s) per week

MIDDLETOWN JOURNAL
PO BOX 490
MIDDLETOWN, OH 45044-4031
513-705-2525
Fax: 513-423-6940
www.middletown.com
• John Bombatch, Sports Writer
(512) 705-2851
jbombatch@coxohio.com
• Jake Trotter, Sports Editor
(513) 705-2837
jtrotter@coxohio.com
Frequency:
7 time(s) per week

MIDDLETOWN PRESS
2 MAIN ST
MIDDLETOWN, CT 06457
860-347-3331
Fax: 860-347-3380

editor@middletown.com
www.middletownpress.com
• Erika Heyer, Assistant Sports Editor
(860) 347-3331
• Robert Briere, Advertising Director
(860) 347-3331

MIDLAND REPORTER-TELEGRAM
201 EAST ILLINOIS AVENUE
MIDLAND, TX 79701-4852
432-682-5311
800-542-3952
Fax: 432-682-3793
www.mywesttexas.com
• Chuck Evers, Advertising Director
(432) 682-5311
• Len Hayward, Sports Editor
(432) 682-5311
Frequency:
7 time(s) per week

MILFORD DAILY NEWS
COMMUNITY NEWSPAPER COMPANY
MILFORD, MA 01757-3255
508-473-1111
Fax: 508-634-7514
www.milforddailynews.com/
• Art Davidson, Sports Editor
(508) 626-4403
Frequency:
7 time(s) per week

MILWAUKEE JOURNAL SENTINEL
P.O. BOX 661
MILWAUKEE, WI 53203-1309
414-224-2000
800-456-5943
Fax: 414-224-2047
jsbiz@journalsentinel.com
www.jsonline.com
• Lori Nickel, Sports Writer
(414) 224-2310
lnickel@journalsentinel.com
• Louisa Rosenau, Sports Assistant Editor
lrosenau@journalsentinel.com
• Tom Silverstein, Sports Reporter
tsilverstein@journalsentinel.com
• Don Walker, Sports Reporter
dwalker@journalsentinel.com
• Bill Windler, Senior Sports Editor
(414) 224-2173
bwindler@journalsentinel.com
• Bob Wolfley, Sports Columnist
(414) 223-5531
bwolfley@journalsentinel.com
• Dennis Black, Assistant Sports Editor
(414) 224-2342
Frequency:
7 time(s) per week

MINDEN PRESS-HERALD
P.O. BOX 1339
MINDEN, LA 71055-3455
318-377-1866
Fax: 318-377-1895
www.press-herald.com
• Gregg Parks, Sports Editor
(318) 377-1866
gparks@press-herald.com
Frequency:
5 time(s) per week

MINERAL WELLS INDEX
P.O. BOX 370
MINERAL WELLS, TX 76067-5331

940-325-4465
Fax: 940-325-2020
editor@mineralwellsindex.com
www.mineralwellsindex.com
• Craig Holamon, Sports Editor
• Ric Holly, Advertising Director
Frequency:
5 time(s) per week

MINIONDAS
2025 S. MAIN STREET
SANTA ANA, CA 92707-1836
714-668-1010
Fax: 714-668-1013
miniondas@miniondas.com
www.miniondas.com
• Patricia Garcia, Sports Editor
(714) 668-1010
miniondas@miniondas.com
Frequency:
1 time(s) per week

MINNEAPOLIS STAR TRIBUNE
425 PORTLAND AVENUE S
MINNEAPOLIS, MN 55488
612-673-4000
800-827-8742
Fax: 612-673-7774
www.startribune.com
• Dennis Anderson, Sports Editor
(612) 673-4424
danderson@startribune.com

MINOT DAILY NEWS
301 4TH STREET, S.E.
MINOT, ND 58702
701-857-1900
800-735-3119
Fax: 701-857-1907
news@minotdailynews.com
www.minotdailynews.com
• Chris Bieri, Sports Editor
(701) 857-1935
Frequency:
7 time(s) per week

MINUTEMAN-WESTPORT
877 POST ROAD EAST
WESTPORT, CT 06880-5224
203-752-2711
Fax: 203-789-5309
www.westportminuteman.com
• Eric Montgomery, Sports Editor
(203) 789-5761
sports@westportminuteman.com
Frequency:
1 time(s) per week

MISSISSIPPI PRESS
P.O. BOX 849
PASCAGOULA, MS 39567-4136
228-762-1111
800-655-6597
Fax: 228-934-1454
www.gulflive.com/mississippipress/
• J.R. Wittner, Sports Editor
(228) 934-1426
Frequency:
7 time(s) per week

MISSOULIAN
500 SOUTH HIGGINS AVENUE
MISSOULA, MT 59801-2736
406-523-5200
800-366-7102
Fax: 406-523-5294

newsdesk@missoulian.com
www.missoulian.com
• Bob Meseroll, Sports Editor
(406) 523-5265
Frequency:
7 time(s) per week

MOBERLY MONITOR-INDEX & DEMOCRAT
218 NORTH WILLIAMS
MOBERLY, MO 65270-1534
660-263-4123
Fax: 660-263-3626
www.moberlymonitor.com
• Chuck Embree, Sports Editor
• Marsha Hargus, Advertising Manager
Frequency:
6 time(s) per week

MODESTO BEE
1325 H STREET
MODESTO, CA 95354
209-578-2330
Fax: 209-578-2207
www.modbee.com
• Ron Agostini, Sports Columnist
(209) 578-2300
• Will Deboard, Sports Columnist
(209) 578-2300
• Joel Hood, Sports Columnist
(209) 238-4574
• Kelly Jones, Sports Writer
(209) 578-2330
• Joe Silva, Sports Columnist
(209) 578-2301
jsilva@modbee.com
• Noel Harris, Assistant Sports Editor
(209) 578-2330
Frequency:
7 time(s) per week

MOHAVE VALLEY DAILY NEWS
2435 MIRACLE MILE
BULLHEAD CITY, AZ 86442
928-763-2505
Fax: 928-763-7820
www.mohavedailynews.com
• Paul Click, Sports Editor
(928) 763-2505
• Jackie Walker, Advertising Manager
(928) 763-2505
Frequency:
6 time(s) per week

MONETT TIMES
505 EAST BROADWAY
MONETT, MO 65708-2333
417-235-3135
Fax: 417-235-8852
www.monett-times.com
• Charles Brady, Sports Editor
sports@monett-times.com
• Robyn Blankenship, Advertising/Marketing Manager
Frequency:
5 time(s) per week

MONITOR
P.O. BOX 3267
MCALLEN, TX 78502
956-683-4000
800-366-4343
Fax: 956-683-4401
news@themonitor.com
www.themonitor.com

• Oscar Gonzalez, Sports Editor
(956) 683-4443
• Brian Sales, Advertising Director
(956) 683-4141
Frequency:
7 time(s) per week

MONROE EVENING NEWS
20 WEST 1ST STREET
MONROE, MI 48161-2333
734-242-1100
Fax: 734-242-3175
www.monroenews.com
• Niles Kruger, Sports Editor
• Jeff Meade, Sports Editor
(734) 240-5783
sports@monroenews.com
• Ron Montri, Sports Editor
(734) 240-5780
Frequency:
7 time(s) per week

MONROE TIMES
1065 4TH AVENUE WEST
MONROE, WI 53566-1318
608-328-4202
800-236-2240
Fax: 608-328-4217
newsclerk@themonroetimes.com
www.themonroetimes.com
• Matt Johnson, Publisher
(608) 328-4202
mpj46@yahoo.com
• Mark Newbitt, Sports Writer
(608) 328-4202
Frequency:
6 time(s) per week

MONTANA STANDARD
25 WEST GRANITE STREET
BUTTE, MT 59701-9213
406-496-5500
800-877-1074
Fax: 406-496-5551
editor@mtstandard.com
www.mtstandard.com
• Bruce Sayler, Sports Editor
(406) 496-5544
• Pat Ryan, Sports Reporter
(406) 496-5544
Frequency:
7 time(s) per week

MONTGOMERY ADVERTISER
425 MOLTON STREET
MONTGOMERY, AL 36104-4250
334-262-1611
Fax: 334-261-1520
www.montgomeryadvertiser.com
• Ron Davidson, Advertising Director
(334) 261-1571
• Brad Zimanek, Sports Editor
(334) 261-1586
bzimanek@gannett.com
Frequency:
7 time(s) per week

MORNING CALL
101 NORTH 6TH STREET
ALLENTOWN, PA 18101
610-820-6500
Fax: 610-820-6693
news@mcall.com
www.mcall.com
• Keith Groller, Senior Sports Reporter
(610) 820-6740

keith.groller@mcall.com
• Ernie Long, Sports Editor
(610) 820-6772
• Stephen Miller, Sports Reporter
(610) 820-6750
• Jeff Schuler, Sports Reporter
(610) 820-6781
• Andre Williams, Sports Reporter
(610) 820-6529
• Mark Wogenrich, Sports Reporter
(610) 820-6588
mark.wogenrich@mcall.com
Frequency:
7 time(s) per week

MORNING HERALD
100 SUMMIT AVENUE
HAGERSTOWN, MD 21740
301-733-5131
Fax: 301-714-0245
news@herald-mail.com
www.herald-mail.com
• Mark Keller, Sports Editor
mkeller@herald-mail.com
Frequency:
7 time(s) per week

MORNING JOURNAL
1657 BROADWAY
LORAIN, OH 44052-3439
440-245-6901
800-765-6901
Fax: 440-245-6912
news@morningjournal.com
www.morningjournal.com
• Ron Beal, Advertising Manager
(440) 245-6901
advertising@morningjournal.com
• Colin Wilson, Sports Editor
(440) 245-6901
Frequency:
7 time(s) per week

MORNING NEWS (ID)
34 NORTH ASH STREET
BLACKFOOT, ID 83221
208-785-1100
Fax: 208-785-4239
www.am-news.com
• Mark High, Sports Editor
(208) 785-1100
Frequency:
6 time(s) per week

MORNING NEWS (SC)
P.O. BOX 100528
FLORENCE, SC 29501
843-317-6397
Fax: 843-317-7292
www.morningnewsonline.com
• Sam Bundy, Sports Editor
(843) 317-7274
• Charlie Price, Advertising Manager
(843) 317-7232
• Justin Driggers, Sports Writer
(843) 317-7262
jdriggers@florencenews.com
Frequency:
7 time(s) per week

MORNING STAR
1003 S. 17TH ST
WILMINGTON, NC 28401
910-343-2000
Fax: 910-343-2227
www.wilmingtonstar.com

• Dan Spears, Sports Editor
dan.spears@starnewsonline.com

MORNING SUN (KS)
P.O. BOX H
PITTSBURG, KS 66762-4038
620-231-2600
800-794-6536
Fax: 620-231-0645
www.morningsun.net
• Cindy Clingan, Advertising Manager
(620) 231-2600
• Brock Sisney, Sports Editor
(620) 231-2600
• Jim Henry, Sports Reporter
(260) 231-2600
Frequency:
7 time(s) per week

MORNING SUN (MI)
711 W PICKARD STREET
MOUNT PLEASANT, MI 48858-1585
989-779-6000
800-616-6397
Fax: 989-779-6051
news@michigannewspapers.com
www.themorningsun.com/
• Jim Lahde, Sports Editor
(989) 779-6061
jlahde@michigannewspapers.com
Frequency:
6 time(s) per week

MORRIS DAILY HERALD
1804 NORTH DIVISION STREET
MORRIS, IL 60450-0749
815-942-3221
Fax: 815-942-0988
news@morrisdailyherald.com
www.morrisdailyherald.com/
• Richard Ponulak, Advertising Manager
(815) 942-3221
• Tim Smith, Sports Editor
(815) 942-3221
tsmith@morrisdailyherald.com
Frequency:
5 time(s) per week
Description:
Community Newspaper

MOSCOW-PULLMAN DAILY NEWS
409 SOUTH JACKSON STREET
MOSCOW, ID 83843
208-882-5561
800-776-4137
Fax: 208-883-8205
briefs@dnews.com
www.dnews.com
• Sandra Kelly, Sports Editor
(208) 882-5561
• Craig Staszkow, Advertising Manager
(208) 882-5561
cstaszkow@dnews.com
• Andrew Nemec, Sports Editor
(208) 882-5561
Frequency:
6 time(s) per week

MOULTRIE OBSERVER
25 NORTH MAIN STREET
MOULTRIE, GA 31768-3861
229-985-4545
Fax: 229-985-3569
www.moultrieobserver.com
• Wayne Grandy, Sports Editor
(229) 985-4545

Frequency:
6 time(s) per week

MOUNT AIRY NEWS
319 N RENFRO STREET
MOUNT AIRY, NC 27030
336-786-4141
Fax: 336-789-2816
www.mtairynews.com
• Thomas Smith, Sports Editor
(336) 719-1920
• Beth Mechum, Sports Editor
(336) 719-1921
Frequency:
7 time(s) per week
Primary Audience:
Mount Airy, Surry County

MOUNT PLEASANT DAILY TRIBUNE
P.O. BOX 1177
MOUNT PLEASANT, TX 75456
903-572-1705
Fax: 903-572-6026
www.dailytribune.net
• Amy Hinton, Advertising Manager
(903) 572-1705
• John Whitten, Sports Editor
(903) 572-1705
Frequency:
6 time(s) per week

MOUNT PLEASANT NEWS
215 WEST MONROE STREET
MOUNT PLEASANT, IA 52641
319-986-5186
Fax: 319-385-8048
pub@mpnews.net
www.mpnews.net
• Billie Allender, Advertising Manager
adv@mpnews.net
• Joe Birkestrand, Sports Editor
Frequency:
5 time(s) per week

MOUNTAIN DEMOCRAT
P.O. BOX 1088
PLACERVILLE, CA 95667-5902
530-622-1255
Fax: 530-622-7894
mtdemo@mtdemocrat.net
www.mtdemocrat.com
• Jerry Heinzer, Sports Writer
• Liz Kane, Sports Editor
(530) 344-5079
• Ian Balentine, Advertising Manager
(530) 344-5048
ibalentine@mtdemocrat.net
Frequency:
4 time(s) per week

MOUNTAIN MAIL
P.O. BOX 189
SALIDA, CO 81201
830-539-6691
888-539-1880
Fax: 719-539-6630
mtnmail@chaffe.net
www.themountainmail.com
• Randa Bess, Classified Manager
(719) 539-6691
• Denise Ronald, Sports Writer
(830) 539-6691
• Vickie Vigil, Advertising Director
Frequency:
5 time(s) per week

MOUNTAIN PRESS
P.O. BOX 4810
SEVIERVILLE, TN 37876-1943
865-428-0746
Fax: 865-453-4913
editor@themountainpress.com
www.themountainpress.com
• Jason Davis, Sports Editor
(865) 428-0748
Frequency:
7 time(s) per week

MUNDO HISPANICO
1927 PIEDMONT CIRCLE SUITE B
ATLANTA, GA 30324-4820
404-881-0441
Fax: 404-881-6085
editorial@mundohispanico.com
www.mundohispanico.com
• Marta Garcia, Sports Editor
(404) 881-0441
Frequency:
1 time(s) per week

MURRAY LEDGER AND TIMES
1001 WHITNELL STREET
MURRAY, KY 42071
270-753-1916
Fax: 270-753-1927
mlt@murrayledger.com
www.murrayledger.com
• Tommy Dillard, Sports Editor
(270) 753-1916
sports@murrayledger.com
Frequency:
6 time(s) per week

MUSKEGON CHRONICLE
981 3RD STREET
MUSKEGON, MI 49443
231-722-3161
Fax: 231-728-3330
www.muskegonchronicle.com
• Tom Kendra, Sports Editor
(231) 725-6363
• Kevin Newton, Advertising Director
(231) 725-6311
Frequency:
7 time(s) per week

NAPA VALLEY REGISTER
1615 SECOND STREET
NAPA, CA 94559
707-226-3711
Fax: 707-224-3963
www.napanews.com
• Marty James, Sports Editor
(707) 256-2223
• Norma Kostecka, Advertising Director
(707) 226-3711
Frequency:
7 time(s) per week

NAPERVILLE SUN
495 N COMMONS DRIVE
SUITE 200
AURORA, IL 60504
630-978-8880
Fax: 630-416-5163
www.napersun.com
• Joni Blackman, Sports Writer
(630) 416-6728
jonihb@aol.com
• R.J. Gerber, Sports Editor
(630) 978-8175

Frequency:
3 time(s) per week

NAPLES DAILY NEWS
1075 CENTRAL AVENUE
NAPLES, FL 34102
239-263-3161
888-262-3161
Fax: 239-263-4816
www.naplesnews.com
• Sis Berube, Classified Manager
(239) 263-4718
• Greg Hardwig, Sports Editor
(239) 263-4767
gshardwig@naplesnews.com
• Bob Sandy, Advertising Sales Director
(239) 435-3433
rhsandy@naplesnews.com
Frequency:
7 time(s) per week

NATCHEZ DEMOCRAT
503 NORTH CANAL STREET
NATCHEZ, MS 39120-2902
601-442-9101
Fax: 601-442-7315
newsroom@natchezdemocrat.com
www.natchezdemocrat.com
• Adam Daigle, Sports Editor
(601) 445-3632
Frequency:
7 time(s) per week

NATCHITOCHES TIMES
PO BOX 448
NATCHITOCHES, LA 71458
318-352-3618
Fax: 318-352-7842
www.natchitochestimes.com
• Al Guidry, Sports Editor
(318) 352-3618
• Charles Norman, Advertising Manager
(318) 352-3618
advertising@natchitochestimes.com
Frequency:
5 time(s) per week

NEBRASKA CITY NEWS-PRESS
823 CENTRAL AVENUE
NEBRASKA CITY, NE 68410-2409
402-873-3334
Fax: 402-873-5436
www.ncnewspress.com
• Kathy Kaufman, Advertising Manager
(402) 873-3334
• Kirt Manion, Sports Editor
(402) 873-3334
kmanion@ncnewspress.com
Frequency:
5 time(s) per week

NEIGHBORS
1405 BROADWAY
SCOTTSBLUFF, NE 69361-3151
308-632-9000
800-846-6102
Fax: 308-632-9001
news@starherald.com
www.starherald.com
• Jeff Fielder, Sports Editor
(308) 632-9050
sports@starherald.com
Frequency:
1 time(s) per week

NEVADA APPEAL
PO BOX 2288
CARSON CITY, NV 89701
775-882-2111
800-221-8013
Fax: 775-887-2420
www.nevadaappeal.com/
• Darrell Moody, Sports Reporter
(775) 881-1281
• Gloria Thomas, Advertising Director
(775) 881-1262
Frequency:
7 time(s) per week

NEVADA DAILY MAIL AND SUNDAY HERALD
131 SOUTH CEDAR STREET
NEVADA, MO 64772-3309
417-667-3344
Fax: 417-667-7475
editorial@nevadadailymail.com
www.nevadadailymail.com
• Kari Vincent, Advertising Manager
composing@nevadadailymail.com
• Eric Wade, Sports Writer
ewade@nevadadailymail.com
Frequency:
5 time(s) per week

NEW CASTLE NEWS
27 MERCER STREET
NEW CASTLE, PA 16101
724-654-6651
Fax: 724-654-5976
www.ncnewsonline.com
• Kayleen Cubbal, Sports Editor
(724) 654-6651
• Ed Gaydos, Advertising Manager
(724) 654-6651
advertising@ncnewsonline.com
• Ron Poniewasz, Sports Writer
(724) 654-6651
rponiewasz@ncnewsonline.com
Frequency:
6 time(s) per week

NEW HAVEN REGISTER
40 SARGENT DRIVE
NEW HAVEN, CT 06511-6111
203-789-5200
800-925-2472
Fax: 203-865-7894
business@nhregister.com
www.newhavenregister.com
• Sean Barker, Sports Editor
(203) 789-5700
sbarker@nhregister.com
Frequency:
7 time(s) per week

NEW JERSEY HERALD
P.O. BOX 10
NEWTON, NJ 07860
973-383-1500
Fax: 973-383-8477
newsroom@njherald.com
www.njherald.com
• Jim Dente, Sports Editor
(973) 383-1253
• Mitch Mayer, Advertising Manager
(973) 383-1010
mmayer@njherald.com
• James Conrad, Sports Writer
(973) 383-1250
jconrad@njherald.com
Frequency:
6 time(s) per week

NEW MEXICAN
202 EAST MARCY STREET
SANTA FE, NM 87501-2021
505-983-3303
800-873-3362
Fax: 505-986-9147
newsroom@sfnewmexican.com
www.santafenewmexican.com
• Laura Harding, Classified Manager
(505) 986-3009
lharding@sfnewmexican.com
• Pancho Morris, Sports Writer
(505) 986-3045
• Virginia Sohn, Advertising Director
(505) 986-3006
ginny@sfnewmexican.com
• Tommy Trujillo, Sports Editor
(505) 986-3060
Frequency:
7 time(s) per week

NEW YORK DAILY CHALLENGE
1195 ATLANTIC AVENUE
BROOKLYN, NY 11216-2600
718-636-9500
Fax: 718-857-9115
challengegroup@yahoo.com
www.challenge-group.com
• Kyle Bostic, Sports Editor
Frequency:
5 time(s) per week

NEW YORK DAILY NEWS
450 WEST 33RD STREET
NEW YORK, NY 10001
212-210-2100
Fax: 212-643-7831
news@edit.nydailynews.com
www.nydailynews.com
• Leon Carter, Sports Editor
(212) 210-2348

NEW YORK POST
1211 AVENUE OF THE AMERICAS
NEW YORK, NY 10036-8790
212-930-8271
Fax: 212-930-8540
letters@nypost.com
www.nypost.com
• Larry Brooks, Sports Writer
(212) 930-8000
larry.brooks@nypost.com
• Mark Cannizzaro, Sports Reporter
mcannizzaro@nypost.com
• Dave Curtis, Sports Reporter
(212) 930-8280
• Mark Everson, Sports Writer
(212) 930-8000
• Ed Fountaine, Sports Reporter
• Greg Gallo, Sports Executive Editor
(212) 930-8700
sports@nypost.com
• Jay Greenberg, Sports Reporter
jgreenberg@nypost.com
• Mark Hale, Sports Reporter
mark.hale@nypost.com
• Fred Kerber, Sports Writer
(212) 930-8700
Fred.Kerber@nypost.com
• Kevin Kernan, Sports Reporter
kevin.kernan@nypost.com
• George King, Sports Reporter
(212) 930-8700
george.king@nypost.com
• Brian Lewis, Sports Reporter
(212) 930-8700
brian.lewis@nypost.com

• Dan Martin, Sports Reporter
(212) 930-8700
dan.martin@nypost.com
• Ken Moran, Sports Columnist
(212) 930-8700
sports@nypost.com
• Phil Mushnick, Sports Columnist
(212) 930-8271
phil.mushnick@nypost.com
• Paul Schwartz, Sports Reporter
(212) 930-8700
paul.schwartz@nypost.com
• Joel Sherman, Sports Writer
(212) 930-8700
sports@nypost.com
• Andy Soltis, Sports Reporter
• Anthony Stabile, Sports Reporter
• Mike Vaccaro, Sports Columnist
(212) 930-8700
sports@nypost.com
• Peter Vecsey, Sports Columnist
• George Willis, Sports Columnist
(212) 930-8700
sports@nypost.com
Frequency:
7 time(s) per week

NEW YORK SUN
105 CHAMBERS STREET
NEW YORK, NY 10007-1093
212-406-2000
Fax: 212-608-7348
newsdesk@nysun.com
www.nysun.com
• Jonathan Mahler, Sports Columnist
• Wallace Matthews, Sports Writer
(212) 901-2681
• Paul Gardner, Sports Reporter
(212) 406-2000
Frequency:
5 time(s) per week

NEW YORK TIMES
620 EIGHTH AVENUE
NEW YORK, NY 10036-3959
212-556-1234
Fax: 212-556-3815
letters@nytimes.com
www.nytimes.com
• Dave Anderson, Sports Columnist
(212) 556-7371
sports@nytimes.com
• Judy Battista, Sports Reporter
sports@nytimes.com
• Howard Beck, Sports Reporter
• John Branch, Sports Columnist
• Clifton Brown, Sports Reporter
(212) 556-7371
sports@nytimes.com
• Dave Caldwell, Sports Reporter
(212) 556-7371
• Murray Chass, Sports Columnist
(212) 556-7371
• Christopher Clarey, Sports Reporter
• Karen Crouse, Sports Reporter
sports@nytimes.com
• Larry Dorman, Sports Reporter
sports@nytimes.com
• Joe Drape, Sports Reporter
(212) 556-7371
drape@nytimes.com
• Stuart Elliott, Advertising Columnist
(212) 556-1234
• Gerald Eskenazi, Sports Reporter
(212) 556-7450
• Ray Glier, Sports Writer
(212) 556-7371
sports@nytimes.com

• Damon Hack, Sports Reporter
(212) 556-7371
• Tyler Kepner, Sports Writer
(212) 556-7371
kepner@nytimes.com
• Jeff Klein, Sports Reporter
• Tom Jolly, Sports Editor
sports@nytimes.com
• Sandy Keenan, Deputy Sports Editor
• Brandon Lilly, Sports Writer
(212) 556-7371
sports@nytimes.com
• Frank Litsky, Sports Reporter
(212) 556-7371
sports@nytimes.com
• Jere Longman, Sports Reporter
(212) 556-7371
sports@nytimes.com
• Juliet Macur, Sports Reporter
(212) 556-7371
macur@nytimes.com
• Carl Nelson,
(212) 556-3647
• Bill Pennington, (212) 556-7371
Sports Reporter
sports@nytimes.com
• Steve Popper, Sports Writer
(212) 556-7371
sports@nytimes.com
• William C. Rhoden, Sports Columnist
• Liz Robbins, Sports Writer
(212) 556-7371
sports@nytimes.com
• Ben Shpigel, Yankees Reporter
• Richard Sandomir, Sports Reporter
sandomir@nytimes.com
Frequency:
7 time(s) per week

NEWNAN TIMES-HERALD
16 JEFFERSON STREET
NEWNAN, GA 30263
770-253-1576
news@newnan.com
times-herald.com
• Doug Gorman, Sports Editor
(770) 683-1781
• Jeff Armstrong, Sports Writer
• Katie Atwood, Multimedia Sales Specialist
(770) 683-1747
Frequency:
7 time(s) per week

NEWPORT BEACH COSTA MESA DAILY PILOT
330 WEST BAY STREET
COSTA MESA, CA 92627
714-966-4600
Fax: 714-966-4667
dailypilot@latimes.com
www.dailypilot.com
• Barry Faulkner, Sports Writer
barry.faulkner@latimes.com
• James Lee, Sports Editor
(714) 966-4616
james.lee@latimes.com
Frequency:
6 time(s) per week

NEWPORT DAILY EXPRESS
P.O. BOX 347
NEWPORT, VT 05855
802-334-6568
Fax: 802-334-6891
www.newportvermontdailyexpress.com
• Ken Wells, Sports Editor
(802) 334-6568
• Ellen Howell, Advertising Manager

Frequency:
5 time(s) per week

NEWPORT DAILY NEWS
101 MALBONE ROAD
NEWPORT, RI 02840-1340
401-849-3300
Fax: 401-849-3306
editor@newportri.com
www.newportdailynews.com
• Scott Barrett, Sports Editor
(401) 849-3300
sports@newportri.com
• Rick McGowan, Sports Reporter
(401) 849-3300
Frequency:
6 time(s) per week

NEWPORT INDEPENDENT
2408 HIGHWAY 67 NORTH
NEWPORT, AR 72112-2324
870-523-5855
800-439-8466
Fax: 870-523-6540
news@newportindependent.com
www.newportindependent.com
• Ken Duvall, Sports Editor
Frequency:
5 time(s) per week

NEWPORT PLAIN TALK
145 EAST BROADWAY
NEWPORT, TN 37822
423-623-6171
Fax: 423-625-1995
info@newportplaintalk.com
www.newportplaintalk.com
• Paul Meador, Sports Editor
(423) 623-6171
Frequency:
5 time(s) per week

NEWS & ADVANCE
101 WYNDALE DRIVE
LYNCHBURG, VA 24501
434-385-5555
800-275-8831
Fax: 434-385-5538
www.newsadvance.com
• Chris Morris, Sports Editor
(434) 385-5528
• Joy Monopli, Advertising Director

NEWS & OBSERVER
P.O. BOX 191
RALEIGH, NC 27601-1331
919-829-4500
800-365-6115
Fax: 919-836-2840
forum@newsobserver.com
www.newsobserver.com
• Gary Schwab, Senior Sports Editor
(919) 829-4552
• Lorenzo Perez, Assistant Sports Editor
(919) 829-4643
• Tim Stevens, Sports Reporter
(919) 829-8910
• Caulton Tudor, Sports Columnist
(919) 829-8946
Frequency:
7 time(s) per week

NEWS & RECORD
P.O. BOX 20848
GREENSBORO, NC 27420

336-373-7000
800-553-6880
Fax: 336-373-7382
www.news-record.com
• Tony Martinette, Advertising Director

NEWS CHIEF
300 WEST LIME STREET
PO BOX 408
LAKELAND, FL 33802
863-802-7508
Fax: 863-802-7577
news@newschief.com
www.newschief.com
• Eroca Filmore, Advertising Director
(863) 421-5504
• Matt Cote, Sports Reporter
Frequency:
7 time(s) per week

NEWS DAILY
P.O. BOX 368
JONESBORO, GA 30236-3514
770-478-5753
Fax: 770-954-0282
www.news-daily.com
• Doug Gorman, Sports Editor
(770) 478-5753
Frequency:
7 time(s) per week

NEWS DEMOCRAT JOURNAL
1405 NORTH TRUMAN
FESTUS, MO 63028
636-931-6636
800-931-6636
Fax: 636-931-2638
sitehelp@stltoday.com
www.stltoday.com
• Don Reed, Sports Editor
dreed@post-dispatch.com
Frequency:
2 time(s) per week

NEWS HERALD
P.O. BOX 1940
PANAMA CITY, FL 32401-2330
850-747-5000
Fax: 850-747-5097
news@pcnh.com
www.newsherald.com
• Pat McCann, Sports Executive Editor
(850) 747-5068
pmccann@pcnh.com
Frequency:
7 time(s) per week

NEWS JOURNAL (DE)
950 WEST BASIN ROAD
NEW CASTLE, DE 19720
302-324-2500
800-235-9100
Fax: 302-324-5509
www.delawareonline.com
• Betty An Dobek, Classified Manager
(302) 324-2932
bdobek@delewareonline.com
• Martin Frank, Sports Reporter
(302) 324-2500
mfrank@delawareonline.com
• Ron Fritz, Sports Editor
(302) 324-2919
rfritz@delawareonline.com
• Buddy Hurlock, Sports Reporter
• Jack Ireland, Sports Reporter
(302) 324-2808

jireland@delawareonline.com
• Doug Lesmerises, Sports Reporter
(302) 324-2500
• Kristian Pope, Sports Writer
(302) 734-7946
• Kevin Tresolini, Sports Reporter
(302) 324-2807
ktresolini@delawareonline.com
Frequency:
7 time(s) per week

NEWS JOURNAL (OH)
70 WEST 4TH STREET
MANSFIELD, OH 44903-1676
419-522-3311
800-472-5547
Fax: 419-521-7415
www.mansfieldnewsjournal.com
• Rob McCurdy, Sports Reporter
(419) 521-7241
rmccurdy@gannett.com
• Scott Miller, Advertising Manager
(419) 521-7329
• Jon Spencer, Sports Columnist
(419) 521-7239
jspencer@gannett.com
Frequency:
7 time(s) per week

NEWS LEADER
P. O. BOX 59
STAUNTON, VA 24402
540-885-7281
800-793-2459
Fax: 540-885-1904
news@newsleader.com
www.newsleader.com
• Hubert Grim, III, Sports Editor
(540) 213-9131
hgrimiii@newsleader.com
• Jim McCloskey, Advertising Manager
(540) 213-9144
Frequency:
7 time(s) per week

NEWS PRESS
211 W. 9TH ST
STILLWATER, OK 74074
405-372-5000 EXT 201
800-364-5000
Fax: 405-372-3112
editor@stwnewspress.com
www.stwnewspress.com
• Roger Moore, Sports Editor
sports@stwnewspress.com

NEWS SUN
2383 NORTH DELANY ROAD
WAUKEGAN, IL 60087
847-336-7000
Fax: 847-249-7202
www.suburbanchicagonews.com
• Jeff Bonato, Sports Editor
(847) 249-7231
• Darren Day, Sports Writer
(847) 249-7244
• Bob Ulmer, Advertising Director
(847) 249-7210
Frequency:
6 time(s) per week

NEWS TRIBUNE
1950 SOUTH STATE STREET
TACOMA, WA 98405-2817
253-597-8742
800-388-8742

Fax: 253-597-8274
newstips@thenewstribune.com
www.thenewstribune.com
• Darrin Beene, Sports Writer
(253) 597-8656
• Dave Boling, Sports Columnist
(253) 597-8440
• Larry LaRue, Sports Reporter
(253) 597-7000
• John McGrath, Sports Columnist
(253) 552-7000
• Todd Milles, Sports Reporter
(253) 597-8442
• Don Ruiz, Sports Columnist
(253) 597-8808
Frequency:
7 time(s) per week

NEWS-BANNER
125 NORTH JOHNSON STREET
BLUFFTON, IN 46714-1907
260-824-0224
Fax: 260-824-0700
www.news-banner.com
• Paul Beitler, Sports Editor
(260) 824-0224
• Jean Bordner, Advertising Manager
Frequency:
6 time(s) per week

NEWS-COURIER
P.O. BOX 670
ATHENS, AL 35612
256-232-2720
800-844-5480
Fax: 256-233-7753
www.enewscourier.com
• Ashley Hargrove, Sports Editor
(256) 232-2720
Frequency:
5 time(s) per week

NEWS-DISPATCH
121 WEST MICHIGAN BOULEVARD
MICHIGAN CITY, IN 46360-3274
219-874-7211
800-489-9292
Fax: 219-872-8511
news@thenewsdispatch.com
www.thenewsdispatch.com/
• Isis Cains, Advertising Manager
(219) 874-7211
icains@thenewsdispatch.com
• Adam Parkhouse, Sports Editor
(219) 874-7211
aparkhouse@thenewsdispatch.com
• Drew White, Sports Writer
(219) 874-7211
Frequency:
7 time(s) per week

NEWS-ENTERPRISE
408 WEST DIXIE AVENUE
ELIZABETHTOWN, KY 42701-2433
270-769-1200
Fax: 270-765-7318
ne@thenewsenterprise.com
www.thenewsenterprise.com
• Chuck Jones, Sports Editor
(270) 769-1200
cjones@thenewsenterprise.com
• Josh Claywell, Sports Writer
(270) 769-1200
Frequency:
6 time(s) per week

NEWS-GAZETTE
15 MAIN STREET
CHAMPAIGN, IL 61820-3625
217-351-5252
Fax: 217-351-5291
www.news-gazette.com
• Jim Rossow, Sports Editor
Frequency:
7 time(s) per week

NEWS-HERALD (PORT CLINTON)
PO BOX 550
PORT CLINTON, OH 43452-1012
419-734-3141
800-636-6906
Fax: 419-734-1850
www.portclintonnewsherald.com/apps/pbcs.
dll/frontpage
• David Barth, Advertising Manager
(419) 734-7501
• Josh Chapin, Sports Editor
jchapin@fremont.gannett.com
• Aaron Smith, Sports Editor
(419) 734-3141
Frequency:
6 time(s) per week

NEWS-HERALD (WILLOUGHBY)
7085 MENTOR AVENUE
WILLOUGHBY, OH 44094-7932
440-951-0000
800-947-2737
Fax: 440-975-2836
editor@news-herald.com
www.news-herald.com
• Scott Kendrick, Sports Editor
(440) 951-0000
sports@news-herald.com
Frequency:
7 time(s) per week

NEWS-ITEM
707 NORTH ROCK STREET
SHAMOKIN, PA 17872-4930
570-644-6397
Fax: 570-648-7581
nieditor@ptd.net
www.newsitem.com
• Jennifer Crone, Classified Manager
(570) 644-6397
• Chris Nagy, Sports Editor
(570) 644-6397
Frequency:
6 time(s) per week

NEWS-PRESS (FL)
2442 DR MARTIN LUTHER KING JR. BLVD
FORT MYERS, FL 33901-3987
941-335-0200
Fax: 941-957-5276
www.news-press.com
• Ed Reed, Sports Editor
(239) 335-0357
ereed@fortmyer.gannett.com
• Bob Carlson, Advertising Director
bcarlson@fortmyer.gannett.com

NEWS-PRESS (OK)
211 WEST 9TH STREET
STILLWATER, OK 74074-4406
405-372-5000
800-364-5000
Fax: 405-372-3112
news@stwnewspress.com
www.stwnewspress.com

• Roger Moore, Sports Editor
(405) 372-5000
sports@stwnewspress.com
Frequency:
7 time(s) per week

NEWS-RECORD
P.O. BOX 3006
GILLETTE, WY 82716-3301
307-682-9306
800-447-4539
Fax: 307-686-9306
news@gillettenewsrecord.com
www.gillettenewsrecord.com
• Kathy Brown, Sports Editor
(307) 682-9306
• Cher Rhoades, Advertising Manager
(307) 682-9306
Frequency:
6 time(s) per week

NEWS-REVIEW
P.O. BOX 1248
ROSEBURG, OR 97470
541-672-3321
Fax: 541-673-5994
www.oregonnews.com
• John McDermott, Sports Reporter
(541) 957-4219
• Rob McCallum, Sports Reporter
(541) 957-4221
• Tom Eggers, Sports Editor
(541) 957-4220
teggers@nrtoday.com
• Pat Bridges, Advertising Director
(541) 957-4250
Frequency:
6 time(s) per week

NEWS-SENTINEL
600 WEST MAIN STREET
FORT WAYNE, IN 46802-1408
260-461-8222
800-444-3303
Fax: 260-461-8817
www.news-sentinel.com\ns
• Tom Davis, Sports Editor
(260) 461-8240
• Blake Sebring, Assistant Sports Editor
(260) 461-8497
• Don Converset, Assistant Sports Editor
(260) 461-8346
Frequency:
6 time(s) per week

NEWS-STAR
411 NORTH 4TH STREET
MONROE, LA 71201
318-362-0289
800-259-7788
Fax: 318-362-0273
news@thenewsstar.com
www.thenewsstar.com
• Jerit Roser, Sports Writer
(318) 362-0234
• Christina Pierce, Advertising Director
(318) 362-0214
christina.pierce@monroe.gannett.com
Frequency:
7 time(s) per week

NEWS-TIMES
333 MAIN STREET
DANBURY, CT 06810-5818

203-744-5100
Fax: 203-792-8730
www.newstimes.com
• Brian Koonz, Sports Reporter
(203) 731-3379
sports@newstimes.com
• Bob Reigeluth, Sports Reporter
(203) 731-3379
sports@newstimes.com
• Jason Sonski, Sports Editor
(203) 731-3377
sports@newstimes.com
• James Stout, Sports Reporter
(203) 731-3377
sports@newstimes.com
• Edward Flink, Sports Writer
(203) 731-3379
sports@newstimes.com
Frequency:
7 time(s) per week

NEWSDAY
235 PINELAWN ROAD
MELVILLE, NY 11747-4226
631-843-2020
Fax: 631-843-2953
bizeditor@newsday.com
www.newsday.com
• Barbara Barker, Contributing Sports
Columnist
(631) 843-2020
barbara.barker@newsday.com
• Neil Best, Sports Reporter
(631) 843-3891
neil.best@newsday.com
• Bill Bleyer, Boating Reporter
• Margaret Corvini, Sports Editor
(631) 843-3435
margaret.corvini@newsday.com
• Ken Davidoff, Sports Writer
(631) 843-2020
• Michael Dobie, Sports Reporter
(631) 843-4839
Michael.Dobie@newsday.com
• Bill Eichenberger, Sports Deputy Editor
(631) 843-4842
• Joe Gergen, Sports Columnist
(631) 843-2020
• Bob Glauber, Sports Columnist (NFL)
(631) 843-3890
bglaubs2@aol.com
• Mark Herrmann, Sports Columnist
(631) 843-2826
• Jon Heyman, Sports Columnist (Baseball)
(631) 843-2810
jonhheyman@aol.com
• Johnette Howard, Sports Columnist
(631) 843-2810
• Aileen Jacobson, Advertising Writer
(631) 843-2960
• John Jeansonne, Sports Reporter
(631) 843-4836
• Mark LaMonica, Sports Writer
(631) 843-2020
mark.lamonica@newsday.com
• Dave Lennon, Sports Reporter (Yankees)
(631) 843-2810
• Greg Logan, Sports Correspondent
(631) 843-2823
• Steven Marcus, Sports Reporter
steve.marcus@newsday.com
• Raymond J. McCutcheon, Advertising Vice
President
• Jason Molinet, Sports Reporter (High
School)
(631) 843-4830
• Paul Moran, Sports Reporter (Horse
Racing)

(631) 843-2810
pmoran1686@aol.com
• Marty Noble, Sports Reporter (Baseball Mets)
(631) 843-2810
dw5254@aol.com
• Monty Phan, Advertising Reporter
(631) 843-2436
• Shaun Powell, Sports Columnist
(631) 843-3892
• Gregg Sarra, (631) 843-2810
Assistant Sports Editor
gregg.sarra@newsday.com
• Elaine Sung, Sports Assistant Editor
(718) 575-2554
• Dave Whitehorn, Deputy News Sports Editor
(631) 843-4820
• Steve Zipay, Sports Media Columnist
(631) 251-6657
steve.zipay@newsday.com
Frequency:
7 time(s) per week

NEWTON DAILY NEWS
200 1ST AVENUE EAST
NEWTON, IA 50208-3716
641-792-3121
Fax: 641-791-7104
newsroom@newtondailynews.com
www.newtondailynews.com
• Jeff Holschuh, Advertising Manager
(641) 792-3121
jholschuh@newtondailynews.com
• Andrew Potter, Sports Editor
(641) 792-3121
ndnsports@newtondailynews.com
Frequency:
6 time(s) per week

NEWTON KANSAN
P.O. BOX 268
NEWTON, KS 67114-2117
316-283-1500
Fax: 316-283-2471
news@thekansan.com
www.thekansan.com
• Joni Regnier, Advertising Manager
(316) 283-1500
• Mark Schnabel, Sports Editor
(316) 283-1500
mark.schnabel@thekansan.com
Frequency:
6 time(s) per week

NIAGARA GAZETTE
PO BOX 549
NIAGARA FALLS, NY 14303-1141
716-282-2311
Fax: 716-286-3895
niagara-gazette.com/
• Jonah Bronstein, Sports Writer
(716) 282-2311
Frequency:
7 time(s) per week

NORFOLK DAILY NEWS
525 NORFOLK AVENUE
NORFOLK, NE 68701
402-371-1020
800-672-8351
Fax: 402-371-5802
www.norfolkdailynews.com
• Larry Bartscher, Advertising Director
(402) 371-1020
• Jay Prauner, Sports Editor

(402) 371-1020
jprauner@norfolkdailynews.com
Frequency:
6 time(s) per week

NORMAN TRANSCRIPT
215 E. COMANCHE ST
PO DRAWER 1058
NORMAN, OK 73070-1058
405-366-3530
Fax: 405-366-3516
www.normantranscript.com
• Andy Rieger, Managing Editor
(405) 366-3543
editor@normantranscript.com
• Justin Harper, Sports Editor

NORTH COUNTY JOURNAL
7751 NORTH LINDBERGH BOULEVARD
HAZELWOOD, MO 63042
314-972-1111
Fax: 314-831-7643
www.stltoday.com
• Mike Elder, Sports Editor
(314) 972-1111
Frequency:
2 time(s) per week

NORTH COUNTY TIMES
207 EAST PENNSYLVANIA AVENUE
ESCONDIDO, CA 92025-2808
760-745-6611
Fax: 760-745-3769
editor@nctimes.com
www.nctimes.com
• Eric Breier, Assistant Sports Editor
(760) 740-3548
ebreier@nctimes.com
• Rick Hoff, Sports Writer
(760) 740-3545
hoff@nctimes.com
• Howard Wahl, Retail Advertising Manager
(760) 740-5435
hwahl@nctimes.com
• Bill Williamson, Advertising Director
(760) 740-3506
bwilliamson@nctimes.com
Frequency:
7 time(s) per week

NORTHEAST MISSISSIPPI DAILY JOURNAL
1242 SOUTH GREEN STREET
TUPELO, MS 38804
662-842-2611
800-264-6397
Fax: 662-842-2233
www.djournal.com
• Gene Phelps, Sports Editor
(662) 678-1593
• Parrish Alford, Collegiate Sports Reporter
(662) 678-1600
parrish.alford@djournal.com
Frequency:
7 time(s) per week

NORTHEAST TIMES
2512 METROPOLITAN DRIVE
TREVOSE, PA 19053-6738
215-355-9009
Fax: 215-355-4857
www.northeasttimes.com
• Sheil Kapadia, Sports Editor
(215) 854-2455
Frequency:
1 time(s) per week

NORTHERN VIRGINIA DAILY
152 NORTH HOLLIDAY STREET
STRASBURG, VA 22657-2143
540-465-5137
800-296-5137
Fax: 540-465-6155
www.nvdaily.com
• Brian French, Sports Editor
(800) 465-5137
Frequency:
6 time(s) per week

NORTHERN WYOMING DAILY NEWS
201 NORTH 8TH STREET
WORLAND, WY 82401-2614
307-347-3241
Fax: 307-347-4267
www.wyodaily.com
• Dustin Fuller, Advertising Manager
ext a
ads@wyodaily.com
• Judy Lockhart, Sports Editor
sports@wyodaily.com
Frequency:
5 time(s) per week

NORTHWEST ARKANSAS TIMES
212 NORTH EAST AVENUE
FAYETTEVILLE, AR 72701-5225
479-442-1700
800-803-8144
Fax: 479-442-1714
www.nwaonline.com
• Heath Allen, Sports Reporter
(479) 571-6419
• Kay Hunton, Classified Manager
(479) 571-6435
• Joe West, Sports Reporter
• Terry Wood, Sports Editor
(479) 442-1700
sports@nwaonline.com
Frequency:
7 time(s) per week

NORTHWEST FLORIDA DAILY NEWS
P.O. BOX 2949
FORT WALTON BEACH, FL 32547
850-863-1111
800-755-1185
Fax: 850-863-7834
news@nwfdailynews.com
www.nwfdailynews.com
• Travis Downey, Sports Editor
(850) 863-1111
• Patrick Flynn, Sports Writer
• Adam Rosenburg, Sports Reporter
• John Whitehead, Advertising Manager
Frequency:
7 time(s) per week

NORTHWEST HERALD
7717 SOUTH ROUTE 31
CRYSTAL LAKE, IL 60014-8196
815-459-4122
800-589-8910
Fax: 815-459-5640
www.nwherald.com
• Eric Olson, Sports Editor
eolson@nwherald.com
Frequency:
7 time(s) per week

NORTHWEST-SIGNAL
595 EAST RIVERVIEW AVENUE
NAPOLEON, OH 43545-1865

419-592-5055
Fax: 419-592-9778
www.northwestsignal.net
• Sally Heaston, Advertising Manager
ads@northwestsignal.net
• Jeff Ratcliff, Sports Editor
jeffr@northwestsignal.net
Frequency:
5 time(s) per week

NORWALK REFLECTOR
61 EAST MONROE STREET
NORWALK, OH 44857-1532
419-668-3771
Fax: 419-668-2424
www.goreflector.com
• Michael Greco, Sports Editor
(419) 668-3771
• Don Hohler, Sports Writer
• John Ringenberg, Advertising Manager
(419) 668-3771
Frequency:
6 time(s) per week

NOVOYE RUSSKOYE SLOVO
861 BAY RIDGE AVENUE
BROOKLYN, NY 11220
718-648-3511
Fax: 718-648-3047
www.inforeklama.com
• Alex Orlov, Sports Editor
• Leena Varskay, Advertising Manager
(646) 218-6900
Frequency:
6 time(s) per week

NOWY DZIENNIK/POLISH DAILY NEWS
333 WEST 38TH STREET
2ND FLOOR
NEW YORK, NY 10018-2914
212-594-2266
Fax: 212-594-2383
www.dziennik.com
• Jerry Gierusvczak, Sports Editor
(212) 594-2266
Frequency:
7 time(s) per week, Daily

O.C. WEEKLY
1666 NORTH MAIN STREET SUITE 500
SANTA ANA, CA 92701
714-550-5900
Fax: 714-550-5903
letters@ocweekly.com
www.ocweekly.com
• Steve Lowery, Sports Editor
Frequency:
1 time(s) per week

OAK RIDGER
P.O. BOX 3446
OAK RIDGE, TN 37830-7076
865-482-1021
Fax: 865-220-5460
www.oakridger.com
• Tank Johnson, Sports Editor
(865) 220-5508
Frequency:
5 time(s) per week

OAKLAND PRESS
48 WEST HURON STREET
PONTIAC, MI 48342-2101
248-332-8181
Fax: 248-332-8885
www.theoaklandpress.com

• Pat Caputo, Sports Columnist
(248) 745-4682
• Dana Gauruder, Sports Columnist
(248) 745-4673
• Paula Pasche, Sports Writer
(248) 745-4682
paula.pasche@oakpress.com
• Jeff Kuehn, Sports Editor
(248) 745-4682
jeff.kuehn@oakpress.com
• Keith Dunlap, Sports Reporter
(248) 745-4674
Frequency:
7 time(s) per week

OAKLAND TRIBUNE
7677 OAKPORT STREET
OAKLAND, CA 94607
510-208-6300
800-488-2070
Fax: 510-208-6477
www.oaklandtribune.com
• Mario Dianda, News Editor
• Steve Herendeen, Sports Editor
(510) 208-6462

OBSERVER (NY)
10 EAST 2ND STREET
DUNKIRK, NY 14048-0391
716-366-3000
Fax: 716-366-2389
editorial@observertoday.com
www.observertoday.com
• Craig Harvey, Sports Editor
(716) 366-3000
sports@observertoday.com
Frequency:
7 time(s) per week

OBSERVER (OR)
1406 5TH STREET
LA GRANDE, OR 97850
541-963-3161
800-422-3110
Fax: 541-963-7804
news@lagrandeobserver.com
www.lagrandeobserver.com
• Paul Harder, Sports Editor
(541) 963-3161
sports@lagrandeobserver.com
• Ted Kramer, Publisher
• Casey Kellas, Sports Writer
(541) 963-3161
• Joe Sova, Sports Reporter
(541) 963-3161
Frequency:
5 time(s) per week
Primary Audience:
Union and Wallowa Counties

OBSERVER-DISPATCH
221 ORISKANY PLAZA
UTICA, NY 13501
315-792-5000
Fax: 315-792-5033
www.uticaod.com
• Anne Delaney, Sports Writer
(315) 792-4963
• Ronald Moshier, Sports Reporter
(315) 792-5031
rmoshier@uticaod.com
• Francis Perritano, Sports Editor
(315) 792-5007
fperrita@uticaod.com
• John Pitarresi, Sports Writer
(315) 792-5032
jpitarresi@uticaod.com

Frequency:
7 time(s) per week

OBSERVER-REPORTER
122 SOUTH MAIN STREET
WASHINGTON, PA 15301-4904
724-222-2200
800-222-6397
Fax: 724-225-2077
www.observer-reporter.com
• Chris Dugan, Assistant Sports Editor
(724) 222-2200
dugan@observer-reporter.com
• Mike Kovak, Sports Reporter
(724) 222-2200
mkovak@observer-reporter.com
• Dale Lolley, Sports Reporter
(724) 222-2200
dlolley@observer-reporter.com
• Matt Miller, Advertising Manager
(724) 222-2200
mtmiller@observer-reporter.com
• Chris Dugan, Sports Editor
(724) 222-2200
dugan@observer-reporter.com
• Joe Tuscano, Assistant Editor
(724) 222-2200
jtuscano@observer-reporter.com
Frequency:
7 time(s) per week

OCEAN COUNTY OBSERVER
8 ROBBINS STREET
TOMS RIVER, NJ 08753-7629
732-349-3000
Fax: 732-557-5758
observer@app.com
www.injersey.com/observer
• Matt Underwood, Sports Editor
(732) 349-3000
munderwood@app.com
Frequency:
6 time(s) per week

ODESSA AMERICAN
222 EAST 4TH STREET
ODESSA, TX 79761-5122
432-337-6262
800-375-4661
Fax: 432-333-7742
www.oaoa.com
• Chris Gove, Sports Assistant Editor
(432) 333-7791
Frequency:
7 time(s) per week

OKLAHOMAN
9000 NORTH BROADWAY
OKLAHOMA CITY, OK 73114-3708
405-475-3311
Fax: 405-475-3183
www.newsok.com
• Mike Baldwin, Sports Writer
(405) 475-3314
• Jenni Carlson, Sports Columnist
(405) 475-4125
• Ed Godfrey, Sports Writer
(405) 475-3159
• John Helsley, Sports Writer
(405) 475-3313
• Joe Hite, Classified Manager
• Scott Munn, Sports Assistant Editor
(405) 475-3313
• John Rohde, Sports Writer
• Todd Schoenthaler, Sports News Assistant
• Mike Sherman, Sports Editor
• Darla Smith, Sports Coordinator (Day)

dsmith@oklahoman.com
• Berry Tramel, Sports Columnist
 btramel@oklahoman.com
• John White, Display Advertising Manager
(405) 475-3392
Frequency:
7 time(s) per week

OLATHE NEWS
514 SOUTH KANSAS AVENUE
OLATHE, KS 66061
913-764-2211
800-467-2720
Fax: 913-764-2251
www.theolathenews.com
• Tod Palmer, Sports Editor
(913) 764-2211
Frequency:
6 time(s) per week

OLEAN TIMES HERALD
639 NORTON DRIVE
OLEAN, NY 14760-1402
716-372-3121
800-722-8812
Fax: 716-373-6397
news@oleantimesherald.com
www.oleantimesherald.com
• Jim Melaro, Sports Editor
(716) 372-3121
jmelaro@oleantimesherald.com
• Charles Pollock, Sports Managing Editor
(716) 372-3121
cpollock@oleantimesherald.com
Frequency:
7 time(s) per week

OLNEY DAILY MAIL
206 WHITTLE AVENUE
OLNEY, IL 62450
618-393-2931
Fax: 618-392-2953
editor@olneydailymail.com
www.olneydailymail.com
• Ray McGrew, Advertising Manager
• Justin Hatten, Sports Editor
(618) 393-2931
Frequency:
6 time(s) per week

OLYMPIAN
P.O. BOX 407
OLYMPIA, WA 98507
360-754-5420
800-869-7080
Fax: 360-357-0202
news@theolympian.com
www.theolympian.com/
• Frank Bauer, Advertising Manager
(360) 754-5461
• Cindy Broome, Classified Manager
(360) 754-5447
• Adam Thaler, Sports Assistant Editor
(360) 704-6868
athaler@theolympian.com
• Gail Wood, Sports Reporter
(360) 754-5432
• Megan Wochnick, Sports Reporter
(360) 754-5473
Frequency:
7 time(s) per week

OMAHA WORLD-HERALD
1334 DODGE STREET
OMAHA, NE 68102-1138

402-444-1000
800-284-6397
Fax: 402-345-4547
news@owh.com
www.omaha.com
• Lee Barfknecht, College Sports Reporter
(402) 444-1024
• Marjie Ducey, State College Sports Writer
(402) 444-1000
marjie.ducey@owh.com
• Rich Kaipust, College Sports Reporter
(402) 444-1000
• Mike Kelly, Sports Columnist
• Elizabeth Merrill, Sports Reporter
(402) 444-1000
• Mike Patterson, High School Sports
Reporter
(402) 444-1000
mike.patterson@owh.com
• Steve Pivovar, College Sports Reporter
(402) 444-1026
• Larry Porter, Sports Writer
(402) 476-3132
• Stu Pospisil, High School Sports Writer
(402) 444-1000
stu.pospisil@owh.com
• Craig Sesker, Sports Reporter
(402) 444-1000
• Tom Shatel, Sports Columnist
 (402) 444-1000
tom.shatel@owh.com
• Mitch Sherman, College Sports Writer
(402) 444-1000
• Steve Sinclair, Sports Editor
(402) 444-1000
• Kevin White, High School Sports Reporter
(402) 444-1000
• Dave Winegarden, Advertising Director
(402) 444-1406
Frequency:
7 time(s) per week

ORANGE COUNTY REGISTER
625 NORTH GRAND AVENUE
SANTA ANA, CA 92701-4347
714-796-7000
Fax: 714-796-3681
www.ocregister.com
• Carlos Arias, Sports Reporter
(949) 606-3602
• Janis Carr, Sports Reporter
• Kevin Ding, Sports Reporter
• Damian Dottore, Sports Reporter
(714) 796-5050
• Steve Fryer, Sports Reporter
(714) 796-2245
sfryer@ocregister.com
• Ryan Hammill, Sports Reporter
• Lee Jenkins, Sports Reporter
• Robert Kuwada, Sports Reporter (UCLA)
• Eric La Pack, Sports Editor
(949) 454-7391
• Michael Lev, Sports Reporter
(714) 796-7804
• Bill Plunkett, Sports Reporter
 (714) 796-5050
bplunkett@ocregister.com
• Scott Reid, Sports Reporter
(714) 932-1809
sreid@ocregister.com
• Marcia Smith, Sports Reporter
(714) 796-2259
• Mark Whicker, Sports Reporter
• Randy Youngman, Sports Columnist
(714) 796-5050
• Curtis Zupke, Sports Reporter
Frequency:
7 time(s) per week

ORANGE LEADER
200 FRONT STREET
ORANGE, TX 77630
409-883-3571
Fax: 409-883-6342
editorial@orangeleader.com
www.orangeleader.com
• Kim Dwyer, Advertising Manager
• Van Wade, Sports Editor
(409) 721-2817
sports@orangeleader.com
Frequency:
7 time(s) per week

OREGONIAN
1320 SOUTHWEST BROADWAY
PORTLAND, OR 97201-3499
503-221-8100
800-826-0376
Fax: 503-227-5306
www.oregonlive.com/oregonian
• Geoffrey Arnold, Sports Reporter
(503) 221-8556
garnold@oregonian.com
• Rachel Bachman, Sports Reporter
(503) 221-4373
• Jim Beseda, Sports Reporter
(503) 221-8380
• Molly Blue, Sports Writer
(503) 294-7608
• Paul Buker, Sports Reporter
(503) 221-8167
• John Canzano, Sports Columnist
(503) 294-5065
• Aaron Fentress, Sports Writer
(503) 221-8211
afentress@oregonian.com
• Joe Freeman, Sports Writer
(503) 294-5183
joefreeman@oregonian.com
• Ken Goe, Sports Reporter
(503) 221-8040
• Mark Hester, Sports Editor
(503) 221-8548
• John Hunt, Sports Writer
 (503) 294-7643
• John Killen, Sports Editor
(503) 221-8538
• Jeff Manning, Advertising Reporter
(503) 294-7606
jmanning@oregonian.com
• Dennis Peck, Sports Editor
(503) 221-8164
• Jason Quick, Sports Reporter
(503) 221-4372
jquick@oregonian.com
• Mike Tokito, Sports Reporter
(503) 294-7603
• Jerry Ulmer, Sports Reporter
(503) 221-8161
julmer@oregonian.com
• Ryan White, Sports Writer
(503) 412-7024
rwhite@oregonian.com
• Michael Wilson, Sports Copy Editor
(503) 412-7065
Frequency:
7 time(s) per week

ORLANDO SENTINEL
633 NORTH ORANGE AVENUE
ORLANDO, FL 32801-1300
407-420-5000
800-347-6868
Fax: 407-420-5350
www.orlandosentinel.com
• Mike Bianchi, Sports Senior Columnist
(407) 420-5395

mbianchi@orlandosentinel.com
• Todd Adams, Sports Editor
(407) 420-5355
tmadams@orlandosentinel.com
• George Diaz, Sports Columnist
(407) 420-5533
gdiaz@orlandosentinel.com
• Chris Hayes, Production Editor
(407) 420-6178
chays@orlandosentinel.com
• Matt Humphrey, Manager,
Production/Online Sports
(407) 420-5078
mhumphrey@orlandosentinel.com
• Josh Robbins, Sports Reporter
jrobbins@orlandosentinel.com
• Brian Schmitz, Sports Columnist
(407) 420-5063
bschmitz@orlandosentinel.com
• Joe Williams, Sports Reporter
(352) 742-5921
jwilliams@orlandosentinel.com
Frequency:
7 time(s) per week

OSHKOSH NORTHWESTERN
224 STATE STREET
OSHKOSH, WI 54901-4839
920-235-7700
Fax: 920-235-1527
www.oshkoshonline.com
• Rob Ebert, Senior Sports Reporter
(920) 426-6679
• Steve Clark, Sports Editor
(920) 426-6659
sclark@thenorthwestern.com
Frequency:
7 time(s) per week

OSKALOOSA HERALD
1901-A AVENUE WEST
OSKALOOSA, IA 52577-1962
641-672-2581
888-672-2581
Fax: 641-672-2294
www.oskaloosaherald.com
• Jim Gries, Sports Editor
(641) 672-2581
sports@oskyherald.com
• Deb Van Engelenhoven, Advertising
Manager
(641) 672-2581
Frequency:
6 time(s) per week

OTTAWA HERALD
104 SOUTH CEDAR STREET
OTTAWA, KS 66067-2318
785-242-4700
800-467-8383
Fax: 785-242-9420
news@ottawaherald.com
www.ottawaherald.com
• Greg Mast, Sports Editor
sports@ottawaherald.com
Frequency:
6 time(s) per week

OTTUMWA COURIER
213 EAST SECOND STREET
OTTUMWA, IA 52501-2902
641-684-4611
800-532-1504
Fax: 641-684-7326
news@ottumwacourier.com
www.ottumwacourier.com

• James Grob, Sports Editor
(641) 684-4611
sports@ottumwacourier.com
Frequency:
6 time(s) per week

OWATONNA PEOPLE'S PRESS
135 WEST PEARL STREET
OWATONNA, MN 55060
507-451-2840
Fax: 507-451-6020
www.owatonna.com
• Debbie Ensley, Advertising Manager
• Chad Urdahl, Sports Editor
(507) 444-2374
• Derek Sullivan, Sports Editor
(507) 444-2374
Frequency:
6 time(s) per week

OWENSBORO MESSENGER-INQUIRER
1401 FREDERICA STREET
OWENSBORO, KY 42301-4804
270-926-0123
800-633-2008
Fax: 270-685-3446
news@messenger-inquirer.com
www.messenger-inquirer.com
• Jake Jennings, Sports Reporter
(270) 691-7312
• Mark Mathis, Sports Reporter
(270) 691-7313
mmathis@messenger-inquirer.com
• Saye Murry, Advertising Manager
(270) 691-7240
• Scott Hagerman, Sports Editor
(270) 691-7314
shagerman@messenger-inquirer.com
• Harold Martin, Sports Copy Editor
(270) 691-7153
Frequency:
7 time(s) per week

OXFORD EAGLE
916 JACKSON AVENUE
OXFORD, MS 38655-
662-234-4331
Fax: 662-234-4351
news@oxfordeagle.com
www.oxfordeagle.com
• John Davis, Sports Editor
• Anna Zemek, Advertising Manager
Frequency:
5 time(s) per week

PADUCAH SUN
P.O. BOX 2300
PADUCAH, KY 42003-1550
270-575-8600
800-599-1771
Fax: 270-442-8188
www.paducahsun.com
• Steve Millizer, Sports Editor
(270) 575-8663
• Joey Fosko, Sports Reporter
(270) 575-8600
Frequency:
7 time(s) per week

PALISADIAN
626 MCCARTHY DRIVE
NEW MILFORD, NJ 07646
201-385-2000
• Dave Nay, Sports Editor
• Robert Nesoff, Sports Columnist
bobmetnews@aol.com

Frequency:
1 time(s) per week

PALLADIUM-ITEM
1175 NORTH A STREET
RICHMOND, IN 47374-3226
765-962-1575
800-686-1330
Fax: 765-973-4570
palitem@richmond.gannett.com
www.pal-item.com
• Josh Chapin, Sports Editor
(765) 973-4463
Frequency:
7 time(s) per week

PALLADIUM-TIMES
140 WEST FIRST STREET
OSWEGO, NY 13126-1514
315-343-3800
Fax: 315-343-0273
editorial@palltimes.com
www.palltimes.com/
• Mike LeBoeuf, Sports Editor
(315) 343-3800
mleboeuf@palltimes.com
Frequency:
6 time(s) per week

PALM BEACH DAILY NEWS
265 ROYAL POINCIANA WAY
PALM BEACH, FL 33480-4041
561-820-3800
800-432-7595
Fax: 561-655-4594
www.palmbeachdailynews.com
• Linda Goings, Advertising Director
lgoings@pbdailynews.com
• Michael Strauss, Sports Editor
Frequency:
7 time(s) per week

PALM BEACH POST
2751 SOUTH DIXIE HIGHWAY
WEST PALM BEACH, FL 33405-1233
561-820-4100
800-432-7595
Fax: 561-831-4340
pb_metro@pbpost.com
www.palmbeachpost.com
• Brian Biggane, Sports Reporter
(561) 820-4440
brian_biggane@pbpost.com
• Joe Capozzi, Sports Reporter
(561) 820-4814
joe_capozzi@pbpost.com
• Tom D'Angelo, Sports Reporter
(561) 820-4714
tom_dangelo@pbpost.com
• Craig Dolch, Sports Reporter
(561) 820-4467
craig_dolch@pbpost.com
• Steve Dorsey, Sports Writer
(561) 820-4738
steve_dorsey@pbpost.com
• Charles Elmore, Sports Columnist
(561) 820-4811
charles_elmore@pbpost.com
• Dave George, Sports Columnist
(561) 820-4468
dave_george@pbpost.com
• Melanie Gerik-Fordyce, Sports Assistant
Editor
(561) 820-4444
melanie_gerik@pbpost.com
• Willie Howard, Sports Reporter
(561) 820-4715

willie_howard@pbpost.com
• Jorge Milian, Sports Reporter
(954) 327-3506
jorge_milian@pbpost.com
• Robb Olsen, Advertising Vice President
(561) 820-4265
robb_olsen@pbpost.com
• Greg Stoda, Sports Columnist
(561) 820-4717
greg_stoda@pbpost.com
• Alan Tays, Sports Reporter
(561) 820-4813
al_tays@pbpost.com
• Dave Tepps, Sports Deputy Editor
(561) 820-4742
• Edgar Thompson, Sports Reporter
(561) 820-4440
edgar_thompson@pbpost.com
Frequency:
7 time(s) per week

PALO ALTO WEEKLY
450 CAMBRIDGE AVE.
PALO ALTO, CA 94306
650-326-8210
Fax: 650-326-3928
editor@paweekly.com
www.paloaltoonline.com
• Rick Eymer, Sports Assistant Editor
• Keith Peters, Sports Editor
(650) 223-6516
Frequency:
Weekly print; daily online

PAMPA NEWS
403 WEST ATCHISON
PAMPA, TX 79065-6303
806-669-2525
800-687-3348
Fax: 806-669-2520
pamnews1@pan-tex.net
www.thepampanews.com
• Michael J. Stevens, Sports Editor
(806) 669-2525
• Beverly Taylor, Classified Manager
• Redonn Woods, Advertising Manager
(806) 669-2525
Frequency:
6 time(s) per week

PANTAGRAPH
P.O. BOX 2907
BLOOMINGTON, IL 61702-2907
309-829-9411
800-747-7323
Fax: 309-829-7000
newsroom@pantagraph.com
www.pantagraph.com
• Jim Benson, Sports Writer
jbenson@pantagraph.com
• Mike Egenes, Sports Editor
(309) 820-3246
• Randy Kindred, Assistant Sports Editor
(309) 829-9411
rkindred@pantagraph.com
• Randy Reinhardt, Sports Writer
(309) 829-9411
rreinhardt@pantagraph.com
• Randy Sharer, Sports Writer
(309) 829-9411
rsharer@pantagraph.com
Frequency:
7 time(s) per week

PARAGOULD DAILY PRESS
1401 WEST HUNT STREET
PARAGOULD, AR 72450

870-239-8562
Fax: 870-239-8565
www.paragoulddailypress.com
• Mike McKinney, Sports Editor
sports@paragoulddailypress.com
• Angie Spencer, Classified Manager
Frequency:
6 time(s) per week

PARIS DAILY BEACON NEWS
218 NORTH MAIN STREET
PARIS, IL 61944
217-465-6424
800-587-5955
Fax: 217-463-1232
www.parisbeacon.com
• Angie Bierly, Advertising Manager
• Andrew Majors, Sports Editor
(217) 465-6424
Frequency:
6 time(s) per week

PARIS NEWS
P.O. BOX 1078
PARIS, TX 75460
903-785-8744
Fax: 903-785-1263
editor@theparisnews.com
www.theparisnews.com
• Tommy Culkin, Sports Editor
(903) 785-6972
• Klark Byrd, Managing Editor
(903) 785-6960
Frequency:
6 time(s) per week

PARIS POST-INTELLIGENCER
208 EAST WOOD
PARIS, TN 38242-4139
731-642-1162
Fax: 731-642-1165
www.parispi.net
• Laura Dougherty, Advertising Manager
• Tommy Priddy, Sports Editor
Frequency:
5 time(s) per week

PARKERSBURG NEWS
519 JULIANA STREET
PARKERSBURG, WV 26101
304-485-1891
800-642-1997
Fax: 304-485-2061
editorial@newsandsentinel.com
www.newsandsentinel.com
• Jay W. Bennett, Sports Reporter
(304) 485-1891
jbennett@newsandsentinel.com
• Jim Butta, Sports Reporter
jbutta@newsandsentinel.com
• Steve Hemmelgarn, Sports Reporter
(304) 485-1891
shemmelgarn@newsandsentinel.com
• David Poe, Sports Editor
(304) 485-1891
dpoe@newsandsentinel.com
Frequency:
7 time(s) per week

PARSONS SUN
P.O. BOX 836
PARSONS, KS 67357
620-421-2000
800-530-5723
Fax: 620-421-2217

news@parsonssun.com
www.parsonssun.com
• Anthony Cook, Sports Editor
acook@parsonssun.com
• Tisha Mitchell, Advertising Manager
tmitchell@parsonssun.com
Frequency:
6 time(s) per week

PASADENA CITIZEN
102 SOUTH SHAVER STREET
PASADENA, TX 77506
713-477-0221
Fax: 713-477-9090
pasadenacitizen@hcnonline.com
www.yourhoustonnews.com/pasadena
• Rob Avery, Sports Editor
(713) 477-0221
ravery@hcnonline.com
Frequency:
5 time(s) per week

PASADENA/SAN GABRIEL VALLEY JOURNAL-NEWS
1541 NORTH LAKE AVENUE
PASADENA, CA 91104-2374
626-798-3972
Fax: 626-798-3282
pasjour@pacbell.net
www.pasadenajournal.com
• John Rando Rodgers, Sports Editor
Frequency:
1 time(s) per week

PATRIOT LEDGER
400 CROWN COLONY DRIVE
QUINCY, MA 02269-9159
617-786-7333
800-972-5070
Fax: 617-786-7193
www.patriotledger.com/
• Earl Lachance, Sports Editor
(617) 786-7057
• Eric McHugh, Sports Writer
(617) 786-7057
• Rick Seto, Sports Writer
(617) 786-7058
• Mike Fine, Sports Reporter
(617) 786-7058
Frequency:
6 time(s) per week

PATRIOT-NEWS
P.O. BOX 2265
HARRISBURG, PA 17105-2808
717-255-8100
800-692-7207
Fax: 717-705-3699
citydesk@patriot-news.com
www.pennlive.com
• Nick Horvath, Sports Editor
(717) 255-8404
• Michael Bullock, Sports Reporter
(717) 255-8124
mbullock@patriot-news.com
Frequency:
7 time(s) per week

PAULS VALLEY DAILY DEMOCRAT
108 SOUTH WILLOW STREET
PAULS VALLEY, OK 73075
405-238-6464
Fax: 405-238-3042
pvpub@swbell.net
www.paulsvalleydailydemocrat.com

• Mike Arie, Sports Editor
(405) 238-6464
marie@pvdemocrat.com
• Sara Fisher, Advertising Manager
sfisher@pvdemocrat.com
Frequency:
5 time(s) per week

PEKIN DAILY TIMES
20 SOUTH 4TH STREET
PEKIN, IL 61554
309-346-1111
800-888-6397
Fax: 309-346-1446
www.pekintimes.com/
Frequency:
6 time(s) per week

PENINSULA DAILY NEWS
P.O. BOX 1330
PORT ANGELES, WA 98362-2205
360-452-2345
800-826-7714
Fax: 360-417-3521
news@peninsuladailynews.com
www.peninsuladailynews.com
• Brad LaBrie, Sports Editor
(360) 417-3525
Frequency:
6 time(s) per week

PENINSULA GATEWAY/GATEWAY PLUS
3555 ERICKSON STREET
GIG HARBOR, WA 98335-1268
253-851-9921
Fax: 253-851-3939
www.gateline.com
• Neil Pierson, Sports Editor
(253) 853-9246
Frequency:
2 time(s) per week

PENSACOLA NEWS JOURNAL
P.O. BOX 12710
PENSACOLA, FL 32502
850-435-8500
800-288-2021
Fax: 850-435-8633
afail@pnj.com
www.pensacolanewsjournal.com
• Bob Heist, Sports Editor
(850) 435-8546
Frequency:
7 time(s) per week

PERRY DAILY JOURNAL
714 DELAWARE
PERRY, OK 73077-6425
580-336-2222
Fax: 580-336-3222
• Scott Barber, Sports Editor
Frequency:
5 time(s) per week

PHAROS-TRIBUNE
PO BOX 210
LOGANSPORT, IN 46947-3154
574-722-5000
800-676-4125
Fax: 574-732-5070
ptnews@pharostribune.com
www.pharostribune.com
• Beau Wicker, Sports Editor
beau.wicker@pharostribune.com
Frequency:
7 time(s) per week

PHILADELPHIA DAILY NEWS
P.O. BOX 7788
PHILADELPHIA, PA 19130-4015
215-854-5900
800-222-2765
Fax: 215-854-5910
www.philly.com/dailynews/
• Josh Barnett, Sports Editor
(215) 854-5212
• Les Bowen, Professional Football Reporter
(215) 854-4133
• Bill Conlin, Sports Columnist
(215) 854-5700
bill1chair@aol.com
• Bob Cooney, Sports Reporter
(215) 854-5900
• Sam Donnellon, Sports Columnist
(215) 854-4550
• Bernard Fernandez, Sports Writer
(215) 854-5700
• Bill Fleischman, Assistant Sports Editor
(215) 854-5705
• Paul Hagen, National Baseball Reporter
(215) 854-4550
• Marcus Hayes, Sports Writer
(215) 854-5700
hayesm@phillynews.com
• Rich Hofmann, Sports Columnist
(215) 854-5130
• Phil Jasner, Basketball Reporter
(215) 854-5700
• Dick Jerardi, Sports Reporter/Columnist
(215) 854-5700
• Pat McLoone, Sports Executive Editor
(215) 854-5700
• Ed Moran, Sports Business Writer
(215) 854-5940
• Ted Silary, High School Sports Reporter
(215) 854-5900
• John Smallwood, Sports Columnist
(215) 854-5847
• Paul Vigna, Sports Reporter
(215) 854-5900
Frequency:
6 time(s) per week

PHILADELPHIA INQUIRER
400 NORTH BROAD STREET
PHILADELPHIA, PA 19130-4015
215-854-2000
Fax: 215-854-5099
www.philly.com
• Don Beideman, Sports Reporter
(610) 701-7613
• Bob Brookover, Professional Football Reporter
(215) 854-2577
• Sam Carchidi, Sports Reporter
(215) 854-5181
• Deirdre Childress, Sports Deputy Editor
• Frank Fitzpatrick, Sports Reporter
(215) 854-5068
• Bob Ford, Sports Reporter
(215) 854-5842
• Mel Greenberg, Sports Reporter
(215) 854-5725
• Bill Iezzi, Sports Writer
• Jim Jenks, Sports Editor
• Mike Jensen, Sports Writer
(215) 854-4489
mjensen@phillynews.com
• Joe Juliano, Sports Writer
(215) 854-4494
• Joe Logan, Sports Writer
(215) 854-5604
• Bill Lyon, Sports Columnist
(215) 854-5508
• Sheil Kapadia, Sports Editor

(215) 854-2455
• Ashley McGeachy Fox, Sports Writer
• Tom McGurk, Sports Reporter
(215) 854-5721
• Gary Miles, Sports Deputy Editor
(215) 854-4487
gmiles@phillynews.com
• Marc Narducci, Sports Reporter
(856) 779-3325
• Rick O'Brien, Sports Reporter
(215) 854-4550
• Tim Panaccio, Sports Writer
(215) 854-2847
• Rob Parent, Sports Writer
(610) 313-8025
• Ray Parrillo, Sports Writer
(215) 854-2743
• John Quinn, Sports Deputy Editor
• Shannon Ryan, Sports Reporter
(610) 701-7607
• James T. Salisbury, (215) 854-4983
Sports Writer
• Don Sapatkin, Sports Writer
(610) 313-8246
• Michael Cu Schaeffer, Sports Assistant Editor
(215) 854-2537
• Mike Schaffer, Sports Assistant Editor
(215) 854-2537
• Pete Schnatz, Sports Writer
(215) 854-5817
• Phil Sheridan, Sports Columnist
(215) 854-2844
Frequency:
7 time(s) per week

PHILADELPHIA NEW OBSERVER
1520 LOCUST STREET SUITE 700
PHILADELPHIA, PA 19102
215-545-7500
Fax: 215-545-5548
www.pnonews.com
• Walter Davis, Sports Editor
bblessed1983@yahoo.com
Frequency:
1 time(s) per week

PHILADELPHIA TRIBUNE
526 SOUTH 16TH STREET
PHILADELPHIA, PA 19146-1565
215-893-4050
Fax: 215-735-3612
info@phillytrib.com
www.phillytrib.com
• Chris Murray, Sports Editor
(215) 893-5790
Frequency:
3 time(s) per week

PHOENIX
POTTSTOWN, PA 19464
610-933-8926
Fax: 610-933-1187
editor@phoenixvillenews.com
www.phoenixvillenews.com
• Barry Sankey, Sports Writer
• Jason Wolf, Sports Editor
Frequency:
6 time(s) per week

PILOT NEWS
PO BOX 220
PLYMOUTH, IN 46563-2135
574-936-3101
800-933-0356
Fax: 574-936-3844
www.thepilotnews.com/

- James Costello, Sports Editor
sports@thepilotnews.com
Frequency:
6 time(s) per week

PIONEER
PO BOX 455
BEMIDJI, MN 56619
218-333-9200
Fax: 218-333-9819
news@bemidjipioneer.com
www.bemidjipioneer.com
- Mary Default, Classified Manager
classifieds@bemidjipioneer.com
- Jim Carrington, Sports Editor
(218) 751-3740
sports@bemidjipioneer.com
- Pat Miller, Sports Reporter
(218) 751-3740
sports@bemidjipioneer.com
- Jaclyn King, Advertising Manager
jking@bemidji.com
Frequency:
6 time(s) per week

PIQUA DAILY CALL
310 SPRING STREET
PIQUA, OH 45356-2334
937-773-2721
Fax: 937-773-2782
editorial@dailycall.com
www.dailycall.com
- Rob Kiser, Sports Editor
(937) 773-2721
rkiser@dailycall.com
- Leiann Stewart, Advertising Manager
(937) 440-5252
Frequency:
6 time(s) per week

PITTSBURGH POST-GAZETTE
34 BOULEVARD OF THE ALLIES
PITTSBURGH, PA 15222-1204
412-263-1100
800-228-6397
Fax: 412-263-1313
editors@post-gazette.com
www.post-gazette.com
- Shelly Anderson, Reporter
(412) 263-1721
shanderson@post-gazette.com
- Gene Collier, Sports Columnist
(412) 263-1283
gcollier@post-gazette.com
- Ron Cook, Sports Columnist
(412) 263-1525
rcook@post-gazette.com
- Chuck Finder, Sports Columnist
(412) 263-1724
cfinder@post-gazette.com
- Teresa Lindeman, Retail Reporter
(412) 263-2018
tlindeman@post-gazette.com
- Paul Meyer, Sports Writer
(412) 263-1144
pmeyer@post-gazette.com
- Jerry Micco, Assistant Managing
Editor/Sports
(412) 263-3052
jmicco@post-gazette.com
- Carl Remensky, Sports Associate Editor
(412) 263-1607
cremensky@post-gazette.com
- Terry Shields, Assistant Sports Editor
(412) 263-1989
tshields@post-gazette.com
- Bob Smizik, Sports Columnist

(412) 263-1468
bsmizik@post-gazette.com
- Larry Walsh, Snowsports Reporter
(412) 263-1488
lwalsh@post-gazette.com
- Steve Ziants, Sports Writer
(412) 263-1474
sziants@post-gazette.com
Frequency:
7 time(s) per week

PITTSBURGH TRIBUNE-REVIEW
503 MARTINDALE STREET
PITTSBURGH, PA 15212-5705
412-321-6460
800-433-3045
Fax: 412-320-7965
release@tribweb.com
www.pittsburghlive.com
- Rob Biertempfel, Sports Writer
(412) 320-7811
- Jerry DiPaola, Sports Reporter
(412) 320-7997
jdipaola@tribweb.com
- Dave Mackall, Sports Reporter
(412) 380-5617
- Kevin Smith, Executive Sports Editor
(412) 320-7848
- Joe Starkey, Sports Reporter
(412) 320-7810
Frequency:
7 time(s) per week

PLAIN DEALER
1801 SUPERIOR AVENUE
CLEVELAND, OH 44114
216-999-4800
800-688-4802
Fax: 216-999-6354
www.plaindealer.com
- Elton Alexander, Sports Reporter (College)

(216) 999-4370
ealexander@plaind.com
- Roger Brown, Sports Writer
rbrown@plaind.com
- Mary Kay Cabot, Sports Reporter
(Football)
(216) 999-4370
mcabot@plaind.com
- Dave Campbell, Metro Sports Editor
(216) 999-4335
dcampbell@plaind.com
- Bob Dolgan, Sports Writer
(216) 999-3540
- Eddie Dwyer, Sports Writer
(216) 999-4677
edwyer@plaind.com
- Bob Fortuna, High School Sports Writer
(216) 999-4665
- Pat Galbincea, Sports Writer
pgalbincea@plaind.com
- Tony Grossi, Sports Reporter
(216) 999-4670
- Roy Hewitt, Sports Editor
(216) 999-4101
rhewitt@plaind.com
- Bruce Hooley, Sports Writer
- Paul Hoynes, Sports Reporter
(216) 999-5158
phoynes@plaind.com
- Bill Livingston, Sports Columnist
(216) 999-4672
- Dennis Manoloff, Sports Writer
(216) 999-4664
dmanoloff@plaind.com
- Joe Maxse, Sports Writer
(216) 999-5168

jmaxse@plaind.com
- Jack McDermott, Sports Writer
jmcdermott@plaind.com
- Rich Medeiros, Advertising Director
(216) 999-4350
rmedeiros@plaind.com
- Bob Migra, Sports Writer
(440) 324-3793
- Mike Peticca, Sports Writer
(215) 999-6177
mpeticca@plaind.com
- Marcia Pledger, Business Columnist
(216) 999-4813
mpledger@plaind.com
- Bob Roberts, Sports Reporter
(216) 999-5754
- Tim Rogers, Reporter
(330) 376-7309
- Mary Schmitt Boyer, Sports Reporter
(216) 999-4668
mschmitt@plaind.com
- Bud Shaw, Sports Columnist
- George Sweda, (216) 999-5809
Sports Reporter
- Branson Wright, Sports Writer
(216) 999-4671
Frequency:
7 time(s) per week

PLAINSMAN
49 3RD STREET, S.E.
HURON, SD 57350-2015
605-352-6401
800-859-3045
Fax: 605-352-7754
editor.plainsman@midconetwork.com
www.plainsman.com
- Mike Carroll, Sports Writer
(605) 353-7435
mcarroll.plainsman@midconetwork.com
- Darian Dudrick, Sports Editor
(605) 353-7425
Frequency:
6 time(s) per week

PLANO STAR COURIER
P.O. BOX 860248
PLANO, TX 75074
972-398-4200
www.planostar.com
- Geoff Blaine, Sports Editor
- Brian Porter, Sports Editor
(972) 398-4200
- Derek Price, Media News Editor
Frequency:
5 time(s) per week

POCONO RECORD
511 LENOX STREET
STROUDSBURG, PA 18360-1516
570-421-3000
800-756-4237
Fax: 570-424-2625
newsroom@poconorecord.com
www.poconorecord.com
- Peter L. Berry, Advertising Director
(570) 420-4372
- Mike Kuhns, Sports Editor
(570) 420-4389
mkuhns@poconorecord.com
Frequency:
7 time(s) per week

PONCA CITY NEWS
300 NORTH 3RD STREET
PONCA CITY, OK 74601

580-765-3311
Fax: 580-762-6397
news@poncacitynews.com
www.poncacitynews.com
• Fred Hilton, Sports Writer
(580) 765-3311
sports@poncacitynews.com
• Everett Lockwood, Advertising Manager
(580) 765-3311
ads@poncacitynews.com
Frequency:
6 time(s) per week

PORTAGE DAILY REGISTER
P.O. BOX 470
PORTAGE, WI 53901-2113
608-742-2111
Fax: 608-742-8346
pdr-news@capitalnewspapers.com
www.wiscnews.com/portagedailyregister/
• Dan Larson, Sports Reporter
(608) 745-3512
dlarson@capitalnewspapers.com
• Travis Houslet, Sports Editor
(608) 745-3518
thouslet@capitalnewspapers.com
Frequency:
6 time(s) per week

PORTERVILLE RECORDER
115 EAST OAK AVENUE
PORTERVILLE, CA 93257-3807
559-784-5000
Fax: 559-784-1172
recorder@portervillerecorder.com
www.portervillerecorder.com
• Doug Moore, Advertising Manager
(559) 784-5000
• Jan Parnell, Classified Manager
(559) 784-5000
• Charles Whisnand, Sports Editor
(559) 784-5000
Frequency:
6 time(s) per week

PORTLAND PRESS HERALD, MAINE SUNDAY TELEGRAM
390 CONGRESS STREET
PORTLAND, ME 04101-3514
207-791-6650
Fax: 207-791-6920
communitynews@pressherald.com
www.pressherald.com
• Paul Betit, Sports Reporter
• Sue Burtchell, Advertising Manager
(207) 791-6213
• Glenn Jordan, Sports Reporter
(207) 791-6425
gjordan@mainetoday.com
• Joe Grant, Sports Editor
(207) 791-6480
jgrant@mainetoday.com
• Kevin Thomas, Sports Writer
(207) 791-6411
kthomas@mainetoday.com
Frequency:
7 time(s) per week

PORTLAND TRIBUNE
6605 S.E. LAKE ROAD
PORTLAND, OR 97222
503-226-6397
Fax: 503-226-7023
www.portlandtribune.com
• Steve Brandon, Sports Editor
(503) 546-5144

Frequency:
2 time(s) per week

PORTSMOUTH HERALD
111 MAPLEWOOD AVENUE
PORTSMOUTH, NH 03801-3715
603-436-1800
800-439-0303
Fax: 603-433-5760
news@seacoastonline.com
www.seacoastonline.com/news/index.htm
• Frank Coppola, Sports Editor
(603) 436-1800
fcoppola@seacoastonline.com
• Mike Zhe, Sports Writer
(603) 436-1800
mzhe@seacoastonline.com
Frequency:
7 time(s) per week

POST AND COURIER
134 COLUMBUS STREET
CHARLESTON, SC 29403
843-577-7111
Fax: 843-937-5579
www.postandcourier.com
• Phil Bowman, High School Sports Reporter
(843) 577-7111
• Tommy Braswell, Outdoors Writer
(843) 937-5580
• David Caraviello, Sports Reporter
• Jeff Hartsell, Sports Reporter
(843) 577-7111
• Mike Mooneyham, Sports Columnist
(843) 577-7111
• Keith Namm, Sports Reporter
Frequency:
7 time(s) per week

POST REGISTER
333 NORTHGATE MILE
IDAHO FALLS, ID 83401-2529
208-522-1800
Fax: 208-529-9683
www.postregister.com
• Ken Clements, Retail Advertising Manager
(208) 522-1800
• Jeff Pinkham, Sports Editor
(208) 542-6772
prsports@postregister.com
• Paul Lambert, Sports Reporter
(208) 542-6770
• Ron Lee, Advertising Director
(208) 522-1800
• Robyn Steins, Sports Reporter
(208) 522-1800
Frequency:
7 time(s) per week

POST-BULLETIN
18 1ST AVENUE, S.E.
ROCHESTER, MN 55904-3722
507-285-7600
Fax: 507-285-7666
news@postbulletin.com
www.postbulletin.com
• Craig Swalboski, Sports Editor
(507) 285-7721
swal@postbulletin.com
Frequency:
6 time(s) per week

POST-CRESCENT
P.O. BOX 59
APPLETON, WI 54911

920-933-1000
800-236-6397
Fax: 920-733-1945
pcnews@postcrescent.com
www.wisinfo.com/postcrescent/index.shtml
• Mike Sherry, Sports Editor
(920) 993-1000
msherry@postcrescent.com
• Brett Christopherson, Sports Reporter
(920) 993-1000
bchristopherson@postcrescent.com
Frequency:
7 time(s) per week

POST-JOURNAL
15 WEST 2ND STREET
JAMESTOWN, NY 14702-5215
716-487-1111
Fax: 716-664-3119
editorial@post-journal.com
www.post-journal.com
• Debbie Brunner, Advertising Manager
(716) 487-1111
dbrunner@post-journal.com
• Scott Kindberg, Sports Assistant Editor
(716) 487-1111
skindberg@post-journal.com
• Jim Riggs, Sports Editor
(716) 487-1111
jriggs@post-journal.com
Frequency:
7 time(s) per week

POST-STANDARD, SYRACUSE HERALD-JOURNAL, SYRACUSE HERALD AMERICAN
CLINTON SQUARE
BOX 4915
SYRACUSE, NY 13221-4915
315-470-0011
800-765-3231
Fax: 315-470-3187
• Bud Poliquin, Sports Columnist
• Bob Snyder, Sports Columnist

POST-STAR
P.O. BOX 2157
GLENS FALLS, NY 12801
518-792-3131 EXT 3220
800-724-2543
Fax: 518-761-1255
obits@poststar.com
www.poststar.com
• Greg Brownell, Sports Editor
(518) 792-3131
brownell@poststar.com
• Warren Alber, Sports Reporter
(518) 792-3131
Frequency:
7 time(s) per week

POST-TRIBUNE (IN)
1433 E. 83RD AVE
GARY, IN 46410-6307
219-648-3000
Fax: 219-648-3236
posttrib.suntimes.com/
• Mark Lazerus, Sports Editor
(219) 648-3140
• Rick Cains, Advertising Director
(219) 648-3189
rcains@post-trib.com

POST-TRIBUNE (MO)
210 MONROE STREET
JEFFERSON CITY, MO 65101-3210

573-636-3131
Fax: 573-636-7035
news@newstribune.com
www.newstribune.com
• Debbie Kiser, Advertising Manager
(573) 761-0226
dkiser@newstribune.com
• Tom Rackers, Sports Editor
(573) 636-3131
sports@newstribune.com
Frequency:
7 time(s) per week

POTEAU DAILY NEWS
804 NORTH BROADWAY
SUITE C
POTEAU, OK 74953-3503
918-647-3188
800-495-6397
Fax: 918-647-8198
www.poteaudailynews.com
• Samantha Hess, Advertising Director
(918) 647-3188
• David Seeley, Sports Editor
sports@poteaudailynews.com
Frequency:
5 time(s) per week

POTOMAC NEWS
PO BOX 351
MANASSAS, VA 20108
571-333-1538
www.insidenova.com/
• Dave Fawcett, Sports Editor
(703) 530-3911
dfawcett@insidenova.com
• Robert Daski, Sports Reporter
(703) 530-3913
• Dave Utnik, Sports Reporter
(703) 530-3914
dutnik@insidenova.com
Frequency:
7 time(s) per week

POUGHKEEPSIE JOURNAL
P.O. BOX 1231
POUGHKEEPSIE, NY 12602
845-437-4800
Fax: 845-437-4921
www.poughkeepsiejournal.com
• Jan Dewey, Advertising Director
(845) 437-4975
jdewey@poughkee.gannett.com
• Dan Pietrafesa, Sports Editor
(845) 437-4849
Frequency:
7 time(s) per week

PRENSA GRAFICA
121 NW 38 COURT
MIAMI, FL 33126
305-649-6267
Fax: 305-649-6300
• Orestes Llana, Sports Editor
Frequency:
1 time(s) per week

PRESS & SUN-BULLETIN
33 LEWIS ROAD
BINGHAMTON, NY 13905
607-798-1234
800-365-0077
Fax: 607-798-1113
www.pressconnects.com
• Charlie Jaworski, Sports Executive Editor
(607) 798-1191

bgmsports@gannett.com
• Jodie Riesbeck, Advertising Director
(607) 798-1100
JRIESBEC@binghamt.gannett.com
• Dave Schultz, Sports Assistant Editor
(607) 798-1191
Frequency:
7 time(s) per week

PRESS DEMOCRAT
427 MENDOCINO AVENUE
SANTA ROSA, CA 95401
707-546-2020
Fax: 707-521-5330
www.pressdemocrat.com
• Phil Barber, Sports Reporter
(707) 526-8672
pbarber@pressdemocrat.com
• Lowell Cohn, Sports Reporter
(707) 521-5486
• Jeff Fletcher, Sports Reporter
jeff_fletcher@pacbell.net
• Bruce Meadows, Sports Reporter
(707) 521-5263
• Bob Padecky, Sports Reporter
(707) 521-5490
• Bill Pinella, Sports Assistant Editor
(707) 526-8500
• Robert Rubino, Sports Reporter
Frequency:
7 time(s) per week

PRESS DISPATCH-TRIBUNE
P.O. BOX 28100
GLADSTONE, MO 64188
816-454-9660
Fax: 816-414-3331
www.kccommunitynews.com
• Kevin Goodwin, Sports Editor
(816) 454-9660
Frequency:
2 time(s) per week

PRESS JOURNAL
14522 SOUTH OUTER FORTY ROAD
TOWN AND COUNTRY, MO 63017
314-821-1110
Fax: 314-821-0843
www.stltoday.com
• Greg Uptain, Sports Editor
(314) 821-1110
guptain@yourjournal.com
Frequency:
2 time(s) per week

PRESS OF ATLANTIC CITY
11 DEVINS LANE
PLEASANTVILLE, NJ 08232
609-272-7000
Fax: 609-272-7224
newstips@pressofac.com
www.pressofac.com
• John Celestino, Advertising Director
(609) 272-7047
• Michael McGarry, Sports Writer
(609) 272-7185
mmcgarry@pressofac.com
• Mark Melhorn, Sports Assistant Editor
(609) 272-7179
mmelhorn@pressofac.com
• Michael Shepherd, Sports Editor
(609) 272-7180
• Kathy Waldron, Classified Manager
(609) 272-7002
Frequency:
7 time(s) per week

PRESS REPUBLICAN
170 MARGARET STREET
PLATTSBURGH, NY 12901
518-561-2300
800-288-7323
Fax: 518-561-3362
www.pressrepublican.com
• Robert Goetz, Sports Editor
(518) 565-4124
• George Rock, Advertising Manager
grock@pressrepublican.com
Frequency:
7 time(s) per week

PRESS-ENTERPRISE (CA)
3512 14TH STREET
RIVERSIDE, CA 92501
951-684-1200
Fax: 951-368-9024
news@pe.com
www.pe.com
• Jim Alexander, Sports Reporter
(951) 368-9543
• David Ammenheuser, Sports Editor
(951) 368-9520
• Sue Barry, Advertising Vice President
(951) 368-9201
• Luis Bueno, Sports Columnist
• Joe Hamelin, Sports Writer
(909) 368-9527
• Eric Johnson, Sports Columnist
(951) 368-9530
ejohnson@pe.com
• Eric Johnson, Sports Writer
(951) 368-9530
• Jeff Parenti, Sports Assistant Editor
(951) 368-9523
• Jeff Parenti, Sports Assistant Editor
(909) 368-9523
• Gregg Patton, Sports Columnist
(951) 368-9597
• Kevin Pearson, Sports Reporter
 (951) 368-9525
• Broderick Turner, Sports Writer
(951) 368-9542
Frequency:
7 time(s) per week

PRESS-ENTERPRISE (PA)
3185 LACKAWANNA AVENUE
BLOOMSBURG, PA 17815-3329
570-784-2121
800-228-3483
Fax: 570-784-9226
www.pressenterpriseonline.com
• Sandra Sterner, Advertising Manager
(570) 387-1234
news@pressenterprise.net
• John Medeiros, Sports Editor
(570) 784-2121
sports@pressenterprise.net
Frequency:
7 time(s) per week

PRESS-REGISTER
401 NORTH WATER STREET
MOBILE, AL 36602-2600
251-219-5400
800-239-1340
Fax: 251-219-5799
www.al.com
• Steve Hall, Classified Manager
(251) 219-5503
• Randy Kennedy, Sports Editor
(251) 219-5689
Frequency:
7 time(s) per week

PRESS-TELEGRAM
300 OCEANGATE
LONG BEACH, CA 90802-1329
562-435-1161
800-436-3676
Fax: 562-437-7892
ptnews@presstelegram.com
www.presstelegram.com
• Jennifer Lemon, Advertising Director
(562) 499-1378
• Bob Keisser, Sports Columnist
(562) 435-1161
• Doug Kirkorian, Sports Columnist
(562) 499-1338
Frequency:
7 time(s) per week

PRINCETON DAILY CLARION
100 NORTH GIBSON
PRINCETON, IN 47670-1855
812-385-2525
Fax: 812-386-6199
news@pdclarion.com
www.pdclarion.com
• Tom Guest, Advertising Manager
• Pete Swanson, Sports Editor
(812) 385-2525
Frequency:
5 time(s) per week

PROGRESS-INDEX
15 FRANKLIN STREET
PETERSBURG, VA 23803-4514
804-732-3456
Fax: 804-861-9452
newsroom@progress-index.com
www.progress-index.com
• Tom Dozier, Sports Editor
(804) 722-5151
• Mike Gochenour, Advertising Manager
(804) 722-5137
Frequency:
7 time(s) per week

PROVIDENCE JOURNAL
75 FOUNTAIN STREET
PROVIDENCE, RI 02902
401-277-7000
888-697-7656
breakingnews@providencejournal.com
www.providencejournal.com
• Bill Corey, Sports Editor
(401) 277-7125
bcorey@providencejournal.com
Frequency:
7 time(s) per week

PUBLIC OPINION
77 NORTH 3RD STREET
CHAMBERSBURG, PA 17201
717-264-6161
800-782-0661
Fax: 717-264-0377
business@publicopinionnews.com
www.publicopiniononline.com
• Ginny Harriger, Advertising Director
(717) 262-4710
• Ed Gotwals, Sports Editor
(717) 262-4755
egotwals@publicopinionnews.com
Frequency:
6 time(s) per week

PUEBLO CHIEFTAIN
825 WEST SIXTH STREET
PUEBLO, CO 81003-2313

719-544-3520
800-279-6397
Fax: 719-544-5897
newsroom@chieftain.com
www.chieftain.com
• Bernie Schutz, Advertising Director
(719) 546-2277
• Judy Hildner, Sports Editor
(719) 404-2765
jhildner@chieftain.com
• Joe Cervi, Sports Writer
(719) 404-2769
jcervi@chieftain.com
Frequency:
7 time(s) per week

QUAD-CITY TIMES
500 EAST 3RD STREET
DAVENPORT, IA 52801-1708
563-383-2244
800-437-4640
Fax: 563-383-2370
www.qctimes.com
• Don Doxsie, Sports Editor
(563) 383-2280
ddoxsie@qctimes.com
Frequency:
7 time(s) per week

QUINCY HERALD-WHIG
130 SOUTH 5TH STREET
QUINCY, IL 62301-3916
217-223-5100
800-373-9444
Fax: 217-223-9757
www.whig.com
• Don O'Brien, Sports Editor
(217) 221-3365
Frequency:
7 time(s) per week

RAPID CITY JOURNAL
507 MAIN STREET
RAPID CITY, SD 57701
605-394-8300
800-843-2300
Fax: 605-394-8462
news@rapidcityjournal.com
www.rapidcityjournal.com
• Andrew Cutler, Sports Editor
(605) 394-8291
• Brad Slater, Advertising Director
(605) 394-8331
Frequency:
7 time(s) per week

RAVALLI REPUBLIC
232 WEST MAIN STREET
HAMILTON, MT 59840
406-363-3300
800-640-2010
Fax: 406-363-1767
editor@ravallirepublic.com
www.ravallirepublic.com
• Erin Hollern, Sports Editor
(406) 363-3300
Frequency:
5 time(s) per week

READING EAGLE
P.O. BOX 582
READING, PA 19601-4029
610-371-5000
800-633-7222
Fax: 610-371-5098

news@readingeagle.com
www.readingeagle.com
• Terry Bickhart, Sports Editor
(610) 371-5061
• Darryl Grumling, Sports Reporter
(610) 371-5072
• Steve Patton, Sports Reporter
(610) 371-5097
spatton@readingeagle.com
• Mike Berres, Sports Writer
(610) 371-5000
Frequency:
7 time(s) per week

RECORD (CA)
P.O. BOX 900
STOCKTON, CA 95201
209-943-6397
800-606-9741
Fax: 209-547-8186
newsroom@recordnet.com
www.recordnet.com/
• Tony Acosta, Sports Copy Editor
(209) 546-8290
tacosta@recordnet.com
• Jason Anderson, Sports Reporter
(209) 546-8283
janderson@recordnet.com
• Patsy Prato, Classified Manager
(209) 546-8213
• Jagdip Dhillon, Sports Reporter
(209) 546-8292
jdhillon@recordnet.com
• Lori Gilbert, Sports Columnist
(209) 546-8284
lgilbert@recordnet.com
• Scott Linesburgh, Sports Reporter
(209) 546-8281
• Pete Ottesen, Sports Reporter
(209) 546-8269
pottesen@recordnet.com
• Sam Smith, Assistant Sports Editor
(209) 546-8289
sports@recordnet.com
Frequency:
7 time(s) per week

RECORD (NJ)
150 RIVER ST
HACKENSACK, NJ 07601
201-646-4000
Fax: 201-646-4428
www.bergen.com
• mitch Krugel, Sports Editor
• Rhona Bronson, Director Marketing
Services

RECORD (NY)
501 BROADWAY
TROY, NY 12181
518-270-1295
Fax: 518-270-1202
www.troyrecord.com
• Kevin Moran, Sports Editor
• Joan Marro Harris, Advertising Director

RECORD SEARCHLIGHT
1101 TWIN VIEW BOULEVARD
REDDING, CA 96003-1531
530-225-8210
800-666-2772
Fax: 530-225-8236
editor@redding.com
www.redding.com
• Nathan Zeliff, Sports Editor
(530) 474-3267

Frequency:
7 time(s) per week

RECORD-ARGUS
10 PENN AVENUE
GREENVILLE, PA 16125
724-588-5000
800-542-3100
Fax: 724-588-4691
argusnews@rrbiznet.com
• Whendy Kozminski, Sports Editor
(724) 588-5000
argussports@rrbiznet.com
• Jim Rust, Advertising Manager
(724) 588-5000
argusads@rrbiznet.com
Frequency:
6 time(s) per week

RECORD-COURIER
P.O. BOX 1201
RAVENNA, OH 44266-2254
330-296-9657
800-560-9657
Fax: 330-296-2698
editor@recordpub.com
www.recordpub.com
• Tom Nader, Sports Editor
(330) 296-9657
tnader@recordpub.com
Frequency:
7 time(s) per week

RECORD-HERALD
30 WALNUT STREET
WAYNESBORO, PA 17268-1644
717-762-2151
Fax: 717-762-3824
news@therecordherald.com
www.therecordherald.com
• Dennis Shockey, Advertising Manager
(717) 762-2151
• Lee Goodwin, Sports Editor
(717) 762-2151
sports@therecordherald.com
Frequency:
6 time(s) per week

RECORD-JOURNAL
11 CROWN STREET
MERIDEN, CT 06450-5713
203-235-1661
Fax: 203-639-0210
newsroom@record-journal.com
www.record-journal.com
• Bryant Carpenter, Sports Editor
(203) 317-2208
bcarpenter@record-journal.com
• John Pettit, Sports Writer
(203) 317-2238
• Kimberley Boath, Director Advertising
(203) 317-2300
Frequency:
7 time(s) per week

RECORDER
ONE VENNER ROAD
AMSTERDAM, NY 12010-5617
518-843-1100
800-453-6397
Fax: 518-843-1338
news@recordernews.com
www.recordernews.com
• Paul Antonelli, Sports Editor
• Kevin McClary, Advertising Manager

Frequency:
7 time(s) per week

REDLANDS DAILY FACTS
700 BROOKSIDE AVENUE
REDLANDS, CA 92373
909-793-3221
Fax: 909-793-9588
www.redlandsdailyfacts.com
• Fred Board, Advertising Director
(909) 793-3221
• Kevin Trudgeon, Sports Editor
(909) 793-3221
Frequency:
6 time(s) per week

REGISTER NEWS
911 BROADWAY
MOUNT VERNON, IL 62864-4008
618-242-0113
Fax: 618-242-8286
mtv@intrnet.net
register-news.com
• Todd Adams, Sports Editor
• Janie Daniels, Classified Manager
(618) 242-0113
Frequency:
6 time(s) per week

REGISTER-GUARD
P.O. BOX 10188
EUGENE, OR 97408
541-485-1234
Fax: 541-683-7631
www.registerguard.com
• Ron Bellamy, Sports Editor
(541) 485-1234 •
ron.bellamy@registerguard.com
• Michael Raz, Advertising Director

REGISTER-HERALD
P.O. BOX 2398
BECKLEY, WV 25801-3822
304-255-4400
800-950-0250
Fax: 304-256-5625
www.register-herald.com
• Gary Fauber, Sports Assistant Editor
(304) 255-4400
gfauber@register-herald.com
• Charles Jessup, Advertising Manager
(304) 255-4425
• Dave Morrison, Sports Editor
(304) 255-4475
Frequency:
7 time(s) per week

REGISTER-MAIL
140 SOUTH PRAIRIE STREET
GALESBURG, IL 61401-4605
309-343-7181
800-747-7181
Fax: 309-342-5171
tmartin@register-mail.com
www.register-mail.com
• Doris Medhurst, Advertising Manager
(309) 343-7181
• Mike Trueblood, Sports Editor
(309) 343-7181
mtrueblood@register-mail.com
Frequency:
7 time(s) per week

REIDSVILLE REVIEW
1921 VANCE STREET
REIDSVILLE, NC 27320-3254

336-349-4331
Fax: 336-342-2513
news@reidsvillereview.com
www.reidsvillereview.com
• Steve Canulli, Sports Editor
Frequency:
5 time(s) per week

RENO GAZETTE-JOURNAL
P.O. BOX 22000
RENO, NV 89502
775-788-6200
800-648-5048
Fax: 775-788-6458
www.rgj.com
• Charle Carlson, Sports Editor
(775) 788-6345
ccarlson@rgj.com
• Dan Hinxman, Sports Reporter
(775) 327-6346
dhinxman@rgj.com
Frequency:
7 time(s) per week

RENSSELAER REPUBLICAN
117 NORTH VAN RENSSELAER STREET
RENSSELAER, IN 47978-2651
219-866-5111
888-729-2454
Fax: 219-866-3775
daily@rensselaerrepublican.com
www.rensselaerrepublican.com
• Don Hurd, President
• Harley Tomlinson, Sports Editor
daily@rensselaerrepublican.com
Frequency:
6 time(s) per week

REPORTER
916 COTTING LANE
VACAVILLE, CA 95688-9338
707-448-2200
Fax: 707-447-7405
thereporter.com
• Eliav Applebaum, Sports Reporter
(707) 453-8157
sports@thereporter.com
• Matt Miller, Sports Production Editor
(707) 453-8156
sports@thereporter.com
• Tim Roe, Sports Editor
(707) 453-8158
sports@thereporter.com
• Derek Wilson, Sports Reporter
(707) 453-8141
sports@thereporter.com
Frequency:
7 time(s) per week

REPORTER-TIMES
50 SOUTH JEFFERSON STREET
MARTINSVILLE, IN 46151
765-342-3311
Fax: 765-342-1446
www.reporter-times.com
• Steve Page, Sports Editor
(765) 342-3311
• Matthew Swanson, Advertising Director
(765) 342-3311
Frequency:
7 time(s) per week

REPOSITORY
500 MARKET AVENUE SOUTH
CANTON, OH 44702-2112

330-580-8544
Fax: 330-454-5745
letters@cantonrep.com
www.cantonrep.com
• Andy Call, Sports Reporter
(330) 580-8346
• Donald J. Detore, Sports Editor
(330) 580-8344
• Todd Porter, Sports Reporter
(330) 580-8340
todd.porter@cantonrep.com
Frequency:
7 time(s) per week

REPUBLIC
333 2ND STREET
COLUMBUS, IN 47201-6709
812-372-7811
800-435-5601
Fax: 812-379-5711
editorial@therepublic.com
www.therepublic.com
• Kirk Johannesen, Sports Editor
(812) 379-5632
kjohannesen@therepublic.com
• Bret Kroger, Advertising Director
(812) 379-5764
bkroger@therepublic.com
Frequency:
7 time(s) per week

REPUBLICAN & HERALD
122 MAHANTONGO STREET
POTTSVILLE, PA 17901-3008
570-622-3456
Fax: 570-628-6092
www.schuylkill.com
• Leroy Boyer, Sports Editor
lboyer@republicanherald.com
• Michael A. Joyce, Advertising Manager
• James Riotto, Classified Manager
Frequency:
6 time(s) per week

REPUBLICAN AND REPUBLICAN SUNDAY
1860 MAIN STREET
SPRINGFIELD, MA 01103-1000
413-788-1000
Fax: 413-788-1301
news@repub.com
www.masslive.com
• Joe Deburro, Sports Editor
(413) 788-1117
• Maureen Thorpe, Classified Manager
(413) 788-1000
Frequency:
7 time(s) per week

REPUBLICAN-AMERICAN
389 MEADOW STREET
WATERBURY, CT 06702-1808
203-574-3636
800-992-3232
Fax: 203-596-9277
www.rep-am.com
• Lee Lewis, Sports Editor
llewis@rep-am.com
• Andrew Pape, Classified Manager
(203) 574-3636
apape@rep-am.com
Frequency:
7 time(s) per week

REVIEW TIMES
113 EAST CENTER STREET
FOSTORIA, OH 44830-2905
419-435-6641
Fax: 419-435-9073
rtnews@reviewtimes.com
www.reviewtimes.com
• Scott Cottos, Sports Editor
(419) 435-6641
scottcottos@reviewtimes.com
Frequency:
6 time(s) per week

RICHMOND TIMES-DISPATCH
P.O. BOX 85333
RICHMOND, VA 23219
804-649-6000
Fax: 804-819-1216
news@timesdispatch.com
www.timesdispatch.com
• Jack Berninger, Sports Editor
(804) 649-6445
• Vic Dorr, Reporter
(804) 649-6442
• David Hamlin, Section Editor
(804) 649-6109
• Mike Harris, College Sports Writer
(804) 649-6839
• Jerry Lindquist, Sports Reporter
(804) 649-6323
• Bob Lipper, Sports Columnist
(804) 649-6555
• John O'Connor, College Sports Writer
(804) 649-6233
joconnor@timesdispatch.com
• John Packett, Sports Reporter
(804) 649-6313
• Tim Pearrell, Sports Reporter
(804) 649-6965
tpearrell@timesdispatch.com
• Nate Ryan, Sports Reporter
(804) 649-6851
• Heather Tucker, Sports Assistant Editor
(804) 649-6456
• Arthur Utley, Sports/Golf Writer
(804) 649-6559
• Jeff White, College Sports Writer
(804) 649-6838
• Paul Woody, Sports Columnist
(804) 649-6444
Frequency:
7 time(s) per week

RIDGWAY RECORD
20 MAIN STREET
RIDGWAY, PA 15853
814-773-3161
Fax: 814-776-1086
record@shop-right.com
www.ridgewayrecord.com
• Darlene Coder, Advertising Manager
• Jim Peterson, Sports Editor
richwayrecord@shop-right.com
Frequency:
6 time(s) per week

ROANOKE TIMES
P.O. BOX 2491
ROANOKE, VA 24010-2491
540-981-3100
800-346-1234
Fax: 540-981-3346
www.roanoke.com
• Mark Berman, Sports Reporter
(540) 981-3125
mark.berman@roanoke.com
• Ray Cox, Sports Reporter

(540) 381-1672
• Doug Doughty, Sports Reporter
(540) 981-3129
• Laurence Hammack, Public Integrity Reporter
(540) 981-3100
laurence.hammack@roanoke.com
• Randy King, Sports Reporter
(540) 981-3100
• Aaron McFarling, Sports Columnist
(540) 981-3222
aaron.mcfarling@roanoke.com
• Jim Reedy, Local News Reporter
(540) 981-3100
• Michael Stowe, Managing Editor
(540) 981-3100
• Belinda Harris, Librarian
Frequency:
7 time(s) per week

ROBESONIAN
P.O. BOX 1028
LUMBERTON, NC 28358-5538
910-739-4322
Fax: 910-739-6553
www.robesonian.com
• Curt Vincent, Sports Editor
(910) 739-4322
• Willis Jacobson, Sports Writer
(910) 739-4322
Frequency:
7 time(s) per week

ROCHESTER SENTINEL
118 EAST 8TH STREET
ROCHESTER, IN 46975-1508
574-223-2111
800-686-2112
Fax: 574-223-5782
news@rochsent.com
www.rochsent.com
• Val Tsoutsouris, Sports Editor
(574) 224-5326
• Karen Vojtasek, Advertising Manager
(574) 223-2111
Frequency:
6 time(s) per week

ROCKDALE CITIZEN
969 SOUTH MAIN STREET
CONYERS, GA 30012
770-483-7108
Fax: 770-483-5797
www.rockdalecitizen.com
• Jeff Gillespie, Sports Editor
(770) 483-7108
Frequency:
7 time(s) per week

ROCKFORD REGISTER STAR
99 EAST STATE STREET
ROCKFORD, IL 61104-1009
815-987-1350
800-383-7827
Fax: 815-987-1365
www.rrstar.com
• Greg Newell, Sports Assistant Editor
(815) 987-1203
• Lani Renneau, Advertising Director
(815) 987-1320
• Randy Ruef, Sports Editor
(815) 987-1203
sports@rrstar.com
• Mike DeDoncker, Sports Reporter
(815) 987-1382
Frequency:
7 time(s) per week

ROCKLAND JOURNAL-NEWS
200 NORTH ROUTE 303
WEST NYACK, NY 10994
845-578-2402
Fax: 845-578-2477
74514.3620@compuserve.com
www.nynews.com
• John Humenn, Sports Editor
(845) 578-2464
jhumenn@thejournalnews.com
• Enedina Vega, Advertising Director
(845) 578-2320
Frequency:
7 time(s) per week

ROCKY MOUNT TELEGRAM
800 TIFFANY BOULEVARD
ROCKY MOUNT, NC 27804-5713
252-407-9966
Fax: 252-446-4057
www.rockymounttelegram.com
• Jennifer Brown, Classified Manager
(252) 407-9926
• Mike Schuttinga, Advertising Manager
(252) 407-9922
• Ben Jones, Sports Editor
(252) 407-9959
Frequency:
7 time(s) per week

ROCKY MOUNTAIN NEWS
101 WEST COLFAX AVENUE
DENVER, CO 80218
303-954-5000
800-345-7461
Fax: 303-954-2841
www.insidedenver.com
• Sam Adams, Sports Columnist
(303) 954-2623
• Michael Bialas, Assistant Sports Editor
(303) 954-5281
• B.G. Brooks, College Sports Reporter
(303) 954-5466
• Lynn DeBruin, Sports Reporter
sports@rockymountainnews.com
• Jack Etkin, Sports Reporter
(303) 892-2921
sports@rockymountainnews.com
• Barry Forbis, Sports Editor
(303) 954-5100
• Randy Holtz, Sports Reporter
(303) 892-5439
sports@rockymountainnews.com
• Kevin Huhn, Deputy Sports Editor
(303) 954-5100
• Dave Krieger, Sports Columnist
(303) 954-5000
• Clay Latimer, Sports Reporter
(303) 892-2596
• Bernie Lincicome, Sports Columnist
(303) 954-2411
• Aaron Lopez, Sports Reporter
(303) 892-5388
• Lee Rasizer, Sports Reporter
(303) 892-5100
• Tracy Ringolsby, Sports Reporter
(303) 892-2843
• Rick Sadowski, Sports Reporter
(303) 892-2587
• Scott Stocker, Sports Reporter
(303) 954-5275
• Chris Tomasson, Sports Reporter
(303) 892-5100
• Gerry Valerio, Sports Editor (High School)
(303) 892-2848
• Bob Willis, Assistant Sports Editor
(303) 892-5100

Frequency:
7 time(s) per week

ROLLA DAILY NEWS
P.O. BOX 808
ROLLA, MO 65401-3243
573-364-2468
Fax: 573-341-5847
www.therolladailynews.com/
• Seth Sowers, Sports Editor
(573) 364-2468
• Lonna Stephenson, Advertising Manager
(573) 364-2468
Frequency:
6 time(s) per week

ROME NEWS-TRIBUNE
305 EAST 6TH AVENUE
ROME, GA 30162-6007
706-291-6397
Fax: 706-234-6478
www.romenews-tribune.com
• Trip Hatley, Advertising Manager
(706) 290-5217
• Jim O'Hara, Sports Editor
(706) 290-5258
• David Dawson, Sports Writer
(706) 291-6397
Frequency:
7 time(s) per week

ROSWELL NEIGHBOR
10930 CRABAPPLE ROAD SUITE 9
ROSWELL, GA 30075
770-993-7400
Fax: 770-518-6062
www.neighbornewspapers.com
• Carten Cordell, Sports Editor
Frequency:
1 time(s) per week

RUSHVILLE REPUBLICAN
219 NORTH PERKINS STREET
RUSHVILLE, IN 46173-1851
765-932-2222
Fax: 765-932-4358
www.rushvillerepublican.com
• Aaron Kirchoff, Sports Editor
(765) 932-2222
• Marilyn Land, Advertising Manager
Frequency:
6 time(s) per week

RUSTON DAILY LEADER
212 WEST PARK AVENUE
RUSTON, LA 71270-
318-255-4353
Fax: 318-255-4006
www.rustonleader.com
• O. K. Davis, Sports Editor
• Jeanie McCartney, Advertising Manager
jeanie@rustonleader.com
Frequency:
6 time(s) per week

RUTLAND HERALD
P.O. BOX 668
RUTLAND, VT 05701-4027
802-747-6133
800-498-4296
Fax: 802-773-0311
pressrelease@rutlandherald.com
www.rutlandherald.com
• Chuck Clarino, Sports Writer
(802) 747-6121
• Bob Fredette, Sports Editor

(802) 747-6121
• Glenda Hawley, Advertising Director
(802) 747-6121
Frequency:
7 time(s) per week

SACRAMENTO BEE
P. O. BOX 15779
SACRAMENTO, CA 95816-6816
916-321-1000
800-284-3233
Fax: 916-321-1109
www.sacbee.com
• Debbie Arrington, Sports Reporter
(916) 326-5514
• Gregg Bell, Sports Senior Writer
(916) 321-1096
• Marcos Breton, Sports Senior Writer
(916) 321-1096
mbreton@sacbee.com
• Victor Contreras, Assistant Sports Editor
(916) 321-1000
• Joe Davidson, Sports Senior Writer
(916) 321-1280
jdavidson@sacbee.com
• Larry Hicks, Sports Assistant Editor
(916) 321-5519
• Scott Howard-Cooper, Sports Senior Writer
(916) 321-1210
• Mark Kreidler, Sports Columnist
(916) 321-1149
• Mark McDermott, Sports Writer
(916) 326-5525
• Martin McNeal, Sports Senior Writer
(916) 326-5516
• Tom Negrete, Assistant Managing Ed., Sports and Busin
(916) 321-1171
• Nick Peters, Sports Senior Writer
• John Schumacher, Sports Senior Editor
(916) 326-5523
• Quwan Spears, Sports Reporter
(916) 326-5517
• Ailene Voisin, Sports Senior Writer
(916) 321-1208
• Barbara Zumwalt, Sports Deputy Editor
(916) 321-1190
Frequency:
7 time(s) per week

SAGINAW NEWS
100 SOUTH MICHIGAN AVENUE
SUITE 3
SAGINAW, MI 48602
989-752-7171
800-875-6397
Fax: 989-752-3115
metro@thesaginawnews.com
www.mlive.com/saginaw
• Paul Neumeyer, Sports Topic Editor
(989) 372-2503
• Hugh Bernreuter, Assistant Sports Editor
(989) 752-7171
Frequency:
7 time(s) per week

SAINT CLOUD TIMES
3000 NORTH 7TH STREET
SAINT CLOUD, MN 56303-3108
320-255-8700
800-759-7653
Fax: 320-255-8775
sctimes@cloudnet.com
www.sctimes.com
• Dave DeLand, Sports Editor
(320) 255-8771

Frequency:
7 time(s) per week

SAINT LOUIS AMERICAN
4242 LINDELL BOULEVARD
SAINT LOUIS, MO 63108-2927
314-533-8000
Fax: 314-533-0038
stlamer@mvp.net
www.stlamerican.com
• Earl Austin, Sports Editor
eaustin@stlamerican.com
Frequency:
1 time(s) per week

SAINT LOUIS ARGUS
4595 MARTIN LUTHER KING DRIVE
SAINT LOUIS, MO 63113
314-531-1323
Fax: 314-531-1324
www.stlouisargus.com
• Charles Edwards, Sports Editor
Frequency:
1 time(s) per week

SAINT LOUIS POST-DISPATCH
900 NORTH TUCKER BOULEVARD
SAINT LOUIS, MO 63101-1069
314-340-8000
800-365-0820
Fax: 314-340-3050
metro@post-dispatch.com
www.stltoday.com
• Bryan Burwell, Sports Columnist
(314) 340-8185
• William Coats, Sports Reporter
(314) 340-8189
• Stu Durando, Sports Reporter
(314) 340-8232
sdurando@post-dispatch.com
• Derrick Goold, Sports Reporter
(314) 340-8170
dgoold@post-dispatch.com
• Roger Hensley, Sports Deputy Editor
(314) 340-8301
rhensley@post-dispatch.com
• Rick Hummel, Sports Reporter
(314) 340-8199
rhummel@post-dispatch.com
• Joe Lyons, Sports Reporter
(314) 946-3903
jlyons@post-dispatch.com
• Bernie Miklasz, Sports Columnist
(314) 340-8192
• Kathleen Nelson, Sports Reporter
(314) 340-8233
• Dan O'Neill, Sports Columnist
(314) 340-8186
• Donald Reed, Sports Deputy Editor
(314) 340-8313
dreed@post-dispatch.com
• Kenneth Roberts, Sports Reporter
(618) 257-0745
• Joe Strauss, Sports Reporter
(314) 340-8170
• James Thomas, Sports Reporter
(314) 340-8197
jthomas@post-dispatch.com
• Tom Timmermann, Sports Reporter
(314) 340-8190
ttimmermann@post-dispatch.com
• James Woodworth, Sports Copy Editor
(314) 340-8165
Frequency:
7 time(s) per week

SAINT PAUL PIONEER PRESS
345 CEDAR STREET
SAINT PAUL, MN 55101-1014
651-222-1111
Fax: 651-228-5500
www.twincities.com
• Thom Fladung, Editor/Vice President
• Rick Alonzo, Sports Reporter
(Timberwolves)
(651) 222-5539
• Mike Bass, Sports Editor
(651) 228-5108
• Bruce Brothers, Sports Reporter/Running
Columnist
(651) 228-5518
• Kevin Cusick, Sports Deputy Editor
(651) 228-5471
kcusick@pioneerpress.com
• Tim Leighton, Sports Reporter (High
School)
(651) 228-5598
• Jeff Hruza, Sports Clerk
(651) 228-5155
• John Pluym, High School Sports Editor
(651) 228-5239
Frequency:
7 time(s) per week

SALAMANCA PRESS
36 RIVER STREET
SALAMANCA, NY 14779-1474
716-945-1644
Fax: 716-945-4285
salpressnews@verizon.net
www.salamancapress.com
• Darren Riethmiller, Sports Editor
• Casey Stockman, Advertising Manager
salpressads@verizon.net
• Brian Jewell, Sports Editor
(716) 945-1644
salpressnews@verizon.net
Frequency:
5 time(s) per week

SALEM NEWS
161 NORTH LINCOLN AVENUE
SALEM, OH 44460-2903
330-332-4601
Fax: 330-332-1441
www.salemnews.net
• B.J Lisko, Sports Editor
(330) 332-4601
Frequency:
7 time(s) per week

SALINA JOURNAL
333 SOUTH 4TH STREET
SALINA, KS 67402
785-823-6363
800-827-6363
Fax: 785-827-6363
www.saljournal.com
• Bob Davidson, Sports Editor
(785) 822-1404
Frequency:
7 time(s) per week

SALINAS CALIFORNIAN
123 WEST ALISAL STREET
SALINAS, CA 93901
831-424-2221
800-300-6397
Fax: 831-754-4104
www.salinascalifornian.com
• Joey Delgado, Sports Editor
(831) 754-4265
jdelgado@salinas.gannett.com

• Janine Perkingson, Advertising Director
(800) 300-6397
• Dave Nordstrand, Sports Columnist
(831) 754-4268
dnordstrand@thecalifornian.com
Frequency:
6 time(s) per week

SALISBURY POST
131 WEST INNES STREET
SALISBURY, NC 28144-4338
704-633-8950
800-633-8957
Fax: 704-639-0003
news@salisburypost.com
www.salisburypost.com
• Mark Bee, Advertising Director
(704) 633-8950
• Ronnie Gallagher, Sports Editor
(704) 797-4287
sports@salisburypost.com
Frequency:
7 time(s) per week

SALT LAKE TRIBUNE
90 SOUTH 400 WEST, SUITE 700
SALT LAKE CITY, UT 84111-1924
801-257-8742
Fax: 801-257-8525
letters@sltrib.com
www.sltrib.com
• Michael Anastasi, Sports Managing Editor
(801) 257-8905
• Jay Drew, Sports Reporter
(801) 257-8906
• Kurt Kragthorpe, Sports Writer
(801) 257-8916
• Michael Lewis, Sports Reporter
(801) 257-8903
• Steve Luhm, Sports Reporter
(801) 257-8913
• Gordon Monson, Sports Columnist
(801) 257-8923
gmonson@sltrib.com
• Martin Renzhofer, Sports Reporter
(801) 257-8908
• Lya Wodraska, Sports Writer
(801) 257-8907
Frequency:
7 time(s) per week

SAMPSON INDEPENDENT
P.O. BOX 110
CLINTON, NC 28328-4426
910-592-8137
Fax: 910-592-8756
www.clintonnc.com
• Wanda Buckner, Advertising Manager
(910) 592-8137
• Billy Todd, Sports Editor
(910) 592-8137
Frequency:
6 time(s) per week

SAN ANGELO STANDARD TIMES
P.O. BOX 5111
SAN ANGELO, TX 76903-5838
325-653-1221
Fax: 325-659-8173
www.sanangelostandardtimes.com
• Charles Bryce, Sports Editor
(325) 653-1221
Frequency:
7 time(s) per week

SAN ANTONIO EXPRESS-NEWS
P.O. BOX 2171
SAN ANTONIO, TX 78287-2171
210-250-3105
800-555-1551
Fax: 210-250-3121
citydesk@express-news.net
www.mysanantonio.com/expressnews
• Jennifer Bellis, Sports Reporter
(210) 250-3391
• Jerry Briggs, Assistant Sports Editor
(210) 250-3000
jbriggs@express-news.net
• Al Carter, Deputy Sports Editor
(210) 250-3000
• Raul Dominguez, Sports Reporter
(210) 250-3362
• Mike Finger, Sports Columnist (College)
(210) 250-3000
mfinger@express-news.net
• David Flores, Sports Columnist
(210) 250-3356
• Tim Griffin, Sports Columnist
• Buck Harvey, Sports Columnist
(210) 250-3372
bharvey@express-news.net
• John Hines, High School/Prep Sports
Reporter
(210) 250-3364
• David King, Sports Reporter (Baseball,
high schools)
(210) 250-3000
• LeAnna Kosub, Assistant Sports Editor
(210) 250-3000
lkosub@express-news.net
• Johnny Ludden, Sports Reporter (NBA)
(210) 250-3369
jludden@express-news.net
• Dan McCarney, Sports Columnist (Soccer)

(210) 250-3351
dmccarney@express-news.net
• Mike Monroe, NBA Sports Writer
(210) 250-3000
mikemonroe@express-news.net
• Richard Oliver, Sports Columnist
(210) 250-3390
• Tom Orsborn, Sports Reporter
(210) 250-3367
torsborn@express-news.net
• Harry Page, Sports Reporter
(210) 250-3000
• Steve Quintana, Assistant Managing
Editor/Sports, Online
(210) 250-3000
• Lee Scheide, Sports Reporter (Minors)
(210) 250-3000
• Ron Henry Strait, Sports Columnist
(210) 250-3358
• Mark Wangrin, Sports Writer (College)
(210) 250-3000
• John Whisler, Sports Columnist (Boxing,
golf)
(210) 250-3392
jwhisler@express-news.net
• Brent Zwerneman, Sports Writer
(210) 250-3000
bzwerneman@express-news.net
Frequency:
7 time(s) per week

SAN BERNARDINO SUN
399 NORTH D STREET
SAN BERNARDINO, CA 92401
909-889-9666
Fax: 909-885-8741
www.sbsun.com

• Louis Brewster, Sports Editor
(909) 386-3865
louis.brewster@sbsun.com
• Paul Oberjuerge, Sports Columnist
(951) 386-3849
paul.oberjuerge@sbsun.com
• Gene Pearlman, Advertising Director
gene.pearlman@sbsun.com
Frequency:
7 time(s) per week

SAN DIEGO UNION-TRIBUNE
350 CAMINO DE LA REINA
SAN DIEGO, CA 92108-0565
619-299-3131
800-244-6397
Fax: 619-293-1896
www.signonsandiego.com
• Kevin Acee, Sports Reporter
(619) 293-1857
• Nick Canepa, Sports Columnist
(619) 293-1397
• Bill Center, Boating Reporter
(619) 293-1851
• Chris Jenkins, Sports Reporter
(619) 293-1267
• Tod Leonard, Sports Reporter
(619) 293-1858
• Don Norcross, Sports Reporter
(619) 293-1858
• Tim Sullivan, Sports Columnist
(619) 293-1033
• Jay Posner, Sports Editor
(619) 293-1834
• Edward Zieralski, Sports Reporter
(619) 293-1225
Frequency:
7 time(s) per week

SAN FRANCISCO CHRONICLE
901 MISSION STREET
SAN FRANCISCO, CA 94103
415-777-7100
Fax: 415-543-7708
metro@sfchronicle.com
www.sfgate.com/chronicle
• John Crumpacker, Sports Reporter
(415) 777-7201
• Thomas Fitzgerald, Sports Reporter
(415) 777-7201
tfitzgerald@sfchronicle.com
• Bruce Jenkins, Sports Columnist
(415) 777-7169
bjenkins@sfchronicle.com
• Allen Johnson, Sports Copy Editor
ajohnson@sfchronicle.com
• Ron Kroichick, Sports Reporter
(415) 777-7201
• Steve Kroner, Sports Columnist
(415) 777-8415
skroner@sfchronicle.com
• Mike Massa, Sports News Editor
mmassa@sfchronicle.com
• Scott Ostler, Sports Columnist
(415) 777-7031
sostler@sfchronicle.com
• Alan Saracevic, Sports Editor
asaracevic@sfchronicle.com
• Henry Schulman, Sports Writer
hschulman@sfchronicle.com
• John Shea, Sports Reporter
jshea@sfchronicle.com
• Susan Slusser, Sports Reporter
(415) 777-8859
sslusser@sfchronicle.com
• Mark Smoyer, Deputy Sports Editor
• Tom Stienstra, Sports Reporter
tstienstra@sfchronicle.com

Frequency:
7 time(s) per week

SAN FRANCISCO EXAMINER
450 MISSION STREET 5TH FLOOR
SAN FRANCISCO, CA 94105
415-826-1100
866-733-7323
Fax: 415-359-2766
www.examiner.com
• Paul Ingegneri, Advertising Vice President
(415) 359-2809
• Chad Morelli, Sports Reporter
(415) 359-2855
• Jason Phillips, Advertising Director
(415) 359-2629
• Eric White, Sports Reporter
(415) 359-2637
• Rick Barry, Sports Columnist
(415) 995-6830
Frequency:
5 time(s) per week

SAN GABRIEL VALLEY DAILY TRIBUNE
1210 NORTH AZUSA CANYON ROAD
WEST COVINA, CA 91790-1003
626-962-8811
800-788-1200
Fax: 626-856-2758
news.tribune@sgvn.com
www.sgvtribune.com
• Steve Ramirez, Sports Columnist
(626) 962-8811
• Doug Spoon, Sports Editor
(626) 962-8811
Frequency:
7 time(s) per week

SAN JOSE MERCURY NEWS
750 RIDDER PARK DRIVE
SAN JOSE, CA 95190
408-920-5000
800-870-6397
Fax: 408-288-8060
business@mercurynews.com
www.mercurynews.com
• Elliott Almond, Sports Reporter
(408) 920-5865
• Daniel Brown, Sports Reporter
(408) 920-5000
• Victor Chi, Sports Reporter
(408) 920-5720
• Dennis Deisenroth, Sports Copy Editor
(408) 920-5354
• David Early, Sports Reporter
(408) 920-5836
• Mark Emmons, Sports Columnist
(408) 920-5745
• Dennis Georgatos, Sports Reporter
(408) 920-5434
• Mark Gomez, Sports Reporter
(408) 920-5354
• Mike Guersch, Sports Deputy Editor
(408) 920-5648
• Bud Geracie, Sports Executive Editor
(408) 920-5389
sports@mercurynews.com
• Chris Haft, Sports Reporter
• Bruce Hammel, Sports Copy Editor
(408) 920-5354
• Gary Hoh, Sports Copy Editor
(408) 920-5354
• Chris Hutchison, Sports Copy Editor
(408) 920-5354
• Tim Kawakami, Sports Columnist
(408) 920-5442
• Greg Keraghosian, Sports Copy Editor

(408) 920-5354
• David Kiefer, Sports Reporter
• Ann Killion, Sports Columnist
(408) 920-5805
• Dennis Knight, High School Sports
Reporter
(408) 920-5899
• Darryl Matsuda, Assistant Sports Editor
(408) 920-5215
• Laurence Miedema, Sports Reporter
lsmiedema@mercurynews.com
• Richard Parrish, Sports Copy Editor
(408) 920-5354
• Eric Pinkela, Sports Copy Editor
(408) 920-2709
• Sal Pizarro, Sports Editor
(408) 920-5473
spizarro@mercurynews.com
• David Pollak, (408) 920-5940
Sports Writer
• Mark Purdy, Sports Columnist
(408) 920-5092
• Darren Sabedra, Sports Writer
(408) 920-5815
dsabedra@mercurynews.com
• Ken Stutz, Sports Copy Editor
(408) 920-5354
• Randy Sumimoto, Sports Copy Editor
(408) 920-5354
• Pam Tso, Sports Copy Editor
(408) 920-2704
Frequency:
7 time(s) per week

SAN MATEO COUNTY TIMES
477 NINTH AVENUE
SAN MATEO, CA 94402
650-348-4321
800-843-6397
Fax: 650-348-4446
www.sanmateocountytimes.com
• Glenn Reeves, Sports Editor
(650) 348-4345
Frequency:
6 time(s) per week

SANDUSKY REGISTER
314 WEST MARKET STREET
SANDUSKY, OH 44870-2410
419-625-5500
800-466-1243
Fax: 419-625-3007
www.sanduskyregister.com
• Dan Angelo, Sports Editor
(419) 625-5500
• Josh DeSonne, Sports Writer
(419) 625-5500
• Nabil Shaheen, Sports Writer
(419) 625-5500
• Mark Yocum, Advertising Director
Frequency:
7 time(s) per week

SANFORD HERALD
P.O. BOX 100
SANFORD, NC 27330-3916
919-708-9000
800-849-5677
Fax: 919-708-9001
obits@sanfordherald.com
www.sanfordherald.com
• Alex Poblogar, Sports Editor
(919) 718-1222
• Doug Rowe, Advertising Director
(919) 718-1259
Frequency:
6 time(s) per week

SANTA BARBARA NEWS-PRESS
P. O. BOX 1359
SANTA BARBARA, CA 93101-2203
805-564-5200
800-654-3292
Fax: 805-966-6258
businessnews@newspress.com
www.newspress.com
• Gerry Spratt, Sports Editor
(805) 564-5173
• Mark Patton, Sports Columnist
(805) 564-5117
mpatton@newspress.com
Frequency:
7 time(s) per week

SANTA CRUZ SENTINEL
207 CHURCH STREET
SANTA CRUZ, CA 95060
831-423-4242
Fax: 831-429-9620
editorial@santacruzsentinel.com
www.santacruzsentinel.com
• Arlene Hudson, Advertising Manager
(831) 429-2442
• Jess Mitchell, Advertising Director
(831) 429-2432
• Tom Moore, Sports Editor
Frequency:
7 time(s) per week

SANTA FE NEW MEXICAN
202 E. MARCY
SANTE FE, NM 87501
505-995-3885
Fax: 505-986-3067
www.sfnewmexican.com
• Robin McKinney, Chief Exectuive
Officer/Editor & Publisher
• Robert McKinney, Editor & Publisher
• Ty Ransdell, General Manager

SANTA MARIA TIMES
P.O. BOX 400
SANTA MARIA, CA 93455
805-739-2228
Fax: 805-928-5657
www.santamariatimes.com
• Elliott Stern, Sports Editor
(805) 739-2235
• Kenny Cress, Sports Reporter
(805) 739-2237
Frequency:
7 time(s) per week

SARASOTA HERALD-TRIBUNE
1741 MAIN STREET
SARASOTA, FL 34236-7824
941-361-4800
Fax: 941-361-4699
www.newscoast.com
• John Brockmann, Sports Reporter
(941) 957-5177
• Mark Cardon, Weekend Sports Editor
(941) 957-5176
• Doug Fernandes, Sports Writer
(941) 957-5179
doug.fernandes@heraldtribune.com
• Bill Herald, Sports Columnist
(941) 957-5172
• Mic Huber, Assistant Sports Editor
(941) 957-5170
mic.huber@heraldtribune.com
• Scott Peterson, Sports Editor
(941) 957-5172
scott.peterson@heraldtribune.com
• Jerry Reed, Sports Editor

(941) 957-5184
• Jody Royce, Sports Reporter
(941) 361-4860
Frequency:
7 time(s) per week

SAVANNAH MORNING NEWS
P.O. BOX 1088
SAVANNAH, GA 31405-1108
912-236-9511
800-533-1150
Fax: 912-234-6522
www.savannahnow.com
• Noell Barnidge, Sports Reporter
(912) 652-0347
noell.barnidge@savannahnow.com
• Sean Coughlin, Assistant Sports Editor
(912) 652-0348
coughlin@savannahnow.com
• Tim Guidera, Sports Writer
(912) 652-0352
tim.guidera@savannahnow.com
• Don Heath, Sports Writer
(912) 652-0353
dheath@savannahnow.com
• Anthony Stastny, Sports Editor
anthony.stastny@savannahnow.com
• Jim Thomas, Sports Writer
(912) 652-0350
jimt@savannahnow.com
Frequency:
7 time(s) per week

SCOTTSDALE TRIBUNE
6991 EAST CAMELBACK ROAD SUITE
A10
SCOTTSDALE, AZ 85251
480-970-2330
Fax: 480-970-2360
www.scottsdaletribune.com
• Scott Bordow, Sports Columnist
(480) 898-6598
• Betsy Goreham, Advertising Director
(480) 898-6500
• Bob Romantic, Sports Editor
(480) 898-6538
Frequency:
7 time(s) per week

SEATTLE POST-INTELLIGENCER
2601 ELLIOT AVENUE
SUITE 300A
SEATTLE, WA 98121
206-448-8036
Fax: 206-448-8190
citydesk@seattlepi.com
www.seattlepi.com
• Scott Anderson, Sports Copy Editor
(206) 448-8372
• Clare Farnsworth, Sports Reporter
(206) 448-8016
• John Hickey, Sports Reporter
(206) 448-8004
• John Levesque, Sports Columnist
(206) 448-8330
• Michael McLaughlin, Sports Reporter
(206) 448-8187
• Ted Miller, Sports Columnist
(206) 448-8017
• Jim Moore, Sports Columnist
(206) 448-8013
• Keith Olson, Sports Copy Editor
(206) 448-8375
• Dan Raley, Sports Reporter
(206) 448-8008
• Nick Rousso, Sports Editor
(206) 448-8211

• Steve Rudman, Sports News Editor
(206) 448-8379
• Art Thiel, Sports Columnist
(206) 448-8009
• Molly Yanity, Sports Reporter
(206) 448-8295
Frequency:
7 time(s) per week

SEATTLE TIMES
1120 JOHN STREET
SEATTLE, WA 98109-5321
206-464-2111
Fax: 206-464-2261
newstips@seattletimes.com
www.seattletimes.com
• Percy Allen, Sports Reporter
(206) 464-2278
pallen@seattletimes.com
• Bob Condotta, Sports Reporter
(206) 515-5699
bcondotta@seattletimes.com
• Jayda Evans, Sports Reporter
(206) 464-2067
jevans@seattletimes.com
• Steve Kelley, Sports Columnist
(206) 464-2176
• Bill Reader, Sports Assistant Editor
(206) 464-2416
breader@seattletimes.com
• Don Shelton, Sports Assistant Editor
(206) 464-8284
dshelton@seattletimes.com
• Larry Stone, Sports Columnist
(206) 464-3146
lstone@seattletimes.com
• Bud Withers, Sports Reporter
(206) 464-8281
bwithers@seattletimes.com
Frequency:
7 time(s) per week

SEDALIA DEMOCRAT
700 S MASSACHUSETTS AVE
SEDALIA, MO 65301-4548
660-826-1000
Fax: 660-826-2413
news@sedaliademocrat.com
www.sedaliademocrat.com
• Zana Meek, Advertising Manager
(660) 826-1000
zanam@sedaliademocrat.com
• Kyle Smith, Sports Editor
(660) 826-1000
Founded:
1868
Frequency:
Tuesday - Saturday
Publications:
Sedalia Democrat, Plainsman and
Whiteman Warrior

SEGUIN GAZETTE-ENTERPRISE
1012 SCHRIEWER ROAD
SEGUIN, TX 78155-7473
830-379-5441
Fax: 830-379-8328
www.seguingazette.com
• Tucker Stephenson, Sports Editor
(830) 379-5441
sports@seguingazette.com
Frequency:
5 time(s) per week

SELMA TIMES-JOURNAL
1018 WATER AVE
SELMA, AL 36701-4617

334-875-2110
Fax: 334-872-4588
news@selmatimesjournal.com
www.selmatimesjournal.com/
• Dale Constance, Sports Editor
(334) 875-2110
• Griffin Pritchard, Sports Writer
(334) 875-2110
Frequency:
6 time(s) per week

SEMINOLE PRODUCER
121 NORTH MAIN STREET
SEMINOLE, OK 74868-4627
405-382-1100
Fax: 405-382-1104
www.seminoleproducer.com
• Mike Gifford, Advertising Manager
ads@seminoleproducer.com
• Josh Griffin, Sports Editor
sports@seminoleproducer.com
Frequency:
5 time(s) per week

SENTINEL
64 DOWNTOWN PLAZA
FAIRMONT, MN 56031-
507-235-3303
Fax: 507-235-3718
news@fairmontsentinel.com
• Kathy Ratcliff, Advertising Manager
kathy@fairmontsentinel.com
• Charlie Sorrells, Sports Editor
illinoisroots@yahoo.com
Frequency:
6 time(s) per week

SENTINEL AND ENTERPRISE
808 MAIN STREET
FITCHBURG, MA 01420
978-343-6911
888-842-3633
Fax: 978-342-1158
news@sentinelandenterprise.com
www.sentinelandenterprise.com
• Ross Edwards, Sports Reporter
(978) 343-6911
• Chad Garner, Sports Editor
(978) 343-6911
Frequency:
7 time(s) per week

SENTINEL-RECORD
300 SPRING STREET
HOT SPRINGS NATIONAL, AR 71901-4148
501-623-7711
Fax: 501-623-2984
mark@hotsr.com
www.hotsr.com
• Penny Thornton, Advertising Director
(501) 623-7711
pthornton@wehco.com
• Bob Wisener, Sports Editor
Frequency:
7 time(s) per week

SENTINEL-TRIBUNE
P.O. BOX 88
BOWLING GREEN, OH 43402-1329
419-352-4611
Fax: 419-354-0314
local_news@sentinel-tribune.com
www.sentinel-tribune.com
• Jack Carle, Sports Editor
(419) 352-4611
sports@sentinel-tribune.com

• Rob Davenport, Advertising Manager
(419) 352-4611
ads@sentinel-tribune.com
Frequency:
6 time(s) per week

SF WEEKLY
185 BERRY STREET LOBBY 4, SUITE 3800
SAN FRANCISCO, CA 94107-1701
415-536-8100
Fax: 415-541-9096
www.sfweekly.com
• Matthew Smith, Sports Columnist
Frequency:
1 time(s) per week

SHAWANO LEADER
1464 EAST GREEN BAY STREET
SHAWANO, WI 54166-2258
715-526-2121
800-236-2105
Fax: 715-524-3941
editor@shawanoleader.com
www.shawanoleader.com
• Cory Dellenbach, Sports Editor
Frequency:
6 time(s) per week

SHAWNEE NEWS-STAR
P.O. BOX 1688
SHAWNEE, OK 74801-6913
405-273-4200
800-332-2305
Fax: 405-273-4207
newsroom@news-star.com
www.news-star.com
• Fred Fehr, Sports Editor
(405) 273-4200
• Sherry Lankford, Advertising Manager
(405) 214-3950
Frequency:
6 time(s) per week

SHEBOYGAN PRESS
632 CENTER AVENUE
SHEBOYGAN, WI 53081-4621
920-457-7711
800-686-3900
Fax: 920-457-0178
www.sheboygan-press.com
• Pete Barth, Sports Editor
(920) 453-5156
Frequency:
7 time(s) per week

SHELBY STAR
P. O. BOX 48
SHELBY, NC 28150-5452
704-484-7000
Fax: 704-484-0805
www.shelbystar.com
• Alan Ford, Sports Editor
(704) 484-7000
alanford@shelbystar.com
Frequency:
7 time(s) per week

SHELBY SUN TIMES
7508 CAPITAL DRIVE
GERMANTOWN, TN 38138-0801
901-755-7386
Fax: 901-755-0827
• Buck Patton, Sports Editor
(901) 755-7386

Frequency:
1 time(s) per week

SHELBY-UTICA NEWS
13650 11 MILE ROAD
WARREN, MI 48089-1422
586-498-8000
Fax: 586-498-9627
www.candgnews.com
• Susan Shanley, Sports Editor
(586) 498-1048
sshanley@candgnews.com
Frequency:
1 time(s) per week

SHELBYVILLE NEWS
123 EAST WASHINGTON STREET
SHELBYVILLE, IN 46176-1463
317-398-6631
800-362-0114
Fax: 317-398-0194
shelbynews@shelbynews.com
www.shelbynews.com
• Dennis Bonner, Advertising Manager
(317) 398-6631
• Jeff Brown, Sports Editor
(317) 398-6631
jbrown@shelbynews.com
Frequency:
6 time(s) per week

SIDNEY DAILY NEWS
1451 NORTH VANDERMARK ROAD
SIDNEY, OH 45365
937-498-8088
800-688-4820
Fax: 937-498-5991
www.sidneydailynews.com
• Ken Barhorst, Sports Editor
(937) 498-5960
Frequency:
6 time(s) per week

SIDNEY SUN TELEGRAPH
1136 ILLINOIS
SIDNEY, NE 69162
308-254-2818
Fax: 308-254-3925
• Doug Law, Sports Reporter
(308) 254-2818
Frequency:
5 time(s) per week

SIERRA VISTA HERALD
102 FAB AVENUE
SIERRA VISTA, AZ 85635-1741
520-458-9440
Fax: 520-459-0120
www.svherald.com
• Matt Hickman, Sports Editor
(520) 458-9440
• Paul Manhufe, Advertising Manager
(520) 515-4630
• Bruce Bourquin, Sports Reporter
(520) 458-9440
Frequency:
6 time(s) per week

SIGNAL
24000 CREEKSIDE ROAD
VALENCIA, CA 91355-1726
661-259-1234
Fax: 661-254-8068
www.the-signal.com
• Grant Gordon, Sports Editor
(661) 259-1234

Frequency:
7 time(s) per week

SILVER CITY DAILY PRESS & INDEPENDENT
300 WEST MARKET
SILVER CITY, NM 88061
505-388-1576
Fax: 505-388-1196
www.thedailypress.com
• Vince Cong, Sports Editor
• Wanda Sleep, Classified Manager
(505) 388-1576
• Mikey Torrez, Advertising Manager
(505) 388-1576
Frequency:
6 time(s) per week

SIOUX CITY JOURNAL
P.O. BOX 118
SIOUX CITY, IA 51101-
712-293-4250
800-397-9820
Fax: 712-279-5059
www.siouxcityjournal.com
• Steven Allspach, Sports Writer / Columnist
(712) 293-4250
• Bob Carruth, Advertising Manager
(712) 293-4320
• Terry Hersom, Sports Editor
(712) 293-4250
Frequency:
7 time(s) per week

SKAGIT VALLEY HERALD
1000 EAST COLLEGE WAY
MOUNT VERNON, WA 98273-5624
360-424-3251
800-683-3300
Fax: 360-428-0400
www.skagitvalleyherald.com
• Jeannette Kales, Classified Manager
(360) 424-3251
• Trevor Pyle, Sports Reporter
(360) 416-2156
• Dan Ruthemeyer, Sports Editor
(360) 424-3251
Frequency:
7 time(s) per week

SLIDELL SENTRY-NEWS
364 PONTCHARTRAIN DRIVE SUITE B
SLIDELL, LA 70458-4816
985-643-4918
Fax: 985-649-0254
www.slidellsentry.com
• Mary Christopher, Retail Advertising Manager
(985) 643-4918
• David Purdum, Sports Editor
(985) 643-4918
Frequency:
6 time(s) per week

SOUTH BEND TRIBUNE
225 WEST COLFAX AVENUE
SOUTH BEND, IN 46626-1001
574-235-6161
Fax: 574-236-1765
sbtnews@sbtinfo.com
www.southbendtribune.com
• Bill Bilinski, Sports Editor
(574) 235-6331
bbilinski@sbtinfo.com
• Al Lesar, Assistant Sports Editor
alesar@sbtinfo.com

• Eric Hansen, Notre Dame Beat Writer
ehansen@sbtinfo.com
• Matt Ingle, Sports Writer
mingle@sbtinfo.com
• Jason Kelly, Sports Reporter
(547) 235-6152
jkelly@sbtinfo.com
• Matt Kopsea, Sports Reporter
(574) 235-6161
mkopsea@sbtinfo.com
• Al Lesar, Sports Assistant Editor
(574) 235-6318
alesar@sbtinfo.com
• Steve Lowe, Sports Reporter
(574) 235-6161
stevelowe@sbtinfo.com
• Forrest Miller, Sports Writer
(574) 235-6161
wmiller@sbtinfo.com
• Tom Noie, Sports Writer
(574) 235-6161
tnoie@sbtinfo.com
• Bob Oppenheim, Michigan High School Sports Reporter
 (574) 235-6161
roppenheim@sbtinfo.com
• Curt Rallo, Sports Reporter
(574) 235-6161
crallo@sbtinfo.com
• Louie Stout, Sports Correspondent
(574) 235-6332
• Jack Walkden, Sports Reporter
(574) 235-6161
jwalkden@sbtinfo.com
Frequency:
7 time(s) per week
Circulation:
75,000 daily; 100,000 Sunday

SOUTH CITY JOURNAL
4210 CHIPPEWA STREET
SAINT LOUIS, MO 63116
314-664-2700
Fax: 314-664-8533
southnews@yourjournal.com
www.stltoday.com
• Scott Fitzgerald, Sports Editor
(314) 664-2700
sfitzgerald@yourjournal.com
Frequency:
1 time(s) per week

SOUTH COUNTY JOURNAL
4210 CHIPPEWA STREET
SAINT LOUIS, MO 63116
314-664-2700
Fax: 314-664-8533
www.stltoday.com
• Scott Fitzgerald, Sports Editor
(314) 664-2700
sfitzgerald@yourjournal.com
Frequency:
2 time(s) per week

SOUTH COUNTY NEWS
2045 GRANT STREET
SELMA, CA 93662-3508
559-896-1976
Fax: 559-896-9160
mmiyamoto@pulitzer.net
www.selmaenterprise.com
• Will Goldbeck, Sports Reporter
(559) 896-1976
Frequency:
1 time(s) per week

SOUTH FLORIDA SUN-SENTINEL
200 EAST LAS OLAS BOULEVARD
FORT LAUDERDALE, FL 33301-2293
954-356-4000
Fax: 954-356-4680
sfeedback@sun-sentinel.com
www.sun-sentinel.com
• Craig Barnes, College Sports Reporter
(954) 356-4000
• Mike Berardino, College Sports Reporter
(954) 356-4635
• Charles Bricker, Sports Columnist
(954) 356-4000
• Dave Brousseau, Sports Reporter
(954) 356-4649
• Christy Cabrera, High School Sports Writer
(954) 356-4000
• Tom Christensen, Assistant Sports Editor
(954) 356-4682
• Michael Cunningham, Sports Reporter
• Bonnie DiPacio, Sports Coordinator (Day)
(954) 356-4644
• Harvey Fialkov, Sports Reporter
(954) 356-4865
hfialkov@sun-sentinel.com
• Dave Heeren, Sports Reporter
(954) 356-4635
• Ted Hutton, Sports Writer
 (954) 356-4635
 thutton@sun-sentinel.com
• Dave Hyde, Sports Columnist
(954) 356-4650
dhyde@sun-sentinel.com
• Dave Joseph, Sports Columnist
(954) 356-4635
djoseph@sun-sentinel.com
• Omar Kelly, Sports Reporter
(954) 356-4000
• Alex Marvez, Sports Writer
(954) 356-4000
• Randall Mell, Sports Columnist
rmell@sun-sentinel.com
• Randy Mell, Sports Writer (Golf)
• Shandel Richardson, Sports Reporter
• Sharon Robb, High School Sports Editor
(954) 356-4000
srobb@sun-sentinel.com
• Juan Rodriguez, Sports Writer (Baseball)
(954) 356-4635
• Jeff Rusnak, Sports Columnist
(954) 356-4635
• Michael Russo, Sports Columnist
(954) 356-4635
• Ethan Skolnick, Sports Columnist
(954) 356-4000
eskolnick@sun-sentinel.com
• Sarah Talalay, Sports Business Writer
(954) 356-4173
stalalay@sun-sentinel.com
• Steve Waters, (954) 356-4648
Sports Writer (Outdoors)
swaters@sun-sentinel.com
• Brian White, Sports Editor
(954) 356-4653
• Ira Winderman, Sports Writer (Basketball)
iwinderman@sun-sentinel.com
Frequency:
7 time(s) per week

SOUTH SIDE JOURNAL
4210 CHIPPEWA STREET
SAINT LOUIS, MO 63116
314-664-2700
Fax: 314-664-8533
www.stltoday.com
• Scott Fitzgerald, Sports Editor
(314) 664-2700

Frequency:
2 time(s) per week

SOUTHBRIDGE EVENING NEWS
25 ELM STREET
SOUTHBRIDGE, MA 01550-2605
508-764-4325
800-367-9898
Fax: 508-764-8015
www.southbridgeeveningnews.com
• Jean Ashton, Advertising Manager
(508) 764-4325
jashton@stonebridgepress.com
• David Forbes, Sports Editor
(508) 764-4325
Frequency:
5 time(s) per week

SOUTHEAST MISSOURIAN
P.O. BOX 699
CAPE GIRARDEAU, MO 63701-7330
573-335-6611
800-877-1210
Fax: 573-334-7288
news@semissourian.com
www.semissourian.com
• Jeff Breer, Reporter
(573) 335-6611
• Toby Carrig, Sports Editor
(573) 335-6611
• Donna Denson, Advertising Manager
(573) 335-6611
ddenson@semissourian.com
Frequency:
7 time(s) per week

SOUTHERN ILLINOISAN
P.O. BOX 2108
CARBONDALE, IL 62902-1283
618-351-5000
Fax: 618-529-3774
news@TheSouthern.com
www.southernillinoisan.com
• Les Winkeler, Sports Editor
(618) 351-5000
Les.Winkeler@TheSouthern.com
Frequency:
7 time(s) per week

SOUTHSIDE REPORTER
2203 SOUTH HACKBERRY
SAN ANTONIO, TX 78210-4199
210-534-8848
Fax: 210-534-7134
www.primetimenewspapers.com
• Gabe Farias, Sports Editor
(210) 534-8848
Frequency:
1 time(s) per week

SOUTHTOWN STAR
6901 WEST 159TH STREET
TINLEY PARK, IL 60477-1789
708-633-6700
Fax: 708-633-5999
news@southtownstar.com
www.southtownstar.com
• Phil Arvia, Sports Columnist
(708) 633-5949
• John O'Brien, Sports Ass't Managing
Editor
(708) 633-5931
• John O'Brien, Sports Editor
(708) 633-5931
Frequency:
6 time(s) per week

SOUTHWEST CITY JOURNAL
4210 CHIPPEWA STREET
SAINT LOUIS, MO 63116
314-664-2700
Fax: 314-664-8533
www.stltoday.com
• Scott Fitzgerald, Sports Editor
(314) 664-2700
Frequency:
2 time(s) per week

SOUTHWEST COUNTY JOURNAL
4210 CHIPPEWA STREET
SAINT LOUIS, MO 63116
314-664-2700
Fax: 314-664-8533
www.stltoday.com
• Scott Fitzgerald, Sports Editor
(314) 664-2700
Frequency:
2 time(s) per week

SOUTHWEST DAILY NEWS
716 EAST NAPOLEON STREET
SULPHUR, LA 70663-3402
337-527-7075
Fax: 337-528-3044
www.sulphurdailynews.com
• David Folser, Sports Editor
• Suzanne Peveto, Advertising Director
(337) 527-7075
swtdaily@yahoo.com
• Jonathan Manning, Sports Editor
(337) 527-7075
Frequency:
6 time(s) per week

SOUTHWEST NEWS-HERALD
6225 SOUTH KEDZIE AVENUE
CHICAGO, IL 60629-3304
773-476-4800
Fax: 773-476-7811
www.swnewsherald.com
• Tom Danz, Sports Editor
(773) 476-4800
Frequency:
1 time(s) per week

SOUTHWEST TIMES
P.O. BOX 391
PULASKI, VA 24301-4608
540-980-5220
Fax: 540-980-3618
editor@southwesttimes.com
www.southwesttimes.com
• Vanessa Young, Advertising Director
• David Bissett, Sports Editor
(540) 980-5220
sports@southwesttimes.com
Frequency:
6 time(s) per week

SOUTHWEST TIMES RECORD
3600 WHEELER AVENUE
FORT SMITH, AR 72901
479-785-7700
888-274-3992
Fax: 479-784-0413
www.swtimes.com
• Scott Faldon, Sports Editor
(479) 784-0469
• John Speck, Advertising Director
Frequency:
7 time(s) per week

SPARTANBURG HERALD-JOURNAL
P.O. BOX 1657
SPARTANBURG, SC 29306-2334
864-582-4511
800-922-4158
Fax: 864-594-6350
www.goupstate.com
• Burke Noel, Sports Editor
(864) 562-7241
• Kathy Towell, Advertising Manager
(864) 562-7350
Frequency:
7 time(s) per week

SPECTRUM
275 EAST SAINT GEORGE BOULEVARD
SAINT GEORGE, UT 84770-2954
435-674-6200
800-748-5489
Fax: 435-674-6265
aperkins@thespectrum.com
www.thespectrum.com
• Bob Hudson, Sports Editor
(435) 674-6250
Frequency:
7 time(s) per week

SPENCER DAILY REPORTER
310 EAST MILWAUKEE STREET
SPENCER, IA 51301-4569
712-262-6610
Fax: 712-262-3044
news@spencerdailyreporter.com
• Nate Shaughnessy, Sports Editor
sports@spencerdailyreporter.com
• Randy Cauthron, Managing Editor
Frequency:
5 time(s) per week

SPIRIT
510 PINE STREET
PUNXSUTAWNEY, PA 15767-1404
814-938-8740
Fax: 814-938-3794
composing@punxsutawneyspirit.com
www.punxsutawneyspirit.com
• Adam Pavock, Sports Editor
sports@punxsutawneyspirit.com
Frequency:
6 time(s) per week

SPOKESMAN-REVIEW
P.O. BOX 2160
SPOKANE, WA 99201-1006
509-459-5000
800-789-0029
Fax: 509-459-5482
www.spokesmanreview.com
• Steve Bergum, Sports Writer
(509) 927-2177
• John Blanchette, Sports Columnist
(509) 459-5509
• Gil Hulse, Sports Assistant Editor
(509) 459-5510
• Joe Palmquist, Sports Editor
(509) 459-5503
joep@spokesman.com
• Nick Eaton, College Sports Writer
(509) 990-9630
Frequency:
7 time(s) per week

SPORTS EYE
18 INDUSTRIAL PARK DRIVE
PORT WASHINGTON, NY 11050-4621

516-484-3300
800-568-7907
Fax: 516-484-6104
• Jack Cohen, Publisher
• Derrick N/A, Editor
• Tina Vitello, Advertising Manager
Frequency:
7 time(s) per week

SPRINGFIELD NEWS-LEADER
651 BOONVILLE
SPRINGFIELD, MO 65806
417-836-1100
800-695-1969
Fax: 417-837-1381
directory.ozarksnow.com
• Jeff Majeske, Sports Editor
• Rhonda Barlow, Advertising Director

SPRINGFIELD NEWS-SUN
P.O. BOX 3090
SPRINGFIELD, OH 45503-4202
937-328-0300
Fax: 937-328-0328
newssuneditor@coxohio.com
www.springfieldnewssun.com
• Rob Mercer, Advertising Director
(937) 328-0240
rmercer@coxohio.com
• Kermit Rowe, Sports Editor
(937) 328-0300
krowe@coxohio.com
Frequency:
7 time(s) per week

ST. ALBANS MESSENGER
P.O. BOX 1250
SAINT ALBANS, VT 05478-2503
802-524-9771
Fax: 802-527-1948
news@samessenger.com
www.samessenger.com/
• Jeremy Read, Advertising Manager
• Josh Kaufmann, Sports Editor
(802) 524-9771
Frequency:
6 time(s) per week

ST. AUGUSTINE RECORD
1 NEWS PLACE
SAINT AUGUSTINE, FL 32086
904-829-6562
Fax: 904-819-3558
www.staugustinerecord.com
• Justin Barney, Sports Editor
(904) 819-3492
• Dawn Ginnane, Advertising Director
(904) 819-3440
Frequency:
7 time(s) per week

ST. CHARLES JOURNAL
4212 NORTH SERVICE ROAD
SAINT PETERS, MO 63376
636-946-6111
Fax: 314-657-3354
www.yourjournal.com
• Russell Korando, Sports Editor
Frequency:
3 time(s) per week

ST. JOSEPH NEWS-PRESS
825 EDMOND STREET
SAINT JOSEPH, MO 64501-2737
816-271-8500
800-779-6397

Fax: 816-271-8692
photo@npgco.com
www.stjoenews-press.com/
• Brent Briggemann, Sports Writer
(816) 271-8553
• Scott Dochterman, Sports Editor
(816) 271-8577
• Clark Grell, Sports Assistant Editor
(816) 271-8555
• Tim Weddle, Advertising Director
(816) 271-8510
• Eddie Burns, Sports Reporter
(816) 271-8558
Frequency:
7 time(s) per week

ST. LOUIS POST-DISPATCH
900 N. TUCKER BLVD
ST. LOUIS, MO 63101
314-340-8000
Fax: 314-340-3070
www.post-dispatch.com
• Tom Rees, Vice President/Director of Advertising
• Cameron Hollway, Sports Director/High School

ST. PETERSBURG TIMES
490 FIRST AVENUE SOUTH
ST. PETERSBURG, FL 33701-4204
727-893-8111
800-333-7505
Fax: 727-893-8675
www.tampabay.com
• Damian Cristodero, Sports Writer
(727) 893-8662
cristodero@sptimes.com
• Antonya English, Sports Writer
(727) 893-8123
english@sptimes.com
• Dona Hankins, Sports Night Editor
(727) 893-8401
hankins@sptimes.com
• Bob Harig, Sports Writer
(727) 893-8806
harig@sptimes.com
• Brant James, Sports Writer
(727) 893-8111
• Tom Jones, Sports Writer
(727) 893-8111
sptsnews@sptimes.com
• Roy LeBlanc, Sports Editor
(727) 893-8925
• Rodney Page, Sports Writer
(727) 893-8818
• Frank Pastor, Sports Writer
(727) 893-8123
pastor@sptimes.com
• Scott Purks, Sports Writer
(813) 226-3353
purks@sptimes.com
• Bob Putnam, Sports Writer
(727) 445-4169
putnam@sptimes.com
• Gary Shelton, Sports Columnist
(727) 893-8805
• Mike Stephenson, Sports Editor
(727) 893-8201
• Rick Stroud, Sports Writer
(727) 893-8123
stroud@sptimes.com
• Marc Topkin, Sports Writer
(727) 893-8801
topkin@sptimes.com
• John Cotey, Sports Writer
(727) 893-8123
cotey@sptimes.com

Frequency:
7 time(s) per week

STAMFORD ADVOCATE
75 TRESSER BOULEVARD
STAMFORD, CT 06901-3304
203-964-2200
Fax: 203-964-2345
letters.advocate@scni.com
www.stamfordadvocate.com
• Bob Kennedy, Sports Editor
(203) 964-2275
Frequency:
7 time(s) per week

STANDARD DEMOCRAT
205 S NEW MADRID ST
SIKESTON, MO 63801-2953
573-471-1137
800-675-6980
Fax: 573-471-6981
standem@yahoo.com
www.standard-democrat.com
• Shawn Crawford, Classified Manager
(573) 471-4141
class@standard-democrat.com
• Derek James, Sports Editor
news@standard-democrat.com
• Deanna Nelson, Advertising Manager
(573) 471-4141
Frequency:
6 time(s) per week

STANDARD-EXAMINER
PO BOX 12790
OGDEN, UT 84404
801-625-4200
Fax: 801-625-4299
cityed@standard.net
www.standard.net
• Chris Miller, Executive Sports Editor
(801) 625-4261
sports@standard.net
• Brad Roghaar, Advertising Manager
(801) 625-4310
• Jasen Asay, College Sports Reporter
(801) 625-4260
Frequency:
7 time(s) per week

STANDARD-JOURNAL
21 NORTH ARCH STREET
MILTON, PA 17847
570-742-9671
Fax: 570-742-9876
newsroom@standard-journal.com
www.standard-journal.com
• Chris Brady, Staff Writer
(570) 742-9671
sports@standard-journal.com
Frequency:
6 time(s) per week

STANDARD-SPEAKER
21 NORTH WYOMING STREET
HAZLETON, PA 18201-6068
570-455-3636
800-843-6680
Fax: 570-455-4244
editorial@standardspeaker.com
www.standardspeaker.com
• Ron Kollar, Sports Editor
(570) 455-3636
sports@standardspeaker.com
• Bruce Leonard, Classified Manager

• Gary Yacubeck, Advertising Director
(570) 455-3636
Frequency:
7 time(s) per week

STANDARD-TIMES
P.O. BOX 5912
NEW BEDFORD, MA 02740-6228
508-979-4440
800-286-9876
Fax: 508-997-7491
newsroom@s-t.com
www.southcoasttoday.com
• Jonathan Comey, Sports Editor
(508) 979-4442
Frequency:
7 time(s) per week

STAR NEWS
296 THIRD
CHULA VISTA, CA 91910
619-427-3000
Fax: 619-426-6346
info@thestarnews.com
www.thestarnews.com
• Phillip Brents, Sports Editor
(619) 427-3000
Frequency:
1 time(s) per week

STAR PRESS
P.O. BOX 2408
MUNCIE, IN 47305-1620
765-747-5717
800-783-7827
Fax: 765-213-5858
news@thestarpress.com
www.thestarpress.com
• Phil Beebe, Sports Editor
(765) 213-5730
pbeebe@muncie.gannett.com
• Brian Saparnis, Sports Assistant Editor
(765) 213-5811
• Rob Sullivan, Sports Reporter
(765) 213-5816
rsullivan@muncie.gannett.com
• Mary Young, Advertising Director
(765) 213-5711
myoung@muncie.gannett.com
• Doug Zaleski, Sports Reporter
(765) 213-5813
dzaleski@muncie.gannett.com
Frequency:
7 time(s) per week

STAR TRIBUNE
425 PORTLAND AVENUE
MINNEAPOLIS, MN 55488-1511
612-673-4000
800-827-8742
Fax: 612-673-4359
www.startribune.com
• Rachel Blount, Sports Columnist
(612) 673-4389
rblount@startribune.com
• Dennis Brackin, Sports Team Leader
(612) 673-1740
• Mark Craig, Sports Reporter
(612) 673-7011
mcraig@startribune.com
Frequency:
7 time(s) per week

STAR-BANNER
P.O. BOX 490
OCALA, FL 34474-7052

352-867-4010
800-541-2171
Fax: 352-867-4018
www.ocala.com
• Eric Barnes, Sports Editor
(352) 867-4143
• Mike Hodge, Sports Writer
Frequency:
7 time(s) per week

STAR-BEACON
4626 PARK AVENUE
ASHTABULA, OH 44005-2100
440-998-2323
Fax: 440-998-7938
www.starbeacon.com
• Karl Pearson, Staff Writer
(440) 998-2323
• Don McCormack, Sports Editor
(440) 998-2323
donmac@suite224.net
• Bob Ettinger, Staff Writer
(440) 998-2323
Frequency:
7 time(s) per week
Circulation:
20,000

STAR-COURIER
105 EAST CENTRAL BOULEVARD
KEWANEE, IL 61443-2245
309-852-2181
800-397-7827
Fax: 309-852-0010
editor@starcourier.com
www.starcourier.com
• Brian Murphy, Sports Editor
(309) 852-2181
Frequency:
6 time(s) per week

STAR-DEMOCRAT
29088 AIRPARK DRIVE
EASTON, MD 21601-7000
410-822-1500
Fax: 410-770-4019
stardem@chespub.com
www.stardem.com
• Derek Coleman, Sports Reporter
(410) 770-4095
• David Fike, Advertising Manager
(410) 770-4040
• Kevin George, Sports Assistant Editor
(410) 770-4095
• Bill Haufe, Sports Editor
(410) 770-4095
bhaufe@chespub.com
• Sil Morrison, Classified Manager
(410) 770-4054
Frequency:
6 time(s) per week

STAR-GAZETTE
201 BALDWIN STREET
ELMIRA, NY 14901-3002
607-734-5151
800-836-8970
Fax: 607-733-4408
www.stargazette.com
• Roger Neumann, Sports Editor
(607) 271-8242
• Andrew Legare, Sports Editor
(607) 734-5151
alegare@stargazette.com
Frequency:
7 time(s) per week

STAR-HERALD
1405 BROADWAY
SCOTTSBLUFF, NE 69361-3151
308-632-9000
800-846-6102
Fax: 308-632-9001
news@starherald.com
www.starherald.com
• Jeff Fielder, Sports Editor
(308) 632-9000
Frequency:
6 time(s) per week

STAR-LEDGER
1 STAR-LEDGER PLAZA
NEWARK, NJ 07102-1200
973-392-4040
Fax: 973-392-1886
www.nj.com/starledger
• Fred Aun, Outdoors Writer
(973) 392-4040
• Richard Chere, Sports Reporter (Hockey)
• Dave D'Alessandro, Basketball Columnist
(973) 392-4203
ddalessandro@starledger.com
• Chris D'Amico, Deputy Managing
Editor/Production
(973) 392-5732
• Sid Dorfman, Sports Columnist
(973) 392-4023
• Matthew Futterman, Sports Business
Reporter
(973) 392-1732
mfutterman@starledger.com
• Jim Hague, Sports Reporter
(201) 955-0016
ogsmar@aol.com
• Jerry Izenberg, Sports Columnist
jizenberg@starledger.com
• Kevin Manahan, Sports Reporter
kmanahan@starledger.com
• Steve Politi, Sports Writer
(973) 392-4023
spoliti@starledger.com
Frequency:
7 time(s) per week

STAR-TELEGRAM (FORT WORTH)
400 W. 7TH St
FORT WORTH, TX 76102
817-390-7400
Fax: 817-390-7789
www.star-telegram.com
• Paul Harral, Editorial Director
• Celeste Williams, Sports Editor
(817) 390-7697
Description:
Covers Sports local and national. Rangers
Cowboys High School Football College
Sports Mavericks/NBA Stars/Pro Hockey
Motorsports Horse Racing Rodeo/Horse

STAR-TRIBUNE
170 STAR LANE
CASPER, WY 82604-2883
307-266-0550
Fax: 307-266-0568
www.casperstartribune.net
• Ron Gullberg, Sports Editor
(307) 266-0573
Frequency:
7 time(s) per week

STARKVILLE DAILY NEWS
316 UNIVERSITY DRIVE
STARKVILLE, MS 39759

662-323-1642
Fax: 662-323-6586
www.starkvilledailynews.com
• Don Foster, Sports Editor
Frequency:
7 time(s) per week

STATE
P.O. BOX 1333
COLUMBIA, SC 29202-4814
803-771-8465
800-288-2727
Fax: 803-771-8430
biznews@thestate.com
www.thestate.com
• Gerald Davis, Sports Assistant Editor
(803) 771-8442
• Bob Gillespie, Golf Columnist
(803) 771-8304
• Craig McHugh, Sports Editor
(803) 771-8450
• Jim McLaurin, Sports Writer
(803) 771-8542
• Rick Millians, Executive Sports Editor
(803) 771-8450
• Ron Morris, Sports Columnist
(803) 771-8432
• David Newton, Sports Senior Writer
(803) 548-3769
• Patrick Obley, Sports Reporter
(803) 771-8465
• Joe Person, Sports Reporter
(803) 771-8496
• Bob Spear, Sports Columnist
Frequency:
7 time(s) per week

STATE GAZETTE
294 HIGHWAY 51 BYPASS
DYERSBURG, TN 38024
731-285-4091
Fax: 731-285-9747
www.stategazette.com
• Mike Smith, Sports Editor
(731) 285-4091
msmith@stategazette.com
Frequency:
6 time(s) per week

STATE JOURNAL-REGISTER
1 COPLEY PLAZA
SPRINGFIELD, IL 62701
217-788-1300
800-397-8757
Fax: 217-788-1372
sjr@sj-r.com
www.sj-r.com
• Robert Burns, Sports Writer
(217) 788-1546
• Dave Kane, Sports Writer
dave.kane@sj-r.com
• Marcia Martinez, Sports Writer
marcia.martinez@sj-r.com
• Hal Pilger, Sports Writer
• Jim Ruppert, Sports Editor
• Tim Stacy, Advertising Manager
(217) 788-1300
• John Supinie, Sports Writer
• Tom Tillman, Display Advertising Manager
(217) 788-1359
Frequency:
7 time(s) per week

STATEN ISLAND ADVANCE
950 FINGERBOARD ROAD
STATEN ISLAND, NY 10305-1453

718-981-1234
Fax: 718-981-5679
editor@siadvance.com
www.silive.com
• Carmine Angioli, Sports Editor
(718) 816-2803
angioli@siadvance.com
• Tom Flannagan, Sports Columnist
(718) 816-2582
• Stephen Hart, Sports Columnist
(718) 981-2241
Frequency:
7 time(s) per week

STATESMAN JOURNAL
P.O. BOX 13009
SALEM, OR 97301-3734
503-399-6611
Fax: 503-399-6706
newsroom@statesmanjournal.com
www.statesmanjournal.com/apps/pbcs.dll/fr
ontpage
• James Day, Sports Editor
(503) 399-6801
jday@statesmanjournal.com
• Teresa Kepplinger, Advertising Director
(503) 399-6648
tkepling@statesmanjournal.com
Frequency:
7 time(s) per week

STATESVILLE RECORD & LANDMARK
222 EAST BROAD STREET
STATESVILLE, NC 28677-5325
704-873-1451
Fax: 704-872-3150
news@statesville.com
www.statesville.com
• Jon Dunham, Advertising Director
(704) 873-1451
• Bill Kiser, Sports Editor
(704) 873-1451
• Jason Bullard, Sports Editor
(704) 873-1451
Frequency:
7 time(s) per week

STEPHENVILLE EMPIRE-TRIBUNE
590 SOUTH LOOP
STEPHENVILLE, TX 76401-4224
254-965-3124
Fax: 254-965-4269
www.empiretribune.com
• John Menzies, Sports Editor
(254) 965-3124
sports@empiretribune.com
Frequency:
6 time(s) per week

STEVENS POINT JOURNAL
P.O. BOX 7
STEVENS POINT, WI 54481-2855
715-344-6100
Fax: 715-344-7229
spj@coredcs.com
www.stevenspointjournal.com
• Chris Schulte, Sports Editor
(715) 845-0700
cschulte@gannett.com
• Scott Williams, Sports Reporter
(715) 345-2282
scott.williams@cwnews.net
• Nathan Vine, Sports Reporter
(715) 345-2281
nvine@stevenspoint.gannett.com
Frequency:
7 time(s) per week

STILLWATER GAZETTE
1931 CURVE CREST BOULEVARD
STILLWATER, MN 55082
651-439-3130
Fax: 651-439-4713
www.stillwatergazette.com/
• Stuart Groskreutz, Sports Editor
(651) 796-1107
Frequency:
5 time(s) per week

STUTTGART DAILY LEADER
111 WEST 6TH STREET
STUTTGART, AR 72160-4243
870-673-8533
800-244-3966
Fax: 870-673-3671
www.stuttgartdailyleader.com
• Patrick Geans, Sports Editor
(870) 673-8533
Frequency:
5 time(s) per week

SUFFOLK NEWS-HERALD
P.O. BOX 1220
SUFFOLK, VA 23434-5323
757-539-3437
Fax: 757-539-3000
www.suffolknewsherald.com
• Earl Jones, Advertising Director
(757) 934-9607
• Andrew Giermak, Sports Editor
(757) 934-9614
Frequency:
6 time(s) per week

SULLIVAN DAILY TIMES
115 WEST JACKSON AVENUE
SULLIVAN, IN 47882-1505
812-268-6356
800-264-6356
Fax: 812-268-3110
• Rick Curl, Sports Editor
• Matt Wilson, Sports Editor
(812) 268-6356
Frequency:
5 time(s) per week

SULPHUR SPRINGS NEWS-TELEGRAM
401 CHURCH STREET
SULPHUR SPRINGS, TX 75482-2681
903-885-8663
800-245-2149
Fax: 903-885-8768
cityed@ssecho.com
www.ssnewstelegram.com/
• Bobby Burney, Sports Editor
(903) 885-8663
sportsed@ssecho.com
• Johnie Hargrave, Advertising Manager
Frequency:
6 time(s) per week

SUMMIT DAILY NEWS
40 WEST MAIN STREET
FRISCO, CO 80443
970-668-3998
Fax: 970-668-0755
news@summitdaily.com
www.summitdaily.com
• Christine Holaday-Schriock, Classified
Manager
(970) 668-9937
cschriock@cmnm.org
• Devon O'Neil, Sports Editor
(970) 668-3998

• Adam Boffey, Sports Editor
(970) 668-3998
Frequency:
7 time(s) per week

SUN (CA)
399 N. D ST
SAN BERNARDINO, CA 92401
909-889-9666
Fax: 909-384-0327
www.sbcsun.com
• Paul Oberjuerge, Sports Editor
• Glenn Rabinowitz, Managing Editor

SUN (MD)
501 N. CALVERT ST
BALTIMORE, MD 21278
410-332-6000
Fax: 410-269-4224
www.sunspot.net
• Ron Fritz, Sports Editor
ron.fritz@baltsun.com

SUN (WA)
545 5TH STREET
BREMERTON, WA 98337-1413
360-377-3711
Fax: 360-377-9237
• Annette Griffus, Sports Reporter
(360) 792-9224
agriffus@kitsapsun.com
• Nathan Joyce, Sports Reporter
(360) 792-9209
njoyce@kitsapsun.com
• Chuck Stark, Sports Editor
(360) 792-9231
Frequency:
7 time(s) per week

SUN CHRONICLE
P.O. BOX 600
ATTLEBORO, MA 02703
508-222-7000
Fax: 508-236-0462
www.thesunchronicle.com
• Mark Farinella, Sports Reporter
• Dale Ransom, Sports Reporter
Frequency:
7 time(s) per week

SUN JOURNAL
3200 WELLONS BOULEVARD
NEW BERN, NC 28562
252-638-8101
Fax: 252-638-4664
www.newbernsj.com
• Randy Jones, Sports Editor
(252) 638-8101
Frequency:
7 time(s) per week

SUN NEWS
P.O. BOX 406
MYRTLE BEACH, SC 29577-6700
843-626-8555
800-568-1800
Fax: 843-626-0356
sneditors@thesunnews.com
www.thesunnews.com
• Al Blondin, Sports Reporter Golf
(843) 626-0284
• Shane Bowen, Sports Editor
(843) 626-0302
• Terry Massey, Columnist
(843) 626-0371

Frequency:
7 time(s) per week

SUN-GAZETTE
6408 EDSALL ROAD
ALEXANDRIA, VA 22312
703-738-2520
Fax: 703-738-2530
news@sungazette.net
www.sungazette.net
• David Facinoli, Sports Editor
(703) 738-2533
sports@sungazette.net
Frequency:
1 time(s) per week

SUN-SENTINEL
200 E. LAS OLAS BLVD
FORT LAUDERDALE, FL 33301-2293
954-356-4000
Fax: 954-356-4676
www.sun-sentinel.com
• Fred Turner, Sports Editor

SUNDAY GAZETTE-MAIL
1001 VIRGINIA ST E.
CHARLESTON, WV 25301
304-348-4827
Fax: 304-348-4847
wvgazette.com
• Mitch Vingle, Sports Editor

SUNDAY NEWS
P.O. BOX 1328
LANCASTER, PA 17603
717-291-8811
800-809-4666
Fax: 717-291-4950
www.lancasteronline.com
• James Hersh, Sports Editor
(717) 291-8699
• Dave Byrne, Sports Reporter
(717) 291-8699
Frequency:
1 time(s) per week

SUPERIOR TELEGRAM
424 W FIRST ST
DULUTH, MN 55802
editorial@superiortelegram.com
www.superiortelegram.com
• Ken Olson, Sports Writer
(715) 395-5023
Frequency:
Tuesday and Friday

SWEETWATER REPORTER
112 WEST THIRD STREET
SWEETWATER, TX 79556
325-236-6677
Fax: 325-235-4967
editor@sweetwaterreporter.com
www.sweetwaterreporter.com
• Ron Howell, Sports Writer
Frequency:
6 time(s) per week
Circulation:
3,400

TAHOE DAILY TRIBUNE
3079 HARRISON AVENUE
SOUTH LAKE TAHOE, CA 96150-7931
530-541-3880
Fax: 530-541-0373

editor@tahoedailytribune.com
www.tahoedailytribune.com/
• Steve Yingling, Sports Editor
(530) 542-8010
Frequency:
5 time(s) per week

TALLADEGA DAILY HOME
4 SYLACAUGA HIGHWAY
TALLADEGA, AL 35160
256-362-1000
Fax: 256-299-2192
news@dailyhome.com
www.dailyhome.com
• Pam Adamson, Advertising Director
(256) 299-2140
padamson@dailyhome.com
• Alta Bolding, Classified Manager
(256) 299-2150
abolding@dailyhome.com
• Sandy Carden, Retail Advertising Manager
(256) 299-2141
scarden@dailyhome.com
• Will Heath, Sports Editor
• Austin Moore, Sports Assistant Editor
amoore@dailyhome.com
• Bran Strickland, Sports Editor
(256) 299-2132
bstrickland@dailyhome.com
Frequency:
6 time(s) per week

TALLAHASSEE DEMOCRAT
P.O. BOX 990
TALLAHASSEE, FL 32301-2695
850-599-2100
800-777-2154
Fax: 850-599-2295
www.tallahassee.com
• Randy Beard, Executive Sports Editor
(850) 599-2160
rbeard@tallahassee.com
• Jack Corcoran, Sports Reporter
(850) 599-2172
• Steve Ellis, Senior College Sports Writer
(850) 599-2100
sellis@tallahassee.com
• Ike Morgan, Sports Editor
(850) 599-2297
• Clair Murraine, Sports Reporter
(850) 599-2317
scmurraine@tallahassee.com
Frequency:
7 time(s) per week

TAMPA TRIBUNE
200 S PARKER STREET
TAMPA, FL 33606
813-259-7655
800-527-2718
Fax: 813-259-8148
sports@tampatrib.com
www.tbo.com
• Kim Pendery, MLB/Rays/Auto Racing/Colleges
(813) 259-8406
kpendery@tampatrib.com
• Doug Jacobs, Prep
(813) 259-7615
djacobs@tampatrib.com
• Joanne Korth, NFL, Bucs, NHL/Lightning
(813) 259-7998
jkorth@tampatrib.com
• Roy Cummings, Sports Reporter
(813) 259-7859
RCummings@tampatrib.com
• Bob D'Angelo, Sports Copy Editor

rdangelo@tampatrib.com
• Eddie Daniels, Sports Writer / Pasco County
(813) 259-7600
EDaniels@tampatrib.com
• Eddie Daniels, Sports Reporter
(813) 948-4274
edaniels@tampatrib.com
• Mick Elliott, Columnist
(813) 259-7341
melliott@tampatrib.com
• Erik Erlendsson, Sports Writer
(813) 259-7600
eerlendsson@tampatrib.com
• Tony Fabrizio, Auto Racing Reporter
(813) 259-7655
afabrizio@tampatrib.com
• Martin Fennelly, Sports Columnist
(813) 259-7352
mfennelly@tampatrib.com
• Carter Gaddis, Sports Reporter
(813) 259-7979
cgaddis@tampatrib.com
• Mike Garbett, Sports Copy Editor
mgarbett@tampatrib.com
• Mike Harris, Team Leader/Local Sports
(813) 259-7302
mharris@tampatrib.com
• Joe Henderson, Sports Writer
(813) 259-7861
JHenderson@tampatrib.com
• Doug Jacobs, Deputy Sports Editor
(813) 259-7600
djacobs@tampatrib.com
• Barb Jiannetti, Sports Copy Editor
BJiannetti@tampatrib.com
• Joey Johnston, Sports Writer
(813) 259-7711
jjohnston@tampatrib.com
• Ira Kaufman, Sports Reporter
(813) 259-7655
ikaufman@tampatrib.com
• Joey Knight, Sports Reporter
(813) 948-4202
jknight@tampatrib.com
• Rozel Lee, Sports Reporter
RLee@tampatrib.com
• Brett McMurphy, Sports Reporter
(813) 259-7928
bmcmurphy@tampatrib.com
• Mike Pennetti, Sports Team Leader
MPennetti@tampatrib.com
• Wes Phillips, Sports Copy Editor
wphillips@tampatrib.com
• Nick Pugliese, (813) 259-7854
Sports Senior Editor
DPugliese@tampatrib.com
• Anwar Richardson, Sports Reporter
arichardson@tampatrib.com
• Matt Severance, Sports Editor
(813) 259-7064
mseverance@tampatrib.com
• Katherine Smith, Sports Writer
(813) 259-7600
ksmith@tampatrib.com
• Alan Snel, Sports Business Writer
(813) 259-7850
ASnel@tampatrib.com
• Andy Staples, Sports Writer
(813) 259-7600
astaples@tampatrib.com
Frequency:
7 time(s) per week

TAYLOR DAILY PRESS
211 WEST 3RD STREET
TAYLOR, TX 76574-3518

512-352-8535
Fax: 512-352-2227
www.taylordailypress.net
• Maurine Stutler, Classified Manager
• Jeremy Weber, Sports Editor
• Don Wilson, Advertising Manager
• Brian Smith, Sports Editor
(512) 352-8535
Frequency:
5 time(s) per week

TELEGRAM & GAZETTE
20 FRANKLIN STREET
WORCESTER, MA 01615
508-793-9100
800-678-6680
Fax: 508-793-9281
newstips@telegram.com
www.telegram.com
• Bill Ballou, Sports Reporter
(508) 793-9350
sports@telegram.com
• Bud Barth, Sports Reporter
(508) 793-9350
sports@telegram.com
• Rich Garven, Sports Reporter
(508) 793-9350
sports@telegram.com
• Dave Greenslit, Sports Editor
(508) 793-9375
• Nick Manzello, Sports Columnist
sports@telegram.com
• Phil O'Neill, Sports Reporter
(508) 793-9350
sports@telegram.com
• Jennifer Toland, Sports Reporter
(508) 793-9350
sports@telegram.com
Frequency:
7 time(s) per week

TELEGRAPH (IL)
111 EAST BROADWAY
ALTON, IL 65606
618-463-2500
800-477-1447
Fax: 618-463-9829
telegraph_pub@hotmail.com
www.thetelegraph.com
• Pete Hayes, Sports Editor
(618) 463-2565
phayes93@hotmail.com
• Greg Shashack, Sports Assistant Editor
gshashack@hotmail.com
Frequency:
7 time(s) per week

TELEGRAPH (NE)
621 NORTH CHESTNUT STREET
NORTH PLATTE, NE 69101-4131
308-532-6000
800-753-7092
Fax: 308-532-9268
editor@nptelegraph.com
www.thenptelegraph.com
• Job Vigil, Sports Editor
(308) 532-6000
jvigil@nptelegraph.com
Frequency:
6 time(s) per week

TELEGRAPH (NH)
17 EXECUTIVE DR
HUDSON, NH 03051
603-594-6576
Fax: 603-882-2681
www.nashuatelegraph.com

• Alan Greenwood, Sports Editor
• Steve Daly, Asst Sports Director

TELEGRAPH HERALD
801 BLUFF STREET
DUBUQUE, IA 52001-4661
563-588-5611
800-553-4801
Fax: 563-588-5745
thonline@wcinet.com
www.thonline.com
• Clete Campbell, Sports Reporter
(563) 588-5623
• Steve Fisher, Advertising Director
(563) 588-5754
• Troy Johnson, Sports Reporter
(563) 588-5626
• Jim Leitner, Sports Editor
(563) 588-5783
jleitner@wcinet.com
• Bill Speltz, Sports Reporter
(563) 588-5632
Frequency:
7 time(s) per week

TEMPLE DAILY TELEGRAM
10 SOUTH 3RD STREET
TEMPLE, TX 76501-7619
254-778-4444
800-460-6397
Fax: 254-771-3516
www.temple-telegram.com
• Gary Garner, Advertising Manager
(254) 778-4444
• Stan Thomas, Classified Manager
(254) 778-4444
tdt@vvm.com
• Greg Willi, Sports Editor
(254) 778-4444
Frequency:
7 time(s) per week

TENNESSEAN
1100 BROADWAY
NASHVILLE, TN 37203
615-259-8000
Fax: 615-259-8093
newstips@tennessean.com
www.tennessean.com
• Joe Biddle, Sports Columnist
(615) 259-8255
jbiddle@tennessean.com
• Larry Taft, Sports Editor
(615) 259-8352
• Chip Cirillo, Sports Reporter
(615) 664-2194
ccirillo@tennessean.com
• David Climer, Sports Columnist
(615) 259-8020
dclimer@tennessean.com
• John Glennon, Sports Reporter
(615) 259-8262
jglennon@tennessean.com
• Mike Jones, Deputy Sports Editor
(615) 259-8013
mjones@tennessean.com
• Jeff Lockridge, Sports Reporter
(615) 259-8023
• Bryan Mullen, Sports Writer
(615) 259-8017
• Mike Organ, Sports Reporter
(615) 259-8021
morgan@tennessean.com
• Maurice Patton, Sports Reporter
(615) 259-8018
mpatton@tennessean.com
• Kevin Procter, Sports Reporter

(615) 259-8014
kprocter@tennessean.com
• Jim Wyatt, Sports Reporter
(615) 259-8015
Frequency:
7 time(s) per week

TERRELL TRIBUNE
150 9TH STREET
TERRELL, TX 75160
972-563-6476
Fax: 972-563-0340
ttrib@swbell.net
www.terrelltribune.com
• Kent Miller, Sports Editor
• Nicole Petet, Advertising Manager
ttribads@swbell.net
Frequency:
6 time(s) per week

TEXARKANA GAZETTE
PO BOX 621
TEXARKANA, TX 75501-5655
903-794-3311
Fax: 903-794-3315
www.texarkanagazette.com
• Louie Avery, Sports Writer
(903) 794-3311
• Johnny Green, Sports Editor
(903) 794-3311
• Rick Meredith, Advertising Manager
(903) 794-3311
• James Williams, Sports Editor
(903) 794-3311
Frequency:
7 time(s) per week

THE ADVERTISER
221 JEFFERSON ST
LAFAYETTE, LA 70501
337-289-6303
Fax: 337-289-6443
www.acadiananow.com
• Brady Aymond, Sports Writer
(337) 289-6357
• Kevin Foote, Sports Editor
(337) 289-6317

AEGIS, THE
139 NORTH MAIN STREET
SUITE 203
BEL AIR, MD 21014
410-838-4400
888-879-1710
Fax: 410-838-7867
news@theaegis.com
www.baltimoresun.com/news/maryland/harford/aegis
• Randy McRoberts, Sports Editor
(410) 332-6718
rmcroberts@theaegis.com
Frequency:
7 time(s) per week

THE ARGUS
37468 FREMONT BLVD
FREMONT, CA 94536
510-353-7027
Fax: 510-353-7029
bangcirc@bayareanewsgroup.com
www.insidebayarea.com/argus/
• Mike Lefkow, Sports Editor
(925) 943-8149
mlefkow@bayareanewsgroup.com
Frequency:
7 time(s) per week

THE STAR
118 WEST 9TH STREET
AUBURN, IN 46706-2225
260-925-2611
800-717-4679
Fax: 260-925-2625
www.kpcnews.com
• Mark Murdock, Sports Editor
(260) 925-2611
Frequency:
7 time(s) per week

THE TRIANGLE TRIBUNE
115 MARKET STREET
SUITE 360-G
DURHAM, NC 27701
919-688-9408
Fax: 919-688-2740
editor@triangletribune.com
www.triangletribune.com
• Bonitta Best, Sports Editor/Managing Editor
Frequency:
1 time(s) per week
Description:
Weekly newspaper
Year Founded:
1998

THREE RIVERS COMMERCIAL-NEWS
PO BOX 130
THREE RIVERS, MI 49093
269-279-7488
Fax: 269-279-6007
www.threeriversnews.com
• Marnie Apa, Advertising Manager
marnie@threeriversnews.com
• Scott Hassinger, Sports Reporter
(269) 279-7488
scott@threeriversnews.com
Frequency:
6 time(s) per week

TIFTON GAZETTE
211 NORTH TIFT AVENUE
TIFTON, GA 31793
229-382-4321
Fax: 229-387-7322
www.tiftongazette.com
• Tom Mark, Sports Editor
(229) 382-4321
• Darrin Wilson, Advertising Manager
Frequency:
6 time(s) per week

TIMES (IN)
601 45TH AVENUE, W.
MUNSTER, IN 46321-2875
219-933-3200
800-589-3331
Fax: 219-933-3249
newstips@nwi.com
www.nwi.com
• Mike Clark, Assistant Sports Editor
(219) 933-3200
Frequency:
7 time(s) per week

TIMES (LA)
222 LAKE STREET
SHREVEPORT, LA 71101-3738
318-459-3270
800-551-8892
Fax: 318-459-3301
www.shreveporttimes.com

• Scott Ferrell, Sports Editor
(318) 459-3300
sferrell@gannett.com
• Brian Vernellis, Sports Reporter
(318) 459-3300
bvernellis@gannett.com
Frequency:
7 time(s) per week

TIMES AND DEMOCRAT
1010 BROUGHTON STREET, S.E.
ORANGEBURG, SC 29115-5955
803-534-3352
Fax: 803-533-5526
news@timesanddemocrat.com
www.timesanddemocrat.com
• Thomas Grant, Sports Senior Reporter
(803) 533-5547
• John Weiss, Advertising Manager
(803) 533-5542
Frequency:
7 time(s) per week

TIMES ARGUS
P.O. BOX 707
BARRE, VT 05641-2504
802-479-0191
Fax: 802-479-4032
news@timesargus.com
www.timesargus.com
• Derek Armstrong, Sports Editor
(802) 479-0191
• David Cousins, Advertising Manager
(802) 479-0191
Frequency:
7 time(s) per week

TIMES DAILY
P.O. BOX 797
FLORENCE, AL 35630-5440
256-766-3434
Fax: 256-740-4717
www.timesdaily.com
• Gregg Dewalt, Sports Editor
(256) 740-5748
• Jeff McIntyre, Assistant Sports Editor
(256) 740-5737
Frequency:
7 time(s) per week

TIMES GAZETTE
209 SOUTH HIGH STREET
HILLSBORO, OH 45133-1444
937-393-3456
Fax: 937-393-2059
www.timesgazette.com
• Lori Boatman-Roush, Sports Editor
• Sharon Kersey, Advertising Manager
Frequency:
6 time(s) per week

TIMES GEORGIAN
901 HAYS MILL ROAD
CARROLLTON, GA 30117-9576
770-834-6631
Fax: 770-834-9991
bbrowning@times-georgian.com
www.times-georgian.com
• Corey Cusick, Sports Editor
(770) 834-6631
• Tim Holder, Advertising Director
tholder@times-georgian.com
Frequency:
6 time(s) per week

TIMES HERALD (MI)
911 MILITARY STREET
PORT HURON, MI 48061-5009
810-985-7171
800-462-4057
Fax: 810-989-6294
timesherald@gannett.com
www.thetimesherald.com
• Lori Driscoll, Advertising Director
(810) 989-6236
ldriscoll@gannett.com
• Jim Wymer, Sports Editor
(810) 989-6267
Frequency:
7 time(s) per week

TIMES HERALD (PA)
410 MARKLEY STREET
NORRISTOWN, PA 19401-4617
610-272-2501
800-887-2501
Fax: 610-272-0660
shuskey@timesherald.com
www.timesherald.com
• Tim Fonde, Sports Editor
(610) 272-2500
• Tom Kerrane, Sports Writer
(610) 272-2232
Frequency:
7 time(s) per week

TIMES HERALD RECORD
40 MULBERRY STREET
MIDDLETOWN, NY 10940
845-341-1100
Fax: 845-343-2170
www.th-record.com
• Kevin Gleason, Sports Columnist
(845) 346-3193
kgleason@th-record.com
• Douglas Mohart, Sports Editor
(845) 346-3191
dmohart@th-record.com
• Kathleen Passineau, Retail Advertising
Manager
(845) 346-3013
• Justin Rodriguez, Sports Reporter
(845) 346-3192
jrodriguez@th-record.com
Frequency:
7 time(s) per week

TIMES JOURNAL
811 GREENHILL BOULEVARD NW
FORT PAYNE, AL 35967
256-845-2550
800-348-4637
Fax: 256-845-7459
www.times-journal.com
• Lew Gilliland, Sports Editor
(256) 304-0053
• Gloria Jackson, Advertising Manager
(256) 304-060
Frequency:
5 time(s) per week

TIMES LEADER
15 N. MAIN ST
WILKES-BARRE, PA 18711
570-829-7101
Fax: 570-831-7319
• Kurt Knapek, Sports Editor
• Paul Graham, Advertising Director

TIMES NEWS
1ST & IRON STREETS
LEHIGHTON, PA 18235
610-377-2051
Fax: 610-826-9608
tnsports@tnonline.com
www.tnonline.com
• Rod Heckman, Sports Reporter
(610) 377-2051
rheckman@tnonline.com
• Ed Hedes, Managing Sports Editor
(610) 377-2051
• Emmett McCall, Sports Reporter
(610) 377-2051
emccall@tnonline.com
• Linda Moyer, Classified Manager
(610) 377-2051
lmoyer@tnonline.com
Frequency:
6 time(s) per week

TIMES OBSERVER
P.O. BOX 188
WARREN, PA 16365-2412
814-723-8200
Fax: 814-723-6922
editorial@timesobserver.com
www.timesobserver.com
• Jon Sitler, Sports Editor
(814) 723-8200
jsitler@timesobserver.com
Frequency:
6 time(s) per week

TIMES RECORD
3 BUSINESS PARKWAY
BRUNSWICK, ME 04011-1302
207-729-3311
800-734-6397
Fax: 207-729-5728
news@timesrecord.com
www.timesrecord.com/
• George Almasi, Sports Editor
(207) 504-8240
• John Bamford, Advertising Manager
(207) 729-3311
Frequency:
5 time(s) per week

TIMES RECORD NEWS
1301 LAMAR STREET
WICHITA FALLS, TX 76301
940-767-8341
800-627-1646
Fax: 940-767-1741
choatet@wtr.com
www.timesrecordnews.com
• Lee Anderson, Sports Reporter
(940) 720-3470
• Nick Gholson, Sports Editor
(940) 720-3470
Frequency:
7 time(s) per week

TIMES RECORDER
34 SOUTH 4TH STREET
ZANESVILLE, OH 43701-3417
740-452-4561
800-866-7326
Fax: 740-450-6780
www.zanesvilletimesrecorder.com
• Dave Weidig, Sports Editor
dweidig@nncogannett.com
Frequency:
6 time(s) per week

TIMES UNION
645 ALBANY SHAKER ROAD
ALBANY, NY 12211
518-454-5694
800-724-0775
Fax: 518-454-5628
tusports@timesunion.com
www.timesunion.com
• James Alan, Sports Writer
(518) 454-5062
jallen@timesunion.com
• Bill Callen, Executive Sports Editor
(518) 454-5560
• Pete Dougherty, Sports Columnist
(518) 454-5416
pdougherty@timesunion.com
• Kathleen A. Hallion, Advertising Director
(518) 454-5568
khallion@timesunion.com
Frequency:
7 time(s) per week

TIMES-COURIER
2110 WOODFALL DRIVE
CHARLESTON, IL 61920
217-345-7085
Fax: 217-345-7090
editorial@jg-tc.com
www.jg-tc.com
• Brian Nielsen, Sports Editor
(217) 238-6865
sports@jg-tc.com
Frequency:
6 time(s) per week

TIMES-HERALD
222 NORTH IZARD STREET
FORREST CITY, AR 72335-3324
870-633-3130
Fax: 870-633-0599
fctimes@thnews.com
www.thnews.com
• Fred Conley, Sports Reporter
(870) 633-3130
• Jim Wirski, Advertising Manager
(870) 633-3130
Frequency:
5 time(s) per week

TIMES-LEADER
200 SOUTH 4TH STREET
MARTINS FERRY, OH 43935-1312
740-633-1131
800-244-5671
Fax: 740-633-1122
timesleader@timesleaderonline.com
www.timesleaderonline.com/
• Robert Kapral, Sports Editor
(740) 633-1131
bkapral@timesleaderonline.com
• Kevin Kolanski, Advertising Manager
(740) 633-1131
Frequency:
6 time(s) per week

TIMES-MAIL
813 16TH STREET
BEDFORD, IN 47421-3822
812-275-3355
800-782-4405
Fax: 812-275-4191
tmnews@tmnews.com
www.tmnews.com
• Jeff Bartlett, Sports Writer
(812) 277-7284
jeff@tmnews.com
• Sean Duncan, Sports Editor
(812) 277-7283
sean@tmnews.com
Frequency:
7 time(s) per week

TIMES-NEWS
132 FAIRFIELD STREET WEST
TWIN FALLS, ID 83301-5842
208-733-0931
Fax: 208-734-5538
www.magicvalley.com
• Joe Paisley, Sports Editor
Frequency:
7 time(s) per week

TIMES-PICAYUNE
3800 HOWARD AVENUE
NEW ORLEANS, LA 70125
504-826-3279
Fax: 504-826-3812
www.timespicayune.com
• Peter Barrouquere, Sports Writer
(504) 826-3803
• John Deshazier, Sports Columnist
(504) 826-3279
• Jeff Duncan, Sports Columnist (NFL)
(504) 826-3405
• Peter Finney, Sports Columnist
(504) 826-3802
• Bob Fortus, Sports Columnist (Horse Racing)
(504) 826-3279
• Joy Hirdes, Sports Writer
(504) 826-3807
• Ted Lewis, Sports Reporter
(504) 826-3405
• Lori Lyons, Sports Reporter
(504) 826-3405
• David Meeks, Sports Editor
(504) 826-3279
• Marty Mule, Sports Writer
(504) 826-3279
• John Reid, Sports Columnist
(504) 826-3279
• Fred Robinson, Sports Reporter
(504) 826-3279
• Larry Simpson, Sports Writer
(504) 826-3279
• Jimmy Smith, Sports Writer
(504) 826-3814
• Mike Strom, Sports Reporter
(504) 826-3787
• Billy Turner, Sports Editor (High School)
(504) 826-3405
• Brian Allee-Walsh, Sports Writer
(504) 826-3279
Frequency:
7 time(s) per week

TIMES-REPORTER
629 WABASH AVENUE, N.W.
NEW PHILADELPHIA, OH 44663-4145
330-364-5577
Fax: 330-364-8416
www.timesreporter.com
• Jack Clay, Advertising Director
• Hank Keathley, Sports Columnist
(330) 364-8426
sports@timesreporter.com
• David Whitmer, Sports Editor
(330) 364-5577
david.whitmer@timesreporter.com
Frequency:
7 time(s) per week

TIMES-REPUBLICAN
135 WEST MAIN STREET
MARSHALLTOWN, IA 50158-5843
641-753-6611
800-542-7893
Fax: 641-753-7221
www.timesrepublican.com
• Ross Thede, Sports Editor
(641) 753-6611
rthede@timesrepublican.com
Frequency:
7 time(s) per week

TIMES-STANDARD
930 6TH STREET
EUREKA, CA 95501
707-441-0500
Fax: 707-441-0501
editor@times-standard.com
www.times-standard.com
• Ray Hamill, Sports Editor
(707) 441-0528
• Brad Botkin, Sports Writer
(707) 441-0500
Frequency:
7 time(s) per week

TIMES-TRIBUNE
149 PENN AVENUE
SCRANTON, PA 18503
570-348-9100
800-228-4637
Fax: 570-348-9135
www.scrantontimes.com
• Ed Christine, Sports Editor
Frequency:
7 time(s) per week

TIMES/NORTHWEST INDIANA
1111 GLENDALE BLVD
VALPARAISO, IN 46383
219-462-5151
Fax: 219-465-7298
www.nwitimes.com
• Greg Smith, Sports Editor
• Debbie Anslm, Advertising Director

TIPTON COUNTY TRIBUNE
116 SOUTH MAIN STREET
SUITE A
TIPTON, IN 46072-1832
765-675-2115
Fax: 765-675-4147
tiptontribune@elwoodpublishing.com
www.elwoodpublishing.com
• Michael Brown, Director of Marketing
• Michelle Gormon, Sports Editor
(765) 675-2115
tiptonsports@elwoodpublishing.com
Frequency:
6 time(s) per week

TODAY IN PEACHTREE CITY
210 JEFF DAVIS PLACE
FAYETTEVILLE, GA 30214
770-461-6317
Fax: 770-460-8172
www.fayettedailynews.com
• Cindy Morley, Sports Reporter
(770) 461-6317
• Joyce Wojcik, Advertising Director
(770) 461-6317
Frequency:
5 time(s) per week

TODAY'S NEWS HERALD
2225 WEST ACOMA BOULEVARD
LAKE HAVASU CITY, AZ 86403-2907
928-453-4237
Fax: 928-855-2637
news@havasunews.com
www.havasunews.com
• Steve Stevens, Advertising Manager
• Ric Swats, Sports Editor
(928) 453-4237
sports@havasunews.com
Frequency:
5 time(s) per week

TONAWANDA NEWS
P.O. BOX 668
NORTH TONAWANDA, NY 14120-6809
716-693-1007
Fax: 716-693-8573
www.tonawanda-news.com/
• Jack Karlis, Sports Editor
(716) 693-1000
• Tom Meranto, Advertising Manager
(716) 693-1000
• Ernie Green, Sports Editor
(716) 693-1000
Frequency:
7 time(s) per week

TOPEKA CAPITAL-JOURNAL
616 SOUTHEAST JEFFERSON STREET
TOPEKA, KS 66607-1120
785-295-1111
800-777-7171
Fax: 785-295-1230
news@cjonline.com
www.cjonline.com
• Leslie Palace, Advertising Sales Manager
• Kurt Caywood, Sports Columnist
(785) 295-1188
kurt.caywood@cjonline.com
• Roger Brokke, Director of Advertising
• Jennifer Burkhart, New Media/Sports
Editor

TRAVERSE CITY RECORD-EAGLE
120 WEST FRONT STREET
TRAVERSE CITY, MI 49684-2202
231-946-2000
Fax: 231-946-8273
• Denny Chase, Sports Editor
(231) 933-1494
Frequency:
7 time(s) per week

TRENTON TIMES
500 PERRY ST
TRENTON, NJ 08618
609-989-5454
800-753-3088
Fax: 609-394-2819
www.nj.com/times
• Jim Gauger, Sports Editor
• Diane M. Day, Advertising Director

TRENTONIAN
600 PERRY STREET
TRENTON, NJ 08618-3934
609-989-7800
800-825-7653
Fax: 609-393-6072
editor@trentonian.com
www.trentonian.com
• Matt Osborne, Sports Editor
• Lorie German, Advertising Manager
(609) 989-7800

• Joe O'Gorman, Sports Writer
jogorman@trentonian.com
Frequency:
7 time(s) per week

TRI-CITY HERALD
107 NORTH CASCADE STREET
KENNEWICK, WA 99336-3851
509-582-1500
800-874-0445
Fax: 509-582-1510
news@tri-cityherald.com
www.tri-cityherald.com
• Jeff Morrow, Sports Editor
(509) 582-1507
• Rene Ferran, Sports Writer
(509) 582-1526
Frequency:
7 time(s) per week

TRI-STATE DEFENDER
203 BEALE STREET, SUITE 200
MEMPHIS, TN 38103
901-523-1818
Fax: 901-578-5037
editorial@tri-statedefender.com
www.tri-statedefender.com
• William Little, Sports Editor
Frequency:
1 time(s) per week

TRI-VALLEY HERALD
127 SPRING STREET
PLEASANTON, CA 94588
925-734-8600
Fax: 925-416-4850
www.insidebayarea.com/trivalleyherald
• Cecil Conley, Sports Reporter
(925) 734-8600
• Steve Herendeen, Sports Reporter
• Dennis Miller, Sports Editor (Local)
• Billy Ortiz, Sports Reporter
(925) 416-4833
Frequency:
7 time(s) per week

TRIBUNE (CA)
3825 SOUTH HIGUERA STREET
SAN LUIS OBISPO, CA 93406
805-781-7800
800-456-8449
Fax: 805-781-7905
newsroom@thetribunenews.com
www.thetribunenews.com
• Melissa Geisler, Sports Editor
(805) 781-7991
Frequency:
7 time(s) per week

TRIBUNE (FL)
600 EDWARDS ROAD
FORT PIERCE, FL 34982-6230
772-461-2050
Fax: 772-461-4447
www.tcpalm.com
• Mike Graham, Sports Editor
(772) 692-8987
mike.graham@scripps.com
Frequency:
7 time(s) per week

TRIBUNE CHRONICLE
240 FRANKLIN STREET
WARREN, OH 44482-5711
330-841-1738
888-550-8742

Fax: 330-841-1717
www.tribune-chronicle.com
• Dave Burcham, Sports Editor
• Mike McClain, Sports Reporter
(330) 841-1738
sports@tribune-chronicle.com
Frequency:
7 time(s) per week

TRIBUNE, SCRANTON TIMES
149 PENN AVE
SCRANTON, PA 18503
570-348-9100
Fax: 570-348-9135
www.nepanews.com
• Ed Christine, Sports Editor
• Steve Sauder, Advertising Manager

TRIBUNE-DEMOCRAT
425 LOCUST STREET
JOHNSTOWN, PA 15907
814-532-5050
800-473-0998
Fax: 814-539-1409
tribdem@tribune-democrat.com
www.tribune-democrat.com
• Mike Elswick, Sports Editor
• Hugh Hudnall, Director of
Marketing/Advertising/Marketing
• Eric Kropsnyder, Sports Editor
(814) 532-5085

TRIBUNE-STAR
222 SOUTH 7TH STREET
TERRE HAUTE, IN 47807-3601
812-231-4200
800-783-8742
Fax: 812-231-4234
community@tribstar.com
www.tribstar.com
• Andy Amey, Sports Reporter
(812) 231-4277
andy.amey@tribstar.com
• Todd Golden, Sports Editor
(812) 231-4272
todd.golden@tribstar.com
• David Hughes, Sports Reporter
(812) 231-4224
david.hughes@tribstar.com
• Craig Pearson, Sports Reporter
(812) 231-4276
craig.pearson@tribstar.com
• James Willis, Sports Reporter
(812) 231-4357
james.willis@tribstar.com
Frequency:
7 time(s) per week

TROY DAILY NEWS
224 SOUTH MARKET STREET
TROY, OH 45373-3327
937-335-5634
Fax: 937-335-3552
www.tdn-net.com
• David Fong, Sports Editor
(937) 440-5251
• Leann Stewart, Advertising Manager
Frequency:
7 time(s) per week

TROY TIMES
13650 11 MILE ROAD
WARREN, MI 48089-1422
586-756-8800
Fax: 586-498-9627
www.candgnews.com

• Susan Shanley, Sports Editor
(586) 498-8000
sshanley@candgnews.com
Frequency:
1 time(s) per week

TRUTH
421 SOUTH SECOND STREET
ELKHART, IN 46516-3238
574-296-5904
Fax: 574-293-8324
www.etruth.com
• Bill Beck, Sports Editor
(574) 294-1661
• Anthony Anderson, Assistant Sports Editor
(574) 296-5904
Frequency:
7 time(s) per week

TRYON DAILY BULLETIN
16 NORTH TRADE STREET
TRYON, NC 28782-3012
828-859-9151
Fax: 828-859-5575
news@tryondailybulletin.com
www.tryondailybulletin.com
• Mike Edwards, Advertising Manager
(828) 859-9151
• Joey Millwood, Sports Editor
Frequency:
5 time(s) per week

TUCSON CITIZEN
4850 SOUTH PARK AVENUE
TUCSON, AZ 85714-1637
520-573-4561
800-754-9332
Fax: 520-573-4590
www.tucsoncitizen.com
• Dan Adams, Advertising Vice President
(520) 573-4415
danadams@tucson.com
• Ken Brazzle, Sports
(520) 573-4561
• Shelly Lewellen, Sports Reporter
• John Moredich, Sports Reporter
(520) 573-4561
• Dave Petruska, Sports Reporter
(520) 573-4635
Frequency:
6 time(s) per week

TULARE ADVANCE-REGISTER
388 EAST CROSS AVENUE
TULARE, CA 93274-2854
559-688-0521
Fax: 559-688-5580
tularenews@gannett.com
www.tulareadvanceregister.com
• Kevin McCusker, Sports Editor
(559) 735-3295
kmccuske@visalia.gannett.com
Frequency:
6 time(s) per week

TULSA WORLD
318 SOUTH MAIN
TULSA, OK 74103-3401
918-583-2161
800-999-6397
Fax: 918-581-8353
www.tulsaworld.com
• Mike Brown, College Sports Reporter
(918) 581-8390
mike.brown@tulsaworld.com
• Matt Doyle, Sports Writer

(918) 581-8316
• John Ferguson, Sports Writer
(918) 581-8358
• Mark Foster, Sports Reporter
(918) 581-8355
• Bill Haisten, Sports Reporter
(918) 581-8397
bill.haisten@tulsaworld.com
• Glenn Hibdon, Reporter
(918) 581-8396
• John Hoover, College Sports Writer
(918) 581-8384
• Lynn Jacobsen, Sports Reporter
(918) 581-8461
• John Klein, Senior Sports Columnist
(918) 581-8368
john.klein@tulsaworld.com
• Barry Lewis, Sports Writer
(918) 581-8355
barry.lewis@tulsaworld.com
• Tom Morris, Advertising Manager
(918) 581-8512
• Dan O'Kane, Sports Reporter
(918) 581-8391
• Sam Powell, Sports Writer
(918) 581-8357
• Patrick Prince, Sports Assistant Editor
(918) 581-8355
patrick.prince@tulsaworld.com
• Dave Sittler, Sports Writer
(918) 583-2161
• Mike Strain, Sports Editor
(918) 581-8356
• Nate Allen, Sports Reporter
(918) 583-2161
Frequency:
7 time(s) per week

TUSCALOOSA NEWS
315 28TH AVENUE
TUSCALOOSA, AL 35402
205-722-0220
Fax: 205-722-0187
news@tuscaloosanews.com
www.tuscaloosanews.com
• Cecil Hurt, Sports Editor
(205) 722-0225
cecil.hurt@tuscaloosanews.com
• Harold Stout, Sports Editor
(205) 722-0228
Frequency:
7 time(s) per week

TYLER MORNING TELEGRAPH
410 WEST ERWIN STREET
TYLER, TX 75702-7133
903-596-6397
Fax: 903-595-0335
news@tylerpaper.com
www.tylerpaper.com/
• Phil Hicks, Sports Editor
(903) 596-6275
sports@tylerpaper.com
• Art McClelland, Advertising Director
• Clint Buckley, Sports Reporter
(903) 596-6292
sports@tylerpaper.com
Frequency:
7 time(s) per week

TYRONE DAILY HERALD
1067 PENNSYLVANIA AVENUE
TYRONE, PA 16686-1514
814-684-4000
Fax: 814-684-4238
dherald@verizon.net

• Kylie Hyde, Advertising Manager
• Bob Miller, Sports Editor
dheraldsports@verizon.net
Frequency:
6 time(s) per week

UNION
464 SUTTON WAY
GRASS VALLEY, CA 95945
530-273-9561
Fax: 530-477-4292
www.theunion.com
• Craig Dennis, Advertising Director
(530) 477-4265
• Brian Hamilton, Sports Editor
(530) 477-4240
brianh@theunion.com
• Stacy Hicklin, Sports Reporter
(530) 477-4244
Frequency:
6 time(s) per week

UNION CITY DAILY MESSENGER
613 JACKSON STREET
UNION CITY, TN 38261
731-885-0744
Fax: 731-885-0782
ucdm@ucmessenger.com
www.ucmessenger.com
• Gloria Chesteen, Advertising Manager
(731) 885-0744
• Mike Hutchens, Sports Editor
mhutch@ucmessenger.com
• Glenda Lingford, Classified Manager
(731) 885-0744
Frequency:
5 time(s) per week

UNION DAILY TIMES
P.O. BOX 749
UNION, SC 29379-7705
864-427-1234
Fax: 864-427-1237
www.uniondailytimes.com
• Brian Whitmore, Sports Editor
(864) 427-1234
Frequency:
6 time(s) per week

UNION DEMOCRAT
84 SOUTH WASHINGTON STREET
SONORA, CA 95370
209-532-7151
800-786-6466
Fax: 209-532-6451
newsroom@uniondemocrat.com
www.uniondemocrat.com
• Kevin Sauls, Sports Editor
Frequency:
5 time(s) per week

UNION LEADER
100 WILLIAM LOEB DRIVE
MANCHESTER, NH 03109-5309
603-668-4321
Fax: 603-668-0382
www.theunionleader.com
• John Hussey, Sports Writer
• Kevin Provencher, Sports Writer
• Vin Sylvia, Sports Editor
(603) 668-4321
Frequency:
7 time(s) per week

UNION-NEWS, SUNDAY REPUBLICAN
1860 MAIN ST
SPRINGFIELD, MA 01101
413-788-1210
Fax: 413-788-1259
• Wayne Phaneuf, Executive Editor
• Joseph Deburro, Sports Editor

UNION-RECORDER
165 GARRETT WAY
MILLEDGEVILLE, GA 31061-2318
478-452-0567
Fax: 478-453-1449
www.unionrecord.com
• Ross Couch, Sports Editor
(478) 453-1465
newsroom@unionrecorder.com
Frequency:
5 time(s) per week

URBANA DAILY CITIZEN
220 EAST COURT STREET
URBANA, OH 43078-1805
937-652-1331
Fax: 937-652-1336
www.urbanacitizen.com
• Steve Stout, Sports Editor
(937) 652-1337
Frequency:
6 time(s) per week

USA TODAY
7950 JONES BRANCH DRIVE
MCLEAN, VA 22108
703-854-3400
800-872-0001
Fax: 703-854-2079
editor@usatoday.com
www.usatoday.com
• Kevin Allen, Ice Hockey Columnist
(703) 854-6519
kmallen@usatoday.com
• Mel Antonen, Sports Reporter
(703) 854-3739
mantonen@usatoday.com
• Deborah Barrington, Senior Sports
Assignment Editor
(703) 854-3400
dbarrington@usatoday.com
• Peter Barzilai, Baseball Assignment Editor
(703) 854-5954
pbarzilai@usatoday.com
• Jarrett Bell, Professional Football Reporter
(703) 854-3738
jbell@usatoday.com
• Hal Bodley, Professional Baseball
Columnist
(302) 378-7766
hbodley@usatoday.com
• Greg Boeck, Sports Reporter
(480) 659-6958
gboeck@usatoday.com
• Erik Brady, Sports Features Reporter
(703) 854-3707
ebrady@usatoday.com
• Mike Brehm, Ice Hockey Assignment
Editor
(703) 854-6519
mbrehm@usatoday.com
• Christine Brennan, Sports Columnist
(703) 854-3400
cbrennan@usatoday.com
• Mary Burn, Sports Editor
(703) 854-3731
mburn@usatoday.com
• Jack Carey, Sports Writer
(703) 854-3687

jcarey@usatoday.com
• Reid Cherner, Sports Senior Editor
(703) 854-3694
rcherner@usatoday.com
• Matt Cimento, Sports Assignment Editor
(703) 854-3746
mcimento@usatoday.com
• Oscar Dixon, Sports Editor
(703) 854-3690
• David DuPree, Sports Reporter
(410) 964-3690
ddupree@usatoday.com
• Andy Gardiner, Sports Writer
(215) 854-8013
agardiner@usatoday.com
• Gary Graves, Sports Reporter
(703) 854-3710
ggraves@usatoday.com
• Michael Hiestand, Sports Reporter
(703) 854-5420
mhiestand@usatoday.com
• Bruce Horovitz, Advertising Reporter
(703) 854-3473
bhorovitz@usatoday.com
• Chris Jenkins, Sports Reporter
• Janice Lloyd, Senior Sports Assignment
Editor
(703) 854-6514
jlloyd@usatoday.com
• Mike Lopresti, Sports Columnist
(765) 962-0989
mjl5853@aol.com
• Monte Lorell, Sports Managing Editor
(703) 854-3743
mlorell@usatoday.com
• Vicki Michaelis, (703) 570-8777
Sports Reporter
vmichaelis@usatoday.com
• Malcolm Moran, Sports Reporter (College)
mmoran@usatoday.com
• Tom O'Toole, Sports Editor (Collegiate)
(703) 854-7629
totoole@usatoday.com
• Dick Patrick, College Sports Reporter
(703) 854-6518
dpatrick@usatoday.com
• Tom Pedulla, Sports Reporter
(703) 854-3400
tpedulla@usatoday.com
• Jerry Potter, Sports Reporter
(703) 854-5317
jpotter@usatoday.com
Frequency:
5 time(s) per week

VAIL DAILY
40780 HIGHWAY 6 & 24
AVON, CO 81620
970-949-0555
Fax: 970-949-7094
newsroom@vaildaily.com
www.vaildaily.com
• Chris Freud, Sports Editor
(970) 949-0555
sports@vaildaily.com
• Andrea Palm-Porter, Advertising Director
Frequency:
7 time(s) per week

VALLEJO TIMES-HERALD
440 CURTOLA PARKWAY
VALLEJO, CA 94590
707-644-1141
800-600-1141
Fax: 707-643-0128
www.timesheraldonline.com
• Ken Hart, Sports Editor
(707) 553-6837

• Heidi Hoffman, Advertising Director
(707) 553-6811
• J.P. Hoonstra, Sports Writer
• Brad Kvederis, Sports Writer
• Timothy Scott, Sports Writer
Frequency:
7 time(s) per week

VALLEY CITY TIMES-RECORD
146 3RD STREET, N.E.
VALLEY CITY, ND 58072
701-845-0463
Fax: 701-845-0175
vctr@daktel.com
www.times-online.com
• Tony Lam, Sports Editor
Frequency:
5 time(s) per week

VALLEY COURIER
401-407 STATE AVENUE
ALAMOSA, CO 81101-2645
719-589-2553
Fax: 719-589-6573
www.alamosanews.com
• Lloyd Engen, Sports Editor
Frequency:
5 time(s) per week

VALLEY INDEPENDENT
EASTGATE 19
MONESSEN, PA 15062
724-684-5200
800-564-9000
Fax: 724-684-2603
www.valleyindependent.com
• Brian Herman, Sports Editor
(724) 684-2667
• Karen Strickland, Advertising Manager
Frequency:
6 time(s) per week

VALLEY MORNING STAR
P.O. BOX 511
HARLINGEN, TX 78550-7711
956-430-6200
Fax: 956-430-6231
www.valleystar.com
• Mary Lou Davis, Classified Manager
(956) 430-6222
• Buddy Green, Sports Editor
(956) 430-6200
• David Favila, Sports Editor
(956) 430-6200
Frequency:
7 time(s) per week

VALLEY NEWS
24 INTERCHANGE DRIVE
WEST LEBANON, NH 03784-2002
603-298-8711
800-874-2226
Fax: 603-298-0212
news@vnews.com
www.vnews.com
• Dave Corriveau, Sports Reporter
• Greg Fennell, Sports Reporter
(603) 298-8711
• Bob Hookway, Sports Reporter
(603) 298-8711
• Don Mahler, Sports Editor
(603) 298-8711
imaginedon@aol.com
• Richard Wallace, Advertising Manager
(603) 298-8711
rwallace@vnews.com

• Bruce Wood, Sports Reporter
(603) 298-8711
Frequency:
7 time(s) per week

VALLEY NEWS DISPATCH
4TH AVENUE & WOOD STREET
TARENTUM, PA 15084
724-224-4321
800-698-2553
Fax: 724-226-4677
vndnews@tribweb.com
www.valleynewsdispatch.com
• Kevin Smith, Executive Sports Editor
• Melanie Murray, Advertising Manager
(724) 226-7701
Frequency:
7 time(s) per week

VALLEY NEWS TODAY
702 WEST SHERIDAN
SHENANDOAH, IA 51601
712-246-3097
800-369-3097
Fax: 712-246-3099
editorial@valleynewstoday.com
www.valleynewstoday.com
• Kevin Slater, Sports Editor
Frequency:
5 time(s) per week

VALLEY TIMES-NEWS
220 NORTH 12TH STREET
LANETT, AL 36863-6422
334-644-1101
Fax: 334-644-5587
news@valleytimes-news.com
www.valleytimes-news.com
• Phillip Jones, Advertising Manager
(334) 644-8110
• Scott Sickler, Sports Editor
(334) 644-8106
sports@valleytimes-news.com
Frequency:
5 time(s) per week

VENTURA COUNTY STAR
P.O. BOX 6711
VENTURA, CA 93003
805-650-2900
800-660-6211
Fax: 805-482-6167
www.venturacountystar.com
• Larry Ames, Sports Editor
(805) 655-5818
lames@venturacountystar.com
• Mike Blackwell, Sports Ass't Managing
Editor
(805) 655-5821
• Bob Buttitta, Sports Reporter
(805) 655-5860
bbuttitta@venturacountystar.com
• Jim Carlisle, Sports Writer
(805) 655-1740
jcarlisle@venturacountystar.com
• Joe Curley, Sports Writer
(805) 655-5820
jcurley@venturacountystar.com
• Derry Eads, Sports Reporter
• Ben Kwasney, Sports Copy Editor
(805) 655-5820
• David Lassen, Sports Reporter
• Rhiannon Potkey, Sports Writer
(805) 655-5828
rpotkey@VenturaCountyStar.com
• Rich Romine, Sports Writer
(805) 496-8316

• Jonathan Catalini, Sports Copy Editor
(805) 655-5819
Frequency:
7 time(s) per week

VERNON DAILY RECORD
3214 WILBARGER STREET
VERNON, TX 76384
940-552-5454
800-234-9014
Fax: 940-553-4823
www.vernonrecord.com/
• Kathy McClellan, Sports Editor
(940) 552-5454
• Jim Surber, Advertising Manager
advertising@vernonrecord.com
Frequency:
6 time(s) per week

VICKSBURG POST
P.O. BOX 821668
VICKSBURG, MS 39180
601-636-4545
Fax: 601-634-0897
www.vicksburgpost.com
• David Gillis, Advertising Director
(601) 636-4545
• Sheila Mantz, Advertising Manager
(601) 636-4545
smantz@vicksburgpost.com
• Sean Murphy, Assistant Managing Editor -
Sports
(601) 636-4545
Frequency:
7 time(s) per week

VICTORIA ADVOCATE
311 EAST CONSTITUTION
VICTORIA, TX 77901-8140
361-575-1451
Fax: 361-574-1220
newsroom@vicad.com
www.victoriaadvocate.com
• Coy Slavik, Sports Editor
Frequency:
7 time(s) per week

VIDA NEWSPAPER
130 PALM DR
OXNARD, CA 93030
805-483-1008
Fax: 805-483-6233
vidanews@aol.com
• Ramon Arceo, Sports Editor
(805) 483-1008
Frequency:
1 time(s) per week

VILLAGER
1600 LAKEFRONT CIRCLE
THE WOODLANDS, TX 77380-3633
281-367-5309
800-659-6997
Fax: 281-363-3299
villageditor@hcnonline.com
www.hcnonline.com
• Kim Richardson, Sports Editor
• Corey Turner, Sports Editor
(281) 367-5309
cturner@hcnonline.com
Frequency:
1 time(s) per week

VINCENNES SUN-COMMERCIAL
PO BOX 396
VINCENNES, IN 47591-2910

812-886-9955
800-876-9955
Fax: 812-885-2235
vscnews@suncommercial.com
www.suncommercial.com/
• Dave Staver, Sports Editor
(812) 886-9955
dstaver@suncommercial.com
• Tom Graham, Sports Reporter
(812) 886-9955
tgraham@suncommercial.com
Frequency:
6 time(s) per week

VINDICATOR
P.O. BOX 780
YOUNGSTOWN, OH 44503-1136
330-747-1471
Fax: 330-747-6712
news@vindy.com
www.vindy.com
• Rob Todor, Sports Editor
(330) 747-1471
sports@vindy.com
• John Bassetti, High School; Prep Sports
Staff Writer
(330) 747-1471
sports@vindy.com
Frequency:
7 time(s) per week

VIRGINIAN REVIEW
128 NORTH MAPLE AVENUE
COVINGTON, VA 24426-1545
540-962-2121
Fax: 540-962-5072
virginianreview@aol.com
www.alleghanyhighlands.com/
• Mark Pifer, Sports Editor
(540) 962-2121
• Donna Via, Classified Manager
vrclassifieds@yahoo.com
Frequency:
6 time(s) per week

VIRGINIAN-PILOT
150 WEST BRAMBLETON AVENUE
NORFOLK, VA 23510-2018
757-446-2000
800-446-2004
Fax: 757-446-2531
elizabeth.simpson@pilotonline.com
www.pilotonline.com
• Bryan Black, Sports Team Leader
(757) 446-2376
• Vicki Friedman, Sports Writer
(757) 446-2039
• Michael Keech, Sports Assistant Editor
• James Miller, Sports Writer
(757) 446-2372
ed.miller@pilotonline.com
• Bob Molinaro, Sports Columnist
(757) 446-2373
• Patricia Peterson, Sports Assistant Editor
(757) 446-5434
• Charles Riebel, Sports Editor
(757) 446-2369
• Thomas Robinson, Sports Columnist
(757) 446-2518
• Larry Rubama, Sports Writer
(757) 446-2273
larry.rubama@pilotonline.com
• Tom White, Sports Team Leader
(757) 446-2360
tom.white@pilotonline.com
Frequency:
7 time(s) per week

VISALIA TIMES-DELTA
330 STREET, N.W.
VISALIA, CA 93291-6010
559-735-3200
Fax: 559-735-3399
news@visaliatimesdelta.com
www.visaliatimesdelta.com
• Mark Daniels, Classified Manager
• Mark Devaughn, Sports Reporter
(559) 735-3289
visalianews@mindinfo.com
• Konan Hauser, Advertising Director
(559) 735-3235
• Kevin Mcusker, Sports Editor
(559) 735-3200
news@visaliatimesdelta.com
• Andrew Bettencourt, Sports Reporter
(559) 688-0521
abettenc@visalia.gannett.com
Frequency:
6 time(s) per week

WABASH PLAIN DEALER
123 WEST CANAL STREET
WABASH, IN 46992-3042
260-563-2131
800-659-6321
Fax: 260-563-0816
www.wabashplaindealer.com
• Aaron Turner, Sports Editor
Frequency:
6 time(s) per week

WACO TRIBUNE-HERALD
P.O. BOX 2588
WACO, TX 76701-1906
254-757-5701
Fax: 254-757-0302
letters@wacotrib.com
www.wacotrib.com/
• Carla D'Andrea, Advertising Director
(254) 757-5788
• Kim Gorum, Sports Editor
(254) 757-5713
• Ann Marie Penrod, Classified Manager
(254) 757-5867
• Brice Cherry, Sports Columnist
(254) 757-5714
bcherry@wacotrib.com
Frequency:
7 time(s) per week

WAKEFIELD DAILY ITEM
26 ALBION STREET
WAKEFIELD, MA 01880-2803
781-245-0080
Fax: 781-246-0061
www.wakefielditem.com
• Jim Southmayd, Sports Editor
(781) 245-0080
Frequency:
5 time(s) per week

WALL STREET JOURNAL
1211 AVENUE OF THE AMERICAS
NEW YORK, NY 10036
212-416-2000
800-568-7625
Fax: 212-416-2653
nywireroom@dowjones.com
www.wsj.com
• Conor Dougherty, Sports Reporter
(212) 416-3917
conor.dougherty@wsj.com
• Erin Friar, Sports News Editor
(212) 416-3999
erin.friar@wsj.com

• Allen John, Sports Columnist
• Brian Steinberg, Advertising Reporter
(212) 416-3155
brian.steinberg@wsj.com
• Russell Adams, Sports Writer
(212) 416-2000
russell.adams@wsj.com
Frequency:
5 time(s) per week

WALLA WALLA UNION-BULLETIN
112 1ST STREET, S.
WALLA WALLA, WA 99362-0306
509-525-3300
Fax: 509-525-1232
www.union-bulletin.com
• Jay Brodt, Advertising Director
• Jim Buchan, Sports Editor
(509) 525-3300
Frequency:
6 time(s) per week

WARREN WEEKLY
13650 11 MILE ROAD
WARREN, MI 48089
586-756-8800
Fax: 586-498-9627
jhorn@candgnews.com
www.candgnews.com
• Susan Shanley, Sports Editor
(586) 498-8000
sshanley@candgnews.com
Frequency:
1 time(s) per week

WASHINGTON DAILY NEWS
217 NORTH MARKET STREET
WASHINGTON, NC 27889-4949
252-946-2144
Fax: 252-946-9797
news@wdnweb.com
www.wdnweb.com
• Brenda Foster, Classified Manager
(252) 946-2144
classified@wdnweb.com
• Ray McKerthan, Sports Editor
• Kevin Travis, Sports Editor
(252) 946-2144
Frequency:
7 time(s) per week

WASHINGTON EXAMINER
6408 EDSALL ROAD
ALEXANDRIA, VA 22312-6410
703-846-8324
Fax: 703-846-8366
www.dcexaminer.com
• Dan Rubin, Sports Editor
(703) 846-8335

WASHINGTON POST
1150 15TH STREET, N.W.
WASHINGTON, DC 20071
202-334-6000
800-627-1150
Fax: 202-334-5417
national@washpost.com
www.washingtonpost.com
• Mark Asher, Sports Staff Writer/College Sports
• Josh Barr, High School Sports Reporter
(202) 334-7350
• Matt Bonesteel, Editorial Assistant/Sports
(202) 334-6000
bonesteelm@washpost.com

WASHINGTON TIMES
3600 NEW YORK AVENUE, N.E.
WASHINGTON, DC 20002-1947
202-636-3000
Fax: 202-636-8906
www.washtimes.com
• Bob Cohn, Sports Writer
(202) 636-3260
• Dan Daly, Sports Columnist
• Barker Davis, College Sports Reporter
(202) 636-8892
• Donna De Marco, Advertising Reporter
(202) 636-4884
• David Elfin, Sports Reporter
(202) 636-3269
• David Fay, Sports Reporter (Hockey)
(202) 636-3260
• Jody Foldesy, Sports Reporter
(202) 636-4932
• Mike Harris, Sports Editor
(202) 636-4865
• John Haydon, Sports Reporter
(202) 636-3093
• Dick Heller, Sports Columnist
(202) 636-3260
• Tom Knott, Sports Columnist
(202) 636-3260
• Thom Loverro, Sports Columnist
(202) 636-3260
• John Mitchell, Sports Reporter (Pro Basketball)
(202) 636-3260
• Rick Snider, Sports Reporter (Pro Football)
(202) 636-3260
• Patrick Stevens, Sports Reporter
(202) 636-3000
• Mark Zuckerman, Sports Reporter
(202) 636-3000
Frequency:
7 time(s) per week

WATERBURY REPUBLICAN-AMERICAN
P.O. BOX 2090
WATERBURY, CT 06722
203-574-3636
Fax: 203-596-9277
releases@rep-am.com
www.rep-am.com
• Tom Talarico, Sports Editor
(203) 574-3636
ttalarico@rep-am.com
• Lee Lewis, Executive Sports Editor
(203) 574-3636
llewis@rep-am.com
• Roger Cleaveland, Sports Reporter
(203) 574-3636
rcleaveland@rep-am.com

WATERLOO-CEDAR FALLS COURIER
P.O. BOX 540
WATERLOO, IA 50701
319-291-1400
800-798-1702
Fax: 319-291-2069
www.wcfcourier.com
• Kelly Beaton, Sports Writer
(319) 291-1456
• Kevin Evans, Sports Editor
(319) 291-1469
• Sean Hylton, Sports Writer
(319) 291-1428
• Jim Nelson, Sports Writer
(319) 291-1521
• Doug Newhoff, Sports Editor
(319) 291-1467
• David Tansey, Advertising Manager
(319) 291-1403

Frequency:
6 time(s) per week

WATERTOWN DAILY TIMES
P.O. BOX 140
WATERTOWN, WI 53094-7623
920-261-4949
Fax: 920-261-5102
news1@wdtimes.com
www.wdtimes.com
• Judy Christian, Advertising Manager
• Kevin Wilson, Sports Editor
(920) 261-4949
news@wdtimes.com
• Adam Burdsall, Sports Reporter
(920) 261-5161
Frequency:
6 time(s) per week

WATERTOWN PUBLIC OPINION
P.O. BOX 10
WATERTOWN, SD 57201-2311
605-886-6901
800-658-5401
Fax: 605-886-4280
news@thepublicopinion.com
www.thepublicopinion.com/
• Roger Merriam, Sports Editor
(605) 886-6903
rogerm@thepublicopinion.com
Frequency:
6 time(s) per week

WAUSAU DAILY HERALD
800 SCOTT STREET
WAUSAU, WI 54403-4951
715-842-2101
800-477-4838
Fax: 715-848-9360
www.wausaudailyherald.com
• Sandy Falk, Advertising Director
(715) 845-0621
sfalk@smgpo.gannett.com
• Mark Multer, Sports Editor
(715) 845-0701
mmulter@wdhprint.com
Frequency:
7 time(s) per week

WAXAHACHIE DAILY LIGHT
200 WEST MARVIN
WAXAHACHIE, TX 75165-3040
972-937-3310
Fax: 972-937-1139
www.thedailylight.com
• John Hicks, Sports Editor
(972) 937-3310
• Jenniffer Kestersen, Advertising Manager
Frequency:
6 time(s) per week

WAYCROSS JOURNAL-HERALD
400 ISABELLA STREET
WAYCROSS, GA 31501-3637
912-283-2244
Fax: 912-285-5255
www.wjhnews.com
• Larry Purdom, Sports Editor
(912) 283-2244
sports@wjhnews.com
• Gary Keels, Sports Reporter
(912) 283-2244
Frequency:
6 time(s) per week

WEATHERFORD DEMOCRAT
512 PALO PINTO STREET
WEATHERFORD, TX 76086
817-594-7447
Fax: 817-594-9734
www.weatherforddemocrat.com
• Tommy Brown, Sports Editor
(817) 594-7447
sports@weatherforddemocrat.com
Frequency:
6 time(s) per week

WEEKEND
3612 NORTH MARTIN LUTHER KING
DRIVE
MILWAUKEE, WI 53212-4134
414-265-5300
Fax: 414-265-1536
editorial@communityjournal.net
www.communityjournal.net
• Tom Mitchell, Sports Editor
(414) 265-5300
Frequency:
1 time(s) per week

WELLINGTON DAILY NEWS
113 WEST HARVEY STREET
WELLINGTON, KS 67152-3840
620-326-3326
Fax: 620-326-3290
www.wgtndailynews.com
• Rick Horn, Advertising Manager
• Ryan Metzen, Sports Editor
(620) 326-3326
Frequency:
5 time(s) per week

WELLSVILLE DAILY REPORTER
159 NORTH MAIN STREET
WELLSVILLE, NY 14895-1149
585-593-5300
Fax: 585-593-5303
editor@wellsvilledaily.com
www.wellsviledaily.com
• Oak Duke, Advertising Manager
oduke51895@aol.com
• Jim Sweet, Sports Writer
(585) 593-5300
• Heather Matta, Sports
(585) 593-5300
Frequency:
6 time(s) per week

WENATCHEE WORLD
14 NORTH MISSION STREET
WENATCHEE, WA 98801-2250
509-663-5161
800-572-4433
Fax: 509-665-1183
www.wenworld.com
• Nick Babcock, Sports Editor
(509) 664-7145
Frequency:
6 time(s) per week

WEST BEND DAILY NEWS
100 SOUTH 6TH AVENUE
WEST BEND, WI 53095-3309
262-306-5000
800-924-3142
Fax: 262-338-1984
www.dailynewsol.com
• Lois Evans, Advertising Manager
(262) 306-5070
• Keith Schmidt, Sports Editor
(262) 306-5051

Frequency:
6 time(s) per week

WEST CENTRAL TRIBUNE
2208 TROTT AVENUE, SW
WILLMAR, MN 56201
320-235-1150
Fax: 320-235-6769
kboldan@wctrib.com
www.wctrib.com
• Jesse Fuchs, Sports Reporter
• Rand Middleton, Sports Reporter
Frequency:
1 time(s) per week

WEST COUNTY TIMES
4301 LAKESIDE DRIVE
RICHMOND, CA 94806
510-758-8400
Fax: 510-262-2776
www.contracostatimes.com
• Phil Jensen, Sports Writer
(510) 262-2739
Frequency:
7 time(s) per week

WEST HAWAII TODAY
75-5580 KUAKINI HIGHWAY
KAILUA KONA, HI 96740
808-329-9311
800-355-3911
Fax: 808-329-3659
wht@aloha.net
www.westhawaiitoday.com
• Joe Ferraro, Sports Editor
(808) 329-9311
• Gloria Fleming, Advertising Manager
Frequency:
6 time(s) per week

WEST PLAINS DAILY QUILL
P.O. BOX 110
WEST PLAINS, MO 65775-2753
417-256-9191
Fax: 417-256-9196
www.westplainsquill.com
• Carla Bean, Advertising Manager
• Dennis Crider, Sports Editor
(417) 256-9191
wpqnews@centurytel.net
Frequency:
5 time(s) per week

WEST VALLEY VIEW
200 WEST WIGWAM BOULEVARD
LITCHFIELD PARK, AZ 85340-4636
623-535-8439
Fax: 623-935-2103
www.westvalleyview.com
• Mike Russo, Sports Editor
(623) 535-8439
• Justin Doom, Sports Writer
(623) 535-8439
Frequency:
1 time(s) per week

WHEELING NEWS-REGISTER
1500 MAIN STREET
WHEELING, WV 26003-2826
304-233-0100
Fax: 304-232-1399
mccabe@theintelligencer.net
www.news-register.net
• Nick Bedway, Sports Editor
Frequency:
6 time(s) per week

WICHITA EAGLE
825 EAST DOUGLAS AVENUE
WICHITA, KS 67202-3512
316-268-6000
800-825-6397
Fax: 316-268-6627
wenews@wichitaeagle.com
www.kansas.com
• Joanna Chadwick, Sports Reporter
(316) 268-6270
• Duane Frazier, Sports Reporter
(316) 268-6296
• Adam Knapp, Sports Reporter
(316) 268-6284
• Dan Loving, Sports Assistant Editor
(316) 269-6706
• Bob Lutz, Sports Columnist
(316) 268-6597
• Jeff Parson, Sports Reporter
(316) 268-6398
• Scott Paske, Sports Reporter
(316) 268-6513
• Rick Plumlee, Sports Reporter
(785) 842-4479
• Kirk Seminoff, Sports Editor
(316) 268-6278
Frequency:
7 time(s) per week

WICHITA FALLS TIMES RECORD NEWS
1301 LAMAR ST
WICHITA FALLS, TX 76307
940-767-8341
800-627-1646
Fax: 940-767-1741
• Nick Gholson, Sports Editor
• Monica Bartling, Advertising Director

WILLIAMSON DAILY NEWS
100 EAST 3RD AVENUE
WILLIAMSON, WV 25661-3620
304-235-4242
Fax: 304-235-0730
editor@williamsondailynews.com
www.williamsondailynews.com
• Joshua Ball, Sports Editor
(304) 235-4242
jball@williamsondailynews.com
Frequency:
7 time(s) per week

WILLIAMSPORT SUN-GAZETTE
P.O. BOX 728
WILLIAMSPORT, PA 17701-6102
570-326-1551
Fax: 570-326-0314
news@sungazette.com
www.sungazette.com
• Ben Brigandi, Sports Editor
(570) 326-1551
bbrigandi@sungazette.com
Frequency:
7 time(s) per week

WILMINGTON NEWS JOURNAL
47 S. SOUTH STREET
WILMINGTON, OH 45177-2231
937-382-2574
Fax: 937-382-4392
info@wnewsj.com
www.wnewsj.com
• Sarah Clark, Sports Editor
(937) 382-2574
sclark@wnewsj.com
Frequency:
6 time(s) per week

WILMINGTON STAR NEWS
1003 SOUTH 17TH STREET
WILMINGTON, NC 28401
910-343-2000
800-222-2385
Fax: 910-343-2227
www.starnewsonline.com
• Dan Spears, Sports Editor
dan.spears@starnewsonline.com
Frequency:
7 time(s) per week

WILSON DAILY TIMES
P.O. BOX 2447
WILSON, NC 27893-4611
252-243-5151
Fax: 252-243-7501
editor@wilsondaily.com
www.wilsondaily.com
• Tom Ham, Sports Editor
(252) 265-7809
hammer@wilsondaily.com
• Wayne Johnson, Advertising Manager
(252) 265-7858
wjohnson@wilsondaily.com
• Paul Durham, Assistant Sports Editor
(252) 265-7808
paul@wilsondaily.com
Frequency:
6 time(s) per week

WINCHESTER STAR
2 NORTH KENT STREET
WINCHESTER, VA 22601
540-667-3200
800-296-8639
Fax: 540-667-1649
news@winchesterstar.com
www.winchesterstar.com
• Ben Brooks, Sports Editor
(540) 667-3200
• John Parkinson, Advertising Manager
(540) 665-4950
Frequency:
6 time(s) per week

WINCHESTER SUN
P.O. BOX 4300
WINCHESTER, KY 40391-1900
859-744-3123
Fax: 859-745-0638
www.winchestersun.com
• Kim Hays, Advertising Director
(859) 744-3123
• Keith Taylor, Sports Editor
(859) 744-3123
Frequency:
6 time(s) per week

WINFIELD DAILY COURIER
201 EAST 9TH STREET
WINFIELD, KS 67156-2817
620-221-1050
Fax: 620-221-1101
www.winfieldcourier.com
• Tracy McCue, Sports Editor
• Marsha Wesseler, Advertising Manager
Frequency:
6 time(s) per week

WINONA DAILY NEWS
PO BOX 5147
WINONA, MN 55987
507-453-3500
800-328-2182
Fax: 507-453-3517

news@winonadailynews.com
www.winonadailynews.com
• Jeff Bersch, Sports Editor
(507) 453-3528
• Tom Kelly, Advertising Director
Frequency:
7 time(s) per week

WINSTON-SALEM JOURNAL
P.O. BOX 3159
WINSTON-SALEM, NC 27101-2805
336-727-7308
800-642-0925
Fax: 336-727-7315
www.journalnow.com
• Tommy Bowman, Sports Reporter
(336) 727-7320
• Bill Cole, College Sports Reporter
(336) 727-7310
• Dan Collins, Sports Reporter
(336) 727-7323
• John Dell, Sports Writer
(336) 727-4081
jdell@wsjournal.com
• John Delong, Sports Reporter
(336) 727-7324
• Phil Hrichak, Sports Editor
(336) 727-4080
• Dan Kibler, Outdoors Writer
(336) 727-7383
• Mason Linker, Sports Columnist
(336) 727-7326
• Terry Oberle, Sports Editor
(336) 727-7321
Frequency:
7 time(s) per week

WISCONSIN STATE JOURNAL
P.O. BOX 8056
MADISON, WI 53713-1248
608-252-6100
800-362-8333
Fax: 608-252-6119
www.madison.com/wsj/
• Eric Anderson, Assistant Sports Editor
(608) 252-6177
• Andy Baggot, College Sports Reporter
(608) 252-6175
• Vic Feuerherd, Sports Reporter
(608) 252-6175
• Perry Hibner, Sports Assistant Editor
(608) 252-6190
• Tom Mulhern, Sports Reporter
(608) 252-6169
• John Nolan, Sports Copy Editor
(608) 252-6168
jnolan@madison.com
• Jesse Osborne, Sports Reporter
(608) 252-6176
• Greg Sprout, Sports Senior Editor
(608) 252-6171
gsprout@madison.com
• Jason Wilde, Sports Reporter
(680) 252-6176
• Nick Zizzo, Sports Reporter
(680) 252-6167
nzizzo@madison.com
Frequency:
7 time(s) per week

WOODWARD NEWS
904 OKLAHOMA AVENUE
WOODWARD, OK 73801-4660
580-256-2200
Fax: 580-254-2159
www.woodwardnews.net
• Johnny McMahan, Sports Editor

Frequency:
6 time(s) per week

WORLD
350 COMMERCIAL STREET
COOS BAY, OR 97420
541-269-1222
800-437-6397
Fax: 541-267-0294
theworldnews@theworldlink.com
www.theworldlink.com
• John Gunther, Sports Editor
(541) 269-1222
jgunther@theworldlink.com
• Bob Reitz, Advertising Manager
(541) 269-1222
Frequency:
6 time(s) per week

WYOMING TRIBUNE-EAGLE
702 WEST LINCOLN WAY
CHEYENNE, WY 82001-4359
307-634-3361
Fax: 307-633-3189
www.wyomingnews.com
• Scott Nulph, Sports Editor
(307) 634-3361
Frequency:
7 time(s) per week

XENIA DAILY GAZETTE
30 SOUTH DETROIT STREET
XENIA, OH 45385-0400
937-372-4444
Fax: 937-372-1951
wbaker@xeniagazette.com
www.xeniagazette.com
• Josh Brown, Sports Editor
pgirton@xeniagazette.com
• Barbara Vandeventer, Advertising
Manager
bvandeventer@xeniagazette.com
Frequency:
6 time(s) per week

YAKIMA HERALD-REPUBLIC
114 N. FOURTH ST
YANKIMA, WA 98901
509-248-1251
Fax: 509-577-7767
www.yakima-herald.com
• Jamie Stickel, Advertising Director
• Mike Anderson, Sports Editor

YANKTON DAILY PRESS & DAKOTAN
319 WALNUT STREET
YANKTON, SD 57078
605-665-7811
800-743-2968
Fax: 605-665-1721
sports@yankton.net
www.yankton.net
• James Cimburek, Sports Editor
(605) 665-7811
james.cimburek@yankton.net
• Cathy Sudbeck, Advertising Sales
• Jeremy Hoack, Assistant Sports Editor
(605) 665-7811
Frequency:
6 time(s) per week
Teams:
University of South Dakota-NCAA Division I,
and Mount Marty College - NAIA

YORK DAILY RECORD/YORK SUNDAY NEWS
1891 LOUCKS ROAD
YORK, PA 17408-9708
717-771-2000
800-788-9675
Fax: 717-771-2009
news@ydr.com
www.ydr.com
• Chris Otto, Sports Editor
(717) 771-2000
• Frank Bodani, Sports Reporter
(717) 771-2104
fbodani@ydr.com
• Bryan Kelley, Advertising Director
Frequency:
6 time(s) per week

YORK DISPATCH
205 NORTH GEORGE STREET
YORK, PA 17401-1107
717-854-1575
Fax: 717-843-2958
www.yorkdispatch.com
• Steve Heiser, Sports Editor
(717) 854-1575
sheiser@yorkdispatch.com
Frequency:
6 time(s) per week

YORK NEWS-TIMES
327 PLATTE AVENUE
YORK, NE 68467
402-362-4478
800-334-4530
Fax: 402-362-6748
news@yorknewstimes.com
www.yorknewstimes.com/
• Ken Kush, Sports Editor/Writer
• SJ Munoz, Sports Editor/Writer
• Steve Moseley, Sports Editor/Writer
Frequency:
6 time(s) per week

YUMA DAILY SUN
2055 ARIZONA AVE
PO BOX 271
YUMA, AZ 85364
928-539-6880
Fax: 928-782-7369
www.yumasun.com
• Ross Priest, Sports Editor
• Lisa Miller, Advertising Director

Magazines

3-D TIMES ARCHERY MAGAZINE
5158 MAIN STREET
LUCEDALE, MS 39452
800-891-5558
Fax: 601-766-9626
www.3-dtimes.com
• Royce Armstrong, Editor
Frequency:
8 time(s) per year
Description:
Publication is a source for archery news,
competitions, short schedules, interviews,
and profiles of top shoots and tournament
results.

48 DEGREES NORTH
6327 SEAVIEW AVENUE, N.W.
SEATTLE, WA 98107

206-789-7350
Fax: 206-789-6392
www.48north.com
• Rich Hazelton, Editor
• Karen Higginson, Associate Editor
• Chuck Streatch, Publisher
Frequency:
1 time(s) per month
Description:
Publication includes information for boating
enthusiasts in Washington, Oregon, Idaho,
Alaska, and British Columbia.

ACADEMIC-ATHLETIC JOURNAL/N4A NATIONAL OFFICE
1630 LYNDON FARM COURT
LOUISVILLE, KY 40233
502-992-8000
Fax: 502-992-8001
www.nfoura.org
• Kathi Ley, N4A National Office Director
Description:
Provides professional research and position
papers to the NAAAA (National Association
of Academic Advisors) for Athletics
membership regarding professional
academic-athletic advising.
Circulation:
300
Sports:
General
Primary Audience:
Association membership
Frequency:
Semiannual
Publishing Company:
NAAAA/Athletic Guidance Center.

ACTION PURSUIT GAMES
4201 VANOWEN PLACE
BURBANK, CA 91505
818-845-2656
800-332-3330
Fax: 818-845-7761
www.cfwgroup.com
• Dan Reeves, Editor
(573) 674-4040
• Gabe Frimmel, Advertising Director
(818) 845-2656
• Curtis F. Wong, Publisher
(818) 845-2656
Frequency:
1 time(s) per month
Description:
Publication covers the sport of paintball for
players of all levels; contains articles on
technology, safety issues, play techniques,
tournaments, and news.

ADIRONDACK SPORTS & FITNESS
15 COVENTRY DRIVE
CLIFTON PARK, NY 12065-1747
518-877-8788
Fax: 518-877-0619
info@adksports.com
www.AdKSports.com
• Mona Caron, Editor
• Darryl Caron, Publisher
(518) 877-8788
Frequency:
1 time(s) per month
Description:
Regional monthly active lifestyle magazine
and producer of summer/winter sports expos
in upstate New York.

ADVENTURE CYCLIST
150 EAST PINE
MISSOULA, MT 59802-4515
406-721-1776
800-755-2453
Fax: 406-721-8754
info@adventurecycling.org
www.adventurecycling.org
• Mike Deme, Editor
(406) 721-1776
Frequency:
9 time(s) per year
Description:
Publication is a bicycle travel magazine with emphasis on destinations.

ADVENTURE SPORTS OUTDOORS
201 GLORIA PARKWAY
WASHIONTON, IL 61571
309-437-2247
877-778-4868
Fax: 309-925-4868
www.asomagazine.com
• Cathy Canterbury, Publisher
(309) 925-7313
• Andy Bugos, Publisher
(309) 437-2247
asoandyb@gmail.com
Frequency:
1 time(s) per month
Description:
Print and online publication geared toward outdoor sporting.
Year Founded:
1996.

AIKIDO TODAY MAGAZINE
1420 NORTH CLAREMONT BOULEVARD
CLAREMONT, CA 91711-3528
909-624-7770
Fax: 909-398-1840
www.aiki.com
• Susan Perry, Editor-in-Chief
(909) 624-7770
Frequency:
6 time(s) per year
Description:
Publication is a martial arts magazine.

ALASKA HORSE JOURNAL
4311 EAST CRANE ROAD
WASILLA, AK 99654
907-376-4470
Fax: 907-376-4470
www.alaskahorsejournal.printroom.com
• Sandy Shacklett, Editor
• Sandy Shacklett, Advertising Manager
• Sandy Shacklett, Publisher
Frequency:
1 time(s) per month
Description:
Publication provides horse enthusiasts with information on all breeds of horses and all disciplines.

AMERICAN BOWLER
5301 SOUTH 76TH STREET
GREENDALE, WI 53129
414-421-6401
Fax: 414-321-8356
americanbowler@bowl.com
www.bowl.com
• Rory Gillespie, Editor
(414) 321-8310
Frequency:
4 time(s) per year

AMERICAN CHEERLEADER
110 WILLLIAM STREET
NEW YORK, NY 10038
212-265-8890
Fax: 212-265-8908
editors@americancheerleader.com
www.americancheerleader.com
• Marisa Walker, Managing Editor
(212) 265-8890
• Joanna Harp, Publisher
(646) 459-4806
• Sheila Noone, Editorial Director
(212) 265-8890
• Jennifer Smith, Senior Editor
(646) 459-4832
• Brittany Geragotelis, Associate Editor
(212) 265-8890
Frequency:
6 time(s) per year
Description:
Publication is written for cheerleaders; features articles on competitions, fitness and exercise, fashion, and footwear.

AMERICAN FARRIERS JOURNAL
16655 W. WISCONSIN AVE
BROOKFIELD, WI 53005
262-782-4480
800-645-8455
Fax: 262-782-1252
info@lessitermedia.com
www.lessitermedia.com
• Jeremy McGovern, Executive Editor/Publisher
• Patrick Sharpe, VP, Audience Development
(262) 777-2406
psharpe@lessitermedia.com
• Mike Lessiter, President
(262) 777-2403
mlessiter@lessitermedia.com
• Frank Lessiter, Editor
Frequency:
8 time(s) per year
Description:
Publication is a hands-on magazine for professional farriers.

AMERICAN FOOTBALL MONTHLY
840 US HIGHWAY 1
NORTH PALM BEACH, FL 33408
561-627-3393
800-537-4271
Fax: 561-627-5275
www.americanfootballmonthly.com
• Rex Lardner, Managing Editor
(561) 627-3393
• Travis Davis, Advertising Manager
(561) 627-3393
• Travis Davis, Publisher
(561) 627-3393
• Jeff Case, Associate Editor
(561) 627-3393
Frequency:
1 time(s) per month
Description:
Publication targets football coaches at all levels.

AMERICAN QUARTER HORSE RACING JOURNAL
1600 QUARTER HORSE DRIVE
AMARILLO, TX 79104
806-376-4888
Fax: 806-349-6400
aqhajrnl@aqha.org
www.aqharacing.com

• Jennifer Hancock, Editor
(806) 376-4888
• Richard Chamberlain, Senior Staff Writer
(806) 376-4888
richc@aqha.org
• Jim Jennings, Publication Executive Director
• Jim Persinger, Advertising Manager
(806) 378-4386
Frequency:
1 time(s) per month
Description:
Publication focuses on Amercian Quarter Horse racing.

AMERICAN SAILOR
5 DOCK SQUARE
KENNEBUNKPORT, ME 04046
207-967-0866
800-877-2451
Fax: 401-683-0840
www.olyc.com/ussailing
Frequency:
10 time(s) per year
Description:
Magazine is the official publication of the U.S. Sailing Association.

AMERICAN SNOWMOBILER
21027 CROSSROADS CIRCLE
WAUKESHA, WI 53187-1612
262-796-8776
Fax: 262-798-6468
www.amsnow.com
• Mark Savage, Editor
(262) 796-8776
msavage@kalmbach.com
• Mark Savage, Executive Editor
(262) 796-8776
msavage@kalmbach.com
• Mark Boncher, Associate Editor
(262) 798-6453
Frequency:
6 time(s) per year
Description:
Publication provides complete news updates about snowmobiling, and other articles relevant to the sport.

AMERICAN SPORTS
PO BOX 6100
ROSEMEAD, CA 91770
626-292-2222
Fax: 626-292-2221
am@asntv.com
• Steve Roquet, Editor
Publishing Company:
American Sports Network, Inc.
Frequency:
Monthly
Primary Audience:
Consumer
Sports:
Prep, collegiate, professional
Circulation:
5% non-paid subscr contr, 95% paid subscr.
Description:
General sports, recreational sports magazine.

AMERICAN TURF MONTHLY
299 EASTSHORE ROAD SUITE 204
GREAT NECK, NY 11023
516-773-4075
800-645-2240
Fax: 516-773-2944

editor@americanturf.com
www.americanturf.com
• Howard Rowe, Senior Editor
• James Corbett, Editor-in-Chief
• Allen Hakim, Publisher
publisher@americanturf.com
Frequency:
1 time(s) per month

AMERICAN WINDSURFER
10 BAYVIEW BUSINESS PARK
GILFORD, NH 03247
603-293-2727
Fax: 603-293-2723
editor@americanwindsurfer.com
www.americanwindsurfer.com
• John Chao, Editor
(603) 293-2721
Frequency:
6 time(s) per year
Description:
Publication is geared toward windsurfers of
all degrees of skill.

ANVIL'S RING
6690 WENTWORTH SPRINGS ROAD
GEORGETOWN, CA 95634
530-333-2687
Fax: 530-333-2689
www.sebastianpublishing.com
• Rob Edwards, Editor
• Rob Edwards, Publisher
Frequency:
4 time(s) per year
Description:
Publication is directed at professional and
hobby blacksmiths in the United States and
abroad.

APPALOOSA JOURNAL
2720 WEST PULLMAN ROAD
MOSCOW, ID 83843-4000
208-882-5578
Fax: 208-882-8150
journal@appaloosa.com
www.appaloosa.com
• Diane Rice, Editor
(208) 882-5578
• Katie Elliott, Advertising Director
(208) 882-5578
advertising@appaloosa.com
• Diane Rice, Associate Editor
(208) 882-5578
Frequency:
1 time(s) per month

ARABIAN HORSE WORLD
1316 TAMSON DRIVE SUITE 101
CAMBRIA, CA 93428-3328
805-771-2300
Fax: 805-927-6522
www.ahwmagazine.com
• Denise Hearst, Publisher
(805) 771-2302
• Lynn Anderson, Advertising Manager
Frequency:
1 time(s) per month
Description:
Publication focuses on the positive rewards
of worldwide involvement with the Arabian
bred horse.

AREA AUTO RACING NEWS
PO BOX 8547
TRENTON, NJ 08610-3603

609-888-3618
Fax: 609-888-2538
news@aarn.com
www.aarn.com
• Lenny H. Sammons, Publisher
lhs@aarn.com
• Tim Hogue, Advertising Director
• Earl Krause, Asst Editor
earl@aarn.com
Frequency:
1 time(s) per week
Description:
Publication covers both local and national
automobile racing events.

ARIZONA, THE STATE OF GOLF
7226 NORTH 16TH STREET SUITE 200
PHOENIX, AZ 85020-5255
602-944-3035
Fax: 602-944-3228
www.azgolf.org
• Peter Wofford, Editor
(843) 856-3290
peterwofford@comcast.net
Frequency:
6 time(s) per year
Description:
Publication deals with regional golf
amateurs in the state of Arizona and
features stories and profiles of the players.

ATHLETIC BUSINESS
4130 LIEN ROAD
MADISON, WI 53704
608-249-0186
800-722-8764
Fax: 608-249-1153
editors@athleticbusiness.com
www.athleticbusiness.com
• Sue Searls, Publisher
(608) 249-0186
• Brad Zaugg, Publisher
(608) 249-0186
editors@athleticbusiness.com
• Marvin Bynum, Assistant Editor
(608) 249-0186
editors@athleticbusiness.com
Frequency:
1 time(s) per month
Description:
Publication is geared toward operators of
athletic and fitness programs and facilities.

ATHLETIC MANAGEMENT
31 DUTCH MILL ROAD
ITHACA, NY 14850
607-257-6970
Fax: 607-257-7328
info@momentummedia.com
www.momentummedia.com
• Mark Goldberg, Publisher
(607) 257-6970
mg@momentummedia.com
• Eleanor Frankel, Editor-in-Chief
(607) 257-6970
• Dave Dubin, Circulation Director
(607) 257-6970
• Don Anderson, Production Manager
(607) 257-6970
Publishing Company:
Momentum Media.
Frequency:
6 time(s) a year
Circulation:
30,037.
Nature of Service:
Articles discuss topics in the field including

working with coaches, marketing and
fundraising strategies, Title IX and other
legal issues, starting new sports,
understanding today's student-athletes, and
much more.
Primary Audience:
Athletic administrations at high school and
college levels.
Sports:
Most.

ATHLETICS ADMINISTRATION
24651 DETROIT ROAD
WESTLAKE, OH 44145
440-892-4000
Fax: 440-892-4007
jwork@nacda.com
www.nacda.com
• Julie Work, Editor
jwork@nacda.com
• Craig Baroncelli, Publisher
(859) 226-4678
• Michael Cleary, Executive Editor
(440) 892-4000
Frequency:
8 time(s) per year
Description:
Publication features articles on the
administration of collegiate athletics.

ATHLON SPORTS COMMUNICATIONS
2451 ATRMWY BUILDING 2
SUITE 320
NASHVILLE, TN 37203
615-327-0747
800-ATHLON-8
Fax: 615-327-1149
www.athlonsports.com
• Charlie Miller, Managing Editor
• Robert T. Doster, III, Senior Editor
• Mitch Light, Editor
• Scott Garrettt, President, Advertising Sales
• Roger Di Silvestro, Chairman/Chief
Executive Officer
• Scott Garrett, Advertising Sales Director
• Troy Childers, Director Circulation
Publishes:
Eastern Football, Southeastern Football,
The Really Big 12, Southwest Football, Big
12 Football, PAC-10 Football, Western
Football, Atlantic Coast Football, Athlon's
Pro Football, Athlon's Inside Saturday,
Athlon's Pro Baseball, Athlon's College, Pro
Basketball, Golf.

ATLANTA SPORTS AND FITNESS
MAGAZINE
3535 PIEDMONT ROAD
ATLANTA, GA 30305
404-843-2257
Fax: 404-843-1339
www.atlantasportsmag.com
• Beth Weithzman, Editor
(404) 870-0123
• Scott Thompson, Director
(404) 843-2257
• JoAnn Carroll, Art/Production Manager
(404) 843-2257
Frequency:
1 time(s) per month
Description:
Articles related to amateur sports and health
and fitness topics.

ATLANTIC RACQUET PRESS
11 BUXTON
EAST WINDSOR, NJ 08520

609-371-3737
Fax: 609-448-6642
www.atlanticracquetpress.com
• Judith F. Arnold, Editor
Frequency:
4 time(s) per year
Description:
Publication contains articles on tennis in the Mid-Atlantic states.

AVID GOLFER MAGAZINE
7200 SOUTH ALTON WAY
SUITE B-180
CENTENNIAL, CO 80112
720-493-1729
Fax: 720-482-0784
info@coloradoavidgolfer.com
www.coloradoavidgolfer.com
• Jon Rizzi, Editor
(720) 493-1729
jon@coloradoavidgolfer.com
• Allen J. Walters, Publisher
(720) 493-1729
allen@coloradoavidgolfer.com
Frequency:
2 time(s) per month
Description:
Publication provides information of interest to professional and amateur golfers.

BACK COUNTRY MAGAZINE
P.O. BOX 190
JEFFERSONVILLE, VT 05464
802-644-6606
Fax: 802-644-6328
www.backcountrymagazine.com
• Adam Howard, Editor
howie@backcountrymagazine.com
Frequency:
4 time(s) per year

BACKPACKER MAGAZINE
33 E. MINOR ST
RODALE PRESS, PA 18098
610-967-8296
Fax: 610-967-8181
www.backpacker.com or
www.bpbasecamp.com
• Jonathan Dorn, Executive Editor
• Eric Zinczenko, Publisher
Publishing Company:
Rodale Press
Frequency:
Nine times annually
Primary Audience:
Consumer
Sports:
Backpacking, hiking, paddle sports, cross country skiing.
Circulation:
NA.
Description:
Devoted to information and features relating to self-propelled wilderness travel.

BALLOON LIFE
P.O. BOX 7
LITCHFIELD, CT 06759
860-567-2061
Fax: 206-935-3326
blarney007@aol.com
www.balloonlife.com
• Michael P Murphy, Editor
• William G Armstrong, Publisher
(203) 629-1241
Frequency:
1 time(s) per month

Description:
Publication covers issues of interest to hot air ballooning enthusiasts.

BALLS AND STRIKES SOFTBALL MAGAZINE
2801 NORTHEAST 50TH STREET
OKLAHOMA CITY, OK 73111-7203
405-424-5266
Fax: 405-424-4734
info@softball.org
www.softball.org
• Brian McCall, Editor
(405) 425-3463
bmccall@softball.org
• Julie Eversgerd, Associate Editor
(405) 425-3431
• Brian McCall, Editor-in-Chief
(405) 425-3463
• Brian McCall, Publisher
(405) 425-3463
Frequency:
2 time(s) per year
Description:
Publication is geared toward amateur softball enthusiasts.

BARREL HORSE NEWS
2112 MONTGOMERY STREET
FORT WORTH, TX 76107
817-731-7867
Fax: 817-737-9266
www.barrelhorsenews.com
• Teri Lee, Managing Editor
• Trisha Johnson, Editorial Coordinator
(817) 737-6397
• Glory Ann Kurtz, Executive Editor
(817) 731-7867
gloryann.kurtz@cowboypublishing.com
• Carl Mullins, Publisher
(817) 731-7867
carl.mullins@cowboypublishing.com
• Patty Tiberg, General Manager
(817) 731-7867
patty.tiberg@cowboypublishing.com
Frequency:
1 time(s) per month
Description:
Publication focuses on barrel racing.

BASEBALL AMERICA
4319 SOUTH ALSTON AVENUE
SUITE 103
DURHAM, NC 27713
919-682-9635
800-845-2726
Fax: 919-682-2880
letters@baseballamerica.com
www.baseballamerica.com
• Will Lingo, Co-Editor in Chief
(919) 682-9635
• Lee Folger, President
(919) 682-9635
• John Manuel, Co-Editor in Chief
(919) 682-9635
Frequency:
26 times yearly.
Description:
A full-service media division of Source InterLink and Grind Media with in-depth coverage of every level of baseball, including; high school, college, the minor leagues and major league baseball.

BASEBALL DIGEST
990 GROVE STREET
EVANSTON, IL 60201-4370

847-491-6440
Fax: 847-491-0459
www.centurysports.net
• Bob Kuenster, Editor
• Norman Jacobs, Publisher
Frequency:
1 time(s) per month
Description:
Publication focuses on baseball players, managers, rosters, statistics, trades, player profiles, and schedules.

BASKETBALL TIMES
P.O. BOX 1269
PINEHURST, NC 28370
910-295-5559
Fax: 910-295-6566
www.basketballtimes.com
• John Akers, Editor
• Nanci Donald, Publisher
Frequency:
1 time(s) per month
Description:
Publication contains information about college, junior college, women's coverage and high school basketball, as well as recruiting and the NBA.

BAY & DELTA YACHTSMAN
4090 SOUTH MCCARRAN BOULEVARD
UNIT-E
RENO, NV 89502
775-353-5100
800-878-7886
Fax: 775-353-5111
www.yachtsforsale.com
• Don Abbott, Co-Publisher & Editor
(775) 353-5100
Frequency:
1 time(s) per month
Description:
Publication contains articles on power and sail boats.

BEDTIME STORIES FOR YOUNG ATHLETES
1060 MAIN STREET
SUITE 307
RIVER EDGE, NJ 07661
201-342-3663
800-580-9663
Fax: 201-342-2258
info@stayinthezone.com
www.stayinthezone.com

BEHIND THE WHEEL
30301 BRIGHT AVENUE
FAYETTEVILLE, TN 37334-1013
931-438-5765
Fax: 931-433-8480
www.btwonline.net
• Sam Holbrooks, Publisher & Editor
(931) 438-5765
• Sam Holbrooks, Publisher
Frequency:
34 time(s) per year
Description:
Publication is geared toward racing professionals and enthusiasts.

BETWEEN THE TOUCHLINES
13540 LAKE CITY WAY N.E. SUITE 3
SEATTLE, WA 98125
206-367-2420
Fax: 206-367-2636
www.varsitycommunications.com

• Luciano Pastor, Editor
(423) 559-1150
• Luciano Pastor, Publisher
(423) 559-1150
Frequency:
3 time(s) per year

BICYCLE RETAILER AND INDUSTRY NEWS
25431 CABOT ROAD SUITE 204
LAGUNA HILLS, CA 92653
949-206-1677
Fax: 949-206-1675
www.bicycleretailer.com
• Megan Tomkins, Editor-in-Chief
• Marc Sani, Publisher
msani@bicycleretailer.com
• Lynette Carpiet, Managing Editor
(949) 206-1677
Frequency:
18 time(s) per year
Description:
Publication is a news magazine for the bicycle industry; focuses on trends, finance, management, and new products.

BICYCLING
33 EAST MINOR STREET
EMMAUS, PA 18098-0099
610-967-8722
Fax: 610-967-8960
bicycling@rodale.com
www.bicycling.com
• Christine Bucher, Senior Editor
(610) 967-8273
christine.bucher@rodale.com
• Michael Frank, Deputy Editor
michael.frank@rodale.com
• Steve Madden, Editor-in-Chief
(212) 573-0229
steve.madden@rodale.com
• Susan G. Snyder, Advertising Business Manager
(610) 259-4082
• William Strickland, Executive Editor
bill.strickland@rodale.com
Frequency:
11 time(s) per year
Description:
Publication features information of interest to cycling enthusiasts.

BIKE
33046 CALLE AVIADOR
SAN JUAN CAPISTRANO, CA 92675-4704
949-496-5922
Fax: 949-496-7849
www.bikemag.com
• Mike Ferrentino, Editor
(949) 661-5158
• Derek DeJonge, Publisher
(949) 661-5153
• Ron Ige, Editor
• Lou Mazzante, Managing Editor
(949) 661-5191
Frequency:
6 time(s) per year
Description:
Publication is geared toward the mountain biking enthusiast.

BILLIARDS DIGEST
122 SOUTH MICHIGAN AVENUE SUITE 1506
CHICAGO, IL 60603

312-341-1110
Fax: 312-341-1469
www.billiardsdigest.com
• Mason King, Editor
(312) 341-1110
• Mike Panozzo, Publisher
mikep@billiardsdigest.com
• Mike Shamos, Contributing Editor
• Ruth Welte, Assistant Editor
(312) 341-1110
Frequency:
1 time(s) per month
Description:
Publication contains information on billiards.

BLACK ATHLETE SPORTS NETWORK
421 W. 144TH ST
NEW YORK, NY 10031
212-926-0402
ceo@blackathlete.net
www.blackathlete.net
• Roland Rogers, Chief Executive Officer
Sports Service Founded:
1999
Nature of Sports Service:
E-Zine - Source for information and breaking news stories about Black athletes at all levels from around the globe. Black writers, from across the country, provide sports coverage about the Black athlete, past, present, and future. Site features include daily updates, weekly columns, audio broadcasts, free email, and chat.

BLACK BELT
300 NORTH CONTINENTAL BOULEVARD SUITE 65
EL SEGUNDO, CA 90245
310-356-4100
800-423-2874
Fax: 661-257-3028
www.aimmedia.com
• Robert Young, Executive Editor
(661) 257-4066
• Robert Young, Sports Executive Editor
(661) 257-4066
Frequency:
1 time(s) per month
Description:
Publication focuses on martial arts.

BLACK TENNIS MAGAZINE
PO BOX 210767
DALLAS, TX 75211
214-339-7370
Fax: 214-339-7370
marcus.freeman.tennis@airmail.net
www.btmag.com
• Olando Temple, Editor-in-Chief
Frequency:
4 time(s) per year
Description:
A quarterly sports magazine centered around tennis and related activities with subscribers located in major cities of the USA, Europe, Africa, Australia and South America.

BLADES ON ICE
7040 NORTH MONA LISA ROAD
TUCSON, AZ 85741-2633
520-575-1747
888-525-8605
Fax: 520-575-1484
azpublish@aol.com
• Gerri Walbert, Executive Editor
boimag1@aol.com

Frequency:
6 time(s) per year
Description:
National and international figure skating information; events, interviews, photos.
Circulation:
10,000 - 20,000

BLOOD-HORSE
3101 BEAMOUNT CENTER CIRCLE
LEXINGTON, KY 40513
859-278-2361
800-866-2361
Fax: 859-276-6743
admin@bloodhorse.com
www.bloodhorse.com
• Dan Liebman, Managing Editor
• Stacy V. Bearse, Publisher
sbearse@bloodhorse.com
• Jim Cox, Advertising Director
(859) 276-6792
jcox@bloodhorse.com
• Ray Paulick, Editor-in-Chief
Frequency:
1 time(s) per week
Description:
Publication offers information on legal, economic, and operational aspects of the Thoroughbred horse industry.

BLUE WATER SAILING
747 AQUIDNECK AVENUE SUITE 201
MIDDLETOWN, RI 02842
401-847-7612
888-800-7245
Fax: 401-845-8580
george@bwsailing.com
www.bwsailing.com
• George Day, Editor
• George Day, Publisher
• Greg Jones, Senior Editor
greg@bwsailing.com
• Alice Noble, Managing Editor
alice@bwsailing.com
• Sandy Parks, Advertising Manager
sandy@bwsailing.com
• Jen Brett, Managing Editor
(401) 847-7612
jen@bwsailing.com
Frequency:
10 time(s) per year
Description:
Publication focuses on gear and seamanship for off-shore sailors.

BMX PLUS
25233 ANZA DRIVE
VALENCIA, CA 91355
661-295-1910
Fax: 661-295-1278
www.bmxplusmag.com
• Adam Booth, Editor
• Roland Hinz, Publisher
Frequency:
1 time(s) per month
Description:
Publication features information on bicycling for a teenage audience.

BOAT & MOTOR DEALER
6600 WEST TOUHY AVENUE
NILES, IL 60714
847-647-2900
Fax: 847-647-1155
webmaster@prestonpub.com
www.boatmotordealer.com

• Jerry Koncel, Editor
(847) 647-2900
jkoncel@prestonpub.com
• Janice S. Gordon, Publisher
(847) 647-2900
jgordon@prestonpub.com
• Jerry Koncel, Managing Editor
jkoncel@prestonpub.com
• Adolfo Mendez, Managing Editor
(847) 647-2900
Frequency:
11 time(s) per year
Description:
Publication covers information of interest to boat and motor dealership owners and marine suppliers; includes coverage of retail operations.

BOAT BROKER OUTDOOR
1910 ALEX HOLDEN WAY
JUNEAU, AK 99801-9384
907-789-4144
Fax: 907-789-0987
www.outdoorsak.com
• Amanda Gragert, Editor
(907) 789-4144
Frequency:
1 time(s) per month
Description:
Publication contains information of interest to commercial, sport, and recreational boaters in Alaska, including equipment and services.

BOAT U.S. MAGAZINE
880 SOUTH PICKETT STREET
ALEXANDRIA, VA 22304-4606
703-461-2864
Fax: 703-461-2845
www.boatus.com
• Bernadette Bernon, Consulting Editor
bbernon@boatus.com
• Elaine Dickinson, Managing Editor
• Michael Vatalaro, Executive Editor
mvatalaro@boatus.com
Frequency:
6 time(s) per year
Description:
Advocate for recreaional boats providing over half million members with government representation, programs and money-saving services.
Circulation:
over 500,000

BOATING
460 NORTH ORLAND AVENUE
WINTER PARK, FL 32789
407-628-4802
Fax: 407-628-7061
www.boatingmag.com
• Randy Steele, Editor
• Daniel Long, Technical Editor
(212) 767-4820
• Wade Luce, Publisher
(323) 954-4853
• Nancy Nisselbaum, Executive Editor
(212) 767-4813
• David Seidman, Executive Features Editor
(212) 767-6030
Frequency:
1 time(s) per month
Description:
Publication is geared toward powerboat enthusiasts.

BOATING INDUSTRY
6420 SYCAMORE LANE SUITE 100
MAPLE GROVE, MN 55369
763-383-4448
Fax: 763-383-4499
www.boating-industry.com
• Matt Gruhn, Editor
(763) 383-4402
• Matt Gruhn, Publisher
• Matt Gruhn, Sports Editor
• Liz Walz, Executive Editor
Frequency:
6 time(s) per year
Description:
Publication is geared toward the international boating industry; contains trend analysis about manufacturers, sales merchandising, international legislation.

BOATING LIFE
460 NORTH ORLANDO AVENUE SUITE 200
WINTER PARK, FL 32789
407-628-4802
Fax: 407-628-7061
www.boatinglifemag.com
• Randy Vance, Editor
• John McEver, Jr., Publisher
(407) 571-4682
john.mcever@worldpub.net
• Robert Stephens, Executive Editor
(407) 571-1131
• Chris Tauber, Senior Writer
(407) 571-1164
• Sue Whitney, Managing Editor
(407) 571-1146
Frequency:
7 time(s) per year

BOATING WORLD
11782 COWAN
SUITE A
IRVINE, CA 92614-6045
949-660-6150
Fax: 949-660-6172
www.boatingworld.com
• Kristina Ackermann, Managing Editor
(949) 660-6150
• Alan Jones, Executive Editor
• Jeffrey Fleming, Associate Publisher
(949) 660-6150
• Duncan McIntosh, Publisher
Frequency:
8 time(s) per year
Description:
Publication is written for active families that own trailerable power boats up to 36 feet in length; contains articles on new boats and marine products, safety, navigation, and maintenance

BONNEVILLE RACING NEWS
6489 WEST STETSON AVENUE
HEMET, CA 92545-9711
951-926-2277
Fax: 951-926-4619
• Wendy Jeffries, Editor
(951) 926-2277
• Wendy Jeffries, Advertising Manager
Frequency:
10 time(s) per year
Description:
Publication is aimed at automobile hot rodders and land speed racers.

BOSTON HANNAH INTERNATIONAL
274 MADISON AVE
9TH FLOOR
NEW YORK, NY 10016
212-889-8191
Fax: 312-284-5864
www.bostonhannah.com
• Kevin Harrington, Chief Executive
• Charles Ford, Managing Editor
• Phillip Lau, Art Director
Frequency:
Annual

BOWLERS JOURNAL INTERNATIONAL
122 SOUTH MICHIGAN AVENUE SUITE 1506
CHICAGO, IL 60603
312-341-1110
Fax: 312-341-1469
www.bowlersjournal.com
• Jim Dressel, Editor
(312) 341-1110
• Mike Panozzo, Publisher
mikep@billiardsdigest.com
Frequency:
1 time(s) per month
Description:
Publication covers the bowling industry.

BOWLING CENTER MANAGEMENT
122 SOUTH MICHIGAN AVENUE SUITE 1506
CHICAGO, IL 60603
312-341-1110
Fax: 312-341-1469
www.bcmmag.com
• Mike Mazek, Editor
• Barbara Peltz, Advertising Manager
(312) 341-1110
• Michael Mazek, Editor
(312) 341-1110
Frequency:
11 time(s) per year
Description:
Publication contains instructional and interpretive articles on bowling equipment, maintenance, management, promotions, and products.

BOWLING WORLD
900 SOUTH WINCESTER BOULEVARD
SUITE 11
SAN JOSE, CA 95128-2932
925-215-2242
Fax: 408-366-0847
readit@bowlingworld.com
www.bowlingworld.com
• Donna Hazel, Managing Editor
• Nicole Martindill, Assistant Editor
Frequency:
1 time(s) per month

BOXING USA
1 OLYMPIC PLAZA
COLORADO SPRINGS, CO 80909-5746
719-866-4506
Fax: 719-635-3246
www.usaboxing.org
• Julie Goldsticker, Editor
(719) 866-2304
Frequency:
4 time(s) per year
Description:
Publication focuses on Olympic style boxing in the United States.

BULLPEN
1770 BRUNSWICK PIKE
TRENTON, NJ 08638
609-695-1434
Fax: 609-695-2505
www.baberuthleague.org
• Colleen Higgins, Editor
colleen@baberuthleague.org
• Rosemary Schoellkopf, Editor
(609) 695-1434
rosemary@baberuthleague.org
Frequency:
4 time(s) per year
Description:
Publication focuses on baseball and softball; contains information on programs, clinic notes, promotions, and membership.

BUSCH NORTH SCENE
542 PLEASANT POND ROAD
TURNER, ME 04282
207-224-2060
Fax: 207-224-2060
soup@neracing.com
www.neracing.com
• George Campbell, Editor
Frequency:
2 time(s) per month
Description:
Publication focus intended for auto racing enthusiasts in the Northeast area.

CAL-HI SPORTS
2780 SKYPARK DRIVE SUITE 475
TORRANCE, CA 90505
310-791-1142
800-660-1334
Fax: 310-257-4444
www.studentsports.com
• Mark Tennis, Editor
(209) 463-9050
• Andy Bark, Publisher
Frequency:
1 time(s) per week
Description:
Publication covers high school sports.

CALIFORNIA BOWLING NEWS
2606 WEST BURBANK BOULEVARD
BURBANK, CA 91505-2303
562-807-3600
Fax: 818-845-6321
news@californiabowlingnews.com
www.californiabowlingnews.com
• Carol Mancini, Publisher
• Lillian Oak, Advertising Manager
Frequency:
1 time(s) per week
Description:
Publication covers bowling news.

CALIFORNIA DIVING NEWS
P.O. BOX 11231
TORRANCE, CA 90510-1231
310-792-2333
Fax: 310-792-2336
mail@saintbrendan.com
www.saintbrendan.com
• Dale Sheckler, Editor
dale@saintbrendan.com
• Mary L. Reed, Associate Editor
• Dale Sheckler, Advertising Sales
• Kim Sheckler, Executive Editor
kim@saintbrendan.com
• Dale Sheckler, Publisher
Frequency:
1 time(s) per month

Description:
Publication is dedicated to California diving; covers dive sites, diving gear, underwater photography, and special events.

CALIFORNIA HOCKEY & SKATING
701 DE LONG AVENUE SUITE I
NOVATO, CA 94945-3224
415-898-5414
Fax: 415-892-6484
hockeyskate@aol.com
• Reggie Winner, Editor
hockyskate@aol.com
• Bill Schoen, Publisher
bill@winecountryguide.com
• Reggie Winner, Managing Editor

CALIFORNIA THOROUGHBRED
201 COLORADO PLACE
ARCADIA, CA 91007-2604
626-445-7800
Fax: 626-574-0852
www.ctba.com
• Rudi Groothedde, Managing Editor
(626) 445-7800
Frequency:
1 time(s) per month
Description:
Publication contains information of interest to Thoroughbred horse breeders, trainers, and racing in the state of California.

CALIFORNIA TRACK AND RUNNING NEWS
583 D'ONOFRIO DRIVE SUITE 203
MADISON, WI 53719
608-827-0806
Fax: 608-827-0811
ssmedit@aol.com
www.caltrack.com
• Christine Jhonson, Editor
• Larry Eder, Group Publisher
(920) 560-8112
stanederjr@aol.com
• Larry Eder, Publisher
(920) 560-8112
Frequency:
1 time(s) per month
Description:
Publication is a complete guide to running and racing; includes feature articles and race results.

CANOE & KAYAK MAGAZINE
10526 NORTHEAST 68TH STREET SUITE 3
KIRKLAND, WA 98033-7004
425-827-6363
800-692-2663
Fax: 425-827-1893
www.canoekayak.com
• Jim Marsh, Advertising Manager
(425) 827-6363
• Scott Waidelich, Advertising Operations
(425) 827-6363
Frequency:
6 time(s) per year
Description:
Publication is North America's resource for canoeing and kayaking.

CASCADE HORSEMAN
1301 ESPLANADE AVENUE
KLAMATH FALLS, OR 97601-5902
541-885-4460
Fax: 530-842-6787

cascade.magazines@heraldandnews.com
www.cascadehorseman.com
• Rod Dowse, Editor
• Rod Dowse, General Manager
Frequency:
1 time(s) per month

CHESAPEAKE BAY MAGAZINE
1819 BAY RIDGE AVENUE SUITE 180
ANNAPOLIS, MD 21403-2896
410-974-8870
Fax: 410-267-6924
www.boatingonline.net
• Tim Sayles, Editor
(410) 974-8870
• Jane Meneely, Managing Editor
(410) 263-2662
• Richard J. Royer, Publisher
(410) 263-2662
Frequency:
1 time(s) per month
Description:
Publication focuses on boating in the Chesapeake Bay region.

CHICAGO DISTRICT GOLFER
11855 ARCHER AVENUE
LEMONT, IL 60439
630-257-2005
Fax: 630-257-2088
info@cdga.org
www.cdga.org
• Cathy Miles-Ralston, Editor
cralston@cdga.org
• Robert Markionni, Executive Director
(630) 685-2303
rmarkionni@cdga.org
• Mia Brown, Editor
(630) 685-2324
mbrown@cdga.org
Frequency:
6 time(s) per year

CHICAGO SPORTS PROFILE
4711 GOLF ROAD SUITE 900
SKOKIE, IL 60076-1234
847-673-0592
Fax: 847-673-0633
www.sportsprofilesplus.com
• Paula Blaine, Editor
• Paula Blaine, Publisher
• Lisa A. Levine, President
(847) 673-0592
Frequency:
4 time(s) per year
Description:
Publication is written for the general sports fan; includes information about coverage and movie releases.

CHICAGO'S AMATEUR ATHLETE
7840 NORTH LINCOLN AVENUE SUITE 204
SKOKIE, IL 60077
847-675-0200
Fax: 847-675-2903
chicagorun@aol.com
www.chicagoaa.com
• Brenda Barrera, Editor
• Eliot Wineberg, Publisher
Frequency:
10 time(s) per year
Description:
Publication contains information on running, cycling, and various other sports.

CHICAGOLAND GOLF
6825 HOBSON VALLEY DRIVE SUITE 204
WOODRIDGE, IL 60517
630-719-1000
Fax: 630-719-1030
chicagolandgolf@aol.com
• Phil Kosin, Editor-in-Chief
• Phil Kosin, Publisher
• Joanne Miller, Assistant Editor
(630) 719-1000
chicagolandgolf2@aol.com
Frequency:
15 time(s) per year
Description:
Publication covers the national and regional golfing scene; includes information on tours, events, vacation spots, health, and golfers.

CHRISTIAN MOTORSPORTS ILLUSTRATED
RR 3, BOX 120A
COLUMBIA CROSS ROADS, PA 16914
570-549-2282
888-548-2282
Fax: 570-549-3366
cpo7@loving-hearts.org
www.christianmotorsports.com
• Roland Osborne, Publisher
Frequency:
4 time(s) per year
Description:
Publication focuses on motorsports venues.

CHRONICLE OF THE HORSE
108 THE PLAINS ROAD
MIDDLEBURG, VA 20117
540-687-6341
Fax: 540-687-3937
staff@chronofhorse.com
www.chronofhorse.com
• John Strassburger, Editor
(540) 687-6341
• Robert L. Banner, Jr., Publisher
(540) 687-6341
rbanner@chronofhorse.com
• Trisha Booker, Managing Editor
(540) 687-6341
tbooker@chronofhorse.com
• Beth Rasin, Assistant Editor
(540) 687-6341
bethr@chronofhorse.com
Frequency:
1 time(s) per week
Description:
Publication is geared toward the horse lover; covers horse shows, combined training events, steeplechase racing, dressage, fox hunting, and endurance riding.

CIRCLE TRACK & RACING TECHNOLOGY MAGAZINE
9036 BRITTNAY WAY
TAMPA, FL 33619
863-644-0449
Fax: 813-675-3559
www.circletrack.com
• Larry Jewett, Editor
(813) 675-3525
• Raquel Jerkins, Managing Editor
(813) 675-3536
Frequency:
1 time(s) per month
Description:
Publication covers circle track auto racing and events, technical articles, personalities, and includes information and entertainment columns.

CITY SPORTS MAGAZINE
444 S. CEDROS AVE, #185
SOLANA BEACH, CA 92075
858-793-2711
Fax: 858-793-2710
bfit@competitor.com
www.citysportsmag.com
• Lois Schwartz, Publisher/Photo Ed/Event Sales
• Bob Babbitt, Publisher
• John Smith, Publisher/Advertising Director
• Diana Babb, Senior Editor
Publishing Company:
National Sports Network
Description:
Provides guides, destination articles and trend pieces with a
Frequency:
11 times annual
Primary Audience:
Consumer
Sports:
Active lifestyle sports such as bicycling, running, skiing, hiking; travel; family activities
Circulation:
75,000 in Northern California. Contr non-paid.

CITYSPORTS MAGAZINE
2220 FILLMORE STREET
SAN FRANCISCO, CA 94115
858-793-2711
Fax: 858-793-2710
www.citysportsmag.com
• Diana Babb, Senior Editor
diana@competitor.com
• Diana Babb, Sports Senior Editor
diana@competitor.com
• Bob Babbitt, Publisher
bob@competitor.com
• John Smith, Advertising Director
(858) 793-2711
john@competitor.com
• John Smith, Publisher
(858) 793-2711
john@competitor.com
Frequency:
11 time(s) per year

CLIMBING
0326 HIGHWAY 133 SUITE 190
CARBONDALE, CO 81623-1571
970-963-9449
Fax: 970-963-9442
www.climbing.com
• Jeff Achey, Managing Editor
(970) 704-2602
• Al Crolius, Publisher
(949) 661-5107
• John Dicuollo, Advertising Director
Frequency:
8 time(s) per year
Description:
Publication is geared toward rock climbers, ice climbers, and mountaineers.

COACHES REPORT
141 LAURIER AVE W.
STE 300
OTTAWA, ON, CANADA K1P 5J3
613-235-5000
Fax: 613-235-9500
www.coach.ca
• Sheila Robertson, Editor
Description:
The official publication of the Canadian

Professional Coaches Association. In-depth articles on various injuries, nutrition, strategy, psychology, special topics, physical training (ex. physiology, biomechanics, strength), testing (physical, psychological), and administration. The magazine examines current issues, profiles top Canadian coaches, and provides a unique perspective on the changing world of sport.
Circulation:
3,000
Sports:
General
Primary Audience:
Top level coaches
Frequency:
Four times annually
Publishing Company:
Coaching Association of Canada

COACHING MANAGEMENT
31 DUTCH MILL ROAD
ITHACA, NY 14850
607-257-6970
Fax: 607-257-7328
info@momentummedia.com
www.athleticsearch.com
• Eleanor Frankel, Editor-in-Chief
(607) 257-6970
info@momentummedia.com
• Mark Goldberg, Publisher
(607) 257-6970
info@momentummedia.com
• Mark Goldberg, Publisher
(607) 257-6970
mg@momentummedia.com
• Jim Catalano, New Products Editor
(607) 257-6970
info@momentummedia.com
Frequency:
6 time(s) per year
Description:
Publication focuses on maintaining and managing athletic departments and coaching staffs at high schools and colleges.

COLLEGE & PRO FOOTBALL NEWSWEEKLY
150 MAIN STREET SUITE 11
PORT WASHINGTON, NY 11050
516-883-4550
800-368-7907
Fax: 516-484-6104
bobbabowski@aol.com
www.cpsn.com
• Vic DeNicola, Editor-in-Chief
• Jack Cohen, Publisher
• Tina Vitello, Advertising Manager
Frequency:
1 time(s) per week
Description:
Publication covers college and professional football.

COLLEGIATE BASEBALL
2515 NORTH STONE AVENUE
TUCSON, AZ 85705-4530
520-623-4530
Fax: 520-624-5501
editor@baseballnews.com
www.baseballnews.com
• Lou Pavlovich, Jr., Editor
lou@baseballnews.com
• Diane Pavlovich, Advertising Director
diane@baseballnews.com

Frequency:
14 time(s) per year
Description:
This tabloid-sized newspaper covers college and high school baseball across the nation. Includes National polls, All-Americans, features and news stories on players and coaches and instructional baseball articles. The paper was started in 1958 as a result of an idea by a group of college baseball coaches.

COLORADO GOLF MAGAZINE
559 2ND AVENUE
CASTLE ROCK, CO 80108-9214
303-688-5853
pade@coloradogolf.com
www.coloradogolf.com
• Timothy Pade, Publisher & Editor
(303) 688-5853
pade@coloradogolf.com
• Timothy Pade, Publisher
Frequency:
4 time(s) per year
Description:
Publication is written for golfers; contains information on travel, instruction, and tournaments.

COMPETITOR
444 SOUTH CEDROS AVENUE SUITE 185
SOLANA BEACH, CA 92075-1917
858-793-2711
Fax: 858-793-2710
www.competitor.com
• Bob Babbitt, Editor
(858) 793-2711
bob@competitor.com
• Diana Babb, Senior Editor
diana@competitor.com
• Bob Babbitt, Publisher
bob@competitor.com
• John Smith, Advertising Manager
(858) 793-2711
john@competitor.com
Frequency:
11 time(s) per year

COMPETITOR MAGAZINE
605 BELVEDERE ROAD SUITE 9
WEST PALM BEACH, FL 33405
561-838-9060
Fax: 561-838-9037
www.competitor.com
• Rebecca Heaton, Editor
Frequency:
11 times per year
Description:
Active Sports Magazine for runners, cyclists, swimmer, mountain bikers and active people.
Circulation:
50,000

CONQUISTADOR
PO BOX 1922
SANTA YNEX, CA 93460
805-688-8318
888-882-6446
Fax: 267-821-1043
www.conquistador.com
• Charlotte Dickey, Editor
(805) 350-1232
Frequency:
6 time(s) per year
Description:

Publication features information on horse breeding, history, riding, and training.

COULOIR
P.O. BOX 2349
TRUCKEE, CA 96160
530-582-1884
Fax: 530-582-1887
www.couloirmag.com
• Craig Dostie, Editor
Frequency:
3 time(s) per year
Description:
Publication for skiers and snowboarders; includes coverage of backcountry riding.

CRITTENDEN GOLF
3990 OLD TOWN AVENUE
SUITE C-205
SAN DIEGO, CA 92110
800-211-1697
Fax: 619-374-1979
www.crittendengolf.com
• Jim Dunlap, Editor-in-Chief
(858) 503-7568
• Jack Crittenden, Publisher
(858) 503-7786
Frequency:
1 time(s) per month
Description:
Publication contains news for owners, developers, and managers of golf courses.

CROSS COUNTRY SKIER
17280 PIONEER ROAD
CABLE, WI 54821-4743
715-798-5500
800-827-0607
Fax: 715-798-3599
info@crosscountryskier.com
www.crosscountryskier.com
• Ron Bergin, Publisher & Editor
(715) 798-3599
ron@crosscountryskier.com
• Lou Dzierzak, Executive Editor
Frequency:
4 times per year
Description:
Publication is geared toward the cross-country skiing enthusiast; focuses on touring, travel, technique, lifestyle, and fitness.
Primary Audience:
Nordic ski/lifetyle enthusiast
Circulation:
30,000
Publications:
Nordic Skiing

CRUISING WORLD
55 HAMMARLUND WAY
MIDDLETOWN, RI 02842
401-845-5100
Fax: 401-845-5180
editorial@sailingworld.com
www.cruisingworld.com
• John Burnham, Editor
(401) 845-5106
• Sally Helme, Publisher
(401) 845-5105
• Gary Jobson, Editor-at-Large
(410) 263-4630
jobsonsailing@compuserve.com
• Elaine Lembo, Managing Editor
• Tim Murphy, Executive Editor
• Jason White, Associate Publisher
(401) 845-5155

Frequency:
1 time(s) per month
Description:
Publication focuses on sailing and seamanship.

CUTTING HORSE CHATTER
260 BAILEY AVENUE
FORT WORTH, TX 76107
817-244-6188
Fax: 817-244-2015
www.nchacutting.com
• Alan Gold, Editor
(817) 244-6188
• Shawn McCoy, Advertising Manager
(817) 244-6188
Frequency:
1 time(s) per month
Description:
Publication contains articles on horse care, veterinary advice, riding tips, and NCHA event Courage.

DESERT BOWLER
8925 NORTH 43RD AVENUE SUITE 2
PHOENIX, AZ 85051-3642
623-435-0867
800-347-1229
Fax: 623-937-9377
• Herb Grassl, Editor
herb@senecapublishing.com
• Herb Grassl, Advertising Manager
herb@senecapublishing.com
• Herb Grassl, Publisher
Frequency:
1 time(s) per month
Description:
Publication contains bowling industry news.

DIRT RAG
3483 SAXONBURG BOULEVARD
PITTSBURGH, PA 15238-1100
412-767-9910
800-762-7617
Fax: 412-767-9920
dirtrag@dirtragmag.com
www.dirtragmag.com
• Michael Browne, Editor
• Chris Cosby, Advertising Coordinator
• Chris Cosby, Advertising Manager
• Maurice Tierney, Publisher
• Karen Brooks, Editor
(412) 767-9910
Frequency:
7 time(s) per year
Description:
Publication targets mountain bike enthusiasts.
Primary Audience:
Cyclists

DOLPHIN DIGEST
8033 NORTHWEST 36TH STREET
MIAMI, FL 33166-6644
305-594-0508
800-334-4005
Fax: 305-594-0518
digest@curtispub.net
www.dolphindigest.net
• Andrew Cohen, Editor
acohen@curtispub.net
• Thomas Curtis, Publisher
newtcurtis@curtispub.net
• Alain Poupart, Associate Editor
(305) 594-0508
Frequency:
26 time(s) per year

Description:
Publication features the Miami Dolphins football team and the National Football League.

DRAG RACER MAGAZINE
265 SOUTH ANITA DRIVE SUITE 120
ORANGE, CA 92868-3310
714-939-9991
Fax: 714-939-9909
www.dragracermag.com
• Randy Fish, Editor
(714) 939-9991
Frequency:
6 time(s) per year

DRAG REVIEW
9 1/2 EAST MAIN STREET
NORWALK, OH 44857
419-663-6666
Fax: 419-663-4472
comments@ihra.com
www.ihra.com
• Pam Marchyshyn, Managing Editor
(419) 660-4214
• Kimberly Parsons, Production Designer
(419) 660-4215
kparsons@ihra.com
• Tom Roman, Advertising Manager
(860) 489-7516
thomasroman@aol.com
Frequency:
2 time(s) per month
Description:
Publication is the membership magazine of the International Hot Rod Association; covers IHRA national and regional drag races, as well as races run by or on IHRA sanctioned strips.

DRESSAGE TODAY
656 QUINCE ORCHARD ROAD
SUITE 600
GAITHERSBURG, MD 20878-1409
301-977-3900
Fax: 301-990-9015
dtletters@aol.com
www.equisearch.com
• Patricia Lasko, Editor
(301) 977-3900
• Susan M Harding, Publisher
(301) 977-3900
Frequency:
1 time(s) per month
Description:
Publication focuses on dressage.

DUSTY TIMES
20761 PLUMER STREET
CHATSWORTH, CA 91311-4408
818-882-0004
Fax: 818-882-0090
www.dustytimes.com
• John Calvin, Editor/Publisher
(818) 882-0004
Frequency:
1 time(s) per month
Description:
Publication covers off-road racing and rallying around the world.

EAGLES DIGEST
8033 NORTHWEST 36TH STREET
MIAMI, FL 33166-6644
305-594-0508
800-334-4005
Fax: 305-594-0518
www.eagles.com
• Dave Spadaro, Editor
(215) 463-2500
• Thomas Curtis, Publisher
(305) 594-0508
newtcurtis@curtispub.net
• Kenneth Keidel, Advertising Manager
(305) 594-0508
Frequency:
2 time(s) per month
Description:
Publication focuses on the Philadelphia Eagles football team.

EASTERN BASKETBALL
P.O. BOX 1269
PINEHURST, NC 28370
910-295-5559
Fax: 910-295-6566
www.basketballtimes.com
• Nanci Donald, Publisher
Frequency:
11 time(s) per year
Description:
Publication contains information of interest to fans of high school and college basketball on the East Coast, including commentary and profiles.

EMPLOYEE SERVICES MANAGEMENT
2211 YORK RD, STE 207
OAK BROOK, IL 60523-2371
630-368-1280
Fax: 630-368-1286
• Patrick B. Stinson, Publisher
• Rene Mulay, Editor
• Alison Bashian, Marketing Manager
Description:
Provides information, trends to persons responsible for administration of employee services and recreation programs - wellness programs, discount programs, pre-retirement planning, fitness facilities, hobby clubs, community service projects, child/elder care, and employee stores.
Circulation:
5,000. 65% association membership, 15% paid subscr, 10% contr non-paid.
Sports:
General
Primary Audience:
Association membership
Frequency:
10 times annually
Publishing Company:
Employee Services Management

ENSIGN
1504 BLUE RIDGE ROAD
RALEIGH, NC 27607-3906
919-821-0892
888-367-8777
Fax: 888-304-0813
www.theensign.org
• Yvonne Hill, Editor
(919) 821-0892
• Kelly Anderson, Associate Editor
Publications:
The Ensign (quarterly print publication);
USPS Compass (monthly e-mail newsletter)
Description:
The Ensign is a nonprofit boating safety and education organization. Our members are sailors, powerboaters and paddleboaters. We publishes articles of general interest to recreational boaters, including maintenance

articles, product reviews, and safe-boating information.
Primary Audience:
Members of U.S. Power Squadrons
Circulation:
40,000
Sports:
Sailing, Power Boating, Paddle Sports

ENTERTAINMENT LAW REPORTER
2118 WILSHIRE BLVD, #311
SANTA MONICA, CA 90403-5784
310-829-9335
Fax: 310-829-9335
www.entertainmentlawreporter.com
• Lionel Sobel, Editor
Description:
Edits periodical that reports recent developments in sports law.

EPM LICENSING LETTER SOURCEBOOK
19 W 21ST STREET
#303
NEW YORK, NY 10010
212-941-0099
888-852-9467
Fax: 212-941-1622
www.epmcom.com
• Riva Bennett, Chief Operating Officer
• Ira Mayer, Publisher
• Michele Jensen, Vice President of Marketing
• Melissa Trosterman, Marketing Coordinator
mtrosterman@epm.com
• Loretta Netzer, Circulation Manager
• Ben Jurin, Associate Editor, The Licensing Letter
Publishing Company:
EPM Communications, Inc.
Frequency:
Annual
Primary Audience:
Licensing business executives
Sports:
General
Circulation:
NA.
Description:
Directory of licensing agents, products, and manufacturers.

EQUESTRIAN
4047 IRON WORKS PARKWAY
LEXINGTON, KY 40511
859-258-2472
Fax: 859-231-6662
www.usef.org
• Brian Sosby, Editor-in-Chief
(859) 225-6923
editor@ahsa.org
• Scott Carling, Advertising Manager
(859) 225-6928
scarling@uses.org
Frequency:
10 time(s) per year
Description:
Publication is an equestrian guide.

EQUIERY
PO BOX 610
LISBON, MD 21765-0610
410-489-7826
Fax: 410-489-7828
info@equiery.com
www.equiery.com

• Tracy McKenna, Associate Publisher
(410) 489-7826
tracy.mckenna@equiery.com
• Katherine Rizzo, Editor
(410) 489-7826
katherine.rizzo@equiery.com
• Carrie Hull, Executive Director, Maryland Horse Council
(410) 489-7826
chull@mdhorsecouncil.org
• Neil Agate, President, Maryland Horse Council
nagate@mdhorsecouncil.org
Frequency:
1 time(s) per month
Description:
Publication features information for horsemen; covers trainers, riding programs, breeding facilities, association news, services, and sales.

EQUINE JOURNAL
103 ROXBURY STREET
KEENE, NH 03431
603-357-4271
800-742-9171
Fax: 603-357-7851
www.equinejournal.com
• Kathleen Labonville, Managing Editor
(603) 357-4271
• Lynn Jenkins, Advertising
(603) 357-4271
Frequency:
1 time(s) per month
Description:
Publication contains news and feature articles for people who ride horses competitively or for recreation.

EQUINE TIMES
331 EAST BELL
CAMDEN, MI 49232-9613
517-368-0365
800-222-6336
Fax: 517-368-5131
www.equine.com
• Cindy Bealer, General Manager
Frequency:
1 time(s) per month
Description:
Publication is for horse enthusiasts.

EQUUS
656 QUINCE ORCHARD ROAD SUITE 600
GAITHERSBURG, MD 20878-1409
301-977-3900
Fax: 301-990-9015
equuslts@aol.com
www.equisearch.com
• Laurie Prinz, Editor
(301) 977-3900
• Bob Kliner, Advertising Manager
(301) 977-3900
• Christine Barakat, Assignments Editor
(301) 977-3900
Frequency:
1 time(s) per month
Description:
Publication focuses on horse health care and training.

ERNIE SAXTON'S MOTORSPORTS SPONSORSHIP MARKETING
1448 HOLLYWOOD AVENUE
LANGHORNE, PA 19047-7417
215-752-7797
Fax: 215-752-1518

esaxton144@aol.com
www.saxtonsponsormarket.com
• Marilyn Saxton, Editor
(215) 752-2392
msaxton188@aol.com
• Joe McHugh, Account Executive
• Ernie Saxton, Publisher
Frequency:
1 time(s) per month
Description:
Publication focuses on sponsorship, marketing, and promotion through motor sports.

ESPN OUTDOORS/B.A.S.S.
5845 CARMICHAEL RD
MONTGOMERY, AL 36117
334-272-9530
Fax: 334-279-7148
www.bassmaster.com
• Dean Kessel, Vice President and General Manager
• Jeff Long, Director of Finance, Operations & Administrat
Publishing Company:
ESPN Productions - B.A.S.S., LLC.
Frequency:
10 times annually with 2 special issues.
Primary Audience:
Consumer
Sports:
Boating, fishing, hunting
Circulation:
550,000+.
Description:
Provides information of interest to outdoor sports participants.

ESPN THE MAGAZINE
19 EAST 34TH STREET
NEW YORK, NY 10016-4303
212-515-1000
Fax: 212-515-1290
www.espnmag.com
• Alison Overholt, General Editor
(212) 515-1000
• Shaun Assael, Senior Writer
(212) 515-1000
Shaun.Assael@espnmag.com
• Gary Belsky, Editor
(212) 515-1089
• Jerry Bembry, Senior Writer
(212) 515-1012
• Jeff Bradley, Senior Writer
(212) 515-1000
• Chris Broussard, Senior Writer
• Ric Bucher, Senior Writer
(212) 515-1000
• Chris Collins, Publisher
(212) 515-1136
• Luke Cyphers, Senior Editor-at-Large
(212) 515-1000
• Bruce Feldman, Senior Writer
(212) 515-1000
bruce.feldman@espnmag.com
• Neil Fine, Executive Editor
 (212) 515-1006
• David Fleming, Senior Writer
(212) 515-1000
david.fleming@espnmag.com
• Tom Friend, Senior Writer
(212) 515-1000
• Peter Gammons, Senior Writer
(212) 515-1000
• L.Z. Granderson, General Editor
(212) 515-1012
• John Gustafson, Contributing Writer

(212) 515-1000
• John Hassan, Senior Editor
(860) 766-4878
• John Hassan, Sports Senior Editor
(860) 766-4878
• Gary Hoenig, Editor in Chief
(212) 515-1030
• Sue Hovey, Senior Deputy Editor
(212) 515-1031
• E.J. Hradek, Senior Writer
(212) 515-1059
• Roxanne Jones, Senior Editor
(212) 515-1016
• Tim Keown, Senior Writer
(212) 515-1000
tim.keown@espnmag.com
• Ivan Maisel, Sports Senior Writer
• Steve Malley, (212) 515-1000
Sports Editor
• J.B. Morris, Senior Editor
(212) 515-1042
john.b.morris@espn3.com
• Jon Pessah, Deputy Editor
(212) 515-1000
• Perry Van Der Meer, Managing Editor
• Glen Waggoner, Executive Editor
(212) 515-1004
glen.waggoner@espn3.com
• Glen Waggoner, Sports Deputy Editor
Description:
ESPN targets young, active men whose lifestyles include watching sports, attending games, and participating in all kinds of athletics. The editorial focus plays off the news and includes what will happen in sports and which match-ups and young players to watch. Covers sports news. Focuses on baseball, hockey, basketball and foot ball, but also features articles on sports like in-line skating, bicycling and snowboarding.
Circulation:
1,900,000
Frequency:
Bi-weekly.

EXECUTIVE GOLFER
2171 CAMPUS DRIVE SUITE 330
IRVINE, CA 92612-1422
949-752-6474
Fax: 949-752-0398
www.executivegolfermagazine.com
• Joyce Stevens, Managing Editor
joyce@executivegolfermagazine.com
• Shaun Mehr, Advertising Director
• Edward F. Pazdur, Director
edward@executivegolfermagazine.com
• Mark Pazdur, Publisher
mpazdur@aol.com
Frequency:
6 time(s) per year
Description:
Publication focuses on golf resorts and golf communities; includes annual guides to golf resorts, golf communities, CEO interviews, and a private country club guest policy directory.

FACILITIES & EVENT MANAGEMENT MAGAZINE
152 MADISON AVE
SUITE 802
NEW YORK, NY 10016
646-580-1860
Fax: 212-578-8398
• Michael Caffin, Managing Editor
Description:
Covers the sports facility and event market

place.
Circulation:
31,000. Contr non-paid.
Sports:
General
Primary Audience:
CEO's, General Managers, Executive
Directors, Entertainment, sports and
convention facilities.
Frequency:
Bi-monthly
Publishing Company:
Bedrock Communications, Inc.

FAIRWAYS
77 EAST CENTER STREET
SUITE B
PROVO, UT 84606
801-360-2440
randy@fairwaysmag.com
www.fairwaysmag.com
• Randy Dodson, Publisher
randy@fairwaysmag.com
• Garrit Johnson, Art Director
Garrit@Fairwaysmag.com
Frequency:
4 time(s) per year
Description:
Founded in 1992, Fairways magazine is the
official publication of the Utah Golf
Association.

FANTASY SPORTS
700 E STATE ST
IOLA, WI 54990-0001
715-445-2214
888-457-2873
Fax: 715-445-4087
www.krause.com
• Greg Ambrosius, Editor
(715) 445-2214
• Dean Listle, Publisher
Frequency:
6 time(s) per year
Description:
Publication is geared toward fans of fantasy
baseball, football, basketball, golf, and
hockey.

FAR POST
13540 LAKE CITY WAY N.E. SUITE 3
SEATTLE, WA 98125
206-367-2420
Fax: 206-367-2636
www.varsitycommunications.com
• Earl Starkoff, Publisher
(800) 643-6061
Frequency:
4 time(s) per year

FIELD & STREAM MAGAZINE
TWO PARK AVE, 10 TH FL
NEW YORK, NY 10016
212-779-5000
Fax: 212-686-6877
www.fieldandstream.com
• Thomas Ott, Group Publisher
• Slaton White, Editor
• Stephen Crow, Advertising Director
Fishing Sponsor:
2003 Co-Title - Wal-Mart FLW Tour; 2004
Field & Stream Big Bass Contest.
Nature of Service:
Lifestyle magazine of the outdoors, focusing
on the fishing/hunting experience and man's
relationship with nature. Editorial covers
conservation and environmental issues as

well as sports current events and ethics. In
addition, magazine has a strong literary
tradition. Editorial also informs enthusiasts
of products, techniques, and locales to
support an outdoor lifestyle.
Publishing Company:
Times Mirror Magazines, Inc.
Frequency:
Monthly.
Primary Audience:
Consumer.
Sports:
Hunting, fishing.
Circulation:
2,007,901. 97% paid subscr, 3% newsstand.

**FITNESS BUSINESS CANADA
MAGAZINE/FITNESS TRAINER CANADA
MAGAZINE**
30 MILL POND DR
RR #3
GEORGETOWN, CANADA L7G 4S6
905-873-0850
888-920-6537
Fax: 905-873-8611
fbc@fitnet.ca
www.fitnet.ca
• Lori Longwell, Advertising Manager
• Graham Longwell, Editor/Publisher
fbc@fitnet.ca
Publishing Company:
Mill Pond Publishing Inc.
Frequency:
Bimonthly.
Primary Audience:
Fitness providers in Canada.
Sports:
Health & Fitness.
Circulation:
Fitness Business 8,000, Fitness Trainer
15,000

FITNESS INFORMATION TECHNOLOGY
1137 VAN VOORHIS RD
CHELSEA SQUARE, STE 32
MORGANTOWN, WV 26505
304-599-3483
800-477-4348
Fax: 304-599-3482
• Andrew Ostrow, FIT President
(304) 599-3483
• Drew Krantz, Marketing Associate
(304) 599-3483
• Julie B. Burrell, Editor
(304) 599-3483
Publishing Company:
Fitness Information Technology, Inc.
Frequency:
4 times a year.
Nature of Service:
Academic publication in sport marketing
worldwide.
Primary Audience:
College.

FLORIDA GOLF NEWS
301 3RD STREET, N.W. SUITE 216
WINTER HAVEN, FL 33881
863-401-9744
Fax: 863-401-9542
www.flgolfnews.com
• Ed Travis, Editor
golfscribe@tampabay.rr.com
Frequency:
1 time(s) per month
Description:
Publication contains information of interest

to golfing enthusiasts in the state of Florida,
including coverage of events and equipment
reviews.

FLORIDA GREEN
P.O. BOX 65
JENSEN BEACH, FL 34958
772-334-7515
800-732-6053
Fax: 772-334-6015
flgrn@aol.com
www.floridagcsa.com
• Larry Keiffer, Publication Manager
(863) 398-4057
• Marie Roberts, Advertising Manager
Frequency:
4 time(s) per year
Description:
Publication contains information on golf
course management.

FLORIDA HORSEMEN
12788 WEST FOREST HILL BOULEVARD
SUITE 1
WELLINGTON, FL 33414
561-793-7606
Fax: 561-793-6090
www.horsemenonline.com
• Joshua Manning, Editor
news@gotowncrier.com
Frequency:
9 time(s) per year

**FLORIDA SPORTS & FITNESS
MAGAZINE**
102 DRENNEN ROAD
ORLANDO, FL 32806
407-816-9596
888-352-5484
Fax: 407-816-9373
www.floridamagazine.com
• E. Douglas Cifers, Publisher
dcifers@floridamagazine.com
• Elizabeth Ashton, Administrative
Coordinator
(407) 816-9596
• Susan Cerulean, Writer
(407) 816-9596
Frequency:
1 time(s) per year

FLORIDA SPORTSMAN
2700 SOUTH KANNER HIGHWAY
STUART, FL 34994
772-219-7400
Fax: 772-219-6900
www.floridasportsman.com
• Herb Allen, Department Editor
(772) 219-7400
• Karl Wickstrom, Editor-in-Chief
(772) 219-7400
• Blair Wickstrom, Publisher
(772) 219-7400
• Bob Mitchell, Marketing Director
• Eric Wickstrom, Internet Editor
(772) 219-7400
editor@floridasportsman.com
• Vic Dunaway, Senior Editor
(772) 219-7400
• Jeff Weakley, Editor
(772) 219-7400
jeff@floridasportsman.com
Description:
Edited for more than 48 million visitors and
residents of Florida, the Bahamas, and the
American tropics. Content is directed to the
ardent sportsman who fishes, hunts, boats,

camps, swims and creates a vast consumer area. Editorial philosophy is geared to these active devotees and the full enjoyment of the natural resources. Articles prepared by Florida's best known outdoors experts emphasize the how-to and where-to approach.

Circulation:
114,066
Sports:
Outdoor sports
Primary Audience:
Consumer
Frequency:
Monthly.
Publishing Company:
Primedia, Inc.

FLORIDA TENNIS
1760 NORTHWEST 107TH AVENUE
PEMBROKE PINES, FL 33026-2806
954-431-4069
800-779-4069
Fax: 954-438-7330
fltennis@aol.com
• Jim Martz, Editor
• Gary Ferman, Managing Editor
Frequency:
1 time(s) per month
Description:
Publication features tennis news in Florida.

FOOTBALL DIGEST
990 GROVE STREET
EVANSTON, IL 60201-4370
847-491-6440
800-334-4005
Fax: 847-491-0459
www.centurysports.net
• William Wagner, Editor
(847) 491-6440
• Norman Jacobs, Publisher
(847) 491-6440
njacobs@centurysports.net
Frequency:
10 time(s) per year
Description:
Publication covers professional football; includes interviews, stats, reports, rosters, and predictions.

FOOTBALL NEWS
8033 NORTHWEST 36TH STREET
SUITE 438
DORAL, FL 33166-6644
305-594-0508
Fax: 305-594-0518
Frequency:
20 time(s) per year
Description:
Publication covers college and professional football.

FOOTWEAR PLUS
8 WEST 38TH STREET
NEW YORK, NY 10120
646-278-1550
Fax: 646-278-1553
www.footwearplusonline.com
• Greg Dutter, Editor-in-Chief
(646) 278-1550
• Thomas Hudson, Jr., Publisher
• Caroline Diaco, Publisher
(646) 278-1550
• Petra Guglielmetti, Asoaciate Fashion Editor

• Kristen Koba, Associate Fashion Editor
• Caletha Crawford, Associate Editor
Publishing Company:
Wickstrom Publishers, Inc.
Frequency:
Monthly except for bi-monthly-April/May; November/December.
Primary Audience:
Trade
Sports:
All Sports.
Description:
The fashion magazine of the footwear industry.

FORE
3740 CAHUENGA BOULEVARD
NORTH HOLLYWOOD, CA 91604-3502
818-980-3630
Fax: 818-980-1808
www.scga.org
• Robert D. Thomas, Editor
(818) 980-3630
• Katie Denbo, Assistant Editor
(818) 980-3630
• Robert D. Thomas, Publisher
(818) 980-3630
• Teri Silvi, Communications/Marketing Specialist
(818) 980-3630
• Timmie High, Production Supervisor
(818) 980-3630
Frequency:
6 time(s) per year
Description:
Publication contains golf news and information focusing on California amateur golf; includes features on resorts, tours, and new products.

FREESKIER
1630 30TH STREET SUITE 272
BOULDER, CO 80301
303-449-2165
Fax: 303-449-2427
www.freeskier.com
• Patrick Crawford, Editor
(303) 449-8212
• Bradford Fayfield, Publisher
(303) 449-5100
bradford@freeskier.com
• Christopher Jerard, Advertising Manager
(303) 449-2165
Frequency:
4 time(s) per year
Description:
Publication is a lifestyle magazine for skiers between the ages of 18 and 34; showcases today's new, youthful ski movement.

GATER RACING PHOTO NEWS
206 FERNCLIFF AVENUE
LIVERPOOL, NY 13088-6410
315-457-0175
Fax: 315-457-0346
www.gaternews.com
• Joseph Patrick, Editor
(315) 457-0175
• Joseph Patrick, Advertising Manager
• Joseph Patrick, Publisher
Frequency:
37 time(s) per year
Description:
Publication covers oval track auto racing and is a regional trade newspaper for sports personnel and fans.

GATOR BAIT
PO BOX 14022
GAINESVILLE, FL 32604
352-372-1215
800-782-3216
Fax: 352-371-9420
www.gatorbait.net
• Marty Cohen, General Manager/Editor
• Guerry Smith, Assistant Editor
• Laura Cohen, Web Editor
• J.L. Kirby, Staff Writer
Description:
Features and information about all sports at the University of Florida.
Circulation:
21,000
Sports:
All sports at the University of Florida
Primary Audience:
Consumer
Frequency:
32 times annually
Publishing Company:
Florida Sports News, Inc.

GOLD SHEET
4717 VAN NUYS BOULEVARD
SHERMAN OAKS, CA 91403
800-798-4653
Fax: 323-273-5932
www.goldsheet.com
• Mort Olshan, Founder/Chairman
• P. Carl Giordano, Managing Editor
Description:
Analysts and commentators of college and pro football and basketball handicapping.
Circulation:
102,712.34% paid subscr, 66% newsstand.
Sports:
Football & Basketball
Primary Audience:
Consumer
Frequency:
Weekly Sept-April
Publishing Company:
Olshan Enterprises, Inc.

GOLF BUSINESS
291 SEVEN FARMS DRIVE 2ND FLOOR
CHARLESTON, SC 29492
843-881-9956
Fax: 843-881-9958
www.golfbusiness.com
• Rodney Foushee, Editor
(843) 881-9956
• Bill Gurney, Director
(843) 881-9956
• Joe Rice, Publisher
(843) 881-9956
Frequency:
1 time(s) per month
Description:
Publication focuses on golf course management.

GOLF CONNOISSEUR MAGAZINE
8988-L SOUTH SHERIDAN ROAD SUITE 360
TULSA, OK 74133
918-492-0660
Fax: 918-492-0680
www.golfconnoisseur.com
• James A. Frank, Editor-in-Chief
(212) 222-0033
Frequency:
4 time(s) per year

GOLF COURSE MANAGEMENT
1421 RESEARCH PARK DRIVE
LAWRENCE, KS 66049-3858
785-832-4431
800-472-7878
Fax: 785-832-3665
www.gcsaa.org
• Bunny Smith, Managing Editor
(785) 832-4490
• Ed Hiscock, Editor In Chief
(785) 832-4431
• Seth Jones, Senior Associate Editor
(785) 832-3682
• Angela Nitz, Senior Associate Editor
Frequency:
1 time(s) per month
Description:
Publication is geared toward golf course
superintendents; includes news, features,
and research.

GOLF COURSE NEWS
4012 BRIDGE AVENUE
CLEVELAND, OH 44113
216-961-4130
Fax: 216-961-0364
www.golfcourse.com
• Kevin Gilbride, Publisher
(330) 657-2889
kgilbride@gie.net
• John Walsh, Managing Editor
(216) 961-4130
jwalsh@gie.net
Frequency:
1 time(s) per month
Description:
Publication focuses on golf course
management for superintendents, owners,
architects, developers, and suppliers.

GOLF DIGEST
20 WESTPORT ROAD
WILTON, CT 06897
203-761-5100
Fax: 203-761-5129
editor@golfdigest.com
www.golfdigest.com
• Roger Schiffman, Managing Editor
(203) 761-5237
roger.schiffman@golfdigest.com
• Max Adler, Assistant Editor
(203) 761-5344
max.adler@golfdigest.com
• Tom Bair, Publisher
(212) 286-3856
tom.bair@golfdigest.com
• Mike O'Malley, Executive Editor
(203) 761-5234
mike.omalley@golfdigest.com
• Craig Bestrom, Senior Editor
(203) 761-5224
craig.bestrom@golfdigest.com
Frequency:
1 time(s) per month
Description:
Publication offers instruction and features
for all golfers from beginners to experienced
players.

GOLF FOR WOMEN
20 WESTPORT ROAD 7TH FLOOR
WILTON, CT 06897
212-286-2888
Fax: 212-286-5340
www.golfforwomen.com
• Susan K. Reed, Editor
(212) 286-3905

• Samantha Hallock, Assistant Editor
(212) 286-3906
• Johnette Howard, Contributing Writer
• Janine Hughes, Managing Editor
(212) 286-3908
• Sally Jenkins, Contributing Writer
• Argy Koutsothanasis, Contributing Writer
(212) 286-3941
• Kate Meyers, Contributing Writer
• Lee Slattery, Publisher
(212) 286-2498
• Stina Sternberg, Senior Editor
(212) 286-3934
stina.sternberg@golfforwomen.com
• Stina Sternberg, Sports Senior Editor
(212) 286-3934
• Sarah Turcotte, Assistant Editor
(212) 286-3954
sarah.turcotte@golfforwomen.com
• Sarah Turcotte, Sports Assistant Editor
(212) 286-3954
• Dana White, Executive Editor
(212) 286-4360
Frequency:
6 time(s) per year
Description:
Publication focuses on golf subjects for
women.

GOLF GEORGIA
121 VILLAGE PARKWAY BUILDING 3
MARIETTA, GA 30067-4061
770-955-4572
800-949-4742
Fax: 770-955-1156
sbower@levelparmedia.com
www.gsga.org
• Stan Awtrey, Editor
• Shannon Bower, Publisher
Frequency:
6 time(s) per year
Description:
Publication targets private and public golf
club members; focuses on golf-related news
and activities around the state, including
competitions, new course openings, and
other items of interest.

GOLF ILLUSTRATED
15115 SOUTH 76TH EAST AVENUE
BIXBY, OK 74008
918-366-6191
Fax: 918-366-6512
www.golfillustrated.com
• Jason Sowards, Editor
(918) 366-6191
• Gerald W. Pope, Publisher
(918) 366-6191
Frequency:
4 time(s) per year
Description:
Publication is a lifestyle magazine for
advanced golfers.

GOLF MAGAZINE
2 PARK AVENUE 10TH FLOOR
NEW YORK, NY 10016-5675
212-779-5000
Fax: 212-779-5522
www.golfonline.com
• Robert Sauerhaft, Managing Editor -
Equipment
(212) 779-5064
• Dave Allen, Senior Associate Editor
(212) 779-5051
• Lorin Anderson, Managing Editor
(212) 779-5514

• Connell Barrett, Senior Editor
• David Clarke, Editor-in-Chief
• David Dusek, Associate Editor
(212) 779-5016
• Carl Mehlhope, Associate Publisher
(212) 779-5000
• Greg Midland, Associate Editor
(212) 779-5567
• Peter Morrice, Executive Editor
• Ron Mulliken, Advertising Director
• Jack Nicklaus, Special Contributor
• Evan Rothman, Executive Editor
• Alan Bastable, Senior Associate Editor
(212) 522-8630
alan_bastable@golf.com
Frequency:
1 time(s) per month
Description:
Publication is written for golf enthusiasts.

GOLF NEWS
10 NORTH NEWNAN STREET
JACKSONVILLE, FL 32202-3322
904-356-2466
Fax: 904-353-2628
admin@baileypub.com
www.baileypub.com
• James Bailey, Publisher
• Fred Seely, Editorial Director
(904) 356-2466
• Melanie White, Advertising Manager
Frequency:
1 time(s) per month
Description:
Publication features information of interest
to golf enthusiasts.

GOLF ON CAPE COD
143 A UPPER COUNTY ROAD
DENNIS PORT, MA 02639
508-398-6101
Fax: 508-398-4711
www.golfoncapecod.com
• Paul Reiss, Editor
(508) 398-6101
• Paul Reiss, Publisher
(508) 398-6101
Frequency:
4 time(s) per year
Description:
Publication covers regional courses,
players, and tournaments.

GOLF PRODUCT NEWS
217 MOUNTAIN BROOK DRIVE SUITE 201
MARIETTA, GA 30064
678-355-1007
www.golfproductnews.com
• Jack Bacot, Editor-in-Chief
(843) 437-5473
• Laurie Dee Dovey, Contributing Editor
• Peter W. Finney, Jr., Contributing Editor
pfinney@clarionherald.org
• Dan Gleason, Contributing Editor
• Robert Nitkewicz, Publisher
rnitkewicz@bellsouth.net
• Jack O'Leary, Contributing Editor
• Barbara Sabella, Contributing Editor
• John Torsiello, Contributing Editor
• Bill Varner, Contributing Editor
Frequency:
8 time(s) per year
Description:
Publication focuses on the golf products and
accessories industry.

GOLF RANGE TIMES
2807 NORTH PARHAM ROAD SUITE 107
RICHMOND, VA 23294
804-379-5760
Fax: 804-282-5780
www.golfrangetimes.com
• James E. Turner, Editor
• Betty Jo Bass, Advertising Manager
(804) 360-0158
• Virginia Sowers, Managing Editor
virginia.sowers@douglasmurphy.com
• James E. Turner, Publisher
Frequency:
7 time(s) per year
Description:
Publication focuses on the golf range business.

GOLF TIPS
12121 WILSHIRE BOULEVARD SUITE 1200
LOS ANGELES, CA 90025
310-820-1500
Fax: 310-820-2793
www.warnerpublishing.com
• Mike Chwasky, Editor
• Steve Werner, Publisher
Frequency:
1 time(s) per month
Description:
Publication provides golf instruction.

GOLF TRAVELER
2575 VISTA DEL MAR DRIVE
VENTURA, CA 93001
805-667-4100
800-765-1912
Fax: 805-667-4217
info@golfcard.com
www.golfcard.com
• Ken Cohen, Editor
Frequency:
6 time(s) per year
Description:
Publication contains information on affiliated Golf Card resorts, accommodations, golf courses, the senior PGA tour, golfing techniques, and developments in equipment and sportswear.

GOLF VIEWS
P.O. BOX 620999
LITTLETON, CO 80162
303-797-8700
Fax: 303-797-1119
www.golfviews.com
• Karl O'Keefe, Editor
• Karl O'Keefe, Publisher
Frequency:
9 time(s) per year
Description:
Publication is geared toward the golf pro.

GOLF WORLD
20 WESTPORT ROAD
WILTON, CT 06897
203-761-5100
Fax: 203-761-5129
golfworld@golf.com
www.golfdigest.com
• Geoff Russell, Features Editor
(203) 761-5253
geoff.russell@golfworld.com
• Mark Furlong, Publisher
(212) 286-4120
mark.furlong@golfdigest.com

• Ron Sirak, Managing Editor
(203) 761-5260
ron.sirak@golfworld.com
• Jerry Tarde, Editor-in-Chief
(203) 761-5225
jerry.tarde@golfdigest.com
• John Antonini, Senior Editor of Tour Talk
(203) 761-5254
john.antonini@golfworld.com
Frequency:
48 time(s) per year
Description:
Publication is geared toward amateur and professional golfers; reports on PGA and LPGA tours and tournaments as well as college golf.

GOLFDOM
7500 OLD OAK BOULEVARD
CLEVELAND, OH 44130-3369
440-243-8100
Fax: 440-891-2675
www.golfdom.com
• Frank Andorka, Managing Editor
(440) 891-2708
• Larry Aylward, Editor in Chief
(216) 706-3737
laylward@questex.com
• Patrick Roberts, Publisher
(440) 891-2609
proberts@questex.com
Frequency:
1 time(s) per month
Description:
Publication delivers technical information on golf course maintenance topics, case studies, news, columns, and opinions.

GOLFER
59 EAST 72ND STREET
NEW YORK, NY 100021
212-867-7070
Fax: 212-867-8550
thegolfer@thegolfermag.com
www.thegolfermag.com/
• Cliffard Blodgett, Managing Editor
cliffard@thegolfermag.com
• H. Kevan Pickens, Editor-in-Chief
kevan@thegolfermag.com
• H. Kevan Pickens, Publisher
kevan@thegolfermag.com
• Colin Sheehan, Senior Editor
(212) 867-7070
colin@thegolfermag.com
• John Clarke, Jr., Managing Editor
(212) 867-7070
Frequency:
6 time(s) per year
Description:
Publication is a golf lifestyle magazine with tournament coverage, course selections and country club updates. Also provides new equipment reviews and suggests spas & restaurants for readers.

GOLFWEEK
1500 PARK CENTER DRIVE
ORLANDO, FL 32835
407-563-7000
Fax: 407-563-7077
email@golfweek.com
www.golfweek.com
• David Seanor, Editor
dseanor@golfweek.com
• Jeff Babineau, Deputy Editor
(407) 563-7046
jbabineau@golfweek.com

• Beth Ann Baldry, Senior Writer
(407) 563-7041
bbaldry@golfweek.com
• Jay Coffin, Staff Writer
(407) 563-7043
jcoffin@golfweek.com
• Craig Horan, Managing Editor
(407) 563-7030
choran@golfweek.com
• Martin Kaufmann, Assistant Editor
(407) 563-7044
mkaufmann@golfweek.com
• Bradley S Klein, Staff Writer
(860) 243-3296
bklein@golfweek.com
• Jim Nugent, Publisher
(407) 563-7014
jnugent@golfweek.com
• David Seanor, Editorial Director
• James Achenbach, Associate Editor
(760) 863-4377
jachenbach@golfweek.com
Frequency:
1 time(s) per week
Description:
Publication contains information of interest to golf enthusiasts, including pro golf news, commentary, amateur and college news, rankings, business news, and America's best courses.

GOLFWEEK'S SUPERINTENDENT NEWS
1500 PARK CENTER DRIVE
ORLANDO, FL 32835
407-563-7000
Fax: 407-563-7076
esoderstrom@golfweek.com
www.golfweek.com
• James E. Nugent, Publisher
jnugent@golfweek.com
Frequency:
2 time(s) per month
Description:
Publication is a golf management magazine.

GOWDY PRINTCRAFT PRESS
22 N. SIERRA MADRE
COLORADO SPRINGS, CO 80903
719-634-1593
Fax: 719-632-0762
• Tex Stuart, Director
Description:
The Fort Carson Mountaineer newspaper since 1942 The Air Force Academy Academy Spirit newspaper since 1959 The Schriever Air Force Base Satellite Flyer newspaper since 1999 The Peterson Air Force Base Space Observer And the P3 Sports Guide series since 1990

GRASSROOTS MOTORSPORTS
P.O. BOX 1568
ORMOND BEACH, FL 32175
386-239-0523
888-676-0573
Fax: 386-239-0573
www.grassrootsmotorsports.com
• David Wallens, Editor
• Marjorie Suddard, Editor
(386) 673-4148
marjorie@grassrootsmotorsports.com
• Timothy P. Suddard, Publisher
• Noelle Omer, Editorial Assistant
(386) 673-4148
Frequency:
6 time(s) per year

GRAY'S SPORTING JOURNAL
735 BROAD ST
AUGUSTA, GA 30901
978-462-6335
Fax: 978-462-6445
www.grayssportingjournal.com
• William S. Morris, Publisher
• David C. Foster, Editor-in-Chief
• James Babb, Editor
(706) 722-6060
jrbabb@verizon.net
Description:
Explores the sophisticated outdoor
adventurer's world of hunting, fishing and
conservation through literature, fine sporting
photography, art and travel.
Publishing Company:
Morris Communications, Inc.
Circulation:
NA.
Sports:
Flyfishing, fishing, bird hunting, big game
hunting
Primary Audience:
Consumer
Frequency:
Six times annually plus Annual Expedition
and Guide Books.

GREAT LAKES BOATING MAGAZINE
1032 NORTH LA SALLE
CHICAGO, IL 60610
312-266-8400
Fax: 312-266-8470
www.greatlakesboating.com
• Karen Malonis, Managing Editor
• F. Ned Dikmen, Publisher
• Karen Malonis, Sports Managing Editor
Frequency:
6 time(s) per year
Description:
Publication focuses on recreational boating
on the Great Lakes.

GREYHOUND REVIEW
729 OLD HIGHWAY 40
ABILENE, KS 67410
785-263-4660
Fax: 785-263-4689
nga@ngagreyhounds.com
www.ngagreyhounds.com
• Tim Horan, Managing Editor
• Gary Guccione, Executive Editor
garyg@ngagreyhounds.com
Frequency:
12 time(s) per year
Description:
Publication contains articles from greyhound
racetracks and breeding farms throughout
the country. Aimed towards the professional
greyhound racing.

H.O. ZIMMAN
SEAPORT LANDING
152 THE LYNNWAY
LYNN, MA 01902
781-598-9230
Fax: 781-599-4018
www.hozinc.com
• Joshua A. Zimman, President
• David Zimman, Advertising Director
• Dan Vinton, Director of Business
Development
Description:
Publishes over 200 magazines which
include: U.S. Open Tennis Magazine,

Tennis Championships Magazine, U.S.
Soccer, The Olympian.

HACHETTE FILIPACCHI MEDIA
1633 BROADWAY
NEW YORK, NY 10019
212-767-6000
Fax: 212-767-5602
• Nick Matarazzo, Sr. VP/Director Group
Publisher Automotive Group
• Nicolas Ricci, Senior Vice President, Sales
& Marketing
• Tony Catalano, Vice President National
Sales Manager
• Lucilla Sitra, Regional Sales
• Adam Meyerson, Regional Sales Director
• Pete Beckenbach, Regional Sales Director
• Lawrence Peters, Managing Director,
Director Response Advertis
Description:
Publishes wide range of consumer
magazines.

**HAND GLIDING & PARA GLIDING
MAGAZINE**
P.O. BOX 1330
COLORADO SPRINGS, CO 80901
800-616-6888
Fax: 719-632-6417
www.ushga.org
• C. J. Sturtevant, Editor
Frequency:
1 time(s) per month

HEALTH & FITNESS MAGAZINE
5001 WOODWAY
SUITE 1404
HOUSTON, TX 77057
713-552-9991
Fax: 713-552-9997
www.healthandfitnessmag.com
• Rod Evans, Editor
(713) 552-9991
• Pat Monfrey, Publisher
(713) 552-9991
Frequency:
1 time(s) per month
Description:
Publication contains information on nutrition,
exercise, sports, and beauty for the
residents of the greater Houston area.

HEARTLAND BOATING
319 NORTH 4TH STREET
SUITE 650
ST LOUIS, MO 63102-1998
314-241-4310
800-366-9630
Fax: 314-241-4207
info@heartlandboating.com
www.heartlandboating.com
• Lee C Braff, Editor
(314) 241-4310
lbraff@heartlandboating.com
• Greg Klohr, Advertising Sales Manager
(314) 241-4310
greg@heartlandboating.com
• H. Nelson Spencer, Publisher
(314) 241-4310
Frequency:
8 times per year, March - October
Description:
Publication focuses on freshwater
recreational boating.
Circulation:
10,000
Primary Audience:

Recreational boat owners in the South and
the Mid-West.

HECKLER MAGAZINE
1915 25TH STREET
SACRAMENTO, CA 95814
916-456-2300
888-897-6247
Fax: 916-444-8972
info@heckler.com
www.heckler.com
• Brad Oates, Co-Editor
(916) 456-2300
Frequency:
7 time(s) per year
Description:
Publication contains articles about
snowboarding, skateboarding, and music.

HIGH SURF ADVISORY
P.O. BOX 789
HALEIWA, HI 96712
808-551-9397
Fax: 808-637-4701
www.highsurfadvisory.com
Frequency:
8 time(s) per year
Description:
Publication is a surfing magazine for
enthusiasts in Hawaii.

HOMETOWN GOLF
9933 ALLIANCE ROAD
CINCINNATI, OH 45242
513-794-4100
Fax: 513-794-4140
mmurphy@reachusa.com
www.cincygolf.com
• Ed Letsinger, Managing Editor
(513) 794-4177
eletsinger@reachusa.com
Frequency:
6 time(s) per year
Description:
Publication features local golf stories and
information in the Greater Cincinnati area.

HOOF BEATS
6130 S SUNBURY ROAD
WESTERVILLE, OH 43081
614-224-2291
877-800-8782
Fax: 614-222-6791
hoofbeats@ustrotting.com
www.hoofbeatsmagazine.com
• Dan Leary, Executive Editor
(614) 224-2291
hoofbeats@ustrotting.com
• Kim French, Editor
(570) 506-9948
hoofbeats@ustrotting.com
• Gena Gallagher, Art Director/Production
Manager
ggalla@ustrotting.com
• Paul Ramlow, Copy Editor
Frequency:
1 time(s) per month
Description:
Publication offers news and practical
information for owners, trainers, drivers, and
fans of standardbred racing and breeding.

HOOK
209 SOUTH MARSHALL STREET
MARSHFIELD, MO 65706-2142

417-468-7000
Fax: 417-859-6075
editor@hookmagazine.com
www.hookmagazine.com
• Dana Marlin, Editor
• Dana Marlin, Advertising Manager
• Dana Marlin, Publisher
Frequency:
6 time(s) per year
Description:
Publication covers all aspects of antique and classic tractor pulling.

HOOP
355 LEXINGTON AVENUE
NEW YORK, NY 10017-6603
212-697-1460
Fax: 212-286-8154
• Tony Gervino, Editor
mwong@pspsports.com
• Ming Wong, Managing Editor
mwong@pspsports.com
Frequency:
8 time(s) per year
Description:
Publication focuses on professional basketball.

HORSE
3101 BEAMOUNT CENTER CIRCLE
LEXINGTON, KY 40513
859-278-2361
800-866-2361
Fax: 859-276-6706
admin@thehorse.com
thehorse.com
• Kim Herbert, Editor
• Michelle Adaway, Advertising Manager
(859) 276-6701
• Stacy V. Bearse, Publisher
• Jim Cox, Advertising Director
(859) 276-6792
Frequency:
1 time(s) per month
Description:
Publication provides practical information on all aspects of horse breeding, training, and related business, with a focus on health/veterinary topics.

HORSE & RIDER
656 QUINCE ORCHARD ROAD
SUITE 600
GAITHERSBURG, MD 20878
301-977-3900
Fax: 301-990-9015
equineeditor@equinetwork.com
www.horseandrider.com
• Darrell Dodds, Editor
(940) 479-4600
Frequency:
1 time(s) per month
Description:
Publication focuses on Western style training and horse care for competitive riders, horse owners, and recreational riders.

HORSE ILLUSTRATED
3 BURROUGHS
IRVINE, CA 92618
949-855-8822
Fax: 949-855-3045
www.animalnetwork.com
• Moira Harris, Editor
(949) 855-8822
• Liz Moyer, Managing Editor

(949) 855-8822
• Norman Ridker, President
• Pat Trowbridge, Publisher
(213) 385-2222
Frequency:
1 time(s) per month
Description:
Publication is geared toward horse owners.

HORSE NEWS
8 MINNEAKOING
FLEMINGTON, NJ 08822
908-782-4747
Fax: 908-782-6572
www.horsenewsonline.com
• Shaneen Kohler, Editor
(908) 782-4747
horsenews@hcdemocrat.com
• Lillian Shupe, Senior Contributing Editor
Frequency:
1 time(s) per month

HORSE OF DELAWARE VALLEY
PO BOX 223
UNIONVILLE, PA 19375-0223
610-793-1425
Fax: 610-793-3119
www.horsedelval.com
• Sara Cavanagh, Editor
• H. L. Schwartz, Publisher
• Deb Vandenberg, Advertising Manager
Frequency:
1 time(s) per month
Description:
An equine publication.

HORSE WORLD
730 MADISON STREET
SHELBYVILLE, TN 37160-3519
931-684-8123
Fax: 931-684-8196
www.horseworld.net
• Bonnie Vannatta, Editor
• Christy Parsons, Editor
• Christy Parsons, Publisher
Frequency:
1 time(s) per month
Description:
Publication reports on horse shows.

HORSEMAN'S JOURNAL
P.O. BOX 202290
AUSTIN, TX 78720-2290
859-259-0451
Fax: 512-249-7446
hj@nationalhbpa.com
www.hbpa.org
• Richard Glover, Managing Editor
(512) 246-9100
Frequency:
4 time(s) per year
Description:
Magazine is the official publication of the Horsemen's Benevolent Protective Association; provides news and information helpful to owners, trainers, and breeders of race horses.

HORSEMAN'S NEWS
34311 DEPORTOLA ROAD
TEMECULA, CA 92592
951-303-3900
Fax: 951-303-3905
horsemannew@aol.com
www.horsemansnews.com

• Virginia McClintock, Editor
virginia@horsemansnews.com
• Virginia McClintock, Publisher
virginia@horsemansnews.com
Frequency:
1 time(s) per month
Description:
Publication provides information to professional horsemen in the western United States.

HOW TO AVOID CHOKING GET MENTALLY TOUGH AND STAY IN THE ZONE
1060 MAIN STREET
SUITE 307
RIVER EDGE, NJ 07661
201-342-3663
800-580-9663
Fax: 201-342-2258
info@stayinthezone.com
www.stayinthezone.com

HOW TO BOWL IN THE ZONE WITH SPORTS PSYCHOLOGY
1060 MAIN STREET
SUITE 307
RIVER EDGE, NJ 07661
201-342-3663
800-580-9663
Fax: 201-342-2258
info@stayinthezone.com
www.stayinthezone.com

HOW TO GET INTO THE ZONE IN JUST ONE MINUTE
1060 MAIN STREET
SUITE 307
RIVER EDGE, NJ 07661
201-342-3663
800-580-9663
Fax: 201-342-2258
info@stayinthezone.com
www.stayinthezone.com

HOW TO LOWER YOUR GOLF SCORE WITH SPORT PSYCHOLOGY AND SELF-HYPNOSIS
1060 MAIN STREET
SUITE 307
RIVER EDGE, NJ 07661
201-342-3663
800-580-9663
Fax: 201-342-2258
info@stayinthezone.com
www.stayinthezone.com

HUNTER & SPORT HORSE
12204 COVINGTON ROAD
FORT WAYNE, IN 46814
260-625-4030
Fax: 260-625-3480
hshhorse@aol.com
www.hunterandsporthorsemag.com
• Laura Allen, Editor
(260) 625-4030
• Lisa Allen, Publisher
• Kerry Scarbrough, Advertising Manager
(260) 625-4030
HSHHorse@aol.com
Frequency:
6 time(s) per year
Description:
Publication covers issues of interest to the sport horse enthusiast, including dressage, combined training, and hunter/jumper.

IEG SPONSORSHIP REPORT
350 NORTH ORLEANS
SUITE 1200
CHICAGO, IL 60654
312-944-1727
800-834-4850
Fax: 312-944-1897
ieg@sponsorship.com
www.sponsorship.com
• Lesa Ukman, Executive Editor
• Jim Andrews, Executive Vice President /
Content Strategy
• William Chipps, Senior Editor
• Penny Perrey, Vice President Marketing
Description:
Your online source for news and articles
covering sponsorship of sports, music,
festivals, the arts and causes. Who
sponsors what and why. How companies
evaluate sponsorship. Majority (about 70%)
of editorial deals specifically with sports
sponsorship. Corporate contacts and phone
numbers listed with each article.
Circulation:
100% paid subscription
Sports:
General
Primary Audience:
Corporate sponsors, rightsholders, agencies
and event producers
Frequency:
24/7 online access
Publishing Company:
IEG, Inc.

ILLINOIS RACING NEWS
111 SHORE DRIVE
BURR RIDGE, IL 60527
630-887-7722
Fax: 630-887-1958
info@midwestoutdoors.com
www.illinoisracingnews.com
• Joan Colby, Editor/Advertising Manager
(630) 887-7722
• Cheryl Magana, Sales Representative
(630) 887-7722
CherylMagana@aol.com
Frequency:
1 time(s) per month
Description:
Publication features Thoroughbred racing
and breeding news.

INDIANA BASKETBALL HISTORY
1 HALL OF FAME COURT
NEW CASTLE, IN 47362-2941
765-529-1891
Fax: 765-529-0273
info@hoopshall.com
• Roger Dickinson, Publisher
roger@hoopshall.com
Frequency:
4 time(s) per year
Description:
Publication contains historic photos and
articles on Indiana basketball.

INPLAY
12501 SOUTH ISIS AVENUE
HAWTHORNE, CA 90250
310-643-6455
800-872-2976
Fax: 310-643-5310
soccernow@ayso.org
www.soccer.org
• David Frickman, Sports Editor
(800) 872-2976

davidfrickman@ayso.org
• David Frickman, Sports Editor
(310) 643-6455
• Sean Hilferty, Publication Coordinator
(310) 643-6455
Frequency:
4 time(s) per year
Description:
Publication is geared toward soccer
coaches and referees.

INSIDE INDIANA
3901 EAST HAGAN STREET
BLOOMINGTON, IN 47401
812-334-9722
800-282-4648
Fax: 812-334-9756
www.insideiu.com
• Ed Magoni, Editor
(812) 334-9722
• Ken Bikoff, Editor
(812) 334-9722
Description:
Publication covers sports at the University of
Indiana.

INSIDE KUNG-FU
4201 VANOWEN PLACE
BURBANK, CA 91505
818-845-2656
800-332-3330
Fax: 818-845-7761
www.cfwenterprises.com
• Dave Cater, Editor
(818) 845-2656
Frequency:
1 time(s) per month
Description:
Publication covers the world of kung-fu.

INSIDE SPORTING GOODS
770 BROADWAY
NEW YORK, NY 10003-9595
646-654-4997
Fax: 646-654-5005
• Robert E. Carr, Editor
(646) 654-4997
Publishing Company:
VNU.
Frequency:
48 times a year.
Primary Audience:
Sporting Goods Trade and Investors.
Primary Audience:
Manufacturers, Retailers, Merchandisers
Frequency:
48 times, annually, delivered by fax or
e-mail.
Publishing Company:
Bill Communications.

INSIDE TENNIS
2220 MOUNTAIN BOULEVARD
SUITE 200
OAKLAND, CA 94611
510-530-2200
Fax: 510-530-1483
www.insidetennis.com
• William G. Simons, Editor
simons@insidetennis.com
• Matt Cronin, Senior Editor
(510) 530-2200
• Richard Osborn, Associate Editor
• William G. Simons, Publisher
simons@insidetennis.com
Frequency:
1 time(s) per month

INSIDE TEXAS RUNNING
2470 GRAY FALLS DRIVE
SUITE 110
HOUSTON, TX 77077-1909
281-759-0555
800-441-9837
Fax: 713-935-0559
www.insidetexasrunning.com
• Lance Phegley, Editor
(281) 759-0555
• Lee Sheffer, Production Manager
Frequency:
1 time(s) per month
Primary Audience:
Road runners and marathon runners.
Circulation:
10,000
Description:
We are a publisher of a magazine devoted
to roadracing and multi-sports (i.e. triathlon).

INSIDE TRIATHLON
1830 NORTH 55TH STREET
BOULDER, CO 80301-2700
303-440-0601
Fax: 303-444-6788
www.insidetri.com
Frequency:
1 time(s) per month
Description:
Publication provides complete coverage of
the triathlon and duathlon.

INTERNATIONAL AEROBATICS CLUB, INC.
3000 POBERENZY ROAD
OSHKOSH, WI 54902-8939
920-426-4800
800-843-3612
Fax: 920-426-6579
iac@eaa.org
www.iac.org
Frequency
12x/year

INTERNATIONAL FIGURE SKATING
420 BOYLSTON STREET 5TH FLOOR
BOSTON, MA 02116
508-756-2595
800-437-5828
Fax: 617-536-0102
www.ifsmagazine.com
• Susan Wessling, Editor-in-Chief
swessling@madavor.com
• Susan Fitzgerald, Publisher
(508) 756-2595
sfitzgerald@madavor.com
• Jeff Wolk, Owner
(508) 756-2595
jwolk@madavor.com
• Kathleen Bangs, Staff Writer
(617) 536-0100
Frequency:
6 time(s) per year
Description:
Publication is a international news magazine
for the sport of figure skating.

INTERNATIONAL GYMNAST
3214 BART CONNER DRIVE
NORMAN, OK 73072-2406
405-447-9988
Fax: 405-447-5810
www.intlgymnast.com
• Dwight Normile, Editor
(405) 447-9988

- Ben Fox, Advertising Manager
(405) 364-5344
- Paul Ziert, Publisher
(405) 364-5344
paul@intlgymnast.com
- John Crumlish, Web Site Editor & Staff Writer
(405) 447-9988
jcrumlish@intlgymnast.com
Frequency:
10 time(s) per year
Description:
Publication covers gymnastics for serious competitors, coaches, judges, and enthusiasts; contains information on international competitions, interviews, training tips, and nutrition.

INTERNATIONAL JOURNAL OF SPORT NUTRITION
1607 NORTH MARKET STREET
CHAMPAIGN, IL 61820
217-351-5076
800-747-4457
Fax: 217-351-2674
journals@hkusa.com
www.humankinetics.com
- Ronald Maughan, Co-Editor
r.j.maughan@lboro.ac.uk
- Priscilla Clarkson, Editorial Board Member
- Rainer Martens, Publisher
rainerm@hkusa.com
- Jack Wolowiec, Managing Editor
(217) 351-5076
Frequency:
4 time(s) per year
Description:
Publication focuses on the nutritional aspects of human physical and athletic performance; includes experimental and experiential evidence on all aspects of athletic ability.

INTERNATIONAL JOURNAL OF ATHLETIC THERAPY AND TRAINING
1607 NORTH MARKET STREET
CHAMPAIGN, IL 61820
217-351-5076
800-747-4457
Fax: 217-351-2674
journals@hkusa.com
www.humankinetics.com
- Gary Wilkerson, Editor
(423) 425-5394
gary-wilkerson@utc.edu
- Greg Reed, Journal Director
(423) 757-1733
- Margery Kane, Journal Managing Editor
Frequency:
6 time(s) per year
Description:
Publication is written for sports healthcare providers.

INTERNATIONAL TENNIS WEEKLY
201 ATP BOULEVARD
PONTE VEDRA BEACH, FL 32082-3211
904-285-8000
Fax: 904-285-5966
www.atptennis.com
- Alex Kennison, Editor
- Alex Kennison, Editor-in-Chief
Frequency:
1 time(s) per week
Description:
Publication features news, information, and statistics concerning ATP Tour players and competitions.

INTERSCHOLASTIC ATHLETIC ADMINISTRATION
PO BOX 690
INDIANAPOLIS, IN 46206
317-972-6900
Fax: 317-822-5700
www.nfhs.org
- Bob Kanaby, Publisher
- Treva Dayton, Editor
- Judy Thomas, Advertising Director
Description:
Professional journal for high school athletic administrators. Also the official organ for the National Interscholastic Athletic Administrators Association.
Circulation:
6,250. 95% paid subscr, 5% non-paid contr.
Sports:
General
Primary Audience:
High school athletic administrators
Frequency:
Quarterly
Publishing Company:
National Federation of State High School Associations

IRISH SPORTS REPORT
225 WEST COLFAX AVENUE
SOUTH BEND, IN 46626-1000
574-235-6469
Fax: 574-235-6091
isr@irishsportsreport.com
www.irishsportsreport.com
- Bill Bilinski, Editor
(574) 235-6331
bbilinski@sbtinfo.com
- Jennifer Gaby, General Manager
(574) 235-6073
- Eric Hansen, Managing Editor
(574) 235-6470
ehansen@sbtinfo.com
- David Ray, Publisher
(574) 235-6241
dray@sbtinfo.com
- Jeff Carroll, Staff Writer
(574) 235-6161
jcarroll@sbtinfo.com
Frequency:
21 time(s) per year
Description:
Publication covers all Notre Dame sports, especially football.

JET SPORTS
27142 BURBANK
FOOTHILL RANCH, CA 92610
714-751-8695
Fax: 631-427-4498
- Rick Lake, Editor
Frequency:
6 time(s) per year
Description:
Publication features news about personal watercraft racing activities sanctioned by the International Jet Sports Boating Association; includes personality profiles of racers, previews of regional clubs, and racing activities.

JOURNAL OF APPLIED SPORT PSYCHOLOGY
DEPARTMENT OF PHYSICAL EDUCATION, HEALTH AND SPORT STUDIES
PHILLIPS HALL
MIAMI UNIVERSITY, OH 45056
513-529-2728
weinber@muohio.edu
www.aaasponline.org/journal.html#eddy
- Robert S. Weinberg, Editor
- Bonnie Berger, Associate Editor of Health Psychology
- Karen Cogan, Associate Editor/Clinical Counseling
- Trent Petrie, Associate Editor/Clinical Counseling
- Robert Eklund, Associate Editor/Performance Psychology
- Thelma Horn, Associate Editor/Social Psychology
Description:
Official journal of the Association for the Advancement of Applied Sport Psychology. Articles and information of interest to sport psychology researchers, practitioners, and coaches.
Circulation:
1,000. Association membership.
Sports:
General
Primary Audience:
Sport psychologists, counselors, coaches, athletes
Frequency:
Twice annually
Publishing Company:
Allen Press

JOURNAL OF ATHLETIC TRAINING
2952 STEMMONS FREEWAY
DALLAS, TX 75247-6103
214-637-6282
800-879-6282
Fax: 214-637-2206
www.nata.org/jat/
- Chris Ingersoll, Editor
- Leslie Neistadt, Managing Editor
(706) 494-3322
- Christopher Ingersoll, Editor-in-Chief
(214) 637-6282
Frequency:
4 time(s) per year
Description:
Publication is geared toward athletic trainers, allied health personnel, students, and physicians participating in sports medicine.

JOURNAL OF LEGAL ASPECTS OF SPORT
WICHITA STATE UNIVERSITY
CAMPUS BOX 16
1845 FAIRMOUNT
WITCHITA, KS 67260-0016
316-978-3340
Fax: 316-798-5451
mary.myers@wichita.edu
www.law.marquette.edu/jw/jlas
- Paul M. Anderson, Editor
- Rebecca Mowrey, Book Review Editor
Description:
Official journal of the Society for the Study of Legal Aspects of Sport & Physical Activity.
Publishing Company:
Scott Printing & Binding.
Frequency:
3 times annually.
Primary Audience:
Association membership.
Sports:

General.
Circulation:
325

JOURNAL OF SPORT BEHAVIOR
JOURNAL OF SPORT BEHAVIOR OFFICE
DEPARTMENT OF PSYCHOLOGY
307 UNIVERSITY BOULEVARD N, UCOM
1000
MOBILE, AL 36608-0002
251-460-6371
Fax: 251-460-6320
chauff@southalabama.edu
www.journalofsportsbehavior.org
• Caitlyn Hauff, Co-Editor
(251) 460-7698
chauff@southalabama.edu
• Benjamin Hill, Co-Editor
(251) 341-3079
bdhill@southalabama.edu
Frequency:
4 time(s) per year
Description:
Publication features original, empirical
investigations and theoretical papers dealing
with studies of social behavior in the areas
of games and sport.

JOURNAL OF SPORT HISTORY
PO BOX 1026
LEMONT, PA 16851-1026
814-238-1288
Fax: 814-238-1288
www.nassh.org
• Ronald A. Smith, Secretary/National
(814) 238-1288
• Melvin Adelman, Editor
(703) 993-2057
Description:
Contains scholarly articles on sport history.
Circulation:
1,000. 100% association membership.
Sports:
General
Primary Audience:
Association membership
Frequency:
Three times annually
Publishing Company:
North American Society for Sport History

JOURNAL OF SPORT MANAGEMENT
1607 NORTH MARKET STREET
CHAMPAIGN, IL 61820
217-351-5076
800-747-4457
Fax: 217-351-2674
humank@hkusa.com
www.humankinetics.com
• Jake Jaquet, Journal Director
• Jennifer Davis, Managing Editor
(217) 351-5076
Publishing Company:
Human Kinetics Publishers, Inc.
Frequency:
Quarterly
Primary Audience:
Professionals, scholars and students of
sport management
Sports:
General
Circulation:
1062
Description:
Journal for North American Society for Sport
Management. Includes theoretical and
applied articles pertaining to all areas of

sport management including athletic
administration, recreation, and leisure.

JOURNAL OF THE PHILOSOPHY OF SPORT
1607 N. MARKET ST
CHAMPAIGN, IL 61820
217-351-5076
800-747-4457
Fax: 217-351-2674
www.kinetics.com
• Greg Reed, Journal Director
• Jeff King, Managing Editor
• J.S. Russell, JPS Editor
Publishing Company:
Human Kinetics Publishers, Inc.
Frequency:
Annual
Primary Audience:
Association membership
Sports:
General
Circulation:
512
Description:
Includes critical reviews of work completed
and philosophic discussions about the
philosophy of sport. Published annually for
the Philosophic Society for the Study of
Sport.

JUCO REVIEW
1755 TELSTAR DRIVE
SUITE 103
COLORADO SPRINGS, CO 80920
719-590-9788
Fax: 719-590-7324
www.njcaa.org
• Mary Ellen Leicht, Editor
Publishing Company:
NJCAA
Frequency:
Monthly, Sept-May
Primary Audience:
Association membership
Sports:
General
Circulation:
3,750. 100% association membership.
Description:
Includes articles about college sports,
including basketball, baseball, football,
volleyball, soccer, tennis. Highlights National
Championship events.

JUICE SOUND, SURF SKATE MAGAZINE
2633 LINCOLN BOULEVARD 411
SANTA MONICA, CA 90405
310-399-5336
juicesss@aol.com
www.juicemagazine.com
• Jim Murphy, Sports Editor
Frequency:
6 time(s) per year
Description:
Publication features underground music,
skateboarding, snowboarding, and surfing;
includes lifestyle features, and investigative
journalism.

JUNIOR BASEBALL
14 WOODWAY LANE
WILTON, CT 06897
203-210-5726
888-487-2448
Fax: 408-475-3055

editor@juniorbaseball.com
www.juniorbaseball.com
• Jim Beecher, Publisher/Editor
Frequency:
6 time(s) per year
Description:
'America's Youth Baseball Magazine' for
players, ages 7-17, their parents, and
coaches.
Year Founded:
1996
Publications:
Junior Baseball Magazine and Youth
Baseball Star e-zine.

KART MARKETING INTERNATIONAL
PO BOX 101
WHEATON, IL 60189
630-653-7368
Fax: 630-653-2637
karting@msn.com
www.e-kmi.com
• Darrell Sitarz, President/Chief Executive
Officer
(630) 653-7368
karting@msn.com
• Craig Ellsworth, Marketing Manager
(630) 653-7368
karting@msn.com
• Len Manley, Sales Director
(859) 983-9234
lenmanley27@aol.com
Nature of Service:
Advertising and Marketing
Publication:
Contains information of interest to people
involved with go-karting and
go-karting-related businesses.
Frequency:
6 time(s) per year

KEEPING IN TOUCH
13540 LAKE CITY WAY N.E. SUITE 3
SEATTLE, WA 98125
206-367-2420
Fax: 206-367-2636
www.varsitycommunications.com
• Earl Starkoff, Publisher
(800) 643-6061
els730@aol.com
Frequency:
3 time(s) per year

KING PANIAGUA
518 5TH AVE
NEW YORK, NY 10036
212-869-7007
Fax: 212-869-7009
• Joseph A. Paniagua, Vice President
• John Mas, Vice President Marketing
Description:
Publishes variety of bilingual magazines in
baseball, boxing, and soccer serving the
Hispanic market.

LA GOLF MAGAZINE
1451 QUAIL STREET SUITE 208
NEWPORT BEACH, CA 92660-2741
949-833-7601
Fax: 949-833-9895
www.churmpublishing.com
• Eric Marson, Editor
(949) 833-7601
• Steven Churm, Publisher
(949) 833-7601

LACROSSE MAGAZINE
113 WEST UNIVERSITY PARKWAY
BALTIMORE, MD 21210-3301
410-235-6882
Fax: 410-366-6735
• Paul Krome, Editor
(410) 235-6882
• Kira Muller, Director of Advertising Sales
(410) 235-6882
kmuller@uslacrosse.org
• Bill Tanton, Senior Associate Editor
(410) 235-6882
Frequency:
12 times per year
Description:
Monthly magazine celebrating the lacrosse life style, on and off the field, and delivered to an affluent, acid and active readership.
Primary Audience:
Youth through High School. 91% of audience is age 24 or less.

LATE MODEL DIGEST
P.O. BOX 340
MURPHY, NC 28906
828-837-9539
Fax: 828-837-7718
www.latemodeldigest.net
• Jim Carson, Editor
(828) 837-9539
• Brian McLeod, Publisher
Frequency:
24 time(s) per year
Description:
Publication reports on late model stock car racing on pavement.

LATITUDE 38
15 LOCUST AVENUE
MILL VALLEY, CA 94941-2805
415-383-8200
Fax: 415-383-5816
editorial@latitude38.com
www.latitude38.com
• John Riise, Managing Editor
(415) 383-8200
• John Arndt, Advertising Sales
(415) 383-8200
john@latitude38.com
• Rob Moore, Senior Editor
(415) 383-8200
• Richard Spindler, Executive Editor
(415) 383-8200
richard@latitude38.com
• Richard Spindler, Publisher
(415) 383-8200
richard@latitude38.com
• Andy Turpin, Senior Editor
(415) 383-8200
Description:
Publication is geared toward those with an interest in sailing.

LATITUDES & ATTITUDES
270 PORTFINO WAY SUITE 510
REDONDO BEACH, CA 90277
310-798-3445
888-893-7245
Fax: 310-798-3448
www.latsandatts.net
• Sue Morgan, Editor
• Bob Bitchin, Publisher & Co-Editor
(310) 798-3445
bbftw@aol.com
• Mike Sweeney, Advertising Director
(727) 224-2116

Frequency:
6 time(s) per year
Description:
Publication focuses on sailing and long-distance cruising.

LEAGUE OF AMERICAN BICYCLISTS MAGAZINE
1612 K STREET NORTH WEST SUITE 800
WASHINGTON, DC 20006-2802
202-822-1333
Fax: 202-822-1334
bikeleague@bikeleague.org
www.bikeleague.org
• Elizabeth Preston, Editor
(202) 822-1333
Frequency:
4 time(s) per year
Description:
Publication is a membership magazine of the League of American Bicyclists; focuses on bicycle education, advocacy, and recreation.

LETS PLAY HOCKEY
2721 EAST 42ND STREET
MINNEAPOLIS, MN 55406-3061
612-729-0023
Fax: 612-729-0259
letsplay@letsplayhockey.com
www.letsplayhockey.com
• Dave McMahon, Editor
• Doug Johnson, Publisher
Frequency:
29 time(s) per year
Description:
Publication covers the world of hockey; includes information on the professional sport, equipment, and the media surrounding hockey.

LETS PLAY SOFTBALL
2721 EAST 42ND STREET
MINNEAPOLIS, MN 55406-3061
612-729-0023
Fax: 612-729-0259
www.letsplaysoftball.com
• Dave McMahon, Editor-in-Chief
• Doug Johnson, Publisher
Frequency:
2 time(s) per month
Description:
Publication is written for softball enthusiasts.

LICENSING BOOK
1501 BROADWAY, STE 500
NEW YORK, NY 10036-5503
212-575-4510
Fax: 212-575-4521
www.licensingbook.com
• Andy Krinner, Publisher
• Jennifer Jaronczak, Advertising Director
• Jim Silver, Group Publisher
Publishing Company:
Adventure Publishing Group, Inc.
Frequency:
Monthly
Primary Audience:
Retailers, Licensors, Licensees, Manufacturers
Sports:
General
Circulation:
22,000. 100% contr non-paid.
Description:
Reports on all aspects of consumer-based

licensed properties and licensing activity in the U.S. and abroad. Sports licensing prominently featured.

LIFESTYLE MEDIA
100 WILLIAM STREET
23RD FLOOR
NEW YORK, NY 10038
646-459-4800
Fax: 646-459-4900
• Robe Holmes, Chief Executive Officer / Chairman
• Peter Cipriano, EVP Finance and Operations
Products:
Magazines

LIGHT SPORT AND ULTRALIGHT FLYING MAGAZINE
1085 BAILEY AVENUE
CHATTANOOGA, TN 37404-2802
423-629-5375
Fax: 423-629-5379
www.ultralightflying.com
• Sharon Wilcox, Editor-in-Chief
(423) 629-5375
• Tracy Knauss, Publisher
• David Prestridge, Advertising Manager
Frequency:
1 time(s) per month
Description:
Publication is written for people who fly ultralight and light sport aircraft.

LINKS MAGAZINE-THE BEST OF GOLF
10 POPE AVENUE EXECUTIVE PARK
SUITE 202
HILTON HEAD ISLAND, SC 29928
843-842-6200
Fax: 843-842-6233
www.linksmagazine.com
• Allen Allnoch, Features Editor
(843) 842-6200
• Richard Cerame, Associate Editor
(843) 842-6200
• Andrew Clifford, Marketing Art Director
(203) 977-8600
• David Gould, Editor
(843) 842-6200
• Jack Purcell, Jr., Publisher
(843) 842-6200
jpurcell@linksmagazine.com
• Elaine Yeager, Advertising Coordinator
(843) 842-6200
Frequency:
7 time(s) per year
Description:
Publication contains information of interest to golf enthusiasts, including profiles of new courses.

LIVING ABOARD MAGAZINE
PO BOX 668
3
REDONDO BEACH, CA 90277
888-893-7245
Fax: 310-798-3448
www.livingaboard.com
• Judy Behler, Advertising Manager
• Fred C. Walters, Publisher
• Sam Bruce, Assistant Editor
(512) 892-4446
Frequency:
6 time(s) per year
Description:
Publication focuses on how to make the

move from land to water and make life on board more enjoyable.

LOG
4918 NORTH HARBOUR DRIVE SUITE 201
SAN DIEGO, CA 92106
619-226-1608
800-841-4377
Fax: 619-226-0573
www.thelog.com
• Jane Hascher, Editor
(619) 226-1608
• Duncan McIntosh, Publisher
(619) 226-1608
Frequency:
26 time(s) per year
Description:
Publication focuses on boating news and is published in three separate editions as follows: San Diego Log; Orange County & Los Angeles Log; and the Ventura & San Francisco Log.

LONG BOARD MAGAZINE
110 EAST PALIZADA SUITE 301
SAN CLEMENTE, CA 92672
949-366-8282
Fax: 949-366-8280
lngdmag@aol.com
www.longboardmag.com
• Guy Motil, Publisher
lngbdmag@aol.com
Description:
Publication covers surfing.

LONG ISLAND GOLFER MAGAZINE
22 WEST NICHOLAS STREET
HICKSVILLE, NY 11801-3806
516-822-5446
800-564-2445
Fax: 516-822-5446
ligolfer@aol.com
www.longislandgolfermagazine.com
• Paul Smith, Managing Editor
• John J. Glozek, Jr., Publisher
Frequency:
6 time(s) per year
Description:
Publication is written for golf enthusiasts; contains instructional articles, human interest stories, and features on destinations for golf vacations.

LOWRIDER BICYCLE
2400 KATELLA AVENUE 11TH FLOOR
ANAHEIM, CA 92806
714-939-2400
Fax: 714-978-6390
info@lowridermagazine.com
www.lowridermagazine.com
• Ralph Fuentes, Editor
• John Jarasa, Publisher
Frequency:
4 time(s) per year
Description:
Publication is a custom bicycle magazine.

MAINE BOATS & HARBORS
218 SOUTH MAIN STREET
PO BOX 566
ROCKLAND, ME 04841
207-594-8622
Fax: 207-593-0026
editor@maineboats.com
www.maineboats.com

• John K. Hanson, Publisher
john@maineboats.com
• Polly Saltonstall, Editor
(207) 594-8622
editor@maineboats.com
Frequency:
6 time(s) per year
Description:
Publication focuses on boating in Maine.

MAINE COASTAL NEWS
966 NORTH MAIN STREET
WINTERPORT, ME 04496
207-223-8846
888-333-8379
Fax: 207-223-9004
igmatats@aol.com
www.mainescoast.com
• Jon B. Johansen, Editor
• Jon B. Johansen, Publisher
Frequency:
18 time(s) per year
Description:
Publication covers yachting, commercial fishing, and the maritime history of Maine.

MARC TIMES RACING NEWS
5845 MOUNT VERNON AVENUE
PORTAGE, MI 49024
269-345-7086
Fax: 269-345-6397
www.marctimes.com
• Dick Beebe, Editor-in-Chief
• Dick Beebe, Publisher
Frequency:
1 time(s) per week
Description:
Publication covers all forms of motorized sports, with emphasis on auto racing and stock car racing, from street stocks to the NASCAR Winston Cup and Indy Cars.

MARINA DOCK AGE
6600 WEST TOUHY AVENUE
NILES, IL 60714-4516
847-647-2900
Fax: 847-647-1155
ppreston@prestonpub.com
www.prestonpub.com
• Jerry Koncel, Editor
jkoncel@prestonpub.com
• Janice S. Gordon, Publisher
(847) 647-2900
jgordon@prestonpub.com
Frequency:
8 time(s) per year
Description:
Publication is geared toward owners and operators of marinas; covers marina management, government regulations, and environmental issues.

MARINE BUSINESS JOURNAL
330 NORTH ANDREWS AVENUE
2ND FLOOR
FORT LAUDERDALE, FL 33301-1020
954-522-5515
Fax: 954-522-2260
www.marinebusinessjournal.com
• Marilyn Mower, Editor
(954) 522-5515
• Bill Ando, Senior Editor
(954) 522-5515
bill@southernboating.com
• Kellie Mackenroth, Marketing & Circulation Manager
kellie@southernboating.com

Frequency:
Quarterly
Description:
Publication is a resource guide for the marine industry.

MARINER
601 NORTH BRIDGE STREET
ELKTON, MD 21921
410-398-3311
Fax: 410-398-4044
www.themariner.net
• Chris Knauss, Editor
(410) 482-7503
• Jeffrey Mezzatesta, Publisher
Frequency:
24 time(s) per year
Description:
Publication contains information on pleasure boating in the Chesapeake Bay area, including coverage of local events.

MARINER'S LOG
17511 EL CAMINO REAL SUITE 148
HOUSTON, TX 77058
281-488-1108
Fax: 281-286-0750
www.thecitizenonline.com
• Chuck Hlava, Editor
(281) 488-1108
chlava@hcnonline.com
• Sharon Rickel, Publisher
(281) 488-1108
srickel@hcnonline.com
Frequency:
1 time(s) per month
Description:
Publication is written for boating enthusiasts.

MARYLAND SOCCER NEWS
13540 LAKE CITY WAY N.E. SUITE 3
SEATTLE, WA 98125
206-367-2420
Fax: 206-367-2636
www.varsitycommunications.com
• Jay Goldstein, Editor
(410) 987-7898
Frequency:
4 time(s) per year

MATERIAL MATTERS
21-00 STATE ROUTE 208
FAIR LAWN, NJ 07410
800-665-2456
Fax: 201-796-5206
golfproductnews.com
• Ruth Rasche, Editor
(352) 332-1252
• Steve Stramm, Publisher
(352) 332-1252
Frequency:
5 time(s) per year
Description:
Publication features apparel for golf players.

MEDIA SPORTS BUSINESS
126 CLOCK TOWER PLACE
CARMEL, CA 93923-8734
831-624-1536
Fax: 831-625-3225
www.kagan.com
• Robin Flynn, Analyst
• Larry Gerbrandt, Analyst
• Sharon Armbrust, Analyst
• Derek Baine, Analyst
• John Mansell, Analyst

- Ian Olgeirson, Analyst
- Richelle Elberg, Analyst
- Deana Myers, Analyst

Publishing Company:
Paul Kagan Associates, Inc.
Frequency:
Monthly
Primary Audience:
Sports media executives
Sports:
General
Circulation:
100% paid subscr.
Description:
Newsletter dealing with sports media rights fees, cable TV syndication opportunities and developments, regional sports network census, ratings, viewership data, team valuations, etc.

MEN'S JOURNAL
1290 AVE OF THE AMERICAS, 2ND FL
NEW YORK, NY 10104
212-484-1616
Fax: 212-484-3435
www.mensjournal.com
- Jann S. Wenner, Editor-in-Chief
- Bob Wallace, Editor

Description:
Focuses on features covering sports travel, fitness and adventure of interest to the active male. Covers sporting equipment reviews, new products, and other information relating to the market.
Circulation:
225,000. 90% newsstand, 10% paid subscr.
Sports:
Outdoor, recreational sports
Primary Audience:
Consumer
Frequency:
Monthly
Publishing Company:
Straight Arrow Publishers, Inc.

METRO SPORTS NEW YORK
259 WEST 30TH STREET 3RD FLOOR
NEW YORK, NY 10001
212-563-7329
Fax: 212-563-7573
www.metrosportsny.com
- Jeremy Shweder, Managing Editor
- Doug Kaplan, Publisher
(312) 421-1551
- Jeremy Shweder, Editorial Director

Frequency:
1 time(s) per month
Description:
Publication focuses on sports, recreation, and travel.

METRO SPORTS NY
259 W. 30TH STREET
3RD FLOOR
NEW YORK CITY, NY 10001
212-563-7329
Fax: 212-563-7573
www.metrosportsny.com
- Doug Kaplan, President/Publisher
- Melanie Stuparyk, Managing Editor
- Michelle Mullin, Sales Vice President

Description:
Encourages and inspires readers' commitments to sports and fitness. Offers sound enlightened advice on life in the active mode. Includes leading aerobics and fitness consumer events in the Northeast;

Boston fitness events.
Circulation:
130,000 total. New York Metro: 80,000; Boston: 50,000. 90% contr non-paid, 5% paid subscr, 5% association membership.
Sports:
Skiing, tennis, aerobics, running, cycling, triathlons, in-line skating, fitness
Primary Audience:
Consumer
Frequency:
10 times annually
Publishing Company:
Tate House Enterprises, Inc.
Additional Offices:
164 Brattle St, Cambridge, MA 02138. 617 492-0636; FAX: 617 492-0756. Connecticut Office: 415 Howe Ave, Shelton, CT 06484. 203 924-0141; FAX: 203 924-8434. Washington/Baltimore Office: 2779 N. Wakefield St, Arlington, VA 22207. 703 528-4154; FAX: 703 528-4239

METRO SPORTS WASHINGTON
4405 EAST WEST HIGHWAY SUITE 206B
BETHESDA, MD 20814
202-289-4551
Fax: 301-907-0973
metrosportsdc.com
- Jeremy Shweder, Editor
- Doug Kaplan, Publisher

Frequency:
1 time(s) per month
Description:
Publication focuses on sports, recreation, and travel.

MICHIGAN GOLFER
P.O. BOX 7007
GRAND RAPIDS, MI 49510-7007
734-507-0241
www.webgolfer.com
- Art McCafferty, Editor
- Art McCafferty, Advertising Manager

Frequency:
6 time(s) per year

MICHIGAN LINKS
24116 RESEARCH DRIVE
FARMINGTON HILLS, MI 48335
248-478-9242
Fax: 248-478-5536
www.gam.org
- Tonia Branch, Publisher & Editor
(248) 478-9242
tbranch@gam.org
- Ed Peabody, Publisher
(248) 691-1800
epeabody@hourdetroit.com

Frequency:
6 time(s) per year
Description:
Publication is devoted to the most active golfers in the state of Michigan.

MICHIGAN SNOWMOBILER
P.O. BOX 417
EAST JORDAN, MI 49727-0417
231-536-2371
Fax: 231-536-7691
www.michsnowmag.com
- Lyle Shipe, Editor-in-Chief
- Lyle Shipe, Advertising Manager
- Lyle Shipe, Publisher

Frequency:
6 time(s) per year

Description:
Publication features information about snowmobiles and related activities.

MICHIGAN SOCCER
13540 LAKE CITY WAY N.E. SUITE 3
SEATTLE, WA 98125
206-367-2420
Fax: 206-367-2636
www.varsitycommunications.com
- Scott Leader, Editor

Frequency:
4 time(s) per year

MID OHIO GOLFER
5255 SINCLAIR ROAD
COLUMBUS, OH 43229-7513
614-848-4653
Fax: 614-848-3838
- Phil Shie, Editor
- Max Brown, Publisher

Frequency:
18 time(s) per year
Description:
Publication serves golfers throughout central Ohio and the surrounding area.

MID-ATLANTIC THOROUGHBRED
30 EAST PADONIA ROAD SUITE 303
TIMONIUM, MD 21093
410-252-2100
Fax: 410-560-0503
info@marylandthoroughbred.com
www.marylandthoroughbred.com
- Joe Clancy, Editor
(410) 252-2100
editor@marylandthoroughbred.com

Frequency:
Monthly
Description:
Publication contains information of interest to Thoroughbred owners, breeders, and trainers in Maryland, New Jersey, North Carolina, Pennsylvania, Delaware, Virginia, and West Virginia.
Primary Audience:
Thoroughbred breeders, owners, trainers and enthusiasts in the Mid-Atlantic region.

MID-SOUTH HORSE REVIEW
16814 HIGHWAY 64
SOMERVILLE, TN 38068-6156
901-465-4042
800-869-7941
Fax: 901-465-5493
www.midsouthhorsereview.com
- Don Dowdle, Publisher

Frequency:
1 time(s) per month

MID-STATES RACING NEWS
719 DES MOINES STREET
WEBSTER CITY, IA 50595-2117
515-832-3713
Fax: 515-832-4531
www.mrnol.com
- Howard Mellinger, Publisher
(515) 832-6043

Frequency:
34 time(s) per year
Description:
Publication is an auto racing magazine; publishes weekly April-September and monthly October-March.

MIDWEST RACING NEWS
1001 LISBON AVENUE
MILWAUKEE, WI 53222
262-238-6397
800-432-4212
Fax: 262-242-9450
www.mrnol.com
• Brian Gapinski, Editor
• Ken Ubert, Publisher
Frequency:
1 time(s) per week
Description:
Publication contains auto racing news.

MIDWEST SOCCER NEWS
4030 MOUNT CARMEL-TOBASCO SUITE 317
CINCINNATI, OH 45255
800-511-1574
Fax: 513-688-0526
hammerhead.net/newpublishing.html
• Beverly Spearman, Staff Writer
Frequency:
4 time(s) per year

MIGALA REPORT
247 W. SCOTT STREET
SUITE 208
CHICAGO, IL 60610
312-932-4002
Fax: 312-932-9177
www.migalareport.com
• Dan Migala, Founder/Publisher
• Katie Migala, Customer Service
Nature of Sports Service:
Electronic newletter which provides sports industry executives with information and trends for ticketing and sponsorship issues.
Sports Service Founded:
2003

MINNESOTA GOLFER
6550 YORK AVENUE, SOUTH SUITE 211
EDINA, MN 55435
952-927-4643
800-642-4405
Fax: 952-927-9642
wp@mngolf.org
www.mngolf.org
• W.P. Ryan, Editor
(952) 345-3966
wp@mngolf.org
Frequency:
4 time(s) per year
Description:
Association publication that contains stories, profiles, and features on the Minnesota golf scene, including tournament information, results, and where to play.
Circulation:
80,000

MINNESOTA HOCKEY JOURNAL
6160 SUMMIT DRIVE
MINNEAPOLIS, MN 55422
763-595-0808
Fax: 763-595-0016
info@tpgsports.com
www.tpgsports.com
• Greg Anzelc, Editor
(763) 595-0808
• Greg Ancelz, Editor
(763) 595-0808
Frequency:
5 time(s) per year

MINNESOTA SOCCER TIMES
12510 NORTH EAST 33RD AVENUE
SUITE 301
SEATTLE, WA 98125
206-367-2420
Fax: 206-367-2636
www.varsitycommunications.com
• Charles Beene, Editor
(206) 367-2420
charles@varsitycommunications.com
Frequency:
8 time(s) per year
Description:
Publication contains association news, coaching tips, and tournament updates.

MISSISSIPPY IN TOUCH
13540 LAKE CITY WAY N.E. SUITE 3
SEATTLE, WA 98125
206-367-2420
Fax: 206-367-2636
www.varsitycommunications.com
• Earl Starkoff, Publisher
(800) 643-6061
els730@aol.com
Frequency:
4 time(s) per year

MOD-STOCK COMPETITION
360 B STREET
IDAHO FALLS, ID 83402
208-524-7000
800-638-0153
Fax: 208-522-5241
info@snowest.com
www.snowest.com
• Lane Lindstrom, Editor
(208) 542-2234
lindstrm@snowest.com
• Steve Janes, Publisher
(208) 542-2214
stevejanes@snowest.com
• Ryan Harris, Assistant Editor
(208) 542-2243
rharris@snowest.com
Frequency:
1 time(s) per year
Description:
Publication contains technical information on all aspects of performance snowmobiling, as well as new product news for the performance snowmobile community.
Circulation:
36,000

MORGAN HORSE
4066 SHELBURNE ROAD
SUITE 5
SHELBURNE, VT 05482-7521
802-985-4944
Fax: 802-985-8897
magazine@morganhorse.com
www.morganhorse.com
• Stephen Kinney, Editorial Director
(802) 985-4944
stephen@morganhorse.com
Frequency:
1 time(s) per month
Description:
Publication aims to promote the Morgan horse and the activities of Morgan owners and AMHA members.

MOTOR BOATING
18 MARSHALL STREET
SUITE 114
NORWALK, CT 06854-2237

203-299-5900
Fax: 203-299-5951
www.motorboating.com
• John Wooldridge, Managing Editor
(212) 649-4127
• Jeanne Craig, Executive Editor
(203) 299-5958
• Dan Fales, Editor-at-Large
(207) 372-8598
danfales@verizon.net
• Brad Kovach, Senior Associate Editor
Frequency:
1 time(s) per month
Description:
Publication is written for boating enthusiasts; includes information on purchasing, maintaining, and enjoying boats.

MOTORACING
P.O. BOX 1203
PLEASANTON, CA 94566-0120
925-846-7728
800-585-3559
76067.1750@compuserve.com
www.usmotoracing.com
• John Kelly, Publisher & Editor
(925) 846-7728
• Patricia J. Kelly, Advertising Manager
• John F. Kelly, Jr., Editor-in-Chief
• John F. Kelly, Jr., Publisher
Frequency:
1 time(s) per month
Description:
Publication covers Western United States sports car road races, oval track races; both pavement and dirt surfaces.

MOUNTAIN BIKE
2509 WEST EMPIRE AVENUE SUITE 2
BURBANK, CA 91504-3320
610-967-8722
Fax: 610-967-8960
www.mountainbike.com
• Jennifer Sherry, Senior Editor
• Robert Davidowitz, Group Publisher
(212) 573-0354
• Nicholas Freedman, Publisher
(610) 967-7544
mbelectro@earthlink.net
• Matt Phillips, Senior Editor
(818) 953-8732
• Susan G. Snyder, Advertising Business Manager
(610) 259-4082
Frequency:
1 time(s) per month
Description:
Publication focuses on off-road bicycling adventure, techniques, equipment, and racing.

MOUNTAIN BIKE ACTION
25233 ANZA DRIVE
VALENCIA, CA 91355
661-295-1910
800-767-0345
Fax: 661-295-1178
www.mbaction.com
• Jody Weisel, Features Editor
(661) 295-1910
• Ryan Cleek, Assistant Editor
(661) 367-2150
• Richard Cunningham, Editor-at-Large
(661) 295-1910
• Carrie Greer, Executive Assistant
• Carrie Greer, Office Manager
• Roland Hinz, Publisher

(661) 295-1910
• John Ker, Assistant Editor
(661) 295-1910
• Jimmy Mac, Editor
(661) 295-1910
• Jim McIlvain, Editor
(661) 367-2145
• Robb Mesecher, Advertising Manager
(661) 367-2105
• Mark Thomas, Advertising Executive
(661) 295-1910
Frequency:
1 time(s) per month
Description:
Publication is written for all-terrain bicycle enthusiasts.

MOUNTAIN BIKING
9509 VASSAR AVENUE UNIT A
CHATSWORTH, CA 91311
818-700-6868
Fax: 818-700-6282
www.mtbiking.com
• Alan Davis, Editor
(818) 700-6868
Frequency:
1 time(s) per month

MOUNTAIN ZONE
316 OCCIDENTAL AVE S.
STE 400
SEATTLE, WA 98104
206-839-8719
800-644-5236
Fax: 206-625-0271
info@mountainzone.com
www.mountainzone.com
• Tim O'Mara, President
Description:
Online magazine focusing on all mountain sports activities, including cybercasting of all types of mountain sports events.

MOUNTAINEER LAKES & MOUNTAINS
ROUTE 3 FAIRGROUNDS ROAD
PLYMOUTH, NH 03264-9803
603-536-1311
800-491-4612
Fax: 603-536-8940
www.record-enterprise.com
• Leigh Sharps, Editor
Frequency:
1 time(s) per week
Description:
Publication focuses on ski tours.

MUSCULAR DEVELOPMENT
690 ROUTE 25A
SETAUKET, NY 11733
631-751-9696
Fax: 631-751-9699
editor@musculardevelopment.com
www.musculardevelopment.com
• Steve Blechman, Editor
• Steve Blechman, Editor-in-Chief
• Adam Ginsberg, Advertising Manager
(631) 751-9696
Frequency:
1 time(s) per month
Description:
Publication features Sports Nutrition training and performance.

MUSHING MAGAZINE
PO BOX 1195
WILLOW, AK 99688

907-495-2468
Fax: 907-479-3137
editor@mushing.com
www.mushing.com
• Mary Haley, Managing Editor
• Amanda Byrd, Managing Editor
(907) 458-0888
editor@mushing.com
Frequency:
6 time(s) per year
Description:
Publication provides information and entertainment content covering the sports of dogsledding, skijoring, carting, dog packing, and weight pulling.

NAIA
23500 W. 105TH ST
OLATHE, KS 66051
913-791-0044
Fax: 816-595-8301
khenry@naia.org
www.naia.org
• Steve Baker, President/Chief Operating Officer
• Jim Carr, Chief Operating Officer
• Mark Chiarucci, Director Corporate Sponsorships Regional Dire
• Natalie Cronkhite, Director of Championships
Circulation:
7,500. 95% association membership, 5% paid subscr.
Sports:
General - collegiate
Primary Audience:
Association membership
Frequency:
Monthly (11 times yearly)
Publishing Company:
NAIA

NASCAR ILLUSTRATED
120 WEST MOREHEAD STREET
SUITE 320
CHARLOTTE, NC 28202-1826
704-973-1300
800-883-7323
Fax: 704-973-1303
• Jon Gunn, Managing Editor
• Steve Waid, Executive Editor
(704) 973-1329
• Steve Waid, Publisher
(704) 973-1329
• Mark Ashenfelter, Associate Editor
(704) 973-1300
Frequency:
1 time(s) per month
Description:
Publication features Winston Cup racing reports, profiles, interviews, and photo spreads.

NASCAR MAGAZINE
1801 WEST INTERNATIONAL SPEEDWAY BLVD
DAYTONA BEACH, FL 32114
386-253-0611
Fax: 386-239-8615
www.nascar.com
• Paul Schaefer, Editor
(386) 947-6788
pschaefer@nascar.com
Frequency:
1 time(s) per month
Description:
Magazine is the official membership

publication of the National Association for Stock Car Racing.

NATIONAL CROQUET CALENDAR
718 EAST JACKSON STREET
MONMOUTH, OR 97361-1814
503-838-5697
• Garth Eliassen, Publisher & Editor
(503) 838-5697
• Garth Eliassen, Publisher
Frequency:
6 time(s) per year
Description:
Publication covers the world of championship croquet; includes news, results, schedules of events, and strategy analysis.

NATIONAL DRAGSTER
P.O. BOX 5555
GLENDORA, CA 91740-4694
626-963-8475
Fax: 626-335-4307
www.nhra.com
• Phil Burgess, Editor
(626) 963-8475
• Vicky Walker, Managing Editor
(626) 963-7695
vwalker@nhra.com
Frequency:
1 time(s) per week
Description:
Publication serves the drag racing industry.

NATIONAL HAWKEYE RACING NEWS
180 EAST 5TH ST
PO BOX 720
VINTON, IA 52349-2500
319-472-4763
800-472-4006
Fax: 319-472-3117
www.hawkeyeracingnews.com
• Jim Morrison, Editor
(319) 472-4763
• Debbie Madorin, Publisher & Editor
(319) 472-4763
• Kathy Root, Publisher
Frequency:
33 time(s) per year
Description:
Hawkeye Racing news is a Midwestern based publication in its 45th year of publication. From Sprints and Midgets to Late Models to Modifieds to Short Tracks to entry-level divisions we cover it all. We offer our readers 33 issues a year and we are weekly from April until October.

NATIONAL PAL COPSNKIDS CRONICLES
618 N. U.S. HWY 1, STE 201
N. PALM BEACH, FL 33408
561-844-1823
Fax: 561-863-6120
copnkid1@aol.com
• Brad Hart, Associate Director/Sports
Description:
Communications from national to locals (PAL). Subjects covered - latest information in the sports world, fundraising programs, events, tournaments, success stories - sport page editorial.
Circulation:
147,756. 80% association memb, 20% contr non-paid.
Sports:
General
Primary Audience:

Association membership, corporate and local community coaches, law enforcement agencies/departments, national associations, media
Frequency:
Quarterly
Publishing Company:
Natl Assn of Police Athletic Leagues

NATIONAL SPEED SPORT NEWS
6509 HUDSPETH ROAD
HARRISBURG, NC 28075
704-455-2531
Fax: 704-455-2605
www.nationalspeedsportnews.com
• Mike Kerchner, Managing Editor
(704) 455-8050
mikek@nationalspeedsportnews.com
• Chris Economaki, Editor In Chief
(704) 455-2531
• Mike Kerchner, Associate Editor
(704) 455-2531
mikek@nationalspeedsportnews.com
• Michael Parra, Advertising Director
(704) 455-2531
mparra@nationalspeedsportnews.com
• Jim Savas, Publisher
(704) 455-2531
Frequency:
1 time(s) per week
Description:
Covers all professional motorsports in U.S. plus F-1
Circulation:
35,000
Primary Audience:
Motorsports fans and participants
Sport:
Automobile racing

NBA INSIDE STUFF
355 LEXINGTON AVENUE
NEW YORK, NY 10017-6603
212-697-1460
Fax: 212-286-8154
t.gervino@pspsports.com
www.nba.com
Frequency:
6 time(s) per year
Description:
Publication is the official teen magazine of the NBA, providing coverage of the league for fans aged 12 to 19.

NCAA NEWS
700 W. WASHINGTON
INDIANAPOLIS, IN 46206-6222
317-917-6222
Fax: 317-917-6831
news_editorial@ncaa.org
www.ncaa.org
• P. Da Pickle, Editor
• Jack L. Copeland, Managing Editor
Description:
Primary means of communication for NCAA with its more than 1,000 member institutions, organizations and conferences, as well as the news media and other persons interested in staying abreast of developments in college athletics. Covers hard news of all NCAA activities and includes administrative content important to all athletic administrators and coaches, as well as classified employment advertising for positions in athletics.
Circulation:
25,000. 100% paid.

Sports:
NCAA sponsored sports
Primary Audience:
Association membership
Frequency:
Weekly except biweekly in summer
Publishing Company:
National Collegiate Athletic Association

NET NEWS
450 NORTHRIDGE PARKWAY
SUITE 202
ATLANTA, GA 30350
770-650-1102
800-536-5669
Fax: 770-650-2848
www.knowatlanta.com
• Laura Newsome, Editor
(770) 650-1102
• John Hanna, Publisher
• John Hanna, Advertising Manager/Publisher
(770) 650-1102
hanna@knowatlanta.com
Frequency:
6 time(s) per year
Description:
Publication contains information about the Atlanta Lawn Tennis Association and its members; includes articles on new products, tennis camps, tennis resorts, tennis communities, preventive medicine, and nutrition.

NEW ENGLAND SPORTS
11 HASKAL STREET
SUITE 2
BEVERLY, MA 01915
978-236-1001
Fax: 978-236-1061
www.metrosportsboston.com
• Rebecca Delaney, Editor
• Jeff Banowetz, Editorial Director
• Doug Kaplan, President/Publisher
Frequency:
1 time(s) per month

NEW ENGLAND WINDSURFING JOURNAL
P.O. BOX 371
MILFORD, CT 06460-0371
203-876-2001
Fax: 203-876-2868
newjournal@aol.com
www.worldwindsurf.com
• Peter Bogucki, Advertising Director
(203) 876-2001
• Peter Bogucki, Advertising Director
• Peter Bogucki, Publisher
Frequency:
9 time(s) per year
Description:
Publication contains windsurfing news.

NEW YORK METS INSIDE PITCH
505 SOUTH DUKE STREET SUITE 504
DURHAM, NC 27701-3153
919-688-0218
800-421-7751
Fax: 919-682-1532
comanpub@comanpub.com
• Bryan Hoch, Managing Editor
(201) 483-3520
metsinsidepitch@aol.com
Frequency:
1 time(s) per month
Description:

Publication includes player features, historical articles, and complete team and individual statistics.

NEW YORK SPORTS & NEWS DIGEST
217 W. FULTON ST
LONG BEACH, NY 11561
516-432-7074
Fax: 516-432-7074
• Robert Elkin, Editor
Description:
Covers all national sports, especially New York and New Jersey; features on players; flashbacks in sports.
Circulation:
50,000+. Newsstand and paid subscription.
Sports:
High School, College, Professional.
Primary Audience:
Consumer.
Frequency:
Monthly.

NEW YORK TIMES SYNDICATION
620 8TH AVENUE
FRNT 5
NEW YORK, NY 10168
212-556-4063
Fax: 212-499-3382
www.nytsyn.com
• Cristian Edwards, President
(212) 499-3300
• Michael Oricchio, Managing Editor
(212) 499-3300
• Tim Hilchey, Deputy Managing Editor
(212) 499-3300
• Lawrence Paul, Executive Editor
(212) 499-3300
Description:
Newspaper syndication of sports stories, graphics and photos from THE NEW YORK TIMES and other U.S. and international sources.

NFHS NEWS
PO BOX 690
INDIANAPOLIS, IN 46206
317-972-6900
Fax: 317-822-5700
www.nfhs.org
• Robert Kanady, Executive Director
• Bruce L. Howard, Director of Pulications and Communications
• Judy Thomas, Director of Marketing
Description:
Details NFS and member state association programs and services; promotes professional growth and image of high school coaches, officials and athletic directors and serves the interests of interscholastic athletic programs of 20,000 member high schools accordingly.
Circulation:
12,000 95% association memb, 5% contr non-paid.
Sports:
General
Primary Audience:
Association membership (State High School Associations; National Federation of Speech and Music Organizations)
Frequency:
Nine issues annually
Publishing Company:
National Federation of State High School Associations

NIRSA JOURNAL
4185 SOUTHWEST RESEARCH WAY
CORVALLIS, OR 97333-1067
541-766-8211
Fax: 541-766-8284
sarah@nirsa.org
www.nirsa.org
• Sarah Hubart, Managing Editor
(541) 766-8211
sarah@nirsa.org
Frequency:
2 time(s) per year
Description:
Publication is written for recreational sports administrators.

NORDIC NETWORK
PO BOX 818
WOODSTOCK, VT 05091
802-236-3021
ccsaa@xcski.org
• Reese Brown, Editor
(802) 236-3021
reese@xcski.org
Frequency:
4 time(s) per year

NORTH AMERICAN PYLON
P.O. BOX 1203
PLEASANTON, CA 94566-0120
925-846-7728
800-585-3559
76067.1750@compuserve.com
www.napylon.com
• John F. Kelly, Jr., Editor
• Patricia Kelly, Business Manager
(925) 846-7728
• John F. Kelly, Jr., Publisher
Frequency:
1 time(s) per month
Description:
Publication covers sports car autocrossing and automotive time trial events in the United States and Canada.

NORTH CAROLINA YOUTH SOCCER
12510 NORTH EAST 33RD AVENUE
SUITE 300
SEATTLE, WA 98125
206-367-2420
Fax: 206-367-2636
www.varsitycommunications.com
• Charles Beene, Editor
(206) 367-2420
charles@varsitycommunications.com
Frequency:
6 time(s) per year

NSGA RETAIL FOCUS
1601 FEEHANVILLE DRIVE
MOUNT PROSPECT, IL 60056
847-296-6742
Fax: 847-391-9827
info@nsga.org
www.nsga.org
• Larry Weindruch, Editor
(847) 296-6742
lweindruch@nsga.org
• Paul M. Prince, Advertising Manager
(847) 296-6742
• Larry Weindruch, Publisher
(847) 296-6742
• Paul M Prince, Editorial
(800) 815-5422
Frequency:
6 time(s) per year
Description:

Publication is geared toward top level executives of sporting goods retail companies.

OCEAN NAVIGATOR
58 FORE STREET
PORTLAND, ME 04101-4502
207-772-2466
Fax: 207-772-2879
editors@oceannavigator.com
www.oceannavigator.com
• Tim Queeney, Editor
(207) 772-2466
tqueeney@oceannavigator.com
• Alex Agnew, Publisher
(207) 772-2466
aagnew@oceannavigator.com
Frequency:
8 time(s) per year
Description:
Publication focuses on offshore and coastal voyaging techniques, procedures, and equipment; also covers meteorology, astronomy, and oceanography for mariners.

OFFSHORE
500 VICTORY ROAD
QUINCY, MA 02171
617-221-1400
Fax: 617-847-1871
www.boatingonline.net
• Gaelen Phyfe, Managing Editor
• Joe Myerson, Senior Editor
• Richard Royer, Publisher
• Kendra Sousa, Advertising Director
Frequency:
1 time(s) per month
Description:
Publication contains articles about boats and boating in the Northeast.

OHIO SOCCER
13540 LAKE CITY WAY N.E. SUITE 3
SEATTLE, WA 98125
206-367-2420
Fax: 206-367-2636
www.varsitycommunications.com
• Kay Catlett, Editor
(330) 659-0989
oysan@aol.com
Frequency:
5 time(s) per year

OHIO STANDARDBRED
12555 BENNER ROAD
RITTMAN, OH 44270-9703
330-925-3040
Fax: 330-927-6890
trogdon@apk.net
www.tradingpostnewspapers.com
• Mike Trogdon, Managing Editor
(330) 722-6322
mtrogdon@thepostnewspapers.com
• Bruce Trogdon, President/Publisher
(330) 925-3040
btrogdon@thepostnewspapers.com
Frequency:
1 time(s) per week
Description:
Publication covers Ohio harness racing.

OREGON CYCLING MAGAZINE
455 WEST 1ST AVENUE
EUGENE, OR 97401-2276

541-686-9885
Fax: 541-344-1197
www.catoregon.org
• Karl Benedek, Editor
Frequency:
10 time(s) per year
Description:
Publication covers information of interest to bicycling enthusiasts in Oregon, including touring, racing, commuting, and mountain biking.

OREGON GOAL LINES
12510 NORTH EAST 33RD AVENUE
SUITE 301
SEATTLE, WA 98125
206-367-2420
Fax: 206-367-2636
www.varsitycommunications.com
• Charles Beene, Editor
(206) 367-2420
charles@varsitycommunications.com
Frequency:
7 time(s) per year
Description:
Publication features articles that bring readers reliable news and information about soccer.

OUTDOOR AMERICA MAGAZINE
707 CONSERVATION LANE
GAITHERSBURG, MD 20878
301-548-0150
800-453-5463
Fax: 301-548-0146
general@iwla.org
www.iwla.org
• Paul Hansen, Executive Director
• Jason McGarvey, Editor
Publishing Company:
NA
Frequency:
Quarterly
Primary Audience:
Association membership
Sports:
Fishing, hunting, camping, hiking, canoeing, winter sports
Circulation:
40,000. 95% association memb, 5% other.
Description:
Contains articles on nationwide conservation issues plus features on outdoor recreation.

OUTDOOR LIFE
TWO PARK AVE
10TH FL
NEW YORK, NY 10016
212-779-5000
800-227-2224
Fax: 212-779-5366
olmagazine@aol.com
www.outdoorlife.com
• Todd Smith, Editor-in-Chief
(212) 779-5090
• Camille Rankin, Senior Managing Editor
(212) 779-5244
• Colin Moore, Executive Editor
(212) 779-5246
• John Snow, Articles Editor
(212) 779-5258
• Frank Miniter, Senior Editor/New Products
(212) 779-5254
• John Taranto, Associate Editor/Midwest & West Regions
(212) 779-5101

• Will Snyder, Associate Editor/East & South Regions
(212) 779-5401
• Joi Harvey, Senior Administrative Assistant
(212) 779-5090
Publishing Company:
Time, Inc.
Frequency:
9 issues per year.
Circulation:
925,000.
Primary Audience:
Hunters, Fishermen.

OUTSIDE MAGAZINE
400 MARKET ST
SANTA FE, NM 87501
505-989-7100
Fax: 505-989-4700
www.outsidemag.com
• Lawrence J. Burke, Chairman/Editor-In-Chief
• Hal Espen, Editor
Description:
Active outdoor lifestyle magazine dedicated to inspiring people to enjoy fuller, more rewarding lives through year-round editorial coverage of the participatory sports, travel, adventure, people, politics, art and literature of the world outside.
Circulation:
NA.
Sports:
Year-round sports
Primary Audience:
Consumer
Frequency:
Monthly
Publishing Company:
Mariah Publications Corp.

OUTSIDE PITCH
722 LIGHT STREET
BALTIMORE, MD 21230-3850
410-234-8888
Fax: 410-234-1029
www.outsidepitch.com
• David Hill, Editor
(410) 234-8888
• Robert Peregoy, Advertising Manager
• David Simone, Publisher
(410) 234-8888
Frequency:
9 time(s) per year
Description:
Publication features articles on the Baltimore Orioles baseball team.

PACIFIC NORTHWEST GOLFER
355 118TH AVENUE S.E. SUITE 100
BELLEVUE, WA 98005
206-526-1238
Fax: 206-343-4784
www.pngamedia.com
• Paul Ramsdell, Editor
(206) 343-4788
• John Bodenahmer, Publisher & Editor
(206) 526-1238
Frequency:
4 time(s) per year
Description:
Publication focuses on topics of interest to golfers in the northwestern United States.

PACKER REPORT
112 MARKET STREET
SUN PRAIRIE, WI 53590
608-837-2200
Fax: 608-825-3053
packredted@aol.com
www.packerreport.com
• Todd Korth, Editor
(920) 497-6500
packrepted@aol.com
• Art Daley, Columnist
(920) 497-7225
packrepted@aol.com
• Johnny Gray, Columnist
gray24@tds.net
• Lee Remmel, Columnist
(920) 497-6500
remmell@packers.com
Frequency:
26 time(s) per year
Description:
Publication contains information of interest to fans of the National Football League in general, and the Green Bay Packers in particular.

PADDLER
735 OAK
STEAMBOAT SPRINGS, CO 80487
970-879-1450
Fax: 970-870-1404
editor@aca-paddler.org
www.paddlermagazine.com
• Jeff Moag, Managing Editor
(970) 879-1450
• Eugene Buchanan, Editor-in-Chief
(970) 879-1450
• Eugene Buchanan, Publisher
(970) 879-1450
• Kevin Thompson, Advertising Director
(970) 879-1450
Frequency:
6 time(s) per year
Description:
Publication is a resource for paddle sports enthusiasts from beginner to expert; includes advice for those who paddle flat water and white water in canoes, kayaks, rafts, sit-on tops, wave skis, and surf skis.

PAINT HORSE JOURNAL
2800 MEACHAM BOULEVARD
FORT WORTH, TX 76137
817-834-2742
Fax: 817-222-8466
www.painthorsejournal.com
• Jessica Smith, Managing Editor
Frequency:
1 time(s) per month
Description:
Publication features articles for horse enthusiasts interested in riding, training, breeding or racing American Paint horses.

PAINTBALL MAGAZINE
4201 VANOWEN PLACE
BURBANK, CA 91505
818-845-2656
Fax: 818-845-7761
www.paintball.com
• Jessica Sparks, Editor
(818) 845-2656
• Gabe Frimmel, Advertising Manager
(818) 845-2656
Frequency:
6 time(s) per year
Description:

Publication features news and events for the paintball enthusiast.

PANASTADIA INTERNATIONAL
STADIUM CENTRE II, HALL FARM HOUSE
9 HIGH ST
CASTLE DONINGTON
DERBYSHIRE, ENGLAND DE74 2PP
www.panstadia.com
• Julian A. Radley,
• Tony Chakraborty, Editor
• Katie Else, Marketing Director
Description:
Journal covering the international sports facility industry.
Frequency:
4 times a year

PAR EXCELLANCE MAGAZINE
10401 WEST LINCOLN AVENUE SUITE 207
WEST ALLIS, WI 53227-1255
414-327-7707
414-327-4146
Fax: 414-327-4146
www.golfparexcellence.com
• Neal Kotlarek, Editor
• Doug Neumann, Publisher
• Doug Newmann, Publisher
Frequency:
5 time(s) per year
Description:
Publication reviews golf courses in the Midwest and other golf related activities or travel.

PARACHUTIST
1440 DUKE STREET
ALEXANDRIA, VA 22314-3403
703-836-3495
Fax: 540-604-9741
uspa@uspa.org
www.uspa.org
• Nancy Koreen, Managing Editor
(703) 836-3495
nkoreen@uspa.org
• Chris Needels, Executive Director
• Kevin Gibson, Editor In Chief
(703) 836-3495
kgibson@uspa.org
Frequency:
1 time(s) per month
Description:
Publication includes articles on safety issues, current events, instructional methods, and association business.

PARKS & RECREATION
22377 BELMONT RIDGE RD
ASHBURN, VA 20148-4501
703-858-0784
Fax: 703-858-0794
www.nrpa.org
• Rachel Roberts, Editor
(703) 858-2175
• Tracey Ellis, Advertising Director
(703) 858-2176
• Maya Avrasin, Associate Editor
(703) 858-2145
Publishing Company:
National Recreation & Park Association.
Frequency:
12 times a year.
Circulation:
23,000.
Nature of Service:
A national, non-profit association dedicated

to advancing parks, recreation and environmental conservation efforts that enhance the quality of life for all people.
Primary Audience:
Park, Parks and Recreation.
Sports:
Professionals.

PASSAGEMAKER-THE TRAWLER AND OCEAN MOTORBOAT MAG
105 EASTERN AVENUE SUITE 103
ANNAPOLIS, MD 21403
410-990-9086
888-487-2953
Fax: 410-990-9094
onlineorders@passagemaker.com
www.passagemaker.com
• Bill Parlatore, Editor
editor@passagemaker.com
• Eileen Nonemaker, Advertising Director
(410) 990-9086
eileen@passagemaker.com
• Candace Orsetti, Associate Editor
(410) 990-9086
candace@passagemaker.com
• Laurene Parlatore, Publisher
(410) 990-9086
Laurene@passagemaker.com
Frequency:
6 time(s) per year
Description:
Publication offers news and information on ocean motorboats and recreational trawlers.

PENNSYLVANIA EQUESTRIAN
40 STREET NORTH LINE STREET
LANCASTER, PA 17602
717-509-9800
Fax: 717-509-0297
debbie@paequestrian.com
www.pennsylvaniaequestrian.com
• Stephanie Lawson, Editor
paequest@aol.com
• Debbie Hocke, Advertising Manager
• Stephanie Lawson, Publisher
paequest@aol.com
Frequency:
6 time(s) per year
Description:
Publication is written for horse owners and equestrian enthusiasts throughout Pennsylvania and neighboring states.

PERFORMANCE RACING INDUSTRY
31706 SOUTH COAST HIGHWAY
LAGUNA BEACH, CA 92651-0327
949-499-5413
Fax: 949-499-0410
mail@performanceracing.com
www.performanceracing.com
• Meredith Kaplan Burns, Managing Editor
(949) 499-5413
meredithk@performanceracing.com
• John Kilroy, Vice President & Editor
(949) 499-5413
• Steve Lewis, Publisher
Frequency:
1 time(s) per month
Description:
Trade magazine focusing on auto racing.

PGA TOUR PARTNERS
12301 WHITEWATER DRIVE SUITE 260
MINNETONKA, MN 55343-4104
952-988-7244
800-688-7611
Fax: 952-936-9169

mail@pgatourpartners.com
www.pgatourpartners.com
• Tom Stine, Editor
• Seth Hoyt, Publisher
Frequency:
6 time(s) per year
Description:
Publication contains articles on golf skills for professionals.

PHILADELPHIA GOLFER
290 COMMERCE DRIVE
FORT WASHINGTON, PA 19034-2400
215-542-0200
Fax: 215-643-9475
www.montgomerynews.com
• Dave Holloway, Sports Editor
(215) 542-0200
dholloway@montgomerynews.com
• Betsy Wilson, Publisher
(215) 628-8330
Frequency:
1 time(s) per month
Description:
Publication offers regional golf information.

PITCH
13540 LAKE CITY WAY, N.E. SUITE 3
SEATTLE, WA 98125-3665
206-367-2420
Fax: 206-363-9099
www.varsitycommunications.com
Frequency:
1 time(s) per month

PLAY ON: WASHINGTON STATE YOUTH SOCCER NEWS
500 SOUTH 336TH STREET SUITE 10
FEDERAL WAY, WA 98003
253-476-2237
Fax: 253-925-1830
playon@wsysa.com
www.varsitycommunications.com
• Erin Freehan, Editor
• Leslie Groce, Contact
(253) 476-2237
leslie@wsysa.com
Frequency:
10 time(s) per year
Description:
Publication contains association news, coaching tips, and tournament updates.

POLO PLAYERS EDITION
3500 FAIRLANE FARMS ROAD SUITE 9
WELLINGTON, FL 33414-8746
561-793-9524
Fax: 561-793-9576
info@poloplayersedition.com
www.poloplayersedition.com
• Gwen Rizzo, Editor
gwen@poloplayersedition.com
• Judy Doyle, Advertising Manager
• Gwen Rizzo, Publisher
gwen@poloplayersedition.com
Frequency:
1 time(s) per month
Description:
Publication focuses on lifestyle, game coverage, action photos, and how-to-do articles related to polo.

PONTOON & DECK BOAT
360 B STREET
IDAHO FALLS, ID 83402

208-524-7000
Fax: 208-522-5241
info@snowest.com
www.pontoon.net
• Brady Kay, Editor
• Mike Harris, Publisher
Frequency:
8 time(s) per year
Description:
Publication is a boating magazine for pontoon and deck boat owners, dealers, and manufacturers.

PONY BASEBALL AND SOFTBALL
1951 PONY PLACE
WASHINGTON, PA 15301
724-225-1060
Fax: 724-225-9852
info@pony.org
www.pony.org

POWDER
33046 CALLE AVIADOR
SAN JUAN CAPISTRANO, CA 92675
949-496-5922
Fax: 949-496-7849
www.powdermag.com
• Tom Bie, Editor
(949) 661-5155
Frequency:
7 time(s) per year
Description:
Publication is geared toward advanced skiers.

POWER & MOTORYACHT
260 MADISON AVENUE 8TH FLOOR
NEW YORK, NY 10016
212-726-4300
Fax: 212-726-4310
www.primedia.com
• Elizabeth Britten, Associate Editor
(917) 256-2278
• Eileen Mansfield, Managing Editor
(917) 256-2277
• Dennis O'Neil, Publisher
(917) 256-2292
• Richard Thiel, Editor-in-Chief
(917) 256-2267
Frequency:
1 time(s) per month
Description:
Publication covers issues of interest to owners of powerboats.

POWERBOAT
1691 SPINNAKER DRIVE SUITE 206
VENTURA, CA 93001-4378
805-667-4100
800-738-5571
Fax: 805-667-4336
info@powerboatmag.com
• Gregg Mansfield, Editor
gregg@powerboatmag.com
• Jason Johnson, Managing Editor
jason@powerboatmag.com
• Jerry Nordskog, Publisher
(805) 667-4100
Frequency:
11 time(s) per year
Description:
Publication is for the performance-conscious boater; contains technical articles, race coverage, personality profiles, water skiing, recreational boating, and performance evaluations.

PRACTICAL HORSEMAN
656 QUINCH ORCHID ROAD SUITE 600
GAITHERSBURG, MD 20878-1409
301-977-3900
800-829-3340
Fax: 301-990-9015
www.equisearch.com
• Sandy Oliynyk, Editor
(301) 977-3900
Frequency:
1 time(s) per month
Description:
Publication focuses on English-style
horseback riding.

PRICE MEDIA
10002 AURORA AVENUE N
#36
SEATTLE, WA 98133
206-418-0747
800-935-1083
Fax: 206-418-0746
info@outdoorsnw.com
• Carolyn Price, Publisher/Sales
• Greg Price, Associate Publisher
• Matthew Butler, Sales Associate
• Kristen Carlton, Editor
• Laurie Scholleart, Art Director
Publishing Company:
Price Media, Inc.
Primary Audience:
Consumer
Sports:
Outdoor, non-mainstream
Circulation:
40,000 per Month.
Description:
News and features about outdoor individual
pursuits and non-mainstream outdoor
sports, including places to go in the Pacific
Northwest. Publishes a calendar of sport
events in the Northwest.

PRIMEDIA
3585 ENGINEERING DRIVE
SUITE 100
NORCROSS, GA 30092
678-421-3000
800-216-1423
www.primedia.com
Description:
Publishes wide range of consumer sports
and special interest publications.

PRO FOOTBALL WEEKLY
302 SAUNDERS ROAD
RIVERWOODS, IL 60015
847-940-1100
800-331-7529
Fax: 847-940-1108
www.profootballweekly.com
• Hub Arkush, Co-Publisher & Editor
(847) 405-7750
• Hub Arkush, Publisher
• Mike Holbrook, Managing Editor
• Keith Schleiden, Managing Editor
(847) 405-7707
• Hub Arkash, Sports Editor
(847) 940-1100
Frequency:
1 time(s) per week
Description:
Publication features previews, reviews,
upcoming events, and postgame coverage.

PROFESSIONAL BOATBUILDER
NASKEAG ROAD
BROOKLIN, ME 04616
207-359-4651
Fax: 207-359-8920
proboat@proboat.com
www.proboat.com
• Paul Lazarus, Editor
• Carl Cramer, Publisher
(207) 359-4651
Frequency:
6 time(s) per year
Description:
Publication covers a wide range of subjects
of importance to the boatbuilding industry.

PRORODEO SPORTS NEWS
101 PRO RODEO DRIVE
COLORADO SPRINGS, CO 80919-
719-593-8840
Fax: 719-548-4889
www.prorodeo.com
• Sean Daniels, Properties VP
• Neal Reid, Editor
• Kendra Santos, Communications Director
Frequency:
26 time(s) per year
Description:
The PRCA, headquartered in Colorado
Springs, Colo, is the largest and oldest
professional rodeo-sanctioning body in the
world. The recognized leader in ProRodeo,
the PRCA is committed to maintaining the
highest standards. The PRCA, a
membership-based organization, sanctions
approximately 600 rodeos annually, and
there are nearly 30 million fans in the U.S.
The PRCA showcases the world's best
cowboys in premier events through the
Wrangler Million Dollar Tour presented by
Justin Boots, and its subsequent Justin
Boots Playoffs, the PRCA Xtreme Bulls Tour
presented by B&W Trailer Hitches; and the
world-renowned Wrangler National FInals
Rodeo. Act

PROFESSIONAL SPORTS PUBLICATIONS
355 LEXINGTON AVE, 9TH FL
NEW YORK, NY 10017
212-697-1460
Fax: 212-286-8154
www.pspsports.com
• Thom Hering, Chief Operating Officer
• Kevin Hahn, Executive Vice President of
Sales/Marketing
• Amy Ehrlich, Vice President/Marketing
Services
• Neil A. Farber, Vice President
• Paul Abramson, Vice President of National
Accounts
Description:
Publishes game day magazines, including
HOOP magazine, the official publications of
the NBA. Other properties include Major
League Baseball programs, National
Hockey League programs, TOUCHDOWN
ILLUSTRATED (college football), COLLEGE
HOOPS ILLUSTRATED (college
basketball), program magazines for 9 major
College Bowl games. Licensed custom
publisher of the United States Olympic
Committee. Also provides sports marketing
and professional services.

QUARTER HORSE NEWS
2112 MONTGOMERY STREET
FORT WORTH, TX 76107-4517
817-737-6397
Fax: 817-737-9266
www.quarterhorsenews.com
• Glory Ann Kurtz, Editor
(817) 737-6397
gloryann.kurtz@cowboypublishing.com
• Carl Mullins, Publisher
(817) 737-6397
carl.mullins@cowboypublishing.com
• Patty Tiberg, General Manager
(817) 737-6397
patty.tiberg@cowboypublishing.com
Frequency:
2 time(s) per month
Description:
Publication is written for the Quarter horse
industry; includes news about reining,
cutting, barrel racing, western pleasure
shows, sales, and futurities.

RACE PLACE
16888 SAINT ANDREWS DRIVE
POWAY, CA 92064-1135
858-485-9806
Fax: 858-485-9805
www.raceplace.com
• Rose Reilly, Editor
Frequency:
6 time(s) per year
Description:
Publication provides participants, event
organizers, and businesses with a bimonthly
reference schedule of all Southern California
and selected regional running, walking,
endurance, and recreational events.

RACER
16842 VON KARMAN SUITE 125
IRVINE, CA 92606
714-259-8240
800-999-9718
Fax: 949-417-6750
comments@racer.com
www.racer.com
• Dyanne Gilliam, Managing Editor
(949) 417-6700
dgilliam@racer.com
• Andrew Crask, Executive Editor
(949) 417-6700
acrask@racer.com
• Laurence Foster, Editor In Chief
(949) 417-6700
lfoster@racer.com
• Ian Havard, Publisher
(949) 417-6700
Frequency:
1 time(s) per month
Description:
Publication focuses on top level international
auto racing.

RACING WHEELS
5212 NORTH EAST SAINT JOHNS ROAD
VANCOUVER, WA 98661
360-892-5590
888-892-2574
Fax: 360-892-8021
www.racingwheels.net
• Dale Redinger, Editor
• Dale Redinger, Advertising Manager
Frequency:
40 time(s) per year
Description:

Publication is geared toward oval track auto racers and enthusiasts.

RACQUETBALL MAGAZINE
1685 WEST UINTAH ST
COLORADO SPRINGS, CO 80904-2921
719-635-5396
Fax: 719-635-0685
hizzett@usra.org
www.usaracquetball.com
• Jim Hiser, Publisher
(719) 635-5396
jhiser@usra.org
• Heather Izzett, Editor
(719) 635-5396
hizzett@usra.org
Frequency:
6 time(s) per year

RAIDER FAN MAGAZINE
22888 GRAND STREET
HAYWARD, CA 94541
510-881-1860
Fax: 510-881-7603
www.raiderfanmagazine.com
• Tim Del Rosario, Editor
Frequency:
2 time(s) per month
Description:
Publication is for fans of the Oakland Raiders football team.

RECREATION SPORTS & FITNESS
825 OLD COUNTRY ROAD
WESTBURY, NY 11590
516-334-3030
Fax: 516-334-8958
ebmpubs2@aol.com
www.ebmpubs.com
• Paul Ragusa, Features Editor
(516) 334-3030
Description:
Publication provides the latest-breaking news about the ever-changing fitness market; includes interviews with people who make it work.

RECREATIONAL SPORTS JOURNAL
4185 SW RESEARCH WAY
CORVALLIS, OR 97333
541-766-8211
Fax: 541-766-8284
nirsa@nirsa.org
www.nirsa.org
• Kent Blumenthal, Executive Director
• Lynn Jamieson, Editor
Publishing Company:
National Intramural Recreational Sports Association
Frequency:
Two times annually
Primary Audience:
Association membership
Sports:
General
Circulation:
3,400. 80% association membership.
Description:
Devoted solely to recreational sports: aquatic programs, extramural sports, fitness programs, informal sports, instructional programs, intramural sports, outdoor recreation, special events, special populations, sport clubs, and facility development and management. Content includes approximately 8 articles, special

features, advertising and professional editorials.

REDLEGS WEEKLY
100 MAIN STREET
CINCINNATI, OH 45202
513-765-7000
Fax: 513-765-7027
www.cincinnatireds.com
• Ralph Mitchell, Editor
rmitchell@reds.com
Frequency:
1 time(s) per month
Description:
Publication is the official newsletter of the Cincinnati Reds.

REFEREE MAGAZINE
2017 LATHROP AVENUE
RACINE, WI 53405
262-632-8855
Fax: 262-632-5460
referee@referee.com
www.referee.com
• Barry Mano, Publisher
(262) 632-8855
• Patrick Miles, Advertising Manager
• Bill Topp, Editor-in-Chief
(262) 632-8855
Frequency:
1 time(s) per month
Description:
Publication contains information of interest to officials, fans, athletes, and school administrators involved in amateur sports.

REFEREE MAGAZINE
PO BOX 161
FRANKSVILLE, WI 53126-0012
262-632-8855
Fax: 262-632-5460
www.referee.com
• Barry Mano, Publisher
• Patrick Sharp, VP Marketing & Business Development
• Bill Topp, VP Publishing & Management Services
Publishing Company:
Referee Enterprises, Inc.
Primary Audience:
Referees, sports officials
Sports:
All major sports
Circulation:
35,000. 55% paid association subscr, 45% paid subscr.
Description:
Provides a balanced look at events that involve sports officials; informs officials about their colleagues' activities.

RIDE MAGAZINE
728 CHERRY STREET
CHICO, CA 95928
530-343-9994
Fax: 530-343-4218
www.ridemagazine.com
• Diana Bishop, Editor
(530) 343-9994
• Dan Swofford, Publisher
dan@ridepublishing.com
Frequency:
1 time(s) per month
Description:
Publication offers articles and information on horse shows, as well as other equestrian topics.

RING
6198 BUTLER PIKE
SUITE 200
BLUE BELL, PA 19422
215-643-6385
Fax: 215-628-3571
www.kappapublishing.com
• Stuart Saks, Assistant Vice President
• Vincent Bellissima, Advertising Manager
Year Founded:
1922
Description:
The sport of Boxing.
Frequency:
Monthly.

RINKSIDE
60 EAST 42ND STREET SUITE 1405
NEW YORK, NY 10165-0721
212-697-0530
Fax: 212-697-0533
• Keith Loria, Editor
• Alan Adams, Contributing Writer
• Lucas Akroyd, Contributing Writer
• Don Cherry, Senior Contributing Editor
• Jim Connelly, Contributing Writer
• Robert F. Corrao, Publisher
• Stan Fischler, Contributing Editor
• Shirley Fischler, Contributing Writer
• Brett Friedlander, Contributing Writer
• Bruce Garrioch, Contributing Writer
• Jay Greenberg, Contributing Writer
• John Kreisen, Contributing Writer
• Dave Luecking, Contributing Writer
• Joe Starkey, Contributing Writer
• Ralph Vacchiano, Contributing Writer
Frequency:
6 time(s) per year

ROCHESTER GOLF WEEK
2535 BRIGHTON HENRIETTA TOWN LINE ROAD
ROCHESTER, NY 14623-2711
585-427-2468
Fax: 585-427-8521
golfweek@frontiernet.net
www.golfweekrochester.com
• Dave Eaton, Editor
• George Morgenstern, Publisher
golfweekrochester@frontiernet.net
Frequency:
1 time(s) per week
Description:
Publication contains news and features about golf and travel related information.

ROCKY MOUNTAIN SPORTS
2525 15TH STREET
SUITE 1-A
DENVER, CO 80211
303-477-9770
Fax: 303-477-9747
• Mary Thorne, Publisher
• Jeff Banowetz, Editorial Director
(303) 477-9770
• Rebecca Heaton, Editor
Publishing Company:
Rocky Mountain Sports Publishing Company, Inc.
Frequency:
Monthly
Primary Audience:
Consumer
Sports:
Individual endurance sports - running, in-line, bicycling, triathlons
Circulation:

80,000. 1% paid subscr, 99% contr non-paid.
Description:
Covers running, Adventure travel, paddling, rock climbing, cycling, in-line skating, triathlons, skiing and health club activities in the Colorado area.

RODALE'S SCUBA DIVING
6600 ABERCORN STREET SUITE 208
SAVANNAH, GA 31405-5800
912-351-0855
Fax: 912-351-0890
www.scubadiving.com
• Robert S. Butler, Editor
(912) 351-6226
• Dane Farnum, Publisher
(912) 351-6233
Frequency:
11 time(s) per year
Description:
Publication contains information of interest to recreational diving enthusiasts, including advice on equipment and travel.

RSV/REVENUES FROM SPORTS VENUES
PO BOX 240854
MILWAUKEE, WI 53224
414-354-0966
• Jim Grinstead, Editor/Publisher
Publishing Company:
Mediaventures
Frequency:
Weekly.
Primary Audience:
Team and venue owners, marketing management, marketing consultants, architects, contractors, premium service vendors, management companies.
Description:
A weekly news service focusing on issues dealing with stadium and arena revenues.

RUGBY
36 W. 84TH ST.
9-B
NEW YORK, NY 10024
917-538-3567
rugbymag@aol.com
www.rugbymag.com
• Edward F. Hagerty, Publisher
(917) 538-3567
rugbymag@aol.com
• Ed Hagerty, Editor
(212) 787-1160
rugbymag@aol.com
Frequency:
1 time(s) per month
Description:
Publication focuses on worldwide rugby events and unions.

SADDLE HORSE REPORT
730 MADISON STREET
SHELBYVILLE, TN 37160-3519
931-684-8123
Fax: 931-684-8196
www.horseworld.net
• Diana Davidson, Editor
• Bob Funkhouser, Executive Editor
• Christy Howard Parsons, Publisher
• Richard T. Hudgins, Advertising Manager
Frequency:
1 time(s) per week
Description:
Publication reports on American

Saddlebred, Hackney Pony, and Morgan horse shows and association news, as well as personalities, instruction, and horse facilities.

SAIL MAGAZINE
98 NORTH WASHINGTON STREET
BOSTON, MA 02114
617-720-8600
800-745-7245
Fax: 617-723-0911
www.sailmag.com
• Peter Nielsen, Editor
(617) 720-8601
• Charles Mason, Executive Editor
(617) 720-8637
cmason@sailmag.com
• Josh Adams, Publisher
(617) 720-8605
jadams@sailmag.com
• Bill Springer, Senior Editor
(617) 720-8607
• Amy Ullrich, Managing Editor
(617) 720-8629
Frequency:
1 time(s) per month
Description:
Publication is written for sailors of all types.

SAILING MAGAZINE
125 EAST MAIN STREET
PORT WASHINGTON, WI 53074-
262-284-3494
800-236-7444
Fax: 262-284-7764
gretas@sailingmagazine.net
www.sailingmagazine.net
• William F Schanen, Publiser/Editor
• Jane Farnham, Production Director
Frequency:
1 time(s) per month
Description:
Publication features information of interest to sailing enthusiasts.

SAILING WORLD
55 HAMMARLUND WAY
MIDDLETOWN, RI 02842
401-845-5100
Fax: 401-845-5180
editorial@sailingworld.com
www.sailingworld.com
• David Reed, Editor
dave.reed@sailingworld.com
• John Burnham, Editor-in-Chief
• Gary Jobson, Editor-at-Large
(410) 263-4630
• Michelle Roche, Classified Manager
• Jason White, Associate Publisher
(401) 845-5155
• Tony Bessinger, Associate Editor
(401) 845-5107
Frequency:
10 time(s) per year
Description:
Publication is written for sailing enthusiasts, with an emphasis on sailboat racing and performance cruising.

SAND SPORTS
2950 AIRWAY AVENUE
COSTA MESA, CA 92626-6031
714-979-2560
Fax: 714-979-3998
msommer@hotvws.com
www.sandsports.net

• Mike Sommers, Editor
(714) 979-2560
• Linda Dill, Advertising Director
(714) 979-2560
• Newell Dunn, Associate Editor
(714) 979-2560
• Skip Coiner, Art Director
(714) 979-2560
Frequency:
5 time(s) per year
Description:
Publication targets recreational, off-road vehicle owners and businesses.

SANTANA
15548 GRAHAM STREET
HUNTINGTON BEACH, CA 92649-1609
714-379-3070
Fax: 714-379-9976
santanarag@aol.com
• Kitty James, Editor
Frequency:
1 time(s) per month
Description:
Publication contains information of interest to boating enthusiasts, including Cruising, Yacht Racing, Learning to Sail, and Boat Maintenance.

SCHOLASTIC COACH & ATHLETIC DIRECTOR MAGAZINE
225 REGENCY COURT
BROOKFIELD, WI 53045
262-782-4480
800-645-8455
Fax: 262-786-5564
www.coachad.com
• Bruce Weber, Publisher
ext 6370
• Herman L. Masin, Editor
ext 6371
• Kevin Newell, Managing Editor
ext 4792
• Michael Wallace, Marketing Manager
ext 6131
Description:
Athletic professionals constantly seek the competitive edge. That's why they demand Coach & A.D. It provides what no other resource offers - in depth coverage of all sports and unbeatable advice from the best coaches around.
Circulation:
52,826. 88% paid subscr, 12% non-paid subscr contr.
Sports:
General.
Primary Audience:
HS/college coaches, athletic directors.
Frequency:
10 times annually.
Publishing Company:
Scholastic Inc.

SEA KAYAKER
6012 SEAVIEW AVENUE NORTH WEST
SEATTLE, WA 98107-2657
206-789-9536
Fax: 206-781-1141
www.seakayakermag.com
• Chris Cunningham, Editor
(206) 789-9536
• Michael Collins, Publisher
(206) 789-9536
• Paul Riek, Advertising Manager
(206) 789-6413

Frequency:
6 time(s) per year
Description:
An invaluable resource for novice and experienced touring kayakers. Every issue covers destinations, navigation of coastal and inland waters, safety, technique, and the latest in kayaks and gear. Focuses on the promotion of kayaking that ensures the safety of the paddler and the preservation of the fragile marine environment.

SEA MAGAZINE
17782 COWAN SUITE A
IRVINE, CA 92614
949-660-6150
Fax: 949-660-6172
www.goboatingamerica.com
• Holly Simpson, Managing Editor
(949) 660-6150
• Jeffrey Fleming, Associate Publisher
(949) 660-6150
• Duncan McIntosh, Publisher
• Stephanie Porter, Assistant Editor
(949) 660-6150
Frequency:
1 time(s) per month
Description:
Publication covers recreational boating in the 13 western states, with emphasis on power boating.

SHARING THE VICTORY
8701 LEEDS ROAD
KANSAS CITY, MO 64129-1680
816-921-0909
Fax: 816-921-8755
stv@fca.org
www.gospelcom.net
• Jill Ewert, Managing Editor
(816) 892-1156
jewert@fca.org
• Les Steckel, Publisher
• Dal Shealy, Publisher
(816) 921-0909
dshealy@fca.org
Frequency:
9 time(s) per year
Description:
Publication serves the Fellowship of Christian Athletes.

SHOW CIRCUIT MAGAZINE
1911 FOOTHILL BOULEVARD SUITE 300
LA VERNE, CA 91750-3511
909-392-8089
Fax: 309-365-8879
showcmag@aol.com
www.showcircuit.com
• Kitty Bowe Hearty, Editor-in-Chief
Description:
Publication features news and articles concerning equestrian competition in the United States.

SIERRA MAGAZINE
85 SECOND ST, 2ND FL
SAN FRANCISCO, CA 94105-3441
415-977-5500
Fax: 415-977-5799
sierra.letters@sierraclub.org
www.sierraclub.org
• Joan Hamilton, Editor-in-Chief
• Robert Schildgen, Managing Director
• Kristi Rummel, National Advertising Director

Description:
Official magazine of the Sierra Club. Definitive voice of the environmental movement. Color photography, editorial informs readers about environmental issues.
Circulation:
500,000. 97% association membership, 2% newsstand, 1% paid subscr.
Sports:
Hiking, rafting, camping, skiing
Primary Audience:
Consumer
Frequency:
Bimonthly
Publishing Company:
Sierra Club

SILENT SPORTS
717 10TH STREET
WAUPACA, WI 54981-1934
715-258-5546
Fax: 715-258-8162
www.silentsports.net
• Joel Patenaude, Editor
(715) 258-5546
• Scott Turner, Publisher
(715) 258-5546
• Jim Wendt, Advertising Manager
(715) 258-5546
• Greg Marr, Editor-in-Chief
(715) 258-5546
Frequency:
1 time(s) per month
Description:
Publication provides information and features stories on self-propelled recreation such as bicycling, paddlesports, cross country skiing, running, and inline skating.

SKATEBOARDER MAGAZINE
33046 CALLE AVIADOR
SAN JUAN CAPISTRANO, CA 92675-4704
949-661-5141
Fax: 949-496-7849
www.skateboardermag.com
• Lauralyn Loynes, Managing Editor
(949) 661-5113
• Roger Harrell, Associate Publisher
(949) 661-5186
• Brian Peech, Editor-in-Chief
Frequency:
6 time(s) per year
Description:
Publication profiles skateboarding culture; includes new moves, features on prominent professionals, and entertaining columns.

SKATING
20 1ST STREET
COLORADO SPRINGS, CO 80906
719-635-5200
Fax: 719-635-9548
memberservices@usfigureskating.org
www.usfigureskating.org
• Laura Fawcett, Editor
lfawcett@usfigureskating.org
• Jenny Driscoll, Assistant Editor
jdriscoll@usfsa.org
Frequency:
10 time(s) per year
Description:
Publication features news and profiles from the world of figure skating.

SKI AREA MANAGEMENT
45 MAIN STREET, N.
WOODBURY, CT 06798-2915

203-263-0888
Fax: 203-266-0452
www.saminfo.com
• Jennifer Rowan, Publisher
jenn@saminfo.com
• Olivia Rowan, Associate Publisher
(508) 655-6408
olivia@saminfo.com
• Sharon Walsh, Advertising Manager
(508) 655-6408
sharon@saminfo.com
• Nils Ericksen, Technical Editor
(203) 263-0888
Frequency:
6 time(s) per year
Description:
Publication targets owners and operators of ski resorts; focuses on lift systems, cross-country skiing, trail grooming, risk management, show mailing, marketing, and foodservice.

SKI MAGAZINE
929 PEARL STREET SUITE 200
BOULDER, CO 80302
303-448-7600
Fax: 303-448-7638
editor@skimag.com
www.skimag.com/skimag
• Kendall Hamilton, Editor
(303) 448-7615
• Kim Beekman, Managing Editor
(303) 448-7683
• Samantha Berman, Senior Editor
(303) 448-7600
• Greg Ditrinco, Executive Editor
(303) 448-7641
• Maureen Drummey, Sports Assistant Editor
• Kate Richardson, Assistant
(303) 448-7610
Frequency:
11 time(s) per year
Description:
Ultimate Insiders Guide to Ski Life focusing on travel, family and gear.

SKI PATROL
133 SOUTH VAN GORDON STREET
SUITE 100
LAKEWOOD, CO 80228
303-988-1111
Fax: 303-988-3005
www.nsp.org
• Stephen M. Over, Executive Director
• Jim Schnebly, Assistant Editor
• Wendy Schrupp, Associate Editor
(303) 988-1111
Frequency:
3 time(s) per year

SKI RACING
1830 NORTH 55TH STREET
BOULDER, CO 80301-2700
303-440-0601
800-552-1558
Fax: 303-444-6788
www.skiracing.com
• Eric McCollom, Features Editor
• Don Cameron, Editor-in-Chief
• Andy Hawk, Advertising Manager
(303) 440-0601
• Andy Hawk, Associate Publisher
(303) 440-0601
• Alex Pasquariello, Managing Editor
Frequency:
20 time(s) per year

Description:
Publication is an international journal of ski competition.

SKIER NEWS
P.O. BOX 77327
WEST TRENTON, NJ 08628-6327
609-882-1111
Fax: 609-882-2700
www.skiernews.com
• Dave Leonardi, Publisher
Frequency:
4 time(s) per year
Description:
Publication focuses on timely topics for skiers around the country; includes information on fitness, technical information, and destinations.

SKIING
929 PEARL STREET
BOULDER, CO 80302
303-448-7600
Fax: 303-442-6321
www.skiingmag.com/skiing
• Marc Peruzzi, Editor-in-Chief
(303) 448-7623
• Mike Kessler, Executive Editor
(303) 448-7658
• Jamie Pentz, Publisher
(303) 448-7650
• Evelyn Spence, Articles Editor
(303) 448-7667
Frequency:
7 time(s) per year

SKIING HERITAGE
499 TOWN HILL ROAD
NEW HARTFORD, CT 06057-2516
203-263-2176
Fax: 203-266-0452
www.skiinghistory.org
• Dick Needhan, Editor
Frequency:
3 time(s) per year
Description:
Publication is the official journal of the International Skiing History Association.

SKIING TRADE NEWS
929 PEARL STREET
BOULDER, CO 80302-5108
303-448-7600
Fax: 303-442-6321
www.mountainsportsmedia.com
• Bill Grout, Editor
(303) 448-7663
• Andy Clurman, Publisher
• Andrew Clurman, Publisher
(303) 448-7600
Frequency:
2 time(s) per year
Description:
Publication covers the retail ski industry, ski specialty shops, mass merchandise sporting goods chains, and manufacturers of consumer ski equipment and fashion.

SKYDIVING
1725 NORTH LEXINGTON AVENUE
DELAND, FL 32724-2148
386-736-4793
editor@skydivingmagazine.com
www.skydivingmagazine.com
• Sue Clifton, Editor-in-Chief
sue@skydivingmagazine.com

• Michael Truffer, Publisher
michael@skydivingmagazine.com
Frequency:
1 time(s) per month
Description:
Publication focuses on the equipment, events, people, places, and techniques of sport parachuting.

SLAM
1115 BROADWAY
8TH FLOOR
NEW YORK, NY 10010
212-462-9550
800-333-6411
Fax: 212-620-7787
www.slamonline.com
• Susan Price, Managing Editor
(212) 462-9635
• Robert Jackson, Editor-at-Large
(773) 324-7790
• Ryan Jones, Editor-in-Chief
• Dennis Page, Publisher
(212) 462-9550
• Khalid Salaam, Associate Editor
(212) 462-9659
• Russ Bengtson, Editor-in-Chief
(212) 807-7100
Frequency:
6 time(s) per year
Description:
Publication is a consumer magazine devoted to all aspects of basketball; includes pro, college, high school, and playground ball.

SLAP MAGAZINE
1303 UNDERWOOD AVENUE
SAN FRANCISCO, CA 94124-3308
415-822-3083
888-520-9099
Fax: 415-822-8359
www.slapmagazine.com
• Mark Whitely, Editor
• Eben Sterling, Advertising Director
eben@thrashermagazine.com
Frequency:
1 time(s) per month
Description:
Publication centers around skateboarding; covers youth culture, music, art, fashion, and fun.

SNOW GOER
3300 FERNBROOK LANE
SUITE 200
PLYMOUTH, MN 55447
763-383-4400
800-848-6247
Fax: 763-383-4499
www.snowgoer.com
• Tim Erickson, Editor
(763) 383-4400
• Andy Swanson, Managing Editor
(763) 383-4400
• Mark Rosacker, Associate Publisher
Snow Goer Magazine
The recognized leader in snowmobiling magazines, Snow Goer procides everything the enthusiast wants to know; from how-to modifications, new product evaluations, snowmobile desintations, events, and standings: this is the magazine for snow power sports.

SNOWBOARDER MAGAZINE
33046 CALLE AVIADOR
SAN JUAN CAPISTRANO, CA 92675-4704
949-496-5922
Fax: 949-496-7849
www.snowboardermag.com
• Pat Bridges, Editor
(949) 661-5197
• Mike Nusenow, Publisher
(949) 661-5110
Frequency:
8 time(s) per year
Description:
Publication covers issues of interest to snowboarding enthusiasts.

SNOWEST
360 B STREET
IDAHO FALLS, ID 83402
208-524-7000
800-657-0135
Fax: 208-522-5241
info@snowest.com
www.snowest.com
• Lane Lindstrom, Editor
(208) 542-2234
• Steve Janes, Publisher
(208) 542-2214
• Ryan Harris, Tech Editor
(208) 542-2243
rharris@snowest.com
Frequency:
6 times per year
Description:
Publication contains information on snowmobiling in the western mountains, including vacation ideas, racing coverage, and other winter activities of interest to snowmobile enthusiasts. Specializes in how-to ride, what-to ride and where-to ride in the west.
Circulation:
36,000

SNOWTECH MAGAZINE
630 HIAWATHA CIRCLE NORTH WEST
ALEXANDRIA, MN 56308-8117
320-763-5411
Fax: 320-763-1775
www.snowtechmagazine.com
• Jim Beilke, Editor
jim@snowtechmagazine.com
• Jim Beilke, Publisher
jim@snowtechmagazine.com
• Kevin Beilke, Managing Editor
(320) 763-5411
kevin@snowtechmagazine.com
Frequency:
5 time(s) per year
Description:
Publication provides information on all aspects of snowmobiling.

SOARING
PO BOX 2100
HOBBS, NM 88241-2100
575-392-1177
Fax: 575-392-8154
feedback@ssa.org
www.ssa.org
• Denise Layton, Features Editor
(505) 392-1177
• Denise Layton, Managing Editor
(505) 392-1177
Frequency:
1 time(s) per month
Description:

Publication contains general, safety, technical, and recreational material related to the sport of soaring.

SOCCER CALIFORNIA
12510 NORTH EAST 33RD AVENUE
SUITE 300
SEATTLE, WA 98125
206-367-2420
Fax: 206-367-2636
www.varsitycommunications.com
• Charles Beene, Editor
(206) 367-2420
charles@varsitycommunications.com
Frequency:
6 time(s) per year
Description:
Publication is aimed at soccer coaches and administrators; includes coaching tips and tournament information.

SOCCER IN NEVADA
13540 LAKE CITY WAY N.E. SUITE 3
SEATTLE, WA 98125
206-367-2420
Fax: 206-367-2636
www.varsitycommunications.com
• Andrea Thompson, Editor
(702) 870-3024
usysny@aol.com
Frequency:
4 time(s) per year

SOCCER JR.
557 BROADWAY
NEW YORK, NY 10012 3999
212-343-6830
Fax: 212-343-4808
www.soccerjr.com
• Mark Wright, Editor
(212) 343-6199
• Anthony Guido, Managing Editor
• Bill Kelchner, Publisher
(212) 343-6443
Frequency:
6 time(s) per year
Description:
Publication is written for children ages 8-14 who are active athletes.

SOCCER NEW JERSEY
13540 LAKE CITY WAY N.E. SUITE 3
SEATTLE, WA 98125
206-367-2420
Fax: 206-367-2636
www.varsitycommunications.com
• Charles Beene, Editor
Frequency:
4 time(s) per year

SOCCER NOW
12501 SOUTH ISIS AVENUE
HAWTHORNE, CA 90250-4149
310-643-6455
800-872-2976
Fax: 310-643-5310
soccernow@ayso.org
www.soccer.org
• Melissa Sterzick, Editor
(310) 643-6455
melissasterzick@ayso.org
Frequency:
4 time(s) per year
Description:
Publication focuses on the players and volunteers of the American Youth Soccer

Organization; includes articles on general membership, news, volunteers, players and events in the world of soccer.

SOCCER OHIO SOUTH
4114 198TH STREET SOUTHWEST
SUITE 5
LYNNWOOD, WA 98046-5008
425-412-7070
888-367-6420
Fax: 425-412-7082
stephens@varsitycommunications.com
www.varsitycommunications.com
• Scott Leader, Editor
Frequency:
4 time(s) per year

SOCIOLOGY OF SPORT JOURNAL
1607 N. MARKET ST
CHAMPAIGN, IL 61820
217-351-5076
800-747-4457
Fax: 217-351-2674
www.humankinetics.com
• Jake Jaquet, Journal Director
• Chad Hoffman, Advertising Sales Manager
Publishing Company:
Human Kinetics Publishers, Inc.
Frequency:
Quarterly
Primary Audience:
Association membership, sport sociologists
Sports:
General
Circulation:
997
Description:
Journal of the North American Society for the Sociology of Sport, focuses on the understanding of human behavior within the context of sport and physical activity. Includes research articles on sociology of sport, teaching innovations and research notes and book reviews.

SOUNDINGS
10 BOKUM ROAD
ESSEX, CT 06426-1500
860-767-3200
Fax: 860-767-0642
soundings@soundingspub.com
www.soundingsonline.com
• William Sisson, Editor
(860) 767-3200
sisson@soundingspub.com
• Mark Hoag, Advertising Manager
• Rich Armstrong, Associate Editor
(860) 767-3200
r.armstrong@soundingspub.com
Frequency:
1 time(s) per month
Description:
Publication focuses on recreational boating.

SOUNDINGS:TRADE ONLY
10 BOKUM ROAD
ESSEX, CT 06426-1152
860-767-3200
Fax: 860-767-0642
editorial@tradeonlytoday.com
www.tradeonlytoday.com
• Tom Hubbard, Editor
t.hubbard@tradeonlytoday.com
• Joann Goddard, Staff Writer
j.gaddard@soundingspub.com
• Mark Hoag, Advertising Director
m.hoag@tradeonlytoday.com

• Esther Pope, Editorial Assistant
(860) 767-3200
e.pope@soundingspub.com
• Melanie Winters, Associate Editor
m.winters@tradeonlytoday.com
Frequency:
1 time(s) per month
Description:
Publication contains business news on the boating industry.

SOURCE INTERLINK MEDIA
831 S DOUGLAS STREET
EL SEGUNDO, CA 90245
310-531-5962
Fax: 310-531-9374
www.sourceinterlinkmedia.com
• Rick Stark, Vice President, Sales
(310) 531-5076
• Carol McGovney, Sales Support Manager
(310) 531-5962

SOUTHERN BOATING MAGAZINE
330 NORTH ANDREWS AVENUE
2ND FLOOR
FORT LAUDERDALE, FL 33301
954-522-5515
Fax: 954-522-2260
sboating@southernboating.com
www.southernboating.com
• Marilyn Mower, Editor
(954) 522-5515
marilyn@southernboating.com
• Bill Ando, Senior Editor
(954) 522-5515
bill@southernboating.com
• Kellie Mackenroth, Marketing & Circulation Manager
kellie@southernboating.com
Frequency:
1 time(s) per month
Description:
Publication is geared toward yachtsmen in the southern United States and the Caribbean; focuses on sailing, cruising, maintenance, and destinations.
Primary Audience:
Marine and Boating Industry enthusiasts.

SOUTHERN HORSEMAN
3839 OLD HIGHWAY 45 NORTH
MERIDIAN, MS 39301
601-693-6607
Fax: 903-297-2264
www.southernhorseman.com
• Thelma Thompson, Editor
• Tracy Thompson, Executive Editor
Frequency:
1 time(s) per month
Description:
Publication is dedicated to the horse showman and breeder.

SOUTHERN MOTORACING
1049 NORTHWEST BOULEVARD
WINSTON-SALEM, NC 27101-1171
336-723-5227
Fax: 336-722-3757
• Hank Schoolfield, Editor
• Hank Schoolfield, Publisher
• Don Wilson, General Manager
Frequency:
25 time(s) per year
Description:
Publication focuses on stock car racing.

SOUTHWEST HORSE TRACK
P.O. BOX 222
MORGAN MILL, TX 76465
254-965-9667
Fax: 254-965-3936
www.trackmagazine.com
• Ben Hudson, Editor
• Ben Hudson, Publisher
Frequency:
11 time(s) per year
Description:
Publication focuses on racing news, breeding, and training.

SPECIAL EVENTS MAGAZINE
23805 STUART RANCH RD, STE 235
MALIBU, CA 90265
310-317-4522
800-543-4116
Fax: 310-317-9644
www.specialevents.com
• Lisa Perrin, Publisher
• Lisa Hurley, Editor
• Natasha Garber, Senior Editor
• Cindy Dell'Amico, West/Midwest Sales Manager
• Diane McGee, East Coast Sales Manager
Frequency:
Monthly
Primary Audience:
Individuals and companies involved in producing and/or managing events
Sports:
General
Circulation:
25,675
Description:
Focuses on hospitality activities related to events, including sports events.

SPEEDHORSE-THE RACING REPORT
1903 48TH AVENUE
NORMAN, OK 73072
405-573-1050
Fax: 405-573-1059
speedhorse@coxinet.net
www.speedhorsemagazine.com
• Andrew Golden, Editor-in-Chief
• Andrew Golden, Advertising Manager
• Connie Golden, Publisher
Frequency:
1 time(s) per week
Description:
Publication is for Quarter horse racing owners and breeders.

SPONSORSHIP REPORT
PO BOX 378
STATION MAIN
CAMPBELLFORD, CANADA K0L 1L0
705-653-1112
Fax: 705-653-1113
www.sponsorship.ca
• Mark Sabourin, Publisher/Editor
Sports Service Founded:
1988
Primary Audience:
Sponsoring companies, advertising agencies, sports marketers, etc.
Sports:
General.
Description:
The aim of the newsletter is to foster successful partnerships between Canadian corporations and arts groups, sports organizations, charities, government initiatives, events, and festivals.

SPONSORVISION
39 VISTA MIRAGE WAY
RANCHO MIRAGE, CA 92270
253-223-9119
Fax: 253-566-6771
• Michael Jensen, Chief Executive Officer
Sports Service Founded:
1995
Nature of Sports Service:
Publisher of comprehensive sponsorship marketing publications and printed resources to for-profit and nonprofit corporations, organizations, agencies, foundations, events and venues internationally

SPORT HISTORY REVIEW
1607 NORTH MARKET STREET
CHAMPAIGN, IL 61820
217-351-5076
800-747-4457
Fax: 217-351-2674
journals@hkusa.com
www.humankinetics.com
• Don Morrow, Editor
(519) 661-4128
donmor@uwo.ca
• Rainer Martens, Publisher
rainerm@hkusa.com
• Rohn Koester, Managing Editor
(217) 351-5076
Frequency:
2 time(s) per year
Description:
Publication is devoted to promoting the study of all facets of sports.

SPORT JOURNAL
ONE ACADEMY DRIVE
DAPHNE, AL 36526
251-626-3303
Fax: 251-626-8829
sportjournal@ussa.edu
www.thesportjournal.org
• Thomas P Rosandich, Publisher
president@ussa.edu
• Kelly E Flanagan, Editor
• Jordan Moon, Associate Editor
jmoon@ussa.edu
Frequency:
4 time(s) per year
Description:
The Sport Journal, is a publication of the United State Sports Academy. It is designed to further the knowledge of sport by allowing professionals in the field to publish articles at this site.

SPORT PSYCHOLOGIST
1607 N. MARKET ST
CHAMPAIGN, IL 61820
217-351-5076
800-747-4457
Fax: 217-351-2674
www.humankinetics.com
• Jake Jaquez, Journal Director
• Chad Hoffman, Advertising Sales Manager
Publishing Company:
Human Kinetics Publishers, Inc.
Frequency:
Quarterly
Primary Audience:
Sport psychologists, coaches, trainers
Sports:
General
Circulation:
1,205

Description:
Journal of the International Society of Sport Psychology. Provides forum for dissemination of applied sport psychology information to practitioners. This journal will focus on issues pertaining to application of this information to coaches and athletes. International in scope and receptive to nontraditional or nonscientific methodologies.

SPORT SCENE:FOCUS ON YOUTH PROGRAMS
PO BOX 140
HUDDLESTON, VA 24104
336-407-2157
800-767-4916
www.naysi.com
• Jack Hutslar, Publisher/Editor
• Sally Hutslar, Education Consultant
• Roman Perez Villejo, Mexico
Description:
Focus on youth programs. Consulting services. Program development objectives. Training. Management ideas. Leadership & Coaching. Program expansion. Lectures. For leaders and parents who work with tots, children and teens. All sports. Youth development. Latest methods, Do's and Don'ts, Safety, Fitness, Health. Mission is to help make sport, recreation, fitness and youth activities more positive.
Circulation:
1,000-15,000. 70% paid by NAYSI, 10% paid subscr, 20% other.
Sports:
General
Primary Audience:
Youth leaders, coaches, teachers, parents, community leaders involved with tots, children and teens
Frequency:
Quarterly or more frequently as direct mail piece for business and industry
Publishing Company:
North American Youth Sport Institute
Founded:
1979

SPORT SUPPLEMENT
ONE ACADEMY DRIVE
DAPHNE, AL 36526
251-626-3303
Fax: 251-626-8829
aodom@ussa.edu
sportsupplement.org/
• Thomas P. Rosandich, Publisher
(251) 626-3303
• Brian Wallace, Assistant Editor
(251) 626-3303
bwallace@ussa.edu
• Enrico Esposito, Editor
(251) 626-3303
Frequency:
4 time(s) per year
Description:
The Sport Supplement, an electronic document, is a publication of the United States Sports Academy. It is designed to further knowledge about issues of sport, fitness and health for professionals as well as anyone seeking knowledge and information in this field.

SPORTBUSINESS GROUP
ELIZABETH HOUSE
39 YORK RD, 6TH FL
LONDON, ENGLAND SE1 7NQ
copydesk@sportbusiness.com
www.sportbusiness.com
• Ben Cawford, Managing Director
• Kevin Roberts, Managing Editor
• Richard Rusell, Editorial
Director/Broadcast
Description:
International coverage of news about
sponsorship, marketing agencies, sports
facilities, sports events and sanctioning
bodies, sports broadcasting developments,
athletes, sports business personalities, and
sports event sites.
Publishing Company:
Sport Business International

SPORTING GOODS BUSINESS
770 BROADWAY
NEW YORK, NY 10003
800-562-2706
Fax: 646-654-5365
www.adweek.com
• Hilary Cassidy, Environmental Reporter
(800) 562-2706
• Mark Sullivan, Group Publisher
(646) 654-4981
• Robert E. Carr, ISG News Editor
(646) 654-4997
• Judy Leand, Executive Editor
(800) 562-2706
• Cara Griffin, Managing Editor
(646) 654-5006
cgriffin@sportsonesource.com
• Tom Ryan, Business/Licensing Editor
(646) 654-5384
Publishing Company:
VNU.
Frequency:
Monthly.
Primary Audience:
Sporting Goods Trade.

SPORTING GOODS INTELLIGENCE
442 FEATHERBED LANE
GLEN MILLS, PA 19342
610-459-4040
800-328-6397
Fax: 610-459-4010
www.sginews.com
• Jon Bogert, Editor
Frequency:
Weekly/Daily
Description:
Publication features news and analysis
concerning the international sporting goods
industry.

SPORTING KID MAGAZINE
240 PROSPECT PL
UNIT E1
ALPHARETTA, GA 30005
678-297-3903
Fax: 678-297-0704
• Tina D'Aversa-Williams, Publisher
• Michael J. Pallerino, Editor

SPORTING NEWS
10176 CORPORATE SQUARE DRIVE
SAINT LOUIS, MO 63132-2924
314-997-7111
Fax: 314-997-0765
editors@sportingnews.com
www.sportingnews.com

• Steve Greeberg, Managing Editor
• John D. Rawlings, Editorial Director
• Ken Rosenthal, Sports Senior Writer
(410) 602-8193
• Pete Spina, Publisher
(646) 424-2227
Frequency:
1 time(s) per week
Description:
Publication is a sports weekly focusing on
baseball, football, basketball, and hockey
coverage.

SPORTING NEWS
10176 CORPORATE SQUARE DR
#200
ST. LOUIS, MO 63132-2924
314-997-7111
Fax: 314-997-0765
www.sportingnews.com
• C. Richard Allen, President and Chief
Executive Officer
• John D. Rawlings, Senior Vice
President/Editorial Director
• Peter A. Spina, Vice President/Publisher
Publishing Company:
The Sporting News
Frequency:
Weekly
Primary Audience:
Consumer
Sports:
Major League Baseball, College and Pro
Football, College and Pro Basketball, Pro
Hockey and NASCAR.
Circulation:
600,000. 95% paid subscr, 5% newsstand.
Description:
Features and articles of interest to sports
fans, including statistical summaries,
updates of trades, etc.

SPORTS 'N SPOKES MAGAZINE
2111 E. HIGHLAND, STE 180
PHOENIX, AZ 85016-4702
602-224-0500
888-888-2201
Fax: 602-224-0507
snsmagaz@aol.com
www.sportsnspokes.com
• Cliff Crase, Editor
• Sherri Shea, Marketing Director
Publishing Company:
Paralyzed Veterans of America
Frequency:
8X per year.
Primary Audience:
Consumer
Sports:
Wheelchair sports
Circulation:
10,000
Description:
Covers wheelchair competitive sports and
recreation primarily for the spinal cord
injured, amputee or polio, plus some
congenital defects; cerebral palsy, spina
bifida.

SPORTS AFIELD
15621 CHEMICAL LANE
HUNTINGTON BEACH, CA 92649
714-373-4910
Fax: 714-894-4949
letters@sportsafield.com
www.sportsafield.com

• Diana Rupp, Editor-in-Chief
(714) 373-4910
letters@sportsafield.com
• Sid Evans, Editor
(714) 373-4910
letters@sportsafield.com
• Ludo J. Wurfbain, Chief Eexecutive Officer
Field Sports Publicat
(714) 373-4910
Publishing Company:
Field Sports Publications.
Frequency:
9 times a year.
Circulation:
50,000.
Nature of Service:
Magazine.
Primary AudienceL
Men 35-65.
Sports:
Hunting.

SPORTS ARIZONA MAGAZINE
67 EAST WELDON AVENUE SUITE 240
PHOENIX, AZ 85012
480-970-6999
888-553-7979
Fax: 602-279-8061
www.sportsaz.com
• Curt Blakeney, Editor
(602) 279-6375
• Joel Harnett, Publisher
Frequency:
6 time(s) per year
Description:
Publication focuses on professional, college,
and amateur sports of all kinds in Arizona.

SPORTS BUSINESS JOURNAL
1166 AVENUE OF THE AMERICAS
14TH FLOOR
NEW YORK, NY 10036
212-500-0700
Fax: 212-500-0701
• Abraham Madkour, Executive Editor
(704) 973-1511
amadkour@sportsbusinessjournal.com
• Ross Nethery, Managing Editor
(704) 973-1437
methery@sportsbusinessjournal.com
• Rob Knapp, Assistant Managing
Editor/News
(704) 973-1416
rknapp@sportsbusinessjournal.com
• David Bourne, Special Reports Editor
(704) 973-1417
dbourne@sportsbusinessjournal.com
Description:
Sports Business Journal provides coverage
of the deals, trades, contracts, and
boardroom power plays that shape the
rapidly changing sports landscape. Regular
columns cover every aspect of the industry,
from media and marketing to finance,
facilities, and labor.
Founded:
In 1999.

SPORTS COLLECTORS DIGEST
700 EAST STATE STREET
IOLA, WI 54990
715-445-2214
888-457-2873
Fax: 715-445-4087
www.krause.com

- Dean Listle, Publisher and Advertising Director
- TS O'Connell, Editor

Publishing Company:
Krause Publications, Inc.
Frequency:
Weekly
Primary Audience:
Consumer/Trade
Sports:
All sports
Circulation:
48,000
Description:
Covers news of the collecting hobby with special focus for the dealer, investor and advanced collector. Marketplace offers widest variety of sports collectibles and baseball cards available. Includes columns, sports card show listings and updated sports card price guide in each issue.

SPORTS EDGE MAGAZINE
240 PROSPECT PL
UNIT E1
ALPHARETTA, GA 30005
678-297-3903
Fax: 678-297-0704
www.sportsedgemag.com
- Tina D'Aversa-Williams, Publisher
- Michael J. Pallerino, Editor
- John Agoglia, Fitness Editor
- Roy Wallack, Outdoor Editor
- Mike Fickes, Retail Editor
- Dinah Ledford, Circulation & Reader Service Manager

SPORTS ILLUSTRATED
TIME-LIFE BUILDING
NEW YORK, NY 10020-1393
212-522-1212
Fax: 212-522-4543
www.si.com
- Terry McDonell, Managing Editor
(212) 522-1650
- Connie Aitcheson, Reporter
(212) 522-1212
- Kelli Anderson, Senior Writer
(212) 522-1212
- Lars Anderson, Staff Writer
(212) 522-7510
- Chris Ballard, Staff Writer
(212) 522-2665
- Michael Bamberger, Senior Writer
(212) 522-0028
- Michael Bamberger, Sports Senior Writer
(212) 522-0028
- David Bauer, Deputy Managing Editor
(212) 522-2210
- Mark Bechtel, Senior Editor
(212) 522-1278
- Michael Bevans, Executive Editor
(212) 522-3334
- Trisha Blackmar, Associate Editor
(212) 522-0073
- John Ed Bradley, Special Contributor
(212) 522-2747
- Sheila Buckley, Publisher
- Larry Burke, Sports Senior Editor
(212) 522-1130
- Stephen Cannella, Senior Editor
(212) 522-1212
- Stephen Cannella, Staff Writer
- Brian Cazeneuve, Staff Writer
(212) 522-8227
brian_cazeneuve@time-inc.com
- Brian Cazeneuve, Staff Writer
(212) 522-8227

- Jeffri Chadiha, Senior Writer
(212) 522-1212
- Bobby Clay, Senior Editor
(212) 522-1212
- Seth Davis, Staff Writer
(212) 522-6431
- Frank Deford, Senior Contributing Editor
(212) 522-1212
- Richard Deitsch, Special Projects Editor
(212) 522-2929
- Richard Demak, Chief of Reporters & Senior Editor
(212) 522-3962
- Nunyo Demasio, Staff Writer
- George Dohrmann, Staff Writer
(212) 522-1212
- Michael Farber, Senior Writer
(212) 522-4165
- Luis Fernando Llosa, Reporter
(212) 522-0847
- Rob Fleder, Sports Executive Editor
(212) 522-8388
- Dick Friedman, Senior Editor
(212) 522-1212
dick_friedman@time-inc.com
Frequency:
1 time(s) per week
Description:
Publication is devoted to total in depth sports news coverage through articles, interviews, and photography. Also provided is information on recreation and leisure activities for both participants and spectators

SPORTS ILLUSTRATED FOR KIDS
135 WEST 50TH STREET
NEW YORK, NY 10020
212-522-3112
Fax: 212-467-1669
www.sikids.com
- Norman Pearlstine, Editor
- Andre Carter, Chief Reporter
(212) 522-0402
andre_carter@timeinc.com
- Andre Carter, Sports Reporter
- Neil Cohen, Managing Editor
(212) 522-4876
- Ellen Cosgrove-Labrecque, Sports Associate Editor
(212) 522-8164
- Jerry Craft, Editorial Director
- Erin Egan, Sports Senior Editor
(212) 522-5829
- Gary Gramling, Editorial Assistant
- Scott Hendrickson, Advertising Director
- Bill Hinds, Contributing Writer
(212) 522-3112
- Ted Keith, Sports Reporter
- Peter King, Assistant Managing Editor
- Peter King, Sports Ass't Managing Editor
- Shawn Nicholls, Associate Producer
(212) 522-3112
- Timothy Pitt, Editorial Director
- John Rolfe, Senior Editor
(212) 522-1847
- Sachin Shenolikar, Chief of Reporters
- Justin Tejada, Senior Editor/SI Kids.com
(212) 522-5829
justin_tejada@timeinc.com
- Justin Tejada, Editor
(212) 522-8853
- David Watt, Publisher
(212) 522-7789
dave_watt@timeinc.com
Frequency:
13 time(s) per year
Description:

Publication is a sports magazine for young people ages 8-14.

SPORTS JOURNAL
UNITED STATES SPORTS ACADEMY
ONE ACADEMY DRIVE
DAPHNE, AL 36526-7055
251-626-3303
Fax: 251-626-3874
- Thomas P. Rosandich, Publisher
(251) 626-3303
- Kelly Flanagan, Assistant Editor
(251) 626-3303
Description:
An electronic journal, is a publication of the United States Sports Academy in cooperation with the International Coaches Association and the International Association of Sports Academies. It is designed to further the knowledge of sport by allowing professionals in the field to publish articles at this site.

SPORTS MARKETING LETTER COMPANY
89 PAUL PL
FARFIELD, CT 06824
203-259-3890
- Brian J. Murphy, Publisher/Editor
Description:
Publishes the daily email briefing Sports Industry Daily, covering all aspects of the sports industry, and allied industries.
Circulation:
NA.
Sports:
All
Primary Audience:
High level executives in sports related industry.
Frequency:
Daily
Publishing Company:
Published by the The Sports Marketing Letter Company.

SPORTS PAGES
THE OAST HOUSE
PARK ROW
FARNHAM, SURREY, ENGLAND GU9 7JH
+44-1252 737333
Fax: +44-1252 737333
info@sportspages.com
www.sportspages.com
- Rich Johnson, Chief Editorial Officer
- Rick Scott, Chief Executive Officer
Sports Service Founded:
1997
Nature of Sports Service:
Online collection of articles and direct links to the sports sections of the major papers in the U.S. and those in and around cities with major league professional teams.

SPORTS PROFILES
4711 GOLF ROAD
SUITE 900
SKOKIE, IL 60076
800-725-9423
800-725-9423 ext 10
info@sppsports.com
- Lisa Levine, President
- Allen Redman, Chief Financial Officer
- Deborah Levine, Vice President

SPORTS REPORTER
527 THIRD AVE (3RD AVE)
BOX 327
NEW YORK, NY 10016
800-305-9604
Fax: 212-683.-1012
• Joe Lazzaro, Editor
Description:
Provides in-depth analysis of all football and basketball games.
Circulation:
30,000
Sports:
Football, basketball, baseball
Primary Audience:
Consumer
Frequency:
Weekly
Publishing Company:
Sports Reporter

SPORTS TRAVELER
1803 WEST 95TH ST., STE 101
CHICAGO, IL 60643
888-654-7755
Fax: 773-881-0389
www.sportstraveler.net
• Anbritt Stengele, Owner
Primary Audience:
Women interested in outdoor-oriented sports
Frequency:
6 times annually
Publishing Company:
Sports Traveler
Advertising Sales Office:
101 E. 52nd St, 9th Floor, New York, NY 10022. 212 759-1357; FAX: 212 759-1282

SPORTSCAR
16842 VON KARMAN AVENUE SUITE 125
IRVINE, CA 92606
949-417-6700
800-722-7140
Fax: 714-259-1502
sportscar@racer.com
www.racer.com
• Richard James, Editor
rjames@racer.com
• Celia Shambaugh, Advertising Manager
(949) 417-6700
cshambaugh@racer.com
Frequency:
1 time(s) per month
Description:
Publication reports on the motor sports activities of the membership, including event reports, results, photos of professional racing, amateur road racing, and road rallies.

SPORTSONE SOURCE
2151 HAWKINS STREET
SUITE 200
CHARLOTTE, NC 28203
704-987-3450
800-950-1314
Fax: 704-987-3455
www.sgdealer.com
• Bob Carr, Editor
(646) 654-4997
Frequency:
1 time(s) per week
Description:
Publication contains marketing and financial news for the sporting goods industry.

SPORTSTRAVEL MAGAZINE
11835 W. OLYMPIC BLVD #1265
LOS ANGELES, CA 90064
310-577-3700
877-577-3700
Fax: 310-577-3715
info@schneiderpublishing.com
www.schneiderpublishing.com
• Timothy Schneider, Publisher
tim.schneider@schneiderpublishing.com
• Lisa Furfine, Associate Publisher
• Jason Gewirtz, Managing Editor
• Rita Burris, Client Services Manager
(877) 577-3700
• Martha Romero, Office Manager
(877) 577-3700
Year Founded:
1997
Nature of Sports Service:
Publishers of SportsTravel and Association News magazines and producers of the TEAMS Conference & Expo.
Circulation:
16,000+
Frequency:
10 time(s) per year

SQUASH MAGAZINE
6001 1ST AVENUE
SUITE 500
SEATTLE, WA 98104
206-748-0085
Fax: 206-748-0277
www.squashmagazine.com
• Jay D. Prince, Publisher
editor@squashmagazine.com
• Ryan Lewis, Director of Operations
ryan@squashmagazine.com
• Paul Hueregue, Design Director
• James Zug, Senior Writer
Description:
The magazine for the sport of Squash.

STADIA MAGAZINE
THE GRAIN STORE
127 GLOUCESTER RD
BRIGHTON, ENGLAND BN1 4AF
44-(0) 1273 601-900
Fax: 44-(0) 1273 601 973
www.stadia.tv
• Ian Nuttall, Managing Director
• Sam Wibrew, Publications Director
• Tim Sewell, Publications Manager
• Mark Bisson, Deputy Editor
Publishing Company:
Broadcast Publishing Ltd.
Frequency:
Quarterly.

STEELERS DIGEST
3000 SOUTHWEST 148TH AVENUE
SUITE 112
MIRAMAR, FL 33027-4181
305-594-0508
800-334-4005
Fax: 305-594-0518
digest@curtispub.net
www.steelersdigestonline.com
• Andrew Cohen, Co-Editor
(412) 481-1846
• Thomas Curtis, Publisher
newtcurtis@curtispub.net
• Bob Labriola, Co-Editor
(412) 481-1846
Frequency:
26 time(s) per year
Description:

Publication is a sports magazine devoted to the Pittsburgh Steelers.

STOCK CAR RACING
9036 BRITTANY WAY
TAMPA, FL 33619
863-644-0449
800-333-2633
Fax: 813-675-3559
www.primedia.com
• Larry Cothren, Editor
• Jana Huss, Managing Editor
(813) 675-3529
Frequency:
1 time(s) per month
Description:
Publication reports on stock car racing; includes personality profiles, technical articles, and race reports.

STRATEGIES: A JOURNAL FOR PHYSICAL AND SPORT ED
1900 ASSOCIATION DRIVE
RESTON, VA 20191-1599
703-476-3400
800-213-7193
Fax: 703-476-8316
strategies@aahperd.org
www.aahperd.org
• Carrie Nygaard, Editor
(703) 476-3451
Frequency:
6 time(s) per year
Description:
Publication provides how-to information for physical and sport educators.

STREET & SMITH'S SPORTSBUSINESS DAILY
120 W MOREHEAD STREET
SUITE 104
CHARLOTTE, NC 28202
704-973-1515
Fax: 704-973-1501
editorial@sportsbusinessdaily.com
www.sportsbusinessdaily.com
• Abraham Madkour, Executive Editor
(704) 973-1511
• Rick Ellington, Managing Editor
(704) 973-1528
rellington@sportsbusinessdaily.com
• Bill Magrath, Media Relations Manager
(704) 973-1515
billm@sportsbusinessdaily.com
• Beverly Padgett, Director of Circulation
(704) 973-1455
bpadgett@sportsbusinessdaily.com
Publishing Company:
Street & Smith's Sports Group.
Frequency:
Daily
Sports:
Sports Business - all sports.
Circulation:
30,000
Nature of Services:
We provide decision-makers in the sports industry with comprehensive, real-time Sports Business News, summarizes industry news reported by more than 500 media outlets in the U.S. and abroad. We also offer relevant original features of in-depth analysis of the industry's latest trends.
Publications:
Morning Buzz; Closing Bell; Sports Business Daily.

STREET & SMITH'S SPORTS GEAR
120 W. MOREHEAD STREET
CHARLOTTE, NC 28202-1844
704-973-1300
Fax: 704-973-1576
annuals@streetandsmiths.com
www.streetandsmiths.com
• Mike Kallay, Publisher
• Scott Smith, Managing Editor
• Patrick Wood, Advertising Director
• Amy Taylor, Senior Marketing Manager
• Jim Penegar, Circulation General Manager
Description:
Brings you great-looking sport collectibles that you can use at home, at the office or at the tailgate.

STREET & SMITH'S SPORTSBUSINESS JOURNAL
120 W. MOREHEAD STREET
SUITE 310
CHARLOTTE, NC 28202
704-973-1400
800-829-9839
Fax: 704-973-1401
help@sportsbusinessjournal.com
www.sportsbusinessjournal.com
• Richard Weiss, Publisher
(704) 973-1410
rweiss@sportsbusinessjournal.com
• Abraham Madkour, Executive Editor
(704) 973-1511
amadkour@sportsbusinessjournal.com
• Jerry Kavanagh, New York Bureau Chief
(212) 500-0714
jkavanagh@sportsbusinessjournal.com
• Martin Bounds, VP Business Development
(704) 973-1413
mbounds@sportsbusinessjournal.com
• Paige Montgomery, Circulation Director
(212) 500-0710
pmontgomery@sportsbusinessjournal.com
• Tom Stinson, Assistant Managing Editor
(704) 973-1424
tstinson@sportsbusinessjournal.com
• David Broughton, Research Director
(704) 973-1433
dbroughton@sportsbusinessjournal.com
• Mark Mensheha, Assistant Managing Editor
(704) 973-1427
mmensheha@sportsbusinessjournal.com
• Jake Kyler, Copy Editor
(704) 973-1436
jkyler@sportsbusinessjournal.com
• Rob Knapp, Assistant Managing Editor/News
(704) 973-1416
rknapp@sportsbusinessjournal.com
Publishing Company:
Street & Smith Sport Group.
Frequency:
49 times a year; Audience 54,400; Annual subscription $254 USD.
Primary Audience:
Sports industry executives, business executives, team leagues and broadcast media.
Sports:
All.
Nature of Service:
Sports Business Journal provides the critical news and information sports industry leaders need to complete, negotiate and succeed. Every issue features coverage of the deals, trades, contracts and board room power plays that shape the rapidly changing sports industry. Regular columns cover

every aspect of the sports industry from media and marketing to finance and facilities.
Circulation:
17,000

STRIKER-WEST
13540 LAKE CITY WAY, N.E. SUITE 3
SEATTLE, WA 98125-3665
607-962-9923
Fax: 206-367-2636
www.varsitycommunications.com
• Charles Beene, Editor
(607) 962-9923
Frequency:
4 time(s) per year
Description:
Publication is the official magazine of the New York State West Youth Soccer Association; contains association news, coaching tips, and tournament updates.

STUDENT SPORTS
2780 SKYPARK DRIVE
TORRANCE, CA 90505
310-791-1142
800-660-1334
Fax: 310-257-4444
www.studentsports.com
• Mark Tennis, Editor
(209) 463-9050
• Andy Bark, Publisher
• Mark Tennis, Editorial Vice President
(209) 463-9050
• Brent Eads, Editor
(310) 791-1142
Frequency:
10 time(s) per year
Description:
Publication covers sports at the high school level.

SURF NEWS
485 EAST 17TH STREET SUITE 202
COSTA MESA, CA 92627
949-548-6740
Fax: 949-548-5572
surfnewsed@aol.com
• Bill Sharp, Editor
• Bill Sharp, Publisher
Frequency:
1 time(s) per month
Description:
Publication focuses on the beach lifestyle in Southern California; geared toward surfers, as well as people who enjoy the beach.

SURFER
33046 CALLE AVIADOR
SAN JUAN CAPISTRANO, CA 92675-4704
949-496-5922
Fax: 949-496-7849
www.surfermag.com
• Chris Mauro, Editor
(949) 661-5115
• Jake Howard, Associate Editor
(949) 661-5130
• Rick Irons, Publisher
(949) 661-5112
Frequency:
1 time(s) per month
Description:
Publication focuses on information of interest to surfing enthusiasts.

SURFER TRAVEL REPORT
33046 CALLE AVIADOR
SAN JUAN CAPISTRANO, CA 92675-4704
949-496-5922
Fax: 949-496-7849
www.surfermag.com
• Luke Seile, Editor
(949) 661-5108
Frequency:
1 time(s) per month
Description:
Publication is a travel guide for surfers.

SURFING
950 CALLE AMANECER SUITE C
SAN CLEMENTE, CA 92673
949-492-7873
Fax: 949-498-6485
www.surfingthemag.com
• Don Meek, Publisher
• Hagan Kelley, Associate Editor
• James Lynch, Advertising Manager
Frequency:
1 time(s) per month
Description:
Publication provides information on equipment, destinations, and competitions for surfers.

SWIMMING WORLD & JUNIOR SWIMMER
2744 EAST GLENROSA AVENUE
PHOENIX, AZ 85015
928-284-4005
800-345-7946
Fax: 928-284-2477
swimworld@swiminfo.com
www.swiminfo.com
• Bob Ingram, Editor
bobi@swiminfo.com
• Toni Blake, Advertising Manager
(310) 379-2278
• Richard Deal, Publisher
• Phillip Whitten, Editor-in-Chief
(480) 874-9364
philw@swiminfo.com
Frequency:
1 time(s) per month
Description:
Publication contains information of interest to children and young adults involved in competitive swimming.

T & L GOLF
1120 AVENUE OF THE AMERICAS 11TH FLOOR
NEW YORK, NY 10036-6700
212-642-1965
Fax: 212-642-1960
www.tlgolf.com
• Jonathan Lesser, Editor
(212) 642-1934
• John Atwood, Editor
• John Atwood, Editor-in-Chief
• Felice Kaplan, Managing Editor
(212) 382-1965
• Jonathan Lesser, Sports Associate Editor
(212) 642-1934
• John P. Newport, Sports Senior Editor
(212) 642-1938
• John Rodenburg, Publisher
(212) 536-2030
Frequency:
6 time(s) per year
Description:
Publication contains information for golfers who also appreciate fine living and elegance.

TEAM MARKETING REPORT
660 WEST GRAND AVENUE
CHICAGO, IL 60611
312-829-7060
Fax: 847-256-2594
tmr.nelix.com/Resources.asp
• Dan Migala, Executive Editor
(312) 202-6551
• Michael Lane, Managing Editor
• Kurt Hunzeker, Director of Business
Development and Marketin
• Meghann Dunlap, Project Manager
Publishing Company:
Team Marketing Report Inc.
Frequency:
Monthly
Primary Audience:
Sports teams, sports venues, sports
TV/radio sales execs, sports marketing
agencies, corporate sponsors, auto
racing/tennis/golf promoters
Sports:
Professional and Collegiate Sports
Circulation:
NA.
Description:
Monthly newsletter reporting innovative and
successful marketing activities of sports
marketers, corporate sponsors and sports
marketing agencies. Provides in-depth
details of new ideas to help marketers,
sponsors and agencies increase sales and
exposure through sports marketing.
Exclusive and original research advertising
rates, ticket prices and examining consumer
attitudes towards sports and sponsors
included in each issue. Other features
include columns by prominent sports
marketing executives, sponsor news,
personnel changes within the sports
marketing field.

TENNIS
79 MADISON AVENUE 8TH FLOOR
NEW YORK, NY 10016
212-636-2700
Fax: 212-636-2720
editors@tennis.com
www.tennis.com
• Stephen Tignor, Managing Editor
stignor@tennismagazine.com
• Peter Bodo, Senior Editor
(212) 636-2714
• Chris Evert, Publisher
cevert@tennismagazine.com
• Norb Garrett, Editorial Director
ngarrett@tennismagazine.com
• Tony Lance, Associate Editor
(212) 636-2731
• Jon Levey, Senior Editor
(212) 636-2719
jlevey@tennis.com
• James Martin, Senior Editor
(212) 636-2708
jmartin@tennismagazine.com
• Jeff Williams, Publisher
jwilliams@tennismagazine.com
• Mark Woodruff, Editor-at-Large
Frequency:
1 time(s) per month
Description:
Publication features information of interest
to tennis enthusiasts.

TEXAS COACH
2553 HIGHWAY 35, S.
SAN MARCOS, TX 78666

512-392-3741
Fax: 512-392-3762
www.thsca.com
• Sheryl Honeycutt, Editor
(512) 392-3741
sherylhoneycutt@thsca.com
Frequency:
9 time(s) per year
Description:
Publication is geared toward coaches at
educational institutions throughout Texas.

TEXAS COACH MAGAZINE
1011 E. 53 1/2 ST
AUSTIN, TX 78751
512-454-6709
Fax: 512-454-3950
www.thsca.com
• Sheryl Honeycutt, Editor
Publishing Company:
Texas High School Coaches Association
Frequency:
Nine times annually
Primary Audience:
Texas high school coaches and coaches in
neighboring states
Sports:
General
Circulation:
16,200. 81% association membership, 19%
non-paid contr.
Description:
Concerned with coach's job as a coach in
his or her sport as well as to make the
coaching profession more professional.
Editorial covers all phases of each sport.

TEXAS FOOTBALL
546 E. MAIN STREET
LEXINGTON, KY 40505
859-226-4678
Fax: 859-226-4567
• Logan Lawton, Collegiate Sports Director
(859) 226-4342
• David Nunnery, Print Advertising Director
(859) 226-4678
• Matt Briggs, Circulation/Fulfillment
Specialist
(866) 313-4678
• Adam Hochfelder, Magazine Executive
Director
(888) 484-4678
• Jake Shaw, Managing Editor
(972) 392-5849
Description:
Sports magazine in the State of Texas that
covers all levels of football programs in the
Lone Star State whether it be High School
Level, College Level, Or Professional Level.
Frequency:
Annually.

TEXAS GOLFER MAGAZINE
4920 CENTER STREET
HOUSTON, TX 77027
877-536-1088
Fax: 713-680-0138
www.texasgolfermagazine.com
• Wayne Morkovsky, Editor
Frequency:
1 time(s) per month
Description:
Publication provides tournament and
competition information about golf in
southern Texas.

TEXAS RUNNER & TRIATHLETE
713-935-0555
Fax: 713-935-0559
www.texasrunnertriathlete.com
• Lance Phegley, Editor
Frequency:
1 time(s) per month
Primary Audience:
Runners and triathletes
Circulation:
6,000

TEXAS THOROUGHBRED
1016 LA POSADA SUITE 130
AUSTIN, TX 78752
512-458-6133
Fax: 512-453-5919
denisb@texasthoroughbred.com
www.texasthoroughbred.com
• Denis Blake, Editor
• David Hooper, Executive Director
davidh@texasthoroughbred.com
• Judy Rosson, Advertising Manager
(512) 458-6133
judyr@texasthoroughbred.com
Frequency:
9 time(s) per year
Description:
Publication contains information of interest
to Thoroughbred horse breeders, trainers,
and racing in the state of Texas.

THE AMERICAN JOURNAL OF SPORTS MEDICINE
• Bruce Reider, Editor
Description:
First published in 1972, the Journal is the
official publication of AOSSM.

THRASHER SKATEBOARD MAGAZINE
1303 UNDERWOOD AVENUE
SAN FRANCISCO, CA 94124-3308
415-822-3083
888-520-9099
Fax: 415-822-8359
mail@thrashermagazine.com
www.thrashermagazine.com
• Jake Phelps, Editor
jake@thrashermagazine.com
• Dean Huitrado, Advertising Director
dean@slapmagazine.com
• Edward H. Riggins, Publisher
• Eben Sterling, Advertising Director
eben@thrashermagazine.com
Frequency:
1 time(s) per month
Description:
Publication fuses on the excitement of
top-level skateboarding with reader
participation, hard edged music, and lots of
attitude.

TOUCHLINE-EASTERN PENNSYLVANIA
13540 LAKE CITY WAY N.E. SUITE 3
SEATTLE, WA 98125-3665
206-367-2420
Fax: 206-363-9099
www.varsitycommunications.com
• Charles Beene, Editor
(206) 367-2420
• Peter Paige, Publisher
(215) 321-9822
repete@paige2.com
Frequency:
4 time(s) per year
Description:
Publication features articles that bring

readers reliable news and information about soccer.

TRACK & FIELD NEWS
2570 W. EL CAMINO REAL
SUITE 480
MOUNTAIN VIEW, CA 94040-1306
650-948-8188
Fax: 650-948-9445
business@trackandfieldnews.com
www.trackandfieldnews.com
• E. Garry Hill, Editor
(650) 948-8188
gh@trackandfieldnews.com
• Ed Fox, Publisher
ef@trackandfieldnews.com
• Jon Hendershott, Associate Editor
• Tom Jordan, Advertising Manager
• Sieg Lindstrom, Managing Editor
(650) 948-8188
sl@trackandfieldnews.com
• Janet Vitu, Publisher
Frequency:
1 time(s) per month
Description:
Publication covers all track events from high school to the Olympics; includes news and results of major meets; interviews with leading athletes, profiles, photos, performance lists, records, rankings and opinion columns.

TRACK COACH
2570 EL CAMINO REAL
MOUNTAIN VIEW, CA 94040-1306
650-948-8188
Fax: 650-948-9445
www.trackandfieldnews.com
• Russ Ebbets, Editor
(650) 948-8188
spinedoctor229@hotmail.com
• Ed Fox, Publisher
(650) 948-8188
ef@trackandfieldnews.com
Frequency:
4 time(s) per year
Description:
Publication provides technical information on track and field for coaches.

TRAILER BOATS
20700 BELSHAW AVENUE
CARSON, CA 90746-3510
310-537-6322
Fax: 310-537-8735
www.trailerboats.com
• Ron Eldridge, Editor
(310) 537-6322
• Ron Eldridge, Executive Editor
• Jim Hendricks, Associate Publisher
(310) 537-6322
• Wiley Poole, Publisher
• Steve Quinlan, Editor
• Dan Armitage, Field Editor
(310) 537-6322
Frequency:
11 time(s) per year
Description:
Publication covers issues of interest to owners and prospective buyers of trailerable power boats.

TRAINING AND CONDITIONING
31 DUTCH MILL ROAD
ITHACA, NY 14850
607-257-6970
Fax: 607-257-7328

info@momentummedia.com
www.athleticsearch.com
• Mark Goldberg, Publisher
(607) 257-6970
mg@momentummedia.com
Frequency:
9 time(s) per year
Description:
Publication is written for people who are involved in training and conditioning competitive athletes at all levels.

TRANSWORLD BUSINESS
353 AIRPORT ROAD
OCEANSIDE, CA 92054-1203
760-722-7777
800-788-7020
Fax: 760-722-0653
www.twsnow.com
• Sean O'Brien, Editor In Chief
(760) 722-7777
• Brad McDonald, President
(760) 722-7777
• Jamey Stone, Advertising Director
(760) 722-7777
• Kristina Ackermann, Associate Editor
(760) 722-7777
Frequency:
6 time(s) per year
Description:
Publication is written for snowboard retailers; includes news, analysis, trends, technical studies, and company profiles.

TRANSWORLD SKATEBOARDING
353 AIRPORT ROAD
OCEANSIDE, CA 92054-1203
760-722-7777
800-334-8152
Fax: 760-722-0653
www.skateboarding.com
• Eric Stricker, Editor
(760) 722-7777
• Carleton Curtis, Managing Editor
(760) 722-7777
• Skin Phillips, Editor-in-Chief
(760) 722-7777
• Jamey Stone, Advertising Director
(760) 722-7777
Frequency:
1 time(s) per month
Description:
Publication contains interviews with pro-skaters, contest coverage, and columns on improving skating skills.

TRIAD GOLF TODAY
P.O. BOX 11784
WINSTON-SALEM, NC 27106
336-924-1619
Fax: 336-922-9449
www.triadgolf.com
• Steve Williams, Editor
(336) 349-2739
editor@triadgolf.com
• Jay Allred, Publisher
Frequency:
8 time(s) per year
Description:
Publication offers in-depth news and features about the local golfing community.

TROTTINGBRED
60 GULF ROAD
GOUVERNEUR, NY 13642

315-287-2294
Fax: 315-287-5010
www.trottingbred.com
• Kathy Denesha, Editor
Frequency:
6 time(s) per year

TUFF STUFF PUBLICATIONS
700 E. STATE ST
IOLA, WI 54990
715-445-2214
800-345-3168
Fax: 715-445-4087
www.tuffstuff.com
• Dean Listle, Publisher
• Rocky Landsverk, Editorial Director
Description:
Comprehensive information (magazines, books, online) about sports and non-sports/entertainment player trading cards, autographs, and memorabilia, including prices, card evaluations, player interviews and industry trends. Also publishes fantasy guides for participants in football and baseball rotisserie leagues.
Circulation:
130,000
Sports:
Baseball, basketball, football, hockey
Primary Audience:
Trading cards & sports memorabilia.
Frequency:
Monthly
Publishing Company:
Tuff Stuff Publications, Inc.

TV SPORTSFILE
PO BOX 4159
ANNA MARIA, FL 34216
941-778-5960
800-876-6604
Fax: 941-778-2895
www.gouldmedia.com
• Barry Gould, Publisher
• Dantia Gould, Editor
Publishing Company:
Gould Media.
Frequency:
Twice Weekly
Description:
Fax/E-mail newsletter dealing with televised sports events, broadcasting organizations and executives, also publishes netSports tracking activities of organizations involved with sports content and e-commerce on the Internet. Annual research reports include Television Sports Rights and Net Sports, 2000.

TWIN CITIES SPORTS
P.O. BOX 1203
PRIOR LAKE, MN 55372
952-440-4898
Fax: 952-440-3628
www.twincitiessports.com
• Jeff Banowetz, Editor
• Doug Kaplan, Publisher
(312) 421-1551
Frequency:
11 time(s) per year
Description:
Publication promotes participation in grass-roots and amateur sports in Minnesota and the Midwest; emphasis is on running, cycling, in-line skating, triathlon, volleyball, hiking, canoeing, kayaking,

aerobics, skiing, snowboarding, and snowshoeing.

UNDERCURRENT
3020 BRIDGEWAY
SUITE 201
SAUSALITO, CA 94965-1439
415-289-0501
800-326-1896
Fax: 415-289-0137
www.undercurrent.org
• Ben Davison, Editor
(415) 289-0501
bendavison@aol.com
• Ben Davison, Publisher
bendavison@aol.com
Frequency:
11 time(s) per year
Description:
Publication is geared toward the recreational scuba diver; includes safety tips, equipment reviews, and reviews of international diving resorts.

UNDERSEA JOURNAL
30151 TOMAS
RANCHO SANTA MARGARI, CA 92688
949-858-7234
800-729-7234
Fax: 949-267-1267
journal@padi.com
www.padi.com
• Susan Tate, Editor
(949) 858-7234
Frequency:
4 time(s) per year

UNITED STATES SPORTS ACADEMY
ONE ACADEMY DRIVE
DAPHNE, AL 36526
251-626-3303
Fax: 251-626-8829
academy@ussa.edu
www.ussa.edu
• Thomas Rosandich, President/Chief Executive Officer
• Andrea Jordan, Assistant Dean of Administration and Finance
(251) 626-3303
• Annita Alldredge, Finance Director
(251) 626-3303
Description:
The United States Sports Academy is an independent, non-profit, accredited, special mission sports university created to serve the nation and the world with programs in instruction, research and service. The role of the Academy is to prepare men and women for careers in the profession of sports.
Year Founded:
1972

USA CYCLING NEWSLETTER
210 USA CYCLING POINT
SUITE 100
COLORADO SPRINGS, CO 80919-2215
719-434-4200
Fax: 719-434-4300
membership@usacycling.org
www.usacycling.org/media/
• Steve Johnson, Chief Executive Officer
• Sean Petty, Chief Operating Officer
• Todd Sowl, Chief Financial Officer
• Susan Diller, Membership Director
Frequency:
Monthly
Description:

Publication focuses on bicycle racing; contains USA Cycling news, race coverage and results, feature articles, and information on training and coaching; includes race schedules.

USA GYMNASTICS
PAN AMERICAN PLAZA
201 SOUTH CAPITOL AVENUE
INDIANAPOLIS, IN 46225-1000
317-237-5050
800-345-4719
Fax: 317-237-5069
www.usa-gymnastics.org
• Adrienne Willy, Marketing Coordinator
awilly@usagym.org
• Steven Penny, President
spenny@usa-gymnastics.org
• Luan Peszek, Publisher
(317) 829-5645
lpeszek@usa-gymnastics.org
• Robert Colarossi, Publisher
(317) 237-5050
Frequency:
6 time(s) per year
Description:
Publication is designed to educate readers on fitness, health, safety, technique, trends, and personalities related to the gymnastics and fitness field.

USA HOCKEY MAGAZINE
1775 BOB JOHNSON DRIVE
COLORADO SPRINGS, CO 80906
719-576-8724
Fax: 719-538-1160
usah@usahockey.org
www.usahockeymagazine.com
• Harry Thompson, Editor-in-Chief
(719) 576-8724
harryt@usahockey.org
Frequency:
10 time(s) per year
Description:
Publication is the official magazine of USA Hockey, and is written for registered players, coaches, officials, parents and volunteers; includes human interest stories, instructional pieces, and pages devoted to children.

USA ROLLER SPORTS MAGAZINE
4730 SOUTH STREET
LINCOLN, NE 68506-1256
402-483-7551
Fax: 402-483-1465
www.usarollersports.org
• Kellie Habeeb, Editor
(402) 483-7551
Frequency:
6 time(s) per year
Description:
Publication contains articles on roller skating for athletes who compete in this sport.

USA TODAY SPORTS WEEKLY
7950 JONES BRANCH DRIVE
MCLEAN, VA 22108-0605
703-854-3400
800-872-1415
Fax: 703-854-2034
sportsweekly@usatoday.com
www.usatoday.com
• Tim McQuay, Managing Editor
(703) 854-6456
tmcquay@usatoday.com
• Lee Ivory, Publisher
(703) 854-5630

livory@usatoday.com
• Lee Ivory, Publisher
(703) 854-8014
livory@usatoday.com
• Bob Nightengale, Columnist
(703) 854-5630
bobnighte@aol.com
• Paul White, Senior Writer
(703) 854-3756
• Chris Colston, Baseball Reporter
(703) 854-3723
ccolston@usatoday.com
Frequency:
1 time(s) per week
Description:
Publication covers major league, minor league, and college baseball.

USA WEIGHTLIFTING
1 OLYMPIC PLAZA
COLORADO SPRINGS, CO 80909-5764
719-866-4508
Fax: 719-866-4741
usaw@usaweightlifting.org
www.usaweightlifting.org
• Phil Andrews, Chief Executive Officer/General Secretary
(719) 866-3386
Phil.Andrews@usaweightlifting.org
• Brad Suchorski, Membership Manager
(719) 866-3227
Membership Requirements:
No requirements - there are memberships of all kinds and dues related to each membership type.
Description:
USA Weightlifing is the national governing body for olympic weightlifting in the United States. USAW is a member of the US Olympic Committee and of the International Weightlifting Federation.

USDF CONNECTION
220 LEXINGTON GREEN CIRCLE SUITE 510
LEXINGTON, KY 40503
859-971-2277
Fax: 859-971-7722
connection@usdf.org
www.usdf.org
• Jennifer Bryant, Editor
(610) 344-0116
jbryant@usdf.org
Frequency:
1 time(s) per month
Description:
Publication is the membership magazine of the United States Dressage Federation and is dedicated to education, recognition of achievement, and promoting the sport of dressage.

USROWING
201 SOUTH CAPITOL AVENUE
INDIANAPOLIS, IN 46225-1068
317-237-5656
Fax: 317-237-5646
members@usrowing.org
www.usrowing.org
• Brett Johnson, Editor
(317) 237-5656
brett@usrowing.org
Description:
Publication covers rowing in the United States; includes event results, nutrition, fitness, technique, and instructional articles.

VELO NEWS
1830 NORTH 55TH STREET
BOULDER, CO 80301-2700
303-440-0601
Fax: 303-444-6788
www.velonews.com
• Kip Mikler, Editor
• Steve Brawley, Advertising Manager
(303) 440-0601
• Ted Costantino, Publisher
(303) 440-0601
Frequency:
20 time(s) per year
Description:
Publication focuses on bicycle racing and race stories; includes columns on business, components, European news, off-road racing, training and physiology, personality interviews, and a complete calendar and results of North American events.

VERMONT SOCCER ASSOCIATION NEWS
13540 LAKE CITY WAY N.E. SUITE 3
SEATTLE, WA 98125
206-367-2420
Fax: 206-367-2636
www.varsitycommunications.com
• Charles Beene, Editor
(206) 367-2420
Frequency:
4 time(s) per year

VERMONT SPORTS TODAY
35 SOUTH MAIN STREET RIVER ROAD HOLDINGS
HANOVER, NH 03755
603-643-1441
Fax: 603-643-4644
www.vtsports.com
• Kathryn Carter, Managing Editor
(802) 244-5796
• Chris Blau, Publisher
(603) 643-1441
Frequency:
1 time(s) per month
Description:
Publication reports on individual aerobic sports in Vermont and the surrounding area.

VINTAGE BECKETT SPORTS COLLECTIBLES
15850 DALLAS PKWY
DALLAS, TX 75248
972-991-6657
Fax: 972-991-8930
www.beckett.com
• James Beckett, Owner
• Mark Harwell, President
Description:
Includes action-packed pages featuring price guides for and articles about: autographed sports collectibles, game-used apparel and equipment, sports cereal boxes, championship tickets and more.
Circulation:
43,494. 85% newsstand, 15% paid subscr.
Sports:
Major and minor league baseball, college football and basketball cards
Primary Audience:
Consumer
Frequency:
Monthly
Publishing Company:
Beckett Publications, Inc.

VINTAGE MOTORSPORT
5151 SOUTH LAKELAND DRIVE
SUITE 15
LAKELAND, FL 33813-2556
415-898-5776
800-626-9937
Fax: 415-898-3756
drandy@vintagemotorsport.com
www.vintagemotorsport.com
• D. Randy Riggs, Editor-in-Chief
drandy@vintagemotorsport.com
• Randy Riggs, Editor in Chief
(863) 607-9701
drriggs@vintagemotorsport.com
Frequency:
6 time(s) per year
Description:
Publication focuses on vintage motor racing and motor racing history.

VISIBILITY
P.O. BOX 628
DALY CITY, CA 94017-0628
650-583-8492
Fax: 650-583-0614
croseusoac@aol.com
www.underwater-society.org
• Carol Rose, Editor
Frequency:
5 time(s) per year
Description:
Publication covers underwater sports; includes skin and scuba diving, diving safety, diving education, and marine ecology.

VOICE OF THE HAWKEYES
P.O. BOX 187
IOWA CITY, IA 52244.
319-530-2272
888-474-8669
Fax: 319-665-3699
voiceofthehawkeyes@yahoo.com
www.voiceofthehawkeyes.com
• Todd Brommelkamp, Editor
Frequency:
25 time(s) per year
Description:
Publication focuses on sports at the University of Iowa.

VOICE OF THE TENNESSEE WALKING HORSE MAGAZINE
250 NORTH ELLINGTON PARKWAY
LEWISBURG, TN 37091-2835
931-359-1567
800-467-0232
Fax: 931-270-8743
www.twhbea.com
• Dan Butt, Managing Editor
• Sarah Gee, Staff Writer
(931) 359-0590
• Richard Hudgins, Advertising Manager
(931) 359-1567
Frequency:
11 time(s) per year
Description:
Publication gives information about events for the Tennessee Walking Horses.

VOLLEYBALL MAGAZINE
420 BOYLSTON STREET 5TH FLOOR
BOSTON, MA 02116
617-536-0100
800-876-2509
Fax: 617-536-0102
www.volleyballmag.com

• Mike Miazga, Editor
mmiazga@madavor.com
Frequency:
1 time(s) per month
Description:
Publication provides information on the entire indoor and outdoor volleyball sport; includes instruction, how-to articles, training, fitness, court strategies, and coaching.

WAKE BOARDING MAGAZINE
460 NORTH ORLANDO AVENUE SUITE 200
WINTER PARK, FL 32789-3150
407-628-4802
Fax: 407-628-7061
www.wakeboardingmag.com
• Luke Woodling, Managing Editor
(407) 628-4802
• Jason Bingham, Advertising Manager
(407) 628-4802
• Jim Emmons, Associate Publisher
(407) 628-4802
• John McEver, Jr., Publisher
(407) 571-4682
john.mcever@worldpub.net
• Kevin Michael, Senior Editor
(407) 628-4802
Frequency:
8 time(s) per year
Description:
Publication includes instructional tips and photographs for water sports fans, particularly wake boarders.

WALKING HORSE REPORT
730 MADISON STREET
SHELBYVILLE, TN 37160-3519
931-684-8123
Fax: 931-684-8196
admin@walkinghorsereport.com
www.walkinghorsereport.com/
• Jennifer Styskal, Editorial Director
• Jeffrey Howard, Publisher
jhoward@horseworld.net
Frequency:
1 time(s) per week
Description:
Publication covers walking horse shows and major events.

WATER SKI
460 NORTH ORLANDO AVENUE SUITE 200
WINTER PARK, FL 32789-3150
407-628-4802
800-879-0495
Fax: 407-628-7061
editor@waterskimag.com
www.worldpub.net
• Todd Ristorcelli, Editor
• John McEver, Jr., Publisher
(407) 571-4682
Frequency:
9 time(s) per year

WATER SKIER
1251 COW ROAD
POLK CITY, FL 33868
863-324-4341
800-533-2972
Fax: 863-325-8259
www.usawaterski.org
• Scott Atkinson, Editor
(863) 324-4341
satkinson@usawaterski.org
• Steve Utt, Advertising Manager

Frequency:
7 time(s) per year
Description:
Publication features information of interest to water skiing enthusiasts.

WATERCRAFT WORLD
6420 SYCAMORE LANE SUITE 100
MAPLE GROVE, MN 55369
805-667-4100
800-848-6247
Fax: 805-667-4336
• Lee Hetherington, Publisher
• Meghan Orazen, Advertising Sales Manager
morazen@affinitygroup.com
Frequency:
6 time(s) per year
Description:
Publication is geared toward personal watercraft enthusiasts.

WEIDER PUBLICATIONS
21100 ERWIN ST
WOODLAND HILLS, CA 91367
818-884-6800
Fax: 818-884-0371
www.fitnessonline.com
• Eric Weider, President
Description:
Publishes several magazines in the health and fitness field, including FLEX, LIVING FIT, MEN'S FITNESS, MUSCLE & FITNESS, SENIOR GOLFER, and SHAPE.
New York Address:
451 Park Ave South, New York, NY 10016.
212 251-0640; FAX: 212 251-0641

WESTERN GUIDE TO SNOWMOBILING
360 B STREET
IDAHO FALLS, ID 83402
208-524-7000
800-638-0135
Fax: 208-522-5241
www.snowest.com
• Lane Lindstrom, Editor
(208) 542-2234
• Ryan Harris, Assistant Editor
(208) 542-2243
rharris@snowest.com
Frequency:
1 time(s) per month
Description:
The exclusive most useful reference guide in print for western snowmobile vacation information. Aimed towards snowmobilers.
Circulation:
26,258

WESTERN HORSEMAN
3850 NORTH NEVADA AVENUE
COLORADO SPRINGS, CO 80907-5339
719-633-5524
Fax: 817-737-9266
edit@westernhorseman.com
www.westernhorseman.com
• A. J. Mangum, Editor
aj.mangum@westernhorseman.com
• Fran Smith, Managing Editor
(719) 633-5524
fran.smith@westernhorseman.com
• Randy Witte, Publisher
r.witte@westernhorseman.com
Frequency:
1 time(s) per month
Description:
Publication is a general interest horse

magazine with emphasis on the training, care, and use of horses for work and pleasure, particularly in the American West.

WESTERN OUTDOOR NEWS
PO BOX 73370
SAN CLEMENTE, CA 92673
949-366-0030
Fax: 949-366-0804
• Robert Twilegar, President
• Pat McDonell, Editor
• Joe Higgins, Advertising Manager
Description:
Covers fishing and hunting news in California and Arizona, plus Baja.
Circulation:
74,990. 81% paid subscr, 8% newsstand, 11% contr non-paid.
Sports:
Hunting, fishing, related outdoor recreation
Primary Audience:
Consumer
Frequency:
52 times annually
Publishing Company:
Western Outdoor Publications

WESTERN OUTDOORS
PO BOX 2027
NEWPORT BEACH, CA 92659-1027
949-546-4370
Fax: 949-662-3486
• Robert S. Twilegar, President/Chief Executive Officer
• Joe Higgins, Publisher
• Pat McDonnell, Editorial Director
Description:
Features articles on fishing and hunting techniques, where-to-go and current events affecting sportsmen in the 11 western states, Baja, Alaska, Hawaii and Western Canada.
Circulation:
130,000. 95% paid subscr, 5% other.
Sports:
Hunting, fishing, related outdoor recreation
Primary Audience:
Consumer
Frequency:
Nine times annually
Publishing Company:
Western Outdoor Publications

WHEELIN' SPORTSMAN
770 AUGUSTA ROAD
EDGEFIELD, SC 29824-1510
803-637-3106
Fax: 803-637-0034
www.nwtf.org
• Karen Lee, Editor
• Chasiti Kirkland, Managing Editor
(803) 637-3106
Frequency:
4 time(s) per year
Description:
Publication features tips, secrets, and information on sports pertaining to the disabled members of the NWTF.

WINDSURFING
460 NORTH ORLANDO AVENUE SUITE 200
WINTER PARK, FL 32789-3150
407-628-4802
888-259-6753

Fax: 407-628-7061
www.worldpub.net
• Eddy Patracelli, Editor
(407) 628-4802
• David Combe, Publisher
(805) 403-8095
Frequency:
8 time(s) per year
Description:
Publication is geared toward windsurfing enthusiasts.

WINDY CITY SPORTS
1450 WEST RANDOLPH
CHICAGO, IL 60607
312-421-1551
Fax: 312-421-1454
www.windycitysports.com
• Doug Kaplan, President/Publisher
• Kate Bongiovanni, Managing Editor & Web Site Editor
(312) 421-1551
Sports Service Founded:
1992
Publication:
Our first issue was printed in 1987. Covers amateur athletics in the Chicago area; focuses primarily on running, cycling, and in-line skating.
Frequency:
1 time(s) per month

WINGFOOT
1303 HIGHTOWER TRAIL SUITE 101
ATLANTA, GA 30350
770-650-1102
Fax: 770-650-2848
www.knowatlanta.com
• Riley McDermid, Editor
(770) 650-1102
• Craig Dekshenieks, Publisher
(770) 650-1102
• Michelle Bourg, Co-Editor & Features Writer
(404) 231-9064
Frequency:
9 time(s) per year

WISCONSIN GOLFER
333 BISHOP'S WAY SUITE 104
BROOKFIELD, WI 53005
262-786-4301
Fax: 262-786-4202
info@wsga.org
www.wsga.org
• John Hughes, Editor
killer@aol.com
• John Hughes, Publisher
killer@aol.com
• Rick Pledl, Associate Editor
Frequency:
6 time(s) per year
Description:
Publication provides information and resources for golfers in the state of Wisconsin.

WISCONSIN SOCCER POST
13540 LAKE CITY WAY N.E. SUITE 3
SEATTLE, WA 98125
206-367-2420
Fax: 206-367-2636
www.varsitycommunications.com
• Kelly Ross, Editor
(414) 545-7227
kross@wysa.org

Frequency:
4 time(s) per year

WOLFPACKER
PO BOX 2331
DURHAM, NC 27702
919-688-0218
Fax: 919-682-1532
www.thewolfpacker.com
• Stuart Coman, Publisher
• Scott Vogelsburg, Editor
• Dave Searcy, Advertising
Director/Marketing Director
Publishing Company:
Coman Publishing Company, Inc.
Frequency:
20 times annually
Primary Audience:
NC State sports fans
Sports:
General - North Carolina State sports
Description:
Covers NC State sports exclusively,
including features about athletes, coaches,
provides coverage of events in which NC
State participates, information pertaining to
team lineups and player statistics.

WOLVERINE
PO BOX 1304
ANN ARBOR, MI 48106
734-996-9092
Fax: 734-996-8196
www.thewolverine.com
• Stuart Coman, Publisher
• John Borton, Editor
Description:
Covers Michigan sports exclusively,
including features about athletes, coaches,
coverage of events in which Michigan
participates, information pertaining to team
lineups and player statistics.
Circulation:
16,000. 95% paid subscr, 5% newsstand.
Sports:
General
Primary Audience:
U. of Michigan sports fans
Frequency:
25 times annually
Publishing Company:
Coman Publishing Company, Inc.

WOMEN'S PRO RODEO NEWS
1235 LAKE PLAZA DRIVE
COLORADO SPRINGS, CO 80906
719-576-0900
Fax: 719-576-1386
www.horseworlddata.com
• Tim Gentry, Editor
• Glory Ann Kurtz, Editor
(719) 576-0900
Frequency:
1 time(s) per month

WOODENBOAT
86 GREAT COVE
BROOKLIN, ME 04616
207-359-4651
Fax: 207-359-8920
woodenboat@woodenboat.com
www.woodenboat.com
• Matthew P. Murphy, Editor
(207) 359-4651
matt@woodenboat.com
• Carl Cramer, Publisher

(207) 359-4651
• Tom Jackson, Associate Editor
tom@woodenboat.com
• Mike O'Brien, Senior Editor
(207) 359-4651
• Jonathan A. Wilson, Editor-in-Chief
(207) 359-4651
jon@woodenboat.com
• Sarah Bray, Editorial Assistant
(207) 359-4651
Frequency:
6 time(s) per year
Description:
Publication provides information on the
design, building, care, preservation, and use
of wooden boats.

**WORLD WIDE SPORTS RADIO
NETWORK**
22 DORFER LANE
NESCONSET, NY 11767
631-965-4990
www.worldwidesportsradio.com
• Errol Marks, CEO/Editor/Host
(631) 965-4990
e.marks@sportsonthego1.com
Frequency:
1 time(s) per month
Description:
All professional sporting events in New
York, New Jersey and national major
sporting events.

WSS EXECUTIVE SEARCH
7755 CENTER AVENUE
SUITE 1100
HUNTINGTON BEACH, CA 92647
714-848-1201
Fax: 714-848-5111
info@WSSExecutiveSearch.com
www.WSSExecutiveSearch.com
• Becky Heidesch, Founder & Chief
Executive Officer
• Mary Lou Youngblood, Chief Operating
Officer
Description:
WSS Executive Search, a division of
Women Sourcing Soltions, is a WBENC
certified, women-owned business
specializing in women and minority sourcing
solutions. WSS partners with their clients to
provide them with sourcing solutions to
solve their most challenging diversity hiring
efforts. WSS specializes in the sports,
financial and technology industry.
Nature of Service:
WSS customizes their recruitment and
management process for each client. By
offering personalized sourcing solutions,
WSS matches qualified professional
candidates with top-tier companies who are
often challenged in their industry in finding
women and minority candidates. WSS has
years of experience assisting companies in
reaching their diversity goals and
empowering candidates to realize their
career dreams!
Primary Audience:
Corporate America, specialty companies in
the sports, financial and technology sectors.
Candidate pool: Mid-management to
Executive Level.
Sports
All.

YACHTING
PO BOX 420235
PALM COAST, FL 32142-0235
203-299-5900
800-999-0869
Fax: 401-845-5180
www.yachtingnet.com
• John Wooldridge, Managing Editor
(203) 299-5900
• Peter Janssen, Editorial Director
• Don Wallace, Executive Editor
• John Young, Publisher
(212) 779-5263
Frequency:
1 time(s) per month
Description:
Publication is written for the active sailor or
powerboater.

YACHTS INTERNATIONAL
1850 SOUTHEAST 17TH STREET SUITE
310
FORT LAUDERDALE, FL 33316
954-761-8777
Fax: 954-761-8890
• Jamie Welch, Editor
• Michel Karsenti, Publisher
Frequency:
6 time(s) per year
Description:
Publication features information on yachts
40 feet and longer.

YOUTH SPORTS JOURNAL
2050 VISTA PKWY
W. PALM BEACH, FL 33411
561-684-1141
800-729-2057
Fax: 561-684-2546
nays@nays.org
www.nays.org
• Fred C. Engh, President/Chief Executive
Officer
• Greg Bach, Editor/Communication Director
• Nathan Washer, Director Education
Description:
Official publication of the National Youth
Sports Coaches Association. Covers news,
programs, tips relating to sports, innovative
products, safety and drug awareness
programs. Provides product information and
advertising geared toward the organized
youth sports programs.
Publishing Company:
National Youth Sports Coaches Assn
Frequency:
Quarterly
Primary Audience:
NYSCA membership, coaches, and parents
involved in youth sports, recreation
professionals (municipal and military),
YMCA, YWCA, CYO, Boys Clubs, etc.
Sports:
Baseball, Softball, Football, Basketball,
Soccer, Volleyball, Ice Hockey, Flag
Football, Cheerleading, Ringette
Circulation:
140,600+.

ZONE TENNIS
1060 MAIN STREET
SUITE 307
RIVER EDGE, NJ 07661
201-342-3663
800-580-9663
Fax: 201-342-2258

info@stayinthezone.com
www.stayinthezone.com
• Jay Granat, Psychotherapist/Founder
(201) 342-3663

Sports Business Directories

ATHLETIC DIRECTORY
20622 OTTAWA ROAD
APPLE VALLEY, CA 92308
760-247-4717
• Dick Sauers, Publisher/Editor
Description:
Covers information and features about
coaching, fitness and other subjects of
interest to athletic coaches. Includes listings
of coaching books and manuals and also
includes interviews with coaches about
techniques and methods used in coaching.
Also publishes Sports Psychology
newsletter on a quarterly basis.
Circulation:
NA.
Sports:
General
Primary Audience:
Coaches
Frequency:
Six times annually
Publishing Company:
Scholastic Resources Unlimited

ATHLETIC GUIDE PUBLISHING
509 SOUTH CENTRAL AVENUE
FLAGLER BEACH, FL 32136-1050
386-439-2050
800-255-1050
flaglernet@gmail.com
www.prepschoolhockeyguide.com
• Tom Keegan, Publisher/Editor
(386) 439-2050
flagernet@gmail.com
• Sharyn Keegan, Production Manager
• Bryan Mitchell, Graphic Design
Description:
Publishes annual guides covering pro
hockey, college hockey, prep school
hockey, junior hockey.
Publishing Company:
Athletic Guide Publishing.
Circulation:
10,000
Frequency:
Annual.
Sports:
College Hockey.

BASEBALL BLUEBOOK, LLC
8373 N CEDAR HILLS LANE
FAIR GROVE, MO 65648
417-833-6550
Fax: 417-833-9911
dj@baseballbluebook.com
www.baseballbluebook.com
• Jodi Wubbena, Publisher
• Dennis Wubbena, Publisher
Baseball Bluebook - Professional Edition
Annual publication. Lists Major League,
Minor League and Independent League
personnel, contact information, schedules,
and scouts. Available spiral bound or in a
3-ring binder
Baseball Bluebook - College Edition
Annual publication. Lists Division I, II, & III,
NAIA, and JUCO personnel, contact

information, and schedules; includes
conference informationand prospects.
Available spiral bound or in a 3-ring binder.

BLUE BOOK OF COLLEGE ATHLETICS
P O BOX 931
MONTGOMERY, AL 36101
334-263-4436
Fax: 334-263-4437
www.athleticpubco.com
• John A. Dees, Jr., Publisher
• Chris Beasley, Marketing Director
Publishing Company:
Athletic Publishing Company
Frequency:
Annually
Primary Audience:
Executives and coaches of educational
institutions
Circulation:
13,000 100% paid subscription
Description:
Includes listings for all senior, junior and
community colleges in the United States and
Canada; male and female colleges. Lists
address, phone, fax numbers. Listings
include school name, coaches listed by
sport, stadium size and school colors.
Sports:
General

**CLELL WADE COACHES DIRECTORY,
INC.**
701 MAIN STREET
CASSVILLE, MO 65625
417-847-2783
Fax: 417-847-5920
www.coachesdirectory.com
• Karan Nickle, Publisher/Editor/Advertising
Sales Director
Publishing Company:
Clell Wade Coaches Directory, Inc.
Frequency:
Annually
Primary Audience:
Athletic administrators, coaches, institutions,
and team sporting goods companies
Sports:
General
Circulation:
70,000. 69% paid subscr. 31% non-paid
contr.
Description:
Provides high school and college
enrollment, school colors, nicknames,
telephone numbers and names of current
coaching personnel in 38 separate
directories, covering the U.S. and Canada.

DEGREES IN SPORTS
7010 E CHAUNCEY LANE
PHOENIX, AZ 85054
480-905-8480
Fax: 480-905-7231
info@degreesinsports.com
www.degreesinsports.com
• Randy Just, National Account Manager
(480) 905-8480
Description:
Online directory of Sport Management
Degrees in the United States.

**EPM LICENSING LETTER
SOURCEBOOK, THE**
160 MERCER ST, 3RD FL
NEW YORK, NY 10012-3212

212-941-0099
888-852-9467
Fax: 212-941-1622
www.epmcom.com
• Riva Bennett, Chief Operating Officer
• Ira Mayer, Publisher
• Michele Jensen, Vice President of
Marketing
• Melissa Trosterman, Marketing
Coordinator
mtrosterman@epm.com
• Loretta Netzer, Circulation Manager
• Ben Jurin, Associate Editor, The Licensing
Letter
Publishing Company:
EPM Communications, Inc.
Frequency:
Annual
Primary Audience:
Licensing business executives
Sports:
General
Circulation:
NA.
Description:
Directory of licensing agents, products, and
manufacturers.

FOOTBALL GREEN BOOK
310 W. WALNUT STREET
SPRINGFIELD, MO 65806
417-866-3464
800-909-0010
Fax: 417-866-3469
www.sportdirectories.com
• Michelle Johnson, Editor
• Joe Terry, Associate Editor
• Jeff Schrag, Publisher
Frequency:
Annual Publications.
Description:
The Football Green Book is a
comprehensive directory of every team in
the sport in the US and Canada: college,
pros; administration, coaching; contracts;
conferences,bowl games, and more.
Primary Audience:
Coaches, Scouts, Agents.

**GAISF CALENDAR OF INTERNATIONAL
SPORTS COMPETITIONS**
4, BD DU JARDIN EXOTIQUE
MONTE CARLO, MONACO 98000
www.agfisonline.com
• Jean C. Schupp, Publisher
Description:
Contains long-term calendar for each sport,
the programs of the Olympic and regional
Games, and the May/November calendar in
chronological order.
Circulation:
NA.
Sports:
General.
Primary Audience:
Sports Business Executives, Sports
Organizations, Sports Media
Frequency:
Semi-annually (May 1, Nov 1).
Publishing Company:
General Association of International Sports
Federations.

GLOBAL SPORTS PRODUCTIONS
16810 CRYSTAL DRIVE EAST
ENUMCLAW, WA 98022

310-454-9480
www.sportsbookempire.com/
• Ed Kobak, President
• Bistro Loving, VP Operations
• Barbara Boldtmann, Vice President
• Greg Andrews, VP of Business Operations
Publishing Company:
Global Sports Productions. Publisher of sport reference books. Publisher of sport magazines.
Description:
Global Sports Productions; 464 page reference directory with 7,500+ listings that includes addresses, telephone & fax numbers, cable & telex numbers, websites, e-mail addresses and contact persons from international and national sports organizations in addition to federations, leagues, teams, clubs, and global publications.
Frequency:
Annually
Primary Audience:
Industry
Sports:
General/International
Publications:
International Sports Directory, Sports Logo Guide, Sports Hall of Oblvion, The Guide to a Sports Career, Sports Address Bible, The Baseball Autograph Collector's Guide, The Celebrity Address Directory Guide, The Encyclopedia of Sports Business Contacts, The NACDA Collegiate Sports Directory and the Dream Job in Sports Publicity, Promotions & Marketing.

HOCKEY BLACK BOOK
PO BOX 400
WOODMERE, NY 11598
917-327-9500
Fax: 201-567-4514
HockeyBlackBook@aol.com
www.HockeyBlackBook.com
• David Kolb, Publisher
Hockey Black Book
Annual publication. Includes in-depth information on professional, amateur, collegiate, and junior hockey leagues; associations, media, organizations; schedules, arenas, staff, and contact information.

IEG SPONSORSHIP SOURCEBOOK
640 NORTH LA SALLE STREET
SUITE 600
CHICAGO, IL 60610-3777
800-834-4850
Fax: 312-458-7111
ieg@sponsorship.com
www.sponsorship.com
• Jon Ukman, Publisher
• Lesa Ukman, President
• Meg Pound, Advertising Sales Director
• Penny Perrey, Associate Publisher
• Laren Ukman, General Manager
• Maureen Gilroy, Marketing Director
Description:
Lists 3,000 major sports events and properties available for sponsorship. Directory listings include contact, address and phone of each event plus budget, attendance, prior sponsors. Events indexed by category, location, date, budget and attendance. Also includes index of sponsors and the properties they tie into, industry yellow pages and event marketing agencies,

sports organizations and industry suppliers.
Frequency:
Annually.
Publishing Company:
IEG, Inc.

ILLINOIS COACHES DIRECTORY
1311 LITTLE JOHN DRIVE
ELGIN, IL 60120
847-742-6262
• Ken Olson, Publisher/Editor
Description:
Contains complete listings for all boys' and girls' high school, college and junior college coaches in Illinois, giving name, address, phone, sports coached, enrollment of school, school colors, nickname of teams, conference.
Circulation:
6,000. 100% paid subscr.
Sports:
General
Primary Audience:
Athletic institutional executives/coaches
Publishing Company:
Illinois Coaches Directory

INTERNATIONAL AUDARENA GUIDE
P O BOX 15158
NORTH HOLLYWOOD, CA 91606-5158
818-487-4582
800-562-2706
Fax: 818-487-4550
www.billboard.com/bbcom/index.jsp
• Brian Kennedy, Vice President Integrated Sales
bkennedy@billboard.com
• Derek Senter, Advertising Director Digital/Consumer Brands
dsentner@billboard.com
• Arkady Fridman, Inside Sales Manager
afridman@billboard.com
Description:
The International AudArena Guide provides complete data on over 4,300 venues worldwide, including Amphitheaters, Arenas, Stadiums, Sports facilities, Concert Halls and New Constructions including complete listings of companies offering services to the touring industry in the Facility Buyer's Guide. AudArena International Guide includes: contact names; phone and fax numbers; email and Website addresses; market population; facility capacities and staging configurations in addition to rental fees and Ticketing Rights.
Publishing Company:
Billboard Store; 310 pages; published October 2004; unit price $99.00; Item# BLBDD35.
Sports:
General
Frequency:
Annually

INTERNATIONAL HANDBOOK FOR THE SPORTING GOODS INDUSTRY
LA MAISON DU SPORT
PO BOX 480
VERBIER, SWITZERLAN CH-196
info@wfsgi.org
www.wfsgi.org
• Anne Gorgemans, Publisher
Description:
Includes, but not limited to, directory of senior WFSGI officials, sports event and trade show calendar, and directory of

member organizations.
Circulation:
NA.
Sports:
General
Primary Audience:
Sporting Goods Manufacturers
Frequency:
Annually
Publishing Company:
World Federation of the Sporting Goods Industry

INTERNATIONAL KARTING INDUSTRY BUYER'S GUIDE
PO BOX 101
WHEATON, IL 60189
630-653-7368
Fax: 630-653-2637
karting@msn.com
• Darrell E. Sitarz, Publisher/President/CEO
(630) 653-7368
karting@msn.com
• Jim Logan, Sales Manager
(630) 653-7368
karting@msn.com
Frequency:
Annually
Primary Audience:
Trade
Sport:
Go Karting
Circulation:
10,000 (60% subscriber, 40% newstand)
Description:
A directory of products and services with nearly 350 categories and more than 2,000 company entries. Each entry includes the company name, address, contact name, phone, fax numbers, web site, and email addresses. Included are manufacturers, safety equipment and apparel, insurance carriers, ticketing, track designers and tools.

NATIONAL DIRECTORY OF COLLEGE ATHLETICS ONLINE & APP
PO BOX 450640
CLEVELAND, OH 44145
216-465-2914
info@collegiatedirectories.com
www.collegiatedirectories.com
• Kevin Cleary, General Manager
Publishing Company:
Collegiate Directories, Inc.
Year Founded:
1969 & 1991
Frequency:
Annual
Primary Audience:
Coaches, Athletic Directors
Sports:
All
Description:
Spiral bound directory lists over 2,100 junior and senior colleges that compete in intercollegiate athletics. Contact information available for every college coach and athletic administrator in the U.S. and Canada. Official publication of the National Association of Collegiate Directors of Athletics (NACDA). For men's and women's sports, contains names, addresses and telephone numbers of all college athletic officials including athletic directors, coaches, sports information directors, athletic business managers and athletic trainers,

and includes two major editorial features dealing with all aspects of college athletics.

NATIONAL DIRECTORY OF HIGH SCHOOL COACHES
2540 EAST FIFTH STREET
MONTGOMERY, AL 36107
334-263-4436
Fax: 334-263-4437
• John Al Dees, Publisher
• Chris Al Beasley, Jr., Marketing Director
Publishing Company:
Athletic Publishing Co.
Frequency:
Annually
Primary Audience:
Executives and coaches of athletic institutions
Sports:
General
Circulation:
18,000. 100% paid subscr.
Description:
Provides listings for 19,500 schools and over 240,000 coaches throughout the U.S.

NSGA BUYING GUIDE
1601 FEEHANVILLE DRIVE
SUITE 300
MT. PROSPECT, IL 60056-6035
847-296-6742
800-815-5422
Fax: 847-391-9827
info@nsga.org
www.nsga.org
• James Faltinek, President/Chief Executive Officer
• Paul Prince, Vice President/Business Development
• Cyndi Boehm, MIS Manager/Editor
Publishing Company:
National Sporting Goods Association
Frequency:
Annually
Primary Audience:
Retail, manufacturing trade
Sports:
General
Circulation:
3,000 Members only.
Desription:
Buying guide for retailers and dealers.

RECREATIONAL SPORTS DIRECTORY
NIRSA
4185 SOUTHWEST RESEARCH WAY
CORVALLIS, OR 97333-1067
541-766-8211
Fax: 541-766-8284
nirsa@nirsa.org
www.nirsa.org
• Kent Blumenthal, Executive Director
• Sarah Hubert, Editor
• Carole Hobrock, Advertising Manager
Publishing Company:
Natl Intramural-Recreational Sports Association/NIRSA
Frequency:
Annually
Primary Audience:
Association membership
Sports:
General
Circulation:
2,000. 80% association membership, 10% contr non-paid, 10% other.
Description:

Listing of colleges, universities, community-junior colleges, military installations. Includes personnel and areas of responsibility, facility managers, sport clubs, intramurals, fitness, instructional programs, outdoor recreation, informal sports, aquatics, extramural sports, individuals with disabilities, special events, and wellness. Includes buyers guide.

REVENUES FROM SPORTS VENUES
2813 HARBOR LIGHTS DRIVE
NASHVILLE, TN 37217
615-367-4241
• Jim Grimstead, Editor/Publisher
• Linda Mansur, Editor/Publisher
Publishing Company:
Mediaventures
Frequency:
Annually
Primary Audience:
Team and venue owners, marketing management, marketing consultants, architects, contractors, premium service vendors, management companies.
Sports:
General
Description:
A directory listing prices and providing analysis for signage, luxury suites, club seats, advertising placements, ticket prices and naming rights deals in addition to number of concession stands and caterer information.

SALESMAN'S GUIDE
2807 NORTH PARHAM ROAD
SUITE 200
RICHMOND, VA 23294
804-762-9600
Fax: 804-217-8999
www.douglaspublications.com
• Alan Douglas, President
• Frank Finn, VP/Editor-in-Chief
Sports:
General
Primary Audience:
Manufacturing, wholesale trade
Frequency:
Annually
Publishing Company:
Douglas Publishing
Description:
Composed of a diverse array of companies, including manufacturers, retailers, marketing agencies and companies. Over 12,000 firms who purchase premiums and incentives are listed, as well as the 20,000 decision-markers that plan to purchase ad specialties, corporate gifts and awards, sales incentives and safety incentives.
Circulation:
5,000. 100% paid subscr.

SPORT INFORMATION RESOURCE CENTER/SIRC
180 ELGIN STREET
SUITE 1400
OTTAWA, ON, CANADA K2P 3K3
613-231-7472
800-665-6413
Fax: 613-231-3739
webmaster@sirc.ca
www.sirc.ca
• Debra Gassewitz, President/CEO
• David Roberts, COO
• Jean-Michel Johnson, Director of Indexing

Services
• Linda Wheeler, Director Product Development
Sports Service Founded:
1973
Nature of Sports Service:
Database producer of sport, fitness and sports medicine information. Organization has been identifying, organizing and communicating sport and fitness information and providing it through a variety of products and services. These include SPORTDiscus, SIRCDetective, SIRCRetriever, SIRCExpress and SIRCUIT.Our subscribers range from universities, libraries and hospitals to coaches, athletes, professors and medical practitioners worldwide.

SPORTING GOODS & ACTIVEWEAR BUYERS DIRECTORY
2807 NORTH PARHAM ROAD
SUITE 200
RICHMOND, VA 23294
804-762-9600
Fax: 804-217-8999
www.douglaspublications.com
• Alan Douglas, President
• Frank Finn, VP/Editor-in-Chief
Sports:
General
Primary Audience:
Manufacturing, wholesale trade
Frequency:
Annually
Publishing Company:
Douglas Publishing
Description:
Includes information about more than 18,400 buyers and executives, including those who purchase sporting goods equipment, accessories, activewear, resortwear, surfwear and swimwear.

SPORTS BUSINESS RESOURCE GUIDE & FACT BOOK
1166 AVENUE OF THE AMERICAS
14TH FLOOR
NEW YORK, NY 10036
212-500-0700
Fax: 212-500-0701
www.sportsbusinessdaily.com/journal
• Derick Moss, Editor
(703) 973-1434
derickmoss@sportsbusinessjournal.com
• Laurie Garrison, Copy Editor, Sports Business Awards Coordinator
(703) 973-1331
lgarrison@sportsbusinessjournal.com
• Ryan Baucom, Associate Editor
(703) 973-1419
rbaucom@sportsbusinessjournal.com
Description:
The Resource Guide & Fact Book is a comprehensive, detailed, reference covering the business of sports. With contacts, addresses, phone numbers, sponsorship information, naming rights, and media rights for more than 8,900 listings, and 60,000 individual contacts, it is a must-have for sports executives.

SPORTS MARKET PLACE DIRECTORY
4919 ROUTE 22
AMENIA, NY 12501
518-789-8700
800-562-2139

Fax: 518-789-0545
www.sportsmarketplace.com
• Richard Gottlieb, President
• Leslie Mackenzie, Publisher
• Laura Mars-Proietti, Editorial Director
Publishing Company:
Grey House Publishing
Frequency:
Annual.
Primary Audience:
Sports executives in advertising, marketing, sales, sponsorships, public relations, events, media, facilities and sports law. Sports management programs and career seekers.
Sports:
General
Circulation:
1,000
Description:
Provides comprehensive listing of organizations and business firms including associations, college athletic conferences, professional sports leagues and teams, sports publications, sports promotion and marketing firms, sports broadcasting firms, sports market and information data services, sports equipment, apparel and footwear manufacturers, colleges and universities with Sports Management Degree Programs. Also available on GOLD online.

THE FOOTBALL GREEN BOOK
310 W WALNUT STREET
SPRINGFIELD, MO 65806
417-866-3464
800-909-0010
Fax: 417-866-3469
www.sportdirectories.com
• Michelle Johnson, Editor
• Joe Terry, Associate Editor
• Jeff Schrag, Publisher
Frequency:
Annual Publications.
Description:
The Football Green Book is a comprehensive directory of every team in the sport in the US and Canada: college, pros; administration, coaching; contracts; conferences,bowl games, and more.
Primary Audience:
Coaches, Scouts, Agents.

THE SPORT SUMMIT SPORTS BUSINESS DIRECTORY
6550 ROCK SPRING DRIVE
SUITE 500
BETHESDA, MD 20817-1126
301-493-5500
800-EJK- EXPO
Fax: 301-493-5705
www.sportsummit.com
• Jim Farlenza, VP/Executive Director Sports Division
• Jamie Attanasia, Managing Editor
Published By:
E.J. Krause & Associates, Inc. 8th Edition, Annual Publication, Topic: Sports Informational.
Description:
A comprehensive annual guide to over 9,000 companies and organizations and 25,000 executives involved in sports marketing, events, media, sponsorship, facilities, manufacturing, teams, finance, law and more. The Sports Business Directory is available in two forms: the traditional Print

Version, and Online Version, with a powerful search engine to help you find the decision-makers in the sports industry, and daily updates to ensure the accuracy of the listings included.

WESTERN SPORTS GUIDE
3992 DONIPHAN DRIVE
EL PASO, TX 79922
915-584-7791
Fax: 888-584-7791
• Emily Anderson, Owner
Description:
Publishes high school directories listing sports, coaches, nicknames, addresses, etc. States covered: Texas, California-Nevada-Hawaii, Arizona-New Mexico, Arkansas-Louisiana, Washington-Oregon-Alaska (Pacific Northwest), Idaho-Wyoming-Montana, Colorado-Utah, Mississippi-Alabama, Oklahoma-Kansas, South Carolina.
Circulation:
Texas-5,600; Cal/Nev-1,600; others 300-800 per edition. Total all editions-10,800. 95% paid subscr, 3% contr non-paid, 2% other.
Sports:
General
Primary Audience:
Coaches, officials, trade
Frequency:
Annually
Publishing Company:
Craftsman Publications, Inc.

Media Production

44 BLUE PRODUCTIONS, INC.
4040 VINELAND AVE, STE 105
STUDIO CITY, CA 91604
818-760-4442
Fax: 818-760-1509
reception@44blue.com
www.44blue.com
• Rasha Drachkovitch, Founder (818) 760-4442
Nature of Sports Service:
National. Syndicated and cable TV programmer. Current properties include Discovery Sport, weekly series; Future Stars in Sport, hosted by Mike Schmidt; The History of College Football, The History of College Basketball, and other programs.

ACTION SPORTS ADVENTURE
322 8TH AVE
NEW YORK, NY 10001
212-375-7622
866-473-5264
Fax: 212-807-9201

AOL SPORTS
1100 AVE OF THE AMERICAS
H11
NEW YORK, NY 10036
212-512-1648
800-937-2212
Fax: 212-512-1751
• Tim Armstrong, Chairman/Chief Executive Officer, AOL
Sports Service Founded:
1990
Marketing & Consulting Services:
Pay-Per-View Programming development and acquisition; purchase of sports

properties for marketing and broadcasting.
Description:
Offers sports scores, as well as sports news, including fantasy sports information.

ASA PRODUCTIONS
5210 E. 65TH ST
INDIANAPOLIS, IN 46220
317-579-7777
Fax: 317-579-7774
www.asaproductions.com
• Scott Kemper, Partner/Creative
• Rich Airis, Partner/Creative

BASEBALLVIDEOS.COM
502 ANCHORAGE LANE
HOUSTON, TX 77079
888-907-0790
Fax: 281-368-1630
www.baseballvideos.com
Nature of Sports Service:
National. Producer and distributor of sports home videocassettes and programming. Current sports video cassettes include: Baseball Skills and Drills; and You and Your Horse.

BASSMASTERS, THE
5845 CARMICHAEL RD
MONTGOMERY, MN 36117
334-272-9530
Fax: 334-279-7148
www.bassmaster.com
• Diehl Unger, Executive Producer
• Dave Precht, Executive Producer
• Mike Harris, Consultant Account Manager
• Don McPherson, Advertising Director
• Ken Woodard, Vice President/Advertising
Nature of Sports Service:
National. TV program producer/packager. Programs feature B.A.S.S. tournament highlights and how-to of bass angling.

BMORE SPORTS
1430 JOH AVENUE
BUILDING M
BALTIMORE, MD 21227
410-247-2345
gandracchio@ptcintl.com
www.bmoresports.com or www.ptcintl.com
Nature of Services:
Bmore Sports is a manufacturer of a variety of game-day promotional products including sports leather binders and jotters, wood ticket boxes, custom coolers and dog tag collectibles.
Year Founded:
1980

BO GANZ PRODUCTIONS
1701 LASHLEY ST
LONGMONT, CO 80504
303-772-9273
Fax: 303-772-9273
boganz@peakpeak.com
• Bo Ganz, Products/Director
Nature of Sports Service:
National. Film and video production company, specializing in sports categories.

BOMBO SPORTS & ENTERTAINMENT
41 MADISON AVE
NEW YORK, NY 10010
212-685-9080
Fax: 212-685-9088

• Bob Potter, Chief Executive Officer/Managing Partner
Sports Service Founded:
1984
Nature of Sports Service:
Develops sports film documentaries on teams and individual athletes.

CALAMARI VIDEO
2973 HOWELL AVE
SANTA CLARA, CA 95051
408-241-1231
• Lon McEachern, Partner
• Amy Smolens, Partner
Nature of Sports Service:
International. TV, video production company. Produces promotional and marketing videotapes, video news releases, and corporate and sports training tapes for events, teams and products.

CAPPY PRODUCTIONS INC.
118 E. 57TH ST, 3RD FL
NEW YORK, NY 10022
212-249-1800
Fax: 212-439-9165
cappyprod@hotmail.com
• Bud Greenspan, President
• Nancy Beffa, Vice President/Executive Vice President
• Bruce Beffa, Senior Producer
• Sydney Thayer, Coordinator Production
Nature of Sports Service:
National. TV film production. Broad production capabilities. Production credits include The Olympiad series; Numero Uno series; Wilma (movie of the week); The Glory of their Times; Olympic Vignettes (4-7 minute documentary spots); Time Capsule: The 1932 Los Angeles Olympics; Time Capsule; The 1932 Los Angeles Olympics; Time Capsule: The 1936 Berlin Olympics. This Day in Sports 16 Days of Glory, The Official Film of the 1984 Los Angeles Olympic Games; The Official Olympics; 16 Days of Glory; The Official Film of the 1988 Seoul Olympics; 16 Days of Glory; The Official Film of the Days of Glory; The Official Film of the 1992 Barcelona Olympics

CBS SPORTS COLLEGE NETWORK
28 EAST 28TH STREET
NEW YORK, NY 10016
• Patricia Power, Senior Vice President of Operations
• Barbara Shulman, Senior Vice President and General Counsel
• Kelly Dunne, Vice President of Creative Services
• Joseph Salerno, Vice President of Midwest Affiliate Sales
Sports Service Founded:
2002
Nature of Sports Service:
Cable network devoted exclusively to college sports, including a significant commitment to women's sports. Network was co-founded by Brian Bedol, Stephen Greenberg and Chris Bevilacqua. Mr. Bedol and Mr. Greenberg were co-founders of Classic Sports Network.

CENTER CITY FILM & VIDEO
1501-1503 WALNUT STREET
PHILADELPHIA, PA 19102
215-568-4134
www.ccfv.com

• Brian Iseley, Vice President/General Manager
• Melanie Macready, Account Executive
Nature of Sports Service:
National. Remote TV production, post production. Capabilities for sports programs, sports production.

CISNEROS MEDIA DISTRIBUTION
305-507-6837
msomoza@cisneros.com
www.cisnerosmediadist.com
• Miguel Somoza, North America/Asia Sales Director
Nature of Sports Service:
International. Program distributor. Program offerings include El Boxeador.

CLEAR CHANNEL BROADCASTING
621 MAINSTREAM DR, STE 230
NASHVILLE, TN 37228
615-742-6100
800-346-9467
Fax: 615-742-6124
www.clearchannel.com
• Bob Pittman, Chief Executive Officer
Nature of Sports Service:
National. Radio program producer/packager, broadcaster, program distribution. Current properties include: U. of Florida football and basketball; Penn State football and basketball; Texas A&M football and basketball; and Iowa State University football and basketball.

CLTV - CABLE CHANNEL
200 YORK RD
OAK BROOK, IL 60521
630-368-4000
Fax: 630-368-4468
cltv.trb.com

CNBC
2200 FLETCHER AVE
FT. LEE, NJ 07024
201-585-2622
800-788-CNBC
Fax: 201-585-6244
www.cnbc.com
• Mark Hoffman, President/Chief Executive Officer

COLONY SPORTS
CORNER OLD ROUTE 9 & MIDDLEBUSH RD
WAPPINGERS FALLS, NY 12590
845-297-5645
Fax: 845-297-3262
• Michael McCartney, Executive Producer
• Hugh Taylor, Director
Nature of Sports Service:
Regional. Program producer, broadcaster for Cable TV. Provides package of Marist College men's basketball events.

CORE DIGITAL
330 S. RIVER DR
TEMPE, AZ 85281
480-707-1000
Fax: 480-707-1010
• Jonae Taylor, VP Sales/Marketing
• Stephanie Brooks, Sales
Nature of Sports Service:
Mobile production company. Mobile Unit capable of simultaneous production of both HD and Standard 601 signals.

Sports Service Founded:
1983

COWEN MEDIA
277 FAIRFIELD ROAD
SUITE 304
FAIRFIELD, NJ 07004
973-575-1234
Fax: 973-575-1238
www.cowenmedia.com
• Robert Cowen, President
• Karen Cowen, Vice President
Nature of Service:
A full service media company that provides superior quality television/video production, editing and consulting to the sports industry. Winner of 10 EMMY awards.
Clients:
Cardinal Health, CSTV, ESPN, ESPN Classic, Fazoli's, Hunter Public Relations, LPGA Tour, Maui Invitational, Northern California Golf Association, Octagon Marketing, The Sporting News, United States Golf Association

COX COMMUNICATIONS
1400 LAKE HEARN DR NE
ATLANTA, GA 30319
404-843-5000
Fax: 404-843-5777
www.cox.com
• Patrick J Esser, President
• James O. Robbins, President/Chief Executive Officer/Director
• John F. Dyer, Senior Vice President/Operations
• William Farina, Vice President Advertising Sales
• Ellen M. East, Vice President Communications/Investor Relati
• Joseph Rooney, Vice President Marketing

CTV TELEVISION NETWORK LTD.
9 CHANNEL NINE CT
SCARBORO, ON, CANADA M1S 4B5
416-332-5000
Fax: 416-299-2342
www.ctv.ca
• Lance Brown, Sports Director
• Virginia Gibberd, Director Production Operations
• Rick Brace, Vice President

CWI PRODUCTIONS, INC.
PO BOX 442
UNIONVALE, PA 19375
610-793-0979
Fax: 203-762-0207
info@healthyaging.net
www.healthyaging.net
Nature of Sports Service:
National. Sports film, video producer. Specializes in corporate-sponsored sports programming for television distribution. Full-service production company handling television syndication as well. Have produced programs on professional bicycle racing. Olympic race walking, running Olympic wrestling, equestrian, exercise/fitness, skiing, aging and athletes.

DYNOCOMM SPORTS TV
9675 4TH ST N.
ST. PETERSBURG, FL 33702
949-361-2063
Fax: 949-361-1716

- George E. Orgera, President
- Robert W. Eisenstaedt, Vice President
- Jeffrey Green, Senior Producer
- Connie Vizaro, Operations Manager

Nature of Sports Service:
National. Program producer/packager, distributor for Broadcast and Cable TV. On-site sponsor arrangements since 1982. Event promotion, broadcast production and syndication, airings in syndication and on ESPN and Fox Sports Net. Programs include OP pro Surfing Championship; World Cup of Sailboarding; Super Bowl of Motocross; Hawaiian International Billfish Tournament; Pro Bodyguard Championship; World Jet Ski Finals; Curacao Open Sailboard Championships, Pro Skateboard Championship: Team USA Skydiving Team Tour-Rep of China; Fiji Pro Surfing Championships; Another Classic Summer; ESPN Classic Summer; ESPN's A Day at the Beach; Budweiser Islamo

ESPN REGIONAL TELEVISION
11001 RUSHMORE DR
CHARLOTTE, NC 28277
704-973-5000
Fax: 704-973-5090
www.espn.com
- Arnie Sgalio, Director Big 10 Programs
- Chuck Gerber, Executive VP/General Manager
- Pete Derzes, Senior VP University Marketing/Program

Nature of Sports Service:
National. Regional. Local. Program producer and distributor. Syndicating programming includes: Philadelphia 76ers, IMSA racing and Top Rank boxing for ESPN; coaches show for University of Kansas and Iowa State; NCAA Championship week on ESPN; and college basketball games for various conferences, including Big Eight, Big West, Great Midwest, Sun Belt, Southern Missouri Valley, Midwestern Collegiate, Ohio Valley, Big 10, Big East, also produces various sports specials.

FOX SPORTS NET SOUTHWEST
100 E. ROYAL LANE, STE 200
IRVING, TX 75039
972-868-1800
Fax: 972-868-1678
foxsports.com
- Jon Heidtke, Vice President/General Manager

Nature of Sports Service:
Regional. Cable and satellite TV sports network. Current programs: Houston Astros home and road games; Texas Rangers home and road games; Dallas Mavericks home a road games; San Antonio Spurs home and road games; Dallas Stars home and road games; Houston Aeros home and road games; Dallas Burn home and road games; Dallas Cowboys weekly programming; Texas high school sports; College football-featuring the Big 12, Conference USA, Pac-10, SEC, Southland Football League; College basketball-featuring the big 12, Pac-10 and WAC; FOX Sports News; Fight Time on FOX; professional boxing; early round PGA coverage; Texas Special Olympics; weekly hunting

FREEDOM SPORTS NETWORK/DELCOM MARKETING GROUP
2055 ANGLO DR, STE 201
COLORADO SPRINGS, CO 80918
719-264-8112
Fax: 719-264-8243
- Ron Delorenzo, President

Nature of Sports Service:
National. Full service packager, syndicator and distributor. Provides television production of events needed separately. Experienced in NFL Football (games & weekly shows), college football, college basketball, hockey, golf, tennis, bowling, rodeo and various anthologies.

GOLF CHANNEL, THE
7580 GOLF CHANNEL DRIVE
ORLANDO, FL 32819
407-363-4653
www.golfchannel.com
- Mike McCarley, President
- Jeff Dilley, Chief Financial Officer
- Robert Greenway, SVP Production/Programming/Ops
- Gene Pizzolato, SVP Advertising Sales
- Kevin Byrnes, Vice President Advertising Sales
- John Houde, Vice President New Media
- R. Andy Murphy, Vice President Network Operations
- Mark Oldham, Vice President Tournament Affairs
- Christine Sullivan, Vice President Marketing
- Tony Tortorici, Vice President Production

Description:
National. Cable Television programmer offering 24-hour, 7 basic service. Live coverage of the PGA Tour, Champions Tour, LPGA, Nationwide, European and Australian Tours. Programming also includes: GOLF TALK LIVE, a call -in interview show with golfers. GOLF CHANNEL ACADEMY LIVE, a call-in instructional show. GOLF CENTRAL, a live news show, PROFILE OF A PRO, PASSAGE TO PARADISE, a golf travel program. The GOLF CHANNEL ACADEMY, an instructional series

GOLF MARKETING BY BIGGS
120 WEBSTER STREET
SUITE 216
LOUISVILLE, KY 40206
502-585-2299
Fax: 502-585-3574
- Biggs Tabler, President

Nature of Sports Service:
Properties include: The National Horse Show, the Tennessee Walking Horse Show, and Thoroughbreds. Tabler Communications specializes in media buying using Regional Sports Networks.

GOULD ENTERTAINMENT CORPORATION
101 W. 57TH ST
NEW YORK, NY 10019
212-586-5760
- Michael J. Gould, President

Nature of Sports Service:
National. Cable TV programmer. TV syndicator, packager, consultant. Current programs: A Man Named Lombardi.

GRAVITY TELEVISION & SPORTS MARKETING
450 BRYANT STREET
SAN FRANCISCO, CA 94107-1303
415-495-5515
andi@gravity.com
www.gravity.com
- Amit Kapur, Founder/Chief Executive Officer
- Jim Benedetto, Chief Technology Officer

HUNTERDON GROUP, INC.
5 LEXINGTON RD
ANNANDALE, NJ 08801
908-730-0369
- Mark Dau, President

Sports Service Founded:
1998

Nature of Sports Service:
Sports television production company specializing in live-event and taped programs.

IMPACT SPORTS
7322 E. BROADWAY AVE
SPOKANE, WA 99212-1135
509-924-7768
Fax: 509-924-7668
buck@indirect.com
www.tnb.net/impactsports
- Gary Knudson, President
- Murray Walden, Vice President
- Paul Sorensen, Chief Executive Officer

Nature of Sports Service:
Regional/National. TV, radio program producer and broadcaster. Current properties include Washington State U. football, basketball, baseball; Arizona State football, basketball and baseball; Arizona High School football, basketball, baseball championships; AA/AAA Boys/Girls basketball championships; statewide championships; Washington Trust cycling championships; Eastern Washington U. football and basketball; U. of Arizona, signage; USC/UCLA/San Diego State marketing reps; Big 12 Football Show TV - 7 states. Tacoma Raniers AAA baseball; State B broadcasts; Mike Price Coaches Show; Big Sky football/basketball games; Olympic swimming championsh

INTERNATIONAL MANAGEMENT GROUP (IMG)
200 5TH AVENUE
7TH FLOOR
NEW YORK, NY 10010
212-489-8300
Fax: 646-558-8399
www.img.com
- Michael J Dolan, Ph.D., Chairman/Chief Executive Officer

Nature of Sports Service:
National. Program production. Live coverage of sports, special events; institutional films - taped segments and programs; syndicated films; rights representation. TWI is IMG's subsidiary television production company

London Office:
TWI House, 23 Eyot Gardens, London, W6 9TR Great Britain. 44.81.846 8070; FAX: 44.81.746 5334

INTERNATIONAL SPORTS COMMUNICATIONS
230 NEW YORK AVE
HUNTINGTON, NY 11743
631-351-5878
Fax: 631-351-5875
jalbert@jalbertfilm.com
www.jalbertfilm.com
• Joe Jay Jalbert, President
• Carol Randel, Syndication Manager
Year Founded:
1970

INTERSPORT, INC.
20 W KINZIE STREET
SUITE 1600
CHICAGO, IL 60610
312-661-0616
Fax: 312-661-0622
www.intersportnet.com
• Mark Adamle, President, Sales
• David Boblink, Chief Financial Officer
Signature Events:
College Football All-Star Challenge (ESPN)
College Slam Dunk and Three-Point
Basketball Championships. (ESPN) The
ARETE Awards (CBS), Liberty Mutual
Coach of the Year Series (ABC)
Services:
Original sports and entertainment
programmins, event marketing and
corporate and fan hospitality

IPAYATTENTION LLC
203-329-0707
harvey@ipayattention.com
www.ipayattention.com
• Harvey Rubin, Executive
Sports Service Founded:
1994
Nature of Sports Service:
National. Arranges for sports events to be
produced for network and cable network
programs, including arranging the deal,
complete production, and coordination of all
elements including budgeting and financial
business planning. Events produced
include: PGA Chattanooga Classic; World
Cup Skeleton, Luge and Bobsled; National
Grand Champions of Dog Shows. Also
provides network program development and
consultation services.

ITV SPORT
THE NETWORK CENTER
200 GRAY'S INN RD
LONDON, ENGLAND WC1X 8HF
www.itv.com
• Adrian Chiles, Chief Presenter
Nature of Sports Service:
International. Commercial broadcasting
network in the United Kingdom.

JALBERT PRODUCTIONS, INC.
230 NEW YORK AVE
HUNTINGTON, NY 11743
631-351-5878
Fax: 631-351-5875
www.jalbertfilm.com
• Joe Jay Jalbert, President
• Carol Randel, Vice President Syndication
Sales
• Jay Jalbert, Vice President Production
Services
Nature of Service:
Producer of sports TV programs,
commercials, motivational videos,

syndicator of summer and winter sports
shows.

JFM SPORTS, INC.
20 SEARS DR
LAKE PLACID, NY 12946
518-523-3593
Fax: 518-523-1774
www.bobsleigh.com
• John F. Morgan, President

LEARFIELD SPORTS
2400 DALLAS PARKWAY
SUITE 500
PLANO, TX 75093
469-241-9191
Fax: 469-241-0110
www.learfieldsports.com
• Andy Rawlings, Executive VP/COO
(469) 241-9191
arwalings@learfield.com
• Greg Brown, President-Learfield Sports
(469) 241-9191
gbrown@learfield.com
• Keith Sampson, Executive Producer
Nature of Sports Service:
Regional. Over-the-air radio/TV program
producer, broadcaster, program distributor.
Produces and distributes collegiate sports in
Big 12, Big Ten, ACC and PAC-10. Men's
football and basketball for U. of Alabama,
Clemson U., U. of Colorado, Indiana U., U.
of Iowa, U. 0of Memphis, U. of Missouri, U.
of North Carolina, Oklahoma State U., U. of
Oklahoma, Oregon State U., Syracuse U.,
and Villanova U.

LEWIS PRODUCTIONS INC., BUTCH
250 W. 57TH ST, STE 311
NEW YORK, NY 10019
212-582-4344
Fax: 212-582-4346
Services:
Sports Productions and Promotions
Nature of Sports Service:
Program producer/packager. Boxing
promotions and client representation.
Sports Service Founded:
1886

LINCOLN FINANCIAL MEDIA
3340 PEACHTREE ROAD NE
SUITE 1430
ATLANTA, GA 30326
404-239-7211
• Edward Hull, President
• Jeff E. Tennant, Vice President/Sales &
Marketing
• Powell Kidd, Assistant Vice
President/Technology Operation
• Jimmy Rayburn, Vice
President/Operations Manager
Nature of Service:
Regional Television produces, syndicates
and sells ACC and SEC football and
basketball throughout the region. 10 ACC
Football Telecasts, 12 SEC Football
Telecasts, 32 ACC Basketball Telecasts, 33
SEC Basketbal Telecasts.

MAIN EVENTS
772 UNION BLVD
TOTOWA, NJ 07512
973-200-7050
Fax: 973-200-7061

knewman@mainevents.com
www.mainevents.com
• Jolene Mizzone, Vice President of
Operations

MEDIA VISTA PRODUCTIONS
500 Railway Avenue
Campbell, CA 85008
408-282-1960
Fax: 408-549-9870
www.mediavista.com
• Peter Liebengood, Founder
• Cassandra Bellantoni, Owner/Executive
Producer
Nature of Sports Service:
National. Television production. Specializes
in sports news and events.

MEDIALINK WORLDWIDE
6430 SUNSET BLVD, STE 1100
LOS ANGELES, CA 90028
323-465-0111
Fax: 323-465-9230
jshulman@medialink.com
www.medialink.com
• Michael E. Kassan, Founder
Additional Offices:
Atlanta, Chicago, Dallas, London, New York,
Washington, DC

MOFFETT PRODUCTIONS, INC.
16140 KUYKENDAHL ST, STE 126
HOUSTON, TX 77068
281-440-0044
Fax: 281-580-3227
info@moffett.com
www.moffett.com
• Bill Moffett, President
(281) 440-0044
bill@moffett.com
• Layne Belchic, Vice President
(281) 440-0044
• Joe Krath, Vice President/Creative
Director
(281) 440-0044
joe@moffett.com
Nature of Service:
Radio & TV Production Company. Leading
producer for Sporting Events, Sporting
Equipment and Promotional
Advertisements.

MOTOR SPORTS RADIO
C/O SPORTCOM ASSOCIATES
80 ZEVAN RD
JOHNSON CITY, NY 13790
607-770-9165
Fax: 607-770-9165
• Paul Kaminski, General Manager
Nature of Sports Service:
Produces Radio shows dealing with motor
sports.

MOTORSPORTS MEDIA GROUP
3455 PEACHTREE INDUSTRIAL BLVD,
#305
DULUTH, GA 30096-9102
770-662-8334
Fax: 770-458-0276
Nature of Sports Service:
National. Full-service producers of television
and video programming, focusing on racing.
Lineup includes 30-minute magazine shows,
behind-the-scenes coverage, team and
event coverage, corporate and sponsor
promotions, and television broadcast

production services. Current properties include: Racers, Checkered Past, This Week at Road Atlanta, Lanier Raceweek, Vintage and Historical Documentary Series; and many other series and documentary concepts. IMAGE Magnification (IMAG) at races is a specialty.

MOUNTAINEER SPORTS NETWORK
WVU COLISEUM, ROOM 107
MORGANTOWN, WV 26505
304-293-2821
Fax: 304-293-4105
www.msnsportsnet.com
Nature of Sports Service:
Regional. Regional program producer. Produces West Virginia University football and basketball games for radio (60 stations) and television (7 stations). Also produces Mountaineer Magazine, a weekly football show (TV) and Mountaineer Jammin, a weekly television basketball show.

NASCAR COUNTRY
181 N. HARBOR DR
DAVIDSON, NC 28036
704-987-8454
Fax: 704-896-3441
• Sid Morris, President/Chief Executive Officer
• Mike Helton, Chief Operating Officer
Nature of Sports Service:
Produces shows and news highlighting NASCAR.

NATIONAL FILM BOARD OF CANADA
350 5TH AVE, STE 4820
NEW YORK, NY 10118
212-629-8890
Fax: 212-629-8502
Nature of Sports Service:
Distributor of award-winning films and videos. Current properties include Chuvalo vs Ali, a documentary depicting the Battle of Toronto boxing match of 1966; King of the Hill, about black Canadian Hall-of-Famer Ferguson Jenkins; Baseball Girls, a documentary on the history of womens participation in the largely male dominated worlds of baseball and softball; The Rocket, a profile of legendary Montreal Canadian Maurice Richard; The Sweater, an animated short about boyhood passion for hockey; Path of the Paddle, series of four films which give clear-cut, well-illustrated explanations of paddling techniques.

NATIONAL MOBILE TELEVISION PRODUCTIONS, INC.
2740 CALIFORNIA ST
TORRANCE, CA 90503
310-782-9945
Fax: 310-782-9949
• Dave Cooper, Vice President Saless
• Michael Fillner, Sales
• Frank Coll, National Vice President of Operations
• Stephanie Hampton, Director of Operations
Nature of Sports Service:
National and international. Television productions. Full Service video production company specializing in remote television production. Supplies mobile television production facilities, production personnel, technical crews and transmission for live and live-to-tape sporting events. Provides

facilities, producers, directors, graphics, design and consultation and editing. Current productions include NBA, NFL, NHL, CFL. Major League Baseball productions: Executive producers for Colorado Rockies; regional, national and international production services for major sporting events including auto racing, baseball, basketball, boxing, bowling, boxing

NCAA
BROADCASTING
PO BOX 6222
INDIANAPOLIS, IN 46206
317-917-6222
Fax: 317-917-6807
jmichiaels@ncaa.org
www.ncaa.com
• Greg Weitekamp, Director of Broadcasting
(317) 917-6265
gweitekamp@ncaa.org
• Chris Fitzpatrick, Associate Director of Braodcasting
cfitzpatrick@ncaa.org
• Frank Rhodes, Associate Director of Broadcasting
frhodes@ncaa.org
• Jeramy Michiaels, Associate Director of Broadcasting
jmichiaels@ncaa.org
Nature of Sports Service:
National. Produce various NCAA Championship Events for national cable networks and syndication. Produce NCAA :30 PSA's for NCAA championship Events. Sell television rights to local stations that air NCAA championship events. License and sell stock NCAA Championship footage.

NFL FILMS
1 NFL PLAZA
MOUNT LAUREL TOWNSHIP, NJ 08054
856-222-3500
• Howard Katz, Chief Operating Officer
• Barry Wolper, Chief Operating Officer
• Hal Lipman, Vice President/Production Director
• Jim Jorden, Vice President/Producers
Nature of Sports Service:
National. Program producer. Provides pre-recorded videotapes and full range production facility and capabilities. Specific programs include: Football Follies Series; NFL Crunch Course; The NFL's Greatest Games; Super Bowl Highlight series; and individual annual team highlights.

NORTH AMERICAN MEDIA GROUP, INC.
12301 WHITEWATER DR
MINNETONKA, MN 55343
952-988-7117
800-688-7611
Fax: 952-936-9169
• Russell M. Nolan, Vice President/Group Publisher
• Rich Sundberg, Publisher (North American Hunter)
• Rich Sundberg, Publisher (North American Fisherman)
• Seth Hoyt, Publisher (PGA Tour Partners)
Nature of Sports Service:
National. Produces outdoor sports programming. Current properties: North American Outdoors, portraying all types of hunting and fishing, appearing on ESPN. Also publishes NORTH AMERICAN HUNTER, NORTH AMERICAN

FISHERMAN, PGA TOUR PARTNERS magazines. How To and Gardening How To magazines.

P.A.S.S. SPORTS
550 W. LAFAYETTE BLVD
DETROIT, MI 48231-3040
313-222-7277
Fax: 313-223-2299
• Jeffrey H. Genthner, General Manager
• Karen Kanigowski, Business Manager
• Keith Allo, Executive Producer
• Tom Maclean, General Sales Manager
Nature of Sports Service:
Regional. Cable TV program producer. Carries Detroit Tigers, Detroit Pistons, Detroit Red Wings, local Michigan universities and other selected amateur and professional events.

PETER ROGERES, INC LTD
1800 N. HIGHLAND AVE, STE 100
LOS ANGELES, CA 90028
323-962-1778
Fax: 323-962-7174
• Stephen M. Rodgers, Chief Executive Officer
• Tay Dall, Distribution Associate
Nature of Sports Service:
National. Sports TV program syndicator. Current programs: Championship Wrestling; White Search, Skiing.

PLATINUM ENTERTAINMENT PARTNERS II
4310 S. CAMERON, STE 4
LAS VEGAS, NV 89103
702-252-3900
Fax: 702-252-4300
• Andrew Fonfa, Chief Executive Officer
• Bill Lastra, President
• Cheryl E Cohen, Vice President/Executive Producer
• Patrick Mauro, Hospitality/Production

PROMARK TELEVISION
500 S. PALM CANYON DR, #220
PALM SPRINGS, CA 92264
760-322-7776
800-266-6662
Fax: 310-276-3208
www.promarktv.com
• David Levine, President
Nature of Sports Service:
National. Sports TV program syndicator.

RAI, ITALIAN RADIO & TELEVISION SYSTEM
1350 AVE OF THE AMERICAS, 21ST FL
NEW YORK, NY 10019
212-468-2500
Fax: 212-765-1956
• Mario Bona, President
Nature of Sports Service:
International. Program producer, broadcaster, distributor for cable, Over-The-Air TV and Over-The-Air Radio. Italian Radio & TV system. Produces, broadcasts and distributes sports programming (originating in Italy). In the U.S., broadcasts Italian League soccer. Current properties include: Italian soccer leagues A & B; Italian basketball league; Italian rugby league; rugby.

ROBBINS MEDIA
375 GREENWICH ST
NEW YORK, NY 10013
212-661-7670
Fax: 212-656-1997
info@robbinsmedia.com
www.robbinsmedia.com
• Shawn Robbins, Producer/Director
Description:
Robbins Media is an award winning full
service production company specializing in
creative images and ideas for a diverse
range of clients. Collaborates closely with
networks, marketing, public relations, and
advertising agencies by giving them a full
service creative sports production arm
capable of any size project.

ROGERS SPORTSNET, INC.
PO BOX 9, STATION O
TORONTO, ON, CANADA M4A 2M9
877-288-7767
www.sportsnet.ca

RUFFOLO COMMUNICATIONS
9 MIDWAY DR
WILLOWBROOK, IL 60527
630-887-7361
Fax: 630-887-7361
trcomm@aol.com
• Jeff Ruffolo, President
Nature of Sports Service:
National. Programmer, distributor, marketer
of regular season, championship and tour
events of professional and collegiate athletic
programming for radio and television.

SFM ENTERTAINMENT
800 WESTCHESTER AVENUE
SUITE N-345
RYE BROOK, NY 10573
212-790-4496
Fax: 212-398-5738
www.sfment.com
• Stanley Moger,
Co-Founder/President/Chief Executive
Office5r
• Michael Maizes, Senior Vice
President/In-House Counsel

SNTV
5 LONGWALK ROAD
STOCKLEY PARK
LONDON, UB11 1FE
+44-203 314 5770
planning@sntv.com
www.sntv.com
• Andrew Parkinson, Editor
(44-) 0-8233-5
aparkinson@imgworld.com
Description:
Sports news video agency, providing six
bulletins a day of action, highlights and
breaking news, gathered 24 hours a day,
365 days of the year.

SONIFI SOLUTIONS
3900 W. INNOVATION ST
SIOUX FALLS, SD 57107
605-988-1000
888-563-4363
hotelsupport@sonifi.com
www.sonifi.com
• Steven Truckenmiller, Senior VP
Programming & Content Management

Frequency:
Daily.
Primary Audience:
Hotel guests.
Sports:
All available leagues.
Nature of Service:
Distribution of live sports packages into
hotel rooms on a pay-per-view basis.

SPEED CHANNEL NETWORK, INC.
1220 WEST WT HARRIS BOULEVARD
CHARLOTTE, NC 28262-8536
704-501-5700
Fax: 704-731-2197
www.speedtv.com
• Todd Siegel, Senior Vice President of
Advertising Sales
(212) 822-8681
• Bobby Akin, Vice President Integrated
Sales/Marketing
• Nancy MacDonald, Director, Marketing &
Promotions
(704) 501-5790
Description:
Speed Channel, a member of the FOX
Sports Media Group, recognized
experimental marketing as an opportunity to
build awareness of the network and boost
their SPEED Fanatic program, a group of
passionate motorsports fans.

SPORTS BYLINE USA
300 BROADWAY, STE 8
SAN FRANCISCO, CA 94133
415-434-8300
800-783-7529
Fax: 415-391-2569
byline@pacbell.net
www.sportsbyline.com
• Ron Barr, CEO
xhighflyer@aol.com
• Darren Peck, President
dpeck@sportsbyline.com
• Ira Hankin, Production Director
• Jessizo Geich, Traffic Director
• James Homs, Web Developer

**SPORTS ILLUSTRATED
TELEVISION/SITV**
1271 AVE OF THE AMERICAS, 21ST FL
C/O SPORTS ILLUSTRATED
NEW YORK, NY 10020
212-522-2845
Fax: 212-522-0138
Nature of Sports Service:
1994. SITV produces television
programming for distribution in broadcast
network and non-traditional formats.

SPORTSBLAST
94209 RESEDA BLVD
NORTHRIDGE, CA 91324
818-882-7297
Fax: 818-882-7563
• Peter Kjenaas, Producer
Marketing & Consulting Services:
SportsBlast specializes in animation.
Produces The Kelly's an animated series
that evolves around auto sports. SportsBlast
has signed a deal with Turner sports
Interactive for the animated series.
Sports Service Founded:
1994

SPORTVISION
4410 NORTH RAVENSWOOD AVE
CHICAGO, IL 60093
773-293-4300
Fax: 773-293-2155
info@sportvision.com
www.sportvision.com
• Ryan Zander, Baseball, Motorsports
• Hank Adams, Chief Executive Officer
• Stan Honey, President/Chief Technology
Officer
• Rich Magid, Cheif Financial Officer
• Mike Jakob, Chief Operating Officer
• Steve Roberts, EVP/Business
Development
• David Goldberg, EVP, Corporate
Development
• Marv White, EVP, Development and Field
Engineer
• Barry Schliesmann, EVP Interactive
Technology
• Tom Worcester, EVP Sales and Marketing
• Russell Quy, VP Media
Prduction/Executive Producer
Sports Service Founded:
1998
Nature of Sports Service:
Develop products and applications that
enhance the fan's experience on television,
the Internet and convergence platforms.
Organization's fan-centric technology
applications allow broadcasters, sports
leagues, teams and internet sites to enrich
content. Creators of 1st and 10 electronic
first down line for television.

**STEINFELD PRODUCTIONS, INC.,
ROBERT**
18031 ROCK BRANCH DR
DALLAS, TX 75287
972-868-1718
Fax: 972-868-1678
• Robert Steinfeld, President
Nature of Sports Service:
National. Program producer/packager.
Producer and director of live sports events
including NBA basketball, Major League
Baseball, NCAA basketball and other
events. Associated with Home Sports
Entertainment and ESPN Sports Networks.
Also produces, markets and distributes Tom
House instructional baseball videos.

STELLARTV-SPORTS
2327 N. VERDUGO RD
GLENDALE, CA 91208
818-240-9581
Fax: 831-401-2627
www.stellartv.com
• Rinny Manzano, Vice President

**THE PHOENIX COMUNICATIONS GROUP,
INC.**
3 EMPIRE BLVD
S. HACKENSACK, NJ 07606
201-807-0888
Fax: 201-807-0272
• Tom L. Filip, Public Relations/Event
Services
(201) 807-0888
• James E. Holland, President
ext 470
• Geoffrey W. Belinfante, Senior
VP/Executive Producer
ext 460
• Richard Domich, Senior VP
Sales/Marketing

• Jean-Marie Cap, Senior VP Finance/Administration
• Tim Roberts, VP News Service

THE SPORTS AND ENTERTAINMENT COMPANY LLC
2525 15TH STREET
SUITE 1-B
DENVER, CO 80211
303-427-3200
Fax: 303-427-3201
info@sports-entco.com
www.sports-entco.com
• Jon J. Franklin, JD, President & Chief Executive Officer
jonf@sports-entco.com
• Briar Sangiuliano, JD, MBA, VP Marketing
(720) 352-3101
briars@sports-entco.com
• Andrew Madigan, MBA, Operations Director
(303) 427-3200
andrewm@sports-entco.com
• Brian Harris, Events Director
(303) 427-3200
brianh@sports-entco.com
• Nina Kim, Marketing Manager
(303) 427-3200
ninak@sports-entco.com
Description:
On site event activation; video production; athlete management.
Clients:
Barilla pasta; Rip It Energy Fuel; Golden Gloves Boxing; World Series of Boxing; Tuff shed marketing; television rights sales for extreme sports, skiing & snowboarding.

TIMELINE VIDEO
ONE BRIDGE ST
IRVINGTON, NY 10533
914-591-7360
Fax: 914-591-7461
www.timelinevideo.com
• Diane Cricchio, President/Creative Director
diane@timelinevideo.com
• Sean LaGamma, Managing Director
sean@timelinevideo.com
Clients Include:
Lucent Technologies, IBM, Minolta.
Nature of Sports Service:
A full service production company. Produces film and video for special events, documentaries, new product introductions, corporate image campaigns, video news releases, commercials, etc.

TRANSMEDIA GROUP
240 West Palmetto Park Road
Suite 300
Boca Raton, FL 33432
561-750-9800
Fax: 561-750-4660
pr@transmediagroup.com
www.transmediagroup.com
• Thomas Madden, Chairman & Chief Executive Officer

TRZ COMMUNICATIONS INC.
4682 STATE ROUTE 43
KENT, OH 44240
800-846-4630
Fax: 800-846-4632
staff@trz.cc
www.trz.cc

• Thomas R. Zawistowski, Chief Executive Officer
• Mike Wilt, Director Team Relations
Nature of Sports Service:
National, Radio program distributor, Live telephone broadcast systems - play-by-play of college, NBA, NFL, NHL, Major League Baseball and auto racing from flagship radio stations.

U.S. OLYMPIC COMMITTEE BROADCASTING DIVISION
ONE OLYMPIC PLAZA
COLORADO SPRINGS, CO 80909
719-578-4740
Fax: 719-632-0250
www.usoc.org
• Mark Jones, Senior Director of Communications
(719) 866-2226
• Lindsay Hogan, Senior Director of Communications
(719) 866-4566
• Beth Bourgeois, Director, Communications
• Patrick Sandusky, Chief Communications & Public Affairs Officer
Nature of Sports Service:
National. Over-The-Air and cable program placement for the U.S. Olympic Committee and National Governing bodies. Involves the U.S. Olympic Committee and its member organizations. Programming includes the U.S. Olympic Festivals, major NGB national and international events. Offers a full-service off-line and on-line production house to service members of the Olympic Family with all aspects of video and audio needs, and serves as a clearing house for vintage Olympic footage and non-Olympic competitions for 41 sports within the United States.

VIDEO SPORTS, INC.
PO BOX 10
DELMAR, NY 12054
518-439-1998
800-USA-1996
Fax: 888-872-2024
• Jonathan Fishbein, President
(518) 439-1998
Nature of Service:
World's largest selection of figure skating videos.
Sports:
Figure skating.

VILCOM
88 VILCOM CENTER
CHAPEL HILL, NC 27514
919-968-4811
800-318-7103
Fax: 919-968-3748
• Jim Heavner, President
• Bob Woodruff, Chief Financial Officer/Executive Vice Presid
• Dean Linke, Vice President/Sales/Marketing
• Tim Noonan, Marketing Director Tar Heel Sports
Nature of Sports Service:
Retains broadcast rights (TV & Radio) to the University of North Carolina athletic programs. Programs include men's basketball and football. Also included is: coaches shows, ACC Hotline show, game programs and web site.

WALLACH ENTERTAINMENT
1400 BRAERIDGE DRIVE
BEVERLY HILLS, CA 90210
310-278-4574
Fax: 310-273-0548
wallach1@sbcglobal.net
• George Wallach, President
(310) 278-4574
wallach1@sbcglobal.net
Nature of Sports Service:
National. Cable TV programmer, syndicator. Produces sports-related shows for national cable and syndication.

WEBB ELECTRONICS
1410 WESTWAY CIRCLE
CARROLLTON, TX 75005
972-242-5400
Fax: 972-245-4517
www.webbelectronics.com
Sports Service Founded:
1986

WEST GLEN COMMUNICATIONS, INC.
1430 BROADWAY
NEW YORK, NY 10018-3396
212-921-2800
800-325-8677
Fax: 212-944-9055
www.westglen.com
• Stanley S. Zeitlin, President
• Mark Dembo, Senior Vice President/Marketing
• Annette Minkalis, Senior Vice President/Broadcast
• John Summerlin, Senior Vice President/Production
• Cathy Boje, Vice President/Operations
Nature of Sports Service:
National. Specializes in developing targeted media networks for audio, video and multi-media program distribution to television, radio and specialized audiences such as schools, clubs, and civic organizations. Services include production and audience development, VNRs, PSAs, satellite media tours, B-roll, web casting, video conferencing, customized feedback and reporting.

WINNERCOMM, INC.
6120 S. YALE, 2ND FL
TULSA, OK 74136
918-496-1900
Fax: 918-496-8606
www.winnercomm.com
• Tom Bergstrand, Sports Sales
• Chris Lincoln, Executive Vice President
• Doug Wren, Executive Vice President/Programs/Production
• Bill Flesher, Executive Vice President
Description:
Founded 1981. A full service video production company and one of the largest independent packagers of programming of the ESPN networks.
Nature of Sports Service:
National. Program producer. Racing To The Kentucky Derby, Racing To The Breeders' Cup; 2Day At The Races; Racehorse Digest; Wrangler World of Rodeo; America's Horse; American Championship Harness Series; Under Wild Skies; Cabela's Sportsman's Quest; Major League Soccer, BASS Masters, World Championship Fishing, In Search of Fly Water.

WORLD WIDE SKI CORPORATION
312 AABC
SUITE I
ASPEN, CO 81611-2568
970-925-7864
Fax: 970-925-7882
Nature of Service:
National, Full service producer/distributor of Ski television programming. Ski industry marketing consulting.

Sports Radio Networks

AMERICAN URBAN RADIO NETWORKS
42 PARK AVE SOUTH
14TH FL
NEW YORK, NY 10016
212-883-2100
Fax: 212-297-2571
www.aurn.com
• Jerry. Lopes, President, Program Operations & Affiliations
• Barry Feldman, Vice President Research
(212) 883-2104
bfeldman@aurn.com
• Shanta Manickam, Manager of Marketing and Digital Services
(21-) 83-2121
Nature of Sports Service:
National. Radio broadcasting network.

AROUND THE RINGS
1776 PEACHTREE ST, STE 436 N
ATLANTA, GA 30309
404-874-1603
Fax: 404-874-3248
www.AroundTheRings.com
• Ed Hula, Founder
Comment@AroundTheRings.com
• Sheila S. Hula, Publisher
Sheila@AroundTheRings.com
• Brian Baker, Director Of Business Development
• Kathy Kuzcka, Circulation
Kathy@AroundTheRings.com
Description:
Full Service news agency, specializing in Olympic coverage, Radio production, specializing in reporting. Publication is the leading publication focusing on business of the Olympic movement.

CAPITOL BROADCASTING COMPANY
2619 WESTERN BLVD
PO BOX 12800
RALEIGH, NC 27606
919-890-6000
Fax: 919-890-6095
webmaster@cbc-raleigh.com
www.capitolnet.com
• James F. Goodmon, President/CEO
(919) 821-8504
jgoodmon@cbc-raleigh.com
• James F. Goodmon, Jr., Vice President CBC New Media Group
(919) 821-8605
jgoodmon@cbcnewmedia.com
• George W Habel, III, Vice President Radio Networks/Sports/99.9 The Fan
(919) 687-6531
Nature of Sports Service:
Produces play by play broadcasts, and coaches shows.

CORUS RADIO
CKNW 980AM
700 W. GEORGIA ST, STE 2000
VANCOUVER, BC, CANADA V7Y 1K9
604-331-2711
888-399-9898
Fax: 604-331-2722
www.cknw.com
• Mike Searson, Director of Sales
• Raila Gutman, Marketing Manager
• Tamara Von Dohren, Promotional Coordinator
Nature of Sports Service:
National (Canadian). 24-hour regional/national news and sports satellite service (Canada-Wide). B.C. Lions (CFL); Vancouver Canucks (NHL).

COX MEDIA GROUP
6205 PEACHTREE DUNWOODY RD
ATLANTA, GA 30328
678-645-0000
Fax: 678-645-5002
www.coxmediagroup.com
• Bill Hoffman, President
• Kim Guthrie, Senior Vice President of Radio
• Richard J. Reis, Senior Vice President Radio Operations
• Donna Hall, Senior Vice President Marketing & Client Solu
• Nick Peluso, Senior Vice President Radio Operations
Nature of Sports Service:
National. Cox Media Group is an integrated broadcasting, publishing, direct marketing and digital media company.

DIALGLOBAL, INC.
CANDLER TOWER
220 W 42ND STREET
NEW YORK, NY 10036
212-967-2888
888-435-7450
www.dialglobal.com
• Spencer Brown, Chief Executive Officer
• Ken Williams, President
• Marty Damin, Vice President Sports Sales
• Ed Quagliariello, Head of New York Sales
Nature of Sports Service:
National. An independent radio network, offering formats, prep, sports programming, music, jingles,imaging and advertising. Current sports programming: NFL, NBC Sports Radio, NCAA and Golf.

ESPN NETWORK
935 MIDDLE ST
BRISTOL, CT 06010
860-766-2000
Fax: 860-766-2213
www.espn.go.com
• John Skipper, President
Nature of Sports Service:
Worldwide. Covers a wide array of sporting events, shows, interviews and sports talk.

ESPN ON ABC
545 MIDDLE STREET
BRISTOL, CT 06010
860-766-2000
espn.go.com/espntv/onair/index
• John Skipper, Executive Vice President Content
• Steve Downs, Senior Vice Presidnt Programming
• Steve Anderson, Vice President Products

Nature of Sports Service:
National. Radio broadcasting network.

MOTOR RACING NETWORK/MRN
555 MRN DRIVE
CONCORD, NC 28027
704-262-6700
Fax: 704-262-6811
www.motorracingnetwork.com
• David Hyatt, President
• Chris D'Aprile, Director
• John Singler, News Director
• Lauren Schweppe, Associate Producer
Nature of Sports Service:
National. Produces radio broadcasts for NASACAR Sprint Cup, NASCAR Nationwide Series, NASCAR Camping World Truck Series, NASCAR K&N Pro Series, NASCAR Whelen Modified Tour and GRAND-AM Road Racing.

PREMIERE RADIO NETWORKS
15260 VENTURA BOULEVARD
SHERMAN OAKS, CA 91403
818-377-5300
Fax: 818-377-5333
www.premiereradio.com
• Steve Lehman, Chairman and Chief Executive Officer
• Jennifer Leimgruber, Senior Vice President of Programming
Nature of Sports Service:
National. Radio Network - sports talk programs.

WESTWOODONE
CANDLE TOWER
220 W 42ND ST
NEW YORK, NY 10036
212-641-2888
888-435-7450
www.westwoodone.com
• Paul Caine, Chief Executive Officer and Director
• Chris B Corcoran, Vice President/Affiliate Management
• Marty Damin, Vice President/Sales Sports
Nature of Sports Service:
National. Leader in live play-by-play radio sports. Sports line-up includes NCAA football and basketball, Men's Basketball Tournament and Final Four; regular season NFL football, the Playoffs and the Super Bowl; College World Series; Frozen Four; the Masters and the Olympics.

YAHOO! SPORTS RADIO
5353 W ALABAMA
STE 415
HOUSTON, TX 77056
713-479-5300
www.yahoosportsradio.com
• David Gow, CEO
• Craig Larson, Program Director
(713) 479-5373
• Josh Vexker, Affiliate Relations Director
(713) 479-5358
• John M Cravens, VP Operations/Stations Operations
• Matt Nahigian, Sports Director
mnahigian@sportingnews.com
• Ryan Williams, Sports Director
• Randy Merkin, Executive Producer
• Jennifer Hadden, Executive Producer
• Kelly Murphy, Host Appearances
• Beth Roncke, Marketing Manager

Nature of Sports Service:
National. 24-hour sports radio network with over 430 affiliated stations. Organization also operates Boston's Sporting News Radio 1510, WWZN The Zone, New York's 620 WSNR,Sporting News Radio, Los Angeles KMPC 1540 Sporting News Radio and 820 WCSN, Chicago's Sporting News. Broadcasts are streamed live through www.sportingnews.com.

Sports Radio Programs, Local

1500 ESPN SPORTSTALK
3415 UNIVERSITY AVENUE
MINNEAPOLIS, MN 55414
651-647-1500
877-615-1500
Fax: 651-649-1515
www.1500espn.com
• Brad Lane, Programming
• Ryan Giles, Promotions
• Bernie Laur, Online Sales
Description:
Talk Radio. Sports programming: M-F SportsTalk 3-4pm, Sports center/All Night 12-4pm, Sports Center/AM 4-5am; Saturday SportsTalk 10-12pm and Sunday SportsTalk 10-12pm.

970 WATH
300 COLUMBUS ROAD
PO BOX 210
ATHENS, OH 45701
740-593-6651
Fax: 740-594-3488
www.970wath.com
• Dave W Palmer, President
palmer@wxtq.com
• Thom Williams, Station and General Sales Manager
twilliams@wxtq.com
• Marianne Williams, National Sales Manager/Special Events
mwilliams@wxtq.com
• Bob Beyette, News Director
news@wxtq.com
Description:
Commentary, Sports. Monday, Tuesday, Wednesday, Thursday, Friday at 6:00PM for 1 hour. Program is a sports call-in show.

CBS PHILLY - SPORTSRADIO 94WIP
400 MARKET ST - 9TH FL
PHILADELPHIA, PA 19106
215-625-9460
wippromotions@cbsradio.com
• Andy Bloom, Operations Manager
(215) 625-6570
• Spike Eskin, Program Director
(215) 625-6568
spike@cbsphilly.com
• Ruby Ross, General Sales Manager
(215) 625-6530
suby.ross@cbsradio.com
• Vince Gambino, Local Sales Manager
(215) 625-6579
vince.gambino@cbsradio.com
• Cindy Webster, Marketing Director
(610) 668-5952
cswebster@cbs.com
Description:
News, Sports and Weather. Sports updates

include: local, Phillies, Sixers, Flyers, Eagles, Wings, Wing Bowl.

CHARLESTON SPORTS RADIO
60 MARK FIELD DRIVE
SUITE 4
CHARLESTON, SC 29407
843-763-6631
Fax: 843-766-1239
ted@kirkmanbroadcasting.com
www.charlestonsportsradio.com
• Ted Byrne, Operations Manager
Description:
Sports Talk Radio. Call-In, Commentary, Current Events, Entertainment, Information, Interview, Sports, Talk, Traffic.

CHIEFS RADIO NETWORK
5800 FOXRIDGE DRIVE
6TH FL
MISSION, KS 66202
913-514-3000
Fax: 913-514-3004
rich.mcardle@cumulus.com
www.kcchiefsradio.com
• Mark Sullivan, President General Manager
(913) 514-3121
mark.sullivan@cumulus.com
• Rich McArdle, Radio Network Sales Manager
rich.mcardle@cumulus.com
Description:
Sports. Talk. Exclusive radio home of Chiefs Gameday coverage.

GATOR IMG SPORTS NETWORK
3909 W. NEWBERRY ROAD
STE D
GAINESVILLE, FL 32607
352-375-4683
www.gatornetwork.com
• Mick Hubert, Broadcast Announcer
Nature of Sports Service:
Play-by-Play action of Florida Gators Football.

HY-VEE RADIO COACHES CORNER
700 MAIN STREET SUITE 211
PELLA, IA 50219
641-842-3161
Fax: 641-842-5606
www.kniakrls.com
Description:
Interview, Play-by-Play, Talk. Monday at 7:00 PM for 1 hour. Program interviews local high school and college coaches.

IDAHO SPORTS TALK
1419 WEST BANNOCK STREET
BOISE, ID 83702
208-336-3670
Fax: 252-473-1584
www.ktik.com
Description:
Call-In, Commentary, Entertainment, Interview, Sports, Talk. Monday-Friday at 3:00PM for 2.00 hours. Team coverage: Idaho Steelheads hHockey and Boise Hawks baseball.

KGSO 1410 SPORTS RADIO
1632 S MAIZE ROAD
WICHITA, KS 67209
312-721-8484
Fax: 316-721-8276
www.kgso.com

• Harry Finch, General Manager
• Lisa Bryce, Business Manager
• Greg Steckline, Owner
Description:
Wichita's premier 24-hour all-sports radio station.
Format:
All sports

LET'S TALK RACING
700 MAIN STREET SUITE 211
PELLA, IA 50219
641-842-3161
Fax: 641-842-5606
kniakrls@kniakrls.com
www.kniakrls.com
• Derek Cardwell, Host
sportsdude61@hotmail.com
Description:
Interview, Play-by-Play, Talk. Saturday at 11:00AM for 30 minutes. Program features informative talks with sprint car drivers, owners, and promoters.

LET'S TALK SPORTS
3755 KARICIO LANE SUITE 2C
PRESCOTT, AZ 86303
928-445-8289
800-264-5449
Fax: 928-442-0448
www.kqna.com
• Sanford Cohen, Host
Description:
Call-In, Interview, Play-by-Play, Talk. Friday at 4:00PM for 2.00 hours. Program focuses on local and national sports.

LOCKED ON SPORTS
351 ELLIOTT AVENUE WEST SUITE 300
SEATTLE, WA 98119
206-494-2000
800-726-0950
Fax: 206-494-2969
jaykelly@clearchannel.com
www.kjram.com
• John Fure, Producer
(206) 494-2000
johnfure@clearchannel.com
• David Locke, Host
davidlocke@clearchannel.com
Description:
Call-In, Commentary, Entertainment, Interview, Play-by-Play, Sports, Talk. Monday, Tuesday, Wednesday, Thursday, Friday at 7:00PM for 4.00 hours.

LONE STAR FISHING
1080 BALLPARK WAY
ARLINGTON, TX 76011-5164
817-543-5400
Fax: 817-543-5572
krldeditor@cbs.com
www.krld.com
• Brian Hughes, Host
(817) 543-5455
tofishtx@aol.com
Description:
Call-In, Commentary, Educational, Information, Interview, News, Sports, Talk, Traffic, Weather. Sunday, Saturday at 5:00AM for 1 hour. Program focuses on fishing.

LOOSE CANNONS
9660 GRANITE RIDGE DRIVE
SAN DIEGO, CA 92123-2657

818-559-2252
800-776-1690
Fax: 858-522-5768
www.xtrasports690.com
Description:
Call-In, Interview, Sports, Talk. Monday, Tuesday, Wednesday, Thursday, Friday at 9:00AM for 4.00 hours. Program is a sports talk show.

MICHIGAN RADIO NETWORK
325 SOUTH WALNUT
LANSING, MI 48933
517-484-4888
Fax: 517-484-1389
• Dennis Mellott, President/General Manager
(517) 484-4888
• Rob Baykian, News Director
(517) 484-4888
Nature of Sports Service:
Covers University of Michigan (Wolverines) sports; Local Sports, Central Michigan University Football, Michigan Racing Network, Michigan State University/MSU Football.
Football:
NFL - Detroit Lions.

NORTH STAR BROADCASTING
1356 MACKINAW AVENUE
CHEBOYGAN, MI 49721
231-627-2341
Fax: 231-627-7000
mary@nsbroadcasting.com
www.nsbroadcasting.com
• Mary Reynolds, General Manager/VP Sales & Marketing
mary@nsbroadcasting.com
Description:
Play-by-Play, Sports, Talk.

RACING ROUNDUP
418 NORTH CENTER STREET
CORRY, PA 16407
814-664-8694
800-513-1370
Fax: 814-664-8695
power1370@yahoo.com
www.wwcb.com
• Kevin Thomas, Host/Producer/Program Director
Description:
Interview, Sports, Talk. Saturday at 10:00AM for 30 minutes. Program features information on regional and NASCAR auto racing events.

SOUL EXPRESSION
1000 ASU DRIVE BOX 269
ALCORN STATE, MS 39096
601-877-6290
Fax: 601-877-2213
www.alcornstateuniversity.com
• Charles Edmond, Sports Director
(601) 877-2480
Description:
Call-In, Interview, News, Play-by-Play, Sports. Sunday, Monday, Tuesday, Wednesday, Thursday, Friday, Saturday at 6:00AM for 8.00 hours.

SPORTS NIGHT
9660 GRANITE RIDGE DRIVE
SAN DIEGO, CA 92123-2657

818-559-2252
800-776-1690
Fax: 858-522-5768
www.xtrasports690.com
• Lee Hamilton, Host
(818) 559-2252
leehamilton@clearchannel.com
Description:
Call-In, Interview, Play-by-Play, Sports, Talk. Monday, Tuesday, Wednesday, Thursday, Friday at 4:00PM for 4.00 hours. Program features sports commentary and interviews.

SPORTS OPEN LINE
1 SOUTH MEMORIAL DRIVE
SAINT LOUIS, MO 63102
314-621-2345
Fax: 314-444-3230
kmox@kmox.com
www.kmox.com
• Mike Grimm, Host
(314) 444-1872
mdgrimm@cbs.com
• Ron Jacober, Sports Director
(314) 444-3275
Description:
Call-In, Interview, Sports, Talk. Sunday, Monday, Tuesday, Wednesday, Thursday, Friday, Saturday at 6:00PM for 2.00 hours. Program is a sports talk show with interviews and listener participation.

SPORTS RADIO KJR
190 QUEEN ANNE AVE N
SEATTLE, WA 98109
206-286-9595
Fax: 206-494-2969
jaykelly@clearchannel.com
www.sportsradiokjr.com
• Dick Fain, Sports Director
Description:
Call-In, Interview, Play-by-Play, Sports, Talk.

SPORTS RAP
24 EAST MEADOW STREET SUITE 1
FAYETTEVILLE, AR 72701-5320
479-521-5566
Fax: 479-521-4968
anita.cowan@cumulus.com
• Chuck Barrett, Executive Producer/Host
(479) 521-5329
Description:
Sports. Monday, Tuesday, Wednesday, Thursday, Friday at 4:00PM for 2.00 hours.

SPORTS TALK
P.O. BOX 13048 SFA
NACOGDOCHES, TX 75962
936-468-4000
www.sfasu.edu/ksau
• Sherry Williford, Executive Producer
(936) 468-4001
Description:
Call-In, Sports, Talk. Tuesday, Thursday at 5:30PM for 30 minutes. Program gives listeners a chance to call in and express opinions or make predictions about a wide range of sporting events.

SPORTS TALK/THE TICKET
20450 NW 2ND AVENUE
MIAMI, FL 33169-2505
305-521-5100
877-790-1015
Fax: 305-521-1416
www.theticketmiami.com

• Larry Most, General Manager
(305) 521-5234
• Scott Prichett, Director Of Marketing
• Donna Mairs, National Sales Manager
• Von Freeman, National Sales Manager
• Eric Stenger, Promotions Director
• Victoria Aguirre, Traffic Director
• Marc Budine, Interactive/Online Sales Manager
(305) 521-5231
Description:
Call-In, Commentary, Entertainment, Sports. Team coverage: Miami Marlins, Miami Dolphins, Miami HEAT, Miamia Hurricanes, FL Int'l University and Florida Panthers.

SPORTS TO THE MAX
625 2ND AVENUE SOUTH
MINNEAPOLIS, MN 55402
612-370-0611
Fax: 612-370-0159
www.wccoradio.com
• Jimmy Erickson, Producer
(612) 370-0665
jerickson@wccoradio.cbs.com
• Mike Max, Host
(612) 375-7264
mmax@wccoradio.cbs.com
Description:
Sports, Talk. Monday, Tuesday, Wednesday, Thursday, Friday at 6:00PM for 3.00 hours.

SPORTS ZOO
4695 SOUTH MONACO STREET
DENVER, CO 80237-3403
303-713-8415
Fax: 303-713-8424
www.850koa.com/
• Scott Hastings, Host
(303) 713-8585
scotthastings@clearchannel.com
• Alan Jackson, Sports Director
(303) 713-8689
alanjackson@clearchannel.com
• Dave Logan, Host
(303) 713-8689
davelogan@clearchannel.com
• Lois Melkonian, Host
(303) 713-8585
loismelkonian@clearchannel.com
Description:
Sports, Talk. Monday, Tuesday, Wednesday, Thursday, Friday at 3:10PM for 3.00 hours.

SPORTSBEAT
2000 WEST LOOP STREET SUITE 300
HOUSTON, TX 77027-3510
713-212-8000
Fax: 713-212-8958
www.ktrh.com
• Carl Dukes, Host
carldukes@clearchannel.com
Description:
Commentary, Play-by-Play, Sports, Talk. Monday, Tuesday, Wednesday, Thursday, Friday at 5:00PM for 3.00 hours. Program focuses on local and national sports.

SPORTSLINE
1749 NORTH 2ND STREET
ABILENE, TX 79603
325-673-1455
Fax: 915-673-3485
www.abileneradio.com
• Al Pickett, Producer

Description:
Call-In, Play-by-Play. Monday, Tuesday, Wednesday, Thursday, Friday at 5:00PM for 1 hour. Program discusses the world of sports and incorporates listener input.

SPORTSPHONE 68 WITH LARRY KRUEGER
55 HAWTHORNE STREET SUITE 1000
SAN FRANCISCO, CA 94105-3914
415-995-6800
Fax: 415-995-6907
www.knbr.com
• Tony Salvadore, General Manager
Description:
Call-In, Commentary, Current Events, Information, Interview, News, Sports, Talk. Monday, Tuesday, Wednesday, Thursday, Friday at 7:00PM for 3.00 hours. Program covers the latest sports news and human interest stories.

SPORTSTALK
2601 NICHOLASVILLE ROAD
LEXINGTON, KY 40503-3307
859-422-1000
Fax: 859-422-1038
• Tom Leach, Host/Producer
(859) 422-1096
tomleach@clearchannel.com
• Jim Tirey, Host/Producer
jimtyree@clearchannel.com
Description:
Play-by-Play. Monday, Tuesday, Wednesday, Thursday, Friday at 4:00PM for 3.00 hours. Program is a sports show, featuring local, regional, and national guests.

SUTER ON SATURDAYS
4404 SOUTHEAST NAPOLEON STREET
IOWA CITY, IA 52240
319-354-1242
Fax: 319-354-1921
kcjjam@aol.com
www.1630kcjj.com
• Tom Suter, Host/Producer
suterman7@aol.com
Description:
Call-In, Play-by-Play, Talk. Saturday at 9:00AM for 1 hour. Program discusses the world of sports and takes listener call-ins.

THE ADAM GOLD SHOW
5000 FALLS OF NEUSE RD STE 308
SUITE 308
RALEIGH, NC 27609-5480
919-875-9100
Fax: 919-875-9080
www.850thebuzz.com
• Adam Gold, Host
(919) 875-9100
• Joe Ovies, Producer
Description:
Call-In, Commentary, Entertainment, Interview, News, Sports, Talk. Monday, Tuesday, Wednesday, Thursday, Friday at 3:00PM for 3.00 hours.

THE D-103 MORNING SHOW
P.O. BOX 98
DOVER FOXCROFT, ME 04426
207-564-2642
Fax: 207-564-8905
www.zoneradio.com

• Toby Nelson, Sports Director
(207) 990-2800
Description:
Call-In, Commentary, Current Events, Entertainment, Full Service, Information, Interview, Magazine,. Sunday at 7:00AM for 3.00 hours; Monday, Tuesday, Wednesday, Thursday, Friday, Saturday at 6:00AM for 3.00 hours. Program is a news, entertainment, and mu

THE FISHING REPORT WITH BRIAN HOFFMAN
55 HAWTHORNE STREET SUITE 1100
SAN FRANCISCO, CA 94105-3906
415-995-6800
Fax: 415-995-6867
sports@knbr.com
www.knbr.com
• Brian Hoffman, Host/Producer
Description:
Call-In, Interview, Sports, Talk. Sunday at 6:00AM for 1 hour. Program features news and information for sport fishing enthusiasts.

THE FRED HONSBERGER SHOW
1 GATEWAY CENTER
PITTSBURGH, PA 15222
412-575-2200
Fax: 412-575-2424
www.kdkaradio.com
• Paul Alexander, Sports Anchor
(412) 575-2328
Description:
Call-In, News, Sports, Talk, Weather. Monday, Tuesday, Wednesday, Thursday, Friday at 3:00PM for 3.00 hours. Program covers current events and news.

THE GARY RADNICH SHOW
55 HAWTHORNE STREET SUITE 1100
SAN FRANCISCO, CA 94105-3906
415-995-6800
Fax: 415-995-6867
sports@knbr.com
www.knbr.com
• Gary Radnich, Sports Host
• Patrick Connor, Producer
(415) 995-6935
Description:
Call-In, Entertainment, News, Sports, Talk, Weather. Monday, Tuesday, Wednesday, Thursday, Friday at 6:00AM for 3.00 hours. Program features news, entertainment, and sports coverage.

THE GOLF SHOW
1819 PEACHTREE ROAD N.E. SUITE 700
ATLANTA, GA 30309-1849
404-367-0640
800-776-4638
Fax: 404-367-6401
www.wgst.com
• Danny McNulty, Host
Description:
Call-In, Sports, Talk. Sunday at 7:00AM for 2.00 hours.

THE INSIDE TRACK
93351 OVERSEAS HIGHWAY
TAVERNIER, FL 33070
305-852-9085
Fax: 305-852-2304
davedonahue@clearchannel.com
www.keysradio.com

• Ed McClean, Host
edmcclean@clearchannel.com
Description:
Call-In, Interview, Sports, Talk. Tuesday at 6:30PM for 1 hour. Program features a weekly update on the world of motorsports and interviews with drivers.

THE JAMIE AND GREGG SHOW
27675 HALSTED ROAD
FARMINGTON HILLS, MI 48331
248-324-5800
Fax: 248-848-0272
www.wdfn.com
• Jon Klimczuk, Producer
jonklimczuk@clearchannel.com
• Jamie Samuelsen, Host
jamiesamuelsen@clearchannel.com
Description:
Sports, Talk. Monday, Tuesday, Wednesday, Thursday, Friday at 6:00AM for 3.00 hours.

THE JOHN CORBY SHOW
50 EAST RIVERCENTER BLVD. SUITE 1200
COVINGTON, KY 41011
614-486-6101
800-610-9886
Fax: 614-487-2559
stevekonrad@clearchannel.com
www.wtvn.com
• Joe Bradley, Producer
(614) 487-2534
joebradley@clearchannel.com
• John Corby, Host
(614) 487-6428
johncorby@clearchannel.com
Description:
Call-In, Sports, Talk. Saturday at 12:30PM for 2.00 hours.

THE MARK MADDEN SHOW
400 ARDMORE BOULEVARD
PITTSBURGH, PA 15221-3019
412-731-1250
Fax: 412-244-4596
www.espnradio1250.com
• Mark Madden, Host
mark.madden@abc.com
Description:
Call-In, Commentary, Sports, Talk. Monday, Tuesday, Wednesday, Thursday, Friday at 4:00PM for 4.00 hours.

THE MIKE TRIVISONNO SHOW
6200 OAK TREE BOULEVARD 4TH FLOOR
INDEPENDENCE, OH 44131
216-520-2600
Fax: 216-524-3200
www.wtam.com
• Marty Allen, Sports Producer
(216) 520-2600
• Mike Snyder, Sports Director
(216) 642-4636
• Mike Trivisonno, Sports Host
(216) 520-2600
trivshow@wtam.com
Description:
Call-In, Current Events, Sports, Talk. Monday, Tuesday, Wednesday, Thursday, Friday at 3:00PM for 4.00 hours.

THE MORNING SHOW
121 SUB BASE
ST THOMAS, U.S. VIRGI 00802
340-774-1340
Fax: 340-776-1316
pottley@wsta.com
www.wsta.com
• Bob Wilmer, Sports Host
Description:
Call-In, Commentary, Current Events,
Educational, Entertainment, Full Service,
Information, Intervie. Sunday at 7:00AM;
Monday, Tuesday, Wednesday, Thursday,
Friday, Saturday at 7:00AM for 4.00 hours.

THE POWER PLAY
3911 SOUTH 1ST STREET
ABILENE, TX 79605
325-676-7711
800-588-5326
Fax: 325-676-3851
shayhill@clearchannel.com
www.keanradio.com
• Rudy Fernandez, Program Director
(325) 676-7711
rudyfernandez@clearchannel.com
• Chaz McGuire, Host
chazmcguire@clearchannel.com
Description:
Call-In, Interview, Play-by-Play. Monday,
Tuesday, Wednesday, Thursday, Friday at
5:00PM for 2.00 hours. Program focuses on
sports.

THE RAZOR & MR. T
55 HAWTHORNE STREET SUITE 1100
SAN FRANCISCO, CA 94105-3906
415-995-6800
Fax: 415-995-6867
www.knbr.com
• Jennifer Violet, Executive Producer
Description:
Call-In, Current Events, Entertainment,
Information, Interview, Sports, Talk, Traffic.
Monday, Tuesday, Wednesday, Thursday,
Friday at 3:00PM for 4.00 hours. Program is
a talk show with emphasis on sports and
entertainment; includes news and sports
update

THE SPORTS TABLE
134 4TH AVENUE
HUNTINGTON, WV 25701
304-525-7788
Fax: 304-525-3299
billcornwell@clearchannel.com
800wvhu.com
• Paul Swann, Host
Description:
Call-In, Play-by-Play, Talk. Sunday,
Monday, Tuesday, Wednesday, Thursday,
Friday, Saturday at 6:30PM for 30 minutes.
Program is a collection of network and local
sports talk, plus national, regional, and local
team play-by-plays.

UNSPORTSMANLIKE CONDUCT
5011 CAPITOL AVENUE
OMAHA, NE 68132
402-342-2000
Fax: 402-342-7041
• Kevin Kugler, Host/Sports Director
(402) 977-9215
• Neil Nelkin, Program Director
(402) 977-9294
• Mike'l Severe, Host
(402) 977-9217

Description:
Call-In, Sports, Talk. Monday, Tuesday,
Wednesday, Thursday, Friday at 3:00PM for
3.00 hours.

WBFH RADIO
4200 ANDOVER ROAD
BLOOMFIELD HILLS, MI 48302-2000
248-341-5690
Fax: 248-341-5679
www.wbfh.fm
• Pete Bowers, Station Manager
Description:
Sports talk show "Sportscan" - Call-In,
Interview, News, Play-by-Play, Talk. Monday
at 8:00PM for 1 hour. Program discusses
regional sports.

WEEKDAY SPORTSBEAT
300 WEST JEFFERSON BOULEVARD
SOUTH BEND, IN 46601-1513
574-233-3141
Fax: 574-289-7382
www.wsbt.com
• Rick Carter, Host
(574) 472-8254
wsbtnews@wsbt.com
• Darin Pritchett, Host/Producer
(574) 282-2696
pritchett@wsbt.com
Description:
Call-In, Entertainment, Interview, Sports,
Talk. Monday, Tuesday, Wednesday,
Thursday, Friday at 5:15PM for 1.00 hours.
Program focuses on national and local
sports.

WILLTIME MOTORSPORTS
1711 EAST WABASH ROAD
PERU, IN 46970
765-473-4448
Fax: 765-473-4449
waru@sbcglobal.net
• Justin Howard, Program Director
waru@sbcglobal.net
Description:
Interview, Sports, Talk. Monday at 7:00PM
for 1 hour. Program focuses on motorsports
news and events.

Sports Radio Programs, National

CHET COPPOCK
190 NORTH STATE STREET 9TH FL
CHICAGO, IL 60601
312-984-0890
800-224-2004
Fax: 312-591-8900
wls.feedback@wlsam.com
www.wlsam.com
• Chet Coppock, Host
• Donna Baker, Vice President/Market
Manager
donna.baker@cumulus.com
• Tracy Slutzkin, Program Director
• Michael Mann, Sales Manager
• Lorraine Lynn, Promotions Director
Description:
Talk radio; news, weather, sports and traffic
reports.

COLLEGE FOOTBALL CENTER
ESPN PLAZA
935 MIDDLE ST
BRISTOL, CT 06010-1001
860-766-2000
800-999-9985
Fax: 860-589-5523
www.espn.com
• Mo Davenport, SVP and General Manager
• Bob Picozzi, News Anchor
• Matt Murphy, SVP Broadband and
Interactive Sales
• Rob Adamski, ESPN Event Production
Description:
Commentary, Talk. Live play-by-play of
seasonal games, "College GameDay"
football analysis, "ESPNU College Football"
podcast and road trips on "The Herd" and
"SVP & Russillo."

COLLEGE GAMEDAY
ESPN PLAZA
935 MIDDLE ST
BRISTOL, CT 06010-1001
860-766-2000
800-999-9985
Fax: 860-766-2213
collegegameday@espnradio.com
www.espn.com
• Rece Davis, Host
• Jay Bilas, Analyst
• Digger Phelps, Analyst
• Jalen Rose, Analyst
Description:
Commentary, Interview, Talk. Program
features sports news, game analysis,
conversations with sports newsmakers, and
previews of upcoming games. Saturday - first
hr begins at 10AM ET on ESPNU continuing
at 11AM on ESPN with a one-hour edition at
8PM on ESPN.

COUNTDOWN TO KICKOFF
935 MIDDLE STREET
BRISTOL, CT 06010-1001
860-766-2000
Fax: 860-589-5523
www.espn.com
• Keith Goralski, Senior Producer
• Stosh Cienki, Associate Producer
countdown@espnradio.com
Description:
Talk. Sunday at 11:00AM for 2.00 hours.
Program features analysis of upcoming NFL
games.

ESPN RADIO - SUNDAY GAMENIGHT
935 MIDDLE STREET
BRISTOL, CT 06010-1001
860-766-2000
800-999-9985
Fax: 860-589-5523
www.espn.com
• Sean Tyman, Producer
• Doug Gottlieb, Host
gamenight@espnradio.com
Description:
Call-In, Interview, Talk. Sunday at 7:00PM
for 4.00 hours. Program features sports
scores, interviews with sports figures, and
game analysis.

ESPN THE MAGAZINE
935 MIDDLE STREET
BRISTOL, CT 06010-1001

860-766-2000
Fax: 860-589-5523
www.espn.com
• Melissa Jacobs, Producer
• Dan Lebatard, Host
(305) 376-3498
Description:
Call-In, Commentary, Magazine, Sports, Talk. Sunday at 7:00AM for 4.00 hours. Program features analysis of the week in sports and a look at the coming week.

GAMEDAY
935 MIDDLE STREET
BRISTOL, CT 06010-1001
860-766-2000
800-999-9985
Fax: 860-589-5523
gameday@espn.com
www.espn.com
• Bill Rodman, Executive Producer
• Jack Arute, Reporter
Description:
Call-In, Commentary, Current Events, Educational, Entertainment, Information, Interview, Investigati. Monday at 4:00PM for 3.00 hours; Tuesday at 4:00PM for 3.00 hours; Wednesday at 4:00PM for 3.00 hours; Thursday at 4:00PM for 3.00 hours; Friday at 4:00P

GAMENIGHT
935 MIDDLE STREET
BRISTOL, CT 06010-1001
860-766-2000
Fax: 860-766-2213
www.espn.com
• Louise Cornetta, Senior Producer
gamenight@espnradio.com
• Chuck Wilson, Host
gamenight@espnradio.com
• Doug Gottleib, Host
gamenight@espnradio.com
Description:
Call-In, Commentary, Interview, Talk. Monday at 7:00PM for 4.00 hours; Tuesday at 7:00PM for 4.00 hours; Wednesday at 7:00PM for 4.00 hours; Thursday at 7:00PM for 4.00 hours; Friday at 7:00PM for 4.00 hours. Program features the latest scores, news updat

HILL & SCHLERETH
ESPN PLAZA
935 MIDDLE ST
BRISTOL, CT 06010
860-766-2000
800-999-9985
Fax: 860-589-5523
www.espnradio.com
• Mike Hill, Host
• Mark Schlereth, Host
• Steve Anderson, EVP/News, Talent & Content Operations
• Mo Davenport, SVP and General Manager
• Michelle Lynch, Event Operations Producer
Description:
Talk. Sports weeknights 7PM - 10PM ET.

INDIANA SPORTS TALK
1 EMMIS PLAZA SUITE 400
INDIANAPOLIS, IN 46204-2902
317-266-9422
800-800-3044
Fax: 317-684-2008
www.wibc.com

• Bob Lovell, Host
(317) 684-4179
bob@indianasportstalk.com
Description:
Commentary, News, Talk. Monday at 7:00PM; Tuesday at 7:00PM; Wednesday at 7:00PM; Thursday at 7:00PM; Friday at 7:00PM. Program features local and national sports news.

LATE GAMENIGHT
935 MIDDLE STREET
BRISTOL, CT 06010-1001
860-766-2000
Fax: 860-766-2213
www.espn.com
• Louise Cornetta, Program Director
gamenight@espnradio.com
• Bob Valvano, Host
gamenight@espnradio.com
Description:
Call-In, Commentary, Interview, Talk. Monday at 11:00PM for 4.00 hours; Tuesday at 11:00PM for 4.00 hours; Wednesday at 11:00PM for 4.00 hours; Thursday at 11:00PM for 4.00 hours; Friday at 11:00PM for 4.00 hours. Program features the latest scores, news

MIKE AND MIKE IN THE MORNING
ESPN PLAZA
935 MIDDLE ST
BRISTOL, CT 06010-1001
860-766-2000
800-999-9985
Fax: 860-589-5523
www.espnradio.com
• Mike Greenberg, Host
• Mike Golic, Host
Description:
Call-In, Commentary, Current Events, Entertainment, Information, News, Panel Discussion, Sports, Tal. M-F, 6AM-10AM.

MIKE NORTH
4334 MARTINGALE LN NW
ACWORTH, GA 30101-3873
770-917-8228
www.foxsports.com
• Mike North, Host
Description:
Talk. Sunday 8:00PM-1:00AM. Program features the latest sports news, as well as Mike's winning picks for the upcoming games of the weekend.

MONDAY MORNING RACING REFRESHER
1801 WEST INTERNATIONAL SPEEDWAY BOULEVA
DAYTONA BEACH, FL 32114-1215
386-947-6400
Fax: 386-947-6716
www.mrnradio.com
Description:
Information, News. Monday at 6:45AM. Program features a recap of the previous weekend's NASCAR events.

NASCAR LIVE
1801 WEST INTERNATIONAL SPEEDWAY BOULEVA
DAYTONA BEACH, FL 32114-1215
386-947-6400
Fax: 386-947-6716
www.mrnradio.com

• Steve Blevins, Producer
sblevins@mrnradio.com
• Eli Gold, Host
Description:
Talk. Tuesday at 7:00PM for 1 hour. Program features NASCAR racing news and features.

NASCAR TODAY
1801 WEST INTERNATIONAL SPEEDWAY BOULEVA
DAYTONA BEACH, FL 32114-1215
386-947-6400
Fax: 386-947-6716
www.mrnradio.com
• Steve Blevins, Producer
sblevins@mrnradio.com
• Joe Moore, Host
Description:
Interview, News. Monday at 4:45PM; Tuesday at 4:45PM; Wednesday at 4:45PM; Thursday at 4:45PM; Friday at 4:45PM. Program features race results, driver interviews, and news from the NASCAR circuit.

NASCAR USA: COUNTRY MUSIC AT THE SPEED OF SOUND
1801 WEST INTERNATIONAL SPEEDWAY BOULEVA
DAYTONA BEACH, FL 32114-1215
386-947-6400
Fax: 386-947-6716
www.mrnradio.com
Description:
Entertainment, Interview, Music, Talk. Sunday at 9:00AM. Program features music, artist interviews, race previews, and NASCAR news; airs live on Sunday mornings.

SPORTS BIZ
1490 DAYTON AVENUE P.O. BOX 4826
GREENWICH, CT 06831-9998
203-422-2800
800-249-8852
Fax: 203-422-2288
www.businesstalkradio.net
• Fred Wallin, Host
sportsfred@aol.com
Description:
Talk. Saturday at 7:00PM for 2.00 hours. Program focuses on the financial aspect of the sports industry.

SPORTS BYLINE
300 BROADWAY SUITE 8
SAN FRANCISCO, CA 94133
415-434-8300
800-783-7528
Fax: 415-391-2569
byline@pacbell.net
www.sportsbyline.com
• Ron Barr, CEO
xhighflyer@aol.com
• Darren Peck, President
dpeck@sportsbyline.com
Description:
Call-In, Commentary, Information, Interview, Sports, Talk. Monday at 10:00PM for 3.00 hours; Tuesday at 10:00PM for 3.00 hours; Wednesday at 10:00PM for 3.00 hours; Thursday at 10:00PM for 3.00 hours; Friday at 10:00PM for 3.00 hours. Program features int

SPORTS BYLINE WEEKEND
300 BROADWAY SUITE 8
SAN FRANCISCO, CA 94133
415-434-8300
800-783-7528
Fax: 415-391-2569
www.sportsbyline.com
• Ron Barr, CEO
xhighflyer@aol.com
• Darren Peck, President
dpeck@sportsbyline.com
Description:
Call-In, Commentary, Interview, Sports,
Talk. Sunday at 10:00PM for 3.00 hours;
Saturday at 10:00PM for 3.00 hours.

SPORTS CALL
125 WEST END AVENUE 6TH FLOOR
NEW YORK, NY 10023-6387
212-456-5185
Fax: 212-456-5150
abcradio@abc.com
www.abcradio.com
• Mike Rizzo, Executive Director
(212) 456-5185
michael.rizzo@abc.com
Description:
Interview, Talk. Sunday, Monday, Tuesday,
Wednesday, Thursday, Friday, Saturday
Program is an audio feed to affiliate stations
airing throughout the day.. Program features
sports news, talk, and game highlights.

**SPORTS OVERNIGHT AMERICA
WEEKEND**
300 BROADWAY SUITE 8
SAN FRANCISCO, CA 94133
415-434-8300
800-783-7528
Fax: 415-391-2569
www.sportsbyline.com
• Ron Barr, CEO
xhighflyer@aol.com
• Darren Peck, President
dpeck@sportsbyline.com
Description:
Call-In, Sports, Talk. Sunday at 1:00AM for
5.00 hours; Saturday at 1:00AM for 5.00
hours. Program offers listeners the
opportunity to discuss today's results and
hot sports topics and debate tomorrow's
possibilities, while also presenting the day's
score

SPORTS TALK
3710 LANDMARK DRIVE SUITE 100
COLUMBIA, SC 29204-4062
803-790-4300
800-956-7266
Fax: 803-790-4309
www.sportstalkgolive.com
• Carlton Green, Producer
• Phil Kornblut, Host
(803) 790-4300
• Tom Jackson, General Manager
(803) 790-4307
• Kevin McCrarey, Host
Description:
Call-In, Information, Interview, Sports, Talk.
Monday at 6:00PM for 2.00 hours; Tuesday
at 6:00PM for 2.00 hours; Wednesday at
6:00PM for 2.00 hours; Thursday at 6:00PM
for 2.00 hours; Friday at 6:00PM for 2.00
hours. Program features the latest sports ne

THE DAN PATRICK SHOW
935 MIDDLE STREET
BRISTOL, CT 06010-1001
860-766-2000
Fax: 860-589-5523
www.espn.com
• Dan Patrick, Host
danpatrickshow@espnradio.com
Description:
Commentary, Interview, Talk. Monday at
1:00PM for 3.00 hours; Tuesday at 1:00PM
for 3.00 hours; Wednesday at 1:00PM for
3.00 hours; Thursday at 1:00PM for 3.00
hours; Friday at 1:00PM for 3.00 hours.
Program features guest athletes, coaches,
entertainers,

THE GOLF SHOW
935 MIDDLE STREET
BRISTOL, CT 06010-1001
860-766-2000
Fax: 860-589-5523
www.espn.com
• Dave Zaslowsky, Producer
• Bob Stevens, Host
(860) 766-2000
Description:
Commentary, Talk. Sunday at 6:00AM for 1
hour. Program takes a look at the latest
professional golf news.

THE JIM ROME SHOW
15260 VENTURA BOULEVARD SUITE 500
SHERMAN OAKS, CA 91403-5307
818-377-5300
Fax: 818-995-8079
webmaster@premierradio.com
www.premierradio.com
• Travis Rodgers, Producer
(818) 461-5426
• Jim Rome, Host
(800) 636-8686
Description:
Call-In, Interview, Talk. Monday at 9:00AM
for 3.00 hours; Tuesday at 9:00AM for 3.00
hours; Wednesday at 9:00AM for 3.00
hours; Thursday at 9:00AM for 3.00 hours;
Friday at 9:00AM for 3.00 hours. Program
presents sports commentary and analysis
with an ou

THE KEVIN WHEELER SHOW
1935 TECHNY ROAD SUITE 18
NORTHBROOK, IL 60062
847-509-1661
800-224-2004
Fax: 847-509-1677
www.sportingnewsradio.com
• Brad Robinson, Producer
(847) 400-3137
• Kevin Wheeler, Host
(847) 400-3137
Description:
Call-In, Interview, Talk. Sunday at 1:00AM
for 4.00 hours; Saturday at 2:00AM for 4.00
hours. Program features game previews
from sports personalities and experts.

THE NFL ON ESPN RADIO
935 MIDDLE STREET
BRISTOL, CT 06010-1001
860-766-2000
Fax: 860-589-5523
www.espn.go.com/radio
• Mike Urrunaga, Producer
Description:
Sports. Sunday at 1:00PM for 6.00 hours.

Program features analysis and discussions
of professional football.

THE RICK BALLOU SHOW
1935 TECHNY ROAD SUITE 18
NORTHBROOK, IL 60062
847-509-1661
800-224-2004
Fax: 847-509-1677
www.radio.sportingnews.com
• Matt Nahigian, Program Director
(847) 400-3075
• Rick Ballou, Host
(847) 400-3132
Description:
Call-In, Interview, Talk. Monday at 10:00PM
for 4.00 hours; Tuesday at 10:00PM for 4.00
hours; Wednesday at 10:00PM for 4.00
hours; Thursday at 10:00PM for 4.00 hours;
Friday at 10:00PM for 4.00 hours. Program
features sports analysis and lively interview

TONY BRUNO SHOW
1935 TECHNY ROAD SUITE 18
NORTHBROOK, IL 60062
800-565-1540
800-224-2004
Fax: 847-509-1677
radio.sportingnews.com/shows/tony_bruno
• Tony Bruno, Host
• Mark Willard, Co-Host
Description:
Talk. Monday at 8:00AM for 4.00 hours;
Tuesday at 8:00AM for 4.00 hours;
Wednesday at 8:00AM for 4.00 hours;
Thursday at 8:00AM for 4.00 hours; Friday
at 8:00AM for 4.00 hours. Program features
the latest sports news.

WE ARE THERE SATURDAY
15260 VENTURA BOULEVARD SUITE 500
SHERMAN OAKS, CA 91403 5339
818-461-8291
Fax: 818-461-8219
www.foxsports.com
• Michael Coover, Producer
mcoover@premiereradio.com
Description:
Call-In, Talk. Saturday at 12:00PM for 8.00
hours. Program features sports news and
commentary.

WEEKEND GAMENIGHT
935 MIDDLE STREET
BRISTOL, CT 06010-1001
860-766-2000
800-999-9985
Fax: 860-766-2213
www.espn.com
• Chuck Wilson, Host
gamenight@espnradio.com
• Louise Cornetta, Senior Coordinating
Producer
gamenight@espnradio.com
Description:
Call-In, Commentary, Interview, Talk.
Sunday at 7:00PM for 4.00 hours; Saturday
at 7:00PM for 6.00 hours. Program features
the latest scores, news updates, and lively
conversation with sports stars.

WORLD OF RACING
1801 WEST INTERNATIONAL SPEEDWAY
BOULEVA
DAYTONA BEACH, FL 32114-1215

386-947-6400
Fax: 386-947-6716
www.mrnradio.com
• Amanda Trautman, Producer
• David Hyatt, Director
dhyatt@mrnradio.com
• Ned Jarrett, Host
• Mike Storms, Executive Producer
Description:
Talk. Monday at 7:00AM; Tuesday at
7:00AM; Wednesday at 7:00AM; Thursday
at 7:00AM; Friday at 7:00AM. Program
focuses on racing personalities.

Sports Satellite Radio

BSKYB
6 CENTAURS BUSINESS PARK
GRANT WAY
ISLEWORTH
MIDDLESEX, ENGLAND TW7 5QD
phx.corporate-ir.net/phoenix.zhtml?c=10401
6&p=irol-corphome
• Tim Mason, Program Manager
• Roger Moody, Deputy Director Sports
Description:
International. Satellite broadcasting
services.

PROSTAR ENTERTAINMENT NETWORK
12831 ROYAL DR
STAFFORD, TX 77477
281-240-1399
800-967-7827
Fax: 281-240-1447
• John C. Parks, President
• Scott Hoffman, Vice President
Nature of Sports Service:
National. Ad supported sports service, via
satellite, offering 16 hours of programming
focusing on sports videos (Sports Video
TV-SVTV), designed for sports bars, night
clubs, colleges, military bases, taverns,
country clubs and commercial
establishments. Programming includes
sports highlights, Tribune media's Sports
Plus and News Plus service, SportsTicker,
and pay-per-view events, sports fantasy and
trivia.

SIRIUS XM RADIO INC.
1221 AVENUE OF THE AMERICAS
36TH FLOOR
NEW YORK, NY 10020
212-584-5100
www.sirius.com
• Mark Redmond, President & Chief
Executive Officer
• Paul Cunningham, Senior VP, Sales &
Marketing
• Mark Knapton, Senior VP, Call Centre
Ops. & Customer Loyalty
Recent Sposorships:
NFL

Sports Radio Stations

107.9 THE BULL
1011 N LINCOLN STREET
WEST POINT, NE 68788
402-372-5423
800-422-3664

Fax: 402-372-5425
www.kticradio.com
• Dwight Lane, Station Manager
• Tom McMahon, Sports Director
Description:
Music, News, Sports.
Frequency:
107.9 fm

1210 THE TICKET
FLINN BRDCASTING
6080 MT. MORIAH
MEMPHIS, TN 38115
901-375-9324
Fax: 901-375-5889
www.flinn.com
• Dan Frazier, Sales/Promotions Sports 56
• Bill Grafeman, Talent Director Sports 56
Nature of Sports Service:
24 Hour Sports.

1320 WAMR
282 N AUBURN RD
VENICE, FL 34292
941-388-3936
Fax: 941-388-3720

1390AM AND 97.1FM THE POINT
P. O. BOX 71
MIDDLEPORT, OH 45760
740-992-6485
866-374-5888
Fax: 740-992-6486
office@wyvk.com
• Rick Ash, Director
(740) 992-6485
office@wyvk.com
• Brenda Merritt, General Manager
(740) 992-6485
Description:
Music, News, Sports. Broadcasting high
school, collegiate and professional sports.

1510 THE ZONE
308 VICTORY ROAD
QUINCY, MA 02171
617-237-1200
Fax: 617-237-1177
www.revolutionboston.com
• Mike Kellogg, General Manager
• Bill Flaherty, Director of Sales
• Anthony Pepe, Director of Marketing
• Tod Rosensweig, Director of
Communications
Nature of Sports Service:
24 Hour Sports.

850 KOA RADIO
4695 S. MONACO ST
DENVER, CO 80237
303-713-8000
Fax: 303-713-8735
www.850koa.com
• Lee Larsen, General Manager
• Larry Zimmer, Sports Director
Nature of Sports Service:
24 Hour Sports Radio.
Baseball:
MLB - Colorado Rockies.
College Sports:
Football - University of Colorado.
Football:
NFL - Denver Broncos.

930 AM THE FOX
11700 CENTRAL PKWY
JACKSONVILLE, FL 32224
904-596-7320
• Jack O'Brien, General Sales Manager
Nature of Sports Service:
24 Hour Sports.
NCAA:
Florida Gators.

96.5 KHMX MIX
3050 POST OAK BOULEVARD
12TH FLOOR
HOUSTON, TX 77056
713-968-1000
Fax: 713-968-1044
• Buddy Scott, Program Director
• Tim Sutherland, Promotion Director

AM 620 WZON THE SPORTS ZONE
861 BROADWAY
BANGOR, ME 04402
207-990-2800
Fax: 207-990-2444
www.zoneradio.com
• Dale Duff, Program Director/WZON
• Clem Labree, Sports Reporter
• Scott Sassone, Sports Reporter

AM 850 THE BUZZ SPORTS RADIO
5000 FALLS OF NEUSE RD
STE 308
RALEIGH, NC 27609
919-875-9100
Fax: 919-875-9080
www.850thebuzz.com
• Brian Maloney, General Manager
• Jarrett Whaley, Sports Sunday/Producer
• Tim Chasteen, Production
Manager/Producer
ESPN:
Affiliate.
NCAA:
Duke University East Carolina University,
North Carolina State University.
NFL:
Carolina Panthers.

AM 950 THE FAN
7800 EAST ORCHARD ROAD
SUITE 400
GREENWOOD VILLAGE, CO 80111
303-321-0950
Fax: 303-676-6294
www.1043thefan.com
Sports Teams Covered:
Colorado Avalanche (NHL), Denver Nuggets
(NBA), Denver Pioneers (University of
Denver NCAA), Air Force Falcons.

AMI NEWS, SAN FRANCISCO/NEW YORK
50 VASHELL WAY, STE 200
ORINDA, CA 94563-3020
925-254-4456
800-736-0370
Fax: 925-254-7923
www.onthesnow.com;
www.mountainsports.com
• Rob Brown, President
• Chad Dyer, Internet Director
Nature of Sports Service:
National. Radio producer/news bureau;
world wide web producer. Regional reports
on participation sports and recreational
activities on a national level. Most reports
have immediacy factor and are updated by

phone. Seasonal services include condition reports on skiing, fishing, camping, beach and water sports. Also reports from major events on behalf of sponsoring companies.

AUTOZONE
123 S. FRONT STREET
MEMPHIS, TN 38103
901-495-6500
800-850-6050
Fax: 901-495-8300
www.autozone.com
• Lynn Campbell, Marketing Director
Media Sponsor:
ESPN Radio Question of the Game brought to you by AutoZone

CJCL
777 JARVIS ST
TORONTO, ON, CANADA M4Y 3B7
416-935-0590
Fax: 416-935-8288
www.fan590.com
• Scott Metcalfe, Sports Director
• Nelson Millman, Program Director
Auto Sports:
Indy Car Racing, NASCAR.
Baseball:
MLB - Sunday Night Game of the Week;
Playoffs - ALCS, NLCS, World Series.
Basketball:
NBA - Toronto Raptors.

ESPN 1490 THE FAN
3438 N COUNTRY CLUB
TUCSON, AZ 85716
520-795-1490
Fax: 520-327-2260
• Diane Frisch, General Manager
• Darla Thomas, Operations Manager
• LarVin Cassmin, Marketing Director
• Jody Oehler, On-Air Personality
Baseball:
MLB - Colorado Rockies.
College Sports:
Basketball - Women's Arizona State University.
Football:
NFL - San Francisco 49ers.

ESPN RADIO 1000
190 N. STATE ST
CHICAGO, IL 60601
312-980-1000
Fax: 312-332-3776
www.am1000.com
• Bob Snyder, General Manager
• Mitch Rosen, Program Director
Shows:
The ESPN Morning Show, with Mike Golic & Mike Greenberg; Tony Kornheiser; Dan Patrick; McNeil, Jurko & Harry; Chicago Bulls Basketball; ESPN Gamenight; AllNight With Todd Wright; ESPN Gameday; Bears NFL Game Day Parlay; Silvy on Sports; The Point After with Peggy Kusinski; Talking Baseball, With Bruce Levine; RPM Now; ESPN Magazine.

ESPN RADIO 1250 PITTSBURGH
400 ARDMORE BOULEVARD
PITTSBURGH, PA 15221
412-731-1250
Fax: 412-244-4596
www.1250espn.com

• Mike Thompson, General Manager
• David Waugaman, National Sales Manager
(412) 244-4555
Primary Audience:
Men 18-49.

ESPN RADIO 920
8755 W. FLAMINGO
LAS VEGAS, NV 89147
702-876-1460
Fax: 702-876-6685
• John Hanson, Program Director
• Derek Roy, Promotions Director
Nature of Sports Service:
24 Hour Sports.

ESPN990 SPORTS RADIO
PO BOX 608
MASSILLON, OH 44648
330-837-9900
Fax: 330-837-9844
espn@espn990.com
www.espn990.com
• Ray Jeske, Station Contact
ray@espn990.com
• Donovan Resh, II, Media Contact
donresh@gmail.com
Nature of Sports Service:
Radio.
Football:
NFL/CBS Radio.
College Sports:
Basketball, Football.
Primary Audience:
Male.
Sports:
Local and ESPN Cincinnati Reds, Columbus Blue Jackets.

KAAN-AM
HIGHWAY 69 SOUTH
BETHANY, MO 64424
660-425-6380
800-892-5959
Fax: 660-425-8148
• Stuart Johnson, Program/Sports Director
Description:
Music, News, Sports.

KAAN-FM
HIGHWAY 69 SOUTH
BETHANY, MO 64424
660-425-6380
800-892-5959
Fax: 660-425-8148
• Stuart Johnson, News/Sports Director
• Mike Mattson, Advertising Manager
Description:
Music, News, Sports.

KAAQ-FM
1210 WEST 10TH STREET
ALLIANCE, NE 69301-2804
308-762-1400
800-584-9310
Fax: 308-762-7804
www.doubleqcountry.com
• Mike Glesinger, Sports Director
mike.glesinger@eagleradio.net
• Kevin Horn, News Director
Description:
Music.

KABZ-FM
2400 COTTONDALE LANE
LITTLE ROCK, AR 72202-2020
501-661-1037
800-477-1037
Fax: 501-664-5871
www.kabzfm.com/
• Tanya Hatfield, Promotions Director
• Randy Rainwater, Sports Director
(501) 661-1037
randy@1037thebuzz.com
Description:
Music, Talk.

KACC-FM
3110 MUSTANG RD
ALVIN, TX 77511-4807
281-388-4675
Fax: 281-388-4910
• Mark Moss, Program Director
(281) 388-4675
Description:
Music, News, Sports.

KACI-AM
502 WASHINGTON
THE DALLES, OR 97058-2217
541-296-2211
Fax: 541-296-2213
www.kaciamfm.com
• Rick Cavagnaro, Advertising Manager
(541) 386-5111
• Greg LeBlanc, News Director
Description:
Music, News, Talk.

KACI-FM
502 WASHINGTON
THE DALLES, OR 97058-2217
541-296-2211
Fax: 541-296-2213
www.kaciamfm.com
• Rick Cavagnaro, Advertising Manager
(541) 386-1511
• Greg LeBlanc, News Director
Description:
Music, News.

KACQ-FM
505 NORTH KEY AVENUE
LAMPASAS, TX 76550
512-556-6193
Fax: 512-556-2197
• Ronnie Witcher, General Manager
• Debra Witcher, Owner
Description:
Music, News, Sports.

KADA-AM
1019 NORTH BROADWAY
ADA, OK 74821-0609
580-332-1212
Fax: 580-332-0128
kada@wilnet1.com
• Mike Manos, Program Director
(580) 332-1212
Description:
Music, News, Sports.

KAGJ-FM
150 EAST COLLEGE AVENUE
EPHRAIM, UT 84627
435-283-7000
Fax: 435-283-7424
www.snow.edu

- Paul Sorensen, News/Sports Director
(435) 283-7439
jonny_54@hotmail.com
- Leslie Nixon, News and Sports Director
(435) 283-7000

KAIR-AM
P.O. BOX G
ATCHISON, KS 66002-0197
913-367-1470
800-367-9370
Fax: 913-367-7021
kairbri@hotmail.com
- Jim Ervin, Advertising Manager
- Brian Hagen, News Director
Description:
Music, News, Sports.

KALE-AM
830 NORTH COLUMBIA CENTER
BOULEVARD SUIT
KENNEWICK, WA 99336
509-783-0783
Fax: 509-735-8627
- Don Morin, General Manager
don.morin@nnbradio.com
- Kris Edwards, Program Director
(509) 783-0783
Description:
Music.

KALV-AM
ROUTE 1, BOX 53
ALVA, OK 73717-9706
580-327-1430
Fax: 580-327-1433
- Craig Killman, News Director
- Todd Miller, Sports Director
tmiller87@sbcglobal.net
Description:
Music, News, Sports.

KAML-FM
2810 SOUTHERN DRIVE
GILLETTE, WY 82716
607-686-2242
Fax: 307-686-7736
theedge@basinsradio.com
www.basinsradio.com/KAML/index.html
- Gina Decker, News Director
ginad@basinsradio.com
Description:
Music, News, Sports.

KANE-AM
2316 EAST MAIN
NEW IBERIA, LA 70560-4032
337-365-3434
Fax: 337-365-9117
kane@kane1240.com
- Jeff Botts, Program Director
jeff@kane1240.com
Description:
Music, News, Sports.

KAPB-FM
520 CHESTER STREET
MARKSVILLE, LA 71351-2844
318-253-9331
Fax: 318-253-5262
kapbfm@yahoo.com
- Pamela Couvillion, General Manager
- Mike Neck, Sports Director

KAQX-FM
1006 WEST MARINE DRIVE
ASTORIA, OR 97103
503-325-2911
Fax: 503-325-5570
- Zetty Mckay, News Director
(503) 325-2911
Description:
Music, News, Sports.

KATA-AM
5640 SOUTH BROADWAY
EUREKA, CA 95503
707-442-2000
Fax: 707-443-6848
kata1340.com
- J.B. Mathers, News & Sports Director
(707) 442-2000
Description:
ESPN sports talk radio
Frequency:
1340 AM
Description:
Sister stations KFMI, KKHB, KRED, KGOE

KAUR-FM
2001 SOUTH SUMMIT AVENUE
SIOUX FALLS, SD 57197
605-274-0770
800-727-2844
Fax: 605-336-5299
- Alex Beck, General Manager
(605) 336-4388
Description:
Music, News, Sports.

KAYS-AM
2300 HALL STREET
HAYS, KS 67601
785-625-2578
Fax: 785-625-3632
www.kaysradio.com
- Mike Cooper, Program Director
(785) 625-2578
- Todd Lynd, Advertising Manager
- Gerard Wellbrock, Sports Director
(785) 625-2578
gerard.wellbrock@eagleradio.net
Description:
Music.

KAZA-AM
765 STORY ROAD SUITE 120
SAN JOSE, CA 95122
408-881-1290
Fax: 408-881-1292
- Ruby Carrasco, Promotion Director
Description:
Music, News, Sports.

KBCR-AM
2110 MOUNT WERNER ROAD
STEAMBOAT SPRINGS, CO 80487-9011
970-879-2270
Fax: 970-879-1404
www.kbcr.com
- Tom Palmer, Sports Director
Description:
Music, News, Sports, Talk.

KBCR-FM
2110 MOUNT WERNER ROAD
STEAMBOAT SPRINGS, CO 80487-9011
970-879-2270
Fax: 970-879-1404
www.kbcr.com

- Dave Lancaster, Sports Director
Description:
Music.

KBEE-FM
434 BEARCAT DRIVE
SALT LAKE CITY, UT 84115-2520
801-485-6700
Fax: 801-487-5369
www.b987.com
- Ginger Buchanan, Promotions Director
- Tammy Rodgers, News Director
(801) 493-8689
- Bryce Taylor, Advertising Manager
(801) 464-8514
Description:
Music, News, Sports.

KBEL-AM
P.O. BOX 418
IDABEL, OK 74745-0418
580-286-6642
Fax: 580-286-6643
kbel96fm@aol.com
- Paul Box, Program Director
Description:
Educational, Music, News, Sports, Talk.

KBER-FM
434 BEARCAT DRIVE
SALT LAKE CITY, UT 84115-2520
801-485-6700
Fax: 801-487-5369
- Kelly Hammer, Program Director
khammer5@hotmail.com
Description:
Music, News, Sports.

KBFI-AM
327 MARION AVENUE
SANDPOINT, ID 83864-1723
208-263-2179
888-263-2013
Fax: 208-267-5594
- Mike Brown, News Director
Description:
Music, News, Sports.

KBFS-AM
707 HA ROADING STREET
BELLE FOURCHE, SD 57717-0787
605-892-2571
Fax: 605-892-2573
www.kbfs.com
- Karl Grimmelmann, General Manager
Description:
Music, News, Sports.

KBGG-AM
4143 109TH ST
URBANDALE, IA 50322-7925
515-331-9200
Fax: 515-278-4117
www.1700thechamp.com
Description:
Educational, Music, News, Talk.

KBHU-FM
1200 UNIVERSITY P.O. BOX 9665
SPEARFISH, SD 57799-0001
605-642-6265
Fax: 605-642-6272
www.bhsu.edu/studentlife/organizations/kbhu

• Scott Holbert, Sports Director
• Cody Oliver, News Director
kbhufm@hotmail.com
Description:
Music, News, Sports.

KBIX-AM
315 STATE STREET SUITE 910
MUSKOGEE, OK 74401-6350
918-682-9700
800-540-5369
Fax: 918-682-6775
www.bossjock.com
• Matt Hutson, Sports Director
(918) 492-2660
• David Stephens, General Manager
(918) 492-2660
stephens@kxoj.com
Description:
Talk.

KBIZ-AM
209 SOUTH MARKET
OTTUMWA, IA 52501-2924
641-682-4535
Fax: 641-684-5892
• Mike Buchanan, News Director
Description:
Music, News, Sports, Talk.

KBLJ-AM
116 DALTON AVENUE
LA JUNTA, CO 81050-1352
719-384-5456
Fax: 719-384-5450
kblj@rural-com.com
• Pat McGee, Sports Director
(719) 384-5456
Description:
Music, News, Talk.

KBLP-FM
204 SOUTH MAIN
LINDSAY, OK 73052-5634
405-756-4438
Fax: 405-756-2040
• Jason Wollenberg, News Director
Description:
Music, News, Sports, Talk.

KBND-AM
711 NORTHEAST BUTLER MARKET
ROAD
BEND, OR 97701
541-382-5263
Fax: 541-388-0456
www.kbnd.com
• Kenn Brown, Advertising Manager
• Mike Cheney, General Manager
Description:
News, Talk.

KBRX-FM
251 NORTH JEFFERSON STREET
ONEILL, NE 68763
402-336-1612
Fax: 402-336-3585
scott@kbrx.com
www.kbrx.com
• Michael Wiiest, Sports Director
(402) 336-1612
sports@kbrx.com
• Scott Poese, General Manager
(402) 336-1612
scott@kbrx.com

Description:
Music, News.

KBSF-AM
P.O. BOX 127
SPRINGHILL, LA 71075-0127
760-322-7890
Fax: 760-322-5493
Description:
Music, News, Sports.

KBST-AM
608 JOHNSON STREET
BIG SPRING, TX 79720-2851
432-267-6391
Fax: 432-267-1579
www.kbst.com
• Mike Henery, News Director
(432) 267-6397
news@kbst.com
• Kris Moore, Advertising Manager
kris@kvst.com
• Tom Ruiz, Sports Director
onair@kbst.com
Description:
Music.

KBUN-AM
502 BELTRAMI AVENUE, N.W.
BEMIDJI, MN 56601-1656
218-444-1500
Fax: 218-751-8091
production@pbbroadcasting.com
• Kevin Jackson, Sports Director
kjackson@pbbroadcasting.com
• Mardy Karger, News Director
Description:
Music, News, Sports.

KBUN-AM SPORTS RADIO
502 BELTRAMI AVE
BEMIDJI, MN 56601
218-444-1500
Fax: 218-751-8091
• Lou Buron, General Manager
• Kevin Jackson, Pro General Manager
Director
kjackson@pbbroadcasting.com
• Peggy Hanson, General Sales Manager
Baseball:
MLB - Minnesota Twins.
Football:
NFL - Minnesota Vikings.
College Sports:
Basketball, Football - University of
Minnesota.

KBVU-FM
BUENA VISTA UNIVERSITY
STORM LAKE, IA 50588
712-749-1220
kbvu@bvu.edu
www.edgebvu.edu
• Fred Seel, General Manager
Description:
Music, News, Sports.

KBYR - TALK 700
1007 W. 32ND AVE
ANCHORAGE, AK 99503
907-562-3456
Fax: 907-273-3189
• Jerry Beaver, General Manager
• Sam Adams, Sports Director
Nature of Sports Service:
News/Sports/Talk.

College Sports:
University of Alaska Anchorage Hockey.

KCBS-AM
865 BATTERY STREET
SAN FRANCISCO, CA 94111
415-765-4000
Fax: 415-765-4080
www.kcbs.com
• Justin Erickson, Advertising Sales Rep
(415) 765-4036
• Hal Ramey, Sports Director
(415) 765-4112
• Steve Bitker, Sports Anchor
(415) 765-4000
kcbsnews@cbs.com
Description:
News.

KCCL-FM
1436 AUBURN BOULEVARD
SACRAMENTO, CA 95815
916-646-4000
Fax: 916-648-6020
www.kool1019.fm
• Don Langsford, Promotion Director
(916) 648-6012
Description:
Music, News, Sports.

KCFS-FM
1101 WEST 22ND STREET
SIOUX FALLS, SD 57105-1600
605-331-6691
Fax: 605-331-6615
www.thecoo.edu/misc/kcfs
• Justin Whitcomb, General Manager
kcfs@usiouxfalls.edu
Description:
Music, News, Sports.

KCFV-FM
3400 PERSHALL RD
SAINT LOUIS, MO 63135-1408
314-513-4472
Fax: 314-513-4217
www.stlcc.cc.mo.us/fv/kcfv
• Mike Grayson, Sports Director
stew8@hotmail.com
• Ben James, News Director
Description:
Educational, Music, News, Sports.

KCHS-AM
P.O. BOX 351
TRUTH OR CONSEQUENCE, NM 87901
505-894-2400
Fax: 505-894-3998
www.gpkmedia.com
• Patrick Kohs, News/Sports Director
• Patrick Kohs, Sports Director
Description:
Music.
Year Founded:
1946

KCII-AM
110 EAST MAIN STREET
WASHINGTON, IA 52353
319-653-2113
Fax: 319-653-3500
kcii@kciiradio.com
www.kciiradio.com
• Drew Shradel, Sports Director
Description:
Music.

KCII-FM
110 EAST MAIN STREET
WASHINGTON, IA 52353
319-653-2113
Fax: 319-653-3500
kcii@kciiradio.com
www.kciiradio.com
• Jeremy Aitken, News Director
• Matt Veto, Sports Director
Description:
Music.

KCKX-AM
1665 JAMES STREET
WOODBURN, OR 97071-3644
503-769-1460
Fax: 503-981-3561
www.cowboy-country.com
• Dorecia Luce, Program Director
Description:
Music.

KCLA-AM
920 COMMERCE ROAD
PINE BLUFF, AR 71601
870-534-8978
Fax: 870-534-8984
• Andy Hodges, General Manager
Description:
Music, News, Sports.

KCLV-AM
2112 THORNTON
CLOVIS, NM 88101-4130
505-763-4401
Fax: 505-769-2564
kclv@hotmail.com
• Roy Norman, Advertising Manager
(505) 763-4401
• Roy Norman, Program Director
kclvradio@hotmail.com
Description:
Music, News, Sports.

KCMC
PO BOX 6397
TEXARKANA, TX 75505
903-793-1137
Fax: 903-792-4261
• Mike Simpson, General Manager
• Al Hanna, Sports Director
Nature of Sports Service:
Local. 24 Hour sports programming.
Baseball:
MLB - Texas Rangers.
College Sports:
Football - Texas A&M.
Football:
Dallas Cowboys.

KCOB-AM
1801 NORTH 13TH AVENUE EAST
NEWTON, IA 50208
641-792-5262
Fax: 641-792-8403
www.kcobradio.com
• Frank Liebl, Advertising Manager
• Randy Van, News Director
• Terry Walter, Sports Director
Description:
Music.

KCOW-AM
1210 WEST 10TH STREET
ALLIANCE, NE 69301

308-762-1400
800-584-9310
Fax: 308-762-7804
www.kcowradio.com
• Mike Glesinger, Sports Director
mike.glesinger@eagleradio.net
• Kevin Horn, News Director
• John Jones, Advertising Manager
Description:
Music, News, Sports.

KCRH-FM
25555 HESPERIAN BOULEVARD
HAYWARD, CA 94545-2447
510-723-6954
www.kcrh.net
• Ted Guiness, Sports Editor
Description:
Educational, Music, News, Sports.

KCRV-AM
777 HIGHWAY 84 WEST
CARUTHERSVILLE, MO 63830
573-333-1370
800-552-1055
Fax: 573-333-1371
Description:
Music, News, Sports.

KCSI-FM
1991 IRONWOOD AVENUE
RED OAK, IA 51566
712-623-2584
800-766-5274
Fax: 712-623-2583
kcsifm@yahoo.com
• Jerry V. Dietz, Program Director
Description:
Music, News, Sports, Talk.

KCTI-AM
615 SAINT PAUL STREET
GONZALES, TX 78629
830-672-3631
800-266-8531
Fax: 830-672-9603
• L. D. Decker, News Director
(830) 672-3631
ld44bigjake@hotmail.com
• Joe Haynes, Advertising Manager
(830) 672-3631
Description:
Music, News, Sports.

KCUB-AM
575 WEST ROGER ROAD
TUCSON, AZ 85705-2616
520-887-1000
Fax: 520-887-7585
www.fox1290.com/
• Carole Mendoza, Promotion Manager
Description:
Music, News.

KCUL-AM
200 WEST INTERSTATE 20
MARSHALL, TX 75672-9708
903-935-2500
Fax: 903-938-9730
• Mike Duncan, Program Director
Description:
Music, News, Sports, Talk.

KCUL-FM
200 WEST INTERSTATE 20
MARSHALL, TX 75672
903-935-2500
Fax: 903-938-9730
• Mike Duncan, Program Director
Description:
Music, News, Sports.

KCYL-AM
505 NORTH KEY AVENUE
LAMPASAS, TX 76550
512-556-6193
Fax: 512-556-2197
• Ronald K. Witcher, General Manager
Description:
Music, News, Sports.

KDAK-AM
859 MAIN STREET
CARRINGTON, ND 58421-1257
701-652-3151
Fax: 701-652-2916
• Dave Reed, General Manager
kdakam@daktel.com
Description:
Music, News, Sports.

KDBS-AM
1515 JACKSON STREET
ALEXANDRIA, LA 71301-6934
318-443-7454
Fax: 318-442-2747
• Cindy B Goode, News Director
(318) 443-7454
cindydickey@clearchannel.com
Description:
News, Talk.

KDCR-FM
498 4TH AVENUE, N.E.
SIOUX CENTER, IA 51250-1606
712-722-0885
Fax: 712-722-6244
kdcr@dordt.edu
www.kdcr.dordt.edu
• John Slegers, News Director
jslegers@dordt.edu
Description:
Music, News, Sports.

KDDR-AM
412 MAIN AVENUE
OAKES, ND 58474-1637
701-742-2187
Fax: 701-742-2009
• Tim Ost, General Manager
Description:
Music, News, Sports.

KDEX-AM
20487 STATE HIGHWAY 114 EAST
DEXTER, MO 63841
573-624-3545
Fax: 573-624-9926
kdex1@sbcglobal.net
• Joe Bowling, News Director
kdex1@sbcglobal.net
• Jim La Brot, Sports Director
kdex1@sbcglobal.net
Description:
Music, News, Sports.

KDIX-AM
119 2ND AVENUE, WEST
DICKINSON, ND 58601
701-225-5133
800-934-1230
Fax: 701-225-4136
kdix@kdix.net
www.kdix.net
• Rod Kleinjan, Sports Director
rod@kdix.net
• Jim Dahl, Associate Sports Director
(701) 225-5134
dahl@kdix.net
• Mike Renner, Rodeo Director
(701) 225-9662
mike@kdix.net
Description:
Music and Sports
Sports Discussed:
Football, Baseball, Basketball, Track,
Volleyball and Golf
Frequency:
1230 AM

KDJS-AM
730 NORTHEAST HIGHWAY 71
WILLMAR, MN 56201
320-231-1600
Fax: 320-235-7010
www.k-musicradio.com/index.html
• Bev Ahlquist, News Director
• Doug Hanson, Promotions Manager
csmdrhanson@yahoo.com
• Randy Quitney, Sports Director
Description:
Music, News, Sports.

KDJW-AM
1721 AVONDALE AVENUE
AMARILLO, TX 79106-4516
806-331-2826
Fax: 806-358-9285
kdjw_production@yahoo.com
www.kdjw.com
• Ron Slover, General Manager
(806) 358-9280
kdjw-production@yahoo.com
Description:
Music.

KDKB-FM
1167 WEST JAVELINA AVENUE
MESA, AZ 85206-4706
480-897-9300
Fax: 480-491-9482
www.kdkb.com
• Matt Spaetzel, Promotions Director
• Todd Walsh, Sports Director
Description:
Music.

KDLR-AM
P.O. BOX 190
DEVILS LAKE, ND 58301-0190
701-662-2161
Fax: 701-662-2222
kdlrkdvl@stellarnet.com
• Mark Beighley, Sports Director
(701) 662-7563
• Curt Teigen, General Manager
kzzyprod@stellarnet.com
Description:
Music.

KDOM-AM
1450 NORTH HIGHWAY 60/71
WINDOM, MN 56101-2018
507-831-3908
800-950-5366
Fax: 507-831-3913
www.kdomradio.com
• Dirk Abraham, News/Sports Director
Description:
Music, News, Sports.

KDOM-FM
1450 NORTH HIGHWAY 60/71
WINDOM, MN 56101-2018
507-831-3908
800-950-5366
Fax: 507-831-3913
www.kdomradio.com
• Dirk Abraham, News/Sports Director
Description:
Music, News, Sports.

KDSJ-AM
745 MAIN STREET
DEADWOOD, SD 57732-1015
605-578-1826
Fax: 605-578-1827
kdsj@deadwood.com
www.kdsj980.com
• Pam Bachs, Advertising Manager
• Ryan Reider, Program Director
Description:
Music, News, Sports.

KDUS-AM 1060 SPORTS
1900 W. CARMEN ST
TEMPE, AZ 85283
602-260-1060
Fax: 480-838-0252
• Chuck Artigue, General Manager
• Henry Lopez, Program Director
• Fred Pandrok, Marketing Director
• Mark Randall, Promotions Director
Nature of Sports Service:
24-hour sports radio programming station
part of the Sporting News Radio.
Football:
NFL - Arizona Cardinals
Ice Hockey:
NHL - Phoenix Coyotes

KDUZ-AM
20132 HIGHWAY 15
HUTCHINSON, MN 55350
320-587-2140
Fax: 320-587-5158
www.kduz.com
• Joel Niemeyer, Sports Director
(320) 587-2140
• Mark Wodarczyk, News Director
news@kduz.com
Description:
Music, News, Sports, Talk.

KDWA-AM
514 VERMILLION STREET
HASTINGS, MN 55033-1941
651-437-1460
Fax: 651-438-3042
www.kdwa.com
• Nick Ridley, News Director
news@kdwa.com
• Nick Tuckner, Sports Director
sports@kdwa.com
Description:
Music, News, Sports.

KDWN
1 MAIN ST
CARE OF : PLAZA HOTEL
LAS VEGAS, NV 89101
702-385-7212
800-338-8255
www.kdwn.com
• Claire Reis, General Manager
• Buzz Jones, Sports Director
Nature of Sports Service
Local. Sports/News/Talk radio programming.
Baseball:
MLB - Los Angeles Dodgers.

KDXL-FM
6425 WEST 33 ROAD STREET
SAINT LOUIS PARK, MN 55426-3403
952-928-6299
Fax: 952-928-6206
• Charlie Fiss, News Director
Description:
Music, News, Sports.

KEES-AM
1001 EAST SOUTH EAST LOOP 323
SUITE 455
TYLER, TX 75701
903-593-2519
Fax: 903-597-8378
• Paul Gleiser, Owner
(903) 593-2519
rogergray@ktbb.com
• Roger Gray, News Director
(903) 593-2519
rogergray@ktbb.com
• David Smoak, Sports Director
(903) 593-2519
smoaky@ktbb.com
Description:
Talk.

KELA
1635 S GOLD
CENTRALIA, WA 98531
360-736-3321
Fax: 360-736-0150
www.kelaam.com
• John Dimeo, General Manager
(360) 736-3321
johndimeo@clearchannel.com
• Ryan Trotter, Sports Director
ryantrotter@clearchannel.com
• Steve Richert, Operations Manager
steverichert@clearchannel.com
• Harland Forrest, General Sales Manager
harlandforrest@clearchannel.com
Nature of Sports Service
News, Talk, Sports.
Baseball:
MLB - Seattle Mariners.
College Sports:
Basketball - University of Washington;
Football - University of Washington,
Washington State University.
Football:
NFL - Seattle Seahawks.
Pro Basketball:
Seattle Sonics

KELO-AM
500 SOUTH PHILLIPS AVENUE
SIOUX FALLS, SD 57104
605-331-5350
Fax: 605-336-0415
www.keloam.com
• Greg Belfrage, News Director
(605) 271-5867

Description:
Music, News.

KELY-AM
PO BOX 151465
ELY, NV 89315
775-289-2077
Fax: 775-289-6997
kelynews@gmail.com
www.kely1230.com
• Howard Tenke, Program Director
Description:
News, Sports, Talk
Frequency:
1230 am

KEOL-FM
ONE UNIVERSITY BOULEVARD
LA GRANDE, OR 97850-2899
541-962-3333
keol@eou.edu
www.eou.edu/keol
• Steven Kalb, Program Director
Description:
Music, News, Sports.

KEOM-FM
2600 MOTLEY DRIVE
MESQUITE, TX 75150-3840
972-882-7560
Fax: 972-882-7569
www.keom.fm
• Steve Glenn, Sports Director
(972) 882-7379
sglenn@mesquiteisd.org
• James Griffin, Station Manager
Description:
Music, News, Sports.

KERN
1400 EASTON DR, STE 144
BAKERSFIELD, CA 93309
661-328-1410
Fax: 661-328-0873
www.liveradio.com
• Roger Fessler, General Manager
• Jon Zimmery, Program Director
Nature of Sports Service:
Local. 24-hour sports radio programming.
College Sports:
Basketball - Cal State University.
Football:
Oakland Raiders.

KERX-FM
1915 CHURCH STREET
BARLING, AR 72923
479-484-7285
800-680-2261
Fax: 479-484-7290
tommy@pearsonbroadcasting.com
• Tommy Craft, Advertising Manager
• Derek Ruscin, Program Director
(479) 484-7285
Description:
Music, News, Sports.
Sports Discussed:
College Football, NFL, College Basketball
Frequency:
96.3 fm

KESN-FM
2221 LAMAR, E.
ARLINGTON, TX 76006-7419

817-640-3776
Fax: 903-455-3692
www.espn1033.com
• Keri Korzeniewski, President
(817) 695-0893
• Scott Masteller, Program Director
(817) 640-3776
Description:
Music.

KETR-FM
2600 SOUTH NEAL
COMMERCE, TX 75429-4504
903-886-5848
800-882-5387
Fax: 903-886-5850
• Kevin Jefferies, News Director
(903) 886-5334
Description:
Music, News, Sports.

KEWI-AM
102 WEST SOUTH
BENTON, AR 72015-3777
501-778-6677
Fax: 501-778-7717
www.kewi690.com
• Jim Landers, Sports Director
Description:
Music, News, Sports.

KEYG-AM
58053 SPOKANE BOULEVARD
NORTHEAST
GRAND COULEE, WA 99133
509-633-2020
Fax: 509-633-1014
www.thedamsite.com
• Mark Wheeler, Advertising/General
Manager
(509) 662-3842
mwheeler@genext.net
Description:
Music, News.

KEZM-AM
208 S HUNTINGTON STREET
SULPHUR, LA 70663
337-527-3611
Fax: 337-527-0213
kezm1310am@structurex.net
• Bruce Merchant, Program/Sports Director
Description:
Sports/Talk Radop
Year Founded:
1955

KFAN SPORTS RADIO
1600 UTICA AVENUE SOUTH
SUITE 400
ST. LOUIS PARK, MN 55416
651-417-3000
Fax: 952-417-3001
www.kfan.com
• Doug Westerman, Program Director
• Greg Swedberg, Operations Manager
• Mick Anselmo, General Manager
Nature of Sports Service:
Local. 24-hour sports radio programming.
Has exclusive rights to broadcast Minnesota
Tiberwolves games.

KFCR-AM
145 MOUNT RUSHMORE ROAD
CUSTER, SD 57730

605-673-5327
Fax: 605-673-3079
• Gary Baker, General Manager
Description:
Music, News, Sports.

KFFX-FM
1420 C OF E DRIVE
EMPORIA, KS 66801-2585
620-342-1400
800-279-1964
Fax: 620-342-0804
kvoe@kvoe.com
• Jeff O'Dell, News Director
• Greg Rahe, Sports Director
raheg@kvoe.com
Description:
Music, News, Sports.

KFGE-FM
4343 O STREET
LINCOLN, NE 68510-1753
402-475-4567
800-444-5546
Fax: 402-479-1411
www.FroggY981.com
• Steve Albertsen, Program Director
• John Bishop, Sports Director
(402) 475-4567
• Mark Halverson, Market Manager
Description:
Music.

KFLD
2621 W. A ST
PASCO, WA 99301
509-547-9791
Fax: 509-547-8509
• Scott Souhrada, General Manager
• Tim O'Rourke, Program Director
Nature of Sports Service:
Local. 24-hour sports radio programming.
Baseball:
Seattle Mariners.
College Sports:
Basketball, Football - Washington State
University.
Ice Hockey:
NHL.

KFLS-AM
1338 OREGON AVENUE
KLAMATH FALLS, OR 97601
541-882-4656
Fax: 541-884-2845
www.kflsradio.com
• Jim Estabrook, News Director
(541) 882-4656
jim@klamathradio.com
Description:
Music, News, Sports.

KFLW-FM
P.O. BOX 1131 SRB
WAYNESVILLE, MO 65583
573-336-5359
800-336-5399
Fax: 573-336-5809
www.kflw99.com
• Jamie Turner, News Director
Description:
Music, News.

KFML-FM
16405 HEAVEN ROAD
LITTLE FALLS, MN 56345

320-632-5414
800-568-7249
Fax: 320-632-2571
ads@fallsradio.com
www.fallsradio.com
• Rod Grams, Program Director
(320) 632-5414
Description:
Music, News, Sports.
Year Founded:
1985

KFMO-AM
804 SAINT JOE DRIVE
PARK HILLS, MO 63601
573-431-1000
800-959-5366
Fax: 573-431-0850
news@b104fm.com
• Greg Alan, Sports Director
(573) 431-1000
sports@b104fm.com
• Greg Camp, Promotions Director
(573) 431-1000
greg@b104fm.com
• Gib Collins, News Director
(573) 431-2000
gib@b104fm.com
Description:
Music, News, Sports, Talk.

KFMT-FM
P. O. BOX 669
FREMONT, NE 68026-0669
402-721-5012
Fax: 402-721-5023
www.kfmt.com
• Rich Ray, Sports Director
(402) 721-5012
• Barry Reker, Advertising Manager
(402) 721-5012
Description:
Music, News, Sports.

KFNS-AM
8045 BIG BEND BOULEVARD
WEBSTER GROVES, MO 63119
314-962-0590
Fax: 314-962-7576
www.kfns.com
• Jason Komito, Marketing/Promotion
Manager
• Rob Weingarten, Program Director
Description:
News, Sports, Talk.

KFNS-AM SPORTS RADIO
8045 BIG BEND BLVD, STE 200
ST. LOUIS, MO 63119
314-962-0590
Fax: 314-962-7576
kfns.com
• Mike Claiborne, Program Director/Sports
Director
Nature of Sports Service:
Local. 24-hour sports radio programming.
College Sports:
Football - Notre Dame University.
Football:
St.. Louis Rams.

KFNZ
434 BEARCAT DR
SALT LAKE CITY, UT 84115
801-485-6700
Fax: 801-485-6611

• Eric Hauenstein, General Manager
• Jeff Rickard, Program Director
• Eric Ray, Operations Manager
Nature of Sports Service:
Local. 24-hour sports radio programming.
Baseball:
Minor League - Pacific Coast
League/PCL/Salt Lake Buzz.
Basketball:
NBA - Utah Jazz.
Football:
NFL - Denver Broncos.

KFOR-AM
3800 CORNHUSKER HIGHWAY SUITE 11
LINCOLN, NE 68504
402-466-1234
Fax: 402-467-4095
www.kfor1240.com
• Dale Johnson, News Director
(402) 466-1234
• Chuck Stevens, Sports Director
(402) 466-1234
Description:
Music, News, Sports.

KFSR-FM
5201 NORTH MAPLE
FRESNO, CA 93740
559-278-2598
Fax: 559-278-6985
kfsrfresno@hotmail.com
www.csufresno.edu/MCJ/kfsr-fm.htm
• Guy Haberman, Sports Director
Description:
Music, News, Sports.

KFTM-AM
P. O. BOX 430
FORT MORGAN, CO 80701-4105
970-867-5674
Fax: 970-542-1023
• Wayne Johnson, Owner
wayne@kftm.net
• John Waters, Sports Director
Description:
Music.

KFXN-AM
1600 UTICA AVENUE SOUTH SUITE 400
MINNEAPOLIS, MN 55416
952-417-3000
Fax: 952-417-3001
www.thescore690.com/main.html
• Chad Abbott, Program Director
chadabbott@clearchannel.com
• Mick Anselmo, Vice President
(952) 417-3020
mickanselmo@clearchannel.com
Description:
Music, News, Sports.

KFXX SPORTS RADIO 910 THE FAN
0700 SW BANCROFT ST
PORTLAND, OR 97239
503-223-1441
Fax: 503-222-6909
www.kfxx.com
• Suzanne Loseth, Marketing/Promotions
Director
• Meghan Olsen, Marketing/Promotions Mgr
LINEUP:
The Herd, Jim Rome, Dan Patrick Show,
The Big Show, Tee In'it up.

KFYN-AM
P.O. BOX 248
BONHAM, TX 75418-0248
903-583-3151
800-828-5396
Fax: 903-583-2728
• Jeff Davis, News Director
• Laura Kelso, Advertising Manager
(903) 583-4901
Description:
Music, News, Sports.

KGAL-AM
P.O. BOX 749
LEBANON, OR 97355-9642
541-451-5425
888-920-5746
Fax: 541-451-5429
www.kgal.com/
• Weldon Greig, News Director
news@kgal.com
• Radio Ray, Sports Director
(541) 926-8683
production@kgal.com
Description:
News, Talk, Sports
Frequency:
1580 AM
Sports Discussed:
All

KGBR-FM
29795 ELLENSBURG AVENUE SUITE-E
GOLD BEACH, OR 97444
541-247-7211
Fax: 541-247-4155
dale@kgbr.com
www.kgbr.com
• Bill Bailey, News Director
(541) 247-7418
bill@kgbr.com
• Randy Robbins, Sports Announcer
randy@kgbr.com
• Dale St. Marie, Owner, General Manager
Description:
Music, News, Sports.
Sports Discussed:
Gold Beach High School football.
Frequency:
92.7 fm

KGEO-AM SPORTS RADIO
1400 EASTON DR, STE 144
BAKERSFIELD, CA 93309
661-328-1410
800-840-5376
Fax: 661-328-0873
www.liveradio.com
• Roger Fessler, General Manager
• Jon Zimney, Sports Director
Nature of Sports Service:
Local. 24-hour sports radio programming.
Baseball:
MLB - San Francisco Giants.
Ice Hockey:
NHL - Anaheim Mighty Ducks.

KGFW-AM
2223 CENTRAL AVENUE
KEARNEY, NE 68847-5346
Fax: 308-237-0312
www.kgfw.com
• Bill Boyer, Operations Manager
(308) 698-2100
• John McDonald, General Manager
(308) 698-2100

Description:
News, Talk.
Year Founded:
1927

KGGG-FM
106 NORTH MAIN
HUTCHINSON, KS 67501-5219
620-665-5758
800-300-1061
Fax: 620-665-6655
ksku@ourtownusa.net
• Cliff Shank, General Manager
• Cliff Shank, Sports Director
Description:
Music, News, Sports.

KGHL-AM
222 NORTH 32ND STREET 10TH FLOOR
BILLINGS, MT 59101
406-238-1000
800-607-5445
Fax: 406-238-1038
790kghl.com/
• Jeff Howell, Program Director
(406) 238-1099
Description:
Music, News, Sports.

KGHS-AM
PO BOX 591
INTERNATIONAL FALLS, MN 56649-2317
218-283-3481
Fax: 218-283-3087
kghsksdm@northwind.net
www.ksdmradio.com
• Jerry Franzen, News Director
production@ksdmradio.com
• Roger Jerome, Sports Director
(218) 283-3481
Description:
Music, News, Sports, Talk.

KGMM ""THE GAME"" 1280 SPORTS
3911 S. FIRST
ABILENE, TX 79605
915-676-7711
Fax: 915-676-3851
www.keanradio.com
• Dean Minnick, General Manager
(915) 676-7111
• Jay Barry, Sports Director
(915) 676-7711
Auto Sports Sponsor:
Indianapolis 500.
Baseball:
MLB - Texas Rangers; World Series.
Basketball:
NBA - Draft; NBA - Finals.
College Sports:
NCAA Football - Texas A&M; NCAA
Basketball - Men's Tournament.
Equestrian:
Kentucky Derby.
Football:
NFL - Dallas Cowboys; Sunday & Monday
Night Football; Super Bowl.

KGNB-AM
1540 LOOP 337 NORTH
NEW BRAUNFELS, TX 78130
830-625-7311
800-594-2056
Fax: 830-625-7336
www.bradio.com

• David Ferguson, News Director
(830) 625-7311
Description:
Music, News, Sports.

KGPQ-FM
279 MIDWAY ROUTE
MONTICELLO, AR 71655
870-367-6854
800-367-8527
Fax: 870-367-9564
• P. Q. Gardner, Owner
Description:
Music.

KGRG-FM
12401 SOUTHEAST 320TH STREET
AUBURN, WA 98092-3622
253-833-9111
Fax: 253-288-3439
www.kgrg.com
• Eric Lucz, Program Director
Description:
Music, News, Sports.

KGSP-FM
8700 RIVER PARK DRIVE BOX 2
PARKVILLE, MO 64152-4358
816-741-2000
Fax: 816-741-4911
• Steve Youngblood, General Manager
Description:
Music, News, Sports.

KGVL-AM
1517 WOLFE CITY DRIVE
GREENVILLE, TX 75401-2111
903-455-1400
Fax: 903-455-5485
www.kgvlradio.com
• Bubba Knoetzes, News Director
kgblradio@hotmail.com
Description:
Music, News, Sports.

KHBT-FM
2196 MONTANA AVENUE
HUMBOLDT, IA 50548
515-332-4100
Fax: 515-332-2723
www.thebolt977.com
• Joe Hassett, Sports Director
• Duren Watts, News Director
Description:
Music, News, Sports.

KHHO-AM
645 ELLIOTT AVENUE WEST SUITE 300
SEATTLE, WA 98119
206-494-2000
richmoore@iheartmedia.com
www.sportsradioKJR.com
• Michelle Grosenick, General Manager
(206) 285-2295

KHKC-FM
P.O. BOX 810
ATOKA, OK 74525-0810
580-889-3392
Fax: 580-889-9308
• Ricky Chase, Program Director
khkc103@yahoo.com
Description:
Music, News, Sports.

KHMX-FM
24 GREENWAY PLAZA
SUITE 1900
HOUSTON, TX 77046
713-881-5100
Fax: 713-212-8965
www.khmx.com
• Buddy Scott, Program Director
(713) 830-8035
buddyscott@clearchannel.com
• Tim Sutherland, Marketing Director
(713) 212-8190
timsutherland@clearchannel.com
Description:
Music, News, Sports.

KHOP-FM
1581 CUMMINS DRIVE SUITE 135
MODESTO, CA 95358-6402
209-766-5000
800-548-0951
Fax: 209-522-2061
www.khop.com
• Geoff Silvius, Promotions Manager
(209) 523-7756
Description:
Music, News, Sports.

KHTK 1140 SPORTS RADIO
5244 MADISON AVE
SACRAMENTO, CA 95841
916-338-8700
Fax: 916-338-8777
• Mike Remy, Program Director
(916) 338-9226
• Michael Hernandez, General Sales
Manager
(916) 338-8781
• Jason Ross, Sports Director
(916) 338-9250
Nature of Sports Service:
Local. Sports radio programming.
College Sports:
Basketball - Sacramento State University;
Football - UC Davis.
Football:
NFL - Oakland Raiders.

KHTR-FM
1101 OLD WAWAWAI ROAD
PULLMAN, WA 99163
509-332-6551
Fax: 509-332-5151
khtr@aol.com
www.hot104.net
• Evan Ellis, News Director
• Rod Schwartz, Advertising Manager
(509) 595-1244
Description:
Music.

KHUB-AM
P.O. BOX 669
FREMONT, NE 68026-0669
402-721-1340
Fax: 402-721-5023
www.kfmt.com
• Jessica Meistrell, News Director
(402) 721-1340
• Rich Ray, Sports Director
(402) 721-1340
• Barry Reker, Advertising Manager
Description:
Educational, News, Sports, Talk.

KHYL-FM
1440 ETHAN WAY SUITE 200
SACRAMENTO, CA 95825-2214
916-929-5325
Fax: 916-925-0118
www.v1011fm.com
• Sonia Jackson, Promotions Director
soniajackson@clearchannel.com
Description:
Music, News, Sports, Talk.

KICE-AM
969 SOUTHWEST COLORADO
BEND, OR 97702
541-382-5611
Fax: 541-389-7885
www.kxux.com
• R.L. Garrigus, News Director
(541) 617-5286
rl@bendradiogroup.com
Description:
Music, News.

KICS-AM
500 EAST J STREET
HASTINGS, NE 68901
402-462-5101
Fax: 402-461-3866
www.espnsuperstation.com
• Wayne Specht, General Manager
• Mike Will, Sports Director
(402) 463-1230
• Doug Duda, Sports Director
(308) 236-9900
Description:
News, Talk.

KIFG-AM
406 STEVENS STREET
IOWA FALLS, IA 50126
641-648-4281
Fax: 641-648-4606
• Jay Knoll, News Director
(641) 648-4281
kifg@iafalls.com
• T.J. Norman, Sports Director
kifg@iafalls.com
Description:
Educational, Music, News, Sports, Talk.

KIFG-FM
406 STEVENS STREET
IOWA FALLS, IA 50126
641-648-4281
Fax: 641-648-4606
• Jay Knoll, News Director
(641) 648-4281
kifg@iafalls.com
• T.J. Norman, Advertising/Sports Director
kifg@iafalls.com
Description:
Educational, Music, News, Sports, Talk.

KIGS-AM
6165 LACEY BLVD
HANFORD, CA 93230-8812
559-582-0361
Fax: 559-582-3981
info@kigs.com
www.kigs.com
• Tony Vieira, General Manager & News Director
(559) 582-0361
• Eduardo Paim, Sports Director
(559) 582-0361
info@kigs.com

Description:
Music, News, Sports.

KIIX-AM
1612 LA PORTE AVENUE
FORT COLLINS, CO 80521
970-482-5991
888-212-9418
Fax: 970-482-5994
jeffersonchase@clearchannel.com
www.1410kiix.com
• Rich Bircumshaw, Sports Director
richbircumshaw@clearchannel.com
Description:
Music, News, Sports, Talk.

KIKR-AM
755 SOUTH 11TH STREET SUITE 102
BEAUMONT, TX 77701
409-833-9421
Fax: 409-833-9296
jbernard2@gt.rr.com
• Jay Bernard, Program Director

KILI-FM
P.O. BOX 150
PORCUPINE, SD 57772
605-867-5002
Fax: 605-867-5634
lakotaco@gwtc.net
www.lakotamall.com
• Wilson Two Lance, Program Director
(605) 867-5059
Description:
Music, News, Sports.

KILT AM 610 SPORTS RADIO
HOUSTON, TX
713-572-7767
www.sportsradio610.com
Basketball:
NBA - Houston Rockets, WNBA - Houston Comets.
College Sports:
NCAA - Texas Longhorns.
Football:
NFL - Houston Texans.

KIMX-FM
302 SOUTH 2ND STREET SUITE 202
LARAMIE, WY 82070-3650
307-745-5208
Fax: 307-745-8570
• Jim O'Reilly, Program Director
Description:
Music, News, Sports.

KINI-FM
P. O. BOX 499
SAINT FRANCIS, SD 57572-0419
605-747-2291
Fax: 605-747-5791
kinifm@gwtc.net
www.gwtc.net/~kinifm
• Bernard Whiting, Jr., General Manager
• Jay Claymore, Sports Anchor
(605) 747-2291
kinifm@gwtc.net
Description:
Music, News, Sports.

KIPA-AM
688 KINOOLE STREET SUITE 112
HILO, HI 96720-3868

808-935-6858
Fax: 808-443-0888
• Chip Begay, Sports Director
Description:
Music, News, Sports.

KIT
4010 SUMMIT VIEW
YAKIMA, WA 98908
509-972-3461
Fax: 509-972-3540
• Dave Aamodt, General Manager
• Brian Teegarden, Sports Director
Office Address:
114 S. 4th St, Yakima, WA 98901.
Nature of Sports Service:
News, Sports, Talk.
Baseball:
MLB - Seattle Mariners.
Basketball:
NBA - Seattle Supersonics.
Football:
NFL - Seattle Seahawks.

KITO-AM
402 NORTH WILSON
VINITA, OK 74301
918-256-2255
Fax: 918-256-2633
kitoamfm@yahoo.com
• Leona Boyd, Advertising Manager
• Dave Boyd, Program Director
Description:
Music, News, Sports.

KITO-FM
402 NORTH WILSON
VINITA, OK 74301
918-256-2255
Fax: 918-256-2633
kitoamfm@yahoo.com
• Dave Boyd, Program Director
Description:
Music.

KJAK-FM
PO BOX 6490
LUBBOCK, TX 79493
806-745-6677
Fax: 806-745-8141
www.kjak.com
• Woody Van Dyke, General Manager
(806) 745-3347
Description:
Provider of live High School games on the radio in Texas.
Year Founded:
1978

KJBZ-FM
902 EAST CALTON ROAD
LAREDO, TX 78041-6359
956-724-9800
Fax: 956-724-9915
• Carny Guerra, Program Director
Description:
Music, News, Sports.

KJCK-FM
US HIGHWAY 77 AND WEST ASH
JUNCTION CITY, KS 66441
785-762-5525
Fax: 785-762-5387
www.kjck.com
• Ed Klimek, Advertising Manager
• Dewey Terrill, News/Sports Director

Description:
Music, News.

KJFF-AM
1026 PHONEX DRIVE
FESTUS, MO 63028-0368
636-937-7642
Fax: 636-937-3636
www.kjff.com
• Ryan Reinheimer, Sports Director
• Matt West, News Director
Description:
Educational, News, Sports, Talk.

KJFM-FM
615 GEORGIA STREET
LOUISIANA, MO 63353-0438
573-754-5102
Fax: 573-754-5544
kjfmradio@yahoo.com
www.kjfmeagle102.net
• Thom Sanders, General Manager
(573) 324-0303
• Marianne Everhart, Operations Manager
(573) 324-0303
kjfmradioeagle102@yahoo.com
Description:
Mainstream country music.
Frequency:
102.1 fm

KJIM-AM
4367 WOODLAWN ROAD
DENISON, TX 75021-8037
903-893-1197
• Bob Allen, Advertising Manager/News
Director
Description:
Music, News.

KJIN-AM
P. O. BOX 2068
HOUMA, LA 70364
985-851-1020
Fax: 985-872-4403
• Glen Gomez, News Director
Description:
Music, News, Sports.

KJJJ-FM
1845 MCCULLOCH BOULEVARD SUITE
A-14
LAKE HAVASU CITY, AZ 86403
928-855-9336
Fax: 928-855-9333
www.kjjjfm.com
• Steve Greeley, Owner
Description:
Music, News, Sports.

KJNO-AM
3161 CHANNEL DRIVE SUITE 2
JUNEAU, AK 99801
907-586-3630
Fax: 907-463-3685
www.kjno.com
• Roy Paschal, President
Description:
Music.

KJOC-AM SPORTS RADIO
1229 BRADY ST
DAVENPORT, IA 52803
563-326-2541
Fax: 563-326-1819

• Scott Dailey, Program Director/Sports
Director
Nature of Sports Service:
Local. 24-hour sports radio programming.
Baseball:
MLB - Chicago White Sox, Chicago Cubs.
College Sports:
Football - Iowa State University; Basketball -
Iowa State University.
Football:
NFL - Chicago Bears.

KJR/KHHO SPORTS RADIO
351 ELLIOTT
SEATTLE, WA 98119
206-286-9595
800-829-0950
Fax: 206-494-2102
www.kjram.com

KJSK-AM
1418, 25 STREET
COLUMBUS, NE 68601-2820
402-564-2891
800-900-3511
Fax: 402-564-1999
www.kjsk.com
• Kara Asmus, Advertising Manager
(402) 564-9101
• Dean Johnson, Program Director
• James Nickel, Program Director; Sports
Director
(402) 564-2891
Description:
Educational, News, Sports, Talk.

KKFN
1095 S. MONACO PKWY
DENVER, CO 80224
303-321-0950
Fax: 303-333-5313
www.sportsradio.com/fan
• Bob Call, General Manager
• Tim Spence, Sports Director
Nature of Sports Service:
Local. 24-hour sports radio programming.
College Sports:
Basketball, Football - Colorado State
University.
Ice Hockey:
NHL - Colorado Avalanche.

KKIA-FM
145 OLD CREEK ROAD
STORM LAKE, IA 50588-7525
712-732-9200
877-220-3261
Fax: 712-732-3095
themoose@pionet.net
• Matt Fisher, News/Sports Director
Description:
Music, News, Sports.

KKIN-AM
37208 US HIGHWAY 169
AITKIN, MN 56431
218-927-2100
800-450-5546
Fax: 218-927-4090
kkinradio@embarqmail.com
• Tom Martin, Sports Director
Description:
Music, News, Sports, Talk.
Format:
All sports

Frequency:
94.3 Weekly sports show, 'Sports Call.'

KKLZ-FM
1455 EAST TROPICANA AVENUE SUITE
800
LAS VEGAS, NV 89119-8326
702-739-9600
Fax: 702-736-8447
• Kelly Hawkins, Promotion Director
(702) 730-0345
• Dennis Mitchell, News Director
(702) 739-9600
Description:
Music, News, Sports.

KKML-AM
6805 CORPORATE DRIVE SUITE 130
COLORADO SPRINGS, CO 80919
719-593-2700
Fax: 719-593-2727
• Jim Arthur, Program Director
(719) 593-2706
• Brenda Goodrich, General Manager
(719) 593-2766
• Jim Ryan, News Director
(719) 593-2774
Description:
Music.

KKNN-FM
315 KENNEDY AVENUE
GRAND JUNCTION, CO 81501
970-242-7788
Fax: 970-243-0567
www.coloradowest.com
• Tommy Rocker, Program Director
(970) 241-9595
• Kevin Wodlinger, Marketing Manager
(970) 242-7788
• Kim Gordon, PSA Director/Sports
(970) 242-7788
Description:
Music, News, Sports.

KKRC-FM
PO BOX 513
MONTEVIDEO, MN 56265
320-269-8815
Fax: 320-269-8449
• Deanna Hodge, Manager/News Director
(320) 269-8815
deekdma@yahoo.com
• Perry Sacharpason, Sports Director

KKRF-FM
204 SOUTH DIVISION STREET
STUART, IA 50250-5021
515-523-1107
Fax: 515-465-3952
www.realcountryonline.com
• Ben Keller, News Director
productiontok107@yahoo.com
• Sue Thomsen, Advertising Manager
suetrealcountry@yahoo.com
Description:
Music, News, Sports.

KKSJ-FM
3225 AMBASSADOR CAFFERY PARKWAY
LAFAYETTE, LA 70506-7214
337-993-5500
Fax: 337-993-5510
bdaigle@pittmanbroadcasting.com
Description:
Music, News, Sports.

KKTX-FM
3810 BROOKSIDE DRIVE
TYLER, TX 75701-9420
903-581-0606
Fax: 903-581-2011
• Craig Reininger, General Manager
(903) 581-0606
craigreininger@clearchannel.com
Description:
Music, News, Sports.

KKZN-AM
4695 SOUTH MONACO STREET
DENVER, CO 80237-3403
303-713-8000
Fax: 303-713-8509
www.thezone760.com
• Andy Lindahl, Sports Producer
andylindahl@clearchannel.com
Description:
Music, News, Sports, Talk.

KLAC-AM
3400 OLIVE AVENUE, W.
BURBANK, CA 91505-5544
818-559-2252
Fax: 818-260-9335
www.am570radio.com
• Kiyo Knight, Office Manager
kiyoknight@clearchannel.com
Description:
Music.

KLAY
10025 LAKEWOOD DR, SW
TACOMA, WA 98499
253-581-0324
Fax: 253-581-0326
klayrad@wol.com
• Clay Huntington, General Manager/Sports
Director
• Bob McCluskey, Sales Manager
• Bruce Bond, Producer
• Walker Mattson, Traffic
• Nick Winter, Engineering Executive
• Evan Brown, Human Resources Manager
Nature of Sports Service:
24-hour sports, talk and news radio
programming station.
College Sports:
Basketball, Football.

KLAY-AM
10025 LAKEWOOD DRIVE SUITE B
TACOMA, WA 98499-3878
253-581-0324
Fax: 253-581-0326
klay1180@blarg.net
www.klay1180.com
• Lynn Benson, News Director
radiolynnbenson@aol.com
Description:
Music, News, Sports.

KLBJ-AM
8309 NORTH IH 35
AUSTIN, TX 78753
512-832-4000
877-590-5525
Fax: 512-832-4081
www.590klbj.com
• Ed Clements, Sports Director
(512) 832-4028
• Todd Jeffries, News Director
Description:
News, Talk.

KLCI-FM
32215 124TH STREET
PRINCETON, MN 55371
612-389-1300
800-850-1061
Fax: 763-389-1359
• Troy Edwards, Program Director
Description:
Music, News, Sports, Talk.

KLCK-AM
514 SOUTH COLUMBUS
GOLDENDALE, WA 98620
509-773-3300
Fax: 509-773-3301
• Nettie Cramer, News Director
(541) 296-9102
Description:
Music, News, Sports.

KLEB-AM
11603 HIGHWAY 308
PO BOX 1350
LAROSE, LA 70373
985-798-7792
Fax: 985-798-7793
klrz@cajunnet.com
www.klrzfm.com
• Jerry Gisclair, Owner
klrz@mobiletel.com
• Brennan Matherne, News/Sports Director
bmatherne@klrzfm.com
Description:
Music.

KLGA-FM
P.O. BOX 160
ALGONA, IA 50511-0160
515-295-2475
Fax: 515-295-3851
• Vic Doane, Sports Director
• Chuck Shockley, News Director
Description:
Music.

KLGR-FM
639 WEST BRIDGE STREET
REDWOOD FALLS, MN 56283
507-637-2989
Fax: 507-637-5347
klgr@mchsi.com
www.klgram.com
• Randy Clausen, Sports Director
• Laura Olson, News Director
Description:
Music.

KLIF-FM
1109 HUDSON LANE
MONROE, LA 71201-6003
318-388-2323
Fax: 318-388-0569
la105@bayou.com
www.la105.com
• Gene Ponti, Sports Director
gino@bayou.com
• John Reynolds, News Director
jreynolds@bayou.com

KLIK-AM
3605 COUNTRY CLUB DRIVE
JEFFERSON CITY, MO 65109-1070
573-893-5100
800-500-9107
Fax: 573-893-8330
www.klik1240.com

• Brian Wilson, Program Director
(573) 893-5100
Description:
Music, News, Sports, Talk.

KLIN
4343 O STREET
LINCOLN, NE 68510
402-475-4567
800-444-5546
Fax: 402-479-1411
www.broadcasthouse.com
• Mark Halverson, General Manager
• John Bishop, Sports Director
Nature of Sports Service:
News, Sports, Talk.
College Sports:
Baseball, Basketball, Football - University of
Nebraska.

KLLC-FM
865 BATTERY STREET 3RD FLOOR
SAN FRANCISCO, CA 94111-1503
415-765-4097
800-400-3697
Fax: 415-781-3697
studio@radioalice.com
www.radioalice.com
• Greg Nemitz, Vice President
• Denise St. Louis, Promotions Director
(415) 765-4137
Description:
Music, News, Sports.

KLOE-AM
3023 WEST 31ST
GOODLAND, KS 67735-0569
785-899-2309
Fax: 785-899-3062
www.kloe.com
• Curtis Duncan, News Director
(785) 899-2309
• Andrew Melia, Sports Director
Description:
Music, News, Sports, Talk.

KLOG-AM
506 COWLITZ WAY WEST
KELSO, WA 98626
360-636-0110
Fax: 360-577-6949
news@klog.com
www.klog.com
• Kirc Roland, News/Sports Director
Description:
Music.

KLOL-FM
2000 WEST LOOP SOUTH SUITE 300
HOUSTON, TX 77027
713-212-8000
Fax: 713-212-8101
mega101houston.com/
• Laurent Fouilloud, News Director
laurentfouilloud@clearchannel.com
Description:
Music, News, Sports.

KLRM-FM
33374 VERNONIA HIGHWAY
SCAPPOOSE, OR 97056
805-922-1041
Fax: 805-928-3069
www.air1radio.com
• David Pierce, Program Director
david@klove.com

Description:
Music, News, Sports.

KLSS-FM
402-19TH STREET, SW
MASON CITY, IA 50401-6435
641-423-8634
Fax: 641-423-8206
www.klssradio.com
• Bob Fisher, News Director
Description:
Music.

KLSX-FM
3580 WILSHIRE BOULEVARD
LOS ANGELES, CA 90010-2501
213-383-4222
Fax: 213-386-3649
www.fmtalki.com
• David Saverino, Advertising Manager
Description:
Music, Talk.

KLTF-AM
16405 HAVEN RD
LITTLE FALLS, MN 56345
320-632-5414
800-568-7249
Fax: 320-632-2571
www.fallsradio.com
• Rod Grams, Program Director
• Al Windsperger, Sports Director
Description:
Music, News, Sports.

KLUP-AM
9601 MCALLISTER FREEWAY SUITE 1200
SAN ANTONIO, TX 78216
210-344-8481
877-630-5757
Fax: 210-340-1213
www.klup.com
• Milton Glueck, Account Manager
(210) 344-8481
• Baron Wiley, Program Director
(210) 344-8481
Description:
Music, News.

KLVI-AM 560
2885 I-10 EAST
BEAVMONT, TX 77702
409-896-5555
Fax: 409-896-5599
klvi@klvi.com
www.klvi.com
• Harold Mann, News/Sports Director
• Jim Love, Program Director
jimlove@clearchannel.com
Teams:
Houston Texans; Lamar University.
Nature of Sports Service:
24-hour sports radio programming station.

KLXS-FM
106 WEST CAPITOL AVENUE
PIERRE, SD 57501-2018
605-224-1240
Fax: 605-224-0095
• John P. Saboor, President
• Brent Nelson, Vice President
• Kevin Coulthart, Vice President Events
• Jonathan Baran, Lake County Sports
Marketing Manager
• Chad Baransky, Osceola County Sports
Marketing Manager

• Jennifer Lastik, Orange County Sports
Marketing Manager
• Jason Maderer, Volusia County Sports
Marketing Manager
• Keith Station, Seminole County Sports
Marketing Manager
• Bob Deglauries, Sports Director
• Tony Mangan, News Director
Description:
Music.

KLZZ-FM
640 SOUTHEAST LINCOLN AVENUE
SAINT CLOUD, MN 56304
320-251-4422
Fax: 320-251-1855
lee@wjon.com
1037theloon.com/
• David Engberg, General Manager
Description:
Music.

KMA-AM
209 NORTH ELM
SHENANDOAH, IA 51601
712-246-5270
800-234-5622
Fax: 712-246-5275
www.kmakkbz.com/kma/
• Lee Hughes, Sports Director
(712) 246-5270
• Mike Peterson, News Director
(712) 246-5270
Description:
Music, News, Sports.

KMAV-FM
1000 MAIN STREET SOUTH WEST
PO BOX 216
MAYVILLE, ND 58257
701-786-2335
Fax: 701-786-2268
news@kmav.com
www.kmavradio.com
• Mary Keating, Owner/Sales Manager
mary@kmav.com
• Dan Keating, General Manager/Sports
Director
dan@kmav.com
Description:
Music, News, Sports.

KMEM-FM
326 EAST JEFFERSON
MEMPHIS, MO 63555-1100
660-465-7225
800-748-7875
Fax: 660-465-2626
mdenney@kmemfm.com
• Rick Fischer, News Director
(660) 465-2716
rfischer@kmemfm.com
• Donnie Middleton, Sports Director
Description:
Music, News, Sports.

KMFY-FM
507 SOUTHEAST 11TH STREET
GRAND RAPIDS, MN 55744-3950
218-326-3446
Fax: 218-326-3448
• Bill Betz, Sports Director
• Kenn Fideldy, News Director
Description:
Music.

KMHI-AM
1871 CANYON CREEK ROAD
MOUNTAIN HOME, ID 83647-3747
208-587-8424
Fax: 208-587-8425
• Alvin Lee Powers, Sports Director
(208) 537-8424
Description:
Educational, News, Sports, Talk and local
sports broadcasts
Sports Discussed:
local high school baseball, softball, football,
volleyball, basketball, wrestling and
American Legion Baseball
Frequency:
Daily

KMIS-AM
1303 SOUTHWEST DRIVE
KENNETT, MO 63857
573-888-4616
Fax: 573-888-4991
ktmo@i1.net
• Monte Lyons, Program Director
(573) 888-4616
Description:
Music, News.

KMJ
1071 W. SHAW
FRESNO, CA 93711
559-266-5800
www.kmj580.com
• Al Smith, General Manager
• Bill Woodward, Sports Director
Office Address:
1110 E. Olive, Fresno, CA 93744.
Nature of Sports Service:
News, Talk, Sports.

KMLB
1109 HUDSON LANE
MONROE, LA 71201
318-388-2323
800-259-1440
Fax: 318-388-0569
kmlb@bayou.com
• Bob Holladay, General Manager
• Greg Gulyas, Sports Director
Nature of Sports Service:
News, Talk, Sports.
Auto Sports:
NASCAR.
Baseball:
CBS - MLB.
Basketball:
Louisiana State University/LSU; Final Four.
College Sports:
Baseball - Northeast Louisiana University;
Football:
Notre Dame University, Louisiana State
University/LSU.
Football:
NFL - CBS.

KMMJ
3205 W. NORTH FRONT ST
GRAND ISLAND, NE 68802
308-382-2800
Fax: 308-382-6701
kmmj@aol.com
• Brad Fossberg, Sports Director
Nature of Sports Service:
News, Talk.

KMND-AM
11300 HIGHWAY 191 BUILDING 2
MIDLAND, TX 79707
432-563-9300
Fax: 432-563-3823
• Robie Burns, Program Director
(432) 563-5499
Description:
Music, News, Sports.

KMNS-AM
1113 NEBRASKA STREET
SIOUX CITY, IA 51105-1438
712-258-5595
Fax: 712-252-2430
kmnsnews@clearchannel.com
www.620kmns.com
• Curtis Anderson, Sports Director
(712) 224-5487
curtisanderson@clearchannel.com
• Rick Schorg, General Manager
rickschorg@clearchannel.com
Description:
Music.

KMOX
ONE MEMORIAL DR
ST. LOUIS, MO 63102
314-621-2345
Fax: 314-444-3230
kmoxspt@kmox.com
www.kmox.com
• Ron Jacober, Sports Director
(314) 444-+187
rdjacober@cbs.com
• Tom Langmyer, VP/General Manager
(314) 444-3285
telangmyer@cbs.com
• Steve Moore, Program Director
(314) 444-3286
swmoore@cbs.com
Baseball:
MLB - St. Louis Cardinals.
College Sports:
Basketball - St. Louis University; University
of Missouri. Football - University of Missouri.
Football:
NFL/CBS.
Nature of Sports Service:
News, talk & sports.
Primary Audience:
Men & women between 35-64 years old.

KMPC-AM
2800 28TH STREET
SUITE 308
SANTA MONICA, CA 90405
213-487-1300
Fax: 310-452-5950
• Roger Nadel, VP/General Manager
• Tim Parker, Program Director
(310) 664-2384

KMRS-AM
P.O. BOX 570
MORRIS, MN 56267-0570
320-589-3131
Fax: 320-589-2715
• Paul Schwarz, News Director
Description:
Music, News, Sports.

KMSA-FM
1175 TEXAS AVENUE
GRAND JUNCTION, CO 81501-7605

970-248-1240
Fax: 970-248-1708
www.kmsa.com
• Ryan Gruwell, Sports Director
Description:
Music, News, Sports.

KMSR-AM
1000 MAIN STREET WEST
MAYVILLE, ND 58257
701-786-2335
Fax: 701-786-2268
news@kmavradio.com
www.kmavradio.com
• Dan Keating, General Manager/Sports
Director
dan@kmav.com
• Mary Keating, Owner/Sales Manager
mary@kmav.com
Description:
Station carries NBC sports talk, including
the Dan Patrick and Colin Cowherd shows,
NFL football, NCAA football and basketball.

KMUN-FM
COAST COMMUNITY RADIO
PO BOX 269
ASTORIA, OR 97103
503-325-0010
Fax: 503-325-3956
www.kmun.org
• David Hammock, General Manager
Description:
Educational, Full Service, Music, News.

KMVP 860 AM SPORTS RADIO
5300 N. CENTRAL AVE
PHOENIX, AZ 85012
602-277-5687
Fax: 602-241-6810
• Chris Gallu, General Manager
• Kevin Ray, Program Director/Sports
Director
• Doug Cannon, Assistant Program Director
Nature of Sports Service:
24-hour sports radio programming station.

KMVP-AM
201 EAST JEFFERSON STREET
PHOENIX, AZ 85004
602-514-8333
Fax: 602-514-8303
newsradio620@ktar.com
www.kmvp.com
• Mike Golic, Sports Host
(888) 729-3776
• Mike Greenberg, Sports Host
(888) 729-3776
• Kevin Ray, Sports Director
(602) 514-8333

KNBR 1050
55 HAWTHORNE ST
SUITE 1100
SAN FRANCISCO, CA 94105-3914
415-995-6800
Fax: 415-995-6867
www.knbr.com
• Lee Hammer, Program Director
Football:
NFL - Oakland Raiders.
College Sports:
NCAA - Stanford Cardinal.
Basketball:
NBA - Golden State Warriors.
Baseball:

MLB - Oakland Athletics.
Auto Sports:
NASCAR.

KNBR RADIO
55 HAWTHORNE STREET
SUITE 1000
SAN FRANCISCO, CA 94105-3914
415-995-6800
Fax: 415-995-6907
www.knbr.com
• Tony Salvadore, General Manager
• Lee Hammer, Program Director
(415) 995-6385
Nature of Sports Service:
24-hour sports radio programming station.
Baseball:
MLB - San Francisco Giants, Oakland
Athletics.
Basketball:
NBA - Golden State Warriors.
Football:
NFL - Oakland Raiders. San Francisco
49'ers.
Ice Hockey:
NHL - San Jose Sharks.

KNBU-FM
7TH & DEARBORN STREETS
BALDWIN CITY, KS 66006
785-594-6451
Fax: 785-594-3570
communication@bakeru.edu
• Ann Rosenthal, General Manager
(785) 594-6451
Description:
Music, News, Sports.

KNDK-FM
9453 HIGHWAY 1
LANGDON, ND 58249-9398
701-256-1080
Fax: 701-256-1081
www.kndk1080.com
• Jake Kulland, Sports Director
kndk1080@utma.com
• Bob Simmons, News Director
(701) 256-1080
kndk1080@utma.com
Description:
Music.

KNEB RADIO
PO BOX 239
SCOTTSBLUFF, NE 69363
308-632-7121
888-632-5653
Fax: 308-635-1079
www.kneb.com
• Craig Larson, Station Manager
• Rob Barney, Sports Director
(308) 632-7121
Baseball:
MLB - Kansas City Royals.
College Sports:
Baseball, Men's & Women's Basketball,
Football, Volleyball - University of
Nebraska-Lincoln; NCAA.
Football:
NFL - Denver Broncos.
Ice Hockey:
NHL - Colorado Avalanche.

KNEB-FM
1928 EAST PORTAL PLACE
SCOTTSBLUFF, NE 69361

308-632-7121
Fax: 308-635-1079
www.kneb.com
• Rob Barney, Sports Director
• Barbara Martinson, Advertising Manager
• Kevin Mooney, News Director
Description:
Music.

KNEI-AM
14 WEST MAIN STREET
WAUKON, IA 52172
563-568-3476
Fax: 563-568-3391
knei@netins.net
• Chuck Bloxham, News Director
Description:
Music.

KNES-FM
627 WEST COMMERCE
FAIRFIELD, TX 75840
903-389-5637
Fax: 903-389-7172
texas99@texas99.com
www.knesfm.com
• Buzz Russell, Sports/Program Director
(903) 389-5637
buzzman@texas99.com
Description:
Music, News, Sports, Talk.

KNIM-AM
1618 SOUTH MAIN
MARYVILLE, MO 64468
660-582-2151
800-748-1496
Fax: 660-582-3211
www.knimmaryville.com
• Matt Gaarder, News Director
Description:
Music, News, Sports.

KNML - ALBUQUERQUE
500 4TH STREET NW
ALBURQUERQUE, NM 87102
505-767-6700
888-922-0610
Fax: 505-767-6767
• Milt McConnell, General Manager
• Ian Martin, Program Director
Nature of Sports Service:
All Sports Station. Broadcasts: Notre Dame
Football (College NCAA I), College
Basketball, New Mexico Scorpions (Western
Professional Hockey League/Minor League
Hockey.

KNOX
OLD BELMONT RD, SOUTH
PO BOX 13638
GRAND FORKS, ND 58208-3638
701-775-4611
Fax: 701-772-0540
• Linn Hodgson, General Manager
• Paul Roberts, Sports Director
Office Address:
Old South Belmont Road, Grand Forks, ND
58208.
Nature of Sports Service:
News, Sports, Talk.
Baseball:
MLB - Minnesota Twins.
College Sports:
Football - Notre Dame; Basketball -
University of North Dakota.

KNPT-AM
906 ALDER STREET, S.W.
NEWPORT, OR 97365
541-265-2266
Fax: 541-265-6397
news@ybcradio.com
www.knptam.com/
• Kiera Morgan, News Director
• Bob Spangler, Sports Director
(541) 265-2266
Description:
Music, News, Sports.

KNWD-FM
P.O. BOX 3038
NATCHITOCHES, LA 71497-0010
318-357-4180
Fax: 318-357-4398
knwd9876@aol.com
www.nsula.edu/knwd
• Brad Hartley, General Manager
nad9876@aol.com
Description:
Music, News, Sports, Talk.

KNX-AM
5670 WILSHIRE BOULEVARD
LOS ANGELES, CA 90036-5679
323-900-2070
Fax: 323-964-8329
knxnews@cbsradio.com
www.knx1070.com
• Steve Grad, Sports Reporter
(323) 900-2070
Description:
News.

KNZR-AM
3651 PEGASUS DRIVE SUITE 107
BAKERSFIELD, CA 93308-6836
661-393-1900
Fax: 661-393-1915
www.knzr.com
• Michael Briggs, Promotions Director
• Otis Warren, Advertising Manager
Description:
News, Talk.

KOAK-AM
1991 IRONWOOD AVENUE
RED OAK, IA 51566
712-623-2584
800-766-5274
Fax: 712-623-2583
kcsifm@yahoo.com
• Jerry V. Dietz, Program Director
Description:
Music, News, Sports, Talk.

KOFE-AM
201 NORTH 8TH STREET
SAINT MARIES, ID 83861-1869
208-245-1240
Fax: 208-245-6525
www.koferadio.com
• Theresa Plank, General Manager
Description:
Music, News, Sports.

KOGT-AM RADIO
PO BOX 1667
ORANGE, TX 77631
409-863-4381
Fax: 409-883-7996
www.kogt.com

• Gary Stelly, General Manager/Sports
Director
Nature of Sports Service:
Sports, News, Country Music.
Baseball:
MLB - Texas Rangers.
College Sports:
Basketball, Football - Texas A&M.

KOHI-AM
36200 PITTSBURG ROAD
SUITE C
SAINT HELENS, OR 97051-0398
503-397-1600
877-397-1632
Fax: 503-397-1601
kohi.radio@gmail.com
www.am1600kohi.com
• Marty Rowe, General Manager
• Phil Dietz, Sports Director
Description:
Local sports and Western OR University
football and 49er Football
Teams:
St. Helens, Scappoose, WOU, San
Francisco 49ers

KOHS-FM
175 SOUTH 400 EAST
OREM, UT 84058-6382
801-224-9236
• Kenneth B. Seastrand, Station Manager
Description:
Music, News, Sports.

KOKB-AM
P.O. BOX 2509
PONCA CITY, OK 74602
580-765-2485
Fax: 580-767-1103
bill@eteamradio.com
www.eteamradio.com
• Bill Coleman, Owner/News Director
(580) 765-2485
Description:
Music, News, Sports.

KOKC-AM
400 EAST BRITTON ROAD
OKLAHOMA CITY, OK 73114
405-478-5104
Fax: 405-793-0514
• Ken Johnson, News Director
Description:
Music.

KOMO 1000 AM RADIO
140 FOURTH AVE
NORTH SEATTLE, WA 98109
206-404-4000
Fax: 206-404-4422
• J.shannon Sweatte, Group Head
• Bill Swartz, Sports Director
• Rob Dunlop, General Manager
• Bill Aanenson, General Sales Manager
• Alyson Soma, Promotions Director
• Wanda Hutton, UW Husky Sports
Coordinator
• Paul Duckworth, Program/News Director
Nature of Sports Service:
News.
College Sports:
Basketball, Football - University of
Washington.

KONA-AM
2823 WEST LOUIS STREET
PASCO, WA 99301
509-547-1618
Fax: 509-546-2678
www.konaradio.com
• Michael McDonnal, Sports Director
• Dennis Shannon, News Director
Description:
Music, News, Sports, Talk.

KOOC-FM
608 MOODY LANE
TEMPLE, TX 76504
254-773-5252
Fax: 254-773-0115
• Brian Mack, Program Director
(254) 773-5252
Description:
Music, News, Sports.

KORN-AM
319 NORTH MAIN STREET
MITCHELL, SD 57301-2611
605-996-1073
Fax: 605-996-6680
www.sbcradop.com
• J.P. Skelly, News Director
Description:
Music, News, Talk.

KOVC-AM
136 CENTRAL AVENUE, NORTH
VALLEY CITY, ND 58072
701-845-1490
Fax: 701-845-1245
dcountry@daktel.com
• Ryan Cunningham, Sports Director
• Kerry Johnson, Advertising Manager
• Ronnie Lee, Program Director
Description:
Music, News, Sports.

KOVO-AM
26 WEST CENTER SUITE 101
PROVO, UT 84601
801-818-1074
Fax: 801-818-3308
• Randy Rogers, General Manager
(801) 412-6040
Description:
Music.

KOWB-AM
3525 SOLDIER SPRINGS ROAD
LARAMIE, WY 82070
307-745-4888
800-352-5249
Fax: 307-742-4576
www.kowb1290.com
• Dave Geist, Program Director
(307) 745-9242
• Keri Eakins, KOWB Sports Assistant
(307) 745-4888
• David Settle, Operations Manager &
Sports Director
(307) 745-4888
davidsettle@gapbroadcasting.com
Description:
News/talk.
Sports Discussed:
National, regional and local.
Frequency:
1290 am

KOY-AM
4686 EAST VAN BUREN STREET
SUITE 300
PHOENIX, AZ 85008
602-374-6000
Fax: 480-966-7435
www.am1230koy.com
• Joe Puglise, Market Manager
joepuglise@clearchannel.com
Description:
Music.

KOZB-FM
5445 JOHNSON ROAD
BOZEMAN, MT 59718
406-587-9999
Fax: 406-587-5855
• Les Clay, News Director
Description:
Music, News.

KOZN-AM
5011 CAPITOL AVENUE
OMAHA, NE 68132
402-342-2000
Fax: 402-342-7041
• Ken Searnaw, General Manager

KPEL-AM
1749 BERTRAND DRIVE
LAFAYETTE, LA 70506-2054
337-233-6000
Fax: 337-234-7360
• Mike Grimsley, General Manager
(337) 233-6000
• Bernadette Lee, News Director
(337) 233-6000
bernie.lee@regentcomm.com
• Jay Walker, Sports/Program Director
(337) 233-6000
Description:
News.

KPEL-FM
1749 BERTRAND DR
LAFAYETTE, LA 70506-2054
337-232-2242
Fax: 337-234-7360
steve.peloquin@regentcomm.com
www.espn1420.com
• Bernadette Lee, News Director
(337) 232-2242
bernie.lee@regentcomm.com
• Jay Walker, Sports Director
(337) 232-2242
Description:
News, Talk.

KPLY
255 W. MOANA LANE, STE 208
RENO, NV 89509
775-829-1964
Fax: 775-825-3183
• Mike Bushey, Program Director
Nature of Sports Service:
Local. 24 Hour Sports.
Baseball:
MLB - San Francisco Giants.
Football:
NFL - Oakland Raiders.
Ice Hockey:
NHL - San Jose Sharks.

KPOK-AM
11 1/2 NORTH MAIN STREET
BOWMAN, ND 58623

701-523-3883
Fax: 701-523-3885
www.kpokradio.com
• Tim Trumbal, Advertising Manager
• Tim Norman, News Director
Description:
Music.

KPRB-FM
231 MAIN STREET
FORT MORGAN, CO 80701-2148
970-867-7271
888-556-5747
Fax: 970-867-2676
thesting@b106.com
www.b106.com
• John Beltran, Sports Director
(970) 867-7271
john@necolorado.com

KPSI-AM
2100 EAST TAHQUITZ-CANYON WAY
PALM SPRINGS, CA 92262
760-325-2582
Fax: 760-322-3562
• Gregg Aratin, Advertising Manager
(760) 325-2582
• Lisa Giles, Promotion Manager
(760) 325-2582
Description:
News, Talk.

KPTT-AM
2900 SUTRO STREET
RENO, NV 89512-1616
775-329-9261
Fax: 775-323-1450
• Steve Diamond, News Director
(775) 329-9261
steved@lotusradio.com
• Don Morchand, Sports Director
(775) 329-9261
• Raina Weathers, Advertising Sales
Director
rainarocks@aol.com

KPUG-AM
2219 YEW STREET ROAD
BELLINGHAM, WA 98229
360-734-9790
Fax: 360-733-4551
www.kpug1170.com
• Doug Lang, Program Director
Description:
News, Sports.

KQAD-AM
1140 150TH AVENUE
LUVERNE, MN 56156
507-283-4444
Fax: 507-283-4445
www.kqad.net
• Matt Crosby, News Director
• Bruce Thalhuber, Sports Director
Description:
Music, News, Sports.

KQAL-FM
P.O. BOX 5838
WINONA, MN 55987
507-453-2222
Fax: 507-453-5226
www.kqal.org/
• Asafsina Yildiz, Program Director
Description:
Music, News, Sports.

KQLL - AM
5801 E. 41ST
TULSA, OK 74135
918-664-2810
Fax: 918-665-0555
• Allen McGlaughlin, General Manager
• Chris Plank, Operations Manager
• Gerry Wilburn, Local Sales Manager
• Bruce Simons, Network Sales Manager
Nature of Sports Service:
Local. 24 Hour Sports.
Baseball:
Minor League - Texas Baseball League/AA - Tulsa Drillers.
College Sports:
Basketball, Football - Tulsa University.
Football:
NFL - Dallas Cowboys.

KQWC-AM
1020 EAST 2ND STREET
WEBSTER CITY, IA 50595-0550
515-832-1570
800-958-2417
Fax: 515-832-2079
www.kqradio.com
• Mary Harris, General Manager/Advertising Director
(515) 832-1570
• Rhonda Martin, Business Manager
(515) 832-1570
• Pat Powers, News Director
(515) 832-1570
• Chris Lockwood, Program Director
(515) 832-1570
Description:
Music, News, Sports, Talk.

KRAN
514 E. BELLEVUE
ATWATER, CA 95301
209-358-9723
Fax: 209-358-9793
• Kelly Leonard, General Manager
• Yolanda Navarro, Program Director
Baseball:
MLB - San Francisco Giants.
College Sports:
Basketball, Football.
Football:
NFL - Oakland Raiders, San Francisco 49ers.

KRDO SPORTS RADIO 1240AM
3 S. 7TH ST
COLORADO SPRINGS, CO 80905
719-632-1515
Fax: 719-635-8455
• Neil Klockziem, General Manager
• Mike Lewis, Operations/Sports Director
(719) 575-6245
• Jim Totum, Afternoon Talk Show Host
(719) 575-6248
Nature of Sports Service:
Sports, Talk.
Baseball:
MLB - Chicago Cubs; Minor League - Pacific Coast League/AAA - Colorado Springs Sky Sox.

KRDZ-AM
32992 U.S. HIGHWAY 34
WRAY, CO 80758
970-332-4171
Fax: 970-332-4172
www.krdz.com

• Wayne Johnson, Owner
(970) 867-5674
• Robert Lovell, Sports Director KRDZ 1440 AM
(970) 630-8615
Description:
Music, News, Sports.
Sport Broadcasts
We cover Wray High School sports and carry Denver Nuggets and Colorado Avalanche games.

KREI-AM
1401 KREI BOULEVARD
FARMINGTON, MO 63640-0461
573-756-6476
Fax: 573-756-9127
mymoinfo.com
• Scott Kubala, Program Director
(573) 756-6476
• Tim Ryan, Sports Director
(573) 756-6476
Description:
Music, News, Sports.

KRFO-FM
245 18TH STREET SOUTHEAST
OWATONNA, MN 55060
507-451-2250
Fax: 507-451-8837
www.krfo.com
• John Connor, Advertising Manager
• Loren Hart, Program Director
Description:
Music, News, Sports.

KRFS-AM
RR 2, BOX 149
SUPERIOR, NE 68978-9802
402-879-3207
Fax: 402-879-4741
• Cory Kopsa, Advertising Manager/News & Sports Director
krfsfm@yahoo.com
Description:
Music, News, Sports.

KRFX-FM
4695 SOUTH MONACO STREET
DENVER, CO 80237-3403
303-713-8000
Fax: 303-713-8743
• Lee Larsen, Senior Vice President
(303) 694-6300
leelarson@clearchannel.com
• Rich Goins, Sports Director
(303) 713-8000
richgoins@clearchannel.com
Description:
Music, News, Sports.

KRHC-AM
5526 HIGHWAY 281 NORTH
MARBLE FALLS, TX 78654-0639
830-693-5551
Fax: 830-693-5107
www.khlb.com
• Art D'Lugach, News Director
• Art D'Lugach, Sports Director
Description:
Music.

KRJB-FM
312 WEST MAIN STREET
ADA, MN 56510-1252

218-784-2844
800-569-4171
Fax: 218-784-3749
krjbada@loretel.net
krjb.outbackpc.net/
• Jim Birkemeyer, Advertising Manager
• Dennis Roux, News Director
Description:
Music, News, Sports.

KRKO-AM
2707 COLBY AVENUE #1380
EVERETT, WA 98201-3528
425-304-1381
Fax: 425-304-1382
rkonews@krko.com
www.krko.com
• Ed Ramirez, Advertising Manager
• Tony Stevens, Program Director
(425) 304-1381
tony.stevens@krko.com
Description:
News, Talk.
Frequency:
1380 am

KRKR-FM
3800 CORNHUSKER HIGHWAY SUITE 11
LINCOLN, NE 68504
402-466-1234
Fax: 402-467-4095
www.knetfm.com
• Dale Johnson, News Director
(402) 466-1234
Description:
Music, News, Sports.

KRMD-AM
3109 ALEXANDER STREET
SHREVEPORT, LA 71104-4628
318-865-5173
Fax: 318-865-3657
cumulus.shreveport@cumulus.com
www.krmd.com
• C J Jones, General Manager
(318) 865-5173
• Tony King, News Director
(318) 603-4730
Description:
Music.

KRNB-FM
621 NORTHWEST 6TH STREET
GRAND PRAIRIE, TX 75050-5555
972-263-9911
972-558-0007
Fax: 972-558-0010
www.broadcast.com/radio/urban/krnb
• Jack Hines, News Director
Description:
Music, News, Sports.

KROD
4150 PINNACLE ST, STE 120
EL PASO, TX 79902
915-544-8864
Fax: 915-532-6342
www.krod.com
• Brad Dubow, General Manager
• Steve Kaplowitz, Sports Director
Nature of Sports Service:
Sports, Talk, News.
Baseball:
Minor League/Texas Baseball League/AA - El Paso Diablos.
College Sports:

Football - University of Texas Longhorns.
Football:
NFL - Dallas Cowboys.
Ice Hockey:
Minor League/Western Professional Hockey
League - El Paso Buzzards.

KROF-AM
1749 BERTRAND DRIVE
LAFAYETTE, LA 70506-2054
337-233-6000
Fax: 337-234-7360
• Bernadette Lee, Program Director
(337) 233-6000
bernie.lee@regentcomm.com
Description:
Music, News, Sports.

KROX-AM
208 SOUTH MAIN STREET
CROOKSTON, MN 56716
218-281-1140
Fax: 218-281-5036
kroxam@hotmail.com
www.kroxam.com/
• Frank Fee, Advertising Manager/Sports
Director
ffee@rrv.net
• Maryann Simmons, News Director
maryann_simmons@hotmail.com
Description:
Music, News, Sports.

KRSC-FM
1701 WEST WILL ROGERS BOULEVARD
CLAREMORE, OK 74017
918-343-7669
Fax: 918-343-7592
www.rsu.edu
• Cathy Coomer, General Manager
(918) 343-7571
Description:
Music, News, Sports.

KRSY-AM
P.O. BOX 2710
ALAMOGORDO, NM 88310
505-437-1505
Fax: 505-437-5566
www.snmradio.com
• Les Henke, Advertising Manager
• Phillip Runnels, General Manager
(505) 437-1505
Description:
Music.

KRVL-FM
1021 EAST MAIN SUITE 200
KERRVILLE, TX 78028-3553
830-896-1230
Fax: 830-792-4142
www.krvl.com
• Monte Spearman, General Manager
Description:
Music, News.

KRYS-FM
501 TUPPER LANE
CORPUS CHRISTI, TX 78417
361-289-0111
Fax: 361-289-5035
frankedwards@clearchannel.com
www.krysfm.com
• Frank Edwards, Program
Director/Promotion Manager
(361) 289-0111

frankedward@clearchannel.com
• Mike Lind, Advertising Manager
mikelind@clearchannel.com
Description:
Music, News, Sports.

KSAL
PO BOX 80
SALINA, KS 67402
785-823-1111
Fax: 785-823-2034
• Jerry Hinrikus, General Manager
• Bruce Steinbrock, Sports Director
Nature of Sports Service:
Sports, Talk, News.
Baseball:
MLB - Kansas City Royals.
College Sports:
Basketball, Football - Kansas State
University; CBS.
Football:
NFL.

KSBL-FM
414 EAST COTA STREET
SANTA BARBARA, CA 93101-1624
805-879-8300
Fax: 805-879-8430
peterbie@clearchannel.com
• Lin Aubuchon, Promotion Director
(805) 879-8306
linaubuchon@clearchannel.com
Description:
Music, News, Sports.

KSCU-FM
SANTA CLARA UNIVERSITY
500 EL CAMINO ROAD
SANTA CLARA, CA 95053
408-554-4414
Fax: 408-985-5728
info@kscu.org
www.kscu.org
• Jason Magrisso, Sports Director
Description:
Music, News, Sports.

KSDM-FM
519 3RD STREET
INTERNATIONAL FALLS, MN 56649-2317
218-283-2622
888-283-1041
Fax: 218-283-3087
kghsksdm@northwinds.net
www.ksdmradio.com/
• Jerry Franzen, News Director
production@ksdmradio.com
• Roger Jerome, Sports Director
Description:
Music, News, Sports.

KSDR-AM
3 EAST KEMP AVENUE SUITE 300
WATERTOWN, SD 57201-6480
605-886-5747
800-234-5793
Fax: 605-886-2121
www.ksdr.com
• Heather Lentz, Promotions Director
(605) 882-1480
• Shari Wirkus, News Director
(605) 882-1480
Description:
Music, News, Sports.

KSEG-FM
5345 MADISON AVENUE
SACRAMENTO, CA 95841-3141
916-334-7777
Fax: 916-339-4559
www.eagle969.com
• Lizann Hunt, Promotion Director
(916) 334-7777
Description:
Music, News, Sports.

KSEI-AM
544 NORTH ARTHUR STREET
POCATELLO, ID 83204-3002
208-233-2121
800-726-5734
Fax: 208-234-7682
www.am930ksei.com
• Sean McCoy, News Director
Description:
News, Talk.

KSEK-AM
P.O. BOX 383
PITTSBURG, KS 66762
620-232-9912
800-215-3853
Fax: 620-232-5550
• Mike Snow, Program Director
Description:
Music, News, Talk.

KSFN-AM
6655 WEST SAHARA AVENUE SUITE
D-110
LAS VEGAS, NV 89146-0851
702-889-7300
Fax: 702-889-7373
www.spike1140.com/
• Jack Landreth, Program Director
• Derek Sante, Promotions Coordinator
Description:
Educational, News.

KSFT-AM
4104 COUNTRY LANE
SAINT JOSEPH, MO 64506
816-233-8881
Fax: 816-279-8280
Description:
Music.

KSGL-AM
3337 WEST CENTRAL AVENUE
WICHITA, KS 67203
316-942-3231
Fax: 316-942-9314
• Terry Atherton, Program Director
Description:
Educational, Music, News, Talk.

KSHE-FM
800 ST. LOUIS UNION STATION
SAINT LOUIS, MO 63103-2256
314-621-0095
Fax: 314-621-3428
www.kshe95.com/
• Tony Busekrus, Promotions Director
(314) 613-7714
• John Cooper, News Director
(314) 613-7865
• John Ulett, Sports Director
(314) 621-0095
Description:
Music, News, Sports.

KSHP-AM
2400 SOUTH JONES BOULEVARD SUITE 3
LAS VEGAS, NV 89146-3127
702-221-1200
Fax: 702-221-2285
mail@kshp.com
www.kshp.com
• Brett Grant, General Manager
(702) 221-1200
Description:
Talk.

KSIS-AM
2209 SOUTH LIMIT
SEDALIA, MO 65301
660-826-1050
800-748-8354
Fax: 660-827-5072
www.ksdl.com
• Danny Hampton, News Director
(660) 826-1050
Description:
Music, News, Talk.

KSIX-AM
710 BUFFALO STREET SUITE 608
CORPUS CHRISTI, TX 78401
361-882-5749
800-765-8810
Fax: 361-884-1204
• Bill Doerner, Station Manager
Description:
Music, News.

KSJS-FM
132 HUGH GILLIS HALL
SAN JOSE, CA 95192-0094
408-924-4548
Fax: 408-924-4558
www.ksjs.org
• Swen Johnson, Sports Director
Description:
Music.

KSJX-AM
501 WOOSTER AVENUE #C
SAN JOSE, CA 95116
408-280-1515
Fax: 408-280-1585
ksjx1500@fbcglobal.net
• Andrea Yamazaki, Advertising Sales
andreay@mrbi.net
Description:
Music, News, Sports.

KSKI-FM
201 SOUTH MAIN STREET
HAILEY, ID 83333
208-726-5324
877-725-5754
Fax: 208-726-5459
kskiprogramming@yahoo.com
www.kski.com
• Scott Anderson, General Manager
• Jody Zarkos,
(802) 726-7118
Description:
Music.

KSKU-FM
10 EAST 5TH AVENUE
HUTCHINSON, KS 67501
620-665-5758
800-300-1061
Fax: 620-662-5758

• Lucky Kidd, News/Sports Director
• Cliff Shank, Sports Director
(316) 665-5758
Description:
Music, News, Sports.

KSKY-AM
6400 NORTH BELTLINE ROAD SUITE 110
IRVING, TX 75063
214-561-9660
Fax: 214-561-9662
kskyradio@aol.com
www.ksky.com
• David Darling, Program Director
Description:
Music, News, Sports.

KSMO-AM
800 SOUTH MAIN STREET
SALEM, MO 65560-1637
573-729-6117
Fax: 573-729-7337
ksmoski@fidnet.com
www.ksmoradio.com
• Melba Headrick, Advertising Manager
ksmoradio@ksmoradio.com
• Stan Stevens, News Director
ksmoradio@ksmoradio.com
Description:
Music, News, Sports.

KSSK-AM
650 IWILEI ROAD SUITE 400
HONOLULU, HI 96817-4822
808-550-9200
Fax: 808-550-9510
www.ksskradio.com
• Jamie Hartnett, Promotions Director
(808) 550-9200
jamiehartnett@clearchannel.com
Description:
Music, News, Sports.

KSSR-AM
2818 WILL RODGERS DRIVE
SANTA ROSA, NM 88435
505-472-5777
Fax: 505-472-5777
kssrradio@yahoo.com
• Gabe Esquibel, Program Director
kssrradio@hotmail.com
Description:
Music, News, Sports.

KSUE-AM
3015 JOHNSTONVILLE ROAD
SUSANVILLE, CA 96130-8739
530-257-2121
800-366-9162
Fax: 530-257-6955
www.theradionetwork.com
• Scott Blackwood, Sports Director
scott@theradionetwork.com
Description:
Music.

KSVP-AM
317 WEST QUAY
ARTESIA, NM 88210-2158
505-746-2751
800-530-4855
Fax: 505-748-3748
www.ksvpradio.com
• Jamie Reynolds, News Director
news@ksvpradio.com

Description:
News, Talk.

KSWH-FM
1100 HENDERSON STREET
ARKADELPHIA, AR 71999
870-230-5185
Fax: 870-230-5046
kswh@hsu.edu
• Derrell Young, Sports Director
Description:
Music, News, Sports.

KTBB-AM
1001 EAST SOUTHEAST LOOP 323 SUITE 455
TYLER, TX 75701
903-593-2519
Fax: 903-597-8378
www.ktbb.com
• Jack Benner, Promotions Manager
• Roger Gray, Program Director
(903) 593-2519
rogergray@ktbb.com
• David Smoak, Sports Director
(903) 593-2519
smoaky@ktbb.com
Description:
News, Talk.

KTBK-FM
3500 MAPLE AVENUE SUITE 1300
DALLAS, TX 75219-3931
214-526-7400
Fax: 214-525-2525
www.theticket.com
• Jimmy Christopher, News Director
(214) 520-4423

KTCC-FM
1255 SOUTH RANGE
COLBY, KS 67701-4007
785-462-3984
Fax: 785-462-4600
• Corey Sorenson, General Manager
(785) 462-3984
Description:
Music, News, Sports.

KTCK/THE TICKET
3500 MAPLE AVE, STE 1310
DALLAS, TX 75219
214-526-7400
Fax: 214-525-2525
www.theticket.com
• Dan Bennett, General Manager
• Mark Followill, Sports Director
Nature of Sports Service:
Local. 24-hour sports radio programming.
College Sports:
Basketball - Texas Christian University/TCU;
Football - Texas Tech.

KTCV-FM
5929 WEST METALINE
KENNEWICK, WA 99336-1494
509-734-3621
Fax: 509-734-3609
dailed@ksd.org
www.ktcv.net
• Ed Dailey, General Manager
(509) 947-5785
Description:
Music, News, Sports.

KTEM
68 MOODY LANE
TEMPLE, TX 76504
254-773-5252
Fax: 254-773-0115
• Mark McLain, Program Director/Sports
Nature of Sports Service:
News, Sports, Talk.
Baseball:
MLB - Houston Astros.
College Sports:
Basketball, Football - Baylor Bears.
Football:
NFL - Dallas Cowboys.
Ice Hockey:
Minor League - Western Professional
Hockey League/WPHL - Central Texas
Stampede.

KTGR-AM
3215 LEMONE INDUSTRIAL BOULEVARD
SUITE 2
COLUMBIA, MO 65201
573-875-1099
Fax: 573-875-2439
• Shelley Tucker, News Director
(573) 875-1099
shelleyt@zrgmail.com

KTHN-FM
116 DALTON AVENUE
LA JUNTA, CO 81050
719-384-5456
Fax: 719-384-5450
kblj@rural-com.com
www.angelfire.com/cokbzzkblj
• Pat McGee, Sports Director
(719) 384-5456
Description:
Music.

KTIK SPORTS RADIO 1350
251 S. CAPITOL BLVD
BOISE, ID 83702
208-377-5845
Fax: 208-375-9248
jeff@ktik.com
www.ktik.com
• Jeff Caves, General Manager
• Pat Metzger, Sports Director
Nature of Sports Service:
Local. 24-hour sports radio programming.
Baseball:
Major League Baseball/MLB.
College Sports:
Basketball, Football.

KTIX-AM
2003 NORTHWEST 56TH DRIVE
PENDLETON, OR 97801
541-278-2500
Fax: 541-276-1480
• John Thomas, News/Sports Director
(541) 278-2500
Description:
News, Talk.

KTKC-FM
P.O. BOX 127
SPRINGHILL, LA 71075-0127
760-322-7890
Fax: 760-322-5493
• Ernest Pickens, Station Manager
epickings@hotmail.com
Description:
Music, News, Sports.

KTKR
6222 NW I H 10
SAN ANTONIO, TX 78201
210-736-9700
800-383-9624
Fax: 210-735-8811
www.ticketsports.com
• Bob Cohen, General Manager
• Jay Howard, Sports Director
Nature of Sports Service:
Local. 24-hour sports radio programming.
Baseball:
MLB - Texas Rangers.
College Sports:
Basketball - University of Texas; Football:
Texas Tech.
Football:
NFL.

KTMC-AM
1801 EAST GENE STAIPE BOULEVARD
MCALESTER, OK 74502-1068
918-423-1400
Fax: 918-423-7119
newsnan@mcalesterradio.com
• John Yates, News Director
(918) 429-2768
newsman@mcalesterradio.com
Description:
Music, News, Sports.

KTMT-AM
1438 ROSSANLEY DRIVE
MEDFORD, OR 97501-1751
541-779-1550
Fax: 541-776-2360
www.espn580.com
• Devin Harpole, Program Director
(541) 779-1550
Description:
Sports.

KTON-AM
P.O. BOX 1387
BELTON, TX 76513-5387
254-939-9377
Fax: 254-939-9458
• James Harrison, General Manager
cdavis940@vvm.com
Description:
Music, News, Sports.

KTRH-AM
2000 WEST LOOP SOUTH
HOUSTON, TX 77027-3510
713-212-8740
Fax: 713-212-8957
ktrh@aol.com
www.ktrh.com/main.html
• Melissa Brezner, Promotion Manager
• Ted DeLuca, Sports Director
(713) 212-8740
• Bryan Erickson, News Director
bryanerickson@clearchannel.com
Description:
News, Sports.

KTRS-AM
638 WEST PORT PLAZA DRIVE
SAINT LOUIS, MO 63146-3106
314-453-5500
888-550-5877
Fax: 314-453-9704
news@ktrs.com
www.ktrs.com/

• Jim Holder, Sports Director
(314) 453-5544
• Brian Kelly, News Director
(314) 453-5500
news@ktrs.com
• Craig Unger, Station Manager
(314) 453-5500
cunger@ktrs.com
Description:
News, Talk.

KTRS-FM
150 NICHOLS AVENUE
CASPER, WY 82601
307-266-5252
Fax: 307-235-9143
ktwo@clearchannel.com
www.kisscasper.com
• Vicki Daniels, News Director
vickidaniels@clearchannel.com
Description:
Music, News, Sports.

KTTT-AM
1418 25TH STREET
COLUMBUS, NE 68601
402-564-2866
800-651-5568
Fax: 402-564-2867
• Jim Dolezal, Sports Director
• Dean Johnson, Program Director
Description:
Music.

KTXT-FM
JOURNALISM BUILDING ROOM 201
LUBBOCK, TX 79409-0011
806-742-3916
Fax: 806-742-3906
pat.cates@ttu.edu
www.ttu.edu/~ktxt
• Josh Justice, Station Manager
(806) 742-3914
ktxtfm@yahoo.com
Description:
Music, News, Sports.

KTZN-AM
800 EAST DIMOND BOULEVARD SUITE
3-370
ANCHORAGE, AK 99515-2058
907-522-1515
Fax: 907-743-5184
anchorage@clearchannel.com
• Sezy Gerow, Marketing Director
(907) 743-5134
sezygerow@clearchannel.com

KUBL-FM
434 BEARCAT DRIVE
SALT LAKE CITY, UT 84115-2520
801-485-6700
Fax: 801-487-5369
www.kbull93.com
• Ed Hill, Program Director
(801) 464-8559
Description:
Music, News, Sports.

KUCD-FM
650 IWILEI ROAD SUITE 400
HONOLULU, HI 96817-5086
808-550-9200
Fax: 808-550-9510
jamiehyatt@clearchannel.com

• Christine Yasuma, Promotion Director
christineyasuma@clearchannel.com
Description:
Music, News, Sports.

KUKU-AM
983 US HIGHWAY EAST 160
WEST PLAINS, MO 65775
417-256-5976
Fax: 417-256-2208
www.ozarknewstalk.com
• Gary Lee, Program Director
• Tom Marhefka, Owner
Description:
Music, News, Sports.

KUPI-AM
854 LINDSAY BOULEVARD
IDAHO FALLS, ID 83402-1820
208-522-1101
Fax: 208-522-6110
www.kupi.com
• John Balginy, News Director
• James Garshow, Sports Director
Description:
Music, Sports.

KURE-FM
1199 FRILEY HALL
AMES, IA 50012-0001
515-294-4332
Fax: 515-294-8093
kure@iastate.edu
www.public.iastate.edu/~stu_org/kure
• Katie Pfeiffer, Program Director
Description:
Music, News, Sports.

KUSJ-FM
608 MOODY LANE
TEMPLE, TX 76504
254-547-8889
Fax: 254-773-0115
• Bourdon Wooten, General Manager
(254) 547-8889
Description:
Music, News, Sports.

KVAC-AM
260 CEDAR AVENUE
FORKS, WA 98331
360-374-6233
Fax: 360-374-6852
Description:
Music, News, Sports.

KVCU-AM
CAMPUS BOX 207
BOULDER, CO 80309
303-492-5031
Fax: 303-492-1369
www.radio1190.org
• Hunter Mancheck, Sports Director
• Schervin Revaie, Promotion Director

KVHT-FM
210 WEST 3RD STREET
YANKTON, SD 57078
605-665-2600
Fax: 605-665-8875
sports@kvht.com
www.kvht.com
• Joe Van Goor, Sports Director
(605) 665-2600

Description:
Music, News, Sports.

KVIV-AM
6060 SURETY DRIVE
SUITE 100
EL PASO, TX 79905
915-565-2999
Fax: 915-562-3156
www.kviv1340.com
• Jesus Cruz, Program Director
Description:
Music, News, Sports.

KVOE-FM
1420 C OF E DRIVE
EMPORIA, KS 66801-2585
620-342-1400
800-279-1964
Fax: 620-342-0804
kvoe@kvoe.com
• Jeff O'Dell, News Director
• Greg Rahe, Sports Director
raheg@kvoe.com
Description:
Music, News, Sports.

KVOL AM/FM
PO BOX 3345
LAFAYETTE, LA 70502
337-232-1311
Fax: 337-233-3779
• Mary Galyean, General Manager
• Keith Leblanc, Program Director
• Jill Johnson, Station Sales Manager
Nature of Sports Service:
Sports, Talk Radio.
College Sports:
Baseball, Basketball, Football - Louisiana
State University/LSU.

KVON-AM
1124 FOSTER ROAD
NAPA, CA 94558
707-252-1440
888-252-1440
Fax: 707-226-7544
www.kvon.com
• Tracy Green, Office Manager
tracy@kvon.com
• Ira Smith, Sports Director
(707) 252-1440
ira@kvon.com
Description:
News, Talk.

KVOX-AM
1020 SOUTH 25TH STREET
FARGO, ND 58103-2312
701-237-5346
Fax: 701-235-4042
psa@kfgo.com
• Tank McNamara, Sports Director
• Paul Jurgens, News Director
Description:
Music, News, Sports.

KVRH-FM
7600 COUNTY ROAD 120
SALIDA, CO 81201-9423
719-539-2575
Fax: 719-539-4851
www.vtinet.com/kvrh
• Mike Kerrigan, Sports Director
Description:
Music.

KVTI-FM
4500 STEILACOOM BOULEVARD SW
TACOMA, WA 98499-4098
253-589-5884
Fax: 253-589-5797
www.i91.ctc.edu
• John Mangan, Program Director
Description:
Music, News, Sports.

KVTK-AM
210 WEST 3RD STREET
YANKTON, SD 57078
605-665-2600
Fax: 605-665-8875
www.kvtk.com
• Joe Van Goor, Sports Director
(605) 665-2600
sports@kvht.com
Description:
Sports.

KWAK-AM
1818 SOUTH BUERKLE STREET
STUTTGART, AR 72160
870-673-1595
800-737-5925
Fax: 870-673-8445
• Scott Siler, Sports Director
sasiler@yahoo.com
Description:
Music, News, Sports.

KWCR-FM
2188 UNIVERSITY CIRCLE
OGDEN, UT 84408-2188
801-626-6450
Fax: 801-626-6550
881weberfm.org
• Ashlie Johansen, General Manager
(801) 626-7424
• Nate Martinez, Sports Director
(801) 626-8817
Description:
Music, News, Sports.

KWDM-FM
1140 35TH STREET
WEST DES MOINES, IA 50266-2138
515-226-2660
Fax: 515-226-2609
kwdmradio@aol.com
www.kwdm.fm.net
• Brian D. Christensen, General Manager
Description:
Educational, Music, Sports.

KWFS-FM
2525 KELL BOULEVARD SUITE 200
WICHITA FALLS, TX 76308-1064
940-763-1111
Fax: 940-322-3166
www.lonestar103.com
• Chris Walters, Program Director
(940) 763-1111
chriswalters@clearchannel.com
Description:
Music, News, Sports.

KWHI-AM
P. O. BOX 1280
BRENHAM, TX 77833
979-836-3655
Fax: 979-830-8141
www.kwhi.com

• Frank Wagner, News Director
(979) 836-3655
news@kwhi.com
• Carolyn Warmke, Advertising Manager
(979) 836-3655
• Ed Pothul, Sports Director
(979) 836-3655
doc@kwhi.com
Description:
Music, News, Sports.

KWIK
PO BOX 998
POCATELLO, ID 83204
208-233-1133
Fax: 208-232-1240
• Mike Hudson, General Manager
• Gary Shockley, Sports Director
Nature of Sports Service:
Local. 24 Hour Sports Station.
College Sports:
Basketball, Football - Idaho University.

KWIQ-AM
11768 KITTLESON ROAD
MOSES LAKE, WA 98837-9720
509-765-1761
Fax: 509-765-8901
www.kwiq.com
• Gary Patrick, General Manager
(509) 663-1586
gary.patrick@morris.com
Description:
Music, News, Sports.

KWKH
6341 WESTPORT AVE
SHREVEPORT, LA 71129
318-688-1130
Fax: 318-687-8574
• Barney Cannon, Sports Director
Office Address:
6341 Westport Ave, Shreveport, LA 71130.
Nature of Sports Service:
News, Sports.
College Sports:
Basketball, Football - Louisiana State
University/LSU.

KWKH-AM
6341 WESTPORT AVENUE
SHREVEPORT, LA 71129-2415
318-688-1130
800-551-1130
Fax: 318-687-8574
www.kwkh1130.com
• John Lee, News Director
johnlee@clearchannel.com
Description:
Music, News, Sports.

KWMO-AM
511 WEST 5TH STREET
WASHINGTON, MO 63090
636-239-5432
Fax: 636-239-9735
studio@kslq.com
www.kwmo.net
• Chris Dieckhaus, News/Promotions
Director
(636) 239-6800
chris@kslq.com
Description:
Music, News.

KWNO-FM
752 BLUFFVIEW CIRCLE
WINONA, MN 55987-2515
507-452-4000
800-584-6782
Fax: 507-452-9494
winonaradio.com/cdcountry/
• Darryl Smelser, News Director
• Paul Van Beek,
(507) 452-4000

KWRD-AM
1101 KILGORE DRIVE
HENDERSON, TX 75652
903-655-1800
Fax: 903-655-1808
www.mykpxi.com
• Esther Melton, General Manager
Description:
Music, News, Sports.

KWSL-AM
1113 NEBRASKA STREET
SIOUX CITY, IA 51105-1438
712-258-5595
Fax: 712-252-2430
www.radio-works.com
• Curtis Anderson, Program/Sports Director
(712) 224-5487
curtisanderson@clearchannel.com
Description:
Music, News, Sports.

KWSN-AM
500 SOUTH PHILLIPS AVENUE
SIOUX FALLS, SD 57104-6825
605-331-5350
Fax: 605-336-0415
www.kwsn.com
• Greg Belfrage, News Director
(605) 271-5867
Description:
News, Talk.

KWTO-FM
3000 EAST CHESTNUT EXPRESSWAY
SPRINGFIELD, MO 65802-2528
417-862-3751
Fax: 417-869-7656
manager@radiospringfield.com
www.ktxrfm.com
• R. J. McAllister, News Director
(417) 862-5600
news@radiospringfield.com
• Art Hains, Sports Director
(417) 862-5600
Nature of Service:
All Sports

KWTS-FM
2501 4TH AVENUE
CANYON, TX 79016-0001
806-651-2797
Fax: 806-651-2818
kwtsgm@gmail.com
www.wtamu.edu/kwts
• Tony Collins, Sports Director
kwtssports@gmail.com
• Teresa Dunn, Sports Co-Director
kwtssports@gmail.com
• Ricky Mariscal, Program Director
(806) 651-2801
kwtspd@gmail.com
Description:
Educational, Music, News, Sports, Talk.
Sports Discussed:

West Texas A&M University sports, National
sports, Local Sports
Frequnecy:
91.1

KWTX THE TICKER 1460AM
314 W. HWY 6
WACO, TX 76712
254-776-3900
Fax: 254-772-8708
• Michael Oppenheim, General Manager
• Rick May, Program Director
Nature of Sports Service:
24-hour sports radio programming station.

KXCA-AM
1525 SOUTHEAST FLOWERMOUND
ROAD
LAWTON, OK 73501
580-355-1050
Fax: 580-355-1056
trebor1380@hotmail.com
1380theticket.4t.com
• Joy Chapman, General Manager
(580) 355-1050
Description:
Music.

KXDL-FM
221 CENTRAL AVENUE SUITE 6
LONG PRAIRIE, MN 56347
320-732-2164
Fax: 320-732-2284
hotrodfm@rea-alp.com
www.kxdlhotrodradio.com/
• Cliff Cline, News Director
Description:
Music, News, Sports.

KXIC-AM
3365 DUBUQUE STREET NORTHEASST
IOWA CITY, IA 52240
319-354-9500
Fax: 319-354-9504
royjustis@clearchannel.com
www.kxic.com
• Brent Balbinot, Sports Director
brentbalbinot@clearchannel.com
• Roy Justis, News Director
(319) 354-9500
Description:
News, Talk.

KXKX-FM
800 PCA ROAD
WARRENSBURG, MO 64093-9275
660-826-1050
800-748-7969
Fax: 660-827-5072
www.kxkx.com
• Danny Hampton, News Director
(660) 826-1050
Description:
Music, News, Sports.

KXLS-FM
PO BOX 952
ENID, OK 73702-0952
580-242-5957
Fax: 580-242-1390
• Geoff Haxton, News Director
(580) 237-1390
• Chad McKee, Sports Director
Description:
Music, News, Talk.

KXLY-AM
500 WEST BOONE AVENUE
SPOKANE, WA 99201-2404
509-324-4004
Fax: 509-327-3932
news4@kxly.com
www.kxly.com
• Gina Mauro, Promotions Manager
• Jerry Post, Assignment Editor
(509) 324-4004
• Kirstin Votava, Marketing Director
• Rick Lukens, Sports Anchor
(509) 324-4000
Description:
News, Talk.

KXMO-FM
609 NORTH FRANKLIN
CUBA, MO 65453
573-885-0953
Fax: 573-364-5161
kxmo@misn.com
• Lee Buhr, Sports Director
• Joe Munsell, General Manager
(573) 364-2525

KXOW-AM
208 BUENA VISTA ROAD
HOT SPRINGS NATIONAL, AR 71913
501-525-4600
Fax: 501-525-4344
klaz@power1.net
• Eddie Tarpley, Advertising Manager
Description:
Music.

KXOX-FM
1801 HOYT LANE
SWEETWATER, TX 79556-2663
325-236-6655
888-869-5969
Fax: 325-235-4391
www.members.tripod.com/~tatzel/wurm/kxox.ht
• Richard Ferguson, Sports Director
• Jeff Stein, News Director
Description:
Music.

KXPS-AM
1321 NORTH GENE AUTRY TRAIL
PALM SPRINGS, CA 92262-7992
760-322-7890
Fax: 760-322-5493
www.1010kxps.com
• Sara Regalado, Marketing Director

KXTA AM
3400 RIVERSIDE DR, #800
BURBANK, CA 91505
818-295-6400
Fax: 818-295-6475
• Roy Laughlin, General Manager
• Bill Lally, Sports Director
Nature of Sports Service:
Local. 24 Hour sports.
Basketball:
2002 signed a five year rights-fee deal with the Los Angeles Clippers.

KXTQ-AM
9800 UNIVERSITY AVENUE
LUBBOCK, TX 79423-4917
806-745-3434
Fax: 806-748-1949
dcampbell@ramarcom.com

• Jeff Klotzman, News Director
(806) 745-3434
jklotzman@ramarcom.com
Description:
Music, News, Sports.

KXTQ-FM
9800 UNIVERSITY AVENUE
LUBBOCK, TX 79423
806-745-3434
Fax: 806-748-1949
• Tony Samarripa, Program Director
(806) 745-3434
tsamarripa@ramarcom.com
Description:
Music, News, Sports.

KYAL-AM
2448 EAST 81ST STREET
SUITE 5500
TULSA, OK 74137-4248
918-492-2660
Fax: 918-492-8840
www.kxoj.com
• Bob Thornton, Program Director
bobt@kxoj.com
Description:
Music.

KYBG-AM SPORTS RADIO
5660 GREENWOOD PLAZA BLVD, STE 400
ENGLEWOOD, CO 80111-2402
303-721-9210
Fax: 303-721-1435
• Rob Quinn, General Manager
• Malcolm McClain, General Sales Manager
Nature of Sports Service:
Local. 24-hour sports radio programming.

KYCN-AM
450 EAST POLE
WHEATLAND, WY 82201
307-322-5926
Fax: 307-322-9300
kycn-kzew.com/
• Derek Barton, News Director
(307) 322-5926
Description:
Music, News, Sports.

KYCX-FM
1006-B MILAM
MEXIA, TX 76667-2527
254-562-5328
Fax: 254-562-6729
www.kycx.com
• David Campbell, Sports Director
kycxsports@aol.com
• Jan Phillips, News Director
Description:
Music.

KYMN-AM
200 DIVISION STREET SUITE 260
NORTHFIELD, MN 55057
507-645-5695
Fax: 507-645-9768
contact@kymnradio.net
www.kymnradio.net
• Tor Ingstad, General Manager
Description:
Music, News, Talk.
Frequency:
1080 am

KYMO-AM
390 SOUTH HIGHWAY 102
EAST PRAIRIE, MO 63845
573-649-3597
Fax: 573-649-3983
• Michael Bennett, News Director
• Barney L. Webster, Advertising Manager
(573) 472-1080
Description:
Music.

KYTC-FM
402 19TH STREET, SW
MASON CITY, IA 50401-6435
641-423-8634
800-598-2858
Fax: 641-423-8206
www.klssradio.com
• Bob Fisher, News Director

KZEP SPORTS RADIO
427 9TH ST
SAN ANTONIO, TX 78215
210-226-6444
Fax: 210-225-5736
• Jay Levine, General Manager
• Chris Winston, Pro General Manager Director
• Gary Isaacs, General Sales Manager
Nature of Sports Service:
Local. 24-hour sports radio programming.

KZEW-FM
450 EAST COAST
WHEATLAND, WY 82201-0248
307-322-5926
Fax: 307-322-9300
www.kycn-kzew.com/
• Derek Barton, News Director
• Catherine Smith, Advertising Manager
Description:
Music, News, Sports.

KZMQ-AM
2700 LANE 37 1/2
GREYBULL, WY 82426-9521
307-578-5000
Fax: 307-527-5045
www.bighornradio.com/
• Roger Gelder, Chief Operating Officer
• Thom Huge, News Director
(307) 578-5019
Description:
Music, News, Sports.

KZMX-AM
WINDCAVENUE ROAD
HOT SPRINGS, SD 57747-0611
605-745-3637
Fax: 605-745-3517
kzmxrealcountry@email.com
• Gary Baker, News Director
Description:
Music, News, Sports.

KZNM-FM
2600A CAMINO ENTRADA
SANTA FE, NM 87505-9291
505-878-0980
Fax: 505-878-0098
• Rene Leon, Program Director
(505) 878-0980
dj977lobo@aol.com
Description:
Music, News, Sports.

KZXY-FM
12370 HESPERIA ROAD SUITE 17
VICTORVILLE, CA 92392
760-241-1313
Fax: 760-241-0205
• Chris Price, Advertising Manager
(760) 241-1313
chrisprice@clearchannel.com
Description:
Music, News, Sports.

MAGNUM BROADCASTING
PO BOX 448
PORTAGE, WI 53901
608-742-1000
Fax: 608-742-1688
www.magnumbroadcasting.com
• Ed Kramer, General Manager
• Brett Mathison, Program Director
Baseball:
MLB - Milwaukee Brewers (night games).

MARSHALL RADIO
1414 EAST COLLEGE DRIVE
MARSHALL, MN 56258-2027
507-532-2282
Fax: 507-532-3739
info@marshallradio.net
www.marshallradio.net
• Dan Paluch, News Director
Description:
Music, News, Sports.

MOTOR RACING NETWORK/MRN
555 MRN DRIVE
CONCORD, NC 28027
704-262-6700
Fax: 704-262-6811
www.motorracingnetwork.com
• David Hyatt, President
• Chris D'Aprile, Director
• Johns Singler, News Director
• Lauren Schweppe, Associate Producer
Nature of Sports Service:
National. Produces radio broadcasts for NASCAR Sprint Cup, NASCAR Nationwide Series, NASCAR Camping World Truck Series, NASCAR K&N Pro Series, NASCAR Whelen Modified Tour and GRAND-AM Road Racing.

NEWSRADIO 1270 WFLA
325 JOHN KNOX RD, BLDG G
TALLAHASSEE, FL 32303
850-422-3107
Fax: 850-383-0747
www.wnls.com
• Judy Bailey, VP/General Manager Clear Channel
• Rick Flagg, News Director
• J.L Dunbar, Program Director
Nature of Sports Service:
24 News and Sports.

POWELL BROADCASTING
2000 INDIAN HILLS DRIVE
SIOUX CITY, IA 51104
712-239-2100
Fax: 712-239-3346
www.kscj.com
• Dennis Bullock, General Manager
• Tim Meacham, Sports Director
(712) 239-2100
• Justin Barker, Production/Promotions Director
(712) 239-2100

Nature of Sports Service:
Sports, Talk, News.
Baseball:
Minor League, American Association, IND - Sioux City Explorers.
College Sports:
Basketball, Football - University of Iowa; Basketball - NAIA Women's Division 2 National Championship (Basketball).

SNOCOUNTRY MOUNTAIN REPORTS
10 WATER STREET
SUITE 300
LEBANON, NH 03766
603-443-8812
Fax: 603-443-8838
info@snocountry.org
www.snocountry.com
• Tom Cottrill, President
• Chuck Devine, Director of Broadcast Operations
(603) 443-8810
chuck.devine@snocountry.org
• Rob Werneer, Sales Representative West, Midwest
(415) 305-7439
rob.werner@snocountry.org
• Andrew Davis, Radio Program Director
(603) 443-8823
andrew.davis@snocountry.org
• Sean Malaguti, Office Manager
(603) 443-8801
sean.malaguti@snocountry.org
• Bill Wadell, Web Developer
(604) 443-8822
bill.waddell@snocountry.org
• Tom Horrocks, Marketing Communications Manager
(603) 443-8825
tom.horrocks@snocountry.org
Nature of Sports Service:
SnoCountry, a not-for-profit trade association, collects and distributes snow conditions and ski resort information, serving media outlets, including web sites, regional and national radio networks. SnoCountry also provides snow sport marketing and event management services

SPORTS 56 WHBQ
6080 MT. MORIAH
MEMPHIS, TN 38115
901-375-9324
Fax: 901-794-0041
www.sports56whbq.com

SPORTS RADIO 1080 THE FAN/KFXX
0700 SW BANCROFT
PORTLAND, OR 97239
503-250-1080
866-358-1080
Fax: 503-223-6909
www.1080thefan.com
• Dennis Glasgow, Program Director
(503) 535-0363
• Jack Hutchison, General Manager
(503) 535-0370
jhutchison@entercom.com
• Erin Hubert, Vice President/Market Manager
(503) 535-0366
• Liz Kay, Promotions Director
(503) 535-0497
• Sam Hicks, General Sales Manager
(503) 535-0259
Nature of Service:
Local. 24-hour sports radio programming.

Year Founded:
1991
Baseball:
MLB - Seattle Mariners.
College Sports:
NFL, MLB, NCAA Football/Basketball, NBA, BCS, March Madness

SPORTS RADIO 1260-AM WNDE
6161 FALL CREEK RD
INDIANAPOLIS, IN 46220
317-257-7565
Fax: 317-253-6501
www.wnde.com
• Rick Green, General Manager
• Buzz Casey, Program Director
• Mark Patrick, Sports Director
• Lee Anne Brooks, General Sales Manager
• Tad Williams, Promotions Director
Nature of Sports Service:
24 Hour Sports.

SPORTS RADIO 1510 KGA
1601 EAST 57TH AVENUE
SPOKANE, WA 99223-3026
509-448-1000
Fax: 509-448-7015
www.1510kga.com
• Pat Kenney, Producer
(509) 448-1000
• Toby Howell, Program Director
(509) 448-1000
thowell@radiospokane.com
• Jessica Foxx, Promotions Director
(509) 448-1000
jfoxx@radiospokane.com
Description:
Talk.
Teams:
Gonzaga University, Spokane Chiefs, Spokane Indians, GSL FB & BB, NCAA BB & FB, NFL

SPORTS RADIO 810/WHB-AM
UNION BRDCASTING INC.
6721 W. 121ST ST
OVERLAND PARK, KS 66209
913-344-1500
Fax: 913-344-1599
www.810whb.com
• Chad Boeger, General Manager/Program Director
• Kevin Kietzman, Sports Director
• Todd Leabo, Asst Sports Director
Football:
NFL - Kansas City Chiefs.
College Sports:
NCAA - University of Kansas, Kansas State, Missouri Tigers, UNKC Kangaroos.
Baseball:
MLB - Kansas City Royals.

SPORTS RADIO 97.1 THE FAN
605 S FRONT STREET
SUITE 300
COLUMBUS, OH 43215
614-460-3850
Fax: 614-460-3757
www.971thefan.com
• Keith Britton, Producer
(614) 460-3850
• Jay Taylor, Program Director
(614) 460-3829
• Scott Torgerson, Sports Director
(614) 460-3701
• Chris Spielman, Host, The Big Show

- Bruce Hooley, Host, The Big Show
- Scott Torgerson, Host, Common Man & The Torg
- Mike Ricordati, Host, Common Man & The Torg

Nature of Sports Service:
24 Hour Sports. ESPN radio network
Ice Hockey:
NHL - Columbus Blue Jackets.

SPORTS TALK 790 THE ZONE (ATLANTA)
3350 PEACHTREE RD, STE 1610
ATLANTA, GA 30326
404-237-0079
Fax: 404-231-5923
- Matt Edgar, Program Director
(404) 564-4433
- Adam Klug, Executive Producer/Operations Director
(404) 237-0079
- Andrew Saltzman, President/General Manager
(404) 2237-007
- Stephen Shapiro, President/Talk Show Host
(404) 237-0079
- Leslie Smith, Promotions Director
(404) 237-0079
- Evan Crocker, General Sales Manager
(404) 237-0079
- D'Ree Harris, Business Manager
(404) 237-0079
- Chris Young, National Sales Manager
(404) 237-0079
Station Covers:
Auto Racing, Boxing, Golf, MLB, NFL, NHL, NBA, NCAA Football, NCAA Men's & Women's Basketball, Olympics, Soccer, Tennis, WNBA.
Frequency:
Daily.
Primary Audience:
Men 25-54
Sports:
All Sports.
Nature of Service:
Sports Talk Radio.

SPORTS TALK 980
8750 BROOKVILLE RD
SILVER SPRING, MD 20910
301-231-7798
Fax: 301-949-0142
- Marty Sheehan, Director of Sales

SPORTSRADIO 1460 KENO
8755 W. FLAMINGO
LAS VEGAS, NV 89147
702-876-1460
Fax: 702-876-6685
- Tony Bonnici, General Manager
- Jesse Leeds, General Sales Manager
- Art Breyfogle, Sports Sales Manager
- John Hanson, Program Director
Nature of Sports Service:
24 Hour Sports.

STAR 610 KILT SPORTS RADIO
24 GREENWAY PLAZA, STE 1900
HOUSTON, TX 77046
713-881-5100
houston.cbslocal.com
- Dickie Rosenfeld, General Manager
- Moose Rosenfeld, Local Sales Manager
Nature of Sports Service:
Local. 24-hour sports radio programming.

STILLWATER RADIO
408 EAST THOMAS AVENUE
STILLWATER, OK 74075
405-372-7800
Fax: 405-372-6969
stillwaterradio@coxinet.net
www.stillwaterradio.net
- Rex Holt, Sports Director
(405) 372-7800
- Bill Van Ness, News Director
Description:
We broadcast all Oklahoma State Men's and Women's sports since 1947. Also Stillwater High School and area high school broadcasts. We also cover Coaches Shows and a Daily Sports Talk Show.

TALK 1450 WMIQ RADIO
101 E. KENT
IRON MOUNTAIN, MI 49801
906-774-4321
Fax: 906-774-7799
talk1450wmiq@uplogon.com
- Veronica Roberts, General Manager
- Mike Carr, Sports Director
- Neal Peterson, Operations Manager
- Tom Hill, News Director
- Kevin Lynch, Production Director
- Randy Van Gasse, Colon Commentary
Nature of Sports Service:
News/Sports/Talk.
Circulation:
10,000
Primary Audience:
Men between 25-54 years old.
Sports:
Local, College & Pro.

TEAM 1200 SPORTS RADIO
87 GEORGE ST
OTTAWA, ON, CANADA K1N 9H7
613-729-1200
Fax: 613-739-4040
- Chris Gordon, Program Director
Nature of Sports Service:
24-Hour sports radio station. Carries play-by-play coverage for the Ottawa Senators, Ottawa 67's and Ottawa Lynx.

THE FAN 590
77 JARVIS ST
TORONTO, ON, CANADA M4Y 3B7
416-935-0590
Fax: 416-413-4116
www.fan590.com
LINEUP:
Marsden and Landry, The Bullpen, The Big Show, Prime Time Sports.
Baseball:
MLB - Toronto Blue Jays.
Basketball:
Toronto Raptors.
Football:
AFL - Toronto Phantoms, CFL - Toronto Argonauts,.
Ice Hockey:
NHL - Toronto Maple Leafs.
Lacrosse:
Toronto Rock.
Soccer:
Toronto Lynx.

THE GAME 730 AM/WVFN
3420 PINE TREE
LANSING, MI 48911

517-394-7272
Fax: 517-394-3388
- Rob Striker, General Manager
rob.striker@ctcomm.com
- Kelly Norton, Director Sales
kelly.norton@ctcomm.com
- Tony Conley, Program Director
tony.conley@ctcomm.com
- Mychal Grenawalt, Senior Account Executive
mychal.grenawalt@ctcomm.com
- Kim Lozinc, GSM
kim.lozinc@ctcomm.com
Nature of Sports Service:
Local. 24-hour sports radio programming.

THE TICKET SPORTSRADIO 1310
3090 OLIVE STREET
WEST VICTORY PLAZA SUITE 400
DALLAS, TX 75219
214-526-2400
Fax: 214-520-4343
www.dfwradio.com

THE ZONE SPORTS RADIO 1300 AM
705 N. LAMAR BLVD
AUSTIN, TX 78703
512-684-7300
Fax: 512-684-7441
www.sportsradio1300.com
- Lise Hudson, Director of Sales
- Chuck Meyer, Program Director
- Marc Hoenig, Promotions Director
Nature of Sports Service:
24 Hour Sports.

TICKET760 KTKR
KTKR-AM
6222 NW IH-10
SAN ANTONIO, TX 78201
210-736-9700
Fax: 210-736-9738
www.ticketsports.com
- Nate Lundy, Program Director
natelundy@clearchannel.com
- Walter Pasacrita, Sports Director
- Jim Forsyth, News Director
jimforsyth@clearchannel.com
- Tim Merryman, Executive Producer
- Eric Gray, Afternoon Producer
ericgray@clearchannel.com
- Matt Martin, Vice President Market Manager
mattmartin@clearchannel.com

WAAV-AM
3233 BURNT MILL DRIVE SUITE 4
WILMINGTON, NC 28403
910-251-9228
Fax: 910-762-0456
www.980waav.com/
- Rhonda Bellamy, News Director
(910) 332-2196
- Jennifer McLean, Advertising Manager
(910) 332-2142
Description:
Music, News, Sports.

WABI-AM
184 TARGET INDUSTRIAL CIRCLE
BANGOR, ME 04401-5113
207-947-9100
Fax: 207-942-0839
www.b97hits.com
- George Hale, Program/Sports Director
(207) 947-9100

georgehale@clearchannel.com
• Larry Pierce, Marketing Manager
larrypierce@clearchannel.com
Description:
Music.

WABO-AM
6746 HIGHWAY 184 WEST
WAYNESBORO, MS 39367-0507
601-735-4331
Fax: 601-735-4332
www.wabo105.com
• Jamie Heathcock, Program Director
Description:
Music, News, Sports.

WACA-AM
11141 GEORGIA AVENUE SUITE 301
WHEATON, MD 20902-4637
301-942-3500
Fax: 301-942-7798
www.radioamerica.net
• Herbert Baires, Sports Director
(301) 942-3500
• Alejandro Carrasco, President
(301) 942-3500
• Samuel Galvez, News Director
(301) 942-3500
• Wilson Romero, Sports Director
Description:
Music.

WACK 1420-AM HOMETOWN SPORTS
187 VIENNA RD
PO BOX 292
NEWARK, NY 14513
315-331-1420
Fax: 315-331-7101
wacknewsroom@gmail.com
www.1420wack.com
• John Tickner, General Manager
• Dick Reeves, Program Director
amdrive@rochester.rr.com
• Rus Jeffrey, News Director
(315) 381-7100
1420wack@rochester.rr.com
• John Oerleth, Local Sales Manager
• Larry Ann Evans, Producer
Nature of Sports Service:
News, Sports covering Rochester New York,
and the Fingerlake Region. Primary
audience age is from 25 through 54 years
old.
Auto Sports:
NASCAR.
Baseball:
MLB - New York Yankees.
College Sports:
Syracuse University Football & Basketball.
Football:
NFL - Buffalo Bills; CBS Sunday & Monday
Nights.
Ice Hockey:
NHL - Playoffs.

WADR-AM
239 GENESEE STREET SUITE 500
UTICA, NY 13501-3412
315-797-0803
Fax: 315-797-7813
adamgerstenhaber@clearchannel.com
www.starsradionetwork.com
• Brian Delaney, General Manager
briandelaney@clearchannel.com
Description:
Music, News, Sports.

WAEL-AM
GUANAJIBO HOMES
CALLA RAMIREZ PABON #600
MAYAGUEZ, PUERTO RIC 00682-1100
787-832-4560
Fax: 787-805-0800
• Luis Pirallo, Program Director
Description:
Music, News, Sports.

WAIK-AM
51 NORTH PRAIRIE STREET
GALESBURG, IL 61401-4613
309-342-3161
Fax: 309-342-0199
www.misslink.net/waik
• Dick Shimmin, News Director
(309) 342-3164
• Rob Strack, Sports Director
Description:
Music.

WAIT-AM
130 SOUTH JEFFERSON SUITE 200
CHICAGO, IL 60661
224-805-6868
Fax: 847-509-1677
wait@relevantradio.com
www.relevantradio.com
• Matt Nahigian, Program Director
(847) 400-3075

WAJZ-FM
6 JOHNSON ROAD
LATHAM, NY 12110-5641
518-786-6600
Fax: 518-786-6610
www.jamz963.com
• Rob Ryan, Program Director
Description:
Music, News, Sports.

WAKQ-FM
206 NORTH BREWER STREET
PARIS, TN 38242
731-642-7100
Fax: 731-644-9367
www.kf99kq105.com/
• Terry Hailey, President/Program Director
Description:
Music, News, Sports.

WAKR-AM
1795 WEST MARKET STREET
AKRON, OH 44313
330-869-9800
800-994-9973
Fax: 330-864-6799
www.wakr.net
• Ed Esposito, News Director
(330) 869-9800
• Joyce Lagios, Marketing/Promotion
Director
(330) 869-9800
jlagios@rcrg.net
Description:
Music, News, Sports.

WALS-FM
3905 PROGRESS BOULEVARD
PERU, IL 61354
815-224-2100
Fax: 815-224-2066
• Stuart Hall, News Director
• Jared White, Sports Director

(815) 224-2100
radio1@theramp.net

WAMV-AM
132 SCHOOL ROAD
AMHERST, VA 24521
434-946-9000
888-946-1420
Fax: 434-946-2201
wamv1420@aol.com
www.wamvradio.com
• Robert K. Langstaff, Advertising
Manager/Program Director
wamradio@aol.com
Description:
Music, News, Sports.

WAMW-AM
104 EAST MAIN STREET
WASHINGTON, IN 47501-2908
812-254-6761
Fax: 812-254-3940
• Taylor Brown, News Director
Description:
Music, News.

WAMW-FM
104 EAST MAIN STREET
WASHINGTON, IN 47501-2908
812-254-6761
Fax: 812-254-3940
www.wamwamfm.com
• Taylor Brown, News Director
Description:
Music, News, Sports.

WAPX-FM
AUSTIN PEAY STATE UNIVERSITY
CLARKSVILLE, TN 37044
931-648-7200
Fax: 931-648-5992
Description:
Music, News, Sports.

WAQE-AM
1859 21ST AVENUE
RICE LAKE, WI 54868-9502
715-234-9059
800-236-3698
Fax: 715-234-6942
info@waqe.com
• Ken Denucci, News Director
Description:
Music, News, Sports.

WAQE-FM
1859 21ST AVENUE
RICE LAKE, WI 54868-9502
715-234-9059
800-236-3698
Fax: 715-234-6942
info@waqe.com
• Ken Denucci, News Director
Description:
Music, News, Sports.

WAQI-AM
800 DOUGLAS ROAD
CORAL GABLES, FL 33134-3187
305-447-1140
Fax: 305-442-7676
www.univision.com
• Sarvelio Del Valle, Sports Director
(305) 447-1140

Description:
News, Talk.

WARK-AM
880 COMMONWEALTH AVENUE
HAGERSTOWN, MD 21740-6836
301-733-4500
800-222-9279
Fax: 301-733-0040
www.warx.com
• Mike Krafthofer, News Director
(301) 733-4500
Description:
Music, News, Sports, Talk.

WARM-AM
600 BALTIMORE DRIVE 2ND FLOOR
WILKES BARRE, PA 18702-7901
570-824-9000
800-447-5000
Fax: 570-820-0520
www.590warm.com
• Brian Hughes, News Director
Description:
Music, News, Sports.

WASU-FM
332 WEY HALL
BOONE, NC 28608-0001
828-262-3170
Fax: 828-262-2543
• Richard Davis, General Manager
(828) 262-3170
• Bryce Johnson, Sports Director
(828) 262-3170
Description:
Music, News, Sports.

WATA-AM
738 BLOWING ROCK ROAD
BOONE, NC 28607
828-264-2411
Fax: 828-264-2412
info@wecr1023.com
• David Blank, News Director
(828) 264-2411
Description:
Music, News, Sports.

WAUD-AM
2514 SOUTH COLLEGE STREET SUITE
104
AUBURN, AL 36830
334-887-9999
888-984-4379
Fax: 334-826-9599
info@thetiger.fm
• Chris Bailey, General Manager
chrisb@thetiger.fm
• Kevin Jackson, Program Director
kevin@thetiger.fm
• Bob Sanders, Advertising Manager
(334) 887-3401
• Bob Sanders, Sports Director
(334) 887-3401
Description:
Educational, Music, News, Sports, Talk.

WAUK ALL SPORTS RADIO
1801 CORAL DR
WAUKESHA, WI 53186
262-544-6800
Fax: 262-544-1705
wauk1510@execpc.com
www.doubleplay1510.com

• Ken Heinlein, Station Manager
• Scott Aebly, Pro General Manager Director
• Bill Johnson, Program Director
Nature of Sports Service:
Local. 24-hour sports radio programming.

WAVL-AM
P.O. BOX 277
APOLLO, PA 15613-0277
724-478-4020
www.praise910.com/
• Jeff Bogaczyk, News Director
Description:
Music, News, Sports, Talk.

WAVT-FM
212 SOUTH CENTER
POTTSVILLE, PA 17901
570-622-1360
Fax: 570-622-2822
news@pbcradio.com
www.pbcradio.com
• James A. Bowman, Advertising Manager
• Chad Gerber, Program Director
(570) 622-1360
Description:
Music, News, Sports.

WAVV-FM
11800 EAST TAMIAMI TRAIL
NAPLES, FL 34113-7909
239-775-9288
Fax: 239-793-7000
• Walt Tiburski, General Manager
w.tiburski@wavv101.com
Description:
Music. 2 minute sports report. M-F 7:30 &
8:30

WAXL-FM
501 OLD STATE ROAD
HUNTINGBURG, IN 47542
812-683-1215
Fax: 812-683-5891
waxl@psci.net
• Jim Anderson, News Director
(812) 683-1215
• Kurt Gutgsell, Sports Director
(812) 683-1215
wbdc@psci.net

WAXO-AM/FM
217 COMMERCE STREET, W.
LEWISBURG, TN 37091-3337
931-359-6641
Fax: 931-270-9290
www.waxo.com
• Tim Atkinson, News Director
• Troy Cashion, Sports Director
(931) 359-6641
Description:
Music, News, Sports. Monday - Friday at
7:15 a.m. CST.

WAYC-FM
134 EAST PITT STREET 2ND FLOOR
BEDFORD, PA 15522-1311
814-623-1000
Fax: 814-623-9692
• Keith Bagley, News Director
• Jay B. Cessna, Sports Director
Description:
Music.

WAYN-AM
1223 ROCKINGHAM ROAD
ROCKINGHAM, NC 28379
910-895-4041
Fax: 910-895-4993
wayninc@aol.com
• Jim Smith, News/Sports Director
Description:
Music.

WAYY-AM
944 HARLEM AVENUE
ALTOONA, WI 54720-1127
715-832-1530
800-866-9299
Fax: 715-832-5329
• Bruce Butler, Promotions Manager
• Dave Craig, Sports Director
davec@maverick-media.ws
• Dan Lea, News Director
• George Roberts, Advertising Manager
Description:
News, Talk.

WAYZ-FM
10960 JOHN WAYNE DRIVE
GREENCASTLE, PA 17225
717-597-9200
800-758-0838
Fax: 717-597-9210
www.wayz.com
• Scott Douglas, News Director
Description:
Music, News.

WAZZ-AM
3012 HIGHWOOD BLVD. #201
RALEIGH, NC 27604
910-484-1490
Fax: 910-323-5635
www.am1490wazz.com/
• Mac Edwards, Vice President
(910) 486-2002
mac@bbgi.com
• Val Jones, News Director
(910) 486-2085
Description:
Music, News, Sports.

WBAG-AM
1745 BIRCH BRIDGE ROAD
BURLINGTON, NC 27217
336-226-1150
Fax: 336-226-1180
• Bill Huff, Sports Director
• Harry Myers, News Director
Description:
Music, News, Sports, Talk.

WBAL RADIO
3800 HOOPER AVE
BALTIMORE, MD 21211
410-338-6570
Fax: 410-366-4166
www.wbal.com
• Ed Kiernan, General Manager
• Steve Melewski, Sports Director
• Jeff Beauchamp, Vice President/Station
Manager
Nature of Sports Service:
News, Talk, Sports.
Baseball:
MLB - Baltimore Orioles.
College Sports:
University of Maryland - Basketball,
Football.

WBAX-AM
149 PENN AVENUE
SCRANTON, PA 18503
570-346-6555
Fax: 570-346-6038
www.wejl-wbax.com/
• Ruth Miller, News Director
(570) 207-8583
Description:
Music.

WBBB-FM
3012 HIGHWOODS BOULEVARD
SUITE 201
RALEIGH, NC 27604
919-876-9600
Fax: 919-882-1746
info@curtismedia.com
www.radio961.com
• Jim Defontes, News Director
(919) 876-0674

WBBP-AM
250 EAST RAINES ROAD
MEMPHIS, TN 38109
901-278-7878
Fax: 901-344-0038
www.bbless.org/wbbp.home.htm
• G. E. Patterson, General Manager
Description:
Music, News, Sports.

WBCK - BATTLE CREEK
390 GOLDEN AVE
BATTLE CREEK, MI 49015
263-963-5555
Fax: 269-963-5185
• Jack McDervitt, General Manager
• Ken Ervin, Sports Director
Baseball:
MLB - Detroit Tigers.
Ice Hockey:
NHL - Detroit Red Wings.

WBCK-AM
390 GOLDEN AVENUE
BATTLE CREEK, MI 49015
269-963-5555
Fax: 269-963-5185
www.am930wbck.com
• Tim Collins, General Manager/Operations
Director
(269) 963-5555
• Ken Ervin, Sports Director
Description:
Radio: AM930, Football: NFL-Detroit Lions,
Football and Basketball: NCAA Michigan
State University

WBCN-FM
83 LEO BURMINGHAM PARKWAY
BOSTON, MA 02135
617-746-1400
Fax: 617-746-1408
www.wbcn.com
• Mark Hannon, General Manager
(617) 746-1400
Description:
Music.

WBCR-FM
700 COLLEGE STREET
PO BOX 39
BELOIT, WI 53511-5509
608-363-2402
Fax: 608-363-2718

wbcrmanager@gmail.com
www.beloit.edu/wbcr
• James Lynch, Program Director
Description:
Music, News, Sports.

WBCV-AM
P.O. BOX 68
BRISTOL, TN 37621-0068
423-968-5221
Fax: 423-968-7711
www.wbcv.com
• Cecil Reed, Program Director
Description:
Music, News, Sports.

WBDG-FM
1200 GIRLS SCHOOL ROAD, N.
INDIANAPOLIS, IN 46214-3403
317-244-9234
Fax: 317-243-5506
• Jon Easter, Station Manager
(317) 244-9234
• Jason Adamson, Sports Director
(317) 244-9234
Description:
Music, News, Sports.

WBEC
211 JASON ST
PITTSFIELD, MA 01201
413-499-3333
Fax: 413-442-1590
• Joseph Gallagher, Owner
• Curt Preisser, Sports Director
• Laura Freed, Owner
Office Address:
211 Jason St, Pittsfield, MA 01202.
Nature of Sports Service:
News, Talk, Sports.
Baseball:
MLB - Boston Red Sox.
Basketball:
NBA Playoffs.
Football:
NFL - New England Patriots.
Ice Hockey:
NHL - Boston Bruins.

WBES-AM
817 SUNCREST PLACE
CHARLESTON, WV 25303-2302
304-342-3136
Fax: 304-342-3118
• Darrell Daniels, News Director
• John Dickensheets, Sports Director
Description:
Music.

WBET-AM
70808 SOUTH NOTTAWA ROAD
STURGIS, MI 49091-9731
269-651-2383
Fax: 269-659-1111
• Tom Duke, Account Executive
(269) 651-2383
tduke@wbetfm.com
• Mike Stiles, News Director
mstiles@wmshradio.com
Description:
ESPN Radio 1230

WBEX-AM
45 WEST MAIN STREET
CHILLICOTHE, OH 45601-3104

740-773-3000
Fax: 740-774-4494
www.wbex.com
• Dan Ramey, Sports Director
danraney@clearchannel.com
• Mike Smith, News Director
Description:
Music, News, Sports, Talk.

WBFD-AM
134 EAST PITT STREET 2ND FLOOR
BEDFORD, PA 15522-1311
814-623-1000
Fax: 814-623-9692
• Keith Bagley, News Director
• Jay B. Cessna, President/Sports Director
Description:
Music.

WBFN-AM
390 GOLDEN AVENUE
BATTLE CREEK, MI 49015
269-963-5555
Fax: 269-963-5185
www.battlecreekradio.com
• Tim Collins, Program Director
(269) 963-5555
timcollins@clearchannel.com
Description:
Radio: AM 1400, Basebal: MLB-Detroit
Tigers, Ice Hockey: NHL-Detroit Red Wings

WBGG-AM
200 FLEET STREET
PITTSBURGH, PA 15220
412-937-1441
800-788-1067
Fax: 412-937-0323
www.970theburgh.com
• Bob McLaughlin, Program Director
(412) 919-8455
bobmclaughlin@clearchannel.com
Description:
Music.

WBGN-AM
901 LEHMAN AVENUE SUITE 1
BOWLING GREEN, KY 42101
270-843-0107
Fax: 270-782-0767
www.1340wbgn.com/
• Brad Hogan, Station Manager
Description:
Music, News, Sports.

WBGO-FM
54 PARK PLACE
NEWARK, NJ 07102-4302
973-624-8880
Fax: 973-824-8888
jazz88@wbgo.org
www.wbgo.org
• Doug Doyle, News Director
(973) 624-8880
ddoyle@wbgo.org
• Dorthaan Kirk, Promotion Manager
(973) 624-8880
dkirk@wbgo.org
Description:
Music, News, Sports.

WBHB-AM
601 WEST ROANOKE DRIVE
FITZGERALD, GA 31750
229-423-2077
Fax: 229-386-9866

• Brian Peters, Sports Director
Description:
Music.

WBHR-AM
1010 2ND STREET NORTH
SAUK RAPIDS, MN 56379
320-252-6200
Fax: 320-252-9367
www.660wbhr.com
• Gary Hoppe, Program Director
Description:
Music.

WBIG-AM
620 NORTH EOLA ROAD
AURORA, IL 60502
630-851-5200
Fax: 630-851-5286
mail@wbig1280.com
www.wbig1280.com
• Steve Marten, General Manager
(630) 851-5200
• Gerry Clarke, Sports Marketing
(630) 851-5200
• Ryan Gatenby, Program Director
(630) 851-5200
Description:
Music.
Description: Teams Sponsored
Chicago Bulls, Chicago Bears, Chicago
White Sox, Kane County Cougers(Cubs
Affiliate), Chicago Soul soccor

WBIZ-AM SPORTS RADIO
619 CAMERON ST
EAU CLAIRE, WI 54703
715-830-4000
Fax: 715-835-9680
• Rick Hencley, General Manager
• Dan Michaels, Program Director
• Mike Sullivan, Sports Director
• Kelly Lafky, Sales Manager
Nature of Sports Service:
Local. 24-hour sports radio programming.

WBLA-AM
512 PEANUT ROAD
ELIZABETHTOWN, NC 28337-8811
910-862-3184
Fax: 910-872-0100
www.wgqr1057.com
• Lee Hauser, Advertising Manager
• Al Radlein, Program Director
Description:
Music, News, Sports.

WBLJ-AM
613 SILVER CIRCLE
DALTON, GA 30721
706-278-5511
Fax: 706-278-9917
www.wbljl230.com
• Randal Davidson, Sports Director
randaldavidson@clearchannel.com
Description:
Music.

WBLK-FM
14 LAFAYETTE SQUARE SUITE 1300
BUFFALO, NY 14203-1928
716-852-9393
800-828-2191
Fax: 716-852-9390
www.wblk.com

• Chris Reynolds, Program Director
• Catherine Roberts, Promotion Director
Description:
Music, News, Sports.

**WBNS AM/FM - 1460 ESPN COLUMBUS &
97.1 THE FAN**
605 S FRONT STREET
SUITE 300
COLUMBUS, OH 43215
614-460-3850
Fax: 614-460-3757
www.971thefan.com
• Jay Taylor, Program Director
(614) 460-3829
• Todd Markiewicz, Director of Sales
(614) 460-2816
Description:
Founded in 1976, the station offers classic
country music, news, sports and local sports
play-by-play, Minnesota TWins, NFL
football, NCAA football and basketball.
Baseball:
Cleveland Indians
Football:
Monday Night Football
Hockey:
NHL - Columbus Blue Jackets
College Sports:
Basketball/Football - Ohio State University

WBNV-FM
740 EAST MAIN STREET
BARNESVILLE, OH 43713
740-425-9268
Fax: 740-432-1991
www.yourradioplace.com
• Reuben Perdue, Program/Sports Director
(740) 432-5605
Description:
Music, Sports.

WBOB-AM 1160 SPORTS RADIO
3656 EDWARDS RD
CINCINNATI, OH 45208
513-533-2500
Fax: 513-533-2527
• John Rohm, General Manager
• Doug Kidd, Interim Pro General
Manager/Director
• Roy Seransky, Sales Manager
• Ron James, Promotions Director
• Patti Marshall, Marketing Director
Nature of Sports Service:
Local. 24-hour sports radio programming.
Baseball:
MLB - Cincinnati Reds..
College Sports:
NCAA DIV I Xavier Musketeers, NCAA DIV I
Cincinnati Bearcats, NCAA Div I University
of Kentucky Wildcats,
Football:
NFL - Cincinnati Bengals.
Ice Hockey:
American Hockey League/AHL - Cincinnati
Mighty Ducks;

WBPZ-AM
21 EAST MAIN STREET
LOCK HAVEN, PA 17745-2443
570-748-4038
Fax: 570-748-0092
• John Lipez, Advertising Manager
• Mark Sohmer, News Director
Description:
Music.

WBRK 1340AM RADIO
100 NORTH ST
PITTSFIELD, MA 01201
413-442-1553
Fax: 413-445-5294
• Chip Hodgkins, General Manager
• Bob Shade, Sports Director
Baseball:
MLB - New York Yankees; Minor League -
Northern League - Berkshire Black Bears.
Basketball:
NBA - Boston Celtics.

WBRY-AM
P. O. BOX 7
WOODBURY, TN 37190
615-563-2313
Fax: 615-563-6229
askus@wbry.com
www.wbry.com
• Doug Combs, General Manager
dcombs@wbry.com
• Keith Ready, Sports Director
(615) 563-2313
askus@wbry.com
Description:
Music, News, Sports, Talk.

WBTI-FM
808 HURON AVENUE
PORT HURON, MI 48060-3705
810-982-9000
Fax: 810-987-9380
• Bill Gilmer, News Director
bgilmer@radiofirst.net
• Dennis Stuckey, Sports Director
(810) 982-9000
Description:
Music, News.

WBTM-AM
710 GROVE STREET
DANVILLE, VA 24541-1704
434-797-4290
Fax: 434-797-3918
wbtm1330@wbtm1330.com
www.wbtm1330.com/
• Carol Metz, Promotion Manager
• Chuck Vipperman, News Director
(434) 797-4290
Description:
Music, News, Sports, Talk.

WBUK-FM
667 WEST MARKET STREET
LIMA, OH 45801
419-223-2060
Fax: 419-229-3888
reneescott@clearchannel.com
www.wbuk.com
• Sou Boudriex, Advertising Sales
souboudrie@clearchannel.com
• Jeff Gunter, News Director
(419) 223-2060
jeffgunter@clearchannel.com
• Mike Mullen, Athletics Senior Editor/Sports
Director
mikemullen@clearchannel.com
• Todd Walker, Sports Director
toddwalker@clearchannel.com

WBUT-AM
252 PILLOW ST
BUTLER, PA 16001

724-287-5778
Fax: 724-282-9188
www.insidebutlercounty.com
• Bob Cupp, Sports Director
bobcupp@bcrnetwork.com
Sponsors:
Pittsburgh Steelers, Pittsburgh Pirates,
Pittsburgh Penguins, Pitt Panthers as well
as local high school leagues.

WBVP-AM
1316 7TH AVENUE
BEAVER FALLS, PA 15010-4217
724-846-4100
Fax: 724-843-7771
www.wbvp-wmba.com
• Bob Barrickman, Sports Director
• Pat Septak, News Director
Description:
Music, News, Sports, Talk.

WBXX-FM
390 GOLDEN AVENUE
BATTLE CREEK, MI 49015
269-963-9595
Fax: 269-963-5185
www.softrock953.com
• Tim Collins, General Manager/Operations
Director
(269) 963-5555
• Nathan Adams, Overnight DJ/Sports
Anchor
(269) 963-5555
NathanAdams@clearchannel.com
• Jeff Cassidy, Program Director
(269) 963-5555
Description:
Radio: FM95.3, Football and Basketball:
NCAA University of Michigan

WBYL-FM
1559 WEST 4TH STREET
WILLIAMSPORT, PA 17701-5650
570-327-1400
Fax: 570-327-8156
kthomas@clearchannel.com
• Ken Sawyer, Sports Director
ksawyer@clearchannel.com
• Tom Scott, Promotion Manager
tscott@clearchannel.com
• Kathy Thomas, News Director
(570) 327-1400
Description:
Music.

WBYT-FM
237 WEST EDISON ROAD SUITE 200
MISHAWAKA, IN 46545-3137
574-258-5483
800-285-8646
Fax: 574-258-0930
www.b100.com
• Sahar Charisse, News Director
(574) 258-5483
Description:
Music, News, Sports.

WBZ-AM
1170 SOLDIERS FIELD ROAD
BOSTON, MA 02134
617-787-7000
Fax: 617-254-6383
www.wbz.com
• Peter Casey, News Director
(617) 787-7246
• Ted Jordan, Vice President

• Laurie Lamper, Promotions Director
(617) 787-7196
• Tony Nesbitt, Sports Executive Producer
(617) 787-7266
• Gil Santos, Sports Director
• Alan Segel, Sports Anchor (Weekend)
Description:
News, Talk.

WBZD-FM
1685 FOUR MILE DRIVE
WILLIAMSPORT, PA 17701-1938
570-323-8200
Fax: 570-323-5075
www.wbzd.com
• John Finn, News Director
• Bob Pawlikowski, Advertising Manager
bobp@aol.com
Description:
Music, News, Sports.

WBZE-FM / WGLF.FM/ WWLD.FM / WHBX.FM
3411 WEST THARPE STREET
TALLAHASSEE, FL 32303-1139
850-201-3000
Fax: 850-561-8903
www.mystar98.com
Description:
Radio Stations : Music, News, Sports.
Sport Broadcasts:
Announces for FSU Volleyball, FSU and
FAMU Basketball, and FAMU Football

WCAO-AM
1829 REISTERSTOWN ROAD SUITE 420
BALTIMORE, MD 21208-6320
410-366-7600
Fax: 410-467-0011
www.heaven600.com
• Yvonne Morton, News Director
(410) 261-7257
Description:
Music, News, Sports, Talk.

WCBG-AM
10960 JOHN WAYNE DRIVE
GREENCASTLE, PA 17225
717-597-9200
800-758-0838
Fax: 717-597-9210
• Scott Douglas, News Director
Description:
Music, News, Sports, Talk.

WCBL-FM
P. O. BOX 387
BENTON, KY 42025
270-527-3102
Fax: 270-527-5606
www.bellsouth.net
• Sam Rickman, News Director
wcbl@bellsouth.net
• Jeff Waters, Sports Editor
(270) 527-3102
wcbl@bellsouth.net
Description:
Music.

WCBT-AM
3 EAST 1ST STREET
WELDON, NC 27890-1503
252-536-3115
Fax: 252-538-0378
www.wcbt1230.com

• Les Atkins, News Director
• Mark Matthews, Sports Director
Description:
Sports.

WCCO
625 2ND AVE S.
SUITE 200
MINNEAPOLIS, MN 55402
612-370-0611
Fax: 612-370-0683
www.wcco.com
• Mike Max, Announcer
• Jay Dailey, GSM
• Lindsey Peterson, APD
Nature of Sports Service:
Local, 24-hour full-service programming.
Broadcast station of the Minnesota
Timberwolves and St. Thomas University.

WCCP
PO BOX 1560
CLEMSON, SC 29633
864-654-0606
800-499-1049
Fax: 864-654-9328
• George Clement, General Manager
• Tommy Powell, Sports Director
Nature of Sports Service:
Sports/70's Music.
Baseball:
MLB - Atlanta Braves.
College Sports:
Baseball, Basketball, Football - Clemson
University.
Football:
NFL - Carolina Panthers.

WCCW-AM
RADIO CENTER-WCCW 300
SUITE 450
TRAVERSE CITY, MI 49684
231-946-6211
Fax: 231-946-1914
brianh@wccw.fm
• Annie Mac, News Director
• Brian Hale, ESPN Manager
(231) 946-6211
Description:
Music, News, Talk. ESPN Radio 1310 AM

WCDK-FM
2307 PENNSYLVANIA AVENUE
WEIRTON, WV 26062
304-723-1430
800-926-8255
Fax: 304-723-1688
• Tammie Beagle, News Director
(304) 723-1444
Description:
Music.

WCDO-AM
75 MAIN STREET
SIDNEY, NY 13838-1138
607-563-3588
Fax: 607-563-7805
www.wcdofm.com
• Rob Ray, News Director
rob@wcdofm.com
• Craig Stevens, Advertising Manager
craig@wcdofm.com
Description:
Music, News, Sports.

WCEM-AM
2 BAY STREET
CAMBRIDGE, MD 21613-0237
410-228-4800
Fax: 410-228-0130
www.mtsline.com
• Norm Elliott, News Director
(410) 228-4800
normelliott@hotmail.com
• Shan Shariff, Sports Director
Description:
Music, News, Sports.

WCFM-FM
WILLIAMS COLLEGE
WILLIAMSTOWN, MA 01267
413-597-3265
Fax: 413-597-2259
wcfmbd@wso.williams.edu
wcfm.williams.edu
• Adam Ain, General Manager
adam.s.ain@williams.edu
• Helena Johnson, Sports Director
(413) 597-3265
99mkm@williams.edu
Description:
Music, News, Sports, Talk.

WCFW-FM
318 WELL STREET
CHIPPEWA FALLS, WI 54729-1563
715-723-2257
Fax: 715-723-8276
• Patricia Bushland, Advertising Manager
• Roland Bushland, General Manager
Description:
Music, News, Sports.

WCGQ-FM
1820 WYNNTON ROAD
COLUMBUS, GA 31904
706-327-1217
Fax: 706-322-1077
www.q1073.com
• D.J. Jones, Sports Director
(404) 762-9942
• Chuck Thompson, Promotions Manager
Description:
Music, News, Sports.

WCHC-FM
COLLEGE OF THE HOLY CROSS
WORCESTER, MA 01610-2322
508-793-2475
Fax: 508-793-2471
www.holycross.edu/wchc
• Chris Delvicio, Program Director
Description:
Music, News, Sports.

WCHO-AM
1535 NORTH STREET
WASHINGTON COURT HOU, OH
43160-1111
740-335-0941
Fax: 740-335-6869
wwww.cho.com
• Dan Latham, General Manager
danlatham@clearchannel.com
• Randy L. Young, Sports Director
(740) 335-0941
randallyoung@clearchannel.com
Description:
Music.

WCHO-FM
1535 NORTH STREET
WASHINGTON COURT HOU, OH
43160-1111
740-335-0941
Fax: 740-335-6869
www.washingtonch.com
• Ed Helt, News Director
carlstaffan@clearchannel.com
• Randy L. Young, Sports Director
(740) 335-0941
randallyoung@clearchannel.com
Description:
Music.

WCJW-AM
3258 MERCHANT ROAD
WARSAW, NY 14569-0251
585-786-8131
Fax: 585-786-2241
• Jenny Snow, News Director
news@wcjw.com
Description:
Music, News, Sports.

WCKY-AM
8044 MONTGOMERY ROAD
SUITE 650
CINCINNATI, OH 45236
513-686-8300
800-749-9326
Fax: 513-241-0358
www.wcky.com/main.html
• Mike Kenney, General Manager
mikekenney@clearchannel.com
Description:
News, Talk.

WCLG-FM
343 HIGH STREET
MORGANTOWN, WV 26505
304-292-2222
Fax: 304-292-2224
www.wclg.com
Description:
Music

WCLH-FM
84 W. S. STREET
WILKES BARRE, PA 18766
570-408-4169
Fax: 570-408-5908
• Ariel Cohen, Assistant Marketing Director
(570) 408-4169
• Renee Loftus, Station Manager
(570) 408-4169
Description:
Educational, Music, News, Sports.

WCLN-AM
118 EAST MAIN STREET
CLINTON, NC 28328
910-592-8949
Fax: 910-592-3732
www.odies1170.com
• Thomas Elliott, Program Director
fly@oldies1170.com
Description:
Music, News, Sports.

WCLO-AM
1 SOUTH PARKER DRIVE
JANESVILLE, WI 53545-3928
608-752-7895
Fax: 608-752-4438

programming@wclo.com
www.wclo.com
• Tim Bremel, Program Director
(608) 752-7895
• Al Fagerli, Sports Director
(608) 752-7895
sports@wclo.com
• Mike O'Brien, Advertising Manager
mobrien@wclo.com
Description:
Music.

WCLT-AM
674 JACKSONTOWN ROAD, SOUTHEAST
HEATH, OH 43056
740-345-4004
Fax: 740-345-5775
www.wclt.com
• Eric Brown, News Director
• Tom Bunyard, General Sales Manager
(740) 345-4004
Description:
Sports radio programming.
Teams sponsored:
Ohio State Buckeyes, Columbus Blue
Jackets, Cleveland Indians, and High
School sports.

WCNC-AM
911 PARSONAGE STREET EXTENDED
ELIZABETH CITY, NC 27906-1246
252-335-4379
Fax: 252-338-5275
www.wcnc1240.com
• Sam Walker, Program/Sports Director
Description:
Music, News, Sports.

WCNC-AM / WZBO-AM
911 PARSONAGE EXTENDED
ELIZABETH CITY, NC 27909
252-335-4379
Fax: 252-338-5275
www.ecri.net
• Sam Walker, News Director
(252) 335-4379
Description:
Music, News, Sports.
Teams:
UNC Tarheels, Carolina Panthers,
Westwood One National Coverage NFL,
NCAA coverage of ACC and Big East.

WCOS
316 GREYSTONE BOULEVARD
COLUMBIA, SC 29210
803-343-1100
Fax: 803-748-9267
www.975wcos.com
• Steve Patterson, General Manager
• Kevin Cohen, Sports Director
Office Address:
56 Radio Lane, Columbia, SC 29210.
Nature of Sports Service:
Local. 24-hour sports radio programming.
Auto Sports:
NASCAR.
Baseball:
MLB - Atlanta Braves.

WCSL
PO BOX 370
CHERRYVILLE, NC 28021
704-435-3297
Fax: 704-435-1217

- Calvin Hastings, General Manager/Sales
- Andy Foster, Sports Director/Music
- Milton Baker, Office Manager
- Tim Biggerstaff, Product Director
- Larry Seagle, News Director
- Terresa Hastings, Traffic Director

Office Address:
1416 Shelby Hwy, Cherryville, NC 28021.
Nature of Sports Service:
Country; Sports.
Baseball:
MLB - Atlanta Braves.
College Sports:
Basketball, Football - University of North Carolina Tarheels.
Football:
NFL - Carolina Panthers.

WCSL-AM
1416 SHELBY HIGHWAY
CHERRYVILLE, NC 28021
704-735-8071
877-638-7234
Fax: 704-435-1217
www.superstations.net
- Tim Biggerstaff, Program Director
- Larry Seagle, Sports Director
Description:
Music, News, Sports.

WCST-AM
440 RADIO STATION LANE
BERKELEY SPRINGS, WV 25411-4108
304-258-1010
Fax: 304-258-1010
- Mike Fagan, Promotion Manager/Sports Director
- Virgil Ruppenthal, Program Director
Description:
Music, News, Sports.

WCTA-AM
114 SOUTH JOHNSON STREET COURT SQUARE
ALAMO, TN 38001-0246
731-696-2781
Fax: 731-696-5006
- Billy Williams, General/Advertising Manager
Description:
Music, News, Sports.

WCTK-FM
75 OXFORD STREET SUITE 402
PROVIDENCE, RI 02905
401-467-4366
800-365-1037
Fax: 401-941-2795
www.wctk.com
- Rick Everett, Program Director
(401) 467-4366
reverett@hallradio.com
- Jamie Prevost, Promotion Manager
Description:
Music.

WCUM-AM
1862 COMMERCE DRIVE SUITE 2
BRIDGEPORT, CT 06605
203-335-1450
Fax: 203-337-1220
radiocumbre1450@aol.com
www.radiocumbre.com
- Migdalia Colon, Vice President
Description:
Music, News, Sports.

WCVM-FM
6200 EAST STATE ROAD 120
HOWE, IN 46746
260-562-3276
Fax: 260-562-2252
www.effectradio.com
- Banner Kidd, General Manager

WCWT-FM
500 EAST FRANKLIN STREET
CENTERVILLE, OH 45459-5714
937-439-3558
Fax: 937-439-3574
- Bob Romond, Program Director
Description:
Music, News, Sports.

WCYJ-FM
51 WEST COLLEGE STREET
WAYNESBURG, PA 15370-1258
724-627-8191
www.waynesburg.edu
- Amy Sigmund, News Director
Description:
Music, News, Sports.

WDAE-AM 620
4002 GANDY BLVD
TAMPA, FL 33611
813-839-9393
Fax: 813-831-3299
www.620wdae.com
- Dave Reinhart, General Manager
- Scott Chase, Program Director
Office Address:
1416 Shelby Hwy, Cherryville, NC 28021.
Nature of Sports Service:
Local. 24-hour sports station.

WDAS-AM
23 WEST CITY AVENUE
BALA CYNWYD, PA 19004
610-617-8500
Fax: 610-617-8501
joetamburro@clearchannel.com
www.wdasam.com/main.html
- Erica Speed, Promotion Director
- Joe Tamburro, Program Director
Description:
Music, News, Sports.

WDBO-AM
4192 NORTH JOHN YOUNG PARKWAY
ORLANDO, FL 32804-2620
321-281-2030
Fax: 407-290-1076
news@wdbo.com
580wdbo.com/
- Scott Anez, Sports Director
(321) 281-2030
Description:
Music, News, Sports.

WDBQ-AM
5490 SARATOGA ROAD
DUBUQUE, IA 52002-2593
563-583-6471
Fax: 563-583-4535
- Scott Lindahl, General Manager
Description:
Music, News, Sports.

WDDD-AM
1822 NORTH COURT
MARION, IL 62959

618-997-8123
Fax: 618-993-2319
brucefasol@clearchannel.com
- Bruce Fasol, Sports Director
(618) 997-8123
- April Ruebke, News Director
(618) 997-8123
aprilruebke@clearchannel.com
Description:
Music, News, Sports.

WDDD-FM
1822 NORTH COURT STREET
MARION, IL 62959
618-997-8123
Fax: 618-993-2319
rock105@accessus.net
www.w3dcountry.com/main.html
- Bruce Fasol, Sports Director
(618) 997-8123
- April Ruebke, News Director
(618) 997-8123
aprilruebke@clearchannel.com
Description:
Music.

WDDK-FM
1271-B EAST BROAD STREET
GREENSBORO, GA 30642-2335
706-453-4140
Fax: 706-453-7179
- Chip Lyness, Advertising Manager
Description:
Music, News, Sports.

WDEL-AM
P.O. BOX 7492
WILMINGTON, DE 19810
302-478-8898
Fax: 302-479-1532
wdelnews@wdel.com
www.wdel.com
- Janette Johnson, Marketing/Promotion Director
(302) 478-2700
- Don Voltz, Sports Director
(302) 478-8898
- Len Holmquist, Sports Reporter
(302) 478-8898
Len@wdel.com
Description:
News, Talk.

WDFN
2930 E. JEFFERSON
DETROIT, MI 48207
313-259-5440
Fax: 313-259-9079
www.wdfn.com
- Peter Connolly, General Manager
- Jamie Samuelson, Sports Director
Office Address:
2909 Woodbridge, Detroit, MI 48207.
Nature of Sports Service:
Local. 24-hour sports radio programming.
Baseball:
CBS Package.
College Sports:
Basketball - NCAA; Football - University Notre Dame.
Football:
Westwood One package.

WDFN - 1130 AM THE FAN
27675 Halsted Road
Farmington Hills, MI 48331

248-848-1130
Fax: 248-848-1422
www.wdfn.com
• Dave Pugh, General Manager
• Rona Danziger, Program Director
• Ellen Sawyer, Promotion and Marketing Director
• Matt Dery, Sports Director
LINEUP:
Jamie Samuelson, Mike Stone, Bob Wojnowski, Matt Dery. Brandon Tierney, Greg Brady (not from the Brady Bunch), Sabrina Black, Mark Spindler, Sean Baligian.

WDHC-FM
440 RADIO STATION LANE
BERKELEY SPRINGS, WV 25411-4108
304-258-1010
Fax: 304-258-1976
• Mike Fagan, Promotion Manager/Sports Director
• Virgil Ruppenthal, Program Director
Description:
Music, News, Sports.

WDKD-AM
51 COMMERCE STREET
SUMTER, SC 29151
803-775-2321
Fax: 803-773-4856
• Dave Baker, Program Director
(803) 775-2321
dave@vfastlink.com
• Derrick Rheims, Sports Director
Description:
Music, News, Sports.

WDKX-FM
683 EAST MAIN STREET
ROCHESTER, NY 14605-2740
585-262-2050
Fax: 585-262-2626
wdkx@wdkx.com
www.wdkx.com
• Andre Marcel, Program Director
• Mike Paz, Sports Editor
• Tariq Spence, Sports Director
Description:
Music, News, Sports.

WDLB
1712 NORTH CENTRAL AVENUE
MARSHFIELD, WI 54449
715-384-2191
800-236-1065
Fax: 715-387-3588
www.wdlbwosq.com
• Ken Rajek, General Manager
• Gene Delisio, Sports Director
(715) 384-2191
gene@wdlbwosq.com
• Arnie Peck, Sales Manager
(715) 384-2191
• Scott Johnson, Program Director
(715) 384-2191
Nature of Service:
Local over 100 high school events per year.
Year Founded:
1947
Basketball:
Marquette
Football:
NFL doubleheader on Sunday, college game of the week
Office Address:

1712 North Central Ave, Marshfield, WI 54449.

WDLZ-FM
1714 WEST MAIN STREET
MURFREESBORO, NC 27855-0038
252-398-4111
Fax: 252-398-3581
frankk_00@hotmail.com
• Frank Knapper, Program Director
(252) 398-5688
Description:
Music.

WDNE-FM
WASHINGTON & DAVIS
ELKINS, WV 26241
304-636-1300
Fax: 304-636-2200
wdne@wvradio.com
• Zoe Ludski, News Director
Description:
Music, News, Sports.

WDOE-AM/FM
P.O. BOX 209
DUNKIRK, NY 14048-0209
716-366-1410
Fax: 716-366-1416
chautauquatoday.com
• Dan Palmer, Sports Director
dan@WDOE1410.com
• David Rowley, News Director
news@wdoe1410.com
Description:
Music, News, Sports, Talk.

WDOG-FM
2447 AUGUSTA HIGHWAY
ALLENDALE, SC 29810-0442
803-584-3500
Fax: 803-584-0202
wdog935@aol.com
www.wdog.fm
• Carl Gooding, Station Manager
wdog93@aol.com
Description:
Music.

WDOR-FM
P. O. BOX 549
STURGEON BAY, WI 54235
920-743-4411
Fax: 920-743-2334
• Roger Levendusky, News Director
(920) 743-4411
roger@wdor.com
• Chad Michaels, Sports Director
(920) 743-4411
chad@wdor.com
• Eddy Allen, General Manager
(920) 743-4411
eddy@wdor.com
Description:
Music, News, Sports, Talk.
Year Founded:
1947

WDOW-AM
26914 MARCELLUS HIGHWAY
DOWAGIAC, MI 49047-7444
269-782-5106
Fax: 269-782-5107
q92radio@yahoo.com
www.wdow.net
• Joe Jason, General Manager

Description:
Music, News, Sports.

WDPN-AM
393 SMYTH AVENUE NE
ALLIANCE, OH 44601-1562
330-821-1111
800-743-9293
Fax: 330-821-0379
• Charlotte Franko, Promotions Manager
• Clint Marshall, News Director
clint@q92radio.com
Description:
Music.

WDSL-AM
431 EATON ROAD
MOCKSVILLE, NC 27028-2582
336-751-9375
Fax: 336-751-5025
wdsl1520am@yahoo.com
• Garry Tilley, News Director
wdslradio@hotmail.com
Description:
Music, News, Sports.

WDSM SPORTS RADIO 710
715 E. CENTRAL ENTRANCE
DULUTH, MN 55811
218-722-4321
Fax: 218-722-5423
• Mark Fleischer, Sports Director/Program Director
Nature of Sports Service:
News and sports radio programming.
College Sports:
Basketball - Univ of Wisconsin, Basketball & Football.
Football:
NFL - Green Bay Packers.

WDSM-AM
715 EAST CENTRAL ENTRANCE
DULUTH, MN 55811-5596
218-722-4321
800-388-2428
Fax: 218-722-5423
www.wdsm.am/
• Roxanne Charles, General Manager
(218) 722-4321
• Mark Fleischer, Program/Sports Director
(218) 722-4321
• Dave Strandberg, News Director
(218) 722-4321
kdalnews@mwcradio.com
Description:
News, Sports.

WDUN-AM
P.O. BOX 10
GAINESVILLE, GA 30501-1706
770-532-9921
800-552-9386
Fax: 770-532-0506
www.wdun.com
• Jeff Hart, Sports Director
• John W. Jacobs, III, Owner
• Judd Hickinbotham, News/Sports Anchor
(770) 532-9921
Description:
Music, News, Talk.

WDUX-AM/FM
200 TOWER ROAD
WAUPACA, WI 54981

715-258-5528
Fax: 715-258-7711
• Jack Barry, News/Sports Director
wdux@waupacaonline.net
Description:
Radio station broadcasting sports.

WDUX-FM
200 TOWER ROAD
WAUPACA, WI 54981
715-258-5528
Fax: 715-258-7711
wduxnews@waupacaonline.net
• Jack Barry, News Director
wdux@waupacaonline.net
• Jack Barry, Sports Director
wdux@waupacaonline.net
Description:
Educational, Music, News.

WDZN-FM
220 PACA STREET
CUMBERLAND, MD 21502
301-724-6000
Fax: 301-724-0617
www.disney.com
• Warren Gregory, Owner
(301) 724-0001
• Robin Jones, Program Director
(818) 955-6761
Description:
Music, News, Sports.

WEAI-FM
2161 OLD STATE ROAD, E.
JACKSONVILLE, IL 62650-6380
217-245-7171
Fax: 217-245-6711
weai@weai.com
www.weai.com
• Jerry Symons, Sports Director
• Gary Scott, General Manager
gscott@wlds.com
Description:
Music, News, Sports. Music format with
extensive coverage of Cardinal baseball and
over 270 local games a year.
Sports Discussed:
Cards-local
Frequency:
107.1

WEAQ-AM
944 HARLEM AVENUE
ALTOONA, WI 54720-1127
715-832-1530
800-866-9299
Fax: 715-832-5329
• Dave Craig, Sports Director
• Dan Lea, News Director
Description:
Music.

WEAS-FM
214 TELEVISION CIRCLE
SAVANNAH, GA 31406-4519
912-961-9000
888-567-0102
Fax: 912-961-7070
www.e93.com
• Lydis Syed, Advertising Manager
(912) 961-9000
Description:
Music, News, Sports.

WEDM-FM
9651 EAST 21ST STREET
INDIANAPOLIS, IN 46229-1706
317-532-6301
Fax: 317-532-6199
• Daniel J. Henn, General Manager
Description:
Music, News, Sports.

WEDO-AM
1985 LINCOLN WAY
MCKEESPORT, PA 15131
412-664-4431
Fax: 412-664-1236
• William Korch, News Director
Description:
Music, News, Sports, Talk.

WEEB-AM
1650 MIDLAND ROAD
SOUTHERN PINES, NC 28388
910-692-7440
Fax: 910-692-7372
steve@weeb990.com
www.weeb990.com
• Steve Adams, News/Sports Director
Description:
News, Talk.

WEEI SPORTS RADIO
20 GUEST ST, THIRD FL
Brighton, MA 02135-2040
617-779-3500
Fax: 617-779-3557
www.weei.com
• Jim Rushton, Advertising
• Kerry Collins, Promotions
• Beverly Tilden, Integrated Marketing
Director

WEEO-AM
37 SOUTH MAIN STREET
CHAMBERSBURG, PA 17201
717-709-0801
Fax: 717-709-0802
Description:
Music.

WEEU-AM
34 NORTH 4TH STREET
READING, PA 19601-3943
610-376-7335
800-323-8800
Fax: 610-376-7756
weeu@weeu.com
www.weeu.com
• Mitch Gerhart, Sports Director
mgerhart@weeu.com
• Paul Roberts, Sports Talk Show Host
proberts@weeu.com
Description:
Talk, News, Sports.
Sports Discussed:
All Philadelphia Eagles and Phillies affiliate
Frequency:
830 AM

WEEX-AM
107 PAXINOSA ROAD, W.
EASTON, PA 18040
610-258-6155
Fax: 610-258-6292
www.espnlv.com
• Tom Fallon, Program Director
(610) 829-5528
• K. J. Zabali, Promotion Manager

Description:
Music.

WEIU-FM
600 LINCLON AVENUE
CHARLESTON, IL 61920
217-581-6116
Fax: 217-581-6650
hitmix@weiu.net
• Jeff Owens, Program/Sports Director
(217) 581-6954
jeff@weiu.net
Description:
Educational, Music, News, Sports, Talk.

WEJL-AM
149 PENN AVENUE
SCRANTON, PA 18503-2022
570-346-6555
Fax: 570-346-6038
www.wejl-wbax.com/main.htm
• Ruth Miller, News Director
(570) 207-8583
Description:
Music, News, Sports.

WEKS-FM
1523 KELL LANE SUITE 1
GRIFFIN, GA 30224-8878
770-412-8700
Fax: 770-412-8080
www.bear92.com
• Carl Pruett, Advertising Sales
• Chuck Tarkinton, Sports Director
• Stan Watson, Promotion Director
• Wanda Wilson, Office Manager

WEKT-AM
P.O. BOX 577
ELKTON, KY 42220-0577
270-265-5636
Fax: 270-265-5637
• Marshall Sidebottom, General/Advertising
Manager
wektam1070@yahoo.com
Description:
Music, News, Sports.

WEKX-FM
522 MAIN STREET
WILLIAMSBURG, KY 40769-1127
606-549-1027
Fax: 606-549-5565
wekx@bellsouth.net
www.hit102fm.com
• Rick Campbell, Program Director

WELM-AM
1705 LAKE STREET
ELMIRA, NY 14901-1220
607-733-5626
Fax: 607-733-5627
• E. D. Crum, Advertising Manager
(607) 733-5626
• Mike Jacobs, News Director
• Bob Michaels, Sports Director
(607) 733-5626
• Donna Van Debogart, Promotions
Manager
(607) 733-5626
Description:
Music, News, Sports.

WELW-AM
PO BOX 1330
WILLOUGHBY, OH 44096
440-946-1330
888-769-1330
Fax: 440-953-0320
www.welw.com
Description:
Talk and sports events
Sports Discussed:
Local high school and collegiate game coverage; Lake County Captains minor league baseball coverage

WEMJ-AM
COUNTRY CLUB ROAD VILLAGE W.
GILFORD, NH 03247
603-524-1323
Fax: 603-528-5185
• Allan Harrison, News/Programming Director
Description:
Sports, Talk.

WENE
320 NORTH JENSEN ROAD
VESTAL, NY 13850
607-584—5800
Fax: 607-584-5900
1430theteam.com
• Jon Scaptura, Program Director
jonscaptura@clearchannel.com
• Joanne Aloi, General Manager
joannealoi@clearchannel.com
• Jim Free, Operations Manager
jimfree@clearchannel.com
• Michele Page Vojtisek, Sales Manager
(607) 584-5800
Year Founded:
1947
Frequency:
1430 KHz.
Primary Audience:
Men 25-54.
Baseball:
MLB - New York Yankees

WENG
PO BOX 1908
ENGLEWOOD, FL 34295
941-474-3231
888-434-1530
Fax: 941-475-2205
kenb@wengradio.com
www.wengradio.com
• Ken Birdsong, General Manager
• Rich Spedaliere, Sports Director
• Kyle Turner, Program Director
Nature of Sports Service:
News, Sports.
Basketball:
Orlando Magic
College Sports:
Basketball; Football - Florida State University, Miami University, Notre Dame University.
Football:
NFL - Tampa Bay Buccaneers, Miami Dolphins.

WENK-AM
1729 NAILLING DRIVE
UNION CITY, TN 38261-2003
731-885-1240
Fax: 731-885-3405
www.1240wenk.com

• Robin Francis, Sports Director
(731) 885-1240
• Terry Hailey, Advertising Manager/Program Director
Description:
Music, Talk.

WEPG-AM
105 NORTH ASH AVENUE
SOUTH PITTSBURG, TN 37380
423-837-8001
Fax: 423-837-8002
• Will Rodgers, News Director
willthevoiceman@aol.com
• Charles Rodgers, Owner
Description:
Music, News, Sports.

WERQ-FM
1705 WHITEHEAD ROAD
BALTIMORE, MD 21207
410-332-8200
Fax: 410-944-7182
www.92q.com
• Latoya Dixon, Promotions Director
(410) 907-0368
ladixson@radio-one.com
• Victor Starr, Program Director
(410) 332-8200
vstarr@radio-one.com
Description:
Music, News, Sports.

WEST-AM
436 NORTHAMPTON STREET
EASTON, PA 18042
610-258-9378
Fax: 610-250-9675
westnews1@verizon.net
www.am1400west.net
• Dick Hammer, Sports Director
• Pamela Richetta, Promotion Manager
richetta@verizon.net
Description:
Music, News, Sports.

WEVR-AM
178 RADIO ROAD
RIVER FALLS, WI 54022-8255
715-425-1111
• T. J. Campbell, News Director
Description:
Music, News, Sports.

WEVR-FM
178 RADIO ROAD
RIVER FALLS, WI 54022-8255
715-425-1111
• Carol Hanten, General Manager
Description:
Music, News, Sports.

WFAN SPORTS RADIO
345 HUDSON STREET
10TH FLOOR
NEW YORK, NY 10014
212-314-9200
877-337-6666
www.wfan.com
• Lee Davis, General Manager
• Eric Spitz, Program Director
• Theresa Beyer, Director of Marketing
• Brian Rooney, Promotions Manager
• Thomas Mansusi, General Sales Manager
Nature of Sports Service:
24-hour sports radio programming focusing

on New York metro area teams.
Baseball:
New York Mets
Basketball:
New York Knicks, New Jersey Nets
Football:
New York Giants
Ice Hockey:
New York Rangers, New Jersey Devils

WFAT-FM
6021 SOUTH WESTNEDGE AVENUE
KALAMAZOO, MI 49002
269-327-7600
Fax: 269-327-0726
www.wfat.com
• Jim Whelan, News Director
Description:
Music, News, Sports.

WFDF 910AM RADIO
6317 TAYLOR DR
FLINT, MI 48507
810-238-7300
Fax: 810-238-7310
• Nancy Dymond, General Manager
Nature of Sports Service:
News, Sports.
Basketball:
NBA - Detroit Pistons.
College Sports:
Basketball, Football - University of Michigan.
Football:
NFL - Detroit Lions.
Golf:
Local Coverage.

WFEB
1209 MILLERVILLE RD
SYLACAUGA, AL 35150
256-245-3281
Fax: 256-245-3050
• Bruce Carr, General Sales Manager/Sports Director
Nature of Sports Service:
News, Sports.
Baseball:
MLB - Atlanta Braves.
College Sports:
Baseball, Basketball, Football - University of Alabama.

WFEB-AM
1209 MILLERVILLE HIGHWAY
SYLACAUGA, AL 35150-0450
256-245-3281
Fax: 256-245-3050
www.wfeb1340.com
• Bruce Carr, Sports Director
Description:
Music, News, Sports, Talk.

WFFC-FM
ROUTE 40
FERRUM, VA 24088
800-868-9797
Fax: 540-365-4203
wffc@ferrum.edu
www.ferrum.edu/wffc
• Robert Glass, News Director
(800) 868-9797
rglass@ferrum.edu
Description:
Music, News, Sports.

WFFF-AM
P.O. BOX 550
COLUMBIA, MS 39429-0550
601-736-1360
Fax: 601-736-1361
• Ronnie Geiger, Sports Director
Description:
Music, News, Sports.

WFGN-AM
470 LEADMINE ROAD
GAFFNEY, SC 29340-4037
864-489-9430
Fax: 864-489-9440
• Eddie Bridges, Program Director
Description:
Music, News, Sports.

WFHR
645 25TH AVE N.
WISCONSIN RAPIDS, WI 54495
715-424-1300
800-424-9459
Fax: 715-424-1347
• Miles Knuteson, General Manager
• Terry Stake, Sports Director
Office Address:
645 25th Ave. North, Wisconsin Rapids, WI
54495.
Baseball:
MLB - Milwaukee Brewers.
College Sports:
Basketball, Football - University of
Wisconsin.
Football:
NFL - Green Bay Packers.

WFIN RADIO
551 LAKE CASCADES PKWY
FINDLAY, OH 45840
419-422-4545
Fax: 419-422-6736
wfin@wfin.com
www.wfin.com
• Sandra J. Kozlevcar, General Manager
• Chris Miller, Sports Director
Nature of Sports Service:
News.
Baseball:
MLB - Cleveland Indians.
College Sports:
Basketball, Football - Ohio State University.

WFIS-AM
1318 NORTH MAIN STREET
FOUNTAIN INN, SC 29644
864-963-5991
Fax: 864-963-5992
wfis16@aol.com
• Joe Lastringer, President/Sports & News
Director
• David Rich, Advertising Manager
contagioustalk@aol.com
Description:
Music, News, Sports.

WFLF-AM
2500 MAITLAND CENTER PARKWAY
SUITE 401
MAITLAND, FL 32751-4122
407-916-7800
Fax: 407-661-1940
www.540wfla.com
• Tom Morgan, Sports Director
tommorgan@clearchannel.com

Description:
News, Talk.

WFMB-AM SPORTS RADIO 1450
3055 S. 4TH ST
SPRINGFIELD, IL 62703
217-528-3033
Fax: 217-528-5348
sportsradio1450@sportsradio1450.com
www.sportsradio1450.com
• Kevin O'Dea, General Manager
• Jeff Hofmann, News Director
Nature of Sports Service:
24-hour sports.
Baseball:
MLB - Chicago Cubs.
Basketball:
NBA - Chicago Bulls.
Football:
NFL - Chicago Bears.

WFMQ-FM
1 CUMBERLAND SQ
LEBANON, TN 37087-3408
615-444-2562
800-467-0562
Fax: 615-444-2569
www.cumberland.edu
Description:
Music, News, Sports.

WFNR
7080 LEE HIGHWAY
RADFORD, VA 24141
540-731-6006
Fax: 540-633-2998
www.nrvtoday.com
• Ron Walton, General Manager
• Steve Gore, Sports Editor
• Rick Watson, Sports Director
• Scott Stevens, Program Director
Nature of Sports Service:
Local. Sports, News, Talk.
Auto Sports:
Indianapolis 500; Brick Yard 400.
Baseball:
MLB - Atlanta Braves.
College Sports
Football - University of Virginia.
Football:
NFL - Washington Redskins.

WFNR-AM
7080 LEE HIGHWAY
RADFORD, VA 24141-8503
540-731-6000
Fax: 540-633-2998
• Wes Watson, News Director
(540) 731-6015
Description:
News, Talk.

WFNZ-AM 610 SPORTS RADIO
1520 SOUTH BLVD, STE 300
CHARLOTTE, NC 28203
704-319-9369
Fax: 704-319-3933
www.wfnz.com
• Bill Schoening, General Manager
• DJ Stout, Operations Manager
Nature of Sports Service:
Local. 24-hour sports radio programming.

WFPR-AM
200 EAST THOMAS STREET
HAMMOND, LA 70401-3316

985-345-0060
Fax: 985-345-1110
• Ken Benitez, News Director
(985) 878-2265
Description:
Music, News, Sports, Talk.

WFRD-FM
DARTMOUTH COLLEGE 3RD FLOOR
HANOVER, NH 03755-0957
603-646-3313
Fax: 603-643-7655
wdcr-wfrd@dartmouth.edu
www.dartmouth.edu/community/broadcast/w
frd
• Vikash Reddy, Program Director
Description:
Music, News, Sports.

WFRM-AM
9 SOUTH MAIN STREET
COUDERSPORT, PA 16915
814-274-8600
Fax: 814-274-0760
whks@verizon.net
• Jason Saulter,
(814) 274-8600
• Pat Kostur,
(814) 642-7004
Description:
Radio station broadcasting High School
sports, locally produced Sports Talk
programming and Pittsburgh Pirates
baseball.

WFRX-AM
1822 NORTH COURT
MARION, IL 62959
618-997-8123
Fax: 618-993-2319
brucefasol@clearchannel.com
wfrx-ampet.ip2m.com
• Bruce Fasol, Sports Director
(618) 997-8123
• April Ruebke, News Director
(618) 997-8123
aprilruebke@clearchannel.com
• Art Smith, Advertising Manager
artsmith@clearchannel.com
Description:
Music, News, Sports.

WFSE-FM
COMPTON HALL ROOM 102
EDINBORO, PA 16444
814-732-2641
timothychizmar@yahoo.com
www.edinboro.edu/cwis/wfse/
• Randy Schriber, General Manager
eupmetal@hotmail.com
• Rob Smith, Sports Director
wfsepsadept@hotmail.com
Description:
Music, News, Sports.

WFTG-AM
534 TOBACCO ROAD
LONDON, KY 40743
606-864-2148
Fax: 606-864-0645
• Brian Sizemore, News Director
(606) 280-2749
Description:
Music.

WFUV-FM
441 EAST FORDHAM ROAD
BRONX, NY 10458
718-817-4550
Fax: 718-817-5595
thefolks@wfuv.org
www.wfuv.org
• Bob Ahrens, Sports Producer
(718) 817-4550
bahrens@wfuv.org
• John Platt, Marketing Director
johnplatt@wfuv.org
• Julianne Welby, News Director
(718) 817-4557
Description:
Music, News, Sports.

WFXE-FM
2203 WYNNTON ROAD
COLUMBUS, GA 31906
706-576-3565
Fax: 706-576-3683
www.foxie105.com
• Carlos Williams, Sports Director
Description:
Music.

WFYY-FM
450 STATE ROUTE 204
SELINSGROVE, PA 17870
570-374-8819
800-871-9456
Fax: 570-374-7444
www.y106.fm
• Peggy Chamberlain, News Director
(570) 374-5711
maxmedianews@yahoo.com
Description:
Music, News, Sports.

WGAB
1180 MAPLE LANE
NEWBURGH, IN 47630
812-451-2422
• Don Davis, General Manager
• Nick Patrick, Director
Nature of Sports Service:
Local. 24-hour sports radio programming.

WGAD
750 WALNUT ST
GADSDEN, AL 35901
256-546-1611
Fax: 256-547-9062
www.wgad.com
• Mike McGowan, General Manager
(256) 546-1611
• Angie Strawn, General Sales Manager
(256) 546-1611
• Scott Chambers, News Director
(256) 546-1611
Nature of Service:
News, Talk, Sports.
Primary Audience:
Adults 25-64.
Sports:
Braves Baseball, Alabama
Football/Basketball, High School Football.

WGAD-AM
PO BOX 1350
GADSDEN, AL 35902-1350
256-546-1611
Fax: 256-547-9062
www.wgad.com

• Dave Hedrick, President
(256) 546-1611
• Mike Hathcock, Sports Director
(256) 546-1611
Description:
Music, News, Sports, Talk.

WGAI-AM
PO BOX 1408
ELIZABETH CITY, NC 27906-1408
252-335-4371
Fax: 252-441-8063
• Mike Smith, General Manager
(252) 449-6074
Description:
Music, News, Sports, Talk.

WGAN
420 WESTERN AVE
SOUTH PORTLAND, ME 04106
207-774-4561
Fax: 207-774-3788
• Cary Pahigian, General Manager
• Doug Tribou, Program Director
Nature of Sports Service:
News, Talk, Sports.

WGAN-AM
420 WESTERN AVENUE
SOUTH PORTLAND, ME 04106
207-774-4561
Fax: 207-774-3788
www.56wgan.com
• Jeff Wade, Program Director
Description:
News, Talk.

WGAP-AM
517 WATT ROAD
KNOXVILLE, TN 37933
865-675-4105
Fax: 865-675-4859
• Alex Carroll, Advertising Manager
• Brian Tatum, News Director
Description:
Music, News, Sports.

WGAW-AM
362 GREEN STREET 362 GREEN STREET
GARDNER, MA 01440
978-632-1332
Fax: 978-630-3011
www.1340.com
• Chris Thompson, General Manager
(978) 630-8700
Description:
Music.

WGBK-FM
4000 WEST LAKE AVENUE
GLENVIEW, IL 60025
847-486-4487
Fax: 847-486-4439
oswald@gbsradio.com
www.glenbrook.k12.il.us/gbsbro/wgbkhome.
htm
• Daniel Oswald, General Manager
Description:
Educational, Music.

WGCM-AM
10250 LORRAINE ROAD
GULFPORT, MS 39503

228-896-5500
Fax: 228-896-0458
gwen@kicker108.com
• Pat McGowan, Program Director
pat@coast102.com
Description:
Music, News, Sports.

WGCY-FM
607 SOUTH SANGAMON AVENUE
GIBSON CITY, IL 60936-1720
217-784-8661
888-784-9429
Fax: 217-784-8677
• Jim Killian, News Director
jimkillian@hotmail.com
Description:
Music, News, Sports.

WGET
1560 FAIRFIELD RD
GETTYSBURG, PA 17325
717-334-3101
Fax: 717-334-5822
www.wget.com
• Cindy Ford, General Manager
• Dave Jackson, Sports Director
Nature of Sports Service:
Country Music, Sports.
Baseball:
MLB - Philadelphia Phillies.
College Sports:
Basketball, Football - Penn State University.
Football:
NFL - Washington Redskins.

WGFR-FM
640 BAY ROAD
QUEENSBURY, NY 12804-1408
518-743-2300
Fax: 518-745-1433
www.wgfr.org
• Kevin Ankeny, General Manager
(518) 743-2300
Description:
Music, News, Sports.

WGGA-AM
1102 THOMPSON BRIDGE ROAD
GAINESVILLE, GA 30501-1706
770-532-9921
800-552-9386
Fax: 770-532-0506
news@wdun.com
am1240wgga.com
• Tony Schiavone, Sports Director
Description:
News, Sports, Talk.

WGH-AM THE SCORE
5589 GREENWICH RD, STE 200
VIRGINIA BEACH, VA 23462
757-497-1310
Fax: 757-671-1010
• William Whitlow, General Manager
• Tony Mercurio, Program Director
• Jason Baker, Sports Sales
• Greg Hastings, Promotions
• Tony Mercurio, Sports Director
Nature of Sports Service:
Local. 24-hour sports radio programming.

WGHB-AM
PIRATE RADIO 1250 & 930
PO BOX 3333
GREENVILLE, NC 27836

252-317-1250
Fax: 252-753-4122
www.pirateradio1250.com
• Wes Hines, News Director
Description:
Music, News, Sports.

WGHT-AM
1878 LINCOLN AVENUE
POMPTON LAKES, NJ 07442-1611
973-839-1500
Fax: 973-839-2400
www.ghtradio.com
• Jonathan Fass, Sports Director
• John Silliman, President
• Debra Valentine, News Director
(973) 839-2424
Description:
Music, News, Sports.

WGL-AM
2000 LOWER HUNTINGTON ROAD
FORT WAYNE, IN 46819-1233
260-747-1511
Fax: 260-747-3999
www.wgl1250.com
• Dean Jackson, Sports Director
• B.J. Steele, Program Director
Description:
Talk.

WGLU-FM
2447 BEDFORD STREET SUITE 101
JOHNSTOWN, PA 15904-1405
814-534-8975
800-539-9458
Fax: 814-266-9212
www.power99online.com
• Mitch Edwards, Sports Director
(814) 534-8975
• Amy Wright, News Director
Description:
Music, News, Sports.

WGLV-FM
140 MAIN STREET
ESSEX JUNCTION, VT 05452
802-878-8885
Fax: 802-879-6835
www.thelightradio.net
• Rick McClary, General Manager
Description:
Music, News, Sports.

WGMA-AM
301 WEST MAIN STREET
SPINDALE, NC 28160-1234
828-287-5150
Fax: 828-287-0081
• Neil Murray, News Director
Description:
Music, News, Sports.

WGMN-AM
3807 BRANDON AVENUE
ROANOKE, VA 24018
540-725-1220
Fax: 540-725-1245
wgmn@clearchannel.com
www.wgmn.cc
• Steve Curtis, Sports Director
(540) 725-1220
stevecurtis@clearchannel.com
• Aaron Roberts, Program Director

WGN-AM
435 NORTH MICHIGAN AVENUE
CHICAGO, IL 60611-4099
312-222-4730
Fax: 312-222-5165
www.wgnradio.com
• Wes Bleed, News Director
• Lori Brayer, Marketing Director
• Dave Eanet, Sports Director
(312) 222-2141
• Mike Ferrin, Sports Producer
(312) 222-4730
• Andy Masur, Sports Reporter
(312) 222-5094
Description:
Music, News, Sports, Talk.

WGNC
1416 SHELBY HWY
CHERRYVILLE, NC 28021
704-435-3297
866-696-5343
Fax: 704-435-1217
netoldies@aol.com
• Calvin Hastings, General Manager/Sales
(704) 435-3297
netoldies@aol.com
• Andy Foster, Sports Director/Music
• Mike Hoyle, Operations Manager/Program
Director
• Anna McGinnis, News Director
• Terresa Hastings, Traffic Director
Baseball:
MLB - Atlanta Braves.
College Sports:
Basketball, Football - University of North
Carolina.
Football:
NFL - Carolina Panthers.

WGOM-AM
820 SOUTH PENNSYLVANIA STREET
MARION, IN 46953
765-664-7396
Fax: 765-668-6767
www.wmri.com
• Jim Brunner, Sports Director
(765) 664-7396
production@wmri.com
• Mike Jenkins, News Director
(765) 664-7396
• David Poehler, Vice President
(765) 664-7396
Description:
News, Sports, Talk.

WGOW-AM
821 PINEVILLE ROAD
CHATTANOOGA, TN 37405-2601
423-756-6141
Fax: 423-266-1652
wgow@wgow.com
www.wgow.com/am
• Kevin West, News Director
(423) 756-6141
• Kenneth Yamada, Advertising Sales
Description:
News, Talk.

WGR 55 SPORTS RADIO
500 CORPORATE PKWY, STE 200
AMHERST, NY 14226
716-843-0060
Fax: 716-832-3080
www.wgr55.com

• Tim Wenger, Operations Manager
• Bob Gaughan, Sports Director
• Andrea Glinski, Promotions Director
Nature of Sports Service:
24 Hour Sports.

WGRE-FM
609 SOUTH LOCUST STREET
GREENCASTLE, IN 46135-2047
765-658-4642
Fax: 765-658-4693
• Wes Anderson, Sports Director
• Lisa Chambers, News Director
Description:
Music, News, Sports.

WGRM-AM
1110 WRIGHT STREET
GREENWOOD, MS 38930
662-453-1240
Fax: 662-453-1241
• Tony Byrd, News Director
Description:
Music, News, Sports.

WGRM-FM
1110 WRIGHT STREET
GREENWOOD, MS 38930
662-453-1240
Fax: 662-453-1241
• Tony Byrd, News Director
Description:
Music, News, Sports.

WHAI-FM/WPVQ
81 WOODWARD ROAD
GREENFIELD, MA 01301
413-774-4301
Fax: 413-773-5637
www.whai.com
• Hugh Maffey, News Director
• Jeff Tirrell, Sports Director
(413) 774-4301
Description:
Music, News, Sports.

WHAN-AM
11337 ASHCAKE ROAD
ASHLAND, VA 23005-0148
804-798-1010
Fax: 804-798-7933
info@whan1430.com
www.whan1430.com
• Skip Andrews, Program Director
• Bill Roberts, Advertising Manager
Description:
Music, News, Sports.

WHB-AM
6721 WEST 121ST STREET
OVERLAND PARK, KS 66209
913-344-1500
Fax: 913-344-1599
www.810whb.com
• Todd Leabo, News Director/Sports VP
toddleabo@810whb.com
Description:
Music, News, Sports, Talk.

WHBC-FM
550 MARKET AVENUE SOUTH
CANTON, OH 44702-2112
330-456-7166
Fax: 330-456-7199

pcook@whbc.com
www.mix941.com
• Pam Cook, News Director
• Jim Johnson, Sports Director
(330) 456-7166
Description:
Music.

WHBG-AM
130 MEDIA LANE
HARRISONBURG, VA 22801
540-434-0331
Fax: 540-432-0129
www.valleyradio.com
• Karl Magenhofer, News Director
Description:
ESPN Satellite Shows

WHBN-AM
2063 SHAKERTOWN ROAD
DANVILLE, KY 40422
859-236-2711
Fax: 859-236-1461
hometownradio@bellsouth.net
• Steve Bertram, Sports Director
(859) 236-2711
• Samantha Irvin, News Director
• Robert Wagner, Sports Director
Description:
Music, News, Sports.
Sports Discussed:
Local High School Teams and University of Kentucky
Frequency:
1420

WHBQ SPORTS 56
SPORTS56 WJBQ
6080 MT. MORIAH
MEMPHIS, TN 38115
901-375-9324
888-360-8255
Fax: 901-794-5356
www.sports56whbq.com
• Dave Green, General Manager
Baseball:
MLB - St. Louis Cardinals, Memphis Redbirds
Basketball:
NBA - Memphis Grizzlies.
College Sports:
Basketball, Football - Ole Miss, Notre Dame Football
Football:
NFL - Tennessee Titans

WHBU 1240
9821 S. 800 W.
DALEVILLE, IN 47334
765-378-2080
Fax: 765-378-2090
www.whbu.com
• Doug Edge, General Manager
• John Fox, Sports Director
• Mike Michael, Program Director
Nature of Sports Service:
News/Sports.
Baseball:
MLB - Chicago White Sox, Chicago Cubs.
College Sports:
Purdue University - Football, Basketball.

WHBU-AM
9821 SOUTH 800 W.
DALEVILLE, IN 47334

765-378-2080
Fax: 765-378-2090
www.indianahoops.com/whbu
• Leland Franklin, Program Director
(765) 378-2080
• Jay Garrison, Sports Director
(765) 288-4403
Description:
News, Sports, Talk.

WHBY-AM
2800 EAST COLLEGE AVENUE
APPLETON, WI 54915-3200
920-733-6639
866-887-1150
Fax: 920-739-0494
whbyam@wcinet.com
www.whby.com
• Bill Scott, Sports Director
(920) 831-5646
• Dave Edwards, Talk Host/Program Director
dedwards@wcinet.com
• Justin Hull, Talk Host
Description:
Talk.
Sports Discussed:
Football, Baseball, basketball, hockey, golf - most all
Frequency:
1150 AM

WHCC-FM
304 STATE ROAD 446
BLOOMINGTON, IN 47401-8837
812-336-8000
Fax: 812-336-7000
whcc105@whcc105.com
www.whcc105.com/
• Jeremy Gray, Sports/News Director
vina4pres04@yahoo.com
• Sheila Stephen, Promotions Director
Description:
Music, News.

WHCY-FM
45 MITCHELL AVENUE
FRANKLIN, NJ 07416
973-827-2525
Fax: 973-827-2135
www.max1063.com
• Alexandra Vallejo, News Director
(973) 823-6170
alexandravallejo@clearchannel.com
Description:
Music, News, Sports.

WHDL-AM
3163 NEW YORK STATE, ROUTE 417
OLEAN, NY 14760-1853
716-372-0161
800-877-9749
Fax: 716-372-0164
• Dick Hannon, Advertising Manager
• Gary Nease, Sports/News Director
Description:
Music.

WHEN
500 PLUM ST, STE 100
SYRACUSE, NY 13204
315-472-9797
Fax: 315-472-2323
www.sybercuse.com/when
• Joel Delmonico, General Manager
• Ted Deluca, Sports Director

Nature of Sports Service:
24-hour sports.
Baseball:
MLB - New York Yankees; Minor League - International League/AAA - Syracuse SkyChiefs.
College Sports:
Basketball, Football, Ice Hockey - Syracuse University.
Football:
NFL - New York Jets.

WHHB-FM
370 HOLLIS ST
HOLLISTON, MA 01746-1135
508-429-0681
www.whhb.com
• Chris Murphy, Advisor
(508) 429-0677
Description:
Music, News, Sports.

WHHS-FM
200 MILL ROAD
HAVERTOWN, PA 19083-3718
610-446-7111
Fax: 610-853-5952
www.whhs.org
• Gail Dornenberg, Sports Director
(610) 446-7111
• Kristy Jost, News Director
Description:
Educational, Music, News, Sports, Talk.

WHIP-AM
2432 HIGHWAY 115
MOORESVILLE, NC 28115-0600
704-664-9447
Fax: 704-664-5551
• Gary Trexler, News Director
Description:
Music, News, Sports.

WHIT
2740 SKI LANE
MADISON, WI 53713
608-273-1000
Fax: 608-271-8182
• Tom Walker, General Manager
• John Sylvester, Operations Manager Program Director
• Chris Krok, Promotions Manager
Nature of Sports Service:
Local. 24-hour sports.

WHKS-AM
42 NORTH MAIN STREET
PORT ALLEGANY, PA 16743
814-642-7004
Fax: 814-642-9491
whks@verizon.net
Description:
Varsity sports, Music, News, Talk

WHOC-AM
1016 WEST BEACON STREET
PHILADELPHIA, MS 39350-3204
601-656-1490
Fax: 601-656-1491
wwslfm@yahoo.com
• Joe Vines, Advertising Manager/News & Sports Director
(601) 656-7102
Description:
Music.

WHOL-AM
1125 COLORADO STREET
ALLENTOWN, PA 18103
610-434-4801
Fax: 484-223-0088
• Alfa Lopez, News Director
(610) 434-4081
Description:
Full Service, Music, News.

WHTC-AM
87 CENTRAL AVENUE
HOLLAND, MI 49423
616-392-3121
Fax: 616-392-8066
www.whtc.com
• Gary Stevens, News Director
Description:
Music, News, Sports, Talk.

WHTG-AM
2355 WEST BANGS AVENUE
NEPTUNE, NJ 07753-4111
732-918-1000
Fax: 732-774-4974
www.g1063.com
• John Dzuiba, General Manager
(732) 774-4755
johnd@g1063.com
Description:
Music, News, Sports.

WHTG-FM
2355 WEST BANGS AVENUE
NEPTUNE, NJ 07753-4111
732-774-4755
Fax: 732-774-7315
www.g1063.com
• Chris Brown, Promotions Director
• Keith Rella, News Director
(732) 774-4755
Description:
Music, News, Sports.

WHTK
207 MIDTOWN PLAZA
ROCHESTER, NY 14604
585-454-4884
Fax: 585-454-5081
www.wham1180.com
• Ken Spitger, General Manager
• Bob Mathews, Sports Director
Nature of Sports Service:
Local. Talk, Sports.
Baseball:
Minor League - International
League/AAA/Rochester Red Wings.
College Sports:
Football - Notre Dame University.

WHTK-AM
207 MIDTOWN PLAZA
ROCHESTER, NY 14604-2016
585-454-3942
Fax: 585-454-5081
• Randy Gorbman, News Director
(585) 454-3942
• Jeff Howlett, General Manager
(585) 454-3942
jeffhowlett@clearchannel.com
Description:
Talk.

WHTL-FM
PO BOX 66
WHITEHALL, WI 54773

715-538-4341
800-823-9485
Fax: 715-538-4360
marty@whtlradio.com
• Marty Little, Program/Sports Director
(715) 538-4341
Description:
Music.

WHTQ-FM
4192 JOHN YOUNG PARKWAY
ORLANDO, FL 32804-2620
407-422-9890
Fax: 407-291-4879
www.whtq.com
• Wes Halliwell, Promotion Manager
(321) 281-2053
Description:
Music, News, Sports.

WHYN-AM
1331 MAIN STREET
SPRINGFIELD, MA 01103-1669
413-781-1011
Fax: 413-734-4434
johnbaicak@clearchannel.com
www.whyn.com
• John Baibak, News Director
(413) 781-1011
johnbaibak@clearchannel.com
Description:
News, Talk.

WIBC
40 MONUMENT CIRCLE
INDIANAPOLIS, IN 46204
317-266-9422
888-240-6397
Fax: 317-684-2021
www.wibc.com
• Tom Severino, General Manager
Football:
NFL - Indianapolis Colts.

WIBM-AM
1700 GLENSHIRE DRIVE
JACKSON, MI 49201-8302
517-787-9546
Fax: 517-787-7517
www.wkhm.com
• Marc Daly, Program Director
• Bruce Goldsen, Owner
bgoldsen@k1053.com
Description:
Music, News.

WIBN-FM
P.O. BOX 25
OXFORD, IN 47971-0025
765-385-2373
Fax: 765-385-2374
www.981wibn.com
• John Balvich, General Manager
(765) 385-2373
• Chris Wagner, Sports Director
(765) 385-2373
Description:
Music, News, Sports.

WIBR
650 WOODALE BLVD
BATON ROUGE, LA 70806
225-926-1106
Fax: 225-928-1606
• Don Nelson, General Manager
• Charles Hanagriff, Sports Director

Nature of Sports Service:
24-hour sports.
Baseball:
MLB - Houston Astros.
College Sports:
Football, CBS; Basketball - Southeastern
Louisiana.
Football:
NFL - CBS Game of the Week.

WIBW AM 580 RADIO
1210 EXECUTIVE DR
TOPEKA, KS 66615
785-272-3456
Fax: 785-228-7282
• Craig Colboch, General Manager
• Greg Sharpe, Program Director/Sports
• Ed O'Donnell, Operations Director
Nature of Sports Service:
Fox Sports Radio.
Baseball:
MLB - Kansas City Royals.

WICK-AM
1049 NORTH SEKOL ROAD
SCRANTON, PA 18504-1040
570-344-1221
Fax: 570-344-0996
www.wick-am.com
• Dean Corwin, News Director
• Mike Remish, Sports Director
Description:
Music.

WICO-AM
919 ELLEGOOD STREET
SALISBURY, MD 21801
410-219-3500
Fax: 410-548-1543
www.wicoam.com
• Bill Reddish, News Director
Description:
News, Talk.

WIGG-AM
959 NORTH MAGNOLIA DRIVE
WIGGINS, MS 39577-3630
601-928-7281
Fax: 601-528-5011
• A. R. Byrd, Advertising Manager
• Tony Coslik, Assignment Editor
Description:
Music, News, Sports.

WIKC-AM
PO BOX 638
BOGALUSA, LA 70427-2229
504-732-4190
Fax: 504-732-7594
• Gardner S. Adams, Jr., General Manager
timberlands@bellsouth.net
Description:
Music, News, Sports, Talk.

WILD-AM
90 WARREN STREET
BOSTON, MA 02119-3259
617-472-9447
Fax: 617-472-9474
www.wildam1090.com
• Rick Anderson, Program Director
(617) 472-9447
randerson@radio-one.com
• Willie Maye, Sports Director
(617) 472-9447
wmaye@radio-one.com

Description:
Music, News, Sports.

WILQ-FM
1685 FOUR MILE DRIVE
WILLIAMSPORT, PA 17701-1938
570-323-8200
800-377-1051
Fax: 570-323-5075
www.wilq.com
• John Finn, News Director
Description:
Music, News, Sports.

WILT-AM
22 SIXTH STREET
STROUDSBURG, PA 18360
570-421-2100
800-570-1013
Fax: 570-421-2040
www.wilk.microserve.net
• Joe Thomas, News Director
(570) 421-2100
Description:
News.

WIMA-AM
667 WEST MARKET STREET
LIMA, OH 45801
419-223-2060
Fax: 419-229-3888
davewoodward@clearchannel.com
www.1150wima.com
• Jeff Gunter, News Director
(419) 223-2060
jeffgunter@clearchannel.com
Description:
News, Talk.

WIMZ-FM
1100 SHARPS RIDGE ROAD
KNOXVILLE, TN 37917
865-525-6000
Fax: 865-525-2000
www.wimz.com
• Terry Gillingham, General Manager
(865) 329-8501
Description:
Music, News, Sports.

WINW-AM
4111 MARTINDALE ROAD, N.E.
CANTON, OH 44705-2727
330-454-3377
Fax: 330-492-5633
• Curtis Perry, General Manager/Promotion
Director
(330) 454-1520
Description:
Music, News, Sports.

WIP SPORTSRADIO 610
441 N. FIFTH ST
PHILADELPHIA, PA 19123
215-922-5000
Fax: 215-922-2434
www.610wip.com
• Marc Rayfield, Vice President/General
Manager
• Tom Bigby, Station Manager/Pro General
Manager
• Jon Latzer, General Sales Manager
• Brian Navy, National Sales Manager
• Will Chapman, Local Sales Manager
Nature of Sports Service:
Local, 24-hour sports radio programming.

WIQB-AM
11640 HIGHWAY 17 BYPASS
MURRELLS INLET, SC 29576
843-651-7869
Fax: 843-651-3197
• Kelly Broderick, Program Director
Description:
Music, News, Sports.

WIRO
134 4TH AVE
HUNTINGTON, WV 25701
304-525-7788
Fax: 304-525-3299
• Judy Jennings-Riffe, General Manager
• Paul Swan, Sports Director
Nature of Sports Service:
Local. 24-hour sports radio programming.

WIRQ-FM
260 COOPER ROAD
ROCHESTER, NY 14617-3049
585-336-3065
Fax: 585-336-2929
• Nick Graveoey, Program Director
finisher@musician.org
Description:
Music, News, Sports.

WIRY-AM
301 CORNELIA STREET
PLATTSBURGH, NY 12901-2308
518-563-1340
Fax: 518-563-1343
wiry@wiry.com
www.wiry.com
• Alan Drake, News/Sports Director
• Ann Tarasavage, Advertising Manager
yoe@yoe.com
• Ducky Drake, News Director; Sports
Director
(518) 563-1340
wiry@wiry.com
Description:
Music, News, Sports.

WISK-FM
1028 ADDERTON STREET
AMERICUS, GA 31709
229-924-6500
Fax: 229-928-2337
www.americusradio.com
• Steve Lashley, Promotion Manager
Description:
Music, News, Sports.

WIUS-AM
815 E 8TH ST
BLOOMINGTON, IN 47408-3842
812-855-7862
Fax: 812-855-1073
www.wius.org
• Carl Gutierez, News Director
• Bryan Scheets, Sports Director
Description:
Music, News, Sports.

WIVQ-FM
3905 PROGRESS BOULEVARD
PERU, IL 61354
815-224-2100
Fax: 815-224-2066
• Cole Studstill, Program Director
• Jared White, Sports Director

WIVV-AM
1409 PONCE DE LEON AVENUE 4TH
FLOOR
SAN JUAN, PUERTO RIC 00907
787-724-1190
Fax: 787-722-5395
radio@therockradio.org
• Ruth Luttrel, General Manager
Description:
Music, News, Sports.

WIXX-FM
P.O. BOX 23333
GREEN BAY, WI 54301
920-435-3771
Fax: 920-444-1155
www.wixx.com
• Jerry Bader, News Director
Description:
Music, News, Sports.

WJAG-AM
309 BRAASCH AVENUE
NORFOLK, NE 68701-4113
402-371-0780
Fax: 402-371-6303
www.wjag.com/
• Jim Curry, News Director
• Joe Tjaden, Sports Director
jtjaden@wjag.com
Description:
Sports

WJAW-FM
PO BOX 708
MARIETTA, OH 45750
800-371-1490
Fax: 740-373-1717
news@morganco.net
www.wjawfm.com
• Andrew Rex, News Director

WJBC
236 GREENWOOD AVENUE
BLOOMINGTON, IL 61704
309-829-1221
Fax: 309-827-8071
newsroom@wjbc.com
www.wjbc.com
• Red Pitcher, General Manager
• Greg Halbleib, Sports Director
• R C McPride, Program Director
Auto Sports:
NASCAR.
Baseball:
MLB - St. Louis Cardinals.
College Sports:
Illinois State and Illinois Wesleyan FB and
BB
Football
NFL - Monday Night Football

WJBO-AM
5555 HILTON AVENUE SUITE 500
BATON ROUGE, LA 70808-2564
225-231-1860
Fax: 225-231-1873
www.wjbo.com
• Robert Lee, News Director
• Jill Stokold, Promotions Director
Description:
News, Talk.

WJCI-AM
129 NORTH GARRARD
RANTOUL, IL 61866

217-893-1460
Fax: 217-893-0884
• Gary Voss, General Manager
whpo@whporadio.com
Description:
Music, Talk.

WJDB-FM
30280 HIGHWAY 43
THOMASVILLE, AL 36784
334-636-4438
800-245-9532
Fax: 334-636-4439
• Ivey Griffin, Marketing/Advertising
Manager
wjdbradio@yahoo.com
Description:
Music, News, Sports.

WJDK-FM
219 WEST WASHINGTON STREET
MORRIS, IL 60450-2146
815-941-1000
Fax: 815-941-9300
• Mike Haensel, News Director
• Larry Nelson, President
(815) 941-1000
Description:
Music, News, Sports.

WJEL-FM
1901 EAST 86TH STREET
INDIANAPOLIS, IN 46240-2347
317-259-5278
• Rob Hendrix, Program Director
(317) 259-5278
Description:
Music, News, Sports.

WJFD-FM, INC.
651 ORCHARD STREET
SUITE 300
NEW BEDFORD, MA 02744
508-997-2929
Fax: 508-990-3893
claudia@wjfd.com
www.wjfd.com
• Manuel Calado, News Director
• Jorge Morais, General Manager
Description:
Music.

WJGA-FM
PO BOX 878
JACKSON, GA 30233
770-775-3151
Fax: 770-775-5153
• Don Earnhart, Sports Director
(770) 775-3151
• Don Earnhart, Sports Director
Description:
Music.

WJJB-AM
779 WARREN AVENUE
PORTLAND, ME 04103-1007
207-773-9695
Fax: 207-761-4406
morningjab@yahoo.com
www.bigjab.com
• Dave Shumacher, Program Director
(207) 773-9695
Description:
Talk.

WJJC-AM
153 BILL ANDERSON BOULEVARD
COMMERCE, GA 30529
706-335-3155
Fax: 706-335-1905
www.nbank.net/net/~wjjc/
• Rick Bennett, Sports Director
• Rob Jordan, Advertisin Sales/Sports
Director

WJJO-FM
2740 SKI LANE
MADISON, WI 53711
608-273-1000
Fax: 608-271-8182
www.wjjo.com
• Randy Hawke, Program Director
(608) 441-3705
randy.hawke@wjjo.com
Description:
Music, News, Sports.

WJJQ-AM
81 EAST MOHAWK DRIVE
TOMAHAWK, WI 54487-8618
715-453-4482
Fax: 715-453-7169
wjjq@wjjq.com
www.wjjq.wjjq.com
• Gregg Albert, Program Director
galbert@wjjq.com
Description:
ESPN Sports Talk Event.
Year Founded:
1984

WJJT-AM
PO BOX 88
230 N FLORENCE AVE
JELLICO, TN 37762
423-494-1582
Fax: 423-784-5991
wjjtradio@gmail.com
www.jellicosgospellight.com
• James Kilgore, President & CEO
(423) 494-1582
• John Blankenship, Jr., General Manager
(606) 524-5123
johnsjsclean@gmail.com
Description:
Gospel music, news, sports and weather

WJOX-AM SPORTS RADIO
244 GOODWIN CREST DR
BIRMINGHAM, AL 35209
205-945-4646
Fax: 205-945-3999
• Terry Bond, General Manager
• Don Leo, Sports Director
Nature of Sports Service:
Local. 24-hour sports radio programming.
Baseball:
MLB - Atlanta Braves.
College Sports:
Baseball, Basketball, Football - Auburn
University.

WJPF-AM
1431 COUNTRY AIRE DRIVE
CARTERVILLE, IL 62918-5118
618-985-4955
800-455-3243
Fax: 618-985-5904
www.wjpf.com
• Mike Reis, Sports Director
(618) 985-4955

• Steve Sine, News Director
• Mike Murphy, Sports Host
(618) 985-4955
mikemu@riverradio.net
Description:
Music, News, Talk.

WJPZ-FM
316 WAVERLY AVENUE
SYRACUSE, NY 13210-2437
315-443-4689
Fax: 315-443-2148
www.z89.org
• Joan Kump, Promotions Director
(315) 443-4689
• Jon Versteeg, News Director
• Andrew Gundling, Sports Director
(315) 443-4689
Description:
Music, News, Sports.

WJR-AM
3011 WEST GRAND BOULEVARD
DETROIT, MI 48202-9816
313-875-4440
800-859-0957
Fax: 313-875-9022
www.wjr.com
• Bridget Burns, Promotion Director
• Steve Courtney, Sports Director
(313) 875-4440
swrap760@hotmail.com
• Dick Haefner, News Director
(313) 873-9850
• Bob Schick, Advertising Sales
(313) 873-9752
• Jim Brandstatter, Sports
(313) 875-4440
Description:
Music, News, Sports.

WJRS-FM
P.O. BOX 800
JAMESTOWN, KY 42629-0800
270-343-4444
Fax: 270-866-2060
• Mike Scales, News Director
Description:
Music, News, Sports.

WJTN-AM
2 ORCHARD ROAD, WEST ELLICOTT
JAMESTOWN, NY 14701-8400
716-487-1151
800-879-7393
Fax: 716-664-9326
www.wjtn.com
• Matt Krieg, Sports Director
(716) 487-1151
• Merrill Rosen, General Manager
(716) 487-1151
Description:
Music, News, Sports.

WJUN-AM
OLD ROUTE 22 EAST
MEXICO, PA 17056
717-436-2135
Fax: 717-436-8155
• Dan Roland, News Director
Description:
Music, News, Sports.

WJVL-FM
1 S PARKER DR
JANESVILLE, WI 53545-3928

608-752-7895
Fax: 608-752-4438
www.wjvl.com
• Tim Bremel, Promotions Director
(608) 752-7895
• Al Fagerli, Sports Director
(608) 752-7895
sports@wclo.com
• Mike O'Brien, Advertising Manager
mobrien@wclo.com
• Stan Stricker, News Director
news@wclo.com
Description:
Music.

WJVS-FM
3254 EAST KEMPER ROAD
CINCINNATI, OH 45241-1540
513-612-5816
Fax: 513-771-4928
• Dave Angeline, News Director
angelind@greatoaks.com
Description:
Music, News, Sports.

WKAN AM 1320
2 DEARBORN SQUARE
KANKAKEE, IL 60901
815-935-9555
Fax: 815-935-9593
www.wkan.com
• Gary Wright, General Manager
• Wyatt McKinstry, Sports Director
• Brendan Michaels, Operations Manager
Nature of Sports Service:
Local coverage of high school, college and professional sports.
Auto Sports:
NASCAR
College Sports:
Basketball, Football - University of Illinois.
Football:
NFL - Chicago Bears.

WKAN-AM
70 MEADOW VIEW CENTER SUITE 400
KANKAKEE, IL 60901-3909
815-935-9555
Fax: 815-935-9593
wkan@staradio.com
www.wkan.com
• Bob Kersmarki, General Manager
• Lee Schrock, Sports Director
Description:
Music, News.

WKAV-AM
1150 PEPSI PLACE SUITE 300
CHARLOTTESVILLE, VA 22901
434-978-4408
Fax: 434-978-0723
lindathomas@clearchannel.com
• Tommie McNeil, Jr., News Director
(434) 978-4408
tommiemcneil@clearchannel.com
Description:
Music.

WKBF-AM
3535 EAST KIMBERLY ROAD
DAVENPORT, IA 52807
563-344-7000
Fax: 563-344-7007
markminnick@clearchannel.com
www.qconline/wkbf.com
• Mark Minnick, News Director

Description:
Music.

WKBH-AM SPORTS RADIO
1407 SECOND AVE N.
LA CROSSE, WI 54602
608-779-9157
Fax: 608-782-8340
• Pat Delaney, Owner
Nature of Sports Service:
Local. 24-hour sports radio programming.
ESPN Radio.

WKBK-AM
69 STANHOPE AVENUE
KEENE, NH 03431-3641
603-352-9230
Fax: 603-357-3926
www.wkbkam.com/
• Bob Lund, Sports Director
(603) 352-9230
• Paul Scheuring, News Director
(603) 352-9230
Description:
Music, News, Sports, Talk.

WKCL-FM
528 COLLEGE PARK ROAD
LADSON, SC 29456-3328
843-553-5420
Fax: 843-553-0636
• Carl Wiggins, Station Manager
(843) 553-8740
wkcl@msn.com
Description:
Music, News, Sports, Talk.

WKDE-FM
200 FRAZIER ROAD
ALTAVISTA, VA 24517-0390
434-369-5588
Fax: 434-369-1632
info@kdcountry.com
www.kdcountry.com
• David Hoehne, Advertising Manager/Sports Director
• Kenny Shelton, Program Director/Promotions Manager
• Dave Haney, Sports Director
(434) 369-1055
info@kdcountry.com
Description:
Music, News.

WKEE-FM
134 4TH AVENUE
HUNTINGTON, WV 25701
304-525-7788
800-544-9533
Fax: 304-525-3299
billcornwell@clearchannel.com
• Bill Cornwell, News Director
• Paul Swann, Sports Director
paulswann@clearchannel.com
Description:
Music, News, Sports.

WKEQ
PO BOX 740
SOMERSET, KY 42502
606-678-5151
Fax: 606-678-2026
• Nolan Kenner, General Manager
• Mike Tarter, Station Manager
Office address:
101 First Radio Lane, Somerset KY 42502.

Nature of Sports Service:
Local. 24-hour sports radio programming.
Baseball:
MLB - Cincinnati Reds.

WKGS-FM
207 MIDTOWN PLAZA
ROCHESTER, NY 14604-0840
585-454-4884
Fax: 585-454-5081
www.kiss1067.com
• Erick Anderson, Program Director
Description:
Music, News, Sports.

WKHS-FM
25301 LAMBS MEADOW ROAD
WORTON, MD 21678
410-778-4249
Fax: 410-778-3802
• Steve Kramarck, Program Director
Description:
Music, News, Sports.

WKIX-FM
2581 US HIGHWAY 70 WEST
GOLDSBORO, NC 27530-1934
919-736-1699
800-849-9582
Fax: 919-736-3876
info@curtismedia.com
www.kixonline.com/
• Thomas Vick, News Director
(919) 736-1699
Description:
Music, News, Sports.

WKJQ-FM 97.3
109 IRON HILL ROAD
PARSONS, TN 38363-0576
731-847-3011
Fax: 731-847-4600
ralphclenney@yahoo.com
• Ralph Clenney, Advertising Manager
ralphclenny@yahoo.com
• Steve Clenney, Program Director
Description:
We are now carrying all our sports on WKJQ-FM 97.3. We do live broadcasts of Tennessee Titans Football, U.T. Vols Football, and local high school Football, Basketbal, Baseball and Softball.
Year Founded:
1990

WKKJ-FM
45 MAIN STREET, W.
CHILLICOTHE, OH 45601-0244
740-773-3000
800-686-9555
Fax: 740-774-4494
newsroom@wkkj.com
www.wkkj.com
• Dan Ramey, Sports Director
(740) 773-3000
danramey@clearchannel.com
• Mike Smith, News/Sports Director
(740) 773-3000
mikesmith2@clearchannel.com
• Tracy Taylor, Advertising Manager
(740) 773-3000
tracytaylor@clearchannel.com
Description:
Music, News.

WKKS-FM
1106 FAIRLANE DRIVE
VANCEBURG, KY 41179-1208
606-796-3031
Fax: 606-796-6186
• Kathy Brown, News Director
Description:
Music, News, Sports.

WKLK-AM
1104 CLOQUET AVENUE
CLOQUET, MN 55720-1620
218-879-4534
888-404-9555
Fax: 218-879-1962
wklk@aol.com
www.wklk.com
• Jake Kachinski, News Director
Description:
Music, News, Sports, Talk.

WKLK-FM
1104 CLOQUET AVENUE
CLOQUET, MN 55720-1620
218-879-4534
Fax: 218-879-1962
wklk@aol.com
www.wklk.com
• Jake Kachinski, Program Director
Description:
Music, News, Sports.

WKLV-AM
P.O. BOX 192
BLACKSTONE, VA 23824
804-292-4146
800-849-4146
Fax: 804-292-7669
bobcatcountryradio.com
• Dennis Royer, General Manager
(804) 292-4146
bobcatcountry@hotmail.com
Description:
Music, News, Sports.

WKNH-FM
KEENE STATE COLLEGE
KEENE, NH 03431-4101
603-358-2734
Fax: 603-358-2131
• John Earl, News Director
(603) 358-2734
Description:
Music, News, Sports.

WKNR SPORTS RADIO
1301 EAST 9TH STREET
SUITE 252
CLEVELAND, OH 44114
216-583-9901
Fax: 216-583-9550
www.espncleveland.com
• Dave Urbach, General Manager
• Steve Legerski, Operations Manager
• Larry Gawthrop, General Sales Manager
• Bob Karlovec, Sports Director
• Jason Yarrow, Promotions Director
Nature of Sports Service:
Local. 24-hour sports radio programming.
Baseball:
MLB - Cleveland Indians.

WKNW-AM
1411 ASHMUN STREET
SAULT SAINTE MARIE, MI 49783

906-635-0995
800-866-8255
Fax: 906-635-1216
www.30below.com
• Dave Watson, News Director
(906) 632-1400
Description:
Music, News, Talk.

WKRK-AM
427 HILL STREET
MURPHY, NC 28906
828-837-4332
Fax: 828-837-8610
www.1320am.com
• Tim Radford, Promotion Manager
tim@1320am.com
• Emma Ramsey, Advertising
Manager/News Director
Description:
Music, News, Sports, Talk.

WKRV-FM
P.O. BOX 100
VANDALIA, IL 62471-2810
618-283-2325
Fax: 618-283-1503
wkrv@sbcglobal.net
www.vandaliaradio.com
• John Harris, Advertising
Manager/Promotions Director
wkrv@sbcglobal.net
• Todd Stapleton, News & Sports Director
(618) 283-2325
wkrv@sbcglobal.net
Description:
Educational, Music, News, Sports, Talk.

WKUB-FM
2132 U.S. HIGHWAY 84
BLACKSHEAR, GA 31516-0112
912-449-3391
Fax: 912-449-6284
wkub@almatel.net
• Brian Blount, Sports Director

WKVG-AM
P.O. BOX 1474
JENKINS, KY 41537-1474
606-832-4655
Fax: 606-832-4656
• Jean Martin, Advertising Manager
wkvg@verizon.net
Description:
Music, News, Sports.

WKVM-AM
415 CALLE CARBONEL
SAN JUAN, PUERTO RIC 00918-2866
787-751-1018
Fax: 787-758-9967
• Alan Corales, General Manager
(787) 751-1013
Description:
Music, News, Sports.

WKVX-AM
P. O. BOX 39
WOOSTER, OH 44691
330-264-5122
800-833-9211
Fax: 330-264-3571
www.wqkt.com
• Mike Breckenridge, Program Director
events@wqkt.com
• Craig Walton, Advertising Manager

• Dan Earich, Sports Announcer
(330) 264-5122
events@wqkt.com
Description:
Music, News, Sports.

WKWF-AM
5450 MACDONALD AVENUE
KEY WEST, FL 33040-5738
305-296-7511
Fax: 305-296-0358
www.keysradio.net
• David Harris, General Manager
(305) 852-9085
daveharris@clearchannel.com
Description:
Music, News, Sports.

WKWZ-FM
70 SOUTH WOODS ROAD
SYOSSET, NY 11791-3204
516-364-5746
Fax: 516-364-5737
bigdave5@aol.com
• David Favilla, General Manager
(516) 364-5736
Description:
Music, News, Sports.

WKXQ-FM
108 EAST MAIN STREET
BEARDSTOWN, IL 62618
217-323-1790
800-704-9200
Fax: 217-323-1705
larry.bostwick@gmail.com
www.kool92.iscool.net
• Kevin Bonnard, General Manager
• Dean Ross, Sports Director
(217) 322-3396
Description:
Music.

WKXW-FM
109 WALTERS AVENUE
TRENTON, NJ 08638-1812
609-771-8181
800-876-9599
Fax: 609-406-7956
www.nj1015.com
• Ray Handel, Promotions Director
• Eric Scott, News Director
ericscot@nj1015.com
Description:
Music, News, Sports, Talk.

WKYR-FM
HWY 90 EAST
BURKESVILLE, KY 42717-0340
270-433-7191
Fax: 270-433-7195
wkyr@mchsi.com
• Don Johnson, News Director
Description:
Music, News, Sports.

WKZO-AM
4200 WEST MAIN STREET
KALAMAZOO, MI 49006
269-345-7121
800-742-6590
Fax: 269-345-1436
www.wkzo.com
• Laura Lehman, News Director
• William J. Wertz, Vice President

Description:
News, Talk.

WKZS-FM
820 RAILROAD STREET
COVINGTON, IN 47932-1357
765-793-4823
Fax: 765-793-4644
newspsa@aol.com
www.kiss1031.com
• Greg Green, News Director/Sports Director
greg@kisscountryradio.com
Description:
Music, News, Sports.

WLAP-AM
2601 NICHOLASVILLE ROAD
LEXINGTON, KY 40503-3307
859-293-0563
Fax: 859-299-9527
www.wlap.com
• Karyn Czar, News Director/Reporter
(859) 293-0563
karynczar@clearchannel.com
Description:
News, Talk.

WLBR-AM
ROUTE 72 NORTH
LEBANON, PA 17046
717-272-7651
Fax: 717-274-0161
• Scott Bradley, Sports Director
• Gordon Weise, News Director
Description:
Music.

WLDY-AM
W8746 HIGHWAY 8
LADYSMITH, WI 54848-9565
715-532-5588
Fax: 715-532-7357
wldywjbl@yahoo.com
• Bob Krejcarek, Sports Director
• Jodi Long, News Director
jo_wldy_news@yahoo.com
• Chris Brooks, Station Manager
Description:
Ladysmith High school sports

WLER-FM
112 HOLLYWOOD DRIVE SUITE 203
BUTLER, PA 16001-4917
724-287-5778
Fax: 724-283-3005
newsdesk@bcrnetwork.com
www.wbut.com
• Victoria Hinterberger, Advertising Manager
vickih@bcrnetwork.com
• Cathy Martin, News Director
frontdesk@bcrnetwork.com
• Ron Willison, Sports Director
Description:
Music, News.

WLEY-AM
P.O. BOX 371300
CAYEY, PUERTO RIC 00737-1300
787-758-1300
Fax: 787-738-7744
• Joe Pagan, Station Manager
Description:
Music, News, Sports.

WLFN-AM
1407 2ND AVENUE NORTH
ONALASKA, WI 54650
608-782-8335
Fax: 608-782-8340
• Pat Smith, Station Manager
Description:
Music, News, Sports.

WLGC
PO BOX 685
GREENUP, KY 41144
606-473-7377
Fax: 606-473-5086
• Rob Scheibly, General Manager
• Kent Robinson, Sports Director
Office Address:
Suite A, Main & Harrison, Greenup, KY
41144.
Nature of Sports Service:
Local. 24-hour sports radio programming.
College Sports:
Basketball - Game of the Week; Football -
Notre Dame.
Football:
NFL Game of the Week/Westwood One.

WLHT-FM
50 MONROE, NW SUITE 500
GRAND RAPIDS, MI 49503
616-451-4800
Fax: 616-451-0113
www.wlht.com
• Bruce Parrott, News/Promotions Director
Description:
Music, News, Sports.

WLKF-AM
404 WEST LIME STREET
LAKELAND, FL 33815
863-682-8184
800-227-9797
Fax: 863-683-2409
news@wpcv.com
www.wlkf.com
• Ed Kirkland, Advertising Manager
(863) 682-8184
Description:
Educational, News, Sports, Talk.

WLKL-FM
5001 LAKELAND BLVD.
MATTOON, IL 61938-5209
217-234-5271
Fax: 217-258-6459
• Ken Beno, Sports Director
(217) 234-5271
kbeno@lakeland.cc.il.us
Description:
Music, News, Sports.

WLKR-AM
10327 MILAN ROAD
MILAN, OH 44846
419-668-8151
800-686-9222
Fax: 419-668-9557
www.wlkrradio.com
• Bill Forthofor, Station Manager
• Mike Jeffries, Program Director
• Scott Truxell, News/Sports Director
Description:
News, Sports.
Frequency:
ESPN Radio Network 1510 am

WLKR-FM
10327 MILAN ROAD
MILAN, OH 44846
419-668-8151
800-686-9222
Fax: 419-609-2679
wlkr@accnorwalk.com
www.wlkrradio.com
• Scott Truxell, News Director
s.truxell@wkfm.com
Description:
Music, News, Sports.

WLLG-FM
7606 NORTH STATE STREET
LOWVILLE, NY 13367-1318
315-376-7500
Fax: 315-376-8549
sales@themoose.net
www.themoose.net
• Brian Best, News Director
(315) 376-7500
Description:
Music, News, Sports.

WLLL-AM
105 WHITE HALL ROAD
LYNCHBURG, VA 24501
434-385-9555
888-224-9809
Fax: 434-385-6073
wlllam930@aol.com
• Fletcher Hubbard, General Manager
(434) 385-4587
wlllam930@aol.com
• Bridgette Marie, Program Director
(434) 385-9555
wlllam930@aol.com
• Savanah Hubbard, Traffic Director
(434) 385-9555
wlllam930@aol.com
Description:
Music, News.
Year Founded:
1996

WLLN-AM
910 MCNEILL STREET 910 MCNEILL
STREET
LILLINGTON, NC 27546
910-893-2811
Fax: 910-893-2811
orlandohenao1@hotmail.com
• Orlando Hemau, Program Director
Description:
Music, News, Sports.

WLLY-AM
210 DEACON STREET
WILSON, NC 27895
252-237-5171
Fax: 252-237-5172
• Wallace Bullock, General Manager
Description:
Music, News, Sports.

WLMD-FM
119 WEST CARROLL STREET
MACOMB, IL 61455
309-833-5561
Fax: 309-833-3460
www.radiomacomb.com
• Beau Spencer, Sports Director
• Mike Weaver, News Director

WLOB-AM
779 WARREN AVENUE
PORTLAND, ME 04103-1007
207-773-9695
Fax: 207-761-4406
newstalkwlob@yahoo.com
• J.J. Jeffrey, Program Director
Description:
Music, News.

WLOH-AM
724 SOUTH COLUMBUS STREET
LANCASTER, OH 43130
740-653-4373
Fax: 470-654-7578
www.wloh.net
• Arlene Bohach, General Manager
Description:
Music, News, Sports.

WLOW-FM
1 SAINT AUGUSTINE PLACE
HILTON HEAD ISLAND, SC 29928-4717
843-785-9569
800-768-7600
Fax: 843-842-3369
www.wlow.com
• Chuck Cannon, Program Director
• Michelle Christensen, Marketing Director
(843) 785-9569
Description:
Music, News, Sports, Talk.

WLQM-FM
320 NORTH FRANKLIN STREET
FRANKLIN, VA 23851
757-562-5650
Fax: 757-562-2345
wlqm@wlqmradio.com
www.wlqmradio.com
• Peter Clark, News Director
• Johnny Hart, Promotions Manager
• Tim Parsons, Sports Director
Description:
Music.

WLRT-AM
2845 NORTH ARMISTEAD AVENUE SUITE C
HAMPTON, VA 23666-1657
757-766-9262
800-296-1490
Fax: 757-766-7439
www.racetalklive.com
• Chuck Hall, Advertising/General Manager
(757) 766-1960
Description:
Music, News, Sports.

WLSC-AM
4164 MAIN STREET
LORIS, SC 29569
843-756-1183
Fax: 843-756-0548
wlscradio@yahoo.com
www.wlsradio.com
• Jerry D. Jenrette, Program Director
Description:
Music, News, Sports, Talk.

WLTP-AM
6006 GRAND CENTRAL AVENUE
VIENNA, WV 26105
304-295-6070
Fax: 304-295-4389
www.wltp.com

• Steve Dougherty, Sports Director
(304) 295-6070
stevedougherty@clearchannel.com
• Lorri Ellman, Advertising Manager
(304) 295-6070
lorriellman@clearchannel.com
• Doug Hess, News Director
(304) 295-6070
douglashess@clearchannel.com

WLUR-FM
WEST WASHINGTON STREET
LEXINGTON, VA 24450-0303
540-458-4017
Fax: 540-458-4079
www.wlu.edu/~wlur
• Jeremy Franklin, Program Director
franklinj@wlu.edu
Description:
Music, News, Sports, Talk.

WLW
1111 ST. GREGORY ST
CINCINNATI, OH 45202
513-241-9597
Fax: 513-665-9700
www.700wlw.com
• Mike Kenney, General Manager
• Tom Horan, Vice President/Sports Marketing
Nature of Sports Service:
News.
Baseball:
MLB - Cincinnati Reds.
College Sports:
Football - University of Cincinnati;
Basketball - University of Cincinnati, Xavier.

WMAM-AM
2880 ROOSEVELT ROAD, N.
MARINETTE, WI 54143
715-735-6631
Fax: 715-732-0125
www.quicksilverbroadcasting.com
• Kit Donaldson, Sports Director
Description:
Talk.

WMBA 1460
1316 7TH AVENUE
BEAVER FALLS, PA 15010
724-846-4100
Fax: 724-843-7771
• Donn Wuycik, General Manager
• Jim Frederick, Sports Director
Nature of Sports Service:
News/Sports.
Baseball:
MLB - Pittsburgh Pirates.
Ice Hockey:
NHL - Pittsburgh Penguins.

WMBE-AM AND WCLB
254 WINNEBAGO DRIVE
FOND DU LAC, WI 54935-2447
920-921-1071
Fax: 920-921-0757
• Chuck Freimund, Sports Director
(920) 921-1071
• Randy Hopper, General Manager
(920) 921-1071
• Mark Kastein, Station Manager
(920) 921-1071
• Bob Nelson, News Director
(920) 921-1071

• Ed Mueller, Sales
(920) 921-1071
Description:
Music, News, Sports.

WMCE-FM
501 EAST 38TH STREET
ERIE, PA 16546-0002
814-824-2261
Fax: 304-472-2571
• William Shannon, Advertising Sales Manager/Program Director
(814) 824-2264
• Steve Warzala, Sports Director

WMCR-FM
237 GENESEE STREET
ONEIDA, NY 13421-2701
315-363-6050
Fax: 315-363-9149
• Todd Emanuelli, Sports Director
wwmcrradio@aol.com
• Vivian Warren, General Manager
Description:
Music.

WMEB-FM
5748 MEMORIAL UNION WMEB FM
ORONO, ME 04469-5748
207-581-4340
Fax: 207-581-4343
www.umaine.edu/wemb
• Mathew Avery, Promotions Director
• Ben Jarvela, Promotion Director
benjamin.jarvela@umit.maine.edu
• Alfred Schulz, Program Director
alfred.schulz@umit.maine.edu
• Dustin Son, Sports Director
dustin.son@umit.maine.edu
Description:
Music, News, Sports.

WMEV-FM
1041 RADIO HILL ROAD
MARION, VA 24354
276-783-3151
800-653-3694
Fax: 276-783-3152
www.fm94.com
• Jim Mabe, Promotions Director
supercountry@fm94.com
• Lynn Rutledge, Program Director
lynnr@fm94.com
Description:
Music, News, Sports.

WMFD-AM
25 NORTH KERR AVENUE SUITE C
WILMINGTON, NC 28405-3403
910-791-3088
800-678-5991
Fax: 910-791-0112
www.am630.net
• Doug Carlisle, News Director
(910) 791-3088
Description:
News, Talk.

WMFR-AM
875 WEST 5TH STREET
WINSTON SALEM, NC 27101
336-777-3900
Fax: 336-777-3915
www.triadsports.com
• Mike Fenley, Program Director
(336) 777-3900

Description:
News, Talk.

WMHW-FM
180 MOORE HALL CENTRAL MICHIGAN UNIV.
MOUNT PLEASANT, MI 48859
517-774-7287
Fax: 517-774-2426
wmhw@cmich.edu
www.cmich.edu
• Peter B. Orlik, General Manager
(517) 774-7279
wmhw@cmich.edu
Description:
Music, News, Sports.

WMIK-AM
NORTH 19TH STREET
MIDDLESBORO, KY 40965
606-248-5842
Fax: 606-248-7660
• Roy Shotton, General Manager
Description:
Music, News, Sports.

WMJI-FM
6200 OAK TREE BOULEVARD 4TH FLOOR
INDEPENDENCE, OH 44131
216-520-2600
800-669-1057
Fax: 216-524-2600
www.wmji.com
• R. C. Bauer, News Director
(216) 520-2600
Description:
Music, News, Sports.

WMJK-FM
1640 CLEVELAND ROAD
SANDUSKY, OH 44870-4357
419-625-1010
888-547-8792
Fax: 419-625-1348
www.wmjkradio.com
• Lisa Rice, General Manager
(419) 625-1010
lisajrice@clearchannel.com
Description:
Music.

WMJZ-FM
3687 SOUTH OTSEGO
GAYLORD, MI 49735
989-732-3446
Fax: 989-732-6202
• Mike Reling, Program Director
Description:
Music, News, Sports.

WMKX-FM
51 PICKERING STREET
BROOKVILLE, PA 15825-1245
814-849-8100
877-634-2765
Fax: 814-849-4585
• Kevin Heinrich, Program Director
(814) 849-8100
Description:
Music, News, Sports.

WMLM-AM
4170 NORTH STATE ROAD
ALMA, MI 48801-9316

989-463-4013
• Greg Siefker, General Manager
Description:
Music, News, Sports.

WMLN-FM
1071 BLUE HILL AVE
MILTON, MA 02186-2302
617-333-0311
Fax: 617-333-6860
• Holly Clark, Promotion Director
(617) 333-0500
• Jadd Naamani, Program Director
(617) 333-2370
• Nick Quinn, Sports Director
Description:
Music, News, Sports.

WMMC-FM
627 1/2 ARCHER AVENUE
MARSHALL, IL 62441
217-826-8017
Fax: 217-826-8519
wmmc106@aol.com
• Lori Spangler, Program Director

WMML-AM
89 EVERTS AVENUE
QUEENSBURY, NY 12804-2040
518-793-7733
Fax: 518-793-0838
www.wink105.com
• John Pratt, Program Director
(518) 793-7733

WMMS-FM
6200 OAK TREE BOULEVARD 4TH FLOOR
INDEPENDENCE, OH 44131
216-520-2600
800-348-1007
Fax: 216-524-2600
www.wmms.com/main.html
• R. C. Bauer, News Director
(216) 520-2600
Description:
Music, News, Sports.

WMNA-AM
P.O. BOX 730
GRETNA, VA 24557-0730
434-656-1234
Fax: 434-656-1235
• Devin Taylor, General Manager
(888) 881-8851
wmna730@hotmail.com
Description:
Music, News, Sports.

WMOI-FM
55 PUBLIC SQUARE
MONMOUTH, IL 61462-1755
309-734-9452
Fax: 309-734-3276
• David Klockenga, General Manager
Description:
Music, News, Sports.

WMOP-AM
343 NORTH EAST 1ST AVENUE
OCALA, FL 34470
352-732-2010
888-777-5765
Fax: 352-629-1614
www.wmop.com

• Adam Reardon, Sports Director
Description:
Music, News, Sports.

WMPX-WMRX AM AND FM
1510 BAYLISS STREET
MIDLAND, MI 48640
989-631-1490
Fax: 989-631-6357
www.wmpxwmrx.com
• Gary Williams, Program/Sports Director
Description:
Music, News, Sports.

WMRC-AM
258 MAIN STREET
MILFORD, MA 01757-2525
508-473-1490
Fax: 508-478-2200
• Edward Thompson, News Director
Description:
Music, News, Sports, Talk.

WMRN-AM
1330 NORTH MAIN STREET
MARION, OH 43302
740-383-1131
Fax: 740-387-3697
bensailor@clearchannel.com
www.wmrn.com
• Ben Failor, News Director
benfailor@clearchannel.com
Description:
Music, News, Sports, Talk.

WMRX-FM
1510 BAYLISS STREET
MIDLAND, MI 48640-1689
989-631-1490
Fax: 989-631-6357
wmpx@sbcglobal.net
• Gary Williams, Program/Sports Director
Description:
Music, News, Sports.

WMSR-AM
1030 OAKDALE STREET
MANCHESTER, TN 37355-2206
931-728-3526
Fax: 931-728-3527
Description:
Music, News, Sports.

WMSS-FM
214 RACE STREET
MIDDLETOWN, PA 17057-2242
717-948-9136
www.wmssfm.com
• Steve Leedy, Sports Director
• John Wilsbach, General Manager
Description:
Music, News, Sports.

WMTL-AM
2160 BRANDENBURG ROAD
LEITCHFIELD, KY 42754
270-259-5692
Fax: 270-259-5693
news@k105.com
• Jared Mitchell, News Director
(270) 259-5692
• David Thompson, Sports Director
(270) 259-5692
Description:
News, Talk.

WMTR-FM
303 NORTH DEFIANCE STREET
ARCHBOLD, OH 43502-1162
419-445-9050
Fax: 419-445-3531
www.961wmtr.com
• Larry Christy, Sports Director
• Mark Knapp, News Director/Promotion
Manager
Description:
Music, News, Sports.

**WMUF 1047FM/97.5AM 1000, WRQR
AM/FM, 94.1 FM**
110 INDIA ROAD
PARIS, TN 38242-1239
731-644-9455
Fax: 731-644-9421
wmuf@bellsouth.net
• Janice Benton, Office Manager
• Howard Mcgill, News Director
radionews@bellsouth.net
• Lance Pierce, Sports Director
(731) 644-9455
wlzk@bellsouth.net
Description:
Educational, Music, News, Sports.

WMUH-FM
2400 CHEW STREET
ALLENTOWN, PA 18104
484-664-3239
Fax: 484-664-3539
wmuh@muhlenberg.edu
www.muhlenberg.edu
• Rich Gensiak, Program Director
Description:
Music, News, Sports.

WMVX-FM
6200 OAK TREE BOULEVARD
INDEPENDENCE, OH 44131
216-520-2600
800-829-1065
Fax: 216-901-8133
www.wmvx.com
• Don Hallett, Program Director
• Mike Snyders, Sports Director
(216) 696-4444
Description:
Music, News, Sports.

WNBH-AM
75 OXFORD STREET SUITE 402
PROVIDENCE, RI 02905
508-979-8003
Fax: 508-979-8009
bobcormier@catcountry.com
www.wnbh.com
• Rick Everett, Program Director
(508) 979-8003
• Ed Pereira, Promotion Manager
Description:
Music, News, Sports.

WNDE
6161 FALL CREEK RD
INDIANAPOLIS, IN 46220
317-257-7565
Fax: 317-253-6501
www.wnde.com
• Mark Patrick, Sports Director
markpatrick@clearchannel.com
Nature of Sports Service:
Local. Sports & Talk radio programming.

Frequency:
1260

WNDH-FM
709 NORTH PERRY STREET
NAPOLEON, OH 43545-1520
419-592-8060
Fax: 419-592-1085
wndh@clearchannel.com
www.wndh1031.com
• David Kleck, News Director
davekleck@clearchannel.com
• David Kleck, Sports Director
davekleck@clearchannel.com
Description:
Music, News, Sports.

WNEG-AM
145 H. ALEXANDER STREET
TOCCOA, GA 30577-1415
706-886-2191
Fax: 706-282-0189
www.wnegradio.com
• Ted Taylor, Sports Director
Description:
Music.

WNER-AM
134 MULLIN STREET
WATERTOWN, NY 13601-3616
315-788-0790
Fax: 315-788-4379
www.wuzz.com
• Nathan Lehman, News Director
(315) 788-0790
morning@790wtny.com
Description:
Music, News, Sports.

WNES-AM
1730 WEST EVERLY BROTHERS
BOULEVARD
CENTRAL CITY, KY 42330
270-754-3000
Fax: 270-754-3710
• Stan Barnett, Advertising Manager
ads@ky-leadernews.com
• Stan Barnett, Program Director
Description:
Music.

WNFL 1140-AM
1420 BELLEVUE STREET
GREEN BAY, WI 54305
920-435-3771
Fax: 920-321-2300
www.wnflam.com
• Dave Edwards, Program Director
(910) 435-3771
• John Maino, Sports Talk Show
(910) 435-3771
• Mark Daniels, Sports Director
(910) 435-3771
Nature of Sports Service:
Talk radio. 1140AM
College Sports:
Football, Basketball.

WNJC-AM
5 POINTS PLAZA
SEWELL, NJ 08080
856-227-1360
Fax: 856-232-9093
www.wnjc1360.com
• John Forsythe, General Manager

Description:
Music, News, Sports.

WNKT-FM
4230 FABER PLACE DRIVE SUITE 100
NORTH CHARLESTON, SC 29405
843-277-1200
800-225-9282
Fax: 843-277-1212
www.catcountry1075.com
• Brian Driver, Program Director
(843) 277-1200
Description:
Music, News, Sports.

WNLS
325 JOHN KNOX RD, BLDG G
TALLAHASSEE, FL 32303
850-422-3107
Fax: 850-383-0747
www.wnls.com
• J.L Dunbar, Program Director
• Brian Willard, Sports Director
• Rick Flagg, News Director
Nature of Sports Service:
24-hour sports.
Baseball:
MLB - Tampa Bay Devil Rays.
College Sports:
Baseball, Men's & Women's Basketball,
Football - Florida State University.
Football:
NFL - Tampa Bay Buccaneers.

WNMH-FM
206 MAIN STREET
NORTHFIELD, MA 01360-1050
413-498-3603
Fax: 413-498-0150
www.nmhschool.org
• Jo Grubman, Station Manager
(413) 498-5470
• Joe Ruscio, Sports Director
jruscio@nmhschool.org
Description:
Music, News, Sports.

WNML AM/FM
4711 OLD KINGSTON PIKE
KNOXVILLE, TN 37919
865-588-6511
Fax: 865-588-3725
sportsanimal99.com
• Mickey Dearstone, Program Director
• Frank Nystrom, Sales Manager
Description:
Music, News and All Sports

WNML-AM
4711 OLD KINGSTON PIKE
KNOXVILLE, TN 37919-5207
865-588-6511
Fax: 865-909-0254
www.sportsanimal99.com/
• Ed Brantley, General Manager
(865) 588-6511
• Mickey Dearstone, Program Director
Description:
News, Talk.

WNNJ-FM
45 MITCHELL AVENUE
FRANKLIN, NJ 07416
973-827-2525
Fax: 973-827-2135
www.wnnj.com

• Ken O'Brien, Program Director
(973) 823-6156
kenobrien@clearchannel.com
Description:
Music, News, Sports.

WNNZ-AM
1331 MAIN STREET
SPRINGFIELD, MA 01103-1669
413-781-1011
Fax: 413-858-1958
www.wnnz.com
• John Baibak, News Director
(413) 734-4432
Description:
Talk.

WNOI-FM
1001 NORTH OLIVE ROAD
FLORA, IL 62839
618-662-8331
Fax: 618-662-2407
www.wnoi.com
• Randy Poole, Advertising Manager
• Bill Thompson, News/Sports Director
Description:
Music, News, Sports.

WNPL-FM
10 MUSIC CIR E SUITE 901
NASHVILLE, TN 37203-4338
615-321-1067
Fax: 615-321-5771
• John Mountz, Program Director
(615) 321-1067
john.mountz@cumulus.com

WNPV-AM
1210 SNYDER ROAD
LANSDALE, PA 19446
215-855-8211
800-355-9678
Fax: 215-368-0180
jnolan@wnpv1440.com
• Jeff Nolan, Sports Director
jnolan@wnpv1440.com
Description:
News, Talk, Sports
Sports Broadcast:
NASCAR, Phillies, Lehigh Valley Iron Pigs,
Penn State Football & Basketball and high
school football broadcasts

WNSR/WMGC RADIO
435 37TH AVE N.
NASHVILLE, TN 37209
615-844-1039
Baseball:
Pacific Coast League: Nashville
College Sports:
Vanderbilt, Belmont University, University of
Tennessee, Tennessee State University.
Football:
NFL - Tennessee Titans.

WNSS-AM
1064 JAMES STREET
SYRACUSE, NY 13203-2704
315-472-0200
Fax: 315-472-1146
• Tom Mitchell, Station Manager
(315) 472-0200
Description:
News.

WNST-AM
1550 HART ROAD
BALTIMORE, MD 21286-1635
410-821-9678
Fax: 410-828-4698
www.nastyone.com
• Paul Kopelke, News Director
(410) 828-8088
Description:
Educational.

WNSV-FM
186 EAST SAINT LOUIS STREET
NASHVILLE, IL 62263
618-327-4444
Fax: 618-327-3716
wnsvfm@charter.net
• Brad Myer, Sports Director
wnsvfm@charter.net
Sports Discussed:
Baseball, football, volleyball, basketball
(local)
Description:
Broadcasts of local high school games in all
previous listed categories.

WNTR
516 WHITE AVE
CUMBERLAND, MD 21502
301-777-5400
Fax: 301-777-5404
www.wntr.com
• Dick Yoder, General Manager
• Pat Sullivan, Promotions Director
Nature of Sports Service:
News, Talk, Sports.
Baseball:
MLB - CBS Package.
College Sports:
Basketball - NCAA Final Four; Notre Dame
University sports.
Football:
NFL - Pittsburgh Steelers.

WNUS-FM
6006 GRAND CENTRAL AVENUE
VIENNA, WV 26105
304-295-6070
Fax: 304-295-4389
www.wnus.com
• Steve Daugherty, Sports Director
(304) 295-6070
steved@clearchannel.com
• Doug Hess, News Director
(304) 295-6070
douglashess@clearchannel.com
• Lori Ullmann, Promotion Manager
Description:
Music.

WNYG-AM
404 ROUTE 109
WEST BABYLON, NY 11704-6214
631-422-5973
Fax: 631-422-5992
www.studentradio1440.com
• Doug Edwards, Program Director
(631) 321-9694
Description:
Music, News, Sports.

WNYY
1751 HANSHAW RD
ITHACA, NY 14850

607-257-6400
Fax: 607-257-6497
www.1470wnyy.com
• Geoff Dunn, Program Director
• Peter Voorhees, Sports Director/ News
Director
• Susan Johnston, Marketing Director
Description:
Progressive talk radio.

WOAI
6222 NW IH 10 W.
SAN ANTONIO, TX 78201
210-736-9700
800-373-9700
Fax: 210-735-8811
• Bob Cohen, General Manager
• Jay Howard, Sports Director
Nature of Sports Service:
News, Talk, Sports.
Baseball:
CBS.

WOBN-FM
COWAN HALL
WESTERVILLE, OH 43081
614-823-1557
Fax: 614-823-1998
• Scott Bacon, Sports Director
• Cat Perlson, News Director
Description:
Music, News, Sports.

WOBT-AM
3616 HIGHWAY 47, N.
RHINELANDER, WI 54501-8819
715-362-1975
Fax: 715-362-1973
www.northwoodsespnsportszone.com
• John Burton, News Director
(715) 362-6140
Description:
Music, News, Sports.

WOES-FM
8989 COLONY ROAD
ELSIE, MI 48831-9724
989-862-4237
Fax: 989-862-4463
• Kevin Somers, Program Director
(989) 862-4237
somers@edzone.net
Description:
Music, News, Sports.

WOFX-AM
1 WASHINGTON SQUARE
ALBANY, NY 12205
518-452-4800
Fax: 518-452-4855
• Chuck Custer, News Director
(518) 452-4847
chuckcuster@clearchannel.com
• Peter Gimblette, Marketing Manager
petergimblette@clearchannel.com
Description:
Music.

WOHS
PO BOX 1590
SHELBY, NC 28151
704-435-3297
Fax: 704-435-1217
• Calvin Hastings, General Manager/Sales
netoldies@aol.com
• Andy Foster, Sports Director/Music

• Terresa Hastings, Office Manager
• Anna McGinnis, News Director
• Lori Deitz, Traffic Director
Office Address:
1511 W. Dixon Blvd, Shelby NC 28151.
Nature of Sports Service:
Country/Sports.
Baseball:
MLB - Atlanta Braves.
College Sports:
Basketball, Football - University of North Carolina.
Football:
NFL - Carolina Panthers.

WOIC-AM
1900 PINEVIEW ROAD
COLUMBIA, SC 29209
803-695-8600
Fax: 803-695-8605
www.woic.com
• Dave Stewart, Program Director
Description:
Music.

WOIZ-AM
PO BOX 561130
GUAYANILLA, PUERTO RIC 00656-3130
787-835-1130
Fax: 787-835-3130
radioantillas@yahoo.com
• Luis A. Rodriguez, III, President/General Manager
(787) 835-3130
radioantillas@yahoo.com
• Manuel Quinonez, Program Director
(787) 835-3130
radioantillas@yahoo.com
• Luis F. Mari, Technical Supervisor
(787) 835-3130
radioantillas@yahoo.com
• Erving Quinonez, Billing Director
(787) 835-3130
radioantillas@yahoo.com
• Rafael Acosta, Chief Executive
(787) 835-3130
radioantillas@yahoo.com
Description:
Music, News, Sports.
Year Founded:
1986

WONN-AM
404 WEST LIME STREET
LAKELAND, FL 33815
863-682-8184
Fax: 863-683-2409
news@wpcv.com
www.wonn.com
• Nancy Cattarius, Station Manager
(863) 682-8184
• Tunie Moss, Promotions Director
(863) 682-8184
• Mike James, Program Director
(863) 682-8184
• Andrea Oliver, News Director
(863) 682-8184
Description:
Music, News, Sports.

WONQ-AM
1033 STATE ROAD 436
SUITE 253
CASSELBERRY, FL 32707-5742
407-830-0800
Fax: 407-260-6100

• George M. Arroyo, Owner/President
• Josi Van Padilla, Sports Director
• Manuel Arroyo, Sports Director
(407) 830-0800
Description:
Music, News, Sports.

WOON-AM
1 SOCIAL STREET
WOONSOCKET, RI 02895-3136
401-762-1240
800-449-1240
Fax: 401-769-8232
studio@onworldwide.com
www.on-radio.com
• Lou Mandeville, Sports Director
(401) 762-1240
Description:
Music, News, Sports.

WOPP-AM
1101 CAMERON ROAD
OPP, AL 36467-2407
334-493-4545
Fax: 334-493-4546
wopp@wopp.com
www.wopp.com
• Joe Adams, Sports Director
(334) 453-4545
• Brett Ballard, Play-By-Play
(334) 453-4545
wopp@wopp.com
• Robert Boothe, General Manager
Frequency:
1290 AM

WORD
501 RUTHERFORD ST
GREENVILLE, SC 29609
864-271-9200
Fax: 864-242-1567
www.newstalkword.com
• Annell Kirkland, General Manager
• John Boone, Program Director/Sports Director
Nature of Sports Service:
Local. News, Talk. Sports radio programming.

WORD-AM
29 DARLINGTON ROAD
GREENVILLE, SC 29609-5313
864-271-6397
Fax: 864-242-1567
• Bob McLain, Program Director
bmclain@entercom.com
Description:
News, Talk.

WORG-FM
1675 CHESTNUT STREET
ORANGEBURG, SC 29115-3327
803-516-8400
Fax: 803-516-0704
www.worg.com
• Stu Wright, Program Director
Description:
Music, News, Sports.

WORW-FM
1799 KRAFFT RD
PORT HURON, MI 48060
810-984-2675
Fax: 810-984-2747
• Carie Mertz, General Manager

Description:
Music, News, Sports.

WORX-FM
1224 EAST TELEGRAPH HILL ROAD
MADISON, IN 47250
812-265-3322
Fax: 812-273-5509
• Scott Davidson, News/Sports Director
manager@worxradio.com
Description:
Music, News, Sports.

WOSO-AM
52 PASEO COVADONGA PELLO
BUILDING C 3RD
SAN JUAN, PUERTO RIC 00901
787-724-4242
Fax: 787-723-9676
• Gary Tuominen, News Director
Description:
Music, News, Sports.

WOSQ-FM
1710 NORTH CENTRAL AVENUE
MARSHFIELD, WI 54449-1514
715-384-2191
Fax: 715-341-9744
Nature of Service:
ESPN Radio, over 100 local high school events per year
Baseball:
ESPN games Saturday and Sunday
Basketball:
Milwaukee Bucks
College Sports:
Wisconsin Football, Men's and Women's Basketball, ESPn Bowl games

WOWO-AM
2915 MAPLES ROAD
FORT WAYNE, IN 46816
260-447-5511
800-333-1190
Fax: 260-447-7546
news@wowo.com
www.wowo.com
• Jim Shovlin, Sports Director
(260) 447-5511
Description:
Radio broadcasting.
Frequency:
1190

WOYL-AM
1411 LIBERTY STREET
FRANKLIN, PA 16323-1696
814-432-2188
Fax: 814-437-9372
mytalkradio@yahoo.com
• Terry Deitz, General Manager
• Joseph Elan, Advertising Manager
joekool95@yahoo.com
• Tim Shaw, Sports Director
Description:
News, Talk.

WPAX-AM
117 REMINGTON AVENUE
THOMASVILLE, GA 31792-5520
229-226-1240
Fax: 229-226-1361
www.wpaxradio.com/
• Mark Brannan, Sports Reporter
• Len Robinson, Advertising Manager

Description:
Music, News, Sports, Talk.

WPCD-FM
2400 WEST BRADLEY AVENUE
CHAMPAIGN, IL 61821-1806
217-351-2450
wpcd@lycos.com
www.parkland.cc.il.us/wpcd
• Dan Hughes, News Director
dhughes@parkland.edu
Description:
Music, News, Sports.

WPCH-AM
500 CAROLINA SPRINGS ROAD
NORTH AUGUSTA, SC 29841
706-396-6000
800-816-1043
Fax: 803-279-0220
janasutter@clearchannel.com
• Charles McNeil, News Director
Description:
Music, News.

WPCV-FM
404 WEST LIME STREET
LAKELAND, FL 33815
863-682-8184
800-227-9797
Fax: 863-683-2409
news@wpcv.com
www.wpcv.com
• Nancy Cattarius, Advertising Manager
• Bob Crews, Sports Director
(863) 682-8184
• Tunie Moss, Promotions Manager
(863) 682-8184
Description:
Music, News, Sports.

WPDM-AM/WSNN-FM
7064 POTSDAM CANTON ROAD
POTSDAM, NY 13676
315-265-5510
Fax: 315-265-4040
www.99hits.com
• Scott Dosztan, News Director
• Chris Engel, Sports Director
Description:
Music.
Year Founded:
1955

WPDR RADIO
PO BOX 300
PORTAGE, WI 53901
608-742-8833
Fax: 608-742-1688
• Ed Kramer, General Manager
• Mike Olson, Program Director
Nature of Sports Service:
Adult Contemporary, News, Talk. ESPN
Sports Talk (weekends)
Basketball:
NBA - Milwaukee Bucks
Baseball:
MLB - Milwaukee Brewers - Day Games.
Football:
NFL - Green Bay Packers.
College Sports:
Basketball, Football, Ice Hockey - University
of Wisconsin.

WPEN-AM
1 BALA PLAZA
BALA CYNWYD, PA 19004-1428
610-667-8500
Fax: 610-664-9610
www.sportstalk950.com
• Art Andrews, News Director
(610) 667-8500
• Tony Bruno, Host - Morning Show
(610) 667-8500
• Bob DeBlois, Station Manager
(610) 667-8500
• Mike Sommers, Program Director
(610) 667-8500
Description:
Music.

WPEZ-FM
544 MULBERRY STREET 5TH FLOOR
MACON, GA 31201-8250
478-746-6286
Fax: 478-742-8061
z937.com/home.php
• John Sheftic, Marketing Manager
Description:
Music, News, Sports.

WPHM-AM
808 HURON STREET
PORT HURON, MI 48060
810-982-9000
Fax: 810-987-9380
www.wphm.com
• Bill Gilmer, News Director
• Al Tyrrell, Advertising Manager
(810) 982-9000
• Dennis Stuckey, Sports Director
Description:
Music, News, Sports, Talk.

WPIC-AM
2030 PINE HOLLOW BOULEVARD
SHARON, PA 16148-2520
724-346-4113
877-872-7737
Fax: 724-981-4545
www.wpic790.com
• Joe Biro, News Director
• Bob Greenburg, Sports Director
(724) 346-4113
bgreenburg@theradiocenter.com
Description:
Music, News, Sports, Talk.

WPIG-FM
3163 NEW YORK STATE, ROUTE 417
OLEAN, NY 14760
716-372-0161
800-877-9749
Fax: 716-372-0164
newsdesk@netsync.net
• Dick Hannon, Advertising Manager
• Gary Nease, News/Sports Director
Description:
Music.

WPKY-AM
108 WEST MAIN STREET
PRINCETON, KY 42445
270-365-2072
Fax: 270-365-2073
• Tom Rogers, General Manager
Description:
Music, News, Sports.

WPLO-AM
239 EZARD STREET
LAWRENCEVILLE, GA 30045-5936
770-237-9897
Fax: 770-237-8769
• Franco Vera, Promotion Director
Description:
Music, News, Sports, Talk.

WPMB-AM
232 SOUTH 4TH STREET
VANDALIA, IL 62471-2810
618-283-2325
Fax: 618-283-1503
• John Harris, Promotions Director
wkrv@sbcglobal.net
• Todd Stapleton, News/Sports Director
tstapleton@cromwellradio.com
Description:
Educational, Music, News, Sports, Talk.

WPMZ-AM
1270 MINERAL SPRING AVENUE
NORTH PROVIDENCE, RI 02904
401-726-8413
Fax: 401-726-8649
wpmz@aol.com
• Tony Mendez, Station Manager
(401) 726-8413
tmendez@poder1110.com

WPOP-AM SPORTS RADIO
10 COLUMBUS BLVD
HARTFORD, CT 06106
860-723-6000
Fax: 860-723-6079
www.espnradio1410.com
• Bob Plant, Program Director
Nature of Sports Service:
Local. 24-hour sports radio programming.

WPPA-AM
212 SOUTH CENTER
POTTSVILLE, PA 17901
570-622-1360
Fax: 570-622-2822
news@pbcradio.com
www.pbcradio.com
• Gene Starr, News Director
(570) 622-1360
• Bill Tidmore, Advertising & Promotion
Manager/Sports Director
Description:
Music, News, Sports.

WPRN-FM
909 WEST PUSHMATAHA STREET
BUTLER, AL 36904
205-459-3222
Fax: 205-459-4140
wprnfm1077@yahoo.com
www.wprnfm.com
• Henry Tyson, Sports Director

WPRO
1502 WAMPANOAY TRAIL
E. PROVIDENCE, RI 02915
401-433-4200
Fax: 401-433-1183
www.wpro.com
• Andrea Scott, General Manager
• Scott Cordischi, Sports Director
• Chris Gardner, Marketing Director
• Donna Callahan, Business Officer
Nature of Sports Service:
News, Talk, Sports.

Baseball:
MLB - Boston Red Sox; Minor League - International League/AA/Pawtucket Red Sox.
College Sports:
Basketball - Providence, Football - Brown University; Ice Hockey - Providence.
Ice Hockey:
NHL - Boston Bruins; Minor League - American Hockey League/AHL/Providence Bruins.

WPRO-AM
1502 WAMPANOAG TRAIL
RIVERSIDE, RI 02915
401-433-4200
Fax: 401-433-5967
wprofm@aol.com
• David Bernstein, News Director
Description:
Music, News, Sports, Talk.

WPRZ-AM
7351 HUNTON STR WARRENTON
WARRENTON, VA 20187
540-349-1250
Fax: 540-349-2726
www.praisecommunications.org
• Sally L. Buchanan, Program Director
sally@wprz.org
Description:
Music, News, Sports.

WPXN-FM
361 NORTH RAILROAD AVENUE
PAXTON, IL 60957-1142
217-379-4333
www.wpxn.com
• Joel Cluver, News Director
• Dan Daugherity, Advertising Manager/Sports Director
wpxn@hotmail.com
Description:
Music, News, Sports.

WQAL-FM
1041 HURON RADIO
CLEVELAND, OH 44115
216-578-0104
Fax: 216-363-7104
www.q104.cbslocal.com/
• Brian Conroy, Promotions Director
bconroy@q104.com
• Jim McIntyre, News Director
(216) 696-0123
jim@wdok.com
Description:
Music, News, Sports.

WQAM 560 SPORTS RADIO
20295 NW 2ND AVE
MIAMI, FL 33169
305-653-6796
Fax: 305-770-1456
• Greg Reed, General Manager
• Bill Mullon, Director of Sports Marketing
• Mike Eckstein, Director Sports Marketing
Nature of Sports Service:
Local. 24-hour sports radio programming. Dolphins (NFL); Miami Hurricanes (NCAA), Marlins (MLB), Florida Panthers (NHL); Miami Heat (NBA).

WQBB-AM
1533 AMHERST ROAD
KNOXVILLE, TN 37909

865-824-1021
Fax: 865-824-1880
www.1040theticket.com
• Bruce Patrick, Program Director
(865) 824-1711
• Chris Protzman, General Manager
(865) 824-1700
Description:
News, Sports, Talk.

WQBX-FM
5310 NORTH STATE ROAD
ALMA, MI 48801
989-463-3175
Fax: 989-463-6674
www.wqbx.com
• Jim Sommerville, Program Director
wqbx@cmsinter.net
• Jim Sommerville, Sports Director
Description:
Music, News, Sports.

WQCM-FM
1250 MARYLAND AVENUE
HAGERSTOWN, MD 21740-7244
301-797-7300
Fax: 301-797-2659
• Mike Holder, Program Director
(717) 263-0813
Description:
Music, News, Sports.

WQDK-FM
443 HIGHWAY 42 WEST
AHOSKIE, NC 27910-9712
252-332-7993
Fax: 252-332-6887
• Don Upchurch, News Director
Description:
Music, News, Sports.

WQEL-FM
403 EAST RENSSELAER STREET
BUCYRUS, OH 44820-2438
419-562-2222
Fax: 419-562-0520
www.wbcowqel.com
• Debra J. Gifford, General Manager
• Jim Radke, Sports Director
Description:
Music, News, Sports.

WQIC-FM
ROUTE 72 NORTH
LEBANON, PA 17046
717-272-7651
Fax: 717-274-0161
• Scott Bradley, Sports Director
• Gordon Weise, News Director
Description:
Music.

WQIO-FM
17421 COSHOCTON ROAD
MOUNT VERNON, OH 43050
740-397-1000
Fax: 740-392-9300
curtisnewland@basbroadcasting.com
www.wqioradio.com
• Curtis Newland, Operations Manager
(740) 397-1000

WQKE-FM
ALUMNI HALL
PLATTSBURGH, NY 12901

518-564-2000
Fax: 518-564-3994
137.142.200.27/wqke/
• Ashley Herington, News Director
• Seth Lindernen, Sports Director
Description:
Music, News, Sports.

WQKR-AM
100 MAIN STREET
PORTLAND, TN 37148
615-325-3250
Fax: 615-325-0803
www.wqkr.com
• Chris Ladd, Advertising Manager
• Chris Ladd, News Director
wqkr@comcast.net
• Chris Ladd, Sports Director
Description:
Music, News, Sports, Talk.

WQKT-FM
186 SOUTH HILLCREST DRIVE
WOOSTER, OH 44691
330-264-5122
800-833-9211
Fax: 330-264-3571
wqkt@aol.com
www.wqkt.com
• Mike Breckenridge, Program Director
events@wqkt.com
• Craig Walton, Advertising Manager
Description:
Music, News, Sports.

WQLA-FM
P.O. BOX 1530
LA FOLLETTE, TN 37766
423-566-1000
Fax: 865-457-5900
q105fm@bellsouth.com
• Cliff Jennings, Owner
q105fm@bellsouth.net
• Frank Scott, Program Director
q105fm@bellsouth.net
Description:
Music, News, Sports.

WQPM-AM
32215 124TH STREET
PRINCETON, MN 55371
763-389-1300
800-850-1061
Fax: 763-389-1359
• Troy Edwards, Program Director
Description:
Music, News, Sports, Talk.

WQSE-AM
201 HALL LANE
WHITE BLUFF, TN 37187
615-797-9785
Fax: 615-797-9788
duanedjwqse@aol.com
www.tngospel.com
• Duane Jeffrey, General Manager
Description:
Music, News, Sports.

WQSN AM 1660
4200 W. MAIN
KALAMAZOO, MI 49006
269-345-7121
800-873-1074
Fax: 269-345-1436
cyanm@wgsn.com

- Stephens C. Trivers, President/General Manager
- Ryan Maguire, Programming/Promotions Director
- Dennis Martin, VP Sales
- Geary Morrill, Chief Engineer
- Tammy Abramowski, Traffic Director
- Melissa Richard, Controller
Nature of Sports Service:
Local and ESPN 24-hour sports radio programming. Jim Rome and 25 hours of local programming weekly. Your local sports leader.
Baseball:
MLB - Chicago Cubs, Chicago White Sox.
College Sports:
Basketball - Michigan State University, Kalamazoo College: Football - Michigan State University, Kalamazoo College.
Football:
NFL - Chicago Bears.
Ice Hockey:
NHL - Detroit Red Wings, UHL - Kalamazoo Wings.
Baseball:
MLB - Chicago Cubs, Chicago White Sox. College - Kalamazoo Kings.
Primary Audience:
Males 25-54 years old.

WQTM
2500 MAITLAND CENTER PKWY, STE 401
MAITLAND, FL 32751
407-916-7800
Fax: 407-916-0329
- Jenny Su Rhodes, General Manager
- Tom Morgan, Sports Director
Nature of Sports Service:
Local. 24-hour sports radio programming.
Baseball:
MLB - Atlanta Braves.
College Sports:
Basketball, Football - University of Florida, University of Central Florida, University of Miami.
Football:
NFL - Miami Dolphins.

WQXI 790
3550 PEACHTREE RD, NE PENTHOUSE
ATLANTA, GA 30326
404-238-3431
Fax: 404-365-9026
- Andrew Saltzman, General Manager
- Matt Edgar, Sports Director
Nature of Sports Service:
Sports radio. Pete Rose Show, Jim Rome, Game Night.

WQXI-AM
3350 PEACHTREE ROAD, N.E.
ATLANTA, GA 30326-1040
404-237-0079
Fax: 404-231-5923
www.790thezone.com
- Leslie Rosetta-Smith, Marketing Director
- Leslie Rosetta-Smith, Promotions Director
- Andrew Saltzman, President
- Steven Shapiro, President
Description:
Music, Talk.

WQXX-FM
129 COLLEGE STREET
WEST LIBERTY, KY 41472-1156

606-784-4141
Fax: 606-743-9557
radio41472@yahoo.com
- Jim Forrest, Program Director
radio412@yahoo.com
Description:
Music, News, Sports.

WRAC-FM
114 MANCHESTER STREET, S.
WEST UNION, OH 45693-1262
937-544-9722
800-326-9722
Fax: 937-544-5523
- Donald J. Bowles, Owner
(937) 544-9722
- Ted Foster, News Director
c103country@yahoo.com
- Gary McClellen, Sports Director
(937) 544-9722
c103country@yahoo.com
Description:
Music, News, Sports.

WRAM-AM
55 PUBLIC SQUARE
MONMOUTH, IL 61462-1755
309-734-9452
Fax: 309-734-3276
- Tom Peterson, News Director
Description:
Music, News, Sports, Talk.

WRAY-AM
1900 WEST BROADWAY
PRINCETON, IN 47670-1095
812-386-1250
Fax: 812-386-6249
- Cliff Ingram, WRAY News Director
(812) 386-1250
cliff@wrayradio.com
Description:
Music, News, Sports.

WRAY-FM
P.O. BOX 8
PRINCETON, IN 47670-1095
812-386-1250
Fax: 812-386-6249
wray@wrayradio.com
www.wrayradio.com
- Cliff Ingram, News Director
(812) 386-1250
cliff@wrayradio.com
- Jeff Lankford, Sports Director
(812) 386-1250
jeff@wrayradio.com
- Lynn Roach, Promotion Director
(812) 386-1250
lynn@wrayradio.com
Description:
Music, News, Contests
Year Founded:
1950

WRCC-FM
390 GOLDEN AVENUE
BATTLE CREEK, MI 49015
269-963-5555
Fax: 269-963-5185
- Tim Collins, Operations Director
(269) 963-5555
- Jeff Jennings, Production Director
(269) 963-5555
- Kit Osborne, General Station Manager
(269) 963-5555

Description:
Radio: FM 104.9, Football and Basketball: NCAA - Michigan Wolverine Football

WRCT-FM
1 WRCT PLAZA
500 FORBES AVENUE
PITTSBURGH, PA 15213
412-621-0728
Fax: 412-268-6549
news@wrct.org
www.wrct.org
- John Ketchpaw, Promotion Director
promotions@wrct.org
- Mike Rossman, Sports Director
sports@wrct.org
- Jason Tagyer, News Director
(412) 621-0728
news@wrct.org
Description:
Music, News, Sports.

WRCU-FM
13 OAK DRIVE
HAMILTON, NY 13346
315-228-7109
Fax: 315-228-7028
wrcu@mail.colgate.edu
www.wrcufm.com
- Darcy Benedict, General Manager
Description:
Music, News, Sports, Talk.

WRDL-FM
ASHLAND UNIVERSITY
ASHLAND, OH 44805-3702
419-289-5157
Fax: 419-289-5329
wrdl@ashland.edu
www.ashland.edu
- Tyler Miller, Sports Director
(419) 289-5157
wrdl@ashland.edu
- Kim Sweet-Buzzard, Program Director
wrdlashland@yahoo.com
- James Hana, Sports Director
(419) 289-5678
wrdl@ashland.edu
Description:
Music, News, Sports.

WRDU-FM
3100 SMOKETREE COURT SUITE 700
RALEIGH, NC 27604-1052
919-878-1500
Fax: 919-876-2929
www.1061rdu.com
- Josh Zach, News Director
joshzach@clearchannel.com
Description:
Music, News, Sports.

WRDW-AM
4051 JIMMIE DYESS PARKWAY
AUGUSTA, GA 30917
706-396-7000
Fax: 706-396-7100
maryliz@wgac.com
www.wrdwam.com
- Ashley Brown, Sports Director
(706) 396-7160

WREK-FM
350 FERST DRIVE, N.W.
ATLANTA, GA 30332-0630

404-894-2468
Fax: 404-894-6872
music.director@wrek.org
www.wrek.org
• Asif Heerji, Sports Editor
sports.director@wrek.org
• Eldon Stegall, Sports Director
(404) 894-2468
sports.director@wrek.org
Description:
Music, News, Sports, Talk.

WREV-AM
3025 WAUGHTOWN STREET SUITE G
WINSTON-SALEM, NC 27107
336-784-9004
Fax: 336-784-8337
www.quepasamedia.com
• Alfonso Fernandez, Station Manager
(336) 784-2774
Description:
Music, News, Sports, Talk.

WRFW-FM
306 N.HALL
RIVER FALLS, WI 54022-2882
715-425-3886
Fax: 715-425-3532
www.pureradio887.com
• Christine Duellman, News Director
• Steve Yeska, Sports Director
Description:
Music, News, Sports.

WRGM SPORTS RADIO 1440
2900 PARK AVE W.
MANSFIELD, OH 44906
419-529-5900
Fax: 419-529-2319
comments@wrgm.com
www.wrgm.com
• Gunther Meisse, General Manager
Nature of Sports Service:
24-hour sports.
Auto Sports:
NASCAR.

WRGS-AM
211 BUREM ROAD
ROGERSVILLE, TN 37857
423-272-2628
Fax: 423-272-0328
www.wrgsradio.com
• Philip Beal, News Director
• Jay Phillips, Sports Director
(423) 272-3900
• J. Phillips, Sports Announcer
(423) 272-2628
stationmanager@wrgsradio.com
Description:
Music, News, Sports.
Sports Discussed:
Cherokee High School football, girls and
boys basketball, baseball and softball.
Frequency:
1370 am & 94.5 fm

WRHU-FM
111 HOFSTRA UNIVERSITY
HEMPSTEAD, NY 11549-1110
516-463-5667
Fax: 516-463-5668
mail@wrhu.org
www.wrhu.org
• Pete McCarthy, Sports Director
sports@wrhu.org

• Jamie Morris, Station Manager
(516) 463-5667
stationmanager@wrhu.org
Description:
Music, News, Sports.

WRIL-FM
P.O. BOX 693
PINEVILLE, KY 40977-0693
606-248-6565
877-724-4792
Fax: 606-248-6569
• Bob Dixon, Sports Director
• Elie Evans, Station Manager
wrilcountry@yahoo.com
Description:
Music, News, Sports.

WRJW-AM
2438 HIGHWAY 43 SOUTH
PICAYUNE, MS 39466-0907
601-798-4835
800-284-5036
Fax: 601-798-9755
www.wrjw.com
• Bo Moeller, News Director
(601) 798-4835
wrjw@charter.net
• Cary Meitzler, Sports Director
(601) 798-4835
wrjw@charter.net
• M. Delores Wood, General Manager
(601) 798-4835
wrjw@charter.net
• Caroline Randolph, Traffic Director
(601) 798-4835
wrjw@charter.net
• Denise Wilson, Public Service/Programs
(601) 798-4835
• Rebecca Barnes, Live Interviews
(601) 799-1900
• Roy Bunales, Music Director
(601) 799-1900
Nature of Service:
Music, News, Sports, Talk.
Year Founded:
1948

WRKD-AM
15 PAYNE AVENUE
ROCKLAND, ME 04841-2117
207-594-9400
Fax: 207-594-2234
matthewthompson@clearchannel.com
• Don Shields, Program Director
(207) 623-9000
donaldshields@clearchannel.com
• Donald Shields, Sports Director
(207) 623-9000
donaldshields@clearchannel.com
Description:
Music.

WRKR-FM
4154 JENNINGS DRIVE
KALAMAZOO, MI 49048
269-344-0111
Fax: 269-344-4223
www.wrkr.com
• Bill Anthony, News Director
• John Sterling, Market Manager
Description:
Music, News, Sports.

WRLS-FM
P.O. BOX 1008
HAYWARD, WI 54843-1008
715-634-4871
Fax: 715-634-3025
wrls@cheqnet.net
• Dick Bender, Sports Director
wrls-radio@cheqnet.net
• Stephanie Holman, News Director
sholman@cheqnet.net
Description:
Music, News, Sports.

WRMS-FM
108 EAST MAIN STREET
BEARDSTOWN, IL 62618-1241
217-323-1790
Fax: 217-323-1705
larry.bosiwick@gmail.com
• Larry Bosiwick, General Manager/Owner
Description:
Broadcasting local and national sports.
Affiliations:
Cubs, White Sox, Bulls, Bears, University of
Illinois, University of Notre Dame and
NASCAR.

WRNA-AM
633 PATTERSON STREET CHINA GROVE
KANNAPOLIS, NC 28083
704-857-1101
Fax: 704-857-0680
carl@fordbroadcasting.com
www.fordbroadcasting.com
• Carl Ford, Program Director
• Carl Ford, Sports Director
Description:
Music.

WRNL-AM
3245 BASIE ROAD
RICHMOND, VA 23228-3404
804-474-0000
800-432-9782
Fax: 804-474-0910
wrnl@clearchannel.com
www.sportsradio910.com
• Gary Hess, Sports Director
(804) 474-0155
garyhess@clearchannel.com
• Deanna Malone, News Director
(804) 474-0440
deannamalone@clearchannel.com
Description:
News, Sports.

WRNX-FM
98 LOWER WESTFIELD STREET
HOLYOKE, MA 01040-2744
413-536-1105
Fax: 413-536-1153
www.wrnx.com
• Glenn Cardinal, General Manager
Description:
Music.

WRRG-FM
2000 5TH AVENUE
RIVER GROVE, IL 60171-1907
708-456-0300
Fax: 708-583-3121
• Kelli Lynch, Program Director
(708) 456-0300
wrrg@aol.com
• Tim McKinney, Sports Director

(708) 456-0300
wrrg@aol.com
Description:
Music, News, Sports.

WRSC
160 CLEARVIEW AVE
STATE COLLEGE, PA 16803
814-238-5085
Fax: 814-238-8993
• Joe Trimarchi, General Manager
(814) 238-5085
• Jeff Byers, Sports Director
(814) 238-5085
ironhead99@hotmail.com
• Dave Shannon, Program Director
(814) 238-5085
Nature of Sports Service:
News.
College Sports:
Basketball, Football, Wrestling - Penn State
University.
Football:
NFL - Pittsburgh Steelers.

WRSE-FM
190 PROSPECT AVENUE
ELMHURST, IL 60126-3271
630-617-3500
Fax: 630-617-3313
www.elmhurst.edu/~jaywaves
• Dave Holder, Program Director
Description:
Educational, Music, News, Sports.

WRSN-FM
3100 SMOKETREE COURT SUITE 700
RALEIGH, NC 27604-1052
919-878-1500
Fax: 919-876-2929
briantaylor@clearchannel.com
www.sunny939.com
• Ken Spitzer, General Manager
(919) 874-9800
kenspitzer@clearchannel.com
• Rob Whiteside, Promotions Manager
robwhiteside@clearchannel.com
Description:
Music, News.

WRSW-AM
216 MARKET STREET, W
WARSAW, IN 46580-2800
574-372-3064
Fax: 574-267-2230
www.wrsw.net
• Roger Grossman, Sports Director
(574) 372-3064
• Jeremy Taylor, News Director
Description:
Music, News, Sports.

WRTK
4040 SIMON RD
YOUNGSTOWN, OH 44512
330-783-1000
Fax: 330-783-0060
• Pat Mulrooney, Program Director/Sports
Nature of Sports Service:
News, Talk, Sports.
Baseball:
MLB - Cleveland Indians.
College Sports:
Baseball, Basketball, Football - Youngstown
State.

Football:
NFL - Pittsburgh Steelers.

WRUC-FM
REAMER CAMPUS CENTER
SCHENECTADY, NY 12308-2311
518-388-6151
Fax: 518-388-6790
wruc.union.edu/wruc/
• Matt Curtain, Sports Director
• Jennifer Mitchell, General Manager
Description:
Educational, Music, News, Sports.

WRUF
3200 WEIMER
GAINESVILLE, FL 32611
352-392-0771
Fax: 352-392-0519
gm@wruf.com
www.wruf.com
• Bob Clarke, Director General Manager
• Steve Russell, Sports Director
• Tom Krynski, News Director
Office Address:
3200 Weimer Hall, University of Florida
Campus, Gainesville, FL 32611.
Nature of Sports Service:
News, Sports, Talk.
Baseball:
CBS.
College Sports:
Baseball - University of Florida, CBS;
Basketball - University of Florida, CBS;
Football - CBS.
Football:
NFL - Miami Dolphins.

WRXL-FM
3245 BASIE ROAD
RICHMOND, VA 23228-3404
804-474-0000
800-345-9436
Fax: 804-474-0168
www.wrxl.com
• Casey Krukowski, Program Director
(804) 474-0000
caseykrukowski@clearchannel.com
Description:
Music, News, Sports.

WRXX-FM
302 SOUTH POPLAR STREET
CENTRALIA, IL 62801-3922
618-533-5700
Fax: 618-533-5737
wrxx@mvn.net
• Aaron Fuchs, Operating Manager
• Brenda Robbins, Promotions Director
Description:
Music.

WSAL-AM
425, 2ND STREET
LOGANSPORT, IN 46947-3410
574-722-4000
Fax: 574-722-4010
www.wsal.com
• Mike Montgomery, Sports Director
• Joe Ulery, News Director
Description:
Music, News, Talk.

WSB-AM
1601 WEST PEACHTREE STREET, N.E.
ATLANTA, GA 30309-2663

404-897-7500
Fax: 404-897-7593
newstips@wsbradio.com
www.wsbradio.com
• Dave Baker, Executive Sports
Producer/Weekend Host
(404) 897-6282
dave.baker@wsbradio.com
• Michael Dobson, Promotions Director
(404) 897-7556
• Larry Munson, Sports Host
• Tony Schiavone, Sports Reporter
(404) 897-7500
Description:
News, Talk.

WSBU-FM
PO BOX O
SAINT BONAVENTURE, NY 14778-2294
716-375-2307
Fax: 716-375-2583
wsbu@sbu.edu
wsbufm.net/p_cms.php?page_type=default&
CID=7
• Jen Anderson, Promotion Director
• Jeremy Noeson, Sports Director
• Elise Witz, News Director
Description:
Music.

WSCR THE SCORE SPORTSRADIO 670
455 N CITYFRONT PLAZA
CHICAGO, IL 60611
312-245-6000
Fax: 312-245-6072
www.wscr670am.com
• Mitch Rosen, Sports Director
• Rod Zimmerman, VP/General Manager
• Jackie Spencer, Director of Marketing
Nature of Sports Service:
24-hour sports radio programming.
Baseball:
MLB - CBS.
College Sports:
Basketball, Football - University of Illinois.

**WSDM-FM/WBOW-AM ESPN SPORTS
RADIO**
1301 OHIO STREET
TERRE HAUTE, IN 47807
812-234-9770
Fax: 812-238-1576
www.espnsportsradio.com
• Scott Jones, Station Director
(812) 234-9770
Description:
ESPN Radio
Teams:
High school: Northview, Terre Haute North,
Terre Haute South, and West Vigo College:
Indiana State University, Purdue University,
and Butler University Professional: Indiana
Pacers

WSDP-FM
46181 JOY ROAD
CANTON, MI 48187-1316
734-416-7732
Fax: 734-416-7763
www.wsdpradio.com
• Bill Keith, General Manager
• Mike Schaffer, Sports Director
Description:
Educational, Music, News, Sports.

WSEW-FM
2 RIDGE ROAD
NEW DURHAM, NH 03855
603-859-9170
Fax: 603-859-8172
www.wsew.org
• Sharon Malone, Operations Manager
(603) 859-9170
smalone@wsew.org
Description:
Music, News, Sports.

WSFN-AM
7515 BLYTHE ISLAND HIGHWAY
BRUNSWICK, GA 31523
912-264-6251
Fax: 912-264-9991
www.thefansportsradio.com
• Gary Moss, Program Director
(912) 264-6251
wsfnradio@yahoo.com
• Kevin Willis, Sports Director
(912) 264-6251
wsfnradio@yahoo.com
Description:
Georgia's # 1 sports station. Featuring
ESPN Radio along with 4 hours of local,
regional sports programing.
Teams:
Atlanta Braves, Atlanta Falcons, Atlanta
Hawks, SECÃ†and ACCC sports.

WSFN-AM SPORTS RADIO
875 E. SUMMIT
MUSKEGON, MI 49444
231-733-2126
Fax: 231-739-9037
• Jill Gossett, General Manager
• Scott Siembida, Pro General Manager
Director
Nature of Sports Service:
Local. 24-hour sports radio programming.

WSHN-AM
3375 MERRIAM STREET
MUSKEGON, MI 49444
231-924-4700
800-386-9746
Fax: 231-924-9746
www.funcountry.com
• Jon Russell, News Director
• Jon Russell, Sports Director
Description:
Music, News, Sports.

WSHR-FM
212 SMITH ROAD
LAKE RONKONKOMA, NY 11779-2229
631-471-1400
Fax: 631-471-1408
wshr@sachem.edu
www.wshr.com
• Mark Laura, General Manager
mlaura@sachem.edu
Description:
Music, News, Sports.

WSHW-FM
PO BOX 545
FRANKFORT, IN 46041-0545
765-659-3338
800-447-4463
Fax: 765-659-3338
www.wshw.com
• Bern Kaspar, Chief Executive Officer
(765) 654-7000

• Mike Reppert, News Director
• Greg Garrett, Sports Host
(765) 659-3338
Description:
Music, News, Sports.

WSIF-FM
1328 COLLEGIATE DRIVE
WILKESBORO, NC 28697
336-838-6179
Fax: 336-838-6277
• Al DeLachica, General Manager
(336) 838-6222
Description:
Music, News, Sports.

WSIG-FM
1866 EAST MARKET STREET SUITE 325
HARRISONBURG, VA 22801
540-432-1063
Fax: 540-433-9267
• Steve Walker, Program Director
Description:
Music, News, Sports.

WSJB-FM
278 WHITE BRIDGE ROAD
STANDISH, ME 04084-5270
207-893-7914
Fax: 207-893-7873
wyates@sjcme.edu
www.stjosephscollege.edu
• Bill Yates, General Manager
Description:
Music, News, Sports.

WSJM-AM
580 EAST NAPIER AVENUE
BENTON HARBOR, MI 49022
269-925-1111
Fax: 269-925-1011
aweston@wsjm.com
www.wsjm.com
• Joe Eauganno, Advertising Manager
(269) 925-1111
• Jim Gifford, Program Director
(269) 925-1111
gifford@wsjm.com
• Phil McDonald, Sports Director
Description:
Music, News, Talk.

WSKW
PO BOX 159, MIDDLE RD
SKOWHEGAN, ME 04976
207-474-5171
Fax: 207-474-3299
• Jason Roberts, General Manager/Program
Director/Sports Director
Nature of Sports Service:
Local. 24-hour sports radio programming.
ESPN Affiliate

WSLI-AM
5 TWELVE OAK CIRCLE SUITE A
JACKSON, MS 39209-6563
601-922-9307
888-848-9754
Fax: 601-922-5051
www.wslisports.com
• Bryan Eubank, General Manager
eubie@supersport930.com
Description:
Music, News, Sports.

WSLJ-FM
SAINT LAWRENCE UNIVERSITY
CANTON, NY 13617
315-229-5356
800-388-6758
Fax: 315-229-5373
radio@ncpr.org
www.ncpr.org
• Martha Foley, News Director
(315) 229-5304
martha@ncpr.org
Description:
Music, News.

WSLL-FM
SAINT LAWRENCE UNIVERSITY
CANTON, NY 13617
315-229-5356
800-388-6758
Fax: 315-229-5373
radio@ncpr.org
www.ncpr.org
• Martha Foley, News Director
(315) 229-5304
martha@ncpr.org
Description:
Music, News.

WSLO-FM
SAINT LAWRENCE UNIVERSITY
CANTON, NY 13617
315-229-5356
800-388-6758
Fax: 315-229-5373
radio@ncpr.org
www.ncpr.org
• Martha Foley, News Director
(315) 229-5304
martha@ncpr.org
Description:
Music, News.

WSMG-AM
1004 ARNOLD ROAD
GREENEVILLE, TN 37743
423-638-3188
Fax: 423-638-1979
wgrv@greeneville.com
www.greeneville.com/wsmg
• Leroy Moon, Advertising Manager
• Bobby Rader, News Director
• Bobby Rader, Sports Director
Description:
Music, News, Sports.

WSMI-AM
PO BOX 10
LITCHFIELD, IL 62056
217-532-5921
Fax: 217-532-2431
wsmi@wsmiradio.com
www.wsmiradio.com
• Kevin Talley, Promotions Director
• Terry Todt, Program Director
• Terry Todt, Sports Director
Description:
Music, News, Sports.

WSMK-FM
925 NORTH 5TH STREET
NILES, MI 49120-1601
616-683-4343
Fax: 269-683-7759
• Jeff Ryder, Program Director
(269) 683-4343

Description:
Music, News, Sports.
Year Founded:
1990

WSNV-FM
3807 BRANDON AVENUE S.W. SUITE
2350
ROANOKE, VA 24018
540-725-1220
Fax: 540-725-1245
www.j935.com
• Tammy Cazap, Advertising Manager
• Steve Cross, Program Director
stevecross@clearchannel.com
Description:
Music, News, Sports.

WSOU-FM
400 SOUTH ORANGE AVENUE
SOUTH ORANGE, NJ 07079-2646
973-761-9768
800-895-9768
Fax: 973-761-7593
wsou@shu.edu
www.wsou.net
• John Brickley, Sports Director
brickljo@shu.edu
• Aleks Tasic, News Director
(973) 313-6110
tasicale@shu.edu
• Brian Ciano, Sports Director
(973) 761-9768
wsousports@hotmail.com
Description:
Music, News, Sports.

WSPD
125 S. SUPERIOR ST
TOLEDO, OH 43602
419-244-8321
Fax: 419-242-2846
• Andy Stuart, General Manager
• Mellisa Richards, Marketing Director
Nature of Sports Service:
News, Sports, Talk.
Baseball:
MLB - Detroit Tigers.
College Sports:
Basketball, Football - University of Toledo.
Football:
NFL - Detroit Lions.

WSQR-AM
1851 COLTONVILLE ROAD
SYCAMORE, IL 60178-2663
815-899-1000
Fax: 815-899-9000
• Bob Costigan, News Director
Description:
Music, News, Sports.

WSRN-FM
500 COLLEGE AVENUE
SWARTHMORE, PA 19081-1306
610-328-8335
Fax: 610-328-8000
www.wsrnfm.org
• John C. Williams, General Manager
(610) 328-8340
Description:
Music, News, Sports.

WSRW-AM
5675 STATE ROUTE 247
HILLSBORO, OH 45133

937-393-1590
Fax: 937-393-1611
www.wsrwam.com
• Damon Scott, Program Director
damonscott@clearchannel.com
Description:
Music, News, Talk.

WSRW-FM
5675 STATE ROUTE 247
HILLSBORO, OH 45133
937-393-1590
Fax: 937-393-1611
www.wsrw.com
• Damon Scott, Program Director
damonscott@clearchannel.com
Description:
Music, News, Sports.

WSSO-AM
601 2ND AVENUE NORTH
COLUMBUS, MS 39701
662-327-1183
Fax: 662-328-1122
chris.doughty@cumulus.com
• Greg Benefield, General Manager
(662) 327-1183
Description:
Music, News, Talk.

WSTP-AM
P. O. BOX 4157
SALISBURY, NC 28145
704-636-3811
Fax: 704-637-1490
newsradio1490@yahoo.com
www.1490wstp.com
• Mark Brown, News Director
• Howard Platt, Sports Director
(704) 636-3811
Description:
Music, News.

WSYL-AM
P.O. BOX 519
SYLVANIA, GA 30467-0519
912-564-7461
Fax: 912-564-7462
• Ann Jones, Advertising Manager
Description:
Music, News, Sports.

WSYY-AM
LAKE ROAD
PO BOX 1240
MILLINOCKET, ME 04462
207-723-9657
Fax: 207-723-5900
calendar@themountain949.com
www.angelfire.com/me2/wsyyfm/index.html
• Michael Hale, Advertising Manager
mhale@themountain949.com
• Michael Hale, News Director
mhale@themountain949.com
• Michael Hale, Sports Director
mhale@themountain949.com
Description:
Music, News, Sports.

WTAD-AM
329 MAINE STREET
QUINCY, IL 62301
217-224-4102
Fax: 217-224-4133
www.wtad.com

• Mary Griffith, News Director
(217) 224-4102
mgriffith@staradio.com
Description:
News, Talk.

WTAW
2700 E. BYPASS, STE 5000
COLLEGE STATION, TX 77840
979-846-1150
Fax: 979-846-1933
www.wtaw.com/wtaw
• Ben Downs, General Manager
• Tom Turbiville, Sports Director
Nature of Sports Service:
News, Sports.
Baseball:
MLB - Houston Astros, CBS Baseball.
College Sports:
Football - University of Texas, CBS NCAA;
Baseball - Texas A&M; Basketball -
University of Texas, Texas A&M.
Football:
NFL - Dallas Cowboys.

WTBU-AM
BOSTON UNIVERSITY
BOSTON, MA 02215-2422
617-353-6401
Fax: 617-353-6403
wtbu@bu.edu
www.wtburadio.com/
• Matt Blanchette, Sports Director
sports@wtburadio.com
• Eden Kasle, News Director
news@wtburadio.org
Description:
Music, News, Sports.

WTCC-FM
P.O. BOX 9000
SPRINGFIELD, MA 01102-9000
413-746-9822
Fax: 413-755-6305
www.wtccfm.org
• Mark Lee, Program Director
(413) 746-9822
Description:
Music, News, Sports.

WTCH-AM
1456 GREENBAY STREET, E.
SHAWANO, WI 54166
715-524-2194
Fax: 715-524-9980
www.wtcham960.com
• Doug Erdman, News Director
(715) 524-2194
• Andy Richards, Sports Director
Description:
Music, News, Sports.

WTCO-AM
50 FRIENDSHIP PIKE
CAMPBELLSVILLE, KY 42718
270-789-2401
Fax: 270-789-1450
www.wtcoldies.com
• Marty Bagby, News Director
• Marty Bagby, Sports Director
Description:
Music, News, Sports.

WTCQ-FM
1501 MOUNT VERNON ROAD
VIDALIA, GA 30474

912-537-9202
Fax: 912-537-4477
www.vidaliacommunications.com
• Collins Knighton, Sports Director
(912) 537-9202
• Martin McIntyre, Advertising Manager
Description:
Music.

WTCR-AM
134 4TH AVENUE
HUNTINGTON, WV 25701
304-525-7788
800-938-1033
Fax: 304-525-3299
billcornwell@clearchannel.com
www.havejoy.com
• Clint McElroy, Program Director
Description:
Music, News, Sports.

WTDK-FM
2 BAY STREET
CAMBRIDGE, MD 21613
410-228-4800
Fax: 410-228-0130
• Norm Elliott, News Director
(410) 228-4800
normelliott@hotmail.com
Description:
Music, News, Sports.

WTDY AM 1670
PO BOX 2058
MADISON, WI 53701
608-273-1000
Fax: 608-271-8182
• Tom Walker, General Manager
• John Sylvester, Operations
Manager/Program Director
• Chris Krok, Promotions Director
Nature Sports Service:
Sports and Talk Radio.

WTEM SPORTS RADIO
8750 BROOKVILLE RD
SILVER SPRING, MD 20910
301-231-7798
• Kristin Lewis, Asst Promotions Dir
Nature of Sports Service:
Local and National. 24-hour sports radio
programming.

WTGG-FM
200 EAST THOMAS STREET
HAMMOND, LA 70401
985-542-9844
Fax: 123-456-5679
ewdowdy@yahoo.com
www.tang965.com
• Ellise Dowdy, Promotions Director
(985) 345-0030
• Roger Gill, Sports Director
(985) 345-0060
• T. J. Maggio, Program Director
tjinthemorning@yahoo.com

WTGZ-FM
2514 SOUTH COLLEGE STREET SUITE
104
AUBURN, AL 36830
334-887-9999
888-984-4379
Fax: 334-826-9599
info@thetiger.fm
www.thetiger.net

• Kevin Jackson, Promotion Director

WTIG-AM
P.O. BOX 608
MASSILLON, OH 44647-9513
330-837-9900
Fax: 330-837-9844
espn@espn990.com
www.espn990.com
• Bill Caples, Sports Director
(330) 837-9900
espn@espn990.com
• Donovan Resh, Program Director
(330) 837-9900
espn@espn990.com
Description:
Music, News, Sports.

WTIV-AM
900 WATER STREET
MEADVILLE, PA 16335
814-724-1111
Fax: 814-333-9628
• Doug Metheney, News Director
radio@zoominternet.net
Description:
Music, News, Sports.

WTKG-AM
77 MONROE CENTER STEET, N.W. SUITE
1000
GRAND RAPIDS, MI 49503-2912
616-459-1919
Fax: 616-242-6599
www.wtkg.com
• Rich Jones, News Director
(616) 459-1919
richajones@clearchannel.com
Description:
Music, News.

WTKT-AM
600 CORPORATE CIRCLE
HARRISBURG, PA 17110
717-540-8800
800-500-9993
Fax: 717-671-9973
billmead@clearchannel.com
www.kool993.com
• Ron Roy, General Manager
ronroy@clearchannel.com
Description:
Music.

WTKY-FM
341 RADIO STATION ROAD
TOMPKINSVILLE, KY 42167
270-487-6119
Fax: 270-487-8462
• Bernice Whittimore, General Manager
• Bernice Whittimore, President
Description:
Music, News, Sports.

WTLC-FM
21 EAST SAINT JOSEPHS STREET
INDIANAPOLIS, IN 46204
317-266-9600
Fax: 317-328-3870
www.wtlc.com/contactus.asp
• Terri Durrett, News Director
tdurrett@radio-one.com
• Kay Feeney-Caito, Promotions Director
• Lakisha Knight, Promotions Director
(317) 266-9600

Description:
Music, News, Sports, Talk.

WTLX-FM
100 STODDART
BEAVER DAM, WI 53916-0902
920-885-4949
800-369-1005
Fax: 920-885-2152
• Evan Cohen, Program Director
(920) 885-4949
• Keith Williams, Sales Manager
(608) 245-9859
Description:
Music, News, Sports.

WTMJ
720 E. CAPITOL DR
MILWAUKEE, WI 53212
414-332-9611
Fax: 414-967-5298
www.620wtmj.com
• Carl Moll, Director Network Operations
• Tom Sheridan, General Sales Manager
• Jon Schweitzer, Senior VP/General
Manager
Nature of Service:
News and score reporting for the bowling
community in the greater Buffalo/Niagara
Falls region.
Baseball:
MLB - Milwaukee Brewers.
Basketball:
NBA-Milwaukee Bucks
College Sports:
Basketball, Football - University of
Wisconsin.
Football:
NFL - Green Bay Packers.
Publishing Company:
Westside News, Inc.
Primary Audience:
Bowling Community.
Frequency:
Weekly during bowling season.
Sports:
Bowling.
Circulation:
2,100

WTNS-FM
114 NORTH 6TH STREET
COSHOCTON, OH 43812
740-622-1560
Fax: 740-622-7940
• Ken Smailes, News Director
• Tom Thompson, Advertising Manager
Description:
Music, News, Sports.

WTNY-AM
134 MULLIN STREET
WATERTOWN, NY 13601-3616
315-788-0790
Fax: 315-788-4379
ltz93@hotmail.com
www.790wtny.com
• Nathan Lehman, News Director
(315) 788-0790
• George Nehr, Promotions Director
Description:
Music, News, Sports, Talk.

WTOD-AM
3225 ARLINGTON AVENUE
TOLEDO, OH 43614-2427

419-725-5700
Fax: 419-385-2902
• Brian Olsen, General Manager
• Tim Roberts, Advertising Manager
(419) 725-5700
Description:
Music, News, Sports.

___

WTON-AM
304 WEST BEVERLEY STREET
STAUNTON, VA 24401-4207
540-885-5188
800-978-2794
Fax: 540-885-1240
• Patrick Hite, News Director
(540) 885-5188
• J. G. Ratcliff, Owner
(540) 885-5188
Description:
Music.

___

WTOP-FM
3400 IDAHO AVENUE, N.W.
WASHINGTON, DC 20016-3046
202-895-5000
Fax: 202-895-5149
www.wtopnews.com
• Dave Johnson, Sports Director
(202) 895-5068
djohnson@wtopnews.com

___

WTOU-AM
1867 WEST MARKET STREET
AKRON, OH 44313-6901
330-836-4700
Fax: 330-836-5321
marvindurant@clearchannel.com
• Tom Duresky, News Director
tomduresky@clearchannel.com
Description:
Music.

___

WTPA-FM
2300 VARTAN WAY
HARRISBURG, PA 17110-9720
717-238-1041
800-946-5104
Fax: 717-234-7780
www.wtpafm.com
• John Paul Shaffer, News Director
Description:
Music, News, Sports.

___

WTPR-AM
206 NORTH BREWER STREET
PARIS, TN 38242
731-642-7100
Fax: 731-644-9367
www.wenkwtpr.com
• Terry Hailey, Advertising Manager
• Terry Hailey, News Director
(731) 642-7100
Description:
Music, News, Sports.

___

WTRN-AM
WASHINGTON AVENUE AND 1ST
STREET
TYRONE, PA 16686
814-684-3200
Fax: 814-684-1220
amnnet@aol.com
www.wtrn.net
• Jean Dixon, News Director
• Rich Saupp, Sports Director

___

Description:
Music, News, Sports, Talk.

___

WTRP-AM
806 NEW FRANKLIN ROAD
LAGRANGE, GA 30240-1844
706-884-7022
706-884-9877
Fax: 706-884-8612
www.wtrp.com
• Michael Buchanan, Sports Anchor
• Jennifer Jones, Advertising Sales

___

WTRS-FM
3357 SOUTHWEST 7TH STREET
OCALA, FL 34474
352-732-9877
Fax: 352-622-6675
www.wtrs.fm
• Sam Gerace, Advertising Manager
Description:
Music, News, Sports.

___

WTSX-FM
15 NEVERSINK DRIVE
PORT JERVIS, NY 12771
845-856-5185
888-967-9879
Fax: 845-856-4757
wtsx@frontiernet.net
www.wtsx.com
• Bob O., News Director
bobomorningshow@yahoo.com
Description:
Music, News, Sports.

___

WTTF-AM
167 MAIN STREET
TIFFIN, OH 44883
419-447-9883
Fax: 419-447-2212
www.wttf.com
• John Spahr, Operations Manager
• Steve Shoffner, News Director
• Jon Kerns, Sports Director

___

WTTR-AM
101 WTTR LANE
WESTMINSTER, MD 21158
410-848-5511
Fax: 410-876-5095
news@wttr.com
www.wttr.com
• Mark Woodworth, News Director
(410) 848-5511
news@wttr.com
• Charles Beckhardt, Sports Director
(410) 848-5511
info@wttr.com
Description:
Music, News, Sports, Talk.

___

WTXM-FM
P.O. BOX 3848
MARYVILLE, TN 47720
865-525-6000
Fax: 865-525-2000
www.knoxoldies.com/
• Brad Jeffries, Program Director
Description:
Music, News, Sports.

___

WTZN-AM
170 REDINGTON AVENUE
TROY, PA 16947

___

570-297-0100
800-326-9445
Fax: 570-297-3193
www.wiggle100.com/
• David Rockwell, News Director
news@wiggle100.com
Description:
Music.

___

WTZX-AM
520 NORTH SPRING STREET
SPARTA, TN 38583-1305
931-836-1055
Fax: 931-836-2320
donhoward@clearchannel.com
Description:
Music, News, Sports.

___

WUCZ-FM
104 Z COUNTRY LANE
CARTHAGE, TN 37030
615-735-1350
Fax: 615-735-0381
www.1041theranch.net
• Jim West, Sports Director
• John Wood, Sportsnuts Host
• Dennis Banka, Station Owner
dennis@1041theranch.net
Description:
Sports talk show dedicated to our local high
school football teams, with segments
dedicated to the Tennessee Volunteers and
the Tennessee Titans.
Sports Discussed:
Primary: local high school football;
Secondary: College & NFL Football,
Tennessee Titans and Tennessee
Volunteers, other sports as needed.
Frequency:
Sportsnuts airs Thrusday nights from August
thru November (High School Football
Season) from 6-8pm Central Time.

___

WUMP 730
PO BOX 389
ATHENS, AL 35612
256-830-8300
Fax: 256-232-6842
www.730ump.com
• Bill Dunnavant, General Manager
• Peter Thiele, Operations Manager/Sports
Director
Nature of Sports Service:
24 Hour sports.
Auto Sports:
NASCAR.
Baseball:
MLB Atlanta Braves.
College Sports:
Football, Basketball - Auburn University.

___

WUNR-AM
160 NORTH WASHINGTON STREET
BOSTON, MA 02114-2120
617-367-9003
Fax: 617-367-2265
• Velma May, News Director
Description:
Full Service, Music, News.

___

WUPR-AM
P.O. BOX 868
UTUADO, PUERTO RIC 00641-0868
787-894-2460
Fax: 787-894-4955
• Jose Martinez Giraud, General Manager

Description:
Music, News, Sports, Talk.

WUSB-FM
S.U.N.Y. AT STONY BROOK
STONY BROOK, NY 11794
631-632-6501
Fax: 631-632-7182
www.wusb.org
• Curt Hylton, Sports Director
(631) 632-6501
• Morton Mecklosky, News Director
(631) 751-2577
mecklom@sunysuffolk.edu
Description:
Music, News, Sports.

WUSI-FM
1100 LINCOLN DRIVE ROOM 1003 MAIL
CODE 6
CARBONDALE, IL 62901
618-453-4343
Fax: 618-453-6186
jeff.williams@wsiu.org
• Mike Zelten, Program Director
(618) 453-5020
Description:
Music, News, Sports.

WUVA-FM
1140 ROSE HILL DRIVE
CHARLOTTESVILLE, VA 22903-5128
434-817-6880
Fax: 434-977-3775
• Tanisha Thompson, Program Director
Description:
Music, News, Sports.

WVAC-FM
110 SOUTH MADISON STREET
ADRIAN, MI 49221-2518
517-265-5161
Fax: 517-264-3331
• Joe Elardo, Sports Director
• Ben McDuffee, News Director
Description:
Music, News, Sports.

WVBU-FM
P.O. BOX C-3956
LEWISBURG, PA 17837-2029
570-577-1174
Fax: 570-577-1174
wvbu@bucknell.edu
www.orgs.bucknell.edu/wvbu/
• Heather Franz, News Director
Description:
Music, News, Sports.

WVCH-AM
308 EAST DUTTONMILL ROAD
BROOKHAVEN, PA 19015-1109
610-872-8861
Fax: 610-872-8865
wvch@juno.com
www.wvch.com
• William Fenton, General Manager
(610) 279-9000
wvchtraffic@juno.com
Description:
Music.

WVEE-FM
1201 PEACHTREE STREET NORTHEAST
SUITE 80
ATLANTA, GA 30361-3500
404-898-8900
Fax: 404-898-8909
www.v-103.com
• Monique Davis, Marketing Director
• Monique Davis, Promotion Director
• Denise Meriwether, Promotions Assistant
• Denise Meriwether, Promotions
Coordinator
• Olivia Seymore, Promotions Coordinator
Description:
Music, News, Sports.

WVEI-AM
181 MORELAND STREET
WORCESTER, MA 01609
508-752-5611
Fax: 508-752-1006
• Jason Wolfe, Program Director
(617) 779-3541
Description:
Sports, Talk.

WVGM-AM
3305 OLD FOREST ROAD
LYNCHBURG, VA 24501
434-385-8298
Fax: 434-385-8991
• Tex Meyer, General Manager
(434) 385-8298
texmeyer@clearchannel.com

WVLZ-AM
802 SOUTH CENTRAL AVENUE
KNOXVILLE, TN 37902-1207
865-546-4653
Fax: 865-637-7133
• Gormon Collins, General Manager
Description:
Music.

WVMJ-FM
SETTLERS GREEN ROUTE 16
NORTH CONWAY, NH 03860
603-356-8870
Fax: 603-356-8875
office@wmwv.com
www.valley1045.com
• Ron Frizzel, General Manager
ronfrizzel@aol.com
Description:
Music, News, Sports.

WVMW-FM
2300 ADAMS AVENUE
SCRANTON, PA 18509-1514
570-348-6202
Fax: 570-961-4769
www.marywood.edu/departments/commarts/
WVMW.html
• Jessica Young, News Director
Description:
Music, News.

WVRY-FM
402 BNA DRIVE SUITE 400
NASHVILLE, TN 37217
615-367-2210
Fax: 615-367-0758
www.solidgospel.com
• Vance Dillard, Program Director
(615) 367-2210

Description:
Music, News, Sports.

WVUM-FM
P.O. BOX 248191
CORAL GABLES, FL 33146
305-284-3131
Fax: 305-284-3132
info@wvum.org
www.wvum.org
• Jeremy Marks-Peltz, Sports Director
sports@wvum.org
Description:
Music, News, Sports.

WVXU-FM
1223 CENTRAL PARKWAY
CINCINNATI, OH 45214
513-352-9170
800-230-3576
Fax: 513-745-1004
wvxu@wvxu.org
www.wvxu.org
• Ann Thompson, News Director
(513) 745-3780
Description:
Educational, Music, News, Sports.

WWAG-FM
1680 STATE ROAD 1071
TOMPKINSVILLE, KY 42167
606-287-9924
1079fm@prtcnet.org
• Sherry Handy, Program Director

WWBF-AM
1130 RADIO ROAD
BARTOW, FL 33830-7600
863-533-0744
Fax: 863-533-8546
www.wwbf.com
• Susan Thornburg, Office Manager
susan@wwbf.com
• Tom Thornburg, Sports Director
tom@wwbf.com
Description:
Music, News, Sports.

WWCD-FM
503 SOUTH FRONT STREET SUITE 101
COLUMBUS, OH 43215-5666
614-221-9923
Fax: 614-227-0021
webmaster@cd101.com
www.cd101.com
• Randy Malloy, Marketing Director
(614) 221-9923
randym@cd101.com
• Randy Malloy, News Director
(614) 221-9923
randym@cd101.com
Description:
Music, News, Sports.

WWDW-FM
3 EAST 1ST STREET
WELDON, NC 27890
252-536-3115
Fax: 252-538-0378
• Les Atkins, News Director
• Mark Matthews, Sports Director
• Amy Moran, Advertising Sales Manager
(252) 538-9790
amymoran@yahoo.com

WWEL-FM
P.O. BOX 1988
LONDON, KY 40743
606-864-2148
Fax: 606-864-0645
www.1039thewolf.com
• Jerry Deaton, News Director
• Trevor Grigsby, Sports Director
• Frances Wilhoit, Account Executive
• Frances Wilhoit, Advertising Manager
• Frances Wilhoit, Promotions Manager
• Terry Harris, Sports Director
(606) 864-2148
Description:
Music.

WWFG-FM
351 TILGHMAN ROAD
SALISBURY, MD 21804-1126
410-742-1923
800-664-3764
Fax: 410-742-2329
salisburyproduction@clearchannel.com
www.delmarvaradio.com
• Brian Cleary, Program Director
(410) 572-6781
briancleary@clearchannel.com
Description:
Music, News, Sports.

WWIS-AM
W11573 TOWN CREEK ROAD
BLACK RIVER FALLS, WI 54615
715-284-4391
Fax: 715-284-9740
wwis@wwisradio.com
www.wwisradio.com
• Brian Brawner, Sports Director
• Bob Gabrielson, General Manager
Description:
Music.

WWIZ-FM
4040 SIMON ROAD
YOUNGSTOWN, OH 44512
330-783-1000
Fax: 330-783-0060
www.realrock104.com/
• Jim Loboy, News Director
(330) 783-1000
Description:
Music.

WWKA-FM
4192 NORTH JOHN YOUNG PARKWAY
ORLANDO, FL 32804
407-298-9292
Fax: 407-290-1076
www.k92fm.com
• Amy Jean Thompson, Promotion Director
(321) 281-2023
Description:
Music, News, Sports.

WWKC-FM
4988 SKYLINE DRIVE
CAMBRIDGE, OH 43725
740-432-5605
Fax: 740-432-1991
www.yourradioplace.com
• W. Grant Hafley, General Manager
• Reuben Perdue, Sports Director
(740) 432-5605
Description:
Music.

WWKY-FM
P.O. BOX 1310
MADISONVILLE, KY 42431
270-825-9779
Fax: 270-825-3260
• Keith Farrell, Account Executive
• Stephanie Vandygriff, Operations Manager
Description:
Music, News, Sports. Carries University of Kentucky's football and men's basketball games, Webster county high school games, as well as the NFL's Tennessee Titans games.
Publications:
High school football and high school basketball schedules.

WWL
1450 PAYDRAS ST
NEW ORLEANS, LA 70112
504-593-6376
Fax: 504-593-1850
• Johnny Andrews, Vice President/General Manager
• Buddy Deliberto, Sports Director
Nature of Sports Service:
News, Sports.
Baseball:
Minor League - Pacific Coast League/PCL/New Orleans Zephyrs.
College Sports:
Basketball, Football - Louisiana State University/LSU, Tulane.
Football:
NFL - New Orleans Saints.

WWLU-FM
LINCOLN UNIVERSITY
LINCOLN UNIVERSITY, PA 19352-0999
610-932-8300
Fax: 610-932-1905
Description:
Music, News, Sports, Talk.

WWTM
181 MORELAND ST
WORCESTER, MA 01609
508-836-9223
wwtm@hotmail.com
• Bruce Mittman, General Manager
• Chuck Perks, Program Director/Sports Director
Nature of Sports Service:
Local. 24-hour sports radio programming.
Baseball:
MLB - New York Yankees.
Basketball:
NBA Finals.
College Sports:
Basketball, Football - Holy Cross.
Ice Hockey:
NHL - Boston Bruins; Stanley Cup Finals.

WWTN-FM
10 MUSIC CIRCLE, E.
NASHVILLE, TN 37203-4338
615-291-7279
800-738-9986
Fax: 615-291-7268
www.997wtn.com
• Blake Fulton, Sports Director
(615) 291-7279
• John Mountz, Program Director
• Lisa Valasquez, Promotions Director
(615) 321-1067

Description:
News, Sports, Talk.

WWVA-AM
1015 MAIN STREET
WHEELING, WV 30309
304-232-1170
Fax: 304-234-0041
www.newsradio1170.com
• Johnson Nixon, News Director
(304) 232-1170
johnsonnixon@clearchannel.com
• John Simonson, Sports Director
(304) 232-1170
johnsimonson@clearchannel.com
• Missy Tchappat, Advertising Director
• Missy Tchappat, Promotion Director
(304) 232-1170
missytchappat@clearchannel.com
Description:
News, Talk.

WXBD-AM
1909 EAST PASS ROAD SUITE D-11
GULFPORT, MS 39507
228-388-2001
Fax: 228-896-9736
• Suzanne Kelly, News Director
(228) 388-2001
mikesuzanne@hotmail.com
Description:
Music, News, Sports.

WXDU-FM
DUKE UNIVERSITY
DURHAM, NC 27708-0689
919-684-2957
Fax: 919-684-3260
wxdu@duke.edu
www.wxdu.duke.edu/
Description:
Music, News, Sports.

WXDX-AM
27675 HALSTED ROAD
FARMINGTON HILLS, MI 48331
248-324-5800
Fax: 248-848-0371
mschroeder@clearchannel.com
www.wxdx1310.com
• Mary Ann Schroeder-Barr, News Director
maryannschroeder@clearchannel.com

WXKS-FM
99 REVERE BEACH PARKWAY
MEDFORD, MA 02155
781-396-1430
Fax: 781-290-0722
www.kissfm.com
• Bill Costa, News Director
billcosta@clearchannel.com
• Dennis O'Heron, Promotion Manager
dennisoheron@clearchannel.com
Description:
Music, News, Sports.

WXLU-FM
SAINT LAWRENCE UNIVERSITY
CANTON, NY 13617
315-229-5356
800-388-6758
Fax: 315-229-5373
radio@ncpr.org
www.ncpr.org

• Martha Foley, News Director
(315) 229-5304
martha@ncpr.org
Description:
Music, News.

WXTB-FM
4002 GANDY BOULEVARD
TAMPA, FL 33611-3410
813-832-1000
Fax: 813-832-1090
www.98rock.com
• Meg Heimstead, Promotions Coordinator
• Mike Oliviero, Promotion Director
mikeoliviero@clearchannel.com
Description:
Music, News, Sports.

WXXA-AM
4000 NUMBER 1 RADIO DRIVE
LOUISVILLE, KY 40218-4514
502-479-2222
Fax: 502-479-2225
www.wwky.com
• Ted Werbin, News Director
(502) 479-2201
tedwerbin@clearchannel.com
Description:
Music, News, Sports.

WXYT-AM
26495 AMERICAN DRIVE
SOUTHFIELD, MI 48034-6114
248-455-7350
Fax: 248-455-7369
www.wxyt.com
• Deb Spadafora, Promotions Director
daspadafora@cbs.com
• Dan Zampillo, Program Director
(248) 455-7350
Description:
Talk.

WYBF-FM
610 KING OF PRUSSIA ROAD
RADNOR, PA 19087-3623
610-902-8457
Fax: 610-902-8285
• Justin Hallman, Sports Director
(610) 902-5115
jjh722@cabrini.edu
• Krista Mazzeo, General Manager
(610) 902-8360
themazzspazz@hotmail.com
Description:
Educational, Music, News, Sports, Talk.

WYNT-FM
1330 NORTH MAIN STREET
MARION, OH 43302
877-472-3464
Fax: 740-387-3697
stevescott@clearchannel.com
www.majic959.com
• Ben Failor, News Director
benfailor@clearchannel.com
• Jeff Ruth, Sports Director
(877) 472-3464
jeffruth@clearchannel.com
Description:
Music, News, Sports, Talk.

WYRQ-FM
16405 HAVEN ROAD
LITTLE FALLS, MN 56345-2630

320-632-2992
800-568-7249
Fax: 320-632-2571
www.fallsradio.com
• Rod Grams, Program Director
(320) 632-5414
• Al Windsperger, Sports Director
(320) 632-2992
ads@fallsradio.com
Description:
Music, News, Sports.
Year Founded:
1980

WYSL-AM
P. O. BOX 236
AVON, NY 14414-9791
585-346-3000
Fax: 585-346-0450
info@wysl1040.com
www.wysl1040.com
• Robert Savage, News Director
savage@wysl1040.com
• Joe Centanni, Weekend And Sports
Producer
(585) 346-3000
info@wysl1040.com
Description:
News, Talk.

WYTI-AM/FM
275 GLENNWOOD DRIVE
ROCKY MOUNT, VA 24151-0430
540-483-9955
Fax: 540-483-7802
wyti@wytiradio.com
www.wytiradio.com
• Susan Mullins, Vice President
Description:
Music, News, Sports.
Year Founded:
1957

WYXC-AM
1410 HIGHWAY 411 NE
CARTERSVILLE, GA 30121-5115
770-382-1306
Fax: 770-936-1967
• Chip Rogers, Owner
Description:
Music, News, Sports.

WYXY-FM
20 N.W. 3RD STREET
EVANSVILLE, IN 47708
812-424-8284
Fax: 812-426-7928
• Tim Huelfing, General Manager
Description:
Music, News, Sports.

WYYZ-AM
268 HOOD ROAD
JASPER, GA 30143-0280
706-692-4100
Fax: 706-692-4012
wyyz1490@aol.com
• Tania Clark, Station Manager
(706) 692-4100
radiomom@etcmail.com
Description:
Music, News, Sports, Talk.

WZBB-FM
10899 VIRGINIA AVENUE
BASSETT, VA 24055

618-564-2171
Fax: 618-564-3202
• Craig Richards, Program Director
crichards@wzbbfm.com
Description:
Music, News, Sports.

WZBO-AM
911 PARSONAGE STREET EXTENDED
ELIZABETH CITY, NC 27909
252-338-0196
Fax: 252-338-5275
www.ecri.net
• Chris Ling, Advertising Manager
(252) 441-2109
• Rick Loesch, Advertising Manager
rloesch@ecri.net
• Rick Loesch, Owner
rloesch@ecri.net
• Sam Walker, News Director
Description:
Music, News, Sports, Talk.

WZCT-AM
1111 EAST WILLOW STREET
SCOTTSBORO, AL 35768
256-574-1330
Fax: 866-506-7181
www.southerngospelam1330.com/
• Rob Carlile, Sports Director
Description:
Music, News, Sports.

WZLX-FM
800 BOYLSTON STREET, SUITE 2450
BOSTON, MA 02199-8001
617-267-0123
Fax: 617-421-9305
www.wzlx.com/
• Chachi Loprete, Marketing Director
• Chachi Loprete, Promotions Coordinator
• Patrick Murray, News Director
(617) 267-0123
• Tank Sferruzza, Sports Director
(617) 267-0123
Description:
Music, News, Sports.

WZMR-FM
6 JOHNSON ROAD
LATHAM, NY 12110-5610
518-786-6600
Fax: 518-786-6610
www.albanyedge.com
• Kevin Callahan, Program Director
(518) 786-6675
Description:
Music, News, Sports.

WZNJ-FM
1028 HIGHWAY 80, E.
DEMOPOLIS, AL 36732-3712
334-289-1400
Fax: 334-289-2156
• Amy Ward, Sports Director
Description:
Music, News, Sports.

WZTM
11300 4TH ST, STE 318
ST. PETERSBURG, FL 33716
727-871-1819
• Rob Weingarten, Program Director
• Al Dukes, Sports Director
• Tom Connolly, Executive Producer

Nature of Sports Service:
Local. 24-hour sports radio programming.
Baseball:
MLB - New York Yankees.
College Sports:
Baseball - University of South Florida;
Basketball - University of South Florida,
Florida State, Football - University of South
Florida, Florida State.
Football:
NFL - Jacksonville Jaguars.

WZVN-FM
6405 OLCOTT AVENUE
HAMMOND, IN 46320
219-462-6111
Fax: 219-989-8516
www.hitsandfavorites.com
• Laura Waluszko, News Director
(219) 462-6111
Description:
Music, News, Sports.

WZXL-FM
8025 BLACKHORSE PIKE BAYPORT ONE,
SUITE
WEST ATLANTIC CITY, NJ 08232
609-484-8444
Fax: 609-646-6331
www.wzxl.com
• Steve Raymond, Program Director
Description:
Music, News, Sports.

WZZE-FM
P.O. BOX 5001
CONCORDVILLE, PA 19331-0004
610-459-8100
Fax: 610-459-4431
• Mark Smith, Program Director
(610) 459-8100
Description:
Music, News, Sports.

WZZT-FM
3101 FREEPORT ROAD
STERLING, IL 61081
815-625-3400
Fax: 815-625-6940
wsdr@theramp.net
• Cathy Wagner, Promotion Director
wsdrsd@theramp.net
• Brian Zschiesche, Program Director
(815) 625-3400
wsdrtm@theramp.net

XTRA SPORTS 910
645 E MISSOURI AVE, STE 119
PHOENIX, AZ 85012
602-798-9340
Fax: 602-798-9364
www.xtrasports910.com
• Susan Karis-Madigan, General Manager
Nature of Sports Service:
Local. 24-hour sports radio programming.

XTRA SPORTS RADIO (690 AM)
610 S. ARDMORE AVE
LOS ANGELES, CA 90005
213-385-0101
Fax: 213-427-7905
www.xtrasports690.com
• Greg Ashlock, General Manager
• Brian Blackmore, Sports Director
Nature of Sports Service:
Regional. 24-hour sports radio

programming. for all of Southern California.
Baseball:
ESPN Radio; CBS Baseball, World Series,
Playoffs.
Basketball:
Los Angeles Clippers; NBA Radio.
College Sports:
University of California Los Angeles (UCLA).
Arena Football League
Los Angeles Avengers.

XTRA SPORTS RADIO 1150 AM
610 S. ARDMORE AVE
LOS ANGELES, CA 90005
213-520-1150
800-522-1150
Fax: 213-427-7278
• Roy Laughlin, General Manager
• Bic Jacobs, Program Director
• Dan Kieley, Program Director
Nature of Sports Service:
Regional. 24-hour sports radio
programming, includes Los Angeles
Dodgers and UCLA.

Sports Television, Cable & Broadcasting

ABC SPORTS, INC.
47 W. 66TH STREET
13TH FLOOR
NEW YORK, NY 10023
212-456-7777
Fax: 212-456-2381
www.abcsports.com
• John Skipper, President, ESPN, Inc.

ANN LIGUORI PRODUCTIONS, INC.
3 PINE GROVE COURT
WESTHAMPTON, NY 11977-1324
631-325-8573
www.annliguori.com
• Ann Liguori, President/Executive
Producer/Host
Nature of Sports Service:
National. Cable TV producer, distributor and
broadcaster. Produces, sells and distributes
Sports Innerview with Ann Liguori, a weekly
show on Fox Sports networks, Ann also
hosts weekly, 5-hour, live sports call-in show
on WFAN - NY.

AUTOTRADER.COM, INC
3003 SUMMIT BLVD
SUITE 200
ATLANTA, GA 30319
404-568-8000
800-353-9350
Fax: 404-568-3060
www.autotrader.com
• Jimmy Hayes, Chairman
• Dallas Clement, Executive Vice
President/Chief Financial Offi
• Edward Smith, CTO
Football Media Sponsor:
NFL - broadcast sponsorship of Monday
Night Football on ABC, NFL Live on ESPN2,
and Sunday Night Football on ESPN
College Sports Media Sponsor:
TV broadcasts of NCAA basketball games
on CBS
Football Media Sponsor:
Superbowl Advertiser

BLACK ENTERTAINMENT TELEVISION
1 BET PLAZA
1235 WEST STREET NORTHEAST
WASHINGTON, DC 20018-1211
202-608-2000
Fax: 202-608-2589
www.bet.com
• Debra L Lee, Chairman/Chief Executive
Officer
• Paxton Baker, President, BET Event
Productions
• Vicky Free, EVP Marketing/Chief
Marketing Officer
• Stephen Hill, President, Music
Programming
Nature of Sports Service:
National. Cable TV
Programmer/broadcaster.

CABLE NEWS NETWORK/CNN
ONE CNN CENTER
ATLANTA, GA 30348
404-827-1700
Fax: 404-827-1099
www.cnn.com
• Jeff Zucker, President
• Janet Rolle, EVP/Chief Marketing Officer
• Ken Jautz, President, CNN US
Nature of Sports Service:
National. Cable TV 24-hour news station.
Sports news presented several times a day
with a 30-minute daily wrap-up during the
evenings; periodic features on sports
figures,. sports events. Heavy sports
programming on weekends.

**CANADIAN BROADCASTING
CORPORATION/CBC**
181 QUEEN STREET
OTTAWA, ON, CANADA K1Y 1E4
613-288-6000
866-306-4636
Fax: 613-288-6245
www.cbc.ca
• Hubert Lacroix, President/Chief Executive
Officer
• Hubert Lacroix, President/CEO/Director
• Johanne B Charbonneau, Vice
President/CFO
• Kirstine Stewart, Executive Vicep
President
• Sylvain Lafrance, EVP French Services
Nature of Sports Service:
National. Broadcasting network. Sales
function includes national, regional and
market-by market sales.
Notes:
CBC has been awarded Canadian
broadcast rights for the next three Olympic
games

CBS SPORTS
51 W. 52ND STREET
NEW YORK, NY 10019-6188
212-975-4321
Fax: 212-975-4516
www.cbscorporation.com
• David Berson, President, CBS Sports
• Summer Redstone, Executive Chairman
• Shari Redstone, Vice Chairman
• Joseph Ianniello, Executive Vice
President/CFO
• Doug Rousso, CTO/CIO
• Gil Schwartz, EVP/Chief Communications
Officer
• Peter Dunn, President, CBS Television
Studios

• David Berson, EVP, CBS Sports/President, CBS College Sports
Nature of Sports Service:
National. TV network.

COMCAST SPORTSNET BAY AREA
370 3RD STREET
2ND FLOOR
SAN FRANCISCO, CA 94107
415-296-8900
www.csnbayarea.com
• Ted Griggs, President, Comcast SportsNet Bay Area
• Janet Fern, Senior Vice President/General Manager
• April Silvia, Director of Programming
• Brad Nau, Executive Producer
Nature of Sports Service:
Regional. Cable TV programmer. Current properties: Oakland A's baseball, San Francisco Giants baseball, Golden State Warriors basketball, San Jose Sharks hockey, the University of California and Stanford sports, San Jose Earthquakes soccer, Oakland Raiders football, San Francisco 49ers football.

COMCAST SPORTSNET NEW ENGLAND
42 3RD AVENUE
BURLINGTON, MA 01803-4414
617-933-9300
• Laura Hannon, Director, Comcast SportsNet New England
Nature of Sports Service:
Regional. Cable TV programmer. Current programs: Boston Celtics, New England Revolution, Boston Cannons, Maine Red Claws.

COX CABLE - SAN DIEGO
5159 FEDERAL BOULEVARD
SAN DIEGO, CA 92105
619-262-1122
Fax: 619-266-5046
www.cox.com/sandiego
• James Robbins, President/CEO
• Jacqui Vines, Vice President
• William Geppert, Senior Vice President
Nature of Sports Service:
Regional. Cable TV programmer. Broadcasts San Diego Padres games, San Diego State University Aztecs and other sports events to cable TV subscribers.

ESPN CLASSIC SPORTS NETWORK
935 MIDDLE STREET
BRISTOL, CT 06010-1099
860-585-2000
Fax: 860-585-2213
www.espnclassic.com
• George C Bodenheimer, President
• Christine Driessen, Chief Financial Officer
• Bob Regina, Director
Nature of Sports Service:
National. Cable TV network. Features classic sports programming, series documentaries, original productions.

ESPN TELEVISION
ESPN PLAZA
935 MIDDLE ST
BRISTOL, CT 06010
860-766-2000
www.espn.go.com
• John D Skipper, President
• Jodi Markley, Senior Vice President,

International Programm
• Michael Hill, Vice President/General Manager
• David Weiler, Vice President of Productions Operations
• Carol Pandiscia, Senior Vice President Of Technology, Business
• Tim Orcutt, Vice President of Tax
• Steve Anderson, EVP, News, Talent, and Content Operations
• Paul Richardson, SVP Human Resources
• David Pahl, Senior Vice President/General Counsel
• Tony Waggoner, Senior Vice President/Controller
• David Casamona, Director
• Linda Moore, Senior Director, Business Administration
• Christina Lemay, Associate Director
• Jessica Martin, Director of Marketing
• Mike Soltys, Director of Communications
• Tomas Casabal, Producer
• Andy Bronstein, Senior Director, On Air Promotions & Developm
• Mark Groeschner, Creative Director
• Brian Burns, VP Strategic Business Plan & Development
• Tim Bunnell, SVP International Programming & Marketing
Nature of Sports Service:
National. Cable TV Network, Sports coverage around the clock, including events, specials, news and information and lifestyle programming. ESPN, Inc. includes: ESPN, ESPN International, ESPN2, ESPN Enterprises, ESPNET, ESPN Radio Network, and ESPN Classic

---

EVENT SPECIALIST OF NEW ORLEANS
400 N. PETERS ST
VIEUX CARRE, SUITE 209
NEW ORLEANS, LA 70130
504-525-1115
877-917-1115
Fax: 504-525-1118
info@eventsno.com
www.eventsno.com
• Renee E. Ganucheau, President
(504) 525-1115
renee@eventsno.com
• Kimberly Zibilich, Sales Manager
(504) 525-1115
Services:
A destination Management Company specializing in arranging transportation, theme parties, entertainment, spouse programs, tours, hotel bookings and more
Clients:
AeroSpace General Counsel's Group, American Express Meetings & Incentives, American Institute of Chemical Engineers, BTI-Kuoni Event Solutions, CIMBAR Performance Minerals, Cole-Parmer Instrument Company, CRG Events, ECC Construction & Debris Removal Services, Entergy Corporation, EXXON-MOBIL, GMAC, Genesys Corporation, Hughes Network, Incentive Holland, The Innovation Group, International Association of Chiefs of Police, Laticrete International Inc., LA/MS Hospice & Palliative Care Organization, Microsoft, Milligan Events, Morris Meetings & Incentives, National Association of Gaming Regulators, National Association of State Boards of Account
Event Management Services:
Complete hotel negotiations for groups,

entertainment, special events, speakers, tours, transportation.

FOX SPORTS ASIA
151 LORONG CHUAN
03-01
NEW TECH PARK, Singapore 556741
656-488-6500
Fax: 656-488-6470
www.foxsportsasia.com
• Ward Platt, President, Fox International Channels Asia Pacific
• Peter Hutton, Senior Vice President of Sports, Fox Internat
Nature of Sports Service:
Organization is joint venture between STAR TV and Fox International Channels. It is the official Asian station of the English Premier League.

FOX SPORTS INTERNATIONAL
TUDOR HOUSE
35 GRESSE ST
LONDON, ENGLAND W1T 1QY
+44-(0) 207 462 3400
info@foxsports.co.uk
• David Flowers, Director
• Richard Battista, Director
Nature of Sports Service
Operates the programming services Fox Soccer Channel and Fox Sports Middle East, as well as syndicating sports content worldwide.

FOX SPORTS NET ARIZONA
455 NORTH 3RD STREET
SUITE 290
PHOENIX, AZ 85004-2193
602-257-9500
Fax: 602-257-0848
www.foxsportsarizona.com
• Rebecca O'Sullivan, Vice President
• Ed Olsen, General Sales Manager
• Kathy Goodenough, On Air Presentation Manager
• Elizabeth Zall, National Sales Manager
• David Soble, Local Sales Manager
• Mike Connelly, Manager
• Amy Sun, Marketing Staff
Nature of Sports Service:
Regional. Cable TV broadcaster/programmer. Current properties include: Arizona Diamondbacks, Phoenix Coyotes, PAC-10, football and basketball, Arizona State University, University of Arizona, and FOX Sports News. An affiliate of FOX Sports Net.

FOX SPORTS NET CHICAGO
350 N. ORLEANS STREET
SUITE S1-100
CHICAGO, IL 60654
312-222-6000
csnchicagowebsite@comcastsportsnet.com
www.csnchicago.com
Nature of Sports Service:
Regional. Cable TV programmer. Basic cable sports network serving Iowa, Illinois and Indiana. Covers Chicago Bulls, Chicago Cubs, Bears, Blackhawks and White Sox; also college games from Notre Dame, DePaul, Northwestern, the Big 10, Missouri Valley Conference, plus high school events and championships. Also, professional golf and tennis, auto and horse racing, and sports talk shows.

FOX SPORTS NET DETROIT
26555 EVERGREEN ROAD
SUITE 90
SOUTHFIELD, MI 48076-4232
248-723-2000
Fax: 248-226-9740
www.foxsportsdetroit.com
• Greg Hammaren, Vice President/General Manager
• Karen Kanigowski, Manager
Nature of Sports Service:
Regional. Cable TV broadcaster/programmer. An affiliate of FOX Sports Net.

FOX SPORTS NET FLORIDA
500 EAST BROWARD BOULEVARD
SUITE 105
FT. LAUDERDALE, FL 33394
954-375-3634
Fax: 800-369-0073
infoFL@foxsports.net
www.foxsportsflorida.com
• Steve Tello, Vice President/General Manager
Nature of Sports Service:
Regional. Cable TV network.

FOX SPORTS NET MIDWEST
THE ANNEX BUILDING
700 ST. LOUIS UNION STATION
SUITE 300
ST. LOUIS, MO 63103
314-206-7000
Fax: 314-206-7070
midwest@foxsports.net
www.foxsportsmidwest.com
Nature of Sports Service:
Regional. Cable TV network. Current properties: St. Louis Cardinals, St. Louis Blues, Missouri Valley Conference basketball, Missouri Tigers sports, St. Louis Billikens men's basketball, Kansas State Wildcats basketball, Nebraska Cornhuskers basketball

FOX SPORTS NET NORTH
ONE MAIN STREET SOUTHEAST
SUITE 600
MINNEAPOLIS, MN 55414
612-486-9500
Fax: 612-486-9513
fsnnorthinfo@foxsports.net
www.foxsportsnorth.com
Nature of Sports Service:
Regional. 24-Hour sports cable channel - regional program producer, broadcaster. Metro feed (50-mile radius surrounding Minneapolis); Non-metro feed - cable companies in Minnesota, North Dakota, South Dakota, Iowa and parts of Wisconsin. Produces and distributes Minnesota Twins baseball; University of Minnesota and Big 10 basketball, volleyball and gymnastics; hockey; local college football; U. of Minnesota and WCHA hockey.

FOX SPORTS NET SOUTH
1175 PEACHTREE STREET, N.E.
SUITE 200
ATLANTA, GA 30361
404-230-7300
fssouth@foxsports.com
www.foxsportssouth.com
Nature of Sports Service:
Regional. Cable TV programmer. Owned and operated affiliate of FOX Sports Net.

Coverage includes Atlanta Braves (MLB), Atlanta Hawks (NBA), Atlanta Dream (WNBA), Southeastern Conference, Atlantic Coast Conference, Conference USA, Southern Conference, Big South Conference.

FOX SPORTS NET WEST
1100 SOUTH FLOWER STREET
SUITE 2200
LOS ANGELES, CA 90015-2125
213-743-7800
www.foxsportswest.com
• Kathryn Cohen, General Manager
• Julien Quattlebaum, Vice President
• Andy Hubsch, Vice President of Finance
• Debbie Chavez, Director of Financial Reporting
• Ron Gralnik, Coordinating Producer
• Brad Kitchen, Management Information Systems Director
Nature of Sports Service:
Regional. Serves 4.8 million subscribers in Southern California, Nevada and Hawaii. Properties include: C.D. Chivas USA (MLS), Los Angeles Angels of Anaheim (MLB), Los Angeles Kings (NHL), Big West Conference(NCAA), West Coast Conference (NCAA)

FOX SPORTS NETWORKS/FOX SPORTS NET
10201 W. PICO BOULEVARD
BUILDING 103
LOS ANGELES, CA 90035
310-369-1000
Fax: 212-354-6902
www.foxsports.com
• David Hill, Chairman/CEO
• Ed Goren, Vice Chairman
• Randy Freer, Co-President/Co-COO
• Eric Shanks, Co-President/Co-COO
• Doug Sellars, EVP Production/Executive Producer
• George Greenberg, EVP Programming & Production
• Mark Silverman, President, The Big Ten Network
• Robert Thompson, President, FOX National Cable Sports Networks
• Gary Hartley, Executive Vice President, Graphics
• Ray Bahrami, Senior Vice President, Sales
• Dennis Welsh, Vice President, Sales & Marketing
• Mike Gammone, Vice President of Advertising Sales
• Guy Weaton, Vice President/General Manager
• Sheila Bruce, Vice President, Sales
• Roy Seinfeld, Network Vice President
• Lauren Halpern, Vice President Sales Manager
• Natalie Murray, Vice President, Regional Sales Manager
• Tom Maney, Senior Vice President Advertising Sales
• Chris Tzianabos, Vice President, Sales & Marketing
• Raul De Quesada, Vice President, Marketing Communications
• Aaron Lowenberg, Vice President, Sales
• Dan Carlin, Vice President, Programming & Research
• Joe Viele, Vice President, Marketing Sales
• John Chalton, Vice President, Finance
• Jerry Carstens, Finance Director

Sports Service Founded:
2002
Nature of Sports Service:
Reaches over 78 million homes through its 21 regional sports channels, and it serves as the first truly national, regional and local supplier of sports programming. Fox Sports Net serves as the cable TV home to 70 of the 80 MLB, NHL and NBA teams based in the United States, and produces over 4,000 live events each year.

FOX SPORTS OHIO
9200 SOUTH HILLS BOULEVARD
SUITE 200
BROADVIEW HEIGHTS, OH 44147-3520
440-746-8000
Fax: 440-746-8700
www.foxsportsohio.com
• Charlie Knudson, Sales Executive
• Jeanmarie Fucci, Director of Marketing
• Steve Pawlowski, Communications Manager
• Melissa Simon, Production Manager
• John Kautz, Production Manager
• Janiak Bill, Finance Executive
• Steve Liverani, Principal
Nature of Sports Service:
Regional. Cable TV network.
Major Professional Teams:
Cleveland Cavaliers (NBA), Cincinnati Reds (MLB), Columbus Blue Jackets (NHL), Columbus Crew (MLS).
Other Professional Teams:
Lake Erie Monsters (AHL)

FOX SPORTS PRIME TICKET
1100 SOUTH FLOWER STREET
SUITE 2200
LOS ANGELES, CA 90015-2125
213-743-7800
www.foxsportswest.com
• Kathryn Cohen, General Manager
• Andy Hubsch, Vice President of Finance
• Julien Quattlebaum, Vice President
• Debbie Chavez, Director of Financial Reporting
• Ron Gralnik, Coordinating Producer
Nature of Sports Service:
Regional. Sports Network serves 2.1 million subscribers in Southern California and Nevada. Properties include: Los Angeles Dodgers, Los Angeles Clippers, Mighty Ducks of Anaheim, Live horse racing, Local high school sports, UCLA & USC athletic events, Xtra Live with Steve Mason & John Ireland and Fox Sports News.

FX NETWORKS, LLC
10201 WEST PICO BOULEVARD
BUILDING 103
LOS ANGELES, CA 90035
310-369-1000
Fax: 310-969-4688
www.fxnetworks.com
• John Landgraf, President/General Manager
• Nick Grad, EVP Original Programming
• Murray Jurgeleit, Managing Director
• Chuck Saftler, Executive Vice President
• Gerard Bocaccio, Senior Vice President, Advertising Sales
• Chris Carlisle, Senior Vice President, Marketing
• Julie Piepenkotter, Research Senior Vice President
• Todd Schoen, Senior Vice President

Affiliate
• Eric Shiu, Vice President, Marketing Advertising
• Rick Haskins, Vice President of Marketing
• Scott Groneman, Vice President of Research
• Bruce Lefkowitz, Executive Vice President of Advertising
• Colette Wilson, Manager
• Derek Kuhn, Senior Director, Marketing & Business
• Audrey Capin, Director, Sales Research
• Leslie Hathaway, Director of Operations
• Jason Phipps, Director of Online Media
• Todd Heughens, Creative Director
• Monica Koyama, New Media Director
Nature of Sports Service:
National cable TV network with several hours of programming devoted to sports, particularly college football, college basketball and major league baseball.

GALAVISION
605 THIRD AVENUE
12TH FL
NEW YORK, NY 10158
212-455-5200
Fax: 212-867-6710
corporate.univision.com
• Haim Saban, Chairman
• Randel A. Falco, President/Chief Executive Officer/Director
• Andrew W. Hobson, Senior Executive Vice President/CFO
• Peter H. Lori, EVP/Controller/Chief Accounting Officer
• Roberto Llamas, EVP/Chief Human Resources Officer
• Jessica Rodriguez, Executive Vice President of Program Schedulin
• Keith G. Turner, President of Sales & Marketing
• Tonia O'Connor, President, Distribution Sales & Marketing
• Rick Alessandri, Senior Vice President, Business Development
• Richard Pacheco, Senior Vice President
• Rick Resnick, Vice President, Sports Marketing
Nature of Sports Service:
National. International. Cable network, with U.S. broadcast affiliates, broadcasting from Mexico to U.S., Europe, Northern Africa, Central and South America. Currently offers wrestling and boxing. Also offers ECO hour which includes results and summary of international sports events.

GLOBAL TELEVISION NETWORK, LTD.
289 GREAT RD
SUITE 307
ACTON, MA 01720-4766
978-264-9921
Fax: 978-264-9457
www.globaltv.com
• James A. Barisano, III, President
• Jackie Normand, General/Technical
• Al Viator, General/Technical
Nature of Sports Service:
National, International. Producer and distributor of automotive television series and automotive special reports.

HBO SPORTS
1100 AVE OF THE AMERICAS
NEW YORK, NY 10036

212-512-1000
Fax: 212-512-1182
www.hbo.com
• Ken Herschman, President, HBO Sports
• Shelley Wright Brindle, EVP, Domestic Network Distribution
• Pamela Levine, EVP, Marketing
• Joe Tarulli, Senior Vice President, Finance
• Sandra Chiles, Senior Vice President & GM, Affiliate Sales
• Barbara Thomas, Senior Vice President, Operations
• Stanley Fertig, Senior Vice President
• Royce Battleman, Senior Vice President, Business Affairs
• Melissa R. Barnett, Senior Vice President, Network Business Affai
• John Micale, Vice President, Sports Production
• Gena Desclos, Vice President, Post Production
• Gavin Doyle, Vice President, Finance
Nature of Sports Service:
National. Cable TV programmer, network. Live televised programming and special events, magazine shows, retrospectives and highlight shows.

IN STORE SPORTS NETWORK
130 WEST 29TH STREET
NEW YORK, NY 10001
212-631-9800
Fax: 212-807-9297
skushner@mediaplace.us
www.mediaplace.us
• Scott Kushner, Chief Operating Officer
(212) 631-9800
skushner@mediaplace.us
• Jeremy Hopwood, Creative Director
(212) 631-9800
jhopwood@mediaplace.us
Nature of Sports Service:
Operators of the In-Store Sports Network. National Closed Circuit television network broadcasting in sport specialty retail, locations.

KING SPORTS & ENTERTAINMENT NETWORK, DON
501 FAIRWAY DRIVE
DEERFIELD BEACH, FL 33441-1865
954-418-5800
www.donkingtv.com
• Don King, President
• John Meehan, Vice President, Finance
• Celia Tuckman, Secretary

MADISON SQUARE GARDEN NETWORK/MSG
TWO PENNSYLVANIA PLAZA
FLOOR 19
NEW YORK, NY 10121-1703
212-465-6000
Fax: 212-465-6498
www.msg.com
• Michael Bair, President
• Jerry Passaro, SVP, TV Network Operations & Distribution
• Bobby Brown, Co-Director, Network Operations
• Michael Phillips, Co-Director, Network Operations
Nature of Sports Service:
National, Regional. Cable TV sports programming network. Reaches more than 6.5 million homes through 245 affiliates in New York, New Jersey, Connecticut, and

Pennsylvania. Programming includes the New York Knickerbockers, New York Liberty, New York Rangers, New York Red Bulls, Buffalo Sabres, college basketball, college football, boxing, tennis, horse racing and more from Madison Square Garden and arenas around the country.

NBC SPORTS DIVISION
30 ROCKEFELLER PLAZA
NEW YORK, NY 10112
212-664-4444
Fax: 212-664-4085
www.nbc.com
• David Neal, EVP, NBC Olympics/Executive Producer, NBC Sports
• Mark H. Lazarus, President, NBC Sports
• Jonathan D. Miller, President of Programming, NBC Sports & VERSUS
• Dick D Ebersol, Chairman, NBC Universal Sports & Olympics
Nature of Sports Service:
National. Network.

NEW ENGLAND SPORTS NETWORK/NESN
480 ARSENAL STREET
BUILDING 1
WATERTOWN, MA 02472
617-536-9233
Fax: 617-536-7814
www.nesn.com
• John Henry, Principal Owner
• Sean McGrail, President
• Vanessa Brown, Managing Director
• Peter Plaehn, Vice President, Marketing
• Thomas C. Werner, Chairman
• Michael Narracci, Senior Coordinating Director
• Erik Haugen, Director of Program Development & Acquisition
• Holly Burgess, Manager
• Rick Booth, Creative Director
• Greg Mize, Promotions Coordinator
• Joel Feld, VP of Programming/Executive Producer
• Jamie Wentworth, Information Technologies Director
• Mary Overlan, Director, Finance
Nature of Sports Service:
Regional. A 24 hour, regional cable TV sports service. NESN delivers exclusive coverage of over 90 Boston Red Sox games each season including spring training coverage; Boston Bruins hockey including Stanley Cup playoff action from the TD BankNorth Garden; Pawtucket Red Sox baseball; ECAC Football Game of the Week; major conference college football, basketball baseball and volleyball; professional golf, tennis volleyball, auto racing, boxing, beach volleyball, soccer bowling and skiing; plus NESN SportsDesk, the network's morning sports news program.

NIPPON TELEVISION NETWORK CORPORATION
1-6-1 HIGASHI SHIMBASHI
MINATO-KU
TOKYO, JAPAN 105-7444
+81-3-6215-1111
www.ntv.co.jp
• Noritada Hosokawa, Chairman/President
Nature of Sports Service:
International. Commercial broadcasting network. Owns the Tokyo Verdy soccer team.

OUTSIDE TELEVISION
33 RIVERSIDE AVENUE
4TH FLOOR
WESTPORT, CT 06880
203-221-9240
Fax: 203-221-9283
www.outsidetelevision.com
Nature of Sports Service:
National. Creates and distributes outdoor lifestyle and resort-based sports programs such as Northface Expeditions, Outside Today, and Outside Television Presents.

PETRY MEDIA
200 PARK AVENUE
NEW YORK, NY 10017
212-230-5600
• Val Napolitano, President/CEO
(212) 230-5710
• Cindy Yantis, Vice President Group Sales Manager
• Rich Quigley, Manager
Nature of Service:
Media sales for live regional feed of Atlantic Coast Conference, Southeast Conference, Western Athletic Conference and Mountain West Conference NCAA Division 1 football and basketball.

PETRY TELEVISION
1 PENNSYLVANIA PLAZA
55TH FLOOR
NEW YORK, NY 10119
212-230-5600
Fax: 212-230-5876
• Val Napolitano, President & CEO, Petry Television
• Steve Berlin, Chief Financial Officer
• Steve Capozzoli, Senior Vice President/Managing Director
• Maureen Tillman, Vice President, Information Services
• Debbie Carter, Vice President/General Manager
• Kara D'Amato, Director of Creative Services
• Erica L. Grundfast, Vice President & Director of Human Resources
Nature of Sports Service:
Regional. TV advertising sales. Sales of sponsorships and promotions.

ROOT SPORTS NORTHWEST
3626 156 AVENUE SOUTHEAST
BELLEVUE, WA 98006
425-641-0104
Fax: 425-641-9811
northwest@rootsports.com
northwest.rootsports.com
• Liz Serrette, Principal
• Wayne Moss, Crew Coordinator
Nature of Sports Service:
Regional. Cable TV network. Provides programming for cable and other delivery systems throughout the Pacific Northwest in the states of Washington, Oregon, Idaho, Alaska, and Montana. Home of PAC-10 and Big Sky conferences, featuring college football, men's and women's basketball, baseball and a variety of Olympic sports and Fox Sports News. Professional sports include: the Seattle Mariners, Seattle Sounders, Portland Timbers, and pre-season Seattle Seahawks football.

ROOT SPORTS PITTSBURGH
323 NORTH SHORE DRIVE
SUITE 200
PITTSBURGH, PA 15212
412-316-3800
Fax: 412-316-3892
pittsburgh@rootsports.com
www.rootsports.com
Nature of Sports Service:
Regional. Program distributor for Cable TV. Provides coverage of Pittsburgh Pirates, Pittsburgh Steelers, and Pittsburgh Penguins; Big East basketball, Northeast Conference basketball, ACC basketball, Big 12 women's basketball, Pac-10 basketball, California University of Pennsylvania football and basektball, WPIAL high school football.

ROOT SPORTS ROCKY MOUNTAIN
2300 15TH ST
SUITE 300
DENVER, CO 80202
720-898-2700
rockymountain@rootsports.com
rockymountain.rootsports.com/
Nature of Sports Service:
Regional. Cable TV network. Current properties: Colorado Rockies, Utah Jazz, Denver Pioneer's men's ice hockey, Mountain West Conference, Conference USA, Western Athletic Conference, Big Sky Conference, and Big 12 Conference.

ROOT SPORTS UTAH
2300 15TH STREET
SUITE 300
DENVER, CO 80202
720-898-2700
rockymountain@rootsports.com
www.rootsports.com
Nature of Sports Service:
Regional. Cable TV network. Utah Jazz and other regional cable sports; TV broadcast of Utah Jazz games.

SPIKE TV
2600 COLORADO AVENUE
SANTA MONICA, CA 90404
310-907-2400
spike-feedback@spike.com
www.spiketv.com
• Jon Taffer, Owner
• Bjorn Rebney, Chief Executive Officer
• David Schwarz, Vice President, Communications
• Sammy Goldsmith, Accounts Payable
Nature of Sports Service:
National. Cable TV network. Programming focused on males ages 18-34.
Notes:
Formerly TNN, The National Network and The Nashville Network.

TELEMUNDO
2290 WEST 8TH AVENUE
HIALEAH, FL 33010
305-884-8200
Fax: 305-889-7980
www.telemundo.com
• Emilio Romano, President
• Javier Maynulet, Chief Financial Officer
• Susan Solano Vila, Executive Vice President, Marketing
• Mimi Belt, Vice President
• Dan Lovinger, EVP, Advertising Sales & Integrated Marketing
• Peter E. Blacker, EVP, Digital Media &

Emerging Business
• Margaret Lazo, Vice President, Human Resources
• Jorge Hidalgo, Senior Executive Vice President, Sports
Nature of Sports Service:
National. TV Network for Hispanic audience.

THE SCORE TELEVISION NETWORK
370 KING ST WEST
SUITE 435
TORONTO, ON, CANADA M5V 1J9
416-977-6787
Fax: 416-977-0238
• John Levy, Chairman of the Board

THE SPORTS NETWORK
2200 BYBERRY ROAD
SUITE 200
HATBORO, PA 19040
215-441-8444
Fax: 215-441-5767
www.sportsnetwork.com

TSN - THE SPORTS NETWORK
9 CHANNEL NINE CT
SCARBOROUGH, ON, CANADA M1S 4B5
416-332-5000
Fax: 416-332-7656
audiencerelations@tsn.ca
www.tsn.ca
Nature of Sports Service:
National (Canadian). 24-hour Cable TV sports channel, distributed on cable in Canada. Covers all major and minor sports in Canada.

TURNER SPORTS, INC.
1015 TECHWOOD DRIVE
ATLANTA, GA 30303
404-827-1700
Fax: 404-827-5212
news.turner.com/section display.cfm?section id=31
• Lenny Daniels, Executive Vice President/Chief Operating Officer
• Jon Diament, Executive Vice President, Sales & Marketing
• Sigal Moshe, Chief Information Officer
• Jackie Adams, Director, Marketing Promotions
• Zandra Teagle, Director, Finance & Accounting

UNIVISION TELEVISION NETWORK
9495 NORTHWEST 4141ST STREET
MIAMI, FL 33178
305-471-8277
www.univision.com
• Evelyn Ramirez, Vice President
• Rodrigo Salazar, Chief Financial Officer
• Eddy Davis, Director
• Sunil Vora, Controller
Nature of Sports Service:
National. Spanish language TV network. Live televised programming and special events.

USA NETWORK
30 ROCKEFELLER PLAZA
NEW YORK, NY 10112
212-664-4444
Fax: 212-664-6365
www.usanetwork.com
• Bonnie Hammer, Chairman
• Chris McCumber, Co-President

- Jane Blaney, EVP Programming, Acquisitions, Scheduling
- Jeff Wachtel, EVP, Original Programming
- Beth Roberts, EVP, Business Affairs, NBC Universal Cable

VIP COVERAGE, LLC
52 QUICKS LANE
KATONAH, NY 10536
914-767-0900
Fax: 914-232-3359
- Ben Harvey, Executive Producer
Year Founded:
2001
Nature of Service:
Three unique golf-related.

WHEELSTV
289 GREAT ROAD
SUITE 301
ACTON, MA 01720
978-264-4333
Fax: 978-264-9547
contact@wheelstv.net
wheelstvnetwork.com
- Jim Barisano, Chairman/CEO
- Lehel Reeves, President/Head Of Business Development
- Theresa Carlo, CFO
Nature of Sports Service:
National. Cable TV network. All auto sports, all the time. Creates and distributes exclusive original content for internet portals, websites, 3G mobile platforms, IPTV networks, OEM showrooms, VOD, and cable systems.

YANKEES ENTERTAINMENT & SPORTS NETWORK/YES
THE CHRYSLER BUILDING
405 LEXINGTON AVE
36TH FLOOR
NEW YORK, NY 10174-3699
646-487-3600
Fax: 646-487-3612
www.yesnetwork.com
- John Filippelli, President, Production & Programming
- Michael Wach, EVP, Advertising Sales
- Ed Deleney, Vice President, Operations
- Nicole Zussman, Vice President, Human Resources
- Jason Feneque, Senior Director of Sales & Marketing
- Reji Mathew, Director, Information Technology
Sports Service Founded:
2001

Sports Television Pay Per View

HBO SPORTS
212-512-1208
www.hbo.com/sports

INTEGRATED SPORTS MARKETING
8909 COMPLEX DRIVE
SUITE A
SAN DIEGO, CA 92123
858-836-0133
Fax: 858-836-0134
dm@ismsports.net
www.ismsports.net

- David Miller, President
dm@ismsports.net
- Cheryl Lemox, Senior Vice President, Marketing & Promotions
- Doug Sampson, Vice President, Operations & Creative Service
doug@ismsports.net
- Kyle Mellor, Account Executive
- Cassie Mnutz, Event Manager
- Deanna Samson, Human Resources/Accounting Director

M-NET TELEVISION
251 OAK AVENUE
FERNDALE
RANDBURG, SOUTH AFRI 2194
+27-011-289-2222
083-900-3788
Fax: +27-011-577-4901
enquiries@multichoice.co.za
www.mnet.dstv.com
- Tom Vosloo, Chairman
- Basil Sgourdos, Chief Financial Officer
- Imtiaz Patel, CEO, Supersport
- Eben Greyling, CEO, Pay-TV Platforms
- Antoine Adries Roux, CEO, Internet Operations
Nature of Sports Service:
International. Pay TV service.

SHOWTIME SPORTS
1633 BROADWAY, 15TH FL
NEW YORK, NY 10019
212-708-1600
Fax: 212-708-1217
www.sho.com
- Matthew C. Blank, Chairman/Chief Executive Officer
- Donald Buckley, EVP, Program Marketing, Digital Services
- Tim Delaney, Senior Vice President
- Geof Rochester, Senior Vice President, Marketing
- Nancy Glauberman, Senior Vice President, Business Development
- Jock McLean, Sports Vice President
Nature of Sports Service:
National. Pay-Per-View television programmer and distributor. Showtime Networks inlcude: Showtime, The Movie Channel and FLIX. Showtime also produces their own shows.

TIGERVISION
LSU ATHLETICS ADMINISTRATION BUILDING
BATON ROUGE, LA 70803
225-578-8001
www.LSUsports.net/tigervision
Nature of Sports Service:
Regional. Broadcaster, distributor (Pay-Per-View). TigerVision game broadcasts are on Pay-Per-View basis only. Other shows, including coaches shows and sports reports, are shown on both over-the-air and cable TV.

WILEN MEDIA CORPORATION
5 WELLWOOD AVE
E FARMINGDALE, NY 11735
631-439-5000
Fax: 631-439-4536
www.wilenmedia.com
- Richard Wilen, Chairman
- Darrin Wilen, President
- Corey Wilen, Executive Vice President
- John Diaz, Executive Vice President/Sales

Nature of Sports Service:
National. Provides video program promotions for Pay-Per-View sports to affiliates and publishes regional sports programming guides of SportsChannel, Prism and the New England Sports Network. Also authorized distributor of all print materials for PPV sporting events. Also publishes TV Blueprint, a national cable television publication.

Sports Television Programs, Local

13 SPORTS JAM
1000 NORTH MERIDIAN STREET
INDIANAPOLIS, IN 46204-1015
317-636-1313
Fax: 317-632-6720
13news@wthr.com
www.wthr.com
- Dave Calabro, Host
(317) 655-5754
dcalabro@wthr.com
Description:
Sports. Sunday at 11:20PM for 40 minutes.

27 SPORTS SPECTRUM
2851 WINCHESTER ROAD
LEXINGTON, KY 40509-4801
859-299-0411
Fax: 859-293-1578
news@wkyt.com
www.wkyt.com
- Barbara Carden, Program Director
- Dick Gabriel, Sports Director
(859) 566-1330
news27@wkyt.com
- David Patrick, Producer
Description:
Sports. Saturday at 11:20PM for 40 minutes. Program features information on local sports.

5 SPORTS LIVE
1100 BANYAN BOULEVARD
WEST PALM BEACH, FL 33401-5000
561-655-5455
800-930-9766
Fax: 561-653-5719
newstips@wptv.com
www.wptv.com
- Ben Becker, Sports Director
(561) 653-5729
bbecker@wptv.com
- Ben Becker, Producer
(561) 653-5729
bbecker@wptv.com
Description:
Sports. Sunday at 11:30PM for 30 minutes.

ARKANSAS OUTDOORS
350 SOUTH DONAGHEY STREET
CONWAY, AR 72034
800-662-2386
Fax: 501-682-4122
outdoors@aetn.org
www.aetn.org/arkansasoutdoors/
- Jim Holmes, Producer
(800) 662-2386
Description:
Educational, Interview, News. Thursday at 7:30PM for 30 minutes. Program covers

topics of hunting, fishing, hiking, canoeing, and outdoor recreation.

BEARS KICK OFF LIVE
205 NORTH MICHIGAN AVENUE 2ND FLOOR
CHICAGO, IL 60601-5922
312-565-5532
Fax: 312-819-1332
www.foxchicago.com
• Corey McPherrin, Sports Anchor
(312) 565-5498
• John Eskra, Executive Producer
(312) 565-5478
Description:
Commentary, Interview. Sunday Program airs during football season.. Program is a sports talk show highlighting the Chicago Bears.

BIG BOARD SPORTS
15 NORTH PEARL STREET
ALBANY, NY 12204-1800
518-436-4791
800-999-9698
Fax: 518-434-0659
comments@wnyt.com
www.wnyt.com
• Rodger Wyland, Anchor
(518) 207-4818
rwyland@wnyt.com
• Rodger Wyland, Producer
(518) 207-4818
rwyland@wnyt.com
Description:
Interview, Talk. Sunday at 11:25PM for 30 minutes.

BIG SPORTS X-TRA
3701 SOUTH PEORIA
TULSA, OK 74105-3263
918-743-2222
800-727-5574
Fax: 918-748-1436
news@kjrh.com
www.kjrh.com
• Al Jerkens, Anchor
(918) 748-1539
jerkens@kjrh.com
• Al Jerkens, Producer
(918) 748-1539
jerkens@kjrh.com
Description:
Sports. Sunday at 10:30PM for 30 minutes.

BUCS ZONE
4045 NORTH HIMES AVENUE
TAMPA, FL 33607
813-354-2828
877-833-2828
Fax: 813-878-2828
news@wfts.com
www.wfts.com
• Al Keck, Anchor
(813) 354-2800
akeck@wfts.com
• Oscar Angulo, Producer
(813) 354-2843
news6tips@wfts.com
Description:
News, Sports, Weather. Sunday at 11:30PM for 30 minutes. Program recaps the week's sports events.

CAROLINA SPORTS FRIDAY
ONE JULIAN PRICE PLACE
CHARLOTTE, NC 28208-5211
704-374-3500 (ext 1)
Fax: 704-374-3889
assignmentdesk@wbtv.com
www.wbtv.com
• Delano Little, Host
dlittle@wbtv.com
Description:
Commentary, Sports, Talk. Friday at 11:35PM for 30 minutes. Includes in-depth segments on high school sports as well as coverage of college and professional sports.

EXTRA POINTS
3310 BISSONNET STREET
HOUSTON, TX 77005-2114
713-666-0713
Fax: 713-664-0013
ktrkwwwnews@abc.com
abc13.com/
• Tim Melton, Host
• Matthew Moore, Producer
matthew.moore@abc.com
Description:
Magazine. Saturday at 5:00PM for 30 minutes. Program is a weekly sports wrap-up show.

FIRST 4 SPORTS - SATURDAY
4 BROADCAST PLACE
JACKSONVILLE, FL 32207-8613
904-399-4000
Fax: 904-393-9822
jaxnews@news4jax.com
www.news4jax.com
• Chris Mullholland, Producer
(904) 399-4000
producer@wjxt.com
• Sean Woodland, Anchor
Description:
Sports. Saturday at 11:20PM for 15 minutes.

FIRST 4 SPORTS - SUNDAY
4 BROADCAST PLACE
JACKSONVILLE, FL 32207-8613
904-399-4000
Fax: 904-393-9822
jaxnews@news4jax.com
www.news4jax.com
• Sean Woodland, Anchor
• Matt Kingston, Producer
Description:
Sports. Sunday at 11:20PM for 20 minutes.

FISH MASTERS
1772 CALLE JOAQUIN
SAN LUIS OBISPO, CA 93405-7210
805-541-6666
Fax: 805-541-5142
ksby@ksby.com
www.ksby.com
Description:
Educational, Entertainment, Magazine, Music, Talk. Saturday at 1:00AM for 30 minutes. Program is a fishing and outdoor entertainment show.

FLY FISHING WITH GLEN BLACKWOOD
301 WEST FULTON STREET
GRAND RAPIDS, MI 49504-6430
616-331-6666
800-442-2771
Fax: 616-331-6625
www.wgvu.org

• Bill Cuppy, Producer
cuppyb@gvsu.edu
• Glen Blackwood, Host
(616) 331-6625
Description:
Educational. Thursday at 9:30PM for 30 minutes. Program features fly fishing tips for beginners and experts.

FOURTH DOWN ON FOUR
1024 NORTH RAMPART STREET
NEW ORLEANS, LA 70116-2406
504-529-4444
Fax: 504-529-6470
www.wwltv.com
• Juan Kincaid, Host
(504) 529-6297
Description:
Interview, Sports. Sunday at 10:35PM for 30 minutes.

FOX 13 SPORTS PAGE
5020 WEST AMELIA EARHART DRIVE
SALT LAKE CITY, UT 84116-2853
801-532-1300
Fax: 801-537-5335
www.fox13.com
• Mike Runge, Anchor
Description:
Interview, Talk. Sunday at 9:30PM for 30 minutes.

FOX 59 OVERTIME
1440 NORTH MERIDIAN
INDIANAPOLIS, IN 46202-2305
317-632-5900
Fax: 317-687-6532
fox59.trb.com
• Allen Beckner, Producer
(317) 632-5900
• Tracy Forner, Anchor
(317) 687-6573
• Chris Hagan, Sports Broadcaster
(317) 687-6559
• Greg Kathary, Producer
(317) 632-5900
Description:
News, Talk. Sunday at 10:35PM for 30 minutes.

FOX SPORTS SUNDAY
400 NORTH GRIFFIN STREET
DALLAS, TX 75202-1901
214-720-4444
Fax: 214-720-3263
www.kdfw.com
• Kevin Morrell, Producer
• Mike Doocy, Host
(214) 720-3164
Description:
Call-In, Talk. Sunday at 10:00PM for 30 minutes.

FOX SPORTS XTRA
4261 SOUTHWEST FREEWAY
HOUSTON, TX 77027-7201
713-479-2600
Fax: 713-479-2859
www.fox26.com
• Keith Calkins, Host
(713) 479-2841
Description:
Sports. Sunday at 9:30PM for 30 minutes. Program is a sports talk show.

GV SPORTS
301 WEST FULTON STREET
GRAND RAPIDS, MI 49504-6430
616-331-6666
800-442-2771
Fax: 616-331-6625
www.wgvu.org
• Phil Lane, Producer
(616) 331-6791
lanep@gvsu.edu
Description:
Interview. Monday at 6:00PM for 30 minutes. Program features interviews with sports team coaches at Grand Valley State University and highlights of the week's games.

HIGH SCHOOL SPORTS FOCUS
2102 COMMERCE DRIVE
SAN JOSE, CA 95131-1804
408-953-3636
Fax: 408-953-3610
www.kicu.com
• Mike Sklut, Host
Description:
Interview. Sunday at 7:00PM for 1 hour; Saturday at 12:00PM for 30 minutes.

INSTANT REPLAY
1408 NORTH STREET MARY'S STREET
SAN ANTONIO, TX 78215-1739
210-351-1200
Fax: 210-351-1328
news@ksat.com
• Greg Simmons, Host
gsimmons@ksat.com
Description:
Entertainment, Interview, News, Play-by-Play, Sports. Sunday at 10:30PM for 30 minutes. Program offers sports recaps, one-on-one interviews, and sports-related features.

KTLA SPORTS ONLINE
5800 SUNSET BOULEVARD
LOS ANGELES, CA 90028
323-460-5500
Fax: 323-460-5333
www.ktla.com
• Tom Klimasz, Weekend Producer
(323) 460-5907
• Damon Andrews, Host
(323) 460-5443
• Ted Green, Producer
(323) 460-5907
Description:
News, Sports. Sunday, Saturday at 10:40PM for 20 minutes.

MAXIMUM SPORTS
4335 NORTHWEST LOOP 410
SAN ANTONIO, TX 78229-5136
210-442-6318
Fax: 210-377-4758
kabbtv@kabb.com
www.kabb.com
• Chuck Miketinac, Host
(210) 442-6318
maxsport@kabb.com
Description:
Sports. Sunday at 9:30PM for 30 minutes.

NBC 5 SPORTS SUNDAY
NBC TOWER 454 NORTH COLUMBUS DRIVE
CHICAGO, IL 60611-5555

312-836-5555
Fax: 312-527-4238
www.nbc5.com/
• O'Meara McCormick, Sports Producer
(312) 836-5665
Description:
Commentary, Interview, Talk. Sunday at 10:35PM for 30 minutes. Program features a recap of the week in sports.

OKLAHOMA SPORTS BLITZ
302 SOUTH FRANKFORT STREET
TULSA, OK 74120-2422
918-732-6000
Fax: 918-732-6185
www.kotv.com
• John Holcomb, Host
(918) 732-6146
Description:
Information, Sports. Sunday at 10:30PM for 40 minutes.

OUTSIDE THE LINES
ESPN PLAZA
BRISTOL, CT 06010
866-377-6685
Fax: 860-766-2422
otlstoryideas@espn.com
sports.espn.go.com/espn/otl/index
• George Bodenheimer, President
• Christine Driessen, EVP & CFO
• Chuck Pagano, EVP & CTO
• Gary Hoenig, GM & Editorial Director, ESPN Publishing
• Kevin Ball, Director of Editorial Content & Copy Chief

PADRES MAGAZINE
1370 INDIA STREET 2ND FLOOR
SAN DIEGO, CA 92101-3418
619-266-5061
Fax: 619-595-0168
www.4sd.com
• Jerry Coleman, Host
(619) 266-5061
• Jason Bott, Coordinating Producer
• Jane Mitchell, Reporter
Description:
Interview, Talk. Sunday, Monday, Tuesday, Wednesday, Thursday, Friday, Saturday Airtime varies; approximately 30 minutes.. Program profiles San Diego Padres players on and off the field.

Q IT UP SPORTS
1813 WESTLAKE AVENUE NORTH
SEATTLE, WA 98109-2706
206-674-1313
Fax: 206-674-1777
tips@q13.com
www.kcpq.com
• Dan Devone, Host
• Colin Resch, Producer
cresch@kcpq.com
Description:
Commentary, Talk. Sunday at 10:35PM for 30 minutes. Program analyzes the week in sports.

RICH BRENNER'S SPORTS SUNDAY
2005 FRANCIS STREET
HIGH POINT, NC 27263-1865
336-841-8888
Fax: 336-841-8051
news@wghp.com
www.fox8wghp.com

• Rich Brenner, Sports Anchor
• Rich Brenner, Host
• Rich Brenner, Producer
• Kevin Connolly, Anchor
(336) 821-1166
kconnolly@wghp.com
Description:
Sports. Sunday at 10:30PM for 30 minutes. Program covers local and national sports.

SPORTS CENTRAL
6121 SUNSET BOULEVARD
LOS ANGELES, CA 90028-6423
323-460-3000
Fax: 323-460-3733
kcbstvnews@cbs.com
www.kcbs-tv.com/
• Jim Hill, Sports Anchor
jhill@channel2000.com
Description:
Interview, Play-by-Play, Sports. Sunday Airtime varies to accommodate special programming.; Saturday Airtime varies to accommodate special programming.. Program is a weekend sports show covering local and national athletic events.

SPORTS EXTRA
5151 WISCONSIN AVENUE N.W.
WASHINGTON, DC 20016-4124
202-895-3000
Fax: 202-895-3133
www.fox5dc.com
• Dave Feldman, Host
Description:
Commentary, Talk. Sunday at 11:00PM for 30 minutes. Program features analysis of the week in sports.

SPORTS FINAL
1001 VAN NESS AVENUE
SAN FRANCISCO, CA 94109-6982
415-441-4444
Fax: 415-561-8136
4listens@kron4.com
www.kron4.com
• Gary Radnich, Sports Director
Description:
Interview, Talk. Sunday at 11:30PM for 30 minutes. Program features sporting news and interviews.

SPORTS FINAL EDITION
550 WEST LAFAYETTE BOULEVARD
DETROIT, MI 48226-3123
313-222-0444
Fax: 313-222-0592
assignmentdesk@wdiv.com
www.clickondetroit.com/
• Fred McLeod, Anchor
(313) 222-0500
fredm@clickondetroit.com
• Fred McLeod, Producer
(313) 222-0504
fredm@clickondetroit.com
• Bernie Smilovitz, Sports Anchor
bernies@wdiv.com
Description:
Interview, Sports, Talk. Sunday at 11:35PM for 35 minutes. Program is a sports show with in-depth coverage of the week's action.

SPORTS JAM
4466 NORTH JOHN YOUNG PARKWAY
ORLANDO, FL 32804-1939

407-521-1200
Fax: 407-298-2122
desk@wkmg.com
www.wkmg.com
• Todd Lewis, Host
Description:
Play-by-Play, Sports. Sunday, Saturday at
11:30PM for 30 minutes. Program is a
sports wrap-up-show.

SPORTS LINE LIVE
3556 LIBERTY AVENUE
SPRINGDALE, AR 72762
479-361-2900
888-777-9392
Fax: 479-361-2323
www.safetv.org
• Grant Hall, Host
• Noreen Dueck, Program Director
• Carlos Pardeiro, Producer
carlosp@ipa.net
• Rick Schaeffer, Host
Description:
Call-In, Interview, News, Sports, Talk.
Thursday at 9:00PM for 1 hour. Program is a
call-in talk show.

SPORTS LOCKER
1950 NORTH MERIDIAN
INDIANAPOLIS, IN 46202-1304
317-923-8888
Fax: 317-931-2242
newsdesk@wishtv.com
www.wishtv.com
• Jimmy Shumar, Producer
• Anthony Calhoun, Anchor
(317) 921-8686
• Stacey Thorne, Executive Producer
(317) 956-8540
• Chris Widlic, Anchor
(317) 921-8536
cwidlic@wishtv.com
Description:
Interview, Talk. Sunday, Saturday at
11:22PM for 38 minutes. Program features
sports updates and topical discussions.

SPORTS NIGHT
511 WEST ADAMS STREET
PHOENIX, AZ 85003-1608
602-257-1234
Fax: 602-262-0181
foxde602@fox.com
• Jude Lacava, Host
• Neil Wolf, Producer
Description:
Interview, News, Sports. Sunday at 9:30PM
for 30 minutes.

SPORTS PAGE
624 WEST MUHAMMAD ALI BOULEVARD
LOUISVILLE, KY 40203-1915
502-584-6441
Fax: 502-589-5559
news@fox41.com
www.fox41.com
• Gary Montgomery, Host
(502) 561-7711
gmontgomery@fox41.com
Description:
Interview, Sports. Saturday at 12:30PM for
30 minutes.

SPORTS PLUS
7020 HEATHERHILL RD
BETHESDA, MD 20817

301-229-5401
Description:
Sports, Talk. Sunday at 10:35PM for 1 hour.
Program is a sports talk show.

SPORTS RAP LIVE
99 DANVILLE CORNER ROAD
AUBURN, ME 04210-8693
207-782-1800
Fax: 207-783-7371
wmtw@wmtw.com
www.wmtw.com
• Norm Karkos, Anchor
nkarkos@wmtw.com
• Norm Karkos, Sports Director
nkarkos@wmtw.com
Description:
Call-In, Commentary, News, Sports. Monday
at 7:00PM for 1 hour.

SPORTS SUNDAY
8181 SOUTHWEST FREEWAY
HOUSTON, TX 77074-1705
713-222-2222
Fax: 713-771-4930
desk@kprc.com
www.kprc.com
• Patsy Harris, Program Director
(713) 778-4751
• Patsy Harris, Producer
(713) 778-4751
Description:
News, Sports. Sunday at 10:20PM for 50
minutes.

SPORTS XTRA
1401 79TH STREET
CAUSOUTHEASTWAY
MIAMI, FL 33141-4104
305-795-2777
800-845-7777
Fax: 305-795-2746
newsdesk@wsvn.com
www.wsvn.com
• Steve Shapiro, Host
(305) 795-2777
sshapiro@wsvn.com
• Mike DiPasquale, Host
(305) 795-2777
mdipasquale@wsvn.com
Description:
Commentary, Talk. Sunday at 11:00PM for
30 minutes. Program analyzes the week in
sports.

SPORTS ZONE
500 CIRCLE SEVEN DRIVE
GLENDALE, CA 91201-2331
818-863-7777
Fax: 818-863-7080
www.abc7.com
• Stan Radford, Producer
(818) 863-7649
stan.r.radford@abc.com
• Mike Parker, Producer
(818) 863-7648
mike.b.parker@abc.com
Description:
Commentary, Interview. Monday at 9:00PM
for 1 hour. Program airs only during football
season.

SPORTSBEAT SATURDAY
BROADCAST HOUSOUTHEAST 55 N. 300
W.
SALT LAKE CITY, UT 84180-1109

801-575-5555
Fax: 801-575-5830
feedback@ksl.com
www.ksl.com
• Tom Kirkland, Anchor
(801) 575-5500
tom.kirkland@ksl.com
Description:
Sports. Saturday at 10:30PM for 30 minutes.

SPORTSBEAT SUNDAY
BROADCAST HOUSOUTHEAST 55 N. 300
W.
SALT LAKE CITY, UT 84180-1109
801-575-5555
Fax: 801-575-5830
feedback@ksl.com
www.ksl.com
• Tom Kirkland, Anchor
(801) 575-5555
tom.kirkland@ksl.com
Description:
Sports. Sunday at 10:30PM for 30 minutes.

SPORTSFINAL
10 MONUMENT ROAD
BALA CYNWYD, PA 19004-1712
610-668-5510
Fax: 610-668-3700
wcaudesk@nbcuni.com
www.nbc10.com
• John Clark, Anchor
(610) 668-5534
Description:
Sports. Sunday at 11:35PM for 30 minutes.

SPORTSLINE
81 BARBER GREENE ROAD
DON MILLS, ON, CANADA M3C 2A2
416-446-5311
800-387-8001
Fax: 416-446-5447
newstips@globaltv.com
www.globaltv.com
• Don Martin, Host
(416) 446-5463
dmartin@globaltv.ca
• Jim Tatti, Host
sportsline.tor@globaltv.ca
Description:
News, Sports. Sunday, Monday, Tuesday,
Wednesday, Thursday, Friday, Saturday at
11:30PM for 35 minutes. Program features
sports highlights and commentary.

SPORTSLINE LIVE
721 BROADWAY
KINGSTON, NY 12401-3449
845-339-6397
800-824-3302
Fax: 845-339-6210
www.rnntv.com
• Kevin Connors, Sports Director
(845) 339-6397
kconnors@rnntv.com
• Kevin Connors, Host
(845) 339-6397
• Kevin Connors, Producer
(845) 339-6397
Description:
Call-In, Interview, Sports, Talk. Monday at
8:30AM for 30 minutes; Tuesday,
Wednesday, Thursday, Friday at 8:30PM for
30 minutes. Program covers sports issues.

SPORTSWRAP AT 10:45
2 JACK LONDON SQUARE
OAKLAND, CA 94607-3727
510-834-1212
Fax: 510-272-9957
www.bayinsider.com
• Joe Fonzi, Anchor
(510) 874-0242
• Fred Inglis, Reporter
(510) 874-0164
• Pete Lupetti, Sports Editor
(510) 874-0252
Description:
News, Sports. Sunday, Saturday at
10:45PM for 15 minutes.

SUNDAY SPORTS EXTRA
3501 FARNAM STREET
OMAHA, NE 68131
402-346-6666
800-688-2431
Fax: 402-233-7888
sixonline@wowt.com
www.wowt.com
• Ross Jernstrom, Producer
(402) 346-6666
sixonline@wowt.com
Description:
Information, Sports. Sunday at 10:35PM for
30 minutes.

SUNDAY SPORTS FINAL
15000 SOUTHWEST 27TH STREET
MIRAMAR, FL 33027-4147
305-379-6666
Fax: 954-622-6107
newsroom@nbc6.net
www.nbc6.net
• Guy Rawlings, Host
(954) 622-6355
• Joe Rose, Host
(954) 622-6359
• Alex Suarez, Producer
(954) 622-6357
alex.suarez@nbc.com
Description:
Commentary, Interview, Talk. Sunday at
11:20AM for 40 minutes. Program analyzes
the week in sports.

SUNDAY SPORTS REPLAY
1422 NEW BRITAIN AVENUE
WEST HARTFORD, CT 06110-1632
860-521-3030
800-523-9848
Fax: 860-521-4860
www.wvit.com
• Kevin Nathan, Anchor
• Don Laviano, Producer
(860) 521-3030
• Kevin Nathan, Sports Anchor
Description:
News, Sports. Sunday at 11:20PM for 20
minutes.

SUNDAY SPORTS SPECIAL
613 WOODIS AVENUE
NORFOLK, VA 23510-1017
757-625-1313
Fax: 757-628-6220
www.wvec.com
• Brian Smith, Host
(757) 628-6217
bsmith@wvec.com
Description:
Sports. Sunday at 11:20PM for 15 minutes.

THE FOX 8 10:00 PM WEEKEND NEWS
2005 FRANCIS STREET
HIGH POINT, NC 27263-1865
336-841-8888
Fax: 336-841-8051
news@wghp.com
www.fox8wghp.com
• Jeff Varner, Anchor
• Alan Hobbs, Producer
(336) 841-1139
Description:
News, Sports, Weather. Sunday, Saturday
at 10:00PM for 30 minutes. 30 minute news
broadcast.

THE SCORE
5233 BRIDGE STREET
FORT WORTH, TX 76113
214-750-1111
888-654-5888
Fax: 214-696-9011
news@ktvt.com
www.cbs11tv.com
• Dandy Killeen, Producer
dandyk@ktvt.com
• Babe Laufenberg, Anchor / Sports Director
(214) 750-1111
babel@ktvt.com
Description:
Commentary, Talk. Sunday at 10:20PM for
30 minutes. Program highlights sports
scores and news.

WALL TO WALL SPORTS
770 TWIN RIVERS DRIVE
COLUMBUS, OH 43215
614-460-3700
Fax: 614-460-2891
www.wbns10tv.com
• Dom Tiberi, Host
(614) 460-3950
dom.tiberi@10tv.com
Description:
Sports. Sunday at 11:35PM for 25 minutes.

WBZ SPORTS FINAL
1170 SOLDIERS FIELD ROAD
BOSTON, MA 02134-1004
617-783-4444
Fax: 617-254-6383
www.cbs4boston.com
• Jackie Connally, Producer
(617) 787-7338
jaconnally@boston.cbs.com
Description:
Sports, Talk. Sunday at 11:35PM for 30
minutes.

Sports Television Programs, National

AROUND THE HORN
935 MIDDLE STREET
BRISTOL, CT 06010-1001
860-766-2000
800-999-9985
Fax: 860-766-2213
espn_inc@espn.com
www.espn.com
Description:
Information, Interview, Sports. Monday at
5:00PM for 30 minutes; Tuesday at 5:00PM
for 30 minutes; Wednesday at 5:00PM for
30 minutes; Thursday at 5:00PM for 30

minutes; Friday at 5:00PM for 30 minutes.
Program features a discussion of the day's
hot-butto

AZTEC SPORTS WEEKLY
1370 INDIA STREET 2ND FLOOR
SAN DIEGO, CA 92101-3418
619-266-5061
Fax: 619-595-0168
www.4sd.com
• Jason Bott, Producer
• Dennis Morgigno, Station Manager
Description:
Sports, Talk. Sunday, Monday, Tuesday,
Wednesday, Thursday, Friday, Saturday
Airtime varies; approximately 30 minutes..
Program focuses on San Diego State
University football and basketball.

BASEBALL TONIGHT
935 MIDDLE STREET
BRISTOL, CT 06010-1001
860-766-2000
800-999-9985
Fax: 860-766-2213
espn_inc@espn.com
www.espn.com
• Brian Kenny, Host
(860) 766-4816
brian.kenny@espn.com
• Chris Berman, Host
(860) 766-2147
chris.berman@espn.com
• Jay Levy, Senior Coordinating Producer
jay.levy@espn.com
• Karl Ravech, Anchor
karl.ravech@espn.com
• Karl Ravech, Host
karl.ravech@espn.com
• Ed Schimmel, Coordinating Producer
ed.schimmel@espn.com
• Mark Simon, Reporter
Mark.A.Simon@espn.com
• Norby Williamson, Managing Editor
(860) 766-2419
norby.williamson@espn.com
Description:
Commentary, Interview, Talk. Sunday,
Monday, Tuesday, Wednesday, Thursday,
Friday, Saturday Program airs daily March
through November for 60 minutes; airs
weekly November through March for 60
minutes; airtimes vary.. Program presents
the latest news from

BOB COSTAS NOW
1100 AVENUE OF THE AMERICAS
NEW YORK, NY 10036-6712
212-512-1000
Fax: 212-512-1751
www.hbo.com
• Rick Bernstein, Executive Producer
(212) 512-1438
rick.bernstein@hbo.com
• Bob Costas, Host
bob.costas@hbo.com
• Nick Dolan, Sports Director
(212) 512-1576
nick.dolan@hbo.com
• Ross Greenburg, Executive Producer
(212) 512-1013
ross.greenburg@hbo.com
Description:
Commentary, Current Events, Information,
Interview. Wednesday at 11:00PM for 1
hour. Program features interviews with
notable sports figures and celebrities.

BOXEO TELEMUNDO
2470 WEST 8TH AVENUE
HIALEAH, FL 33010-2020
305-884-8200
Fax: 305-884-6715
correo@telemundo.com
www.telemundo.com
• Robert Pardo, Producer
(305) 884-9640
• Rene Giraldo, Host
(305) 882-8782
• Jessi Losada, Host
(305) 884-9683
• Guillermo Santa Cruz, Sports Director
(305) 882-8796
• Eli Velazquez, Executive Producer
(305) 889-7348
evelazquez@telemundo.com
Description:
Sports. Sunday, Monday, Tuesday,
Wednesday, Thursday, Friday, Saturday
Program airs on Saturday; time varies..
Program features live coverage of major
boxing matches.

CHARGERS PREVIEW
1370 INDIA STREET 2ND FLOOR
SAN DIEGO, CA 92101-3418
619-266-5061
Fax: 619-595-0168
www.4sd.com
• Michael Saks, Producer
(619) 263-9251
• Billy Ra Smith, Host
Description:
Magazine, Sports. Sunday, Monday,
Tuesday, Wednesday, Thursday, Friday,
Saturday Airtime varies; approximately 30
minutes..

EMPIRE SPORTS REPORT
795 INDIAN CHURCH ROAD
WEST SENECA, NY 14224-1205
716-558-8444
800-357-3939
Fax: 716-558-8430
www.empiresports.com
• David Tasca, Producer
Description:
News, Play-by-Play, Talk. Sunday at
10:30PM for 1 hour; Monday at 10:30PM for
1 hour; Tuesday at 10:30PM for 1 hour;
Wednesday at 10:30PM for 1 hour;
Thursday at 10:30PM for 1 hour; Friday at
10:30PM for 1 hour; Saturday at 10:30PM
for 1 hour. Program fea

ESPN
545 MIDDLE STREET
BRISTOL, CT 06010-1001
860-766-2000
www.espn.com
• Trey Wingo, Anchor
(860) 766-4852
trey.wingo@espn.com
• John Anderson, Anchor
(860) 766-7239
john.anderson@espn.com
• Chris Berman, Anchor
(860) 766-2147
newseditors@espn.com
• Bruce Bernstein, Coordinating Producer
(860) 766-2156
bruce.bernstein@espn.com
• James Bowdon, Coordinating Producer
(860) 766-2675
james.bowdon@espn.com

• Linda Cohn, Anchor
(860) 766-2148
linda.cohn@espn.com
• Rece Davis, Anchor
(860) 766-2372
rece.davis@espn.com
• Rece Davis, Reporter
(860) 766-2372
rece.davis@espn.com
• Mark Gross, Assistant Managing Editor
(860) 766-7865
• Geoff Herman, Coordinating Producer
(860) 766-2552
geoff.herman@espn.com
• Brian Kenny, Anchor
(860) 766-4816
• Suzy Kolber, Anchor
suzy.kolber@espn.com
• Craig Lazarus, Senior Coordinating
Producer
(860) 766-2126
craig.lazarus@espn.com
• Steve Levy, Anchor
steve.levy@espn.com
• Jay Levy, Coordinating Producer
(860) 766-4457
jay.levy@espn.com
• Bob Ley, Anchor
otlweekly@espn.com
• Mark Malone, Reporter
• Julie Mariash, Coordinating Producer
(860) 766-2694
julie.mariash@espn.com
• Kenny Mayne, Anchor
(860) 766-2455
kenny.mayne@espn.com
• Chris McKendry, Anchor
(860) 766-4970
chris.mckendry@espn.com
• Mike McQuade, Coordinating Producer
(860) 766-2133
mike.mcquade@espn.com
• Dan Patrick, Anchor
• Bill Perry, Coordinating Producer
(860) 766-4872
• Bill Pidto, Anchor
(860) 766-2687
• Mark Preisler, (860) 766-7391
Coordinating Producer
• Gus Ramsey, Coordinating Producer
(860) 766-4568
• Karl Ravech, Anchor
karl.ravech@espn.com
• Tom Reilly, Coordinating Producer
(860) 766-2157
• Dave Revsine, Anchor
(860) 766-4066
• Ed Schimmel, Coordinating Producer
(860) 766-2118
Description:
Commentary, Talk. Sunday, Monday,
Tuesday, Wednesday, Thursday, Friday,
Saturday Program airs for 90 minutes;
airtimes vary.. Program features the latest
sports news, scores, game previews and
highlights, as well as sports history,
statistics, and trivia.

FRONT ROW
70 BROOKLINE AVENUE
BOSTON, MA 02215-3403
617-536-9233
Fax: 617-536-7814
sports@nesn.com
www.nesn.com
• Todd Kerrissey, Producer
tkerrissey@nesn.com
• Tom Caron, Host

tcaron@nesn.com
• Tom Larson, Assignment Reporter
• Steve Sera, Executive Producer
Description:
Sports. Sunday at 12:30PM for 30 minutes;
Monday at 5:00PM for 30 minutes; Tuesday
at 5:00PM for 30 minutes; Wednesday at
5:00PM for 30 minutes; Thursday at 5:00PM
for 30 minutes; Friday at 5:00PM for 30
minutes. Program covers New England
sports.

FUTBOL TELEMUNDO
2470 WEST 8TH AVENUE
HIALEAH, FL 33010-2020
305-884-8200
Fax: 305-884-6715
correo@telemundo.com
www.telemundo.com
• Eli Velazquez, Executive Producer
(305) 889-7348
evelazquez@telemundo.com
• Guillermo Santa Cruz, Sports Director
(305) 882-8796
• Alejandro Blanco, Host
(305) 889-7373
• Andres Cantor, Host
(305) 889-7143
axcantor@telemundo.com
Description:
Sports. Sunday, Monday, Tuesday,
Wednesday, Thursday, Friday, Saturday
Airs on Sunday; times vary.. Program offers
live coverage of international soccer games.

HALLS OF FAME
TWO PENN PLAZA
NEW YORK, NY 10121-0091
212-465-6741
Fax: 212-465-4489
www.msgnetwork.com
• Francis X. Healy, Executive Producer
(212) 465-5926
• Francis X. Healy, Host
(212) 465-5926
Description:
Interview, Talk. Sunday, Monday, Tuesday,
Wednesday, Thursday, Friday, Saturday
Program airs weekly for 30 minutes; air
times vary.. Program features in-depth
discussions with athletes from a variety of
sports, all of whom are Hall of Fame
inductees in th

HIGH SCHOOL WEEKLY
4 PENN PLAZA
NEW YORK, NY 10001-2819
212-465-5949
Fax: 212-465-5944
www.msgnetwork.com
• Mike Quick, Producer
msgnetpr@msgnetwork.com
• Gene Golda, Associate Producer
gene.golda@thegarden.com
• Mike Quick, Host
msgnetpr@msgnetwork.com
Description:
Magazine. Thursday at 7:00PM for 30
minutes. Program features expanded
coverage of high school sports throughout
the fall and winter.

HOCKEY HOTLINE
795 INDIAN CHURCH ROAD
WEST SENECA, NY 14224-1205
716-558-8444
800-357-3939

Fax: 716-558-8430
www.empiresports.com
• Chrisanne Bellas, Producer
(716) 558-8470
• Chrisanne Bellas, Host
(716) 558-8470
• Mike Robitaille, Host
Description:
Commentary, Interview, News, Talk.
Sunday, Monday, Tuesday, Wednesday,
Thursday, Friday, Saturday Program airs
after each Buffalo Sabres game during the
NHL season, for 60 minutes..

INSIDE THE NFL
1100 AVENUE OF THE AMERICAS
NEW YORK, NY 10036-6712
212-512-1000
Fax: 212-512-1751
www.hbo.com/infl/
• Rick Bernstein, Executive Producer
(212) 512-1438
rick.bernstein@hbo.com
• Bob Costas, Host
bob.costas@hbo.com
• Dave Harmon, Coordinating Producer
(212) 512-5606
dave.harmon@hbo.com
• Brian Hyland, Coordinating Producer
(212) 512-1017
brian.hyland@hbo.com
Description:
Interview, Talk. Thursday at 8:00PM for 1
hour. Program covers the latest news in pro
football, reviews game highlights, and
features interviews and league history.

MONDAY NIGHT COUNTDOWN
935 MIDDLE STREET
BRISTOL, CT 06010-1001
860-766-2000
800-999-9985
Fax: 860-766-2422
espn_inc@espn.com
www.espn.com
• Stewart Scott, Host
(860) 766-2686
• Bob Rauscher, Senior Coordinating
Producer
(860) 766-2113
bob.rauscher@espn.com
• Melissa Stark, Correspondent
• Ed Werner, Reporter
Description:
Commentary, Interview, Talk. Monday at
7:00PM for 2.00 hours. Program features an
in-depth preview of the week's Monday
Night Football game, along with the latest
NFL news, Sunday game highlights, and a
look at the week's upcoming games; does
not air off-

NBA 2NIGHT
935 MIDDLE STREET
BRISTOL, CT 06010-1000
860-766-2000
Fax: 860-766-2422
www.espn.com
Description:
Magazine. Sunday, Monday, Tuesday,
Wednesday, Thursday, Friday, Saturday
Program airs weeknights for 30 minutes
during basketball season; airtimes vary..
Program features the latest news from the
NBA, as well as game highlights and
analysis.

NBA INSIDE STUFF
450 HARMON MEADOW BOULEVARD
SECAUCUS, NJ 07094-3618
201-865-1500
800-635-4438
Fax: 201-865-8989
www.nba.com
• Ahmad Rashad, Executive Producer
(201) 974-6691
Description:
Talk. Sunday, Monday, Tuesday,
Wednesday, Thursday, Friday, Saturday
Program airtime varies.. Program features
NBA news and interviews with NBA figures.

NBA TODAY
935 MIDDLE STREET
BRISTOL, CT 06010
860-766-2000
800-999-9985
Fax: 860-585-2400
espn_inc@espn.com
www.espn.com
• David Aldridge, Reporter
(202) 997-0035
• Barry Sacks, Senior Coordinating
Producer
(860) 766-2187
Description:
Interview, Talk. Tuesday at 5:00PM for 30
minutes. Program features NBA news, plus
game highlights and previews.

NESN SPORTSDESK
70 BROOKLINE AVENUE
BOSTON, MA 02215-3403
617-536-9233
Fax: 617-536-7814
sports@nesn.com
www.nesn.com
• Jamie Parker, Producer
• Hazel Mae, Anchor
Description:
News. Monday at 5:00AM for 4.00 hours;
Tuesday at 5:00AM for 4.00 hours;
Wednesday at 5:00AM for 4.00 hours;
Thursday at 5:00AM for 4.00 hours; Friday
at 5:00AM for 4.00 hours. Program covers
the latest news in New England sports.

NESN SPORTSDESK: THE WEEKEND EDITION
70 BROOKLINE AVENUE
BOSTON, MA 02215-3403
617-536-9233
Fax: 617-536-7814
sports@nesn.com
www.nesn.com
• Jamie Parker, Producer
• Hazel Mae, Anchor
Description:
News. Sunday at 6:00AM for 6.00 hours;
Saturday at 6:00AM for 6.00 hours. Program
reviews the week in New England sports.

NFL 2NIGHT
935 MIDDLE STREET
BRISTOL, CT 06010-1001
860-766-2000
800-999-9985
Fax: 860-585-2400
espn_inc@espn.com
www.espn.com
• Trey Wingo, Host
trey.wingo@espn.com
• Hank Goldberg, Reporter
(860) 766-2000

• Suzy Kolber, Reporter
suzy.kolber@espn.com
• Andrea Kremer, Reporter
(818) 569-7500
• Sal Paolantonio, Reporter
sal.paolantonio@espn.com
• Bob Rauscher, Senior Coordinating
Producer
(860) 766-2113
bob.rauscher@espn.com
• Ed Werder, Reporter
werdere@espn.com
Description:
Commentary, Information, Interview.
Tuesday at 7:30PM for 30 minutes;
Wednesday at 7:30PM for 30 minutes;
Thursday at 7:30PM for 30 minutes; Friday
at 7:30PM for 30 minutes; Saturday at
7:30PM for 30 minutes. Program provides
daily NFL news, discusses cur

NFL COUNTDOWN
935 MIDDLE STREET
BRISTOL, CT 06010-1001
860-766-2000
800-999-9985
Fax: 860-585-2400
espn_inc@espn.com
www.espn.com
• Bob Rauscher, Senior Coordinating
Producer
(860) 766-2113
bob.rauscher@espn.com
Description:
Interview, Talk. Sunday at 11:00AM for 2.00
hours. Program features football pre-game
analysis along with updates and special
reports.

NFL PRIMETIME
935 MIDDLE STREET
BRISTOL, CT 06010-1001
860-766-2000
800-999-9985
Fax: 860-585-2400
espn_inc@espn.com
www.espn.com
• Bill Fairweather, Producer
• Chris Berman, Host
(860) 766-2147
chris.berman@espn.com
• Bob Rauscher, Senior Coordinating
Producer
(860) 766-2113
Description:
Commentary, Talk. Sunday at 7:30PM for 30
minutes. Program features football game
highlights.

ONE-ON-ONE WITH JANE MITCHELL
1370 INDIA STREET 2ND FLOOR
SAN DIEGO, CA 92101-3418
619-266-5061
Fax: 619-595-0168
www.4sd.com
• Jane Mitchell, Producer
jane.mitchell@cox.com
• Jane Mitchell, Host
jane.mitchell@cox.com
Description:
Interview, Talk. Sunday, Monday, Tuesday,
Wednesday, Thursday, Friday, Saturday
Airtime varies; approximately 30 minutes..
Program features in-depth personal profiles
of Padres stars and other local celebrities,
business people and athletes.

PRIME TIME PADRES
1370 INDIA STREET 2ND FLOOR
SAN DIEGO, CA 92101-3418
619-266-5061
Fax: 619-595-0168
www.4sd.com
• Jason Bott, Producer
(619) 266-5061
• Tim Flannery, Host
• Jane Mitchell, Reporter
• Dennis Morgigno, Station Manager
• Argy Stathopulos, Reporter
(619) 266-5024
Description:
Sports, Talk. Sunday, Monday, Tuesday,
Wednesday, Thursday, Friday, Saturday
Schedule varies; airs 15 to 30 minutes..
Program previews San Diego Padres
baseball.

REAL SPORTS WITH BRYANT GUMBEL
1100 AVENUE OF THE AMERICAS
NEW YORK, NY 10036-6712
212-512-1000
Fax: 212-512-1751
www.hbo.com/realsports
• Kirby Bradley, Senior Producer
(212) 512-1469
kirby.bradley@hbo.com
• Rick Bernstein, Executive Producer
(212) 512-1438
rick.bernstein@hbo.com
• Rick Bernstein, Sports Director
(212) 512-1438
rick.bernstein@hbo.com
• Frank Deford, Correspondent
frankdeford@hbo.com
• Bernard Goldberg, Correspondent
(212) 512-1000
• Ross Greenburg, Executive Producer
(212) 512-1013
ross.greenburg@hbo.com
• Bryant Gumbel, Host
(212) 512-5235
Description:
Interview, Talk. Thursday at 10:00PM for 1
hour. Program presents in-depth and
investigative reports covering issues from
the sports world.

REPUBLICA DEPORTIVA
9405 NORTHWEST 41ST STREET
MIAMI, FL 33178-2301
305-471-3900
Fax: 305-471-4236
www.univision.net
• Fernando Fiore, Host
(305) 471-4070
Description:
Commentary, Interview, Play-by-Play,
Sports, Talk. Sunday at 11:00AM for 2.00
hours. Program features interviews, the
latest scores, and highlights of sporting
events of interest to an Hispanic audience.

SPORTS CONNECTION
700 CARILLION PARKWAY
SUITE 9
SAINT PETERSBURG, FL 33716
727-329-2400
888-437-1239
Fax: 727-329-2434
www.baynews9.com
• Chris Elias, Producer
• Rock Riley, Host
• Elliott Wiser, General Manager

Description:
Call-In, Interview, Sports, Talk. Program
features live sports commentary and
analysis.

SPORTS CORNER
4270 WEST MARDON AVENUE
LAS VEGAS, NV 89139-5854
702-361-2191
800-336-2225
Fax: 818-352-3229
www.cableradionetwork.com
• Jack Roberts, Executive Producer
• Jennifer Horn, Marketing Vice President
• Michael Horn, President
• Rod Myers, Host
Description:
Call-In, Sports, Talk. Sunday at 5:00PM for
2.00 hours; Monday at 5:00PM for 1 hour;
Tuesday at 5:00PM for 1 hour; Wednesday
at 5:00PM for 1 hour; Thursday at 5:00PM
for 1 hour; Friday at 5:00PM for 1 hour.
Program features audience call-in and guest
inte

SPORTS LATENIGHT
160 WELLS AVENUE
NEWTON, MA 02459-3302
617-630-5000
Fax: 617-630-5057
newsdesk@necn.com
www.necn.com
• Chris Collins, Anchor
(617) 630-5000
ccollins@necn.com
Description:
Sports. Monday at 11:00PM for 30 minutes;
Tuesday at 11:00PM for 30 minutes;
Wednesday at 11:00PM for 30 minutes;
Thursday at 11:00PM for 30 minutes; Friday
at 11:00PM for 30 minutes. Program
features highlights and scores from around
the various sports l

SPORTS ON 1
75 NINTH AVENUE 6TH FLOOR
NEW YORK, NY 10011-7006
212-379-3311
Fax: 212-379-3575
www.ny1.com
• Kevin Garrity, Sports Anchor
• Marc Weingarten, Sports Director
Description:
Call-In, Interview, Sports, Talk. Sunday at
11:30PM for 1 hour; Monday at 11:30PM for
1 hour; Tuesday at 11:30PM for 1 hour;
Wednesday at 11:30PM for 1 hour;
Thursday at 11:30PM for 1 hour; Friday at
11:30PM for 1 hour; Saturday at 11:30PM
for 1 hour. Pro

SPORTS PAGE
2000 YORK ROAD SUITE 114
OAK BROOK, IL 60523-8863
630-368-4000
Fax: 630-368-4468
www.cltv.com
• L. J. Tabano, Producer
• Mike Bloomberg, Host
• Lou Canellis, Host
Description:
Call-In. Monday at 9:00PM for 1 hour;
Tuesday at 9:00PM for 1 hour; Wednesday
at 9:00PM for 1 hour; Thursday at 9:00PM
for 1 hour; Friday at 9:00PM for 1 hour;
Saturday at 9:00PM for 1 hour.

SPORTS REPORTERS II
935 MIDDLE STREET
BRISTOL, CT 06010-1001
860-766-2000
800-999-9985
Fax: 860-766-2213
espn_inc@espn.com
www.espn.com
• Joe Valerio, Producer
jovaler@optonline.net
Description:
Information, News, Talk. Tuesday at 7:30PM
for 30 minutes. Program features a panel
discussion of the day's hottest sports news.

SPORTSCENTURY
935 MIDDLE STREET BUILDING 7
BRISTOL, CT 06010-1001
860-585-2000
Fax: 860-766-2213
www.espn.com
Description:
Magazine. Monday at 8:00PM for 1 hour;
Tuesday at 8:00PM for 1 hour; Wednesday
at 8:00PM for 1 hour; Thursday at 8:00PM
for 1 hour; Friday at 8:00PM for 1 hour.
Program profiles the lives of sports legends
of the 20th century.

**THE SPORTS PAGE WITH LOU
CANELLIS**
2000 YORK ROAD SUITE 114
OAK BROOK, IL 60523-8863
630-368-4000
Fax: 630-368-4468
www.cltv.com
Description:
Call-In, Commentary, Interview. Sunday at
9:00PM for 1 hour. Program features games
and humor along with sports news and
analysis.

THE SPORTS REPORTERS
5 MINUTE MAN HILL
WESTPORT, CT 06880-6523
860-766-2000
800-999-9985
Fax: 203-226-3561
www.espn.com
• Joe Valerio, Producer
jovaler@optonline.net
• John Saunders, Host
jovaler@optonline.net
Description:
Commentary, Panel Discussion. Sunday at
10:00AM for 30 minutes. Program features
discussions of current sports issues.

Sports Satellite Television

CAPITOL SPORTS NETWORK
2619 WESTERN BOULEVARD
RALEIGH, NC 27606
919-890-6000
Fax: 919-890-6095
www.cbc-raleigh.com
• James F. Goodmon, President/Chief
Executive Officer
• Daniel P. McGrath, Vice President
• James F. Goodmon, Jr., Vice President,
CBC New Media Group
• Michael Goodmon, Vice President, Real
Estate
• Ardie Gregory, Vice President/GM,
WRAL-FM

• George Habel, Vice President, Radio Networks/Sports 99.9 Th
• Angie Emerline, Vice President, Human Resources
• Steve Hammel, Vice President/GM, WRAL-TV
• Thomas McLaughlin, Assistant Treasurer
• Robert Matheny, Vice President, Police & Innovation

Nature of Sports Service:
Capitol Broadcasting Company, Inc. is a diversified communications company that owns and/or operates WRAL-TV, WRAL Digital, WRAZ-TV, WRAZ Digital, WRAL-FM, WRAL-HD2, WCMC-FM, WCMC-HD1, WDNC-AM, WCMC-HD2, WCMC-HD3, WCLY-AM, WCMC-HD4, Microspace, CBC New Media Group and Wolfpack Sports Properties (a joint venture with Learfield Sports) in Raleigh, NC; WJZY-TV and WMYT-TV in Charlotte, NC; WILM-TV and Sunrise Broadcasting in Wilmington, NC; The Durham Bulls Baseball Club in Durham, NC; and real estate interests including the American Tobacco Project and Diamond View office buildings in Durham, NC.

Additional Office:
229 N. Church St, Charlotte, NC 28202.

DIRECTV, INC.
2230 E. IMPERIAL HWY
EL SEGUNDO, CA 90245
310-964-5000
888-238-7177
800-531-5000
Fax: 877-580-2148
www.directv.com
• Michael White, Chairman/President/CEO
• Joseph A. Bosch, Executive Vice President/Chief HR Officer
• Brian B. Churchill, EVP/President, DIRECTV Latin America
• Patrick T. Doyle, Executive Vice President/Chief Financial Officer
• Larry D. Hunter, Executive Vice President/General Counsel
• Romulo C. Pontual, EVP/Chief Technology Officer
• Fazal Merchant, Senior Vice President/Treasurer
• John F. Murphy, SVP/Controller/Chief Accounting Officer
• Ellen Filipiak, Senior Vice President, Customer Care

Baseball Sponsor:
MLB, Minor League
Auto Sports Sponsor:
NASCAR
Basketball Sponsor:
NBA
Football Sponsor:
NFL
Ice Hockey Sponsor:
NHL

DISH NETWORK
9601 SOUTH MERIDIAN BOULEVARD
ENGLEWOOD, CO 80112
303-723-1000
800-333-3474
888-743-5750
Fax: 303-723-1399
www.dish.com
• Charlie Ergen, Co-Founder/Chairman of the Board
• Joseph Clayton, President/Chief Executive

Officer
• Michael Kelly, President of Blockbuster, L.L.C.
• Jim DeFranco, Co-Founder/EVP/Special Advisor to the CEO
• W. Erik Carlson, Executive Vice President, Operations
• Tom Cullen, Executive Vice President, Corporate Developme
• R. Stanton Dodge, EVP, General Counsel & Secretary
• Bernie Han, EVP/Chief Operating Officer
• Robert Olsen, EVP/Chief Financial Officer
• Dave Shull, EVP/Chief Commercial Officer
• Amir Ahmed, Senior Vice President, Sales & Distribution
• Vivek Khemka, Senior Vice President, Product Management
• Mike McClaskey, Senior Vice President, Chief Information Offi
• James Moorhead, Senior Vice President, Chief Marketing Office
• Brian Neylon, SVP, Sales Planning, Administration & Direct
• Warren Schlichting, Senior Vice President, Ad Sales

FOX SPORTS DIRECT
100 EAST ROYAL LANE
SUITE 250
IRVING, TX 75039
972-868-1400
800-766-6746
Fax: 972-868-1616
www.foxsports.com
• Glenn Gurgiolo, President
Description:
The nation's leading distributor of sports programming to the residential and commercial satellite dish marketplace by providing, NBA, NHL, MLB and NCAA action on more than 20 Regional Sports Networks via C-Band and Direct Broadcast Satellite (DBS). Networks represented: nine (9) FOX Sports Net regional networks, eight (8) from Sports Channel, plus Madison Square Garden, NESN, PASS Sports, HTS, Midwest Sports Channel, and Sunshine Network. Additional sports programming represented includes NFL Sunday Ticket and the Golf Channel.

NASCAR
1 DAYTONA BOULEVARD
DAYTONA BEACH, FL 32114
386-253-0611
www.nascar.com
• Brian Z. France, Chairman/CEO
• Mike Helton, President
• Steve Phelps, Chief Marketing Officer
• Jim O'Connell, Chief Sales Officer/VP, Corporate Marketing
• Todd Wilson, Chief Financial Officer
• Gary Crotty, General Counsel
• Ed Bennett, SVP/Chief Administrative Officer
• Sabrina Macias, Director, Brand & Consumer Marketing Communic
• Chris Tropeano, Senior Manager, Business Communications
• Jon Schwartz, Senior Director, Business & Brand Communicati
• David Higdon, Managing Director, Integrated Marketing Comm.
• Jim Cassidy, Vice President
• Zane Stoddard, Vice President
• Kim Brink, Vice President

Products & Services:
The National Association for Stock Car Auto Racing, Inc. (NASCAR) is the sanctioning body for one of North America's premier sports. NASCAR races are broadcast in more than 150 countries and in 20 languages. In the U.S., races are broadcast on FOX, TNT, ABC/ESPN/ESPN2, SPEED, Motor Racing Network Radio, PRN Radio, and Sirius XM Satellite Radio. NASCAR fans are among the most brand-loyal in all of sports, and as a result more Fortune 500 companies participate in NASCAR than any other sport. NASCAR consists of three national series (the NASCAR Sprint Cup Series, NASCAR Nationwide Series, and NASCAR Camping World Truck Series), four regional

---

RFDTV
3201 DICKERSON PIKE
NASHVILLE, TN 37207
615-227-9292
patrick@rfdtv.com
www.rfdtv.com
• Patrick Gottsch, Founder/President
• Raquel Gottsch, EVP, Corporate Communications
• Gatsby Gottsch, EVP, Finance
• Randy Bernard, Chief Executive Officer
• Ed Frazier, Chief Operating Officer
• Steve Campione, Chief Financial Officer
• Michael E. LaBroad, Chief Marketing Officer

Nature of Sports Service:
RFD-TV is home to the most comprehensive lineup of agricultural-based programs ever assembled on one channel. Shows from around the world give agriculture professionals and hobbyists the widest variety of news and information available. Horses on RFD-TV is America's only daily block of high-quality and exclusive programs dedicated to the horse owner and horse lover, featuring the world's most respected and popular equine clinicians, breed features, competitions & event coverage. People who lvoe and respect the land make up the largest share of the RFD-TV audience. RFD-TV covers this growing market with a wide variety of programs and featu

---

SHERIDAN BROADCASTING NETWORK
960 PENNSYIVANIA AVENUE
SUITE 200
PITTSBURGH, PA 15222
412-456-4086
800-456-4211
Fax: 412-456-4040
• Ty Miller, Director of Sports
• Jerry Lopes, President
Description:
National. Satellite distribution company.

SPORTS NEWSATELLITE
3 EMPIRE BOULEVARD
SOUTH HACKENSACK, NJ 07606
201-807-0888
Fax: 201-807-9007
• Joseph L. Podesta, Chairman
• James E. Holland, President
• Geoff Belinfante, Senior Vice President/Executive Producer
• Rich Domich, Senior Vice President/Sales/Marketing
• Jeanmarie Cap, Senior Vice President

• Tim Roberts, Vice President/Sports News Director
Description:
National. Program producer, distributor, syndicator. Produces sports news feeds for all NBC affiliates. Current properties include: Play It Up (For MSG Network).

STAR GROUP LIMITED
8th FLOOR, ONE HARBOURFRONT, 18 TAK FUNG STREET
HUNGHOM
KOWLOON
HONG KONG,
corp-aff@startv.com
www.startv.com
• James Murdoch, Chariman/Chief Executive Officer
• Bruce Churchill, President/Chief Operating Officer
• Gary Walrath, Executive Vice President, STAR Group Limited
• Steve Askew, Executive Vice President/STAR Group Ltd.
Description:
International. Satellite programming network.

THE SPORTS NETWORK
2200 BYBERRY ROAD
SUITE 200
HATBORO, PA 19040
215-441-8444
Fax: 215-441-5767
www.sportsnetwork.com
• Mickey Charles, CEO/President
• Ken Zajac, Director of Sales
• Steve Cwikowitz, Account Executive
• Bernie Greenberg, Client Relations Coordinator
Nature of Sports Service
TSn is the largest privately owned international sports information company in North America and possibly, the world, servicing hundreds and hundreds of clients whose range multiplies that to, literally, millions of viewers/users worldwide. TSN covers the gamut of sports information, ranging from NFL to Rugby, MLB to Cricket and virtually everything in between.

VERESTAR
3040 WILLIAMS DRIVE
SUITE 500
FAIRFAX, VA 22031
703-206-9000
Fax: 703-573-3522
• David Garrison, Chairman/Chief Executive Officer
• David Kagan, President/Chief Operating Officer
Description:
National, International. Satellite transmission service for sports programmers to broadcast and cable industries. Verestar has 11 satellite network access points, with gives them access to over 60 different satellites and manages 70 transponders.

Sports Television Stations

CLEAR CHANNEL ENTERTAINMENT, INC.
200 E BASSE ROAD
SAN ANTONIO, TX 78209

210-822-2828
Fax: 310-867-7001
www.clearchannel.com
• Mark P. Mays, Chairman
• Randall T. Mays, Vice Chairman
• Robert W. Pittman, CEO/Director
• Thomas W. Casey, Executive Vice President/Chief Financial Offi
• Robert H. Walls, Executive Vice President/General Counsel
• John E. Hogan, Chairman/CEO, Media & Entertainment
• Bob Stohrer, President
• Scott D. Hamilton, Senior Vice President/Chief Accounting Office
• Drew Fisher, Senior Vice President, Information

COX SPORTS/CHANNEL 9
17602 N. BLACK CANYON HWY, STE 111
PHOENIX, AZ 85023
602-866-0072
Fax: 602-547-8039
• Suzee Smith-Everhard, Director Televideo

GOLF CHANNEL, THE
7580 COMMERCE CENTER DRIVE
ORLANDO, FL 32819
407-363-4653
Fax: 407-363-7976
www.thegolfchannel.com
• Mike McCarley, President
• Jeff Dilley, Chief Financial Officer
• Robert Greenway, SVP Production/Programming/Ops
• Gene Pizzolato, SVP Advertising Sales
• Kevin Byrnes, Vice President Advertising Sales
• John Houde, Vice President New Media
• R. Andy Murphy, Vice President Network Operations
• Mark Oldham, Vice President Tournament Affairs
• Christine Sullivan, Vice President Marketing
• Tony Tortorici, Vice President Production
Description:
National. Cable Television programmer offering 24-hour, 7 basic service. Live coverage of the PGA Tour, Champions Tour, LPGA, Nationwide, European and Australian Tours. Programming also includes: GOLF TALK LIVE, a call -in interview show with golfers. GOLF CHANNEL ACADEMY LIVE, a call-in instructional show. GOLF CENTRAL, a live news show, PROFILE OF A PRO, PASSAGE TO PARADISE, a golf travel program. The GOLF CHANNEL ACADEMY, an instructional series

KABC-TV
500 CIRCLE SEVEN DRIVE
GLENDALE, CA 91201-2331
818-863-7500
Fax: 818-863-7080
www.abclocal.go.com/kabc
• Bill Burton, Vice President
(818) 863-7261
• Rob Fukuzaki, Sports Anchor
(818) 863-7500
• Mike Parker, Sports Producer
(818) 863-7649
stan.r.radford@abc.com
• Stan Radford, Sports Producer
(818) 863-7649
stan.r.radford@abc.com

KAII-TV
88 PIIKOI STREET
HONOLULU, HI 96814-4245
808-591-2222
Fax: 808-593-8479
www.khon.com
• Kanoa Leahey, Sports Director
(808) 591-6359
• Darlene Lee, Executive Assistant
• John Veneri, Sports Anchor
(808) 591-4289

KAMR-TV
1015 FILLMORE STREET, S.
AMARILLO, TX 79101-0751
806-383-3321
Fax: 806-349-9083
news@kamr.com
www.kamr.com
• Jeff Barger, Sports Director
(806) 383-3321

KAPP-TV
P.O. BOX 10208
YAKIMA, WA 98902-1208
509-453-0351
Fax: 509-453-3623
kappnews@kapptv.com
www.kapptv.com
• Brad Reierson, Sports Director
(509) 453-0351

KARE-TV
8811 OLSON MEMORIAL HIGHWAY
MINNEAPOLIS, MN 55427-4762
763-546-1111
Fax: 763-546-8606
kare11@kare11.com
www.kare11.com
• Randy Shaver, Sports Director/Anchor
(763) 546-1111
rshaver@kare11.com
• Tim Stanko, Marketing Vice President
• Tim Stanko, Promotion Vice President
• Tim McNiff, Sports Anchor
(763) 546-1111

KARK-TV
1401 WEST CAPITOL AVENUE
LITTLE ROCK, AR 72201-2940
501-340-4444
Fax: 501-375-1961
news4@kark.com
www.kark.com
• Dean Hinson, President
• Mark Rushing, Sports Anchor
(501) 340-4525
• Bo Mattingly, Sports Anchor
(501) 340-4444

KATV-TV
PO BOX 77
LITTLE ROCK, AR 72201-3801
501-324-7777
Fax: 501-324-7899
tv7@katv.com
www.katv.com
• Paul Eells, Sports Director
(501) 324-7529
peells@katv.com
• Tim Vahsholtz, Promotions Director
(501) 324-7807
tvahsholtz@katv.com
• Steve Sullivan, Sports Anchor/Reporter
(501) 324-7777

KAUZ-TV
P.O. BOX 2130
WICHITA FALLS, TX 76309
940-322-6957
Fax: 940-761-3331
www.kauz.com/
• Adam Ostrow, Sports Director
aostrow@kauz.com
• Charlie Bartlett, Sports Reporter/Anchor

KBCI-TV
140 NORTH 16TH STREET
BOISE, ID 83702
208-472-2222
Fax: 208-472-2211
news@kbcitv.com
www.2news.tv/
• Vince Trimboli, Sports Director
(208) 472-2222
• Andrew Marden, Weekend Sports Anchor
(208) 489-1243

KBIM-TV
214 NORTH MAIN STREET
ROSWELL, NM 88201-4723
505-622-2120
Fax: 505-623-6606
• Mickey Winfield, Sports Director

KBMT-TV
525 INTERSTATE 10 SOUTH
BEAUMONT, TX 77701-3708
409-833-7512
Fax: 409-835-1617
• Dave Hofferth, Sports Director
• Will Norman, Promotions Director

KBSH-TV
2300 HALL STREET
HAYS, KS 67601-3062
785-625-5277
Fax: 785-625-1161
cwalker_kbsh@yahoo.com
• Gerard Wellbrock, Sports Anchor
(785) 625-2578

KBTX-TV
PO BOX 3730
BRYAN, TX 77802-4305
979-846-7777
800-752-5289
Fax: 979-846-1888
news@kbtx.com
www.kbtx.com
• Jon Boaz, Advertising Manager
(979) 595-1580
• Darryl Bruffett, Sports Director
(979) 846-7777
bruffett@kbtx.com

KCAL-TV
6121 SUNSET BOULEVARD
LOS ANGELES, CA 90028
323-460-3000
Fax: 323-460-3733
kcbstvnews@cbs.com
www.kcal9.com/
• Jim Hill, Sports Reporter
• Alan Massengale, Sports Anchor

KCBS-TV
6121 SUNSET BOULEVARD
LOS ANGELES, CA 90028-6423
323-460-3000
Fax: 323-460-3733

kcbstvnews@cbs.com
www.kcbs-tv.com/
• Steve Hartman, Sports Reporter
• Jim Hill, Sports Director
jhill@channel2000.com

KCCW-TV
720 HAWTHORNE STREET
ALEXANDRIA, MN 56308-1866
320-763-5166
800-934-5226
Fax: 320-763-4991
www.kcco-tv.com
• Stacy Steinhagen, Sports Director
(320) 763-7189

KCEC-TV
777 GRANT STREET
DENVER, CO 80203
303-832-0050
800-725-8454
Fax: 303-318-6252
www.univision.com
• Luis Canela, Sports Director
(303) 832-0050
lcanela@entravision.com

KCEN-TV
PO BOX 6103
TEMPLE, TX 76503-6103
254-773-6868
Fax: 254-859-5831
news@kcentv.com
www.kcentv.com
• Steve Iandoli, Sports Director
(254) 859-5481
• Tyler Hedrick, Sports Reporter
(254) 773-6868

KCFW-TV
P.O. BOX 857
KALISPELL, MT 59901-4937
406-755-5239
Fax: 406-752-8002
news@kcfw.com
www.nbcmontana.com
• Matt Seigel, Sports Director
• Martin Ross, Sports Director
(406) 755-5239

KCNC-TV
1044 LINCOLN STREET
DENVER, CO 80203-2714
303-830-6464
Fax: 303-830-6380
kcncnews@cbs.com
www.kcncnews4.com
• Steve Cox, Executive Sports Producer
(303) 830-6464
scox@cbs.com

KCOP-TV
1999 SOUTH BUNDY DRIVE
LOS ANGELES, CA 90025
310-584-2000
Fax: 310-584-2024
www.mynetworktv.com
• Rod Cohen, Sports Assignment Editor
(310) 584-2030
• Rod Cohen, Sports Producer
(310) 584-2030
• Steve Jahnke, Sports Director
• Rick Garcia, Sports Anchor
(310) 584-2369

KCPQ-TV
1813 WESTLAKE AVENUE, NORTH
SEATTLE, WA 98109-2706
206-674-1305
Fax: 206-674-1713
tips@q13.com
www.kcpq.com
• Dan Devone, Sports Anchor
• Tony Ventrella, Sports Anchor
• Bill Wixey, Sports Anchor
(206) 674-1305

KCRA-TV
3 TELEVISION CIRCLE
SACRAMENTO, CA 95814-0794
916-444-7316
Fax: 916-441-4050
www.kcra.com
• Ron Hyde, Sports Director
(916) 325-3294
rbhyde@hearst.com
• Chris Lango, Sports Writer
(916) 444-7316
clango@hearst.com

KCRG-TV
501 2ND AVENUE, S.E.
CEDAR RAPIDS, IA 52401
319-398-8422
800-332-5443
Fax: 319-368-8505
newsreleases@kcrg.com
www.kcrg.com
• John Campbell, Sports Director
(319) 398-8325
john.campbell@kcrg.com
• Scott Saville, Weekend Sports
Anchor/Reporter
(319) 398-8422
Scott.Saville@kcrg.com
• Shawn Terrell, Sports Reporter
(319) 365-9999
shawn.terrell@kcrg.com
• David Welsh, Promotions Director
david.welsh@kcrg.com

KCTV-TV
4500 SHAWNEE MISSION PARKWAY
FAIRWAY, KS 66205
913-677-5555
Fax: 913-677-7135
kctv5@kctv5.com
www.kctv5.com
• Ken Bauer, Promotions Director
(913) 677-7129
kbauer@kctv5.com
• Leif Lisec, Sports Anchor

KDAF-TV
8001 JOHN W. CARPENTER FREEWAY
DALLAS, TX 75247
214-252-9233
Fax: 214-252-3379
www.kdaf.com
• Dave Crome, Sports Anchor
(214) 252-9233
• Bob Irzyk, Sports Anchor
(214) 252-9233

KDF-TV
409 SOUTH STAPLES
CORPUS CHRISTI, TX 78401
361-886-6100
Fax: 361-886-6175
newsroom@kristv.com
www.kristv.com

• Art Mack, Sports Director
(361) 886-6172
amack@kristv.com
• Adela Paradero, Promotions Assistant
Director
(361) 886-6100
aparadero@kristv.com
• Adela Paradero, Promotions Director
(361) 886-6100

KDFW-TV
400 NORTH GRIFFIN STREET
DALLAS, TX 75202-1901
214-720-4444
Fax: 214-720-3263
www.kdfwfox4.com/
• Mike Doocy, Sports Anchor
(214) 720-3164
mdoocy@foxtv.com
• Max Morgan, Sports Anchor
(214) 720-3158
mmorgan@foxtv.com
• Nita Wiggins, Sports Reporter
(214) 720-3187
nwiggins@foxtv.com
• Chris Yates, Sports Reporter
(214) 720-4444
cyate032@foxtv.com

KDIN-TV
PO BOX 6450
JOHNSTON, IA 50131
515-281-4500
800-532-1290
Fax: 515-242-4113
www.iptv.org
• Jerry Grady, Sports Director
(515) 242-3111
• Dan Miller, Executive Director
(515) 242-3123
• Pat Rowan, Sports Director
(515) 281-4500

KDKA-TV
1 GATEWAY CENTER
PITTSBURGH, PA 15222
412-575-2200
Fax: 412-575-2871
newsdesk@kdka.com
www.kdka.com
• Mike Bukovcan, Sports Director
• Greg Jena, Promotions Director
(412) 575-2508
• Mike Zappone, Sports Director
• Bob Pompeani, Sports Director
(412) 575-2200

KDLH-TV
246 LAKE AVENUE, S.
DULUTH, MN 55802-1511
218-720-9600
Fax: 218-720-9660
www.northlandsnewscentre.com.com
• Christi Corbett, Promotion Manager
(218) 733-0303
• Chris Earl, Sports Director
(218) 720-9626
• Joe Dufek, Sports Anchor
(218) 727-9600

KDLT-TV
3600 SOUTH WESTPORT AVENUE
SIOUX FALLS, SD 57106-6325
605-361-5555
800-727-5358
Fax: 605-361-3982

news@kdlt.com
www.kdlt.com
• Mark Kitterman, Promotions Director
• Mark Ovenden, Sports Director
(605) 361-5555
sports@kdlt.com
• Jason Anschutz, Sports Anchor
(605) 361-5555
info@kdlt.com

KDRX-TV
4625 SOUTH 33RD PLACE
PHOENIX, AZ 85040-2861
602-268-2648
Fax: 602-470-0810
• Franciscio Romero, Sports Director
(602) 470-0507

KDTV-TV
50 FREMONT STREET 41ST FLOOR
SAN FRANCISCO, CA 94105-2240
415-538-8000
Fax: 415-538-8053
www.univision.net
• Tony Lopez, Sports Director
(415) 538-8010
• Sandra Thomas, Executive Director
(415) 538-8003
sthomas@univision.net

KECI-TV
340 WEST MAIN STREET
MISSOULA, MT 59802-4149
406-721-2063
Fax: 406-549-6507
news@keci.com
www.keci.com
• Kristian Read, Sports Director

KERO-TV
321 21ST STREET
BAKERSFIELD, CA 93301
661-637-2320
Fax: 661-323-5538
www.turnto23.com
• Joseph Fernandez, Sports Director
(661) 637-2323
• Steve McEvoy, Marketing Director
(661) 637-2323
• Steve Taylor, Promotions Director
(661) 637-2323
• Bryce Anslinger, Weekend Sports
Anchor/News Reporter
(661) 637-2320

KESQ-TV
42-650 MELANIE PLACE
PALM DESERT, CA 92211
760-773-0795
Fax: 760-773-5128
www.kesq.com
• Brad Hoffman, Sports Anchor
(760) 773-0795
bhoffman@kesq.com
• Brad Hoffman, Sports Reporter

KETK-TV
4300 RICHMOND ROAD
TYLER, TX 75703-1201
903-581-5656
800-594-5385
Fax: 903-561-2459
www.ketknbc.com/
• Danny Elzner, Sports Director
(903) 581-5656

• Danny Elzner, Sports Director
(903) 581-5656

KETV-TV
2665 DOUGLAS STREET
OMAHA, NE 68131
402-978-8954
Fax: 402-978-8931
www.ketv.com
• Jon Schuetz, Sports Director
(402) 345-7777
• Jon Schuetz, Sports Director
• Mike Sigmond, Sports Anchor
• Matt Schick, Weekend Sports Anchor
(402) 978-8954

KEVN-TV
2000 SKYLINE DRIVE
RAPID CITY, SD 57701
605-394-7777
Fax: 605-348-9128
news@kevn.com
www.fox7.blackhills.com
• Jamie Zepp, Sports Director
(605) 394-7777
sports@kevn.com

KEZI-TV
2975 CHAD DRIVE
EUGENE, OR 97408-7344
541-485-5611
Fax: 541-342-1568
kezi@kezi.com
www.kezi.com
• Carolyn S. Chambers, Chief Executive
Officer
• Scott Chambers, President
• Joe Giansante, Sports Director
(541) 485-5611
• Sam Adams, Sports Reporter
(541) 485-5778

KFBB-TV
3200 OLD HAVRE HIGHWAY
BLACK EAGLE, MT 59414-1139
406-453-4377
Fax: 406-727-9703
kfbb@kfbb.com
www.kfbb.com
• Jason Nitschke, Sports Director
(406) 453-4370
newsroom@kfbb.com

KFDA-TV
7900 BROADWAY DRIVE
AMARILLO, TX 79108
806-383-1010
Fax: 806-381-9859
newsroom@newschannel10.com
www.newschannel10.com
• Joyce Austin, Advertising Manager
jaustin@newschannel10.com
• Jason Zielinski, Sports Reporter; Weekend
Anchor
(806) 383-1010
sports10@newschannel10.com
• Jeff Barger, Sports Director
(806) 383-1010
sports10@newschannel10.com

KFDM-TV
2955 INTERSTATE 10, E.
BEAUMONT, TX 77702-7128
409-892-6622
Fax: 409-892-6622

news@kfdm.com
www.kfdm.com
• Mike Friedman, Sports Director
(409) 895-4672
• Rix Garey, Advertising Manager
(409) 899-5544
rgarey@kfm.com
• Gina Hinson, Promotions Director
(409) 895-4628

KFDX-TV
P. O. BOX 4000
WICHITA FALLS, TX 76309
940-692-6273
Fax: 940-692-1441
kfdx@kfdx.com
www.kfdx.com
• Susan Knowles, Sports Director
(940) 692-1414

KFMB-TV
7677 ENGINEER ROAD
SAN DIEGO, CA 92111-1515
858-571-8888
Fax: 858-560-0627
yourstories@kfmb.com
www.kfmb.com
• John Howard, Sports Anchor
(858) 571-8888
jhoward@kfmb.com
• Kyle Kraska, Sports Director/Anchor
(858) 571-8888
kkraska@kfmb.com

KFOR-TV
PO BOX 14068
OKLAHOMA CITY, OK 73114-7515
405-424-4444
Fax: 405-478-6337
4warn@kfor.com
www.kfor.com
• Bob Barry, Sports Director
(405) 478-6366

KFSM-TV
PO BOX 369
FORT SMITH, AR 72901
479-783-3131
Fax: 479-783-1965
www.kfsm.com/
• Mike Irwin, Sports Director
(479) 783-3131

KFVE-TV
150 B PUUHALE ROAD
HONOLULU, HI 96819
808-847-3246
Fax: 808-845-3616
www.khnl.com
• Jim Leahy, Sports Director

KFYR-TV
P.O. BOX 1738
BISMARCK, ND 58501-4004
701-255-8105
Fax: 701-255-8220
news@kfyrtv.com
www.kfyrtv.com
• Lee Timmerman, Sports Director
(701) 255-8105
sports@kfyrtv.com

KGAN-TV
P.O. BOX 3131
CEDAR RAPIDS, IA 52402-2152

800-222-5426
800-222-5426
Fax: 319-395-0987
newsreleases@kgan.com
www.kgan.com
• Ruth Barnett, Promotions Manager
(319) 395-9060
rbarnett@kgan.com
• Kevin Hall, Sports Director
(800) 222-5426
• Jared Aarons, Sports Anchor
(319) 395-9060

KGMV-TV
1534 KAPIOLANI BOULEVARD
HONOLULU, HI 96814-3715
808-973-5462
Fax: 808-941-8153
www.kgmvnews.com
• Liz Chun, Sports Director
(808) 218-7696

KGO-TV
900 FRONT STREET
SAN FRANCISCO, CA 94111-1427
415-954-7926
Fax: 415-956-6402
abc7listens@kgo-tv.com
www.abc7news.com
• Bill Bacigalupi, Advertising Sales
• Larry Beil, Sports Anchor
larry.beil@abc.com
• Martin Wyatt, Sports Director
martin.wyatt@abc.com
• Mike Shumann, Sports Anchor
(415) 954-7926
mike.shumann@abc.com

KGPE-TV
4880 NORTH 1ST STREET
FRESNO, CA 93726-0514
559-222-2411
Fax: 559-225-5305
newsdesk@cbs47.tv
www.47tv.com
• Paul Loeffler, Sports Director
(559) 222-2411
paulloeffler@clearchannel.com
• George Takata, Sports Anchor
(559) 222-2411
georgetakata@clearchannel.com
• Rick Turner, Promotion Director
rickturner@clearchannel.com

KGTV-TV
4600 AIR WAY
SAN DIEGO, CA 92102-2528
619-527-6397
Fax: 619-527-0369
10news@10news.com
www.kgtv.com
• Jeff Cawley, Sports Director
(619) 237-6324
jeff_cawley@10news.com
• Wendy Simmons, Promotions Manager
wendy_urushima-simmons@10news.com
• Ben Higgins, Sports Anchor
(619) 527-6397
ben_higgins@10News.com

KGW-TV
1501 SW JEFFERSON STREET
PORTLAND, OR 97201-2549
503-226-5000
Fax: 503-226-5059

newsdesk@kgw.com
www.kgw.com
• Joe Becker, Sports Anchor
(503) 226-5000
• Ron Pivo, Sports Director

KHAS-TV
P.O. BOX 578
HASTINGS, NE 68901
402-463-1321
Fax: 402-463-6551
www.khastv.com/
• Ed Littler, Sports Director
• Scott Abraham, Sports Anchor
(402) 463-1321

KHNL-TV
150-B PUHALE ROAD
HONOLULU, HI 96819-2233
808-847-3246
Fax: 808-845-3616
www.khnl.com
• Russell Yamanoha, Sports Anchor

KHON-TV
88 PIIKOI STREET
HONOLULU, HI 96814-4245
808-591-4278
Fax: 808-593-2418
news@khon.com
www.khon.com
• John Veneri, Weekend Sports Anchor
(808) 591-4278
jveneri@khon.com
• Kanoa Leahey, Sports Director
(808) 591-4278

KHOU-TV
1945 ALLEN PARKWAY
HOUSTON, TX 77019-2506
713-526-1111
Fax: 713-520-7763
assignments@khou.com
www.khou.com
• Butch Alsandor, Sports Anchor
(713) 284-8781
balsandor@khou.com
• Carleton Cole, Sports Producer
(713) 521-4375
• Matt Musil, Sports Reporter
assignments@khou.com
• Gifford Nielsen, Sports Director/Anchor
(713) 284-8708

KHQA-TV
301 SOUTH 36TH STREET
QUINCY, IL 62301
217-222-6200
800-929-3518
Fax: 217-228-3164
khqa@khqa.com
www.khqa.com
• Chris Duerr, Sports Director
cduerr@khqa.com
• Kurt LaBelle, Sports Anchor
(217) 222-6200
klabelle@khqa.com
• Tyler Fulghum, Weekend Sports
Anchor/Reporter
(217) 222-6200
tfulghum@khqa.com

KICU-TV
2102 COMMERCE DRIVE
SAN JOSE, CA 95131-1804

408-953-3636
Fax: 408-953-3610
www.kicu.com
• Jeff Holub, Promotion Director
(510) 874-0542
• Mike Sklut, Anchor - High School Sports
Focus
(408) 953-3636
• Mike Sklut, Sports Producer
(408) 953-3636
• Brodie Brazil, Sports Reporter
(408) 953-3636

KIEM-TV
5650 SOUTH BROADWAY
EUREKA, CA 95503-6905
707-443-3123
Fax: 707-268-8109
kiem-tv.com
• Manny Machado, Sports Director
(707) 443-3123

KIII-TV
5002 SOUTH PADRE ISLAND DRIVE
CORPUS CHRISTI, TX 78411-4416
361-986-8300
Fax: 361-986-8311
news@kiiitv.com
www.kiiitv.com
• Dan McReynolds, Sports Director
(361) 986-8394

KIIN-TV
6450 CORPORATE DRIVE
JOHNSTON, IA 50131-1636
515-242-3100
800-532-1290
Fax: 515-242-4113
www.iptv.org
• Jerry Grady, Sports Director
(515) 242-3111
• Dan Miller, Executive Director
(515) 242-3123

KIMA-TV
2801 TERRACE HEIGHTS DRIVE
YAKIMA, WA 98901-1455
509-575-0029
Fax: 509-575-5526
tvnews@kimatv.com
www.kimatv.com
• Alan Sillence, Sports Director
(509) 575-0029
sillence@kimatv.com

KIMT-TV
112 NORTH PENNSYLVANIA AVENUE
MASON CITY, IA 50401-3404
641-423-2540
800-323-4883
Fax: 641-423-9309
www.kimt-tv.com
• Greg Berry, Sports Director
(641) 421-2620
• Jerome Risting, Promotion Director
(641) 421-2624
jristing@kimt.com

KING-TV
333 DEXTER AVENUE NORTH
SEATTLE, WA 98109-5107
206-448-3850
Fax: 206-448-4525
newstips@king5.com
www.king5.com

• Greg Bailey, Sports Anchor
• Michael King, Sports Reporter
• Katie Love, Promotion Coordinator
(206) 448-3890
• Paul Silvi, Sports Director/Anchor
(206) 448-3946
psilvi@king5.com
• D. J. Wilson, Advertising Sales Director
(206) 448-3882
• Lisa Gangel, Sports Reporter
(206) 448-3850

KION-TV
1550 MOFFETT STREET
SALINAS, CA 93905-3342
831-422-3500
800-321-5222
Fax: 831-422-9365
newstips@kion46.com
www.kion46.com
• Brent Calvin, Promotion Director
(831) 784-6401
brentcalvin@clearchannel.com
• Omar Ruiz, Sports Director
(831) 784-6411
omarruiz@clearchannel.com
• Hunter Finnell, Sports Director
(831) 784-1702
hunterfinnell@clearchannel.com

KIRO-TV
2807 THIRD AVENUE
SEATTLE, WA 98121
206-728-8308
800-777-5476
Fax: 206-441-4840
newstips@kirotv.com
www.kirotv.com
• Gaard Swanson, Sports Director
(206) 728-8308

KITV-TV
801 SOUTH KING STREET
HONOLULU, HI 96813
808-535-0400
Fax: 808-536-8993
www.kitv.com
• Rob DeMello, Sports Anchor (Weekend)
(808) 535-0400
• Robert Kekaula, Sports Anchor
(808) 535-0400

KIVI-TV
1866 EAST CHISHOLM DRIVE
NAMPA, ID 83687-6805
208-336-0500
Fax: 208-381-6681
news@todays6.com
www.todays6.com
• Joe Hughes, Sports Director
(208) 381-6855
jhughes@todays6.com

KJCT-TV
8 FORESIGHT CIRCLE
GRAND JUNCTION, CO 81505
970-245-8880
Fax: 970-245-8249
news8@kjct8.com
www.kjct8.com
• Josh Mitelman, Sports Director
jmitelman@kjct8.com
• Spencer Linton, Sports Reporter
(970) 245-8880
slinton@kjct8.com

KJRH-TV
P.O. BOX 2
TULSA, OK 74105-3263
918-743-2222
800-727-5574
Fax: 918-748-1436
news@kjrh.com
www.teamtulsa.com
• Marty Carpenter, Sports Reporter
sports@kjrh.com
• Al Jerkens, Sports Director
(918) 748-1539
jerkens@kjrh.com
• Jason Shackelford, Sports Reporter
(918) 743-2222
shackelford@kjrh.com
• Cayden McFarland, Sports Anchor
(918) 743-2222
news@kjrh.com

KKTV-TV
3100 NORTH NEVADA
COLORADO SPRINGS, CO 80907-5325
719-634-2844
Fax: 719-634-3741
ddownie@kktv11news.com
www.kktv.com
• Michelle Hughes, Promotions Manager
(719) 634-2844
mhughes@kktv11news.com
• Jesse Kurtz, Weekend Sports Anchor
(719) 634-2844
• John Owens, Sports Director
(719) 634-2844
jowens@kktv11news.com

KLAS-TV
3228 CHANNEL 8 DRIVE
LAS VEGAS, NV 89109-9000
702-792-8870
Fax: 702-792-2977
newsdesk@klastv.com
www.klastv.com
• Chris Maathuis, Sports Anchor
(702) 792-8895
cmaathuis@klastv.com
• Dave McCann, Sports Director
(702) 795-8896
• Michael Berk, Sports Reporter
(702) 792-8870

KLKN-TV
3240 S 10TH ST
LINCOLN, NE 68502-4401
402-434-8000
888-221-5556
Fax: 402-436-2236
8@klkntv.com
www.klkntv.com/
• Jon Wofford, Sports Director
(402) 436-2251
jwofford@klkntv.com

KMBC-TV
1049 CENTRAL STREET
KANSAS CITY, MO 64105-1619
816-760-9260
Fax: 816-421-4163
www.kmbc.com
• John Crumley, Sports Director
(816) 221-9999
jcrumley@hearst.com
• Len Dawson, Sports Anchor
ldawson@hearst.com
• Karen Kornacki, Sports Anchor/Reporter
(816) 760-9260
kkornacki@hearst.com

• Karen Kornacki, Sports Reporter
kkornacki@hearst.com
• Bill Pikus, Sports Anchor
(816) 221-9999
• Andy Fales, Weekend Sports Anchor
(816) 760-9260

KMEX-TV
5999 CENTER DRIVE
LOS ANGELES, CA 90045
310-216-3434
Fax: 310-348-3493
www.kmex.com
• Luis De La Parra, Promotions Director
(310) 348-3580
• Alejandro Luna, Sports Anchor
(310) 348-3478
aluna@univision.net
• Francisco Pinto, Sports Anchor
(310) 348-3497

KMGH-TV
123 SPEER BOULEVARD
DENVER, CO 80203-3417
303-832-7777
Fax: 303-832-0119
dennews@thedenverchannel.com
www.kmgh.com
• Lionel Bienvenu, Sports Anchor
(303) 832-0136
lionel_bienvenu@thedenverchannel.com
• Steve Gottsegen, Weekend Sports Anchor
(303) 832-7777
steve_gottsegen@kmgh.com
• Bobby Hayden, Sports Director
(303) 832-0169
bobby_hayden@kmgh.com
• Jay Maloney, Promotions Manager
(303) 832-0295
jay_maloney@kmgh.com
• Phil Aldridge, Sports Reporter
(303) 832-7777
phil_aldridge@thedenverchannel.com

KMIR-TV
72920 PARKVIEW DRIVE
PALM DESERT, CA 92260
760-568-3636
Fax: 760-341-7029
www.kmir6.com
• Cal Ahlers, Sports Anchor
(760) 568-3636

KMIZ-TV
501 BUSINESS LOOP 70 EAST
COLUMBIA, MO 65201-3909
573-449-0917
Fax: 573-875-7078
news@kmiz.com
www.kmiz.com
• Beau Baehnan, Sports Director
(573) 449-0917
sports@kmiz.com
• Beau Baehman, Sports Director
(573) 449-0917

KMOV-TV
ONE MEMORIAL DRIVE
SAINT LOUIS, MO 63102-2425
314-444-6333
Fax: 314-621-4775
pressrelease@kmov.com
www.kmov.com
• Dan Dillon, Promotions Director
(314) 444-3330
• Steve Savard, Sports Director

ssavard@kmov.com
• Jeff Skversky, Sports Anchor/Reporter
(314) 444-6333

KMPH-TV
5111 MCKINLEY AVENUE, E.
FRESNO, CA 93727-1985
559-453-8850
Fax: 559-255-9626
newsdesk@kmph.com
www.kmph.com
• Ken Felder, Advertising Manager
(559) 255-2600
kfelder@kmph.com
• Ralph Wood, Weeknight Sports Anchor
(559) 453-8850
rwoood@kmph.com
• Heidi Watney, Weekend Sports Anchor
(559) 453-8850
hwatney@kmph.com

KMSP-TV
11358 VIKING DRIVE
EDEN PRAIRIE, MN 55344-7238
952-946-5767
Fax: 952-942-0455
www.kmsp.com
• Jeff Grayson, Sports Director
• Dawn Mitchell, Weekend Sports
Anchor/Reporter
(952) 946-5767

KMTR-TV
3825 INTERNATIONAL COURT
SPRINGFIELD, OR 97477-1086
541-746-1600
Fax: 541-747-3429
newsdesk@kmtr.com
www.nbc16.com
• Dave Wenda, Sports Director
(541) 746-1600

KMTV-TV
10714 MOCKINGBIRD DRIVE
OMAHA, NE 68127
402-592-3333
Fax: 402-593-2737
news@km3news.com
www.kmtv3.com
• Ken Dudzik, Marketing Director
• Travis Justice, Sports Director
(402) 592-3333

KMVT-TV
1100 BLUE LAKES BOULEVARD, N.
TWIN FALLS, ID 83301-3305
208-733-1100
Fax: 208-733-4649
jmartin@kmvt.com
www.kmvt.com
• Eric Geller, Sports Director
(208) 733-6407
• Paul Johnson, Promotions Manager

KNBC-TV
3000 WEST ALAMEDA AVENUE
BURBANK, CA 91523
818-840-4444
Fax: 818-840-3535
knbc.desk@nbcuni.com
www.knbc.com
• Bob Long, Vice President
• Fred Roggin, Sports Director/Anchor
(818) 840-4444
fred.roggin@nbc.com
• Charlie Rosene, Senior Sports Producer

(818) 840-4444
• Kevin Applebaum, Sports Producer
(818) 840-4444

KNOE-TV
1400 OLIVER ROAD
MONROE, LA 71201
318-388-8888
Fax: 318-388-0070
knoetv@bayou.com
www.knoe.com
• Aaron Dietrich, Sports Director
(318) 388-8888
• Bill Elliott, Marketing Director
(318) 388-8888
• Bill Elliott, Promotions Manager

KNSD - NBC 7/39
8330 ENGINEER RD
SAN DIEGO, CA 92111
619-231-3939
Fax: 619-578-0202
www.nbcsandiego.com
• Phyllis Scwartz, President/General
Manager
• Jim Laslavic, Sports Director
Sports Covered:
All Major and minor league sports. Local
teams: San Diego Chargers San Diego
Padres San Diego Spirit San Diego Gulls
San Diego Sockers San Diego Riptide
University of San Diego Toreros SDSU
Aztecs UCSD Tritons.

KNSD-TV
225 BROADWAY
SAN DIEGO, CA 92101
619-578-0201
Fax: 619-578-0202
pressinquiries@nbcsandiego.com
www.nbcsandiego.com
• Jim Laslavic, Sports Director
(858) 279-3939
• Phyllis Schwartz, President

KNTV-TV
2450 NORTH FIRST STREET
SAN JOSE, CA 95110-2613
408-432-4780
Fax: 408-432-4425
newstips@nbc11.com
www.nbc11.com
• Craig Fierro, Sports Producer
(408) 432-4780
• Raj Mathai, Sports Director/Anchor
(408) 432-4780
raj.mathai@nbcuni.com
• Raj Mathai, Sports Director
(408) 297-8780
raj.mathai@nbc.com
• Jim Sanders, Vice President

KNXV-TV
515 NORTH 44TH STREET
PHOENIX, AZ 85008-6511
602-685-6397
Fax: 602-685-6363
assignmentdesk@abc15.com
www.phoenix360.com
• Craig Fouhy, Sports Director
(602) 273-1500
cfouhy@abc15.com

KOAA-TV
530 COMMUNICATIONS CIRCLE
COLORADO SPRINGS, CO 80905-1744

719-632-5030
Fax: 719-295-6677
news@koaa.com
www.koaa.com
• Richard Bouchez, Promotions Manager
(719) 544-5781
• Lee Douglas, Sports Director

KOAM-TV
2950 NORTHEAST HIGHWAY 69
PITTSBURG, KS 66762-0659
620-231-0400
Fax: 417-624-3158
www.koamtv.com
• Chad Plein, Sports Director
(620) 231-0400
• Danny Thomas, President
(620) 231-0400
dwthomas@koamtv.com

KOAT-TV
P.O. BOX 25982
ALBUQUERQUE, NM 87107-4501
505-884-6324
Fax: 505-884-6282
koatdesk@hearst.com
www.thenewmexicochannel.com
• Bob Brown, Sports Director
(505) 884-6330
rbrown@hearst.com

KOBI-TV
125 SOUTH FIR STREET
MEDFORD, OR 97501-3115
541-779-5555
Fax: 541-779-5564
www.localnewscomesfirst.com
• Scott Gee, Promotion Director
sgee@kobi5.com
• Jordan Mason, Sports Director
(541) 842-4294
• Joe Camarlinghi, Sports Director
(541) 779-5555

KOCT-TV
3801 CARLISLE BOULEVARD, N.E.
ALBUQUERQUE, NM 87107
505-884-7777
Fax: 505-884-6282
koatdesk@hearst.com
www.thenewmexicochannel.com
• Bob Brown, Sports Director

KODE-TV
1928 WEST 13TH STREET
JOPLIN, MO 64801-3839
417-623-7260
Fax: 417-623-3736
www.kode-tv.com
• Brett Newtson, Sports Director
(417) 623-7260
• Bruce Vonde-Harr, Sports Director
(417) 623-7260

KOKI-TV
2625 SOUTH MEMORIAL DRIVE
TULSA, OK 74129
918-388-5100
Fax: 918-388-0516
news@fox23.com
www.fox23.com
• Deedra Determan, Marketing Director
• Ron Terrell, Sports Director
(918) 388-5263
rterrell@fox23.com

KOLR-TV
2650 EAST DIVISION STREET
SPRINGFIELD, MO 65803-5228
417-862-1010
Fax: 417-866-6397
www.ozarksfirst.com
• Dan Lucy, Sports Director
(417) 862-1010
dlucy@kolr10.com

KOMO-TV
140 4TH AVENUE NORTH
SEATTLE, WA 98109-4932
206-404-4145
Fax: 206-404-4422
tips@komo4news.com
www.komotv.com
• Colleen Brown, President
(206) 404-7000
• Eric Johnson, Sports Director
(206) 404-4145
ericj@komotv.com
• Eric Johnson, Sports Director
ericj@komotv.com
• Randa Minkarah, Marketing Director
rminkarah@komotv.com
• Derek Agnew, Sports Reporter
(206) 404-4000
dereka@komotv.com

KOMU-TV
5550 HIGHWAY 63, S.
COLUMBIA, MO 65201
573-882-8888
Fax: 573-884-5353
news@komu.com
www.komu.com
• Chris Grevino, Sports Director
• Monica Stoneking, Promotions Assistant
• Eric Blumberg, Sports Anchor; Reporter
(573) 882-8888

KOSA-TV
4101 EAST 42ND STREET
SUITE J7
ODESSA, TX 79762
432-580-5672
Fax: 432-580-8010
news@cbs7.com
www.cbs7.com/
• Whitney Harding, Sports Director
(915) 580-6397

KOTV-TV
PO BOX 6
TULSA, OK 74120-2422
918-732-6000
Fax: 918-732-6185
www.kotv.com
• John Holcomb, Sports Director
(918) 732-6146
• Donita Quesnel, Promotions Director
(918) 732-6070
bquesnel@kotb.com
• Mike Wolfe, Weekend Sports Anchor
(918) 732-6000

KOVR-TV
2713 KOVR DRIVE
WEST SACRAMENTO, CA 95605-1600
916-374-1313
Fax: 916-374-1304
news@kovr.com
www.kovr13.com
• Steve Harris, Promotions Manager
(916) 374-1429

• Jennifer Krier, Sports Anchor (Weekend)
• Arran Andersen, Sports Anchor
(916) 374-1313

KOVT-TV
3801 CARLISLE BOULEVARD, N.E.
ALBUQUERQUE, NM 87107
505-884-7777
Fax: 505-884-6282
koatdesk@hearst.com
• Bob Brown, Sports Director

KPIC-TV
P.O. BOX 1345
ROSEBURG, OR 97470-2955
541-672-4481
Fax: 541-672-4482
kpic4news@kpic.com
www.kpic.com
• Jason Hink, Sports Director
(541) 672-4481
• Connie Williamson, Advertising Manager
(541) 672-4481

KPIX-TV
855 BATTERY STREET
SAN FRANCISCO, CA 94111-1503
415-765-8610
Fax: 415-765-8916
newsdesk@kpix.com
www.kpix.com/
• Dennis O'Donnell, Sports Anchor
(415) 765-8610
newsdesk@kpix.com
• Dennis O'Donnell, Sports Director
• Rick Quan, Sports Anchor
(415) 765-8643

KPLR-TV
2250 BALL DRIVE
SAINT LOUIS, MO 63146
314-213-2222
Fax: 314-447-6430
www.kplr11.com
• Rich Gould, Sports Director
(314) 447-6438
• David Maul, Promotions Director
(314) 447-6359

KPNX-TV
1101 NORTH CENTRAL AVENUE
PHOENIX, AZ 85004-1818
602-257-1212
Fax: 602-257-6619
assignmentdesk@12news.com
www.kpnx.com
• Barry Orr, Sports Director
• Joe Pequeno, Sports
Producer/Reporter/Anchor
(602) 257-1212
• Bruce Cooper, Weekend Sports Reporter
(602) 257-1212

KPRC-TV
P.O. BOX 2222
HOUSTON, TX 77074-1705
713-778-4950
Fax: 713-771-4930
hounews@click2houston.com
www.click2houston.com/
• Katherine Harvin, Marketing Director
(713) 778-4831
kfuller@kprc.com
• Steve Mark, Sports Anchor
smark@click2houston.com
• Randy Mcilvoy, Sports Anchor

rmcilvoy@kprc.com
• Edward Ortelli, Advertising Manager
(713) 778-4893
• Michael Stewart, Promotions Director
(713) 778-4739
• Keith Norton, Sports Reporter
(713) 778-4950

KPRY-TV
300 NORTH DAKOTA AVENUE
SIOUX FALLS, SD 57104
605-336-1300
800-955-5739
Fax: 605-336-7936
ksfy@ksfy.com
• Eric Thorstenson, Sports Director
(605) 336-1300
ethorstenson@ksfy.com

KPTM-TV
4625 FAMAM STREET
OMAHA, NE 68132-3222
402-558-4200
Fax: 402-554-4279
news42@kptm.com
www.kptm.com/
• JJ Davis, Sports Director
(402) 558-4200
• Jeff Radcliffe, Sports Reporter
(402) 558-4200
• Donna Ridgley, Promotions Director
(402) 554-4232

KPTV-TV
14975 NW GREENBRIER PARKWAY
BEAVERTON, OR 97006-5731
503-906-1249
Fax: 503-548-6920
kptvnews@kptv.com
www.kptv.com/
• Tim Becker, Sports Director
(503) 906-1249
tbecker@kptv.com
• Matt Hyatt, Promotion Manager

KPVI-TV
902 EAST SHERMAN
POCATELLO, ID 83204-0667
208-232-6666
Fax: 208-233-6678
newsroom@kpvi.com
www.kpvi.com/
• Dave Reichelt, Sports Director
• Brad Shellgren, Sports Director
(208) 232-6666

KQCA-TV
58 TELEVISION CIRCLE
SACRAMENTO, CA 95814-0750
916-447-5858
Fax: 916-554-4663
www.kqcachannel.com
• Ron Hyde, Sports Director
(916) 325-3294

KRBC-TV
4510 14TH STREET, S.
ABILENE, TX 79605-4737
325-692-4242
Fax: 325-692-8265
www.krbc.tv
• Amanda Campbell, Promotions Director
(325) 692-4242
• Caden McFarland, Sports Director
• John Wilson, Sports Director
(325) 692-4242

KRCR-TV
755 AUDITORIUM DRIVE
REDDING, CA 96001-0920
530-243-7777
800-222-5727
Fax: 530-243-9382
www.krcrtv.com
• Mike Mangas, Sports Director
• Damae Thompson, Promotion Manager
• Eric Natkin, Sports Director
(530) 243-7777

KREM-TV
4103 SOUTH REGAL STREET
SPOKANE, WA 99223-7737
509-448-2000
Fax: 509-448-6397
newsdesk@krem.com
www.krem.com
• Tom Hudson, Sports Director
(509) 838-7370

KRGV-TV
NEWSCHANNEL 5
WESLACO, TX 78596
956-631-5555
Fax: 956-973-5001
www.newschannel5.tv
• Dave Brown, Sports Director
(956) 631-5555
dave@klgv.com

KRIS-TV
P.O. BOX 840
CORPUS CHRISTI, TX 78401
361-886-6100
Fax: 361-886-6175
newsroom@kristv.com
www.kristv.com
• Art Mack, Sports Director
(361) 886-6172
• Sean Horejs, Weekend Sports Anchor
(361) 886-6100

KRIV-TV
4261 SOUTHWEST FREEWAY
HOUSTON, TX 77027-7201
713-479-2600
Fax: 713-479-2859
www.myfoxhouston.com/
• Mark Berman, Sports Director
(713) 479-2600

KRON-TV
1001 VAN NESS AVENUE
SAN FRANCISCO, CA 94109-6982
415-561-8905
Fax: 415-561-8136
www.kron4.com
• Mark Antonitis, Vice President
• Jason Applebaum, Sports Producer
• Vernon Glenn, Sports Anchor
(415) 561-8905
• Dave Guingona, Sports Producer
(415) 561-8633
• Deb McDermot, President
(615) 369-7222

KRQE-TV
13 BROADCAST PLAZA SW
ALBUQUERQUE, NM 87104-1056
505-243-2285
Fax: 505-842-8483
newsdesk@krqe.com
www.krqe.com/

• Mike Powers, Sports Director
(505) 764-5240
• Mike Powers, Sports Director
(505) 764-5214
• Van Tate, Weekend Sports
Anchor/Reporter
(505) 243-2285
van.tate@krqe.com

KRTV-TV
3300 OLD HAVRE HIGHWAY
BLACK EAGLE, MT 59414-1079
406-791-5400
800-823-5788
Fax: 406-791-5479
krtvnews@krtv.com
www.krtv.com
• Heath Heggem, Sports Director
heath@krtv.com

KSBW-TV
P.O. BOX 81651
SALINAS, CA 93901-3339
831-758-8888
Fax: 831-422-0124
www.theksbwchannel.com
• Dennis Lehnen, Sports Director
(831) 758-8888

KSBY-TV
1772 CALLE JOAQUIN
SAN LUIS OBISPO, CA 93405-7210
805-541-6666
Fax: 805-597-8520
news@ksby.com
www.ksby.com
• Dave Alles, Sports Director/Anchor
(805) 541-6666
• Ryan Bennett, Sports Anchor
• Madeline Palaszewski, Promotion Director
(805) 597-8471

KSDK-TV
1000 MARKET STREET
SAINT LOUIS, MO 63101
314-421-5055
Fax: 314-444-5164
newstips@ksdk.com
www.ksdk.com
• Rene Knott, Sports Director
(314) 421-5055
• Frank Cusumano, Sports Reporter
(314) 421-5055

KSFY-TV
300 NORTH DAKOTA AVENUE
SIOUX FALLS, SD 57104
605-336-1300
800-955-5739
Fax: 605-336-2067
news@ksfy.com
www.ksfy.com/
• Erik Thorstenson, Sports Director
(605) 336-1300
ethorstenson@ksfy.com

KSHB-TV
4720 OAK STREET
KANSAS CITY, MO 64112-2236
816-932-4141
800-818-5742
Fax: 816-932-4145
desk@kshb.com
www.kshb.com

• Jack Harry, Sports Director
(816) 932-4141
harry@nbcactionnews.com

KSL-TV
5 TRIAD CENTER
SALT LAKE CITY, UT 84180-1109
801-575-5555
Fax: 801-575-5830
feedback@ksl.com
www.ksl.com
• Tom Kirkland, Sports Director
(801) 575-5555
tom.kirkland@ksl.com

KSNF-TV
PO BOX 1393
JOPLIN, MO 64802
417-781-2345
Fax: 417-782-2417
www.fourstateshomepage.com
• Eric Knecht, Sports Anchor
(417) 781-2345
• Debora Palmer, Advertising Manager
(417) 781-2345
• Morgan Vance, Sports Ancor
(417) 781-2345

KSNT-TV
PO BOX 2700
TOPEKA, KS 66618
785-582-4000
Fax: 785-582-4783
27news@ksnt.com
www.ksnt.com
• Lance Veeser, Sports Anchor
(785) 582-3222
• Lance Veeser, Sports Director
(785) 582-3222
• Adam Alter, Sports Reporter
(785) 582-4000

KSTP - KSTP 5/ABC
3415 UNIVESITY AVE
SAINT PAUL, MN 55114
651-646-5555
Fax: 651-642-4409
www.kstp.com
• Ed Piette, Vice President/General Manager
• Joe Schmit, Sports Director

KSTS-TV
2450 NORTH FIRST STREET
SAN JOSE, CA 95131-1125
408-435-0327
Fax: 408-434-1046
info@ksts.com
www.ksts.com/
• Ramon Diaz, Sports Director
(408) 435-0327
noticias@ksts.com

KSTU-TV
5020 AMELIA EARHART DRIVE
SALT LAKE CITY, UT 84116-2853
801-532-1300
Fax: 801-536-1325
www.myfoxutah.com
• Mike Runge, Sports Director
• Rick Aaron, Sports Director
(801) 536-1313

KSWO-TV
P.O. BOX 708
LAWTON, OK 73501

580-355-7000
Fax: 580-357-3811
news@kswo.com
www.kswo.com
• Nathan Thompson, Sports Director
(580) 355-7000
• Todd Young, Promotions Director
tyoung@kswo.com
• Mike Straub, Sports Reporter
(580) 355-7000
mstraub@kswo.com

KTAL-TV
3150 NORTH MARKET STREET
SHREVEPORT, LA 71107-4005
318-629-6000
Fax: 318-629-7171
www.newschannel6.tv
• Dave Schwartz, Sports Director
(318) 629-6000
• Scott Thomas, Advertising Manager
(318) 629-6000

KTBC-TV
119 EAST 10TH STREET
AUSTIN, TX 78701
512-476-7777
Fax: 512-495-7060
www.fox7.com
• Dave Cody, Sports Director
(512) 495-7708

KTIV-TV
3135 FLOYD BOULEVARD
SIOUX CITY, IA 51108-1465
712-239-4100
800-234-5848
Fax: 712-239-2621
ktivnews@ktiv.com
www.ktiv.com
• Brad Pautsch, Sports Director
(712) 239-4100
bpautsch@ktiv.com
• Mike Orlando, Weekend Sports Anchor
(712) 239-4100

KTLA-TV
5800 SUNSET BOULEVARD
LOS ANGELES, CA 90028
323-460-5500
Fax: 323-460-5333
www.ktla.com
• Damon Andrews, Sports Director/Anchor
(323) 460-5500
• Damon Andrews, Sports Director
(323) 460-5443
• Mark Brinks, Sports Writer
(323) 460-5907
• Ted Green, Sports Writer
(323) 460-5907

KTMD-TV
1235 NORTH LOOP WAY SUITE 125
HOUSTON, TX 77008-6405
713-974-4848
Fax: 713-266-6397
www.ktmd.com
• Lester Gretsh, Sports Director
• Carlos Munoz, Sports Reporter

KTNV-TV
3355 SOUTH VALLEY VIEW BOULEVARD
LAS VEGAS, NV 89102-8216
702-871-3345
Fax: 702-876-2237

ktnvnewsdesk@ktnv.com
www.ktnv.com
• Dennis Evans, Sports Anchor
(702) 257-8323
devans@ktnv.com
• Doug Kezirian, Sports Director
(702) 871-3345
dkezirian@ktnv.com

KTRE-TV
P.O. BOX 729
LUFKIN, TX 75902-0729
936-853-5873
Fax: 936-853-3084
ktrenews@ktre.com
www.ktre.com
• Shawn Clynch, Sports Director
(936) 853-5873
sClynch@ktre.com
• Mike Wiggins, Promotion Manager
mwiggins@ktre.com

KTRK-TV
P.O. BOX 13
HOUSTON, TX 77005-2114
713-666-0713
Fax: 713-664-0013
ktrk.newsalerts@abc.com
abc13.com/
• Bob Allen, Weekday Sports Director
(713) 663-4536
• Tim Melton, Weekend Sports Anchor
(713) 666-0713
• Bob Slovak, Weekend Sports Anchor
(713) 666-0713

KTTC-TV
6301 BANDEL ROAD NW
ROCHESTER, MN 55901-8798
507-280-5105
800-288-1656
Fax: 507-288-6324
www.kttc.com
• Pat Lund, Sports Director
(507) 280-5105

KTTV-TV
1999 SOUTH BUNDY DRIVE
LOS ANGELES, CA 90025-5235
310-584-2025
Fax: 310-584-2023
www.myfoxla.com
• Rod Cohen, Sports Producer
• Jennifer Gould, Sports Anchor
(310) 584-2030
• Rick Garcia, Sports Director
(310) 584-2261

KTUU-TV
701 EAST TUDOR ROAD
ANCHORAGE, AK 99503
907-762-9202
Fax: 907-563-3318
news_desk@ktuu.com
www.ktuu.com
• John Carpenter, Sports Director
(907) 762-9229
jcarpenter@ktuu.com

KTVB-TV
P.O. BOX 7
BOISE, ID 83706-1162
208-321-5614
800-559-7277
Fax: 208-375-7770

ktvbnews@ktvb.com
www.ktvb.com
• David Augusto, Sports Director
(208) 321-5614
daugusto@ktvb.com
• Kristi Edmunds, Marketing Director
kedmunds@ktvb.com
• P. J. Laws, Promotion Director
(208) 375-7277

KTVE-TV
200 PAVILION ROAD
WEST MONROE, LA 71292
318-323-1972
Fax: 318-322-0926
www.region10.com
• Chris Mycoskie, Sports Director
(318) 323-1972
• Esther Phillips, Promotions Manager

KTVH-TV
P.O. BOX 6125
HELENA, MT 59601
406-457-1212
Fax: 406-442-5106
www.ktvh.com
• Al Marks, Sports Director
amarks@ktvh.com
• Alan Marks, Sports Director
(406) 457-1212

KTVI-TV
2250 BALL DRIVE
SAINT LOUIS, MO 63146
314-213-2222
800-920-0222
Fax: 314-647-8960
ktvinews@foxtv.com
www.fox2now.com
• Rob Desir, Sports Reporter
• Susan Edwards, Executive Director
ktvinews@foxtv.com
• Martin Kilcoyne, Sports Director/Anchor
(314) 647-2222

KTVK-TV
5555 NORTH SEVENTH AVENUE
PHOENIX, AZ 85013-1701
602-207-3333
Fax: 602-207-3477
3tvnews@azfamily.com
www.azfamily.com
• Todd Kelly, Sports Director
todd_kelly@azfamily.com
• Brad Cesmat, Sports Reporter
(602) 207-3333

KTVM-TV
BOX 5268
BOZEMAN, MT 59715
406-586-0296
Fax: 406-586-0554
news@ktvm.com
www.ktvm.com/montana_news.php
• Steve Dent, Sports Director
(406) 586-0296

KTVN-TV
4925 ENERGY WAY
RENO, NV 89502-4105
775-861-4290
Fax: 775-861-4246
producers@ktvn.com
www.ktvn.com
• J. K. Metzker, Sports Director
(775) 861-4229

jmetzker@ktvn.com
• Garrett Dearborn, Weekend Sports Anchor
(775) 861-4290
gdearborn@ktvn.com

KTVT-TV
PO BOX 2495
FORT WORTH, TX 76113
817-451-1111
888-654-5888
Fax: 817-457-1897
news@ktvt.com
www.cbs11tv.com
• Dandy Killeen, Sports Director
dandyk@ktvt.com
• Babe Laufenberg, Sports Anchor
(817) 451-1111
• Chris Bullock, Sports Producer
(817) 586-7440
chrisb@ktvt.com

KTVU-TV
2 JACK LONDON SQUARE
OAKLAND, CA 94607-3727
510-874-0242
Fax: 510-451-2610
www.ktvu.com
• Mark Ibanez, Sports Director
(510) 874-0254
• Greg Rando, Advertising Writer
(510) 874-0375
• Joe Fonzi, Weekend Sports Anchor
(510) 834-1212

KTVX-TV
2175 WEST 1700 SOUTH
SALT LAKE CITY, UT 84104-4200
801-975-4401
800-766-1776
Fax: 801-973-4176
www.4utah.com
• Wesley Ruff, Sports Director
(801) 975-4444
wesley@abc4.com
• Wesley Ruff, Sports Director
(801) 975-4428
wruff@abc4.tv
• Dana Greene, Sports Reporter
(801) 975-4401
dana@abc4.com

KTVZ-TV
62990 OB RILEY ROAD
BEND, OR 97701
541-383-2121
800-331-8821
Fax: 541-382-1616
ktvz@ktvz.com
www.ktvz.com
• Vic Quick, Sports Director
sports@ktvz.com

KTXL-TV
4655 FRUITRIDGE ROAD
SACRAMENTO, CA 95820-5201
916-454-4548
Fax: 916-739-0559
fox40.trb.com/
• Jim Crandell, Sports Director
(916) 454-4548

KTXS-TV
P. O. BOX 2997
ABILENE, TX 79601
325-677-2281
800-588-5897

Fax: 325-672-5307
levesque@ktxs.com
www.ktxs.com
• David Caldwell, Promotions Manager
(325) 677-2281
• Jorge Montoya, Advertising Manager
(325) 677-2281
• Mark Rogers, Sports Anchor
(325) 677-2281

KUSA-TV
500 EAST SPEER BOULEVARD
DENVER, CO 80203-4187
303-871-1499
Fax: 303-698-4700
news@9news.com
www.9news.com
• Steve Carter, Promotions Director
(303) 871-1855
• David Hunt, Sports Executive
Producer/Sports Directo
(303) 871-1499
david.hunt@9news.com

KUTV-TV
299 SOUTH MAIN STREET
SALT LAKE CITY, UT 84111
801-973-3000
Fax: 801-973-3349
news@kutv2.com
www.kutv.com
• Jeremy Castro, Sports Director
(801) 973-3327
castroje@kutv2.com
• John Greene, Marketing Director
(801) 973-3001
greenejr@kutv2.com
• Dan Sheldon, Sports Anchor/Reporter
(801) 973-3000

KUVN-TV
2323 BRYAN STREET SUITE 1900
DALLAS, TX 75201
214-758-2300
800-494-5886
Fax: 214-758-2351
noticias23dfw@univision.net
www.univision.net
• Louis Hernandez, Advertising Sales
Director
• Mario Montez, Sports Director
(214) 758-2344

KVAL-TV
P.O. BOX 1313
EUGENE, OR 97405
541-342-4961
Fax: 541-342-5436
kvalnews@kval.com
www.kval.com
• Todd McKim, Sports Director

KVBC-TV
1500 FOREMASTER LANE
LAS VEGAS, NV 89101-1103
702-657-3150
Fax: 702-657-3152
www.kvbc.com
• Mitch Roberts, Sports Director
(702) 657-3150
• Rick Strasser, Sports Reporter/Director
(702) 657-3150

KVIA-TV
4140 RIO BRAVO
EL PASO, TX 79902-1002

915-496-7777
Fax: 915-532-0505
kvia@kvia.com
www.kvia.com
• Rick Cabrera, Sports Director
• Trini Parada, Promotions Assistant
• Raul Martinez, Sports Director
(915) 496-7777

KVII-TV
ONE BROADCAST CENTER
AMARILLO, TX 79101-4328
806-373-1787
Fax: 806-371-7329
pronews7@kvii.com
www.kvii.com
• Lee Baker, Sports Director
(806) 373-1787
lbaker@kvii.com
• Lee Baker, Sports Reporter
(806) 373-1787
lbaker@kvii.com
• Lisa Schmidt, Promotion Director
(806) 373-1787
lschmidth@kvii.com
• Lisa Schmidt, Promotions Manager
(806) 373-1787
lschmidt@kvii.com
• Paul Tubbs, Sports Reporter

KVLY-TV
P.O. BOX 1878
FARGO, ND 58103
701-237-5211
800-450-5844
Fax: 701-237-5396
news@kvlytv11.com
www.kvlytv11.com
• Scott Peters, Sports Director
(701) 237-5211

KVMD-TV
28202 CABOT ROAD
SUITE 300
LAGUNA NIGUEL, CA 92677
760-366-9881
888-550-5862
Fax: 949-365-5709
www.kvmdtv.com
• Larry Peterson, General Manager
• Larry Peterson, Program Director

KVOA-TV
P.O. BOX 5188
TUCSON, AZ 85705-6539
520-624-2477
Fax: 520-884-4644
www.kvoa.com/
• Dan Ryan, Sports Director
• Jay Campbell, Sports Reporter
(520) 624-2477

KVUE-TV
PO BOX 9927
AUSTIN, TX 78757-8026
512-459-6521
Fax: 512-533-2233
news@kvue.com
www.kvue.com
• Mike Barnes, Sports Director/Anchor
(512) 459-2065

KVVU-TV
25 TV 5 DRIVE
HENDERSON, NV 89014

702-436-8256
Fax: 702-436-2507
5newsdesk@kvvu.com
www.ktvutv.com
• Dave Hall, Sports Anchor
(702) 436-8256
dhall3@kvvu.com
• Terri Peck, Marketing Director
• Kevin Bolinger, Sports Director
(702) 435-5555
kbolinger@kvvu.com

KWAB-TV
11320 COUNTY ROAD 127, WEST
MIDLAND, TX 79711
432-567-9999
Fax: 432-567-9993
• Donna Cooper, Account Executive
(432) 567-9999
dkcooper@kwes.com
• Scott Shields, Sports Director
(432) 567-9999
• Kathy Swindler, Promotions Director
(432) 567-9999

KWES-TV
11320 COUNTY ROAD 127, WEST
MIDLAND, TX 79711
432-567-9999
Fax: 432-567-9993
www.kwes.com
• Donna Cooper, Account Executive
(432) 567-9999
dkcooper@kwes.com
• Scott Shields, Sports Director
(432) 567-9999
• Kathy Swindler, Promotions Director
(432) 567-9999

KWEX-TV
411 EAST DURANGO
SAN ANTONIO, TX 78204-1309
210-227-4141
Fax: 210-227-0469
www.univision.net
• Jorge Rodriguez, Sports Director
(210) 242-7467
• Jaime Becerril, Sports Anchor
(210) 227-4141

KWGN-TV
6160 SOUTH WABASH WAY
GREENWOOD VILLAGE, CO 80111
303-740-2855
Fax: 303-740-2803
cw2.trb.com/
• Chris Riva, Sports Director
(303) 740-2855
• Mark Soicher, Sports Anchor
• Rob Venuski, Promotions Director
• Lisa Holbrook, Weekend Sports Anchor
(303) 740-2855

KWNB-TV
P.O. BOX 220
KEARNEY, NE 68848-0220
308-743-2494
Fax: 308-743-2644
• Becky Miller, Promotions Director
• Matt Schick, Sports Director
• Anita Wragge, Promotions Director
awragge@nebraska.tv

KWQC -TV6
805 BRADY ST
DAVENPORT, IA 52803

563-383-7000
Fax: 563-383-7131
www.kwqc.com
• Thom Cornelis, Sports Director
• Jim Graham, Vice President/General
Manager
• Trish Tague, Marketing Director
Affiliate:
CBS.
Neilsen Market:
90

KWQC-TV
805 BRADY STREET
DAVENPORT, IA 52803-5211
563-383-7048
Fax: 563-383-7131
news@kwqc.com
www.kwqc.com/
• Jeff Bilyeu, Promotions Director
(563) 383-7075
• Thom Cornelis, Sports Director
(563) 383-7037

KWTV-TV
7401 NORTH KELLEY AVENUE
OKLAHOMA CITY, OK 73111-8420
405-841-9956
Fax: 405-841-9989
tv9@aol.com
www.newsok.com
• Dean Blevins, Sports Director
(405) 841-9956
• Joyce Reed, Vice President
• Mike Thomas, Marketing Director

KWTX-TV
P.O. BOX 2636
WACO, TX 76712-3976
254-776-1330
Fax: 254-776-4010
news@kwtx.com
www.kwtx.com
• Matt Iazzetti, Sports Director
(254) 741-5833
matt.iazzetti@kwtx.com

KWWL-TV
500 EAST FOURTH STREET
WATERLOO, IA 50703-5798
319-291-1200
Fax: 319-291-1255
www.kwwl.com/
• Rick Coleman, Sports Anchor/Reporter
(319) 291-1200
rcoleman@kwwl.com
• Raivan Hall, Promotions Assistant
(319) 291-1200
rhall@kwwl.com
• Matthew Hundley, Promotions Manager
(319) 291-1200

KXAM-TV
908 WEST MARTIN LUTHER KING JR.
AUSTIN, TX 78701
512-476-3636
Fax: 512-469-0630
news36@kxan.com
www.kxan.com
• Roger Wallace, Sports Director
(512) 476-3636
roger.wallace@kxan.com

KXAS - NBC 5
PO BOX 1780
FORT WORTH, TX 76101-1780

800-232-5927
Fax: 817-654-6325
www.kxas.com
• Tom O'Brien, General Manager
• Susan Tully, News Director
• Scott Murray, Sportscaster

KXAS-TV
P.O. BOX 1780
FORT WORTH, TX 76103-1400
817-429-5555
Fax: 817-654-6325
nbc5i@nbc.com
www.nbc5i.com
• Derek Castillo, Sports Anchor (Weekend)
• Derek Castillo, Sports Reporter
• Newy Scruggs, Sports Director
(817) 654-6326
newy.scruggs@nbc.com
• Susan Tully, Vice President

KXII-TV
P. O. BOX 1175
SHERMAN, TX 75090-1935
903-892-8123
Fax: 903-892-4623
firstnews@kxii.com
www.kxii.com
• David Reed, Sports Director; Anchor
(903) 892-8123
david.reed@kxii.com
• Mark Paasschen, Weekend Sports Anchor
(903) 892-8123
mvp@kxii.com

KXJB-TV
4302 13TH AVENUE S.W.
FARGO, ND 58103-3313
701-282-0444
Fax: 701-282-9331
www.cbs4you.com
• Rich Lodewyk, Sports Director

KXLF-TV
1003 SOUTH MONTANA STREET
BUTTE, MT 59701-2839
406-496-8400
Fax: 406-782-8906
www.kxlf.com
• Shane Eqing, Sports Director
(406) 496-6427
• Aslan Hodges, Sports/News Reporter
(406) 496-8400
• Lennie Ambrose, Sports Anchor
(406) 496-8475
Description:
The above personnel also serve KBZK-TV in Bozeman, MT, which is a sister station to KXLF. A sports segment is part of the 5:30 p.m. and 10:00 p.m. newscast of KXLF/KBZK.

KYIN-TV
6450 CORPORATE DRIVE
JOHNSTON, IA 50131-1636
515-242-3100
800-532-1290
Fax: 515-242-4113
www.iptv.org
• Jerry Grady, Sports Director
(515) 242-3111

KYTV-TV
P.O. BOX 3500
SPRINGFIELD, MO 65807-2443

417-268-3200
Fax: 417-268-3364
www.ky3.com/
• Peggy LaComfora, Promotion Manager
placomfora@ky3.com
• Peggy LaComfora, Promotions Manager
• Ned Reynolds, Sports Director
(417) 268-3200
nreynolds@ky3.com
• Joe Hickman, Weekend Sports Anchor/Reporter
(417) 268-3200
jhickman@ky3.com

KYW-TV
1555 HAMILTON STREET
PHILADELPHIA, PA 19106-2517
215-977-5300
Fax: 215-977-5658
newsdesk@cbs3.com
www.cbs3.com
• Todd Ballantyne, Marketing Manager
ballantyne@kyw.com
• Steve Bucci, Sports Reporter
(215) 238-4660
bucci@kyw.com
• Gary Cobb, Sports Anchor (Weekend)
(215) 238-4612
cobb@kyw.com
• Michael Colleran, Vice President
colleran@kyw.com
• Beasley Reece, Sports Director
(215) 238-4700

LE RESEAU DES SPORTS (RSD) INC.
1755 BLVDRENE-LEVESQUE EST, BUR 300
MONTREAL, QUEBEC, CANADA H2K 4P6
514-599-2244
Fax: 514-599-2299
www.rds.ca
• Gerrry Frappier, President/General Manager
(514) 599-2244
• Francois Messier, Vice President Programming
(514) 599-2244
• Michel Gagnon, Vice President Marketing
(514) 599-2244
• Claude Dugre, Vice President Operations
• Lino Bramucci, Vice President Sales
Nature of Sports Service:
Regional. Cable TV broadcaster. 24-hour French sports channel featuring major and minor league sports and news shows.

OUTDOOR CHANNEL
43445 BUSINESS PARK DR
STE 103
TEMECULA, CA 92590-3670
800-770-5750
Fax: 909-699-6313
info@outdoorchannel.com
www.outdoorchannel.com
• Andrew J. Dale, President/Chief Executive Officer
• Jake Hartwick, Executive Vice President
• Wade Sherman, Vice President Business Development
• Amy Hendrickson, Vice President/Affiliate Sales/Marketing
Nature of Sports Service:
Features quality programming designed to educate and entertain sportsmen of all skill levels. The channel promotes the traditional outdoor activities that are a vital part of our

national heritage including fishing, hunting and shooting sports.

TBO (WFLA) NEWS CHANNEL 8
200 S. PARKER ST
TAMPA, FL 33606
813-259-8010
www.tbo.com
• Kirk Read, General Manager
• Ray Trigony, Regonal Sales Manager
• Sabina Espinet, Production Team Leader
• Karen Barr, Technical Manager
• Carl Lisciandrello, Weather/Sports Team Leader
• Marty Strasen, Weather/Sports Producer

WAAY-TV
1000 MONTE SANO BOULEVARD, S.E.
HUNTSVILLE, AL 35801-6137
256-533-3131
Fax: 256-533-5191
newsroom@waaytv.com
www.waaytv.com
• T.W. Starr, Sports Director
(256) 533-3131
starr@waaytv.com
• Hugh Keeton, Sports Reporter
(256) 533-3131
keeton@waaytv.com

WAFB-TV
844 GOVERNMENT ST
BATON ROUGE, LA 70802-6030
225-383-9999
Fax: 225-379-7891
news@wafb.com
www.wafb.com
• Jacques Doucet, Sports Anchor
jdoucet@wafb.com
• Steve Schneider, Sports Anchor
(225) 383-9999
sschneider@wafb.com
• James Verrett, Sports Anchor
jverrett@wafb.com

WAFF-TV
1414 MEMORIAL PARKWAY, N.W.
HUNTSVILLE, AL 35801-5933
256-533-6397
Fax: 256-534-4101
news@waff.com
www.waff.com
• Will Kennedy, Sports Reporter
wkennedy@waff.com
• Lee Meredith, Vice President
justaminute@waff.com
• Kristen Talent, Sports Reporter
ktalent@waff.com
• Mike Aweau, Sports Producer
(256) 533-6397
maweau@waff.com

WAGA-TV
1551 BRIARCLIFF ROAD, N.E.
ATLANTA, GA 30306-2217
404-875-5555
Fax: 404-898-0169
newstipsatlanta@foxtv.com
www.fox5atlanta.com
• Chip Zeller, Sports Executive Producer
(404) 875-5555
czell593@foxtv.com
• Karen Graham, Weekend Sports Anchor/Reporter
(404) 875-5555
karen.graham@foxtv.com

WAGT-TV
P.O. BOX 1526
AUGUSTA, GA 30901-1212
706-826-0001
800-924-8639
Fax: 706-724-4028
www.nbcaugusta.com
• Chris Kane, Sports Director
• Buddy Miller, Advertising Manager
(706) 826-0026
• Darien Wernig, Sports Anchor
• Stan Byrdy, Sports Director
(706) 826-0026

WAKA-TV
3251 HARRISON ROAD
MONTGOMERY, AL 36109
334-271-8888
800-467-0424
Fax: 334-244-6444
news@waka.com
www.waka.com
• Dee Jackson, Sports Director
(334) 271-8888
• Kayla Anderson, Sports Anchor
(334) 271-8888

WALA-TV
1501 FATCHEL PAIGE DRIVE
MOBILE, AL 36602-2614
251-434-1010
Fax: 251-434-1023
www.fox10tv.com
• Matt Pumo, Advertising Manager
• Eric Richey, Sports Director
(251) 434-1084
• Rob Lehocky, Sports Anchor; Reporter
(251) 434-1010
rob.lehock@fox10tv.com

WALB-TV
1709 STUART AVENUE
ALBANY, GA 31707-1701
229-446-1010
Fax: 229-446-4000
www.walb.com
• Robert Hydrick, Sports Director
(229) 446-4042
robert.hydrick@walb.com

WAOW-TV
1908 GRAND AVENUE
WAUSAU, WI 54403-6870
715-842-2251
800-236-9269
Fax: 715-848-0195
www.waow.com
• Bryon Graff, Sports Director

WAPT-TV
P.O. BOX 10297
JACKSON, MS 39209-9634
601-922-1652
Fax: 601-922-8993
www.wapt.com
• Tony Bahou, Sports Anchor
(601) 922-1652

WATE - 6 WATE
1306 BROADWAY, NE
KNOXVILLE, TN 37917
865-637-6666
Fax: 865-523-3561
www.wate.com
• Jan Wade, General Manager
• Jim Wogan, Sports Director

Affiliation:
CBS.
Neilsen Market:
63
Sports:
All.
Local Sports:
KnoxPreps (High School) Sports. University
of Tennessee Men's & Women's Sports.

WAVE-TV
725 S. FLOYD STREET
LOUISVILLE, KY 40203-2337
502-561-4150 EXT 3
800-800-9283
Fax: 502-561-4105
newsrelease@wave3.com
www.wave3.com
• Kent Taylor, Sports Director
(502) 561-4126
ktaylor@wave3tv.com
• Bob Domine, Sports Anchor
(502) 585-2201
bdomine@wave3tv.com

WAVY-TV
300 WAVY STREET
PORTSMOUTH, VA 23704-5200
757-393-1010
Fax: 757-399-7628
newsdesk@wavy.com
www.wavy.com
• Bruce Rader, Sports Director
(757) 673-5370
• Judy Triska, Promotion Manager
(757) 396-6164
• Chris Francis, Sports Anchor
(757) 397-8279

WB 32
10255 SW ARCTIC DR
BEAVERTON, OR 97005
503-644-3232
Fax: 503-626-3576
• Russel Cameron, Executive
Producer/Fishing The West
russc@wb32tv.com
• Steve Dant, General Manager
Nature of Sports Service:
National. Program producer and syndicator.
Current programs: Fishing The West,
Northwest Hunter.

WBAL-TV
3800 HOOPER AVENUE
BALTIMORE, MD 21211-1313
410-467-3000
Fax: 410-338-6526
www.thewbalchannel.com
• Gerry Sandusky, Sports Director/Anchor
(410) 467-3000
gsandusky@hearst.com
• Pete Gilbert, Sports Reporter
(410) 467-3000

WBAY - WBAY-TV 2
115 S. JEFFERSON ST
GREEN BAY, WI 54301
920-432-3331
Fax: 920-432-7808
www.wbay.com
• Tom McCarey, News Director
• Don Carmichael, General Manager
Nielsen Rank:
69
Affiliate:

ABC.
Sports:
University of Wisconsin Green Bay Men's
and Women's Local High School Sports.
Professional Teams:
Green Bay Packers NFL Green Bay Blizzard
Arena Football League.

WBAY-TV
115 SOUTH JEFFERSON STREET
GREEN BAY, WI 54301-4534
920-432-3331
800-242-8090
Fax: 920-432-1190
wbay@wbay.com
www.wbay.com/
• Chris Roth, Sports Director
(920) 438-3257

WBBH - NBC 2
3719 CENTRAL AVE
FORT MYERS, FL 33901
239-261-8820
www.nbc-2.com
• Darrel Adams, News Director
• Steven Pontius, Executive Vice
President/General Manager
Sports:
All.
Nielsen Market:
81
Affiliate:
NBC.

WBBH-TV
3719 CENTRAL AVENUE
FORT MYERS, FL 33901
239-939-2020
Fax: 239-939-3244
nbc2news@nbc-2.com
www.nbc-2.com
• Lori Grimaldi, Marketing Director
(239) 939-2020
• Dan Sheldon, Sports Anchor (Weekend)
• Grant Lodes, Weekend News and Sports
Anchor
(239) 939-2020

WBBJ-TV
346 MUSE STREET
JACKSON, TN 38301-3620
731-424-4515
Fax: 731-424-9299
7news@wbbjtv.com
www.wbbjtv.com
• Bart Barker, Sports Director
• Bret Barker, Sports Anchor
(731) 424-4515

WBBM-TV
630 NORTH MCCLURG COURT
CHICAGO, IL 60611-4536
312-202-2222
Fax: 312-202-3878
wbbm.programming@cbs.com
www.cbs2chicago.com
• Steve Goldberg, Sports Producer
(312) 202-2642
sjgoldberg@cbs.com
• Megan Mawicke, Sports Reporter
(312) 202-3601
mamawicke@cbs.com
• Norm Potash, Sports Producer
(312) 202-2653
nppotash@cbs.com
• Sabert Bardo, Sports Reporter

(312) 202-2222
sdbardo@cbs.com

WBFS-TV
8900 NORTHWEST 18TH TERRACE
MIAMI, FL 33172
954-523-3333
Fax: 305-628-3448
wfornews@wfor.cbs.com
www.cbs4.com
• Jim Berry, Sports Director

WBKB-TV
1390 NORTH BAGLEY STREET
ALPENA, MI 49707
989-356-3434
800-824-1092
Fax: 989-356-4188
www.wbkbtv.com
• Barbara Bowen, Advertising Manager
• Mark Kunz, Sports Director
• Jeff Schaffer, Sports Director
(989) 356-3434
wbkbsports@yahoo.com

WBMA-TV
800 CONCOURSE PARKWAY SUITE 200
BIRMINGHAM, AL 35244-1889
205-403-3340
Fax: 205-403-3329
www.abc3340.com
• Mike Raita, Sports Director
(205) 982-3988
markr@abc3340.com

WBNG-TV
560 COLUMBIA DRIVE
JOHNSON CITY, NY 13790
607-729-8812
Fax: 607-729-4022
actionnews@wbngtv.com
www.wbng.com
• Brendan Oreilly, Sports Director
(607) 584-7283
wbng@wbngtv.com

WBOY-TV
904 PIKE STREET, W.
CLARKSBURG, WV 26301-2555
304-623-3311
Fax: 304-623-9269
news@wboy.com
www.wboy.com
• Greg Chandler, Sports Reporter
(304) 623-3311

WBRZ-TV
1650 HIGHLAND ROAD
BATON ROUGE, LA 70802-7018
225-387-2222
Fax: 225-336-2346
www.wbrz.com
• Michael Cauble, Sports Director
(225) 387-2222

WBZ-TV
1170 SOLDIERS FIELD ROAD
BOSTON, MA 02134-1004
617-787-7000
Fax: 617-254-6383
www.wbztv.com
• Steve Burton, Sports Reporter
(617) 787-7344
sjburton@boston.cbs.com
• Jackie Connally, Sports Producer
(617) 787-7338

jaconnally@boston.cbs.com
• Alice Cook, Sports Reporter
(617) 787-7340
• Bob Lobel, Sports Anchor
(617) 787-7022
• Dan Roche, Sports Reporter

WCAU-TV
10 MONUMENT ROAD
BALA CYNWYD, PA 19004-1712
610-668-5510
Fax: 610-668-3700
www.nbc10.com
• Howard Eskin, Sports Anchor (Weekend)
• Via Sikahema, Sports Anchor
• Colin Macaulay, Sports Producer
(610) 668-5660

WCAX-TV
30 JOY DRIVE
SOUTH BURLINGTON, VT 05403-6118
802-652-6300
Fax: 802-652-6399
channel3@wcax.com
www.wcax.com
• J. J. Cioffi, Sports Director
(802) 652-6340
sports@wcax.com

WCBI-TV
201 5TH STREET, S.
COLUMBUS, MS 39701-5729
662-327-4444
800-844-9224
Fax: 662-329-1004
news@wcbi.com
www.wcbi.com
• Susan Bell, Promotions Manager
• Jeff Shepard, Sports Director
(662) 327-4444
• Drew Powell, Sports Director
(662) 327-4444

WCBS-TV
524 WEST 57TH STREET
NEW YORK, NY 10019-2902
212-975-4321
Fax: 212-975-9387
desk@cbs2ny.com
wcbstv.com/
• Duke Castiglione, Sports Anchor
• Chris Scaglione, Sports Executive
Producer
• Chris Wragge, Sports Correspondent
• John Discepolo, Sports Anchor/Reporter
(212) 975-4321

WCCB-TV
1 TELEVISION PLACE
CHARLOTTE, NC 28205-7038
704-372-1800
Fax: 704-358-4841
www.foxcharlotte.tv
• Kelli Bartik, Sports Reporter/Anchor
(704) 632-7517

WCCO-TV
90 SOUTH 11TH STREET
MINNEAPOLIS, MN 55403-2414
612-339-4444
Fax: 612-330-2767
www.wcco.com/
• Carry Clancy, Sports Producer
• Greg Littman, Sports Director
• Wendy McMahon, Promotions Director
• Mike Max, Sports Reporter

(612) 339-4444
mmax@cbs.com

WCFN-TV
118 WEST EDWARDS
SPRINGFIELD, IL 62704
217-544-3691
Fax: 217-544-3818
news@wcia.com
www.wcia.com
• Jason Elliott, Sports Director
(217) 373-3656

WCHS-TV
1301 PIEDMONT ROAD
CHARLESTON, WV 25301-1426
304-346-5358
Fax: 304-345-1849
news@wchstv.com
www.wchstv.com
• Paul Fox, Promotions Director
(304) 346-5358
pfox@wchstv.com
• Alan Frank, Regional Manager
(412) 931-5300
afrank@sbgnet.com
• Josh Lewis, Sports Anchor
(304) 346-5358
jlewis@wchstv.com
• Mark Martin, Sports Director
(304) 346-5358
mmartin@wchstv.com
• Kennie Bass, Sports Reporter
(304) 346-5358
kbass@wchstv.com

WCIA-TV
509 SOUTH NEIL STREET
CHAMPAIGN, IL 61820
217-373-3650
Fax: 217-373-3663
news@wcia.com
illinoishomepage.net
• Peter Carlson, Promotions Manager
(217) 373-3638
promotions@wcia.com
• Jason Elliott, Sports Director
(217) 373-3650
news@wcia.com
• Aaron Bennett, Sports Reporter
(217) 356-8333

WCIV-TV
888 ALLBRITTON BOULEVARD
MOUNT PLEASANT, SC 29464-3033
843-881-4444
Fax: 843-849-2507
desk@wciv.com
www.wciv.com
• Josh Morton, Sports Director
(843) 881-4444

WCJB-TV
6220 NORTHWEST 43RD STREET
GAINESVILLE, FL 32653-3334
352-377-2020
Fax: 352-371-0747
tv20news@wcjb.com
www.wcjb.com
• Joe Girvan, Sports Director
(352) 377-2020
• Hank Astengo, Weekend Sports
Anchor/Weekday Sports Rep
(352) 377-2020

WCNC - NBC6
1001 WOOD RIDGE CENTER DR
CHARLOTTE, NC 28217
704-329-0898
Fax: 704-357-4980
www.nbc6.com
• Stuart Powell, Vice President/General Manager
• Chuck Howard, Sports Director
• Keith Connors, Executive News Director
Professional Sports:
Carolina Panthers, (NFL), Carolina Hurricanes (NHL), Carolina Cobras (Arena Football League), NASCAR.
Network Affiliate:
NBC.
Nielsen Markett:
28

WCNC-TV
1001 WOOD RIDGE CENTER DRIVE
CHARLOTTE, NC 28217-1902
704-329-3636
Fax: 704-357-4975
www.wcnc.com
• Chuck Howard, Sports Director
• Greg Bailey, Sports Director
(704) 329-3636

WCPO-TV
1720 GILBERT AVENUE
CINCINNATI, OH 45202-2311
513-721-9900
Fax: 513-721-7717
newsdesk@wcpo.com
www.cincinow.com
• Paul Harper, Promotions Assistant Director
• Sheila Obermeyer, Promotion Director
• John Popovich, Sports Director
(513) 852-4078
jpopovich@wcpo.com
• Lisa Cornwell, Weekend Sports Anchor/Reporter
(513) 721-9900
lisa.cornwell@wcpo.com

WCSC-TV
2126 CHARLIE HALL BOULEVARD
CHARLESTON, SC 29414-5832
843-402-5755
Fax: 843-402-5744
talkback@live5news.com
www.wcsc.com
• Craig Birnbach, Sports Anchor
(843) 402-5750
cbirnbach@live5news.com
• Craig Birnbach, Sports Director
(843) 402-5750
cbirnbach@live5news.com
• Andy Pruitt, Sports Reporter
(843) 402-5755
apruitt@live5news.com
• Bob Behanian, Sports Reporter
(843) 402-5755

WCSH-TV
1 CONGRESS SQUARE
PORTLAND, ME 04101-3801
207-828-6666
800-464-1213
Fax: 207-828-6630
newscenter@wcsh6.com
www.wcsh6.com
• Bruce Glasier, Sports Director
(207) 828-6666

WCVB-TV
5 TV PLACE
NEEDHAM, MA 02494-2302
781-449-0400
Fax: 781-449-6681
www.thebostonchannel.com
• Mike Lynch, Sports Anchor
(781) 449-0400
mlynch@hearst.com
• Mike Dowling, Sports Reporter
(781) 433-4703

WDAF-TV
3030 SUMMIT STREET
KANSAS CITY, MO 64108-3312
816-753-4567
Fax: 816-561-4181
news@wdaftv4.com
www.wdaftv4.com/
• Frank Boal, Sports Director
(816) 753-4567

WDAM-TV
2362 HIGHWAY 11
MOSELLE, MS 39459
601-544-4730
Fax: 601-584-9302
info@wdam.com
www.wdam.com
• Jim Cameron, Vice President
• Brenda Parker, Promotions Director
bparker@wdam.com
• Mitchell Williams, Sports Director
(601) 544-4730

WDAZ-TV
2220 SOUTH WASHINGTON STREET
GRAND FORKS, ND 58201-6346
701-775-2511
Fax: 701-746-4507
• Angela Cary, Promotions Director
• Pat Sweeney, Sports Director
(701) 775-2511

WDBJ-TV
P.O. BOX 7
ROANOKE, VA 24017
540-344-7000
Fax: 540-344-5097
news@wdbj7.com
www.wdbj7.com
• Mike Stevens, Sports Director
(540) 985-3623
mstevens@wdbj7.com
• Grant Kittelson, Sports Reporter
(540) 344-7000
gkittelson@wdbj7.com

WDEF
3300 BROAD ST
CHATTANOOGA, TN 37408
423-785-1257
Fax: 423-785-1273
www.wdef.com
• Cathy Gugerty, General Manager
• John Appicello, Sports Director
Office Address:
3300 Broad St, Chattanooga, TN 37401.
Nature of Sports Service:
Local. 24-hour sports radio programming.
Baseball:
MLB - Atlanta Braves.
College Sports:
Basketball, Football - University of Tennessee.

Football:
NFL - Carolina Panthers.

WDEF-TV
3300 BROAD STREET
CHATTANOOGA, TN 37408-3061
423-785-1200
Fax: 423-785-1273
www.wdef.com
• Rick Nyman, Sports Director
(423) 785-1277
• Jason Law, Weekend Sports Anchor/Reporter
(423) 785-1200

WDIV-TV
550 WEST LAFAYETTE BOULEVARD
DETROIT, MI 48226-3123
313-222-0500
Fax: 313-222-0592
assignmentdesk@wdiv.com
www.clickondetroit.com
• Fred Mcleod, Sports Reporter
fredm@clickondetroit.com
• Bernie Smilovitz, Sports Anchor & Director
(313) 222-0504
bernies@clickondetroit.com
• Katrina Hancock, Sports Anchor
(313) 222-0500
khancock@clickondetroit.com

WDJT-TV
809 S. 60TH STREET
MILWAUKEE, WI 53214-3363
414-607-8140
Fax: 414-777-5802
newsdesk@cbs58.com
www.cbs58.com
• Rock Rote, Sports Director
(414) 607-8140
• Ryan Nolan, Sports Reporter
(414) 607-8140

WEAR-TV
P.O. BOX 12278
PENSACOLA, FL 32506-3230
850-455-4599
Fax: 850-455-8972
newsroom@weartv.com
www.weartv.com
• Dan Shugart, Sports Director
(850) 455-4599
dshugart@weartv.com
• Mac McAllister, Sports Producer/Photographer
(850) 455-4599

WEAU-TV
P.O. BOX 47
EAU CLAIRE, WI 54701-4551
715-835-1313
Fax: 715-832-3476
weau@weau.com
www.weau.com
• Emily Edwards, Promotions Director
• Bob Gallaher, Sports Director
(715) 835-1313
bob.gallaher@weau.com
• Paige Pearson, Weekend Sports Anchor
(715) 835-1313
paige.pearson@weau.com

WECT-TV
322 SHIPYARD BOULEVARD
WILMINGTON, NC 28412

910-791-6681
Fax: 910-791-9535
newsproducers@wect.com
www.wect.com
• Bob Bonner, Sports Director
(910) 791-6681

WEEK-TV
2907 SPRINGFIELD ROAD
EAST PEORIA, IL 61611-4878
309-698-3737
Fax: 309-698-2070
news25@week.com
www.week.com
• Lee Hall, Sports Director
(309) 698-3737
lhall@week.com
• Mike Dimmick, Weekend Sports Anchor
(309) 698-3737
mdimmick@week.com

WEHT-TV
800 MARYWOOD DRIVE
HENDERSON, KY 42420-2431
812-424-9215
800-879-8542
Fax: 270-827-0561
www.abc25.com
• Mellissa Marks, Promotion Director
(812) 424-9215
• Lance Wilkerson, Sports Director
(800) 879-8574
• Drew Amman, Sports Anchor
(800) 879-8575

WENY-TV
474 OLD ITHACA ROAD
HORSEHEADS, NY 14845-7212
607-739-3636
Fax: 607-796-6171
www.weny.com
• Neille Gissune, Sports Director
(607) 739-3636
• Cory Hepola, Sports Director
(607) 739-3636

WESH-TV
1021 NORTH WYMORE ROAD
WINTER PARK, FL 32789-1717
407-645-2222
Fax: 407-539-7948
www.newschannel2000.com
• Pat Clarke, Sports Director
(407) 645-2222
pclarke@hearst.com
• Robert Fein, Vice President

WETM-TV
P.O. BOX 1207
ELMIRA, NY 14901
607-733-5518
Fax: 607-733-4739
news@wetmtv.com
www.wetmtv.com/
• Ed Bak, Sports Director
(607) 733-5518

WEWS-TV
3001 EUCLID AVENUE
CLEVELAND, OH 44115-2516
216-431-5555
Fax: 216-431-3666
news@newsnet5.com
www.newsnet5.com
• Tony Burke, Sports Producer
(216) 431-3441

burke@wews.com
• Chris Miller, Sports Director
miller@wews.com
• Andy Baskin, Sports Director
(216) 431-3700
abaskin@wews.com

WFAA-TV
606 YOUNG STREET
DALLAS, TX 75202-4895
214-748-9631
Fax: 214-977-6585
news8@wfaa.com
www.wfaa.com/
• Jim Glass, Promotions Director
• Dale Hansen, Sports Anchor
(214) 977-6214
dhansen@wfaa.com
• Gina Miller, Sports Reporter
(214) 748-9631
• David Muscari, Vice President
dmuscari@wfaa.com
• George Riba, Sports Director
(214) 977-6255
griba@wfaa.com
• Joe Trahan, Sports Reporter
jtrahan@wfaa.com

WFIE-TV
P.O. BOX 1414
EVANSVILLE, IN 47720
812-426-1414
Fax: 812-428-2228
www.14wfie.com
• Mike Blake, Sports Director
(812) 433-3404
mblake@14wfie.com

WFLA-TV
P.O. BOX 1410
TAMPA, FL 33606
813-221-5788
800-824-1695
Fax: 813-225-2770
news@wfla.com
www.wfla.com
• Dave Cook, Sports Producer
• J.P. Peterson, Sports Anchor
• Dan Lucas, Sports Reporter
(813) 221-5788
dlucas@wfla.com

WFLD TV CHANNEL 32 CHICAGO/FOX
205 N. MICHIGAN AVE
CHICAGO, IL 60601
312-565-5532
Fax: 312-819-1332
www.foxchicago.com
• Debra Juarez West, News Director

WFLD-TV
205 NORTH MICHIGAN AVENUE
CHICAGO, IL 60601-5922
312-565-5532
Fax: 312-565-5517
www.myfoxchicago.com
• Jill Carlson, Sports Anchor
• John Eskra, Sports Producer
(312) 565-5478
• James Marketti, Promotion Vice President
• Corey McPherrin, Sports Anchor
(312) 565-5529
• John Nuck, Vice President
(312) 565-5607

WFMJ-TV
101 WEST BOARDMAN STREET
YOUNGSTOWN, OH 44503-1305
330-744-8821
800-488-9365
Fax: 330-742-2472
news@wfmj.com
www.wfmj.com
• Mike Ackelson, Anchor
(330) 744-8611
• Dana Balash, Sports Director
(330) 744-8611
• Mike Case, Sports Anchor
(330) 744-8611
• Joe Romano, Promotions Director
(330) 744-8611
• Jack Stevenson, Marketing Director

WFMY-TV
P.O. BOX TV-2
GREENSBORO, NC 27405
336-379-9369
800-237-1615
Fax: 336-230-0971
news@wfmy.com
www.digtriad.com/news/
• Greg Kerr, Sports Director
(336) 379-5780
gkerr@wfmy.gannett.com

WFMZ-TV
300 EAST ROCK ROAD
ALLENTOWN, PA 18103-7519
610-791-1111
Fax: 610-791-9994
news@wfmz.com
www.wfmz.com
• Dean Dallman, Advertising Coordinator
(610) 798-4000
• Troy Hein, Sports Reporter
(610) 791-1111
• Dave Taveriner, Promotion Director
(610) 798-4000

WFRV-TV
P.O. BOX 19055
GREEN BAY, WI 54301
920-437-5411
Fax: 920-437-5769
www.wfrv.com
• Larry McCarren, Sports Director
(920) 437-5555
• Burke Griffin, Sports Anchor
(920) 437-5411
burke.griffin@wfrv.com

WFSB-TV
3 CONSTITUTION PLAZA
HARTFORD, CT 06103-1807
860-244-1700
Fax: 860-728-0263
newsdesk3@wfsb.com
www.wfsb.com
• Dina Falco, Sports Director
newsdesk3@wfsb.com
• Robert Montesi, Marketing Director
(860) 244-1736
newsdesk3@wfsb.com
• John Holt, Weekend Sports
Anchor/Reporter
(860) 244-1700
john.holt@wfsb.com

WFTS-TV
4045 NORTH HIMES AVENUE
TAMPA, FL 33607-6651

877-833-2828
Fax: 813-870-2828
newstips@wfts.com
www.wfts.com
• Oscar Angulo, Sports Producer
oangulo@wfts.com
• Al Keck, Sports Director
(813) 354-2800
akeck@wfts.com
• Donna Wilson, Promotion Director
dwilson@wfts.com
• Donna Wilson, Promotions Director
dwilson@wfts.com
• Dan Eassa, Sports Reporter/Producer
(877) 833-2828
deassa@wfts.com

WFTV-TV
490 EAST SOUTH STREET
ORLANDO, FL 32801-2816
407-841-9000
Fax: 407-481-2891
news@wftv.com
www.wftv.com
• Dan Hellie, Sports Director
• Zach Klein, Weekend Sports
Anchor/Weekday Sports Rep
(407) 841-9000
news@wftv.com
Description:
Monday, Tuesday, Wednesday, Thursday,
Friday at 4:30AM for 2.00 hours.

WGAL-TV
P.O. BOX 7127
LANCASTER, PA 17603-3824
717-393-5851
Fax: 717-295-7457
www.wgal.com
• Mike Hostetler, Sports Anchor
(717) 393-5851
mhostetler@hearst.com
• Pat Principe, Sports Director; Anchor
(717) 393-5851
pprincipe@hearst.com

WGBA-TV
1391 NORTH ROAD
GREEN BAY, WI 54313-9099
920-494-2626
800-800-6619
Fax: 920-494-9550
www.nbc26.com
• Ted Stefaniak, Sports Director
• John Burton, Sports Anchor
(920) 494-2626
jburton@nbc26.com
Sports Discussed:
All
Description:
News time.

WGCL-TV
425 14TH STREET, N.W.
ATLANTA, GA 30318-7965
404-327-3200
Fax: 404-327-3004
www.cbs46.com/
• Mark Harmon, Weekend Sports Anchor
(404) 327-3250
mharmon@mdp.com
• Sylvia McDonald, Sports Director
(404) 327-3250
• Corey Anderson, Sports
Producer/Reporter/Anchor
(404) 327-3250
Corey.Anderson@cbs46.com

WGEM-TV
P.O. BOX 80
QUINCY, IL 62301
217-228-6600
Fax: 217-228-6670
www.wgem.com
• Shawn Dickerman, Promotion Director
(217) 228-6632
sdickerman@wgem.com
• Ben Marth, Sports Director
(217) 228-6615
bmarth@wgem.com
• Ben Marth, Sports Reporter
(217) 228-6615
bmarth@wgem.com
• Bree Stewart, Sports Anchor
bstewart@wgem.com
• Tyler Tomlinson, Sports Anchor
(217) 228-6600

WGGB-TV
1300 LIBERTY STREET
SPRINGFIELD, MA 01104
413-733-8840
Fax: 413-788-7640
assignmentdesk@wggb.com
www.wggb.com/
• Jim Cline, Sports Reporter
(413) 733-4040
jcline@sbgnet.com
• Scott Coen, Sports Director
(413) 733-8840
scoen@sbgnet.com

WGME-TV
1335 WASHINGTON AVENUE
PORTLAND, ME 04103-3638
207-797-1313
Fax: 207-878-3505
www.wgme.com/
• Dave Eid, Sports Director
deid@wgme.sbgnet.com
• Dave Eid, Sports Reporter
(207) 797-1313
deid@wgme.sbgnet.com

WGN-9 CHICAGO'S CW
2501 WEST BRADLEY PLAZA
CHICAGO, IL 60618-4718
773-528-2311
Fax: 773-528-6050
www.wgntv.com
• Marty Wilke, Vice President/General
Manager
(773) 883-3383
• Bill Herriott, Director Sports Sales
(773) 883-3429
• Errol Gerber, Director Sales
(773) 883-3285
• Ken Reiner, Director Programming
• Bob Vorwald, Director Production
Baseball Sponsor:
MLB - Chicago Cubs, Chicago White Sox.
Basketball Sponsor:
NBA - Chicago Bulls.

WGXA-TV
599 MARTIN LUTHER KING JR.
BOULEVARD
MACON, GA 31201-3367
478-743-0742
800-592-4240
Fax: 478-745-6057
www.fox24.com
• Pete Cataldo, Sports Director
(478) 745-2424
• Marc Nash, Promotions Manager

(478) 745-2424
• Chace Ambrose, Sports
Reporter/Photographer
(478) 743-0742

WHAM-TV
4225 WEST HENRIETTA ROAD
ROCHESTER, NY 14623
585-334-8700
Fax: 585-359-1570
news@13wham.com
www.iknowrochester.com
• Mike Catalana, Sports Director
(585) 334-8700
mcatalana@13wham.com

WHBQ-TV
485 SOUTH HIGHLAND STREET
MEMPHIS, TN 38111-4398
901-320-1313
Fax: 901-323-0092
www.fox13whbq.com
• John Koski, Vice President
(901) 320-1310
• David Lee, Sports Director
(901) 320-1345
• Paul Sloan, Promotion Director
(901) 320-1311
fox13news@foxtv.com
• Greg Gaston, Sports Anchor/Reporter
(901) 320-1313

WHDH-TV
7 BULFINCH PLACE
BOSTON, MA 02114
617-725-0777
Fax: 617-723-6117
7news@whdh.com
www.whdh.com/
• Fred Nutter, Sports Director
(617) 725-0777
fnutter@whdh.com
• Joe Amorosino, Sports Director
(617) 725-0756
jamorosino@whdh.com

WHIO-TV
1414 WILMINGTON AVENUE
DAYTON, OH 45420-1543
937-259-2111
Fax: 937-259-2001
7online@whiotv.com
www.whiotv.com
• Mike Hartsock, Sports Director
(937) 259-2142
• Margaret Brosko, Sports Anchor
(937) 259-2111

WHIZ-TV
629 DOWNARD ROAD
ZANESVILLE, OH 43701-5108
740-452-5431
Fax: 740-452-6553
news@whizamfmtv.com
www.whizamfmtv.com
• Hank Littick, President
(740) 452-5431
hankcl@whizamfmtv.com
• Aaron Spragg, Sports Director

WHKY-TV
P.O. BOX 1059
HICKORY, NC 28602-1103
828-322-5115
Fax: 828-322-8256

news@whky.com
www.whky.com
• Jason Savage, Sports Director
(828) 322-5115
jsavage@whky.com

WHLA-TV
821 UNIVERSITY AVENUE
MADISON, WI 53706-1412
608-263-2121
800-422-9707
Fax: 608-263-1952
www.wpt.org
• Deb Piper, Sports Director
(608) 263-4222
piper@wpt.org

WHMB-TV
10511 GREENFIELD AVENUE
NOBLESVILLE, IN 46060
317-773-5050
Fax: 317-776-4051
www.lesea.com
• Dennis Kasey, Sports Director
(317) 773-5050
dkasey3535@aol.com

WHME-TV
61300 SOUTH IRONWOOD ROAD
SOUTH BEND, IN 46614
574-291-8200
Fax: 574-291-9043
www.lesea.com
• Charles Freeby, Sports Director
(574) 231-5260

WHNT-TV
P.O. BOX 19
HUNTSVILLE, AL 35801-4903
256-533-1919
800-533-8819
Fax: 256-536-9468
www.whnt.com
• Judy Cornelius, Promotions Manager
(256) 533-1919
• Lori Miller, Marketing Director
lori.miller@whnt.com
• John Pearson, Sports Director
(256) 533-1919

WHO-TV
1801 GRAND AVENUE
DES MOINES, IA 50309-3309
515-242-3500
Fax: 515-242-3796
news@whotv.com
www.whotv.com
• Tim Gardner, Promotions Director
(515) 242-3500
tim.gardner@whotv.com
• Keith Murphy, Sports Director
(515) 242-3739
keith.murphy@whotv.com
• Chris Hassel, Sports Reporter/Anchor
(515) 242-3500

WHOI-TV
500 NORTH STEWART STREET
CREVE COEUR, IL 61610
309-698-1919
Fax: 309-698-4819
www.hoinews.com
• James Care, Promotions Producer
(309) 698-1919
• Jim Mattson, Sports Director
(773) 838-7878

WHRM-TV
821 UNIVERSITY AVENUE
MADISON, WI 53706-1412
608-263-2121
800-422-9707
Fax: 608-263-1952
www.wpt.org
• Deb Piper, Sports Director
(608) 263-4222
piper@wpt.org

WHTM-TV
P.O. BOX 5860
HARRISBURG, PA 17110-2226
717-236-2727
Fax: 717-236-1263
news@abc27.com
www.abc27.com
• John Appicello, Sports Reporter
(717) 236-2727
• Betty Fish, Promotions Manager
• Gregg Mace, Sports Director
(717) 236-2727

WHWC-TV
821 UNIVERSITY AVENUE
MADISON, WI 53706-1412
608-263-2121
800-422-9707
Fax: 608-263-1952
www.wpt.org
• Deb Piper, Sports Director
(608) 263-4222
piper@wpt.org

WIAT - CBS 42
2075 GOLDEN CREST DR
BIRMINGHAM, AL 35209
205-322—4200
Fax: 205-320-2722
newsrelease@cbs42.com
www.wiat.com
• J.D. Huey, Vice President/General
Manager
• Tod Buccelli, Marketing/Promotion Director
• Larry Ragan, News Director
Major Sports:
Major Sports Covered links to
sportsline.com.
Affiliate:
CBS.
Neilsen Market:
39

WICU-TV
3514 STATE STREET
ERIE, PA 16508
814-454-5201
Fax: 814-455-0703
www.wicu12.com
• Mike Ruzzi, Sports Director
(814) 454-5201
• Jay Puskar, Weekend Sports Anchor
(814) 454-5201

WIFR-TV
2523 NORTH MERIDIAN ROAD
ROCKFORD, IL 61101
815-987-5300
Fax: 815-965-0981
talkto23@wifr.com
www.wifr.com
• Mike Garrigan, anchor
(815) 987-5300
mike.garrigan@wifr.com

WILX-TV
500 AMERICAN ROAD
LANSING, MI 48911-5978
517-393-0110
Fax: 517-393-9180
news@wilx.com
www.wilx.com/
• Tim Staudt, Sports Director
(517) 393-0110
tim.staudt@wilx.com
• Dan Hedman, Sports Reporter
(517) 393-0110
dan.hedman@wilx.com

WINK-TV
2824 PALM BEACH BOULEVARD
FORT MYERS, FL 33916-1503
239-334-1131
800-886-6397
Fax: 239-334-0744
www.winktv.com
• Clayton Ferraro, Sports Director
(239) 334-1131
• Brian Simon, Sports Director

WIS-TV
P.O. BOX 367
COLUMBIA, SC 29201-3722
803-799-1010
Fax: 803-758-1155
countonwis@wistv.com
www.wistv.com
• Rick Henry, Sports Director
(803) 799-1010
rhenry@wistv.com

WISC-TV
7025 RAYMOND ROAD
MADISON, WI 53719-5053
608-273-3333
Fax: 608-271-0800
www.channel3000.com
• Eric Franke, Sports Director
(608) 277-5241
efranke@wisctv.com
• George Johnson, Sports Director
(608) 273-3333
gjohnson@wisctv.com

WISH-TV
1950 NORTH MERIDIAN STREET
INDIANAPOLIS, IN 46202-1304
317-923-8888
Fax: 317-931-2242
newsdesk@wishtv.com
www.wishtv.com
• Chris Widlic, Sports Director
cwidlic@wishtv.com
• Derek Daly, Sports Reporter
(317) 923-8888

WITN-TV
P.O. BOX 468
WASHINGTON, NC 27889
252-946-3131
Fax: 252-946-0558
• Billy Weaver, Sports Director
(252) 946-3131
• Brian Meador, Sports Reporter
(252) 946-3131

WIVB-TV
2077 ELMWOOD AVENUE
BUFFALO, NY 14207
716-876-7333
Fax: 716-874-8173

newsroom@wivb.com
www.wivb.com
• Dennis Williams, Sports Director
(716) 874-4410

WIXT-TV
5904 BRIDGE STREET
EAST SYRACUSE, NY 13057-2941
315-446-9999
Fax: 315-446-0045
wixttv9@aol.com
www.wixt.com
• Steven Insanti, Sports Director
steveninsanti@clearchannel.com

WJBK-TV
16550 WEST NINE MILE ROAD
SOUTHFIELD, MI 48075-4705
248-395-3692
Fax: 248-557-1199
fox2newsdesk@foxtv.com
www.myfoxdetroit.com
• Dana McDaniel, Vice President
(248) 557-2000
• Glenn Therrien, Sports Executive Producer
(248) 522-5257
gther257@foxtv.com
• Ryan Ermanni, Sports
Anchor/Reporter/Producer
(248) 395-3692
ryan.ermanni@foxtv.com

WJFW-TV
3217 COUNTY HIGEWAY
RHINELANDER, WI 54501
715-365-8812
Fax: 715-365-8810
www.wjfw-nbc12.com
• Matt Thompson, Sports Director
(715) 365-8812

WJHG-TV
8195 FRONT BEACH ROAD
PANAMA CITY BEACH, FL 32407-4820
850-234-7777
Fax: 850-233-6647
wjhg@wjhg.com
www.wjhg.com
• Scott Rossman, Sports Director
(850) 234-7777
scott.rossman@wjhg.com
• Adam Roland, Sports/News Reporter
(850) 234-7777
adam.roland@wjhg.com

WJHL-TV
P.O. BOX 1130
JOHNSON CITY, TN 37601-5730
423-926-2151
800-606-9545
Fax: 423-926-9080
www.wjhl.com
• Kenny Hawkins, Sports Director
(423) 434-4544
khawkins@wjhl.com

WJLA-TV
1100 WILSON BOULEVARD
ARLINGTON, VA 22209
703-236-9555
Fax: 703-236-2331
newsdesk@wjla.com
www.wjla.com
• Tim Brant, Sports Anchor
(703) 236-9555
• Stan Melcon, Promotions Director

(703) 236-9552
smelcon@wjla.com
• Howard Zeiden, Marketing Director
(703) 236-9552
hzeiden@wjla.com

WJTV-TV NEWS CHANNEL 12
1820 TV ROAD 1820
JACKSON, MS 39204-4148
601-372-6311
Fax: 601-372-8798
www.wjtv.com
• Jeff Platt, Sports Anchor/Reporter
(601) 944-4920
• Jason Hurst, Sports Anchor/Reporter
(601) 944-4921

WJW-TV
5800 SOUTH MARGINAL ROAD
CLEVELAND, OH 44103-1040
216-431-8888
888-847-6397
Fax: 216-391-9559
www.fox8cleveland.com
• Dan Coughlin, Sports Reporter
(216) 431-8888
• John Telich, Sports Reporter
(216) 432-4248

WJXT-TV
4 BROADCAST PLACE
JACKSONVILLE, FL 32207-8613
904-399-4000
Fax: 904-393-9822
jaxnews@news4jax.com
www.news4jax.com
• Sam Kouvaris, Sports Director
(904) 399-4000
• John Dunlap, Sports Anchor/Reporter
(904) 399-4000

WJZ-TV
3725 MALDEN AVENUE
BALTIMORE, MD 21211-1322
410-466-0013
Fax: 410-578-0642
newsroom@wjz.com
www.wjz.com
• Mark Viviano, Sports Director
(410) 466-0013
• Mike Pupo, Sports Producer
(410) 466-0013
pupom@wjz.com

WKBN-TV
3930 SUNSET BOULEVARD
YOUNGSTOWN, OH 44512
330-782-1144
Fax: 330-782-3504
newsroom@wkbn.com
www.wkbn.com
• Ryan Allison, Sports Director
(330) 782-1144
newsroom@wkbn.com

WKBW-TV
7 BROADCAST PLAZA
BUFFALO, NY 14202-2611
716-845-6100
800-770-9645
Fax: 716-856-8784
news@wkbw.com
www.wkbw.com
• John Disciullo, Promotion Director
(716) 840-7860
johndis@wkbw.com

• John Murphy, Sports Director
(716) 840-7796
• Ginger Geoffery, Sports Anchor
(716) 845-6100

WKEF-TV
45 BROADCAST PLAZA
DAYTON, OH 45408
937-263-4500
Fax: 937-268-5265
www.daytonsnewssource.com
• Ray Crawford, Sports Director
(937) 262-1422
rcrawford@sbgnet.com
• Ryan Brant, Sports Director
(937) 262-1423

WKMG-TV
4466 JOHN YOUNG PARKWAY
ORLANDO, FL 32804-1939
407-521-1200
Fax: 407-298-2122
desk@wkmg.com
www.local6.com
• Todd Lewis, Sports Director
(407) 521-1215
• Kim Peoples, Marketing Director
(407) 521-1333
kpeoples@wkmg.com
• David Pingalore, Sports Anchor/Reporter
(407) 521-1200

WKOW-TV
5727 TOKAY BOULEVARD
MADISON, WI 53719-1219
608-273-2727
Fax: 608-274-9569
news@wkowtv.com
www.wkowtv.com/
• Jill Genter, Promotion Manager
(608) 274-1234
• Jay Wilson, Sports Director
• Paul Garcia, Sports Anchor/Reporter
(608) 273-2727

WKRC-TV
1906 HIGHLAND AVENUE
CINCINNATI, OH 45219-3109
513-763-5500
Fax: 513-421-3820
www.wkrc.com
• Dennison Keller, Sports Reporter
• Elbert Tucker, Vice President
(513) 763-5447
• Brad Johansen, Sports Anchor
(513) 763-5500
bjohansen@wkrc.com

WKRN-TV
441 MURFREESBORO ROAD
NASHVILLE, TN 37210
615-248-7200
Fax: 615-248-7329
news@wkrn.com
www.wkrn.com
• John Dwyer, Sports Director
(615) 369-7240
sports@wkrn.com
• Mike Sechrist, President
news@wkrn.com
• Connie Sullivan, Advertising Manager
(615) 369-7222
• Tim Hardiman, Sports Producer
(615) 369-7200
timhardiman@wkrn.com

WKTV-TV
P.O. BOX 2
UTICA, NY 13503-0002
315-793-3475
Fax: 315-733-4893
newslink2@wktv.com
www.wktv.com
• Jason Powles, Sports Director/Sports Anchor
(315) 733-0404

WKYC-TV
1333 LAKESIDE AVENUE
CLEVELAND, OH 44114-1134
216-344-3300
Fax: 216-344-7493
news@wkyc.com
www.wkyc.com
• Mike Cairns, Sports Reporter
• Jim Donovan, Sports Director
(216) 344-3406
jimdonovan@wkyc.com
• Joe Brown, Sports Reporter
(216) 344-3300
joebrown@wkyc.com

WKYT-TV
P.O. BOX 55037
LEXINGTON, KY 40509-4801
859-299-2727
Fax: 859-299-2494
www.wkyt.com
• Dick Gabriel, Sports Director
(859) 566-1330
dick.gabriel@wkyt.com
• Rob Bromley, Sports Anchor
(859) 299-2727
Rob.Bromley@wkyt.com

WLBT-TV
715 SOUTH JEFFERSON STREET
JACKSON, MS 39201-5622
601-948-3333
Fax: 601-355-7830
news@wlbt.com
www.wlbt.com
• Jackie Ellens, Promotions Director
jackiee@wlbt.net
• Rob Jay, Sports Director
(601) 948-3333
rob@wlbt.net
• Chuck Stinson, Sports Reporter
(601) 948-3333
chuck@wlbt.net

WLEF-TV
821 UNIVERSITY AVENUE
MADISON, WI 53706-1412
608-263-2121
800-422-9707
Fax: 608-263-9763
www.wpt.org
• Deb Piper, Sports Director
(608) 263-4222
piper@wpt.org

WLFI-TV
2605 YEAGER ROAD
WEST LAFAYETTE, IN 47906
765-463-1800
800-877-9534
Fax: 765-463-7979
newsroom@wlfi.com
www.wlfitv18.com
• Clayton Duffy, Sports Director
(765) 463-1800

• Deb McMahan, Promotions Director
(765) 237-5046
• Gage Butterbrodt, Sports Anchor
(765) 463-1800

WLIO-TV
1424 RICE AVENUE
LIMA, OH 45805-1949
419-228-5909
Fax: 419-225-6109
newsrelease@wlio.com
www.wlio.com
• Kevin Creamer, President/General Manager
(419) 228-8835
kevin@wlio.com
• Jeff Fitzgerald, News Director
fitz@wlio.com
• Jayson Geiser, Sports Director
jgeiser@wlio.com

WLS-TV
190 NORTH STATE STREET
CHICAGO, IL 60601-3302
312-750-7777
Fax: 312-899-8019
www.abc7chicago.com
• Emily L. Barr, President
• Jeff Blanzy, Weekend Sports Anchor
(312) 750-7777
• Mark Giangreco, Sports Director
(312) 750-7777
• Tom Hebel, Promotions Manager
• Mike Johnson, Sports Producer
• Brad Palmer, Sports Reporter
• Jim Rose, Sports Anchor
(312) 750-7777

WLS-TV CHANNEL 7 ABC (CHICAGO)
WLS TV
190 N. STATE ST.
CHICAGO, IL 60601
312-750-7777
Fax: 312-899-8019
www.abc7chicago.com
• Jennifer Graves, News Director
• Ben Koff, Marketing Account Executive

WLTV-TV
9405 NORTHWEST 41ST STREET
MIAMI, FL 33178-2301
305-471-3900
Fax: 305-471-3948
www.univision.net
• Manny Delafe, Sports Director
(305) 471-4362

WLVI-TV
75 MORRISSOUTHEASTY BOULEVARD
BOSTON, MA 02125-3316
617-265-5656
Fax: 617-265-0063
www.wb56.com
• Mike Ratte, Sports Director

WLWT-TV
1700 YOUNG STREET
CINCINNATI, OH 45210
513-412-5000
Fax: 513-412-6121
www.channelcincinnati.com
• Ken Broo, Sports Director
(513) 412-5089
• Jonathan Killian, Promotion Manager
(513) 412-5650
• George Vogel, Executive Sports Producer

(513) 412-5000
• George Vogel, Sports Director
(513) 412-5088

WMAQ TV CHICAGO
454 N. COLUMBUS DR, 1ST FL
CHICAGO, IL 60611-5514
312-836-5555
Fax: 317-527-5925
www.nbc5.com
• Larry Wert, NBC 5 President and General Manager
• Vicky Burns, News Director
• Sharon Brooks Buchanan, National Sales Manager
• Patricia Golden, VP/Dir Sls
• Toni Falvo, Dir Research Marketing and Press

WMAQ-TV
454 NORTH COLUMBUS DRIVE
CHICAGO, IL 60611-5555
312-836-5555
Fax: 312-527-5925
www.nbc5.com
• Jody Bajor, Marketing Manager
(312) 836-5551
jody.bajor@nbc.com
• Ryan Baker, Weekend Sports Anchor/Reporter
(312) 836-5555
• Tony Capriolo, Sports Executive Producer
(312) 836-5665
tony.capriolo@nbc.com
• V. Hannes, Sports Host
• Peggy Kusinski, Sports Reporter
(312) 836-5555
marion.brooks@nbc.com
• Mark Schanowski, Sports Reporter
• Frank Whittaker, Vice President
(312) 836-5654
frank.whittaker@nbc.com

WMAZ-TV
1314 GRAY HIGHWAY
MACON, GA 31211-1904
478-752-1313
Fax: 478-752-1429
eyewitnessnews@13wmaz.com
www.13wmaz.com
• Jeff Dudley, Marketing Manager
jdudley@13wmaz.com
• David Solano, Sports Director
(478) 752-1393
• Suzanne Lawler, News/Sports Anchor/Reporter
(478) 752-1313

WMBB-TV
613 HARRISON AVENUE
PANAMA CITY, FL 32401
850-769-2313
Fax: 850-769-8231
www.wmbb.com
• Christian Ashley, Sports Director
• Kyle Burger, Sports Director
(850) 769-2313

WMC-TV
1960 UNION AVENUE
MEMPHIS, TN 38104-4031
901-726-0555
Fax: 901-278-7633
www.wmcstations.com
• Jarvis Greer, Sports Director
(901) 726-0568

jgreer@wmctv.com
• Carrie Anderson, Sports Reporter
(901) 726-0555

WMGM-TV
1601 NEW ROAD
LINWOOD, NJ 08221-1116
609-927-4440 EXT 200
Fax: 609-926-8875
www.nbc40.net
• Pete Thompson, Sports Director
(609) 927-4440
• Rob Brennan, Weekend Sports Anchor
(609) 927-4440

WMTW-TV
P.O. BOX 8
AUBURN, ME 04210-8693
207-782-1800
Fax: 207-782-2165
news8wmtw@hearst.com
www.wmtw.com/
• Norm Karkos, Sports Director
• Dave Guthro, Sports Anchor/Reporter
(207) 782-1800

WMUR-TV
100 SOUTH COMMERCIAL STREET
MANCHESTER, NH 03101
603-669-9999
800-257-5151
Fax: 603-641-9005
news@wmur.com
www.thewmurchannel.com
• Jason King, Sports Anchor
(603) 669-9999
• Jamie Staton, Sports Anchor
(603) 669-9999
jstaton@hearst.com
• Naoko Funayama, Sports
Anchor/Reporter/Producer
(603) 669-9999
nfunayama@hearst.com

WNBC-TV
30 ROCKEFELLER PLAZA
NEW YORK, NY 10112-0002
212-664-4444
Fax: 212-664-2994
newstips@wnbc.com
www.wnbc.com
• Bruce Beck, Weekend Sports Anchor
(212) 664-2903
Bruce.Beck@nbcuni.com
• Len Berman, Sports Anchor
(212) 664-4990
• Len Berman, Sports Director
newstips@wnbc.com
• Anna Carbonell, Vice President
newstips@wnbc.com
• Otis Livingston, Morning Sports Anchor
(212) 664-4444

WNCN-TV
1205 FRONT STREET
RALEIGH, NC 27609-7526
919-836-1717
Fax: 919-836-1687
www.nbc17.com
• Josh Adams, Sports Producer
(919) 836-1717
• Maryann Balbo, Marketing Director
(919) 835-6223
• Penn Holderness, Sports Reporter/Anchor
(919) 836-1717

WNEM-TV
P.O. BOX 531
SAGINAW, MI 48607
989-758-2044
800-522-9636
Fax: 989-758-2111
wnem@wnem.com
www.wnem.com
• Scott Kuhl, Sports Director
• Darryl Sellers, Sports Anchor/Reporter
(989) 758-2044

WNJU-TV
2200 FLETCHER AVENUE 6TH FLOOR
FORT LEE, NJ 07024
201-969-4047
Fax: 201-969-4120
www.telemundo47.com/index.html
• Veronica Contreras, Sports Anchor
veronica.contreras@nbcuni.com

WNWO-TV
300 SOUTH BYRNE ROAD
TOLEDO, OH 43615-6217
419-535-0024
Fax: 419-535-8936
news@nbc24.com
www.nbc24.com
• Jim Tichy, Sports Anchor
jtichy@nbc24.com
• Jim Tichy, Sports Director
• Ryan Fowler, Sports
Reporter/Videographer
(419) 535-0024

WNYW-TV
205 EAST 67TH STREET
NEW YORK, NY 10021-6089
212-452-3808
Fax: 212-452-5512
www.myfoxny.com
• Lou Albanese, Sports Senior Producer
(212) 452-3784
lou.albanese@foxtv.com
• Ken Ashley, Promotion Director
• Scott Matthews, Vice President
fox5news@hotmail.com

WOAI-TV
P.O. BOX 2641
SAN ANTONIO, TX 78205-1321
210-226-4444
Fax: 210-224-9898
www.woai.com
• David Chancellor, Sports Anchor/Reporter
(210) 226-4444
• Don Harris, Sports Anchor
(210) 476-1036
• Brooks Hogg, Vice President

WOFL-TV
35 SKYLINE DRIVE
LAKE MARY, FL 32746-6202
407-644-3535
Fax: 407-741-5189
www.fox35wofl.com
• Eric Clinkscales, Sports Anchor
• Eric Clinkscales, Sports Reporter
• Rick Snyder, Promotion Manager
• Thomas Forester, Sports Anchor
(407) 644-3535

WOI-TV
3903 WESTOWN PARKWAY
WEST DES MOINES, IA 50266

515-457-1026
800-858-5555
Fax: 515-457-1025
www.woi-tv.com
• Ray Cole, President
• Doug Sawyer, Promotions Manager
(515) 457-9645
• John Walters, Sports Director
• Eric Murphy, Weekend Sports Anchor
(515) 457-1026

WOIO-TV
1717 EAST 12TH STREET
CLEVELAND, OH 44114-3230
216-771-1943
800-929-0132
Fax: 216-436-5460
19tips@woio.com
www.woio.com
• Brian Duffy, Sports Anchor/Reporter
(216) 781-1900

WOLO-TV
P.O. BOX 4217
COLUMBIA, SC 29223-7209
803-754-7525
Fax: 803-691-4015
www.wolo.com
• Jeff Floyd, Promotions Manager
(803) 754-7525
• Tim Hill, Sports Director
(803) 754-7525

WOWT-TV
3501 FARNAM STREET
OMAHA, NE 68131
402-346-6666
800-688-2431
Fax: 402-233-7888
sixonline@wowt.com
www.wowt.com
• John Chapman, Sports Anchor
(402) 346-6666
john.chapman@wowt.com
• Merlyn Klaus, Sports Producer
(402) 346-6666
merlyn.klaus@wowt.com
• Dave Webber, Sports Director
dave.webber@wowt.com

WPBN-TV
8513 M-72 WEST
TRAVERSE CITY, MI 49684
231-947-7770
800-968-7770
Fax: 231-947-0354
www.tv7-4.com
• Jerome Helminiak, Sports Director
(231) 995-5832
• Greg Johnson, Promotions Manager
(231) 995-5900
• Thom Pritz, Advertising Manager
(231) 995-5810
• Jayson Geiser, Sports Anchor/Reporter
(231) 947-7770

WPDE-TV
1194 ATLANTIC AVENUE
CONWAY, SC 29526
843-234-9733
800-698-4733
Fax: 843-234-9739
www.wpdetv.com
• Rich Chrampanis, Sports Director
(843) 234-9733
• Billy Huggins, Vice President

WPHL-TV
5001 WYNNEFIELD AVENUE
PHILADELPHIA, PA 19131-2504
215-878-1700
Fax: 215-879-7682
www.wb17.com
• Matt Biondi, Sports Anchor (Weekend)
• Wendy Kaiser, Promotion Director
(215) 883-3355
• Sabrina Pacifico, Publicity Coordinator
(215) 878-3334

WPIX-TV
220 EAST 42ND STREET
NEW YORK, NY 10017-5529
212-210-2411
Fax: 212-210-2591
cw11.trb.com
• Betty Ellen Berlamino, Vice President
(212) 210-2650
• Lolita Lopez, Sports Weekend Anchor
(212) 949-1100
• Sal Marchiano, Weeknight Sports Anchor
(212) 210-2411
• Bob Taute, Sports Director

WPLG-TV
3900 BISCAYNE BOULEVARD
MIAMI, FL 33137-3786
305-325-2370
Fax: 305-325-2480
newsdesk@wplg.com
www.local10.com
• Jimmy Cefalo, Sports Director
(305) 325-2484
• Henry Amor, Sports Producer
(305) 325-2370

WPMI - NBC 15
661 AZALEA RD
MOBILE, AL 36609
251-602-1500
Fax: 251-602-1547
• Pat Greenwood, Sports Director
• Sharon Moloney, Vice President/General
Manager
Alabama Collegiate Sports:
Alabama Athletics Auburn Athletics
University of South Alabama Spring Hill
College University of Mobile.
Neilsen Market:
62
Affiliate
NBC.
Professional Sports Teams:
New Orleans Saints (NFL), Mobile Reverlers
(National Basketball Development League).
Mobile BayBears (Southern League/AA)
NASCAR Atlanta Braves (MLB) Mobile
Wizards (Arena Football League).

WPNE-TV
821 UNIVERSITY AVENUE
MADISON, WI 53706
800-422-9707
Fax: 608-263-9763
comments@wpt.org
www.wpt.org
• Deb Piper, Sports Director
(608) 263-4222
piper@wpt.org

WPRI-TV
25 CATAMORE BOULEVARD
EAST PROVIDENCE, RI 02914-1203

401-438-7200
Fax: 401-431-1012
desk@wpri.com
www.wpri.com/
• Patrick Little, Sports Director
(401) 438-7200
plittle@wpri.com
• Robb Garofalo, Sports Anchor
(401) 438-7200
rgarofalo@wpri.com

WPTV-TV
1100 BANYAN BOULEVARD
WEST PALM BEACH, FL 33401-5000
561-653-5700
800-930-9766
Fax: 561-653-5719
newstips@wptv.com
www.wptv.com
• Ben Becker, Sports Director
newstips@wptv.com
• Jay Gilmore, Sports Reporter/Anchor
(561) 653-5700

WPTY-TV
2701 UNION AVENUE EXTENSION
MEMPHIS, TN 38112
901-323-2430
800-346-3030
Fax: 901-452-1820
www.abc24.com
• Greg Gaston, Sports Director
(901) 321-7617
greggaston@clearchannel.com
• Ari Bergeron, Sports Anchor/Reporter
(901) 323-2430

WPVI-TV
4100 CITY LINE AVENUE
PHILADELPHIA, PA 19131-1610
215-878-9700
Fax: 215-581-4530
cyber6@abc.com
www.wpvi.com
• Rebecca Campbell, President
• Paula McDermott, Marketing Director
(215) 581-4570
• Keith Russell, Sports Reporter/Weekend
Sports Anchor
(215) 878-9700
• Kevin Russell, Sports Reporter
• Caroline Welch, Promotion Director
• Jamie Apody, Sports Reporter/Anchor
(215) 878-9700

WPXI-TV
4145 EVERGREEN ROAD
PITTSBURGH, PA 15214-4025
412-237-1100
800-237-9794
Fax: 412-237-4900
assignments@wpxi.com
www.wpxi.com
• John Fedko, Sports Director
(412) 237-1212
• Karen Lah, Promotions Director
(412) 237-1101
klah@wpxi.com

WQAD-TV
3003 PARK 16TH STREET
MOLINE, IL 61265-6060
309-764-8888
Fax: 309-764-5763
news@wqad.com
www.wqad.com

• Dan Burich, Sports Director
(309) 736-3325
• Mick Moninghoff, Sports Director
(309) 764-8888

WRBL-TV
1350 13TH AVENUE
COLUMBUS, GA 31901-2303
706-324-6397
Fax: 706-323-0841
news@wrbl.com
www.wrbl.com
• Stuart Webber, Sports Director
(706) 324-6397

WRC-TV
4001 NEBRASKA AVENUE, N.W.
WASHINGTON, DC 20016-2733
202-885-4000
Fax: 202-885-4104
www.nbc4.com
• Wally Bruckner, Sports Reporter
(202) 885-4111
• Jeff Greenberg, Sports Producer
(202) 885-4870
• Joe Schreiber, Senior Sports Producer
(202) 885-3026
• Donna Weston, Promotions Vice President
donna.weston@nbcuni.com
• Nicole Zaloumis, Sports Reporter
• Lindsay Czarniak, Weekend Sports
Anchor/Reporter
(202) 885-4000

WRCB-TV
900 WHITEHALL ROAD
CHATTANOOGA, TN 37405-3247
423-267-5412
Fax: 423-756-3148
news@wrcbtv.com
www.wrcbtv.com
• Randy Smith, Sports Director
(423) 267-5412

WREG-TV
803 CHANNEL 3 DRIVE
MEMPHIS, TN 38103-4603
901-543-2333
800-766-3973
Fax: 901-543-2167
news@wreg.com
www.wreg.com
• Glenn Carver, Sports Director
(901) 543-2333

WRGB-TV
1400 BALLTOWN ROAD
SCHENECTADY, NY 12309-4301
518-381-4988
Fax: 518-346-6249
news@cbs6albany.com
www.wrgb.com
• Doug Sherman, Sports Director
(518) 381-4988
• Tim Mack, Weekend Sports Anchor
(518) 381-4988

WRIC TV-8
301 ARBORETUM PLACE
RICHMOND, VA 23236-3464
804-330-8888
Fax: 804-330-8883
www.wric.com
• Tom Best, General Manager
• Dan Klintworth, Station Manager
• Bill Foy, News Director

Neilsen Rank:
60
Affiliate:
ABC.
Sports:
All.
Richmond Sports Teams:
Richmond Braves (Minor League Baseball)
Richmond Kickers (Soccer) Richmond
Renegades (Minor Lg Hockey) Richmond
Speed (Arena Football Lg)..

WRIC-TV
301 ARBORETUM PLACE
RICHMOND, VA 23236-3490
804-330-8888
Fax: 804-330-8883
news@wric.com
www.wric.com
• Chip Tarkenton, Sports Director
(804) 330-8888
• Dawn Davenport, Weekend Sports
Anchor; Reporter
(804) 330-8888

WRNN-TV
721 BROADWAY
KINGSTON, NY 12401-3449
845-339-6397
800-824-3302
Fax: 845-339-6210
www.rnntv.com
• Kevin Connors, Sports Director
(845) 339-6397

WSAW-TV
1114 GRAND AVENUE
WAUSAU, WI 54403-6688
715-845-4211
Fax: 715-845-2649
news@wsaw.com
www.wsaw.com
• Mike Jacques, Sports Director
(715) 845-4211
mjacques@wsaw.com
• John Allee, Sports Reporter
(715) 845-4211
jallee@wsaw.com

WSAZ-TV
P.O. BOX 2115
HUNTINGTON, WV 25701
304-690-3069
800-426-1075
Fax: 304-208-3065
joe.wallace@wsaz.com
www.wsaz.com
• Matt Jaquinte, Advertising Manager
(304) 690-3003
matt.jaquinte@wsaz.com
• Keith Morehouse, Sports Director
(304) 697-4780
keith.morehouse@wsaz.com

WSB-TV
1601 WEST PEACHTREE STREET, N.E.
ATLANTA, GA 30309-2641
404-897-6270
Fax: 404-897-7370
assignmentdesk@wsbtv.com
www.wsbtv.com
• Chuck Dowdle, Sports Anchor
(404) 897-6270
• Kevin Gerke, Sports Producer
(404) 897-7745

• Barry Sinnock, Promotions Director
(404) 897-7454

WSBK-TV
1170 SOLDIERS FIELD ROAD
BOSTON, MA 02134-1004
617-787-7000
Fax: 617-254-6383
tv38.com
• Angie Kucharski, Vice President
(617) 746-8353
• Bob Lobel, Sports Director
(617) 787-7000
• Julio Marenghi, President
(617) 787-7123

WSBT-TV
300 WEST JEFFERSON BOULEVARD
SOUTH BEND, IN 46601-1513
574-233-3141
800-872-3141
Fax: 574-288-6630
wsbtnews@wsbt.com
www.wsbt.com
• Charlie Adams, Sports Director
(574) 472-8119
nwsrm@wsbt.com
• Tom Lebuzienski, Advertising Manager
tom@wsbt.com
• Peter Byrne, Sports Anchor
(574) 233-3141
pmbyrne@wsbt.com

WSEE-TV
1220 PEACH STREET
ERIE, PA 16501
814-455-7575
Fax: 814-454-2564
www.35wsee.com
• Gary Drapcho, Sports Director
(814) 455-7575

WSFA-TV
P.O. BOX 251200
MONTGOMERY, AL 36105
334-284-5276
Fax: 334-613-8303
www.wsfa.com
• Edith Parten, Marketing Director
• Edith Parten, Promotions Director
• Jeff Shearer, Sports Director
(334) 284-5276
jshearer@wsfa.com

WSIL-TV
1416 COUNTRY AIR DRIVE
CARTERVILLE, IL 62918
618-985-2333
Fax: 618-985-6482
newsdesk@wsiltv.com
www.wsil3.com
• Darren Kinnard, Sports Director
sports@wsiltv.com

WSLS-TV
P.O. BOX 10
ROANOKE, VA 24011
540-981-9126
800-800-9757
Fax: 540-343-2059
news@wsls.com
www.wsls.com
• Justin Ditmore, Sports Director
(540) 981-9126

WSMV-TV
5700 KNOB ROAD
NASHVILLE, TN 37209-4523
615-353-4444
Fax: 615-353-2343
news@wsmv.com
www.wsmv.com
• Tim Hall, Promotions Manager
(615) 353-2203
thall@wsmv.com
• Rudy Kalis, Sports Director
(615) 353-4444
rkalis@wsmv.com
• Brad Hopkins, Sports Reporter/Host
(615) 353-4444

WSNS-TV
454 NORTH COLUMBUS DRIVE
CHICAGO, IL 60614-3877
312-836-3000
Fax: 312-836-3232
TelemundoChicagoAssignment@telemundo
.com
www.telemundochicago.com
• Oscar Guzman, Sports News Anchor
(312) 836-3000
TelemundoChicagoAssignment@telemundo
.com

WSOC-TV
P.O. BOX 34665
CHARLOTTE, NC 28206-2733
704-335-4871
Fax: 704-335-4736
assignment@wsoc-tv.com
www.wsoctv.com
• Harold Johnson, Sports Reporter
(704) 335-4746
assignment@wsoc-tv.com
• Jarod Latch, Sports Reporter
(704) 335-4871

WSPA-TV
P.O. BOX 1717
SPARTANBURG, SC 29303-6637
864-576-7777
Fax: 864-595-4600
newschannel7@wspa.com
www.wspa.com
• Bill Shatten, Advertising Manager
(864) 587-4455
• Bill Shatten, Marketing Manager
(864) 587-4455
• Pete Yanity, Sports Director
pyanity@wspa.com
• Ken Griner, Sports Photographer
(864) 576-7777

WSVN-TV
1401 79TH STREET CAUSEWAY
MIAMI, FL 33141-4104
305-795-2777
800-845-7777
Fax: 305-795-2746
www.wsvn.com
• Mike DiPasquale, Sports Anchor
(305) 795-2777
• Jim Goodman, Sports Producer
• Steve Shapiro, Sports Anchor
(305) 795-2777
sshapiro@wsvn.com
• Steve Shapiro, Sports Reporter
(305) 795-2777
• Donovan Campbell, Sports
Reporter/Anchor
(305) 795-2777

WTAP-TV
1 TELEVISION PLAZA
PARKERSBURG, WV 26101-5373
304-485-4588
800-300-9827
Fax: 304-422-3920
news@wtap.com
www.wtap.com
• Joyce Ancrile, Promotion Manager
• James Wharton, Sports Director
(304) 485-6397
• Chris Brett, Weekend Sports Anchor
(304) 485-4588

WTEN NEWS 10/ABC
341 NORTHERN BLVD
ALBANY, NY 12204
518-436-4822
Fax: 518-426-4792
www.wten.com
• Bob Peterson, General Manager
• Dan Murphy, Sports Director
• Terry Kowalski, Marketing & Promotions
Director
Affiliate:
ABC.
Neilsen Rank:
56
Sports:
All.

WTEN-TV
341 NORTHERN BOULEVARD
ALBANY, NY 12204-1001
518-436-4822
Fax: 518-426-4792
news@wten.com
www.wten.com
• Terry Kowalski, Marketing Director
• Terry Kowalski, Promotions Director
• Dan Murphy, Sports Director
• Jamie Seh, Sports Reporter
(518) 436-4822

WTEV-TV
11700 CENTRAL PARKWAY
JACKSONVILLE, FL 32224-2600
904-642-3030
Fax: 904-642-5665
www.wtev.com
• Barry Buetel, Sports Director
barrybuetel@clearchannel.com

WTHI-TV
918 OHIO STREET
TERRE HAUTE, IN 47807
812-232-9481
Fax: 812-232-8953
action10news@wthitv.com
www.wthi.com
• Liam McHugh, Sports Director
(812) 232-4953
• Dick Telezyn, Advertising Manager
(812) 232-9481
dtelezyn@wthitv.com

WTHR-TV
P.O. BOX 1313
INDIANAPOLIS, IN 46204-1015
317-636-1313
Fax: 317-632-6720
www.wthr.com
• Dave Calabro, Sports Director
(317) 655-5754
dcalabro@wthr.com
• Rich Nye, Weekend Morning Sports

Anchor
(317) 636-1313
rnye@wthr.com
• Don Hein, Sports Reporter
(317) 636-1313
dhein@wthr.com

WTIC-TV
1 CORPORATE CENTER
HARTFORD, CT 06103-3290
860-527-6161
Fax: 860-727-0158
fox61.trb.com/
• Rich Coppola, Sports Director
(860) 723-2068
rcoppola@fox61.com

WTKR-TV
720 BOUSH STREET
NORFOLK, VA 23510-1502
757-446-1352
Fax: 757-446-1376
desk@wtkr.com
www.wtkr.com
• Ted Alexander, Sports Director
(757) 446-1361
ted.alexander@wtkr.com

WTMJ-TV
720 EAST CAPITOL DRIVE
MILWAUKEE, WI 53212-1308
414-332-9611
Fax: 414-967-5378
news@todaystmj4.com
www.todaystmj4.com
• Lance Allan, Sports Anchor
(414) 967-5368
jallan@todaystmj4.com
• Gregg Schraufnagel, Marketing Manager
(414) 332-9611
• Erick Weber, Sports Reporter (Football
NFL)

WTNH-TV
8 ELM STREET
NEW HAVEN, CT 06510-2006
203-784-8888
Fax: 203-789-2010
news8@wtnh.com
www.wtnh.com
• Noah Finz, Sports Director
(203) 784-8888
• Paul Spingola, Promotions Director
• Mary Lee Weber, Marketing Director

WTOC-TV
P.O. BOX 8086
SAVANNAH, GA 31405
912-234-6397
Fax: 912-232-4945
www.wtoctv.com
• Rick Snow, Sports Director
(912) 234-1111
• Tiffany Greene, Sports Reporter
(912) 234-6397
tiffanygreene@wtoc.com

WTOL-TV
730 NORTH SUMMIT STREET
TOLEDO, OH 43604-1808
419-248-1111
800-248-9865
Fax: 419-244-7104
news@wtol.com
www.wtol.com

• Gary Albers, Promotion Manager
(419) 248-1170
galbers@wtol.com
• Gary Albers, Promotions Manager
(419) 248-1170
galbetrs@wtol.com
• Dan Cummins, Sports Director
(419) 248-1111
dcummins@wtol.com

WTOM-TV
8518 M-72 WEST
TRAVERSE CITY, MI 49684
231-947-7770
800-968-7770
Fax: 231-947-0354
www.tv7-4.com
• Jerome Helmeniak, Sports Director
(231) 995-5863

WTOV-TV
9 RED DONLEY PLAZA
MINGO JUNCTION, OH 43938
740-282-0911
800-288-0799
Fax: 740-282-0439
www.wtov.com
• Sherry Hansen, Promotions Manager
(740) 282-0911
shansen@wtov.com
• Don Sloan, Sports Director
(740) 282-0911
dsloan@wtov.com

WTRF-TV
96 16TH STREET
WHEELING, WV 26003-3660
304-232-7777
800-777-9873
Fax: 304-232-4975
www.wtrf.com
• Scott Nolte, Sports Director
(304) 230-6293
snolte@wtrf.com
• Mike Anthony, Sports Anchor
(304) 230-6286

WTSP-TV
P.O. BOX 10000
SAINT PETERSBURG, FL 33702-1908
727-577-1010
Fax: 727-576-6924
10news@tampabays10.com
www.wtsp.com
• John Nugent, Sports Director
(617) 474-5513
• Justin Allen, Sports Anchor/Reporter
(727) 577-1010

WTTG-TV
5151 WISCONSIN AVENUE, N.W.
WASHINGTON, DC 20016-4124
202-244-5151
Fax: 202-895-3133
wttg.desk@foxtv.com
www.fox5dc.com
• Dave Feldman, Sports Anchor
• Dave Feldman, Sports Director
• Lou Holder, Weekend Sports Anchor
(202) 244-5151

WTVC-TV
4279 BENTON DRIVE
CHATTANOOGA, TN 37406
423-756-5500
Fax: 423-757-7400

news@newschannel9.com
www.newschannel9.com
• Ronnie Minton, Marketing Director
rminton@newschannel9.com
• Darrell Patterson, Sports Director
(423) 757-7332
darrell@newschannel9.com

WTVD-TV
411 LIBERTY STREET
DURHAM, NC 27701-3407
919-687-2212
Fax: 919-687-4373
wtvdassignmentdesk@abc.com
www.abc11tv.com
• Drew Smith, Sports Director
• Mark Armstrong, Sports Anchor
(919) 687-2212
mark.armstrong@abc.com

WTVF-TV
474 JAMES ROBERTSON PARKWAY
NASHVILLE, TN 37219-1212
615-244-5000
Fax: 615-244-9883
newsroom@newschannel5.com
www.newschannel5.com
• Hope Hines, Sports Anchor
(615) 244-5223
hhines@newschannel5.com
• Hope Hines, Sports Director
(615) 244-5223
• Mark Howard, Sports Anchor
mhoward@newschannel5.com
• Mark Howard, Sports Reporter
mhoward@newschannel5.com
• Eric Yutzy, Sports Reporter
(615) 244-5000
sports@newschannel5.com
• Eric Yutzy, Sports Reporter
sports@newschannel5.com
• Kami Carmann, Sports Reporter
(615) 244-5000
sports@newschannel5.com

WTVH-TV
980 JAMES STREET
SYRACUSE, NY 13203-2503
315-425-5555
Fax: 315-425-0129
www.wtvh.com
• Kevin Maher, Sports Director
(315) 477-4637
• Rishi Barran, Sports Anchor
(315) 425-5555

WTVJ-TV
15000 SOUTHWEST 27TH STREET
MIRAMAR, FL 33027-4147
954-622-6000
Fax: 954-622-6107
newsroom@nbc6.net
www.nbc6.net
• Maria Khalil-Pagani, Promotions Manager
• Guy Rawlings, Sports Anchor
(954) 622-6355
• Joe Rose, Sports Anchor
(954) 622-6359
• Adam Kuperstein, Sports Anchor/Reporter
(954) 622-6000

WTVM-TV
P.O. BOX 1848
COLUMBUS, GA 31906-2931
706-324-6471
Fax: 706-322-7527

newsleader@wtvm.com
www.wtvm.com
• Adelaide Kirk, Advertising Manager
akirk@wtvm.com
• Dave Platta, Sports Director
dplatta@wtvm.com
• David Platta, Sports Director
(706) 322-5734
dplatta@wtvm.com

WTVO-TV
1917 NORTH MERIDIAN ROAD
ROCKFORD, IL 61101-9215
815-963-5413
Fax: 815-963-0029
newsdesk@wtvo.com
www.wtvo.com
• Scott Leber, Sports Director/Weekday
Anchor - 5, 6 &
(815) 963-5413
sports@wtvo.com
• Vince Conway, Weekend Sports
Anchor/Reporter
(815) 963-5413
vconway@wtvo.com

WTVT-TV
3213 WEST KENNEDY BOULEVARD
TAMPA, FL 33609-3006
813-876-1313
Fax: 813-871-5815
www.myfoxtampabay.com/myfox/
• Chip Carter, Sports Director
(813) 870-9733
• Chris Field, Sports Anchor
(813) 870-7105
• Mike House, Promotions Director
• Carrie Schroeder, Promotions Director

WTVW-TV
477 CARPENTER STREET
EVANSVILLE, IN 47708-1027
812-424-7777
800-511-6009
Fax: 812-421-7289
www.wtvw.com
• Mark McVicar, Sports Director
(812) 433-5572
• Doug Kufner, Sports Anchor/Reporter
(812) 424-7777

WTVY-TV
P.O. BOX 1089
DOTHAN, AL 36303
334-792-3195
Fax: 334-712-7452
www.wtvynews4.com
• Brad Sherwood, Sports Director
(334) 712-7419
• Kelly O'Donnell, Sports Anchor
(334) 792-3195

WTXF-TV
330 MARKET STREET
PHILADELPHIA, PA 19106-2706
215-925-2929
800-220-6397
Fax: 215-982-5494
www.foxphiladelphia.com
• Larry Fernchick, Marketing Director
(215) 925-2929
• Don Tollefson, Sports Director
(215) 925-7085
• Tom Sredenschek, Senior Sports
Producer
(215) 925-2929

WUAB-TV
1717 EAST 12TH STREET
CLEVELAND, OH 44114-3230
216-771-1943
800-929-0132
Fax: 216-436-5460
19tips@woio.com
www.wuab.com
• Rob Boenau, Marketing Director
(216) 367-7111
rboenau@woio.com
• Chuck Galeti, Sports Reporter/Anchor
(216) 771-1943
cgaleti@woio.com

WUSA-TV
4100 WISCONSIN AVENUE, N.W.
WASHINGTON, DC 20016-2810
202-895-5999
Fax: 202-364-6163
www.wusa9.com
• Brett Haber, Sports Director
(202) 895-5999
• Levan Reid, Sports Anchor (Weekend)

WVEC-TV
613 WOODIS AVENUE
NORFOLK, VA 23510-1017
757-625-1313
Fax: 757-628-5855
www.wvec.com
• Scott Cash, Sports Director
(757) 628-6215
scash@wvec.com
• Matt Earl, Promotion Manager
(757) 625-1313

WVII-TV
371 TARGET INDUSTRIAL CIRCLE
BANGOR, ME 04401-5721
207-945-6457
800-499-9844
Fax: 207-945-6864
www.wvii.com
• Gene Hardin, Promotions Director
• Ted Lombardi, Sports Director
(207) 945-6457

WVIT-TV
1422 NEW BRITAIN AVENUE
WEST HARTFORD, CT 06110-1632
860-521-3030
800-523-9848
Fax: 860-521-4860
newstips@nbc30.com
www.wvit.com/
• Kevin Nathan, Sports Anchor
• Persefone Contos, Sports Anchor
(860) 521-3030

WVLT-TV
P.O. BOX 59088
KNOXVILLE, TN 37919-4815
865-450-8880
Fax: 865-584-1978
wvltnews@wvlt-tv.com
www.volunteertv.com
• Dino Cartwright, Promotions Director
dino.cartwright@wvlt-tv.com
• Rick Russo, Sports Director
(865) 450-8880
rick.russo@wvlt-tv.com
• Daryl Hobby, Sports Anchor/Reporter
(865) 450-8880
daryl.hobby@wvlt-tv.com

WVTM-TV
1732 VALLEY VIEW DRIVE
BIRMINGHAM, AL 35209-1251
205-558-7300
800-947-6397
Fax: 205-323-3314
www.nbc13.com
• Rob Carlin, Sports Anchor
(205) 933-1313
• Jim Dunaway, Sports Director
(205) 933-1313
• Don Hawes, Sports Director
(205) 558-7300
dhawes@wvtm.com

WVUT-TV
1200 NORTH 2ND STREET
VINCENNES, IN 47591-2325
812-888-4135
Fax: 812-882-2237
• Tony Cloyd, Sports Director
(812) 888-5283
tcloyd@vinu.edu

WWAY-TV
615 NORTH FRONT STREET
WILMINGTON, NC 28402-3325
910-762-8581
Fax: 910-762-8367
www.wwaytv3.com
• Gene Motley, Sports Director
(910) 762-8581

WWBT-TV
P.O. BOX 12
RICHMOND, VA 23225-6116
804-230-1212
Fax: 804-230-2789
newsroom@nbc12.com
www.nbc12.com
• Eileen Cowel, Promotions Director
ecowel@nbc12.com
• Ben Hamlin, Sports Director
(804) 230-1212
bhamlin@nbc12.com
• Paula Hersh, Marketing Director
phersh@nbc12.com
• Nancy Kent, Vice President

WWLP-TV
ONE BROADCAST CTR.
CHICOPEE, MA 01013
413-786-2200
Fax: 413-377-2263
news@wwlp.com
www.wwlp.com
• Anna Giza, Promotion Manager
agiza@wwlp.com
• William M. Pepin, President
(413) 377-2236
bpepin@wwlp.com
• Rich Tettemer, Sports Director
(413) 786-2200
rtettemer@wwlp.com

WWMT-TV
590 WEST MAPLE STREET
KALAMAZOO, MI 49008-1926
269-388-9339
Fax: 269-388-8322
desk@wwmt.com
www.wwmt.com/
• Ed Kengerski, Sports Director
(269) 388-9339
ekengerski@wwmt.com

WWOR-TV
9 BROADCAST PLAZA
SECAUCUS, NJ 07096-2913
201-330-2215
Fax: 201-330-3844
www.my9ny.com/
• Rich Bagala, Sports Producer
(201) 330-2245
• Scott Matthews, Vice President
• Russ Salzberg, Sports Anchor
(201) 330-2215

WWSB-TV
1477 10TH STREET
SARASOTA, FL 34236-4048
941-923-8840
Fax: 941-923-8709
wwsbnews@wwsb.tv
www.wwsb.com
• Kevin Negandhi, Sports Anchor
(941) 923-8840
knegandhi@wwsb.tv
• Don Brennan, Sports Director
(941) 923-6397
dbrennan@wwsb.tv

WWTV-TV
22320 130TH AVENUE
TUSTIN, MI 49688-8564
231-775-3478
800-782-7910
Fax: 231-775-3671
webmaster@9and10news.com
www.9and10news.com
• Tessia Clix, Promotions Director
tessiaclix@9and10news.com
• Mario Iacobelli, Owner
(231) 775-3478
marioiacobelli@9and10news.com
• Brian Lawson, Sports Director
(231) 775-3478
brianlawson@9and10news.com
• Luke Notestine, Sports Reporter/Anchor
(231) 775-3478
LukeNotestine@9and10news.com

WWUP-TV
22320 130TH AVENUE
TUSTIN, MI 49688-8564
231-775-3478
800-782-7910
Fax: 231-775-3671
webmaster@9and10news.com
www.9and10news.com
• Tessia Clix, Promotions Director
tessiaclix@9and10news.com
• Mario Iacobelli, Owner
(231) 775-3478
marioiacobelli@9and10news.com
• Brian Lawson, Sports Director
(231) 775-3478
brianlawson@9and10news.com
• Aaron Mills, Sports Director
(231) 775-3478
AaronMills@9and10news.com

WXIA-TV
1611 WEST PEACHTREE STREET, N.E.
ATLANTA, GA 30309-2641
404-873-9114
Fax: 404-881-0675
news@11alive.com
www.11alive.com
• Fred Kalil, Sports Anchor
(404) 873-9145
• Fred Kalil, Sports Director
(404) 873-9114

• Kristy Revero, Sports Producer
krevero@wxia.gannett.com
• Sam Crenshaw, Weekend Sports Anchor
(404) 873-9114

WXOW-TV
3705 CTH25
LA CRESCENT, MN 55947
507-895-9969
Fax: 507-895-8124
wxow@wxow.com
www.wxow.com
• Scott Emerich, Sports Director
• Laramie McClurg, Promotions Manager
• Brian Schumacher, Advertising Manager

WXVT-TV
3015 EAST REED ROAD
GREENVILLE, MS 38703-9452
662-334-1500
800-489-9988
Fax: 662-378-8122
www.wxvt.com
• Beverly Ford, Promotions Director
(662) 334-1500
• Stephen Robinson, Sports Anchor;
Reporter
(662) 334-1500
• Tony Byrd, Sports Anchor
(662) 334-1500

WXXA-TV
28 CORPORATE CIRCLE
ALBANY, NY 12203-5121
518-862-0995
Fax: 518-862-0930
www.fox23news.com
• Rich Becker, Sports Director
(518) 862-0995
richbecker@clearchannel.com
• Scott Marlock, Sports Anchor / Reporter
(518) 822-0995
• Dani Stein, Sports Reporter /
Photographer
(518) 862-0995
Teams Covered:
NY Giants, Jets, Bills, Patriots, Siena,
UAlbany and Syracuse athletics, Union and
RPI athletics, NY Yankees, Mets, Red Sox,
NY Rangers, Isles, Sabres and Bruins, NY
Knicks and Nets

WYLN-TV
1057 TENTH STREET, E.
HAZLETON, PA 18201
570-459-1869
888-499-5635
Fax: 570-459-1383
www.wylntv.com
• Tim Thompson, Sports Director
(570) 459-1869

WYMT-TV
199 BLACK GOLD BOULEVARD
HAZARD, KY 41701
606-436-5757
Fax: 606-439-3760
www.wymtnews.com
• Brian Milam, Sports Director
(606) 436-5757
• Jeff Archer, Sports Reporter
(606) 436-5757

WYTV-TV
3930 SUNSET BOULEVARD
YOUNGSTOWN, OH 44512

330-782-1144
Fax: 330-782-3504
jmarling@wytv.com
www.wytv.com
• Bob Hannon, Sports Director
• Bill Castrovince, Sports Reporter
(330) 788-4046

WZBN-TV
2600 EAST STATE STREET EXTENSION
HAMILTON, NJ 08619
609-587-2500
Fax: 609-587-0011
www.wzbn.com
• Greg Angelillo, Sports Reporter
(609) 587-2500

WZVN-TV
3719 CENTRAL AVENUE
FORT MYERS, FL 33901-8220
239-939-2020
Fax: 239-939-4801
www.abc-7.com
• Jason Kurtz, Sports Director
• Jason Kurz, Sports Director
(239) 939-2020

WZZM-TV
WZZM 13 BOX Z
GRAND RAPIDS, MI 49544-1601
616-785-1313
Fax: 616-785-1301
news@wzzm13.com
www.wzzm13.com/
• Henry Wofford, Sports Director
• Tom Clyde, Weekend Sports Reporter
(616) 785-1313

Sports on the World Wide Web

BLEACHER REPORT
info@bleacherreport.com
www.bleacherreport.com
• Bill McCandless, VP of Video
Programming and Production
• Dave Finocchio, Founder, VP of Content
• Dave Nemetz, Founder, VP of Business
Development
• Sam Parnell, Founder, VP of Engineering
• Joe Yanarella, Editor-in-Chief
Description:
b/r is an online medium for expert sports
writers to provide opinion and analysis of all
of the major US sports, including College,
MMA, Wrestling, and Motorsports, Cricket
and Rugby; content is provided by
thousands of professional sports writers,
and syndicated on CBSSports.com, the LA
Times, NHL.com, Hearst Newspapers,
USAToday.com, and Telegraph.co.uk. The
site also has the b/r Blog, as well as local
editions. Online subscriptions available.
Become a fan on Facebook, or follow on
Twitter
8330

CHICAGO TRIBUNE SPORTS
435 NORTH MICHIGAN AVE
CHICAGO, IL 60611
312-222-3478
800-874-2863
Fax: 312-828-9392
www.chicagosports.com

• Stuart W Courtney, Breaking Sports Editor
• Joel Boyd, Source Editor, Sports
• Tim Bannon, Deputy Sports Editor
• Christopher Boghossian, Sports Source
Editor
Description:
Focusing on 6 professional teams and
Illinois high school sports, site pools Tribune
Company media resources (Chicago
Tribune, WGN-TV, WGN Radio, and CLTV)
and others to deliver fast, accurate and
interesting sports news for Chicago sports
fans.

E-SPORTS MEDIA GROUP, INC.
3505 N. NORDICA
CHICAGO, IL 60634
773-736-7556
Fax: 775-263-1497
www.esportsmediagroup.com
• Dustin Klein, Publisher
• Rick Capone, Managing Editor
Features:
A growing number of contributing authors
covering a wide variety of topics, an online
sports wear super store with thousands of
products, daily polls and contests, trivia and
quotes, interactive games and fantasy
leagues, and a portal (gateway/search
engine) to other quality sports web sites on
the Internet.
Description:
Owned by VSM, operator of e-sports! web
site: www.e-sports.com, powered by a
community of sports fans, athletes, coaches
and sports media personalities.

GLOBAL REACH SPORTS
PO BOX 1417
WILLISTON, VT 05495
828-279-1674
Fax: 828-279-1674
info@globalreachsports.com
www.globalreachsports.com
• Geoff Elder, Co-Founder and Chief
Technology Officer
• Katherine Ross, Co-Founder and Creative
Director
• Stacy Luther, Director of Internet
Development
Sports Service Founded:
1999
Description:
Organization offers Web site design and
development, e-commerce solutions,
content management, integrative software
development, and participatory community
tools and features. The organization's
mission is to increase participation and
services across an entire sport, starting with
grassroots development on up to
professional and elite-level performance.
Parent organization of BikeResults.com.

GUESTMVP
104 W 4TH STREET
SUITE 301
ROYAL OAK, MI 48067
888-483-7868
Nature of Services:
GuestMVP powered by Konsyerzh, LLC. is
the newest revolutionary device for the
sports industry which maximizes the fan
experience while providing sponsors with an
interactive advertising portal - guests have
the ability to order food and beverage,
purchase merchandise, view instant replays,

see live stats, search for local attractions,
and much more.

INTERNET SPORTS AWARDS
EXCALIBUR MARKETING GROUP
4258 GERMANNA HWY, STE D-1
LOCUST GROVE, VA 22508
540-972-4690
Fax: 540-972-4691
www.isportsnet.com
Description:
Reaches over 18 million sports fans a year.
Allows fans to vote for various awards.

IVRNET
1338-36TH AVENUE NE
CALGARY, AB, CANADA T2e 6T6
403-538-0400
800-351-7227
Fax: 403-538-2621
www.ivrnet.com
• David L Snell, President/Chief Executive
Officer
• Chris D Groot, Vice President/Sales &
Marketing
• Marcel Jacques, Senior Developer
• Frank Nemeth, Director and Developer
Description:
Organization specializes in the design and
implementation of web-enabled league
management software for recreational
sports leagues.

MYTEAM.COM
400 UNICORN PARK, SUITE 300
WOBURN, MA 01801
781-376-9944
Fax: 781-376-8158
www.myteam.com
• Darko Dejanovic, Chief Executive Officer
• John Frascotti, President/Chief Operating
Officer
• David Block, Director
Technology/Development
• John Feldmeier, Director Product
Development
• John Young, Vice President/Strategic
Projects
• Reed Thompson, National Organization
Initiatives
Description:
My Team is an online center for amateur
sports.

ONLINE SPORTS
2060 WINERIDGE PLACE, SUITE C
ESCONDIDO, CA 92029
760-839-9363
800 856-2638
Fax: 760-839-9370
www.onlinesports.com
• Mike Farkas, President/Owner
• Chris Haupt, Chief Technology Officer
Nature of Sports Service:
National. On-line sports service. Serves as
showplace for sports and recreation
products and services on the Internet. Links
to thousands of sports equipment, apparel,
collectibles and services available online.
Companies can list services or products
directly for sale, or for promotional
purposes.

ROTOWORLD
www.rotoworld.com

• Rick Cordella, Senior VP & General Manager, Digital Media
Nature of Sports Service:
Provider of Internet-based sports and financial games w/ over 30 games including full fantasy sports competitions, salary cap games, sports stock market simulations, pick'em style games and financial stock market simulations. 2 million members.

SI.COM
ONE CNN CENTER
ATLANTA, GA 30303
404-878-1600
Fax: 404-878-0011
www.si.com
• Matt Bean, Managing Editor
• Joey Trotz, Vice President, Operations, CNNSI,COM

SOCCER365.COM
3029 6TH AVE, SOUTH
BIRMINGHAM, AL 35233
205-323-3755
Fax: 205-323-2355
www.soccer365.com
• David Fleenor, Contributor

SPORTS NETWORK, THE
2200 BYBERRY RD
SUITE 200
HATBORO, PA 19040
215-441-8444
Fax: 215-441-5767
• Ken Zajac, Director of Sales
(215) 441-8444
• Bernie Greenberg, Sales
(215) 441-8444
bgreenberg@sportsnetwork.com
• Steve Cwitkowitz, Sales
(215) 441-8444
scwitkowitz@sportsnetwork.com
Description:
Organization offers real-time sports wire service furnishing sports content on a 24/7 basis using state-of-the-art technology. The data includes scores, trends, analysis, news, features, statistics, pre- and post-game reports, box scores, and historical data.

SPORTS STANDINGS, INC.
2514 TARPLEY RD, STE 104
CARROLLTON, TX 75006
972-416-8657
Fax: 972-478-7957
info@sportsstandings.com
Description:
The premier Internet athletic connection for amateur sports organizers, leagues and teams.

SPORTS XCHANGE, THE
PO BOX 918
NOVATO, CA 94948
415-897-8555
• Frank Cooney, President
Description:
National. Bulletin board information exchange service covering professional sports leagues. Information is submitted by beat writers and columnists across the country for each professional sport. Each participating group (NBA, NFL, MLB, etc.) has ability to exchange stories or features daily and in-depth notes weekly. Information

remains on-line throughout the season and past seasons are archived. Participants have access to daily personnel moves and can download current rosters. Service is open to any group desiring to exchange information on a regular basis. Minimum of ten participants per group is preferred.

SPORTSNET
21 CHARLES ST
WESTPORT, CT 06880
800-226-7633
Fax: 203-226-7633
sales@sportsnet.com
www.sportsnet.com
Description:
National. Computerized trading card/information network. Services include SportsNet, SportsNet Stadium, SportsNet Today Magazine, SportsNet's Electronic Price Guide.

SPORTSNUTS, INC.
THE TOWERS AT SOUTH TOWNE, #2
10421 SOUTH 400 WEST, SUITE 550
SALT LAKE CITY, UT 84095
801-816-2500
Fax: 801-816-2599
• Chene Gardner, Chief Financial Officer
Description:
A leader in providing unique solutions to the challenges faced by athletes and the organizations in which participate. Helps organize and manage a wide variety of sports events providing online registration, event sponsorship, event coordination, online and offline promotion, and merchandise sales.

SPORTSPILOT, INC.
2514 TARPLEY RD
SUITE 104
CARROLLTON, TX 75006
214-472-3410
888-516-7249
Fax: 214-472-2641
www.sportspilot.com
• Ron Toupal, Chief Executive Officer
• Brad Cook, Founder
• Tim Adkison, Sales Manager
Description:
An Internet based company that provides Amateur Sport Organizations with sports office automation services, automated scorekeeping and real-time sports news and stats.

SPORTSWIRE/BUSINESS WIRE
44 MONTGOMERY STREET
39th FLOOR
SAN FRANCISCO, CA 94104
415-986-4422
800-381-9473
mike@bizwire.com
www.businesswire.com
• Cathy Baron Tamraz, Chairman/Chief Executive Officer
• Scott D. Goll, Editor
Description:
The leading source for full-text breaking news releases, multimedia and regulatory filings for companies and groups throughout the world.

STATS
2775 SHERMER ROAD
NORTHBROOK, IL 60062
847-583-2100
Fax: 847-583-2600
sales@stats.com
www.stats.com
• Gary Walrath, Chief Executive Officer

STAY IN THE ZONE
1060 MAIN STREET
SUITE 307
RIVER EDGE, NJ 07661
201-342-3663
800-580-9663
Fax: 201-342-2258
info@stayinthezone.com
www.stayinthezone.com
• Jay P. Granat, Founder
Description:
Blog focusing on sport psychology; resources, publications, and products for self-help.

TEAMLINK.COM, INC
200 NORTH COBB PARKWAY
SUITE 140
MARIETTA, GA 30062
770-514-0077
800-599-9402
Fax: 770-604-9520
www.tmlk.com
• David Supple, Chief Operating Officer
• Heather Voight, Vice President/Collegiate Initiatives
Description:
Offers sports media professionals and team staffers access to team generated sports information from over 500 professional and collegiate sports organizations. This information is delivered to you via fax or e-mail the instant it is available or can be viewed directly from the site via the TeamLink Viewer.

THE ACTIVE NETWORK, INC.
1020 PROSPECT STREET
SUITE 250
LA JOLLA, CA 92037
858-551-9916
Fax: 858-551-7619
www.active.com
Description:
Active.com offers a one-stop shop for maintaining healthy lifestyles or setting and achieving fitness goals. THe site offers an online database of more than 100,000 events and activities in over 50 sports in 5,00 cities nationwide, from 5k runs to marathons to cycling races and triathlons. Finding events is easy and online registration makes participation fast and convenient.

THEPIT.COM
245 MAIN STREET
4TH FLOOR
WHITE PLAINS, NY 10601
866-374-8266
Fax: 212-376-0699
customer.service@thepit.com
www.thepit.com
Description:
An online marketplace that buys, sells or trades sport cards.

TURNER SPORTS
ONE CNN CENTER
ATLANTA, GA 30303
404-827-1700
www.turner.com
• David Levy, President
Description:
Exclusive producer of NASCAR.com.

VEGASINSIDER.COM
675 GRIER DRIVE
LAS VEGAS, NV 89119
702-892-0670
800-211-4759
Fax: 702-892-0682
www.vegasinsider.com
• Joseph Pesta, Webmaster
Description:
National. Sports information provider; on-line database sports service. Sports information service providing on-line database devoted to sports and horse racing. Including: Scores, standings, statistics, historical data, analysis, news, odds, and more updated and available 24 hours, seven days a week. Compatible with existing electronic, broadcasting newsroom systems. Customization available for individual markets, media, and promoters; also markets professional handicapping software for football and basketball.

YAHOO! SPORTS
701 FIRST AVENUE
SUNNYVALE, CA 94089
408-349-3300
Fax: 408-349-3301
www.sports.yahoo.com
• David Filo, Co-Founder
• Jerry Yang, Co-Founder
• Marissa Myer, Chief Executive Officer, President, Director
• Adam Cahan, SVP of Mobile and Emerging Products
• Henrique De Castro, Chief Operating Officer
• David Dibble, Executive Vice President, Technology & Operat
• Mikie Rosen, Senior Vice President, Global Media & Commerc
• Jay Rossiter, Executive Vice President, Platforms
• Kathy Savitt, Chief Marketing Officer
Baseball Sponsor:
MLB - San Francisco Giants.
Basketball Sponsor:
EA Sports Maui Classic.

5

sports sponsors

Sports Sponsorship

In 2016, the total North American sponsorship market was approximately 22 billion U.S. dollars.[1] According to ESP Properties, 106 companies allocated at least $15 million[2] to spending on properties of all types, including the arts, festivals, causes, entertainment, and sports, with professional and amateur leagues and teams, and "mega" events such as the Super Bowl,[3] accounting for 70 percent of the total, or $16 billion. Overall, sponsorship spending continued to rise in 2016, even as many of the top spenders (including three of the top four: PepsiCo, Anheuser-Busch InBev and Coca-Cola)[4] decreased their spending, and a trend toward activation spending over fee spending strengthened.[5]

In 2019, Talent Backer reported an annual North American spend of $24.2 billion, with beverage, auto, sport apparel and telecommunications companies comprising the top-spenders[6]. Key marketing partners were, not surprisingly, the National Football League (NFL), National Basketball Association (NBA), and Major League Baseball (MLB), with Major League Soccer (MLS), golf, tennis, and motorsports close behind. Big-budget spenders Pepsi, Nike, Anheuser-Busch InBev, and Coca Cola took the top slots.

In 2020, global sports sponsorship was projected to fall a whopping $17.2 billion due to the COVID-19 pandemic.[7] However, the National Football League (NFL) defied expectations with sponsorship revenue across the league soaring to $1.62 billion, a rise of 10 percent over the 2019/20 season. Naming rights deals for two new stadiums and new league-level sponsorships were key contributors to the revenue growth.[8] This growth continued across the major sports, with the NBA setting a record in the 2020-21 season, despite a late start and shorter season[9].

By 2023, with the pandemic largely behind us, Statista estimated the global sports sponsorship market to be worth $97.35 billion USD. Moreover, they estimated that the industry would continue to grow at a rate of 8.68 percent annually until 2030, with a value of almost $190 billion USD.[10] In 2023, the NFL alone accounted for $2.35 billion USD in team sponsorship, an increase of 15 percent.

By 2024, the sports sponsorship market was valued at $64.1 billion USD, with an estimated jump to a whopping $144.9 billion USD by 2034.[11] Of all types of sponsorship, broadcast dominated at 34.5% due to its prominent visibility during major events. Football was the primary sport for sponsors, at 35.2% of the sport segment measured, due to its popularity around the world and sizable fanbase. In terms of the sponsors themselves, the automotive industry led the pack at 29.7% of their segment, thanks to strong brand awareness and ads that connected with audiences. Finally, North America was the leading region for sports sponsorships, contributing $22.11 billion USD, being an epicenter of both major sports leagues and large corporate sponsors.

[1] Statista. "North American sponsorship spending by property type from 2009 to 2018 (in billion U.S. dollars)." Statista.com. https://www.statista.com/statistics/196893/sponsorship-spending-by-property-type-since-2009.

[2] IEG. "Number of companies in ESP rankings shrinks." Sponsorship.com. http://www.sponsorship.com/Report/2017/09/18/Number-Of-Companies-In-ESP-s-Top-Sponsor-Rankings-.aspx.

[3] Statista. "North American sponsorship spending by property type from 2009 to 2018 (in billion U.S. dollars)." Statista.com. https://www.statista.com/statistics/196893/sponsorship-spending-by-property-type-since-2009.

[4] ESP Properties. (2017). *Top Sponsors Report*.

[5] Ibid.

[6] Talent Backer. "Biggest sports sponsorship deals in the USA." Talentbacker.com. https://talentbacker.com/2020/04/biggest-sports-sponsorship-deals-in-the-usa.

[7] Two Circles. "Sponsorship spend to fall $17.2bn; Financial Services by $5.7bn." Twocircles.com. https://twocircles.com/gb-en/articles/projections-sponsorship-spend-to-fall-17-2bn.

[8] SportsPro. "Study: NFL defies Covid-19 as sponsorship revenue soars to US$1.62bn." Sportspromedia.com. https://www.sportspromedia.com/news/nfl-sponsorship-revenue-2020-allegiant-sofi-stadium-gambling.

[9] IEG. "Sponsorship is a Slam Dunk for the NBA 2020-21 Season." Sponsorship.com. www.sponsorship.com/About/Announcements/Sponsorship-is-a-Slam-Dunk-for-the-NBA-2020-21-Sea.aspx.

[10] Statista. "Size of sports sponsorship market worldwide in 2022, with a forecast for 2023 and 2030." Statista.com https://www.statista.com/statistics/269784/revenue-from-sports-sponsorship-worldwide-by-region.

[11] Market.us. "Global Sports Sponsorship Market Size, Share, Growth Analysis By Type of Sponsorship." Market.us. https://market.us/report/sports-sponsorship-market.

Basketball Sponsors - Womens National Basketball Association

AT&T INC., 725
BANK OF AMERICA CORPORATION, 725
COCA-COLA COMPANY, 727
EA SPORTS, 1213
ENTERPRISE HOLDINGS, INC., 727
EXXON MOBIL CORPORATION, 727
KIA MOTORS AMERICA, 729
NIKE, 730
PAPA JOHN'S INTERNATIONAL, 731
T-MOBILE USA, 733
TARGET STORES, 733
TOYOTA MOTOR SALES, U.S.A., 734
UNDER ARMOUR, 734

Boating Sponsors

AMJ CAMPBELL, 924
NAUTICA INTERNATIONAL, 1166

Bowling Sponsors

BOWLING PROPRIETORS' ASSOCIATION OF AMERICA, 65
PEPSICO, INC., 731

Canoeing Sponsors

AMJ CAMPBELL, 924
CLIF BAR, 1116

College Sponsors

AMERICAN EXPRESS COMPANY, 725
ANHEUSER-BUSCH INBEV, 725
ARAMARK CORPORATION, 1066
AT&T INC., 725
AUTOTRADER.COM, INC, 673
BANK OF AMERICA CORPORATION, 725
CAPITAL ONE FINANCIAL, 726
CHEVRON CORPORATION, 727
COCA-COLA COMPANY, 727
COMCAST CORPORATION, 727
CUTTER AND BUCK, INC., 1121
DIRECTV, INC., 686
EA SPORTS, 1213
ENTERPRISE HOLDINGS, INC., 727
GREATER FORT LAUDERDALE CONVENTION & VISITORS BUREAU, 234
HARMON TRAVEL SERVICE, 926
HEALTHSOUTH REHABILITATION, 920
HOLLAND & KNIGHT, 884
JACKSONVILLE AND THE BEACHES CONVENTION AND VISITORS BUREAU, 236
JEDC SPORTS AND ENTERTAINMENT DIVISION/JACKSONVILLE FLORIDA, 237
KIA MOTORS AMERICA, 729
MACY'S, CALIFORNIA, 1232
MCDONALD'S CORPORATION, 729
MERCEDES-BENZ USA, 730
MICROSOFT CORPORATION, 730
NATIONWIDE FINANCIAL SERVICES, 730
NIKE, 730
NISSAN NORTH AMERICA, 730
PAPA JOHN'S INTERNATIONAL, 731
PEPSICO, INC., 731
PGA TOUR, 108
PNC FINANCIAL SERVICES, 731

RAWLINGS SPORTING GOODS COMPANY INC., 1180
RICHARD PETTY DRIVING EXPERIENCE, 18
SHERWIN-WILLIAMS CO., 732
SIRIUS XM RADIO, 732
ST. AUGUSTINE, PONTE VEDRA & THE BEACHES VISITORS & CONVENTION BUREAU, 246
SUBWAY RESTAURANTS, 733
TICKET760 KTKR, 635
TICKETS.COM, 933
TOOLBOX STUDIOS, 814
TOPPS COMPANY, INC., 1202
U.S. ARMY ALL-AMERICAN BOWL, 203
VERIZON COMMUNICATIONS, 734
WELLS FARGO & CO, 735
WILSON SPORTING GOODS COMPANY, 1210
WRIGHT STATE UNIVERSITY NUTTER CENTER, 1020
YUM! BRANDS, 735
96.5 KHMX MIX, 611

Curling Sponsors

CAPITAL ONE FINANCIAL, 726
TIM HORTONS, 733

Cycling Sponsors

CANNONDALE BICYCLE CORPORATION, 1113
CLIF BAR, 1116
THE EMIRATES GROUP, 733
H-E-B, 1229
LANDS' END, INC., 1154
LEADING BRANDS, 1155
OCEAN PACIFIC APPAREL CORPORATION, 1170
POWERCRANKS, 1176
SAMSUNG ELECTRONICS NA, 732
SCHWINN CYCLING & FITNESS, 1186
SPEEDPLAY, INC., 1192
VANS, INC., 1240
VF CORPORATION, 734

Diving Sponsors

COLORADO DISPLAY SYSTEMS, 1118
COLORADO TIME SYSTEMS, 1118
KAISER FOUNDATION HEALTH PLAN, 729

Endurance Sports Sponsors

BANK OF AMERICA CORPORATION, 725
CHEVRON CORPORATION, 727
COCA-COLA COMPANY, 727
FOOT LOCKER, INC., 1228
NATIONAL BASKETBALL ASSOCIATION DEVELOPMENT LEAGUE, 59
NATIONWIDE FINANCIAL SERVICES, 730
NIKE, 730
NISSAN NORTH AMERICA, 730
UNDER ARMOUR, 734
UNITED CONTINENTAL HOLDINGS, 734
WELLS FARGO & CO, 735

Equestrian Sponsors

BESSEMER TRUST, 767
BLUE RIBBON BLANKETS, 1219
BMO FINANCIAL GROUP, 726

THE EMIRATES GROUP, 733
LAS VEGAS CONVENTION & VISITORS AUTHORITY, 238
SAP AMERICA, INC., 732
USA CANOE/KAYAK, 208

Exercise/Fitness Sponsors

ASICS AMERICA CORPORATION, 1100
GNC CORPORATION, 1138

Extreme Games (X-games) Games Sponsors

MONSTER BEVERAGE CORPORATION, 730
SONY COMPUTER ENTERTAINMENT AMERICA, INC., 1191

Facility Sponsors

AMERICAN AIRLINES, 725
AMERICAN EXPRESS COMPANY, 725
ANHEUSER-BUSCH INBEV, 725
AT&T INC., 725
BANK OF AMERICA CORPORATION, 725
BELL CANADA, 725
BUDWEISER CANADA, 726
CITIGROUP, INC., 727
COCA-COLA COMPANY, 727
FEDEX CORPORATION, 728
FORD MOTOR COMPANY, 728
HONDA CANADA INC., 728
IBM, 728
J.P. MORGAN CHASE, 728
LUCAS OIL, 729
MERCEDES-BENZ USA, 730
METLIFE, 730
NRG ENERGY, 731
PAPA JOHN'S INTERNATIONAL, 731
PEPSICO, INC., 731
PNC FINANCIAL SERVICES, 731
ROGERS COMMUNICATIONS, 731
SCOTIABANK, 732
SHERWIN-WILLIAMS CO., 732
T-MOBILE USA, 733
TARGET STORES, 733
TD CANADA TRUST, 733
TELUS CORPORATION, 733
TOYOTA MOTOR SALES, U.S.A., 734
3M, 725
UNITED CONTINENTAL HOLDINGS, 734
WELLS FARGO & CO, 735
YUM! BRANDS, 735

Fishing Sponsors

AQUASPORT CORPORATION, 1099
BASS PRO SHOPS, 1217
COLEMAN COMPANY INC., 1117
FIELD & STREAM MAGAZINE, 559
TOYOTA MOTOR SALES, U.S.A., 734
WALMART INC., 734
WOOLRICH, INC., 1211
ZEBCO, 1212

Football Sponsors

ALLSTATE INSURANCE, 725
AMJ CAMPBELL, 924
ANTIGUA GROUP, INC., 1099

ARAMARK CORPORATION, 1066
AUTOTRADER.COM, INC, 673
BOSTON PIZZA, 726
COCA-COLA COMPANY, 727
CUTTER AND BUCK, INC., 1121
DIRECTV, INC., 686
EA SPORTS, 1213
GENERAL MOTORS, 728
GREATER FORT LAUDERDALE CONVENTION & VISITORS BUREAU, 234
HEALTHSOUTH REHABILITATION, 920
HOLLAND & KNIGHT, 884
J.P. WISER'S, 729
JACKSONVILLE AND THE BEACHES CONVENTION AND VISITORS BUREAU, 236
JEDC SPORTS AND ENTERTAINMENT DIVISION/JACKSONVILLE FLORIDA, 237
KIA MOTORS AMERICA, 729
LG ELECTRONICS USA, 729
MACY'S, 729
MAJESTIC ATHLETIC WEAR LIMITED, 1159
MARRIOTT INTERNATIONAL, 729
MCDONALD'S CORPORATION, 729
NATIONWIDE FINANCIAL SERVICES, 730
OLD DUTCH FOODS, 731
PEPSICO, INC., 731
REEBOK CANADA INC., 1181
SCOTIABANK, 732
SIRIUS XM RADIO, 732
ST. AUGUSTINE, PONTE VEDRA & THE BEACHES VISITORS & CONVENTION BUREAU, 246
STANLEY BLACK & DECKER, 732
SUBWAY RESTAURANTS, 733
TELUS CORPORATION, 733
TICKET760 KTKR, 635
TIM HORTONS, 733
TOOLBOX STUDIOS, 814
TOPPS COMPANY, INC., 1202
TOYOTA MOTOR SALES, U.S.A., 734
WILSON SPORTING GOODS COMPANY, 1210

Football Sponsors - National Football League

ADIDAS AMERICA, 725
ANHEUSER-BUSCH INBEV, 725
AT&T INC., 725
AUTOTRADER.COM, INC, 673
BANK OF AMERICA CORPORATION, 725
BMW OF NORTH AMERICA, LLC, 726
BOSE CORP., 726
BRIDGESTONE AMERICAS, 726
CHARTER COMMUNICATIONS, 727
CHEVRON CORPORATION, 727
COCA-COLA COMPANY, 727
DELTA AIR LINES, 727
DIRECTV, INC., 686
EA SPORTS, 1213
FEDEX CORPORATION, 728
LOWE'S, 729
MACY'S, CALIFORNIA, 1232
MARS NORTH AMERICA, 729
MCDONALD'S CORPORATION, 729
MERCEDES-BENZ USA, 730
MICROSOFT CORPORATION, 730
MILLERCOORS, 730
NESTLE USA, 730
NEW ERA CAP, CO, 730
NIKE, 730
NISSAN CANADA, 730
NRG ENERGY, 731
PAPA JOHN'S INTERNATIONAL, 731
PEPSICO, INC., 731
PNC FINANCIAL SERVICES, 731

PROCTER & GAMBLE COMPANY, 731
SAP AMERICA, INC., 732
SIRIUS XM RADIO, 732
SIRIUS XM RADIO INC., 611
SUBWAY RESTAURANTS, 733
TOPPS COMPANY, INC., 1202
TOYOTA MOTOR SALES, U.S.A., 734
3M, 725
UNITED CONTINENTAL HOLDINGS, 734
VERIZON COMMUNICATIONS, 734
VISA USA, 734
WELLS FARGO & CO, 735
YUM! BRANDS, 735

Games Sponsors

HYUNDAI MOTOR AMERICA, 728
PEPSICO, INC., 731

Golf Sponsors

AMERICAN HONDA MOTOR CO., 725
ANTIGUA GROUP, INC., 1099
ASERTA SPORTS, 1100
BEARCOM GROUP, 1105
CALLAWAY GOLF, 1113
CAPITAL ONE FINANCIAL, 726
CLEVELAND GOLF COMPANY, 1116
CLUB CAR, INC., 1117
CLUB GLOVE, 1117
COCA-COLA COMPANY, 727
CUTTER AND BUCK, INC., 1121
THE EMIRATES GROUP, 733
FOOTJOY, 1134
G III SPORTS, 1135
GOLF CLEARING HOUSE/NATIONAL GOLF SALES REPRESENTATIVES ASSOCIATION (NGSA), 101
KIA CANADA, 729
MASTERCARD, 729
NATIONWIDE FINANCIAL SERVICES, 730
PING, INC., 1174
PRICEWATERHOUSECOOPERS, 760
ROLEX WATCH USA, 732
TOP-FLITE COMPANY, 1202
WALMART INC., 734

Golf Sponsors - Champions Tour

ANHEUSER-BUSCH INBEV, 725
CLUBCORP, 100
ENTERPRISE HOLDINGS, INC., 727
IBM, 728
MASTERCARD, 729
NIKE, 730
PEPSICO, INC., 731
UNITED PARCEL SERVICE OF AMERICA, INC./UPS, 734
WELLS FARGO & CO, 735
WILSON SPORTING GOODS COMPANY, 1210

Golf Sponsors - LPGA Tour

ANHEUSER-BUSCH INBEV, 725
BEARCOM GROUP, 1105
CALLAWAY GOLF, 1113
COCA-COLA COMPANY, 727
ENTERPRISE HOLDINGS, INC., 727
IBM, 728
KIA MOTORS AMERICA, 729
PEPSICO, INC., 731

PROCTER & GAMBLE COMPANY, 731
ROLEX WATCH USA, 732
TOYOTA MOTOR SALES, U.S.A., 734
UNDER ARMOUR, 734

Golf Sponsors - PGA Tour

AMERICAN EXPRESS COMPANY, 725
ANHEUSER-BUSCH INBEV, 725
AT&T INC., 725
BMW OF NORTH AMERICA, LLC, 726
CALLAWAY GOLF, 1113
CAPITAL ONE FINANCIAL, 726
CHEVRON CORPORATION, 727
COCA-COLA COMPANY, 727
DELL TECHNOLOGIES, 727
ENTERPRISE HOLDINGS, INC., 727
G III SPORTS, 1135
HYUNDAI MOTOR AMERICA, 728
IBM, 728
MASTERCARD, 729
MERCEDES-BENZ USA, 730
METLIFE, 730
NIKE, 730
NORTHWESTERN MUTUAL LIFE, 731
PEPSICO, INC., 731
PRICEWATERHOUSECOOPERS, 760
ROCKET MORTGAGE, 731
ROLEX WATCH USA, 732
SAMSUNG ELECTRONICS NA, 732
SIRIUS XM RADIO, 732
SONY CORP. OF AMERICA, 732
SUBWAY RESTAURANTS, 733
TOP-FLITE COMPANY, 1202
TOYOTA MOTOR SALES, U.S.A., 734
3M, 725
U.S. BANCORP, 734
UNDER ARMOUR, 734
UNITED PARCEL SERVICE OF AMERICA, INC./UPS, 734
WELLS FARGO & CO, 735
WILSON SPORTING GOODS COMPANY, 1210
WORLD GOLF VILLAGE, 119
ZURICH AMERICAN INSURANCE CO., 735

Gymnastics Sponsors

OLD DUTCH FOODS, 731
VISA USA, 734

Handball Sponsors

ADIDAS AMERICA, 725

High School Sports Sponsors

RAWLINGS SPORTING GOODS COMPANY INC., 1180
SPORT CHEK, 732

Ice Hockey Sponsors

AMERICAN EXPRESS COMPANY, 725
AMERICAN SPECIALTY, 773
AMJ CAMPBELL, 924
ARAMARK CORPORATION, 1066
BAUER NIKE HOCKEY, INC., 1105
BOSTON PIZZA, 726
COCA-COLA COMPANY, 727
DODGE, 727

HONDA CANADA INC., 728
J PATTON SPORTS MARKETING, 790
JOFA HOCKEY/THE HOCKEY COMPANY, 1150
KIA CANADA, 729
MCDONALD'S CORPORATION, 729
MEIGRAY GROUP, 1233
NATIONWIDE FINANCIAL SERVICES, 730
OT SPORTS, 1172
PEPSICO, INC., 731
PRO SPECIALTIES GROUP, 1177
SAP AMERICA, INC., 732
SHERWIN-WILLIAMS CO., 732
SUBWAY RESTAURANTS, 733
TELUS CORPORATION, 733
TOPPS COMPANY, INC., 1202
TOYOTA MOTOR SALES, U.S.A., 734
VERIZON COMMUNICATIONS, 734
ZURICH AMERICAN INSURANCE CO., 735

Ice Hockey Sponsors - National Hockey League

AMERICAN HONDA MOTOR CO., 725
AMJ CAMPBELL, 924
ANHEUSER-BUSCH INBEV, 725
BOSTON PIZZA, 726
BRIDGESTONE AMERICAS, 726
CANADIAN TIRE, 726
CAPITAL ONE FINANCIAL, 726
COCA-COLA COMPANY, 727
DELTA AIR LINES, 727
DIAGEO NORTH AMERICA, 727
DRAFTKINGS, INC., 727
EA SPORTS, 1213
ENTERPRISE HOLDINGS, INC., 727
FORD MOTOR COMPANY OF CANADA, 728
HONDA CANADA INC., 728
MARRIOTT INTERNATIONAL, 729
MASTERCARD, 729
MCDONALD'S CORPORATION, 729
NATIONWIDE FINANCIAL SERVICES, 730
NEW ERA CAP, CO, 730
NORTHWESTERN MUTUAL LIFE, 731
PAPA JOHN'S INTERNATIONAL, 731
PEPSICO, INC., 731
PNC FINANCIAL SERVICES, 731
SAP AMERICA, INC., 732
SCOTIABANK, 732
SIRIUS XM RADIO, 732
SPORT CHEK, 732
SUBWAY RESTAURANTS, 733
T-MOBILE USA, 733
TD CANADA TRUST, 733
TOYOTA MOTOR SALES, U.S.A., 734
U.S. BANCORP, 734
UNDER ARMOUR, 734
VERIZON COMMUNICATIONS, 734
VISA USA, 734
WELLS FARGO & CO, 735

Inline Skating Sponsors

BAUER NIKE HOCKEY, INC., 1105

Lacrosse Sponsors

ADIDAS AMERICA, 725
MOHAWK INTERNATIONAL LACROSSE, 1163
PEPSICO, INC., 731
SUBWAY RESTAURANTS, 733
TELUS CORPORATION, 733
WELLS FARGO & CO, 735

Martial Arts Sponsors

BOSTON PIZZA, 726
LAS VEGAS CONVENTION & VISITORS AUTHORITY, 238
OKINAWAKENPODSSI.COM, 846

Media Sponsors

AUTOTRADER.COM, INC, 673
AUTOZONE, 612
BOSTON HANNAH INTERNATIONAL, 553

Motorcycle Sponsors

THE EMIRATES GROUP, 733
LAS VEGAS CONVENTION & VISITORS AUTHORITY, 238
MONSTER BEVERAGE CORPORATION, 730
OCEAN PACIFIC APPAREL CORPORATION, 1170
WELLS FARGO & CO, 735

NCAA Sponsors

ADIDAS AMERICA, 725
ALLSTATE INSURANCE, 725
AMERICAN EXPRESS COMPANY, 725
AT&T INC., 725
BURGER KING, 726
COCA-COLA COMPANY, 727
COMCAST CORPORATION, 727
HOLLAND & KNIGHT, 884
JACKSONVILLE AND THE BEACHES CONVENTION AND VISITORS BUREAU, 236
MCDONALD'S CORPORATION, 729
MERCEDES-BENZ USA, 730
MICROSOFT CORPORATION, 730
NATIONWIDE FINANCIAL SERVICES, 730
NIKE, 730
NISSAN NORTH AMERICA, 730
NORTHWESTERN MUTUAL LIFE, 731
PAPA JOHN'S INTERNATIONAL, 731
PEPSICO, INC., 731
PGA TOUR, 108
SHERWIN-WILLIAMS CO., 732
SIRIUS XM RADIO, 732
ST. AUGUSTINE, PONTE VEDRA & THE BEACHES VISITORS & CONVENTION BUREAU, 246
SUBWAY RESTAURANTS, 733
TICKET760 KTKR, 635
TOOLBOX STUDIOS, 814
TOYOTA MOTOR SALES, U.S.A., 734
UNITED PARCEL SERVICE OF AMERICA, INC./UPS, 734
VERIZON COMMUNICATIONS, 734
WELLS FARGO & CO, 735
YUM! BRANDS, 735

Olympic Sponsors

ADIDAS AMERICA, 725
AMJ CAMPBELL, 924
BELL CANADA, 725
BMW OF NORTH AMERICA, LLC, 726
BP AMERICA, 726
BRIDGESTONE AMERICAS, 726
BURTON SNOWBOARDS, 1112
CANADIAN TIRE, 726
COCA-COLA COMPANY, 727
COMCAST CORPORATION, 727
DELTA AIR LINES, 727
EA SPORTS, 1213
FOOT LOCKER, INC., 1228
GENERAL ELECTRIC, 728
THE HERSHEY CO., 733
KIA MOTORS AMERICA, 729
MONDELEZ INTERNATIONAL, 730
PROCTER & GAMBLE COMPANY, 731
SAMSUNG ELECTRONICS NA, 732
SWATCH GROUP, 733
TICKETS.COM, 933
TOYOTA MOTOR SALES, U.S.A., 734
UNITED CONTINENTAL HOLDINGS, 734
VISA USA, 734
ZURICH AMERICAN INSURANCE CO., 735

Racquetball Sponsors

EKTELON, 1128

Rodeo Sponsors

MONSTER BEVERAGE CORPORATION, 730

Rugby Sponsors

EA SPORTS, 1213
THE EMIRATES GROUP, 733
HEINEKEN USA, 728
MASTERCARD, 729
SAMSUNG ELECTRONICS NA, 732
UNDER ARMOUR, 734

Running Sponsors

ADVOCARE INTERNATIONAL, 725
ASICS AMERICA CORPORATION, 1100
BMO FINANCIAL GROUP, 726
BROOKS, 1110
DELTA AIR LINES, 727
ENTERPRISE HOLDINGS, INC., 727
FILA USA, 1132
FOOT LOCKER, INC., 1228
GNC CORPORATION, 1138
H-E-B, 1229
KAISER FOUNDATION HEALTH PLAN, 729
NISSAN NORTH AMERICA, 730
POWERCRANKS, 1176
SAUCONY, 1185
SCOTIABANK, 732
TD CANADA TRUST, 733
UNITED CONTINENTAL HOLDINGS, 734
WELLS FARGO & CO, 735

Sailing Sponsors

THE EMIRATES GROUP, 733
SAP AMERICA, INC., 732
SAUCONY, 1185
VANGUARD SAILBOATS, 1207

Shooting/Hunting Sponsors

WOOLRICH, INC., 1211

Skateboard Sponsors

MONSTER BEVERAGE CORPORATION, 730
OCEAN PACIFIC APPAREL CORPORATION, 1170
RED BULL NORTH AMERICA, 731
VANS, INC., 1240

Ski Sponsors

ATOMIC SKI USA, 1101
CANADIAN TIRE, 726
COLUMBIA SPORTSWEAR COMPANY, 1118
FILA USA, 1132
OLD DUTCH FOODS, 731
RELIABLE RACING SUPPLY, INC., 1181
SPORT CHEK, 732
VISA USA, 734

Snowboard Sponsors

BURTON SNOWBOARDS, 1112
MONSTER BEVERAGE CORPORATION, 730
OCEAN PACIFIC APPAREL CORPORATION, 1170
OLD DUTCH FOODS, 731
RED BULL NORTH AMERICA, 731
SPORT CHEK, 732
VANS, INC., 1240
VISA USA, 734

Snowmobile Sponsors

CANADIAN TIRE, 726
RED BULL NORTH AMERICA, 731

Soccer Sponsors

ADVOCARE INTERNATIONAL, 725
AMERICAN EXPRESS COMPANY, 725
AMJ CAMPBELL, 924
ANTIGUA GROUP, INC., 1099
BARCLAYS, 725
BERKSHIRE HATHAWAY, INC., 726
BURGER KING, 726
CANADIAN TIRE, 726
THE EMIRATES GROUP, 733
ENTERPRISE HOLDINGS, INC., 727
FEDEX CORPORATION, 728
FILA USA, 1132
GNC CORPORATION, 1138
HEINEKEN USA, 728
HYUNDAI MOTOR AMERICA, 728
IBM, 728
KIA CANADA, 729
KIA MOTORS AMERICA, 729
KROGER, 729
MASTERCARD, 729
MCDONALD'S CORPORATION, 729
MICROSOFT CORPORATION, 730
NESTLE USA, 730
NISSAN NORTH AMERICA, 730
PNC FINANCIAL SERVICES, 731
SAMSUNG ELECTRONICS NA, 732
SAP AMERICA, INC., 732
TARGET STORES, 733
UMBRO U.S.A., 1205
VISA USA, 734
YAHOO! SPORTS, 715

Soccer Sponsors - Major League Soccer

ADIDAS AMERICA, 725
ALLSTATE INSURANCE, 725
ANTIGUA GROUP, INC., 1099
BMO FINANCIAL GROUP, 726
DRAFTKINGS, INC., 727
KIA CANADA, 729
KROGER, 729
MONDELEZ INTERNATIONAL, 730
NRG ENERGY, 731
SAP AMERICA, INC., 732
SIRIUS XM RADIO, 732
SPORT CHEK, 732
TARGET STORES, 733
TIM HORTONS, 733
TOYOTA MOTOR SALES, U.S.A., 734
UMBRO U.S.A., 1205
VOLKSWAGEN GROUP OF AMERICA, 734
YAHOO! SPORTS, 715

Softball Sponsors

RAWLINGS SPORTING GOODS COMPANY INC., 1180
RINGOR, 1182

Special Olympics Sponsors

KIA MOTORS AMERICA, 729
MICROSOFT CORPORATION, 730
UNITED CONTINENTAL HOLDINGS, 734

Squash Sponsors

DUNLOP/MAXFLI/SLAZENGER GROUP AMERICAS, 1126
J.P. MORGAN CHASE, 728

Surfing Sponsors

OCEAN PACIFIC APPAREL CORPORATION, 1170
RED BULL NORTH AMERICA, 731
VANS, INC., 1240

Swimming Sponsors

AQUA SPHERE US, 1099
COLORADO DISPLAY SYSTEMS, 1118

Tennis Sponsors

AMERICAN EXPRESS COMPANY, 725
BMW OF NORTH AMERICA, LLC, 726
CITIGROUP, INC., 727
FILA USA, 1132
HYUNDAI MOTOR AMERICA, 728
IBM, 728
J.P. MORGAN CHASE, 728
KIA MOTORS AMERICA, 729
MASTERCARD, 729
PENN RACQUET SPORTS, 1173
PORSCHE CARS NORTH AMERICA, 1175
ROGERS COMMUNICATIONS, 731
ROLEX WATCH USA, 732
SAP AMERICA, INC., 732
WILSON SPORTING GOODS COMPANY, 1210

Track & Field Sponsors

BROOKS, 1110
FOOT LOCKER, INC., 1228
REEBOK CANADA INC., 1181
VISA USA, 734

Triathlon Sponsors

AQUA SPHERE US, 1099
CLIF BAR, 1116
IRONMAN PROPERTIES, 178
IRONMAN WETSUITS, 1148
KAISER FOUNDATION HEALTH PLAN, 729
PANAMA CITY BEACH CONVENTION & VISITORS BUREAU, INC., 243
POWERCRANKS, 1176
SAUCONY, 1185

Volleyball Sponsors

ASICS AMERICA CORPORATION, 1100
MIKASA SPORTS USA, 1163
THE ORIGINAL BALL BAG LLC, 1171
SAMSUNG ELECTRONICS NA, 732
WILSON SPORTING GOODS COMPANY, 1210

Walking Sponsors

GNC CORPORATION, 1138

Water Polo Sponsors

CAPITAL ONE FINANCIAL, 726
COLORADO TIME SYSTEMS, 1118
MIKASA SPORTS USA, 1163

Water Ski Sponsors

COLEMAN COMPANY INC., 1117

Wrestling Sponsors

ASICS AMERICA CORPORATION, 1100
LAS VEGAS CONVENTION & VISITORS AUTHORITY, 238
MONSTER BEVERAGE CORPORATION, 730
SAMSUNG ELECTRONICS NA, 732

Yacht Sponsors

NAUTICA INTERNATIONAL, 1166
SAUCONY, 1185
TOMMY HILFIGER, 1239
YAHOO! SPORTS, 715

Youth Sports Sponsors

BERKSHIRE HATHAWAY, INC., 726

DODGE, 727
LOWE'S, 729
MCDONALD'S CORPORATION, 729
SAMSUNG ELECTRONICS NA, 732
TIM HORTONS, 733

TOYOTA MOTOR SALES, U.S.A., 734

Sports-Related

3M
3M CENTER
ST. PAUL, MN 55144-1000
888-364-3577
www.3m.com
• William Brown, Chair & Chief Executive Officer
• John P. Banovetz, Exec. VP, Chief Tech. Officer
Sales:
$25,575B (2024)
Recent Sponsorships:
SkillsUSA; 3M Young Scientist Challenge - Discovery Education; NOBEL Media; University of Minnesota (3M Arena).
Golf Sponsor:
PGA 3M Open
Football Sponsor:
NFL Minnesota Vikings (Official Science Partner)

ADIDAS AMERICA
ADIDAS VILLAGE
5055 N GREELEY AVENUE
PORTLAND, OR 97217
800-982-9337
Fax: 800-982-9337
customerservice@shopadidas.com
www.adidas-group.com/en/group/headquarters
• Bjorn Gulden, Chief Executive Officer & Global Brands
• Mathieu Sidokpohou, Executive Board Member, Global Sales
Sales:
$24.7B (2024)
Recent Sponsorships:
Mercedes-AMG Petronas F1 Team; Esports World Cup (EWC)
Baseball Sponsor:
Minor League
Handball Sports:
EHF Champions League
College Sports:
NCAA Football, College Bowl
Lacrosse Sponsors:
National Lacrosse Classic; Premier Lacrosse League; Myles Jones
Soccer Sponsor:
Major League Soccer
Football Sponsor:
NFL, Indoor League

ADVOCARE INTERNATIONAL
2800 TELECOM PKWY
RICHARDSON, TX 75082
800-542-4800
www.advocare.com
• Christina Helwig, CEO
• Todd Mallon, CFO
Sales:
$75M (2024)
Recent Sponsorships:
FC Dallas; Rock 'n' Roll Running Series; Hendrick Motorsports; Mayhem Classic

ALLSTATE INSURANCE
2775 SANDERS ROAD
NORTHBROOK, IL 60062
800-255-7828
invrel@allstate.com
www.allstate.com
• Thomas J. Wilson, Chair, President & CEO

Sales:
$64.11B (2024)
Football Sponsor:
Allstate Sugar Bowl; Southeastern Conference (SEC); College Football Playoff
Soccer Sponsor:
U.S. Soccer, Major League Soccer (MLS); Mexican National Team (Federacion Mexicana de Futbol/FMF) and CONCACAF

AMERICAN AIRLINES
DALLAS-FORTH WORTH, TX
800-433-7300
www.aa.com
• Robert Isom, CEO & President
Sales:
$54.2B (2024)
Facility Sponsor:
American Airlines Center, Dallas, TX
Basketball Sponsor:
NBA Dallas Mavericks; Dallas Stars; Texas Rangers

AMERICAN EXPRESS COMPANY
WORLD FINANCIAL CENTER
200 VESEY STREET
NEW YORK, NY 10285-3106
1-800-869-3016
www.americanexpress.com
• Stephen Squeri, Chairman & CEO
Sales:
$65.9B (2024)
Basketball Sponsor:
NBA Boston Celtics; Brooklyn Nets; Chicago Bulls; Los Angeles Lakers; and Miami Heat.
Facility Sponsor:
American Express community stadium, Falmer, UK; Staples Center; United Center
Tennis Sponsor:
US Open;
Soccer Sponsor:
MLS Los Angeles Galaxy, Real Salt Lake
Hockey Sponsor:
NHL Chicago Blackhawks, Los Angeles Kings
Golf Sponsor:
PGA of America

AMERICAN HONDA MOTOR CO.
1919 TORRANCE BLVD
TORRANCE, CA 90501-2746
800-999-1009
Fax: 310-783-3023
www.honda.com
• Kazuhiro Takizawa, President & CEO, Honda Motor Co.
• Toshiaki Mikoshiba, Chairman & CEO, American Honda Motor Co.
Sales:
$138.25B (2024)
Baseball Sponsor:
Little League Baseball & Softball; Toronto Blue Jays
Golf Sponsor:
The Honda Classic
Ice Hockey Sponsor:
NHL; Hockey Hall of Fame

ANHEUSER-BUSCH INBEV
250 PARK AVE
NEW YORK, NY 10177
800-342-5283
Fax: 314-577-2900
media.relations@ab-inbev.com
www.anheuser-busch.com
• Michel Doukeris, CEO

Sales:
$59.768B (2024)
Baseball Sponsor:
MLB; Minor; Busch Stadium
Basketball Sponsor:
NBA
College Sponsor:
NCAA; College Bowl
Football Sponsor:
NFL
Golf Sponsor:
PGA
Hockey Sponsor:
NHL

AT&T INC.
208 S AKARD STREET
DALLAS, TX 75202
210-821-4105
www.att.com
• John T. Stankey, CEO
Sales:
$122.3B (2024)
Golf Sponsor:
PGA
College Sponsor:
NCAA
Facility Sponsor:
AT&T Center; AT&T Stadium; Jones AT&T Stadium; AT&T Performing Arts Center
Basketball Sponsor:
NBA; WNBA
Football Sponsor:
NFL, Dalls Cowboys home stadium

BANK OF AMERICA CORPORATION
100 NORTH TRYON STREET
CHARLOTTE, NC 28202
www.bankofamerica.com
• Brian Moynihan, Chairman & CEO
• Dean Athanasia, President, Regional Banking
• Paul M. Donofrio, Vice Chair
• Alastair Borthwick, Chief Financial Officer
• Geoffrey S. Greener, Chief Risk Officer
Sales:
$101.89B (2024)
Auto Sports Sponsor:
NASCAR
Football Sponsor:
NFL; Bank of America Stadium
Basketball Sponsor:
WNBA; NBA
College Sponsor:
NCAA; College Bowl; NCAA Bank of America Arena at Hec Edmundson Pavilion
Running Sponsor:
Bank of America Chicago Marathon

BARCLAYS
125 S WEST S
WILMINGTON, DE 19801
www.barclays.com
• Nigel Higgins, Group Chairman
• C.S. Venkatakrishnan, Group CEO
Sales
$35M-$40M
Soccer Sponsor:
Barclays FA Women's Super League; Premier League

BELL CANADA
1 CARREFOUR
ALEXANDER-GRAHAM-BELL
BUILDING A, 4TH FLOOR
VERDUN, QC, CANADA H3E 3B3

1-888-932-6666
Fax: 514-766-5735
bcecomms@bce.ca
www.bce.ca
• Mirko Bibic, President & CEO, BCE and
Bell Canada
Basketball Sponsor:
Toronto Raptors
Facility Sponsor:
TIFF Bell Lightbox
Other:
Canadian Olympic/Paralympic Committees,
Bell Let's Talk, TIFF

BERKSHIRE HATHAWAY, INC.
3555 FARNAM STREET
OMAHA, NE 68131
www.berkshirehathaway.com
• Warren E. Buffett, Chief Executive Officer
Sales:
$608.77B (2024)
Sponsor:
Pennsauken Youth Soccer Club

BMO FINANCIAL GROUP
100 KING ST WEST
TORONTO, ON, CANADA M5X 1A1
1-844-837-9228
www.bmo.com
• Darryl White, Chief Executive Officer
Soccer Sponsor:
MLS (Vancouver Whitecaps; Toronto FC;
CF Montreal)
Other:
Calgary Stampede, Stratford Festival,
Canada Army Run; Pride & Remembrance
Run; Navy Bike Ride; Royal Manitoba
Winter Fair; Canadian Western Agribition;
Farmfair International; Banff Marathon;
Orchestre Symphonique de Montreal,
Toronto Argos; The Santa Claus Parade;
BMO International Film Festival of South
Asia; Walk so Kids Can Talk; International
Plowing Match and Rural Expo (IPM); BMO
Vancouver Marathon; BMO Nations' Cup
and Equestrian Sport

BMW OF NORTH AMERICA, LLC
300 CHESTNUT RIDGE ROAD
WOODCLIFF LAKE, NJ 07677-7731
1-800-831-1117
www.bmwusa.com
• Sebastian Mackensen, President & CEO
  ext 4232
Total Spend:
$25M-$30M
Tennis Sponsor:
BMW Malaysian Open
Golf Sponsor:
PGA Tour BMW Championship
Sponsor:
U.S Olympic Committee, U.S Paralympics,
U.S Speedskating, USA Bobsled and
Skeleton, USA Swimming, USA Track and
Field
Football Sponsor:
NFL Atlanta Falcons, Houston Texans

BOSE CORP.
THE MOUNTAIN RD
FRAMINGHAM, MA 01701
508-879-7330
1-800-869-2114
www.bose.com
• Lila Snyder, Chief Executive Officer

Sales:
$3B (2023)
Football Sponsor:
NFL
Auto Motorsports Sponsor:
Formula 1; Mercedes-AMG Petronas
Motorsport
Sponsor:
261 Fearless

BOSTON PIZZA
85 PROLOGIS BLVD, UNIT 4
MISSISSAUGA, ON, CANADA L5W 0G4
905-848-2700
bostonpizza.com
• Jim Treliving, Chairman
• Michael Harbinson, President
Baseball Sponsor:
Toronto Blue Jays
Hockey Sponsor:
AHL, Hockey Canada, OHL, NHL (Calgary
Flames; Edmonton Oilers; Vancouver
Canucks; Winnipeg Jets), WHL
Other:
UFC

BP AMERICA
4101 WINFIELD RD
WARRENVILLE, IL 60555
281-366-2000
800-333-3991
bpconsumer@bp.com
www.bp.com
• Murray Auchincloss, Chief Executive
Officer
• Gordon Birrell, EVP, Production &
Operations
Sales:
$194.629B (2024)
Baseball Sponsor:
MLB Seattle Mariners.
Sponsor:
U.S Olympic Committee; U.S Paralympics;
BP MS 150 Bike Ride

BRIDGESTONE AMERICAS
200 4TH AVENUE S
NASHVILLE, TN 37201
615-937-1000
800-543-7522
Fax: 615-937-3621
www.bridgestoneamericas.com
• Paolo Ferrari, President and CEO,
Bridgestone Americas
• Scott Damon, Chief Operating Officer
Sales:
$6.3B (2024)
Sports Sponsorships:
Worldwide Olympic and Paralympic Games;
NFL; NHL; Bridgestone Arena.
Motorsports Sponsor:
Bridgestone World Solar Challenge (WSC);
Fireston Racing
Motor Show Sponsor:
Global Auto Show
Other Sponsors:
Rock the Crop Concert Sweepstakes.

BUDWEISER CANADA
207 QUEEN'S QUAY WEST
SUITE 299
TORONTO, ON, CANADA M5J 1A7
416-361-5050
800-268-2337
Fax: 416-361-5200
www.budweiser.ca

• Marcelo Michaelis, President, Labatt
Canada
Other:
Budweiser Stage (Ontario Place)

BURGER KING
5505 BLUE LAGOON DR
MIAMI, FL 33126
866-394-2493
www.bk.com
• Tom Curtis, President
Sales:
$1.3B (2023)
Sponsorships:
Stevenage Football Club (EFL); FIFA;
NCAA

CANADIAN TIRE
2180 YONGE STREET
TORONTO, ON, CANADA M4P 2V8
416-480-3000
Fax: 416-480-3970
www.canadiantire.ca
• Greg Hicks, President & CEO
• Darren Myers, CPA, CMA, Exec.
Vice-Pres. & CFO
• Susan O'Brien, Chief Brand & Customer
Officer
Auto Sports Sponsor:
NASCAR
Hockey Sponsor:
NHL
Amateur Sport Sponsor:
Canadian Olympic/Paralympic Committee,
Canadian Soccer Association, Skate
Canada, Hockey Canada, Alpine Canada,
Canada Snowboard
Other:
Canadian Tire Jumpstart Charities;
Canadian Sports Hall of Fame; Canada
Games

CAPITAL ONE FINANCIAL
1680 CAPITAL ONE DRIVE
MCLEAN, VA 22102
703-448-3747
877-383-4802
www.capitalone.com
• Richard D. Fairbank, Chairman & CEO
Sales:
$10.2B (2024)
Recent Sponsorships:
Capital One Orange Bowl
Baseball Sponsor:
Major League Baseball (MLB).
Basketball Sponsor:
NBA New Orleans Hornets, Washington
Wizards, Capital One Arena; Women's
Basketball Coaches Association
College Sponsor:
Capital One Cup; College Football Playoff
Hockey Sponsor:
NHL Washington Capitals
Curling Sponsor:
Capital One Cup (curling), Capital One
Grand Slam of Curling, ASHAM World
Curling Tour
Sponsor:
USA Water Polo

CATERPILLAR INC.
510 LAKE COOK RD
SUITE 100
DEERFIELD, IL 60015
309-675-2337
www.cat.com

• Jim Umpleby, Chairman and CEO
Sales:
$64.8B (2024)
Motorsports Sponsor:
NASCAR

CHARTER COMMUNICATIONS
400 WASHINGTON BLVD
STAMFORD, CT 06902
203-905-7800
888-438-2427
corporate.charter.com
• Chris Winfrey, Chairman and CEO
• Jessica Fischer, Chief Financial Officer
Sales:
$55.5B (2024)
Auto Sports Sponsor:
NASCAR, IndyCar, NHRA
Sponsor:
NBA Los Angeles Lakers and Sparks.

CHEVRON CORPORATION
6001 BOLLINGER CANYON ROAD
SAN RAMON, CA 94583
925-842-1000
www.chevron.com
• Michael K. Wirth, Chairman and CEO
Sales:
$196.9B (2024)
Golf Sponsor:
Ladies Professional Golf Association
(LPGA)
Baseball Sponsor:
Minor League. MLB Atlanta Braves, San
Francisco Giants
Sponsor:
NFL Tampa Bay Buccaneers, Denver
Broncos, New Orleans Saints.
Basketball Sponsor:
NBA Los Angeles Lakers, New Orleans
Pelicans.
Endurance Sports Sponsor:
Chevron Houston Marathon

CITIGROUP, INC.
388 GREENWICH ST
NEW YORK, NY 10013
800-285-3000
Sponsorship@citi.com
www.citigroup.com
• Jane Fraser, Chief Executive Officer,
Citigroup
Sales:
$81.1B (2024)
Recent Sponsorships:
Ryder Cup; Aston Martin's F1 team;
ATP/WTA tennis event.
Facility Sponsor:
Citi Field, New York, NY - MLB New York
Mets

COCA-COLA COMPANY
ONE COCA-COLA PLAZA
ATLANTA, GA 30313
800-438-2653
www.coca-colacompany.com
• James Quincey, CEO
• Henrique Braun, President and COO
Sales:
$47.06B (2024)
Auto Sports Sponsor:
NASCAR
College Sponsor:
NCAA
Basketball Sponsor:
NBA; WNBA

Golf Sponsor:
PGA; LPGA
Hockey Sponsor:
NHL
Other Sponsors:
American Idol; BET Network; Olympic
Games
Canadian Sponsors:
Canadian Olympic Committee (Team
Canada); Canada Soccer; Calgary Flames
(NHL); Montreal Canadiens (NHL); Ottawa
Senators (NHL); Special Olympics Canada;
Toronto Blue Jays (MLB); Toronto Football
Club (MLS); Toronto Maple Leafs (NHL);
Toronto Marlies (AHL); Toronto Raptors
(NBA); Winnipeg Jets (NHL)

COMCAST CORPORATION
COMCAST CENTER
1701 JOHN F. KENNEDY BOULEVARD
PHILADELPHIA, PA 19103
corporate.comcast.com
• Brian L. Roberts, Chair & CEO
• Michael J. Cavanagh, President
• Jason S. Armstrong, Chief Financial
Officer
• Dalila Wilson Scott, EVP & Chief Diversity
Officer
Sales:
$123.7B (2024)
Recent Sponsorships:
USA Olympic Team (LA28)
College Sponsor:
NCAA; College Bowl; March Madness
Baseball Sponsor:
MLB Chicago Cubs, Chicago White Sox
Basketball Sponsor:
NBA
Hockey Sponsor:
NHL

DELL TECHNOLOGIES
ONE DELL WAY
ROUND ROCK, TX 78682
investor_relations@dell.com
www.dell.com
• Michael S. Dell, Chair & CEO
• Bill Scannell, President, Global Sales &
Customer Operations
Sales:
$88.4B (2024)
Recent Sponsorships:
McLaren Automotive
Golf Sponsor:
PGA Tour

DELTA AIR LINES
1030 DELTA BLVD
ATLANTA, GA 30320-6001
404-715-2600
800-221-1212
www.delta.com
• Ed Bastian, Chief Executive Officer
• Glen W. Hauenstein, President
Sales:
$61.6B (2024)
Recent Sponsorships:
Olympic Games (Team USA; LA28);
Paralympic Games
Golf Sponsors:
LPGA
Baseball Sponsor:
NY Mets
Basketball Sponsor:
NBA; LA Lakers; WNBA
College Sponsor:
NCAA

Football Sponsor:
NFL
Hockey Sponsor:
NHL

DIAGEO NORTH AMERICA
396 ALHAMBRA CIRCLE
CORAL GABLES, FL 33134
203-229-2100
www.diageo.com
• Debra Crew, Chief Executive Officer
• Sally Grimes, President, North America
Sales:
$20.269B (2024)
Football Sponsor:
NFL

DODGE
1000 CHRYSLER DRIVE
AUBURN HILLS, MI 48326
248-576-5741
Fax: 248-512-1811
www.dodge.ca
• Matt McAlear, Brand CEO
Other:
Dodge Caravan Kids (hockey)

DRAFTKINGS, INC.
222 BERKELEY ST
5TH FLOOR
BOSTON, MA 02116
support@draftkings.com
www.draftkings.com
• Jason Robins, Chief Executive Officer &
Co-Founder
• Matt Kalish, President, DraftKings North
America & Co-Founder
Sales:
$4.77B (2024)
Sponsor:
Boston Red Sox-MLB; MLS; NASCAR;
NHL; CFL; PGA; WNBA; UFC

ENTERPRISE HOLDINGS, INC.
600 CORPORATE PARK DR
ST. LOUIS, MO 63105
855-266-9565
www.enterprise.com
• Chrissy Taylor, President & Chief
Executive Officer
• Andrew C. Taylor, Executive Chair
Sales:
$35B (2023)
Transportation Sponsor:
Disney
Soccer Sponsor:
UEFA Europa League
College Sponsor:
NCAA
Golf Sponsor:
DP World Tour
Hockey Sponsor:
NHL

EXXON MOBIL CORPORATION
3525 DECKER DR
BAYTOWN, TX 77520
972-940-6000
www.exxonmobil.com
• Darren W. Woods, Chairman and CEO
• Neil A. Chapman, Senior Vice President
• Kathryn A. Mikells, Senior Vice President
& Chief Financial Officer
• Jack P. Williams, Senior Vice President
Sales:
$349.6B (2024)

Recent Sponsorships:
NBA; WNBA
Auto Sports Sponsor:
NASCAR

FCA US, LLC
1000 CHRYSLER DRIVE
AUBURN HILLS, MI 48326
800-247-9753
www.chrysler.com
• Christine Feuell, CEO
• Carlos Zarlenga, COO, North America
Sales:
$5.9B (2024)
Recent Sponsorships:
Formula 1.

FEDEX CORPORATION
3650 HACKS CROSS RD
MEMPHIS, TN 38125
901-369-3600
800-463-3339
www.fedex.com
• Frederick W. Smith, Founder, Chairman & CEO
• Raj Subramaniam, President and COO
• John W. Dietrich, Executive Vice President & CFO
Sales:
$87B (2024)
Soccer Sponsors:
UEFA Champions League
Football Sponsor;
NFL.
Facility Sponsor:
Fedex Forum (Memphis, TN)
Auto Sports Sponsor:
NASCAR

FORD MOTOR COMPANY
1 AMERICAN ROAD
DEARBORN, MI 48126
1-800-392-3673 (US)
1-800-565-3673 (CAN)
www.ford.com
• Jim Farley, CEO
• William Clay Ford, Executive Chair
Sales:
$185B (2024)
Facility Sponsor:
Ford Field, Detroit, MI; Ford Center, Evansville, IN

FORD MOTOR COMPANY OF CANADA
THE CANADIAN ROAD
P.O. BOX 2000
OAKVILLE, ON, CANADA L6J 5E4
www.ford.ca
• Bev Goodman, President and CEO
Basketball Sponsor:
Toronto Raptors
Hockey Sponsor:
Toronto Maple Leafs

GENERAL ELECTRIC
1 NEUMANN WAY
CINCINNATI, OH 45215
407-378-6203
www.ge.com
• H. Lawrence Culp, Jr., Chairman & CEO
Sales:
$68B (2023)
Motorsports Sponsor:
Formula 1
Other:
Olympic Games

GENERAL MOTORS
100 RENAISSANCE CTR
DETROIT, MI 48243
www.gm.com
• Mary T. Barra, Chair and CEO
• Daniel E. Berce, Sr. VP & President/CEO, GM Financial
• Marissa West, EVP & President, North America
• Arden Hoffman, SVP, Global Human Resources
• Gerald Johnson, EVP, Global Manufacturing & Sustainability
• Tony Cervone, SVP, Global Communications
Sales:
$267.92B (2024)
Recent Sponsorships:
Southwestern Athletic Conference (2021-2024); 48th annual Bayour Classic, New Orleans (football)

GOODYEAR TIRE & RUBBER CO., THE
200 INNOVATION WAY
AKRON, OH 44316
330-796-2121
800-321-2136
Fax: 330-796-2222
corporate.goodyear.com
• Mark Stewart, Chairman, CEO and President
• Ryan Waldron, President, Americas
Sales:
$18.9B (2024)
Recent Sponsorships:
NCAA Goodyear Cotton Bowl.
Auto Sports Sponsor:
NASCAR; NHRA
Baseball Sponsor:
Goodyear Ballpark, Phoenix, AZ.

HEINEKEN USA
360 HAMILTON AVE
SUITE 1103
WHITE PLAINS, NY 10601
914-681-4100
www.heinekenusa.com
• Maggie Timoney, President and CEO
• Marc Busain, President Americas
Sales:
$32.6B (2024)
Soccer Sponsor:
UEFA Champions League
Rudgy Sponsor:
Rugby World Cups
Golf Sponsor:
PGA
Auto Motorsports Sponsor:
Formula 1, Formula E

HILTON HOTELS
7930 JONES BRANCH DR
MCLEAN, VA 22102
703-883-1000
1-800-HILTONS
Fax: 310-205-7880
www.hilton.com
• Christopher J. Nassetta, President and CEO
christopher.nassetta@hilton.com
Sales:
$16.5B (2024)
Motorsports Sponsor:
McLaren-Honda (Formula 1)

HONDA CANADA INC.
180 HONDA BLVD
MARKHAM, ON, CANADA L6C 0H9
888-946-6329
www.honda.ca
• Jean Marc Leclerc, President & CEO
Auto Sports Sponsor:
Honda Indy (Toronto)
Hockey Sponsor:
NHL
Other:
Hockey Hall of Fame, Make-A-Wish Canada

HYUNDAI MOTOR AMERICA
10550 TALBERT AVENUE
FOUNTAIN VALLEY, CA 92708
800-633-5151
consumeraffairs@hmausa.com
www.hyundaiusa.com
• Jose Munoz, President & CEO, Hyundai Motor North America
Sales:
$122.1B (2024)
Recent Sponsorships:
SoFi Stadium (Hollywood Park - Los Angeles Rams and Los Angeles Chargers).
Archery Sponsor:
Korea Archery Association since 1985
Soccer Sponsor:
FIFA World Cup since 2002
Auto Motor Sponsor:
World Rally Championship (WRC) since 2014
Tennis Sponsor:
Australian Open

IBM
NEW ORCHARD ROAD
ARMONK, NY 10504
914-499-1900
800-426-4968
Fax: 914-765-6021
www.ibm.com
• Arvind Krishna, Chairman & CEO
Sales:
$62.75B (2024)
Golf Sponsor:
The PGA Masters; Augusta National Women's Amateur
Tennis Sponsor:
US Open; Wimbleton
Facility Sponsor:
Mercedes-Benz Stadium, Atlanta, GA
Soccer Sponsor:
MLS Los Angeles FC

J.P. MORGAN CHASE
270 PARK AVE
FLOOR 34
NEW YORK, NY 10017-2014
212-270-6000
www.jpmorganchase.com
• Jamie Dimon, Chairman and CEO
• Mary Callahan Erdoes, CEO, Asset and Wealth Management
• Douglas B. Petno, CEO, Commercial Banking
Sales:
$162.4B (2024)
Recent Sponsorships:
MSG Sports; MSG Entertainment; US Open Tennis (extension)
Squash Sponsor:
Tournament of Champions
Tennis Sponsor:
US Open Tennis Championships
Facility Sponsor:

Lord's Cricket Ground, London; Amalie Arena, Tampa, FL; Amway Center, Orlando, FL

J.P. WISER'S
225 KING ST W
SUITE 1100
TORONTO, ON, CANADA M5V 3M2
416-479-2400
www.jpwisers.com
• Nicolas Krantz, President & Chief Executive Officer
Other:
ESPN Fantasy Football, Women of Influence

KAISER FOUNDATION HEALTH PLAN
1 KAISER PLAZA
OAKLAND, CA 94612
510-271-5800
Fax: 510-271-6493
healthy.kaiserpermanente.org
• Gregory A. Adams, Chair & CEO
Sales:
$100.8B (2023)
Basketball Sponsor:
NBA; WNBA; NBA D-League; USA Basketball

KIA CANADA
180 FOSTER CRESCENT
MISSISSAUGA, ON, CANADA L5R 4J5
905-755-6250
877-542-2886
Fax: 866-267-7424
www.kia.ca
• Sungwon Kwon, President & CEO
Soccer Sponsor:
FIFA, Toronto FC
Hockey Sponsor:
CHL (Saint John Sea Dogs, 2022 Memorial Cup)
Athlete Sponsor:
David Hearn (PGA)
Other:
Special Olympics

KIA MOTORS AMERICA
111 PETERS CANYON ROAD
IRVINE, CA 92606
949-468-4800
888-542-6334
Fax: 949-468-4515
kiamedia.com
• Sean Yoon, President and CEO
• Eric Watson, VP, Sales Operations
Recent Sponsorships:
Olympic Games, 2018; Special Olympics, 2018; Summer Olympics, 2024
Basketball Sponsor:
NBA; Kia NBA Tip-Off; Kia All-Star MVP; Kia NBA Performance Awards; WNBA
College Sports Sponsor:
College Football Hall of Fame
Soccer Sponsor:
FIFA World Cup; UEFA Europa League; MLS
Tennis Sponsor:
Australian Open

KROGER
1014 VINE STREET
CINCINNATI, OH 45202-1100
513-762-4000
www.thekrogerco.com
• Rodney McMullen, CEO

Sales:
$150B (2023)
Recent Sponsorships:
FC Cincinnati (MLS)
Auto Sports Sponsor:
NASCAR, Indy Racing

LG ELECTRONICS USA
201 JAMES RECORD RD SW
HUNTSVILLE, AL 35824
201-816-2000
800-243-0000
Fax: 201-816-0636
www.lg.com
• Thomas Yoon, CEO, LG Electronics North America
Recent Sponsorships:
NCAA; Turner Sports; CBS Sports; FA (Football Association)
Basketball Sponsor:
Los Angeles Lakers, Toronto Raptors
Hockey Sponsor:
Toronto Maple Leafs, Toronto Marlies (AHL)
Soccer Sponsor:
Toronto FC, English Premier League

LOWE'S
1000 LOWE'S BLVD
MOORESVILLE, NC 28117
704-758-2917
800-445-6937
800-985-6937
community@lowes.com
www.lowes.com
• Marvin R. Ellison, President and CEO
• Brandon Sink, Chief Financial Officer
• Tony Cioffi, President and CEO, Canada
Sales:
$86.38B (2023)
Sponsor:
Boys & Girls Club of America; NFL; NBA; MLS

LUCAS OIL
3610 RIVER CROSSING PKWY
INDIANAPOLIS, IN 46240
951-270-0154
800-342-2512
Fax: 951-270-1902
lucasoil.com
• Lucas Forrest, Founder, President & CEO
Facility Sponsor:
Lucas Oil Stadium (Indianapolis)
Motorsports Sponsor:
Eight racing series, Lucas Oil Speedway (Missouri)

MACY'S
151 W 34TH ST
NEW YORK, NY 10001
513-579-7000
Fax: 513-579-7555
www.macys.com
• Tony Spring, President & CEO
• Adrian V. Mitchell, Chief Financial Officer
Sales:
$25.3B (2023)
Event Sponsor:
Macy's Thanksgiving Day Parade; SEC football

MARRIOTT INTERNATIONAL
7750 WISCONSIN AVENUE
BETHESDA, MD 20814

301-380-3000
www.marriott.com
• Anthony Capuano, President & CEO
• Leeny Oberg, Chief Financial Officer
Sales:
$25.1B (2024)
Recent Sponsorships:
FC Bayern; NHL Toronto Maple Leafs

MARS NORTH AMERICA
6885 ELM STREET
MCLEAN, VA 22101
703-821-4900
www.mars.com
• Poul Weihrauch, CEO
• Loic Moutault, President, Global Petcare
• Claus Aagaard, Chief Financial Officer
• Stephanie Straub, Vice President & General Counsel
• Rebecca Snow, Vice President, People & Organization
Sales:
$50B (2024)
Recent Sponsorships:
MLB Washington Nationals
Football Sponsor:
NFL

MASTERCARD
2000 PURCHASE ST
PURCHASE, NY 10577
914-249-2000
www.mastercard.com
• Michael Miebach, CEO
• Linda Kirkpatrick, President, North America
Sales:
$28.2B (2024)
Recent Sponsorships:
Rugby World Cup
Soccer Sponsor:
UEFA Champions League; Brazilian National Team; Boca Juniors (Argentina); River Plate (Argentina); NYC Football Club
Golf Sponsor:
PGA TOUR; APGA TOUR; Open Championship
Baseball Sponsor:
MLB; MLB Advanced Media; MLB Boston Red Sox, Chicago Cubs, Los Angeles Dodgers, New York Yankees
Hockey Sponsor:
NHL Montreal Canadiens, Toronto Maple Leafs
Tennis Sponsor:
The Miami Open; The Australian Open

MCDONALD'S CORPORATION
110 N CARPENTER ST
CHICAGO, IL 60607
corporate.mcdonalds.com
• Chris Kempczinski, President & CEO
• Joe Erlinger, President, McDonald's USA
• Katie Beirne Fallon, EVP & Chief Global Impact Officer
• Mark Ostermann, VP, Strategic Alignment & Chief of Staff
• Ian Borden, Chief Financial Officer
• Morgan Flatley, Global Chief Marketing Officer
• Heidi Capozzi, Exec. VP & Global Chief People Officer
Sales:
$25.49B (2023)
Recent Sponsorships:
23XI Racing (2022)
Basketball Sponsor:

Maine McDonald's All-Star Basketball Games; All American Games
Football Sponsor:
NFL
Ice Hockey Sponsor:
NHL; AtoMc (minor hockey)
College Sports Sponsor:
NCAA, Bowl Games
Baseball Sponsor:
MLB, Minor League

MERCEDES-BENZ USA
303 PERIMETER CENTER NORTH
ATLANTA, GA 30346
www.mbusa.com
• Dmitris Psillakis, President & CEO
Recent Sponsorships:
Mercedes-Benz Stadium, Atlanta, GA, 2018;
Mercedes-Benz Dealer Championships
Baseball Sponsor:
Minor League
Golf Sponsor:
PGA Championship
Football Sponsor:
NFL
College Sponsor:
NCAA, Bowl Games

METLIFE
METLIFE BUILDING
200 PARK AVENUE
NEW YORK, NY 10166
www.metlife.com
• Michael A. Khalaf, CEO
Sales:
$14.5B (2024)
Golf Sponsor:
PGA; Metlife MatchUp Houston Open
Baseball Sposnor:
MLB
Facility Sponsor:
MetLife Stadium; NFL New York Giants,
New York Jets

MICROSOFT CORPORATION
ONE MICROSOFT WAY
REDMOND, WA 98052
425-882-8080
Fax: 425-706-7329
www.microsoft.com
• Satya Nadella, Chief Executive Officer
• Brad Smith, President and Chief Legal Officer
Sales:
$245.12B (2024)
Recent Sponsorships:
Special Olympics; Women's Soccer, Seattle Reign FC
College Sports Sponsor:
NCAA, March Madness
Auto Sports Sponsor:
NASCAR
Football Sponsor:
NFL

MILLERCOORS
250 S WACKER DRIVE
CHICAGO, IL 60606
info@molsoncoors.com
www.millercoors.com
• Gavin Hattersley, President & Chief Executive Officer
• Kevin Doyle, President, Sales & Distributor Operations
Sales:
$13.7B (2024)

Recent Sponsorships:
Dallas Cowboys (NFL; extension)
Baseball Sponsor:
MLB - Colorado Rockies
Basketball Sponsor:
NBA

MONDELEZ INTERNATIONAL
905 WEST FULTON MARKET
SUITE 200
CHICAGO, IL 60607
847-943-4000
www.mondelezinternational.com
• Dirk Van de Put, Chief Executive Officer
Sales:
$36.4B (2024)
Recent Sponsorships:
NBA; Olympic Games (Team USA)
Soccer Sponsor:
MLS

MONSTER BEVERAGE CORPORATION
1 MONSTER WAY
CORONA, CA 92879
866-322-4466
info@monsterbevcorp.com
www.monsterbevcorp.com
• Hilton Schlosberg, Chairman and CEO
Sales:
$1.81B (2024)
Recent Sponsorships:
Monster Energy Cup Series; Monster Energy Boarderstyle Tour; PBR Monster Energy Tour; Monster Energy AMA Supercross
Auto Motorsports Sponsor:
NASCAR
Sponsor:
Ultimate Fighting Championship (UFC)

NATIONWIDE FINANCIAL SERVICES
1 NATIONWIDE
COLUMBUS, OH 43210
1-877-669-6877
www.nationwide.com
• Kirt Walker, Chief Executive Officer
• Tim Frommeyer, Executive Vice President & Chief Financial Officer
Sales:
$60.3B (2023)
Golf Sponsor:
Memorial Tournament
Running Sponsor:
Nationwide Better Health Columbus Marathon
Baseball Sponsor:
Minor League, Columbus Clippers
College Sponsor:
Central Intercollegiate Athletic Association Tournament; Ohio State University athletics
Football Sponsor:
NFL
Hockey Sponsor:
NHL, Columbus Blue Jackets

NESTLE USA
1812 NORTH MOORE ST
ARLINGTON, VA 22209
1-800-225-2270
www.nestleusa.com
• Martin Thompson, CEO, Nestle USA
Sales:
$101.4B (2024)
Baseball Sponsor:
MLB
Basketball Sponsor:

NBA
Football Sponsor:
NFL
Soccer Sponsor:
Manchester City F.C. (Premier League)

NEW ERA CAP, CO
160 DELAWARE AVENUE
BUFFALO, NY 14202
716-604-9193
877-632-5950
Fax: 716-604-9299
www.neweracap.com
• Christopher H. Koch, CEO
Sales:
$2B (2024)
Recent Sponsorships:
Schmidt Peterson Motorsports; NBA Brooklyn Nets
Auto Motor Sponsor:
IndyCar
Baseball Sponsor:
MLB; Minor League
Hockey Sponsor:
NHL
Basketbal Sponsor:
NBA
Football Sponsor:
NFL

NIKE
1 BOWERMAN DR
BEAVERTON, OR 97005
503-671-6453
800-344-6453
www.nike.com
• Elliot Hill, Chief Executive Officer
• Philip H. Knight, Chairman Emeritus
• Mark Parker, Executive Chairman
Sales:
$51.36B (2024)
Baseball Sponsor:
MLB
Basketball Sponsor:
NBA; WNBA; NBA D-League; FIBA
Running Sponsor:
Bank of America Chicago Marathon
Football Sponsor:
NFL
Golf Sponsor:
PGA; Champions Tour; LPGA

NISSAN CANADA
5290 ORBITOR DRIVE
MISSISSAUGA, ON, CANADA L4W 4Z5
800-387-0122
www.nissan.ca
• Trevor Longley, President
Auto Sports Sponsor:
Nissan Micra Cup
Football Sponsor:
NFL

NISSAN NORTH AMERICA
ONE NISSAN WAY
FRANKLIN, TN 37067
615-725-1000
800-647-7261
www.nissanusa.com
• Jeremie Papin, Senior Vice President, CFO
Sales:
$66.1B (2024)
Recent Sponsorships:
Univision Deports/Mexican National Team; London Marathon

Auto Motor Sponsor:
Pirelli World Challenge
College Sponsor:
NCAA; College Bowl
Endurance Sports Sponsor:
Marine Corps Marathon

NORTHWESTERN MUTUAL LIFE
720 E WISCONSIN AVE
MILWAUKEE, WI 53202-4797
414-271-1444
866-950-4644
www.northwesternmutual.com
• Jim Gerend, President and CEO
Sales:
$38B (2024)
College Sports Sponsor:
NCAA
Golf Sponsor:
PGA Champion Tour
Hockey Sponsor:
NHL St. Louis Blues

NRG ENERGY
910 LOUISIANA ST
HOUSTON, TX 77002
713-537-3000
www.nrg.com
• Laurence S. Coben, President & CEO
Sales:
$28.13B (2024)
Recent Sponsorships:
Coachella Valley Music & Arts Festival
Basketball Sponsor:
NBA (2)
Facility Sponsor:
NRG Stadium (Houston, NFL)
Football Sponsor:
NFL (8)
Soccer Sponsor:
MLS (2)

OLD DUTCH FOODS
100 BENTALL ST
WINNIPEG, MB 55113
800-351-2447
www.olddutchfoods.ca
• Steve Aanenson, President
Sales:
$130M (2024)
Football Sponsor:
Winnipeg Blue Bombers
Other:
MS Society Ontario; The Outdoor Adventure
& Travel Show; World Ski & Snowboard
Festival

ORACLE CORPORATION
2300 ORACLE WAY
AUSTIN, TX 78741
800-392-2999
www.oracle.com
• Lawrence J. Ellison, Co-Founder,
Executive Chairman & CTO
• Safra A. Catz, Chief Executive Officer
Sales:
$53B (2024)
Sponsor:
F1

PAPA JOHN'S INTERNATIONAL
2002 PAPA JOHN'S BLVD
LOUISVILLE, KY 40299
www.papajohns.com
• Todd Penegor, President & Chief
Executive Officer

Sales:
$4.85B (2024)
Recent Sponsorships
Ending official sponsorship of the NFL, but
will continue sponsoring NFL teams locally;
EFL
Baseball Sponsor:
MLB
Basketball Sponsor:
NBA and WNBA
College Sponsor:
NCAA; March Madness
College Bowl Games Sponsor:
Sheraton Hawai'i Bowl, Texas Bowl
Facility Sponsor:
NCAA Papa John's Cardinal Stadium,
Louisville, KY
Hockey Sponsor:
NHL Tampa Bay Lightning

PEPSICO, INC.
700 ANDERSON HILL RD
PURCHASE, NY 10577
914-253-2000
800-433-2652
www.pepsico.com
• Ramon L. Laguarta, Chairman & CEO
• Jim Andrew, EVP & Chief Sustainability
Officer
Sales:
$86.39B (2024)
Recent Sponsorships:
NBA (renewed); NCAA's SWAC
(Southwestern Athletic Conference)
Auto Sports Sponsor:
NASCAR; USAR
Baseball Sponsor:
MLB
Basketball Sponsor:
NBA
Bowling Sponsor:
PBA
College Sponsor:
NCAA; Bowl Games
Facilities Sponsor:
Auto Club Speedway of Southern California;
NBA/NHL Pepsi Center, Denver, CO; USHL
Pepsi Coliseum, Indianapolis, IN
Football Sponsor:
NFL; AF2; CIFL
Golf Sponsor:
LPGA Tour; PGA Tour
Hockey Sponsor:
NHL; AHL; CHL
Lacrosse Sponsor:
NLL

PNC FINANCIAL SERVICES
300 5TH AVE
PITTSBURGH, PA 15222
888-762-2265
www.pnc.com
• William S. Demchak, Chairman, President
and CEO
• Robert Q. Reilly, Chief Financial Officer
• E. William Parsley, Chief Operating Officer
• Kieran J. Fallon, Chief Risk Officer
Sales:
$5.44B (2024)
Recent Sponsorships:
Verizon IndyCar Series; No. 9 Honda, 2018;
NFL New York Giants, 2016
College Sponsor:
NCAA
Facility Sponsor:
MLB PNC Park, Pittsburgh, PA; AAA PNC
Field, Moosic, PA; NCAA PNC Arena,

Raleigh, NC
Football Sponsor:
NFL
Hockey Sponsor:
NHL; Carolina Hurricanes
Soccer Sponsor:
Racing Louisville FC (National Women's
Soccer League)

PROCTER & GAMBLE COMPANY
2 P&G PLAZA
CINCINNATI, OH 45202
513-983-1100
us.pg.com
• John M. Moeller, Executive Chairman of
the Board
Sales:
$120.54B (2024)
Recent Sponsorships:
NFL, 2018-2023
Golf Sponsor:
LPGA; Walmart NW Arkansas
Championship
Olympic Sponsor:
Team U.S.A.

RED BULL NORTH AMERICA
1740 STEWART STREET
SANTA MONICA, CA 90404
310-393-4647
Fax: 310-230-2361
www.redbull.com
• Chris Hunt, Chief Executive Officer
Sales:
$1.71B (2024)
Extreme Sports Sponsor:
BMX, Motocross, Windsurfing,
Snowboarding, Skateboarding, Surfing

ROCKET MORTGAGE
1050 WOODWARD AVE
DETROIT, MI 48226-1906
800-476-2538
www.rocketmortgage.com
• Dan Gilbert, Chairperson
Sales:
$1.8B (2024)
Recent Sponsorships:
Rocket Mortgage Classic (PGA Tour) -
extended through 2027.
Basketball Sponsor:
Cleveland Cavaliers
Football Sponsor:
Detroit Lions
Golf Sponsor:
PGA, Rickie Fowler
Hockey Sponsor:
Detroit Red Wings
Motorsports Sponsor:
NASCAR, Ryan Newman

ROGERS COMMUNICATIONS
333 BLOOR ST EAST
TORONTO, ON, CANADA M4W 1G9
416-935-3548
1-888-764-1771
1-514-734-7699
www.rogers.com
• Tony Staffieri, President & CEO
Baseball Sponsor:
Toronto Blue Jays
Facility Sponsor:
Rogers Centre (Toronto)
Tennis Sponsor:
Rogers Cup
Other:

Writers' Trust of Canada, United Way, Canadian Women's Foundation

ROLEX WATCH USA
665 FIFTH AVENUE
NEW YORK, NY 10022
212-758-7700
Fax: 212-980-2166
www.rolex.com
• Luca Bernasconi, President & CEO
Sales:
$11.5B (2024)
Golf Sponsor:
PGA/LPGA, The Masters, U.S. Open, U.S. Women's Open, The Open, The Ryder Cup, The Presidents Cup, The Solheim Cup
Motorsports Sponsor:
Formula 1, FIA World Endurance Championship, The 24 Hours of Le Mans
Tennis Sponsor:
Wimbledon, Australian Open
Other:
Salzburg Festival, Teatro alla Scala, Royal Opera House, Metropolitan Opera, Opera National de Paris

SAMSUNG ELECTRONICS NA
85 CHALLENGER RD
RIDGEFIELD PARK, NJ 07310
201-229-4000
1-800-726-7864
info.seca@samsung.com
www.samsung.com
• JH Han, Vice Chairman & CEO
• Jong-Hee Han, President & CEO
Sales:
$75.8T (2024)
Sponsor:
Olympic Games; Youth Olympics; IAAF World Championships in Athletics; IAAF World Indoor Championships in Athletics; FINA World Aquatic Championships; UCI Track Cycling World Cup; World Rowing Championships; Volleyball World League; AFC Asia Cup; Africa Cup of Nations; NBA; NBA Summer League; MLB; PGA Championship; Samsung World Championship; NASCAR; Super Rudgy

SAP AMERICA, INC.
SAP LABS, INC.
3410 HILLVIEW AVE
PAOLO ALTO, CA 94304
650-849-4000
800-872-1727
www.sap.com
• Christian Klein, Chief Executive Officer
Sales:
$36.98B (2024)
Baseball Sponsor:
MLB New York Yankees
Basketball Sponsor:
FC Bayern Basketball; NBA
Equestrian Sponsor:
CHIO Aachen; Black Horse One GmbH; EquiRatings Limited; International Equestrian Federation
Hockey Sponsor:
Alder Mannheim Hockey Club; NHL; NHL New York Rangers; SAP Center - NHL San Jose Sharks
Football Sponsor:
NFL New York Giants, New York Jets, San Francisco 49ers
Sailing Sponsor:
World Sailing Series
Soccer Sponsor:

FC Bayern Basketball
Tennis Sponsor:
WTA

SCOTIABANK
SCOTIA PLAZA
40 KING STREET WEST
TORONTO, ON, CANADA M5H 1H1
416-947-7660
800-472-6842
www.scotiabank.com
• L. Scott Thomson, President & CEO
Hockey Sponsor:
NHL, Hockey Day in Canada; Scotiabank Community Hockey Sponsorship Program; Scotiabank Hockey Club; Scotiabank Road Hockey to Conquer Cancer; Rogers Hometown Hockey presented by Scotiabank; Scotiabank Girls HockeyFest
Baseball Sponsor:
Minor League
Football Sponsor:
CFL (Edmonton Eskimos; Hamilton Tiger-Cats; Winnipeg Blue Bombers; BC Lions; Calgary Stampeders)
Facility Sponsor:
Scotiabank Arena (Toronto), Scotiabank Saddledome (Calgary)
Other:
FitSpirit Celebrations; Scotiabank Rat Race; Scotiabank Skaters Program; Scotiabank Road Hockey to Conquer Cancer (in support of the Princess Margaret Cancer Foundation); Rogers Hometown Hockey; Scotiabank Community Hockey Sponorship Program

SHELL OIL COMPANY
150 N DAIRY ASHFORD RD
HOUSTON, TX 77079
713-767-5300
832-337-2000
www.shell.us
• Wael Sawan, CEO
Sales:
$323.183B (2024)
Auto Sports Sponsor:
NASCAR, Ferrari, Ducati

SHERWIN-WILLIAMS CO.
101 W PROSPECT AVENUE
CLEVELAND, OH 44101
1-800-474-3794
www.sherwin-williams.com
• Heidi Petz, President & CEO
Sales:
$23.09B (2024)
Baseball Sponsor:
Los Angeles Angels
Hockey Sponsor:
CHL
Facility Sponsor:
Indianapolis Motor Speedway
Motorsports Sponsor:
NASCAR

SIRIUS XM RADIO
1221 AVENUE OF THE AMERICAS
36TH FLOOR
NEW YORK, NY 10020
1-888-539-7474
www.siriusxm.com
• Jennifer Witz, Chief Executive Officer
Sales:
$8.7B (2024)
Auto Racing Sponsor:

IRL; NASCAR
Soccer Sponsor:
MLS
Golf Sponsor:
PGA
Football Sponsor:
NFL, CFL
Baseball Sponsor:
MLB; Minor Leagues
College Sponsor:
NCAA
Basketball Sponsor:
NBA
Hockey Sponsor:
NHL

SONY CORP. OF AMERICA
25 MADISON AVENUE
NEW YORK, NY 10010
212-833-6722
Fax: 212-833-6956
www.sony.com
• Karen L. Halby, Vice President, Sony USA
SCA.CSR@sony.com
Sales:
$86.4B (2024)
Golf Sponsor:
Sony Open (extended to 2026)

SPORT CHEK
824 41ST AVENUE NE
CALGARY, AB, CANADA T2E 3R3
403-717-1400
1-877-977-2435
www.sportchek.ca
• T.J. Flood, President
Baseball Sponsor:
Toronto Blue Jays
Basketball Sponsor:
Toronto Raptors
Hockey Sponsor:
NHL (Calgary Flames; Edmonton Oilers; Ottawa Senators; Toronto Maple Leafs; Vancouver Canucks; Winnipeg Jets)
Soccer Sponsor:
MLS (Toronto FC; Vancouver Whitecaps FC)
Amateur Sport Sponsor:
Canadian Olympic/Paralympic Committee, Hockey Canada, Alpine Canada, Canada Snowboard
Other:
Canadian Sports Hall of Fame; Canada Games; Kamloops Marathon; SickKids Great Camp Adventure

STANLEY BLACK & DECKER
1000 STANLEY DR
NEW BRITAIN, CT 06053
860-225-5111
CorporateRequest@sbdinc.com
www.stanleyblackanddecker.com
• Donald Allan, Jr., Chief Executive Officer
Sales:
$15.4B (2024)
Baseball Sponsor:
Major League Baseball (MLB)
Motorsports Sponsor:
NASCAR; NHRA racing
Soccer Sponsor:
English Premier League (EPL); FC Barcelona (FCB)
Extreme Sports Sponsor:
Skateboarding, Snowboarding, Bull Riding, Mountain Biking, Motocross, BMX Flatland, BMX

SUBWAY RESTAURANTS
325 BIC DRIVE
MILFORD, CT 06461-3059
203-877-4281
800-888-4848
www.subway.com
• Carrie Walsh, Interim Chief Executive Officer
Sales:
$9.98B (2024)
Recent Sponsorships:
National Football League (NFL); Guild Esports
Baseball Sponsor:
Little League

SUNOCO
8020 PARK LANE
SUITE 200
DALLAS, TX 75231
832-234-3600
800-786-6261
www.sunoco.com
• Joseph Kim, President and CEO
Sales:
$5.27B (2024)
Motorsport Sponsor:
NASCAR; eNASCAR iRacing World Championship Series; Richmond Raceway

SWATCH GROUP
SEEVORDSTADT 6
BIEL/BIENNE, 2502
41 32 343 6811
Fax: 41-32 343 6911
www.swatchgroup.com
• Nick Hayek, Jr., CEO
Sales:
$7.89B (2024)
Sponsors:
FISU (International University Sports Federation); Olympic Games (Tokyo); Formula One

T-MOBILE USA
12920 SE 38TH STREET
BELLEVUE, WA 98006
425-378-4000
1-855-760-0626
Fax: 425-378-4040
www.t-mobile.com
• Mike Sievert, CEO
Sales:
$81.4B (2024)
Facility Sponsor:
T-Mobile Arena, Paradise, NV
Baseball Sponsor:
MLB; Little League
Basketball Sponsor:
NWBA National Tournament
Ice Hockey Sponsor:
NHL; Vegas Golden Knights

TARGET STORES
1000 NICOLLET MALL
MINNEAPOLIS, MN 55403
612-304-6073
www.target.com
• Brian Cornell, Chair & CEO
• Katie Boylan, EVP & Chief Communications Officer
• Michael Fiddelke, Chief Operating Officer
Sales:
$107.4B (2023)
Soccer Sponsor:
MLS (through 2024), Minnesota United FC;

US Youth Soccer; US Soccer Foundation
Baseball Sponsor:
MLB (Minnesota Twins)
Basketball Sponsor:
NBA (Minnesota Timberwolves); WNBA (Minnesota Lynx)
Facility Sponsor:
MLB Target Field, Minneapolis, MN; NBA/WNBA Target Center, Minneapolis, MN

TD CANADA TRUST
TORONTO-DOMINION CENTRE
66 WELLINGTON ST W
TORONTO, ON, CANADA M5K 1A1
416-869-1144
www.td.com
• Bharat Masrani, Chief Executive Officer, TD Bank Group
Running Sponsors:
TD Beach to Beacon 10K; TD Five Boro Bike Tour; US Biathlon; TD Mayor's Cup (Boston Pro Cycling)
Basketball Sponsor:
NBA (Boston Celtics)
Hockey Sponsor:
NHL (Boston Bruins)
Baseball Sponsor:
MILB (Greenville Drive; Somerset Patriots)
Facility Sponsor:
TD Garden (Boston), TD Place (Ottawa); TD Stage at the Peace Center (Greenville); TD Convention Center (Greenville); TD Cener for the Performing Arts (Philadelphia); TD Arena (College of Charleston's men's and women's basketball and volleyball teams, Charleston)
Other Sponsors:
James Moody Democracy of Jazz Festival

TELUS CORPORATION
510 W GEORGIA ST
23RD FLOOR
VANCOUVER, BC, CANADA V6B 0M3
604-697-8044
888-811-2323
Fax: 604-899-1289
www.telus.com
• Darren Entwhistle, President & CEO
• Doug French, EVP & CFO
Football Sponsor:
CFL (BC Lions; Calgary Stampeders; Edmonton Elks; Hamilton Tiger-Cats; Montreal Alouettes); Canadian Football League (Ottawa Redblacks)
Hockey Sponsor:
Calgary Flames (NHL); Brandon Wheat Kings (WHL); Baie-Comeau Drakkar (Quebec Major Junior Hockey League); Rimoushki Oceanic (QMJHL); Ottawa 67's (Ontario Hockey League); Red Deer Rebels (Western Hockey League)
Lacrosse Sponsor:
Calgary Roughnecks (National Lacrosse League)
Other Sponsors:
Laval Rouge et Or (Universite Laval, Quebec City); Spruce Meadows (Calgary)

THE EMIRATES GROUP
800-777-3999
www.emirates.com
• Tim Clark, President, Emirates Airline
Sales:
$32.62B (2022-23)
Motorsports Sponsor:
Formula 1

Rugby Sponsor:
Emirates Airline Dubai Rugby Sevens; Cape Town Sevens; RWC (Rugby World Cup); World Rugby referees; Emirates Lions; UAE Rugby Federation
Tennis Sponsor:
U.S. Open; ATP Tour; Roland Garros tournament; Dubai Tennis Championship; Australia Open
Soccer Sponsor:
AC Milan; Arsenal FC; Asian Football Confederation; Olympiacos FC; Olympique Lyonnais; Real Madrid; S.L. Benfica; The Emirates FA Cup
Equestrian Sponsor:
Dubai World Cup Carnival
Golf Sponsor:
European Tour; Hong Kong Open
Cricket Sponsor:
International Cricket Council; Durham County Cricket Club; Lancashire County Cricket Club
Cycling Sponsor:
UAE Team Emirates
Sailing Sponsor:
Emirates Team New Zealand; America's Cup World Series Portsmouth

THE HERSHEY CO.
100 CRYSTAL A DRIVE
HERSHEY, PA 17033
717-534-4200
1-800-468-1714 (US/CA)
Fax: 717-534-6550
www.hersheys.com
• Michele Buck, President & CEO
Sales:
$11.2B (2024)
Olympic Sponsor:
Michael Phelps; Katie Ledecky; Caeleb Dressel (U.S.)

TIM HORTONS
EXCHANGE TOWER
130 KING ST WEST
SUITE 300
TORONTO, ON, CANADA M5X 2A2
888-601-1616
www.timhortons.com
• Axel Schwan, President
Baseball Sponsor:
Toronto Blue Jays
Basketball Sponsor:
Toronto Raptors
Football Sponsor:
CFL (BC Lions; Calgary Stampeders; Edmonton Eskimos; Hamilton Tiger-Cats; Montreal Alouettes; Saskatchewan Roughriders; Toronto Argonauts; Winnipeg Blue Bombers)
Hockey Sponsor:
NHL (Montreal Canadiens; Toronto Maple Leafs; Calgary Flames; Vancouver Canucks; Ottawa Senators; Winnipeg Jets; Edmonton Oilers), CHL, CWHL, Hockey Hall of Fame
Soccer Sponsor:
Toronto FC; Montreal Impact; Vancouver Whitecaps FC
Other:
Curling Canada, Tim Hortons Brier, Tim Hortons Roar of the Rings (Canadian Olympic Curling Trials)

TOYOTA MOTOR SALES, U.S.A.
800-331-4331
Fax: 310-468-7814
www.toyota.com/usa
• Tetsuo Ogawa, President & CEO
• Mark Templin, EVP & Chief Operating Officer
• Christopher P. Reynolds, EVP & Chief Strategy Officer
Recent Sponsorships:
10-year Olympic sponsor, 2015; Paralympic Foundation
Auto Racing Sponsor:
NASCAR
Baseball Sponsor:
MLB; Minor Leagues; Michaels Toyota Youth Baseball
Basketball Sponsor:
NBA; WNBA; NBDL
College Sports Sponsor:
NCAA, Bowl Games, Broadcast sponsor
Facility Sponsor:
NBA Toyota Center, Houston, TX; NFL Toyota Stadium, Georgetown, KY; AF2/WHL Toyota Center, Kennewick, WA; AIFL/NAHL Town Toyota Center, Wenatchee, WA; CHL/AIFA Tim's Toyota Center, Prescott Valley, AZ; MLS/MLL Toyota Park, Bridgeview, IL; NBA/NHL Toyota Sports Center, El Segundo, CA
Football Sponsor:
NFL; AF2
Fishing Sponsor:
B.A.S.S.
Golf Sponsor:
PGA Tour; LPGA Tour
Hockey Sponsor:
AHL; CHL; NHL
Soccer Sponsor:
MLS
Toyota Canada Sponsorships:
Canada Basketball; Wheelchair Basketball Canada; Canada Soccer; Canada Snowboard; Freestyle Canada; Senior Women's National Basketball Team; Senior Women's National Wheelchair Basketball Team; Senior Men's National Wheelchair Basketball Team; Women's National Soccer Team

U.S. BANCORP
800 NICOLLET MALL
MINNEAPOLIS, MN 55402
651-466-3000
800-872-2657
www.usbank.com
• Andrew Cecere, Chair, President & CEO
Sales:
$27.46B (2024)
Recent Sponsorships:
Collin Morikawa (PGA Tour), 2021
Facility Sponsor:
U.S. Bank Stadium (NFL)

UNDER ARMOUR
1020 HULL ST
BALTIMORE, MD 21230
888-727-6687
mediarelations@underarmour.com
about.underarmour.com
• Kevin Plank, President & CEO
• David E. Bergman, Chief Financial Officer
• Eric Liedtke, Brand President
• Kara Trent, President of the Americas
• Yassine Saidi, Chief Product Officer
• Shawn Curran, Chief Supply Chain Officer

Sales:
$5.683B (2021)
Recent Sponsorships:
Cancelled its sponsorship with Southampton FC (EPL) and NFL
Baseball Sponsor:
MLB; Samsung Lions (KBO League); Rakuten Monkeys (Chinese Professional Baseball League)
Basketball Sponsor:
NBA; WNBA
Golf Sponsor:
PGA; LPGA
Endurance Sports Sponsor:
Chevron Houston Marathon
Auto Racing:
Hendrick Motorsports; Mick Schumacher, Haas F1 Team

UNILEVER USA
2407 QUALITY WAY
JONESBORO, AR 72401
800-298-5018
www.unileverusa.com
• Hein Schumacher, Chief Executive Officer
• Herrish Patel, President, Unilever USA
Sales:
$13B (2023)
Auto Motorsports Sponsor:
NASCAR

UNITED CONTINENTAL HOLDINGS
233 SOUTH WACKER DRIVE
CHICAGO, IL 60606
newsroom.united.com
• Scott Kirby, Chief Executive Officer
• Brett J. Hart, President
Sales:
$57.1B (2024)
Baseball Sponsor:
MLB Chicago Cubs, Chicago White Sox, Kansas City Royals
Football Sponsor:
NFL Chicago Bears, Cleveland Browns, Denver Broncos, Houston Texans, Kansas City Chiefs, New Orleans Saints, New York Giants, New York Jets, Tampa Bay Buccaneers, Washington Redskins
Facility Sponsor:
United Center, Chicago, IL; NBA Chicago Bulls; NHL Chicago Blackhawks
Other Sponsor:
U.S. Olympic Committee; U.S. Paralympics

UNITED PARCEL SERVICE OF AMERICA, INC./UPS
55 GLENLAKE PKWY NE
ATLANTA, GA 30328
800-742-5877
www.ups.com
• Carol B. Tome, Chief Executive Officer
• Nando Cesarone, President, U.S. Operations
Sales:
$91.07B (2024)
Auto Sports Sponsor:
NASCAR
College Sponsor:
NCAA
Golf Sponsor:
PGA; The Masters; The Open Championship

VERIZON COMMUNICATIONS
ONE VERIZON WAY
BASKING RIDGE, NJ 07920-1097

www.verizon.com
• Hans Vestberg, Chief Executive Officer
• Leslie Berland, EVP & Chief Marketing Officer
Sales:
$134.79B (2024)
Baseball Sponsor:
MBL, Minor League
Basketball Sponsor:
NBA
College Sponsor:
NCAA; College Bowl
Football Sponsor:
NFL
Hockey Sponsor:
NHL; AHL

VF CORPORATION
1551 WEWATTA ST.
DENVER, CO 80202
336-424-6000
www.vfc.com
• Bracken Darrell, President & CEO
Sales:
$10.45B (2024)
Cycling Sponsor:
Colorado Classic
Brands:
The North Face; Timberland; Smartwool; Icebreaker; Altra

VISA USA
900 METRO CENTER BLVD
FOSTER CITY, CA 94404
800-847-2911
www.visa.com
• Ryan McInerney, Chief Executive Officer
• Frank Cooper, III, Chief Marketing Officer
• Jack Forestell, Chief Product & Strategy Officer
• Chris Suh, Chief Financial Officer
• Paul D. Fabara, Chief Risk & Client Services Officer
Sales:
$35.93B (2024)
Auto Sports Sponsor:
NASCAR
Football Sponsor:
NFL
Ice Hockey Sponsor:
NHL; NHLPA
Olympics Sponsor:
Olympic & Paralympic Games (through 2032); Team: Sarah Nurse (Ice Hockey); Max Parrot (Snowboard); Justine Dufour-Lapointe (Freestyle Skiing); Mac Marcoux (Para apline skiing)
Soccer Sponsor:
FIFA

VOLKSWAGEN GROUP OF AMERICA
2200 WOODLAND POINTE AVE.
HERNDON, VA 20171
248-754-5000
www.volkswagengroupofamerica.com
• Kjell Gruner, CEO & President
Sales:
$73B (2024)
Recent Sponsorships:
U.S. Soccer (2021)

WALMART INC.
702 SW 8TH STREET
BENTONVILLE, AR 72716

800-925-6278 (US)
800-328-0402 (CAN)
walmart.com
• Doug McMillon, President & CEO
Sales:
$680.99B (2025)
Recent Sponsorships:
Joe Martin Stage Race, 2022; Red Bull
Racing (Formula One)
Golf Sponsor:
Walmart NW Arkansas Championship
(LPGA)
Fishing Sponsor:
Walmart FLW Tour (fly-fishing)

WELLS FARGO & CO
420 MONTGOMERY STREET
SAN FRANCISCO, CA 94103
800-869-3557
800-956-4442
www.wellsfargo.com
• Charles W. Scharf, President & CEO
• Michael P. Santomassimo, Senior EVP &
Chief Financial Officer
Sales:
$82.3B (2024)
Recent Sponsorships:
US Motorcycle Coaching Association
(USMCA)

Facility Sponsor:
Wells Fargo Arena, Des Moines, IA
Football Sponsor:
NFl
College Sponsor:
NCAA; College Bowl
Golf Sponsor:
PGA; Wells Fargo Championship
Baseball Sponsor:
MLB Colorado Rockies; Minor League
Basketball Sponsor:
NBA (Philadelphia 67ers)
Endurance Sports Sponsor:
St. George Marathon; Grandma's Marathon
Hockey Sponsor:
NHL (Philadelphia Flyers)
Lacrosse Sponsor:
Philadelphia Wings, National Lacrosse
League (NLL)

YUM! BRANDS
1441 GARDINER LANE
LOUISVILLE, KY 40213
502-874-8300
www.yum.com
• David Gibbs, Chief Executive Officer
Sales:
$7.076B (2023)
Recent Sponsorships:

NFL; NCAA; FCS Division 1 College
Football Championship
Facility Sponsor:
KFC Yum! Center, Louisville, KY - Louisville
Cardinals (men's and women's basketball);
American Airlines Center, Dallas, TX
Basketball Sponsor:
NBA Dallas Mavericks
Baseball Sponsor:
MLB; MLB Cleveland Indians

ZURICH AMERICAN INSURANCE CO.
1299 ZURICH WAY
SCHAUMBURG, IL 60196-1056
800-382-2150
info.source@zurichna.com
www.zurichna.com
• Kristof Terryn, Chief Executive Officer
Hockey Sponsor:
Swiss National Team
Golf Sponsor:
PGA
Other:
World Economic Forum, Zurich
Vitaparcours, Zurich Marato de Barcelona,
German Olympic Team

6

professional services

A

A.D.D. MARKETING AND ADVERTISING, 771
A.P. SWANN INSURANCE SERVICES LLC, 766
A.V. CONCEPTS, 819
AAI SPORTS INC. & AAI INTERNATIONAL, INC., 823
ABBOTT MANAGEMENT GROUP, 823
ABES & BAUMANN, 861
ABRAHAM, WATKINS, NICHOLS, SORRELS, MATTHEWS & FRIEND, 861
ACC PROPERTIES, 771
ACCESS SPORTS MEDICINE & ORTHOPAEDICS, 918
ACCU-STATS VIDEO PRODUCTIONS, 819
ACENTECH INC., 819
ACKERMAN, VALERIE B., 861
ACME MASCOTS, INC., 771
ACTION INK, INC., 771
ACTION MEDIA/VISION ENTERTAINMENT, 749
ACTION SPORTS AMERICA, 771
ACTION SPORTS INTERNATIONAL, 771
ACTION SPORTS MEDIA, 771
ACTIVE ALERT, 819
ACTIVE INTERNATIONAL, 766
AD CETERA SPORTS CELEBRITIES, 824
ADAMS & REESE, 861
ADAMSKI MOROSKI MADDEN & GREEN LLP, 861
ADELMAN, DANIEL W., 861
ADKINS, M. DOUGLAS, 861
ADLER & BLASS, 861
ADLINK, 771
ADRENALIN, INC., 772
ADVANCED ATHLETIC REPRESENTATION, 824
ADVANCED ORTHOPEDICS AND SPORTS MEDICINE INSTITUTE, 918
ADVANCED PROMOTIONAL CONCEPTS, INC., 772
ADVANTAGE MARKETING GROUP, INC., 749
ADVERTISING WORLD SERIES, 750
AEGIS SCIENCES CORPORATION, 918
AET LASERS, 750
AKIN & RANDOLPH AGENCY, 824
ALAN TAYLOR COMMUNICATIONS, INC., 772
ALCOX, PATRICK, 862
ALEXANDER & ASSOCIATES, P.C. MARY, 862
ALL AMERICAN AMATEUR BASEBALL ASSOCIATION, 928
ALL PRO SPORTS & ENTERTAINMENT, 824
ALL TERRAIN PRODUCTIONS, INC., 772
ALL-CITY SPORTS MARKETING, 772
ALL-PRO SOFTWARE, 928
ALLEN CONSULTING, INC., 772
ALLIED SPECIALTY INSURANCE, 766
ALLMAN & MITZNER, LLC, 862
ALLOY MARKETING & PROMOTION, 772
ALLOY MEDIA & MARKETING, 772
ALPHA & OMEGA MOUNTED SECURITY PATROL, 765
ALSTRAR INC. SPORTS & ENTERTAINMENT, 824
AMATEUR SPORTS GROUP, INC., 824
AMATEUR SPORTS TRAVEL GROUP, INC, 924
AMBAC ASSURANCE CORPORATION, 767
AMBROSE LAW GROUP, LLP, 862
AMERICA OUTDOORS/AO, 924
AMERICA'S SCHOOLS PROGRAM, 767
AMERICAN ACADEMY OF ORTHOPAEDIC SURGEONS, 918
AMERICAN ACADEMY OF PODIATRIC SPORTS MEDICINE, 918
AMERICAN ADVERTISING SERVICES, INC./SPORTS MARKETING DIVISION, 750
AMERICAN COLLEGE OF SPORTS MEDICINE, 918
AMERICAN COLLEGE OF VETERINARY SPORTS MEDICINE AND REHABILITATION, 918
AMERICAN DREAMS, 772
AMERICAN GRAPHITI, 750
AMERICAN HOLE 'N ONE, 773
AMERICAN MARKETING AND MOTORSPORTS GROUP, 750
AMERICAN MEDICAL SOCIETY FOR SPORTS MEDICINE, 918
AMERICAN ORTHOPAEDIC FOOT & ANKLE SOCIETY, 918
AMERICAN ORTHOPAEDIC SOCIETY FOR SPORTS MEDICINE, 918

AMERICAN OSTEOPATHIC ACADEMY OF SPORTS MEDICINE, 919
AMERICAN PHYSICAL THERAPY ASSOCIATION, 919
THE AMERICAN PHYSIOLOGICAL SOCIETY, 923
AMERICAN SPECIALTY, 773
AMERICAN SPECIALTY INSURANCE & RISK SERVICES, INC., 773
AMERICAN SPORTS DATA, INC., 773
AMERICAN SPORTS MEDICINE INSTITUTE, 919
AMJ CAMPBELL, 924
AMTRAK, 925
ANAPOL, SCHWARTZ, WEISS, COHAN, FELDMAN & SMALLEY, P.C., 862
ANDERSON & TUCKER, 862
ANDREA KIRBY COACHES, INC., 747
ANDREWS INSTITUTE FOR ORTHOPAEDICS & SPORTS MEDICINE, 919
ANDREWS KURTH LLP, 862
ANDREWS SPORTS MEDICINE & ORTHOPEDIC CENTER, 919
ANSLOW, ESQ., RICHARD I., 824
ANTHONY TRAVEL, INC., 925
AON ENTERTAINMENT, 767
APUNIX COMPUTER SERVICES, 819
AQUARIUS SPORTS AND ENTERTAINMENT, 773
ARANDA GROUP, 824
ARCTIC SPORTS, 825
ARNET, WILLIAM F., 862
ARTHROSCOPY ASSOCIATION OF NORTH AMERICA, 919
ASAP SPORTS, 819
ASCENSION ENTERPRISES INC., 825
ASHFORD & WRISTON, 862
ASPEN ORTHOPAEDIC ASSOCIATES, 919
ASSANTE SPORTS MANAGEMENT GROUP, 825
ASSURED GUARANTY CORPORATION, 767
ATH-ELITE MANAGEMENT SERVICES, 825
ATHERTON COMMUNICATIONS, LP, 750
ATHLETES ADVANCE, 930
ATHLETIC RESOURCE MANAGEMENT, INC., 825
ATHLETICO PHYSICAL THERAPY, 919
AUDIO VISUAL CONFERENCE TECHNOLOGIES, 819
AULTMAN, TYNER, ET AL, 863
AURA360 VENTURES, 774
AUSTIN SPORTS MEDICINE, 919
AUTO SPORTS MARKETING GROUP, 774
AVIS RENT A CAR SYSTEM, 925
AXELROD, BARRY, 825

B

BAIZLEY, DONALD, 863
BAKER & DANIELS, 863
BAKER & MCKENZIE, 863
BAKER SPORTS MANAGMENT, 825
BAKER, DAVID L., 863
BALTIMORE, BRYON, 863
BAMBOO WORLDWIDE, 774
BANSHEE MUSIC, 774
BARNES MARKETING, INC., 826
BARNNETT, HOWARD D, 826
BARRETT SPORTS GROUP, 774
BARRETT, WILLIAM A., 863
BARTH, BERUS & CALDERON, LLP, 864
BASSFORD, LOCKHART, TRUESDELL & BRIGGS, P.A., 864
BATE, PETERSON, DEACON, ZINN & YOUNG, LLP, 864
BATTLE, MICHAEL RAY, 826
BAUM, ETENGOFF & BUCKLEY, 864
BDA SPORTS MANAGEMENT, 826
BDS MARKETING, INC., 774
BEACON ORTHOPAEDICS & SPORTS MEDICINE, 919
BEALL & BURKHARDT, 864
BEAR ENTHUSIAST MARKETING GROUP, 775
BEAR FOOT SPORTS, 750
BEAUTYMAN ASSOCIATES, P.C., 865
BECHTA, JACK D./JB SPORTS, 826
BECKER & POLIAKOFF, P.A., 865
BECKER, WILLIAM F.X., 865
BENDELOW LAW FIRM, 865
BENJAMIN, GLEN, 826
BENNETT GLOBAL MARKETING GROUP, 775

BERMAN, HOWARD E., 865
BERNARD M. RESNICK, ESQ, P.C., 865
BERNARD, PAMELA J., 865
BERNARD, WILLIAM DAVID, 865
BERRY & HOMER, 775
BERRY, ROBERT C., 866
BERSHAD, LAWRENCE, 866
BERTHELSEN, RICHARD, 826
BERTUZZI, LAWRENCE, 866
BESSEMER TRUST, 767
BEST IN SPORTS, 826
BEVERLY HILLS SPORTS COUNCIL, 866
BEWI PRODUCTIONS, INC., 750
BFG COMMUNICATIONS, 775
BIG TEN ATHLETIC CONFERENCE, 826, 292
BIKE TAHOE, 827
BILLBOARD TRAY, 775
BINGHAM MCCUTCHEN LLP, 866
BIRDZERK!, 775
BKB LTD., 775
BLACK, WILLIAM D., LAW OFFICES OF, 866
BLACKBOURN, LISLE W., 866
BLACKMAN & RABER, LTD., 827
BLACKROCK, 767
BLACKSTAR SPORTS MANAGEMENT, INC., 827
BLACKWELDER, MURRAY, 827
BLAIR, ROBERT W., 866
BLALOCK COMPANY, JANE, 750
BLANC, DAVID, 867
BLECHER & COLLINS, 867
BLIMP WORKS, INC., 776
BLIMPWORKS, 776
BLUE BIRD CORPORATION, 925
BLUMENFELD AND ASSOCIATES PR, INC., 776
BLYTHE, DONOVAN A., 827
BMK SPORTS, 751
BOARDWALK, 776
BODDICKER SPORTS MANAGEMENT, 827
BOEHM, STEVE B., 867
BOESCHE MCDERMOTT LLP, 867
BOLLINGER INSURANCE, 767
BONHAM GROUP, INC., 776
BORTZ MEDIA & SPORTS GROUP, INC., 776
BOSCH, GERARD R., 867
BOSE CORPORATION, 819
BOSE MCKINNEY & EVANS LLP, 867
BOUTIN, DENTINO, GIBSON, DI GIUSTO, HODELL, INC., 867
BOZELL WORLDWIDE, 776
BRADLEY & GMELICH, 867
BRANDBUILDERS, 776
BREAUX, PAUL P., 868
BRENNAN, PATRICK CAVANAUGH, 868
BRIAN J. MURPHY CONSULTANT, 776
BRICK, ADAM, 868
BRICKER & ECKLER, 868
BRICKEY JAMES N. L.C., 868
BRIDGES, HAROLD A., 868
BRIGGS, BUCK, 868
BRITTEN MEDIA, 751
BRONSKILL & CO., 819
BROTMAN WINTER FRIED COMMUNICATIONS, INC., 751
BROWN, HALL, SHORE & MCKINLEY LLP, 868
BROWN, J. MICHAEL, 868
BRUNINI, GRANTHAM GROWE & HEWES, P.L.L.C, 868
BRUNO, CHRISTOPHER J., 869
BRYANT-FIELDS, REGINA, 869
BRYENTON, GARY L., 869
BUCHANAN INGERSOLL ROONEY, 869
BUCHANAN INGERSOLL ROONEY PC, 869
BUNTING, ELIZABETH C., 869
BURELSON, PATE & GIBSON, L.L.P., 869
BURFORD, LLL, CHRIS W., 870
BURG & ELDREDGE, P.C., 870
BURGOYNE, ROBERT A., 870
BURNS ENTERTAINMENT & SPORTS MARKETING, INC, 820
BURT, JR., EDWARD C., 870
BURWASH INTERNATIONAL, PETER, 751
BUSBANK, 925
BUSINESS ARENA, INC., 827
BUSINESS LAW VENTURES, 870
BUTLER. JAMES D., P.A., 870
BUTZEL LONG, A PROFESSIONAL CORPORATION, 870
BWD GROUP LLC, 767

Executive Search Services

ANDREA KIRBY COACHES, INC.
14364 NOLEN LANE
CHARLOTTE, NC 28277
704-541-4842
800-831-3883
Fax: 704-541-4816
www.andreakirby.com
Clients:
Sports Figures
Description:
Media workshops for players and management focusing on interview skills and media relationships. Also, skills for presentations and appearances. Broadcast coaching and evaluation for play-by-play and color commentators, announcers, and studio talent. Offers personal and team workshops for players, managers, coaches and front office personnel. Broadcast talent coach for networks and local stations.
Sports Service Founded:
1985

CHASEAMERICA, INC.
300 PARK AVENUE
17TH FLOOR
NEW YORK, NY 10022
646-706-7300
800-491-4980
• David E. Stefan, Chief Executive Officer
• Maria Dennison, President
Nature of Sports Service:
Executive search, M&A and management consulting services for sports apparel, footwear and equipment manufacturers, golf course and residential developers, hotels, spas, stadiums and other athletic facilities.

CORPORATE EXECUTIVE SERVICES
6 HUTTON CENTRE DRIVE
SUITE #1280
SOUTH COAST METRO, CA 92707
714-836-6742
Fax: 714-836-6816
www.corporateexecutive.com
• Warren Tempero, Chief Executive Officer
Services:
Provides career counseling and job placement firm for Corporate Executives in Southern California
Sports Service Founded:
1961
Description:
Executive search firm specializing in $40,000 - $200,000 accounting/financial/banking, technical - computer related, medical, legal and manufacturing.

CREATIVE GROUP
10 ALMADEN BOULEVARD
SUITE 900
SAN JOSE, CA 95113
408-961-2975
888-846-1668
Fax: 408-271-9487
san.jose@creativegroup.com
www.creativegroup.com
Description:
Expertise in creative staffing of freelance professionals. Provides freelance creative, advertising, marketing and Internet professionals to companies on a project basis. Creative Group for consultants who possess expertise in: Internet design, direct marketing, e-marketing and media relations

EASTMAN & BEAUDINE, INC.
7201 BISHOP ROAD
SUITE 220
PLANO, TX 75024
972-312-1012
• Bob E. Beadine, President & Chief Executive Officer
Services:
One of the country's leading executive searches for sports/entertainment/media, collegiate sports, marketing, board of directors, hospitality and leisure, technology/e-business, retail, manufacturing/operations, financial services.
Description:
Recognized as the premier search firm in sports recruiting. Exclusive affiliated partners in nine major cities throughout Europe and the Far East.
Year Founded:
1967

EXECUTIVE LEVELS INTERNATIONAL, LLC
4938 HAMPDEN LANE
#430
BETHESDA, MD 20814
301-320-3080
Fax: 831-306-3080
moreinfo@executivelevels.com
www.executivelevels.com
Nature of Service:
Performance based full service executive search firm specializing in management and executives for the following areas: Corporate Sports Properties, Media, Entertainment Sports Facilities, Live Event Producers, Professional Teams, All Leagues, Governing Bodies, Sports Apparel, Footwear, Sports Marketing and Advertising, Corporate Marketing, Sporting Goods, Consumer Goods: Manufacturers and Retailers, Online & Fantasy Related Sports, Arena Sports, College Athletics, Information Technology, E-Business, ECommerce, Networking, Telecommunications, Wireless, Internet, IT Consulting, Management Consulting, Media.
Year Founded:
1995

EXECUTIVE SPORTS PLACEMENT
74-923 HIGHWAY 111
#186
INDIAN WELLS, CA 92210
888-884-0495
Sports Service Founded:
1997
Services:
Placement of people in the sports industry.
Description:
Executive search and career consulting firm providing professional services in executive recruitment, career planning and resume preparation for entry to senior level management personnel.

GAME FACE, INC.
PO BOX 330
LEHI, UT 84043
503-523-8381
www.gamefaceinc.com
• Robert Cornilles, Founder/CEO
Description:
A sports executive training firm that specializes in enhancing sales and revenue, customer service, and personnel skills development for professional sports clubs, intercollegiate athletic departments, and individual executives.
Clients:
Clients include over 400 major and minor league professional sports organization, intercollegiate athletic departments, and fortune 1000 corporations.
Founded:
1995

GENERAL SPORTS TURF SYSTEMS
400 WATER STREET
SUITE 250
ROCHESTER, MI 48307
248-601-2200
Fax: 248-601-2400
www.generalsports.com
• Andrew D. Appleby, Chairman
• Robert Heinrich, Senior Vice President
• Ryan Copacia, Manager
• Shawn Vellek, Sales Representative
• Tyler Ingle, Controller

GRANT ASSOCIATES
301 SAYRE DRIVE
PRINCETON, NJ 08540-5826
609-514-8674
Fax: 212-684-4607
• David Grant, President
Nature of Service:
Executive recruiting, licensing management, sports/event promotion, strategic corporate growth consulting, U.S. market development.
Year Founded:
1997
Sports Service Founded:
1997

HEALTHANDWELLNESSJOBS.COM
3402 ENGLEWOOD DRIVE
PEARLAND, TX 77584
281-794-7879
www.healthandwellnessjobs.com
• Scott Hankosky, Chief Executive Officer
Services:
Provides health and wellness professionals national exposure to employment opportunities.
Nature of Sports Service:
A job posting web site for employers to post positions for Exercise Physiologist, Physical Therapist, Athletic Trainers, Personal Trainers, Academic Professors, Aerobic Instructors, Aquatic Instructors, Massage Therapist, Sports Administrators & Management and other health and wellness professionals.

HRESHKO CONSULTING GROUP
850 US HIGHWAY ONE
SUITE 2
NORTH BRUNSWICK, NJ 8902
732-545-9000
Fax: 732-545-0080
info@hcgusa.com
www.hcgusa.com
• Frank Hreshko, Managing Partner
Sports Service Founded:
1991
Marketing & Consulting Services:

Retained executive search firm specializing in recruiting, accounting, finance, licensing, sales, marketing, and senior management professionals for sporting goods manufacturers, professional sports teams and professional sports leagues and associations.

KORN/FERRY INTERNATIONAL
1900 AVENUE OF THE STARS
SUITE 2600
LOS ANGELES, CA 90067
310-552-1834
www.kornferry.com
• Paul C. Reilly, Chairman/Interim President, EMEA
(310) 843-4130
paul.reilly@kornferry.com
• Gary D. Burnison, CEO
(310) 226-2613
gary.burnison@kornferry.com
• Stephen Giusto, Executive Vice President/Chief Financial Offi
Services:
Premier provider of executive human capital solutions, with services ranging from corporate governance and CEO recruitment to executive search, middle-management recruitment and Leadership Development Solutions (LDS).
Description:
World-wide executive search firm with 71 offices in 40 countries. Specializes in assisting organizations locate high-caliber senior management in all aspects of the Sports Industry Including: Professional Sports, Collegiate Sports, Sporting Goods, Sports Finance, and Sports Technology

MICA SPORTS
759 BLOOMFIELD AVENUE
SUITE 207
WEST CALDWELL, NJ 7006
973-618-9979
Fax: 973-618-9629
info@micasports.com
www.micasports.com
• Michelle Beidner, Co-Founder
michelle@micasports.com
• Caryn Snerson, Pricipal
(973) 618-9979
caryn@micasports.com
Sports Service Founded:
1999.
Nature of Service:
An executive search and placement firm servicing the national sports marketing industry. Concentrating exclusively on sports marketing opportunities, from corporate sponsorship and promotions to events, public relations, business development, sales, media, product licensing and more.

NEXT LEVEL EXECUTIVE SEARCH
24 CATHEDRAL PLACE
SUITE 500
SAINT AUGUSTINE, FL 32084
904-810-5177
866-810-5177
Fax: 904-810-6855
info@nextlevelexecutive.com
www.nextlevelexecutive.com
• Michael Garnes, President
Founded:
2003
Description:

Next Level Executive Search (NLES), is a focused global search firm specializing in recruitment and placement in the sports industry. The firm's functional areas of specialization are: sales, marketing, sponsorship and partnership leaders. The sectors NLES serves are companies, corporate sponsors and partnerships, associations, governing bodies, sports media, colleges, and professional teams and leagues.
Clients:
Retained and contingency executive search firm. Clients confidential

RUSSELL REYNOLDS ASSOCIATES, INC.
200 PARK AVENUE
SUITE 2300
NEW YORK, NY 10166-0002
212-351-2000
Fax: 212-370-0896
info@russellreynolds.com
www.russellreynolds.com
• Jim Bagley, Associate
jbagley@russellreynolds.com
• James Carpenter, Associate
Description:
A global executive recruitment and management assessment firm that delivers solutions to organizational challenges through the recruitment of exceptional leaders. Excels in finding uniquely qualified leaders for clients in all major markets.

SEARCH SYNERGY INC.
3004 NE 26TH AVENUE
PORTLAND, OR 97212-3547
503-288-2400
www.searchsynergy.com
• Ross Regis, Founder/President
• Ross Regis, Founder/President
(503) 288-2400
• Julie Yochim, Database Manager
Nature of Service:
Executive search firm specializing in mid-to-executive level positions within the sporting goods, outdoor, and action sports industries, for the product segments of footwear, apparel and equipment.

SPENCER STUART
353 N CLARK ST
CHICAGO, IL 60654
312-822-0080
Fax: 312-822-0116
www.spencerstuart.com
• Kenneth V Eckhart, Manager/Consultant
• Susan J. Baldwin, Consultant
Nature of Sports Service:
Firm offers management consulting and executive searches, specializing in finding top-level executives and board directors. Firm has nearly 300 consultants, who operate from 50 offices in 24 countries.

SPORT SEARCH.MVP GROUP
2990 E NORTHERN AVENUE
SUITE B101
PHOENIX, AZ 85028
602-485-5555
Fax: 602-458-3435
mt@sportsearch.net
www.sportsearch.net
• Marty McEvoy, Managing Director-International
martym@sportsearch.net

• Mark Tudi, President/Founder
mt@sportsearchonline.com
Services:
A premier Executive Search/Recruiting and Human Resource Consulting firm, sourcing the critical layer of management, completely focused in the Sports, Recreation and Entertainment Industries which provides retained executive search, customized recruiting assignments, on-line career management program, and sports & entertainment human resources forum

SPORTS GROUP INTERNATIONAL
7317 SPYGLASS WAY
SUITE 400
RALEIGH, NC 27615
919-855-0226
Fax: 919-855-0793
sgisearch@aol.com
www.sgisearch.com
• Joseph A. White, President
(919) 855-0226
sgisearch@aol.com
• Joseph White, President
(919) 855-0266
sgisearch@aol.com
• Dave Reinhart, Vice President
(413) 587-0022
• Rod Jahner, Vice President
(919) 435-7579
rjahner@gmail.com
• Alison White, Executive Search Consultant
(704) 466-0899
awhite.sgi@gmail.com
Nature of Service:
Retained Executive Search firm serving sporting goods, performance athletic footwear and apparel industries. Disciplines in which Sports Group International conducts search assignments include sales, marketing, product design, product development, supply chain management, international sales and marketing, general management, and sports marketing. Client scope is global. Sports Group International conducts search assignments in the USA, Canada, and overseas.
Year Founded:
1989

SPORTS GUIDES, LLC
13901 N 73RD STREET
SUITE 219
SCOTTSDALE, AZ 85281
480-948-8885
Description:
Assisted thousands of individuals in their pursuit of a career in the sports industry as well as thousands of companies to find the perfect employee. Offers many services such as job listings, a resume bank, industry contact, industry overviews, job description, salary information and chat sessions.

SPORTSEARCH, INC.
2990 E NORTHERN AVENUE
SUITE B101
PHOENIX, AZ 85028-4838
602-485-5555
Fax: 602-485-3435
www.sportsearchonline.com
• Mark Tudi, President
(602) 485-5555
mt@sportsearch.net
• Marty McEvoy, Managing Director
martym@sportsearch.net

• John Byrne, Search Consultant
john@sportsearch.net
• Mark Williamson, Manager Of Marketing Operations
mark@sportsearch.net
• Andy Sandler, Partner
Services:
Executive Search/Recruiting and Human Resource Consulting firm, sourcing the critical layer of management, completely focused in the Sports Recreation and Entertainment Industries, on a global basis.

STRATEGIC RESOURCES
19125 N CREEK PARKWAY
SUITE 120
BOTHELL, WA 98011
425-688-1151
Fax: 425-732-2112
corporate@strategicresources.com
www.strategicresources.com
• Ted Warren, President/Senior Partner
tedwarren@strategicresources.com
• Ted Warren, President and Senior Partner
tedwarren@strategicresources.com
• Marcus Williams, Vice President
mwilliams@strategicresources.com
• David Castelblanco, Vice President
dcastelblanco@strategicresources.com
• Daniela Chetan, Vice President
dchetan@strategicresources.com
• Allen Barron, Affiliated Partner
adb@strategicresources.com
Services:
National executive search firm specializing in senior-level executive search and Board of Director appointments. Also offers introductory services for M&A or strategic alliance.
Sports Service Founded:
1998
Nature of Sports Service:
Executive search firm recruiting for positions in middle to upper level management specializing in the sports industry. Services provided to professional leagues, stadium/arena operations, sporting goods manufacturers, sports marketing firms and sports broadcast media.

TALON GROUP INTERNATIONAL D/B/A/MANAGEMENT RECRUITERS OF MERCER ISLAND
9725 SE 36TH STREET
SUITE 312
MERCER ISLAND, WA 98040
206-232-0204
Fax: 206-232-6172
denise@mrmi.com
www.mrmi.com
• Vince Holt, President
(206) 232-0129
• Vanica Salvacruz, Project Coordinator
(206) 232-1624
• Cheryl Cho, Director of Footwear
(206) 232-5047
cheryl@mrmi.com
• Jim Dykeman, Executive Recruiter
(206) 232-0211
• Denise Holt, Manager Administration
(206) 232-7051
denise@mrmi.com
• Vince Holt, President
(206) 232-0129
Sports Service Founded:
1980
Nature of Sports Service:
Specialize in employee placement in the

wholesale apparel and footwear industry. Placements with major athletic and casual footwear and apparel companies such as Adidas, And 1, L.L. Bean, Brooks Sports, Diesel, XOXO, Mecca, Nautica, Reef Brazil and Teva. Positions include Product Design, Product Development, Marketing, Sales, and Sourcing.

TEAMWORK CONSULTING, INC.
22550 MCCAULEY ROAD
SHAKER HEIGHTS, OH 44122
216-360-1790
Fax: 216-292-9265
info@teamworkonline.com
www.teamworkconsulting.com
• Buffy Filippell, President
(216) 360-1790
Services:
Retained executive search firm focusing on mid-level to senior-level positions in the sports and live event industry.

THE GOULD GROUP
1471 ROUTE 9
ROME EXECUTIVE PLAZA
CLIFTON PARK, NY 12065
518-371-3052 EXT 301
Fax: 518-371-3953
www.thegouldgroup.net
• Tom Gould, Owner
Services:
Assists firms in sourcing outstanding performers in the field of sales management
Description:
Our professional placement assists firms in sourcing outstanding performers in the field of sales management. Works with client, companies and candidates throughout the United States.

TMP. WORLDWIDE/MONSTER GLOBAL HEADQUARTERS
622 THIRD AVENUE
39TH FLOOR
NEW YORK, NY 10017
212-351-7000
Fax: 646-658-0541
• Sal Iannuzzi, Chairman/Chief Executive Officer
• Tim Yates, EVP/CFO
Services:
A global online careers and recruitment resource, known for connecting quality job seekers at all levels with leading employers across all industries and offers employers innovative technology and superior services that give them more control over the recruiting process.
Description:
Retained executive search firm servicing active apparel, sporting goods, athletic footwear and retail sports related companies. Recruit for positions from CEO to middle management sales, marketing, manufacturing, sourcing, finance and other functional areas.

TURNKEY SPORTS & ENTERTAINMENT
9 TANNER STREET
SUITE 8
HADDONFIELD, NJ 8033
856-685-1450
Fax: 856-685-1451
www.turnkeyse.com
• Len Perna, President/Chief Executive Officer

• Patrick Kuhlen, Marketing Director
• Haynes Hendrickson, Senior Vice President
• Michael Mayle, Vice President Information Technology
• Melissa Dean, Senior Vice President
• Dan Rossetti, Senior Vice President/Turnkey Search
Year Founded:
1996
Nature of Services:
Turnkey provides agency clients, brand clients and property clients comprehensive solutions that include marketing intelligence services in addition to recruitment services in the areas of live events, sports, sports media and entertainment.

WORK IN SPORTS
7010 E CHAUNCEY LANE
SUITE 115
PHOENIX, AZ 85054
480-905-7221
Fax: 480-905-7231
support@WorkInSports.com
www.WorkInSports.com
• John Mellor, President/Chief Executive Officer
jmellor@WorkInSports.com
• Jason Backs, EVP/Chief Operations Officer
• Robert Oakley, VP Interactive Marketing/Client Services
amyeaton@WorkInSports.com
• Amy Eaton, Director Employer Relations
Nature of Services:
WorkInSports.com provides job board and employment resource services in the sports industry, working with teams, leagues, facilities, sponsors, agencies and other sports related organizations.
Year Founded:
2000

Event Planning & Services

ACTION MEDIA/VISION ENTERTAINMENT
2200 W ORANGEWOOD AVENUE
SUITE 230
ORANGE, CA 92868
949-789-7439
Fax: 949-789-7444
www.actionmediallc.com
• Rick Stark, Event Sales And Marketing
(989) 789-7439
Services:
Action Media and its subsidiary Vision Entertainment is an integrated marketing and event production company that provides a unique, powerful gateway to the potent, yet elusive Gen X-Y audience. Provides compelling original concepts and turn-key solutions for an extensive list of clients.
Event Management Services:
Creates and manages sports events for snowboarding, skateboarding and wakeboarding.

ADVANTAGE MARKETING GROUP, INC.
10030 N MACARTHUR BOULEVARD
SUITE 195
IRVING, TX 75063
972-869-2244
Fax: 847-952-3348
www.amgsports.com

• Werner Scott, President/Chief Executive Officer

ADVERTISING WORLD SERIES
8117 MANCHESTER AVENUE
SUITE #198
PLAYA DEL REY, CA 90293
310-740-2195
michael@adworldseries.com
www.adworldseries.com
• Michael Meiches, Founder/Commissioner
(310) 740-2195
michael@adworldseries.com
Sports Service Founded:
1981
Event Management Services:
Produces Advertising Softball World Series Tournament for advertising media, and corporate teams plus other corporate events. Sponsored by Sports Illustrated.

AET LASERS
8124 NORRIS LANE
BALTIMORE, MD 21222
410-355-2055
800-771-7938
Fax: 410-355-2054
moreinfo@imageengineering.com
www.imageengineering.com
Event Management Services:
Special events and spectaculars, featuring lasers, lights pyro, and special effects, designed to enhance appeal and interest in sports events, as well as providing a unique, high profile vehicle for corporate sponsors.
Services:
Laser displays for events including: corporate, sporting, festival, broadcast media. Shows may include: pyrotechnics, confetti, intelligent lighting and CO2 for a fully integrated, turn-key production. Other services: hardware design, manufacturing, permanent installation. Created world's largest inflatable projection screen, the ITV.

Clients:
Anheuser Busch, Apple Computer, AT&T, Baltimore Blast, Boston Red Sox, Boy Scouts of America - Naitonal Jamboree, British Luxury Council, British Airways, Brooklyn Bridge - 120th Anniversary, Cannon, City of Peshtigo, WI, City of Rockville, MD, Coca-Cola, Detroit Red Wings, Digital Equipment Corporation, Discovery Channel, Fairfax, VA, Florida Sun Coast Dome, Ford Motor Company, General Motors, Georgia-Pacific
Sports Service Founded:
1979.

AMERICAN ADVERTISING SERVICES, INC./SPORTS MARKETING DIVISION
121 CHESTNUT STREET
PHILADELPHIA, PA 19106
215-923-9100
Sports Service Founded:
1986
Services:
Offers public relations, advertising, and marketing services which includes Sales Presentations, Commercials, Product Demonstrations, Training Tapes, and Shooting.
Athlete Management Services:
Promotion, contract negotiation, representation, accounting, legal and related services.
Event Management Services:
Full event management, including planning, sponsorship, traffic promotion and ticket

---

sales, program books, exhibit areas, post event merchandising sales.
Marketing & Consulting Services:
Subsidiary of advertising agency, fully staffed to provide publicity and advertising services.

AMERICAN GRAPHITI
101 TREMONT STREET
BOSTON, MA 02108-5004
617-426-6668
Fax: 617-848-8950
elleng@americangraphiti.com
www.americangraphiti.com
• Ellen Gitelman, President
elleng@americangraphiti.com
Services:
Offers Public Relations and Marketing services.
Event Management Services:
Manages all aspects of events. Designs sponsorship programs, secures media sponsors, creates promotions, handles press and publicity, and obtains celebrity endorsements and appearances. Develops events from scratch or brings added value and fresh ideas to existing events.
Sports Service Founded:
1987

AMERICAN MARKETING AND MOTORSPORTS GROUP
26 GARDEN STREET
NEW YORK MILLS, NY 13417
315-736-8834
• Ralph Stoppiello, President/New Business Manager
• Dale Stoppiello, Vice President

ATHERTON COMMUNICATIONS, LP
705 BOSTON POST ROAD
GUILFORD, CT 6437
203-604-0028
Fax: 203-604-0028
www.athertoncommunications.com
• R. Kent Atherton, Founder/President
(203) 604-0028
Year Founded:
1994
Event Management Services:
Develops, produces and manages sports events for network broadcast including major college basketball invitational, The John R. Wooden Classic, Jet Jam (a 3 day extreme water sport and concert event, featuring professional personal watercraft racing), competing on the IJSBA tour and professional wakeboarding. Designs sponsorship opportunities with strategic marketing components to introduce advertising, merchandising and licensing rights.

AUTO SPORTS MARKETING GROUP
PO BOX 491
CLARKS SUMMIT, PA 18411
570-586-2198
Fax: 570-586-2198
sales@kidracers.com
www.kidracers.com
• Oscar Koveleski, Founder/Designer
Nature of Service:
50 years of organizing, managing events, contests, auto races (SCAA races at Pocono Raceway) model cars, slot cars, R/C cars, Battery Ride Ons, for SCCA, IMSA, NASCAR, IRL, SVRA, tracks and

---

shows. Now offers consultant services for hire performed by hand picked special ops personnel. References include food industry, auto industry, toy industry, hobby industry, sanctioning bodies, track management.
Sports Service Founded:
1980
Athlete Management Services:
Auto racing sponsors.
Event Management Services:
Auto racing event promotion.
Brands:
Ferrari Monza, McLaren MK2, McLaren MK6, McLaren MK8B, 1914 Stutz Bearcat, Baby Ferrari 250, Type 52 Baby Bugatti Replica, Bugatti Vise

---

BEAR FOOT SPORTS
20 TOWNE DRIVE
PMB #200
BLUFFTON, SC 29910
843-757-8520
www.bearfootsports.com
• Mark Weisner, President/Founder
Sports Service Founded:
1991
Services:
Sports marketing and special event producer. Source for Adult Soccer Six Tournaments and Road Races. Publishes Coastal Sport & Wellness and provides Consultant Services for soccer, running and festival event planners.
Marketing & Consulting Services:
Consults with corporations with regard to corporate sponsorships, advertising and sales promotion related to sports and sports events. Also publishes COASTAL SPORT and WELLNESS. Corporate event planning.
Clients Include:
Universal Studios, Valsport, Select Sport, Tenet Health Systems, Nova Care, Hargray Communications, Pepsi, Old Navy.

BEWI PRODUCTIONS, INC.
240 BEAR HILL ROAD
SUITE 201
WALTHAM, MA 2451
781-890-3234
Fax: 781-890-0534
www.bewisports.com
• Bernard E. Weichsel, Founder/President
Nature of Service:
Producer of Ski and Snowboard Expos, Active Sports Events, Specialty Winter Promotions and The New England Youth Sports Festival.
Sports Service Founded:
1979
Clients:
U.S. Ski Team and other non-profit Organizations
Event Management Services:
Complete production services - creation, implementation and on-site. Produces consumer snowsports expos in Boston; Denver. Specialists in skiing, outdoor wintertime activities. And the all new: New England Youth Sports Festival.

BLALOCK COMPANY, JANE
197EIGHTH STREET - FLAGSHIP WHARF
BOSTON, MA 2129
617-225-0008
800-466-1133
Fax: 617-621-8630

mbedrosian@jbcgolf.com
www.cowen-design.com/JBC
• Jane Blalock, President/Chief Executive Officer
• Jenn Shedd, Merchandise
jshedd@jbcgolf.com
• Mark Keaney, Sponsorship Sales
mkeaney@jbcgolf.com
• Megan Gardner, Marketing Opportunities
mgardner@jbcgolf.com
Services:
Produces top-quality, innovative golf programs and events.
Marketing & Consulting Services:
Primary focus in the area of golf. Specialists in corporate outings; creation and development of corporate programs; conference entertainment in golf, tennis and skiing. Organizer and creator of senior tournament featuring LPGA legends.
Event Management Services:
Organizers of the Gillette LPGA Golf Clinics and the Cadillac Golf Series for Women.
Sports Service Founded:
1990

BMK SPORTS
1207 BRIDGEWAY
SAUSALITO, CA 94965
415-289-5700
• Barry Mackay, Owner
• Rick Raducha, Owner
Services:
Sports Promotions
Sports Service Founded:
1970
Event Management Services:
Manages with SJAM ATP Tour Event, San Jose Arena, annually in February.

BRITTEN MEDIA
2322 CASS ROAD
TRAVERSE CITY, MI 49684
855-763-8204
Fax: 231-941-8299
• Paul Britten, President
Services:
Maker of unique banners, flags, and event solutions.
Clients:
University of Notre Dame, Tournament of Roses, ANC Sports, Anheuser-Busch, Indian Wells Tennis Center, Infineon Raceway, Atlanta Motor Speedway, Nasdaq 100 Tennis Open, Choice Hotels International, IMG, Dover Downs Entertainment, Gateway International Speedway, Bristol Motor Speedway, John Deer, Subaru of America, Crownline Boats, ATP Tennis, Paralyzed Veterans of America, Labatt USA, Mercedes-Benz Fashion Week, Pearle Vision, Purina, General Motors Corporation, Clear Channel Entertainment, General Growth Properties, Simon Property Group and Daytona International Speedway
Description:
Specializes in banner graphics.

BROTMAN WINTER FRIED COMMUNICATIONS, INC.
111 PARK PLACE
FALLS CHURCH, VA 22046
703-534-4600
Fax: 703-536-2255
• Charlie Brotman, Board Chairman/Chief Executive Officer/Founder

• Steve Winter, President/Chief Operating Officer
swinter@bwfcom.com
• Kenny Fried, Executive Vice President
kfried@bwfcom.com
• Brian Bishop, Vice President
Services:
Specializes in public and media relations, promotions, public service, community service, grass roots community outreach, special event management, artwork production, advertising and marketing campaigns.
Clients:
Booze Allen Classic Golf Tournament, DC United, D.C. Sports & Entertainment Commission, Legg Mason Tennis Classic, U.S. Soccer Foundation, RFK Stadium, California Tortilla, Bamboo Club, Coyote Ugly, Gordon Biersch Brewery Restaurant, Brasserie Les Halles, Starbucks, Tysons Corner Center, Foot Locker, Fahrney's Pens, Dulles Town Center, Hair Cuttery, Mervis Diamond Importers, DukesFest, Help the Homeless Walkathon, Sallie Mae 10K Road Race, McDonald's McSoccer Fest, Discovery Communications, Sport and Health Clubs, JK Moving and Storage, Mr. Wash's Brushless Car Wash, DC United's Kicks for Kids, Sallie Mae Fund, Hoop Dreams, Special Love, Most

---

BURWASH INTERNATIONAL, PETER
4200 RESEARCH FOREST DRIVE
SUITE 250
THE WOODLANDS, TX 77381
281-363-4707
800-255-4707
Fax: 281-292-7783
pbihq@pbitennis.com
www.pbitennis.com
• Chris Dyer, Chief Executive Officer
• Karen Kruse, Chief Financial Officer
• Chris Reid, Vice President
• Dave E. Neuhart, Tennis Director
• Chris Myrold, Director
Tennis Management Services:
Contracts with hotels, clubs and resorts all over the world to direct tennis operations. Also provides coaching services to national tennis teams in different countries, as well as on an individual basis to tournament players. Also manages and designs tennis facilities.
Event Management Services:
Produces International Tennis Show featuring entertainment and instruction. Produces tournaments, celebrity events, convention programs, grand openings.
Services:
Managing Professional Tennis Management and Staffing Hotels, Resorts and Clubs.
Products:
High Performance Tennis Apparel

CABELA'S SPORTSMAN'S QUEST
ONE CABELA DRIVE
SIDNEY, NE 69160
308-255-1347
800-243-6626
corporate@cabelas.com
www.cabelas.com
• Dennis Highby, Chief Executive Officer
Services:
Producer of competitive fishing, archery and sportsmen's events across the United States.

Clients:
People who enjoy the outdoor lifestyle
Event Management Services:
Develops and conducts shooting, angling, and outdoor sports promotions with participant and spectator appeal to hunters and anglers. Events include fishing tournaments, sporting clays, archery, sporting dogs, game calling, and all other related interests. Media exposure includes television coverage, a national radio network nation-wide and a magazine that is published six times a year. National sponsors include: Cabela's, Chevy Suburban-Tahoe, Starcraft, LaCrosse Footwear, VISA USA and Illinois DNR/DCCA.

CADWALADER, WICKERSHAM & TAFT
ONE WORLD FINANCIAL CENTER
NEW YORK, NY 10281
212-504-6000
Fax: 212-504-6666
www.cadwalader.com
• Marc A. Tolchin, Associate/Real Estate Finance
(212) 504-6019
marc.tolchin@cwt.com
• Andrew M. Troop, Partner/Financial Restructuring
(212) 504-6760
andrew.troop@cwt.com
Clients:
Financial Institutions, Industrial and Service Corporations, Governmental, Health Care and Not-For-Profit Entities, Individual Clients and Closely Held Companies
Description:
Project finance as been an integral component to the Firm's practice. Experience and expertise in ship, aircraft, electrical power generation, and sports arena financing. Represented banks financing the construction and renovation of the Golden State Warriors Arena, Oakland Raiders Coliseum, and Pasadena Rose Bowl.

CALIFORNIA CITYSPORTS/EVENT DIVISION
john@competitor.com
www.competitor.com
• John Smith, National Advertising Director
john@competitor.com
• Justin Sands, Regional Account Manager
justin@competitor.com
• Kelly Trimble, National Event Managing
kelly@competitor.com
• Geoff Barnett, Marketplace Advertising
geoff@competitor.com
Services:
Creates and manages sports events, focusing on lifestyle sports.

CAMEO MARKETING, INC
49 FARM VIEW DRIVE #302
SUITE 302
NEW GLOUCESTER, ME 4260
207-688-4580
Fax: 207-688-4581
www.cameomarketinginc.com
• Bob Tiernan, President
(207) 688-4580
• Bonnie Tirenan, COO
• Catriona Sumner, Director Account Services

Description:
Specializes in developing and managing sports, entertainment cause-related and media based event programs, Promotions and sponsorships. Cameo utilizes, mobile marketing and event execution.
Clients:
America Online, Castrol North America, United States Smokeless Tobacco, MCI / WorldCom Telecommunications, Schwans Sales Enterprises / Red Baron Frozen Pizza, Friendsly's Restaurant Corporation, Looking Glass Technologies, Ray Ban / Bausch & Lomb, Cadbury Beverages, Dynamix/Sierra Online, USPA & IRA, Hasbro Toys, Colgate Palmolive, Merryll Lynch Media, American Express / IDS Financial

CARD STUNTS BY KIVETT PRODUCTIONS
2543 SAINT HEATHER WAY
ORLANDO, FL 3206
407-342-0752
joe@cardstunts.com
www.cardstunts.com
• Joe Kivett, Owner
(407) 342-0752
joe@cardstunts.com
Founded:
1991
Nature of Service:
Audience participation flip card stunts

CARSON EVENTS INTERNATIONAL, INC.
323 LEWIS STREET
KETCHUM, ID 83340
208-726-5990
info@carsonevents.com
www.carsonevents.com
• Kathy Carson, President
• Paul Carson, Chief Executive Officer
• Dave Miglia, Operations Manager
• Art Daves, Vice President Operations/New Business
Services:
Event Management - Creation and concept design, Project management, Athlete liaison, Public relations, Venue procurement and site development, Vendor relations and contracting, Master scheduling, Staffing, Logistics and equipment management, Budgeting and accounting; Promotions - Merchandise programs, Product sampling, Consumer interactive programs, Celebrity endorsements, Public relations, Charity tie-ins, Fundraisers; Marketing - Creative elements, Print design and production, Corporate signage, Corporate functions and hospitality, Onsite branding design and production, Market and demographic research, Web element design and integration
Sports Service Founded:
1981

CHAMPIONSHIP MANAGEMENT EVENTS, INC.
307 N EUCLID AVENUE
ONTARIO, CA 91762-3425
909-460-5500
Services:
Sports Promotions and Special Events
Athlete Management Services:
Manages and produces professional PGA Tour and Champions Tour events in Las Vegas.

Marketing & Consulting Services:
Sports marketing programs and consulting for corporate sponsors.

CHAMPIONSHIP SPORTS GROUP
1219 N STUART STREET
ARLINGTON, VA 22201-4809
703-875-9192
Fax: 703-875-9130
• Jonathan Rourke, Owner
Services:
Sports Marketing and Event Management services.

CIVIC ENTERTAINMENT GROUP
450 PARK AVENUE S
FLOOR 5
NEW YORK, NY 10016
212-426-7006
Fax: 212-426-7002
• Parke Spencer, President
Description:
CEG is a full-service event planning and marketing firm. Produces and oversees all elements of promotional events. Not limited to New York, CEG's clients and events are nationwide.

CLEAR CHANNEL ENTERTAINMENT - MOTORSPORTS
4255 MERIDIAN PARKWAY
AURORA, IL 60504
630-566-6100
Services:
Producer and promoter of The Speed Stick presents National Arenacross Series and the Arenacross Series of regional events.
Clients:
Monster Trucks, Grave Digger, Supper Cross, Freestyle Motocross,IHRA, Arenacross, Road Racing, Street Warriorz, Alpinestars, Thor, Snow Cross, Freestyle Snowcross

COMCAST-SPECTATOR
215-336-3600
• Peter A Luukko, President/Chief Operating Officer
Services:
Provides high quality sports and entertainment services anf facilities, provides sports programming for regional cable television.
Marketing & Consulting Services:
Owns the Philadelphia 76ers NBA team and the NHL's Philadelphia Flyers. Comcast Spectator also owns the Wachovia Center and Watchovia Spectrum sports and event arenas, three minor league baseball teams, two soccer teams, one minor league hockey team, and one lacrosse team.

COMPASS COLLECTIVE
165 OTTLEY DRIVE NE
ATLANTA, GA 30324
404-875-6543
Fax: 404-875-7917
www.compasscollective.com
• David Peck, President/Chief Operating Officer
(404) 888-7723
• Robert A. Dailey, VP/Chief Executive Officer
(404) 888-7722
• Scott Hughes, Project Manager
(404) 888-7730

• David Peck, President
(404) 888-7723
• Rob Dailey, VP & CEO
(444) 888-7722
• Greg Oberholtzer, General Manager
(404) 888-7731
Services:
Design: - two and three dimensional design, space planning, technology fulfillment, engineering. Primary expertise: tradeshow exhibits, permanent showrooms, corporate environments, meeting and event properties, museums, kiosks, large-format graphic presentations, banners, tension fabric structures, design conversant with American and European portable/modular exhibit systems. Production - wood, metal and plastics fabrication shops. Tradeshow program management - comprehensive logistics coordination, knowledgeable and responsible on-site supervision, shipping, warehousing. Content development/digital animation - development and production of
Event Marketing Services:
A full-service exhibit designs and fabrication company which specialize in customer service oriented design, fabrication, installation and logistics for product rooms, special events, tradeshow exhibits, specialty retail environments and museums. Provides presence marketing for large scale events, NFL teams and major sponsors.

CONCORD EXPO GROUP
PO BOX 885
EDEN, UT 84310
801-745-8804
Fax: 801-745-8803
conexpogrp@earthlink.net
www.concordexpogroup.com
• Kathy Donnelly, President
Marketing & Consulting Services:
Promotion and management of foreign trade shows, organizing American pavilions at these shows.
Clients:
People who wish to participate in trade shows in foreign countries.

CONE COMMUNICATIONS
855 BOYLSTON STREET
BOSTON, MA 2116
617-227-2111
Fax: 617-523-3955
jbang@coneinc.com
• Jens Bang, President/Chief Executive Officer
(617) 227-2211
jbang@coneinc.com
• Jens Bang, CEO
(617) 939-8324
• Tim Munroe, VP Business Development
(617) 939-8325
tmunroe@ConeComm.com
• Bill Fleishman, President
(617) 939-8340
Services:
Helps companies build their brands and develop a competitive market position through innovative programs that respond to the needs and passions of consumers through Brand Marketing, Cause Branding and Crisis and Issues Management.
Sports Service Founded:
1980
Marketing & Consulting Services:

Specializing in sporting goods marketing communications

CONFERENCE PLANNERS
3600 GIDDINGS ROAD
AUBURN HILLS, MI 48326
248-475-2500
Fax: 248-475-2325
careers@gpj.com
www.gpj.com
• Jeff Rutchik, Executive VP
(617) 535-9912
sales@gpj.com
• Tom Maher, Executive Director, Marketing
tom.maher@gpj.com
Description:
Provider of event management services and web-based registration tools that enable superior event performance.
Services:
Help clients improve event performance, reduce costs and deliver results throught the event portfolio, from tradeshows and conferences to road shows, mobile marketing and sponsorships.

CONVENTURES, INC.
ONE DESIGN CENTER PLACE
BOSTON, MA 2210
617-439-7700
Fax: 617-439-7701
info@conventures.com
www.conventures.com
• Ted Breslin, Vice President & CFO
tbreslin@conventures.com
• Kathleen Chrisom, Vice President, Sales & Marketing
kchrisom@conventures.com
• Dusty S. Rhodes, President
drhodes@conventures.com
• David Choate, Vice President & COO
dchoate@conventures.com
Nature of Service:
An special event agency focused on integrated event planning, public relations and marketing.
Event Management Services:
Marketing, promotion, publicity and on-site management of sporting events including road races, international soccer tournaments, track and field meets, golf tournaments, tennis celebrity series, exhibitions and seminars.

CORPORATE COMMUNICATIONS, INC.
108 S UNION STREET
ROCHESTER, NY 14607
585-262-3430
Fax: 585-262-3436
email@corp.com
www.corporatecomm.com
• Terry Palis, President
• Gil Fuqua, President
Services:
Full service advertising, marketing and public relations company that helps improve client's market share, positioning and corporate/public image.
Event Management Services:
Full service advertising, marketing, public relations, promotions, sponsor procurement and events administration. Consulting services available on per-project/event basis, as well as for entire event management.
Marketing & Consulting Services:
Marketing and consulting services for all

---

areas of event management and business promotion.

COSTANTE GROUP SPORTS & EVENT MARKETING, LLC
4741 CENTRAL STREET
SUITE 117
KANSAS CITY, MO 64112
210-213-8792
don@costantegroup.com
www.costantegroup.com
• Don Costante, President
(210) 213-8792
don@costantegroup.com
• Kyle Hamrick, Producer and Video Specialist
• Zach Dierks, Producer, writer and editor
• Beth Roche, Client Services Specialist
• MIke Behymer, Business Development
• Jason Lodato, Event Management Speciaist
• Kasey Schweitzer, Event Presentation
• Don Costante, Event Presentation & Production Specialist
Nature of Service:
The Costante Group offers a comprehensive solution for every aspect of athletic or corporate event production, designed to integrate seamlessly with your existing team in whatever capacity necessary. If specialized training or advice is all your staff requires, the Costante Group provides strategic consultations. If you're seeking more inclusive services, again, the Costante group steps up to meet your challenge.
Clients:
Jordan Brand Classic, NBA Entertainment, U.S. Army All-American Bowl
Year Founded:
2007

CREATIVE FACTOR, INC.
9805 HORTON RD. SW
CALGARY, ALBERTA, CANADA T2V 2X5
403-301-0811
403-719-3844
Fax: 403-301-0889
info@creativefactor.ca
www.creativefactor.ca
• Lynne DuVivier, President
Event Management Services:
Sales promotion, premium, and advertising specialty company that specializes in event and sports promotions. Provides custom manufacturing, imprinting, packaging, fulfillment, etc.

CREATIVE GROUP, INC.
619 N LYNNDALE DRIVE
APPLETON, WI 54914
920-739-8850
800-236-2800
Fax: 920-739-8817
webmaster@creativegroupinc.com
www2.creativegroupinc.com
• Ron Officer, President/CEO
• Janet Traphagen, EVP, Sales
Description:
Expertise includes: Event planning, Meetings, sponsorship hospitality and event public relations programs. Works with clients on incentive programs with the ability to be flexible. Offers planning, imaginative promotion, reliable administration and budget management.
Services:
Provides a variety of marketing services

---

specializing in building and managing incentive programs and planning corporate meetings and events. It also offers personal travel services including travel planning and emergency services that benefit from the company's large corporate travel business.

DEBOW COMMUNICATIONS, LTD.
350 W 31ST STREET
NEW YORK, NY 10001-2726
212-239-3000
Fax: 212-977-8376
info@debow.com
www.debow.com
• Thomas J. DE Bow, Owner
Services:
Creates, develops and implements effective integrated marketing solutions such as advertising programs, nationwide survey of real estate professionals, employee voluntary benefit enrollment program, corporate asset retention program, marketing program, on-line shopping and financial communications program.
Sports Service Founded:
1976
Event Management Services:
Creates and manages sports events with experience in billiards, football, and golf.
Marketing & Consulting Services:
Full service agency experienced in all facets of marketing strategy and communications, public relations, and advertising, including implementation services such as copy, art, and design.

DRIVER CONNECTION/RAPID RACEWAYS
161 WOODFORD AVENUE
UNIT 55
PLAINVILLE, CT 06062
860-793-1888
Fax: 860-229-3970
Services:
Provides renting of race cars as well as weekly competition events for every age and skill level. Features two state of the art racetracks supported by complete inventory of beginner cars to high performance cars, as well as parts and accessories for either the amateur or professional racer. Also features monthly major racing events.
Services:
Motorsports Marketing and Promotions
Clients:
Work with speedways, businesses and corporations in the field of sponsorship, marketing and promotions
Services:
Event Management Services: Development and organization of advertising, sponsorship, and entertainment programs at events, speedways, charity functions, trade shows, car shows, autograph sessions, etc.
Marketing & Consulting Services: Specializes in the development and fulfillment of advertising and promotional programs for businesses and corporations utilizing motorsports to build sales, improve credibility while strengthening brand loyalty to accomplish business goals
Services:
Event Management Services: Development and organization of advertising, sponsorship, and entertainment programs at events, speedways, charity functions, trade shows, car shows, autograph sessions, etc.

Marketing & Consulting Services: Specializes in the development and fulfillment of advertising and promotional programs for businesses and corporations utilizing motorsports to build sales, improve credibility while strengthening brand loyalty to accomplish business goals

Event Management Services: Development and organization of advertising, sponsorship, and entertainment programs at events, speedways, charity functions, trade shows, car shows, autograph sessions, etc.

What We Offer: Weekly Slot Car Events, Birthday Parties, Club Racing, Track & Car Rentals, Parts & Supplies, 1/24th and 1/32nd Scale Cars. We also feature monthly major racing events perfect for both the amateur and professional.

DSL GLOBAL EVENT MARKETING
94 VALLEY ROAD
MONTCLAIR, NJ 7042
336-924-1141
Fax: 336-924-1152
Description:
Specializes in mobile marketing tours, special events, event sponsorships and media events.
Services:
Provides integrated event marketing, development, consulting, and management services.
Clients:
The Upper Deck Company and Sony

EAGLE INTERNATIONAL TENTS & AIR DOMES
5620 E SHEA BOULEVARD
SCOTTSDALE, AZ 85254
480-219-9400
www.ei-tents.com
• Buford J. Dowell, Owner/Founder
• Rav.Buford Dowell, Founder
• Shannon Dowell, Associate
Services:
Offers a wide variety of products and services such as Giant Pole Tents, Frame Tents, Clear Span, Air Dome and like portable structures.
Event Management Services:
Agency for the design & production of pole & metal frame tents, clear span portable structures, large air supported dome - arenas, sports covers for tennis - golf - soccer - hockey - basketball - volleyball - football - ice skating - skateboarding - driving ranges - storage - pools.

EDELMAN SPORTS/EVENT MARKETING
200 E RANDOLPH STREET
63RD FLOOR
CHICAGO, IL 60601
312-240-3000
Fax: 312-240-2900
www.edelman.com
• Daniel J. Edelman, Founder/Chairman
• Richard Edelman, President/Chief Executive Officer
• Richard Edelman, President
Event Management Services:
All phases of public relations and other related activities designed to maximize the value of client-sponsored sports events. Clients include MVP.com.

Sports Service Founded:
1988

ELITE RACING, INC.
9477 WAPLES STREET
SUITE 150
SAN DIEGO, CA 92121
858-450-6510
800-311-1255
Fax: 858-450-6905
www.eliteracing.com
• Tim Murphy, Founder/Chief Executive Officer
Description:
Sports marketing and management company. Elite Racing organizes eight events each year, including the Rock 'n' Roll Marathon and the Carlsbad 5000, the world's fastest 5K.
Services:
Sports and management company that produces world-class running events.
Clients:
Produces Rock 'n' Roll Marathon and Carlsbad 5000

EPIC: STRATEGIC PLANNING & INTEGRATION WORLDWIDE
ATLANTA, GA
770-457-1145
ashaw@epic-usa.com
www.epic-usa.com
• Alan Shaw, Managing Director
• Steve Clark, Former Director
Year Founded:
1996
Description:
Provides strategic (and tactical) event planning & operations services with a focus on planning & execution of major sporting events. Assists corporations, organizing committees and association/federations who sponsor, own/operate and participate in a wide variety of large-scale sporting events, including Olympic Games, FIFA World Cups, Asian Games, Pan Am Games and Commonwealth Games. Established in 1996, by former Olympic/World Cup executive, Alan Shaw and purchased by LeadDog Marketing Group, Inc. in 2007. Core competencies and areas of expertise include: Strategic Planning, Event Ops Planning & Auditing, Venue Management & Ops, Workforce

---

EVENT AUDIO VISUAL GROUP
45053 GRAND RIVER AVENUE
SUITE C
NOVI, MI 48375
800-935-2323
Fax: 800-935-8191
detroit@subrent.com
www.subrent.com
• Bret Tracey, President
(248) 867-4160
btracey@subrent.com
• Keith Solomon, Operations Manager
(248) 240-0519
ksolomon@subrent.com
Services:
Wholesale provider of LCD and DLP Projectors, lenses, video switchers and accessories for rental and resales.
Event Management Services:
Specializes in video displays for indoor and outdoor events.

Sports Service Founded:
1988

EVENTIVE MARKETING
488 MADISON AVE
4TH FLOOR
NEW YORK, NY 10022-5702
212-463-9700
Fax: 212-727-1716
www.eventivemarketing.com
• David Saalfrank, Senior Vice President Business Development
• David Saalfrank, Senior Vice President
• Ernie Kapanke, Vice President
• Raffi Grigorian, CEO
Services:
Event Marketing, Sampling Programs, Sponsorship Activation, Retail-tainment, Mobile Marketing, Multi-Cultural Marketing
Sports Service Founded:
1992
Event Management Services:
Design and implement programs geared toward a demographic audience from an athletes to weekend warriors. Marathons, triathlons, mountain biking or road racing, health clubs or ski resorts. Develops and execute integrated marketing programs that combine brand equity building elements.

EVENTS PROMOTIONS USA
1270 GLEN AVE.
MOORETOWN, NJ 08057
602-840-9005
800-378-6373
Fax: 602-840-9291
• Tim A. Owens, Chief Executive Officer/Event Producer
(602) 840-9005
• Tom G. Tygett, President/Event Producer/Operations Director
(480) 941-1911
Description:
Specializes in working with municipalities and non-profit organizations in the marketing, sales and production of major events on a public/private partnership. Integration includes: event marketing, sponsorship/partnership development, entertainment productions, special event food service and catering management, site management, etc.
Sports Service Founded:
1987

EXTRAORDINARY EVENTS
13425 VENTURA BOULEVARD
SUITE 300
SHERMAN OAKS, CA 91423
818-783-6112
Fax: 818-783-8957
www.extraordinaryevents.net
• Andrea Michaels, President
amichaels@extraordinaryevents.net
• Jon Michaels, EVP Operations
jmichaels@extraordinaryevents.net
• Lauren Arnold, Associate producer
• Mandy Bianchi, Account Manager
• Taylor Black, Senior Account Manager
• Chris Clark, Senior Accoun Executive
• Brad Dawson, CPA-Accounting Manager
• Andrea Michaels, President of Extraordinary Events
amichaels@extraordinaryevents.net
Description:
Specializes in entertainment marketing. Headline entertainment, award

presentations, business theater, gala events, theme events, music and entertainment, product launches, tradesshow-productions sponsorships and sales support, tours and transportation, venues.
Sports Service Founded:
1988

FELD ENTERTAINMENT
8607 WESTWOOD CENTER DRIVE
VIENNA, VA 22182
703-448-4000
Fax: 703-448-4100
information@feldinc.com
www.feldentertainment.com
• Kenneth Feld, Chairman/Chief Executive Officer
• Mike Ruch, Chief Financial Officer
• Julie Robertson, Marketing SVP
• Jason Bitsoff, VP/GM Sponsorship/Strategic Alliance
Event Management Services:
Produces show featuring world-class figure skating and Disney starts showcased by state-of-the-art staging and special effects. Regular tour appears in over 90 markets annually.

FLW OUTDOORS
30 GAMBLE LANE
BENTON, KY 42025
270-252-1000
info@flwoutdoors.com
• Jeff McCoy, Director Public Relations
jeff.mccoy@jacobs-mgmt.com
• Charlie Evans, President

FORESITE SPORTS
234 BRYN MAWR AVENUE
SUITE 101
BRYN MAWR, PA 19010-2133
610-525-8003
888-882-5440
Fax: 610-525-8004
info@foresitesports.com
www.foresitesports.com
Event Management Services:
Full service golf tournament supply firm specializing in hole in one insurance, putting contest coverage, shootout contests, event signage and promotional products.
Services:
Specializes in supplying and organizing golf outings and instructional clinics.

FRANKEL SPORTS GROUP
35 W WACKER DRIVE
CHICAGO, IL 60601
312-220-3200
• Marc Landsberg, Global President
• Bill Rosen, Chief Creative Officer
• Jeff Lupinacci, Chief Financial Officer
• Jenny Cacioppo, EVP/Managing Director
Services:
Sales promotion agency specializes in motivating consumers to buy now.
Clients:
Allstate, AT&T, Coca-Cola, CDC, Cuervo, Dreyers, GM, Mcdonald's, Kellogg's, P&G, Symantec, Visa, Tylenol, United,Whirlpool
Event Management Services:
Develops and implements national, regional and local events. Coordinates and executes cross promotions with event media partners, co-sponsors and athletes. Advertising, New Product Introduction, Brand Positioning,

Packaging, Direct/Database, Marketing, Promotional Products & Services, Employee Communications, Public Relations, Entertainment Marketing, Retail Design and Ethnic Marketing.
Sports Service Founded:
1984
Marketing & Consulting Services:
Sports marketing, strategic development and consultation. Advises corporations currently using or seeking to use sports as a strategic marketing tool. Creates sponsorships and marketing programs, with major sports organizations, leagues, teams, federations and networks. Plans and develops sales promotion, public relations and licensing programs relating to sports marketing.
Services:
Advertising, New Product Introduction, Brand Positioning, Packaging, Direct/Database, Marketing, Promotional Products & Services, Employee Communications, Public Relations, Entertainment Marketing, Retail Design, Ethnic Marketing, Sports Marketing, Event Marketing Sweepstakes, Contests and Games, Fulfillment, Tie-in Partnerships, Kids Marketing, Trade Promotion, Loyalty Programs, Web Design, Marketing Research.
Clients:
Allstate, AT&T Wireless, Coca-Cola, CDC, Clorox, Cuervo, Dreyer's, General Motors, Kellogg's, London Fog, McDonald's, Proctor & Gamble, Symantec, Tylenol, United, Visa, Whirlpool.
Other Locations:
103 Carnegie Center, Suite 106, Princeton, NJ 08540. 609-720-1000; 303 Second Street, South Tower, Fourth Floor, San Francisco, CA 94107. 415-344-6400.

FRONT RUNNER
1665 9TH STREET
WHITE BEAR LAKE, MN 55110
651-653-7401
randy@frontrunnerusa.com
www.frontrunnerusa.com
Nature of Service:
Consulting firm in sport marketing, sports promotion, sports public relations. Specializing in running and fitness sports. President is 3-time U.S. Olympic Distance Runner and 2-time World Champion.
Sports Service Founded:
January 1980

GAMEDAY MANAGEMENT GROUP
315 E ROBINSON STREET
SUITE 505
ORLANDO, FL 32801
407-648-0213
Fax: 407-648-2418
www.gamedaymanagementgroup.com
• Tony Vitrano, President
• Mike Witte, Senior VP Operations
• Mike Witte, Vice President
• Deborah McCandless, Vice President
• Cristine Paull, Vice President
• Jeff Hinton, Director Sales/Marketing
jhinton@gamedaymanagement.com
Nature of Service:
Gameday Management Group specializes in the design and implementation of effective transportation management solutions for sporting and special events. Services

include event traffic plan design and implementation, shuttle system design & ground travel management.
Year Founded:
1994
Clients:
National Football League (Super Bowl), NFL Europa, Major League Baseball, International Speedway Corporation, Daytona International Speedway, California Speedway, Capital One Bowl, Champs Sports Bowl, Arena Football League, Soccer United Marketing, City of Glendale (AZ), University of Florida, University of Central Florida, 2005 Presidential Inauguration, 2004 G8 Summit.

GCI GROUP
200 FIFTH AVENUE
NEW YORK, NY 10010
212-798-9700
Fax: 212-329-9900
jim.joseph@cohnwolfe.com
www.cohnwolfe.com
• Donna Imperato, President/Chief Executive Officer
(212) 789-9800
• Tom Petrosini, EVP/CFO
(212) 789-9857
Services:
Areas of Expertise are Community Relations, Consumer Marketing, Corporate Communications, Events Marketing, Healthcare Communications, Media Relations, Multi-Cultural Marketing, New Product Launches, Public Affairs, Youth Marketing
Services:
Industry Knowledge: Automotive, Beauty & Health, Biotechnology, Consumer Health Products, Diet & Nutrition, Fashion & Apparel, Financial Services, Food & Beverage, Gas & Oil, Government Agencies, Home Entertainment, Home Improvement, Hospitality, Hospitals, Media Organizations, Medical Devices, Over-the-Counter Medications, Payors/Providers, Pharmaceuticals, Retail, Sports Organizations, Technology, Telecommunications, Third Party Organizations, Toys, and Transportation
Sports Service Founded:
1984
Event Management Services:
All facets of event marketing and management.

GIVING BACK FUND
6033 W CENTURY BOULEVARD
SUITE 350
LOS ANGELES, CA 90045
310-649-5222
Fax: 310-649-5070
main@givingback.org
www.givingback.org
• Marc Pollick, Founder/President
• Stephanie Sandler, Senior Vice President
Year Founded:
1997
Description:
To advise and mentor professional athletes, entertainers, business entrepreneurs, and others according to best practices in philanthropy and to leverage celebrity to raise funds for a wide range of charitable causes and important social issues.
Clients:

The Yao Ming Foundation, The Ben Roethlisberger Foundation, The Ben Gordon New Life Foundation, and others

GLOBAL EVENT MAKERS USA
11408 ORCHARD PARK DRIVE
SUITE 311
GLEN ALLEN, VA 23059
804-273-6731
800-476-8368
Fax: 804-273-6732
www.eventmakersusa.com
• Lawrence A. Creeger, Founder/President
(804) 273-6731
Event Management Services:
Rental equipment design, rental installation and management. Includes hospitality area concessions and spectator areas - tenting, heating, lighting, sound, crowd control, equipment for catering.

GLOBAL SPECTRUM
3601 S BROAD STREET
PHILADELPHIA, PA 19148
215-389-9587
Fax: 215-952-5651
tglickman@comcast-spectacor.com
www.global-spectrum.com
• Todd Glickman, Vp Business Development/Client Relations
tglickman@comcast-spectacor.com
• Tom Bradley, Box Office Manager
• Wayne Letson, Facility Engineer
• Todd Glickman, Senior Vp/COO
(215) 389-9587
jpage@comcast-spectacor.com
Nature of Service:
Provides innovative management, marketing, operations and event booking services for public assembly facilities, including arenas, civic and convention centers, stadiums, ice facilities, equestrian centers and theatres.
Marketing & Consulting Services:
Provides innovative, customized management and consulting solutions for the planning, start-up and operation of arenas, stadiums, convention centers and theaters worldwide.

GMR MARKETING
16155 W.STRATTON DR.
NEW BERLIN, WI 53151
262-786-5600
Fax: 262-786-0697
msmathers@gmrlive.com
www.gmrmarketing.com
• Gary Reynolds, Chief Executive Officer/Chairman
• Craig Connelly, President
• Bryan Buske, Chief Operating Officer
• Jay Lenstrom, Chief Marketing Officer
• Mike Boykin, EVP Sports
• Greg Busch, SVP Group Account Director
• Steve Dupee, Senior Director Sports
• Todd Fischer, Account Supervisor
• Tamera Green, Vice President
• David Martin, Account Director
• Dave Mullins, Account Executive
• Jonathan Norman, Sports Director
• Tyson Webber, Senior Account Director
Event Marketing Services:
Organization offers unique blend of event marketing strategic consulting and execution for Fortune 500 clients and brings expertise in key market segments including sports, music, entertainment, ethnic, lifestyle and mobile marketing.
Services:
Creates specialized event marketing programs for sports, music, lifestyle, and mobile marketing campaigns. The company produces product promotions at shopping malls, temporary retail locations, concerts, sports, and lifestyle events. It provides all-inclusive services - from concept and design to construction and site management.
Clients:
Alltel, DaimlerChrysler, Gillette, McDonald's, Microsoft, Miller Brewig Co., Nokia, Unilever and WM Wrigley Jr. Co.
Sports Service Founded:
1979
Clients Include:
Microsoft Corporation, Pepsi, Mercedes Benz, The Miller Brewing Company, Unilever, Intel, Kraft Food, Family Show.

GROUP DYNAMICS
411 US ROUTE
ONE FALMOUTH, ME 4105
207-781-8800
800-626-3539
Fax: 207-781-3841
info@groupdynamicsinc.com
www.groupdynamicsinc.com
• Robert Funk, President
Services:
A full service marketing and promotions company which specializes in the production and promotion of major national and international sporting and entertainment events. Provides operations, advertising, public relations, point-of sale production, marketing, sampling and event management services for major U.S. and International corporations. Organize MISS DANCE DIRLL TEAM COMPETITION.
Sports Service Founded:
1969
Marketing & Consulting Services:
Marketing consultation and sales promotion for sports and segmented marketing.

GROUP FIVE SALES, EVENT & SPORTS MARKETING
8701 MALLARD CREEK ROAD
CHARLOTTE, NC 28262
704-547-0683
Services:
Management Consulting and Event Marketing Services.
Description:
An event marketing company which is evolving to embrace the Internet to assist companies and their agencies to improve their results in the event marketing arena. Their software system that uses the Internet for the evaluation of a proposed event sponsorship in a fraction of the time it traditionally takes. The evaluation provides specific information in relation to the company's marketing goals. Specializing in the sports marketing and evaluation arena.

GUS MACKER BASKETBALL
107 EAST MAIN STREET
SUITE 3
BELDING, MI 48809
616-794-1445
Fax: 616-794-1472
www.macker.com
• Scott McNeal, Founder

Description:
The concept of Gus Macker 3-on-3 basketball tournament is being imitated across the USA but the Macker is still the one-and-only original game that is evolving as the hottest mass participation sport today.
Services:
Organizes 3-on-3 Basketball Tournaments which creates marketing opportunities for the sponsors.
Sports Service Founded:
1974

HAMILTON ASSOCIATES, SEENA
1161 YORK AVENUE
SUITE 12E
NEW YORK, NY 10065-7971
212-308-5368
Fax: 212-753-8742
• Seena Hamilton, President
Services:
Creative, PR-focused marketing firm specializing in the design and promotion of high-profile events, sponsorships, and multi-faceted marketing campaigns that meet a client's objectives.
Event Management Services:
Public relations focused events marketing firm that specializes in developing unique strategies for leveraging corporate sports and entertainment sponsorships with high-profile public relations and promotion programs

HCC SPECIALTY UNDERWRITERS, INC
401 EDGEWATER PLACE
SUITE 400
WAKEFIELD, MA 1880
781-994-6000
800-927-6306
Fax: 781-994-6001
inquiry@hccsu.com
www.hccsu.com
• Bill Hubbard, Chairman
• Marc Idelson, President/Chief Underwriting Officer
midelson@hccsu.com
• Matt Overlan, Chief Financial/Chief Operations Officer
moverlan@hccsu.com
• Mark Barry, Marketing Senior Vice President
mbarry@hccsu.com
Services:
Provides creative insurance solutions utilizing an ever-evolving portfolio of products and continuously expanding capabilities/leading provider of specialty insurance to the promotion marketing, sports and entertainment industries
Services:
Coverage includes disability, accidental death and dismemberment, life medical expense, team catastrophic, kidnap and ransom, and team stop/loss, event cancellation, weather insurance, special event liability insurance, prize indemnity insurance, contractual bonus insurance

HERITAGE CLASSIC FOUNDATION
71 LIGHTHOUSE ROAD
SUITE 4200
HILTON HEAD ISLAND, SC 29928
843-671-2448
800-234-1107

Fax: 843-671-6738
www.heritageclassicfoundation.com
• Simon Fraser, Chairman
• Ed Dowaschinski, VP Finance &
Administration
• Rick Reichel, Treasurer
Sports Service Founded:
1990
Services:
Sponsor of the Verizon Heritage, South
Carolina's only PGA TOUR event to
generate funds for local and state charities
and award grants to the Foundation's
scholars.
Event Management Services:
Manages all aspects of sports events.

HIGHLINE SPORTS & ENTERTAINMENT
12 VAIL ROAD
SUITE 500
VAIL, CO 81657
970-476-6797
Fax: 970-476-6890
www.gohighline.com
• Jeff Brausch, President/Chief Executive
Officer
(970) 476-6797
• James Deighan, Vice President
(970) 476-6797
jamesd@gohighline.com
• Kelli Brausch, Controller
(970) 328-0905
Sports Service Founded:
1996
Event Management Services:
A three-fold company focusing on the
marketing and promotion of sporting events,
media products, and organizations. The
company offers expertise in sponsorship
coordination, event production and
management, event marketing, sales
promotions and public relations.
Events include:
Vail Mogul Mania, Mountain Challenger, Vail
Ultra 100, Fore SOS Par-Tee.
Services:
Leading provider of sports and
entertainment event marketing services. The
company specializes in creating turn-key
event marketing programs and successful
partnerships with many of the world's
leading brands.

HOMESTEAD MIAMI SPEEDWAY
ONE SPEEDWAY BOULEVARD
HOMESTEAD, FL 33035-1501
305-230-5000
866-409-7223
Fax: 305-230-5140
hmstix@homesteadmiamispeedway.com
www.homesteadmiamispeedway.com
• Sherry Adams, Corporate
Partnerships/Hospitality Sponsorship
(305) 230-5209
• Matthew Becherer, President
Event Management Services:
Creates, manages and promotes auto
racing events including, but not limited to,
IndyCar, NASCAR, Formula One.
Services:
Creates, manages and promotes auto
racing events. Home of the Ford 400 and
Ford Championship Weekend, featuring the
finales for the NASCAR NEXTEL Cup,
Busch, and Craftsman Truck Series.

HURRICANE GOLF
203 E LINCOLN HIGHWAY
DEKALB, IL 60115
815-217-0110
866-955-3362
Fax: 815-787-3720
orders@hurricanegolf.com
www.hurricanegolf.com
• Mark Rankin, Sales
• Rob Lopez, Sales
(512) 385-4653
Services:
Event management for sporting events,
production of large scale golf tournaments

ILTIS ASSOCIATES, JOHN
680 N LAKE SHORE DRIVE
SUITE 1328
CHICAGO, IL 60611-4546
312-787-8253
Fax: 312-337-1258
• John Iltis, President
Event Management Services:
Organize sport sponsorships and promote
sports events.
Marketing & Consulting Services:
Licensing; coordination of corporations with
sports events for promotion and
sponsorship.

IMAGE IMPACT
4925 WYACONDA ROAD
ROCKVILLE, MD 20852
301-984-8283
800-336-0966
Fax: 212-208-4677
www.imageimpactinc.com
• Mickey Lawrence, President
• Olie Pirzadeh, President

IMPACT SPORTS, INC.
7322 E BROADWAY
SPOKANE, WA 99212
509-924-7768
Fax: 509-924-7668
www.tnb.net/impact-sports
• Paul Sorensen, Chief Executive Officer
• Gary Knudson, President
• Murray Walden, VP
Services:
A sports marketing company specializing in
college athletics. Produces and markets
radio and television broadcasts, handles
game day promotions and markets on site
signage at collegiate sporting venues.
Event Management Services:
Produces annual sports events in the
Kingdome including the Kingbowl (High
School State Championships), Washington
State University TV, Eastern Washington
University Radio Network, and World Indoor
Paper Airplane Championship; plus,
produces TV and radio sports packages of
high school football and basketball; national
cycling championships.

**IMS PROPERTIES/INDY MOTOR
SPEEDWAY**
4790 W 16TH STREET
INDIANAPOLIS, IN 46222
317-492-6750
sales@brickyard.com
www.indianapolismotorspeedway.com
• Joie Chitwood, President/Chief Operating
Officer
(970) 476-6797

Marketing & Consulting Services:
Representation of the Indianapolis
Speedway Corporation's trademarks for
marketing, licensing, and sponsorship.
Event Management Services:
Manages all aspects of the Indianapolis 500
and the Brickyard 400.
Athlete Management Services:
Represents Indy Racing League drivers and
teams in marketing, licensing, and
sponsorship opportunities.

INTERBIKE
31910 DEL OBISPO STREET
SUITE 200
SAN JUAN CAPISTRANO, CA 92675
240-439-2986
866-221-7934
Fax: 949-226-5686
www.interbike.com
• Andria Klinger, Sales Manager
(949) 226-5745
• Pat Hus, Managing Director
• Sarah Timleck, Marketing Director
• Justin Gottlieb, Director Of
Communications & PR
• Jennie Brewton-Dufur, Art Director
Marketing & Consulting Services:
Produces INTERBIKE, national trade show
for bicycle products. Also publishes
industry-wide bicycle market Interbike
directory.

JAVELIN
1910 LOCUST STREET
ST LOUIS, MO 63103
314-361-1450
Fax: 314-361-1451
hello@javelin-inc.com
www.javelin-inc.com
• Donna Meier, Senior Partner
donnam@javelin-inc.com
• Jen Novak, Senior Partner
jenn@javelin-inc.com
• Jon Maurice, Executive Creative Director
jonm@javelin-inc.com
• Mark Lockwood, VP Bussiness
Development
markl@javelin-inc.com
• Tammy Derigan, Senior Dir of Cultural and
Consumer insights
tammyd@javelin-inc.com
• David Catron, Director of production
davidc@javelin-inc.com
• Mark Lockwood, Vice President Business
Development
(314) 361-1450
markl@javelin-inc.com
Services:
Concept development; creative design and
production; account and budget
management; end-to-end logistics
management/tour scheduling; set, activity
and exhibit design; fabrication and
production; venue/location/event research;
selection, negotiation and sell-in; sampling
goods management/warehousing; field
staffing, training and management; vehicle
leasing/insurance/maintenance/DOT
compliance; & Bulls-i ROI evaluation/project
reporting/recap
Nature of Service:
A worldwide event company specializing in
account specific and in-account events,
collegiate and youth marketing, corporate
events & incentive travel, mall tours, mobile
and custom vehicle tours, publicity stunts,
sampling and street intercept programs,

757

special events, sponsorship solicitation and tie-ins.

JESSEN ASSOCIATES
9931 SW 61ST AVENUE
PORTLAND, OR 97219
503-977-3240
Fax: 503-977-3239
peterjj@peterjessen-gpa.com
www.peterjessen-gpa.com
Services:
Communication and Business Development Consultation
Event Management Services:
Sports event photography company, specializing in professional teams, leagues & events.

KEYLIN & ASSOCIATES
2308 48TH AVENUE SW
SEATTLE, WA 98116
206-933-0339
• Ben Keylin, President
Services:
Marketing, Promotional, Public Relations & Communications
Marketing & Consulting Services:
Serve as marketing consultants to minor and major sports league teams and leagues, including APSL, and Seattle SuperSonics.
Event Management Services:
Produces local and national sporting events including National Cheerleading Championship and the USA Spirit Squad Cheerleading Tour.
Sports Service Founded:
1987

KORFF ENTERPRISES
250 W 57TH STREET
SUITE 1713
NEW YORK, NY 10107
212-691-2200
Fax: 212-691-6009
contact@korffenterprises.com
www.korffenterprises.com
• John Korff, President
john@korffenterprises.com
• Victoria Brumfield, Executive Director
victoria@korffenterprises.com
• Linsey Skalamara, Manager
linsey@korffenterprises.com
• Sarah Labawsky, Event Manager
sarah@korffenterprises.com
Services:
Sports and Special Events Marketing
Event Management Services:
Promotes and manages various types of sporting events.

KPMG CONVENTION, SPORTS & ENTERTAINMENT PRACTICE
100 N TAMPA STREET
SUITE 1700
TAMPA, FL 33602-5145
813-223-1466
Fax: 813-229-3976
www.kpmg.com
• Timothy P Flynn, Chairman Kpmg International
• Michael Andrew, Chairman
• Alan Buckle, Deputy Chairman
Marketing & Consulting Services:
Specializes in development planning and financial consulting for all forms of public assembly facilities worldwide. Services include market studies, operations analysis,

economic impact and financial assistance including valuation services.

MARKETING EVENT PARTNERS
2711 PEACHTREE SQUARE
ATLANTA, GA 30360
404-522-7300
Fax: 404-255-6622
• Dennis Cooper, Chairman
• Paul Cooper, President
• Dominic Hoffman, Director Of Sales & Event Staff
Event Management Services:
Conducts municipal event, management and sports organization management audits. Creates and implements sports events.
Marketing & Consulting Services:
Consults with cities and events regarding bidding procedures. Develops programs and sponsorship activities on behalf of sports organizations.

MASON & MADISON
23 AMITY ROAD
BETHANY, CT 6524
203-393-1101
Fax: 203-393-2813
• Charlie Mason, President/Managing Principal
mikec@javelin-inc.com
• Fran Onofrio, President
Services:
Advertising: Branding, Media, Print, Broadcast, Direct, Collateral & Unconventional
Clients:
Sun Connecticut, New Alliance Bank, Emhart Teknologies, Cookson Electronics, SAS, Bruegger's, Adelphia, Braun, Cucina di Carla, Krispy Kreme, Clear Channel, Orrefors & Sprague
Services:
Public Relation: Research and Planning, Media Relation, Community Relations, Crisis Communication, Media Training, Analyst Relations, Employee Communication, Event Planning, Trade Show Support & Ramp-Up Program
Event Management Services:
Multi-dimensional agency, includes community service, international marketing, interactive & multi-media, trade shows, event planning, media buys, press relations and media placement services. Provides client service in automotive, electronics & instrumentation, consumer products, communications, transportation, utilities, banking & finance, tourism, hospitality, insurance healthcare and travel.

MAX-AIR PRODUCTIONS, INC.
9430 S RAINTREE DRIVE
SANDY, UT 84092
801-944-4849

MILLER & ASSOCIATES, CATHERINE
12 HOLLYWOOD ROAD
CHELSEA, LONDON, ENGLAND SW10 9HY
44-207-3511973
Fax: 619-234-8605
catherine@catherinemiller.com
www.catherinemiller.com
• Catherine Miller, Owner & Director
catherine@catherinemiller.com
• Claudia Kennaugh, Assistant Director

Services:
Advertising, Promotions, Public Relations & Special Events

MIRAMAR EVENTS
1327 LIVINGSTON AVENUE
PACIFICA, CA 94044
650-726-3491
tim@miramarevents.com
www.miramarevents.com
• Timothy R. Beeman, Chairman/Chief Executive Officer
(650) 726-3491
tim@miramarevents.com
Sports Service Founded:
1986
Event Management Services:
Strategic event planning; event management and production; sponsorship packaging and negotiation; TV packaging and negotiation; sponsorship program implementation; advertising and promotion; publicity.
Services:
Media Relations, Marketing/Promotion, Advertising, Project Coordination, Sponsorship Sales Development, Sponsorship Implementation & Strategic Planning

MOBIVITY
58 W BUFFALO
SUITE 200
CHANDLER, AZ 85225
512-522-4710
Fax: 512-639-3375
info@mobivity.com
www.txtstation.com
• Michael Falato, Vice President Sales & Business Development
(512) 535-5381
michael@txtstation.com
• Brook Paterson, Co-Founder
brook@txtstation.com
• Matthew Moulin, Chief Technology Officer
• Dennis Becker, President/CEO
• Michael Falato, SVP of Sales & Business Development
• Brad Dolian, VP,Client Services
• Thi VanAusdal, Technical Lead
• Loyda Drew, Project Manager
Nature of Services:
Txtstation provides integrated campaigns that combine the passion of live broadcasts and events with the ubiquity of mobile messaging allowing broadcasters, event owners, sponsors and general media to communicate with viewers or fans directly through their mobile phones.

MOUNT UNION COLLEGE ANNUAL SPORTS SALES WORKSHOP
1972 CLARK AVENUE
ALLIANCE, OH 44601
800-992-6682
www.mountunion.edu
• Jim Kadlecek, Ph.D., Department Head
(330) 823-4045
• Richard F Giese, Ph.D., President
• James Thoma, Program Coordinator
Degrees Offered:
Sport Business

OVATION ENTERTAINMENT
7337 E SHOEMAN LANE
SCOTTSDALE, AZ 85251

480-946-9711
Fax: 480-941-1420
Services:
Develops and produces family shows and sports and entertainment special events.

PACIFIC SPORTFEST
12932 MOORPARK STREET
UNIT 2
STUDIO CITY, CA 91604
818-784-8077
Fax: 818-688-3863
www.playpsf.com
• Ingrid Moon, President/Chief Executive Officer
(888) 918-4938
Sports Service Founded:
2001
Services:
Event Consulting, Fundraising & Event Promotion
Event Management Services:
Organizes amateur sports events including tournaments, festivals, camps, and clinics. Specializes in women's and girls' sports, but also has co-ed events. Current focus is ice hockey; will be branching into soccer, inline hockey, and rugby.

PANOZ/SANCHEZ GROUP
14175 ICOT BOULEVARD
SUITE 300
CLEARWATER, FL 33760
305-670-4343
Fax: 305-670-4344
www.streetperformance.com
Marketing & Consulting Services:
Administers and manages professional motorsports including the Trans-Am Series.
Services:
Race promoter

PAULETTE WOLF EVENTS & ENTERTAINMENT
1165 N CLARK STREET
SUITE 613
CHICAGO, IL 60610
321-981-2600
Fax: 321-981-3600
events@pwe-e.com
www.pwe-e.com
• Paulette Wolf, Chief Executive Officer
• Jodi Wolf, President
Services:
Concept Development And Event Design, Event Production, Handling of All Logistics, Financial Management/Budgeting, Crowd Control/Security Plan, Organization Plan (Creating Timelines and Schedules), Food and Beverage Operations, Vendor Sourcing And Negotiation, Entertainment Negotiation, Booking and Production, Operational Planning and On Site Logistics, On Site Labour, Staging, Sound, Lighting, Video and Technical Staff, Custom Stage Design and Construction, Meeting Planning, Graphic Design, Blueprinting and Floor Plan Layout, Theme/Decor Design and Coordination, Set Up and Post Event Tear Down, Venue Selection
Clients:
AAML, ABC Sports, Adidas USA, Inc., Advocate Healthcare, AGFA, AIDS Foundation of Chicago, Aladdin Resort Casino, Alliant Foodservice, Allied Fibers, Amate House, American Beauty Association, American Red Cross, American

Tobacco, AMOCO Corporation, Anheuser-Busch, Arlington Park Racetrack, Atlanta Committee For The Olympic Games, Avon, Beatrice Companies, Inc., Beckman-Coulter, Blue Cross/Blue Shield, The Rouse Company, The Borgata, Boyd Gaming, Breeder's Cup, Buena Vista Pictures, Burson Marsteller, Cannon USA, Inc., Catalina Conservancy, Charles Schwab, Chicago Architecture Foundation, Chicago Title & Trust, Children Defense Fund, Chris Cra
Services:
Coordination of City Services (i.e. Street Closure, Permitting, Police, EMT, Trash Removal, Etc.), Hotel Negotiations/Hotel Liaison, Space Management, Secure Celebrity Participation, Fashion Show Creative, Scheduling and Production, Premium Giveaways, Signage/Banners, Coordination and Production of Pyrotechnics, On Site Communications, Coordinate VIP Hospitality, General Liability Insurance From All Vendors, Secure Photographer and Video Services, Linen and Floral Design, Coordinate All Ground Transportation, Hotel, Hospitality and Backline Needs for Entertainment, Destination Management/Ground Transporatation.

PETER JACOBSEN PRODUCTIONS
9400 SW BARNES ROAD
SUITE 550
PORTLAND, OR 97225
503-526-9331
Fax: 503-641-2957
www.peterjacobsensports.com
• Mike Galeski, Executive Vp/ Managing Director
• Mike O'Donnell, Chief Operating Officer
• Monica Cruz, Chief Financial Officer
• Peter Jacobsen, President & Chief Executive Officer
Services:
Sports marketing and event management specializing in golf tournament management, marketing, and sponsorship
Event Management Services:
Specializes in event development, operations, sales, marketing and TV production. Produces and manages events in golf.

PIER 39 MARKET DEVELOPMENT
PIER 39, BEACH STREET & THE EMBARCADERO
STAIRWELL 2, LEVEL 3
SAN FRANCISCO, CA 94119-3730
415-705-5500
www.pier39.com
• Beth Schnitzer, Vice President Strategic Alliance
(415) 705-5500
• Tamara Goddard, Director Strategic Alliance
(415) 705-5500
• Mary Moffett, Partnership Marketing Account Executive
(415) 705-5563
• Katie Gibbs, Sales Executive Partnership Marketing & Sales
(415) 705-5421
• Joe Ngammekchay, Coordinator Partnership Marketing & Sales
(415) 705-5566
• Ruth Tempest, Sales Administrator

Partnership Marketing & S
(415) 705-5565
Sports Service Founded:
1979
Services:
A festival marketplace with more than 110 stores, 13 full-service restaurants with bay views and numerous fun-filled attractions. PIER 39's two-level design complements one of San Francisco's most unique shopping districts, featuring everything from NFL merchandise to jewelry and imported chocolates
Clients:
Coca-Cola, Crystal Geyser Alpine Spring Water, Discover Network, Dreyer's Grand Ice Cream, Shell Vacations Club
Event Management Services:
Official in-house sponsorship agency for Pier 39, its events and attractions and sponsorship representative for multiple high traffic venues in San Francisco. Purpose is to leverage the more than 10.5 million visitors annually to aid sponsors in reaching their marketing goals and objectives through Corporate or Event Sponsorship, Sampling and Display, Product Placement/Introduction or Outdoor Advertisement. Activities include, but are not limited to, Regattas, Hispanic Festival, July 4th Festival, Fleet Week, Snow Party/Ski exhibition. Annual event themes include Family, Civic, Cultural, Patriotic and Seasonal/Holiday Events.

POD PRODUCTIONS
20 BYRON ST
BANGALOW, NSW, 2479
612-6687-0411
Fax: 612-6687-0511
gallery@podproductions.com.au
www.podproductions.com.au
• Sean Watson, Photographer/Creative Director
Description:
Includes professionals with vast experiences in non-profit management, event planning, marketing, professional sports marketing, television production, and public relations.
Products:
Contemporary Image Gallery

PREMIERE RACING
67B FRONT STREET
MARBLEHEAD, MA 1945
781-639-9545
Fax: 781-639-9171
KWInfo@premiere-racing.com
www.premiere-racing.com
• Peter S. Craig, President
Peter@premiere-racing.com
• Jeanne Kleene, Manager
Jeanne@premiere-racing.com
• Alison Sipes, Office Manager
alison@premiere-racing.com
Description:
Management of sailboat regattas.
Services:
Management of sailboat regattas; involved in 2 major events: the January international regatta at Key West, Florida and Miami Race Week; manages other special events such as the Chesapeake stopover of the Volvo Ocean Race, the Drumbeat Regatta and other one-design regattas.

PRICEWATERHOUSECOOPERS
300 MADISON AVENUE
24TH FLOOR
NEW YORK, NY 10017
646-471-4000
• Fax: 646-471-4444
• Bob Mortiz, Chairman, Senior Partner
• Mike Burwell, Operations Leader, Chief Financial Officer
• John Carter, Partner Affairs Leader, Chief Administrator
• Mitch Cohen, Strategic Execution Leader
• Scott Duncan, Marketing And Sales Leader
• Mike Davies, Director of Global Communications
Sponsor:
MLS Houston Dynamo. PGA Fall Finish, PGA Tour, PGA The Player's Championship, Champions Tour, Web.com Tour.

PRIMEDIA
3585 ENGINEERING DRIVE
SUITE 100
NORCROSS, GA 30092
687-421-3000
800-216-1423
Fax: 212-745-0121
• Dean B. Nelson, Chairman
• Charles Stubbs, President/CEO
• Michaelanne Discepolo, EVP, Human Resources
• Charles C. Stubbs, President & CEO
• Kim Payne, Senior Vice President & CFO
• Marlon Starr, Senior Vice President
• Mike Barber, Senior Vice President & Chief Accounting Offi
Services:
PRIMEDIA Enthusiast Media - encompasses the company's consumer magazine brands, including web sites and live events, as well as About.com
Services:
PRIMEDIA Consumer Guides - the country's largest publisher and distributor of free publications including Apartment Guide, New Home Guide and Auto Guide PRIMEDIA Education - empowers millions of students to learn, includes Channel One, a propriety network to secondary schools; Films Media Group, a leading source of education videos; and Interactive Medical Network, a continuing medical education business.
Sports Service Founded:
1988
Event Management Services:
Total implementation of events from creative to on-site direction/management.
Marketing & Consulting Services:
Long and short-range marketing plan development; public relations counsel and direction; media placement; entertainment property and venue negotiation; customized retail/sales promotions; develop, license and merchandise products for distribution and on-site display.

PRO AM TOURNAMENTS
118 E MAPLE AVENUE
SUITE 2
LANGHORNE, PA 19047
800-357-1722
• Dennis M. O'Brien, President/Treasurer

Event Management Services:
Produces local, regional and national sports events.

PRO SPORTS & ENTERTAINMENT
1161 SAN VICENTE BOULEVARD
SUITE 304
LOS ANGELES, CA 90001
310-479-3806
• Paul H. Feller, President/Chief Executive Officer
• Peter Ellsworth, Corporate Sales Manager
• Jay Key, College Sports Marketing/Sales
Nature of Sports Service:
Organization is an owner, producer, promoter, and operator of live entertainment events that generates revenue through selling corporate sponsorship, tickets, corporate hospitality, event merchandise, concessions, and athlete management, representation and endorsements.
Services:
Professional event marketing and management organization that owns, operates, manages, and promotes live sports and entertainment events. Specific services are: Sponsorship, Talent Representation, Marketing, Consultancy, Merchandise, Ticket / Entry, E-Commerce, Team League and Venue Rights, Television
Other Locations:
New York, Los Angeles, Seattle, Maui

PROFORMA SPORTS
810 PIONEER PARKWAY
PEORIA, IL 61615
309-692-6390
Fax: 309-692-6397
jeff.brookes@proforma.com
www.proforma.com/info
• Jeff Brookes, President
(309) 692-6390
jeff.brooke@proforma.com
Description:
Works with sports teams across the country producing their team programs.
Services:
Proforma specializes in serving the graphic communications needs of the sports and entertainment industry by partnering with our clients to develop innovative promotional campaigns, which build and support their brand identity, and most importantly, generate results for their organization and event.

QUICKFOOT
16330 SCENIC CIRCLE FORNEY
FORNEY, TX 75126
469-728-7700
info@quickfoot.com
www.quickfoot.com
Description:
Premier small-sided soccer tournament organizers.

RALEIGH CYCLE
6004 S 190TH STREET
SUITE 101
KENT, WA 98032
253-395-1100
Fax: 253-872-0257
www.raleighusa.com
• Sharon Robinson, CFO
Products:
Raleigh bicycles either for fitness, commuting, racing, or just cruising with

family and friends.
Brands:
Raleigh Performance Comfort Road: Cadent 5.0 2006, Cadent 4.0 2006, Cadent 3.0 2006, Cadent 2.0 2006, and Cadent 1.0 2006. Raleigh Road: Rush Hour 2006, Team 2006, Prestige 2006, Competition 2006, Supercourse 2006, Grand Prix 2006, Grand Sport 2006, Sport 2006, Route 66 2006, Route 24 2006 and Route 1 2006. Raleigh Hybrid: Passage 5.0 2006, Passage 4.0 2006 and Passage 3.0 2006. Raleigh Full Suspension: Phase 2 2006, Phase 1 2006 and Phase 2006. Raleigh MTN Hardtail: Mojave 8.0 2006, Mojave 5.5 2006, Mojave 5.0 2006, Mojave 4.0 2006, Mojave 4.5 2006 and Mojave 2.0 2006. Raleigh Comfort: Venture 5.0 2006, Venture 4.0 2006, Venture 3.0 2006,
Services:
Athlete Management: Bicycle racers/race teams and triathletes
Event Management Services:
Bicycle races.
Year Founded:
1896

RED SAIL SPORTS
PIER 5, THE EMBARCADERO
SUITE 102
SAN FRANCISCO, CA 94111
858-521-8244
877-733-7245
info@redsail.com
www.redsail.com
• Paul Lusk, Chief Operating/Financial Officer
plusk@redsail.com
• Lee Ann Wade, Corporate Marketing Director
lwade@redsail.com
Nature of Service:
Watersports centers, custom-built, luxurious catamarans, scuba diving, snorkeling and instruction, cruise passenger day trips, group travel expertise.

RIBER SPORTS MARKETING GROUP
7442 JAGER COURT
CINCINNATI, OH 45230
513-624-2100
Fax: 513-624-2110
www.ribersports.com
• Burch Riber, Founder
• Sam Riber, President
• Daryl Ellis, Director Of Business Development
• Burch R. Riber, President
Sports Service Founded:
1983
Event Management Services:
Creates, manages sports events. Develops and implements retail promotions based on events. Markets event sponsorships.
clients:
Prilosec OTC, ThermaCare, Pepto-Bismol, Metamucil, Pfizer, R+L Carriers, Sony, P+G BrandSAVER.

RICHLIN GROUP
13428 MAXELLA AVENUE
#278
MARINA DEL RAY, CA 90292
310-641-6477
Fax: 310-641-7250
www.trgolf.com

- Sandra Richlin, Founder/President
(310) 641-6477
- Mark Gallandt, Operations Director
- Stacy Gallandt, Marketing/Public Relations
- Danny Garcia, Director Tournament
Operations
Services:
Organizing golf events
Sports Service Founded:
1990
Event Management Services:
Specializes in producing golf events for
corporations, tour groups, charities, and
individuals. Full service agency includes
management, promotional items, insurance
and fundraising expertise.
Marketing & Consulting Services:
Consultation for sponsorship development.

RMY MANAGEMENT GROUP
5905 NW 54TH CIRCLE
CORAL SPRING, FL 33067
800-409-3813
Fax: 800-409-3813
roger@rmygroup.com
- Roger Yaffe, President
roger@rmygroup.com
Event Management Services:
Turnkey corporate event planning,
association management and golf
operations firm. Manages conferences,
client entertainment and hospitality
functions, sales meetings, incentives and
golf events.
Services:
Association Management, Event Production,
Professional Golf Services

SENIOR TOUR PLAYERS, INC.
1244 BOYLSTON STREET
SUITE 200
CHESTNUT HILL, MA 02467
617-266-3600

SFX/CLEAR CHANNEL ENTERTAINMENT
220 W 42ND STREET
NEW YORK, NY 10036
917-421-4000
Nature of Sports Services:
Producer and promoter of live
entertainment. It produces concerts, touring
Broadway shows, and sports events.
Provides sports marketing and talent
representation service through the SFX
Sports Group.

SHOWPROCO, LLC
2915 BISCAYNE BOULEVARD
SUITE 303
MIAMI, FL 33137
305-893-8771
800-327-3736
Fax: 305-893-8783
www.showproco.com
- Sandra Lafrance, Operations/Productions
(305) 893-8771
- Christine Gomont, Accounting
(305) 893-8771
- Hardy C. C. Katz, Manager
Nature of Service:
Produces trade shows for sports licensed
products and tailgate and picnic products:
the Sports Licensing & Entertainment
Marketplace and the Tailgate/Picnic Show.

SKYSIGNS UNLIMITED
302 3RD STREET
SUITE 7B
NEPTUNE BEACH, FL 32266
904-247-1241
Event Management Services:
Manages corporate balloon programs
nationally and world wide. Creates and
implements ballooning events including the
Balloon Tour America professional hot air
balloon racing circuit.

SMG
300 CONSHOHOKEN STATE ROAD
SUITE 770
WEST CONSHOHOKEN, PA 19428
610-729-7900
Fax: 610-729-1590
www.smgworld.com
- Wes Westley, President and CEO
- Maureen Ginty, Executive VP
- John Burns, Executive VP
- Gregg Caren, Sr.VP
Sports Service Founded:
Sports Service Founded: 1977
Event Management Services:
Production and marketing of sporting
events.
Marketing & Consulting Services:
Stadiums, arenas, theaters, auditoriums and
convention centers under its guidance
worldwide. Divisions include SMG
Productions, Network International, SMG
sports advertising affiliate.

**SOCCER MARKETING & PROMOTIONS,
INC.**
7444 SW 48 STREET
MIAMI, FL 33155
305-669-0101
Fax: 305-669-9979
www.copalatina.com
- Thomas Mulroy, Founder/President
- Paola Mulroy, VP Finance
- Marc Jacquemin, Operations
Director/Tournament Coordinator
- Daniel Prenat, Competition Coordinator
- Rodrigo Oliva, Special Event Corrdinator
Services:
SM&P is a sports marketing firm that
specializes in soccer events, has experience
in the Hispanic market, international games,
also experienced in corporate grass root
implementation.
Clients:
Adidas USA, Inc., American Airline, Amateur
Athletic Union, Anheuser Busch, Campbell's
Soup Co., Chiquita, Dannon, Del Monte
USA, Erima Sportswear, Eurosport,
Gatorade, Hawaiian Punch, Hitachi America
Ltd., Inca Kola, Just Say No Int., Ladeco
Chilean Airlines, Lan Chile Airlines, Master
Card, McDonalds Corp., Mlitre Sports,
Motorola, M&M/Snickers, National Soccer
Coaches Association, Nike, Shout, Soccer
America Magazine, Soccer USA Partners,
South Florida Olympic Committee, Terra
Pro-Beach Soccer, The Academy, The
Sports Authority, The Sports Chalet,
TransAmerican Life, Transitions Optical,
Uniroyal, United States Soccer Federation,
Western U
Description:
SM&P is a sports marketing firm that
specializes in soccer events, has experience
in the Hispanic market, international games,

also experienced in corporate grass root
implementation.

SOUTHWIND KAYAK CENTER
17855 SKY PARK CIRCLE
#A
IRVINE, CA 92614
949-261-0200
800-768-8496
info@southwindkayaks.com
www.southwindkayaks.com
- John Upchurch, General Manager
info@southwindkayaks.com
Event Management Services:
Hosts sports events, focusing on
environmental sports such as kayaking,
canoeing, paddle surfing, etc.; also
manages sea kayaking school and outfitter.

SPECIAL EVENT PRODUCTION
205 INDUSTRIAL DRIVE
CLEMMONS, NC 27012
336-764-2477
800-327-2352
Fax: 336-764-0684
information@sep-sports.com
www.sep-sports.com
Sports Service Founded:
1987
Event Management Services:
Transports, installs and operates portable
electronic displays, scoreboards, video
screens and scoring systems for the PGA
Tour, Champions Tour, LPGA Tour,
Nationwide Tour, ESPN X-Games,
collegiate golf tournaments, celebrity golf
tournaments, multi-sport events, and
individual sports events (racing, waterski,
horse shows, rodeos and promotions).

SPONSORWISE
info@sponsorwise.com
www.sponsorwise.com
- Burt Cummings, Chief Executive Officer
- Richard Raphael, Vice President Sales
- George Rassam, VP
Finance/Administration/CFO
- Russell Hinds, Founder
- Tad Williams, Marketing Director
Description:
Created to provide spohisticated tools need
in today'ssponsorship market. Based on our
collective experiences in corporations,
properties, agencies and the Internet, we set
out to design a platform that actively
supports everyone involved in the process.
Year Founded:
2002
Clients:
AirTran Airways, All State Insurance,
Amtrak, Bacardi, Bombay Sapphire,
Cingular Wireless, Columbia Sportswear,
ExxonMobil, Frontier Airlines, Gateway,
Gillette, Hershey's Food Company, Hyundai
Motor America, Hyundai Motor
Manufacturing/Alabama, Imperial Oil/Esso,
JetBlue Airways, Kawasaki, Kyocera
Wireless, L.G. Mobile Phones, Lexus,
Lowe's Companies, Marriott International,
MasterCard International, Mitsubishi Motors,
Motorola, Nintendo, Qwest
Communications, Reebok, SanDisk,
Staples, Toyota, Verizon Wireless, Wrigley.

SPORTHILL MARKETING
422 SPORT HILL ROAD
EASTON, CT 6612

203-261-5552
Fax: 203-452-2279
www.sporthillmarketing.com
• Bill Tustian, Owner/Founder
• Theresa S. Kelso, Office Manager
• Nancy Riling, Administrative Assistant
Clients:
ESPN, Equitable Life Assurance Co.,
Accessories Magazinne, Ski Magazine,
Skiing Magazine, Smith Corona, Inc.
Event Management Services:
Production, management of special events.

SPORTS AMERICA, INC.
10 S ADAMS STREET
ROCKVILLE, MD 20850
301-762-7100
• Robert J Geoghan, President/Chief
Executive Officer/Founder
(301) 424-1080
• Wayne Ellis, VP Marketing
• Marc B. Steigerwalt, Events Manager
(301) 424-9354
Services:
Full-service event development and
management, including on-site execution,
pre-planning and post-evaluation,
promotion, public relations and all aspects of
project coordination.
Sports Service Founded:
1974
Marketing & Consulting Services:
Creation and management of sports
properties, strategic planning to integrate
sports into the marketing mix and creative
project development.

SPORTS MARKETING GROUP
47 MAIN STREET
#1
KEENE, NH 03431
603-358-5223
Fax: 509-756-3907
Services:
Specializes in international projects for
sports consulting for national/city
governments, corporations and
organizations
Products:
Racing Sportshirt, Polo, Long Sleve,
T-Shirts, Tank Tops, and Posters
Sports Service Founded:
1979
Event Management Services:
Financing, production and management of
major events, exclusively sports or including
sports activities.

SPORTS MEDIA ENTERPRISES
110 PEABODY DRIVE
STOW, MA 1775
978-897-5480
• John Clary, Contact
(978) 897-5480
Services:
Event Management: Organizing committee
for Emerald Isle Classic (Football), other
football games.

SPORTS PLUS
7020 HEATHERHILL ROAD
BETHESDA, MD 20817
301-229-5401
Fax: 301-229-2375
• Sara K. Fornaciari, Event Director
(301) 229-5401

• Greg Chambers, Marketing Services
Director
Services:
Tournament promoter for IGA U.S. Indoors -
WTA Tour tennis event, MS Tennis Classic
in Denver, and the Owl Foundation Tennis
Fundraiser in Florida. Sports Promoters
Managers & Recruiters
Clients:
Express Sports, IGA, Multiple Sclerosis
Society - Colorado Chapter, National, The
Owl Foundation.
Sports Service Founded:
1990

SPORTSECONOMICS LLC
5847 HERON DRIVE
OAKLAND, CA 94618
510-387-0644
Fax: 510-295-2578
info@sportseconomics.com
www.sportseconomics.com
• Daniel Rascher, President
• Heather Rascher, VP
Nature of Services:
SportsEconomics is a professional services
firm that provides a broad range of
consulting services to the sports business
and entertainment communities. In the past
decade, SportsEconomics has provided
economic, financial, and marketing research
analysis to clients in a wide variety of fields
associated with sports. SportsEconomics is
based in the San Francisco Bay Area, but
serves clients throughout the United States
and the world. Our consultants offer
strategic analyses built on a base of intimate
knowledge of the institutions and economic
realities affecting the markets in which our
clients operate. We advise clients on topics
such as the
Description:
Marketing research is only as good as the
data collected. SportsEconomics offers a full
suite of custom business intelligence and
consulting solutions to address clients'
critical business issues and to enhance
organizational performance. Our research
not only provides clients with a better
understanding of the target customers and
markets in which they operate, but also
provides in-depth market analysis and
insight to put that information to optimal use.
We offer research and strategic analyses on
topics including effectiveness of marketing
projects and promotions, demand analysis,
ticket pricing optimization, media market
optimization, faci
Clients:
National Football League; National
Basketball Association; Major League
Baseball; National Hockey League;
American Hockey League; Major League
Soccer; Premier League (Soccer); National
Collegiate Athletic Association (NCAA);
Minor League Baseball Teams; NASCAR,
NHRA, Sports Commissions, PGA Tour.
Year Founded:
1998

SPORTSMARK MANAGEMENT GROUP
781 LINCOLN AVENUE
SUITE 380
SAN RAFAEL, CA 94901
415-461-5801
Fax: 415-461-5804
www.sportsmark.com

• Keith Bruce, Chief Marketing Officer
(415) 461-5801
keith@sportsmark.com
• Steve Skubic, CEO
Nature of Service:
All phases of event management including
creation, development, implementation and
hospitality. Hospitality services include
accomodations, transportation, tickets,
premiums, on-site communications, security,
and other aspects.

SPORTSMITH
5925 S 118TH E AVENUE
TULSA, OK 74146
918-307-2446
888-713-2880
Fax: 918-307-0216
www.sportsmith.net
Sports Service Founded:
1995
Event Management Services:
Develops, sets strategy, and implements
projects for clients utilizing local, regional or
international sports and special events to
promote their company's image and
corporate culture. Packages appropriate
tie-in promotions with media, retailers, and
major corporations. Events include trade
shows, running, walking, golf, water sports,
and track and field events.
Marketing & Consulting Services:
Complete corporate sponsorship planning,
management and on-site execution
including public relations, hospitality,
promotion and evaluation of companies.

SPORTSTARS, INC
1370 AVENUE OF THE AMERICAS
19TH FLOOR
NEW YORK, NY 10019
212-757-4044
Fax: 212-765-4833
marketing@sportstarsnyc.com
www.sportstarsnyc.com
Description:
Member contract advisor, represents
professinoal athletes in contract negotiations
in all major team sports.
Description:
Development and implementation of wide
range of sports-related promotional
programs, including special events,
endorsement programs, and entertainment
functions.

SPORTSVISIONS
29 QUAIL RUN
ORCHARD PARK, NY 14127-4611
716-639-8680
800-683-2880
Fax: 866-235-0566
• Terrence Murzynski, Owner
Nature of Sports Service:
Provides sports glasses that will enhance
what the user wants to see and block out
sunlight.

SPORTSYSTEMS CORPORATION
40 FOUNTAIN PLAZA
BUFFALO, NY 14202
716-858-5000
Fax: 716-858-5479
Services:
Manages all aspects of horse and
greyhound racetrack operations. The largest
owner and operator of pari-mutuel facilities

in the United States. General Concessions: Offers upscale dining and services for suites and club seating areas through its premium catering division, Well Bread Restaurant Services Group, and retail sales through its Fan Zoner division, making Delaware North Companies Delaware North Companies Sportservice a true 'triple threat' operation.

SPURNEY ASSOCIATES, PETER
3701 LELAND STREET
CHEVY CHASE, MD 20015
301-652-7512
• Peter Spurney, President
Event Management Services:
An attraction and sports management firm. Services all segments of event/attraction management. Sets up attractions including from conceptual development, financing, sponsorship, implementation and management. Provides strategic partners with event association.
Sports Service Founded:
1973

SROBA & ASSOCIATES
8401 MAYLAND DRIVE
SUITE A
RICHMOND, VA 23294
804-965-5555
jsroba@sroba.com
• Joseph P Sroba, President
• Vern E. Inge, Jr., Legal Counsel
• Jose Ortega, Director of Player Development
• Miguel Nava, Director of Latin Operations
Sports Service Founded:
1985.
Nature of Sports Service:
Provides guidance and assistance in all areas of private personal and business management. Develops full marketing plans for image development and income generation. Coordinates financial plan, post-career consulting including business acquisition, new business formation, management and development.

STANDOUT SPORTS & EVENTS
205 W MAIN STREET
SOMERVILLE, NJ 08876-2834
908-725-7500
Fax: 908-725-7744
demarsport@aol.com
• John Demartini, President/Chief Executive Officer
Services:
Full Service sports and event company specializing in creating and producing charity fund-raising. Sports events include golf tournaments, dinners, galas, etc.

STARK EVENTS & ASSOCIATIONS
7510 W SUNSET BOULEVARD
LOS ANGELES, CA 90046
323-851-5446
www.starkeventsinc.com
• Rick Stark, Owner
(323) 851-5446
rick@becore.com
Services:
Develops and manages sponsorship and coordinates Extreme Sports Competition events nationally and internationally. Provides assistance to corporate clients and managing efficient sports sponsorships through extreme sports events.

Services:
Event Management : Promotion, production, marketing, and consulting for extreme sports events. Properties include Core Tour National Skate Series, United Skiboard Series, and the King of Dirt BMX Series. Also provides promotion and marketing for college and music events.
Sports Service Founded:
1993

STEINER SPORTS MARKETING
33 LECOUNT PLACE
NEW ROCHELLE, NY 10801
800-759-7267
Fax: 914-632-1102
generalinfo@steinersports.com
www.steinersports.com
• Brandon Steiner, Founder/Chairman/President/CEO
• Steve Weinreb, Managing Director
• Tony Cappa, Chief Financial Officer
• Jared Weiss, Executive Vice President
• Debbie Ebben, Vice President
• Jonathan Wolfsie, Director
Nature of Sports Service:
A full-service sports marketing agency that offers sponsorship consultation, management of consumer and trade promotions, development of point-of-sales materials, development of customer loyalty programs, creation of athlete fantasy experiences for key clients, and implementation of employee incentive programs.
Services:
Provides sportsmarketing services and authentic memorabilia
Products:
Producer of authentic autographed collectibles and the best source for all sports gift needs.
Clients:
Aetna US Healthcare; Alan Taylor Communications; Alcone Marketing Group; American Express; Anheuser-Busch; BBDO; Burson Marsteller; Cannon Business Solutions; Chase; Citi; Coca-Cola; Dannon; Davis Vision; DeMatteo Monness - Security Traders; Diageo Spirits; Kraft General Foods; eBay; ESPN; Fenway Partners - Investment Bankers; Fleishman - Hillard Public Relations; Foot Locker; Ford Motor Company; Gillette; J Brown, LMC Group; J.P. Morgan; Major League Baseball; MasterCard; Merck; Modell's Sporting Goods; New York Merchantile Exchange; Novartis; Schering - Plough; UBS Warburgh; Unilever; Yahoo; YPO; Baseball Athletes; Basketball Athletes; Foo
Sports Fantasy Division:
Offers sports fans the opportunity to meet athletes. The current packages feature players such as Mark Messier, NBA Legends Walt Clyde Frazier and others.
Strategic Sports Marketing & Consulting:
Provides corporations with expertise to help maximize the impact of their sports marketing efforts. Our focus is not only developing integrated marketing strategies, but also to provide a comprehensive program evaluation to determine the return on investment. Marketing, promotion, celebrity talent service with access to over 1,700 athletes available. Provides talent for events, appearances, public relations campaigns and endorsements.

STOWE AREA ASSOCIATION
51 MAIN STREET
PO BOX 1320
STOWE, VT 5672
802-253-7321
877-467-8693
Fax: 802-253-6628
askus@gostowe.com
www.gostowe.com
• Jo Sabel Courtney, Public Relations Manager
(802) 253-7321
Event Management Services:
Creates and manages summer sports events in the Stowe Mountain geographic area.
Services:
Miscellaneous: Child Care, Stowe Kinderhaus Home Day Care, Post Office, Western Union, Library, Meeting and Conferences, Weddings, Claire's Dog Camp, North Country Animal League, Stowe Kid's Stuff

STRATEGIC PLANNING CONCEPTS INTERNATIONAL
515 E FIRST STREET
SUITE A
TUSTIN, CA 92780
714-505-9353
888-895-3871
Fax: 714-505-4417
Andrew@spcintl.net
www.spcintl.net
• Andrew Strenk, President
(714) 505-9353
Andrew@spcintl.net
• Scott Klein, Fieldwork Manager and Research Associate
(714) 505-9353
Scott@spcintl.net
Services:
Provides services for sports facilities. Programs include site location and site analysis, feasibility studies, strategic plans, business plans, financial analysis, design development, entitlement procurement and traffic studies & tax assessments. International retail real estate consulting company: Strategy Formulation, Retail Format Selection, Project Sizing, Project Positioning, Tenant Strategies, Feasibility Studies, Market Analysis, Site Assessment, Evaluation of Conflicting Demographic and Psychodemographic Data, Trade Area Definitions, Cultural Context Assessment, Economic Trend Analysis, Labor Studies, Marketing Strategies, Site Analy
Clients:
Auto Zone, Avatar Development, Carlson Company, Carver Company, City of San Diego, Crumpler and Kruger, Donahue Schriber, Fenton Western, Forest City Development, Fransen Company, Hahn Company, Hechnger Company, Holsman International, Home Depot, Hoyts Cinema Corporation, Kornwasser Friedman, Mexus, Ross Dress for Less, Saks Fifth Avenue, San Diego National Sports Training Foundation, Southwestern Bell, Smart and Final, Sport Floor USA, Staubach Company, Strategic Edge, Thompson and Associates, Warner Bros.

SUMMIT SPORTS & EVENTS
9100 W JEWELL
SUITE 200
LAKEWOOD, CO 80232

763

303-989-4084
Fax: 303-989-0539
• Dan Cramer, President
Description:
Producer and manager of grassroots sporting events for amateur athletes in soccer, basketball and football.
Other Offices:
Atlanta, Boston, Pittsburgh.

TARGET SPORTS MARKETING
2811 UNIVERSITY AVENUE SOUTHEAST
#141050
MINNEAPOLIS, MN 55414
610-688-9233
Fax: 877-768-4164
info@tsmworldwide.com
Nature of Sports Service
A business consultancy and service partner focused on providing market and non-market strategic services to firms competing in the international shooting, hunting, and outdoor recreation industry.

TAYLOR WEST ADVERTISING
4040 BROADWAY
SUITE 302
SAN ANTONIO, TX 78209
210-805-0320
Fax: 205-805-9371
www.taylorwest.com
• Bill West, Chief Executive Officer/Owner
• Pat Roberson, VP/Chief Media Strategist

THE MCCRUM COMPANIES, INC.
3838 OAK LAWN
SUITE 200
DALLAS, TX 75219
214-526-5050
800-411-3756
Fax: 214-526-6050
www.gsrisk.com
• Douglas McCrum, President/Chief Business Officer
Event Management Services:
GSR provides special contingency insurance coverage to event promoters, sports teams, race tracks, broadcasters, agents and sponsors. Products include: prize indemnity for all contests, games and sweepstakes; coverage for cancellation, postponement, curtailment, abandonment or relocation of an event; non-appearance of artist(s), group(s) or teams(s) to cover abandonment of tours, film sessions and other events; failure to telecast pay-per-view, cable or other transmissions due to equipment failure, airwave disruption or pre-emption airtime; death and disgrace to cover costs in employing sports personalities in the promotion of a product, even

THINK TANK COMMUNICATIONS
Am SCHRAGEN WEG 19
POSTFACH 6
VADUZ, LICHTENSTE 9490
423-239-0145
Fax: 423-239-0146
www.thinktankag.com
• Jeffrey J. Stern, President
• Pablo G. Estela, Contact
• Colin Kuchy, Contact
• Manfred Frostner, Contact
Services:
Individual client management, corporate sponsorship and event management,

sponsorship analysis, business partner network. Have offices in Europe and U.S. Organizers of Street Soccer Cup USA, a youth soccer tournament.

TOP RANK
3980 HOWARD HUGHES PARKWAY
SUITE 580
LAS VEGAS, NV 89109
702-732-2717
Fax: 702-733-8232
www.toprank.com
• Robert Arum, Founder/Chairman
Services:
Promotes championship fights and other major boxing matches throughout the world.
Clients:
Represents baseball players in all facets of sports representation / organizes and structures boxing matches

TOURNAMENT SPORTS
185 WEBER STREET S
WATERLOO, ONTARIO, CANADA N2J 2B1
519-888-6500
800-265-2454
Fax: 519-888-6540
info@tournament-sports.com
www.tournament-sports.com
Services:
Production and management services for professional golf events.

TRIPLE CROWN SPORTS
3930 AUTOMATION WAY
FORT COLLINS, CO 80525
970-223-6644
Fax: 970-223-3636
www.triplecrownsports.com
Sports Service Founded:
1982
Services:
Sports: Department for sponsor services include data base listings, research (surveys), publications, media and publicity, accounting service, travel agency. Publishes tournament brochures, direct mailing sales catalogues, event magazines.

TRITON SPORTS ASSOCIATES
325 MANVILLE ROAD
PLEASANTVILLE, NY 10570
914-747-5066
Fax: 914-747-5033
• Gordon Saint-Denis, President
• Ashish Raythatha, Principal
Services:
Services include Mergers and Acquisitions; Placement of Debt
Sports Service Founded:
2002
Nature of Sports Service:
Organization specializes in execution of complex transactions within the sports industry and maximizing the efficiency of the capital structure and operations of clients' sports properties. Services include Mergers and Acquisitions; Placement of Debt and Equity; Financial and Transactional Advisory; Restructuring, Turnaround, and Bankruptcy; Venue and Franchise Valuation; and Operational Advisory.

UBS FINANCIAL SERVICES
1285 AVENUE OF THE AMERICAS
NEW YORK, NY 10019

212-649-8000
www.ubs.com
• Marcel Ospel, Chairman
• Stephan Haeringer, Executive Vice Chairman
• Marco Suter, Executive Vice Chairman
• Rosemary Berkery, Vice Chairman of UBS Wealth Management Americ
• Bob McCann, CEO UBS Group Americas
• Dan Cochran, Chief Operating Officer, Wealth management
• John Dalby, Chief Financial Officer and Chief Risk Office
• Jonathan Eisenberg, General Counsel
• Paula Polito, Client Strategy Officer
• Anita Sands, Head of Change Leadership
Services:
Provides a full spectrum to institutional and corporate clients, governments and financial intermediaries globally.
Description:
Assists municipalities, government agencies, non-profit organizations and private entities in structuring, underwriting, trading and distributing tax-exempt and taxable bonds. The Group also provides a secondary market for these securities and develops and markets various financial products.

ULTRAFIT-USA
PO BOX 629
HILLIARD, OH 43026
614-332-5205
www.ultrafit-usa.com
• Jeff Sheard, President
(614) 332-5205
• Abby Sheard, Marketing
(614) 260-1452
Services:
Athlete Management: Sports marketing and management.
Services:
Event Management: Produces and coordinates triathlons and biathlons and other special event.
Sports Service Founded:
1985

UNITED RENTALS
5 GREENWICH OFFICE PARK
GREENWICH, CT 6831
203-622-3131
800-877-3687
Fax: 203-622-6080
www.unitedrentals.com
• Michael J Kneeland, President/Chief Executive Officer
• William B. Plummer, CEO/CFO
Event Management Services:
Manufactures, designs, coordinates and provides the rental of power generation, electrical distribution, portable air conditioning and mobile electric resistive heat for sporting events world wide. Also carries a line of complete catering kitchens, food trucks and mobile dish washing trucks for rental. Capable of servicing any size event. Provides professional service and technical advice. Complete turn-key operation.
Sports Service Founded:
1960

VAIL VALLEY FOUNDATION
90 BENCHMARK ROAD
SUITE 300
AVON, CO 81620
970-949-1999
888-920-2787
Fax: 970-949-9265
info@vvf.org
www.vvf.org
• Ceil Folz, President
• Heidi Elzinga, Assistant To President
helzinga@vvf.org
Nature of Service:
Through the organization of educational, cultural, historical, artistic and athletic performances, events and attractions for the education and benefit of the community. Providing the community with athletic educational and cultural events to enhance the quality of life in the Vail Valley.
Year Founded:
1981
Event Management Services:
World Cup Ski Racing, Pro-Am Ski Event/Fundraiser, Invitational Snowboard Event

VELOCITY SPORTS & ENTERTAINMENT
230 E AVENUE
NORWALK, CT 06855
203-831-2000
Fax: 203-831-2300
• Ed Beamon, CEO
(973) 285-9332
• Michelle Berg, Senior Vice President, Group Director
(973) 285-9332
Nature of Service:
Velocity Sports Management is a full-service, community minded, international sports marketing firm specializing in the concept, packaging, marketing and management of professional cycling teams and athletes. In addition, we provide the management of all related initiatives including on-site product demonstrations and sampling, athlete appearances for retail and corporate functions, and quantifying sponsorship effectiveness. Our mission is to maximize corporate and brand exposure by creating synergy between sponsors, consumers and the healthy, high-energy atmosphere that professional cycling creates.
Year Founded:
1994

WALSH ENTERPRISES, BOB
233 - 6TH AVENUE N
SEATTLE, WA 98109
206-903-6850
Fax: 206-903-6851
• Bob Walsh, President/Chief Executive Officer
Sports Service Founded:
1992
Services:
Event Management, Marketing & Consulting: Overall event planning, sponsorship development, creative direction, day-of-event management. Press and public relations direction and coordination.
Marketing & Consulting Services:
Specialists in the development of strategic affinity/lifestyle marketing programs for the corporate sector.

Other Location:
20 Telavi Street, Tbilisi, GA 38003.

WIRZ & ASSOCIATES
665-A NORTH TRAIL
STRATFORD, CT 6614
203-380-9931
203-858-4890
Fax: 612-465-5349
BWirz2@gmail.com
www.wirzandassociates.com
• Bob Wirz, Founder/President
(203) 858-4890
BWirz2@gmail.com
Services:
Sports: Full service media planning, publicity and management. Sports specialists experienced from amateur to major league All Star and World Series.
Clients:
American Baseball Coaches Association, Art Spaces, Inc., Bantam Doubleday Dell Publishing, Baseball America magazine, Bob's Stores, The City of NOrfolk, Virginia, Continental Basketball Association, Denver Baseball Commission, eNewsRelease.com, Fairfield Univ., Federacion Internationale De Volleyball, Glaucoma Foundation, Howe Sportsdata International, IBM, Independent Professional Baseball, Jessica Howard, Just For Men Haircolor (Combe, Inc.), Little League Baseball, Inc., Major League Baseball, MCI, National Adult Baseball Association, New Haven County Cutters, Northern League, Oscar Mayer, Panini, Prodigy, Rotisserie League Baseball.
Sports Service Founded:
1985
Marketing & Consulting Services:
Wide-ranging public relations and marketing services in all sports.

WOHL & COMPANY
1630 JOSEPHINE
NEW ORLEANS, LA 70130
504-528-9900
www.wohlco.com
• Amy Wohl, Founder
Event Management Services:
On site event management.
Marketing & Consulting Services:
Full services as they relate to the sports event being managed, including consultation with the sports sanctioning organization.

WOMEN'S SPORTS LEGENDS
PO BOX 537
SAUSALITO, CA 94966-0537
415-331-7100
Fax: 415-331-7102
netres1@aol.com
www.wslegends.com
• Pam Shriver, President
Services:
Event Management: Athlete-owned sports promotion company, specializing in corporate events, tournaments and merchandising.
Sports Service Founded:
1995

WORLD BASKETBALL OPPORTUNITIES
W326 N9586 PERADELL CT
HARTLAND, WI 53029
262-966-9660
Fax: 262-966-9661
www.worldbasket.com

• Scott Woltzen, Contact
Services:
Marketing & Consulting: Independent scouting services provided for regional, national, and international professional and collegiate basketball games.
Services:
Event Management: Scheduling of inbound international men's and women's basketball games. Athlete Management: Representation of basketball players (male and female) from comprehensive contract negotiations, tax planning, financial planning, marketing, and summer sports camps to management of free agent camps to provide exposure to pro and international scouts.

WORLD GOLF HOSPITALITY
9755 DOGWOOD ROAD
SUITE 110
ROSWELL, GA 30075
770-998-3123
877-288-6719
Fax: 770-998-5515
• Brendan Lillis, President/CEO
• Martin Willis-Jackson, Chief Financial Officer
• Jess Taylor, Chief Operating Officer
• Aubrey Proud, Business Development
Nature of Service:
To offer the finest quality service to corporations in need of event, meeting, incentive, travel, hospitality and golf products.
Year Founded:
1992
Clients:
Absolut Vodka, The Absolut Spirits Company, Golf Magazine, Bridgestone, Level, Georgia-Pacific, AIG, Jim Beam, Coca-Cola

WORLD SPORTS GROUP, LTD.
419 E 57TH STREET
SUITE 9A
NEW YORK, NY 10022-3060
212-260-5001
Fax: 212-412-9022
• Rey Olsen, President

Event Security

ALPHA & OMEGA MOUNTED SECURITY PATROL
2906 W SOUTHLAKE BOULEVARD
SOUTHLAKE, TX 76092
817-379-6607
Fax: 817-379-5993
info@mountedpatrol.com
www.mountedpatrol.com
• Frank Keller, Founder/CEO
(817) 379-6607
info@mountedpatrol.com
• John DeRouen, Sr. Vice President, General Manager, A&O
(817) 379-6607
john.derouen@gmail.com
• Bruce Smith, VP of Operations, National Recruiting Directo
(817) 312-0164
equinesafety@aol.com
Description:
Pioneer of private mounted horse patrols in North America. Provides mounted patrol

services to stadiums, arenas, auditoriums etc. Troopers specialize in weaponless security.

Services:
consulation for site selection and layout, advance work, tour security, review of staffing plans, on-site management of security teams, threat assessment, development of emergency response plans for multiple scenarios, analysis of manpower needs, integration of security plans with local law enforcement officials, emergency evacuation planning, consulation on people and package screening, consulation on venue surveillance needs and options, post-event evaluation and follow up plans, venue assessment and security planning.

Clients:
world cup soccer, super bowl xxviii houston,tx, united center chicago, il, bonnaroo music and camping festival, rothbury music festival, langerado music festival, phish music and camping festivals, virgin music festival, town and country village houston, tx, market street the woodlands township,tx, law enforcement units, g-8 summit savannah,ga, merriweather post pavilion, chronicle pavilion.

CONTEMPORARY SERVICES CORPORATION
17101 SUPERIOR STREET
NORTHRIDGE, CA 91325
818-885-5150
Fax: 818-885-0609
www.csc-usa.com
• Damon Zumwalt, CEO
dzumwalt@csc-usa.com
• Jim Granger, President
jgranger@csc-usa.com
• Mark Camillo, Sr. Vice President, Strategic Planning
• Mark Glaser, Sr. Vice President, Operations
• James H. Service, Vice President, General Counsel
• Jay Brock, Vice President, Operations
• Bruce Wagner, Vice President, Operations

Description:
CSC is the world leader in fully-managed event staffing, crowd management, security, and guest services for both the entertainment and sporting event industries. CSC's 42 years of experience have resulted in a loyal and esteemed client base, including more than 100 stadiums and arenas, over 70 universities and colleges, more than 20 convention centers, and numerous clients in the MLB, MLS, NBA, NFL, NHL, and NASCAR. CSC also has experience providing services to the world's largest special events, including the U.S. Open, 29 Super Bowls, 7 Olympic Games, 4 Presidential Inaugurations, and 2 World Cups.

Services:
Crowd management, security, ticket taking, ushering, parking services, box office services, and consulting.

GARDA WORLD
1101 WILSON BOULEVARD
SUITE 1725
ARLINGTON, VA 22209
703-253-8080
Fax: 703-592-1500
www.garda-world.com

• Lemarque Sheppard, President
• Steve Casteel, SVP, International Business Development
• Obie R Moore III, Seinor Vice President
• Rob Shuster, Senior Vice President
• Ray O'Hara, Senior Vice President
• Rolando P. Soliz, General Director
• Nicole A. Watson, Vice President Business Development
• Kevin Coughenour, Chief Information Officer
• Brent Wegner, General Counsel
• Christina Mansfield, Vice President Human Resources

Sports Service Founded:
1984.

Services:
Management: Help security professionals & event managers plan for, manage and respond to risks during events - including annual shareholders' meetings, sales conferences, product road shows, publicity events, conventions, and large-scale parties.

Services:
Event Integrity, Workplace Integrity, Litigation Integrity, Travel Integrity, Property Integrity, Product Integrity

Athlete Management Services:
Security services for athletes and their families, such as residential security surveys, personal protection.

Event Management Services:
All types of security services for sports events.

Marketing & Consulting Services:
Advises corporations on security-related issues pertaining to events, athletes and sponsorship programs.

WACKENHUT SPORTS SECURITY
910 PAVERSTONE DRIVE
RALEIGH, NC 27615
561-622-5656
800-922-6488
www.g4s.com
• Grahame Gibson, COO/Divisional President Security
• Drew Levine, President Security Services
• William Hill, President Consulting & Investigation Services
• Susanne Jorgensen, Chief Financial Officer
• Julie Payne, Svp & General Counsel
• Dr. Michael Goodboe, Vp Human Resources/Corporate Learning Officer
• Brian McCabe, Chief Information Officer
• John Connolly, Chairman
• Nick Buckles, Group Chief Executive
• Trevor Dighton, Chief Financial Officer

Services:
Provides security, safety, crowd management, admissions, ushers, parking and related services to sports and entertainment venues throughout the United States.

Financial Services

A.P. SWANN INSURANCE SERVICES LLC
980 N MICHIGAN AVENUE
SUITE 1377
CHICAGO, IL 60611
312-274-0950
877-277-9266
Fax: 312-274-0955

info@apswann.com
www.apswann.com

Description:
nationally licensed insurance brokerage. A.P. Swann provides the ability and the experience to bring a vast array of surety bonds and insurance products,to both individual consumers and businesses.

specialties
meeting the unique needs of consumers seeking efficient, on-demand product purchase, and carriers desiring a cost-effective sales and delivery channel for low premium, low profit margin products.

ACTIVE INTERNATIONAL
ONE BLUE HILL PLAZA
PEARL RIVER, NY 10965
845-735-1700
800-448-7233
Fax: 845-735-0717
www.activeinternational.com
• Alan Elkin, Co-Founder/Chief Executive Officer
• Arthur Wagner, Co-Founder/President
• Richard Vendig, EVP/Chief Financial and Administrative Officer
• Fredrick Fuest, President, International Division
• Alan Brown, Evp Worldwide Media
• Elysa Gonzalez, Svp Marketing
• Barry M. Green, Evp Sales
• Sharon Marshall, General Counsel
• Jim Porcarelli, Chief Strategy Officer
• Thomas Ruderman, Chief Human Resource Officer
• Stu Allen, Svp Business Services
• Alan Elkin, Founder/CEO
• Mark Ordover, Evp Global Real Estate & Financial Assets

Description:
Enables a company to fund their sponsorship property without additional money. Offers customized corporate trading programs to assist in financing their racing team, golf outing, naming rights or sports and event sponsorships.

Services:
Provides a wide range of ways to help clients meet their business needs which includes advertising, printing, shipping and packaging, sports events marketing, etc.

ALLIED SPECIALTY INSURANCE
10451 GULF BOULEVARD
TREASURE ISLAND, FL 33706
727-367-6900
800-237-3355
Fax: 727-367-1407
rdaprile@alliedspecialty.com
www.alliedspecialty.com
• David Gallace, Contact
dgallace@alliedspecialty.com
• Rick D'Aprile, Contact
rdaprile@alliedspecialty.com
• Mark Jones, Contact
mjones@alliedspecialty.com
• Carol Perkins, Contact
cperkins@alliedspecialty.com

Services:
Provider of insurance solutions, which includes amusement facility, motorsports, outdoor amusement and specialty insurance.

Marketing & Consulting Services:
Specialists in sports and venue insurance needs, including but not limited to coverage of spectator and participant legal liability for

athletic events, tenant-user liability programs for venue lessees, and group accident medical coverage for athletic teams and associations.

AMBAC ASSURANCE CORPORATION
ONE STATE STREET PLAZA
NEW YORK, NY 10004
212-658-7470
800-221-1854
Fax: 212-509-9190
www.ambac.com
• Michael A. Callen, Chair/Interim CEO
• Sean T. Leonard, Svp/CFO
• Douglas C. Renfield-Miller, Evp Europe & Asia/Pacific
• Diana N. W. Adams, President and Chief Executive Officer
• Robert B. Eisman, Senior Managing Director and Chief Accounting
• Stephen M. Ksenak, Senior Managing Director, General Counsel and
• David Trick, Senior Managing Director, Chief Financial Off
• Michael Fitzgerald, Managing Director (212) 208-3222
Description:
Primarily engaged in insuring municipal and structured finance obligations and is the successor of the oldest municipal bond insurance company. Financial guarantee insurance written by AMBAC, guaranteed payment when due of the principal and interest on the obligations insured. AMBAC has been assigned Triple A claims paying ability ratings from the 3 major rating agencies.
Services:
Primarily engaged in insuring municipal and structured finance obligations and is the successor of the oldest municipal bond insurance company. Financial guarantee insurance written by AMBAC, guaranteed payment when due of the principal and interest

AMERICA'S SCHOOLS PROGRAM
PO BOX 236
ATWOOD, CA 92601
800-345-4025
Fax: 951-344-8279
www.americas-schools.org/home.php
• Don Baird, Sponsorships,Partnerships,Media Relationships
(800) 345-4025
• Vijay Kotrappa, Programs/General Information
(800) 345-4025
Marketing & Consulting Services:
Engaged in the business of generating additional discretionary revenues for schools, including high schools, grammar schools and community colleges via six primary revenue sources: corporate sponsors; an affinity credit card program; financial services; logo-licensing; non-logo licensing; and direct marketing.

AMERICAN HOLE 'N ONE
55 SCOTT STREET
BUFORD, GA 30518
800-499-2257
Fax: 770-271-4006
golf@ahno.net
www.americanholeinone.net

Services:
Leading resource for hole in one insurance, custom showroom promotions, sports risk insurance and superior sign packages

AON ENTERTAINMENT
707 WILSHIRE BOULEVARD
SUITE 2600
LOS ANGELES, CA 90017
213-630-3200
Fax: 213-627-6155
www.aon.com
• Mary Greening, Contact
Services:
All types of insurance services for the sports industry/creator innovative solutions in insurance and risk management, human capital consulting, and insurance underwriting to help clients

ASSURED GUARANTY CORPORATION
31 W 52ND STREET
NEW YORK, NY 10019
212-974-0100
Fax: 212-581-3268
info@fsa.com
www.assuredguaranty.com
• Robert P Cochran, Chairman/Chief Executive Officer
• Sean W McCarthy, President/Chief Operating Officer
• Joseph W Simon, Chief Financial Officer
• Bruno Deletre, Evp/Member Executive Committee
• Michele Colin, Head Risk Management
Services:
Triple A rated insurer of municipal bonds guaranteeing all types of general obligations and revenue bonds in both the new issue and secondary markets. Organization provides full service to the municipal market from its New York headquarters and regional area

BESSEMER TRUST
630 5TH AVENUE
NEW YORK, NY 10111
212-708-9100
Fax: 212-265-5826
www.bessemer.com
• George A. Wilcox, Jr., President
• Marc D Stern, Chief Executive Officer
• Rebecca H Patterson, Chief Investment Officer
Services:
Official Private Banking and Wealth Management Partner of NTRA/Breeders' Cup Limited.

BLACKROCK
60 STATE STREET
BOSTON, MA 02109
617-357-1200
800-531-0131
Fax: 617-951-9919
www2.blackrock.com
• Laurence Fink, Chairman/Chief Executive Officer
• James Rohr, Board Member
• Kenneth Dunn, Board Member
• Laurence D. Fink, Chairman and Chief Executive Officer
• Philipp Hildebrand, Vice Chairman
• Kendrick R. Wilson III, Vice Chairman
• Barbara Novick, Vice Chairman
• Robert S. Kapito, President
• Robert W. Fairbairn, Senior Managing

Director
• Peter R. Fisher, Senior Managing Director
Description:
A new division within Private Client Group. Provides investment management for professional athletes.
Services:
Provides risk management, investment system outsourcing and financial advisory services to a growing number of institutional investors

BOLLINGER INSURANCE
101 JFK PARKWAY
SHORT HILLS, NJ 07078
973-467-0444
800-526-1379
Fax: 973-921-2876
www.bollingerinsurance.com
• Lori Windolf Crispo, Senior Executive Vice President, Sports Division
(800) 526-1379
lori@bollingerinsurance.com
• John A. Windolf, Chairman/CEO
Description:
Bollinger is a leading provider of Sports Insurance products and risk management services in all 50 states. Insuring Amateur Sports Organizations has been our specialty for over 60 years. Bollinger provides a full array of coverages through A rated insurance companies for sports organizations and sports facilities.
Sports Service Founded:
1944
Year Founded:
1876

BWD GROUP LLC
45 EXECUTIVE DRIVE
PLAINVIEW, NY 11803
516-327-2700
www.bwdgroup.com
Sports Service Founded:
1929
Services:
Insurance products, risk management services and benefit programs for a diverse and distinguished clientele; sports and entertainment insurance; commercial and personal lines, individual and employee benefits, financial planning, consulting, program administration and claims services

CARPENTER, PETERSEN & ASSOCIATES - CPA'S
26020 TOWNE CENTRE DRIVE
FOOTHILL RANCH, CA 92610
949-951-3200
Fax: 949-951-3210
info@cpcpas.com
www.cpcpas.com
• John Carpenter, Owner
• David Petersen, Owner
Services:
Financial Statement consulting and preparation at all traditional levels, Tax Planning and compliance, Consulting Services, Accounting and Bookkeeping, and Industries and Professions Served
Description:
Provides financial and estate planning, money management services, income tax planning and preparation for over 30 years.

CHARLES SCHWAB & CO.
211 MAIN STREET
SAN FRANCISCO, CA 94105
415-667-1009
888-403-9000
800-435-4000
www.schwab.com
• Chuck Schwab, Founder
• Carol Benz, Investment Advisor
• Carolyn Clayton, Team Member
• Kirk Larson, Team Member
• Mike Dewitt, Management Team
Services:
Official investment firm of the PGA Tour, Champions Tour, and US Ski Team.

DELOITTE & TOUCHE LLP
100 KIMBALL DRIVE
PARSIPPANY, NJ 07054-2176
973-602-6000
Fax: 973-602-5050
www.deloitte.com

ERNST & YOUNG
5 TIMES SQUARE
NEW YORK, NY 10036-6530
212-773-3000
Fax: 212-773-6350
www.ey.com
• James Turley, Chairman/Chief Executive Officer
• John Ferraro, COO
Services:
Auditing, financial planning, accounting and consulting services for corporate involvement in sports franchises, sports facility management, or event management. Special purpose and compliance examinations; valuations and appraisals; tax planning

GAGLIARDI INSURANCE SERVICES
1302 LINCOLN AVE
SUITE 202
SAN JOSE, CA 95125
408-414-8100
800-995-9768
Fax: 408-414-8199
sales@gsportsinsurance.com
www.gisins.com
• Dominic Gagliardi, President
• Nicholas Gagliardi, Vp Sales / Marketing
• David Abhraham, VP
• MIchelle Valdivia, Director of Operations
• Patricia Chavez, Customer Service
• Rick Dukelow, Sales Representative
rdukelow@gsportsinsurance.com
Services:
Develop custom plans for organizations in specialty markets such as amateur and professional sports, special events, entertainment, prize indemnification, camps and conferences, and facilities
Description:
Providers of specialty insurance relating to sports and entertainment. Offer services in Sports Risk Management and Sports Leadership consultation. Experienced provider of league insurance, camp insurance and school athletic coverage.

JEFFREY M. BROOKS & CO, INC.
21207 CHAGRIN BOULEVARD
CLEVELAND, OH 44122
216-295-9530
Fax: 216-591-1656
• Jeffrey M Brooks, President

JPMORGAN CHASE BANK, N.A.
20201 E JACKSON DRIVE
SUITE 420
INDEPENDENCE, MO 64057
816-795-2914
866-281-9557
Fax: 816-795-2909
michael.a.dailey@chase.com
www.jpmorganchase.com
• Michael A. Dailey, Branch Manager
(816) 795-2914
michael.a.dailey@chase.com
• James A Bell, Audit Committee
• Laban P Jackson, Chairman of Audit Committee
• Stephen Burke, Compensation & Management Development Committ
• William C Weldon, Chairman of Corporate Governance & Nominating
• Crandall C Bowles, Chairman of Public Responsibilty Committee
• James S Crown, Chairman of Risk Policy Committee
• Jamie Dimon, Chairman/Executive Committee
Description:
Specializes in providing mortgage loans, rookie lines of credit, equity lines, and pre-bonus lines of credit to professional athletes, family members, staff of athletic departments, as well as coaches. Also offers educational seminars on credit management and restoration, as well as identity theft protection.

K & K INSURANCE GROUP
1712 MAGNAVOX WAY
PO BOX 2338
FORT WAYNE, IN 46804
260-459-5000
800-237-2917
800-637-4757
Fax: 260-459-5800
lorena.hatfield@kandkinsurance.com
www.kandkinsurance.com
• Dan Johnson, Program Manager
• Stacie Helton, Underwriter
• Sheila Morton, Sales Director
• Lorena Hatfield, Marketing Resources Manager
(260) 459-5663
Nature of Service:
Provides quality, professional commercial insurance products and services to virtually every aspect of the sports markets served, including professional and amateur sports teams, leagues, associations, events, facilities, coaches, camps, and clinics. Considered the leading provider of specialty sports, leisure and entertainment insurance in the industry.

M R COMART
450 FASHION AVENUE
SUITE 1701
NEW YORK, NY 10123
212-563-3100
Nature of Sports Service:
Organization offers all traditional accounting services, but with an emphasis on areas like royalties, taxation and advances that are unique and critical to entertainment and sports professionals.

MARCEL V. KUPER, CPA/PFS, CFE
500 W PALATINE ROAD
WHEELING, IL 60090

847-215-8630
Fax: 847-215-8632
mvkcpa@aol.com
www.ltplanning.com
• Marcel V Kupen, President
mvkruper@aol.com
Nature of Service:
Asset protection, cash management, business management, estate planning, investment management, risk management, retirement planning. In addition, representation for the Internal Revenue Service, tax preparation, fraud prevention and detection. A fee-based financial planner. We sell no products, and offer representation throughout the United States.
Services:
Corporate Web Application, e-Government Web Application, Customer Relation Management, Citizen Relation Management, Content Management for Complex Organizations, Content Management for Less Complex Organizations, Subscription-based Broadcast Email System, e-Government Preparation.
Year Founded:
1980

MARSH & MCLENNAN
1166 AVENUE OF THE AMERICAS
NEW YORK, NY 10036
212-345-5000
www.mmc.com
• Oscar Fanjul, Director
• Leslie M Baker, Jr., Board of Directors
• Zachary W. Carter, Director
• Daniel S. Glaser, Director
• H. Edward Hanway, Director
Services:
Risk and Insurance Services and Risk Consulting and Technology
Marketing & Consulting Services:
Insurance brokerage firm providing consulting and transactional services in the management of risk for enterprises throughout the world, with offices in 70 countries.

MBIA INSURANCE CORPORATION
113 KING STREET
ARMONK, NY 10504
914-273-4545
info@mbia.com
www.mbia.com
• Cliff Corso, Managing Director
(914) 273-4545
• Anthony McKiernan, Managing Director
(914) 765-3611
• John Dare, Managing Director Structured Finance and St
(914) 765-3777
• Greg Diamond, Managing Director Head of Investor Relation
(914) 765-3190
• Kevin Brown, Managing Director Corporate Communications
(914) 765-3428
• Tom Jordan, Managing Director
(914) 765-3428
Services:
Global Public Finance, Global Structured Finance, Asset Management, Revenue Finances
Description:
A leading insurer of municipal bonds and structured finance transactions. A leading provider of investment management

services to the public sector. MBIA Insurance Corporation has a claims-paying rating of Triple-A from Moody's Investors Service, Inc., Standard & Poor's Ratings Group and Fitch Investors Service, L.P.

MOAG & COMPANY
323 WEST CAMDEN STREET
SUITE 400
BALTIMORE, MD 21201
410-230-0105
Fax: 410-230-0547
www.moagandcompany.com
• John A Moag, Jr., Chairman/Chief Executive Officer
jmoag@moagandcompany.com
• Thomas F Lang, Vice President
tlang@moagandcompany.com
• Marsha Russell, Administrator
mrussell@moagandcompany.com
• Nathaniel Wilson, Analyst
nwilson@moagandcompany.com
• Lauren Moag, Analyst
Description:
Dedicated team of investment bankers serving the sports, media and entertainment industries in ways that only a boutique firm can.
Sports Service Founded:
2001

MOODY'S INVESTORS SERVICE
ONE FRONT STREET
SUITE 1900
SAN FRANCISCO, CA 94111
212-553-1653
Fax: 415-274-1726
clientservices@moodys.com
www.moodys.com
Description:
Currently maintains over 40,000 ratings involving more than 20,000 local entities of government throughout the U.S. and Canada.
Services:
Provides independent credit ratings, research and financial information to the capital markets.

MZ SPORTS
3000 ATRIUM WAY
SUITE 101
MT LAUREL, NJ 08054-3910
856-778-9400
Fax: 856-778-8478
www.mzsports.com
• Mitchell H Ziets, President/Chief Executive Officer
Description:
Develops creative solutions for clients, due to an understanding of finance and sports, tremendous access to capital, both debt and equity and a developed web of relations with team, league and public officials, the financial community, architects, attorneys, tax advisors, consultants and other project vendors. These relationships are drawn upon to obtain for clients state-of-the-art information and ideas.
Services:
Acquisition Finance, Facility Finance, Lease Negotiation, Capital Structuring
Clients:
Anaheim Angels, Anaheim Mighty Ducks, City of Anaheim, Arena Football League, City of Arlington, Atlanta Falcons, Atlanta Hawks, Atlanta Thrashers, and Philps

Arena, Boston Red Sox, Buffalo Sabres, Camden Couty Improvement Authority, Cleveland Cavaliers, Florida Marlins, Georgia Force, City of Grant Prairie, Hamilton County, Indiana University of Pennsylvania, Kansas City Royals, Los Angeles Dodgers, City of Los Angeles, City of Louisville, Middlesex County, Milwaukee Brewers, Minnesota Vikings, State of Minnesota, Minor League Baseball, New York City, NJ Sports and Exposition Authority - Giants Stadium, City of Oakland, Philadelphia City, Ph

NEUBERGER BERMAN
53 STATE STREET
SUITE 1303
BOSTON, MA 02109
212-476-8800
800-877-9700
866-497-4240
Fax: 781-796-2953
www.nb.com
Services:
Advisory Services (individuals), Advisory Services (institutions), Broker Advised Products, Close-End Funds, Institutional Separate Accounts, Mutual Funds(individuals), Mutual Funds (institutions), Private Asset Management, Professional Investor Clearing Services, Trust and Investment Management(individuals), Wealth and Fiduciary Services (individuals)
Description:
Offers a wide spectrum of investment products for a full range of clients, both individuals and institutional. Includes tax and financial planning, fiduciary services and financial advocacy for viturally any circumstances or need.

PARK LANE - INVESTMENT BANKING SERVICES
2029 CENTURY PARK E
SUITE 437
LOS ANGELES, CA 90067
310-201-8496
Fax: 310-388-5799
www.prkln.com
• Andrew W Kline, Founder and MD
• Carlos Silva, MD
• James A Shortill, Director,Sports Media
• Robert Fasulo, Director, Corporate Development-Internationa
• Tarlin Ray, Director,Entreprenuer in Residence
• Mark Abdou, Head General Counsel
• Chris Stuart, Principal, Sports Licensing & Estates
Nature of Service:
Park Lane is the preeminent small and middle market, investment bank providing clients with world class athletics corporate finance and M&A services. We advise clients when buying and selling sports related businesses and professional teams. Raise capital for emerging leagues and businesses involved in sports.

PATRICK M. CAPOZZI, CPA
3831 S PARK AVENUE
BLASDELL, NY 14219
716-824-4111
Fax: 716-825-6807
• Patrick Capozzi, Owner

Nature of Sports Service:
Financial services for professional athletes. Investment counseling, income tax planning and preparation.

PUBLIC FINANCIAL MANAGEMENT
ONE KEYSTONE PLAZA
SUITE 300
HARRISBURGH, PA 17101-2044
717-232-2723
Fax: 717-233-6073
www.pfm.com
• Dean Kaplan, Managing Director
Description:
Specializes in lease negotiations, financial planning and debt management, maintains an active strategic consulting and investment management practice.
Clients:
Alaska Industrial Economic Development Authority; Arizona State University; Arizona School Facilities Board; Salt River Project; Arkansas State Highway Commission; California Asset Management Program; City and County of San Francisco; City of Anaheim; City of Newport Beach; City of Roseville; City of San Diego; Contra Coast Transportation Authority.

SADLER & COMPANY, INC.
3014 DEVINE ST.
PO BOX 5866
COLUMBIA, SC 29250-5866
800-622-7370
800-622-7370
Fax: 803-256-4017
sport@sadlersports.com
www.sadlersports.com
• John Sadler, President
(800) 622-7370
john@sadlerco.com
Description
Sadler & Company specializes in providing insurance solutions for the sports and recreation industries. Client base includes 12 national sports organizations and over 7000 community sports organizations such as teams & leagues, camps, outdoors, special events, health clubs, etc.

SADLER AND COMPANY INC
3014 DEVINE ST.
PO BOX 5866
COLUMBIA, SC 29250-5866
800-622-7370
800-622-7370
Fax: 803-256-4017
sport@sadlersports.com
www.sadlersports.com
• John Sadler, President
(800) 622-7370
john@sadlerco.com

SPORTS COVERAGE
5535 MILITARY PARKWAY
DALLAS, TX 75227
972-698-7329
888-844-3420
Fax: 214-381-4585
www.kentex.com
Sports Service Founded:
1988
Products:
America sports products
Brands:
America SP., JC Penney, NFL, Collegiate, NHL

Marketing & Consulting Services:
Provides insurance coverage for college athletic programs and sports camps, as well as disability income insurance for individual amateur and professional athletes and coaches.
Event Management Services:
Provides liability coverage for sports events.

SPORTSINSURANCE.COM
PO BOX 1155
LAKE PLACID, NY 12946
866-889-4763
Fax: 866-467-8770
info@SportsInsurance.com
www.sportsinsurance.com
• Mark DiPerno, President
mark@sportsinsurance.com
Nature of Sports Service:
Insurance organization focusing only on the Sport, Special Event, Prize and Contingency Markets.
Sports Service Founded:
1997

TIAA CREF
PO BOX 1259
CHARLOTTE, NC 28201
800-842-2252
www.tiaa-cref.org
• Edward J. Grzybowski, Senior Managing Director, Chief Investment Of
Description:
Provides long-term financing in the construction and operational phases of projects worldwide, including major and minor league sports facilities, infrastructure, power, energy, telecommunications, and industrial operations.
Services:
Provides national financial services and retirement services in the academic, research, medical and cultural fields

TREATY OAK BANK
101 WESTLAKE DRIVE
AUSTIN, TX 78746
512-617-3600
888-387-3289
Fax: 512-617-3697
• Jeff Nash, President
• Coralie Pledger, Chief Financial Officer
• Randy Meeks, Executive Vice President
• Sheila Bostick Jagger, Senior Vice President
• Tommy Clark, Senior Vice President
• Steve Blackburn, Vice President
Nature of Sports Service:
Tax Strategy and Preparation, Small Business Consulting, Financial and Retirement Planning, Investment advisory, Asset management, Employee Benefits (Life, Health, Disability, 401k), Insurance & Annuities, Estate planning.

WELLS FARGO
1 NORTH JEFFERSON AVENUE
ST LOUIS, MO 63101-2205
877-879-2495
Fax: 314-955-2890
www.wachoviasecurities.com
Description:
The largest full services national securities firm. Services include: underwriting, financial advisory and private placement as well as, on-going services for public (state and local government) and private entities. Developed a sports and entertainment group.

WELLS FARGO INSURANCE INC.
10 S. WACKER
CHICAGO, IL 60606
312-920-9177
866-226-7342
Fax: 312-423-2508
• Ellen Sievert, National Director Of Communications
• Julien Smiley, Regional managing director
• Laura Schupbach, Executive VP
• Kevin Kenny, Executive VP Head of Insuarnce Brokerage
• H. David Wood, Executive VP Head of Insuarnce Operations Off
Services:
Provides insurance brokerage, administrative services, and financial and consulting services with a unique blend of big-broker clout and local-broker service.

Marketing & Consulting Services

16W MARKETING, LLC
75 UNION AVENUE
RUTHERFORD, NJ 7070
201-635-8000
bnelson@16wmarketing.com
www.16wmarketing.com
• Ralph Vuono, Senior Director
(201) 635-8004
rvuono@16wmarketing.com
• Janice Miceli, VP
(201) 635-8005
jmecili@16wmarketing.com
• Kerry Kelly, Ass. To Partner
(201) 635-8006
kkelly@16wmarketing.com
• Shawn Flannelly, Manager - Business Develpment
(201) 635-8007
sflannelly@16wmarketing.com
• Brian Nelson, Vp
(201) 635-8003
bnelson@16wmarketing.com
• Ralph Vuono, VP
(201) 635-8004
rvuono@16wmarketing.com
Nature of Service:
Sports Marketing firm specializing in talent marketing, corporate consulting, league/team services and corporate hospitality.

20/20 SPECIAL MARKETS
4650 BAKER STREET
CINCINNATI, OH 45212
513-561-9920
Fax: 513-569-0189
www.2020specialmarkets.com
Services:
Sales and marketing
Clients:
All-Clad Metalcrafters; J.A. Henckels; Enclume Design; Francis Francis

360 MANAGEMENT, LLC
8000 E DRIVE
SUITE 201
MIAMI, FL 33141
Fax: 734-372-6431
www.360mgt.com
• Morgan Menahem, Managing Director
morgan@360mgt.com
Services:
Serves as a managing and marketing representative for athletes and firms in the sporting world, with an emphasis in tennis; from sponsors to media and broadcasters.
Clients:
Tony Parker (Basketball); Jeanne-Marie Busutill (Golf); Jean-Francois Bachelot (Tennis); Ansley Cargill (Tennis); Peter Luczak (Tennis); Cyril Saulnier (Tennis); Christophe Rochus (Tennis); Lindsay Lee-Walters (Tennis)
Sports Service Founded:
2002
Sponsors Consulting & Sport Events:
Involved in the valuation of sponsors' partnership investments in various events as well as providing services, such as consulting for marketing plans specificaly designed for companies involved in the world of sports.

361o EXPERIENTIAL
633 N ST CLAIR STREET
CHICAGO, IL 60611-3234
312-425-5053
inquiries@dfcbx.com
www.361experiential.com
• Brad Back, Senior Vice President Group Management Director
• Shannon Babcock, Management Director

4LICENSING CORPORATION
767 3RD AVENUE
17TH FLOOR
NEW YORK, NY 10017
212-758-7666
Fax: 212-754-5481
www.4licensingcorp.com
• Jay Emmett, Board of Directors
• Bruce M. Foster, Executive VP/CFO
Services:
Specializes in the areas of TV production and distribution, home video production, merchandise licensing, media planning and buying, music development, and Web site development.

A TEAM
232 MADISON AVENUE
NEW YORK, NY 10016
212-239-0499
Fax: 212-239-0575
acohen@ateampromo.com
www.theateamagency.com
• Andrew Cohen, Chief Executive Officer
(212) 239-0499
acohen@ateampromo.com
• Tom Sato, Executive VP
(212) 239-0499
• Bernie Lee, VP West Coast
blee@ateampromo.com
• Rick Krisburg, VP Account Director
rkrisburg@ateampromo.com
• Patti Villegas, Sr. Account Director
pvillegas@ateampromo.com
Description:
Strategic planning/concept development, creative development/execution, account management, event marketing and direct marketing.
Services:
Provides marketing services that helps

strengthen and emphasize their client's brand image and unique attributes.
Clients:
Jaguar, Weight Wathcers, HIghfalls, Volvo, Skyy Spirits, Ricola, Vitamin Water, H-E-B
Other Location:
8001 Irvine Center Drive, 4th Floor, Irvine CA 92618. 949-754-3022; FAX: 949-754-4001.

A.D.D. MARKETING AND ADVERTISING
6600 LEXINGTON AVENUE
LOS ANGELES, CA 90038
323-790-0500
Fax: 323-790-0240
www.addmarketing.com
• Scott Leonard, CEO
• Elizabeth Baudoin, Client relation
• Lauren LeBlanc, Marketing and Advertising
Description:
Marketing Consultants, Advertising & Promotional Product Dealers.
Services:
Specializes in developing communication solutions that seamlessly span from traditional to non-traditional.
Clients:
ABC Entertainment, America Online, Boost Mobile, Dreamworks, EA, ESPN, Fox Sports, Full Tilt Poker, Gravity Games, Haribo Gummie Bears, Head and Shoulders Shampoo, Levi's, Lexus, Mazda, Milk Processing Board, MTV, NBC Sports, Nestle, Nike, Nokia, Pantene, Paramount, Pringles, Razor Scooter, Sony, Toyota, Zumiez

AAA FLAG & BANNER
8955 NATIONAL BLVD
LOS ANGELES, CA 90034
310-836-3200
855-218-3300
Fax: 310-836-7253
sales@aaaflag.com
www.aaaflag.com
• Jay Jacoby, Representative
Nature of Services:
AAA Flag & Banner manufacturers and installs custom displays, banners and flags for Major Sporting Events and Fortune 500 Companies throughout the United States-services include concept creation, banner, sign and flag design, logos and corporate identity, layout and composition, marketing materials and event pageantry consultation.

AAI SPORTS INC. & AAI INTERNATIONAL, INC.
16000 DALLAS PARKWAY
SUITE 300
DALLAS, TX 75248
972-739-8401
Fax: 972-739-8495
gbass@aaisports.com
www.aaisports.com

ACC PROPERTIES
4512 WEYBRIDGE LANE
PO DRAWER ACC
GREENSBORO, NC 27407
336-854-8787
Fax: 336-854-8797
feedback@theacc.org
www.theacc.com

• John D Swofford, Commissioner
• Jeff Elliott, Finance/Administration
• Amy Yakola, Public Relations/Marketing
• Lynne Herndon, Director Of Business Operations
Marketing & Consulting Services:
Marketing Venture managed by ACC television partners Raycom Sports and Jefferson Pilot Sports & Entertainment. Serves to consolidate Conference-related marketing opportunities into a one-stop shopping format that will enhance the Raycom and Jefferson Pilot television packages. Oversees marketing, advertising merchandising, licensing and promotional opportunities for the Atlantic Coast Conference.

ACME MASCOTS, INC.
PO BOX 23831
BROOKLYN, NY 11202
718-722-7900
Fax: 718-770-7678
• Wayde Harrison, Development Director
• Bonnie Erickson, Creative Director
Services:
Provides a powerful character design, production, product development, and art direction and animation.
Clients:
Burger King, Swatch, AT&T, Sharp Electronics, American Dairy Association, Procter & Gamble, Budweiser, McDonald's, Montreal Expos, Hiroshima Carp, Chicago, White Sox, Philadelphia Phillies, New York Yankees, New Jersey Nets, Houston Rockets, Washington Wizards, Philadelphia 76ers, Orlando Magic, Charlotte Hornets, Kansas City Chiefs, Jacksonville Jaguars, Bell Telephone Company, TV Pilots, General Motors, State of Alaska, Sigma Marketing, Colorforms, Applause, Hasbro, Knickerbocker, etc.
Sports Service Founded:
1978
Marketing & Consulting Services:
Producers of Sport Consulting, design, construction and merchandising of mascot characters.

ACTION INK, INC.
14607 SAN PEDRO AVENUE
SUITE 130
SAN ANTONIO, TX 78232
210-490-1900
Fax: 210-490-1930
actionink@sbcglobal.net
www.actioninkresumes.com
• Tony Oliva, Contact
Year Founded:
1984
Description:
Offers complete resume preparation with writers who are degreed and have management, sales, personnel, and military experience.

ACTION SPORTS AMERICA
5263 PLACENTIA PARKWAY
SUITE 13
LAS VEGAS, NV 89118
610-832-7500
Fax: 612-465-1669
www.giantjersey.com
• Doug Verb, Founder & President
• Sam Sheckman, Vice President

(917) 767-7505
sam@giantjersey.com
Founded:
1983
Clients:
NHL, Scout Sports & Entertainment, Vegas Golden Knights
Nature of Service:
Sales promotion and event creation/management firm.

ACTION SPORTS INTERNATIONAL
4945 PRESIDENTS WAY
WESTWOOD GATEWAY
TUCKER, GA 30084
770-696-2575
Fax: 817-665-0047
• Jennifer Reese, Chief Operating Officer
Marketing & Consulting Services:
Corporate and non-profit sports organization marketing, event management, sports art production and marketing, athlete appearances, athletic fund raising, innovative marketing concepts. Dealer Kodak Dynamic Imaging.
Services:
Specializes in capturing an athlete's most memorable images through digital and film photography.

ACTION SPORTS MEDIA
3401 RUSS CIRCLE
SUITE E
ALCOA, TN 37701
865-379-0625
Fax: 865-379-9653
• Gordon Whitener, Chief Executive Officer
(865) 379-0625
• Jerry Felix, Chief Financial Officer
(865) 379-0625
Description:
A full service collegiate sports marketing company specializing in game day multimedia.
Clients:
The University of Alabama, The University of Iowa, Kansas State University, University of Kentucky/Rupp Arena, The University of Mississippi, Mississippi State University, Oklahoma State University, Oregon State University, Purdue University, The University of South Carolina, The University of Tennessee, The University of Texas, Texas A&M Uneversity, Gaderbilt University, University of Washington, Washington State University

ADLINK
WESTWOOD GATEWAY
11150 SANTA MONICA BOULEVARD
SUITE 1000
LOS ANGELES, CA 90025
310-477-3994
Fax: 310-477-8139
www.adlink.com
• Lisa Palmer, General Manager/Sales
Description:
Sells Television advertising in Los Angeles California encompassing 44 Cable Networks. Offer advertisng opportunities through marketing programs. Adtag - With Adtag, you can customize your commercials for unique geographic groups within the Los Angeles market. Adcopyâ‚¢ Adcopy enables advertisers to sell different products to different market segments by running

multiple commercials simultaneously, all with one buy.

ADRENALIN, INC.
54 W 11TH AVENUE
DENVER, CO 80204
888-454-8888
888-757-5646
Fax: 303-454-8889
info@goadrenalin.com
www.goadrenalin.com
• Daniel S Price, President
(303) 454-8888
dprice@goadrenalin.com
• Bryan Kimbell, Vice President, Partnership & Strategy
(303) 454-8888
• Rick A Fillmon, Principal/Vice President Business Operations
(303) 454-8888
rfillmon@goadrenalin.com
Nature of Service:
Specializes in sports branding and marketing solutions. Develops and expands brands for sports and entertainment organizations.
Clients:
Altitude Sports Network,American Alpine Club, AEG, Broomfield Event Center, Chicago Fire, Cleveland Indians, Colorado Avalanche, Colorado Mammoth, Continental Basketball Assoc., Dallas Mavericks, Denver Broncos, Fox Sports Rocky Mountain, Gilco Sports & Entertainment Marketing, Gold Crown Foundation, Harlem Globetrotters, London Knights, Los Angeles Avengers, Major League Baseball Players Alumni Assoc., Major League Soccer, Memphis Redbirds, Metro Denver Sports Commission, National Basketball Association, National Hockey League, NYC2012, Phoenix Coyotes, Pikes Peak International Raceway, Sixth Man Solutions, Seattle Sonics, Team Builder Allia
Marketing & Consulting Services:
Specialize in designing logos, team uniforms, retail promotional materials, event tickets, advertising campaigns, game programs and brand architecture.
Year Founded:
1997

ADVANCED PROMOTIONAL CONCEPTS, INC.
2802 N HOWARD AVENUE
TAMPA, FL 33607
813-254-6600
Fax: 813-254-3526
apctampa@aol.com
www.apcpromotions.com
• Barbara Baker, Chief Executive Officer/President
Services:
Designs, negotiates and implements complete turn-key marketing services to clients such as Product Sampling, Product Demonstrations, Couponing, Mobile Marketing, Creative / Production, Point of Sale, Point of Sale Placement, Contests/ Games, Promotion Planning, Sweepstakes / Fulfillment, Retail Merchandising, Name Generation, Sponsorship Negotiations, Premium Give-A-Ways, Field Research and Ethnic Marketing.
Clients:
Seagram Americas / Diageo, The Andrew Jergens Company, Universal Studios / CITYWALK, GMC / Cadillac, Con Agra

Grocery Products, Clairol, Inc., Florida's Natural Growers, Gerber Products Co., Schering-Plough (Coppertone), The Rockport Co., Thomas J. Lipton Co., United Distillers, MCI Communications, Nutrogena, Ocean Spray Juices, Optyl, Inc. (Carrera), Procter and Gamble Co., Sara Lee Corp., Holiday Inn Worldwide, Jim Beam Brands Co., Joseph E. Seagram & Sons, MCA Music Group, M&M Mars, Whittle Communications, LP, General Motors Corp. (Cadillac), Van Camp's / Con Agra, R.J. Reynolds Tobacco Co. / Nabisco, Hiram Walker Group, Tech Data Corporat

ALAN TAYLOR COMMUNICATIONS, INC.
350 FIFTH AVENUE
EMPIRE STATE BUILDING
SUITE 3800
NEW YORK, NY 10118
212-714-1280
Fax: 212-695-5685
• Tony Signore, Chief Executive Officer and Managing Partner
(212) 714-1280
• Mark Beal, Contact
Services:
Provides a full range of public relations services that build brands and drive business.
Clients:
Gillette, MasterCard International, Yahoo!, Ameriquest, Best Western International, Inc., Duracell, Smirnoff, US Smokeless Tobacco, The History Channel, Reebok International, Levitra, AT&T Bank of America, Diageo North America Inc., Eight O'Clock Coffee, General Mills, Nestle Purina Petcare Company, GlaxoSmithKline/Schering Plough - Levitra, Pacific Health Laboratories, Inc., Staples, Pitney Bowes, Combe Inc., Sara Lee, Warner Bros., Boys Clubs of New York, Ironman Triathlon World Championships, JPMorgan Chase Corporate Challenge, The Miami Project to Cure Paralysis, International Tennis Hall of Fame, JPMorgan Chase, Pacific Life Open, Pilot

ALL TERRAIN PRODUCTIONS, INC.
2675 WEST GRAND AVENUE
CHICAGO, IL 60612
312-421-7672
www.allterrain.net
• Brook Jay, Co-President
• Sarah Eck-Thompson, Co-President
Year Founded:
1998
Description:
A hybird company of event management, field marketing & promotion and technical production.

ALL-CITY SPORTS MARKETING
1431 BROADWAY
11TH FLOOR
NEW YORK, NY 10018
212-221-7690
Fax: 212-719-9251
Sports Service Founded:
1995
Products:
Apparel and accessories
Marketing & Consulting Services:
Full service organization designed to handle three areas: manufacturing, marketing and media services.

Other Location:
85 NE Loop 410, Suite 600, San Antonio TX 78216. 800-235-8774; FAX: 210-341-2050.

ALLEN CONSULTING, INC.
89 MIDDLETOWN ROAD
HOLMDEL, NJ 07733
732-946-2711
Fax: 732-946-8032
Sylvia@allenconsulting.com
www.allenconsulting.com
• Sylvia Allen, Founder
sylvia@allenconsulting.com
Marketing & Consulting Services:
Advises on sponsorship development including developing marketing partners and strategic alliances, tailoring sports marketing programs and event sponsorship to best meet client needs, objectives and designing programs to achieve sales objectives. On-site event and sports sponsorship and sales training.

ALLOY MARKETING & PROMOTION
77 N WASHINGTON STREET
8TH FLOOR
BOSTON, MA 02114
617-723-8929
Fax: 617-723-2188
info@ampagency.com
www.ampagency.com
• Gary Colen, President & CEO
• Steve McCall, Partner
• Erica Melia, Senior VP of Accounts Management
• Joel Breen, Digital Account Director
Services:
Provides urban, youth, and multicultural promotional marketing services, focuses grassroots marketing, promotional events, and web design and offers market research services to clients.

ALLOY MEDIA & MARKETING
10 ABEEL ROAD
CRANBURY, NJ 8512
609-655-8878
Fax: 609-395-0737
• Matthew Diamond, Chief Executive Officer/Managing Partner
• Chris Cassino, Vp
• Jodi Smith, VP of Public relations
• Gary Colen, President Of Agency
• James K. K. Johnson, COO/President/Co-Founder
Description:
Media and marketing arm of Alloy, Inc. Specializes in college and teen marketing. Sources include: MarketSource Corporation, CASS Communications, YouthStream Media, Market Place Media and others to provide sales and marketing solutions targeting young adults.
Clients:
MarketSource Youth Division, CASS Communications, YouthStream Media, Market Place Media and others to provide sales and marketing solutions targeting young adults.

AMERICAN DREAMS
3950 KOVAL LANE
SUITE 3029
LAS VEGAS, NV 89109
702-732-1971
Fax: 702-732-2815
www.usdreams.com

• Jim Bickford, President

Description:
To help celebrities and athletes share their stories and wisdom across America through the following: Books, Speeches, Seminars/Workshops, Speakers Bureau, Events, Foundation, TV Series and Web Site.

Products:
Books

Brands:
The Present Collage - Bill Gates, Quote, Reflections Of A Changing Era, From Homeless To Multi-Millionaire, Scaling The Summit Forward, Onward, Upward, Bouncing Back From Black Monday, High School Dropout To High Tech CEO, Turning Weakness Into Strength, From Iron Lung, To Illiterate, To Self-Made Millionaire, Community Hero, American Entrepreneur, The Building Of Lucy's Cafe El Adobe, Hollywood Style, Fairy Tales Can Come True, Constructing A Better America, You've Got To Have A Goal Bigger Than You Are, The Journey To Freedom, Soaring To Success, I Am Focusing On God, Family And Domino's Pizza, I'm Proud To Be An American.

Services:
Conducts motivatiohal speeches, seminars/workshops, speakers bureau, and TV series.

AMERICAN HOLE 'N ONE
55 SCOTT STREET
BUFORD, GA 30518
770-271-1065
800-822-2257
Fax: 770-271-4006
info@ahno.net
www.americanholeinone.net

Services:
Leading resource for hole in one insurance, custom showroom promotions, sports risk insurance and superior sign packages

---

AMERICAN SPECIALTY
142 N MAIN STREET
ROANOKE, IN 46783
260-672-8800
800-245-2744
Fax: 260-672-8835
amerspec@amerspec.com
www.amerspec.com
• Drew Smith, Chief Marketing Official
(260) 673-1234

Description:
Providing insurance and risk management services to the Sports and Entertainment Industry.

AMERICAN SPECIALTY INSURANCE & RISK SERVICES, INC.
142 N MAIN STREET
PO BX 309
ROANOKE, IN 46783-0309
260-672-8800
800-245-2744
Fax: 260-672-8835
amerspec@amerspec.com
www.amerspec.com
• Tony Wittwer, SVP / Chief Marketing Officer
(260) 672-8800

Services:
Provides opportunities in management, marketing, underwriting, insurance service,

risk consulting, crisis management, security, information services, finance, claims management, administration, regulatory compliance, and public relations - integrating it into one comprehensive program designed to protect the assets and enhance the financial performance of clients.

Clients:
Associations, organizing committees, events, facilities, intercollegiate and interscholastic organizations, sanctioning bodies, amusement, theme and water parks, family entertainment centers, carnivals, pari-mutuel facilities, venues, special and ancillary events, race teams, tracks, sponsors, drivers, driving schools and professional athletes.

Marketing & Consulting Services:
Provides a portfolio of specialized and risk management services for the sports and entertainment industry, including risk management insurance, claims management, loss control, and technology services.

Sports Service Founded:
1989

AMERICAN SPORTS DATA, INC.
51009 ARRIETA COURT
FORT MILL, SC 29707
914-461-3271
Fax: 914-461-3131
sportsdata@comporium.net
• Harvey Lauer, President

Services:
Provides syndicated and custom research to a wide array of major corporations, media and industry associations

Clients:
Adidas USA, Inc., Amateur Athletic Foundation, Bauer USA, Inc., Boston Consulting Group, Casio, Inc., Converse, Inc., Deutsche Banc, DDB Needham Worldwide, Nokia, Procter & Gamble, Sears, Roebuck & Co., Universal Gym Equipment, Wrangler

Sports Brand Intelligence Report:
Syndicated study of 186 U.S. sports brands. Awareness and ownership analyzed by demographics, product ownership, sports participation, magazine readership and sports viewership.

Health Club Trend Report:
Annual syndicated study of consumer behavior.

Sports Media Index:
Syndicated tracking study of athlete recognition, magazine readership, in-person spectator sports, TV sports viewership.

Sports Equipment Monitor:
Annual syndicated tracking study of consumer awareness of 24 sporting goods categories.

Athletic Footwear Monitor:
Tri-annual syndicated tracking study of the athletic footwear market.

American Sports Analysis:
Annual syndicated tracking study of sports participation monitoring 58 sports/activities.

AQUARIUS SPORTS AND ENTERTAINMENT
9801 WASHINGTONIAN BLVD
SUITE 310
GAITHERSBURG, MD 20878

301-604-2606
Fax: 240-328-6051
firstinitialLastname@aquarius-se.com
aquarius-se.com
• Marc Bluestein, President, Founder
(240) 547-3498
mbluestein@aquarius-se.com
• Jeff Goldscher, Executive VP, Marketing & Creative
jgoldscher@aquarius-se.com
• Sara Blum, VP, Finance & Operations
sblum@aquarius-se.com
• Eric Goldscher, Client Services Director
(240) 547-3483
egoldscher@aquarius-se.com
• Samantha Hooker, Client Services Coordinator
shooker@aquarius-se.com

Description:
Sports and entertainment marketing firm that provides sponsorship consulting, sponsorhsip sales representation, corporate hospitality, and event and promotional marketing.

Nature of Services:
Sponsorship Consulting; Activation Consulting Services; Property Representation; Corporate Hospitality; Athlete Marketing; Entertainment Marketing

---

ARAMARK CORPORATION
1101 MARKET STREET
PHILADELPHIA, PA 19107
215-238-3000
800-272-6275
Fax: 215-238-3333
www.aramark.com
• Joseph Neubauer, Chairman
• L Frederick Sutherland, Executive Vice President/Chief Financial Officer
• Cathy Schlosberg, Vice President, Marketing/Education
• David Freireich, Media Relations Coordinator, Sports Entertainment
• Eric Foss, President

Baseball:
MLB; Minor League

College Sponsor:
NCAA; College Bowl

Basketball Sponsor:
NBDL

Football Sponsor:
Indoor League

Hockey Sponsor:
AHL

ARBITRON, INC.
9705 PATUXENT WOODS DRIVE
COLUMBIA, MD 21046
410-312-8000
www.arbitron.com
• Neal Bonner, Director, Custom Research
(410) 312-8594
neal.bonner@arbitron.com

Nature of Services:
Arbitron Inc., a media and marketing research firm serving the radio, television, cable, and advertising industries, measures network and local-market radio audiences across the United States by surveying the retail, media and product patterns of consumers and providing application software used for analyzing media audience and marketing information data.

**ATLANTA INTERNATIONAL
CONSULTING GROUP, INC. (AICG)**
1401 PEACHTREE STREET
SUITE 500
ATLANTA, GA 30309
404-872-4884
Fax: 404-870-0440
sales@aicginc.com
www.aicginc.com
Services:
Specializes in creating programs that
increase brand awareness, improve market
share, and boost product profitability of
clients through graphic design, printing,
specialty merchandise and fulfillment
services.
Services:
Graphic Design &Creative Direction,
Custom Illustration & Artwork (Sports &
Entertainment), Project Management,
Corporate & Brand Identity (Logo
Development), POS/POP & Custom
Packaging (Restaurant & Food Industry;
Retail), Sales Collateral Support &
Promotion (Desktop Publishing and
Brochures), Internet Design &
Implementation
Clients:
The Coca-Cola Company, Coca-Cola
Enterprises, Bellsouth Corporation,
McDonald's Corporation, AOL/Turner, S.C.
Johnson, ARAMARK, MCI WorldCom
Athlete Management Services:
Exclusive representation of leading sports
personalities. Representation of select
entertainment properties. Full-service sports
marketing firm for professional and amateur
athletics. Provides career management
consulting, contract advisement,
endorsements, financial planning,
promotions, entertainment representation
and full-service merchandising.
Marketing & Consulting Services:
Provides strategic and tactical consultation
in general sports marketing consultation,
professional development, special segment,
general market development, ethnic
marketing development (African American,
Hispanic, and Asian), youth marketing and
female marketing development. Marketing
representation for entertainers, musicians
and broadcasters. Provides financial
services through strategic alliances and
affiliated company.
Event Management Services:
Creates grassroots or
made-for-TV-sports/entertainment oriented
events from concept to completion.
Develops and implements integrated
programs to assist clients in promoting their
products and/or services. Full public
relations and advertising capabilities,
arranging for sponsorship of both new and
existing sports events, developing tie-in
promotions for such sponsorships, complete
management of event. Experienced in
targeting particular sales objectives through
sports promotions. Develops event-driven
sales promotion campaigns for corporate
clients. Provides complete strategic
planning, project management and
promotional support services.

AURA360 VENTURES
28 DANFORTH STREET
SUITE 210
PORTLAND, ME 04101

207-699-2360
Fax: 207-699-2929
info@360mediaventures.com
www.aura360.com
• Lauren Panarese St. Clair, Marketing
Director
• Parker Swenson, Properties Coordinator,
Event Manager
• Ken Hess, Media Manager, Editor
• William Caswell, Editor & Videographer
• Rufus Frost, Managing Director
• Cathy Cooper, Partner, Production And
Content
• Jessie Nickerson, Manager/Corporate
Admin
Nature of Service:
Provides clients innovative brand integrated
marketing services including property
creation and development, property
representation, event management, TV
production and consultation.
Clients:
Jeep, Columbia Sportwear Company, Red
Bull, Honda, Lucas Oil Products Inc., BF
Goodrich, Gillette, Amstel, Absolut Vodka,
Sony, Rossignol, etc.

Next generation content marketing. Aura360
specializes in animating client brands
through innovative event and media
properties and related marketing ventures.

AUTO SPORTS MARKETING GROUP
PO BOX 491
CLARKS SUMMIT, PA 18411
570-586-2198
Fax: 570-586-2198
• Oscar Koveleski, Founder/Designer
Nature of Service:
50 years of organizing, managing events,
contests, auto races (SCAA races at
Pocono Raceway) model cars, slot cars,
R/C cars, Battery Ride Ons, for SCCA,
IMSA, NASCAR, IRL, SVRA, tracks and
shows. Now offers consultant services for
hire performed by hand picked special ops
personnel. References include food
industry, auto industry, toy industry, hobby
industry, sanctioning bodies, track
management.
Sports Service Founded:
1980
Athlete Management Services:
Auto racing sponsors.
Event Management Services:
Auto racing event promotion.
Brands:
Ferrari Monza, McLaren MK2, McLaren
MK6, McLaren MK8B, 1914 Stutz Bearcat,
Baby Ferrari 250, Type 52 Baby Bugatti
Replica, Bugatti Vise

BAMBOO WORLDWIDE
30 NORTH RACINE
SUITE 300
CHICAGO, IL 60607
773-227-4848 EXT x 105
Fax: 773-227-2509
tracyt@bambooinc.com
www.bambooexperience.com
Description:
Marketing Consulting Services.
Services:
Provides strategic consulting, creative
development and turnkey execution creating
marketable experiences in the fields of retail

design, costumer service, organizational
development and sales force training.

BANSHEE MUSIC
5000 S TOWNE DRIVE
NEW BERLIN, WI 53151
262-501-2726
Fax: 262-786-0687
info@bansheemusic.com
• John Canaday, Director of Sports
Marketing
• Jen DeBuhr, Digital Music Manager
• Chris Hanson, Musician
• Steve Knill, Manager
• Gary Reynolds, Member
• Kelly Schwanke, Manager
Nature of Services:
Banshee Music provides marketing services
that focus on artist development, music
publishing/administration, music producers
for film and TV including sound design for
professional and college sports teams,
content development, music licensing, live
touring and creating brand marketing
campaigns around a music platform.

BARNES MARKETING, INC.
15510 ROCKFIELD BOULEVARD
SUITE C
IRVINE, CA 92618
949-768-2942
Fax: 949-768-0630
info@barnesmarketing.com
www.barnesmarketing.com
Sports Service Founded:
1974
Services:
Specializes in marketing and consulting and
event management services in motorsports
marketing and race team sponsorship
including comprehensive sales packages
provided for potential sponsors, media
coordination, and public relations and
athlete management services which
includes speaking engagements, personal
appearances, product endorsements, radio
and television, movies.
Athlete Management Services:
Speaking engagements, personal
appearances, product endorsements, radio
and television, movies.

BARRETT SPORTS GROUP
1219 MORNINGSIDE DRIVE
SUITE 101
MANHATTAN BEACH, CA 90266
310-802-8775
Fax: 310-802-8777
www.barrettsports.com
• Joshua C Cohen, Manager
jcc@barrettsports.com
Sports Service Founded:
2000
Services:
Provides high-quality and value-added
consulting services such as in market
demand, financial feasibility and economic
impact analysis; finance; valuation;
negotiations; operations; and politics and
strategic planning to the sports and
entertainment industry. Sports management
consulting firm.

BDS MARKETING, INC.
10 HOLLAND
IRVINE, CA 92618

949-472-6700
www.bdsmktg.com
Services:
Provides sales promotion, field marketing, retail demonstrations/trainings and interactive services to clients.
Event Management Services:
Pavilion activities including product sampling, premium distribution, games and hospitality tents, IMSA Tour, LPGA Tour, NASCAR Nextel Cup Series.

BEAR ENTHUSIAST MARKETING GROUP
4520 E THOUSAND OAKS BOULEVARD
SUITE 200
WESTLAKE VILLAGE, CA 91362
818-371-7950
Fax: 818-371-7956
• Bruce Bear, President/Chief Executive Officer
• Rick Hauser, Senior Vice President/Account Director
• Jason Bear, Senior Account Executive
• Amy Brown, Public Relations Accounts Supervisor
(818) 865-6464
Nature of Service:
Fully integrated marketing, advertising and public relations agency focused on the marketing needs of global and regional enthusiast brands.
Sports Service Founded:
1962
Clients:
Suzuki Marine, Dogloo, Body Glove, Trijicm, Buck Knives, Bowtech, Outdoor Products, Fiocdai, Corona Clipper, Marinco, Mothwing, Wiley X, Warn Industries, and Vivitar
Marketing & Consulting Services:
Advertising agency with 40+ years of branding experience and marketing expertise in sporting goods, hunting/fishing, outdoor boating, hardware, automotive and pet industries.

BENNETT GLOBAL MARKETING GROUP
1050 WINTER STREET
SUITE 1000, BAY COLONY CORPORATE CENTER
WALTHAM, MA 2451
781-839-7390
Fax: 781-530-3605
info@bennettglobal.com
• Jeffrey Bennett, Founder/President/Chief Executive Office
(781) 839-7390
jeff@bennettglobal.com
• Sean Barror, Partner
sean@bennettglobal.com
• Benjamin Sturner, Marketing Director
(781) 888-3530
ben@bennettglobal.com
• Leigh Chodos, Business Technology Development Director
leigh@bennettglobal.com
Nature of Sports Service:
Full-service marketing agency that specializes in sponsorship programs, naming rights, licensing rights and content distribution.
Sports Service Founded:
2003
Clients:
Dunkin Donuts, Reebok, Dunlop and Nike; world renowned sports franchise Manchester United Football Club and tennis sensations Anna Kournikova; leading music labels RCA and BMG Heritage of BMG Entertainment; and global Internet portal Terra Lycos.

BERRY & HOMER
2035 RICHMOND STREET
PHILADELPHIA, PA 19125
215-425-0888
Fax: 215-425-2701
info@berryandhomer.com
www.berryandhomer.com
• James Ely, Vice President Sales & Marketing
info@berryandhomer.com
Nature of Services:
Berry & Homer provides turnkey graphic imaging systems services, specializing in printed graphic and visual communications, tradeshow displays and materials, banners, double sided graphics, backlit displays, stadium & stage graphics - large format prints up to 150 feet long.
Locations:
Additional branch office at: 4390 Parliament Place, Suite G, Lanham, MD, 20706; (Phone) 888-459-0888, 301-459-4500, (Fax) 301-459-9813.

BFG COMMUNICATIONS
6 ANOLYN
HILTON HEAD ISLAND
BLUFFTON, SC 29910
843-837-9115
Fax: 843-837-9225
info@bfgcom.com
www.bfgcom.com
• Kevin Meany, President
(843) 837-9115
• Neil Arlett, Account Director
(843) 837-0057
• Jill King, Production Director
(843) 837-0022
• Scott Seymour, VP, Chief Creative officer
• Sloane Kelly, Director of Interactive strartegy
• Steve Hamilton, VP Of Account Services
• Larry McGearty, Chief Creative Strategists
• Kyle Langley, Chief Research Officer
Services:
A full service marketing firm; handles everything from mobile marketing to the internet.
Clients:
Bailey's Irish Cream, Century 21 Real Estate, BC Wines, Alleton Rum, Guiness Brewing, Hyatt, Malibu Run, RTI Software. TGI Friday's Blenders.

BGA NEW MEDIA
230 PARK AVENUE
NEW YORK, NY 10169
212-808-3093
Marketing & Consulting Services:
Services range from B2B marketing to cutting-edge creative design. Specifically includes design, video production, branding, e-commerce, sponsorship sales, and strategic planning.

BILLBOARD TRAY
4355 COBB PARKWAY
SUITE J517
ATLANTA, GA 30339
678-444-4120
• Stephen Weinberger, CEO
Nature of Services:
Billboard Tray is THE walking billboard that delivers food with your advertising and promotional messages simultaneously to affluent, brand-loyal, and desireable spectators in marquee sports and entertainment venues nationwide.

BIRDZERK!
3715 KLONDIKE LANE
LOUISVILLE, KY 40218-1712
502-458-4020
800-219-0899
Fax: 502-458-0867
info@theskillvillegroup.com
www.birdzerk.com
• Dominic Latkovski, Owner
• Brennan Latkovski, Owner
brennan@theskillvillegroup.com
• Stephanie Fish, General Manager
stephanie@theskillvillegroup.com
Nature of Service:
The wildest, craziest show in sports featuring BirdZerk!, Zerk Jr., BabyZerk!, and BallZerk!
Year Founded:
1992
Sports Service Founded:
1992
Event Marketing Services:
Traveling mascot company.
Clients:
2002 AAA All-Star Game (Oklahoma City, OK), 2001 Southern League All-Star Game (Sevierville, TN), 2000 AAA All-Star Game (Rochester, NY), 2000 Southern League All-Star Game (Greenville, SC), 1999 AA All-Star Game (Mobile, AL), 1999 South Atlantic League All-Star Game (Salisbury, MD), 1998 AAA All-Star Game (Norfolk, VA), 1998 AAA World Series (Las Vegas, NV), 1998 NAIA Women's Final Four (Jackson, TN), 1994 California League All-Star Game (Adelanto, CA), 1994 AAA All-Star Game (Nashville, TN), 1993 Florida League All-Star Game (St. Petersburg, FL), 1991 AAA All-Star Game (Louisville, KY), Aberdeen Arsenal, Aberdeen Ironbirds.

BKB LTD.
PO BOX 4184
ENGLEWOOD, CO 80155
303-694-2202
Fax: 303-694-2278
www.bkbltd.com
• Kelley Creigh, President
(303) 694-2202
creigh@theendresultco.com
• Creigh Kelley, President
creigh@bkbltd.com
Services:
Provides the latest computerized Winning Time chip timing technology, creates a management plan and time line for a brand new recreational sporting event, manages recreational sporting events - from initial concept to full-race day staffing and equipment, provides event management and timing services for convention special events, assist with media contacts, direct-mail, and email campaigns, helps with brochure production and placement
Clients:
Houston Marathon, Runnin' of the Green 7K, Cozumel Marathon, and Colorado Springs Race for the Cure
Sports Service Founded:
1979.
Event Management Services:

Provides radio, TV, and public announcers for cycling, running events, triathlons.

BLIMP WORKS, INC.
156 BARNES AIRSHIP DRIVE
STATESVILLE, NC 28625
704-876-2378
Fax: 704-876-1251
www.theblimpworks.com
• Tracy Barnes, President/Designer
• Mollie Cook, Sales/Service Representative
• Tracey Barnes, President
Nature of Service:
Blimp Works advertising blimps and balloon products are ideal for outdoor advertising, grand openings, trade shows, marketing displays, promotional exhibits, promotional blimps, parade balloons, height visibility, indoor, outdoor attention.

BLIMPWORKS
9955 W ST MARTINS ROAD
FRANKLIN, WI 53132
414-305-3145
Fax: 414-425-8095
www.rcblimp.net
• Scott Fisher, President/Owner
Sports Service Founded:
1994
Event Mangement Services:
Blimp sales and marketing of radio-controlled indoor and outdoor advertising airship and cold-air inflatable, fethered blimps, Aerostats. tunnels and other shapes, for use at sporting events, games, arenas and sports fan-oriented fanfests.

BLUMENFELD AND ASSOCIATES PR, INC.
1877 BROADWAY
SUITE 100
BOULDER, CO 80302
203-326-1200
www.blumenfeldpr.com
• Jeff Blumenfeld, President
requests@blumenfeldpr.com
Year Founded:
1980
Nature of Service:
Special events, public relations and Web content.
Publications:
ExpeditionNews.com

BOARDWALK
116 N MARYLAND AVENUE
#220
GLENDALE, CA 91206
818-548-5639
Fax: 818-548-5931
www.boardwlk.com
• Kevin Walker, Account Supervisor
(818) 566-7007
info@boardwlk.com
• Harriet Breitborde, Creative Director
(818) 566-7007
Sports Service Founded:
1990
Services:
A branding, design and advertising agency that specializes in developing advantageous communication between sports/entertainment properties and their many constituencies.
Clients:
Anschutz Entertainment Group, Honda

Racing, Los Angeles Dodgers, NASCAR, NFL Properties, STAPLES Center, Tony Hawk

BONHAM GROUP, INC.
6400 S FIDDLER'S GREEN CIRCLE
PLAZA TOWER ONE, SUITE 1600
SUITE 1600
GREENWOOD VILLAGE, CO 80111
303-592-4290
Fax: 303-592-4293
www.bonham.com
• Dean Bonham, Founder
(303) 592-4290
• Rob Vogel, President/Chief Operating Officer
(303) 592-4290
• David Ehrlich, EVP
(303) 592-4290
• Shawn Bradley, VP/Chief Operating Officer
(303) 592-4290
• Dick Albair, Vice President of Sales
Services:
Sponsorship evaluation, strategic consulting, market research, sponsorship sales, negotiation
Clients:
Adidas, Mervyn's, Ameriquest Mortgage Company, Miller Brewing Company, Bank of America, Motorola, Best Western National Car Rental, Boeing, Nationwide, Carolinas Healthcare, NEC, Centrix Financial, New York Life, Champ Sports, O2, Chick-fil-A, Office Depot, CITGO, Pacific Life, Corel Corporation, PETCO Animal Supplies, Datatix, Piedmont Hospital, Dell, PNC Bank, Delta Air Lines, Qwest, DeWalt, Reebok, DIRECTV, Schick, DSW Shoe Warehouse, Sears, Ericsson, Sprint, Enterprise Rent-a-Car, Suzuki Motor Corporation, FedEx, Target, General Mills, Tosco, Grainger, US Bank, IBM, U.S. Cellular, Invesco Funds, Verizon, Jeep, Xcel Energy, JPMorgan Chase
Services:
Naming rights analysis, TBG Property Analysis, sponsorship analysis, media analysis, soft drink analysis, and other analysis such as internet, food and beverage contracts, on-site events, and vendor relationships.
Marketing & Consulting Services:
Development of marketing plans, market analysis. Media analysis, food and beverage analysis, leverage sponsor benefits.
Clients:
Corporations, Entertainment Properties, Collegiate Properties, Sports Properties, Cultural Properties, Development Properties, Municipalities.

BORTZ MEDIA & SPORTS GROUP, INC.
5105 DTC PARKWAY
SUITE 200
GREENWOOD VILLAGE, CO 80111
303-893-9902
Fax: 303-893-9913
info@bortz.com
www.bortz.com
• Mark C Wyche, Managing Director
• Arthur B Steiker, Managing Director
• Arthur M Steiker, Managing Director
• Jim Trautman, Managing Director
• Mark Wyche, Managing Director
Description:
A 25 year leader in providing revenue enhancing services to the business of

sports. Offers an aray of services to assist professional and collegiate clients competing more effectively in the rapidly changing sports world.
Nature of Services:
Media rights assessment, business plans/launch support for new national and regional sports networks, ticket pricing/gate revenue maximization and league scheduling
Clients:
Major League Baseball (MLB), National Basketball Association (NBA), National Hockey League (NHL), PGA Tour, Big East Conference, PAC-10 Conference and many individual franchises.
Media Consulting:
Offers financial analysis, market research and technological assessment to commercial broadcasters, cable television operators and programmers, wireless cable operators, new media, and Internet companies.

BOZELL WORLDWIDE
1022 LEAVENWORTH
OMAHA, NE 68102
402-965-4300
Fax: 402-965-4399
info@bozell.com
www.bozell.com
• Robin Donovan, Managing Principal/Administration
rdonovan@bozell.com
Marketing & Consulting Services:
Public relations services.
Services:
Advertising Agencies, Advertising, Marketing and Direct Mail
Clients:
ShopVac, Plymouth and Chrysler

BRANDBUILDERS
PO BOX 1087
TENAFLY, NJ 07670-5087
201-266-8130
Fax: 973-575-6001
www.brandbuildersllc.com
• Richard L. Brown, President
• Jeff Brown, Manager
Services:
Provider of best premiums, promotional products, ideas and professional services and direct-factory source of promotional needs
Year Founded:
1982
Clients:
American Airlines, American Express, Castrol Motor Oil, Citibank, Coca Cola, Colgate, Days Inn, Dun & Bradstreet, FILA, Harrah's, Harvey's, Hyatt Hotels, JVC, Lever Brothers, M&M Mars.
Event Management Services:
Provides variety of imprinted apparel items i.e. embroidered shirts, caps, etc., for events. Also provides site selection, travel, other event management services.

BRIAN J. MURPHY CONSULTANT
PO BOX 99
SOUTHPORT, CT 6490
203-259-3890
Fax: 203-255-1787
• Brian J Murphy,
(203) 259-3890

Services:
Provides in-depth information about all types of sponsorship and sports marketing activities, provides covering of auto sports, team and individual sports events and sponsor activities
Consulting Services:
Provides objective opinions and analysis on sports-themed promotions, advertising, public relations, and all other areas of sports marketing. In-person consultation and/or written reports available.

CANAAN PUBLIC RELATIONS
75 S BROADWAY
SUITE 470
WHITE PLAINS, NY 10601
914-304-4080
Fax: 914-304-4083
• Lee Canaan, Founder
• Jed Canaan, President/CEO
Sports Service Founded:
1977
Services:
Media Relations, Audience Identification, Promotions, Marketing, Special Events, Launches and Openings, Press Conferences, Video News Releases, Audio News Releases, MAT Stories, Satellite Media Tours, Media Training, Press Releases/Press Kits/Speech Writing, Internal/External Communications (brochures, newsletters, etc.), Website Creation, Crisis Management, Printing, Photography

---

CARAT NORTH AMERICA
150 E 42ND ST
SUITE 14
NEW YORK, NY 10017
212-591-9100
Fax: 212-252-1250
mark.mylan@carat.com
www.carat.com
Description:
A multi-faceted marketing firm. An international marketing/media firm. Very versatile in approach and execution. Carat originates from Europe, and handles complex initiatives. Markets business/brand to consumer as well as Business to Business.
Services:
Carat delivers communications and media solutions and markets business/brand to consumer as well as Business to Business solutions such as advertiser-funded programming, barter, business to business, communication planning, communication strategy, communication/consumer insight, customer relationship management, data planning, event, face-to-face, interactive, international services, marketing management analysis, media buying, media planning, outdoor, product placement, sponsorship, and sport
Clients:
Adidas, Boost Mobile, Bank One, Festina Watches, Hyatt, Hyundai Motor America, Kia Motors America, New Line Cinema, Orbitz, Pernod, Ricard Philips Electronics, Rational Software, Siebel, TiVo, Warner-Lambert, Pfizer, RadioShack, and Philips, Midas, and Alberto-Culver

---

CATALYST COMMUNICATION
1515 WALNUT
SUITE 300
BOULDER, CO 80302
303-444-5545
800-444-5548
Fax: 303-444-0440
Info@catacom.com
www.catacom.com
• Lynn Guissinger, Chief Financial Officer/Legal
• Beth Prehn, Project-Ateer
• Billy Edward, List Magician
Services:
Advertising, communications and marketing agency, with specialty in cycling and fitness.

CATALYST MARKETING INTERNATIONAL
203-454-3168
bzappi@catalystnow.com
www.catalystnow.com
• Bob Zappi, Chief Executive Officer/Marketing Catalyst
(203) 256-5644
bzappi@catalystnow.com
Marketing & Consulting Services:
Integrated Marketing, Strategic Promotions, e-business, Co-marketing Strategic Partnerships, Person to Person, Mobile Mmarketing.
Description:
Catalyst approaches marketing with a Person to Person philosophy. Catalyst maintains a presence at events utilizing e-marketing and consumer data applications on site.
Services:
Integrated Marketing, Strategic Promotions, e-business, Co-marketing Strategic Partnerships, Person to Person Mobile Marketing.

CBS COLLEGIATE SPORT PROPERTIES
15320 E. MARIETTA
SUITE 2
SPOKANE VALLEY, WA 99216
509-892-4720
Fax: 509-892-4720
• Doug Paschal, Vice President/General Manager
(704) 541-5812
• Bill Cartwright, VP/Director Business Development
(605) 333-0417
• David Johnson, Director Sales/Marketing
• Rich Klein, Director Collegiate Properties
(434) 977-0239

CDM ENTERPRISES, INC.
4273 SANTOLINA WAY
MURRELLS INLET, SC 29576
843-357-3240
www.cdmenterprisesinc.com
Services:
Handles corporate licensing and consulting, for both the licenser and licensee, secures and consults on latest trends.

CELEBRITY FOCUS, INC.
1115 DEERFIELD RD
DEERFIELD, IL 60015
847-682-1234
ricbachrach@celebrityfocus.com
www.celebrityfocus.com
• Ric Bachrach, Chief Executive Officer

Nature of Services:
Provides celebrity sports and entertainment talent consultation and procurement services for corporations, public relations firms, advertising agencies and associations.
Year Founded:
1987
Clients:
Bustin & Company, Cohn & Wolfe, Edelman, Fallon McElligott, Fleishman Hillard, Golin Harris, Italia Advertising, Ketchum Public Relations, Leo Burnett, Lippe Taylor, Manning Selvage & Lee, Ogilvy Adams & Rinehart, Porter Novelli, Presence Euro RSCG, Rapp Collins, Publicis Consultants, Dig Communications, Marina Maher, R F Binder Dorland Communications
Marketing & Consulting Services:
Represents advertising, marketing, public relations agencies and corporations seeking athletes and celebrities for promotional services and endorsements.

CENERGY SPORTS & ENTERTAINMENT
728 MAIN STREET
EAST AURORA, NY 14052
716-652-7400
Fax: 716-652-7161
• John D Cimperman, Managing Partner
• Duncan Shaw, Partner Agency Development
Services:
Offers a full range of sports and entertainment marketing services for professional sports teams, entertainment venues, municipalities, and brands.
Clients:
Agressive Skate Association (ASA), Bernie Kosar Enterprises, Charter Communications, Cleveland Indians, Court TV, DSR Motorsports, Meyer Products, Minnesota Twins, NASCAR Members Club, Ohio Historical Society, Superstation WGN, Toronto Blue Jays, Turner Network Television (TNT), Western Reserve Historical Society, World's Sports Center (Charlotte, NC), International Children's Games (Cleveland, 2004).

CHAMPIONS WORLD
250 MOONACHIE AVENUE
SUITE 102
MOONACHIE, NJ 07074
201-229-0175
Fax: 407-997-4503
• Charlie Stillitano, Chief Executive Officer
(201) 229-0175
• Frank Campagna, Special Assistant Chief Executive Office
(201) 229-0175
• Lino DiCuollo, Legal SVP/Finance
• Tim Kassel, SVP Administration
Services:
Provides unparalleled marketing, merchandising and operating expertise primarily in international football and other sports related events.

CHESTNUT COMMUNICATIONS INC.
15 E PUTNAM AVENUE
#3290
GREENWICH, CT 06830
203-629-9098
Services:
Creates marketing and advertising

campaigns using sports personalities; recommends appropriate personalities for campaigns, negotiates terms, schedules appearances, etc.

CHOICE MARKETING SPORTSCARDS
369 TURNER INDUSTRIAL WAY
ASTON, PA 19014
610-494-1270
800-999-CHOICE (2464)
Fax: 610-494-8074
www.choicesportscards.com/
• Scott Smith, Vice President Sales & Operations
Nature of Services:
We design, print and package custom trading cards for sports teams and businesses nationwide.

CINI-LITTLE INTERNATIONAL
20251 CENTURY BOULEVARD
SUITE 375
GERMANTOWN, MD 20874
301-528-9700
Fax: 301-528-9711
www.cinilittle.com
• William V Eaton, Principal
(626) 441-1700
weaton@cinilittle.com
• Theodore E. Farrand, President/COO
tfarrand@cinilittle.com
• Kathleen M. Held, Vice President of Marketing & Business Dev.
kheld@cinilittle.com
• Michael W. Perigard, Director of CAD
mperigard@cinilittle.com
Year Founded:
1971.
Nature of Service:
Clients from all over the world have been coming to Cini-Little for over 50 years to find creative solutions for Foodservce, Laundry and Solid Waste/Recycling projects. Whether it be a management/operations issue, a remodeling or a new facility, Cini-Little has provided successful, operational and financial solutions to support clients in achieving their goals and objectives.
Representative Corporate Clients:
3-Com; Adobe Systems, Inc.; Allen-Bradley; Allstate Insurance Company; Alza Corporation; Anixter International, Inc.; Blue Cross Blue Shield; British Petroleum; Chase Mortgage Corporation; Cisco Systems, Inc.; Credit Suisse/First Boston; Debevoise & Plimpton; Discover Financial Services; Electronic for Imaging; Exxon Mobil; Fannie Mae; GAP, Inc.; Goldman Sachs; Hewlett Packard; Honda of America; IBM; International Monetary Fund; La Salle Bank Corporation/ABM AMRO Plaza; Lehman Brothers; MBNA America; Motorola; Oracle Corporation; Owens Corning; Philips Medical Systems; Principal Financial Group; QVC; Sherman & Sterling; The World Bank; Toys R

CLEAR BLUE MARKETING NETWORK
135 N OLD WOODWARD AVENUE
BIRMINGHAM, MI 48009
248-644-0800
todd@clearblue.biz
www.clearblue.biz
• Todd Smith, Founder/President/Chief Executive Office
todd@clearblue.biz

Description:
A full service marketing, event development and management firm. The organization researches targeted audiences, customers and media. They work understand the client needs and the atmosphere surrounding them. They look at communication as an event. This is used to develop more dynamic events or presentations. They also have the capabilities to organize press/trade show events.
Services:
Experiential Marketing, Public Relations, Branding, Launch Strategy, Online Communications

CLUB MARKETING AND MANAGEMENT SERVICES
5730 SOUTH
1050 EAST
OGDEN, UT 84405
801-390-3726
Fax: 888-541-0951
clubdoc@cms-clubweb.com
www.cms-clubweb.com
• Mark Davis, President
Services:
Offers personal consultations, training, marketing, advertising and multimedia publications services to independent club owners and operators run profitable clubs.
Description:
Sports and health club business advisors.

CMI
220 EAST 23RD STREET
SUITE 305
NEW YORK, NY 10010
212-598-4567
Fax: 212-598-4566
www.cminyc.com
Clients:
Coca-Cola, R.J. Reynolds, Kodak, Animal Planet, J. Walter Thompson, CMS, Revlon.

COHN & WOLFE
200 FIFTH AVENUE
NEW YORK, NY 10010
212-798-9700
Fax: 212-329-9900
resumes@cohnwolfe.com
www.cohnwolfe.com
• Donna Imperato, President/Chief Executive Officer
(212) 798-9800
donna.imperato@cohnwolfe.com
• Michael O'Brien, President/General Manager
• Tom Petrosini, Chief Financial Officer
Services:
Strategic marketing public relations firm creating, building and protecting the world's most prolific brands through corporate communications, product launches and positioning, sponsorships, special events, analyst relations, public affairs and more.
Clients:
Hampton Inn, Absolut, Chevron, Pfizer, Embassy Suites Hotel, Internet Security System, Lego, Tilley Endurables, ADP, UCP, Interwoven, Hilton, Aventis, The Medicines Company, Visa, Taco Bell, Epson, Endo Pharmaceuticals, Spirit Airlines, Pioneer Sound.Vision.Soul, Emcor, Samsung, Merck, LG Electronics, Colgate
Marketing & Consulting Services:
Provides counsel, creates sports

sponsorship programs and executes public relations strategies designed to enhance media exposure, brand awareness, identity and image: Develops media programs for sports organizations as well as corporate and brand marketing initiatives.
Other Offices:
Dallas, London, Sydney.

COLLEGIATE LICENSING COMPANY
1075 PEACHTREE STREET
SUITE 3300
ATLANTA, GA 30309
770-956-0520
Fax: 770-955-4491
accounting@clc.com
www.clc.com
• Bill Battle, Founder / Chairman
wrb@clc.com
• Pat Battle, President / Chief Executive Officer
pbattle@clc.com
Services:
Brand Protection (Trademark Enforcement, Hologram Labeling, Labor Code Compliance); Brand Management (Brand Control Systems, Types of Licenses); Brand Development (Apparel and Non-Apparel Marketing, Retail Marketing, Promotional Licensing, Championship and Post-Season Licensing, Creative Services, External Communications)
Clients:
Colleges and Universities (Alabama A&M University, Alabama at Birmingham, The University of Alabama, The University of Alaska Anchorage, University of Alaska, University of Albany SUNY, University at Appalachian State University Arizona, The University of Arkansas Fayetteville, University of Arkansas Pine Bluff, University of Arkansas State University, Auburn University, Baylor University, Boise State University, Boston College, Boston University, Brigham Young University, California State University Northridge, California State University Sacramento, Central Florida, University of, Central Washington University Cincinnati, University of Cita

COLLEGIATE LICENSING COMPANY/CLC
1075 PEACHTREE STREET
SUITE 3300
ATLANTA, GA 30309
770-956-0520
Fax: 770-955-4491
iCLCcomments@clc.com
www.clc.com
• Bill Battle, Founder/Chairman
• Pat Battle, President/Chief Executive Officer
• Derek Eiler, Chief Operating Officer
• Doug Whitlock, President
Services:
Provides Accounting, Legal and Enforcement, Licensing Administration, Retail Marketing, Public Relations, and Promotional Licensing
Clients:
Alabama A&M University, The University of Alabama-Birmingham, The University of Alabama, University of Alaska-Anchorage, University of Alaska, University at Albany SUNY, Appalanchin State University, The University of Arizona, University of Arkansas Fayetteville, Univerity of Arkansas Pine

Bluff, Arkansas State University, Auburn University, Baylor University, Boise State University, BostonCollege, Boston University, Brigham Young University, California State University Northridge, California State University Sacramento, University of Central Florida, Central Washington Universiy, University of Cincinnati, The Citadel, Clemson University, Col

Sports Service Founded:
1983

Marketing & Consulting Services:
Serves as collegiate licensing firm representing over 160 colleges, universities, bowls and conferences and the NCAA. Assists groups with retail and promotional licensing opportunities. Partner with CollegeGear.com.

COLOGNE INTERNATIONAL TRADE FAIRS
8700 WEST BRYN MAWR AVE.
SUITE 640 NORTH
CHICAGO, IL 60631
773-326-9920
Fax: 773-714-0063
info@koelnmessenafta.com
www.koelnmessenafta.com
• Mette Petersen, President & Managing Director
• Ken Dickerson, Sales & Project Manager
• Rita Dommermuth, Sales & Project Manager

Sports Service Founded:
1982

Marketing & Consulting Services:
Represents the SPOGA Sports and Camping Equipment Trade Fair in Germany.

COLONIAL LIFE & ACCIDENT INSURANCE COMPANY
PO BOX 100195
COLUMBIA, SC 29202-3195
803-798-7000
800-325-4368
Fax: 803-213-7243
www.coloniallife.com
• Randall C Horn, President/CEO
• Dan Hughey, SVP National Sales

Facility/College Sports:
2004/12 year title - U. South Carolina's Basketball Arena.

COMSCORE MEDIA METRIX
7 PENN PLAZA
10TH FLOOR
NEW YORK, NY 10001-3967
212-497-1700
866-276-6972
Fax: 212-497-1701
www.comscore.com
• Magid M Abraham, President/Chief Executive Officer/Co-Founder
• Kenneth Tarpey, Chief Financial officer
• Serge Matta, President, Commercial Solutions
• Cameron Meierhoefer, Chief Operating Officer
• Gian M Fulgoni, Executive Chairman/Co-Counder

CONNECTIONS CONSULTING
1745 JEFFERSON DAVIS HIGHWAY
SUITE 612
ARLINGTON, VA 22202
703-416-6414

• Charlene Lefkowitz, Contact
Description:
Sports Marketing & Special Events.

CONSOLIDATED GRAPHICS
5858 WESTHEIMER
SUITE 200
HOUSTON, TX 77057
713-787-0977
Fax: 713-787-5013
www.cgx.com
• Ryan C. Farris, President
• Michael B. Barton, EVP/Chief Administrative Officer
• Aaron T. Grohs, National Sales & Marketing
• Joe R H. Davis, Chairman/CEO
• Jon C Biro, EVP, CFO
• Jim Cohen, EVP,Mergers and Acquisition
• M.Grae Griffin, EVP,Human Resources
• Aaron T Grohs, EVP, Sales and Marketing

Nature of Services:
Consolidated Graphics (CGX) offers web printing, industry-leading digital printing services, a rapidly growing number of fulfillment centers and proprietary Internet-based technology solutions.

Year Founded:
1985

COPELAND COMPANY, INC., HAL
5646 MILTON STREET
SUITE 330
DALLAS, TX 75206
214-361-8788
Fax: 214-361-5467
hecopeland@aol.com
• Harry E. Copeland, President
• Ann B. Copeland, Vice President

Services:
Public relations counsel and services, including sports authors for talk shows; marketing sports events, speech writing and ghostwriting for executives, coaches and athletes.

Description:
Ticket promotion and sponsor sales for sports team seasons and events, including publicity, advertising and media trade agreements.

CORNELL SPORTS MARKETING
CORNELL UNIVERSITY ATHLETICS
TEAGLE HALL, CAMPUS ROAD
ITHACA, NY 14853
607-255-6680
Fax: 607-255-2969
jwh33@cornell.edu
www.cornellbigred.com

CORPORATE SPORTS MARKETING GROUP/ATLANTA OFFICE
2120 RANGE ROAD
CLEARWATER, FL 33765
727-669-6972
866-550-5580
Fax: 727-669-2591
• Christopher King, Chairman/Chief Executive Officer
• Kevin Kieman, SVP Sales, Clearwater
• Christopher King, Chairman and CEO
• Holly King, Executive Vice President,Finance
• Carver Donaldson, Vice president, Sales
• Sheri Richards, Vice President, Cloent Relations

Description:
Sports related sponsorship and advertising opportunities for its clients, Major League Sports Advertising.
Clients:
MLB, NASCAR, NHL.

CORPORATE VISIONS
7-11 S BROADWAY
SUITE 406
WHITE PLAINS, NY 10601
914-761-9602
Fax: 914-761-9607
Services:
Domestic and International Promotional Products and Premium Development and Sourcing, GWP/PWP Programs (Gift with purchase and Purchase with Purchase Programs), Brand Building, New Product Launches, Marketing and Promotional Program Consulting, Sales/Trade Incentives, Corporate Gifts
Description:
Bayer Pharmaceuticals, Bear Stearns, Breitling, Bristol-Myers Squibb Pharmaceuticals, Clairol Inc. (Herbal Essences,Aussie,Revitalique, Ultress, Nice'n Easy), NY Presbyterian Hospital, Cosmair/Ralph Lauren, Ebel, Eileen Fisher, Equitable Distributors, Inc., Good Housekeeping, Graham Windham, JP Morgan Chase, Jaeger Le Coultre, John Frieda, Judicial Title, Insurance, Manhattan Reporting Company, Matrix Essentials, MeadJohnson,Nutritionals, Mondera.com, Pepperidge, Farm, Redbook, Verizon, Warburg Pincus

Description:
To design innovative promotional programs that provide clients with the highest level of creativity and service in the business.
Sports Service Founded:
1989

CREATIVE SOLUTIONS GROUP
1250 N CROOKS
CLAWSON, MI 48017
248-288-9700
Fax: 248-288-0700
info@csgnow.com
www.csgnow.com
Description:
A full service marketing agency. Services include: Event marketing, trade show and auto show exhibits, product cutaways, animated displays, rental systmes and show management.
Services:
Provides Event Marketing, Trade Show and Auto Show Exhibits, Product Cutaways and Animated Displays, Rental Systems, Business Theater and Show Management.

CSMG INTERNATIONAL, LTD
20 W KINZIE
SUITE 1000
CHICAGO, IL 60610
312-242-2700
Fax: 312-242-2707
• Harry Hoopis, Chairman
• Henry Thomas, President
• Marty Pereira, Chief Operating Officer
• Ginger Gorden, Chief Financial Officer
• Andrew Stroth, Executive Vice President, Talent Marketing
• Nova Lanktree, Executive Vice President, Marketing Services

- Scott Pucino, Executive Vice President, Baseball
- Fletcher N Smtih, III, Executive Vice President, Football
- Kennard McGuire, Executive Vice President, Sports
- Melvin Roman, Vice President, Latin American Operations Bas

Nature of Service:
Talent management, talent marketing, corporate consultancy, event marketing and media production. International sports consulting and sports marketing. Offers personal financial planning and comprehensive individual tax services for professional athletes.

Year Founded:
1981

Locations:
Chicago, Houston, Columbia, South Carolina, Atlanta, Scottsdale AZ.

CT MARKETING
10 WREN CT
MORRISTOWN, NJ 7960
973-267-6587
888-653-2645
Fax: 973-267-2490
www.ctmarketing.com
Description:
Advanced technology for market data and collection. Technology developed to handle event registration and management online. Build and manage a custom database also creates Web-based systems for inventive program tracking and award fulfillment.

CURTIS BIRCH, INC.
1547 10TH STREET
SUITE A
SANTA MONICA, CA 90401
310-394-2020
Fax: 310-496-1309
www.curtisbirch.com
- Richard Yelland, Founder/Director/Photographer
(310) 450-2020
richardy@curtisbirch.com
Year Founded:
2000.
Services:
Produces highly effective advertising, design, PR and marketing solutions from conception to execution, for major regional and national clients.
Clients:
Fox Sports, Fuel TV, Hot Wheels/Mattel, the Life Rolls Foundation, Surgi Count Medical.
Nature of Service:
Creative boutique providing full-service ad agency, public relations, and marketing services with a specialty in action and outdoor sports.

CUSTOM BUSINESS SOLUTIONS, INC.
12 MORGAN
IRVINE, CA 92618
949-380-7674
Fax: 949-380-7644
info@cbs-posi.com
www.cbs-posi.com
- Art Julian, Founder and CEO
(949) 609-6708
- Michael Block, Chief Financial Officer
(949) 609-6709
- Joseph Castillo, VP, Software Development

(800) 551-7674
- Rom V. Krupp, VP, Bisiness Development
(214) 924-1249
- Tammy Brown, VP, Support Services
(949) 609-6778
- Gary Henderson, Chief Technical Officer
Description:
Providing a cost efficient method to accommodate our clients with the products and services they need to make their businesses successful.
Services:
Complete POSitouch training, re-training and software upgrades, internet services, automated pooling, web-basedemail, consolidated reports, advanced POS system, INetBlock
Clients:
The Cheesecake Factory, Stars, Ruby's Diner, Pat & Oscar's Restaurant, Riva Grill On the Lake, Ogden Entertainment, Sbarro

DANIEL BLACKMAN CONSULTING
7637 OAKBORO DRIVE
LAKE WORTH, FL 33467
561-965-1350
- Daniel Blackman, Chief Product Officer
Description:
Specializing in the use of computers and information systems by sport organizations.

DAXKO
600 UNIVERSITY PARK PLACE
SUITE 500
BIRMINGHAM, AL 35209
205-437-1400
877-729-4786
Fax: 205-437-0225
sales@daxko.com
www.daxko.com

DIRECTION
213 W INSTITITE PLACE
SUITE 506
CHICAGO, IL 60610-3128
312-943-2202
Fax: 312-943-2218
www.directiontourmarketing.com
- Micah Taylor, Nationwide Account Manager
(773) 404-4402
- Todd Kasten, Partner
- Joe Shanahan, Partner
- Chess Hubbard, Web Designer
Description:
Full service marketing company. Services Include: Retail marketing and promotion, Lifestyle Marketing, College and university marketing, event production, Graphic design, event promotion and market research.
Clients:
Chicago Department of Cultural Affairs, String Cheese Incident/ Sci-Fidelity Records, Museum of Contemporary Art, Clear Channel Entertainment, Kaiju Big Battel, Jam Productions, Resfest Digital Film Festival, Mayor's Office of Special Events; Chicago, Metro/Smart Bar/Double Door, Broadway in Chicago (Chicago's Leading Stage Producer), Quiksilver Clothing
Sports Service Founded:
1999.
Other Locations:
New York, Chicago.

DISSON SKATING
1420 BEVERLY ROAD
SUITE 350
MCLEAN, VA 22101
202-364-8500
Fax: 202-364-1997
- Stephen Disson, President/Founder/Chief Executive Officer
- Stephen Disson, Director of Events
(703) 962-6640
- Pete Bockelman, Director of Operations & Sponsorships
(703) 962-6625
- Alyssa Shane, Director of Events
(202) 903-0887
Nature of Services:
Disson Skating was founded by the company's President, Stephen Disson, a sports marketing veteran who has been in the business since 1976. Formerly with Disson, Furst & Partners, as well as the D&F Group and ProServ. He has created and produced over 100 events for NBC, CBS, USA Network, ESPN, Style Network, Universal HD and Bravo.
Sports Service Founded:
1989.

DOM CAMERA ASSOCIATES, INC./NATIONAL ADVERTISING NETWORK
630 THIRD AVENUE
NEW YORK, NY 10017
212-370-1130
Fax: 212-370-1201
www.domcameracompany.com
- Dom Camera, Principal
- Jeanine Domich, Owner
Marketing, Media & Consulting Services:
Provides sports marketing, media buying and consulting services.
Event Management Services:
Planning, development and execution.
Sports Service Founded:
1985

DON JAGODA ASSOCIATES, INC.
100 MARCUS DRIVE
MELVILLE, NY 11747
631-454-1800
Fax: 631-454-1834
www.dja.com
- Bruce Hollander, Executive Vice President
- Larry Berney, Chief Operating Officer
- Bruce Hollander, Executive Vice President
Description:
Award winning marketing services and sales promotion agency. Specializing in sweepstakes, contests, instant win games and social media promotions.
Clients:
A&E Televeision Network Agency, AARP, ABS-CBN, ACH Foods, ADI, Aeropostale, America Online, Inc., American Express, Ann Taylor, Apple & Eve, Applebees (NY & NJ), Astoria Federal Savings Bank, AT&T, Atlantic Bank, Best Western International, kay Jewelers, Kayser-Roth Corp., Key Foods Stores, Lime, Minolta, Neutrogena, Newsday, NFO Plog, Nikon Inc, Olympus America, Pepsi-Cola Company, Canon USA
Promotion/Marketing Services
Award-winning promotion planning & strategy; creative & production; sweepstakes, contests & games; refunds & premium programs; merchandise & travel incentive programs; club/loyalty/frequency

programs; interactive/Internet promotions; database & telemarketing services; direct response & fulfillment services.

Sports Service Founded:
1962.
Other Locations:
4370 Tujunga Avenue, Suite 330, Studio City, CA 91604. 818-508-3000; FAX: 818-508-3034, 8125 Monetary Drive, Suite G-5, West Palm Beach, FL 33404. 561-840-3333; FAX: 561-840-7772.

DORNA USA, LLC
800 THIRD AVENUE
28TH FLOOR
NEW YORK, NY 10022-7604
212-699-8400
Fax: 212-986-0927
lvillafane@vanwagner.com
• Michael J Levine, President
(212) 699-8603
mlevine@vanwagner.com
• Cliff Kaplan, President, Advertising and Sponsorship S
(212) 699-8525
ckaplan@vanwagner.com
• John Haegele, Chief Operating Officer
(212) 699-8625
jhaegele@vanwagner.com
• John Massoni, Executive VP Operations & Partner
Chicago Office:
601 S. Chaddick Drive, Wheeling, IL 60090. 847 465-8500; FAX: 847 465-8515
Services:
Offers national advertisers prominent Placements within the game action in full-view of the television cameras via its Dorna rotational signage systems; optimal Reach through a diverse offering of Media and Sponsorship Sales opportunities for any demographic; and Consulting and Management services for advertisers needing the Delivery of well-crafted strategic plans.
Marketing & Consulting Services:
Full service sports marketing organization specializing in rotational signage, sponsorship sales, hospitality, and event management and promotion. Marketing agreement in place with over 90 professional and college properties in North America. Signage is utilized along the courts, fields and rinks of the NBA, MLB, NHL and NCAA. Also provides custom-built fascia signage for stadiums and areas. Sports Promotion division, based in Virginia, promotes, organizes, and markets sports events in college football and basketball, and pre-season NBA and MLB games.
22 NBA Basketball Teams:
Atlanta Hawks, Boston Celtics, Chicago Bulls, Cleveland Cavaliers, Dallas Mavericks, Denver Nuggets, Detroit Pistons, Golden State Warriors, Houston Rockets, Los Angeles Clippers, Los Angeles Lakers, Miami Heat, Milwaukee Bucks, Minnesota Timberwolves, New Jersey Nets, New York Knicks, Orlando Magic, San Antonio Spurs, Utah Jazz, Memphis Grizzlies, Washington Wizards.
7 NHL Hockey Teams:
Calgary Flames, Carolina Hurricanes, Dallas Stars, Detroit Red Wings, Minnesota Wild, New York Islanders, Pittsburgh Penguins.
16 MLB Baseball Teams:
Anaheim Angels, Atlanta Braves, Chicago White Sox, Cincinnati Reds, Detroit Tigers,

Florida Marlins, Houston Astros, Kansas City Royals, Milwaukee Brewers, Minnesota Twins, New York Mets, Oakland A's, Pittsburgh Pirates, St. Louis Cardinals, Tampa Bay Devil Rays, Texas Rangers.
Clients Include:
Ace Hardware, American Express, Anheuser Busch, Armitron, AT&T, AutoZone, carsdirect.com, Coca Cola, Datek Online, Dean Witter, Discovery Channel, Dunkin Donuts, FootAction, FootLocker, Finish Line, GEICO, hoopstv.com, IBM, Kraft, MasterCard, McDonalds, Office Depot, Office Max, Pepsi, Pfizer, Powerbar, Sears, Subway, True Value and Volkswagen

DRAFTWORLDWIDE
633 N SAINT CLAIR STREET
CHICAGO, IL 60611-2897
312-425-5000
Fax: 312-944-3566
• Howard Draft, Executive Chairman
• Tod Tilford, Chief Creative Officer
• Daniel Bowens, Executive Creative Director
• Micheal Fassnacht, President
Services:
Specializes in many disciplines including Direct Marketing, Promotional/Retail Marketing, Interactive Marketing, Media, Data Technology Services, Direct-To-Consumer Healthcare Marketing, Customer Specific Marketing, Emerging Media, Multi-cultural Marketing.
Description:
Marketing communications, branding, direct marketing, promotions and retail.

DSN RETAILING TODAY
425 PARK AVENUE
SUITE 6
NEW YORK, NY 10022
212-756-5000
800-274-6951
Fax: 212-756-5209
• Tim Craig, Editor-in-Chief
(212) 756-5000
• Bernadette Casey, Executive Editor
(212) 756-5000
Products:
Business and finance magazine targeted to retail professionals from CEOs to store managers, in all incudsty, including sports.

DUFFY JENNINGS COMMUNICATIONS
SILICON VALLEY
SAN FRANCISCO, CA 94404
408-896-6900
duffy@duffyjennings.com
www.duffyjennings.com
• Tim Harrington, CEO
Services:
Offers Strategic Counsel, Public Relations, Media Relations, Media Coaching, Writing-Editing, Press Releases, Brand Messaging, Reputation Management, Employee Communications, Community Affairs, Press Conferences, Trade Shows, Publishing
Description:
Full service public relations firm and marketing communications agency.

DVC WORLDWIDE
210 HEADQUARTERS PLAZA
MORRISTOWN, NJ 7960-6855

973-775-6700
Fax: 973-775-6703
Services:
Specializes in global marketing, communications and digital solutions. Utilizes advertising, merchandising and co-marketing. Integrates promotional, interactive, experiental, relationship and healthcare marketing.

ELITE INTERNATIONAL SPORTS MARKETING, INC.
1049 BRISTOL MANOR DRIVE
BALLWIN, MO 63011
636-891-8028
Fax: 314-621-4449
• Jackie Joyner-Kersee, President
(314) 621-4448
• Della Gray, Operations Director
• Valerie Foster, Executive Assistant
Services:
Event Management: Create, plan, organize and execute special events. Marketing & Consulting: Specialized client research and development; program development; activity scheduling and travel coordination; and public relations.
Clients:
Football - Terry Fair, Ernest Blackwell, Matt Sherman, Baseball - Brian Jordan, Robert Kersee, Track & Field - Jackie Joyner-Kersee, Gail Devers, Greg Foster, Amy Acuff

ENDURANCE SPORTS MARKETING GROUP
801 MAIN STREET
SUITE 025
LOUISVILLE, CO 80516
303-926-1017
Fax: 425-920-5306
• Craig Mintzlaff, Principle
• Maggie Arnold, Directors Asst. Marketing & Registration
• Josh Caves, Sales & Field Marketing
• Jeff Stoner, Event Execution
Description:
Specializes in cycling and fitness expos held in conjunction with the countries largest bicycling, running, triathlon and fitness events.
Services:
Groundzero Sports specialty lies in producing, managing and promoting all aspects of the countries largest sports and fitness expos allowing race promoters and organizers to focus on what they do best - the race.

ENTRY MEDIA, INC.
127 W FAIRBANKS AVENUE
SUITE 417
WINTER PARK, FL 32789
407-678-4446
Fax: 407-679-1658
info@entrymedia.com
www.entrymedia.com
• Martin Hering, Founder/President
• Kenny Pober, Vice President, New York Market Manager
(212) 297-6400
Description:
Originator, manufacturer and marketer of Turnstile Advertising with Turnstile AdSleeve Armcovers. Converts ordinary turnstile units into revenue generators.

ENVIRONMENTAL OUTDOOR EDUCATION & RECREATION
29 WESTWOOD TERRACE
DEDHAM, MA 2026
617-326-2543
• David P Hodgdon, President/Executive Director
Sports Service Founded:
1966
Marketing & Consulting Services:
Recreational and educational consulting service including environmental analysis, Nordic skiing and mountain bike trail use, design, site evaluation, staff training, safety, workshops, etc. Historic, environmental and trail designation, documentation. State, national, world level capabilities. Also lecturer and photographer in out-of-doors for such activities as snow shoeing, ski touring, alpine and ski mountaineering, hiking, winter camping and survival, rock climbing, avalanche, training in the above listings.

EQUISURE INC,.
13790 E RICE PLACE
AURORA, CO 80015
303-614-6961
800-752-2472
Fax: 303-614-6967
www.equisure-inc.com
• Lesher Diane, Executive Vice President ext 302
Services:
Official Insurance Provider to United States Equestrian Federation members.

ESPN ABC SPORTS CUSTOMER MARKETING AND SALES
77 W 66TH STREET
NEW YORK, NY 10023
212-456-3654
www.espncms.com
• Ed Erhardt, President
Nature of Sports Service:
Provides detailed analysis on audience data, usage trends, industry news, and advertising case studies for customers looking to create a customized advertising plan.

EVENT STRATEGY GROUP
4070 BUTLER PIKE
#800
PLYMOUTH MEETING, PA 19462
610-260-2550
info@esg.us
www.esg.us
• Norman Aamodt, President/Chief Executive Officer
(610) 260-2551
• Renee Scullin, VP Event Management
(610) 260-2552
• Stefanie Turco, Strategic Development VP
(610) 260-2555
sturco@eventstrategygroup.com
• Pam Zelinski, Business Manager
(610) 260-2550
• Kathleen McKeever, Sr.Event Manager
(610) 260-2554
• Jennifer Scand, Sr.Event Manager
(610) 260-2556
• Melissa Edwards, Sr.Event Manager
(610) 260-9389
Description:
Full service marketing and sponsorship agency. Develops integrated and sponsorship programs. Their model is broken down five key components: strategic planning, information management, integrated maketing, event management and sponsorship marketing. Extensive experience in tradeshow management and hosted event management.
Clients:
Sungard, Plumtreet, QRS, Sungard Securities Processing, serena, dvHr Partnership, Lincoln Financial Group, siteRock, K Rain, Siebel eBusiness, Coalition of Commercial Real Estate Associations, SeeBeyond, Ecom, Ziff Davis Media, GVFHRA, T-SIG, IDS Scheer Business Process Excellence

EVENTNET USA
1129 SE 4TH AVENUE
FORT LAUDERDALE, FL 33316
954-467-9898
Fax: 954-467-8252
info@EventNetUsa.com
www.eventnetusa.com
• Jill B Benson, Director,Business Development
• Allison Wurstle, Associate Director, Business Development
• Joel Benson, Founder/Chief Executive Officer
(954) 467-9898
joelb@eventnetusa.com
• Ira Jaffe, Senior Vice President, Account Services
Services:
Specializes in mobile marketing, custom exhibit building, mall radio, pop-up marketing stores, targeted consumer sampling, spirit field services, targeted shows, mall billboards, guerrilla marketing, shopping malls.
Clients:
Adidas, Allstate Insurance, AARP, Almay, American Airlines, American Express, American Red Cross, American Tourister, Amoco Motor Club, Apple Computers Inc., Armstrong, AT&T, Barnes-Hind Inc., Best Buy, Better Homes & Gardens, Black & Decker, Blimpie, BMW, Boost, Borden, Inc., Bounty Microwave, Butterfingers, CBS Television, California Olive, California Pistachio, California Prune, Campbell Soup, Canon, Chevrolet, Citibank, Clairol, Inc., Coca Cola, Colgate, Converse, Coppertone, Corning, Dr. Pepper, DeBeers Diamonds, Discover Card, Disney Corp., Dole, Dove, Duncan Hines, Eastman Kodak, ELLE Magazine, Equal, Eureka, Ford Tractor, Frito Lay
Sports Service Founded:
1976
Promotional Tours:
CBS Sports Challenge, Apple Open House, Reebok Pump-up and Air-out campaign, NBA America's Tour, Olympic Games, the Turner Goodwill Games, the NBA All-Star Games, Major League Baseball, and the NFL Super Bowl Tour to malls, stadiums, and fairs.

EVENTORS
1030 N STATE STREET
SUITE 1-M
CHICAGO, IL 60610
312-944-6667
eventors@aol.com
• Jane E. Canepa, Owner
Sports Service Founded:
1976

Services:
Event Management Services: events, marketing and public relations company that focuses on special events
Event Management Services:
Public relations, promotion sponsorship, and event management of special events.

EXCALIBUR MARKETING GROUP
4258 GERMANNA HIGHWAY
SUITE D-1
LOCUST GROVE, VA 22508
540-972-4690
Fax: 540-972-4691
www.isportsnet.com
Sports Service Founded:
1992
Services:
Full service sports marketing firm specializing in all levels of the football industry, athlete management services, professional services, sports agents, market research services. Owns and operates the Dick Butkus Football Internet site (www.dickbutkus.com), dedicated to all levels of football. Also owns and operates Internet Sports Awards. Represents over 20 NFL Hall of Fame players available for corporate marketing programs.
Athlete Management Services:
Represents over 20 NFL Hall of Fame players available for corporate marketing programs.

EXCLUSIVE SPORTS MARKETING, INC.
6421 CONGRESS AVE
SUITE 103
BOCA RATON, FL 33487
561-241-3801
Fax: 561-241-3805
• Chris Colgan, President
(561) 241-3801
• Linda Meyer, VP of Finance
(561) 241-3801
• Chris Carusone, Event Director
• Stevn J Tebon, CEO
• Katty Peraza, Design
Services:
Sports and event marketing/management which include road races, skating events, open water swims, and kids' events.
Clients:
Publix Supermarkets, Coca-Cola, PepsiCo, Anheuser-Busch, Gatorade, Toyota, Buick, Nike, Sunshine Network, Yamaha, Holiday Inn, Marriott, Ocean Properties, and Club Med.
Sports Service Founded:
1986
Nature of Sports Service:
Recreational based sports marketing firm.

EXHIBIT ENTERPRISES
1400 S LIVERNOIS
ROCHESTER HILLS, MI 48307
800-582-9250
800-582-9250
Fax: 248-601-9901
interest@eeiglobal.com
www.eeiglobal.com
• David M Gentile, Founder/Chairman
interest@eeiglobal.com
• Derek M Gentile, President/Chief Executive Officer
interest@eeiglobal.com
• Kirk A Brien, VP and General Manager
• Simon Fairweather, CCO

Services:
Specializes in major builds, permanent installations, private exhibitions, mobile marketing, animation, finishing and cut aways, modular displays, digital and large format graphics, trade shows and exhibits, e-business solutions and event services

Clients:
BMW, GM ElectroMotive, BorgWarner, Visteon, Delphi, Dodge, Mini, Bendix, Eaton, Alcoa, Mitsubishi Electric, Daimler Chrysler, Rolls Royce, Detroit Zoological Institute, Ford Motor Company, GM Power Train, JTC Corporation, American Axle& Manufacturing, FAG, Wacker Ceramics, DTE Energy, DTE Energy Technologies

Description:
A globally-minded provider of creative marketing experiences. Curent reputation includes the auto industry, healthcare, aerospace and consumer goods. Increased capacity and service for both national and mobile business to business event groups. Utilizes animations/cutaways and large format graphics.

Sports Service Founded:
1981

FENWAY SPORTS GROUP
82 BROOKLINE AVENUE
BOSTON, MA 02215
617-226-6300
Fax: 617-226-6484
info@fenwaysportsgroup.com
www.fenwaysportsgroup.com
• Sam Kennedy, President
• Charles H. Steedman, Executive Vice President
• Jay Monahan, Executive Vice President
• Mark I. Lev, Co-Managing Director

Marketing & Consulting Services:
Specializes in development sponsorship and marketing programs for consumer product and industry-related companies seeking to leverage their sponsorships in auto racing.

FIELDHOUSE, INC.
1220 116TH AVENUE NE
SUITE 200
BELLEVUE, WA 98004
425-458-4200
877-232-9785
Fax: 425-467-0800
customerservice@fieldhouse.net
www.fieldhouse.com
• Carl Lombardi, Jr., President/Founder
• Carl Lombardi Jr., Founder
• Carl Lombardi Jr., Founder ext 203

Nature of Service:
Fieldhouse Store is a complete apparel, merchandise and fundraising site which offers the following services: Retail Store, Presale Online Bulk Ordering, Fan Poster, One Source, Tickets, Season Passes, Local Market and My Store

Year Founded:
2003

Marketing & Consulting Services:
Fieldhouse provides merchandise solutions to teams and leagues across the nation. Our benefits are our no-hassle bulk buying experience, and our free web stores for team logo wear.

FIRST PLUS SPORTS MARKETING
1600 VICEROY DR.
SUITE 325
DALLAS, FL 75235
954-475-2001
Fax: 954-475-8392
www.bizapedia.com/fl/FIRSTPLUS-SPORTS-MARKETING-INC.html
• Green Eric, Vice President
• Marino Daniel Cjr, Chief Executive Officer/President
• Phillips Daniel T, Director
• Jim Roundtree, CFO

Services:
Marketing and consulting; represents professional athletes for marketing and endorsements.

FITPRO LIFESTYLE CONSULTANTS
121 HUBLEY MILL LAKE ROAD
UPPER TANTALLON, NS, CANADA B3Z 1E8
902-402-5466
866-4-FITPRO
Fax: 902-826-7230
• Paul Griffith, President
• Chris Tremblay, Director of Operations and Partner
• Sue Griffith, Consultant
• Paul Griffith, President and CEO

Description:
Is a health and lifestyle company that provides services to individuals, teams and organizations. We offer fitness programming and practical lifestyle management tools to assist individuals with thier personal goals and objectives.

FLAIR COMMUNICATIONS
214 W ERIE STREET
CHICAGO, IL 60654
312-943-5959
800-621-8317
Fax: 312-943-6049
• Allyn Miller, President
• Lee F Flaherty, Chief Executive Officer
• Kevin Kennedy, EVP
(312) 943-5959
• Bob Walz, Chief Operating Officer

Services:
Sales Promotion and Specialized Marketing Services; specializes in consumer brand marketing; develops program targeting consumers to brands and then build the relationship; utilizes the internet, events, instore promotions or home; PowerHouse marketing, account specific marketing, promotional media creating and buying, matchmaker database and tie-ins, ten-point plan to cut cost, incremental volume estimates and ROI models.

Description:
Specilizes in consumer brand marketing. Develops program targeting consumers to brands and then build the relationship. Utilizes the internet, events, ins tore promotions or home. Independently owned, results-oriented strategic planning and integrated marketing company handles everything from sponsorships, special events and grassroots field marketing.

Revenue:
$23.70 M

FRANKLIN COVEY
2200 W PARKWAY BOULEVARD
SALT LAKE CITY, UT 84119
801-817-5001
888-576-1776
800-827-1776
Fax: 801-817-8313
info@franklincovey.com
www.franklincovey.com
• Robert A Whitman, Chairman/Chief Executive Officer
• Stephen D. Young, Chief Financial Officer
• Scott Miller, Chief Marketing Officer
• Robert A. W. Whitman, Chairman
• Stephen Covey, Executive Vice President/Education/Training
• Todd R. Davis, Executive Vice President, Chief People & Oper

Services:
Franklin Covey is the global leader in effectiveness training,productivity tools,and assessment services and organizations,teams and indivduals.FranlinCovey helps companys succeed by unleashing the power of the work force to focus on top business priorities. FranlinCovey has 2,000 associates in 35 offices in 95 countries.

FULL HOUSE SPORTS MARKETING
FULL HOUSE
3215 GOLF ROAD #112
DELAFIELD, WI 53018
866-280-0637
866-280-0637
Fax: 312-360-0002
office@fillthehouse.com
www.fillthehouse.com
• Ron Contorno, President

Nature of Service:
Season tickets/Mini-plans, Group Sales, Consumer/Residential Databases, Subscription Files, Enthusiasts, Opt-In Email Databases

Clients:
Nashville Predators, Feld Entertainment, Washington Capitals, Providence Bruins, Comcast Spectacor, Harlem Globetrotters, Chicago Wolves, Louisiana IceGators, Los Angeles Galaxy, Milwaukee Bucks, Houston Comets, Toronto Raptors, New Orleans Saints, Minnesota Timberwolves, Grand Rapids Rampage, Oklahoma State University, Pittsburgh Pirates, Dayton Dragons, Houston Astros, Lexington Legends, Disney Sports Attractions, Maywood Park, DTE Energy Music Theatre, Memphis Grizzlies, Chicago Fire, Detroit Pistons, Chicago Blackhawks, Jacksonville Jaguars, Columbus Blue Jackets, Rochester Americans, Mandalay Sports Entertainment, Grand Rapids Griffins,

FURMAN, INC., ANTHONY M.
250 W 57TH STREET
SUITE 1501
NEW YORK, NY 10107
212-956-5666
Fax: 212-956-5703
info@furmansports.com
www.furmansports.com
• Anthony Furman, President
tony@furmansports.com
• Joyce Keating, Office Manager
• Linda Torel, Account Consultant
• Evelyn Pate, Senior Account Consultant

Services:
Sports Marketing and Public Relations; marketing and consulting services which include programming, consultation and public relations activities to introduce clients

to sports marketing and to enlarge and direct clients already having involvement.
Accounts Have Included:
American Express Travel Related Services, AT & T, Beneteau, Inc., Corning Optics, Ice Follies, International Toy Center, Knickerbocker Cup, Lake Placid Film Forum, National Powerboat Association, New Jersey Special Olympics, Ski New Hampshire, Sportcraft, Vail Resorts, Hunter Mountain Resort, Wham-O Manufacturing Co., Woman's Pro Skiing, Liberty Cup, North Cove Yacht Harbor, Ski Utah Association.
Sports Service Founded:
1966
Marketing & Consulting Services:
Programming, consultation and public relations activities in sports to introduce clients to sports marketing and to enlarge and direct clients already having involvement with sports.

FUSE
431 PINE STREET
PO BOX 4509
BURLINGTON, VT 05406-4509
802-864-7123
Fax: 802-864-2595
www.fusemarketing.com
• Bill Carter, Partner
• Brett Smith, Partner
• Issa Sawabini, Partner
• Julie C. Jatlow, Executive Director
Nature of Service:
A full-service youth culture marketing agency with capabilities in the following areas: Consulting, Event Marketing, Communications, Research, Creative Services
Sports Service Founded:
1995
Marketing & Consulting Services:
A promotional agency that connects corporate brands with the youth market through alternative sports such as snowboarding, wakeboarding, skateboarding, surfing, mountain biking, and BMX. Services include consultation and PR services, event sponsorship and management, athlete representation and promotion, and research services.
Clients:
180s, Association of Surfing Professionals, Battle Born Records, Billabong, Bula, Burton Snowboards, Dew Action Sports Tour, Dreaming Tree Films, Eastern Mountain Sports, Eastman Kodak, ESPN X Games Skateparks, Ford Motor Company, Motorola, Mountain Dew (Pepsi), Mr. Green (Pepsi), NBC Olympics, Polo Ralph Lauren, Powerpuff Girls (Cartoon Network), Quiksilver, Right Guard (Gillette), Sea-Doo (Bombardier Recreational Products), Sierra Mist (Pepsi), Ski-Doo (Bombardier Recreational Products), Slim Jim (Con Agra Foods), Stowe Mountain Resort, TAG Body Spray, Tony Hawk Clothing (Kohl's Department Stores), Toy Wishes, US Open Snowboarding Champion

GAGE MARKETING GROUP
10000 HIGHWAY 55
PLYMOUTH, MN 55441
763-595-3800
Fax: 763-595-3871

info@gage.com
www.gage.com
• Gregg Sampson, SVP Business Development/Media Relations
(763) 595-3846
businessdevelopment@gage.com
• Colleen Christensen, Project Manager
• Tom Belle, President, CEO
Nature of Service:
Promotional marketing programs in sports, including but not limited to Internet marketing.
Year Founded:
1992
Clients:
Alcoa Building Products, Allergan, American Express, Buca di Beppo Restaurants, Chino Latino Restaurant, Canon, Deli Express, Del Monte, ESPN, Formica, General Mills, Gerber, Goodyear, H J Heinz, Haagen Dazs, Healthy Choice, Hewlett Packard, Hunt Wesson, Kaiser Permanente, Knudson, Lee Jeans, Maxtor, M&M/Mars, Meredith, Nabisco, Orville Redenbacher, Pillsbury, Potlatch Corporation, Schwan's, Snapple, Steelcase, Toto USA, Trus Joint MacMillan, UPM-Kymmene, Whirlpool
Other Location;
4701 Von Karman, First Floor, Newport Beach, CA 92660

GAME DAY COMMUNICATIONS
700 W PETE ROSE WAY
CINCINNATI, OH 45203
513-929-4263
Fax: 513-929-0245
jreau@gamedaypr.com
www.gamedaypr.com
• Betsy Ross, President
bross@gamedaypr.com
Clients:
Anthony Munoz Foundation, Cincinnati Bengals, Cincinnati Flying Pigs Marathon, Cincinnati Kings and hart productions.

GAZELLE GROUP
475 WALL STREET
PRINCETON, NJ 08540
609-921-1300
Fax: 609-921-2332
gazelle@gazellegroup.com
www.gazellegroup.com
• Rick Giles, Founder/President
Description:
Represents, creates and consults across sports, entertainment and cultural activities. Committed to developing prioritiezed business plans that achieve its clients' marketing and financial goals.
Services:
Professional athlete and coach representation, sponsorship representation and sales, corporate endorsements, personal appearances and motivational speaking, advertising, promotions and publicity, program production and advertising sales, conceptualization and development of individual events and series, merchandising and licensing, project and event implementation, rights acquisition, hospitality implementation and sales, creation of Internet presence, TV rights, packaging, representation and sales, signage and electronic imaging, budgeting
Clients:
Alliant Energy, American Airlines, Anaconda, Anheuser-Busch, AT&T

Wireless, Big Y Supermarkets, Champion, Chevrolet, Cingular, Clear Channel, Coca-Cola, Continental Airlines, Crown Oil, Dell, Dish Network, First Union/Wachovia, First USA Bank, Fleet Bank, Foot Locker, Gillette, GlaxoSmithKline, Health Net, Infiniti, IKON, Legg Mason, Merrill Lynch, Microsoft, Mohegan Sun, New York Life, Nike, Ocean Spray, Oldsmobile, Orbitz.com, Papa John's, Pennsylvania Lottery, Pepsi Cola, PNC Bank, Sony Playstation/, 989 Sports, Sports Illustrated, TIAA-CREF, Toyota, U.S. Marines, Warburg Pincus, Warrior Lacrosse, White Castle, Zebra Pen, Roto-Rooter, Roya
Sports Service Founded:
1994

GENESCO SPORTS ENTERPRISES, INC.
1845 WOODALL RODGERS FREEWAY
SUITE 1250
DALLAS, TX 75205-5412
214-826-6565
Fax: 214-826-6494
www.genescosports.com
• Charlie Torano, Co-Founder/Director
• John Tatum, Co-Founder/Director/Partner
• Mark Tatum, EVP
Description:
Sports Marketing Agency. Our mission is deceptively simple: to grow business by efficiently and effectively leveraging sports.
Services:
Sports marketing, negotiations and media, activation and execution of sports sponsorship programs
Clients:
Pepsi, Mountain Dew, Fortune magazine, Small World, Haggar Clothing, and awards.com
Sports Service Founded:
1994

GEOMETRY GLOBAL
636 11TH AVENUE
NEW YORK, NY 10036
212-537-3700
Fax: 212-537-3737
www.g2.com
• Jay Farrell, President
(312) 299-8500
• Toby Hoare, Chairman
• Steve Harding, Global Chief Executive
Nature of Service:
Local event marketing. Develops customized events to complement localized brand marketing strategies. Concentration on grass roots participatory events, such as bicycling, beach volleyball, running, multi-sport, walking and youth sports.
Sports Service Founded:
1988
Clients:
Past and Present Clients: Dannon, Kraft/Nabisco, Yoo-Hoo, Dairy Management, Beef Council, Bic Pen, Guinness, Hewlett-Packard, Darden, Del Monte, FedEx, Kiwi, ABC News, Spectrum Brands, NBA Basketball, Scotties, Dr.Pepper/7-Up, Jose Cuervo, Smuckers, Avaya, Gerber, Nokia & The Knockout Group

GEORGE P. JOHNSON COMPANY
3600 GIDDINGS ROAD
AUBURN HILLS, MI 48326
248-475-2500
Fax: 248-475-2325

careers@gpj.com
www.gpj.com
• Robert Vallee, Sr., Chairman
• Laurence Vallee, President
• Robert G. Vallee, Jr, Chief Executive Officer
• David Drews, EVP/Chief Financial Officer
• Jeff Rutchik, Executive VP
(617) 535-9912
• Tom Maher, Executive Director, Marketing
Clients:
CISCO, IBM, Rotary, Siebel, Saturn, Ford, Reebok, Scion, Acura, Lexus, Toyota, Honda
Description:
Specializes in integrated event marketing. Utilizes creative services, event marketing, event management and production. Incorporates event analysis and strategy to creative direction and design, architectural engineering and production and entertainment hospitality.
Other Locations:
18500 Crenshaw Boulevard, Torrance, CA 90504. 310-965-4300; FAX: 310-965-4696, 48 Wall Street, Suite 1100, New York, NY 10005. 212-918-4595; FAX: 212-918-4596, 999 Skyway Road, Suite 300, San Carlos, CA 94070. 650-226-0600; FAX: 650-226-0601.

GFK CUSTOM RESEARCH NORTH AMERICA
200 LIBERTY STREET
5TH FLOOR
NEW YORK, NY 10281
212-240-5300
Fax: 212-240-5353
www.gfkamerica.com
• Debra Pruent, Chief Operations Officer
• Thomas J. Finkle, Chief Client Services Officer
Services:
Offers a full spectrum of research products, strategic models and consulting services to address clients' key business needs on a global basis.
Sports Marketing Research:
Conducts research to test and evaluate all types of sports marketing and related activities. Custom marketing research of all types to answer specific objectives relating to events, promotions, personalities, ad campaigns, imagery, audience, demographics, attitudes, sponsorship, sampling and overall effectiveness. Weekly national and regional omnibus services available. Overnight custom research services.

GIGUNDA GROUP
540 N COMMERCIAL STREET
MANCHESTER, NH 3101
603-314-5000
Fax: 603-314-5001
info@gigundagroup.com
www.gigundagroup.com
• Ryan FitzSimons, Founder/Chief Executive Officer
(603) 491-3523
ryan@gigundagroup.com
• Dan Dewey, Chief Financial Officer
• Scott Schoessel, Sales VP/New Business Development
(603) 340-1940
• Michael B. Petran, Creative VP
michael_petan@gigundagroup.com

Description:
Provides marketing services to clients targeting the college crowd. Services include placement the Fall Welcome Gift(product samples, student offers) and In Your Face Memo Boards(small billboards).
Services:
Experiential / Mobile / Event / Field / Trade Marketing; Sponsorship Activation - Music / Sports / Entertainment; Brand Enhancement & Consultation — Strategy / Ideation / Positioning; Retail Activation / RetailTainment / EngageTainment; Trade & Consumer Hospitality Parties / VIP Packages; Viral / Interactive / Word-of-Mouth; PR / Stunts / Buzz; Product Sampling / Demonstration; Trade Shows & Sales Meetings - Design / Development / Execution. Total Program Management - Strategy, Design, Creation; Execution, Reporting; Field Staffing / Training / Management / CDL Drivers; Vehicle Design / Build Outs /Graphic Wraps /Procurement; Promotional Des
Clients:
Procter & Gamble, Kellogg's, Kraft/Nabisco, Campbell's, Cadbury Schweppes, Nestle, Just Born and TastyKake.
Other Locations:
Chicago, St. Louis, Denver.
Current projects:
Kroger 300. Formerly known as The Collegue Kit. Develops mobile marketing programs that clients visibility.

GILT EDGE SOCCER MARKETING, LLC
321 JEFFERSON STREET
FLOOR 2
CHICAGO, IL 60563
312-600-9710
contact@giltedgesoccer.com
www.giltedgesoccer.com
• John Guppy, Founder/President
(312) 600-9710
jguppy@giltedgesoccer.com
• Scott Hutchison, Managing Director/Partner
Description:
Marketing solutions agency for brand seeking to connect with the soccer consumer. We work with corporate, media, and industry brands.

GLOBAL PRODUCTIONS
550 POST OAK BOULEVARD
HOUSTON, TX 77027
713-681-5898
888-381-2861
Fax: 713-681-5220
service@globalindustrial.com
www.globalindustrial.com
Sports Service Founded:
1999
Marketing & Consulting Services:
An independent group of companies providing their clients with international reach and local implementation in the areas of public relations, sponsorship, and event marketing & management. Global has offices in the US, England, France, Italy, Spain, UAE and Japan.

GLOBAL SPORTS & ENTERTAINMENT
300 N CONTINENTAL BOULEVARD
SUITE 140
EL SEGUNDO, CA 90245

310-414-2690
Fax: 310-414-2693
admin@globalsports-ent.com
www.globalsports-ent.com
• Nick Zaccagnino, Founder & President
• Julie Matz, Senior Talent Producer
• Evan Levy, Senior Event Manager/Talent Producer
• Cindy Katz, Talent Producer
• Ben Weiss, Athlete Relations/Jr. Talent Producer
Sports Service Founded:
1996
Marketing & Consulting Services:
Represents clients in all aspects of sports marketing. Develops or assists in the implementation of strategic marketing campaigns. Designs promotional campaigns to generate interest in targeted demographic groups. Promotes image enhancement and generates publicity for athletes and celebrities.

GO WITH A PRO, INC.
38 MILLER AVENUE P M B 241
MILL VALLEY, CA 94941
415-383-3907
www.gowithapro.com

GOLDEN BEAR INTERNATIONAL, INC.
11780 US HIGHWAY ONE
SUITE 500
NORTH PALM BEACH, FL 33408-3007
561-227-0300
Fax: 561-227-0548
www.nicklaus.com
• Jack Nicklaus, Chairman/Chief Executive Officer
• Bill O'Leary, President Landscape Design Services
Sports Service Founded:
1970
Marketing & Consulting Services:
Corporate services provided by eight operating divisions include: sports marketing and consulting; special events; television, video production and publishing; licensing and merchandising; public relations and promotion.
Services:
Marketing and Communications, Plan Documents, Specifications and Details, Computer Modeling, Landscape Design Services and Renovation Services.

GOLDEN BOY PROMOTIONS
626 WILSHIRE BOULEVARD
SUITE 350
LOS ANGELES, CA 90017
213-489-5631
Fax: 213-489-9048
info@goldenboypromotions.com
www.goldenboypromotions.com
• Oscar De La Hoya, President
(213) 489-5631
• Richard Schaefer, Chief Executive Officer
(213) 489-5631
Nature of Sports Service:
National boxing promotions firm.

GOLF SCORECARDS, INC
9735 SW SUNSHINE COURT
SUITE 700
BEAVERTON, OR 97005
503-352-0281
800-238-7267
Fax: 503-226-4501

information@golfscorecards.com
www.golfscorecards.com
• Cynthia Grant, President
(503) 352-0283
• Byron Grant, General Manager
(503) 352-0284
byron@golfscorecards.com
Products:
Quality design and printing: scorecards, yardage guides, other golf printed materials.

GOLFUTURES, INC.
7373 N SCOTTSDALE ROAD
SUITE B-100
PHOENIX, AZ 85253
480-315-8401
877-440-5360
Fax: 480-905-8705
www.golfutures.com
Services:
An employment service, serving both employers looking for golf educated personnel, as well as individuals searching for golf employment opportunities within the golf industry.
Marketing & Consulting Services:
Provides a variety of publishing and advisory services related to employment opportunities in the golf industry.
Sports Service Founded:
1991

GORILLA MARKETING, INC.
4100 FLAT ROCK DRIVE, #A
RIVERSIDE, CA 92505-5866
951-353-8133
800-464-6745
Fax: 951-353-1647
info@gorillamarketing.net
www.gorillamarketing.net
• Chris Arranaga, Chief Executive Officer/Sales
chris@gorillamarketing.net
• Bryce Arranaga, Art Department
• Rosslyn Forrester, Sales
• Joe Kalish, Sales
• Chris Arranaga, Owner & President
(951) 353-8133
chris@gorillamarketing.net
Services:
Delivers quality products and competitive prices along with unparalleled customer service.
Marketing & Consulting Services:
Promotional item supplier, stadium give-aways.

GRAND SLAM SPORTS MARKETING
625 MISSION VALLEY ROAD
NEW BRAUNFELS, TX 78132
830-625-5911
Fax: 830-625-5966
www.legendsoftennis.com
• Louanne Fischer, Director of Sales
Services:
Provides celebrity entertainment for tennis events to corporations, charity organizations, clubs, resorts, and tournaments. The company specializes in corporate outings and hospitality, charity events, club and resort programs, tournaments and product endorsements.
Event Management Services:
Event marketing through tennis events. Involved in setting up corporate events, sponsorship, endorsements, club and charity events.

GRANT ASSOCIATES
301 SAYRE DRIVE
PRINCETON, NJ 08540-5826
609-514-8674
Fax: 609-514-8673
• David Grant, President
Nature of Service:
Executive recruiting, licensing management, sports/event promotion, strategic corporate growth consulting, U.S. market development.
Year Founded:
1997
Sports Service Founded:
1997

GRAVITY TELEVISION & SPORTS MARKETING
1315 OAKRIDGE STREET
PO BOX 8189
FORT COLLINS, CO 80525
970-845-7979
Fax: 970-845-7991
• Mark Schelde, Founder/President
(970) 845-7979
• Amit Kapur, CEO and Co Founder
• Jim Benedetto, CTO and Co-founder
• Steve Pearman, CPO and Co-founder
• Chris Bissell, Chief Software Architect
• Karl Rinderknecht, VP Business Development
Year Founded:
1998
Nature of Service:
A full service sports and entertainment company specializing in program development, strategic consulting, negotiation, planning, budgeting, activation and fulfillment. Gravity's biggest asset is the ability to create efficient and unique solutions in marketing & promotions, events & sponsorships and television production. Gravity has proven experience with national sponsorships like the PGA TOUR and NASCAR down to local sponsorships such as the San Francisco Giants and The Ski Tour. Gravity has extensive experience with the major sport governing bodies and their respective teams, athletes and events. Gravity is headquartered in Beaver Creek, C
Clients:
Charles Schwab & Company, World Championship Sports Network (WCSN), and Visionbytes. Past recent projects included Gillett Evernham Motorsports and Discovery HD Theater.

GRAVITY TELEVISION & SPORTS MARKETING
450 BRYANT STREET
SAN FRANCISCO, CA 94107-1303
415-495-5515
• Amit Kapur, CEO and Co Founder
• Jim Benedetto, CTO and Co-founder
• Steve Pearman, CPO and Co-Founder
• Chris Bissell, Chief Software Architect
• Karl Rinderknecht, VP Business Development
Year Founded:
1998.
Nature of Service:
A full service sports and entertainment company specializing in program development, strategic consulting, negotiation, planning, budgeting, activation and fulfillment. Gravity's biggest asset is the ability to create efficient and unique solutions in marketing & promotions, events & sponsorships and television production. Gravity has proven experience with national sponsorhsips like the PGA TOUR and NASCAR down to local sponsorships such as the San Francisco Giants and The Ski Tour. Gravity has extensive experience with the major sport governing bodies and their respective teams, athletes and events. Gravity is headquartered in Beaver Creek,
Clients:
Charles Schwab & Company, World Championship Sports Network (WCSN), and Visionbytes. Past recent projects included Gillett Evernham Motorsports, and Discovery HD Theater.

HACHI INTERNATIONAL
444 PARK AVENUE S
7TH FLOOR
NEW YORK, NY 10016
212-696-1399
Fax: 212-696-1491
• Cammallere Kristi, Contact
Marketing Services:
Promotional, premium, ad specialty company. Sports Division sells promotional items of professional teams and college athletic programs.
Services:
Specializes in high perceived value gift ideas and direct sourced items from China. Advertising, Marketing and Sales, Player Development, Promotional Products, Premium Gifts: Catalog Merchandis Programs, Custom Design - Direct Import, Advertising Specialties, Award Programs, Redemption, Corporate Gifts, Direct Mail - Fulfillment.

HALO BRANDED SOLUTIONS
1980 INDUSTRIAL DRIVE
STERLING, IL 61081
815-625-0980
Fax: 815-632-6900
moreinfo@halo.com
www.halo.com
• Marc Simon, Chief Executive Officer and Director
• Jack Mewhirter, President
• Dale Moir, SVP - Information Technology, Programs O
• Dale Limes, Sales VP
Description:
Distributor of promotional marketing products and advertising specialities.
Services:
Effective in building brands through branded merchandise: an experienced sales force, online solutions, a diligent merchandising team, convenient distribution facilities, friendly customer service, marketing support, and the most efficient order processing technology in the industry.

HANG TEN INTERNATIONAL LICENSING CALIFORNIA CORPORATION
1400 BROADWAY
18TH FLOOR
NEW YORK, NY 10018
217-763-9200
Fax: 858-391-3386
info@hangten.com
www.hangten.com
• Paul Epner, Chief Executive Officer/President

- Michael Wakeman, General Manager
- Craig Kalter, Marketing VP

Products:
Accessories, activewear, boys, denim, hosiery / underwear / loungewear, sportswear, swimwear and all types of casual sportswear.

Marketing & Consulting Services:
Licensing agency for the Hang Ten, Lightning Bolt, Ozzy and Cinderella brands.

HDS PROMOTIONAL MARKETING
1140 E WASHINGTON STREET
SUITE 206
PHOENIX, AZ 85034
602-635-6400
800-952-5339
Fax: 602-254-1212
info@hdsideas.com
www.hdsideas.com
- Scott Nash, General Partner
(602) 635-6387
- Ryan Niggel, COO
- Martin Bohinski, CFO
- Kelly Chiccitt, VP of Marketing
- Mark Algeri, VP of Sales
- Joss Witzel, Director Of Operations
- Michele Fausti, Assistant to CEO
- Howard Schwartz, Founder and CEO

Nature of Services:
Team Shop Premiums produces products for staff use, game day giveaways as well as sponsor and sports related gifts.

HEIDRICK & STRUGGLES
233 SOUTH WACKER DRIVE
WILLIS TOWER - SUITE 4200
CHICAGO, IL 60606-6303
312-496-1200
Fax: 312-496-1686
www.heidrick.com
- Joe Bailey, Managing Partner - Global Sport Leadership
(212) 551-3412
jbailey@heidrick.com
- John S Wood, Vice Chairman & Managing Partner
- Eric Olson, Managing Partner
- Rusty o' Kelley, Managing Partner
- Gareth McIlroy, Managing Partner

Description:
The world's first Leadership Advisory firm, blending executive search & leadership consulting. Heidrick & Struggles actively solves business problems for their clients every day. Through their leadership advisory framework, they help companies attract, develop and retain the world's most talented individuals. For nearly 60 years, they have helped the world to be better led.

Nature of Service:
The group serves as the trusted advisor on effective leadership and solving complex problems involving vision, strategy, and talent management. Our clients are selected from owners, boards, companies, associations, federations and government entities which are or have aspirations to become peak performance organizations in the global industry of sport. There is no other firm that offers this combined service of leadership consultation and executive search, known as Leadership Advisory.

HILL AND KNOWLTON PUBLIC RELATIONS
825 THIRD AVENUE
NEW YORK, NY 10022
212-885-0300
Fax: 212-885-0570
www.hillandknowlton.com
- Paul Taaffe, Chairman & Chief Executive Officer
(212) 885-0300
paul.taaffe@hillandknowlton.com
- Tony Burgess-Webb, Chief Marketing Officer/EV
- Juan Capello, President and Managing Partner, Latin America
(212) 885-0334
- Mike Coates, President and Chief Executive Officer, H
(416) 413-4606
- Ian Bailey, Executive Vice President & General Manager

Event Management Services:
Event promotion/coordination; event publicity.

Services:
Public relations firm with services that range from marketing communications, corporate reputation management to political lobbying. Caters to the technology and health industries.

Clients:
Microsoft, Intel, Allied Bakeries, Ambev - Cerveceria Rio, Ariel P&G, baidu.com, Boots Nurofen, British Horseracing, Debswana, First Alert - Carbon Monoxide, Geox Respira, Heal Florida Healthcare, HP Elle, HP Photo Big Bang, i.Dolphin, International Truck, Labatt Sterling, Lock&Lock, London 2012, Lucky Loonie, Motorola Razr, Pacific Gas & Electric, Pfizer Detrol, SCIO, Sega Sonic, Smithsonian, Starbucks Muan Jai, The Maldives, The Palm, UK Trade & Investment, Ziggs

Marketing & Consulting Services:
Spokesperson identification/training.

Other Locations:
222 Merchandise Mart Plaza, Chicago, IL 60654. 312-255-1200; FAX: 312-255-3554, 808 Travis, Suite 2100, Houston, TX 77002. 713-752-1900; FAX: 713-752-1930, 10 Corporate Park, Suite 200, Irvine, CA 92606. 949-223-2300; FAX: 949-752-2130, 700 NE Multnomah, Suite 975, Portland, OR 97232. 503-248-9468; FAX: 503-274-7689, 2127 Fifth Avenue, Seattle, WA 98121. 206-728-1100; FAX: 206-728-1106, 421 W Riverside, Suite 450, Spokane, WA 99201. 509-744-3350; FAX: 509-744-3355, 106 E College Avenue, Suite 730, Tallahassee, FL 32301. 850-22-4100; FAX: 850-222-0075

HIVE
507 KING STREET E
UNIT 16
TORONTO, ONTARIO, CANADA M5A1M3
416-203-1339
www.thehive.ca

Services:
Advertising and promotion of the wares and services of others namely, conceiving, preparing, directing, and carrying out marketing promotions for others and conceiving, preparing, directing and carrying out advertising campaigns for others by: conceiving, preparing, directing and carrying out events, meetings, and travel for others, advertising and promotion of wares and services of others, by mailings and printed

matter for direct mail, print advertising, or outdoor media, dissemination on the internet, production of advertising messages for radio, television and the internet, copywriting, art direction, and concept generation

HOPE-BECKHAM, INC.
17 EXECUTIVE PARK DRIVE
SUITE 600
ATLANTA, GA 30329
404-636-8200
Fax: 404-636-0530
info@hopebeckham.com
www.hopebeckham.com
- Paul Beckham, Chairman
- Bob Hope, President, Co-Founder
bhope@hopebeckham.com
- Tom Hughes, Vice President
- Michael King, Vice President
- Garet Hayes, Vice President
- Ann Nelson, Vice President Finance/Administration
anelson@hopebeckham.com
- Dick Stevens, Managing Director Event Marketing
- Chad Wallace, Project Director
- Dave Van Voorhis, Director Business Development

Nature of Service:
Public Relations, Event Marketing, Media Relations, Consulting and Web Integration.

Year Founded:
1994

Marketing & Consulting Services:
Consults on operations and marketing with leagues, teams, events and corporations on programming, financial and marketing issues with television and communications companies.

Clients:
Acuity, General Motors, Arcapita, Georgia Lottery Corporation, Atlanta Spirit LLC, Heavy Inc., Atlanta Sports Council, Help A Child Smile, BIKE - A division of Russell Corporation, Honduras Outreach Inc., Jones Day, Bugaboo Creek Steakhouse, LPGA (Ladies Professional Golf Association), Caribou Coffee, Learning Disabilities Association of Georgia, Channel One Network, McCormick & Schmick's Seafood Restaurant, ChoicePoint, Mount Bethel Christian Academy, Church's Chicken, Overtime Magazine, Coca-Cola Company, Southern Company, Comcast Cable Communications, Trinity House, Feld Entertainment, Women's Sports Foundation, Fisher & Phillips, Flagstar

HORROW SPORTS VENTURES
6800 SW 40TH STREET
SUITE 174
MIAMI, FL 33155
561-743-6408
Fax: 305-559-6737
info@horrowsports.com
www.horrowsports.com
- Rick Horrow, President
rhorrow@horrowsports.com
- Karla Swatek, Vice-President

Services:
Advisor to Teams and Leagues, Universities, Government Agencies, and Not-for-Profit Organizations. Experts in all aspects of Public/Private Partnership Financing. Also, providers of solutions for complex team and entertainment facility development projects including coordination

of public infrastructure objectives.
Clients:
NFL, NASCAR, Baltimore Orioles, New York Mets, National Association of Proffesional Baseball Leagues, CBS Sportsline USA, State of Virginia/ Virginia Tourism Corporation, Great White Shark Enterprises, Alabama Sports Foundation/City of Birmingham/Jefferson County Civic Center Authority, Hampton Roads Partnership, Metropolitan Richmond Business Foundation, Cleveland Indians, Columbus (OHIO) Community Development Council, Ladies Professional Golf Association and International Management Group.
Marketing & Consulting Services:
Specializes in serving in the creation of sports organizations and sports teams; facility development services for sports teams; and evaluating markets for expansion for sports organizations, leagues and teams.

HOST COMMUNICATIONS, INC.
546 E MAIN STREET
LEXINGTON, KY 40508
859-226-4678
imgassociations@imgworld.com
• Thomas J. Stultz, Senior Vice President/Managing Director
• David Bertram, VP National Priorities
• Tim Campbell, Vice President Sponsorship Sales - Western US
• Steve Cornwell, Executive Vice President Operations
• Lisa Fluty, Chief Information Officer
• Lawton Logan, Executive Vice President Sales
Nature of Service:
Creates opportunities for corporations to connect with specific audiences, who ultimately impact their growth and success.
Year Founded:
1972
College Bowl Game Sponsor:
Gator Bowl Foundation - The Patch Partner

HOST MANAGED EVENTS
546 E MAIN STREET
LEXINGTON, KY 40508
859-226-4678
imgassociations@imgworld.com
• Thomas Stultz, Senior Vice President/Managing Director
• David Bertram, VP National Priorities
• Dave Cawood, EVP, Administration and Collegiate Marke
• Tim Campbell, VP Media
Event Consulting Services:
Organization excels at staging and producing large, participatory grassroots sporting events domestically and internationally, and creating fully integrated marketing platforms, interactive events, tours, sampling programs, mobile marketing units, golf projects and fan fest events. Organization owns the NBA Hoop-It-Up, the official 3-on-3 basketball tour of the NBA, and Got Milk? 3v3 Soccer Shootout, the official 3v3 tour of Major League Soccer. Other projects include producing the NCAA Hoop CIty interactive events at the Men's Final Four and Women's Final Four, as well as at Frozen Fest during the Division I Men's Ice Hockey Championship.
Services:
One of the top five in the world of sports

marketing. The company offers significantly diverse services with operating areas that include Collegiate Marketing and the NCAA, Association Management, Printing & Publishing, Radio and Television.

> **Clients:**
> Alltel, Coca Cola Deloitte & Touche, Dodge, Foot Locker, got milk?, IBM, Kraft Foods, New Balance, Pevonia Botanica, Methode Physiodermie, State Farm Insurance, Toys R Us

HUGHES SPORTS MARKETING
1141 S 7TH STREET
ST LOUIS, MO 63104
314-571-6300
Fax: 314-571-6300
• Jim Schnurbusch, Contact
Services:
Brand Positioning and Planning, Corporate Identity, Direct Marketing, Graphic Design, Guerrilla Marketing, Interactive Media Media Relations and Planning, Non-traditional Advertising (ambient and created media), Public Relations, Sales Promotion, Traditional Advertising (print, radio, TV), Web Site Design and Development

IEG, LLC
350 NORTH ORLEANS STREET
SUITE 1200
CHICAGO, IL 60654
312-944-1727
800-834-4850
Fax: 312-944-1897
www.sponsorship.com
• Jim Andrews, Senior Vice President, Content Strategy
• Shan Riggs, Vice President, IEG Client Solutions
Services:
IEG is the leading provider of consulting, valuation, measurement, research and training to the global sponsorship industry. IEG's sponsorship objective is to maximize sponsorship revenue for properties and maximize return on investment for sponsors.
Sports Service Founded:
1982
Marketing & Consulting Services:
From Sponsorship Valuation and Sponsorship Consulting Services to newsletters, conferences and customized research, IEG has the knowledge and resources to take yor sponsorship efforts to the next level. Because IEG neither sells sponsorship nor manages sponsors programs, they offer unbiased analysis and recommendations. IEG helps properties determine what their sponsorships are worth and hot to retain and grow current partnerships. As well as helps sponsors select the right opportunity, measure their sponsorship ROI and research their competitors' sponsorships.
Clients:
Dallas Cowboys, FIFA World Cup, NFL, MLS, U.S. Open Cycling Championship, Chicago Blackhawks, Miami Heat, Diageo, JPMorgan Chage, ING

IGNITION, INC.
101 MARIETTA STREET NW
6TH FLOOR
ATLANTA, GA 30303
678-701-0369
Fax: 678-701-0393

• Mark Driscoll, Founder
(678) 701-0369
• John Piester, Executive Vice President
• Susan Driscoll, Founder
• Dill Driscoll, Founder
• Mikey Hersom, Owner and President
• Cindy A Hersom, Owner and CMO
• Andi McWhorter, Chief Financial officer
• Amanda Daniels, VP
Services:
On the street activations, sampling programs, mobile tours, sponsorship management, motosports. Hospitality programs include design, development and implementation, merchandise, signage and promotion.
Other Locations:
3 Harvest Lane, Tinton Falls, NJ 07724. 732-578-0035; FAX: 732-578-0089, 130 Taconic Business Park Road, Manchester, VT 05255. 802-366-8200; FAX: 802-366-8220
Clients:
Coca-Cola, Fanta, Burger King, Delta, AT&T, eBay, Sprite, CNN, Southern Fried Football, Discovery Channel, Banquet, John Deere, Microsoft, Indy Racing Gear

IMAGE MARKETING
1428 ORCHARD LAKE DRIVE
CHARLOTTE, NC 28270
704-849-2288
Fax: 704-849-2292
imarkinc@aol.com
• Don Doby, President/Media Relations
Marketing & Consulting Services:
Represents sponsors with respect to their involvement in auto sports.

IMAGES USA
1320 ELLSWORTH INDUSTRIAL BOULEVARD
BLDG. C
ATLANTA, GA 30318
404-892-2931
Fax: 404-892-8651
• Robert L McNeil, Jr., President/Chief Executive Officer
• Robert L. McNeil, President & CEO
• John Lockyer, EVP Finance/Business Management, Chief Operat
• Maria M. Moffitt, Vice President, Director of Client Services
• Juan Quevedo, Director Market Intelligence
• Shawn Arthur, Creative Director
• Hank Ernest, Director Public Relations
Nature of Service:
International and domestic advertising, ethnic marketing, public relations, market research and event marketing and consulting
Year Founded:
1989
Event Management Services:
Provides event coordination, including advertising for corporate sponsorship, specialized promotions, and a wide range of corporate hospitality services. Represents sports events for sponsorship sales and marketing.
Clients:
Army/ROTC, EPA, Georgia Lottery, Goody Products, Atlanta DeKalb, Cox Communications, Sprint, American Institute for Managing Diversity, Fulton County Arts Council, Scientific Games, CDC, DHR

Georgia Department of Human Resources, Coca-Cola, McDonalds, United States Environmental Protection Agency, Compucredit, Roche, Wachovia

IMPACT MANAGEMENT GROUP, INC.
124 W CAPITOL AVENUE
SUITE 1886
LITTLE ROCK, AR 72201
501-244-9600
Fax: 501-244-9601
• Richard Bearden, Partner
bearden@img-partners.com
• Terry Benham, Owner & President
Marketing & Consulting Services:
Broad range of professional services for corporations interested in using sports or event marketing to increase sales and awareness of their products. Also offers consulting and administrative assistance to sports organizations, including sales and marketing planning, multimedia sales representation and expense reduction activities. Impact Management Group has teamed up with Integrated Sports Partners, for a consortium of 6 NCAA Div I Conferences. IMG also administers Kentucky High School sports awards program.
Sports Service Founded:
1992

IMPRESS SPORTS INC
7800 THE BLUFFS
SUITE C
ATLANTA, GA 30336
678-391-6217
Fax: 678-428-0018
• Richard Wheeler, President
• Danny Jasiczek, Vice President Sales
Marketing & Consulting Services:
Specializing in the production and distribution of custom point-of-sale displays, in-store signs, pennants, banners, posters, growth-charts, and more.
Description:
ImPress Sports is a print production company focused on providing small to large quantity promotional materials for sports, event and product marketers. ImPress Sports offers creative development, production and distribution of custom point-of-sale, posters, standees, banners, growth posters, collateral, merchandisers, pennant strings and more.

INFOUSA
1020 E 1ST STREET
PAPILLION, NE 68046
402-593-4500
800-835-5856
Fax: 402-331-1505
ir@infousa.com
www.infousa.com
• Edward C Mallin, President
• Bill L. Fairfield, President/CEO
• Mark Puljan, VP Central Region
• Jason Morris, Regional Manager Mid Market Solutions
Nature of Services:
InfoUSA is a provider of sales leads, mail, email and telemarketing lists that helps companies manage their sales databases through standardizing, updating, and enhancing their current systems with valuable, insightful information.

INNOVATIVE MARKETING CONSULTANTS
4284 SHORELINE DRIVE
SPRING PARK, MN 55384
952-252-1254
877-674-8206
Fax: 952-417-8146
info@imcsuccess.com
www.imcsuccess.com
• Shane Erickson, President/Chief Executive Officer
• Paul Higgins, Operations Manager
• Paul Yahnke, National Sales Manager
• Adam Tschida, Senior Account Executive
adam@imcsuccess.com
• Robert Ed, Marketing Specialist
robert@imcsuccess.com
Nature of Services:
Innovative Marketing Consultants manufactures on-premise promotional marketing products for a variety of industries including Sports Marketing (Sports Beads), the Retail and Beverage Markets, and Casinos.

INSIGHT SPORTS MANAGEMENT CO, LLC
8941 MILLER LANE
VIENNA, VA 22180
703-255-6588
Fax: 301-371-8095
• Anne Cook, Director, Club Operations
Marketing & Consulting Services:
Provides staffing, programming and marketing services to tennis facilities in the Mid-Atlantic region. Tennis event design, promotion and management. Full range of tennis club membership promotions and sales efforts.

INTEGRITY SPORTS MARKETING, MEDIA & MANAGEMENT
228 ROUNDWAY DOWN
PO BOX 1064
DAVIDSON, NC 28036
704-896-8181
Fax: 704-896-8441
www.is3m.com
• Pat Millen, President, Chief Executive Officer
(704) 896-8181
• S. G. Pat Millen, President/CEO
Services:
Consultants to the soccer industry, ISM provides strategic planning guidance, creation and implementation for television, print, video, digital and web-oriented projects.
Clients:
US Youth Soccer, NSCAA, ACOG, FIFA, CONCACAF, Caribbean Football Union, NCAA, WUSA, ACC, Big East, Adidas, MLS, Eurosport, Quokka Sports
Sports Service Founded:
1992
Event Management Services:
ISM is a multimedia sports marketing consulting firm with an emphasis on soccer.

INTERFERENCE
611 BROADWAY
SUITE 819
NEW YORK, NY 10012
212-995-8553
info@interferenceinc.com
www.interferenceinc.com

• Sam Tr Ewen, Chief Executive Officer
• Michael Glickman, Event Marketing President
(212) 995-8553
Description:
Specializes in Guerilla/street marketing. Works to develop non-traditional Ad/marketing campaigns designed to grab the attention of others. Their style is considered alternative and unique in grabbing the attention of the consumers and forming a brand message.

INTERNATIONAL SPORTS MARKETING CONSULTANTS, LTD.
HAYBARN HOUSE
118 SOUTH STREET
DORKING, SURREY, ENGLAND RH4 2EZ
44-1306-743322
Fax: 44-1306-743007
jobs@ismsearch.com
www.ismsearch.com
• Jack McMahon, President
• Fred Steinberg, VP
Marketing & Consulting Services:
A full service agency with worldwide sports sponsorship experience. Provides strategic planning and program development for the integration of sports into a company's mainstream communications operation. ISMC develops and implements all aspects of event creation and management including negotiations, advertising, promotion, media relations and research. ISMC has extensive experience in Olympic games marketing and operations, the application of information technology for scoring and statistics, as well as sports-oriented Web Site development and marketing.
Sports Service Founded:
1994

INTERNATIONAL SPORTS PROPERTIES, INC.
540 N TRADE STREET
WINSTON-SALEM, NC 27101
336-831-0700
Fax: 336-768-7681
www.imgcollege.com
• Ben Sutton, Jr., Chairman of the Board/Chief Executive Officer
• Rick Barakat, Vice President
• Dan Barrett, Associate Regional Vice President
• Matthew Carlomagno, Vice President, Human Resources
• Ben C. Sutton Jr., President
Nature of Service:
General sports marketing work, event management, sales driven, handles sponsorship sales activities on behalf of broadcast media, colleges, college conferences, facilities, corporations, etc.
Year Founded:
1992
Clients:
Virginia Tech, Wake Forest University, Marshall University, University of Cincinnati, Georgia Tech, Southern Miss, Ohio University, Vanderbilt University, University of Alabama, University of Missouri, Syracuse University.

INTROMARK INC
217 NINTH STREET
PITTSBURG, PA 15222

800-851-6030
888-648-4332
Fax: 412-338-0497
licensing@intromark.com
www.intromark.com
Services:
Patent referral, submission of
invention/ideas to industries for reviews.
Offers inventors and entrepreneurs a variety
of seminars, presentations and panel
discussions to help pursue ideas.

INVENTION TECHNOLOGIES
2655 LE JEUNE ROAD
SUITE 550
CORAL GABLES, FL 33134-5846
786-437-8801
800-940-9020
Fax: 305-255-4515
info@invent-tech.com
Services:
Offers strategic marketing and global
representation of inventors in the sale or
license of their new product concepts;
assists in the comprehensive research and
documentation of product ideas and utilize
aggressive and creative promotional
techniques to introduce these ideas to
industry; Handles all subsequent follow-up
and negotiations with interested parties with
the intent of securing a licensing agreement.

IRWIN BROH RESEARCH
1011 E TOUHY AVENUE
SUITE 450
DES PLAINES, IL 60018
847-297-7515
Fax: 847-297-7847
www.irwinbroh.com
• David L. Waitz, President/Chief Executive
Officer
dwaitz@irwinbroh.com
• Thomas E. Jackowiak, Vice President
(847) 297-7515
• Robert J. Rowe, Executive Vice President
browe@irwinbroh.com
General Description:
Irwin Broh Research is a full-service
marketing research firm based in Des
Plaines, Illinois. For over 45 years, they
have been providing insight to a wide variety
of clients who want to know what their
customers and prospects are thinking.
Sports Services Founded:
1971
Market Research & Consulting:
Specializing in the leisure time industry.
Services include focus group research,
market analyses, acquisition studies, sales
forecasting, customer satisfaction, new
product potential, market segmentation,
awareness & usage, advertising research,
retail site location and more. In-house
facilities include focus group center,
telephone interviewing center and data
processing department.
Sporting Goods Market Database:
All major sports covered. Source is the
annual consumer survey for NSGA'S THE
SPORTING GOODS MARKET report.
Covers 63 individual sporting goods items,
more than 20 sport categories. Other
syndicated reports available for golf,
sporting goods equipment, and sports
footwear.

J PATTON SPORTS MARKETING
3450 RIVERGREEN COURT
DULUTH, GA 30096
770-612-0400
Fax: 770-612-0439
questions@jpattonsports.com
Auto Sports:
Indianapolis Motor Speedway - Digital Asst
Management Services, Online Artwork
Approval Systems, Holographic Brand
Protection
Ice Hockey:
ECHL - Corporate Sponsor - Exclusive
Supplier of Hologram Products.
The Collegiate Licensing Company:
Digital Asset Management Services,
holographic Brand Protection
National Hockey League:
Digital Asset Management Services, Online
Artwork Approval System
NASCAR:
Online Artwork Approval System
PGA Tour:
Digital Assest Management Services,
Holographic Brand Protection

JACK ROUSE ASSOCIATES
600 VINE STREET
SUITE 1700
CINCINNATI, OH 45202
513-381-0055
Fax: 513-381-2691
www.jackrouse.com
• Keith James, President
kjames@jackrouse.com
• Jack Rouse, Chief Executive Officer
• Shawn McCoy, VP Marketing & Business
Development
smccoy@jackrouse.com
• Amy Merrell, Chief Operating Officer
• Brian Donahue, Senior Project Director
• Randy Smith, Senior Project Director
Nature of Sports Service:
Creates attractions at sports venues
designed to enhance fans' experiences and
increase per caps revenue. Attractions
include halls of fame, museums, interactive
games/exhibitory, retail. Works with sponsor
companies to design sponsored
entertainment areas.
Services:
Provides a full range of planning, design,
media and production management
services.
Clients:
American Royal Museum and Visitor Center,
Chisholm Trail Heritage Center, Columbus
Zoo Pachyderm Exhibit, Enginuity, Texas
Wild! at the Fort Worth Zoo, Fort Siloso at
Sentosa Island, The National Underground
Railroad Freedom Center, All About You,
Cincinnati Museum of Natural History and
Science, Head First! Theater at
HealthSpace Cleveland, Journey to the
Model T, The Arab American National
Museum, Public Landing Gallery at The
Cincinnati History Museum, The Wyoming
Territorial Prison and End-of-Tracks Town,
Western North Carolina Nature Center,
AEGIS Theater, The National Park Service
Washington Monument Interpretive Center,
African Rift Va
Current Projects:
Atlanta Braves Plaza & Scout's Alley;
Cincinnati Reds Museum & Hall of Fame;
Dayton USA; Green Bay Packers Hall of
Fame; Jack Nicklaus Museum; University of
Kentucky Basketball Museum; Ohio State

University Hall of Fame; San Diego Padres
Plaza.

JACKSON DAWSON MOTOR SPORTS
2 TASK INDUSTRIAL COURT
GREENVILLE, SC 29607
864-272-3000
800-722-3234
Fax: 864-272-3040
customer.service@jacksonmg.com
www.jacksonmg.com
Marketing & Consulting Services:
Locates sponsors for drivers, teams, and
sports events. Also produces decals for
sponsors, teams and events. Primary
specialty is motorsports.
Event Management Services:
Hospitality, catering and other services
involved in the implementation of sports
events. Display and promotion tours and
program implementation.

JHG TOWNSEND
6215 FERRIS SQUARE
SUITE 210
SAN DIEGO, CA 92121
888-246-2396
www.jhg.com
• Alex Benjamin, VP Finance & Operations
• Jayne Hancock, President/CEO
• Lisa Kendall, VP Business Partnerships
• Liya Sharif, VP Public Relations & Brand
Strategy
• Mary Fechtig, President/CEO
• Elizabeth E Cooper, Co-Founder
• Alex Benjamin, SVPof Finance &
Operations
• Cindy Subido, SVP
• Jacob Shea, EVP of Interactive &
technology
Nature of Services:
JHG is a San Diego-based marketing
agency serving the media, entertainment,
sports, and technology sectors that
integrates marketing strategy, branding,
public relations, interactive services, mobile
technology, and metrics to propel client
companies to success in the changing
marketplace.

JOYCE JULIUS AND ASSOCIATES, INC.
1225 EISENHOWER PLACE
SUITE 3
ANN ARBOR, MI 48108
734-971-1900
877-302-6389
Fax: 734-585-3451
www.joycejulius.com
• Cindy Shevrovich, President
• Robert Cotman, Chief Executive Officer
• Leslie Butler, Comptroller
• Jeff Meeson, IIT Director
• Laura Webb, Vice President Sales
(734) 971-1900
• Eric Wright, Vice President
Research/Development
(734) 971-1900
• Cathie Joynt, Account Representative
(734) 971-1900
• David Yott, Managing Editor-Series
Reports
(734) 971-1900
• Raymond Howland, Managing
Editor-Special Reports
(734) 971-1900
Services:
Provides comprehensive documentation of

in-broadcast brand exposure during sports, special event, and entertainment television programming. Provides complete impression measurement of a sponsorship program.
Sports Service Founded:
1985
Clients:
ABC, AFL, AMA, Anaheim Ducks, AVP, Bank of America, Baylor University, Best Buy, Boston Red Sox, Calgary Exhib. & Stamp., Callaway, CBS, CFL, Champ Car, Chicago Rush, Cotton Bowl Committee, DaimlerChrysler, Detroit Lions, Eastman Kodak, ESPN, FedEx, Ford Motor Company, Fox, General Motors, GMR Marketing, Gold Eagle Company, Golf Channel, Gr. Phoenix Visit & Conv., Holiday Inn, IMG, IRL, J. Walker Thompson, Just Marketing, Latham Entertainment, Live Nation, Miami Heat, Millsport LLC, MLB, Momentum World Wide, NASCAR, National Geographic, NBA, NBC, NCAA, N.O./Okh C. Hornets, NFL, NHL, Octagon, Orlando Predators, Palace of Auburn Hills, PGA Tour
Marketing & Consulting Services:
Consultation for corporate sponsors their current programs and available program options evaluating. Recommendations based on corporate marketing objectives. With marketing research service, NTIV can provide pre and post event media analysis, assistance with graphic design and placement for optimum exposure.

JTR PRODUCTIONS
1515 MARLBOROUGH DRIVE
PO BOX 3056
ANN ARBOR, MI 48104-6222
734-994-0138
JTRProductions@sbcglobal.net
www.jtrproductions.com
• John T. Reid, President
(734) 994-0138
jreid66206@aol.com
Sports Service Founded:
1991
Event Management Services:
Produces football games for black colleges. Specialists in all aspects of game coordination, production and marketing.

JUMPIN' JACK SPORTS
333 OCEAN BOULEVARD
HAMPTON BEACH, NH 03842
603-957-6222
www.jumpinjacksjava.com
• Jack Fleming, President
College Bowl Game Sponsor:
College - University of North Carolina through 2007-2008.

JUST MARKETING INTERNATIONAL
10960 BENNETT PARKWAY
ZIONSVILLE, IN 46077
317-344-1900
Fax: 317-344-1901
info@justmarketing.com
www.justmarketing.com
• Zak Brown, Founder, CEO
Nature of Service:
Strategic consultation, Research and evaluation; Sponsorship development, negotiation and management; Integrated promotion planning and execution; Event creation, Marketing and management;

Hospitality and corporate entertainment; Customized driving events.

K & S PROMOTIONS
34 BAREFOOT HILL ROAD
SHARON, MA 2067
781-784-0100
• Bob Myerson, President
(781) 784-0100
Marketing & Consulting Services:
Develops and implements sports promotions including corporate hospitality, sports celebrity appearances, memorabilia give-aways etc. Frequently utilized for client entertaining, sales incentives, and sweepstakes.

KAGAN WORLD MEDIA
40 RAGSDALE DRIVE
SUITE 250
MONTEREY, CA 93940
831-624-1536
800-307-2529
Fax: 831-641-0961
www.snl.com
• Paul Kagan, Chairman/Chief Executive Officer
• Harvey Kraft, Marketing Director
• John Mansell, Senior Analyst/Consultant
• Robin Flynn, Senior Consultant
Products:
Databooks, Newsletters, Conferences on Kagan's CD, Industry Reports, Kagan Events
Services:
Appraisals and Consulting
Sports Service Founded:
1969
Marketing & Consulting Services:
Appraisals and valuations of sports teams and sports media interests.

KARLITZ & CO.
570 SEVENTH AVENUE
SUITE 1004
NEW YORK, NY 10018
646-289-8900
Fax: 646-289-8911
info@karlitz.com
www.karlitz.com
• Herb Karlitz, President/Founder
hkarlitz@karlitz.com
• Herb Karlitz, President
(646) 289-8901
hkarlitz@karlitz.com
Sports Service Founded:
1995
Services:
Entertainment/Lifestyle and Event Marketing
Clients:
A Better Chance, American Airlines, American Film Institute, AT&T, Cendant, Children Uniting Nations, CIT, Coca-Cola, Cohn & Wolfe, Entertainment Industry Foundation, Glaxo Smith Kline, IBM, Kraft Foods, The March of Dimes, Morgan Stanley, Nabisco, Napa Valley Vintners Association, The New York Times, The Rusty Staub Foundation, Scholarship America, Sentient Jet, Serta, Sony, Stamps.com, U.S. Postal Service, Vespa
Marketing & Consulting Services:
Serves in a continuing advisory capacity with clients relating to sports marketing involvement and sponsorship.

KART MARKETING INTERNATIONAL, INC
PO BOX 101
WHEATON, IL 60187
630-746-4164
Fax: 630-653-2637
karting@msn.com
• Darrell Sitarz, President/CEO
• Darrell Sitarz, President, CEO
• Len Manley, Sales
(859) 983-9234
Description:
Marketing for Go-Kart Industry (Motorsports); Trade Show Producer (Kart Expo International); News and Information website.
Sports Service Founded:
1990
Publications:
KARTING INDUSTRY BUYER'S GUIDE; KART MARKETING INTERNATIONAL (KMI).

KATZ MEDIA GROUP, INC/RADIO
125 W 55TH STREET
NEW YORK, NY 10019
212-424-6000
Fax: 212-424-6110
www.katz-media.com
• Stu Olds, Chief Executive Officer
(212) 424-6780
• Robert Damon, Chief Financial Officer
(212) 424-6880
• David Prager, Chief Information Officer
(212) 424-6704
• Theresa Frasca, Public Relations Manager
(312) 755-3817
Services:
Advertising
Sports Service Founded:
1992
Event Management Services:
Develops and implements integrated sports communication programs utilizing properties in the NFL, NBA, MLB, NHL and Division I college football and basketball to assist clients in achieving specific sales and marketing goals. Services include customized media, merchandising, and promotion.
Marketing & Consulting Services:
Exclusive broadcast marketing representative of college and professional sports franchises. Provides account servicing and consulting from concept to completion on national, regional and local sports marketing programs.

KCA ENTERPRISES INC
124 N MAIN STREET
ASHLAND CITY, TN 37015
615-792-2664
800-805-5654
• Jim Jackson, President
(800) 805-5654
Services:
Providing fund raising ideas and logoed products

KCSA PUBLIC RELATIONS WORLDWIDE
880 THIRD AVENUE
6TH FLOOR
NEW YORK, NY 10022
212-682-6300
Fax: 212-697-0910
www.kcsa.com
• Herbert L. Corbin, Founding Partner
hcorbin@kcsa.com

• Jeffrey Corbin, Managing Partner/Chief Executive Officer
jcorbin@kcsa.com
• Todd Fromer, Managing Partner/Investor Relations
tformer@kcsa.com
Services:
Corporate guidance, integrated financial/investor relations, and sophisticated business and consumer marketing communications services.
Sports Service Founded:
1952
Event Management Services:
Manages all aspects of sports event for public relations and marketing purposes - experienced in motorsports sponsorships, Pay-Per-View sports and entertainment, running, basketball, wrestling, all major league sports, sports publishing, corporate sponsorship and promotions. Works with organizations, corporations, publications, broadcasting, retail/apparel and travel related companies.
Clients:
Investor Relations Clients: 4Kids Entertainment, Inc. - (NYSE: KDE), Acies Corp. - (OTC BB: ACIE), ADDvantage Technologies Group, Inc - (Amex: AEY), Alexander & Baldwin, Inc. - (NASDAQ: ALEX); American Scientific Resources; American Stock Exchange; Arbitron Inc. - (NYSE: ARB); Authentidate - (NASDAQ: ADAT); Axiom Global Partners; Deutsche Telekom - (NYSE: DT); Dewey Electronics Corporation - (NASDAQ: DEWY); Docucorp International, Inc. - (NASDAQ DOCC); EVCI Career Colleges Holding Corp. - (NASDAQ: EVCI); General Steel Holdings Inc. - (OTC BB: GSHO.OB); Global Traffic Network

---

KETCHUM NEW YORK
1285 AVENUE OF THE AMERICAS
FOURTH FLOOR
NEW YORK, NY 10019
646-935-3900
ray.kotcher@ketchum.com
www.ketchum.com
• Rob Flaherty, Senior Partner/President
• Rob Flaherty, Senior Partner, CEO
rob.flaherty@ketchum.com
• Ray Kotcher, Senior Partner & Chairman
(646) 935-3902
ray.kotcher@ketchum.com
Description:
Ketchum Sports Network (KSN) - KSN creates and manages sponsorship programs. Organizations they have worked with includes but is not limited to: National Football League/NFL, College Football, NASCAR, Major League Baseball/MLB, Olympic Games, Professional Soccer, Golf, Tennis and boating.
Services:
Brand marketing, Corporate communications, Food and nutrition communications, Healthcare communications, Media relations and strategy, Communications training and message development, Issues and crisis management, Change management consulting services, Entertainment marketing, Sports marketing, Multicultural marketing, Investor relations
Specialties:
Brand Marketing, Corporate, Food & Nutrition, Healthcare, Media Relations, Communications Training & Message

Development, Issues & Crisis Management, Investor Relations, Ketchum Design, Ketchum Productions, Account Planning & Research, Knowledge Center, Concentric Communications, KEM(Ketchum Entertainment Marketing), Media Strategy, Creative Specialty Services, Global Research, Sports Marketing

---

KEYSTONE MARKETING, INC.
709 NORTH MAIN STREET
WINSTON-SALEM, NC 27101
336-777-3473
Fax: 336-354-0047
www.keystonemarketing.net
• Roger Bear, Chairman
• David Scheumann, President
• Candy Borreson, Marketing SVP
• Mike Grice, President/Chief Creative Officer
(336) 354-0038
Services:
Research, Multimedia design and production, Graphic design services
Clients:
Kraft Foods, The Hershey Company, NTN Bearings, Checkers Restaurants, Jim Beam Brands, Dremel, Toyota Motor Sales USA, Inc.
Marketing & Consulting Services:
Complete sports marketing services including promotion, sponsorship consulting and management, account specific marketing, hospitality and public relations.
Event Management Services:
Manages sports marketing programs for the Planters' and Life Savers' Divisions of Nabisco Foods, Reckitt & Coleman, Rhodes Furniture, The Pfizer Company, Schneider National Trucking, Mallory Ignitions, Manager of Clarence Rose, PGA Tour. Heilig-Meyers Company, and golf activities for Northern Telecom. Also manages marketing efforts for Show Car programs for Heilig-Meyers Furniture and Barbasol Race Teams.
Sports Service Founded:
1989
Clients:
Kraft Foods, Jim Beam Brands, Pfizer, Hershey Foods Corporation, US Army, NVE Pharmaceuticals, Dremel, NTN Bearings, Toyota Motor Sales USA

KIKU OBATA & COMPANY
6161 DELMAR BOULEVARD
SUITE 200
ST LOUIS, MO 63112-1203
314-361-3110
www.kikuobata.com
• Kiku Obata, President
(314) 505-8414
kiku_obata@kikuobata.com
• Kevin Flynn, EVP
(314) 505-8418
kflynn@kikuobata.com
• David Leavey, Senior Architect
(314) 505-8440
dleavey@kikuobata.com
Year Founded:
1977
Description:
An expert at crafting fan experiences. For over thrity years, we have created strategies and design for sports, entertainment and retail brands and destinations around the world.

Clients:
Scottrade Center, Palace of Auburn Hills, St. Louis Cardinals, Sports Service, Comerica Park, Coors Field, AC St. Louis, Carolina Panthers, Target, Eco Shoppe, Whole Foods and Brown Shoe

---

KIVETT PRODUCTIONS
2543 SAINT HEATHER WAY
ORLANDO, FL 3206
407-342-0752
joe@cardstunts.com
www.giantamericanflag.com
• Joe Kivett, President
(407) 342-0752
joe@cardstunts.com
Services:
Kivett Productions manufactures giant American flags for major sporting events.
Founded:
1991
Clients Include:
NFL, MLB, NASCAR, NBA, NHL, NCAA, MLS, Coca-Cola, Nike, Pepsi, Home Depot, Australian Football League, Canadian Football League

---

KLINGE & ASSOCIATES, JOHN G.
25 STURGES HIGHWAY
WESTPORT, CT 6880
203-255-0829
• John G. Klinge, President
Sports Service Founded:
1986
Event Management Services:
Sponsor selection.
Marketing & Consulting Services:
Market analysis, media analysis, consumer research, sports premiums, promotions (trade and consumer), sports collectibles (cards, posters).

KNOX SPORTS MARKETING
13063 W LINEBAUGH AVENUE
TAMPA, FL 33626
813-891-6653
Fax: 813-891-6768
kmcmahon@knoxsports.com
• Paul Sickmon, President
(813) 891-6653
psickmon@knoxsports.com
• Kaitlyn McMahon, New Business Manager
(813) 891-6653
kmcmahon@knoxsports.com
• Jennifer Hope, Director, Client Services
(813) 891-6653
jhope@knoxsports.com
• Morgan Swem, Social Media Manager
(813) 891-6653
mswem@knoxsports.com
Specialties:
We assist clients in negotiating their sports sponsorships. Our expertise gives us the ability to think outside the box and create unique ways to meet our client's goals through the passionate fan base of sports teams and events.
Number of Members:
Four
Clients:
84 Lumber, Atlantic Coast Bank, BI-LO, CCM, Cirde K, Farm Bureau Insurance (Florida, Virginia, Texas, South Carolina), Huntington Bank, Hunters Kane's Furniture, Land o' Frost, Surgery Partners, St. Petersburg Times, Nash Finch.

LATINO SPORTS MARKETING, LLC
1901 FOURTH AVENUE
SUITE 300
SAN DIEGO, CA 92101
619-255-1027
Fax: 619-255-1504
• Anthony Eros, Chief Executive Officer and President
Description:
Full service marketing and consulting firm that creates vital relationships between companies and Latinos via sports.
Services:
Strategy/Consulting, Event Management
Clients:
Copa Tecate, U.S. Army, PGA Tour, Cartel Impacto, Inc., Curb Cup, Novamex, Sonrics, Latino Basketball Tournament, Host Communications, Heineken USA

LEADDOG MARKETING GROUP
440 9TH AVENUE
17TH FLOOR
NEW YORK, NY 10001
212-488-6530
Fax: 212-741-5013
www.leaddogmarketing.com
• Dan Mannix, President/CEO
(212) 488-6530
• Karen A Shnault, Sr.VP and Account Management
(212) 488-6530
• Lisa Hyman, Sr.VP and Integrated marketing
(212) 488-6530
• Donna Providenti, COO
(212) 488-6530
• JG Robilotti, Sr. VP, Client Services
(212) 488-6530
• Dan Jahn, VP, Brand Promotions
(212) 488-6530
• John Inguagiato, CFO
(212) 488-6530
Services:
Event Management and Production, Event Marketing, Magazine/Media Events, Sports Marketing, Promotions/Sweepstakes, Mobile Marketing, Design and Interactive Services.
Nature of Sports Service:
An independently-owned, NYC based full-service event marketing and brand promotion agency of 65 passionate people with satellite offices in Los Angeles, Chicago, Atlanta, Boston and Austin.LeadDog produces all aspects of consumer-focused experiences from ideation to execution, houses a full in-house design team and pays particular attention to developing turnkey strategies that deliver measurable results and align well with our clients' objectives.
Clients:
World Wrestling Entertainment, InStyle Magazine, American Cancer Society

LEADING IMAGE
54 KINGS FERRY ROAD
MONTROSE, NY 10548
914-739-5562
Fax: 914-739-5808
lsolomon@computer.net
• Lawrence Solomon, President
lsolomon@computer.net
Sports Service Founded:
1993
Marketing & Consulting Services:
Full range of sports, sporting goods and health and fitness marketing and promotion, public relations including publicity, new product introductions, strategic planning, special events, corporate sponsorships/celebrity endorsements, identity/image programs, infomercials, trade show/convention exhibit videos, VNR's, advertising, sales and marketing materials (print and video), marketing communications, internet marketing and World Wide Web ad design.
Other Office:
54 Main St., Terrytown, NY 10591 (Ph) 914-333-0722 (Fax) 914-333-0721.

LEIGH STOWELL & COMPANY
91 SOUTH JACKSON STREET
SUITE 4735
SEATTLE, WA 98194
206-727-2700
888-896-1641
Fax: 206-727-2898
main@stowellco.com
www.stowellco.com
• Leigh Stowell, Chief Executive Officer
• Sandy Schlee, EVP
• Craig Cripps, National Sales Director
Services:
Ascertainment, Market Roll-Out, Presentation Coaching, Market Visit Training, Weekly Video Email Training, Anytime Web-Based Software Training, Advanced Sales Skills Training, Visits with Key Clients and Agencies
Consulting Services:
Taking customized research to the next level integrating it around organizational objectives. Tactically assists North American sports, entertainment, and media organizations in the areas of sales, marketing, promotions, and business development based on proprietary annual surveys.
Sports & Entertainment:
Local customized research delivered in interactive software for sales, marketing, advertising, and promotional strategies. Conduct segmentation studies and measure sports fan behaviors and attitudes. Focus on customer preferences and behavior in measuring event attendance, ticket purchases, media consumption, and product purchases. Also can analyze corporate, venue, talent, and brand attitudes. Discovering everything about customers and non-customers in local markets.

LESTER SPORTS & ENTERTAINMENT
PO BOX 481
HOPEWELL, NJ 08525
609-466-7905
Fax: 609-466-7562
pam.lester@lestersports.com
www.lestersports.com
• Pamela R. Lester, President
pam.lester@lestersports.com
Nature of Service:
Provides consulting services to the sports, entertainment, and licensing and merchandising industries, including, sports management and marketing, licensing and merchandising television.

LICENSING RESOURCE GROUP, INC.
442 CENTURY LANE
SUITE 100
HOLLAND, MI 49483
616-395-0676
Fax: 616-395-2517
www.lrgusa.com
• J. Lewis Hardy, President/CEO
(336) 896-7907
lewis@lrgusa.com
• Richard L. Rademaker, Founder/Chairman
(616) 395-0676
dick@lrgusa.com
• Gene Wandling, EVP/Chief Financial Officer
(319) 351-1776
gene@lrgusa.com
Nature of Service:
Provides its clients with the very best in service, from core management needs such as day-to-day administration, royalty management, compliance and enforcement, to marketing, merchandising, design and brand development.
Sports Service Founded:
1991
Clients:
University of Akron, University of Alabama in Huntsville, Alabama State University, Arizona State University, Austin Peay State University, Bemidji State University, Big East Conference, Bowling Green State University, Bradley University, Butler University, Cal State Fullerton, Cal State San Marcos, University of California Davis, University of California Santa Barbara, Campbell University, Canisius College, Case Western Reserve University, University of Central Arkansas, Central Colegiate Hockey Association, Central Connecticut State University, Central Michigan University, Charleston Southern University, Colorado College.
Marketing & Consulting Services:
Full service management company for college trademark licensing programs, including colleges, college conferences and college sports associations.

LIVE WIRE SPORTS GROUP
1260 N HANCOCK STREET
SUITE 105
ANAHEIM, CA 92807
714-777-7850
Fax: 714-777-7851
• Bill Hodson, Director
Nature of Services:
Advertising/Marketing, Custom Publishing, Digital Media, Sponsors Events, Media Planning/Buying, Market Research, Pilot Programs, Public Relations, Sports Management, Sponsor Development
Sports Service Founded:
2002

LOWENSTEIN EVENT MARKETING GROUP
11200 VALLEY HEIGHTS DRIVE
OWINGS MILLS, MD 21117
443-870-3657
Fax: 443-870-3547
info@lowensteinevents.com
www.lowensteinevents.com
• Lance Lowenstein, President
lance@lowensteinevents.com
• Barbara Bozzuto, Partner
Services:
Handles special event management, marketing and promotions, sponsorship packaging, and traveling tours.

MACKEY MARKETING GROUP, INC.
12 POWDER SPRINGS STREET
SUITE 220
MARIETTA, GA 30064
770-423-9593
info@mackeymarketing.com
www.mackeymarketing.com
• Brian C. Mackey, President
Services:
Specializes in event management,
preparation, execution and publicizing of
motorsports sponsorships.

MAKAI EVENTS AND PROMOTIONS
211 NEVADA STREET
EL SEGUNDO, CA 90245
310-546-9585
Fax: 310-321-7933
info@makaiinc.com
www.makaiinc.com
• Robbie Thain, President/Founder
• Linda Rosenberg, VP of Client Services
• Andrea Rackley, VP of Client Services
• Robbie Thain, Founder/President
Services:
Event Planning and Production, Guerilla
Marketing, Product Sampling, Development
and Execution of Promotional Campaigns,
Warehouse Services and Equipment Rental,
Integrated Media Services, Production
services, Complete Creative Services,
Cultural Marketing.
Nature of Sports Service:
Ch@lk T@lk is an online reporting system
that gives clients real-time access to the
events as the programs roll out.

MANDALAY ENTERTAINMENT COMPANY
4751 WILSHIRE BOULEVARD
3RD FLOOR
LOS ANGELES, CA 90010
323-549-4300
Fax: 323-549-9844
www.mandalay.com
• Peter Guber, Chairman/Chief Executive
Officer
peterg@mandalay.com
• Paul Schaeffer, Vice Chairman/CEO
(323) 956-2400
pauls@mandalay.com
• Hank Stickney, Chief Executive Officer
• Ken Stickney, Managing Director
• Jon Spoelstra, President
Sports Service Founded:
1995
Services:
Specialize in managing professional sports
franchises and venues throughout the
country.
Clients:
Frisco Roughriders, Dayton Dragons, Erie
Seawolves, Hagerstown Suns, Las Vegas
51s
Marketing & Consulting Services:
Movie production company that is using
sports and specifically minor league
baseball teams as a vehicle to create new
entertainment channels, as well new
markets for sponsors and advertisers to hit
regional markets. Interested in producing
sports movie productions. Owns the Dayton
Dragons and Lake Elsinore Storm. Provides
consulting services for TodaySports.com.

MARATHON
4655 S COACH DRIVE
TUCSON, AZ 85714-3467

520-202-2400
Fax: 520-202-2409
• Sue Brooks, President
• Susan Brooks, Owner
• Sharon Shearman, Consultant
Services:
A non-traditional marketing agency,
specializing in event marketing, sponsorship
sales, sponsorship activation, and non-profit
event consulting.
Clients:
Chrysler, The Event, Ronald McDonald
House Charities, The K Sean Elliot Charity
Golf Classic, and Wildcat Dream Foundation
Sports Service Founded:
1986
Event Management Services:
Tournament sales, coordination,
sponsorship and promotion for auto sports,
golf, tennis, football, basketball, and other
sports in the Tucson and Phoenix areas.
Marketing & Consulting Services:
Works with companies/products to develop
an event or arrange special promotions
within an existing event.

MARKET REACH
1010 WASHINGTON BOULEVARD
STAMFORD, CT 6901
203-352-0700
jtighe@market-reach.net
• Jim Tighe, President
(203) 257-6451
Services:
Specializes in event marketing, mobile
marketing, mall marketing, retailtainment,
sponsorship activation, hispanic sampling,
college sampling, guerilla marketing and
product sampling.
Clients:
Qwest, Campbell's, Dannon, Hersheys,
Hewlett Packard, American Express,
Duracell, Pillsbury, Pfizer, Starbucks Coffee,
AT&T, Yoohoo, Chock Fullo Nuts, Procter &
Gamble, Kraft,SC Johnson, AZO, Orangina,
and BIC

MARKETING ARM
1999 BRYAN STREET
SUITE 1800
DALLAS, TX 75201
214-259-3200
Fax: 214-259-3201
info@themarketingarm.com
www.themarketingarm.com
• Gregg Hamburger, Chief Integration
Officer
• Jennifer Henry, Chief Financial Officer
• Ray Clark, Founder/CEO
• Dan Belmont, President
Year Founded:
1993
Sports Service Founded:
1975.
Description:
A network of marketing services agencies
building brands through emotionally
powerful platforms,including sports,
entertainment, music, events, promotions,
and cause marketing. Based in Dallas, The
Marketing Arm operates within Omnicom
Group Inc (NYSE: OMC) and serves as the
umbrella brand for four best-in-class
agencies: Millsport, Davie Brown
Entertainment, USMP, and ipsh.

MARKETING CONNECTIONS
712 N WELLS STREET
SUITE 200
CHICAGO, IL 60610
312-587-1465
Fax: 312-587-9883
www.mktgconnections.com
• Patrick Va Den Heuvel, Marketing Director
(312) 587-1465
pvanden@mktgconnections.com
Services:
Full service marketing agency that
specializes in live field marketing. Offers
pass-through pricing and online reporting.
Clients:
RJ Reynolds, Gatorade, Kellogg Co.

MARKETING DRIVE WORLDWIDE
800 CONNECTICUT AVENUE
3RD FLOOR E
NORWALK, CT 06854
203-857-6100
Fax: 203-834-1786
info@marketingdrive.com
www.marketingdrive.com
• Michael Harris, CEO, President
(203) 857-6100
Services:
Provides the full spectrum of promotional
marketing services such as strategic
planning, national and regional promotions,
co-marketing, channel marketing, retail
menu marketing, promotional services,
co-op advertising, co-op media, site
development, e-marketing, CD and DVD
authoring and design, customer acquisition
programs, customer retention and loyalty
programs, and database management;
Interactive and Direct Response Services
Marketing & Consulting Services:
Assists clients to create national promotions,
convert national sponsorships to local market
promotions, create account-specific promotions
and co-marketing programs.
Sports Service Founded:
1996

MARKETING WERKS
130 E RANDOLPH STREET
SUITE 2400
CHICAGO, IL 60601
312-228-0800
Fax: 312-228-0801
www.marketingwerks.com
• Betty Newman, President
• Scott Moller, VP
• Jason Vargas, Marketing Director
• T. J. Nolan, Sales Director
Services:
Event management, integrated experiential
marketing; event, mobile and sports
marketing; creative sampling solutions;
brand launches, PR and media support;
retail and sales promotion.
Clients:
Discover Card/ESPN Tailgate Tour,
Hershey's Kissmobile Tour, LEGO Bionicle
Find the Power Tour, Schick Shave Shack
Tour, Snapple Dye Hard Tour,

MARLIN ENTERTAINMENT GROUP, LTD
1720 POST ROAD E
WESTPORT, CT 06880
203-255-6100 EXT x 28
Fax: 203-255-6103
• Neal Frank, President
(203) 255-6100

Services:
Contest/Sweepstakes, Design/Production, Event Marketing/Tours, Entertainment Marketing, Cause Marketing, Sampling Programs, Guerilla/Buzz Marketing and Incentive/Loyalty Marketing ServicesProvides concept development, game play and design, registration, bonding, compliance, independent judging, online creative and hosting, and management, staffing, and event/tour production for mobile tours, mall tours, nightlife marketing, college events, fairs, festivals, and health clubs.

Clients:
We, Purina, MTV, History Channel, American Express, Comedy Central, Knowledge TV, GTE, MasterCard, Universal, A&E Network, Paramount, SEGA Channel, US West, NINTENDO, USWEST, VH1, ABC Family, Finlandia, Sci Fi, AMC, USA Network, Teen People, Sony, TAO, Toon Disney, Ragdoll, Ovation, NCC, NFL, The Weather Channel, CERTS, TCM, Music First, Game Show, Coca Cola, HBO, NBC Universal, and SOAP

Areas of Specialization:
Ambush, Cause, College, Entertainment Tie-ins, Experimental, Field Marketing, Interactive, Mall events, Mobile Marketing, Partnership Marketing, PR Stunts, Street Teams, Sponsorship Activation, Sweepstakes/Contests, Tours & Events

---

MATTEL SPORTS PROMOTION DEPARTMENT
333 CONTINENTAL BOULEVARD
MI-0836
EL SEGUNDO, CA 90245-5012
310-252-2000
Fax: 310-252-3866
corporate.mattel.com
• Daniel Roddick, Director
Description:
Program implementation center;develops and executes sports events and educational programs for flying disc(Frisbee) and foot bag play.

MAZZ MARKETING, INC.
287 COURTLAND AVENUE
BRIDGEPORT, CT 6605
203-260-4932
Fax: 866-209-1305
Wayne@WayneMazzoni.com
• Wayne Mazzoni, President
(203) 260-4932
wayne@waynemazzoni.com
• Gale Mazzoni, Marketing
mazzmarketing@aol.com
Company Description:
Helps high school athletes and their parents in their search for the right college, athletic program and athletic scholarships.
Nature of Service:
College recruiting seminars; Baseball Camps for high school athletes, consulting for high school athletes, books on getting college scholarships for high school athletes.
Products:
Books, video and apparel to learn more about the process in an effort to handle the process by themselves, camps, books, serminars, consulting.

MEDIA VISIONS
5875 OLD LEEDS ROAD
BIRMINGHAM, AL 35210
205-324-4600
800 254-0876
Fax: 205-324-4688
www.mediavisions.com
• Michael K Cruce, Founder/President

MEDIAMARK RESEARCH INC./MRI
75 NINTH AVENUE
5TH FLOOR
NEW YORK, NY 10011
212-884-9200
800-310-3305
Fax: 212-884-9339
• Kathi Love, President/Chief Executive Officer
(212) 884-9257
• Alain Tessier, Chairman
(212) 884-9261
• Ian Jack, EVP/Chief Operating Officer
(212) 884-9252
• Ann Ma Kelly, VP/Marketing & Strategic Planning
(212) 884-9204
Magazine Research Product Volumes:
All major participation/spectator sports. Demographic/media cross-tabulated by sports annually. Cost depends upon purchaser.
Services:
Consumer Targeting, Brand Trial Loyalty, Promotional Opportunities, and Trade Marketing

---

MERCURY SPORTS MANAGEMENT
222 BLOOMINGDALE ROAD
WHITE PLAINS, NY 10605
914-683-0146
Fax: 914-683-1408
• Jay Schulthess, President
(914) 683-0146
Marketing & Consulting Services:
Provides management services to NASCAR drivers. Consulting services to corporate auto racing sponsors. Coordinates and manages NASCAR licensing programs for companies. Provides hospitality and public relations services.
Specialty:
Auto Sports.
Clients:
Auto Sports, Nascar drivers, corporate auto racing sponsors

METRO SIGNS ADVERTISING, INC.
4608 SCHUFF AVENUE
LOUISVILLE, KY 40213
502-452-2561
800-441-0627
Fax: 502-473-1286
www.1-metro.com

MILLSPORT, LLC
320 POST ROAD
DARIEN, CT 6820
203-662-4500
Fax: 203-662-9456
• Bob Basche, Chairman
(203) 662-4505
• Dan Belmont, President
(203) 662-4500
• Mike Bartelli, SVP-Millsport Motorsports Division
(704) 262-6461
• Andrew Robinson, Senior Vice President

---

(214) 259-3200
• Daniel G. Belmont, President
• Andrew Robinson, Vice President
• Lisa Markham, Senior Vice President
• Mike Bartelli, Senior Vice President
Clients:
Frito-Lay, NASDAQ, Sunoco, Taco Bell, AT&T, WalMart, Wells Fargo, Yahoo!, Pepsi International, Tylenol, Elizabeth Arden
Sports Service Founded:
1975
Description:
The sports sponsorship and motorsports consulting and activation division of The Marketing Arm. Founded in 1975 as one of the first sports marketing agencies in the US, Millsport helps clients build maketing advantage and drive business results utilizing sports marketing assets. Based in Stamford, Conn, with offices in Dallas (1999 Bryan Street, Suite 1800, Dallas, TX 75201, Phone: 214-259-3200, Fax: 214-259-3201), Chicago, and Los Angeles, Millsports services include brand strategy, property/media acquisition, integrated program modeling, multi-channel activation, hospitality, promotions, and evaluation. ROI analytics.

MOBIVITY
58 W BUFFALO
SUITE 200
CHANDLER, AZ 85225
512-522-4710
Fax: 512-639-3375
sales@txtstation.com
www.txtstation.com
• Michael Falato, Director Sales & Business Development
• Brook Paterson, Chief Financial Officer/Director
• Matthew Moulin, Chief Technology Officer
• Dennis Becker, President/CEO
• Michael Falato, SVP of Sales & Business Development
• Brad Dolian, VP,Client Services
• Thi VanAusdal, Technical Lead
• Loyda Drew, Project Manager
Nature of Services:
Txtstation provides integrated campaigns that combine the passion of live broadcasts and events with the ubiquity of mobile messaging allowing broadcasters, event owners, sponsors and general media to communicate with viewers or fans directly through their mobile phones.

MODAK ILLUSTRATIONS
4225 JONATHAN LANE
CUMMING, GA 30130
828-368-8601
800-645-8165
• Ken Modak, Artist
Description:
Individuals and sports organizations have sought out Modak's art talent.
Services:
Ken Modak is an artist whose ability to capture the likeness of individuals is exceptional. Many individuals and sports organizations have sought out Modak's art talent. Working primarily in a color pencil technique, Ken feels this medium allows him to best capture the feeling and detail he looks for in his photo-realistic style. Ken's knowledge of airbrush offers a perfect complement to his pencil technique.

Clients:
Atlanta Falcons, Atlanta Junior Golf Association, Coca-Cola, Country Music Singer - Tracy Lawrence, Fellowship of Christian Athletes, GTE Customer Networks, PGA BellSouth Classic. Colleges: Cleveland State, Florida, Florida State, Gannon, Georgia, Georgia Southern, Georgia Tech, Kentucky, Notre Dame, Youngstown State

MOMENTUM IMC COMPANY
250 HUDSON STREET
2ND FLOOR
NEW YORK, NY 10013
646-638-5400
www.momentumww.com
Description:
Events and sponsorship unit of the advertising agency McCann-Erickson North America
Clients:
AT&T, General Motors, Coca-Cola, Anheuser-Busch, Black & Decker, Sega of America

MOTORSPORT CONCEPTS, LLC
2677 E. HWY 224
UNIT 11
DENVER, CO 80229
303-286-9498
motorsportconcepts@gmail.com
www.motorsport-concepts.com
Marketing & Consulting Services:
Provide marketing consulting, event hospitality and coordination. Assist drivers with obtaining sponsorship for motorsport events.

MOUNTAIN NEWS CORPORATION
50 VASHELL WAY
SUITE 400
ORINDA, CA 94563
925-254-4456
Fax: 925-254-7923
info@mountainnews.com
www.mountainnews.com
Sports Service Founded:
1978
Marketing & Consulting Services:
Operates a separate recreation division which represents a number of outdoor recreation manufacturers, associations and consumer show expositions with respect to all facets of public relations, advertising and sales promotion.

MULTI-AD
1720 W DETWEILLER DRIVE
PEORIA, IL 61615
309-692-1530
Fax: 309-692-8378
info@multiad.com
www.multi-ad.com
• Brian Jeske, Vice President, Sports Operations
(770) 421-6461
• Joe Dalfonso, Sports Consultant
(800) 348-6485
jdalfonso@multiad.com
• John F. Kocher, President
Year Founded:
1945
Sports Service Founded:
1990
Description:
Sports printer specializing in programs, media guides, trading cards, promotional material. Design, mailing, and warehouse offered as well.

MURPHY & ORR EXHIBITS
564 MAIN STREET
FOREST PARK, GA 30297
404-366-2537
Fax: 404-366-2585
www.murphy-orr.com
• Art Hammerstrom, Account Executive
Nature of Services:
Murphy & Orr offers turnkey, custom exhibit and display services including design and space planning, exhibit and graphic fabrication, interactive exhibit development, as well as installation and updating services.
Year Founded:
1946

NATIONAL ASSOCIATION OF SPORTS COMMISSIONS
9916 CARVER ROAD
SUITE 100
CINCINNATI, OH 45242
513-281-3888
Fax: 513-281-1765
info@SportsCommissions.org
www.SportsCommissions.org
• Don Schumacher, CSEE, Executive Director
(513) 281-3888
don@sportscommissions.org
• Beth Hecquet, CMP, Meetings & Events Director
(513) 281-3888
beth@sportscommissions.org
• Elizabeth Chaney, Director of Member Services
(513) 281-3888
elizabeth@sportscommissions.org
Clients Include:
The National Association of Sports Commissions (NASC) is a non-profit membership based association for professionals in the sports event travel industry. Members include organizations that attract sporting events to their community (i.e. sports commissions and convention and visitors bureaus), event owners, and vendors and suppliers to the sports event industry.
Nature of Service:
The NASC provides networking opportunities, professional development, and industry best practices to sports event industry professionals. Nearly 550 organizations across the United States, Canada, and Puerto Rico are members of the NASC.
Sports Organization
For more than 20 years the National Association of Sports Commissions (NASC), a non-profit, 501(c) 3, membership based association, has served the sports event industry as its premier networkinf organization. The NASC is able to assit you in every way possible to meet all of your domestic and international event needs.

NATIONAL HOLE-IN-ONE ASSOCIATION
1840 N GREENVILLE AVENUE
SUITE 178
RICHARDSON, TX 75081-1898
972-808-9001
800-527-6944
888-527-6944
Fax: 972-808-9012
hio@hio.com
www.hio.com
Services:
Provider of golf-event prize services and offers the most complete hole-in-one promotion package which includes promotional materials.
Description:
We offer promotional programs to build traffic to your dealership through prize indemnification. Programs include golf, direct mail key matching, weather, basketball, football, baseball, hockey and fishing.

NATIONAL MEDIA GROUP, INC.
545 FIFTH AVENUE
SUITE 640
NEW YORK, NY 10017
212-424-0100
Fax: 212-867-1116
• Michael Goldberg, Chief Executive Officer
• Sid Schechter, Chief Operating Officer
• Adam M. Poe, Sales and Marketing Director
• Tina Gargiulo, Event Marketing Director
Services:
NMG and its affiliated agencies work with their clients to create integrated marketing platforms and campaigns incorporating one or more of the following elements sports sponsorship tie-ins, public relations, event management, consumer promotions, television production.
Clients:
IBM, Schick, AT&T, Nike, American Express, Reebok, Lucent Technologies, Nestle, Sony, Dodge, Saturn, Schering-Plough, Warner-Lambert, Pfizer, Prudential Securities, EA Sports, KSwiss, Acclaim Entertainment, Fila, and Ocean Spray.
Year Founded:
1980
Description:
Sports marketing, Talent Representaton, Official Marketing Agency for NBA Coaches Association
Association Marketing:
Integrating sports personalities into sales and marketing platforms for corporate sponsors. Our creativity and contacts with some of the most high profile individuals in sports affords our clients the opportunity to leverage the assets of professional sports properties.
Event Marketing:
Maintains strategic relationships with experienced affiliated event management companies to implement affinity programs and insure the quality controls required for the event marketing components of our campaigns to achieve the established objective.
College Marketing:
The activities that NMG integrates into the college promotions are created by programming experts currently employed on college campuses throughout the United States who also serve our clients as supervisors on a regional level.
Talent and Television Production:
Has developed an in-depth knowledge of the television industry and a solid relationship with the major televison sports broadcast networks.

NATIONAL OUTDOOR SPORTS ADVERTISING
1200 POTOMAC STREET, NW
WASHINGTON, DC 20007-3211
202-965-9850
• W Micheal Gretschel, President

NATIONAL SCHOLASTIC ATHLETICS FOUNDATION, INC.
112 WIDGEON WAY
BRIDGEVILLE, DE 19933
919-414-8619
info@nationalscholastic.org
www.nationalscholastic.org
• James I. Spier, Executive Director
Description:
To support the development of junior age (under 20 years of age) athletes.
Sports Service Founded:
1990

NATIONAL SPORTING GOODS ASSOCIATION (NSGA)
1601 FEEHANVILLE DRIVE
SUITE 300
MOUNT PROSPECT, IL 60056
847-296-6742
800-815-5422
Fax: 847-391-9827
info@nsga.org
www.nsga.org
• Matt Carlson, President & Chief Executive Officer
Services:
The world's largest sporting good trade association consisting of retailers, suppliers, sales agent, media and industry associates. Provides cost-saving services, information, and education for its members on a wide variety of sports also serves as the voice of the retailer/dealer, speaking out on issues that affect sporting goods retailers/dealers.
Fitness in America:
Analyzes adult frequent participants in seven fitness activities — aerobic, exercising, bicycling, calisthenics, exercise walking, exercising with equipment, running and swimming.
Lifestyle Characteristics of Sporting Consumers:
Using PRIZM analysis developed by Claritas, this report provides a versatile geo-demographic analysis of consumer purchasers of sporting goods. It addresses such questions as, Who are our target consumers?; Where do they live and shop?; How can we best reach them?. PRIZM clusters are organized into 12 broad social groups. In addition to analysis by individual product, product groupings are analyzed, e.g., all exercise equipment, in addition to home gyms, treadmills, etc. This report contains demographics on population, type of residence, household type (family, non-family, singles, etc.), size of HH, education and occupation of HH head.
Cost of Doing Business Survey:
Survey relates business costs for sporting goods stores. Contains income statements and productivity ratios by retail sales volume, number of stores, region, full line vs. specialty and team business. Productivity ratios included are: sales per employee, profit per employee, sales per total selling square foot, profit per total selling square foot and inventory turnover. Survey is free to NSGA retail members.

Cost to non-members is $1,250.00.
Sport Equipment Expenditures:
Equipment expenditures presented for 28 sports. NSGA Brand Share Report: based on consumer recall of most recent purchase, NSGA Brand Share Studies report market share for 63 products. List of products available from NSGA. Cost is $425 for first product report, $375 for second, $275 for each additional report.
Year Founded:
1929

NATIONAL SPORTS FORUM
7290 NAVAJO ROAD
SUITE 204
SAN DIEGO, CA 92119
619-469-4101
Fax: 619-469-4007
info@sports-forum.com
www.sports-forum.com
• Ron Seaver, President
(619) 469-4101
r.seaver@sports-forum.com
• Erin Mooney, Communications Coordinator
(619) 469-4101
• Linsay Campbell, Operations Coordinator
(619) 469-4101
lindsay@sports-forum.com
• Bob Voight, Vice President
(619) 469-4101
• Lindsay Campbell, Director of Operations
(619) 469.4101
• Erin Mooney, Director of Communications
(619) 469.4101
• Ryan Heidrich, Marketing Department
(619) 469.4101
• Nick Gilbert, Assistant Coordinator
Nature of Service:
Produce international team and event marketing, promotions and sales conferences that bring together top team executives from both professional and collegiate sports along with leading corporate sponsors, advertisers and agencies for the purpose of networking, idea sharing and learning.
Sports Service Founded:
1994
Clients:
Budweiser, Winstead, Seachrest & Miuick, Picture U Promotion, Txtstation, Garden Fresh Restarants.
Marketing & Consulting Services:
Full service promotion and marketing agency, creating developing and executing national regional and local sponsorship campaigns within teams, sports and events.

NELLIGAN SPORTS MARKETING, INC.
150 CLOVE ROAD
LITTLE FALLS, NJ 07424
973-812-5900
Fax: 973-812-8111
• T.J. Nelligan, Chairman / Chief Executive Officer
tjn@nelligansports.com
• Tim Hofferth, President / Chief Operating Officer
timh@nelligansports.com
• Mike Palisi, SVP
mikep@nelligansports.com
• TJ Nelligan, Chairman and CEO
(973) 812-5900
tjn@nelligansports.com
• Tim Hofferth, President and Chief Operating Officer

(803) 945-2000
timh@nelligansports.com
• Mike Palisi, Executive Vice President
(973) 812-5900
mike@nelligansports.com
• Tom Varga, Senior Vice President
(973) 812-5900
tomv@nelligansports.com
• Mark Devine, Regional Senior Vice President
(973) 812-5900
mdevine@nelligansports.com
Sports Service Founded:
1999
Services:
Provides sales and marketing expertise for sports properties worldwide
Clients:
Hess, Geico, Lincoln Mercury, MBNA, Pepsi, Aeropostale, Philips, Cooper Tires, Cingular Wireless, Toyota, Nextel, 7-Up, Verizon Wireless, Gatorade, Prudential Financial, Pizza Hut, Oxford Health Plans, Frontier, AMTRAK, Hilton, U.S. Army, Coca-Cola, OppenheimerFunds, ING Finacial Institutions, Pontiac, Bank of America, US Airways, Wendy's Hamburger

NETWORK FOUNDATON TECHNOLOGIES (NFT)
818 NELSON AVENUE
RUSTON, LA 71272
318-257-5432
888-262-9611
Fax: 318-257-5283
www.nft-tv.com
• Mike O'Neal, Founder/Chief Scientist
• Marcus Morton, Co-Founder/President
• Mike o' Neal, Founder and Chief Scientist
Nature of Services:
Network Foundation Technologies (NFT) provides streaming media technology services that harness the power of distributed computing to bring the economics of traditional broadcasting to the world of online webcasting.

NEW JERSEY SPORTS PRODUCTIONS, INC./DBA MAIN EVENTS
772 UNION BOULEVARD
TOTOWA, NJ 07512
973-200-7050
Fax: 973-200-7061
dtremblay@mainevents.com
www.mainevents.com
• Jolene Mizzone, Vice President, Operations
• Kim Newman, Sports Scene Distributor
• Ellen Haley, Public Relations

NEW TIER COMMUNICATIONS
15875 N GREENWAY-HAYDEN LOOP
SUITE 109
SCOTTSDALE, AZ 85260
480-922-1711
Fax: 480-922-1733
www.newtier.com
• Michael D. Rossman, President & Chief Executive Officer
• Mark Malenfant, VP Sales
• Steve Graber, Production Manager
Description:
Provides an integrated suite of multimedia applications enabling clients to broadcast real-time marketing messages to consumers registered on the new Tier Network.
Nature of Services:

Services include development of interactive multimedia development, web site development, print and display advertising, video and audio production, screen savers and animation.

Clients:
IBM, Ticketmaster, TECO Energy, Adelphia, Ohio Health, Verizon Electronics, Fox Sports Net, SBC, Union Bank of California, US Bank, American West Airlines, TD Waterhouse, Solo, Philips, D.C. Lottery, Major Leage Baseball, National Basketball Assoc., National Hockey League, National Football League, Collegiate, Specialty, Southwest Airlines, Royals, Astros, Brewers, Cardinals, University of Utah, Emerald Downs.

Year Founded:
1994

NEWMAN COMMUNICATIONS
20 GUEST STREET
SUITE 150
BRIGHTON, MA 02135
617-254-4500
Fax: 617-923-2616
www.newmancom.com
• Bob Newman, Founder
• Robert K Newman, President
• Elise Bogdan, VP/Client Services Director
Services:
Provides public relations services specializes in literary publicity and corporate public relations necessary for planning a public relations campaigns that target specific media for any topic, and to any market.
Description:
Founded 1991. NC is a national publicity/media relations firm with a focus on sports publicity. Many clients are former athletes or sports authors.

NEXT LEVEL SPORTS, INC.
24 CATHEDRAL PLACE
SUITE 500
SAINT AUGUSTINE, FL 32084
904-810-5177
Fax: 904-810-6855
www.nextlevelsports.net
• Michael L. Garnes, Founder/President
Nature of Service:
Next Level Sports, Inc. (NLS) is a career management, job placement and consulting firm to college graduated 'scholar' student-athletes. We provide a wide range of career counseling, planning, assessment and consulting services for college and university student-athletes to help them make a seamless transition from the world of college to the business world. NLS provides 'real life' skills and proven job hunting tools through presentations, seminars and workshops. Our programs give student-athletes a laser-like focus on how to approach, develop, manage and execute effective job search with an implementation plan. We help them to level the pla
Year Founded:
1991
Consulting and Seminar Topics:
Clarifying career focus, Networking, Creating resumes and letters, Analyzing income potential, Understanding the job market, Maximizing personal apperance, Evaluating and negotiating offers. NLS

seminars are offered individually or as a series. We can also customize seminars to address the specific concerns or needs of your student-athletes.

NEXT MARKETING
2820 PETERSON PALACE
NORCROSS, GA 30071
770-225-2200
Fax: 770-225-2300
info@nextmarketing.com
www.nextmarketing.com
• Henry Rischitelli, President
• Pat Conreaux, SVP, Creative Director
• Tim Leaumont, EVP, Finance and Agency Business
Nature of Service:
Whether a brand is targeting large audiences or singling out influencers, Next Marketing creates brand experiences that make profound and lasting impressions. Event marketing, sponsorship activation, guerilla marketing, on-premise sampling and retail demonstrations are just a few areas of Next Marketing's expertise.
Year Founded:
1993
Clients:
U.S. Air Force, Air National Guard, General Motors, Community Coffee, HPE, HPI, Cox, General Tire, CDW, Webber Stevens and Ford amongst others.

NFL BUSINESS VENTURES
280 PARK AVENUE
NEW YORK, NY 10017
212-450-2000
Fax: 212-681-7573
• Roger Goodell, EVP/Chief Operating Officer
• Gary Gertzog, SVP, Business Affairs/General Counsel
• John Collins, SVP Marketing/Entertinment Programming
• Anthony Noto, Chief Financial Officer
• Kimberly A. Williams, CFO
• James W. Fields, Senior Strategic Analyst
• Paul J. Tagilabue, Consultant

NIELSEN SPORTS
85 BROAD STREET
NEW YORK, NY 10004
646-654 5000
800-864-1224
Fax: 646-654-8593
www.nielsensports.com
• Barbara Zidovsky, Director, Marketing
• Dan O'Toole, Director, New Products
• Earl Jeff, Account Manager
• Sara Erichson, General Manager, National Services
• Stephen Master, Vice President, Operations Manager Nielsen Sp
Description:
Nielsen Sports, a division of Nielsen Media Research, specializes in creating best practices for the sports sponsorship industry. Nielsen Sports is committed to providing information that is results-oriented and objective for both buyers and sellers of sports sponsorships.
Sponsorship Scorecard:
Launched in January 2005, Sponsorship Scorecard is a service that measures television audience exposure to sponsor-placed media in all televised sporting events.

FANLinks:
The FANLinks service identifies changes in brand purchase habits of sports fans.
Nielsen Sports Quarterly:
Quarterly publication that is dedicated to best practices for the sports sponsorship industry. Topics include industry articles, scorecards, buyer insights, recent announcements, and glossary of terms.
Nielsen Media Research:
Provides media research and marketing services for sports and major events. Services include national and local television information services for networks and affiliates, independent stations, syndicates, cable networks and systems, advertisers and agencies.

NORDIC GROUP INTERNATIONAL
2727 NELSON ROAD
SUITE A107
LONGMONT, CO 80503
303-579-4739
Fax: 303-652-1709
jonathan@nordicgroupinternational.com
www.nordicgroupinternational.com
• Jonathan Wiesel, Principal
jonathan@nordicgroupinternational.com
• Jonathan Wiesel, Principal
(303) 579-4739
jonathan@nordicgroupinternational.com
Year Founded:
1981.
Clients:
Cross Country Ski Areas Association, NH, Viking Nordic, VT, Methow Valley Sport Trails Association, WA, Town of Breckenridge, CO, Breckenridge Nordic, CO, Crested Butte Nordic Council, CO, Eggshells in the Coffee (dude ranch seminars), CO, Great Glen Trails Outdoor Center, NH, Winding Trails Cross Country, CT and others
Nature of Service:
Site evaluations; Feasibility studies; Resort planning; Operations audits; Business planning; Four-season trail and facility design and construction; Recreation development; Staff selection and training; Program development; Marketing; Operations; Research; Approvals and permitting

---

NUVISIONS
259-263 GOFFLE ROAD
HAWTHORNE, NJ 7506
741-327-1650
888-239-3365
Fax: 949-752-9137
• George Carter, VP, Marketing
• Billy Carter, VP, Multi-Media
• Dominic Symes, Partner/Creative Director
Services:
Provides advertising, catalogue production, identity development, packaging and digital photography.
Other Location:
80 S. Yesler Way, Ste 310, Seattle, WA 98104.
Marketing & Consulting Services:
Advertising and design studio for footwear, sporting goods, outdoor, apparel & fitness products. Emphasis is on advertising, catalogue production, identity development, packaging and digital photography.

O'CONNOR COMMUNICATIONS
333 WARWICK ROAD
LAKE FOREST, IL 60045
847-615-5462
Fax: 847-615-5465
jimo@oconnorpr.com
• James O'Connor, President
(847) 615-5462
jimo@oconnorpr.com
• Jim O'Connor, President
• Lynda O'Connor, President
Year Founded:
1989
Nature of Service:
TV and Radio interviews, Website content,
Speech writing, Press kits, Sales literature,
Newsletters, Blogs, Seminar planning, New
Product releases, Feature Stories, Case
Studies, Trade Show support, Brochures.

**OCTAGON MARKETING NORTH
AMERICA**
800 CONNECTICUT AVENUE
2ND FLOOR
NORWALK, CT 06854
203-354-7400
Fax: 203-354-7600
www.octagon.com
• Rick Dudley, President/CEO
• Phil D Picciotto, Founder & President
• Jeff Shifrin, President
• Lisa Murray, EVP
• Sean Nicholls, MD
• Simon Wardle, Chief Stratergy Officer
• Joan Cusco, President
Description:
Octagon is the world's largest sports and
entertainment representation and marketing
agency. Now affiliated with Ken Lindner &
Associates to provide clients with
multi-platform representation, and
world-class services.

OCTAGON SPORTS
7100 FOREST AVENUE
SUITE 201
RICHMOND, VA 23226
804-285-4200
Fax: 804-285-4224
www.octagon.com
• Giff Breed, Managing Director
Golf/Outdoors
• Phil De Picciotto, Founder & President
• Lisa Murray, Executive Vice President &
Chief Marketing Of
• Simon Wardle, Chief Strategy Officer
• Rick Dudley, President & CEO
Nature of Service:
Octagon is uniquely poised to provide full
service marketing solutions across the
global platform. Octagon offers client
expertise in the following areas: Angler
Representation (endorsements, clinics,
outings, appearances, licencing), Event
Management (event ownership, creation &
implementation), Sales/Property
Management (package development &
sponsorship management), Consulting
(strategic sponsorship selection, contract
negotiation, field marketing and
implementation).

OKLAHOMA EVENTS, INC.
6465 AVONDALE DRIVE
NICHOLS HILLS, OK 73116
405-842-4141
Fax: 405-842-9674

• Lee Al Allan Smith, President
Services:
Full service event marketing & advertising
Sports Service Founded:
1990
Event Management Services:
Full service event marketing & management
company, active in hockey, NBA,
equestrian, and other sports.

OLYMPIA ENTERTAINMENT, INC.
2211 WOODWARD AVENUE
4TH FLOOR
DETROIT, MI 48201
313-471-3200
Fax: 313-471-3259
Info@olympiaentertainment.com
www.olympiaentertainment.com
• Steve Facione, SVP
Services:
Provides Advertising Sales/Corporate
Partnerships, Event Booking and
Development, Event, Facility & Team
Marketing, including Publicity, Group
Services, Sponsorship Sales, Promotions,
Merchandising, Graphics, Subscriber
Services, and Ticketing, Hospitality,
Broadcasting, Merchandising, Food and
Beverage Services, Specialty Food
Concepts, Corporate Hospitality, Building
Operations: Security, Parking, Maintenance,
Public Assembly, Facility Management,
Sports Administration, Management
Consulting, and Customized Business
Communications & Presentations

Sports Service Founded:
1982
Event Management Services:
Manages Joe Louis Arena and Cobo Arena in
Detroit, MI.
Marketing & Consulting Services:
Provides full marketing, management, sales,
and booking services for Joe Louis Arena and
Cobo Arena.

ONEWORLD COMMUNICATIONS
2001 HARRISON STREET
SAN FRANCISCO, CA 94110
415-355-1935
Fax: 415-355-0295
info@owcom.com
www.owcom.com
• Jonathan Villet, Director, Strategic &
Creative Services
• Jonathan Villet, President & Founder
jonathan.villet@owcom.com
• Mark Allen, Lead Account Supervisor
• Dave Wren, Public Relations, Copywriting
• Rose Tash, Art Director
• Alex Uncapher, Online Advertising Media
Planner and Buyer
• Susan Barnes, Social Marketing/Social
Media Manager
• Jonathan Villet, Founder, President
Services:
Full Service Communications Programs,
from Planning to Evaluation, Strategic
Planning, Positioning and Branding,
Corporate Identity, Logo, Style, Marketing
Organizational Development and Training,
Call Center Service, Results Tracking and
Analysis, Copywriting, Graphic Design,
Website Design and Internet Services,
Photography, Video Production, Radio and
Television Commercials, Public Service
Announcements, Displays and Conference
Booths, Printing and Duplication, Print,

Broadcast, Outdoor, Transportation, Web,
Creative Production, Media Research and
Analysis, Negotiation, Purchasing and
Placement Tracking, Direct Mail and
Fulfillment, Respon
Clients:
UNICEF, UNFPA Zimbabwe Press kit, IFAD,
Atlanta Journal Constitution, The Age &
Good Weekend Magazine, Australia, FAO
Photo Library: permanent collection,
Gourmet Magazine Australia, St. Stephens
School, Rome, New Sociey, England,
Pinto-Peira Brazil newspaper, Brazil,
Australian Photography Yearbook, The Best
of The Age, 1980 & 1981, 125 Years The
Age Newspaper, Australia

ONSPORT STRATEGIES
8540 COLONNADE CENTER DR
RALEIGH, NC 27615-3052
919-256-1600
Fax: 919-256-1601
• Gary R Stevenson, President/Chief
Executive Officer
Description:
Consulting practice dedicated to helping its
clients leverage their investment in sports
ownership, sports marketing, and sports
television and new media.
Sports Service Founded:
1999
Clients:
American Express, National Basketball
Association(NBA), PGA Tour, Simon Brand
Ventures, Total Sports

ORIGINAL MEGAFAN
17410 MINNETONKA BOULEVARD
SUITE 164
MINNETONKA, MN 55345
952-334-4402
Fax: 952-473-2078
jonrichie@comcast.net
www.theoriginalmegafan.com
• Jon Richie, President
Nature of Services:
The MegaFan takes an ordinary,
non-revenue driving concession container
and combines it with a classic sports icon to
transform it into the ideal container for
popcorn, peanuts or chips.

OUTDOOR SPORTS MARKETING GROUP
822 LOCUST STREET
HENDERSONVILLE, NC 28792
866-893-8676
Fax: 866-336-542
info@outdoorsportsmarketing.com
www.outdoorsportsmarketing.com
Services:
Provides emerging and extreme sports
marketing and development. Offers funding
and sponsorship acquisition.

PAC-10 PROPERTIES
1021 W PICO BOULEVARD
BUILDING 103
SUITE 2146
LOS ANGELES, CA 90035
310-369-0598
Fax: 310-557-4455
www.pac-10.org
• Thomas C. Hansen, Commissioner
• Mitch Huberman, SVP, Fox Sports
Enterprises/Pac-10 Prope
(310) 369-0598
mhuberman@foxsports.net

• Renee Cohen, Marketing Manager
(310) 369-0083
• Shawn Culver, Account Executive
(310) 369-0631
Sports Service Founded:
1996
Marketing & Consulting Services:
Joint venture between FOX Sports Net and the Pac-10 collegiate conference. Manages all aspects of Conference marketing, including licensing, merchandising, publications and special events. Coordinates with Fox Sports Net Sales in developing integrated marketing platforms for advertisers targeting adults 18-24 and 25-54 in some of the strongest DMA's (Demographics) in the country.
Services:
Manages all aspects of Conference marketing, including licensing, merchandising, publications and special events.
Clients:
Champion, Classic Sportswear, Electronic Arts, Fotoball, Killian Athletics, Nutmeg Mills, Sony, Spotlight, Stadium Sports, Whirley, Gear For Sports

PAOLISSO & ASSOCIATES, INC.
9051 BALTIMORE NATIONAL PIKE
ELLICOTT CITY, MD 21042
410-465-8930
• Paul Paolisso, President
Services:
Offers Sponsorship sales and event marketing. Produces sports programming for syndication, cable and non-broadcast use. Packages and markets sports properties and events

PARADIGM CONSULTING
26 RADCLIFFE DRIVE
GETZVILLE, NY 14068
716-688-1808
stephen@paradigmconsulting.ca
www.paradigmconsulting.ca
Services:
Provides business development, strategic planning, marketing and process consulting to indoor and outdoor sports and entertainment facility owners, operators, and developers of municipal, private and intercollegiate venues.

PATTERSON SPORTS VENTURES
2206 E LINCOLN DRIVE
SUITE 102
PHOENIX, AZ 85016
602-468-9700
Coach@Carlette.com
www.carlette.com
• Jack Sullivan, Creative Director
• Carlette Patterson, Founder/CEO
coach@carlette.com
• Dr. ralph Pim, 3D Coach
• Jackie R. Hutt, Player Development
• Elizabeth Lennon, Sports Life coach
Services:
Assists professional athletes develop, design and implement a Game Plan for life after the League. Specializes in marketing, management and special events, which includes, broadcast rights packaging, sponsorship sales, corporate imaging, board development, and community outreach and education.
Clients:

The Robert Wood Johnson Foundation, The Sports Philanthropy Project, The Athlete Legacy Network, Arizona State University, Phoenix Suns, Arizona Cardinals, Grand Canyon State Games, Fox Sports Net Arizona, Channel 3/Arizona Family.com, Arizona Republic, The Arizona Interscholastic Association, Arizona Tourism and Sports Authority, Cox Communications, Arizona Department of Health Services/Tobacco Education & Prevention Program, Blue Cross Blue Shield Arizona, Gatorade, Arizona Department of Commerce - Office of Sports Promotion, and Tempe Sports Authority
Sports Service Founded:
1998
Nature of Sports Service:
A full-service agency specializing in marketing, management and special events. Organization focus is on youth and community based sports programs and initiatives. Also has extensive experience in broadcast rights packaging, sponsorship sales, corporate imaging, board development, and community outreach and education. Expanded business to include life coaching for athletes transitioning from the League to life and adults transitioning from success to significance.

PCA WORLDWIDE, INC.
23 MALA COMPRA ROAD
PALM COAST, FL 32137
386-446-8721
PCAF@PCAFhq.org
www.pcafhq.org
Marketing & Consulting Services:
A full service sports marketing, public relations and ad agency specializing in unique golf products & video production. Exclusive agent and lobbyist for the Tour Caddies Association Worldwide. Diverse, integrated marketing opportunities & database marketing.

PCGCAMPBELL
3200 GREENFIELD
SUITE 280
DEARBORN, MI 48120
313-336-9000
www.pcgcampbell.com
• David Scheinberg, President/Chief Executive Officer
(313) 336-9000
• John Scodellaro, Chief Financial Officer
(313) 336-9000
• Cheryl Kohs, Vice President Event Management
(313) 336-9000
• Kevin Kennedy, Vice President Public Relations
(313) 203-7108
Nature of Service:
Product marketing; public relations such as mass media and business-to-business publicity, corporate goodwill and community presence programs, professional sports media relations, product launches, event and program publicity.

PENN STATE SPORTS MARKETING
621 MAINSTREAM DRIVE, SUITE 230
NASHVILLE, TN 37228
615-742-6100
800-346-9467
Fax: 615-742-6124

PERFORMANCE PROMOTIONS SPORT PROMOTIONS
2010 NE 7TH AVENUE
PO BOX 350067
DANIA, FL 33004
954-462-3235
Fax: 954-462-3240
• David Benson, Operations Director
Sports Service Founded:
1986
Marketing & Consulting Services:
Specializes in motorsports marketing. Handles all aspects of sponsorship from inception to implementation, providing all services from publicity to team management.

PERFORMANCE RESEARCH
25 MILL STREET
QUEEN ANNE SQUARE
NEWPORT, RI 02840
401-848-0111
Fax: 401-848-0110
www.performanceresearch.com
• Jed Pearsall, President
jed@performanceresearch.com
• Bill Doyle, VP
bill@performanceresearch.com
• Marc Porter, Observational Research Manager
mporter@performanceresearch.com
• Larry Shannon-Missal, Reports Manager
Services:
Provide consulting services in order to maximize spending and ensure an appropriate match between corporate marketing objectives and proposed sponsorship packages such as On-Site/Event Research, Telephone Research, Focus Groups, On-Line Research, Web-based Sponsorships, Observational Research, Research in a box, Interantional Research and Sponsorship Consulting
Clients:
Cirque de Soleil, Daytona Properties, ESPN, Head of the Charles Regatta, Indy Racing League MLS, NCAA, Simon Properties, TNT, WTA,WTT WWE, X Games, Anheuser-Busch, AT&T, Bank of America, BF Goodrich, BP Amoco, Clorox, Coca-Cola, Colgate-Palmolive, Coors Brewing Company, Country Financial, Discover Card, Ford, General Foods, General Mills, General Motors, Harley Davidson, Hartford Insurance, Honda, Hyundai, KeyCorp, Kimberly Clark, Kodak, Lowes, Masterfoods, MCI Worldcom, Miller Brewing Company, Motorola, Nestle, Nike, Nissan, NTL, Ocean Spray, Pepsi-Cola, Philips Electronics, RJR, Saturn, Saucony, SmithKline Beecham, Sperry Topsider
Custom/Syndicated Studies:
Full-Service evaluation of cost, reach and impact of corporate sponsored sports and special events through proprietary and syndicated research studies. Focus group research of targeted sports audiences.
Consulting Services:
Provide consulting services related to event selection in order to maximize spending and ensure an appropriate match between corporate marketing objectives and proposed sponsorship packages.
Other Location:
95 Wilton Road, STE 375, London, UK IBZ; Phone: +44(0) 149I-410-822 Fax: +44(0) 20-7401-9234

Year Founded:
1985

PGI, INC.
220 WEST 42ND STREET
10TH FLOOR
NEW YORK, NY 10036
646-445-7000
Fax: 646-445-7001
• Lee Rubenstein, President/Chief
Operating Officer
• Cindy Bell, EVP Meeting Services
Services:
The development of event marketing plans, sponsorship packages, sales strategies and solicitation plans for event or sports properties. Creation, design and management of promotional event concepts, displays and attractions and hospitality facilities for corporations and sports properties.
Event Management Services:
Creation, design and management of promotional event concepts, displays and attractions and hospitality facilities for corporations and sports properties.
Sports Service Founded:
1989
Other Location:
Atlanta Office: 5775 Peachtree Dunwoody Road, Bldg B, Ste 260, Atlanta, GA 30342; 404 256-1336; FAX: 404 256-1922

PHILLIPS MARKETING
1001 COOPER PT. RD. SW
SUITE 140-#189
OLYMPIA, WA 98502
360-596-9092
Fax: 360-596-9093
www.phillipsmarketing.net
• Robert B. Phillips, President
Sports Service Founded:
1989
Marketing & Communication Services:
Marketing, advertising, public relations, sales promotion, direct marketing, research, sales motivation, specializing in sports and sporting goods.

PHOTO FILE
333 NORTH BEDFORD ROAD
SUITE 130
MOUNT KISCO, NY 10549
914-375-6000
800-346-1678
Fax: 914-375-6009
customerservice@photofile.com
www.photofile.com
• Charles Singer, President
• Bill Cook, Chief Financial Officer
• Bryan Reilly, Photo Editor
Sports Service Founded:
1987
Services:
Manufactures licensed sports photography.
Clients:
Major League Baseball, the NBA and WNBA, NHL, NFL, and their respective player associations, as well as thousands of individual athletes.
Products:
Double Mat Mounted 8x10 Photos, Framed 8x10 Photos, Custom 11 x 14 and 16 x 20 Enlargements, Photoramics (12 x 36) Photos and Milestone & Memories-Double Matted Triple Image Commemorative.
Marketing & Consulting Services:

Specializes in the marketing and sales of sports photography, licensing with all major sports organizations including MLB, NFL, NBA, NHL, NASCAR in photos, key chains, plaques, and posters. Extensive photo library. Develops sports marketing and promotional programs for corporate clients through PF marketing services.

PITCH PR
39-43 BREWER STREET
LONDON, ENGLAND W1F 9UD
+44-(0) 20 7494 1616
Fax: 20-7437-5262
info@pitch.co.uk
www.pitch.co.uk
• Henry Chappell, Managing Director
henry@pitchpr.co.uk
Year Founded:
2001
Services:
Innovative public relations and marketing company specializing in representing sports-related clients - be it sponsorship activation, personalities, sponsorship consultancy and campaigns for clients. consumer PR, sponsorship activation, corporate PR, sports PR, personalities, sponsorship consultancy

PLAYMAKER SPORTS ADVISORS
500 GRANT STREET
SUITE 5000
PITTSBURGH, PA 15219-2507
412-454-5000
Fax: 412-281-0717
phinfo@pepperlaw.com
www.pepperlaw.com
• Chuck Greenberg, President/Chief Executive Officer
Description:
Provides corporate, litigation and regulatory legal services to leading businesses, governmental entities, non-profit organizations and individuals throughout the nation and the world.
Services:
Assists owners and prospective owners of sports franchises with sports transaction structuring and negotiations
Other Locations:
100 Renaissance Center, 36th Floor, Detroit, MI 48243; Phone: 313-259-7110; 1180 Avenue of the Americas, 14th Floor, New York, NY 10036; Phone: 212-899-5090; 5 Park Plaza, Suite 1700, Irvine, CA 92614; Phone: 949-567-3500; Hamilton Square, 600 Fourteenth Street NW, Washington, DC 20005; Phone: 202-220-1200; Hercules Plaza, STE 5700, 1313 Market Place, P.O. Box 1709, Wilmington, DE 19899; Phone: 302-777-6500

PLB SPORTS
PENN CENTER W
BUILDING 3, SUITE 411
PITTSBURGH, PA 15276
412-787-8800
877-PLB-SPRT
Fax: 412-787-8745
info@plbsports.com
www.plbsports.com
• Ty Ballou, President
(412) 322-9409
info@plbsports.com
• Melissa Heher, Marketing VP

(412) 787-8800
info@plbsports.com
Description:
Marketer of Flutie Flakes named after Doug Flutie of the Buffalo Bills, and Ed's End Zone O's - A cereal named after Ed McCaffrey of the Denver Broncos.
Products:
Food products featuring athletes from the NFL, MLB, NBA, and NHL. Most recognized for the development and launch of Flutie Flakes for Doug Flutie and the Doug Flutie Foundation for Autism. Manages every aspect of its sports products from product development, sourcing through retail sales, marketing and public relations.
Brands:
Dan Marino, Ben Roethlisberger, David Ortiz, Carmelo Anthony, Doug Flutie, Ed McCaffrey, Pedro Martinez, Jerome Bettis, Bettis The Bus Barbecue Sauce, Bettis The Bus Mustard, Bettis The Bus Peanut Butter, Bettis The Bus Salsa, Bettis TheBus Pickles, Bucs Mustard, Buffalo Bills Mustard, Buffalo Bills Mustard, Dawg Pound FoodLine, Dilger'sDijon Mustards, Ed McCaffrey's Eddie Mac&Cheese, Ed McCaffrey'sEndzone O's, Elway's Comeback Crunch, Falcons Mustard, Flutie Flakes, Flutie Flakes, Flutie Flakes SuperCharged, Flutie Fruitie, Grid Iron Fruit Snacks, Hines Ward 86 Steak Sauce, Holcomb's Hometown BBQ Sauce, Holcomb's Hometown Mustards, HotRod's
Sports Service Founded:
1996

POC MEDIA SPORTS & ENTERTAINMENT DIVISION
511 LINDSEY DRIVE
PATRICK O' CONNOR
WAYNE, PA 19087
610-636-5805
Fax: 610-971-0261
www.pocmedia.com
• Ashley Downey, General Manager
• Pat O'Connor, Contact
(610) 636-5805
pat.oconnor@pocmedia.com
Services:
Integrated Marketing and Branding Initiatives, Development of Web Site, Multimedia and Interactive Marketing Communications Tools, Event Management, Planning and Staging and Non-Traditional Promotion for the Entertainment Industry

PORTER NOVELLI
250 GREENWICH STREET
36TH FLOOR
NEW YORK, NY 10007
212-601-8000
Fax: 212-601-8101
Darlan.Monterisi@porternovelli.com
www.porternovelli.com
• Anthony T Viceroy, President/Chief Financial Officer
(212) 601-8311
anthony.viceroy@porternovelli.com
• Gary Stockman, CEO
(212) 601-8114
gary.stockman@us.porternovelli.com
• Mike Gehb, Chief Financial Officer
mike.gehb@porternovelli.com
• Greg Waldron, Chief Talent Officer
greg.waldron@porternovelli.com
• Karen Van Bergen, CEO

Marketing & Consulting Services:
Public relations firm.
Services:
Strategic Planning & Research, Media & Influencer Relations, Multicultural, Alliance Building, Advertising & Corporate Identity, Direct Marketing, Interactive, Sports Marketing, CRM, Crisis & Issues
Clients:
Dannon, Gillette, Kellogg, Nissan, Schering-Plough, Tambrands and Wrigley's.
Sports Service Founded:
1972

PORTER PERFORMANCE SYSTEMS
PO BOX 5584
EUGENE, OR 97405
541-342-6875
kayporter1@comcast.net
www.thementalathlete.com
• Kay Porter, Owner
(541) 342-6875
kayporter1@comcast.net
Sports Service Founded:
1983
Description:
Author, The Mental Athlete, Inner Training for Peak Performance, 2nd Edition (2000).
Marketing & Consulting Services:
Conducts sports psychology and mental training for peak performance seminars/workshops/clinics for athletes, teams, coaches and youths. General motivational speaking programs for companies and groups. Also offers wide range of seminars specializing in corporate fitness, mental training for peak performance, team building, customer relations, peak sales performance, conflict resolution and thriving on change. Also offers individual counseling/consultations for athletes and coaches.

POWER IMAGES
2333 STIRLING ROAD
FT LAUDERDALE, FL 33312
954-966-0260
800-207-9486
Fax: 954-963-2971
service@powerimages.com
• Mark Gompertz, SVP Video Services
(954) 966-0260
mark@medialab.tv
• Nadine Floyd, Jr, President, Operations
Services:
Provides design, digital photography and on demand printing, event signage and web sites. Provides video production services to corporations and television. Staging and production for on-site meetings and events.
Clients:
Power Images Media Lab produces marketing support materials for a large and prestigious client base. A partial list includes The Miami Dolphins, Spherion, Arby's, Motorola, DHL, Revlon, Concord Camera, Hunter Douglas, LaSalle Brokers, Convergsys, The Hackett Group

PREMIER PARTNERSHIPS
1148 4TH STREET
SANTA MONICA, CA 90403
310-656-2500
Fax: 310-656-2590
www.premierpartnerships.com
• Alan Rothenberg, Chairman
Alan@PremierPartnerships.com

• Randy Bernstein, President/Chief Operating Officer
Randy@PremierPartnerships.com
• Christopher Pepe, Western Operations VP
• Todd Parker, Eastern Operations VP
Todd@PremierPartnerships.com
• Alan I. Rothenberg, Chairman
• Randy Bernstein, President & CEO
• Jeff Marks, Managing Director
• Stephanie Cheng, Vice President, Marketing Services
• Todd Ferderer, Director, Finance
Nature of Sports Service:
Agency formed by top soccer executives that focuses on including sponsorship, marketing, naming rights and venue management.
Services:
Stadium/Venue Naming Rights Sales, Sports, Entertainment & Civic Sponsorship Sales, Broadcast Media & Internet Sales, Premium Ticket and Suite Sales, Sponsorship Sales Training Counsel on Prospective Opportunities, Sponsorship Analyses, Sponsorship Negotiation, Program Implementation Stadium/Venue Naming Rights, Sponsorship of stadium or property
Clients:
Rose Bowl, Major League Soccer, NBA, SUM, Pizza Hut Park, The Bard Capital Challenge, Hunt Sports Group, Los Angeles Dodgers, Kroenke Sports Enterprises, Clippers, Los Angeles Angels, Minnesota Timberwolves, Minnesota Twins, Lowes, MasterCard, Yahoo, Rochester Rhino Soccer, Worcester IceCats, Colorado Rapids, FC Dallas, The Fresno Grizzlies, Sacramento RiverCats, HBCU, Jacksonville, NAIA, Toronto Argonauts, North Texas Soccer, Music Center Speaker Series, Long Beach International Marathon, HOK, ASA Events, BlackHawk Marketing, Hoop It Up, Milwaukee Bucks, USL, Full, NTRA, Starfire Sports
Other Location:
New York

PREMIER SPORTS MANAGEMENT, INC.
7450 W 130TH STREET
SUITE 360
OVERLAND PARK, KS 66214
913-681-6990
Fax: 913-681-8864
www.premiersportsonline.com
• Gary Heise, President/Chief Operating Officer
gheise@premiersportsonline.com
• Lamar Hunt, Owner Sports Franchises
Marketing & Consulting Services:
Provides a full-service menu of marketing and communications services to sports properties, encompassing professional, amateur, corporate and private sectors. Services include sports marketing and promotions, event management, public relations, video production, creative services.
Services:
Provides a full-service include event management, marketing/communications, sponsorships, video production, and creatice services
Clients:
National Football League, Major League Soccer, National Collegiate Athletic Association (NCAA), Top Regional Clients:Kansas City Chiefs (NFL), Dallas

Cowboys (NFL), Kansas City Wizards (MLS), Dallas Burn (MLS), Kansas City Royals (MLB), Big 12 Conference and University of Missouri. Corporate Sports Partners: Gatorade, Nike, New York Life, Pro Player, Nickelodeon, Associated Wholesale Grocers, Cellular One, Southwestern Bell, Time-Warner, Midland Dairy Association and American Airlines

PRINCE MARKETING GROUP
18 CARILLON CIRCLE
LIVINGSTON, NJ 7039
973-325-0800
800-987-7462
800-98-PRINCE
Fax: 973-243-0037
helpdesk@princemarketinggroup.com
www.princemarketinggroup.com
• Darren Prince, President/CEO
dprince@princemarketinggroup.com
• Steve Simon, Vice President and Talent representation
• Nicholas Cordasco, Talent representation
• Reggie Dance, Contact
• Daren Prince, President and CEO
(212) 585-0973
Nature of Service:
Full service sports and celebrity marketing firm. Public Appearances, Product Placement, Autograph Signing Sessions, Charity Events, Fantasy Camps and Tournaments available for athletes, Grand Openings and Promotions, Licensing and Product Endorsements, Motivational Speakers, Print Advertisements and Commercials and Voice-overs
Sports Service Founded:
1998
Clients:
Earin 'Magic' Johnson, Dennis Rodman, Hulk Hogan, Joe Frazier, Evel Knievel, Roy Jones Jr, Vinny Pazienza, Dave Winifield, Jenny McCarthy, Carmen Electra, Pamela Anderson, Nicollette Sheridan, Stacy Kiebler, Vince Neil, Marcus Schenkenberg, Brande Roderick, Symone Maree, Dave Prowse, Corbin Bernsen, Chuck Zito.

PRO MOTION, INC.
18405 EDISON AVENUE
CHESTERFIELD, MO 63005
314-997-0101
Fax: 314-997-6831
info@promotion1.com
www.promotion1.com
• Steve Randazzo, President
steve.randazzo@promotion1.com
Services:
Assist agencies in putting their Clients' products in the hands of potential customers where they live, work and play. Create the link between a Brand's advertising and its purchase with live commercials.
Clients:
Bandai, Gundam Invasion, Black & Decker, PartyMate Party Patrol, SnakeLight Tour, Bud Light, Bubble Zone, Maxim XXposure, Budweiser, NASCAR Brew Crew Challenge, SAM's CLUB Road Show, Wal-Mart and SAM's Club Grand Openings, Winner's Circle, Busch, Big Jake Million, Dollar Fish, Know Your Busch Racing
Description:
An independent, event/field/mobile marketing agency. Initiates personal encounters between consumers and products.

Sports Service Founded:
1995

PRO-REP, INC.
PO BOX 13176
CHESAPEAKE, VA 23325
757-222-9977
Fax: 330-308-8410
www.pro-rep.com
• Corinne Mastronardi, President
• Ellis Gillespie, Player Relations VP
• Loretta Journey, Accounting Manager
• Christopher Zambar, Player Protective Services Vice President
Description:
Full service marketing agency.
Services:
Corporate services include providing professional athletes for: Player Appearances, Player Endorsements, Speaking Engagements, Autographed Collectibles. Contract Negotiation, Pursuance of Endorsement Opportunities, Marketing and Public Relations (Public Persona Development, Press Conferences, Press Releases), Financial Analysis (Budget Structuring, Income Tax Planning and Preparation, Insurance Coverage Analysis, Retirement Planning), Personal Services (Supervised off-season conditioning and diets; Concierge services, including temporary housing, transportation rentals, event tickets, limousine service)
Other Location:
South Florida Mid-Atlantic, PO Box 21234, Fort Lauderdale, FL 33335. 877-776-7376

PROFESSIONAL SPORTS MARKETING, INC.
2300 W WHITE AVENUE
MCKINNEY, TX 75071
214-544-0500
Fax: 214-544-0505
psm@professionalsportsmarketing.com
www.professionalsportsmarketing.com
• Kent Kramer, President
psm@professionalsportsmarketing.com
• Kurt Kramer, VP
Services:
Research, Creative Planning, Project Design and Implementation, Event Production and Staging, Sponsorship Evaluation and Negotiation, Sponsorship Sales, Public and Media Relations, Program Evaluation and Incentive Sports Travel. Totally integrated sports concept for sports events marketing, promotional programs, setup merchandising and advertising. Sports marketing consulting for corporate clients. Sports incentive travel programs including development and production of corporate.
Services:
Sport Marketing and Advertising
Clients:
Fritolay, Pepsi, Trimega, Ash Almond Associates
Sports Service Founded:
1985
Event Management Services:
Advertising and sales promotion. Specializes in special project events including project design, creative planning, research and event production, sponsorship evaluation and negotiation, public and media relations, program evaluation, incentive travel at major sporting events.

PROJECT SPORTS MARKETING
412 E MADISON STREET
SUITE 1218
TAMPA, FL 33602
813-442-4049
Fax: 509-756-3907
• Robert M. Bruni, Vice President Sales
(813) 442-4007
• Alan Weiss, Marketing Executive
(813) 442-4003
• Gabriel Guerrero, Sports Property Manager
(813) 442-4009
• Zach Levine, Creative Director
(813) 442-4006
Services:
Specializing in sports promotions, public relations and marketing services, including consultation with firms pursuing sports marketing strategies.
Event Management Services:
Event sponsorship negotiations.
Sports Service Founded:
1988

PROMARK ADVERTISING, INC.
3030 RED HILL AVENUE
COSTA MESA, CA 92626
714-641-1973
Fax: 714-641-3540
www.promarkadvertisinginc.com
• Brad Pilz, President
• David Major, Account Services
• Brad Pilz, President
Services:
Planning, development and activation of mobile marketing programs, product demonstrations, dealer/retail promotions, contests, sweepstakes, hospitality and special events, creative development and production of exhibit properties, signage, specialty advertising, promotional materials, tour logistics, event staffing, venue and sponsorship negotiation.
Description:
National promotional field-marketing company. Their expertise is in the development and implementation of strategic, fully integrated, experiential mobile marketing programs.
Sports Service Founded:
1981
Industry Expertise:
Automotive, motorcycles, marine, automotive aftermarket, consumer electronics, food and beverage

PROMONDE
12 CROMBIE STREET
SALEM, MA 1970
978-744-2654
• David Pelletier, President
(781) 639-8369
• Roland J. Regan Jr, Principal
(781) 639-8369
Marketing & Consulting Services:
A sports marketing and events development management firm. Events include the Mayors Cup racing series. Ride America, and Action Lounge. ProMonde provides strategic market planning, sponsorship development, experiential marketing events, investment analysis, public relations, media negotiations, etc. The organization also represents entertainers and or athletes. Affiliated with the Cuban Charitable Classics CCC. CCC is a 501C3 charitable entity

which promotes and directs sporting events in Cuba for Cuban charity.

PROMOSPORT
76 CLARK ROAD
PO BOX 985
STOWE, VT 5672
802-253-5155
Fax: 802-253-9240
www.promosport.com
Sports Service Founded:
1981.
Marketing & Consulting Services:
Advises and performs independent contractor projects for sports marketing companies and public relation agencies; Event management and promotion; marketing and communication services for sports events.

PROMOTION EVENT & HOSPITALITY EXCHANGE
17212 N SCOTTSDALE ROAD
SUITE 1272
SCOTTSDALE, AZ 85255
480-699-8766

PROPERTYPORT
580 WHITE PLAINS ROAD
SUITE 620
TARRYTOWN, NY 10591
914-729-7231
866-729-7355
Fax: 914-729-7201
www.property-port.com
• Chris Thompson, Vice President Valuation Services
• Mark F. Rockefeller, Board Chairman/CEO
Nature of Sports Services:
Organization is an application service provider to consumer marketing companies and their agencies that assists in crunching down the time consuming and costly offline processes that impede sponsorship evaluation. The mission of SponsorAid is to provide the necessary analytics that facilitate sponsorship proposal decision-making and negotiation for both sponsors and properties.
Sports Service Founded:
2001

PROSPORTS MVP
225 E. CHEYENNE MOUNTAIN BOULEVARD
SUITE 202
COLORADO SPRINGS, CO 80906
719-227-3920
Fax: 719-227-3922
general@prosportsmvp.com
www.prosportsmvp.com
• David Chavez, President, CEO
dchavez@prosportsmvp.com
• Mark Morley, Vice President
• Brian Lee, Director
blee@prosportsmvp.com
Nature of Service:
Pro Sports MVP is a full-service marketing firm that specializes in events and promotions which features sports and entertainment personalities. We also provide marketing services for over one thousand of the sports world's most recognizable and enduring athletes as well as a host of Hollywood stars.
Year Founded:
1998

PSP SPORTS MARKETING
519 EIGHTH AVENUE
NEW YORK, NY 10018
212-697-1460
Fax: 212-286-8154
www.pspsports.com
• Martin Lewis, Executive Vice President
Business Development
(301) 315-0181
mlewis@pspsports.com
• David Gerschwer, Executive VP
(212) 697-1460
dgerschwer@pspsports.com
• Doug Kimmel, Marketing and Promotions
VP
dkimmel@pspsports.com
Services:
Provides marketers with a menu of fully
integrated services and marketing solutions
including print media, golf properties, sports
marketing services, custom publishing,
corporate hospitality and online media.
Clients:
Becks, Suzuki, Century 21, Thompson's
Waterseal
Sports Service Founded:
1971
Marketing & Consulting Services:
Full-service marketing agency handling the
development and implementation of a wide
range of sports-related promotional
programs, including sweepstakes, special
events, consumer promotions, point of sale,
sampling, single sponsor publications,
corporate hospitality and trade incentives.
Uniquely capable of coordinating
promotional programs with leading
professional and collegiate sporting events
across the country.
Other Locations:
New England Region: 151 Merrimac Street
#200, Boston, MA 02114. 617-367-5955;
FAX: 617-367-5831, Southeast Region:
3226 Leslie Lane, Atlanta, GA 30345.
770-414-9810; FAX: 770-414-9813, Midwest
Region: 20 North Wacker Drive, Suite 1330,
Chicago, IL 60606. 312-899-8098; FAX:
312-899-1252, Southwest Region: 12870
Hillcrest Road H226, Dallas, TX 75230.
972-387-2055; FAX: 972-387-2061, West
Region: 5200 West Century Boulevard,
Suite 810, Los Angeles, CA 90045.
310-410-5280; FAX: 310-342-7159

PUBLICIS DIALOG CHICAGO
111 E WACKER DRIVE
CHICAGO, IL 60601
312-552-4600
Fax: 312-552-4650
• Rose Ann Anschuetz, President / Chief
Executive Officer
(312) 522-4602
• Paul Fullmer, Chairman
(312) 373-7090
Description:
Full service public relations organization &
consultancy.
Services:
Research and strategic planning, media
relations, issues management, investor
relations, event and contest management,
and culinary services.
Clients:
ABC Radio, Abbott Labs, American
Express, Centers for Disease Control and
Prevention, Church and Dwight, ConAgra,
Geyser Peak Winery, Hewlett-Packard,
Microsoft, Nestlâ€š, Principal Financial

Group, Purina, Safeway Supermarkets,
Samsung, Siemens, Travelweb,
UnitedHealthcare, United Soybean Board,
Whirlpool
Other Location:
Washington DC

PUBLICIS NEW YORK
950 3RD AVENUE
7TH FLOOR
NEW YORK, NY 10001
212-279-6950
Fax: 212-279-5560
www.publicis-usa.com
• Gill Duff, President / Chief Executive
Officer
• Debbie Yount, Chief Executive Officer
(212) 279-5815
• David Corr, EVP / Executive Creative
Director
david.corr@publicis-usa.com
• Marta LaRock, EVP / Brand Planning
Director
Services:
Creates highly acclaimed advertising
campaigns such as research and strategic
planning, media relations, issues
management, investor relations, event and
contest management, and culinary services
to a wide range of industries.
Clients:
Ad Council, Amstel Light, Bermuda Tourism,
BMW, Citizen, The Coca-Cola Company,
Coinstar, Computer Discount Warehouse,
COnsumer Electronics Association,
Cranberry Marketing Committee, Urves,
Denny's, DISH Network, FujiFilm, General
Mills, GlaxoSmithKline, Hazelnut Council,
Heifer International, Heineken,
Hewlett-Packard, ISE, Kraft, L'Orâ€šal,
Legg Mason, Marriot Hotels, Nestlâ€š,
Pernord Ricard, Power BAr, Procter &
Gamble, Real Networks, Ross Products,
Safeco, Sanofi-Aventis, Sara Lee, Siemens,
Simon Property Group, TBS, T-Mobile,
Thomson/RCA, Tumi, UBS, United Soybean
Board, United Way, Vault, Washington's
Lottery, Whirlpool, Wyeth
Marketing & Consulting Services:
Advertising and marketing communications.

PUBLICITY MATTERS
14644 MCKNEW ROAD
BURTONSVILLE, MD 20866
301-385-2090
www.publicitymatters.net
Services:
Full service public relations such publicity,
media relations, media buying and media
tours specializing in entertainment and
sports events.

QUALITY REPETITION, THE
611 OLD WILLETS PATH
HAUPPAUGE, NY 11788-4105
631-232-1588
Services:
Provides guidance to athletes in all
professional sports to create balanced
physique that is more resistant to incidence
and/or severity of on-the-field injury and
improve physical ability to compete in
specific sports.
Sports Service Founded:
1988

R. PANIAGUA, INC.
9 E 38TH STREET
SUITE 901
NEW YORK, NY 10016
212-679-6755
Fax: 212-679-6757
www.rpaniagua.com
• Ralph Paniagua, President
(212) 679-6755
• Ralph A Paniagua Jr., President & CEO
Services:
Provides quality, integrated,
media-leveraged Latino marketing
community programs, tracks record of
tying-in promotional marketing efforts with
publishing, broadcast and grassroots
programs that deliver measurable results to
corporate partners.
Sports Service Founded:
1988
Athlete Management Services:
Promotion of Latino sports personalities for
corporate sponsors, tying in with major
sporting events and community projects.
Promoters of major world Champion title
fights on pay-per-view and closed circuit.
Major League Baseball/stadium tie-ins,
including the New York Yankees.
Event Management Services:
Manages events at baseball and other
sports stadiums and sports facilities, small
and large in capacity. Extensively involved
in promotional events in the Hispanic
market. Creates grassroots corporate
promotional campaigns for boxing, baseball
and soccer events. Broadcast rights holders
of the Baseball Winter Leagues Caribbean
World Series (TV, Cable).
Marketing & Consulting Services:
Hispanic marketing tied to retail and all
levels of sports, including professional, on a
regional and national level. Also provides
international sports marketing. Creates and
implements sports media and programs that
increase the self-worth of Latinos, while
delivering measurable success for corporate
partners.

R.B. ROBERTSON & COMPANY
1350 COLLEGE POINT
WINTER PARK, FL 32789-5700
407-647-3963
800-835-7212
Fax: 407-644-1374
www.rbrobertson.com
• Randall B Robertson, President / Chief
Executive Officer
(407) 647-3963
Sports Service Founded:
1987
Services:
Organization offers solutions to corporations
to leverage golf events, specialize in
corporate events, charity events, business
golf seminars, and major championship
hospitality.
Clients:
EMC, Fannie Mae, Golfweek, ITG Inc.,
Jefferies & Company, JPMorgan Chase,
Lanny Wadkins, Marriott, McKesson HBOC,
Pfizer Consumer Healthcare,
Schering-Plough Corporation, Terrabrook,
Trammell Crow Company, Thomas Weisel
Partners
Services:
Corporate Events, Major Championships
Hospitality, The Masters, Celebrity

Appearances, Business Golf Seminars, Charity Events

RACING ENTERPRISES MOTOCROSS
13223 BLACK MOUNTAIN ROAD
SUITE 1-176
SAN DIEGO, CA 92129
858-484-1441
Fax: 858-484-7056
www.remsatmx.com
• Frank Thomason, President
Services:
Promotes motocross racing
Description:
Helps promote pro and amateur riders from across the world.
Event Management Services:
Promotes motocross racing at Carlsbad Raceway.
Sports Service Founded:
1986

RADIAN 1
824 W.SUPERIOR STREET
SUITE 205
CHICAGO, IL 60642
312-492-9333
Fax: 312-372-0682
www.robinsonmaites.com
• Alan Maites, President
• Ryan Jarol, Vice President, Account director
• Paul Woolf, Vice President, Strategy and planning
• Bob Neff, Executive Creative Director
• Lowell Wallace, Account Director,Strategy
Marketing & Consulting Services:
Full service, fully integrated sports and events consulting. Program development, execution and sponsorship sales.
Services:
Involvement and Action Incentives, Sales and Retailer Programs, Account-Specific Programs, Co-Marketing Programs, Merchandising, Site Design, Online Training/Education, E-mail Campaigns, On/Off Line Integration, Offline to Online Traffic Drivers, Text Message Marketing, Interactive Kiosks, Database Marketing - Development & Maintenance, Design and Modeling, Response Analysis, Direct Mail, List Acquisition, Relationship Marketing, Lead Generation and Qualification, Cross Sell and Upsell Marketing, Meeting and Convention ROI Optimization, Sports/Entertainment, Mobile Marketing, Sponsorship Activation and Leveraging, Product Sampling and Demonst
Clients:
BMG, Clorox, DHL, Discover Financial Services, MB Financial Bank, Minuteman International, Nakano, Nestle, Rand McNally, Sara Lee Intimates, Verizon Communications, Visa, World Space, Make A Wish Foundation, Big Brothers/Big Sisters, Better Business Bureau

RADIUS GROUP, INC.
545 E WESTFIELD BOULEVARD
INDIANAPOLIS, IN 46220
317-205-3500
Fax: 317-205-3501
• Kevin A. Davey, President
Description:
Manufacturer and martketers of die-cast replics vehicles for sporting and other evetns. Among recent custom die-cast

projects include: Indianapolis 500, Indy Racing League, NASCAR, Minor Baseball, Kentucky Derby and more.

RAYCOM SPORTS
1900 W MOREHEAD STREET
SUITE 200
CHARLOTTE, NC 28208
704-378-4400
www.raycomsports.com
• Ken Haines, President / Chief Executive Officer
(704) 378-4400
khaines@raycomsports.com
• De Cordell, Sales and Marketing VP / ACC Properties
dcordell@raycomsports.com
• Brian Flajole, Golf & Business Development VP
(916) 645-7200
bflajole@raycomsports.com
• Ken Haines, President & CEO
• Jimmy Rayburn, Chief Operating Officer
• George Johnson, Senior Vice President
• Rob Reichley, Executive Producer
Services:
Leader in marketing, producing and distributing sports program and creating, managing and distributing special events

RCA GROUP EVENT MARKETING + MANAGEMENT
2310 W 75TH STREET
PRAIRIE VILLAGE, KS 66208
913-384-8920
Fax: 913-384-8921
www.rcagroup.com
• Russ Cline, President
russ@rcagroup.com
• Tom Boehm, Administration and Finance EVP
tom@rcagroup.com
• Mike Mathis, Operations EVP
• David Pulford, EVP
Services:
A sports and entertainment production/promotion company which provides turnkey event production/activation, sponsor management and marketing promotions services.
Marketing & Consulting Services:
Consults with businesses on marketing and managing sponsorships, sports and entertainment involvement.
Event Management Services:
Marketing, management and promotion firm providing event production, marketing, promotion, and operations for entertainment and sports events.
Clients Include:
ESPN, Inc., International Tennis Federation, Kansas City Chiefs Football Club, Inc., United States Tennis Association.
Year Founded:
1984

REESE SPORTS
955 BERKSHIRE BOULEVARD
WYOMISSING, PA 19610
610-378-1835
Fax: 610-378-1676
info@reeseadv.com
• Matt Golden, Managing Partner
(610) 378-1835
matt@reeseadv.com
• Greg Purcell, Director Brand Strategy/Managing Partner

Sports Service Founded:
1980
Marketing & Consulting Services:
Full service advertising, marketing and public relations agency. Areas of concentration include automotive racing, bicycling, boating, exercise/fitness, golfing, motorcycling, skiing, and tennis.

RELAY SPORTS AND ENTERTAINMENT MARKETING
222 MERCHANDISE MART PLAZA
SUITE 4-160B
CHICAGO, IL 60654
312-297-1212
Fax: 312-297-1401
• Wally Hayward, Chief Executive Officer
(312) 297-1400
• John Dolan, Chief Operating Officer
(314) 569-1977
• Jeannette Mueller, Chief Financial Officer
(314) 743-4718
• Tim Mauer, EVP/Managing Director
(312) 297-1400
Services:
Specializes in event production, mobile marketing, on-premise promotion, product sampling, trade shows and conventions, corporate hospitality, grassroots tournaments
Sponsorship Services:
League partnership, consumer promotions, made for tv-events, integrated sponsorship, athlete endorsement, motorsports
Year Founded:
2001
Other Locations:
303 E Wacker Drive, Chicago, Il 60601. 312-297-1423; FAX: 312-297-1401, 1675 Broadway, 3rd Floor, New York, NY 10019. 212-468-3916; FAX:212-468-4383, 1230 Peachtree Street NE, Suite 1825, Atlanta, GA 30309, 5200 Lankershim Boulevard, Suite 800, North Hollywood, CA 91601. 818-753-7268
Nature of Sports Service:
Provides strategic consulting and idea generation, program leveraging and management, and on-site event execution for its world-class brands. Expertise includes field marketing and research measurement, development and production of merchandising materials, event research/evaluation, event production and management, venue signage, naming rights, made-for-TV events, athlete endorsements, mobile marketing, mall tours, product sampling, hospitality, concert tours, equipment design and fabrication, and network sponsorships.
Clients:
Allstate, Anheuser-Busch, U.S. Army, Better Homes & Gardens, Coca-Cola, Delta Airlines, Hallmark, LEGO, McDonald's, MSN.IT, Nike, Nintendo and Ralston Purina.

RHINO SPORTS MARKETING
550 POST OAK BOULEVARD
SUITE 450
HOUSTON, TX 77027
713-681-6711
Fax: 713-681-5220
thensey@rhinomarketing.cc
www.rhinoworldwide.com
• Thomas Hensey, Head of USA Operations
thensey@rhinomarketing.cc
• Philip Lay, Head of UK Operations

Nature of Sports Service:
An independent consultancy specializing in sports marketing, sponsorship consultancy and sales, event marketing and management.
Services:
Consultancy (target audience analysis, role within the marketing mix, media evaluation, opportunity fit & analysis, sponsorship search and negotiation, contract advice, future projections), Sponsorship Management & Exploitation, Sponsorship sales. Event Marketing, Event Management (Plans and budgets, construction, planning apparovals, project management, emergency services, media management and contracts, security, ticketing, hospitality
Clients:
KrisBrown's KickClub, Red Bull Master Class, Final 5, Shell Houston Open, Houston Golf Association, Giff Nielson/Roger Clemens Day of Golf For Kids

RHYS MILLEN RACING
17492 APEX CIRCLE
HUNTINGTON BEACH, CA 92647
714-847-2158
Fax: 714-848-6821
sales@rmrproducts.com
www.rodmillenstore.com

RMG3 EAST COAST
1801 W INTL SPEEDWAY BOULEVARD
DAYTONA BEACH, FL 32114
386-681-6124
www.rmg3.com
• Kevin Hindson, Vice President Marketing/Communications
(704) 377-7477
• Matt Heisley, VP Sales
(704) 377-7477
Services:
A full-service media, marketing and merchandising agency, providing such services as web site development, e-commerce consultation, and sponsorship solicitation.
Clients:
Alltel, Arena Football League, FIFA, Ford, FoxSports.com, Masterfoods, Mazda, MSNBC, National Guard, Speedway Motorsports (SMI), Speed Channel, US Men's National Soccer Team Players Association and West Coast Conference.
Sports Service Founded:
1998

ROBUSTELLI SPORTS MARKETING
1717 NEWFIELD AVE
STAMFORD, CT 06903
203-322-2790
Fax: 203-912-6487
www.rcsltd.com
• Richard Robustelli, Chairman/President
• Paul Salvatore, Chief Executive Officer
(203) 352-0500
• Dan DeFrancesco, Corporate Travel Management Division
(203) 352-0505
• Jim Robustelli, President
Sports Service Founded:
1958
Services:
Sports Marketing (sports related promotions, client entertainment, celebrity appearances, special event Ticketing), Merchandise

Services, Motivation, Multimedia.
Event Management Services:
Sales meetings, incentive programs, celebrity appearances, sports related retail and trade promotions, sports memorabilia and major sporting event travel.
Business Revenue:
$10.60 M

ROUND ROBIN SPORTS
1415 N DEARBORN PKWY
SUITE 16C
CHICAGO, IL 60610
312-337-3790
Fax: 312-337-3996
• Robin Monsky, President
Nature of Services:
Provides media relations services to the sports industry

ROWLAND COMPANY
1675 BROADWAY
3RD FLOOR
NEW YORK, NY 10019
212-527-8800
Fax: 212-527-8924
• Steve Bryant, Managing Director
• Maryanne Caruso, Senior Vice President
Services:
Public relations services for sporting goods, sports marketing and sports sponsorship clients.

RPR SPORTS & ENTERTAINMENT, LLC
23 VREELAND ROAD
FLORHAM PARK, NJ 7932
973-360-0600
Services:
Product placement/brand placement and seamless brand/ brand message integrations in feature films, television, and world-class events. Strategically and seamlessly integrate brands into the scripts of tomorrow's blockbuster films.

RSR PARTNERS
600 STEAMBOAT ROAD
GREENWICH, CT 06830
203-618-7000
Fax: 203-618-7011
info@rsrpartners.com
www.rsrpartners.com
• Cameron Smith, Senior Associate, Global Sport Leadership
(301) 675-8855

RUDER/FINN SPORTS, INC.
301 E 57TH STREET
NEW YORK, NY 10022
212-593-6400
info@ruderfinn.com
www.ruderfinn.com
• David Finn, Chairman
• Michael Schubert, Chief Innovation Officer
• Louise Harris, Chief Global Strategist
• Scott Schneider, Chief Digital Officer
• Rachel Spielman, Global Head of Corporate Communications
(212) 593-6400
spielmanr@ruderfinn.com
• Emmanuel Tchividjian, Chief Ethics Officer
• John McInerney, Director, Consumer Affairs
• Jen Long, Director, Technology & Innovation

Nature of Sports Service:
A leading independent communications agency whose expertise includes corporate reputation management, branding, cultural and social issues, and intent-driven social media.

SADLER & COMPANY, INC.
3014 DEVINE ST.
PO BOX 5866
COLUMBIA, SC 29250-5866
800-622-7370
800-622-7370
Fax: 803-256-4017
www.sadlersports.com
• John Sadler, President
(800) 622-7370
Description
Sadler & Company specializes in providing insurance solutions for the sports and recreation industries. Client base includes 12 national sports organizations and over 7000 community sports organizations such as teams & leagues, camps, outdoors, special events, health clubs, etc.

SAXTON COMMUNICATIONS INC.
1448 HOLLYWOOD AVENUE
LANGHORNE, PA 19047-7417
215-752-7797
Fax: 215-752-1518
ESAXTON144@AOL.COM
www.saxtonsponsormarket.com
• Ernie Saxton, President/Publisher
• Marilyn Saxton, Treasurer
• Joe McHugh, Advertising Staff
Nature of Sports Service:
A motorsports sponsorship firm specializing in marketing, public relations, representation, and media relations

SCA PROMOTIONS, INC.
3030 LBJ FREEWAY
SUITE 300
DALLAS, TX 75234
214-860-3770
888-860-3770
Fax: 214-860-3723
scainfo@scapromo.com
www.scapromotions.com
• Robert D. Hamman, Founder/President/Chief Executive Office
info@scapromo.com
• Susan Hatfield, Marketing Director
(214) 860-3712
Services:
Jumbo prize coverage for contests, games and other promotional programs, including sports contests, gaming promotions, retail contests, brand marketing programs and media promotions, Guarantees for athlete performance incentives
Clients:
BEN Marketing Group, Don Jagoda, Promotion Group Central, The Integer Group, The Properties Group, Ventura Associates, Inc., Daimler Chrysler, Harley Davidson, Mazda Motors of America, Inc., Mazda Motors of America, Inc., Nissan North America, Inc., Toyota Motor Sales, Bally's Las Vegas, Caesars Atlantic City, Foxwoods Resort Casino, Harrah's, MGM Grand Detroit Casino, Venetian Resort Hotel, Harvard University, Ohio University, Texas Tech University, University of Arkansas, University of California-Berkeley, University of Hawaii, Adidas American,

Blockbuster Inc., Hasbro Interactive, Sony Electronics, Inc., WM Wrigley, American Express Financ

Services:
Over-redemption protection for coupons and premium offers, Internet and e-commerce promotions, Packaged services where they provide both the prize and materials to help with the setup

Sports Service Founded:
1986

Event Management Services:
Contingent prize coverage, up to $1 million in cash, of contests and sweepstakes, contractual bonus awards, player incentives and other promotional games; specializing in sporting events. Contests such as football toss and kick, basketball shots, hockey shots, grand slam home runs, race tracks, fishing tournaments, golf, track and field, bowling, soccer, etc. Contractual incentive bonuses with PGA, LPGA, Champion player; NHL teams and NASCAR drivers. Also specializes in promotional contests for radio/TV stations and publications associated with sports and sporting events.

Marketing & Consulting Services:
Provides consultation to sponsors, advertisers, direct marketers, manufacturers, event planners, and sports teams for design, planning, and implementation of promotional contests and sweepstakes. Advises clients in contest design and prize structuring, as well as the latest concepts in promotional contests.

Clients:
Advertising/Promotions, Automotive, Casinos & Lotteries, Colleges and Universities, Consumer Products, Financial Services, Food & Beverage, Insurance, Internet, ESPN, Media, Non-Profit, Sports, Technology & Telecommunications, Microsoft Corporation

SCARBOROUGH SPORTS MARKETING
770 BROADWAY
NEW YORK, NY 10003
646-654-8400
855-80-SCARB
Fax: 646-654-8450
info@scarborough.com
www.scarborough.com
• Bob Cohen, President/Chief Executive Officer
• Brian Condon, Executive VP, Commercial Development
• Yvonne McHugh, Director of Marketing and Communications
• Steve Seraita, Executive VP Sales
• Diana Illiano, Public Relations & Event Coordinator
• Cary McFarland, Account Executive
• Tom Reutter, Account Manager

Nature of Service:
Provides consumer insights on sports fan avidity; multi-media measures including sports viewing and listening on a local, regional and national level. Scarborough measures over 1,700 categories and brands, as well as media, demographics and lifesytles of consumers. Corporate sponsorhsip information including fans' shopping and product/service usage.

SCHEERGAME SPORTS DEVELOPMENT
3127 W WISCONSIN AVENUE
MILWAUKEE, WI 53208

414-908-4252
Fax: 414-908-4259

SCREEN WORKS
2201 W. FULTON STREET
CHICAGO, IL 60612
312-243-8265
800-294-8111
Fax: 312-243-8290
screens@thescreenworks.com
www.thescreenworks.com
Services:
Creative Web site development and the maintenance

SEATS 3D
1150 BALLENA BOULEVARD
SUITE 250
ALAMEDA, CA 94501
510-521-0720
Fax: 510-521-3972
www.seats3d.com
• Steve Stonehouse, Senior VP Sales
• Jeff Sherratt, Director Business Development
• David Schwartz, Chief Operations Officer/Chief Technology Officer
• Richard H. Sherratt, Chairman of the Board/Chief Executive Officer
Nature of Services:
Using 3D visualizations of sports venues, Ballena Technologies creates realistic seating visuals to improve the online ticketing experience by familiarizing potential customers with a facility, creating excitement, sales, and customer satisfaction.

SFX/CLEAR CHANNEL COMMUNICATIONS
200 EAST BASSE ROAD
SAN ANTONIO, TX 78209-8328
210-822-2828
www.clearchannel.com
• Lowry Mays, Chairman of the Board
LLowryMays@clearchannel.com
• Mark Mays, Chief Executive Officer
MarkPMays@clearchannel.com
• Randall Mays, President and Chief Financial Officer
(210) 822-2828
RandallTMays@clearchannel.com
• Andrew W Levin, EVP and Chief Legal Officer
AndyLevin@clearchannel.com
Sports Service Founded:
1978
Marketing & Consulting Services:
Events and promotion, public relations/marketing communications for sports firms, associations, organizations and magazines, feature articles, brochures, news releases and newsletters on all aspects of sports medicine and participatory sports emphasizing prevention and treatment of athletic injuries; and athletic health/fitness research.

SHERRY GROUP INC.
TWO SYLVAN WAY
PARSIPPANY, NJ 7054
973-984-3000
Fax: 973-984-3088
• J. Gr Sherry, Chief Executive Officer
Services:
Public relations and sports marketing services for events, companies, institutions

and individuals.
Clients:
Adams USA, Akadema, Amer Sports, Cendant Hotel Group, Commonfund, Danskin, Edgewood Country Club, Edwin Watts Golf, Fender Footwear, GlaxoSmithKline, Higher One, Hollow Brook Golf Club, LG Electronics, Marriot Golf, Tennis Industry Association, The Peninsula, Promised Land Dairy, Roche Sports, Smith & Wesson, Snickers (Masterfoods), State Fair Meadowlands, Suunto USA, USA Fencing, Waeve Corporation, Wilson Golf, Wenger NA
Sports Service Founded:
1992
Marketing & Consulting Services:
Public relations and sports marketing services for events, companies, institutions and individuals.

SHOP
3195A AIRPORT LOOP
COSTA MESA, CA 92626
714-434-7467
Fax: 714-435-3599
• Nick Adcock, Contact
Services:
Provides a global view into the world of alternative sports marketing. Specializes in authentic and credible creative, promotional and marketing executions to the youth market.
Sports Service Founded:
1985

SHOT BLOCK PROMOTIONS
11 WESTFIELD ROAD
NATICK, MA 1760
508-651-7900
Sports Service Founded:
1992
Event Management Services:
Onsite promotions for amateur or semi-pro events and corporate promotions.Live event announcing and sponsor promotions.

SIGNATURES NETWORK
2 BRYANT STREET
SUITE 300
SAN FRANCISCO, CA 94105
415-247-7400
800-673-6136
Fax: 415-247-7407
info@signaturenetworks.com
www.signaturesnetwork.com
• Dell Furano, Chief Executive Officer
dfurano@signaturesnet.com
• Phil Cussen, President/ Chief Operating Officer
pcussen@signaturesnet.com
• Rick Fish, EVP, Artist Relations
rfish@signaturesnet.com
• Django Bayless, SVP, New Media Technology/ Artist Relation
dbayless@signaturesnet.com
Services:
SN holds the rights to market and license more than 125 superstars, artists, celebrities and entertainment properties.
Clients:
Aaron Carter, Alicia Keys, Bobby Brown, Bonnie McKee, Boyz II Men, Britney Spears, Kanye West, Kenny G, Kylie Minogue, Luther Vandross, Madonna, O-Town, The Monkees, Usher, Adan Chalino Sanchez, Gloria Estefan, Jennifer Lopez, Jon Secada,

Luis Miguel, Mana, Marc Anthony, Shakira, Thalia, American Idols, Blues Brothers, Bridge School Benefit, Chicago, Curious George, Guys and Dolls, Happy Tree Friends, Hatewear, House of Blues, John Belushi, Mavericks, Peter Pan, Robin Williams, The English Roses, The Osbourne Family, Yellow Submarine, Alan Parsons, Alice Cooper, Barbra Streisand, Billy Idol, Billy Joel, Black Sabbath, Bruce Springsteen, Dan F
Sports Service Founded:
1993

SILVERMAN MEDIA & MARKETING GROUP
2761 ELLEN RD
BELLMORE, NY 11710
516-781-1668
Fax: 516-679-1614
smmgsports@aol.com
www.silverman-media.com
• Ira H Silverman, President
(516) 495-5280
• Erica Quagliata, Account Executive
(516) 495-5280
Description:
Areas of service: public relations, integrated marketing, special event creation management, celebrity representation and charitable foundations. We are nationally recognized for our creativity, placement success, writing skills. Primary areas of specialization include: sports leagues, associations, charities, foundations, events, teams, venues, Halls of Fame, sponsors, equipment, toys, games, players (active and retired), sportscasters, managers, coaches, sports marketing, companies, agents, etc.
Services:
Public Relations, Integrated Marketing, Special Event Creation and Management, Celebrity/Personal Representation, Charitable Foundations, Creative Services.
Clients:
16W Marketing, Leslie Allen Foundation, Alzheimer's Association, Crohn's Colitis Foundation of America (CCFA), Tariq Abdul-Wahad, Current NBA Player, Leslie Allen, Retired WTA Tennis Player, Len Berman, WNBC-TV Sports Anchor, Bill Boggs, TV Personality.
Other Location:
245 5th Avenue, Room 64, New York, NY 10016. 212-686-5983
Year Founded:
1996

SILVERMAN SPORTS CONSULTANTS
900 PINE HALLOW ROAD
MOUNT PLEASANT, SC 29464
843-881-3383
Fax: 843-881-3387
• Stuart Fetter, Chief Executive Officer
Services:
Full-service provider of sales consulting and financial services for sporting goods retailers.
Sports Service Founded:
1945
Marketing & Consulting Services:
Full-service provider of sales consulting & financial services for sporting goods retailers.

SIMMONS MARKET RESEARCH BUREAU/SMRB
230 PARK AVENUE S
3RD FLOOR
NEW YORK, NY 10003
212-863-4500
Fax: 212-863-4495
• Evan Goldfarb, EVP, Media Services
(760) 992-9061
EvanG@smrb.com
• Chistopher Lubniewski, Managing VP, Media Services
(212) 863-4560
ChrisL@smrb.com
• Gary Warech, Managing VP, Media Services
(212) 863-4566
GaryW@smrb.com
• Jeromy Gabor, VP, Media Services
(212) 863-4554
JeremyG@smrb.com
Services:
Provides companies and advertising agencies with the critical marketing information, needed to target their products, brands and media to today's consuming public, including Adult Study (NCS/NHCS), Teens Study, Tweenz Study, Youth Study, Kids Study, Hispanic Study, Household Study, Gay and Lesbian Consumer Study, Simmons Local, Segmentation Systems, Database Integration, and Custom Research.

> **Study of Media and Markets:**
> All major sports covered. Sample size: 23,555 adults. Provides number/demographic characteristics of sports participants and spectators as well as their frequency of participation/attendance, equipment purchases and media exposure. Conducted annually, latest report - Oct, 1997. Subscription fee depends on size of company. More detailed information (brand preferences, attitudes, etc.) can be obtained via custom re-contact of 12,000 respondents, eliminating screening costs.
> **Other Location:**
> 700 West Hillsboro Blvd., Bldg 4-201, Deerfield Beach, FL 3441; Phone: 954-427-4104; Fax: 954-427-3760

SLAM DUNK TO THE BEACH
ATTN: ROBERT F JACOBS
PO BOX 0133
FELTON, DE 19943
302-430-7526
Fax: 302-430-3865
www.slamdunktothebeach.com
• Robert F. Jacobs, Executive Director/Chief Executive Offic
Services:
Marketing & Consulting: Creates and manages Slam Dunk To The Beach National Holiday Basketball Invitational for high school basketball teams, as well as Slam Dunk To The Beach National Golf Invitational and Rockin' The Rim National Amateur Basketball Invitational.
Sports Service Founded:
1990

SLOANE VISION UNLIMITED
305 MADISON AVENUE
SUITE 1337
NEW YORK, NY 10017
212-922-0555
Fax: 212-922-1306
• Glenn Hendricks, VP Business Development/Licensing

(212) 922-0555
• Dave Landesberg, Director oF Licensing
Nature of Service:
Strategic targeting and product planning, Contract negotiations, Product concept development, Hand-in-hand working relationships with Licensors and Licensees, Billing, collections and Royalty reporting, Integrated retail progams, Cross-marketing and Licensing opportunities, Quality control, Worldwide program implementation.
Sports Service Founded:
1939
Clients:
Chicken Soup for the Soul, DQ, J-14, Little League Baseball, Little Trees, Slinky Brand, TV Guide, Woman's World, Stuckeys
Marketing & Consulting Services:
Exclusive Worldwide Licensing agency for Little League Baseball.

SMART INDUSTRIES
1901 BELL AVENUE
SUITE 12
DES MOINES, IA 50315
515-265-9900
800-553-2442
Fax: 515-265-3148
www.smartind.com
Services:
Strategic planning and marketing services related to sports events, including, demand analysis, program development, financial feasibility, corporate sponsorship, and organization and staffing plans. Creates sponsorship collateral materials, sponsorship development, and media planning.

SME BRANDING
298 FIFTH AVENUE
5TH FLOOR
NEW YORK CITY, NY 10001
212-924-5700
Fax: 212-924-1941
www.smebranding.com
• Edward O'Hara, Chairman/Senior Partner
(212) 924-5700
• Frederick S. Popp, CEO/Partner
(212) 924-5700
Year Founded:
1989.
Sports Service Founded:
1988
Services:
With over 2000 brand building solutions provided to sports, higher education, and corporate clients worldwide, SME has an unparalleled insight as to how brands must be built and communicated for maximum success. This experience is applied to each client engagement with highly successful results, increasing client revenue and building brand value.
Clients:
Adidas,Akebono, Amateur Softball Association, Anheuser-Busch, Anna Kournikova, Appalachian State University, Arena Football League, Asahi Beer, Atlanta Hawks, Atlanta Thrashers, Auburn University, Australian Football League, Bakersfield Blitz, Baltimore Bayhawks, Baylor University, Binghamton University, Boston Bruins, Boston Cannons, Boston College, The Boys Club of New York, Brand Asset Valuator, Brickyard 400, Brigham Young University, Cal State University -

Northridge, Calgary Flames, California Cougars, Cadbury Schweppes, Cameron University, Canadian Football League, Chicago Rush, Chinese Football League, Churchill Downs, Classic Sports

---

SMITH ASBURY, INC.
225 N LIMA STREET
SUITE 6
SIERRA MADRE, CA 91024
626-836-3300
Fax: 626-836-5500
info@smithasbury.com
www.smithasbury.com
• Greg Asbury, Principal
• Judy Smith Asbury, Founder
Services:
Delivers compelling marketing solutions through the use of strategic planning, identification of critical messages and target audiences, production of impactful designs, illustrations, and copywriting. Provides Strategic marketing, print design, e-marketing, and public relations.

SOCCER MARKETING & PROMOTIONS, INC.
7444 SW 48 STREET
MIAMI, FL 33155
305-669-0101
Fax: 305-669-9979
www.copalatina.com

SOCCER SPHERE
11140 ROCKVILLE PIKE (151)
ROCKVILLE, MD 20852
301-231-8022
Fax: 301-231-5261
ramsaysoccer@yahoo.com
• Graham Ramsay, President
(301) 231-8022
ramsaysoccer@yahoo.com
Description:
Specializing in both commercial and educationsl spheres of soccer marketing/consultancy activities worldwide
Year Founded:
1978

SPEEDWAY GROUP, INC.
19706 ONE NORMAN BOULEVARD
SUITE B12
CORNELIUS, NC 28031
704-904-4141
Fax: 704-987-5055
legal@speedwaygroup.com
www.speedwaygroup.com
• Mike Schriefer, President
Services:
Motorsports marketing and management group specializing in all forms of motorsports including INDYCAR and NASCAR Racing. Services include driving personnel for off-road or on-track demonstrations, ride and drives, driver training, sponsorship, and hospitality.

SPIKE/DDB PRODUCTIONS
55 WASHINGTON STREET
SUITE 650
BROOKLYN, NY 11201
718-596-5400
Fax: 718-596-7256
info@spikeddb.com
www.spikeddb.com

• Spike Lee, Chairman
slee@spikeddb.com
• Bola Esho, Account Supervisor
dwade@spikeddb.com
• Chad Mclean, Assistant Account Executive
• Felix Messina Jr., Account Executive
• Leah Hamilton, Senior Art Producer
• Jeison Rodriguez, Senior Art Director
Services:
Develops strategic and production of advertising and marketing programs. Develops and executes television, radio and print advertisements.
Clients:
Chanel, Pepsi, New York Knicks, Royal Caribbean, NFB, Clean&Clear, Exxon Mobil, Essence, Tanqueray, Doritos, State Palm Insurance, Frito Lay, Alltel, Foxwoods, Usta, TNT, Mountain Dew

---

SPONSORLOGIC, INC.
PO BOX 3728
MOORESVILLE, NC 28117
704-664-1714
Fax: 704-794-95796
www.sponsorlogic.com
• Mel Poole, President
(704) 788-9915
Year Founded:
1997.
Description:
Full service sponsorship management, coaching and sales agency
Clients:
National Electrical Contractors Assn, National Apartment Association, Sports Business Journal and Assn for Manufacturing Technology.

SPONSORSHIP RESEARCH INTERNATIONAL USA
230 E AVENUE
NORWALK, CT 06855
203-831-2061
Fax: 203-831-2301
hello@teamsri.com
www.teamsri.com
• Julie Zdziarski, EVP
(203) 831-2061
julie.zdziarski@teamsri.com
• Jeff Eccleston, VP
(203) 831-2060
jeff.eccleston@teamsri.com
Services:
Provides Event/Spectator Research, Custom Telephone Research, Web-based Research, Ethnography and Observation Research, Qualitative Research, Corporate Hospitality Evaluations, Impressions Analysis, Media Exposure and Valuation, and Property Valuation.
Clients:
ADT Security Services, Allstate, American Century, American Express, Anheuser-Busch, Bank One, Bell Sports, Canon, Cingular Wireless, Citizens Bank, Coca-Cola, ConAgra Foods, Delta Airlines, Eli Lilly, FedEx, Gateway Computers, Gillette, Hallmark, IBM, monster.com, Motorola, New Balance, Nike, Nissan, Nokia, Norelco, Pfizer, Philips, Reebok, Sprint, Sunoco, Texaco, The Home Depot, UBS, Wired Magazine, VISA, AFL, Dew Action Sports Tour, NASCAR, NBA, New York Jets, New York Mets, MLS, NFL, NTRA, New York Road Runners, San Francisco 49ers, US Open Tennis Series,

WWE, AEG, Digitas, Edelman Public Relations, GMR Marketing, IMG, Jack Morton
Description:
Experience in spectator surveys, national sponsorship tracking studies, and national and international TV and press exposure reports, custom qualitative and quantitative sponsorship research.
Year Founded:
1996

SPORT & SOCIAL CLUBS OF THE U.S.
770 N HALSTED
SUITE #306
CHICAGO, IL 60622
312-850-8196
Fax: 312-850-3138
www.chicagosportandsocialclub.com
• Jason Erkes, President
• Chris Hastings, VP
Services:
Creates and sponsors events
Number of members:
15,000 participants.
Publications:
TAKE ACTION, 6 times annually.
Membership Requirements:
Dues of $30 per year.
Description:
Founded 1989. Event planning focusing on grass roots events. Over 150,000 participants in 20 cities across the U.S.

SPORT MANAGEMENT RESEARCH INSTITUTE
6965 EL CAMINO REAL
SUITE 105-228
CARLSBAD, CA 92009
954-389-9095
858-779-9291
info@go-smri.com
www.go-smri.com
• Kathleen A. Davis, President
kdavis@go-smri.com
• Sandy Keehn, Operations Director
skeehn@go-smri.com
Description:
Conducts all phases of market research projects. Works with sponsoring sports organizations the purpose, scope and methods for the project are determined. Marketing research projects data on: Sponsorship Impact, Service Deliver Assessment, Demographic Profiles, Event Satisfaction, Cross Event Preferences, Community Support/Public Relations. Marketing research projects conducted at consecutive annual events or intervals throughout a season. Research also includes trend analysis and industry comparisons.
Clients:
Giants Stadium, Florida Marlins, Florida Panthers, Cleveland Browns Coca-Cola Company, San Diego Chargers, San Diego Padres, University of Southern California, U.S. Tennis Open, USTA, Montreal Expos, NFL, AVP Tour, Super Bowls XXIV - XXVI.

SPORT SCAN INFO
2151 HAWKINS STREET
SUITE 200
CHARLOTTE, NC 28203
704-987-3450
Fax: 704-987-3455

sportscan@sportsonesource.com
www.sportscaninfo.com
Description:
Provider of weekly point-of-sale information on athletic footwear, apparel, licensed products, team sports equipment, outdoor products, golf, tennis, fitness equipment, inline skating and other sporting goods to the nation's leading retailers, manufacturers, financial institutions, sport agents and other interested third parties.
year founded
1989

SPORTAMERICA
PO BOX 95030
SALT LAKE, UT 84095
801-253-3360
800-467-7885
customerservice@sportamerica.com
www.sportamerica.com
• John W Scott, Chief Executive Officer
(801) 253-3360
john@sportAmerica.com
Marketing & Consulting Services:
Athletic educational and motivational products. Specializes in production, distribution and promotion of sports videos, books, camps, and clinics. Products focus on work ethic - from fundamentals, mental training, and fitness to X's and O's, skill development, team training, and individual workouts. Produces motivational audio products for business through the medium of the following sports: Basketball, golf, soccer, baseball, football, volleyball and fitness products.
Sports Service Founded:
1990

SPORTS & ENTERTAINMENT DIRECT, INC
2470 WINDY HILL ROAD
SUITE 300
MARIETTA, GA 30067
770-952-0025
Marketing & Consulting Services:
A promotional direct marketing company specializing in distribution of samples and advertising messages at major sports and entertainment events. Provides advertisers direct-to-sports-fan marketing programs through co-op fan bag distribution or solo sampling at major sports events.

SPORTS & FITNESS INDUSTRY ASSOCIATION
8505 FENTON STREET
SUITE 211
SILVER SPRING, MD 20910
301-495-6321
Fax: 301-495-6322
info@sfia.org
• Cove Tom, President & CEO
Description:
Trade association of leading sports and fitness brands.

SPORTS ADVERTISING NETWORK, INC.
366 N BROADWAY
JERICHO, NY 11753-2025
516-942-4215
• John Fugazy, VP
Services:
Sells advertising for professional teams, covering all aspects of professional team advertising media including broadcast, print,

signage, official sponsorships and promotions. Also provides media buying services for advertisers to gain access to sports venue.

SPORTS BUSINESS GROUP
1800 S PACIFIC COAST HIGHWAY
SUITE 24
REDONDO BEACH, CA 90277-6161
310-316-8825
Fax: 310-316-8826
info@sportsbusinessgroup.com
www.sportsbusinessgroup.com
• David M Carter, Founder/Business Consultant
david.carter@sportsbusinessgroup.com
• David M. Carter, Founder
david.carter@sportsbusinessgroup.com
• Jeff Marks, Senior Marketing Executive
jeff.marks@sportsbusinessgroup.com
Description:
Founded as a means to service the dynamic and increasingly volatile Southern California sports and entertainment industries. Provides consulting recommendations and advice to a broad range of corporations, the legal community, venues, the public sector, the media and academia. Is favorably and uniquely positioned as the premier provider of strategic marketing services for the sports industry.
Services:
Develops and implements business solutions for companies and organizations seeking strategic direction in the areas of sports marketing and management.
Year Founded:
1999

SPORTS BUSINESS RESEARCH NETWORK
PO BOX 2378
PRINCETON, NJ 08543
609-896-1996
Fax: 609-896-1903
richard@sbrnet.com
www.sbrnet.com
• Richard A Lipsey, President
(609) 896-1996
richard@sbrnet.com
Nature of Sports Service:
Provide marketing research on the sporting goods industry and a database of sixteen trade publications with articles indexed by subject and keyword. Market research information includes participation trends, consumer expenditures, import data, attendance data. Covers equipment, footwear, and apparel.

SPORTS DISPLAY
30051 COMMERCIO
RANCHO SANTA MARGARITA, CA 92688
800-854-3476
800-854-3476
Fax: 949-589-9247
www.sportsdisplay.com
• Janet Willingham, Recruiting Department Administrator
Sports Service Founded:
1977
Services:
International company specializing in advertising sales to businesses. Creates organization designs, builds and installs activity and information centers in over 4000 golf courses, tennis clubs, racquetball

facilities and fitness centers across North America.

SPORTS INTERNATIONAL, INC.
9375 WASHINGTON BOULEVARD
LAUREL, MD 20723
301-575-9400
800-555-0801
Fax: 301-575-9439
www.footballcamps.com
• Chuck Bollweg, President
Sports Service Founded:
1982. Specializes in football camps for kids ages 8-18 hosted by NFL players past and present. Total marketing packages include: Supervision, location and player-position literature. Provides full coverage for all facets of camps.
Services:
Specializes in football camps for kids ages 8-18 hosted by NFL players past and present. Total marketing packages include: Supervision, location and player-position literature. Provides full coverage for all facets of camps.

SPORTS MANAGEMENT WORLDWIDE
1100 NW GLISAN STREET
SUITE 2B
PORTLAND, OR 97209
503-445-7105
888-95-AGENT
877-SMWW-Now
Fax: 503-445-9392
info@smww.com
www.smwwagency.com
• G. Lynn Lashbrook, President
(503) 407-2959
lynn@smww.com
• Liz Lashbrook, Executive Director
• Bill Kent, Director Operations
• John Print, Director of Soccer
• Trisonya Abraham, Director of Basketball
• Joe Bonahoom, Director of Baseball
Description:
Candidates complete an eight week SMW course, top performing students are offered the opportunity to stay on as Agent Advisors with Sports Management Worldwide.
Nature of Services:
New Agent Advisors have immediate access to the extensive infrastructure of the company, including certified professional sports team contract negotiations, financial planners, insurance counseling, accounting services, and marketing/endorsement resources for the athletes they represent.

SPORTS MARKET RESEARCH GROUP, INC.
1443 BEACON STREET
APT 808
BROOKLINE, MA 02446
617-277-5660
Nature of Service:
Creates consumer survey reports on bicycles, fitness equipment, Inline skates, ice hockey skates and golf equipment for U.S.
Year Founded:
1990

SPORTS MARKETING & ENTERTAINMENT, INC
11640 SAN VICENTE BOULEVARD
SUITE 204
LOS ANGELES, CA 90049

310-207-2233
800-288-0758
Fax: 310-207-0330
info@smenet.com
www.smenet.com
• Corey Shapoff, President/Chief Executive Officer
(310) 207-2233
cshapoff@smenet.com
• Matt Barnett, EVP
mbarnett@smenet.com
Services:
Secures entertainment, keynote speakers, and sports personalities for many of the world's most notable Fortune 500 companies.
Clients:
AFLAC, AMI, CONOCO, DirecTV, GTE, Ingram Alliace, Lucent Technologies, MCI, Merck, Nordstrom, Prudential, Sprint, Tyson, Warburg Dillon Read, etc.
Marketing & Consulting Services:
Provides sports personalities for personal appearances to corporations.
Sports Service Founded:
1991

SPORTS MARKETING ADMINISTRATORS
140 STREET ANDREWS WAY
ETTERS, PA 17319
717-932-0252
rick@sportsmarketingadmin.com
www.sportsmarketingadmin.com
Nature of Service:
Sports marketing company that creates and maintains sports websites and assists companies administer their sports marketing plans.

SPORTS MARKETING INTERNATIONAL
11 RAVEN ROAD
GLOUCESTER, MA 01931-0738
978-283-2030
• Bruton Smith, Chairman/Chief Executive Officer
Sports Service Founded:
1993
Marketing & Consulting Services:
International marketing; promotional planning and development; international communications; product development; product sourcing and logistics; full design services; international inventory movement; and sales and financial planning focusing on the tennis industry.

SPORTS MARKETING SURVEYS USA
6650 W INDIANTOWN ROAD
SUITE 220
JUPITER, FL 33458
561-427-0647
Fax: 561-427-0648
info@sportsmarketingsurveysusa.com
www.sportsmarketingsurveysusa.com
• Keith Storey, Vice President
(561) 427-0647
• Brandon Mason,
• Carolyn Houston,
• Stephen Proctor, Chairman
• Keith Storey, Vice President
(561) 427-0647
Keith.storey@sportsmarketingsurveysusa.com
Nature of Sports Service:
An independent company providing a specialist market research service to the sports and leisure industry. Provides full range of traditional and innovative market research techniques on a local, national, and international level.
Services:
Offers media research and market research, and also provides publications and consultancy service.
Clients:
Tennis: Wilson, Prince, Dunlop, Head, Yonex, Babolat, Volkl, United States Tennis Association, Tennis Industry Association Golf: Taylor Made, Callaway, Nike, Titleist/Cobra Cycling: Specialized, Giro Sport Design, Mavic, Michelin, Trek Snowsports: Snowsports Industries America, Salomon, K-2, Ride, Dalbello, Head, Dynastar, Nordica Soccer: adidas, Puma, Nike, Brine Hockey: National Hockey League, Mighty Ducks of Anaheim, Carolina Hurricanes, Washington Capitals, Chicago Blackhawks, Atlanta Thrashers, Columbus Bluejackets Baseball: Anaheim Angels Darts: Unicorn Rugged Outdoor Apparel: Salomon, Helly Hansen, Duofold Rugged Outdoor Footwear.

SPORTS PLACEMENT SERVICE INC
330 WEST 11TH STREET
SUITE 105
LOS ANGELES, CA 90015-2230
213-744-1308
Fax: 213-765-1871
www.sportsplacement.com
• Harlan Werner, President/Chief Executive Officer
Services:
Represents and markets the name, likeness and character of world-renowned, retired athletes, through Commercial Endorsement, Celebrity Placement, Public Speaking, Special Events, Licensing, Autograph Signing, Corporate Events.

SPORTS PROFILES
4711 GOLF ROAD
SUITE 900
SKOKIE, IL 60076
800-725-9423
800-725-9423 ext 10
info@sppsports.com
Description:
A promotions and publishing company that develops retail promotions and corporate entertainment.
Publications:
CHICAGO SPORTS PROFILES MAGAZINE, CALIFORNIA SPORTS PROFILES MAGAZINE.
Services:
Develops retail promotions and corporate entertainment.
Year Founded:
1983.

SPORTS RESEARCH CONSULTANTS
13 TERRACE CIRCLE
APT 2B
GREAT NECK, NY 11021-4145
516-487-0664
• Warren M. Shapiro, President
Nature of Sports Service:
Custom sports research of all types to answer specific objectives relating to sports promotions, personalities, and campaigns.

SPORTSALES
PO BOX 386025
BLOOMINGTON, MN 55438-6025
952-881-5280
800-466-4946
Fax: 866-733-9918
sportsales@aol.com
www.sportsalesinc.com
• David Rubinstein, President
Sports Service Founded:
1989
Marketing & Consulting Services:
Services include advertising and promotion sales, sports franchise consulting, corporate sponsor promotions, and purchasing and marketing of sports broadcast media.
Products:
Oudoor Gears
Brands:
Viking, Acorn

SPORTSCORP LTD.
875 N MICHIGAN AVENUE
SUITE 2325
CHICAGO, IL 60611
312-649-1799
888-296-1900
Fax: 312-649-1197
• Marc S. Ganis, President
Products and Services:
Sports facility development and consultation. Sells portable debit-card devices for concessions at St. Louis Rams
Clients/Brands:
St. Louis Rams, NCAA Final Four / FastBreak Concession Card
Sports Service Founded:
1984

SPORTSECONOMICS LLC
61 LOMBARDY LANE
ORINDA, CA 94563
510-387-0644
Fax: 510-295-2578
info@sportseconomics.com
www.sportseconomics.com
• Daniel A. Rascher, P.H.D., President
Nature of Sports Service
A professional services firm that provides a broad range of consulting services to the sports business and entertainment communities.

STARCOM MEDIAVEST GROUP
35 W WACKER DRIVE
CHICAGO, IL 60601
312-220-3535
Fax: 312-220-6530
• Laura Desmond, CEO
Services:
Starcom MediaVest Group encompasses an integrated network of nearly 3,800 contact architects specializing in media management, internet + digital communications, response media, entertainment marketing, sports sponsorships, event marketing and multicultural media
Description:
Mediavest researches and buys advertising space while Starcom provides media planning and marketing services.
Year Founded:
2000.

STEINER SPORTS MARKETING
145 HUGUENOT STREET
NEW ROCHELLE, NY 10801
914-307-1000
800-759-7267
Fax: 914-365-6428
generalinfo@steinersports.com
www.steinersports.com

STRATBRIDGE, INC.
BLANCHARD HOUSE
SUITE 304
249 AYER ROAD
HARVARD, MA 01451
978-772-4647
Fax: 617-977-8630
www.stratbridge.com
• Matthew Marolda, Founder/Chief Executive Officer
• Andrew H. Palmer, Strategy & Sales/Marketing
• Thomas L. Doorley, III, Strategy & Growth/Board of Directors
• Anthony J. Marolda, Strategy & Planning/Board of Directors
• Michael T. Horvath, Strategic Alliances/Board of Directors
Nature of Services:
StratBridge provides analytic solutions that enable professional sports managers to perform exhaustive diligence research at the touch of a button - StratBridge.net, a platform product, is a Web-native system that seamlessly extracts data from internal and external sources, regardless of format, and then visually renders it in high-resolution plasma displays.

STRATEGIC INSIGHT, LLC
11209 N. 26TH STREET
PHOENIX, AZ 85028
480-499-0466
info@strategicinsight.com
www.strategicinsight.com
• W. Lee Steele, President
lee@strategicinsight.com
Services:
Provide clients with practical, market-based, customer-oriented solutions designed to achieve specific sales and marketing goals
year founded
1991
Marketing & Consulting Services:
Specializing in maximization of clients' sales and marketing efforts in the sporting goods industry, through long range strategic planning, market research, new product development, trade and consumer promotions, communication plans, and internet marketing.
Internet Marketing:
We design and manage Pay-Per-Click Search Engine Ad Campaigns designed to generate a steady stream of pre-qualified sales prospects ready to buy your product or service. No ad budget is too big or too small.

STREET CHARACTERS, INC.
2-2828 18TH STREET NE
CALGARY, ALBERTA, CANADA T2E 7B1
888-627-2687
Fax: 403-250-3846
topdog@mascots.com
www.mascots.com
• Glenn Street, President
topdog@mascots.com

• Aubrey Fishman, Marketing Director
• Brendan Whitty, Concept Artist
Services:
Designs, manufactures, trains and manages mascot characters. Specialists in the manufacture of highly active, durable mascots for sports teams.
Notes:
888-MASCOTS and mascots.com are licensed trademarks of Street Characters, Inc.
Sports Service Founded:
1987
Clients Include:
MLB - Minnesota Twins, Pittsburgh Pirates; Texas Rangers; NFL - Arizona Cardinals, Denver Broncos, Detroit Lions, Houston Texans, Seattle Seahawks; NHL - Calgary Flames, Chicago Blackhawks, New York Islanders; NCAA - Georgetown University, Iowa State University, University of Nebraska, UNLV, San Jose State University.

STRIKE TEN ENTERTAINMENT, INC.
615 SIX FLAGS DRIVE
ARLINGTON, TX 76011
800-871-7869
Fax: 817-649-1918
striketen@bpaa.com
www.stemarketing.com
• John Berglund, President
(800) 871-7869
john@bpaa.com
• Toby Brown, Director
• Frank DeSocio, Vice President Sales/Activation
(316) 636-9494
frank@stemarketing.com
• Henry Lewczyk, Vice President Marketing/Research
(800) 871-7869
henry@bpaa.com
• John Harbuck, Executive Vice President/Managing Partner
(404) 606-2410
john@stemarketing.com
Nature of Service:
Centralized bowling marketing, bowling management, television, communications, merchandising, bowling promotions, bowling trade shows and events company representing the Bowling Proprietors Association of America, Strike Ten Entertainment and Strike Ten Select.

SUCCESS PROMOTIONS
14440 S OUTER FORTY ROAD
CHESTERFIELD, MO 63017
314-878-1999
Fax: 314-878-6663
• Colleen Wadley, Project Coordinator
• Andrea Everett, Customer Service
• Brandon Everett, Sales
• Chris Hahs, Sales Executive
• Dave Lois, Sales Executive
• Diana Everett, President
• Chad Everett, Sales Manager
Nature of Services:
Success Promotions provides professional sports with functional, retail-quality promotion merchandise to increase traffic, retain clientele and extend brand impressions long after an event.

SUMMIT SPORTS GROUP
3970 SADDLE ROCK ROAD
COLORADO SPRINGS, CO 80918
719-264-8112
Fax: 719-264-8243
www.summitsportsgroup.com
• Ron De Lorenzo, Founder/Owner/President
ron_summitsports@msn.com
Year Founded:
1986.
Sports Service Founded:
1986.
Services:
Provides advertising and marketing programs to reach golfers, both in Colorado and on a national scale.
Event Management Services:
Provides marketing, promotional, merchandising and broadcast plans for events, as well as for companies using the events as promotion/marketing vehicles.

SUPERLATIVE GROUP, INC.
26600 DETROIT ROAD
SUITE 250
CLEVELAND, OH 44145
216-592-9400
Fax: 216-592-9405
info@superlativegroup.com
www.superlativegroup.com
• Myles Gallagher, President and CEO

SWANSON COMMUNICATIONS
1025 VERMONT AVENUE NW
SUITE 1005
WASHINGTON, DC 20005
202-783-5500
Fax: 202-783-5516
contact@swansonpr.com
www.swansonpr.com
• Kelly Swanson, President
kswanson@swansonpr.com
• Lisa Milner, Manager
• Janet Cassar, Account Executive
Description:
Founded in 1997 and based in Washington DC, Swanson Communications is passionate about creating powerful communications strategies. They are experts in their field and a small agency by design. The agency establishes unique relationships with each of our clients while we develop and customize comprehensive marketing and communications plans that maximize investment and cut unnecessary costs. They maintain their client's integrity and keep them in the news through efficient follow-up strategies, commitment to market research, and active media contact. By forming solid partnerships, they generate positive public perception of their clients and
Clients:
HBO Sports/HBO Pay-Per-View™, Golden Boy Productions, Floyd Mayweather, Caron Butler (Dallas Mavericks), Bernard Hopkins, Washington Freedom
Nature of Services:
Public Relations, Marketing and Promotions, Event Planning and Management, and Research and Development

TAILWIND SPORTS/CYCLING DIVISION
88 KEARNEY STREET
4TH FLOOR
SAN FRANCISCO, CA 94108

415-705-6000
Fax: 415-705-6005
• Bill Stapleton, Chief Executive Officer
• Dan Osipow, General Manager /
Operations Director
Description:
Sports marketing firm that owns United
States Postal Pro Cycling Team, which is
lead by six timer tour de France winner
Lance Armstrong. The company is
expanding into cycling event management.

**TAYLOR RESEARCH & CONSULTING
GROUP, INC.**
500 MARKET STREET
PORTSMOUTH, NH 03801
603-422-7600
Fax: 603-422-7610
www.thetaylorgroup.com
• Scott Taylor, President
• Peter Fondulas, EVP
• Jason LaMountain, Senior
Communications Consultant
• Scott Taylor PhD., President
• Jason Grucel, Communications
Director/Research Consultant
jasong@thetaylorgroup.com
• Jason Lamountain, Senior Methodologist
• Joseph Hickey, Tracking Studies
Director/Senior Research Con
• J. Scott Taylor, Client Service
director/Research Consultant
Nature of Sports Service:
Estimates audience size and price/demand
relationships for major pay-per-view events;
analyzes brand equity of professional sports
leagues; provides market estimates of
sports licensed products; and identifies key
target markets for clients.
Services:
Provides qualitative and quantitative market
and opinion research and consulting
services to businesses in a variety of
industries

TBA ENTERTAINMENT CORPORATION
220 WEST 42ND STREET
10TH FLOOR
NEW YORK, NY 10036
646-445-7000
Fax: 646-445-7001
• Robert Geddes, Chief Executive Officer
• Lee Rubenstein, President/COO
• Jeff Kline, Business Affairs EVP
• Paula Balzer, CEO
Sports Service Founded:
1984
Clients:
Herbalife, SAP, Bristol-Myers Squibb,
Motorola
Marketing & Consulting Services:
Specializing in managing merchandise
concessions for sporting events and
concerts.
Other Locations:
Los Angeles, London, Nashville, Chicago,
San Diego, Salt Lake City, Atlanta, Omaha,
Seattle.

TEAM FLORIDA MARKETING
PO BOX 13515
GAINESVILLE, FL 32604
352-372-1215
800-782-3216
Fax: 352-372-8944
• Dwight Johnson, President

Services:
Marketing representative for Florida Athletic
Coaches Association, the College Sports
Publishers Association (CSPA) and other
Florida sports properties. Full service firm
specializing in sports publishing,
sponsorship sales, event management and
promotion
Sports Service Founded:
1992

TEAM SPORTS, INC.
6228 STATE STREET
WAUWATOSA, WI 53213
414-431-0559
Fax: 262-431-0585
www.teamsportsinc.com
• Tom Schuler, Director
tjsplow@aol.com
• Jack Hirt, Events Director
Services:
Provides team management and marketing
service for some of the nation's most
prestigious cycling and multisport team and
events
Sports Service Founded:
1992
Marketing & Consulting Services:
Sports management for corporate
sponsored team sports. Manages
Volvo/Cannondale Mountain Bike Racing
Team, Saturn Cycling Team, and the
Rollerblade Racing Team.

TELE-SPORTS, INC.
PO BOX 232
ALLENTOWN, NJ 08501
800-410-9800
www.tele-sports.com
Marketing & Consulting Service:
Specializes in sports telemarketing and
consulting for professional teams and
organizations. Sells season and mini plan
packages, sponsorship packages,
appointment setting, and event
management.

THE CHAPEL HILL NORTH GROUP
GLENN, MI
KENNETT SQUARE, PA 45140
877-887-0972
Fax: 267-908-9101
www.chapelhillnorth.com
• Stephen Frank, Contact
Services:
market and industry analyses, competitor
analysis, due diligence services.
Sports Service Founded:
2001
Nature of Sports Service:
assist organizations in understanding their
competitive landscape in terms of
competitors' costs structure and strategy.

THE KING PARTNERSHIP
1210 TRINITY ROAD
RALEIGH, NC 27607
919-828-2990
• George King, Chief Executive Officer
(919) 719-1319
• Jenny Martin, Account Director
Marketing & Consulting Services:
Full service advertising and sports
marketing agency with experience in season
ticket campaigns, sponsorship sales, team
representation and event management.
Services:

Provides marketing services, including
media planning and placement, public
relations and radio production.

THE Q SCORES COMPANY
1129 NORTHERN BLVD
SUITE 404
MANHASSET, NY 11030
516-365-7979
Fax: 516-365-9351
info@qscores.com
www.qscores.com
• Steven Levitt, President
steven@qscores.com
Nature of Service:
SPORTS Q: National survey on the
familiarity and appeal Q SCORES of 500
active and retired sports personalities,
among a sports fan audience, aged 12-64.
Nature of Service:
PERFORMER Q: National survey on the
familiarity and appeal Q SCORES of over
1700 performers, including major sports
personalities.
Year Founded:
1963

THE ROWERS' CODE
P.O. BOX 99613
SEATTLE, WA 98139
201-703-1020
855-ROW-CODE
Fax: 201-797-8769
info@rowerscode.com
www.rowerscode.com
• Rollinson Jane, President and CEO
• Marilyn Krichko, Founding Partner
• Jane Rollinson, Team Member
• Michael Roney, Sales and Marketing
(201) 703-1020
mr@michaelroney.net
Description of Sports Organization:
The Rowers' Code program includes both
rowing and indoor elements- the ultimate in
teambuilding impact. It is designed to let
individuals, teams and leaders experience
what it takes to pull together as a team. In
this workshop you experience rowing with
your fellow team members in a 60-foot
Olympic-style boat, and then are challenged
to apply the Rowers' Code to your sitation at
work, allowing your team to achieve
unprecedented success. The Rower's Code
is a simple, actionable set of behaviors
about teamwork and communication that
can be applied to every workplace scenario.
It is based on the premise that every
Teams:
Sessions available coast to coast.
Publications:
Book: The Rowers' Code: A Business
Parable. How to Pull Together as a Team-
And Win! Hardcover: 224 pages Publisher:
Career Press ISBN-10: 1601631650
ISBN-13: 978-1601631657

**THE SPORTS & FITNESS INDUSTRY
ASSOCIATION (SFIA)**
8505 FENTON STREET
SUITE 211
SILVER SPRING, MD 20910
301-495-6321
Fax: 301-495-6322
info@sfia.org
www.sfia.org
• Tom Cove, President/Chief Executive
Officer

(202) 775-1762
• Gregg Hartley, VP
(202) 349-9411
• Andrea Cernich, Communications Director
(202) 349-9415
• Chris Strong, Business Development Director
(202) 349-9413
• Robert Puccini, Chairman President, Mizuno USA
• Tom Cove, President & CEO, SFIA
• Chris Clawson, Secretary/Treasurer
• Carlos Ferraro, President Unisource Global Solutions
• Jon Letzler, President & CEO Augusta Sportswear Group
• Robert Parish, President & GM Jarden Team Sports

Services:
Sporting goods equipment, sports apparel, athletic footwear

Clients:
Outdoor Adventure Series Day Hiker Insoles, AquaSkipper, Golf Radar Timing Device, Spenco Medical, Inventist, Sports Sensors Inc.

Sports Equipment Monitor:
Brand recognition and ownership of 186 sports brands; $795. Monitors 24 types of sports equipment purchases; $365.

SGMA Marketing Expenditures Study:
Comprehensive report on manufacturers spending for communications, merchandising, promotion and other marketing expense items. A total of thirty items are reported by company size, major product, retail classes of trade. Report available at cost of $300 ($125 to SGMA members).

SGMA Sports Participation Index by ASD:
An abridged version of the American Sports Analysis sports participation study, available only to SGMA members free of charge. The 75-page report focuses on frequent sports participants.

SGMA Sports Apparel Market Index:
Detailed unit and dollar purchases by sex, retail channel of distribution for sweat pants, sweat shirts, shorts, thermals, athletic socks, jackets, swimwear, and sport shirts plus active sports report - three times per year. Annual demographic report. Free to SGMA members, $495 for four reports to non-members.

SGMA Athletic Footwear Market Index:
Tracking study of athletic footwear at retail. Total trends and separate trends for women, men and children. Trends by shoe type, price point, retail outlet, sale vs. regular price, primary use. Annual report on demographics of purchases. Free to SGMA members, $495 for non-members for four reports.

Recreation Market Report:
Statistical summary of manufacturers' shipments in wholesale dollars for the sporting goods/recreation industry and its products. Free.

Executive Compensation Study:
Report on compensation trends for key executives and middle managers employed by sporting goods companies. Based upon 120-plus company experiences totaling almost 700 positions.

Industry Financial Study:
Reports on overall industry sales trends and manufacturer's financial performance as measured by 26 key financial ratios.

Monthly U.S. Imports Report:
Major source for statistical report on flow of sporting goods to and from the U.S. Details volume trade from countries. Narrative summary and graphs show trends free to SMGA, every six months.
Other Location:
1150 17th Street, NW, STE 407, Washington, DC 20036; Phone: 202-775-1762

STRATEGIC AGENCY, THE
70 WEST 36TH STREET
10TH FLOOR
NEW YORK, NY 10018
212-869-3003
info@thestrategicagency.com
www.thestrategicagency.com
Description:
The primary goal is to influence your consumers' purchasing behavior. To do this, we must transfer equity between your brand and a relevant sports property. Here is the step-by-step process we use to facilitate this transfer: Client Research, Property Alignment, Activation, Management and Measurement.
Services:
Provide strategic method on how the sports marketplace can be leveraged to effectively help a brand achieve its objectives.
Clients:
Carolina Panthers, Russell Athletic, Fox Sports, Western Union, The History Channel, Gulf Oil, New England Patriots/Foxboro Stadium, GlaxcoSmithKline, OfficeMax, Merck, Bank of America, AltaVista.
Other Location:
One Baltimore Place, Suite 350, Atlanta, GA 30308. 404-885-9696; FAX: 404-885-9449.

TICKETMASTER
880 W. SUNSET BLVD
WEST HOLLYWOOD, CA 90069
213-639-6100
Fax: 213-386-1244
www.ticketmaster.com
• Michael Rapino, President & CEO
• Nathan Hubbard, Chief Executive Officer of Ticketing
Nature of Service:
Provides event ticket sales, marketing and distribution through Internet, phone, and retail outlets, along with online auctions, fan club ticketing, and venue-authorized fan resale ticketing services.
Brands:
TicketsNow; TicketExchange; Ticketmaster
Marketing & Consulting Services:
Works with professional and college sports teams to develop new programs designed to expand ticket sales by helping with marketing ideas and actual sales of tickets using outlets, telephones and Internet.
Sports Service Founded:
1995; Merged with Live Nation on January 25, 2010, creating Live Nation Entertainment, Inc

---

TNS SPORT - NORTH AMERICA
100 PARK AVENUE
4TH FLOOR
NEW YORK, NY 10017
212-991-6194
Fax: 914-684-6078

info-us@tns-global.com
www.tns-us.com
• Eric Salama, Global CEO
• MIke Gettle, Chief Financial Officer and Chief Operating o
• James Brooks, Global Operations Director
• Matthew Froggatt, Chief development Officer
• Tracy Schoenadal, VP
(203) 618-8621
tracy.schoenadel@intersearch.tnsofres.com
Description:
Leading provider of sports and sponsorship research. The only sports research company able to offer the complete research solution on a global scale, setting the industry standards utilising the latest research techniques and technologies. Regarded as a leader in evaluating sponshorships, providing customised, impartial and actionable research to over 200 of the World's leading corporate sponsors, teams, agencies, events and sports.

TOOLBOX STUDIOS
454 SOLEDAD STREET
SUITE 100
SAN ANTONIO, TX 78205
210-225-8269
877-225-8205
Fax: 210-225-8200
info@toolboxstudios.com
www.toolboxstudios.com
• Rob Simons, President
(210) 225-8269
• Kathy Babb, Account Manager
(210) 225-8269
• Ron Herrera, Account Executive
(210) 225-8269
Nature of Service:
Toolbox Studios is a communication design firm that specializes in delivering creative solutions for highly complex marketing challenges. We offer strategy, design and execution services all under one roof. While we employ some of the most creative, award-winning minds in the industry, we are also uniquely staffed and equipped to execute any concept in virtually any medium - from podcast to broadcast, from outdoor boards to banner ads, from web design to web press. We are experts in branding, corporate identities, websites, advertising and publications. Our clients represent industries as diverse as financial services, youth media, museums, s
Year Founded:
1996

TOTAL SPORTS ENTERTAINMENT
PO BOX 5635
DEPERE, WI 54115
800-962-2471
Fax: 608-788-3864
info@yourtse.com
www.totalsportsentertainment.com
• Robert Masewicz, Founder/Owner
bob@totalsportsentertainment.com
• Bob Masewicz, Owner, Chief Consultant
(80) 962-24
• John Brostrom, Chief Executive Officer
(80) 962-24
• Chris Mahal, Account Executive
Nature of Service:
Sports entertainment and promotions consulting company specializing in video board installation, training, and gameday entertainment enhancement. Developers of

TSE GameTime game management computer program.

TRACK RECORD ENTERPRISES
11500 OLYMPIC BOULEVARD
OLYMPIC PLAZA BUILDING, SUITE 400
LOS ANGELES, CA 90064
310-839-1996
• Tom Mills, President
(310) 839-1996
Sports Service Founded:
1979
Services:
Music production and marketing company
Marketing & Consulting Services::
Full service sports marketing firm involved in hundreds of events, programs and projects featuring Olympians from the Southern California Olympians' alumni organization and a host of official sponsors, suppliers and licensees.

TRIPLE CROWN PRODUCTIONS
700 CENTRAL AVENUE
LOUISVILLE, KY 40208-1200
502-636-4405
triplecrown@kyderby.com
• Robert L. Evans, President
• Edward P. Seigenfeld, EVP
• Joseph A. De Francis, VP - Treasurer
• C. St Duncker, Secretary
Services:
Event Management Services spacilizes in horseracing events.
Sports Service Founded:
1985
Event Management Services:
Company incorporated by Churchill Downs, Inc., the Maryland Jockey Club of Baltimore City and the New York Racing Association to coordinate marketing, sponsorship sales, publications, public relations and promotions for the Triple Crown (Kentucky Derby, Preakness Stakes, Belmont Stakes).

TSE SPORTS & ENTERTAINMENT
14 PENN PLAZA
SUITE 925
NEW YORK, NY 10122
212-695-9480
877-621-5243
Fax: 212-564-8098
www.tseworld.com
• Robert Tuchman, President
(212) 695-9480
• Brett Sklar, SVP
(877) 621-5243
• Andy Robb, Operations Director
(212) 695-9480
Services:
Provides marketing programs to reach and engage customers by leveraging the power of sports & entertainment to bring their brand messages to life. Provides athlete/celebrity talent for appearances, events, promotions, public relations projects and endorsements.
Services:
Specializes in working with corporations to provide them with marketing programs that reach and engage their customers by leveraging the power of sports & entertainment to bring their brand messages to life. Focuses on Corporate Hospitality, Sales Promotions & Sweepstakes, Meeting & Event Planning, Athlete/ Celebrity Marketing, and Corporate Consulting.

Clients:
Anheuser-Busch, Bacardi Martini, Brown Forman, Coors, Deer Park, Geyser Peak Winery, InBev/Labatt USA, Miller Brewing Company, Diageo, Schieffelin & Somerset, Triarc Beverages, ABC Sports, Conde Nast Publications, Fox Network, GQ Magazine, HBO, NBC, ESPN, Maxim Magazine; Castrol, Daimler Chyrsler, ExxonMobil, Ford Motor Co., General Motors, Lexus, Pennzoil Products, Toyota; American Express, Bank of America, Merrill Lynch, JP Morgan Chase, KPMG, Bear Stearns, Hartford Financial, Morgan-Stanley Dean Whitter, AT&T, EMC, Ericsson, Hewlett-Packard, Lucent Technologies, Microsoft, IBM, Sony, Verizon; Bayer Corp., BIC USA, Bristol-Myers, Campbell's
Sports Travel:
Specializes in travel packages to major sporting events.
Athlete Management Services:
Provides athlete/celebrity talent for appearances, events, promotions, public relations projects and endorsements.
Event Management Services:
Specializes in providing hospitality and promotional services with multi-level involvement including consumer, trade and retail sales.
Promotional Services:
Specializes in fully integrated marketing promotions.

TSI SPORTS, INC.
2342 DANBURY LN
GAINESVILLE, GA 30507
678-717-1200
800-465-3461
Fax: 770-534-2233
golf@tsisports.com
www.tsisports.com
• Jennifer Sanders, Vice President
Description:
A leading, nationwide hole-in-one and promotional contest insurance company.
Services:
TSI Sports provides prize insurance services for hole-in-one and promotional contests, sweepstakes and games of chance and skill. The 800-Hole-in-1 brand is synonymous with quality and service. TSI Sports also has the latest in graphic and sign-making technology to put the promotional sponsors proudly in the spotlight. This includes printed fabric banners, signs and tabledrapes and direct UV printed signs on hard surfaces.

TURNKEY SPORTS & ENTERTAINMENT
9 TANNER STREET
SUITE 8
HADDONFIELD, NJ 08033
856-685-1450
Fax: 856-685-1451
www.turnkeyse.com
• Haynes Hendrickson, Senior Vice President - Turnkey Intelligence
• Kyle Mathiot, VP
• Michael Mayle, Chief Technical Officer
• Patrick Kuhlen, VP,Product Designing and marketing
• David Stys, SVP, Product Development
• Mellisa Dean, Chief Financial officer
• Len Perna, President
• Haynes Hendrickson, President, Turnkey Intelligence

Year Founded:
1996

UMBRELLA ENTERTAINMENT GROUP
1110 EUGENIA PLACE
SUITE 300
CARPINTERIA, CA 93013-2082
800-553-6637
Fax: 805-684-7808
info@airshownetwork.com
www.airshownetwork.com
• Jim Breen, President/Founder
(805) 684-0155
jim@airshownetwork.com
Services:
Develops and executes marketing campaigns for specific events which involves customer research, development of a marketing strategy, and design and implementation of all aspects of that strategy.
Clients:
Knudsen's, Kraft, Red Baron Pizza, Pontiac, Kodak, Metlife
Marketing & Consulting Services:
Creates, develops and executes relationship marketing strategies with key target audiences; specializes in college, air shows, military, family special events and recreation; sampling and coupon programs.
Event Management Services:
Creates events, develops sponsorships, provide turn-key services for these events.
Sports Service Founded:
1988

UNITED SPORTS ASSOCIATES/USA
170 ATLANTIC AVENUE
SWAMPSCOTT, MA 1907
781-477-0240
Fax: 781-598-4285
www.unitedsportsassociates.com
• Phil Sloan, Founder/President
(781) 477-0742
phil@unitedsportsassociates.com
• Craig Calcasola, VP/Director of Events
(781) 477-0240
Description:
Develops and implements customer based sales initiatives. Produces and promotes proprietary sponsorship event properties. Plans and develops grassroots corporate hospitality programs. Manages and monitors audience acqusition strategies.
Year Founded:
2003

UNITED STATES SPORTS ACADEMY
ONE ACADEMY DRIVE
DAPHNE, AL 36526
251-626-3303
800-223-2668
Fax: 251-625-1035
academy@ussa.edu
www.ussa.edu
• Thomas Rosandich, President/CEO
Services:
An independent, non-profit, special mission school of sport offering sport-specific, degree-granting residential and online distance learning programs to students, teachers and administrators around the world.
Nature of Services:
Offers Bachelor's, Master's, and Doctoral degrees and Continuing Education programs.

Sports Service Founded:
1972

UPSTARES MEDIA
184 S LIVINGSTON AVENUE
SUITE 9126
LIVINGSTON, NJ 07039
973-968-6666
Fax: 973-556-1999
stares@upstaresmedia.com
www.upstaresmedia.com
• Barry Roberts, President/CEO
Clients:
AT&T, KFC, Bright House Networks, Charter
Communications, Target, Unilever, Sprint,
Six Flags, Absolut, Makers Mark, Discovery
Networks, Disney, VISA, PETCO,
Coca-Cola, Wellpoint, Verizon, Sunglass
Hut, Toyota, Sony, Nationwide, Hilton,
Kellogg's, Bank of America, and many more

USA COACHES CLINICS, INC.
4800 FALL BROOK DRIVE
COLUMBIA, MO 65203-9133
573-445-3843
800-COACH-13
Fax: 573-445-4224
www.usacoaches.com
• Bob Murrey, President, Owner
• Earl Hopper, Clinic Director
(314) 991-8600
• Craig Harbaugh, Director Sales/Operations
(314) 991-8600
Nature of Service:
Providing meetings set up to help coaches
improve, and offers a sports library with
books, and videos.
Year Founded:
1989
Marketing & Consulting Services:
Conducts seminars for high school coaches
for basketball, football, track and field,
baseball and volleyball. Also markets library
of coaching books and videos, sold by mail
order.

USA TODAY/SPORTS MARKETING
7950 JONES BRANCH DRIVE
MCLEAN, VA 22108-0605
703-854-3400
800-872-7073
accuracy@usatoday.com
www.usatoday.com
• Brent Jones, Reader Editor
(800) 872-7073
accuracy@usatoday.com
Services:
Sports Event Marketing Services
Marketing & Consulting Services:
Creates, evaluates and complements
advertising programs of USA Today's major
sports advertising accounts. Also develops
integrated programs with various leagues,
associations and numerous other
sports-driven clients.
Sports Service Founded:
1987

USADATA.COM
477 MADISON AVENUE
SUITE 1220
NEW YORK, NY 10017
212-679-1411
800-599-5030
800-395-7707
Fax: 212-679-8507

info@usadata.com
www.usadata.com
• Ric Murphy, President/Chief Executive
Officer
(212) 679-1411
rmurphy@usadata.com
• Bruce Meberg, VP
(212) 679-1411
bmeberg@usadata.com
• Dominic Leclaire, List Integration Partner
dleclaire@usadata.com
Services:
Leading provider of Sales Leads and
On-Demand 1-to-1 Marketing Automation
solutions for customer acquisition and
relationship management for a wide range
of companies.
Clients:
A.I.G,A.D.P,A.D.T,All Nations
Church,American Cancer Society,Bankers
Life,Big Planet,BMW Excluservice,Bonetics
Corporation,Capital Financial,Castle
Press,Centers for Advanced
Medicine,Corcoran,Custom Exteriors,
Inc.,E.F.I,Farmers Insurance,Federal
Reserve Bank of Atlanta,Flexeprint,FX
STUDIOS,Hover Round,Hussman Corp.,JP
Morgan Chase,Kelley Solutions,Met
Life,Modern Postcard,Money Mailer,Morgan
Stanley,Nationwide,New England
Financial,New York Golf Center,New York
Life,Nu-Ear,Pinnacle Development
Partners,Press-Sense,RE/MAX,Restaurant.
com,Spectrum Bank,Sprint PCS,State Farm
Insurance,State University of New
York,Tampa Bay Buccaneers.
Products:
USADATA's application automate and
improve sales processes for organizations
ranging from networks of thousands of
decentralized users to a single, centralized
user.

VELOCITY SPORTS & ENTERTAINMENT
230 E AVENUE
NORWALK, CT 06855
203-831-2000
Fax: 203-831-2300
• David Grant, Principal
(203) 831-2000
grant@teamvelocity.com
• Alex Nieroth, Principal
(203) 831-2000
nieroth@teamvelocity.com
• Mike Reisman, Principal
(203) 831-2000
reisman@teamvelocity.com
• Harlan Stone, Principal
(203) 831-2000
stone@teamvelocity.com
• Bob Wilhelmy, Principal
Services:
Marketing agency specializing in helping
clients maximize the value of their sports
and entertainment sponsorship marketing
efforts. Assists clients in sponsorship
marketing process including strategic
planning, negotiation, program
development, leveraging, execution,
customer hospitality and pre-/post-event
evaluation.
Clients:
IBM, FedEX, Cingular Wireless, Texaco,
Novartis, The New York Times and
NASCAR
Description:
Sponsorship and event marketing agency.

VENUEWORKS
4611 MORTENSEN ROAD
SUITE 111
AMES, IA 50014
515-232-5151
888-232-5151
Fax: 515-663-2022
info@venuworks.com
www.venuworks.com

VISION PRO SPORTS, INC.
80 RIVER STREET
3RD FLOOR
HOBOKEN, NJ 7030
201-792-4111
Marketing & Consulting Services:
A full service creative marketing agency that
specializeds in the youth, sports and
entertainment industries.

**VISION SPORTS & ENTERTAINMENT
PARTNERS**
330 MADISON AVENUE
9TH FLOOR
NEW YORK, NY 10017
212-983-7250
look@vision.com
www.vision.com
• Billy Glennon, Group CEO
• Gerald Adams, Co-Founder and group
Director
• Charles Spinosa, Group Director
• Matthew Hancocks, Group Director
• Gianluca Romano, Group Director
• Graeme Toolin, Chief Financial Officer
Services:
Sports and Marketing firm and sports
agency for professional hockey players

**WASHINGTON SPORTS &
ENTERTAINMENT**
601 F STREET NW
WASHINGTON, DC 20004
202-628-3200
Fax: 202-661-5063
www.verizoncenter.com
• Abe Pollin, Chairman
• Susan O'Malley, President
• Brian Cawley, Director, Corporate
Marketing
• Judy Holland, SVP, Community Relations
Services:
Oversees marketing operations of
Washington Capitals, MCI Center, and the
Washington Wizards. Handles all aspects of
arena, event and team corporate
sponsorships, radio and TV sales, suite
sales, signage and other entertainment and
sports marketing.
Sports Service Founded:
1995

WEBER SHANDWICK WORLDWIDE
919 THIRD AVENUE
NEW YORK, NY 10022
212-445-8000
www.webershandwick.com
• Jack Leslie, Chairman
jleslie@webershandwick.com
• Harris Diamond, Chief Executive Officer
• Andy Polansky, President, Weber
Shandwick Worldwide
apolansky@webershandwick.com
• Colin Byrne, Chief Executive Officer,
Weber Shandwick
cbyrne@webershandwick.com

Description:
Public relations and communications management firm.

WILKINSON GROUP
330 PRIMROSE ROAD
SUITE 205
BURLINGAME, CA 94010
650-375-7888
Fax: 650-340-8067
david@twgsponsorship.com
• David G. Wilkinson, President/Chief Executive Officer
(650) 375-7888
david@twgsponsorship.com
• Krista Semotiuk, VP
(650) 375-7888
krista_semotiuk@twgsponsorship.com
• Louise M. Felsher, SVP Event Marketing
(650) 375-7883
lfelsher@twgsponsorship.com
Services:
Create marketing programs based on strategies and built around events, sponsorships or lifestyle activities; entertainment, media, sport and cause properties that are owned by clients for true equity positioning; Create communications strategies that make direct contact with target markets in a focused manner; Add a textured, human element to corporate brands through alignment with lifestyle activities; Stretch investments by creating alliances (corporate, media, cause) that decrease implementation costs; Generate a direct return on investment for the sponsor clients; Generate a direct return on investment for the sponsor clients; Drive custo
Clients:
Air Canada, Air Jamaica, Air New Zealand, Akamai, Ast Computers, Bank of America, Best Buy, Brugal, California Overnight, Canadian Imperial Bank of Commerce, Cisco Systems, Citibank, Clorox (Brita), Coca-Cola Canada, Gateway, Hewlett-Packard, Intel, Invensys, Jergens (Biore), Manulife Financial, Pacific Bell, Panasonic, Pepsi, Petro Canada, PG & E, Proctor & Gamble, Reuters, Sears Roebuck & Co, Teleglobe Canada, The New Power Company, Wells Fargo, etc.
Sports Service Founded:
1982
Marketing & Consulting Services:
Sponsorship marketing seminars and consulting for corporations; corporate sponsorship consulting services; educational materials; event creation and production, propert, representation and sales.

WINDY CITY SPORTS
1450 W RANDOLPH STREET
CHICAGO, IL 60607
312-421-1551
Fax: 312-421-1454
www.windycitysports.com
• Doug Kaplan, President/Publisher
• Kate Bongiovanni, Associate Editor
Sports Service Founded:
1992

WOLF GROUP-NY
4401 FAIR LAKES COURT
SUITE 310
FAIRFAX, VA 22033
703-502-9500
Fax: 703-502-3970
info@thewolfgroup.com
www.thewolfgroup.com
• Leonard S Wolf, Managing Partner
l.wolf@thewolfgroup.com
• Robert D. Len, Director
• Dale Mason, Senior International Tax Manager
• Robert D. Len, Partner
blen@thewolfgroup.com
• Dale Mason, International Tax Director and Chief Operatin
• Sharif Mahfouz, Global Tax Director
• Michael Goodson, Chief Investment Officer
• Leonard S. M. Wolf, Director
Description:
Fully integrated, brand-centric organization with services in advertising, corporate branding, interactive marketing, media buying and planning, direct response, sales promotion and public relations.
Services:
Offers a full range of marketing communications services, including advertising, strategic planning, sales promotion, direct response, public relations, package design, directory marketing and interactive.
Clients:
Aamco, Canandaigua Wine Company, Haagen-Dazs, HSBC Bank USA, I LOVE NY, Scotts Company.
Other Locations:
Toronto, Cleveland, Atlanta, Buffalo, Rochester NY

WOLF GROUP-OH
10860 KENWOOD ROAD
CINCINNATI, OH 45242
513-891-9100
800-222-4045
Fax: 513-792-3533
www.wolfgrp.com
• Steve Zweig, President
• Stuart Glassman, EVP
Services:
Provides promotional marketing development of sports programs in the promotion of client's name and/or products. Full service and turn-key consumer and trade promotions utilizing sports events, media vehicles, premiums and sweepstakes.
Sports Service Founded:
1984
Other Location:
New York

WORLD CLASS SPORTS
5777 W CENTURY BOULEVARD
SUITE 1070
LOS ANGELES, CA 90045
310-665-9400
Fax: 310-665-9844
wcsagent@pacbell.net
www.worldclass-sports.com
• Don Franken, President
wrldclssprts@earthlink.net
• Andrew Woolf, Vice President
(310) 665-9400
wcsagent@pacbell.net
Nature of Service:
Sports talent agency, sports celebrity agency and sports speakers bureau. Began in 1982. Professional and Olympic athletes,
legends and current stars.
Sports Service Founded:
1982
Marketing & Consulting Services:
Through Franken Enterprises advises recommends and creates sports events around a client's marketing objectives. Creates fully integrated sports marketing opportunities to increase client visibility and sales.
Clients:
Pepsi, All Sport - Jerry Rice, Steve Young, Hallmark - Bill Walton, Sprint - Dick Butkus, Larry Czonka, Deacon Jones, ESPN Extreme Games - Evel Knievel, Kellogg's - Marion Jones, Ariba Computers - Marion Jones, Gunze of Japan - Mike Piazza, American Express - Evelyn Ashford, American Express - Billy Mills, Got Milk - Bob Burnquist, Mission Foods - Shannon Miller, Dean Witter Reynolds - Bob Mathias, Bayer Agriculture - Nolan Ryan, California Dept. of Transportation - Joe Montana, Panasonic - Nadia Comaneci, Sports Illustrated - Deacon Jones and Conrad Dobler, Black Star Bears Beer - Rollie Fingers, Glaxo - Jim Ryun, Glaxo - Bob Beamon, Dermik

WORLD PROMOTIONAL PRODUCTS, INC.
17751 SKY PARK CIRCLE
SUITE F
IRVINE, CA 92614
800-705-7796
Fax: 949-221-0693
• Chris Tyler, Vice President
Description:
World Promotional Products provides logo and imprinted merchandise - services of which include graphic and creative design, screen print and embroidery.
Clients:
World Promotional Products works with many NBA, MLB, NHL and Fortune 500 companies.
Nature of Services:
Trade Shows; Employee Incentives; Events and Meetings; New Product Launches; Brand Marketing Initiatives; Award Programs; Golf and Charity Events.

WORLD SPORTS & MARKETING
460 N. ORLANDO AVE
SUITE 200
WINTER PARK, FL 32789
407-628-4802
Fax: 407-628-7061
www.wakeboardingmag.com

WSS EXECUTIVE SEARCH
7755 CENTER AVENUE
SUITE 1100
HUNTINGTON BEACH, CA 92647
714-848-1201
Fax: 714-848-5111
www.wssexecutivesearch.com
• Becky Heidesch, Founder & Chief Executive Officer
• Mary Lou Youngblood, Sr.Partner
Clients:
Anaheim Angels, Hyundai Motor America, Oshman's Sporting Goods, Gart Sports, WNBA, Alta Dena Dairy, LPGA, Scudders Private Investment Counsel, Monster, 24 Hour Fitness, Sports Illustrated for Women, American Express, ESPN, Health Magazine,

817

Executive Women's Golf Association, Vans, Golf Digest Companies, Golf Channel, Burton Snowboards, O'Neil, SELF Magazine, Healthsouth, WNBA LA Sparks, Black Women in Sport Foundation, Association for Women in Sports Media, WUSA San Diego Spirit, California Interscholastic Federation, etc.

Description:
WSS Executive Search, a division of Women Sourcing Soltions, is a WBENC certified, women-owned business specializing in women and minority sourcing solutions. WSS partners with their clients to provide them with sourcing solutions to solve their most challenging diversity hiring efforts. WSS specializes in the sports, financial and technology industry.

Nature of Service:
WSS customizes their recruitment and management process for each client. By offering personalized sourcing solutions, WSS matches qualified professional candidates with top-tier companies who are often challenged in their industry in finding women and minority candidates. WSS has years of experience assisting companies in reaching their diversity goals and empowering candidates to realize their career dreams!

Primary Audience:
Corporate America, specialty companies in the sports, financial and technology sectors. Candidate pool: Mid-management to Executive Level.

Sports
All.

WTS INTERNATIONAL
3200 TOWER OAKS BOULEVARD
SUITE 400
ROCKVILLE, MD 20852
301-622-7800
800-229-8262
Fax: 301-622-3373
wts@wtsinternational.com
www.wtsinternational.com
• Gary J. Henkin, President
(301) 622-7800
ghenkin@wtsinternational.com
• Ralph Newman, Chief Operating Officer
(301) 622-7800
rnewman@wtsinternational.com

Services:
One of the world's leading spa, fitness, and leisure consulting and management firms. WTS provides: conceptual and strategic planning; feasibility and needs assessment studies; design consultation and space plan development; pre-opening services; and turnkey management or operational consulting. Services spas, athletic and tennis facilities, and leisure complexes of all types and sizes throughout the United States and abroad.

Clients:
The Sanderling Spa Resort and Spa, Ashburn Village Sports Pavilion, Wyndham Sugar Bay Resort and Spa, PGA Tour Spa Laterra, Al Corniche Club, The Spa at Southern Highlands, Peter Island Resort and Spa, Hilton San Francisco Spa Fusion, Piedmont Community

Sports Service Founded:
1973

Marketing & Consulting Services:
Provides management, consulting services, personnel selection and program development for health/fitness facilities and spas of all types and sizes.

WUNDERMAN
285 MADISON AVENUE
NEW YORK, NY 10017
212-941-3000
Fax: 212-627-8342
www.wunderman.com
• Daniel Morel, Chairman/Global Chief Executive Officer
• Stewart Pearson, Chief Executive Officer/Wunderman EMEA

Services:
Promotional marketing programs. Achieves defined client objectives through the strategic and tactical application of sports as an integrated marketing medium, accomplished through programs that produce measurable results against brand objectives on nation

Clients:
American Institute of Certified Public Accountants, Astra-Zeneca, Canada Post, Caterpillar, Citibank, Coca-Cola, Danone, Diageo, Ford, Gannett, Hewlett-Packard, Hotels.com, Jaguar, Johnnie Walker, Land Rover, Lincoln Mercury, Lufthansa, M&G Investments, Mazda, Microsoft, Pfizer, Royal Canadian Mint, Royal Marsden Hospital, Sears, Star Alliance

XA, THE EXPERIENTIAL AGENCY
333 HUDSON STREET
SUITE 203
NEW YORK, NY 10013
646-688-6381
Fax: 212-274-1788
www.experientialagency.com
• Valerie Morel, EVP Marketing
(212) 625-9191
• Amanda Puck, Director Business Development/Public Relation
(312) 397-9100

Year Founded:
1989.

Clients:
ABN AMRO, Accenture, Aegis Insurance, Alberto-Culver, American Council of Life Insurers, Ameritech, Amoco, Anchor Food Products, Aramark, Astrazeneca, Avenue Q, Bank Calumet, Bank One, Biora, Black Clawson, Bristol-Myers Squibb, Burberry, Capri Capital Advisors, Cellular One, Chicago Stock Exchange, Citadel Investment Group, Clinical Insights, ComEd, Coors Brewing, Del Monte, Discount Tire Company, Enterprise Rent-A-Car, Ernst & Young, Eurex, ewireless, Exelon, Fairmont Hotels, The Fashion Group, Fleet Mortgage, Gardner Publishing, Chicago Gateway Green, GE Capital, General Growth Properties, Gilead Sciences, GlaxoWellcome, Goldman Sachs, Hea

Nature of Service:
Event Strategy Design/Production: Event Concepts, Design & Production, Multimedia Content Development, Talent Buying & Management, Celebrity Wrangling, Guest Management, Destination Management, Data Capture & Measurement; Non-Traditional Marketing, Public Relations, Event Promotion.

YESAWICH, PEPPERDINE, BROWNE & RUSSELL
423 S KELLER ROAD
SUITE 100
ORLANDO, FL 32810-6121
407-875-1111
Fax: 407-875-1115
pyesawich@mmgyglobal.com
www.mmgyglobal.com
• Peter C. Yesawich, President/Chief Executive Officer
peter_yesawich@ypbr.com
• Larry Tolpin, President/Chief Creativer Officer
(407) 875-1111
larry_tolpin@ypbr.com
• Gary Sain, EVP/Chief Marketing Officer
(407) 875-1111
gary_sain@ypbr.com
• Clayton A. Ried, CEO & President
• Hugh McConnell, CFO & Executive Vice President
• Stewart Colowin, Executive Vice President
• Jeff Huggins, Senior Vice President

Sports Service Founded:
1993

Services:
Marketing, advertising and public relations agency that delivers extraordinary results for its clients through proprietary consumer insights, surprising strategies, big ideas and bold creative executions.

Clients:
Aero Mexico, Frontier, Mexicana, USAirways, Western Pacific Airlines, Dardens- Seasons 52, Ruth's Chris Steakhouse; Financial/Investment Banking: American Express, Bear Stearns and Company, Discover Card, MasterCard International, Merrill Lynch; Gaming: Bally Gaming, Belle Casinos, Caesar's Palace, Casino Rouge, Florida Lottery, Foxwoods Casino Resort, Grand Casinos, Hard Rock Hotels & Casinos, Hyatt Casinos, Wynn Las Vegas, etc.

Marketing & Consulting Services:
Advertising, public relations, marketing firm specializing in golf.

ZIP CELEBRITY, INC.
ONE COMMERCIAL WHARF WEST
BOSTON, MA 02110
617-350-5518
Fax: 508-647-5101
info@zipcelebrity.com
www.zipcelebrity.com

Description:
To match celebrity casting with corporate identity and goals. At the same time, we make sure that a portion of every talent fee goes to worthy charities. We give you the opportunity to match the true celebrity with your brands.

Services:
Matches celebrity casting with corporate identity and goals

ZOOPERSTARS!
PO BOX 36061
LOUISVILLE, KY 40233
502-458-4020
800-219-0899
Fax: 502-458-0867
www.zooperstars.com
• Brennan Latkovski, Co-Owner
(502) 458-4020
brennan@zooperstars.com

• Stephanie Fish, General Manager
stephanie@zooperstars.com
General Description:
Crazy Animals. Funny Stuff. Hilarious
Routines. The hottest entertainment act in
sports with characters such as LeBronco
James, Peyton Manatee, Ken Giraffey, Jr.,
Tiger Woodschuck, Elephant Presley,
Barack Ollama, Mia Hammster, Snail
Earnhardt, Jr., Whale Gretzky, Shaquille
O'Seal, Clammy Sosa, and other funny
friends in a show the audience will love.
Year Founded:
1998
Sports Service Founded:
1998
Event Marketing Services:
An independent traveling troupe of inflatable
mascots that perform during special events
and half-time shows.
Clients:
Aberdeen Ironbirds, Adirondack Frostbite,
Aguascalientes Railroadmen, Akron Aeros,
Alabama Slammers, Albany Conquest,
Albuquerque Dukes, Albuquerque Isotopes,
Alexandria Aces, Altoona Curve, Amarillo
Dillas, Arizona Rattlers, Arkansas
RiverBlades, Arkansas Twisters, Asheville
Tourists, Atlantic 10 Conference, Auburn
Doubledays, Auburn University, Augusta
Greenjackets, Augusta Lynx, Bakersfield
Blitz, Bakersfield Condors, Bellarmine
University, Big League World Series, Billings
Mustangs, Binghamton Mets, Binghamton
Senators, Birmingham Barons, Boise
Hawks, Boise Power Series, Boston Celtics,
Bowie BaySox, Brevard County Manatees.

Technical Services

A.V. CONCEPTS
1917 W 1ST STREET
TEMPE, AZ 85281
866-927-7590
800-473-6828
Fax: 480-894-8376
www.avconcepts.com
• Nick Smith, Owner/Founder
• Fred Mandrick, Owner/Founder
Nature of Service:
A provider of audio/video staging services
including planning, technical support,
coordination and execution of video audio
and lighting for an event.
Year Founded:
1987
Other Locations:
7365 Mission Gorge Road, Suite A, San
Diego, CA 92120; we also have office
locations in Los Angeles, Scottsdale,
Phoenix and Tucson.

ACCU-STATS VIDEO PRODUCTIONS
PO BOX 299
BLOOMINGDALE, NJ 07403
800-828-0397
Fax: 973-838-5771
accustats@accu-stats.com
www.accu-stats.com
Services:
Offers Professional Billiard Video Plays;
Also offers professional instructional videos.
Description:
Offers the best in professional billiard
videos. Instructional videos by Buddy Hall,
Grady Matthews, Bill Incardona, Mike

Massey and Pat Fleming. Collections of
books, instructional and biographical,
essential to the avid pool and billiard fans.

ACENTECH INC.
33 MOULTON STREET
CAMBRIDGE, MA 02138
617-499-8000
Fax: 617-499-8074
info@acentech.com
www.acentech.com
• David Bowen, Senior Consultant
dbateman@acentech.com
• Carl Rosenberg, Principal
• Eric Wood, Principal
• J. Christopher Jaffe, Principal Consultant
• Christopher Savereid, Principal
Services:
Offers sound system design, mechanical
noise and vibration control services,
architectural acoustics, and video system
design for sports facilities.
Nature of Sports Service:
Full service acoustical consulting firm.
Sound system design, mechanical noise
and vibration control services, architectural
acoustics, and video system design for
sports facilities.
Description:
Kenyon College Athletic Facility, Gambier
OH; Quinnipiac College Recreation Center,
Hamden CT; University of Maryland
Recreation Center, College Park, MD

ACTIVE ALERT
15120 ENTERPRISE COURT
SUITE 100
CHANTILLY, VA 20151
703-227-9690
Fax: 703-803-3299
aasolutions@spectrarep.com
www.activeaccess.com
• Terrence Thomas, Interactive Marketing
Manager
• Rodger Metchori, Sales Director
Nature of Services:
BIA Information Network offers
ActiveAccess, a private-label desktop
application that gives a sports team a direct
pipeline to fans to deliver the information
they crave - scores, game videos, updated
gameday information, local weather, and
much more.

APUNIX COMPUTER SERVICES
17150 VIA DEL CAMPO
SUITE 308
SAN DIEGO, CA 92127
858-673-8649
800-827-8649
Fax: 858-673-8640
support@apunix.com
• Peter Berens, Founder/President
Peter.Berens@apunix.com
• Sylvia Berens, Founder/VP
Services:
Develops Kiosks and Photo ID systems.
Offers instant issue employee photo ID
system (which interfaces to time and
attendance systems) and can be use to
create VIP or season ticket holder cards.
Description:
Develops Kiosks and Photo ID systems.
Offers instant issue employee photo ID
system (which interfaces to time and
attendance systems) and can be used to
create VIP or season ticket holder cards.

Apunix's kiosk is the first Java touch screen
multimedia kiosk.
Year Founded:
1981

ASAP SPORTS
225 BROADWAY
SUITE 700
NEW YORK, NY 10007
212-385-0297
info@asapsports.com
www.asapsports.com
• Peter P Balastrieri, CEO
(212) 385-0297
peter@asapsports.com
• Jeri Gargano, VP,Managing Director
(631) 425-2701
jeri@asapsports.com
• Vasili Timofeev, Director,Finance
(212) 385-0297
basil@asapsports.com
• Jaime Morrocco,
Director,Technology,Quality Control and
Huma
(503) 317-8664
jaime@asapsports.com
Description:
Provides transcrpits and soundclips of press
conferences at major sporting events
around the world.

**AUDIO VISUAL CONFERENCE
TECHNOLOGIES**
2 BARNES ST
PATTERSON, NJ 7501
973-345-5211
Description:
Provides professional audio visual services
to convention centers and meeting facilities.
Provides complete on-site audio/visual and
business center departments. Specialists in
operating and maintaining audio/visual
systems.

BOSE CORPORATION
100 THE MOUNTAIN ROAD
FRAMINGHAM, MA 01701-9168
508-879-7330
800-999-2673
Fax: 508-820-3465
www.bose.com
• Sherwin Greenblatt, President
• Shari Goldman, Marketing Assistant
Services:
Develops total sound systems for any size
facility.
Description:
Develops total sound systems for any size
facility.

BRONSKILL & CO.
55 FIELDWAY RD
TORONTO, ON, CANADA M8Z 3L4
416-703-8689
Fax: 416-703-0740
info@bronskill.com
www.bronskill.com
• Michael Regan, President
(602) 722-5837
• Reg Bronskill, Chairman/CEO
Services:
Event creation, environmental design and
entertainment.

BURNS ENTERTAINMENT & SPORTS MARKETING, INC
820 DAVIS STREET
SUITE 222
EVANSTON, IL 60201
847-866-9400
Fax: 847-491-9778
Bob.Williams@burnsent.com
www.burnsent.com
• Bob Williams, Chief Executive Officer
• Doug Shabelman, President
• Marc Ippolito, President/General Counsel
Services:
Burns Entertainment provides talent procurement services, linking entertainment and sports celebrities and properties with corporations, agencies, not-for-profits, colleges and associations. Provides leveraging experience and industry savvy to negotiate and execute deals in entertainment and sports. Also provides a propietary, state-of-the-art database to over 20,000 celebrities and properties for any request.
Sports Service Founded:
1970.

CALIFONE INTERNATIONAL, INC.
1145 ARROYO AVENUE
A
SAN FERNANDO, CA 91340
818-407-2400
800-722-0500
Fax: 818-407-2405
www.califone.com
• Roscoe Anthony, President
• Chase Stone, VP, Eastern Sales
• Terry Davis, VP, Central Sales
• Mike Morse, VP, Western & International Sales
Products:
Califone manufactures a full line of educationally-focused audio/visual products including installed and portable PA's, wireless products,megaphones, multimedia player/recorders, document cameras, and computer peripherals for school uses.

CCI SOLUTIONS
1247 85TH AVENUE, SE
OLYMPIA, WA 98501
360-943-5378
800-426-8664
800-562-6006
Fax: 360-754-1566
info@ccisolutions.com
• Ronald L Simonson, Principal Consultant
(800) 426-8664
indepth@ccisolutions.com
• Joe Brannberg, Project Manager
(800) 426-8664
indepth@ccisolutions.com
• Rick Boring, Systems Consultant
(800) 426-8664
indepth@ccisolutions.com
• Greg Hearns, Systems Consultant
(800) 426-8664
indepth@ccisolutions.com
• Ronald L. Simonson, P.E., Principal Consultant
• Mark Pearson, Senior Systems Consultant
• Greg Hearns, Senior Systems Consultant
• Rick Boring, Senior Systems Consultant
Services:
Offers audio-visual consulting, products, technical systems and expertise; Offers custom solutions which includes: public and corporate facilities services, worship facilities services, retail product sales, cassette/CD duplication and replication services, architectural consulting, equipment rental, and equipment repair.
Description:
Develops and installs high definition arena sound systems. Exclusive source for the high definition KB-8 Arena audio system.
Clients Include:
Gund Arena, Cleveland OH; America West Arena, Phoenix AZ; Key Arena, Seattle WA; MCI Center, Washington DC

COACH D*A*V*E
1700 N HIGHLAND AVENUE
SUITE H-648
HOLLYWOOD, CA 90028
818-508-7578
Sports Service Founded:
1981. D*A*V*E is an acronym for Definitive Audio Video Education. Prepares athletes for endorsements and broadcasting, working one-on-one teaching fundamentals that help to develop greater marketability. Focuses on media training, oral presentation skills, speech therapy, image development, personal appearances, audio/video techniques, TV and radio commercials, endorsement training.

COMMUNITY PROFESSIONAL LOUDSPEAKERS
333 E 5TH STREET
CHESTER, PA 19013-4511
610-876-3400
800-523-4934
Fax: 610-874-0190
info@communitypro.com
www.communitypro.com
• Grace Paoli, Marketing Communications Manager
gpaoli@communitypro.com
Year Founded:
1968.
Nature of Service:
Supplier of professional sound systems for forty years.
Brands:
(Loudspeakers) Cloud Series; CPL; CSV; DnD Series; Horns & Drivers; I/O Series; iBox; M-Class; MVPII; R-Series; Solutions; STS; T-Class; Tandem Drive; WET; XLTE; (Electronics) DXP4800 Digital Controller; (Software) ULYSSES; (Discontinued Products) CBA/CBS; CSV8; CSV; CSX; DSC52 Digital Controller; MVP; SC21.1 System Controller; TANDEM DRIVE; VLF218; XLT; XLTPRO

EVENT AUDIO VISUAL GROUP
50888 CENTURY COURT
WIXOM, MI 48393
800-935-2323
Fax: 800-935-8191
detroit@subrent.com
www.subrent.com

GENUONE
3 COPLEY PLACE
SUITE 201
BOSTON, MA 02116
617-226-3000
866-436-8663
Fax: 617-226-3001
www.opsecsecurity.com
• Jeffrey Unger, Chief Executive Officer/Director
• Donn Worby, Chief Financial Officer
• Thomas Taylor, SVP Operations and Engineering
• Stephen Polinsky, VP of Sales
Description:
Provider of security technologies and solutions that enable companies to protect their products and value chain from counterfeiting, grey-market diversion, warranty fraud and intellectual property theft in the physical world and on the internet.
Brands:
SourceGuard, GenuNet, GenuGuard
Sports Service Founded:
1998.

GLOBAL SPECTRUM
41-B NEW LONDON TURNPIKE
SUITE 107
Glastonbury, CT 6033
860-657-0630
Fax: 860-657-0761
frusso@global-spectrum.com
www.global-spectrum.com
• Peter Luukko, President/Chief Operating Officer
• Frank E. Russo Jr, SVP, Sales and Client Services
frusso@global-spectrum.com
• John Page, SVP/Chief Operations Manager
jpage@global-spectrum.com
• Frank E. M. Russo Jr., Sr. Vice President
• Todd Glickman, Vice President
Clients:
Pre-opening clients Wachovia Center - Philadelphia, Pennsylvania; John Labatt Centre - London, Ontario; University of South Carolina Carolina Center - Columbia, South Carolina; The Budweiser Events Center at the Ranch - Loveland, Colorado; Bank United Center - Coral Gables, Florida; Overland Park Convention Center - Overland Park, Kansas; University of Rhode Island Ryan Center & Bradford R. Boss Arena - Kingston, Rhode Island; Old Dominion University Ted Constant Convocation Center - Norfolk, Virginia; Palm Beach County Convention Center - West Palm Beach, Florida; Hy-Vee Hall, Des Moines, Iowa; St. Charles Convention Center, St. Charles, Mis
Event Management Services:
Computer software for event scheduling, settlement, accounting, ticketing, fundraising.
Sports Service Founded:
1994
Other Location:
3601 South Broad Street, Philadelphia, PA 19147. 215-389-9587; FAX: 215-952-5651; 41B New London Turnpike, Glastonbury, CT 06033, Phone: 860-657-0630; 780 94th Avenue North, STE 107, St. Petersburg, FL 33702, Phone: 727-456-1170

GOLF SCORECARDS, INC
9735 SW SUNSHINE COURT
SUITE 700
BEAVERTON, OR 97005
503-352-0281
800-238-7267
Fax: 503-226-4501
information@golfscorecards.com
www.golfscorecards.com
• Cynthia Grant, President
(503) 352-0283

• Byron Grant, General Manager
(503) 352-0284
byron@golfscorecards.com
Products:
Quality design and printing: scorecards,
yardage guides, other golf printed materials.

GRIP SALES & SERVICE TRAINING
2900 SE MARTINS STREET
PORTLAND, OR 97202
503-939-3927
Fax: 203-724-4331
www.gripinc.com
• Bret Polvorosa, President/Chief Executive
Officer
Nature of Sports Services:
Help organization to generate more revenue
and greater customer retention.

HENDERSON ENGINEERS INC.
8345 LENEXA DRIVE
SUITE 300
LENEXA, KS 66214
913-742-5000
Fax: 913-742-5001
info@hei-eng.com
www.hei-eng.com
• Russ L. Olsen, President
(913) 384-1261
• Ian Wolfe, VP
(913) 384-1261
• Brian Kubicki, VP
(913) 384-1261
• George Damon, Senior Associate
(913) 384-1261
Services:
Provides a wide range of consulting and
design services for all facility types.
Consulting includes noise control, video
playback, video production,
television-distribution and multimedia
systems design, and commissioning
services.
Clients:
Athletics: GM Place, Vancouver Canada;
Van Andel Arena, Grand Rapids, MI; Bob
Devaney Arena, University of Nebraska -
Lincoln; St. Charles Arena, St. Charles, MS;
Gwinnett Arena, Duluth, Georgia; Memorial
Coliseum, Fort Wayne, IN; MGM Grand
Arena, Las Vegas, NV; Office Depot Center,
Fort Lauderdale, FL; The Pyramid,
Memphis, TN; Sovereign Center Arena,
Reading, PA; Tyson Events Center Arena,
Sioux City, Iowa; Dean Smith Center Arena,
Chapel Hill, NC; America West Arena,
Phoenix, AZ; Seabury Convocation and
Recreation Center, Berea, Kentucky;
Earlham Student Activities Center,
Richmond, IN; Marietta College, Marietta,
OH; Fulton and Susie Coll
Clients include:
Van Andel Arena, Grannett Civic & Cultural
Center Arena, GM place, Dean Smith
Center, Devaney Arena
Sports Service:
Provides a wide range of consulting and
design services for all facility and venue
types. Our services include architectural
acoustics, facility analysis, sound & ALV
design, noise & vibration control, TV
distribution system design, systems
commissioning, expert testimony.

INFORMATION & DISPLAY SYSTEMS, INC.
10275 CENTURION COURT
JACKSONVILLE, FL 32256
904-645-8697
Fax: 904-645-8496
marketing@ids-sports.com
www.ids-sports.com
• Rallis Pappas, President
• David Lunghino, VP
Services:
Technology vendor to the sports industry.
Services focused on scoring/results
systems, display, TV production, web
production.
Sports:
Golf, Tennis, Basketball, hockey, Skiing,
Olympics, Action Sports, Racing, Fighting

INNOVATIVE ELECTRONIC DESIGNS, INC.
9701 TAYLORSVILLE ROAD
LOUISVILLE, KY 40299
502-267-7436
Fax: 502-267-9070
info@iedaudio.com
www.iedaudio.com
• Jason Kleiman, Inside Sales Manager
• Mark Lewellyn, Sales and Marketing
Director
• Matt Gray, Applications Engineer
• Rod Rupp, Applications Engineer
Brands:
500 Announcement Control Systems, 500
Visual Information Systems, 8000 Series
Totally Integrated Processing System, 6000
Series Power Amplifier Systems, 3200
Series Digital Signal Processing Systems,
4400 and 4800 Series Automatic Mixers
Description:
Design and manufacturer of
computer-controlled audio processing
systems, including the 8000 series (TIPS
Total Integrated Processing System) and
the UDAPS-universal digital audio
processing systems featuring all-digital
equalizing, delay, attenuation, mixing, and
routing. Other products include the 500ACS
announcement control system, 4000 Series
automatic microphone mixer systems,
4400/4800 stand-alone mixer systems, 5000
audio processing systems, 6000 power
amplifier system, and 540 ambient analysis
system. Applications include arenas and
stadiums.

JHG TOWNSEND
6215 FERRIS SQUARE
SUITE 210
SAN DIEGO, CA 92121
888-246-2396
• Alex Benjamin, VP Finance & Operations
• Chris Hassett, VP Communications
• Lisa Kendall, VP Business Partnerships
• Liya Sharif, VP Public Relations & Brand
Strategy
• Mary Fechtig, President/CEO
• Elizabeth E Cooper, Co-Founder
• Alex Benjamin, SVPof Finance &
Operations
• Cindy Subido, SVP
• Jacob Shea, EVP of Interactive &
technology
Nature of Services:
JHG is a San Diego-based marketing
agency serving the media, entertainment,
sports, and technology sectors that
integrates marketing strategy, branding,

public relations, interactive services, mobile
technology, and metrics to propel client
companies to success in the changing
marketplace.

M.B.I. PRODUCTS CO., INC.
801 BOND STREET
ELYRIA, OH 44035-3118
440-322-6500
Fax: 440-322-1900
sales@mbiproducts.com
www.mbiproducts.com
• Emily Hoke, Marketing Director
sales@mbiproducts.com
• Andrew Ungar, Advertising Manager
sales@mbiproducts.com
• C. Boyd, Advertising Manager
sales@mbiproducts.com
• Chris Kysela, Sales
sales@mbiproducts.com
Brands:
Cloud-Lite Acoustical Baffles, Colorsonix
Wall Panels, Lapendary Panels, San Pan
Sanitary Panels, Shadow-Coustic Pads,
Specialty Products (Colorsonix Floater
Panel, Nubby Ceiling Panel, Rebounder
Panel, Sound Stop Blanket)
Description:
Facilities - sound absorbers for arenas. High
performance acoustical products that reduce
reverberation and echo.

MODERNFOLD, INC.
215 W NEW ROAD
GREENFIELD, IN 46140
800-869-9685
Fax: 866-410-5016
info@modernfold.com
• Troy Pavy, Marketing
• Frank Mecklenburg, Customer Service
Manager
fmecklenburg@modernfold.com
• Dan Popplewell, North East US Sales
Manager
• Steve Molone, North Central US Sales
Manager
Brands:
Acousti-Seal operable partitions, Audio-Wall
accordion partitions, Soundmaster
accordion doors/partitions, ultra-seal, and
moveable glass walls.
Description:
Owners and managers of arenas,
convention centers, stadiums and theaters.
Manufacturer of Modernfold movable wall
systems, a complete line of acoustically
operable partitions and accordion doors in a
broad range of panel sizes and fabric finish
options.

NEW TIER COMMUNICATIONS
15875 N GREENWAY HAYDEN LOOP
SUITE 109
SCOTTSDALE, AZ 85260
480-922-1711
Fax: 480-922-1733
• Michael D. Rossman, President & Chief
Executive Officer
• Mark Malenfant, VP Sales
• Steve Graber, Production Manager
Description:
Provides an integrated suite of multimedia
applications enabling clients to broadcast
real-time marketing messages to consumers
registered on the new Tier Network.
Nature of Services:
Services include development of interactive

multimedia development, web site development, print and display advertising, video and audio production, screen savers and animation.

Clients:
IBM, Ticketmaster, TECO Energy, Adelphia, Ohio Health, Verizon Electronics, Fox Sports Net, SBC, Union Bank of California, US Bank, American West Airlines, TD Waterhouse, Solo, Philips, D.C. Lottery, Major Leage Baseball, National Basketball Assoc., National Hockey League, National Football League, Collegiate, Specialty, Southwest Airlines, Royals, Astros, Brewers, Cardinals, University of Utah, Emerald Downs.

Year Founded:
1994

ONE-ON-ONE SPORTS CONSULTANTS
4250 ALBANY DRIVE APT
SUITE F109
SAN JOSE, CA 95129
408-261-8480
Fax: 408-985-8341
jgr03@aol.com
• Jim Reardon, President
jgr03@aol.com
Nature of Sports Service:
Technical advisors.

PELTON MARSH KINSELLA
901 CARLETON DRIVE
RICHARDSON, TX 75081
214-814-5940
Fax: 206-495-1706
info@pmkconsultants.com
www.pmkconsultants.com
• Mollie Prince, Marketing Manager
• David E Marsh, VP
• Usman Bhatti, Principal - PMK International
• Dan Saenz, Acoustical Consultant
Manufacturer
Acoustics, theatrical planning, systems design including sound reinforcement, theatrical lighting, scoreboards, rigging, audio/visual and broadcast systems.

PHYSICIANS FOR QUALITY
808 W BLUEBONNET DRIVE
SAN MARCOS, TX 78666
800-284-3627
800-284-3627
Fax: 512-233-0642
Kim@PFQ.com
www.physiciansforquality.com
Description:
Founded 1987. Specialize in medical & fitness software consulting.

PILSON COMMUNICATIONS, INC.
160 KING STREET
CHAPPAQUA, NY 10514-3433
914-861-9216
• Neal H Pilson, President
Clients:
NASCAR, the International Olympic Committee, the Rose Bowl, UBS Bank, the Arena Football League and others
Sports Service Founded:
1995
Marketing & Consulting Services:
Active in all areas of sports television, media and marketing, providing representation, negotiation, consulting and packaging

services for U.S. and international companies, organizations and associations.

PLAYING FIELD PROMOTIONS LLC
277 S FOREST STREET
DENVER, CO 80246
303-377-1109
800-966-1380
www.playingfieldpromotions.com
Description:
Athlete marketing and sports consulting with regard to athletes. Clients such as: Dusty Baker, Sean Casey, Drott Nixon, and Joe Mauer. Broadcasters John Miller, Kirby Puckett.

POC MEDIA SPORTS & ENTERTAINMENT DIVISION
511 LINDSEY DRIVE
MANOR HOUSE SUITE 301
WAYNE, PA 19087
610-636-5805
Fax: 610-971-0261
www.pocmedia.com
• Ashley Downey, General Manager
• Pat O'Connor, Contact
(610) 636-5805
pat.oconnor@pocmedia.com
Services:
Integrated Marketing and Branding Initiatives, Development of Web Site, Multimedia and Interactive Marketing Communications Tools, Event Management, Planning and Staging and Non-Traditional Promotion for the Entertainment Industry

RAPIDTRON
3151 AIRWAY AVENUE
Bldg Q
COSTA MESA, CA 92626
949-798-0652
866-817-0127
Fax: 949-474-4550
www.rapidtron.com
• John Creel, President/Chief Executive Officer
• Peter Dermutz, Chief Technology Officer
• Larry Williams, Chief Operating Officer
• Chris Perkins, VP Sales & Marketing, Resorts
Brands:
AX 500 Smart Access Terminal, Panic Arms, Smart AX 500 reader, Smart Hand Held, Paper RFID Ticket, Smart Card, Printer, Smart TVM

SMITH, FAUSE, MCDONALD, INC.
351 8TH STREET
SAN FRANCISCO, CA 94103
415-255-9140
800-461-0660
Fax: 415-255-9180
info@sfmi.com
www.sfmi.com
• Peter A. McDonald, Principal/Founder/President
info@sfmi.com
• Kenneth R. Fause, Principal/VP
info@sfmi.com
• Ray Enriquez, Project Engineer
info@sfmi.com
Clients:
Partial list of organizations from Local Government (City of Berkeley, City of Phoenix, etc.); School and Community College Districts (Dublin Schools, Liberty Union high School District, etc.); Federal

(Sandia National Labs); Developers (Cabot, Cabot & Forbes, Hines, etc.); Institutions (San Francisco Archdiocese, etc.); Corporations (Del Monte, Compaq, etc.); and Architects, Engineers and Constructions Managers (ADP, HMC Group, etc.)
Description:
Projects include college, NBA, NFL and NHL facilities.
Description:
Independent consulting services in acoustics, sound and MATV systems, broadcast and media facilities, large screen video displays, and event facilities for arenas and stadiums.

SPL INTEGRATED SOLUTIONS
6301 BENJAMIN ROAD
SUITE 101
TAMPA, FL 33634
813-884-7168
800-282-6733
Fax: 410-992-0758
sales@avispl.com
www.avispl.com
• Ashley Downey, General Manager
• Chad Gillenwater, Vice Chairman
• John Zettel, CEO
• Peter Grabowski, Chief Financial Officer
• Steve Benjamin, Executive VP
• Don Mastro, EVP, Sales
• Doug Carnell, EVP of Operations
• Martin Schaffel, Executive Chairman
Description:
Integrates audio and video systems, large-display videoconferencing systems, multimedia systems and large scale audio and video systems at sports venues. Has installed AV systems in over 40 professional sports stadiums and arenas.

SPORTS COMMUNICATIONS GROUP, LLC
831 HUNTERS GLN
ROCKWALL, TX 75032
972-772-8867
Marketing & Consulting Services:
Provides comprehensive communications support from experienced sports PR veterans for athletes, sports management firms, golf industry businesses and corporations with sports marketing initiatives. SCG has built its foundation in golf, but is currently exploring opportunities to expand into team sports.

SPORTS MEDIA CHALLENGE
7300 CARMEL EXECUTIVE PARK DRIVE
SUITE 120
CHARLOTTE, NC 28226
704-541-5942
800-929-4386
Fax: 704-541-5943
info@sportsmediachallenge.com
www.sportsmediachallenge.com
• Kathleen Hessert, Certified Speaking Professional
(704) 541-5942
khessert@sportsmediachallenge.com
• Joshua Baer, Chief Technology Consultant
Services:
Media Training, Crisis Communications, Public Speaking, Reputation Management, Online Word of Mouth and Conversation Tracking
Clients:
ASSOCIATIONS: American Football

Coaches Association (AFCA), Black Coaches Association (BCA) College Sports Information Directors Association (CoSIDA), National Association of Collegiate Directors of Athletics (NACDA), Women's Basketball Coaches' Association (WBCA), NBA Coaches Associaiton; COLLEGES: Bowling Green UNiversity, Michigan State University, San Diego State University, University of Colorado, University of Connecticut, University of Florida, University of Maryland, University of North Carolina, University of Nortre Dame, University of Tennessee, University of Texas, University of Washington; ATHLETES, COACHES & PROFESSIONALS: Derek

---

SPORTS SYSTEMS SERVICES, INC.
2160 N CENTRAL ROAD
SUITE 104
FORT LEE, NJ 7024
201-429-9270
Fax: 201-585-3014
ContactUs@SportsSystems.com
www.sportssystems.com
• Jim Daigle, President
(201) 429-9288
Jim@SportsSystems.com
• Barb Hyde, VP of Operations
(201) 429-9280
barb.hyde@sportssystems.com
Sports Service Founded:
1987
IT Services:
Event sponsors and hospitality clients use our GuestPass to enchance guest communications and simplify complex or high-levelinvitation-registration for events. Companies with sponsorship or purchased tickets needing to increase usage (hence ROI) use our TicketTracker service to improve marketing, policy compliance, usage tracking and overall return on these investments. Our PressPass service is the far and away leader in online event accreditation management, serving nearly 1,100 worldwide events in 2010,
Clients:
Most of our clients are the major sports marketing agencies- Agencies like IMG, Octagon, Genesco, Velocity/Team Epic, GMR and others rely on us because this is our core service - which helps them deliver their core service better.

SYNCHRON
15095 W 116TH STREET
OLATHE, KS 66062
913-338-4800
800-279-3874
Fax: 913-323-6049
www.synchron.com.hk
• Ben Cascio, Founder/President/Chief Executive Office
Description:
Provides audio conference calling services to sports organizations, teams and businesses world-wide. From an ad-hoc conference call for an impromptu meeting, to a Question-and-Answer session for a nation-wide press conferences.
Clients:
Microsoft, Starwood Hotels, Clear Channel and several other Fortune 2000 companies.
Year Founded:
1990

VENUE 1
489 DEVON PARK DRIVE
SUITE 310
WAYNE, PA 19087-1809
610-977-7700
• Jay T. Snider, Chairman/Chief Executive Officer
info@venueone.com
• Steve Weiss, President
info@venueone.com
• Jay R. Halbert, Chief Financial Officer/General Counsel
info@venueone.com
• Paul C. Frascella, Chief Operating Officer
Description:
Sports, entertainment, & recreational facility solutions. Designs facility management software. Enabling an arena/venue to keep track of all phases of facility management from ticket sales to concessions. Enables the customer to maintain fiscal control of concessions, suites, premium seat services, vending and retail operations.
Products:
Offer comprehensive, integrated venue management software and hardware solutions to the sports and entertainment sections.
Brands:
Tangent POS, FrontLine, TicketManager

WRIGHTSON, JOHNSON, HADDON & WILLIAMS, INC.
4801 SPRING VALLEY ROAD
SUITE 113
DALLAS, TX 75244
972-934-3700
Fax: 972-934-3720
info@wjhw.com
www.wjhw.com
• Jack Wrightson, Founder / Managing Principal
• Bill Haddon, Founder / Managing Principal
• Chris Williams, Founder / Managing Principal
• William B. Haddon, Co-Founder/Managing Principal
info@wjhw.com
• Jim Faber, Senior Associate
info@wjhw.com
Services:
Wrightson, Johnson, Haddon & Williams, Inc. is a 38-person M/WBE Certified firm offering state-of-the-art design services and consulting in audio, visual, video & scoring displays, broadcast provisions & video production, acoustics & noise control, theatre planning, lighting & rigging, distributed TV & satellite, video surveillance & access control, and tel/data structured cabling. Our strengths lie in the combined talents of our principals and employees, our diverse technical and business skills, and experience accrued over the years from hundreds of successfully completed projects.
Clients:
We have a diverse range of project types including large sporting arenas and stadia, aviation, airports, health care facilities, high-tech edicational learning environments and athletic facilities, high-end performance arts, theatre and entertainment spaces, municipal facilities, and worship spaces.

Sports Agents

2X, INC.
413 SUNLIGHT WAY
CANON CITY, CO 81212
208-699-7696
Fax: 719-623-0020
jeanne@2xinc.com
www.2xinc.com
• Jeanne McNutty-King, Owner/Agent
jeanne@2xinc.com
Nature of Service:
Represents female athletes in all sports.
Services:
Full service sports agency representing women athletes.
Sports Service Founded:
1998

AAI SPORTS INC. & AAI INTERNATIONAL, INC.
16000 DALLAS PARKWAY
SUITE 300
DALLAS, TX 75248
972-739-8401
Fax: 972-739-8495
gbass@aaisports.com
www.aaisports.com
• George A Bass, Jr., Chief Executive Officer/President
gbass@aaisports.com
• George Bass, Partner
(972) 739-8490
gbass@aaisports.com
Services:
AAI's broad spectrum of services includes contract negotiation, commercial endorsements, marketing, media and public relations, as well as, an impressive range of services related to financial, business management, and tax preparation.
Clients:
Thomas Adams, Cory Alexander, Derrick Bryant, Jose Manuel Calderon, Larry Davis, KennyDye, Rick Hughes, Larry Johnson, Fredrik Jonzen, Federic Kammerichs, Mario Kasun, Pete Mickeal, Tyrone Nesby, Luis Scola, Tony Smith, Aaron Swinson, Nem Sovic, Tremaine Wingfield, John Woods, Angie Ball, Keisha Brown, Swin Cash, Camille Cooper, Katrina Crenshaw, Grace Daley, Helen Darling, Claudia Maria Das Neves, Keitha Dickerson, Adriana Dos Santos, Simone Edwards, Barbara Farris, Shauzinski Gortman, Julia Goureva, Dale Hodges, Kedra Holland-Corn, Joy Holmes-Harris, Shannon Johnson, Carolyn Jones-Young, Helen Luz, Clarisse Machanguana, Hamchetou Maiga, Izi

---

ABBOTT MANAGEMENT GROUP
14 BEACON STREET
SUITE 814
BOSTON, MA 2108
617-723-4874
Fax: 617-723-8198
nabbott97@gmail.com
• Neil F Abbott, Founder/Partner
• Brittany Forgues, Associate
Services:
Offers: Pre-Draft Preparation, Off-Ice Training and Development, Contract Negotiation, Financial Management, Marketing/Public Relations, Insurance, Tax and Estate Planning and Post-Career Planning

Clients:
Some of Abbott Management's more successful clients include: Jeremy Roenick, Sergei Samsonov, Kyle McLaren, Mariusz Czerkawski, P.J. Axelsson, Nils Eksman
Description:
Contract negotiation, post career planning, investment contract negotiation, arbitration hearings, federal/state/international tax filings, provides securities advice, provides investment advice, licensing, endorsement exploration, tort actions/litigation.

AD CETERA SPORTS CELEBRITIES
2905 N SUMMIT AVENUE
MILWAUKEE, WI 53211-3441
414-967-7767
Fax: 414-967-7769
Nature of Service:
Provides a wide variety of personalities for just about any promotion or occasion. From product or service endorsements to appearances at corporate gatherings and grand openings, autograph signings to speaking engagements, Ad Cetera can find the perfect celebrity for your event.

ADVANCED ATHLETIC REPRESENTATION
5920 SAINT LAURENT DRIVE
AGOURA HILLS, CA 91301
818-889-3933
www.advanceathletics.com
• Michael C Moline, Chief Executive Officer
• Mike Mosa, Partner
Services:
All phases of athlete representation including contract negotiation, long-range planning, financial planning, and post-career counseling.

AKIN & RANDOLPH AGENCY
ONE GATEWAY CENTER
SUITE 2600
NEWARK, NJ 07102
973-353-8409
Fax: 973-353-8417
info@akinandrandolph.com
www.akinandrandolph.com
• Wanda Akin, Founder/Agent
(212) 581-7100
info@akinandrandolph.com
• Frank D. McIntyre, Sports Agent
(212) 581-7100
info@akinandrandolph.com
• Wanda Akin, Sports Agent, Literary Agent, General Agent a
Description:
Full representation firm for athletes.
Services:
Review contracts with editors, publishers, record producers and sports organizations, Negotiate all aspects of contracts to obtain the most beneficial terms, Create book proposals and other image packages, Negotiate/shop foreign book rights, Review book proposals and submit same to publishers for review and bid, Receive and review payment to clients and distribute advances and royalties, Represent small publishers on business/transactional matters, Obtain recording contracts and film deals, Arrange media exposure through television, radio and magazine interviews
Clients:
Clients include Literary Division, Small

Press, Film, Music/Recordings, Broadcast/TV, Sports

ALL PRO SPORTS & ENTERTAINMENT
36 STEELE STREET
THE SMITH CENTER, SUITE 100
DENVER, CO 80206
303-320-4004
800-783-4776
Fax: 303-320-4019
www.apse.net
• C. Lamont Smith, Founder/President
(303) 320-4004
• Peter J. Schaffer, Sports Agent
(303) 320-4004
• Grant Wittenwyler, Golf Director
(303) 320-4004
grantapse@comcast.net
Services:
All phases of athlete management, including contract negotiation, financial planning, post-career planning, endorsements, etc.
Clients:
Barry Sanders, LeCharles Bentley, Jonathan Kaye, Jerome Bettis, Aaron Smith, Shane Bertsch, Eddie George, David Diehl, Scott Petersen, Braylon Edwards, Antonio Bryant, Brian Kortan, Lito Sheppard, Jesse Palmer, Ben Portie, Samari Rolle, Mike Anderson, Chris Sessler, Derrick Mason, Dexter Jackson, John Restino, Jason Gildon, Rudi Johnson, Tom Woodard, Chad Brown, Willie Roaf, Troy Riddle, Trevor Pryce, Mike Rucker, Gavin Morgan, Tra Thomas, Marques Anderson, Josef Marha, Jason Ball, Tony Bryant, Tomas Divisek, Colin Branch, Trung Canidate, Michal Sykora, Bryce Fisher, Mario Edwards, Denise Plante, Ray Green, Quinten Griffen, Vic Lombardi, Kell

ALSTRAR INC. SPORTS & ENTERTAINMENT
25 REGAL DRIVE
NEW ROCHELLE, NY 10804
914-576-1943
Fax: 914-673-1282
Services:
Handles marketing and public relations for businesses, organizations, athletes and companies.

AMATEUR SPORTS GROUP, INC.
201 W. BALTIMORE STREET
SUITE 119
FIRST MARINER ARENA
BALTIMORE, MD 21201
410-962-7070
866-696-5425
Fax: 410-962-8777
www.asgsports.com
• Scott Westcoat, Director
(410) 962-7070
• Jonathan Reid, Operations Director
(443) 277-3125
• Damian Orencel, Event Specialist
(443) 834-6860
• Kerrie Eisenhauer, Senior Event Specialist
(410) 962-7070
• Sergio Luna, Multicultural Event Specialist
(410) 962-7070
• Denny Gordon, Event Specialist
(410) 962-7070
bullets52@aol.com
• Rob Spigone, DCU Event Specialist
(410) 962-7070
thebigspig@aol.com

• Scott Westcoat, President/CEO
• Derek Wilson, Executive Vice President, derek@asgevents.com
• Keith Finnegan, Director of Operations & Personnel
• Geoff Stinson, ASG Digital Event Specialist
(410) 962-7070
• Warren Westcoat, Director of Enviroevents
• Charles Allen, Director of ASG Logistics
• Kristin Dempsey, Director of ASG Fulfillment
Services:
Event Management, Event Production, Event Consulting, Marketing/Promotions
Marketing & Consulting Services:
Event Management and Production, Full In-House Digital Media Division, Event Marketing, Warehouse/Fulfillment Services.
Event Management Services:
Full event management, including planning, sponsorship, traffic promotion and ticket sales, program books, exhibit areas, post event merchandising sales.
Athlete Management Services:
Promotion, contract negotiation, representation, accounting, legal and related services.
Sports Service Founded:
1994
Clients:
Ravens Fan Zone, Soccer Celebration, Maryland Pepsi Pride, US Soccer Federation, McDonald's McSoccerfest, DC United's Just 4 Kicks, Soccer Seats, MSYSA, Sand Duels, LAXFEST, Hoop it Up, Copa Sears, Kicks Against Breast Cancer, Twenty Plus Entertainment, TerraGol Beach Soccer, Legacy Cup Soccer Tournament.

ANSLOW, ESQ., RICHARD I.
195 ROUTE 9 S
2ND FLOOR
MANALAPAN, NJ 7726
732-409-1212
Fax: 732-577-1188
info@anslowlaw.com
• Richard I. Anslow, Managing Partner
(732) 409-1212
• Gregg E. Jaclin, Partner
(732) 409-1212
Services:
Securities, Business & Corporate, Real Estate, Wills & Estates, Sports & Entertainment
Description:
Contract negotiation, post career planning, investment contract negotiation, arbitration hearings, federal/state/international tax filings, licensing, endorsement exploration.

ARANDA GROUP
724 OLD YORK ROAD
JENKINTOWN, PA 19046-2833
215-576-6666
877-272-4033
Fax: 215-884-0356
www.arandagroup.com
• Arthur Rosenberg, President
(215) 576-6666
arthur@aranda.com
• Steven Rosenberg, VP/Chief Operating Officer
(215) 576-6666
steven@aranda.com
• Arthur Rosenberg, Chairman of the Board

- Bill Alsberg, Associate VP
- Jacki Simmons, VP/Bookeeping
- Joanne Keller, Registered Investment Assistant
- Tom Gallagher, Investment Assistant
- Erica Gurian, Client Services

Services:
Financial management firm; agents for professional athletes and others.
Description:
Contract negotiation.

ARCTIC SPORTS
353 HUNTINGTON TURNPIKE
BRIDGEPORT, CT 6610
203-371-8326
Fax: 203-373-9655
- Rick Piccirillo, Owner
(203) 371-8326
Sports Service Founded:
1994.
Services:
Represents athletes who desire to play abroad, handling all phases of contract negotiations, team placement and sponsorship opportunities.

ASCENSION ENTERPRISES INC.
PO BOX 301033
ARLINGTON, TX 76007-1033
817-633-7612
Fax: 817-633-7612
www.ascensionentinc.com
- Darren Deloatche, Founder
Year Founded:
1995
Services:
Contract Negotiation, Performance Enhancement, Marketing Services, Personal Services, Post-Athletic Career Planning, Continuing Education
Clients:
Eddie Moore, Omari Hand, Keyon Whiteside, Justin Brown, Troy Fleming, Mark Jones, Steve Mascorro, Anthony Hines, Delvin Hughley, Eric Houle, Jerome Braziel, George Hudson, D'Wayne Taylor,
Descripton:
Full service representation and management organization for professional athletes and entertainers.

ASSANTE SPORTS MANAGEMENT GROUP
2 QUEEN STREET EAST
19TH FLOOR
TORONTO, CANADA M5C 3G7
416-348-9994
888-348-9994
Fax: 416-364-2969
service@assante.com
www.assante.com
- Murray Oxby, Director Communications
(416) 681-3254
- James E. Ross L.L.B, Senior Vice President,Wealth and Estate Plan
- Robert J. Dorrell CIIM,FCSI, Senior Vice President and Distribution Servic
- Steven J. C. Donald FCA, FCPA, President
OTHER LOCATIONS:
151 Yonge Street, 9th Floor, Toronto, Ontario, Canada M5C 2W7; Phone: 416-645-4000; Fax: 416-645-4005; 360 Main Street, STE 1900, Winnipeq, Manitoba, Canada R3C 3Z3; Phone: 204-957-1730; Fax: 204-947-2103

Description:
Our goal is to simplify and enhance the lives of our clients by serving as their primary financial advisor, managing their assets and lifestyle needs from the day we begin our relationship with them, through succeeding generations.

ATH-ELITE MANAGEMENT SERVICES
300 N MAIN STREET
BOWLING GREEN, OH 43402
419-352-4650
Fax: 419-354-4550

ATHLETIC RESOURCE MANAGEMENT, INC.
1100 RIDGEWAY LOOP ROAD
SUITE 500
MEMPHIS, TN 38120
901-761-8503
Fax: 901-763-3762
www.sextonsports.com
- Jim Sexton, President
(901) 763-4900
- Rick Landrum, Vice President
(901) 761-8505
- Jim Dutton, Director of Client Develoment
(901) 763-4900
- John Haur, Director of Marketing
(901) 763-4900
Services:
Sports agency representing NFL and Major League Baseball stars, golf and sports broadcasters.
Nature of Sports Services:
Athlete represenatation.

ATLANTA INTERNATIONAL CONSULTING GROUP, INC. (AICG)
1401 PEACHTREE STREET
SUITE 500
ATLANTA, GA 30309
404-872-4884
Fax: 404-870-0440
sales@aicginc.com
www.aicginc.com
Services:
Specializes in creating programs that increase brand awareness, improve market share, and boost product profitability of clients through graphic design, printing, specialty merchandise and fulfillment services.
Services:
Graphic Design &Creative Direction, Custom Illustration & Artwork (Sports & Entertainment), Project Management, Corporate & Brand Identity (Logo Development), POS/POP & Custom Packaging (Restaurant & Food Industry; Retail), Sales Collateral Support & Promotion (Desktop Publishing and Brochures), Internet Design & Implementation
Clients:
The Coca-Cola Company, Coca-Cola Enterprises, Bellsouth Corporation, McDonald's Corporation, AOL/Turner, S.C. Johnson, ARAMARK, MCI WorldCom
Athlete Management Services:
Exclusive representation of leading sports personalities. Representation of select entertainment properties. Full-service sports marketing firm for professional and amateur athletics. Provides career management consulting, contract advisement,

endorsements, financial planning, promotions, entertainment representation and full-service merchandising.
Marketing & Consulting Services:
Provides strategic and tactical consultation in general sports marketing consultation, professional development, special segment, general market development, ethnic marketing development (African American, Hispanic, and Asian), youth marketing and female marketing development. Marketing representation for entertainers, musicians and broadcasters. Provides financial services through strategic alliances and affiliated company.
Event Management Services:
Creates grassroots or made-for-TV-sports/entertainment oriented events from concept to completion. Develops and implements integrated programs to assist clients in promoting their products and/or services. Full public relations and advertising capabilities, arranging for sponsorship of both new and existing sports events, developing tie-in promotions for such sponsorships, complete management of event. Experienced in targeting particular sales objectives through sports promotions. Develops event-driven sales promotion campaigns for corporate clients. Provides complete strategic planning, project management and promotional support services.

AXELROD, BARRY
2236 ENCINITAS BOULEVARD
SUITE A
ENCINITAS, CA 92024
760-753-0088
Fax: 760-436-7399
baxy@msn.com
- Barry Axelrod, Owner
(760) 753-0088
Services:
Marketing of professional athletes and other sports-related entities.
Clients:
Legal, personal and financial management of professional and amateur athletes.
Sports Service Founded:
1977

BAKER SPORTS MANAGMENT
1750 MONTGOMERY STREET
1ST FLOOR
SAN FRANCISCO, CA 94111
415-433-3355
Fax: 415-433-4522
steve@bakersports.com
www.bakersports.com
- Stephen Baker, Owner
Description:
Contract negotiation, marketing, and endorsements.
SERVICES:
Sports Management
Clients:
Jeff Garcia, Ken Harvey, Brian Mitchell, Ray Brown, Kailee Wong, Nnamdi Asomugha, Eric Johnson, Jamie Winborn, Casey Moore, JT O'Suvillivan, Paul Smith, Adimchinobe Echemandu, Courtney Anderson, Brett Pierce, Will Svitek, Matt Giordano, Jon Ritchie, Greg Clark, Mike Croel & Shante Carver

BARNES MARKETING, INC.
1401 DOVE STREET
STUDIO 520
NEWPORT BEACH, CA 92660
949-553-0820
Fax: 949-768-0630
info@barnesmarketing.com
www.barnesmarketing.com
Sports Service Founded:
1974
Services:
Specializes in marketing and consulting and event management services in motorsports marketing and race team sponsorship including comprehensive sales packages provided for potential sponsors, media coordination, and public relations and athlete management services which includes speaking engagements, personal appearances, product endorsements, radio and television, movies.
Athlete Management Services:
Speaking engagements, personal appearances, product endorsements, radio and television, movies.

BARNNETT, HOWARD D
333 S MAIN STREET
POCATELLO, ID 83204
208-233-0845
Fax: 208-233-1304
www.hteh.com
• Howard D Burnett, Partner
(208) 233-0845
info@hawleytroxell.com
• Susan Olson, Executive Director
(208) 344-6000
solson@hawleytroxell.com
Description:
Contract negotiation, investment contract negotiation, federal/state/international tax filings.
Services:
Provides quality legal solutions for Business & Finance, Litigation, Real Estate, Employment, Construction & Environmental Matters.

BATTLE, MICHAEL RAY
1801 LARKHILL LANE
RICHMOND, VA 23235
804-323-5041
Nature of Sports Service:
All phases of athlete representation including contract negotiation, long-range planning, financial planning, and post-career counseling.

BDA SPORTS MANAGEMENT
700 YGNACIO VALLEY ROAD
SUITE 330
WALNUT CREEK, CA 94596
925-279-1040
Fax: 925-279-1060
www.bdasports.com
• Bill A. Duffy, President/Chief Executive Officer
• Kevin Bradbury, Player Representation VP
• Merle Scott, Player Representative
• Bill Duffy, Chairman and CEO
• Billy Kuenzinger, President and General counsel
• Julie Neuman, Chief Financial Officer
• Shauna Smith, VP Client Relations
• Kevin Brabury, Sr. VP, Player Relations
• Michael Conley, Agent
• Todd Ramasar, Agent

Other Locations:
1000 North Kingsbury Street #105, Chicago, IL 60610; Phone: 312-467-9027; 655 Amsterdam Avenue, Uniondale, NY 11553; Phone:925-279-1040; 7402 SW 64th Place, Portland, OR 97219; Phone: 503-245-8989; 870 Commonwealth Avenue, STE 100, Venice, CA 90291; Phone: 310-581-4509
Services:
Draft Preparation & Positioning, Contract Negotiation, Career Management, Investment Planning, Global Management & Post-Career Guidance Sponsor Relations, Media Relations, Fan Relations, Camps & Clinics, Special Projects, Player Relationship, Family Relationship, Team Relationship & Role as Mentor/Role Model
Clients:
Carmelo Anthony, Leandro Barbosa, Andris Biedris, Zarko Cabarkapa, Anthony Carter, Speedy Claxto, Antonio Davis, Juan Dixon, Chris Duhon, Francisco Elson, Raymond Felton, Jeff Foster, Drew Gooden, Devin Green, Chuck Hayes, Mike James, Marko Jaric, Freddy Jones, Yao Ming, Steve Nash, Rasho Nesterovic, Michael Olowokandi, Travis Outlaw, Tayshaun Prince, Joel Przybilla, Zeljko Rebraca, Kareem Rush, Hakim Warrick, Louis Williams, Dorell Wright, Troy Bell, Jay Williams, Toby Bailey, Miroslav Beric, Andrew Betts, Ruben Boumtje-Boumtje, Yiannis Bouroussis, Louis Bullock, Robert Conley, Taylor Coppenrath, Vladimir Dasic, Bennett Davidson, Obinna Ekez

BECHTA, JACK D./JB SPORTS
7660 FAY AVENUE
SUITE H-502
LA JOLLA, CA 92037
858-454-9005
800-800-4775
Fax: 858-454-2330
sportsagent@NFLAdvisor.com
www.nfladvisor.com
• Jack D Bechta, Owner
Jack@NFLAdvisor.com
• Dominique Brutsche, Assistant
dominique@nfladvisor.com
Services:
Personalized pre-draft game plan; All Star and combine preparation; Coordination of individual pre-draft workouts; Pre-draft marketing, highlight films, and personalized assets; Draft day events coordination; Contract negotiations; Personal training
Clients:
Jonathan Babineaux, Matt Bowen, Tyrone Carter, Kerry Carter, Jared Clauss, Earl Dotson, Tim Dwight, Zeron Flemister, Kelly Gregg, Al Harris, Renaldo Hill, Brody Liddiard, Pete Lougheed, Jermane Mayberry, Mat McBriar, Larry Moore, Gene Mruczkowski, Scott Mruczkowski
Nature of Sports Service:
All phases of athlete representation including contract negotiation, long-range planning, financial planning, and post-career counseling.

BENJAMIN, GLEN
6 GLODE CT
AIRMONT, NY 10952
845-352-1449
Description:
Contract negotiation.

BERTHELSEN, RICHARD
280 PARK AVENUE
NEW YORK, NY 10017
212-450-2000
Fax: 212-681-7573
www.nfl.com
• Troy Vincent, President
tvincent@nfl.com
• Jerome Mertens, President
jmertens@nfl.com
• Harold Henderson, Labor Relation EVP
hhenderson@nfl.com
• Steve Bornstein, Media EVP
sbornstein@nfl.com
Services:
Collective bargaining agent for all players employed by clubs of the National Football League, governed by a volunteer board of active NFL players elected by their teammates on each team.
Description:
Represents sports organizations.

BEST IN SPORTS
138 RIVER ROAD
SHATTUCK OFFICE CENTER
ANDOVER, MA 01810
978-725-3581
Fax: 978-725-3582
• Thomas McLaughlin, Sports Agent
• Dwight Robinson, Sports Agent
Nature of Sports Service:
Athlete representation including contract negotiation, long-range planning, post-career counseling, endorsements contracts, European contracts.

BEVERLY HILLS SPORTS COUNCIL
9595 WILSHIRE BOULEVARD
SUITE 1010
BEVERLY HILLS, CA 90212
310-858-1935
Fax: 310-550-7980
• Daniel Lozano, Partner
• Rick Thurman, Chief Financial Officer
• Jeff Borris, General Counsel
Description:
Full representation of professional baseball players.
Services:
Professional sports club and promoter

BIG TEN ATHLETIC CONFERENCE
1500 W HIGGINS ROAD
PARK RIDGE, IL 60068-6300
847-696-1010
Fax: 847-696-1150
www.bigten.org
• James E Delany, Commissioner
jdelany@bigten.org
• Brad Traviolia, Associate Commissioner - Chief Operating
btraviolia@bigten.org
• Rich Falk, Associate Commissioner
rfalk@bigten.org
• James A. Delany, Commissioner
• Brad Travioliia, Deputy Commissioner
• Diane Dietz, Chief communications officer
• Wendy Fallen, Associate Commissioner
• Julie Suderman, Controller
Services:
Provide in excess of $63 million in athletic scholarship aid to 7,500 men and women student-athletes to compete for 25 championships, 12 for men and 13 for women. Conference institutions sponsor more than 250 athletic programs.

Description:
Represents sports organizations.

BIKE TAHOE
PO BOX 673
ZEPHYR COVE, NV 89448
775-586-9566
ty@biketahoe.org
www.biketahoe.org
• Ty Polastri, President
Founded:
2013
Clients Include:
State of Nevada, City of South Lake Tahoe, Sierra Nevada Media Group, The Tahoe Fund, Lake Tahoe Visitors Authority, El Dorado County, Zephyr Cove Lodge, Lakeside Inn, Hyatt Hotel, Flume Trail Bikes, South Shore Bikes, Tahoe Chamber of Commerce, North Lake Tahoe Resort Association
Nature of Service:
Multi-channel marketing, promotion and education using sport as a vehicle to drive consumers to business as to affect regional economic and environmental sustainability.

BLACKMAN & RABER, LTD.
123 E 54TH STREET
SUITE 9C
NEW YORK, NY 10022-4507
212-593-1803
Services:
Advertising Agency
Sports Service Founded:
1964
Athlete Management Services:
Consults with lawyers and agents on player endorsement negotiations. Placement of sports personalities in advertising and promotions.
Event Management Services:
Full service sales promotion agency. Creates sweepstakes and contests, celebrity and special events. Negotiates sponsorships and licenses.
Marketing & Consulting Services:
Acts as talent consultants for advertising agencies specializing in sports campaigns. Assists with sales and trade incentive programs, advertising and promotional campaigns, and casting sports personalities.

BLACKSTAR SPORTS MANAGEMENT, INC.
2556 LAKESHORE BOULEVARD W
TRONTO, ONTARIO, CANADA M8V 1G1
416-399-6473
Fax: 416-252-4487
• Maurice C Martin, Agent
Nature of Sports Service:
All phases of athlete representation including contract negotiation, long-range planning, financial planning, tax service, endorsements and post-career counseling.
Clients Include:
Represents players from the National Football League (NFL), Arena Football League and Canadian Football League.

BLACKWELDER, MURRAY
IOWA STATE UNIVERSITY
1750 BEARDSHEAR HALL
AMES, IA 50011
515-294-4111
800-262-3810
Fax: 515-294-2592

contact@iastate.edu
www.iastate.edu
• Gregory L Geoffroy, President
(515) 294-2042
president@iastate.edu
• Elizabeth Hoffman, EVP/Provost
• Thomas L. Hill, Student Affairs VP
(515) 294-4420
tomhill@iastate.edu
• Warren R. Madden, Business and Finance VP
(515) 294-1530
wmadden@iastate.edu
Services:
Provides education services to their students.

BLYTHE, DONOVAN A.
595 INDUSTRIAL ROAD
SAN CARLOS, CA 94070
650-595-7797
donovan@blythesbasketball.com
www.blythesbasketball.com
• Donovan A Blythe, Director
(650) 341-3998
donovan@blythesbasketball.com
Nature of Sports Service:
All phases of athlete representation including contract negotiation, long-range planning, financial planning, and post-career counseling.

BODDICKER SPORTS MANAGEMENT
8333 DOUGLAS AVENUE
SUITE 975
DALLAS, TX 75225
214-369-9655
Fax: 214-369-9681
• Daniel J Boddicker, President
Nature of Sports Service:
All phases of athlete representation including contract negotiation, long-range planning, financial planning, and post-career counseling.

BUSINESS ARENA, INC.
4720 MONTGOMERY LANE
SUITE 1010
BETHESDA, MD 20814
301-656-4800
Fax: 301-907-9494
• George Mavrikes, Sports Agent
Nature of Sports Service:
All phases of athlete representation including contract negotiation, long-range planning, financial planning, and post-career counseling.
SERVICES:
Contract Negotiations, Financial Services, Endorsements, Tax Advice - Referrals Only, Career Counseling, Post Career Counseling, Estate Planning, Marketing

CAFLISCH, ROBERT J.
301 SOUTH BEDFORD STREET
SUITE 7
MADISON, WI 53703
608-257-8280
Fax: 608-255-6010
www.ritzcaflisch.com
• Peter B. Ritz, Lawyer
• Robert J. Caflisch, Lawyer
Description:
Licensing, endorsement exploration.
Services:
Licensing, endorsement exploration.

CAMPBELL, JOHN RUSSELL (RUSS)
1901 SIXTH AVENUE N
SUITE 1500
BIRMINGHAM, AL 35203-4642
205-251-8100
Fax: 205-226-8799
rcampbell@balch.com
www.balch.com
• Russ Campbell, Partner
• Patrick Strong, Associate
Services:
Antitrust, Appellate, Business Litigation, Casualty Litigation, Civil Rights Litigation, Class Action Litigation, Coal and Fossil Fuels, Condemnation, Land Use and Water Rights, Construction, Consumer Financial Services, Corporate & Securities, Corporate Governance, Creditors Rights & Bankruptcy, Economic Development Incentives, Education, Employee Benefits & Executive Compensation, Energy, Energy and Utility Litigation, Energy Litigation, Finance, Lending and Leasing, Financial Institution Formations, Mergers & Acquisitions, Financial Institutions, Financial Products & Services, Financial Services Litigation, Financial Services Regulatory. R
Nature of Sports Service:
All phases of athlete representation including contract negotiation, long-range planning, and post-career counseling.
Other Locations:
1275 Pennsylvania Avenue, NW, 10th Floor, Washington, DC 20004; Phone: 202-347-6000; 40l East Capital Street, STE 200, Jackson, MS 3920l; Phone: 601-961-9900

CARDIOKICKBOXING.COM
91-1013 WAIPAA STREET
EWA BEACH, HI 96706-6499
808-457-7164
marcus.devalentino@cardiokickboxing.com
www.cardiokickboxing.com
• Marcus DeValentino, Program Director
marcus.devalentino@cardiokickboxing.com
• Frank Thiboutot, Cardio Kickboxing Creator
Description:
Created in 1992 as a fitness alternative and to preserve the integrity of the sport of kickboxing.

CAREER SPORTS & ENTERTAINMENT
150 INTERSTATE N PARKWAY SE
ATLANTA, GA 30339
770-955-1300
Fax: 770-226-5560
www.careersports.com
• Matt Kramer, Director Public Relations
(770) 955-1300
mkramer@careersports.com
• Lonnie Cooper, CEO
Sports Service Founded:
1986
Description:
Full service client representation, marketing and media services agency.
Clients:
Bellsouth, Cingular Wireless, The Home Depot, Kellogg Company, Aflac, Larry Coker, Bobby Cox, Billy Donovan, Mike Fratello, Paul Hewitt, Tom Izzo, Eddie Jordan, Nate Mcmillan, Sam Mitchell, Doc Rivers, Kelvin Sampson, Mark Slonaker, Reggie Theus, Isiah Thomas, Lennie Wilkens, Brian Winters, Randy Walker

Clifford Warren, Brent Abernathy, Russ Adams, Michael Barrett, Kyle Davies, Mark DeRosa, Wes Helms, Richard Lewis, Kerry Ligtenberg, Ron Mahay, Mike Maroth, John Smoltz, TJ Tucker, Billy McCarthy, Briah Moehler, Derek Wathan, Roland Thatcher, Nick Cassini, Paul Claxton, David Denham, Ryuji Imada, Franklin Langham, Lee Williams, Allen Bestwic

Athlete Management Services:
Negotiation of player contracts - baseball, basketball and football.

Marketing & Consulting Services:
Endorsement marketing, personal appearances, speaking engagements, promotion of sports clinics. Internal & consumer promotions, event management, sponsorship negotiation and fulfillment.

CAREY, MICHAEL
SPORTS PERSONALITIES INC
16 TERRI RD
FRAMINGHAM, MA 1701
508-877-6150

Services:
Contract negotiation.

CASTLEREAGH, INC.
320 BUFFALO AVENUE
FREEPORT, NY 11520
516-379-2122
Fax: 516-379-2386
www.castlereaghpress.com

Sports Service Founded:
1992.

Services:
Commercial printers

Athlete Management Services:
Manages talent for appearances and endorsements.

Event Managment Services:
Represents corporations for event day sponsorships.

Marketing & Consulting Services:
Produces and markets sports memorabilia and collectibles; produces and manages theme travel related to DreamWeek and Fantasy Camp programs for golf and baseball.

CELEBRITY CONNECTIONS, L.L.C.
29 TROTTER LANE
NEWINGTON, CT 06111-5334
860-667-8290

Services:
Manages special events; handles athlete appearances and endorsements. Provides creative and cause marketing, entertainment and event management services. Serves as celebrity clearinghouse for charity events, providing celebrity personal appearances, talent development, and sport

Sports Service Founded:
1992

Athlete Management Services:
Handles athlete appearances and endorsements. Provides creative and cause marketing, entertainment and event management services. Serves as celebrity clearinghouse for charity events, providing celebrity personal appearances, talent development, and sports marketing. Specialty is niche marketing to African-American and Latino businesses.

CELEBRITY MARKETING GROUP
1701-1/2 BANKS
SUITE 1
HOUSTON, TX 77098
713-522-2230
• Mary Beggins, President

Services:
Provides public relations and administrative services to athletes. Specializes in endorsement opportunities, unique promotions, speaking engagements, personal appearances, merchandising and entertainment representation.

Sports Service Founded:
1993.

CELEBRITY SUPPLIERS OF LAS VEGAS
2756 N GREEN VALLEY PARKWAY
SUITE 449
LAS VEGAS, NV 89014-2100
702-451-8090
www.celebritysuppliers.com
• A.J. Sagman, President
(561) 362-0079
info@entertainmentservices.com
• Steve Rosenthal, Sales Manager
(561) 362-0079
info@entertainmentservices.com
• D. Manning, Marketing Director

Marketing & Consulting Services:
Supplying Half-time Visual Performers, TV Celebrities and Singing Impersonators for Teams Worldwide.

Services:
Provides top name performers, singers, dance bands, Motown bands, singing groups, oldies groups, disco groups, comedians, variety acts, magicians, jugglers, Celebrities, Speakers, Celebrity Athletes, musical and corporate entertainment for various types of events and venues worldwide.

Sports Service Founded:
1985

Other Location:
Boca Raton, FL. 561-362-0079

CENTRAL VIRGINIA SPORTS MANAGEMENT
117 SKYLARK DRIVE
DANVILLE, VA 24541
434-799-6426
Fax: 434-797-8857
• Kenneth Lewis, Sports Agent

Nature of Sports Service:
All phases of athlete representation including contract negotiation, long-range planning, financial planning, and post-career counseling.

CENTURY CITY SPORTS & ENTERTAINMENT
23679 CALABASAS ROAD
SUITE 151
CALABASAS, CA 91302
818-591-0295
Fax: 818-591-1140
• Ronald Glickman, Sports Agent

Nature of Sports Service:
All phases of athlete representation including contract negotiation, long-range planning, financial planning, and post-career counseling.

CHAMPIONSHIP GROUP, INC.
PO BOX 80489
ATLANTA, GA 30366

770-457-5777
info@champgrp.com
www.ChampionshipGroup.com
• Ardy Arani, CEO/Managing Director
• Larry Lubin, EVP Strategic Innovation
(770) 457-5777
• Roy Barudin, EVP Brand Development
(770) 457-5777
• Ray Curtis, Chief Financial Officer
(770) 936-3600
• Jeff Martin, Creative Services Director
(770) 457-5777

Year Founded:
1980

Services:
A strategic sports marketing and promotion resource with a twenty-eight year track record of creating innovative, high-impact business building campaigns, leveraged sponsorships, retail activation and lifestyle marketing programs for corporate clients.

Athlete Management Services:
Sports marketing and promotions for corporate clients with motorsports and lifestyle marketing.

Event Management Services:
Sports and special event marketing specialists. Develops and manages corporate sports promotion campaigns within motorsports, action sports, lifestyle and special events. Award winning strategy, flawless execution.

CHASE AMERICA
300 PARK AVENUE
17TH FLOOR
NEW YORK CITY, NY 10022
646-706-7300
800-491-4980
Fax: 561-491-5001
• David E Stefan, Jr., Chief Executive Officer / Palm Beach Office
(561) 491-5000
• Maria Dennison, President Corporate Office (New York)
• John Roy, Managing Director / Palm Beach Office

Services:
Executive search firm specializing in the home building industry.

Clients:
Fortune 500 companies to include chemical, mineral, oil and gas companies, land development, PUD, golf course communities and golf resort properties; home builders and land developers, commercial and multi-family real estate, the sports market place.

Sports Service Founded:
1996. Provides the highest quality professional education and image relations program for the emerging and professional athlete. Recognizes and meets the demands placed on the athlete's celebrity status; brings the best talent on the issues. Locations in New York, Palm Beach, Chicago, San Diego and Atlanta (Corporate Office).

CLARKE, ALLEN R.
40 N CENTRAL AVENUE
SUITE 1900
PHOENIX, AZ 85004
602-262-5311
Fax: 602-262-5747
www.lrlaw.com

• Jose A Cardenas, Chairman and Partner
(602) 262-5790
• Kenneth Va Winkle Jr, Managing Partner
(602) 262-5357
Kvanwinkle@lrlaw.com
Description:
Contract negotiation, tort actions/litigation.
Services:
Appeals, Arbitration and Mediation, Banking and Lending, Bankruptcy, Broker/Dealer, Commercial Litigation, Construction, Corporate and Securities, Creditor's Rights, Criminal Defense, Government Regulation and Corporate Compliance, E-Discovery & Data Management, Education and Schools, Employee Benefits, Environmental and Natural Resources, Finance, Gaming, Government Contracts, Government Relations and Admnistrative, Health Care, Indian Affairs Law, Insurance, Intellectual Property, Labor and Employment, Mergers and Acquisitions, Personal Injury, Products Liability, Professional Liability and Discipline, Real Estate.

CLAYTON, LORINZO
43 THIRD AVENUE
WESTBURY, NY 11590
516-334-2767
Fax: 516-334-7282
Services:
All phases of athlete representation including contract negotiation, long-range planning, financial planning, and post-career counseling.

CLEAR CHANNEL ENTERTAINMENT, INC.
200 E BASSE ROAD
SAN ANTONIO, TX 78209
210-822-2828
Fax: 310-867-7001
www.clearchannel.com
• Randall T Mays, President/Chief Financial Officer
randalltmays@clearchannel.com
• John Hogan, CEO
Marketing & Consulting Services:
Integrates all components of the marketing mix to develop and implement full-service plans that meet the clients objectives. Expertise includes corporate consulting, stadium and arena naming rights, team and venue services, sponsorship sales, media sales, property marketing, retail licensing and merchandising, online strategies and public relations.
Services:
Promoters and producers of live entertainment events including music concerts, theatrical performances, and specialized motor sports events. Also provides event sponsorship and advertising.
Athlete Management Services:
Offering full-service representation of athletes, coaches and broadcasters. Services include contract negotiation and all marketing endeavours, including endorsements, licensing, promotions, charitable activities, speaking engagements and personal appearances.
Event Management Services:
Providing turnkey event development and management for a wide array of sports including tennis, golf, thoroughbred racing, soccer, figure skating and motor sports.
Television:

Develops, produces and distributes television and theatrical productions to meet the converging needs of sports and entertainment clients, including concept development and network negotiations. Organization has ongoing relationships with virtually every major broadcast and cable network and movie studio.

CMG WORLDWIDE
10500 CROSSPOINT BOULEVARD
INDIANAPOLIS, IN 46256
317-570-5000
Fax: 317-570-5500
www.cmgww.com
• Greg Thompson, Chief Operating Officer
• Maria Gejdosova, Vice President, Finance & Acquisitions
• Mark Roesler, Chairman/Chief Executive Officer
• Greg Thompson, COO
• Mark Vo Roesler, Chairman & CEO
Sports Service Founded:
1971
Services:
Worldwide representative of a wide range of athletic organizations, athletes, and estates. Negotiates personal appearances.
Services:
Merchandise Licensing, Advertising/Promotional Licensing, Brand Development/Extension, Sponsorship Negotiation, Professional Contract Negotiation, Product/Service Endorsements, Speakers Bureau, Personal Appearances, Autograph Signings, Interviews, Intellectual Property Strategies and Branding Services, Infringement, Policing and Enforcement Services, Domain Names Recovery and Internet Issues, Expert Witness Services, Consulting and Negotiation Services, Speakers, Lecturers and Presenters for Conferences, Programs and Commentary, Software Design for Licensing and Marketing Companies, Web Development, Media Asset Management, Hardware Support
Clients:
Marilyn Monroe, James Dean, Sophia Loren, Ingrid Bergman, Ivana Trump, Lana Turner, Bette Davis, Tyrone Power, Errol Flynn, Montgomery Clift, Sir Laurence Olivier, Rock Hudson, Helen Hayes, Jean Harlow, Ginger Rogers, Josephine Baker, Lou Jacobs, Matthew Stymie Beard,Jr., George Spanky McFarland, William 'Buckwheat' Thomas,LillianGish,AlanLadd, Bettie Page, Telly Savalas, Peter Sellers, Jayne Mansfield, Marty Feldman, Mickey Rooney, Lee Strasberg, Tennessee Ernie Ford, Liza Minnelli, Carmen Miranda, Sharon Tate, Hedy Lamarr, Victoria Fuller, Redd Foxx, Gene Siskel, Holly Madison, Bridget Marquardt, Kendra Wilkinson,Dorothy Dandridge, Walter M
Consulting, Auction/Merchandise, Event Services:
Rights and Clearances, Auction, Location Shoots, Receptions/Event Venue, Exhibits.
Athlete Management Services:
Worldwide representative of a wide range of athletic organizations, athletes, and estates. Negotiates personal appearances.
Marketing & Consulting Services:
Provides management, marketing and advertising consultation for professional athletes.
Other Location:

8560 Sunset Boulevard, 10th Floor
Penthouse, West Hollywood, CA 90069.
310-651-2000; FAX: 317-570-5500.

COLEMAN, DENNIS M.
800 BOYLSTON ROAD
PRUDENTIAL TOWER
BOSTON, MA 02199-3600
617-951-7000
Fax: 617-951-7050
www.ropesgray.com
• Dennis M Coleman, Partner
(617) 951-7361
dennis.coleman@ropesgray.com
• Mark V Nuccio, Partner
(617) 951-7368
mnuccio@ropesgray.com
Services:
All phases of athlete representation including contract negotiation, long-range planning, financial planning, and post-career counseling.
Clients:
National sports associations and foundations; Athletic footwear and licensed apparel manufacturers; A professional sports franchise; Coaches; Colleges and universities; and Sports marketing organizations.

CONDON, TOM
801 W 47TH STREET
SUITE 200
KANSAS CITY, MO 64112-1253
• Tom Condon, Lawyer
Services:
Personalized Representation, Contract Negotiation, Marketing and Endorsements, IMG Academies, Financial Services

CONSOLIDATED MANAGEMENT GROUP, INC.
237 PARK AVENUE
NEW YORK, NY 10017
212-551-3514
Services:
All phases of athlete representation including contract negotiation, long-range planning, financial planning, and post-career counseling.

CONWAY, MICHAEL W.
4 CAMPUS DRIVE
2ND FLOOR
PARSIPPANY, NJ 07054
973-285-3600
Fax: 973-285-3666
www.sfr1.com
• Michael W Conway, Financial Planner/Principal
(973) 285-3640
mconway@sfr1.com
• Nancy Chung, Director of Client Services
(973) 292-3710
• Joseph F Rowek, Vice President
(973) 285-3688
jrowek@sfr1.com
• Steven R Weinman, CPA, MBA, APC, Chairman of the Board & Chief Investment Offi
(973) 285-3660
Services:
Separate divisions showcase specific strategies for sports stars and other celebrities, insurance planning for families and individuals, equities management that leaves no stone unturned, and wealth

counseling that helps their clients make a difference in their communities

COOPER & COOPER LLD
1080 W. SHAW
SUITE 105
FRESNO, CA 93711
559-442-1650
Fax: 559-442-1659
joe@coopllp.com
• Joseph D Cooper, Member
(559) 442-1650
• Leah Ann Alcazar, Attorney
Year Founded:
1994.
Sports Service Founded:
1994.
Description:
Civil and insurance, which represents athletes and organizations.

CORBETT, KEVIN
220 JUANA AVENUE
SAN LEANDRO, CA 94577
510-357-4970
Fax: 510-357-1032

CORPORATE SPORTS INCENTIVES, INC.
7 NEW ENGLAND EXECUTIVE PARK
SUITE 610
BURLINGTON, MA 01803
800-627-7547
800-627-7545
Fax: 781-229-8886
• Marc H. Matthews, President/Chief Executive Officer
Services:
Marketing and consulting
Services:
Provides prepaid experience tickets to corporate and retail buyers offering first class access to a nationwide network of participating golf courses, ski resorts, movie theaters, and spas throughout the United States and Canada

CORRELL, P. KENT
102 E 10TH STREET
NEW YORK, NY 10003
212-475-3070
Fax: 212-475-2378

COTHERN, JOHN
1301 E MAIN STREET
MIDDLE TENNESSEE STATE UNIVERSITY
MURFREESBORO, TN 37132-0001
615-898-2300
Fax: 615-898-5671
www.mtsu.edu
• Sidney A McPhee, President
smcphee@mtsu.edu
• Kaylene Gebert, EVP/ Provost
(615) 898-2880
kgebert@mtsu.edu
• John W. Cothern, SVP
• Robert K Glenn, VP Student Affairs
Services:
Educational Services
Clients:
Students

CRACIUN III, JOSEPH
COLDWELL BANKER
27271 LAS RAMBLAS, SUITE 231
MISSION VIEJO, CA 92691

949-367-2082
Fax: 949-367-2080

CRAIGHILL, FRANCIS H., III
7950 JONES BRANCH DRIVE
SUITE 700N
MCLEAN, VA 22107
703-905-3300
Fax: 703-905-4495
www.octagon.com
• Kathy Connors, Director of Strategic Communications, At
• Lance Hill, VP
Description:
Contract negotiation, post career planning, endorsement exploration.
Services:
Contract negotiations; Marketing initiatives and endorsement programs; Public relations and charity involvement; Financial planning, wealth advisory and asset management; Television opportunities; Content creation; Property development; Event management; Speaking engagements
Clients:
NFL Hall of Famer and Super Bowl Champion John Elway; 8-time Olympic medalist Michael Phelps; Women's Soccer Icon Mia Hamm; Hot new musical act IL Divo; British Royalty The Duchess of York

CRANFORD, MICHAEL J.
913 WASHINGTON AVENUE
MACON, GA 31201
478-746-0704
Fax: 478-746-0927
• J. Michael Cranford, Law Attorney
(478) 746-0704
• Teresa M. Cranford, Paralegal/Mediator
(478) 746-0704
Services:
criminal defence of misdemeanor,DUI and felony cases. as well as personal injury and tort cases. including motorcycle related, automobile, pedestrian, premise liability and medical malpractice.

CRAVEN, JAMES B., III
349 W MAIN STREET
LIBERTY MARKET BUILDING
PO BOX 1366
DURHAM, NC 27701
919-688-8295
Fax: 919-688-7832
• James B. Craven III,
Description:
Contract negotiation.

CRAWFORD LAW OFFICES
253 ALMENDRA AVENUE
LOS GATOS, CA 95030
408-395-9898
Fax: 408-395-4335
dcrawfordlaw@aol.com
www.dcrawfordlaw.com
• Dawson G. Crawford, Attorney
dcrawford@dcrawfordlaw.com
Description:
Business Litigation; Estate Planning; Business Transactions; Probate; Estate Litigation; Sports Law.

CRONSON TEAM, THE
336 W END AVENUE
SUITE 15A
NEW YORK, NY 10023

212-362-3322
• Don Cronson, President
Services:
Contract negotiation, post career planning, arbitration hearings, federal/state/international tax filings, provides investment advice, licensing, endorsement exploration and all other forms of financial management.

CROWE & DUNLEVY
20 N BROADWAY
SUITE 1800
OKLAHOMA CITY, OK 73102
405-235-7700
Fax: 405-239-6651
taylort@crowedunlevy.com
www.crowedunlevy.com
• Kevin D Gordon, Director
(405) 239-6619
kevin.gordon@crowedunlevy.com
• William G Paul, Advisory Director
(405) 239-6676
bill.paul@crowedunlevy.com
• D Ke Meyers, Chairman
(405) 235-7729
meyersd@crowedunlevy.com
• Clyde A Muchmore, Chairman Appellate Practice
(405) 235-7734
muchmore@crowedunlevy.com
• Zachary W. Allen, Director
(405) 235-7728
zach.allen@crowedunlevy.com
• Elliot P. Anderson, Associate
(918) 592-9844
elliot.anderson@crowedunlevy.com
Services:
represents clients in all aspects of the general practice of law, including complex business transactions, litigation in both state and federal courts, natural resource law, and all types of alternative dispute resolution

CURRAN, RICHARD
REPRESENTATION INC
411 TIMBER LANE
DEVON, PA 19333
610-964-1062
Fax: 610-964-1007
Description:
Represents Hockey players.
Editor's note:
Mr. Curran also owns the Orr Hockey Group.

CURTIN, THOMAS R.
4 HEADQUARTERS PLAZA
PO BOX 1991
MORRISTOWN, NJ 07962
973-292-1700
Fax: 973-292-1767
• Thomas R. Curtin, Managing Partner
Description:
Contract negotiation, arbitration hearings, tort actions/litigation.

CURTIS MANAGEMENT GROUP
10500 CROSSPOINT BOULEVARD
INDIANAPOLIS, IN 46256
317-570-5000
Fax: 317-570-5500
www.cmgworldwide.com
• Greg Thompson, Chief Operating Officer
• Maria Gejdosova, Vice President, Finance & Acquisitions
• Mark Roesler, Chairman/Chief Executive

Officer
- Greg Thompson, COO
- Mark Vo Roesler, Chairman & CEO

Sports Service Founded:
1971
Services:
Worldwide representative of a wide range of athletic organizations, athletes, and estates. Negotiates personal appearances.
Services:
Merchandise Licensing, Advertising/Promotional Licensing, Brand Development/Extension, Sponsorship Negotiation, Professional Contract Negotiation, Product/Service Endorsements, Speakers Bureau, Personal Appearances, Autograph Signings, Interviews, Intellectual Property Strategies and Branding Services, Infringement, Policing and Enforcement Services, Domain Names Recovery and Internet Issues, Expert Witness Services, Consulting and Negotiation Services, Speakers, Lecturers and Presenters for Conferences, Programs and Commentary, Software Design for Licensing and Marketing Companies, Web Development, Media Asset Management, Hardware Support
Clients:
Marilyn Monroe, James Dean, Sophia Loren, Ingrid Bergman, Ivana Trump, Lana Turner, Bette Davis, Tyrone Power, Errol Flynn, Montgomery Clift, Sir Laurence Olivier, Rock Hudson, Helen Hayes, Jean Harlow, Ginger Rogers, Josephine Baker, Lou Jacobs, Matthew Stymie Beard,Jr., George Spanky McFarland, William 'Buckwheat' Thomas,LillianGish,AlanLadd, Bettie Page, Telly Savalas, Peter Sellers, Jayne Mansfield, Marty Feldman, Mickey Rooney, Lee Strasberg, Tennessee Ernie Ford, Liza Minnelli, Carmen Miranda, Sharon Tate, Hedy Lamarr, Victoria Fuller, Redd Foxx, Gene Siskel, Holly Madison, Bridget Marquardt, Kendra Wilkinson,Dorothy Dandridge, Walter M
Consulting, Auction/Merchandise, Event Services:
Rights and Clearances, Auction, Location Shoots, Receptions/Event Venue, Exhibits.
Athlete Management Services:
Worldwide representative of a wide range of athletic organizations, athletes, and estates. Negotiates personal appearances.
Marketing & Consulting Services:
Provides management, marketing and advertising consultation for professional athletes.
Other Location:
8560 Sunset Boulevard, 10th Floor Penthouse, West Hollywood, CA 90069. 310-651-2000; FAX: 317-570-5500.

DAVIS, HOWARD E. (BEN)
6655 FIRST PARK TEN BOULEVARD
SUITE 250
SAN ANTONIO, TX 78213
210-738-8080
800-401-4619
Fax: 210-738-8088
- Howard E. Davis, Founder
(210) 738-8080
irish-x@att.net
Services:
Handles legal cases

DAVIS, TODD
10271 W PICO BOULEVARD
LOS ANGELES, CA 90064
310-277-4700
Fax: 310-201-0967
Description:
Represents professional sports teams.

DEKAI ENTERPRISES
440 RAMSEY ROAD
YARDLEY, PA 19067
215-321-4323
Fax: 215-321-3175
- Linda Bodley, VP
Nature of Sports Service:
All phases of athlete representation including contract negotiation, long-range planning, financial planning, and post-career counseling.
Services:
Contract Negotiations, Endorsements, Career Counseling, Post Career Counseling, Public Relations

DELL, DONALD L.
5335 WISCONSIN AVENUE NW
SUITE 850
WASHINGTON, DC 20015
202-721-7200
Fax: 202-721-7201
www.experiencebest.com
Nature of Services:
Sports marketing; television, events and representation

DENNIS CONNER SPORTS, INC.
2525 SHELTER ISLAND DRIVE
SUITE E
SAN DIEGO, CA 92106
619-523-5131
Fax: 619-263-1495
- Dennis Conner,
Sports Service Founded:
1987.
Services:
Management, marketing and operations of large scale sailing, and related events including The America's Cup.
Marketing & Consulting Services:
Fundraising and sports.

DEPERSIA, ROBERT
35 KINGS HIGHWAY E
SUITE 102
HADDONFIELD, NJ 08033-2009
856-795-9688
Fax: 856-795-7944
info@depersialaw.com
www.depersialaw.com

DOMANN & PITTMAN
5 BURR OAKS CT
BOLINGBROOK, IL 60440-1285
630-783-9498
Fax: 630-783-9821
- Craig E. Domann, Co-founder
- Drew Pittman, Co-founder
Services:
Contract Negotiations, Marketing, Financial Guidance, Player Management, Career Transition, Vets Free Agency Contract Negotiation, Preparation for All-Star Games, Combine Training, Pre-draft Marketing
Clients:
Shaunard Harts, Quintin Williams, Billy Bajema, Marion Barber III, David Barrett,

William Bartee, Jarrod Baxter, Monty Beisel, Ryon Bingham, Marc Boerigter, Alfonso Boone, Marko Cavka, Chris Chester, Tony Curtis, Trey Darilek, Glenn Earl, Makoa Freitas, Gilbert Gardner, Kelvin Garmon, Eric Ghiaciuc, Bobby Gray, MIke Green, Eric Green, Brock Gutierrez, Tyjuan Hagler, Ryan Hannam, Nick Hardwick, Drew Hodgdon, Jeb Huckeba, Frisman Jackson, Jeno James, Adrian Jones, Brandon Jones, Chris Kuper, Michael Lehan, Ryan Lilja, Kevin Mathis, David McMillan, Mike MInter, Jason Murphy, Chad Owens, Derek Pagel, Domata Peko, Duke Preston, John Standeford, Re
Sports Service Founded:
1991.
Other Office:
J. Drew Pittman, 2905 Maple Ave, Dallas, TX 75201. 214 855-1411; FAX: 214 954-1523

DRIVER CONNECTION/RAPID RACEWAYS
161 WOODFORD AVENUE
UNIT 55
PLAINVILLE, CT 06062
860-793-1888
Fax: 860-229-3970

EASTERN ATHLETIC SERVICES
11350 MCCORMICK ROAD
SUITE 800
EXECUTIVE PLAZA 1
HUNT VALLEY, MD 21031
410-229-0080
Fax: 443-212-5594
www.easfootball.com
- Anthony Agnone, Board of Directors
- Edward G Johnson, Board of Director
- Richard M Rosa, Board of Director
- Howard S Shotsky, Contract Researcher/Analyst
Services:
Combine Preparation/Pre-Draft Counseling, Contract Reviews and Negotiations, Player Marketing, Endorsements and Promotions, Financial Reviews and Planning, Tax Planning and Preparation, Insurance Planning, Personal Banking, Day-to-Day Needs
Clients:
John Abraham, Jason Babin, Tim Bulman, Trent Cole, Bill Conaty, Will Demps, Jason Fabini, Michael Gaines, Cornelius Griffin, Andrew Hoffman, Bhawoh Jue, Patrick Kerney, Dan Koppen, David Macklin, Sean McHugh, Antwan Odom, Shaun OHara, Jeffery Posey, Casey Rabach, Chris Roberson, Bryan Scott, Jamie Sharper, Chris Snee, Jerald Sowell, Michael Strahan, Kyle VandenBosch, Chris Villarrial, Bracy Walker, Rian Wallace, Reggie Wells, Ernest Wilford, Bobbie Williams
Description:
Contract negotiation, investment contract negotiation, federal/state/international tax filings, provides investment advice, endorsement exploration.
Year Founded:
1978

ECLIPSE SPORTS MANAGEMENT
675 SEMINOLE AVENUE
ATLANTA, GA 30307
404-853-5088
404-841-8223

• Scott Greenspun, Co-Founder/Principal
Services:
Sports and Event Marketing

EDELIN, KENTON S.
1200 BRADDOCK PLACE
SUITE 211
ALEXANDRIA, VA 22314
703-683-3961
Fax: 703-683-9696
marketing@mccuemortgage.com
www.mccuemortgage.com
• Kenton S Edelin, President
Nature of Sports Service:
All phases of athlete representation
including contract negotiation, long-range
planning, financial planning, and post-career
counseling.

EDGE SPORTS INTERNATIONAL, INC.
1410 TECHNY ROAD
NORTHBROOK, IL 60062
847-291-4333
Fax: 847-498-6215
kreiter@edgesportsintl.com
www.edgesportsintl.com
• Keith Kreiter, President
kreiter@edgesportsintl.com
• Alessandro Barbalich, International
Director
• Micheal Elman, General Counsel
• Keith Kreiter, Founder/CEO
• Greg Haenke, Vice President
Sports Service Founded:
1994.
Services:
Contract Negotiation, Wealth Management
& Life Planning Service, The Marketing
Edge, Media Relations
Clients:
Maciej Lempe, Orien Greene, Kendall Gill,
Marcello Hurtas, George Weah, Garrett
Jones, Marcus Nettles, Jose Nieves
Description:
Athlete representation, marketing &
consulting firm advising top athletes and
corporations worldwide. Edge has been
recognized as an industry leader in strategic
marketing/branding campaigns. Business
advisory arm counsels all athletes on
creating a wealth preservation strategy
insulating players with best in class service
providers.
Athlete Management Services:
Manages careers of professional athletes in
all sports, offering a package of services
including contract negotiation,
marketing/public relations, legal counsel,
financial planning, product endorsement
contract negotiations, and arranging for
public appearances.
Marketing & Consulting Services:
Consults with corporations seeking to
expand business through sports promotion,
marketing, public relations, and licensing.
Develops marketing plans and strategy
implementation.
Clients include:
Rafer Alston, Cedric Ceballos, Mark
Dalesandro, Matt Williams, Cathy Turner.

ELLIS, JIM
239 S FIFTH STREET
KENTUCKY HOME LIFE BUILDING, SUITE
1800
LOUISVILLE, KY 40202-3233

502-583-5547
Fax: 502-736-8150
Description:
Contract negotiation, endorsement
exploration, tort actions/litigation/criminal
law.

ELS MANAGEMENT INC.
39633 DORCHESTER CIRCLE
CANTON, MI 48188
734-446-4003
Fax: 734-727-0525
• Everett L. Stone, President
Nature of Sports Service:
All phases of athlete representation
including contract negotiation, long-range
planning, financial planning, and post-career
counseling.
Services:
Contract Negotiations, Endorsements, Tax
Advice - Referrals Only, Career Counseling,
Post Career Counseling, Marketing

ENTER SPORTS MANAGEMENT
FIVE CONCOURSE PARKWAY
SUITE 3000
ATLANTA, GA 30328
770-350-8011
Fax: 770-350-8012
info@enter-sports.com
www.enter-sports.com
• Hadley Engelhard, President
(770) 350-8011
hadley@enter-sports.com
• Michael McGarvey, VP Marketing
• Ira Pernsley, Player Development
(770) 350-8011
irap@enter-sports.com
• James Story, Marketing & Player
Development
(770) 350-8011
pstory@enter-sports.com
Services:
Contract Negotiations;
Marketing/Endorsements; Financial
Services; Legal/Personal Services; and
Conditioning/Training
Clients:
Travis Henry, Running Back, Buffalo Bills;
Dorsey Levens, Running Back, Philadelphia
Eagles; Dewayne Robertson, Defensive
Tackle, New York Jets; Phillip Daniels,
Defensive End, Washington Redskins;
Tyrone Poole, Cornerback, New England
Patriots; Nick Harper, Cornerback,
Indianapolis Colts; Roosevelt Williams,
Cornerback, Washington Redskins; Allen
Rossum, Defensive Back/Returner, Atlanta
Falcons; Kenyatta Jones, Offensive Tackle,
Washington Redskins; Donte' Curry,
Linebacker, Detroit Lions; Robert Mathis,
Defensive End/ Linebacker, Indianapolis
Colts; Nick Maddox, Running Back, Carolina
Panthers;Joe Hamilton, Quarterback,
Indianapolis Colts

ESTES, PETER R.
7108 EVANSTON ROAD
SPRINGFIELD, VA 22150
703-451-1254
Description:
Contract negotiation.

EUROSPORT ENTERPRISES, INC.
4810 JEAN TALON WEST
SUITE 203

QUEBEC
MONTREAL, CANADA H4P 2N5
514-875-1500
Fax: 514-875-2180
contactus@bamstrategy.com
www.bamstrategy.com
• Andrew Hertzog, President
(514) 369-2233
ahertzog@hllaw.ca
Nature of Service:
Full service sports agency, representing
men and women basketball players from the
United States and Canada. Handles
basketball players ready to play overseas,
as an alternative approach to gaining the
experience to enter the NBA.
Year Founded:
1993

EXCALIBUR MARKETING GROUP
827 EASTOVER PARKWAY
LOCUST GROVE, VA 22508
540-972-7388
Fax: 540-972-4691
www.isportsnet.com
Sports Service Founded:
1992
Services:
Full service sports marketing firm
specializing in all levels of the football
industry, athlete management services,
professional services, sports agents, market
research services. Owns and operates the
Dick Butkus Football Internet site
(www.dickbutkus.com), dedicated to all
levels of football. Also owns and operates
Internet Sports Awards. Represents over 20
NFL Hall of Fame players available for
corporate marketing programs.
Athlete Management Services:
Represents over 20 NFL Hall of Fame
players available for corporate marketing
programs.

FAMILIE
2052CORTE DEL NOGAL
SUITE 150
CARLSBAD, CA 92011
760-602-6200
Fax: 760-602-9800
info@wgmllc.com
www.wmgllc.com
• Steve Astephen, Principal Action Sports
steve@thefamilie.com
• Cris Whittaker,
(760) 602-6200
• Casey Wasserman, Chairman and CEO
• Arn Tellem, Vice Chairman
• David Kogan, Managing director
• Dean Christopher, Chief Financial officer
• Denise Durante, Co-managing Director of
Consulting Division
• Elizabeth Lindsey, Co-Managing Director
of Consulting Division
• John Brody, Managing Director
Services:
Marketing, public relations, creative,
licensing, trend research and consulting.
Clients:
ESPN, Disney, Nike ACG, Jakks Pacific,
Nestle, and DonJoy among others
Athlete Management:
Geared toward action sports athletes.
Handles all phases of athlete management,
contracts, endorsement opportunities, etc.
Public Relations & Marketing:
Develops public relations campaigns that

includes extensive media coverage for products, athletes and event properties.

FAZZONE & BAILLIE
ONE TOWN CENTER
CHESHIRE, CT 6410
203-250-2222
Fax: 203-250-7388
info@fazzoneryan.com
www.fazzoneryan.com
• Joanne M Ryan, Attorney
(203) 250-2222
jryan@fazzoneryan.com
• Anthony J Fazzone, Attorney
afazzone@fazzoneryan.com
• Joanne M Ryan, Attorney
jryan@fazzoneryan.com
• Phillip Ricciuti, Attorney
pricciuti@fazzoneryan.com
Description:
Contract negotiation, post career planning, investment contract negotiation, arbitration hearings, federal/state/international tax filings, endorsement exploration, tort actions/litigation.
Services:
Real Estate Law, Business Services, Estate Planning, Estate and Probate Administration, Elder Law, Zoning and Land Use, Civil Litigation, Family Law

FEHR, STEVEN A.
204 W LINWOOD BOULEVARD
KANSAS CITY, MO 64111-1328
816-561-3755
Description:
Contract negotiation.
Services:
Labor and Employment Relations Attorneys, Probation Services, Professional Services.

FELDMAN, OSCAR
STONEBRIDGE W
41000 WOODWARD AVENUE
BLOOMFIELD HILLS, MI 48304
248-258-1616
Fax: 248-258-1439
feldman@butzel.com
www.butzel.com
• Richard E Rassel, Director, Global Client Relations
(313) 225-7014
rassel@butzel.com
• Philip J Kessler, President and Shareholder
(313) 225-7018
• Keefe A Brooks, VP and Shareholder
(248) 593-3010
brooks@butzel.com
• Richard B. C Brosnick, VP and Shareholder
brosnick@butzel.com
Description:
Represents professional sports teams. NBA - Detroit Pistons basketball.
Services:
Independent law firm, innovative solutions and advice. The firm strives to be on the cutting edge of new developments including advanced technology and manufacturing, e-commerce, internet law, intellectual property and cross-border operations and transactions.
Clients:
The firm's clients come from many business sectors, including automotive, manufacturing, banking and financial

services, retail and wholesale distribution, insurance, professional services, health care, advertising, media, publishing, technology and computers, marine, transportation, construction, utilities and real estate.

FENTRESS, A. LEE
7950 JONES BEACH DR.
SUITE 700N
MCLEAN, VA 22107
703-905-3300
Fax: 703-905-4495
www.octagon.com
• Phil de Picciotto, Founder and President
• Rick Dudley, President & CEO
• Jeff Shifrin, President
• Lisa Murray, Executive Vice President Chief Marketing Offi
• Sean Nicholls, Managing Director
• Simon Wardle, Chief Strategy Officer
• Jeff Ehrenkranz, Managing Director
Description:
Contract negotiation, post career planning, endorsement exploration.
Services:
Contract negotiations, Marketing initiatives and endorsement programs, Public relations and charity involvement, Financial planning, wealth advisory and asset management, Television opportunities, Speaking engagements, Content creation, Property development, Event management

FINAL KICK MARKETING GROUP, INC.
2865 LYNNHAVEN DRIVE, C3
VIRGINIA BEACH, VA 23451
757-481-3400
800-789-6888
www.finalkick.com
Services:
Seeks endorsements for clients with equipment manufacturers, licensed goods, trading card companies, corporations; arranges personal appearances, television appearances, commercial deals, infomercials, speaking engagements; and conducts training.
Represents professional and amateur athletes, Olympians and celebrities. Specializes in creating product media awareness of clients and the products they endorse. Services include contract negotiations, career management, tax preparation and post-career preparations.
Marketing & Consulting Services:
Seeks endorsements for clients with equipment manufacturers, licensed goods, trading card companies, corporations; arranges personal appearances, television appearances, commercial deals, infomercials, speaking engagements; and conducts a training and fitness program.
Athlete Management Services:
Represents professional and amateur athletes, Olympians and celebrities. Specializes in creating product media awareness of clients and the products they endorse. Services include contract negotiations, career management, tax preparation and post-career planning.
Sports Service Founded:
1996

FINAL KICK SPORTS
2865 LYNNHAVEN DRIVE
VIRGINIA BEACH, VA 23451
757-481-3400
800-789-6888
Fax: 757-481-3461
www.finalkick.com

Services:
Seeks endorsements for clients with equipment manufacturers, licensed goods, trading card companies, corporations; arranges personal appearances, television appearances, commercial deals, infomercials, speaking engagements; and conducts training.
Represents professional and amateur athletes, Olympians and celebrities. Specializes in creating product media awareness of clients and the products they endorse. Services include contract negotiations, career management, tax preparation and post-career preparations.
Marketing & Consulting Services:
Seeks endorsements for clients with equipment manufacturers, licensed goods, trading card companies, corporations; arranges personal appearances, television appearances, commercial deals, infomercials, speaking engagements; and conducts a training and fitness program.
Athlete Management Services:
Represents professional and amateur athletes, Olympians and celebrities. Specializes in creating product media awareness of clients and the products they endorse. Services include contract negotiations, career management, tax preparation and post-career planning.
Sports Service Founded:
1996

FIRST DOWN PROMOTIONS
595 INDUSTRIAL ROAD
SAN CARLOS, CA 94070
650-595-7797
fdpromo@aol.com
• John Paye, President/Chief Executive Officer
(650) 326-7797
• Danielle Donahue, Marketing-Promotions VP
• Kristin Larios, Marketing And Promotions
Sports Service Founded:
1989.
Event Management Services:
Organizes and promotes the Benefit Basketball Association, a collection of NFL athletes who play basketball for charity. Manages celebrity golf tournaments, football clinics and softball fund-raisers.
Marketing & Consulting Services:
Promotes and markets products to directly increase sales and serve as product advertising.

FIRST STRING MANAGEMENT
85 ELLESMERE ROAD
UNIT 31
SCARBOROUGH, CANADA ON M1R 4B7
416-447-5991
• Kevin E. Fitzpatrick, Sports Agent
Nature of Sports Service:
All phases of athlete representation including contract negotiation, long-range planning, financial planning, and post-career counseling.

FITNESS PERFORMANCE CENTERS
280 ROUTE 513
SUITE V & W
GLEN GARDENER, NJ 08826
908-638-4687
Fax: 847-562-0386
s.cavitch@comcast.net
fitnessperformancecenter.com
• Robert Garza, Trainer
(847) 562-4386
• Michael Carnevali, Personal Trainer
• Shawn Cavitch, Owner

FOSTER & EASLEY SPORTS MANAGEMENT GROUP
13701 42ND AVENUE NE
SEATTLE, WA 98125
206-362-7780
800-326-3031
Fax: 206-362-0478
• Cameron Foster, President
• Kenny Easley, VP
• Courtney Foster, VP
Services:
Sports Promotions & Special Events. All phases of athlete representation including contract negations, commercial endorsements and tax planning. Member of NFLPA, NBAPA,CFLPA.
Clients:
Tom Ackerman, Archie Anderson, Kenyan Branscomb, Anthony Calvillo, Derrick Fenner, Napolean Kaufmann, Leon Neal
Description:
All phases of athlete representation including contract negations, commercial endorsements and tax planning. Member of NFLPA, NBAPA,CFLPA.

FRAZIER & FRAZIER
2399 UNIVERSITY BLVD.
4TH FLOOR
HOUSTON, TX 77005
713-655-7100
Fax: 713-655-7150
www.frazierlawhouston.com
• Kyle Frazier, Partner
• Bill Frazier, Partner
(281) 407-7910
Description:
Contract negotiation, post career planning, federal/state/international tax filings, investment advice, endorsement exploration, tort actions/litigation.

FRIED & COMPANY, P.C.
700 THIRTEENTH STREET NW
SUITE 990
WASHINGTON, DC 20005
202-331-3900
Fax: 202-331-3905
• Jeffrey Fried, President
• Nathan Peake, Sports Management Director
• Tanisha Howard, Sports/Entertainment Management
• Kiyo Ohen, Attorney
Description:
Athlete Management, contract negotiation, post career planning, licensing, endorsement commercialization, teaches sports law, Federal/state/International tax filings, Representing professional sports teams, Investment advice.

FUHRO, HANLEY & BEUKAS
36 MOUNTAINVIEW BOULEVARD
WAYNE, NJ 07470
973-686-1000
• Brian Fuhro, Esquire
Services:
Legal Services
Description:
Contract negotiation, post career planning, investment contract negotiation, arbitration hearings, federal/state/international tax filings, represents professional sports teams, provides securities advice, provides investment advice, licensing, endorsement exploration, tort actions/litigation.

FUTURE FOR KIDS
6991 E CAMELBACK ROAD
SUITE B - 100
SCOTTSDALE, AZ 85251
480-947-8131
Fax: 480-947-3729
info@futureforkids.org
www.FutureforKIDS.org
• Rodney Smith, President/Founder
info@futureforkids.org
• Beth Albrecht, Project Director/Grant Coordinator
info@futureforkids.org
• Sheehan McAuley, Program Director
info@futureforkids.org
• Madoona Bistany, Executive Director
• Regina LaPlante, Program Coordinator
• Becki Stephens, Office Assistant
• Bennett Conklin, Board Chair
• Michael Bankston, Vice Chair
• Tim Hyde, Secretary
Sports Service Founded:
1990.
Services:
Provides at-risk youth with mentorship and education through sports camps and technology centers.
Athlete Management Services:
Sports marketing firm specializing in the placement of past and present athletes and coaches for speaking engagements, appearances and endorsements.

GANIM ENTERPRISES
6449 LAKE TRAIL DRIVE
WESTERVILLE, OH 43082-8795
614-890-6073
Fax: 614-890-9986
• Doug Ganim, President
(614) 890-6073
ganim@earthlink.net
Sports Service Founded:
1984
Athlete Management Services:
Full professional representation of male and female racquetball players.
Event Management Services:
Sports marketing specialists in racquetball. Event production, administration and promotion nationwide. Professional, semi-pro and amateur events on both regional and national level.
Marketing & Consulting Services:
Sports marketing and consulting services offered with an emphasis in the sport of racquetball. Sponsorship procurement, industry consulting, and other specialized services available.

GARDA WORLD
5870 TRINITY PARKWAY
SUITE 300
CENTERVILLE, VA 20120
703-592-1400
Fax: 703-592-1500
www.vanceglobal.com
• Drew T. Ladau, President
• Steven W. Casteel, SVP, Intenational Business Development
• Oliver Westmacott, President and COO
• Pete Dordal Jr, Senior Vice President
• Adrian Blanchette, VP, Operations
• James Grimshaw, VP, Business Process and Integration
• Joe Hogan, Director, Emerging Markets
• Caroline Passey, Director, Marketing

Services:
Risk Analysis and Planning, Business Intelligence and Due Diligence, Uniformed Protection, Education and Training, Executive Protection, Contingency Planning and Response, Litigation Support, Labor Unrest Protection, Security and Intelligence in High-Risk Markets, Protection, Investigation, Monitoring and Compliance, Digital Security and Investigation
Sports Service Founded:
1984.
Nature of Sports Service:
Security services for athletes and their families.
Other Office:
Rio Nilo 74'4; Col Cuauhtemoc; Mexico, DF 06500. 525 514 2044

GARY PLAYER GROUP, INC
3930 RCA BOULEVARD
SUITE 3001
PALM BEACH GARDENS, FL 33410
561-624-0300
Fax: 561-624-0304
info@garyplayer.com
www.garyplayer.com
• Scott Ferrell, Gary Player Design President
(561) 624-0300
• Tim Smith, Gary Player Enterprises President
(561) 624-0300
Services:
Golf Course Design Service, Enterprises Service, Management Services & Golf Academy
Products:
Apparel, Accessories & Headwear, Golf Shoes, Equipment & Golf Accessories, Books, Videos & CDs, Special Items & Gifts & Memorabilia

GAUSDEN, THOMAS
ONE BREWERS WAY
MILWAUKEE, WI 53214
414-902-4400
Fax: 414-933-5474
www.milwaukeebrewers.com
Description:
Represents professional sports teams.

GAYLORD SPORTS MANAGEMENT
13845 N NORTHSIGHT BOULEVARD
SUITE 200
SCOTTSDALE, AZ 85260
480-483-9500
Fax: 480-483-9598
info@gaylordsports.com
• Steve Loy, Chief Executive Officer
(480) 483-9500
sloy@gaylordsports.com
• E.K. Gaylord, II, Chairman
(480) 483-9500
• David Yates, EVP/Chief Operating Officer
dyates@gaylordsports.com
• Steve Loy, President
• David Yates, Senior VP
• Jon Hartigan, Chief Financial Officer
Nature of Sports Service:
A full-service professional management company with the proven ability to manage the careers of some of the best professional golfers in the world. Provides services for contract negotiations, corporate marketing and consulting, corporate outings and television and event opportunities.

Specializes in the sport of golf.
Services:
Talent Representation, Corporate Sports Consulting, Media and Public Relations & Event Management (Tommy Bahama Challenge)
Clients:
Rich Beem, Mark Calcavecchia, Jim Carter, DavidGossett, Dudley Hart, Matt Hansen, Frank Lickliter II, Billy Mayfair, Rocco Mediate, Phil Mickelson, Ryan Moore, Arron Oberholser, Jeff Overton, Craig, Perks, Tom Pernice, Jr., Scott Piercy, Heath Slocum, Boyd Summerhays, Nick Watney, Jeremy Anderson, Ricky Barnes, Todd Demsey, Craig Lile, Bryce Molder, Chris Nallen, Chez Reavie, Tom Scherrer, Hale Irwin, Darren Clarke, David Howell, Stephen Leaney, Graeme McDowell, Paul McGinley, Peter O'Malley, Craig Parry, Lee Westwood, Robert Hamilton, Lee Williamson, Beth Bauer, Catherine Cartwright, Rachel Hetherington, Brittany Lang, Cristie Kerr.

GEM GROUP
3 GATEAWAY CENTER
SUITE 1200
401 LIBERTY AVENUE
PITTSBURG, PA 15222
412-471-2885
800-242-8923
Fax: 412-471-2891
www.gemgroup.com
• Chuck Corcoran, Entertainment VP
(310) 843-3142
CCorcoran@gemgroup.com
Services:
Full service marketing communications agency specializing in Sport and Entertainment.
Areas of Sports Expertise:
Motorsports, soccer, horse raising, olympics, collegiate sports, tennis, figure skating, sailing, cricket, golf, rugby league, ice hockey, rugby union.
Services Include:
Contract negotiation, asset management, athlete recruitment, sponsorship consulting, promotion marketing, director marketing, public relations, internet, point-of-sale, hospitality services, event PR, media relations, special events, sampling, field marketing and alliance marketing.

GENERAL SPORTS TURF SYSTEMS
400 WATER STREET
SUITE 250
ROCHESTER, MI 48307
248-601-2200
Fax: 248-601-2400
www.generalsports.com
• Andy Appleby, Chairman/CEO
• Laurie Alpers, Director of administration and finance
• Melissa Priester, Director of Client Service
• Josh Hartman, Director of sales and marketing
• Lee Stacey, Executive Vice president
• Andrew D L. Appleby, Chairman and CEO
Services:
Executive Placement, Consulting Services, Hospitality & Event Management, Naming Rights & Sponsorships, Team Acquisition

GEORGE SPADORO
ONE BOLAND DRIVE
WEST ORANGE, NJ 07052

973-325-1500
Fax: 973-325-1501
info@wolffsamson.com
www.wolffsamson.com
• George Spadoro, Partner
(973) 530-2113
Nature of Sports Service:
All phases of athlete representation including: Marketing the athlete to professional teams, contract negotiation, endorsements, merchandising, tax/financial planning and post-career counseling.
Services:
Handles legal matters in the following practice areas: Corporate/Business, Administrative, Banking, Litigation, Labor, Commercial Real Estate, Creditors Rights, Partnerships, Mergers and Acquisitions, Municipal Law, Public and Private Real Estate Redevelopment.

GLASS, INC, KEITH
69 BROAD STREET
SUITE B
RED BANK, NJ 07701
732-741-9339
Fax: 732-741-3090
otgentertainment.net
• Laura Renae, Coordinator
(908) 741-9339
• Chuck Iarussi, Overseas/Placement Services
Services:
Legal Services
Clients:
Dale Ellis, Marty Conlon
Description:
Contract negotiation, endorsements, appearances & marketing.

GLOBAL ATHLETE MANAGEMENT ENTERPRISES
21031 VENTURA BOULEVARD
PENTHOUSE, 12TH FLOOR
WOODLAND HILLS, CA 91364
818-999-9127
Fax: 818-999-3354
• Jeffrey A. Slott, President/Agent/General Legal
• Nancy Hoover, Secretary/Director Operations
Description:
Offers legal and agent services to professional athletes.

GLOBAL SPORTS MARKETING & EVENTS
2432 W PEORIA AVENUE
SUITE 1163
PHOENIX, AZ 85034
602-943-6605
Services:
Marketing & Consulting Services: Sports sponsorship sales, event marketing, public relations, promotions, and athlete marketing.
Services:
Event Management Services: Full event management from consulting to full production.
Marketing & Consulting Services:
Sports sponsorship sales, event marketing, public relations, promotions, and athlete marketing.

GLOBAL SPORTS PRODUCTIONS, LTD.
16810 CRYSTAL DRIVE E
ENUMCLAW, WA 98022

310-454-9480
Fax: 253-874-1027
• Ed Kobak, President
edkobak@yahoo.com
Products:
Sports marketing and publishing firm that specializes in producing sports reference books and directories from around the world
Brands:
The Sports Address Bible & Almanac, Mascots!, The Celebrity Address Directory and Autograph Collector's Guide, The International Sports Directory, The Encyclopedia of Minor League Football, Sports Logo Guide, The National Directory of College Athletics, The Dream Job, The Career Guide to Sports Administration & The Encyclopedia of Sports Business Contacts

GOEPEL, ROBERT
1400 MAIN STREET
RACINE, WI 53403
262-637-5100
Fax: 262-637-8353
goepel@execpc.com
Services:
Legal Services
Description:
Contract negotiation, arbitration hearings, endorsement exploration, tort actions/litigation.

GOLDEN BEAR SPORTS MANAGEMENT
11780 US HIGHWAY ONE
N PALM BEACH, FL 33408
561-227-0300
Fax: 561-626-4104
• Keenan Delaney, Marketing Director
• Jack Nicklaus, Chief Executive Officer
• Steve Nicklaus, Designer
Sports Service Founded:
1991.
Services:
Design services include Marketing & Communications; Plan Documents; Specifications and Details; Computer Modeling; Landscape Design Services; and Renovation Services.
Marketing & Consulting Services:
All phases of contract negotiation, financial management and planning for professional golfers.

GOWLING LAFLEUR HENDERSON
1600, 421 7TH AVENUE SW
CALGARY, ALBERTA, CANADA T2P 4K9
403-298-1000
Fax: 403-263-9193
webmaster@gowlings.com
www.gowlings.com
• Kenneth J. Warren, Managing Partner
(403) 298-1000
kenneth.warren@gowlings.com
• Greg Peterson, Partner
(403) 292-9812
• James S. Peacock, Partner
(403) 298-1011
• Kerry R. Powell, Partner
(403) 292-9805
kerry.powell@gowlings.com
Services:
Aboriginal Law; Administrative & Public; Advertising; Banking Litigation; Business Law Charities & Not-For-Profit; Civil Fraud, Commercial Litigation; Construction Law; Copyright; Corporate Finance; Securities &

Public M&A; Defamation & Media;
Employment & Labour; Environmental;
Estates & Trusts; Family; Financial
Regulatory Law; Financial Services;
Franchise and Distribution Law;
Government Relations and Regulatory
Affairs; Government Services; Immigration;
Insurance; Professional Liability; Intellectual
Property Litigation; Natural Resources;
Occupational Health & Safety; Patent
Prosecution; Privacy; Real Estate & Urban
Development; Recover
Description:
Provides a full complement of legal services
to national and international clients.

GRAND SLAM III
7160 ZIONSVILLE ROAD
INDIANAPOLIS, IN 46268
317-575-5900
Services:
Marketing Consultant Professional Athelete
Management

GRANT ASSOCIATES
301 SAYRE DRIVE
PRINCETON, NJ 08540-5826
609-514-8674
Fax: 609-514-8673
• David Grant, President
Nature of Service:
Executive recruiting, licensing management,
sports/event promotion, strategic corporate
growth consulting, U.S. market
development.
Year Founded:
1997
Sports Service Founded:
1997

GREG DAWLEY
1900 AVENUE OF THE STARS
SUITE 2350
LOS ANGELES, CA 90067
310-551-1700
Fax: 310-277-7062
Services:
Civil litigation and counseling in
business-related matters, business torts,
including banking, insurance, title insurance
and real estate
Description:
Tort actions/litigation, real estate contract
representative.

GROUP II COMMUNICATIONS
1311 W FOREST HOME AVENUE
FRANKLIN, WI 53132
414-425-2080
Fax: 414-425-7682
customerservice@groupii.com
www.groupii.com
• Laura Manion, Business Development
tom.feeney@groupii.com
• Tim Leahy, Client Services
tim.leahy@groupii.com
Services:
Merchandising services

GUNSTER, YOAKLEY & STEWART, P.C.
777 S FLAGLER DRIVE
SUITE 500 E
WEST PALM BEACH, FL 33401-6194
561-655-1980
800-749-1980
Fax: 561-655-5677

contact@gunster.com
www.gunster.com
• Stephen F. McDermott, Chief Financial
Officer/Chief Operations
(561) 650-0527
smcdermott@gunster.com
• H. William Perry, Managing Shareholder
(561) 650-0640
hperry@gunster.com
• Grant Sagear, Director of Information
Services
(561) 804-4354
gsagear@gunster.com
• William A. Adams, Shareholder
• David Atkinson, Practice Leader
• Davis D. Balz, Associate
Description:
Post career planning, licensing,
endorsement exploration.
Services:
Provide services to client relating to:
Corporate, Private Wealth Services,
Litigation Department, Real Estate Services
Clients:
Arvida/JMB Partners JM Family Enterprises,
Inc. SBA Communications Corporation,
AutoNation, Inc. J.P. Morgan Chase & Co.
Seven Springs Golf Club, Bank of America,
N.A. Jupiter Island Club Smiths Industries
PLC, Bankrate, Inc. Kellstrom Aerospace,
LLC Sonesta Hotels & Resorts, Boca Raton
Resort and Club Lee Munder Capital Group
The St. Joe Company, Capital City Bank
Group, Inc. Levenger Company Starwood
Hotels & Resorts, Chiquita International, Inc.
Lykes Bros., Inc. Teva Pharmaceutical Citrix
Systems, Inc. Murray Goodman Company
Todhunter International, Inc., First Citizens
Bank & Trust Park Avenue BBQ
Restaurants.
Areas of Practice:
Financial Services, Corporate Transactions,
Employment Law, Immigration, Land Use &
Environmental, Leisure & Resorts, Private
Wealth Services, Real Estate, Securities,
Mergers & Acquistions, Taxation &
International Taxation, Technology Law,
Urban Development, Litigation.

GURWIN, DAVID A.
301 GRANT STREET
ONE OXFORD CENTRE
20TH FLOOR
PITTSBURGH, PA 15219-1410
412-562-8800
Fax: 412-562-1041
info@bipc.com
www.buchananingersoll.com
• Thomas L. VanKirk, Chief Executive
Officer and Managing Dir
(412) 562-8875
vankirktl@bipc.com
• David A. Gurwin, Entertainment
Chair/Media Law Group/Technology
(412) 440-4493
david.gurwin@bipc.com
• Edward Jo Allera, Board of Director
(412) 562-8875
vankirktl@bipc.com
• John A. E. Barbour, CEO & Chairman of
the Board
(412) 392-2087
• Patrick C. Keane, Executive Shareholder
(703) 838-6522
• Steven E. Bizar, Executive Shareholde
(215) 665-3826
• Wendelynne J. Newton, Executive
Shareholder

(412) 562-8932
• Thomas S. Giotto, Executive Shareholder
(412) 392-2068
• Nolan W. Kurtz, Chief Operating Officer
(717) 237-4807
• Miles H. Simon, Chief Financial Officer
(412) 562-1809
Description:
Contract negotiation, post career planning,
investment contract negotiation, represents
professional sports teams, licensing,
endorsement exploration, represents college
athletic departments, represents sports
organizations.
Clients:
ABN Amro Bank N.V., Amerisourcebergen
Corp., Avecia, Bacardi, Ltd., Bank of
America, Bayer BioScience, N.V., Black Box
Corporation, Bush Brothers and Company
Catholic Health East, Cendant Corporation,
CFA Institute, Chevron, Children's Hospital
of Pittsburgh, Citigroup Inc., City of New
York, Concurrent Technologies Corporation,
Dale Carnegie & Associates Inc., Deere &
Co., Equitable Resources, Hearst-Argyle
Television Inc., Hershey Company, JER
Revenue Services, J.E. Robert Companies,
Johns Mansfield, J.P. Morgan Chase, Knoll
Inc., KV Pharmaceutical Company, Merck &
Company, Merrill Lynch, National City,
Oceania Cruises, Payment Protection S
Year Founded
1850
Other Locations:
One Chase Manhattan Plaza, 35th Floor,
New York, NY 10005; Phone:
212-440-4400; 1776 K Street, NW STE 800,
Washington, DC 20006; Phone:
202-452-7900; Sun Trust Finance Center,
401 East Jackson Street, STE 2500,
Tampa, FL 33602; Phone 813-222-8180;
First National Bank Center, 401 West A
Street, STE 1900, San Diego, CA 92101;
Phone: 619-578-5000

GWINN & ROBY
1201 ELM STREET
4100 RENAISSANCE TOWER
DALLAS, TX 75270
214-698-4100
Fax: 214-747-2904
• Robert R Roby, Managing Partner
(214) 698-4198
• Robert A Gwinn, Of Counsel
(214) 698-4101
Services:
Represents both publicly and privately-held
corporations as well as individuals in
matters that include healthcare, HMO, and
medical malpractice defense; product
liability; complex multi-district class actions;
medical device and pharmaceutical
litigation; commercial litigation; construction
litigation; legal malpractice; securities
litigation; employment litigation on behalf of
management; insurance defense and
coverage matters; automobile litigation;
aviation litigation; general negligence
litigation; premises liability; family law; and
workers' compensation matters.
Clients:
Acme Trucking Company, Alcoa, Allstate,
Amarillo Globe News, American Red Cross,
American Welding Society, Baxter, Brinker
International, Bristol Hotel Co, Brookshire
Grocery Company, Brown & Brown, Inc.,
California State Auto Association, Carter
BloodCare, Inc., Coca-Cola Enterprises,

Inc., Coffee Memorial Blood Center, Comcast, ConocoPhillips, ContiBeef, L.L.C., Core Data Resources, Inc., Covenant Health System, Cracker Barrel, Crawford and Co., Delphi Automotive Systems, Eastern Livestock, L.L.C., EMCARE, Inc., Empire Fire & Marine Insurance Co., Fireman's Fund Insurance Cos., Friona Industries, L.P., General Motors, Grove, Worldwide, Guid
Nature of Sports Service:
All phases of athlete representation including contract negotiation, long-range planning and post-career counseling.

HACKLER, KENNETH P.
1700 SW COLLEGE AVENUE
TOPEKA, KS 66621-0001
785-670-1010
Fax: 785-233-2780
www.washburn.edu
• Jerry B. Farley, President
• Ron Wasserstein, VP for Academic Affairs
wasserstein@washburn.edu
• Wanda B. Hill, VPfor Administration and Treasurer
• Denise C. Ottinger, VP for Student Life
ottinger@washburn.edu
Description:
Represents college athletic departments.
Services:
Provides High Academic Standards in a Small Class Environment, Committed To Student Success, Well Funded and Affordable and Technologically Sophisticated Environment

HAITBRINK, RICHARD F.
5208 ARGENTINE BOULEVARD
KANSAS CITY, KS 66106
913-328-1100
Fax: 913-287-1919
Services:
Promotion of tennis events, professional and amateur, and corporate and fund raising events. Consulting services for tennis promoters, tennis clubs, resorts and corporate departments seeking to utilize tennis events in marketing strategy. Serves as Executive Director for the National Interscholastic Tennis Coaches Association.

HALL OF FAME SPORTS, INC.
14 BEACH DRIVE
PO BOX 2386
DARIEN, CT 6820
203-655-1023
Fax: 203-655-0799
www.halloffamesports.com
Athlete Management Services:
Manages business affairs of professional athletes.
Marketing & Consulting Services:
Provides marketing, promotional material and photographic services for organizations with specific public relations objectives.

HAMAKAWA, CURT L.
1 OLYMPIC PLAZA
COLORADO SPRINGS, CO 80909-5760
719-866-4852
Fax: 719-866-2029
www.usolympicteam.com
• Jim Scherr, Chief Executive Officer
• Jeff Benz, General Counsel
• Walter Glover, Interim Chief Financial Officer

• Larry Buendorf, Chief Security Officer
Larry.Buendorf@usoc.org
Services:
Organizes sports events, programs and training centers to athletes
Description:
Amateur sports representation.

HAMBRIC SPORTS MANAGEMENT
3131 MCKINNEY AVENUE
SUITE 875
DALLAS, TX 75204
214-720-7179
Fax: 214-720-7787
www.hambricsports.com

HEALY, PAUL J.
1830 ATLANTIC BOULEVARD
HEALY, STONE & ZAHLER BUILDING
JACKSONVILLE, FL 32207
904-391-0029
Fax: 904-399-4540
contactus@paulhealylaw.com
www.paulhealylaw.com
• Paul J. Healy, Attorney
Nature of Service:
All phases of athlete representation including contract negotiation, long-range planning, financial planning, and post-career counseling.
Year Founded:
1994

HERBERT L. RUDOY LTD.
230 W SUPERIOR STREET
SUITE 510
CHICAGO, IL 60654-3584
312-654-1717
Fax: 312-266-4220
chisport@aol.com
www.interperformances.com
• Herbert Rudoy, President
• Arturo Ortega, CEO
Services:
Contract negotiation.

HINSHAW & CULBERSON LLP
3200 N CENTRAL AVENUE
SUITE 800
PHOENIX, AZ 85012-2428
602-631-4400
Fax: 602-631-4404
www.hinshawlaw.com
• Donald L Mrozek, Chairman
(312) 704-3111
dmrozek@hinshawlaw.com
• J. William Roberts, Managing Partner
(312) 704-3918
broberts@hinshawlaw.com
Nature of Sports Service:
All phases of athlete representation including contract negotiation, long-range planning, financial planning, and post-career counseling.
Services:
Construction Law, Corporate & Business Law, Environmental, Government, Health Care, Insurance Services, Labor & Employment, Litigation, Professional Liability, School Law

HINSHAW & CULBERTSON
222 N LASALLE STREET
SUITE 300
CHICAGO, IL 60601

312-704-3000
Fax: 312-704-3001
• Donald L. Mrozek, Chairman
(312) 704-3111
dmrozek@hinshawlaw.com
• J. William Roberts, Managing Partner
(312) 704-3918
broberts@hinshawlaw.com
Services:
Recruiting, retaining and promoting its attorneys and staff members regardless of gender, race, ethnicity, national origin, physical ability, religion or personal background
Nature of Sports Service:
All phases of athlete representation including contract negotiation, long-range planning, financial planning, and post-career counseling.

HORROW, RICK
6800 SW 40TH STREET
SUITE 174
MIAMI, FL 33155
561-743-6408
Fax: 305-559-6737
info@horrowsports.com
www.horrowsports.com
• Rick Horrow, President
• Karla Swatek, VP
• Brian Finkel, Creative Director
• Betty Curbelo, Administrative assistant
Services:
Development and implementation of facilities, properties, and projects for communities, development entities, leagues, franchises, and other businesses. Organizes virtually every sport. Site selection, lease negotiations, public/private partnership financing and project implementation are just some of the services HSV provides to leagues, sanctioning organizations and teams.

HS INTERNATIONAL
9871 IRVINE CENTER DRIVE
IRVINE, CA 92618
949-753-9153
Fax: 949-753-9253
info@hsi.net
www.hsi.net
• Daniel Escamilla, Track and Field
daniel@hsi.net
• Emanuel Hudson, Track & Field/Football/Tennis, Attorney at La
((94)) 753-91
Description:
To assist top athletes in their quest to accomplish personal goals. Represents and assists clients and athletes in business ventures, including athletic endorsements, public and media relations, marketing and legal services.
Services:
Provide expert training and guidance along with specialized management and counseling

HUEBNER, ROBERT E. P.A.
2090 STADIUM DRIVE
SUITE A
BOZEMAN, MT 59715
406-586-4311
Services:
Represents and assists clients and athletes in a wide range of ventures including: Speed Training, Athletic Endorsements, Contract

Negotiations, Image and Brand Enhancement, Legal Services, Public and Media Relations Marketing, Events Scheduling, Logistics Management and Retirement Planning
Description:
Contract negotiation. Land Use; Government; Sports Law.

HURSEY, RALPH MICHAEL
100 SE THIRD AVENUE
9TH FLOOR
FT. LAUDERDALE, FL 33394
954-761-8600
Fax: 954-463-6643
Services:
All phases of athlete representation including contract negotiation, long-range planning, financial planning, and post-career counseling.

ICON SPORTS MANAGEMENT
3916 CLOCK POINTE TRAIL
SUITE 101
STOW, OH 44224-2932
330-945-4234
Fax: 330-945-4371

IMAGE CIRCLE, THE
19 W 34TH STREET
PENTHOUSE FLOOR
NEW YORK, NY 10001
212-874-7394
Fax: 212-874-6607
www.dinahdayimagecoach.com
• Dinah Day, Chief Executive Officer
(646) 339-9955
Nature of Service:
Provides self-image and communication skills training. Group and individual workshops customized for athletes, coaches, and media spokespeople focusing on interpersonal skills, self-image awareness and public speaking, press for sucess training and improved overall confidence.
Sports Service Founded:
1985.
Clients:
Con Edison of New York, Inc., Continental Airlines, Baer Marks & Upham LLP, Avon Products, Inc., Pitney Bowes, Inc., American Express, Right Management Consultants, International Management Group, JPMorgan Chase, NCAA Division 1 Universities, Credit Suisse First Boston, RLR Associates, Lehman Brothers, Affiliations/Associations/Partnerships, Association of Fashion and Image Consultants, The Outplacement Institute, International Association of Career Management Professionals, The Fashion Group, International, Screen Actors Guild, Relapse Prevention Specialists, Publications

---

IMG
1360 E 9TH STREET
SUITE 100
CLEVELAND, OH 44114
216-522-1200
Fax: 216-522-1145
web.feedback@imgworld.com
www.imgworld.com
• Micheal J. Dolan, Chairman & CEO
• Chuck Bennett, President, IMG Golf/Tennis
• Michel Masquelier, President, IMG Media

• George Pyne, President, IMG Sports & Entertainment

Teams:

IMG CHICAGO
626 W JACKSON BLVD
SUITE 650
CHICAGO, IL 60661
312-275-8200
Fax: 312-327-2303
www.imgworld.com
• Theodore J Forstmann, Chairman/CEO
• Chuck Bennett, President IMG Golf, Tennis,Fashion and Event
• Michel Masquelier, President IMG Media
• Michael J J Dolan, President/CEO
• George Pyne, President IMG Sports & Entertainment
Description:
IMG connects brands to global opportunities in sports, fashion and media

IMG FOOTBALL
123 W 8TH STREET
LAWRENCE, KS 66044
785-312-7555
Fax: 785-312-7557
www.imgworld.com
• Theodore J Forstmann, Chairman/CEO
• Chuck Bennett, President IMG Golf, Tennis,Fashion and Event
• Michel Masquelier, President IMG Media
• Michael J J Dolan, President/CEO
• George Pyne, President IMG Sports & Entertainment
Description:
IMG connects brands to global opportunities in sports, fashion and media.

IMG LOS ANGELES/IMG X SPORTS
2049 CENTURY PARK E
SUITE 2480
LOS ANGELES, CA 90067
424-653-1960
Fax: 424-653-1914
www.imgworld.com
• Theodore J Forstmann, Chairman/CEO
• Chuck Bennett, President IMG Golf, Tennis,Fashion and Event
• Michel Masquelier, President IMG Media
• Michael J J Dolan, President/CEO
• George Pyne, President IMG Sports & Entertainment
Description:
IMG connects brands to global opportunities in sports, fashion and media.

IMPACT SPORTS MANAGEMENT
114-116 CURTAIN ROAD
1ST FLOOR
LONDON, ENGLAND EC2A 3AH
44-20-8905 1133
Fax: 44-20-8905-1020
impact-sports.com
• Mitchell Frankel, President
(407) 393-1475
Nature of Service:
Contract negotiation, endorsements and marketing for professional NFL, MLB and NBA athletes.

IMS SPORTS
2051 SAN ELIJO AVENUE
CARDIFF, CA 92007
Fax: 760-487-1368
• Circe Wallace-Hetzel, Sports Agent
(760) 487-1341
• Linnea Gibson, Sports Agent
(760) 487-1341
• Ashby Sorensen, Sports Agent
(760) 487-1342

• Peter A. Golden,
golden@goldenew.com
Services:
Full-service agency which represents more than 40 alternative sports athletes.
Services:
Talent management to event operations, from broadcast ownership to retail development
Clients:
Evan Hernandez, Jereme Rogers, Mike Taylor, Pat Channita, Paul Rodriguez, Ryan Sheckler, Tyler Adams Hawkins, Jake Brown, Lyn-Z Adams Hawkins, Rune Glifberg, Alexis Waite, Hana Beaman, Janna Meyen, Jeremy Jones, Jimi Tomer, Travis Rice, Wyatt Caldwell, Brad Gerlach, Jamie Sterling, Megan Abubo, Mike Losness, Taylor Knox, Dayne Kinnaird, Drake McElroy, Mary Osborne, Mike Carter, Fabiola Da Silva, Allan Cooke, Jamie Bestwick, Steve McCann
Sports Service Founded:
2000

INNOVATIVE SPORTS MARKETING & MANAGEMENT
720 MONROE STREET
SUITE #E303
HOBOKEN, NJ 7030-6352
201-610-0200
Fax: 201-610-9260

INTEGRATED SPORTS MANAGEMENT
6015 MIDDLEWATER CT
COLUMBIA, MD 21044
410-740-1147
Fax: 410-992-4999
Services:
Contract Negotiation and Business Management; Personality Marketing, Endorsements and Tax Refund Preparation; Combine and Draft Preparation; Preparation for Team Interviews; Real Estate Acquisition and Financing; Acquisition of Necessary Insurance; Assistance in Obtaining a Line of Credit; Individual Estate and Gift Tax Planning; Bank Account Reconciliation and Management; Post Sports Career Development
Nature of Sports Service:
All phases of athlete representation including contract negotiation, long-range planning, financial planning, and post-career counseling. Certified Athlete Agents in Florida, Tennessee and Mississippi. Member of the NFLPA since 1987. Associate member of Sports Lawyers Association.

INTEGRITY SPORTS PLAYER MANAGEMENT
26000 W 12 MILE ROAD
SOUTHFIELD, MI 48034
248-355-1727
800-887-6370
Fax: 248-355-5674
• Kevin T. Granader, President/Special Counsel
• Storm T. Kirschenbaum, VP/General Counsel
• Tim Walton, Founder
• Eugene Brown, Player Personnel VP
Services:
Asset Management, Securities Recordkeeping and Safekeeping, Annual Tax Information, Monthly Accounting

Statement, Cash Flow Projections, Financial and Estate Planning, Real Property Management, Estate and Insurance Planning, Risk Management, Retirement Planning, Income Tax Returns for Federal, State and City Taxing Authorities, Assistance in Buying/Selling Homes, Cars and Other Assets, High School and College Tuition Management Planning, Public Relations, Corporate Association, Merchandising, Equipment and Relocation Services

Clients:
Jermaine Brock, Nick DeBarr, Dan DeMent, Sean Dobson, Travis Gulick, Brian Hertel, Jared Hoerman, Tim Keinath, Gary Kinnie, Adam Moreno, Scott Koerber, Kevin Olore, Mike Prochaska, Johnny Poss, Dustin Shafer, Aaron Shrewsbury, Adam Sokoll, Doug Stasio, Chuck Van Robays, Chad Wiles, Joseph Yarbrough, Ruth Riley, Willie Burton, Clay Tucker, Bill Flowers, Ernest Jones, Earl Stephens, Adrian Jones, Victor Hobson, Marko Cavka, Stanley Wilson, David McMillan, Akarika Dawn, Jamar Landrom, Brian Alford, Bennie Blades, Brian Blades, Jovon Burkes, Tommie Boyd, Kevin Bryant, Mill Coleman, Lional Dalton, Dorsett Davis, Fred Foggie, Ricky Foggie, Dan Gibb

Nature of Service:
Full service sports representation firm. Represent athletes in Baseball, Football, Basketball, Hockey, Golf and Entertainers.

INTERNATIONAL CREATIVE MANAGEMENT, INC.
10250 CONSTELLATION BOULEVARD
LOS ANGELES, CA 90067
310-550-4000
careersla@icmpartners.com
www.icmtalent.com
• Jeffrey Berg, Chairman/Chief Executive Officer
jberg@icmtalent.com
• Jeffrey Berg, President
• Edward Limato, Co-President
• Chris Silbermann, Co-President
• Richard B. Levy, Chief Business Development Officer

Services:
Represents creative and technical talent in the fields of motion pictures, television, publishing, music, live performance, commercials and new media

Clients:
Allure, Amerie, Ashanti, Avant, DJ Beverley Bond, Bone Thugs N Harmony, Cam'ron, Case, Cash Money Millionaires, Crazy Al Cayne, Chico DeBarge, Mobb Deep, DJ Clue, DMX, Drag-On, En Vogue, Faith Evans, Fabolous, Fat man Scoop, Funk Master Flex, Anthony Hamilton, David Hollister, Joe, Patti LaBelle, Lil' Mo', Jennifer Lopez, Lost Boyz, LS-1, Memphis Bleek, Mr. Cheeks, Mystikal, Nas, New Edition, Nivea, Rah Digga, Ray J, Ron G, Royce Da 5'9, Ruff Endz, Ruff Ryders, Eric Sermon, Beanie Sigel, Smilez and Southstar, Special K 6 & Teddy Ted, Styles, Keith Sweat, The Lox, Usher

Sports Service Founded:
1975

Athlete Management Services:
Represent sports personalities for national television commercials and endorsements. Top athletes have been booked by this agency and have appeared in ads for Coca Cola, Gillette Right Guard, Pepsi, Nike, and many other products.

Other Locations:
40 West 57th Street, New York, NY 10019; Phone: 212-556-5600; 4-6 Soho Square, London WID 3PZ, England; Phone: 011-44-207-432-0800

Marketing & Consulting Services:
Marketing and management services for athlete clients involved with television commercials.

INTERPERFORMANCES, INC.
230 W SUPERIOR STREET
SUITE 510
CHICAGO, IL 60654
312-654-1717
Fax: 312-266-4220
chrisport@aol.com
www.interperformances.com
• Luciano Capicchioni, President/Co-Chief Executive Officer
info@interperformances.com
• Luciano Capicchioni, President and Chief Executive Officers
• Manel Bosch, CEO Worldwide Operations
• Patricia A. Levine, Executive Administrator
• John Kern, Legal Counsel
• Herb Rudoy, President/Co-CEO

Other Office:
Via degli Aceri, 14, Gualdicciolo, 47892 Republic of San Marino, (Europe) 378 911007; Fax: 378 911008.

Services:
Full-service Marketing, Media Relations Advice, Public Relations, Post-Career Planning and Representation of Athletes, Corporations, Teams, Events, and Sponsors.

Clients:
Albert Alfonso, Amagou Pape-Philippe, Anderson Christian, Andriuskevicius Martynas, Angelopoulos Nikos, Angulo Alberto, Angulo Lucio, Argiropoulos Nikos, Baloggiannis Giorgos, Barcenas Enrique, Barlos Nikos, Barycz Wojciech, Becirovic Sani, Becka Pavel, Benevelli Andrea, Bianchi Alessandro, Bianco Gustavo, Blanda Marco, Bossini Thomas, Boudouris Nikos, Brana Carlos, Brkic David, Bryan Sylvere, Bueno Antonio, Caceres Juan, Callahan Dan, Carretta Luca, Causin Alberto, Cazorla Carlos, Cei Saverio, Charisis Kostas, Cinciarini Daniele, Coffin Mike, Coldebella Claudio, Conti Andrea, Cortesi Simone, Corvo Giuseppe, Cresnik Matej, Cusin Marco, D'Ayal

Description:
Full-service Marketing and Representation of Athletes, Corporations, Teams, Events, and Sponsors.

INTRASPORT MANAGEMENT GROUP
LEESBURG, VA 22075
703-861-0771
Fax: 703-777-2873
• Michael Draine, Sports Agent
• Caroline Roney, Attorney

Nature of Sports Service:
All phases of athlete representation including contract negotiation, long-range planning, financial planning, and post-career counseling.

IRWIN SPORTS MANAGEMENT, LLC
720 S GAY STREET
KNOXVILLE, TN 37902
865-637-5566
877-994-7946
Fax: 865-637-8819
• Timothy E. Irwin, President
(865) 637-5566
• Beth H. Riley, Office Manager

Services:
All phases of athlete representation including contract negotiation, long-range planning, financial planning, and post-career counseling.

Clients:
Josh Burr, Tyson Clabo, Brennan Curtin, William dela Houssaye, Brad Hoover, Luke Lawton, Josh Mallard, Steve McKinney, Nick McNeil, Ben Nelson, Constantin Ritzmann, Larry Turner, Todd Yoder, Madison Hedgecock, Kelly Griffeth, Jonas Crafts, Amos Lamb, Brett Hodge, Brian Sump, Mike Woolridge

---

JACKSON WALKER LLP
777 MAIN STREET
SUITE 2100
FORT WORTH, TX 76102
817-334-7200
Fax: 817-334-7290
www.jw.com
• T. Michael Wilson, Firmwide Managing Partner
(214) 953-6020
mwilson@jw.com
• Albon O. Head, Jr., Managing Partner
(817) 334-7230
ahead@jw.com
• Jaymie D. Bell, Chief Marketing Officer
(214) 953-5812
jbell@jw.com
• Richard A. Herlan, Chief Financial Officer
(214) 953-5834
rherlan@jw.com
• Gail R. Horne, Administrator Dallas/Fort Worth
(214) 953-5879
ghorne@jw.com
• Sharon H. Kasachkoff, Director Operations
(214) 953-6048
skasachkoff@jw.com
• Steven W. McHargue, Chief Information Officer
(214) 953-5810
smchargue@jw.com

Nature of Service:
The firm regularly represents clients in such areas as corporate and securities, litigation, intellectual property, health care, labor and employment, legislative and regulatory, real estate, tax and estate planning, technology, bankruptcy, aviation and international law.

Year Founded:
1887

Clients:
Fortune 500 companies, multi-national corporations, major financial institutions, and a wide range of publicly traded corporations and closely held businesses.

Other Locations:
100 Congress Avenue, Suite 1100, Austin, Texas 78701; Bank of America Plaza, 901 Main Street, Suite 6000, Dallas, TX 75202; 1401 McKinney Street, Suite 1900, Houston, Texas 77010; 301 W. Beauregard Avenue, Suite 200, San Angelo, Texas 76903; Weston Centre, 112 E. Pecan Street, Suite 2400, San Antonio, Texas 78205.

JAMES CLIBANOFF BASKETBALL SERVICES
PO BOX 3267
MAPLE GLEN, PA 19002
215-793-4516
Fax: 215-793-4517
www.worldbasket.com
• Jim Clibanoff, President

JONES, IRIS
9430 RESEARCH BOULEVARD
ECHELON 1V, SUITE 400
AUSTIN, TX 78731
512-343-4564
Fax: 512-343-2351
Nature of Sports Service:
All phases of athlete representation including contract negotiation, long-range planning, financial planning, and post-career counseling.

JORDAN SPORTS MANAGEMENT - (LA)
2900 WESTFOLD DR, SUITE 200
BATON ROUGE, LA 70827
225-295-5624
Fax: 225-771-3272
Nature of Sports Service:
All phases of athlete representation including contract negotiation, long-range planning, financial planning, and post-career counseling.

JOSEPH ATHLETIC MANAGEMENT
104 W NORTHWOOD STREET, SUITE F
GREENSBORO, NC 27401
336-275-0863
800-826-7658
Fax: 336-275-6071
Nature of Sports Service:
All phases of athlete representation including contract negotiation, long-range planning, financial planning, and post-career counseling.

JUCKETT SPORTS & ENTERTAINMENT
3119 OAKES AVENUE
EVERETT, WA 98201
425-339-1559
Fax: 425-252-0798
staff@juckett.com
Sports Service Founded:
1986
Athlete Management Services:
International professional athlete representation, contract negotiation, world wide and regional endorsements, commercials, infomercials, personal appearances, speaking presentations and training, legal counsel.
Marketing & Consulting Services:
Marketing strategies provided for individual celebrity talent depending on area of recognition and location of talent. Legal counseling provided as needed. Sponsors road to Winning program.

KARIZMA SPORTS, LLC.
66 PROSPECT STREET
MANCHESTER, NH 3104
603-627-4666
Fax: 603-634-4347

KATZ MEDIA CORPORATION
125 W 55TH STREET
NEW YORK, NY 10019

212-424-6000
Fax: 513-721-3077
www.katz-media.com
• Stu Olds, Chief Executive Officer
• Robert Damon, CFO
Nature of Sports Service:
All phases of athlete representation including contract negotiation, long-range planning, financial planning, and post-career counseling.

KAUFFMAN SPORTS MANAGEMENT GROUP
5565 ADELINA COURT
SUITE 200
AGOURA HILLS, CA 91301
310-456-5400
818-991-1300
steve@kauffmansports.com
www.kauffmansports.com
• Steve Kauffman, Founder/President
• Larry Kauffman, Vice President of Finance
• Spencer Breecker, Partner
• John Hammond, General Manager
• Donnie Walsh, President of Basketball Operations
• Mike Born, Director of NBA Scouting
• Mike Bratz, Director of Player Personnel
• Steve Kauffman, Founder and President
steve@kauffmansports.com
Description:
Contract negotiation, post career planning, arbitration hearings, federal/state/international tax filings, provides investment advice, licensing, endorsement exploration.

KC SPORTS MANAGEMENT, INC.
23702 HARBOR VISTA DRIVE
SUITE 200
MALIBU, CA 90265
310-456-5400
Fax: 239-337-5364
Description:
All phases of athlete representation including contract negotiation, long-range planning, financial planning, and post-career counseling.

KCB SPORTS MARKETING
4000 ISLAND BOULEVARD
AVENTURA, FL 33160
kcbsportsmarketing.com
• Robert Bailey, Member
Description:
KCB is a full service marketing and athlete representation agency. Services include: endorsement exploration, personal appearnces, television and media appearances, radio, commercials, memorbilia products and show appearances.

KELLY ENTERPRISES, JIM
8207 MAIN STREET
SUITE 1
WILLIAMSVILLE, NY 14221
716-204-1212
Fax: 716-204-0999
dstupski@jimkelly.com
www.jimkelly.com
Sports Service Founded:
1986
Event Management Services:
Manages golf tournaments, camps, etc., working with athletes and corporate sports sponsors.

Athlete Management Services:
Provides contract negotiation and corporate sponsorship services.

KELMAN, LORIA, WILL HARVEY & THOMPSON
17000 W 10 MILE ROAD
SUITE 100
SOUTHFIELD
DETROIT, MI 48075
313-961-7363
Fax: 313-961-8875
• Charles Chomet, Attorney
• James Harvey, Attorney
• Alan Posner, Attorney
• Ann Thompson, Attorney

KING PRODUCTIONS, INC., DON
501 FAIRWAY DRIVE
DEERFIELD BEACH, FL 33441
954-418-5800
800-883-2288
Fax: 954-418-0166
www.donking.com
• Don King, President/Chief Executive Officer
Sports Service Founded:
1976
Athlete Management Services:
Handles athlete endorsements, promotional aspects for commercials, product endorsements.
Event Management Services:
Promotes and arranges for promotion of sports events of all types, specializing in boxing.

KIRKPATRICK, CRAWFORD
5300 MEMORIAL DRIVE, SUITE 520
HOUSTON, TX 77007
713-523-9500
Fax: 713-861-0079
• Crawford Kirkpatrick, Attorney

LAMPROS & ROBERTS CONSULTING
235 W. MAIN STREET
LOS GATOS, CA 95030
408-358-1125
800-841-7767
• Nick J Lampros, Member
• Jerry W. W. Roberts, Member
Description:
Contract negotiation, arbitration hearings, federal/state/international tax filings, endorsement exploration.

LANDMARK SPORT GROUP
10990 WILSHIRE BOULEVARD
LOS ANGELES, CA 90024
310-966-4101
Fax: 905-949-4984
admin@landmarksport.com
www.landmarksport.com
• Elliott Kerr, President
• Sharon Podatt, Director
• Adrian Sciarra, Director
• Lisa Dichiera, Director Of Advocacy
• Brian Hogg, Director
Sports Service Founded:
1987
Marketing & Consulting Services:
Advises clients on the most efficient way to utilize sports event marketing for commercial purposes. Advise clients already using sports event marketing on how to maximize investment. Assists corporations

to determine speaker objectives and matches with speaker/personality to fulfill role of speaker.
Event Management Services:
Develops and implements all aspects of major sporting events on full-service, turn-key basis. Consultation, acquisition of sponsors, event coordination and management, negotiations with TV, facility contracts, etc.
Athlete Management Services:
Contract negotiation, financial management and endorsement negotiation services.
Clients:
Olympic Winter Athletes, Olympic Summer Athletes, Professional Athletes, Motivational Speakers. Event Management of the Mississauga Marathon, Oakville Half Marathon, and the Jane Rogers Championship Mississauga.

LANKTREE SPORTS CELEBRITY NETWORK, INC.
440 NORTH WELLS STREET
CHICAGO, IL 60610
312-266-9558
Fax: 312-242-2707
Sports Service Founded:
1991
Marketing & Consulting Services:
Comprehensive supplier of athletes for commercial and personal appearance projects from casting to negotiations.

LATIMER, TRACIE K.
11801 SW SECOND STREET
FT. LAUDERDALE, FL 33325
954-473-4964
Nature of Sports Service:
All phases of athlete representation including contract negotiation, long-range planning, financial planning, and post-career counseling.

LAW OFFICES OF JOSEPH R. CRUSE JR.
5541 DART COURT
SUITE 210
AGOURA HILLS, CA 91301
818-699-6282
Fax: 310-598-3876
• Joseph Cruse, Attorney at Law
(562) 833-5800
jcruse@jcruselaw.com
Founded:
1993
Services:
Handles legal matter in the following practice areas: Intellectual Property, Entertainment Law, Sports, Trademarks, Copyrights and Contracts

LEGACY SPORTS GROUP
500 NEWPORT CENTER DRIVE
SUITE 800
NEWPORT BEACH, CA 92660
949-720-8700
Fax: 949-720-1331
info@legacy-agency.com
www.legacy-agency.com
• Gregory Genske,
(949) 720-8700
Description:
Contract negotiation, post career planning, arbitration hearings, and endorsement exploration.
Services:
A sports representation firm acting for

professional athletes in a variety of sports, with emphasis on baseball and football. Legacy Sports Group also represents a number of media and other entertainment industry figures.

LINKS MANAGEMENT GROUP
PO BOX 2552
READING, RG4 8FR
44-1189-545045
Fax: 972-381-4228
info@linkmanagementgroup.com
www.linkmanagementgroup.com
• David K Parker, President
Athlete Management Services:
All phases of representation including endorsements, charity events, and other aspects of management, representing PGA Tour, Champions Tour, Nationwide Tour and LPGA Tour players.
Sports Service Founded:
1992

LISS, ARTHUR Y.
39400 N WOODWARD AVENUE
SUITE 200
BLOOMFIELD HILLS, MI 48304
248-647-9700
Fax: 248-647-0638
www.lissfirm.com
• Arthur Y Liss, Attorney
(248) 647-9700
• Jacqueline Benyo, Legal Assistant
Nature of Sports Service:
All phases of athlete representation including contract negotiation, long-range planning, financial planning, and post-career counseling.

LLOYD, ROBERT V.
10303 JASPER AVENUE
SUITE 1400
EDMONTON, ALBERTA, CANADA T5J 3N6
780-429-6220
Fax: 780-429-4453
www.ogilvie.com
Services:
Post career planning, arbitration hearings, federal/state/international tax filings.

LUMSDEN & MCCORMICK, LLP
369FRANKLIN ST
THE CYCLORAMA BUILDING
BUFFALO, NY 14202
716-856-3300
888-586-7336
Fax: 716-856-2524
www.lumsdencpa.com
• Louis Cercone, Jr., Partner
(716) 856-3300
• Dennis A. A Castiglia, Partner, Investment Management
(716) 856-3300
• Dale B. B Demyanick, Partner, Tax Planning
(716) 856-3300
• Michael J. J Grimaldi, Partner, Health Care Organizations
(716) 856-3300
Nature of Sports Service:
All phases of athlete representation including contract negotiation, long-range planning, financial planning, and post-career counseling, accounting and tax and consulting services.
Year Founded:
1952

Sports Service Founded:
1985

LYLES, FREDERICK T.
3613 ADAVALE DRIVE
PLANO, TX 75025
972-335-8130
Nature of Sports Service:
All phases of athlete representation including contract negotiation, long-range planning, financial planning, and post-career counseling.

Other locations:

M.D. GILLIS & ASSOCIATES LTD.
154 EARL STREET
KINGSTON, ONTARIO, CANADA K7L 2H2
613-548-4917
Fax: 613-548-3991
• Michael Gillis, Agent
(613) 548-4917
• Dan Palango, Agent
(416) 816-3257
Services:
Organization is a sports representation firm catering exclusively to professional hockey players.
Clients:
Pavel Bure (NHL); Ulf Dahlen (NHL); Mathew Dandenault (NHL); Bobby Holik (NHL); Sergei Krivokrasov (NHL); Markus Naslund (NHL); Marcus Ragnersson (NHL); and Pat Verbeek (NHL).
Nature of Sports Service:
Organization is a sports representation firm catering exclusively to professional hockey players.
Clients Include:
Pavel Bure (NHL); Ulf Dahlen (NHL); Mathew Dandenault (NHL); Bobby Holik (NHL); Sergei Krivokrasov (NHL); Markus Naslund (NHL); Marcus Ragnersson (NHL); and Pat Verbeek (NHL).

MADIGAN CAPITAL MANAGEMENT
PO BOX 8
MONMOUTH BEACH, NJ 07750-1130
732-571-3132
• Ray Clark, Founder/CEO
• Dan Belmont, President, Sports
Services:
Athlete Management: Financial management, contract negotiation, marketing. Event Management: Product endorsement, corporate affiliations, golf outings.
Marketing & Consulting Services:
Product endorsement.

MAIN EVENTS
772 UNION BOULEVARD
TOTOWA, NJ 07512
973-200-7050
Fax: 973-200-7061
jmizzone@mainevents.com
www.mainevents.com
• Jolene Mizzone, Vice President of Operations
jmizzone@mainevents.com
• Kim Newman, Sports Scene Distributions
knewman@mainevents.com
• Ellen Haley, Public Relations
ehaley@mainevents.com
Year Founded:
1978
Description:
Professional boxing promotion
Clients:
Professional boxers

MAJOR LEAGUE BASEBALL PLAYERS ASSOCIATION
12 E 49TH STREET
24TH FLOOR
NEW YORK, NY 10017
212-826-0808
Fax: 212-752-4378
feedback@mlbpa.org
mlbplayers.mlb.com
• Donald M. Fehr, Executive Director/General Counsel
• Martha Child, Managing Officer
• Judy Heeter, Director Business Affairs/Licensing
• Greg Bouris, Director Communications
Services:
Contract negotiation.

MAKE IT HAPPEN SPORTS
108 N MAIN STREET
SUITE 800
SOUTH BEND, IN 46601
574-232-3025
Fax: 574-234-3363
• Andre B. Gammage, Sports Agent
Services:
All phases of athlete representation including contract negotiation, long-range planning, financial planning, and post-career counseling.

MANAGEMENT ONE
7925A N ORACLE ROAD
#114
TUCSON, AZ 85704
513-651-1610
888-921-6663
Fax: 800-860-1984
info@management-one.com
• James M. Gould, Managing Partner
James.Gould@TheWalnutGroup.com
Services:
General Counsel for retail, service and manufacturing industries

MANAGEMENT PLUS ENTERPRISES, INC.
6100 CENTER DRIVE
SUITE 900
LOS ANGELES, CA 90045
310-426-7500
888-483-2652
Fax: 310-426-8010
• Leonard Armato, President
Sports Service Founded:
1988.
Marketing & Consulting Services:
Representation of professional athletes in marketing negotiation activities.

MARKETFORCE ONE, INC.
22353 SWEET JASMINE
THE SUMMIT
WOODLAND HILLS, CA 91367
818-279-2167
866-990-4440
Fax: 818-346-3105
www.bobpritchard.com
• Robert G. Pritchard, Chief Executive Officer
• Susan Aird, Personnel Management
Services:
Business & marketing strategies, Planning and implementation, Direct marketing, Strategic Partner, Finance Acquisition, Marketing for prolonged, sustainable growth (domestic & global), Marketing Audits,

Complete business audits, Advertising, Complete business audits, Advertising, Consumer purchasing benefit, customer service and added value programs, Project management, Research, Sales Promotion, Cause Related Marketing, Sponsorship management, Event management, Training & keynote addresses
Clients:
Formula One Motor Racing, Legends of Tennis, McEnroe, Borg., Skins Golf with Norman, Nicklaus., Pro-beach Volleyball, Katarina Witt 18 Olympians Tour, World Freestyle Skiing Championships, World Series Cricket, Los Angeles International Track Meet, Association of Surfing Professionals, World Masters Games, Indy Car Racing, Oakland Raiders, World Heavyweight Champion, Evander Holyfield
Athlete Management Services:
Representation of athletes for corporate endorsements including sales promotions and public relations.
Other Office:
142 Cathedral St. Sydney New South Wales 2011 Australia
Sports Service Founded:
1978 (1986 in U.S.).
Event Management Services:
Marketing, sponsorship management, event management, television production, procurement and distribution, sport and special event related promotions; event staging hospitality, licensing.
Marketing & Consulting Services:
Lifestyle sponsorship packaging and solicitation. Corporate sponsorship management, sales promotion, public relations, web site production, video production.

MARKETING ARM
1999 BRYAN STREET
18TH FLOOR
DALLAS, TX 75201
214-259-3200
Fax: 214-259-3201
info@themarketingarm.com
www.themarketingarm.com
• Ray Clark, Founder/CEO
• Dan Belmont, President, Sports
Services:
Athlete Management: Financial management, contract negotiation, marketing. Event Management: Product endorsement, corporate affiliations, golf outings.
Marketing & Consulting Services:
Product endorsement.

MASTERPLAN GROUP INTERNATIONAL
122 S MICHIGAN AVENUE
SUITE 1220
CHICAGO, IL 60603
312-880-0340
Fax: 312-880-0346
www.masterplangroup.com
• Joseph D Wright, President/Chief Executive Officer
• Steve Raquel, Director Marketing
Services:
Contract Negotiations, Preparing the Athlete, Diet Assessment, Marketing the Athlete, Financial and Tax Management, Endorsements, Media and Community Relations, Relocation Assistance, Personal Organization

Clients:
National Football League, NFL Europe, Motorsports
Sports Services Founded:
1990
Nature of Sports Service:
Contract and endorsement negotiations; comprehensive financial management services focused on risk management and preservation of wealth; tax planning; public relations; personal, professional, and post-career counseling.

MATTGO ENTERPRISES, INC.
185 E 85TH STREET
APARTMENT 18G
NEW YORK, NY 10028-2146
212-427-4444
• Matt V Merola, President
(212) 427-4444
Services:
Representation of professional athletes in off-the-field activities, excluding investments.
Sports Service Founded:
1968.

MAUPIN, TAYLOR, P.A.
301 FAYETTEVILLE STREET
SUITE 1700
RALEIGH, NC 27601
919-981-4000
Fax: 919-981-4300
www.williamsmullen.com
• Julious P Smith, Jr., Chairman/Chief Executive Officer
(804) 783-6408
jsmith@williamsmullen.com
• Keith M. Kapp, Vice President
(919) 981-4024
kkapp@williamsmullen.com
• William P Barrett, Staff
(919) 981-4043
• David D. W Addison, Partner
Services:
Labor and employment, environmental law and real estate
Description:
Contract negotiation, endorsement exploration.

MAX-AIR PRODUCTIONS, INC.
9430 S RAINTREE DRIVE
SANDY, UT 84092
801-944-4849
• Craig Peterson, President
Services:
Pioneered ski jumping and trampoline shows and offers acrobatic thrill show entertainment tosporting events, state and county fairs, amusement parks and special events worldwide. The company has expanded into snowboarding and big air jumping and leads the market with the latest ramp and air bag innovations.
Event Management Services:
Design, production and implementation of regional and national sponsorship and marketing programs, including grass roots product sampling and distribution programs, extreme sport shows, events and competitions. Owns and operates the MAX-AIR SKI SHOW, the Vertical Thrill Show Tour and Splash! Aerial Ski and Snowboard water ramp competition series.
Marketing & Consulting Services:
Specializes in providing corporate marketing

opportunities and strategies through, turn-key, event-driven sales promotion campaigns for corporate clients. Provides project management, public relations and promotional support services.

MAXIMUM SPORTS MANAGEMENT
6435 W JEFFERSON BOULEVARD
#197
FORT WAYNE, IN 46804
888-494-3330
Fax: 800-631-4380
www.maximumsports.com
• Rebecca Flaherty, General Manager
• Eugene Parker, Contract Advisor
Nature of Services:
All phases of athletes representation including contract negotiation, long-range planning, financial planning, and post-career counseling.
Services:
Based in Roanoke, Indiana, it is a sports representation firm with a significant client list of football athletes. The range of sports agency services includes negotiation of player contracts, performance bonuses and endorsement and marketing contracts and assists in linking professional athletes to endorsement, marketing and public relations opportunities.

MAXIMUM SPORTS MARKETING
196 N MAIN STREET
ROANOKE, IN 46783
260-672-9480
Fax: 260-672-1310
• Eugene Parker, Chief Executive Officer
Services:
All phases of athlete representation including contract negotiation, long-range planning, financial planning, and post-career counseling.

MCCARTHY TETRAULT
40 ELGIN STREET
THE CHAMBERS
SUITE 1400
OTTAWA, CANADA K1P 5K6
613-238-2000
Fax: 613-563-9386
info@mccarthy.ca
www.mccarthy.ca
• W. Lain Scott, Chair and Chief Executive Officer
(416) 601-7686
• Kenneth C. Morell, COO/Nationel Leader, Markets
(416) 601-7585
Services:
One of Canada's most prestigious law firms. Provides its clients with ready access to legal and related professional resources and representation on a national and international basis. offers legal services in communications, information technology, intellectual property, Internet and e-commerce, among other fields.
Description:
Represents college athletic departments, endorsement exploration.

MCCLELLAN SPORTS MANAGEMENT GROUP
20321 SW BIRCH STREET
SUITE 203
NEWPORT BEACH, CA 92660
949-752-6151

Services:
Sports Club/Manager/Promoter
Sports Service Founded:
1990
Athlete Management Services:
Sponsorship procurement; contract negotiation; legal and financial advising; career planning and development.
Event Management Services:
Event organization/planning; marketing strategies; advertising and promotion; sponsorship procurement.
Marketing & Consulting Services:
Organizational development; administration, etc.

MCCOY & ASSOCIATES, LLC
2381 E STADIUM BOULEVARD
ANN ARBOR, MI 48104
734-769-0001
Fax: 734-769-0056
info@mccoyandassociates.com
www.mccoyandassociates.com
• Robert McCoy,
Services:
Legal services office
Nature of Sports Service:
All phases of athlete representation including contract negotiation, long-range planning, financial planning, and post-career counseling.

MCSHERRY, JR., WILLIAM J.
1675 BROADWAY
NEW YORK, NY 10019
212-484-3900
Fax: 212-484-3990
www.arentfox.com
• Jerrold S Abeles, Partner
• Jennifer Allen, Associate
Services:
Sports practice is one of the most experienced in the country. Serves as counsel to sports team franchises and provides legal advice to numerous purchasers and sellers of professional football, basketball, hockey and soccer teams, as well as team tennis.
Clients:
Charlotte Bobcats NBA franchise, the Washington Mystics WNBA franchise and the Charlotte Sting WNBA franchise.
Description:
Arbitration hearings, represents professional sports teams, licensing, tort actions/litigation.

MD STADIUM AUTHORITY
333 W CAMDEN STREET
SUITE 500
BALTIMORE, MD 21201
410-333-1560
877-637-8234
800-735-2258
Fax: 410-333-1888
www.mdstad.com
• Frederick W Puddester, Chairman
• Michael J. Frenz, Executive Director
• Gregory Smith, Chief Operating Officer
• Francoise Ca Hubschman, President
Year Founded:
July 1, 1986
Services:
Operation of baseball and football stadiums as well as other facilities.

MEDIA VISTA PRODUCTIONS
500 RAILWAY AVENUE
#306
CAMPBELL, CA 95008
408-282-1960
Fax: 408-549-9870
www.mediavista.com
• Peter Liebengood, President
• Cassandra Bellantoni, Executive Producer and Creative Director
• Gary Hinderliter, Engineering and Technology
• Jeanine Herrera, Graphic Artist and Designer
Services:
Specializes in Corporate Communications, provides on-camera talent, original music and production team to broadcast productions and various multimedia.
Clients:
Petroglyph, Mount Hermon Christian Conference Center, ADAC Laboratories, Dreamsports, Air Systems Inc., Lucent Technologies, Rentals.com, Naprotek, Inc., Hyatt San Jose, CPS, Graniterock, Santa Clara Valley Water District, NeoMagic Corporation, Featherlite Exhibits, Informatica, All Van Transportation, COM 21, ebay, Exodus, Santa Clara County Parks, SFS, The Business Journal, Casto Travel Inc., BJS.
Marketing & Consulting Services:
Provides image development training to athletes and sports personalities. Clients are trained on how to make the media work for them and to increase endorsement opportunities. Broadcast program features one-on-one coaching to assist athletes considering or making the transition from playing field to the broadcast booth.
Athlete Management Services:
Procures endorsements, personal appearances, and spokesperson roles for professional and amateur athletes. Creates and negotiates contracts for athlete marketing opportunities on a local, regional, national and global basis.
Sports Service Founded:
1991

MID-SOUTH SPORTS MANAGEMENT
• Stanley Morgan, President
(901) 523-2535
• Tim Jumper, Director of Basketball Operations
• Jay Laney, Chief Operating Officer
Sports Service Founded:
1995
Description:
All facets of athlete representation.
Services:
Athlete representation primarily in basketball.

MIDDLEBROOKS, WILLIAM T.
707 SE THIRD AVENUE
SUITE 600
FORT LAUDERDALE, FL 33316
954-462-4500
800-688-1054
Fax: 954-462-6597
info@middlebrookslaw.com
www.middlebrookslaw.com
Nature of Sports Service:
All phases of athlete representation including contract negotiation, long-range planning, financial planning, and post-career

counseling.
Services:
Full-service law firm, specializing in Insurance Law, Medical Malpractice Law, Personal Injury Law, and Product Liability Law.

MILLER CANFIELD SPORTS
150 W JEFFERSON
SUITE 2500
DETROIT, MI 48226
313-963-6420
Fax: 313-496-7500
www.millercanfield.com
• Michael W Hartmann, Chief Executive Officer
(313) 496-7554
hartmann@millercanfield.com
• David A. Robson, Office Manager
(313) 496-7575
robson@millercanfield.com
• Thomas Phillips, Managing Director
(517) 483-4902
phillipst@millercanfield.com
• Amanda Va Dusen, Managing Director
(313) 496-7512
vandusen@millercanfield.com
• Irene B. Hathaway, Resident Director
• James M. Angyan, Paralegal
Services:
Biggest and longest established law firm in Michigan. Makes use of dispute resolution, information technology, and many other innovative approaches in helping its clients solve their legal problems.
Description:
All phases of athlete management included but not limited to: Contract negotiations, business and career planning, estate planning, federal and state tax planning, protection of intellectual property.

MILLER, J. BRUCE
605 W MAIN STREET
LOUISVILLE, KY 40202-2921
502-587-0900
Fax: 502-587-9008
• J Br Miller,
Description:
Contract negotiation.
Services:
Practices in the following areas of law: Civil and Commercial Litigation, Corporate Law, Sports and Entertainment Law, Governmental Law; Administrative Law and Health Care Law.
Clients:
Arvin Industries, Inc.; Buena Vista Distribution Co. (California/Kentucky); Columbia Pictures Industries, Inc. (California/Kentucky); D.A. Enterprises, Inc.; Derby Industries, Inc. (Kentucky); Dollar General Corporation, Inc.; Don King Productions, Inc.; Houghton Mifflin Co.; Humana, Inc.; Kentucky State Racing Commission; LGâ€™ Energy Corporation; Louisville (City of); Mabex Universal Film Corporation, Inc.; Maker's Mark Distillery; MGM/United Artists Communications Co.; Motion Picture Association of America; Paitco, Inc.; NTS Development, Inc.; Orion Pictures Distribution Corp.; Packaging Un-Limited, Inc.; R.Gene Smith Investments; Spectronic

---

MILLS, JR., ALVIN J.
1919 14TH STREET
ST# 410
PO BOX 187
BOULDER, CO
303-443-7770
• A Ja Mills Jr,
Services:
All phases of athlete representation including contract negotiation, long-range planning, financial planning, and post-career counseling.

MITNICK, CRAIG R.
35 KINGS HIGHWAY E
HADDONFIELD, NJ 8033
856-427-9000
Fax: 856-427-0360
Description:
Contract negotiation, post career planning, investment contract negotiation, provides securities advice, provides investment advice, licensing, endorsement exploration, tort actions/litigation.
Services:
Specializing in State and Federal Criminal Defense. Preparation and Trial of Litigated Criminal Matters, the majority of which are venued in Superior Court and Federal Court. Extensive Knowledge and Experience involving indicatable/felony offenses, and Federal organized crimes, including all major crime prosecutions
Clients:
Matthew Lovett

MONFORE GROUP, INC
620 14TH STREET
SUITE C
TUSCALOOSA, AL 35402
205-750-8102
Fax: 205-750-8120
www.monforegroup.com
• Robert Monfore,
rwm@monforegroup.com
Services:
Contract negotiation, post career planning, investment contract negotiation, provides investment advice.

MORRIS INTERNATIONAL
120 PARK AVE
SUITE 6
NEW YORK, NY 10017
917-663-2000
Fax: 704-896-3441
info@morrisinternational.com
www.morrisinternational.com
• Rick Hendrick, President
• Jaceb Olczak, Chief Financial Officer
Description:
The only AAAA advertising agency specializing in motorsports marketing and new product development has offered its clients a full range of professional expertise, including strategic planning, negotiations with teams, drivers & sanctioning bodies, car design, team management, public relations and event hospitality.
Services:
Morris International is the only AAAA advertising agency specializing in motorsports marketing and new product development. Morris International has offered its clients a full range of professional expertise, including strategic planning, negotiations with teams, drivers and

sanctioning bodies, car design, team management, public relations and event hospitality. The company develops strategies that capture events, partnerships and media.
Clients:
AC-Delco, Alpha Sailboards, Anchorage Marine, Anheuser Busch, Busch Beer, Natural Light, Apache Stove Company, Apex Machine Tool Company, Tom Blackaller, Blue Bell, Inc./Wrangler Jeans, Boy Scouts of America, Buck Baker Driving School, Charlotte Motor Speedway, Charlotte Orioles, Cigarette Racing Boats, Consolidated Coin Caterers Corporation, Corning Glass Works/ Chameleon Sunglasses, Craftsman Motorsports, Dale Earnhardt Fan Club, Darlington International Raceway, Daytona International Speedway, Dixie Boat Company, Econo Lodges of America, Inc., John Force, GMAC, Grand National Scene, Grand National Illustrated, Griggs Publishing Company.
Sports Service Founded:
1971

NATIONAL FOOTBALL LEAGUE
280 PARK AVENUE
NEW YORK, NY 10017
212-450-2000
Fax: 212-681-7573
www.nfl.com
• Roger Goodell, NFL Commissioner
• Joe Browne, EVP Communications
• Jay E. Moyer, Special Counsel
• Troy Vincent, President-NFL Players Association
Services:
The exclusive collective bargaining agent for all players employed by clubs of the National Football League
Description:
Represents sports organizations.

NATIONAL FOOTBALL LEAGUE-LEGAL/NFL
280 PARK AVENUE
NEW YORK, NY 10017
212-450-2000
Fax: 212-681-7599
www.nfl.com
• Harold Henderson, EVP-NFL Management Council
• Dennis L. Curran, SVP/General Counsel-NFL Management Counc
Sponsors:
Merck-Zocor cholesterol reduction drug.
Services:
Represents all NFL Players

NATIONAL SPORTS AGENCY
5 LAKEVIEW COURT
LAKE SAINT LOUIS, MO 63367
636-265-1300
800-753-1245
Fax: 636-265-1303
• Harold C. Lewis, President
• Kevin J. Omell, VP / General Counsel
• Jonathan M. Caplin, Marketing and Player Relations Director
• Patty A. Midkiff, Controller
Nature of Sports Service:
All phases of athlete representation including contract negotiation, long-range planning, financial planning, and post-career counseling.
Clients:

Kenderick Allen, David Bowens, Kevin Carter, Shawn Cody, Travis Hall, Anthony Herron, Darrell Lee, CJ Mosley, Josh Buhl, Marlon Greenwood, Edgerton Hartwell, Bart Scott, Ellis Hobbs, Kevin House, Siddeeq Shabazz, Frank Walker, Bennie Anderson, Thomas Barnett, Jason Brown, Rob Hunt, Bo Lacy, Fred Miller, David Allen, Nehemiah Broughton, ReShard Lee, Josh Scobey, Joe Smith, Derek Abney, James Adkisson, Richard Alston, Cortez Hankton, Harry Williams, Zach Hilton, Ben Steele, Roland Williams, Mike Scifres, Steve Atwater, Lewis Bush, Boby Christian, D Marco Farr, Mike Gruttadauria, Michael Jones, Randy Jordan, Max Lane, Stump Mitchell

NATIONAL SPORTS MANAGEMENT INC.
2425 E CAMELBACK
SUITE 1000
PHOENIX, AZ 85016
602-808-0404
Fax: 602-808-8788
www.nsmsports.com
• Todd Eley, President-Basketball
• George Sotos, President-Marketing
(602) 808-0404
• Ted Kritza, VP-Basketball
(602) 808-0404
• Michael Giorgio, Co-Owner, Agent
• John Massaroni, Co-Owner, General Counsel, Agent
• Tony Giorgio, Marketing Specialist
• Doug Lilly, Consultant / Agent
• David Segui, Baseball Consultant
Services:
Contract negotiation, post career planning, investment contract negotiation, arbitration hearings, federal/state/international tax filings, provides investment advice, endorsement exploration.
Year Founded:
1960

NATIONWIDE SPEAKERS BUREAU
1801 CENTURY PARK E
SUITE 460
LOS ANGELES, CA 90067
310-273-8807
Fax: 310-432-1181
• Jim Abott, Speaker
• Ed Adler, Vice President
Description:
Lecture Agency
Services:
Resource for booking speakers for conferences and special events, and talent for endorsements, product introductions and media tours
Clients:
AON Risk Services, Wal-Mart, kodak, lexus, mutual of omaha, hilton hotels, the national association of realtors, kinko's, the million dollar round table and fidelity investments.

NEOSTAR SPORTS AND ENTERTAINMENT
510 SHOTGUN ROAD
SUITE 520
SUNRISE, FL 33326
954-475-9311
Fax: 954-475-8392
www.neostarsportsandent.com
• Ralph Stringer, President / Chief Executive Officer
Sports Service Founded:
1989

Athlete Management Services:
Represents professional athletes for marketing and endorsement.
Event Management Services:
Production and management of sports and special events promotions, including celebrity golf tournaments, 3-on-3 basketball.
Marketing & Consulting Services:
Evaluates sports marketing and endorsement opportunities for corporations in all areas.
Description:
Corporate sports marketing consultants.

NEWPORT BEACH
8000 W IH 10
SUITE 725
SAN ANTONIO, TX 78230-3868
210-342-9310
Services:
Contract negotiation, endorsement exploration.

NHLPA: NATIONAL HOCKEY LEAGUE PLAYERS' ASSOCIATION
10 BAY STREET
SUITE 1200
TORONTO, ONTARIO, CANADA M5J 2N8
416-313-2300
Fax: 416-313-2301
www.nhlpa.com
Products:
Player Apparel, Collectibles, fantasy games, jersey customizers, novelties, player greetings, Printed Products, Trading Cards and video games.
Brands:
ccm/sport maska, activa consumer promotions corp.,enterplay llc, highland mint, mcfarlane toys,team beans, the promotions factory,beneway oy, chatham kent cyclones, espn, fantasy sports network, fantasy sport services, the sporting news, yahoo.com, all canadian emblem corporation, exclusive pro sports, great plains marketing, airborne entertainment, aminco international (usa) inc, burris, neiman & assosiates, frameworth sports marketing, gamewear, inglasco, minnesota wild hockey club, sababa toys, sports fx international cooperation,strat-o-matic game company inc., the meisner gallery inc., upi marketing inc.,wincraft inc., allstar greetings

OCTAGON ATHLETE REPRESENTATION (AGENTS)
800 CONNECTICUT AVENUE
2ND FLOOR
NORWALK, CT 06854
203-354-7400
Fax: 703-905-4495
www.octagon.com
• Rick Dudley, President /Chief Executive Officer
rick.dudley@octagon.com
• Phil De Picciotto, President-Athlete Representation
phil.depicciotto@octagon.com
• Chris Guinness, President-Octagon Television
• Mike Liut, Managing Director-Octagon Hockey
Services:
Career management/guidance, Contract negotiations, Marketing and endorsements, Team relations, Public relations, Charitable

activities, Financial planning and services
Clients:
Justin Leonard (golf), Davis Love III (golf), Anna Kournikova (tennis), Martina Hingis (tennis), Steffi Graf (tennis), Jana Novotna (tennis), Mark Philippoussis (tennis), Gustavo Kuerten (tennis), Amelie Mauresmo (tennis), David Robinson (basketball), Jerry Stackhouse (basketball), Sheryl Swoopes (basketball), Sergei Fedorov (hockey), Gareth Southgate (soccer), Ben Clarke (rugby), Steve Waugh (cricket), Jeanette Lee (billiards)
Description:
Contract negotiation, post career planning, arbitration hearings, federal/state/international tax filings, provides securities advice, provides investment advice, licensing, endorsement exploration. Sports marketing consulting agency.

OCTAGON ATHLETES & PERSONALITIES DIVISION
7950 JONES BRANCH DRIVE
SUITE 700N
MCLEAN, VA 22107
703-905-3300
• Nicola Murphy, Director Marketing, Athlete & Property Marketing
• Lisa Murray, Executive Vice President
• Sean Nicholas, Managing Director
• Simon Wardle, Chief Strategy Officer
• Rick Dudley, CEO, President
• Phillip DM DePicciotto, Founder and President, Octagon Worldwide
• Jeff Shirin, President, Octagon Marketing America
Services:
Athlete representation, financial consultancy, event management, property representation, tv rights sales and distribution, tv production and archive, rights ownership, and licensing and merchandising.

OCTAGON FOOTBALL
832 SANSOME STREET
1ST FLOOR
SAN FRANCISCO, CA 94111
415-318-4311
Fax: 415-646-0215
footballinfo@octagon.com
www.octagonfootball.com
• Mike Sullivan, Managing Director
• Ken Landphere, Director
Services:
All phases of athlete representation including contract negotiation, long-range planning, financial planning, and post-career counseling.

OCTAGON SPORTS
7231 FOREST AVENUE
SUITE 103
RICHMOND, VA 23226
804-285-4200
Fax: 804-285-4224
www.octagongolf.com
• Giff Breed, Managing Director Golf/Outdoors
• Phil De Picciotto, Founder & President
• Lisa Murray, Executive Vice President & Chief Marketing Of
• Simon Wardle, Chief Strategy Officer
• Rick Dudley, President & CEO

Nature of Service:
Octagon is uniquely poised to provide full service marketing solutions across the global platform. Octagon offers client expertise in the following areas: Angler Representation (endorsements, clinics, outings, appearances, licencing), Event Management (event ownership, creation & implementation), Sales/Property Management (package development & sponsorship management), Consulting (strategic sponsorship selection, contract negotiation, field marketing and implementation).

OKINAWAKENPODSSI.COM
91-1013 WAIPAA STREET
EWA BEACH, HI 96706-6499
808-457-7164
marcus.devalentino@okinawakenpodssi.com
www.OkinawaKenpoDSSI.com
• Marcus DeValentino, Program Director
marcus.devalentino@OkinawaKenpoDSSI.com
Nature of Service:
Promotes martial arts, training, certification, fitness and produces DVDs.

OLSEN, THOMAS
19000 MCCARTHER BOULEVARD
SUITE 500
IRVINE, CA 92612
714-440-7919
• Thomas Olsen, Attorney
Nature of Sports Service:
All phases of athlete representation including contract negotiation, long-range planning, financial planning, and post-career counseling.

OLSHER GROUP
2700 N MILITARY TRAIL
SUITE 210
BOCA RATON, FL 33431
561-338-7200
Nature of Sports Service:
All phases of athlete representation including contract negotiation, long-range planning, financial planning, post-career counseling, marketing & television.
Services:
Metal building industry

OUTSIDE THE BOX MARKETING, INC
ST MARY'S STREET
COUNTY HOUSE
WORCESTER, ENGLAND WR1 1HB
797-388-6417
Fax: 480-348-9678
• Scott Bartle, President
Sports Service Founded:
2000
Services:
Athlete representation, event management, sponsorship/marketing consulting.

OWENS, BRIGMAN
3524 K STREET NW
WASHINGTON, DC 20007-3503
202-625-3330
Fax: 202-337-0475
• Brigman Owens, Attorney

P.S. STARGAMES
40 SALEM STREET
SUITE 7
LYNNFIELD, MA 01940
781-224-9655
Fax: 781-224-9656
www.stargamesinc.com
• Jerry Solomon, President/Chief Executive Officer
(781) 224-9655
jerry@stargamesinc.com
• Michael Kerrigan, Director-Business Development/Affiliate
mstargames@aol.com
• Jess Smyser, Administrative Assistant
(781) 224-9655
Services:
Produces live and made-for-television sporting events
Year Founded:
1994
Description:
All phases of athlete representation including contract negotiation, long-range planning, and post-career counseling.
Clients Include:
Athletes: Nancy Kerrigan, Ivan Lendl, Vania King. Properties: Halloween on Ice, Nancy Kerrigan's World of Skating, Countdown to Draft Day, A New Year's Tradition: The Pure Bowl, Live the Dream: The Texas Longhorns Magical March: National Champions: The Story of the 2006 Florida Gators

PAIGE & RICE
9701 APOLLO DRIVE
SUITE 245
UPPER MARLBORO, MD 20774
301-925-4404
Fax: 301-925-4820
• Tony Paige, President/Chief Executive Officer
(301) 925-4404
• Kevin Glover, VP
(301) 925-4404
• Rodney Rice, Chief Financial Officer/Partner
(301) 925-4404
• Cherise Rhyns, Player Relations Director
(301) 925-4404
Description:
We are committed to conducting business with professionalism, honesty and integrity. Which is complimented by a full service approach to management that includes contract negotiation, marketing for endorsements, financial advising, investment counseling and career counseling.
Services:
All phases of athlete representation including contract negotiation, long-range planning, financial planning, and post-career counseling.

PALACE SPORTS & ENTERTAINMENT, INC.
6 CHAMPIONSHIP DRIVE
AUBURN HILLS, MI 48326
248-377-0100
Fax: 248-377-2154
www.palacenet.com
• Tom Gore, Owner
• Dennis Mannion, President
• Jeffrey Ajluni, Vice President
Description:
Owns and operates the NBA's Detroit

Pistons, the WNBA's Detroit Shock, and the NHL's Tampa Bay Lightning.

PAOLI & SHEA, P.C.
257 W FRONT STREET
SUITE A
PO BOX 8131
MISSOULA, MT 59801
406-542-3330
800-816-9699
Fax: 406-542-3332
contact@paoli-law.com
www.paoli-law.com
• David R. Paoli, Member
• James Je Shea, Member
• Heather M. Latino, Associate
• Lance P. Jasper, Associate
Nature of Sports Service:
All phases of athlete representation including contract negotiation, long-range planning, financial planning, and post-career counseling.
Services:
Handles litigaton needs of clients in areas of Federal Employers' Liability Act (FELA), Serious injury and death cases, Product liability, Medical malpractice, Insurance, Criminal defense, and Employment disputes.

PENTRUST FINANCIAL SERVICES
3160 CAMINO DEL RIO S
B309
SAN DIEGO, CA 92108-3813
619-521-1458
• Joe E. Outlaw, President / Chief Executive Officer
Nature of Sports Service:
All phases of athlete representation including contract negotiation, long-range planning, financial planning, and post-career counseling.

PERFORMANCE SPORTS & ENTERTAINMENT
4615 SW FREEWAY
HOUSTON, TX 77027
713-965-0330
Services:
All phases of athlete representation including contract negotiation, long-range planning, financial planning, and post-career counseling.

PETER GREENBERG & ASSOCIATES
200 MADISON AVENUE
SUITE 2225
NEW YORK, NY 10016
212-334-6880
Fax: 212-334-6895
• Peter E. Greenberg, President
Services:
Sports promoter and managers, contract negotiation, post career planning, arbitration hearings, endorsement exploration and promotional marketing, specializing in baseball

PETER S. BRADLEY, ATTORNEY & COUNSELOR AT LAW
PO BOX 10904
NAPA, CA 94559
707-253-8838
Fax: 707-253-2962

- Brad S. Peter, Attorney & Owner
(707) 287-2661
- Mike Schumacher, Member
Description:
Contract negotiation, post career
counseling, investment planning, arbitration
hearings, federal/state/international tax
filings, endorsement exploration, tort
actions/litigation, estate planning, family law,
business law.
Services:
Offers a complete list of career, financial,
and image development services in the
sports management field.
Year Founded:
1978

PETER SPORTS MANAGEMENT
PO BOX 10904
NAPA, CA 94581
707-253-8838
Fax: 707-253-2962
team_psm@sbcglobal.net
- Brad S. Peter, Managing Partner/Principal
Owner
(707) 287-2661 m
- Mike Schumacher, Member
Nature of Sports Service:
All phases of athlete representation
including contract negotiation, investment
planning, arbitration hearings,
federal/state/international tax filings,
endorsement exploration, tort
actions/litigation. Well known for its
mentoring program - personal assistance,
support and individual off season training
programs with former professional athletes.
Year Founded:
1983
Services:
Offers a complete list of career, financial,
and image development services in the
sports management field.

PGA 20/20
100 PGA TOUR BOULEVARD
PONTE VEDRA BEACH, FL 32082
904-285-3700
Fax: 904-273-3512
www.pgatour.com

PHS, LTD.
401 WASHINGTON AVENUE
SUITE 902
TOWSON, MD 21204
410-296-2929
Fax: 410-296-2121
phsltd@abs.net
- Pam Shriver, Owner
- Marc Kantrowitz, Managing Director
Description:
Represents professional tennis player Pam
Shriver.

PINNACLE ENTERPRISES, INC.
20121 S 172ND PLAZA CIRCLE
SPRINGFIELD, NE 68059-7186
402-677-3546
Fax: 703-893-3504
www.wiapt.com
- W D Denny Minami, President
- Peter M. Hill, Chairman/Chief Executive
Officer
- Robert C. Morris, Founder / VP
- Brian L. Jo Katz, President
Services:
Management, Marketing Communications,

Leasing and Acquisitions, Development,
Consulting
Sports Service Founded:
1988
Athlete Management Services:
Primarily represents golf professionals in all
business opportunities including, but not
limited to: corporate and product
endorsements; personal, corporate and
tournament appearances; financial
management. Also works with major
athletes in professional yachting, tennis,
football, and with network sportscasters.
Event Management Services:
Provides turn-key management and
consulting in areas of sports (especially golf)
event conception, organization and
implementation including, but not limited to:
production, marketing and sponsor sales,
financial management, public relations and
operations. Specializes in procurement of
professional golfers for event appearances.
Marketing & Consulting Services:
Specializes in serving designers,
manufacturers and distributors of golf
products worldwide. Critical and progressive
intelligence in manufacturing, retail
operations and wholesale marketing for
established and start-up golf products and
ventures. Expertise in product development
and analysis, market analysis, market
strategy and business development.

PLAYBOY ENTERTAINMENT GROUP
2706 MEDIA CENTER DRIVE
LOS ANGELES, CA 90065
323-276-4000
Fax: 323-276-4050
www.playboyenterprises.com
- Bob Meyers, Executive Vice
President/President Media
- Jeffrey M. Jenest, EVP
- Scott N. Flanders, CEO
- Kristin Patrick, Chief Marketing Officer
- Rachel Sagan, Executive Vice President
- Matthew A. Nordby, Executive Vice
Principal
Event Management Services:
Represents 75 Playboy Playmates,
organized into 22 different sports teams, for
celebrity promotions for corporations, event
promoters, advertisers and charities.

PLAYPRO MANAGEMENT, INC.
1325 FRANKLIN AVENUE
SUITE 545
GARDEN CITY, NY 11530
516-741-0747
Fax: 516-741-1592
- Lloyd M. Friedland, President
Nature of Services:
Personal management services for
professional athletes and broadcast
professionals. Provides contract negotiation,
endorsements, financial and personal
planning, post career planning, and personal
counseling services.
Sports Service Founded:
1992.

**POITINGER REDMOND LYONS KURA &
WALKER**
2735 CRAWFIS BOULEVARD
SUITE 100
FAIRLAWN, OH 44333-2878

330-864-1144
Fax: 330-864-3002
www.prlkw.com
- Michael D. Poitinger, Shareholder
- James E. Redmond,
- Richard W. Lyons,
- Michael R. Kura,
Services:
Offers financial services such as fee-based
financial, estate and non-qualified executive
planning, charitable giving techniques, life
and disability insurance, mutual funds and
annuities and lifetime settlements.
Description:
Contract negotiation, post career planning,
provides investment advice, licensing,
endorsement exploration. Specialty is
Financial Planning. Seeks opportunities to
design creative solutions to both personal
and business financial matters.

POLK, MARLIN A.
1650 FARNAM STREET
THE OMAHA BUILDING
OMAHA, NE 68102-2186
402-346-6000
Fax: 402-346-1148
www.kutakrock.com
Nature of Sports Service:
All phases of athlete representation
including contract negotiation, long-range
planning, financial planning, and post-career
counseling.
Services:
Antitrust, Arbitrage Rebate Compliance,
Banking and Commercial Lending,
Bankruptcy, Blue Sky, Construction,
Corporate, Corporate Finance, Emerging
Companies, Employee Benefits,
Employment Law, Environmental Law,
Federal Practice and National Security Law,
Government Contracts, Government
Relations, Health Care Insurance,
Intellectual Property and Technology Law,
Litigation, Public Finance, Real Estate and
Commercial Practice, Securities Law,
Securities Litigation, Arbitration and
Regulatory, Structured Finance, Tax, Tax
Credits, Workouts and Surveillance

PONTON, WILLIE
PO BOX 2738
NEWPORT NEWS, VA 23609
757-988-0554
Nature of Sports Service:
All phases of athlete representation
including contract negotiation, long-range
planning, financial planning, and post-career
counseling.

PORTER WRIGHT
41 S HIGH STREET
HUNTINGTON CENTER
COLUMBUS, OH 43215-6194
614-227-2000
800-533-2794
Fax: 614-227-2100
www.porterwright.com
- Robert W. Trafford, Managing Partner
(614) 227-2149
rtrafford@porterwright.com
- Robert S. Anderlen, Attorney
(216) 443-2554
- Jon M. Anderson, Attorney
(614) 227-2154
- William E. Arthur, Attorney

(614) 227-2056
warthur@porterwright.com
Nature of Sports Service:
All phases of athlete representation including contract negotiation, long-range planning, post-career counseling, endorsements, business transactions, estate planning (wills, etc.), and tax counseling.
Other Locations: :
250 East Fifth Street, STE 2200, Cincinnati, OH 45202; Phone 513-381-4700; 925 Euclid Avenue, STE 1700, Cleveland, OH 44115; Phone: 216-443-9000; One Dayton Centre, STE 1600, One South Main Street, Dayton, OH 45402; Phone: 937-449-6810; 5801 Pelican Bay Boulevard, STE 300, Naples, Fl 34108; Phone: 239-593-2900; 1919 Pennsylvania Avenue, NW, STE 500, Washington, DC 20006; Phone: 202-778-3000

POSITION SPORTS MARKETING
4852 E BASELINE RD.
SUITE 105
MESA, AZ 85206
480-248-6645
Fax: 480-240-5887
www.positionsports.com
• Kevin Foley, President
Sports Service Founded:
1975
Athlete Management Services:
Represents professional athletes for licensing, personal appearances.
Marketing & Consulting Services:
Consults, develops and executes sports promotion programs for corporations.

PPI MARKETING
15660 NORTH DALLAS PARKWAY
SUITE 1250
DALLAS, TX 75248
972-388-5300
800-937-5107
Fax: 972-388-5315
www.ppimarketing.com
• Roger Staubach, Founder/Partner
• Otis Birdsong, Events Director/Promotions
• Roz Cole, President
(972) 388-5307
• Kristopher Cumnock, Vice Persident, Creative Services, Event Mark
(972) 388-5304
• Tommy Finn, Vice President, Corporate Partnerships
(972) 388-5308
• Mary Barnes Knox, Vice President, Talent Marketing
(972) 388-5306
• Ward Eastman, Vice president, Strategic Alliances
(972) 388-5305
Sports Service Founded:
1993
Athlete Management Services:
Negotiates athlete/celebrity endorsement contacts.
Services:
Helps customize an alliance with one or any number of legends to fit client specific goals, strategies and objectives. Resource for business and motivational speakers, sports personalities and celebrities, entertainers and bands.
Marketing & Consulting Services:
Speakers bureau and sports celebrity

marketing firm. Specializes in marketing athletes and celebrities; plus scheduling public speakers and entertainers for a variety of events.

PREMIER MANAGEMENT GROUP
700 EVANVALE COURT
CARY, NC 27518
919-363-5105
Fax: 919-363-5106
evan@pmgsports.com
www.pmgsports.com
• Evan Morgenstein, President/Chief Executive Officer
(919) 363-5105
evan@pmgsports.com
• Bobby Brewer, Vice President
(520) 743-3979
bobby@pmgsports.com
• Laura Cutler, Corporate Communications Director
(919) 363-5105
laura@pmgsports.com
• Steven Weinreb,
(919) 363-5105
steven@pmgsports.com
• Kelsey Morgan,
(919) 363-5105
kelsey@pmgsports.com
Sports Service Founded:
1997
Sports Organization:
As an eliste marketing agency, PMG's goal is to create a space in the industry that is completely unique in the world of sports marketing throughits creativity and innovation. With over 35 exclusive Olympic and celebrity clients, PMG's goal is to provide each client with the same level of professional representation and service. Additionally, PMG is an industry leader in providing corporate consulting services. Each client, whether an athlete or a corporation, is treated with a personal touch.

PREMIERE MANAGEMENT
410 30TH AVENUE EAST
SUITE 107
ALEXANDRIA, MN 56308
320-762-6555
Fax: 903-297-8832
Premiere@premieremanagement.com
www.premiermanagement.com
• DuWayne Johnson, President
(320) 762-6555
djohnson@premiermanagement.com
Services:
Asset/Liability Management, Strategic Planning, Productivity Improvement, Financial Analysis and Reporting, Branch Acquisition/Mergers, Internal Control Programs, Leadership Development/Team Building, and Policy Writing
Clients:
First National Bank of Volga, Republic Bank, Duluth, MN, Independent Community Bankers of South Dakota, BankStar Financial, Elkton, SD, Reliabank, Estelline, SD
Nature of Sports Service:
All phases of athlete representation including contract negotiation, long-range planning, financial planning, and post-career counseling.

PRESKILL ROBERT
500 AIRPORT BLVD
SUITE 100
BURLINGAME, CA 94010
415-377-3919
preskilllaw@hotmail.com
• Robert Preskill, Founder
Services:
Provides assistance in licensing, purchase and sale of media-based or entertainment-based properties, and also in the areas of franchising, commercial leasing, purchase and sale of businesses and business assets, and trademark registration.
Description:
Publishing, entertainment, intellectual property, licensing agreements, sports law.

PRINCE MARKETING GROUP
18 CARILLON CIRCLE
LIVINGSTON, NJ 07039
973-325-0800
800-987-7462
800-98-PRINCE
Fax: 973-243-0037
helpdesk@princemarketinggroup.com
www.princemarketinggroup.com
• Darren Prince, President/CEO
dprince@princemarketinggroup.com
• Steve Simon, Vice President and Talent representation
• Nicholas Cordasco, Talent representation
• Reggie Dance, Contact
• Daren Prince, President and CEO
(212) 585-0973
Nature of Service:
Full service sports and celebrity marketing firm. Public Appearances, Product Placement, Autograph Signing Sessions, Charity Events, Fantasy Camps and Tournaments available for athletes, Grand Openings and Promotions, Licensing and Product Endorsements, Motivational Speakers, Print Advertisements and Commercials and Voice-overs
Sports Service Founded:
1998
Clients:
Earin 'Magic' Johnson, Dennis Rodman, Hulk Hogan, Joe Frazier, Evel Knievel, Roy Jones Jr, Vinny Pazienza, Dave Winifield, Jenny McCarthy, Carmen Electra, Pamela Anderson, Nicollette Sheridan, Stacy Kiebler, Vince Neil, Marcus Schenkenberg, Brande Roderick, Symone Maree, Dave Prowse, Corbin Bernsen, Chuck Zito.

PRIORITY SPORTS
325 N LA SALLE
SUITE 650
CHICAGO, IL 60654
312-664-7700
Fax: 312-664-5172
info@prioritysports.biz
www.prioritysports.biz
• Mark Bartelstein, Founder/Chief Executive Officer
mbart13@prioritysports.biz
• Brad Ames, President
• Rick Smith, President, Team Operations & General Cou
ricks@prioritysports.biz
• Jeff Roth,
jeffr@prioritysports.biz
• Mike Mccartney, Football Operations Director

- Aaron Mintz,
- Kenny Zuckerman, President, Athlete Representation
kennyz@prioritysports.biz
- Mark Bartelstein, CEO & Founder
Services:
Represents professional athletes in contract negotiations, endorsements, licensing, personal appearances. Provides clients with general career management and post-career planning. Consults businesses and organizations in all aspects of promotion and sponsorship.
Clients:
Robert Gallery, Marvel Smith, Kurt Warner, Kevin Mawae, Domanick Davis, Brad Hopkins, Alan Faneca, Jake Delhomme, Levi Jones, Adam Timmerman, Tory James, Olin Kreutz, Jon Jansen, Brandon Stokley
Sports Service Founded:
1985

PRIORITY SPORTS & ENTERTAINMENT
325 N LA SALLE
SUITE 650
CHICAGO, IL 60654
312-664-7700
Fax: 312-664-5172
info@prioritysports.biz
www.prioritysports.biz
- Mark Bartelstein, Founder/Chief Executive Officer
mbart13@prioritysports.biz
- Brad Ames, President
- Rick Smith, President, Team Operations & General Cou
ricks@prioritysports.biz
- Jeff Roth,
jeffr@prioritysports.biz
- Mike Mccartney, Football Operations Director
- Aaron Mintz,
- Kenny Zuckerman, President, Athlete Representation
kennyz@prioritysports.biz
- Mark Bartelstein, CEO & Founder
Services:
Represents professional athletes in contract negotiations, endorsements, licensing, personal appearances. Provides clients with general career management and post-career planning. Consults businesses and organizations in all aspects of promotion and sponsorship.
Clients:
Robert Gallery, Marvel Smith, Kurt Warner, Kevin Mawae, Domanick Davis, Brad Hopkins, Alan Faneca, Jake Delhomme, Levi Jones, Adam Timmerman, Tory James, Olin Kreutz, Jon Jansen, Brandon Stokley
Sports Service Founded:
1985

PRO FOOTBALL ASSOCIATES
10808 DEPOT STREET
WORTH, IL 60482
708-448-3768
Description:
All phases of athlete representation.

PRO FOOTBALL MANAGEMENT
434 NINTH STREET
SAN FRANCISCO, CA 94103
301-717-1748
Fax: 301-881-8642
- Michael Bernstein, Sports Agent

PRO IMAGE, INC.
4401 O'DONNELL STREET
THE CANTON TRADE CENTER
BALTIMORE, MD 21224
410-675-6775
Fax: 410-675-6776
- John Wright, President
Services:
Provides event services, including development, production, promotions, and management for a variety of related fields such as: Graphic Design, Archtecture, Promotions, Talent Negotiations, Entertainment and Marketing
Clients:
The Baltimore Orioles, The University of Maryland, The Baltimore Sun Newspaper, Helix Health Services, The Johns Hopkins University, The Rite Aid Corporation, The Center Club, The National Aquarium, The Maryland Science Center, The Washington Capitals, Signet Bank, The Hyatt Regency Hotel, The Baltimore Zoo, The Office of the Governor of Maryland, The Office of the Mayor of Baltimore, WBAL-TV 11, The Best Western Corporation, Towson University, Bayer Aspirin, The Baltimore Ravens, The Baltimore Arena, The Pier Six Concert Pavilion, etc.
Description:
All phases of athlete representation including contract negotiation, long-range planning, financial planning, and post-career counseling.

PRO PLAYER REPS (PPR, INC.)
34208 AURORA RD.
SUITE 250
CLEVELAND, OH 44139
440-665-1713
Fax: 440-498-1220
info@playersrep.com
www.playersrep.com
- Jerry Lastelick, Attorney
(972) 247-4327
Services:
Serves as Entertainment lawyers
Other Office:
PO Box 29333, Dallas, TX 75229-0333. 972 620-8050; 800 989-7377; FAX: 972 241-6430.
Sports Service Founded:
1989
Athlete Management Services:
Contract negotiation, legal services, general career management for professional athletes in football, basketball, baseball, and representation of Champions Tour golfers.
Marketing & Consulting Services:
Product endorsements, corporate outings, personal appearances, and special engagements.

PRO SPORT MANAGEMENT
8355 E HARTFORD DRIVE
SUITE 105
SCOTTSDALE, AZ 85255
480-368-8434
Fax: 480-368-1905
www.prosportmanagement.com
- Geoff Ogilvy, Representative Player
- Aaron Baddeley, Representative Player
Golfers Represented:
Stephen Allan, Aaron Baddeley, Henrik Bjornstad, Maria Boden, Matthew Goggin, Richard Johnson, Jeff Klauk, Geoff Ogilvy, Craig Spence, Henrik Stenson.

Services:
Provides player management services including career management, endorsement negotiations, secretarial services, personal and professional development
Clients:
Aaron, Baddeley, Anders Hansen, Lisa Holm, Steven Jeppesen, Jeff Klauk, John Klauk, Amanda Moltke-Leth, James Oh, Geoff Ogilvy, Aron Price, Craig Spence, Iben Tinning

PRO SPORT MANAGEMENT, INC.
8355 E. HARTFORD DRIVE
SUITE 105
SCOTTSDALE, AZ 85255
480-368-8434
Fax: 480-368-1905
www.prosportmanagement.com
- John F. Geletka, Sports Agent
Services:
Offers all phases of athlete representation including contract negotiation, long-range planning, financial planning, and post-career counseling.

PRO STAR MANAGEMENT, INC.
312 WALNUT STREET
1600 SCRIPPS CENTER
CINCINNATI, OH 45202
513-762-7676
Fax: 513-721-4628
Prostar@fuse.net
www.prostarmanagement.com
- Joe Bick, President
(513) 762-7676
prostar@fuse.net
- Joe Bick, President, Founder
Prostar@fuse.net
Services:
Representation of professional athletes (primarily baseball players) and media personalities. Services include contract negotiations, financial planning and management, endorsements and merchandising.
Year Founded:
1986.

PROFESSIONAL KICKING SERVICES, INC.
3121 JARBRIDGE WAY
SPARKS, NV 89434
775-626-5425
Fax: 775-626-3217
- Ray Pelfrey, Owner/Chief Executive Officer
- Rob Pelfrey, President
- Dusty Apocotos, Senior Staff Instructor
Services:
PKS is football's leading developer of college scholarship talent at all levels. Specific services are: Player Infor Database, Private Lessons, Pro/Free Agent Program
Services:
Provides Player Info Database, private lessons, and pro/free agent program. Creates Kicking shoes, accessories and training gear, and instructional videos.
Sports Service Founded:
1975
Athlete Management Services:
National kicking camps - college, high school free agents. NFL, private pro development program.

PROFESSIONAL SPORTS CONSULTANTS, INC.
ONE NORTHFIELD PLAZA
NORTHFIELD, IL 60093
847-441-1842
Fax: 847-441-1843
• Francis J. Murtha, President
• Matthew F. Murtha, VP, Stadium/Structures
• Brian Roy, VP, Marketing
Services:
Contract negotiations and financial management for the professional athlete and entertainer. Consulting services for the acquisition and sale of professional sports franchises and sports related assets.

PROFESSIONAL SPORTS MANAGEMENT GROUP
800 UNIVERSITY W
WINDSOR, ON, CANADA N9A 5R9
519-252-7771
Fax: 519-259-1831
www.prosportsmanagement.com
• Patrick J. Ducharme, Sports Agent
• Edward Ducharme, Sports Agent
Services:
Offers all phases of athlete representation including contract negotiation, long-range planning, financial planning, and post-career counseling.
Nature of Sports Service:
All phases of athlete representation including contract negotiation, long-range planning, financial planning, and post-career counseling.

PROFESSIONAL SPORTS MARKETING, INC.
2300 W WHITE AVENUE
SUITE 102
MCKINNEY, TX 75071
214-544-0500
Fax: 214-544-0505
www.professionalsportsmarketing.com
• Kent Kramer, President
psm@professionalsportsmarketing.com
• Kurt Kramer, VP
Services:
Research, Creative Planning, Project Design and Implementation, Event Production and Staging, Sponsorship Evaluation and Negotiation, Sponsorship Sales, Public and Media Relations, Program Evaluation and Incentive Sports Travel. Totally integrated sports concept for sports events marketing, promotional programs, setup merchandising and advertising. Sports marketing consulting for corporate clients. Sports incentive travel programs including development and production of corporate.
Services:
Sport Marketing and Advertising
Clients:
Fritolay, Pepsi, Trimega, Ash Almond Associates
Sports Service Founded:
1985
Event Management Services:
Advertising and sales promotion. Specializes in special project events including project design, creative planning, research and event production, sponsorship evaluation and negotiation, public and media relations, program evaluation, incentive travel at major sporting events.

PROFESSIONAL SPORTS PLANNERS
9140 IRVINE CENTER DRIVE
IRVINE, CA 92618
949-752-1010
Fax: 949-833-7960
www.prosportsplanners.com
• Michael M. Watkins, President
(949) 752-1010
• J.D. Sanchez, Esq, Sports Attorney
Year Founded:
1985.
Services:
Provides complete contract negotiations, tax and billing services, investment guidance, product endorsement, arbitration and free agency.
Sports Service Founded:
1985.

PROFESSIONAL SPORTS PLANNING
909 FANNIN STREET
TWO HOUSTON CENTER, SUITE 2090
HOUSTON, TX 77010
713-659-2255
800-698-8680
Fax: 713-655-9545
• Carl C. Poston III, Agent
• Kevin D. Poston, President/CEO
Services:
Provides advice and representation for professional athletes.
Clients:
LaVar Arrington, Charles Woodson and Ty Law
Description:
Contract negotiation.

PROFILES SPORTS, INC.
3340 PEACHTREE ROAD, NE
16TH FLOOR
ATLANTA, GA 30326
404-842-7800
Fax: 404-842-7801
• Pat Dye, Jr., President
• Bill Johnson, Executive Vice President
billj500@aol.com
• Michael Perrett, VP Client Development/Marketing
• Chandra Vitale, COO/Executive Assistant to Pat Dye, Jr.
• Randi Chapman, Director Client Services
• Kevin McGuire, Director Marketing
Nature of Service:
At ProFiles, we want our clients to have more than just memories when they leave the game. We want them to be financially secure and prepared for life's challenges after sports.
Clients:
Jeff Backus, Fred Beasley, Michael Bennett, Keith Brooking, Mark Brown, Reggie Brown, Shawn Bryson, Tim Carter, Dexter Coakley, Antonio Cochran, Cosey Coleman, Rod Coleman, Russell Davis, Mike Degory, Heath Evans, Robert Geathers, Charles Grant, David Greene, Roman Harper, Garrison Hearst, Steve Herndon, Montrae Holland, Rueben Houston, Tommy Jackson, Sean Jones, Calvin Pace, Jermaine Phillips, Mike Pucillo, Kelvin Pritchett, Izell Reese, Tony Richardson, Victor Riley, Dennis Rolland Jr., Justin Smiley, Jon Stinchcomb, Matt Stinchcomb, Demarcus Ware, Marcus Washington, Benjamin Watson, Fred Weary, Charlie Whitehurst, Ben Wilkerson.

PROFORMA SPORTS
810 W. PIONEER PARKWAY
PEORIA, IL 61615
309-692-6390
Fax: 309-692-6397
jeff.brookes@proforma.com
www.proforma.com/info

PROMOTION ASSOCIATES GROUP, INC.
3545 E LAYTON AVENUE
CUDAHY, WI 53110
414-747-1711
Fax: 414-747-1714

PROREPS AGENCY, INC./SPORTS STAR
2338 NW PROFESSIONAL DRIVE
CORVALLIS, OR 97330-3881
541-754-1440
Fax: 541-758-4019
• William B. Heck, Sports Agent
Nature of Sports Service:
All phases of athlete representation including contract negotiation, long-range planning, financial planning, and post-career counseling.

PROSTAR ENTERPRISES, INC.
5340 NE 32ND AVENUE
FORT LAUDERDALE, FL 33308
954-202-7792

PROTECT MANAGEMENT CORP.
30699 RUSSELL RANCH ROAD
SUITE 210
WESTLAKE VILLAGE, CA 91362
818-889-2121
Fax: 818-889-2141
www.protectmanagement.com
• Gary Wichard, President/ Chief Executive Officer
• Michael Sasson, VP / Certified MLB Agent
• Jason Chinn, Public Relations/Marketing
• Jason Chinn, Vice President
• Jess Richman, Media and Marketing
• Beth Acker, Execuitve Assistant
Services:
Contract negotiations combined with marketing and public relations services.
Clients:
NFL Client: Jason Taylor, Terrell Suggs, Dwight Freeney, Keith Bulluck, Adam Archuleta, JP Losman, Teddy Lehman, Darren Howard, Tebucky Jones, Dyson Kevin, Stephen Alexander, Eric Hicks, Kevin Curtis, Andre Dyson, Kevin Mitchell, Justin Fargas, Chris Cooley, Brian Jennings, Cliff Russell, Brandon Moore, Johnnie Morant, Tommy Kelly, Grant Wiley, Travis Johnson and Darren Sproles. NBA Client: Wally Szczerbiak. MLB Client: Eric Byrnes, Justin Miller, Scott Cassidy, Jason Hart, Cody McKay, Matt Duff, John Gall, Dee Haynes, Nunez Jose, Gerald Laird and Josh Schmidt. Entertainment Client: Brian Bosworth.

QUATRINI, JAY
30 OLD BURLINGTON STREET
LONDON, ENGLAND W1S 3NL
+44-20-7468-2600
Fax: +44-20-7437-8216
• Vincent Calcara, Associate
(207) 468-5590
• Catherine Baker, Professional Support Lawyer
(207) 468-2713

• Michelle Brown, Associate
(207) 468-5571
• Vincenza Calcara, Associate
(207) 468-5590
Services:
Provides leagal services through its five departments, Company & Commercial, Litigation, Property, Employment and Private Client.
Clients:
ABTA, Agnes b, Aardman Animations, Armor Holdings Inc., Ask Central, Baker Street Media Finance Ltd, Barclays Bank plc, Bespoke Couture/Ozwald Boateng, Brand Connection Ltd, British Airways, British Greyhound Racing Board, Broadway Communications Ltd, Business Systems Group Holdings Plc, Capital Radio, Centaur Communications Ltd, Charlton Down Developments Ltd, CIT Group, Contender Entertainment Group, Counterpoint Systems Ltd, Derwent Valley Holdings Plc,Dorling Kindersley Ltd,Dune,Ed Victor Ltd, English & Pockett, Epson Europe Ltd, Express Newspapers,First Title Insurance Plc, French Connection Group plc, Fuller Smith & Turner, FX Corpora
Description:
Contract negotiation, represents professional sports teams, licensing, endorsement exploration, teaches sports law.

R.L.R. ASSOCIATES, LTD.
7 W 51ST STREET
4TH FLOOR
NEW YORK, NY 10020
212-541-8641
Fax: 212-541-6052
sgould@rlrassociates.net
www.rlrassociates.net
• Robert L. Rosen, President
rrosen@rlrassociates.net
• Gary I. Rosen, EVP
grosen@rlrassociates.net
• Craig Foster, VP
cfoster@rlrassociates.net
• Robert Rosen, Owner
• Eric Winchel, Manager
• Robert Lewis Rosen, President
Services:
Offers services on career management, talent marketing, content development and content rights sales.
Clients:
PGA, PGA Tour, America's Most Wanted, National Cheerleaders Association, CDT, NCSSE, Kelly Atkinson, Cathy Barreto, David Blatt, Peter Bleckner, Mike Cohen, Jennifer Danska, Chip Dean, Bob Fishman, Earl Freiman, Sandy Grossman, Jim Jennett, Jeff Kay, David Kiviat, Bob Matina, Jeff Mitchell, John Moore, Eric Neuhaus, April Rouge, etc.
Sports Service Founded:
1964
Athlete Management Services:
Full-service representation including, but not limited to, contract negotiation, financial and career planning, and endorsement opportunities for sports broadcasting executives and on-air professionals, sports associations, and sports authors, nationally and internationally.
Event Management Services:
Negotiates domestic and international television license fees and arranges for television sponsorship of events.

Marketing & Consulting Services:
Represents and negotiates television contracts for sportscasters, directors and producers.
Clients Include:
Dave Barnett (Announcer - ESPN), Tim Brando (CBS Sports), Bill Daughtry (Host, SportsDesk - MSG), Marques Johnson (FOX Sports Net), Ralph Kiner (Mets), Bob Ley (ESPN), Verne Lundquist (Turner Sports, CBS Sports), Tim McCarver (FOX Sports, SF Giants), Billy Packer (CBS Sports, ESPN), Gary Thorne (ESPN), Joe Torre (Mgr - NY Yankees).

RAD & ASSOCIATES
58 PARKWAY W
MOUNT VERNON, NY 10552
914-668-7898
Fax: 914-668-2575
rad58phd@aol.com
• Dick Dolce, President
• Glenn L Dolce, VP
Services:
Develops and provides licensing and merchandising consultation to professional athletes for product endorsements, promotions and media strategies.
Sports Service Founded:
1987
Athlete Management Services:
Develops and provides licensing and merchandising consultation to professional athletes for product endorsements, promotions and media strategies.
Event Management Services:
Secures corporate sponsorship for sports/special events. Manages, handle all aspects including licensing, merchandising and event concession sales in connection with event.
Marketing & Consulting Services:
Serve as consultant to national governing bodies, organizations, corporations and major manufacturers interested in achieving or maintaining specific licensing, merchandising or sales promotion goals through the use of sports. Consulting services include licensing feasibility, program objectives, licensing plans, policies and procedures. Assists manufacturers in search, evaluation, negotiation and acquisition of sport licenses.

RALEIGH CYCLE
6004 S 190TH STREET
SUITE 101
KENT, WA 98032
253-395-1100
800 222-5527
Fax: 253-872-0257
www.raleighusa.com
• Sharon Robinson, CFO
Products:
Raleigh bicycles either for fitness, commuting, racing, or just cruising with family and friends.
Brands:
Raleigh Performance Comfort Road: Cadent 5.0 2006, Cadent 4.0 2006, Cadent 3.0 2006, Cadent 2.0 2006, and Cadent 1.0 2006. Raleigh Road: Rush Hour 2006, Team 2006, Prestige 2006, Competition 2006, Supercourse 2006, Grand Prix 2006, Grand Sport 2006, Sport 2006, Route 66 2006, Route 24 2006 and Route 1 2006. Raleigh Hybrid: Passage 5.0 2006, Passage

4.0 2006 and Passage 3.0 2006. Raleigh Full Suspension: Phase 2 2006, Phase 1 2006 and Phase 2006. Raleigh MTN Hardtail: Mojave 8.0 2006, Mojave 5.5 2006, Mojave 5.0 2006, Mojave 4.0 2006, Mojave 4.5 2006 and Mojave 2.0 2006. Raleigh Comfort: Venture 5.0 2006, Venture 4.0 2006, Venture 3.0 2006,
Services:
Athlete Management: Bicycle racers/race teams and triathletes
Event Management Services:
Bicycle races.
Year Founded:
1896

RAWLINGS, GEORGE R.
325 W MAIN STREET
SUITE 1700, WATERFRONT PLAZA
LOUISVILLE, KY 40202
502-587-1279
800-928-1279
Fax: 502-584-8580
Services:
Provides all phases of athlete representation including contract negotiation, long-range planning, financial planning, and post-career counseling.

RELLIHAN, JERRY J.
895 E WALNUT STREET
RAYMORE, MO 64083
816-322-6777
Fax: 816-322-6719
jerry@rellihanlaw.com
www.rellihanlaw.com
• Jerry Rellihan, Contact
jerry@rellihanlaw.com
Year Founded:
1984.
Services:
Provides legal assistance on Estate Planning.
Description:
Contract negotiation.

REMICK, LLOYD Z.
1650 MARKET STREET
56TH FLOOR
ONE LIBERTY PLACE
PHILADELPHIA, PA 19103-7334
215-790-1155
Fax: 215-575-3801
www.zanemanagement.com
• Lloyd Zane Remick, President/Chief Executive Officer
(215) 790-1155
remick@braverlaw.com
Nature of Service:
Provides personal management, contract negotiation, expert witness testimony, event planning, hospitality & tourism, appearances & endorsements and accounting & tax services for Boxing, Football, Music, Authors, Movies and Television.
Year Founded:
1978

REYNOLDS SPORTS MANAGEMENT
3850 VINE STREET
SUITE 230
RIVERSIDE, CA 92507
951-784-6333
Fax: 951-784-1451
Info@Reynoldssports.com
www.reynoldssports.com

- Larry Reynolds, Founder/President
- Patrick Murphy, COO
- Mike Dillon, Executive Vice President
- Terry Jones, Vice President of Baseball Operations
- Doreen Hurtado, Director of Client Services
- Erika Moore, Executive Assistant / Director of Special Pro
- Larry Reynolds, President/CEO

Description:
Contract negotiation, post career planning, arbitration hearings, endorsement exploration, tort actions/litigation.

Services:
Provides assistance on Contract negotiation, Salary arbitration, Marketing and endorsement development, Income tax preparation assistance, Financial management coordination, Secondary career planning and management, Web page development and maintenance and Real estate and personal property purchasing assistance.

Clients:
Major League Roster: (40 man) Reggie Abercrombie: Florida Marlins,Boof Bonser: Minnesota Twins, Chad Cordero: Washington Nationals, Matt Diaz: Atlanta Braves, Carl Everett: Seattle Mariners, Joey Gathright: Tampa Bay Devil Rays, Chad Gaudin: Oakland Athletics, aTroy Hawkins: Baltimore Orioles, Ryan Howard: Philadelphia Phillies, Torii Hunter: Minnesota Twins, Scott Tyler: Florida Marlins, B.J. Upton: Tampa Bay Devil Rays and Mitch Wylie: NY Mets. Minor League Roster: Nick Bourgeois: Seattle Mariners, Ryan Christianson: Tampa Bay Devil Rays, Thomas Diamond: Texas Rangers, Clint Everts: Washington Nationals, Kiel Fisher: Philadelphia Phillies

---

RICE & RICE
100 E LINCOLNWAY
SUITE 1
VALPARAISO, IN 46383
219-462-0809
800-303-7423
Fax: 219-531-8644
www.riceandrice.com
- Bruce N. Adams, Partner
- Bruce Mi Rice, Attorney

Description:
Contract negotiation.

Services:
Provides legal assistance on Family Law.

RICHARD HOWELL SPORTS MANAGEMENT, INC.
2964 PEACHTREE ROAD
SUITE 330
ATLANTA, GA 30305
404-842-1556
Fax: 404-842-1586
- Richard S. Howell, Sports Agent

Nature of Sports Service:
Provides a full range of agency services to professional athletes including team contract negotiations, marketing endorsements and career counseling.

RILEY & HURLEY, P.C.
19853 W OUTER DRIVE
SUITE 100
DEARBORN, MI 48124

313-565-1330
Fax: 313-565-1318
rfrpc@rileyhurley.com
www.rileyhurley.com
- Robert F. Riley, Partner
rriley@rileyhurley.com
- William C. Hurley, Partner
whurley@rileyhurley.com

Services:
Represents sports associations and organizations; litigation, arbitration and negotiations.

RILEY, WILLIAM T., JR.
500 E PRATT STREET
SUITE 200
BALTIMORE, MD 21202
410-783-4900
Fax: 410-727-0460
www.reznickgroup.com
- William T. Riley Jr, Managing Principal
(410) 783-4900
- Ryan Duckworth, National Conferences/Events
(404) 497-8960

Services:
All phases of athlete representation including contract negotiation, long-range planning, financial planning and income tax planning and preparation.

Clients:
Corporate Executives, Business Owners and Enterpreneurs; Government Professionals; Healthcare Administrators; Leadership and Investors; Nonprofit Professionals

---

RMI/ATLANTA
2498 JETT FERRY ROAD
SUITE 100
ATLANTA, GA 30338
770-399-9668
Fax: 770-391-9518
- Doug Messerlie, Founder
- Greg Thornton, Marketing Assistant

Services:
Research and Analysis, Marketing, Promotional ans Sponsorship Management, Event Management and Customer Entertainment, Public Relations, Media & Communications, Measurements and Return on Investment Documentation, Sponsorship Opportunities

Clients:
AT&T Racing, Siemens, Burger King, Dynoject, Ericsson, Dassault Systemes, PPG Industries, Perrier, Motorola Racing, Mighty, Turner, Cartoon Network, Caterpillar, Rotozip, Sylvania 300, Superchips, MSD Ignition, Stanley

Marketing & Consulting Services:
Creates and implements sports marketing strategies for corporations desiring to promote their products and services through auto racing, events and related activities, including event management, public relations, promotions, research analysis and sponsor relations.

Sports Service Founded:
1989

ROSENBLATT, GERALD F.
2049 CENTURY PARK E
SUITE 3180
LOS ANGELES, CA 90067
310-393-5345

- Gerald F. Rosenblatt, Attorney
gerrysmusiclaw@aol.com

Services:
Contract negotiation, endorsement exploration. Represents athletes and entertainers.

ROSENHAUS SPORTS MANAGEMENT
6400 ALLISON ROAD
MIAMI BEACH, FL 33141-4540
305-936-1093
Fax: 305-864-3731
www.rosenhaussports.com
- Drew Rosenhaus, Chief Executive Officer
drosenhaus@aol.com

Services:
Contract negotiation, investment contract negotiation, provides investment advice.

Clients:
Clinton Portis (NFL Denver Broncos), Jeremy Shockey (NFL NY Giants), Wiillis McGahee (NFL Bullfalo Bills).

RUDER/FINN SPORTS, INC.
301 E 57TH STREET
NEW YORK, NY 10022
212-593-6400
www.ruderfinn.com
- David Finn, Chairman
- Kathy Bloomgarden, Chief Executive Officer
- Michael Schubert, Chief Innovation Officer

Services:
Health care marketing activities, developing a premier position in science programming, Corporate Relations, Public Affairs, Government Affairs, Professional and Financial Services, Investor Relations, Consumer/Product Marketing, Lifestyle Marketing, High Tech, Visual Technology, Design/Publishing, Crisis Communications, Travel/Hospitality, International

Services:
National network of event managers and promotional specialists help maximize sponsor identification with sporting events. Contacts with national and local print and broadcast media offers combination of event experience and publicity background. Aids clients in identifying which sports and events best fit marketing needs. Strong association with athletes and sports organizations gives R/F an ad hoc panel of experts to routinely approach for consulting services.

Sports Service Founded:
1986

Marketing & Consulting Services:
Aids clients in identifying which sports and events best fit marketing needs. Strong association with athletes and sports organizations gives R/F an ad hoc panel of experts to routinely approach for consulting services.

Other Offices:
Chicago,Washington DC, Beijing, Guangzhou, Hong Kong, Shanghai, Singapore, London and paris.

RUNGE, JOHN B.
2011 E. LAMAR BOULEVARD
SUITE 200
ARLINGTON, TX 76006
817-336-5355
Fax: 817-336-0432
www.rungefirm.com
Description:
Contract negotiation.

SAMMS, GREGORY A.
225 ALCAZAR AVENUE
CORAL GABLES, FL 33134
786-953-5802
Fax: 305-446-3538
sammslaw@gmail.com
www.gregsamms.com
Services:
All phases of athlete representation
including contract negotiation, long-range
planning, financial planning, and post-career
counseling.

SANDERS, FREDRIC M.
120 BROADWAY
NEW YORK, NY 10271
212-810-2400
Fax: 212-810-2410
• Fredric M. Sanders, Partner
(212) 810-2400
Description:
Tax specialist.

SAXTON COMMUNICATIONS INC.
1448 HOLLYWOOD AVENUE
LANGHORNE, PA 19047-7417
215-752-7797
Fax: 215-752-1518
ESAXTON144@AOL.COM
www.saxtonsponsormarket.com
• Eric Saxton, Member
(267) 934-7286
ESAXTON144@AOL.COM
Other Offices:
Daytona Beach, FL; Norristown, PA
Sports Service Founded:
1970
Athlete Management Services:
Sponsorship representation, public relations,
marketing, preparation of support materials
(kits, releases, etc.), program books
created, sponsorship and marketing
consultation.
Event Management Services:
Brings together motorsports events and
participants with sponsors, public relations,
publicity, program books, newsletters,
advertising, promotion.
Marketing & Consulting Services:
Advising clients on how they can fit into
motorsports with sponsorship,
merchandising and promotional programs.
Publishes ERNIE SAXTON'S
MOTORSPORTS SPONSORSHIP
MARKETING NEWS, a monthly newsletter
on marketing and sponsorship in
motorsports.
Clients Include:
Eastern Motorsports Press Association,
Grandview Speedway, Rising Star
Publishing, Pennzoil Motorsports Show,
Martin Brothers Tractor Racing Team,
Ranger Joe Cyphen Monster Truck Team.

SCHAEFFER, RICHARD L.
8700 HEARTH STONE WAY
GRAND LEDGE, MI 48837
517-627-6530
Services:
Contract negotiation, post career planning,
investment contract negotiation, arbitration
hearings, endorsement exploration, tort
actions/litigation.

SCHIFF HARDIN LLP
233 S WACKER DRIVE
6600 SEARS TOWER
CHICAGO, IL 60606
312-258-5500
Fax: 312-258-5600
www.schiffhardin.com
• Thomas W. Abendroth, Partner
(312) 258-5600
tabendroth@schiffhardin.com
• John F. Adams, Counsel
(312) 258-5541
jadams@schiffhardin.com
Description:
Represents professional sports teams
(Chicago Bears).
Services:
Represents professional sports teams
(Chicago Bears).
Year Founded:
1864
Other Locations:
Washington DC, New York NY, Lake Forest
IL, Atlanta GA

SCHOEPPLER, KURT J.
1360 E 9TH STREET
IMG CENTER
SUITE #100
CLEVELAND, OH 44114-1737
216-522-1200
Fax: 216-522-1145
martin.jolly@imgworld.com
www.imgworld.com
• Ian Todd, President
• Theodore J. Forstmann, Chairman/CEO
tforstmann@imgworld.com
• Robert Ryder, EVP and Chief Financial
Officer
rryder@imgworld.com
• Alastair Johnston, Co-Chief Executive
Officer
ajohnston@imgworld.com
Services:
Contract negotiation.
Other Locations:
IMG MODELS, 304 Park Avenue South,
Penthouse North 12th Floor, New York, NY
10010; Phone: 212-253-8884; 20 Guest
Street, STE 400, Brighton Landing East,
Brighton, MA 02135; Phone: 617-783-9032;
5301 Wisconsin Avenue, NW, STE 425,
Washington, DC 20015; Phone:
202-964-8500; W - 2370 One PPG Place,
pittsburgh, PA 15222; Phone:
412-391-4927; 175 Bloor Street East, STE
400, South Tower, Toronto, Ontario, CAN
M4W 3R8; Phone: 416-960-5312; 2 Bryant
Street, STE 150, San Francisco, CA 94105;
Phone: 415-227-8000; 150 Athambra Circle,
STE 825, Coral Gables, Fl 33134; Phone:
305-446-220

SCHULEFAND, KEITH
1301 N. FOREST ROAD
WILLIAMSVILLE, NY 14221
716-568-4453
888-499-1552
Fax: 716-565-1575
schulefand@hotmail.com
www.schulefandlawoffice.com
• Keith Schulefand, Esquire
(716) 632-5919
schulefand@hotmail.com
Services:
All phases of athlete representation
including contract negotiation, long-range

planning, financial planning, and post-career
counseling.

SCOTT BORAS CORPORATION
2100 MAIN STREET
SUITE 300
IRVINE, CA 92714
949-833-1818
Fax: 949-833-1816
• Scott Boras, President and Owner
Services:
Agent for professional baseball players. It
represented many of the highest-paid
players in baseball.

SCRIMMAGE LINE SPORTS
917 E 543 ROAD
LAWRENCE, KS 66047
785-295-6275
Fax: 785-266-7819
• Aaron G. Hove, Sports Agent
Nature of Sports Service:
All phases of athlete representation
including contract negotiation, long-range
planning, financial planning, and post-career
counseling.

SEA BROWN & ASSOCIATES
9200 BASIL COURT
SUITE 203
LANDOVER, MD 20785
301-322-8907
Fax: 301-322-4583
Services:
All phases of athlete representation
including contract negotiation, long-range
planning, financial planning, and post-career
counseling.

SENIOR MANAGEMENT GROUP
125 STRAFFORD AVE
SUITE 112
WAYNE, PA 19087
610-293-1500
Fax: 610-293-1504
www.seniormg.com
• Brett W. Senior, Senior Partner
(610) 941-0770
Brett@seniormg.com
• D. Ch Le Vine, Financial Services Director
(610) 941-0770
• Susan W. O'Donnell, Attorney
(610) 941-0770
• Terri V. McGrath, Manager
(610) 941-0770
tmcgrath@seniormg.com
Description:
Representing hundreds of professional
athletes, coaches and management/owners
from the sports industry.
Services:
Legal, tax, accounting and investment
advisory services to actively and objectively
advocate the clients' interest in the
marketplace - delivering superior service,
performance and fiduciary peace of mind
Clients:
Joe Paterno: Penn State University Head
Coach; Bill Parcells: Dallas Cowboys Head
Coach; Robbie Gould: Placekicker, Chicago
Bears; Frank Chamberlin: Linebacker,
Houston, Texas; Jamie Bestwick: BMX
X-Games Champion

SENIOR TOUR PLAYERS, INC.
1244 BOYLSTON STREET
SUITE 200
CHESTNUT HILL, MA 02467
617-266-3600
Services:
Represents and arranges for the services of the Champions Tour Golf Professionals. Events include corporate and charity pro-ams, speaking engagements, clinics, and golf community developments.
Services:
Event Management: Total golf event management and design; sponsorship sales. Marketing & Consulting: Specializes in residential golf course communities providing full marketing and consulting services in all aspects of the project including market studies, financial presentations, design, etc.

SENNET, CHARLES J.
435 N MICHIGAN AVENUE
TRIBUNE COMPANY
STE 600
CHICAGO, IL 60611
312-222-9100
Fax: 312-222-4206
www.tribune.com
• Samuel Zell, Chairman/Chief Executive Officer
• Chandler Bigelow, CFO
• Crane H. Kenney, SVP/General Counsel & Secretary
(312) 222-9100
• Thomas D. Leach, SVP, Development
(312) 222-9100
Services:
Publishing and broadcasting.
Description:
Contract negotiation, represents professional sports teams, licensing.

SFX SPORTS GROUP
5335 WISCONSIN AVENUE NW
SUITE 850
WASHINGTON, DC 20015
202-686-2000
Fax: 202-686-5050
www.sfxsports.com
• James R. Steiner, President
• David Falk, Chairman and Chief Executive Officer
• Tim J. Hoy, Executive Officer
• John Mascatello, President SFX Golf
• Bud Martin, Senior Vice President, SFX Sports
• Jim Lehman, Senior Vice President, SFX Golf
Nature of Service:
Provides full-service representation to its athlete clients. Our services include contract negotiation and all 'off-the-field' business and marketing endeavors, including endorsements, licensing, financial planning, promotions, charitable pursuits, speaking engagements, and personal appearances.
Events:
American Century Golf Championships, Heineken Classic, The Minnesota Golf Show, Rock-N-Racquets, Bob Hope Chrysler Classic, Legg Mason Tennis Classic, NFL Sporting Clays Team Challenge, Scholarship America Showdown.
Clients:
Jerry Rice, Cadillac Williams, Pedro Martinez, David Ortiz, Andre Agassi, Andy

Roddick, Tom Lehman, and Andrew Bogut are just a few of the many top names in sports who choose SFX.

SFX SPORTS GROUP, INC.
5335 WISCONSIN AVENUE, NW
SUITE 850
WASHINGTON, DC 20015
202-686-2000
Fax: 202-686-5050
• Tim J. Hoy, Executive Officer
• David J Falk, Chairman and Chief Executive Officer
Services:
Baseball: Negotiation of Baseball Contracts (including winter ball, where appropriate); Representation in Salary Arbitration; Development and Updating of a Budget and Financial Plan; Preparation of All Tax Returns; Negotiation of Off-field Contracts, Including Product Endorsements & Appearances; Day-to-Day Personal & Financial Assistance
year founded:
1999
Nature of Sports Services:
Sports Marketing firm and talent agency representing athletes.

SHANNON PROFESSIONAL MANAGEMENT
313 N BIRCH AVENUE
SANTA ANA, CA 92701
714-542-3592
Services:
All phases of athlete representation including contract negotiation, long-range planning, financial planning, and post-career counseling.

SHAPIRO MANAGEMENT
2147 N BEACHWOOD DRIVE
LOS ANGELES, CA 90068
323-469-9452
Fax: 801-653-6571
burtjay@mail.com
www.burtshapiro.com
• Burt J. Shapiro, President
(323) 469-9452
burtjay@mail.com
Services:
Represents on-air broadcasters (anchors, sportscasters, weathercasters, reporters, hosts) news managers, producers,etc., represents actors, comedians, sports personalities, writers, directors, producers, etc.
Clients:
Ray Brune——Exec. Prod./ABC's World News Now, Sr Prod/KTLA-TV;Lisa Darr——Actress——numerous series, pilots, guest starring roles; Natasha Pavlova——numerous guest starring roles; Dorothy Malone——Oscar winning actress; Amy Jacobson——Reporter/WMAQ-TV; Jim Von Fleet——Weathercaster/WOFL-TV; Tim Brando——Host/Anchor, Play-by-Play/ESPN; Karie Ross——Anchor/Reporter/ESPN, Sports News Network, WTVJ-TV; Lola Martinez——Weather Anchor/CNN Int.; Hiram Enriquez——Host/Anchor/Reporter/CNN en Espanol; Max Bretos——Play-by-Play/Fox Sports Net; Mauricio Guevara——Play-by-Play/Fox Sports Net; Naibe Reynoso——Host/Radio Visa,Rep/Anchor/ KWGN-TV; Ricardo Fernan

Marketing & Consulting Services:
Sports management, marketing and leisure time marketing. Consultant to corporations and advertising agencies interested in achieving or maintaining specific marketing or sales promotions through the use of sports.
Event Management Services:
Summer camps, clinics, coordinates programs to assist companies in promoting their products and/or services.
Athlete Management Services:
Contract negotiation, appearances, endorsements, commercials, athlete career management and planning, theatrical planning, as well as financial management. In addition, represents sports broadcasters with network and local stations.
Sports Service Founded:
1986

SHAW SPORTS & ENTERTAINMENT
4819 S PARK AVENUE
HAMBURG, NY 14075
716-648-3020
Fax: 716-648-3730
www.shawsports.net
• Joseph H. Shaw, President
Nature of Sports Service:
All phases of athlete representation including contract negotiation, long-range planning, financial planning, and post-career counseling.

SHEEHY, NEIL K.
7760 FRANCE AVENUE SOUTH
SUITE 1100
MINNEAPOLIS, MN 55435
612-340-0261
neilksheehy@msn.com
• Neil K. Sheehy, Lawyer/Sports Agent
(612) 340-0261
NeilKSheehy@msn.com
• Timothy K. Sheehy, NHLPA Certified Agent
(508) 624-4556
tksheehy@aol.com
Description:
Contract negotiation, Endorsements, Career Advertisement
Services:
Represents professional athletes and media personalities, negotiates rookie contracts for first round draft choices in all four major sports- hockey, basketball, baseball and football.
Clients:
Sheehy Hockey, LLC.

SHEPLEY AGENCY
3109 W 6TH STREET
SUITE A
LAWRENCE, KS 66049
785-865-5200
Fax: 785-865-0643
• Vickie Shepley,
(785) 865-5200
Description:
Contract negotiation.
Services:
Insurance Carriers

SHERMAN SPECIALTY COMPANY
300 JERICHO QUADRANGLE
SUITE 240
JERICHO, NY 11753

516-861-6420
800-645-6513
Fax: 516-861-1034
info@ShermanSpecialty.com
Products:
Toys and gifts with sports logos and designs.

SHOENFELT SPORTS MANAGEMENT
2109 PERKINS ROAD
BATON ROUGE, LA 70808
225-336-4300
800-291-8452
Fax: 225-336-4350
info@shoenfeltlaw.com
• Oscar Shoenfelt, Owner/Sports Agent
(225) 336-4300
• Katie Shoenfelt, Partner
Services:
Medical malpractice, personal injury & sports law firm
Clients:
Dwayne Missouri; Rufus Porter; and Willie Williams, Ervin Johnson and Stanley Roberts

---

SIMS, JR. JAMES A.
760 LONGRIDGE ROAD
OAKLAND, CA 94610
510-444-4974
Fax: 510-834-4456
JamesASims@aol.com
www.simssports.com
• James A. Sims Jr, President/Principal
(510) 444-4974
JamesASims@aol.com
• Jeremy Veit, Player Relations Administrator
(510) 444-4974
JMVeit@aol.com
Services:
Full-service sports management firm dedicated to providing the absolute highest quality representation possible Contract, Negotiation and Legal Services, Financial and Investment Monitoring, Tax Services and Estate Planning, Marketing, Endorsements and Public Relations, Combine Preparation, Career and Business Planning, Talent Development, Charitable and Philanthropic Services, Event Planning and Coordination.
Clients:
Partial List of Players Represented in the NFL, Jamal Anderson, Eugene Wilson, Takeo Spikes, Rob Burnett, Tully Banta-Cain, La'Roi Glover, Deltha O'Neal, BJ Tucker, DeJuan Green, Wendell Hunter, Johnny Johnson, First Rounders, Andre Rison, Leonard Renfro, Takeo Spikes, Deltha O'Neal, Second Rounders, Robert Blackmon, Bruce Walker, Anthony Cook, Dedric Mathis, Jeremy Newberry, Eugene Wilson, Middle & Late Rounders, Fred Beasley, Leonardo Carson, Troy Dumas, Sam Garnes, Kahlil Hill, Monty Montgomery, Pro Bowlers, Jamal Anderson, Robert Blackmon, Rob Burnett, Johnny Johnson, La'Roi Glover, Larry Whingham.

SMITH MOORE LEATHERWOOD, LLP
300 N GREENE STREET
SUITE 1400
GREENSBORO, NC 27401
336-378-5200
Fax: 336-378-5400
www.smithmoorelaw.com

• Erik Albright, Attorney
(336) 378-5368
erik.albright@smithmoorelaw.com
• Alan W. Duncan, Business Litigation
Nature of Sports Service:
Mr. Albright has represented sports organizations and individuals for 20 years. He represents collegiate conferences, professional sports franchises, sports venues, and event organizers. He previously represented professional football and baseball players.

SMITHERMAN, RODGER
2029 2ND AVENUE N
BIRMINGHAM, AL 35203
205-322-0012
Fax: 205-324-2000
rodger.smitherman@alsenate.gov
• Rodger Smithermanq, Senator
(205) 322-3768
rodger.smitherman@alsenate.gov

SPAIN & GILLON, LLC
2117 2ND AVENUE N
THE ZINSZER BUILDING
BIRMINGHAM, AL 35203
205-328-4100
Fax: 205-324-8866
www.spain-gillon.com
• David S. Maxey, Partner
(205) 581-6232
dsm@spain-gillon.com
• Scott B. Hannon, System Administrator/Webmaster
• Jarrod Br Bazemore, Partner
(205) 581-6235
jbb@spain-gillon.com
• Steve R. Burford, Partner
(205) 581-6247
• Jarrod B. Bazemore, Attorney
• Brian V. Cash, Attorney
• James E. Ferguson, III, Attorney
(205) 581-6289
jef@spain-gillon.com
• Samuel H. Frazier, Of Counsel
(205) 581-6225
shf@spain-gillon.com
• Frederick M. Garfield, Partner
(205) 581-6259
fmg@spain-gillon.com
Services:
Administrative Law, Appellate Practice, Arbitration and Mediation Services, Bankruptcy, Business, Corporate Law & Litigation, Civil Liability, Class Actions, Commercial Transactions, Commercial Transportation Litigation, Construction, Consumer Fraud and Bad Faith, Corporate Taxation, Environmental & Toxic Tort Claims, ERISA, Errors & Omissions Defense, Estate Planning and Administration of Estates, Fidelity & Surety, General Insurance Matters, Governmental, Health & Hospital, Labor and Employment, Life and Health Insurance Defense, Medical & Professional Malpractice, Mergers and Acquisitions, Pharmaceuticals and Medical Devices.

SPARTA GROUP MEDIA/COACHES, INC.
140 LITTLETON ROAD
SUITE 100
PARSIPPANY, NJ 07054
973-335-0550
Fax: 973-335-2148

Frontdesk@thespartagroup.com
thespartagroup.com
• Craig E. Fenech, President
• Michael Nicotera, Senior Partner, Director of Baseball Operatio
miken@thespartagroup.com
• Gene Casaleggio, Senior Partner, Director of Player Developmen
Genec@thespartagroup.com
• William R. Boyd, Chief Financial Officer
Billb@thespartagroup.com
Clients:
Coaches: John Calipari (NCAA), Fran Fraschilla (NCAA)
Media Personalities: Mike Breen, Mike Francesa, John Sterling, Suzyn Waldman
Description:
All phases of athlete management.

SPITZ, ROBERT J.
204 N SAN ANTONIO AVENUE
ONTARIO, CA 91762
909-395-0909
Fax: 909-395-9535
TPLaw@aol.com
www.robertspitzlaw.com
• Robert J. Spitz, Attorney
tplaw@aol.com
Year Founded:
1975
Description:
Legal services, contracts and negotiations

SPORT MANAGEMENT, INC.
5805 CHANDLER COURT
WESTERVILLE, OH 43082
614-899-9476
Marketing & Consulting Services:
Sports marketing and management agency representing athletes, venues and teams in regard to sale promotions and sponsorship procurement.

SPORTRUST ASSOCIATES INTERNATIONAL
823 22ND STREET
SANTA MONICA, CA 90403
310-829-1747
Fax: 310-315-0424
• Ronald M. Del Duca Jr, Sports Agent
Nature of Sports Service:
All phases of athlete representation including contract negotiation, long-range planning, financial planning, and post-career counseling.

SPORTS & SPONSORSHIPS, INC.
4000 HOLLYWOOD BOULEVARD
SUITE 755
SOUTH HOLLYWOOD, FL 33021
954-334-5930
Fax: 954-206-0360
info@sportsandsponsorships.com
www.sportsandsponsorships.com
• Scott Becher, President
scott@sportsandsponsorships.com
Services:
Strategic Planning, Representation, Event Marketing
Clients:
Bristol-Myers Squibb Company, Cancun, Clairol, Skis Dynastar, Sports, FPL, Foot Locker, Fox Sports, Gillette, Hershey's, Sprint, FIFA, Florida Marlins, Crock Pot, Major League Baseball, NASCAR, NFL, NHL, NCAA

SPORTS BUSINESS ASSOCIATES, LLC
3 BENTLEY DRIVE
FRANKLIN LAKES, NJ 7417
201-697-2436
Fax: 201-581-0277
• James Santomier, Jr, PhD, Founder
(203) 697-2436
Description:
Provides critical intelligence to the sport
industry and educational community
worldwide. It offers a portfolio of in-depth
reports and publications focusing on
marketing, sponsorship, hospitality, media
and broadcasting, new media, finance,
globalization, licensed merchandise, and
sport business education, as well as sport
and country specific reports.

SPORTS IMPACT, INC.
60 E 42ND STREET
SUITE 726
NEW YORK, NY 10165-0721
212-697-0530
Fax: 212-697-0533
• Robert F. Corrao, Chairman/Chief
Executive Officer
Services:
Offers sports celebrities as hosts of
promotional events.
Other Address:
14 Diane Court, Katonah, NY 10536
Budget:
$1,000,000-$2,499,999
Sports Service Founded:
1984
Event Management Services:
Incorporates promotional opportunities in
advertising packages.
Marketing & Consulting Services:
Produces and publishes magazines (NBA
and NHL teams), distributed within the
arenas and directly to season ticket holders
homes.

SPORTS LINK, INC.
2033 W MCDERMOTT DRIVE
SUITE # 320-260
ALLEN, TX 75013
972-608-8818
888-727-7332
Fax: 972-608-8805
• Kyle Kramer, Founder
Services:
provides services and systems to maximize
the usage and investments of companies
that own or want to own season tickets,
luxury suites of that sponsor teams and
events.
year founded
1998

SPORTS LOOP
500 LAKE COOK ROAD
SUITE 350
DEERFIELD, IL 60015
847-797-0900
Fax: 888-253-5997
• Roy D. Kessel, President/General Counsel
• Pete Force, VP-Business Development
• John Rudnick, VP-Technology
• John Morrison, Sports Management
Associate
Services:
professional representation for athletes and
entertainers, event management, sports
marketing, corporate consulting, brand
management, and hospitality services.

Description:
full service sports and entertainment firm
providing innovative and sound approaches
to meeting its clients objectives.

SPORTS MANAGEMENT AND MARKETING, INC.
1481 DOMINION COURT
PITTSBURGH, PA 15241
412-257-1900
Fax: 412-257-5939
SMMI@aol.com
www.sportsmmi.com
• John I. Nubani, President
SMMI@aol.com
• William Parise, Football Manager
SMMI@aol.com
• Jack Pierce, Track and Field Manager
SMMI@aol.com
Services:
Contract negotiations, Personal
development of the athlete, Sports
Promotions and Special Events
Clients:
Track and Field: Ibrahim Aden, Tacita Bass,
Kameisha Bennett, Brahim Boulami, Khalid
Boulami, Christian Cantwell, Lachlan
Chrisholm, Jearl Miles Clark, Karol Damon,
Dawn Ellerbe, Lindel Frater, Joe Greene,
Abdelkader Hachlaf, MaryJayne Harrelson,
Micah Harris, Kenny Harrison, Mohammed
El Hattab, Aubrey Herring, Godfrey Herring,
Nick Hysong, Denis Kholev, Kris Kuehl, Jeff
Laynes, Nathan Leeper, Kevin Little, Jud
Logan, Brian Miller, Virginia Miller, Maurice
Mitchell, Emily Morris, Justin Norberg, Tracy
O'Hara, Kjersti Platzer, Shanelle Porter,
Mike Power, Connie Price-Smith, Rachid
Ramzi, Todd Riech, Sean Robbins, Karol
Rovelto, Tim Rusan, Sco

SPORTS MANAGEMENT GROUP WORLDWIDE, INC./SMGW
4041 UNIVERSITY DRIVE
SUITE 400
FAIRFAX, VA 22030
703-273-4640
Fax: 703-273-1130
www.smgwinc.com
• Dominick A Pilli, President and Chief
Contract Advisor
dominick.pilli@gmail.com
Description:
SMGW, Inc. is a premier sports marketing
and management firm consisting of clients
from the major professional sports leagues
and their respective Hall of Fames.
Year Founded:
1988
Nature of Services:
Contractional negotiations, representation
agreements and marketing agreements.
Clients:
Clients originate from the major sports
leagues and associations, not limited to
MLB, NFL, NHL, NBA, and the Golf, Tennis,
Soccer and Olympic areas.

SPORTS PERSONALITIES, INC.
3328 COMMERCIAL AVENUE
NORTHBROOK, IL 60062
508-877-6150
847-272-7892
info@personalitiesinc.com
www.personalitiesinc.com
• Michael Carey, President

Services:
All facets of athlete agency representation
and management, including financial and
marketing negotiations and contracts.

SPORTS STARS INTERNATIONAL, INC.
18485 MACK AVENUE
GROSSE POINTE FARMS
DETROIT, MI 48236-3242
313-886-9140
Fax: 313-886-0559
info@SportsStarsInternational.com
www.sportsstarsinternational.com
• Peter J. Huthwaite, President
Services:
Represent professional athletes in football,
basketball, ice hockey, baseball, tennis. All
phases of representation - negotiations,
endorsements, financial planning and
consulting.
Sports Services Founded:
1968.

SPORTS WEST FOOTBALL
27084 GRANDVIEW AVENUE
HAYWARD, CA 94542
510-888-9211
Fax: 510-581-6512
• Angelo Wright, President
(510) 553-7031
Services:
Contract negotiation

SPORTSTARS, INC
1370 AVENUE OF THE AMERICAS
19TH FLOOR
NEW YORK, NY 10019
212-757-4044
Fax: 212-765-4833
www.sportstarsnyc.com

SPORTSWORLD CONSULTANTS
14 SUPREME COURT
GAITHERSBURG, MD 20878
301-977-3735
• Leonard J. Levy, President
(301) 977-3735
Services:
Representation of athletes, including
promotion, contract negotiation, and tax and
financial services.
Sports Service Founded:
1984.

STANLEY & ASSOCIATES
200 12TH STREET
SUITE 800
ARLINGTON, VA 22202
703-310-5570
Fax: 703-310-5560
• Phil O. Nolan, Chairman/President/CEO
• Brian J. Clark, Executive Vice
President/CFO/Treasurer
• Scott D. Chaplin, General
Counsel/Secretary/Senior Vp
• Tom R. Fradette, Cheif Accounting
Officer/Corporate Controller

STEPHENS SPORTS MANAGEMENT INC.
111 CENTER STREET
SUITE 300
LITTLE ROCK, AR 72201
501-377-2000
800-643-9691
Fax: 501-377-2470
www.stephens.com

• Kevin M. Scanlon, President
Services:
Contract negotiation, financial management, etc.
Sports Service Founded:
1987.

STERN, DAVID J.
590 FIFTH AVENUE
NEW YORK, NY 10036
212-515-6221
800-826-7050
Fax: 212-826-6197
dstern@nba.com
www.nba.com
• David J. Stern, Commissioner
Description:
Contract negotiations.

STINGER SPORTS GROUP
1200 S RESERVE STREET
SUITE F
MISSOULA, MT 59801
406-542-0119
Fax: 406-728-4631
• Ken Staninger, Owner/President
(406) 542-0119
• Ken Staninger, Member
(406) 544-3497
• Abdul Noah, Contect
(480) 234-5689
Description:
All phases of athlete representation.
Services:
All phases of athlete representation including talent evaluation, preparation for the draft, counseling, contract negotiations, public appearance and endorsements, and selectivity.

STITES & HARBISON
250 W MAIN STREET
SUITE 2300
LEXINGTON, KY 40507-1758
859-226-2300
Fax: 859-253-9144
general@stites.com
www.stites.com
• Marjorie A. Farris, Member
(502) 779-8258
mfarris@stites.com
• Stephen G. Allen, Member
(859) 226-2257
sallen@stites.com
Nature of Sports Service:
All phases of athlete representation including contract negotiation, long-range planning, financial planning, and post-career counseling.
Services:
Administrative Law, Airport Law, Alternative Dispute Resolution, Antitrust and Consumer Protection Litigation, Appellate Advocacy, Aviation Litigation, Bankruptcy, Business Expansions, Relocations, Joint Ventures & Government Incentive Procurement, Business Litigation, Capital Markets Lending, Charitable and Non-Profit Organizations, Civil Litigation, Class Action Defense, Commercial Disputes-Contracts and Business Torts, Commercial Finance, Community Development and Revitalization, Company Failure, Rehabilitation and Liquidation, Company Management, Governance and Control Litigation, Complex/Large Transaction Litigation Computer Law.

Clients:
AEGON USA Investment Management, Inc., Alcan Aluminum Corporation, The Alliance of Community Hospices & Palliative Care Services, Inc., Alternative Healthcare System, Inc., Ambrake Corporation, American Electric Power, American Institute of Steel Construction, Inc., Anthem Inc., Appriss, Inc., Aqua Tex, ArchVision, Ashland Inc., The Beck Group, BellSouth Corporation, Belo Corp., Bluegrass Conservancy, Robert Bosch Corporation, Boston Scientific Corporation, BrainstormUSA, LLC, Brown-Forman Corporation, Caldwell Tanks, Inc., Cingular Wireless, Columbus (Ohio) Airport Authority, Commonwealth Land Title Insurance Company, The Cordish Company.

STRIVERS GROUP
1100 INDUSTRIAL BOULEVARD
SUITE 3
SAN CARLOS, CA 94070
650-508-8078
Fax: 650-508-4411
• Kelly Cook, President
Services:
Represents professional athletes in contract negotiations, financial guidance, post-career exploration, development, and endorsement.
Sports Service Founded:
1989

SUNDHEIM, GEORGE M., III
DOTY SUNDHEIM & GILMORE
260 SHERIDAN AVENUE, SUITE 200
PALO ALTO, CA 94306
650-327-0100
Fax: 650-327-0101
duf@dotysund.com
www.dslaw.com
• Stanley E Doty, Partner
stan@dotylaw.com
• Annette Barlow, Partner
annette@dotylaw.com
Nature of Sports Service:
All phases of athlete representation including contract negotiation, long-range planning, financial planning, and post-career counseling.
Services:
Business Law, Employment Law and Real Estate Law.

SUNWEST SPORTS
7883 N PERSHING AVENUE
STOCKTON, CA 95207
209-952-9922
Fax: 209-951-3216
• Frank Bauer, President
(805) 773-0367
Services:
All phases of athlete representation.
Description:
All phases of athlete representation.

SUPERSTAR MANAGEMENT, INC.
7633 SUNKIST DRIVE
OAKLAND, CA 94605-3024
510-839-5400
Fax: 510-638-8889
info@superstarmanagement.com
www.superstarmanagement.com
• Abdul Jalil, President/Chief Executive Officer
(510) 839-5400

jalil@superstarmanagement.com
• Ian Faux, VP/Chief Operating Officer
info@superstarmanagement.com
• Kyle Peck, Sports Division
Services:
Provides PRE-DRAFT CONSULTATION. Utilizing the preseason, and post-season industry scouting reports, they market, push, and promote your interest to the selected pro teams they have determined are the best fit for you. SSM assesses the factors of ability and current production of Athlete, publicity and exposure quotient, level of competition, past performance of athlete, ability, needs and financial condition of the selected teams, public acceptance and marketability, desire of athlete, winning team, character and mental toughness, geographical preference of professional team.
Clients:
Muhammad Ali, Brian Taylor, U.S. Rep. J.C. Watts, Warner Bros. Records, Deion Sanders, Byron Stewart, Delvin Williams, Giant Records, Kareem Abdul-Jabbar, M.C. Hammer, Capitol Records, Lyman Bostock, Evander Holyfield, Spencer Haywood, Cliff Robinson
Nature of Sports Service:
Specialties include promoting, representing, advising, negotiating, and arbitrating contracts in the sports and entertainment field.

SYNERGY SPORTS INC.
14001 DALLAS PARKWAY
SUITE 1200
DALLAS, TX 75240
972-934-6562
Fax: 972-934-6508
gglick@synergysportsinc.com
www.synergysportsinc.com
Services:
NFL Pre-Combine Training, NBA Pre-Camp Training, Post-Combine Training, Market Research, Evaluation of Client Position, Development of Negotiation Position and Strategy, Education of Client Regarding Negotiations in Professional Leagues, Interface and Negotiate with Professional Team, Interface with Players Association, Contract Injury and Non-Injury Grievance Issues, Enforcement of Player Agreements, Coordination of Individual Workouts with Professional Teams, Specialized Weight, Speed, Flexibility and Strength Training, Post-Season Orthopedic Evaluations, Nutritional Consultations, Weight Loss Programs, Massage Therapy, Acupuncture and Chi
Sports Service Founded:
1997

TAFT, STETTINIUS & HOLLISTER
425 WALNUT STREET
SUITE 1800
CINCINNATI, OH 45202-3957
513-381-2838
Fax: 513-381-0205
webmaster@taftlaw.com
www.taftlaw.com
• Stephen M. Nechemias, Partner
(513) 357-9392
nechemias@taftlaw.com
• Marcia Voorhis Andrew, Partner
(513) 357-9671
andrew@taftlaw.com

Description:
Represents professional sports teams.
Services:
Offers legal services in areas of: (1) Business and Finance (which handles general business, corporate, mergers, and acquisitions, securities, private and public financing, real estate, banking, and insurance matters); (2) Laborand Employment; (3) Litigation (which includes bankruptcy, environmental and workers' compensation subgroups; and (4) Tax, Probate and Estate Planning.
Clients:
Businesses and individuals engaged in manufacturing, banking, finance, insurance, distribution, television and radio, professional sports, health care, advanced technology, energy, transportation, and real estate, as well as the New Economy.
Year Founded:
1924
Other Locations:
Twelfth Floor, 21 East State Street, Columbus, Ohio 43215-4221. 614-221-2838; FAX: 614-221-2007, 1717 Dixie Highway, Suite 340, Covington, Kentucky 41011-4704. 513-331-2838; FAX: 513-381-6613, 3500 BP Tower, 200 Public Square, Cleveland, Ohio 44114-2302. 216-241-2838; FAX: 216-241-3707, 110 North Main Street, Suite 900, Dayton, Ohio 45402-1786. 937-228-2838; FAX: 937-228-2816

TAGGART, WALTER J.
299 N SPRING MILL ROAD
VILLANOVA, PA 19085
610-519-7010
Fax: 610-519-5672
www.law.villanova.edu
• Nicole Garafano, Events Director
(610) 519-7066
garafano@law.villanova.edu
• Wendy C. Barron, Assistant Dean, Financial Aid
(610) 519-7015
• April ma Barton, Assistant Dean, Academic Computing
(610) 519-5201
• Colleen Belz, Alumni Relations Director
(610) 519-7036
cbelz@law.villanova.edu
• April Barton, Director for Academic Computing
(610) 519-5201
barton@law.villanova.edu
• Colleen Belz, Director of Development
(610) 519-7036
cbelz@law.villanova.edu
• Anthony Cancelli, Director of Business and Support Services
(610) 519-7833
cancelli@law.villanova.edu
• Elizabeth Dunn, Associate Director of Public Service Careers
(610) 519-7228
• Christopher Dwyer, Associate Dean Finance & Administration
(610) 519-7083
• Diane Edelman, Director of International Programs and Associ
(610) 519-7047
edelman@law.villanova.edu
Description:
Contract negotiation.
Services:

Provides professional education that teaches student a probono legal service.

TALENT SPORTS MANAGEMENT
11141 ROSSER ROAD
DALLAS, TX 75229
214-369-2255
Fax: 210-417-4080
• Wollace DeSouza, Agent

TAYLOR, TODD
20 N BROADWAY
SUITE 1800
OKLAHOMA CITY, OK 73102
405-235-7700
Fax: 405-239-6651
taylort@crowedunlevy.com
www.crowedunlevy.com
• Jimmy Goodman, Director
(405) 235-7717
jimmy.goodman@crowedunlevy.com
• Lisa L. Rose, Director, HR and Administration
(405) 235-7777
lisa.rose@crowedunlevy.com
• Robb Pethick, Manager, Administrative Services
(918) 592-9826
rob.pethick@crowedunlevy.com
• Gail Huneryager, Director of Business Development and Marketin
(405) 239-6691
gail.huneryager@crowedunlevy.com
• Tom Keifer, Executive Director
(405) 235-7711
tom.keifer@crowedunlevy.com
• Jeanette Stanton, Business Development Manager
(405) 239-5481
jeanette.stanton@crowedunlevy.com
• Terry Hunter, IT Manager
(405) 239-6670
terry.hunter@crowedunlevy.com
Description:
Contract negotiation.
Services:
Practice areas include administrative and regulatory practice, alternative dispute resolution, antitrust, appellate practice, aviation/aircraft, bankruptcy and creditors' rights, commercial real estate, construction industry, corporate and securities/mergers and acquisitions, employee benefits and ERISA, energy law, environmental, financial institutions and finance, franchising and distribution, healthcare, healthcare litigation, hospitality industry, entertainment and gaming, initiative petition, insurance, intellectual property.

TERRIE WILLIAMS AGENCY
382 CENTRAL PARK W # 7R
SUITE 17U
NEW YORK, NY 10025
212-316-0305
Fax: 212-749-8867
www.terriewilliams.com
• Terrie M. Wiliams, President
Services:
Marketing & Consulting
Clients:
Andre Harrell, Daryl Simmons/Silent Partner Prod., Master P, George Howard, Janet Jackson, Miles Jaye, Kid n' Play, Donna McElroy, Rene McLean, Charnett Moffet, Eddie Murphy, Heavy D, Keith Sweat, Take 6, Jermaine Dupri, Russell Simmons, Boyz

---

II Men, Carl Anderson, Anita Baker, Kathleen Battle, Bobby Brown, Miles Davis, Will Downing, Family Stand, Full Force, Richie Havens, Najee, Jay Hoggard, Lionel Richie, Sean Puffy Combs, NYC Grammy Committee, ASCAP, A Rage in Harlem/Miramax, The Inkwell/Touchstone, Cadence/Republic Pictures, The Five Heartbeats/20th Century Fox, House Party/New Line Cinema, The Meteor Man/MGM, Sarafina/Miramax, Tales fro

---

THEOFANOUS, PAUL
106 W 74TH STREET
NEW YORK, NY 10023
212-874-3043
Fax: 212-874-3997
• Paul Theofanous, President
Description:
Represents professional tennis players and professional hockey players.

THOMPSON HINE
3900 KEY CENTER
127 PUBLIC SQUARE
CLEVELAND, OH 44114-1291
216-566-5500
877-628-5500
Fax: 216-566-5800
www.thompsonhine.com
• Mark S Floyd, Vice Chair, Labor & Employment Practice
(216) 566-5836
• Robert B. Ford, Partner
(216) 566-5603
Nature of Sports Service:
Handles sports entertainment services, represents strategic investor in syndicated sports media content site.
Clients:
Alltel, Anthem Blue Cross/Blue Shield, Avery Dennison, Bank One Corporation, BIC Corporation, CH Energy Group, Central Hudson Gas & Electric Corporation, Charter One Bank FSB, Chemed, Davey Tree Expert Company, Duke Realty Corp., Eaton Corporation, Energizer/Eveready, Executive Jet Aviation, FirstMerit Corporation, FlowServe Corporation, Ford Motor Company, Ford Motor Credit, Forest City Enterprises, Inc., Formica Corp., Goodrich Corporation, Goodyear Tire and Rubber Co., Hobart Corporation, Howard Hanna Smythe Cramer, Indiana Insurance Co., Jo-Ann Stores, Inc., Kelly Services, Inc., KeyCorp/KeyBank, Lexis Nexis, Limited Brands, MeadWestvaco

---

THOMSON, WILLIAM R.
201 ONEAL STREET
BELTON, SC 29627-1410
864-338-7168
Fax: 864-338-7168
• William R. Thomson, Attorney
Description:
Contract negotiation.
Services:
Legal Services (Real Estate Law)

TOP NOTCH SPORTS MANAGEMENT
7324 SW FREEWAY
SUITE 349
HOUSTON, TX 77074
713-995-4681
800-903-9004
Fax: 713-995-4685

• Leroy M. Daniels, NFLPA Certified Contract Advisor/Agent
Nature of Sports Service:
All phases of athlete representation including contract negotiation, long-range planning, financial planning, and post-career counseling.

TRUE NORTH SPORTS MANAGEMENT
55 TABOR PLACE
SOUTH BURLINGTON, VT 05403
802-233-3478
info@truenorthsportsmgt.com
www.truenorthsportsmgt.com
• Erica Vessey, President/CEO
(802) 233-3478
info@truenorthsportsmgt.com
• Erica MacConnell, Marketing Director
(802) 233-3478
erica@kensowles.com
Description:
A full service athlete management and sports promotion company representing athletes and businesses in a variety of action sports. Contract negotiation, post career planning, endorsement exploration, represents sports organizations. Turn Key sports promotions and events.

TUDOR, DAVID F.
1047 MAPLE AVENUE
PO BOX 1775
NOBLESVILLE, IN 46060-2837
317-773-0600
Fax: 317-773-0610
Description:
Contract negotiation.

U/S SPORTS ADVISORS
250 EAST 96TH STREET
SUITE 450
INDIANAPOLIS, IN 46240
317-569-0300
Fax: 317-569-0393
dmartin@ussportsadvisors.com
www.ussportsadvisors.com
• Ungar Ken, President
(317) 569-0381
kungar@ussportsadvisors.com
• Krissi Edgington, Vice President of Marketing
(317) 569-0202
kedgington@ussportsadvisors.com
• Teri Toler, Vice President, Administration
(317) 569-0351
• David Martin, Vice President, Business Development
(704) 904-7872
dmartin@ussportsadvisors.com
• Ronda Hite, Controller
(317) 569-0220
rhite@ussportsadvisors.com

U/S Sports Advisors is a privately owned sports and entertainment marketing agency. Since 2006, our agency has served as a partner and strategic advisors to sponsors, leagues, governing bodies, teams, and athletes. We are known for our steadfast belief in their goals and our commitment to showcasing their brands in authentic and unexpected ways. Our experience in the sports and entertainment industries help clients connect to markets and fan bases that constantly change. We like to win. That's why we play smarter. We'll help you play smarter.

UNIVERSAL SPORTS ASSOCIATES, INC.
12 S FIRST AVENUE
ST. CHARLES, IL 60174
630-377-7430
800-321-7430
Fax: 630-584-3081
• Tom Selakovich, President
Nature of Sports Service:
All phases of athlete representation including contract negotiation, long-range planning, financial planning, and post-career counseling.

UPDIKE, THEODORE R.
4600 S MILL AVENUE
SUITE 130
TEMPE, AZ 85282-6758
602-820-4489
Fax: 602-820-8225
• Theodore R. Updike, Attorney

VANTAGE SPORTS MANAGEMENT
PO BOX 3140
WINTER PARK, FL 32790-3140
407-628-3131
Fax: 407-628-3121
• Scott Siegel, President
• Jeffrey Siegel, Chairman
• Alex Chehansky, Managing Director, Business Development
• Davey Johnson, Senior Advisor, Baseball
Services:
Client Management, Strategic Alliances, Sports and Event Marketing

VECTOR SPORTS MANAGEMENT LTD. CO.
417 KELLER PARKWAY
KELLER, TX 76248-2302
817-337-4494
Services:
Contract Negotiation, Career Management, Commercial Development, Training
Sports Service Founded:
1989

WALDON, GROUP THE
560 WHITE PLAINS ROAD
TARRYTOWN CORPORATE CENTER
TARRYTOWN, NY 10591
914-332-9700
Fax: 914-332-0020
office@waldenmed.com
www.waldenmed.com
• James A. W. Walden, Founder
• Richard S. Cohen, President
• Merle Symes, Leader
• Daniel J. Doyle, Chief Executive
• Steve Steiber, Executive
Services:
Guides the careers of such athletes and entertainers

WALLACH ENTERTAINMENT
1400 BRAERIDGE DRIVE
BEVERLY HILLS, CA 90210
310-278-4574
Fax: 310-273-0548
wallach1@sbcglobal.net
• George Wallach, President
Services:
Contract negotiation, appearances, endorsements, commercials, athlete career management and planning, theatrical planning, as well as financial management; Summer camps, clinics. Designs programs

to assist companies in promoting their products and/or services; Advises, advertising agencies and companies on use of athletes, as well as obtaining athletes for such organizations. Also produces movies and TV sport shows.

WARREN ASSOCIATES
2901 BRIGHTON ROAD
PITTSBURGH, PA 15212
412-766-5757
Fax: 412-766-6993
www.warrenassociates.net
• Mark Bolster, President
(412) 734-3757
Services:
Provide the highest quality production services in photography
Clients:
Fortune 500 companies like Heinz, Disney, and PPG, to non-profit organizations including The Smithsonian and National Geographic, and entertainment businesses such as Universal Studios, IMG, the NFL, and ESPN.

WEG & MEYERS
52 DUANE STREET
2ND FLOOR
FEDERAL PLAZA
NEW YORK, NY 10007
212-227-4210
Fax: 212-349-6702
• Dennis T. D'Antonio, Partner
• Joshua L. Mallin, Partner
• William H. Parash, Partner
Nature of Sports Service:
All phases of athlete representation including contract negotiation, long-range planning, financial planning, and post-career counseling.
Services:
Represent the large and small property owners in suits against third parties who are responsible for causing damage to property, the representation of public adjusters and insurance brokers in suits against insurance companies and the prosecution of claims against insurance brokers in cases where their negligence has caused or contributed to coverage issues in connection with a policyholder's claim.
Clients:
Tishman-Speyer Realty Helmsley-Spear Inc., Witkoff Group Manocherian Real Estate Developers, Industrial Acoustics Co. William Zeckendorf, T.I.I. Industries Harry Macklowe, Adelphi University National Hockey League, The Gitano Group, Inc. Bank Leumi, Allou Distributors New York National Bank, Kenar Enterprises, Ltd. Proskauer, Rose, Goetz & Mendelsohn, LLP, Oleg Cassini Sol G. Atlas Realty Company, Inc, Berkshire Bank American Rice, Inc., Newmark & Co. Real Estate, Inc. Ranch One, Inc. and Ben Arnold-Sunbelt Beverage Company

WEINER LESNIAK LLP
629 PARSIPPANNY ROAD
PO BOX 438
PARSIPANNY, NJ 07054
973-403-1100
Fax: 973-403-0010
VFarrow@weinerlesniak.com
www.weinerlesniak.com

• Paul M Weiner, Senior Partner/Managing Partner
pweiner@weinerlesniak.com
• Raymond J Lesniak, Senior Partner/Corporate Law Department
rlesniak@weinerlesniak.com
• Howard E. Brecher, Partner/Tort Defense Division Head
hbrechner@weinerlesniak.com
• Louis I. Karp, Partner
lkarp@weinerlesniak.com
Nature of Sports Service:
All phases of athlete representation including contract negotiation, long-range planning, financial planning, and post-career counseling.
SERVICES:
Legal services to both the established business and the emerging technology company.

WEISS, ARTHUR B.
777 FRANKLIN AVENUE
SUITE 2
FRANKLIN LAKES, NJ 7417
201-891-6030
888-741-3206
Fax: 201-848-0311
• Arthur B. Weiss, Partner
Description:
Contract negotiation, appearances, endorsements, legal service, public relations.
Clients:
Football: Wayne Chrebet, Arlen Harris, Stephen Bowen, Devale Ellis, Mike Barr, Chas Gessner, Leon Johnson, Glen Foley, Dave Fiore, Gary Reasons, Blake Costanzo.

WHITE, STANLEY R.
10716 POT SPRING ROAD
COCKEYSVILLE, MD 21030
410-628-7543
Description:
Contract negotiation, arbitration hearings, endorsement exploration.

WIDENER UNIVERSITY SPORT MANAGEMENT
WIDENER UNIVERSITY ONE UNIVERSITY PLACE
CHESTER, PA 19013
610-499-1182
888-943-3637
888-WIDENER
Fax: 610-499-4614
bvlarson@widener.edu
www.widener.edu
• Brian Larson, Coodinator/ Sport Management
(610) 499-1182
brlarson@widener.edu
• Greg Cermignano, Faculty
(610) 499-4311
• Joe Fuhr, Faculty
(610) 499-1172
• Nicholas P. Trainer, Chairman
(610) 499-4512
• John H. Tilelli Jr., Vice Chair
• James T. Harris, President
• Joseph J. Baker, MBA, Senior Vice President for Administration and
(610) 499-4156
jjbaker@widener.edu
• Marcine Pickron-Davis, PhD, Chief Community Engagement and Diversity Offi
(610) 499-4566

Nature of Service:
Widener's Sport Management program is one of the most rigorous and longest established program in the region. It is housed in the AAC5B-accredited School of Business Administration. Working with such teams as the Philadelphia Phillies, Sixers, Flyers and Eagles.
Year Founded:
1995
Description:
Academic, undergraduate program that works closely with industry experts from professional sport teams (Philadelphia Flyers; Philadelphia 76ers; Philadelphia Eagles; Philadelphia Union; Philadelphia Phillies), semipro teams (Wilmington Blue Rocks), retailers(Dick's Sporting Goods) and sporting goods manufacturer(Gore Tex).

WILDMAN, JOSEPH L.
1188 BISHOP STREET
SUITE 1811
HONOLULU, HI 96813-3307
808-521-5297

WILLIAMS & CONNOLLY
725 TWELFTH STREET, NW
WASHINGTON, DC 20005
202-434-5000
Fax: 202-434-5029
info@wc.com
• Richard M. Cooper, Partner
(202) 434-5466
rcooper@wc.com
• David E. Kendall, Partner
(202) 434-5145
dkendall@wc.com
• Jerry L. Shulman, Partner
(202) 434-5510
jshulman@wc.com
• James L. Tanner Jr, Partner
(202) 434-5104
jtanner@wc.com
Nature of Sports Service:
All phases of athlete representation including contract negotiation, long-range planning, financial planning, and post-career counseling.
Services:
Provide general business advice and representation, for assistance in negotiating contracts, leases, and league structures, for specific advice on how to structure their businesses to avoid controversy, and to represent them in major litigation/arbitration disputes. Also includes radio, television, and cable broadcast agreements; stadium leases; stadium construction agreements; advertising and sponsorship agreements; and player arbitration; Provides legal services.

WITLIN PROFESSIONAL MANAGEMENT
7805 SW 6TH COURT
PLANTATION, FL 33324
954-473-4500
Fax: 954-473-1970
barrywitlin@gmail.com
• Barry Witlin, President
(954) 473-4500
barrywitlin@gmail.com

WONG, STANTON
733 BISHOP STREET
SUITE 2675
HONOLULU, HI 96813
808-536-3826
Fax: 808-536-3828
• Leighton Wong, President
(808) 536-3826
Services:
Contract negotiation

WOOLF ASSOCIATES, INC.
101 HUNTINGTON AVENUE
BOSTON, MA 2199
617-437-1212
Services:
Represents professional athletes and entertainment personalities

WORLD SPORTS GROUP, LTD.
419 E 57TH STREET
SUITE 9A
NEW YORK, NY 10022-3060
212-260-5001
Fax: 212-412-9022

WORLDWIDE SPORTS MANAGEMENT
45-14 30TH AVENUE
ASTORIA, NY 11103
718-204-2078
Fax: 718-204-2097
info@nysalamina.com
www.nysalamina.com

YEE & DUBIN LLP
725 S FIGUEROA STREET
SUITE 3085
LOS ANGELES, CA 90017-5430
213-892-7420
Fax: 213-892-7421
info@yeedubin.com
www.yeedubin.com
• Donald H. Yee, Partner
• Stephen L. Dubin, Partner
Description:
Contract negotiation; represents professional sports athletes and coaches; licensing; endorsement exploration; sports business consulting.

ZANE MANAGEMENT, INC.
1650 MARKET STREET
ONE LIBERTY PLACE, 56TH FL00R
PHILADELPHIA, PA 19103-7334
215-790-1155
Fax: 215-575-3801
lzr@braverlaw.com
www.zanemanagement.com
• Lloyd Zane Remick, President
• Christopher J. Cabott, Co-Founder
• Christopher J. Cabott, Associate Attorney
Services:
Provides Personal Management, Legal-Expert Contract Negotiation and Advice, Expert Witness Testimony Hospitality, Tourism & Event Planning, Appearances & Endorsements, Accounting & Tax Services, Teamwork; Soliciting and attracting sponsorships; Representing corporations in virtually all of their celebrity sales promotional and marketing needs.
Clients:
Merrill Reese, Lisa Natson p/k/a Golden Girl, Pat Ciarrochi, Marc Howard, Phil Andrews, Phil Jasner, Monica Malpass,Joyce Evans, John Valerio, Lisa

Thomas-Laury, Vernon Odom, Wally Kennedy, Dina Bair, Andrew Colton, Nicole Fox, Denise James, Laura Jones, Don Polec, Kathy Levine

Sports Attorneys

ABES & BAUMANN
810 PENN AVENUE
5TH FLOOR
PITTSBURGH, PA 15222-3614
412-228-4786
Fax: 412-765-0906
www.abesbaumann.com
• Edward Jaffee Abes, Esquire
eja@abesbaumann.com
• Thomas C Baumann, Esquire
tcb@abesbaumann.com
• Edward Jaffee Abes, Partner
(412) 228-4786
• Susan Paczak, Esquire
sp@abesbaumann.com
• Thomas C. Baumann, Partner
(412) 228-4786
• James R. Burn Jr., Associate
(412) 228-4786
• Douglas A. Williams, Associate
(412) 228-4786
Description;
Law Firm concentrating in representing Workers' Compensation claimants in Pennsylvania.
Services:
Representing professional athletes in Worker's Compensation saces including, but not limited to football, hoceky, baseball and soccer players.
Clients:
Members of NFLPA, PHPA, NHLPA, MLBPA and others

ABRAHAM, WATKINS, NICHOLS, SORRELS, MATTHEWS & FRIEND
800 COMMERCE STREET
HOUSTON, TX 77002
713-222-7211
713-587-9668
Fax: 713-225-0827
www.abrahamwatkins.com
• Nick C. Nichols, Partner
(713) 222-7211
nnichols@abrahamwatkins.com
• Randall Owen Sorrels, Partner
(713) 222-7211
• Randall Ow Sorrels, Partner
(713) 222-7211
rsorrels@abrahamwatkins.com
• David P. Matthews, Partner
(713) 222-7211
dmatthews@abrahamwatkins.com
Services:
Provides legal services representing individuals and families who suffer catastrophic injuries and wrongful death
Description:
Tort actions/litigation.
Year Founded:
1951

ACKERMAN, VALERIE B.
645 5TH AVENUE
OLYMPIC TOWER
NEW YORK, NY 10022
212-407-8000
Fax: 212-750-9622
www.wnba.com
• Laurel J. Richie, President
(212) 407-8000
• Christine Godleski, Chief Operating Officer
• Renea€š Brown, Chief of Basketball Operations and Player Rel
• Todd DeMoss, Senior Director, Basketball Operations
• Dipali Ottaviani, Director, WNBA Team Business Development:
• Dina Skokos, Director, WNBA Communications
• Patrick Mulrenin, Director
Description:
Represents NBA.
Services:
Legal Services
Clients:
NBA

ADAMS & REESE
701 POYDRAS STREET, ONE SHELL SQUARE
SUITE 4500
NEW ORLEANS, LA 70139
504-581-3234
Fax: 504-566-0210
www.adamsandreese.com
• Charles P Adams Jr, Managing Partner
(601) 353-3234
charles.adams@arlaw.com
• M. Ann Huckstep, Chairman/Executive Committee
(205) 250-5009
ann.huckstep@arlaw.com
• Robert M Shofstahl, Chief Administrative Officer
(225) 615-8400
• Paul J Lassalle, Chief Financial Officer
(225) 615-8400
paul.lassalle@arlaw.com
Description:
Contract negotiation, arbitration hearings, endorsement exploration, tort actions/litigation.
Other Locations:
450 Laurel Street, STE 1900, Baton Rouge, LA 70801; Phone: 225-336-5200; Concord CÃ†enter, 2100 Third Avenue North, STE 1100, Birmingham, AL 35203; Phone: 205-250-5000; One Houston Center, 1221 McKinney, STE 4400, Houston TX 77010; 713-652-5151; 111 East Capitol Street, STE 350, Jackson, MS 39201; Phone: 601-353-3234; One St. Louis Street, STE 4500, Mobile, AL 33602; Phone: 251-433-3234; Market Square North, 401 9th Street, STE 610 South, Washington, DC 20004; Phone: 202-737-3234

ADAMSKI MOROSKI MADDEN & GREEN LLP
6633 BAY LAUREL PLACE
AVILA BEACH, CA 93424
805-543-0990
Fax: 805-543-0980
info@ammcglaw.com
• Steven J Adamski, Partner/Co-Founder
• Martin P. Moroski, Partner/Co-Founder
• Thomas J. Madden III, Partner
• Thomas D. Green, Partner
• Steven J. Adamski, Partner
(805) 543-0990
• Martin P. Moroski, Partner/Co-Founder
(805) 543-0990

• Thomas J. Madden, Partner
• John Nicholson, Partner
• David Cumberland,
(805) 543-0990
• Raymond A. Biering, Partner
(805) 543-0990
Description:
Business Litigation; Commercial Litigation; Insurance Litigation; Real Property Litigation; Intellectual Property Litigation; Sports Law; Construction Defect Litigation; Product Liability Litigation.
Other Locaation:
1200 Vine Street, Paso Robles, CA 93446; Phone: 805-238-2300

ADELMAN, DANIEL W.
27 ELM STREET
NEW HAVEN, CT 06510
203-777-5007
Fax: 203-782-9830
heidi@adelmanlawct.com
www.adelmanlawct.com
• Daniel W. Adelman, President
(203) 777-5007
adelaw@aol.com
• Anne E. Epstein, Partner
adelaw@aol.com
Services:
Contract negotiation, arbitration hearings.
Description:
Family law

ADKINS, M. DOUGLAS
1601 ELM STREET
SUITE 3000
THANKSGIVING TOWER
DALLAS, TX 75201-4761
214-999-3000
Fax: 214-999-4667
www.gardere.com
• M. D. Adkins, Partner
(214) 999-4444
dadkins@gardere.com
• Michael A. Abbott, Partner
(713) 276-5571
mabbott@gardere.com
• James F Adama, Partner
(214) 999-4846
• Stephen Good, Managing Partner
(214) 999-4216
sgood@gardere.com
Other Locations:
One American Center, STE 3000, 600 Congress Avenue, Austin, TX 78707; Phone: 512-542-7000; Fax: 512-542-7100; 1601 Elm Street, STE 3000, Dallas, TX 75201; Phone: 214-999-3000; Fax: 214-999-4667; 1000 Louisiana, STE 3400, Houston, TX 77002; Phone: 713-276-5500; Fax: 713-276-5555;
Services:
Legal Services

ADLER & BLASS
89 FIFTH AVENUE
SUITE 902
NEW YORK, NY 10003
212-465-1718
Fax: 212-629-4005
• Norman Blass, Attorney
• Jonathan Blass, Attorney
Services:
Contract negotiation

ALCOX, PATRICK
75 PUBLIC SQUARE
SUITE 650
CLEVELAND, OH 44113
216-575-1560
Fax: 216-241-4851
• Patrick Alcox, Attorney/Owner
Services:
NFLPA worker's compensation panel
Cleveland Browns, Workers Compensation,
Sports Injury, Social Security Disability,
Personal Injury.

ALEXANDER & ASSOCIATES, P.C. MARY
44 MONTGOMERY STREET
SUITE 1303
SAN FRANCISCO, CA 94104
866-802-9497
877-454-9315
Fax: 415-433-5440
www.maryalexanderlaw.com
• Mary E. Alexander, Attorney/Principal
• Jennifer L. Fiore, Associate
• Mary E. Alexander, Attorney
• Sophia M. Aslami, Attorney
Description:
Courtroom preparation is the tademark of
our successful trial firm and we use
innovative courtroom exhibits to help juries
understand even the most complex legal
cases. Because the firm's strength has been
in innovation, creativity and preparation we
have been able to achieve an outstanding
record of success.
Services:
Legal Services

ALLMAN & MITZNER, LLC
1775 SHERMAN STREET
21ST FLOOR
DENVER, CO 80203
303-293-9393
Fax: 303-293-3130
www.allman-mitzner.com
• Robert L. Allman, Attorney
rallman@allman-mitzner.com
• John P. Mitzner, Attorney
Description:
NFLPA workers' compensation panel.
Services:
Legal Services

AMBROSE LAW GROUP, LLP
222 SW COLUMBIA STREET
SUITE 1670
PORTLAND, OR 97201-6616
503-222-0552
Fax: 503-222-0984
www.ambroselaw.com
• Christopher Ambrose, Attorney
crambrose@ambroselaw.com
• Janis K Alexander, Chief Operating Officer
(503) 222-0552
jkalexander@ambroselaw.com
• David R. Ambrose, Attorney
drambrose@ambroselaw.com
Services:
Legal Services

**ANAPOL, SCHWARTZ, WEISS, COHAN,
FELDMAN & SMALLEY, P.C.**
1710 SPRUCE STREET
PHILADELPHIA, PA 19103
215-735-1130
866-735-2792
Fax: 215-735-2211
www.anapolschwartz.com

• Nathaniel E. Ehrlich, Attorney
(610) 375-2750
nehrlich@anapolschwartz.com
• Alan Schwartz, Shareholder
(215) 735-0330
aschwartz@anapolschwartz.com
• Thomas R Anapol, Shareholder
(215) 790-4572
tanapol@anapolschwartz.com
• Sol H. Weiss, Shareholder
(215) 735-2098
sweiss@anapolschwartz.com
Services:
Arbitration hearings, tort actions/litigation.
Represents injured and terminated
professional athletes in collective bargaining
contract grievances, and in claims resulting
from their injuries.
Year Founded:
1977
Other Locations:
1900 Delancy Place, Philadelphia, PA
19103; Phone: 215-735-1130; 920 Trenton
Road, Fairless Hills, PA 19030; Phone:
215-945-6799; 1040 Kings Highway North,
STE 304, Cherry Hill, NJ 08034; Phone:
856-482-1600; 146 North 6th Street,
Reading, PA 19601; Phone: 610-375-2750;
334 West Front Street, Media, PA 19063;
Phone: 610-892-3714

ANDERSON & TUCKER
2101 FIFTH AVENUE N
PO BOX 360
ST. PETERSBURG, FL 33713
727-323-8886
800-458-6811
Fax: 727-323-3252
• Donald C. Anderson, Attorney
(727) 323-8886
• John V. Tucker, Attorney
(727) 323-8886
• Shannon Black, Staff
• Angela Jensen, Staff
• Stanice Anderson, Owner
• Mike Tucker, Owner
Services:
Legal Services

ANDREWS KURTH LLP
450 LEXINGTON AVENUE
NEW YORK, NY 10017
212-850-2800
Fax: 212-850-2929
webmaster@andrewskurth.com
www.andrewskurth.com
• Howard Ayers, CEO/Managing Partner
(713) 220-4044
• David Barbour, Partner
Corporate/Securities
(214) 659-4444
dbarbour@andrewskurth.com
• Richard Caldwell, Partner Litigation
(713) 220-4712
• Jason S Brookner, Partner
(214) 659-4457
• Andrew Feiner, Partner
(212) 850-2883
• Donna D Kim, Partner
(212) 850-2818
• Jessica Chue, Associate
(212) 850-2841
• Mathew A Gray, Associate
(212) 850-2834
• Rinat Hafizov, Associate
(212) 850-2810
• Brian M Clarke, Associate
(212) 850-2825

Services:
Provides services for corporate litigation,
bankruptcy reorganization, labor and
employment, environmental, real estate,
public law, securitization, benefits/executive
compensation, antitrust, corporate/securities
and a host of other legal problems.
Clients:
Clients includes private individuals and
corporations such as: Texas Water Dev.
Board, Texas Public Finance Authority,
Texas State Affordable Housing Corp., Univ.
of Houston, Harris County, City of Houston,
Houston Independent School Dist.,
Goldman Sachs, JP Morgan Securities,
Morgan Stanley, UBS Financial Services,
Coastal Securities, First Southwest
Company, Morgan Keegan & Co. and RBC
Dain Rauscher.

ARNET, WILLIAM F.
1100 CARRIE FRANCKE DRIVE
277 UNIVERSITY HALL
COLUMBIA, MO 65211-3020
573-882-2121
icshelpdesk@umsystem.edu
www.umsystem.edu
• Gary Forsee, President
(573) 882-2011
• Gordon H. Lamb, Executive Vice President
• Natalie Krawitz, Finance and
Administration VP
(573) 882-3611
krawitzn@umsystem.edu
• Stephen J. Owens, General Counsel
(573) 882-3211
owenssj@umsystem.edu
• Katharine S. Bunn, Counsel
(573) 882-3211
bunnk@umsystem.edu
• Susan M. Gardner, Counsel
(573) 882-3211
• Nancie D. Hawke, Counsel
(573) 882-3211
hawken@umsystem.edu
Services:
Learning institution committed to discover,
disseminate, preserve, and apply
knowledge. Promotes learning and fosters
innovation to support economic
development, and advances the health,
cultural, and social interests.
Description:
Represents college athletic departments.

ASHFORD & WRISTON
1099 ALAKEA STREET
ALII PLACE SUITE 1400
HONOLULU, HI 96813
808-539-0400
Fax: 808-533-4945
atty@awlaw.com
www.ashfordwriston.com
• A. Ja Wriston Jr, Of Counsel
(808) 539-0412
jwriston@awlaw.com
• Paul S. Aoki, Partner
(808) 539-0467
• Kirk W. Caldwell, Partner
(808) 539-0461
• Rosemary T. Fazio, Partner
(808) 539-0415
rfazio@awlaw.com
Services:
Provides legal expertise with emphasis in all
aspects of real property law and civil
litigation.
Clients:

Barnwell Industries, Bank of Hawaii, Dept. of Hawaiian Homelands, Finance Realty Co., Ltd., First Hawaiian Bank, Ford Motor Credit Corp., Hawaii Credit Union League, Hawaii Medical Services Assoc., Hawaii Reserves, Inc., Hawaii State Federal Credit Union, Kahua Ranch Ltd., Kamehameha Investment Corp., Kamehameha Schools, Kaneohe Ranch, Knudsen Trust, McCandless Ranch, Old Republic Title Co., Parker Ranch, Queen Liliuokalani Trust, The Queen Emma Foundation, Queen's Medical Center, State of Hawaii, Roman Catholic Church in the State of Hawaii, The Rehabilitation Hospital of the Pacific, Territorial Savings & Loan Association.

AULTMAN, TYNER, ET AL
315 HEMPHILL STREET
PO DRAWER 750
HATTIESBURG, MS 39403
601-583-2671
Fax: 601-583-2677
• Thomas W. Tyner,
Description:
Contract negotiation, licensing, endorsement exploration, tort actions/litigation.

BAIZLEY, DONALD
201 PORTAGE AVENUE
SUITE 2200
WINNIPEG, MB, CANADA R3B 3L3
204-957-1930
855-483-7529
Fax: 204-940-0570
info@tdslaw.com
www.tdslaw.com
• P. Mi Sinclair, Q.C., Managing Partner
(204) 934-2493
pms@tdslaw.com
• David J. Bailey, Executive Director
(204) 934-2500
djb@tdslaw.com
• Ainslie Brown, Comptroller
(204) 934-2510
ainslie@tdslaw.com
• Linda Balance, HR Administrator
(204) 934-2424
linda@tdslaw.com
Services:
Provides law services in the following areas: aboriginal, administrative, alternative dispute resolution, business, construction, environmental, family, financial services, government and regulatory, insolvency, bankruptcy, insurance, intellectual property, labor and employment, litigation, natural resources and energy, property development, municipal, securities, taxation, sports and entertainment, technology and trusts, estates and fiduciary obligations.

BAKER & DANIELS
300 N MERIDIAN STREET
SUITE 2700
INDIANAPOLIS, IN 46204-1750
317-237-0300
800-382-5426
Fax: 317-237-1000
webmaster@bakerd.com
www.bakerdaniels.com
• Brian K. Burke, Chair/Chief Executive Officer
(317) 237-1242
Brian.Burke@bakerd.com
• Melanie S. Green, Director of Business

Development & Marketing
(317) 237-1334
melanie.green@bakerd.com
• Thomas C. Fox, Legal Administrator
(260) 460-1712
Tom.Fox@bakerd.com
• Jacqueline K. Kost, Legal Personnel Director
(317) 237-1105
Jacqueline.Kost@bakerd.com
Description:
Represents professional sports teams (Seattle Mariners).
Services:
Provides an array of integrated services in the following fields of legal services, medical technology, public affairs and federal relations.
Clients:
Alimentation Couche-Tard Inc., American Commercial Lines, Borg/Warner Inc., Bridgestone Corp., Bunge North America, Inc., Central Indiana Corporate Partnership, Circle K, Citizens Gas & Coke Utility, City of Indianapolis, Clarian Health Partners, Cummins Inc., Eli Lilly and Co., Fleetwood Ent., Guidant Corp., Indiana Dept. of Insurance, Indiana Univ., Indianapolis Bond Bank, Indianapolis Public Schools, Integra Bank Corp., JP Morgan Chase & Co., Kimball International Inc., Lear Corpo., Lehman Brothers, Lilly Endowment, Mac's Convenience Stores Inc., Mittal Steel USA, Inc., National Org. of Life and Health Insurance Guaranty Associations, Pinna
Other Locations:
600 East 96th Street, STE 600, Indianapolis, IN 46240; Phone: 317-569-9600; 111 East Wayne Street, STE 800, Fort Wayne, IN 46802; Phone: 260-424-8000; First Bank Building, 205 West Jefferson Blvd, STE 250 South Bend, IN 46601; Phone: 574-234-4149; 317 West Franklin Street, Elkhard, IN 46515; Phone: 574-296-6000; 805 15th Street, NW, STE 700, Washington, DC 2005; Phone: 202-312-7440

BAKER & MCKENZIE
130 E RANDOPLH DRIVE
ONE PRUDENTIAL PLAZA SUITE 2500
CHICAGO, IL 60601
312-861-8800
Fax: 312-861-8823
• John Conroy, Chairman
• David P. Hackett, Partner Chicago
(312) 861-6640
david.p.hackett@bakernet.com
• Nicholas F. Coward, Partner Washington DC
(202) 452-7021
nicholas.f.coward@bakernet.com
• Eduardo C. M. Leite, Chairman of execuitve board
• Raymundo E. Enriquez, Partner
• Greg C Walters, Global COO
• Peter Engstorm, Legal Counsel
• Michael Campbell, Global director of knowledge
Description:
Arbitration hearings, endorsement exploration.
Services:
Provides legal services in the following areas: antittrust & trade, banking & finance, corporate, dispute resolution, employment, insurance, intellectual property, international/commercial, IT/communications, major projects & project

finance, pharmaceuticals & healthcare, real estate, construction, environment & tourism and tax matters.
Other Location:
One Prudential Plaza, STE 2500, Chicago, IL 60601; Phone: 312-861-8800

BAKER, DAVID L.
1000 E UNIVERSITY AVENUE
LARAMIE, WY 82071
307-766-1121
www.uwyo.edu
• Thomas Buchanan, President
(307) 766-4121
tombuch@uwyo.edu
• Andrew Hansen, ACE Fellow
(307) 766-4121
hansen@uwyo.edu
• Shannon Sanchez, Executive Administrative Assistant
(307) 766-4121
sanchez@uwyo.edu
• Kellie A. Southards, President's Staff Associate
(307) 766-4122
ksouth@uwyo.edu
• Janet Lowe, Interim VP-Fiscal Admin
• Mark A. Collins, Interim VP-Operations
• Katy Hudson, Coord Financial Services
• Jeffery Greenwald, Manager
• Sheralyn Farnham, Analyst Executive
• Joshua Decker, Manager-Real Estate Ops
Description:
Represents college athletic departments.
Services:
Provider of baccalaureate and graduate education, research, and outreach services.

BALTIMORE, BRYON
10088-102 AVENUE
2401 TD TOWER
EDMONTON, ALBERTA, CANADA T5J 2Z1
780-426-4660
Fax: 780-426-0982
lawyers@mccuaig.com
www.mccuaig.com
• Bryon Baltimore, Lawyer
(780) 441-3418
bbaltimore@mccuaig.com
• Robert M. Curtis, Lawyer
(780) 426-4660
rcurtis@mccuaig.com
• Branny M. Schepanovich, Lawyer
(780) 441-3404
bschepanovich@mccuaig.com
• Robert M. Curtis, Lawyer
rcurtis@mccuaig.com
Services:
Provides high quality legal services to individual, corporate and institutional clients in the following fields of expertise: aboriginal, corporate/commercial, employment, immigration & citizenship, labour, litigation, municipal, real estate, administrative, criminal, family law, intellectual property, landlord & tenant, mediation/ADR, personal injury and wills & estate law.
Clients:
Bryon Baltimore serves as certified agent for National Hockey Leage Player's Association.

BARRETT, WILLIAM A.
LAKE MERRITT PLAZA
1999 HARRISON ST.

SUITE 1700
OAKLAND, CA 94612-4700
510-465-7100
Fax: 510-465-8556
www.mcinerney-dillon.com
• William A. Barrett, Partner
(415) 558-4169
• Stacey Bales, Firm Administrator
Services:
Provides business & commercial legal
services

BARTH, BERUS & CALDERON, LLP
333 CITY BOULEVARD W
SUITE 2050, CITY TOWER
ORANGE, CA 92868-2944
714-704-4828
800-548-8564
Fax: 714-704-1513
www.hmbfinlaw.com
• Harry M. Barth, Senior Partner
(714) 704-4828
• Joy Gi Berus, Partner
(714) 704-4828
• David R. Calderon, Attorney
(714) 704-4828
• Bradley G. Barth, Associate
Attorney/Notary Public
(714) 704-4828
• Harry M. Barth, Founding Member/Senior
Partner
(714) 704-4828
harry@barthattorneys.com
• David R. Calderon, Partner
(714) 704-4828
david@barthattorneys.com
• David M. Huynh, Associate
(714) 704-4828
• Matthew Amaro, Associate
(714) 704-4828
• Chris Barsness, Attorney/Finance &
Business Management Consul
(714) 704-4828
• Darry C. Sheetz, Of Counsel
(949) 553-0300
Description:
Provides individual, family and business
clients with legal representation that
concentrates on asset protection planning.
We address our client's immediate concerns
while anticipating and safeguarding their
long-term business, financial and personal
interests. Our clientele includes individuals
as well as many leading companies in the
healthcare, manufacturing and food-related
industries.
Clients:
Seminars conducted: Banfield Charter
Practice, Pet Hospitals/Petsmart, Burger
King - Dallas/Fortworth Burger King
Franchisee Association,Burger King -
Mid-America Burger King Franchisee
Association, Burger King - Mid-Atlantic
Burger King Association, Burger King -
National Franchisee Association
Conventions,Burger King - Northern
California Burger King Franchisee
Association,Burger King - Northwest Burger
King Franchisee Association,Burger King -
Southern California Burger King Franchisee
Association,Burger King - Southwest Burger
King Franchisee Association, Burger King -
Texas Franchisee Association.

BASSFORD, LOCKHART, TRUESDELL & BRIGGS, P.A.
33 S SIXTH STREET
SUITE 3800
MINNEAPOLIS, MN 55402-3707
612-333-3000
Fax: 612-333-8829
info@bassford.com
www.bassford.com
• Gregory P. Bulinski, Managing
Partner/Chief Operating Officer
(612) 376-1610
greg@bassford.com
• Rebecca Egge Moos, Chief Executive
Officer
(612) 376-1611
beckym@bassford.com
• Kevin P. Hickey, Chief Financial Officer
(612) 376-1620
kevinh@bassford.com
• Gregory P. J. Bulinski, Chief Executive
Officer
(612) 376-1610
gbulinski@bassford.com
• Mark R. Whitmore, Chief Operating
Officer/Managing Partner
(612) 376-1603
mwhitmore@bassford.com
• Michael A. Klutho, Chief Financial Officer
(612) 333-3000
mklutho@bassford.com
• Christopher R. Morris, Management
Committee Member
(612) 376-1627
cmorris@bassford.com
• Kelly A. Putney, Management Committee
Member
(612) 376-1605
kputney@bassford.com
• Robin Ann Williams, Management
Committee Member
(612) 376-1631
rawilliams@bassford.com
• Jessica A. Gerhardson, Operations
Manager
(612) 376-1642
jgerhardson@bassford.com
Services:
Provides a broad range of litigation services
including: admiralty and maritime law,
alternative dispute resolution, appellate
practice, commercial litigation, construction
law, environmental law, ERISA liability,
Trust and estate, FDCPA, FCRA and
privacy issues, health care and risk
management, hospital law, insurance,
intellectual property, labor and employment,
liquor liability, medical device, motor vehicle
and no-fault, municipal, non-competition,
trade secret and related claims, personal
injury, products liability, professional ethics
and liability, securities, shareholder and
related corporate litigation and
telecommunications.
Clients:
National recognized manufacturing
corporations, insurance companies,
healthcare providers.
Description:
Contract negotiation. Products Liability;
Commercial Litigation; Insurance Litigation;
Employment Litigation

BATE, PETERSON, DEACON, ZINN & YOUNG, LLP
888 S FIGUEROA STREET
15TH FLOOR
LOS ANGELES, CA 90017

213-362-1860
Fax: 213-362-1861
• David H. Bate, Attorney
(231) 362-1860
• John W. Peterson, Attorney
• Linda Va Winkle Deacon, Attorney
• Harry A. A. Zinn, Attorney
(213) 362-1860
hzinn@yzblaw.com
• Julie A. Young, Attorney
(213) 362-1860
jyoung@yzblaw.com
• David H. Bate, Attorney
(213) 362-1860
dbate@yzblaw.com
• Lester F. Aponte, Attorney
(213) 362-1860
laponte@yzblaw.com
• Patricia M. Berry, Attorney
(213) 362-1860
pberry@yzblaw.com
• Stephanie M. Saito, Attorney
(213) 362-1860
ssaito@yzblaw.com
• Nirma Shivayi, Attorney
(213) 362-1860
nshivayi@yzblaw.com
Description:
Employment and Labor Law, Commercial
Litigation, Business Law, Real Estate,
Construction Law, Sports Law.
Services:
Represents clients in all aspects of
employment and labor law and general
business, insurance, securities, real estate
and construction litigation.

BAUM, ETENGOFF & BUCKLEY
900 WASHINGTON STREET
VANCOUVER, WA 98660
360-693-2002
800-845-3099
Fax: 360-693-1407
• Mark Baum, Attorney
(360) 693-2002
Nature of Sports Service:
All phases of athlete representation
including contract negotiation, long-range
planning, financial planning, and post-career
counseling.
Services:
Provides legal services in the fields of
personal injury, family law and others.

BEALL & BURKHARDT
1114 STATE STREET
SUITE 200
LA ARCADA BUILDING
SANTA BARBARA, CA 93101-2716
805-966-6774
Fax: 805-963-5988
ArtyC@aol.com
beallandburkhardt.com
• William C. Beall, Partner
• Eric W. Burkhardt, Partner
Services:
Represent creditor, debtor and trustee
clients in bankruptcy
Clients:
Camarillo Community Bank and Bryant Sons
Jewelers
Description:
Contract negotiation, represents
professional sports teams, sports law, tort
actions/litigation.

BEAUTYMAN ASSOCIATES, P.C.
1201 BETHLEHEM PIKE
FLOURTOWN, PA 19031
215-836-7000
Fax: 215-836-6886
mbeauty@beautyman.com
www.beautyman.com
• Michael J. Beautyman, Chairperson
(215) 836-7000
michael@beautyman.com
• Stephen Alvstad, Counsel
• Robert J Nolan,
• Jodi R Adelizzi,
Description:
All phases of athlete representation
including contract negotiation, long-range
planning, financial planning, and post-career
counseling.
Services:
General Practice, all Courts. Insurance Law,
Estate Planning, Personal Injury, Family
Law, Taxation and Probate.

BECKER & POLIAKOFF, P.A.
1 EAST BROWARD BOULEVARD
SUITE 1800
FORT LAUDERDALE, FL 33301
954-987-7550
800-432-7712
Fax: 954-985-4176
care@bplegal.com
www.becker-poliakoff.com
• Alan S. Becker, Founding Shareholder
(954) 985-4127
• Gary A. Poliakoff, Founding Shareholder
(954) 985-4150
Services:
Provides a full range of legal services
including asset protection and estate
planning, homeowner and community
association law, civil and complex
commercial litigation, administrative law,
bancruptcy and creditors' rights, securities
law and litigation, custom and international
trade.
Clients:
AT&T, Broward County Schools, CBS
SportsLine.com, CVS Pharmacy, Florida
Memorial College, Engle Homes, Harley
Davidson, InterParfums, Inc., Isle of Capri
Casinos, Boston Proper, Miami Dade
County Schools, Miami Dade County, IKON
Office Solutions, Palm Beach County, Perry
Slingsby Systems, Inc., Raleigh Enterprises,
Ryder, Sprint PCS, TeleDanmark, Tishman
Speyer Properties, Inc., Ultimate Software
Group, Inc., Westin Diplomat Resort Hotel
Nature of Sports Service:
Entertainment Law; Sports Law; Intellectual
Property Law; Technology.

BECKER, WILLIAM F.X.
260 E JEFFERSON STREET
POTOMAC VALLEY BANK BUILDING, 2ND
FLOOR
ROCKVILLE, MD 20850-2333
301-340-6966
Fax: 301-309-6653
• William F. Becker, Attorney
(301) 340-6966
wfxbecker@aol.com
• Chelsea Drew, Legal Assistant
Nature of Sports Service:
All phases of athlete representation
including contract negotiation, long-range
planning, financial & estate planning,
post-career counseling. Licensed attorney in

Maryland, District of Columbia and West
Virginia.

BENDELOW LAW FIRM
1707 NORTH MAIN ST.
SUITE 301
LONGMONT, CO 80501
303-837-9600
Fax: 303-860-0311
www.bendelow.net
• Edward M. Bendelow, Managing Partner
(303) 837-9600
tedbendelow@bendelow.net
• Kenneth R. Hope, Attorney
(303) 837-9600
• Peter Scott, Attorney
(303) 837-9600
• Scott Watson, Attorney
(303) 837-9600
Description:
Experts in all aspects of commercial law,
real estate, land use and development,
water law, intellectual property. business
transactions and litigation. Represent
individuals, partnerships, business
governments and associations of all sizes
and types on issues small and large.
Services:
Business & Commercial Law, Contracts,
Business Organizations, Construction Law,
DUI/DWI, Entertainment, Sports & Leisure
Law, Environmental Law, Estate Planning,
Wills, Family Law, Divorce, Intellectual
Property Law, Trademarks, Litigation &
Appeals, Natural Resource Law, Real
Estate Law, Land Use and Zoning, Taxation
Law
Clients:
American Cancer Society, American Historic
Motorcycle Racing Association, American
Power Boat Association, Chenango
Homeowners Association, Sports Car Club
of America, Telluride Mountain Title
Company, Rocky Mountain Forest Products,
Sigma Dynamics
Other Location:
101 East Colorado Avenue, #201A, PO Box
726, Telluride, CO 81435; Phone:
970-728-4300; 79050 US Highway 40, STE
202C, PO Box 67, Winter Park, CO 80482;
Phone: 970-726-0600

BERMAN, HOWARD E.
1250 CENTRAL PARK AVENUE
YONKERS, NY 10708
914-423-8880
Fax: 914-423-8964
• Howard Berman, Partner
(914) 423-8880
• John P. Farrauto, Partner
(914) 423-8880
• Richard G. Fontana, Attorney
Services:
All phases of athlete representation
including contract negotiation,
endorsements, estate planning and legal
representation.

BERNARD M. RESNICK, ESQ, P.C.
TWO BALA PLAZA
SUITE 300
BALA CYNWYD, PA 19004
610-660-7774
bmresnick@gmail.com
www.bernardresnick.com
• Bernard M. Resnick, Sports Attorney

Description:
Entertainment law firm
Services:
Full-service entertainment, communications
and sports law firm which concentrates on
transactional work in various facets of the
entertainment industry.
Clients:
The Philadelphia Orchestra; Susan Milan;
The Budapest String Quartet; Piffaro, Ex
Umbris, and Fortune's Wheel; Peter Richard
Conte; Vitalij Kuprij; and The Amernet String
Quartet; Dave Mason; The Rembrandts;
Pink; Us3; The Alan Parsons Project, The
Cuffs, Pornosonic, Blink, The Naked Apes,
V.A., Peekaboo, Janita, Raje Shwari,
Anthrophobia, aboyandagirl, Autumn, Pete
Palladino, The Badlees, and Electron Love
Theory; Rich Gavalis (Bloodhound Gang);
and Chord Recordings, Tazmania Records,
Metropolitan Records, Dancesport Sounds
USA, DRP Records, BMP/Put It On A Disk
Records, 215 Records, Krush Unit, Inc.,
Chocolate Fireguard Music, Ltd., Ultimae

BERNARD, PAMELA J.
123 TIGERT HALL
PO BOX 113125
GAINESVILLE, FL 32611-3257
352-392-3261
Fax: 352-392-4387
www.generalcounsel.ufl.edu
• Pamela Bernard, VP/General Counsel
(352) 392-1358
pbernard@ufl.edu
• Karon Grabel, Senior Administrative
Assistant
(352) 392-1358
karon@ufl.edu
• James Be Machen, President
• Jamie Lewis Keith, Vice President and
General Counsel
jlkeith@ufl.edu
• Barbara C. Wingo, Associate Vice
President and Deputy General C
wingo@ufl.edu
• Amy M. Hass, Associate Vice President
and Deputy General C
amhass@ufl.edu
• Michael W. Ford, Sr. University Counsel
for Tax, Corporations
mwford@ufl.edu
Description:
Represents college athletic departments.
Services:
provides legal advice and representation to
the University of Florida, its component units
and affiliated entities, and to its employees
while acting within the scope and course of
their employment.
Clients:
Units and entities of University of Florida

BERNARD, WILLIAM DAVID
101 N COLUMBIA STREET
CHAPEL HILL, NC 27514-3502
919-968-1111
Fax: 919-968-1444
wbernard@brownandbunch.com
www.brownandbunch.com
• William Bernard, Partner
Services:
Contract negotiation, arbitration hearings,
represents professional sports teams,
endorsement exploration, tort
actions/litigation. Commercial Law;

Residential and Commercial Real Estate; Mediation.

BERRY, ROBERT C.
140 COMMONWEALTH AVENUE
CHESTNUT HILL, MA 02467
617-552-8550
Fax: 617-552-2615
bclawadm@bc.edu
www.bc.edu
• Robert Berry, Professor Emeritus
(617) 552-4360
• Filippa Ma Anzalone, Professor/Library and Computing Services
(617) 552-6809
filippa.anzalone@bc.edu
Services:
Prepares students to be among the best in law profession, both by giving them a thorough knowledge of the foundations of law through an extensive array of required and elective courses, and by encouraging them to think creatively in real-world situations, through advocacy programs, clinical programs, and student publications
Clients Include:
Impact Sports.
Description:
Contract negotiation, teaches sports law, handles publicity & private issues.

BERSHAD, LAWRENCE
SETON HALL UNIVERSITY SCHOOL OF LAW
ONE NEWARK CENTER
1109 RAYMOND BOULEVARD
NEWARK, NJ 7102
973-642-8500
888-415-7271
Fax: 973-642-8876
lawwebmaster@shu.edu
law.shu.edu
• Lawrence Bershad, Law Professor
(973) 642-8810
bershala@shu.edu
• Michelle Adams, Law Professor
(973) 642-8197
adamsmch@shu.edu
• Erik Lillquist, Vice Dean & Professor of Law
(973) 642-8844
erik.lillquist@shu.edu
• Terry Dealmedia, Assistant Dean for Administration and Finance
(973) 642-8732
terry.dealmeida@shu.edu
• Rose Marie Martins, Administrative Assistant to the Vice Dean & A
(973) 642-8378
rose.martins@shu.edu
• Gisele Joachim, Dean of Enrollment Management
(973) 642-8475
gisele.joachim@shu.edu
• Katya Valasek, Associate Director of Admissions
(973) 642-8848
katherine.valasek@shu.edu
• Mimi Huang, Associate Director of Admissions
(973) 642-8737
mimi.huang@shu.edu
Description:
Teaches sports law.
Services:
Educates health lawyers and health care professionals through its three degree programs: the Juris Doctorate with a

concentration in health law (J.D.), the Master of Laws in Health Law (LL.M.), and the Masters of Science in Jurisprudence (M.S.J.). The program's faculty engages in original empirical and analytical research on emerging issues in health law and policy, and the program serves the wider community through frequent lectures and symposia

---

BERTUZZI, LAWRENCE
600 - 60 COLUMBIA WAY
MARKHAM, ON, CANADA L3R 0C9
905-415-6700
866-348-2432
Fax: 905-415-6777
markham@millerthomson.com
www.millerthomson.ca
• Lawrence Bertuzzi, Partner
(905) 415-6750
• Gerald D. E Courage, Chairman
• Paul Brace, Partner
(905) 415-6703
pbrace@millerthomson.com
• Peter McKelvey, Chief Operating Officer
• Chris Issar, Chief Financial Officer
• Richard Van Dyk, Chief Information Officer
• Katrina Stevens, National Director, Human Resources
• Monique Wijgerse, Chief Marketing & Business Development Office
Services:
Provides a complete range of business law, advocacy and personal legal services to Canadian and international corporations, entrepreneurs, institutions, governments and not-for-profit organizations

---

BEVERLY HILLS SPORTS COUNCIL
131 S. RODEO DRIVE
SUITE 100
BEVERLY HILLS, CA 90212
310-858-1872
Fax: 310-550-7980
info@bhscouncil.com
bhscouncil.com
• Daniel Lozano, Partner
• Rick Thurman, Chief Financial Officer
• Jeff Borris, General Counsel
Description:
Full representation of professional baseball players.
Services:
Professional sports club and promoter

BINGHAM MCCUTCHEN LLP
THREE EMBARCADERO CENTER
SAN FRANCISCO, CA 94111-4067
415-393-2000
Fax: 415-393-2286
• Jay S. Zimmerman, Chairman
(415) 393-2080
• Donn P. Pickett, Partner
(415) 393-2082
• William A. Bachman, Chief Operating Officer
(617) 951-8216
• Sherri Bracken, Regional Director of Administration
(212) 705-7856
Services:
Endorsement exploration; provides a variety of legal services in areas of Corporate, Finance and Litigation law

---

BLACK, WILLIAM D., LAW OFFICES OF
ONE E CAMELBACK ROAD
SUITE 550
PHOENIX, AZ 85012
602-910-6144
888-349-3599
Fax: 602-265-3685
• William D. Black, Attorney/Principal
(602) 265-2211
• William D. Black, Attorney
• Bill Black, Attorney
• Stephen J. McFarlane, Of Counsel
• Robert E. Wisniewski, Of Counsel
• William D. J. Black, Founding Attorney
Year Founded:
1979
Services:
Personal Injury, Wrongful Death, Medical Malpractice, Workers Compensation, Employment Concerns, Intellectual Property Law, Computer Law, Restaurant & Liquor License Law, Hotel & Travel Law, Entertainment & Sports Law, Real Estate Law, Communications Law, 1st Amendment Law, General Business Law, Commercial Litigation

---

BLACKBOURN, LISLE W.
354 SEYMOUR COURT
ELKHORN, WI 53121
262-723-3220
Fax: 262-723-5091
godfrey@godfreylaw.com
www.godfreylaw.com
• Lisle Blackbourn, Attorney
(262) 723-3220
lblackbourn@godfreylaw.com
• Lisle W. Blackbourn, President & Managing Partner
(262) 723-3220
• Patrick S. DeMoon III, Associate
(262) 723-3220
• Michael J. Frazier, Associate
(262) 723-3220
• Kim A. Howarth, Partner
(262) 723-3220
• James P. Howe, Associate
(262) 723-3220
• Theodore N. Johnson, Partner
(262) 723-3220
• Robert C. Leibsle, Senior Partner
(262) 723-3220
Description:
Personal injury.
Services:
General Corporate Representation, Labor Negotiations, Arbitration, Financial & Commercial Transactions, Business & Financial Planning, Employment Law and Practices, Trademarks, Trade Names and Licensing Agreements, Business Succession Planning, Personal Injury, Commercial, Employment Litigation, General Business Litigation, Product Liability, etc.

BLAIR, ROBERT W.
1155 DAIRY ASHFORD
SUITE 103
HOUSTON, TX 77079
281-870-9991
Fax: 281-870-9969
rwblair1@aol.com
• Robert Blair, Attorney
(281) 275-4275
Services:
Personal Injury, Business Disputes, Real Estate, Wills, Estates

Description:
Federal/state/international tax filings.

BLANC, DAVID
222 SE DORION AVENUE
PO BOX 218
PENDLETON, OR 97801
541-276-3331
800-994-3331
Fax: 541-276-3148
www.corey-byler.com
• David Blanc, Attorney
(541) 276-3331
blanc@corey-byler.com
• Steven H Corey, Attorney
corey@corey-byler.com
Services:
Civil Litigation, Estate Planning, Elder Law,
Personal Injury, Divorce & Custody, Real
Estate, Agricultural Law, Zoning & Land
Use, Condemnation, Business, Water Law,
Wills, Probate & Trusts

BLECHER & COLLINS
515 S FIGUEROA STREET
SUITE 1750
LOS ANGELES, CA 90071
213-622-4222
Fax: 213-622-1656
www.blechercollins.com
• Maxwell M. Blecher, Attorney/Founding
Partner
(213) 622-4222
• Harold R. Collins, Jr, Attorney/Founding
Partner
(213) 622-4222
• John E E. Andrews, Attorney/Partner
(213) 622-4222
• Howard K Alperin, Attorney/Partner
• Gary M Joye, Attorney/Partner
• Alyson C Decker, Attorney/Partner
• William Hsu, Attorney/Partner
• Donald R Pepperman, Attorney/Partner
• Kristen M Peters, Attorney/Partner
Services:
Antitrust, complex commercial litigation,
class actions, professional malpractice,
intellectual property.

BOEHM, STEVE B.
1275 PENNSYLVANIA AVEUE, NW
WASHINGTON, DC 20004-2415
202-383-0100
Fax: 202-637-3593
steven.boehm@sablaw.com
• Steven B. Boehm, Attorney/Partner
(202) 383-0176
steven.boehm@sablaw.com
• Miranda K. Davis, Associate
(404) 853-8242
miranda.davis@sutherland.com
Nature of Sports Service:
All phases of athlete representation
including contract negotiation, long-range
planning, financial planning, and post-career
counseling.
Services:
Represents national and regional financial
service organizations in connection with the
establishment and operation of public and
private open and closed-end investment
funds; assists insurance company and other
financial services clients with the design and
implementation of a variety of
investment-oriented insurance products,
including SEC-registered and unregistered

variable life insurance products and other
variable annuities

BOESCHE MCDERMOTT LLP
110 W 7TH STREET
SUITE 900
TULSA, OK 74119
918-583-1777
866-483-1777
Fax: 918-592-5809
• Bradley Beasley, Attorney
bbeasley@bme-law.com
• Michael Forsman, Attorney
• David Johnson, Attorney
Year Founded:
1927

BOSCH, GERARD R.
111 N 6TH STREET
READING, PA 19601
610-478-2000
Fax: 610-376-5610
Nature of Sports Service:
All phases of athlete representation
including contract negotiation, long-range
planning, financial planning, and post-career
counseling. Assists universities in
investigating violations of NCAA rules and
regulations.

BOSE MCKINNEY & EVANS LLP
111 MONUMENT CIRCLE
SUITE 2700
INDIANAPOLIS, IN 46204
317-684-5000
Fax: 317-684-5173
webmaster@boselaw.com
www.boselaw.com
• Craig E. Pinkus, Partner/Co-Chair of the
Intellectual Pro
(317) 684-5358
cpinkus@boselaw.com
• Lisa McKinney Goldner, Co-Chair
Environmental Law
(317) 684-5124
lgoldner@boselaw.com
Services:
provides a full-range of legal services to
privately owned businesses, publicly traded
companies, high-tech organizations, and
governmental entities
Clients:
Automotive Finance Corporation,
Association of Indiana Life Insurance
Companies, BMW Constructors, Inc.,
Brownsburg Community School Corporation,
Chip Ganassi Racing Teams, Inc., Cinram,
Inc., City of Indianapolis, Community
Bankers Association of Indiana, Crowe
Chizek and Company, LLP, Emmis
Communications Corporation, Endress +
Hauser, Fall Creek Regional Waste District,
First Indiana Bank, Hillenbrand Industries,
Indiana Bankers Association, Indiana Pork
Producers Association, Indiana Soybean
Board, Inc., Indiana University
Anesthesiology Associates, Indiana Water &
Wastewater Association, Indianapolis Colts,
Inc., Johnson County REMC
Description:
Tort actions/litigation, represents college
athletic departments, dispute resolution.
Other Locations:
2700 First Indiana Plaza, 135 North
Pennsylvania Street, Indianapolis, IN 46204;
Phone: 317-684-5000; 700 North One
Lafayette Center, 1120 20th Street NW,

Washington, DC 20036; Phone:
202-973-1229

**BOUTIN, DENTINO, GIBSON, DI GUISTO,
HODELL, INC.**
555 CAPITOL MALL
SUITE 1500
SACRAMENTO, CA 95814
916-321-4444
Fax: 916-441-7597
info@boutinjones.com
www.boutinjones.com
• Stephen F. Boutin, Founder
(916) 321-4444
• William Dentino, Principal
(916) 321-4444
• Chris Gibson, Principal
(916) 321-4444
• Jennifer E Lloyd, Paralegal
(916) 321-4444
• Elizabeth D Pullen, Paralegal
(916) 321-4444
epullen@boutinjones.com
• Sheryl S Stuckey, Paralegal
(916) 321-4444
sstuckey@boutinjones.com
• Penny R Brown, Attorney
(916) 321-4444
pbrown@boutinjones.com
• Kevin C Davis, Attorney
(916) 321-4444
• Chris Gibson, Attorney
(916) 321-4444
• B.J Susich, Attorney
(916) 321-4444
Services:
Entity formation and consultation, corporate
transactions, intellectual property, real
estate, secured transactions, taxation,
estate planning, and litigation
Description:
General business law, joint ventures, real
estate, taxation, estate planning, sports,
mergers, acquisitions.

BRADLEY & GMELICH
700 N BRAND BOULEVARD
10TH FLOOR
GLENDALE, CA 91203
818-243-5200
Fax: 818-243-5266
info@bglawyers.com
www.bglawyers.com
• Barry A. Bradley, Attorney/Managing
Partner
(818) 243-5200
bbradley@bglawyers.com
• Thomas Gmelich, Attorney/Partner
(818) 243-5200
tgmelich@bglawyers.com
• Mirth White, Associate
(818) 243-5200
• John K. Flock, Associate
(818) 243-5200
• Robert A. Crook, Associate
(818) 243-5200
• Lindy M. Bradley, Partner
(818) 243-5200
• Gary J. Bradley, Partner
(818) 243-5200
• Jonathan A. Ross, Partner
(818) 243-5200
• Barry A. Bradley, Managing partner
(818) 243-5200
Services:
General civil litigation, Private security,
Inadequate Security Liability, Premises
Liability Litigation, Sports & Recreational

Injury, Employment Law, Commercial Business Litigation, Construction Claims & Litigation, Alternative Dispute Resolution
Clients:
Brownyard Claims Management, Inc., Certain Underwriters at Lloyds of London, Connecticut Specialty Insurance Company, Crawford & Company, First Financial Insurance Company, Frontier Pacific Insurance Company, Great American Insurance Company, Hartford Insurance Company, Kemper Insurance Company, National American Insurance Company of California, Royal Insurance Company, Schifrin, Gagnon & Dickey, Inc., Specialty Risk Services, Inc., USF&G Insurance Company, Zurich Insurance Company, Albertsons/ Lucky Stores, Inc., Allied Protection Services, American Stores, Inc., Arden Realty, Inc., Armguard Security, Auburn Hills Racquet & Fitness Club

BREAUX, PAUL P.
3525 BANK DRIVE
ST GABRIEL, LA 70776-4616
225-642-5532
• Phil Breaux, Attorney
• Robert Hornstein, Attorney
Nature of Sports Service:
All phases of athlete representation including contract negotiation, long-range planning, financial planning, and post-career counseling.

BRENNAN, PATRICK CAVANAUGH
324 E WISCONSIN AVENUE
MILWAUKEE, WI 53202
414-476-8707
• Brennan Patrick Cavanaugh, Attorney
Services:
Personal injury lawyer
Description:
Contract negotiation, endorsement exploration, criminal law litigation specialist.

BRICK, ADAM
GEORGETOWN UNIVERSITY
MCDONOUGH ARENA
WASHINGTON, DC 20057
202-687-5414
Fax: 202-687-5366
www.georgetownuniversity.com
• Adam Brick, Senior Associate Athletic Director Legal

BRICKER & ECKLER
100 S THIRD STREET
COLUMBUS, OH 43215-4291
614-227-2300
Fax: 614-227-2390
info@bricker.com
www.bricker.com
• Richard Simpson, Managing Partner
(614) 227-2354
rsimpson@bricker.com
• Richard King, Chief Operating Officer
(614) 227-2393
rking@bricker.com
• Charlotte Patin, Chief Information Officer
(614) 227-8882
cpatin@bricker.com
• Steve Odum, CFO
sodum@bricker.com
• Faith Williams, Administrative Partner
fwilliams@bricker.com
• Richard King, COO
rking@bricker.com

• Kurt Tunnell, Managing Partner
ktunnell@bricker.com
• Ahmad Sinno, CIO
asinno@bricker.com
Description:
Represents college athletic departments, individuals, as well as corporations, nonprofit organizations, government, agencies, health care facilities, school districts, and municipalities.

BRICKEY JAMES N. L.C.
8000 MARYLAND AVE
SUITE 750
CLAYTON, MO 63105
314-863-6178
Fax: 314-725-7075
• James N. Brickey, Attorney

BRIDGES, HAROLD A.
444 S FLOWER STREET
SUITE 2400
LOS ANGELES, CA 90071-2953
213-236-0600
800-333-4297
Fax: 213-236-2700
www.bwslaw.com
• Harold Bridges, Attorney
(213) 236-0600
• Lisa Arias, Secretary
Services:
All phases of athlete representation including contract negotiation, long-range planning, financial planning, and post-career counseling.
Year Founded:
1927
Other Locatons:
2310 East Ponderosa Drive, STE 25, Camarillo, CA 93010; Phone: 805-987-3468; Fax: 805-482-9834; 5 Park Plaza, Ste 1280, Irvine, CA 92614; Phone: 949-863-3363; Fax: 949-863-3350; 3403 Tenth Street, STE 300, PO Box 1609, Riverside, CA 92501; Phone: 951-788-0100; Fax: 951-788-5785; 701 B Street, Ste 1790, San Diego, CA 92101; Phone: 619-615-6672; Fax: 619-615-6673; 96 North Third Street, STE 620, San Jose, CA 95112; Phone 408-299-0422; Fax: 408-299-0429

BRIGGS, BUCK
CORNELL LAW SCHOOL
MYRON TAYLOR HALL
ITHACA, NY 14853-4901
607-255-4299
Fax: 607-255-7193
rfr4@cornell.edu
www.lawschool.cornell.edu
• Thomas R Bruce, Director Legal Information Institute
• Richard F. Robinson, Associate Dean for Administration and Finance
(607) 255-4299
rfr4@cornell.edu
• Richard D. Geiger, Associate Dean, Communications & Enrollment
(607) 255-5141
rdg9@cornell.edu
• Peter Cronin, Associate Dean for Alumni Affairs & Developme
(607) 255-3373
pc253@cornell.edu
• Martha Fitzgerald, Director of Communications
(607) 255-6596
mpf28@cornell.edu

• Anne Lukingbeal, Associate Dean and Dean of Students
(607) 255-5839
al50@cornell.edu
• Diane Cross, Director
(607) 255-1311
dsr2@cornell.edu
• William Buckley Briggs, Adjunct Professor of Law
(607) 254-4765
william.briggs@nfl.com
Description:
Teaches sports law.

BROWN, HALL, SHORE & MCKINLEY LLP
3031 W MARCH LANE
SUITE 230
STOCKTON, CA 95219
209-477-8171
888-583-7178
Fax: 209-477-2549
• Jerry Hall, Partner
(209) 477-8171
• Reed K Scott, Attorney
• John Conger, Attorney
• John McKinley, Attorney
• Dennis Shore, Attorney
• Scott L J. Harper, Attorney
Nature of Service:
Real Estate; Business and Corporate Law; Commercial Law; Partnerships; Estate Planning; Sports Law; Entertainment Law; International Business Law; Intellectual Property; Civil Litigation, Sports Agency Law, Trademark infringement.
Year Founded:
1984
Sports Service Founded:
2002

BROWN, J. MICHAEL
500 W JEFFERSON STREET
PNC PLAZA, SUITE 2600
LOUISVILLE, KY 40202-2898
502-589-5235
Fax: 502-589-0309
Description:
Contract negotiation.
Other Locations:
2525 West End Avenue, STE 1500, Nashville, TN 37203; Phone: 615-244-0020; 1600 Lexington Financial Center, 250 West Main Street, Lexington, KY 40507; Phone: 859-233-2012; The Renaissance Center, 1715 Aaron Brenner Drive, STE 800, Memphis, TN 38120; Phone 901-537-1000; 918 State Stree, Bowling Green, KY 42102; Phone: 270-842-1050; 101 West Spring Street, New Albany, IN 47150; Phone: 812-945-3561

BRUNINI, GRANTHAM GROWE & HEWES, P.L.L.C
190 E CAPITOL STREET
SUITE 100
PO DRAWER 119
JACKSON, MS 39201
601-948-3101
Fax: 601-960-6902
www.brunini.com
• Stephen Carmody, Attorney
(601) 960-6890
scarmody@brunini.com
• Christopher A. Shapley, Attorney
(601) 960-6875

Description:
Labor and Employment; Litigation; Workers Compensation; Sports Law.
Services:
Handles a wide range of cases, including litigation involving complex commercial transactions, mass torts, construction disputes, employment discrimination, products liability, medical malpractice, breach of contract, antitrust, securities fraud, business torts, taxation, white collar crime, and environmental issues
Clients:
AES Corporation, Aetna Casualty and Surety, Adora Networks, Air2Lan, Allen Canning Company, Amerada Hess Company, American General, American Home Shield, Inc., Amoco Business Services, AmSouth Bank, Anderson-Tully Company, Apache Corporation, Aquila Energy, ARAMARK, Astec Industries, Inc., AT&T Corp., Athlon Pharmaceuticals, Inc., Ball-Foster Glass Company, Barksdale Bonding and Insurance, Inc., Beazer East, Inc., Beverly Enterprises, Birds Eye Foods, Blue Cross & Blue Shield of Mississippi, BOC Group, Inc., BP Amoco, Brothers of the Sacred Heart, Brown and Williamson Tobacco Corp., Browning-Ferris Industries, Inc., Allied Waste Industries, B
Other Location:
1710 Jackson Avenue, Pascagula, MS 39567; Phone: 228-696-0040

BRUNO, CHRISTOPHER J.
855 BARRONE STREET
NEW ORLEANS, LA 70113
504-525-1335
800-966-1335
Fax: 504-581-1493
info@brunobrunolaw.com
www.brunobrunolaw.com
• Christopher J. Bruno, Partner/Attorney
(504) 525-1335
• Joseph M. Bruno, Managing Partner
(504) 525-1335
info@brunobrunolaw.com
Nature of Sports Service:
All phases of athlete representation including contract negotiation, long-range planning, financial planning, and post-career counseling.

BRYANT-FIELDS, REGINA
555 CALIFORNIA STREET
SUITE 2000
SAN FRANCISCO, CA 94104
415-772-1200
Fax: 415-772-7400
www.brownwoodlaw.com
Services:
Contract negotiation, arbitration hearings, represents professional sports teams, endorsement exploration.
Clients:
Clients include numerous Fortune 100 and 500 companies in a wide range of industries and business sectors, governments, banks, insurance and financial institutions, professional firms, foundations, institutions, associations and individuals.
Description:
Contract negotiation, arbitration hearings, represents professional sports teams, endorsement exploration.

BRYENTON, GARY L.
1900 E 9TH STREET
3200 NATIONAL CITY CENTER
CLEVELAND, OH 44114-3482
216-621-0200
Fax: 216-696-0740
info@bakerlaw.com
www.bakerlaw.com
• R. St Kestner, Executive Partner
(216) 861-7558
skestner@bakerlaw.com
• Alec Wightman, Executive Partner
(614) 462-2636
awightman@bakerlaw.com
• John M. Gherlein, Partner/Chairperson, Business
(216) 861-7398
jgherlein@bakerlaw.com
• Ronald G. Linville, Partner/Chairperson, Employment and Labo
(614) 462-2647
rlinville@bakerlaw.com
• R. Steven Kestner, Executive Partner
(216) 861-7558
skestner@bakerlaw.com
Description:
Contract negotiation, post career planning, investment contract negotiation, arbitration hearings, federal/state/international tax filings, represents professional sports teams (Cleveland Indians), provides securities advice, licensing, tort actions/litigation.
Other Locations:
666 Fifth Avenue, New York, NY 10103; Phone: 212-589-4200; Washington Square, STE 1100, 1050 Connecticut Avenue, NW, Washington, DC 20036; Phone: 202-861-1500; 333 South Grand Avenue, STE 1800, Los Angeles, CA 90071; Phone: 213-975-1600

BUCHANAN INGERSOLL ROONEY
301 GRANT STREET
ONE OXFORD CENTER, 20TH FLOOR
PITTSBURGH, PA 15219-1410
412-562-8800
Fax: 412-562-1041
www.bipc.com
• Arthur J. Rooney II, Of Counsel
(412) 392-2000
• Edwin L. Klett, Senior Lawyer/Shareholder
• William H. Schorling, Shareholder
(412) 392-2114
• Robert J. Tyler Jr, Executive Director & Chief Financial Off
Services:
Areas of practice include Bankruptcy and Insolvency Practice, Corporate Practice, Gaming Practice, General Liability Defense Practice, Government Affairs Practice, Higher Education Practice, International Business Practice, Labor and Employment Practice, and Real Estate Practice.
Description:
Contract negotiation, represents professional sports teams, corporate law, government affairs.

BUCHANAN INGERSOLL ROONEY PC
301 GRANT STREET
20TH FLOOR, ONE OXFORD CENTRE
PITTSBURGH, PA 15219-1410
412-562-8800
Fax: 412-562-1041
www.klettrooney.com
• Peter P. Ackourey, Shareholder
(609) 987-6807
peter.ackourey@bipc.com

• Nolan W. Kurtz, Executive Director/Practice Operations
(717) 237-4807
nolan.kurtz@bipc.com
• Virginia L. O'Hare, Firm Administrator
• Daniel F. Duffy Jr, Information Systems Director
• Susan A. Yohe, Managing Shareholder
• Allyson J. Singel Aldous, Associate
(412) 0562-182
allyson.aldous@bipc.com
• Lynn J. Alstadt, Shareholder
(412) 562-1632
lynn.alstadt@bipc.com
• Christopher A. Amar, Associate
(412) 562 8394
christopher.amar@bipc.com
• Bruce A. Americus, Shareholder
(412) 562-8885
bruce.americus@bipc.com
• Margaret B. Angel, Shareholder
(412) 562-3982
margaret.angel@bipc.com
Description:
Represents college athletic departments.
Services:
Provides a full-service, general commercial law services to corporations and other business entities through interdisciplinary practice.
Clients:
Clients range from leading Fortune 500 companies and closely-held businesses to numerous colleges and universities, hospitals and other health care institutions, banks and other financial establishments, software and technology companies, minority businesses, charitable and community organizations, and a National Football League team.

BUNTING, ELIZABETH C.
910 RALEIGH ROAD
PO BOX 2688
OFFICE OF THE PRESIDENT
CHAPEL HILL, NC 27514
919-962-1000
www.northcarolina.edu
• Erskine B. Bowles, President
(919) 962-9000
• Jeffrey R. Davies, Chief of Staff
(919) 962-1591
• Jane Morton, Executive Assistant to the President
(919) 962-4622
• Tom Ross, President
(919) 962-9000
cparrish@northcarolina.edu
• Joni Worthington, Associate VP, Communications/Special Ass
(919) 962-4629
worthj@northcarolina.edu
• Celeste Parrish, Executive Assistant to the President
(919) 962-4622
• Kathy Jones, Administrative Assistant
(919) 962-462
kjones@northcarolina.edu
Description:
Represents college athletic departments.
Services:
Offers high quality education for the graduate and undergraduate studies.

BURELSON, PATE & GIBSON, L.L.P.
900 JACKSON STREET
SUITE 300
DALLAS, TX 75202

214-871-4900
Fax: 214-871-7543
www.bp-g.com
• John E. Agnew, Member
(214) 871-4900
jagnew@bp-g.com
• Timothy A. Duffy, Member
(214) 871-4900
tduffy@bp-g.com
• Michael P. Gibson, Partner
(214) 871-4900
mgibson@bp-g.com
• John E. E. Collins, Attorney
(214) 871-4900
jcollins@bp-g.com
• Paul Lund, Attorney
(214) 871-4900
plund@bp-g.com
• Tom Pappas, Attorney
(214) 871-4900
tpappas@bp-g.com
• John E. Agnew, Attorney
(214) 871-4900
jagnew@bp-g.com
• Carl D. Medders, Attorney
(214) 871-4900
cmedders@bp-g.com
Services:
Represents and advises clients in the areas
of criminal defense, especially white collar
crime, family law, personal injury,
bankruptcy, tax, business litigation, labor
and employment law, estate planning,
probate, real estate, and insurance defense.

BURFORD, LLL, CHRIS W.
800 S BROADWAY
SUITE 400
WALNUT CREEK, CA 94596
925-937-4950
Fax: 925-937-0104
Services:
Licensing, endorsement exploration,
represents sports organizations, tort
actions/litigation, college conference
representative.

BURG & ELDREDGE, P.C.
40 INVERNESS DRIVE E
ENGLEWOOD, CO 80112
303-792-5595
888-895-2080
Fax: 303-708-0527
info@burgsimpson.com
www.burgsimpson.com
• Michael S. Burg, Founder/Shareholder
(303) 792-5595
mburg@burgsimpson.com
• Peter W. Burg, Shareholder
(303) 792-5595
pburg@burgsimpson.com
• Alan K. Simpson, Shareholder
(307) 527-7891
asimpson@burgsimpson.com
• Scott J. Eldredge, Shareholder
(303) 792-5595
seldredge@burgsimpson.com
Services:
Athlete representation including contract
negotiation, marketing, endorsements,
estate planning and post career counseling.
Other Locations:
227 Massachusetts Avenue, NE, STE 1,
Washington, DC 20002; Phone:
202-544-7600; 1135 14th Street, Cody, WY
82424; Phone: 307-527-7891; 7920 Belt
Line Road, STE 650, Dallas, TX 75254;
Phone: 972-934-1313; 2415 East

Camelback Road, STE 700, Phoenix, AZ
85016; Phone: 602-508-6040

BURGOYNE, ROBERT A.
801 PENNSYLVANIA AVENUE NW
MARKET SQUARE
SUITE 500
WASHINGTON, DC 20004-2623
202-662-0200
Fax: 202-662-4643
info@fulbright.com
www.fulbright.com
• Robert A. Burgoyne, Partner
(202) 662-4513
rburgoyne@fulbright.com
• Danny Kim, Partner
• Selina Coleman, Senior Associate
(202) 662-4536
• Tracy DeMarco, Associate
(202) 662-4653
• Mark Thomas Emery, Senior Associate
(202) 662 0210
• Robert Owen, Partner
(212) 318-3070
rowen@fulbright.com
Description:
Represents college athletic departments.

BURT, JR., EDWARD C.
2583 WHITNEY AVENUE
HAMDEN, CT 06518
203-248-2182
Fax: 203-248-9466
www.burtlaw.us
• Edward C Burt, Attorney
• Christine Burt, Attorney
Description:
Contract negotiation.

BUSINESS LAW VENTURES
400 CAPITOL MALL
SUITE 900
SACRAMENTO, CA 95814
916-475-1272
Fax: 916-780-9838
info@businesslawventures.com
• Brent Lawrence, Chief Executive
Officer/Managing Attorney
(916) 475-1272
brent@businesslawventures.com
• John Rosenbaum, Corporate Atorney
(916) 475-4212
john@businesslawventures.com
• Zuzana Bednarova, Business
Development
(916) 475-1272
zuzana@businesslawventures.com
• Jordan Miller, Law Clerk
(916) 475-1272
jordan@businesslawventures.com
• Cindy Salwlyers, Bookkeeping
(916) 475-1272
cindi@businesslawventures.com
• Brent Lawrence, JD, MBA, Managing
Atorney
brent@businesslawventures.com
Services:
Mergers & Acquisitions, Real Estate (joint
ventures and financing), Corporate Law
Services (formation of Corporations and
LLCs), Business Plans (including Marketing
Plans), Assistance of early stage high-tech
companies, Negotiation and Preparation of
Contracts
Clients:
Sierra BG Office Supplies & Printing,
California Family Fitness, Peabodys Coffee,

FDI Collateral Management, PDF
Development, Valley Air Express, Inc.,
TESCO Controls, Inc., Kiff Analytical, LLC,
CWNet.com, RF Olmo & Associates,
Air-Trak, ASK International, AP Thomas
Construction, Jewel Fine Wines, TechCoire,
Coastline Construction Corporation,
Software Contract Solutions, Indicium
Technologies, Heron Innovators, Murieta
Health Club and others.
Nature of Sports Service:
All phases of athlete representation
including contract negotiation, long-range
planning, financial planning, and post-career
counseling. 1) Mergers & Acquisitions, (2)
Corporate Securities, (3) Business Planning
and Contracts, and (4) Real Estate
Development.
Year Founded:
1998

BUTLER. JAMES D., P.A.
591 SUMMIT AVENUE
JERSEY CITY, NJ 7306
201-653-1676
Fax: 201-653-3673
• James D. Butler, Attorney
• Alexander T. West, Associate
• Paul A. Liggio, Counsel
Description:
NFLPA. Handles the New York Giants/Jets
workers compensation. Risk Management;
Self-Insurance Law; Products Liability Law;
Toxic Substances Law; Environmental Law;
Construction Law; Transportation Law;
Admiralty Law; Aviation Law; Sports Law.

**BUTZEL LONG, A PROFESSIONAL
CORPORATION**
41000 WOODWARD AVENUE
SUITE 200
STONERIDGE WEST BUILDING
BLOOMFIELD HILLS, MI 48304
248-258-1616
Fax: 248-258-1439
info@butzel.com
www.butzel.com
• Keefe A. Brooks, VP/Shareholder
(248) 593-3010
• James C. Bruno, VP/Shareholder
(313) 225-7024
bruno@butzel.com
• Carey A. DeWitt, VP/Shareholder
(313) 225-7056
dewitt@butzel.com
• Richard B. W. Brosnick, VP/Shareholder
brosnick@butzel.com
Services:
Admiralty, Marine and Waterfront
Development Practice,
Advertising/Marketing Law Practice,
Alternative Dispute Resolution Philosophy
and Practice, Appellate Practice, Bond
Practice, Business Litigation Practice,
Business, Corporate and Taxation Practice,
China Practice, Commercial and Industrial
Property Assessment Appeals, Commercial
Lending and Workout Practice, Commercial
Workout and Bankruptcy Practice,
Condemnation and Zoning Law Practice,
Corporate Compliance, Internal
Investigations and Criminal Defense, Family
Law Practice, Financial Institutions Practice,
Employee Benefits Practice, etc.
Description:
Represents sports organizations.
Other Locations:
150 West Jefferson, Ste 100, Detroit, MI

48226; Phone: 313-225-7000; Fax: 313-225-7080; 110 West Michigan, Ste 1100, Lansing, MI 48933; Phone: 517-372-6622; Fax: 517-372-6672; 350 South Main Street, Ste 300, Ann Arbor, MI 48104; Phone: 734-995-3110; Fax: 734-995-1777; 25 West 8th Street, Ste 200, Holland, MI 49423; Phone: 616-396-8860; Fax: 616-396-1771; 1200 North Federal Highway, Ste 420, Boca Raton, FL 33432; Phone: 561-368-2151; Fax: 561-368-4668; 801 Laurel Oak Drive, Ste 705, Naples, FL 34108; Phone: 239-593-1647; Fax: 239-593-1648

C. JAY ROBBINS
5115 HAMPTON BLVD.
NORFOLK, VA 23529
757-683-3144
Fax: 757-683-5041
www.odu.edu
• C. Ja Robbins, Special Assistant Attorney General/Gener
Description:
Represents college athletic departments.

CALIFORNIA WESTERN SCHOOL OF LAW
225 CEDAR STREET
SAN DIEGO, CA 92101
619-239-0391
Fax: 619-525-7092
www.cwsl.edu
• Jan Stiglitz, Law Professor/Co-Director, Innocence Pro
(619) 525-1697
jstiglitz@cwsl.edu
• William J. Aceves, Law Professor/Director, International Le
(619) 515-1589
waceves@cwsl.edu
• Richard J Finkmore, Law Professor/Director, Louis M. Brown P
(619) 525-1687
tbarton@cwsl.edu
• Neils B. R. Schaumann, Dean
• Deborah Williams, Executive Assistant
Services:
Teaches sports law arbitration.

CALLAHAN, ROBERT E.
4041 MACARTHUR BOULEVARD
SUITE 350
NEWPORT BEACH, CA 92660
949-252-4615
Fax: 949-252-4616
rec@rcallahanlaw.com
• Robert Callahan, Attorney at Law
Nature of Services:
Legal Counsel
Clients include:
Big West Conference, Golden State Athletic Conference, Pacific Sports LLC

CAMPBELL, ROBERT G.
2049 CENTURY PARK E
SUITE 2800
LOS ANGELES, CA 90067
310-284-2200
Fax: 310-284-2100
www.coxcastle.com
• Robert G. Campbell, Senior Counsel
(310) 284-2259
rcampbell@coxcastle.com
• Paul N. Dubrasich, Senior Counsel
(415) 262-5120
pdubrasich@coxcastle.com

• Edward C. Dygert, Senior Counsel
(949) 260-4642
edygert@coxcastle.com
• Ted M. Handel, Senior Counsel
(310) 284-2262
thandel@coxcastle.com
Services:
Represents and assists businesses, institutions, and individuals in all aspects of the real estate, finance, and construction industries, including, acquisitions and dispositions, affordable housing, bankruptcy, workouts and commercial remedies, commercial leasing, construction, development risk management, environmental, finance, institutional investments, International and Emerging markets, joint venture, labor and employment, land use and entitlements, litigation, property management, residential, resort and hospitality properties, retail development, and tax and estate planning.
Nature of Sports Service:
All phases of athlete representation including contract negotiation and post-career counseling.

CANTOR, DAVID MICHAEL P.C., LAW OFFICES OF
2141 E BROADWAY ROAD
SUITE 220
TEMPE, AZ 85282
480-858-0808
888-822-6867
• David Michael Cantor, Attorney
Description:
Criminal Practice and General Civil Litigation before State and Federal Courts. Criminal Defense, Driving While Intoxicated, Traffic Violations, Felonies, Drug Offenses, Sexual Offenses, Assault and Battery, Manslaughter, Murder, Capital Offenses, Sports Law, with emphasis in Trial and Appellate Practice.
Services:
Provides service in areas of Criminal Law, DUI/DWI, Entertainment, Sports & Leisure Law, Immigration & Naturalization Law, Litigation & Appeals, Motor Vehicle Accidents — Plaintiff, Personal Injury — Defense, Personal Injury — Plaintiff, Traffic Violations, and White Collar Crimes.

CARDWELL, VICTOR
10 S JEFFERSON STREET
SUITE 1400
ROANOKE, VA 24011
540-983-7600
800-552-4529
Fax: 540-983-7711
www.woodsrogers.com
• Heman Ma III, Principal
(540) 983-7654
marshall@woodsrogers.com
• Victor O. Cardwell, Principal
(540) 983-7529
cardwell@woodsrogers.com
• Nicholas C. R. Conte, Chairman of the Board
• Thomas Bagby, President
(540) 983-7766
bagby@woodsrogers.com
• George Leloudis, Executive Director
(540) 983-7779
gleloudis@woodsrogers.com
• Paula Hess, Director of Human Resources
(540) 983-7534

phess@woodsrogers.com
• Lillian Crites, Marketing Director
(540) 983-7579
lcrites@woodsrogers.com
• Charles Helvey, IT Director
(540) 983-7572
chelvey@woodsrogers.com
• Cindi Harris, Accounting Manager
(540) 983-7573
charris@woodsrogers.com
Description:
Litigation, Sports and Entertainment Law.
Services:
Legal Representation
Other Locations:
823 East Main Street, Suite 1200, Richmond, VA 23219; Phone: 804-343-5020; 825 Kemper Street, Lynchburg, VA 24501; Phone: 434-846-4040; 530 Main Street, STE 201, Danville, VA 24541; Phone: 434-797-8200

CARNEY & TROUPE
185 DEVONSHIRE ST.
SUITE 802
BOSTON, MA 2110
617-426-9797
Fax: 617-426-3816
• Gerard B. Carney, Attorney/Partner
Services:
Legal Representation
Description:
NFLPA workers' compensation panel. Handles workers' compensation for the New England Patriots.

CARTWRIGHT LAW FIRM, THE
222 FRONT STREET
5TH FLOOR
SAN FRANCISCO, CA 94111
415-433-0444
888-433-0440
Fax: 415-433-0449
www.cartwrightlaw.com
• Robert Cartwright, Partner
Services:
A personal injury law firm dedicated to providing high quality, aggressive legal representation to victims of personal injury.

CASHATT, BRENT A.
501 S.W. 7TH STREET
SUITE J
DES MOINES, IA 50309-2200
515-244-4300
Fax: 515-244-2650
lbabich@babichgoldman.com
www.babichgoldman.com
• Brent Cashatt, Attorney
• Leslie Babich, Attorney
• Todd E. Babich, Attorney
• Michael J. Carroll, Attorney
Description:
Contract negotiation, arbitration hearings, endorsement exploration, tort actions/litigation and financial planning.
Services:
Family Law; Domestic Relations; Litigation; Conflict Resolution; Mediation Services

CASTILLO, ANGEL
815 MORAGA DRIVE
LOS ANGELES, CA 90049
310-471-3000
Fax: 310-471-7990
ssmall@lsl-la.com
www.lsl-la.com

- Angel F. Castillo, Attorney
(310) 471-3000
acastillo@lsl-la.com
- Charles M. Levy, Attorney
(310) 471-3000
clevy@lsl-la.com
- Steven G. Small, Attorney
ssmall@lsl-la.com
- Tom Lallas, Attorney
tlallas@lsl-la.com
Services:
Represents commercial lenders

CELLI & ASSOCIATES
130 WEST LANCASTER AVENUE
SUITE 201
WAYNE, PA 19087
610-525-5380
Fax: 610-527-7659
rcelli@cellilaw.com
www.cellilaw.com
- Michael G. Celli, Jr, Attorney
Nature of Sports Service:
All phases of athlete representation
including contract negotiation, long-range
planning, financial planning, and post-career
counseling.

CHAPMAN & CUTLER
111 W MONROE STREET
FLOOR 13
CHICAGO, IL 60603-4080
312-845-3000
Fax: 312-701-2361
www.chapman.com
- Richard A Cosgrove, Chief Executive
Partner
(312) 845-3738
cosgrove@chapman.com
- Ann E. Acker, Partner
acker@chapman.com
- Daniel Johnson, Chief Operating Partner
- Kimberly L. Ahlgrim, Partner
ahlgrim@chapman.com
- Adrienne Ancheta, Associate
ancheta@chapman.com
- Anna M. Anderson, Associate
aanderso@chapman.com
- Laura E. Appleby, Associate
appleby@chapman.com
Services:
Asset Securitization, Banking, Bankruptcy,
Restructuring and Workouts, Commercial
Litigation and Dispute Resolution, Corporate
Counseling, Corporate Finance and
Securities, Intellectual Property, Investment
Companies, Lease Finance, Public Finance,
Real Estate and Environmenta, Sports
Finance, Taxation, Trusts and Estates,
Utility Finance
Clients:
World's largest banks, insurance
companies, investment banks, corporate
and governmental issuers, investors and
credit providers.
Description:
Contract negotiation, investment contract
negotiation.
Other Locations:
595 Market Street, STE 2600, San
Francisco, CA 94105; Phone:
415-541-0500; 50 South Main Street, Salt
Lake City, UT 84144; Phone: 801-533-0066

CHASEN & BOSCOLO CHARTERED
7852 WALKER DRIVE
SUITE 300
GREENBELT, MD 20770
301-220-0050
Fax: 301-474-1230
www.chasenboscolo.com
- Gerald Herz, Attorney
(301) 220-0050
- Benjamin T. Boscolo, Attorney
(301) 220-0050
- Barry Chasen, Attorney
- Thomas Teodori, Attorney
- Barry M Chasen, Attorney
- Gerald Herz, Attorney
- W. David Falcon, Attorney
- Matthew J. Peffer, Attorney
- Michael D Reiter, Attorney
- Kevin H Stillman, Attorney
Services:
Represents professional athletes in disability
and worker's compensation claims

CHERNESKY, RICHARD
10 N LUDLOW STREET
1100 COURTHOUSE PLAZA SW
DAYTON, OH 45402
937-449-2800
Fax: 937-449-2821
www.dinsmore.com
- Richard J. Chernesky, Managing Partner
(937) 449-2800
- Edward M. Kress, Attorney
(937) 449-2800
- Richard A. Broock, Attorney
- Suellen J. Young, Executive Director
- Kenneth L. Crooks, Chief Financial Officer
- Jennifer A. Davenport, Director of
Marketing
- Christopher Flaherty, Chief Business
Development Officer
- Stephanie Higgins, Director of Human
Resources & Employee Benefi
- Mary Jo Merkowitz, Director of Library
Services
- Frederick Caspar, Attorney
Description:
Business Law,Mergers & Acquisitions,
Litigation, Estate Planning.
Services:
Corporate law, strategic planning, tax
analysis, and litigation
Clients:
AAA Miami Valley Advantage Per Diem
Staffing, LLC AK Steel Architectural
Resources Corporation The Aristocrat
Products Mfg. Co. Audi of America, Inc. The
Berry Company Better Business Bureau of
Dayton/Miami Valley, Inc. Bradstreet &
Company, Inc. Bri Lyn, Inc. Brown Industrial,
Inc. CBS Personnel Services, LLC Central
State University Foundation CFA Holding,
Inc. Chiropractic Health & Wellness Center,
Inc. Church of the Messiah The Connor
Group CSA Nutrition Services, Inc. Day
International, Inc. Dayton Christian School,
Inc. The Dayton Heart Center, Inc. The
Dayton-Montgomery County Port Authority
Digital Concepts, Inc. Digitron, Inc.
Year Founded:
1988

CINDRICH & COMPANY
552 WASHINGTON AVENUE
PITTSBURGH, PA 15106
412-429-1250
Fax: 412-429-1260

info@cindrich.com
www.cindrich.com
- Ralph E. Cindrich, Founder
(412) 429-1250
ralph@cindrich.com
- Gregory P. Diulus, Attorney
(412) 429-1250
gregory@cindrich.com
- Brian Ayrault, Attorney/Contract Advisor
brian@cindrich.com
- John Bermudez, Executive Director
john@cindrich.com
Services:
Assists clients in all football career related
areas; deals with every significant company
in the sporting goods, apparel and trading
card industry; career counseling; media
relations; legal advice and assistance; tax
advice and preparation of tax returns;
financial planning; represented Pro Football
players from every team in the NFL and CFL
Clients:
Rookies: Greg Esligner, Erik Gill, Bruce
Gradkowski, Ryan LaCasse, Matt Lentz,
Chris Morris, Jonathan Orr, Kai Parham,
John Ritcher, Jason Spitz, Ative NFL clients:
Eugene Baker, Ladell Betts, Martin Bibla,
Jeff Blake, Jamaal Branch, Zach Bray,
Ethan Brooks, Lang Campbell, Ben Claxton,
Enoch DeMar, Daryl Dixon, Jeff Dugan,
Mike Echols, Eric Edwards, James Farrior,
Matt Farrior, Mike Flynn, Kynan Forney,
John Paul 'JP' Foschi, Hank Fraley, Steven
Gibbs, Tarik Glenn, Brian Griese, Michael
Hawthorne, Ronney Jenkins, Adrian Klemm,
Justin Kurpeikis, Mike Labinjo, Rien Long,
Rasheed Marshall

CLARDY, DON S.
55 BEATTIE PLACE
ONE LIBERTY SQUARE, SUITE 1200, PO
BOX 10589
SUITE 1200
GREENVILLE, SC 29601
864-271-9580
Fax: 864-271-7502
www.gwblawfirm.com
- Henry Mi Gallivan, Managing Shareholder
(864) 271-5341
mgallivan@gwblawfirm.com
- W. Howard Boyd, Jr., Shareholder
(864) 271-5343
hboyd@gwblawfirm.com
- Arthur L. Howson Jr, Shareholder
(864) 271-5352
ahowson@gwblawfirm.com
- Freda G. Lark, Human Resources
Manager
(864) 271-5392
flark@GWBLawfirm.com
- Jeanette Behrens, Operations Assistant
(864) 271-5432
jbehrens@GWBlawfirm.com
- Tiffany Breeden, Billing & Collections
Manager
(864) 241-7020
tbreeden@GWBlawfirm.com
- Kevin Dehlinger, Marketing Director
(864) 271-5369
kdehlinger@GWBlawfirm.com
- Kira DeLoache, Accounting Director
(864) 271-5388
kdeloache@GWBlawfirm.com
- Freda Lark, Human Resources Director
(864) 271-5392
flark@GWBlawfirm.com
- Rick Phillips, Operations Director

(864) 271-5393
rphillips@GWBlawfirm.com
Description:
Corporate law, Business Law, Estate Planning, Trusts & Estates.
Services:
Litigation, Administrative Law, Business and Commercial Law, Alternative Dispute Resolution
Clients:
ACE USA, AETNA, Air Products Polymers, L.P., American International Group, Baxter Healthcare Corporation, Bayer Corporation, BBA Nonwovens, Bell-Air, LLC, Blue Cross Blue Shield of South Carolina, BP America, Inc., Canal Insurance Company, Centex Homes, Central Carolina Bank, City of Greenville, CNA Insurance Companies, Coca-Cola Bottling Company Consolidated, CoLinx, LLC, Companion Healthcare, Companion Technologies, Crown Cork & Seal, CSX Transportation, Inc., DIRECTV, Inc., Dycos Staffing, Inc., The Dow Chemical Company, Empire Fire & Marine Insurance, Engelhard Corporation, ESIS, Genuine Parts Company, GMAC Insurance, Greenville Airport C

CLARK, CAROL
1544 OLD ALABAMA ROAD
ROSWELL, GA 30076
770-804-0400
800-275-7171
Fax: 770-643-4080
www.mccalla.com
• Carol V. Clark, Attorney
(770) 804-0400
carol.clark@mccalla.com
• Timothy L. Geraghty, Attorney
(770) 804-0400
Services:
Contract negotiation

CLAYBORNE, COURTNEY
4020 JACKSON BOULEVARD
PO BOX 6900
RAPID CITY, SD 57709-6900
605-348-7300
800-998-3998
Fax: 605-348-4757
JohnsonEiesland@Rushmore.com
www.johnsoneiesland.com
• Courtney R. Clayborne, Attorney (Past)
• Glen H. Johnson, Attorney/Partner
gjohnson22@aol.com
• Gregory A. Eiesland, Attorney/Partner
geiesland@aol.com
• Kenneth R. Dewell, Attorney/Associate
Description:
Business Law, Commercial Litigation, Workers Compensation.
Services:
Laywer, Rapid City, SD, injury, Rapid City, medical, automobile, attorney, Rapid City, criminal, malpractice, Contracts, insurance, Defense, Rapid City

CLINARD, KEITH ASHFORD
ONE W FOURTH STREET
PO BOX 84
WINSTON-SALEM, NC 27101
336-721-3600
Fax: 336-721-3660
www.wcsr.com
• Keith A. Clinard, Attorney
(336) 721-3631
KClinard@wcsr.com

• William Sullivan, Senior Partner
(336) 721-3506
WSullivan@wcsr.com
• Deborah Hylton, Partner
DHylton@wcsr.com
• James B. Hunt Jr, Partner
JHunt@wcsr.com
Services:
Contract negotiation, arbitration hearings, tort actions/litigation.
Other Locations:
1401 Eye Street NW, 7th Floor, Washington, DC 20005; 8065 Leesburg Pike, 4th Floor, Tysons Corner, VA 22182; One Atlantic Center, STE 3500, 1201 West Peachtree Street, Atlanta, GA 30309

COHEN, ROBERT M.
4 FANEUIL HALL SQUARE
3RD FLOOR
BOSTON, MA 2109-1632
617-523-0505
• Robert M. Cohen, Founder
(617) 523-0505
• Steven D. Weil, Partner
(617) 523-0505
• Janet B. Fierman, Founding Partner
(617) 523-0505
• Thomas W. Evans, Partner
(617) 523-0505
• Robert M Cohen, Partner
Services:
Provides comprehensive business, real estate and litigation services
Clients:
Restaurants: Applebee's, Boston Market, Cinnabon, Inc., D'Angelos, Inc., Fuddruckers, Inc., McDonald's Corporation, Papa Gino's, Inc.; Retail & Service Companies: BÆ'loise-Holding, Bridgestone/Firestone, Dancing Deer Baking Company, Exxon/Mobil, HP, Kinkos, Inc., MBNA America Bank, N.A., Mercator Assurances S.A., Pitney Bowes, Zeltia S.A.; Real Estate: AIMCO, Alcourt Management Corporation, AvalonBay Communities, DMC Management Company, The Dolben Company, Inc., ELAW Corporation, Forest City, Homes Incorporated, Stuart Family Trust, Trammell Crow Company
Description:
Sports law.

COHN, WILLIAM A.
291 GERMANTOWN BEND COVE
CORDOVA, TN 38018
901-757-5557
888-LAWVOL1
Fax: 901-757-5535
info@cohnlawfirm.com
www.cohnlawfirm.com
• William Cohn, Principal Attorney
(901) 757-5557
info@cohnlawfirm.com
• Jeremy A. A Davis, Associate Attorney
Year Founded:
1981.
Sports Service Founded:
1985.
Nature of Service:
Focuses on personal injury, auto accidents, DUI, medical malpractice, family law, Real Estate Law, Bunkruptcy, Business Law, Account Collections, Social Security Disability and Sports Law.

COLE, DAYTON T.
BB DOUGHETHY ADMINISTRATION BUILDING
3RD FLOOR
PO BOX 32126
BOONE, NC 28608-2126
828-262-2000
Fax: 828-262-2556
www.appstate.edu
• Dayton T. Cole, University Attorney
(828) 262-2751
coledt@appstate.edu
• Dr. Kenneth E. Peacock, The Chancellor
• Dr. Lori Gonzalez, The Provost
• Cathy Bates, Chief Information Officer
• Charlie Cobb, Director of Athletics
• Hank Foreman, Associate Vice Chancellor for University Comm
• Lori Gonzalez, Provost & Executive Vice Chancellor
• Patrick McCoy, Director of Human Resources
Description:
Represents college athletic departments.

COLLINS, MESEREAU, REDDOCK & YU, LLP
10390 SANTA MONICA BOULEVARD
SUITE 220
LOS ANGELES, CA 90025
310-789-1177
Fax: 310-861-1007
info@mesereauyu.com
www.mesereauyu.com
• Susan C. Yu, Attorney
• Thomas A. Mesereau, Jr, Attorney
• Susan C Yu, Attorney
Services:
Litigation, criminal cases (state and federal court), civil rights, personal injury and sports/entertainment law, fraud, unfair competition, securities fraud, employment, breach of contract.

COMODECA, JAMES A.
255 E FIFTH STREET
SUITE 1900
CINCINNATI, OH 45202
513-977-8200
800-934-3477
Fax: 513-977-8141
info@dinslaw.com
• Alan H. Abes, Partner
(513) 977-8149
alan.abes@dinslaw.com
• James A. Comodeca, Partner
(513) 977-8358
jim.comodeca@dinslaw.com
Services:
Provides quality legal counsel to our clients
clients:
Public and private corporations to charitable organizations and encompass healthcare providers, local and state governments, financial institutions, real estate evelopers, franchisors and distributors and pharmaceutical companies.
Description:
General Litigation; Medical Malpractice Defense; Sports/Entertainment Law; Products Liability Defense.
Other Locations:
Lexington Financial Center, 250, West Main Street, STE 1400, Lexington, KY 40507; Phone: 859-425-1000; The Grant Building, 330 Grant Street, STE 2415, Pittsburgh, PA 15219; Phone: 412-281-5000

CONBOY, JOSEPH B.
1802 HARTFORD AVENUE
LUBBOCK, TX 79409-0004
806-742-3990 EXT 226
Fax: 806-742-1629
info.law@ttu.edu
www.law.ttu.edu
• Jon Whitmore, President
(806) 742-2121
• Jennifer S. Bard, Director of the Health
Law Program
(806) 742-3990
• Martha McDaniel, Senior Business
Assistant
(806) 742-3990
martha.mcdaniel@ttu.edu
• Dan Runge, Asst. Director, Admissions
(806) 742-3990
Description:
Teaches sports law.

CONBOY, MELISSA L.
317 MAIN BUILDING
113 JOYCE CENTER
NOTRE DAME, IN 46556
574-631-5000
Fax: 574-631-8212
newsinfo@nd.edu
www.nd.edu
• John Jerkins, President
(574) 631-3903
newsinfo@nd.edu
• Jack L Swarbrick, University Vice
President/Director of Athleti
(574) 631-6107
• Missy Conboy, Senior Deputy Athletics
Director
(574) 631-6107
• John Heisler, Senior Associate A.D./Media
& Broadcast Relat
• Tom Nevala, Senior Associate Athletics
Director
(574) 631-6107
• Jill Bodensteiner, Associate Athletics
Director
(574) 631-6107
• Michael Danch, Associate Athletics
Director
(574) 631-6107
• Jim Fraleigh, Associate Athletics Director
(574) 631-6107
Services:
Represents college athletic departments
NCAA Compliance.

CONNELL, MARY ANN
2094 OLD TAYLOR ROAD
SUITE 200
5 UNIVERSITY OFFICE PARK
OXFORD, MS 38655
662-236-0055
Fax: 662-236-0035
mconnell@mayomallette.com
www.mayomallette.com
• J. Ca Mayo Jr, Partner
(662) 236-0055
cmayo@mayomallette.com
• Pope S. Mallette, Partner
(662) 236-0055
pmallette@mayomallette.com
Description:
Represents college athletic departments.
Services:
Provides outstanding legal services to local,
regional and national clients from its offices
located in north Mississippi
Clients:
Amphenol Corporation, Baptist Memorial

Health Care Corporation, Copeland
Corporation, Emerson Electric Company,
First National Bank of Oxford, Grisanti Ford,
Inc., Grisanti Rebel Motors, Inc.,
Johnston-Tombigbee Furniture
Manufacturing Company

CONNER & WINTERS, P.L.L.C.
4000 ONE WILLIAMS CENTER
TULSA, OK 74172-0148
918-586-5711
www.cwlaw.com
• John R. Elrod, Partner
(479) 582-5711
jelrod@cwlaw.com
• Greg S. Scharlau, Partner
(479) 582-5711
gscharlau@cwlaw.com
• Charles E. Scharlau, Jr, Attorney
(479) 582-5711
cscharlau@cwlaw.com
• Victor F. Di Albert, Partner
(405) 272-5733
• P. Bradley Bendure, Partner
(918) 586-8521
bbendure@cwlaw.com
• Mark H. Bennett, Partner
(405) 272-5718
• Mark G. Berman, Partner
(918) 586-8961
mberman@cwlaw.com
• Gary L. Betow, Partner
(918) 586-5714
gbetow@cwlaw.com
• Debbie L. Blackwell, Partner
(918) 586-8970
• Terri Chadick, Of counsel
(479) 582-5711
Description:
Services extend from general, personal and
business counseling to highly specialized
assistance and advice. The firm offers a full
range of legal services in each of our offices
with regard to banking, real estate, trusts,
probate, estate planning, litigation, income,
gift taxation law and corporate finance.
Year Founded:
1933
Other Locations:
1627 I Street, NW STE 900, Washington,
DC 20006; Phone: 202-887-5711; 1000
Louisana, STE 1301, Houston, TX 77002;
Phone: 713-355-5711; 1700 One
Leadership Square, 211 North Robinson,
Oklahoma City, OK 73102; Phone:
405-272-5711

COOK & FRANKE S.C.
660 E MASON STREET
MILWAUKEE, WI 53202
414-271-5900
Fax: 414-271-2002
• Steven L Nelson, Attorney
(414) 227-1220
• Jeffrey JP Conta, Attorney
(414) 227-1226
• Lawrence Clancy, Attorney
(414) 227-1207
• Paul D. Cranley, Attorney
(608) 251-0404
Services:
Contract negotiation, represents
professional sports teams (Milwaukee
Admirals).
Clients:
Companies and individuals working in the
electronics, manufacturing, communications,
utility and construction engineering,

architectural, design and construction,
commercial real estate, sports and
entertainment industries.

COOLEY, GODWARD, LLP
101 CALIFORNIA STREET
5TH FLOOR
SAN FRANCISCO, CA 94111-5800
415-693-2000
Fax: 415-693-2222
www.cooley.com
• Gian-Michele A Marca, Partner
(415) 693-2148
gmamarca@cooley.com
• Stephen Neal, Chairman
• Joe Conoroy, CEO
• Mark Pitchford, Administrative and Legal
Practice Partner
• Warren Martin, COO
• Gordon C Atkinson, Partner
(415) 693-2088
Services:
Represents professional sports teams.
Other Locatons:
380 Interlocken Crescent, STE 900,
Bloomfield, CO 80021; Phone:
720-566-4000; One Freedom Square,
Reston Tower Center, 11951 Freedom
Drive, Reston, VA 20190; Phone:
703-456-8000

CORBETT & STEELMAN
18200 VON KARMAN AVENUE
SUITE 900
IRVINE, CA 92612-1023
949-553-9266
Fax: 949-553-8454
www.corbettandsteelman.com
• Bruce R. Corbett, Attorney
• Ken E. Steelman, Attorney
• Richard B. Spector, Attorney
• Christine Vaughn, Office Administration
Services:
Business litigation, entertainment litigation,
media, sports law.

**COWAN, DEBAETS, ABRAHAMS &
SHEPPARD, LLP**
41 MADISON AVENUE
34TH FLOOR
NEW YORK, NY 10010
212-974-7474
Fax: 212-974-8474
cdas@cdas.com
www.cdas.com
• Timothy Debaets, Partner
(212) 974-7474
tdebaets@cdas.com
• Anne C. Baker, Partner
(212) 974-7474
abaker@cdas.com
• Frederick P. Bimbler, Partner
fbimbler@cdas.com
Description:
Sports Law, Motion Picture; Television;
Publishing.
Services:
Entertainment law, publishing, art law,
copyright, trademark, and litigation
Clients:
Well-known organizations and individuals in
motion pictures, television, book publishing,
the visual arts and sports.

CRIVELLO, CARLSON, MENTKOWSKI S.C.
710 N PLANKINTON AVENUE
SUITE 500
MILWAUKEE, WI 53203
414-271-7722
Fax: 414-271-4438
www.milwlaw.com
• Nick Kotsonis, Attorney
(414) 271-7722
nkotsonis@milwlaw.com
• Donald H. Carlson, Attorney
(414) 271-7722
Description:
Contract negotiation.
Services:
Provides Trial, Appellate, Mediation and Arbitration Services in the following areas: Architectural and Engineering Litigation, Civil Rights Litigation, Commercial and Corporate Litigation, Construction Litigation, Electrical Accidents, Electronic Media and Privacy Law, Employee Benefits/ ERISA, Employment Law, Environmental Litigation, Errors and Omissions, Fire and Explosion, Fraudulent Insurance Claims, Industrial Accidents, Insurance Bad Faith Defense, Insurance Coverage Litigation, Labor Law, Legal Malpractice Defense, Libel, Slander and Defamation, Management Labor Relations, Mechanical Accidents

CROAK, FRANCIS R.
660 E MASON STREET
STE 300
MILWAUKEE, WI 53202
414-271-5900
Fax: 414-271-2002
• Francis R. Croak, Shareholder
• Lawrence Clancy, Attorney
(414) 227-1207
• Jeffrey JP Conta, Attorney
(414) 227-1226
Services:
Contract negotiation, represents professional sports teams (Milwaukee Admirals).
Clients:
Companies and individuals working in the electronics, manufacturing, communications, utility and construction engineering, architectural, design and construction, commercial real estate, sports and entertainment industries.

CULLEN, WESTON, PINES & BACH LLP
122 W WASHINGTON AVENUE
SUITE 900
MADISON, WI 53703-2718
608-807-0752
Fax: 608-251-2883
www.cwpb.com
• Lee Cullen, President/Attorney
(608) 251-0101
cullen@cwpb.com
• Carol Grob, Partner
(608) 251-0101
grob@cwpb.com
• Curt F. Pawlisch, Partner
pawlisch@cwpb.com
Services:
Includes labor and employment, energy and telecommunications, governmental relations, family law, civil and criminal litigation, and business and commerce
Description:
Contract Negotiation.

DALTON, MICHAEL
2200 ROSS AVENUE
SUITE 5200
DALLAS, TX 75201
214-665-3600
Fax: 214-665-3601
www.gtlaw.com
• Michael Dalton, Shareholder
(214) 665-3628
• Eric W Buether, Shareholder
(214) 665-3664
Services:
Provides advice and counsel to industry leaders worldwide

DANIELS, ERIC D.
280 TRUMBULL STREET
HARTFORD, CT 06103-3597
860-275-8200
Fax: 860-275-8299
ml@rc.com
www.rc.com
• Nancy A. Hayes, Operation Officer
(860) 275-8368
• Peter M. Merriman, Financial Officer
(860) 275-8368
• Wystan M. Ackerman, Partner
(860) 275-8388
wackerman@rc.com
• Shannon Holden, Legal Administrative Assistant
(860) 541-2645
sholden@rc.com
• Benjamin B. Adams, Member
(860) 275-8271
• Adam Anderson, Associates
(860) 275-8352
aanderson@rc.com
• Stephen W. Aronson, Partner
(860) 275-8281
saronson@rc.com
• Eileen P. Baldwin, Member
(860) 275-8277
ebaldwin@rc.com
Services:
Provides Trial, Appellate, Mediation and Arbitration Services in the following areas: Architectural and Engineering Litigation, Civil Rights Litigation, Commercial and Corporate Litigation, Construction Litigation
Description:
Contract negotiation.

DAVIS & KUELTHAU, S.C.
111 E KILBOURN AVENUE
SUITE 1400
MILWAUKEE, WI 53202
414-276-0200
lbevan@dkattorneys.com
www.dkattorneys.com
• Charles I. Henderson, Attorney/Shareholder
(414) 225-1479
chenderson@dkattorneys.com
• Lee A. M Bevan, Local Office Administrator
(414) 225-7503
lbevan@dkattorneys.com
• Dillon J. Ambrose, Associate
(414) 225-1410
dambrose@dkattorneys.com
• Patrick M. Bergin, Shareholder
(414) 225-7563
pbergin@dkattorneys.com
• James E. Braza, Shareholder
(414) 225-1421
jbraza@dkattorneys.com

• Rodney W. Carter, Shareholder
(262) 792-2405
rcarter@dkattorneys.com
• Peter W. Bruce, Of Counsel
(414) 225-1437
pbruce@dkattorneys.com
• Dianne S. Cauble, Of Counsel
(414) 225-1436
dcauble@dkattorneys.com
Description:
Contract negotiation, arbitration hearings, federal/state/international tax filings, represents professional sports teams, endorsement exploration, tort actions/litigation, representing sports arenas and event sponsors.
Other Locations:
10 East Doty Street, STE 600, Madison, WI 53703; Phone: 608-280-8235; 318 South Washington Street, suite 300 Green Bay, WI 54301; Phone: 920-435-9378; 219 Washington Avenue,Oshkosh, WI 54901; Phone: 920-233-6050 605 North 8th Street, STE 610, Sheboygan, WI 53081; Phone: 920-451-1461; 300 North Corporate Drive, STE 150, Brookfield, WI 53045; Phone: 262-792-2400;

DAVIS & WILKERSON
5113 SW PARKWAY
SUITE 115
AUSTIN, TX 78735
512-482-0614
Fax: 512-482-0342
www.dwlaw.com
• David M. Davis, Director/Shareholder
(512) 482-0614
• Kevin Reed, VP
(512) 482-0614
• Leonard W Woods, Secretary/Treasurer
• Robert L Hargett, Director
Services:
All phases of athlete representation including contract negotiation, long-range planning, financial planning, and post-career counseling. Construction Litigation; First and Third Party Insurance Litigation; Products Liability.
Other Location:
1110 East Holland, Alpine, TX 79803; Phone: 432-837-5547
Year Founded:
1985

DEE, PAUL T.
5821 SAN AMARO DRIVE
PO BOX 248167
CORAL GABLES, FL 33146
305-284-2680
Fax: 305-284-2193
athleticdirector@miami.edu
www.hurricanesports.collegesports.com
• Paul T. Dee, Intercollegiate Athletics Director
(305) 284-2673
athleticdirector@miami.edu
• Blake James, Athletics Director
• Chris Freet, Associate AD
• Tony Hernandez, Deputy AD/Business Operations
• Jennifer Strawley, Sr Associate AD
Description:
Represents college athletic departments.

DEKAJLO LAW
1975 HEMPSTEAD TURNPIKE
SUITE 101
EAST MEADOW, NY 11554
516-542-9300
Fax: 516-542-9303
dekajlo@aol.com
dekajlo.com
• Oleh Dekajlo, Managing Partner
(516) 542-9300
• Orest R. Dekajlo, Attorney
(516) 542-9300
Services:
Tort actions/litigation.

DEMAYO, LAW OFFICES OF MICHAEL L.L.P.
1211 EAST MOREHEAD ST
CHARLOTTE, NC 28204
704-333-1000
877-529-1222
Fax: 704-333-6677
• Michael A. DeMayo, Principal/Founder
michael@demayolaw.com
• Michael J. McGinley, Chief Operating Officer
Nature of Service:
Represents auto accidents, workers' compensation, medical malpractices, personal injury and mass torts, social security disability, nursing home negligence, wrongful death, motocycle accidents, tractor trailer accidents, serious brain and spinal cord injuries. Guide our clients through the legal and financial challenges that they face after they are injured in a dignified and responsible manner.
Year Founded:
1992
Other Locations:
321 3rd Avenue NW, Hickory, NC 28601; 406 S Sutherland Avenue, Monroe, NC 28112

DENUNE, III, RALPH
5580 MONROE STREET
TOLEDO, OH 43560
419-885-3597
Fax: 419-885-3861
• John J. Callahan, Attorney
(419) 885-3597
• John F. McCarty, Attorney
(419) 885-3597
• Ralph De III, Attorney
(419) 885-3597
• John J. McHugh III, Attorney
(419) 885-3597
Services:
Provides Legal Services.

DEUTCH, ALLAN H
7670 N PORT WASHINGTON ROAD
STE 200
MILWAUKEE, WI 53217
414-247-9958
Fax: 414-247-9959
alan.deutch@deutch.com
www.deutch.com
• Alan H. Deutch, Attorney
alan.deutch@deutch.com
• Monte E. Weiss, Attorney
monte.weiss@deutch.com
• Alan H. Deutch, Attorney
• James L. McAlister, Attorney
• Nichole King, Legal Assistant
• G. Brighum, Legal Assisatant

Clients:
Real Estate Related: Re/Max Realty 100, Re/Max Preferred, Capitol Title, Inc. Title 100, Inc, Re/Max Executive Homes, Inc, American Southern Insurance Co., Home Insurance Co., Utah Fire and Home Insurance Co, Investors Insurance Co, Rupnow Homes, Bradley J. Kimmel Homes, M & M Home Builders, Meadow Homes, North Meadows, Park Meadows, Forest Hill Village, Cloisters of Greenforest Computer Related: Innovative Software, Ltd, Web Emporium, LLC, Paramount Optical Laboratories, Allen-Knox Studios, Crownpoint Timesharing, Multiple Listing Service, Inc. Insurance Defense: Amerisure Insurance Company, American Family Insurance, American Southern Insur
Description:
Contract negotiation, teaches sports law, represents professional sports teams, licensing, endorsement exploration, tort actions/litigation, represents sports organizations.

DEWALD, SCOTT D.
201 EAST WASHINGTON
SUITE 1200
PHOENIX, AZ 85004
602-262-5311
Fax: 602-262-5747
clientservices@lrlaw.com
www.lewisandroca.com
• Scott D. DeWald, Partner
(602) 262-5333
Sdewald@lrlaw.com
• Nathalie M Daum, Marketing Director
(602) 528-4588
clientservices@lrlaw.com
Description:
Represents professional sports teams, provides securities advice, licensing.

DIFILIPPO, JAMES
2001 E FOURTH STREET
SUITE 104
SANTA ANNA, CA 92705
714-543-1770
• James Difilippo, Contact
description
real estate.

DINSMORE
101 S FIFTH STREET
2500 NATIONAL CITY TOWER
LOUISVILLE, KY 40202-3175
502-540-2300
Fax: 502-585-2207
• Donna King Perry, Managing Partner
(502) 581-8085
dperry@whf-law.com
• Glen Bagby, Partner
(859) 244-7100
gbagby@whf-law.com
Services:
Real property, probate, products liability, securities, health and hospital, medical malpractice, tax law, sports law and entertainment law.
Clients:
Norton Healthcare, CARITAS, Catholic Health Initiatives, CNA Pro, Chubb Insurance Company, Design Professionals Insurance Company, Interstate Insurance Company, Philadelphia Insurance Company, Pharmacists Mutual Insurance Company, Liberty Mutual Underwriters and AIG,

American Commercial Lines Holdings LLC/Jeffboat LLC, Anderson Wood Products,Bank One Corporation,Baptist Healthcare Systems, Brown-Forman Corporation, CARITAS Medical Center, CARITAS Peace Center, CARITAS Home Health, Catholic Health Initiatives, Center for Women and Families, Colgate-Palmolive Company, Ford Motor Company, Hill's Pet Nutrition, Kentucky Restaurant Association P

DREW, ECKL & FARNHAM, LLP
880 W PEACHTREE STREET
PO BOX 7600
ATLANTA, GA 30309
404-885-1400
Fax: 404-876-0992
jreale@deflaw.com
www.deflaw.com
• John P. Reale, Partner
(404) 885-6404
Description:
Civil, corporate or individual cases.
Services:
Provides company a wide variety of practice areas, including Civil rights/municipal liability, commercial law, construction law, employment and labor law, environmental law, federal workers' compensation, general liability, insurance coverage, major property subrogation, medical malpractice, nursing home litigation, personal injury, premises liability, products liability, professional athletes/ entertainment, professional liability, propety insurance, reinsurance, transportation cargo, transportation trucking, workers' compensation.
Year Founded:
1983

DRINKER BIDDLE
191 N WACKER DRIVE
SUITE 3700
CHICAGO, IL 60606-1698
312-569-1000
Fax: 312-569-3000
www.drinkerbiddle.com
• Harold L. Kaplan, Chairman/Partner
(312) 569-1204
• David L. Wolfe, Partner
(312) 569-1313
dwolfe@gcd.com
• Edwin A. Getz, Partner in Charge
• Matthew Farley, Counsel
(212) 248-3150
• Mark D. Nelson, Partner
(312) 569-1326
Services:
Practices and industries include Corporate Law, Corporate Restructuring & Financial Institutions, Customs and International Trade, Government Relations, Health, Higher Education, Indian Tribal Governments, Intellectual Property, Litigation, Pharmaceuticals, Real Estate, Wealth Planning & Philanthropy.
Clients:
Client base includes Fortune 1000 and middle market companies, investment advisory firms, financial institutions, hospitals and health care providers, universities, governmental entities, manufacturing companies and emerging technology companies.
Description:
Contract negotiation, post career planning, investment contract negotiation,

federal/state/international tax filings, licensing, endorsement exploration.

DUANE MORRIS LLP
750 B STREET
SUITE 2900
SAN DIEGO, CA 92101-4681
619-744-2200
Fax: 619-744-2201
www.duanemorris.com
• Charles J. O'Donnell, Chief Operating Officer
(215) 979-1450
CJODonnell@duanemorris.com
• Michael A. Gillen, Tax Accounting Director
(215) 979-1635
MAGillen@duanemorris.com
• Mary Fa Robinson, Human Resources Director
(215) 979-1290
• Marianne F M. Adriatico, Partner
(619) 744-2212
• P.Blake Allen, Partner
(619) 744-2231
• Ann K Bradley, Partner
(619) 744-2269
akbradley@duanemorris.com
• David A Charapp, Partner
(619) 744-2251
• Richard C kim, Partner
(619) 744-2294
RCKim@duanemorris.com
• Lisa H Chung, Associate
(619) 744-2272
• Courtney L Baird, Associate
(619) 744-2285
CLBaird@duanemorris.com
Clients:
From Fortune 500 companies to small entrepreneurial ventures, from public entities to individuals; domestic and international clients ranging from large multinational corporations to closely held entrepreneurial businesses.
Description:
Business law, business litigation, college and university law, commercial law, commercial litigation, sports law, trademarks, trademark licensing.
Other Locations:
1667 K Street, NW, Washington, DC 20006; Phone: 202-776-7800;380 Lexington Avenue, New York, NY 10168: Phone: 211-692-1000; 470 Atlantic Avenue, STE 500, Boston, MA 02210; Phone: 617-289-9200; 3200 Southwest Freeway, STE 3150, Houston, TX 77027; Phone: 713-402-3900

DUKE LEGAL COUNSEL
310 BLACKWELL STREET
4TH FLOOR, BOX 104124
DURHAM, NC 27710
919-684-3955
Fax: 919-684-8725
ogc-info@duke.edu
www.ogc.duke.edu
• Pamela J. Bernard, Vice President and General Counsel
pam.bernard@duke.edu
• Mark D. Gustafson, Deputy Counsel
• Kate S. Hendricks, Deputy Counsel for Duke University
kate.hendricks@duke.edu
• Ann E. Bradley, Associate University Counsel
ann.bradley@duke.edu

• Henry L. Cuthbert, Associate University Counsel
henry.cuthbert@duke.edu
Description:
Represents college athletic departments.

DURANTE, CHARLES J.
1007 N ORANGE STREET
NINTH FLOOR
PO BOX 2207
WILMINGTON, DE 19801
302-658-9141
Fax: 302-658-5614
• Charles J. Durante, Partner
(302) 888-6280
• Burton A. Amernick, Partner
(202) 331-7111
• D. Ro Casey, IS/Operations Manager
• Burton A. Amernick, Partner
(202) 331-7111
burton.amernick@novakdruce.com
• Richard C. Auchterlonie, Partner
(713) 571-3400
richard.auchterlonie@novakdruce.com
• Joseph W. Bain, Partner
(561) 847-7800
joseph.bain@novakdruce.com
• R. James Balls, Partner
(202) 572-0319
james.balls@novakdruce.com
• Katherine M. Basile, Partner
(408) 414-7330
katherine.basile@novakdruce.com
• Michael Bell, Partner
(202) 331-7111
michael.bell@novakdruce.com
• Jeffrey B. Bove, Partner
(302) 888-6241
jeff.bove@novakdruce.com
Other Location:
1990 M Street NW, STE 800, Washington, DC 20036; Phone: 202-331-7111
Services:
Provides wide range of legal disciplines in the fields of Intellectual Property, Commercial, Corporate, and Business Law, Transaction Services, International Trade Commission, Bankruptcy, Mergers and Acquisitions
Clients:
International, national and local corporate and individual clients.

EBERLE, BERLIN, KADING, TURNBOW & MCKLVEEN
1111 W JEFFERSON STREET SUITE 530
PO BOX 1368
BOISE, ID 83701
208-344-8535
Fax: 208-344-8542
webmaster@eberle.com
www.eberle.com
• R.M. Turnbow, Attorney
rturnbow@eberle.com
• William J. McKlveen, Attorney
wmcklveen@eberle.com
• Warren E. Jones, Attorney
wjones@eberle.com
• Thomas R. Linville, Attorney
tlinville@eberle.com
Services:
Provides Legal Services.
Clients:
Ada County Highway District; Agri-Beef Co.; AT&T; Bank United of Texas; Cessna Aircraft Co.; Chase Manhattan Leasing & Co.; C.I.T. Group Equipment Financing, Inc.; Citicorp Naitonal Services, Inc.; CRI

Advantage, Inc.; The Dosen Companies; Deloitte & Touche; Employers Resource Management Company; First Banks; Franklin Building Supply Company; New Holland, North America; General Electric Co.; Investors Property Management; Edward D. Jones & Co.; Key Bank National Association; Key Corp Leasing, Ltd.; DcDonnell Douglas Corporation; OX Ranch; Phillips Petroleum; Piper Jaffrey, Inc.; Prudential Securities; Shearson/American Express

---

ECKERT SEAMANS
600 GRANT STREET
US STEEL TOWER 44TH FLOOR
PITTSBURGH, PA 15219-2788
412-566-6000
Fax: 412-566-6099
info@eckertseamans.com
www.eckertseamans.com
• Timothy P. Ryan, Chief Executive Officer
(412) 566-5990
tryan@eckertseamans.com
• Scott D. Cessar, Attorney in Charge
scessar@eckertseamans.com
• Dan Abeles, Member
(412) 566-1295
dabeles@eckertseamans.com
• Jennifer Adams, Associate
(412) 566-6859
jadams@eckertseamans.com
• Brij K. Agarwal, Member
(412) 566-6183
bagarwal@eckertseamans.com
• Kevin P. Allen, Member
(412) 566-6866
kpallen@eckertseamans.com
• Kathryn C. Arbogast, Associate
(412) 566-6088
karbogast@eckertseamans.com
• Daniel C. P. Abeles, Member
(412) 566-1295
dabeles@eckertseamans.com
Clients:
Any local, regional, national or international corporations, individual, entrepreneurial, start-up, nonprofit and government clients.
Description:
Provides legal services to sports, entertainment and arts industry clients throughout the country. General representation of professional and college sports organizations. Advises on a number of sports-related issues, including player contracts and other labor law matters, broadcasting agreements, trademark, copyright and merchandising issues, as well as general corporate, finance and litigation matters
Other Locations:
1747 Pennsylvania Avenue, NW, STE 1200, Washington, DC 20006; Phone: 202-659-6600; Fax: 202-659-6699; The Towne Center, 4 East 8th Street, STE 200, Wilmington, DE 19801; Phone: 302-425-0430; Fax: 302-425-0432; U.S Steel Tower, 600 Grant Street, 44th Floor, Pittsburgh, PA 15219; Phone: 412-566-6000; Fax 412-566-6099; 1515 Market Street, 9th Floor, Philadelphia, PA 19102; Phone: 215-851-8400; Fax: 215-851-8383; 213 Market Street, 8th Floor, Harrisburg, PA 17101; Phone: 717-237-6000; Fax: 717-237-6019; 2400 Cranberry Square, 2nd Floor, Morgantown, WV 26508; Phone: 304-594-1000; Fax: 304-594-1181

ECKSTEIN LAW FIRM
1515 POYDRAS ST.
SUITE 2195
NEW ORLEANS, LA 70112
504-527-0701
Fax: 504-566-0040
• Michael Eckstein, Member
Description:
Provides individual and corporate tax
planning, closely held business law, estate
and gift taxation, entrepreneurial business
law, professional sports law, real estate tax
practice, tax controversy work at city, state
and federal level, high-tech/venture capital
concerns, communication businesses,
representation of professional athletes,
licensing, mergers and acquisitions

EDELSTEIN, LAIRD & SOBEL
9255 SUNSET BOULEVARD
SUITE 800
LOS ANGELES, CA 90069
310-274-6184
Fax: 310-274-6185
Sobel@elsentlaw.com
www.elsentlaw.com
• Gerald F. Edelstein, Counsel/Attorney
Sobel@elsentlaw.com
• Peter Laird, Partners
Sobel@elsentlaw.com
• William R. Sobel, Partner
Sobel@elsentlaw.com
• Peter Laird, Partner
• Gerald. F. Edelstein, Partner
Services:
Provide clients with responsive service,
quality legal work, the highest degree of
confidentiality, and value.

EFRON, MORTON L.
5246 HOHMAN AVENUE
FIFTH FLOOR
HAMMOND, IN 46320
219-931-5380
Fax: 219-933-3180
mort@efronlaw.com
www.efronlaw.com
• Morton L. Efron, Attorney
(219) 931-5380
mort@efronlaw.com
• Marissa McDermott, Attorney
(219) 931-5380
Description:
Legal representation, including investment
advice.
Services:
Provides expert legal skills and advice.
Year Founded:
1938

EGAN, ROBERT T.
33 EAST EUCLID AVENUE
ONE CENTENNIAL SQUARE
HADDONFIELD, NJ 08033
856-795-2121
Fax: 856-795-0574
webmaster@archerlaw.com
www.archerlaw.com
• Robert T. Egan, Partner
(856) 354-3079
regan@archerlaw.com
• Clint B. Allen, Associate
(856) 354-3017
callen@archerlaw.com
• Frank D. Allen, Partner
(856) 354-3075
fallen@archerlaw.com

• Robert. T. A. Egan, Partner
(856) 354-3079
regan@archerlaw.com
• Lynne Abraham, Partner
(215) 246-3113
labraham@archerlaw.com
• Kenneth E. Ahl, Partner
(215) 246-3132
kahl@archerlaw.com
• Clint B. Allen, Partner
(856) 354-3017
callen@archerlaw.com
• Frank D. Allen, Partner
(856) 354-3075
fallen@archerlaw.com
• James S. Asali, Partner
(215) 246-3112
jasali@archerlaw.com
• William M. Aukamp, Partner
(302) 356-6630
waukamp@archerlaw.com
Description:
Contract negotiation.
Services:
Provides highest quality, result-driven legal
services to corporate and individual clients.
Clients:
Alliant Tech Systems, Associated Press,
Avaya Inc., Bancroft Neurohealth,
Bridgestone/Firesone Inc., Capital Blue
Cross, City of Philadelphia, COIM USA, Inc.,
Cooper Hospital/UMC, Coriell Institute for
Medical Research, Crown cork & Seal,
Co.,Inc., Cumberland Farms, Inc., Cybex
International, Delaware River Port Authority,
Exxon Mobil Corporation, Fifth Third Bank,
First American Marketing Corp., Gannett,
Inc., Gloucester County College, Goucester
County Imrprovement Authority, Hale Trailer
Brake & Wheel, Heritage Building Group,
Holman Enterprises, Hunterdon Medical
Center, Lockheed-Martin Corp., Main Line
Health System, Morgan Stanley DW

EHRHARDT, CHARLES W.
425 W JEFFERSON STREET
BK ROBERTS HALL, ROOM 205
TALLAHASSEE, FL 32306-1601
850-644-3400
Fax: 850-644-5487
www.law.fsu.edu
• Charles W. Ehrhardt, Emeritus Professor
(850) 644-5240
ehrhardt@law.fsu.edu
• Talbot D'Alemberte, President
Emeritus/Professor
(850) 644-0800
Description:
Teaches sports law.

ELSWIT, LAWRENCE S.
1 SILBER WAY
BOSTON, MA 2215
617-353-2000
Fax: 617-353-5529
lelswit@bu.edu
www.bu.edu
• Robert A. Brown, President
(617) 353-2200
president@bu.edu
• Elizabeth B. Green, Executive Assistant to
the President
(617) 353-2200
ebgreen@bu.edu
• Nancy K. Baker, Assistant to the President
(617) 353-2466
nbaker@bu.edu

• Tammy Egan, Administrative Manager
(617) 353-2200
tegan@bu.edu
Services:
Represents college athletic departments.

ELY, BETTINI, ULMAN & ROSENBLATT
3200 N CENTRAL AVENUE
SUITE 1930
PHOENIX, AZ 85012
602-230-2144
800-303-2144
Fax: 602-264-9337
eburlaw@eburlaw.com
www.eburlaw.com
• Herbert L. Ely, Attorney
Herbely@eburlaw.com
• Ronald Ozer, Attoney
(602) 230-2144
ronozer@eburlaw.com
• Alicia Funkhouser, Attoney
(602) 230-2144
afunkhouser@eburlaw.com
• Jenna Mandraccia, Attoney
(602) 230-2144
jenna@eburlaw.com
• Herb Ely, Attoney
(602) 230-2144
herbely@eburlaw.com
• Joseph M. M. Bettini, Attorney
(602) 230-2144
JoeBettini@eburlaw.com
• Walter R. R. Ulman, Attorney
(602) 230-2144
WaltUlman@eburlaw.com
• Burt Rosenblatt, Attoney
(602) 230-2144
burt@eburlaw.com
Services:
Specialists in personal injury, wrongful
death, workers' compensation cases,
medical malpractice, construction cases,
product liability cases by the Arizona Board
of Legal Specialization

EMERICK, WILLIAM E.
300 MAIN STREET
SUITE 900
PO BOX 1010
LAFAYETTE, IN 47902-1010
765-423-1561
Fax: 765-742-8175
www.stuartlaw.com
• William E. Emerick, Partner
(765) 428-7061
wee@stuartlaw.com
• Anthony S Benton, Partner
(765) 423-1561
asb@stuartlaw.com
• Nina B Kirkpatrick, Partner
nbk@stuartlaw.com
• James P Pratt, Firm Administrator
jep@stuartlaw.com
Description:
Represents college athletic departments.
Services:
Handles complex issues in nearly any area
of the law, banking and creditors rights,
business counselling, business
transactions, buying and selling
businesses, design and construction law,
education law, employment law,
environment law, estates and trusts, health
care law, insurance law, intellectual property
law, litigation, real estate, development and
zoning, taxation
Other Location:
8888 Keystone Crossing, STE 640,

Indianapolis, IN 46240; Phone:
317-574-7245

EMPLOYMENT LAW MANAGERS
225 E MASON STREET
SUITE 502
MILWAUKEE, WI 53202
414-276-0600
• James D. Thorne, President
Description:
Contract negotiation, post career planning,
investment contract negotiation, arbitration
hearings, federal/state/international tax
filings, provides investment advice,
licensing, endorsement exploration.

ENG & WOODS
903 E ASH STREET
COLUMBIA, MO 65201
573-874-4190
877-888-2345
Fax: 573-874-4192
info@engandwoods.com
www.engandwoods.com
• Patrick J. Eng, Partner
info@engandwoods.com
• Matthew B. Woods, Partner
info@engandwoods.com
• Larry M. Woods, Partner
info@engandwoods.com
• Patrick J. F. Eng, Senior Partner
• Matthew B. Woods, Senior Partner
• Douglas Pugh, Partner
info@engandwoods.com
• Thad R. Mulholland, Partner
• Jonathan D. McQuilkin, Partner
• Andrew D. Popplewell, Partner
• Adam Dowling, Associate
Description:
Contract negotiation.
Services:
Practice includes representing people who
are injured in auto accidents, by dangerous
or defective products, through the fault or
negligence of another person or at work:
criminal law, family law, probate law, and
general and commercial business law,
personal wills, damage lawsuits of all types,
product liability cases, auto accidents,
workers compensation cases and routine
consultations with business clients
Year Founded:
1953

ETTER, MCMAHON, LAMBERSON & CLARY, P.C.A.
618 W RIVERSIDE AVENUE
BANK OF WHITMAN BUILDING
SUITE 210
SPOKANE, WA 99201-0401
509-747-9100
Fax: 509-623-1439
ettermcmahon@ettermcmahon.com
www.ettermcmahon.com
• William F. Etter, Member
(509) 747-9100
ettermcmahon@ettermcmahon.com
• Michael J. McMahon, Member
(509) 747-9100
ettermcmahon@ettermcmahon.com
• Stephen M. Lamberson, Member
ettermcmahon@ettermcmahon.com
• William F. F. Etter, Managing Member
(509) 747-9100
• Michael J. McMahon, Member
(509) 747-9100
• Stephen M. Lamberson, Member

(509) 747-9100
• Raymond F. Clary, Member
(509) 747-9100
• Carl J. Oreskovich, Member
(509) 747-9100
• Ronald A. Van Wert, Member
(509) 747-9100
• Daniel E. Stowe, Associate
(509) 747-9100
Services:
Contract negotiation, post career planning,
investment contract negotiation,
endorsement exploration, tort
actions/litigation. Alcohol, Beverage Law,
Construction Law, Domestic Relations Law,
Estate Planning, Real Estate Law. Medical
Malpractice

EVANS, ESQ., THOMAS S.
110 WEST FAYETTE STREET
ONE LINCOLN CENTER
SYRACUSE, NY 13202-1355
315-218-8000
Fax: 315-218-8100
rhole@bsk.com
www.bsk.com
• Thomas S. Evans, Senior Member
(315) 218-8217
tevans@bsk.com
• John D. Allen, Attorney
(315) 343-9116
jdallen@bsk.com
• S. Pa Battaglia, Attorney
(315) 218-8277
sbattaglia@bsk.com
• Richard D. M. Hole, Chairman of the
Management Committee
(315) 218-8210
rhole@bsk.com
• Jordan C. Alaimo, Senior Counsel
(585) 362-4720
jalaimo@bsk.com
• John R. Aldrich, Member (Partner)
(518) 533-3240
jaldrich@bsk.com
• Jeffrey F. Allen, Senior Counsel
(585) 362-4709
jeffreyallen@bsk.com
• John D. Allen, Member (Partner)
(315) 218-8250
jdallen@bsk.com
• Kathleen M. Bennett, Member (Partner)
(315) 218-8631
kbennett@bsk.com
• Paul J. Avery, Associate
(315) 218-8238
pavery@bsk.com
Description:
Contract negotiation, arbitration hearings,
licensing, tort actions/litigation, represents
college athletic departments. NCAA
infractions and compliance matters.

FAGUE, TERENCE L.
33 W FIRST STREET
SUITE 600
DAYTON, OH 45402
937-223-8177
Fax: 937-223-6705
www.coollaw.com
• Douglas M. Ventura, Chief Operating
Officer
(937) 449-5545
ventura@coollaw.com
• Matthew L. Rauch, COO and CFO
(937) 449-1637
• Alan J. Gusky, Controller
(937) 223-8177

• Russell W. Jacox, IT Manager
(937) 223-8177
jacox@coollaw.com
• Elaine F. Reinert, Applications Support
(937) 223-8177
Services:
Litigation: Business Litigation, Employment
Litigation, Real Estate Litigation. Represents
college athletic departments.
Description:
Represents college athletic departments.

FANEUIL, ROBERT A.
175 HIGHLAND AVENUE
NEEDHAM HEIGHTS, MA 2494
781-444-3838
Fax: 781-449-8240
RAF3838@aol.com
• Robert A. Faneuil, Attorney
(781) 444-3838
Services:
All phases of athlete representation
including contract negotiation, long-range
planning, financial planning, and post-career
counseling.
Clients:
Global Companies, LLC, Alliance Energy
Corp., The Education Resources Institute,
PMI Mortgage Insurance Co., New York
State Higher Education Service Corp.
Other Office:
Ritz Carleton Hotel, 2 Commonwealth Ave,
STE 15D, Boston, MA 02116

FENNEMORE CRAIG, A PROFESSIONAL CORPORATION
2394 EAST CAMELBACK ROAD
SUITE 600
PHOENIX, AZ 85016-3249
602-916-5000
Fax: 602-916-5999
tberg@fclaw.com
www.fclaw.com
• Amy Abdo, Director
(602) 916-5399
aabdo@fclaw.com
• Bryan A. Albue, Director
(602) 916-5311
balbue@fclaw.com
• Scott L. Altes, Director
(602) 916-5323
saltes@fclaw.com
• Amy Abdo, Director
(602) 916-5399
aabdo@fclaw.com
• Robert D. Anderson, Director
(602) 916-5455
randerso@fclaw.com
• Gregory L. Adams, Associate
(602) 916-5474
gadams@fclaw.com
• Todd M. Allison, Associate
(602) 916-5391
tallison@fclaw.com
• Scott K. Ames, Of Counsel
(602) 916-5339
sames@fclaw.com
• Karen A. Curosh, Of Counsel
(602) 916-5458
kcurosh@fclaw.com
Other Locations:
One South Church Avenue, STE 1000,
Tucson, AZ 85701; Phone: 520-879-6800;
1891 North Mastick Way, STE A, Nogales,
AZ 85621; Phone: 520-761-4215; 1221
North Street, STE 801, Lincoln, NE 68508;
Phone: 402-323-6200

Services:
Substantial business practice covers real estate, finance, public offerings, private placements, corporate reorganizations, mergers and acquisitions, dispositions, entity formation, intellectual property, estate planning, government relations and numerous other practice areas.
Clients:
7-Eleven Inc.,Allied Waste Industries, Inc., America West Arena, Apple Computer Inc., Arizona Cattle Growers' Association, Arizona Sports & Tourism Authority (AZSTA), Arizona-American, Water Company, Avnet, Inc., Banner Health Arizona, BNSF Railway Company, The, Bridgestone-Firestone, Cendant Corporation, Christian Care, Circle G Property Development LLC, ConocoPhillips Company, D.R. Horton - Continental Series, DMB Associates, Inc., Eurofresh, Exact Flow/Flow Dynamics Inc.,Fairfield Investments Inc., FINOVA Group Inc., First Magnus Financial Corporation, Florida, State of, Giant Industries Inc., Gila River Power LP, Glendale, City of, Harlem

FERGUSON, BRIG GEN/USA RET., MICHAEL L.
4300 BAYOU BOULEVARD
SUITE 13
PENSACOLA, FL 32503
850-477-0660
Fax: 850-477-4510
• Michael Ferguson, Partner

FERNANDEZ, SANTIAGO/SENIOR VP/GENERAL COUNSEL LOS ANGELES DODGERS, LLC
1000 ELYSIAN PARK AVENUE
LOS ANGELES, CA 90012
323-224-1507
Fax: 323-224-1269
www.dodgers.com
• Sam Fernandez, Senior Vice President and General Counsel
Services:
Contract negotiation, represents professional sports teams, licensing.

FIDELIS COUNSEL ASSOCIATES
23 LACEWOOD COURT
OTTAWA, ONTARIO, CANADA K2E 7E2
613-226-8130
Fax: 613-224-3422
• Ed Ratushny, Agent
(613) 226-8130
• Rolland Hedges, Agent
(613) 795-9435
Services:
Contract negotiation, arbitration hearings, teaches sports law.
Year Founded:
1990

FIERBERG, IRA M. LAW OFFICES OF
1334 PARK VIEW AVENUE
SUITE 100
MANHATTAN BEACH, CA 90266-3788
323-546-8181
Fax: 310-546-8180
• Ira M. Fierberg, Member
• Craig S. Sunada, Member
Description:
Personal Injury, including Vehicular, Slip and Fall, Major Bodily Injury, Dog Bites, Wrongful Death. General Civil Litigation in

all State and Federal Courts, Trial, Business Litigation, Sports Law, Motor Racing Sports Representation and Motor Racing Consulting.

FILLENWARTH DENNERLINE GROTH & TOWE
429 E VERMONT STREET
SUITE 200
INDIANAPOLIS, IN 46202
317-353-9363
Fax: 317-351-7232
glohman@fdgtlaborlaw.com
www.fdgtlaborlaw.com
• William R. Groth, Attorney/Partner
wgroth@fdgtlaborlaw.com
Services:
NFLPA workers' compensation panel for the Indianapolis Colts.

FINKELMEIER LAW FIRM
36 E SEVENTH STREET
SUITE 1660
CINCINNATI, OH 45202-4453
513-621-9921
(866) 781-5692
Fax: 513-621-9923
finkelmeier@fuse.net
www.finkelmeierlaw.com
• Louis J. Finkelmeier, Attorney at Law
• William I. Farrell, Partner/Attorney
(513) 621-9921
billfarrell@fuse.net
Services:
Workers Compensation, Sports Injury, Social Security Disability and Probate Law.

FLY, WILLIAM L.
601 UNIVERSITY DRIVE
SAN MARCOS, TX 78666-4684
512-245-2111
www.txstate.edu
• William L. Fly, Staff
(512) 245-2530
• Denise M. T. Trauth, President
Description:
Represents college athletic departments.

FOGELGAREN, FORMAN & BERGMAN
277 BROADWAY
ROOM 1701
NEW YORK, NY 10007
212-962-1200
Fax: 212-608-5935
fofoberg@aol.com
• Eric I. Fogelgaren, Partner
(212) 962-1200
• Jonathan Forman, Partner
(212) 962-1200
• Robert Bergman, Partner
(212) 962-1200
Description:
Panel attorneys for NFLPA
Teams:
NY Jets and NY Giants

FOLEY & LARDNER
777 E WISCONSIN AVENUE
SUITE 3800
VEREX PLAZA
MILWAUKEE, WI 53202-5306
414-271-2400
Fax: 414-297-4900
www.foley.com
• Ralf-Reinhard Boer, Partner
(414) 297-5609

rboer@foley.com
• Mary K. Braza, Partner/Practice Chair
(414) 297-5505
mbraza@foley.com
• Irwin P. Raij, Partner/Practice Co-Chair
iraij@foley.com
• Linda E. A. Benfield, Office Managing Partner
(414) 297-5825
lbenfield@foley.com
• Thomas N. Landgraf, Director, Administration and Operations,
(414) 297-5454
tlandgraf@foley.com
• Joshua A. Agen, Senior Counse
(414) 297-5703
jagen@foley.com
Nature of Service:
Recognized for its thorough understanding of complex sports issues, Foley & Lardner LLP is trusted by professionals in all aspsects of the sports industry. The firm represents professional franchises and leagues, amateur and collegiate teams, owners, stadium operators, sponsors, promoters, developers and sporting goods manufacturers. With an inside view of the sports world, our attorneys have the perspective and knowledge to help clients identify and respond to emerging trends in the industry. The firm's attorneys are experienced in antitrust, public affairs, litigation, intellectual property, public finance, real estate, and labor and employ

FOSTER, DON
260 S BROAD STREET
PHILADELPHIA, PA 19102-5003
215-568-6060
Fax: 215-568-6603
www.klehr.com
• Don P Foster, Partner
(215) 569-4646
• Richard M Beck, Partner
(215) 569-2299
• Keith W Kaplan, Partner
(215) 569-4143
• Heather I Levine, Partner
(215) 569-4398
Services:
Workers Compensation
Clients:
NFLPA workers' compensation panel
Other Locations:
919 Market Street, STE 100, Wilmington, DE 19801; Phone: 302-426-1189; 457 Hadonfield Road, STE 510, Cherry Hill, NJ 08002; Phone: 856-486-7900

FOSTER, SWIFT, COLLINS & SMITH, P.C.
313 S WASHINGTON SQUARE
LANSING, MI 48933-2114
517-371-8100
Fax: 517-371-8200
www.fosterswift.com
• Kimberly P. Hafley, Director of Marketing & Recruitment
• Charles E. Barbieri, Shareholder
(517) 371-8155
CBarbieri@fosterswift.com
• Judith A. P. Salminen, Director of Human Resources
(248) 538-6324
pasker@fosterswift.com
Services:
General Trial and Appellate Practice in all State and Federal Courts. Administrative Practice, Banking, Insurance, Corporation,

Real Estate, Municipal, Labor, Tax, Estate Planning, Probate, ESOPs, Employee Benefits, Environmental, Election, Oil and Gas, Immigration, Motor Carrier, Transportation, Licensing, Public Utility and Securities Law, Litigation, Products Liability, Professional Malpractice, Health and Hospital Law, International, Intellectual Property, Insurance Insolvency, Workers' Compensation, Aviation Law, Construction, Agricultural Law.

FOX & SPILLANE, LLP
1880 CENTURY PARK E
SUITE 1004
LOS ANGELES, CA 90067-1623
310-229-9300
Fax: 310-229-9380
• Jay Spillane, Attorney/Partner
• Gerard P Fox, Attorney/Partner
• Donald S Engel, Attorney
• Donald L Zachary, Attorney
Services:
Business litigation, copyright, trademark, intellectual property, media, sports.

FRANK, MONTE E.
158 DEER HILL AVENUE
DANBURY, CT 06810
203-792-2771
Fax: 203-791-8149
cw@cohenandwolf.com
www.cohenandwolf.com
• Monte E. Frank, Principal
(203) 792-2771
mfrank@cohenandwolf.com
• Martin J. Albert, Principal
(203) 337-4121
malbert@cohenandwolf.com
• Richard L. Albrecht, Principal
(203) 368-0211
ralbrecht@cohenandwolf.com
• David A. Ball, Principal
(203) 368-0211
dball@cohenandwolf.com
Services:
All phases of athlete representation including contract negotiation, long-range planning, financial planning, and post-career counseling.
Year Founded:
1951
Other Locations:
1115 Broad Street, Bridgeport, CT 06604; Phone: 203-368-0211; 112 Prospect Street, Stamford, CT 06904; Phone: 203-964-9907; 190 Main Street, Westport, CT 06880; Phone: 203-222-1034

FRANKEL, PAUL D.
520 MADISON AVENUE
1030 SPITZER BLDG
TOLEDO, OH 43604
419-255-5111
419-255-3883
Fax: 419-255-3231
www.paulfrankellaw.com
Services:
Contract negotiation, endorsement exploration.

FRANKFURT, KURNIT, KLEIN & SELZ, P.C.
488 MADISON AVENUE
10TH FLOOR
NEW YORK, NY 10022

212-980-0120
Fax: 212-593-9175
www.fkks.com
• Michael Frankfurt, Senior Partner/Founder
(212) 826-5555
mfrankfurt@fkks.com
• Jeffrey A. Greenbaum, Partner in Advertising, Marketing
• Michael Williams, Partner
(212) 826-5587
mwilliams@fkks.com
• Thomas D. Selz, Founding Partner
(212) 826-5535
• Cameron Myler, Associate
(212) 826-5545
• Edward Rosenthal, Partner
(212) 826-5524
erosenthal@fkks.com
Nature of Service:
All phases of athlete management. Contract negotiation, arbitration/litigation, intellectual property, trademark (U.S. and International) issues for athletes, agents and organizations. Represents athletes, sports related sponsorship, licensing/merchandising, television producers.
Year Founded:
1977

FRILOT, PARTRIDGE, KOHNKE & CLEMENTS, L.C.
1100 POYDRAS STREET
SUITE 3700
NEW ORLEANS, LA 70163
504-599-8000
Fax: 504-599-8100
contact@Frilot.com
• Miles Clements, Partner
(504) 599-8004
mclements@frilot.com
• Angela M. M. Bowlin, Partner
(504) 599-8215
abowlin@frilot.com
Description:
Contract negotiation, provides investment advice, licensing, tort actions/litigation. Admiralty and Maritime Law; Commercial Litigation; Construction Litigation; Energy; Environmental Litigation; Professional Liability; Entertainment and the Arts; Mass Torts; Litigation; Sports Law.

FULBRIGHT & JAWORSKI.L.L.P.
555 S FLOWER STREET
FORTY-FIRST FLOOR
LOS ANGELES, CA 90071
213-892-9200
Fax: 213-892-9494
www.fulbright.com
• Harry L. Hathaway, Counsel
(213) 892-9336
hhathaway@fulbright.com
• Peter H. Mason, Partner-In-Charge
(213) 892-9233
pmason@fulbright.com
Services:
Legal Services
Additional Offices United States:
Austin TX, Dallas, TX; Houston, TX; Los Angeles, CA; Minneapolis, MN; New York, NY, San Antonio, TX; Washington, D.C
Other Offices:
Hong Kong, London, Munich.
Year Founded:
1919
Description:

Our specifics deal with litigation, corporate, energy, intellectual, property, health law, public finance, international arbitration

GARVEY & STODDARD
634 W MAIN STREET
MADISON, WI 53703
608-256-1003
Fax: 608-256-0933
• Edward Garvey, Shareholder/Founder
• Kathleen McNeil, Shareholder
• Pamela McGillivray, Shareholder
• Christa Westerberg, Associate
Year Founded:
1997.
Services:
Teaches sports law, attorney training.
Description:
Emphasizing environmental, labor, employment, civil rights, Indian, local government, land, US and public interest law.

GARVEY, SCHUBERT & BARER
100 WALL STREET
20TH FLOOR
NEW YORK, NY 10005-3708
212-431-8700
Fax: 212-334-1278
www.gsblaw.com
• John K. Hoerster, Chairman
(206) 464-3939
jhoerster@gsblaw.com
• Keven J. Davis, Owner
(212) 431-8700
• Lucinda D. Fernald, Executive Director
(206) 464-3939
cfernald@gsblaw.com
• Hillary H. L. Hughes, Owner
(212) 965-452
hhughes@gsblaw.com
• Andrew J. Goodman, Owner
(212) 965-4534
agoodman@gsblaw.com
• Matthew R. Schneider, Managing Director
(202) 298-1787
mschneider@gsblaw.com
• Seymour H. Bucholz, Of Counsel
(212) 965-4531
sbucholz@gsblaw.com
• MaryLyn R. Carabello, Associate
(212) 965.4509
mcarabello@gsblaw.com
• Je Jun Moon, Of Counsel
(212) 965-4524
jmoon@gsblaw.com
Description:
Contract negotiation, arbitration hearings, represents professional sports teams, licensing, endorsement exploration, tort actions/litigation, represents college athletic departments, represents sports organizations. Represents a large and diverse array of clients in the arts, entertainment and sports industries, both regionally and nationally.
Other Locations:
11th Floor, 121 SW Morrison Street, Portland, OR 97204; Phone: 503-228-3939; 18th Floor, Second & Seneca Building, 1191 Second Avenue, Seattle, WA 98101; Phone: 206-464-3939; 5th Floor Flour Mill Building, 1000 Potomac Street, NW, Washington, DC 20007; Phone: 202-965-7880

GEIGER & KEEN LLP
5405 N. PERSHING AVENUE
SUITE 2A
BUILDING C
STOCKTON, CA 95207
209-948-0434
Fax: 209-948-9451
www.bgrn.com
• Dennis Do Geiger, Partner
(209) 948-0434
• Laureen J. Keen,
(209) 948-0434
lkeen@bgrn.com
• Timothy J. Kooy,
(209) 948-0434
Description:
Contract negotiation, tort actions/litigation.
General Civil and Trial Practice.
Corporation, Probate, Estate Planning,
Family Law, Estate Planning, Family Law,
Banking, Real Property, Public Districts,
Creditors' Bankruptcy and Commercial
Transactions.

GOBER LAW FIRM
3200 WEST END AVENUE
SUITE 500
NASHVILLE, TN 37203-1322
615-783-2874
800-634-6237
Fax: 615-783-1606
www.goberlaw.com
• Gary Gober, Principal Attorney/Founder
(800) 634-6237
Description:
NFLPA. Handles workers compensation for
the Tennessee Titans.
Clients:
Tennessee Titans and NFLPA.

GOLD, KEVIN M., ESQUIRE
ONE SOUTH MARKET SQUARE
M&T BANK BUILDING, 12TH FLOOR, PO
BOX 1146
HARRISBURG, PA 17108-1146
717-862-4534
Fax: 717-238-8623
• Kevin Gold, Administrative Chair
(717) 237-6702
• Richard E. Artell, Chairperson
(717) 237-6717
Description:
Representation of professional football
players.
Services:
Player Representation Services, Negotiation
of the Player Contract, Counseling,
Financial Management and Planning,
Personal Training, Marketing, Career
Planning
Clients:
NFLA players

GOLDMAN, LEE
4001 W. MCNICHOLS ROAD
DETROIT, MI 48221-3038
313-596-0264
Fax: 313-596-0280
www.udmercy.edu
• Lee Goldman, Law Professor
(313) 596-0203
goldmanl@udmercy.edu
• Antoine M. Garibaldi, Ph.D., President
(313) 993-1455
Description:
Teaches sports law.

GOLDSMITH, JAMES A.
1660 W 2ND STREET
SUITE 1100
CLEVELAND, OH 44113-1448
216-583-7000
Fax: 216-583-7001
infocleveland@ulmer.com
www.ulmer.com
• James Cowan, Executive Director
jcowan@ulmer.com
• Robert Horvath, Chief Financial Officer
• Sam Shipley, Chief Information Officer
• Jennifer Lawry Adams, Partner
(216) 583-7052
jadams@ulmer.com
• John M. Alten, Partner
(216) 583-7354
• Mary Forbes Lovett, Partner
(216) 583-7074
mlovett@ulmer.com
Description:
Contract negotiation, post career planning,
federal/state/international tax filings.
Other Locations:
600 Vine Street, STE 2800 Cincinnati, OH
45202; Phone: 513-698-5000; Fax:
513-698-500l; 88 East Broad Street, STE
1600, Columbus, OH 43215; Phone:
614-229-0000; Fax: 614-229-0001; One
North Franklin Street, STE 1825, Chicago,
IL 60606; Phone: 312-324-8000; Fax:
312-324-8001

GOPLERUD, III, C. PETER
2621 CARPENTER AVENUE
27TH & CARPENTER, OPPERMAN HALL
DES MOINES, IA 50311
515-271-2824
1-800-44-DRAKE x2824
Fax: 515-271-1958
www.law.drake.edu
• Allan W. Vestal, Dean
Description:
Teaches and consults in sports law, author.

GORDON, GEORGE B.
401 QUEEN CITY AVENUE
UNIVERSITY COUNSEL OF ALABAMA
SYSTEM OFFICE
TUSCALOOSA, AL 35487
205-348-5681
Description:
Represents college athletic departments.

GOWEN, GEORGE W.
1359 BROADWAY
SUITE 600
NEW YORK, NY 10018
212-682-8811
Fax: 212-661-7769
DBM@dunnington.com
www.dunnington.com
• Marvin M Brown, Partner
mbrown@dunnington.com
• John T Dunlap, Partner
jdunlap@dunnington.com
• George W Gowen, Partner
• Michael J Kopcsak, Partner
Services:
Corporate, Estates, Trusts and Private
Clients, Immigration, Litigation and
Arbitration, Not-For-Profit, Religious and
Charitable Institutions, Real Estate and
Construction, Taxation
Description:
Represents sports organizations.

GRASSIA, ESQ., THOMAS C.
5 COMMONWEALTH ROAD
NATICK, MA 01760-1526
508-653-0054
Services:
Contract negotiation, post career planning,
endorsement exploration.

GREENBERG TRAURIG, LLP
54 STATE STREET
6TH FLOOR
ALBANY, NY 12207
518-689-1400
Fax: 518-689-1499
info@gtlaw.com
www.gtlaw.com
• Henry W. Holmes Jr, Counsel
(310) 586-7858
• Paola A. Abello, Associate
(305) 579-0500
• Tricia A. Asaro, Shareholder
(518) 689-1400
• Michael A. Berlin, Shareholder
(212) 801-6424
• Christopher A. Cernik, Shareholder
(518) 689-1400
• Mark F. Glaser, Shareholder
• Michael J. Grygiel, Shareholder
(518) 689-1400
• Hugh E. Hackney, Shareholder
(214) 665-3676
Services:
Artist and professional athlete management
and representation.
Description:
Contract negotiation, post career planning,
arbitration hearings, represents professional
sports teams, licensing, endorsement
exploration.
Specialty:
All phases of Motion pictures, television,
sports.

GULAS LAW FIRM, P.C.
2031 SECOND AVENUE N
BIRMINGHAM, AL 35203
205-297-0005
877-453-4852
Fax: 205-879-1247
www.gulasandstuckey.com
• Ike Gulas, Attorney
• Jason Stuckey, Attorney
Services:
Personal Injury, Auto, truck or motor vehicle
accident, Wrongful Death, Pharmaceutical,
Drug or Medication Matters, Class actions or
mass torts, Dangerous Products,
Ephedra-related matters, Zyprexa use,
Trucking, 18-wheeler accidents, Duragesic,
Ortho-Evra, Vioxx, Unsafe Toys,
Antidepressants, Car and tire defects

HAILE, SHAW & PFAFFENBERGER, P.A.
660 US HIGHWAY ONE
3RD FLOOR
NORTH PALM BEACH, FL 33408
561-627-8100
Fax: 561-622-7603
clientservices@hsplaw.com
www.haileshaw.com
• Robert G. Haile, Jr., Lawyer
rhaile@hsplaw.com
• David M. Shaw, Lawyer
dshaw@hsplaw.com
• William J. Pfaffenberger, Lawyer
wpfaffenberger@hsplaw.com
• Robert G. Haile Jr., Partner

- David M. Shaw, Partner
- Phillip M. Dicomo, Partner
- John Flanigan, Partner
- Lawrence C. Griffin, Partner
- Gerald L. Principe, Partner

Services:
Areas of practice include Trust and Estate Planning and Administration, Corporate Law and Business Planning, Real Estate Development, Environmental and Land Use, and Commercial and Civil Litigation

Description:
Contract negotiation, post career planning, investment contract negotiation, arbitration hearings, licensing, endorsement exploration, tort actions/litigation.

HANSEN, STEVEN W.
BELLFLOWER
LAKEWOOD, CA 90712-1347
562-866-6228
www.swhlaw.com
- Steven W. W. Hansen, Attorney

Other Locations:
1573 Indian Summer Road, San Marcos, CA 92069; Phone: 562-866-6228; 507 Sylvan Avenue, Mountain View, CA 94041; Phone 562-866-6228

Services:
Product Liability Defense / Sports Litigation Defense, Premises Liability Defense, Professional Liability Defense, Insurance Coverage and Bad Faith, Governmental Liability, Contract General Counsel/Third Party Administrator (TPA) services, Newsletter

---

HARBOUR, SMITH, HARRIS & MERRITT
404 N GREEN AT MAGRILL STREET
LONGVIEW, TX 75606-2072
903-757-4001
888-757-4001
Fax: 903-753-5123
emerritt@harbourlaw.com
www.harbourlaw.com
- Thomas W. Reardon, Esquire
(903) 757-4001
- John M Smith, Attorney
(903) 757-4001
- Jerry S Harris, Attorney
(903) 757-4001
jharris@harbourlaw.com
- Edward L Merritt, Attorney
(903) 757-4001
emerritt@harbourlaw.com
- Jessica M LaRue, Associate
(903) 757-4001
jlarue@harbourlaw.com

Services:
Contract negotiation, represents professional sports teams, endorsement exploration, tort actions/litigation.

Clients:
Regions Bank (formerly Longview National Bank) Spring Hill State Bank, Community Bank, General Accident Fire & Life Assurance Co.; Highlands Insurance Co.; Zurich-American Insurance Co.; Commercial Union Insurance Co.; State Farm Insurance Co.; ACE U.S.A. (formerly CIGNA Property & Casualty); ESIS, Inc.; Safeco Insurance Co.; Dairyland County Mutual Insurance Co.; Kemper Insurance Group; Mid-Continent Casualty Co.; National Surety Corp.; Ranger-Pan American Insurance Group; Sentry Insurance Co.; Scottsdale Insurance Co.; Nationwide Insurance; Farmland Insurance; Reliance Insurance

Company; State & County Mutual Insurance Co.

HARRIS, ALAN E.
235 MONTGOMERY STREET
RUSS BUILDING
17TH FLOOR
SAN FRANCISCO, CA 94104
415-954-4400
Fax: 415-954-4480
www.fbm.com
- Alan E Harris, Counsel
(415) 954-4424
aharris@fbm.com
- John R Epperson, Special Counsel
(415) 954-4942
jepperson@fbm.com

Services:
Practices and Industries, Bankruptcy and Creditors' Rights, Business Litigation, Business Transactions, Construction, Employment, Environmental Law, Family Wealth, Hospitality, Insurance Coverage, Intellectual Property and Technology, Private Clients, Product Law, Real Estate, Securities, Tax, White Collar Crime.

Description:
Arbitration hearings, federal/state/international tax filings, licensing, tort actions/litigation.

HASLER, FONFARA AND MAXWELL, LLP
KEY BANK BUILDING, 6TH FLOOR, PO BOX 2267
FORT COLLINS, CO 80522
970-493-5070
Fax: 970-493-9703
www.hfglawfirm.com
- Timothy W Hasler, Attorney
- Joseph H Fonfara, Attorney
- Michael A Maxwell, Attorney
- Timothy L Goddard, Attorney

Description:
NFLPA workers' compensation panel, Denver Broncos. Estate Planning; Estate Administration; Business Law; Real Estate; Worker's Compensation.

HAUS & ROMAN, LLP
148 E WILSON STREET
SUITE 200
MADISON, WI 53703-3423
608-257-0420
Fax: 608-257-1383
hrbllp.com
- William Haus, Attorney/Partner

Services:
Worker's compensation

Clients:
NFLPA workers' compensation panel.

HAZLETT, WILKES & BAYHAM
310 S WILLIAMS BOULEVARD
SUITE 305
TUCSON, AZ 85711
520-790-9663
- Thomas Bayharm, Attorney/Partner
- James M Wilkes, Attorney/Partner
- Carl E. Hazlett, Attorney/Partner

HEAD, ALBON O., JR.
777 MAIN STREET
SUITE 2100
FORT WORTH, TX 76102

817-334-7200
Fax: 817-334-7290
www.jw.com
- Albon O Head Jr, Managing Partner
(817) 334-7230
ahead@jw.com
- Gail R. Horne, Administrator
(214) 953-5879
ghorne@jw.com

Services:
Antitrust, Appellate, Bankruptcy, Business Transactions, Corporate and Securities, Eminent Domain, Immigration, Intellectual Property, International, Labor and Employment, Litigation, Public Finance, Regulatory and Legislative, Tax

Description:
Represents professional sports teams (Texas Rangers).

HERMAN, HERMAN, KATZ & COTLAR, L.L.P.
820 O'KEEFE AVENUE
NEW ORLEANS, LA 70113
504-581-4892
Fax: 504-561-6024
info@hhkc.com
www.hhkc.com
- Leonard A Davis, Attorney/Partner
(504) 581-4892
ldavis@hhkc.com
- Maury, A. Herman, Founder
(504) 581-4892
- Morton. H. Katz, Founder
(504) 581-4892
- Steven. J. Lane, Attorney
(504) 581-4892
- Leonard. A. Davis, Attorney
(504) 581-4892
- James. C. Klick, Partner
(504) 581-4892
- Stephen. J. Herman, Attorney
(504) 581-4892
- Russ M. Herman, Founder
(504) 581-4892

Description:
Contract negotiation, arbitration hearings, represents professional sports teams, licensing, endorsement exploration, tort actions/litigation, represents sports organizations. Corporate Law; Commercial Law; Class Actions; Personal Injury; Business Litigation; Railroad Crossing and Derailment.

HERSHNER, HUNTER, ANDREWS, NEILL & SMITH L,L,P.
180 E 11TH AVENUE
EUGENE, OR 97401
541-686-8511
Fax: 541-344-2025
contact@hershnerhunter.com
www.hershnerhunter.com
- David N. Andrews, Attorney
contact@hershnerhunter.com
- William D. Brewer, Attorney
contact@hershnerhunter.com
- Melissa F. Busley, Attorney
contact@hershnerhunter.com
- Nancy K. Cary, Attorney
contact@hershnerhunter.com
- Jeffrey S. Cook, Firm Administrator
- Nancy Parks, Accounting Manager
- Crystal Harder, I.T. Manager

Services:
Contract negotiation, federal/state/international tax filings, licensing, endorsement exploration.

Corporate Law; Estate Planning; Business Planning; Probate; Trust Administration; Tax Disputes.

HICKS, JERRY
2728 N. HARWOOD STREET
500 WINSTEAD BUILDING
DALLAS, TX 75201
214-745-5400
Fax: 214-745-5390
ksullivan@winstead.com
www.winstead.com
• W. Mike Baggett, Chairman
Emeritus/Shareholder
(214) 745-5303
mbaggett@winstead.com
• Thomas R. Helfland, Chief Operating
Officer
(214) 745-5342
thelfand@winstead.com
Nature of Sports Service:
Serves as lead counsel to a number of
professional sports teams, international
venue management companies, and
governmental authorities responsible for the
financing, developing, and operation of
sports venues.
Project/Clients:
Reliant Stadium for the Houston Texans
NFL franchise, SBC Center for thr San
Antonio Spurs NBA franchise, New Houston
downtown arena for the Houston Rockets
and Houston Aeros, Sydney Olympic Arena
for a management company, Various
European arena venue; Appellate, Banking
& Credit Transactions, Bankruptcy,
Biotechnology, Business Restructuring,
Construction, Corporate / Securities, Crisis
Management, Emerging Business, Energy,
Environmental, ERISA / Employee Benefits,
Financial Institutions, Government Relations
/ Public Policy, Insurance, Intellectual
Property, International, Labor &
Employment, Litigation / Dispute Resolution,
Nanotechnology

HITCHCOCK LAW FIRM
1465 ARCADE STREET
THE BARRISTER BUILDING
ST. PAUL, MN 55106
651-772-3401
Fax: 651-772-2115
• Edward J. Hitchcock, Attorney
(651) 772-3401
ehitchcock@hitchcocklaw.com
• Gene E Adkins, Attorney
(651) 772-3401
gadkins@hitchcocklaw.com
• Ralbern B Hitchcock, Attorney
rhitchcock@hitchcocklaw.com
• Gene E. Adkins, Attorney
• Edward J. Hitchcock, Attorney
• Raebern B. Hitchcock, Attorney
• Drew S. Slagle, Attorney
Services:
Represent and advise clients in the areas of
estate planning, probate and trust
administration, general litigation, and sports
law
Description:
Contract negotiation, post career planning,
investment contract negotiation, arbitration
hearings, endorsement exploration, tort
actions/litigation.

HODARI, AJILI
52 E GAY STREET
COLUMBUS, OH 43215
614-464-6400
Fax: 614-464-6350
www.vssp.com/hodari.html
• W. Jonathan Airey, Partner
(614) 464-6346
• Raymond D. Anderson, Partner
(614) 464-6447
rdanderson@vssp.com
Nature of Sports Service:
All phases of athlete representation
including contract negotiation, long-range
planning, financial planning, and post-career
counseling.
Services:
Represents clients in litigation, business and
personal transactions involving virtually
every legal subject
Other Locations:
First National Tower, 106 South Main Street,
Akron, OH 44308; Phone: 330-245-1153;
277 South Washington Street, STE 310,
Alexandria, VA 22314; Phone:
703-837-6999; Atrium Two, STE 2000, 22l
EAst Fourth Street, Cincinnati, OH 45201;
Phone: 513-723-4000; 2100 One Cleveland
Center, l375 East 9th Street, Cleveland, OH
44114; Phone: 216-479-6100; 1828 L Street
NW, 11th Floor, Washington, DC 20036;
Phone; 202-467-8800

HOLLAND & KNIGHT
100 N TAMPA STREET
SUITE 4100
TAMPA, FL 33602
813-227-8500
Fax: 813-229-0134
fgrady@hklaw.com
www.hklaw.com
• Rod Anderson, Partner
(813) 227-6721
rod.anderson@hklaw.com
• Douglas A. Wright, Attorney
(813) 227-6536
doug.wright@hklaw.com
• Mark D. Austin, Associate
(813) 227-6535
mark.austin@hklaw.com
• Frederick J. Grady, Partner
(813) 227-6705
fred.grady@hklaw.com
• Bradford Kimbro, Partner
(813) 227-6660
brad.kimbro@hklaw.com
• Sylvia Stephens, Business Manager
sylvia.stephens@hklaw.com
College Sports/Football:
Gator Bowl Associaton, Chairman's Club
Member.
Services:
Efficient and responsive legal representation
anywhere in the world.
Newsletter:
Sports Law Subscription based.
Specialty:
Litigation - Commercial; Sports - Collegiate
Administration and Compliance; Education;
Government Contracts; Litigation -
Commercial: Construction and Design; Drug
and Medical Devices; Litigation -
Commercial: Entertainment. Taxation - State
and Local; Taxation: Federal; Sports
Practice.

HOLLER, J. EDWARD
1777 BULL STREET
COLUMBIA, SC 29201
803-765-2968
Fax: 803-252-8290
Services:
Contract negotiation, investment contract
negotiation, endorsement exploration, tort
actions/litigation - criminal.

HOLMES, RICH
4200 FIFTH AVENUE
PITTSBURGH, PA 15260
412-624-4141
Fax: 412-624-6688
usenate@pitt.edu
www.pitt.edu
• Irene Hanson Frieze, Professor
(412) 624-4336
frieze@pitt.edu
• Michael R. Pinsky, Vice President
mrpinsky@pitt.edu
• Ellen Ansell, Secretary
eansell@pitt.edu
• Nicholas G. Bircher, Immediate Past
President
ngbircher@pitt.edu
Description:
Represents college athletic departments.

HORLEN, HOLT & HOLLAS PLLC
2700 RUDDER FREEWAY, S
SUITE 5300
COLLEGE STATION, TX 77845-8142
979-696-1923
Fax: 979-696-2206
• Stephen R. Hollas, Attorney/Partner
Services:
All phases of athlete representation
including contract negotiation, long-range
planning, financial planning, and post-career
counseling.

HUGHES & LUCE
111 CONGRESS AVENUE
SUITE 900
AUSTIN, TX 78701
512-482-6800
Fax: 512-482-6859
• Edward O. Coultas, Partner
(512) 482-6823
• Philip M. Slinkard, Partner
(512) 482-6803
• Robert H Mow Jr, Partner
Clients:
Hillwood Development Corporation,
Electronic Data Systems, National Heritage
Insurance Company, SBC Communications,
H. Ross Perot, Sr., American Airlines,
Blockbuster, Dell, Dillard's, Ericsson,
Hillwood Development Corporation, Holly
Corporation, McAfee, VarTec Telecom,
Wal-Mart Stores, Worldspan, Sammons
Enterprises
Description:
Contract negotiation, arbitration hearings,
represents professional sports teams.
Other Location:
1717 Main Street, Ste 2800, Dallas, TX
75201; Phone: 214-939-5500

**HUNEGS, STONE, LENEAVE, KYAS &
THORNTON, P.A.**
1000 12 OAKS CENTER DRIVE
SUITE 101
WAYZATA, MN 55391

612-568-0243
800-787-3453
Fax: 612-339-5150
www.hlklaw.com
• Richard Hunegs, Attorney
rhunegs@hlklaw.com
• Cortney S. LeNeave, Attorney
cleneave@hlklaw.com
• Cortney LeNeave, Attorney
• Randal W. LeNeave, Attorney
• Richard L. Carlson, Attorney
(612) 568-0243
• Richard J. Dinsmore PC, LLO, Attorney
(612) 568-0243
• Katie D. Figgins, Attorney
(612) 568-0243
• Richard G. Hunegs, Attorney
(612) 568-0243
• William Kvas, Attorney
(612) 568-0243
Description:
NFLPA. Handles the Minnesota Vikings
workers compensation.
Services:
Handle a variety of personal injury and
occupational illness claims
Other Location:
1000 Second Avenue, STE 3310, Seattle,
WA 98104; Phone: 206-448-7172;
800-525-3352

**HUNT, ORTMANN, PALFFY & ROSSELL,
INC.**
301 N LAKE AVENUE
7TH FLOOR
PASADENA, CA 91101
626-440-5200
Fax: 626-796-0107
info@huntortmann.com
www.huntortmann.com
• Omel A. Nieves, Shareholder
(626) 440-5200
nieves@huntortmann.com
• Richard Mah, Principal
(626) 440-5200
mah@huntortmann.com
• Lawrence P Lubka, Principal
lubka@hobpr.com
• Richard E Blasco, Principal
blasco@hobpr.com
Clients:
City of Los Angeles, Alameda Corridor East,
Metropolitan Water District of Southern
California (MWD), Charles Pankow Builders,
Ltd., Sachs Electric Company, ACCO
Engineered Systems, R. D. Olson
Construction, W.E. O'Neil Construction Co.,
Tishman International Companies, Marcor
Environmental, Malcolm Drilling, Skidmore
Contracting Corporation, The Converse
Professional Group, Penhall Company, Los
Angeles County Metropolitan Transportation
Authority (MTA), City of Oxnard, Advanced
Structures, Inc., Building Industry Credit
Association, Salick Healthcare, Inc.,
Peterson Bros. Construction, Parr Lumber
Company, A. E. Schmidt Environmental,
Tetra
Description:
Contract negotiation, investment contract
negotiation, arbitration hearings,
federal/state/international tax filings,
licensing.

HUTCHISON, Q.C., J. MICHAEL
108-1218 WHARF STREET
VICTORIA, BC, CANADA V8W 1T8

250-388-6666
Fax: 250-389-0400
mhutchqc@bclawfirm.com
www.bclawfirm.com
Description:
Endorsement exploration, tort
actions/litigation, represents college athletic
departments, represents sports
organizations, player group and individual
athletes.

IAN C. PULVER
479 BEDFORD PARK AVENUE
TORONTO, ONTARIO, CANADA M5M 1K2
819-923-1034
Fax: 416-785-8032
ian@willsportsgroup.com
willsportsgroup.com
• Ian C. Pulver, Attorney
(416) 907-9801
Services:
Works in varied disciplines as labour law,
product licensing and community relations.
Description:
Represents sports organizations, tort
actions/litigation, Associate Counsel-NHL
Players Association.

IBACH, JOHN R.
1301 RIVERPLACE BOULEVARD
SUITE 1500
JACKSONVILLE, FL 32207
904-398-3911
Fax: 904-396-0663
bibach@rtlaw.com
www.rtlaw.com
• A. Gr Allen, Shareholder
(904) 346-5799
gallen@rtlaw.com
• Heather Ra Ambrose, Associate
(904) 346-5731
hambrose@rtlaw.com
Nature of Sports Service:
All phases of athlete representation
including contract negotiation, long-range
planning, financial planning, and post-career
counseling.
Clients:
Acosta Sales Co., Advanced Disposal
Services, Inc., Agri Dynamics, Inc., Alfred I.
Dupont Hospital for Children, American
Bio-Tech, Inc., American Coolair
Corporation, AmSouth Bank, Anchor Health
Centers, Ascom Energy Systems, Inc.,
Atlantic Coast Asphalt Company, Atlantic
States Bank, Bank of New York, The,
Bartram Park, Ltd., BB&T, Inc., Ben Carter
Properties, LLC, Borland - Groover Clinic,
P.A., BPB America, Inc., Bremer Brace,
Bremer Group, Brooks Health System,
Brownfields Properties, LLC, Burkhardt
Distributing Company, Celotex Corporation,
Centex Homes Corporation of Florida,
Chicago Title Insurance Company, City of
Clearwater, Florida
Other Location:
170 Malaga Street, STE A, St. Augustine,
FL 32084; Phone: 904-8241-0879
Year Founded:
1905

IRVING, PAUL H.
11355 W OLYMPIC BOULEVARD
LOS ANGELES, CA 90064
310-312-4000
Fax: 310-312-4224

pirving@manatt.com
www.manatt.com
• Paul Irving, Co-Chairman
(310) 312-4196
pirving@manatt.com
• Valentin G. Aguilar, Partner
(310) 312-4313
vaguilar@manatt.com
• Keith M. Allen Niesen, Partner
(310) 312-4105
kallen-niesen@manatt.com
• Dinesh R. Badkar, Associate
(310) 312-4266
dbadkar@manatt.com
Description:
Represents professional sports teams,
licensing, endorsement exploration.
Services:
Advertising, Marketing & Media; Antitrust;
Banking & Financial Industry; Bankruptcy &
Financial Restructuring; Corporate &
Finance; Energy, Environment & Resources;
Government & Regulatory; Healthcare;
Insurance; Intellectual Property & Internet;
Employment & Labor; Litigation;
Entertainment; Real Estate & Land Use;
Tax, Benefits & Global Compensation; and
Venture Capital & Technology.
Clients:
The Coca-Cola Company, Diageo North
America, Den-Mat Corporation/Rembrandt
Oral Care Products, D.L. Blair,
DreamWorks, Dyson, Energizer Holdings, E.
& J. Gallo Winery, Eveready Battery
Company, Inc., Expedia, General Mills, Inc.,
Harley-Davidson, Jamba Juice,
Kimberly-Clark Corporation, Martin Agency,
MasterCard International, Mattel, Inc., Mead
Johnson, Miller Brewing Company, Papa
John's International, Inc., Reader's Digest
Association, Inc., Schick Manufacturing,
Inc., Thane International, Tommy Hilfiger,
UniWorld Group, Inc., Yahoo! Inc., Zila
Nutraceuticals, Amresco Commercial
Finance, Bank of America Corp., California
National Bank.
Other Locations:
121 State Street, Albany, NY 12207; Phone:
518-432-5990; 7 Times Square, New York,
NY 10036; Phone: 212-790-4500; 695 Town
Center Drive, 14th Floor, Costa Mesa, CA
92626; Phone: 714-371-2500; 1001 Page
Mill Road, Building 2, Palo Alto, CA 94304;
Phone: 650-812-1300; 1215 K Street, STE
1900, Sacramento, CA 95814; Phone:
916-552-2300; One Metro Center, 700 12th
Street, NW, STE 1100, Washington, DC
20005; Phone 202-585-6500.

ISAAC, BRANT, LEDMAN & TEETOR
250 E BROAD STREET
SUITE 900
COLUMBUS, OH 43215-3742
614-221-2121
Fax: 614-365-9516
www.isaacbrant.com
• Timothy E. Miller, Attorney
• Scyld D. Anderson, Attorney
• Donald Anspaugh,
• Douglas C. Boatright,
Services:
Trial, Appellate & Federal Practice, General
Business, Corporate, Estate Planning,
Probate, Guardianship, Real Estate,
Employment, Family, Negligence, Personal
Injury, Transfusion-Related AIDS, Civil
Arson, Insurance Defense, Insurance,
Professional Malpractice, Premises Liability,

Products Liability, Carrier Liability, Motor Sports Law, Commercial including Banking, Securities & OSHA Litigation, Risk Management
Nature of Sports Service:
All phases of athlete representation including contract negotiation, long-range planning, financial planning, and post-career counseling.

ISRAEL, FRIEDBERG & KORBATOV L.L.P.
11601 WILSHIRE BOULEVARD
SUITE 2200
LOS ANGELES, CA 90025
310-553-2200
Fax: 310-553-2280
www.ifklaw.com
• Igor Korbatov, Attorney
• James A. Friedberg, JFriedberg@ifklaw.com
• Igor Korbatov, IKorbatov@ifklaw.com
• Rudy Valner, Of Counsel
• Samuel Israel, Attorney
sisrael@ifklaw.com

JAFFE, RAITT, HEUER & WEISS, PC
500 GRISWOLD
SUITE 2400
DETROIT, MI 48226
313-961-1200
Fax: 313-961-1205
www.jaffelaw.com
• Arthur A. Weiss, Attorney
(248) 351-3000
aweiss@jaffelaw.com
• Joel Alam, Attorney
(248) 351-3000
jalam@jaffelaw.com
• Christopher A. Andreoff, Member
(248) 351-3000
candreoff@jaffelaw.com
• Patrice S. Arend, Member
(248) 351-3000
parend@jaffelaw.com
Description:
Contract negotiation, post career planning, investment contract negotiation, arbitration hearings, federal/state/international tax filings, endorsement exploration, tort actions/litigation. Business Planning Law; Federal, State and Local Taxation Law.
Other Locations:
300 Park Street, STE 285, Birmingham, MI 48009; Phone: 248-540-1300; 201 South Main Street, STE 300, Ann Arbor, MI 48104; Phone: 734-222-4776

JANZER, JEROME M.
1000 N WATER STREET
SUITE 1700
MILWAUKEE, WI 53202
414-298-1000
800-553-6215
Fax: 414-298-8097
www.reinhartlaw.com
• Chad M. Anthony, Associate
(414) 298-8393
canthony@reinhartlaw.com
• Amy E. Arndt, Attorney
(414) 298-8300
aarndt@reinhartlaw.com
Description:
Post career planning, endorsement exploration, real estate investment.
Services:

Appellate, Banking and Finance, Bankruptcy and Creditors' Rights, Business Law, Computer & Technology, Crisis Management and Business Continuity, Employee Benefits, Entertainment Law, Environmental, Estate Planning, Executive Compensation, Government Relations, Health Care, Intellectual Property, International, Labor & Employment, Litigation, OSHA, Product Distribution and Franchise Law, Real Estate, Securities, Tax, Telecommunications and Energy
Other Locations:
22 East Mifflin Street, Madison, WI 53703; Phone: 608-229-2200; W233 North 2080 Ridgeview Parkway, Waukesha, WI 53188; Phone: 262-951-4500

JASEN & JASEN
69 DELAWARE AVENUE
SUITE 700
BUFFALO, NY 14202
716-848-9500
716-472-4444
www.jasenlaw.com
• Peter Jasen, Nsel, Couber
(716) 848-9500
lawyers@jasenlaw.com
• Mark M. Jasen, Member
(716) 848-9500
Nature of Sports Service:
All phases of athlete representation including contract negotiation, long-range planning, financial planning, and post-career counseling.
Services:
Provides high quality, responsive, cost effective and efficient legal services such as Auto/Motorcycle Accidents, Construction Accidents, Work Injuries, Neck/Back/Spine Injuries, Paraplegic, Quadriplegic, Paralysis, Wrongful Death, Boat Accidents, Railroad Accidents, Broken, Bones/Fractures, Head & Brain Injuries, Defective Products, Scaffold/Fall Injuries

JASPER, PATRICIA M.
405 HILGARD AVENUE
3149 MURPHY HALL
LOS ANGELES, CA 90024-1405
310-825-4321
Fax: 310-206-2390
www.ucla.edu
• Gene Block, Chancellor
(310) 825-2151
chancellor@conet.ucla.edu
• Gene G. Block, Chancellor
• Carole Goldberg, Vice Chancellor
Description:
Represents college athletic departments.
Services:
Provides cost-effective and high-quality business support and administrative services to campus customers such as buying, facilities & operations, finance, hospitality, housing, human resources, public safety, technology and travel & transportation.

JEANNIE BAUMGARTNER
2 PENNSYLVANIA PLAZA
14TH FLOOR
NEW YORK, NY 10121
212-465-6000
Fax: 212-465-6549
newyorkrangers@thegarden.com
www.newyorkrangers.com

• Glen Sather, President / General Manager
• Mike Golub, SVP-Marketing and Business Operations
• Jeanie Baumgartner, VP-Marketing
• Rana Dershowitz, VP-Legal and Business Affairs
Description:
Represents professional sports teams.

JENKENS & GILCHRIST PC
500 N AKARD
SUITE 1830
DALLAS, TX 75201
214-965-0776
Fax: 214-965-0780
Services:
Administrative & Legislative, Antitrust, Bankruptcy, Construction, Corporate & Securities, Energy, Environmental & Administrative Advocacy, ERISA, ESOP, Estate Planning, Financial Institutions, Financial Services, Franchise & Distribution, Health, Immigration, Intellectual Property, International, Labor & Employment, Litigation, Real Estate, Tax, Technology, Transportation, White Collar
Description:
Contract negotiation, investment contract negotiation, arbitration hearings, federal/state/international tax filings, represents professional sports teams, provides securities advice, licensing, endorsement exploration, tort actions/litigation.

JENKINS & JONES
910 17TH STREET NW
SUITE 800
WASHINGTON, DC 20006-2606
202-223-2484
Fax: 202-331-3759
• Charles R. Jones Jr, Partner
(202) 223-2484
Services:
Contract negotiation, post career planning, investment contract negotiation, Provides investment advice, endorsement exploration.

JERNIGAN LAW FIRM
2626 GLENWOOD AVENUE
SUITE 330
CAROLINA PLACE BUILDING
RALEIGH, NC 27608
919-833-0299
800-849-4478
(888) 877-3956
Fax: 919-256-2595
www.jernlaw.com
• Leonard T. Jernigan, Jr., Attorney
ltj@jernlaw.com
Description:
Practice focuses on people injured or disabled, auto accidents, defective products, on the job injuries, workers compensation claims, exposure to asbestor and toxic substances.

JOHNSON & BELL
33 W MONROE STREET
SUITE 2700
CHICAGO, IL 60603-5404
312-372-0770
Fax: 312-372-9818
info@jbltd.com
www.johnsonandbell.com

• William V. Johnson, President / Shareholder
(312) 984-0218
johnsonw@jbltd.com
• John W. Bell, VP / Shareholder
(312) 984-0241
bellj@jbltd.com
• Jack T. Riley, VP / Shareholder
(312) 984-0269
rileyj@jbltd.com
• John A. Childers, VP / Shareholder
(312) 984-0262
childersj@jbltd.com
• John. W. Bell, Vice President
• Katherine J. Adamany, Associate
• Thomas J. Andrews, Shareholder
(312) 984-0239
• Joann T. Angarola, Shareholder
(312) 984-0201
• William G. Beatty, Shareholder
(312) 984-0232
• Daniel R. Bedell, Associate
(312) 984-0206
Services:
Apellate, Aviation litigation, Business Litigation & Practice, Complex/Class Litigation, Employment Law/ERISA, Environmental, Financial Crimes, general Negligence & Premises Liability, Hospitality Law & Medical Liability, National Coordinating Counsel, Product Liability, Professional Liability Defense, Title Insurance Defense, Toxic tort/Continuous Exposure, Trucking & transportation Law, Additional Practice Groups
Other Locations:
STE A, 9000 Indianapolis Blvd., Highland, IN 46322; Phone: 219-923-5250; Fax: 219-923-6170; 325 Washington Street, STE 200, Waukegan, IL 60085; Phone: 847-662-7458; Fax: 847-662-7366
Year Founded:
1975

KAISER, RONALD A.
TEXAS A & M UNIVERSITY
156 FRANCIS HALL, CAMPUS 2261
FRANCIS HALL, SUITE 156
COLLEGE STATION, TX 77843-2261
979-845-3211
Fax: 979-845-0446
www.tamu.edu
• Jeffrey S. Vitter, EVP / Provost
(979) 845-4016
provost@tamu.edu
• R.Bowen A. Loften, President
(979) 845-5303
rkaiser@tamu.edu
• Karan Watson, EVP for academic affairs
• B.J. Crain, VP for finance and CFO
• Eric Hyman, Athletic Director
Clients:
Bookstore, Department of Student Life-Off-campus, Department of Residence Life-On-campus, Food Services, Health Plan Provider, Housing Information, Memorial Student Center, Memorial Student Center Box Office, Print 'n' Copy, Student Counseling Services, Student Health Services, Transportation, University Police, University Writing Center
Description:
Teaches sports law.

KALIS, CHRISTOPHER A.
5160 VILLAGE CREEK DRIVE
SUITE 100
PLANO, TX 75093

214-871-6005
Fax: 214-871-6050
chriskalis@kalislaw.com
• Christopher I. Kalis, Lawyer
(214) 871-6005
chriskalis@kalislaw.com
Nature of Sports Service:
All phases of athlete representation including contract negotiation, long-range planning, financial planning, and post-career counseling.
Services:
Commercial Disputes, Trade Secret Protection, Non-compete Agreements, Athletes & Entertainers, Employment Disputes, Personal Injuries, Defective Products, Insurance Claims, Wrongful Death

---

KANAI, MARK A.
1101 15TH STREET
PO BOX 791
MODESTO, CA 95354
209-527-3650
Fax: 209-527-5518
mark@kanai-law.com
www.kanai-law.com
• Mark A. A. Kanai, Member
(906) 043-545
mark@kanai-law.com
Description:
Estate Planning, Trusts and Estates, Living Trusts, Elder Law, Financial Planning, Retirement Planning, Wealth Preservation, Business Law, Employment Law, Corporate Law, Partnership Law, Buying and Selling of Businesses, Closely Held Business Law, Emerging Growth Companies, Family Business Successions, Real Estate, Broadcast Radio, Sports Law.

KAPLAN, GARY L.
25 TAMALPAIS AVENUE
SUITE C
SAN ANSELMO, CA 94960
415-721-7584
• Gary L. Kaplan,
Services:
Areas of practice include Personal Injury and Civil Litigation, Estate Planning and Probate, Labor and Employment Law, Commercial and Educational Loan Law, and Arbitration and Mediation

---

KARSNER & MEEHAN P.C.
128 DEAN STREET
TAUNTON, MA 2780
508-822-6600
877-684-0345
Fax: 508-822-8006
info@karsnermeehan.com
www.karsnermeehan.com
• James K. Meehan, Attorney
• Mark R. Karsner, Esquire
• David O. DeAbreu, Esquire
• Colleen C. G. Karsner, Attorney
(508) 822-6600
cck@karsnermeehan.com
• Mark R. Karsner, Attorney
(508) 822-6600
mrk@karsnermeehan.com
• James K. Meehan, Attorney
(508) 822-6600
jkm@karsnermeehan.com
• Robert C. Shea, Attorney
(508) 822-6600
rcs@karsnermeehan.com
• Karen L. Medeiros, Attorney

(508) 822-6600
klm@karsnermeehan.com
Description:
NFLPA. Handles workers compensation for the New England Patriots.
Services:
Areas of practice include Personal Injury, Workers' Compensation, Civil Litigation, Criminal Law, Wills & Estates, and Business Formation

---

KATZ, TELLER, BRANT & HILD
255 E FIFTH STREET
2400 CHEMED CENTER
CINCINNATI, OH 45202-4724
513-721-4532
Fax: 513-762-0000
ktbh@katzteller.com
www.katzteller.com
• Reuven J. Katz, Lawyer
(513) 977-3417
rkatz@katzteller.com
• Jerome S. Teller, Lawyer
(513) 977-3453
jteller@katzteller.com
• Andrew R. Berger, Attorney
(513) 977-3478
jcassity@katzteller.com
• Joel S. Brant, Attorney
(513) 977-3473
vschornak@katzteller.com
• Robert E. Brant, Attorney
(513) 977-3405
jcassity@katzteller.com
• Joseph A. Brant, Of Counsel
(513) 977-3408
jabrant@katzteller.com
• Adam D. Colvin, Attorney
(513) 977-3423
acolvin@katzteller.com
• Tedd H. Friedman, Attorney
(513) 721-4532
tfriedman@katzteller.com
Services:
Areas of practice include Creditors' Rights and Bankruptcy, Domestic Relations and Family Law, Employee Benefits and Retirement Planning, Employment Law, Entertainment and Sports Law, Estate and Wealth Planning, Finance and Lending, General Business and Tax Matters, Health Care, Information Technology and e-Business, Insurance, Litigation, Probate, Real Estate and Environmental, Securities Law, and Title Insurance

---

KAY & MERKLE
100 THE EMBARCADERO
PENTHOUSE
SAN FRANCISCO, CA 94105-1217
415-357-1200
Fax: 415-512-9277
www.kaymerkle.com
• Steven Kay, Lawyer
(415) 357-1200
stevenkay@kmlaw100.com
• Walter F F. Merkle, Lawyer
(415) 357-1200
wmerkle@kmlaw100.com
• Steven Kay, Attorney
• W.Bruce Bercovich, Attorney
• John W Merkle, Attorney
• Lionel T. Aiken, Attorney
• Alan J Silver, Attorney
• Douglas A Marshall, Attorney
Services:
Areas of practice include business litigation,

professional sports law, estate planning, entertainment law, and business law.

KEITH O. GREGORY
434 FAYETTEVILLE STREET MALL
SUITE 2030
RALEIGH, NC 27601
919-647-9728
877-297-6842
Fax: 919-832-4777
attykeithgregory@aol.com
• Keith O. Gregory, Member
attykeithgregory@aol.com
Services:
Areas of practice include Criminal Law, Driving While Intoxicated, Drug Crimes, Felonies, Homicide, Sexual Assault, Traffic Violations, Personal Injury, Automobile Accidents and Injuries, Wrongful Death, Divorce, Entertainment Law, Music Law, Sports Contracts, Separation Agreements, and Wills

KELLEY, MCELWEE & SCHMIDT, P.A.
2025 NORTH THIRD STREET
SUITE 150
PHOENIX, AZ 85004
602-230-1118
Fax: 602-230-9622
theresem@azfamilylaw.com
www.azfamilylaw.com
• Therese R. McElwee, Member
(602) 230-1118
theresem@azfamilylaw.com
• Brian E. Kelley, Member
(602) 230-1118
briank@azfamilylaw.com
• Paul G. Schmidt, Member
(602) 230-1118
pauls@azfamilylaw.com
Services:
Areas of practice include Complex Divorce, Prenuptial / Postnuptial Agreements, Mediation & Arbitration, Domestic Relations, and Child Custody Issues

KENYON & KENYON (DC OFFICE)
1500 K STREET NW
SUITE 700
WASHINGTON, DC 20005-1257
202-220-4200
Fax: 202-220-4201
www.kenyon.com
• Gwen Bey, Chief Administrative Officer
(212) 908-6396
• John S. Barry, Chief Financial Officer
(212) 908-6468
• Kerstin Isaacs, Public Relations and Communications Mana
(212) 908-6853
• Kathleen S. Lynn, Professional Recruiting Director
(212) 908-6177
Services:
Provides litigation, prosecution, licensing and counseling services relating to patents, trademarks, copyrights, trade secrets and related matters, such as unfair business and unfair trade practices.
Other Office:
One Broadway, New York, NY 10004; Phone: 212-425-7200; 333 West San Carlos Street, STE 600, San Jose, CA 95110; Phone: 408-975-7500

KING & KELLEHER
4 EMBARCADERO CENTER
17H FLOOR
SAN FRANCISCO, CA 94111-4158
415-781-2888
Fax: 415-781-3011
• Edward V. King, Member
(415) 781-2888
evking@kingandkelleher.com
• Dirk V. Ausdall, Associate
(901) 868-914
• Alvin Lindsay, Associate
(415) 781-2888
• Edward B. Vincent King, Jr., Partner
(905) 879-374
Description:
Litigation, Patents, Intellectual Property, Securities, Antitrust, Sports, Entertainment.
Services:
Areas of practice include Copyright, Patent & Trademark Attorneys, Corporate Business Attorneys, and Professional Services

KIRKPATRICK, WILLIAMS & MEEKS, L.L.P.
500 BROADWAY PLACE
SUPERIOR FEDERAL BUILDING, SUITE 404
LITTLE ROCK, AR 72201-3343
501-372-0401
Fax: 501-372-5277
• Joseph E. Kilpatrick Jr, Member
(501) 372-0401
• Aylmer G. Ge Williams, Member
(501) 372-0401
• Richard A. Smith, Managing Partner
• Charles H. Crocker, Associate
• W.Russell Meeks, Of Counsel

KORNBURG, HOWARD CRAIG
10880 WILSHIRE BOULEVARD
SUITE 1840
LOS ANGELES, CA 90024
310-474-5588
866-685-7259
Fax: 310-474-1078
www.kornberglawfirm.com
• Howard C. Kornberg, Sole Practitioner
hck@kornberglaw.com
Description:
Civil litigation, sports law, entertainment law, intellectual property, medical malpractice.
Services:
Areas of practice include Pedestrian & Bicycle Accidents; Elder Abuse; Birth Injuries; Dog bites; Slip and Fall Injuries; Trucking & Bus Accidents; Construction Site Accidents; Medical Malpractice; Sexual Harassment; Bad Faith Denial of Insurance Benefits; Motorcycle Accidents; Nursing Home Negligence; Death Claims; Burn Injuries; Fractures, Paralysis, Spinal Injuries; Aviation Accidents; Defective Products; Legal Malpractice; Civil Rights/Discrimination; and Fraud Claims.

KORZENIOWSKI, WALTER, ESQ.
688 WASHINGTON STREET
SOUTH EASTON, MA 2375
508-238-6200
Fax: 508-238-2899
walterkorzeniowski@hotmail.com
www.walterklaw.com
Description:
Handles workmans' compensation for the New England Patriots.

Services:
Provides legal services

KUPELIAN, ORMOND & MAGY
25800 NORTHWESTERN HIGHWAY
SUITE 950
SOUTHFIELD, MI 48075
248-357-0000
Fax: 248-357-7488
• Peter B. Kupelian, Lawyer
(248) 351-8351
• Peter B. P. Kupelian, Attorney
• David M. Blou, Associate attorney
Services:
Serves clients worldwide through the following departments: Litigation, Business and International, Commercial Property, and Municipal Law and Litigation.
Description:
Contract negotiation, licensing, endorsement exploration, tort actions/litigation.

LAING, DEAN P.
111 E WISCONSIN AVENUE
SUITE 1400
MILWAUKEE, WI 53202
414-276-5000
Fax: 414-276-6581
webmaster@wilaw.com
www.wilaw.com
• Jean M. Ansay, Lawyer
(262) 284-3407
jean.ansay@wilaw.com
• Dean P. Laing, Lawyer
(414) 276-5000
Services:
Areas of practice include Bankruptcy and Creditors Rights; Business Acquisitions and Dispositions; Business Succession Planning; Commercial Litigation; Commercial Transactions; Construction Law; Corporations, Partnerships and Limited Liability Companies; Divorce, Custody and Marital Property Agreements; E-Commerce and Telecommunications Law; Employee Benefits and ERISA; Employment and Labor Law; Estate Planning and Probate; Intellectual Property Law; Municipal, Zoning and Administrative Law; Personal Injury and Products Litigation; Qualified Plans and Executive Compensation; Real Estate and Construction Law; Securities and Franchise Law; Tax
Description:
Contract negotiation, tort actions/litigation. Litigation; Products Liability; Personal Injury.
Other Location:
1329 West Grand Avenue, STE 200, PO Box 306, Port Washington, WI 53074; Phone: 262-284-3407
Year Founded:
1973

LAMPART, ABE
55 SECOND STREET
SUITE 1700
SAN FRANCISCO, CA 94105-3493
415-227-0900
Fax: 415-227-0770
www.buchalter.com
• Peter G. Bertrand, Shareholder
(415) 227-0900
pbertrand@buchalter.com
• Jonathan Y. Hawkins, Sr administrative director
• Kristy Sessions, HRM

- Judith Gordon, Marketing director
- David Bustle, Director of IT
Description:
Investment contract negotiation, represents sports organizations, arbitration hearings, provides securities advice, provides investment advice, endorsement exploration.
Services:
Provides transactional and litigation support for established and evolving businesses in the following practice areas: Bank and Finance; Business Practices; Insolvency; Intellectual Property; Labor & Employment; Litigation; Pro Bono; Real Estate; Tax.
Other Locations:
601 S Figueroa Street, STE 2400, Los Angeles, CA 90017; Phone: 213-891-0700; Fax: 213-896-0400; 18400 Von Karman Avenue, STE 800, Irvine, CA 92612; Phone: 949-760-1121; Fax: 949-72-0182; Anderson Brody Buchalter Nemer, 4600 East Shea Blvd., STE 100, Phoenix, AZ 85028; Phone: 602-234-0563; Fax: 602-234-2952

LAMPLEY, NATHANIEL
301 EAST FOURTH STREET
SUITE 3500
GREAT AMERICAN TOWER
CINCINNATI, OH 45202
513-723-4000
Fax: 513-723-4056
nlampley@vorys.com
www.vorys.com
- Terri Reyering Abare, Partner
(513) 723-4001
- TerriReyering Abare, Partner
(513) 723-4001
- T. Gregory Apocotos, Partner
(513) 723-8581
- Melvin A. Bredre, Partner
(513) 723-4023
- David E. Barnes, Paralegal
(513) 723-4815
- Jessica K. Baverman, Associate
(513) 723-4092
jkbaverman@vorys.com
- Eric B Bond, Associate
(513) 723-4824
- William P. DG Baldwin, Partner
(513) 723-4030
Nature of Sports Service:
All phases of athlete representation including contract negotiation, long-range planning, financial planning, and post-career counseling.
Services:
Areas of practice include Intellectual Property; International Law; Labor and Employment; Litigation; Probate and Estate Planning; Taxation, Technology; and Toxic Tort.

LANG, XIFARAS & BULLARD
115 ORCHARD STREET
NEW BEDFORD, MA 02740
508-992-1270
Fax: 508-993-8696
sfweiner@lxblaw.com
www.lxblaw.com
- Scott W. Lang, Attorney
(508) 992-1270
- Scott W. D. Lang, Attorney
swlang@lxblaw.com
- Peter C. Bullard, Attorney
(508) 992-1270
pcbullard@lxblaw.com

- Susan Forgue Weiner, Attorney
(508) 992-1270
sfweiner@lxblaw.com
- Jennifer L. Davis, Attorney
(508) 992-1270
- Gigi D. D. Tierney, Attorney
(508) 992-1270
gdtierney@lxblaw.com
Description:
Providing quality legal services to families and businesses in the Greater New Bedford area.
Areas of Practice:
Administrative Law, Business Law, Consumer Protection, Employee Benefits, Estate Administration, Estate Planning, Family Law, Employment Law, Labor Law, Litigation, Personal Injury, Real Estate, Social Security, Workers' Compensation.

LATSHA DAVIS & MCKENNA, P.C.
1700 BENT CREEK BOULEVARD
SUITE 140
MECHANICSBURG, PA 17050
717-620-2424
Fax: 717-620-2444
www.ldylaw.com
- Latsha L. Kimber, Principal/Managing Shareholder
klatsha@ldylaw.com
- Kevin M. McKenna, Esq., Shareholder
(610) 524-8454
Description:
Tort litigation; sports law; workers' compensation

LATTINVILLE, ROBERT H.
7700 FORSYTH BOULEVARD
SUITE 1100
ST. LOUIS, MO 63105
314-863-0800
Fax: 314-863-9388
www.stinson.com
- John W. Moticka, St. Louis Co-Managing Partner
(314) 259-4562
jmoticka@stinson.com
- Charles G. Misko, St. Louis Co-Managing Partner
(314) 259-4570
cmisko@stinsonmoheck.com
Services:
Areas of practice include real estate law, mergers & acquisitions, labor & employment, business litigation, financial services, health care, sports law, and products liability.

   Nature of Sports Service:
   All phases of athlete representation including contract negotiation, estate planning, endorsements, financial planning, compliance matters, licensing matters and post-career counseling.

LAURIA TOKUNGA GATES & LINN, LLP
1755 CREEKSIDE OAKS
#240
SACRAMENTO, CA 95833
916-492-2000
Fax: 916-492-2500
www.ltglaw.net
- Anthony D. Lauria, Lawyer
alauria@ltglaw.net
- Mark D. Tokunga, Lawyer
- Scott A. Linn, Lawyer
- Scott Andre, Sports Lawyer

Description:
Civil Practice, Construction Law, Insurance Defense, Medical Malpractice, Personal Injury, Products Liability, Bad Faith, Recreation/Sports Law.

LAW OFFICE OF DONALD J STANTON
1185 WASHINGTON STREET
SUITE 6
NEWTON, MA 2465
617-964-1341
Fax: 617-964-6910
d4stanton@aol.com
- Donald J. Stanton, Esquire
(617) 964-1341
d4stanton@aol.com
Services:
Legal Services
Description:
Contract negotiation, arbitration hearings, represents professional sports teams, tort actions/litigation, estate planning.

LAW OFFICE OF WILLIAM D HOCHBERG
222 THIRD AVENUE N
EDMONDS, WA 98020
425-744-1220
Fax: 425-744-0464
info@hochberglaw.net
www.hochberglaw.net
- Bill Hochberg, Attorney
- Lillian Kaufer, Paralegal
Year Founded:
1996
Description:
Represents injured professional athletes in Washington State.
Nature of Services:
Workers' compensation claims, social security, disability, and personal injury claims.

LAYMAN, MICHAEL L.
268 NEWMAN AVENUE
HARRISONBURG, VA 22801
540-433-2121
800-394-1646
Fax: 540-433-7296
info@layman-nichols.com
www.layman-nichols.com
- Michael L. Layman, Attorney/CPA
mlayman@layman-nichols.com
- Michael L. M. Layman, Attorney
- Lenora Fowler, Legal Secretary
- Carol B. Boutillier, Office Administrator
Services:
Areas of practice include tax planning, estate and business succession planning, elder law, wills and trusts, estate administration, qualified retirement plans, real estate, tax-deferred exchanges, representation of closely-held businesses, including professional practices, health law, charitable planning, and employee benefits.

LEADBETTER, RONALD C.
527 ANDY HOLT TOWER
527 ANDY HOLT TOWER
KNOXVILLE, TN 37996-0184
865-974-1000
Fax: 865-974-4811
chancellor@utk.edu
www.utk.edu
- Susan Martin, Vice Chancellor Academic Affairs
- Jimmy G. Cheek, Chancellor

(865) 974-3265
chancellor@utk.edu
Services:
Prides itself on adding value to
Tennessee—by educating its students,
doing research and creative work that
improves quality of life, and reaching out to
share expertise with Tennesseans.
Description:
Represents college athletic departments.

LEDBETTER, BEVERLY E.
ONE PROSPECT STREET
CAMPUS BOX 1860
PROVIDENCE, RI 2912
401-863-1000
Fax: 401-863-1199
SAC@brown.edu
www.brown.edu
• Ruth Simmons, President
(401) 863-2234
president@brown.edu
• Christina Paxson, President
Services:
A leading Ivy League institution with a
distinctive undergraduate academic
program, a world-class faculty, outstanding
graduate and medical students, and a
tradition of innovative and rigorous
multidisciplinary study.
Description:
Represents college athletic departments.

LEFKOWITZ, PAUL
55 PUBLIC SQUARE
SUITE 1950
CLEVELAND, OH 44113
216-621-8484
(800) 621-1062
Fax: 216-771-1632
www.climacolaw.com
• John R. Climaco, Founder
(216) 522-0265
jrclim@climacolaw.com
• John A. Peca, Managing Principal
(216) 522-0991
japeca@climacolaw.com
Services:
Areas of practice include Litigation,
Commercial Law, Municipal Law,
Employment Law, and Class Actions
Description:
NFLPA workers' compensation panel.

LEVIN, PAPANTONIO, THOMAS, MITCHELL, ECHSNER & PROCTOR, P.A.
316 S BAYLEN STREET
SUITE 600
PO BOX 12308
PENSACOLA, FL 32591
850-435-7000
888-435-7001
Fax: 850-435-7020
contact@levinlaw.com
www.levinlaw.com
• Brian Barr, Shareholder
• Robert Smith, Administrator
Nature of Sports Service:
All phases of athlete representation
including contract negotiation, long-range
planning, financial planning, and post-career
counseling.
Services:
Areas of practice include Personal Injury;
Medical Malpractice; Mass Tort / Product
Liability; Commercial Litigation; Insurance
Bad Faith; Workers' Compensation; Criminal

Law; Nursing Home Abuse; Environmental
Litigation.

LEVINSON, FRIEDMAN, P.S.
1001 FOURTH AVENUE
SUITE 4131
SEATTLE, WA 98154
206-624-8844
800-448-8008
Fax: 206-624-2912
www.admiralty.com
• Robert M. Kraft, Partner
(206) 624-8844
rmk@admiralty.com
• Lance E. Palmer, Partner
(206) 624-8844
Services:
Handles personal injury trials.
Clients:
Represents clients in following areas:
construction site injury; automobile injury;
motorcycle injury; workplace injury;
pedestrian injury; slip and fall injury; cruise
ship injury; fisherman injury; admiralty law;
maritime law; pharmaceutical injury;
fen-phen injury; wrongful death; product
liability; railroad injury; toxic products;
mesothelioma; redux injury; PPA Injury;
asbestosis.
Nature of Sports Service:
All phases of athlete representation
including contract negotiation, long-range
planning, financial planning, and post-career
counseling.
Year Founded:
1929

LEVY, HERMAN M.
500 EL CAMINO REAL
SANTA CLARA, CA 95053
408-554-4000
Fax: 408-554-5095
hlevy@scu.edu
www.scu.edu
• Paul Locatelli, Chancellor
• Lucia Albino Gilbert, Provost
Description:
Arbitration hearings, teaches sports law.
Services:
Areas of practice include arbitration
hearings and sports law.

LEWIS AND ROCA LLP
201 EAST WASHINGTON
SUITE 1200
PHOENIX, AZ 85004
602-262-5311
Fax: 602-262-5747
clientservices@lrlaw.com
www.lrlaw.com
• Emily Bayton, Partner
(602) 262-5768
ebayton@lrlaw.com
Other Locations:
One South Church Avenue, STE 700,
Tucson, AZ 85401; Phone: 520-622-2090;
Fax: 520-622-3088; 3993 Howard Hughes
Parkway, STE 600, Las Vegas, NV 89109;
Phone: 702-949-8200; Fax: 702-949-8398;
201 Third Street, NW, STE 1950,
Albuquerque, NM 87102; Phone:
505-764-5400; Fax: 505-764-5480
Services:
Areas of practice include Antitrust and Trade
Regulation, Appeals, Arbitration and
Mediation, Bankruptcy, Broker/Dealer,
Commercial Litigation, Construction,

Corporate and Securities, creditor's Rights,
Criminal Defense, Government Regulation
and Corporate Compliance, E-Discovery &
Data Management, Education and Schools,
Employee Benefits, Environmental and
Natural Resources, Finance, Gaming,
Government Relations and Administrative,
Healthcare, Indian Affairs Law, Insurance,
Intellectual Property, Labor and
Employment, Legal Risk Evaluation,
Mergers and Acquisitions, Personal Injury,
Products Liability

LEWIS, KING, KRIEG & WALDROP, P.C.
620 MARKET STREET
ONE CENTRE SQUARE, FIFTH FLOOR
PO BOX 2425
KNOXVILLE, TN 37901
865-546-4646
Fax: 865-523-6529
www.lewisking.com
• Charles B. Lewis, Lawyer
(865) 546-4646
• John K King, Lawyer
(865) 546-4646
jking@lewisking.com
• Richard W. Kreig, Lawyer
(865) 546-4646
Dkrieg@lkkwc.com
• Loy W Waldrop, Lawyer
(865) 546-4646
lwaldrop@lkkwc.com
Services:
Areas of practice include Appellate,
Arbitration, Aviation, Banking, Bankruptcy,
Business Organization and Litigation,
Casualty Defense, Construction and Surety
Law, Copyright and Trademark, Corporate,
Criminal, Domestic, Education,
Employment, Fire Loss, Health Care,
Insurance, Landlord/Tenant, Mediation,
Military, Municipal, Personal Injury, Products
Liability, Professional Liability, Regulatory,
Real Estate, Workers' Compensation, and
Zoning
Other Location:
Suntrust Bank Building, 201 Fourth Avenue
North, STE 1500, PO Box 198615,
Nashville, TN 37219; Phone: 615-259-1366

LIBRETT, FRIEDLAND & LIEBERMAN
1325 FRANKLIN AVENUE
SUITE 545
GARDEN CITY, NY 11530-1701
516-874-3523
866-427-5413
Fax: 516-741-1592
lfriedland@lfllaw.com
www.lfllaw.com
• Lloyd M. Friedland, Attorney
(516) 741-1040
lfriedland@lfllaw.com
• Richard A. Librett, Attorney
(516) 741-1040
rlibrett@lfllaw.com
• Edward L. Lieberman, Attorney
(516) 741-1040
elieberman@lfllaw.com
Year Founded:
1978
Description:
Contract negotiation, real estate, and
general practice law firm.

LICARI & WALSH, L.L.C.
322 E. MAIN STREET
SUITE 2B
BRANFORD, CT 06405
203-752-1450
Fax: 203-752-1401
www.licariwalsh.com
• Christopher M. Lucari, Member
(203) 752-1450
clicari@licari-walsh.com
• John M. Walsh Jr, Member
(203) 752-1450
jwalsh@licari-walsh.com
• Craig L. Manemeit, Associate
cmanemeit@licari-walsh.com
• Gary P. Sklaver, Counsel
gsklaver@licari-walsh.com
Services:
Areas of practice include: Personal Injury
(Automobile Collisions, Premises Liability,
Product Liability, Medical Malpractice,
Wrongful Death), Business Torts and
Commercial Litigation, Labor and
Employment Law, Workers' Compensation,
Small Business Law, Consumer Law,
Criminal Law, Real Estate (Commercial and
Residential), Wills and Probate.

**LIEBMANN, CONWAY, OLEJNICZAK &
JERRY**
231 S ADAMS STREET
PO BOX 23200
GREEN BAY, WI 54301
920-437-0476
Fax: 920-437-2868
www.lcojlaw.com
• Thomas M. Olejniczak, Partner
• Herbect C. Liebmann III, Partner
• Geogory B. Conway, Partner
• Gregory Mi Conway, Attorney
Services:
Areas of practice include Adoptions,
Bankruptcy and Creditors' Rights,
Commercial Litigation, Computer and
Internet Law, Construction, Corporate/
Business Law, Development, Leasing,
Environment Issues, Estate/Retirement,
Planning and Probate, Hospital and Health
Care Law, Insurance Coverage/Defense,
Intellectual Property, Labor Employment
Matters, Litigation and Trials,
Meditation/Arbitration, Mergers/
Acquisitions, Municipal Law, Non-Profit
Institutions, Municipal Law, Non-Profit
institutions, Personal Injury Claims, Real
Estate and Construction, Tax, and Pension
and Employee Benefit Planning
Description:
Represents professional sports teams. On
the Board of Directors for the Green Bay
Packers.
Year Founded:
1976

LINDNER & MARSACK, S.C.
411 E WISCONSIN AVENUE
SUITE 1800
MILWAUKEE, WI 53202
414-273-3910
Fax: 414-273-0522
www.lindner-marsack.com
• Gary A. Marsack, President/Senior
Shareholder
(414) 273-3910
gmarsack@lindner-marsack.com
• Robert E. Schreiber, Jr., VP/Shareholder
(414) 273-3910
rschreiber@lindner-marsack.com

• Jonathan T. Swain, Board of Directors
jswain@lindner-marsack.com
• Chelsie D. R. Allan, Attorney
• Douglas M. Feldman, Attorney
• Alan M. Levy, Attorney
• Gary A. Marsack, Attorney
• John E. Murray, Attorney
• David C. Mckone, Attorney
Services:
Representation Matters (Maintaining
Non-Union Status, Union Organizing
Campaigns), Collective Bargaining and
Contract Administration (Labor Contract
Negotiations, Mediation, Interest Bargaining
(Win-Win), Public Sector Interest Arbitration,
Contract Interpretation, Discipline,
Grievance Handling, Arbitration), Labor
Dispute (Strike Preparations, Managing the
Labor Disputes, Public Relations and the
Labor Dispute), General Labor Matters
(General Consultation, Strategy
Development, OSHA and Safety and Health
Matters, WARN Act - Plant Closings - Mass
Layoffs), Labor Litigation (NLRB and
Related State Labor Agencies, Unfair Labor
Practice Matter

LOPEZ & FANTEL
2292 WEST COMMODORE WAY
SUITE 200
SEATTLE, WA 98199
206-322-5200
Fax: 206-322-1979
clopez@lopezfantel.com
• Carl Taylor Lopez, President
Services:
All phases of athlete representation
including contract negotiation, long-range
planning, financial planning, and post-career
counseling.

LOPEZ, PAT P.
6363 N SWAN ROAD
SUITE 151
TUCSON, AZ 85718
520-792-4800
Fax: 520-529-4262
rusingandlopez@aol.com
www.rusingandlopez.com
• Michael J. S. Rusing, Attornry
(520) 792-4800
mrusing@rusingandlopez.com
• Patricio P. Lopez III, Attorney
plopez@rusingandlopez.com
Clients:
AIMCO Properties, Alphagraphics, America
Online, Arizona Board of Regents, Arizona
Electric, Power Cooperative, Bank of
America, Big 5 Corp., Bob's Custom
Roofing, Brush Ceramic Products, Brush
Wellman Inc., Capin Car Wash, Charter
Funding, Chicanos por la Causa, Chubb
Group of Insurance Companies, Cintas
Citizens Transport and Storage, Cox
Communications, El Coronado Ranch,
Electronic Data Systems, Fairfield Homes,
First Magnus Financial Corporation,
Fresenius Medical Care North America,
Frontier Towing, Inc., Gates Learjet, Goettl
Air Conditioning, Inc., Guarantee Mutual
Life, Hydro Geo Chem, Jack in the Box, Inc.,
La Causa Construction, In
Nature of Sports Service:
All phases of athlete representation
including contract negotiation, long-range
planning, financial planning, and post-career
counseling.

LUBIN & ENOCH, P.C.
349 N 4TH AVENUE
PHOENIX, AZ 85003-1505
602-234-0008
Fax: 602-626-3586
www.lubinandenoch.com
• Nicholas J. Enoch, Attorney
• Stanley Lubin, Member
• Nicholas J. Enoch, Partner
• Jarrett J. Haskovec, Member
Services:
Areas of practice include Labor and
Employment Relations, Civil Service,
Employment Discrimination, Administrative
Law, and Arbitration. Civil Trial and
Appellate Practice
Clients:
Arizona State AFL-CIO; Local Unions 2859
& 3954, American Federation of
Government Employees, AFL-CIO; Local
Union 3190, American Federation of State,
County & Municipal Employees, AFL-CIO;
Local Union 93, American Postal Workers
Union, AFL-CIO; Community Legal Services
Attorney Union; Locals 266, 387, 570, 640,
769 and 1116, International Brotherhood of
Electrical Workers, AFL-CIO; Engineers and
Associate Employees of KTVK; United Farm
Workers, AFL-CIO; Professional Fire
Fighters of Arizona & Local Unions I-60,
3066, 3560, 3573, 3690, 3878, 3924 &
4191; International Association of Fire
Fighters, AFL-CIO

**LYNCH, GILARDI & GRUMMER, A
PROFESSIONAL CORPORATION**
170 COLUMBUS AVENUE
5TH FLOOR
SAN FRANCISCO, CA 94133
415-397-2800
Fax: 415-397-0937
www.lgglaw.com
• Kenneth F. Vierra, Partner
(415) 397-2800
• Robert T. Lynch, Partner
(415) 397-2800
Services:
Areas of practice include Commercial
Litigation & Advice Products Liability
Litigation, Construction Law & Litigation,
Professional Liability Litigation, Directors'
and Officers' Liability Real Estate Law and
Litigation, Employment Litigation and Advice
Sports Law & Athlete Representation,
Insurance Law And Litigation Toxic Tort and
Areas of practice include Environmental
Liability, and Intellectual Property
Transportation Law
Nature of Sports Service:
Sports Law, Real Estate, Landlord and
Tenant Law, Employment Law, Litigation,
Directors and Officers Liability.

MACDONALD, JAMES
709 S. DEAKIN STREET
PO BOX 442321
MOSCOW, ID 83844-2321
208-885-4977
888-884-3246
Fax: 208-885-5709
info@uidaho.edu
• James S. Macdonald, Professor
(208) 885-7947
jimmymac@uidaho.edu
• Michele Bartlett, Director, Development
(208) 364-4044
bartlett@uidaho.edu

Services:
Teaches sports law.

MAHONE, GLENN R.
435 SIXTH AVENUE
PITTSBURGH, PA 15219
412-288-3131
Fax: 412-288-3063
www.reedsmith.com
• Glenn R. Mahone, Partner
(412) 288-4240
gmahone@reedsmith.com
• Gary A. Sokulski, Chief Operating Officer
(412) 288-4232
gsokulski@reedsmith.com
Services:
All phases of athlete representation including contract negotiation, long-range planning, financial planning, and post-career counseling.
Clients:
Advertising Research Foundation, AMION Advertising & Marketing International Network, ANA, Bank of America, Caithness Energy, CIT, Dominion Resources, Inc., Federated Investors, FPL Energy LLC, GMAC, H.R. Block, ICOM International Communications Network, Interpublic Group, JPMorgan Chase, Key Bank, MAGNET Advertising Agency Network, Mellon Financial Corporation, Merck, Inc., National Penn, NiSource, Inc., Ocâ€š, Ocwen, Pfizer, Inc., PNC Bank, Sony Corporation of America, Sony Electronics Inc., Sony Pictures Entertainment, Starwood Capital Group, TAAN Transworld Advertising Agency Network, Wachovia, Wells Fargo, N.A., WWP Wordwide Partners

---

MAJOR LEAGUE BASEBALL PROPERTIES
75 NINTH AVENUE
5TH FLOOR
NEW YORK, NY 10011
212-931-7800
866-800-1275
Fax: 212-949-5654
www.mlb.com
• Allan H. Selig, Commissioner of Baseball
• Robert A DuPuy, President/Chief Operating Officer
• Sandy Alderson, Executive VP of Baseball Operations
• Carmen Julia Hunt, Information Contact Person
• Jonathan Mariner, EVP,Finance
• Tim Brosnan, EVP,Business
Description:
The licensing agent for all of the Major League Baseball entities the Office of the Commissioner of Baseball, the American and National Leagues of Professional Baseball Clubs, the individual Major League Baseball clubs and their affiliated and related entities. MLBP secures protection for and enforces the intellectual property rights of all of the Major League Baseball entities against infringers and counterfeiters worldwide.

MALLOY, DOROTHY A.
800 E. LANCASTER AVENUE
206 TOLENTINE HALL, VILLANOVA UNIVERSITY
VILLANOVA, PA 19085
610-519-4500
Fax: 610-519-7875

ogc@villanova.edu
www.villanova.edu
• Dorothy A. Malloy, VP/General Counsel
(610) 519-7857
dorothy.malloy@villanova.edu
• Debra Fickler, Deputy General Counsel
(610) 519-7857
debra.fickler@villanova.edu
Services:
Represents college athletic departments.

MANATT, PHELPS & PHILLIPS, LLP
7 TIMES SQUARE
NEW YORK, NY 10036
212-790-4500
Fax: 212-790-4545
wbernstein@manatt.com
www.manatt.com
• Mathew S. Rosengart, Partner
(212) 790-4565
mrosengart@manatt.com
• William S. Bernstein, Partner
(212) 830-7282
wbernstein@manatt.com
Services:
Areas of practice include Advertising, Marketing & Media, Antitrust, Appellate, Banking & Financial Industry, Bankruptcy & Financial Restructuring, Corporate & Finance, Criminal Defense & Investigations, Employment & Labor, Energy, Environmental & Natural Resources, Entertainment, Financial Services, Government & Regulatory, Healthcare Industry, Insurance Industry, Intellectual Property & Internet, International Trade & Policy, Litigation, Mergers & Acquisitions, Not-for-Profit Organizations, Real Estate & Land Use, Tax, Employee Benefits & Global Compensation, Unfair Competition Litigation, and Venture Capital & Technology
Clients:
The Coca-Cola Company, Diageo North America, Den-Mat Corporation/Rembrandt Oral Care Products, D.L. Blair, DreamWorks, Dyson, Energizer Holdings, E. & J. Gallo Winery, Eveready Battery Company, Inc., Expedia, General Mills, Inc., Harley-Davidson, Jamba Juice, Kimberly-Clark Corporation, Martin Agency, MasterCard International, Mattel, Inc., Mead Johnson, Miller Brewing Company, Papa John's International, Inc., Reader's Digest Association, Inc., Schick Manufacturing, Inc., Thane International, Tommy Hilfiger, UniWorld Group, Inc., Yahoo! Inc., Zila Nutraceuticals, Amresco Commercial Finance, Bank of America Corp., California National Bank, Cit
Description:
All phases of athlete representation including contract negotiation, long-range planning, financial planning, and post-career counseling.

MANDEL, IRWIN,
1901 W MADISON STREET
UNITED CENTER
CHICAGO, IL 60612-2459
312-455-4000
Fax: 312-455-4189
sth@bulls.com
www.chicagobulls.com
• Jerry Reinsdorf, Chairman
• Irwin Mandel, SVP, Financial & Legal
Services:
Represents professional sports teams.

MANNING, MARDER, KASS, ELLROD, & RAMIREZ
801 S FIGUEROA STREET
15TH FLOOR
LOS ANGELES, CA 90017
213-624-6900
Fax: 213-624-6999
• Anthony J. Ellrod, Partner
(213) 624-6900
aje@mmker.com
• Steven D. Manning, Partner
(213) 624-6900
sdm@mmker.com
Other Locations:
1 Park Plaza, Suite 500 Irvine, CA 92614 Phone: (949) 440-6690 Fax: (949) 474-6691; 550 W C Street, Suite 1900 San Diego, CA 92101 Phone: (619) 515-0269 Fax: (619) 515-0268; One California Street, Suite 1100 San Francisco, CA 94111 Phone: (415) 217-6990 Fax: (415) 217-6999; 14362 N Frank Lloyd Wright Boulevard, Suite 2300 Scottsdale, AZ 85260 Phone: (480) 477-5269 Fax: (480) 477-5268, 801 S Figueroa Street, 15th Floor, Los Angeles, CA 90017 Phone: (213) 624-6900 Fax: (213) 624-6999.
Description:
Insurance defense and coverage, business and commercial law, business transactions, sports and recreation, employment, wage and hour, professional, errors and omissions, appellate law, workers compensation, general civil defense, medical malpractice defense, construction defect, real estate litigation and transactions, police civil liability, government fort liability, immigration law.

MARGOLIS EDELSTEIN
170 S INDEPENDENCE MALL W
THE CURTIS CENTER
SUITE 400E
PHILADELPHIA, PA 19106-3337
215-922-1100
Fax: 215-922-1772
mail@margolisedelstein.com
www.margolisedelstein.com
• Joseph S. Bekelja, Partner
(215) 931-5807
jbekelja@margolisedelstein.com
• Peter D. Bludman, Partner
(215) 931-5879
pbludman@margolisedelstein.com
• Joseph S. Bekelja, Partner
(215) 931-5807
jbekelja@margolisedelstein.com
• Gordon Gelfond, Partner
(215) 931-5812
• Alan Wm. Margolis, Partner
(215) 931-5802
• Donald M. Davis, Partner
(215) 931-5813
ddavis@margolisedelstein.com
• William Longo, Partner
(215) 931-5861
wlongo@margolisedelstein.com
• Mark N. Cohen, Partner
(215) 931-5848
Other Location:
Curtis Center, 4th Floor, Independence Square West, 601 Walnut street, Philadelphia, PA 19106; Phone: 215-922-1100
Services:
Automobile and Trucking Litigation, Aviation Litigation, Complex/Environmental/Toxic Tort Litigation, Construction Defect

Litigation, Domestic Relations/Marital Law, Employment Practices Liability, ERISA and Employee Benefit Litigation, Fidelity and Surety Law, General Liability, Insurance Coverage, Insurance Fraud, Municipal Liability, Product LIability, Professional Liability, Worker's Compensation
Clients:
ACE Insurance Group, Allied Waste Industries, Inc., American International Group, Inc., Arch Insurance Group, Best Buy Company, Broadspire Services, Budget Rent-A-Car Corporation, CAMICO Mutual Insurance Co., Crawford & Company, Delta Air Lines, Inc., Erie Insurance Group, Federal Express Corporation, GAB Robins North America, Inc., Gallagher Bassett Services, General Star Management Company, Great American Insurance Company, Guideone Insurance Co., J & J Snack Food Corporation, K&K Insurance Group, Kingsway Insurance Group, Lennox International, Inc, Liberty Mutual Insurance Company, Navigators Insurance, New Jersey Manufacturers Insurance

MARISCAL, WEEKS, MCINTYRE & FRIELANDER, P.A.
2901 N CENTRAL AVENUE
SUITE 200
PHOENIX, AZ 85012
602-285-5000
Fax: 602-285-5100
• Gary L. Birnbaum, Managing Director
(602) 285-5009
• Ann Eastepp, Director of Administration
(602) 285-5050
Description:
General Civil Trial and Appellate Practice in all State and Federal Courts and Administrative Bodies. Corporate and Securities, Probate, Real Estate, Personal Injury, Insurance, Eminent Domain, Construction, Estate Planning, Family, Taxation, Health Care, Municipal, Native American, Administrative, Commercial, Financial Institution and Secured Lending, Bankruptcy, Employment, Environmental, Sports, Trademark and Intellectual Property, Title Insurance and Escrow Law, Professional Malpractice Defense, Alternative Dispute Resolution (Arbitration/Mediation).

MARKS, MARKS & KAPLAN
55 W MONROE STREET
SUITE 3300
CHICAGO, IL 60603
312-332-5200
Fax: 312-332-2952
• Arnee J Eisenberg, Partner
• Howard D. Galper, Partner
• Gilbert W. Gordon, Partner
• Spencer J. Marks, Partner
Services:
Civil Litigation, Commercial Litigation, Corporate and Business, Employee Benefits, Employee Relations, Estate Planning, Info Tech Law, Real Estate Law
Description:
NFLPA workers' compensation panel. Handles worker's compensation for the Chicago Bears. Complex Civil Litigation; Medical Malpractice; Class Actions; Professional Athletes' Injury Litigation; Appellate Practice; Sports Law.

MARRONE, ROBINSON, FREDERICK & FOSTER
111 N FIRST STREET
SUITE 300
BURBANK, CA 91502
818-841-1144
Fax: 818-841-0746
info@mrfflaw.net
www.mrfflaw.net
• Phillip R. Marrone, Member
• J. Alan Frederick, Member
• Thomas A. Foster, Attorney
• Gary D. Ellington, Attorney
Services:
All phases of athlete representation including contract negotiation, long-range planning, financial planning, and post-career counseling.
Clients:
Acceptance Risk Managers, Inc., Admiral Insurance Company, Argonaut Insurance Company, City of Burbank, Collier-Keyworth Company, Columbia Pictures Industries, Inc., Columbia Records, Dyna-Span Corporation, Emhart Industries, Inc., Epic Records, Euro Reinsurance Company, Farmers Insurance Exchange, Fireman's Fund, Fireman's Insurance of Washington, D.C., Fremont Indemnity Company, Guaranty National Companies, Hyster Company, Investor's Insurance Group, L.A. Turf Club Incorporated, Leader Insurance Company, Magna Entertainment Corp., MCA Inc., Maxon Industries, Mustang Claim Service, Inc., NACCO Materials Handling Group, Inc., National Contine

MARSHALL, JR., HARRISON L.
201 N TRYON STREET
C/O SMITH, HELMS, MULLISS & MOORE
CHARLOTTE, NC 28202
704-343-2000
Fax: 704-343-2300
Services:
Represents college athletic departments.

MATHEWSON, ALFRED D.
1117 STANFORD NE
ALBUQUERQUE, NM 87131-0001
505-277-2146
Fax: 505-277-9958
mathewson@law.unm.edu
• Paul Biderman, Director - Institute of Public Law
(505) 277-8789
biderman@unm.edu
• Daniel Ortega, Director, International Law Programs
(505) 277-5723
ortega@law.unm.edu
Description:
Teaches sports law.

MAZZOTTA LAW OFFICES
24 WOODVILLE AVENUE
PITTSBURGH, PA 15220
412-471-0300
Fax: 412-471-3476
dmazzotta@mazzottalaw.com
www.mazzottalaw.com
• Donald S. Mazzotta, Attorney
dmazzotta@mazzottalaw.com
Services:
All phases of athlete representation including contract negotiation, long-range planning, financial planning, post-career counseling and all legal representation.

MCAFEE, ARTHUR
2021 L STREET NW
SUITE 600
WASHINGTON, DC 20036
202-463-2200
800-372-2000
Fax: 202-835-9775
Services:
Staff Counsel with the NFL Players Association.

MCBRIDE, B. GARY
FOUR SEAGATE
SUITE 400
TOLEDO, OH 43604-2622
419-241-2201
Fax: 419-241-8599
• B. Gary McBride, Partner
(419) 252-6231
• Joel A Levine, Counsel
(419) 252-6274
Services:
Represents college athletic departments. Special Education Law; School Law; Labor Relations Law.

MCCAREINS, R. MARK
35 W WACKER DRIVE
CHICAGO, IL 60601-9703
312-558-5600
Fax: 312-558-5700
www.winston.com
• R. Mark McCareins, Partner
(312) 558-5902
• Janis N Acosta, Partner
(312) 558-3711
Services:
Litigation, Corporate and Financial, Labor and Employment Relations, Tax, Real Estate, Intellectual Property, Governmental Relations and Regulatory Affairs, Energy, Environmental, Employee Benefits and Executive Compensation, Pro Bono, Health Care, Maritime and Admiralty, Trust and Estates
Clients:
Ameritech Corp., Tropicana Products, Inc., Abbott Laboratories, Monsanto Company, Hallmark Cards, Titan Wheel Co., Spiegel Co., The Marmon Group, Smurfit-Stone Container Co., Windmere Corp., Gannett Co., Hyatt Hotel Corp., Hinckley & Schmitt Co., Keebler Company, Western Union Corp., Luxottica Group (LensCrafters, Inc.), The Interlake Corp., Barr Laboratories, Dell Computer Co., Universal Outdoor, Marsulex Corp., Waste Management Corp., New Archery Products, Summation Legal Technologies, Integrated Machinery Systems, Inc. and Metals Service Center Institute.
Description:
Endorsement exploration, represents sports organizations, tort actions/litigation.
Other Locations:
333 South Grand Avenue, Los Angeles, CA 90071; 200 Park Avenue, New York, NY 10166; 101 California Street, San Francisco, CA 94111; 1400 L Street NW, Washington, DC 20005

MCCARTY & PRY
1655 W MARKET STREET
SUITE 400
AKRON, OH 44313
330-864-6611

Services:
All phases of athlete representation including contract negotiation, long-range planning, financial planning, and post-career counseling.

MCCLOUD, BARBARA
1450 JAYHAWK BOULEVARD
THE UNIVERSITY OF KANSAS
245 STRONG HALL
LAWRENCE, KS 66045-7535
785-864-2700
Fax: 785-864-4617
www.ku.edu
• Bernadette A. Gray-little, University chancellor
(785) 864-3131
chancellor@ku.edu
• Jeffrey Vitter, Executive Vice Chancellor, Provost
((78)) 864-49
jsv@ku.edu
Services:
Represents college athletic departments.

MCCULLOCH, JOSEPH M. JR.
1426 RICHLAND STREET
2ND FLOOR
COLUMBIA, SC 29201
803-779-0005
Fax: 803-779-0666
www.lawyers.com
• Joseph M. McCulloch Jr, Member
Description:
Represents college athletic departments.Criminal Defense; Driving While Intoxicated; Drug Crimes; Civil Litigation; Personal Injury; Wrongful Death.

MCDONALD, FLEMING, MOORHEAD & FERGUSON, GREEN & SMITH
25 W GOVERNMENT STREET
PENSACOLA, FL 32502-5813
850-477-0660
Fax: 850-477-4510
www.pensacolalaw.com
• Bruce A. McDonald, Founding Partner
• Edward P. Fleming, Partner
Description:
Develops agreements for sports organizations and individuals.
Services:
Personal Injury and Wrongful Death, Insurance Litigation, Mediation, Business Litigation, Construction Litigation, Real Estate Law, Real Estate Development, Community Association Law, Land Use, Planning and Zoning, Real Estate Closing, Probate, Business Law.

MCDONALD, SNYDER & WILLIAMS P.C.
1004 LIGONIER STREET
LATROBE, PA 15650
724-539-3511
Fax: 724-539-3527
mswlaw.lawoffice.com
• Gene E. McDonald, Attorney
(724) 539-3511
mswlaw@adelphia.net
• Donald J. Snyder Jr, Attorney
(724) 539-3511
• Robert P. Lightcap, Attorney
(724) 539-3511
• James J. Conte, Attorney
(724) 539-3511
Services:
Banking and Finance Law, Business and

Commercial Law, Estate Planning, Family Law, Insurance Law, Municipal Law, Construction Law, Litigation and Appeals, Personal Injury Law, Real Estate Law, Eminent Domain Law and Workers' Compensation Law.
Description:
Endorsement exploration represents sports organizations, tort actions/litigation.

MCGUIREWOODS
101 W MAIN STREET
SUITE 9000
NORFOLK, VA 23510-1655
757-640-3700
Fax: 757-640-3701
www.mcguirewoods.com
• Robert L. Burrus, Jr., Partner/Chairman Emeritus
(804) 775-4306
• William J. Strickland, Managing Partner
(804) 775-4350
wstrickland@mcguirewoods.com
Services:
Commercial Litigation, Complex Products Liability & Mass Tort Litigation, Corporate Services, Financial Services, Health Care & Pharmaceuticals, International Group, Labor & Employment, Real Estate & Environmental, Taxation & Employee Benefits, Technology & Business
Nature of Sports Service:
All phases of athlete representation including contract negotiation, long-range planning, financial planning, and post-career counseling.
Clients Include:
Baltimore Ravens, Virginia Baseball Stadium Authority.
Other Locations:
Washington Square, 1050 Connecticut Avenue NW, STE 1200, Washington, DC 20036; Phone 202-857-1700; 1324 Avenue of the Americas, Seventh Floor, New York, NY 10105; Phone: 212-548-2100; The Proscenium, 1170 Peachtree Street NE, STE 2100 Atlanta, GA 30309; Phone: 404-443-5500

MCINNIS, MALCOLM C.
1720 VOLUNTEER BOULEVARD
262 STOKELY ATHLETICS CENTER
KNOXVILLE, TN 37996-0184
865-974-1000
Fax: 865-974-4811
chancellor@utk.edu
www.utk.edu
• Jimmy G Cheek, Chancellor
(865) 974-3265
chancellor@utk.edu
• Malcolm C. McInnis, Staff
Services:
Represents college athletic departments.

MCKENNA, LONG & ALDRIDGE, LLP
ONE MARKET PLAZA
SPEAR TOWER, 24TH FLOOR
SAN FRANCISCO, CA 94105
415-267-4000
Fax: 415-267-4198
cvolz@mckennalong.com
• Frank Kendo Berfield, Counsel
(415) 267-4048
fberfield@mckennalong.com
• Christopher Wood, Partner
(415) 267-4140
cwood@mckennalong.com

• S. Da Anderson, Executive Director
danderson@mckennalong.com
• Thomas Wardell, Corporate
(404) 527-4990
twardell@mckennalong.com
• Lynne Blair, Partner
(415) 267-4115
lblair@mckennalong.com
• Michelle Jackson, Partner
(415) 267-4132
mjackson@mckennalong.com
• John Vaughn, Partner
(619) 595-8030
jvaughn@mckennalong.com
• Daniel Hoye, Of Counsel
(415) 267-4055
dhoye@mckennalong.com
• Jennifer Lee, Partner
(415) 267-4126
jlee@mckennalong.com
• Lisa Oberg, Partner
(415) 267-4175
loberg@mckennalong.com
Services:
Offered in three areas: Corporate, Real Estate Finance and Development and Debt Restructuring and Bankruptcy. MLA's traditional Corporate practice ranges from day-to-day counseling to mergers & acquisitions to tax planning. Additionally, assist clients with conducting internal investigations and creating governance and regulatory compliance programs. The Corporate teams focus on helping clients meet their business objectives, while minimizing legal costs and complications.
Clients:
Serve local, regional, national and international clients, Fortune 500 corporations, private corporations, governmental agencies, non-profits, and high net worth individuals including: Affiliated Computer Computer Services, Inc., AFLAC, Inc., Agilent Technologies Inc., AGL Resources Inc., AT&T Corporation, Ball Corporation, Bank of America, NA, The Boeing Company, City of Atlanta, Canadian-American Business Council, Cisco Systems, Inc., Coca-Cola Enterprises Inc., Delta Air Lines, Inc., Dow AgroSciences LLC, Duke Energy Corporation, Eon Labs, Inc., General Motors Corporation, GMAC Commercial Mortgage Corporation, Hewlett-Packard Company
Other Locations:
303 Peachtree Street NE, Suite 5300, Atlanta, GA 30308. 404-527-4000; FAX: 404-527-4198, 1875 Lawrence Street, Suite 200, Denver, CO 80202. 303-634-4000; FAX: 303-634-4400, 444 South Flower Street, 8th Floor, Los Angeles, CA 90071-2901. 213-688-1000; FAX: 213-243-6330, 28 South Waterloo Road, Suite 101; Devon, PA 19333. 610-687-9750; FAX: 610-687-9755, Symphony Towers, 750 B Street, Suite 3300, San Diego, CA 92101-8105. 619-595-5400; FAX: 619-595-5450, 1900 K Street NW, Washington, DC 20006-1108. 202-496-7500; FAX: 202-496-7756

MCKENZIE, W. SHELBY
451 FLORIDA STREET
8TH FLOOR, CHASE TOWER S
BATON ROUGE, LA 70801
225-387-3221
Fax: 225-346-8049

info@taylorporter.com
www.taylorporter.com
• W. Shelby McKenzie, Partner
(225) 381-0243
shelby.mckenzie@taylorporter.com
• W. Arthur Abercrombie, Jr., Jr., Attorney
(225) 381-0259
arthur.abercrombie@taylorporter.com
Description:
Represents college athletic departments.
Clients:
Represent a variety of clients including established public and private companies, banks, insurance companies, governmental agencies, partnerships, individuals, estates, and not-for-profit organizations.

MCLOUGHLIN, STEPHEN J., LAW OFFICE OF
2555 RICHMOND AVENUE
STATEN ISLAND, NY 10314
718-983-1500
• Stephen J. McLoughlin PC, Attorney
Services:
Contract negotiation, post career planning, arbitration hearings, federal/state/international tax filings, provides investment advice.

MCPHERSON & KALMANSOHN
1801 CENTURY PARK E
24TH FLOOR
LOS ANGELES, CA 90067
310-553-8833
Fax: 310-553-9233
• Edwin F. McPherson, Attorney/Partner
• Mark E. Kalmansohn,
• Asha Dhillon,
• Anita Stephan,
Services:
Represents numerous film, television and stage actors, professional athletes, screenwriters, directors, producers, stunt professionals, stunt Coordinators, authors, recording artists, musicians, songwriters, composers, record producers and engineers, personal managers, talent agents, business managers, attorneys, record companies, independent production companies, and major studios
Clients:
Music (Artists) - Stevie Nicks, The Beach Boys, Dan Fogelberg, Earth, Wind & Fire, Lou Rawls, Natalie Cole, Limp Bizkit, Fred Durst, Linkin Park, Weezer, Mya, Shakira, Jane's Addiction, Perry Farrell, Tool, Backstreet Boys, Porno For Pyros, Blink 182, Poison, Bret Michaels, Great White, Meat Loaf, Dr. Dre, Rage Against The Machine, Smash Mouth, Staind, Rufus, Ricky Martin, Santana, Megadeth, Faith No More, Russ Freeman, Wu Tang Clan, The The, Shai, Jeff Trott, Jonathan Butler, David Roback, Nashville Pussy, Record Labels - Interscope Records, Interscope Music, Death Row Records, Time Warner, Warner Music, Flawless Records, Priority Records
Nature of Sports Service:
All phases of athlete representation including contract negotiation, endorsements, and entertainment crossover.

MEYER, DARRAGH, BUCKLER, BEBENEK & ECK, PLLC
600 GRANT STREET
US STEEL TOWER

SUITE 4850
PITTSBURGH, PA 15219
412-261-6600
Fax: 412-471-2754
info@mdbbe.com
www.mdbbe.com
• Marie M. Jones, Attorney-at-Law
(412) 553-7103
mjones@mdbbe.com
• Eric N. Anderson, Executive Committee Member
(412) 553-7071
eanderson@mdbbe.com
• Daniel C Lawson, Executive Committee Member
(412) 553-7033
dlawson@mdbbe.com
• Dean Passodelis, Executive Committee Member
(412) 553-7145
dpassodelis@mdbbe.com
Nature of Sports Service:
All forms of litigation, including employment matters and contractual issues, with respect to athletes and sports organizations, including the representation of student athletes regarding their right to participate in sports.
Other Locations:
114 South Main Street, Greensburg, PA 15601. 724-836-4840; FAX: 724-836-0532, 120 Lakemont Park Boulevard, Altoona, PA 16602. 814-941-4600; FAX: 814-941-4605
Year Founded:
1913

MEYER, SUOZZI, ENGLISH & KLEIN
1350 BROADWAY
SUITE 501
PO BOX 822
NEW YORK, NY 10018
212-239-4999
800-734-0565
Fax: 212-239-1311
www.msek.com
• Barry J. Peek, Member
(212) 239-4999
bpeek@msek.com
• Linda E. Rodd, Of Counsel
(212) 239-4999
lrodd@msek.com
Description:
Contract negotiation, post career planning, arbitration hearings, provides investment advice, licensing, endorsement exploration, teaches sports law, tort actions/litigation.
Clients:
Allan Schneider Associates, Commerce, America's Most Convenient Bank, Conservation Services Group (CSG)
Year Founded:
1960

MEYER, UNKOVIC & SCOTT, LLP
535 SMITHFIELD STREET
SUITE 1300
HENRY W. OLIVER BUILDING
PITTSBURGH, PA 15222
412-456-2800
800-434-7765
Fax: 412-456-2864
postmaster@muslaw.com
www.muslaw.com
• Debra Z. Anderson, Counsel
(412) 456-2818
dza@muslaw.com
• W. Grant Scott, Partner
(412) 456-2893

wgs@muslaw.com
• Richard G. Kotarba, Partner
(412) 456-2841
rgk@muslaw.com
• Robert Mauro, Managing Partner
(412) 456-2826
rm@muslaw.com
• Joseph E. Bartoszewicz, Attorney
(412) 456-2865
jeb@muslaw.com
• Nicholas J. Bell, Attorney
(412) 456-2524
njb@muslaw.com
• Thomas A. Berret, Attorney
(412) 456-2828
tab@muslaw.com
• Peter J. Borghetti, Attorney
(412) 456-2817
pjb@muslaw.com
• Robert E. Dauer, Jr., Attorney
(412) 456-2835
red@muslaw.com
Description:
Contract negotiation.

MIDDLEBERG RIDDLE GROUP
909 POYDRAS STREET
SUITE 1400
NEW ORLEANS, LA 40112
504-525-7200
Fax: 504-581-5983
AdminNewOrleans@midrid.com
www.midrid.com
• Ira J. Middleburg, Managing Partner
imiddleb@midrid.com
• Dominic J. Gianna, Chair, Litigation Services
• Edie Koonce, Administrator
(214) 220-6300
adminneworleans@midrid.com
• Carol Riddle, Administrator - Dallas
admindallas@midrid.com
• Darci Johnson, Director of Human Resources
(214) 220-6300
hrdallas@midrid.com
Services:
Contract negotiation. Environmental and Toxic Tort Law; Insurance Coverage Law; Drug and Medical Device Litigation; Product Liability.
Year Founded:
1980
Other Locations:
717 North Harwood, Suite 2400, Dallas, TX 75201. 214-220-6300, 450 Laurel Street, Suite 1101, Baton Rouge, LA 70809-1101. 225-381-7700

MILLER, KAGAN RODRIGUEZ AND SILVER, P.A.
515 N FLAGLER DRIVE
SUITE 1425
NORTH BRIDGE CENTRE
WEST PALM BEACH, FL 33401
561-833-1860
800-761-6577
Fax: 561-833-8848
www.mkrs.com
• H. George Kagan, Equity Partner
georgek@mkrs.com
• Robert J. Rodriguez, Equity and Managing Partner
• K. Kay Dodd, Attorney

MILLER, PEARSON, GLOE, BURNS, BEATTY & PARRISH, P.L.C.
301 W BROADWAY
PO BOX 28
DECORAH, IA 52101
563-382-4226
Fax: 563-382-3783
www.millerlawdecorah.com
• Marion L Beatty, Lawyer
Services:
Provides legal services; practices in the following areas of law: General Practice, all Courts. Insurance Law, Estate Planning, Personal Injury, Family Law, Taxation and Probate
Clients:
Luther College; Decorah Community School District; Winneshiek County Memorial Hospital; Community First National State Bank; Viking State Bank; Waukon State Bank; Farmland Insurance Co.; Allied Mutual Insurance Co.; Royal Insurance Co.; Ohio Casualty Insurance Co.; Iowa Farm Mutual Insurance Cos.; Employers Mutual Liability Insurance Co. of Wisconsin; Continental Casualty Co.; Employers Mutual Casualty Co.; Employers Mutuals of Wausau, Wisconsin; Firemans Fund Group; Hawkeye Security Insurance Co.; The Atlantic Co.; Continental Insurance Co.; Iowa Mutual Insurance Co.; Motor Club of America; Auto Owners Insurance Co.; General Casualty; Grinne
Description:
Emphasis on personal injury, insurance law, estate planning, family law, taxation and probate. Represents college athletic departments.
Year Founded:
1940

MILLING BENSON WOODWARD, L.L.P.
909 POYDRAS STREET
SUITE 2300
NEW ORLEANS, LA 70012
504-569-7000
Fax: 504-569-7001
www.millinglaw.com
• Leon J. Bechet, Partner
(504) 549-7146
lbechet@millinglaw.com
• Hilton S. Bell, Managing Partner
(504) 569-7000
hbell@millinglaw.com
• J. Ti Betbeze, Partner
(504) 569-7196
jbetbeze@millinglaw.com
• Richard E. Santora, Partner
rsantora@millinglaw.com
Description:
Entertainment Law, Environmental, Governmental Relations, Health Care, Hospital Law, Intellectual Property, International, Labor, Legislative Practice, Mergers, Acquisitions, Oil and Gas, Professional Liability, Public Utility, Real Estate, Regulatory, Securities, Sports, Taxation, Tax Exempt Organizations, Technology, Telecommunications, Torts, Transportation, Trusts and Estates Law, Utility Law.
Year Founded:
1896
Other Locations:
101 La Rue France, Suite 200, Lafayette, LA. 337-232-3929; FAX: 337-233-4957, 214 Third Street, Suite 2B, Baton Rouge, LA. 225-291-7300; FAX: 225-291-4524

MINGLE, JAMES J.
GARDEN AVENUE
300 CCC BUILDING
ITHACA, NY 14853
607-255-5124
Fax: 607-255-2794
counsel-web@cornell.edu
counsel.cornell.edu
• James J. Mingle, Counsel/Secretary
(607) 255-3903
jjm19@cornell.edu
• David J. D. Skorton, President
Services:
Handles all aspects of the University's legal services including litigation, real property, commercial law, trusts and estates, tax, employment, legal-policy issues and corporate legal advice to both the University administration and the University Board of Trustees
Description:
Represents college athletic departments.

MIZELL, CATHERINE
719 ANDY HOLT TOWER
1331 CIRCLE PARK
KNOXVILLE, TN 37996-0170
865-974-6538
Fax: 865-974-3074
bot.tennessee.edu
• Catherine Mizell, VP/General Counsel/Secretary
(865) 974-3245
cmizell@tennessee.edu
• Don C. Stansberry, Vice Chair
• Charles C. Anderson, Jr, Finance and Administration Chair
• Joe DiPietro, President
• Spruell Driver, Jr, Academic Affairs and Student Success (Chair)
• D. Crawford Gallimore, Member
• Bill C Haslam, Chair
Services:
Represents college athletic departments.

MONTGOMERY, MCCRACKEN, WALKER & RHODAS, LLP
1105 N MARKET STREET
SUITE 1500
WILMINGTON, DE 19801
302-504-7800
800-572-6697
Fax: 302-504-7820
info@mmwr.com
www.mmwr.com
• James G. McMillan, III, Associate
(302) 504-7879
• Virginia P. Sikes, Partner - PA
(215) 772-7275
• Louis A. Petroni, Partner - NJ
(856) 488-7757
lpetroni@mmwr.com
• Richard M M. Donaldson, Partner - DE
(302) 504-7840
• Sidney S Liebesman, Partner
(215) 772-7279
• Richard G Placey, Partner
(302) 504-7880
rplacey@mmwr.com
• Natalie D Ramasey, Partner
(215) 772-7354
nramsey@mmwr.com
• Joanne T Semeister, Partner
(215) 772-7747
jsemeister@mmwr.com
• Mark A Fink, Of Counsel
(302) 504-7811

• Laurie A Krepto, Associate
(215) 772-7410
Areas of Specialization:
Litigation, corporate and securities, labor and employment law, tax, trust and estates, and antitrust. Practices in intellectual property, e-commerce and web-based business, computer and information technology, class action defense, toxic, long-term care, and sports law.
Other Locations:
123 South Broad Street, Avenue of the Arts, Philadelphia, PA 19109. 215-772-1500; FAX: 215-772-7620, Liberty View, 457 Haddonfield Road, Suite 600, Cherry Hill, NJ 08002. 856-488-7700; FAX:856-488-7720, One Westlakes, Suite 200, 1235 Westlakes Drive, Berwyn, PA 19312. 610-889-2210; FAX: 610-889-2220.
Year Founded:
1912

MORRISON & FOERSTER LLP
370 SEVENTEENTH STREET
5200 REPUBLIC PLAZA
DENVER, CO 80202-5638
303-592-1500
Fax: 303-592-1510
info@mofo.com
www.mofo.com
• Randall J. Fons, Partner
(303) 592-2257
rfons@mofo.com
• Eric Elliff, Managing Partner - CO
(303) 592-2240
• A. Ma Olson, Managing Partner - CA
(213) 892-5362
aolson@mofo.com
• Mika L. Mayer, Partner
(650) 813-4298
mmayer@mofo.com
• Randall J. Fons, Managing Partner
(303) 592-2257
rfons@mofo.com
• Jordan Eth, Partner
(415) 268-7126
jeth@mofo.com
• Mark C. Zebrowski, Partner
(858) 720-5162
mzebrowski@mofo.com
• Craig D. Martin, Managing Partner
(415) 268-7681
cmartin@mofo.com
• Daniel R. Kahan, Associate
(703) 760-7306
dkahan@mofo.com
• Sherman W. Kahn, Of Counsel
(212) 468-8023
skahn@mofo.com
Description:
Corporate finance, project finance, institutional lending, financial services, real estate. Entertainment and Sports Law.
Clients:
Charles Schwab Corporation, Chiron Corporation, The Clorox Company, Converge Medical, Inc., Digirad Corporation, Dynavax Technologies Corporation, EchoStar Communications Corporation, El Paso Corporation, Forward Ventures, Fujitsu Limited, GE Consumer Finance, The Hartford Financial Services Group, Inc., Hershey Foods Corporation, Hitachi, Ltd., JPMorgan Chase & Co., Kaiser Foundation Health Plan, Inc./Kaiser Foundation Hospitals, Kerr-McGee Corporation, Korn/Ferry International, LNR Property Corporation, Lucasfilm Ltd., Medtronic, Inc.,

New York University, Nextel Communications, Inc., Nikon Corporation, Novell, Inc., Oracle Corporation
Other Locations:
5200 Republic Plaza, 370 Seventeeth Street, Denver, Colorado 80202-5638. 309-592-1500; FAX: 303-592-1510, 555 West Fifth Street, Suite 3500, Los Angeles, California 90013-1024. 213-892-5200; FAX: 213-892-5454, 1290 Avenue of the Americas, New York, New York 10104-0050. 212-468-8000; FAX: 212-468-7900, 1650 Tysons Boulevard, Suite 300, McLean, Virgina 22102. 703-760-7700; FAX: 703-760-777, 2000 Pennsylvania Avenue NW, Suite 5500, Washington, DC 20006-1888. 202-887-1500; FAX: 202-887-0763

MORTON & MCGOLDRICK, P.S.
820 A STREET
SUITE 600, PO BOX 1533
TACOMA, WA 98402
253-627-8131
Fax: 253-272-4338
bvmm@bvmm.com
www.bvmm.com
• Marc H. Cochran, Attorney
mhcochran@bvmm.com
• James H. Morton, Member
jhmorton@bvmm.com
• DAVID McGOLDRICK, Member
dmcgoldrick@bvmm.com
Services:
Contract negotiation, investment contract negotiation, arbitration hearings, federal/state/international tax filings. Tax Law; Estate Planning Law; Pension and Profit Sharing Law; Corporations Law; Securities Law.
Clients:
Apple, Bank of America Corporation, Beckman Coulter, Inc., Beijing Organizing Committee for the Games of the XXIX Olympiad, Calpine Corporation, Capital One Financial Corporation, The Columbia State Bank, Kemper Insurance Group, Chubb Group of Insurance Companies, Transport Insurance Company, Anglo American Insurance Co., McDonald's Corp., The Southland Corp., CRST Trucking Company, Markel Insurance Company, Cole & Weber (advertising agency), Edge Learning Institute, Inc., Cablecraft, Inc., Western Surety Co., Tacoma Telco Credit Union, Swanson-McGoldrick, Inc. (Realtor), Brandrud Manufacturing Company, Inc., Tacoma Cemeteries

---

MUNGO AND ASSOCIATES, P.C.
155 W CONGRESS
SUITE 404
DETROIT, MI 48226
313-963-0407
Fax: 313-963-0200
• Leonard Mungo, Regional Field Director
(313) 963-0407

MURPHY & DESMOND, S.C.
33 E MAIN STREET
SUITE 500
PO BOX 2038
MADISON, WI 53703
608-257-7181
877-619-5742
Fax: 608-257-2508

email@murphydesmond.com
www.murphydesmond.com
• Tim R. Valentyn, President/Managing Shareholder
(608) 268-5599
tvalentyn@murphydesmond.com
• Harvey L. Wendel, Member
(608) 268-5578
hwendel@murphydesmond.com
Services:
All phases of athlete representation including contract negotiation, endorsement exploration, long-range planning, financial planning, and post-career counseling. Business Law; Real Estate; Sports Law; Entertainment Law.

MURRAY & MURRAY
2 CENTER PLAZA
SUITE 620
BOSTON, MA 02108
617-720-4411
Fax: 617-723-5370
• Vincent A. Murray Jr, Founding Member
vmurray@murraylawoffice.com
• Dino R. Santangelo, Associate
• Vincent A. H. Murray, Attorney
Services:
Contract negotiation.
Year Founded:
1975

NEW YORK YANKEES/BUSINESS OFFICE
E 161ST STREET
BRONX, NY 10451
718-293-4300
Fax: 718-681-1051
newyork.yankees.mlb.com
• Lonn A. Trost, COO
• Harold Z. Steinbrenner, Managing General Partner/Co-Chair
Services:
Represents sports organizations, arbitration hearings, represents professional sports teams, licensing, tort actions/litigation.

NIXON, PEABODY
437 MADISON AVENUE
NEW YORK, NY 10022-7039
212-940-3000
Fax: 212-940-3111
• Arthur Rosner, Office Managing Partner
(212) 940-3023
arosner@nixonpeabody.com
• Elizabeth Kennedy, Office Administrator
(518) 427-2657
ekennedy@nixonpeabody.com
• Andrew Glincher, Office Managing Partner
(617) 345-1222
• Susan Roney, Office Managing Partner
(716) 853-8101
sroney@nixonpeabody.com
• Lorraine McDonough, Office Adminstrator
(716) 853-8106
lmcdonough@nixonpeabody.com
• Mark Shea, Marketing Contact
(585) 263-1141
mshea@nixonpeabody.com
Services:
Include emerging and middle-market businesses, national and multinational corporations, financial institutions, public entities, educational and not-for-profit institutions, and individuals.
Other Locations:
100 Summer Street, Boston, MA 02110;

Phone: 617-345-1000; one Embarcadero Center, San Francisco, CA 94111; Phone: 415-984-8200; 401 9th Street, NW, STE 900, Washington, DC 20004; Phone: 202-585-8000; two penn center 1500 jfk blvd ste 200 philadelphia, pa 19102 phone: 215-854-4096; one citizens plaza providence, ri 02903; phone: 401-454-1000.

NORONHA-ADVOGADOS CONSULTING
AV. ANTONIO AUGUSTO AGUIAR
LISBOA, PORTUGAL 1050-021
21-389-4178
Fax: 21-389-4179
noadlis@noronhaadvogados.com.br
www.noronhaadvogados.com.br
• Alexandre Laender Delgando, Director Stock Market/Insurance
• Durval De. Goyos, Senior partner, Partner and President
dng@noronhaadvogados.com.br
• Robert E. Williams, Partner-International Tax Dept
rew@noronhaadvogados.com.br
• Jun Zhang, Director
• Sherry Liu, Partner
• Stephen Logan, Partner
• Ramma Luthra, Partner
• Joao Campos, Partner
Description:
Mergers and Acquisitions, Contracts, Corporations, Competition, Antitrust Law, Sports and Entertainment Law and Internet Law.
Services:
Offers a broad variety of legal services to clients with activities in the industrial, financial, commercial and service areas. It is capable and equipped to adequately assist the clients in the many different aspects of business law, particularly in the areas of aviation; banking, finance and insurance; corporate; contracts; environmental; international business transactions; labor; civil and tax litigation; maritime; mergers and acquisitions; mining, energy and oil; public administration; intelectual property; real estate; securities; taxation; trade; international tax planning; anti-trust; entertainment, internet and electronic commerce.

NORTH, PURSELL, RAMOS & JAMESON, PLC
414 UNION STREET
SUITE 1850
BANK OF AMERICA PLAZA
NASHVILLE, TN 37219
615-255-2555
Fax: 615-255-0032
• Michael F. Jameson, Lawyer
(615) 255-2555
mjameson@nprjlaw.com
• Edward A Hadley, Lawyer
(615) 255-2555
ehadley@nprjlaw.com
• Michael F. Jameson, Lawyer
(615) 255-2555
mjameson@nprjlaw.com
• Phillip North, Lawyer
(615) 255-2555
pnorth@nprjlaw.com
• Ronald H. Pursell, Lawyer
(615) 255-2555
rpursell@nprjlaw.com
• Ramos A. Gregory, Lawyer
(615) 255-2555
aramos@nprjlaw.com

• Lauren J. Smith, Lawyer
(615) 255-2555
lsmith@nprjlaw.com
• Renee L. Stewart, Lawyer
(615) 255-2555
rstewart@nprjlaw.com
Description:
NFLPA. Handles workers' compensation for the Tennessee Titans.
Services:
Areas of practice include, but are not limited to, civil trial practice, labor law, medical malpractice defense, commercial litigation, sports law, products liability, taxation, real estate, and general business and corporate law.
Clients:
Current clients includes (listed alphabetically) : Auto Owners' Insurance Company; Castle Recording Studio, Inc.; Castle Publishing, Inc.; National Football League Players' Association; Professional Hockey Players' Association; State Volunteer Mutual Insurance Company; Tennessee Urgent Care Associates; Tepro, Inc.; and The Yasuda Fire & Marine Insurance Company of America.

OBERMAYER, REBMANN, MAXWELL & HIPPEL, LLP
200 LOCUST STREET
SUITE 400
HARRISBURG, PA 17101-1508
717-234-9730
Fax: 717-234-9734
ark.clouser@obermayer.com
www.obermayer.com
• Louis B. Kupperman, Partner
(215) 665-3146
louis.kupperman@obermayer.com
• Martin Weinberg, Partner and Chairman
(215) 665-3196
martin.weinberg@obermayer.com
• Walter W Cohen, Attorney
(717) 234-9730
walter.cohen@obermayer.com
• Robart C Jubelirer, Attorney
(814) 942-3333
robert.jubelirer@obermayer.com
• Kevin J Kehner, Attorney
(717) 234-9730
kevin.kehner@obermayer.com
• Jay Evans, Attorney
(412) 288-2473
jay.evans@obermayer.com
• Bruce C Fox, Attorney
(412) 566-1500
bruce.fox@obermayer.com
• Beth Kirkpatrick, Attorney
(412) 288-2474
beth.kirkpatrick@obermayer.com
Description:
Certified contract advisor with the National Football League Players Association. Represents professional athletes in contract negotiations with professional sports teams. Also handles Major League Baseball Players.
Services:
Offers particular depth in the following practice areas: health, energy and utility, environmental, municipal finance, technology, employment, business and litigation, including criminal defense.
Year Founded:
1904
Other Locations:
One Penn Center, 19th Floor, 1617 John F

Kennedy Boulevard, Philadelphia, Pennsylvania 19103-1895. 215-665-3000; FAX: 215-665-3165, One Mellon Center, 500 Grant Street, Suite 5240, Pittsburg, Pennsylvania 15219-2502. 412-566-1500; FAX: 412-566-1508, 20 Brace Road, Suite 300, Cherry Hill, New Jersey 08034-2634. 856-795-3300; FAX: 856-795-8843, 1170 E Landis Avenue, Suite B, Vineland, New Jersey 08360-4230. 856-696-4600; FAX: 856-696-0501, 3 Mill Road, Suite 306A, Wilmington, Delaware 19806. 302-655-9094; FAX: 302-658-8051

OCTAGON ATHLETE REPRESENTATION (ATTORNEYS)
7950 JONES BRANCH DRIVE
SUITE 700N
MCLEAN, VA 22107
703-905-3300
Fax: 703-905-4495
www.octagon.com
• Rick Dudley, President/Chief Executive Officer
• Phil de Picciotto, President, Athletes & Personalities
Services:
Helps clients reach their customers by leveraging relevant sports and entertainment content based on the company's proven expertise in: 1) Engagement marketing: consulting, events, promotions, public relations and property representation; 2) Athletes & personalities: management and procurement; 3) Television: rights, production, sales, distribution; and new media strategies, and; 4) Music and entertainment: management and production.
Description:
Endorsement exploration.

ORLANDO & ASSOCIATES
ONE WESTERN AVENUE
GLOUCESTER, MA 01930
978-283-8100
800-696-7111
Fax: 978-283-8507
firm@orlandoassociates.com
www.orlandoassociates.com
• Joseph M. Orlando, Lawyer
(978) 283-8100
jmorlando@orlandoassociates.com
• Joseph Orlando, Attorney
Services:
Specializes in personal injury litigation, with an emphasis on maritime personal injury law, but also including wrongful death and land-based personal injury tort law.

ORRICK, HERRINGTON & SUTCLIFFE LLP
777 S FIGUEROA STREET
SUITE 3200
LOS ANGELES, CA 90017-5855
213-629-2020
Fax: 213-612-2499
www.orrick.com
• Ralph H Baxter, Jr., Partner
(415) 773-5650
ralphbaxter@orrick.com
• J. Pe Coll Jr, Partner
(212) 506-3790
pcoll@orrick.com
• Karen G Johnson-McKewan, Partner
(415) 773-5917
kjohnson-mckewan@orrick.com

• Felicia B Graham, Partner
(202) 339-8486
fgraham@orrick.com
Description:
Maintains a substantial legal practice in the area of public finance for 100 years. Recognized as one of the nations leading counsel, acts as underwriters counsel, issuer counsel, swap/derivative counsel, and lender counsel in connection with the issuance of tax-exempt bonds. Maintains an active practice in advising public power entities, investor owned utilities and independent power producers on matters related to energy re-regulation.
Other Locations:
Orrick Building, 405 Howard Street, San Francisco, CA 94105; Phone: 415-773-5700; Fax: 415-773-5759; Washington Harbour, 3050 K Street NW, Washington, DC 20007; Phone: 202-339-8400; Fax: 202-339-8500; 666 Fifth Avenue, New York 10103; Phone: 212-506-5000; Fax: 212-506-5151; 400 Capital Mall, STE 3000, Sacramento, CA 95814; Phone: 916-447-9200

OSBORN MALEDON, P.A.
2929 N CENTRAL AVENUE
THE PHOENIX PLAZA, TWENTY-FIRST FLOOR
PHOENIX, AZ 85012-2793
602-640-9000
Fax: 602-640-9050
webmaster@omlaw.com
www.omlaw.com
• William J. Maledon, Lawyer
(602) 640-9331
wmaledon@omlaw.com
• Lynne C. Adams, Attorney
(602) 640-9348
ladams@omlaw.com
• Yaser Ali, Attorney
(602) 640-9349
• Jonathan F. Ariano, Attorney
(602) 640-9311
jariano@omlaw.com
• Ronda Beckerleg Thraen, Attorney
(602) 640-9303
• Maureen Beyers, Attorney
(602) 640-9305
mbeyers@omlaw.com
• John L. Blanchard, Attorney
(602) 640-9304
jblanchard@omlaw.com
• Timothy A. Nelson, Attorney
(602) 640-9388
nelson@omlaw.com
Description:
Intellectual Property; Mergers, Acquisitions and Divestitures; Probate; Products Liability; Professional Liability; Real Estate; Regulatory Law; Securities; Sports Law; Technology Business Startups; Technology Licensing; Technology and Science; Technology Transfers; Trusts and Estates.
Services:
Provides litigation, business and general counsel solutions for clients in the Southwest and nationwide.

PACKMAN, NEUWAHL & ROSENBERG
1500 SAN REMO AVENUE
SUITE 125
CORAL GABLES, FL 33146
305-665-3311
Fax: 305-665-1244

info@pnrlaw.com
www.pnrlaw.com
• Malcolm H. Neuwahl,
Shareholder/Attorney
(305) 665-3311
• Michael Rosenberg, Partner/Associate
(305) 665-3311
info@pnrlaw.com
Services:
Services provided: Estate Planning; General
Taxation; International Taxation; Real
Estate, Transactional and Commercial
Practice; Immigration; Technology and
Personal Service; Education.
Nature of Sports Service:
All phases of athlete representation
including contract negotiation, long-range
planning, financial planning, and post-career
counseling.

PATTON BOGGS
2550 M STREET, NW
WASHINGTON, DC 20037
202-457-6000
Fax: 202-457-6315
www.pattonboggs.com
• Thomas Hale Boggs, Jr.,
Chairman/Partner
(202) 457-6040
• Edward J Newberry, Partner
(202) 457-5285
enewberry@pattonboggs.com
• Mary Be Bosco, Partner
(202) 457-6420
• Thomas S Hale Boggs, Jr., Chairman
(202) 457-6310
• Donald V. Moorehead, Vice Chairman
• Edward J. Newberry, Managing Partner
Services:
Administrative and Regulatory, Antitrust,
Appropriations, Bankruptcy and
Restructuring, Business, Corporate Finance,
Defense and National Security, Employment
Law, Energy, Environmental, Health and
Safety, Estate Planning and Wealth
Preservation, Federal Marketing, Firm
Overview, Food and Drus, Government
Contracts, Health Cate, Housing,
Immigration, Intellectual Property,
International Trade and Transactions,
Litigation and Dispute Resolution, Mergers
and Acquisitions, Middle East Practice,
Municipal Representation, Native American
Affairs, Political Law, Postal Regulation,
Public Policy and Lobbying, Real Estate,
Securities, Tax, Telecommun
Description:
Legislative, political and legal representation
of private and public entities interested in
the development or redevelopment of sports
stadiums and arenas, including the public
and/or private financing of stadiums, lease
negotiations and drafting, economic
generators, subcontracting with
disadvantaged business entities, and state,
local and federal tax issues.
Year Founded:
1962
Other Locations:
701 West 5th Avenue, STE 700, Anchorage,
AK 99501; Phone: 907-263-6300; 2001
Ross Avenue, STE 3000, Dallas, TX 75201;
Phone: 214-758-1500; 1660 Lincoln Street,
STE 1900, Denver, CO 80264; Phone:
303-830-1776; Phone303-830-1776; 8484
Westpark Drive 9th Floor, McLean, VA
22102; Phone: 703-744-8000

PELLETTIERI RABSTEIN AND ALTMAN
100 NASSAU PARK BOULEVARD
SUITE 111
PRINCETON, NJ 8540
609-520-0900
800-432-5297
Fax: 609-452-8796
pra@pralaw.com
www.pralaw.com
• Tom Smith, Attorney
• Gary E. Adams, Lawyer
• Stephanie Testa, Marketing Coordinator
(609) 520-0900
• Gray E. Adams, Attorney
Services:
Specializes in Personal Injury & Accident;
Medical Malpractice & Negligence; Workers
Compensation & Disability; Class Action and
Mass Tort; Divorce Litigation; Child Custody;
Wills and Estate Planning; Tax Litigation;
Elder Law; Real Estate; Criminal Law;
Business Litigation; Contract Disputes;
Shareholder & Partnership Disputes;
Insurance Claims, Business Torts; Business
Formation & Planning; Commerial Real
Estate Litigation; Land Use; Labor &
Employment.
Clients Include:
NCAA Div 1 Conference, The Northeast
Conference, Metro Atlantic Athletic
Conference, Atlantic 10 Conference, West
Coast Conference and Patriot League,
National Association of Sports Officials,
Little League Baseball.
Year Founded:
1929

PERKINS COIE LAW FIRM
1201 THIRD AVENUE
SUITE 4900
SEATTLE, WA 98101-3099
206-359-8000
Fax: 206-359-9000
www.perkinscoie.com
• Nancy Williams, Managing Partner
NWilliams@perkinscoie.com
• Shylah R. Alfonso, Partner
(206) 359-3980
SAlfonso@perkinscoie.com
• Dannon Allbee, Associate
(206) 359-3496
• Anastasia K. Anderson, Associate
(206) 359-6760
• Stephen E. Arnett, Partner
(206) 359-6351
SArnett@perkinscoie.com
Services:
Provides national and international legal
counsel and representation to leading
aerospace, high-technology, manufacturing,
natural resource, transportation and
industrial companies as well as financial
institutions. Also offers clients
business-oriented advice in every major
area of commercial and regulatory law,
litigation, estate planning and trust services.

PHILLIPS & AKERS PC
3200 SW FREEWAY
SUITE 3200
HOUSTON, TX 77027
713-552-9595
Fax: 713-552-0231
www.phillipsakers.com
• Brock C. Akers, Shareholder
(713) 877-2555
• Michael Phillips, Shareholder

(713) 552-9595
• Joe M. Allen, Associate
Services:
Practice areas include General Liability;
Retailer Liability; Premises Liability and
Security Cases; Healthcare Liability
Defense; Non-Subscribers' Actions;
Products Liability; Truck Litigation;
Insurance Litigation; Appellate; Labor and
Employment; Commercial Litigation;
Environmental Litigation; Consumer
Litigation; and Oil
Field/Construction/Industrial.
Description:
Contract negotiation, post career planning,
investment contract negotiation, arbitration
hearings, provides investment advice,
endorsement exploration, tort
actions/litigation.
Year Founded:
July 4, 1982

PIASECKI, MARK J.
511 S ST JOSEPH STREET
SOUTH BEND, IN 46601
574-233-7052
Fax: 574-233-7052
• Marl J. Piasecki, Lawyer
Description:
Contract negotiation, post career planning,
federal/state/international tax filings, tort
actions/litigation.
Services:
Areas of practice include Civil Litigation,
Wills and Estates, and Business

PIERCE & HUGHES P.C.
17 VETERANS SQUARE
PO BOX 604
MEDIA, PA 19063-3217
610-566-9111
Fax: 610-566-0191
info@piercehughes.com
www.pierceandhughes.com
• Michael P. Pierce, Attorney
mppierce@piercehughes.com
• Paul Gordon Hughes, Attorney
pghughes@piercehughes.com
Services:
Handles legal matters in the following
practice areas: Family Law, Divorce, Child
Custody, Child Support, Domestic Violence,
Visitation Rights, Personal Injury,
Automobile Accidents, Slip and Fall,
Wrongful Death, Medical Malpractice,
Municipal Law, Workers Compensation,
Social Security Disability, Unsafe Products,
Consumer Law, Consumer Fraud, Civil
Practice, Negligence, Criminal Law, Driving
While Intoxicated, Drug Crimes, Juvenile
Crimes, Parole and Probation, Traffic
Violations, White Collar Crime, Trusts and
Estates, Wills and Probate, Employment
Law.
Description:
Pierce & Hughes is a boutique law firm with
a focus on the sports world and a passion
for serving those who excel in it.

PIPER MARBURY RUDNICK & WOLFE
203 N LASALLE STREET
SUITE 1900
CHICAGO, IL 60601-1293
312-368-4000
Fax: 312-236-7516
info@dlapiper.com

• Louis S Cohen, Partner
(312) 368-2171
• Deborah E Jennings, Partner/Chairman, Environmental Practice
(202) 861-3842
deborah.jennings@dlapiper.com
• Paul A Tiburzi, Managing Partner
(410) 580-4273
paul.tiburzi@dlapiper.com
• John G McJunkin, Managing Partner
(703) 773-4154
Services:
Provides an extensive range of legal services through seven global practice groups as follows: Commercial, Corporate and Finance, Human Resources, Legislative and Regulatory, Litigation, Real Estate, Technology, Media and Communications.
Description:
Full service national law firm. Sports facilities development proactive group has extensive experience representing and advising municipalities, counties, states and other political entities, professional sports teams, underwriters and financial consultants in connection with stadium and arena development, financing, construction, use and operation.
Other Locations:
One International Place, 21st Floor, Boston, MA 02110; Phone: 617-406-6000; 400 Capital Mall, STE 2400, Sacramento, CA 95814; Phone: 916-930-3200; 1221 South MoPac Expressway, STE 400, Austin, TX 78746; Phone: 512-457-7000; 1251 Avenue of the Americas, New York, NY 10020; Phone: 212-835-6000; One Liberty Place, I650 Market Street, STE 4900, Philadelphia, PA 19103; Phone: 215-656-3300; 117 Bay Street, Easton, MD 21601; Phone: 410-820-4460

POLSINELLI, SHALTON, FLANIGAN, SUELTHAUS PC
900 W. 48TH PLACE
SUITE 900
KANSAS CITY, MO 64112
816-753-1000
Fax: 816-753-1536
info@polsinelli.com
www.polsinelli.com/
• W. Russell Welsh, Chairman/Chief Executive Officer
(816) 360-4342
wrwelsh@polsinelli.com
• Jack M Epps, Partner
(913) 234-7455
jeppes@polsinelli.com
• Ron Patterson, Chief Operating Officer
rpatterson@polsinelli.com
• Julian Arredondo, Chief Financial Officer
jarrrendo@polsinelli.com
Nature of Sports Service:
All phases of athlete representation including contract negotiation, long-range planning, financial planning, and post-career counseling.
Other Locations:
100 South Fourth Street, STE 1100, St Louis, MO 63102; Phone: 314-889-8000; 400 Madison Avenue Suite 16C, New York NY 10017; Phone: 212-684-0199; 555 12th Street NW, STE 710, Washington, DC 20004; Phone: 202-783-3300.
Year Founded:
1972

POTTORFF, JAMES P. JR.
1450 JAYHAWK BLVD
LAWRENCE, KS 66045
785-864-2700
Fax: 785-864-4120
question@ku.edu
www.ku.edu
• James P. Pottorff, University General Counsel
(785) 864-3276
jpottorff@ku.edu
• Bernadette Gray E. Little, University Chancellor
rhemenway@ku.edu
• Jeffery Vitter, Executive Vice Chancellor and Provost
• Doug Girod, Executive Vice Chancellor
• Timothy Caboni, Vice Chancellor forPublic Affairs
Description:
Represents college athletic departments.
Services:
A major public research and teaching institution that operates through a diverse, multicampus system.

PRESTON, GATES & ELLIS
925 FOURTH AVENUE
SUITE 2900
SEATTLE, WA 98104-1158
206-623-7580
Fax: 206-623-7022
kim.church@klgates.com
www.klgates.com
• Cabrelle M. Abel, Associate, Seattle
(206) 370-7812
• Ramona M. Emerson, Managing Partner, Seattle
(206) 370-6748
• Jennifer S. Addis, Associate
(206) 370-8068
• Heidi Eckel Alessi, Partner
(206) 370-7983
• Carley Daye Andrews, Partner
(206) 370-7661
• James A. Andrus, Partner
(206) 370-8329
• Theodore J. Angelis, Partner
(206) 370-8101
• David A. Bateman, Partner
(206) 370-6682
Services:
Practice Areas: 1) Advocacy and Disputes: Appellate, Constitutional and Governmental Litigation; Commercial Litigation; Competition Law and Economic Regulation; Document Analysis Technology Group; Government Contracts, Construction and Procurement Policy; Intellectual Property Litigation; Labor, Employment and Benefits. 2) Policy and Infrastructure: Energy and Utilities; Environmental, Land Use and Natural Resources; Global Telecom and Media; Maritime; Policy and Public Law; Public Finance; School Districts. 3) Transactions: Alternative Investment Management; Asia; Business Law; Corporate Securities/Mergers and Acquisitions
Description:
Contract negotiation, represents professional sports teams, endorsement exploration, tort actions/litigation.
Other Locations:
601 West Riverside Avenue, STE 1400, Spokane, WA 99201; Phone: 509-624-2100; 55 Second Street, STE 1700, San Francisco, CA 94105; Phone:

415-882-8200; 420 L Street, STE 400, Anchorage, AK 99501; Phone: 907-276-1969; 222 SW Columbia Street, STE 1400, Portland, OR 97201; Phone : 503-228-3200

PRINCE YEATES
15 WEST SOUTH TEMPLE
SUITE 1700
SALT LAKE CITY, UT 84101
801-524-1000
Fax: 801-524-1098
ronm@pyglaw.com
www.princeyeates.com
• Adam S. Affleck, Lawyer
• Wilford A. Beesley III, Lawyer
• Wilford A. Beesley, Lawyer
• Richard L. Blanck, Lawyer
Services:
The firm provides a full range of services with a particular focus on the practice of business, litigation, real estate, bankruptcy and employment law.

QUINN, JAMES W.
767 FIFTH AVENUE
ROOM 3501
NEW YORK, NY 10153
212-310-8000
Fax: 212-310-8007
www.weil.com
• James W. Quinn, Senior Partner
(212) 310-8385
james.quinn@weil.com
• Brad D. Scott, Executive Director
(212) 310-8271
• Scott Green, Chief Administrative Officer
(212) 310-6883
• Norman LaCroix, Chief Financial Officer
(212) 310-8359
Nature of Sports Service:
Arbitration hearings, represents professional sports players associations, licensing, represents other sports related organizations, teaches sports law, tort actions/litigation, anti-trust, and collective bargaining.
Services:
Areas of practice include Business Finance & Restructuring, Banking & Finance, Capital Markets, Corporate Governance, Mergers & Acquisitions, Private Equity, Real Estate Transactions & Finance, Structured Finance/Derivatives, Tax, Trusts & Estates, Litigation/Regulatory, Antitrust/Competition, Appellate, Bankruptcy Litigation, Complex Commercial Litigation, Employment, Financial Services, Global Dispute Resolution, Intellectual Property & Media, International Trade, Patent Litigation, Product Liability/Mass Tort/Environmental, and Securities/Corporate Governance

---

RAGSDALE, RICHARD A.
619 RIVER DRIVE
SUITE 200
ELMWOOD, NJ 7407
201-791-7797
Fax: 609-683-9501
www.nj-lawyer.com
• Richard A. Ragsdale, Managing Member
(609) 924-7179
richard.ragsdale@verizon.net
• Robert A. Sochor, Partner
(201) 791-7797
• Leonard E. Schwartz, Partner
(973) 301-1900

• Kenneth R. Cohen, Partner
(973) 301-1900
Services:
Provides expertise in the following areas: Negotiating and closing a complete range of commercial transactions, including business acquisitions and sales, commercial real estate leases and sales, and sophisticated lending arrangements; Taxation: federal, state, individual and corporate; Estate planning and taxation, estate administration, probate litigation and elder law; Asset Protection. Using limited liability companies, asset protection trusts and other creative planning techniques to preserve assets from the potential claims of creditors, State and Federal taxing authorities, and other governmental authorities.
Description:
Investment contract negotiation, represents sports organizations, provides investment advice, licensing, endorsement exploration, represents college athletic departments, sports complex.

RAUCH, JR., MARTIN W.
8742 MISTY CREEK DRIVE
SARASOTA, FL 34241
941-927-2722
Fax: 941-371-8388
martyrauch@aol.com
Services:
Provides services in contract negotiation, arbitration hearings, endorsement exploration, tort actions/litigation, and sports management

RAWLE LAW OFFICES
1339 CHESTNUT STREET ONE S PENN SQUARE
THE WIDENER BUILDING, 16TH FLOOR
PHILADELPHIA, PA 19107
215-575-4200
Fax: 215-563-2583
info@rawle.com
www.rawle.com
• John T. Donovan, Partner
(215) 575-4254
jdonovan@rawle.com
• Timothy J. Abeel, Partner
(215) 575-4280
tabeel@rawle.com
• Joshua Bachrach, Partner
(215) 575-4261
• Timothy J. S. Abeel, Partner
(215) 575-4280
tabeel@rawle.com
• Thomas A. Kuzmick, Partner
(215) 575-4262
tkuzmick@rawle.com
• John H. McCarthy, Partner
(215) 575-4359
jmccarthy@rawle.com
• Fred B. Buck, Partner
(215) 575-4317
fbuck@rawle.com
• William J. Carr, Partner
(215) 575-4221
wcarr@rawle.com
• Cynthia M. Certo, Partner
(215) 575-4284
• Maureen E. Daley, Partner
(215) 575-4293
mdaley@rawle.com
Services:
Represents manufacturers of industrial, commercial and consumer products; drug, pharmaceutical and chemical

manufacturers; life, health and disability insurers and ERISA plans; owners and architects, prime contractors, general contractors, sub-contractors and construction managers; nationally known retail chains; and bus and trucking companies. Defends insurers in coverage actions and prosecute declaratory judgment actions on their behalf; municipalities, hospitals and public authorities; attorneys, accountants, architects and other professionals; shipowners here and abroad; nearly every industry, service and profession.

RAWLINGS, WILLIAM R.
11576 S STATE STREET
BUILDING 401
DRAPER, UT 84020-7122
801-553-0505
877-456-0505
Fax: 801-495-2122
www.brawlingslaw.com
• William R. Rawlings, Lawyer
(866) 329-0208
• Kenneth L. Christensen, Lawyer
(801) 553-0505
Services:
Areas of practice include business and commercial law, criminal defense, probate and estate administration, and a broad range of other legal matters.
Nature of Sports Service:
All phases of athlete representation including contract negotiation, long-range planning, financial planning, and post-career counseling.

REDWINE, THOMAS R.
116 S CROCKETT
SHERMAN, TX 75090
903-893-2133
Fax: 903-893-7889
• Thomas R. Redwine, Lawyer
(903) 893-2133
• John R. Mabary, Lawyer
(903) 893-2133
• Victoria E. Ingham, Partner
(903) 893-2133
• Bob Fleming, Lawyer
(903) 893-2133
Services:
Area of practice include contract negotiation, post career planning, investment contract negotiation, provides securities advice, provides investment advice, and endorsement exploration.

REED SMITH
225 FIFTH AVENUE
PITTSBURGH, PA 15222
412-288-3131
Fax: 412-288-3063
www.reedsmith.com
• Gregory B. Jordan, Global Managing Partner
(412) 288-4124
gjordan@reedsmith.com
• Gary A. Sokulski, Chief Operating Officer
(412) 288-4232
gsokulski@reedsmith.com
• David S. Egan, Chief Marketing Officer
(412) 288-4276
degan@reedsmith.com
• Kevin C. Abbott, Partner
(412) 288-3804
kabbott@reedsmith.com

• Gregory B. Jordan, Global Managing Partner
• Colleen T. Davies, Global Head of Legal Personnel
• Michael B Pollack, Global Head of Strategy
• Roger J. Parker, Europe, Middle East & AsiaManaging Partner
• David J. Boutcher, Chair of Business & Finance Department
• Alexander Y. Thomas, Chair of Litigation Department
Services:
Areas of practice include Advertising & Marketing, Advocacy, Antitrust, Competition & Regulatory Litigation, Appellate, Arbitration, Associations, Aviation Litigation, Banking, Bankruptcy and Commercial Restructuring, Benefits, Class Action Defense, Communications, Construction, Corporate Services (U.K.), E-commerce, Employment, Energy & Natural Resources, Environmental Law, Executive Compensation, Export, Customs & Trade, Financial Services, Financial Services Litigation, Financial Services Regulatory, Fraud, French Group, German Group, Government Contracts, Government Relations, Health Care, Higher Education, Homeland Security, Immigration
Description:
Represents college athletic departments.
Other Locations:
599 Lexington Avenue, 29th Floor, New York, NY 10022; Phone: 212-521-5400; 1301 K Street NW, STE 1100, East Tower, Washington DC 20005; Phone: 202-414-9200; 355 South Grand Avenue, STE 2900, Los Angeles, CA 90071; Phone: 213-457-8000

REED SMITH LLP
599 LEXINGTON AVENUE
22ND FLOOR
NEW YORK, NY 10022
212-521-5400
Fax: 212-521-5450
www.reedsmith.com
• Gregory B. Jordan, Global Managing Partner
(412) 288-4124
gjordan@reedsmith.com
• Michael Pollack, Partner
(215) 851-8182
mpollack@reedsmith.com
• Thomas R. Amlicke, Partner
(212) 549-0341
tamlicke@reedsmith.com
• Douglas Wood, Partner
(212) 549-0377
dwood@reedsmith.com
• Jennifer L. Achilles, Associate
(212) 521 5412
jachilles@reedsmith.com
• James Andriola, Partner
(212) 205-6003
jandriola@reedsmith.com
• Jill N. Averett, Associate
(212) 205-6005
javerett@reedsmith.com
• Jason Barr, Associate
(212) 521-5428
jbarr@reedsmith.com
• Arnold L. Bartfeld, Partner
(212) 205-6008
abartfeld@reedsmith.com
• Oliver Beiersdorf, Partner
(212) 549 0415

obeiersdorf@reedsmith.com
• John B. Berringer, Partner
(212) 205-6010
jberringer@reedsmith.com
Description:
Representing sports organizations.
Services:
Areas of practice include Advertising &
Marketing, Advocacy, Antitrust, Competition
& Regulatory Litigation, Appellate,
Arbitration, Associations, Aviation Litigation,
Banking, Bankruptcy and Commercial
Restructuring, Benefits, Class Action
Defense, Communications, Construction,
Corporate Services (U.K.), E-commerce,
Employment, Energy & Natural Resources,
Environmental Law, Executive
Compensation, Export, Customs & Trade,
Financial Services, etc
Other Location:
375 Park Avenue, Suite 17, New York, New
York 10152-1799

REICH, ROBERT S.
345 PARK AVENUE
NEW YORK, NY 10154
212-407-4000
Fax: 212-407-4990
www.loeb.com
• David S. Schaefer, Managing
Partner/Co-Chair
(212) 407-4848
• Kenneth B. Anderson, Partner
(212) 407-4856
• Roger M. Arar, Partner
(212) 407-4906
rarar@loeb.com
• Michael D. Beck, Partner
(212) 407-4920
mbeck@loeb.com
Other Locations:
10130 Santa Monica Boulevard, STE 2200,
Los Angeles, CA 90067; Phone:
310-282-2000; 321 North Clark Street, STE
2300, Chicago, Il 66610; Phone:
312-464-3100; 1906 Acklen Avenue,
Nashville, TN 37212; Phone: 615-749-8300
Services:
Areas of practice include corporate and
securities, litigation, entertainment and
media, finance, real estate, intellectual
property, private equity, employment,
advertising and promotions, and tax and
wealth services.

REINHART, BOERNER, VAN DEUREN S.C.
1000 N WATER STREET
SUITE 1700
MILWAUKEE, WI 53202
414-298-1000
800-553-6215
Fax: 414-298-8097
dsisson@reinhartlaw.com
www.reinhartlaw.com
• Richard A. Van Deuren, Chairman
(414) 298-8103
rvandeur@reinhartlaw.com
• Meg S. Pekarske, Shareholder
(608) 229-2216
mpekarsk@reinhartlaw.com
• James A. Pellegrini, Shareholder
(262) 951-4500
jpellegr@reinhartlaw.com
• David G. Hanson, Shareholder
(414) 298-8324
dhanson@reinhartlaw.com

• Wesley D. Anderson, Health Care
Attourney
wanderson@reinhartlaw.com
• Joseph J. Balistreri, Real Estate/Banking &
Finance Attourney
jbalistreri@reinhartlaw.com
• Thomas Burnett, Litigation Attourney
tburnett@reinhartlaw.com
• William R. Cummings, Real Estate
Attourney
tburnett@reinhartlaw.com
Description:
Contract negotiation.
Services:
Areas of practice include Appellate, Banking
and Finance, Bankruptcy and Creditors'
Rights, Business Law, Computer &
Technology, Crisis Management and
Business Continuity, Employee Benefits,
Entertainment Law, etc
Clients:
Resolute Systems, Allen-Edmonds, WTC,
Historic King Place, Sargento Cheese,
Carmelite Sisters, Riley Construction, GIC
Management, Inc., The Alliance, Ruud
Lighting, Skil-Tech of Madison, Inc.
Other Locations:
22 East Mifflin Street, Madison, WI 53703;
Phone: 608-229-2200; Phone:
608-229-2200; Ridgeview, Waukesha, WI
53188; Phone: 262-951-4500

REITER, ARNOLD E.
2 N BAYARD LANE
BOX 915
MAHWAH, NJ 7430
201-818-2333
Fax: 201-825-1509
Description:
Contract negotiation, post career planning,
investment contract negotiation, arbitration
hearings, federal/state/international tax
filings, licensing, endorsement exploration,
teaches sports law, tort actions/litigation.

RICHARDSON, DEAN
245 WINTER STREET SE
SALEM, OR 97301
503-370-6282
Fax: 503-370-6375
law-admission@willamette.edu
• Carol Long, Dean/Professor
(503) 370-6285
clong@willamette.edu
• Ann Nicgorski, Associate Dean &
Associate Professor of
(503) 370-6285
anicgors@willamette.edu
• Jerry D. Gray, Associate Dean
jgray@willamette.edu
• Dean Richardson, Professor
(503) 370-6410
drichard@willamette.edu
Services:
Provides comprehensive understanding of
the law, along with highly refined skills in
problem-solving, research and writing.
Offers a strong, integrated curriculum -
enhanced by extensive opportunities for
research and study.
Description:
Contract negotiation, post career planning,
arbitration hearings, endorsement
exploration, teaches sports law.

RIDENOUR, HIERDON, HARPER & KELHOFFER P.L.L.C.
201 N CENTRAL AVENUE
CHASE TOWER
SUITE 3300
PHOENIX, AZ 85004
602-254-9900
Fax: 602-254-8670
www.rhlfirm.com
• Kurt Peterson, Member
(602) 254-9900
• Robert R. Beltz, Member
(602) 254-9900
• Jeffrey A. Bernick, Member
(602) 254-9900
• William G. Ridenour, Member
(602) 254-9900
Services:
Provides services in the following areas of
law: Alternate Dispute Resolution; Federal,
State and Local Taxation; Appellate
Advocacy Department; Government
Operations and Affairs; Banking,
Commercial Finance and Real Estate
Finance Group; Insurance and Financial
Services; Industry Regulation; Bankruptcy
Practice Group; Labor and Employment
Section; Business Services Group;
Legislative and Government Affairs
Services; Captive Insurance and Alternative
Risk Transfer; Municipal Liability;
Commercial Litigation; Personal Injury and
Insurance Defense Litigation; Construction
Litigation Real Estate Practice Group; and
Estate Planning Group
Nature of Sports Service:
All phases of athlete representation
including contract negotiation, long-range
planning, financial planning, and post-career
counseling. Commercial Transactions;
Banking; Real Estate Law; Leasing;
Mortgages.

RISMAN, MARC D.
10120 S EASTERN
SUITE 200
HENDERSON, NV 89052
702-388-8100
Fax: 702-492-4992
www.calneva-law.com
• Marc D. Risman, Lawyer
(702) 388-8100
Description:
Founded in 1979. Specializes in contract
negotiation, arbitration hearings, and
litigation in legal matters concerning boxing,
motor sports. and amateur athletics.
Services:
Practicing Intellectual Property, Sports Law,
Entertainment Law, Travel Law, Business
Law; Personal Injury, Gaming Law,
Trademarks, and Trade Names.
Publications:
Law of Boxing, Professionalism in the
Olympics, TAC Trust Fund, Legal aspects of
Major International Sporting Events,
Sports-Law Resolution of Disputes and
Litigation, Endorsement Contracts, Special
Event Security and Premises Liability

ROBINSON, WATERS & E'DORISIO
1099 18TH STREET
26TH FLOOR
DENVER, CO 80202
303-297-2600
Fax: 303-297-2750
info@rwolaw.com
www.rwolaw.com

• Otto K. Hilbert, III, Attorney
(303) 297-2600
ohilbert@rwolaw.com
• Stephen L. Waters, Attorney
(303) 297-2600
swaters@rwolaw.com
• John W. O'Doresio Jr, Shareholder
jodorisio@rwolaw.com
• Jeffrey A. Bartholomew, Shareholder
jbartholomew@rwolaw.com
Nature of Sports Service:
All phases of athlete representation
including contract negotiation, long-range
planning, financial planning, and post-career
counseling. Arbitration; Civil Litigation; Labor
and Employment; Securities Litigation;
White Collar Crime.

ROLAND, LENORA, R.
2000 TOWN CENTER
SUITE 900
SOUTHFIELD, MI 48075
248-355-0300
800-967-1234
Fax: 248-936-1971
info@sommerspc.com
• Leonard B. Schwartz, Lawyer
(248) 746-4064
lschwartz@sommerspc.com
• William M Brukoff, Senior Shareholder
(248) 746-4067
wbrukoff@sommerspc.com
• Steven J. Schwartz, Lawyer
(248) 746-4042
sjschwartz@sommerspc.com
• Norman S. Sommers, Lawyer
(248) 355-0300
nsommers@sommerspc.com
Nature of Sports Service:
All phases of athlete representation
including contract negotiation, long-range
planning, financial planning, and post-career
counseling.
Services:
Areas of practice include
ADR/Mediation/Arbitration, Age
Discrimination, Appellate Litigation, Auto
Negligence, Aviation Crash Litigation, Birth
Trauma, Business Litigation, Business
Transactions Law Civil Rights, Construction
Accidents, Corporate/Business
Transactions, Divorce/Family Law,
Employment and Labor Litigation, Estate
Planning/Probate, Medical Malpractice,
Mold Litigation/Toxic Torts

ROLLINS, RON
310 GROVELAND AVENUE
MINNEAPOLIS, MN 55403
612-874-8550
Fax: 612-874-9362
• David E. Krause, Attorney
(612) 874-8550
• Ronald L. Rollins, Partner
(612) 874-8550
• James B. Hovland, Lawyer
(612) 874-8550
Services:
Areas of practice include Products Liability,
Personal Injury, Transportation Law, Labor
Law, Pharmaceutical Law, Commercial Law,
Corporate Law, and Civil Law
Description:
NFLPA workers' compensation panel.

ROSENTHAL, ROBERT E.
787 MUNRAS AVENUE
PO BOX 1111
SUITE 200
MONTEREY, CA 93940
831-649-5551
Fax: 831-649-0272
info@brklegal.com
• Thomas P. Bohnen, Member
(831) 649-5551
• Douglas K. Dusenbury, Member
(831) 649-5551
• Roger D. Bolgard, Partner
(831) 649-5551
rbolgard@redshift.com
• Thomas P. J. Bohnen, Associate
• Robert E. Rosenthal, Partner
• Andrew Kreeft, Partner
• Roger D. Bolgard, Associate
• Catherine J. Lee, Associates
• Sergio H. Parra, Associate
• Laura L. Franklin, Associate
Services:
Areas of practice include Commercial
Litigation, Family Law, Sports Law, Personal
Injury, Creditor Rights, Business Litigation,
Legal Malpractice, Real Property Litigation,
Entertainment Law, onstruction Litigation,
Collections, Criminal Law, Business
Transactions,and Medical Malpractice
Description:
Contract negotiation.

ROSS, STEPHEN F.
504 E PENNSYLVANIA AVENUE
CHAMPAIGN, IL 61820
217-333-0931
Fax: 217-244-1478
admissions@law.uiuc.edu
www.law.uiuc.edu
• Stephen F. Ross, Professor
sross@law.uiuc.edu
• Bruce P. M. Smith, Dean
• Margareth Etienne, Associate dean for
academic affairs
• John Rossi, Executive assistant dean
• Heather Ball, Director of events
• Jenny Carroll, Director of alumni relations
Description:
Teaches sports law.

ROUND, BRYAN E., ESQ.
PO BOX 480465
KANSAS CITY, MO 64148-0465
816-943-8383
Description:
NFLPA. Handles workers compensation for
the Kansas City Chiefs.

ROZIER LAW FIRM, P.C.
315 TOMBIGBEE STREET
1ST FLOOR
ST.JACKSON, MS 39201-4600
601-948-2779
Services:
Areas of practice include Personal injury,
Porbate, Property, Real Estate, Sports Law,
Torts, Wills and Estates, and Federal and
State Workers Compensation.

RUBENSTEIN, MARK A.
UNIVERSITY OF CALIFORNIA
545 STUDENT SERVICES BUILDING
BERKELEY, CA 94720- 1900
510-642-3580
Fax: 510-643-1420

www.haas.berkeley.edu/groups/finance/rubi
nste.html
• Steven Glazer, Of Counsel
• Mark A. Rubenstein, Member
• John D. Albright, Associate
• Eileen M. Burger, Associate
Services:
Handles legal matters in different practice
areas such as General Civil Practice before
State and Federal Courts, Real Estate,
Corporation, Commercial and Banking,
Personal Injury, Commercial Litigation,
Planning and Zoning Trials and Appeals.
Description:
Contract negotiation, licensing,
endorsement exploration, tort
actions/litigation.

RUBIN, ERIC M.
1201 CONNECTICUT AVENUE, NW
SIXTH FLOOR
SUITE 200
WASHINGTON, DC 20036
202-861-0870
Fax: 202-429-0657
www.rwdhc.com
• Frederick D. Cooke, Jr., Attorney
fcooke@rwdhc.com
• Walter E. Diercks, Esquire
wdiercks@rwdhc.com
• Eric M. Rubin, Esquire
• Steven J. Stone, Esquire
sstone@rwdhc.com
Services:
Areas of practice include Antitrust and Trade
Regulation, Banking, Business
Transactions, Communications, Corporate
Law and Governance, Criminal Law, Estate
Planning and Administration, Government
Relations, Homeland Security, litigation,
Media, Municipal Law, Outdoor Advertising,
and Real Estate and Land Use
Description:
Represents professional sports teams.

RUBIN, MICHAEL D.
611 ANTON BOULEVARD
SUITE 1400
COSTA MESA, CA 92626-1931
714-641-5100
Fax: 714-546-9035
learnmore@rutan.com
www.rutan.com
• Michael D. Rubin, Partner
(714) 641-3423
MRubin@rutan.com
• L. Ski Harrison, Partner
(714) 662-4641
sharrison@rutan.com
Services:
Areas of practice include: Business
Litigation, Competitive Business and
Advertising Practices,
Condemnation/Property Valuation,
Construction Law, Corporate/Securities,
Education Law, Employment/Labor,
Environmental, Financial Practices,
Intellectual Property/Technology, Land
Use/Natural Resources, Life Sciences,
Municipal & Government Agency Law, Real
Estate, Tax, Trusts/Estates
Description:
Represents sports facilities, equipment
manufacturers.
Year Founded
1906
Other Location:

50 West San Fernando Street, STE 320,
San Jose, CA 95113; Phone: 408-289-8777;
Fax: 408-289-8778

RUTGERS-NEWARK ATHLETICS
42 WARREN STREET
NEWARK, NJ 07102-1807
973-353-5474
Fax: 973-353-1431
www.rutgersnewarkathletics.com
• Mark Griffin, Director of Athletics
• Mary Stadelmann, Associate Director of
Athletics/Senior Woman
(973) 353-1460
mary.stad@rutgers.edu
Description:
Arbitration hearings.

RUXIN, ROBERT H.
676 ELM STREET
CONCORD, MA 1742
978-371-1732
Fax: 978-369-6223
• Richard W. Kazmaier Jr, President / Chief
Executive Officer
• Robert H. Ruxin, VP / General Counsel
Services:
Offering advisory services since 1975 to
sports product and sports marketing clients.

SAFFREN & WEINBERG
815 GREENWOOD AVENUE
SUITE 22
JENKINTOWN, PA 19046
215-576-0100
Fax: 215-576-6288
• Marc A. Weinberg, Lawyer / Partner
• Kenneth S. Saffren, Partner
Services:
All phases of athlete representation
including contract negotiation, long-range
planning, financial planning, and post-career
counseling.

SAPIR, EDDIE L., THE HONORABLE
1300 PERDIDO STREET
SECOND FLOOR WEST
NEW ORLEANS, LA 70112
504-658-1000
Fax: 504-658-1068
www.nocitycouncil.com
• Arnie Fielkow, Vice President
(504) 658-1060
afielkow@cityofno.com
• Stacy Head, President
• Jonathan Harris, Chief of staff
• Catrina Simmons, Executive administrative
assistant and schedu
• Barbara Lacen-keller, Director of
constituent services
• Greg Malveaux, Personal assistant

SASSOON & CYMROT LLP
84 STATE STREET
8TH FLOOR
BOSTON, MA 02109
617-720-0099
Fax: 617-720-0366
info@sassooncymrot.com
www.sassooncymrot.com
• Lewis Sassoon, Lawyer
lsassoon@sassooncymrot.com
• Jeffrey Cymrot, Lawyer
jcymrot@sassooncymrot.com
• William R Moriarty, Lawyer
• Anthony M. S Ambriano, Attorney

Services:
Provides local and multinational business
clients legal services on civil litigation, real
estate, bankruptcy and insolvency, business
and personal estate planning, bad debt
collection, divorce, construction, hotel and
restaurant, personal injury/tort claims and
patent and intellectual property

SAUER, JR., RUSSELL F.
355 S GRAND AVENUE
LOS ANGELES, CA 90071-1560
213-485-1234
Fax: 213-891-8763
www.lw.com
• Manuel A. Abascal, Partner
(213) 891-7889
manny.abascal@lw.com
• James L. Arnone, Partner
(213) 891-8204
james.arnone@lw.com
• LeeAnn Black, Chief Operating Officer
(212) 906-1218
leeann.black@lw.com
• Adrian F. Davis, Chief Attourney
Development Officer
(415) 616-8335
adrian.davis@lw.com
• James E. Dow, Chief Real Estate Officer
(619) 238-2800
• Joshua S. Friedlander, Chief Human
Resources Officer
(212) 906-1286
josh.friedlander@lw.com
• Rod Harrington, Chief Administrative
Officer
(004) 420-7710
• Alfred Harutunian, Chief Financial Officer
(213) 891-7253
alfred.harutunian@lw.com
Description:
Offers sophisticated corporate finance,
mergers and acquisitions, company
representation and corporated governance,
private equity and investment funds,
restructuring, internal investigations,
intellectual property, and venture and
technoloby transactions practices. Litigation
department comprises commercial,
securities and professional liability, antitrust,
employment, insurance coverage, white
collar and toxic tort. Finance department
includes practice groups involved in all
phases of lending work for banks and other
lending insitututions and for borrowers,
insolvency and creditors rights, project
finance and public and tax-exempt finance
Other Locations:
Riverside Center, 275 Grove Street, 4th
Floor, Newton, MA 02466; Phone:
617-663-5700; Sears Tower, STE 5800, 23
South Wacker Drive, Chicago, IL 60606;
Phone: 312-876-7700; 885 Third Avenue,
STE 1000, New York, NY 10022; Phone:
212-906-1200; 555 Eleventh Street, NW,
STE 1000, Washington, DC 20004; Phone:
202-637-2200; Two Freedom Square, 11955
Freedom Drive, STE 500, Reston, VA
20190; Phone: 703-456-1000; 505
Montgomery Street, STE 200, San
Francisco 94111; Phone: 415-391-0600

SCARINCI HOLLENBECK
1100 VALLEY BROOK AVENUE
PO BOX 790
LYNDHURST, NJ 07071-0790
201-896-4100
Fax: 201-896-8660

info@sh-law.com
www.sh-law.com
• Peter Moeller, Director Marketing &
Communications
• Donald Scarinci, Managing Partner
(201) 896-4100
dscarinci@scarincihollenbeck.com
• Sheri K. Siegelbaum, Chair-Public Law
Group
ssiegelbaum@njlegalink.com
Description:
Founded in 1988, Scarini Hollenbeck is a
general practice law firm practice law firm
focusing on real estate, business law,
environmental and land use, public law,
labor and employment law and litigation.
Nature of Service:
Legal industry.

SCHAFFER, S. ANDREW
70 WASHINGTON SQUARE S
NEW YORK, NY 10012
212-998-1212
Fax: 212-995-3048
www.nyu.edu
• John Sexton, President
(212) 998-2345
john.sexton@nyu.edu
• David W. McLaughlin, Provost
david.mclaughlin@nyu.edu
Services:
Represents college athletic departments.

SCHILL, JR., GILBERT E.
901 E CARY STREET
ONE JAMES CENTER
RICHMOND, VA 23219-4030
804-775-1000
Fax: 804-775-1061
www.mcguirewoods.com
• Gilbert E. Schill Jr, Partner
(804) 775-4345
gschill@mcguirewoods.com
• John V. Cogbill III, Managing Partner
(804) 775-4383
Description:
Represents college athletic departments.
Services:
Areas of practice include Complex Products
Liability & Mass Tort Litigation, Corporate
Services, Financial Services, Health Care &
Pharmaceuticals, International Group, Labor
& Employment, Real Estate & Benefits,
taxation & Employee Benefits, and
Technology & Business

SCHINE, JULIANEL, ANTONUCCI
830 POST ROAD E
WESTPORT, CT 6880
203-226-6861
Fax: 203-226-6866
• Francis Antonucci, Lawyer

SCHOENI, K. ROGER
201 E FIFTH STREET
PNC CENTER
SUITE 800
CINCINNATI, OH 45202-4190
513-381-0656
Fax: 513-381-5823
info@kplaw.com
www.kohnenpatton.com
• K. Roger Schoeni, Partner
(513) 381-0656
rschoeni@kplaw.com
• Peggy M. Barker, Partner
(513) 381-0656

pbarker@kplaw.com
• Joseph Beech, Partner
jbeech@kplaw.com
• Colleen M. Blandford, Partner
cblandford@kplaw.com
• John L. Campbell, Partner
jcampbell@kplaw.com
• Anthony J. Caruso, Partner
tcaruso@kplaw.com
• Ann R. Combs, Partner
acombs@kplaw.com
• Rebecca Cull, Partner
rcull@kplaw.com
Services:
Areas of practice include Corporate and Securities, Litigation, Employment Law, Estate Planning and Probate, Banking, Finance and Creditors' Rights, Real Estate and Construction, Government Relations, Franchising and Distribution, Computers and Technology, Tower Mediation, and Tower Land Title
Description:
Contract negotiation, arbitration hearings, federal/state/international tax filings, endorsement exploration, tort actions/litigation. Trial Practice; Products Liability Law.
Other Location:
211 Grandview Drive, STE 236, Fort Mitchell, KY 41017; Phone: 859-341-0009; Fax: 859-341-0344

SCHOONOVER, PAUL D.
4015 MAIN STREET
SUITE 200
DALLAS, TX 75226
214-712-4400
Fax: 815-572-9448
www.vialaw.com
• Paul D. Schoonover, Lawyer
(214) 712-4470
paul@klbf.com
Services:
Bankruptcy, Banking & Financial Institutions, Business Litigation, Commercial Litigation, Corporate & Securities, estate Planning & Probate, Family Law, Fidelity and Surety, Insurance Coverage, Insurance Defense, Labor & Employment, Products Liability, Real estate & Construction, School of Law, Sports & Entertainment, State & Local Government, Taxation

---

SCHUTTS & BOWEN
201 S BISCAYNE BOULEVARD
1500 MIAMI CENTER
MIAMI, FL 33131
305-358-6300
800-325-2892
Fax: 305-381-9982
• Kevin D. Cowan, Partner
(305) 379-9110
kcowan@shutts.com
• Carlos J. Abarca, Lawyer
(305) 347-7324
• Jeannette E. Albo, Partner
(305) 347-7381
Description:
Contract negotiation, endorsement exploration.
Services:
Areas of practice include Administrative Law, Admiralty, Antitrust, Appellate, Aviation, Commercial Finance, Community associations, Compliance Audits, Construction, Corporate, Corporate/Securities, Creditor's Right and

Bankruptcy, Eminent Domain Inverse Condemnation, Environmental, Financial Institutions, Governmental Relations, Health Care, Immigration, Insurance, Insurance Regulatory Practice, Intellectual Property, International Dispute Resolution, Internet, Labor & Employment, Land Use, Litigation, Public Finance and Local Government, Real Property and Development, Taxation, and Trusts and Estates

---

SCOTT A BLACKMUN
1750 E BOULDER STREET
UNITED STATES OLYMPIC TRANING CENTER
COLORADO SPRINGS, CO 80909-5760
719-632-5551
Fax: 719-866-4654
athleteservices@usoc.org
Services:
Amateur sports representation.

SCOTT, DAVID R.
7 COLLEGE AVENUE
WIANTES HALL, ROOM 324
NEW BRUNSWICK, NJ 08901-1259
732-932-7741
732-445-info (4636)
Fax: 732-932-6818
legal@oldqueens.rutgers.edu
www.rutgers.edu
• Richard L. McCormick, President
(732) 932-7454
koncsol@oldqueens.rutgers.edu
• Ralph R. Izzo, Chair
• Gerald C. Harvey, Vice Chair
• Robert Balchi, Ex Officio
• Bruce Fehn, Treasurer
• Leslie A. Fehrenbach, Secretary
• Mary Brennan, Assistant Secretary
Description:
Represents college athletic departments.
Services:
Dedicated to advanced learning, creating new knowledge and contributing to the growing vitality of the state

---

SEEKINGS, MICHAEL
29 MONTAGU STREET
CHARLESTON, SC 29401
843-513-1073
Fax: 843-853-8994
mseekings@leathbouchlaw.com
• Michael S. Seekings, Member
• Francis E. Grimball, Member
(843) 785-6969
Nature of Sports Service:
All phases of athlete representation including contract negotiation, long-range planning, financial planning, and post-career counseling.

SEGAL & LAX
501 FIFTH AVENUE
SUITE 2004
NEW YORK, NY 10017
212-922-0891
800-762-7852
Fax: 212-922-0896
www.segalandlax.com
• Mark Segal, Partner
(212) 922-0891
• Emil Lax, Lawyer
(212) 922-0891
• Patrick D. Gatti,
Services:
Areas of practice include Personal Injury,

Medical Malpractice, Slips & Falls, Motor Vehicle Accidents, Complex Litigation, Wrongful Death Claims, Construction site accidents, Immigration, Catastrophic Brain Injury, Dental Malpractice, Electrical Accidents, Birth Trauma, Serious Injury Claims, Burn Injuries, Defective drugs, and Sports Law
Description:
Contract negotiation, arbitration hearings, endorsement exploration, tort actions/litigation.

SERGEANT, DAVID A.
1728 CENTRAL AVENUE
FORT DODGE, IA 50501
515-576-0333
Fax: 515-955-6388
• David A. Sergeant, Principal
Services:
Areas of practice include contract negotiation, investment contract negotiation, arbitration hearings, endorsement exploration, and sports law.

SHAPIRO, RONALD M.
1340 SMITH AVE
SUITE 200
BALTIMORE, MD 21209
410-779-1341
• Ronald Shapiro, Founder
(410) 779-1341
Nature of Service:
Deal coaching and negotiation consulting.
Clients:
San Antonio Spurs; Brooklyn Nets; Oklahoma City Thunder; Cleveland Browns
Description:
Founded in 2017, Shapiro Advisors is a negotiation deal coaching and consulting company.

SHEFSKY, LLOYD E.
111 E WACKER
SUITE 2800
CHICAGO, IL 60601
312-527-4000
Fax: 312-527-4011
www.shefskylaw.com
• Lloyd Shefsky, Counsel
(312) 836-4001
• Cezar M. Froelich, Partner
(312) 836-4002
cfroelich@shefskylaw.com
• Richard E. Aderman, Partner
(312) 836-4104
raderman@shefskylaw.com
• Sylvia D. Taylor, HRM
• Thomas Dal Compo, Litigation Paregal
• Dan Henderson, Sr litigation paralegal
• Kathy Deane, Firm administrator
• Amy Inlander, Paralegal manager
Description:
Post career planning, investment contract negotiation.
Services:
Areas of practice include Banking and Financial Institution, Bankruptcy, Corporate Finance, Creditors' Rights and Insolvency, Employment Law, Estate Planning and Probate, Government Regulation, Health Car, International Law, Litigation, Mergers & Acquisitions, Real Estate, Securities, and Technology
Clients:
TCB Development Corp.

SHEPHERD, JR., ROBERT E.
28 WESTHAMPTON WAY
UNIVERSITY OF RICHMOND
TC WILLIAMS SCHOOL OF LAW
RICHMOND, VA 23173
804-289-8189
Fax: 804-287-6516
www.law.richmond.edu
• Robert E. Shepherd Jr, Professor
• Margaret I. Bacigal,
Professor/Administrative Director
(804) 289-8950
mbacigal@richmond.edu
• Ronald J. Bacigal, Professor
(804) 289-8194
rbacigal@richmond.edu
• John R. Barden, Head, Reference &
Research Services
(804) 289-8727
Description:
Teaches sports law.

SHERMAN & NATHANSON, A
PROFESSIONAL CORPORATION
9454 WILSHIRE BOULEVARD
A PROFESSIONAL CORPORATION
SUITE 900
BEVERLY HILLS, CA 90212
310-246-0321
Fax: 310-246-0305
rsherman@snlaw.com
www.smnlawfirm.com
• Richard L. Sherman, Partner
(310) 246-0321
• Ken Nathanson, Partner
(310) 246-0321
knate@snmlaw.com
• Sheila Kadisha, Associate
• Abhay Khosla, Associate
• Maria Hall, Associate
• Richard Lloyd Sherman, Managing Partner
Services:
Areas of practice include Business
Litigation, Entertainment Litigation, Real
Estate Litigation, Civil Appeals, Business
Transactions, Employment Law, and
Intellectual Property Litigation

SHERRARD, GERMAN & KELLY
620 LIBERTY AVENUE
28TH FLOOR, TWO PNC PLAZA
PITTSBURGH, PA 15222
412-355-0200
Fax: 412-261-6221
sgk@sgkpc.com
www.sgkpc.com
• David R. Lowe, Shareholder/V.P.
(412) 355-0200
• Robert D. German, Managing Shareholder
(412) 355-0200
rdg@sgkpc.com
• Rita Kelly,
(412) 258-6718
rk@sgkpc.com
• James R. Hankle,
(412) 258-6712
jrh@sgkpc.com
Services:
Areas of practice include Corporate
Services, Retail Financial Services,
Commercial, Industrial and Real Estate
Lending Services, Commercial Credit
Recovery, Consumer Collection,
Commercial Litigation, Litigation
Management, and Estates and Trusts
Services
Nature of Sports Service:
All phases of athlete representation

including contract negotiation, long-range
planning, financial planning, and post-career
counseling.

SHEUERMANN & JONES
701 POYDRAS STREET
41ST FLOOR
NEW ORLEANS, LA 70139
504-525-4361
888-525-4361
Fax: 504-525-4380
joneslaw@nola-law.com
www.nola-law.com
• Blake Jones, Managing Partner
• Arthel J Scheuermann, Partner
Nature of Sports Service:
All phases of athlete representation
including contract negotiation, long-range
planning, financial planning, and post-career
counseling.

SHNEIDMAN, DANIEL L.
SHNEIDMAN LAW SC
PO BOX 442
MILWAUKEE, WI 53201
414-271-8650
Fax: 414-271-1054
Services:
Labor and sports law.

SHOR, ALAN P.
901 W WALNUT HILL LANE
MS 6A-6
IRVING, TX 75038-1003
972-580-5047
Fax: 972-580-5238
CustomerService@zales.com
www.zalecorp.com
• David H. Sternblitz, VP & Treasurer
(972) 580-4000
ir@zalecorp.com
• Sue E. Gove, EVP/Chief Operating Officer
• Mark R. Lenz, Group SVP/Chief Financial
Officer
Description:
Contract negotiation, arbitration hearings,
represents professional sports teams,
licensing, endorsement exploration, tort
actions/litigation, represents sports
organizations.
Brands:
Zales Jewelers, Zales Outlet, Gordon's
Jewelers, Bailey Banks & Biddle Fine
Jewelers, Peoples Jewellers, Mappins
Jewellers, Piercing Pagoda, Zales.com,
BaileyBanksAndBiddle.com

SHOTWELLE, BROWN & SPERRY
1101 ROYAL AVENUE
PO BOX 14140
SUITE A
MONROE, LA 71201-4140
318-388-4700
Fax: 318-388-4736
www.shotwell-law.com
• Marshall T. Napper, Shareholder
(318) 388-4700
mnapper@centurytel.net
• George M M. Wear, Jr, Jr., Shareholder
gmwjr@centurytel.net
Description:
Contract negotiation, tort actions/litigation,
represents college athletic departments,
represents sports organizations.

SHROPSHIRE, KENNETH L.
3730 WALNUT STREET, JON M
HUNTSMAN HALL
6TH FLOOR
SUITE 600
PHILADELPHIA, PA 19104
215-898-1393
Fax: 215-573-2006
sportsbusiness@wharton.upenn.edu
wsb.wharton.upenn.edu/
• Derrick L Hegans, Managing Director
Services:
Areas of practice include arbitration
hearings, speaker, teaches sports law,
author and expert witness

SHUMATE, FLAHERTY & EUBANKS &
BAECHTOLD, P.S.C.
225 W IRVINE STREET
PO BOX 157
RICHMOND, KY 40475
859-623-3049
800-742-5830
Fax: 859-623-6406
www.eblawfirm.com
• Michael F. Eubanks, Lawyer
• James W. Baechtold, Lawyer
Services:
Areas of practice include Litigation, Personal
Injury (Auto Accidents), Workers'
Compensation, Criminal Law, Domestic
Relations, Estates, Probate, General
Practice, Real Estate, and Sports Law
Nature of Sports Service:
All phases of athlete representation
including contract negotiation, long-range
planning, financial planning, and post-career
counseling. Criminal Law; Drugs and
Narcotics; Personal Injury; Workers
Compensation; Sports Law; Probate; Real
Estate.

SICKING, RICHARD A., ESQ
1313 PONCE DE LEON BOULEVARD
SUITE 300
CORAL GABLES, FL 33134-3343
305-446-3700
800-431-4689
Fax: 305-446-4014
sickingpa@aol.com
• Richard A. Sicking, Attorney
Services:
NFLPA workers' compensation panel for the
Miami Dolphins and Tampa Bay
Buccaneers.

SIKORSKI, JR., EDMUND J.
29211 FORD ROAD
GARDEN CITY OFFICE
GARDEN CITY, MI 48135
734-422-2377
Fax: 734-423-1423
Firm@SikorskiLaw.com
www.sikorskilaw.com
Nature of Service:
Represents Michigan High School Athletic
Association.
Year Founded:
1972

SILLS CUMMIS & GROSS P.C.
ONE RIVERFRONT PLAZA
THE LEGAL CENTER
NEWARK, NJ 07102
973-643-7000
Fax: 973-643-6500

sillsmail@sillscummis.com
www.sillscummis.com
• Anthony Caruso, Associate
• Peter A. Cross, Associate
• Lynne Anne Anderson, Member
(973) 643-5686
landerson@sillscummis.com
• Seth M. Apple, Associate
(973) 286-4815
sapple@sillscummis.com
Description:
Sills, Cummis & Gross is a premier law firm representing companies from Fortune 500 to emerging growth. Their entertainment and sports law group has represented artists and performers, coaches and athletes, sports marketing, sports leagues and investment groups involved in sports and entertainment projects.

SIMPSON, JACQUELINE
1360 E 9TH STREET
SUITE 100
CLEVELAND, OH 44114
216-522-1200
Fax: 216-436-3187
jsimpson@imgworld.com
• Jacqueline Simpson, Attorney
Description:
Contract negotiation.

SKODA, MINOTTI & CO.
6685 BETA DRIVE
MAYFIELD VILLAGE
CLEVELAND, OH 44143
440-449-6800
888-201-4484
Fax: 440-646-1615
www.skodaminotti.com
• Robert Barkett, Partner
(440) 449-6800
• Patrick T. Carney, Partner
(440) 449-6800
• Robert E. Coode, Partner
(440) 449-6800
• Kenneth M. Haffey, Partner
(440) 449-6800
khaffey@skodaminotti.com
Description:
Contract negotiation, post career planning, federal/state/international tax filings, represents professional athletes, provides investment advice, endorsement exploration, contract actions/litigation.
Services:
Offers Accounting, Consulting, Financial, Healthcare and Tax Services.

SLAUGHTER, FRED L.
411 W. 4TH STREET
8000 U.S COURTHOUSE
SANTA ANA, CA 92701
741-338-3500
Fax: 310-394-4243
Description:
Contract negotiation, post career planning, arbitration hearings, federal/state/international tax filings, endorsement exploration, teaches sports law, represents sports labor organizations.
Services:
Areas of practice include contract negotiation, post career planning, arbitration hearings, federal/state/international tax filings, endorsement exploration, teaches sports law, and represents sports labor organizations.

SLOTT, JEFFREY LAW OFFICE
21031 VENTURA BOULEVARD
12TH FLOOR
WOODLAND HILLS, CA 91364
818-999-5859
Fax: 818-999-3354
• Jeffrey A. Slott, President/Agent/General Legal
(818) 999-5859
Description:
Offers legal and agent services to professional athletes.
Services:
Legal Services

SMITH & SMITH ATTORNEYS AT LAW
3838 OAK LAWN AVENUE
SUITE 1222
DALLAS, TX 75219
214-522-5571
Fax: 214-522-5009
pview.findlaw.com/view/1970123_1
• Robert B. Smith, Member
• Smith B. Robert, Member
Description:
Endorsement exploration, represents sports organizations, tort actions/litigation.
Services:
Areas of practice include endorsement exploration, represents sports organizations, and tort actions/litigation.

SMITH, CHARLES EDISON
640 NELSON STREET
DURHAM, NC 27707
919-530-6333
Fax: 919-530-6339
www.nccu.edu/law
• Phyliss Craig-Taylor, Professor
(919) 530-6333
pcraigt@nccu.edu
• Marshall Dayan, Professor
(919) 530-7816
mdayan@wpo.nccu.edu
• Jennifer Brobst, Clinical Supervising Lawyer
(919) 530-5371
jbrobst@nccu.edu
• Charles E. Smith, Professor, School of Law
(919) 530-6333
csmith@wpo.nccu.edu
Services:
Offers two programs leading to the Juris Doctor degree: a full-time day program and the only part-time evening program between Atlanta, Georgia, and the metropolitan Washington, DC area.
Description:
Teaches sports law.

SMITH, PAYTON
1201 THIRD AVENUE
SUITE 2200
SEATTLE, WA 98101-3045
206-622-3150
Fax: 206-757-7700
seattle@dwt.com
www.dwt.com
• Greg F Adams, Partner
(206) 757-8000
gregadams@dwt.com
• Keith Gormley Baldwin, Partner
(206) 757-8008
Description:
Represents sports organizations.
Services:

Serves regional, national and international clients, including Washington's largest newspaper, one of the nation's largest banks, leading hospitals and health care providers, retailers, telecommunications and other industry giants, many of which are involved in international transactions.

SOMERS & HODGES
TWO RAVINIA DRIVE
SUITE 310
ATLANTA, GA 30346
770-394-7200
Fax: 770-395-7698
Services:
Areas of practice include Golf industry legal matters; Private Club Law; Computer Software Law; Limited Liability Company; Tax Exempt Organizations; Golf Course Development; Country Club Law; Trade Association Law; and Nonprofit Organizations Law.
Description:
Golf industry legal matters. Private Club Law; Computer Software Law; Limited Liability Company; Tax Exempt Organizations; Golf Course Development; Country Club Law; Trade Association Law; Nonprofit Organizations Law.

SOOY, KATHLEEN T.
1001 PENNSYLVANIA AVENUE, NW
WASHINGTON, DC 20004-2595
202-624-2500
Fax: 202-628-5116
www.crowell.com
• Terry L. Albertson, Partner
(202) 624-2635
talbertson@crowell.com
• Shauna E. Alonge, Partner
(202) 624-2742
salonge@crowell.com
• Paul Alp, Counsel
(202) 624-2747
palp@crowell.com
• Katheryn W. Holmes Johnson, Director, media PR Communications
• Jessica O'Neil, Manager, media PR and communications
• Meredith Reilly, Specialist, PR
Description:
Represents college athletic departments.
Services:
Expertise: Administrative Law/Regulatory; Aerospace; Agriculture; Alternative Dispute Resolution; Antitrust; Appellate Practice; Associations; Automotive; Aviation; Bankruptcy; C&M; Capitolink; C&M International; Chemicals; Class Actions; Construction; Corporate Employee Benefits; Energy; European Practice; False Claims; Forest Products; Government Affairs; Government Contracts; Hazardous Materials; Health Care; Insurance; Intellectual Property; International Arbitration; Investment Management; Labor & Employment; Legislation; Life Sciences; Litigation; Mining; Natural Resources & Environmental; Pharmaceuticals; Plaintiff's Recovery Practice;

SOROY, H. MICHAEL
11766 WILSHIRE BOULEVARD
SUITE 270
LOS ANGELES, CA 90025
310-444-7750
Fax: 310-312-1034

office@soroylaw.com
www.soroy.com
• H Michael Soroy, Firm Founder
(310) 444-7750
hms@soroylaw.com
• Fredrik Gran, Associate
(310) 444-7750
• H. Michael Soroy, Founder
(310) 444-7750
• Peter C Ver. Halen, Of Counsel
(310) 444-7750
• Asa Rosen, Business Operations
Specialist
(310) 444-7750
• Iselin J. Tveitnes, Paralegal
(310) 444-7750
Description:
Entertainment, Sports and Leisure Law.
Services:
Handles cases in the areas of business &
commercial law; business organizations;
contracts; collections; international law;
trademarks; travel, tourism & leisure law;
estate planning; probate & estate
administration; and residential & commercial
real estate.
Year Founded:
1991

SQUIRE, SANDERS & DEMPSEY, LLP
127 PUBLIC SQUARE
4900 KEY TOWER
CLEVELAND, OH 44114
216-479-8500
Fax: 216-479-8780
www.ssd.com
• Frederick R. Nance, Managing Partner
(216) 479-8623
fnance@ssd.com
• Cipriano S. Beredo, III, Partner
(216) 479-8280
cberedo@ssd.com
• Rick Horrow, Counsel
(305) 577-2825
• Stephen Lerner, Partner
(513) 361-1220
slerner@ssd.com
Description:
Founded 1890, Squire, Sanders & Dempsey
LLP has lawyers in 32 offices and 15
countries around the world. With one of the
strongest integrated global platforms and
their longstanding one-firm philosophy,
Squire Sanders provides seamless legal
counsel worldwide. Squire Sanders is ideally
positioned to closely monitor legal
developments that affect athletes, as well as
sports teams, leagues, related businesses
and governments seeking to succeed in an
increasingly global sports and entertainment
marketplace. With a full range of legal
services that assist clients in their
management and marketing efforts, they
have helped organizations and individ
Services:
All forms of dispute resolution including
litigation; bond offerings and project
financings; business, tax and estate
planning issues for the post-career period;
contract negotiations; how to maximize
endorsement opportunities; legal aspects of
marketing and public relations activities; and
protection of image and other intellectual
property

STEARNS WEAVER MILLER
150 W FLAGLER STREET
SUITE 2200

MUSEUM TOWER
MIAMI, FL 33130
305-789-3200
Fax: 305-789-3395
info@stearnsweaver.com
www.stearnsweaver.com
• Alan H. Fein, Shareholder
(305) 789-3416
afein@swmwas.com
• Arturo J. Fernandez, Associate
(305) 789-3296
afernandez@swmwas.com
Nature of Service:
Represents professional sports franchises
and athletes on a variety of subject matters
and litigation.

**STEIN, SPERLING, BENNETT, DE JONG,
DRISCOLL & GREENFEIG, P.C.**
25 W MIDDLE LANE
ROCKVILLE, MD 20850
301-340-2020
800-435-5230
Fax: 301-340-8217
info@steinsperling.com
www.steinsperling.com
• Fred A. Balkin, Principal
(301) 838-3225
fbalkin@steinsperling.com
• Millard S. Bennett, Principal
(301) 838-3203
mbennett@steinsperling.com
• Alexia Ke Bourgerie, Principal
(301) 838-3232
abourgerie@steinsperling.com
• David S. De Jong, Principal
(301) 838-3204
ddejong@steinsperling.com
• Fred Balkin, Principal
(301) 838-3225
fbalkin@steinsperling.com
• Millard Bennett, Principal
(301) 838-3203
mbennett@steinsperling.com
• Jolie Deutschman, Principal
(301) 738-2222
jdeutschman@steinsperling.com
• David Driscoll, Principal
(301) 838-3205
ddriscoll@steinsperling.com
• Monica Harms, Principal
(301) 838-3230
mharms@steinsperling.com
• Micah Bonaviri, Associate
(301) 838-3235
mbonaviri@steinsperling.com
Services:
Concentrates around various practice
groups including business & tax,
employment law, technology & e-commerce,
estate planning & probate, family law, real
property & commercial leasing, criminal law
and injury law.
Description:
Contract negotiation, post career planning,
investment contract negotiation,
federal/state tax filings, IRS audits, appeals
and litigation, endorsement exploration, tort
actions. Tax Law; Tax Controversies; Estate
Planning; Business Law; Professional
Practices; Business Valuation.

STEINBERG, LEIGH
1280 BEACH AVENUE
SUITE 800
NEWPORT BEACH, CA 92660-4258
949-720-9121
Fax: 949-720-1331

• Leigh Steinberg,
Services:
Areas of practice include contract
negotiation, post career planning, arbitration
hearings, and endorsement exploration.

**STEPHEN D. LINETT, ATTORNEY AT
LAW**
1900 AVENUE OF THE STARS
SUITE 1100
LOS ANGELES, CA 90067
310-284-8277
Fax: 310-203-9428
linettemark@aol.com
• Steve Linett, Owner
Services:
Long time Attorney Agent representing
athletes, coaches and sports broadcasters
snce 1980. All phases of athlete
representation including contract
negotiations, financial planning, and
post-career counseling, endorsement and
legal advice.

STIMPERT & FORD, LLP
6300 WILSHIRE BOULEVARD
SUITE 1890
LOS ANGELES, CA 90048-5220
323-782-6782
888-907-3801
Fax: 323-677-2233
info@stimpertford.com
• Daniel P. Stimpert,
(323) 782-6782
dpstimpert@stimpertford.com
• Daniel P. Stimpert, Attorney
• Ian J. J. Ford, Attorney
(323) 782-6782
ianjford@stimpertford.com
Services:
Real Estate Law, Real Estate &
Construction Litigation, Commercial
Collection & Commercial Law, Contract &
Partnership Litigation, Tort Litigation,
Insurance Defense
Clients:
The Arba Group, ICO Investment Group, La
Curacao Business Center, Surety Trust
Deed Services, Mika Company, Glendale
Memorial Hospital and Health Center,
Touring & Tasting Magazine, Lisanti, s.r.l.,
Travertini Paradiso s.r.l., Randolph
International Trading Company, F&A
Cheese/F&A Dairy

STINSON MORRISON HECKER LLP
1850 N CENTRAL AVENUE
SUITE 2100
PHOENIX, AZ 85004
602-279-1600
Fax: 602-240-6925
www.stinson.com
• Michael C. Manning, Partner
(602) 212-8503
mmanning@stinson.com
• James P. Armstrong, Partner
(602) 212-8605
jarmstrong@stinsonmoheck.com
• C. Ta Ashworth, Partner
(602) 212-8626
tashworth@stinsonmoheck.com
• Christian C. M. Beams, Associate
(602) 212-8609
cbeams@stinsonmoheck.com
• Mark D. Hinderks, Managing Partner
(816) 691-2706
mhinderks@stinson.com

• Terry E. Brummer, Chief Operating Officer
(816) 691-3366
tbrummer@stinson.com
• Allison M. Murdock, Deputy Managing
Partner
(816) 691-3138
amurdock@stinson.com
• Doug Doerfler, Chief Financial Officer
(816) 691-3209
ddoerfler@stinson.com
• Vic A. Peterson, Chief Information Officer
(816) 691-2461
vpeterson@stinson.com
Services:
Delivers quality services from business
litigation, commercial finance and business
issues, to complex bankruptcy matters,
intellectual property and media law, and
banking matters.

STOCKTON & HING, P.A.
6609 N SCOTTSDALE ROAD
DEAUVILLE BUILDING
SUITE 202
SCOTTSDALE, AZ 85250
480-447-9649
Fax: 480-483-7721
www.martindale.com
• Robert On Hing, Member
(480) 951-0882
• Gregory Hing, Member
(480) 447-9649
Greg.Hing@azbar.org
• Robert Hing, Member
(480) 447-9649
• Henderson Stockton, Member
Year Founded:
1962.
Clients:
Representative Clients: Alliance of American
Insurers; American Council of Life
Insurance; Amica Mutual Insurance
Company; Arizona Conference Corporation
of Seventh-Day Adventists; Arizona Life &
Disability Insurance Guaranty Fund; Arizona
Property and Casualty Insurance Guaranty
Fund; Chubb Life Insurance Co.; Cities
West Publishing, Inc.; Equitable Insurance
Services; Globe Life & Accident Insurance
Co.; Great Republic Life Insurance Co.;
Northwestern Mutual Life Insurance Co.;
Pilgram Screw Corp.; Rancho Soledad
Nurseries; Senate Insurance Co.; Scottsdale
Athletic Club; Thunderbird Academy; United
American Insurance Company; W.M. Grace.
Sports Service Founded:
1971.
Services:
General Practice. Probate, Estate Planning,
Corporate, Real Estate, Insurance
Regulatory Law and Legislative Law.
General Civil Litigation, Administrative Law,
Sports Law.

STOREY, MOYES
1850 N CENTRAL AVENUE
SUITE 1100
PHOENIX, AZ 85004
602-604-2141
Fax: 602-274-9135
• Jay I. Moyes, Member
(602) 604-2141
jimoyes@lawms.com
• Jeffrey L. Sellers, Member
(602) 604-2141
jlsellers@lawms.com
• William J. Sims III, Member
(602) 604-2141

• Jeffery L. A. Sellers, Attorney
jlsellers@law-msh.com
• Jay I. Moyes, Attorney
jimoyes@law-msh.com
• Keith Hendricks, Attorney
khendricks@law-msh.com
• Jeffery C. Zimmerman, Attorney
jczimmerman@law-msh.com
• Steve Wene, Attorney
swene@law-msh.com
Services:
Counsels clients throughout Arizona and the
Southwest on a broad range of legal
matters.

STRAYER & MIRABILE, P.C.
121 E GREGORY BOULEVARD
KANSAS CITY, MO 64114
816-363-3775
Fax: 816-221-4866
• Craig A. Strayer, Attorney/Partner
Services:
NFLPA workers' compensation panel

STUART LAW FIRM, P.L.L.C
1033 WADE AVENUE
SUITE 202
RALEIGH, NC 27605-1155
919-787-6050
Fax: 919-787-9988
www.stuartlawfirm.com
• James L. Stuart, Principal
(919) 787-6050
jstuart@stuartlawfirm.com
• Catherine R. Stuart, Principal
(919) 787-6050
• Theresa S. Dew, Associate
(919) 787-6050
tdew@stuartlawfirm.com
• Charles C. Kyles, Associate
(919) 787-6050
• James L. Stuart, Member
• Catherine R. Stuart, Member
cstuart@stuartlawfirm.com
• Theresa S. Dew, Member
• Charles C. Kyles, Member
Services:
Areas of practice include Bankruptcy,
Business Law, Dispute
Resolution/Mediation, Housing Finance,
Insurance Regulatory, Intellectual Property,
Municipal Bond Finance, Sports Law,
Tax-Exempt Organizations, Workers
Compensation
Clients:
North Carolina Self-Insurance Guaranty
Association, U.S. Patent and Trademark
Office

SULLIVAN FIRM, LTD., THE
2550 W GOLF ROAD
SUITE 101, THE MEADOWS CORPORATE
CENTER - EAST TOWER
ROLLING MEADOWS, IL 60008-4501
847-228-1100
Fax: 847-228-5199
sullivan@thesullivanfirmltd.com
thesullivanfirmltd.com
• Terry Sullivan, President
thesullivanfirm@aol.com
• Judy Chessick, Member
thesullivanfirm@aol.com
• Nancy J. Nicol, Member
NJN96@aol.com
• Terry D. Sullivan, President
(847) 228-1100
sullivan@thesullivanfirmltd.com

• Michael Sullivan, Associate
(847) 228-1100
thesullivanfirm@aol.com
• Nancy J. Nicol, Associate
(847) 228-1100
nnicol@thesullivanfirmltd.com
• Judy Chessick, Associate
(847) 228-1100
jchessick@thesullivanfirmltd.com
• Martin J. Healy Jr, Counsel
Services:
Areas of practice include Litigation, Criminal
Law, Family Law, Employment Law,
Business Law, DWI and Real Estate
Description:
Contract negotiation.

SULLIVAN OLIVARIO & GIOIA LLP
665 MAIN STREET
SUITE 400
BUFFALO, NY 14202-3706
716-854-5300
Fax: 716-854-5299
• Kevin M. Carter, Attorney
• Horace A. Gioia, Attorney
• Charles H. Dougherty, Attorney
Services:
Areas of practice include General Practice,
Family Law Adoption, Divorce, and Real
Estate Law

**SULLIVAN, WARD, BOME, TYLER &
ASHER, P.C.**
25800 NORTHWESTERN HIGHWAY
1000 MACCABEES CENTER
SOUTHFIELD, MI 48075-8412
248-746-0700
Fax: 248-746-2760
swappc@swappc.com
www.swappc.com
• Anthony A. Asher, Managing Partner
(248) 746-2701
aasher@swappc.com
• Lee C. Patton, Lawyer
(248) 746-2730
lpatton@swappc.com
• Robert E. Sullivan Jr, Lawyer
(248) 746-2738
• Sharon S. Almonrode, Senior Litigation
Attorney/Partner
(248) 746-2732
Services:
Areas of practice include Complex Litigation
& Creditors/Debtors Rights & Remedies,
Business Planning and Licensing, Real
Estate Transactions and Litigation, General
Litigation, Labor (ERISA, Pension, and
Governance), Tax and Estate Planning,
Engineering Architectural Construction,
Specialty Litigation
Clients:
Acura West, AEGON USA/Life Investors
Insurance Company of America, AmerUs
Annuity Group Co, Amurcon Corp, Arvo
Group, LLC, Beztak Land Companies,
Disability Managerment Services, Inc.,
Diversified Chemical Technologies, Inc.,
Franklin Eye Consultants, P.C., Global
Home Care, Inc., Hamon Research-Cottrell,
Inc., Milacron Inc., Senior Benefit Services,
Inc, Shenandoah Life Insurance Company
The General Employees' Retirement System
of the City of Pontiac, The Policemen's &
Firemen's Retirement System of the City of
Pontiac, Valenite LLC, Wedge-Mill Tool,
Inc., American Dental Group; Community
Bank of Dearborn, Cost Plus, Inc., Fifth
Third Bank,

SUNSERI, J. DOUGLAS
3000 18TH STREET
METAIRIE, LA 70002
504-837-1304
888-703-1304
Fax: 504-833-2843
• J. Douglas Sunseri, Lawyer
(504) 837-1304
• Albert J. Nicaud, Lawyer
(504) 837-1304
• Frank Th Fradella, Lawyer
(504) 837-1304
• James G. Washburn, Lawyer
(504) 837-1304
Services:
Areas of practice include General Liability,
Coverage Issues, Worker's Compensation,
Property & Casualty, Auto Liability, and
Employer Liability
Clients:
Continental National Indemnity Company,
Bridgefield Casualty Insurance Company,
The Allen Insurance Group, Risk
Management Services, Inc., The St. Paul
Companies/USF&G, Louisiana State Board
of Home Inspectors, Louisiana Department
of Transportation and Development,
Louisiana Nursing Home
Association-Self-Insured Fund, Louisiana
Employers Safety Association-Self Insured
Fund, Louisiana Retailers Association-Self
Insured Fund, Louisiana Hospital
Association-Self Insured Fund, Hospital
Services of Louisiana, Inc., Ashington
University, Delgado University, The Bottle
Water Company, Vinson Guard Service, B&I
Welding and Consultants, Inc., AppleOn
Description:
Contract negotiation.

SWADOS, ROBERT
ONE CANAL SIDE
125 MAIN STREET
BUFFALO, NY 14203-2887
716-847-8400
Fax: 716-852-6100
www.phillipslytle.com
• Morgan G. Graham, Partner
(716) 847-7070
mgraham@phillipslytle.com
• Frederick G Attea, Partner
(716) 847-7010
fattea@phillipslytle.com
• Thomas C. Bailey, Partner
(716) 847-5410
tbailey@phillipslytle.com
• Robert O. Swados, Special Counsel
(716) 504-5728
rswados@phillipslytle.com
Description:
Represents professional sports teams.
Services:
Areas of practice include Commercial
(Banking & Commercial, Bankruptcy &
Creditors' Rights, Real Estate,
Telecommunications, Public Finance);
Corporate (Corporate and Securities,
Employee Benefits, Immigration, Intellectual
Property, Franchise, Health Care, Tax,
Family Wealth Planning(Family Wealth
Planning); Labor & Employment(Labor &
Employment, Education Law);
Trial(Business Disputes, Antitrust,
Accountants' Liability, Banking/Lender,
Liability, Breach of Contract, Business Torts,
Class Actions,
ConstructionE-Commerce/Computer, Law,
ERISA, Franchise and Distributorship,

Relations, Fraud/RICO, Health Care,
Insurance Coverage.
Clients:
ABB Automation, Inc., Archer Daniels
Midland Company, BlueCross BlueShield of
Western New York, Catholic Health System,
Cello-Pack Corporation, Citibank, N.A.,
Coach, Inc., Davis Ulmer Sprinkler
Company, Inc., DuPont, Emerson Electric
Co., Ford Motor Credit Company, HSBC
Bank USA, National Association, Keybank,
N.A., Nassau County Industrial
Development Agency, National Fuel,
Platinum LLC, Rich Products Corporation,
Sevenson Environmental Services, The
Sovran Companies, UnumProvident
Corporation, W.R. Grace & Co.

SWARBRICK, JR., JACK
UNIVERSITY OF NOTRE DAME
NOTRE DAME, IN 46556
574-631-5000
www.nd.edu
• John B. Swarbrick, Jr., Athletics Director
• John Affleck-Graves, Executive Vice
President
• Terrill D. Albright, Partner
(317) 237-1262
Terry.Albright@bakerd.com
• James A. Aschleman, Partner
(317) 237-1131
Jim.Aschleman@bakerd.com
Services:
Areas of practice include Antitrust, Appellate
Practice, Business Planning, China,
Commercial, Financial and Bankruptcy,
Construction, Corporate Finance, Education
Law, Employee Benefits, Energy and Public
Utilities Environmental Law, Government
Affairs, Health Care, Immigration,
Individual/Family, Insurance and Financial
Services, Intellectual Property International,
Labor and Employment, Life Sciences
Litigation, Medical Device and
Pharmaceuticals, Nonprofit Private Equity,
Venture Capital and Investment
Management, Product Liability, Public
Finance, Real Estate/Land Use, Sports and
Entertainment, Tax, Transportation, Trusts
and Estates
Clients:
Alimentation Couche-Tard Inc. (ACT),
American Commercial Lines, BorgWarner
Inc., Bridgestone Corporation, Bunge North
America, Inc., Central Indiana Corporate
Partnership, Circle K, Citizens Gas & Coke
Utility, City of Indianapolis, Clarian Health
Partners, Cummins Inc., Eli Lilly and
Company, Fleetwood Enterprises, Guidant
Corporation, Indiana Department of
Insurance, Indiana University, Indianapolis
Bond Bank, Indianapolis Public Schools,
Integra Bank Corporation, J.P. Morgan
Chase & Co., Kimball International Inc., Lear
Corporation, Lehman Brothers, Lilly
Endowment, Mac's Convenience Stores
LLC, Mittal Steel USA, Inc.
Description:
Represents major sports events.

**TALLEY, ANTHONY, HUGHES & KNIGHT
L.L.C.**
322 COLUMBIA STREET
PO BOX 340
BOGALUSA, LA 70427
985-732-7151
866-517-8245
Fax: 985-732-1664

info@tahk.net
www.tahk.net
• E. B. Dittmer, II, Attorney
(985) 732-7151
ebd@tahk.net
• Charles M. Hughes Jr, Member
(985) 624-5010
cmhjr@tahk.net
• Craig J. Robichaux, Lawyer/Member
(985) 624-5010
cjr@tahk.net
• Paul S. Hughes, Lawyer
psh@tahk.net
Services:
Handles legal matters in the following
practice areas: General Civil Practice, Trials,
Probate, Real Property, Personal Injury,
Banking and Corporate Law, Environmental
Workers Compensation, Insurance,
Banking, Real Estate, Trusts and Estates,
and Litigation, as well as a general
Corporate and Civil Practice.
Clients:
Aetna Casualty and Surety Co.; Audubon
Insurance Co.; New Hampshire Indemnity
Co.; South Carolina Insurance Co.; Trinity
Insurance Co.; Security Insurance Co.;
Hewitt-Coleman & Associates; Pacific
Marine Insurance Co.; Employers National
Insurance Co.; Louisiana Farm Bureau
Casualty Insurance Co.; Louisiana Farm
Bureau Mutual Insurance Co.; Southern
Farm Bureau Casualty Insurance Co.;
Southern Farm Bureau Mutual Insurance
Co.; Mississippi Farm Bureau Casualty
Insurance Co.; Texas Farm Bureau Casualty
Insurance Co.; Louisiana Insurance
Guaranty Association; State of Louisiana,
Office of Risk Management; Houston
General Insurance Co.
Nature of Sports Service:
All phases of athlete representation
including contract negotiation, long-range
planning, financial planning, and post-career
counseling.

TARSHES, DAVID C.
1201 THIRD AVENUE
SUITE 2200
SEATTLE, WA 98101-3045
206-622-3150
Fax: 206-757-7700
www.dwt.com
• David C. Tarshes, Partner
(206) 622-3150
davidtarshes@dwt.com
• Greg F. Adams, Partner
(206) 622-3150
Description:
Represents professional sports teams, tort
actions/litigation, representation of leagues,
associations, in litigation.
Services:
Areas of practice include Admiralty &
Maritime, Advertising & Marketing Law,
Aircraft Industry, Antitrust, Appellate
Litigation, Business & Corporate, China
Practice/Shanghai Office, Construction,
Corporate Diversity Counseling, Corporate
Finance, Credit Recovery & Bankruptcy,
Education, eHealth/HIPAA, Emerging
Business & Technology, Employment
Related Services, Employee Benefits,
Employment, Employment Litigation,
Immigration Traditional Labor Energy,
Entertainment, Environmental, Estate
Planning, Finance & Commercial Law,
Financial Services, Food & Agriculture,

Government Contracts, Government Investigations & Criminal Defense, Governmental

TAULBEE, GEORGE M.
101 S TRYON STREET
SUITE 4000, BANK OF AMERICA PLAZA
CHARLOTTE, NC 28280-4000
704-444-1000
Fax: 704-444-1111
info@alston.com
www.alston.com
• Kenneth F. Britt, Executive Director
(404) 881-7000
ken.britt@alston.com
• Barbara J. Bryant, Chief Marketing Officer
(404) 881-7901
barbara.bryant@alston.com
• Cathy A. Benton, Chief Human Resources Officer
(404) 881-7202
cbenton@alston.com
• Scott Cotie, Chief Financial Officer
(404) 881-7562
scotie@alston.com
• John F. Baron, Partner in Charge
(704) 444-1434
john.baron@alston.com
• David M. Alban, Senior Associate
(704) 444-1174
david.alban@alston.com
• Malachi Alston, Associate
(704) 444-1129
malachi.alston@alston.com
• Blas P. Arroyo, Partner
(704) 444-1012
blas.arroyo@alston.com
Services:
Provides creative solutions to client challenges and an extraordinary skill base in more than a dozen areas of legal service, including a variety of transactional, litigational, tax, and intellectual property and technology services.
Clients:
Aflac, AIG, ALCOA, Allegiance Healthcare Corporation, Allied Systems, Altana Inc., ARCADIS, Arthritis Foundation, Assurant, Inc., BB&T, Belk Store Services, Inc., BellSouth Corporation, Bertelsmann AG, BGF Industries, Inc., BNP Residential Properties, Inc., Boral Industries, Inc., Borden, Inc., Bose Corporation, Cable News Network, CGW Southeast Partners & Affiliates, Cingular Wireless LLC, Delta Air Lines, Inc., Dimension Date Holdings, Inc., Duke University, Duke University Management Company, Emory Healthcare, Emory University, Genuine Parts Company, Georgia Hospital Association, Georgia-Pacific Corporation, Global Payments Inc., Gold Kist
Description:
Contract and license negotiation, trademark and copyright protection and enforcement (Auto Sports).

THACHER PROFFITT & WOOD
TWO WORLD FINANCIAL CENTER
NEW YORK, NY 10281
212-912-7400
Fax: 212-912-7751
www.tpw.com
• Paul D. Tvetenstrand, Managing Partner
(212) 912-7452
• Kofi Appenteng, Partner
(212) 912-7418

• Robert C. Azarow, Partner
(212) 912-7815
• Charles Do Bethill, Partner
(212) 912-8240
Services:
Designs innovative financial structures and deals for the major financial institutions. Practice focus in New York include Banking, Bankruptcy, Compensation & Benefits, Commercial Lending, M&A, Securities, Municipal Finance, Project Finance, Intellectual Property, Global Finance, International Arbitration, Latin America, Investment Company Act of 1940, Investment Advisers Act of 1940, Litigation & Dispute Resolution, Maritime, Real Estate, Structured Finance
Description:
Tort actions/litigation.

THE FERRARO LAW FIRM
600 BRICKELL AVENUE
38TH FLOOR
MIAMI, FL 33131
305-375-0111
800-275-3332
Fax: 305-379-6222
jlf@ferrarolaw.com
www.ferrarolaw.com
• James L. Ferraro, Shareholder
(305) 375-0111
jlf@ferrarolaw.com
• James L. Ferraro, Attorney/Share Holder
(305) 375-0111
• David A. Jagolinzer, Attorney/ Shareholder
• Juan P. Bauta, Attorney
• Sam Holland, Attorney
Services:
Contract negotiation, arbitration hearings, federal/state/international tax filings, tort actions/litigation.
Year Founded:
1985

THE UNIVERSITY OF TULSA COLLEGE OF LAW
3120 E FOURTH PLACE
TULSA, OK 74104
918-631-2401
Fax: 918-631-3126
www.law.utulsa.edu
• Janet Koven Levit, Dean
(918) 631-2400
janet-levit@utulsa.edu
• Martha Cordell, Assistant Dean for Student Compliance an
(918) 631-2445
martha-cordell@utulsa.edu
• Tom Arnold, Associate Dean for Assessment and Instit
(918) 631-3108
mark-arnold@utulsa.edu
• Ray Yasser, Professor
(918) 631-2442
raymond-yasser@utulsa.edu
• Jason Aamodt, Assistant Dean of Online Legal Education
(918) 631-305
jason-aamodt@utulsa.edu
Services:
Provides a unique student-centered environment designed to foster success at every step of the way from admission to placement
Description:
Contract negotiation, teaches sports law, tort actions/litigation, author.

THIES, DAVID
202 LINCOLN SQUARE
PO BOX 189
URBANA, IL 61803-0189
217-367-1126
Fax: 217-367-3752
www.webberthies.com
• Richard L. Thies, Shareholder
(217) 367-1126
rthies@webberthies.com
• Carl M. Webber, General Practice Lawyer/Member
(217) 367-1126
cwebber@webber.com
• David C. Thies, General Practice Lawyer/Member
(217) 367-1126
dthies@webber.com
• Holten D. Summers, General Practice Lawyer/Member
(217) 367-1126
hsummers@webber.com
Description:
Represents sports organizations.
Services:
Areas of practice include General, Appellate, Trial and Federal Practice, Complex Litigation, Probate, Trust, Family, Corporation, Labor/Employment (Management), Taxation, Real Estate, Zoning, Environmental, Health, Banking and Intellectual Property Law
Clients:
Porter Athletic Equipment Co. (Sporting Goods Mfg.); Village of Thomasboro; Illinois Crop Improvement Assoc.; GMS Management of Illinois, Inc. (Real Estate Development & Leasing); Frasca International; Heatlh Care Service Corporation, d/b/a Blue Cross/Blue Shield of Illinois; Regional Health Resource Center, Inc.; National Council of Teachers of English; Illinois-American Water Company; Durst Cycle.

THOMAS & TEAFF
7911 HERSCHEL AVENUE
SUITE 300
PO BOX 3100
LA JOLLA, CA 92038-3100
858-551-1980
Fax: 858-551-1988
www.lawyers.com
• Teaff F. Robert, Principal
(858) 551-1980
Description:
Entertainment and Sports Law, General Business.
Services:
Areas of practice include General Civil Practice. Estates, Business, Real Property, Negligence, Entertainment and Sports Law, and Personal Injury

THOMAS M. COOLEY LAW SCHOOL
300 S CAPITOL AVENUE
PO BOX 13038
LANSING, MI 48933
517-371-5140
Fax: 517-334-5718
admissions@cooley.edu
www.cooley.edu
• Don LeDuc, President/Dean/Professor
(517) 371-5140
leducd@cooley.edu
• Brent V. Danielson, Chairman of the Board
(517) 371-5140

• Lawrence P. Nolan, Vice Chairman of the Board
(517) 371-5140
• Lawrence P. E. Nolan, Chair
• Louise Alderson, Vice Chair
• Don LeDuc, President and dean
• Cherie L. Beck, Corporate secretary, associate legal counsel
Services:
Focuses on skills training and practical legal education.
Description:
Teaches sports law, torts, product liability.

THOMAS PILACEK & ASSOCIATES
158 TUSKAWILLA ROAD
SUITE 2320
WINTER SPRINGS TOWN CENTER
WINTER SPRINGS, FL 32708
407-278-7243
800-569-8796
Fax: 407-660-8343
• Thomas J. Pilacek, Lawyer
(407) 660-9595
tpilacek@pilacek.com
• John C. Palmerini, Law Clerk
(407) 660-9595
• Deborah C. Brock, Firm Administrator/Paralegal
(407) 660-9595
• Jason Pilacek, Administrative Assistant
(407) 660-9595
Services:
Areas of practice include Private, Public and Federal Sector Employment, Federal & State Litigations, Appeals, Administrative Law & Arbitrations, Contract Preparation and Review, Severance, Non-Compete, and Retirement Agreements, Federal & State Labor, Fair Employment Practice & Civil Rights Laws, Business & Partnership Disputes
Nature of Sports Service:
All phases of athlete representation including contract negotiation, long-range planning, financial planning, and post-career counseling.

THOMAS S. BUSCH
6900 COLLEGE BLVD
SUITE 700
OVERLAND PARK, KS 66211
913-491-5500
Fax: 913-491-3341
www.fulbright.com
• Thomas S. Busch, Member
• Joseph Y. Holman, Member
• Brent A. Mitchell, Attorney
(316) 265-9311
bamitchell@martinpringle.com
• Sam Colville, Member
• Frank Basgall, Attorney
(316) 265-9311
Description:
Sports licensing
Services:
Offers legal assistance in the area of sports organization governance.
Year Founded:
1982

THOMAS, MEANS & GILLIS, P.C.
60 COMMERCE STREET
SUITE 200
PO BOX 5058
MONTGOMERY, AL 36104

334-270-1033
800-626-9684
Fax: 334-260-9396
meansgillislaw.com
• Kenneth L. Thomas, Partner
(334) 270-1033
• Tyrone C. Means, Managing Partner
(334) 270-1033
• H. Le Gillis, Managing Partner
(334) 270-1033
• Quinton S. Seay, Partner
(404) 222-8400
Services:
Legal expertise spans the civil litigation spectrum, including personal injury and wrongful death, insurance law, consumer protection, and workers compensation, labor and employment law, education and government law and civil rights and Constitutional law
Description:
Contract negotiation, tort actions/litigation.

THORSNES, BARTOLOTTA & MCGUIRE
2550 FIFTH AVENUE
11TH FLOOR
SAN DIEGO, CA 92103
619-236-9363
800-577-2922
Fax: 619-236-9653
info@tbmlawyers.com
www.tbmlawyers.com
• Vincent J. Bartolotta Jr, Founding Partner
barlotta@tbmlawyers.com
• John F. McGuire, Jr., Founding Partner
mcguire@tbmlawyers.com
• Kevin F F. Quinn, Partner
quinn@tbmlawyers.com
• Vincent J Bartolotta, Partner
bartolotta@tbmlawyers.com
• John F McGuire, Partner
mcguire@tbmlawyers.com
• Karen R Frostrom, Partner
frostrom@tbmlawyers.com
• Ian Fusselman, Parner
fusselman@tbmlawyers.com
• Michael T Thorsnes, Of counsel
Services:
Services include the areas of Business Litigation, Personal Injury, Construction Defects, Wrongful Death, Medical Malpractice, ERISA, Class Action

TONKON TORP LLP
888 SW FIFTH AVENUE
1600 PIONEER TOWER
PORTLAND, OR 97204
503-221-1440
Fax: 503-274-8779
owen@tonkon.com
www.tonkon.com
• Owen D. Blank, Attorney
(503) 802-2011
owen.blank@tonkon.com
• Ryan M. Bledsoe, Attorney
(503) 802-2120
ryan.bledsoe@tonkon.com
Description:
Contract negotiation, post career planning, investment contract negotiation, arbitration hearings, represents professional sports teams, endorsement exploration. Business, commercial, constitutional, corporate, international, media, real estate, and sports law.
Year Founded:
1974

TREBATOSKI, CHRIS J.
100 E WISCONSIN AVENUE
SUITE 3300
MILWAUKEE, WI 53202
414-271-6560
Fax: 414-277-0656
info@michaelbest.com
www.michaelbest.com
• Thomas E. Obenberger, Managing Partner
(414) 225-4960
teobenberger@michaelbest.com
• David A. Krutz, Chairman, Management Committee
(262) 956-6550
dakrutz@michaelbest.com
• Scott C. Beightol, Partner
(414) 225-4994
scbeightol@michaelbest.com
• Robert J. Johannes, Partner
(414) 225-4954
rjjohannes@michaelbest.com
Description:
Represents professional sports teams.
Services:
Provides complete legal services related to Business, Employment Relations, Health Care, Intellectual Property, Land & Resources, Litigation, Taxation, and Wealth Planning Services.
Clients:
ABS Global, AE Business Solutions, Inc., AMEC Construction Company, American Transmission Company, LLC, Auto Glass Specialists, Inc., Bank of America, Berbee Information Networks Corporation, Blue Cross Blue Shield Association, Cedar Creek Partners LLC, Chicago Metallic Corporation, Clear Channel Outdoor, Inc., Cleary Gull, Coca-Cola Bottling Corp., Conley Publishing Group, Ltd., Derse, Inc., Envirotest Systems Corp., Earth Tech, Ltd., Ecker Enterprises, Inc., The F. Dohmen Company, U.S. Bank, National Association, Fiserv, Inc., Fort James Corporation, Freedom Plastics, Inc., Great Lakes Higher Education Corporation, HK Systems, Inc.

TRIBLER, ORPETT & CRONE
225 W WASHINGTON STREET
SUITE 1300
CHICAGO, IL 60606-3408
312-201-6400
Fax: 312-201-6401
info@tribler.com
www.tribler.com
• Mitchell A. Orpett, Director
(312) 201-6413
maorpett@tribler.com
• Willis R. Tribler, Director
(312) 201-6417
• Michael J. Meyer, Director
(312) 201-6435
mjmeyer@tribler.com
• Jeremy N. H. Boeder, Attorney
Services:
Areas of practice includes General Liability Defense, Labor and Employment, Insurance Coverage, Insurance Agents and Brokers, Construction Law, Directors and Officers Liability, Environmental Law & Toxic Torts, Insurance Insolvency and Regulatory Practice, Legal Malpractice, Medical Malpractice, Municipal Law, Petroleum Industries, Product Liability, Real Estate Agents and Brokers, Reinsurance
Description:
Arbitration hearings, tort actions/litigation.

Year Founded:
1978

VAINISI, JEROME R.
222 N LASALLE STREET
SUITE 300
CHICAGO, IL 60601
312-704-3000
Fax: 312-704-3001
info@hinshawlaw.com
www.hinshawlaw.com
• Paul R. Boken, Executive Managing
Director
(312) 704-3208
pboken@hinshawlaw.com
• Donald L. Mrozek, Chairman
(312) 704-3111
dmrozek@hinshawlaw.com
• Jerome R. Vainisi, Partner
(312) 704-3166
jvainisi@hinshawlaw.com
Nature of Sports Service:
All phases of athlete representation
including contract negotiation, income tax
planning, estate planning,
financial planning, and post-career
counseling, marketing.
Services:
Provides a full-service practice with an
emphasis in commercial litigation, products
and general liability defense litigation,
corporate, environmental and employment
law, as well as the representation of
professionals in their risk management and
liability matters

VAN DER SMISSEN, BETTY
HPER 308
UNIVERSITY OF ARKANSAS
FAYETTEVILLE, AR 72701
Description:
Teaches sports law.
Services:
Provides Health, Physical Education and
Leisure Services education in its 6 major
divisions: Athletic Training; Health
Promotion and Education; Leisure, Youth
and Human Services; Physical Education;
Graduate Studies; and Liberal Arts

VILLARINI & HENRY
16 MAIN STREET
HAMBURG, NY 14075
716-312-1136
888-834-8623
Fax: 716-648-1806
dhenry@villariniandhenry.com
www.villariniandhenry.com
• Robert M. Villarini, Lawyer and Partner
(716) 648-0510
bert@villariniandhenry.com
• Daniel John Henry, Jr., Lawyer & Partner
(716) 312-1136
dhenry@villariniandhenry.com
Services:
Offers high-quality representation based on
a thorough understanding of the area of
Criminal Law, Personal Injury/Negligence
and Sports Law involving Professional
Athletes' injury claims

VINET, MARK
63 DES FRENES
VAUDREUIL-SUR-LE-LAC
QUEBEC, CANADA J7V 8P3
450-510-1102
Fax: 450-510-1095

mark@markvinet.com
www.markvinet.com
• Mark Vinet, Author/Historian/Entertainment
Lawyer
(450) 510-1102
markvinet@videotron.ca
Services:
Teaches college level history, entertainment
business, contracts and copyright law
courses.
Description:
Sports and entertainment law.

**VLADECK WALDMAN ELIAS &
ENGELHARD, P.C.**
1501 BROADWAY
SUITE 800
NEW YORK, NY 10036-5560
212-403-7300
Fax: 212-221-3172
info@vladeck.com
www.vladeck.com
• Debra L. Raskin, Partner
(212) 403-7300
• Anne C. Vladeck, Partner
(212) 403-7327
avladeck@vladeck.com
• Debra L. Raskin, Partner
(212) 403-7300
draskin@vladeck.com
• Ivan D. Smith, Partner
(212) 403-7300
ismith@vladeck.com
Services:
Areas of practice includes Employment,
Labor, Employee Benefits, General
Litigation, Entertainment, Sports and the
Arts, Non-profits and Pro Bono Commitment

VORYS, SATER, SEYMOUR & PEASE
52 E GAY STREET
PO BOX 1008
COLUMBUS, OH 43215
614-464-6400
www.vorys.com
• W. Jonathan Airey, Partner
(614) 464-6346
• Raymond D. Anderson, Partner
(614) 464-6447
rdanderson@vssp.com
• Sandra J. Anderson, Partner
(614) 464-6405
• Julie K. R. Brown, Technology Executive
Manager
(614) 464-5684
crauge@vssp.com
Description:
Contract negotiation, post career planning,
federal/state/international tax filings,
licensing, endorsement exploration, teaches
sports law.
Services:
Areas of practice include Commercial & real
Estate, Corporate & Finance, Energy&
Utility, environment, Government &
Lobbying, Health Care, intellectual Property,
International, Labor 7 Employment,
Litigation, Probate & Estate Planning, Tax,
Technology, and Toxic Tort
Clients:
The Scotts Company, United States Shoe
Corporation, Stringfellow, Tybouts Corner,
ChemDyne, and Fields Brook, Honda of
America, Mfg., Inc., Wendy's International,
Inc., The Limited, Inc., Worthington
Industries, Inc., Bob Evans Farms, Inc., and
Eaton Corporation, Citibank, IBM, Columbia

Gas Transmission Company, Nigerian
National Petroleum Corporation

WAGENHEIM & WAGNER, P.A.
100 SOUTHEAST 3RD AVENUE
7TH FLOOR
ONE FINANCIAL PLAZA
FORT LAUDERDALE, FL 33394
954-564-4800
Fax: 954-564-5121
info@sportsinjurylaw.com
www.sportsinjurylaw.com
• Richard Wagenheim, Lawyer/Partner
(954) 564-4800
richw@sportsinjurylaw.com
• Barbara Wagner, Lawyer/Partner
(954) 564-4800
barbw@sportsinjurylaw.com
Clients:
List of professional athlete clients are
players from the National Football League,
Arena Football League, NFL Europe, Major
League Baseball, Minor League Baseball,
National Hockey League, East Coast
Hockey League, International Hockey
League and Major League Soccer.
Nature of Sports Service:
Workers' compensation injury and disability
claims for professional athletes (members of
NFLPA, AFLPA panel of workers
compensation attorneys) Represent players
from the NFL, AFL, NFLE, Major and Minor
League Baseball, Hockey, Soccer, NHLPA
and PHPA.

WALES, SCOTT A.
9001 N 76TH STREET
SUITE 310
MILWAUKEE, WI 53223-1911
414-357-7555
• Jerome T. Safer, Lawyer
(414) 357-7555
• Martin R. Stein, Lawyer
(414) 357-7555
• Scott A. Wales, Lawyer
(414) 357-7555
• Fredrick J. Safer, Attorney
• Martin R. Stein, Attorney
Services:
Areas of practice include contract
negotiation, endorsement exploration, and
tort actions/litigation

WALL LAW OFFICES, PLLC
4310 N 75TH STREET
SUITE B
SCOTTSDALE, AZ 85251
480-222-3888
Fax: 480-990-7860
Stephen.Wall@azbar.org
• Stephen M. M. Wall, Lawyer
(480) 222-3888
Stephen.Wall@azbar.org
Services:
Areas of practice include DUI/DWI, Extreme
DUI, Aggravated DUI, Vehicular Homicide,
All Criminal Offenses, Motorcycle & Auto
Accidents, Serious Injury and Death

WARE, R. DAVID
504 BUTLER NATIONAL DRIVE
DULUTH, GA 30097
404-402-0204
Fax: 770-813-9776
• Robert Da Ware, Lawyer
(404) 402-0204
rdware@aol.com

Services:
Areas of practice include General Practice and Trial Law, Tort and Insurance Practice, and Local Government Law
Description:
Contract negotiation.

WARSHAFSKY LAW FIRM
839 N JEFFERSON STREET
SUITE 300
MILWAUKEE, WI 53202
414-276-4970
800-728-4970
Fax: 414-276-5533
www.warshafsky.com
• Frank T. Crivello, II, Lawyer
(414) 276-4970
• Ted M Warshafsky, Lawyer
(414) 273-4764
• Merton Rotter, Lawyer
(414) 276-4970
• Michael Tarnoff, Lawyer
(414) 276-4970
• Frank T. Crivello, Lawyer
• Gerald J. Bloch, Lawyer
• John R. Schatzman, Lawyer
Description:
Contract negotiation, endorsement exploration.
Services:
Areas of practice focus on personal injury law, including automobile accidents, medical malpractice, wrongful death and product liability

WATSON, RICHARD
925 EUCLID AVENUE
2000 HUNTINGTON BUILDING
CLEVELAND, OH 44115-1496
216-696-4700
Fax: 216-696-2706
www.spiethbell.com
• J. Talbot Young, Partner
(216) 535-1066
• Richard T Watson, Lawyer
(216) 696-4700
richardtwatson@worldnet.att.net
• James R. Bright, Shareholder
(216) 696-4700
Description:
Represents professional sports teams.
Services:
Areas of practice include Business Law and Tax, Employment Law, Estate Planning & Personal Tax, Labor Law, liquor Control Law, Litigation, and Real Estate

WATTS, STEVEN R.
10 N LUDLOW STREET
1100 COURTHOUSE PLAZA, SW
DAYTON, OH 45402
937-449-2800
Fax: 937-449-2821
www.chklaw.com
• Richard J. Chernesky, Managing Partner
(937) 449-2804
richard.chernesky@dinslaw.com
• Edward M. Kress, Senior Partners
(937) 449-2830
edward.kress@dinslaw.com
• Richard A. Brook, Senior Partner
• Alexander A. R. Arestides, Associate
(937) 463-4935
alexander.arestides@dinsmore.com
• James E. Beyer, Partner
(937) 449-6438
james.beyer@dinsmore.com

• Richard A. Broock, Partner
(93-) 49-2840
richard.broock@dinsmore.com
• Frederick J. Caspar, Partner
(937) 449-2818
fred.caspar@dinsmore.com
• Joshua J. Chernesky, Associate
(937) 449-2811
joshua.chernesky@dinsmore.com
Description:
Contract negotiation.
Services:
Areas of practice include Business Law, Mergers and Acquisitions, Real Estate, Litigation, Securities, Taxation, Regulated Industries, Employment Law Counseling, Compensation, Retirement, and Employee Benefit Plans, Estate Planning and Administration, Probate Law, Banking, Product Liability, and Health Care Law
Clients:
AAA Miami Valley, Advantage Per Diem Staffing, LLC, AK Steel, Architectural Resources Corporation, The Aristocrat Products Mfg. Co., Audi of America, Inc., The Berry Company, Better Business Bureau of Dayton/Miami Valley, Inc., Bradstreet & Company, Inc., Bri Lyn, Inc., Brown Industrial, Inc., CBS Personnel Services, LLC, Central State University Foundation, CFA Holding, Inc., Chiropractic Health & Wellness Center, Inc., Church of the Messiah, The Connor Group, CSA Nutrition Services, Inc., Day International, Inc., Dayton Christian School, Inc., The Dayton Heart Center, Inc., The Dayton-Montgomery County Port Authority, Digital Concepts, Inc.

WEBB, WILLIAM Y.
1735 MARKET STREET
51ST FLOOR
PHILADELPHIA, PA 19103-7599
215-665-8500
Fax: 215-864-8999
www.ballardspahr.com
• Brian Walsh, Partner
(215) 864-8510
walsh@ballardspahr.com
• Arlene J Angelo, Partner
(215) 864-8133
angeloa@ballardspahr.com
• Steven Arbittier, Partner
(215) 864-8125
arbittier@ballardspahr.com
• Lynn Axelroth, Partner
(215) 864-8707
axelroth@ballardspahr.com
Description:
Represents professional sports teams, teaches sports law, mergers and acquisitions.
Services:
Areas of practice include Business and Finance, Construction, Employee Benefits, Energy and Project Finance, Environmental, Housing, Labor, Employment & Immigration, Litigation, Public Finance, Real Estate Leasing, Securities, Secularization, Tax, technology and emerging Companies, Telecommunications, Transactional Finance, Zoning and Land Use
Clients:
Comcast Corporation, Exelon Corporation, Going Global, Greka Energy Corporation, Leading the Way, Puratos Group, The Legal Services Corporation, Tractebel SA, Vision in a Virtual World, Overture to the Future,

The Johns Hopkins University Downtown Center, The Philadelphia Phillies, The Ritz-Carlton, Exelon Corporation, Greka Energy Corporation, Leading the Way, An Urban Village, A League of Their Own.

WEBER & BAER, LLP
2029 CENTURY PARK E
SUITE 1400
LOS ANGELES, CA 90067
310-226-7570
Fax: 310-226-7571
www.weberbaer.com
• Jonathan S. Weber, Member
• Tracy Mi Baer, Member
• Andrew Treger, Member
• Jonathan S. Weber, Attorney
• Tracy Baer, Attorney
• Eric G. Rudin, Attorney
Services:
Provides services in the following areas: personal injury, plaintiffs personal injury, medical malpractice, products liability, negligence, automobile accidents and injuries, wrongful death, nursing home abuse.

WEIL, GOTSHAL & MANGES
767 FIFTH AVENUE
NEW YORK, NY 10153
212-310-8000
Fax: 212-310-8007
www.weil.com
• Stephen J. Dannhauser, Chairman
(212) 310-8326
stephen.dannhauser@weil.com
• Brad D. Scott, Executive Director
(212) 310-8271
brad.scott@weil.com
• Nancy L. Gray, Legal Recruiting Manager
(212) 735-4554
• Elizabeth A. Ventura, Senior director, communications
• Ashley Laputka, PR manager
• Meredith Moore, Director of global diversity
• Naima Walker-fierce, Director of legal recruiting
Description:
Contract negotiation, arbitration hearings, licensing, endorsement exploration, tort actions/litigation.
Services:
Areas of practice include Antitrust/Competition, Banking & Finance, Bankruptcy Litigation, Business Finance & Restructuring, Capital Markets, Complex Commercial, Litigation, Corporate, Corporate Governance, Employment, Financial Services, Global Dispute Resolution, Intellectual Property & Media, International Trade, Litigation/Regulatory, Mergers & Acquisitions, Patent Litigation, Private Equity, Product Liability/Mass Tort/Environmental, Real Estate Transactions & Finance, Securities/Corporate Governance, Structured Finance/Derivatives, Tax, and Trusts & Estates

WEILER, PAUL C.
1563 MASSACHUSETTS AVENUE
CAMBRIDGE, MA 2138
617-495-2955
Fax: 617-496-4865
pweiler@law.harvard.edu
www.law.harvard.edu

- Elena Kagan, Dean
(617) 495-4601
- Paul C. Weiler, Professor of Law
(617) 495-2955
pweiler@law.harvard.edu
- Henry J. Steiner, Director, Human Rights Program
(617) 495-3107
hsteiner@law.harvard.edu
- Paul C. Weiler, Henry J. Friendly Professor of Law
(617) 495-2955
pweiler@law.harvard.edu
Services:
Provides unparalleled opportunities to study law and related disciplines in an energetic and creative learning environment
Description:
Investment contract negotiation, represents sports organizations, teaches sports law.

WEINER, MICHAEL
12 E 49TH STREET
24TH FLOOR
NEW YORK, NY 10017
212-826-0808
Fax: 212-752-4378
feedback@mlbpa.org
www.mlbplayers.com
- Donald M. Fehr, Executive Director
(212) 826-0808
feedback@mlbpa.org
- Michael Weiner, General Counsel
(212) 826-0808
feedback@mlbpa.org
- Judy Heeter, Business Affairs and Licensing Director
(212) 826-080
feedback@mlbpa.org
- Gene Orza, Chief Operating Officer
(212) 826-080
feedback@mlbpa.org
Description:
Assistant General Counsel to Major League Baseball Players Association.
Services:
Aims to encourage citizen participation and direct action; promote economic justice and oppose corporate welfare; resist over-commercialization; foster informed and principled consumers; emphasize fan-friendliness; promote sustainability; cultivate personal and global responsibility; fight for inclusion, equal opportunity and respect for diversity; combat performance-enhancing drug use; encourage respectful fan behavior; resist network control; highlight physical fitness and participation; challenge media fusion with franchises, leagues and governing bodies.

WEISMAN, PAUL
15301 VENTURA BOULEVARD
SUITE # 300
SHERMAN OAKS, CA 91403-3129
818-986-9525
www.lagop.org
- Paul Weisman, Lawyer
(818) 986-9525
pweisman1@socal.rr.com
- Mark Vafiades, Chairman
- Stephen C. Smith, First Vice Chairman
- Arturo Alas, Second Vice Chairman
arturo@lagop.org
Services:
Tax & Sports attorney, estate planning, tax controversy representation, corporate law,

sports law and mediation.
Clients:
BNA Tax Management Portfolio on Federal Tax Collection Procedure 638 2d.
Description:
Taxation Law, Contract negotiation.

WEISS, STEPHEN L.
320 E VIRGINIA AVENUE
PHOENIX, AZ 85004
602-254-1977
888-650-4798
800-358-CATS
email@taylorandassociates.net
www.injuredworker.com
- Richard Taylor, Managing Attorney
(602) 254-2220
richard@taylorandassociates.net
- Thomas C. Whitley, Managing Attorney
(928) 526-4160
thomas@taylorandassociates.net
- Brian A. Weekley, Associate
(602) 254-1977
brian@taylorandassociates.net
- Roger A. Schwartz, Associate
(602) 257-5018
roger@taylorandassociates.net
Services:
Areas of practice include personal injury, workers' compensation, and social secuirty disability
Clients:
Kingman, Bullhead City, Lakeside, Payson, Mesa and Casa Grande
Description:
NFLPA workers' compensation panel.

WEISTART, JOHN C.
210 SCIENCE DRIVE
BOX 90362
DURHAM, NC 27708
919-613-7006
Fax: 919-613-7257
admissions@law.duke.edu
www.law.duke.edu
- David F. Levi, Dean
(919) 613-7006
levi@law.duke.edu
- William Hoye, Associate Dean, Admissions and Financial
(919) 613-8533
hoye@law.duke.edu
- Bruce A. Elvin, Assistant Dean, Career Services
(919) 613-7084
Elvin@law.duke.edu
- Theresa Newman, Associate Dean, Academic Affairs
(919) 613-7133
Newman@law.duke.edu
Description:
Post career planning, arbitration hearings, represents professional sports teams, teaches sports law, consulting.
Services:
Prepares students for responsible and productive lives in the legal profession, and, as a community of scholars, the Law School also provides leadership at the national and international levels in efforts to improve the law and legal institutions through teaching, research and other forms of public service

WELCH & CONDON
1109 TACOMA AVENUE S
PO BOX 1318
TACOMA, WA 98402

253-383-3427
Fax: 253-572-8957
info@welchcondon.com
www.welchcondon.com
- David B. Condon, Co-Founder
(253) 383-3427
dave@welchcondon.com
- Terri L. Herring-Puz, Associate
(253) 383-3427
therring@harbornet.com
Nature of Service:
Focuses on Workers' Compensation Law
Year Founded:
1978

WENDEL, CHRITTON, PARKS, AND DEBARI CHARTERED
5300 S FLORIDA AVENUE
PO BOX 5378
LAKELAND, FL 33813-4921
941-646-5091
Fax: 941-644-3477
- John F. Wendel, President/Shareholder
(941) 646-5091
- Charles P. Chritton, VP/Shareholder
Description:
Investment contract negotiation, represents sports organizations, arbitration hearings, represents professional sports teams, licensing, tort actions/litigation, stadium construction, team/league transactions.

WILLIAMS, BRIAN P.
501 MAIN STREET
SUITE 305, POST OFFICE BOX 3646
EVANSVILLE, IN 47735-3646
812-423-3183
Fax: 812-423-3841
evvlaw@k2d2.com
www.kddk.com
- Alan N. Shovers, Managing Partner
(812) 423-3183
ashovers@kddk.com
- Thomas O. Magan, Managing Partner
(812) 423-3183
shovers@k2d2.com
- Brian P. Williams, Partner
(812) 423-3183
williams@k2d2.com
- Larry R. Downs, Partner
(812) 423-3183
downs@k2d2.com
Description:
Represents college athletic departments.
Services:
Business Law Services, Bankruptcy, Collection & Creditors' Rights Services, Construction Law Services, Economic Development, Law Services, Education Law Services Environmental Law Services, Estate Planning Services, Family Law & Private, Adoption Services, Health Care Law Services, Immigration Law Services, Intellectual PropertyLaw Services, Labor & Employment
Law Services, Litigation & Trial Services, Real Estate Law Services, Tax & Employee Benefits Law Services
Clients:
Deaconess Hospital, Inc., American General Finance, University of Southern Indiana, Cresline Plastic Pipe Co., Inc., Keller Crescent Co., Inc., Red Spot Paint & Varnish Co., Inc., Lewis Bakeries, Inc., Buchta Leasing, Inc., Wabash General Hospital, The Rehabilitation Center, George Koch Sons, Inc., George Koch Sons, Inc., Toyota Motor Corporate Services of North America, Inc., AK Steel Corporation, Kaiser Aluminum Chemical Corporation, Card

Management Corporation, Princeton Mining Company, Inc., Champion Laboratories, Inc., Raben Tire Co., Inc., Tyco Electronics Corporation, Mid-States Rubber Products, Inc., AES Corporation, DSM Engineering.

WILSON, ELSER, MOSKOWITZ ET AL
150 E 42ND STREET
NEW YORK, NY 10017-5639
212-490-3000
Fax: 212-490-3038
info@wilsonelser.com
www.wilsonelser.com
• Mark K. Anesh, Partner
(212) 490-3000
• Tracy J. Abatemarco, Partner
(212) 490-3000
• Bruce Ainbinder, Partner
(212) 490-3000
• Kevie An Aulbach, Partner
(212) 490-3000
• Larry Lum,
(212) 490-3000
larry.lum@wilsonelser.com
• Robert T. Adams,
(212) 490-3000
• Timothy P. Coon,
(212) 490-3000
Services:
Offers counseling, litigation, arbitration and mediation, and other legal services. Represents Fortune 500 companies, including major insurers, and many other commercial, industrial, government and nonprofit entities. Areas of practice include aviation, admiralty and marine, corporate, commercial, professional liability, insurance coverage, general liability, intellectual property, employment, product liability, real estate and construction.
Description:
Contract negotiation, investments, arbitration hearings, representation of professional sports teams, licensing, endorsement exploration, teaches sports law, tort actions/litigation, representation of sports promoters.

WINSTEAD ATTORNEYS
600 TRAVIS STREET
JPMORGAN CHASE TOWER
SUITE 1100
HOUSTON, TX 77002
713-650-8400
Fax: 713-650-2400
cporter@winstead.com
www.winstead.com
• Cindy Graves, Director of Administration
(713) 650-2777
cgraves@winstead.com
• Greg Erwin, Managing Shareholder (Houston)
(713) 650-2781
gerwin@winstead.com
• Herb Albritton, Executive Director (Dallas)
• Allen Fuqua, Chief Marketing Officer (Dallas)
• Glen Pryor, Chief Financial Administrator (Dallas)
• Dominique Anderson, Director of Attorney Recruiting (Dallas)
• Patty Stewart, Director of Human Resources (Dallas)
• Joel Edwards, Director of Information Technology (Dallas)
• Terri L. Lawrence, Director Library & Information Resources (Dal
• Tom Forestier, Managing Shareholder

(713) 650-2749
tforestier@winstead.com
• Cindy Graves, Director of Administration
(713) 650-2777
cgraves@winstead.com
• Zachary B Allie, Associate
(713) 650-2771
zallie@winstead.com
• Frank Amini, Associate
(713) 650-2795
famini@winstead.com
• Kenneth L Anderson, Associate
(713) 650-2648
kanderson@winstead.com
• Holly D Arnold, Associate
(713) 650-2723
harnold@winstead.com
Nature of Services:
The Sports Business and Public Venues Practice at Winstead Attorneys is counsel to major league and minor league teams in the development, operation and management of their franchises.
Clients:
Dallas Cowboys; Houston Texans; San Antonio Spurs; Texas Rangers; Portland Trail Blazers.
Sponsor:
National Sports Forum sponsor and partner.

WOLFE LAW, P.C.
200 W ADAMS STREET
SUITE 2200
CHICAGO, IL 60606
312-727-0403
Fax: 312-727-0406
ken@wolfelawpc.com
www.wolfelawfirmpc.com
• Kenneth Wolfe, President
ken@wolfelawpc.com
Description:
Law firm representing professional athletes in workers' compensation claims.
Year Founded:
2006

WOLOHAN, JOHN T.
953 DANBY ROAD
13 HILL CENTER
ITHACA, NY 14850
607-274-3011
Fax: 607-274-5792
admission@ithaca.edu
www.ithaca.edu
• Thomas R. Rochon, President
(607) 274-3111
president@ithaca.edu
Year Founded:
1893.
Description:
Teaches sports law, tort actions/litigation.

WOMBLE, CARLYLE, SANDRIDGE & RICE, PLLC
ONE W FOURTH STREET
PO BOX 84
WINSTON-SALEM, NC 27101
336-721-3600
Fax: 336-721-3660
mgunter@wcsr.com
www.wcsr.com
• Michael D. Gunter, Lawyer
(336) 721-3607
mgunter@wcsr.com
• Alfred G. Adams, Lawyer
(336) 721-3642
aadams@wcsr.com

• Jean T. Adams, Lawyer
(336) 721-3600
jadams@wcsr.com
• Patrick M. Allen, Lawyer
(336) 721-3574
PAllen@wcsr.com
• Alfred G. Adams, Lawyer
(336) 721-3642
• Jean T. Adams, Lawyer
• Mary Craven Adams, Lawyer
• Reid C. Adams, Lawyer
• Patrick M. Allen, Lawyer
(336) 721-3574
Description:
Contract negotiation, post career planning, federal/state/international tax filings, endorsement exploration.
Services:
Areas of practice include Antitrust, Distribution and Franchise Law; Appellate; Bankruptcy and Creditors' Rights; Capital Markets Business Group; Construction Law; Corporate and Securities; Economic Development; Employee Benefits; Environmental Law and Toxic Tort Litigation; Federal and State Government Affairs; Gaming Law; Government Contracts; Health Care; Insurance, Governmental and Tort Litigation; Intellectual Property; International Trade; Labor & Employment; Patent; Product Liability Litigation; Public Finance; Real Estate; Tax; Telecommunications, Cable & Broadcast; and Trusts & Estates

---

WONG, GLENN M.
121 PRESIDENTS DRIVE
UNIVERSITY OF MASSACHUSETTS
AMHERST, MA 1003
413-545-0441
Fax: 413-577-0642
www.isenberg.umass.edu
• John V. Lombardi, Chancellor/Professor
(413) 545-2211
lombardi@umass.edu
• Lisa Pi Masteralexis, Department Head
(413) 545-5061
lpmaster@sportmgt.umass.edu
• Carol A. Barr, Associate Department Head
(413) 545-5065
cbarr@sportmgt.umass.edu
• Glenn M. Wong, Professor
(413) 545-5053
gwong@sportmgt.umass.edu
Description:
Arbitration hearings, teaches sports law.
Services:
Offers undergraduate, masters and doctoral programs in a growing number of fields.

WOOD & LAMPING LLP
600 VINE STREET
SUITE 2500
CINCINNATI, OH 45202
513-852-6000
Fax: 513-852-6087
www.woodlamping.com
• Thomas M. Woebkenberg, Lawyer
(513) 852-6044
tmwoebkenberg@woodlamping.com
• Edward D. Bender, Lawyer
(513) 852-6000
edbender@woodlamping.com
• Paul R. Berninger, Lawyer
(513) 852-6000
prberninger@woodlamping.com
• Edward D. H. Bender, Partner
(513) 852-6002
edbender@woodlamping.com

- Paul R. Berninger, Partner
(513) 852-6002
- Thomas J. Breed, Partner
(513) 852-6076
tjbreed@woodlamping.com
- Rayan F. Coutinho, Partner
(513) 852-6030
- Susan K. Cliffel, Partner
(513) 852-6040
- Gary J. Davis, Partner
(513) 852-6085
gjdavis@woodlamping.com
Services:
Works in the areas of litigation, business, government and land use, employment law, real estate, probate and estate planning, and domestic relations. Areas of practice include Admiralty, Bankruptcy, Business Reorganization, Civil / Commercial Litigation, Computer Law, Contract Negotiations, Construction, Corporate and Finance, Domestic Relations, Elder Law, Employee Benefits, ERISA, Estate Planning/Probate, Family Law, Health Care / Hospital, Insurance Defense, Financial Institutions/Banking, Labor/Employment, Medicaid Planning, Medical Malpractice, Mergers/Acquisitions, Municipal/Governmental, Personal Injury, Product Liability Defense, Pro
Description:
Contract negotiation.

WOOD, RICHARD
1400 R ST.
LINCOLN, NE 68588
402-472-2111
Fax: 402-472-2038
www.unl.edu
- Harvey S. Perlman, Chancellor
(402) 472-2116
hperlman1@unl.edu
- Richard Wood, VP/General Counsel
(402) 472-1201
Description:
Represents college athletic departments.
Services:
A research leader with a wide array of grant-funded projects aimed at broadening knowledge in the sciences and humanities

WORLEY, JAMES G.
727 E DEAN KEETON STREET
PO BOX 7399
AUSTIN, TX 78705
512-471-1232
Fax: 512-471-8102
www.utexas.edu
- William C. Powers Jr, President
(512) 471-1232
president@po.utexas.edu
- Patricia L. Clubb, VP, Employee & Campus Services
(512) 232-7742
- Richard B. Eason, VP, Resource Development
(512) 475-9609
- Sheldon Ekland-Olson, EVP and Provost
(512) 232-3301
seo@mail.utexas.edu
Description:
Represents college athletic departments.
Services:
From teaching and research to public service, the university's activities support its mission and core purpose: to transform lives for the benefit of society through the core values of learning, discovery, freedom,

leadership, individual opportunity and responsibility

WRIGHT, DOUGLAS A.
100 N TAMPA STREET
SUITE 4100
TAMPA, FL 33602
813-227-8500
Fax: 813-229-0134
www.hklaw.com
- Bradford Kimbro, Executive Partner
(813) 227-6660
brad.kimbro@hklaw.com
- William Dufoe, Partner
(813) 227-6371
william.dufoe@hklaw.com
Nature of Sports Service:
All phases of athlete representation including contract negotiation, long-range planning, financial planning, and post-career counseling.

WYNN & WYNN, P.C.
90 NEW STATE HIGHWAY
RAYNHAM, MA 2767
508-823-4567
800-852-5211
Fax: 508-822-4097
www.wynnandwynn.com
- Thomas J. Wynn, Founding Partner
(508) 823-4567
- Paul F. Wynn, Founding Partner
(508) 823-4567
- John J. O'Day Jr, Founding Partner
(508) 823-4567
- Elizabeth K. Balaschak, Partner
(508) 823-4567
- Paul Wynn, Founding Partner
(508) 823-4567
- Thomas Wynn, Founding partner
(Ext) 435
- Kevin McRoy, Partner
(Ext) 422
- Charles Mulcahy, Partner
(Ext) 423
- William Rosa, Partner
(Ext) 412
- Andrew Toldo, Partner
(Ext) 411
Services:
Areas of practice include Business Litigation, Criminal Law, Insurance Defense, Estate Planning, and Wills, Bankruptcy, Estate Administration, Family and Marital Law, Real Estate, Personal Injury, and Workers' Compensation
Clients:
Fleet National Bank
Description:
NFLPA workers' compensation panel, handles workers' compensation for the New England Patriots.

WYRICK, ROBBINS, YATES & PONTON, L.L.P
4101 LAKE BOONE TRAIL
SUITE 300, THE SUMMIT
RALEIGH, NC 27607-7506
919-781-4000
Fax: 919-781-4865
www.wyrick.com
- Samuel T. Wyrick III, Lawyer
(919) 781-4000
swyrick@wyrick.com
- Larry E. Robbins, Lawyer
(919) 781-4000
lrobbins@wyrick.com

- James M. Yates Jr, Lawyer
(919) 781-4000
jyates@wyrick.com
- Thomas A. Allen, Attorney
Services:
Areas of practice include Appellate Advocacy, Banking Law, Business Law, Commercial Real Estate & Development Community & Homeowners' Associations, Construction Law, Creditors' Rights; Bankruptcy; Loan Work-Outs, Election Law, Employee Benefit, Environmental Law, Estate and Wealth Planning & Probate, Family Law, Franchise Law, Government Contracting Law, Health Care Law, Intellectual Property Protection & Licensing, Labor & Employment Law, Life Sciences & Biotechnology, Litigation, Mergers, Acquisitions & Divestitures, Securities Law, Taxation, Venture Capital & Private Equity Financings
Clients:
Adherex Technologies, Inc., Aeolus Pharmaceuticals, Inc., Argolyn Bioscience, Inc., Arius Pharmaceuticals, Inc., BioDelivery Sciences International, Inc., BioMarck Pharmaceuticals, Ltd, BioStratum, Incorporated, Campbell Alliance Group, Inc., Chelsea Therapeutics, Inc., Container Graphics Corporation, DARA Biosciences, Inc., DarPharma, Inc., Encelle, Inc., Entegrion, Inc., Global Vaccines, Inc., Globus Medical, Inc., emocellular Therapeutics, Inc., Inspire Pharmaceuticals, Inc., Metabolon, Inc., Parion Sciences, Inc., Pentech Pharmaceuticals, Inc., Pharmaceutical Product Development, Inc. (PPD), PharmaNetics, Inc., Respirics, Inc.
Description:
Contract negotiation, tort actions/litigation. Community Association Law, Municipal Law, Creditor's Rights & Collections, Bankruptcy & Workouts, Litigation.

YONKE & POTTENGER, L.L.C.
1100 MAIN ST
SUITE 2450
KANSAS CITY, MO 64105
816-221-6000
877-221-8166
Fax: 816-221-6400
- Michael T. Yonke, Lawyer/Partner
(816) 221-6000
- Jason M. Pottenger, Lawyer/Partner
(816) 221-6000
- Albert J. Yonke, Of Counsel
(816) 221-6000
- Michael T. Yonke, Attorney
- Jason M. Pottenger, Attorney
- Thomas R. Onik, Attorney
- Albert J. Yonke, Attorney
- Tony Miller, Lawyer
(816) 221-6000
Services:
Areas of practice include Motor Vehicle Accidents, Construction Site Accidents, Medical Malpractice, Nursing Home Negligence, Trucking Accidents, Workers Compensation, and Criminal Defense

YOUNGER, TIMOTHY M.
10681 FOOTHILL BOULEVARD
SUITE 280
RANCHO CUCAMONGA, CA 91730
909-980-0630
www.youngerassociates.net
- Timothy M. Younger, Managing Partner
(909) 980-0630

• Melissa M. Thom, Associate
(909) 980-0630
• Timothy M. Younger, Attorney
Services:
Areas of practice include Civil Litigation including Personal Injury, Automobile accidents, Dog bites/attacks, Slip and fall accidents, Defective products, Wrongful death, Employment Law Matters, Workers' Compensation Subrogation, and Insurance Defense
Clients:
Liberty Mutual Insurance, Company Golden Eagle Insurance Corporation, Verizon, Crawford & Company, Southern California Risk Management Associates, Laidlaw Transit, Inc., Daewoo Motor Company, Stephen Daniels Real Estate Group, Zendejas Mexican Restaurants, Sunset Haven, Inc., CMAC Construction Company, Pacific Coast Funding, Michael J. Byrne Mfg. Co., Dean Foods Company, American Home Assurance Company
Description:
Contract negotiation and legal services.

ZIMMERMAN REED, P.L.LP.
1100 IDS CENTER
80 SOUTH 8TH STREET
MINNEAPOLIS, MN 55402
612-341-0400
800-755-0098
Fax: 612-341-0844
www.zimmreed.com
• Charles S. Zimmerman, Founding Partner
(612) 341-0400
• Robert C. Moilanen, Partner
(612) 341-0400
• Timothy J. Becker, Lawyer
(612) 341-0400
• Carolyn G. G. Anderson, Attorney
Services:
Areas of practice include Consumer Fraud, Dangerous & Defective Drugs, Deceptive Insurance Practices, Securities & Investment Fraud, Employment Violations, Wage and Hour Litigation, Environmental & Toxic Torts, Healthcare Litigation, Improper Homeowner Charges, Mortgage Litigation, and Defective Medical Devices
Description:
All phases of athlete representation including contract negotiation, long-range planning, financial planning, and post-career counseling. Class Actions; Products Liability; Consumer Fraud; Mass Torts; Complex Litigation. Investment contract negotiation, represents sports organizations, arbitration hearings, licensing, endorsement exploration, tort actions/litigation, worker's comp.
Year Founded:
1982

Sports Medicine Services

ACCESS SPORTS MEDICINE & ORTHOPAEDICS
www.accesssportsmed.com
Description:
Locations in Exeter, Portsmouth, Plaistow, Raymond, Rochester and Dover.
Specialty:
Orthopaedic and sports medicine care.

ADVANCED ORTHOPEDICS AND SPORTS MEDICINE INSTITUTE
POND VIEW PROFESSIONAL PARK
301 PROFESSIONAL VIEW DRIVE
BUILDING 300
FREEHOLD, NJ 07728
advancedorthosports.com
Year Founded:
2007
Specialty:
Orthopedic and sports medicine care.

AEGIS SCIENCES CORPORATION
515 GREAT CIRCLE ROAD
NASHVILLE, TN 37228
800-533-7052
info@aegislabs.com
www.aegislabs.com
• David L. Black, Chief Executive Officer
• Timothy A. Robert, Chief Science Officer
Services/Products:
AEGIS is a federally certified forensic toxicology laboratory providing services to corporations, colleges & universities, schools, government agencies, families, and individuals. AEGIS products and services will Deter and Detect substance abuse in your organization and, most importantly, Defend against the added costs and liability of drug abuse. Our goal is to provide you with accurate information and quality services that will help you insure a drug-free workplace, school, sports program, or family.
Brands:
Zero-Tolerance Drug Testingr; #9001 Zero-Tolerancer Substance Abuse Prevention Kit; #50277 Ensure Personal Breath Alcohol Tester; #50278 Disposable Mouthpieces; #50278 Disposable Mouthpieces.
Marketing & Consulting Services:
Drug and steroid testing for sports teams, conferences.
Year Founded:
1990

AMERICAN ACADEMY OF ORTHOPAEDIC SURGEONS
9400 W HIGGINS ROAD
ROSEMONT, IL 60018
847-823-7186
Fax: 847-823-8125
www.aaos.org
• Karen L. Hackett, Chief Executive Officer
• Richard J. Stewart, Chief Operating & Financial Officer
• Will Shaffer, Medical Director
Description:
Provides education and practice management services for orthopaedic surgeons.
Year Founded:
1933
Members:
39,000

AMERICAN ACADEMY OF PODIATRIC SPORTS MEDICINE
3121 NE 26TH STREET
OCALA, FL 34470
352-620-8562
info@aapsm.org
www.aapsm.org
• Rita Yates, Executive Director
Description:
Preventing and managing lower extremity

sports and fitness injuries through scientific research, professional education and increasing public awareness.
Year Founded:
1970

AMERICAN COLLEGE OF SPORTS MEDICINE
401 W MICHIGAN STREET
INDIANAPOLIS, IN 46202-3233
317-637-9200
Fax: 317-634-7817
www.acsm.org
• Lawrence E. Armstrong, President
Description:
World's largest sports medicine and exercise science organization.

AMERICAN COLLEGE OF VETERINARY SPORTS MEDICINE AND REHABILITATION
PO BOX F
FORT COLLINS, CO 80522
info@vsmr.org
vsmr.org
• Andris J. Kaneps, President
Description:
A new College of the American Veterinary Medical Association, the ACVSMR was developed to care for athletic and working animals.
Year Founded:
2010

AMERICAN MEDICAL SOCIETY FOR SPORTS MEDICINE
4000 W 114TH STREET
SUITE 100
LEAWOOD, KS 66211
913-327-1415
Fax: 913-327-1491
www.amssm.org
• Jim Griffith, Executive Director
Description:
A forum for primary care non-surgical sports medicine physicians.
Year Founded:
1991

AMERICAN ORTHOPAEDIC FOOT & ANKLE SOCIETY
9400 W HIGGINS ROAD
SUITE 220
ROSEMONT, IL 60018-4975
847-698-4654
800-235-4855
Fax: 847-692-3315
www.aofas.org
• Oster M. Susan, Executive Director
Description:
International organization of more than 2,000 orthopaedic surgeons specializing in treating injuries, diseases and conditions of the foot and ankle.
Year Founded:
1969

AMERICAN ORTHOPAEDIC SOCIETY FOR SPORTS MEDICINE
9400 W HIGGINS ROAD
SUITE 300
ROSEMONT, IL 60018
847-292-4900
877-321-3500
Fax: 847-292-4905
www.sportsmed.org

• Irvin E. Bomberger, Executive Director
Description:
Fosters, promotes, supports and augments investigative knowledge of sports medicine and its many ramifications. Develops and encourages the teaching of the same by developing, publishing and copyrighting educational material and providing specialized training for orthopaedic surgeons and others. Encourages education in allied professions in the prevention, recognition and orthopedic treatment of sports injuries.
Membership Requirements:
Five classifications of membership - Active, Associate, Affiliate, Honorary and Emeritus. Active members must be orthopaedic surgeons who are members of American Academy of Orthopaedic Surgeons or Canadian citizens with similar qualifications, and must meet certain other requirements. Associate members must be orthopaedic surgeons either certified by American Board of Orthopaedic Surgery or eligible for certification or Canadian citizens with similar qualifications, and certain other requirements. Affiliate members are non-members of American Academy of Orthopaedic Surgeons or Canadian members with similar qualifications.
Member Services:
Interim Scientific meetings held each winter in conjunction with the American Academy of Orthopaedic Surgeons. Annual meetings held each summer.
Year Founded:
1972

AMERICAN OSTEOPATHIC ACADEMY OF SPORTS MEDICINE
2424 AMERICAN LANE
MADISON, WI 53704
608-443-2477
Fax: 608-443-2474
www.aoasm.org
• R. Scott Cook, President
• Shawn Kerger, Secretary & Treasurer
Description:
Forum for osteopathic sports medicine physicians.
Year Founded:
1984

AMERICAN PHYSICAL THERAPY ASSOCIATION
1111 NORTH FAIRFAX STREET
ALEXANDRIA, VA 22314-1488
703-684-2782
800-999-2782
Fax: 703-706-8536
www.apta.org
• J. Michael Bowers, Chief Executive Officer
Description:
Organization advancing the practice of physical therapy through education and research.

AMERICAN SPORTS MEDICINE INSTITUTE
833 ST. VINCENT'S DRIVE
SUITE 205
BIRMINGHAM, AL 35205
205-918-0000
www.asmi.org
• Lanier Johnson, Executive Director
(205) 918-2127

Services:
Provides medical education for physicians. Publisher of clinical and biomechanical research, surgical procedures, patient follow-up, and literature reviews, and audio/visual materials.
Year Founded:
1987

ANDREWS INSTITUTE FOR ORTHOPAEDICS & SPORTS MEDICINE
1040 GULF BREEZE PARKWAY
GULF BREEZE, FL 32561
850-916-8700
Fax: 850-916-8709
www.andrewsinstitute.com
• David M. Joyner, Executive Director
Year Founded:
2007
Specialty:
Musculoskeletal treatments and research.

ANDREWS SPORTS MEDICINE & ORTHOPEDIC CENTER
www.andrewssportsmedicine.com
Description:
Locations in Birmingham, Hoover and Pelham, Alabama.

ARTHROSCOPY ASSOCIATION OF NORTH AMERICA
9400 W HIGGINS ROAD
SUITE 200
ROSEMONT, IL 60018
847-292-2262
Fax: 847-292-2268
www.aana.org
• Laura M. Downes, Executive Director
Description:
New techniques and information defining the practice of arthroscopic surgery.
Year Founded:
1981

ASPEN ORTHOPAEDIC ASSOCIATES
0401 CASTLE CREEK ROAD
SUITE 2100
ASPEN, CO 81611
970-925-4141
866-925-4141
Fax: 970-925-4233
www.orthop.com
Specialty:
Orthopedic Sports Medicine

ATHLETICO PHYSICAL THERAPY
625 ENTERPRISE DRIVE
OAK BROOK, IL 60523
630-575-6200
Fax: 630-575-7400
info@athletico.com
www.athletico.com
• Mark Kaufman, President
Description:
Physical and occupational therapy.
Year Founded:
1991

AUSTIN SPORTS MEDICINE
900 W 38TH STREET
SUITE 300
AUSTIN, TX 78705
512-450-1300
www.austinsportsmed.com

Specialty:
Comprehensive care for active life style and sports related injuries.

BEACON ORTHOPAEDICS & SPORTS MEDICINE
513-354-3700
888-773-4353
www.beaconortho.com
Description:
Seven locations in the Cincinnati Tri-State area.
Year Founded:
1988

CAMPBELL CLINIC ORTHOPAEDICS
901-759-3100
www.campbellclinic.com
Description:
Five locations in the Memphis area with after hours urgent care clinics at Germantown and Southaven locations.
Year Founded:
1909

CENTER FOR ATHLETIC MEDICINE
830 W DIVERSEY
SUITE 300
CHICAGO, IL 60614
773-248-4150
Fax: 773-248-4291
www.athleticmed.com
• Preston M. Wolin, Director
• Morgan Wolin, Sports Psychologist
Description:
Team Physicians for the Chicago Fire, DePaul University and University Illinois-Chicago.
Specialty:
Orthopedics/sports medicine; Knee, Shoulder, Elbow.
Year Founded:
1991

CHICAGO ORTHOPAEDICS & SPORTS MEDICINE
CHICAGO, IL
773-433-3130
www.chiorthosports.com
• Franni Huspen, Practice Administrator
Services:
Non-surgical procedures, minimally invasive surgery, traditional surgeries and physical therapy.
Year Founded:
1965

CINCINNATI SPORTSMEDICINE & ORTHOPAEDIC CENTER
10663 MONTGOMERY ROAD
CINCINNATI, OH 45242
513-347-9999
Fax: 513-792-3230
info@csmoc.com
www.cincinnatisportsmed.com
• Frank R. Noyes, Founder & Orthopaedic Surgeon
• Mark G. Siegel, Orthopaedic Surgeon
• Thomas N. Lindenfeld, Orthopaedic Surgeon
• Michelle Andrews, Orthopaedic Surgeon
• Marc T. Galloway, Orthopaedic Surgeon
• Samer S. Hasan, Orthopaedic Surgeon
• Matthew L. Busam, Orthopaedic Surgeon
• Sanjeev Bhatia, Orthopaedic Surgeon

• Rebecca E. Popham, Sports Medicine Physician
Board Certified:
Yes.
Fellowship Trained:
Yes.
Specialization:
Treatment of all musculoskeletal injuries, especially the knees and shoulder.
Services:
Specializes in the treatment of orthopaedic and sports injuries of joints and muscles of the knee, shoulder, elbow, ankle and hip. And internationally renown for its Cincinnati SportsMedicine Research and Education Foundation having published over 200 articles and 50 research studies.
Advanced Treatment:
Include meniscus allegrafts, repairs of the posterior cruciate ligament, repairing and reconstructing artifular cartilage in the knee, and complex knee disorders.
Year Founded:
1985

CLEVELAND CLINIC
9500 EUCLID AVENUE
CLEVELAND, OH 44195
800-223-2273
my.clevelandclinic.org
• Delos Cosgrove, President & Chief Executive Officer
Services/Products:
Services include Aging, Geriatrics, Eldercare, Allergy, Alcohol and Drug Dependency, Arthritis, Asthma, Back and Spine, Blood Disorders (Anemias), Breathing Problems, Bones, Joints, Muscles, Sports Injuries, Brain and Nervous System, Breast Disease, Cancer, Circulation, Colorectal Surgery, Diabetes, Endocrine, and Metabolism, Diabetic Foot Care, Digestive Diseases, including Liver, Ears, Nose, Throat and Mouth, Executive Health, Eyes, Gastric Bypass Surgery, General Surgery including Gall Bladder, Genetics and Inherited Diseases, Hearing Problems, Heart Disease, Hernias, Homecare, In Vitro Fertilization, Incontinence, Infertility, Inherited C
Specialty:
Orthopaedic Sports Medicine.
Year Founded:
1921

COASTAL ORTHOPAEDIC & SPORTS MEDICINE CENTER
www.coastal-orthopaedic.com
Services:
Minimally invasive surgery, sports injuries and rehabilitation, fracture care, viscosupplementation, joint replacement, urgent care, workers' compensation.

D1 SPORTS MEDICINE
www.d1sportsmedicine.com
• Geoffrey Connor, Founder & Medical Director
Description:
Integrated rehabilitation and training for a higher level of function post-injury. Locations in AL, AR, CO, FL, KS, KY, MS, NE, OK, TN and TX.

DISC SPORTS & SPINE CENTER
866-481-3472
discmdgroup.com

Description:
DISC is an integrated multidisciplinary practice with three locations in Southern California and is a medical services provider to the Los Angeles Kings and Red Bull North America.
Services:
Conservative and surgical spine and orthopedic care, interventional pain management, chiropractic care and sports medicine.

DMC ORTHOPAEDICS & SPORTS MEDICINE
DETROIT MEDICAL CENTER
3990 JOHN R STREET
DETROIT, MI 48201
313-745-6035
www.dmc.org
• Joe Mullany, President
Description:
The Detroit Medical Center is a network of nine specialty hospitals and is the healthcare services provider of the Detroit Tigers, Detroit Red Wings and Detroit Pistons.
Year Founded:
1886

DR. CHRIS STANKOVICH
1395 GRANDVIEW AVENUE
SUITE 6
COLUMBUS, OH 43212
614-561-4482
information@drstankovich.com
www.drstankovich.com
• Chris Stankovich,
Services:
Provides athletes, coaches, parents, officials, and entire sport organizations with clinical and applied sport science peak performance training and counseling.

ELITE SPORTS MEDICINE & ORTHOPEDICS
www.eliteorthopaedic.com
• Burton Elrod, Founder
Description:
Elite has five locations in the Nashville area.

FONDREN ORTHOPEDIC GROUP
FONDREN MAIN AT TEXAS ORTHOPEDIC HOSPITAL
7401 MAIN STREET
HOUSTON, TX 77030
713-799-2300
Fax: 713-794-3380
www.fondren.com
Description:
The Group operates many offices in the Greater Houston area. Its main location is at Texas Orthopedic Hospital.
Year Founded:
1973

HEALTHSOUTH REHABILITATION
3660 GRANDVIEW PARKWAY
SUITE 200
BIRMINGHAM, AL 35243
205-967-7116
www.healthsouth.com
• Jay Grinney, President & Chief Executive Officer
• Doug Coltharp, EVP & Chief Financial Officer

• Mark J. Tarr, EVP & Chief Operating Officer
Description:
Network of post-acute healthcare service providers operating in 34 states and Puerto Rico.

ILLINOIS BONE & JOINT INSTITUTE
www.ibji.com
Description:
IBJI provides expert care in every orthopedic specialty at 20 locations throughout Chicago.
Year Founded:
1990

JACKSONVILLE ORTHOPAEDIC HOSPITAL
1325 SAN MARCO BOULEVARD
SUITE 701
JACKSONVILLE, FL 32207
904-346-3465
www.joionline.net
Description:
Sports medicine provider for the Jacksonville Jaguars, JOI operates out of six locations in the Jacksonville area.
Specialty:
Hand, foot & ankle, spine, joint replacement, sports medicine and rehabilitation.

KERLAN-JOBE ORTHOPAEDIC CLINIC
6801 PARK TERRACE
LOS ANGELES, CA 90045
310-665-7200
www.kerlanjobe.com
Specialty:
Sports medicine
Services:
Well known procedures that are available include Tendon Repair; Rotator Cuff Repair and Achilles Tendon Repair; Total Joint Replacement: Shoulder, Hip, Knee; Ligament Reconstructions: Tommy John Procedure and ACLR: Anterior Cruciate Ligament Reconstruction; Arthroscopic Surgery: Joint Debridement, Labral Repair, and Partial Menisectomy

KSF ORTHOPAEDIC CENTER
HOUSTON, TX
281-440-6960
www.ksfortho.com
Description:
Two locations serve Northwest Houston.
Services:
Spine & neck, shoulder, hand & wrist, hip, knee, foot & ankle, elbow and sports medicine.

LEMAK SPORTS MEDICINE & ORTHOPEDICS
720 MONTCLAIR ROAD
SUITE 101
BIRMINGHAM, AL 35213
866-252-3618
info@lemakhealth.com
www.lemaksports.com
• Matthew T. Lemak, Chief Executive Officer
Services:
Ankle, knee, elbow, hip, shoulder, spine, concussion clinics and Tenex Health procedure.

LENOX HILL HOSPITAL
100 E 77TH STREET
NEW YORK, NY 10075
212-434-2000
www.northwell.edu
• Michael J. Dowling, President & Chief Executive Officer
Specialty:
Internal medicine, cardiovascular disease, orthopaedics, sports medicine, otolaryngology/head and neck surgery and maternal/child health.
Services:
Anesthesiology, Cardiothoracic Surgery, Interventional Cardiology, Medicine, Medicine - Dermatology, Medicine - Division of Allergy & Immunology, Medicine - Division of Cardiovascular Disease, Medicine - Division of Critical Care Medicine, Medicine - Division of Emergency Services, Medicine - Division of Endocrinology/Metabolism, Medicine - Division of Gastroenterology, Medicine - Division of Hematology & Medical Oncology, Medicine - Division of Infectious Disease, Medicine - Division of Internal Medicine/Primary Care, Medicine - Division of Nephrology, Medicine - Division of Neurology, Medicine.

MAYO CLINIC SPORTS MEDICINE
600 HENNEPIN AVENUE
MINNEAPOLIS, MN 55403
612-313-0520
sportsmedicine.mayoclinic.org
• Michael Stuart, Co-Director
• Edward Laskowski, Co-Director
• Jonathan Finnoff, Medical Director
Specialty:
Sports medicine
Services:
Sports and musculoskeletal injury prevention and rehabilitation.

MEDICAL CENTER ARLINGTON
3301 MATLOCK ROAD
ARLINGTON, TX 76015
817-465-3241
medicalcenterarlington.com
• Winston Borland, President & Chief Executive Officer
Year Founded:
1976

MEDSTAR UNION MEMORIAL SPORTS MEDICINE
201 E UNIVERSITY PARKWAY
BALTIMORE, MD 21218
410-554-2000
www.medstarunionmemorial.org
• Bradley S. Chambers, President
Services:
Regional center for sports medicine.
Clients:
Official medical team of the Baltimore Ravens.

MEMORIAL MEDICAL CENTER
701 N FIRST STREET
SPRINGFIELD, IL 62781
217-788-3000
www.memorialmedical.com
• Edgar J. Curtis, President & Chief Executive Officer
• Charles D. Callahan, EVP & Chief Operating Officer

• Rajesh G. Govindaiah, SVP & Chief Medical Officer
Services:
Cancer Services, Cardiovascular Services, Emergency Services, General Services, Home Health Care, Imaging Services, Orthopedic & Rehabilitation Services, Outpatient Services, Pediatric Services, Surgical Services, Wellness Programs, Women's Services

METHODIST SPORTS MEDICINE
201 PENNSYLVANIA PARKWAY
SUITE 100
INDIANAPOLIS, IN 46280
317-817-1200
Description:
Official team physicians for the Indianapolis Colts since 1984.
Specialty:
Concussion management, foot & ankle, hand, wrist & elbow, hip, joint replacement & arthritis, knee, pediatric sports medicine, physical medicine & rehabilitation, shoulder, spine, sports performance and workers compensation.
Year Founded:
1984

MICHIGAN ORTHOPAEDIC INSTITUTE
248-663-1927
www.moimd.com

MIDWEST ORTHOPAEDICS AT RUSH
877-632-6637
www.rushortho.com
Description:
Regional center for orthopedic services and team physicians to the Chicago Bulls, Chicago White Sox and Chicago Fire Soccer Club.

NATIONAL ACADEMY OF SPORTS MEDICINE
1750 E NORTHROP BOULEVARD
SUITE 200
CHANDLER, AZ 85286-1744
800-460-6276
Fax: 480-656-3276
www.nasm.org
• Andrew Wyant, President & General Manager
Services:
Assessment, Optimum Performance Training, Recovery & Regeneration, Professional Consulting
Description:
Certification, continuing education and tools for personal trainers.
Member Services:
Job opportunities, referrals, insurance (liability and health), discounts from equipment manufacturers, and travel discounts.
Year Founded:
1987

NATIONAL ATHLETIC TRAINERS' ASSOCIATION
1620 VALWOOD PARKWAY
SUITE 115
CARROLLTON, TX 75006
214-637-6282
Fax: 214-637-2206
www.nata.org
• Dave Saddler, Executive Director

Description:
Professional association of athletic trainers dedicated to enhancing the quality of health care they provide.
Year Founded:
1950
Members:
35,000.

NATIONAL CENTER FOR SPORTS SAFETY
1286 OAK GROVE ROAD
BIRMINGHAM, AL 35209
205-329-7535
866-508-6277
info@SportsSafety.org
www.sportssafety.org
• Lawrence Lemak, Founder
Description:
The NCSS is dedicated to the promotion of injury prevention and safety in youth sports.

NATIONAL SPORTS MEDICINE INSTITUTE
19455 DEERFIELD AVENUE
SUITE 312
LANSDOWNE, VA 20176
703-729-5010
Fax: 703-729-5833
contact@nationalsportsmed.com
www.nationsportsmed.com
Description:
State-of-the-art sports injury evaluation & treatment, diagnostic imaging and physical therapy in Lansdowne, Virginia.
Specialty:
Elbow, shoulder, knee, hip, ankle, sports medicine, wellness & human performance.

NATIONAL STRENGTH AND CONDITIONING ASSOCIATION
1885 BOB JOHNSON DRIVE
COLORADO SPRINGS, CO 80906
719-632-6722
800-815-6826
Fax: 719-632-6367
nsca@nsca.com
www.nsca.com
• Lee Madden, Sr. Director of Administrative Services
Description:
The Association exists to support the practical application of the latest research-based knowledge.
Year Founded:
1978

NEBRASKA ORTHOPAEDIC & SPORTS MEDICINE
CHI ST. ELIZABETH MEDICAL BUILDING
575 SOUTH 70TH STREET
SUITE 200
LINCOLN, NE 68510
402-488-3322
Fax: 402-488-1172
nebraskaortho.com
Services:
Foot & ankle, fracture clinic, general orthopaedics, hand & wrist, joint replacement, shoulder, spine care and sports medicine.

NEW ENGLAND BAPTIST HOSPITAL
125 PARKER HILL AVENUE
BOSTON, MA 02120

617-754-5000
www.nebh.org
• Trish Hannon, President & CEO
• Thomas Gheringhelli, Vice President, Finance
Services:
New England Baptist Hospital is the regional center for orthopedic surgery and musculoskeletal diseases and disorders.
Clients:
NEBH has been the official and exclusive hospital of the Boston Celtics for over 26 years.
Specialty:
Orthopaedic Surgery

NORTHWEST ORTHOPEDICS & SPORTS MEDICINE
350 HERITAGE WAY
SUITE 1200
KALISPELL, MT 59901
406-752-6784
Fax: 406-756-4111
www.kalispellregional.org

NYU LANGONE HOSPITAL FOR JOINT DISEASES
301 E 17TH STREET
NEW YORK, NY 10003
212-598-6000
nyulangone.org
• Robert I. Grossman, Chief Executive Officer
Services:
Provides the highest quality of surgical and therapeutic care in the treatment, rehabilitation, and prevention of musculoskeletal, rheumatic, immunological, neurological, and other related diseases and injuries. Programs and services include Ambulatory Care Services, Center for Arthritis & Autoimmunity, Diabetes Foot and Ankle Center, Harkness Dance Center, Initiative for Women with Disabilities, Occupational and Industrial Orthopedic Center, Osteoporosis Center, Comprehensive Pain Treatment Center, The Center for Children, Adult Orthopedic Service, Adult Reconstructive Services, Foot & Ankle Service, Trauma Fracture Service, Hand Service.
Year Founded:
1905

ORTHOCAROLINA
www.orthocarolina.com
• Daniel Murrey, Chief Executive Officer
• Steve Hendrick, Chief Operating Officer
• Jennifer Schenk, Chief Counsel & Chief Compliance Officer
• Brent Shear, Chief Financial Officer
Description:
Comprehensive musculoskeletal care.
Year Founded:
1922

ORTHOINDY
317-802-2000
orthoindy.com
Description:
Orthopedic practice in Central Indiana with more than 10 locations. Medical services provider to the Indiana Pacers.

ORTHOPAEDIC & SPORTS MEDICINE CENTER OF OREGON
orthosportsmed.com
Services:
Fracture care, joint reconstruction and arthroscopy.

ORTHOPAEDIC AND SPORTS MEDICINE CLINIC OF KANSAS CITY
3651 COLLEGE BOULEVARD
SUITE 100A
LEAWOOD, KS 66211
913-319-7500
www.osmckc.com
Services:
Cartilage restoration and repair, ligament reconstruction of the knee and knee replacement, shoulder surgery and replacement, elbow surgery and platelet rich plasma therapy.

ORTHOPAEDIC RESEARCH OF VIRGINIA
PO BOX 71690
RICHMOND, VA 23255-1690
804-527-5960
Fax: 804-527-5961
www.orv.com
• John F. Meyers, Physician
(804) 285-2300
• William R. Beach, Physician
(804) 285-2300
• Shannon Wolfe, Physician
(804) 285-2300
• Paul E. Caldwell, Physician
Services:
Performs various functions to advance musculoskeletal care, teaching, and research. Sponsors a one year fellowship in arthroscopy and sports medicine for residency-trained orthopaedic surgeons. Maintains a modern cadaver lab fully equipped with traditional and arthroscopic surgical instruments. Sponsors periodic educational programs for practicing orthopaedic surgeons and coordinates team coverage for local high school and collegiate athletic programs.

ORTHOPEDIC & SPORTS MEDICINE SPECIALISTS OF GREEN BAY
2223 LIME KILN ROAD
SUITE 1
GREEN BAY, WI 54311
920-430-8113
800-310-3877
Fax: 920-430-8124
www.osmsgb.com
Specialty:
Orthopedic and rheumatologic care.
Year Founded:
1963

ORTHOPEDIC ASSOCIATES OF HARTFORD
85 SEYMOUR STREET
SUITE 607
HARTFORD, CT 06106-5500
860-549-3210
www.oahct.com
Description:
Physicians providing comprehensive orthopedic and musculoskeletal healthcare.
Specialty:
Orthopedic surgery
Year Founded:
1970

ORTHOPEDIC PHYSICIAN ASSOCIATES
601 BROADWAY
SEATTLE, WA
www.opaortho.com
Description:
Regional center for orthopedic and musculoskeletal care. Medical services provider to the Seattle Mariners and Seattle Seahawks.
Year Founded:
1958

PEACHTREE ORTHOPAEDIC CLINIC
ATLANTA, GA
404-355-0743
www.pocatlanta.com
Description:
POC's clinics, rehabilitation locations and MRI facilities deliver a range of orthopaedic services to the Atlanta community. POC is the orthopaedic care provider to the Atlanta Braves and the Atlanta Hawks.
Year Founded:
1953

PHOENIX ORTHOPEDIC GROUP
602-277-1558
Description:
POG operates orthopedic surgery clinics in Phoenix and Scottsdale.
Specialty:
Orthopedic surgery, osteoporosis and osteoarthritis care, sports medicine and arthroplasty.

RESURGENS SPORTS MEDICINE CENTER
ATLANTA, GA
www.resurgenssportsmedicine.com
Description:
Georgia's largest orthopaedic practice.
Specialty:
Muscle strain, bone fracture, tendinitis, joint or ligament strain/tears, joint dislocation and MCL/ACL injuries.

ROTHMAN INSTITUTE
925 CHESTNUT STREET
5TH FLOOR
PHILADELPHIA, PA 19107
800-321-9999
www.rothmaninstitute.com
• Richard H. Rothman, Founder
• Alexander R. Vaccaro, President
Description:
Rothman Institute has twenty offices in the Greater Philadelphia area.
Specialty:
Sport medicine, rehabilitation, fracture care and orthopaedic oncology.

RUSH UNIVERSITY MEDICAL CENTER - SPORTS MEDICINE PROGRAM
1653 W CONGRESS PARKWAY
CHICAGO, IL 60612
888-352-7874
www.rush.edu
Description:
The pioneering specialists at Rush treat both the most common and the most complex conditions in athletes of all ages.

SLOCUM CENTER FOR ORTHOPEDICS & SPORTS MEDICINE
55 COBURG ROAD
EUGENE, OR 97401

541-485-8111
800-866-7906
Fax: 541-342-6379
www.slocumcenter.com
Specialty:
Ankle, elbow, foot, hand, hip, knee, shoulder, wrist, sports medicine.
Services:
MRI, digital X-ray, bone density/bone health, therapy center, on-site pharmacy.
Year Founded:
1939

SOUTHERN CALIFORNIA ORTHOPEDIC INSTITUTE
6815 NOBLE AVENUE
VAN NUYS, CA 91405
818-901-6600
moreinfo@scoi.com
www.scoi.com
Description:
Regional center for bone, joint and muscle injuries as well as musculoskeletal and spine disorders.
Specialty:
Orthopedic surgery
Services:
Provides a comprehensive range of orthopedic services, including Arthroscopic Surgery Sports Medicine, Worker's Compensation Injuries Knee Surgery, Shoulder Surgery Foot and Ankle Surgery, Hip Surgery Microsurgery and Limb Replantation, Hand and Upper Extremity Surgery, Arthritis Diagnosis and Treatment, Physical Medicine Total Joint Replacement, Fracture and Trauma Care Spinal Surgery & Scoliosis Treatment, Pediatric & Adolescent Orthopedics Electrodiagnostic Evaluations.

SOUTHERN ORTHOPAEDICS & SPORTS MEDICINE
3231 GLYNN AVENUE
BRUNSWICK, GA 31520
912-265-9006
Fax: 912-265-7200
www.sosmga.com
• Burton F. Elrod, Owner
Specialty:
Sports medicine
Services:
Orthopaedic specialties, particularly arthroscopic surgery, sports medicine/athletic injuries, reconstructive surgery of the knee, shoulder and elbow, surgical and non-surgical care of athletic injuries, spine surgery, joint replacement surgery, revision surgery for total joint problems, treatment of fractures, surgery of the hand, upper extremity/repetitive motion problems, and surgery of the foot and ankle.

SPORTS & ORTHOPAEDIC SPECIALISTS
952-946-9777
www.sportsandortho.com
Description:
Orthopedic surgery and sports medicine practice in Minneapolis and medical care provider to the Minnesota Twins.
Year Founded:
1999

SPORTS MEDICINE ASSOCIATES
TEXAS CENTER FOR ATHLETES
21 SPURS LANE
SUITE 300
SAN ANTONIO, TX 78240

210-699-8326
info@smasatx.com
sportsmedsa.com
Specialty:
Sports medicine, orthopaedics, concussion management, ligament repair and joint replacement.

SPORTS PHYSICAL THERAPY SECTION
PO BOX 431
ZIONSVILLE, IN 46077-431
877-732-5009
Fax: 317-669-8276
spts.org
• Mark S. De Carlo, Executive Director
• Mary Wilkinson, Director of Marketing
Description:
A component member of the American Physical Therapy Association, the SPTS is a forum for Association members with an interest in sports PT practice.

SPORTS, ORTHOPEDIC & REHABILITATION MEDICINE ASSOCIATES
650-851-4900
soarmedical.com
Description:
SOAR is a medical care provider for the San Francisco Giants.
Specialty:
Sports medicine, arthroscopy, ligament reconstruction, hand & foot surgery, joint replacement and pediatric and adolescent sports medicine.
Services:
Sports medicine, joint replacement, diagnostic radiology, spine rehabilitation, arthritis treatment and fracture care.

STAY IN THE ZONE
1060 MAIN STREET
SUITE 307
RIVER EDGE, NJ 07661
888-580-9663
Fax: 201-342-2258
stayinthezone.com
• Jay P. Granat, Founder
Description:
Sports psychology programs for athletes from many sports.
Year Founded:
1978
Teams:
High School, College, Professional

STEADMAN HAWKINS CLINIC - DENVER
8200 E BELLEVIEW AVENUE
SUITE 615
GREENWOOD VILLAGE, CO 80111
303-694-3333
Fax: 303-694-9666
www.shcdenver.com
Specialty:
Sports medicine & performance, physical & occupational therapy, upper extremity, hip & knee and foot & ankle.

STOP SPORTS INJURIES
9400 W HIGGINS ROAD
SUITE 300
ROSEMONT, IL 60018
847-655-8660
info@stopsportsinjuries.org
www.stopsportsinjuries.org

Description:
Stop Sports Injuries offers sport specific injury prevention resources for athletes, coaches, parents and healthcare providers.
Year Founded:
2008

TEMPLE ORTHOPAEDICS & SPORTS MEDICINE
MEDICAL OFFICE BUILDING
8815 GERMANTOWN PIKE
SUITE 14
PHILADELPHIA, PA 19118
215-248-9400
Fax: 215-248-9403
ortho.templehealth.org
• Eric J. Kropf, Chair
Specialty:
Regional center for the treatment of musculoskeletal disorders with five offices in the Philadelphia area.
Services:
Arthritis care, athletic care and treatment of spinal disorders as well as fractures, foot and ankle problems and hand, wrist and elbow pain.

TEXAS SPORTS MEDICINE & ORTHOPAEDIC GROUP
214-369-7733
Fax: 214-369-7739
www.txsportsmed.com

THE AMERICAN PHYSIOLOGICAL SOCIETY
9650 ROCKVILLE PIKE
BETHESDA, MD 20814-3991
301-634-7164
Fax: 301-634-7241
www.the-aps.org
• Patricia E. Molina, President
Description:
The Society is dedicated to fostering education, research and the dissemination of information in the physiological sciences.
Year Founded:
1887

THE CARRELL CLINIC
9301 NORTH CENTRAL EXPRESSWAY
TOWER ONE
SUITE 500
DALLAS, TX 75231
214-220-2468
Fax: 469-232-9738
info@carrellclinic.com
www.carrellclinic.com
Specialty:
Pediatric orthopedics, sports injuries and arthroscopy.
Year Founded:
1921

THE ORTHOPAEDIC & SPORTS MEDICINE CENTER
888 WHITE PLAINS ROAD
TRUMBULL, CT 06611
203-268-2882
www.osmcenter.com
Services:
Hand, foot, ankle, knee, spine, hip and shoulder surgery. Joint reconstruction, podiatry and chiropractic care.
Year Founded:
1994

THE ORTHOPEDIC CENTER
410-820-8226
800-464-8226
Fax: 410-820-8405
www.theorthopediccenter.net
Description:
Multidisciplinary bone and joint care.
Year Founded:
1971

THE ORTHOPEDIC SPECIALTY HOSPITAL
5848 S FASHION BOULEVARD
MURRAY, UT 84107
801-314-4100
intermountainhealthcare.org
Services:
Orthopedic, physical therapy, sports medicine and sports training services.

THE STEADMAN CLINIC
181 W MEADOW DRIVE
VAIL, CO 81657
970-476-1100
thesteadmanclinic.com
• J. Richard Steadman, Founder & Managing Partner
• Marc J. Philippon, Managing Partner
Specialty:
Injuries of the knee, hip, shoulder, elbow, hand & wrist, foot & ankle and spine & neck.

THE STONE CLINIC
3727 BUCHANAN STREET
SUITE 300
SAN FRANCISCO, CA 94123
415-563-3110
www.stoneclinic.com

TRI-COUNTY ORTHOPEDICS
THE ADVANCED MEDICAL CENTER
197 RIDGEDALE AVENUE
SUITE 300
CEDAR KNOLLS, NJ 07927
973-538-2334
Fax: 973-829-9174
www.tri-countyortho.com

TRIA ORTHOPAEDIC CENTER
8100 NORTHLAND DRIVE
BLOOMINGTON, MN 55431
952-831-8742
tria.com
Services:
Sports medicine, physical therapy, orthotics & prosthetics, diagnostic imaging, bone densitometry and ambulatory surgery.

TRIHEALTH
619 OAK STREET
CINCINNATI, OH 45206
513-569-6111
www.trihealth.com
Description:
Regional network of sports medicine physicians, physical therapists and trainers. Medical services provider to the Cincinnati Bengals and Cincinnati Reds.

U.S. CENTER FOR SPORTS MEDICINE
333 S KIRKWOOD ROAD
SUITE 200
ST. LOUIS, MO 63122
314-909-1666
Fax: 314-909-7406

UBMD ORTHOPAEDICS & SPORTS MEDICINE
5500 MAIN STREET
SUITE 107
WILLIAMSVILLE, NY 14221
716-204-3200
contact@ubortho.com
www.ubortho.com
Description:
Team doctors to many high school and college teams in Western New York as well as professional teams such as the Buffalo Bills and Buffalo Sabres.

UHZ SPORTS MEDICINE INSTITUTE
786-268-6208
www.uhzsmi.com
Services:
Sports medicine; orthopedic, arthroscopic, knee, shoulder, elbow and ankle surgery.

UK HEALTHCARE ORTHOPAEDICS & SPORTS MEDICINE
800 ROSE STREET
ROOM C101
LEXINGTON, KY 40536
859-257-1000
800-333-8874
ukhealthcare.uky.edu
Description:
UK HealthCare is the brand name of the University of Kentucky's health care system offering advanced patient care to the people of Kentucky.
Year Founded:
1957

UNIVERSITY OF FLORIDA ORTHOPAEDICS & SPORT MEDICINE INSTITUTE
3450 HULL ROAD
GAINESVILLE, FL 32607
352-273-7002
Fax: 352-273-7293
www.ortho.ufl.edu
Description:
Orthopaedic care, rehabilitation and radiological services at the University of Florida College of Medicine.

UPMC SPORTS MEDICINE
200 LOTHROP STREET
PITTSBURGH, PA 15213-2582
412-647-8762
800-533-8762
www.upmc.com
Description:
Sports medicine provider for the Pittsburgh Penguins and Pittsburgh Steelers.
Services:
Athletic training; concussion, imaging, performance, bone & joint services; Young Athlete program.

VIRGINIA INSTITUTE FOR SPORTS MEDICINE
1849 OLD DONATION PARKWAY
VIRGINIA BEACH, VA 23454
757-422-8476
Description:
Providing surgical and non-surgical treatment of adult and pediatric patients.
Year Founded:
2003

WASHINGTON ORTHOPAEDICS & SPORTS MEDICINE
WASHINGTON, DC
www.wosm.com
• Laura Jensen, Chief Executive & Operating Officer

WELLINGTON ORTHOPAEDIC & SPORTS MEDICINE
CINCINNATI, OH
513-232-2663
wellingtonortho.com
Specialty:
Sports medicine, general orthopedics, joint replacement and concussion.
Year Founded:
1968

Sports Travel Services

AMATEUR SPORTS TRAVEL GROUP, INC
3808 OAK FOREST DRIVE
HIGH POINT, NC 27265
336-869-5954
888-541-5810
Fax: 888-541-5810
www.travel4sports.com
Services:
The world's largest sport travel directory aimed directly at youth and adult amateur athletes of all ages. It provides a discount travel source, free of charge for amateur athletes, parents, and coaches and intends to link amateur athletes with national sponsors who will offer discounts on travel, food, goods, and services to enhance and promote the world of amateur sports.

AMERICA OUTDOORS/AO
PO BOX 10847
KNOXVILLE, TN 37939
865-558-3595
800-524-4814
Fax: 865-558-3598
www.americaoutdoors.org
• Julie Kahlfeldt, Executive Director
• Robin Brown, Communications Director
Nature of Service:
A national association representing adventure travel outfitters, tour companies and outdoor educators, the mission of America Outdoors is supporting and developing outfitting businesses in the United States.

AMJ CAMPBELL
100 MILVERTON DRIVE
SUITE 830
MISSISSAUGA, ON, CANADA L5R-4H1
905-795-3785
888-AMJ-MOVE
Fax: 905-670-3787
contact@amjcampbell.com
www.amjcampbell.com
• Bruce D. Bowser, President/Chief Executive Officer
• Denis Cordick, VP Marketing
• Brian Farquhar, EVP Of Operations
• Bruce Bowser, President/CEO
• Dennis Frappier, President, Self Storage and Business develop
• Denis Cordick, VP, Marketing
Services
Official Mover for: BC Lions, Hamilton Tiger Cats, Winnipeg Blue Bombers; Toronto

Maple Leafs; Canada Soccer Association; Toronto Raptors; Western Mustangs; Canadian Curling Association; World Curling Tour.

AMTRAK
60 MASSACHUSETTS AVENUE NE
SUITE 4E-315
WASHINGTON, DC 20002
202-906-3000
800-872-7245
Fax: 202-906-3560
mediarelations@amtrak.com
www.amtrak.com
• Joseph H. Boardman, President/Chief Executive Officer
• Linda Park, National Marketing Group Manager
(202) 906-4825
• Barbara Richardson, Executive Vice President
(202) 906-3610
• Karen Dunn, Media Relations Director
Regional Offices:
West - Oakland, CA; Midwest - Chicago, IL; Northeast - New York; South - New Orleans.

ANTHONY TRAVEL, INC.
7920 BELT LINE ROAD
SUITE 1010
DALLAS, TX 75254
214-363-0073
800-736-6377
Fax: 214-363-1180
www.anthonytravel.com
• Tina Acosta, International Travel Consultant
tinaacosta@anthonytravel.com
• Jean Anthony, Director, Notre Dame Events
• Normajean Baxter, Event Coordinator
normajeanbaxter@anthonytravel.com
• Dee An Bell, Marketing Manager
deeannbell@anthonytravel.com
Services:
Provides personal, professional travel service to all our clients, regardless of the size of the request.

AVIS RENT A CAR SYSTEM
6 SYLVAN WAY
PARSIPPANY, NJ 7054
973-496-3500
800-352-7900
Fax: 973-496-7584
www.avis.com
• Ronald L. Nelson, Chairman/CEO
• David B Wyshner, Sr.Executive VP, Chief Financial Officer
• Larry De Shon, President, EMEA
• Scott Deaver, Executive VP of Strategy
• Thomas M Gartland, President,North America
• Mark J Servodidio, Executive VP and Chief Administrative Officer
• Gerard Insall, Sr.VP and CIO
• Ronald L Nelson, Chairman/Chief Operating Officer
Services:
MLB - New York Yankees Official rental car company

BLUE BIRD CORPORATION
402 BLUE BIRD BOULEVARD
PO BOX 937
FORT VALLEY, GA 31030
478-825-2021
800-486-7122
Fax: 478-822-2467
info@blue-bird.com
www.blue-bird.com
• Drew Hawkins, National Sales Manager
(770) 751-6755
wdhawkin@blue-bird.com
• Chris Payne, Bid and Contracts Administrator
(478) 822-2566
cdpayne@blue-bird.com
• Glenn Wilder, Sales Administration Manager
(478) 822-2904
ghwilder@blue-bird.com
• Phil Horlock, President nad CEO
• John Kwapis, Chief Operating Officer
• Dale Wendell, Senior VP of Global Bus Sales and marketing
• Phil Tighe, Chief Financial officer
• Steve Girardin, President and CEO
Products:
Provides innovative design and manufacturing of school buses, commercial buses and motor coaches.

BUSBANK
200 W ADAMS STREET
SUITE 1100
CHICAGO, IL 60606
312-476-6100
866-428-7226
Fax: 312-577-0947
sales@busbank.com
www.busbank.com/sportstravel/
• William R. Maulsby, President/CEO
• Don Sivesind, Vice President Sales
Nature of Services:
The BusBank is a group and event transportation specialist, services of which includes motorcoaches, school buses, mini buses, executive and sleeper coaches and other specialty vehicles, such as trolleys and double decker buses.

CAREY WORLDWIDE CHAUFFERED SERVICES
4530 WISCONSIN AVENUE NW
WASHINGTON, DC 20016
202-895-1200
800-336-4646
Fax: 904-223-9698
Customercare@carey.com
www.carey.com
• Diane M Ennist, Sr.VP,General Counsel
• Rae D Fawcett, Sr.VP, Organisational Development and Human C
• Sally A Snead, Sr.Vp, Operations
• Joel J Barch, VP, Customer Experience
• Yolanda Carneiro, VP,Sales Development
• Gary L Kessler, President/CEO
• Mitchell J Lahr, Executive VP and Chief Financial Officer
Services:
Official Ground Transportation for the Gator Bowl.

CARLSON TRAVEL NETWORK
701 CARLSON PARKWAY
PO BOX 59159
MINNETONKA, MN 55305
763-212-5000
800-213-7295
Fax: 763-212-6664
info@carlson.com
www.carlson.com
• Marilyn C. Nelson, Chairman
• Curtis C. Nelson, President and Chief Operating Officer
cnelson@carlson.com
• Trudy Rautio, EVP and Chief Financial Officer
trautio@carlson.com
• Jeffrey Balagna, EVP and Chief Information and Customer
jbalagna@carlson.com
Services:
Known as a global leader in the marketing, travel, and hospitality industries.
Brands:
Among the names in the Carlson family of brands and services are: Regent International Hotels r; Radisson Hotels & Resorts r; Park Plaza Hotels & Resorts; Country Inns & Suites By Carlson; Park Innr hotels; Radisson Seven Seas Cruisesr; T.G.I. Friday'sr and Pick Up Stixr restaurants; Carlson Wagonlit Travel; Cruise Holidays; All Aboard Travel; Cruise Specialists; Fly4Less.com; CruiseDeals.com; Results Travel; Carlson Destination Marketing Services; Carlson Leisure Travel Services; SeaMaster Cruisesr; SinglesCruise.comr; CW Government Travel; Carlson Marketingr; Peppers & Rogers Groupr; and Gold Points Reward Network.
Travel Services:
Team travel, special event travel, sports meetings and conventions, special event tour packages.
Sports Service Founded:
1986

CORPORATE AMERICA AVIATION, INC.
PO BOX 1978
BURBANK, CA 91507-1978
818-953-7206
800-521-8585
Fax: 818-563-2368
privatebizjets@aol.com
www.privatebizjets.com
• Daniel A. Darwish, President
Specializes in:
Private aircraft transportation for special events, promotional or personal tours; executive and celebrity travel, late-night flights. Worldwide scope of service.
Year Founded:
1989

FORSYTHE & ASSOCIATES, INC.
7770 FRONTAGE ROAD
SKOKIE, IL 60077
847-213-7000
800-843-4488
info@forsythe.com
www.forsythe.com
• Richard A. Forsythe, Chairman
• William P. Brennan, President
wbrennan@forsythe.com
• Albert L. Weiss, Chief Financial Officer
• William P. Brennan, President & CEO
Event Management Services:
Specializes in providing management of all transportation for sports events, serving the needs of event producers, sponsors and broadcast media. Services include motor pool development, ground transportation and shuttle systems.
Services:
Technology infrastructure solutions provider, technology and business consulting

services, leasing services, and value-added reseller services for all of the leading technology product manufacturers.

Services:
Provides technology and business consulting services, technology leasing services, and value-added reseller services for all of the leading technology product manufacturers.

Clients:
AFLAC, Archipelago, Education Management Corporation, H&R Block, NASDAQ, Outback Steakhouse, Snap-on Incorporated, Trizetto, US Bancorp, Visiting Nurse Service of New York

GO WITH A PRO, INC.
38 MILLER AVENUE P M B 241
MILL VALLEY, CA 94941
415-383-3907
• Tim Fitzpatrick, Cofounder/President/Chief Executive Officer
• Scot Schmidt, Co-Founder/Athlete Relations VP
• Jay Orlando, Co-Founder/Operations VP
• Robert Weaver, Surfing Director
Description:
We offer access to over 100 world-class professionals across a variety of today's most popular outdoor sports including skiing, snowboarding, surfing, climbing and mountain biking.
Services:
Provides a full line of services for companies looking to identify their products and corporate image with an active, exciting lifestyle. GowithaPro not only provides easy web-based access to an incredible pool of elite athletes ranging from Olympic heroes to action sport legends but also offers a complete line of professional services.

HAKINS MEETINGS & INCENTIVES
239 MADISON AVENUE
WYCKOFF, NJ 7481
201-848-7678
800-643-3977
Fax: 201-848-9210
info@hakins.com
www.hakins.com
• Paul Smith, President
psmith@hakins.com
• Florio Gay, VP
• Judy Zanetti, Director of Accounts
Other Locations:
Hakins West, 3541 Calle Gavanzo, Carlsbad CA 92009. 800 869-1873; FAX: 760 634-3219. E-Mail: bginnhakinswest@msn.com; William S. Ginn, Dir Bus Dev
Services:
Provides professional support in the design and execution of exceptionally successful group travel programs, supported by state-of-the-art group travel technology solutions. Delivers sound, value-based solutions to corporations involved in moving groups of people for meetings, incentives, promotions, hospitality, special events or sporting events.
Clients:
Weichert Realtors, Verizon, Ryan Partnership, Action/Emco
Sports Service Founded:
1986
Event Management Services:
Sports hospitality, special events, travel

fulfillment of promotions, meetings, group and individual incentive travel.

HARMON TRAVEL SERVICE
1529 W WASHINGTON STREET
BOISE, ID 83702
208-388-3000
800-627-1315
Fax: 208-388-3003
vacations@harmontravel.com
www.harmontravel.com
• David Harmon, Group Dept Manager
• Mary E Cook, Corporate Dept Manager
• Kathleen Kelley, Accounting Manager
• Amee Bybee, Leisure Travel Consultant
• Anne Connors, Leisure Travel Consultant
• Bob E. Harmon, President, MCC, CTC
BobH@harmontravel.com
• Eleanor Harmon, Co-Founder

LUXECONCIERGE
404 CAMINO DEL RIO S
SUITE 601
SAN DIEGO, CA 92108
619-234-7766
800-964-6887
Fax: 619-234-2587
• Cynthia D. Adkins, Founder/President
• Jennifer Hecker, Operations Director
• Karen S. Somers, Conference Services Director
Services:
Provider of of luxury and corporate concierge services.
Description:
LuxeConcierge is a worldwide full service concierge and travel organization. A complete travel service. Skilled in booking, dinner reservations, local hotspots, tickets for sold out shows and events, car service, rental car booking, corporate travel gifts. Complete coordination and luxury.
Event Packages Include:
Super Bowl. NBA All-Star. Olympics. Final Four. The Masters. Wimbledon. World Series. Daytona 500. Ibiza. Essence Music Fest. Mardi Gras. Carnival. Cannes and more.
Services Include:
Travel Planning, Concierge Services, Event Tickets & Packages, Event Planning, Personal Shopping.

NEW DIRECTIONS
131 OLIVER STREET
BOSTON, MA 02110-3620
617-523-7775
Fax: 617-357-6482
info@newdirections.com
• David D. Corbett, Chief Executive Officer / Director
dcorbett@newdirections.com
• Jeffrey D. Redmond, President / Director
jredmond@newdirections.com
• Patricia B. Baillieul, VP
• Michael D. Jeans, President and Senior Consultant
• David D. Corbett, Founder and Senior Consultant
(617) 624-3333
dcorbett@newdirections.com
• Jeffrey D. Redmond, Partner, Director, and Senior Consultant
(617) 624-3334
• Patricia D. Smith, Senior Vice President
(617) 624.3359
• Samuel C. Pease, Vice President and

Senior Consultant
(617) 624-3302
Description:
Pre-eminent provider of career transition services exclusively for senior-level executives, professionals and their families. Helping clients find and create opportunities that not only meet their near-term career expectations and needs, but also advance their long-term work and life goals.
Year Founded:
1986

SENTIENT
100 GROSSMAN DRIVE
4TH FLOOR
WEYMOUTH, MA 02184
866-307-3684
800-760-4908
Fax: 631-756-0809
anicholas@sentientflight.com
www.sentient.com
• Steve M. Hankin, Chief Executive Officer
(866) 307-3684
• Tom Davis, President and Chief Executive Officer, A
(866) 307-3684
• John Bax, Chief Financial Officer
(866) 307-3684
• Charles Starkowsky, Chief Safety Officer
(866) 307-3684
Services:
Pioneers a unique membership program that offers the most flexible private jet solution for both individuals and corporations.

SEVEN CONTINENTS SPORTS, INC.
2340 S RIVER ROAD
DES PLAINES, IL 60018
847-699-8064
Sports Service Founded:
1985

SKYQUEST CHARTERS
1140 CORPORATE BOULEVARD
RENO, NV 89502-2330
775-746-5555
Fax: 775-746-5551
www.skyquestcharters.com
• Kevin Gustafson, Chief Executive Officer
Services:
Serves tour operators, travel agents, cruise lines, collegiate sports teams and bands, and thousands of football fans. Fortune 500 companies, travel and leisure groups, also make up a small portion of its clientele.

SNOWMOBILE ADVENTURES
PO BOX 4167
DURANGO, CO 81302
970-259-7293
Fax: 970-749-5522
www.snowmobileadventures.com
• Pete Busby, Owner
Description:
Dispatch Snowmobile tours.

SNOWMOBILE ADVENTURES BCD, LC
1240 HARROP STREET
OGDEN, UT 84404-4641
801-394-5448
Description:
Rent our Snowmobiles, and provide guides for snowmobiling and racing.

SPORTS DESTINATION NETWORK, INC.
6501 E GREENWAY PARKWAY
SUITE 103-625
SCOTTSDALE, AZ 85254
480-767-3900
Fax: 480-767-6061
www.sdninc.com
• Dirk Smith, President/Founder
dsmith@sdninc.com
• Michelle McNally, Executive Asst
Services:
Services include: a) Initiate and formulate the site selection process of group events/meetings; b) Deliver collateral materials and SDN comments/information regarding potential hotels; c) Coordinate for client all appointment scheduling for any personal site inspection visits; d) Take responsibility for contract negotiation directly with hotels, yet the client signs the contracts for complete control, and; e) Assist with any ancillary requirements for group meetings (buses, limos, golf tournament, guest speaker, etc).
Clients:
Clients: 1) SPORTS WEAR / EQUIPMENT MANUFACTURERS, DISTRIBUTORS: Adidas America, Converse Sportswear, Easton Sports, Mizuno USA, Rawlings Sporting Goods, Reebok International, Russell Athletic, Taylor Made, The Sports Authority; 2) SPORTS TEAMS: Buffalo Sabres, San Francisco Giants, Sacramento Kings, San Jose Sharks, Seattle SuperSonics, St. Louis Blues, Tampa Bay Devil Rays; 3) SPORTS HEALTH AND FITNESS: American Youth Soccer Association, Gold's Gym Enterprises, HealthSouth; 4) SPORTS SERVICES AND PRODUCTS: H.O.K. Sports Facilities, Sega of America, Sony Signatures, Ticketmaster; 5) SPORTS BROADCASTING & COMMUNICATIONS: KNBR Radio, ESPN Radi
Nature of Sports Service:
A comprehensive sports travel consultant and management company uniquely designed to accommodate members of the sports community. Specializes in group and special projects.
Manufacturing Clients Include:
Adidas America — Professional / recreational sportswear Cleveland Golf — Golf Equipment Manufacturer Converse Sportswear — Professional / recreational sportswear Mizuno USA — Professional / recreational equipment Precept — Golf Equipment Manufacturer Rawlings Sporting Goods — Professional / recreational equipment Reebok International — Professional / recreational sportswear Russell Athletic — Professional / recreational sportswear Taylor Made — Golf Equipment Manufacturer The Sports Authority — Retail outlet chain

SPORTS EXPRESS, LLC
72 SUTTLE STREET
TRAVEL GUEST CARE
SUITE G
DURANGO, CO 81303
970-247-3048
800-357-4174
Fax: 970-385-8680
orders@luggageforward.com
www.sportsexpress.com
• Dave Welz, Media Relations Director
(970) 375-3405

• Jon Trevelise, Chief Executive Officer
• Mike Smedley, Media Relations
(970) 375-3405
Services:
Provides premier luggage and sports equipment delivery service; Partners with leading firms including FedEx, UPS, national and regional airlines and numerous travel, resort and hospitality companies.
Clients:
Partners: West Coast Trends, Inc.; Fairmont Hotels & Resorts; Abercrombie & Kent Destination Clubs; Merrill +; America West Airlines; Northwest Airlines; United Airlines; Aspen/Snowmass; Adventure Cycling Association; The Executive Women's Golf Association; TSE Golf; Tri All 3 Sports.

SPORTS FANTASY TOURS & EVENTS
16633 DALLAS PARKWAY
SUITE 600
ADDISON, TX 75001
214-691-9476
Services:
Offers tours and programs at major sporting events including: Game tickets, Luxury suite rentals and hospitality, Hotel accommodations, Celebrity theme event, Ground transportation, Personalized gift amenities, On-site staffing & coordination; 2) Corporate hospitality events; 3) Consumer promotions (point of sale, sweepstakes, sports team tie-ins); 4) Golf tournament management & coordination; 5) Inter-active sporting events: Basketball Shoot-out, Football Toss, Golf Putting Contests; 6) Sports Celebrities & Professional Players (speakers, meet & greet, chalk talks, insider info); 7) Sales incentive awards; and 8) Trade show promotions.
clients
Sprint, Compaq, Fox SportsNet.
Sports Service Founded:
1994
Marketing & Consulting Services:
Specialists in the development and marketing of Inside The Game sports tour programs.

SPORTS TOUR CLASSICS
11150 SANTA MONICA BOULEVARD
#500
LOS ANGELES, CA 90025
310-777-2525
800-591-9198
Fax: 310-777-2524
info@primesport.com
www.primesport.com
Services:
A leader in the development, sales, and management of premium ticket packages to sold-out sport, concert and cultural events worldwide.
Sports Service Founded:
1989
Nature of Sports Service:
Travel tours for major sporting events. Specializing in incentive programs to major spectator sporting events (tickets, hotel, transportation, celebrity speakers).

SPORTS TRAVEL, INC.
9601 WHITE ROCK TRAIL
SUITE 101
DALLAS, TX 75238-5011
214-341-9777
800-528-5260

Fax: 214-341-8849
info@sportstravelinc.com
www.sportstravelinc.com
• Doug Hill, Sales Representative
(214) 341-9777
doug@sportstravelinc.com
• Tony Liscio II, President
(214) 341-9777
tony@sportstravelinc.com
• Jennifer Babisak, Sales Support
jennifer@sportstravelinc.com
• Tony Liscio II, President
tony@sportstravelinc.com
• Doug Hill, Sales Rep
doug@sportstravelinc.com
• Mary A. Hill, Administration Office
maryann@sportstravelinc.com
Sports Service Founded:
1982
Services:
Coordinates trips for all occasions and for any age group; arranges ski vacations for church groups, Young Life groups, and families.
Nature of Sports Service:
A full service travel agency specializing in ski trips for groups.

THS COMPANY
200 ROUTE 31
SUITE 204
FLEMINGTON, NJ 08822
908-979-0928
888-536-8326
Fax: 908-684-2456
www.thsweb.com
• Tom Berkman, General Manager
(908) 979-0928
• Kelli Orpen, Operations Director
(908) 850-5900
• Briana Chapman, GM Championship Travel
(866) 790-8747
Services:
Offers a complete housing service that makes the booking of rooms easier for the hotels, the teams and the tournament.
Year Founded:
1998
Description of Sport Organization:
The premier sports housing service in the U.S. THS signs $25 million in hotel contracts per year as the official housing service for 80+ regional and national tournaments and championships each year.
Nature of Sports Service:
Provides free professional housing services for sports tournaments and other events. Organization handles all hotel-related responsibilities for an event including the signing of hotel contracts, negotiating headquarters hotel, comp rooms, reservations services, rebates and rebate collection.

TRANSPORTATION MANAGEMENT SERVICES, INC.
2870 PEACHTREE ROAD NW
ATLANTA, GA 30305
404-815-0551
• Tom Hastings, President
Florida Address:
4501 W. Cayuga Ave, Tampa, FL 33614.
813-873-8861; FAX: 813-873-8661
Event Management Services:
Transportation services including tour packaging, hotel accommodations, etc. Also

provides receptive operator and charter bus services.

TSE SPORTS & ENTERTAINMENT
14 PENN PLAZA
SUITE 925
NEW YORK, NY 10122
212-695-9480
877-621-5243
Fax: 212-564-8098
www.tseworld.com
• Robert Tuchman, President
(212) 695-9480
• Brett Sklar, SVP
(877) 621-5243
• Andy Robb, Operations Director
(212) 695-9480
Services:
Provides marketing programs to reach and engage customers by leveraging the power of sports & entertainment to bring their brand messages to life. Provides athlete/celebrity talent for appearances, events, promotions, public relations projects and endorsements.
Services:
Specializes in working with corporations to provide them with marketing programs that reach and engage their customers by leveraging the power of sports & entertainment to bring their brand messages to life. Focuses on Corporate Hospitality, Sales Promotions & Sweepstakes, Meeting & Event Planning, Athlete/ Celebrity Marketing, and Corporate Consulting.
Clients:
Anheuser-Busch, Bacardi Martini, Brown Forman, Coors, Deer Park, Geyser Peak Winery, InBev/Labatt USA, Miller Brewing Company, Diageo, Schieffelin & Somerset, Triarc Beverages, ABC Sports, Conde Nast Publications, Fox Network, GQ Magazine, HBO, NBC, ESPN, Maxim Magazine; Castrol, Daimler Chyrsler, ExxonMobil, Ford Motor Co., General Motors, Lexus, Pennzoil Products, Toyota; American Express, Bank of America, Merrill Lynch, JP Morgan Chase, KPMG, Bear Stearns, Hartford Financial, Morgan-Stanley Dean Whitter, AT&T, EMC, Ericsson, Hewlett-Packard, Lucent Technologies, Microsoft, IBM, Sony, Verizon; Bayer Corp., BIC USA, Bristol-Myers, Campbell's
Sports Travel:
Specializes in travel packages to major sporting events.
Athlete Management Services:
Provides athlete/celebrity talent for appearances, events, promotions, public relations projects and endorsements.
Event Management Services:
Specializes in providing hospitality and promotional services with multi-level involvement including consumer, trade and retail sales.
Promotional Services:
Specializes in fully integrated marketing promotions.

WESTERN SKI PROMOTIONS, INC.
4031 STONE WAY N
PO BOX 75298
SEATTLE, WA 98103
206-634-3620
Fax: 206-363-2114
Services:
Ski reports; European ski tours.

WORLDTEK TRAVEL
ONE AUDUBON
SUITE 400
NEW HAVEN, CT 6511
203-772-0470
800-243-1723
Fax: 203-865-2034
info@worldtek.com
www.worldtek.com
• Vito Luciani, Owner/Chairman
• Peter LeMay, Finance SVP
• Karen LaRose, Marketing and Special Events SVP
• Dave Smith, Operations SVP
dave.smith@worldtek.com
Sports Service Founded:
1969
Services:
Offers comprehensive travel services for associations, colleges, corporations, meetings, universities and vacationers
Marketing & Consulting Services:
Manages travel arrangements for a wide range of sports organizations, teams and trade shows.
Clients Include:
Big Ten Conference, LPGA, NCAA, U.S. Skiing, U.S. Volleyball.

Statistical Services

ALL AMERICAN AMATEUR BASEBALL ASSOCIATION
331 PARKWAY DRIVE
ZANESVILLE, OH 43701
740-453-8531
• Douglas Pollack, President
• Len DiForte, 1st Vp
• Lou Tiberi, 2nd Vp
Services:
Supports and organizes amateur baseball tournaments

ALL-PRO SOFTWARE
333 DOTY STREET
PO BOX 149
MINERAL POINT, WI 53565
608-987-4549
800-776-7859
Fax: 608-987-4553
info@allprosoftware.com
www.allprosoftware.com
Description:
Providing quality sports statics and scheduling software. Offering quality software thats easy to use for coachs, scorekeepers, leagues and tournament directors as well as YMCA's, city park and recs, high school and colleges.
Products:
Quality Sports Statistics and Scheduling Software
Brands:
Coaches, Scorekeepers, League & Tournament Directors as well as YMCAs, City Park & Recs, High Schools and Colleges; StatTrak Address Manager v3.0; StatTrak K-ForCE v3.0; League Scheduler v6.0; Tournament Scheduler Pro; StatTrak for Baseball; StatTrak for Hockey; StatTrak for Volleyball; StatTrak for Soccerl; StatTrak for Football

ELIAS SPORTS BUREAU
500 FIFTH AVENUE
SUITE 2140
NEW YORK, NY 10110
212-869-1530
Fax: 212-354-0980
www.esb.com
• Steve Hirdt, EVP
• Chris Thorn, VP
Services:
Statistical services in the field of professional sports
Clients:
Major League Baseball Records, World Series Records, Championship Series Record, Division Series Records, All-Star Game records, Hall of Fame Records, The Elias Book of Baseball Records
Products:
Offers products on historical research in the field of professional sports
Products:
Offers products on historical research in the field of professional sports
Description:
Founded in 1913. Providing historical research and statistical services in the field of professional sports.
Clients Include:
All the major professional sports leagues in North America, television networks, newspapers and other publications, as well as other providers of new media and web-sites.
Publications:
The Elias Book of Baseball Records.

EQUIBASE COMPANY
821 CORPORATE DRIVE
LEXINGTON, KY 40503-2794
859-224-2860
800-333-2211
Fax: 859-224-2870
feedback@equibase.com
www.equibase.com
• Hank Zeitlin, President/Chief Operating Officer
(859) 224-2860
hzeitlin@equibase.com
• Carlie Ambrose, Manager, Sales and Contract
(859) 224-2868
cambrose@equibase.com
• Connie Brannen, Operations Manager
(859) 224-2854
cbrannen@equibase.com
• Hank Zeitlin, President and Chief Operating Officer
(859) 224-2860
hzeitlin@equibase.com
• Shelby Cook, Online Service Coordinator
(859) 224-2863
scook@equibase.com
• Chris Dawahare, Manager, eBusiness Operations and Developmen
(859) 224-2862
cdawahare@equibase.com
Sports Service Founded:
1991
Products:
Provides the Thoroughbred racetracks of North America with a uniform, industry-owned database of racing information and statistics. Collects past performance information from all Thoroughbred racetracks in North America through a network of chartcallers.
Brands:

Race Programs, Expert Selections, F.A.S.T. Sheets, Performance Cycle, Cycles Lite, FlashNet, Daily Racing Form, Track Bias Reports, SpeedGraph, ClassGraph, Premium Edited Pedigree, Five Generation Pedigree, ChartPlus, Harness Race Information, Harness Racing Products, Virtual Stable, Racing Leaders, All-Time Top 10 Leaders, Top Leaders by Track, Meet Statistics, Wireless Information, New Fan Information; Equibaser Race Programs, Virtual StableT

Nature of Sports Service:
Thoroughbred industry's official database for racing information and statistics. Through a network of chart callers, the company collects past performance information from all thoroughbred race tracks in North America. Its state-of-the-art database in Lexington, Kentucky processes, stores and makes available for retrieval over five million individual race starts containing well over a half billion items of information.

GOLFSTAT
PO BOX 399
BLOOMINGTON, IL 61702-0399
www.golfstat.com
• Mark Laesch, Founder
Description:
Developed and provided free tournament software for college golf tournments. Provides statistical services and software for men's and women's college golf programs. Compiles the MasterCard rankings for the College Golf Foundation and perform on side scoring at their national tournaments. Provides background information and scoring for Intersport Television for their productions of college golf. Created and provide the statistical information used by Golf World magazine in their college golf poll section. Wrote the first points system software for the AJGA.
Services:
Provides statistical services and software development services for college golf tournaments and events. Offers a customized statistical service for college golf teams on the web. Hosts and maintains personalized web pages for teams' and players' statistics
Clients:
Men's Golf Team of University of Alabama, Barry University, Baylor University, Boston College, University of California Riverside, University of Central Florida, Clemson University, Coastal Carolina University, University of Denver, East Tennessee State University, Fresno State University, University of Georgia, Georgia State University, Indiana University, Jacksonville State University, Kent State University, Long Beach State, Louisiana-Monroe, LSU, Mercer University, New Mexico, Savannah College of Art and Design, Southeastern Louisiana University, University of Southern California, University of South Florida, Southern Methodist, St. Mary'

ONNIDAN GROUP, THE
6122 RICKER ROAD
RALEIGH, NC 27610
919-329-7036
Fax: 919-747-4541
www.onnidan.com
• Eric Moore, Managing Editor
(919) 329-7036

Description:
Founded in 1987, The Onnidan Group is a partnership of individuals with backgrounds in sports information, marketing, journalism and telecommunication.
Services:
Statistical services, information brokering, personal computer operations and webite administration.

PLAYER HISTORY.COM
www.playerhistory.com
• Hakon An Winther, Founder
• Christian Holm, Technical Staff
Description:
Consists of a group of idealistic football fans with the intenion to making this web site the best place on the web to find information about players from all around the world as well as statistics about matches.

SPORTS REFERENCE, THE
6757 GREENE ST.
SUITE 315
PHILADELPHIA, PA 19119
215-301-9181
Fax: 800-660-5292
sf@sports-reference.com
www.sports-reference.com
• Sean Forman, Owner
sean-forman@baseball-reference.com
• Justin Kubatko, VP
• Doug Drinen, Football Operations
• Jay Virshbo, Business Development
• Neil Paine, User Affairs Coordinator
Services:
Provides statistical services and information services about baseball.

SPORTSLINE USA, INC./CBS.SPORTSLINE.COM
1401 W CYPRESS CREEK ROAD
FORT LAUDERDALE, FL 33309
954-351-2120
800-771-4616
Fax: 954-771-2807
ir@sportsline.com
www.cbssports.com
• Michael Levy, Founder/President/Chied Executive Office
• Mark J. Mariani, Sales/Marketing President
• Kenneth W. Sanders, Strategic and Financial Planning EVP
• Stephen E. Snyder, Product Development and Operations EVP
Services:
Provides online sports content, community and online sales of sporting equipment and supplies. Sports content includes multimedia sports news, information, entertainment
Clients:
CBSSportsLine.com, FANSTASY Sports, GolfWeb, NFL.com, PGATour.com, NCAA Sports.com
Products:
Fantasy sports products and merchandise
Nature of Sports Service:
Global on-line sports information service and media company. Devoted exclusively to sports information, entertainment and merchandising. Producers of CBS SportsLine. Produce the official League Web sites for Major League Baseball, the PGA Tour, and NFL European League, and serves as the primary sports content

provider for America Online, Netscape, and Excite.

STATS LLC
2775 SHERMER ROAD
NORTHBROOK, IL 60062
847-583-2100
Fax: 847-583-2600
sales@stats.com
www.stats.com
• Gary Walrath, Chief Executive Officer
• Susan Zamachek, Director, Human Resources
• Steve Byrd, Executive Vice President
• Bobby Schur, Executive Vice President
• Allan Spear, Director of Operations
• Brian Orefice, Editorial
• Jim Corelis, AVP, Applications
• Brian Kopp, Vice President, Strategic Planning
• John Sasman, Asst. VP, Commercial Products
• Nick Stamm, Director, Communications
• Greg Kirkorsky, VP- Sales
Nature of Service:
STATS is the world's leading sports technology, data and content company. The company passionately abides by a mission to revolutionize the way sports contests are viewed, understood and enjoyed. STATS' calling card consists of real-time scores, historical sports information, Associated Press editorial content, a turnkey fantasy sports operation and SportVU technology. Today, STATS' worldwide client network of media companies and professional sports leagues and teams utilize a broad spectrum of dynamic in-game broadcast presentations and virtual images, multimedia enhancements and game analysis and tactical coaching tools. STATS is owned join
Year Founded:
1981
Locations:
STATS recently opened satellite offices in Bangalore, Hong Kong and London to join an existing bureau in Mexico City.
Clients:
Professional teams, print and broadcast media, iTV platforms, software developers, fantasy game operators, publishers and interactive and wireless service providers around the globe, Yahoo!, EA Sports, Fox Sports, DIRECTV, CHIEFS

STRATBRIDGE, INC.
BLANCHARD HOUSE
SUITE 304
249 AYER ROAD
HARVARD, MA 1451
978-772-4647
Fax: 617-977-8630
www.stratbridge.com
• Matthew Marolda, Founder/Chief Executive Officer
• Andrew H. Palmer, Strategy & Sales/Marketing
• Thomas L. Doorley, III, Strategy & Growth/Board of Directors
• Anthony J. Marolda, Strategy & Planning/Board of Directors
• Michael T. Horvath, Strategic Alliances/Board of Directors
Nature of Services:
StratBridge provides analytic solutions that enable professional sports managers to perform exhaustive diligence research at the touch of a button - StratBridge.net, a

platform product, is a Web-native system that seamlessly extracts data from internal and external sources, regardless of format, and then visually renders it in high-resolution plasma displays.

TRAKUS, INC.
107 AUDUBON RD
BUILDING 3-10
WAKEFIELD, MA 1880
617-544-6070
Fax: 617-544-6071
info@trakus.com
www.trakus.com
• Bob McCarthy, President/Chief Executive Officer
• Barry Weisbord, Chairman
• Michael Ciacciarelli, Chief Operating Officer
• Patrick Cummings, Business Manager/Director, Racing Information
• Peter Gargalianos, Director, Field Operations
Sports Service Founded:
1997
Brands:
Trakus System 2.0
Nature of Sports Service:
System delivers motion characteristics like speed, acceleration, and impact of a collision. The resulting information will form new class of statistics, on-air graphics and coaching tools. Also creating a new way to record an event, providing a bridge between sports and emerging electronic media like the Internet, digital television, and video games.

Student Athlete Recruiting Services

ATHLETES ADVANCE
35 SALUTATION STREET
SUITE # 3
BOSTON, MA 2109
• Chris Teso, Chief Executive Officer
Description:
Promise to give student athletes exposure to collegiate athletic programs. Puts the power of search agents into the hands of coaches and allow them to search for talent on their own terms and contact the recruits that match their program.
Services:
Intends to be an online stat tracking and athletic community that acts as a conduit between college coach and student-athlete. Bridges geographic barriers that typically prevent a quality athlete from getting the recognition he/she deserves because they come from a small school that seldom elicits the same attention of a larger school. Athletes Advance puts the power of search agents into the hands of coaches and allows them to search for talent on their own terms and contact the recruits that match their program.

CERTIFIED ATHLETE
HOUSTON, TX 66216
913-905-5872
certifiedathlete@gmail.com
www.certifiedathlete.com
Description:
Set out to create a system that would allow

academies to post athlete information and make it available to recruiters. The result of this effort is Certified Athlete.
Services:
A unique online network of athletes, schools, recruiters, and training academies that is revolutionizing the college recruiting process. CertifiedAthlete.com is designed to gain exposure for athletes and provide the tools for recruiters to review more athletes and in greater detail than was previously possible. Certified Athlete's Partner Academies offer Athlete Certifications, providing independent 3rd party tests and opinions.

COLLEGE PROSPECTS OF AMERICA
12682 COLLEGE PROSPECT DRIVE
LOGAN, OH 43138-0269
740-385-6624
888-275-2762
Fax: 740-385-9065
• Tracy Jackson, President & Chief Executive Officer
Year Founded:
1986.
Sports Service Founded:
1986
Services:
CPOA offers the following services:A custom profile form detailing athletic and academic achievements, Mailings of personalized reports to college coaches, Personal guidance throughout the recruiting process, Continuous internet marketing, Financial aid counseling, FAFSA preparation and electronic filing as well as enhancement and preparation of athletic videos for distribution to college coaches.

FIRST JOB IN SPORTS
201 N. ILLINOIS STREET
16TH FLOOR-SOUTH TOWER
INDIANAPOLIS, IN 46204
317-721-8134
Fax: 610-884-1800
www.firstjobinsports.com
• Brad Freeman, Executive Director
Nature of Service:
An online service to college students looking to find an internship or entry-level position in the sports industry. Students are able to insert criteria of positions they are looking for and only show jobs within that certain criteria. members are also able to submit their resume for hundreds of businesses to look at and members can receive daily job alerts directly in their email. Also offers advice regarding resume writing, cover letters, interview techniques, and other valuable information to help members land their first job in the sports industry.
Products:
Sports job board website for college students.

GLOBAL SPORTS CONNEXION
771 WEST END AVENUE
NEW YORK, NY 10025
212-967-0204
Fax: 212-656-1480
info@gsconline.net
www.gsconline.net
• Mark Ozer, Founder/Director
• Mark Ozer, Founder, Chairman
Sports Service Founded:
1990

Nature of Sports Services:
Assists high-level collegiate and professional athletes take advantage of global opportunities through their College Connexion and Tournament Connexion programs; heavy emphasis on Tennis.

NATIONWIDE SPORTS, INC.
1612 SHARON PLACE
CEDAR PARK, TX 78613-3563
512-249-2611
• Jeff Forster, President

NEW ENGLAND INTERACTIVE
3 SUNSET RIDGE
LEXINGTON, MA 2421
617-308-5094
info@NewEnglandInteractive.com
www.newenglandinteractive.com
• David Galehouse, Founder
(781) 862-3180
Products:
Creates and manages both local and national content websites.
Brands:
Varsityedge.com, Golfingnewengland.com, Newenglandathletics.com

RECRUIT, INC.
PO BOX 301
OWINGS MILLS, MD 21117
888-284-9227
Fax: 410-581-9513
Nature of Sports Service:
Recruiting and scouting service for high school athletes desiring to play college sports. Organization creates scouting reports on client athletes that can play at some level in college i.e., Division 1, 2, 3, or NAIA. Organization markets the athlete to the level that would get them the best response from college coaches. 100 scouts throughout the nation that work part and fulltime to find potential college prospects. Scouts are assigned to 20-30 schools to identify potential college prospects in their area. The regional scout interviews a potential college prospect to go over their academic and athletic background.

RECRUIT-ME
805-550-7566
support@recruit-me.com
www.recruit-me.com
• Jon Fugler, Founder
Founded:
2002
Nature of Service:
College recruitment and athletic scholarships.

SPORTS MEDIA CHALLENGE
7300 CARMEL EXECUTIVE PARK DRIVE
SUITE 120
CHARLOTTE, NC 28226
704-541-5942
800-929-4386
Fax: 704-541-5943
info@sportsmediachallenge.com
www.sportsmediachallenge.com
• Kathleen Hessert, Certified Speaking Professional
(704) 541-5942
khessert@sportsmediachallenge.com
• Joshua Baer, Chief Technology Consultant

Services:
Media Training, Crisis Communications, Public Speaking, Reputation Management, Online Word of Mouth and Conversation Tracking
Clients:
ASSOCIATIONS: American Football Coaches Association (AFCA), Black Coaches Association (BCA) College Sports Information Directors Association (CoSIDA), National Association of Collegiate Directors of Athletics (NACDA), Women's Basketball Coaches' Association (WBCA), NBA Coaches Associaiton; COLLEGES: Bowling Green UNiversity, Michigan State University, San Diego State University, University of Colorado, University of Connecticut, University of Florida, University of Maryland, University of North Carolina, University of Nortre Dame, University of Tennessee, University of Texas, University of Washington; ATHLETES, COACHES & PROFESSIONALS: Derek

VISION SPORTS, INC.
13236 WOODSEDGE WAY
CLERMONT, FL 34711-5916
407-654-6277
866-152-6418
Fax: 407-654-6269
• John Harris, Owner/President
Sports Service Founded:
2002
Services:
The College Sports Network for Recruiting High School Athletes
Nature of Sports Service:
Organization brings together student-athletes who are seeking scholarships with colleges that are seeking qualified student-athletes. Clients can monitor which colleges have visited their personal scouting report by using our innovative tracking feature.

Ticket Services

CITYSEATS.COM
1250 24TH STREET N.W 20037-1193
P.O 97180
WASHINGTON, DC 20090-7180
202-293-4800
• Carter Robertson, President and CEO
Nature of Sports Service:
Online marketplace to buy and sell tickets to hundreds of local events. Exchange tickets with other members through classifieds and auctions, or buy discounted tickets available exclusively through CitySeats.com.
Services:
Provides online marketplace to buy and sell tickets to hundreds of local events.

CYBERSEATS.COM
2995 VAN BUREN BOULEVARD
BUILDING A-13, SUITE 228
RIVERDALE, CA 92503-5606
951-637-8050
Fax: 951-637-8054
• Jim Lynskey, General Manager
Nature of Service:
Ticketing application that will allow fans to see the views from the premium locations available in the stadium before they buy. Once fans have viewed the field they can

then choose the exact seats they want, book them and pay for them in one easy transaction.

DESTINET LIMITED
BRADLEY HOUSE
7 PARK FIVE BUSINESS CENTRE,
HARRIER WAY
EXETER, DEVON, ENGLAND EX2 7HU
44-01392-447-200
Fax: 44-01392-447-230
info@destinet.co.uk
www.destinet.co.uk
• Trevor Munday, Managing Director
• Ian Creek, Marketing Manager
Services:
Provides advanced online business solutions.
Clients:
The Royal Bank of Scotland Group Plc (Lombard), IDN Telecom Plc, English Regional Arts Board, Nationwide, Alpha Telecom and MyCallSavings.com
Description:
Delivers a full range of ticket sales service for special events, sporting events and performing arts clients. DESTINET provides an integrated agency/in-house ticketing service utilizing SQL dBASE management, networked Windows/NT and tandem servers.

DI/AN CONTROLS, INC.
530 W STREET
BRAINTREE, MA 02184
781-848-1299
• Robert Kodis, President,Treasurer and Director
Year Founded:
1958
Nature of Service:
Master System, Point of Sale Systems, Food Service Management System.

INTERNATIONAL MICRO SYSTEMS, INC.
200 RACOOSIN DRIVE
SUITE 110
ASTON, PA 19014
800-882-0627
800-882-0627
Fax: 484-574-8874
www.ims-pos.com
• Jeff Harvey, Director of Sales
• Rob Rae, Director of Marketing
Nature of Services:
International Micro Systems provides integrated POS (Point of Sales) and venue management solutions with a strong focus on sports arenas, convention centers, amusement facilities, and colleges/universities - products and services include inventory management, food and beverage POS systems, full-scale venue systems planning, installation and support, and pre-paid concession payment systems through ticketing.

INTERNATIONAL TICKETING ASSOCIATION (INTIX), THE
5868 EAST 71ST STREET
SUITE E 367
INDIANAPOLIS, IN 46220
212-629-4036
Fax: 212-629-8532
info@intix.org
www.intix.org

• Maureen Andersen, President
(212) 629-4036
• Kathleen O'Donnell, Deputy Director
• Mardi Dilger, Board Chair
(305) 480-1620
mdilger@marlins.com
Description:
The International Ticketing Association is a nonprofit membership organization committed to leading the forum for the entertainment ticketing industry. INTIX represents over 1000 ticketing, sales, technology, finance, and marketing professionals who work in arts, sports, and entertainment as well as a full range of public venues and institutions.

INTERTICKET, INC.
2 GLENRIDGE DRIVE
BEDFORD, MA 01730
781-275-5724
info@interticket.com
www.interticket.com

NATIONAL TICKET COMPANY
5562 SNYDERTOWN ROAD
PAXINOSN, PA 17860
570-672-2900
800-829-0829
Fax: 570-672-2999
ticket@nationalticket.com
www.nationalticket.com
• John Conway, VP Sales/Administration
ticket@nationalticket.com
• Ginger Seidel, Advertising/Marketing Coordinator
gseidel@nationalticket.com
Year Founded:
1907
Description:
Manufacturer of tickets and wristbands. Season sheets, books and season wristband books. All printed in the USA!

NEIGHBORHOOD BOX OFFICE
3676 W CALIFORNIA AVENUE
BUILDING D
SALT LAKE CITY, UT 84104
801-887-7000
800-545-5776
Fax: 801-973-4188
www.nbo.com
• Keith A. Guevara, Chairman, Director, President and Chief
• Christopher Foley, Chief Financial Officer
Services:
Distributes and manages gift cards on all three platforms, MasterCard, Visa, and Discover. Provides Proprietary Technology, Transaction Processing, Client Services, Fulfillment, Order Processing, Tech Support, Call Center Support, Risk Management, Reporting, Marketing, Merchant and Mall Personnel Training.
Description:
Ticketing. Develops and markets transaction based interactive ticket & merchandise kiosks. Provides information and customer demographics to venues, promoters and retailers.

OMNICO GROUP
3100 SPRING FOREST ROAD
SUITE 125
RALEIGH, NC 27616

919-747-5700
Fax: 678-747-5799
www.omnicogroup.com
• Marc Bension, President
• Mark Kamiyama, Sales and Marketing SVP
Services:
Provides professional system solutions, service and consultancy for the leisure industry in the United States, North and South America, Europe, Asia and Africa. The world leaders in the design, development, implementation and service of specialized ticketing, concessions and merchandising point of sale systems for the leisure industry.
Description:
A Wembley TicketMaster joint venture, develops P.O.S. systems for stadium and arenas. The concession and merchandise systems include inventory control, suite catering and vending applications.

OPENSEATS, INC.
2805 WESTWOOD AVENUE
NASHVILLE, TN 37212
615-846-6750
866-789-1884
www.openseats.com
• Dan Maclellan, President
Sports Service Founded:
1999
Nature of Sports Service:
An online person-to-person trading community for people who want to buy or sell tickets to local sports and entertainment events.

PACIOLAN SYSTEMS, INC.
5171 CALIFORNIA AVENUE
SUITE 200
IRVINE, CA 92617
866-722-4652
Fax: 949-823-1610
www.paciolan.com
• Kothari Amit, CFO
(949) 823-1611
investors@paciolan.com
• Jane Kleinberger, Chairman
Services:
Online Ticketing, Enterprise Ticketing, Fund Development, Ticket Marketplace, Access Management, PACMail and Group Ticket Window; Implementation, Customer Support, Internet Adoption and eCommerce Services and Hosted Services

---

PEREY TURNSTILES, INC
308 BISHOP AVENUE
BRIDGEPORT, CT 6610
203-333-9400
877-TURNSTILE
Fax: 203-333-9410
perey@turnstile.com
www.turnstile.com
• Ed Hendrickson, VP
ehendrickson@turnstile.com
Products:
Waist High Passimeters, Optical Turnstiles, Drop Arm Turnstiles, Roto Gates, Mass Transit Turnstiles, Waist-High Traffic Control, Wheelchair Access, Automated Ticketing Turnstiles, Ticket Bo-Coin OP-Railings, Custom Designs
Brands:
Model HD (#048), Model HDAC (#136), Model HDACR (#150), Model HDACMR (#150), Model TC (#055), Model HDACR-Optical (#152), Model HDACMR-Optical (#152), Model HD-Optical (#050), Model 151S Drop Arm, Model 151M Drop Arm, Model 49 Drop Arm, Customized Designs, Twin Roto-Gate, SA Roto-Gate, Type AA Roto-Gate, Type B Roto-Gate, Model 110, Model 109, Model 107, Impenetrable AA Roto-Gate, Super Kompak Controller (#055), #20 Traffic Controller, #80 Traffic Controller, Perey Railing, Swing Gate #1255, Swing Gate #1256, PAS-Gate Drop Arm Site, HD-OmniScan (#048), Model 138, Field Upgrade in Progress, Ticket Box, Internal Ticket Box, Kompak Coinpassor, P
Nature of Sports Service:
Turnstiles, automated ticketing support, ADA compliance, and life safety compliance.

QUICK TICK INTERNATIONAL, INC.
12902 HAYNES ROAD
SUITE 4
HOUSTON, TX 77066
832-249-6400
800-231-6144
Fax: 832-249-6424
www.quicktick.com
• Don C. Andrews, President
• Lisa Andrews, Assistant President
Services:
Commercial Ticket Printing

RAZOR GATOR, INC.
4094 GLENCOE AVE
SUITE A
MARINA DEL REY, CA 90292
310-481-3400
800-542-4466
Fax: 310-289-3010
www.razorgator.com
• Doug Knittle, Chief Executive Officer
• David Lord, Chief Operating Officer, President
• Thomas Swalla, Business Development Director
(310) 289-3000
Nature of Sports Service:
A leading secondary ticket distributor that provides its customers with sold-out and hard-to-find tickets to premium sports, concerts and theater events worldwide.
Sports Service Founded:
1958
Services:
Buying and Selling Sold-Out or Hard-to-Find Tickets

SEATS 3D
1150 BALLENA BOULEVARD
SUITE 250
ALAMEDA, CA 94501
510-521-0720
Fax: 510-521-3972
www.seats3d.com
• Steve Stonehouse, Senior VP Sales
• Jeff Sherratt, Director Business Development
• David Schwartz, Chief Operations Officer/Chief Technology Officer
• Richard H. Sherratt, Chairman of the Board/Chief Executive Officer
Nature of Services:
Using 3D visualizations of sports venues, Ballena Technologies creates realistic seating visuals to improve the online ticketing experience by familiarizing potential customers with a facility, creating excitement, sales, and customer satisfaction.

SELECT TICKETING SYSTEMS, INC.
344 W GENESEE STREET
SUITE 102
SYRACUSE, NY 13202
315-479-6663
800-944-7277
Fax: 315-471-2715
• Renee Devesty,
Products:
Ticketing - Designs, installs, and supports Ticket Wizard, PASS and PASS GOLD-software created for ticketing, marketing, and events management.
Description:
Select Technologies Corporation is the largest international vendor of in-house computerized ticketing systems in the world. Over 530 customers use Select's PASS system which operates over 2,000 venues (locations where arts, sports and entertainment events are viewed) around the world.

SPLITSEASONTICKETS, LLC
splitseasontickets.com
• Dan Bartlett, Founder/Owner
• Dan DeMato, Partner
• Brian De Vries, Partner
Nature of Services:
A season ticket sharing web-based service partnering with professional sports teams. SplitSeasonTickets provides: Matcher Service to match existing season ticket holders with share partners; Drafting Service that provides season ticket holders and share partners a simple, efficient way to divide their season tickets; and Partner Extranet access to real-time data and sharing activities. The services benefit the teams by allowing them to participate in providing the services, and track the sharer data.

STUBHUB
199 FREMONT STREET
SAN FRANCISCO, CA 94105
415-222-8400
866.788.2482
Fax: 415-222-8552
www.stubhub.com
• Jeff Fluhr, Co-Founder and Chief Executive Officer
customerservice@stubhub.com
• Carolyn Arend, Chief Financial Officer
customerservice@stubhub.com
• Colin Evans, Sales and Business Development VP
• Chris Tsakalakis, President
• Anne Robie, Director, Human resources
• Brigitte R. Bellan, GM, International
• Danielle Maged, Global Head of Partnership
Nature of Sports Service:
Web site that works as an intermediary between ticket buyers and sellers. Users can see what event tickets are available, purchase tickets or post tickets for sale. Site takes a ten percent listing fee on consummated sales and uses the LiquidSeats technology platform. The LiquidSeats engine enables content sites, team sites and portals to easily integrate a secondary ticket market into their web site.

Services:
Buying and Selling Tickets

TICKET RESERVE, THE
20 N WACKER DRIVE
SUITE 1100
CHICAGO, IL 60606
312-357-4281
888-205-1611
Nature of Sports Service:
Organization utilizes technology to create new revenue streams for professional teams and organizations.
Services:
Seamless integration with teams' and event producers' existing technologies, providing secure transactions, reliable information and convenient use for fans worldwide; The Fan Forward, ConnectingPoint
Products:
Product that lets teams and leagues capitalize on potential contingent events

---

TICKET RETURN INC.
6407 IDLEWILD ROAD
CHARLOTTE, NC 28212
866-858-7876
info@ticketreturn.com
www.ticketreturn.com
• Aaron Clark, Account Executive
Brands:
ProTicket, ProScan, UTicket, UScan, Ustudent

TICKET TO GO, LLC
4124 CENTRAL PIKE
HERMITAGE, TN 37076
615-360-6700
877-282-8942
Fax: 615-874-8005
support@agiletix.com
• Caren Shaffer, President
• Michael Holt, EVP Product Development And Client support Se
• John Lemon, Director, System Implementation and Customer
• Julien McBride, Director, Software and System Development
• Shane A. Burkett, Director, Strategic Marketing
• Richard Steward, EVP Operations/Sales
Nature of Sports Service:
Offers online ticketing, software for box office operations, and portable ticket selling and printing kiosks. Also offers Interactive Voice Response system, allowing

customers to place orders by telephone and listen to pre-recorded information on events, venues and payment and shipping options.
Services:
Full-featured Box Office and Call Center sales, Robust venue and event management, Fully integrated, highly customizable security, Express Sales, Web sales seamless integrated into your website, Kiosk sales, Reserved seating and general admission ticketing, Table seating, Catalog sales, Flexible packaging for season ticket and tour package sales, Group Sales, Unique ticket bar coding, Data mart, data mining and decision support services, Accounting support, 24/7 call center, Fulfillment services, Application and web hosting, System administration management, Implementation, conversion, training services

---

TICKETMASTER
880 W. SUNSET BLVD
WEST HOLLYWOOD, CA 90069
213-639-6100
Fax: 213-386-1244
www.ticketmaster.com
• Michael Rapino, President & CEO
• Nathan Hubbard, Chief Executive Officer of Ticketing
Nature of Service:
Provides event ticket sales, marketing and distribution through Internet, phone, and retail outlets, along with online auctions, fan club ticketing, and venue-authorized fan resale ticketing services.
Brands:
TicketsNow; TicketExchange; Ticketmaster
Marketing & Consulting Services:
Works with professional and college sports teams to develop new programs designed to expand ticket sales by helping with marketing ideas and actual sales of tickets using outlets, telephones and Internet.
Sports Service Founded:
1995; Merged with Live Nation on January 25, 2010, creating Live Nation Entertainment, Inc

---

TICKETS.COM
555 ANTON BOULEVARD
PO BOX 272127
COSTA MESA, CA 92626
714-327-5400
888-397-3400
Fax: 714-327-5410

sales@tickets.com
www.tickets.com
• Larry Witherspoon, Chief Executive Officer
• John Walker, CEO, President
• Daniel Wu, Chief Financial Officer
• Joe Choti, Chief Technology Officer
• Joe DeMots, Senior Vice President of Business Development
• John Rizzi, Senior Vice President of Project Management
• Ed Gow, Vice President of Sales and Marketing
• Doug Lyons, Vice President of Product Marketing
• Danielle Nagao, Vice President of Financial Operations
• Jan Yerzik, Chief Marketing Manager
• Chaeli Walker, Marketing Manager
• John Walker, President, CEO
Description:
Online, offline ticketing software and services.
Baseball Sponsor:
Chicago Cubs, New York Mets

WEBTICKETS.COM
4651 ROSWELL ROAD NE
SUITE F-503
ATLANTA, GA 30342-3051
404-843-1344
800-846-2407
Fax: 404-303-1574
cto@webtickets.com
www.webtickets.com
• Carl White, Chief Ticket Officer
cto@webtickets.com
Services:
Buying and Selling Event Tickets

WORLDWIDE TICKET CRAFT
3606 QUANTUM BLVD
BOYNTON BEACH, FL 33426
954-426-5754
877-426-5754
Fax: 954-426-5761
www.worldwideticketcraft.com
• Erik Covitz, President
• Mark Turner, Vice President of information Systems
• Alan Tonks, Chief Financial Officer
• George Scher, Chief Operations Officer
Description:
Ticket Manufacturer. Designer and developer of event tickets, custom tickets, etc.
Services:
Ticket Printing

7
facilities

Arenas & Stadiums

A.J. MCCLUNG MEMORIAL STADIUM
600 4TH STREET
COLUMBUS, GA 31901
706-653-4500
Fax: 706-653-4549
• Anthony L. Ford, General Manager
Seating Capacity:
15,000

A.J. PALUMBO CENTER
600 FORBES AVENUE
PITTSBURGH, PA 15282
412-396-6632
800-456-0590
Fax: 412-396-5855
harperd1@duq.edu
www.goduquesne.com/facilities/duqu-facil-p
alumbo.html
• Bob Derda, General Manager
Seating Capacity:
4,406

ABILENE CIVIC CENTER
1100 NORTH 6TH STREET
ABILENE, TX 79601
325-676-6211
Fax: 325-676-6343
abilene@abilenetx.com
www.abilenetx.com
Seating Capacity:
2,121

ACADEMIC-ATHLETIC CENTER
195 ACADEMIC-ATHLETIC CENTER
MOREHEAD, KY 40351
606-783-2088
Fax: 606-783-5035
www.msueagles.com
• Randy Stacy, Athletic Media Relations
Director
r.stacy@moreheadstate.edu
• Brian Hutchinson, Director of Athletics
(606) 783-2089
b.hutchinson@moreheadstate.edu
• Rhonda Ferguson, Administrative
Assistant to the AD
(606) 783-2089
r.ferguson@moreheadstate.edu
• Harry Floyd, Athletic Secretary
(606) 783-2088
hbfloyd@moreheadstate.edu
• Peggy Osborne, Faculty Athletics
Representative
(606) 783-2755
p.osborne@moreheadstate.edu
Seating Capacity:
6,500

ADAMS CENTER
32 CAMPUS DRIVE
MISSOULA, MT 59812
406-243-5355
Fax: 406-243-4265
tristin.flint@mso.umt.edu
www.gogriz.com/facilities/
• Brad Murphy, Executive Director
(406) 243-4261
brad.murphy@mso.umt.edu
• Brandon Kress, Assistant Director,
Operations
(406) 243-5357
brandon.kress@mso.umt.edu
• Adrien Wingard, Events & Promotion
Coordinator

(406) 243-5403
adrien.wingard@mso.umt.edu
• Kelsi Plante, Client Technology Support
Manager
(406) 243-5329
kelsi.plante@mso.umt.edu
Seating Capacity:
7,500 sporting events; 6,000 concerts, 7,655
concerts in the round.
Year Founded:
1955

AGGIE MEMORIAL STADIUM
3035 WILLIAMS AVENUE
ROBERTS HALL
LAS CRUCES, NM 88003
575-646-4413
Fax: 575-646-2099
www.nmstatesports.com
• Bobbie Welch, Booking and Marketing
Director
(505) 646-7630
• Gary Rachele, Assistant Director
(505) 646-4413
• Will Lofdahl, Special Events Director
(505) 646-4413
• Barbara A. Welch, Special Events
Coordinator
(505) 646-7525
Seating Capacity:
30,343
Year Founded:
1978

AL F. CANIGLIA FIELD
60TH & DODGE STREET
UNIVERSITY OF NEBRASKA AT OMAHA
OMAHA, NE 68182
402-554-2305
Fax: 402-554-3694
www.omavs.com
• Kevin Brady, Assistant Operations
Coordinator
(402) 554-2606
knbrady@unomaha.edu
Services
Located in the heart of the UNO campus,
the stadium's infield is Field Turf while the
track is a Seal-Flex surface. The stadium is
the home field for the Maverick football
team, and also hosts UNO's outdoor track &
field events.
Seating Capacity
3,0+8

AL G. LANGFORD CHAPARRAL CENTER
3600 NORTH GARFIELD
MIDLAND COLLEGE
MIDLAND, TX 79705
432-685-4500
Fax: 432-685-4740
www.midland.edu
• Mike Stevens, Director
(416) 685-4583
mstevens@midland.edu

ALAMODOME SAN ANTONIO
100 MONTANA STREET
SAN ANTONIO, TX 78203
210-207-3663
Fax: 210-207-3646
dmarketing@alamodome.com
www.alamodome.com
Services:
The Alamodome is what is known as a 'third
generation' facility. It features the very latest
in dome architecture and engineering

technology, with column-free spans for
unobstructed viewing and a curtain wall
system for configuration flexibility. The
Alamodome has 160,000 gross square feet
of contiguous exhibit floor space. The
Alamodome has two 24.5' X 32.5'
Daktronics ProStarr 16.5mm end zone
displays, a center hung arena scoreboard
with four 9' X 12' Daktronics ProStar 10mm
displays, and a brand new dual sided
Daktronics ProStarr 23mm outdoor marquee
located in Parking Lot A.
Seating Capacity:
65,000

ALBANY CIVIC CENTER
100 WEST OGLETHORPE BOULEVARD
ALBANY, GA 31701-6808
229-430-5200
Fax: 229-430-5163
www.albany.ga.us
• Joel Holmes, Director
(229) 430-5222
• Derrell Smith, Deputy Director
(229) 430-5222
• Shanice Howard, Event Manager
(229) 430-1804
• Uy Tram, Administrative Manager
(229) 430-1805
Arena Seating Capacity:
10,240

ALBERT LEA CITY ARENA
701 LAKE CHAPEAU DRIVE
ALBERT LEA, MN 56007
507-377-4374
Fax: 507-377-4336
cityofalbertlea.org/departments/parks-and-re
creation/city-arena/
• Robert Furland, Facility Manager
(507) 377-4374
Services:
The facility is home to the boys and girls
high school hockey teams, the Albert Lea
Figure Skaters, the Albert Lea Youth Hockey
Association and the Waldorf College Hockey
Team.

ALERUS CENTER
1200 42ND STREET SOUTH
GRAND FORKS, ND 58201
701-792-1200
Fax: 701-746-6511
www.aleruscenter.com
• Tami Pearson, Marketing Manager
• Vione Jordheim, Senior Administrative
Assistant
• Wendy Nimens, Business Manager
wnimens@aleruscenter.com
• Jeremy Linstad, Director of Operations
Services
Able to accommodate a variety of sporting
events, the Alerus Center is home to the
University of North Dakota Fighting Sioux
Football team and hosts soccer, wrestling,
basketball, monster trucks, rodeos, and
Super Snowcross. This remarkable facility
has the capacity to host local, regional and
national sporting events.
Seating Capacity
Footbal seating capacity: 13,400 concert
seating capacity: 22,000 145,000 square
feet of exhibit space

ALEX BOX STADIUM
SKIP BERTMAN DRIVE
BATON ROUGE, LA 70803

225-578-8001
800-469-8781
Fax: 225-578-2430
www.lsusports.net
• Ronnie Haliburton, Sr. Associate AD, Facility Management
(225) 578-4712
• Todd Jeansonne, Director of Facilities & Grounds
(225) 578-5519
tjeans2@lsu.edu
• Flo Williams, Manager of Facilities & Grounds
(225) 578-6729
fwilli3@lsu.edu
Services:
Since 1985, it has been the site of four SEC tournaments, 16 NCAA regional tournaments, three NCAA super regional series and one ABCA Hall of Fame tournament. Each year, The Box undergoes facility-improvement projects designed to enhance the comfort and enjoyment of LSU baseball fans.
Seating Capacity:
10,326

ALFOND ARENA
COLLEGE AVENUE
ORONO, ME 04473
207-581-1104
Fax: 207-581-3297
www.goblackbears.com
• Deb Leavitt, Athletic Ticket Manager
(207) 581-2327
• Jason Hoyt, Account Executive
(207) 584-4103
Arena Seating Capacity:
5,712
Year Founded:
1977

ALFRED LAWSON JR. MULTIPURPOSE CENTER
1800 WAHNISH WAY
TALLAHASSEE, FL 32307
850-412-5966
Fax: 850-599-3810
www.famu.edu
• Robert D. Carroll, Director of Multipurpose Facility
(850) 599-8081
Arena Seating Capacity:
8,470

ALLEN COUNTY WAR MEMORIAL COLISEUM
4000 PARNELL AVENUE
FORT WAYNE, IN 46805
260-482-9502
Fax: 260-484-1637
www.memorialcoliseum.com
• Randy Brown, General Manager
(260) 482-9502
rbrown@memorialcoliseum.com
• Bryan Christie, Vice President of Operations
(260) 482-9502
bchristie@memorialcoliseum.com
• Rich Thoma, Plant Facilities Manager
(260) 482-9502
rthoma@memorialcoliseum.com
Services:
Allen County War Memorial Coliseum can be configured with a 1/10 mile paved indoor oval for special events. The facility has most recently been used for an indoor USAC

event.
Seating Capacity:
10,240

ALLSTATE ARENA
6920 NORTH MANNHEIM ROAD
ROSEMONT, IL 60018
847-635-6601
Fax: 847-635-6606
www.rosemont.com/allstate/
• Patrick Nagle, Executive Director
(847) 635-6601
Seating Capacity:
18,500

ALLTEL ARENA
ONE VERIZON ARENA WAY
NORTH LITTLE ROCK, AR 72114
501-340-5660
Fax: 501-340-5668
www.verizonarena.com
• Michael Marion, General Manager
Services:
In addition to being the home court for UALR Basketball, this facility also hosts the Arkansas Twisters Arena Football 2 Team, Ringling Brothers Barnum and Bailey Circus, Champions on Ice Figure Skating exhibition, concerts and a number of other exciting quality attractions.
Seating Capacity:
18,000

ALOHA STADIUM
99-500 SALT LAKE BLVD
HONOLULU, HI 96818
808-483-2500
Fax: 808-483-2823
alohastadium@hawaii.gov
alohastadium.hawaii.gov
• Scott Chan, Stadium Manager
Seating Capacity:
50,000
Teams:
Hawaii Rainbow Warriors, Hawai'i Bowl

ALUMNI COLISEUM
521 LANCASTER AVENUE
RICHMOND, KY 40475
859-622-3654
Fax: 859-622-5108
michael.clark@eku.edu
www.ekusports.com
• Sean Hamilton, General Manager
(859) 622-6372
• Lynn Tyler, Athletics Administrative Coordinator
(859) 622-2120
Stadium Seating Capacity:
6,500

ALUMNI FIELD STADIUM, BOSTON COLLEGE
140 COMMONWEALTH AVENUE
BOSTON COLLEGE ATHLETICS
CHESTNUT HILL, MA 02467
617-552-3000
www.bceagles.com
• Matt Conway, Associate Athletics Director, Operations
(617) 552-6672
conwayml@bc.edu
Stadium Seating Capacity:
45,000

ALUMNI FIELD STADIUM, VIRGINIA MILITARY INSTITUTE
VIRGINIA MILITARY INSTITUTE
116 SMITH HALL
LEXINGTON, VA 24450
540-464-7253
Fax: 540-464-7622
igoec@vmi.edu
www.vmikeydets.com
• Elizabeth Igo, Assistant Athletic Director, Facilities
(540) 464-7266
igopec@vmi.edu
Stadium Seating Capacity:
10,000

AMARILLO CIVIC CENTER COMPLEX
401 SOUTH BUCHANAN
AMARILLO, TX 79101
806-378-4247
amarillociviccenter.com
• Sherman Bass, General Manager
(806) 378-4247
sherman.bass@amarillo.gov
• Bo Fowlkes, Assistant General Manager
(806) 378-9460
bo.fowlkes@amarillo.gov
• Christopher Post, Operations Manager
(806) 378-9480
christopher.post@amarillo.gov
Seating Capacity:
4,870

AMERICAN AIRLINES CENTER
2500 VICTORY AVENUE
DALLAS, TX 75219
214-222-3687
800-745-3000
www.americanairlinescenter.com
Tenant(s):
Dallas Mavericks, Dallas Stars

AMON G. CARTER STADIUM
2850 STADIUM DRIVE
FORT WORTH, TX 76129
817-257-7000
Fax: 817-257-7656
www.gofrogs.com/facilities/tcu-facilities-football.html
• Jay Fields, General Manager
• Sean Conner, Assistant Athletics Director, Ticket Operations
s.conner@tcu.edu
Seating Capacity:
45,000
Team:
Texas Christian University Horned Frogs

ANDY KERR STADIUM
13 OAK DRIVE
HAMILTON, NY 13346
315-228-1000
Fax: 315-228-7008
www.gocolgateraiders.com
• Kenny Copps, Ticket Manager
(315) 228-7600
• Emmett House, Grounds Supervisor
(315) 228-7577
Seating Capacity:
10,221

ANGELS STADIUM OF ANAHEIM
2000 GENE AUTRY WAY
ANAHEIM, CA 92806
714-940-2000
Fax: 714-940-2266

robert.alvarado@angelsbb.com
losangeles.angels.mlb.com/ana/ballpark/
• Billy Eppler, General Manager
• Calvin Ching, Sr. Manager, Stadium
Events & Operations
• Brian Sanders, Sr. Director, Ballpark
Operations
Team:
Los Angeles Angels
Seating Capacity:
45,050

APPALACHIAN POWER PARK
601 MORRIS STREET
SUITE 201
CHARLESTON, WV 25301
304-344-2287
Fax: 304-344-0083
• Ken Fogel, Executive Vice-President
(304) 344-BATS
• Tim Mueller, General Manager
(304) 344-BATS
• Gary Olson, Director of Ticketing
(304) 344-BATS
Sport:
Minor League Baseball
Team:
WV Power - a single A affiliate of the
Pittsburgh Pirates.
Seating Capacity:
4,300

ARIZONA STADIUM
545 NORTH NATIONAL CHAMPION DRIVE
TUCSON, AZ 85721-0096
520-621-2200
Fax: 520-621-9323
www.arizonawildcats.com
• Joe Moeller, General Manager
(520) 626-5538
joe.moeller@imgworld.com
Seating Capacity:
56,029
Tenants:
Arizona Wildcats; Arizona Bowl

ARKANSAS STATE FAIR
2600 HOWARD STREET
LITTLE ROCK, AR 72206
501-372-8341
Fax: 501-372-4197
www.arkansasstatefair.com
• Ralph Shoptaw, President and General
Manager
• Tiffany Wilkerson, Commercial Exhibit
Coordinator
tiffany@asfg.net
• Will Hornburg, Director of Sales &
Promotions
(501) 372-8341
will.h@asfg.net
Arena Seating Capacity:
10,000

ARKANSAS STATE UNIVERSITY
CONVOCATION CENTER
217 OLYMPIC DRIVE
JONESBORO, AR 72401
870-972-3870
Fax: 870-972-3825
www.astateconvo.com
• Tim Dean, Director
(870) 972-3870
timd@astate.edu
• Lesa Carmack, Booking Coordinator
(870) 972-3870
• Haley Stout, Box Office Manager

(870) 972-2781
hstout@astate.edu
• Dennis Timms, Operations Foreman
(870) 972-3870
dennis@astate.edu
Seating Capacity:
10,529
Seating Capacity:
30,000

ARMSTRONG STADIUM
100 EAST QUEEN STREET
HAMPTON, VA 23668
757-727-5641
Fax: 757-728-6995
www.hamptonpirates.com/sports/2006/8/8/a
rmstrongstadium.aspx
• John Jackson, Director of Facilities
(757) 727-5516
john.jackson@hamptonu.edu
• John Brown, Assistant Director of Facilities
(757) 728-6665
john.brown@hamptonu.edu
Seating Capacity:
12,000

ARROWHEAD STADIUM
ONE ARROWHEAD DRIVE
KANSAS CITY, MO 64129
816-920-9300
Fax: 816-924-4570
www.kcchiefs.com
• Tim Hassett, Vice President of Stadium
Operations
• Rocco Mazzella, Stadium Services
Manager
• Brandon Hamilton, Director of Facilities
Tenants:
Kansas City Chiefs
Seating Capacity:
76,416

ARTHUR ASHE STADIUM
124-02 ROOSEVELT AVENUE
FLUSHING, NY 11368
718-760-6200
Fax: 718-592-9488
www.usta.com
Note:
Arthur Ashe Stadium is a part of the USTA
National Tennis Center.
Seating Capacity:
23,771

ASSEMBLY HALL
1001 EAST 17TH STREET
BLOOMINGTON, IN 47408-1590
812-855-2794
Fax: 812-855-0488
iuad@indiana.edu
iuhoosiers.com
• Eric Neuburger, Associate Athletic
Director, Facilities
(812) 855-2127
Seating Capacity:
17,484

AT&T CENTER
ONE AT&T CENTER PARKWAY
SAN ANTONIO, TX 78219
210-444-5140
www.attcenter.com
Seating Capacity:
19,000
Tenant(s) :
San Antonio Spurs (NBA), San Antonio

Stars (WNBA), San Antonio Rampage
(AHL), San Antonio Stock Show & Rodeo
(PRCA).

AT&T FIELD
201 POWER ALLEY
CHATTANOOGA, TN 37402
423-267-2208
Fax: 423-267-4258
web.minorleaguebaseball.com/index.jsp?sid
=t498
• Rick Mozingo, President
rmozingo@lookouts.com
• Steve Sullivan, Director, Food & Beverage
ssullivan@lookouts.com
• Anastasia McCowan, Business & Ticket
Operations Manager
amccowan@lookouts.com
• Alex Tainsh, Marketing & Promotions
Manager
atainsh@lookouts.com
Sport:
Minor League Baseball.
Team:
Chattanooga Lookouts.
Year Founded:
2000
Capacity:
6,362

AT&T PARK
24 WILLIE MAYS PLAZA
SAN FRANCISCO, CA 94107
415-972-2000
Fax: 415-947-2800
sanfrancisco.giants.mlb.com/sf/ballpark
Stadium Seating Capacity:
41,915
Tenant(s) :
San Francisco Giants (MLB).

ATWOOD STADIUM
1700 UNIVERSITY AVENUE
FLINT, MI 48504
810-766-7463
Fax: 810-766-7468
• Thomas W. Ayers, Vice President for
Administration & Finance
(810) 762-9787
Stadium Seating Capacity:
11,000
Arena Seating Capacity:
11,000

AUTOZONE PARK
200 UNION AVENUE
MEMPHIS, TN 38103
901-721-6050
Fax: 901-328-1102
• Craig Unger, General Manager
cunger@cardinals.com
• Gian D'Amico, Ticket Operations Manager
gdamico@cardinals.com
• Mark Anderson, Director of Operations
manderson@cardinals.com
Year Opened:
2000
Team:
Memphis Redbirds.
Capacity:
10,000

AUTZEN STADIUM
2700 MLK JR. BOUELVARD
EUGENE, OR 97401

541-346-4481
Fax: 541-346-5031
tigersoccercamp@yahoo.com
www.goducks.com
• Rob Mullens, Athletic Director
(541) 346-5455
• Mike Duncan, Sr. Associate Athletic
Director, Facilities
(541) 346-5326
Stadium Seating Capacity:
54,000
Team:
University of Oregon Ducks (NCAA)

AVISTA STADIUM
602 NORTH HAVANA STREET
SPOKANE, WA 99202
509-343-6886
Fax: 509-534-5368
mail@spokaneindians.com
• Chris Duff, General Manager
cduff@spokaneindians.com
• Josh Roys, Vice President, Tickets
jroys@spokaneindians.com
• John Tibbett, Stadium Operations
Manager
• Larry Blumer, Assistant Director of
Stadium Operations
Sport:
Baseball
Tenant(s) :
Spokane Indians (NWL)
Year Founded:
1958
Capacity:
6,803

BAKER ATHLETICS COMPLEX
533 WEST 218TH STREET
NEW YORK, NY 10034
212-942-0431
Fax: 212-854-2988
jar14@columbia.edu
www.gocolumbialions.com
• Steve Figueroa, Manager of Facilities
Operations
(212) 851-0113
sf2317@columbia.edu
• Erich Ely, Associate Athletics Director,
Facilities Op.
(212) 854-5911
ee2133@columbia.edu
Stadium Seating Capacity:
17,000

BALLPARK AT HARBOR YARD
500 MAIN STREET
BRIDGEPORT, CT 06604
203-345-4800
Fax: 203-345-4830
info@bridgeportbluefish.com
bridgeportbluefish.com/stadium/
• Frank Boulton, Principal Owner, CEO
• Jamie Toole, General Manager
(203) 416-1705
• Dan Gregory, Director of Stadium
Operations
(203) 416-1704
• Drew LaBoy, Director of Operations
(203) 416-1719
Sport:
Minor League Baseball, Lacrosse
Tenant(s) :
Bridgeport Bluefish (ALPB), Sacred Heart
Pioneers (NCAA).

BANCORP SOUTH ARENA
375 EAST MAIN STREET
TUPELO, MS 38804
662-841-6573
Fax: 662-841-6413
thunt@bcsarena.com
www.bcsarena.com
• Todd Hunt, Executive Director
thunt@bcsarena.com
• Craig Russell, Director of Operations
crussell@bcsarena.com
• Kevan Kirkpatrick, Director of Marketing
kkirkpatrick@bcsarena.com
Arena Seating Capacity:
10,000
Year Founded:
1993

BANK OF AMERICA STADIUM
800 SOUTH MINT STREET
CHARLOTTE, NC 28202
704-358-7000
1-888-297-8673
Fax: 704-358-7619
feedback@panthers.nfl.com
www.panthers.com/stadium
• Jerry Richardson, Owner, Founder
• Dave Gettleman, General Manager
• Matthew Getz, Facility Manager
Stadium Seating Capacity:
75,412
Description:
Home Stadium for the Carolina Panthers.
Owned by:
Carolinas Stadium Corp.

BARCLAYS CENTER
620 ATLANTIC AVENUE
BROOKLYN, NY 11217
917-618-6100
800-745-3000
Fax: 718-942-9595
www.barclayscenter.com
• Brett Yormark, Chief Executive Officer
• Fred Mangione, Chief Operating Officer
• Stephen Rosebrook, General Manager
• Richard Vartigian, Director, Operations
Seating Capacity:
19,000 for shows & events; approximately
17,732 for Brooklyn Nets
Opened:
September 28, 2012
Tenant(s) :
Brooklyn Nets (NBA), New York Islanders
(NHL)

**BASEBALL GROUNDS OF
JACKSONVILLE**
301 A. PHILIP RANDOLPH BOULEVARD
JACKSONVILLE, FL 32202
904-358-2846
Fax: 904-358-2845
www.jaxsuns.com
• Harold Craw, General Manager
harold@jaxsuns.com
• Christian Galen, Director of Field
Operations
christiang@jaxsuns.com
• Weill Casey, Stadium Operations Manager
Tenant(s) :
Jacksonville Suns, Jacksonville Armada FC
Year Founded:
2003
Capacity:
11,000

BASKETBALL CITY
PIER 36 AT 299 SOUTH STREET
NEW YORK, NY 10002
212-233-5050
Fax: 212-233-6161
info@basketballcity.com
www.basketballcity.com
• Bruce Radler, President
bruce@basketballcity.com
• Lee Isenstein, COO, Corporate Events
lee@basketballcity.com
• Christopher Kenny, Director of Youth
Programs
chris@basketballcity.com
Description:
A basketball facility geared toward, league
set ups, and an NBA practice facility.
Equipped with 6 basketball courts on the
main floor, as well as a weight training
facility.
Year Founded:
1997

**BAYONNE VETERANS MEMORIAL
STADIUM**
WEST 26TH STREET
BAYONNE, NJ 07002
201-858-6164
Fax: 201-858-6092
Stadium Seating Capacity:
8,000

BB&T BALLPARK
324 SOUTH MINT STREET
CHARLOTTE, NC 28202
704-274-8300
Fax: 704-274-8330
www.milb.com
• Dan Rajkowski, Chief Operating Officer
danr@charlotteknights.com
• Scotty Brown, General Manager
• Matt Parrott, Head Groundskeeper
Stadium Seating Capacity:
10,200

**BB&T BALLPARK AT HISTORIC
BOWMAN FIELD**
1700 WEST FOURTH STREET
WILLIAMSPORT, PA 17701
570-326-3389
Fax: 570-326-3494
mail@crosscutters.com
www.crosscutters.com
• Doug Estes, VP, General Manager
doug@crosscutters.com
• Gabe Sinicropi, Jr, VP, Marketing & Public
Relations
gabe@crosscutters.com
• Bill Gehron III, Director of Food &
Beverage
bill@crosscutters.com
• Sarah Budd, Director of Ticket
Operations/Community Relations
sarah@crosscutters.com
• Nate Schneider, Director of Partner
Services
nate@crosscutters.com
Sport:
Minor League Baseball.
Tenant(s) :
Williamsport Crosscutters baseball.
Year Founded:
1926
Seating Capacity:
4,200

BB&T CENTER
ONE PANTHER PARKWAY
SUNRISE, FL 33323
954-835-7000
Fax: 954-835-8012
info@floridapanthers.com
www.thebbtcenter.com
• Adam Fullerton, Director, Arena Operations
• Brian Gilner, Operations Manager
• Tom Embrey, Director of Events & Guest Services
Arena Seating Capacity:
20,737
Year Founded:
1998
Nature of Service:
Sports, Entertainment, Concerts, and more.
Tenant(s):
Florida Panthers (NHL).

BC PLACE
777 PACIFIC BOULEVARD
VANCOUVER, BC, CANADA V6B 4Y8
604-669-2300
stadium@bcpavco.com
www.bcplace.com
• Chris May, General Manager
• Anita Sodhi-Cavezza, Director, Business Development & Event Sales
• Wayne Smith, Director, Human Resources & Labour Relations
• Dale Doering, Director, Facility Operations
Owned and Operated:
British Columbia
Year Opened:
1983
Seating Capacity:
54,500
Tenant(s):
BC Lions (CFL), Vancouver Whitecaps FC (MLS)

BEARD-EAVES-MEMORIAL COLISEUM
329 SOUTH DONAHUE DRIVE
AUBURN, AL 36849
334-844-4750
Fax: 334-844-0515
athletics@auburn.edu
www.auburntigers.com
• Jay Jacobs, Director of Athletics
(334) 844-9891
athldir@auburn.edu
• David Benedict, Chief Operating Officer
(334) 844-1411
dpb0013@auburn.edu
• Jeff Steele, Associate Athletic Director, Facilities
(334) 844-2389
steelmj@auburn.edu
• Ben Thomas, Director of Facilities
(334) 844-9176
thomabe@auburn.edu
• Sarah Stallkamp, Manager of Operations
(334) 844-9622
ses0032@auburn.edu
Seating Capacity:
10,500

BEARS & EAGLES RIVERFRONT STADIUM
450 BROAD STREET
NEWARK, NJ 07102
973-848-1000
Fax: 973-621-0095
• Garry Templeton, General Manager

Year Founded:
1999
Capacity:
6,200

BEAVER STADIUM
ONE BEAVER STADUIM
UNIVERSITY PARK
STATE COLLEGE, PA 16802
814-863-1000
www.gopsusports.com
• David M. Joyner, Director of Athletics
(814) 865-1086
Athletic_Director@athletics.psu.edu
• Fran Ganter, Associate Athletic Director for Football Admi
(814) 865-0411
fxg2@psu.edu
• Charmelle Green, Associate Athletic Director/Senior Woman Admi
(814) 865-1104
• Mark Bodenschatz, Associate Athletic Director - Facilities & Op
(814) 863-3489
• Greg Myford, Associate Athletic Director of Business Relat
(814) 865-1757
gjm14@psu.edu
• Joe Battista, Associate Athletic Director of Ice Arena & Ho
(814) 863-203
• Jan Bortner, Assistant Athletic Director
(814) 863-0420
jeb12@psu.edu
Seating Capacity:
106,572
Team:
Pennsylvania State University football.

BEEGHLY GYM
224 WEST SPRING STREET
YOUNGSTOWN, OH 44502
330-941-2962
800-468-6978
Fax: 330-941-3191
ysusports@ysu.edu
ysusports.com/information/facilities/beeghly_center
• Ron Strollo, Executive Director of Intercollegiate Athletics
(330) 941-2385
• Tim Stuart, Assistant Athletic Director
(330) 941-2887
testuart@ysu.edu
• Alvy Armstrong, Head Equipment Manager
(330) 941-3725
adarmstrong@ysu.edu
Seating Capacity:
6,300

BENDER ARENA
4400 MASSACHUSETTS AVENUE NW
WASHINGTON, DC 20016-8005
202-885-3001
Fax: 202-885-3033
walker@american.edu
www.aueagles.com
• Billy Walker, Director of Athletics
(202) 885-3001
walker@american.edu
• Jordan Tobin, Assistant Athletic Director, Facilities
(202) 885-3074
jtobin@american.edu
Arena Seating Capacity:
6,000

BERNARD G. JOHNSON COLISEUM
1964 BOBBY K. MARKS
HUNTSVILLE, TX 77340
936-294-1111
Fax: 936-294-1913
www.gobearkats.com
• Bobby Williams, Athletic Director
(936) 294-4205
bwilliams@shsu.edu
• Greg Hinze, Associate Athletic Director Operations
(936) 294-1725
ghinze@shsu.edu
Coliseum Seating Capacity:
6,110

BERRY EVENTS CENTER
1401 PRESQUE ISLE AVENUE
NORTHERN MICHIGAN UNIVERSITY ATHLETICS
MARQUETTE, MI 49855-5301
906-227-2850
800-682-9797
Fax: 906-227-2855
www.nmuwildcats.com
• Forrest Karr, Director of Athletics
(906) 227-1826
fkarr@nmu.edu
• Carl Bammert, Associate Athletic Director, Facilities
(906) 227-2465
cbammert@nmu.edu
• Kathy Malay, Principal Secretary, Facilities
(906) 227-2851
kmalay@nmu.edu
Seating Capacity:
4,300
Tenant(s):
Northern Michigan Wildcats (Hockey & Basketball).

BETHPAGE BALLPARK
3 COURT HOUSE DRIVE
CENTRAL ISLIP, NY 11722
631-940-3825
Fax: 631-940-3800
info@liducks.com
www.liducks.com
• Frank Boulton, Founder/CEO
• Michael Pfaff, President, General Manager
• Doug Cohen, Assistant General Manager
• Gerry Anderson, Director of Administration
Sport:
Minor League Baseball
Tenant(s):
Long Island Ducks baseball
Year Founded:
2000
Seating Capacity:
6,002

BIG SANDY SUPERSTORE ARENA
ONE CIVIC CENTER PLAZA
HUNTINGTON, WV 25701
304-696-5990
Fax: 304-696-1777
www.bigsandyarena.com
• Rik Edgar, General Manager
(304) 696-5566
redgar@bigsandyarena.com
• Cara Hedrick, Marketing and Sales Manager
(304) 696-5990
• Steve Kessick, Director of Operations
(304) 696-5990
skessick@bigsandyarena.com
• Sherry Sias-Lyell, Finance and Human

Resources Manager
(304) 696-5990
slyell@bigsandyarena.com
Seating Capacity:
9,000
Nature of Service:
Facility can accommodate concerts, flat exhibitions, sales events, seminars, live performances, indoor sporting events including football, basketball, hockey, ice skating, rodeo, motor sports, wrestling. Venue also offers full-service conference center ad
Year Founded:
1977

BILL SNYDER FAMILY STADIUM
1800 COLLEGE AVENUE
BRAMLAGE COLISEUM
MANHATTAN, KS 66502
785-532-6910
1-800-221-CATS
www.kstatesports.com/facilities
• John Currie, Director of Athletics
(785) 532-6912
jcurrie@kstatesports.com
• Clint Dowdle, Chief Of Staff
(785) 532-7056
cdowdle@kstatesports.com
• Scott Garrett, Sr. Associateathletic Director, External Ops.
(785) 532-2880
sgarrett@kstatesports.com
• R.J. Bokelman, Director of Facilities Operations
(785) 532-7601
rjb@kstatesports.com
Team:
Kansas State University
Seating Capacity:
50,000

BILLINGS MUSTANGS PROFESSIONAL BASEBALL CLUB
DEHLER PARK
2611 9TH AVENUE NORTH
BILLINGS, MT 59101
406-252-1241
Fax: 406-252-2968
mustangs@billingsmustangs.com
www.billingsmustangs.com
• Gary Roller, General Manager
groller@billingsmustangs.com
• Chris Marshall, Sr. Director, Corporate Sales
• Matt Schoonover, Sr. Director, Stadium Operations
mschoonover@billingsmustangs.com
• John Barta, Sr. Director, Field Maintenance & Facilities
Seating Capacity:
3,071
Year Founded:
1948

BISMARCK EVENT CENTER
315 SOUTH 5TH STREET
BISMARCK, ND 58504
701-355-1370
Fax: 701-222-6599
www.bismarckeventcenter.com
• Charlie Jeske, General Manager
(701) 355-1370
cjeske@bismarcknd.gov
• Ron Staiger, Operations Director
(701) 355-1381
rstaiger@bismarcknd.gov

Seating Capacity:
10,100
Nature of Service:
Arena, Exhibit Hall, Belle Mehus Theatre.

BLACKHAM COLISEUM
444 CAJUNDOME BOULEVARD
LAFAYETTE, LA 70506
337-482-5393
Fax: 337-482-5830
www.lafayettetravel.com
• Cindy Dermenstein, Convention Services Coordinator
Seating Capacity:
9,800

BLUE CROSS ARENA
ONE WAR MEMORIAL SQUARE
ROCHESTER, NY 14614
585-758-5300
Fax: 585-758-5327
info@bluecrossarena.com
www.bluecrossarena.com
• Jeff E Calkins, General Manager
jcalkins@bluecrossarena.com
Tenant(s) :
Rochester Americans (AHL), Rochester Knighthawks (NLL), Rochester Razorsharks (PBL)
Seating Capacity:
10,669

BLUE CROSS PARK
ONE PORTAGE AVENUE E
WINNIPEG, MB, CANADA R3B 3N3
204-982-2273
Fax: 204-982-2274
contact@goldeyes.com
www.goldeyes.com/blue-cross-park
• Andrew Collier, General Manager
Owners:
Riverside Park Management.
Operators:
Winnipeg Goldeyes Baseball Club Inc.
Year Founded:
1999.
Capacity:
7,461.
Team:
Winnipeg Goldeyes (AA).

BMO FIELD
170 PRINCES' BLVD.
TORONTO, ON, CANADA M6K 3C3
416-263-5700
Fax: 416-815-6050
fanservices@mlse.com
www.bmofield.com
• Michael Friisdahl, President/CEO
Owners:
City of Toronto.
Operators:
Maple Leafs Sports & Entertainment.
Year Opened:
2007
Seating Capacity:
30,991
Tenant(s):
Toronto FC (MLS), Canada men's national soccer team, Canada women's national soccer team, Canada national rugby union team, Toronto Argonauts (CFL).

BOB CARPENTER CENTER
631 SOUTH COLLEGE AVENUE
UNIVERSITY OF DELAWARE
NEWARK, DE 19716
302-831-4016
Fax: 302-831-8653
athletics@udel.edu
www.bluehens.com
• Joe Shirley, Sr. Associate Athletic Director, Facilities
(302) 831-8586
jshirley@udel.edu
• Alica Greco-Walker, Associate Athletic Director, Events & Ops.
(302) 831-8660
agreco@udel.edu
Arena Seating Capacity:
5,100
Organization:
University of Delaware Athletics

BOBBY BOWDEN FIELD AT DOAK CAMPBELL STADIUM
PENSACOLA STREET & STADIUM DRIVE
FLORIDA STATE UNIVERSITY
TALLAHASSEE, FL 32306
850-645-2527
Fax: 850-644-7293
www.seminoles.com/facilities
• Stan Wilcox, Director of Athletics
(850) 644-1079
• Bernie Waxman, Associate Athletics Director, Facilities
(850) 644-9940
bwaxman@fsu.edu
• Ryan Zornes, Assistant Director of Event Management
(850) 228-7589
rzornes@fsu.edu
Seating Capacity:
82,300
Teams:
Florida State University football.

BOBBY DODD STADIUM AT HISTORIC GRANT FIELD
155 NORTH AVENUE NORTHWEST
GEORGIA INSTITUTE OF TECHNOLOGY
ATLANTA, GA 30332
404-894-5400
Fax: 404-894-1300
www.ramblinwreck.com
• Derek Grice, Associate Athletic Director, Facilities
(404) 894-6668
dgrice@athletics.gatech.edu
• Cheryl LaFoy, Director of Event Operations
(404) 894-5431
clafoy@athletics.gatech.edu
• Jackson Matthews, Facilities Manager
(404) 894-5474
jmathews@athletics.gatech.edu
• Doc Hill, Facility Manager, Bobby Dodd Stadium
(404) 894-8490
dhill@athletics.gatech.edu
Stadium Seating Capacity:
55,000

BOBCAT STADIUM
101 BRADDOCK ROAD
FROSTBURG STATE UNIVERSITY
FROSTBURG, MD 21532-2303
301-687-4000
Fax: 301-687-4201

tadell@frostburg.edu
www.frostburgsports.com
• Troy Dell, Athletic Director
(301) 687-4455
• Rubin Stevenson, Associate Athletic
Director
(301) 687-4086
rstevenson@frostburg.edu
Seating Capacity:
4,000
Year Founded:
1974
Track Size:
8 Lane, 400m (42)

BOBCAT STADIUM (MSU)
#1 BOBCAT CIRCLE
MONTANA STATE UNIVERSITY
BOZEMAN, MT 59717
406-994-7117
Fax: 406-994-2278
www.msubobcats.com/sports/2009/9/20/Fac
ilities.aspx
• Peter Fields, Director of Athletics
(406) 994-3499
• Quinn Pacini, General Manager
(406) 994-4244
qpacini@bobcatsportsproperties.com
• Melanie Stocks, Director of Sports
Facilities
(406) 994-6997
Stadium Seating Capacity:
20,767

BOBCAT STADIUM TEXAS STATE
1100 AQUARENA SPRINGS
TEXAS STATE UNIVERSITY
SAN MARCOS, TX 78666
512-245-2114
Fax: 512-245-8387
athletics@txstate.edu
www.txstatebobcats.com
• Jeremy Stolfa, Assistant Athletic Director,
Facilities
(512) 245-2023
stolfa@txstate.edu
• Chris Hannah, Director of Facilities and
Game Ops.
(512) 245-9027
c_h165@txstate.edu
• Cody Farr, Director of Sports Turf
Maintenance
(512) 245-2404
cf24@txstate.edu
Stadium Seating Capacity:
30,000

BOJANGLES' COLISEUM
2700 EAST INDEPENDENCE
BOULEVARD
CHARLOTTE, NC 28205
704-372-3600
Fax: 704-335-3118
www.bojanglescoliseum.com
• Michael Crum, Chief Operating Officer
Permanent Seating Capacity:
8,600

BON SECOURS WELLNESS ARENA
650 NORTH ACADEMY STREET
GREENVILLE, SC 29601
864-241-3800
Fax: 864-250-4939
info@bswarena.com
www.bonsecoursarena.com
• Roger Newton, President / General
Manager

• Randy Collins, Food & Beverage General
Manager
• Beth Paul, Director of Finance and
Administration
• Chris Williams, Operations Manager
• Dwight Rust, Director of Operations
• Rik Knopp, Director of Sales and
Marketing
Seating Capacity:
15,000
Tenant(s) :
Greenville Road Warriors/Swamp Rabbits
(ECHL)

BOONE PICKENS STADIUM
700 WEST HALL OF FAME AVENUE
OKLAHOMA STATE UNIVERSITY
STILLWATER, OK 74078
405-744-7301
877-227-6773
Fax: 405-744-9084
posse@okstate.edu
www.okstate.com/facilities/boone-pickens-st
adium.html
• Shan Rains, Associate Athletic Director,
Facilities Ops.
(405) 744-3012
shan.rains@okstate.edu
• Douglas Beach, Assistant Director of
Athletic Facilities
(405) 744-6142
douglas.beach@okstate.edu
• John Houck, Manager, Cowboy Athletic
Facilities
(405) 780-0004
john.houck@okstate.edu
• Monty Karns, Sr. Associate Athletic
Director, Facilities
monty.karns@okstate.edu
Seating Capacity:
60,218
Tenant(s) :
Oklahoma State Cowboys (NCAA).

BOSSE FIELD
23 DON MATTINGLY WAY
EVANSVILLE, IN 47711
812-435-8686
Fax: 812-435-8688
www.evansvilleotters.com
• Joel Padfield, General Manager
(812) 435-8686
jpadfield@evansvilleotters.com
• Jake Riffert, Director of Operations
(812) 435-8686
• Lance Adler, Sports Turf Manager
(812) 435-8686
• Casie Williams, Controller
Tenant(s) :
Evansville Otters (FL).
Seating Capacity:
5,181

BOUTWELL MUNICIPAL AUDITORIUM
1930 8TH AVENUE NORTH
BIRMINGHAM, AL 35203
205-254-2820
Fax: 205-254-2926
opi@birminghamal.gov
www.birminghamal.gov/about/city-directory/
boutwell-auditorium
• Kevin G. Arrington, Director
(205) 254-2820
• Charlotte Latham, Concessions Supervisor
(205) 254-7762
• Charles Williams, Building Maintenance
Superintendent

(205) 254-7733
• Jesse McElroy, Stage Manager
(205) 254-7761
Seating Capacity:
5,000

BOWEN FIELD
2003 STADIUM DRIVE
BLUEFIELD, WV 24701
304-324-1326
Fax: 304-324-1318
www.milb.com/index.jsp?sid=t517
• George McGonagle, President
(304) 324-1326
• Jeff Gray, General Manager
• Mike White, Director of Fields Operations
Tenant(s) :
Bluefield Blue Jays
Capacity:
3,000

BRADLEY CENTER
1001 NORTH 4TH STREET
MILWAUKEE, WI 53203
414-227-0797
Fax: 414-227-2400
• Brad Harrison, General Manager
(414) 288-1679
brad.harrison@marquette.edu
Seating Capacity:
20,000
Tenant(s) :
Milwaukee Bucks (NBA), Milwaukee
Admirals (AHL), Marquette Golden Eagles
(NCAA).

BRAGG MEMORIAL STADIUM
1835 WAHNISH WAY
TALLAHASSEE, FL 32307
850-599-3000
Fax: 850-599-3810
michael.smith@famu.edu
www.famathletics.com
• Milton Overton, Director of Athletics
(850) 599-3868
• Rose Garrison, Event Manager
(850) 599-3868
rose.garrison@famu.edu
• LaNorris Hayes, Grounds and
Maintenance Staff
(850) 599-3983
Seating Capacity:
25,500

BRAMLAGE COLISEUM
1800 COLLEGE AVENUE
MANHATTAN, KS 66502
785-532-7600
Fax: 785-532-7655
bramlage@ksu.edu
www.kstatesports.com
• John Currie, Director of Athletics
(785) 532-6912
jcurrie@kstatesports.com
• Jim Muller, Director of Facilities
Maintenance
(785) 532-7602
jmuller@kstatesports.com
• Charlie Thomas, Sr. Associate AD, Capital
Project Development
(785) 532-7609
cthomas@kstatesports.com
• Casey Scott, Sr. Associate AD, Operations
& Event Management
(785) 532-5263
caseys@kstatesports.com
• R.J. Bokelman, Director of Facilities

Operations
(785) 532-7601
rjb@kstatesports.com
• Brian Cordill, Director of Event Operations
(785) 532-7713
bcordill@kstatesports.com
Seating Capacity:
12,528

BRENT BROWN BALLPARK
970 W UNIVERSITY PARKWAY
OREM, UT 84058
801-377-2255
Fax: 801-377-2345
www.oremowlz.com
• Rick Berry, General Manager
rick@oremowlz.com
• Julie Hatch, Assistant General Manager
julie@oremowlz.com
Sport:
Baseball
Opened:
2005
Team:
Orem Owlz (Pioneer League); Utah Valley
Wolverines (NCAA)
Seating Capacity:
2,500

BRICK BREEDEN FIELDHOUSE
1 BOBCAT CIRCLE
BOZEMAN, MT 59717
406-994-7117
800-808-5940
mstocks@montana.edu
brickbreeden.com
• Chris Hayden, Director of Operations
(406) 994-4238
christopher.hayden@montana.edu
• Melanie Stocks, Director
(406) 994-6997
mstocks@montana.edu
• Ron Perrin, Director of Concessions
(406) 994-7741
rperrin@montana.edu
Arena Seating Capacity:
8,900

BRIDGESTONE ARENA
501 BROADWAY
NASHVILLE, TN 37203
615-770-2000
Fax: 615-770-2010
www.bridgestonearena.com
• Hugh Lombardi, SVP/General Manager
(615) 770-2002
• Jim Green, Assistant General Manager
(615) 770-2051
Arena Seating Capacity:
20,000
Year Founded:
1996
Tenant(s) :
Nashville Predators

BRIGHT HOUSE NETWORKS STADIUM
4000 CENTRAL FLORIDA BOULEVARD
BUILDING 39
ORLANDO, FL 32816
407-823-3213
adoffice@athletics.ucf.edu
www.ucfknights.com
• Danny White, Director of Athletics
(407) 823-2261
adoffice@athletics.ucf.edu
• Lauren Perez, Director of Executive
Operations

(407) 823-2261
lperez@athletics.ucf.edu
• Tom Snyder, Associate AD, Facilities &
Event Operations
(407) 823-4954
• Matt Oberlin, Director, Event Operations
(407) 823-4299
moberlin@athletics.ucf.edu
• Robert Sample, Director of Sports Turf and
Grounds
(407) 823-4598
rsample@athletics.ucf.edu
Seating Capacity:
44,206
Tenant(s) :
The University of Central Florida

BRINGHURST FIELD
1 BABE RUTH DRIVE
ALEXANDRIA, LA 71301
318-473-2237
Fax: 318-473-2229
• Andrew Aguilar, General Manager
Year Founded:
1933
Capacity:
3,500
Tenant(s) :
Alexandria Aces baseball.

BROADMOOR WORLD ARENA
3185 VENETUCCI BOULEVARD
COLORADO SPRINGS, CO 80906
719-477-2100
Fax: 719-477-2199
www.broadmoorworldarena.com
• Dot Lischick, General Manager
• Tuesday Heslop, Assistant General
Manager
• Claudean Brooks, Executive Assistant
Arena Seating Capacity:
9,000
Year Founded:
1998
Clients:
Colorado College Tigers (NCAA)

BRONCO STADIUM
1910 UNIVERSITY DRIVE
BOISE STATE UNIVERSITY
BOISE, ID 83725
208-426-1000
Fax: 208-426-1998
www.broncosports.com
• Curt Apsey, Executive Director of Athletics
(208) 426-1826
• Bob Carney, Associate Athletic Director,
Facilities & Ops.
(208) 426-2570
robertcarney@boisestate.edu
• Joey King, General Manager
(208) 426-4999
jking@broncosportsproperties.com
• DJ Guimento, Assistant Athletic Director,
Facility Ops.
(208) 426-1513
Stadium Seating Capacity:
76,125

**BROOME COUNTY VETERANS
MEMORIAL ARENA**
ONE STUART STREET
BINGHAMTON, NY 13901
607-778-1528
Fax: 607-778-1528
www.broomearenaforum.com
• Robert Warner, Chairman of the Board

Seating Capacity:
6,925
Tenant(s) :
Binghamton Senators (AHL)

**BROWN COUNTY VETERANS MEMORIAL
ARENA**
2420 NICOLET DRIVE
UNIVERSITY OF WISCONSIN -
GREENBAY
GREEN BAY, WI 54311-7001
920-465-2145
Fax: 920-465-2652
athletics@uwgb.edu
www.greenbayphoenix.com
• Mary Ellen Gillespie, Director of Athletics
(920) 465-2145
• Jeff Krueger, Director of Operations
(920) 465-2189
kruegerj@uwgb.edu
• Brent Tavis, Assistant AD for Events and
Operations
(920) 465-2064
Seating Capacity:
5,248

BROWN STADIUM
235 HOPE STREET
BROWN UNIVERSITY ATHLETICS
PROVIDENCE, RI 02912
401-863-2295
Fax: 401-863-1436
www.brownbears.com
• Jack Hayes, Director of Athletics
(401) 863-2972
• Tom Bold, Sr. Associate Director of
Athletics, Facilities
(401) 863-2295
• AJ Kizekai, Facilities & Operations
Coordinator
(401) 863-1869
• Dave Longo, Manager, Facilities &
Operations
(401) 863-9647
Stadium Seating Capacity:
20,000

BROWNWOOD COLISEUM
500 EAST BAKER
HOWARD PAYNE UNIVERSITY
BROWNWOOD, TX 76801
325-649-8111
Fax: 325-649-8960
achoate@hputx.edu
www.hpusports.com
• John Nickols, Director of Athletics
jnickols@hputx.edu
• Troy Drummond, Associate Director of
Athletics, Operations
(325) 649-8103
tdrummond@hputx.edu
• Abram Choate, Assistant Director of
Athletics, Sports Info.
(325) 649-8111
achoate@hputx.edu
Arena Seating Capacity:
4,000

BRYANT DENNY STADIUM
BOX 870323
UNIVERSITY OF ALABAMA
TUSCALOOSA, AL 35487
205-348-3600
Fax: 205-348-2196
www.rolltide.com
• Bill Battle, Director of Athletics
(205) 348-3600

fgaston@ia.ua.edu
• Brandon Sevedge, Assistant Athletics
Director, Facilities
(205) 348-3573
bsevedge@ia.ua.edu
• Jonathan DeWitt, Director, Athletic
Grounds
Stadium Seating Capacity:
101,821

BRYCE JORDAN CENTER
127 BRYCE JORDAN CENTER
UNIVERSITY PARK, PA 16802
814-865-5555
Fax: 814-863-5705
bjc.psu.edu
• Mark Bodenschatz, Associate Athletic
Director, Facilities
(814) 863-3489
mab163@psu.edu
• Cory Chapman, General Manager
(814) 867-1337
• Shawn Shaible, Athletic Equipment &
Facilities Worker
(814) 865-2723
Arena Seating Capacity:
15,000

BULLDOGS STADIUM
1794 EAST BARSTOW AVENUE
FRESNO, CA 93740
559-431-3647
Fax: 559-278-7003
www.gobulldogs.com
• Jim Bartko, Director of Athletics
(559) 278-3178
athleticdirector@mail.fresnostate.edu
• Thomas Beach, Director of Athletics
• Betsy Mosher, Deputy Director
• Paul Ladwig, Sr.Associate
• John Kriebs, Associate A.d
• Steve Robertello, Associate A.d
• Ryan Reggiani, Assistant A.d
• Betsy Mosher, Sr. Associat AD,
Administration
(559) 879-4876
Stadium Seating Capacity:
41,031
Team:
Fresno State football.

BURGESS-SNOW FIELD AT JSU STADIUM
700 PELHAM ROAD N
JACKSONVILLE, AL 36265
www.jsugamecocksports.com/sports/2008/8
/4/FB_0804082618.aspx
• Greg Seitz, Athletic Director
• John Grass, Head Coach, Football
(256) 782-5365
jsufootball@jsu.edu
Opened:
1947
Team:
Jacksonville State Gamecocks
Seating Capacity:
24,000

BURICH ARENA
950 HARRINGTON STREET SW
HUTCHINSON, MN 55350
320-234-5640
Fax: 320-234-4243
www.hutchinsonprce.com
Arena Seating Capacity:
3,500

BURKE FIELD
9550 16TH STREET NORTH
SAINT PETERSBURG, FL 33716
727-822-6937
800-582-6953
Fax: 727-821-5819
admin@minorleaguebaseball.com
www.minorleaguebaseball.com
• Steve Mullins, Athletic Director
(479) 968-0245
smullins@atu.edu
• Sam Bernabe, Chairman
• Randy Mobley, President
(614) 791-9300
• Branch Rickey, President
(719) 636-3399
• Lee Landers, President (Appalachian
League)
(704) 873-5300
Stadium Seating Capacity:
6,000

BURLINGTON ATHLETIC STADIUM
1450 GRAHAM STREET
BURLINGTON, NC 27217
336-222-0223
Fax: 336-226-2498
info@burlingtonroyals.com
www.burlingtonroyals.com
• Miles Wolff, President
info@burlingtonroyals.com
• Dan Moushon, Vice President
info@burlingtonroyals.com
• Ryan Keur, General Manager
• Miranda Ervin, Assistant General Manager
• Mikie Morrison, Director of Operations

BURLINGTON BEES
2712 MOUNT PLEASANT STREET
BURLINGTON, IA 52601
319-754-5705
Fax: 319-754-5882
www.gobees.com
• Chuck Brockett, General Manager
chuck@gobees.com
• Kim Parker, Assistant General Manager
kim@gobees.com
Arena Seating Capacity:
3,200
Year Founded:
1947

BURTON MEMORIAL COLISEUM
7001 GULF HIGHWAY
LAKE CHARLES, LA 70607
337-721-4090
www.burtoncomplexevents.com
• Jason A. Barnes, General Manager
jbarnes@burtoncomplex.com
• Jared LeBlue, Operations Manager
jleblue@burtoncomplex.com
• Emily Porche, Event Coordinator
eporche@burtoncomplex.com
Arena Seating Capacity:
7000

BUSCH STADIUM
700 CLARK STREET
SAINT LOUIS, MO 63102
314-345-9600
stlouis.cardinals.mlb.com/stl/ballpark
• William O. DeWitt, Jr., Chairman & CEO
(301) 345-9600
• Joe Abernathy, Vice President, Stadium
Operations
(301) 345-9600

Description:
Home of the St. Louis Cardinals, Major
League Baseball team; inaugural game April
10, 2006.
Tenant(s):
MLB - St. Louis Cardinals baseball.
Permanent Seating Capacity:
43,975

BUTLER BOWL
SUNSET AVENUE & WEST 46TH STREET
BUTLER UNIVERSITY
INDIANAPOLIS, IN 46208
317-940-9375
Fax: 317-940-9734
info@butler.edu
www.butlersports.com
• Willis Cheaney, General Manager
(317) 940-8279
wcheaney@butlersportsproperties.com
• Chandler Prince, Manager, Business
Development
(317) 940-8278
cprince@butlersportsproperties.com
Permanent Seating Capacity:
5,647

C.E. GAINES CENTER
601 SOUTH MARTIN LUTHER KING JR.
DRIVE
WINSTON-SALEM STATE UNIVERSITY
WINSTON-SALEM, NC 27110
336-750-2141
Fax: 336-750-8880
wssurams.com
• Tonia Walker, Director of Athletics
(336) 750-2141
• Ariel Germain, Director of Marketing and
Special Events
(336) 750-2936
germaina@wssu.edu
Arena Seating Capacity:
3,200

C.O. BROWN STADIUM
1392 CAPITAL AVENUE NORTHEAST
BATTLE CREEK, MI 49017
269-962-0735
northwoodsleague.com
• Dick Radatz, Jr., Owner
(269) 962-0735
• Anthony Iovieno, General Manager
(269) 962-0735
• Kyle Harvey, Corporate Marketing
Manager
• Andrea Weed, Director of Marketing
• Patrick Bielec, Director of Ballpark
Operations
Stadium Seating Capacity:
4,701

CAJUN FIELD STADIUM
201 REINHARDT DRIVE
LAFAYETTE, LA 70506
337-482-5393
Fax: 337-482-6649
www.ragincajuns.com
• Scott Farmer, Director of Athletics
(337) 482-5393
sfarmer@louisiana.edu
• David Faber, Assistant Athletics Director of
Operations
(337) 482-1835
dfaber@louisiana.edu
Stadium Seating Capacity:
36,900

CAJUNDOME
444 CAJUNDOME BOULEVARD
LAFAYETTE, LA 70506
337-265-2100
Fax: 337-265-2311
www.cajundome.com
• Greg Davis, Director
(337) 265-2100
• Phil Ashurst, Operations Director
(337) 265-2143
Arena Seating Capacity:
11,550

CALFEE PARK
700 SOUTH WASHINGTON AVENUE
PULASKI, VA 24301
540-980-1070
Fax: 540-980-1850
info@pulaskiyankees.net
www.milb.com
• Blair Hoke, General Manager
Arena Seating Capacity:
2,500

CALGARY STAMPEDE
1410 OLYMPIC WAY SE
CALGARY, AB, CANADA T2G 2W1
403-261-0101
Fax: 403-265-7197
info@calgarystampede.com
www.calgarystampede.com
• Joel Cowley, Chief Executive Officer
Description:
Annual rodeo, exhibition, and festival held
every July.
Dates:
July 4-13.
Founded:
1923 (Exhibition and Stampede).

CALIFORNIA MEMORIAL STADIUM
76 CANYON ROAD
BERKELEY, CA 94720-4422
510-642-0580
Fax: 510-642-3399
www.calbears.com
• H. Michael Williams, Director of Athletics
(510) 642-0580
athletic.director@berkeley.edu
• Chris Pezman, Associate AD of Facilities
& Operations
• Matthew Gallagher, General Manager
matthew.gallagher@img.com
• Katie Fontes, Coordinator Sponsor
Services
katie.fontes@img.com
Seating Capacity:
62,467
Teams:
University of California football.

CALIHAN HALL
4001 WEST MCNICHOLS ROAD
UNIVERSITY OF DETROIT MERCY
DETROIT, MI 48221
313-993-1700
Fax: 313-993-2449
www.detroittitans.com
• Robert C. Vowels, Jr., Director of Athletics
(313) 993-1700
vowelsrc@udmercy.edu
• Clifford Sims, Director of Operations
(313) 993-1714
• Tim Fair, Assistant Director of Operatinos
(313) 993-1700
fairtr@udmercy.edu

Arena Seating Capacity:
8,295

CAM HENDERSON CENTER
MARSHALL UNIVERSITY
PO BOX 1360
HUNTINGTON, WV 25715
304-696-5408
Fax: 304-696-6448
www.herdzone.com
• Mike Hamrick, Director of Athletics
(304) 696-5408
• Tom Ponietowicz, Director of Events
(304) 696-7280
ponietowicz@marshall.edu
• Andrew Brown, Director of Facilities
(304) 696-3665
brown613@marshall.edu
Seating Capacity:
62,467

CAMBRIA COUNTY WAR MEMORIAL
326 NAPOLEON STREET
JOHNSTOWN, PA 15901-1704
814-536-5156
800-243-8499
Fax: 814-536-3670
www.warmemorialarena.com/
• Stephen St. John, General Manager
(814) 536-5156
• Karen Gregorchik, Assistant General
Manager
(814) 536-5156
• Brian Levandoski, NCRC Arena Manager
(814) 915-0430
Seating Capacity:
4,001

CAMERON HALL
401 NORTH MAIN STREET
VIRGINIA MILITARY INSTITUTE
LEXINGTON, VA 24450
540-464-7251
Fax: 540-464-7622
www.vmikeydets.com
• Dave Diles, Athletic Director
(540) 464-7251
dilesdl@vmi.edu
Seating Capacity:
5,000

CAMP RANDALL STADIUM
1440 MONROE STREET
UNIVERSITY OF WISCONSIN
MADISON, WI 53711
608-262-1866
800-GO-BADGERS
Fax: 608-265-3036
contactus@uwbadgers.com
www.uwbadgers.com
• Barry Alvarez, Director of Athletics
(608) 262-1866
• Glenn Betts, Building Operations
(608) 262.3354
Tenant(s) :
NCAA - University of Wisconsin football.
Stadium Seating Capacity:
80,321

CAMPANELLI STADIUM
1 FEINBERG WAY
BROCKTON, MA 02301
508-559-7000
Fax: 508-584-1620
roxfun@brocktonrox.com
www.brocktonrox.com

• Chris English, Owner and President
cenglish@brocktonrox.com
• Todd Marlin, General Manager
tmarlin@brocktonrox.com
• Ben Rapaport, Assistant General Manager
Stadium Seating Capacity:
4,750
Year Founded:
2002
Track Type:
Natural grass.

CANADA LIFE CENTRE
300 PORTAGE AVE
WINNIPEG, MB, CANADA R3C 5S4
204-987-7825
info@tnse.com
www.canadalifecentre.ca
• Mark Chipman, Executive Chair, TNSE
• Kevin Donnelly, Sr. Vice President,
Venues & Entertainment
Owners:
True North Sports & Entertainment
Year Opened:
2004
Seating Capacity:
Ice Hockey: 15,321; Concerts: 16,345.
Tenant(s) :
Winnipeg Jets (NHL); Manitoba Moose
(AHL); Winnipeg Sea Bears (CEBL)

CANADA LIFE PLACE
99 DUNDAS STREET
LONDON, ON, CANADA N6A 6K1
519-432-8894
www.canadalifeplace.com
• Tim Leiweke, Chair & CEO, OVG360
• Irving Azoff, Co-Founder, OVG360
Owners:
London Civic Centre Corporation.
Operator:
Global Spectrum
Year Founded:
2002
Seating Capacity:
10,200
Tenant(s) :
London Knights (OHL), London Lightning
(NBL).

CANADIAN TIRE CENTRE
1000 PALLADIUM DRIVE
OTTAWA, ON, CANADA K2V 1A5
613-599-0100
www.canadiantirecentre.com
Owner:
Capital Sports Properties Inc.
Operator:
Canadian Tire
Year Opened:
1996
Seating Capacity:
21,153
Tenant(s) :
Ottawa Senators (NHL); Ottawa Black Bears
(NLL)

CANAL PARK
300 SOUTH MAIN STREET
AKRON, OH 44308
330-253-5151
1-855-977-8225
Fax: 330-253-3300
information@akronrubberducks.com
www.milb.com

• Ken Babby, Owner, CEO
kenbabby@akronrubberducks.com
• Jim Pfander, General Manager
jim@akronrubberducks.com
• Adam Horner, Director, Ballpark
Operations
ahorner@akronrubberducks.com
Sport:
Minor League Baseball.
Team:
Akron Aeros baseball
Year Founded:
1997
Capacity:
7,630

CANTON MEMORIAL CIVIC CENTER
1101 MARKET AVENUE NORTH
CANTON, OH 44702
330-489-3090
Fax: 330-471-8840
www.cantonciviccenter.com
• Blake Schilling, General Manager
blake.schilling@cantonohio.gov
• Geoff Tompkins, Assistant General
Manager
geoff.tompkins@cantonohio.gov
• Steve Meadows, Operations Manager
steve.meadows@cantonohio.gov
• Monica Johnson, Box Office Manager
monica.johnson@cantonohio.gov
• Wilbur Allen, Finance Manager
wilbur.allen@cantonohio.gov
Seating Capacity:
5,200

CAPITAL CITY STADIUM
301 SOUTH ASSEMBLY STREET
COLUMBIA, SC 29201
803-705-4784
Fax: 803-705-4842
www.benedicttigers.com
• Willie Washington, Athletic Director
(803) 705-4734
washingtonw@benedict.edu
• William Hatten, Intramurals and Facilities
Coordinator
(803) 705-4965
hattenw@benedict.edu
Tenant(s) :
Benedict Tigers

CARL WOOTEN STADIUM
PO BOX 430
OKLAHOMA PANHANDLE STATE
COLLEGE
GOODWELL, OK 73939
580-349-2611
800-664-6778
Fax: 580-349-2302
www.opsu.edu
• R. Wayne Stewart, Athletic Director
(580) 349-1408
rwstewart@opsu.edu
Stadium Seating Capacity:
5,000

CARLSON CENTER
2010 2ND AVENUE
FAIRBANKS, AK 99701
907-451-7800
Fax: 907-451-1195
info@carlson-center.com
www.carlson-center.com
• Kristin Baysinger, General Manager
• Adam Powell, Operations Manager
• Camille Relatado, Marketing & Box Office

Manager
• Sarah Nolan, Bookkeeper
Seating Capacity:
4,595
Year Founded:
1990
Tenant(s) :
Alaska Nanooks (WCHA), World Eskimo
Indian Olympics, WWF/WWE
Nature of Service:
Entertainment and sports arena.

CARNIE SMITH
STADIUM/BRANDENBURG FIELD
1701 SOUTH BROADWAY
PITTSBURG STATE UNIVERSITY
PITTSBURG, KS 66762
620-231-7000
800-854-7488
Fax: 620-235-4661
psuinfo@pittstate.edu
www.pittstategorillas.com
• Jim Johnson, Athletics Director
(620) 235-4389
jjohnson@pittstate.edu
• Tom Myers, Associate Athletic Director,
Facilities
(620) 235-4640
ltmyers@pittstate.edu
• Lacie Anderson, Office and Special Events
Manager
(620) 235-4389
landerson@pittstate.edu
Stadium Seating Capacity:
8,343

CARRIER DOME
900 IRVING AVENUE
SYRACUSE UNIVERSITY
SYRACUSE, NY 13244
315-443-4221
888-366-3849
Fax: 315-443-3692
www.carrierdome.com
• Pete Sala, Vice President & Chief
Facilities Officer
(315) 443-4221
pesala@syr.edu
• John DeFrancisco, Facility Systems
Specialist
(315) 443-4221
jadefran@syr.edu
• Lacey Kohl, Operations
• Mark Barbuto, Event Staff Manager
(315) 443-4634
mbarbuto@syr.edu
• Jeremiah Maher, Assistant Athletics
Director, Ticket Sales
(315) 443-2121
Permanent Seating Capacity:
49,262

CARTER FINLEY STADIUM
4600 TRINITY ROAD
RALEIGH, NC 27607
919-515-2101
Fax: 919-515-1161
www.gopack.com
• Jeff Dunlap, Director of Operations
(919) 515-2104
• Deborah A. Yow, Director of Athletics
(919) 515-2109
• Chris Boyer, Deputy Athletic Director,
External Ops.
(919) 513-8085
ccboyer@ncsu.edu
• James Bowling, Carter-Finley Stadium

Facilities
(919) 515-7369
jhbowlin@ncsu.edu
• Christopher Norris, Facilities Maintenance
Supervisor
(919) 515-7369
cwnorris@ncsu.edu
• Nathan Abraham, Assistant Director of
Turf & Grounds
(919) 515-7369
Stadium Seating Capacity:
57,583
Tenant(s) :
North Carolina Wolfpack football (NCAA).

CARVER-HAWKEYE ARENA
1 ELLIOT DRIVE
UNIVERSITY OF IOWA
IOWA CITY, IA 52242-1020
319-335-9743
Fax: 319-335-9333
www.hawkeyesports.com
• Gary Barta, Director of Athletics
(319) 335-9435
gary-barta@uiowa.edu
• Damiam Simcox, Director, Facilities
(319) 335-9410
• Katie Ortmann, Attendant, Facilities
Operations
(319) 335-9406
katie-ortmann@uiowa.edu
Arena Seating Capacity:
15,400
Tenant(s) :
Iowa Hawkeyes men's and women's
basketball, gymnastics, volleyball, and
wrestling

CASHMAN FIELD
850 LAS VEGAS BOULEVARD NORTH
LAS VEGAS, NV 89101
702-943-7200
Fax: 702-386-7214
info@lv51.com
www.lv51.com
• Don Logan, President, COO
(702) 943-7200
dlogan@lv51.com
• Nick Fitzenreider, Vice President,
Operations
fitzstadium@aol.com
• Chip Vespe, Operations Manager
chip@lv51.com
Stadium Seating Capacity:
9,334
Year Founded:
1983

CASPER EVENTS CENTER
200 NORTH DAVID
CASPER, WY 82601
307-235-8400
800-442-2256
Fax: 307-235-8445
www.caspereventscenter.com
• Brett Dovala, Building Manager
(307) 235-8441
• Paul Hanson, Operations Supervisor
(307) 235-8458
• Matt Hinds, Events Coordinator
(307) 235-8449
• Cody Lawson, Maintenance Crew Chief
(307) 235-8434
Arena Seating Capacity:
8,395

CASSELL COLISEUM
675 WASHINGTON STREET SOUTHWEST
BLACKSBURG, VA 24061
540-231-9963
Fax: 540-231-3060
hokipoki@vt.edu
www.hokiesports.com
• Whit Babcock, Director of Athletics
(540) 231-9984
hokipoki@vt.edu
• Tom Gabbard, Sr. Associate Athletics
Director, Facilities
(540) 231-6265
tgabbard@vt.edu
• James Torgersen, Director, Facilities
(540) 231-7584
• Jerry Cheynet, Coordinator, Operations
(540) 231-6067
msoccer@vt.edu
• Pete Pool, Director, Stadium and Fields
(540) 231-6067
ppool@vt.edu
Coliseum Seating Capacity:
10,052

CENTENE STADIUM
1015 25TH STREET NORTH
GREAT FALLS, MT 59401
406-452-5311
Fax: 406-454-0811
voyagers@gfvoyagers.com
www.gfvoyagers.com
• Scott Reasoner, General Manager
(406) 452-5311
scott@gfvoyagers.com
• Matt Coakley, Assistant General Manager
(406) 452-5311
• Scott Lettre, Director of Sales
(406) 452-5311
slettre@gfvoyagers.com
Team:
Great Falls Voyagers
Year Founded:
1969
Capacity:
4,500

BELL CENTRE
1909 AVENUE DES
CANADIENS-DE-MONTREAL
MONTREAL, QC, CANADA H4B 5G0
514-492-1775
855-219-0576
www.centrebell.ca
• Geoff Molson, Owner
Owners:
Groupe CH (Molson family)
Operator:
Evenko
Year Opened:
1996
Seating Capacity:
Hockey: 21,105; Basketball: 22,114;
Concerts: 15,000-19,200; Amphitheatre:
10,000-14,000; Theatre: 5,000-9,000;
Hemicycle: 2,000-3,500; MMA
16,000-23,152
Tenant(s) :
Montreal Canadiens (NHL).

CENTURYLINK CENTER OMAHA
455 NORTH 10TH STREET
OMAHA, NE 68102
402-341-1500
Fax: 402-991-1501
bdrass@creighton.edu
www.centurylinkcenteromaha.com

• Bruce Rasmussen, Athletic Director
(402) 280-2720
bdrass@creighton.edu
• Brandon McCarville, Director of Facilities
brandonmccarville@creighton.edu
• JJ Borecky, Assistant Director of Facilities
jjborecky@creighton.edu
Seating Capacity:
18,975
Owned by:
City of Omaha
Year Opened:
2003
Facility Management:
Metropolitan Entertainment & Convention
Authority.

CESSNA STADIUM
1845 FAIRMOUNT
WICHITA STATE UNIVERSITY
WICHITA, KS 67260-0018
316-978-3265
Fax: 316-978-3336
mediarelations@goshockers.com
www.goshockers.com
• Darron Boatright, Interim Director of
Athletics
(316) 978-5498
dboatright@goshockers.com
• Brad Pittman, Associate Athletic Director,
Facilities & Ops.
(316) 978-5556
bpittman@goshockers.com
• Mike Sandbo, Director of Facilities and
Operations
(316) 978-5512
msandbo@goshockers.com
• Jesse Torres, Director of Equipment
Operations
(316) 978-7471
jtorres@goshockers.com
• Mark Rogers, General Manager
(316) 978-7552
mrogers@goshockers.com
• Sheri Jans, Senior Acount Executive
(316) 978-7554
sjans@goshockers.com
Arena Seating Capacity:
24,000

CFE ARENA
12777 GEMINI BOULEVARD NORTH
ORLANDO, FL 32816
407-823-3070
Fax: 407-823-0248
www.cfearena.com
• Brian Hixenbaugh, General Manager
(407) 823-3070
brian.hixenbaugh@ucf.edu
• Lavar Smith, Assistant General Manager
lavar.smith@ucf.edu
• Mike Terrell, Operations Manager
• Jack Wentzell, Assistant Operations
Manager
jack.wentzell@ucf.edu
• Ryan Fitzgerald, Event Manager
ryan.fitzgerald@ucf.edu
Arena Seating Capacity:
10,072

CHAMPION STADIUM
700 SOUTH VICTORY WAY
LAKE BUENA VISTA, FL 34747
407-938-3500
Fax: 407-938-3442
www.espnwwos.com/complex/champion-stadium

• Vinny O'Leary, Director, Stadium Ops.
Sport:
Minor League Baseball/Major League
Baseball Training.
Tenant(s) :
Atlanta Braves, USSSA Pride (NPF).
Year Founded:
1997
Capacity:
9,500

CHARLES E. SMITH CENTER
600 22ND STREET, NW
GEORGE WASHINGTON UNIVERSITY
WASHINGTON, DC 20052
202-994-6650
Fax: 202-994-6818
gwad@gwu.edu
www.gwsports.com
• Patrick Nero, Director of Athletics
(202) 994-6650
gwad@gwu.edu
• Michael Aresco, Assistant Athletics
Director, Administration
(202) 994-5480
• Andrew Lundt, Assistant Director of
Operations, Facilities
(202) 994-3151
andrew_lundt@gwu.edu
• Autumn Glowacki, Coordinator of
Operations, Events and Facilities
(202) 994-5959
athsched@gwu.edu
Seating Capacity:
5,000
Sports:
Men's & Women's Basketball, Vomen's
Volleyball, Women's Gymnastcs

CHARLES KOCH ARENA
1854 FAIRMOUNT
WICHITA STATE UNIVERSITY
WICHITA, KS 67260
316-978-3456
Fax: 316-978-3345
mediarelations@goshockers.com
www.goshockers.com
• Darron Boatright, Interim Director of
Athletics
(316) 978-5498
dboatright@goshockers.com
• Rege Klitzke, Sr. Associate AD, Business
Ops.
(316) 978-3251
rklitzke@goshockers.com
• Brad Pittman, Associate Athletic Director,
Facilities & Ops.
(316) 978-5556
bpittman@goshockers.com
• Mike Sandbo, Director of Facilities and
Operations
(316) 978-5512
msandbo@goshockers.com
• Jesse Torres, Director of Equipment
Operations
(316) 978-7471
jtorres@goshockers.com
Arena Seating Capacity:
10,506

**CHARLES M. MURPHY ATHLETIC
CENTER**
MURPHY CENTER ROOM G100
MIDDLE TENNESSEE STATE
UNIVERSITY
MURFREESBORO, TN 37132

615-904-8258
Fax: 615-904-8101
rita.whitaker@mtsu.edu
www.mtsu.edu/murphycenter
• Darrell Towe, Director
(615) 904-8258
darrell.towe@mtsu.edu
• Rita Whitaker, Manager
(615) 904-8129
rita.whitaker@mtsu.edu
• Sherrie Murray, Administrative Assistant & Office Manager
(615) 904-8258
sherrie.murray@mtsu.edu
• Chris Gannar, Event Coordinator
(615) 898-5189
chris.gannar@mtsu.edu
Arena Seating Capacity:
11,520

CHARLESTON CIVIC CENTER
200 CIVIC CENTER DRIVE
CHARLESTON, WV 25301
304-345-1500
Fax: 304-345-3492
john.robertson@charlestonwvciviccenter.com
www.charlestonwvciviccenter.com
• John Robertson, General Manager
(304) 345-1500
• Jim Smith, Assistant Manager, Director of Operations
• Betty Tinney, Business Manager
• Anna Campbell, Director of Marketing
(304) 345-1500
Arena Seating Capacity:
13,500
Year Founded:
1959
Nature of Service:
Spectator concert, family events, sporting events, meetings, conventions, banquets.

CHASE FIELD BALL PARK
401 EAST JEFFERSON STREET
PHOENIX, AZ 85004
602-462-6500
Fax: 602-462-6600
ballparktours@dbacks.com
arizona.diamondbacks.mlb.com
• Ken Kendrick, Managing General Partner
(602) 462-6500
• Dave Stewart, SVP & General Manager
(602) 462-6500
• Russ Amaral, VP, Facilities & Event Services
(602) 462-6500
• Bryan White, Director, Event Services
(602) 462-6500
Owned by:
Maricopa County Stadium District.
Seating Capacity:
48,519
Year Founded:
1998
Team:
Arizona Diamondbacks MLB baseball.

CHENEY STADIUM
2502 SOUTH TYLER STREET
TACOMA, WA 98405
253-752-7707
Fax: 253-752-7135
aartman@tacomarainiers.com
www.milb.com/index.jsp?sid=t529
• Aaron Artman, President
(253) 752-7707

aartman@tacomarainiers.com
• Cameron Badgett, Director of Ticket Operations
(253) 752-7707
cbadgett@tacomarainiers.com
• Ryan Schutt, Sr. Director of Ballpark Operations
(253) 752-7707
rschutt@tacomarainiers.com
• Nick Cherniske, Stadium Operations Manager
(253) 752-7707
ncherniske@tacomarainiers.com
Stadium Seating Capacity:
6,800
Year Founded:
1960
Clients:
Tacoma Rainiers Baseball Club

CHESAPEAKE ENERGY ARENA
100 WEST RENO AVENUE
OKLAHOMA CITY, OK 73102
405-602-8700
info@chesapeakearena.com
www.chesapeakearena.com
Seating Capacity:
18,203
Year Founded:
2002
Tenant(s):
Oklahoma City Thunder

CHICKASAW BRICKTOWN BALLPARK
2 SOUTH MICKEY MANTLE DRIVE
OKLAHOMA CITY, OK 73104
Founded:
1998
Team:
Oklahoma City Dodgers
Seating Capacity:
13,066

CHRISTENSEN STADIUM
4300 NORTH LAMESA ROAD
MIDLAND, TX 79706
432-685-4500
Year Founded:
1952
Capacity:
5,000

CHRISTL ARENA
639 HOWARD ROAD
WEST POINT, NY 10996
845-938-6332
Fax: 845-938-8707
www.goarmywestpoint.com
• Boo Corrigan, Director of Athletics
(845) 938-3701
• Steve Tucker, General Manager
(845) 446-2500
stucker@awpsportsproperties.com
• Jillian Mazza, Sponsorship Coordinator
(845) 446-2500
Arena Seating Capacity:
5,043

CHUKCHANSI PARK
1800 TULARE STREET
FRESNO, CA 93721
559-320-4487
Fax: 559-320-1216
info@fresnogrizzlies.com
www.fresnogrizzlies.com

• Derek Franks, President
(559) 320-2524
dfranks@fresnogrizzlies.com
• Andrew Melrose, VP, Partnership Marketing
(559) 320-2502
amelrose@fresnogrizzlies.com
• Andrew Milios, VP, Ticket Sales
(559) 320-2533
amilios@fresnogrizzlies.com
Stadium Seating Capacity:
12,500
Year Founded:
1994, new stadium opened 2002
Nature of Service:
Triple A Affiliate of the Washington Nationals.
Teams:
Fresno Grizzlies

CINCINNATI GARDENS
2250 SEYMOUR AVENUE
CINCINNATI, OH 45212
513-631-7793
Fax: 513-351-5898
info@cincygardens.com
www.cincygardens.com
• Gerry Robinson, Owner/Chairman
• Pete Robinson, President/CEO
(513) 351-3999
• Joe Jagoditz, General Manager
(513) 351-3999
• Greg Waddell, Director of PR/Media Relations
(513) 351-3999
gwaddell@cincygardens.com
• Jerry Henderson, Operations Manager
(513) 351-3999
jhenderson@cincygardens.com
Arena Seating Capacity:
10,208

CITI FIELD
120-01 ROOSEVELT AVENUE
FLUSHING, NY 11368
718-565-1542 EXT 4360
newyork.mets.mlb.com/nym/ballpark
• Fred Wilpon, Chairman of the Board & Chief Executive Officer
• Saul Katz, President
• Jeff Wilpon, Chief Operating Officer
• Sandy Alderson, General Manager
• Sue Lucchi, Vice President, Ballpark Operations
Seating Capacity:
41,922
Team:
New York Mets MLB baseball.

CITIZENS BANK PARK
ONE CITIZENS BANK WAY
PHILADELPHIA, PA 19148
215-463-6000
www.citizensbank.com/ballpark
• Andy MacPhail, President
(215) 463-6000
• David Montgomery, Chairman
(215) 463-6000
• Mike DiMuzio, Director, Operations/Facility
• Eric Tobin, Director, Operations/Events
• Sal DeAngelis, Director, Operations/Security
Year Opened:
2004
Permanent Seating Capacity:
43,651

Tenant(s) :
MLB - Philadelphia Phillies baseball

CIVIC CENTER COMPLEX
701 MAIN STREET
BEAUMONT, TX 77701
409-838-3435
800-782-3081
Fax: 409-838-3715
discoverbeaumont@beaumonttexas.gov
www.discoverbeaumont.com
• Lenny Caballero, Event Facilities Director
• Tommie Minkins, Operations Division
Manager
tminkins@beaumonttexas.gov
• Emily Wheeler, Marketing Division
Manager
ewheeler@beaumonttexas.gov
Arena Seating Capacity:
6,500

CIVIC CENTER OF ANDERSON
3027 MLK JR. BOULEVARD
ANDERSON, SC 29625
864-260-4800
Fax: 864-260-4847
asec@andersoncountysc.org
www.andersonevents.com
• Terry Gaines, Events Coordinator
(864) 260-4800
• Shelly Callahan, Receptionist, Business
Office
(864) 260-4800
Seating Capacity:
3,200

CLASSIC PARK
35300 VINE STREET
EASTLAKE, OH 44095
440-975-8085
Fax: 440-975-8958
www.captainsbaseball.com
• Peter Carfagna, Chairman,
Secretary/Treasurer
• Rita Murphy, Vice Chairman of Captains
Charities
Sport:
Baseball.
Tenant(s) :
Lake County Captains baseball
Capacity:
7,273

CLEMSON MEMORIAL STADIUM
100 PERIMETER ROAD
CLEMSON, SC 29634
864-656-2564
Fax: 864-656-0415
www.clemsontigers.com
• Dan Radakovich, Director of Athletics
(864) 656-1935
• Graham Neff, Deputy Athletics Director
(864) 656-0128
neffg@clemson.edu
• Gary Wade, Assistant Athletic Director of
Facilities
(864) 643-6004
wgary@clemson.edu
Stadium Seating Capacity:
81,500

**CLEVE L. ABBOTT MEMORIAL ALUMNI
STADIUM**
1200 WEST MONTGOMERY ROAD
TUSKEGEE, AL 36088

334-724-4545
Fax: 334-724-4233
www.goldentigersports.com
• Curtis Campbell, Director of Athletics
(334) 724-4545
• Dave Lunn, Manager, Athletics Facilities
and Transportation
Stadium Seating Capacity:
10,000

CMC-NORTHEAST STADIUM
2888 MOOSE ROAD
KANNAPOLIS, NC 28083
704-932-3267
Fax: 704-938-7040
info@intimidatorsbaseball.com
kannapolis.intimidators.milb.com
• Brad Smith, President
• Randy Long, General Manager
rlong@intimidatorsbaseball.com
• Josh Feldman, Director of
Communications
• Darren Cozart, Director of Operations
Sport:
Baseball.
Tenant(s) :
Kannapolis Intimidators baseball.
Year Founded:
1995
Capacity:
4,700

COBO ARENA
1 WASHINGTON BOULEVARD
DETROIT, MI 48226
313-877-8777
Fax: 313-877-8577
www.cobocenter.com
• Thom Connors, Regional Vice President
SMG
• Claude Molinari, General Manager Cobo
Center
• Cedric Turnbore, Director of Operations
• Greg DeSandy Turnbore, Director of Sales
and Event Services
Arena Seating Capacity:
12,141

COCA-COCA FIELD
1 JAMES D. GRIFFIN PLAZA
BUFFALO, NY 14203
716-846-2000
Fax: 716-852-6530
info@bisons.com
www.bisons.com
• Joseph W. Segarra, Vice President, Chief
Operating Officer
• Jonathan A. Dandes, President, Rich
Baseball Operations
• Michael Buczkowski, Vice President,
General Manager
• Tom Sciarrino, Director, Stadium
Operations
• Robert Free, Director of Foodservice
Operations
Seating Capacity:
18,025

COCA-COLA COLISEUM
19 NUNAVUT RD
TORONTO, ON, CANADA M6K 3C3
416-815-5982
Fax: 416-263-3901
www.coca-colacoliseum.com
Owners:
City of Toronto.
Operators:

Maple Leafs Sports & Entertainment Ltd.
Seating Capacity:
Hockey 8,100; Boxing/Wrestling 7,600;
Basketball 8,500; Extreme Sports 5,200
Tenant(s) :
Toronto Marlies (AHL); Toronto Sceptres
(PWHL)

COHEN STADIUM
9700 GATEWAY N. BOULEVARD
EL PASO, TX 79924
915-755-2000
Seating Capacity:
9,725

COLEMAN COLISEUM
BOX 870323
TUSCALOOSA, AL 35487
205-348-3600
Fax: 205-348-2196
www.rolltide.com
• Bill Battle, Athletic Director
(205) 348-3600
• Brandon Sevedge, Assistant Athletics
Director, Facilities
(205) 348-3573
bsevedge@ia.ua.edu
Arena Seating Capacity:
15,383

COLLEGE OF WILLIAM & MARY
751 UKROP WAY
WILLIAMSBURG, VA 23185
757-221-3400
Fax: 757-221-3412
www.tribeathletics.com
• Terry Driscoll, Athletic Director
(757) 221-3332
• Michael Pritchett, Assistant Athletics
Director, Facilities & Ops.
(757) 221-3355
mapritchett@wm.edu
• Adam Andrusyszyn, Assistant Director,
Facilities & Ops.
(757) 221-3345
anandrusyszyn@wm.edu
• Shane Vernarsky, Head Athletic
Equipment Amanager
(757) 221-3335
sjvernarsky@wm.edu
• Vicki Collier, Facilities & Operations
Coordinator
(757) 221-1039
vmcollier@wm.edu
Arena Seating Capacity:
8,600
**Walter J. Zable Stadium Seating
Capacity:**
11,686

COLONIAL LIFE ARENA
801 LINCOLN STREET
COLUMBIA, SC 29208
803-576-9200
Fax: 803-576-9299
www.coloniallifearena.com
• Sid Kenyon, General Manager
(803) 576-9200
• Lexie Boone, Sr. Assistant General
Manager, Director of Ops.
(803) 576-9200
• Curt Derrick, Assistant General Manager,
Director of Ticketing
(803) 576-9200
• Julie Carter, Director of Business
Operations
(803) 576-9200

Year Opened:
2002
Arena Seating Capacity:
18,000
Tenant(s) :
NCAA - University of South Carolina basketball.

COMERICA PARK
2100 WOODWARD AVENUE
DETROIT, MI 48201-3470
313-962-4000
Fax: 301-985-6254
• Michael Illitch, Detroit Tigers Owner/Director
(313) 471-2000
• Al Avila, EVP of Baseball Ops & General Manager
(313) 471-2000
• Brian Skipinski, Director, Park Operations
(313) 471-2000
• Heather Nabozny, Head Groundskeeper
(313) 471-2000
• Ed Goward, Sr Manager, Park Operations
(313) 471-2000
Stadium Seating Capacity:
41,574
Tenant(s) :
MLB - Detroit Tigers baseball.

COMMONWEALTH STADIUM (EDMONTON)
11000 STADIUM ROAD NW
EDMONTON, AB, CANADA T5H 4E2
780-442-5311
311@edmonton.ca
www.edmonton.ca/attractions_events/comm
onwealth-stadium
Owners:
City of Edmonton
Year Opened:
1978
Seating Capacity:
56,302
Tenant(s) :
Edmonton Elks (CFL)

COMMONWEALTH STADIUM (KENTUCKY)
338 LEXINGTON AVENUE
LEXINGTON, KY 40506-0604
859-257-8000
mbarn@uky.edu
www.ukathletics.com
• Mitch Barnhart, Athletics Director
(859) 257-8015
mbarn@uky.edu
• Elizabeth Briggs, Assistant Athletic Director, Premium Seating
(859) 257-1757
elizabeth.briggs@uky.edu
• Kevin Saal, Sr. Associate Athletic Director, Operations
(859) 254-2788
• Donnie Mefford, Assistant Athletic Director, Facilities
(859) 257-7124
donnie.mefford@uky.edu
Seating Capacity:
61,000

COMMUNITYAMERICA BALLPARK
1800 VILLAGE WEST PARKWAY
KANSAS CITY, KS 66111
913-328-2255
Fax: 913-328-5674
www.tbonesbaseball.com

• John Ehlert, Owner
• Matt Fulks, Director of Media Relations
(913) 328-5639
• Adam Ehlert, President
• Chris Browne, General Manager
• John Massarelli, Manager, Director of Baseball Operations
• Kyle Disney, Stadium Operations Coordinator
(913) 328-5655
Tenant(s) :
Kansas City T-Bones baseball.
Seating Capacity:
10,385

CONSOL ENERGY CENTER
1001 FIFTH AVENUE
PITTSBURGH, PA 15219
412-642-1800
Fax: 412-642-1925
info@consolenergycenter.com
www.consolenergycenter.com
• Jay Roberts, General Manager
(412) 642-1893
Seating Capacity:
18,000
Tenant(s) :
Pittsburgh Penguins (NHL).

CONVOCATION CENTER: EMU
799 NORTH HEWITT ROAD
EASTERN MICHIGAN UNIVERSITY
YPSILANTI, MI 48197
734-487-1050
Fax: 734-487-6898
www.emich.edu/bookemu/convo/
• Heather Lyke, Vice President, Director of Athletics
(734) 487-1050
• Mike Malach, Sr. Associate AD for Finance/Operations
(734) 487-7174
michael.malach@emich.edu
• Adam Martin, Director of Facilities and Operations
(734) 487-1050
• Andrew Hensley, Assistant Director of Facilities
(734) 487-1050
ahensle3@emich.edu
Seating Capacity:
8,824
Year Founded:
1998

CONVOCATION CENTER: NIU
1525 WEST LINCOLN HIGHWAY
NORTHERN ILLINOIS UNIVERSITY
DEKALB, IL 60115-2854
815-752-6800
Fax: 815-753-7700
convocenter@niu.edu
www.niuconvo.com
• Sean T. Frazier, Director of Athletics
(815) 753-9473
• John Cheney, Sr. Associate Athletics Director, Facilities
(815) 753-1801
jcheney2@niu.edu
• Kiera Miller, Assistant Athletics Director, Compliance
(815) 753-8339
kmiller4@niu.edu
Arena Seating Capacity:
10,000
Year Founded:
2002

COOLEY LAW SCHOOL STADIUM
505 E MICHIGAN AVENUE
LANSING, MI 48912
517-485-4500
Fax: 517-485-4518
www.lansinglugnuts.com
• Nick Grueser, General Manager
ngrueser@lansinglugnuts.com
• Dennis Busse, Stadium Operations Manager
ext 459
dbusse@lansinglugnuts.com
Founded:
1996
Team:
Lansing Lugnuts
Seating Capacity:
7,527

COORS EVENTS CENTER
950 REGENT DRIVE
BOULDER, CO 80309
303-492-5319
Fax: 303-492-4801
www.cubuffs.com
• Rick George, Athletic Director
(303) 492-6843
rick.george@colorado.edu
• Steve Pizzi, Assistant Athletics Director, Coors Events Center
(303) 492-4749
stephen.pizzi@colorado.edu
• Jason DePaepe, Associate Athletic Director, Facilities
(303) 492-4749
jason.depaepe@colorado.edu
• Marco Amrbiz, Custodail Maintenance Staff, Coords Events Center
(303) 492-4749
Seating Capacity:
11,064

COORS FIELD
2001 BLAKE STREET
DENVER, CO 80205
303-292-0200
Fax: 303-296-2068
colorado.rockies.mlb.com
• Richard L. Monfort, Owner, CEO
• Jeff Bridich, Sr. Vice President & General Manager
• Lenus Lucero, Assistant VP, Balpark Operations
Permanent Seating Capacity:
50,398
Owned by:
State of Colorado.

COPELAND PARK
800 COPELAND AVENUE
LA CROSSE, WI 54603
608-796-9553
Fax: 608-796-9032
info@lacrosseloggers.com
www.lacrosseloggers.com
• Dan Kapanke, Owner
• Chris Goodell, General Manager
• Ben Kapanke, Assistant General Manager
• Elizabeth Kapanke, Director of Merchandising
Sport:
Minor League Baseball.
Tenant(s) :
Lacrosse Loggers baseball (NWL), UW-La Crosse (NCAA).
Year Founded:
2003

Capacity:
3,550

CORN PALACE
604 NORTH MAIN STREET
MITCHELL, SD 57301
605-995-8430
Fax: 605-996-8273
cornpalace.com
• Scott Schmidt, Director
(605) 995-8427
sschmidt@cornpalace.com
Arena Seating Capacity:
3,200

COTTON BOWL/FAIR PARK
3921 MARTIN LUTHER KING JR.
BOULEVARD
DALLAS, TX 75210
214-565-9931
info@bigtex.com
bigtex.com
Seating Capacity:
92,100
Team:
Heart of Dallas Bowl (NCAA)

COW PALACE
2600 GENEVA AVENUE
DALY CITY, CA 94014
415-404-4111
Fax: 415-469-6111
info@cowpalace.com
www.cowpalace.com
• Mara Kopp, President
• Barbara Wanvig, 1st Vice President
• Paul Wattis, 2nd Vice President
• Ken Alstott, CEO
Seating Capacity:
16,500
Year Founded:
1941

COWBOY STADIUM
700 EAST MCNEESE STREET
LAKE CHARLES, LA 70605
337-475-5000
800-622-3352
Fax: 337-475-5202
www.mcneesesports.com
• Bruce Hemphill, Director of Athletics
(337) 475-5563
bhemphill@mcneese.edu
• Steve Gugliucci, Director of Marketing,
Ticket Operations
(337) 475-5208
sgugliucci@mcneese.edu
• Tommy McClelland, Director
Stadium Seating Capacity:
17,410

COWBOYS STADIUM
ONE AT&T WAY
ARLINGTON, TX 76011
817-892-4000
800-745-3000
stadium.dallascowboys.com
• Jeff Stroud, General Manager
• Jud W. Heflin, Director of Planning and
Logistics
• Paul Turner, Director of Event Operations
& Security
• Scott Woodrow, Director of Stadium
Engineering
• Tod Martin, Director of Stadium Projects

Seating Capacity:
80,000
Tenant(s) :
Dallas Cowboys (NFL), Cotton Bowl Classic
(NCAA)

COWELL STADIUM
145 MAIN STREET
DURHAM, NH 03824
603-862-1850
Fax: 603-862-4069
unhwildcats.com
• Marty Scarano, Director of Athletics
(603) 862-2013
marty.scarano@unh.edu
• Jon Danos, Sr. Associate Athletic Director,
External Affairs
(603) 862-4677
jon.danos@unh.edu
• Carrie Kimball, Associate Athletic Director,
Operations
(603) 862-2774
carolynn.kimball@unh.edu
• Ciaran Cullen, Associate Athletic Director,
Business Development
(603) 862-0287
ciaran.cullen@unh.edu
• Jean Mitchell, Athletic Facilities,
Housekeeping Manager
(603) 862-4746
Seating Capacity:
6,500

COWTOWN COLISEUM
121 EAST EXCHANGE AVENUE
FORT WORTH, TX 76164
817-625-1025
888-269-8696
Fax: 817-625-1148
stockyardsrodeo.com
• Hub Baker, General Manager
(817) 625-1025
• Clay Barlow, Facilities Manager
(817) 625-1025
• Nate Krieger, Marketing Director
(817) 625-1025
Coliseum Seating Capacity:
3,418

CRANDON PARK TENNIS CENTER
7300 CRANDON BOULEVARD
KEY BISCAYNE, FL 33149
305-365-2300
www.miamidade.gov/parks/crandon-tennis.a
sp
Seating Capacity:
13,800

CRISLER CENTER
333 EAST STADIUM BOULEVARD
UNIVERSITY OF MICHIGAN
ANN ARBOR, MI 48104
734-647-2583
Fax: 734-764-3221
info@umich.edu
www.mgoblue.com
• Mark S. Schlissel, President
(734) 764-6270
• Rob Rademacher, Executive Sr. Associate
Athletic Director, COO
(734) 647-9763
Seating Capacity:
12,707

**CRYPTO.COM ARENA/ANSCHUTZ
ENTERTAINMENT GROUP**
1111 S FIGUEROA STREET
SUITE 2350
LOS ANGELES, CA 90015
213-742-7100
www.cryptoarena.com
• Dan Beckerman, President & CEO, AEG
• Ross Pebley Jr., Vice President
Former Name:
Staples Center
Tenant(s) :
NBA - Los Angeles Clippers basketball;
NBA - Los Angeles Lakers basketball; NHL -
Los Angeles Kings hockey; WNBA - Los
Angeles Sparks basketball.
Arena Seating Capacity:
Basketball 19,079; Ice Hockey 18,230;
Arena Football 16,096; Boxing/Wrestling
16,000-21,000; Concerts 20,000

DAKOTADOME
414 EAST CLARK STREET
DEPARTMENT OF ATHLETICS
VERMILLION, SD 57069
605-677-5309
Fax: 605-677-5618
www.goyotes.com
• David Herbster, Athletics Director
(605) 677-5943
david.herbster@usd.edu
• Dan Gaston, Sr. Associate Athletic
Director, Operations
• Gary Madsen, Operations Manager
gary.madsen@usd.edu
Stadium Seating Capacity:
10,000

DAMASCHKE FIELD
95 RIVER STREET
ONEONTA, NY 13820
607-432-6326
Fax: 607-432-1965
• Nader John, Assistant GM/Business
Manager
Tenant(s) :
Oneonta Outlaws
Year Founded:
1905

**DARRELL K ROYAL - TEXAS MEMORIAL
STADIUM**
2139 SAN JACINTO BOULEVARD
AUSTIN, TX 78712
512-471-9405
www.texassports.com
• Dave Marmion, Executive Sr. Associate
Athletic Director
(512) 471-4067
• Nick Voinis, Sr. Associate Athletics
Director, Communications
(512) 471-2151
• Ed Goble, Executive Sr. Associate AD,
Facilities
(512) 471-6848
Seating Capacity:
100,119

DAVIS WADE STADIUM AT SCOTT FIELD
90 B.S. HOOD DRIVE
MISSISSIPPI STATE, MS 39762
662-325-2532
Fax: 662-325-7904
www.hailstate.com
• Scott Stricklin, Director of Athletics
(662) 325-0863
scottstricklin@athletics.msstate.edu

• Don Williams, General Manager
(662) 325-4171
dwilliams@learfield.com
• Bobby Tomlinson, Associate AD, Facility
Planning
(662) 325-7452
btomlinson@athletics.msstate.edu
• Jay Logan, Associate AD, Event &
Facilities Management
(662) 325-2877
jlogan@athletics.msstate.edu
Stadium Seating Capacity:
61,337
Year Founded:
1914
Track Type:
Prescription Athletic Turf

DAYTONA BEACH LEISURE SERVICES
301 SOUTH RIDGEWOOD AVENUE
DAYTONA BEACH, FL 32114
386-671-8337
Fax: 386-671-3410
www.codb.us
• Percy Williamson, Director
Permanent Seating Capacity:
10,000

DEAN E. SMITH CENTER
300 SKIPPER BOWLES DRIVE
UNIVERSITY OF NORTH CAROLINA
CHAPEL HILL, NC 27514
919-962-6000
Fax: 919-966-3173
www.goheels.com
• Bubba Cunningham, Athletic Director
(919) 962-6000
bubba.cunningham@unc.edu
• Angie Bitting, Director of Smith Center
(919) 962-6000
abitting@uncaa.unc.edu
• Curt Brossman, Smith Center Operations
Assistant
(919) 962-6000
cbrossman@unc.edu
Permanent Seating Capacity:
21,750

DEE EVENTS CENTER
3870 STADIUM WAY DEPT. 2701
OGDEN, UT 84408
801-626-6817
Fax: 801-626-6490
www.weberstatesports.com
• Jerry Bovee, Director of Intercollegiate
Athletics
(801) 626-6817
• Ron Goch, Associate Athletics Director,
External Operations
(801) 626-6731
• Paul Grua, Director of Athletic
Communications
(801) 626-7414
pgrua@weber.edu
Arena Seating Capacity:
11,500

DEE GLEN SMITH SPECTRUM
7400 OLD MAIN HILL
LOGAN, UT 84322
435-797-1850
Fax: 435-797-2615
john.hartwell@usu.edu
www.utahstateaggies.com
• John Hartwell, Athletics Director
(435) 797-2060
john.hartwell@usu.edu

• Landon Day, General Manager, Aggie
Sports Properties
(435) 797-8991
lday@aggiesportsproperties.com
• Reed Capener, Director of Event
Operations
(435) 797-7186
reed.capener@usu.edu
• Jana Doggett, Deputy Athletics Director,
External Operations
(435) 797-3907
kana.doggett@usu.edu
Stadium Seating Capacity:
10,270

DELL DIAMOND
3400 EAST PALM VALLEY BOULEVARD
ROUND ROCK, TX 78665
512-255-2255
Fax: 512-255-1558
info@rrexpress.com
www.roundrockexpress.com
• Reese Ryan, Owner & CEO
dbowman@rrexpress.com
• JJ Gottsch, Chief Operating Officer
jjgottsch@rrexpress.com
• Tim Jackson, General Manager
tjackson@rrexpress.com
• David Powers, Senior Director, Stadium
Operations
dpowers@rrexpress.com
• Aurelio Martinez, Director, Stadium
Maintenance
amartinez@rrexpress.com
Team:
Round Rock Express
Year Founded:
2000
Capacity:
8,631

DELMAR STADIUM COMPLEX
1900 MANGUM ROAD
HOUSTON, TX 77455
713-957-7700
Fax: 713-957-7704
• Mike Truelove, Stadium Supervisor
Field Seating Capacity:
12,000

**DELTAPLEX ENTERTAINMENT & EXPO
CENTER**
2500 TURNER AVENUE NORTHWEST
GRAND RAPIDS, MI 49544
616-364-9000
Fax: 616-559-8001
events@deltaplex.com
deltaplex.com
• Joel Langlois, President
(616) 364-9000
joel@deltaplex.com
• Erin Spaanstra, Assistant General
Manager & Event Director
(616) 559-7927
erin@deltaplex.com
• Adam Sturt, Operations Manager
(616) 365-5759
operations@deltaplex.com
Arena Seating Capacity:
7,000

DENVER COLISEUM
4600 HUMBOLDT STREET
DENVER, CO 80216
720-865-2475
tad.bowman@denvergov.org
www.denvercoliseum.com

• Tad Bowman, Venue Director
(720) 865-2488
tad.bowman@denvergov.org
• Steve Jorgensen, Guest Services
Manager
(720) 865-2477
steven.jorgensen@denvergov.org
• Jeannette Murrietta, Booking Manager
(720) 865-2484
jeannette.murrietta@denvergov.org
• Jordan Bishop, Assistant Director of
Marketing & Communications
(720) 865-4309
jordan.bishop@denvergov.org
Seating Capacity:
10,500

DEVAULT MEMORIAL STADIUM
BOX 1434
BRISTOL, VA 24203
276-206-9946
Fax: 276-669-7686
gm@bristolbaseball.com
www.bristolbaseball.com
• Mark Young, Vice President of Community
Relations
marky@bristolbaseball.com
• Craig Adams, Vice President of Game Day
Operations
ballparkoperations@bristolbaseball.com
• Lucas Hobbs, Vice President of Marketing
and Communications
marketing@bristolbaseball.com
Seating Capacity:
2,000
Team:
Bristol White Sox

DIAMOND FIELD
3001 NORTH BOULEVARD
RICHMOND, VA 23230
804-359-3866
Fax: 804-359-1373
info@squirrelsbaseball.com
• Chuck Domino, Chief Executive Officer
• Ben Rothrock, Assistant General Manager
of Operations
ben.rothrock@squirrelsbaseball.com
• Steve Pump, Director of Stadium
Operations
steve.pump@squirrelsbaseball.com
• Steve Ruckman, Director of Field
Operations
stever@squirrelsbaseball.com
Tenant(s) :
Richmond Braves baseball
Year Founded:
1985
Capacity:
12,134

DICKEY-STEPHENS PARK
400 WEST BROADWAY STREET
NORTH LITTLE ROCK, AR 72114
501-664-1555
travs@travs.com
• Greg Johnston, Park Superintendent
greg@travs.com
Opened:
April 12, 2007
Team:
Arkansas Travelers
Sport:
Baseball
Seating Capacity:
5,800 fixed seats; 7,200 seating capacity for
baseball

DIDDLE ARENA
1605 AVENUE OF CHAMPIONS
BOWLING GREEN, KY 42101-6412
270-745-3542
www.wkusports.com
• Todd Stewart, Director of Athletics
(270) 745-5276
• Craig Biggs, Associate AD, Administration
(270) 745-5279
craig.biggs@wku.edu
• Lee Forsythe, Assistant Athletic Director,
Facilities
(270) 745-2903
les.forsythe@wku.edu
• Chris Bloomfield, General Manager
(270) 745-6462
chris.bloomfield@imgworld.com
Seating Capacity:
7,326

DODGE PHYSICAL FITNESS CENTER
WEST 119TH STREET & BROADWAY
NEW YORK, NY 10027
212-854-2548
Fax: 212-854-6200
www.gocolumbialions.com
• Bill Ebner, Facilities Operations Director
• Patrick Desir, Manager Of Facilities
Operations
(212) 854-3441
pd2227@columbia.edu
Seating Capacity:
3,405

DODGER STADIUM
1000 ELYSIAN PARK AVENUE
LOS ANGELES, CA 90012
866-800-1275
Fax: 323-224-1269
www.dodgers.com
• Steve Ethier, Sr. Vice President, Stadium
Operations
• Josh Byrnes, Sr. Vice President, Baseball
Operations
• David Edford, Director of Facilities
Permanent Seating Capacity:
56,000
Description:
Home Stadium For: Los Angeles Dodgers
Owned by:
Los Angeles Dodgers

DON MCBRIDE STADIUM
201 NW 13TH STREET
RICHMOND, IN 47374
765-983-7291
Fax: 765-962-7529
Year Founded:
1995
Capacity:
1,787

DONALD E. YOUNG FITNESS CENTER
1200 UNIVERSITY STREET
UNIT 9409
SPEARFISH, SD 57799-9424
605-642-6096
800-255-2478
Fax: 605-642-6539
www.bhsu.edu/StudentLife/YoungCenter.as
px
• Jhett Albers, Director of Athletics
(605) 642-6885
jhett.albers@bhsu.edu
• Melissa Christensen, Assistant Athletic
Director, External Operations
(605) 642-6460

melissa.christensen@bhsu.edu
• Brock Anundson, Assistant Athletic
Director, Facility Operations
(605) 642-6882
brock.anundson@bhsu.edu
• Brock Anundson, Assistant Athletic
Director, Facility Operations
(605) 642-6882
brock.anundson@bhsu.edu
Arena Seating Capacity:
4,000

DONALD L. TUCKER CIVIC CENTER
505 WEST PENSACOLA STREET
TALLAHASSEE, FL 32301
850-645-2527
Fax: 850-644-7293
www.seminoles.com
• Stan Wilcox, Director of Athletics
(850) 644-1079
vcupp@admin.fsu.edu
• Karl Hicks, Deputy Athletics Director,
External Operations
(850) 645-2014
kphicks@fsu.edu
• Brandon Kendrick, Assistant Director of
Facilities
(850) 228-9316
bkendrick@fsu.edu
Seating Capacity:
13,500

**DONALD W. REYNOLDS RAZORBACK
STADIUM**
350 NORTH RAZORBACK ROAD
FAYETTEVILLE, AR 72701
479-575-6533
Fax: 479-575-4904
raztk@uark.edu
www.arkansasrazorbacks.com
• Jeff Long, Vice Chancellor and Director of
Athletics
(479) 575-7641
athldir@uark.edu
• Pat Berger, Director of Sports Turf
(479) 575-6887
pberger@uark.edu
• Chris Freet, Sr. Associate AD, External
Operations
(479) 575-6533
cjfreet@uark.edu
• Chris Pohl, Associate AD, Event
Management
(479) 575-7312
cpohl@uark.edu
• Justin Maland, Associate Athletic Director,
Facilities
(479) 575-6768
jmaland@uark.edu
Seating Capacity:
72,000

**DORT FEDERAL CREDIT UNION EVENT
CENTER**
3501 LAPEER ROAD
FLINT, MI 48503
810-744-0580
Fax: 810-744-2906
www.dorteventcenter.com
• Jeremy Torrey, General Manager
jeremy@dorteventcenter.com
Opened:
1969
Team(s) :
Flint Firebirds (OHL); Waza Flo (MASL)
Seating Capacity:

Hockey 4,021; Boxing 5,109; Concerts
6,469

DOYT PERRY FIELD STADIUM
1610 STADIUM DRIVE
BOWLING GREEN, OH 43403
419-372-2401
Fax: 419-372-0475
ckingst@bgsu.edu
www.bgsufalcons.com
• Chris Kingston, Director of Athletics
(419) 372-7052
ckingst@bgsu.edu
• Jamie Baringer, Assistant AD, Arena
Operations
(419) 372-2764
jbaring@bgsu.edu
• Steve Messenger, Assistant AD,
Operations & Events
(419) 372-7263
smessen@bgsu.edu
• Chuck Spicer, Falcon Sports Properties
General Manager
(419) 372-4007
cspicer@falconsportsproperties.com
Stadium Seating Capacity:
24,000

DOZER PARK
730 SW JEFFERSON STREET
PEORIA, IL 61605
peoria.chiefs.milb.com/index.jsp?sid=t443
Founded:
2002
Team:
Peoria Chiefs
Seating Capacity:
7,500

DR. PEPPER BALLPARK
7300 ROUGHRIDERS TRAIL
FRISCO, TX 75034
972-334-1900
Fax: 972-731-7455
info@ridersbaseball.com
www.ridersbaseball.com
• Chuck Greenberg, CEO & General Partner
• Jason Dambach, General Manager
• Scott Burchett, Chief Operating Officer
• Gina Pierce, Director, Game Entertainment
Sport:
Minor League Baseball.
Tenant(s) :
Frisco RoughRiders (TL), TXU Energy
Winter Games of Texas
Year Founded:
2003

DRAKE STADIUM
2507 UNIVERSITY AVENUE
DES MOINES, IA 50311
515-271-2889
Fax: 515-271-4189
godrakebulldogs.com
• Sandy Hatfield, Director of Athletics
(515) 271-2889
sandra.clubb@drake.edu
• Dave Haskin, Associate Athletic Director,
External Affairs
(515) 271-4628
dave.haskin@drake.edu
• Brady Randall, Assistant Athletic Director,
Operations
(515) 271-3849
brady.randall@drake.edu
• Greg Ellis, General Manager

(515) 271-4894
greg.ellis@img.com
Stadium Seating Capacity:
14,557

DRAKE STADIUM/UCLA
325 WESTWOOD PLAZA
LOS ANGELES, CA 90095
310-825-8699
Fax: 310-206-7047
www.uclabruins.com
• Dan Guerrero, Director of Athletics
ad@athletics.ucla.edu
• Jake Kuennen, Facilities Manager
jkuennen@athletics.ucla.edu
• Mike Dowling, Associate Athletic Director,
Operations
mdowling@athletics.ucla.edu
• Kevin Borg, Assistant Athletic Director,
Facilities
kborg@athletics.ucla.edu
Tenant(s) :
Drake Relays, Drake University football
(NCAA).
Seating Capacity:
14,557

DUDY NOBLE STADIUM, POLK-DEMENT STADIUM
145 LAKEVIEW DRIVE
MISSISSIPPI STATE UNIVERSITY
MISSISSIPPI, MS 39762
662-325-5232
Fax: 662-325-7904
rice@athletics.msstate.edu
www.hailstate.com
• Scott Stricklin, Director of Athletics
(662) 325-0863
• Don Williams, General Manager, Bulldogs
Sports Properties
(662) 325-4171
• Mike Nemeth, Sr. Associate AD,
Administration
(662) 325-2300
Stadium Seating Capacity:
7,200
Year Founded:
1967
Track Type:
Tiflawn 419 Hybrid Bermuda Grass

DUNN CENTER
WINFIELD DUNN CENTER
CORNER OF MARION STREET & DRANE
STREET
ROOM 141417
CLARKSVILLE, TN 37040
931-221-7127
877-861-2778
Fax: 931-221-7980
gov@apsu.edu
letsgopeay.com
• Ryan Ivey, Director of Athletics
(931) 221-7904
iveyr@apsu.edu
• Josh Jorgensen, Assistant Athletics
Director, External Affairs
(931) 221-7672
jorgensenj@apsu.edu
• Bud Jenkins, Facilities Director
(931) 221-7700
jenkinsc@apsu.edu
Arena Seating Capacity:
7,257

DUNN FIELD
546 LUCE STREET
ELMIRA, NY 14904
607-734-2690
Fax: 607-734-0891
www.theelmirapioneers.com
• Don Lewis, Owner
(607) 734-2690
donspioneers@gmail.com
• Robbie Nichols, Owner
(607) 734-2690
generalmanagernichols@yahoo.com
• Chris P. Bacon, Director of Fan
Entertainment
(607) 734-2690

DURHAM BULLS ATHLETIC PARK
409 BLACKWELL STREET
DURHAM, NC 27701
919-687-6500
Fax: 919-687-6560
info@durhambulls.com
www.durhambulls.com
• Mike Birling, General Manager
(919) 687-6500
mbirling@durhambulls.com
• Scott Strickland, Director of Stadium
Operations
(919) 687-6500
sstrickland@durhambulls.com
• Cortlund Beneke, Operations Manager
cbeneke@durhambulls.com
• Peter Wallace, Director of Ticketing
(919) 687-6500
pwallace@durhambulls.com
Sport:
Baseball.
Tenant(s) :
Durham Bulls baseball.
Capacity:
10,000

DUTCHESS STADIUM
1500 ROUTE 9D
WAPPINGERS FALLS, NY 12524
845-838-0094
Fax: 845-838-0014
www.hvrenegades.com
• Jeff Goldklang, President
• Eben Yager, Senior Vice President &
General Manager
eben@hvrenegades.com
• Vicky DeFreese, Director of Business
Operations
vicky@hvrenegades.com
• Jon Basil, Director of Ticket Sales
• Joe Ausanio, Director of Baseball
Operations
joe@hvrenegades.com
Sport:
Baseball.
Tenant(s) :
Hudson Valley Renegades baseball.
Capacity:
4,494

DWYER STADIUM
299 BANK STREET
BATAVIA, NY 14020
585-343-5454
Fax: 585-343-5620
www.muckdogs.com
• Travis Sick, General Manager
(585) 343-5454
• Mike Ewing, Assistant General Manager
(585) 343-5454
• Don Rock, Director of Stadium Grounds

(585) 343-5454
rockhead44@hotmail.com
• Kathy Bills, Director of Merchandising
(585) 454-1001
Sport:
Baseball.
Team:
Batavia Muckdogs
Capacity:
2,600

EAGLEBANK ARENA
4500 PATRIOT CIRCLE
FAIRFAX, VA 22030
www.eaglebankarena.com
• Brad Edwards, Asst. Vice President,
Director of Athletics
bedwards@gmu.edu
• Dave Paulsen, Head Coach, Men's
Basketball
dpaulsen@gmu.edu
• Nyla Milleson, Head Coach, Women's
Basketball
nmilleso@gmu.edu
Team:
George Mason Patriots
Seating Capacity:
10,000

ECCLES COLISEUM
351 WEST UNIVERSITY BOULEVARD
SOUTHERN UTAH UNIVERSITY
CEDAR CITY, UT 84720
435-865-8354
Fax: 435-586-5444
www.suutbirds.com
• Jason Butikofer, Athletic Director
jasonbutikofer@suu.edu
• Andrew Parrish, Chief Operating Officer
andrewparrish@suu.edu
• David Thompson, Director for Business
Operations
(435) 865-8263
davidthompson6@suu.edu
Coliseum Seating Capacity:
8,500

ED & RAE SCHOLLMAIER ARENA
2800 STADIUM DRIVE
FORT WORTH, TX 76109
817-257-7000
Fax: 817-257-7656
www.gofrogs.com
• Chris Del Conte, Director of Intercollegiate
Athletics
• T. Ross Bailey, Sr. Associate Athletic
Director, Facilities
r.bailey@tcu.edu
Seating Capacity:
6,800

ED SMITH STADIUM/SPORTS COMPLEX
2700 12TH STREET
SARASOTA, FL 34237
941-893-6300
Fax: 941-365-1587
baltimore.orioles.mlb.com
• Peter G. Angelos, Chief Executive Officer
• Robert A. Ames, Chief Financial Officer
• Kevin Cummings, Director, Ballpark
Operations
Owned by:
City of Sarasota, Florida
Sport:
Baseball.
Team:
Sarasota Red Sox.

Stadium Seating Capacity:
8,500

EL PASO COUNTY COLISEUM
4100 EAST PAISANO DRIVE
EL PASO, TX 79905
915-534-4229
Fax: 915-532-4048
• Brian Kennedy, President/CEO
bkennedy@elpasosports.us
• James Smith, VP, Director of Operations
jsmith@elpasosports.us
• Thea Chambers, Marketing Director
(915) 494-4907
Fixed Seating Capacity:
5,250

EMENS AUDITORIUM
2000 WEST UNIVERSITY AVENUE
BALL STATE UNIVERSITY
MUNCIE, IN 47306
765-285-1539
Fax: 765-285-3719
emens@bsu.edu
cms.bsu.edu/web/emens/
• Mark Sandy, Director of Intercollegiate
Athletics
(765) 285-5131
• Pat Quinn, Deputy Athletics Director,
Operations
(765) 285-8907
• Chris Ulm, General Manager, Ball State
Sports Properties
(765) 285-1434
Auditorium Seating:
3,575

ENMAX CENTRE
2510 SCENIC DRIVE SOUTH
LETHBRIDGE, AL T1K 1N2
403-320-4040
Fax: 403-327-3620
www.enmaxcentre.ca
• Kim Gallucci, General Manager
(403) 320-4086
• Jordan Dekens, Sales & Marketing
Manager
(403) 320-3807
• Len Overbeeke, Operations Manager
(403) 320-4055
• Becky Little, Events Manager
(403) 320-4119
becky.little@lethbridge.ca
• Jennifer Norsworthy, Account & Ticket
Manager
(403) 328-7361
jennifer.norsworthy@lethbridge.ca
Seating Capacity:
5,479
Tenants:
Lethbridge Hurricanes (WHL)

ERIE INSURANCE ARENA
809 FRENCH STREET
ERIE, PA 16501
814-453-7117
Fax: 814-455-9931
casey@erieevents.com
www.erieinsurancearena.com
• John A. Wells, Executive Director
(814) 453-7117
casey@erieevents.com
• Ray Williams, Director of Sports Facilities
rwilliams@erieevents.com
• Jeff Esposito, General Manager
• Barry Copple, Operations Manager
barry@erieevents.com

Seating Capacity:
9,000
Year Founded:
1983
Nature of Service:
Multi-purpose facility.
Tenant(s) :
Erie BayHawks (NBA D-League), Erie Otters
(OHL).

**ESPN WIDE WORLD OF SPORTS
COMPLEX**
PO BOX 10000
LAKE BUENA VISTA, FL 32830
407-938-3398
Fax: 407-938-3478
www.espnwwos.com/complex/
Date opened:
1997

EVERETT MEMORIAL STADIUM
3802 BROADWAY
EVERETT, WA 98201
425-258-3673
Fax: 425-258-3675
info@aquasox.com
www.aquasox.com
• Danny Tetzlaff, General Manager
dannyt@aquasox.com
• Dustin Coder, Director of Tickets
• Pat Dillon, Director of Corporate
Partnerships
patd@aquasox.com
• Rick Maddox, Director of Food and
Beverage
rickm@aquasox.com
Sport:
Baseball.
Tenant(s) :
Everett Aqua Sox baseball.
Year Founded:
1984
Capacity:
12,000

EXHIBITION PLACE
100 PRINCES' BOULEVARD
TORONTO, ON, CANADA M6K 3C3
416-263-3000
info@explace.on.ca
www.explace.on.ca
• Don Boyle, Chief Executive Officer
DBoyle@explace.on.ca
Owners:
City of Toronto.
Year Opened:
1879.

EXPO NEW MEXICO
300 SAN PEDRO NE
ALBUQUERQUE, NM 87108
505-222-9700
Fax: 505-266-7784
www.exponm.com
• Dan Mourning, General Manager
(505) 222-9700
• Erin Thompson, Deputy Manager
• Ken Salazar, Operations Manager
• Sally Mayer, Senior Manager
Permanent Seating Capacity:
12,000

EXPOCITE
250 WILFRID-HAMEL BLVD
QUÂ☐BEC CITY, QC, CANADA G1L 5A7

418-691-7110
888-866-3976
info@expocite.com
www.expocite.com
• Melissa Coulombe-Leduc, Chair
Owners:
Quebec City.
Operators:
ExpoCite.
Year Founded:
1898

FAIR GROUNDS FIELD
2901 PERSHING BOULEVARD
SHREVEPORT, LA 71109
318-636-5555
Fax: 318-636-5670
Sport:
Baseball
Year Founded:
1986
Seating Capacity:
Stadium/Arena 4,200

FAIR PARK COLISEUM
1012 AVENUE A
LUBBOCK, TX 79408
806-763-2833
Fax: 806-744-5903
info@southplainsfair.com
southplainsfair.com
Sports Arena Seating Capacity:
8,513

FALCON PARK
130 NORTH DIVISION STREET
AUBURN, NY 13021
315-255-2489
Fax: 315-255-2675
info@auburndoubledays.com
www.milb.com/index.jsp?sid=t458
• Mike Voutsinas, General Manager
• Andrew Sagarin, Operations Manager
• Paul Mullin, Sponsorship Services
Manager
Sport:
Baseball.
Tenant(s) :
Auburn Doubledays baseball.
Year Founded:
1995
Capacity:
2,800

FALCON STADIUM
2169 FIELD HOUSE DRIVE
US AIR FORCE ACADEMY
COLORADO SPRINGS, CO 80840-9500
719-333-4008
www.goairforcefalcons.com
• Jim Knowlton, Director of Athletics
(719) 333-4008
• Col. Tony McKenzie, Director of Staff
(719) 333-4008
tony.mckenzie1@usafa.edu
• Mitch Mann, Associate AD, External
Operations
(719) 333-2626
• Gary Sheffield, Stadium Manager
(719) 333-4924
Seating Capacity:
46,692

FAMILY ARENA, THE
2002 ARENA PARKWAY
ST. CHARLES, MO 63303

636-896-4200
Fax: 636-896-4205
info@familyarena.com
familyarena.com
• Jim Knowlton, Director of Athletics
(719) 333-4008
Arena Seating Capacity:
10,467

FANT-EWING COLISEUM
308 WARHAWK WAY
MONROE, LA 71209-9900
318-342-5360
Fax: 318-342-5367
www.ulmwarhawks.com
• Brian Wickstrom, Director of Athletics
(318) 342-5360
• Phil Shaw, Associate Athletics Director,
Internal Ops.
(318) 342-5442
• Kevin VanDerzee, Assistant Athletics
Director, Business Ops.ra
(318) 342-5380
• Joe Domingos, General Manager
(318) 342-3556
jdomingos@warhawksportsproperties.com
Seating Capacity:
7,085

FARGODOME
1800 UNIVERSITY DRIVE NORTH
FARGO, ND 58102
701-241-9100
Fax: 701-237-0987
dome.info@fargodome.com
www.fargodome.com
Seating Capacity:
26,700

FARREL STADIUM
855 SOUTH NEW STREET
WEST CHESTER, PA 19383
610-436-3555
Fax: 610-921-7566
www.wcupagoldenrams.com
• Edward Matejkovic, Director of Athletics
(610) 436-3555
ematejkovic@wcupa.edu
• Terry Beattie, Associate Athletic Director,
Facilities
(610) 436-3317
tbeattie@wcupa.edu
• Chris Frey, Facilities, Operations Manager
(610) 430-4416
cfrey@wcupa.edu
Stadium Seating Capacity:
7,500

FAUROT FIELD AT MEMORIAL STADIUM
MIZZOU ATHLETICS
MIZZOU ARENA
1 CHAMPIONS DRIVE
COLUMBIA, MO 65205
573-882-6501
www.mutigers.com
• Mack Rhoades, Director of Athletics
(573) 882-2055
• Allen Frost, Mizzou Sports Park Facils.
Mgr. - Memorial Stadium
frosta@missouri.edu
• Barry Odom, Head Coach, Football
Seating Capacity:
71,168
Team:
University of Missouri Tigers

FEDEXFIELD
1600 FEDEX WAY
LANDOVER, MD 20785
301-276-6000
Fax: 301-276-6002
www.redskins.com
• Daniel Snyder, Owner
• Scot McCloughan, General Manager
• Dennis Greene, President of Business
Operations
Description:
Home Stadium for the Washington Redskins
Permanent Seating Capacity:
82,000

FENWAY PARK
4 YAWKEY WAY
BOSTON, MA 02215
617-226-6000
Fax: 617-226-6394
events@redsox.com
boston.redsox.mlb.com
• Sam Kennedy, President
(617) 226-6000
• Mike Hazen, Sr. Vice President, General
Manager
(617) 226-6000
• Frank Wren, Sr. Vice President, Baseball
Operations
(617) 226-6000
• Pete Nesbit, Vice President, Ballpark
Operations
(617) 226-6000
• Raquel Ferreira, Vice President, Baseball
Administration
Tenant(s):
MLB - Boston Red Sox baseball.
Permanent Seating Capacity:
37,227

FERRELL CENTER
1500 SOUTH UNIVERSITY PARKS DRIVE
WACO, TX 76706
254-710-1234
Fax: 254-710-1968
www.baylorbears.com
• Ian McCaw, Director of Athletics
(254) 710-1222
• Nick Joos, Executive Associate AD,
External Affairs
(254) 710-3043
nicholas_joos@baylor.edu
• Wes Yeary, Director of Sports Ministries
(254) 710-3027
wes_yeary@baylor.edu
Arena Seating Capacity:
12,000

FIFTH THIRD BALLPARK
4500 WEST RIVER DRIVE NE
COMSTOCK PARK, MI 49321
616-784-4131
800-277-7946
Fax: 616-784-4911
playball@whitecapsbaseball.com
www.fifththirdballpark.com
• Lew Chamberlin, CEO
lchamberlin@whitecapsbaseball.com
• Denny Baxter, Chief Financial Officer
dbaxter@whitecapsbaseball.com
• Chad Sayen, Director of Ticket Sales
chads@whitecapsbaseball.com
• Michael Craven, Operations Manager
mcraven@whitecapsbaseball.com
Sport:
Baseball.
Team:

West Michigan Whitecaps
Year Founded:
1994
Capacity:
9,684

FIFTH THIRD FIELD
220 NORTH PATTERSON BOULEVARD
DAYTON, OH 45402
937-228-2287
Fax: 937-228-2284
dragons@daytondragons.com
dayton.dragon.milb.com
• Robert Murphy, President and General
Manager
teampresident@daytondragons.com
• John Wallace, Sr. Director of Operations
john.wallace@daytondragons.com
• Joe Elking, Director of Facility Operations
• Britt Barry, Sports Turf Manager
Seating Capacity:
7,230
Year Founded:
2000

FIRST AMERICAN BANK BALLPARK
5514 CHAMPIONS DRIVE
MIDLAND, TX 79706
432-520-2255
Fax: 432-520-8326
rockhounds@nwol.net
www.midlandrockhounds.org
• Miles Prentice, President
• Monty Hoppel, General Manager
(432) 520-2255
• Andrew Brown, Director of Ticket
Operations
(432) 520-2255
• Ray Fieldhouse, Assistant General
Manager, Operations
(432) 520-2255
• C.J. Bahr, Director of Stadium Operations
(432) 520-2255
Team:
Midland Rockhounds
Sport:
Baseball
Year Founded:
2002
Capacity:
6,669

FIRST ENERGY STADIUM
100 ALFRED LERNER WAY
CLEVELAND, OH 44114
440-891-5050
Fax: 440-891-5051
www.firstenergystadium.com
• Alec Scheiner, President
• Sashi Brown, Executive Vice President,
Footbal Ops.
• Phil Dangerfield, Vice President, Football
Operations
Stadium Seating Capacity:
67,431
Description:
Home stadium for NFL - Cleveland Browns

FIRSTENERGY STADIUM
1900 CENTRE AVENUE/RT 61 SOUTH
READING, PA 19605
610-375-8469
Fax: 610-373-5868
info@fightins.com
www.milb.com/index.jsp?sid=t522

- Scott Hunsicker, General Manager
- Matt Hoffmaster, Executive Director of Operations
- Kevin Sklenarik, Executive Director of Baseball Operations
- Mike Becker, Executive Director of Tickets
- Eric Scarcella, Director of Public Relations
Sport:
Baseball.
Team:
Reading Phillies
Year Founded:
1951
Capacity:
9,000

FLORENCE CIVIC CENTER
3300 WEST RADIO DRIVE
FLORENCE, SC 29501
843-679-9417
Fax: 843-679-9429
info@florenceciviccenter.com
www.florenceciviccenter.com
- Paul Beard, Jr., Director of Operations
- Tony Rogers, Operations Manager
- Mark Wade, Director of Sales and Marketing
Arena Seating Capacity:
9,736

FNB FIELD
245 CHAMPION WAY
HARRISBURG, PA 17101
717-231-4444
Fax: 717-231-4445
information@senatorsbaseball.com
www.milb.com/index.jsp?sid=t547
- Randy Whitaker, General Manager
(717) 231-4444
whitaker@senatorsbaseball.com
- Tim Foreman, Director of Stadium Operations
(717) 231-4444
Sport:
Minor League Baseball.
Tenant(s):
Harrisburg Senators, Harrisburg City Islanders
Year Founded:
1987
Capacity:
6,187

FOLSOM FIELD
2400 COLORADO AVENUE
BOULDER, CO 80302
303-492-2200
Fax: 303-492-1700
www.cubuffs.com
- Rick George, Athletic Director
(303) 492-6843
rick.george@colorado.edu
- Lance Gerlach, General Manager
(303) 469-9600
lgerlach@buffalosportsproperties.com
- Steve Pizzi, Assistant AD, Coors Events Center
(303) 492-1994
stephen.pizzi@colorado.edu
- Jason DePaepe, Associate AD, Facilities & Operations
(303) 492-1994
jason.depaepe@colorado.edu
Stadium Seating Capacity:
50,183

FORD FIELD
2000 BRUSH STREET
DETROIT, MI 48226
313-262-2000
Fax: 313-262-2808
www.detroitlions.com
- Michael Singer, Sr. Director of Corporate Partnership
- Veronica Bonner, Sr. Manager of Human Resources
- Jared Kozinn, Director of Business Development
- Mark Graham, Director of Ticket Operations
- Fred Reddig, Director of Facilities
Year Opened:
2002
Seating Capacity:
65,000
Tenant(s):
NFL - Detroit Lions football.

FORUM FIELD
84 MECHANIC STREET
PRESQUE ISLE, ME 04769
207-764-0491
Fax: 207-764-2525
theforum@pirec.org
www.pirec.org
Arena Seating Capacity:
4,800

FOSTER FIELD
1600 UNIVERSITY AVENUE
SAN ANGELO, TX 76904
325-942-6587
Fax: 325-947-9480
www.angelosports.com
- James Reid, Interim Director of Athletics
(325) 942-2267
james.reid@angelo.edu
- Troy Hill, Assistant Athletics Director, Sports Medicine
(325) 486-6055
troy.hill@angelo.edu
- Brandon Ireton, Assistant Athletics Director of Athletic Comm.
(325) 942-2378
brandon.ireton@angelo.edu
Arena Seating Capacity:
4,200
Year Founded:
2000
Tenant(s):
Angelo State Rams (NCAA)

FOX CITIES STADIUM
2400 NORTH CASALOMA DRIVE
PO BOX 7464
APPLETON, WI 54912
920-733-4152
Fax: 920-733-8032
info@timberrattlers.com
www.milb.com/index.jsp?sid=t572
- Rob Zerjav, President
rzerjav@timberrattlers.com
- Aaron Hahn, Vice President, Assistant General Manager
ahahn@timberrattlers.com
- Ryan Moede, Director of Tickets
rmoede@timberrattlers.com
- Ron Kaiser, Director of Stadium Operations
- Aaron Johnson, Stadium Operations Manager
Sport
Baseball.

Capacity:
5,900

FRANK ERWIN CENTER
1701 RED RIVER
AUSTIN, TX 78701
512-471-7744
Fax: 512-471-9652
comments@erwin.utexas.edu
www.uterwincenter.com
- John M. Graham, Executive Sr. Associate Athletics Director
(512) 471-4716
john.graham@athletics.utexas.edu
- Thom Ramirez, Assistant Director for Operations
(512) 471-2645
thom.ramirez@athletics.utexas.edu
- Chris Reynolds, General Manager
(512) 471-2646
christopher.reynolds@sodexo.com
Arena Seating Capacity:
16,540

FRANK HOWARD FIELD AT MEMORIAL STADIUM
1 AVENUE OF CHAMPIONS
CLEMSON, SC 29634
800-253-6766
www.clemsontigers.com
- Dan Radakovich, Director of Athletics
(864) 656-1935
danrad1@clemson.edu
- Graham Neff, Deputy Athletics Director
(864) 656-0128
- Dabo Swinney, Head Coach, Football
(864) 656-2796
Seating Capacity:
80,301
Team:
Clemson Tigers

FRANKLIN FIELD
235 SOUTH 33RD STREET
UNIVERSITY OF PENNSYLVANIA
PHILADELPHIA, PA 19104
215-898-6151
Fax: 215-573-2095
www.pennathletics.com
- M. Grace Calhoun, Director of Athletics and Recreation
(215) 898-7215
athdir@pobox.upenn.edu
- Alanna Shanahan, Deputy Director of Athletics
(215) 898-9828
- Roger Reina, Sr. Associate AD, External Affairs
(215) 898-6602
rreina@upenn.edu
- Michael J. Diorka, Associate AD, Facility Management
(215) 898-6121
- Scott Ward, Assistant AD, Operation
(215) 898-6153
sward2@upenn.edu
- Noah Gustkey, Assistant AD, Facilities
(215) 573-4025
gustkey@upenn.edu
Stadium Seating Capacity:
52,958
Team:
University of Pennsylvania football.

FRASER FIELD
365 WESTERN AVENUE
LYNN, MA 01904

781-595-9400
Fax: 781-583-5025
navigatorsgm@gmail.com
www.nsnavs.com
• Bill Terlecky, General Manager
• Ashley Laramie, Assistant General
Manager
• Pete Laven, President, Salvi Sports
Sport:
Baseball.
Tenant(s) :
North Shore Spirit baseball
Year Founded:
1940
Capacity:
3,804

FREEDOM HALL CIVIC CENTER
1320 PACTOLAS ROAD
FREEDOM HALL CIVIC CENTER
JOHNSON CITY, TN 37604
423-461-4855
Fax: 423-461-4867
www.johnsoncitytn.org
• Lisa Chamness, Director
(423) 461-4855
Arena Seating Capacity:
19,200
Year Founded:
1956

FREEMAN COLISEUM
3201 EAST HOUSTON STREET
SAN ANTONIO, TX 78219
210-226-1177
Fax: 210-226-5081
www.freemancoliseum.com
• Derrick Howard, Executive Director
(210) 226-1177
derrickh@freemancoliseum.com
• JC Hrubetz, General Manager
(210) 226-1177
jc@freemancoliseum.com
• John Kinard, Assistant Operations
Manager
(210) 225-2562
johnk@freemancoliseum.com
• Jeanne Janes, Marketing Director
(210) 226-1177
jeanne@freemancoliseum.com
• Anna Harrier, Events Director
(210) 226-1177
annah@freemancoliseum.com
Arena Seating Capacity:
11,700

FRESNO CONVENTION & ENTERTAINMENT CENTER
848 M STREET
2ND FLOOR
FRESNO, CA 93721
559-445-8100
800-788-0836
Fax: 559-445-8110
fresnoconvention-entertainmentcenter@smg
fresno.com
www.fresnoconventioncenter.com
• William Overfelt, General Manager
(559) 445-8150
bill.overfelt@smgfresno.com
• Lyn Higginson, Director of Finance
(559) 445-8152
lyn.higginson@smgfresno.com
• Matt Heinks, Box Office Manager
(559) 445-8200
matt.heinks@smgfresno.com
• Skyla Souza, Event Manager

(559) 445-8171
skyla.souza@smgfresno.com
• Israel Morales, Utility Manager
(559) 445-8169
israel.morales@smgfresno.com
Arena Seating Capacity:
11,300

FRONTIER FIELD
ONE MORRIE SILVER WAY
ROCHESTER, NY 14608
585-454-1001
Fax: 585-454-1056
info@redwingsbaseball.com
www.redwingsbaseball.com
• Naomi Silver, President, CEO & COO
nsilver@redwingsbaseball.com
• Dan Mason, General Manager
dmason@redwingsbaseball.com
• Rob Dermody, Director of Ticket
Operations
rdermody@redwingsbaseball.com
• Jeff Dodge, General Manager, Food &
Beverage
Sport:
Baseball.
Team:
Rochester Red Wings.
Year Founded:
1996
Capacity:
13,500

G. RICHARD PFITZNER STADIUM
7 COUNTY COMPLEX COURT
WOODBRIDGE, VA 22192
703-590-2311
Fax: 703-590-5716
info@potomacnationals.com
www.potomacnationals.com
• Art Silber, Chairman, CEO
• Lani Silber Weiss, President, COO
• Zach Prehn, Vice President, General
Manager
• Chris Bentivegna, Director of Ticket
Operations
• Arthur Bouvier, Director of Stadium
Operations
Stadium Seating Capacity:
6,000
Nature of Service:
Minor League Baseball.

GAINBRIDGE FIELDHOUSE
125 SOUTH PENNSYLVANIA STREET
INDIANAPOLIS, IN 46204
317-917-2500
Fax: 317-917-2599
pacersinsider@pacers.com
www.gainbridgefieldhouse.com
• Herbert Simon, Owner, Chairman and
CEO
• Kevin Pritchard, President, Basketball
Operations
• Mel Raines, CEO
• Andy Arnold, SVP, Facility Operations
Former Names:
Conseco Fieldhouse; Bankers Life
Fieldhouse
Seating Capacity:
Basketball 17,274; Ice Hockey 11,651;
Concerts 19,000
Home Arena for:
NBA-Indiana Pacers; WNBA-Indiana Fever

GARCELON FIELD
130 CENTRAL AVENUE
LEWISTON, ME 04240

207-786-6411
Fax: 207-786-8232
athletics.bates.edu
• Kevin McHugh, Director of Athletics
(207) 786-6341
kmchugh@bates.edu
• Tommy Verdell, Assistant Athletic Director
(207) 786-6357
tverdell@bates.edu
Stadium Seating Capacity:
3,000

GARRETT COLISEUM
1555 FEDERAL DRIVE
MONTGOMERY, AL 36109
334-356-6866
Fax: 334-272-6835
www.thegarrettcoliseum.com
• Bill Hardin, Director of Events and
Marketing
(334) 356-6866
bill@thegarrettcoliseum.com
• Connie Luckie, Office Manager
(334) 356-6866
connie@thegarrettcoliseum.com
Arena Seating Capacity:
10,500

GARY SOUTH SHORE RAILCATS
U.S. STEEL YARD
ONE STADIUM PLAZA
GARY, IN 46402
219-882-2255
Fax: 219-882-2259
www.railcatsbaseball.com
• Pete Laven, President, Salvi Sports
Enterprises
• Brian Lyter, General Manager
blyter@railcatsbaseball.com
• David Kay, Assistant General Manager
(219) 882-2255
dkay@railcatsbaseball.com
• Phil West, Director of Food and Beverage
(219) 882-2255
pwest@railcatsbaseball.com
• Noah Simmons, Head Groundskeeper,
Operations
(219) 331-9833
nsimmons@railcatsbaseball.com
Team:
Gary Southshore Railcats
Year Founded:
2002
Capacity:
6,139

GCS BALLPARK
2301 GRIZZLIE BEAR BOULEVARD
SAUGET, IL 62206
618-337-3000
Fax: 618-332-3625
www.gatewaygrizzlies.com
• Steve Gomric, General Manager
sgomric@gatewaygrizzlies.com
• Kurt Ringkamp, Director of Stadium
Operations
kringkamp@gatewaygrizzlies.com
Sport:
Baseball.
Tenant(s) :
Gateway Grizzlies (Frontier League).
Year Founded:
2002
Seating Capacity:
6,000

GEORGE J. SHERMAN FAMILY-SPORTS COMPLEX
2095 HILLSIDE ROAD
UNIT 1173
STORRS, CT 06269
860-486-2725
Fax: 860-486-3300
athleticdirector@uconn.edu
www.uconnhuskies.com
• David Benedict, Director of Athletics
(860) 486-2725
athleticdirector@uconn.edu
• Neal Eskin, Sr. Associate Director of
Athletics, External
neal.eskin@uconn.edu
• Maureen O'Connor, Associate Director of
Athletics, Business Services
(860) 486-4142
• Evan Feinglass, Associate Director of
Athletics, Facilities
(860) 486-4712
evan.feinglass@uconn.edu
• Tom Murphy, General Manager
(860) 834-3339
tom.murphy@img.com

GEORGE M. STEINBRENNER FIELD
ONE STEINBRENNER DRIVE
TAMPA, FL 33614
813-673-3055
Fax: 813-673-3174
www.steinbrennerfield.com
• C. Vance Smith, Director of Florida
Operations, General Manager
vsmith@yankees.com
• Matt Gess, Assistant General Manager,
Marketing
mgess@yankees.com
• AmySue Manzione, Operations
Coordinator
amanzione@yankees.com
• Jennifer Magliocchetti, Assistant Director,
Ticket Operations
jmagliocchetti@yankees.com
Sport:
Baseball
Tenant(s) :
New York Yankees (spring training), Tampa
Yankees (FSL), Gulf Coast Yankees (GCL)
Year Founded:
1996
Capacity:
11,026

GEORGIA DOME
ONE GEORGIA DOME DRIVE NW
ATLANTA, GA 30313-1591
404-223-9200
Fax: 404-223-8011
• Frank Poe, Executive Director
(404) 223-4000
fpoe@gwcc.com
• Kevin Duvall, Chief Operating Officer
(404) 223-4000
kduvall@gwcc.com
• Carl Adkins, Chief Commercial Officer
(404) 223-4000
cadkins@gadome.com
Tenants:
Peach Bowl (NCAA), Georgia State
Panthers (NCAA)
Permanent Seating Capacity:
80,000

GEORGIA INSTITUTE OF TECHNOLOGY
N AVENUE
GEORGIA INSTITUTE OF TECHNOLOGY
ATLANTA, GA 30332-0255
404-894-2000
Fax: 404-894-4243
finaid@gatech.edu
www.gatech.edu
• Dan Radakovich, Athletic Director
(404) 894-5411
• Mike Edwards, Athletics
Director/Recreation Facilities
Coliseum Seating Capacity:
10,000

GIANT CENTER
550 WEST HERSHEYPARK DRIVE
HERSHEY, PA 17033
717-534-3911
Fax: 717-534-8996
info@hersheypa.com
www.hersheyentertainment.com
• Vikki Hultquist,
(717) 534-8966
vhultquist@hersheypa.com
Seating Capacity:
12,500

GILL COLISEUM
114 GILL COLISEUM
OREGON STATE UNIVERSITY
CORVALLIS, OR 97331
541-737-7373
Fax: 541-737-7363
wecare@oregonstate.edu
www.osubeavers.com
• Todd Stansbury, Vice President, Director
of Athletics
(541) 737-7373
• Zack Lassiter, Deputy Athletics Director,
External Operations
(541) 737-7373
zack.lassiter@oregonstate.edu
• Steve Sullivan, General Manager
(541) 737-8364
ssullivan@beaversportsproperties.com
• Matt Kolasinski, Associate General
Manager
• Jake Gibson, Assistant Athletic Director,
Facilities
(541) 737-1618
Arena Seating Capacity:
9,604

GILLETTE STADIUM
ONE PATRIOT PLACE
FOXBOROUGH, MA 02035-1388
508-384-4378
Fax: 508-384-4339
www.gillettestadium.com
Tenant(s):
New England Patriots (NFL), New England
Revolution (MLS), UMass Minutemen
(NCAA), Boston Cannons (MLL)
Seating Capacity:
65,829

GLASS BOWL STADIUM
2801 WEST BANCROFT STREET
TOLEDO, OH 43606-3390
419-530-2945
Fax: 419-530-4428
www.utrockets.com
Stadium Seating Capacity:
26,248

GLENS FALLS CIVIC CENTER
ONE CIVIC CENTER PLAZA
GLENS FALLS, NY 12801
518-798-0366
Fax: 518-793-7750
www.glensfallscc.com
• Jeff Mead, General Manager
(518) 798-0366
• Alyssa Aufiero, Event Manager
(518) 798-0366
• Avery Giroux, Box Office Manager
(518) 798-0366
• Ron Russell, Operations Manager
(518) 798-0366
• Larry Didio, Assistant Operations Manager
(518) 798-0366
Arena Seating Capacity:
4,794

GOLDEN LION STADIUM
1200 NORTH UNIVERSITY DRIVE
PINE BLUFF, AR 71601
870-575-7950
Fax: 870-575-7880
www.uapblionsroar.com
• Lonza Hardy, Jr., Director of Athletics
(870) 575-7950
• Stephanie Smith-Brown, Athletics
Business Manager
(870) 575-8273
smithbs@uapb.edu
• Carolyn Nance, HPER Complex Facilities
Manager
(870) 575-7184
nancec@uapb.edu
Stadium Seating Capacity:
16,000

GRAYSON STADIUM
1401 EAST VICTORY DRIVE
SAVANNAH, GA 31404
912-712-2482
thesavannahbananas.com
• Jared Orton, President
(336) 675-1066
jared@thesavannahbananas.com
• Marie Gentry, Director of Sponsor Services
(336) 312-3421
marie@thesavannahbananas.com
• Austin Glasscox, Director of Fan
Development
(704) 507-7092
Stadium Seating Capacity:
4,000
Year Founded:
1941
Clients:
Savannah Bananas

GREAT AMERICAN BALLPARK
100 JOE NUXHALL WAY
CINNCINNATI, OH 45202
513-765-7000
cincinnati.reds.mlb.com
• Robert H. Castellini, President and Chief
Executive Officer
• Mike Saverino, Operations Manager
• Tim O'Connell, Vice President of Ballpark
Operations
Seating Capacity:
42,319
Teams:
Cincinnati Reds baseball.

GREAT PLAINS COLISEUM
920 SOUTH SHERIDAN ROAD
LAWTON, OK 73505

580-357-1483
Fax: 580-357-1192
gpc64@swbell.net
www.gpcoliseum.com
• Phillip Humble, Executive Director
(580) 357-1483
gpc64@swbell.net
• Joe Kirk, Office Manager
(580) 357-1483
• Brandy Jaurez, Executive Assistant
Arena Seating Capacity:
3,000

GREENSBORO COLISEUM COMPLEX
1921 WEST GATE CITY BOULEVARD
GREENSBORO, NC 27403
336-373-7400
Fax: 336-373-2170
www.greensborocoliseum.com
• Matt Brown, Managing Director
(336) 373-7400
matt.brown@greensboro-nc.gov
• Scott Johnson, Deputy Director
(336) 373-7449
scott.johnson@greensboro-nc.gov
• Mike Frost, General Manager
(336) 373-7466
mike_frost@comcastspectacor.com
Seating Capacity:
23,500
Team:
UNC Greensboro Men's Basketball

GREYHOUND STADIUM
1500 SOUTH AVENUE K
PORTALES, NM 88130
575-562-2088
Fax: 505-562-2822
athletics@enmu.edu
www.goeasternathletics.com
• Jeff Geiser, Athletic Director
(575) 562-2153
jeff.geiser@enmu.edu
• Karen Doherty, Facilities Coordinator
(575) 562-2153
karen.doherty@enmu.edu
Stadium Seating Capacity:
5,200

HADLOCK FIELD
271 PARK AVENUE
PORTLAND, ME 04102
207-874-9300
Fax: 207-780-0317
seadogs@seadogs.com
www.milb.com/index.jsp?sid=t546
• Charlie Eshbach, President
ceshbach@seadogs.com
• Geoff Iacuessa, Executive Vice President
& General Manager
geoff@seadogs.com
• Chris Cameron, Director of Media
Relations
ccameron@seadogs.com
Arena Seating Capacity:
7,368
Team:
Portland Sea Dogs
Year Founded:
1994

HAMMONS STUDENT CENTER
901 SOUTH NATIONAL AVENUE
SPRINGFIELD, MO 65807
417-836-5240
www.missouristate.edu/hsc

• Keith Boaz, Executive Director
keithboaz@missouristate.edu
• Laree Moore, Associate Director
lareemoore@missouristate.edu
Arena Seating Capacity:
8,846

HAMPTON COLISEUM
1000 COLISEUM DRIVE
HAMPTON, VA 23666
757-838-4203
Fax: 757-838-2595
www.hamptoncoliseum.org
Arena Seating Capacity:
13,800

HANCOCK STADIUM
ILLINOIS STATE UNIVERSITY
CAMPUS BOX 2660
NORMAL, IL 61790-2660
309-438-8000
Fax: 309-438-2220
www.goredbirds.com
• Larry Lyons, Director of Athletics
(309) 438-3636
lelyons@ilstu.edu
• Bryan Goodall, Assistant Athletics
Director, Ticket Operations
(309) 438-8787
bsgooda@ilstu.edu
Arena Seating Capacity:
13,391

HANK AARON STADIUM
755 BOLLING BROTHERS BOULEVARD
MOBILE, AL 36606
251-479-2327
Fax: 251-476-1147
www.mobilebaybears.com
• Chris Morgan, General Manager
• Ari Rosenbaum, Assistant General
Manager
• Matt Baranofsky, Director of Ticket
Operations
• Nathan Breiner, Director of Stadium
Operations
Sport:
Baseball
Team:
Mobile BayBears
Year Founded:
1997
Capacity:
6,000

HARA ARENA
1001 SHILOH SPRINGS ROAD
DAYTON, OH 45414
937-278-4776
Fax: 937-278-4633
www.haracomplex.com
• Rose Cory, General Manager
(937) 278-4776
crose@haracomplex.com
• Karen Wampler, Public Relations Director
(937) 278-4776
harapr@haracomplex.com
• Tom Shade, Food Service Manager
(937) 278-4776
tshade@haracomplex.com
• Kimberly Wampler, Event Coordinator
(937) 278-4776
kswampler@haracomplex.com
Arena Seating Capacity:
5,500

HARBOR PARK
150 PARK AVENUE
NORFOLK, VA 23510
757-622-2222
Fax: 757-624-9090
receptionist@norfolktides.com
www.norfolktides.com
• Ken Young, President
(757) 622-2222
kyoung@norfolktides.com
• Joe Gregory, General Manager
jgregory@norfolktides.com
• Mike Zeman, Director of Stadium
Operations
mzeman@norfolktides.com
• Gretchen Todd, Director of Ticket
Operations
gtodd@norfolktides.com
Sport:
Baseball
Team:
Norfolk Tides
Year Founded:
1993
Capacity:
11,856

HARDER STADIUM
STADIUM ROAD
UNIVERSITY OF CALIFORNIA, SANTA
BARBARA
SANTA BARBARA, CA 93106
805-893-4011
Fax: 805-893-8640
www.ucsbgauchos.com
• John McCutcheon, Director of
Intercollegiate Athletics
(805) 893-8320
jmccutch@athletics.ucsb.edu
• Lee Pike, General Manager, Gaucho
Sports Properties
(805) 893-7875
Permanent Seating Capacity:
17,000

HARRY GROVE STADIUM
21 STADIUM DRIVE
FREDERICK, MD 21703
301-662-0013
Fax: 301-662-0018
info@frederickkeys.com
www.frederickkeys.com
• Dave Ziedelis, General Manager
dziedelis@frederickkeys.com
• Ben Sealy, Director of Ticket Operations
bsealy@frederickkeys.com
• Kari Collins, Director of Stadium
Operations
kcollins@frederickkeys.com
Sport:
Baseball
Tenant(s) :
Frederick Keys baseball
Year Founded:
1990

HARVARD UNIVERSITY - BRIGHT ARENA
65 NORTH HARVARD STREET
HARVARD UNIVERSITY
BOSTON, MA 02163
617-495-3454
Fax: 617-496-2270
harvtix@fas.harvard.edu
www.gocrimson.com
• Bob Scalise, Director of Athletics
(617) 495-2204
scalise@fas.harvard.edu

• Patricia Henry, Sr. Associate Director of
Athletics
(617) 495-2201
pwhenry@fas.harvard.edu
• Patricia Henry, Sr. Associate Director of
Athletics
(617) 495-2201
pwhenry@fas.harvard.edu
Seating Capacity:
3,095

HAYMARKET PARK
403 LINE DRIVE CIRCLE
LINCOLN, NE 68508
402-474-2255
Fax: 402-474-2254
www.saltdogs.com
• Jim Abel, Chairman
• Charlie Meyer, President, General
Manager
(402) 474-2255
charliem@saltdogs.com
• Dave Aschwege, Director of Stadium
Operations
(402) 441-4191
davea@saltdogs.com
• Dan Busch, Assistant Director of Stadium
Operations
(402) 441-4186
danielb@saltdogs.com
• Josh Klute, Athletic Turf Manager
(402) 441-4189
joshk@saltdogs.com
Capacity:
2,500
Year Founded:
2002
Team:
Lincoln Saltdogs
Sport:
Baseball

HEC EDMUNDSON PAVILION
218 GRAVES BUILDING
BOX 354070
SEATTLE, WA 98195-4070
206-543-2210
Fax: 206-616-1761
tickets@u.washington.edu
www.gohuskies.com
• Jennifer Cohen, Athletic Director
huskyad@uw.edu
• Chip Lydum, Associate AD Operations
(206) 616-2026
• Dan Erickson, Director of Events & Guest
Services
(206) 685-2570
dgerick@uw.edu
• Tyler Clay, Facilities Manager
(206) 616-9331
Arena Seating Capacity:
10,000

HEINZ FIELD
100 ART ROONEY AVENUE
PITTSBURGH, PA 15212
412-432-7800
Fax: 412-432-7878
www.steelers.com
• Arthur J. Rooney II, President
• Kevin Colbert, General Manager
• Jim Sacco, Director of Stadium
Management
• Steve Eyerman, Facilities Manager
Owned by:
Sports & Exhibition Authority of Pittsburgh
and Allegheny County.

Tenant(s) :
NFL - Pittsburgh Steelers football; NCAA -
Univ. of Pittsburgh football.
Seating Capacity:
65,000

**HELENA AREA CHAMBER OF
COMMERCE**
225 CRUSE AVENUE
SUITE A
HELENA, MT 59601
406-442-4120
Fax: 406-447-1532
info@helenachamber.com
helenachamber.com
• Cathy Burwell, CEO/President
• Mike Mergenthaler, Vice President
• Margaret Hennen, Office &
Communication Director
Sport:
Baseball
Team:
Helena Brewers
Year Founded:
1939

**HERITAGE FIELD AT MAVERICK
STADIUM**
12000 STADIUM ROAD
ADELANTO, CA 92301
760-246-6287
Fax: 760-246-3197
• Ben Hemmen, General Manager
• Sarah Bosso, Assistant General Manager
• Eric Smith, Stadium Operations Manager
• David Barry, Director of Tickets and
Finance
Sport:
Baseball
Team:
High Desert Mavericks
Year Founded:
1991
Capacity:
3,808

HESTAND STADIUM FAIRGROUNDS
ONE CONVENTION CENTER PLAZA
PINE BLUFF, AR 71601
870-536-7600
Fax: 870-850-2105
pbinfo@pinebluff.com
www.pinebluffcvb.org
• Greg Gustek, Director
(870) 536-7600
• Susie Madsen, Visitor and Group Tour
Information
(870) 536-7600
Seating capacity:
7,000

HI CORBETT FIELD
1 NATIONAL CHAMPIONSHIP DRIVE
TUCSON, AZ 85721-0096
520-621-2200
Fax: 520-327-2371
www.arizonawildcats.com/facilities/hi-corbett
-field.html
• Greg Byrne, Vice President for Athletics
(520) 621-4622
uofaad@arizona.edu
• James Francis, Sr. Associate Director of
Athletics, External Ops.
(520) 621-8001
jfrancis@arizona.edu
• Joe Moeller, General Manager
(520) 626-5538

joe.moeller@imgworld.com
• Suzy Mason, Sr. Associate Director of
Athletics, Facilities
(520) 621-6484
masons@arizona.edu
Stadium Seating Capacity:
9,500

HINKLE FIELDHOUSE
510 WEST 49TH STREET
BUTLER UNIVERSITY
INDIANAPOLIS, IN 46208
317-940-9375
Fax: 317-940-9734
info@butler.edu
www.butlersports.com
• Barry Collier, Director of Athletics
(317) 940-9878
athleticdirector@butler.edu
• Mike Freeman, Associate Athletic Director,
External Ops.
(317) 940-6452
msfreema@butler.edu
• Neal Smith, Assistant Athletic Director,
Facilities
(317) 940-9316
nasmith@butler.edu
Permanent Seating Capacity:
9,100

HIRAM BITHORN STADIUM
AVE FRANKLIN DELANO ROOSEVELT
SAN JUAN, PUERTO RIC 00920
787-725-2110
Fax: 787-725 2133
Permenant Seating Capacity:
18,264
Tenant(s) :
Santurce Crabbers

HOBART ARENA
255 ADAMS STREET
TROY, OH 45373
937-339-2911
Fax: 937-335-0046
www.hobartarena.com
• Ken Siler, Arena Manager
ken.siler@troyohio.gov
• Cheryl Terry, Office Manager
cheryl.terry@troyohio.gov
• Phill Noll, Operations Manager
phill.noll@troyohio.gov
Seating Capacity:
3,782

HOFHEINZ PAVILION
3204 CULLEN BOULEVARD
HOUSTON, TX 77204-6002
713-743-9370
Fax: 713-743-9375
directorofathletics@uh.edu
www.uhcougars.com
• Hunter Yurachek, Vice President for
Athletics
(713) 743-9370
directorofathletics@uh.edu
• Marvin Julich, Jr., Sr. Associate Athletics
Director, External Relatio
mjulich@central.uh.edu
• Jeremy McDonald, Facilities General
Manager
mcdonald-jeremy@aramark.com
• Valerie Roux, S&E General Manager
roux-valerie@aramark.com
Arena Seating Capacity:
8,918

HOFSTRA UNIVERSITY STADIUM & ARENA
245 HOFSTRA NORTHERN BOULEVARD
HOFSTRA UNIVERSITY
HEMPSTEAD, NY 11549
516-463-6633
800-463-7872
Fax: 516-463-6520
www.gohofstra.com
• Jay Artinian, Sr. Associate Director of Athletics Facilities
(516) 463-7931
jay.m.artinian@hofstra.edu
• Ann Baller, Associate Director of Athletic Facilities
(516) 463-6671
• Maria Corvino, Assistant Director of Athletics, Ticket Ops.
(516) 463-8499
Stadium Seating Capacity:
1,600

HOHOKAM STADIUM
1235 NORTH CENTER STREET
MESA, AZ 85201
mesaaz.gov/things-to-do/hohokam-stadium
Year Founded:
1997
Seating Capacity:
10,500
Team:
Spring training home of Oakland Athletics.

HOLMAN STADIUM
67 AMHERST STREET
NASHUA, NH 03064
603-718-8883
Fax: 603-718-1305
info@nashuasilverknights.com
www.nashuasilverknights.com
• Victoria Cookson, General Manager
• Michael Broderick, General Manager
• Cheryl McCardell, Front Office Coordinator
Sport:
Baseball
Team:
Nashua Silver Knights
Capacity:
4,000

HOLT ARENA
550 MEMORIAL DRIVE
POCATELLO, ID 83201
208-282-3398
Fax: 208-233-1553
• George Casper, Director of Events
(208) 282-3398
caspgeor@isu.edu
• Erin Joy Fisk, Director of Ticketing
(208) 282-4093
joyerin@isu.edu
• Julie McKnight, Box Office Manager
(208) 282-3330
mcknjuli@isu.edu
• Mike Dooley, Concession Manager
(208) 282-4170
doolmike@isu.edu
Arena Seating Capacity:
12,000

HOMER BRYCE STADIUM
712 HAYTER STREET
NACOGDOCHES, TX 75962
936-468-3501
Fax: 936-468-7601
sfajacks.com

• Robert Hill, Director of Athletics
(936) 468-4540
• John Branch, Associate Athletic Director, External Affairs
(936) 468-4334
jbranch@sfasu.edu
• Greg Payne, Director of Facilities
(936) 468-4200
Stadium Seating Capacity:
14,575

HOMER STRYKER FIELD
251 MILLS STREET
KALAMAZOO, MI 49048
269-492-9966
Fax: 269-388-8333
northwoodsleague.com/kalamazoo-growlers/team/ballpark
Sport:
Baseball
Tenant(s) :
Kalamazoo Growlers
Year Founded:
1963
Capacity:
4,000

HOMEWOOD FIELD
3400 NORTH CHARLES STREET
BALTIMORE, MD 21218
410-516-7490
Fax: 410-516-5376
www.hopkinssports.com
• Tom Calder, Director of Athletics & Recreation
(410) 516-7490
tcalder@jhu.edu
• Jon Gregory, Assistant Director of Athletics, Facilities
(410) 516-5053
• Brad Mountcastle, Director of Sports Performance and Wellness
(410) 516-6176
bmountcastle@jhu.edu
Stadium Seating Capacity:
8,500
Year Founded:
1906

HONDA CENTER
2695 EAST KATELLA AVENUE
ANAHEIM, CA 92806
714-704-2400
Fax: 714-704-2443
contactus@hondacenter.com
www.hondacenter.com
Owned by:
City of Anaheim
Tenant(s) :
Anaheim Ducks (NHL), Los Angeles Kiss (AFL)
Seating Capacity:
18,900

HOOKER FIELD
450 EAST COMMONWEALTH BOULEVARD
MARTINSVILLE, VA 24112
276-403-5250
Fax: 276-403-5376
www.martinsvillemustangs.com
• Brian McConnell, General Manager
(276) 403-5250
Sport:
Minor League Baseball
Team:
Martinsville Mustangs

Year Founded:
1988
Capacity:
3,200

HOOPER EBLEN CENTER
1100 MCGEE BOULEVARD
TTU BOX 5057
COOKEVILLE, TN 38505
931-372-3940
Fax: 931-372-3114
www.ttusports.com
• Mark Wilson, Director of Athletics
(931) 372-6306
mwilson@tntech.edu
• Matt Dexter, Sr. Facilities and Events Coordinator
(931) 372-3945
mmdexter@tntech.edu
Arena Seating Capacity:
9,280

HOOVER METROPOLITAN STADIUM
100 BEN CHAPMAN DRIVE
HOOVER, AL 35244
205-444-7500
Fax: 205-988-9698
www.hooveral.org
Sport:
Baseball
Team:
Hoover High School football
Year Founded:
1988
Capacity:
10,800

HOWARD C. GENTRY COMPLEX
3500 JOHN A MERRITT BOULEVARD
NASHVILLE, TN 37209
615-963-5000
Fax: 615-963-5911
www.tnstate.edu
• Teresa Lawrence Phillips, Athletics Director
(615) 963-1545
• Wilson Lee, Center For Extended Ed Director
(615) 963-7362
Seating Capacity:
10,500

HOWARD J. LAMADE STADIUM
539 U.S ROUTE 15 HWY
P.O. BOX 3485
S. WILLIAMSPORT, PA 17701
570-326-1971
www.springfieldchallenger.org
Teams:
Little League World Series
Seating Capacity:
40,000

HP PAVILION AT SAN JOSE
525 W SANTA CLARA STREET
SAN JOSE, CA 95113
408-287-9200
800-366-4423
Fax: 408-999-5797
• Goddard Jim, Executive Vice President/General Manager
• Jim Goddard, EVP/General Manager
• Kent Russell, VP Sales/Marketing
• Steve Kirsner, Booking & Events Director
(408) 999-5834

Owned by:
City of San Jose
Seating Capacity:
17,496

HSBC ARENA
ONE SEYMOUR H KNOX III PLAZA
BUFFALO, NY 14203-3096
716-855-4100
Fax: 716-855-4122
info@firstniagaracenter.com
www.firstniagaracenter.com
• Makowski Stan, Director of Arena Operations
• Edward Thompson, Director Concessions
• Christye Peterson, SVP Marketing
• Jennifer Stich, Event Booking Manager
Owned by:
Crossroads Arena L.L.C.
Tenant(s) :
AFL - Buffalo Destroyers Football, NHL - Buffalo Sabres Hockey, NLL - Buffalo Bandits Lacrosse
Permanent Seating Capacity:
20,000. AFL- 18,200

HUMBERT HUMPHREY METRODOME
900 S 5TH ST.
MINNEAPOLIS, MN 55415
612-332-0386
Fax: 612-332-8334
www.msfc.com
• Ted Mondale, CEO/Executive Director
(612) 335-3315
• Steve Maki, Director of Facilities/Engineering
(612) 335-3313
• Mary C. Fox-Stroman, Director of Finance
(612) 335-3311
mary.fox-stroman@msfa.com
• Jennifer Hathaway, Director of Communications
(612) 335-3308
• Bobbi Ellenberg, Events Services Manager
(612) 335-3318
Seating Capacity:
64,000
Teams:
Minneapolis Vikings NFL football.

HUGH MILLS MEMORIAL STADIUM
ALBANY STATE UNIVERSITY
601 NORTH VAN BUREN STREET
ALBANY, GA 31705
229-430-4600
csmith@oceancenter.com
www.oceancenter.com
• John I. Davis, Athletic Director
• Henry Rivers, Sports Medicine Director
• Pam Hill, Concessions Coordinator
Physical Address:
601 N. Van Buren, Albany, GA.
Seating Capacity:
10,000

HUGHES STADIUM (CA)
3835 FREEPORT BOULEVARD
SACRAMENTO, CA 95822
916-558-2111
Fax: 916-558-2030
www.scc.losrios.edu
• Mitchell Campbell, Dean / Athletic Director
• Kathryn E. Jeffery, Ph.D, President
Seating Capacity:
22,240
Owned by:

Metropolitan Sports Commission (City of Minneapolis)

HUGHES STADIUM (CO)
COLORADO STATE UNIVERSITY
FORT COLLINS, CO 80523-0120
970-491-5300
800-491-RAMS
Fax: 970-491-1348
csurams.cstv.com
• Max Doug, Assistant Athletic Director/Facilities
(970) 491-2706
dmax@lamar.colostate.edu
• Paul Kowalczyk, Director of Athletics
(970) 491-3350
karen.taylor@colostate.edu
• Jim McElwain, Head Coach
• Jack Graham, Director of athletics
• Jim Francis, Faculty
• David Crum, Sr.Associate Director
• Doug Max, Sr.Associate Director

HUGHES STADIUM (MD)
1700 E COLD SPRING LANE
BALTIMORE, MD 21251
443-885-3333
Fax: 410-319-4011
info@morgan.edu
www.morgan.edu
• Kevin M. Banks, Vice President for Student Affairs
kevin.banks@morgan.edu
• Tanya V. Rush, Associate Vice President for Student Affairs
tanya.rush@morgan.edu
• Seymour E. Chambers, Chief Judicial Officer
seymour.chambers@morgan.edu
• Marsha M. Price, Administrative Assistant
marsha.price@morgan.edu
• Sharon R. Taylor, Administrative Assistant
Sharon.taylor@morgan.edu
• Floyd Kerr, Athletic Director
Stadium Seating Capacity:
7,500

HULMAN CENTER
200 N SEVENTH STREET
TERRE HAUTE, IN 47809-1902
812-237-3737
800-468-6478
Fax: 812-237-3741
www.indstate.edu/hctaf
• Jennifer Cook, Business Manager
(812) 237-3770
j-cook@indstate.edu
• Jennifer Cook, Facility Marketing/Ticket Sales Manager
• Judith Price, Operations/Event Services Manager
• Julia Kirkpatrick, Administrative Assistant/Reservations
Year Founded:
1973
Arena Seating Capacity:
10,220

HUMPHREY COLISEUM
PO BOX HY
MISSISSIPPI STATE, MS 39762
662-325-4201
Fax: 662-325-7456
www.humphreycoliseum.msstate.edu
• Todd Hunt, Humphrey Coliseum Director
(662) 325-4201

• Duffy Neubauer, Operations Coordinator
(662) 214-4201
Permanent Seating Capacity:
10,500

HUNNICUTT FIELD
205 OLD BLUEFIELD ROAD
PRINCETON, WV 24740
304-487-2000
Fax: 304-487-8762
www.princetonrays.net
• Jim Holland, General Manager
• Mick Bayle, Director - Stadium Operations
• Dewey Russell, President
Arena Seating Capacity:
1,950
Year Founded:
1988
Teams:
Princeton Rays Professional Baseball, Mercer County Public Schools

---

HUNTER WRIGHT STADIUM
800 GRANDBY ROAD
KINGSPORT, TN 37600
423-224-2626
Fax: 423-224-2625
info@kmets.com
web.minorleaguebaseball.com
• Spivey Rick, Kingsport Mets President
• Pat O'Conner, President & CEO
admin@minorleaguebaseball.com
• Stan Brand, Vice President
admin@minorleaguebaseball.com
• Scott Poley, Senior Vice President, Legal Affairs
• Tim Brunswick, Vice President, Baseball & Business Operation
timbrunswick@minorleaguebaseball.com
• Brian Earle, Vice President, BIRCO & Business Services
brianearle@minorleaguebaseball.com
• Tina Gust, Vice President, Business Development
tinagust@minorleaguebaseball.com
• Steve Densa, Executive Director, Communications
Sport:
Baseball
Tenant(s) :
Kingsport Mets baseball
Year Founded:
1995
Capacity:
2,000

HUNTINGTON PARK
330 HUNTINGTON PARK LANE
COLUMBUS, OH 43215
614-462-5250
Fax: 614-462-3271
info@clippersbaseball.com
www.clippersbaseball.com
• Ken Schnacke, President/GM
kschnacke@clippersbaseball.com
Sport:
Minor League Baseball.
Team:
Columbus Clippers.
Seating Capacity:
10,000

HUNTSVILLE STARS
3125 LEEMAN FERRY ROAD
PO BOX 2769
HUNTSVILLE, AL 35801

256-882-2562
Fax: 256-880-0801
info@huntsvillestars.com
web.minorleaguebaseball.com
• Rogers Va Buck, General Manager
tom@huntsvillestars.com
• Pat O'Conner, President & CEO
admin@minorleaguebaseball.com
• Stan Brand, Vice President
admin@minorleaguebaseball.com
• Scott Poley, Senior Vice President, Legal Affairs
• Tim Brunswick, Vice President, Baseball & Business Operation
timbrunswick@minorleaguebaseball.com
• Brian Earle, Vice President, BIRCO & Business Services
brianearle@minorleaguebaseball.com
• Tina Gust, Vice President, Business Development
tinagust@minorleaguebaseball.com
• Steve Densa, Executive Director, Communications
Nature of Service:
Minor League Baseball.
Year Founded:
1985
Nature of Service:
AA affiliated of Milwaukee Brewers.

HURON ARENA
150 5TH STREET SW
HURON, SD 57350
605-353-6970
Fax: 605-353-6973
www.huron.k12.sd.us
• Terry Rotert, Arena Activities Director/Arena Manager
• Colette Habbena, Administrative Assistant
Arena Seating Capacity:
5,448

HUSKY STADIUM
218 GRAVES BUILDING
UNIVERSITY OF WASHINGTON BOX 354070
3910 MONT LAKE BLVD
SEATTLE, WA 98195
206-543-2200
Fax: 206-616-1761
tickets@u.washington.edu
www.gohuskies.com
• Scott Woodward, Athletic Director
(206) 543-2212
huskyad@u.washington.edu
• Chip Lydum, Associate Athletic Director/Facilities &
(206) 543-7373
clydum@washington.edu
• Larry White, Facilities Manager
• Jim Daves, Facilities Manager
(206) 543-2230
• Larry White, Facilities Manager
Year Founded:
1920
Stadium Seating Capacity:
72,500
Track Type:
Synthetic
Track Size:
400 meters
Team:
University of Washington football.

HYSLOP SPORTS CENTER
ROOM 120
2751 2ND AVEUE N STOP 9013
GRAND FORKS, ND 58202-9013
701-777-2237
Fax: 701-777-2285
www.fightingsioux.com
• Steve Brekke, Director of Athletic Development
(701) 777-6426
• Kathleen McCann, Assistant Director
Arena Seating Capacity:
6,000

I WIRELESS CENTER
1201 RIVER DRIVE
MOLINE, IL 61265
309-764-2001
Fax: 309-764-2192
www.iwirelesscenter.com
• Steve R Hyman, Executive Director
(309) 764-2001
• Rocky R Jones, Director Finance
(309) 764-2001
• Brett Cornish, Marketing/Sales Director
• Scott Mullen, Executive Director
(309) 277-1309
• John Watts, Director Operations
Home Arena for:
AF2 - Quad City Steamwheelers.
Arena Seating Capacity:
10,700 Basketball, 9,800 Hockey.

INDEPENDENCE STADIUM
3301 PERSHING BLVD.
LA STATE FAIRGROUNDS
SHREVEPORT, LA 71109
318-673-7758
independencebowl.org
• John Hubbard, Chairman
• Troy J. Broussard, Vice-Chairman
• Kyle McInnis, 1st Vice-Chairman
• Paul Pratt, 2nd Vice-Chairman
• Darin Seal, Treasurer
• Missy Setters, Executive Director
• John Cordaro, Assistant Executive Director for Ticketing an
Seating Capacity:
51,000
Teams:
Independence Bowl football.

INGALLS RINK
20 TOWER PARKWAY
YALE UNIVERSITY
NEW HAVEN, CT 6511
203-432-4747
Fax: 203-432-7772
www.yalebulldogs.com
• Thomas Beckett, Director of Athletics
(203) 432-1414
thomas.beckett@yale.edu
• Jennifer O'Neil, Assistant to the Director
(203) 432-1414
jennifer.oneil@yale.edu
• Dan Silverman, Director of Compliance
(203) 436-8309
daniel.c.silverman@yale.edu
• Amy Backus, Senior Associate Athletics Director for Compl
(203) 432-7668
amy.backus@yale.edu
• Barbara Chesler, Senior Associate Athletics Director for Capit
(203) 432-1437
barbara.chesler@yale.edu
• Francine Georges, Senior Associate

Athletics Director for Human
(203) 432-1442
francine.georges@yale.edu
• Edward Mockus, Senior Associate Athletic Director Facilities
(203) 432-2494
edward.mockus@yale.edu
Arena Seating Capacity:
3,486.00
Year Founded:
1958

INVESCO FIELD AT MILE HIGH STADIUM
1701 BRYANT STREET
SUITE 700
DENVER, CO 80204
720-258-3000
Fax: 720-258-3050
parking@broncos.nfl.net
www.sportsauthorityfieldatmilehigh.com
• Freeman Mac, Stadium Operations VP
• Gail Stuckey, Stadium Operations Director
• Andy Gorchov, Events Director
• Lorraine Spargo, Premium Seat Sales Director
Tenant(s) :
NFL - Denver Broncos football, MLS - Colorado Rapids soccer.
Permanent Seating Capacity:
76,125

INVESTORS GROUP FIELD
315 CHANCELLOR MATHESON RD.
WINNIPEG, MB, CANADA R3T 1Z2
204-784-2583
bbombers@bluebombers.com
Owners:
Winnipeg Blue Bombers; City of Winnipeg; University of Manitoba.
Operators:
Winnipeg Blue Bombers.
Year Opened:
2013.
Seating Capacity:
33,422; expandable to 40,000.
Tenant(s) :
CFL - Winnipeg Blue Bombers. CIS - Manitba Bisons. CJFL - Winnipeg Rifles.

IOWA STATE CENTER
SCHEMAN BUILDING SUITE 102
IOWA STATE UNIVERSITY
AMES, IA 50011-1113
515-294-3347
877-843-2368
Fax: 515-294-3349
iscinfo@iastate.edu
www.center.iastate.edu
• Mark North, Executive Director
• Scott Wycoff, Business Finance Director
• Sara Barr, Marketing Director
• Hilton Coliseum, Management
• Randy Baumeister, Operations Director
Arena Seating Capacity:
15,000
Stadium Seating Capacity:
56,000

IOWA STATE UNIVERSITY ATHLETICS
1800 S 4TH STREET
JACOBSON ATHLETIC BUILDING
AMES, IA 50011-1140
515-294-3662
Fax: 515-294-0558
www.cyclones.com
• Jamie Pollard, Athletic Director
(515) 294-0123

bvelde@iastate.edu
• Rebecca Hornbacher, Women's Soccer Coach
(515) 294-5328
• Bobby Douglas, Wrestling Coach
(515) 294-4643
bobbyd@iastate.edu
• Jamie Pollard, Director of Athletics
(515) 294-0123
jbp@iastate.edu
• Julie Bright, Sr. Assoc. AD/Administration
(Apr) 10
jabright@iastate.edu
• David Harris, Sr. Assoc. AD/Student Services
(Apr) 41
dwh@iastate.edu
• Chris Jorgensen, Sr. Assoc. AD/Facilities, Planning and Manage
(4-0) 07
cjorg@iastate.edu
Stadium Seating Capacity:
15,000

ISOTOPES PARK
1601 AVENIDA CESAR CHAVEZ SE
ALBUQUERQUE, NM 87106
505-924-2255
Fax: 505-242-8899
web.minorleaguebaseball.com
• Young Ken, President
• Daniel Luna, Ticketing Director
• Pat O'Conner, President & CEO
admin@minorleaguebaseball.com
• Stan Brand, Vice President
admin@minorleaguebaseball.com
• Scott Poley, Senior Vice President, Legal Affairs
• Tim Brunswick, Vice President, Baseball & Business Operation
timbrunswick@minorleaguebaseball.com
• Brian Earle, Vice President, BIRCO & Business Services
brianearle@minorleaguebaseball.com
• Tina Gust, Vice President, Business Development
tinagust@minorleaguebaseball.com
• Steve Densa, Executive Director, Communications

ITHACA COLLEGE ATHLETICS
953 DANBY ROAD
ITHACA COLLEGE
ITHACA, NY 14850
607-274-3209
Fax: 607-274-1667
mlindberg@ithaca.edu
www.ithaca.edu
• Ken Kutler, Intercollegiate Athletics Director
(607) 274-3209
kkutler@ithaca.edu
• Ernie McClatchie, Asst Director of Intercollegiate Athletics
(607) 274-5708
emcclatchie@ithaca.edu
• Mike R. Lindberg, Asst Director of Intercollegiate Athletics
(607) 274-3199
mlindberg@ithaca.edu
Stadium Seating Capacity:
5,000
Track Type:
All-Weather (synthetic)
Track Size:
400 Meters.
Tenants:
Ithaca College football.

IWIRELESS CENTER
1 UNIVERSITY CIRCLE
WESTERN ILLINOIS UNIVERSITY
MACOMB, IL 61455
309-298-1190
Fax: 309-298-2009
SID@wiu.edu
www.goleathernecks.com
• Tim Van Alstine, Director of Athletics
(309) 298-1190
• Matt Tanney, Associate Athletics Director
(309) 298-1964
m-tanney@wiu.edu
• Claire Smalzer, Assistant Director of Academic Services
• Chris Wlezien, Interim Director of Compliance
(309) 298-2221
cm-wlezien@wiu.edu
• Becky Schluter, Administrative Assistant to the Associate Athletic
(309) 298-1964
rs-schluter@wiu.edu
• Patrick Osterman, Assistant Athletics Director for Media Services
(309) 298-1133
pr-osterman@wiu.edu
• Nancy Sprouy, Asst. Director Of Athletics, Business Operations
(309) 298-1190
NK-Sprout@wiu.edu
Tenant(s):
NCAA - Western Illinois University football.
Stadium Seating Capacity:
15,368

IZOD CENTER
THE MEADOWLANDS SPORTS COMPLEX
50 STATE ROUTE 120
EAST RUTHERFORD, NJ 7073
201-935-8500
contact@metlifestadium.com
www.izodcenter.com
• Minish Jim, SVP
(201) 460-4203
jminish@njsea.com
• Kathleen Francis, Sales/Marketing & Communications SVP
(201) 842-5010
kfrancis@njsea.com
• Ron Va DeVeen, VP/Associate General Manager
(201) 460-4387
rvandeveen@njsea.com
• Karen Sullivan, Ticketing VP
(201) 842-5325
ksullivan@njsea.com
Arena Seating Capacity:
40,000
Year Founded:
1981
Nature of Service:
Arena.
Tenants:
NJ Devils (NHL), NJ Nets (NBA), Seton Hall Pirates (College Basketball).

J LAWRENCE WALK-UP SKYDOME
PO BOX 15400
FLAGSTAFF, AZ 86011
928-523-3449
Fax: 928-523-7588
• Dave Brown, Skydome Director/Color Commentator
dave.brown@nau.edu
• Steve Holton, Athletic Director/Northern Arizona Unive

Arena Seating Capacity:
16,500

J. LAWRENCE WALKUP SKYDOME
NORTHERN ARIZONA UNIVERSITY
PO BOX 15096
FLAGSTAFF, AZ 86011
928-523-3449
Fax: 928-523-7588
www.nauathletics.com/information/facilities/skydome
• Lisa Campos, Vice President for Intercollegiate Athletics
• Rob Morrison, Director of Facilities
• Jerome Souers, Head Coach, Football
• Jack Murphy, Head Coach, Men's Basketball
• Sue Darling, Head Coach, Women's Basketball
Team:
NAU Lumberjacks
Seating Capacity:
11,230

JACK BRESLIN STUDENT EVENTS CENTER
534 BIRCH ROAD
MICHIGAN STATE UNIVERSITY
EAST LANSING, MI 48824
517-432-1989
800-968-2737
Fax: 517-432-1510
www.breslincenter.com
• Scott H Breckner, Director
• Gavin J Smith, Operations Assistant Director
Permanent Seating Capacity:
15,130

JACK RUSSELL MEMORIAL STADIUM
800 PHILLIES DRIVE
CLEARWATER, FL 33755
727-797-9090
727-781-2224
Fax: 727-447-3924
• Timberlake John, General Manager
• Dianne Gonzalez, Busines Manager/Florida Operations
Sport:
Baseball
Tenant(s):
Clearwater Phillies

JACK SPINKS STADIUM
1000 ASU DRIVE
#510
ALCORN STATE, MS 39096
601-877-6500
Fax: 601-877-3821
asu_sportsinfo@yahoo.com
www.alcornsports.com
• Wiley H Jones, Interim Athletic Director
• LaToya G Shields, Sports Information Director
(601) 877-6466
latoya@alcorn.edu
• Johnny Thomas, Football Coach
• Samuel West, Men's Basketball Coach
Stadium Seating Capacity:
22,500
Arena Seating Capacity:
7,000

JACK TRICE STADIUM
1800 S. 4TH STREET
AMES, IA 50011-1140

515-294-3662
Fax: 515-294-0104
mtodd@iastate.edu
www.cyclones.com
• Julie Bright, Sr. Assoc. AD/Administration
(515) 294-5410
jabright@iastate.edu
• David Harris, Sr. Assoc. AD/Student
Services
(515) 294-3141
dwh@iastate.edu
• Chris Jorgensen, Sr. Assoc. AD/Facilities,
Planning and Manage
(515) 294-0307
cjorg@iastate.edu
• Steve Malchow, Sr. Assoc.
AD/Communications
(515) 294-5095
sdm@iastate.edu
• Frank Nogel, Sr. Assoc. AD/External
Relations
(515) 294-6463
fnogel@iastate.edu
• Jamie Pollard, Director of Athletics
(515) 294-0123
jbp@iastate.edu
• Mike Green, Assoc. Director
(515) 294-2008
mgreen@iastate.edu
Seating Capacity:
55,000
Teams:
Iowa State University football.

JACKIE ROBINSON BALLPARK
110 E ORANGE AVENUE
DAYTONA BEACH, FL 32114
386-257-3172
Fax: 386-257-3382
www.milb.com
• Bill Papierniak, General Manager
• Michael Swope, General Manager
• Pat O'Conner, President / CEO
admin@minorleaguebaseball.com
• Brady Ballard, General Manager
Sport:
Baseball
Team:
Daytona Cubs
Year Founded:
1914
Capacity:
4,000

JACKSONVILLE VETERANS MEMORIAL ARENA
300 A. PHILIP RANDOLPH BOULEVARD
JACKSONVILLE, FL 32202
904-630-3900
howcanwehelp@jaxevents.com
jaxevents.com/venue/veterans-memorial-arena
• Bill McConnell, General Manager
(904) 630-3900
• Sandy Avery, Box Office Manager
(904) 630-3900
savery@smgjax.com
• Val Glanton, Senior Event Manager
• Lyle Klemmt, Senior Operations Manager
(904) 630-3934
lklemmt@smgjax.com
• Alex Alston, Director of Sales & Marketing
(904) 630-4055
alexa@smgjax.com
• Whitney Oxnard, VIP Services Coordinator
(904) 630-3953
woxnard@smgjax.com

Home Arena for:
AF2 - Jacksonville Tomcats.
Coliseum Seating Capacity:
10,276

JACOBS FIELD
2401 ONTARIO STREET
CLEVELAND, OH 44115
216-420-4444
Fax: 216-420-4396
access@website.mlb.com
cleveland.indians.mlb.com
• Lawrence J Dolan, Owner and Chief
Executive Officer
• Scott Sterneckert, Ticket Sales Director
• Jerry Crabb, Ballpark Operations Director
• Gloria Carter, Assistant Ballpark
Operations
• Paul J. Dolan, Chairman/Chief Executive
Officer
• Mark Shapiro, President
• Chris Antonetti, Executive Vice President
& General Manager
• Bob DiBiasio, Senior Vice President,
Public Affairs
• Victor Gregovits, Senior Vice President,
Sales & Business Devel
• Sara Lehrke, Vice President, Human
Resources/Chief Diversi
Permanent Seating Capacity:
42,400
Description:
Home Stadium For: Cleveland Indians.
Owned by:
Gateway Economic Development Corp.

JADWIN GYMNASIUM
PRINCETON UNIVERSITY
PRINCETON, NJ 8544
609-258-3000
Fax: 609-258-4477
www.princeton.edu
• Gary D Walters, Athletic Director
Seating Capacity:
7,500

JAMES A. RHODES ARENA
373 CARROLL STREET
UNIVERSITY OF AKRON
AKRON, OH 44325-5104
330-972-6920
Fax: 330-972-5847
athfac@uakron.edu
www.gozips.com
• Paul Hammond, Assistant Athletic
Director/Facilities O
• Tom Wistrcill, Director of Athletics
(330) 972-7080
krex@uakron.edu
• Mary Lu Gribbschaw, Senior Associate
Athletics Director/Senior Wo
(330) 0972-708
marylu@uakron.edu
• Dan Satter, Senior Associate Athletics
Director for Exter
(330) 972-7468
dsatter@uakron.edu
• J. Dean Carro, Faculty Athletics
Representative
(330) 972-7751
carro1@uakron.edu
• Kathy Rex, Sr. Administrative Assistant to
the Director
(330) 972-6689
krex@uakron.edu
• Kyra Lobbins, Coordinator of Programming

(330) 972-8355
kyralob@uakron.edu
Arena Seating Capacity:
4,984

JAMES E. O'NEILL JR. ARENA
7400 BAY ROAD
SAGINAW VALLEY STATE UNIVERSITY
UNIVERSITY CENTER, MI 48710-0001
989-964-4000
800-968-9500
Fax: 989-964-7389
javogl@svsu.edu
www.svsu.edu
• Mike Watson, Athletic Director
Arena Seating Capacity:
6,000

JAMESTOWN CIVIC CENTER
212 3RD AVENUE NE
JAMESTOWN, ND 58401
701-252-8088
Fax: 701-252-8089
www.jamestownciviccenter.com
• Pam Fosse, Director
(701) 252-8088
pfosse@daktel.com
• Crystal Diestler, Administrative Assistant
cdiestler@daktel.com
• Chastity Mikkelson, Secretary
cmikkelson@daktel.com
Permanent Seating Capacity:
Stadium/Arena 6,500

JAX EVENTS PRESENTED BY SMG
ONE EVER BANK FIELD DRIVE
JACKSONVILLE, FL 32202
904-633-6100
Fax: 904-633-6190
www.jaxevents.com
• Gerry Albert, Senior Vice President of
Stadium Operations
galbert@smgjax.com
• Tracey Evans, Director
• Nan Coyle, Director Marketing
• Sandy Avery, Box Office Manager
(904) 630-3974
savery@smgjax.com
• Barry Milligan, Sales & Marketing Manager
(904) 630-4056
• Christina Castle, Assistant Marketing &
Media Manager
(904) 630-4026
• Angela Green, VIP Services Manager &
Group Sales
(904) 630-3958
Permanent Seating Capacity:
73,000
Home Stadium for:
Jacksonville Jaguars.

JAYNE STADIUM
112 PLAYFORTH PLACE
MOREHEAD STATE UNIVERSITY
MOREHEAD, KY 40351
606-783-2088
800-585-6781
Fax: 606-783-5035
athletics@moreheadstate.edu
www.msueagles.com
• Brian Hutchinson, Athletic Director
b.hutchinson@moreheadstate.edu
• Randy Stacy, Athlete/Media Relations
Director
• Rhonda Ferguson, Administrative
Assistant to the AD
(606) 783-2089

r.ferguson@moreheadstate.edu
• Harry Floyd, Athletic Secretary
(606) 783-2088
hbfloyd@moreheadstate.edu
• Peggy Osborne, Faculty Athletics
Representative
(606) 783-2755
p.osborne@moreheadstate.edu
Stadium Seating Capacity:
10,000

JEKYLL ISLAND SOCCER COMPLEX
700 SOUTHVILLE BEACHVIEW DRIVE
JEKYLL ISLAND, GA 31527
877-453-5955
Fax: 912-635-4004
admin@goldenislesoccer.com
www.goldenislesoccer.com
• Eric Garvey, Soccer Marketing Director
Description:
7 Soccer fields, prescription Bermuda turf,
concession pavilion.

JERRY UHT PARK
110 E 10TH STREET
ERIE, PA 16501
814-456-1300
Fax: 814-456-7520
seawolves@seawolves.com
www.seawolves.com
• Mark Pirrello, Director of Merchandise/Box
Office Manager
mpirrello@seawolves.com
• Amy McArdle, Director of Accounting and
Finance
• Cody Herrick, Director of Ticket Sales
• Dan Torf, Director of Group Sales
• Kevin Forte, Group Sales Coordinator
• Greg Coleman, President
Sport:
Baseball
Team:
Erie Seawolves
Year Founded:
1995
Capacity:
6,000

JOAN C. EDWARDS STADIUM
2001 3RD AVENUE
HUNTINGTON, WV 25755
www.herdzone.com
• Mike Hamrick, Director of Athletics
• Doc Holliday, Head Coach, Football
Seating Capacity:
38,016

JOE AILLET STADIUM
305 WISTERIA STREET
PO BOX 3046
RUSTON, LA 71270-9985
318-257-4111
Fax: 318-257-3757
vandevelde@latech.edu
www.latechsports.com
• Tommy Sisemore, Director Athletic
Facilities
(318) 257-53223
• Derek Dooley, Athletics Director
(318) 257-4547
• Marie Gilbert, Associate A.D./Chief
Financial Officer
(318) 257-3637
mgilbert@latech.edu
• James Liberatos, Faculty Athletics
Representative
(318) 257-4287

jamesl@latech.edu
• Leah Beasley, Associate A.D./Marketing
and Game Management
(318) 257-5332
lbeasley@latech.edu
• Malcolm Butler, Associate A.D./Media
Relations
(318) 257-3145
mbutler@latech.edu
• Mary Kay Hungate, Deputy Athletics
Director - SWA
(318) 257-5654
usmkh@latech.edu
• Bruce Van De Velde, Athletics Director
(318) 257-3247
vendevelde@latech.edu
Seating Capacity:
30200
Tenant(s) :
Louisiana Tech Bulldogs

JOE ALBI STADIUM
4918 W EVERETT
SPOKANE, WA 99205
509-326-4625
Fax: 509-326-0636
• Jeff Robbins, General Manager
Stadium Seating Capacity:
22,000

JOE FABER FIELD
5001 VETERANS DRIVE
SAINT CLOUD, MN 56303
320-240-9798
Fax: 320-255-5228
info@stcloudrox.com
www.stcloudrox.com
• Nelson Jim, Director of Broadcasting
• Scott Schreiner, Vice President &
Co-owner
Scott@StCloudRox.com
• Wes Sharp, General Manager
• Kyle Kohls, Assistant General Manager
• Andy Sailer, Media & Public Relations
Manager
• Scott Schreiner, Co-Owner & VP
scott@stcloudrox.com
Sport:
Collegiate Professional Baseball
Tenant(s) :
St. Cloud River Rats baseball
Year Founded:
1971
Capacity:
2,200

JOE L. REED ACADOME
915 S JACKSON STREET
MONTGOMERY, AL 36104
334-229-4100
800-253-5037
Fax: 334-229-4988
www.alasu.edu
• John Knight, Executive Director of
Marketing & ommunications
• William H. Harris, President
Arena Seating Capacity:
8,000

JOE MARTIN FIELD
1221 POTTER STREET
BELLINGHAM, WA 98229
360-527-1035
bellinghambells.com
• Nick Caples, Vice President of Operations
(360) 746-0406
nick@bellinghambells.com

• Stephanie Morrell, General Manager
(360) 746-0409
stephanie@bellinghambells.com
• Levi Stewart, Sales & Marketing
Coordinator
(360) 527-1035
levi@bellinghambells.com
Capacity:
1,600

JOE O'BRIEN FIELD
136 S SYCAMORE STREET
ELIZABETHTON, TN 37643
423-547-6441
Fax: 423-547-6442
www.milb.com/index.jsp?sid=t576
• Jim Rantz, Director
• David Nanney, Head Groundskeeper
Sport:
Minor League Baseball.
Team:
Elizabethton Twins.
Year Founded:
1974
Capacity:
1,500

JOHN E. TUCKER COLISEUM
1306 N EL PASO AVENUE
RUSSELLVILLE, AR 72801
479-968-0389
Fax: 479-968-0647
kdavis@atu.edu
athletics.atu.edu
• Brent Linker, Athletic Facilities Director
(479) 968-0212
• Steve Mullins, Athletic Director
(479) 968-0245
smullins@atu.edu
• Paul smith, Information Director
(479) 968-0645
psmith@atu.edu
• Kristy Bayer, Administrator
(479) 968-0513
kbayer@atu.edu
• Amy White, Compliance Officer
(479) 968-6071
awhite@atu.edu
• Bryan Fisher, Director of Athletic Relations
(479) 968-0674
bfisher@atu.edu
• Ben Greenberg, Sports Information
Director
bgreenberg@atu.edu
Arena Seating Capacity:
3,500

JOHN F. SAVAGE HALL
2801 W BANCROFT STREET
UNIVERSITY OF TOLEDO
TOLEDO, OH 43606-3390
419-530-4226
800-586-5336
Fax: 419-530-8429
utmarcom@utoledo.edu
www.utoledo.edu
• John Adams, Director, University
Marketing
(419) 530-2676
john.adams@utoledo.edu
• C. Vernon Snyder, Vice President for
Institutional Advancement
(419) 530-4249
• Ron Beczynski, Facilities Director
• Chris Spengler, Director of Advancement
Relations
(419) 530-4927

• Daniel Stong, Major Gifts Officer, Athletics
(419) 530-5525
• Jeff Barton, Director of Development,
College of Pharmacy
(419) 530-5413
• Patricia Keller, Director of Prospect
Research
(419) 530-5409
• Laura Robinson, Senior Major Gift Officer
(860) 989-9652
Arena Seating Capacity:
9,600

JOHN O'QUINN FIELD AT ROBERTSON STADIUM
3100 CULLEN BOULEVARD
UNIVERSITY OF HOUSTON
HOUSTON, TX 77204-6002
713-462-6647
877-268-4275
Fax: 713-743-9449
support@uh.edu
www.uhcougars.com
• Dave Maggard, Athletic Director
• John Robinson, Deputy Athletics Director
• Darren Dunn, Athletics Director
• T.J. Meagher, Associate Athletics Director
for Internal Ope
• DeJuena Chizer, Associate Athletics
Director/SWA
• Barbara Stone, Executive Administrative
Assistant
• Pat A. Streko, Jr., Assistant Vice
President/General Manager
(713) 743-1446
Stadium Seating Capacity:
22,000

JOHN THURMAN FIELD
601 NEECE DR. ROAD
MODESTO, CA 95351
209-572-4487
Fax: 209-572-4490
fun@modestonuts.com
www.modestonuts.com
• Eric Rauber, Director of Group Sales
• Ryan Thomas, Director of Operations
• Alex Margulies, Director of Broadcasting
• Justin McKissick, Director of Public
Relations
• Ed Mack, Assistant General Manager -
Operations
• Tyler Richardson, Assistant General
Manager - Sales & Marketing
• Steven Almanza, Production Manager
• Mike Gorrasi, Executive Vice President-
HWS Baseball
Sport:
Baseball
Team:
Modesto A's
Year Founded:
1952
Capacity:
3,870

JOHNNY RED FLOYD STADIUM
MTSU BOX 20
MURFREESBORO, TN 37132
615-898-2450
Fax: 615-898-5626
www.goblueraiders.com
• Darrell Towe, Director
(615) 494-7699
dtowe@mtsu.edu
• Boniface Amuzu, Operations Coordinator
(615) 898-5189

bamuzu@mtsu.edu
• Todd Wyant, Director, Student Athlete
Enhancement Center
(615) 898-5610
twyant@mtsu.edu
• Wynnifred Counts, Associate
Director/Coordinator of Life Skills
(615) 898-5581
wcounts@mtsu.edu
• Chris Massaro, Director of Athletics
(615) 898-2452
cmassaro@mtsu.edu
• Diane Turnham, Associate Athletic
Director/SWA
(615) 898-2938
dturnham@mtsu.edu
• Graham Neff, Associate Athletic Director
(615) 898-5563
gneff@mtsu.edu
• Zackie Sanderson, Associate Athletic
Director/Business
(615) 898-2207
zsanders@mtsu.edu
Stadium Seating Capacity:
30,788
Sport:
Football

JOHNSON HAGOOD STADIUM
171 MOULTRIE STREET
THE CITADEL FOUNDATION
CHARLESTON, SC 29409
843-953-5277
Fax: 843-953-5124
ron.ginyard@citadel.edu
www.citadelsports.com
• Mike Hoffman, Communications &
Marketing Asst Dir
mhoffma1@citadel.edu
• Noelle Orr Blaney, Director Media
Relations
(843) 953-5353
noelle.orr@citadel.edu
• Larry Leckonby, Director of Athletics
(843) 953-5030
larry.leckonby@citadel.edu
• John McAleer Sr., Associate Athletic
Director/Development
(843) 953-1354
john.mcaleer@citadel.edu
• Kelly Simpson, Associate Athletic
Director/SWA
(843) 953-6604
kelly.simpson@citadel.edu
• Geoff Von Dollen, Associate Athletic
Director/Business
(843) 953-5352
geoff.vondollen@citadel.edu
• Andy Solomon, Associate Athletic
Director/Marketing
(843) 953-6300
solomona@citadel.edu
• Robby Bennett, Assistant Athletic
Director/Ticket Office
(843) 953-7181
robert.bennett@citadel.edu
Stadium Seating Capacity:
21,000

JOKER MARCHANT STADIUM
2125 North Lake Avenue
#A
LAKELAND, FL 33805
863-686-8075
Fax: 863-688-9589
www.milb.com
• Myers Ron, Director of Florida Operations
• Don Miers, Florida Operations Director

Sport:
Baseball
Tenant(s) :
Detroit Tigers; Spring Training Facility
Lakeland Tigers.
Year Founded:
1966, Renovated 2002
Capacity:
8,500

JON M. HUNTSMAN CENTER
1825 E S CAMPUS DRIVE
UNIVERSITY OF UTAH
SALT LAKE CITY, UT 84112-0900
801-581-8171
Fax: 801-581-6670
utahutes.cstv.com
• Chris Hill, Director of Athletics
(801) 581-3508
• Liz Abel, Assistant Athletic Director/Sports
Infor
Basketball Seating Capacity:
15,000

JONES AT&T STADIUM
6TH STREET
BOX 43021
LUBBOCK, TX 79409
806-742-3355
Fax: 806-742-1856
www.texastech.com
• Ron Damron, Associate Athletic
Director/Facility Operations
• Liz Parke, Assistant Athletic
Director/Facility Operations
• Tim Walker, Facilities Manager
• Gerald Myers, Director of Athletics
• Kirby Hocutt, Athletic Director
Coliseum Seating Capacity:
52,000

JONES SBC STADIUM
6TH STREET
TEXAS TECH ATHLETIC DEPARTMENT
LUBBOCK, TX 79409
806-742-3355
Fax: 806-742-7856
www.texastech.com
• Steve Uryasz, Senior Associate Athletic
Director
• Tim Walker, Facilities Manager
• Kirby Hocutt, Athletic Director
• Gerald Myers, Director of Athletics
Stadium Seating Capacity:
50,500

JOSEPH L. BRUNO STADIUM
80 VANDENBURGH AVENUE
TROY, NY 12180
518-629-2287
Fax: 518-629-2299
info@tcvalleycats.com
www.tcvalleycats.com
• Rick Murphy, General Manager
(518) 629-2287
rickmurphy@tcvalleycats.com
• Matt Callahan, Assistant General Manager
(518) 629-2287
matt@tcvalleycats.com
• Ryan Burke, Account Executive
(518) 629-2287
• Chris Chenes, Media/Production Manager
(518) 629-2287
chrischenes@tcvalleycats.com
• Keith Sweeney, Stadium Operations
Manager
(518) 629-2287

• Jessica Kaszeta, Box Office/Ticket
Manager
(518) 629-2287
jessicakaszeta@tcvalleycats.com
• William L. Gladstone, President/Principal
Owner
 ext 21
Stadium Seating Capacity:
4,500.00
Year Founded:
2002
Track Type:
Grass.
Track Size:
L 330, C 400, R 330.

JOSEPH P. RILEY, JR PARK
360 FISHBURNE STREET
CHARLESTON, SC 29403
843-723-7241
Fax: 843-723-2641
admin@riverdogs.com
www.riverdogs.com
• Mike Veeck, President
admin@riverdogs.com
• Dave Echols, VP/General Manager
• John Schumacher, Director of Stadium
Operations
• Marvin Goldklang, Chairman
• Kristen Wolfe, Special Events Manager
• Mike Veeck, President
• Dr. Gene Budig, Co-Owner
• Peter Freund, Co-Owner
• Al Phillips, Co-Owner
• Bill Murray, Director of Fun
• Michael DeAntonio, Director of
Merchandise
Sport:
Baseball
Team:
Charleston River Dogs
Year Founded:
1996
Capacity:
7,880
Sports Organization:
The Charleston RiverDogs are a Minor
League Baseball team who serve as the
Class A Affiliate of the New York Yankees,
and are a proud member of the South
Atlantic League.

**JOYCE ATHLETIC & CONVOCATION
CENTER**
C113 JOYCE CENTER
NOTRE DAME UNIVERSITY
NOTRE DAME, IN 46556
574-631-5030
Fax: 574-631-8596
www.und.com
• Kevin White, Athletics Director
(574) 631-7277
• Patricia Bellia, Faculty Athletics
Representative
(574) 631-3866
• Missy Conboy, Senior Deputy Athletics
Director
(574) 631-6107
• John Heisler, Senior Associate Athletics
Director (Media an
(574) 631-6107
• Jill Bodensteiner, Associate Athletics
Director (Compliance and
(574) 631-6107
• Michael Danch, Associate Athletics
Director (Facilities)
(574) 631-6107

• Jack Swarbrick, University Vice
President/Director of Athleti
(574) 631-6107
Arena Seating Capacity:
11,400

JPS FIELD AT MALONE STADIUM
ULM ATHLETICS
308 WARHAWK WAY
MONROE, LA 71209
318-342-5360
www.ulmwarhawks.com
• Brian Wickstrom, Director of Athletics
• Matt Viator, Head Coach, Football
Seating Capacity:
30,427

JS DORTON ARENA
1025 BLUE RIDGE BOULEVARD
RALEIGH, NC 27607
919-821-7400
Fax: 919-733-5079
claudine.davis@ncagr.gov
www.ncstatefair.org/dorton.htm
• Wyatt V Wesley, Manager
• Claudine Davis, Facility Sales Director
claudine.davis@ncagr.gov
• Pam Moore, Budget and Human
Resources Director
• Dudley Baggett, Landscaping Director
• Ray Frost, Assistant Manager for
Operations
• Peter Green, Maintenance Office Manager
• Angie Crone, Sponsorship Coordinator
Arena Seating Capacity:
5,110
Number of Members:
52
Affiliations:
Carolina Roller Derby, Inc, aWFTA member
Teams:
Carolina Rollergirls- Caroline Rollar Derby,
Inc. Womens Flat Track Derby
Association(WFTDA)
www.carolinarollergirls.com

**JUDY JOHNSON FIELD AT DANIEL S.
FRAWLEY STADIUM**
801 SHIPYARD DRIVE
WILMINGTON, DE 19801
302-777-5772
Fax: 302-777-5657
info@bluerocks.com
www.delawarestadiumcorp.com
• Steve Gold, Field Operations Director
sgold@bluerocks.com
• Jared Forma, Ticket Sales Director
Sport:
Baseball.
Tenant(s) :
Wilmington Blue Rocks baseball.
Year Founded:
1993
Capacity:
6,532

KANSAS COLISEUM
1279 E 85TH STREET
PARK CITY, KS 67147
316-440-0888
Fax: 316-440-0928
www.kansascoliseum.com
• Sam Fulco, Director
Arena Seating Capacity:
11,652

KASEYA CENTER
601 BISCAYNE BOULEVARD
MIAMI, FL 33132
786-777-1000
Fax: 786-777-1600
guestservices@heat.com
www.kaseyacenter.com
• Brian Babin, VP/Assistant General
Manager
Former Names:
American Airlines Arena; FTX Arena;
Miami-Dade Arena
Seating Capacity:
Basketball 19,600; Hockey 14,447; Concerts
5,000-20,021

KAUFFMAN STADIUM
1 ROYAL WAY
PO BOX 419969
KANSAS CITY, MO 64129
816-504-4040
Fax: 816-504-4142
ticketservices@royals.com
kansascity.royals.mlb.com
• Dan Glass, Director Stadium Operations
• Charlie Seraphin, VP Sales & Marketing
• Rob Stoltz, General Manager/Volume
Services
• Tonya Mangels, Marketing/Sales Director
• Allan H. Selig, Commissioner of Baseball
• Tim Brosnan, Executive Vice President,
Business
• Rob Manfred, Executive Vice President,
Economics & League
• Jonathan Mariner, Executive Vice
President and Chief Financial
• John McHale, Jr, Executive Vice
President, Administration & Ch
• Joe Torre, Executive Vice President of
Baseball Operatio
• Frank Robinson, Executive Vice President
of Baseball Developm
Owned by:
Jackson County Sports Authority
Description:
Home Stadium For: Kansas City Royals.
Permanent Seating Capacity:
40,625

KAY RODGERS PARK
4400 MIDLAND BOULEVARD
FORT SMITH, AR 72904
479-783-6176
cindy@kayrodgerspark.com
www.kayrodgerspark.org
• Rebecca, Accounting - Administration
rebecca@kayrodgerspark.com
• Cindy, Futurity - Administration
cindy@kayrodgerspark.com

KELLOGG ARENA
ONE MCCAMLY SQUARE
BATTLE CREEK, MI 49017
269-963-4800
Fax: 269-968-8840
www.kelloggarena.com
• Kevin M. Scheibler, General Manager
(269) 963-4800
• Treasa Sylvester, Finance Director
(269) 963-4800
tsylvester@kelloggarena.com
• Bill Evans, Sports Promotion
• Ben Randels, Operations Manager
(269) 963-4800
brandels@kelloggarena.com
• Lindsay Lerette, Sales and Marketing
Manager

(269) 963-4800
• Jimmy Biggs, Food and Beverage Manager
(269) 963-4800
jbiggs@kelloggarena.com
Permanent Seating Capacity:
6,000

KELLY/SHORTS STADIUM
1200 FRANKLIN STREET
MT. PLEASANT, MI 48859
989-774-4000
Fax: 989-774-7957
cmsports@cmich.edu
www.cmich.edu
• Keith Voeks, Assistant Director
voeks1ke@cmich.edu
• Cal Seelye, Director, Events and Conference Services
seely1ch@cmich.edu
• Chad Garland, Assistant Director, Events and Conference Ser
(989) 774-7675
garla1ce@cmich.edu
• Emily Tritschler, Coordinator, Events and Conference Services
mcclu1es@cmich.edu
• Scott Harrington, Technical Specialist, University Events
(989) 774-3355
harri3sr@cmich.edu
• Connie Camp, SR Specialist Clerk, Bovee University Center,
(989) 774-7477
highe1cl@cmich.edu
• Brittany Cornwell, Graduate Assistant, Events and Conference Ser
cornw1ba@cmich.edu
Stadium Seating Capacity:
Football - 30,000.

KENAN MEMORIAL STADIUM
78 STADIUM DRIVE
UNIVERSITY OF NORTH CAROLINA
CHAPEL HILL, NC 27514
919-962-5555
Fax: 919-966-3173
www.goheels.com
• Dick E Baddour, Athletic Director
(919) 962-6000
dbaddour@uncaa.unc.edu
• Karlton Creech, Sr. Assoc. Athletic Director/Chief of Staff
(919) 843-8432
• Beth Miller, Sr. Associate Athletic Director/Senior Woman
• Paul Pogge, Assoc. Athletic Director/Risk Management
(919) 962-6000
ppogge@uncaa.unc.edu
• Larry Gallo, Exec. Associate Athletic Director
(919) 962-6000
athgallo@uncaa.unc.edu
• Molly Norton, Executive Assistant to Bubba Cunningham
(919) 962-8200
mbnorton@uncaa.unc.edu
• Kathy Griggs, Administrative Assistant
(919) 843-5834
kgriggs@uncaa.unc.edu
• Bubba Cunningham, Athletic Director
(919) 962-8200
bubba.cunningham@unc.edu
Permanent Seating Capacity:
60,000

KENT STATE UNIVERSITY ATHLETICS
PO BOX 5190
KENT, OH 44242
330-672-5974
Fax: 330-672-5978
info@kent.edu
www.kentstatesports.com
• Laing Kennedy, Director of Athletics
(330) 672-3120
lkennedy@kent.edu
• Cynthia Stone, Facilities/Operations Assistant
(303) 672-7493
cstone1@kent.edu
Stadium Seating Capacity:
30,520
Memorial Gym Capacity Seating:
6,327

KEYSPAN PARK
1904 SURF AVENUE
BROOKLYN, NY 11224
718-382-2600
Fax: 718-449-6368
info@brooklyncyclones.com
www.brooklyncyclones.com
• Rebecca Schwartz, Marketing & Entertainment Manager
• Steve cohen, General Manager
steve@brooklyncyclones.com
• Kevin Mahoney, Assistant General Manager
kevin@brooklyncyclones.com
• Gary J. Perone, Director of New Business Development
• Billy Harner, Director of Communications
(718) 382-2610
BHarner@BrooklynCyclones.com
• Greg Conaway, Manager, Ticket Operations
• Danny Diaz, Manager, Group Sales
• Josh Mevorach, Community Relations Manager
(718) 382-2603
Sport:
Baseball
Team:
Brooklyn Cyclones
Year Founded:
2001
Capacity:
8,000

KIBBIE DOME
PO BOX 442307
UNIVERSITY OF IDAHO
MOSCOW, ID 83844
208-885-7928
888-884-3246
Fax: 208-885-2862
info@uidaho.edu
www.govandals.com/
• Scott Gadeken, Head Strength & Conditioning Coach
• Joy Francis, Assistant Manager/Kibbie Dome
Arena Seating Capacity:
8,500
Stadium Seating Capacity:
16,500

KIDD BREWER STADIUM
111 RIVERS STREET
GEORGE M HOLMES CONVOCATION CENTER
BOONE, NC 28608

828-262-2079
Fax: 828-262-2556
www.goasu.com
• Charlie Cobb, Athletic Director
(828) 262-4010
robinsonlk@appstate.edu
• Mike Flynn, Sports Information Director
(828) 262-2268
flynnmh@appstate.edu
• Troy Heustess, Athletics Facilities Coordinator
(828) 262-7768
Stadium Seating Capacity:
18,000

KIMBROUGH MEMORIAL STADIUM
BUFFALO STADIUM ROAD AT I-27
CANYON, TX 79016
806-651-4400
Fax: 806-651-4409
www.gobuffsgo.com
• Ed Harris, Athletic Director
• Kent Johnson, Assoc. Dir for Event Operations
(806) 651-4406
• Patrick O' Brien, President University
(806) 651-2100
pobrien@wtamu.edu
• Michael McBroom, Director of Intercollege Athletics
(806) 651-4400
• David Rausch, Faculty
(806) 651-2423
drausch@wtamu.edu
• John Hasse, Ass.Director
(806) 651-2766
• Debra Carter, Administration
(806) 651-4400
dcarter@wtamu.edu

KIRBY SPORTS CENTER
700 WEST PIERCE STREET
EASTON, PA 18042
610-330-5470
Fax: 610-230-5702
www.goleopards.com
• Bruce McCutcheon, Director of Athletics
(610) 330-5470
mccutchb@lafayette.edu
Arena Seating Capacity:
3,500

KNIGHTS STADIUM
2280 DEERFIELD DRIVE
FORT MILL, SC 29715
704-357-8071
Fax: 704-329-2155
www.charlotteknights.com
• Mike Riviello, Director of Marketing & Advertising
• Kelly Crawford, Ticket Office Coordinator
• Sean Owens, Group Sales Director/Ticket Operations
• Dan Rajkowski, Executive Vice President, Chief Operating Off
• Chris Semmens, Vice President of Sales
• Mark Smith, Vice President of Marketing
• Julie Clark, Director of Special Programs & Events
• Sean Owens, Director of Ticket Sales & Hospitality
• Matt Millward, Director of Ticket Operations
Stadium Seating Capacity:
10,002.00
Nature of Service:
Baseball Entertainment.

KNOLOGY PARK
373 DOUGLAS AVENUE
#A
DUNEDIN, FL 34698
727-733-9302
Fax: 727-734-7661
shelby.nelson@bluejays.com
www.dunedinbluejays.com
• Janette Donoghue, Assistant General
Manager
(727) 738-7019
• Shelby Nelson, Director and General
Manager
(727) 738-7020
shelby.nelson@bluejays.com
• Gayle Gentry, Accounting Manager
(727) 738-7002
gayle.gentry@bluejays.com
Sport:
Baseball.
Team:
Dunedin Blue Jays baseball.
Year Founded:
1990
Capacity:
6,106

**KNOXVILLE CIVIC
AUDITORIUM/COLISEUM**
500 HOWARD BAKER JR AVENUE
PO BOX 2603
KNOXVILLE, TN 37915
865-215-8900
Fax: 865-215-8989
www.knoxvillecoliseum.com
• Dale Dunn, General Manager
(865) 215-1454
• Robbie Sandoval, Assistant General
Manager / Booking
(865) 215-8911
• Greg Mackay, Director of Public Facilities
(865) 215-1454
• Dale Dunn, General Manager
(865) 215-8910
• Doug Simmons, Operations Manager
(865) 215-8931
• Elizabeth Morrow, Box Office Manager
(865) 215-8922
• Salina Garrett, Financial Analyst
(865) 215-8913
• Jamie Cunningham, Executive Secretary
(865) 215-8914
Arena Seating Capacity:
7,000

KNUTE NELSON MEMORIAL FIELD
503 5TH AVENUE W
ALEXANDRIA, MN 56308
320-763-8151
Fax: 320-763-8152
• Shawn Reilly, Owner
(320) 763-8151
• Mitch Kluver, Assistant General Manager
(320) 763-8151
Sport:
Baseball
Tenant(s) :
Alexandria Beetles baseball
Year Founded:
1939, Renovated 1967
Capacity:
1,500

KOHL CENTER
601 W DAYTON STREET
UNIVERSITY OF WISCONSIN
MADISON, WI 53715

608-263-5645
866-788-2482
Fax: 608-265-4700
webmaster@uwbadgers.com
www.uwbadgers.com
• Zach Wagne, General Manager
• Ryan Sedevie, Assistant Director of
Marketing & Promotions
• Barry Alvarez, Administration Director of
Athletics
(608) 262-1866
• Michael Cerniglia, Administration Assistant
To The Athletic Dire
(608) 262-0147
• Sean Frazier, Administration Deputy
Athletic Director
(608) 890-2017
Tenant(s) :
NCAA - University of Wisconsin athletics.
Seating Capacity:
17,230

KYLE FIELD
WELBORN ROAD
TEXAS A&M UNIVERSITY
KOLDUS BLDG
COLLEGE STATION, TX 77843
979-845-5129
Fax: 979-845-6825
webmaster@tamu.edu
www.tamu.edu
• Antonio Cepeda-Benito, Associate Dean of
Faculties
(979) 845-5129
• Eddie J. Davis, Interim President
Arena Seating Capacity:
82,600.00
Year Founded:
1927

L.P. FRANS STADIUM
2500 CLEMENT BOULEVARD NW
HICKORY, NC 28601
828-322-3000
Fax: 828-322-6137
crawdad@hickorycrawdads.com
www.hickorycrawdads.com
• Mark Seaman, General Manager
(828) 322-3000
mseaman@hickorycrawdads.com
• Charlie Downs, Assistant General
Manager of Operations
Team:
Hickory Crawdads
Year Founded:
1993
Seating Capacity:
5,062

LA CROSSE CENTER
300 HARBORVIEW PLAZA
LA CROSSE, WI 54601
608-789-7400
Fax: 608-789-7444
office@lacrossecenter.com
www.lacrossecenter.com
• Art Fahey, Director
(608) 789-7413
afahey@lacrossecenter.com
• Sue Weiman, Business Manager
• Mike Ferris, Sales Representative
• Sue Wieman, Business Manager
(608) 789-7411
• Dave Guepfer, Food and Beverage
Manager
(608) 789-7428
dguepfer@lacrossecenter.com

• Nikki Kimpton, Box Office Supervisor
(608) 789-7426
• Dave Follansbee, Assistant Food and
Beverage Supervisor
(608) 789-7428
• Thao Moua, Accountant/Bookkeeper
(608) 789-7449
Arena Seating Capacity:
8,000

LACKAWANNA COUNTY STADIUM
235 MONTAGE MOUNTAIN ROAD
MOOSIC, PA 18507
570-969-2255
Fax: 570-963-6564
www.lackawannacounty.org
• Jeremy Ruby, General Manager/Red
Barons
(570) 969-2255
• Ann Ma Nocera, Director/Ticket
Operations
• Curt Camoni, Director/Stadium Operations
(570) 969-2255
Sport:
Baseball
Team:
Scranton Wilkes-Barre Red Barons
Year Founded:
1989
Capacity:
10,800

LADD PEEBLES STADIUM
1621 VIRGINIA STREET
PO BOX 66721
MOBILE, AL 36604
251-208-2500
Fax: 251-208-2514
www.laddpeeblesstadium.com
• Paul Christopher, Manager
• Allen Chapman, Director
allen.chapman@hubinternational.com
• Ann Davis, Director
• Richard Davis, Director
davis230@bellsouth.net
• Clyde Dumas, Director
clydedumas@comcast.net
• Thelma Cooke Thrash, Director
thelmathrash@aol.com
• David Wilhelm, Director
• Randy Gould, Chairman
lq6070gm@laquinta.com
Stadium Seating Capacity:
41,000
Team:
Southern Alabama football, Senior and
GMAC Bowls.

LAFAYETE COLLEGE
PIERCE & HAMILTON STREETS
KIRBY SPORTS CENTER
EASTON, PA 18042
610-330-5470
Fax: 610-330-5702
www.goleopards.com
• Bruce McCutcheon, Director of Athletics
mccutchb@lafayette.edu
• George Bright, Associate Director Of
Athletics
Field Seating Capacity:
13,745

LAKE ELSINORE STORM
500 DIAMOND DRIVE
LAKE ELSINORE, CA 92530
951-245-4487
Fax: 951-245-0305

info@stormbaseball.com
www.stormbaseball.com
• Bruce Kessman, VP/Director/Stadium Operations
• Jake Burch, Assistant Director/Stadium Operations
• Gary Jacobs, Owner
• Len Simon, Owner
• Dave Oster, President
doster@stormbaseball.com
• Chris Jones, Chris Jones VP/General Manager
• Tracy Kessman, Assistant General Manager
• Kasey Rawitzer, Account Executive
Sport:
Baseball
Tenant(s) :
Lake Elsinore Storm baseball
Year Founded:
1994
Capacity:
7,866

LAKE OLMSTEAD STADIUM
78 MILLEDGE ROAD
AUGUSTA, GA 30904
706-736-7889
Fax: 706-736-1122
info@greenjacketsbaseball.com
www.greenjacketsbaseball.com
• Tom Denlinger, General Manager
tdenlinger@greenjacketsbaseball.com
• Brandon Greene, Assistant General Manager
bgreene@greenjacketsbaseball.com
• Billy Nowak, Supervisor, Stadium Operations
bnowak@greenjacketsbaseball.com
Year Founded:
1988
Capacity:
4,800
Nature of Service:
Minor league baseball facility.

LAKELAND CENTER
701 W LIME STREET
LAKELAND, FL 33815
863-834-8100
800-200-4870
Fax: 863-834-8101
tlcclientservices@lakelandgov.net
www.thelakelandcenter.com
• Mike LaPan, Executive Director
(863) 834-8133
mike.lapan@lakelandgov.net
• Scott Sloman, Assistant Director
(863) 834-8144
scott.sloman@lakelandgov.net
• Tim Holloway, Client Services Manager
• Scott Sloman, Assistant Director/Booking Director
(863) 834-8144
• Lori Powell, Director of Sales
(863) 834-6116
• Lisa Parker, Sales Administrative Assistant
(863) 834-5110
• Lindsay Hansen, Executive Administrative Assistant
(863) 834-8145
• Jennifer Clark, Box Office Manager
(863) 834-8136
• Shirley Greife, Assistant Box Office Manager
(863) 834-8121

Owned by:
City of Lakeland.
Arena Seating Capacity:
10,000

LAKELAND CENTER, THE
701 W LIME STREET
THE LAKELAND CENTER
LAKELAND, FL 33815
863-834-8100
800-200-4870
Fax: 863-834-8125
tlcinfo@lakelandgov.net
www.thelakelandcenter.com
• Mike LaPan, Executive Director
(863) 834-8133
• Scott Sloman, Assistant Director
• John Oney, Director of Sales
John.Oney@lakelandgov.net
• Jason Refermat, Director Of Markering
Jason.refermat@lakelandgov.net
• Jennifer Clark, Box Office Manager
Jennifer.Clark@lakelandgov.net
• Allison Jones, Director Of Event Services
Allison.Jones@lakelandgov.net
• Steven Collazo, Director Of Event Services
Steven.Collazo@lakelandgov.net
Description:
The Lakeland Center is multi-purpose entertainment complex featuring the 10,000 seat Jenkins Arena, 2,300 seat Youkey Theatre and 100,000 square feet of meeting and exhibition space.
Arena Seating Capacity:
10,000 - Jenkins Arena. 2,300 - Youkey Theatre

LAKEVIEW ARENA
300 WEST BARAGA AVE.
MARQUETTE, MI 49855
906-228-0490
Fax: 906-228-0493
www.mqtcty.org
• Leslie Hugh, Parks/Recreation Director
Permanent Seating Capacity:
3,500

LAKEWOOD BLUECLAWS
2 STADIUM WAY
LAKEWOOD, NJ 8701
732-901-7000
Fax: 732-901-3967
lakewood.blueclaws.milb.com
• Rich Mozingo, Assistant General Manager
(732) 901-7000
• Brandon Marano, General Manager
(732) 901-7000
• Joe Harrington, Assistant General Manager of Ticket Sales
(732) 901-7000
• Amy DeMichele, Marketing Manager
(732) 901-7000
• Andrew Gilberti, Ticket Sales Manager
(732) 901-7000
• Annmarie Clifford, Ticket Sales Manager
(732) 901-7000
Clients:
Lakewood BlueClaws (Professional Baseball)
Nature of Service:
Single-A Affiliate of the Philadelphia Phillies

LAMBEAU FIELD
1265 LOMBARDI AVENUE
GREEN BAY, WI 54304

920-569-7500
Fax: 920-569-7301
www.packers.com
• Ted Eisenreich, Packers Director of Facility Operations
• Tim Connolly, Packers VP Sales/Marketing
• Jim Boettcher, Director of Operations-Levy Restaurants
• Larry L. Weyers, Vice President and Lead Director
• Mark H. Murphy, President
• Daniel T. Ariens, Secretary
• Mark J. McMullen, Treasurer
Owned by:
City of Green Bay
Tenant(s) :
NFL - Green Bay Packers football
Permanent Seating Capacity:
73,128; 166 Private Suites; 6,000 Club Seats

LANE STADIUM/WORSHAM FIELD
122 LANE STADIUM - WEST SIDE
VIRGINIA TECH (0502)
BLACKSBURG, VA 24061
540-231-6796
800-828-3244
Fax: 540-231-3060
hokipoki@vt.edu
www.hokiesports.com
• Jim Weaver, Director Athletics
(540) 231-3977
• Kent Sheets, Facilities Manager
(540) 231-2199
• Tim East, Associate Director of Athletics for External
(540) 231-6600
• Tom Gabbard, Associate Director of Athletics for Internal
(540) 231-6265
tgabbard@vt.edu
• Mike Gentry, Associate Director of Athletics for Athletic
(540) 231-2984
• Mike Goforth, Associate Director of Athletics for Sports Me
(540) 231-6410
ab8631@vt.edu
• Tom Gabbard, Assoc. Director of Athletics, Internal Affair
(540) 231-6265
tgabbard@vt.edu
Stadium Seating Capacity:
66,000
Team:
Virginia Tech football.

LANGLEY EVENTS CENTRE
7888 200 STREET
LANGLEY, BC, CANADA V2Y 3J4
604-882-8800
www.langleyeventscentre.com
Opened:
2009
Capacity:
5,276
Tenant(s) :
Trinity Western Spartans (U Sports), Langley Thunder (BCJALL), BC High School Basketball Championships, Vancouver Giants (WHL), Vancouver Bandits (CEBL), Valley West Gints (BCMML)

LANTZ ARENA
2024 LANTZ ARENA
CHARLESTON, IL 61920

217-581-6408
Fax: 217-581-7001
bvrettberg@eiu.edu
www.eiu.edu
• Rich D McDuffie, Director Athletics
• Rodger D Jehlicka, Associate Athletic
Director
Arena Seating Capacity:
5,200

LAS VEGAS CONVENTION & VISITOR'S AUTHORITY
3150 PARADISE ROAD
LAS VEGAS, NV 89109
702-892-0711
877-847-4858
Fax: 702-386-7126
www.lvcva.com
• Vince Alberta, APR, Vice President of
Public Affairs
(702) 892-7663
PR@lvcva.com
• Joey Campbell, Business Marketing
Manager
(702) 892-7638
• Dawn Christensen, Director of
Communications
(702) 892-2984
• Jeremy Handel, Senior Manager, Public
Affairs
(702) 892-7640
jhandel@lvcva.com
• Courtney Fitzgerald, Public Relations
Manager - Leisure
(702) 892-7686
cfitzgerald@lvcva.com
• Lisa Jacob, Senior Manager, Las Vegas
News Bureau
(702) 892-7641
ljacob@lvcva.com
• Jesse Davis, APR, Director, International
Public Relations
(702) 892-7655
Stadium Seating Capacity:
9,370

LAVELL EDWARDS STADIUM
A-41 ASB
Brigham Young University
PROVO, UT 84602
801-422-4636
Fax: 801-422-0806
marriottcenter@byu.edu
home.byu.edu
• Larry R Duffin, Director
• David Miles, Assistant Director- Booking
Stadium Seating Capacity:
65,000
Team:
Brigham Young University football.

LAWLOR EVENTS CENTER
1500 N VIRGINIA STREET
MAIL STOP 230
LEGACY HALL/MS-264
RENO, NV 89557
775-784-4659
Fax: 775-784-4428
lawlorinfo@yahoo.com
www.unr.edu/lawlor
• Chris Orheim, Facilities/Events
(775) 784-6900
corheim@unr.edu
• Jeff Rabedeaux, Facilities Coordinator
(775) 784-6900
Arena Seating Capacity:
12,400

LAWRENCE A. WIEN STADIUM
411 W 116 STREET
MAIL CODE 1902
NEW YORK, NY 10027
212-854-2538
Fax: 212-854-2988
www.columbia.edu
• Patrick Desir, Manager of Facilities
Operations
(212) 854-3441
pd2227@columbia.edu
• Mark Monty, Director of Athletics
Department
(212) 851-7458
Stadium Seating Capacity:
3,405

LAWRENCE JOEL VETERANS MEMORIAL COLISEUM
2825 UNIVERSITY PARKWAY
WINSTON-SALEM ENTERTAINMENT
SPORTS COMPLEX
WINSTON-SALEM, NC 27105
336-758-2410
Fax: 336-727-2922
jeff.salisbury@img.com
www.ljvm.com
• Benjamin Dame, Complex Director
(336) 725-5635
• Charlie R Vestal, Assistant Director Event
Services
(336) 725-5635
• Benjamin P Dame, Director, Public
Assembly Facilities
(336) 725-5635
• Dewey Williard, Finance Director
(336) 725-5635
• Chuck Webster, Complex Marketing
Director
(336) 725-5635
• Brian Day, Operations Director
(336) 725-5635
• David Sparks, Dixie Classic Fair Director
(336) 725-5635
• Brian Candler, General Manager Aramark
Sports & Entertainmen
(336) 725-5635
• Leigha Cordell, Event Sales Coordinator
(336) 725-5635
Arena Seating Capacity:
15,290
Tenant(s) :
NCAA - Wake Forest University basketball,
SEHL - Winston-Salem Moosehead ice
hockey

LAWRENCE-DUMONT STADIUM
300 S SYCAMORE STREET
WICHITA, KS 67213
316-264-6887
Fax: 316-264-2129
www.wichitawingnuts.com
• Robertson Josh, Asst. GM/Director,
Stadium/Baseball Operations
• David Poppleton, Assistant
Stadium/Baseball Operations

LEE ARENA
1700 SW COLLEGE AVENUE
TOPEKA, KS 66621
785-670-1010
Fax: 785-670-1028
webmaster@washburn.edu
www.washburn.edu
• Loren Ferre, Athletic Director
(785) 670-1794
loren.ferre@washburn.edu

• Gilbert Herrera, Facilities Manager
• Loren Ferre, Director Athletics
• Gene Cassell, Director Sports Information
Stadium Seating Capacity:
3,818

LEE CIVIC CENTER
11831 BAYSHORE ROAD
N FORT MYERS, FL 33917
239-543-8368
Fax: 239-543-4110
swffair@leeciviccenter.com
www.leeciviccenter.com
• Alta Mosley, General Manager
• Simon Train, Operations Manager
• Al Bertoni, Concessions Manager
Arena Seating Capacity:
8,000

LEGION FIELD STADIUM
400 GRAYMONT AVENUE W
BIRMINGHAM, AL 35204-4008
205-254-2391
Fax: 205-254-2515
wegarre@ci.birmingham.al.us
• Melvin Miller, Stadium Manager
melvin.miller@birminghamal.gov
Seating Capacity:
71.594
Team:
University of Alabama football; Papa Johns
Bowl.

LEGION STADIUM COMPLEX
302 WILLARD STREET
WILMINGTON, NC 28401
910-341-7855
Fax: 910-341-7854
amy.beatty@wilmingtonnc.gov
www.wilmingtonnc.gov
• Marian Doherty, Manager
(910) 341-3237
marian.doherty@wilmingtonnc.gov
• Amy Beatty, Concessions & Facilities
(910) 341-4604
amy.beatty@wilmingtonnc.gov
Stadium Seating Capacity:
6,500

LELACHEUR PARK
450 AIKEN STREET
LOWELL, MA 01854
978-459-2255
Fax: 978-459-1674
info@lowellspinners.com
www.lowellspinners.com
• Drew Weber, Owner & CEO
• Tim Bawmann, President & General
Manager
• Jon Healy, Vice President, Ticket
Operations
• Jeff Cohen, Director of Merchandising
• Gareth Markey, Vice President, Facilities
Sport:
Baseball
Tenant(s) :
Lowell Spinners baseball
Year Founded:
1998
Capacity:
5,030

LEWIS AND CLARK PARK
3400 LINE DRIVE
SIOUX CITY, IA 51106

712-277-9467
Fax: 712-277-9406
www.xsbaseball.com
• Ashley Schoenrock, Director of Ticket Sales
• Shane Tritz, General Manager
• Luke Nielsen, Assistant General Manager
• Shane Tritz, General Manager
(712) 277-9467
• Ashley Schoenrock, Assistant General Manager
(712) 277-9467
• Dave Nitz, Director of Broadcasting
d_nitz@hotmail.com
• Julie Stinger, Office Manager
Team:
Sioux City Explorers
Year Founded:
1993
Sport:
Baseball
Seating Capacity:
3,650

LIACOURAS CENTER
1776 N BROAD STREET
PHILADELPHIA, PA 19121
215-204-2400
800-298-4200
Fax: 215-204-2405
www.liacourascenter.com
• Fran Rodowicz, Regional Vice President
(215) 204-2401
• James Grafstrom, Assistant General Manager
(215) 204-2407
• Scott Walcoff, Marketing Manager
(215) 204-2403
Arena Seating Capacity:
10,200
Year Founded:
1997
Nature of Service:
Multi-purpose arena
Tenant(s) :
Temple University Basketball

LIBERTY BOWL MEMORIAL STADIUM
335 S HOLLYWOOD STREET
MEMPHIS, TN 38104
901-729-4344
Fax: 901-678-4134
www.libertybowl.org
• Patti Shannon, Chairman of the Board
• Ray Pohlman, President
• Billy Hicks, Jr, Vice President
• Steve Ehrhart, Executive Director
sehrhart@libertybowl.org
• Perry Winstead, Chief Financial Officer
• Patrick Byrne, Director of Sales and Marketing
Patrick.byrne@libertybowl.org
• Kevin Alexander, Operations Manager
kevin.alexander@libertybowl.org
Seating Capacity
62,384
Team:
Memphis Tigers football.

LINCOLN FINANCIAL FIELD
ONE NOVACARE WAY
PHILADELPHIA, PA 19145
215-463-2500
Contact@lincolnfinancialfield.com
www.lincolnfinancialfield.com
Seating Capacity
68,532

Tenants
NFL - Philadelphia Eagles football; NCAA - Temple University football

LINCOLN PARK STOCKER STADIUM
250 N 5TH STREET
GRAND JUNCTION, CO 81501
970-244-1542
Fax: 970-242-1637
Seating Capacity
5,500
Seating Capacity:
Suplizio Field: 6600

LINDBORG-CREGG FIELD
700 CREGG LANE
MISSOULA, MT 59801
406-543-3300
Fax: 406-543-9463
info@missoulaosprey.com
www.missoulaosprey.com
• Jared Amoss, General Manager Ogren Park Allegiance Field
• Mike Ellis, Executive Vice President
mellis@missoulaosprey.com
• Jeff Griffin, Vice President/General Manager
• Jared Amoss, General Manager-Operations
• Kim Johns, Retail Manager
kimj@missoulaosprey.com
• Grant Warner, Sales Assistant/Account Executive
• Nola Hunter, Office Manager
nhunter@missoulaosprey.com
Sport
Baseball
Team:
Missoula Osprey
Year Founded:
1999
Seating Capacity
2,200

LINDQUIST FIELD
2330 LINCOLN AVENUE
OGDEN, UT 84401
801-393-2400
Fax: 801-393-2473
• Kenny Kppinski, Head Groundskeeper
(864) 656-2308
butch@clemson.edu
• Dave Baggott, President
• Damon Berryhill, Manager
• Doug Mientkiewicz, Hitting Coach
• Bill Simas, Pitching Coach
Seating Capacity
5,000
Sport
Baseball
Team:
Ogden Raptors
Year Founded:
1997

LISTON B. RAMSEY REGIONAL ACTIVITY CENTER
92 CATAMOUNT ROAD
WESTERN CAROLINA UNIVERSITY
CULLOWHEE, NC 28723
828-227-7677
828-227-7677
www.wcu.edu/ramsey/
• Laura Huff, Director of Marketing
• Debbie Hyatt, Box office manager
dhyatt@wcu.edu

• Ryan Fisher, Assistant director of operations
jrfisher@wcu.edu
• Bill Clarke, Director
clarke@wcu.edu
Arena Seating Capacity:
8,100

LLOYD NOBLE CENTER
660 PARRINGTON OVAL
NORMAN, OK 73019-0390
405-325-0311
Fax: 405-325-4583
lnc@ou.edu
www.ou.edu
• Kenny Gajewski, Athletic Facilities
• Greg Smith, Athletic Facilities
• David L. Boren, President
• Kevin McIntyre, Director of Operations
• Loida Haffener-Salmond, Director of Events
Seating Capacity
12,000
Sports Organization
Division 1 arena hosting University of Oklahoma Men's and Women's Basketball, Women's Gymnastics, Graduations, Concerts and any other large event.

LOANMART FIELD
8408 ROCHESTER AVENUE
RANCHO CUCAMONGA, CA 91730
909-481-5000
Fax: 909-481-5005
info@rcquakes.com
www.rcquakes.com
• Brent Miles, President
(909) 481-5000
info@rcquakes.com
• Grant Riddle, Vice President, General Manager
Sport:
Baseball
Team:
Rancho Cucamonga Quakes
Year Founded:
1993
Capacity:
6,588

LOS ANGELES MEMORIAL COLISEUM SPORTS ARENA/STADIUM
3939 S FIGUEROA STREET
LOS ANGELES, CA 90037
213-747-7111
www.lacoliseum.com
• Pat Lynch, General Manager
(213) 265-6317
• Harold Zoubul, General Manager Food/Beverage
(213) 765-6380
• Yrene Asalde, Event Manager
(213) 765-6362
• Jonathan Lee, Director Of Marketing, Filmings Manager
(213) 765-6357
Seating Capacity
93,607
Seating Capacity
16,500

LOS ANGELES TENNIS CENTER
420 CHARLES E YOUNG DRIVE WEST
LOS ANGELES, CA 90095
310-825-4546
www.recreation.ucla.edu

LOUIS BROWN ALTHETIC CENTER
83 ROCKAFELLER ROAD
PISCATAWAY, NJ 8854
732-445-4220
Fax: 732-445-2752
www.scarletknights.com
• Robert E Mulcahy, Athletic Director
(732) 445-8610
Seating Capacity
8,400

LOUISIANA SUPERDOME
SUGAR BOWL DRIVE
NEW ORLEANS, LA 70112
504-587-3663
800-756-7074
Fax: 504-587-3848
ada@superdome.com
www.superdome.com
• Doug Thornton, General Manager
• Danny Vincens, Assistant General
Manager
• David Weidler, Director
Finance/Administration
• Bill Curl, Director Public Relations
Owned by:
State of Louisiana
Description:
NFL - New Orleans Saints football, NCAA -
Tulane University football
Seating Capacity
72,000

LOUISVILLE METRO HALL
601 W JEFFERSON ST.
LOUISVILLE, KY 40202
502-574-3521
Fax: 502-574-0065
• Alvin Hampton, Sales/Marketing Director
Mary Helen Byck Arena Seating Capacity:
6,850

LOUISVILLE SLUGGER FIELD
401 E MAIN STREET
LOUISVILLE, KY 40202
502-212-2287
Fax: 502-515-2255
www.batsbaseball.com
• James Breeding, Director Ticket Sales
jbreeding@batsbaseball.com
• Scott Shoemaker, Director Stadium
Operations
sshoemaker@batsbaseball.com
• Gary Ulmer, President/CEO
gulmer@batsbaseball.com
• Dale Owens, Sr. Vice President of
Corporate Sales
dowens@batsbaseball.com
• Greg Galiette, Sr. Vice President of
Marketing
ggaliette@batsbaseball.com
• Scott Shoemaker, Vice President of
Operations & Technology
sshoemaker@batsbaseball.com
• James Breeding, Vice President of
Business Operations
jbreeding@batsbaseball.com
• Michele Anderson, Controller
manderson@batsbaseball.com
Sport
Baseball
Tenants
Lousville Bats baseball
Year Founded:
2000
Seating Capacity
13,131

LP FIELD
460 GREAT CIRCLE ROAD
NASHVILLE, TN 37228
615-565-4000
Fax: 615-565-4175
www.titansonline.com
• Mike Reinfeldt, Executive Vice President
and General Manager
• Dempsey Henderson, Facilities Manager
• K.S. Adams, Jr., Founder, Owner,
Chairman of the Board, Presid
• Don MacLachlan, Executive Vice
President of Administration an
• Ruston Webster, Executive Vice
President/General Manager
• Elza Bullock, Senior Vice President and
General Counsel
• Lake Dawson, Vice President of Player
Personnel
• Bob Hyde, Vice President of Community
Relations
• Jenneen Kaufman, Vice President/CFO
Tenant(s) :
NFL - Tennessee Titans football.
Stadium Seating Capacity:
68,804

LT SMITH STADIUM
1 BIG RED WAY
WESTERN KENTUCKY UNIVERSITY
BOWLING GREEN, KY 42101
270-745-6062
Fax: 270-745-6187
pam.herriford@wku.edu,
www.wkusports.com
• Camden Wood Selig, Athletic Director
(270) 745-5276
• Craig Biggs, Associate Athletics Director
(270) 745-5729
craig.biggs@wku.edu
• Jim Clark, Associate Athletics Director
(270) 745-5321
jim.clark@wku.edu
• Todd Stewart, Director of Athletics
(270) 745-5276
todd.stewart@wku.edu
• Lindsay Boyden, Assistant AD (Marketing)
(270) 745-6562
• Debbie Carroll, Business Operations
Specialist
(270) 745-5038
debbie.carroll@wku.edu
Stadium Seating Capacity:
17,000

LUCAS OIL STADIUM
500 S CAPITOL AVENUE
INDIANAPOLIS, IN 46225-1117
317-262-8600
Fax: 317-262-5757
losinfo@icclos.com
www.lucasoilstadium.com
• Barney Levengood, Executive Director
(317) 262-3400
• Eric Neuburger, Stadium Director
(317) 262-8600
Seating Capacity:
Football 63,000; Basketball, Conventions,
Concerts, Superbowl, etc 70,000
Tenants:
Indianapolis Colts
Owned by:
Indiana Stadium and Convention Building
Authority (ISCBA) but leased and operated
byt the Capital Improvement Board of
Managers of Marion County (CIB).
Nature of Service:

Large Sports and Convention Arena.
Year Founded:
2008

LYNCHBURG CITY STADIUM
3180 FORT AVENUE
LYNCHBURG, VA 24501
434-528-1144
Fax: 434-846-0768
info@lynchburg-hillcats.com
www.lynchburg-hillcats.com
• Bonnie Roberts, Assistant General
Manager/Hillcats
(434) 528-1144
• Darren Johnson, Director of Sales
• Brad Goodale, Director of Group Sales
• Erik Wilson, Director of Broadcasting
• Ashley Stephenson, Director of
Promotions
• John Hutt, Director of Ticketing
• Paul Sunwall, General Manager
• Rex Angel, President
Sport
Baseball
Team:
Lynchburg Hillcats
Year Founded:
1940
Seating Capacity
4,000
Description:
Minor League professional baseball team,
member of the Class A Advanced Carolina
League.

M.M. ROBERTS STADIUM
118 COLLEGE DRIVE
HATTIESBURG, MS 39406
601-266-5017
www.southernmiss.com
• Bill McGillis, Director of Athletics
• Tim Atkinson, Assistant Athletic Director
(601) 266-5025
• Jay Hopson, Head Coach, Football
(601) 266-4567
Team:
Southern Miss Golden Eagles
Seating Capacity:
36,000

MABEE CENTER ARENA
7777 S LEWIS AVENUE
TULSA, OK 74171
918-495-6400
Fax: 918-495-6478
www.mabeecenter.com
• Tony Winters, General Manager
(918) 495-6404
twinters@oru.edu
• Vick Barker, Operations Director
(918) 495-6406
vbarker@oru.edu
• James D. Smith, Director of Marketing &
Business Development
jasmith@oru.edu
Seating Capacity
11,763

MACKAY STADIUM
RENO, NV
Fax: 775-784-4497
www.nevadawolfpack.com/facilities/mackay-
stadium.html
Seating Capacity:
30,000

MACKEY ARENA
900 JOHN R. WOODEN DRIVE
WEST LAFAYETTE, IN 47907
765-494-3194
800-497-7678
Fax: 765-494-5447
www.purduesports.com
• Steve Simmerman, Snr. Associate
Athletics Director - Facilities
(765) 494-3143
simmerman@purdue.edu
• Paul Horsley, Operations Superintendent
(765) 494-6773
Seating Capacity:
14,264

MADISON SQUARE GARDEN
4 PENNSYLVANIA PLAZA
NEW YORK, NY 10001
212-465-6741
msgfeedback@msg.com
www.thegarden.com
• Dolan L James, Executive Chairman
• Hank Ratner, President, Chief Executive
Officer
• Lawrence Burian, EVP, General Counsel,
Secretary
• Steve Collins, Executive VP Facilities
• Robert Pollichino, Executive Vice
President, Chief Financial Officer
• Barry Watkins, Executive Vice President of
Communications
Seating Capacity:
18,200
Home Arena for:
New York Knicks, New York Rangers, New
York Liberty.

MAGNOLIA FIELD
MISSISSIPPI VALLEY STATE
UNIVERSITY, DEPT. OF ATHLETICS
14000 HIGHWAY 82 WEST
BOX 7246
ITTA BENA, MS 38941
662-254-3550
Fax: 662-254-3639
www.mvsusports.com
• Dianthia Ford-Kee, Director of Athletics
(662) 254-3550
• Lee Smith, Associate Athletic Director &
Head Coach, Softball
(662) 254-3721
• Aaron Stevens, Head Coach, Baseball

**MANNING FIELD AT JOHN L. GUIDRY
STADIUM**
906 EAST 1ST STREET
THIBODAUX, LA 70310
www.geauxcolonels.com
• Rob Bernardi, Director of Athletics
• Tim Rebowe, Head Coach, Football
Team:
Nicholls State Colonels
Seating Capacity:
10,500

MAPFRE STADIUM
ONE BLACK & GOLD BOULEVARD
COLUMBUS, OH 43211-2091
614-447-2739
Fax: 614-447-4109
mapfrestadium.com
• Dan Lolli, Director of Stadium Operations
• Meredith Ley, Stadium Operations
Manager
mley@columbuscrewsc.com
• Jordan Enke, Director of Facilities

Stadium Seating Capacity:
19,968
Tenant(s) :
MLS - Columbus Crew soccer.

MARIUCCI ARENA
1901 4TH STREET SE
MINNEAPOLIS, MN 55455
612-625-8365
Fax: 612-624-5887
www.gophersports.com
• Beth Goetz, Interim Director of Athletics
• Don Lucia, Head Coach, Men's Hockey
• Brad Frost, Head Coach, Women's
Hockey
Seating Capacity:
9,800

MARRIOTT CENTER
500 E UNIVERSITY PARKWAY
PROVO, UT 84602
801-422-2981
byucougars.com/facilities/basketball
• Tom Holmoe, Director of Athletics
(801) 422-1508
• Dave Rose, Head Coach, Men's
Basketball
(801) 422-3612
• Jeff Judkins, Head Coach, Women's
Basketball
(801) 422-1265
Seating Capacity:
20,900

MARYLAND STADIUM
90 STADIUM DRIVE
UNIVERSITY OF MARYLAND
COLLEGE PARK, MD 20742
301-314-7070
www.umterps.com/facilities
• Kevin Anderson, Director of Athletics
(301) 314-7075
dorourke@umd.edu
• Joshua Kaplan, Associate AD, Facilities
Operations & Events
(301) 314-9729
jkap@umd.edu
• P.J. Ellis, Director of Grounds
(301) 314-7383
pellis@umd.edu
Seating Capacity:
51,802
Teams:
University of Maryland football.

MARYVALE BASEBALL PARK
3600 N 51ST AVENUE
PHOENIX, AZ 85031
623-245-5500
www.mlb.com/springtraining
Description:
Spring training home of the Milwaukee
Brewers.
Seating Capacity:
10,000

MATTHEW KNIGHT ARENA
1390 VILLARD STREET
EUGENE, OR 97403
541-346-4461
800-932-3668
www.goducks.com
• Rob Mullens, Athletic Director
Seating Capacity:
12,364

MATTHEWS ARENA
238 ST. BOTOLPH STREET
BOSTON, MA 02115
617-373-2691
www.gonu.com
• Peter Roby, Athletic Director
• Jim Madigan, Head Coach, Men's Hockey
• Dave Flint, Head Coach, Women's Hockey
• Bill Coen, Head Coach, Men's Basketball
• Kelly Cole, Head Coach, Women's
Basketball
Seating Capacity:
6,000

MAVERICK STADIUM
1307 W MITCHELL STREET
ARLINGTON, TX 76019-0079
817-272-2033
Fax: 817-272-2922
www.uta.edu/maverickstadium
• Tom Kloza, Stadium Director
Seating Capacity:
12,500

MCCARTHY STADIUM
1900 W OLNEY AVENUE
PHILADELPHIA, PA 19141
www.goexplorers.com
• Bill Bradshaw, Interim Director of Athletics
(215) 951-1425
• Pat Farrell, Head Coach, Men's Soccer
(215) 951-1993
• Paul Royal, Head Coach, Women's
Soccer
(215) 951-1523
• Candace Taglianetti Bossell, Head Coach,
Women's Lacrosse
(215) 951-1994
Seating Capacity:
7,500

MCCORMICK FIELD
30 BUCHANAN PLACE
ASHEVILLE, NC 28801
828-258-0428
Fax: 828-258-0320
asheville.tourists.milb.com/index.jsp?sid=t57
3
• Brian DeWine, President
• Larry Hawkins, General Manager
• Brandon Reeves, Director, Stadium
Operations
Sport:
Baseball
Team:
Asheville Tourists
Year Founded:
1992
Seating Capacity:
4,100

MCCOY STADIUM
1 COLUMBUS AVENUE
PAWTUCKET, RI 02860
401-724-7300
Fax: 401-724-2140
info@pawsox.com
www.milb.com/index.jsp?sid=t533
• Charles Steinberg, President
• Dan Rea, SVP & General Manager
Sport:
Baseball
Team:
Pawtucket Red Sox
Year Founded:
1942. Renovated 1999

Seating Capacity:
10,031

MCKALE MEMORIAL CENTER
1721 E ENKE DRIVE
TUCSON, AZ 85721
www.arizonawildcats.com
• Greg Byrne, Vice President, Athletics
• Sean Miller, Head Coach, Men's
Basketball
• Niya Butts, Head Coach, Women's
Basketball
Seating Capacity:
14,000

MEADOWLANDS SPORTS COMPLEX
50 STATE HIGHWAY 120
EAST RUTHERFORD, NJ 07073
201-935-8500
www.njsea.com

MEMORIAL COLISEUM
201 AVENUE OF CHAMPIONS
LEXINGTON, KY 40506-0019
www.ukathletics.com/page/facilities-memori
al-coliseum
• Mitch Barnhart, Athletics Director
(859) 257-8015
• Matthew Mitchell, Head Coach, Women's
Basketball
• Tim Garrison, Head Coach, Gymnastics
• Craig Skinner, Head Coach, Volleyball
Seating Capacity:
8,500

MEMORIAL FIELD
4 CROSBY STREET
HANOVER, NH 03755
603-646-1110
www.dartmouthsports.com
• Harry Sheehy, Director of Athletics &
Recreation
• Richard Whitmore, Sr. Assoc. Athl. Dir. of
Facilities & Operations
• Buddy Teevens, Head Coach, Football
Seating Capacity:
11,000

MEMORIAL GYM
210 25TH AVENUE S
NASHVILLE, TN 37240
615-322-1793
www.vucommodores.com
• David Williams, II, Athletics Director
• Kevin Stallings, Head Coach, Men's
Basketball
(615) 322-6530
• Melanie Balcomb, Head Coach, Women's
Basketball
(615) 343-8482
Seating Capacity:
14,326

MEMORIAL GYMNASIUM
GRAMBLING UNIVERSITY
GRAMBLING, LA
www.gram.edu
• Obadiah Simmons, Interim Athletic
Director
(318) 274-2374
• Demetria Keys-Johnson, Head Coach,
Volleyball
(318) 274-3216
Seating Capacity:
2,200

MEMORIAL STADIUM (ILLINOIS)
1402 S FIRST STREET
CHAMPAIGN, IL 61820
217-333-1400
www.fightingillini.com
• Josh Whitman, Director of Athletics
(217) 333-3631
• Lenny Willis, Director of Facilities
(217) 333-2303
• Lovie Smith, Head Coach, Football
Seating Capacity:
60,670
Team:
University of Illinois Fighting Illini

MEMORIAL STADIUM (INDIANA)
1001 E 17TH STREET
BLOOMINGTON, IN 47408
812-855-1966
iuhoosiers.com
• Fred Glass, Vice President & Director of
Athletics
iuad@indiana.edu
• Scott Dolson, Deputy Director of Athletics
sdolson@indiana.edu
• Eric Neuburger, Assoc. Athl. Dir. for
Facilities & Ext. Alliances
• Kevin Wilson, Head Coach, Football
football@indiana.edu
Seating Capacity:
52,929
Team:
Indiana Hoosiers

MEMORIAL STADIUM (KANSAS)
1101 MAINE STREET
LAWRENCE, KS 66045
785-864-3141
www.kuathletics.com
• Sheahon Zenger, Director of Athletics
kuathletics@ku.edu
• Jay Ellis, Assistant Athletic Director -
Facilities
ajellis@ku.edu
• David Beaty, Head Coach, Football
kansasfootball@ku.edu
Seating Capacity:
50,071
Team:
Kansas Jayhawks

MEMORIAL STADIUM (NEBRASKA)
ONE STADIUM DRIVE
LINCOLN, NE 68588
402-472-2263
www.huskers.com
• Shawn Eichorst, Director of Athletics
• Mike Riley, Head Coach, Football
Team:
Nebraska Cornhuskers
Seating Capacity:
85,000

MERRILL FIELD AT YUNEVICH STADIUM
1 SAXON DRIVE
ALFRED, NY 14802
800-541-9229
saxons@alfred.edu
www.alfred.edu
• Paul Vecchio, Athletic Director
(607) 871-2030
vecchio@alfred.edu
• Bob Rankl, Head Coach, Football
(607) 871-2302
ranklr@alfred.edu
• Jason Lockner, Head Coach, Men's
Lacrosse

(607) 871-2890
locknerj@alfred.edu
• Erynn Anderson, Head Coach, Women's
Lacrosse
(607) 871-2628
andersonel@alfred.edu
• Matt Smith, Head Coach, Men's Soccer
(607) 871-2899
smithma@alfred.edu
• Aileen Ascolese, Head Coach, Women's
Soccer
(607) 871-2896
ascolese@alfred.edu
Seating Capacity:
1,355

MESQUITE ARENA
1818 RODEO DRIVE
MESQUITE, TX 75149
972-285-8777
Fax: 972-289-2999
info@mesquiterodeo.com
www.mesquiterodeo.com
Seating Capacity:
5,500
Convention/Expo Center:
35,000 sq. ft.

METRAPARK
308 6TH AVENUE N
BILLINGS, MT 59101
406-256-2400
info@metrapark.com
www.metrapark.com
Rimrock Auto Arena Seating Capacity:
12,000

METRO BANK PARK
245 CHAMPIONSHIP WAY
HARRISBURG, PA 17101
717-231-4444
information@senatorsbaseball.com
www.senatorsbaseball.com
Sport:
Baseball
Team:
Harrisburg Senators, AA affiliate of the
Washington Nationals.
Year Founded:
1987
Seating Capacity:
6,187

MGM GRAND HOTEL & CASINO
3799 LAS VEGAS BOULEVARD SOUTH
LAS VEGAS, NV 89109
877-880-0880
Fax: 702-891-3036
guestservices@lv.mgmgrand.com
www.mgmgrand.com
Year Founded:
1993

MICHIE STADIUM
700 MILLS ROAD
WEST POINT, NY 10996
877-849-2769
www.goarmywestpoint.com
• Boo Corrigan, Director of Athletics
• Jeff Monken, Head Coach, Football
Seating Capacity:
38,000
Teams:
Army Black Knights

MICHIGAN STADIUM
1201 S MAIN STREET
ANN ARBOR, MI 48104-3722
734-647-2583
Fax: 734-764-3221
www.mgoblue.com
• Warde Manuel, Director of Athletics
• Jim Harbaugh, Head Coach, Football
(734) 763-4422
• John Paul, Head Coach, Men's Lacrosse
(734) 763-3679
• Jennifer Ulehla, Head Coach, Women's
Lacrosse
(734) 647-9856
Seating Capacity:
107,601
Team:
University of Michigan Wolverines

MILLER PARK
ONE BREWERS WAY
MILWAUKEE, WI 53214
414-902-4400
milwaukee.brewers.mlb.com
Team:
Milwaukee Brewers
Seating Capacity:
41,900

MILLETT HALL
500 E SYCAMORE STREET
OXFORD, OH 45056
www.miamiredhawks.com
• David Sayler, Director of Athletics
(513) 529-7286
• John Cooper, Head Coach, Men's
Basketball
(513) 529-1650
• Cleve Wright, Head Coach, Women's
Basketball
(513) 529-3300
• Carolyn Condit, Head Coach, Volleyball
(513) 529-6922
Team:
Miami University RedHawks
Seating Capacity:
6,400

MINUTE MAID PARK
501 CRAWFORD STREET
SUITE 400
HOUSTON, TX 77002
houston.astros.mlb.com
Team:
Houston Astros
Seating Capacity:
40,963

**MISSISSIPPI COAST COLISEUM AND
CONVENTION CENTER**
2350 BEACH BOULEVARD
BILOXI, MS 39531
228-594-3700
800-726-2781
Fax: 228-594-3812
www.mscoastcoliseum.com
• Matt McDonnell, Executive Director
• Gregg Blaize, Assistant Executive Director
Seating Capacity:
15,000

**MISSISSIPPI VETERANS MEMORIAL
STADIUM**
2531 NORTH STATE STREET
JACKSON, MS 39216

601-354-6021
www.ms-veteransstadium.com
• Tom Cooper, Event Manager
(601) 345-6021
Seating Capacity:
60,492
Team:
Jackson State University Tigers

MITCHELL HALL GYMNASIUM
1820 PINE STREET
LA CROSSE, WI 54601
608-785-8616
Fax: 608-785-8674
athletics@uwlax.edu
www.uwlathletics.com
• Kim Blum, Director of Athletics
(608) 785-8616
kblum@uwlax.edu
• Jason Murphy, Facilities Director
• Ken Koelbl, Head Coach, Men's
Basketball
• Lois Heeren, Head Coach, Women's
Basketball
• Dave Malecek, Head Coach, Wrestling
• Barbara Gibson, Head Coach, Gymnastics
Seating Capacity:
2,880

MOBILE CIVIC CENTER
401 CIVIC CENTER DRIVE
MOBILE, AL 36602
251-208-7261
www.mobilecivicctr.com
• Bob Brazier, General Manager
(251) 208-2111
• Joe Delaronde, Director of Operations
(251) 208-7937
Seating Capacity:
10,112

MOBY ARENA
951 W PLUM STREET
FORT COLLINS, CO 80523
970-491-5300
800-491-RAMS
www.csurams.com
• Joe Parker, Athletics Director
(970) 491-3350
• Doug Max, Snr. Assoc. Athl. Dir. for
Facilities & Scheduling
• Larry Eustachy, Head Coach, Men's
Basketball
(970) 491-6232
• Ryun Williams, Head Coach, Women's
Basketball
(970) 491-6569
• Tom Hilbert, Head Coach, Volleyball
(970) 491-6410
Team:
Colorado State Rams
Seating Capacity:
8,745

MOHEGAN SUN ARENA
1 MOHEGAN SUN BOULEVARD
UNCASVILLE, CT 06382
888-226-7711
information@mohegansun.com
mohegansun.com
Team:
Connecticut Sun
Seating Capacity:
9,518

MONTAGNE CENTER
4400 SOUTH MLK PARKWAY
BEAUMONT, TX 77705
409-880-1810
Fax: 409-880-1814
www.montagnecenter.com
• Jason Henderson, Director of Athletics
(409) 880-8303
jason.henderson@lamar.edu
• Tic Price, Head Coach, Men's Basketball
(409) 880-8301
tic.price@lamar.edu
• Robin Harmony, Head Coach, Women's
Basketball
(409) 880-2238
robin.harmony@lamar.edu
Team:
Lamar University Cardinals & Lady
Cardinals
Seating Capacity:
10,080

MONTANA EXPOPARK
400 3RD STREET NW
GREAT FALLS, MT 59404
406-727-8900
Fax: 406-452-8955
goexpopark.com
• Randy Bogden, Advisory Board Chairman
Description:
Home of the Montana State Fair, the
Montana ExpoPark is a 133-acre fairground
consisting of exhibition pavilions, a horse
racing track and a multi-purpose sports
arena. The six original, Art Deco buildings
were added to the National Register of
Historic Places.

MOODY COLISEUM
6024 AIRLINE ROAD
DALLAS, TX 75205
214-768-2000
www.smumustangs.com
• Rick Hart, Director of Athletics
(214) 768-4301
rlhart@smu.edu
• Larry Brown, Head Coach, Men's
Basketball
(214) 768-3501
• Lisa Dark, Associate Head Coach,
Women's Basketball
(214) 768-3681
Team:
Southern Methodist University Mustangs
Seating Capacity:
7,000

MOSAIC STADIUM
1700 ELPHINSTONE STREET
REGINA, SK, CANADA S4P 2Z6
306-781-9200
info@real1884.ca
www.realdistrict.ca/venues/mosaic-stadium
Owner:
City of Regina
Operator:
Regina Exhibition Association Ltd.
Opened:
2017
Seating Capacity:
33,350 (expandable to 40,000)
Tenant(s) :
Saskatchewan Roughriders (CFL), Regina
Rams (U Sports), Regina Thunder (CJFL),
Regina Riot (WWCFL)

MOUNTAINEER FIELD AT MILAN PUSKAR STADIUM
1 IRA ERRETT RODGERS DRIVE
MORGANTOWN, WV 26505
www.wvusports.com
• Shane Lyons, Director of Athletics
• April Messerly, Asst. AD for Facilities & Operations
• Dana Holgorsen, Head Coach, Football
Team:
West Virginia Mountaineers
Seating Capacity:
60,000

MULLINS CENTER
200 COMMONWEALTH AVENUE
2ND FLOOR
AMHERST, MA 01003
413-545-3040
www.mullinscenter.com
• Brian Caputo, General Manager
(413) 545-3129
• Sean Dolan, Director of Operations & Asst. GM
(413) 545-3336
• Derek Kellogg, Head Coach, Men's Basketball
• Sharon Dawley, Head Coach, Women's Basketball
• John Micheletto, Head Coach, Ice Hockey
Team:
UMass Minutemen
Seating Capacity:
10,500

MUNICIPAL STADIUM
274 EAST MEMORIAL BOULEVARD
HAGERSTOWN, MD 21740
301-791-6266
Fax: 301-791-6066
info@hagerstownsuns.com
www.hagerstownsuns.com
• Bruce Quinn, President
• Travis Painter, General Manager
• Brian Saddler, Grounds Keeper
Sport:
Baseball
Team:
Hagerstown Suns
Year Founded:
1930

MUSSELMAN STADIUM
300 N WASHINGTON STREET
GETTYSBURG COLLEGE
GETTYSBURG, PA 17325
717-337-6300
Fax: 717-337-6666
tmyers@gettysburg.edu
www.gettysburg.edu
• David Wright, Athletic Director
(717) 337-6530
• Susan Fumagalli, Assistant Director of Athletics
(717) 337-6401
sfumagal@gettysburg.edu
Stadium Seating Capacity:
6,000

MYRL H. SHOEMAKER CENTER
2700 O'VARSITY WAY
SHOEMAKER CENTER, UNIVERSITY OF CINCINNATI
CINCINNATI, OH 45221
513-556-2170
Fax: 513-556-0619
uccheerleading@yahoo.com
www.gobearcats.com
• Mike Thomas, Director of Athletics
(513) 556-4603
bearcat.ad@uc.edu
• Bob Arkeilpane, Deputy Director of Athletics
(513) 556-2449
bob.arkeilpane@us.edu
• David Szymanski, Faculty Athletics Representative
(513) 556-3935
david.szymanski@uc.edu
• Omar Banks, Sr. Associate AD/CFO
(513) 556-0608
• Brendan Fouracre, Sr. Associate AD/Facilities & Operations
(513) 556-3541
brendan.fouracre@uc.edu
• Andy Hurley, Sr. Associate AD/External Relations
(513) 556-9302
• Santa Ono, University President
(513) 556-2201
president@uc.edu
Arena Seating Capacity:
13,176
Nippert Stadium Seating Capacity:
35,000

N.E.C. ARENA BIRMINGHAM
NATIONAL EXHIBITION CENTRE
BIRMINGHAM, ENGLAND B4O 1NT
44-(0) 121 780 4141
Fax: -44-767-3700
info@necgroup.co.uk
www.necgroup.co.uk
• Martin C Angle, Non-Executive Chairman
• Paul Thandi, Chief Executive
• John Hornby, Chief Operating Officer
• Nick Waight, Chief Executive of the Convention Centre
• Kevin Watson, Managing Director Amadeus
• Kathryn James, Managing Director, National Exhibition Centre
• Phil Mead, Managing Director, Arenas
Permanent Seating Capacity:
12,500

NASHVILLE MUNICIPAL AUDITORIUM
417 4TH AVENUE N
NASHVILLE, TN 37201
615-862-6390
Fax: 615-862-6394
www.nashvilleauditorium.com
• Bob Skoney, General Manager
bob.skoney@nashville.gov
• Derrick Pentico, Event Manager
derrick.pentico@nashville.gov
Description:
A multipurpose sports arena and entertainment venue located in downtown Nashville. Houses Musicians Hall of Fame & Museum.
Seating Capacity:
8,000

NASSAU VETERANS MEMORIAL COLISEUM
1255 HEMPSTEAD TURNPIKE
UNIONDALE, NY 11553
www.nassaucoliseum.com
Description:
Multi-purpose indoor arena on Long Island. Until 2015 the Nassau Coliseum was the home of the New York Islanders of the NHL.

Current renovations are expected to be completed in 2017.
Seating Capacity:
18,000

NATIONALS PARK
1500 SOUTH CAPITOL STREET SE
WASHINGTON, DC 20003
202-675-6287
Fax: 202-640-7999
nationals.com
• Theodore N. Lerner, Managing Principal Owner
• Mike Rizzo, General Manager & President of Baseball Operations
Teams:
Washington Nationals
Seating Capacity:
41,546

NATIONWIDE ARENA
200 W NATIONWIDE BOULEVARD
COLUMBUS, OH 43215
614-246-2000
Fax: 614-246-4300
www.nationwidearena.com
Description:
Multi-purpose sports and entertainment revue. Nationwide Arena hosts more than 150 events annually.
Founded:
2000
Team(s):
Columbus Blue Jackets (NFL); Columbus Destroyers (AFL)
Seating Capacity:
20,000

NAVY-MARINE CORPS MEMORIAL STADIUM
550 TAYLOR AVENUE
ANNAPOLIS, MD 21401
410-263-4783
www.navysports.com
• Chet Gladchuk, Director of Athletics
(410) 293-8910
gladchuk@usna.edu
• Tom McKavitt, Assoc. AD, Facilities & Maintenance
(410) 293-8770
• Ken Niumatalolo, Head Coach, Football
(410) 293-2241
• Rick Sowell, Head Coach, Men's Lacrosse
(410) 293-8779
• Cindy Timchal, Head Coach, Women's Lacrosse
(410) 293-8746
timchal@usna.edu
Team:
Navy Midshipmen
Seating Capacity:
34,000

NBT BANK STADIUM
300 NBT BANK PARKWAY
SYRACUSE, NY 13208
315-474-7833
www.syracusechiefs.com
Team:
Syracuse Chiefs
Founded:
1997
Seating Capacity:
11,071

NELSON W. WOLFF MUNICIPAL STADIUM
5757 US HWY 90 WEST
SAN ANTONIO, TX 78227
210-675-7275
Fax: 210-670-0001
sainfo@samissions.com
www.milb.com/index.jsp?sid=t510
• Dave Gasaway, General Manager
Team:
San Antonio Missions
Seating Capacity:
9,200

NEW BRITAIN STADIUM
230 JOHN KARBONIC WAY
NEW BRITAIN, CT 06051
860-826-2337
info@nbbees.com
nbbees.com
• Patrick Day, General Manager
Team:
New Britain Bees
Founded:
1996
Seating Capacity:
6,146

NEWMAN OUTDOOR FIELD
1515 15TH AVENUE NORTH
FARGO, ND 58102
701-235-6161
800-303-6161
Fax: 701-297-9247
redhawks@fmredhawks.com
www.fmredhawks.com
• Brad Thom, President & CEO
• Tim Jallen, Director of Field & Stadium
Operations
tjallen@fmredhawks.com
Founded:
1996
Team:
Fargo-Moorhead RedHawks
Seating Capacity:
4,513

NEYLAND STADIUM
1600 PHILLIP FULMER WAY
SUITE 201
KNOXVILLE, TN 37996
www.utsports.com
• Dave Hart, Director of Athletics
(865) 974-1224
athleticdirector@utk.edu
• Kevin Zurcher, Asst. AD for Athletic
Facilities & Grounds
(865) 974-8479
kzurcher@tennessee.edu
• Butch Jones, Head Coach, Football
Team:
Tennessee Volunteers
Seating Capacity:
102,455

NICKERSON FIELD
285 BABCOCK STREET
BOSTON, MA 02215
617-353-4630
Fax: 617-353-5286
gobu@bu.edu
www.goterriers.com
• Drew Marrochello, Director of Athletics
(617) 353-4631
• Ryan Polley, Head Coach, Men's Lacrosse
(617) 358-0365

• Liz Robertshaw, Head Coach, Women's
Lacrosse
(617) 353-2094
• Neil Roberts, Head Coach, Men's Soccer
(617) 358-3793
• Nancy Feldman, Head Coach, Women's
Soccer
(617) 353-8456
Team:
BU Terriers
Seating Capacity:
10,412

NIPPERT STADIUM
2700 BEARCATS WAY
CINCINNATI, OH 45221
513-556-2287
www.gobearcats.com
• Mike Bohn, Director of Athletics
(513) 556-4603
• Brendan Fouracre, Sr. Assoc. AD,
Facilities & Operations
(513) 556-3541
• Tommy Tuberville, Head Coach, Football
(513) 556-4110
Team:
Cincinnati Bearcats
Seating Capacity:
35,000

NORTH CHARLESTON COLISEUM
5001 COLISEUM DRIVE
NORTH CHARLESTON, SC 29418
843-529-5000
www.northcharlestoncoliseumpac.com
Team:
South Carolina Stingrays (ECHL)
Seating Capacity:
14,000

NOTRE DAME STADIUM
MOOSE KRAUSE CIRCLE
SOUTH BEND, IN 46616
574-631-7356
www.und.com
• Jack Swarbrick, Univ. VP & Director of
Athletics
(574) 631-6107
• Dan Brazo, Facility Manager, Notre Dame
Stadium
(574) 631-7962
Team:
Notre Dame Fighting Irish
Seating Capacity:
80,795

NRG STADIUM
1 NRG PARK
HOUSTON, TX 77054
832-667-1400
Fax: 832-667-1748
www.reliantpark.com/nrg-park-facilities/nrg-stadium
Seating Capacity:
72,000
Teams:
Houston Texans NFL football; Texas Bowl.

NYSEG STADIUM
211 HENRY STREET
BINGHAMTON, NY 13901
607-723-6387
Fax: 607-723-7779
bmets@bmets.com
www.bmets.com

• Jim Weed, General Manager
• Richard Tylicki, Director of Stadium
Operations
Team:
Binghamton Mets
Year Founded:
1992
Seating Capacity:
6,012

O'BRIEN FIELD
GRANT AVENUE & 4TH STREET
CHARLESTON, IL 61920
www.eiupanthers.com
• Tom Michael, Athletic Director
• Kim Dameron, Head Coach, Football
(217) 581-5031
rkdameron@eiu.edu
• Tom Akers, Director, Track & Field
(217) 581-2625
tlakers@eiu.edu
Team:
Eastern Illinois Panthers
Seating Capacity:
10,000

O'NEILL CENTER
43 LAKE AVENUE EXTENSION
DANBURY, CT 06811
203-837-9015
Fax: 203-837-9050
www.wcsuathletics.com/information/Western
_Athletic_Facilties
• Scott Ames, Interim Athletic Director
(203) 837-9014
• Bob Campbell, Head Coach, Men's
Basketball
(203) 837-9017
• Kimberley Rybczyk, Head Coach,
Women's Basketball
(203) 837-9018
rybczykk@wcsu.edu
• Don Ferguson, Head Coach, Women's
Volleyball
(203) 837-9022
fergusond@wcsu.edu
Team:
WestConn Colonials
Seating Capacity:
4,500

O.co COLISEUM
7000 COLISEUM WAY
OAKLAND, CA 94621
510-569-2121
www.coliseum.com
Teams:
Oakland Athletics (MLB); Oakland Raiders
(NFL)
Seating Capacity:
Baseball 35,067; Football 56,057; Soccer
63,132

OCEAN CENTER
101 N ATLANTIC AVENUE
DAYTONA BEACH, FL 32118
386-254-4500
800-858-6444
Fax: 386-254-4512
frontdesk@oceancenter.com
www.oceancenter.com
• Don Poor, Director
dpoor@oceancenter.com
Owner:
Volusia County
Seating Capacity:

Hockey/Arena Football 6,176; Basketball 8,362; Wrestling 8,582

ODEUM EXPO CENTER
1033 NORTH VILLA AVENUE
VILLA PARK, IL 60181
630-941-9292
Fax: 630-832-9183
www.odeumexpo.com
• Phil Greco, President
phil@odeumexpo.com
• Brad Walsh, Facility Manager
brad@odeumexpo.com
Team:
Chicago Blitz (AIF)
Seating Capacity:
Indoor Soccer/Football, Lacrosse 2,500;
Boxing/Wrestling 5,500

OHIO STADIUM
411 WOODY HAYES DRIVE
COLUMBUS, OH 43210
614-292-6330
Fax: 614-292-3585
www.ohiostatebuckeyes.com
• Gene Smith, Athletics Director
• Don Patko, Assoc. AD, Facilities
Operations
• Urban Meyer, Head Coach, Football
Team:
Ohio State Buckeyes
Seating Capacity:
104,944

OKLAHOMA MEMORIAL STADIUM
180 WEST BROOKS
NORMAN, OK 73019
405-325-8000
www.soonersports.com
• Joe Castiglione, Director of Athletics
(405) 325-8208
• Kenny Mossman, Sr. Associate AD,
External Operations
(405) 325-8228
kmossman@ou.edu
• Zac Selmon, Sr. Associate AD, Operations
(405) 325-3396
zacselmon@ou.edu
• Greg Tipton, Sr. Associate AD, Internal
Operations
(405) 325-8379
gtipton@ou.edu
• Eric Barnhart, General Manager
(405) 352-2407
ebarnhart@oussp.com
Seating Capacity:
82,112
Teams:
University of Oklahoma football.

OLYMPIC CENTER
2634 MAIN STREET
LAKE PLACID, NY 12946
518-523-1655
800-462-6236
info@orda.org
www.whiteface.com
Description:
Sports complex in Lake Placid, NY,
comprising a conference center, Olympic
museum, two arenas, and speed skating
and figure skating rinks.

OLYMPIC PARK
4545 PIERRE-DE COUBERTIN AVE
MONTREAL, QC, CANADA H1V 0B2

514-252-4141
Fax: 514-252-6906
po@parcolympique.ca
parcolympique.qc.ca
• Michel Labrecque, CEO
Founded:
1976
Seating Capacity:
56,040
Tenant:
CF Montrâ€šal (MLS)

OMAN ARENA
179 LANE AVENUE
JACKSON, TN 38301
731-425-8580
Fax: 731-425-8589
info@cityofjackson.net
www.cityofjackson.net
Founded:
1967
Seating Capacity:
5,600

ONEOK FIELD
201 NORTH ELGIN AVENUE
TULSA, OK 74120
918-744-5998
Fax: 918-747-3267
mail@tulsadrillers.com
www.tulsadrillers.com
• Mike Melega, President/GM
mike@tulsadrillers.com
• Mark Hilliard, Vice President, Operations
mark@tulsadrillers.com
• Marshall Schellhardt, Stadium Operations
Manager
marshall@tulsadrillers.com
Founded:
2010
Team:
Tulsa Drillers
Seating Capacity:
7,833

ORACLE ARENA
7000 COLISEUM WAY
OAKLAND, CA 94621
510-383-4801
www.coliseum.com
Team:
Golden State Warriors (NBA)
Seating Capacity:
Basketball 19,596; Concert 20,000; Hockey
17,200

ORIOLE PARK AT CAMDEN YARDS
333 WEST CAMDEN STREET
BALTIMORE, MD 21201
410-685-9800
baltimore.orioles.mlb.com/bal/ballpark
• Kevin Cummings, Director, Ballpark
Operations
Team:
Baltimore Orioles (MLB)
Seating Capacity:
45,971

ORLANDO CITRUS BOWL
1 CITRUS BOWL PLACE
ORLANDO, FL 32805
407-440-7000
Fax: 407-440-7001
www.orlandocitrusbowl.com
• Allen Johnson, Executive Director
• Charles P. Leone, Operations Division

Manager
charles.leone@cityoforlando.net
• John Sparks, Stadium Operations
Assistant Division Manager
• Matthew Larsen, Stadium Manager
matthew.larsen@cityoforlando.net
• Ollie Rives, Facility Manager
ollie.rives@cityoforlando.net
Tenant(s) :
Citrus Bowl (NCAA), Florida Classic
(NCAA), Orlando City SC (MLS), Cure Bowl
(NCAA), Orlando Pride (NWSL)
Seating Capacity:
70,000

ORLEANS ARENA
4500 W TROPICANA AVENUE
LAS VEGAS, NV 89103
702-284-7777
888-234-2334
Fax: 702-284-7778
www.orleansarena.com
Team:
Las Vegas Sin (LFL)
Seating Capacity:
9,500

OSCEOLA COUNTY STADIUM
631 HERITAGE PARK WAY
KISSIMMEE, FL 34744
321-697-3201
www.osceolastadium.com
• Erik Anderson, Facility Superintendent
Team:
Astros (GCL)
Seating Capacity:
5,300

OTTAWA STADIUM
300 COVENTRY ROAD
OTTAWA, ON, CANADA K1K 4P5
343-633-2273
Fax: 343-633-2274
contact@ottawatitans.com
www.ottawatitans.com/ottawa-stadium
Founded:
1993
Seating Capacity:
10,332
Team:
Ottawa Titans (FL)

OZARK CIVIC CENTER
320 EAST COLLEGE STREET
PO BOX 789
OZARK, AL 36361
334-774-2618
877-622-2322
civic@ozarkalabama.us
www.ozarkalabama.us
• Lauren Hohbach, Area Supervisor
• Steve Sherrill, Director of Leisure Services
• Kassidy Reeder, Administrative Assistant
Built:
1975
Seating Capacity:
3,600

PACIFIC COLISEUM
PACIFIC NATIONAL EXHIBITION
100 N RENFREW STREET
VANCOUVER, BC, CANADA V5K 5J1
604-253-2311
Fax: 604-251-7753
info@pne.ca
www.pne.ca

• Shelley Frost, President & CEO
Owner:
City of Vancouver
Opened:
1968
Seating Capacity:
Ice hockey: 16,281; Concerts: 17,500

PALACE OF AUBURN HILLS, THE
6 CHAMPIONSHIP DRIVE
AUBURN HILLS, MI 48326
248-377-0100
www.palacenet.com
• Dennis Mannion, President & CEO
• Mario Etemad, EVP, Operations
Team:
Detroit Pistons (NBA)
Seating Capacity:
24,276

PALESTRA, THE
235 SOUTH 33RD STREET
PHILADELPHIA, PA 19104-6322
215-898-6151
Fax: 215-573-2161
www.pennathletics.com
• Calhoun M. Grace, Director of Athletics &
Recreation
• Steve Donahue, Head Coach, Men's
Basketball
• Mike McLaughlin, Head Coach, Women's
Basketball
• Kerry Carr, Head Coach, Women's
Volleyball
• Alex Tirapelle, Head Coach, Wrestling
Team:
Penn Quakers
Seating Capacity:
8,722

PAN AMERICAN CENTER
1810 EAST UNIVERSITY AVENUE
LAS CRUCES, NM 88003
575-646-4413
panam.nmsu.edu
• Mario Moccia, Director of Athletics
moccia@nmsu.edu
• Marvin Menzies, Head Coach, Men's
Basketball
mtrakh@nmsu.edu
• Mark Trakh, Head Coach, Women's
Basketball
mtrakh@nmsu.edu
• Michael Jordan, Head Coach, Volleyball
micjorda@nmsu.edu
Founded:
1968
Team:
New Mexico State Aggies
Seating Capacity:
12,482

PAPA JOHN'S CARDINAL STADIUM
2800 SOUTH FLOYD STREET
LOUISVILLE, KY 40209
• Michael J. Ortman, Stadium Manager
(502) 852-3893
Team:
Louisville Cardinals
Seating Capacity:
56,000

PARKVIEW FIELD
1301 EWING STREET
FORT WAYNE, IN 46802

260-482-6400
Fax: 260-471-4678
www.parkviewfield.com
Sport:
Baseball
Opened:
2009
Team:
Fort Wayne TinCaps
Seating Capacity:
8,100

PARSONS FIELD/FRIEDMAN DIAMOND
178 KENT STREET
BROOKLINE, MA 02446
617-373-2672
Fax: 617-373-8988
gonu.com
• Peter Roby, Athletic Director
• Mike Glavine, Head Coach, Baseball
(617) 373-3657
• Chris Gbandi, Head Coach, Men's Soccer
(617) 373-7581
• Ashley Phillips, Head Coach, Women's
Soccer
(617) 373-2335
Opened:
1930
Team:
Northeastern Huskies
Seating Capacity:
7,000

PAUL BROWN STADIUM
1 PAUL BROWN STADIUM
CINCINNATI, OH 45202
www.bengals.com
• Mike Brown, President
• Katie Blackburn, Executive Vice President
Team:
Cincinnati Bengals
Seating Capacity:
65,535

PAULEY PAVILION
301 WESTWOOD PLAZA
LOS ANGELES, CA 90024
310-825-4546
Fax: 310-825-8664
www.uclabruins.com
• Dan Guerrero, Director of Athletics
• Steve Alford, Head Coach, Men's
Basketball
• Cori Close, Head Coach, Women's
Basketball
• Valorie Kondos Field, Head Coach,
Women's Gymnastics
• John Speraw, Head Coach, Men's
Volleyball
• Michael Sealy, Head Coach, Women's
Volleyball
Team:
UCLA Bruins
Seating Capacity:
13,800

PENDLETON CONVENTION CENTER
1601 WESTGATE
PENDLETON, OR 97801
541-276-6569
800-863-9358
Fax: 541-278-1317
www.pendletonconventioncenter.com
• Kathy Marshall, Operations
kathy.marshall@ci.pendleton.or.us
Seating Capacity:
5,000

PENSACOLA BAY CENTER
201 E GREGORY STREET
PENSACOLA, FL 32502
850-432-0800
www.pensacolabaycenter.com
• Cyndee Pennington, General Manager
cpennington@smgpcola.com
• Scott Cornwell, Director of Operations
scornwell@smgpcola.com
Team:
Pensacola Ice Flyers (SPHL)
Seating Capacity:
Hockey 8,150; Non-hockey 10,000

PEOPLES NATURAL GAS FIELD
1000 PARK AVENUE
ALTOONA, PA 16602
814-943-5400
Fax: 814-943-9050
www.altoonacurve.com
Opened:
1999
Team:
Altoona Curve (EL)
Seating Capacity:
7,210

PEORIA CIVIC CENTER
201 SW JEFFERSON STREET
PEORIA, IL 61602
309-673-8900
www.peoriaciviccenter.com
• Anne Clayton, General Manager
aclayton@peoriaciviccenter.com
• Jason Bain, Operations Manager
jbain@peoriaciviccenter.com
Opened:
1982
Seating Capacity:
Hockey/Indoor Football 9,919; Basketball
11,433; Concerts 12,036

PEORIA SPORTS COMPLEX
16101 N 83RD AVENUE
PEORIA, AZ 85382
623-773-8700
Fax: 623-773-8716
sportscomplex@peoriaaz.gov
peoriasportscomplex.com
Opened:
1994
Team(s) :
Seattle Mariners and San Diego Padres
Seating Capacity:
12,339

PEPSI CENTER
1000 CHOPPER CIRCLE
DENVER, CO 80204
303-405-1100
Fax: 303-575-1920
customerservice@altitudetickets.com
www.pepsicenter.com
• E. Stanley Kroenke, Owner
• Martin Jim, President & CEO
Team(s) :
Denver Nuggets (NBA); Colorado
Avalanche (NHL); Colorado Mammoth
(NLL); Colorado Crush (AFL)
Seating Capacity:
Basketball 19,155; Hockey/Lacrosse
18,007; Arena Football 17,417

PERCIVAL MOLSON MEMORIAL STADIUM
475 PINE AVE W
MONTREAL, QC, CANADA H2W 1S4
514-398-7000
en.montrealalouettes.com/history-stadium
Owner:
McGill University
Year Opened:
1915
Seating Capacity:
23,035
Tenant(s) :
Montreal Alouettes (CFL); McGill Redbirds and Martlets (U Sports)

PERKINS STADIUM
910 WEST SCHWAGER DRIVE
UNIVERSITY OF WISCONSIN
WHITEWATER, WI 53190
262-472-1234
Fax: 262-472-2791
webmaster@uww.edu
www.uww.edu
• Amy Edmonds, Director of Intercollegiate Athletics
(262) 472-4661
• Bob Lanza, Associate AD/Finance & Business Operations
(262) 472-3190
lanzar@uww.edu
• Kirby Mills, Assistant AD/Development
(262) 472-5646
• Chris Lindeke, Director of Athletic Communications
(262) 472-1147
lindekec@uww.edu
• Kay Bradley, Athletic Administrative Assistant
(262) 472-4661
bradlekf@uww.edu
• Reid Gibbs, Assistant Coach/Equipment Room Manager
(262) 472-3189
Year Founded:
1970
Seating Capacity:
11,000

PERSHING CENTER
226 CENTENNIAL MALL S
LINCOLN, NE 68508
402-441-8744
Fax: 402-441-7913
• Tom Lorenz, General Manager
• Derek Andersen, Marketing Director
• Fred McCoy, Operations Director
• Sharon Mandery, Event Services Director
Arena Seating Capacity:
6,818

PETE MARAVICH ASSEMBLY CENTER
PETE MARAVICH ASSEMBLY CENTER
LOUISIANA STATE UNIVERSITY
BATON ROUGE, LA 70803
225-578-8025
Fax: 225-578-8437
athletics@lsu.edu
www.maravichcenter.com
• Brendan Fouracre, Director
(225) 578-8424
bdfour@lsu.edu
• Jeff Campbell, Associate Director
• Nathan Hanson, Assistant Operations Manager
• Dwight Johnson, Assistant Operations Manager

Arena Seating Capacity:
14,500

PETE MATHEWS COLISEUM
700 PELHAM ROAD N
JACKSONVILLE STATE UNIVERSITY
JACKSONVILLE, AL 36265-1602
256-782-5368
800-231-5291
Fax: 256-782-5666
info@jsu.edu
www.jsu.edu
• Pete Conroy, Director
Arena Seating Capacity:
6,000

PETE TAYLOR BASEBALL PARK
THE UNIVERSITY OF SOUTHERN MISSISSIPPI
118 COLLEGE DRIVE
HATTIESBURG, MS 39406-0001
601-266-4468
Fax: 601-266-6595
www.southernmiss.com
• Richard C Giannini, Athletic Director
(601) 266-5422
richard.giannini@usm.edu
• Diane Stark, Senior Associate Athletic Director
(601) 266-5422
• Scott Carr, Associate Athletic Director/External Ope
(601) 266-5017
scott.carr@usm.edu
• Sonya Varnell, Associate Athletic Director/Olympic Spor
(601) 266-5017
sonya.varnell@usm.edu
• Christi Holloway, Chief Financial Officer
(601) 266-5299
• Jeremy McClain, Senior Associate Athletic Director for Extern
(601) 266-5017
• Kent Hegenauer, Senior Associate Athletic Director/Director o
(601) 266-5017
• Brian Morrison, Associate Director of Athletics/Major Gifts
(601) 266-5055
• Jeff Hammond, Athletics Director
(601) 266-5422
Clients:
Colleges, Universities nationwide.
Nature of Service:
Baseball diamond for colleges and universities as part of Institutions of Higher Learning.
Seating Capacity:
37,000

PETERSEN EVENTS CENTER
3719 TERRACE STREET
UNIVERSITY OF PITTSBURGH
PITTSBURGH, PA 15261
412-648-3054
Fax: 412-648-3285
PECHelp@pitt.edu
www.peterseneventscenter.com
• John Abrams, Facilities/Operations Manager
(412) 648-8204
jabrams@athletics.pitt.edu
• Anthony Smith, Operations Manager
• Steve Haught, Accounting Manager
• Jodi Hummert, Events & Guest Services Manager
• Scott Michaels, General Manager

Year Opened:
2002
Arena Seating Capacity:
12,500
Tenant(s) :
University of Pittsburgh basketball.

PETERSON EVENTS CENTER
3719 TERRACE STREET
UNIVERSITY OF PITTSBURGH
PITTSBURGH, PA 15261
412-648-8230
Fax: 412-648-8306
www.pittsburghpanthers.com
• Jeff Long, Athletic Director
(412) 648-8230
• Carol Sprague, Senior Associate Athletic Director
• Mike Pratapas, Senior Associate Athletic Director
• Steve Pederson, Athletic Director
(412) 648-8230
spederson@athletics.pitt.edu
• Donna Sanft, Executive Associate Athletic Director
(412) 648-8209
dsanft@athletics.pitt.edu
• Marcus Bowman, Assistant Athletic Director for Administratio
(412) 648-7181
mbowman@athletics.pitt.edu
• Stephanie Armstrong, Executive Secretary for the Athletic Director
(412) 648-8230
sarmstrong@athletics.pitt.edu
• Sue George, Secretary to Executive Associate AD
(412) 648-8209
sgeorge@athletics.pitt.edu
• Maureen Anderson, Associate Athletic Director, Development
(412) 648-8738
manderson@athletics.pitt.edu
Arena Seating Capacity:
6,798

PGE PARK
1844 SW MORRISON
PORTLAND, OR 97205
503-553-5400
Fax: 503-553-5405
• Ben Hoel, Director, Ticket Operations
Team:
Portland Beavers
Sport:
Baseball
Capacity:
30,500

PHILIP B. ELFSTROM STADIUM
34W002 CHERRY LANE
GENEVA, IL 60134
630-232-8811
Fax: 630-232-8815
info@kanecountycougars.com
www.kccougars.com
• Woleben Mike, President
• Jeff Sedivy, VP/General Manager
• Mary Almlie, Business Manager
• R. Michael Patterson, Senior Director, Ticketing
rmpatterson@kanecountycougars.com
• Douglas Czurylo, Senior Director - Finance and Administration
dczurylo@kanecountycougars.com
• Amy Mason, Director of Ticket Services, Director, Commun

amason@kanecountycougars.com
• Dan Klinkhamer, Director of Security
• Shawn Touney, Director of Public Relations
• Mike Klafehn, Director of Stadium Operations
mklafehn@kanecountycougars.com
• Robin Hull, Business Manager
rhull@kanecountycougars.com
Sport:
Baseball
Team:
Kane Country Cougars
Year Founded:
1991
Capacity:
5,900

PHILIPS ARENA
1 PHILIPS DRIVE
ATLANTA, GA 30303
404-878-3000
Fax: 404-878-3020
www.philipsarena.com
• Bob Williams, President/General Manager
• Danny Ferry, President of Basketball Operations and Genera
• Phil Ebinger, Executive Vice President and Chief Financial
• Scott Wilkinson, Executive Vice President, Chief Legal Officer
• Ailey Penningroth, Senior Vice President and Chief Marketing Off
• Andrew Steinberg, Senior Vice President and Chief Revenue Offic
• Trey Feazell, Senior Vice President and General Manager
Arena Seating Capacity:
Arena Football 18,500; Basketball 20,007; Concerts 21,000; Hockey 18,559.
Arena Football:
Georgia Force.
NBA:
Atlanta Hawks.
NHL:
Atlanta Thrashers.

PHOENIX MUNICIPAL STADIUM
5999 E VAN BUREN
PHOENIX, AZ 85008
602-495-7240
800-550-2827
Fax: 602-392-0225
www.phoenix.gov/parks/sports
• Huss Chad, Groundskeeper
Team:
Oakland Athletics Spring Training.
Year Founded:
1965
Capacity:
8,500

PICO RIVERA SPORTS ARENA
350 SOUTH BIXEL STREET
SUITE 250
LOS ANGELES, CA 90017
213-482-6333
Fax: 213-482-6340
www.lasports.org
• Ralph Hauser, Manager
• Anthony Hauser, Concessions Manager
• Scott L London, Chairman
• David Simon, President
• Karen Brodkin, SVP
• Ben Stilp, Controller
• Mark Meyers, Director of Communications
• Monica Maldonado, Director of Special

Events
• Mona Green, Executive Assistant
Arena Seating Capacity:
4,500.00
Year Founded:
1979
Nature of Service:
Rodeo style arena, catering to the Latin Charro Rodeos.

PINNACLE BANK ARENA
PINNACLE ARENA DRIVE
400 PINNACLE ARENA DRIVE
LINCOLN, NE 68508
402-904-4444
info@pinnaclebankarena.com
www.pinnaclebankarena.com
• Tom Lorenz, General Manager
• Charlie Schilling, Assistant General Manager

PIONEER FIELD
1 UNIVERSITY PLAZA
UNIVERSITY OF WISCONSIN
PLATTEVILLE, WI 53818-3099
608-342-1491
800-362-5515
Fax: 608-342-1576
athletics@uwplatt.edu
www.uwplatt.edu
• Mark Molesworth, Athletic Director
(608) 342-1567
molewom@uwplatt.edu
• Daus Hap, Event Manager
(608) 342-1567
• Curt Fatzinger, PAC/Intramural Director
(608) 342-1568
• Tom Antczak, Head Cross Country Asst. Track
(608) 342-1504
• Ryanne Breckenridge, Asst. Athletic Trainer
(608) 342-6015
• Eric Frese, Head Baseball Coach
(608) 342-1843
• Enzo Fuschino, Head Men's Soccer Coach
(608) 342-1343
• Jeff Gard, Head Men's Basketball Coach
(608) 342-1278
Stadium Seating Capacity:
10,000

PK PARK
2760 M.L. KING JR. BOULEVARD
EUGENE, OR 97405
541-342-5367
Fax: 541-342-6089
info@emeraldsbaseball.com
www.milb.com/index.jsp?sid=t461
• Allan Benavides, General Manager
allan@emeraldsbaseball.com
• Matt Dompe, Assistant General Manager
matt@emeraldsbaseball.com
• Chris Bowers, Event Manager
chris@emeraldsbaseball.com
• Peter Billups, Director of Tickets
peter@emeraldsbaseball.com
Stadium Seating Capacity:
4,000
Year Founded:
2009
Tenant(s) :
Eugene Emeralds, Oregon Ducks

PLASTER SPORTS COMPLEX
901 S NATIONAL AVENUE
SPRINGFIELD, MO 65897
417-836-5000
Fax: 417-836-7660
www.missouristate.edu
• Blackwood Randy, Executive Director
• Brad Brown, Associate Director
• Keith Boaz, Assistant Director
• Randy Blackwood, Executive Director
RandallBlackwood@missouristate.edu
• Laree Moore, Associate Director
• Beverly Nickols, Facility Supervisor
• Keith Boaz, Director
KeithBoaz@missouristate.edu
• Laree Moore, Associate Director
LareeMoore@missouristate.edu
• Melissa Blankenship, Assistant Director
MelissaBlankenship@missouristate.edu
• Brenda O'Connell, Administrative Secretary
BrendaOConnell@missouristate.edu
Stadium Seating Capacity:
16,000

PNC PARK
115 FEDERAL STREET
PNC PARK AT N SHORE
PITTSBURGH, PA 15212
412-323-5000
• Dennis DaPra, Operations VP
• Frank Coonelly, President
• Bryan Stroh, Vice President and General Counsel
• Tyrone Brooks, Director of Player Personnel
• Joe DelliCarri, Director of Amateur Scouting
• Rene Gayo, Director of Latin American Scouting
• Larry Broadway, Director of Minor League Operations
• Bob Nutting, Chairman of the Board
Tenant(s) :
Pittsburgh Pirates

POHLMAN FIELD
2301 SKYLINE DRIVE
PO BOX 855
BELOIT, WI 53511
608-362-2272
Fax: 608-362-0418
snappy@snappersbaseball.com
www.snappersbaseball.com
• Jeff Vohs, General Manager
• Dennis Conerton, Chairman
• Perry Folts, President
• Jeff Klett, VP/Director
• Natalie Tobey, Director of Community Relations
• Mark Inserra, Director of Media Relations
• Bill Czaja, Director, Corporate Sales/Promotions
• Katie Pietrowiak, Director, Tickets/Merchandise
Capacity:
3,501
Year Founded:
1982
Sport:
Baseball
Team
Beloit Snappers

POINT STADIUM
401 MAIN STREET
CITY HALL RECREATION DEPARTMENT
JOHNSTOWN, PA 15901
814-533-2104
Fax: 814-533-2111
• Karl Kittner, Recreation Director
• Rich Horvath, Stadium Manager
Stadium Seating Capacity:
10,500

PONTIAC SILVERDOME
1200 FEATHERSTONE ROAD
PONTIAC, MI 48342
248-338-7000
Fax: 248-499-6754
• Walker Eric, Executive Director
Owned by:
City of Pontiac
Permanent Seating Capacity:
80,311

PRATHER COLISEUM
NSU ATHLETIC FIELDHOUSE
220 S JEFFERSON
NATCHITOCHES, LA 71497
318-357-5251
Fax: 318-357-4221
athleticsinfo@nsula.edu
www.nsudemons.com
• Greg Burke, Athletics Director
(318) 357-5251
burkeg@nsula.edu
• Haley Taitano, Assoc. AD for Ext.
Relats./Sr. Women's Advisor
(318) 357-4278
blounth@nsula.edu
• Doug Ireland, Asst. AD, Media Relations
(318) 357-6467
ireland@nsula.edu
• Mike Jaworski, Director of Development
and Engagement
(318) 357-4295
jaworskim@nsula.edu
• Mike Doty, Director of Athletic Facilities
and Event Mgmt.
(318) 357-6898
dotym@nsula.edu
• Chance Creppel, Asst. Director of
Facilities and Event Mgmt.
(318) 357-4265
creppelc@nsula.edu
Coliseum Seating Capacity:
3,400
Nature of Service:
Basketball and volleyball arena

PRINCE GEORGE'S STADIUM
4101 CRAIN HIGHWAY
BOWIE, MD 20716
301-805-6000
Fax: 301-464-4911
info@baysox.com
www.baysox.com
• Shallcross Brian, General Manager
• Brandan Kaiser, Director of Marketing
• Charlene Fewer, Director of Ticket
Operations
cfewer@baysox.com
• Matt McLaughlin, Director of Corporate
Sponsorships
mmclaughlin@baysox.com
• Darlene Mingioli, Director of Game Day
Staff
dmingioli@baysox.com
• Brian Shallcross, General Manager
bshallcross@baysox.com

• Phil Wrye, Assistant General Manager
pwrye@baysox.com
• Andrew Jackson, Stadium Operations
Manager
Sport:
Baseball
Team:
Bowie Baysox
Year Founded:
1994
Seating Capacity:
10,000

PRINCE WILLIAM CO. STADIUM
7 COUNTY COMPLEX COURT
WOODBRIDGE, VA 22192
703-590-5900
Fax: 703-590-0209
www.pwcparks.org
• Rich Artenian, Director
• Marvin Vann, Sports Marketing
Coordinator
(703) 792-4005
mvann@pwcgov.org

PROGRESSIVE AUTO SALES ARENA
1455 LONDON ROAD
SARNIA, ON, CANADA N7S 1P6
519-332-0330
parksandrecreation@sarnia.ca
Owners:
City of Sarnia.
Year Opened:
1998.
Seating Capacity:
Hockey 4,118 (5,500 with standing room);
Concerts 6,000.
Tenant(s) :
Sarnia Sting (OHL).

PROGRESSIVE FIELD
2401 ONTARIO ST
CLEVELAND, OH 44115
216-420-4487
cleveland.indians.mlb.com
Seating Capacity:
43,345
Teams:
Cleaveland Indians MLB baseball.

PROVOST UMPHREY STADIUM
4400 MLK PARKWAY
LAMAR UNIVERSITY
BEAUMONT, TX 77705
409-880-1715
800-687-9962
Fax: 409-880-7542
www.lamarcardinals.com
• Brad McGowan, Assistant Athletic Director
for Development
(409) 880-1881
• Jason Henderson, Athletic
Director/Compliance Director
(409) 880-8303
jason.henderson@lamar.edu
• Sharon Williams, Executive Associate
(409) 880-2248
Sharon.Williams@lamar.edu
• Scott Reeves, Sport Performance Director
(409) 880-7427
• Joshua Miller, Sport Performance
Assistant
(409) 880-7445
• Billy Tubbs, Athletic Director
(409) 880-2248
billy.tubbs@lamar.edu

Arena Seating Capacity:
17,000. Football; 10,200 Basketball.

QUAD CITIES RIVER BANDITS
209 S GAINES STREET
DAVENPORT, IA 52802
563-324-3000
Fax: 563-324-3109
www.riverbandits.com
• Nick Harvey, Ticket Manager
(563) 333-2737
Sport:
Minor League Baseball, Midwest League,
Class A Affiliate of the Houston Astros.
Year Founded:
1931
Capacity:
5,500

QUALCOMM STADIUM
9449 FRIARS ROAD
SAN DIEGO, CA 92108
619-641-3100
Fax: 619-283-0460
stadium@sandiego.gov
www.sandiego.gov
• Michael McSweeney, Stadium General
Manager
(619) 641-3126
• Michele Kelley, Special Events
Coordinator
(619) 641-3187
Stadium Seating Capacity:
70,000.00
Year Founded:
1967
Clients:
San Diego Chargers, San Diego State
Aztecs.

QUICKEN LOANS ARENA
1 CENTER COURT
CLEVELAND, OH 44115
216-420-2000
800-332-2287
888-894-9424
Fax: 216-420-2101
www.theqarena.com
• Boland Jim, Vice Chairman
• Len Komoroski, President
• Roy Jones, Executive VP/General
Manager
• Edward Markey, Communications VP
• Gordon Gund, Chief Executive Officer
• John Wolf, Chief Financial Officer
• Roy Jones, Executive Vice President
• Sue Katalinas, President
• David Katzman, Vice Chairman
• Rod Hollen, Vice President
Owned by:
Gordon Gund & Gateway Economic
Development Corp.
Permanent Seating Capacity:
20,500
Tenant(s):
AHL - Cleveland Barons ice hockey, NBA -
Cleveland Cavaliers basketball, WNBA -
Cleveland Rockers basketball.

QWEST FIELD
800 OCCIDENTAL AVENUE S
SUITE 100
SEATTLE, WA 98134
206-381-7555
888-NFL-HAWK
Fax: 425-893-5108

customerservice@seahawks.com
www.qwestfield.com
• Jeff Klein, VP/General Manager
Year Opened:
2002
Seating Capicity:
67,000
Team:
Seattle Seahawks NFL football.

RACER ARENA
218 STEWART STADIUM
ATHLETIC DEPARTMENT, MURRAY
STATE UNIVERSITY
MURRAY, KY 42071
270-762-6800
800-272-4678
Fax: 270-762-6814
www.murraystate.edu
• Allen Ward, Athletic Director
(270) 809-3164
• Matt Kelly, Senior associate AD
(270) 809-4424
matt.kelly@murraystate.edu
• Paul Bubb, Associate AD (External affairs)

(270) 809-3369
• Steve Harrell, Associate AD - Compliance
& Administrative Af
(270) 809-3430
Seating Capacity:
5,500

**RALEIGH CONVENTION AND
CONFERENCE CENTER COMPLEX**
500 S SALISBURY STREET
RALEIGH, NC 27601
919-996-8500
Fax: 919-996-8550
www.raleighconvention.com
• Laurie Okun, Director of Sales and
Marketing
• Mickey Barbour, Operations Director
• Dave Chapman, IT Director
• Hazel Cockram, Assistant Director,
Business and Finance
• Doug Grissom, Assistant Director, Outdoor
Events and Festiv
• Mara Craft, National/International
Convention Senior Sale
Permanent Seating Capacity:
3,800

RALEY FIELD
400 BALLPARK DRIVE
W SACRAMENTO, CA 95691
916-376-4700
Fax: 916-376-4710
reception@rivercats.com
www.raleyfield.com
• Matt LaRose, Stadium Operations VP
• Matt Fucile, Stadium Operations Director
Sport:
Baseball
Team:
Sacramento River Cats
Year Founded:
2000
Seating Capacity:
19,111

RALPH ENGELSTAD ARENA
ONE RALPH ENGELSTAD ARENA DRIVE
GRAND FORKS, ND 58203
701-777-4167
Fax: 701-777-6643

fans@theralph.com
www.theralph.com
• Michael Bergeron, Chief Financial Officer
(701) 777-4930
michaelb@theralph.com
• Charlie Muus, Director of Maintenance &
Operations
(701) 777-0807
charliem@theralph.com
• Sadie Steenerson, Administrative
Assistant
(701) 777-6609

RALPH WILSON STADIUM
1 BILLS DRIVE
ORCHARD PARK, NY 14127
716-648-0658
877-228-4257
888-283-4327
Fax: 716-312-8603
www.buffalobills.com
• William G Munson, Operations VP
• Joe Frandina, Vice President, Stadium
Operations
• Russ Brandon, Business
Development/Marketing VP
Permanent Seating Capacity:
73,967
Team:
Home Stadium for the Buffalo Bills
Owned by:
County of Erie

RANGERS BALLPARK
1000 BALLPARK WAY
ARLINGTON, TX 76011
817-273-5222
texas.rangers.mlb.com
Seating Capacity:
49,115
Teams:
Texas Rangers MLB baseball

RANKIN WILLIAMS FIELD HOUSE
100 CAMPUS DRIVE
SOUTHWESTERN OKLAHOMA STATE
UNIVERSITY
WEATHERFORD, OK 73096
580-772-6611
www.swosu.edu/athletics
• Todd Thurman, Athletic Director
todd.thurman@swosu.edu
• Justin Tinder, Sports Information Director
(580) 774-7162
justin.tinder@swosu.edu
Stadium Seating Capacity:
9,000

RAPIDES PARISH COLISEUM
5600 COLISEUM BOULEVARD
ALEXANDRIA, LA 71303
318-442-9581
Fax: 318-442-9582
rapidescoliseum@gmail.com
www.therapidesparishcoliseum.com/
• Don Guillory, Executive Director
Permanent Seating Capacity:
6,000

RATCLIFFE STADIUM
1101 E UNIVERSITY AVENUE
FRESNO, CA 93741
559-442-4600
Fax: 559-489-2281
www.fresnocitycollege.edu

• Susan Yates, Athletic Director
susan.yates@fresnocitycollege.edu
• Tony Cantu, President
• Dr.Tim Woods, VP
• Dr.Chris Villa, VP
• Cheryl Sullivan, VP of Administrative
Services
• Tony A. Cantu, President
Stadium Seating Capacity:
13,500

RAYMOND JAMES STADIUM
4201 N DALE MABRY HIGHWAY
TAMPA, FL 33607
813-350-6500
Fax: 813-673-4312
www.raymondjamesstadium.com
• Mickey Farrell, Dir. of Operations
(813) 350-6507
• Jeanette Baker, Vice President of
Finance/Administration
(813) 350-6517
• Bobby Silvest, Vice President of Marketing
& Communications
(813) 350-6504
• Kennie Sims, Vice President of Golf
Operations
(813) 350-6510
• Kevin Kenny, Director of Golf
(813) 673-4316
• Laura Beuhring, Director of Golf
(813) 641-4374
• Eric Hart, President & CEO
(813) 350-6500
Owned by:
Tampa Sports Authority.
Tenant(s) :
NFL - Tampa Bay Buccaneers football,
NCAA - Outback Bowl football, NCAA -
Univ. of South Florida football, Monster Jam
Permanent Seating Capacity:
65,890

RBC CENTER
1400 EDWARDS MILL ROAD
RALEIGH, NC 27607
919-861-2300
www.lenovocenter.com
• Dave Olsen, EVP & General Manager
Formerly Known As:
Raleigh Entertainment & Sports Arena; RBC
Center; PNC Arena.
Arena Seating Capacity:
Basketball 19,500; Hockey 18,700; Concerts
21,000.
Home Arena for:
NHL - Carolina Hurricanes; ACC - NC State
Wolfpack; ACHA - Governor's Cup.

RE/MAX FIELD
10233 96TH AVENUE NW
EDMONTON, AB, CANADA T5K 0A5
587-802-2244
www.riverhawksbaseball.com/remax-field
Owners:
City of Edmonton
Year Opened:
1995
Seating Capacity:
9,200
Tenant(s) :
Edmonton Riverhawks (WCL)

RED BULL ARENA
600 CAPE MAY STREET
HARRISON, NJ 7029

888-370-7287
fanservices@newyorkredbulls.com
www.newyorkredbulls.com/redbullarena
Seating Capacity:
25,000
Teams:
New York Red Bulls soccer.

RED MC EWEN BASEBALL FIELD
4202 E FOWLER AVENUE
UNIVERSITY OF SOUTH FLORIDA
TAMPA, FL 33620
813-974-2011
Fax: 813-974-4028
help@usf.edu
www.usf.edu
• Carl Carlucci, Chief Financial
Officer/President
• Clark Bruuns, Marketing/Promotions
Manager
• Kelly C Hickman, Event Operations
Assistant Director
• Doug Woolard, Director of Athletics
(813) 974-1442
• Bill McGillis, Executive Associate Director
of Athletics
(813) 974-8930
• Barry Clements, Senior Associate Director
of Athletics / Spor
(813) 974-4144
clements@usf.edu
• Craig Angelos, Associate Director of
Athletics / Compliance
(813) 974-3528
• Scott Glaser, Associate Director of
Athletics / Facilities
(813) 974-3110
sglaser@usf.edu
• Brett Huebner, Associate Director of
Athletics / CFO
(813) 974-3227
• Amy Perkins, Associate Director of
Athletics / SWA / Stude
(813) 974-3007
Stadium Seating Capacity:
3,000

REDBIRD ARENA
CAMPUS BOX 2660
ILLINOIS STATE UNIVERSITY, COLLEGE
AT DELAINE
NORMAL, IL 61790-2660
309-438-2000
Fax: 309-438-3513
www.goredbirds.com
• Cheahon Zenger, Athletic Director
(309) 438-3636
• Gary Friedman, Director of Athletics
(309) 438-3636
• Larry Lyons, Executive Associate Athletics
Director
(309) 438-5626
lelyons@ilstu.edu
• Leanna Bordner, Senior Associate
Athletics Director/SWA
(438) 3639
lkbordn@ilstu.edu
• Cindy Harris, Senior Associate Athletics
Director/Complianc
(309) 438-2677
caharri@ilstu.edu
Arena Seating Capacity:
10,500

REED GREEN COLISEUM
(BASKETBALL)
118 COLLEGE DRIVE
PO BOX 5017, UNIVERSITY OF
SOUTHERN MISSISSIPPI
HATTIESBURG, MS 39406-5142
601-266-6085
Fax: 601-266-4445
• Richard Giannini, Athletic Director
(601) 266-5422
• Scott Carr, Deputy Director of Athletics
(601) 266-5422
scott.carr@usm.edu
• Denis Wiesenburg, Provost
• Bob Pierce, Vice President-Advancement
• Tom Estes, Interim Vice President-Finance
& Administrati
• Frances Lucas, Vice President-Gulf Coast
• Joseph S. Paul, Vice President-Student
Affairs
• Aubrey K. Lucas, Interim President
Arena Seating Capacity:
8,095

RELIANT ASTRODOME
8400 KIRBY LANE
HOUSTON, TX 77054
832-677-1400
Fax: 832-667-1410
guestservices@reliantpark.com
www.reliantpark.com
• Guinn Shea, President
• Eric Jones, Marketing/Sales Director
• Mark Miller, General Manager
• Mary Majorwitz, Client Relations
Coordinator
• Barbara Beaton, Director of Sales
• Justin White, Executive Sales Manager
• Craig Chapman, Event Coordinator
• Ejah Praag, Event Coordinator
Permanent Seating Capacity:
58,000
Owned by:
Harris County

RELIANT ASTRODOME COMPLEX
8400 KIRBY DRIVE
HOUSTON, TX 77054
832-667-1400
Fax: 832-667-1748
guestservices@reliantpark.com
www.reliantpark.com
• Guinn Shey, General Manager
• Mark Miller, GM
• Jeff Gaines, Ass. GM
• Barbara Beaton, Sales Direcor
• Justin White, Executive Sales Manager
• Liz Conner, Contract Manager
• Lydia Parker, Booking Manager
• Pam Jones, Sales Administrative
Event Management Services:
Manages Astrodome/Astrohall/Astroarena.
Sports Complex-trade shows, consumer
shows, and exhibitions.
Seating Capacity:
65,000

RENSSELAER POLYTECHNIC
INSTITUTE/HOUSTON FIELD
110 8TH STREET
TROY, NY 12180-3590
518-276-6000
www.rpi.edu
• Norris Pearson, Manager
(518) 276-6121
• Brian Darby, Operations Supervisor
darbyb@rpi.edu

Seating Capacity:
6,900

RENTSCHLER FIELD
615 SILVER LANE
EAST HARTFORD, CT 6118
860-610-4700
info@rentschlerfield.com
www.rentschlerfield.com
• Michael Fresher, General Manager
Seating Capacity:
40,000
Teams:
Univertisy of Conneticut football; Hartford
Colonials, United Football League

RESER STADIUM
114 GILL COLISEUM
OREGON STATE UNIVERSITY
CORVALLIS, OR 97331
541-737-2547
Fax: 541-737-7895
www.osubeavers.com
• Bob Cheney, Interim Operations Director
• Matt Arend, Ticket Operations Director
Stadium Seating Capacity:
35,000
Team:
Oregon State University football.

REYNOLDS COLISEUM
2500 WARREN CARROLL DRIVE
CAMPUS BOX 8502
WEISIGER BROWN BUILDING
RALEIGH, NC 27695
919-515-3050
Fax: 919-515-1161
www.gopack.com
• Billy Ray Dunn, Manager
(919) 515-2108
brdunn3@unity.ncsu.edu
• David Bowles, Maintainence Supervisor
(919) 515-2108
Arena Seating Capacity:
12,400

RICE STADIUM
6100 MAIN STREET
RICE UNIVERSITY
HOUSTON, TX 77005
713-348-0000
Fax: 713-348-6019
www.riceowls.com
• Chris DelConte, Athletic Director
(713) 348-4077
• Rick Greenspan, Director of Athletics
(713) 348-4077
• Rick Mello, Senior Executive Athletics
Director
(713) 348-8872
• Stacy Mosely, Senior Associate Athletics
Director, SWA
(713) 348-5829
• Dr. Jack Garrett, Senior Associate
AD/Sport Admin. and Support
(713) 348-6921
• Tina Villard, Director of Recreation Center
and Activities
(713) 348-5398
tvillard@rice.edu
• Andy Platt, Associate Athletics
Director/Business & Finan
(713) 348-509
• David Sayler, Sr. Executive Athletics
Director
(713) 348-4077

Arena Seating Capacity:
70,000
Team:
Rice University football.

RICE-ECCLES STADIUM
451 SOUTH 1400 EAST
6TH FLOOR
SALT LAKE CITY, UT 84112
801-581-5445
Fax: 801-585-1417
info@stadium.utah.edu
www.stadium.utah.edu
Seating Capacity:
45,600
Teams:
Utah Utes football.

RICE-TOTTEN STADIUM
MISSISSIPPI VALLEY STATE
UNIVERSITY, DEPT. OF ATHLETICS
14000 HIGHWAY 82 WEST
BOX 7246
ITTA BENA, MS 38941
662-254-3550
Fax: 662-254-3639
www.mvsusports.com
• Dianthia Ford-Kee, Director of Athletics
(662) 254-3550
• Rick Comegy, Head Coach, Football
rick.comegy@mvsu.edu
Seating Capacity:
10,000

RICHARD M BORCHARD REGIONAL
FAIRGROUNDS/SPECTRA
1213 TERRY SHAMSIE BOULEVARD
ROBSTOWN, TX 78380
361-387-9000
Fax: 361-387-9077
jgreen@rmbfairgrounds.com
www.rmbfairgrounds.com
• Jason Green, General Manager
(361) 387-9000
jgreen@rmbfairgrounds.com
Teams:
Hurricane Alley Roller Derby Team
Seating Capacity:
Central Pavilion Arena: 2,000
Year Founded:
2003
Capacity:
4,000
Track Type:
Flat Track

RICHMOND COLISEUM
601 E LEIGH STREET
RICHMOND, VA 23219-1431
804-780-4970
Fax: 804-780-4606
info@richmondcoliseum.net
www.richmondcoliseum.net
• Dwight Johnson, Assistant General
Manager/Director of Operations
(804) 780-4970
djohnson@richmondcoliseum.net
• Lesa Williams, Assistant General Manager
Arena Seating Capacity:
13,523
Home Arena for:
AF2 - Richmond Speed.
Sports Organizations
Richmond Raiders-AIFA-Arena Football;
Arena Racing

RICHMOND COUNTY BANK BALLPARK
75 RICHMOND TERRACE
STATEN ISLAND, NY 10301
718-720-9265
Fax: 718-273-5763
www.siyanks.com
• Brown Robert, Manager, Stadium
Operations
• Dominic Costantino, Tickets Director
• Jane M. Rogers, President, General
Manager
• Kerry Atkinson, Senior Vice President of
Corporate Sales
• Brian Levine, Vice President of Ticket
Sales
• Matt Gulino, Director, Ticket Sales &
Operations
• Tom Phillips, Finance Manager
• Jillian Wright, Manager, Sponsor Services
• Bob Brown, Facility Manager
(718) 313-1345
Sport:
Baseball
Team:
Staten Island Yankees
Year Founded:
2001
Capacity:
6,500

RICKENBRODE STADUIM
800 UNIVERSITY DRIVE
NW MISSOURI STATE UNIVERSITY
MARYVILLE, MO 64468
660-562-1562
Fax: 660-562-1493
www.nwmissouri.edu
• Gene Steinmeyer, Women's Basketball
Coach
(660) 562-1299
• Bob Boerigter, Athletic Director
(660) 562-1306
• James Redd, Athletic Director
• Andy Seely, Sports Information Director
Rickenbrode Stadium Seating Capacity:
7,000
Lampkin Arena Seating Capacity:
3,000

RIPKEN STADIUM
873 LONG DRIVE
ABERDEEN, MD 21001
410-297-9292
Fax: 410-297-6653
www.ironbirdsbaseball.com
• Aaron Mozser, General Manager
(410) 297-9292
• Amy Venuto, Sales Director
(410) 297-9292
• Aaron Moszes, Assistant General
Manager
(410) 297-9292
• Cal H Ripken, Jr., Principal
Owner/Chairman & Founder
• Bill Ripken, CO-Owner/Executive Vice
President
• Amy Venuto, Executive Director
• Brad Cox, Assistant General Manager
• Jason Vaughn, Production & Game
Entertainment Manager
• Christopher Stieber, Account Executive
• Elly Ripken, Accounting Manager
elly@ripkenbaseball.com
Stadium Seating Capacity:
5,800.00
Year Founded:
2002

Clients:
MBNA, Coca-Cola, Baltimore Sun,
Mercantile Bank, ComCast, Wingate Inn,
Close Call America.
Nature of Service:
Baseball Stadium, Event Destination
(Concerts/Shows/Games/etc.)
Teams:
Aberdeen Iron Birds

RIVERFRONT STADIUM
850 PARK ROAD
WATERLOO, IA 50703
319-232-0500
Fax: 319-232-0700
www.waterloobucks.com
• John Marso, Co-Owner
• Dan Corbin, General Manager
(319) 232-0500
• Aaron Rustad, Assistant General Manager
• Kendall Hughson, Asst. GM/Dir of Stadium
Operations
(319) 232-0500
Sport:
Summer collegiate baseball team.
Capacity:
5,000
Teams:
Waterloo Bucks, Northwoods League

RIVERSIDE ARENA
900 HARRINGTON STREET
HUTCHINSON, MN 55350
320-234-5640
Fax: 320-234-4243
Information@ci.hutchinson.mn.us
www.ci.austin.mn.us
• Dale Madison, Chairperson
(507) 433-1881
• Randy Queensland, Vice-Chairperson
• Lindy Rider, Secretary/Treasurer
• Tony Bennett, Director
• Tim Gabrielson, Director
• Marian Clennon, Director
• Steve Leif, Director
Arena Seating Capacity:
3,500.00
Year Founded:
1976
Track Type:
Concrete.
Track Size:
85x200.

ROANOKE CIVIC CENTER
710 WILLIAMSON ROAD
ROANOKE, VA 24016
540-853-2241
Fax: 540-853-2748
• Boyd Mina, Director
• Robyn Schon, Assistant Director
Arena Seating Capacity:
11,000.00
Year Founded:
1971
Clients:
Clear Channel Entertainment/Motorsports,
Outback Concerts, Feld Entertainment.
Nature of Service:
Full-service public assembly facility.

ROBERTS STADIUM (IA)
3201 PETERS AVENUE
SIOUX CITY, IA 51102
712-279-6651
Fax: 712-279-6099

• Ray Rowe, Facility Manager
Stadium Seating Capacity:
7,000

ROBINS CENTER
ROBINS CENTER
UNIVERSITY OF RICHMOND
RICHMOND, VA 23173
804-289-8363
Fax: 804-289-8820
www.cbssports.com
• Jim Miller, Athletic Director
(804) 289-8694
jmiller@richmond.edu
• Ruth M Goehring, Associate Athletic
Director/Events & Fac
• Tanya Cornwell, Ticket Manager
Arena Seating Capacity:
9,171

ROBINS STADIUM
ROBINS CENTER
UNIVERSITY OF RICHMOND
RICHMOND, VA 23173
804-289-8363
Fax: 804-289-8820
athletic@richmond.edu
www.richmondspiders.com
• Jim Miller, Athletic Director
(804) 289-8694
• Keith M Gill, Director of Athletics
(804) 289-8694
athleticdirector@richmond.edu
• Robbie Brinkley, Assistant to the Director
of Athletics
(804) 289-8694
• David Walsh, Deputy Athletic Director
(804) 289-8009
dwalsh@richmond.edu
• Cathy Rossi, Assistant Director of
Athletics/Business
(804) 289-8368
• Bob Black, Assistant Director of
Athletics/Communication
(804) 287-6885
bblack@richmond.edu
Stadium Seating Capacity:
22,319

ROCKFORD AVIATORS
4503 INTERSTATE DRIVE
LOVES PARK, IL 61111
815-885-2255
Fax: 815-885-2204
• Brad Sholes, General Manager
(815) 885-2255
• Rich Austin, Manager
(815) 885-2255
• Jacob Wise, Director of
Media/Broadcasting
(815) 885-2255
Sport:
Baseball.
Team:
Rockford Aviators.
Year Founded:
2001
Seating Capacity:
3,500
Description:
Independent baseball team; member of
Frontier league.

ROGER DEAN STADIUM
4751 MAIN STREET
JUPITER, FL 33458

561-775-1818
Fax: 561-691-6886
f.desk@rogerdeanstadium.com
www.rogerdeanstadium.com
• Jorge Toro, Stadium Building Manager
(561) 630-1852
• Marshall Jennings, Facility Operations
Manager
(561) 630-1854
m.jennings@rogerdeanstadium.com
• Rob Rabenecker, General Manager
(561) 630-1848
• Mike Bauer, General Manager
(561) 630-1840
m.bauer@rogerdeanstadium.com
• Carol McAteer, Executive Assistant to the
General Manager
(561) 630-1850
• Lisa Fegley, Assistant GM
(561) 799-1389
• Melissa Kuper, Assistant GM
(561) 630-1848
m.kuper@rogerdeanstadium.com
• David Vago, Office Manager
(561) 775-1818
• Angie Albert, Accounting Assistant
(561) 630-1849
• Alex Inman, Event Services Manager
(561) 630-1855
Sport:
Baseball
Team:
Jupiter Hammerheads
Year Founded:
1998
Capacity:
6,600

ROGERS ARENA
800 GRIFFITHS WAY
VANCOUVER, BC, CANADA V6B 6G1
604-899-7400
rogersarena.com
Owner:
Aquilini Investment Group.
Year Opened:
1995.
Seating Capacity:
Hockey 18,910; Basketball 19,700; Concerts
19,000.
Tenant(s):
Vancouver Canucks (NHL); Vancouver
Warriors (NLL); Vancouver Titans (OWL).

ROGERS CENTRE
1 BLUE JAYS WAY
TORONTO, ON, CANADA M5V 1J1
416-341-1000
www.mlb.com/bluejays/ballpark
• Colette Watson, President, Rogers Sports
& Media
Owner:
Rogers Communications.
Operator:
Rogers Stadium Limited Partnership.
Year Opened:
1989.
Seating Capacity:
Baseball 39,150; Concerts 10,000-55,000.
Tenant(s):
Toronto Blue Jays (MLB).

ROGERS PLACE
300, 10214 104 AVENUE NW
EDMONTON, AB, CANADA T5J 0H6

780-414-5483
info@rogersplace.com
www.rogersplace.com
• Stuart Ballantyne, President & COO
Owners:
City of Edmonton.
Operators:
Oilers Entertainment Group.
Seating Capacity:
Hockey 18,347; Basketball 19,500; Concerts
20,734.
Tenant(s):
Edmonton Oilers (NHL); Edmonton Oil
Kings (WHL).

ROGERS STADIUM
1 HAYDEN DR.
VIRGINIA STATE UNIVERSITY
PETERSBURG, VA 23806-2096
804-524-5000
Fax: 804-524-5763
www.vsu.edu
• Peggy Davis, Athletic Director
• Andrea C. Tatum, Director of Alumni
Relations
(804) 524-5973
atatum@vsu.edu
• Sharna D. Gannaway, Alumni Relations
Assistant
(804) 524-6935
sgannaway@vsu.edu
Permanent Seating Capacity:
13,500

RON STEPHENS STADIUM
1400 NW DEARBORN AVENUE
LAWTON, OK 73507
580-357-5672
• Jerry Cauthern, Athletic Director
Stadium Seating Capacity:
9,900

ROSE BASKETBALL ARENA
1200 FRANKLIN STREET
CENTRAL MICHIGAN UNIVERSITY
MOUNT PLEASANT, MI 48859
989-774-4000
Fax: 989-774-7957
cmsports@cmich.edu
www.cmich.edu
• Cal Seelye, Director, Events and
Conference Services
seely1ch@cmich.edu
• Chad Garland, Assistant Director, Events
and Conference Ser
(989) 774-7675
• Emily Tritschler, Coordinator, Events and
Conference Services
mcclu1es@cmich.edu
• Scott Harrington, Technical Specialist,
University Events
(989) 774-3355
harri3sr@cmich.edu
• Connie Camp, SR Specialist Clerk, Bovee
University Center,
(989) 774-7477
highe1cl@cmich.edu
• Brittany Cornwell, Graduate Assistant,
Events and Conference Ser
cornw1ba@cmich.edu
Description:
Additional Website:
www.cmuchippewas.com
Arena Seating Capacity:
5,200

ROSE BOWL STADIUM
1001 ROSE BOWL DRIVE
PASADENA, CA 91103
626-577-3100
Fax: 626-405-0992
rosebowlstadium@yahoo.com
www.rosebowlstadium.com
• Darryl Dunn, General Manager
• Larry Madden, CFO
(626) 577-3100
• Charles Thompson, HR Manager
(626) 577-3100
• George Cunningham, Chief Operating
Officer
• Larry Madden, Chief Financial officer
• David Sams, Director of Golf Course
Operations
• Charles Thompson, Corp Communications
• Julie Benavidez, Event Manager
• Paul Engl, Sponsorship Director
Home Stadium for:
NCAA - Rose Bowl, UCLA Bruins Football,
MLS - Los Angeles Galaxy.
Stadium Seating Capacity:
92,542
Description:
Sports/Entertainment stadium

ROSE GARDEN, THE
ONE CENTER COURT
SUITE 150
PORTLAND, OR 97227
503-797-9619
Fax: 503-236-4906
facilitymarketing@rosequarter.com
www.rosegarden.com
• Hubert Erin, EVP
• J Isaac, SVP Business Affairs
• Jim Kotchik, SVP/Chief Financial Officer
• Jim McCue, VP Facility Sales/Marketing
Permanent Seating Capacity:
20,300
Tenant(s) :
NBA - Portland Trail Blazers basketball;
WHL - Portland Winter Hawks hockey.

ROSE QUARTER BOX OFFICE
ONE CENTER COURT
SUITE 150
PORTLAND, OR 97227
503-235-8771
Fax: 503-736-2187
Feedback@RoseQuarter.com
www.rosequarter.com
• Erin Hubert, EVP
• J Isaac, SVP Business Affairs
• Jim Kotchik, SVP/Chief Financial Officer
• Chris Oxley, General Manager
Arena Seating Capacity:
12,000

ROSENBLATT STADIUM
12356 BALLPARK WAY
WERNER PARK
PAPILLION, NE 68046
402-734-2550
Fax: 402-734-7166
www.oroyals.com
• Kyle Fisher, Vice President/Baseball
Operations
• Erich Hover, Ticket Sales
Director/Operations
• Gary Green, Chief Executive Officer
• Martie Cordaro, President and General
Manager
• Laurie Schlender, Assistant General
Manager

• Matthew Rau, Director of Corporate Sales
• Dave Endress, Director of Business
Development
• Mark Nasser, Director of Broadcasting
• Brett Pollock, Director of Baseball
Operations
Sport:
Baseball
Team:
Omaha Royals
Year Founded:
1948
Capacity:
24,000

ROSS-ADE STADIUM
850 BEERING DRIVE
PURDUE UNIVERSITY
W LAFAYETTE, IN 47907
765-496-2005
800-497-7678
Fax: 765-496-1842
www.purduesports.com
• Morgan Burke, Athletic Director
(765) 494-3189
mjb@purdue.edu
• Roger Blalock, Senior Associate Athletic
Director
(765) 494-3203
Stadium Seating Capacity:
62,500

ROY STEWART STADIUM
217 STEWART STADIUM
MURRAY STATE ATHLETICS
MURRAY, KY 42071-3351
270-809-6858
Fax: 270-762-6800
www.goracers.com
• Miles Chambers, Equipment Manager
(270) 809-3430
• Allen Ward, Administration - Director of
Athletics
(270) 809-3164
• Matt Kelly, Administration - Senior
Associate AD
(270) 809-4424
matt.kelly@murraystate.edu
• Paul Bubb, Administration - Associate AD -
External Affa
(270) 809-3369
• Steve Harrell, Administration - Associate
AD - Compliance &
(270) 809-3430
• Velvet Milkman, Administration - Senior
Woman Administrator
(270) 809-5408
vmilkman@murraystate.edu
• Crystal Morrow, Administration - Assistant
to the Athletic Di
(270) 809-3746
crystal.morrow@murraystate.edu
Permanent Seating Capacity:
16,800

ROY WILKINS AUDITORIUM
199 WEST KELLOG BLVD.
SAINT PAUL, MN 55102
651-265-4800
Fax: 651-265-4899
info@xcelenergycenter.com
www.theroy.org
• Jim Ibister, Vice President
(651) 265-4801
• Jim Ibister, General Manager
(651) 265-4801
• Susan Hubbard, Director of Booking and

Administration
(651) 265-4806
• Mark Stoffel, Senior Director of Operations
(651) 265-4807
• Kristina Meier, Director of Box Office
Operations
(651) 726-8264
• Kate Steley, Director of Event
Management and RiverCentre
(651) 265-4810
• John Koehler, Event Manager
(651) 265-4849
• Jill Mastel, Event Manager
(651) 265-4809
Seating Capacity:
10,000

ROYAL FARMS ARENA
201 WEST BALTIMORE STREET
BALTIMORE, MD 21201
410-347-2020
Fax: 410-347-2042
www.royalfarmsarena.com
• Jason Smith, Director of Operations
Arena Seating Capacity:
11,271
Year Founded:
1962
Nature of Service:
Entertainment, sporting events.

RUPP ARENA
430 W VINE STREET
LEXINGTON, KY 40507
859-233-4567
Fax: 859-253-2718
boxoffice@rupparena.com
www.rupparena.com
• Bill Owen, President and CEO
bowen@rupparena.com
• Carl Hall, Director Arena Management
chall@rupparena.com
• Carl Hall, Director of Arena Management
• Cathy Derr, Senior Manager, Arena Events
• Theresa Lloyd, Manager, Arena Events
• Neal Werner, Director of Business Affairs
• Merrill Richardson, Director of Facilities
Administration
• Bob Stoops, Technical Services Manager
Year Founded:
1976
Arena Seating Capacity:
2,300-23,000
Clients Include:
University of Kentucky Men's Basketball,
Clear Channel Entertainment, Lexington
Horsemen, Outback Concerts

RUSHMORE PLAZA CIVIC CENTER
444 N. MT. RUSHMORE ROAD
RAPID CITY, SD 57701
605-394-4111
800-468-6463
Fax: 605-394-6621
gotmine@rushmore.com
www.gotmine.com
• Brian Maliske, General Manager
(605) 394-4115
• Jayne Kraemer, Assistant General
Manager
(605) 394-4115
jaynek@rushmore.com
• Steve Montgomery, Marketing Sales
Manager
• Paul Sterling, Operations Manager
• Tom Barber, Asst operations Manager
• Brian Maliske, General Manager

• Tracy Heitsch, Asst General Manager /
Finance
• Jayne Kraemer, Asst General Manager /
Events
• Tanya Gray, Director of Events Services
• Larry Dale, Life Safety & Events
Coordinator
Arena Seating Capacity:
11,000

RUSSELL E. DIETHRICK JR. PARK
485 FALCONER STREET
RUSSELL E DIETHRICH, JR PARK
JAMESTOWN, NY 14702-0638
716-664-0915
Fax: 716-664-4175
www.jamestownjammers.com
• Matt Drayer, General Manager
• George Sisson, Sales/Marketing Director
Sport:
Baseball
Team:
Jametown Jammers
Year Founded:
1941
Capacity:
3,300

RUTGERS ATHLETIC CENTER
83 ROCKAFELLER ROAD
PISCATAWAY, NJ 08854
732-445-4223
Fax: 732-445-2990
www.scarletknights.com
• McK Williams, Associate Athletic Director
• Tim Pernetti, Athletic Director
(732) 445-7839
ad@scarletknights.com
• Jason Baum, Senior Associate AD,
Communications
(732) 445-4200
jbaum@scarletknights.com
• Geoff Brown, Senior Associate AD/Chief
Marketing Officer
(732) 445-7868
• Doug Fillis, Senior Associate AD,
Administration
(732) 445-7816
• Kate Hickey, Senior Associate AD/Senior
Woman Administrato
(732) 445-7899
khickey@scarletknights.com
• Douglas Kokoskie, Senior Associate AD
for Facilities/Events/Oper
(732) 445-4223
koko@scarletknights.com
• Tim Thiess, Accounting Assistant
Permanent Seating Capacity:
9,000

RYAN CENTER
ONE LINCOLN ALMOND PLAZA
THE RYAN CENTER
KINGSTON, RI 02881
401-788-3200
Fax: 401-788-3210
info@theryancenter.com
www.theryancenter.com
• Ron Petro, Athletic Director
• Diana Zanetto, Director Sales & Marketing
(401) 788-3230
Year Opened:
2002
Tenant(s) :
NCAA - University of Rhode Island
basketball.
Permanent Seating Capacity:

7,571
Team:
Northwestern football

RYAN FIELD
1501 CENTRAL STREET
EVANSTON, IL 60208
847-491-7887
www.nusports.com
• Jim Phillips, Vice President for Athletics &
Recreation
• Scott Arey, Assoc. AD, Facilities
• Pat Fitzgerald, Head Coach, Football
Team:
Northwestern Wildcats
Seating Capacity:
47,130

SAFECO FIELD
1250 1ST AVENUE
SEATTLE, WA 98154
206-346-4000
800-332-3226
Fax: 206-346-4250
www.safeco.com
• Geffrey Craig, Manager
• Jackie Cram, Assistant
Manager/Operations
• Cindy Hum, Assistant Manager/Services
• Moose Clusen, Safeco Site Sales
Stadium Seating Capacity:
47,000
Team:
Seattle Mariners major league baseball.

SAINT JOSEPH CIVIC ARENA
100 N 4TH STREET
SAINT JOSEPH, MO 64501
816-271-4717
800-821-5052
Fax: 816-232-9213
kbrock@stjoemo.org
civicfac@ci.st-joseph.mo.us
• Kathy Brock, Manager Civic Facilities
(816) 271-4717
kbrock@stjoemo.org
• Chad Bumphrey, Operations Supervisor
cbumphrey@stjoemo.org
• Carolyn Thomas, Operations Coordinator
cathomas@stjoemo.org
Arena Seating Capacity:
4,222 concert style; 3,800 basketball style
Year Founded:
1980
Nature of Service:
Multi-use facility hosting events such as
trade shows, banquets, circus, meetings,
basketball, bull riding, roller derby,
conventions, concerts, wrestling,
gymnastics, etc.

SALEM CIVIC CENTER
1001 ROANOKE BOULEVARD
SALEM, VA 24153
540-375-3004
Fax: 540-375-4011
www.salemciviccenter.com
• Harveycutter C. Carey, Director of Civic
Facilities
charveycutter@salemva.gov
• John E Saunders, Assistant Director
• Peggy Dickerson, Sales Director
Arena Seating Capacity:
8,500
Stadium Seating Capacity:
6,100 (Baseball).

Stadium Seating Capacity:
8,000 (Football).

SAM BOYD STADIUM
4505 S MARYLAND PARKWAY
LAS VEGAS, NV 89154
702-895-3011
Fax: 702-895-1099
• Gayle Juneau, Ed.D., Executive Director of
Academic Advising
• Tricia Lozano, M.Ed., Academic Advising
Administration Coordinator
• Roy Hessinger, B.S., Advising Database
Analyst
• Eric Lee, UNLV Transition Advisor
• Janet Hollinger, UNLV Transition Advisor
Stadium Seating Capacity:
42,500
Owned by:
Univ of Nevada, Las Vegas.

SAM LYNN BALLPARK
4009 CHESTER AVENUE
BAKERSFIELD, CA 93301
661-716-4487
Fax: 661-322-6199
• Noren Craig, Stadium Operations Director
• Cricket Whitaker, Ticket Sales Director
• Dan Besbris, Director of Broadcasting and
Media Relations
(424) 248-0866
• Dale Billodeaux, Director of Sales and
Merchandise
• Elizabeth Martin, General Manager
• Philip Guiry, Assistant General Manager
• Mike Candela, Assistant General
Manager, Ticketing
• Megan Murphy, Event and Group Manager
• Brianne Gidcumb, Ticket Sales Manager
Sport:
Baseball
Team:
Bakersfield Blaze
Year Founded:
1941
Capacity:
4,200

**SAMUEL J. PLUMERI FIELD AT MERCER
COUNTY WATERFRONT PARK**
ONE THUNDER ROAD
TRENTON, NJ 8611
609-394-3300
Fax: 609-394-9666
fun@trentonthunder.com
www.trentonthunder.com
• Matt Pentima, Ticket Operations Director
(609) 394-3300
• Will Smith, General Manager/ Chief
Operating Officer
• Eric Lipsman, Senior Vice President of
Corporate Sales and
(609) 394-3300
eric@trentonthunder.com
• Ryan Crammer, Vice President,
Operations
(609) 394-3300
• Matt Pentima, Director of Ticket
Operations
(609) 394-3300
• Bill Cook, Director of Public Relations
(609) 394-3300
• Joe Pappalardo, Director of Merchandising
(609) 394-3300
• Patience Purdy, Director of Community
Relations
(609) 394-3300

Sport:
Baseball
Team:
Trenton Thunder
Year Founded:
1994
Capacity:
6,440

SAN JOSE MUNICIPAL STADIUM
588 E ALMA AVENUE
SAN JOSE, CA 95112
408-297-1435
Fax: 408-297-1453
www.sjgiants.com
• Linda Pereira, Director, Player Relations
(408) 297-1435
• Chris Lampe, Chief Operating Officer
(408) 297-1435
• Mike Wilson, General Manager
(408) 297-1435
markwilson@sjgiants.com
• Zach Walter, Assistant General Manager
(408) 297-1435
• Terry Mylor, Operations
Capacity:
4,000

SANFORD STADIUM
1 SELIG CIRCLE
UNIVERSITY OF GEORGIA, PO BOX 1472
ATHENS, GA 30602
706-542-9036
Fax: 706-542-2980
www.georgiadogs.com/facilities/sanford-sta
dium.html
• Vince Dolley, Athletic Director
• Charles Whittemore, Assistant Athletic
Director/Facilities
• Ray McEwen, Assistant Director/Facilities
• Michael Adams, UGA President
• Jere W. Morehead, Vice Chairman
• Greg McGarity, Director of Athletics
ad@sports.uga.edu
• Frank Crumley, Executive Associate
Athletic Director - Finan
fcrumley@sports.uga.edu
• Carla Williams, Executive Associate
Athletic Director
cwilliams@sports.uga.edu
• Claude Felton, Senior Associate Athletic
Director - Sports C
cfelton@sports.uga.edu
• Alan Thomas, Associate Athletic Director -
External Operat
athomas@sports.uga.edu
Stadium Seating Capacity:
92,746

SAVVIS CENTER
1401 CLARK AVENUE
SAINT LOUIS, MO 63103
314-622-5400
Fax: 314-622-2588
webmaster@scottradecenter.com
www.scottradecenter.com
• Dennis Petrullo, SVP/General Manager
• Fred Corsi, Operations VP
• Dave Coverstone, Human Resources VP
• David Born, Guest Service Director
Arena Seating Capacity:
19,022
Tenant(s) :
NHL - St. Louis Blues ice hockey; NCAA -
Saint Louis University men's basketball

SCHAUMBURG BOOMERS STADIUM
1999 SOUTH SPRINGSGUTH ROAD
SCHAUMBURG, IL 60193
847-461-3695
Fax: 630-493-3501
info@boomersbaseball.com
www.boomersbaseball.com
• Pete Laven, President, General Manager
(847) 461-3695
• Mike Tlusty, Director of Facilities
(847) 461-3695
mtlusty@boomersbaseball.com
• Ryan Kukla, Director of Ticket Operations
(847) 461-3695
Services
It is primarily used for baseball and cricket,
and is the home field of the Schaumburg
Boomers.
Seating Capacity
7,365

**VALUE CITY ARENA/JEROME
SCHOTTENSTEIN CENTER**
555 BORROR DRIVE
COLUMBUS, OH 43210
614-688-3939
800-273-6201
800-ARENA-01
Fax: 614-292-5067
osuarena@osu.edu
www.schottensteincenter.com
• Vicki L Chorman, Associate Director
• Justin Doyle, Manager Marketing
Promotions
• Michael Gatto, Director Events
Administration
• Scott Dickson, Director of Event Services
and Security
• Carolyn Speicher, Guest Services
Manager
• Andy Geiger, Athletics Director
Arena Seating Capacity:
13,276

SCOPE ARENA
201 E BRAMBLETON AVENUE
NORFOLK, VA 23510
757-664-6464
Fax: 757-664-6990
www.sevenvenues.com/about/mission/scop
e
• John Rhamstine, Director
Arena Seating Capacity:
13,800
Home Arena for:
NCAA - Old Dominion University, AF2 -
Norfolk Nighthawks

SCOTIABANK ARENA
40 BAY STREET
TORONTO, ON, CANADA M5J 2X2
416-815-5982
www.scotiabankarena.com
• Michael Friisdahl, President & CEO, Maple
Leaf Sports & Entertainment
• Nick Eaves, Chief Venues & Operations
Officer
Owners & Operators:
Maple Leaf Sports & Entertainment Ltd.
Year Opened:
1999.
Seating Capacity:
Basketball - 19,800; Hockey - 18,800;
Lacrosse - 18,800; Concerts - 19,800;
Theatre - 5,200.
Tenant(s) :
Toronto Maple Leafs (NHL); Toronto

Raptors (NBA); Toronto Marlies (AHL);
Raptors 905 (NBA G League).

SCOTIABANK SADDLEDOME
555 SADDLEDOME RISE SE
CALGARY, AB, CANADA T2G 2W1
403-777-4646
Fax: 403-777-2171
customerservice@calgaryflames.com
www.scotiabanksaddledome.com
• Susan Darrington, VP, Building Operations
• Elizabeth Whittaker, Director, Building
Operations
Owners:
City of Calgary.
Operators:
Saddledome Foundation; Calgary Sports
and Entertainment.
Year Opened:
1983.
Seating Capacity:
19,289.
Tenant(s) :
Calgary Flames (NHL); Calgary Hitmen
(WHL); Calgary Roughnecks (NLL); Calgary
Wranglers (AHL).

SCOTT STADIUM
UVA ATHLETIC DEPT
PO BOX 400825
CHARLOTTESVILLE, VA 22904-4825
434-982-5200
Fax: 434-982-5213
ece3k@virginia.edu
www.virginiasports.com
• Keith Te VanDerbeek, Associate Director
of Athletics for Business Opera
(434) 982-5200
kdv@virginia.edu
• Jon Oliver, Executive Assistant Athletics
Director
(434) 243-5114
jko3b@virginia.edu
• Craig Littlepage, Director of Athletics
(434) 982-5100
• Becky Davis, Executive Assistant
(434) 982-5100
• Jon Oliver, Executive Associate Athletics
Director
(434) 243-5114
• Sharon McCauley, Administrative
Assistant to the Executive Ass
(434) 243-5114
• Jane Miller, Senior Associate Director of
Athletics for Pr
(434) 982-5151
• Kyle Denzel, General Manager
Stadium Seating Capacity:
61,500
Team:
University of Virginia football.

SCOTTSDALE STADIUM
7408 E OSBORN ROAD
SCOTTSDALE, AZ 85251
480-312-2586
Fax: 480-312-2888
tnichols@ScottsdaleAZ.gov
www.scottsdaleaz.gov/stadium
• Clifford Craig, Financial services general
manager
• Jeff Cesaretti, Stadium Co-ordinator
(480) 312-2380
jcesaretti@ScottsdaleAZ.gov
• Stephanie Johnson, Assistant Stadium
Co-ordinator

(480) 312-2856
stejohnson@ScottsdaleAZ.gov
Sport:
Minor League Baseball
Team:
Scottsdale Scorpions.
Year Founded:
1992
Capacity:
3688 Stadium seats; 4500 Bleacher seats;
3012 Berm seats

SEAGATE CENTRE
401 JEFFERSON AVENUE
TOLEDO, OH 43604
419-255-3300
Fax: 419-255-7731
www.toledo-seagate.com
• Carol E DuPuis, Director of Sales and
Marketing
(419) 392-0937
cdupuis@meettoledo.org
• Jim Thielman, Director Operations
• Carol Dupuis, Director
Sales/Marketing/Booking
(419) 392-0937
• Steve Miller, General Manager
(419) 321-5010
• J.T. Theilman, Director of Operations
(419) 321-5025
• Agnes Rock, Director of Finance
(419) 321-5015
• Terry Huerta, Human Resource & Payroll
Manager
(419) 321-5018
• Launren O'neill, Sales Manager
(419) 321-5006
• Michael Mccall, Event Services Manager
(419) 321-5029
Arena Seating Capacity:
7,500

SEC TAYLOR STADIUM
ONE LINE DRIVE
PRINCIPAL PARK
DES MOINES, IA 50309
515-243-6111
800-464-2827
Fax: 515-243-5152
www.iowacubs.com
• Tom Greene, Director Stadium Operations
tgreene@iowacubs.com
• Jim Nahas, VP, Assistant General
Manager
jnahas@iowacubs.com
• Chris Schlosser, Head Groundskeeper
• Michael Gartner, Chairman
mgartner@iowacubs.com
• Sam Bernabe, President / General
Manager
sbernabe@iowacubs.com
• Michael Giudicessi, Corporate Secretary
mikeg@iowacubs.com
• Nate Teut, VP / Assistant General
Manager
(515) 280-2652
natet@iowacubs.com
• Jim Nahas, VP / Assistant General
Manager
(515) 243-6019
jnahas@iowacubs.com
• Sue Tollefson, VP / Chief Financial Office
(515) 243-6015
suet@iowacubs.com
• Deene Ehlis, VP / Director of Broadcast
Operations
(515) 280-2648
dehlis@iowacubs.com

Stadium Seating Capacity:
11,500.00
Year Founded:
1992
Track Type:
Grass.
Track Size:
335-400-335.

SELBY STADIUM
61 S SANDUSKY STREET
DELAWARE, OH 43015
740-368-3200
Fax: 740-368-3751
www.owu.edu
• Roger Ingles, Athletic Director
(740) 368-3738
• Seth McGuffin,
(740) 368-3756
Seating Capacity:
9,800
Sports:
Track & Field, Field Hockey, Football, Track,
Men's & Women's Lacrosse.
Track:
1/4 mile Defango

SHIRK STADIUM
13TH & BERN STREETS
PO BOX 15234
READING, PA 19612
610-921-2381
Fax: 610-921-7566
athletics@alb.edu
www.albright.edu
• Robert J. Beall, President & Chief
Executive Officer
• W. C. Jack Miller, Vice Chair
• Steve George, Athletic Director
• Karen A. Rightmire, Secretary
• John T. Baily, Chair
Stadium Seating Capacity:
9,000

SHOEMAKER CENTER
2600 CLIFTON AVENUE
UNIVERSITY OF CINCINNATI
CINCINNATI, OH 45221
513-556-6000
Fax: 513-556-0601
reccenter@uc.edu
www.uc.edu
• Kendra Violet, Associate Director of
Facilities and Operations
• Francisco Hiawath, Coordinator
Operations/Facilities
• Bob Bauer, Operations/Maintenance
Director
Arena Seating Capacity:
13,164

SHOW ME CENTER
1333 N SPRIGG STREET
CAPE GIRARDEAU, MO 63701
573-651-2297
Fax: 573-651-5054
smc@semo.edu
www.showmecenter.biz
• Ross David, Director
• Greg Talbut, Business Manager
(573) 651-2297
gtalbut@semo.edu
• Brad Gentry, Marketing Director
bgentry@semo.edu
• Jack Davis, Event Supervisor
Arena Seating Capacity:
10,000

Tenant(s) :
NCAA - Southeast Missouri State University
athletics

SHUFORD GYM/STADIUM
625 7TH AVENUE NE
HICKORY, NC 28601
828-328-1741
Fax: 828-328-7329
• Todd Lawing, Associate Athletics Director
• Caroline Cauthen, Director
Shuford Gym Seating Capacity:
3,000
Stadium Seating Capacity:
10,000

SILVER CROSS FIELD
1 MAYOR ART SCHULTZ DRIVE
SILVER CROSS FIELD
JOLIET, IL 60432
815-722-2287
Fax: 815-726-4304
info@jolietslammers.com
www.jolietslammers.com
• Kelly Sufka, Executive Vice
President/General Manager
(815) 774-2885
• Jeff Eckert, Director of Field/Stadium
Operations
Team:
Joliet Jackhammers
Sport:
Baseball
Year Founded:
2003
Capacity:
6,915

SILVIO O. CONTE FORUM
140 COMMONWEALTH AVENUE
CHESTNUT HILL, MA 2467
617-552-8520
Fax: 617-552-4903
gene.d@bc.edu
www.bceagles.com
• Gene DeFilippo, Athletic Director
• Brad Bates, Director of Athletics
(617) 552-4681
• Beth Mahoney, Administrative Assistant to
the Director of A
(617) 552-4680
• John Kane, Senior Associate Athletic
Director
(617) 552-8840
kano@bc.edu
• Jody Mooradian, Senior Associate
Athletics Director - SWA
(617) 552-4801
Arena Seating Capacity:
8,606

SIMMONS FIELD
330 N GLENVIEW AVENUE
MILWAUKEE, WI 53143-3379
414-453-4567
Fax: 414-453-3001
www.wlhs.org
• Jeff Sitz, Athletic - Director
(414) 453-4567
• Ryan Walz, Physical Education/Religion
(414) 453-4567
• Rev. Kenneth Fisher, President
ext 2161
ken.fisher@wlhs.org
Sport:
Baseball
Team:

Kennosha Mammoths
Year Founded:
1933
Capacity:
3,000

SIOUX FALLS ARENA
1201 N W AVENUE
SIOUX FALLS, SD 57104-1334
605-367-7288
800-338-3177
Fax: 605-338-1463
info@sfarena.com
www.sfarena.com
• Russ DeCurtins, General Manager
• Terry Torkildson, General Manager
• Jeff Gortmaker, Director of Operations
• Carmen Giles, Director of Event Services
• Dusty Plaugher, Operations Manager
• Nicole Nogosek, Box Office Manager
• Rick Huffman, Director of Sales & Marketing
• Kelly Zamora, Director of Finance
Arena Seating Capacity:
8,000

SIOUX FALLS STADIUM
1001 N W AVENUE
SIOUX FALLS, SD 57104
605-333-6060
Fax: 605-333-0139
info@sfcanaries.com
www.sfcanaries.com
• John Kuhn, President
• Tom Garrity, President/CEO
• Gary Weckwerth, Managing Partner
garyweck@aol.com
• Jim Loria, Senior Vice President of Corporate Sponsorshi
(605) 336-6060
• Jim Olander, Vice President of Broadcast & Communications
(605) 336-6060
olander@sfstampede.com
• Nate Welch, Vice President of Operations
(605) 336-6060
• Matt Ferguson, Vice President of Ticket Sales
(605) 336-6060
• Kim Hipple, Director of Ticketing
(605) 336-6060
Sport:
Baseball.
Team:
Sioux Falls Canaries.
Year Founded:
1941
Capacity:
4,500

SKY SOX STADIUM
4385 TUTT BOULEVARD
SECURITY SERVICE FIELD
COLORADO SPRINGS, CO 80922
719-597-1449
Fax: 719-597-2491
www.skysox.com
• Rai Henniger, Senior Vice President Marketing & Promotions
• Steve DeLeon, Vice President of Field Operations
Sport:
Baseball
Team:
Colorado Springs Sky Sox
Year Founded:
1988

Capacity:
8,500

SKYHAWK ARENA
15 MT PELIA ROAD
1022 ELAM CENTER
UT MARTIN
MARTIN, TN 38238
731-881-7660
Fax: 731-881-7962
www.utmsports.com
• Kevin Creech, Sales & Marketing Assistant
(731) 881-7694
kcreech@utm.edu
• Phil Dane, Athletics Director
(731) 881-7661
pdane@utm.edu
• Bill Kaler, Assistant Athletics Director/Compliance Offic
(731) 881-7662
bkaler@utm.edu
• Danelle Fabianich, Assistant Athletics Director for Administrati
(731) 881-7663
danellef@utm.edu
• Tracie Moss, Athletics Secretary & Insurance
(731) 881-7660
tmoss@utm.edu
• Trudy Henderson, Administrative Specialist
(731) 881-7630
trudyh@utm.edu
• Joe Lofaro, Sports Information Director
(731) 881-7632
jlofaro@utm.edu
• Bart Belew, Assistant Athletics Director for Athletic Tra
(731) 881-7679
bbelew@utm.edu
Arena Seating Capacity:
6,600

SKYHAWK STADIUM
15 MT PELIA ROAD
1022 ELAM CENTER
UT MARTIN
MARTIN, TN 38238
731-881-7660
Fax: 731-881-7962
www.utmsports.com
• Phil Dane, Athletic Director
(731) 881-7661
pdane@utm.edu
• Danelle Fabianich, Assistant Athletics Director for Administrati
(731) 881-7663
danellef@utm.edu
• Tracie Moss, Athletics Secretary & Insurance
(731) 881-7660
tmoss@utm.edu
• Trudy Henderson, Administrative Specialist
(731) 881-7630
trudyh@utm.edu
• Joe Lofaro, Sports Information Director
(731) 881-7632
jlofaro@utm.edu
• Bart Belew, Assistant Athletics Director for Athletic Tra
(731) 881-7679
bbelew@utm.edu
Stadium Seating Capacity:
7,500

SLEEP TRAIN ARENA
ONE SPORTS PARKWAY
SACRAMENTO, CA 95834
916-928-0000
Fax: 916-928-0727
www.sleeptrainarena.com
Seating Capacity:
17,317
Tenants:
Sacramento Kings

SMITH'S BALLPARK
77 WEST 1300 SOUTH
SALT LAKE CITY, UT 84115
801-350-6900
Fax: 801-485-6818
www.milb.com/index.jsp?sid=t561
• Clark Whitworth, President
(801) 350-6900
• Steve Starks, President, Miller Sports Properties
(801) 350-6900
• Marc Amicone, Vice President, General Manager
Sport:
Baseball.
Tenant(s) :
Salt Lake Bees baseball.
Year Founded:
1994
Capacity:
15,411

SMITH-WILLIS STADIUM
200 LAKELAND DRIVE
JACKSON, MS 39216
601-968-5956
Fax: 601-965-7025
slittle@belhaven.edu
• Aguilar Andrew, Assistant General Manager
• Amanda Stringer, Group Sales/Ticket Marketing Director
Team:
Jackson Senators
Sport:
Baseball

SMITH-WILLS STADIUM
1200 LAKELAND DRIVE
JACKSON, MS 39216
601-362-2294
Fax: 601-362-9577
www.jacksonsenators.com
• Brasfield Craig, VP/General Manager
(601) 362-2294
• Chet Carey, Assistant General Manager/Sales Marketin
(601) 362-2294
• Scott Jacobs, Group Sales Director/Ticket Operations
(601) 362-2294
• Carrie Brasfield, Merchandising Director
(601) 362-2294
Sport:
Baseball
Capacity:
5,200

SMOKIES PARK
3540 LINE DRIVE
KODAK, TN 37764
865-286-2300
Fax: 865-523-9913
info@smokiesbaseball.com
www.smokiesbaseball.com

- Rennie Leon, Director of Marketing Development
- Doug Kirchhofer, President
dkirchhofer@smokiesbaseball.com
- Mick Gillispie, Director, Broadcasting
mgillispie@smokiesbaseball.com
- Lauren Chesney, Director, Community Relations
lchesney@smokiesbaseball.com
- Matt Strutner, Director, Corporate Ticket Development
mstrutner@smokiesbaseball.com
- Ryan M. Cox, Director, Entertainment & Client Services
rcox@smokiesbaseball.com
- Stuart Morris, Director, Field Operations
smorris@smokiesbaseball.com
- Tony DaSilveira, Director, Food and Beverage
tdasilveira@smokiesbaseball.com
Sport:
Baseball
Team:
Tennessee Smokies
Year Founded:
2000
Capacity:
6,412

SMOOTHIE KINGS CENTER
1501 DAVE DIXON DRIVE
NEW ORLEANS, LA 70113
504-587-3663
800-756-7074
www.smoothiekingcenter.com
Team:
New Orleans Pelicans (NBA)
Seating Capacity:
18,500

SOLDIER FIELD
1410 S MUSEUM CAMPUS DRIVE
CAMPUS DRIVE GATE14
CHICAGO, IL 60605
312-235-7000
Fax: 312-235-7030
www.soldierfield.net
- Kate McGregor, Director of Sales & Marketing
- Tim LeFevour, GM
- Michael Ortman, Director of Operations
- Kevin Walsh, Director of Events
- Luca Serra, Director of Sponsership Media
- Marty McAndrew, finance
- Scott Rendell, Event Coordinator
Owned by:
Chicago Park District (City of Chicago)
Tenant(s):
NFL - Chicago Bears football, MLS - Chicago Fire soccer.
Permanent Seating Capacity:
61,500

SOUTH CAROLINA STATE UNIVERSITY
300 COLLEGE STREET NE
ORANGEBURG, SC 29117
803-536-7000
800-260-5956
Fax: 803-533-3988
admissions@scsu.edu
www.scsu.edu
- Carolyn M Free, ASSOCIATE DIRECTOR
- David O. Igiozee, Accountant/Manager
digiozee@scsu.edu
- Angelia P. Jackson, Administrative Assistant
ajackson@scsu.edu

- Gloria Lott, Fiscal Technician
- Gwendolyn Love, Fiscal Technician
glove@scsu.edu
- Kay Snider, Interim Director
ksnider@scsu.edu
- Andrea S. Milford Williams, Project Director
- Charlene Johnson, Director of Athletics
Bulldog Stadium:
2,500
S.H.M Memorial Center Seating Capacity:
2,500

SPACE COAST STADIUM
5800 STADIUM PARKWAY
SUITE 101
VIERA, FL 32940
321-633-9200
Fax: 321-633-4418
www.manateesbaseball.com
- Tom Winters, Chairman
- Jeff Weinhold, Tickets Manager
- Tom Winters, Chairman
- Dewight Titus, Vice Chairman
- Charlie Baumann, President
- Frank Longobardo, Director of Ticketing and Media
(321) 633-9200
- Kelley Wheeler, Director of Business Operations and Finance
(321) 633-9200
- Kevin Soto, Director of Promotions and Community Relation
(321) 633-9200
- Kyle Smith, General Manager
(321) 633-9200
Sport:
Baseball
Team:
Montreal Expos spring training facility; Brevard County Manatees.
Year Founded:
1994
Capacity:
8,100

SPARTAN STADIUM
ONE BIRCH ROAD
JACK BRESLIN STUDENT EVENTS CENTER
E LANSING, MI 48824
517-432-1989
Fax: 517-432-1510
alliance@msu.edu
www.msuspartans.com
- Mark Hollis, Athletic Director
(517) 355-1623
ad@ath.msu.edu
- Greg Ianni, Deputy Athletic Director
(517) 355-5263
ianni@ath.msu.edu
- Shelly Appelbaum, Senior Associate AD
(517) 355-8849
appelbau@ath.msu.edu
- Chuck Sleeper, Senior Associate AD
(517) 432-4611
sleeper@ath.msu.edu
Stadium Seating Capacity:
72,027
Team:
Michigan State University football.

SPECIAL OLYMPICS STADIUM
350 NEW CAMPUS DRIVE
THE COLLEGE AT BROCKPORT
BROCKPORT, NY 14420-2914

716-395-2211
Fax: 716-395-2160
mandriat@brockport.edu
www.brockport.edu
- Mike Andriatch, Sports Information Director
(585) 395-5809
- Lee J. Cohen, Head Athletic Trainer
(585) 395-2251
lcohen@brockport.edu
Stadium Seating Capacity:
10,000

SPECTRUM
7400 OLD MAIN HILL
UTAH STATE UNIVERSITY
LOGAN, UT 84322
435-797-1000
800-488-8108
Fax: 435-797-2615
registrar@usu.edu
www.usu.edu
- Doug Hoffman, Athletic Media Relations Director
(435) 797-3714
doug.hoffman@usu.edu
- Scott Randall, Assistant AD
(435) 797-7186
scott.randall@usu.edu
- Justin Williams, Event Services Manager
(435) 797-2995
justin.williams@usu.edu
Seating Capacity:
Romney Stadium (Football) 25,513; Dee Glen Smith Spectrum (Basketball) 10,270

SPOKANE VETERANS MEMORIAL ARENA
720 W MALLON AVENUE
SPOKANE, WA 99201
509-279-7000
Fax: 509-279-7050
www.spokanearena.com
- Kevin Twohig, General Manager
(509) 279-7002
- Kevin B Twohig, CEO, Spokane Public Facilities District
- Matt Gibson, Arena General Manager
- Stephanie Huff, Hr and Contract Services Manager
- Dave Gebhardt, Operations Manager
- Shardell Shrum, Operations Supervisor
- Casey Booey III, Tech Specialist
cbooey@spokanearena.com
- Monte Koch, Tech Specialist
Arena Seating Capacity:
12,500

SPORTS PAVILION
1925 UNIVERSITY AVENUE SE
MINNEAPOLIS, MN 55455
612-625-3007
Fax: 612-625-7788
dale0099@umn.edu
gophersports.com
- Scott P. Ellison, Associate Athletic Director
(612) 624-4497
ellis004@umn.edu
- Norwood Teague, Director of Athletics
(612) 624-4497
- David Benedict, Executive Associate
(612) 624-4497
- Mike Ellis, Sr. Associate AD
(612) 624-4497
- Beth Goetz, Sr. Associate AD/SWA
(612) 624-4497

Arena Seating Capacity:
5,700

ST JOHN'S UNIVERSITY
8000 UTOPIA PARKWAY
CARNESECCA ARENA, ROOM 157
QUEENS, NY 11439
718-990-6217
Fax: 718-990-2063
webmaster@stjohns.edu
redstormsports.collegesports.com
• Erin McDonnell, Associate Athletics
Director for Facilities and Op
(718) 990-1690
mcdonnee@stjohns.edu
• Neftali Collazo, Associate Athletic
Director/Facilities
(718) 990-5951
collazon@stjohns.edu
• Dennis Myron, Ticket Operations Director
Alumni Hall Seating Capacity:
6,008
Stadium Seating Capacity:
3,000

ST LAWRENCE UNIVERSITY
23 ROMODA DRIVE
CANTON, NY 13617
315-229-5011
800-285-1856
Fax: 315-229-5589
lcania@stlawu.edu
www.stlawu.edu/sports
• Margie Strait, Athletic Director
(315) 229-5784
mstrait@stlawu.edu
• Bob Durocher, Assistant Athletic
Director/Facilities
(315) 229-5870
bdur@stlawu.edu
Field Stadium Seating Capacity:
5,000
Sports Center Seating Capacity:
3,500
Ice Arena:
3,500

ST PAUL SAINTS
360 BROADWAY
SAINT PAUL, MN 55101
651-644-3517
Fax: 651-644-1627
www.saintsbaseball.com
• Derek Sharrer, Executive Vice President /
General Manager
dsharrer@saintsbaseball.com
• Tom Whaley, Executive Vice President
twhaley@saintsbaseball.com
• Chris Schwab, Senior Vice
President/Assistant General Manager
cschwab@saintsbaseball.com
• Sean Aronson, Vice President/Director Of
Broadcasting/Media
saronson@saintsbaseball.com
• Tyson Jeffers, Director Corporate Sales
• Sierra Bailey, Director
Marketing/Promotions
sbailey@saintsbaseball.com
Year Founded:
1993
Team:
St. Paul Saints
Sport:
Baseball
Capacity:
7,210

STABLER ARENA
124 GOODMAN DRIVE
LEHIGH UNIVERSITY
BETHLEHEM, PA 18015
610-758-3770
Fax: 610-866-8070
www.stablerarena.com
• Richard H Fritz, Director of Events
• Allen Biddinger, Facilities/Events Manager
• Ed Barndt, Facilities/Events Manager
• Jason Gall, Facilities/Events Coordinator
Arena Seating Capacity:
6,700

STADE CANAC
100 RUE DU CARDINAL-MAURICE-ROY
QUEBEC, QC, CANADA G1K 8Z1
418-521-2255
877-521-2244
Fax: 418-521-2266
info@capitalesdequebec.com
capitalesdequebec.com
• Charles Demere, President
Operators:
City of Quebec.
Year Opened:
1938; Renovated 1999, 2016.
Seating Capacity:
Baseball 4,300.
Tenant(s) :
Quebec Capitales (FL); Quebec Diamants.

STADE SAPUTO
MONTREAL OLYMPIC PARK
4750 SHERBROOKE STREET E
MONTREAL, QC, CANADA H1V 3S8
514-328-3668
Fax: 514-328-1287
info@cfmontreal.com
en.cfmontreal.com/stadium/stade-saputo
• Joey Saputo, Owner, CF Montreal & Stade
Saputo
• Nicolas Dos Santos Borges, Manager,
Stade Saputo Operations
Owner:
Saputo Inc.
Operator:
CF Montreal.
Year Opened:
2008; Expanded 2012.
Seating Capacity:
19,619.
Tenant(s) :
CF Montreal (MLS)

STAMBAUGH STADIUM
ROOM 1003
ONE UNIVERSITY PLAZA
YOUNGSTOWN, OH 44555
330-941-2962
800-468-6978
Fax: 330-941-3191
ysusports@ysu.edu
www.ysusports.com
• Grant Springer,
(330) 941-3671
• Tom Morella,
(330) 941-2351
tmorella@ysu.edu
Seating Capacity:
Stadium 20,630; Arena 6,300
Tenants:
Youngstown State Athletics
Track:
Becoming an indoor facility

STANFORD STADIUM
625 NELSON RD
STANFORD, CA 94305
650-723-4591
Fax: 650-725-8642
www.gostanford.com
Seating Capacity:
50,000
Teams:
Stanford University football.

STANLEY COVELESKI REGIONAL STADIUM
501 W S STREET
COVELESKI REGIONAL STADIUM
S BEND, IN 46601
574-235-9988
Fax: 574-235-9950
• Peter Argueta, Director of Stadium
Operations
• Alan Levin, Principal Owner
• Tony Wittrock, Sales Director
• Andrew Berlin, Owner
• Joe Hart, President
• Nick Brown, Director of Corporate
Sales/Business Developm
• Cheryl Carlson, Director of Finance and
Human Resources
• Kelly Knutson, Director of Marketing
• Ben Hayes, Director of Food and
Beverage
bhayes@prosportscatering.com
• Peter Argueta, Assistant General Manager
- Operations
Sport:
Baseball.
Team:
South Bend Silver Hawks.
Year Built:
1987
Seating Capacity:
5,000

STANLEY J MARSHALL HPER CENTER
11TH STREET AND 16TH AVENUE
SDSU BOX 2820
BROOKINGS, SD 57007-1497
605-688-5817
Fax: 605-688-5999
• Matt Thorn, Assistant AD
• Erin Breczinski, Athletic Tickets Manager
Arena Seating Capacity:
9,000

STARR RINK
13 OAK DRIVE
HAMILTON, NY 13346
315-228-1000
Fax: 315-824-7544
www.colgate.edu
• Dave Roach, Athletic Director
• Robert D. Cornell, Director
Arena Seating Capacity:
2,200

STATE MUTUAL STADIUM
755 BRAVES BOULEVARD
ROME, GA 30161
706-368-9388
Fax: 706-368-6525
rome.braves@braves.com
www.romebraves.com
• Michael Dunn, General Manager
• Jim Jones, Assistant General Manager
• Eric Allman, Director of Stadium
Operations

- Dave Atwood, Director of Culinary Services
- Brad Smith, Director of Food and Beverage
- Jeff Fletcher, Ticket Manager
- Michael Dunn, General Manager
Team:
Rome Braves
Date:
2003
Capacity:
5,000
Sport:
Baseball

STATE UNIVERSITY OF NEW YORK
102 ALUMNI ARENA
UNIVERSITY OF BUFFALO, DIVISION OF ATHLETICS
BUFFALO, NY 14260
716-645-3141
Fax: 716-645-2438
ub-athletics@buffalo.edu
- Bob Maxwell, Assistant Athletic Director for Facility Operation
(716) 645-3486
rmax@buffalo.edu
- Sue Kurkowski, Director, Facility Operations
(716) 645-3992
kurowski@buffalo.edu
- Linda Billups, Facilities/Events Operations Assistant
- Nicolas Titus, Coordinator Facilities
UB Stadium:
17,200
Stadium Seating Capacity:
4,000
Alumni Arena Seating Capacity:
8,500
Natatorium Seating Capacity:
2,000

STEPHEN C O'CONNELL CENTER
2132 STADIUM ROAD
GAINESVILLE, FL 32611
352-392-5500
Fax: 352-392-7106
scoc-marketing@ufl.edu
www.oconnellcenter.ufl.edu
- Lynda Reinhart, Director
lyndar@ufl.edu
- Jeremy Cynkar, Operations Director
(352) 392-5507
cynkar@ufl.edu
- Renne Musson, Associate Director
(352) 392-5506
musson@ufl.edu
- Anthony Rizo, Production Manager
(352) 392-0408
arizo15@ufl.edu
- Lynda Reinhart, Director
(352) 392-5510
lyndar@ufl.edu
- David Lucier, Assistant Director
(352) 392-5505
dlucier@ufl.edu
Seating Capacity:
11,500
Sports:
Men's & Women's basketball, women's volleyball, women's gymnastics, men's & women's swimming & diving, men's & women's indoor track.
Home Team:
University of Florida Gators

STRAHAN COLISEUM
601 UNIVERSITY DRIVE
SAN MARCOS, TX 78666
512-245-2114
Fax: 512-245-8387
athletics@txstate.edu
www.txstatebobcats.com
- Derek Grice, Facility/Game Operations Director
(512) 245-2023
pg13@txstate.edu
- Adam Alonzo, Assistant Director - Facility & Game Operatio
(512) 245-2404
aa08@txstate.edu
- Larry Teis, Director Of Athletics
(512) 245-2963
lt10@txstate.edu
- Don Coryell, Administration - Associate Athletics Director
(512) 245-2220
dc32@txstate.edu
- Tracy Shoemake, Administration - Associate Athletics Director
(512) 245-2114
ts23@txstate.edu
- Travis Comer, Administration - Associate Athletics Director
(512) 245-2247
tc26@txstate.edu
- Paul Gowens, Administration - NCAA Faculty Representative
(512) 245-3252
pg01@txstate.edu
- Jessica Henry, Support Staff - Administrative Assistant - At
(512) 245-2963
Coliseum Seating Capacity:
7,200

STRAWBERRY STADIUM
SLU 10309
HAMMOND, LA 70402
985-549-2253
Fax: 985-549-3495
sportsinfo@selu.edu
www.lionsports.net
- Andrew Bechae, Facility Director
(985) 549-3419
- Dennis Roland, Head Football Coach
(985) 549-5550
- Bart Bellairs, Athletics Director
(985) 549-2395
athletics@southeastern.edu
- Linda Alford, Administrative Coordinator
(985) 549-5599
- Andrew Bechac, Senior Associate AD for Internal Operations
(985) 549-3419
Andrew.Bechac@southeastern.edu
- Tim Baldwin, Head Golf Coach/Assistant AD for Special Even
(985) 549-5186
- Chris Bentley, Assistant to the AD/Lifeskills and Academic L
(985) 549-3393
cbentley@southeastern.edu
- Mary Kathryn Borland, Assistant AD for Academic Services/SWA
(985) 549-2256
- Carley Cryer, Marketing and Promotions
(985) 549-3227
Stadium Seating Capacity:
8,396

SULLIVAN ARENA
1600 GAMBELL STREET
ANCHORAGE, AK 99501

907-279-0618
Fax: 907-274-0676
www.sullivanarena.com
- Tanya Pont, Marketing Director
- Joe Wooden, General Manager
- Penny McKibbon, Director of Finance
- Tanya Pont, Director of Marketing
- Greg Stubbs, Director of Operations
Permanent Seating Capacity:
8,935

SUN BOWL
151 GLORY ROAD
EL PASO, TX 79908
915-747-5481
Fax: 915-747-5228
dhc@utep.edu
www.utepspecialevents.com/
- Michael Spence, Facility Director
mspence@utep.edu
- Jorge Vazquez, Executive Director of Special Events
(915) 747-5481
vazquezj@utep.edu
- Mike Spence, Director of Special Facilities Management
(915) 747-5481
mspence@utep.edu
- Ricky Nichols, Assistant Director
(915) 747-5481
rlnichols@utep.edu
- Eileen Laidler, Business Manager
(915) 747-5481
eclaidler@utep.edu
- Julian E. Valdes, Marketing Coordinator
(915) 747-5481
jevaldes@utep.edu
- Fernie Mabini, Technical Supervisor
(915) 747-5481
fmabini@utep.edu
- Bradley Serrao, Technical Coordinator
(915) 747-5481
blthomas@utep.edu
Stadium Seating Capacity:
52,000.00
Year Founded:
1963
Clients:
Clear Channel Entertainment, AEG, Stargate, Stone City Attraction.
Nature of Service:
University Venue.

SUN DEVIL STADIUM
500 EAST VETERANS WAY
TEMPE, AZ 85287
480-965-2381
888-786-3857
Fax: 480-965-6006
sundeviltickets@asu.edu
thesundevils.cstv.com
- Jeff O'Connor, Athletic Facilities Manager
(480) 965-0950
jeff.oconner@asu.edu
- Michael Chismar, Senior Associate AD
(480) 965-1287
michael.chismar@asu.edu
- John McClees, Athletic Facilities Maintenance Coordina
- Lyn Music, Facilities/Events Management Director
Owned by:
Arizona State University
Tenant(s):
Arizona State University football, NCAA - Tostitos Fiesta Bowl football game.

Permanent Seating Capacity:
73,379

SUN LIFE STADIUM
2269 NW 199TH STREET
MIAMI GARDENS, FL 33056
305-943-8000
• Stephen M. Ross, Owner/Managing
General Partner
• Tom Garfinkel, President/Chief Executive
Officer
• Jeremy Walls, Sr., Vice President/Chief
Revenue Officer
• Claudia Lezcano, Sr., Vice President,
Chief Marketing Officer
• Terry Howard, Sr., Vice President/Chief
Technology Officer
• Todd Boyan, Vice President/General
Manager, Sun Life Stadium
Tenant(s) :
MLB - Florida Marlins baseball, NFL - Miami
Dolphins football, NCAA - Florida Atlantic
University football, NCAA - FedEx Orange
Bowl football game.
Permanent Seating Capacity:
75,540 (football); 36,331 (baseball).

SUN NATIONAL BANK CENTER
81 HAMILTON AVENUE
ROUTE 129
TRENTON, NJ 08611
609-656-3200
Fax: 609-656-3201
www.sunnationalbankcenter.com
• Claudio Oliveira, General Manager
• Tim Moore, Event Manager
tim_moore@comcastspectacor.com
• Robert Coughlin, Director of Operations
robert_coughlin@comcastspectacor.com
Arena Seating Capacity:
8,600

SUPERIOR DOME
1401 PRESQUE ISLE AVENUE
NORTHERN MICHIGAN UNIVERSITY
MARQUETTE, MI 49855
906-227-2850
800-682-9797
Fax: 906-227-2855
brberube@nmu.edu
www.nmu.edu
• Carl Bammert, Associate
Director-Facilities
• Forrest Karr, Athletic Director
(906) 227-1826
fkarr@nmu.edu
• Steve Reed, Senior Associate Director
(906) 227-1183
sreed@nmu.edu
• Carl Bammert, Associate
Director-Facilities
(906) 227-2465
cbammert@nmu.edu
• Bridget Berube Carter, Associate
Director-Compliance
(906) 227-2371
brberube@nmu.edu
Stadium Seating Capacity:
9,000

SYDNEY ENTERTAINMENT CENTRE
35 HARBOUR STREET
PO BOX K10
DARLING HARBOUR, NSW 2000, 2000
-61-02-9320-4200
Fax: -61-02-9281-2682

• Tegan Pryce, Venue Services Manager
(029) 320-4207
tegan@sydentcent.com.au
• Natalie Cutcliffe, Marketing Manager
• Joe Brex, Business Manager
• Lee Kessler, Events Manager

TACO BELL ARENA
1910 UNIVERSITY DRIVE
BOISE STATE UNIVERSITY
BOISE, ID 83725
208-426-1900
Fax: 208-426-1998
www.tacobellarena.com
• Joyce Grimes, Executive Director
(208) 426-1600
jgrimes@boisestate.edu
• Leslie Pass, Events Assistant Director
(208) 426-1982
lpass@boisestate.edu
• Lisa Cochran, Marketing Director
(208) 426-2546
lcochran@boisestate.edu
• Lisa Cochran, Executive Director
lcochran@boisestate.edu
• Ron Janeczko, Associate Director
Facilities & Production
rjaneczk@boisestate.edu
• Leslie Pass, Assistant Director of Events
lpass@boisestate.edu
• John Roberts, Assistant Director, Booking
and Scheduling
• Micki Courtney, Assistant Director,
Ticketing and Guest Servi
mickicourtney@boisestate.edu
• Alex Satterlee, Office Manager
• Rodney Miller, Production Manager
rodneymiller@boisestate.edu
Seating Capacity:
12,428

TACOMA DOME
2727 EAST D STREET
TACOMA, WA 98421
253-272-3663
Fax: 253-593-7620
info@tacomadome.org
www.tacomadome.org
• Rob Henson, Deputy Director/Booking
Manager
• Hillary Brenner, Marketing Assistant
hbrenner@tacomadome.org
• Beth Sylves, Marketing Manager
(253) 593-7602
• Kim Bedier, Director
• Rob Henson, Booking Manager
• Nancy Green, Administrative Assistant
• Angela Tamajka, Marketing Manager
• Hillary Brenner, Marketing Coordinator
• Jeff Brown, Event Coordinator
Arena Seating Capacity:
23,000
Year Founded:
1983
Events:
Concerts, Exhibitions/Trade Shows, Family
Events, High School Sports

TAD SMITH COLISEUM
908 ALL-AMERICAN DRIVE
UNIVERSITY, MS 38677
662-915-7241
1-800-467-3235
www.olemisssports.com
• Ross Bjork, Director of Athletics
(662) 915-7546
• Joe Swingle, Associate Athletic Director,

Facilities
(662) 915-7508
jswingle@olemiss.edu
• Neal Mead, Assistant Director for Event
Management Ops.
(662) 816-2699
nmead@olemiss.edu
Coliseum Seating Capacity:
8,867

TAMPA BAY TIMES FORUM
401 CHANNELSIDE DRIVE
TAMPA, FL 33602
813-301-6500
Fax: 813-301-1480
sponsorship@tampabaytimesforum.com
• Jay Goulde, Executive Director
• Rob Higgins, Executive Director, Tampa
Bay Sports Commissi
Tenant(s) :
AFL - Tampa Bay Storm football, NHL -
Tampa Bay Lightning hockey.
Permanent Seating Capacity:
20,000

TARGET CENTER
600 FIRST AVENUE N
MINNEAPOLIS, MN 55403-1416
612-673-1600
Fax: 612-673-1370
info@targetcenter.com
www.targetcenter.com
• Kevin McHale, Basketball Operations VP
• Sandy Sweetser, Marketing Director
• Dana Warg, Executive Director
• Ajay Sekhran, Concessions Manager
Description:
Home Arena For: Minnesota Timberwolves.
Permanent Seating Capacity:
19,006

TARGET FIELD
1 TWINS WAY
MINNEAPOLIS, MN 55403
612-375-1366
minnesota.twins.mlb.com
• Alfton Dennis, Operations Director
(612) 335-3314
• Dave Horsman, Senior Director, Ballpark
Operations
davehorsman@twinsbaseball.com
• Lisa Knutson, Event Operations Assistant
lisaknutson@twinsbaseball.com
• Dick Dugan, Security Manager
dickdugan@twinsbaseball.com
• Jim Pohlad, Chief Executive Officer,
Minnesota Twins
• Dave St. Peter, President, Minnesota
Twins
• Terry Ryan, Executive Vice President,
General Manager
• Laura Day, Executive Vice President,
Business Developmen
• Kip Elliott, Executive Vice President,
Business Administra
• Matt Hoy, Senior Vice President,
Operations
Owned by:
Minnesota Ballpark Authority in conjunction
with the Twins-Hennepin County ballpark
legislation.
Tenant(s) :
MLB - Minnesota Twins baseball, NCAA -
University of Minnesota football
Seating Capacity:
39,504

TAYLOR STADIUM
ONE CHAMPIONS DRIVE
COLUMBIA, MO 65211
573-256-4004
Fax: 573-256-4003
www.mutigers.com
• Wendt Gary, President/Co-Owner
• Karen Watson, Office Director/Ticket
Operations
• Melissa Wheeler, Business Affairs Director
(573) 256-4004
• Rick Stonelang, Sales/Marketing Director
Capacity:
3,331
Year Founded:
2002
Team:
Missouri Tigers
Sport:
Baseball

TCF BANK STADIUM
2009 SOUTH EAST UNIVERSITY AVE
MINNEAPOLIS, MN 55455
612-624-8080
Fax: 612-625-0003
www.mygophersports.com
Seating Capacity:
50,000
Teams:
University of Minneapolis Gophers

TD BANKNORTH GARDEN
100 LEGENDS WAY
BOSTON, MA 2114
617-624-1050
Fax: 617-523-7184
customerservice@tdgarden.com
www.tdbanknorthgarden.com
• Rusty Sullivan, Executive Director
(617) 624-1237
rsullivan@dncboston.com
• John Wentzell, SVP/General Manager
• David Splaine, SVP Sales
• Christopher W Maher, VP/Boston Garden
Dev
• John Ratoff, SVP Corporate Partnerships
• Christopher Johnson, VP Corporate
Partnerships
• Caryn Kelly, Client Services Manager
• Michele Savage, Corporate Partnerships
Permanent Seating Capacity:
19,580
Description:
Home Arena For: Boston Bruins, Boston
Celtics.
Owned by:
Delaware North Inc.

TD PLACE
1015 BANK STREET
OTTAWA, ON, CANADA K1S 3W7
613-232-6767
877-489-2849
www.tdplace.ca
• Chris Wynn, Sr. Director, Operations
• Brian Giles, Manager, Facilities
Owner:
The Ottawa Sports and Entertainment
Group.
Operator:
Ottawa Sports and Entertainment Group.
Year Opened:
1908.
Seating Capacity:
9,862.
Tenant(s) :

Ottawa Redblacks (CFL); Atletico Ottawa
(CPL); Ottawa Gee-Gees football (OUA).

TD STATION
99 STATION STREET
SAINT JOHN, NB, CANADA E2L 4X4
506-632-6103
www.harbourstation.ca
• Blair McGauchie, General Manager
Year Opened:
1993, renovated 2005.
Seating Capacity:
Hockey 6,308; Basketball; 6,603; Concert
8,100.
Tenant(s) :
Saint John Sea Dogs (QMJHL)

TD WATERHOUSE CENTRE
600 W AMELIA STREET
ORLANDO CENTROPLEX
ORLANDO, FL 32801-1113
407-849-2000
Fax: 407-849-2329
• Allen Johnson, Executive Director
(407) 849-2012
allen.johnson@cityoforlando.net
• Jon Dorman, Deputy Director
(407) 849-2088
• Tanya Bowley, Marketing Director
(407) 849-2590
tanya.bowley@cityoforlando.net
• Cindy Mitchum, Business Manager
(407) 849-2150
cindy.mitchum@cityoforlando.net
Permanent Seating Capacity:
17,320 AFL 15,595
Tenant(s) :
ACHL - Orlando Seals hockey; NBA -
Orlando Magic basketball; AFL - Orlando
Predators football.

SEMINOLE COUNTY SPORTS TRAINING CENTER
1000 AAA DRIVE
SUITE 200 MS14
HEATHROW, FL 32746
407-665-2900
800-800-7832
Fax: 407-665-2920
dtrosset@seminolecountyfl.gov
www.visitseminole.com
• Sharon Sears, Executive Director
(407) 665-2901
ssears@seminolecountyfl.gov
• Danny Trosset, Sales and Marketing
Manager
(407) 665-2913
dtrosset@seminolecountyfl.gov
• Rosangela Santiago, Senior Staff
Assistant
(407) 665-2908
rsantiago@seminolecountyfl.gov
• Sarah Collins, Customer Service
Representative
(407) 665-2900
SCollins@seminolecountyfl.gov
Year Founded:
1993
Description:
Team Seminole event experts make events
smoth, gratifying, and a memorable
experience. Goal is not to simply meet
expectations, but to go above and beyond
all expectations and make events
extraordinary. Paying attention to the little
things, the team makes certain all
participating teams, coaches, family

members, and spectators want to come
back to Seminole County for the next big
event.

TEAMWORKS CENTERS
30 GREAT ROAD
ACTON, MA 01720
978-287-5533
Fax: 508-287-0211
info@twcenters.com
www.twcenters.com
• Kevin O'Connell, CEO/President
(978) 287-0212
koconnell@twcenters.com
• Peter Corbet, Co-Chief Executive Officer
• Bill Disandro, General Manager/Bay State
Description:
Multi-purpose family and corporate indoor
sports and entertainment complexes
featuring a wide variety of activities such as
sport leagues, tournaments, birthday
parties, instructional programs, corporate
and other special events for all ages. The
faciliti

TED CONSTANT CONVOCATION CENTER
4320 HAMPTON BOULEVARD
NORFOLK, VA 23529
757-683-5762
Fax: 757-683-6544
tedconstantcenter@gmail.com
www.constantcenter.com
• Mike Fryling, General Manager
mike_fryling@comcastspectacor.com
• Chase Hathway, Assistant General
Manager
• Jordan Avant, Director of Events and
Operations
jordan_avant@comcastspectacor.com
• Matthew Gibb, Event Manager
Year Opened:
2002
Tenant(s) :
NCAA - Old Dominion University basketball.
Permanent Seating Capacity:
9,520

TEXAS RANGERS BASEBALL CLUB
1000 BALLPARK WAY
SUITE 400
ARLINGTON, TX 76011
817-273-2222
Fax: 817-273-5110
www.texasrangers.com
• Ryan Nolan, President
(817) 273-5233
mcramer@texasrangers.com
• Rick McLaughlin, Business Operations
EVP
(817) 436-5944
rmclaughlin@texasrangers.com
• Casey Shilts, General Counsel SVP
(817) 273-5235
cshilts@texasrangers.com
• Jeff Cogen, Marketing EVP
(817) 273-5196
jcogen@texasrangers.com
• Jay Miller, Senior Vice President
(817) 273-5233
jmiller@texasrangers.com
Owned by:
City of Arlington
Home Stadium for:
Texas Rangers.
Permanent Seating Capacity:
49,115 (Ballpark in Arlington)

Year Founded:
1972

THE BALLPARK AT JACKSON
4 FUN PLACE
JACKSON, TN 38305
731-988-5299
Fax: 731-988-5246
www.milb.com

THE CROWN COMPLEX
1960 COLISEUM DRIVE
FAYETTEVILLE, NC 28306
910-438-4100
Fax: 910-323-0489
contactus@crowncoliseum.com
www.crowncomplexnc.com
• Karen Long, Chief Executive Officer
• Dionne Hill, Director Of Sales
• Max Speers, Sales Manager
• Karen Long, General Manager
klong@crowncoliseum.com
• Chris Ragland, AGM / Director of
Operations
cragland@crowncoliseum.com
• Lisa Foster, Director of Finance
• Marshall Perry, Director of Marketing &
Sales
• Victor Landry, Director of Event Services
vlandry@crowncoliseum.com
• Rita Perry, Executive Administrative
Assistant to the GM
rperry@crowncoliseum.com
• Chris Ragland, AGM / Director of
Operations
Crown Coliseum Seating Capacity:
13,500
Arena Seating Capacity:
5,500
Tenant(s) :
ACHL - Cape Fear FireAntz ice hockey,
AFL2 - Cape Fear Wildcats indoor football,
NBDL - Fayetteville Patriots basketball.

THE DOME AT AMERICA'S CENTER
901 NORTH BROADWAY
ST. LOUIS, MO 63101
314-342-5036
Fax: 314-621-7729
convention@explorestlouis.com
explorestlouis.com
Permanent Seating Capacity:
66,000
Description:
St. Louis Rams

THE DOME CENTER
2695 EAST HENRIETTA ROAD
HENRIETTA, NY 14467
585-334-4000
Fax: 585-334-3005
• Fran Tepper, Executive Director
Seating Capacity:
4,700

**THE UNIVERSITY OF MONTANA
ATHLETIC DEPARTMENT**
32 CAMPUS DRIVE
UNIVERSITY OF MONTANA-MISSOULA
MISSOULA, MT 59812-8496
406-243-4749
888-666-8262
Fax: 406-243-2264
grizzlymarketing@mso.umt.edu
www.gogriz.com

• Christie Anderson, Director of Marketing
and Promotions
(406) 243-4336
chrisite.anderson@mso.umt.edu
• Jimmy Martinez, Assistant
Director/Facilities
Arena Seating Capacity:
15,400

THE WINNIPEG BLUE BOMBERS
315 CHANCELLOR MATHESON ROAD
WINNIPEG, MB, CANADA R3T 1Z2
204-784-2583
Fax: 204-783-5222
bbombers@bluebombers.com
www.bluebombers.com
• Garth Buchko, President and Chief
Executive Officer
• Jim Bell, Vice-President and Chief
Operating Officer
• Jerry Maslowsky, Vice President of
Marketing & Brand Developme
• Fin Paterson, Vice President and Director
of Sales
• Bill Watchorn, Chairperson - Board of
Directors
• Darren Cameron, Director of
Communications and Media Relation
• Jeffrey Bannon, Director of Marketing
Seating Capacity:
29,503
Playing Surface:
Artificial
Teams:
Winnipeg Blue Bombers

THOMAS ASSEMBLY CENTER
1650 W ALABAMA
PO BOX 3046
RUSTON, LA 71270
318-257-4111
Fax: 318-257-3757
vandevelde@latech.edu
www.latechsports.com
• Tommy Sisemore, Facilities Director
(318) 257-5323
sisemore@latech.edu
• Bruce Van De Velde, Athletics Director
(318) 257-3247
vendevelde@latech.edu
• Marie Gilbert, Associate A.D./Chief
Financial Officer
(318) 257-3637
mgilbert@latech.edu
• James Liberatos, Faculty Athletics
Representative
(318) 257-4287
jamesl@latech.edu
• Leah Beasley, Associate A.D./Marketing
and Game Management
(318) 257-5332
lbeasley@latech.edu
• Malcolm Butler, Associate A.D./Media
Relations
(318) 257-3145
mbutler@latech.edu
• Mary Kay Hungate, Deputy Athletics
Director - SWA
(318) 257-5654
usmkh@latech.edu
• Derek Dooley, Athletics Director
(318) 257-4547
Seating Capacity:
8,000

THOMAS J. DODD MEMORIAL STADIUM
14 STOTT AVENUE
NORWICH, CT 6360
860-887-7962
Fax: 860-886-5996
info@cttigers.com
www.cttigers.com
• Andrew Weber, General Manager
• Eric Knighton, Vice President & Assistant
General Manager
(860) 887-7962
• Eric Knighton, Assistant General Manager
• C J Knudsen, Vice President & General
Manager
(860) 887-7962
• Heather Bartlett, Director of Concessions
and Merchandise
(860) 887-7962
• Bryan Barkley, Director of Facilities and
Turf Management
(860) 887-7962
• Dave Schermerhorn, Director of
Community Relations and Promotion
(860) 887-7962
• Jon Versteeg, Director of Media Relations
(860) 887-7962
• Minna DeGaetano, Accounting Manager
Sport:
Minor League Baseball
Seating Capacity:
6,270
Year Founded:
1995

THOMPSON ARENA
6083 ALUMNI GYM
DARTHMOUTH ATHLETICS
HANOVER, NH 03755-3512
603-646-3074
Fax: 603-646-3348
sportspub@dartmouth.edu
www.dartmouth.edu
• Richard Whitmore, Operations/Facilities
Director
(603) 646-2673
• Randy Meck, Operations/Facilities
Assistant Director
(603) 646-9299
Seating Capacity:
3,500; 4,500 SR.

THOMPSON-BOLING ARENA
1600 PHILLIP FULMER WAY
SUITE 202
KNOXVILLE, TN 37996
865-974-0953
Fax: 865-974-2800
treese@utk.edu
www.tbarena.com
• Tim Reese, Manager
(865) 974-0953
treese@utk.edu
Arena Seating Capacity:
24,451

TICKETRETURN.COM FIELD
1251 21ST AVENUE NORTH
MYRTLE BEACH, SC 29577
843-918-6002
info@myrtlebeachpelicans.com
www.myrtlebeachpelicans.com
• Chuck Greenberg, Chairman and
Managing Partner
chuck@myrtlebeachpelicans.com
• Andy Milovich, President/General Manager
andy@myrtlebeachpelicans.com
• Mike Snow, Assistant General Manager,

Operations
msnow@myrtlebeachpelicans.com
• Corey Russell, Sports Turf Manager
crussell@myrtlebeachpelicans.com
Year Founded:
1999
Permanent Seating Capacity:
6,599
Team:
Myrtle Beach Pelicans

TIGER STADIUM
ATHLETIC ADMINISTRATION BUILDING
5TH FLOOR
PO BOX 25095
BATON ROUGE, LA 70803
225-578-8826
800-469-8781
Fax: 225-578-2430
webmaster@lsu.edu
www.lsu.edu
• Ronnie Haliburton, Associate Athletic
Director
(225) 578-4712
• Skip Bertman, Athletic Director
(225) 578-3600
• David D. Kurpius, Associate Vice
Chancellor for Enrollment Mana
• Norma Riles, Assistant to the Associate
Vice Chancellor fo
nriles@lsu.edu
• Amy Marix, Associate Director - Federal
Aid & Scholarshi
amarix@lsu.edu
• Amy Prejean, Associate Director -
Athletics, Customer Serv
apreje1@lsu.edu
• Christine Day, Associate Director -
Business Unit
ctday@lsu.edu
• Lupe Lamadrid, Associate Director -
Undergraduate Admissions
glamadrid@lsu.edu
• Melanie Thornton, Associate Director -
Technology
mverre2@lsu.edu
Seating Capacity:
92,400
Team:
Louisiana State University football.

TIMES UNION CENTER
51 S PEARL STREET
ALBANY, NY 12207
518-487-2000
Fax: 518-487-2020
www.timesunioncenter-albany.com
• Bob Belber, General Manager
Arena Seating Capacity:
17,000, AFL-13,652.
Tenant(s) :
AF2 - Albany Conquest football, AHL -
Albany River Rats hockey, NLL - Albany
Attack lacrosse.

TOLEDO MUD HENS
406 WASHINGTON STREET
TOLEDO, OH 43604
419-725-4367
Fax: 419-725-4368
webmaster@milb.com
www.milb.com
• Kirk Sausser, Manager Stadium
Operations
• Joe Napoli, President/General Manager
• Neil Neukam, Assistant G.M./Director of
Corporate Partners

• Erik Ibsen, Assistant G.M./Ticket Sales &
Operations
• Pam Alspach, Chief Financial Officer
• Kim McBroom, Chief Marketing Officer
Sport:
Baseball.
Tenant(s) :
Toledo Mud Hens baseball.
Year Founded:
2002
Capacity:
8,500

TOOMEY FIELD
ONE SHIELDS AVENUE
HICKEY GYM 264
DAVIS, CA 95616
530-752-1011
Fax: 530-752-6681
www.ucdavis.edu
• Greg Warzecka, Athletic Director
(530) 752-4557
gwarzecka@ucdavis.edu
• Bob Bullis, Associate Athletic Director
(530) 752-4806
rebullis@ucdavis.edu
• Russell Randall, Event Manager
• P.B Katehi, Chancellor
• Ralph Hexter, Executive Vice Chancellor
• JOhn Meyer, Vice Chancellor
• Shaun Keister, Vice Chancellor
• Claire Pomeroy, Vice Chancellor
• Harris Lewin, Vice Chancellor
Stadium Seating Capacity:
10,111

TOP OF THE THIRD
440 N GIDDINGS STREET
VISALIA, CA 93291
559-625-0480
Fax: 559-739-7732
oaksbaseball@hotmail.com
• Drietz Tom, Head Groundskeeper
• Jennifer Whiteley, General Manager
• John Drigotas, Group Sales Director
• Ira Liebman, Broadcasting & Media
Relations Director
Arena Seating Capacity:
1,612.00
Nature of Service:
Minor League Baseball.
Year Founded:
1998, Recreation Park 1946

TOYOTA CENTER
1510 POLK STREET
HOUSTON, TX 77002
713-758-7200
Fax: 713-758-7315
guestservices@rocketball.com
www.houstontoyotacenter.com
• Hall Doug, General Manager
• Tad Brown, Corporate Development VP
tadb@rocketball.com
Tenant(s) :
AHL - Houston Aeros hockey, NBA -
Houston Rocket basketball, WNBA -
Houston Comets basketball.
Permanent Seating Capacity:
18,500 basketball 17,800 hockey
Year Opened:
2003. Home arena for Houston Rockets.
Owned by:
Harris County-Houston Sports Authority.

TR HUGHES BALLPARK
900 TR HUGHES BOULEVARD
OZZIE SMITH SPORTS COMPLEX
O'FALLON, MO 63366
636-240-2287
Fax: 636-240-7313
www.rivercityrascals.com
• John Kuhn, President
• Lou Siville, Assistant General Manager,
VP of Corporate Sales
• Dan Dial, Executive Vice President &
General Manager
• Ashley Phillips, Sr. Account Executive
(636) 240-2287
• Courtney Oakley, Sr. Director of Ticket
Operations
(636) 240-228-
• Greg Talbott, Director of Broadcast/ Media
Relations
• Jody Sellers, Assistant General Manager/
Director of Corpor
(636) 240-228-
• Mo Stranz, Director of Food & Beverage
(636) 240-228-
• Sheri Livingston, Business Manager
(636) 240-228-
Sport:
Baseball.
Team:
River City Rascals.
Year Founded:
1999
Capacity:
4,989

TRADITION FIELD SPORTS COMPLEX
525 NW PEACOCK BOULEVARD
PORT ST LUCIE, FL 34986
772-871-2115
Fax: 772-785-6878
info@stluciemets.com
www.stluciemets.com
• Paul Taglieri, President & CEO
• Jack Brenner, Clubhouse Manager
• Benny Distefano, Hitting Coach
• Phil Regan, Pitching Coach
• Jose Carreno, Coach
• Ryan Ellis, Manager
Sport:
Baseball
Tenant(s) :
New York Mets Spring Training. St. Lucie
Mets baseball.
Capacity:
7,800
Year Founded:
1988

TRI-CITIES STADIUM
6200 BURDEN BOULEVARD
PASCO, WA 99301
509-544-8789
Fax: 509-547-9570
info@dustdevilsbaseball.com
www.dustdevilsbaseball.com
• Monica Ortega, Vice President/General
Manager
• Brent Miles, President
bmiles@dustdevilsbaseball.com
• Derrel Ebert, Vice President - General
Manager
debert@dustdevilsbaseball.com
• Tim Gittel, Vice President - Business
Operations
tgittel@dustdevilsbaseball.com
• Dan O'Neill, Assistant General Manager -
Tickets

doneill@dustdevilsbaseball.com
• Anne Brenner, Director of Sponsorships
abrenner@dustdevilsbaseball.com
• Andrew Klein, Group Sales Manager
aklein@dustdevilsbaseball.com
• Austin Redman, Ticket Operations
Manager
aredman@dustdevilsbaseball.com
Sport:
Baseball
Team:
Tri-City Dust Devils
Capacity:
3,750
Year Founded:
1995

**TRINITY MOTHER FRANCES ROSE
STADIUM**
609 FAIR PARK DRIVE
TYLER, TX 75701
903-262-1000
Fax: 903-262-1168
www.tylerisd.org
• Danny Long, Athletic Director
(903) 590-4084
• Sharon Roy, Executive Director of Human
Resources
• Nancy Swanson, Executive Director of
Curriculum & Instructio
• Kim Tunnell, Executive Director of
Strategic Planning & Co
• Dawn Parnell, Director of Communications
• Tosha Bjork, Chief Financial Officer
• Cecil McDaniel, Deputy Superintendent
• Darlene Marshall, Executive Director of
Elementary Education
(903) 262-3080
maryellen.reed@tylerisd.org
Stadium Seating Capacity:
11,500.00
Nature of Service:
Football Games, Track Meets.
Track Type:
All weather rubber composite.
Track Size:
7 Lanes.

TROPICANA FIELD
ONE TROPICANA DRIVE
SAINT PETERSBURG, FL 33705
727-825-3137
888-326-7297
Fax: 727-825-3300
www.devilrays.com
• David Auker, Business Operations SVP
• Brian Richeson, Vice President of Sales &
Service
• Rick Nafe, Operations/Facilities VP
• Rick Vaughn, Public Relations VP
Arena Seating Capacity:
42,500
Year Founded:
1995
Team:
Tampa Bay Rays MLB baseball.

TSONGAS CENTER
300 MARTIN LUTHER KING JR. WAY
LOWELL, MA 01852
978-934-5760
Fax: 978-934-5743
www.tsongascenter.com
Opened:
1996
Team:
UMass Lowell River Hawks

Seating Capacity:
6,496

TUCKER STADIUM
1151 STADIUM DRIVE
PO BOX 5057, TENNESSEE TECH
ATHLETICS
COOKEVILLE, TN 38505
931-372-3961
Fax: 931-372-3114
MailAdmin@tntech.edu
www.tntech.edu
• Frank Harrell, Interim Athletic Director
(931) 372-3939
fharrell@tntech.edu
• John Wheeler, Director
(931) 372-3945
bshannon@tntech.edu
• Randy Smith, Assistant Interim Athletic
Director/Faci
Stadium Seating Capacity:
16,500

TUCSON ELECTRIC PARK
2500 E AJO WAY
TUCSON, AZ 85713
520-546-5566
Fax: 520-434-1159
info@kinosportscomplex.com
www.kinosportscomplex.com
• Burke Matthew, Stadium Operations
Director
• David Whatton, Program Manager
(520) 243-6350
david.whatton@pima.gov
Sport:
Baseball.
Team(s) :
Chicago White Sox Spring Training; Arizona
Diamondbacks Spring Training; Tucson
Sidewinders baseball.
Year Founded:
1998
Capacity:
11,000

TULANE UNIVERSITY
6823 SAINT CHARLES AVENUE
NEW ORLEANS, LA 70118
504-865-5000
Fax: 504-862-8961
www.tulane.edu
• Rick Dickson, Executive Director
(504) 865-5569
• Scott S Cowen, President
(504) 865-5201
ssc@tulane.edu
Arena Seating Capacity:
3,600

TURNER FIELD
755 HANK AARON DRIVE SE
ATLANTA, GA 30315
404-522-7630
Fax: 404-614-1329
www.atlantabraves.com
• Larry Bowman, Senior Director Stadium
Operations & Security
• Mike Glisson, Stadium Operations
Manager
Seating Capacity:
50,000
Permanent Seating Capacity:
52,007
Tenants:
Home Stadium For: Atlanta Braves.

Notes:
Site of the 2000 MLB All-Star game.

TURPIN STADIUM
NSU ATHLETIC FIELDHOUSE
220 S JEFFERSON
NATCHITOCHES, LA 71497
318-357-5251
Fax: 318-357-4221
athleticsinfo@nsula.edu
www.nsudemons.com
• Mike Doty, Director of Facilities
(318) 357-6898
dotym@nsula.edu
• Chance Creppel, Asst. Director of
Facilities
(318) 357-4265
creppelc@nsula.edu
• Greg Burke, Director of Athletics
(318) 357-5251
burkeg@nsula.edu
• Haley Taitano, Assoc. AD, External
Relations & Sr. Women's Adv.
(318) 357-4278
blounth@nsula.edu
• Doug Ireland, Asst. AD, Media Relations
(318) 357-6467
ireland@nsula.edu
• Mike Jaworski, Director of Development
and Engagement
(318) 357-4295
jaworskim@nsula.edu
Stadium Seating Capacity:
15,971
Description:
The football stadium for Northwestern State
University. Two local high schools also use
the field for their home football games.
Teams:
Northwestern State Demons Football; High
Schools: Natchitoches Central High School
and St. Mary's High School

TUSKEGEE UNIVERSITY
1200 W. MONTGOMERY ROAD
TUSKEGEE, AL 36088
334-727-8500
800- 622- 6531
Fax: 334-727-5750
www.tuskegee.edu
• Dr. Benjamin F. Payton, President
(334) 727-8501
• Shamima Amin, Chief of Staff
(334) 727-8503
• Luther S. Williams, President
(334) -727-802
• Cecil Lucy, Vice President for Finance
(334) 724-4733
• Gilbert S L. Rochon, President's Office
(334) 727-8501
Seating Capacity
3,000

U.S. CELLULAR CENTER
87 HAYWOOD STREET
ASHEVILLE, NC 28801
828-259-5736
Fax: 828-259-5777
ccorl@ashevillenc.gov
www.uscellularcenterasheville.com
• Chris Corl, General Manager
(828) 259-5452
ccorl@ashevillenc.gov
• Dan Dover, Operations Manager
(828) 259-5741
ddover@ashevillenc.gov
• Cassandra Marcelo, Marketing and Box

Office Coordinator
(828) 259-5739
Seating Capacity:
7,200

UAA SPORTS ARENA
3211 PROVIDENCE DRIVE
UNIVERSITY OF ALASKA-ANCHORAGE
ANCHORAGE, AK 99508
907-786-1250
Fax: 907-786-1142
goseawolves@uaa.alaska.edu
www.goseawolves.com
• Steve Cobb, Athletic Director
(907) 786-1225
ansrc@uaa.alaska.edu
• Nate Sagan, Sports Information Director
(907) 786-1295
• Tim McDiffett, Associate Athletic Director
(907) 786-1307
tim@uaa.alaska.edu
• Steve Cobb, Director of Athletics
(907) 786-1225
srcobb@uaa.alaska.edu
• Dede Allen, Assoc. Athletic Director
(Compliance & Academ
(907) 786-4803
dmallen@uaa.alaska.edu
• Jane Pallister, Assoc. Athletic Director
(Internal Affairs)
(907) 786-1225
jane@uaa.alaska.edu
• Kevin Silver, Assoc. Athletic Director
(WFSC)
(907) 786-4809
kevin.silver@uaa.alaska.edu
• Tlisa Northcutt, Director of Development
(907) 786-1211
tanorthcutt@uaa.alaska.edu
• Margot Ferguson, Marketing Specialist
(907) 786-1307
margot@uaa.alaska.edu
Arena Seating Capacity:
1,500

UAB ARENA
617 13TH STREET S, BRTW 134
BRTW 134
BIRMINGHAM, AL 35294-1160
205-934-7296
Fax: 205-975-8015
BartowArena@uab.edu
www.uab.edu
• Steve Mitchell, Director
(205) 934-7748
Arena Seating Capacity:
8,460
Year Founded:
1987
Nature of Service:
This facility accommodates most of the UAB
athletic teams and is used as the official site
to see Blazer Basketball and Lady Blazer
Basketball and Volleyball. Bartow Arena
seats 8,460 for basketball and there are
other configurations ranging from 1,200 s

UD ARENA
1801 EDWIN C. MOSES BOULEVARD
DAYTON, OH 45408
937-229-1000
Fax: 937-229-4461
info@udayton.edu
udayton.edu
Arena Seating Capacity:
14,000
Nature of Service:

Full service multi-purpose sports and
entertainment facility.
Tenants:
University of Dayton Flyers (NCAA).

UNI-DOME
1227 WEST 27TH ST.
CEDAR FALLS, IA 50614
319-273-2311
877-216-3663
Fax: 319-273-5966
UNIDOME@uni.edu
www.vpaf.uni.edu
• Andre Seoldo, Assistant Athletic Director
(319) 273-6636
andre.seoldo@uni.edu
• Dave Kohrs, Assistant Director for
Facilities
(319) 273-2865
david.kohrs@uni.edu
• Michael Hager, Vice President for
Administration & Financial
(319) 273-2382
michael.hager@uni.edu
• Jan Hanish, Assistant Vice President for
Administration &
(319) 273-3526
jan.hanish@uni.edu
• Jennifer Hansmann, Administrative
Assistant to Vice President
(319) 273-2382
jenny.hansmann@uni.edu
• Brenda Neff, Account Specialist
(319) 273-2383
brenda.neff@uni.edu
• Bruce Rieks, Budget System
Development/Reporting Director
(319) 273-7498
bruce.rieks@uni.edu
Arena Seating Capacity:
24,196
Stadium Seating Capacity:
16,300

UNITED CENTER
1901 W MADISON STREET
CHICAGO, IL 60612
312-455-4500
Fax: 312-455-4511
webmaster@unitedcenter.com
www.unitedcenter.com
• Jim Koehler, General Manager
(312) 455-4501
• Steve Schanwald, Senior Vice President of
Operations
(312) 455-4110
• Terry Savarise, Operations Senior VP
• Terry Savarise, Sr. VP of Operations
• Jim Koehler, General Manger
• Steve Schulze, Chief Information Officer
• Greg Hanrahan, Sr.Director of Premium
Seating
• Jim Bare, Sr.Director Box Office
• Troy Brown, Sr.Director Youth Service
• Valerie Toth, Seating Manger
Owned by:
United Center Joint Venture.
Tenant(s) :
NBA - Chicago Bulls basketball; NHL -
Chicago Blackhawks hockey.
Permanent Seating Capacity:
20,500 (ice hockey); 22,500 (basketball).

UNIVERSITY ARENA
1414 UNIVERSITY BOULEVARD SE
COLLEEN J MALOOF ADMINISTRATION

BUILDING
ALBUQUERQUE, NM 87106
505-925-5500
Fax: 505-925-5955
www.golobos.com
• Scott Dotson, Associate Athletic Director
Facilities
(505) 925-5925
• Jimmy Martinez, Assistant Director
(985) 925-5954
jdmartin@unm.edu
• Jeff Salmond, Head Sports Turf Manager
Arena Seating Capacity:
18,018

UNIVERSITY CENTER
800 GALLOWAY DRIVE
SLU 10309
HAMMOND, LA 70402
985-549-5091
Fax: 985-549-2504
sportsinfo@selu.edu
www.lionsports.net
• Joel Erdmann, Athletic Director
(985) 549-2359
• Bart M Bellairs, Athletics Director
(985) 549-2395
athletics@southeastern.edu
• Linda Alford, Administrative Coordinator
(985) 549-5599
lalford@southeastern.edu
• Andrew Bechac, Senior associate
(985) 549-3419
Andrew.Bechac@southeastern.edu
• Tim Baldwin, Head Golf Coach/Assistant
AD for Special Even
(985) 549-5186
tbaldwin@southeastern.edu
Arena Seating Capacity:
7,500

UNIVERSITY HALL
295 MASSIE RD.
PO BOX 400862
CHARLOTTESVILLE, VA 22903
434-22904-4862
888-575-8497
Fax: 434-243-4959
Linda@rmcevents.com
www.johnpauljonesarena.com
• Liz Flynn, Director of Marketing
(434) 243-4957
• Scott Cornwell, Director Of Operations
(434) 243-2077
Arena Seating Capacity:
8,450

UNIVERSITY OF CHARLESTON
2300 MACCORKLE AVENUE SE
CHARLESTON, WV 25304
304-357-4800
800-995-4682
Fax: 304-357-4781
admissions@ucwv.edu
www.ucwv.edu
• Edwin H Welch, Dr, President
• Dr. Edwin H. Welch, President
(304) 357-4713
edwinwelch@ucwv.edu
Stadium Seating Capacity:
22,000

**UNIVERSITY OF HARTFORD SPORTS
CENTER**
200 BLOOMFIELD AVENUE
W HARTFORD, CT 6117

860-768-5050
Fax: 860-768-4229
www.hartford.edu/athletics/SPORTSCTR//hours.html
• Ted Stavropoulos, Sports Center Director
tstavropo@hartford.edu
• Kelli Cullen, Assistant Facility Director
kcullen@hartford.edu
• Chris Wilk, Assistant Facility Director/Events
• Shaun Krafthofer, Assistant Facility Director/Evening Superviso
krafthofe@hartford.edu
Arena Seating Capacity:
3,545

UNIVERSITY OF KANSAS
1651 NAISMITH DRIVE
SLU 10309
LAWRENCE, KS 66045
785-864-3143
Fax: 785-864-5035
KUAthletics@KU.edu
www.kuathletics.com
• Lew Perkins, Athletic Director
(785) 864-3143
• Debbie Van Saun, Associate Athletic Director/Senior Woman
(785) 864-7903
dvansaun@ku.edu
• John Hadl, Associate Athletic Director/Development
• Chris Howard, Associate Athletics Director
(785) 864-7993
choward1@ku.edu
• Paul Buskirk, Associate Athletics Director - Student Athlet
(785) 864-7960
• Glenn Quick, Associate Athletics Director - Academic and C
(785) 864-7961
• Scott Ward, Ph.D., Associate Athletics Director - Academic and C
(785) 864-7696
• Shanda Hayden, Associate Director, Academic and Career Couns
(785) 864-7695
• Laura Jacobsen, Associate Director, Academic and Career Couns
(785) 864-4035
• Katie Martincich, Associate Director, Academic and Career Couns
(785) 864-7795
Seating Capacity:
50,000

UNIVERSITY OF NORTH TEXAS-COLISEUM
1155 Union Circle
310857
DENTON, TX 76203
940-565-2557
Fax: 940-565-3671
coliseum@unt.edu
• Rick Villarreal, Athletic Director
(940) 565-3646
rick.villarreal@unt.edu
• Steven Bartolotta, Assistant Sports Information Director
(940) 369-8329
• Bill Michael, Football Coach
• Jessica Hulsebosch,, Director of Mean Green Club
(940) 369-8916
• Dan Johnston, Associate Athletic Director, Development
(940) 369-7034
• Andy Williams, Assistant Athletic Director -

Business Operat
(940) 565-4067
• Jamie Adams, Assistant Athletic Director, Marketing & Prom
(940) 369-7169
• Mike Ashbaugh, Senior Associate Athletic Director, Business
(940) 565-2068
• Chaunte Baldwin, Assistant Athletic Director, Student Services
(940) 891-6834
Arena Seating Capacity:
10,000

UNIVERSITY OF PHOENIX STADIUM
1 CARDINALS DRIVE
GLENDALE, AZ 85305
623-433-7102
Fax: 623-433-7199
www.universityofphoenixstadium.com
Seating Capacity:
63,400
Teams:
Arizona Cardinals NFL football.

UNIVERSITY OF PORTLAND
5000 N WILLAMETTE BOULEVARD
CHILES CENTER, THE
PORTLAND, OR 97203-5798
503-943-8000
Fax: 503-943-8082
www.up.edu
• Julie Lapomarda, Sports Information Director
Seating Capacity:
5,000

UNIVERSITY OF WYOMING ARENA-AUDITORIUM
1000 E UNIVERSITY AVENUE
UNIVERSITY OF WYOMING
DEPARTMENT 3414
LARAMIE, WY 82071
307-766-2292
Fax: 307-766-5414
wyosid@uwyo.edu
www.gowyo.com
• Tom Burman, Athletic Director
(307) 766-2292
• Kevin McKinney, Senior Associate AD, External Affairs
(307) 766-2444
kevinm@uwyo.edu
• Tom Burman, Director of Athletics
(307) 766-2292
• Matt Whisenant, Deputy Director of Athletics
(307) 766-5551
mwhise@uwyo.edu
• Molly Moore, Sr. Assoc. AD, Internal Operations/SWA
(307) 766-4092
mmoore30@uwyo.edu
• Phil Wille, Assoc. AD, Academic Services
(307) 766-2391
pwille@uwyo.edu
• Sara Ray, Assoc. AD, Academic Services
(307) 766-2391
sray3@uwyo.edu
• Bill Sparks, Sr. Assoc. AD, Business Operations
(307) 766-5771
bsparks@uwyo.edu
Arena Seating Capacity:
15,028

UNIVERSITY STADIUM
1414 UNIVERSITY BOULEVARD SE
COLLEEN J MALOOF ADMINISTRATION BUILDING
MSC04 2680
ALBUQUERQUE, NM 87131-0001
505-925-5500
Fax: 505-925-5955
www.golobos.com
• Tim Cass, Senior Associate Athletic Director
(505) 925-5508
tcass@unm.edu
• Greg Remington, Associate AD/Media Relations
(505) 925-5925
gregrem@unm.edu
• Rocky Long, Football Coach
• Fran Fraschilla, Men's Basketball Coach
Stadium Seating Capacity:
30,000

UNK SPORTS CENTER
HEALTH AND SPORTS CENTER 102
UNIVERSITY OF NEBRASKA AT KEARNEY
KEARNEY, NE 68849
308-865-8514
Fax: 308-865-8832
www.lopers.com
• Jon McBride, Athletic Director
(308) 865-8332
mcbridejl@unk.edu
• Amy Perko, Associate AD Director
(308) 865-8863
lundgrenjl@unk.edu
Arena Seating Capacity:
5,842

UNLV TICKETS
4505 S MARYLAND PARKWAY
BOX 450003
LAS VEGAS, NV 89154-0003
702-895-3761
866-388-3267
Fax: 702-895-1099
customer.service@unlvtickets.com
www.unlvtickets.com
• Daren Libonati, Arena Director
(702) 895-3761
• Joe Carter, Food & Beverage Director
(702) 895-4172
joe.carter@thomasandmack.com
• Dale Eeles, Corporate Relations Director
• Elizabeth Swallia, Director of UNLVtickets Operations
• Chuck Soberinsky, Director of Ticketing for Thomas & Mack Cente
(702) 895-3905
• Susan Schwartz, Director of Athletic Ticketing
(702) 895-3679
Arena Seating Capacity:
18,500
Owned by:
University of Nevada, Las Vegas.
Boxing Capacity:
19,522
Tenant(s):
AFL - Las Vegas Gladiators football, NCAA - UNLV basketball.

UNM ARENA
1 UNIVERSITY OF NEW MEXICO
COLLEEN J MALOOF ADMINISTRATION BUILDING

MSC04 2680
ALBUQUERQUE, NM 87131-0001
505-925-5500
Fax: 505-925-5955
rita@unm.edu
www.golobos.com
• Tim Cass, Senior Associate Athletic
Director
(505) 925-5508
tcass@unm.edu
• Greg Remington, Associate AD/Media
Relations
(505) 925-5925
gregrem@unm.edu
• Mark Koson, Stadium Manager
• Paul Krebs, Vice-President, Athletics
(505) 925-5510
rita@unm.edu
• Tim Cass, Deputy Athletic Director
(505) 925-5508
tcass@unm.edu
• Janice Ruggiero, Senior Associate
AD/Administration & Senior W
(505) 277-5067
ruggiero@unm.edu
• Kurt Esser, Senior Associate AD/External
(505) 925-5544
kesser@unm.edu
• Henry Villegas, Associate AD/Student
Development
(505) 277-6538
hvillega@unm.edu
• Brad Hutchins, Associate AD/Marketing &
Revenue Generation
(505) 925-5606
hutchins@unm.edu
• Lee De Leon, Associate AD/Development
(505) 925-5919
Stadium Seating Capacity:
30,000

US AIRWAYS CENTER
201 E JEFFERSON STREET
PO BOX 433
ST. PHOENIX, AZ 85004
602-379-7878
800-800-9494
Fax: 602-379-2002
webmaster@phxses.com
• Colangelo Jerry, Chairman/Chief
Executive Officer
• Bob Machen, President
• Paige Peterson, General Manager
• Alvan Adams, VP Facility Manager
Owned by:
City of Phoenix
Home Arena for:
Phoenix Suns, Phoenix Coyotes, Arizona
Rattlers, Phoenix Mercury
Seating Capacity:
Basketball: 19,023; Football: 16,285

US BANK ARENA
100 BROADWAY
CINCINNATI, OH 45202
513-421-4111
Fax: 513-333-3040
info@usbankarena.com
www.usbankarena.com
• Chuck Kemp, General Manager
• Bill Barrett, Director Marketing/Booking
• Matt Dunne, Building Manager
Arena Seating Capacity:
17,000

US CELLULAR ARENA
400 W KILBOURN AVENUE
MILWAUKEE, WI 53203
414-908-6000
800-745-3000
Fax: 414-908-6010
boxoffice@wcd.org
• Richard A Geyer, President/CEO
(414) 908-6050
rgeyer@wcd.org
• David Schneider, Sales Manager
(414) 908-6098
dschneider@wcd.org
• Jason Borders, Event Services Director
(414) 908-6079
jborders@wcd.org
• Donna Hrobsky, Box Office Manager
(414) 908-6035
dhrobsky@wcd.org
• Allan Ray, Technical
(613) 966-2972
Seating Capacity:
Maximum-12,418; Basketball-11,119;
Hockey-9,652; Indoor
Soccer/Football-9,600;
Boxing/Wrestling-12,146; Open Floor
(indoor motorsports, rodeo etc) -8,910.
Tenants:
Milwaukee Wave (Major Indoor Soccer
League); University of Wisconsin-Milwaukee
Panthers Men's Basketball team (NCAA
Division I, Horizon League conference).
Events:
Disney on Ice; Tripoli Shrine Circus;
Universal Cheerleaders competitions

US CELLULAR CENTER
370 1ST AVENUE NE
CEDAR RAPIDS, IA 52401-1197
319-398-5211
Fax: 319-362-2102
info@uscellularcenter.com
www.uscellularcenter.com
• Schoenike Scott, Executive Director
d.herting@uscellularcenter.com
• Terry Dederich, Assistant Executive
Director
• Thomas Fesenmeyer, Director Operations
• Gene Felling, Executive Director
(319) 398-5211
g.felling@uscellularcenter.com
• Taya Roos, Director of Finance
(319) 398-5211
t.roos@uscellularcenter.com
• Scott Piquard, Director of Event
Operations
(319) 398-5211
s.piquard@uscellularcenter.com
• Sarah Mandalinski, Marketing Director
(319) 398-5211
s.madalinski@uscellularcenter.com
• Deena Rupalo, Ticket Office Manager
(319) -398-521
d.rupalo@uscellularcenter.com
• Jason Lester, Event Manager
(319) 398-5211
j.lester@uscellularcenter.com
Seating Capacity:
10,000

US CELLULAR FIELD
333 WEST 35TH ST
CHICAGO, IL 60616
312-674-1000
Fax: 312-674-5103
chicago.whitesox.mlb.com
Seating Capacity:
41,000

Teams:
Chicago White Sox MLB baseball.

USA HOCKEY ARENA
14900 BECK ROAD
PLYMOUTH, MI 48170
734-453-6400
www.usahockeyarena.com
• Scott Monaghan, Sr. Director, Operations
scottm@usahockey.org
• Denise Ronayne, Director of Sales &
Marketing
denise.ronayne@usahockeyarena.org
Seating Capacity:
3,504; 4,500 for concerts.

USF SOCCER STADIUM
4202 EAST FOWLER AVENUE
ATH 100
TAMPA, FL 33620
813-974-2125
Fax: 813-974-4028
www.gousfbulls.com
• Mark Harlan, Director of Athletics
(813) 974-1442
markharlan@usf.edu
• Barry Clements, Deputy Director of
Athletics
(813) 974-4144
clements@usf.edu
• Jocelyn Fisher, Senior Associate Director
of Athletics
(813) 974-6885
jafisher1@usf.edu
• Marquita Armstead, Associate Director of
Athletics/Compliance
(813) 974-4061
marmstead@usf.edu
• Scott Glaser, Senior Associate Director of
Athletics/Facilities
(813) 974-3110
sglaser@usf.edu
• Dan Krone, Director of Facilities
(813) 974-8935
dkrone@usf.edu
Permanent Seating Capacity:
3,000

USF SUN DOME
4202 EAST FOWLER AVENUE
SUN 130
TAMPA, FL 33620
813-974-3111
Fax: 813-905-9813
sundomearena@usf.edu
www.sundomearena.com
• Trent Merritt, General Manager
tmerritt1@usf.edu
• Jack Ligon, Assistant General
Manager/Director of Operations
jligon@usf.edu
• Allison Dobin, Director of Marketing
dobin@usf.edu
• Nicole Williams, Director of Finance
nicolew@usf.edu
• Tom Bradley, Box Office Manager
tbradley2@usf.edu
• Dennis Perez, Senior Operations Manager
dennisperez@usf.edu
• Michele Harhut, Senior Event Manager
mharhut@usf.edu
• Tyler Hine, Operations Manager
tylerhine@usf.edu
• Eric McDade, Event Manager
mcdade@usf.edu
• Wayne Letson, Facility Engineer
wletson@usf.edu

• Whitney Henry, Marketing & Sales
Coordinator
 whitneyhenry@usf.edu
Permanent Seating Capacity:
10,411
Year Founded:
1980
Tenants:
USF Athletics.

**USTA BILLIE JEAN KING NATIONAL
TENNIS CENTER**
FLUSHING MEADOW-CORONA PARK
FLUSHING, NY 11368
718-760-6200
Fax: 718-592-9488
www.usta.com
Description:
The largest public tennis facility in the world
and home to the US Open. Twenty outdoor
and twelve indoor courts.

UTC MCKENZIE ARENA
720 EAST 4TH STREET
DEPT 3403
615 MCCALLIE AVENUE
CHATTANOOGA, TN 37403
423-425-4706
Fax: 423-425-4783
mckenziefan@utc.edu
www.utc.edu/mckenzie-arena
• Obie Webster, Executive Director,
Entertainment & Sports Venues
(423) 425-4706
obie-webster@utc.edu
• Kyle Askew, Technical Director
(423) 425-4746
• Arland Jenkins, Operations Coordinator
(423) 425-4648
• Sandra Farris, Event
Coordinator/Accounting
(423) 425-4030
• Brent McMillan, Box Office Supervisor
(423) 425-5273
Arena Seating Capacity:
11,557
Year Founded:
1982
Nature of Service:
Multi-purpose arena.
Tenant(s) :
University of Tennessee at Chattanooga,
men's & women's basketball.

UTEP SPECIAL EVENTS
151 GLORY ROAD
EL PASO, TX 79908
915-747-5481
Fax: 915-747-7469
events@utep.edu
www.utepspecialevents.com
• Jorge Vazquez, Executive Director
vazquezj@utep.edu
• Mike Spence, Director of Special Facilities
Management
mspence@utep.edu
• Ricky Nichols, Assistant Director
rlnichols@utep.edu
• Julian E. Valdes, Marketing Manager
jevaldes@utep.edu
• Christina Garay, Building Supervisor
cvgaray@utep.edu
Arena Seating Capacity:
12,000
Clients:
AEG, Stardate, Stone City Attractions.

Nature of Service:
University venues

VA MEMORIAL STADIUM
17273 STREET ROUTE 104
CHILLICOTHE, OH 45601
740-773-7117
Fax: 740-773-8338
www.chillicothepaints.com
• Chris Hanners, Owner
• Shirley Bandy, President
• John Wend, Director of Sales &
Marketing/PA Announcer
• Maleine Davis, Director of Finance
• Brian Mannino, Director of Baseball
Operations
• Greg Cypret, Manager
• Jim Miner, Stadium Operations/Clubhouse
Manager
• Toni Diehl, Stadium Supervisor
Capacity:
3,000

VALLEY VIEW CASINO CENTER
3500 SPORTS ARENA BOULEVARD
SAN DIEGO, CA 92110-4919
619-224-4171
Fax: 619-224-3010
info@valleyviewcasinocenter.com
www.valleyviewcasinocenter.com
• Ernie Hahn, General Manager
Seating Capacity:
15,000

**VALUE CITY ARENA/JEROME
SCHOTTENSTEIN CENTER**
555 BORROR DRIVE
COLUMBUS, OH 43210
614-292-3231
800-273-6201
Fax: 614-292-5067
osuarena@osu.edu
www.schottensteincenter.com
• Michael Gatto, Director
(614) 688-5579
• Bredan Buckley, Booking & Scheduling
Director
(614) 688-8400
• Tracy Hedrick, Promotions Director
(614) 247-0008
• Tim Flipovich, Arena Supervisor
(614) 688-5411
• Sarah Reissig, Arena Supervisor
(614) 688-5411
Seating Capacity:
17,500-20,000.

VAN ANDEL ARENA
130 WEST FULTON
GRAND RAPIDS, MI 49503-2601
616-742-6600
Fax: 616-742-6197
webmaster@smggr.com
www.vanandelarena.com
• Richard MacKeigan, General Manager
• Jim Watt, Assistant General Manager
• Lynne Ike, Director of Marketing
(616) 742-6198
• Hilarie Szarowicz, Marketing Manager
hszarowicz@smggr.com
• Kevin Abbott, Operations Manager
• Marcus Scott, Box Office Manager
Year Founded:
1996
Seating Capacity:
12,000.
Nature of Service:

Sports Arena for Arenacross, Basketball,
Football, Wrestling and other events.
Clients Include:
Grand Rapids Griffins - AHL, Harlem
Globetrotters, WWE, Arenacross, Thunder
Nationals, Freestyle.
Tenant(s):
Grand Rapids Griffins - AHL.

VANDERBILT STADIUM
2601 JESS NEELY DRIVE
NASHVILLE, TN 37212
615-322-4653
Fax: 615-343-7064
www.vucommodores.com
• David Williams II, Athletics Director
(615) 343-1107
• Brock Williams, Assistant Vice Chancellor,
Facilities & Game Ops
(615) 343-4411
brock.williams@vanderbilt.edu
• Ed Higgins, Director, Facilities & Game
Operations
(615) 343-2012
ed.higgins@vanderbilt.edu
• Eric Chaffin, Associate Director, Game
Operations & Facilities
(615) 322-1793
eric.chaffin@vanderbilt.edu
Stadium Seating Capacity:
40,550
Team:
Vanderbilt college football.

**VAUGHT-HEMINGWAY
STADIUM/HOLLINGSWORTH FIELD**
908 ALL-AMERICAN DRIVE
PO BOX 1848
UNIVERSITY, MS 38677
662-915-7241
Fax: 662-915-7683
www.olemisssports.com
• Ross Bjork, Director of Athletics
(662) 915-7546
• Joe Swingle, Associate Director, Facilities
& Game Operations
(662) 915-7508
jswingle@olemiss.edu
• Kerry Page, Associate Director, Facilities
& Sports Turf
• Durrell Buford, Associate Superintendent,
Athletics Grounds
Stadium Seating Capacity:
60,580

VERIZON CENTER
601 F STREET NORTHWEST
WASHINGTON, DC 20004
202-628-3200
www.verizoncenter.com
• Ted Leonis, Founder/Chairman/Majoriy
Owner/CEO
• Dick Patrick, Vice Chairman/Chief
Operating Officer
• Raul Fernandez, Vice Chairman
• Sheila Johnson, Vice Chairman
Tenant(s):
NHL - Washington Capitals hockey, NBA -
Washington Wizards basketball.
Owned by:
Monumental Sports & Entertainment
Seating Capacity:
20,000

VERIZON WIRELESS CENTER
ONE CIVIC CENTER PLAZA
MANKATO, MN 56001

1015

507-389-3000
Fax: 507-345-1627
verizonwirelesscentermn.com
• Burt Lyman, Executive Director
(507) 389-3000
• JoAnn Hoffmann, Ticket Office Specialist
(507) 387-8456
• Steve Conover, Operations Manager
(507) 387-8440
Seating Capacity:
5,280

VERMONT LAKE MONSTERS
1 KING STREET FERRY DOCK
BURLINGTON, VT 05401
802-655-4200
Fax: 802-655-5660
info@vermontlakemonsters.com
www.vermontlakemonsters.com
• Raymond C. Pecor Jr., President
• Kyle Bostwick, Vice President
• Nate Cloutier, General Manager
nate@vermontlakemonsters.com
• Joe Doud, Asst. General Manager
nate@vermontlakemonsters.com
Sport:
Minor League Baseball.
Team:
Vermont Expos baseball
Year Founded:
1922
Capacity:
4,000

VERNON KENNEDY FIELD/WALTON STADIUM
203 MULTIPURPOSE BUILDING
500 SOUTH WASHINGTON STREET
WARRENSBURG, MO 64093
660-543-4250
877-729-8266
Fax: 660-543-8034
www.ucmathletics.com
• Jerry Hughes, Athletics Director
hughes@ucmo.edu
• Kathy Anderson, Senior Associate Athletic Director
(660) 543-4310
klanderson@ucmo.edu
• Scott Thomason, Assistant Athletic Director, Facilities
(660) 543-4011
sthomason@ucmo.edu
Stadium Seating Capacity:
12,000

VETERANS MEMORIAL COLISEUM
300 NORTH WINNING WAY
PORTLAND, OR 97227
503-235-8771

VETERANS MEMORIAL COLISEUM (IN)
300 COURT STREET
EVANSVILLE, IN 47708
812-424-5879
Coliseum Seating Capacity:
4,055

VETERANS MEMORIAL STADIUM
2531 NORTH STATE STREET
JACKSON, MS 39216
601-354-6021
Fax: 601-354-6019
www.ms-veteransstadium.com
• Thomas Cooper, Interim Stadium Manager

Stadium Seating Capacity:
60,492

VETERANS MEMORIAL STADIUM (CEDAR RAPIDS)
950 ROCKFORD ROAD SOUTHWEST
CEDAR RAPIDS, IA 52404
319-363-3887
Fax: 319-363-5631
www.kernels.com
• Doug Nelson, Chief Executive Officer
(319) 896-7614
• Scott Wilson, General Manager
(319) 896-7612
• Andrea Brommelkamp, Director of Tickets & Group Sales
(319) 896-7603
• Jesse Roeder, Sports Turf Manager
(319) 896-7637
• Sammy Brzostowski, Ticket Office Manager
(319) 896-7622
Stadium Seating Capacity:
5,300
Year Founded:
2002
Tenant(s) :
Cedar Rapids Kernels.

VICTORY FIELD
501 WEST MARYLAND STREET
INDIANAPOLIS, IN 46225
317-269-3545
Fax: 317-269-3541
www.indyindians.com
• Max B. Schumacher, Chairman/President
(317) 269-3548
• Cal Burleson, Vice President, Baseball & Administrative Affairs
• Randy Lewandowski, General Manager
• Joel Zawacki, Director of Corporate Sales & Marketing
(317) 532-6935
• Tim Hughes, Director of Facilities
(317) 532-6779
• Matt Guay, Director of Tickets & Operations
(317) 532-6784
Sport:
Baseball
Team:
Indianapolis Indians
Year Founded:
1996
Capacity:
14,230

VIKING HALL CIVIC CENTER
1100 EDGEMONT AVENUE
PO BOX 3563
BRISTOL, TN 37620
423-764-4171
423-764-0188
Fax: 423-764-3299
• Darlene Cole, Venue Manager
• Terrie Talbert, Department Manager
• Sarah Rhymer, Box Office Manager
• Eddie Abbott, Operations Manager
• Lisa Beckner, Office Manager
• Terrie Talbert, Department Manager
• Tommy Baker, City Web Master
• Angie Rutherford, Box office Manager
Arena Seating Capacity:
6,200

VINES CENTER
1971 UNIVERSITY BOULEVARD
LYNCHBURG, VA 24515
434-582-2000
866-447-2084
Fax: 434-582-2205
www.liberty.edu
• Jeff Barber, Director of Athletics
jbarber2@liberty.edu
• Mickey Guridy, Senior Associate AD, Internal Operations
maguridy@liberty.edu
• Tim East, Senior Associate AD, External Operations
• Dan Maxam, Assistant Athletics Director, Facilities
• Anna Hutchinson, Assistant Athletics Director, Ticket Operations
Capacity:
8,085

VIRGINIA BEACH SPORTSPLEX
2044 LANDSTOWN CENTRE WAY
VIRGINIA BEACH, VA 23456
757-427-2990
Fax: 757-430-8895
chuck@beachsportsplex.com
www.thevirginiabeachsportsplex.com
• Nick Senti, Contact
Built:
1999
Operated by:
Hometown Sports Management
Seating Capacity:
10,000
Nature of Service:
Color Me Rad, USA Field Hockey, Division 3 College Lacrosse, High School Football, Soccer, Field Lacrosse and Rugby

VIVINT SMART HOME ARENA
301 WEST SOUTH TEMPLE
SALT LAKE CITY, UT 84101
801-325-2000
Fax: 801-325-2516
comments@vivintarena.com
www.vivintarena.com
Permanent Seating Capacity:
20,000
Tenant(s) :
Utah Jazz (NBA)

VOLCANOES STADIUM
6700 FIELD OF DREAMS WAY
NORTHEAST
KEIZER, OR 97303
503-390-2225
Fax: 503-390-2227
info@volcanoesbaseball.com
www.volcanoesbaseball.com
• Jerry Walker, Co-Owner/General Manager
(503) 390-2225
jwalker@volcanoesbaseball.com
• Rick Nelson, Stadium Operations
(503) 390-2225
rnelson@volcanoesbaseball.com
• Jerry Howard, Senior Account Executive
• Bea Howard, Ticket Office
Stadium Seating Capacity:
4,254
Year Founded:
1997
Nature of Service:
Sports facility.
Tenant(s) :
Salem-Keizer Volcanoes, Single A Affiliate of the San Francisco Giants.

VON BRAUN CENTER
700 MONROE STREET
HUNTSVILLE, AL 35801
256-533-1953
Fax: 256-551-2203
vbcinfo@vonbrauncenter.com
www.vonbrauncenter.com
• Steve Maples, Executive Director
stevemaples@vonbrauncenter.com
• Mike Vojticek, Assistant Director
vojticek@vonbrauncenter.com
• Ron Grimes, Director of Operations
rgrimes@vonbrauncenter.com
• Marie Arighi, Director of Sales & Marketing
marighi@vonbrauncenter.com
• Johnny Hunkapiller, Director of Special
Projects
jhunkapiller@vonbrauncenter.com
• Shawn McCown, Director of Finance
smccown@vonbrauncenter.com
• Bruce Mitchell, Director of Food &
Beverage
bmitchell@vonbrauncenter.com
• Byron Clanton, Director of Facilities
bclanton@vonbrauncenter.com
Capacity:
10,000

WAGNER FIELD/KSU
1800 COLLEGE AVENUE
BRAMLAGE COLISEUM
MANHATTAN, KS 66502
785-532-5876
800-221-1187
Fax: 785-532-2004
sportsinfo@k-state.edu
www.kstatesports.com
• Bob Krause, Athletics Director
(785) 532-6912
vpia@ksu.edu
• John Currie, Director of Athletics
(785) 532-6912
• Reid Sigmon, Senior Associate AD/Chief
Operating Officer
(785) 532-6913
• Vicki Jones, Executive Assistant to Athletic
Director
(785) 532-6912
• Jana Buehler, Academic Learning
Specialist
• Jim Muller, Associate Director
jamesbm@ksu.edu
Stadium Seating Capacity:
50,000

WAKE FOREST BASEBALL PARK
401 DEACON BOULEVARD
WINSTON-SALEM, NC 27115
336-758-4620
Fax: 336-759-2042
www.wakeforestsports.com
• Ron Wellman, Director of Athletics
(336) 758-5753
• Steve Adams, Associate AD, Internal
Operations
(336) 758-4908
adamss@wfu.edu
• Pete Fisch, Associate AD, Venue
Management
(336) 758-2659
• Corey Jenkins, Associate AD, Events and
Facilities
(336) 758-6166
Arena Seating Capacity:
6,280
Year Founded:
1956

Nature of Service:
Minor League Baseball.

WALKER ARENA
955 4TH STREET
MUSKEGON, MI 49440
231-726-2939
www.lcwalkerarena.com
• John Vanbiesbrouck, General Manager
• Tim Taylor, President of Business
Operations
• Dan Devowe, Sales Director
Tenant(s) :
USHL - Muskegon Lumberjacks.
Arena Seating Capacity:
5,000

**WALTER J. ZABLE STADIUM AT CARY
FIELD**
100 STADIUM DRIVE
COLLEGE OF WILLIAM & MARY
WILLIAMSBURG, VA 23185
757-221-3400
Fax: 757-221-7691
www.tribeathletics.com
• Terry Driscoll, Athletic Director
(757) 221-3332
• Steve Cole, Associate Athletics Director,
Internal Affairs
(757) 221-3361
slcole@wm.edu
• Chelsey Burk, Assistant Athletics Director,
Business Affairs
(757) 221-3373
cpburk@wm.edu
• Michael Pritchett, Assistant Athletics
Director, Facilities
(757) 221-3355
mapritchett@wm.edu
• Pete Kresky, Director of Corporate Sales
and Sponsorship
(757) 221-3353
pmkres@wm.edu
• Jaime LaBianco, Executive Secretary
(757) 221-3332
jllabi@wm.edu
• Sarah Smith, Administrative Assistant
(757) 221-3327
smsmith@wm.edu
Seating Capacity:
11,686

WAR MEMORIAL AUDITORIUM
800 NORTHEAST 8TH STREET
FORT LAUDERDALE, FL 33304
954-828-5380
Fax: 954-763-1769
rstried@fortlauderdale.gov
www.fortlauderdale.gov/wma
• Karen Newhart, Marketing Specialist
(954) 828-4352
knewhart@fortlauderdale.gov
Seating Capacity:
2,110
Sports:
MMA, Boxing, Wrestling, Karate, Judo,
Gymnastics

WAR MEMORIAL STADIUM
1 STADIUM DRIVE
LITTLE ROCK, AR 72225
501-663-0775
Fax: 501-663-6387
www.wmstadium.com
• Jerry Cohen, Executive Director
• Danny-Joe Crofford, Marketing Director
• J.O. Bailey, Assistant Stadium Manager

• Nancy Toland, Office Manager
• Dinah Soderling, Stadium Fiscal Manager
• Emily Martin, Special Events Manager
Seating Capacity:
54,120
Team:
Arkansas college football.

WAR MEMORIAL STADIUM (WY)
1000 EAST UNIVERSITY AVENUE
UNIVERSITY OF WYOMING
DEPARTMENT 3414
LARAMIE, WY 82071
307-766-2292
Fax: 307-766-6729
www.gowyo.com
• Tom Burman, Director of Athletics
(307) 766-2292
uwad@uwyo.edu
• Matt Whisenant, Deputy Director of
Athletics
(307) 766-5551
mwhise@uwyo.edu
• Kevin McKinney, Senior Associate AD,
External Affairs
(307) 766-2444
kevinm@uwyo.edu
• Bill Sparks, Senior Associate AD,
Business Operations
(307) 766-5771
bsparks@uwyo.edu
• Phil Wille, Associate AD, Internal
Operations
(307) 766-2391
pwille@uwyo.edu
• Tyson Drew, Associate AD, Facility
Operations/Event Management
(307) 766-2007
tdrew@uwyo.edu
• Albert Reiser, Assistant AD, Academic
Services
(307) 766-2075
areiser@uwyo.edu
Stadium Seating Capacity:
29,181
Year Founded:
1950

WAYNE STATE COLLEGE
1111 MAIN STREET
WAYNE, NE 68787
402-375-7520
Fax: 402-375-7271
migrosz1@wsc.edu
www.wscwildcats.com
• Mike Powichi, Athletic Director
• Mike Barry, Associate Athletic Director
(402) 375-7521
mibarry1@wsc.edu
• Steve Schafer, Sports Information Director
Rice Fieldhouse Seating Capacity:
2,500
Memorial Stadium Seating Capacity:
3,500
Sports:
Football, Volleyball, Women's Soccer, Golf,
Cross Country, Basketball, Track and Field,
Baseball, Softball
Track Types:
Mondo Sports Surface: indoor, 160 meters;
Polyurethane: Outdoor, 400 meters

WEEDE ARENA
1701 SOUTH BROADWAY
PITTSBURG STATE UNIVERSITY
PITTSBURG, KS 66762-7504

620-231-7000
Fax: 620-235-4661
psuinfo@pittstate.edu
www.pittstate.edu
• Steve Scott, President
• Jim Johnson, Athletics Director
(620) 235-4389
jjohnson@pittstate.edu
• Dan Wilkes, Associate Athletic
Director/Communications
(620) 235-4147
dwilkes@pittstate.edu
• Tom Myers, Associate Athletic
Director/Facilities
(620) 235-4640
ltmyers@pittstate.edu
• Heidi Johnson, Director of Media Relations
& Promotions
(620) 235-4138
hjohnson@pittstate.edu
Arena Seating Capacity:
6,500

WELLS FARGO CENTER
3601 SOUTH BROAD STREET
PHILADELPHIA, PA 19148
215-336-3600
800-298-4200
www.wellsfargocenterphilly.com
• John Page, President, Wells Fargo
Complex
Owned by:
Ed Snider.
Tenant(s) :
NBA - Philadelphia 76ers Basketball, NHL -
Philadelphia Flyers Hockey.
Permanent Seating Capacity:
19,500

WELSH RYAN ARENA
2705 ASHLAND AVENUE
NORTHWESTERN UNIVERSITY
EVANSTON, IL 60208
847-491-3205
Fax: 847-491-4659
d-robert@northwestern.edu
www.nusports.com
• Jim Phillips, Vice President, Athletics &
Recreation
• Steve Green, Deputy Director of Athletics
(Internal Affairs)
(847) 467-6827
sag411@northwestern.edu
• Carrie Forsman, Director of Facilities
(847) 491-8686
c-forsman@northwestern.edu
• Rachel Gunn, Department Assistant
(847) 467-6827
• Debbie Robert, Administrative Assistant
(847) 491-4795
d-robert@northwestern.edu
Arena Seating Capacity:
8,117

WEST VIRGINIA UNIVERSITY/WVU COLISEUM
3450 MONONGAHELA BOULEVARD
WEST VIRGINIA UNIVERSITY
MORGANTOWN, WV 26505
304-293-5621
Fax: 304-293-4105
www.wvusports.com
• Shane Lyons, Director of Athletics
(304) 293-5621
• Keli Cunningham, Executive Senior
Associate Athletic Director
(304) 293-6758

keli.cunningham@mail.wvu.edu
• Matt Borman, Senior Associate
AD/Executive Director
(304) 293-2294
matt.borman@mail.wvu.edu
• Terri Howes, Senior Associate AD/Sports
Administration
(304) 293-2889
terri.howes@mail.wvu.edu
• Michael Szul, Senior Associate
AD/Business Operations
(304) 293-2101
michael.szul@mail.wvu.edu
• Michael Fragale, Associate Athletic
Director/Communications
(304) 293-2821
michael.fragale@mail.wvu.edu
• April Messerly, Assistant Athletic Director
for Facilities
(304) 293-3056
april.messerly@mail.wvu.edu
Coliseum Seating Capacity:
14,000

WESTERN HALL
1 UNIVERSITY CIRCLE
WESTERN ILLINOIS UNIVERSITY
MACOMB, IL 61455
309-298-1190
Fax: 309-298-2009
www.goleathernecks.com
• Matt Tanney, Director of Athletics
(309) 298-1190
m-tanney@wiu.edu
• Patrick Osterman, Assistant Athletic
Director for Communications
(309) 298-1133
pr-osterman@wiu.edu
• Nancy Sprout, Assistant Athletic Director
for Business Operation
(309) 298-1591
nk-sprout@wiu.edu
Arena Seating Capacity:
5,139
Tenant(s) :
NCAA - Western Illinois University
basketball

WHITAKER BANK BALLPARK
207 LEGENDS LANE
LEXINGTON, KY 40505
859-252-4487
Fax: 859-252-0747
lexington.legends.milb.com
• Shannon Kidd, Director, Stadium
Operations
skidd@lexingtonlegends.com
• Mark Costagliola, Ticket Operations
Manager
mcostagliola@lexingtonlegends.com
Sport:
Baseball
Team:
Lexington Legends
Year Founded:
2001
Seating Capacity:
6,994

WHITTEMORE CENTER ARENA
128 MAIN STREET
DURHAM, NH 03824
603-862-4000
campus.recreation@unh.edu
campusrec.unh.edu/whittemore-center-aren
a

• Marty Scarano, Director of Athletics
(603) 862-2013
marty.scarano@unh.edu
• Steve Metcalf, Deputy Athletic Director
(603) 862-2596
steve.metcalf@unh.edu
• Kate McAfee, Associate Athletic Director
for Event Management
(603) 862-0173
kate.mcafee@unh.edu
• AJ Lewis, Box Office Manager
(603) 862-1763
aj.lewis@unh.edu
Arena Seating Capacity:
6,500

WHITTIER FIELD
9000 COLLEGE STATION
BOWDOIN COLLEGE
BRUNSWICK, ME 04011-8490
207-725-3326
Fax: 207-725-3019
• Tim Ryan, Director of Athletics
(207) 725-3247
tryan@bowdoin.edu
• Alice Wiercinski, Associate Director of
Athletics
(207) 798-4342
awiercin@bowdoin.edu
• Terry Meagher, Associate Athletic Director
(207) 725-3328
tmeagher@bowdoin.edu
• Lynn Ruddy, Associate Athletic Director
(207) 725-3623
lruddy@bowdoin.edu
• James Caton, Assistant AD for
Communications
(207) 725-4254
jcaton@bowdoin.edu
• Micki Manheimer, Sports Information
Associate
(207) 725-3701
mmanheim@bowdoin.edu
Stadium Seating Capacity:
9,000

WILKINS STADIUM
100 EAST UNIVERSITY
OFFICE OF THE PRESIDENT
MAGNOLIA, AR 71753-5000
870-235-4000
Fax: 870-235-5005
www.muleriderathletics.com
• Steve Browning, Director of Athletics
(870) 235-4132
dsbrowning@saumag.edu
• Michael Westbrook, Associate Director of
Athletics for Operations
(870) 235-5090
• Daniel Gallegos, Sports Information
Director
(870) 235-4104
sausid@saumag.edu
Stadium Seating Capacity:
6,000

WILLIAM & MARY HALL
751 UKROP WAY
WILLIAMSBURG, VA 23185
757-221-3340
Fax: 757-221-7691
www.tribeathletics.com
• Terry Driscoll, Athletics Director
(757) 221-3332
• Steve Cole, Associate Athletics Director,
Internal Affairs
(757) 221-3361

slcole@wm.edu
• Chelsey Burk, Assistant Athletics Director, Business Affairs
(757) 221-3373
cpburk@wm.edu
• Tiffany Christian, Assistant Athletics Director, Compliance
(757) 221-7601
ttchristian@wm.edu
• Michael Pritchett, Assistant Athletics Director, Facilities
(757) 221-3355
• Spencer Milne, Assistant Athletics Director, Marketing/Promotions
(757) 221-3356
• Jason Simms, Assistant Athletics Director, Academic Services
(757) 221-3241
jlsimms@wm.edu
• Jaime LaBianco, Executive Secretary
(757) 221-3332
Arena Seating Capacity:
11,300

WILLIAM R. JOHNSON COLISEUM
712 HAYTER STREET
NACOGDOCHES, TX 75962
936-468-4540
www.sfajacks.com
• Robert Hill, Director of Athletics
(936) 468-4540
• Matt Fenley, Associate Athletics Director, Compliance
(936) 468-4570
• John Branch, Associate Athletics Director, External Affairs
(936) 468-4334
jbranch@sfasu.edu
• Rob Meyers, Assistant Athletics Director, Business
(936) 468-4080
rmeyers@sfasu.edu
• Rob McDermand, Assistant Athletics Director, Academic Services
(936) 468-4429
mcdermanrd@sfasu.edu
• Payton Adams, Coordinator of Athletic Operations
(936) 468-5183
• Pam Cole, Administrative Assistant
(936) 468-4540
Coliseum Seating Capacity:
7,200

WILLIAMS ARENA
1925 UNIVERSITY AVENUE SOUTHEAST
MINNEAPOLIS, MN 55455
612-625-3007
Fax: 612-625-7788
icaadmin@umn.edu
www.gophersports.com
• Beth Goetz, Interim Director of Athletics
(612) 624-4497
• Tom McGinnis, Senior Associate AD/CFO
(612) 624-4497
• Marc Ryan, Senior Associate AD
(612) 624-4497
• Jeremiah Carter, Director of Compliance
(612) 626-5480
Arena Seating Capacity:
14,625

WILLIAMS COLLEGE ATHLETICS
22 SPRING STREET
LASELL GYMNASIUM
WILLIAMSTOWN, MA 1267

413-597-4982
Fax: 413-597-4158
webfeedback@williams.edu
athletics.williams.edu
• Harry Sheehy, Chair & Director of Athletics/PE/Recreation
(413) 597-2366
hsheehy@williams.edu
• Bud Fisher, Associate AD/Head Coach of Nordic Skiing
(413) 597-2340
rfisher@williams.edu
• Gary Guerin, Associate Director for Operations
(413) 597-3321
gguerin@williams.edu
• Jennifer Chuks, Assistant Athletic Administrator
(413) 597-4085
Jennifer.E.Chuks@williams.edu
• Lisa Melendy, Athletic Director
(413) 597-3511
lmelendy@williams.edu
Stadium Seating Capacity:
8,000

WILLIAMS STADIUM
1971 UNIVERSITY BOULEVARD
LYNCHBURG, VA 24515
434-582-2100
Fax: 434-582-2205
www.liberty.edu
• Jeff Barber, Director of Athletics
jbarber2@liberty.edu
• Mickey Guridy, Senior Associate Athletics Director
maguridy@liberty.edu
• Tim East, Senior Associate Athletics Director
tmeast@liberty.edu
• Mike Minyard, Associate Athletics Director, Sales & Promotions
• Dan Maxam, Assistant Athletics Director, Facilities
dlmaxam@liberty.edu
Stadium Seating Capacity:
19,200

WILLIAMS-BRICE STADIUM
1125 GEORGE ROGERS BOULEVARD
COLUMBIA, SC 29201
803-777-4202
www.gamecocksonline.com
• Ray Tanner, Athletics Director
• Charles Waddell, Deputy Athletics Director
• Josh Waters, Assistant AD/Marketing
• Duane Grooms, Assistant AD/Facilities Services
• Lance Grantham, Assistant AD/Ticket Operations
Stadium Seating Capacity:
80,250
Team:
University of South Carolina football.

WINGS EVENT CENTER
3600 VANRICK DRIVE
KALAMAZOO, MI 49001
269-345-1125
Fax: 269-345-6584
www.wingseventcenter.com
• Toni Daniels, Director of Sales
• Rob Underwood, Director of Entertainment
runderwood@wingseventcenter.com
• Holly Rinal, Operations Manager
• Emilie Vanderlaan, Special Events Coordinator

Arena Seating Capacity:
5,113

WISCONSIN CENTER DISTRICT
400 WEST WISCONSIN AVENUE
MILWAUKEE, WI 53203
414-908-6000
Fax: 414-908-6010
www.wcd.org
• Russell Staerkel, President/CEO
• Jeffrey Sinkovec, Director of Finance and Accounting
(414) 908-6071
jsinkovec@wcd.org
• Thomas Paul, Director of Information Technology
(414) 908-6090
tpaul@wcd.org
• Trace Goudreau, Director of Sales & Marketing
(414) 908-6072
tgoudreau@wcd.org
• Robert Seefeld, Director of Building Services
(414) 908-6054
rseefeld@wcd.org
• Tony Dynicki, Director of Sports & Entertainment Sales
(414) 908-6084
tdynicki@wcd.org
• Elizabeth Unruh, Sales Manager
(414) 908-6079
eunruh@wcd.org
Description:
A convention center used for basketball, volleyball, gymnastics, fencing and other tournaments.

WISCONSIN-MADISON FIELDHOUSE
1450 MONROE STREET
UNIVERSITY OF WISCONSIN
MADISON, WI 53706
608-262-3354
Fax: 608-265-3036
webmaster@uwbadgers.com
www.uwbadgers.com
• Barry Alvarez, Director of Athletics
• Walter Dickey, Deputy Athletic Director
(608) 265-2973
wjd@athletics.wisc.edu
• Justin M Doherty, Senior Associate Athletic Director
(608) 262-9023
jmd@athletics.wisc.edu
• Terry Gawlik, Senior Associate Athletic Director/SWA
(608) 265-4987
tlg@athletics.wisc.edu
• Mario Morris, Director of Financial Operations
(608) 265-4134
Arena Seating Capacity:
10,600
Tenant(s) :
University of Wisconsin.

WJ HALE STADIUM
3500 JOHN A MERRITT BOULEVARD
NASHVILLE, TN 37209
615-963-5000
www.tsutigers.com
• Teresa L Phillips, Director of Athletics
(615) 963-5034
tphillips@tnstate.edu
• Daniel Kuhn, Director of Operations
(615) 963-2136
dkuhn@tnstate.edu

• Zellina Anderson, Ticket Office Manager
(615) 963-5841
zanderson@tnstate.edu
Stadium Seating Capacity:
10,000
Tenant(s) :
Tennessee State University.

WL ZORN ARENA
121 GARFIELD AVENUE
EAU CLAIRE, WI 54701
715-836-4636
service_center@uwec.edu
www.blugolds.com
• Dan Schumacher, Director of Athletics
(715) 836-5858
schumadj@uwec.edu
• Jill Millis, Assistant Athletic Director,
Sports Information
(715) 836-4184
millisjl@uwec.edu
Year Founded:
1952
Arena Seating Capacity:
2,500

WOLSTEIN CENTER
2000 PROSPECT AVENUE
CLEVELAND, OH 44115
216-687-9292
Fax: 216-687-5450
www.wolsteincenter.com
• Jennifer Kelly, Executive Director
(216) 687-9292
j.r.kelly1@csuohio.edu
• Nicole Taylor, Fiscal Manager
(216) 687-9292
n.m.taylor79@csuohio.edu
• Karey Clarke, Box Office Manager
(216) 687-9292
• Vicki Wetzler, Event Manager
(216) 687-9292
v.wetzler@csuohio.edu
Arena Seating Capacity:
8,500

WORLD WAR MEMORIAL STADIUM
510 YANCEYVILLE STREET
GREENSBORO, NC 27405
336-274-0462
www.greensborosports.org/war-memorial-st
adium
• Billy Edringston, Associate Athletics
Director/Facilities/Operations
Sport:
Baseball
Tenant(s) :
NCAA - North Carolina A&T State University
athletics, Greensboro College athletics.
Year Founded:
1926
Capacity:
7,500

WORTHEN ARENA (WR)
1699 WEST BETHEL AVENUE
BALL STATE UNIVERSITY
MUNCIE, IN 47306
765-285-8708
Fax: 765-285-5353
cms.bsu.edu
• Mark Sandy, Director of Intercollegiate
Athletics
• Daniel P Byrnes, Director, Sports Facilities
& Recreation Services
• Brian Hardin, Deputy Athletics Director

• Karin Lee, Senior Associate Athletics
Director
(765) 285-5127
kalee2@bsu.edu
• Joe Hernandez, Associate Athletics
Director for Sports & Alumni
(765) 285-1282
jhernand@bsu.edu
• Mark Serrao, Assistant Director of
Ticketing & Premium Seating
(765) 285-1474
maserrao@bsu.edu
Permanent Seating Capacity:
11,500
Tenant(s) :
NCAA - Ball State University athletics.

WRIGHT STATE UNIVERSITY RAIDERS
3640 COLONEL GLENN HIGHWAY
SUITE 430
DAYTON, OH 45435-0001
937-775-3498
Fax: 937-775-2060
nutterguest@wright.edu
www.nuttercenter.com
• John Cox, Facilities Manager
(937) 775-4672
john.cox@wright.edu
• Becky Sparks, Business Manager
(937) 775-4785
becky.sparks@wright.edu
• Misty Cox, Booking/Marketing Manager
(937) 775-4674
misty.cox@wright.edu
• Kiley Fleming, Box Office Manager
(937) 775-4786
kiley.fleming@wright.edu
Arena Seating Capacity:
11,200
Arena events:
Southwest Ohio's hottest sports and
entertainment venue.
Tenant(s) :
NCAA - Wright State University athletics.
Founded:
1990
Description:
Location for national touring acts and
sporting events.

WRIGLEY FIELD
1060 WEST ADDISON STREET
CHICAGO, IL 60613-4397
773-404-2827
Fax: 773-404-4129
chicago.cubs.mlb.com
• Alex Sugarman, SVP, Strategy & Ballpark
Operations
• Matt Kenny, Senior Director, Event
Operations
• Patrick Meenan, Senior Director, Facilities
& Procurement
• Miguel DeJesus, Ticket Office Manager
Permanent Seating Capacity:
41,160
Team:
Chicago Cubs MLB baseball.

XCEL ENERGY CENTER
199 WEST KELLOGG BOULEVARD
SAINT PAUL, MN 55102
651-265-4800
Fax: 651-265-4899
info@xcelenergycenter.com
www.xcelenergycenter.com
• Jack Larson, Vice President/General
Manager

• Mark Stoffel, Senior Director Operations
(651) 265-4807
Stadium Seating Capacity:
17,954
Tenant(s) :
NHL - Minnesota Wild ice hockey.

XL CENTER
ONE CIVIC CENTER PLAZA
HARTFORD, CT 06103
860-249-6333
877-522-8499
Fax: 860-241-4226
xlcenterinfo@xlcenter.com
www.xlcenter.com
• Chris Lawrence, General Manager
• Bryan Dooley, Vice President, Corporate
Sales
Permanent Seating Capacity:
15,564
Owned by:
City of Hartford.
Year Founded:
1975
Tenants:
University of Connecticut Men's and
Women's Basketball (NCAA/Big East),
Hartford Wolf Pack (AHL).

YACK ARENA
3131 THIRD STREET
WYANDOTTE, MI 48192
734-324-7292
agarbin@wyandottemi.gov
www.wyandotte.net
• Justin Lanagan, Superintendent
(734) 324-4507
jnlanagan@wyan.org
Description:
Youth hockey and youth figure skating.
Home Teams:
Wyandotte Warriors, Wyandotte Roosevelt
High School Hockey, Wyandotte Figure
Skating Club

YAGER STADIUM AT MOORE BOWL
1700 SW COLLEGE AVENUE
TOPEKA, KS 66621
785-670-1134
Fax: 785-670-1091
www.wusports.com
• Loren Ferre, Director of Athletics
(785) 670-1794
loren.ferre@washburn.edu
• Gil Herrera, Facilities Director
(785) 670-1304
gilbert.herrera@washburn.edu
• Craig Schurig, Head Coach, Football
(785) 670-1340
craig.schurig@washburn.edu
• Chris Jones, Head Coach, Women's
Soccer
(785) 670-1756
Teams:
Washburn University Ichabods football &
Lady Blues soccer.
Seating Capacity:
7,200

YAKIMA COUNTY STADIUM
1220 PACIFIC AVENUE
YAKIMA, WA 98901
509-575-4487
Fax: 509-469-2105
info@pippinsbaseball.com

• Zachary Fraser, President
• Jeff Garretson, General Manager
• Marcus McKimmy, Assistant General Manager
marcus@pippinsbaseball.com
• Andy Jones, Director of Hospitality
andy@pippinsbaseball.com
Stadium Physical Address:
1301 S Fair Ave, Yakima, WA 98901.
Sport:
Baseball
Tenant(s) :
Yakima Valley Pippins baseball
Year Founded & Description:
Club founded in 2014. The Pippins are a member of the 11-team West Coast League, a summer wood-bat collegiate league with teams in Washington state, Oregon and British Columbia.
Arena Seating Capacity:
2,800

YAKIMA VALLEY SUNDOME
1301 SOUTH FAIR AVENUE
YAKIMA, WA 98901
509-248-7160
Fax: 509-248-8093
www.statefairpark.org
• Trent Marquis, Chairman
• Sid Morrison, Vice Chairman
• Greg Stewart, President & General Manager
(509) 248-7160
cwsf@fairfun.com
• Greg Lybeck, Assistant General Manager
(509) 248-7160
gregl@fairfun.com
• Steve Sires, Facilities Manager
steves@fairfun.com
• Willard Nelson, Operations Manager
willardn@fairfun.com
• Ray Mata, Events & Production Manager
raym@fairfun.com
• Ruth Anglin, Fair Activities Manager
• Jill Rodgers, Fair Activities Assistant
jillr@fairfun.com
Arena Seating Capacity:
6,195
Year Founded:
1990

YALE BOWL
20 TOWER PARKWAY
YALE UNIVERSITY
NEW HAVEN, CT 06511
203-432-4747
Fax: 203-432-7772
support.athletics@yale.edu
www.yalebulldogs.com
• Thomas Beckett, Director of Athletics
(203) 432-1414
thomas.beckett@yale.edu
• Christian Bray, Director of Compliance
(203) 432-7668
christian.bray@yale.edu
• Edward Mockus, Senior Associate Athletic Director Facilities
(203) 432-2494
edward.mockus@yale.edu
• Patrick O'Neill, Associate Athletic Director Marketing/Licensing
(203) 432-2205
patrick.oneill@yale.edu
• Jennifer O'Neil, Assistant to the Director
(203) 432-1414
jennifer.oneil@yale.edu
• Francine Georges, Human Resources

Generalist, Athletics
(203) 432-1442
francine.georges@yale.edu
Arena Seating Capacity:
61,466
Year Founded:
November 21, 1914

YALE FIELD
252 DERBY AVENUE
WEST HAVEN, CT 06516
203-432-1423
scott.griffin@yale.edu
www.yalebulldogs.com
• Scott Griffin, General Manager
(203) 432-1423
scott.griffin@yale.edu
Sport:
Baseball
Team:
Yale Bulldogs
Year Founded:
1928
Capacity:
5,000

YANKEE STADIUM
ONE EAST 161ST STREET
BRONX, NY 10451
718-293-4300
Fax: 718-293-8431
newyork.yankees.mlb.com
• Joan Steinbrenner, Vice Chairperson
• Randy Levine, President
• Lonn A Trost, Chief Operating Officer/General Counsel
• Brian Cashman, Senior Vice President, General Manager
• Deborah A Tymon, Senior Vice President, Marketing
• Cindy Kamradt, Stadium Planning & Special Projects Director
• Carol Laurenzano, Stadium Operations Director
Year opened:
2009
Permanent Seating Capacity:
52,325
Description:
Home stadium for New York Yankees.

YOGI BERRA STADIUM
8 YOGI BERRA DRIVE
LITTLE FALLS, NJ 07424
973-746-7434
Fax: 973-655-8006
info@jackals.com
www.jackals.com
• Floyd Hall, Owner and Chairman
  ext 8068
• Gregory L. Lockard, President
• Larry Hall, Executive Vice President
• Jennifer Fertig, Vice President of Finance & Operations
• Jeff Palladino, Director of Group Sales & Ticket Operations
(973) 655-8009
• Jarrett Schack, Group Sales & Operations Coordinator
(973) 655-8038
• Aldo Licitra, Facilities Manager
• Eric McConnell, Concessions Manager
(973) 655-8053
Sport:
Baseball
Tenant(s) :
New Jersey Jackals baseball

Year Founded:
1998
Capacity:
3,784

YOST ICE ARENA
1116 SOUTH STATE STREET
UNIVERSITY OF MICHIGAN
ANN ARBOR, MI 48109
734-764-4600
Fax: 734-764-0247
yostice@umich.edu
www.umich.edu
• Mark S. Schlissel, President
• Andrew Hicks, Facility Manager
adhicks@umich.edu
• Jill Feudi, Business Office Manager
jfeudi@umich.edu
• Trey Garant, Associate Manager
tgarant@umich.edu
• Rob Ramsburgh, Operations Manager
robram@umich.edu
Arena Seating Capacity:
6,603
Tenant(s) :
NCAA - University of Michigan ice hockey.

Race Tracks - Auto

ALABAMA INTERNATIONAL DRAGWAY
1245 CRUMP ROAD
PO BOX 426
STEELE, AL 35987
256-538-7223
Fax: 256-354-5014
www.alabamainternationaldragway.com
• Colins Jason, General Manager/Promoter
Track Type:
Dragstrip

ALABAMA STATE FAIRGROUNDS
2331 BESSEMER ROAD
BIRMINGHAM, AL 35208
205-786-8100
Fax: 205-786-8222
opi@birminghamal.gov
www.informationbirmingham.com
• Leroy R Cowan, Director
State Fair Arena Seating Capacity:
6,000
Birmingham International Speedway Seating Capacity
10,000

ALASKA RACEWAY PARK
3900 ENGLISH BAY DRIVE
WASILLA, AK 99654
907-746-7223
Fax: 907-376-0733
www.akracewaypark.com
• Rickey Rogers, Promoter
Track Length:
1/8 mile.
Track Type:
Dragstrip.

ALL AMERICAN SPEEDWAY
800 ALL AMERICAN CITY BOULEVARD
ROSEVILLE, CA 95678
916-786-2025
Fax: 916-786-2139
info@allamericanspeedway.com
www.allamericanspeedway.com

• Rick Poppert, Director Competition
(916) 786-2025
Track Size:
1/4 mile.
Track Type:
Semi-Banked Oval.

AMAROO PARK
ANNANGROVE ROAD
AUSTRALIAN RACING DRRS CLUB
NSW, 2156
-3-5952 2548
Fax: -61-9678-1184
www.amaroopark.com
• Beck Damon, Member, Ardc Committee

ATLANTA DRAGWAY
500 E RIDGEWAY ROAD
COMMERCE, GA 30529
706-335-2301
Fax: 706-423-9261
www.atlantadragway.com
• Ray Wilkings, General Manager
(706) 335-2301
• Crystal Wilson, Sales& Marketing Manager
(706) 423-9252
cwilson@nhra.com
• Joanne Lineberry, Sales/Marketing
Manager
• Mike Savage, Track Manager
(706) 335-2301
msavage@nhra.com
• Jodee Kennedy, Administrative Assistant
(706) 423-9253
jkennedy@nhra.com
Description:
Drag Racing Track.
Seating capacity:
30,000

ATLANTA MOTOR SPEEDWAY
PO BOX 500
HAMPTON, GA 30228
770-946-4211
877-926-7849
Fax: 770-946-3928
amstix@atlantamotorspeedway.com
www.atlantamotorspeedway.com
• Ed Clark, President/General Manager
(770) 946-3921
• Dave Mullison, Manager
Marketing/Communications
(770) 707-7980
davem@atlantamotorspeedway.com
• Juanita Martin, Assistant to the President
• Greg Walter, VP Sales
(770) 946-3918
gregw@atlantamotorspeedway.com
• Kristi Wilson, Director of Client Services
• Brad Harrison, Web Content Manager
• Allison Fillmore, Corporate Sales Manager
• Nicole Fowler, Sales Executive
Description:
Auto race track.
Series:
NASCAR Nextel Cup Series; NASCAR
Busch Series.

ATMORE DRAGWAY
PO BOX 912
FLOMATON, AL 36441-1915
251-368-8363
Fax: 904-212-6597
karen@atmoredragway.com
www.atmoredragway.com
• Ed Clark, President and General Manager

Size:
1/8 mile
Type of Track:
Dragstrip

AUTO CLUB FAMOSO
33559 FAMOSO ROAD
MCFARLAND, CA 93250
661-399-5351
Fax: 661-399-2608
famosoraceway@gmail.com
www.famosoraceway.com
• Clake Bowser, Operator

CALIFORNIA SPEEDWAY
9300 CHERRY AVENUE
FONTANA, CA 92335
909-429-5000
800-944-7223
Fax: 909-429-5500
sales@autoclubspeedway.com
www.autoclubspeedway.com
• Gillian Zucker, President
• Fritz Maskrey, Senior Director of Corporate
Sales & Marketing
• Jason Klein, Marketing Director
• Gillian Zucker, President
president@autoclubspeedway.com
• Dave Allen, Vice President of Sales and
Marketing
• Otis Greer, Director of Community Affairs
• Art Avila, Director of Accounting
• Fritz Maskrey, Sr. Director of Corporate
Sales & Marketing
• Curt Jacey, Director of Business
Development
• Deanna Ingram, Director of Ticketing
Track Length:
2 miles
Front Straight:
3,100 feet
Back Straight:
2,500 feet
Banking:
11 degrees

BAKERSFIELD SPEEDWAY
PO BOX 82184
BAKERSFIELD, CA 93380-2184
661-393-3373
Fax: 661-393-7085
www.bakersfieldspeedway.com
• Scott Schweitzer, Owner
(661) 393-3373
scott@bakersfieldspeedway.com
Track Type:
High Banked Oval.
Track Size:
1/3 mile.

BANDIMERE SPEEDWAY
3051 S ROONEY ROAD
MORRISON, CO 80465
303-697-6001
800-664-8946
Fax: 303-697-0815
www.bandimere.com
• John C. Bandimere, Jr., President
(303) 697-6001
• John C. Bandimere, III, Executive Vice
President, General Manager
(303) 697-6001
• Larry Crispe, Executive VP Operations
(303) 697-6001
• Sandy Newton, C.F.O.
(303) 697-6001
• Bruce Kamada, Director of

Sales/Sponsorship Developmen
(303) 697-6001
• Debbra Parker, Director of Hospitality
(303) 697-6001
• Paul Lombardi, Food & Beverage Director
(303) 697-6001
Track:
1/4 concrete drag strip
Seating Capacity:
Track: 23,000

BARC LIMITED
THRUXTON CIRCUIT
ANDOVER HAMPSHIRE, ENGLAND SP11
8PN
-44-1264 882200
Fax: 44-1264 882233
info@barc.net
www.barc.net
• Dennis Carter, Chief Executive
dcarter@barc.net
• Trevor Swettenham, Press Officer
press@barc.net
• Dale Wells, Competition Manager
dwells@barc.net
• Mark Jones, Chief Executive
mcurley@barc.net
• Ian Watson, Business Development
Manager
iwatson@barc.net
• Pat Blakney, Thruxton Operations Manage
(012) 4 774918
pat@thruxtonracing.co.uk
• Angie Kew, Membership Secretary
akew@barc.net
• Mark Youngs, Thruxton Catering Manager
(044) 01554 89
pembrey@barc.net
• Tom Jones, Thruxton Facilities Supervisor
(044) 01264 88
tjones@barc.net
Rallycross:
0.9 miles.
Track Length:
1.456 miles.

BARONA SPEEDWAY
1794 WILDCAT CANYON ROAD
LAKESIDE, CA 92040
619-749-8115
Salz944@cox.net
www.baronaspeedway.com
• Jim Scribellito, Promoter
Type of Track:
High-Banked Oval.
Track Length:
1/6 mile.

BATESVILLE MOTOR SPEEDWAY
5090 HEBER SPRINGS ROAD
BATESVILLE, AR 72501
870-251-0011
www.batesvillemotorspeedway.net
• Connie Starr, Ticket sales and Promotions
(870) 613-1337
• Wimp Reed, Technical Support
(870) 251-1566
wreed31@gmail.com
• Starr Mooney, Promoter
Type of Track:
High-Banked Oval.
Track Length:
3/8 mile.

BEACON HILL SPEEDWAY
400 GOBATTI PL
PUEBLO, CO 81008-9667

719-542-2277
www.beaconhillsspeedway.com
• Sparks Dall, Promoter
Type of Track:
Semi-Banked Oval
Track Length:
1/4 mile

BIRMINGHAM INTERNATIONAL RACEWAY
2321 BESSEMER ROAD
BIRMINGHAM, AL 35208
205-781-2471
Fax: 205-424-5537
• Ray Tennyson, Director of Public Relations
• Carolyn Harvey, General Manager
Arena Seating Capacity:
8,000.00
Year Founded:
1914
Track Type
Asphalt.
Track Size
5/8.

BRAINARD INTERNATIONAL RACEWAY
5523 BIRCHDALE ROAD
BRAINERD, MN 56401
218-824-7223
866-444-4455
Fax: 218-824-7240
www.brainerdraceway.com
• Scott Quick, General Manager
Description:
Auto race track.

BRISTOL MOTOR SPEEDWAY & DRAGWAY
151 SPEEDWAY BOULEVARD
BRISTOL, TN 37620
423-989-6933
Fax: 423-764-1646
www.bristolmotorspeedway.com
• Jeff Byrd, President/General Manager
(423) 989-6999
jeff@bristolmotorspeedway.com
• Wayne Estes, VP/Communications & Events
(423) 989-6935
wayne@bristolmotorspeedway.com
• Logan McCabe, VP Marketing
(423) 989-6934
Logan@bristolmotorspeedway.com
• O.Bruton Smith, Chairman
• Jerry Caldwell, General Manager
(423) 989-6912
• DeDe Hash, VP Security /Asset Management
(423) 989-6928
• Julie Bennett, VP General Counsel
(423) 989-6912
• Fred King, VP Finances
(423) 989-6927
• Wayne Estes, VP Events
(423) 989-6935
• Kevin Triplett, VP/Public Affairs
(423) 989-6905
ktriplett@bristolmotorspeedway.com
Series:
NASCAR Nextel Cup Series; NASCAR Busch Series.
Description:
Auto race track.

BUTTONWILLOW RACEWAY PARK
24551 LERDO HIGHWAY
BUTTONWILLOW, CA 93206

661-764-5333
Fax: 661-764-5334
info@buttonwillowraceway.com
www.buttonwillowraceway.com
• Les Phillips, Contact
(661) 764-5333
lesrace@aol.com
• Carrie Hester, Administrator
carrie@buttonwillowraceway.com
• Mike Miserendino, Business Development Manager
mike@buttonwillowraceway.com
• Laura May Booker, Food & Gift Shop Manager

CALEXPO
1600 EXPOSITION BOULEVARD
SACRAMENTO, CA 95815
916-263-3000
877-225-3976
Fax: 916-263-3250
info@calexpo.com
www.calexpo.com
• Norbert J. Bartosik, CEO & General Manager
• Don Henry, Marketing Director
• Jerry Brown, Govenor
• Cynthia Bryant, Director
• Willie Pelote, Director
• Sonney Chong, Director
• Jeffrey Azoff, Dirctor

CANYON SPEEDWAY
9777 W CAREFREE HIGHWAY
PEORIA, AZ 85345
602-258-7223
Fax: 623-465-7131
www.canyonspeedwaypark.com
• Jeff Stafford, Promoter
Track Type:
High-Banked Oval.
Track Length:
3/8 mile.

CAPITOL SPEEDWAY
MILE 75.5 PARKS HIGHWAY
WILLOW, AK 99688
907-495-6420
Fax: 907-495-5819
www.capitolspeedway.org
• Lackey Karen, Owner
• Earl Lackey, Owner
• Michelle Maynor, Business Manager
(907) 354-7223
Track Size:
1/4 mile.
Track Type:
Dragstrip.

CARLSBAD RACEWAY
649 DAISY
ESCONDIDO, CA 92069
760-480-8369
Fax: 760-727-4390
carlsbadraceway@carlsbadraceway.org
www.carlsbadraceway.org
• Jim LeVold, Promoter

CENTERVILLE DRAGWAY PARK INC
10239 DRAGSTRIP LANE
PO BOX 160
CENTERVILLE, AR 72829
479-576-4001
cvdrag@arkwest.com
www.centervilledragway.com

• Wayne Styles, President
• Patty Styles, Promoter
Track Length:
1000 feet.
Track Type:
Dragstrip.

CHARLOTTE MOTOR SPEEDWAY
5555 CONCORD PARKWAY S
CONCORD, NC 28027
704-455-3200
800-455-3267
Fax: 704-455-2547
tickets@charlottemotorspeedway.com
www.charlottemotorspeedway.com
• Marcus Smith, President/General Manager
• Doug Stafford, Executive Vice President
• Jerry Gappens, Promotions/Public Relations VP
• Dan Farrell, Corporate Sales/Marketing Director
Description:
Founded 1960. Auto race track.
Series:
NASCAR Nextel Cup Series; NASCAR Busch Series.
Year Founded:
1960
Seating Capacity:
165,000

CHICAGOLAND SPEEDWAY
500 SPEEDWAY BOULEVARD
JOLIET, IL 60433
815-722-5500
888-629-7223
Fax: 815-724-0520
marketing@chicagolandspeedway.com
www.chicagolandspeedway.com
• Tim Carey, President
• Scott Paddock, President
• John Brokopp, Public Relations/Publicity Director
• Edward Duffy, Chief Executive Officer
• Lori Whalen, Director of Accounting
• Lisa Bhender, Office Coordinator
• Julyn Stiff, Director of Guest Services
• Erin Barry, Hospitality Manager
Description:
Horse race track.
Description:
Horse race track.

YUMA SPEEDWAY PARK
3450 W COUNTY 15TH STREET
YUMA, AZ 85365
620-344-1563
Fax: 520-726-7280
www.cocopahspeedway.com/
Track Type:
Semi-Banked Oval.
Track Length:
3/8 mile.

COLORADO NATIONAL SPEEDWAY
4281 GRADEN BOULEVARD
DACONO, CO 80514
303-665-4173
303-665-4173
Fax: 303-828-2403
info@coloradospeedway.com
www.coloradospeedway.com
• Mindy Harkins, Marketing
(303) 231-9460
• Sue Nordhougen, Track Operations
(303) 828-0116

• Joe Star, Track Photographer
(303) 828-0116
• Randy Wolf, Food And Beverage
(303) 828-0116
• Marc Mooser, Track Announcer
• Darrell Smith, CNS Tech
Description:
Track Operates 28 events running April -
September. Average Attendance 6,300.
Weekly car count exceeds 100. Divisions
include late models, protracts, figure-eight's,
grand american modified, super stocks,
trains.
Description:
Auto race track (3/8 mile paved oval)
hosting the following NASCAR series:
NASCAR Craftsman Truck Series/NASCAR
Nextel Cup Series, Featherlite Southwest
Tour.
Track Size:
3/8 mile
Track Type:
Semi-Banked Oval

COMPETITION PARK MOTOCROSS
96 SUGAR SHACK LANE
BEAR CREEK, NC 27207
919-224-7237
speedcompound@yahoo.com
www.speedcompoundmx.com
• Jim Neese, Rider Development
• Dan Rodgers, Promoter

COSTA MESA SPEEDWAY
88 FAIR DRIVE
PO BOX 3334
COSTA MESA, CA 92674
949-492-9933
Fax: 949-492-2547
www.costamesaspeedway.net
• Brad Oxley, Promoter
• John Creith, Track Staff
Seating Capacity:
8,750

CRAWFORD COUNTY SPEEDWAY
7118 N HIGHWAY 59
VAN BUREN, AR 72956
479-632-2749
Fax: 479-632-4450
www.crawfordcountyspeedway.net
• Donnie Watson, Promoter
Track Type:
Slightly banked, 3/8 of a mile, red clay oval
Seating Capacity:
4,500
Sport:
Stock Car Racing (Modified, Street Stock,
Mini Stock, Grand National, Front Wheel
Drive and 360 E Modified).

**CROFT CLASSIC & HISTORIC
MOTORSPORTS LTD (CCHM)**
WEST LANE
DALTON ON TEES
N YORKSHIRE, ENGLAND DL2 2PN
-44-01325 721815
Fax: -44-01325 721819
www.croftcircuit.co.uk
• Tara Horn, Contact person

CROWLEY'S RIDGE RACEWAY
1708 HIGHWAY 351
PARAGOULD, AR 72450

870-236-3141
Fax: 805-398-0467
www.crraceway.com

CYCLELAND SPEEDWAY
47 NELSON ROAD
OROVILLE, CA 95965
530-342-0063
Fax: 530-892-9213
www.cyclelandspeedway.com
• Moural Lowell, Promoter

DALLAS COUNTY DRAGWAY
3182 COUNTY ROAD 63
PO BOX 110651
SELMA, AL 35211
334-418-6900
• Alexander Marvin, Promoter
Size:
1/8 mile.
Track Type:
Dragstrip

DARLINGTON RACEWAY
1301 HARRY BYRD HIGHWAY
DARLINGTON, SC 29532
843-395-8900
Fax: 843-393-3911
tickets@darlingtonraceway.com
www.darlingtonraceway.com
• Chris Browning, President
• Mac Josey, Vice President & General
Manager
• Josey Mac, Ticket Operations Director
Description:
Founded 1950. NASCAR Auto race track.
Series:
NASCAR Nextel Cup Series NASCARA
Busch Series NASCAR Craftsman Truck
Series

DAYTONA INTERNATIONAL SPEEDWAY
1801 W INTERNATIONAL SPEEDWAY
BOULEVARD
DAYTONA BEACH, FL 32114
386-254-2700
866-472-8725
Fax: 386-257-0281
www.daytonainternationalspeedway.com
• Kenny Kane, Media &Communications
Senior Director
• Robin Braig, President
• Brian Harper, Corporate Sales Senior
Manager
• Debbie Weller, Marketing
Partnerships/Sales Director
Arena Seating Capacity:
170,000 and infield.
Year Founded:
1953
Track Type:
Superspeedway.
Track Size:
2.5 miles, 3.56 mile road course.

DEL MAR SPEEDWAY
1001 N PACIFIC AVENUE
SAN PEDRO, CA 95928
310-547-9898
Fax: 310-547-9900
• Chris Agajanian, Promoter

DELTA SPEEDWAY
1658 S AIRPORT WAY AT CHARTER WAY
STOCKON, CA 95206

1-4-595-8922
Fax: 209-823-2928
info@deltaraceway.com
www.deltaraceway.com
• Mick Evans, President
(209) 239-3079
Nature of Service:
Micro sprint race track, 600 cc multi, 600 cc
Stock, 250 cc, 600 cc Restrictor, Stock
appearing, beginning box stock.
Track Type:
Dirt Oval.
Track Size:
1/8 Mile.

DIXIE SPEEDWAY
150 DIXIE DRIVE
WOODSTOCK, GA 30189
770-926-5315
Fax: 770-926-8339
dixiespeedway@aol.com
www.dixiespeedway.com
• Mickey Swims, President
• Mike Swims, VP
Description:
Founded 1968.
Seating capacity:
10,000.00
Auto Racing:
Sprint cars; stock cars' Hav-A-Tampa late
models.

DOVER INTERNATIONAL SPEEDWAY
1131 N DUPONT HIGHWAY
DOVER, DE 19901
302-883-6500
800-441-7223
Fax: 302-672-0100
info@doverspeedway.com
www.doverspeedway.com
• Denis McGlynn, President/Chief Executive
Officer
• Jerry Miraglia, Dover Motorsports VP
• Jerry Dunning, VP/General Manager
• Mark Rossi, Sales/Marketing VP
• Craig Amhaus, Business Development
Manager
Description:
Auto race track.
Series:
NASCAR Nextel Cup Series; NASCAR
Busch Series; NASCAR Craftsman Truck
Series.

EAST ALABAMA MOTOR SPEEDWAY
4238 US HIGHWAY 80 W
PHENIX CITY, AL 36870
334-297-2594
Fax: 334-297-2699
eams@bellsouth.net
www.eamsdirt.com
• Billy Thomas, President
Description:
Auto race track.
Track Type:
High-Banked Oval.
Size:
3/8 mile.

FAASST MOTORSPORTS INC.
719-761-1372
fmi@faasst.com
www.faasst.com
• Judy Faass, CEO
Track Length:
2.5 miles

Type of Track:
Road course
Founded:
2005
Description:
Faasst Motorsports offers educational driving and racing programs in a race track environment for teens, high performance car owners and novice racers. Faasst is also an authorized dealer of driving gear, racing gear and equipment.
Nature of Service:
Racing Operations - Racing Schools - Product Development - Equipment Sales

FAIRBANKS RACING LIONS
PO BOX 74762
FAIRBANKS, AK 99707
907-452-3833
• Wes Wallace, Promoter
(907) 495-6420
• Nancy Wallace, Promoter
(907) 495-6420
• Jamie Bodenstadt, President
akgrizzly@gci.net
Track Length:
3/8 mile.
Track Type:
Slightly-Banked Oval.

FAIRPLEX
1101 W MCKINLEY AVENUE
POMONA, CA 91768
909-623-3111
Fax: 909-865-3602
info@fairplex.com
www.fairplex.com
• Wendy Talarico, Communications Manager
(909) 865-4263
• Melissa DeMonaco-Tapia, Director of Sales
(909) 865-4042
demonaco@fairplex.com
Description:
Founded 1922. Home of thoroughbred and quarter horse racing during the Los Angeles County Fair each September-October. Horse shows held regularly throughout the year. Also hosts National Hot Rod Association Winternationals (February), and Winston World Fi
Description:
Founded 1922. Home of thoroughbred and quarter horse racing during the Los Angeles County Fair each September-October. Horse shows held regularly throughout the year. Also hosts National Hot Rod Association Winternationals (February), and Winston World Fi
Seating Capacity
10,000

FIREBIRD INTERNATIONAL RACEWAY
20000 S MARICOPA ROAD
BOX 5023
CHANDLER, AZ 85226
602-268-0200
Fax: 520-796-0531
teamfirebirdinfo@aol.com
www.firebirdraceway.com
• Charlie Allen, President
• Franki Buckman, Vice President
• Charlie Allen, President
(602) 268-0200
Track Length:
1.6 mile, 1.2 mile, 1.1 mile.

Track Type:
Road Course (multiple).

FLOMATON SPEEDWAY
913 HWY 113
FLOMATON, AL 36441
251-296-2233
flomaton.racing@gmail.com
www.flomatonspeedway.com
• Jimmy Goodwin, Promoter
• Pete Arnold, Promoter
• Freddie McCall, Track Owner
(850) 554-3848
• Nascar Ron, Promoter
(251) 538-0546
• Micha McCall McCall, Track Operations
• Tim Wood, Chief Technical Inspector
(251) 727-1513
• Bo McCall, Fuel/ Tire Sales
(251) 655-0971
Track Type:
High-Banked Oval.
Size:
1/4 mile.

GATEWAY MOTORSPORTS PARK
700 RACEWAY BOULEVARD
PO BOX 200
MADISON, IL 62060
618-875-7550
866-357-7333
www.gatewaymsp.com
• Denis F McGlynn, president and CEO of Dover Motorsports
• Lenny Batycki, General Manager
• Linda Thornton, Administration Manager
• Curtis Francisco,
• Mike Stambaugh, COO
• Allison Dziadus, Corporate Sales, Hospitality & NHRA
• Jeff Zelenovich, Ticketing Manager
• Mark Fourier, Digital Marketing & Social Media
• Jeanne Lachmiller, Event Planning & Executive Assistant
• Dan Harman, Opertaing Manager
Series:
NASCAR Busch Series; NASCAR Craftsman Truck Series.
Description:
Motorsports facility.

GEORGE RAY'S DRAGSTRIP
485 HIGHWAY 135 S
PARAGOULD, AR 72450
870-236-8247
• Charles Joliffs, Contact
Track Type:
Dragstrip.
Track Size:
1/8 mile.

HALLETT MOTOR RACING CIRCUIT
59901 E 55 ROAD
JENNINGS, OK 74038
918-356-4814
Fax: 918-356-4815
www.hallettracing.com
• Scott Stephens, Contact
(918) 356-4814
• Connie Stephens, Contact Person
(918) 356-4814
Description:
Auto race track. NHRA sanctioned drag racing.

HICKORY MOTOR SPEEDWAY
3130 HIGHWAY 70 SE
NEWTON, NC 28658
828-464-3655
Fax: 828-465-5017
hickorymotor@bellsouth.net
www.hickorymotorspeedway.com
• Kevin Piercy, Promoter
• Alan Kanupp, Race Director
alan91557@yahoo.com
• Scott Kilby, Technical Director
(704) 880-8003
scott.kilby@ecmd.com
• Bobby Everhart, Website
(336) 692-5131
Description:
Auto race track for NASCAR/Busch Grand National Series, Goody's Dash, and Nextel Cup Series.

HOLIDAY RACEWAY
20105 HWY 11
WOODSTOCK, AL 35188
205-938-2123
www.holidayraceway.com
• Jason Beams, Track Promoter
jason@holidayraceway.com
• Chris Batech,
chris@holidayraceway.com
• Jonathan Beams,
jonathan@holidayraceway.com
Track Type:
Dragstrip.
Size:
1/8 mile.

HOLTVILLE AERODOME INTERNATIONAL RACEWAY
2975 E NORRISH ROAD
HOLTVILLE, CA 92250
619-356-4641
Fax: 205-672-2186
• Jeanne Matthews, Promoter

HOMESTEAD MOTORSPORTS COMPLEX
ONE SPEEDWAY BOULEVARD
HOMESTEAD, FL 33035-1501
305-230-5000
866-409-7223
Fax: 305-230-5140
HMSguestservices@homesteadmiamispeedway.com
www.homesteadmiamispeedway.com
• Nathalie Salas, Community Relation Manager
• Hope Mees, Operations/Track Rentals
(305) 230-5174
hmees@homesteadmiamispeedway.com
• Phil de Montmollin, Public Relations
• Matthew Becherer, Track President
• Albert Garcia, Vice President, Operations
• Shawn McGee, Vice President, Sales and Marketing
• Art Cordova, Director, Accounting & Finance
• William Donnay, Director of Facility Operations
• Ali Bradshaw, Director, Ticket Sales
• Kevin Gregory, Director, Marketing
Track Length:
1.5 miles, 8 degrees.

HOMESTEAD-MIAMI SPEEDWAY, LLC
ONE RALPH SANCHEZ SPEEDWAY BOULEVARD
HOMESTEAD, FL 33035-1501

305-230-5000
866-409-7223
Fax: 305-230-5140
HMSguestservices@homesteadmiamispeed
way.com
www.homesteadmiamispeedway.com
• Gray Curtis, President
• Al Garcia, Vice President of Operations
• Mayra Soto, Controller
• Matthew Becherer, Track President
• Albert Garcia, VP/Operations
• Shawn McGee, VP/Sales and Marketing
• Ali Bradshaw, Director,Ticket Sales
• Art Cordova, Director, Accounting &
Finance
• Jay Fraioli, Director, Security
• Kevin Gregory, Director, Marketing
Description:
Founded 1995. Auto race track.
Series:
NASCAR Nextel Cup Series, NASCAR
Busch Series, NASCAR Craftsman Truck
Series, Indy Racing League.

HUNTSVILLE DRAGWAY
502 QUARTER MOUNTAIN ROAD
HARVEST, AL 35749
205-852-4505
Fax: 205-251-7375
www.huntsvilledragway.com
• George Howard, Promoter
Track Type:
Dragstrip
Track Size:
1/8 mile.

HUNTSVILLE SPEEDWAY
357 HEGIA BURROW ROAD
HUNTSVILLE, AL 35803
256-882-9191
Fax: 256-882-9131
huntsvillespeedway@gmail.com
www.huntsvillespeedway.com
• Ben David Atkinson, Promoter
(256) 539-4484
• Elizabeth Lee, General Manager
(256) 882-9191
Arena Seating Capacity:
3,000.00
Year Founded:
1959
Clients:
Racing Divisions: Late Models, Super
Modifieds, Super Streets, Mini Modifieds,
Hobby Cups, Huntsville Buzz, Mini Cups,
Southern All Stars, USCS Winged Sprint
Cars.
Track Type:
High banked asphalt.

I-70 SPEEDWAY
12773 N OUTER ROAD
ODESSA, MO 64070
816-230-0080
Fax: 913-230-8222
I70Speedway@hotmail.com
www.i70speedway.net
• Marc Olson, General Manager
• Craig Hover, Marketing/Public Relations
Director
Track Address:
12773 Outer Road, Odessa, MO 64076
Description:
Auto Racing Facility featuring ASA AcDello
Series and NASCAR weekly racing series.
Hosts the biggest racing events in Missouri,
with a 28-degree bank.

I-76 SPEEDWAY
16359 COUNTY ROAD S
FORT MORGAN, CO 80701
970-867-2101
Fax: 970-867-2101
i76speedway@fmweb.us
www.i-76speedway.com
• Butch Speicher, Owner
(970) 867-2101
Track:
1/4 mile dirt
Seating Capacity:
1,000
Event:
Stock Car races
Description:
The premier destination for sports events in
Chicago's Northwest suburbs, convenient to
downtown Chicago and O'Hare Airport. We
will assist with locating venues and housing.
Our area features a 100,000 sq. ft.
Convention Center, soccer &
baseball/softball fields, local college facilities
and indoor park district complexes.

INDIANAPOLIS MOTOR SPEEDWAY CORPORATION
4790 W 16TH STREET
INDIANAPOLIS, IN 46222
317-492-8500
Fax: 317-492-6482
imspr@brickyard.com
www.indianapolismotorspeedway.com
• George H Anton, President/Chief
Executive Officer
• Joie Chitwood, President/Chief Operations
Officer IMS
• Jeff Belskus, EVP
• Fred Nation, EVP/Corporate
Communications
• David Strahan, Account Executive
Series:
NASCAR Nextel Cup Series; NASCAR
Busch Series; NASCAR Craftsman Truck
Series.
Description:
Owns and operates race track and related
facilities. Home of the Indianapolis 500 (Indy
Racing League); Brickyard 400 (NASCAR);
United States Grand Prix (Formula One).
Publications:
INDIANAPOLIS 500 OFFICIAL PROGRAM,
annual; MAY INDY REVIEW, annual;
BRICKYARD 400 OFFICIAL PROGRAM,
annual; UNITED STATES GRAND PRIX
OFFICIAL PROGRAM, annual; RECORD
BOOK OF INDIANAPOLIS 500, annual;
RECORD BOOK OF BRICKYARD 400,
annual.

INDIANAPOLIS RACEWAY PARK
10267 E US HIGHWAY 136
PO BOX 34300
INDIANAPOLIS, IN 46234
317-291-4090
Fax: 317-291-4220
wcollier@nhra.com
www.lucasoilraceway.com
• Angela Eaton, Business Administration
Director
• Jeff Dakin, Director Operations
• Brad Horn, Communications Manager
Sports Service Founded:
Sports Service Founded: 1960.
Nature of Service:
Motorsports Park.

INTERNATIONAL SPEEDWAY CORPORATION
ONE DAYTONA BOULEVARD
DAYTONA BEACH, FL 32114
386-254-2700
www.internationalspeedwaycorporation.com

JENNERSTOWN SPEEDWAY
224 RACE STREET
PO BOX 230
PO Box 230
JENNERSTOWN, PA 15547
814-629-6677
Fax: 814-629-7121
www.jennerstown.com
• Dave Wheeler, President
(814) 629-6677
• Jen Wheeler, Secretary/Treasurer
(814) 629-6677
• Joseph Dirienzo, Sales/Marketing Director
(814) 629-6677
• Larry Mattingly, General Manager
(814) 629-6677
Arena Seating Capacity:
9,000.00
Clients
Weekly Nascar-sanctioned races, Hooters
Pro Cup 250, ASA, ISMA.
Nature of Service:
Automobile racetrack.
Track Type:
Asphalt.

JULESBURG DRAGSTRIP
98 KANSAS STREET
CHEYENNE, WY 82009
970-631-4490
Fax: 970-474-9999
• Bill Schneider, Promoter
Track Type:
Dragstrip
Track Size:
1/4 mile

KANSAS SPEEDWAY
400 SPEEDWAY BOULEVARD
KANSAS CITY, KS 66111
913-328-3380
866-460-7223
Fax: 913-328-3380
www.kansasspeedway.com
• Jamie Bodenstadt, President
• Greg Fritze, Vice President
• Travis Watson, Business Manager
• Sue Bodenstadt, Treasure
• Jeff Anderson, Secretary
• Anna M Watson, Site Admin
• Jamie Bodenstadt,
(907) 322-8359
• Jamie Bodenstadt, President
akgrizzly@gci.net
Track Type:
Dragstrip.
Track Length:
1/4 mile.

KENNEDY RACEWAY
912 6TH STREET NE
SUITE 10
KENNEDY, AL 35073
205-674-8088
• Kathy Hills, Promoter
Developers:
International Speedway Corp.
Size:
3/8 mile.

Track Type:
High-Banked Oval.

KENTUCKY SPEEDWAY
ONE SPEEDWAY DRIVE
SPARTA, KY 41086
859-578-2300
888-652-7223
Fax: 859-647-4307
www.kentuckyspeedway.com
• Andy Vertrees, Director Operations
• Dan Stuart, Director of Sponsorship
Development & Client Svcs.
dstuart@kentuckyspeedway.com
• Tim Bray, Communications Director
(859) 567-3400
tbray@kentuckyspeedway.com
• Mark Simendinger, GM
mSimendinger@kentuckyspeedway.com
• Karen Bannick, Office Manager
kbannick@kentuckyspeedway.com
• Pam Mylor, Service Coordinator
pmylor@kentuckyspeedway.com
• Kara Spencer, Front Desk
kspencer@kentuckyspeedway.com
• John Cox, VP Of sales
(859) 578-2328
jcox@kentuckyspeedway.com
Series:
Busch Series, Craftsman Truck Series, Indy
Racing League, ARCA RE/MAX Series, Hills
Bros All Pro Series, Goody's Dash Series,
K.O.I.L. Tour.

KERN COUNTY RACEWAY PARK
PO BOX 816
ROSAMOND, CA 93560
805-272-1234
Fax: 805-266-0584
• Rusty Fields, Promoter

KNOXVILLE RACEWAY
1000 N LINCOLN STREET
PO BOX 347
KNOXVILLE, IA 50138
641-842-5431
Fax: 641-842-2899
info@knoxvilleraceway.com
www.knoxvilleraceway.com
• Brian Stickel, General Manager, Promoter
bstickel@knoxvilleraceway.com
Description:
Races most Saturday nights from May to
October. Featured events include 50th
Goodyear Knoxville Nationals provided by
Lucas Oil, 20th Annual Arnold Motor Supply
360 Knoxville Nationals, Lucas Oil Late
Model Knoxville Nationals.
Events:
Knoxville Nationals
Track:
1/2 mile banked dirt oval.

LAKEPORT SPEEDWAY
401 MARTIN STREET
PO BOX 1411
LAKEPORT, CA 95453
707-279-9577
Fax: 707-279-9677
www.lakeportspeedway.com
• Dave Swindell, Promoter
• Danny McIntire, President
Description:
Track Size:
1/4 mile.

LAKESIDE SPEEDWAY
5615 WALCOTT DRIVE
KANSAS CITY, KS 66109
913-299-2040
Fax: 913-299-1105
www.lakesidespeedway.net
• Marc Olson, Owner
Track Size:
3/8 mile.
Track Type:
High-Banked Oval.

LAS VEGAS MOTOR SPEEDWAY/LVMS
7000 LAS VEGAS BOULEVARD N
LAS VEGAS, NV 89115
702-644-4444
800-644-4444
Fax: 702-644-7774
media@lvms.com
www.lvms.com
• Ricky May, Sales/Marketing VP
(702) 632-8241
rmay@lvms.com
• David Stetzer, Vice President of
Operations
(702) 632-8234
dstetzer@lvms.com
• Chris Powell, President/General Manager
(702) 632-8030
cpowell@lvms.com
• O. Bruton Smith, Chairman of the Board
• Chris Powell, President and General
Manager
(702) 644-4444
media@lvms.com
• Bill Soard, Vice President of Finance
(702) 632-8042
wsoard@lvms.com
• David Stetzer, Vice President of
Operations
(702) 632-8234
dstetzer@lvms.com
• Jeff Motley, Vice President of Public
Relations
(702) 632-8266
jmotley@lvms.com
• Kevin Camper, Senior Vice President of
Sales and Marketing
(702) 632-8241
kcamper@lvms.com
• Bobby McKenna, Director of Facility
Operations
(702) 632-8128
bckenna@lvms.com
Series:
NASCAR Nextel Cup Series; NASCAR
Busch Series; NASCAR Craftsman Truck
Series.
Back Straight:
3 degrees.
Front Straight:
8 degrees.
Banking:
Corners: 12 degrees.

LASSITER MOUNTAIN DRAGWAY
PO BOX 934
GARDENDALE, AL 35071
205-849-2778
lassitermountain@gmail.com
www.lassitermountain.net
• John Howard, Track Manager
(205) 849-2778
lassitermountain@gmail.com
• Matt Howard, Advertising
(205) 746-6616

matt.howard58@gmail.com
• Anthony Brown, Promoter
Track Size:
1/8 mile.
Track Type:
Dragstrip.

LEMOORE RACEWAY
1750 HIGHWAY 41
LEMOORE, CA 93245
559-924-2536
Fax: 559-217-8832
info@stoneysllc.com
www.lemooreraceway.com
• Nadine Strauss, Manager
• David Furia, Co-manager
• Danny McIntire, President
Year Founded:
1949
Arena Seating Capacity:
1,800.00
Nature of Service:
Auto Racing.
Track Type:
Asphalt.

LIME ROCK PARK
60 WHITE HOLLOW ROAD
LAKEVILLE, CT 6039
860-435-5000
Fax: 860-435-5010
info@limerock.com
www.limerock.com
• Steve Potter, General Manager/VP
(860) 435-5000
• William McMinn, Marketing/Sales Director
(860) 365-0047
wmcminn@limerock.com
• Petra Willig, Track Sales Manager
(860) 435-5000
• Skip Barber, President and Owner
• Nancy Eppley, Operations Manager
(860) 432-5011
• Donnia A Hamzy, Office Manager
(860) 432-5000
• Rick Roso, Press, PR & Editorial Director
(860) 432-5000
• Georgia Blades, CEO
(860) 432-5000
georgia@limerock.com
• Walter Irvine, Director Business
Development
(860) 432-5000
walter@limerock.com
• Renea Topp, Director of Marketing & PR
(860) 432-5000
Year Founded:
1957
Track Type:
Paved Road Race Track.
Seating Capacity:
Unlimited Hillside viewing.
Track Size:
1.53 Miles.

LOS ANGELES COUNTY RACEWAY
6850 E AVENUE T
PALMDALE, CA 93550
661-533-2224
Fax: 661-533-2226
lacountyraceway@hotmail.com
www.lacr.net
• Bernard Longjohn, Promoter
Track Size:
1/4 mile.
Track Type:
Dragstrip.

MADERA SPEEDWAY
1850 W CLEVELAND AVENUE
MADERA, CA 93637
209-356-1968
Fax: 209-356-1968
tickets@racemadera.com
www.racemadera.com
• Kye Evans, Promoter
(559) 924-2536
• Kenny Shephard, President / GM
(209) 769-9581
kshepherd@racemadera.com
Track Size:
1/8 mile.
Track Type:
Semi-Banked Oval.

MANZANITA SPEEDWAY
3417 W BROADWAY ROAD
PHOENIX, AZ 85041
602-276-7575
Fax: 602-276-2328
• Keith Hall, Promoter
• Ladd Hall, Promoter
Track Type:
Semi-Banked Oval.
Track Size:
1/2 mile and 5/8 mile.

MARBURY DIRT TRACK & KART SHOP
3098 GO KART ROAD
MARBURY, AL 36051
205-755-0465
• Jeff Scott, Promoter
Track Type:
High-Banked Oval.
Track Size:
1/8 mile.

MARTINSVILLE SPEEDWAY
340 SPEEDWAY ROAD
RIDGEWAY, VA 24148
276-956-1543
Fax: 276-956-2820
www.martinsvillespeedway.com
• W. Clay Campbell, President
• Mike Smith, Public Relations Director
(276) 956-1543
msmith@martinsvillespeedway.com
• Karen Parker, Marketing/Business
Development Director
(276) 956-8460
kparker@martinsvillespeedway.com
• Hope Perry, Promotions/Publications
Director
(276) 956-1148
• Karen Parker, VP Marketing
• Rob Gehman, Sr.Director of Accounting
• Henry Williams, Sr.Director of Facility
Operations
• Billy Moore, Track Suprintendent
• Gordon Wilson, Director, Track Operations
Year Founded:
1947
Track Type:
Oval.
Track Size:
.526 mile.

MAZDA RACEWAY LAGUNA SECA
1021 MONTEREY-SALINAS HIGHWAY
SALINAS, CA 93908
831-242-8201
800-327-7322
Fax: 831-373-0533
media@mazdaraceway.com
www.mazdaraceway.com

• Jeanie Sumners, Marketing Manager
(831) 242-8252
jeanie@MazdaRaceway.com
• Steve Fields, Executive Director of
Corporate Development
(831) 277-5798
steve@mazdaraceway.com
• Ann Bixler, Events VP
• Gill Campbell, CEO/General Manager
• Melvyn Record, VP Marketing and Sales
• Ann Bixler, VP Event Operations
• Barry Toepke, VP Communications &
Historic Racing
• Bo Beresiwsky, VP Facility Operations
• Jim Harris, Chief Financial officer
• Steve Fields, Executive Director of
Corporate Development
Description:
Founded 1957. Auto and motorcycle road
race track.

MEMPHIS MOTORSPORTS PARK (MMP)
5500 VICTORY LANE
MILLINGTON, TN 38053
901-969-7223
866-40-77333
Fax: 901-969-8012
www.racemir.com
• Jason Rittenberry, VP/General Manager
(901) 354-2530
• Aaron Hitchcock, Business Development
Manager
• Doug Franklin, Director Public
Relations/Marketing
• Blake Barnes, Ticket Manager
• Daniel Carpenter, Director of Business
Development
• Christi Carson, Corporate Account
Executive
• Jerry Pennington, Corporate Account
Executive
• Jason Rittenberry, General Manager
• Garett Story, Corporate Account Executive
• Pam Kendrick, Vice President & General
Manager
(901) 969-0811
• Paul Cartwright, Director of Operations
(901) 969-0661
• Kate Armitage, Director of Public Relations
& Communication
(901) 969-0667
• Sharon Nix, Concessions & Facility
Manager
(901) 969-0669
• Mike Fry, Maintenance Manager
(901) 969-0668
• Glynn Williford, Account Executive /
Sponsor Relations
(901) 969-0777
• Dan Carpenter, Sponsorship Sales
(901) 969-7223
Series:
NASCAR Busch Series; NASCAR
Craftsman Truck Series.

MERCED FAIRGROUNDS SPEEDWAY
900 MARTIN LUTHER KING JR HIGHWAY
(HIGWAY 59)
MERCED, CA 95301
209-383-3802
Fax: 209-383-3802
• Chuck Griffin, Promoter
(209) 383-3802
ccmrchuck@att.net
• Marylee Griffin, Manager/Treasurer
(209) 383-3802
ccmrmarylee@att.net
• John Bass, Announcer

Track Type:
Semi-Banked Oval.
Track Size:
1/4 mile.
Tracks:
Paved Oval, Dirt Track, Dragstrip, Road
Course.

MESA MARIN RACEWAY
9520 TAFT HIGHWAY
BAKERSFIELD, CA 93311
661-397-7333
Fax: 661-831-2582
• Marion Collins, President/Owner
• Larry Collins, Operations VP
• Judy Salamacha, Public
Relations/Marketing VP
Description:
Auto race track hosting the following
NASCAR racing series: NASCAR West,
Featherlite Southwest Tour, Supertruck,
NASCAR Craftsman Track Series, NASCAR
Winston West, NASCAR Featherlite
Southwest Tour, NASCAR Nextel Cup
Series, Ultra Wheel Spec Trucks, WSMR

**MICHIGAN INTERNATIONAL SPEEDWAY
(MIS)**
12626 US HIGHWAY 12
BROOKLYN, MI 49230-9068
517-592-6666
Fax: 517-592-3848
contact@mispeedway.com
www.mispeedway.com
• Roger Curtis, President
• Keith Karbo, Marketing Director
• Bill Janitz, Public Relations/New Manager
• Roger Curtis, President
• Kelly Daniels, Director of Accounting
• Jennifer Hutchinson, Director of Business
Development
(517) 592-1128
• Sammie Lukaskiewicz, Sr.Director of
Communications
• Karen Hively, Sr.Executive Ass to the
President
• Barry Gibson, Sr.Director of Operations
• Jim Hobbs, Security Director
Description:
Auto race track.
Series:
NASCAR Nextel Cup Series; NASCAR
Busch Series; NASCAR Craftsman Truck
Series.
Year Founded:
1968
Seating capacity:
136,373

MID-OHIO SPORTS CAR COURSE
7721 STEAM CORNERS ROAD
LEXINGTON, OH 44904-0108
419-884-4000
Fax: 419-884-0042
info@midohio.com
www.midohio.com
• Craig Rust, President
crust@midohio.com
• Adam Fisher, Director Of Operations &
Facility
• Kathy Nolan, Business Development
Director
knolan@midohio.com
• Steve Bidlack, Marketing And
Communications Manager
sbidlack@greensavoree.com

Year Founded & Description:
A comprehensive motorsports facility openedin 1962, Mid-Ohio Sports Car Course features a permanent road-racing circuit with two primary configurations: a 2.4-mile, 15-turn; and a 2.25-mile, 13-turn circuit. Located 60 miles north of Columbus and 75 miles south of Cleveland near Mansfeild, the track has been called the most competitive in the U.S. and annually hosts a diversity of locally, regionally and nationally sanctioned racing events for amateur, club and professional drivers and riders.
Track Type:
Permanent road course.
Track Size:
2.4 miles.
Seating Capacity:
Unlimited general admission and approximately 5,000 grandstand seats.
Clients Include:
American Honda Motor Co. Inc; Cooper Tires; Summit Racing; Sunoco.
Nature of Service:
Motorsports entertainment and driving; riding school.

MILWAUKEE MILE
7722 W GREENFIELD AVENUE
W ALLIS, WI 53214
414-453-5761
Fax: 414-453-9920
• Claude Napier, President/CEO
• Steve Jones, General Manager/Chief Operating Officer
• Gary Girard, Operations Director
• Cheryl Kuchinskas, Office Manager/Business Manager
Arena Seating Capacity:
45,000
Track Type:
1 mile paved.
Track Size:
1 mile.
Year Founded:
1903

MITCHELL RACEWAY
4075 PEGER ROAD
FAIRBANKS, AK 99709
907-479-4266
Fax: 907-457-5063
• Jessica Bain, Secretary
(907) 479-5655
• Mark (Doc) Davos, President
Track Type:
Slightly-Banked Oval.
Track Length:
1/4 mile.

MOBILE DRAGWAY
7800 PARK BOULEVARD
IRVINGTON, AL 36544
251-957-3054
MobileDragway@aol.com
www.mobiledragway.com
• Gary Moore, Promoter
(251) 957-3054
Track Size:
1/8 mile.
Track Type:
Dragstrip.

MOBILE INTERNATIONAL SPEEDWAY
7800 PARK BOULVARD
IRVINGTON, AL 36544
251-957-2063
Fax: 251-957-2026
www.mobilespeedway.net
• Bill Roth, Promoter
Track Size:
1/2 mile.
Track Type:
High-Banked Oval.

MONTEZUMA COUNTY FAIRGROUNDS
107 N CHESTNUT
CORTEZ, CO 81321
970-565-1000
• Dante Sena, Promoter
Track Type:
Semi-Banked Oval
Track Size:
3/8 mile

MONTGOMERY MOTORSPORTS PARK (MMP)
2600 N BELT DRIVE
MONTGOMERY, AL 36110
334-260-9660
Fax: 334-260-9320
jim@mmpdragracing.com
www.mmpdragracing.com
• Anthony Oehler, Manager
• Phillips Chris,
• Jim Howard,
Track Size:
1/4 mile.
Track Type:
Dragstrip.

MOUNTAIN VIEW MOTORSPORTS PARK
3692 26TH STREET
BOULDER, CO 80304
970-535-9999
• Andrew Rosen, Promoter
• Travis Rosen, Promoter
Track Size:
1.3 miles
Track Type:
Road Course (9 turns)

MYRTLE BEACH SPEEDWAY(MBS)
455 HOSPITALITY LANE
MYRTLE BEACH, SC 29579
843-236-0500
Fax: 704-886-2410
stevez@mbsspeedway.com
www.myrtlebeachspeedway.com
• Billy Hardee, Owner
• Nick Lucas, Owner
• Bill Hennecy, Track Manager
bhennecy@aol.com
Description:
Auto race track for NASCAR Weekly Racing Series presented by Dodge, Hills Bros All Pro Series, Goody's Dash and SMART Open Wheel Modified.
Seating Capacity:
12,500
Year Founded:
1958
Track Type:
Asphalt.

NASHVILLE SUPERSPEEDWAY
4847-F MCCRARY ROAD
LEBANON, TN 37090
615-547-7500
Fax: 615-547-7575
Info@nashvillesuperspeedway.com
www.nashvillesuperspeedway.com
• Connie Boshers, Director of Administration
• Griffin Colvert, Director Business Development
• Cliff Hawks, General Manager
Nature of Service:
Track Rental, Road Course, Community Events.
Year Founded:
2001
Clients:
NASCAR Busch Series(2), Indy Car Series, NASCAR Craftman Truck Series, 40th Anniversary of the Ford Mustang.
Arena Seating Capacity:
25,000.00

NATIONAL HOT ROD ASSOCIATION
2035 FINANCIAL WAY
GLENDORA, CA 91741
626-914-4761
Fax: 626-963-5360
nhra@nhra.com
www.nhra.com
• Tom Compton, President
• Dallas Gardner, Board Chairman
Track Type:
Dragstrip.
Track Size:
1/4 mile.

NATIONAL ORANGE SHOW EVENTS CENTER
689 S E STREET
SAN BERNANDINO, CA 92408
909-888-6788
Fax: 909-889-7666
info@nosevents.com
www.nosevents.com
• Steve Larsen, General Manager
(909) 888-6788
Type of Track:
Semi-Banked Oval.
Track Size:
1/4 mile.

NATIONAL TRAIL RACEWAY
2650 NATIONAL ROAD SW
HEBRON, OH 43025
740-928-5706
Fax: 740-928-2922
www.nationaltrailraceway.com
• Jim Layton, General Manager
(740) 928-5706
jlayton@nhra.com
• Mike Fornataro, Sales/Marketing Manager
(740) 928-5706
MFornataro@nhra.com
• Christoper Stilwell, Facility and Operations manager
(740) 928-5706
CStilwell@nhra.com
• Janice Hagg, Administrative Assistant
(740) 928-5706
JHagg@nhra.com
Seating Capacity:
12,000
Sports:
National Trail Raceway is a division of NHRA Drag Racing.
Track Type:
1/4 mile drag strip.
Description:
NHRA Drag Race Track

Events:
Chrysler Classic, MOPAR Nationals, NMRA, Buick Performance Nationals, NHRA Unleashed, Jegs Northern Sports Nationals, ET Racing

NEA SPEEDWAY
1512 WOFFORD STREET
JONESBORO, AR 72401
870-935-3749
• Hugh Cornelison, Promoter
• Edna Cornelison, Promoter
Track Type:
Semi-Banked Oval.
Track Size:
1/4 mile.

NELSON LEDGES ROAD COURSE
10342 STATE ROUTE 305
GARRETTSVILLE, OH 44231
330-977-0111
info@nelsonledges.com
www.nelsonledges.com
• Fred Wolf, Manager
(330) 977-0111
Description:
Automobile and motorcycle race track.
Year founded
1958.
Track type and size
Road course; 2.0 miles.
Seating capacity:
10,0000.

NEW HAMPSHIRE MOTOR SPEEDWAY
1122 ROUTE 106 N
LOUDON, NH 3307
603-783-4744
Fax: 603-783-9691
info@nhms.com
www.nhms.com
• O Bruton Smith, Chairman of the Board
• Jerry Gappens, EVP/General Manager
• Susan Colby, VP Guest Services
(603) 783-4744
scolby@nhms.com
• Troy Taylor, VP Sales/Marketing
(603) 783-4744
ttaylor@nhms.com
Track:
1.058 Mile Oval & 1.6 Mile Road Course.
Seating Capacity:
93,521
Year Built:
1989-1990
Events:
Inaugural Sno Bowl (Snowmobile Racing); Annual Vintage Racing Celebration; Annual Loudon Classic (Motorcycle Racing); Annual LENOX Industrial Tools 301 (NASCAR); Annual SYLVANIA 300 (NASCAR).
Description:
NHMS features a wide variety of racing sanctioned by NASCAR, including the NASCAR Sprint Cup Series, NASCAR Nationwide Series, the NASCAR Camping World Truck Series, the NASCAR K&N Pro Series East, and the NASCAR Whelen Modified Tour. The American-Canadian Tour late models compete in an invitation-only event during the September NASCAR SYLVANIA 300 race weekend. Features sanctioned racing with the American SportBike Racing Association, the Championship Cup Series, the Sports Car Club of America, the World Karting Association, the Vintage Racing Group, the

Sidecar Racers Association, and the United States Classic Racing Association.

NORTH ALABAMA SPEEDWAY
12200 HIGHWAY 247
TUSCUMBIA, AL 35674
256-381-0881
northalabamaspeedway@hotmail.com
• Sam Bates, Owner
Track Type:
Dragstrip.
Track Size:
1/8 mile.

NORTHWEST ARKANSAS SPEEDWAY
1804 SLACK STREET
PEA RIDGE, AR 72751
479-451-8636
Fax: 501-451-1900
• Darla Nix, Track operator
• Gary Wilbur, Promoter
• Butch Wilbur, Promoter
Track Size:
3/8 mile.
Track Type:
High-Banked Oval.

OCEAN SPEEDWAY
2601 E LAKE AVENUE
WATSONVILLE, CA 95010
831-662-9466
Fax: 831-668-0708
OceanSpeedway@aol.com
www.oceanspeedway.com
• John Prentice, Promoter
(831) 464-1500

PENTON RACEWAY, INC.
PENTON KARTING KOMPLEX
LAFAYETTE, AL 36862
334-864-0967
• Edge Bill & Debbie, Promoter
(334) 864-9641
• Mike Edge,
(334) 864-9448
Arena Seating Capacity:
1,200.00
Year Founded:
1980
Track Type:
Clay round track.
Track Size:
1/8 mile.

PERRIS AUTO SPEEDWAY
18700 LAKE PERRIS DRIVE
PERRIS, CA 92571
951-940-0134
800-595-4849
Fax: 909-940-0634
openwhchic.kim@aol.com
www.perrisautospeedway.com
• Dan Kazarian, Promoter
Track Type:
High-Banked Oval.
Track Size:
1/2 mile.

PETALUMA SPEEDWAY
PO BOX 6
PETALUMA, CA 94953
707-763-7223
Info@Petaluma-Speedway.com
www.petaluma-speedway.com
• Jim Soares, Promoter

Track Type:
Semi-Banked Oval.
Track Size:
3/8 mile.

PHOENIX INTERNATIONAL RACEWAY
7602 S. AVONDALE BOULEVARD
AVONDALE, AZ 85323
623-772-2000
Fax: 623-932-0416
ticketoffice@phoenixinternationalraceway.com
www.phoenixintlraceway.com
• Bryan Sperber, President
• Marie Jarnlof-Carey, Accounting & Ticketing Operations Direct
• Jim Kofakis, Director Sales
• Bryan Sperber, President
• Jennifer Wentzel, Execuive Assistant
• James Hamilton, Director of Government Affairs
• Marie Isabell, Sr.Director of Business Directions
• Jay Wagner, Director of Ticket Operations
• Gale Powers, Sr.Management Member
• Terrie Ball, Accounting and Payroll Manager
Sponsor
Checker Auto Parts 500.
Description:
Founded 1964. One-mile oval track for auto racing. Stages four events annually, including NASCAR Nextel Cup weekend, Copper World Indy 200, Grand American Road Racing, NASCAR Winter Heat.
Track Address:
7602 S. 115th Ave, Avondale, AZ 85323

PIKES PEAK INTERNATIONAL RACEWAY
16650 MIDWAY RANCH ROAD
FOUNTAIN, CO 80817
719-382-7223
888-306-7223
Fax: 719-382-9180
info@ppir.com
www.ppir.com
• Bob Boileau, President
(719) 382-7223
• Jared Thompson, Track Manager
jared@ppir.com
Special Events:
USAC Silver Crown Championship Series; USAC National Midget Series; NASCAR West Series; ARCA Bondo/Mar-Hyde Series; NASCAR Busch Series; ASA ACDelco Challenge Series; USAC Western States Midget Series; USAC Western States Sprint Car Series; Late Model St
Seating Capacity:
10,000
Track Type:
Oval; Road Course; Autocross Lot; Dirt Road Course
Track Size:
1-Mile Oval; 1.3 Mile Road Course; 12 Acre Autocross Lot; 2-mile Dirt Road Course
Nature of Service:
Homegrown festival and motor-sports events and Facility Rentals

PLACERVILLE SPEEDWAY
100 PLACERVILLE DRIVE
SUITE #3
PLACERVILLE, CA 95667
530-626-3680
Fax: 916-783-7223

placervillespeedwaymedia@yahoo.com
www.placervillespeedway.com
• John Padjen, Sullivan
• Alan Handy, Track Manager
• Mike Andreeta, Director of Competiton
• Cindy Jones, Scorekeeping
• Kristina Coffey, Business Office
• Bill Sullivan, Director of Communications
Track Distance:
1/4 mile.
Track Type:
High-Banked Oval.

PLAZA PARK RACEWAY
1820 W. LACEY BLVD.
HANFORD, CA 93230
559-651-5114
plazaparkraceway@gmail.com
www.plazaparkraceway.com
• Brandon Morse, Promoter
Track Type:
Semi-Banked Oval.
Track Distance:
1/5 mile.

POCONO RACEWAY
PO BOX 500
LONG PONG ROAD
LONG POND, PA 18334
570-646-2300
800-722-3929
Fax: 570-646-2010
www.poconoraceway.com
• Dr Joseph R. Mattioli, Chief Executive
Officer/Chairman
• Rose Mattioli, Secretary/Treasurer
• George Ewald, VP/Track Superintendent
• Daniel Dougherty, VP Track
Services/Leases
Description:
Auto race track.
Sponsors:
Pocono 500; Pennsylvania 500.

PORTLAND INTERNATIONAL RACEWAY
1940 N VICTORY BOULEVARD
PORTLAND, OR 97217
503-823-7223
Fax: 503-823-5896
pir@portlandoregon.gov
www.portlandraceway.com
• E.C. Mueller, Racetrack Manager
Description:
Founded 1961. Auto, on- & off-road
motorcycle racing, drag racing, bicycle
racing, Swap Meets, police training, driver
training, action sports events, runs/walks.
Track Type:
1/4 mile & 1/8 mile drag strips incorporated
in to a Road Course whose track length
without "Festival Turns" is 1.915 miles and
nine turns. With the "Festival Turns" it is
1.967 miles and 12 turns. The track surface
is asphalt with a concrete surface for the
"Festival Turns." There are no banked turns.
Seating Capacity:
18,000 seating plus additional 8,000
General Admission
Clients:
INDYCAR, Pirelli World Challenge, SCCA,
NHRA Summit Series, Cascade Sports Car
Club, Oregon Motorcycle Road Racing
Association, Thursday Night Motocross,
SOVREN, SVRA
Nature of Service:
Portland International Raceway hosts sports
car and motorcycle road racing, INDYCAR,

USAC, NHRA drag racing, motocross,
bicycle racing and running/walking events.
Portland International Raceway is owned
and operated by the City of Portland through
its bureau of Parks and Recreation. The
raceway is operated as an Enterprise Fund,
meaning that it is self-sustaining. Operating
expenses and capital improvements are
covered by the revenues that it generates,
as the raceway receives no general fund tax
dollars. The raceway's varied, year-round
activities bring between 30 and 40 million
dollars into the surrounding community each
year.

PORTLAND SPEEDWAY
9727 N MARTIN LUTHER KING JR
BOULEVARD
PORTLAND, OR 97217
508-285-2881
Fax: 281-447-3915
houevents@aol.com
• Craig Armstrong, General Manager
• Shannon Derrick, Public Relations Director
• Fred Armstrong, Marketing Director
• Kim Mitchell, Administration/Operations
Manager
Description:
Auto race track hosting the NASCAR
Weekly Racing Series, (Friday nights;
April-September), plus the Pennzoil World of
Outlaws sprint car series, Northern Sprint
Tour; Dirt Late Models; National
Championships Flat Track Motorcycles.

PRAIRIE CITY SVRA RACEWAY PARK
191 WALKER LANE
OROVILLE, CA 95965
530-532-1014
Fax: 503-532-9180
info@hangtownmx.com
• Jerry W Ahrens, Promoter
(530) 532-1014
amp@cncnet.com
Track Type:
Semi-Banked Oval.
Track Size:
1/8 mile.

PRESCOTT RACEWAY
5121 HIGHWAY 53 E
PRESCOTT, AR 71857
870-887-3984
Fax: 501-332-4413
jackie-lewis@live.com
www.prescottraceway.net
• Jackie Lewis, Owner
(870) 904-5952
jackie-lewis@live.com
• Velvet Lewis, Owner
(870) 234-2184
Track Size:
1/8 mile.
Track Type:
Dragstrip.

REDWOOD ACRES FAIRGROUNDS
3750 HARRIS STREET
EUREKA, CA 95501
707-445-3037
Fax: 707-445-1583
www.redwoodacres.com
• Richard Olson, Chairman and co-founder
• Terry Coltra, President
tcoltra@ncidc.org
• Cindy Bedingfield, CEO
• Scott Downie,

sdownie@dfg.ca.gov
• Ed Laidlaw,
egllge@yahoo.com
• Meredith Biasca,
• Connie Stewart,
conniestew@humboldt.edu
Type of Track:
Semi-Banked Oval.
Track Length:
3/8 mile.

RICHMOND INTERNATIONAL RACEWAY
600 E LABURNUM AVENUE
RICHMOND, VA 23222
866-455-7223
866-455-7223
Fax: 804-321-3833
ririnfo@rir.com
www.rir.com
• Douglas Fritz, President
• Brett Adams, Senior Operations Director
• Roger Curtis, Seniorr Marketing/Sales
Director
• Dennis Bickmeier, President
• John Moreland, VP, Sales and Marketing
• Justin DuBrueler, Sr.Director Accounting
• Jeff Hedrick, Sr.Director of Operations
• Deborah Clemons, Director of Community
Affairs
• Diane Cahoon, Director of Ticket
Operations
• Louis Gilmore, Director of Business
Developmetn
Arena Seating Capacity:
107,000.00
Clients:
NASCAR Nextel Cup Series, NASCAR
Busch, MASCAR Craftsman Truck, IRL
IndyCar Series.
Track Type:
D-shaped oval.
Track Size:
3/4 mile.

ROAD AMERICA
N7390 STATE HIGHWAY 67
PLYMOUTH, WI 53073
920-892-4576
800-365-7223
Fax: 920-892-4550
info@roadamerica.com
www.roadamerica.com
• George Bruggenthies, General
Manager/President
(920) 892-4576
george@roadamerica.com
• Mary Lo Haen, Marketing
(920) 893-3704
marylou@roadamerica.com
• Gail Bartelt, Corporate Hospitality/Rentals
(920) 892-4576
• Tonya Gosse, Finance
• Gail Barteilt, Hospitality & Track Trends
• Mary L Haen, Marketing & Promotions
• John Ewert, Communications
• Kathy Kiesau, Administration & Retail
• Mike Kertscher, Group Programs &
Schools
• Carson Wilkinson, Safety Director
(920) 892-4576
safety@roadamerica.com
Arena Seating Capacity:
250,000.00
Year Founded:
1955
Clients:
Top professional, amateur motorcycle,

sports car, open wheel, kart series.
Nature of Service:
Road America provides a full service, first class road race facility; anemities include VIP suites, gourmet catering, camping, motor home area, internationally acclaimed permanent road racing track.

ROAD ATLANTA
5300 WINDER HIGHWAY
BRASELTON, GA 30517
770-967-6143
800-849-7223
Fax: 770-967-2668
info@roadatlanta.com
www.roadatlanta.com
• Geoff Lee, President
(770) 967-6143
glee@roadatlanta.com
• Joey Greene, Vice President of Operations
(770) 967-6143
jgreene@roadatlanta.com
• Steve Lanier, Facility Manager
slanier@roadatlanta.com
• Ken Grogan, Director of Security
kgrogan@roadatlanta.com
• Angie Griffin, Corporate Sales Coordinator
agriffin@roadatlanta.com
• Lisa Stewart, Accounting Manager
lstewart@roadatlanta.com
Description:
Road racing track and entertainment facility. Features Professional SportsCar, AMA, NASB & WERA Motorcycles, Vintage and Historic Racing. Operates Driver Training Center offering Advanced Handling and Road Racing courses.

ROCKY HILL SPEEDWAY
312 W BELLVIEW
PORTERVILLE, CA 93257
209-784-4660
Fax: 870-773-2243
WhoWon.com
• Issac Vallejo, Promoter
Track Length:
1/4 mile.
Track Type:
Slightly-Banked Oval.

ROYAL PURPLE RACEWAY
2525 SOUTH FM 565
BAYTOWN, TX 77523
281-383-7223
281-383-2666
Fax: 281-383-3777
media@royalpurpleraceway.com
www.royalpurpleraceway.com/
• Seth Angel, Executive VP/General Manager
• LaRhonda Aron, Director of Business Affairs and Ticketing
laron@royalpurpleraceway.com
• Fern Davis, Director of Sales & Business Development
fdavis@royalpurpleraceway.com
• Nayeli Pacheco, Executive Administrative Assistant & Hospital
npacheco@royalpurpleraceway.com
• Don Neal, Food & Beverage Coordinator
npacheco@royalpurpleraceway.com
• Kenny DeLaughter, Faciliti es Manager
• John Wood, Photographer
• Seth Angel, EVP & General Manager
seth@royalpurpleraceway.com
Description:
Auto race track. NHRA sanctioned drag

racing.
Permanent seating capacity:
30,000

SACRAMENTO RACEWAY PARK (DRAGSTRIP/MX)
5305 EXCELSIOR ROAD
SACRAMENTO, CA 95827
916-363-2653
Fax: 916-368-8772
sacramentoraceway@zetabb.com
www.sacramentoraceway.com
• D. L Smith, Track Owner
nitrofeverracing@zetabb.com
• Cynthiia C Crump, Concession Manager
(916) 708-8811
• Jennifer A Trimp, General Manager
(916) 416-0545
• Tony A Trimp, Events Manager
(916) 416-0545
• Roger Williams, Drag Racing Director
red99nb@yahoo.com
• David Smith, Promoter
(916) 416-1689
• David Smith Jr., Test & Tune
davejr@zetabb.com
• Cindy Crump, Track Rental Info.
sacramentoraceway@zetabb.com
• Ken Breneisen,
Teams Sponsored:
Dragstrip, dirt oval.
Track Size:
1/4 mile.
Teams Sponsored:
SRP ET Drag Racing Finals team NHRA

SANAIR SUPER SPEEDWAY
830 GRAND RANG SAINT-FRANCOIS
SAINT-PIE, QC, CANADA J0H 1W0
450-772-6400
www.sanair.ca
Description:
Motorsports park.

SAND HILL RANCH
50 CAMINO DIABLO ROAD
BRENTWOOD, CA 94513
925-634-3328
prsports@silcon.com
• Tom Anderson, Promoter
Track Size:
1/5 mile.
Track Type:
Semi-Banked Oval.

SEBRING INTERNATIONAL RACEWAY
113 MIDWAY DRIVE
SEBRING, FL 33870
863-655-1442
800-626-7223
Fax: 863-655-1777
info@sebringraceway.com
www.sebringraceway.com
• Tres Stephenson, President and General Manager
(941) 655-1442
tstephenson@sebringraceway.com
• Tres Stephenson, President and GM
• Jesse McClelland, Director of Operations
• Ken Breslauer, Communications Director/Track Historian
(727) 895-3482
sebring12pr@aol.com
• Kristie Scottile, Director of Sales and Amrketing
• David Gourley, Ass Director of Sales and Marketing

• Greg Marcotte, Director of Finance and HR
• Toni Feo, Ass.Director of Finance and HR
Description:
Auto race track.

SECOND CREEK RACEWAY (OVAL)
17010 E 88TH AVENUE
ROUTE 1
BOX 113
COMMERCE CITY, CO 80022
303-371-6661
Fax: 303-371-6662
www.na-motorsports.com/Tracks/CO/Secon dCreek.html
• Bob McClusky, Track Manager
Track Types:
Semi-Banked Oval; Airport Road Course (8 turns)
Track Length:
1/5 mile; 1.7 miles

SHANNONVILLE MOTORSPORT PARK
7047 OLD HIGHWAY #2
PO BOX 259
SHANNONVILLE, ON, CANADA K0K 3A0
613-969-1906
800-959-8955
Fax: 613-966-6890
info@shannonville.com
www.shannonville.com
Description:
Race track.
Long Track:
4.051 km.
Pro Track:
2.47 km.
Fabi Circuit:
2.25 km.
Nelson Circuit:
1.801 km.
Opened:
1979.
Owner(s) :
John Bondar and Steve Gidman.

SHASTA DISTRICT FAIR
1890 BRIGGS STREET
ANDERSON, CA 96007
530-378-6789
Fax: 530-378-6788
• Sciarani Trish, Shasta District Fairgrounds/Chief Execut
• George Wade, Raceway Park Operations General Manager
(530) 378-6789
• Chris Workman, CEO
• Stina Deatley, Representative
• Melanie Silva, Business Assistant
• Ken Scheeler, Maintainace Suprintendent
• Tom Atkinson, Maintainance
Seating Capacity:
3,800

SILVER DOLLAR SPEEDWAY
704 VINE AVENUE
ROSEVILLE, CA 95678
530-891-6535
Fax: 916-891-6535
www.na-motorsports.com
• Alan Padjen, Track Manager
Track Type:
Semi-Banked Oval.
Track Size:
1/4 mile.

SISKAYOU MOTOR SPEEDWAY
1712 FAIRLANE ROAD
YREKA, CA 96097
530-842-2767
Fax: 530-842-4724
siskiyoumotorspeedway@gmail.com
www.siskiyoumotorspeedway.com
• Josh Cullen, President
• Rick Weber, Vice President
• Rebecca Desmond, CEO
• Julie Phillips, Secretary
• Chris Cullen, Director
• Jim Rohn, Director
• Linda Carlin, Treasurer
Track Type:
Semi-Banked Oval.

SONOMA RACEWAY
29355 ARNOLD DRIVE
SONOMA, CA 95476
707-938-8448
800-870-7223
Fax: 707-938-8691
trackinfo@racesonoma.com
www.racesonoma.com
• Frank Gullum, VP Sales
(707) 933-3914
fgullum@infineonraceway.com
• Melvyn Record, VP Marketing
(707) 933-3937
mrecord@infineonraceway.com
• Bobby O'Gorman, Operations Director
(707) 933-3906
• Brad Lawrence, Group Sales
(707) 933-3939
blawrence@infineonraceway.com
Description:
Founded 1988. Auto race track. Features all
types of racing including NASCAR Nextel
Cup, NASCAR West Featherlite Southwest
Tour, and Craftsman Truck Series, AMA
Vintage Motorcycles and superbikes, NHRA
Drag Racing, SCCA Trans-Am, Professional
SportsCar Ra
Series:
NASCAR Nextel Cup Series

SOUTH ALABAMA SPEEDWAY
189 WEST HWY 52
KINGSTON, AL 36453
334-774-3161
speedway.SAS@gmail.com
www.southalabamaspeedway.com
• John Dykes, owner
(334) 774-3161
southalabama@charter.net
• Sandra Dykes, Promoter
• John Dykes,
(334) 774-3161
• MaLeah Hill,
(334) 432-0211
MaLeah.SAS@gmail.com
• Edward Berry, Tech
(334) 379-4457
Track Size:
4/10 mile.
Track Type:
High-Banked Oval.

SOUTH BOSTON SPEEDWAY
1188 JAMES D HAGOOD HIGHWAY
PO BOX 1066
S BOSTON, VA 24592
434-572-4947
877-440-1540
Fax: 434-575-8992

info@southbostonspeedway.com
www.southbostonspeedway.com
• Cathy Rice, General Manager
• Nick Iqdalsky, Sr.VP
• Jenny Morris, Office Assistant
• Helen Barksdale, Office Manager
• Terry Daniels, Maintainace Supritendent
• John A Evans, Speedway Announcer
Description:
Auto race track for NASCAR and NASCAR
All-Pro Series. Hosting NASCAR Hills Bros..
All-Pro Series, ASA Series, ARCA RE/MAX
Series, NASCAR Goody's Dash Series,
Extreme Motor-X, USAR Hooter's Pro Cup
Series, USAC Midgets, NASCAR Craftsman
Truck Series and NA

EL MIRAGE DRY LAKE
2517 SYCAMORE DRIVE
SUITE 353
SIMI VALLEY, CA 93065
805-526-1805
Fax: 805-584-8518
office@scta-bni.org
www.scta-bni.org
• Lonnie Martin, El Mirage Maintenance
Club Liaison
• Scott Andrews, President
(818) 419-8074
Location:
El Mirage, CA

**SOUTHWESTERN INTERNATIONAL
RACEWAY**
12000 S HOUGHTON ROAD
TUCSON, AZ 85747
520-762-9700
Fax: 520-762-9777
sirace97@yahoo.com
• Dennis Scheepstra, Track manager
(520) 429-0397
• Dan Owens, Events
(520) 869-7772
dowens@merlesauto.com
• Paul Smith, Events
(520) 850-0353
Track Size:
1/4 mile.
Track Type:
Dragstrip.

STAFFORD MOTOR SPEEDWAY
55 W STREET
STAFFORD SPRINGS, CT 6076
860-684-2783
Fax: 860-684-6236
www.staffordspeedway.com
• Mark Arute, COO/General Manager
markarute@staffordspeedway.com
• Lisa Arute, Executive Vice President
lisaarute@staffordspeedway.com
• Scott Running, Sr.Director
scottrunning@staffordspeedway.com
• Mike Young, Manager
Description:
Auto race track hosting the following
NASCAR racing series: Busch North Series,
Featherlite Modified Series. Also hosts SK
Modifieds, Late Models, D.A.R.E. Stocks,
U.S. Hot Rods, Monster Trucks, Harley
Davidson Jamboree, Automotive Swap
Meets, and motorcy

SUMMERVILLE SPEEDWAY
1896 CENTRAL AVENUE
SUMMERVILLE, SC 29483-9325

843-761-1428
Fax: 843-761-2772
www.na-motorsports.com/Tracks/SC/Summ
erville.html
• Charlie Powell, Promoter
Description:
Auto race track hosting the following
NASCAR racing series: Slim Jim All Pro
Series, Goody's Dash Series.

SUMMIT POINT MOTORSPORTS PARK
201 MOTOR PARK CIRCLE
PO BOX 190
SUMMIT POINT, WV 25446
304-725-8444
Fax: 304-728-7124
office@bsr-inc.com
www.summitpoint-raceway.com
• Bill Scott, President
Description:
Auto, motorcycle, kart race track.

SYDNEY MOTORSPORT PARK
PO BOX 6747
BLACKTOWN DC, NSW, 2148
61—2 9672 1000
Fax: 61—9672-0208
www.sydneymotorsportpark.com
• Brian Goulding, Race Operations Manager
• Phil Harrison, Marketing Manager
phil@ardc.com.au
• Brian Goulding, Race Operations Manager

TALLADEGA GRAN PRIX RACEWAY
46 PILGRIM LANE
MUNFORD, AL 36268
256-493-0302
Fax: 256-362-3718
www.tgprace.com
• David Upchurch, President
• Michael Upchurch, VP
• Katrina Upchurch, Administrator
katrina@tgprace.com
Track Type:
Road Course (9 turns).
Track Length:
1.3 miles.
Sports:
Motorcycle races, testing, riding schools,
limited car tune & test, driving schools

TALLADEGA SHORT TRACK
4343 SPEEDWAY BVLD
EASTABOGA, AL 36260
256-831-1413
• Lynn Phillips, Promoter
(256) 454-5414
• Alfred Gurley, Promoter
Track Type:
High-Banked Oval.
Track Length:
1/3 mile.

TALLADEGA SUPERSPEEDWAY
3366 SPEEDWAY BOULEVARD
TALLADEGA, AL 35160
877-462-3342
Fax: 256-761-4717
www.talladegasuperspeedway.com
• Kristi R King, Director Public Relations
(256) 761-4705
• Andrew Smith, Public Relations Assistant
(256) 761-4706
Description:
Founded 1969. Tri-oval race track.
Seating Capacity:

With approximately 143,000 grandstand seats and a 212-acre infield, Talladega Superspeedway hosts two major stock car racing weekends each year. The Talladega 500 in April and Alabama 500 in October. Both are NASCAR Nextel Cup Series events.

TEXAS MOTOR SPEEDWAY/TMS
3545 LONE STAR CIRCLE
FORT WORTH, TX 76177
817-215-8500
Fax: 817-491-3749
www.texasmotorspeedway.com
• Eddit Gossage, President/General Manager
• Kenton Nelson, Assistant General Manager
• Kevin Camper, Director of Sales & Bus. Dev.
• Mike Zizzo, Director Public Relations
Sponsor
DIRECTV
Back Straight:
1,330 feet
Front Straight:
2,250 feet
Banking:
24 and 8 degrees

TEXAS MOTORPLEX
7500 W. HIGHWAY 287
ENNIS, TX 75119
972-878-2641
Fax: 972-878-1848
www.texasmotorplex.com
• Ryan Haas, General Manager
• Gregg Griffin, Marketing Services
• Elon Werner, Media Relations Director
• Arthur O'Bright, Marketing Services/Sales
Description:
Founded 1986. Drag racing track.

THE LEGENDARY DARLINGTON
2056 E BOBO NEWSOME HWY
SC 151
HARTSVILLE, SC 29550
843-383-0008
Fax: 843-383-9933
www.darlingtondragway.com
• Bill Wilson, President
(843) 383-0008
Description:
Dragstrip (1/4 mile).
Seating Capacity:
15,000

THOMPSON SPEEDWAY MOTORSPORTS PARK
205 E THOMPSON ROAD
THOMPSON, CT 06277
860-923-2280
Fax: 860-923-2398
oval@thompsonspeedway.com
www.thompsonspeedway.com
• Donald J Hoenig, Owner/Promoter
pitcrew@thompsonspeedway.com
• Russ Dowd, Operations Director/Media Contact
• Donald J Hoeing, President
• D.R Hoeing, VP
• Jeff Zuidema, Race Director
• Russ Dowd, Director of Operations
• Mary Ann Rossi, Office Manager
pitcrew@thompsonspeedway.com
• Richard Sprague, Chief Inspector
• Josh Vanada, Competition Director

Track:
5/8 mile high banked asphalt oval
Seating Capacity:
15,000

THUNDER MOUNTAIN SUPER SPEEDWAY
10151 SPEEDWAY LANE
PO BOX 13
CENTERVILLE, AR 72829
479-576-2593
Fax: 479-576-2432
• Wayne Tidwell, Owner/Promoter
(479) 970-0160
Track Type:
High-Banked Oval.
Track Size:
1/4 mile.

THUNDER RACEWAY, INC.
4701 E DEUCE OF CLUBS
SHOW LOW, AZ 85901
928-978-0428
Fax: 520-532-0170
www.thunderraceway.com
• Bob Livingston, Promoter
(928) 242-1384
Track Size:
1/4 mile.
Track Type:
High-Banked Oval.

THUNDER RIDGE MOTOR SPEEDWAY
1601 49TH AVENUE SW
LANNETT, AL 36863-3655
334-576-7233
Fax: 334-576-7233
Track Length:
1/8 mile.
Track Type:
Banked Oval.

THUNDER VALLEY RACEWAY
JUMPER'S BROOK ROAD
PO BOX 681
BISHOP'S FALLS, NL, CANADA A1V 1W5
205-487-3199
• Floyd Dillard, Promoter
Track Length:
1/4 mile.
Track Type:
Slightly-Banked Oval.

THUNDER VALLEY SPEEDWAY
1588 SHADE CHURCH RD
CENTRAL CITY
CENTRAL CITY, PA 15926
240-382-0526
thundervalleyrace@gmail.com
• Tiffany Trollinger, Contact
• Morgan Padula, General Manager
• Joe Padula, Promoter
• Mark Lashley, Head Flagman
• Mark Moore, Chief Steward
Track Length:
3/8 mile.
Track Type:
Semi-Banked Oval.

THUNDERBOWL RACEWAY
BARDSLEY & K STREET
TULARE, CA 93274
559-688-0909
Fax: 559-687-1957
www.thunderbowlraceway.com

• Steve Faria, Promoter
(559) 688-0909
• Don Sharp, Marketing/Advertising
(559) 734-9246
Track Type:
Oval- Dirt Track (Clay) Big events- World of Outlaws & Torphy Cup
Track Size:
1/3 mile.

THUNDERHILL RACEWAY PARK
5250 HWY
PO BOX 966
WILLOWS, CA 95988
530-934-5588
888-995-7222
Fax: 530-934-8794
office@thunderhill.com
www.thunderhill.com
• David Vodden, Chief Executive Officer/Promoter
(530) 934-5588
dvodden@thunderhill.com
• Shannon Ell, General Manager
(530) 934-5588
shannon@thunderhill.com
• Terry Taylor, Accounting Manager
(530) 934-5588
office@thunderhill.com
• Ray Mudd, Events Manager
(530) 934-5588
ray@thunderhill.com
• Bob Maybell, Facilities Manager
(530) 934-5588
• Terry Taylor, Personnel and Accounting
(530) 934-5588
• Sean Crandall, Maintenance
(530) 330-2188
Year Founded:
1993
Seating Capacity:
On Hills, 10,000.
Track Type:
3 Mile, 15 Turn Road Course.
Track Size:
Six Configurations: 1.0, 1.3, 1.5, 1.7, 1.9 and 3.0 Miles.

TRI CITY SPEEDWAY
5100 NAMEOKI ROAD
PONTOON BEACH, IL 62040
636-448-9111
800-617-9077
Fax: 618-931-3217
tricityspeedway@msn.com
www.tricityspeedway.net
• Anita Ratliff, Contact person
Description:
Dirt track stock car racing.

TUCSON RACEWAY PARK
11955 S HARRISON ROAD
TUCSON, AZ 85747
520-762-9200
Fax: 520-762-5053
www.tucsonracewaypark.com
• David Deery, General Manager
(520) 762-9200
• Mark Ebert, Director
Year Founded:
1968
Track Size:
3/8 mile & 1/4 mile.
Track Type:
Banked-Asphalt Oval.
Seating Capacity:
6,500

TWIN CITY RACEWAY
7075 SHOTGUN DRIVE
KENAI, AK 99611
907-283-9078
• Ed Kobak, Media and Promotions
(907) 260-6292
globalnw@earthlink.net
• Bill Jackson, Promoter
Track Type:
Semi-Banked Oval.
Track Length:
3/8 mile.

VENTURA RACEWAY
10 WEST HARBOUR BLVD.
VENTURA, CA 93001
805-985-5433
Fax: 805-984-3095
info@venturaraceway.com
• Jim Naylor, Promoter
(805) 985-5835
jnaylor@ucnet.com
• Cliff Morgan, General Manager
(805) 985-5433
cmorgan428@hotmail.com
• Mike Sweeney,
mike@venturaraceway.com
Arena Seating Capacity:
4,000.00
Year Founded:
1977
Clients:
Motorsports Teams and Fans.
Nature of Service:
Motorsports Racing weekly series, Ventura
Racing Associates Sprint Cars, VRASR
Sprints Cars, VRA Pony Stocks, VRA
Modifieds, VRA Dwarf Cars, IMCA
Modifieds, USAC Midgets, Focus Midgets,
USAC/CRA 410 Sprint Cars.

WATKINS GLEN INTERNATIONAL
2790 COUNTY ROUTE 16
WATKINS GLEN, NY 14891
607-535-2486
866-461-7223
Fax: 607-535-8918
racing@theglen.com
www.theglen.com
• Kevin Gundaker, Contact
kevin@tricityspeedway.net
• Tammy Gundaker, Contact Person
tammy@tricityspeedway.net
• Brandy Gundaker, Marketing Incharge
Seating Capacity:
4,500
Description:
Founded 1963. Auto race track. Features
Super Stock, Stock, Winged Sprint, Oval
Track and Midget Car Racing.

WESTERN COLORADO DRAGWAY
115 32 RD
GRAND JUNCTION
CLIFTON, CO 81520
970-523-1720
wcdra@hotmail.com
www.wcdra.com
• Doug Styers, President
• Dale Umberger, VP
• Mike McCallum, Executive Board
(970) 260-7430
• Chris McCallum, Executive Board
(970) 986-5401
• John Cozzette, Executive Board
(970) 242-5955
• Bryan Carmack, Executive Board

(970) 523-1720
• Bud Preuss, Executive Board
(970) 250-2217
• Mike Hansen, Treasurer
Track Length:
1/4 mile
Track Type:
Dragstrip

**WILLOW SPRINGS INTERNATIONAL
RACEWAY**
3500 75TH STREET W
ROSAMOND, CA 93560
661-256-6666
Fax: 661-256-9140
info@willowspringsraceway.com
www.willowspringsraceway.com
• Rick Romo, Contact
(661) 256-8974
Physical Address:
3500 75th St West, Rosamond, CA 93560.
Nature of Service:
Auto, motorcycles, and karts racetrack.
Features Sprint Car, Oval Track, Indy Car,
Stock Car, and Midget Car racing.
Seating Capacity:
10,000+.
Publications:
WILLOW SPRINGS SPECTATOR, monthly.

Race Tracks - Equestrian Downs & Parks

ALABAMA STATE FAIRGROUNDS
2331 BESSEMER ROAD
BIRMINGHAM, AL 35208
205-786-8100
Fax: 205-786-8222
opi@birminghamal.gov
www.informationbirmingham.com
• Leroy R Cowan, Director
State Fair Arena Seating Capacity:
6,000
**Birmingham International Speedway
Seating Capacity**
10,000

ALAMEDA COUNTY FAIRGROUNDS
4501 PLEASANTON AVENUE
PLEASANTON, CA 94566
925-426-7600
Fax: 925-426-7599
info@alamedacountyfair.com
www.alamedacountyfair.com
• Janet Lockhart, President
• Dean Schenone, Vice President
Seating capacity racing grandstand:
6,500

ARIZONA EXPOSITION & STATE FAIR
1826 W MCDOWELL ROAD
PHOENIX, AZ 85007
602-252-6771
Fax: 602-495-1302
info@azstatefair.com
www.azstatefair.com

ARKANSAS STATE FAIRGROUNDS
2600 HOWARD STREET
LITTLE ROCK, AR 72206
501-372-8341
Fax: 501-372-4197
www.arkansasstatefair.com

• Ralph Shoptaw, President / General
Manager
Barton Coliseum Seating Capacity:
10,219

ARLINGTON INTERNATIONAL
2200 WEST ELUCID AVENUE
ARLINGTON HEIGHTS, IL 60006
847-385-7500
Fax: 309-792-0522
eaglemotz@aol.com
www.arlingtonpark.com
• Richard Duchossois, Chairman
• Ed Jamison, VP/General Manager
Year Founded:
1973
Seating capacity:
3,500
Nature of Service:
Harness horse race track.

ASSINIBOIA DOWNS
3975 PORTAGE AVENUE
WINNIPEG, MANITOBA, CANADA R3K
2E9
204-885-3330
800-282-8053
Fax: 204-831-5348
info@assiniboiadowns.com
www.assiniboiadowns.com
• Harvey D. Warner, President
(204) 885-3330
info@assiniboiadowns.com
• Norm Elder, Vice President
(204) 885-3330
info@assiniboiadowns.com
• Barry Anderson, Secretary
(204) 885-3330
info@assiniboiadowns.com
• Sharon Gulyas, General Manager
(204) 885-3330
sgulyas@assiniboiadowns.com
Seating capacity:
5,000
Year Founded:
1958
Track Type:
Thoroughbred Dirt Track.
Track Size:
13/16 mile.

ATLANTIC CITY RACE COURSE
4501 BLACK HORSE PIKE
MAYS LANDING, NJ 8330
609-641-2190
Fax: 609-645-8309
www.acracecourse.com
• James J. Murphy, President/General
Manager
• Robert P. Levy, Chief Business
Description:
Founded 1944. Thoroughbred race track.
Seating capacity:
16,000

BAY MEADOWS
901 MARINES ISLAND BOULEVARD
SUITE 125
SAN MATEO, CA 94404
650-573-4600
650-574-7223
Fax: 650-573-4670
www.baymeadows.com
• Jack Liebau, President

BELMONT PARK
3146 MISSION BOULEVARD
PO BOX 90
SAN DIEGO, CA 92109
858-228-9283
Fax: 858-488-4316
www.belmontpark.com
• Nancie No Geller, PRESIDENT
• Terrence Meyoucks, President/Chief Operating Officer
• Alec Ingle, Chief Financial Officer/Asst to the Pres
• Glen Mathes, Director, Communications

BELTERRA PARK
6301 KELLOGG ROAD
CINCINNATI, OH 45230-5237
513-354-8246
800-699-7558
Fax: 513-232-1412
• Jack Hanessian, General Manager
(513) 232-8000
• John Engelhardt, Director, Public Relations
(513) 232-8000
• Vincent Cyster, Simulcast Coordinator
• Ed Vomacka, Secretary, Racing
• Shannon Fink, Group Sales
(513) 354-8246
• Terry Moore, Bookeper
(513) 354-8265
Description:
Thoroughbred horse race track.
Seating capacity:
15,000.00
Nature of Service:
Year-Round Simulcasting.

BERGERON RODEO GROUNDS AND ENTERTAINMENT CENTER
6591 ORANGE DRIVE
DAVIE, FL 33314
954-797-1000
Fax: 954-797-2061
citizens_response@davie-fl.gov
www.davie-fl.gov
• Joan Kovac, Chairperson
• Phillip R. Holste, Intergovernmental Affairs Manager
• Giovanni Moss, Housing and Community Development Director
Seating Capacity:
7,000
Description:
Rentals: 954-797-1163

BETFAIR HOLLYWOOD PARK
1050 S PRAIRIE AVENUE
INGLEWOOD, CA 90301
310-419-1549
Fax: 310-672-4664
www.hollywoodpark.com
• Eual M. Eual, Vice President & General Manager
• Eual Wyatt, General Manager
• Steve Arnold, VP, Finance
• Alan Gutterman, VP, Marketing
Description:
Founded 1938. Thoroughbred horse race track.
Seating capacity:
50,000

BEULAH PARK
3811 SW BOULEVARD
PO BOX 850
GROVE CITY, OH 43123

614-871-9600
Fax: 614-871-0433
www.beulahpark.com
• Charles Ruma, President
• Michael A. Weiss, General Manager
• Vic Mason, Publishing Director
• Jim McKinney, GM
(614) 871-9400
• Gina Schmidt, Coordinator
(614) 871-9400
• Ed Vomacka, Racing Secreatary
(614) 871-9400
• Larry Shipley, Food and Beverage
(614) 871-9400
• Holly Chandler, Admissions Incharge
(614) 871-9400
• David Hardy, Plant Supritendent
(614) 871-9400
Description:
Thoroughbred horse race track, simulcast and banquet facility.
Seating capacity:
9,000

BIG FRESNO FAIR (BFF)
1121 CHANCE AVENUE
FRESNO, CA 93702
559-650-3247
Fax: 559-650-3226
info@fresnofair.com
www.fresnofair.com
• John C C Alkire, Chief Executive Officer
(559) 650-3247
jalkire@fresnofair.com
• Debbie Nalchajian-Cohen, Communications/Media Relations
Arena Seating Capacity:
5,000.00
Year Founded:
1883
Clients:
Local residents, racing enthusists.
Nature of Service:
Horseracing Facility.

BIRMINGHAM RACE COURSE
1000 JOHN ROGERS DRIVE
BIRMINGHAM, AL 35210
205-838-7500
800-998-8238
Fax: 205-838-7407
www.birminghamracecourse.com
• Joe E. O'Neill, Operations Manager
• W. M. Russell, VP, Operations
• S. Le Yates, Chief Financial Officer
• Linda Butler, Human Resources Officer
• Brian Carpenter, Director of Racing
• Elaine Lucas, Director of Mutuels
• Bennie Polo, Manager
• Barabara Hummel, Group Sales
Description:
Horse Racing Track.

CALDER CASINO & RACE COURSE
21001 NW 27TH AVENUE
PO BOX 1808
MIAMI GARDEN, FL 33056
305-625-1311
800-333-3227
Fax: 305-624-6284
customerservice@calderracecourse.com
www.calderracecourse.com
• Tom O'Donnell, President
• John Marshall, General Manager/Vice President
• Michael Cronin, Director, Marketing

Description:
Founded 1972. Sporting event/entertainment facility, thoroughbred race track.
Permanent Seating capacity:
15,000

CALIFORNIA EXPOSITION & STATE FAIR
1600 EXPOSITION BOULEVARD
SACRAMENTO, CA 95815
916-263-3000
877-225-3976
Fax: 916-263-3304
info@calexpo.com
www.calexpo.com
• Marko Mlikotin, Chairman
emanuel@calexpo.com
• Norbert Bartosik, General Manager
(916) 263-3061
nbartosik@calexpo.com
• David Dhillon, Assistant General Manager, Marketing
(916) 263-3219
ddhillon@calexpo.com
• Dave Elliott, Assistant General Manager, Racing
(916) 263-3283
delliott@calexpo.com
• Jerry Brown, Goveror
• Willie Pelote, Director
• Sonney Chong, Director
• Jeffery Azoff, Director
• Rima Barkett, Director
• Rex Hime, Director
Description:
Founded 1854 as an agricultural fair. Offers entertainment and exhibits with broad public appeal.

CALGARY STAMPEDE
1410 OLYMPIC WAY SE
CALGARY, AB, CANADA T2G 2W1
403-261-0101
800-661-1767
www.calgarystampede.com
• Joel Cowley, Chief Executive Officer
Description:
Annual rodeo, exhibition, and festival held every July.
Dates:
July 4-13.
Founded:
1923 (Exhibition and Stampede).

CANTERBURY PARK
1100 CANTERBURY ROAD
SHAKOPEE, MN 55379
952-445-7223
800-340-6361
Fax: 952-496-6400
cbypark@canterburypark.com
www.canterburypark.com
• Randy D. Sampson, President/Chief Executive Officer
• John Harty, VP, Marketing
• Michael J. Garin, VP, Hospitality
• Mark A. Erickson, VP Facilities

CHURCHILL DOWNS
700 CENTRAL AVENUE
LOUISVILLE, KY 40208
502-636-4400
Fax: 502-636-4430
customerservice@kyderby.com
www.churchilldowns.com
• Carl Pollard, Chairman
• Thomas H. Meeker, Chief Executive

Officer/President
• Steve Sexton, President
• Karl Schmitt, SVP Corporate
Communications
• Tricia Amburgey, Senior Director
Sponsorship Sales
Description:
Owns Arlington International Racecourse.

CLINTON RACEWAY
129 BEECH ST
PO BOX 778
CLINTON, ON, CANADA N0M 1LO
519-482-5270
Fax: 519-482-1489
clintonraceway.com
• Jessica Carnochan, Marketing Manager
jessicacarnochan@gmail.com
Description:
Horse race track.

DEL MAR THOROUGHBRED CLUB
2260 JIMMY DURANTE BOULEVARD
DEL MAR, CA 92014
858-755-1141
Fax: 858-792-1477
marys@dmtc.com
www.dmtc.com
• Joe W. Harper, President/General
Manager
(858) 755-1141
joeh@dmtc.com
• Craig R. Fravel, EVP
(858) 755-1141
craig@dmtc.com
• Michael R. Ernst, VP/Chief Financial
Officer
(858) 755-1141
mike@dmtc.com
• Joe Harper, President & GM
joeh@dmtc.com
• Mike Ernst, EVP & CFO
mike@dmtc.com
• Tom Robbins, EVP, Racing & Industry
Realtions
tomr@dmtc.com
• Josh Rubinstein, SVP, Development
josh@dmtc.com
• Craig Dado, SVP, Marketing
(858) 755-1141
craigd@dmtc.com
• Ann Hall, VP Humann resources&
Administration
annh@dmtc.com
• Tim Read, VP, Operations & Collective
Bargain
timr@dmtc.com
Year Founded:
1937
Track Type:
Dirt, Turf.
Track Size:
1 mile dirt, 7/8 turf.

DELAWARE COUNTY FAIR
236 PENNSYLVANIA AVENUE
PO BOX 1278
DELAWARE, OH 43015
740-362-3851
800-335-3247
Fax: 740-363-4132
fair@delawarecountyfair.com
www.delawarecountyfair.com
• Kent Hastings, President
• Gary Must, General Manager
garymust@midohio.net
• Phil Terry, Marketing Director & fair

manager
pterry@littlebrownjug.com
• Steve Vaughn, Grounds
• Jennifer Keysor, Reserve Tickets &
Admissions
• Sheila Hemans, Reserve Tickets &
Admissions
Description:
Harness race track.
Seating capacity:
17,500

DELAWARE PARK RACETRACK & SLOTS
777 DELAWARE PARK BOULEVARD
WILMINGTON, DE 19804
302-994-2521
800-417-5687
Fax: 302-355-1292
programs@delawarepark.com
www.delawarepark.com
• William Rickman, president and general
manager
• Andrew Gentile, General Manager
• Bill Fasy, EVP/Chief Operating Officer
• John Rooney, VP, Finance/Racing

DRESDEN RACEWAY
1244 N STREET
DRESDEN, ONTARIO, CANADA N0P 1M0
519-683-4466
Fax: 519-683-4038
www.windsorraceway.com
• Lorrie Brown, General Manager
• Paul Hawman, Race Secretary
Description:
Harness horse race track.

DUQUOIN STATE FAIR
655 EXECUTIVE DRIVE
DU QUOIN, IL 62832
618-542-1515
Fax: 618-542-1541
www.agr.state.il.us/dq
• John Rednour Jr., Fairground Director
Description:
Home of the World Trotting Derby.

EL COMANDANTE RACE TRACK
ROAD NO 3, KM 15.3
PO BOX 1643
CANOVANAS, PUERTO RIC 00729-1643
787-641-6060
Fax: 787-641-6085
• Juan M. Rivera, President/Chief Executive
Officer
• Alejandro Fuentes, EVP/General Manager
• Carlos A. Pena, VP, Racing Operations
• Stanley Pinkerton, VP/Chief Financial
Officer
Description:
Horse race track.

ELLIS PARK
3300 US HIGHWAY 41
HENDERSON, KY 42420
812-425-1456
800-333-8089
Fax: 812-425-3725
ellispark@ellisparkracing.com
www.ellisparkracing.com
• Ron Geary, Owner/President
• Ron Geary, Owner/President
• Joe Rudisill, General Manager
• Bob Jackson, Operations Manager
• Eric Lemerand, IRM Operations Manager

• Robyn Oglesby, Marketing Manager
• Chad Keown, Food & Beverage Manager
Year Founded:
1922
Description:
Founded 1922. Pari-mutuel wagering on
horse racing; conducts live thoroughbred
racing.
Nature of Service:
Pari-mutuel wagering on horse racing; live
thoroughbred racing.

EMERALD DOWNS
2300 EMERALD DOWNS DRIVE
AUBURN, WA 98001
253-288-7000
888-931-8400
Fax: 253-288-7010
info@emeralddowns.com
www.emeralddowns.com
• Ron Crockett, President
• Bob Fraser, Director, Operations
• Ron Crockett, President
• Jack Hodge, Vice President
• Emerald Downs, Vice President of
Operations
Description:
Thoroughbred horse race track.

EVANGELINE DOWNS
2235 CRESWELL LANE EXTENSION
PO BOX 90270
OPELOUSAS, LA 70570
866-472-2466
877-770-7867
Fax: 337-594-3166
www.evangelinedowns.com
• Mike As Howard, General Manager
• Charles As Jr, VP

EXHIBITION PARK
37 MCALLISTER DRIVE
PO BOX 284
SAINT JOHN, NB, CANADA E2L 3Y2
506-636-2020
Fax: 506-636-6958
blair.macdonald@nb.aibn.com
• Blair MacDonald, Administration
• Paul Gilbride, President
• Frank McCarey, VP
• Williard Jenkins, Treasurer
• J.Charles Swanton, Secretary
• Gerry Lowe, BOD
• Stan Fielding, BOD
Year Founded:
1890
Nature of Service:
Harness race track; part of The Exhibition
Association of the City and County of Saint
John.

EXIBITION PARK - LETHBRIDGE
3401 PARKSIDE DRIVE S
LETHBRIDGE, CANADA ABT1J 4R3
403-328-4491
Fax: 403-320-8139
events@exhibitionpark.ca
www.exhibitionpark.ca
• Rudy Friesen, General Manager
(403) 328-4491
rudy@exhibitionpark.ca
• Rudy Friesen, GM
(403) 328-4491
rudy@exhibitionpark.ca
• Diana DiRocco, Executive Assistant
(403) 328-3201
diana@exhibitionpark.ca

• Bridget Mearns, Developmetn Coordinator
(403) 328-3218
bridget@exhibitionpark.ca
• Bruce Larson, Controller
(403) 328-3203
bruce@exhibitionpark.ca
• Shawn Anderson, Product Supervisor
(403) 317-3207
shawan@exhibitionpark.ca
• Bryan Litchfield, Manager Operations
(403) 894-0418
bryan@exhibitionpark.ca
• Don Young, President
Description:
Thoroughbred, quarter horse race track.
Seating capacity:
3,750

FAIR GROUNDS CORPORATION
1751 GENTILLY BOULEVARD
NEW ORLEANS, LA 70119
504-944-5515
Fax: 504-948-1160
www.fairgroundsracecourse.com
• Bryan G. Krantz, President
• Gordon M Robertson, Director, Mutuels

FAIRMOUNT PARK RACETRACK
9301 COLLINSVILLE ROAD
COLLINSVILLE, IL 62234
618-345-4300
Fax: 314-436-1516
info@fairmountpark.com
www.fairmountpark.com
• Greg Graves, Mutuel Manager
(618) 345-4300
• Nikki Tanner, Group Sales Director
(618) 345-4300
groupsales@fairmountpark.com
• Rajni Kumar, Manager
(618) 345-4300
• Bobby Pace, Racing Secretary
(618) 345-4300
Description:
Founded 1925. Year-round thoroughbred
and harness racing track.
Publications:
THE INSIDE TRACK NEWSLETTER,
quarterly.

FAIRPLEX
1101 W MCKINLEY AVENUE
POMONA, CA 91768
909-623-3111
Fax: 909-865-3602
info@fairplex.com
www.fairplex.com
• Wendy Talarico, Communications
Manager
(909) 865-4263
• Melissa DeMonaco-Tapia, Director of
Sales
(909) 865-4042
demonaco@fairplex.com
Description:
Founded 1922. Home of thoroughbred and
quarter horse racing during the Los Angeles
County Fair each September-October.
Horse shows held regularly throughout the
year. Also hosts National Hot Rod
Association Winternationals (February), and
Winston World Fi
Description:
Founded 1922. Home of thoroughbred and
quarter horse racing during the Los Angeles
County Fair each September-October.
Horse shows held regularly throughout the

year. Also hosts National Hot Rod
Association Winternationals (February), and
Winston World Fi
Seating Capacity
10,000

FINGER LAKES GAMING & RACETRACK
5857 ROUTE 96
PO BOX 25250
FARMINGTON, NY 14425
585-924-3232
Fax: 585-924-3967
smartin@dncinc.com
www.fingerlakesracetrack.com
• Steve Martin, Sr. Director of Marketing and
Gaming
(585) 924-3232
smartin@dncinc.com
• Brad Lewis, Director, Racing
blewis@dncinc.com
• Steve Martin, Director, Publicity/Marketing
smartin@dncinc.com
• Chris Riegle, President and GM
• Vieden Zahariev, Sr.Director of Finance
• Philip Palermo, Director of Operations
• Steve Martin, Sr.Director of Marketing
• Mike Struzyk, Controller
• Charles Petersen, Gaming Manager
• Brian Moore, Director of Marketing
Arena Seating Capacity:
6,000 Seating; 10,000 Total Capacity.
Year Founded:
1962
Track Type:
Dirt, Thoroughbred (no turf course).
Track Size:
1 mile oval.

FINISH LINE MANAGEMENT
1700 JOE YENNI BOULEVARD
KENNER, LA 70065
504-466-8521
Fax: 504-466-3908
• Nick Leggio, Director
Description:
Horse race track.

FONNER PARK
700 E STOLLEY PARK ROAD
PO BOX 490
GRAND ISLAND, NE 68802
308-382-4515
Fax: 308-384-2753
fonnerpark@aol.com
www.fonnerpark.com
• Hugh M. Miner Jr, EVP/Chief Executive
Officer
• Bruce Swihart, Chief Operating Officer
• Todd Otto, Assistantt Manager
Description:
Founded 1954. Thoroughbred horse race
track. Also serves as civic center for
activities throughout the year. Home of the
Hall County Fair.
Seating capacity:
8,000

FOUR STATES FAIR & RODEO
3700 E 50TH STREET
TEXARKANA, AR 71854
870-773-2941
800-776-1836
Fax: 870-772-0713
lisab@fourstatesfair.com
www.fourstatesfair.com
• Jimmy Curtis, Chairman of the Board
(870) 773-2941

• Ken Curtis, Concession Manager
(870) 773-2941
kenc@fourstatesfair.com
• Sharon Hays, Office Manager
(870) 773-2941
sharonh@fourstatesfair.com
• Tammy Turk, Marketing Director
(870) 773-2941
tammy@fourstatesfair.com
Arena Seating Capacity:
6,800.00
Year Founded:
1945
Nature of Service:
Multi-purpose entertainment center,
fairgrounds and RV year-round parking
available.
Track Type:
Ampitheater.

FRASER DOWNS
17755 60TH AVENUE
SURREY, BC, CANADA V3S 1V3
604-576-9141
Fax: 604-576-9821
www.fraserdowns.com
• Chuck Keeling, Vice President Racing
Operations
• Keith Quinlan, Racing Secretary
• Dan Jukich, Simulcast Coordinator
• Francis Penny, Marketing
Manager/Publicist

**FREDERICTON CAPITAL EXHIBIT
CENTRE**
361 SMYTHE STREET
STATION A
FREDERICTON, NB, CANADA E3B 4Y9
506-458-8819
Fax: 506-458-9294
www.frex.ca
• Joe Bilrout, General Manager/Secretary
• Mike Vokey, Executive Director
mvokey@frex.ca
Year Founded:
1827
Nature of Service:
Harness race track; trade and convention
center; ice arena.

FREEHOLD RACEWAY
130 PARK AVENUE
FREEHOLD, NJ 7728
732-462-3800
Fax: 732-462-2920
www.freeholdraceway.com
• Howard Bruno, General Manager
• Mark Rosenthal, Controller
Description:
Located in central New Jersey in the historic
town of Freehold, Freehold Raceway was
established in 1853 and features live
Standardbred barness races for trotters and
pacers from August through early June. Also
open seven days a week and seven nights
year round for thoroughbred and harness
racing simulcasts from tracks throughout
North America.
Track:
1/2 mile harness racetrack

FREMONT CO. FAIRGROUNDS
1004 LEGION ROAD
SIDNEY, IA 51652
712-374-2715
Fax: 712-374-3286
• Doug Doty, Extension Director

Rodeo Arena Seating Capacity:
8,500
Grandstand Seating Capacity:
5,500

GEORGIA INTERNATIONAL HORSE PARK (GIHP)
1996 CENTENNIAL OLYMPIC PARKWAY
CONYERS, GA 30013
770-860-4190
888-860-4224
Fax: 770-602-2500
www.georgiahorsepark.com
• Darlene Partain, Sales Manager
(770) 860-4198
Seating Capacity:
Grand Prix Stadium 8,000 (plus additional);
Charles Walker Arena 25,00 (plus additional)

GREAT CANADIAN GAMING CORPORATION
7485 5TH SIDEROAD
INNISFIL, ONTARIO, CANADA L9S 3S1
705-726-9401
866-915-9400
Fax: 705-726-8364
www.georgiandowns.com
• Chris Roberts, Director of Operations
(705) 726-9401
• Bruce Barbour, Director of Racing Operations
• Linda Prosser, Pari-Mutuel Manager
(705) 726-9401
• Barb Rafuse, Accounting Manger
brafuse@georgiandowns.com
• Jackie Warner, Public Relations
• Dexter Hunte, Security Manager
dhunte@georgiandowns.com
• Peter Musgrove, Facilities/Operations Manager
(705) 726-9401
Arena Seating Capacity:
2,000
Year Founded:
2001
Nature of Service:
Harness Racing, Restaurants, Tele Theatre Lounge, Meetings, Conferences, Slots, Casino.
Tenant(s) :
Ontario Lottery and Gaming Corporation, Slots at Georgian Downs.
Description;
Standardbred Racetrack.

GIANTS STADIUM
50 STATE ROUTE 120
E RUTHERFORD, NJ 7073
201-935-8500
Fax: 201-935-7646
publicaffairs@njsea.com
www.njsea.com
• James Minish, SVP, Stadium/Arena
(201) 460-4204
jminish@njsea.com
• Ron Va Veen, VP/Associate General Manager, Booking/Ev
(201) 460-4387
rvandeveen@njsea.com
• Helen Strus, VP, Stadium/Arena Event Marketing
(201) 460-4355
hstruc@njsea.com
• Eric Stover, AVP, Stadium Ops
(201) 460-4299
estover@njsea.com

Description:
Home of the Hambletonian.

GOLDEN GATE FIELDS (GGF)
1100 EASTSHORE HIGHWAY
BERKELEY, CA 94710
510-559-7330
Fax: 510-559-7460
www.goldengatefields.com
• Jack Liebau, General Manager
Seating capacity:
14,750
Year Founded:
1941
Nature of Service:
Thoroughbred race track.

GRAND RIVER RACEWAY (GRR)
7445 WELLINGTON COUNTY ROAD 21
ELORA, ONTARIO, CANADA N0B 1S0
519-846-5455
Fax: 519-846-0206
info@grandriverraceway.com
www.grandriverraceway.com
• Ted Clarke, General Manager
(519) 846-5455
tclarke@GrandRiverRaceway.com
• Kelly Spencer, Marketing/Communications Manager
(519) 846-5455
kspencer@GrandRiverRaceway.com
• Susan Ellis, Administrative Assistant
(519) 846-5455
sellis@grandriverraceway.com
• Helen Bogl, CFO
(519) 846-5455
hbogl@GrandRiverRaceway.com
• Doug McCaig, Facilities manager
(519) 846-5455
• Diane Twasnick, Race Office
(519) 846-1106
raceoffice@GrandRiverRaceway.com
• Amy Clarke, Gift Shop Manager
(519) 846-5455

GULFSTREAM RACING & CASINO PARK
901 S FEDERAL HIGHWAY
HALLANDALE BEACH, FL 33009
954-454-7000
800-771-8873
Fax: 954-457-6510
www.gulfstreampark.com
• Bernie Hettel, Director of Racing Operations
(954) 457-6138
• David Rovine, Director, Marketing
• Joe Tanenbaum, Director, Communications
• Dennis Testa, Director, Operations
Description:
Manages Gulfstream Horse Race Track sponsorships & special events.

HANOVER RACEWAY
265 5TH STREET
HANOVER, ONTARIO, CANADA N4N 3X3
519-364-2860
Fax: 519-364-7314
hanoverraceway@wightman.ca
www.hanoverraceway.com
• Diane Twasnick, Race Secretary
(519) 846-1106
• Gord Dougan, General Manager
• Linda MacDonald, Food and Beverage Manager

HARRAH'S LOUISIANA DOWNS
8000 E TEXAS STREET
BOSSIER CITY, LA 71111
318-742-5555
800-427-7247
Fax: 318-741-2615
www.harrahslouisianadowns.com
• Lori Megown, Vice President
• Thomas Roberts, General Manager
Description:
Horse race track.

HARRINGTON RACEWAY & CASINO
15 W RIDER ROAD
HARRINGTON, DE 19952
302-398-7223
Fax: 302-398-3056
hri@harringtonraceway.com
www.harringtonraceway.com
• Patricia Key, Chief Operating Officer
pkey@harringtonraceway.com
• James Boese, General Manager
jboese@harringtonraceway.com
• Jim Boese, Director Simulcast/Publicity
Year Founded:
1946
Nature of Service:
Pari-Mutuel harness racing.

HASTINGS RACECOURSE
PNE GATE 8 OR 9
VANCOUVER, BC, CANADA V5K 3N8
604-254-1631
877-677-7702
Fax: 604-251-0411
info@hastingsracecourse.com
www.hastingsracecourse.com
• Mutti Raj, General Manager
• Michael Brown, General Manager
• Geoff Mussellam, Communications Manager
• Raj Mutti, Marketing Manager
Description:
Thoroughbred horse race track.
Seating capacity:
7,800

HAWTHORNE RACE COURSE
3501 S LARAMIE
STICKNEY/CICERO, IL 60804
708-780-3700
Fax: 708-780-3677
www.sportsmanspark.com
• Tim F. Carey, President & General Manager
• Howard Fagan, Director, Marketing
• David Zenner, Director Publicity

HAZEL PARK HARNESS RACEWAY (HPHR)
1650 E 10 MILE ROAD
HAZEL PARK, MI 48030
248-398-1000
Fax: 248-398-5236
hazelparkharness@yahoo.com
hazelparkraceway.com
• Ken Marshall, Director Operations
• Ladd Biro, Race Secretary
• Bernard Hartman, VP
• Mike Bozich, Ass. Director of Operations
• Bobbie Walker, Horseman's bookeeper
• Kathy Deluge, Comptroller
• Mary Matuszak, Plant Suprintendent
• Pete Marvin, Security Director
Description:
Harness horse race track.

Seating capacity:
12,200

HESTAND STADIUM FAIRGROUNDS
420 N BLAKE
PINE BLUFF, AR 71601
870-535-2900
Fax: 870-534-2864
www.pinebluffchamber.com
• Greg Gustek, Director
(870) 536-7600
• Susie Madsen, Visitor and Group Tour
Information
(870) 536-7600
Seating capacity:
7,000

HIALEAH PARK RACING & CASINO
105 E 21ST STREET
PO BOX 158
HIALEAH, FL 33013
305-885-8000
Fax: 305-887-8006
• John J. Brunetti, Chairman
• Janet Diaz, Media & Website Coordinator
Description:
Founded 1925. Thoroughbred race track.
Seating capacity:
32,000

HIAWATHA HORSE PARK & ENTERTAINMENT CENTRE
1730 LONDON LINE
SARNIA, ONTARIO, CANADA N7T 2H2
519-542-5543
Fax: 519-542-3538
info@hiawathahorsepark.com
www.hiawathahorsepark.com
• James R. Henderson, Owner
• Ryan Trusler, General Manager
• Brian Tominson, Chef
• Linda Fisher, Special Event Manager
• Mary Edwards, Bar Manager
• Becky Ramasay, Bookeeper
Sports Organizaton
Dring Range- 27 automated stations and
expansive grass tee deck; 6 beach volley
ball courts; 2 baseball diamonds; F1 Go
Karting

HOLLYWOOD CASINO AT PENN NATIONAL RACE COURSE
777 HOLLYWOOD BOULEVARD
GRANTVILLE, PA 17028
717-469-2211
Fax: 717-469-2910
Fred.Lipkin@pngaming.com
www.hollywoodpnrc.com
• Gary Luderitz, General Manager
(717) 469-2211
• Fred Lipkin, Publicity Director
(717) 469-2211
Description:
Horse race track.

HOOSIER PARK
4500 DAN PATCH CIRCLE
ANDERSON, IN 46013
765-642-7223
800-526-7223
Fax: 765-644-2754
info@hoosierpark.com
www.hoosierpark.com
• Richard B. Moore, President/General
Manager
• Thomas F. Bannon, VP, Communications

• Donna R. Smith, VP, Marketing
• Brian Elmore, General Manager
Arena Seating Capacity:
3,500.00
Year Founded:
1994
Nature of Service:
Horse Racing, Simulcasting.
Track Type:
Standardbred, Thoroughbred, Quarter
Horse.

HUMBOLDT COUNTY FAIR ASSN
1250 FIFTH STREET
FERNDALE, CA 95536
707-786-9511
Fax: 707-786-9450
humcofair@frontiernet.net
www.humboldtcountyfair.org
• Stuart Titus, General Manager
• Ella Robinson, Racing Secretary
• George Vidak, Mutuel Manager

ILLINOIS OFF TRACK BETTING
13148 RIVERCREST DRIVE
CRESTWOOD, IL 60445
708-489-4700
800-826-3344
Fax: 708-672-5932
• Mike Belmonte, General Manager
• Ken Churilla, Marketing
• Michelle Milligan, Group Sales
Description:
1 mile horse racing facility

INDIANA STATE FAIR/FAIRGROUNDS
1202 E 38TH STREET
INDIANAPOLIS, IN 46205
317-927-7500
Fax: 317-927-7695
www.in.gov
• Cindy C. Hoye, Executive Director
(317) 927-7500
• Michelle Leavell, Entertainment & Events
Manager
(317) 927-7530
• Andy Klotz, Publicity Coordinator
Year Founded:
1852
Nature of Service:
Horse, quarter midget auto and motorcycle
race tracks; horse shows, ice skating, figure
skating, and rollerblading.

ISLAND GROVE REGIONAL PARK (IGRP)

501 N 14TH AVENUE
GREELEY, CO 80634
970-350-9390
Fax: 970-350-9344
www.greeleygov.com
• Tom Welch, Facility Manager
(950) 350-9522
• Kathy Dilbeck, Scheduling Coordinator
Pro-Rodeo Arena Seating Capacity:
9,300

ISLE CASINO RACING POMPANO PARK
777 ISLE OF CAPRI CIRCLE
POMPANO BEACH, FL 33069
954-972-2000
800-843-4753
Fax: 954-972-7894
www.pompanopark.com
• Doug Shipley, General Manager and the
Corporate Vice President

• Kathleen Jenny, VP Finance
• Steven Wolf, Director,
Marketing/Communications
• Mark Loewe, Director,
Racing/Simulcasting

JEFFERSON COUNTY FAIRGROUNDS (JCF)
15200 W 6TH AVENUE
SUITE A
GOLDEN, CO 80401
303-271-6600
Fax: 303-271-6606
www.co.jefferson.co.us
• Mark A Danner, Director
mdanner@jeffco.us
• Sherry Burgener, Administrative
Coordinator
• Scott L. Gales, Director

KANSAS STATE FAIR (KSF)
2000 N POPLAR STREET
HUTCHINSON, KS 67502-5562
620-669-3600
800-362-3247
Fax: 620-669-3640
info@kansasstatefair.com
www.kansasstatefair.com
• Lori Mulch, Assistant General Manager
• Denny Stoecklein, General Manager
• Mary Holmes, Director, Special Events
Horse Exhibition Seating Capacity:
1,500
Grandstand Seating Capacity:
10,000

KAWARTHA DOWNS & SPEEDWAY
1382 COUNTY ROAD
SUITE 28
FRASERVILLE, ONTARIO, CANADA K0L
1V0
705-939-6316
Fax: 705-939-6342
race@kawarthadowns.com
www.kawarthadowns.com
• Derek Lynch, Speedway Manager
(705) 939-6316
• Jenn Fraser, Manager of Security Services
(705) 939-6316
Seating capacity:
2,000
Description:
Harness horse race track.

KAY ROGERS PARK
4400 MIDLAND BOULEVARD
FORT SMITH, AR 72904
479-783-6176
800-364-1080
Fax: 479-782-9944
www.kayrogerspark.com
• Rebecca, Accounting - Administration
rebecca@kayrogerspark.com
• Cindy, Futurity - Administration
cindy@kayrogerspark.com

KEENELAND ASSOCIATION, INC
4201 VERSAILLES ROAD
PO BOX 1690
LEXINGTON, KY 40510
859-254-3412
800-456-3412
Fax: 859-255-2484
webmaster@keeneland.com
www.keeneland.com

• Nick C. Nicholson, President/Chief
Executive Officer
• Harvie Wilkinson, VP
• W.B. Ro Beasley, Director, Racing
• Bill Thomason, President and CEO
• Vince Gabbert, VP, COO
• Walt Robertson, VP of Sales
• Brad Lovell, VP, Chief Information Officer
• Rogers Beasley, VP of racing
• Connie V Onselder, VP, CFO
Year Founded:
1936
Nature of Service:
Thoroughbred race course and auction
company.

LAKE COUNTY FAIR
889 S COURT STREET
PO BOX 327
CROWN POINT, IN 46308
219-663-3617
Fax: 219-662-6013
lcfsecretary@lake-county-fair.com
www.lake-county-fair.com
• Bub Wise Roland, President
• Zern Hayden, 1st VP
• Tom Lump, VP
• Arlene Marcinek, Secretary
Horse Arena Seating Capacity:
1,500
Grandstand Seating Capacity:
2,000

LAUREL PARK
ROUTE 198 & RACETRACK ROAD
PO BOX 130
LAUREL, MD 20725
301-725-0400
800-638-1859
Fax: 301-725-4561
info@marylandracing.com
www.laurelpark.com
• Joe De Francis, President/Chief Executive
Officer
• Ron Charles, COO
• Douglas J. Illig, Chief Financial Officer
• John Mooney, President, Racing Services
Year Founded:
1911
Nature of Service:
Thoroughbred race track.

LES BOIS PARK
5610 GLENWOOD STREET
GARDEN CITY, ID 83714
208-258-2177
800-376-3991
Fax: 208-321-4820
• Duayne Dideriksen, General Manager
• Roger White, Director, Racing
• Ron Andreoli, Simulcast Coordinator
• Kerry Lawson, GM
(208) 258-2177
• Tim Thibert, Racing secretary
(208) 258-2181
• Melinda Nothern, Marketing & Public
Relations
(208) 867-5847
Description:
Horse race track.

LOS ALAMITOS RACE COURSE
4961 KATELLA AVENUE
LOS ALAMITOS, CA 90720
714-820-2800
Fax: 714-995-6276

larace@losalamitos.com
www.losalamitos.com
• Ed Allred, Chairman & CEO
eallred@losalamitos.com
• Orlando Gutierrez, Marketing Director &
Media
(714) 820-2690
larace@losalamitos.com
• Jeff TRUE, Director, Marketing
• Ed Allred, Owner
Description:
Horse race track.

MARSHFIELD FAIR
140 MAIN STREET
PO BOX 5
MARSHFIELD, MA 2050
781-834-6629
Fax: 781-834-6750
www.marshfieldfair.org
• Ray McKay, Fair Director
• Carleton Chandler, Secretary/Treasurer
• Leonardo S. LaForest, President
• Richard Harlfinger, Vice President
• William Frugoli, Auditor
Description:
Founded 1867.

MAYWOOD PARK
8600 W N AVENUE
MELROSE PARK, IL 60160
708-343-4800
800-748-5782
Fax: 708-343-2564
www.maywoodpark.com
• Jim Hannon, Director, Public Relations
• Duke Johnston, President
Description:
Horse race track.

METRAPARK
308 6TH AVENUE N
PO BOX 2514
BILLINGS, MT 59103
406-256-2400
800-366-8538
Fax: 406-256-2479
www.metrapark.com
• Wood Faye, President
• Sandra Hawke, Marketing Director
Grandstand Seating:
8,500

MOHAWK RACETRACK
9430 GUELPH LINE
CAMPBELLVILLE, ON, CANADA L0P 1B0
416-675-7223
888-675-7223
Fax: 416-213-2128
jss@woodbineentertainment.com
www.woodbineentertainment.com
• David Willmot, Chairman and Chief
Executive Officer
• Nick Eaves, President
• Jamie Martin, EVP Racing
• Steve Koch, VP Thoroughbred Racing
• Bruce Murray, VP Standardbred Racing
Seating capacity:
7,000
Description:
Harness horse race track.

MOHEGAN SUN POCONO DOWNS
1280 HIGHWAY 315
WILKES-BARRE, PA 18702

570-831-2100
888-878-3696
Fax: 570-823-9407
mythoughts@mohegansunpocono.com
www.poconodowns.com
• Conrad Sonkowiak, VP of Racing
• John Zimich, Public Relations Director
• Dale Rapson, Operations Manager

MONMOUTH PARK
175 OCEANPORT AVENUE
OCEANPORT, NJ 7757
732-222-2100
Fax: 732-571-5240
monmouthinfo@njsea.com
www.monmouthpark.com
• Dennis O. Dowd, SVP, Racing
(201) 842-5027
bgarland@njsea.com
• Robert Kulina, VP/General Manager
(732) 571-5545
bkulina@njsea.com
• Bob Juliano, Director, Facilities
(732) 571-5486
bjuliano@njsea.com
• James Jeamas, VP, Finance
(732) 571-5551
jjeamas@njsea.com
Description:
Thoroughbred horse race track.
Seating capacity:
50,000

MONTICELLO RACEWAY
204 ROUTE 17B
PO BOX 5013
MONTICELLO, NY 12701
845-794-4100
Fax: 845-791-7060
swiles@empireresorts.com
www.monticelloraceway.com
• Cliff Ehrlich, Executive VP & GM
(845) 794-4100
cehrlich@empireresorts.com
• Shawn Wiles, General Manager
(845) 794-4100
swiles@empireresorts.com
• Eric Warner, Director of Racing
(845) 794-4100
• John Manzi, Director, Public Relations
(845) 794-4100
jmanzi@empireresorts.com
Description:
Harness Race Track.

MOUNTAINEER CASINO, RACE TRACK &
RESORT
MOUNTAINEER CIRCLE, ROUTE 2
CHESTER, WV 26034
304-387-8000
800-804-0468
info@mtrgaming.com
www.moreatmountaineer.com
• Tim Ameault, President/Chief Executive
Officer
• Tamara Pettit, Director, Public Relations
• Rosemary Williams, Director of Racing
• Jeffery J Dahl, President and CEO
• John W Bittner, EVP and CFO
• Joseph L Billhimer, EVP and COO
• Fred A Buro, VP and Chief Marketing
Officer
• Steven M Biilik, Chairman
• Rober A Blatt, Vice Chairman
Description:
Founded 1951. Thoroughbred race track
with mini-resort.

Permanent seating capacity:
7,000

NEBRASKA STATE FAIR
1811 WEST 2ND STREET
GRAND ISLAND, NE 68803
308-382-1620
Fax: 308-384-1555
info@statefair.org
www.statefair.org
• Joseph McDermott, Executive Director
• Connie Decker, Ticket Manager
• Jana Kruger, Chairperson
• Joseph McDermott, Executive Director
• Kelly O' Brien, Administrative Assistant
• Chelsey Junqck, Entairtainment Director
• Valerie Brewer, Entairtainment Assistant
• Scott Yound, Maintainance Director
• Bill Angell, Supritenent
Description:
Thoroughbred horse race track. Late model
car races.
Seating capacity:
6,000
Seating Capacity:
1,860

NEW MEXICO STATE FAIR
300 SAN PEDRO NE
ALBUQUERQUE, NM 87108
505-222-9700
Fax: 505-266-7784
www.exponm.com
• Mike Cerletti, General Manager
• Kathy Duffy, Marketing Director
• Dan Mouring, General Manager
• John C Jaramillo, Deputy Manager
• Ken Salazar, Operations Manager
• Sally Mayer, Sr. Manager
• Bill Nordin, CFO
• Alison Haxton, Event Coordinator
Description:
Founded 1938, to hold 17-day agricultural
exposition.

AQUEDUCT
110-00 ROCKAWAY BOULEVARD
PO BOX 90
JAMAICA, NY 11420
718-641-4700
800-221-6266
Fax: 718-843-0054
nyra@nyrainc.com
www.nyra.com
• Barry K K. Schwartz, Chairman/Chief
Executive Officer
• Terrence Meyocks, President/Chief
Operating Officer
• Alec Ingle, Chief Financial
Officer/Assistant to the
• David Skorton, Chairman
• Anthhony J Bonomo, President
• Rick Cotton, EVP
• Michael J Giudice, Sr.M.D
• Michael Dubb, Principal
• Bobby Flay, Team
• Robert Megna, Budget Director
Description:
Thoroughbred horse race track.

NORTHVILLE DOWNS
301 SOUTH CENTER STREET
NORTHVILLE, MI 48167
248-349-1000
800-270-7117
Fax: 248-348-8955
www.northvilledowns.com

• Zayti Margaret, Executive Manager
• Louis E. Carlo, Director, Operations
• Michael Janchick, Race Secretary
Description:
Horse race track.

OAKLAWN JOCKEY CLUB
2705 CENTRAL AVENUE
PO BOX 699
HOT SPRINGS, AR 71901
501-624-4950
800-625-5236
Fax: 501-623-4088
winning@oaklawn.com
www.oaklawn.com
• Charles J. Cella, Owner/President
• Eric Jackson, General Manager
ejackson@oaklawn.com
• Bobby Geiger, Director
Mutuels/Simulcasting
• Craig Holtz, Operations Director
Description:
Founded 1904. Thoroughbred horse race
track.
Seating capacity:
27,000

PAXRACING
3001 STREET ROAD
PO BOX 1000
BENSALEM, PA 19020
215-639-9000
888-238-2946
Fax: 215-639-0337
www.parxracing.com
• Joe Wilson, Chief Operating Officer
• Len Carey, Senior Vice President/Facilities
• Bill Barnes, Director Mutuels
Description:
Founded 1974. Thoroughbred horse race
track.
Seating capacity:
9,400

PENN NATIONAL RACECOURSE
777 HOLLYWOOD BOULEVARD
PO BOX 32
GRANTVILLE, PA 17028
717-469-2211
Fax: 717-469-2910
Fred.Lipkin@pngaming.com
www.hollywoodpnrc.com
• Gary Luderitz, General Manager
(717) 469-2211
• Fred Lipkin, Publicity & Marketing Director
(717) 469-2211
Description:
Thoroughbred horse race track.
Seating capacity:
6,500

PIMA COUNTY FAIR
11300 S HOUGHTON ROAD
TUCSON, AZ 85747
520-762-9100
Fax: 520-762-5005
Office@Pimacountyfair.com
www.pimacountyfair.com
• Jon Baker, Executive Director
(520) 762-9100
Jon@pimacountyfair.com
• Jon Baker, Executive Director
 ext 14
• Bryon Lopez, CFO
• Peggy Bauernfeind, Administrative
Assistant, Interim Events
• Diane McDonald, Accountant

• Launa Rabago, Marketing Manager
(520) 762-9100
launa@pimacountyfair.com
• Phyllis Armbruster, Concession Manager
• Bert Rodriguez, Maintenance Manager
Horse Arena Seating Capacity:
3,000
Livestock Arena Seating Capacity:
3,000
Rodeo Arena Seating Capacity:
3,000
Super Stage Field:
64,000

PIMLICO RACE COURSE
5201 PARK HEIGHTS AVENUE
BALTIMORE, MD 21215
410-542-9400
800-638-3811
Fax: 410-542-1221
info@marylandracing.com
www.pimlico.com
• Karen A. Weiss, Director of Group Sales
(301) 470-5439
• Robert Dipietro, EVP
• James Mango, Chief Operating Officer
• Martin Jacobs, General Counsel
Year Founded:
1870
Nature of Service:
Thoroughbred race track.

PLATTE COUNTY AGRICULTURAL
SOCIETY
822 15 STREET
COLUMBUS, NE 68601
402-564-0133
Fax: 402-564-0990
www.agpark.com
• Gary Wiese, President
• Patty Laska, Office Manager
• Leon Ebel, Mutuels Manager
(402) 564-9711
Seating capacity:
4,000.00
Year Founded:
1941
Track Type:
Dirt.
Nature of Service:
Thoroughbred horse racing. Live from July -
September. Simulcast year-round.

PORTLAND MEADOWS
1001 N SCHMEER ROAD
PORTLAND, OR 97217
503-285-9144
800-888-7576
Fax: 503-737-1038
www.portlandmeadows.com
• William Alempijevic, General Manager
• William Alamplijevlc, General Manager
• Patrick J. Kerrison, Director, Operations
• Cheryl Jones, Director/Off Track
Wagering/OTBs
• Jerry P Kohls, Director of racing
• Kelth Jones, Mutuel Manager
• Kent Hunter, Manager
• Brlan Vierck, Manager of Guest Services
• John McSwain, Security Manager
Description:
Thoroughbred horse race track.
Seating capacity:
5,000

PRAIRIE MEADOWS RACETRACK AND CASINO, INC
1 PRAIRIE MEADOWS DRIVE
PO BOX 1000
ALTOONA, IA 50009
515-967-1000
800-325-9015
chuck.schott@prairiemeadows.com
www.prairiemeadows.com
• Gary Palmer, President / CEO
gary.palmer@prairiemeadows.com
• Ann Atkin, VP Operations
ann.atkin@prairiemeadows.com
• Derron Heldt, Director, Racing
• Tom Manning, Director,
Marketing/Sales/Public Relatio
Year Founded:
1989
Nature of Service:
Horse race track.
Seating capacity:
5,000
Overall capacity:
8,000

QUINTE EX FALL FAIR
18 YEOMAN STREET
BEN BLEECKER BUILDING
BELLEVILLE, ONTARIO, CANADA K8P
3X2
613-968-3266
Fax: 613-968-3956
info@qer.ca
www.qer.ca
• Marilynne Cotten, President
(613) 966-3266
• Liz Muldoon, Second VP
(613) 475-8890

RACEWAY PARK
5700 TELEGRAPH ROAD
TOLEDO, OH 43612
419-476-7751
Fax: 419-476-7979
racewayparkinfo@pngaming.com
• John McNamara, Director of Marketing &
Guest Services
john.mcnamara@pngaming.com
• Craig Laginess, Finance Director
craig.laginess@pngaming.com
• Bruce Patterson, Facilities Director
bruce.patterson@pngaming.com
• Ron Hornyak, Mutuels Manager
ron.hornyak@pngaming.com
• Matt Clark, Simucast Director
matt.clark@pngaming.com
• Mark Loewe, General Manager
Description:
Harness horse race track.
Seating capacity:
5,700

RED MILE, THE
1200 RED MILE ROAD
LEXINGTON, KY 40504
859-255-0752
Fax: 859-231-0217
info@theredmile.com
www.theredmile.com
• Joe Costa, President & CEO
• Donna Bradford, Director Operations
• Nick Salvi, Race Secretary
• Connie Hochstetler, Racing Secretary
• Shannon Cobb, CFO
• Julie Sorrell, Director of Mutuels

REMINGTON PARK
ONE REMINGTON PLACE
OKLAHOMA CITY, OK 73111
405-424-1000
800-456-4244
Fax: 405-425-3234
contact@remingtonpark.com
www.remingtonpark.com
• Frank Stronach, Chairman
• Mike Corey, Chief Steward
• Fred Hutton, Director, Racing
• Matt Vance, Director, Operations
Year Founded:
1988
Nature of Sports Service:
Founded 1988. Thoroughbred, quarter horse
race track.
Seating capacity:
12,000
Publications:
THE REMINGTON POST, monthly during
racing seasons.

RETAMA PARK
1 RETAMA PARKWAY
SELMA, TX 78154
210-651-7000
Fax: 210-651-7097
run@retamapark.com
www.retamapark.com
• Brian P. Brown, Chief Executive Officer
• Joe R. Straus, Jr., Board Chairman
• Larry Craft, Director, Racing
• Jackie F. Hart, Director, Mutuels
Physical Address:
1 Ratama Pkwy, Selma, TX 78265-7535
Description:
Thoroughbred and Quarter Horse race track.

RIDEAU CARLETON RACEWAY
4837 ALBION ROAD
OTTAWA, ON, CANADA K1X 1A3
613-822-2211
Fax: 613-822-1586
www.rcr.net
• Alexei Vidal, Marketing Coordinator
(613) 822-2211
alexei.vidal@hrcottawa.com
• Monica Boudreau, Account Manager
(613) 236-5444
• Kenzie Scott, Account Manager
(613) 236-5444
Year Founded:
1962
Nature of Sports Service:
Harness race track.

ROCKINGHAM PARK
ROCKINGHAM PARK BOULEVARD
PO BOX 47
SALEM, NH 3079
603-898-2311
Fax: 603-893-7284
• Ozzie Cole, Racing Secretary
(603) 898-2311
• Ed Callahan, President/General Manager
(603) 898-2311
• Edward Keelan, VP
(603) 898-2311
• Ed Ca Callahan, President/GM
(603) 898-2311
• Kathleen Brothers, Vp/Mutuel Manager
(603) 898-2311
• John Vitale, Ass.Genaral Manage
(603) 898-2311
• Robert Black, Admissions Director
(603) 898-2311
• Ron Oldeman, TV Control

(603) 898-2311
• Bob Tolman, Comptroller
(603) 898-2311
• Skip Burbine, Money Room Settlement
(603) 898-2311
Year Founded:
1906
Seating capacity:
10,000
Nature of Service:
Thoroughbred horse track.
Track Type:
Harness

ROSECROFT RACEWAY
6336 ROSECROFT DRIVE
FORT WASHINGTON, MD 20744
301-567-4500
Fax: 301-567-9267
www.rosecroft.com
• Scott Warren, Director of Racing &
Simulcasting
• Lisa Watts, VP Mutuels & Operations
• Greg Boehmer, Simulcast Manager
• Christopher M McErlean, VP
christopher.mcerlean@pngaming.com
• Lisa Watts, Director of Operations
lisa.watts@pngaming.com
• Lisa White, Director of Finance
lisa.white@pngaming.com
• Michael Wandishin, Racing Secretary
michael.wandishin@pngaming.com
Description:
Harness horse race track.
Seating capacity:
3,000

RUIDOSO DOWNS RACE TRACK CASINO
26225 US HWY 70
RUIDOSO DOWNS, NM 88346
575-378-4431
Fax: 505-378-4631
info@raceruidoso.com
www.ruidownsracing.com
• R. D. Hubbard, Owner
• Bruce Rimbo, President
• Rick Baugh, General Manager
• Vicki McCabe, Director, Personnel

SAN JOAQUIN COUNTY FAIR
1658 S AIRPORT WAY
STOCKTON, CA 95206
209-466-5041
Fax: 209-466-5739
www.sanjoaquinfair.com
• Mitch Slater, President
• Victoria Salazar, Vice President
• George Vidak, Manager, Mutuel
• Nanett Martin, President
• Tori Verber, President
• Joe Valente, VP
• Sam Fant, BOD
Description:
Thoroughbred, quarter horse race track.
Seating capacity:
5,000

SANDOWN PARK
1810 GLAMORGAN ROAD
PO BOX 2370
SIDNEY, BC, CANADA V8L 3Y3
250-656-1631
Fax: 250-656-7422
• Jackie Ballas, Director, Operations
• Chuck Keeling, General Manager
• Keith Quinlan, Secretary, Racing

Description:
Horse race track.

SANTA ANITA PARK
285 W HUNTINGTON DRIVE
PO BOX 60014
ARCADIA, CA 91007
626-574-7223
888-338-7223
Fax: 626-446-1456
info@santaanita.com
www.santaanita.com
• Charles Ron, President
• Jim McAlpine, Chief Financial Officer
• Chris McCarron, VP and General Manager
• Stuart Zanzille, Marketing Manager
Description:
Founded 1934. Thoroughbred horse race track.
Seating capacity:
26,000

SARATOGA RACETRACK
NYRA
PO BOX 90
JAMAICA, NY 11417
718-641-4700
888-285-5961
Fax: 518-581-4064
info@southernsaratoga.org
www.saratogaracetrack.com
• George Hathaway, Facilities Manager
Description:
Horse race track.

SCIOTO DOWNS
6000 S HIGH STREET
PO BOX 7823
COLUMBUS, OH 43207
614-295-4700
800-723-6967
Fax: 614-295-8871
www.sciotodowns.com
• Ryan T. Edward, President
• Jerry Kalb, Assistant General Manager
• Anne Doolin, Director, Publicity and Marketing
Description:
Harness horse race track.

SIKESTON JAYCEE BOOTHEEL RODEO ARENA
1220 N INGRAM ROAD
PO BOX 5
SIKESTON, MO 63801
573-471-7196
800-455-2855
Fax: 573-471-1540
info@sikestonrodeo.com
www.sikestonrodeo.com
• Jason Pounds, President
• Ron Payne, VP
• Jon Gilmore, Secretary
Seating Capacity:
7,000

SOLANO COUNTY FAIRGROUNDS
900 FAIRGROUNDS DRIVE
VALLEJO, CA 94589
707-551-2000
Fax: 707-642-7947
bdill@scfair.org
www.scfair.org
• Michael Paluszak, General Manager
(707) 551-2000
mpaluszak@scfair.org

• Trina Gonzalez, Executive Assistant to General Manager
• Patrick Skelton, Deputy General Manager
• Michael Passey, GM
• Kim Mini, Events Coordinator
(707) 551-2006
• Eric Burke, Food Department
(707) 551-2014
• Mark Coffman, Security Supervisor
(707) 551-2013
• Rene Edens, Place Manager
(707) 551-2030
Description:
Founded 1940.

SONOMA COUNTY FAIRGROUNDS
1350 BENNETT VALLEY ROAD
PO BOX 1536
SANTA ROSA, CA 95404
707-545-4200
Fax: 707-573-9342
info@sonomacountyfair.com
www.sonomacountyfair.com
• Tawny J. Tesconi, Fair Manager
(707) 545-4200
• Mike Runyan, President
Description:
Horse race track.
Stadium Seating Capacity:
4,000
Track Seating Capacity:
5,000
Track Size:
1.25 miles

SPORTS CREEK RACEWAY
4290 MORRISH ROAD
PO BOX 207
SWARTZ CREEK, MI 48473
810-635-3333
Fax: 810-635-9711
www.sportscreek.com
• Chris Locking, General Manager
Description:
Harness horse race track.

SUFFOLK DOWNS
525 MC CLELLAN HIGHWAY
EAST BOSTON, MA 2128
617-567-3900
800-225-3460
Fax: 617-567-7511
www.suffolkdowns.com
• John Hall, II, President
• Chip Tuttle, Chief Operating Officer
• John Morrissey, Racing Secretary
• Sam Elliott, Assistant Racing Secy
Description:
Thoroughbred horse race track.
Seating capacity:
60,000.00

SULKY TROIS RIVIERES
1850 RUE DE L HIPODROME
PO BOX 1565
TROIS RIVIERES, QC, CANADA G9A 5L6
819-374-6734
Fax: 819-376-4453
• Frenette Benoit, Race Secretary
• Ginette Ricard, SC Field Representative

SUNLAND PARK RACETRACK & CASINO
1200 FUTURITY DRIVE
SUNLAND PARK, NM 88063-9057
505-874-5200
800-572-1142

Fax: 505-589-1518
sunlandinfo@sunland-park.com
www.sunland-park.com
• Harold Payne, Resident Manager
• Adeline Rogers, Director, Marketing
• Linda Robb, Facilities Manager
• Bruce Bruebaker, Director, Human Resource

TAMPA BAY DOWNS
11225 RACETRACK ROAD
TAMPA, FL 33626
813-855-4401
866-823-6967
Fax: 813-854-3539
customerservice@tampabaydowns.com
www.tampabaydowns.com
• Margo Flynn, VP Marketing
Description:
1 mile dirt/turf track

THE DOWNS RACETRACK & CASINO AT ALBUQUERQUE
201 CALIFORNIA STREET NE
ALBUQUERQUE, NM 87108
505-266-5555
Fax: 505-268-1970
michaell@abqdowns.com
www.abqdowns.com
• Craig Smith, General Manager
• Don Cook, Director Racing

THE SHOW PLACE ARENA & PRINCE GEORGE'S EQUESTRIAN CENTER
14900 PENNSYLVANIA AVENUE
UPPER MARLBORO, MD 20772
301-952-7900
Fax: 301-952-8167
showplacearena@pgparks.com
www.showplacearena.com
• Bill Chambers, General Manager
(301) 952-7906
• Nancy Weiman, Marketing Manager
(301) 952-7913
Seating Capacity:
Stadium/Arena 5,500
Sports:
Basketball, horse shows, other
Events:
Capital Challenge Horse Show, Atlantic 10 Women's Basketball Championship, Fall & Spring Home Shows and Concerts. Host of the 2012 CAA Women's Basketball Championship.
Description:
The Show Place Arena and Prince George's Equestrian Center, suburban Washington D.C.'s most versatile sports & entertainment venue - creates a unique setting for sporting events. With flexible seating, concessions, parking, air conditioning, and banquet rooms available. Also available outdoor equestrian lighted show rings, stabling, schooling rings, and secretaries booth with PA system.

THISTLEDOWN RACINO
21501 EMERY ROAD
CLEVELAND, OH 44128
216-662-8600
800-289-9956
Fax: 216-662-5339
www.caesars.com
• Brent D. Reitz, General Manager
• Heather McColloch, Publicity Director
• Greg Davis, Simulcasting
• Bob Hickey, Simulcasting

Description:
Thoroughbred horse race track.
Seating capacity:
7,500

THREE COUNTY FAIR
3 COUNTY FAIR
HAMPSHIRE
NORTHAMPTON, MA 01060-0305
413-584-2237
info@3countyfair.com
www.3countyfair.com
• Alan Jacque, President
Description:
Founded 1818.

**THUNDER RIDGE RACING AND
ENTERTAINMENT COMPLEX**
164 THUNDER ROAD
PRESTONBURG, KY 41653
606-886-7223
Fax: 606-886-7225
asratliff@yahoo.com
www.thunderridgeharness.com
• Ann Reeder, General Manager/President
• Wilma Foley, Mutuels
• Anita Ratliff, GM
Description:
Harness horse race track.

TURF PARADISE
1501 W BELL ROAD
PHOENIX, AZ 85023
602-942-1101
Fax: 602-942-8659
tp@turfparadise.net
www.turfparadise.com
• Jerry Simms, Chairman
• Dave Johnson, VP & Assistant General
Manager
Description:
Horse race track.

TURFWAY PARK
7500 TURFWAY ROAD
PO BOX 8
FLORENCE, KY 41042
859-371-0200
800-733-0200
Fax: 859-647-4730
spinson@tpark.com
www.turfway.com
• Robert N. Elliston, President & CEO
• Clifford Reed, VP/Chief Financial Officer
• Daniel Bach, General Manager
• Rick Leigh, Racing Secretary
• Sherry Pinson, Director of
Communications
• Tyler Picklesimer, Assistant Racing
Secretary
Description:
Horse race track established in 1959.
Stabling for 1,000 horses. One-mile
Polytrack racing surface with quarter-mile
and 6 1/2-furlong chutes. Live racing
December-March. Simulcast racing
year-round.

VERNON DOWNS
4229 STUHLMAN ROAD
VERNON, NY 13476
315-829-2201
877-88-3766
Fax: 315-829-3320
info@vernondowns.com
www.vernondowns.com

• Pete Savage, President
• Paul V. Noyes, Secretary
• James R. Wise, Chief Financial
Officer/Treasurer
• Don Hoover, Director, Racing/Simulcasting

**WESTERN FAIR ENTERTAINMENT
CENTRE**
316 RECTORY STREET
PO BOX 7550
LONDON, ONTARIO, CANADA N5W 53V9
519-438-7203
800-619-4629
Fax: 519-679-3124
• Hugh Mitchell, CEO
• Dave Taylor, Senior Marketing Manager
• Ian Fleaming, Acting Raceway Manager
• Reg Ash, CFO
• Mike Woods, COO
• Michelle Campbell, Chairperson
• Don McCallum, Vice Chairman
• Janet Carr, Member
• Pam Kelly, Assistant Raceway Manager
Description:
Founded 1960. Harness horse race track.
Seating capacity:
4,500

WOODBINE ENTERTAINMENT
555 REXDALE BOULEVARD
PO BOX 156
TORONTO, ON, CANADA M9W 5L2
416-675-7223
888-675-7223
Fax: 416-213-2129
kbm@woodbineentertainment.com
www.woodbineentertainment.com
• David Willmot, Chairman/Chief Executive
Officer
• Nicholas Eaves, President/Chief Operating
Officer

WOODLANDS RACE PARK
9700 LEAVENWORTH ROAD
PO BOX 12036
KANSAS CITY, KS 66109
913-299-9797
Fax: 913-299-9804
www.woodlandskc.com
• Jayme A LaRocca, General Manager
• Howard T. Grace, President
Description:
Quarter horse and thoroughbred horse
racetrack (one-mile Oval).
Seating capacity:
20,000. The Woodlands racing complex is a
dual-horse and greyhound racing facility with
two separate tracks.

WOODSTOCK RACEWAY
851 NELLIS STREET
WOODSTOCK, ON, CANADA N4S 8Z9
519-537-4808
woodstock@gatewaycasinos.ca
woodstock.gatewaycasinos.com
Description:
Harness racing track.

YONKERS RACEWAY
810 YONKERS AVENUE
YONKERS, NY 10704
914-968-4200
Fax: 914-968-4479
www.empirecitycasino.com
• Timothy J J Rooney, President
• Robert J. Galterio, General Manager

• Denis Moran, Assistant General Manager
• Jack Moran, Mutuel Director, Live Racing

Race Tracks - Greyhound

BEST BET
201 MONUMENT ROAD
PO BOX 54249
JACKSONVILLE, FL 32225
904-646-0001
Fax: 904-646-0420
www.bestbetjax.com
• Howard Korman, President
• Jamie Shelton, CFO
jamies@bestbetjax.com
• Howard Korman, President
howardk@bestbetjax.com
• Matt Kroetz, COO
• Deborah Giardina, Executive Director of
Poker
deborahg@bestbetjax.com
• Jesse Hollander, Associate Director
jesseh@bestbetjax.com
• Brett Howard, Room Manager
• Marty Fontes, Race Director
• Howard Korman, CEO
Description:
Greyhound racing track.

BLUFFS RUN
2701 23RD AVENUE
COUNCIL BLUFFS, IA 51501
712-323-2500
800-238-2946
Fax: 712-322-9354
• Weien Peter J, SVP/GM
• Julie Pritchard, Director, Marketing
• Dianne Wegley, Human Resource Director
Description:
Greyhound racing track.

**CORPUS CHRISTI GREYHOUND RACE
TRACK**
5302 LEOPARD STREET
ST.CORPUS CHRISTI, TX 78408
361-289-9333
Fax: 361-289-4307
CCGRT1@yahoo.com
www.corpuschristidogs.com
• Triplett Jacques, General Manager
(361) 289-4301
cccrt@aol.com
• Michelle Gonzalez, Administrative
Assistant
(361) 289-4306
• Jim Austin, Mutuels Manager
(361) 289-4321
• Norman T. Campbell, Simulcast
Coordinator and Decoder
(305) 649-3000
Arena Seating Capacity:
1,952.00
Year Founded:
1990
Track Type:
Greyhound.
Track Size:
1/4 mile.

DAIRYLAND GREYHOUND PARK, INC
5522-104TH AVENUE
KENOSHA, WI 53144
262-657-8200
800-233-3357

Fax: 262-657-8231
dgpinfo@dairylandgp.com
• William O. Agpar, Jr., VP
Operations/General Manager
• Danny Crouch, Director Mutuels/Asst
General Manager
• Paul Lu Jr, Director, Publicity and
Marketing
Description:
Greyhound racing track.

DAYTONA BEACH KENNEL CLUB
960 S WILLAMSON BOULEVARD
PO BOX 11470
DAYTONA BEACH, FL 32114
386-252-6484
Fax: 386-255-6075
breid@dncinc.com
www.daytonagreyhound.com
• Daniel Francati, General Manager
(386) 252-6484
dfrancat@dncinc.com
• Michael Stringer, Asst General
Manager/Food & Beverage Manager
(386) 252-6484
mstringe@dncinc.com
Description:
Greyhound racing track.

DERBY LANE
10490 GANDY BOULEVARD NORTH
SAINT PETERSBURG, FL 33702-2395
727-812-3339
Fax: 727-579-4362
marketg@derbylane.com
www.derbylane.com
• David Tiano, Chief Operations Officer
• Bill Van Hoogen, Director of Racing
• Stephen P. Hlas, Secretary/Treasurer
Description:
Greyhound racing track.

**DUBUQUE GREYHOUND PARK AT
MYSTIQUE**
1855 GREYHOUND PARK ROAD
DUBUQUE, IA 52004-3190
563-582-3647
800-373-3647
Fax: 563-582-9074
joeya@mystiquedbq.com
www.mystiquedbq.com
• Brian Carpenter, Racing Director
(563) 585-2970
brianc@mystiquedbq.com
Seating Capacity:
Grandstand 400; Outdoor 200
Track:
Greyhound Track; 3/19 of a mile, 5/16 of a
mile, 3/8 of a mile, 7/16 of a mile.

FLAGLER DOG TRACK
450 NW 37TH AVENUE
PO BOX 350940
MIAMI, FL 33125
305-649-3000
888-56-MAGIC
Fax: 305-631-4525
info@magiccitycasino.com
www.magiccitycasino.com
• Hutchinson William, General Manager
(305) 649-3000
• Fred Havenick, President and Chief
Executive Officer
(305) 649-3000
Arena Seating Capacity:
2,000
Year Founded

1934
Nature of Service:
For simulcasting, live greyhound racing and
poker.
Track Type:
Sand and Marl greyhound track.

GENEVA LAKES GREYHOUND TRACK
1600 E GENEVA STREET
INTERSTATE 43 HIGHWAY 50
DELAVAN, WI 53115
262-728-8000
800-477-4552
Fax: 262-728-6103
www.genevagreyhounds.com
• Roth Milt, General Manager
• Rebecca Krahn, Mutuel Manager and
Assistant General Man
• Mae Mohr, Director, Racing
Description:
Greyhound racing track.
Seating capacity:
2,950 indoors; 900 outdoors.

GREENETRACK INC.
PO BOX 471
EUTAW, AL 35462
205-372-9318
800-633-5942
Fax: 205-372-0579
www.greenetrackpaysyoumoney.com
• Herlecia Hampton, General Manager
herleciaher@yahoo.com
• Jimmie Paster, Operations Director
gteutowal@aol.com
Seating Capacity:
Track 1,800

GREYHOUND PARK & EVENT CENTER
5100 RIVERBEND AVENUE
POST FALLS, ID 83854
208-773-0545
800-828-4880
Fax: 208-773-2049
ContactUs@GPEventCenter.com
www.gpeventcenter.com
• Oaks Randy, General Manager
Description:
Greyhound racing track.

LINCOLN PARK
100 TWIN RIVER ROAD
LINCOLN, RI 02865
401-723-3200
877-827-4237
Fax: 401-727-4770
• Dan Bucci, General Manager
• Lauren Quinn, Park Supervisor
• Craig Sculos, Marketing Director and
Assistant General
• Gary Liberatore, Director, Racing
Description:
Thoroughbred race track and Greyhound
racing track.
Description:
Thoroughbred race track and Greyhound
racing track.

LUCKY'S CARD ROOM
8300 N NEBRASKA AVENUE
PO BOX 8096
TAMPA, FL 33609
813-932-4313 Ext 301
Fax: 813-932-5048
www.tampadogs.com

• Mike Hater, President/General Manger
• Hillary Fellenz, Marketing
• Theresa Hughes, Racing Secretary
Description:
Greyhound racing track.

**MACON COUNTY GREYHOUND PARK,
INC.**
8680 COUNTY ROAD 40
PO BOX 128
SHORTER, AL 36075
334-727-0540
800-688-2946
Fax: 334-727-0737
www.victoryland.com
• James W. Baker, Raing Manager
• Victory Land, Contact
Description:
Greyhound racing track.

MARDI GRAS CASINO
831 N FEDERAL HIGHWAY
HALLANDALE BEACH, FL 33009
954-924-3200
877-557-5687
Fax: 954-457-4229
www.mardigrascasinofl.com
• Berg Howard, Director, Public Relations
and Marketing

**MEADOWLANDS RACING &
ENTERTAINMENT**
50 STATE ROUTE 120
E RUTHERFORD, NJ 7073
201-935-8500
800-782-2537
Fax: 201-460-4244
www.thebigm.com
• Dennis Dowd, SVP Racing
(201) 460-4183
ddowd@njsea.com
• Chris McErlean, VP Racing Operations
(201) 460-4184
cmcelean@njsea.com
• Vernard Bennett, Assistant VP, Wagering
Guest Services
(201) 460-4115
vbennett@njsea.com
• Marcello Esposito, Assistant VP,
Operations
(201) 842-5034
mesposito@njsea.com
• Darin Zoccali, Director of Racing
Operations
dzoccali@newmracing.com
• Sam McKee, Director of Simulcasting &
TV Production
smckee@newmracing.com
• Mona Vaccarella, Director of HR
mvaccarella@newmracing.com
• James Patalano, Director of Purchasing
jpatalano@newmracing.com
• Jessica Wester, Asst. Director
jwester@newmracing.com
• Bill Kudlacik, Director of Security
bkudlacik@newmracing.com
Arena Seating Capacity:
Track 40,000, Grandstand 25,000,
Clubhouse 10,000.
Year Founded:
1971
Nature of Service:
Harness, Thoroughbred, Simulcasting
Horseracing.
Track Type:
Harness, Thoroughbred, Simulcasting
Horseracing.

**MELBOURNE GREYHOUND PARK &
CLUB 52 POKER**
1100 N WICKHAM ROAD
MELBOURNE, FL 32935
321-259-9800
Fax: 321-259-3437
info@mgpark.com
www.mgpark.com
• Patrick T. Biddix, General Manager
Description:
Greyhound racing track.

**MILE HIGH RACING &
ENTERNTAINMENT**
10750 E LLIFF AVENUE
AURORA, CO 80014
303-751-5918
Fax: 303-289-1640
www.mihiracing.com
• Bruce Seymore, Director Racing
Operations
Description:
Greyhound racing track.

MOBILE GREYHOUND PARK
7101 OLD PASCA GOULA ROAD
PO BOX 43
THEODORE, AL 36582-4011
251-653-5000
800-272-5000
Fax: 251-653-9185
info@pcigaming.com
www.mobilegreyhoundpark.com
• David L. Jones, General Manager
djones1@pcigaming.com
• Paula Justice, Simulcast Director
pjustice@pcigaming.com
• Vivian Reynolds, Group Sales
• Barbara Holt, Mutuels
• Carol Mitchell, Bookeeping
cmitchell@pcigaming.com
• Ellis Hardy, Director of Racing
ehardy@pcigaming.com
• John Rooks, Food Director
Description:
Greyhound racing track.

**NAPLES-FORT MYERS GREYHOUND
TRACK**
10601 BONITA BEACH ROAD
PO BOX 2567
BONITA SPRINGS, FL 34135-2567
239-992-2411
Fax: 239-947-9244
www.naplesfortmyersdogs.com
• Larry Mosher, Director Racing Operations
• James Schwartz, Security Director
(239) 992-2411
• Larry Baldwin, Executive Manager
• Juan Fra, General manager
(239) 992-2411
• Michael Hernandez, Ass.General manger
(239) 992-2411
• David Sonenstahl, Facilities Director
(239) 992-2411
• Cindy Fra, Room Manger
(239) 992-2411
• Bob Dorris, Mutuel Manager
(239) 992-2411
• Tammy Gaida, Admissions Incharge
(239) 992-2411
• Vered Ullman, Office Manager
(239) 992-2411
Description:
Greyhound racing track.

PALM BEACH KENNEL CLUB
1111 NORTH CONGRESS AVENUE
W PALM BEACH, FL 33409
561-683-2222
Fax: 561-471-9114
www.pbkennelclub.com
• Arthur J. Laughlin, General Manager
(561) 683-2222
• Joe Love, Government Affairs
• Micheal Glenn, General Manager
• San Catalfano, Director of Mutuels
• Rick Domian, Racing Director
• Theresa Hume, Publicity Director
• Renne Lampman, HR
• Patrick J Rooney Sr., CEO, President
Description:
Greyhound racing track.

PENSACOLA GREYHOUND TRACK
951 DOG TRACK ROAD
PENSACOLA, FL 32506
850-455-8595
800-345-3997
Fax: 850-453-8883
www.pensacolagreyhoundtrack.com
• Schlikin Nick, General Manager
• Mary Utterbach, Director Racing
Description:
Greyhound racing track.

PHOENIX GREYHOUND PARK
3801 E WASHINGTON STREET
PO BOX 20300
PHOENIX, AZ 85034
602-273-7181
Fax: 602-273-6176
www.phoenixgreyhoundpark.com
• Daniel A. Luciano, General Manager
dluciano@dncinc.com
• Mike Hillard, Director Racing
• Dennis Young, Operations
• Bac Tran, Director Marketing
• Mike Hillard, Racing Director
Description:
Greyhound racing track.
Permanent seating capacity:
6,500

PUEBLO GREYHOUND PARK
3215 LAKE AVENUE
PUEBLO, CO 81004-3895
719-566-0370
Fax: 719-566-0450
www.wembleyco.com
• Rose Steve, General Manager
• Dave Montoya, Mutuel Manager
• Frank Provenza, Marketing Director
Description:
Greyhound racing track.

**SANFORD-ORLANDO KENNEL CLUB,
INC.**
301 DOG TRACK ROAD
LONGWOOD, FL 32750
407-831-1600
Fax: 407-831-3997
info.sokc@pngaming.com
www.sanfordorlandokc.com
• Collins Jack, Track Manager
• Mike Newlin, General Manager
Description:
Greyhound racing track.

SARASOTA KENNEL CLUB, INC.
5400 BRADENTON ROAD
SARASOTA, FL 34234

941-355-7744
Fax: 941-351-2207
info@sarasotakennelclub.com
www.sarasotakennelclub.com
• Collins Jr. Jack, Track Manager
Description:
Greyhound racing track.

SEABROOK PARK
319 NEW ZEALAND ROAD
PO BOX 219
SEABROOK, NH 03874-4119
603-474-3065
866-732-2766
Fax: 603-474-2438
www.seabrookgreyhoundpark.com
• Carney James, President
• Glenn Jones, Racing Secy
• Neil Casey, Director Racing
• Bill Modie, Publicity
• Edward J Keelan, President
• Joseph Carney, General Manager
Description:
Greyhound racing track.

SOUTHLAND PARK
1550 N INGRAM BOULEVARD
PO BOX 2088
I-40 & I-55 Exit 279 A
W MEMPHIS, AR 72301
870-735-3670
800-467-6182
Fax: 870-732-8335
www.southlandgreyhound.com
• Troy Keeping, President/General Manager
(870) 735-3670
tkeeping@dncinc.com
• Gayla Allen, Executive Assistant
(870) 735-3670
gallen@dncinc.com
• Maurice Cummings, Controller
• Troy Keeping, President and GM
• Osi Imomoh, Sr.Director of Operations
• Maureen Finley, Director of Finance
• JIm Wilson, Director of Gaming
• Shane Bolender, Director of Racing
• Bobbi Jones, Marketing
• Estell Wilson, Food Director
Year Founded:
1956
Track Type:
Greyhound Racing.

TUCSON GREYHOUND PARK, INC.
2601 S THIRD AVENUE
TUCSON, AZ 85713
520-884-7576
800-704-5218
Fax: 520-624-9389
info@tucsongreyhound.com
www.tucdogtrak.com
• Tom Taylor, CEO/General Manager
• Joseph Zappala, President/Owner
Description:
Greyhound racing track.

WHEELING ISLAND GAMING, INC.
1 S STONE STREET
WHEELING, WV 26003-2009
304-232-5050
877-946-4373
Fax: 304-231-1834
www.wheelingisland.com
• Campbell R. Lesley, Publicity Director
Description:
Greyhound racing track.

Permanent seating capacity:
3,500

WICHITA GREYHOUND PARK
1500 E 77TH STREET N
VALLER CENTER
WICHITA, KS 67147-0277
316-755-4000
800-535-0482
Fax: 316-755-2405
www.wgpi.com
• Ruffin G Phil, Owner
• Shelli Baker, Interim General Manager/Simulcast
• Todd Dennett, Director Mutuels
• Phillip Ru Jr, Director Operations
Description:
Greyhound racing track.

WOODLANDS, THE
9700 LEAVENWORTH ROAD
PO BOX 12036
KANSAS CITY, KS 66109-3551
913-299-9797
800-695-7223
Fax: 913-299-9804
www.woodlandskc.com
• Jayme LaRocca, General Manager
• Howard T. Grace, President
Description:
Greyhound racing track.

Facility Architects & Developers

360 ARCHITECTURE
300 W 22ND STREET
SUITE 400
KANSAS CITY, MO 64108
816-472-3360
Fax: 816-531-3388
360architects.com
• Tracy Stearns, Senior Principal
• George M. Heinlein, Senior Principal
Nature of Service
Architectural Design, interior design, visioning & strategic design, building & site evaluation, programming & space planning, graphics & way finding, 3D illustration & animation, and sustainability consulting
Clients
Cutler Residence, KC Power & Light, Burnham Square Condominium, Nationwide Arena District, Bernstein-Rein Advertising Atrium, H&R Block Center, Boulevard Brewery Expansion, Johnson County Sunset Drive, Valencia Place/Lockton, IRS Service Center, Midland Loan Services, C3, University of Dayton Arena, American Airlines Arena, Nationwide Arena, Mizzou Arena, New York Sports & Convention Center, Sprint Center, UCF Football Stadium, KCK Baseball, KU Hall Center for the Humanities, Graceland University, Carter Art Center

ABEL BANNISON BUTZ
80 8TH AVENUE
SUITE 1105
NEW YORK, NY 10011
212-206-0630
Fax: 212-645-0048
info@abbnyc.com
www.abbnyc.com

• Terri-Lee Burger, Prinicipal
• John S. Butz, Principal
(212) 206-0630
• Terri-Lee Burger, Registered Landscape Architect
• John S. Butz, Registered Landscape Architect
Services:
Park design, campus planning, and outdoor sports and athletic facility design
Specialties:
Public Parks, Waterfront Parks, Athletic Facilities, Campus Planning and Design, Streetscape Improvements, Master Planning/Site Planning
Projects:
1998-2001 Hudson River Park - Segment 4, New York, NY; 2001 Madison Square Park, New York, NY; 2000 Community Rock Garden, Bronx, NY; 1998 Fountain of Youth Playground, Bronx, NY; 1993 Riverbank State Park, New York, NY; 1991 Broadway Malls, 61st to 168th Street, New York, NY; 1990-1996 East River Esplanade: Phase I - 94th to 103rd Street, Phase II - 63rd to 71st Street, Phase IV - 90th to 94th Street; 1999 Grand Central North End District Streetscape, New York, NY; 1999 47th Street Improvements, Diamond District, New York, NY; 1999 Raul Wallenberg Memorial, New York, NY; 1998 South Broadway, Yonkers, NY; 1995 Citicorp/Court Square, Long Islan

ACKERMAN MCQUEEN ADVERTISING
1601 N W EXPRESSWAY
1100 THE TOWER
OKLAHOMA CITY, OK 73118
405-843-7777
Fax: 405-848-8034
debby-johnson@am.com
www.am.com
• Agnes McQueen, Chief Executive Officer
• Bill Winkler, Chief Financial Officer/Chief Operating
• Edmund O. Martin, Board Chairman
• David Lipson, President
Services:
Marketing, Advertising and Research agency
Clients:
Kerr-McGee Corporation, Juniper Networks, Inc., LeapFrog, BancFirst, Integris Health, Integris Heart Hospital, Caymus Vinyards, WinStar Casinos, OGE Energy Corporation, Air Force Memorial Foundation, TownCenter Booksellers, Chickasaw Nation, Oklahoma Tourism and Recreation Department, Shark Jaw Toys, American Indian Cultural Center, Texas Alliance of Energy Producers, Big Boing Toys, The Oklahoman, Bickel & Brewer, Oklahoma Parks, Resorts & Golf, Oklahoma State Fair, Greater Oklahoma City Chamber of Commerce, Oklahoma Capitol Complex & Centennial Commemoration, River Parks Authority, Xirrus

ADOLFSON & PERTSON, INC.
6701 WEST 23RD STREET
MINNEAPOLIS, MN 55426
952-544-1561
Fax: 952-525-2333
contactMN@a-p.com
www.a-p.com
• David Adolfson, Chairman Emeritus
• Michael C. Peterson, Chief Growth Officer

• Scott A. Weicht, President/Chied Financial Officer
• William Bradford, President/CEO
• Marc W. Boatwright, Seior Vice President
• Mark Dixon, President & Owner
• Kevin Gott, President
Services:
General Construction, Construction Management Services, Design and Build Services, Facilites Maintenance Services. Operates as a contractor of commercial construction
Clients:
CenturyTel,Duke-weeks Realty,Carlson Real Estate Company,SunCor,360Networks,SuperValu, Inc.,Lang Associates,The Trammell Crow Company,The Chute Companies,Prudential Insurance Co.,Wal-Mart,Dayton Hudson Corporation,Target Stores,Amerimar Enterprises,Saks Fifth Avenue,Federated Department Stores,General Growth,REI,Home Depot,JC Penney Corporation,Safeway,Hutchinson Technology, Inc.,Andersen Windows,Control Data Corporation,Donatelle Plastics, Inc.,Cannon,Equipment Company,Green Giant Company,Green Bay Packaging,ADC Telecommunications,Midwest Coca-Cola Bottling,Pepsi-Cola Mid-Wisconsin,Beverage, Inc.,Kaiser Permanente,Howard Young Medical Center

AECOM
800 LA SALLE AVENUE
MINNEAPOLIS, MN 55402
612-376-2000
Fax: 612-376-2271
• Rick Lincicome, Chief Executive Officer
• Welton Becket, Founder
• Jon Buggy, Managing Principal-Healthcare,
• Maggie Walsh, Associate Vice President, Marketing
asktransportation@aecom.com
Service
Architectural and planning services for sport facilities
Client
Alfa Development Corporation, Allina Health System, American University in Cairo, Amtrak Consolidated National Operations Center, Atlanta Braves, Augsburg Fortress Publishers, Bay Area Medical Center, Blue Stream Ventures, Bovis Lend Lease, Bozeman Deaconess Hospital, Brasil Telecom, Buffalo Sabres, Capital Projects, Charlotte Bobcats/Charlotte Sting, Children's National Medical Center, City of Grand Forks, City of Kansas City, City of Sioux City, City Public Service Energy Management Center, Cleveland Cavaliers, Cleveland State University, Crescendo Ventures, Crozer Keystone Health System, Dai-Ichi Resort Company, Drug Enforcement Agency (D
Clients
E*TRADE, East Texas Medical Center, El Paso Diablos, Elon University, ERCOT (Electric Reliability Council of Texas), Federal Reserve Bank of Kansas City, First & Goal Inc. (FGI), Florida Hospital Orlando, Gearworks, Georgetown University Law Center, Gonzaga University, Grand Action Committee, GSA (U.S. General Services Administration), Gustavus Adolphus College, Hae Song Company International Ltd., Hammes Company, Hays Medical

Center, Health Care Systems, Hewlett-Packard, HI-WIRE, Huizenga Holdings Inc., IHMS - Welcare, Indiana Pacers, Iowa State University, JP Morgan Chase H&Q

ALBANESE/BROOKS/ASSOCIATES P.C.
1001 N ALVERNON WAY
SUITE 175
TUCSON, AZ 85711
520-881-4512
Fax: 520-881-7505
• Kim Fernandez, Principal
• Kim Ferranti, Treasurer
• Paty Marquez, Project Architect
• Rob Bass, Project Architect
Services:
Design and master planning of indoor and outdoor recreational facilities. Specialty includes recreation centers and pools
Clients:
City of Tucson, Pima County, United Methodist Church, Lutheran Church of the Ascension, Catalina American Baptist Church, Holy Way Presbyterian Church, Cottonwood Elementary, Mesquite Elementary, Catalina High Magnet School, Sycamore Elementary

ALFRED GOBAR ASSOCIATES
300 S HARBOR BOULEVARD
SUITE 900
ANAHEIM, CA 92805
714-772-8900
Fax: 714-772-8911
www.gobar.com
• Alfred J Gobar, President and Chairman
• Alonzo Pedrin, Principal
• James Wolf, Principal
• Ryan Early, Senior Research Associate
Services:
Consultants that specialize in economic feasibility analyses and market analyses for recreation and mass spectator facilities
Clients:
Kaufman & Broad, Greystone Homes, S & S Construction, Presley Homes, Centex Homes, Lewis Homes, The Irvine Company, Catellus Development Corp., CT Realty Corp., Birtcher, Mission Viejo Company, Del Webb Corporation, Pacific Gulf Properties, Rancho Mission Viejo, Tejon Ranch, Santa Margarita Company, Triquest Development, Rose Hills Company, Pohl-Brown Associates, Polygon Homes, Greystone Homes, Instorage, ICI Development, Majestic Realty, The Koll Company, the Lusk Companies, Wrather Corporation, DoubleTree Inns, TraveLodge, All Seasons Inn

AMERICAN LEISURE CORPORATION
414 AIRPORT EXECUTIVE PARK
NANUET, NY 10954
845-371-5670
Fax: 845-371-5680
www.americanleisure.com
• Steve Kass, Founder/Chief Executive Officer
• Wendy Bosalavage, President
wbosalavage@americanleisure.com
• Terri Barbaria, EVP
• Wendy Bosalavage, President
• Tom Johnston, COO
• Beth Caplan, Chief Financial Officer
bcaplan@americanleisure.com
• Jason D Verney, VP, Operations

• Don Amblo, VP, Operations
• Joann Patrello, VP
Services:
Provides expert assistance and services in the design, development, marketing and management of recreational and lifestyle facilities such as Fitness Clubs, Corporate Fitness Centers, Wellness Centers, Spas, Medical Spas, Golf & Country Clubs, JCC's & YMCA's
Clients:
The Fitness Center at Atlantic Apartments, The Bay Club, BelleFair at Rye Brook, The Bromley Fitness Center, Carlton House Club, The Channel Club, The Estates at Chapel Hill Lifestyle Center & Spa, The Lifestyle Center, Spa & Lake Club at Chapin Estates, The Lifestyle Center at Clinton Green, The Columbia Fitness Center, The Lifestyle Center at Columbus Tower, Connaught Tower Club, The Copley Lifestyle Center, The Lifestyle Center at The Devonshire, The Esplanade Lifestyle Center, The Exchange Fitness Center, Affinia Fitness Spa at The Dumont Hotel, Affinia Wellness Spa at The Benjamin Hotel, The Spa at The Aruba Grand Hotel, The Spa at Ballys at Bally's Casino

AQUATIC DESIGN GROUP, INC.
2226 FARADAY AVENUE
CARLSBAD, CA 92008
760-438-8400
800.938.0542
Fax: 760-438-5251
info@aquaticdesigngroup.com
www.aquaticdesigngroup.com
• Randy Mendoroz, President
Services:
Planning, architecture and engineering services for competitive, recreation and leisure aquatic facilities
Clients:
Four Seasons Hotels, Gravity Fitness Center and Spa at Le Parker Meridien Hotel, Hampton Retreats, The Rock Spa at The Hard Rock Hotel, The Thalossotherapy Spa, Fitness & Tennis Club at The Marbella Hotel, Millenium Hilton Hotel Fitness Center, The Spa & Fitness Center at Ocean Point Hotel, R & A Hotels, The Spa & Salon at The Ritz Carlton San Juan, Sheraton Health Club, Sheraton Manhattan, Sheraton Health Club, Sheraton New York, Starwood Hotels, Sutton Place Hotels, The Spa & Fitness Center at The Victor Hotel, Villa Roma Resort & Country Club, The Spa at The Aruba Grand Hotel, The Spa at Ballys at Bally's Casino Hotel etc

ARC ARCHITECTS
1101 E PIKE STREET
FLOOR 3
SEATTLE, WA 98122
206-322-3322
Fax: 206-322-9323
www.arcarchitects.com
• Dave Rutherford, Principal
• Rex Bond, Principal
• Stan Lokting, Principal
Services:
Provides architectural services such as feasibility studies, master planning, programming, design & construction administration, sustainable design, special needs & diverse communities, and renovations & additions
Clients:

Camp Easter Seals, Lake Sammamish State Park, Port Townsend City Hall, Sammamish Commons, Lake City Library, WSU Agricultural Research & Technology Building, UW Golf Driving Range, South Bellevue Community Center, William Shore Memorial Pool, St. Andrews East Village Housing

ARC ICESPORTS & ENTERTAINMENT
50 S LAWN COURT
ROCKVILLE, MD 20850
301-315-5660
Fax: 301-315-5665
• John Cook, President
(416) 675-7604
Nature of Sports Service:
Developers of hockey and figure skating facilities. Focus on developing ice rinks in the United States

ARCHITECHNICS INC.
510 MAINE STREET
10TH FLOOR
QUINCY, IL 62301
217-222-0554
Fax: 217-223-3361
archeng@architechnicsinc.com
www.architechnicsinc.com
• Anthony E Crane, Partner
• Todd J. Moore, Professional Engineer
• Martin E Meyer, Partner
Description:
Architects providing architectural design as well as utility studies, budget analysis and services for buildings, HVAC, mechanical and electrical components

ARCHITECTS DELAWIE WILKES RODRIGUES BARKER
2265 INDIA STREET
SAN DIEGO, CA 92101
619-299-6690
Fax: 619-299-5513
info@delawie.com
www.delawie.com
• Michael B. Wilkes, Chief Executive Officer
• M. Andrew An Rodrigues, President
• James Barker, VP
• M. Andrew Rodrigues, Principal
• Paul E. Schroeder, Principal
• Frank Ternasky, Principal
• Michael Asaro, Principal
Description:
Architectural planning
Services:
Architecture, Master Planning, Programming & Facilities Analysis, Computer Graphics

ARCHITECTURAL ASSOCIATES, LTD.
5801 WASHINGTON AVENUE
SUITE 203
RACINE, WI 53402
262-886-1700
Fax: 262-886-5885
architect@aaltd.com
www.aaltd.com
• John Murphy, President
johnm@aaltd.com
Description:
Recreation and aquatic centers

ARCHITECTURAL RESOURCES CAMBRIDGE INC.
FIVE CAMBRIDGE CENTER
CAMBRIDGE, MA 2142

617-547-2200
Fax: 617-547-7222
ARCmail@arcusa.com
www.arcusa.com
• Henry S. Reeder, President/Principal
• Colin L. Smith, Principal
• Arthur Cohen, Principal
Services:
Provides professional services in the fields of architecture, planning, and interior design
Clients:
Terry Sanford Institute of Public Policy,John Pappajohn Business Building,Kennedy School of Government,Jaharis Family Center for Biomedical and Nutrition Sciences,Olin Center for Language & Culture,Isenberg School of Management,George S. Dively Executive Education Center, Leeds School of Business Design,Blake Hall Renovation and Addition,Research & Development Building/Manufacturing Building,New Research Building,R&D Facility/Office and Laboratory Renovations,Jaharis Family Center for Biomedical and Nutrition Sciences,Five Mountain Road-Laboratory Conversion,Research Building,Pharmaceutical Production and R&D Expansion,Hauser Center for Nonpr
Description:
Amherst College, Boston University, Boston College, Princeton University, Yale University, Berkshire School, Milton Academy, Noble & Greenough School and Phillips Exeter Academy

BALLARD KING & ASSOCIATES
2743 E RAVENHILL CIRCLE
HIGHLANDS RANCH, CO 80126
303-470-8661
Fax: 303-470-8642
BKA@ballardking.com
www.ballardking.com
• Jeffrey L. King, President & Founding Partner
• Kenneth S. Ballard, President & Founding Partner
• Darin J. Barr, Senior Associate
Services:
Recreation facility planning and operation consultants specializing in needs assessment studies, feasibility reports, design review operations pro formas, marketing plans, audits and operations planning
Clients:
Wheat Ridge Recreation Center, Sylvester Powell Community Center, Red Mountain Multigenerational Center, Greater Plymouth Community Center, Sherwood Family YMCA, The Pointe at Ballwin Commons

BARKER RINKER SEACAT ARCHITECTURE
3457 RINGSBY COURT
UNIT 200
DENVER, CO 80216
303-455-1366
866-646-1980
Fax: 303-455-7457
brs@brsarch.com
www.brsarch.com
• Steve Blackburn, Principal
• Keith Hayes, Principal
• Roz Schneider, Principal
• Craig Bouck, President, CEO
(303) 455-1366
craigbouck@brsarch.com

• Chuck Musgrave, Principal, CFO
(303) 455-1366
• Frank Buono, Principal, CIO
(303) 455-1366
• Katie Barnes, Principal, COO
(303) 455-1366
katiebarnes@brsarch.com
• Dave Hammel, Principal
(303) 455-1366
davehammel@brsarch.com
• Keith Hayes, Principal
(303) 455-1366
keithhayes@brsarch.com
Description:
Program and design of community recreation centers throughout the United States

BERNIER, CARR & ASSOCIATES
327 MULLIN STREET
WATERTOWN, NY 13601
315-782-8130
Fax: 315-782-7192
kreinhardt@thebcgroup.com
www.thebcgroup.com
• Bernard H Brown Jr, Chief Executive Officer
• Rick W. Tague, President
rtague@thebcgroup.com
• Bernard H Brown, CEO
• Pamela S Beyor, Chairperson
• Rick W Tague, President
• Mari L Cecil, VP
• Shawn M Travers, Principal
• Lynette Beck, Marketing Director
• Mickey G Lehman, VP

BETA DESIGN GROUP, INC.
2534 ROYAL PL
C
GRAND RAPIDS, MI 49503
770-491-9250
800-235-6299
Fax: 616-235-6393
• Doug Brant, President
• Liz English, Marketing Director
• Carolyn DuBuis, Human Resources Director
Description:
Comprehensive architectural, mechanical and electrical design services including interior design, site planning, community planning, graphic design construction administration and civil engineering

BLUNDEN BARCLAY ROBBIE ASSOCIATES ACHITECTS
200 PUBLIC SQUARE
BP TOWER, SUITE 200
CLEVELAND, OH 44114
216-566-7888
Fax: 216-566-9023
• Robert A Barclay, President, Marketing, Human Resources
Description:
Athletic facilities including gymnasiums, fitness centers, field houses and outdoor education facilities.

BMK ARCHITECTS
323 CENTRAL AVENUE
SARASOTA, FL 34236
941-365-6056
Fax: 941-955-2592
• Darrell Mclain, President/Principal
• Charles Kuykendall, SVP/Principal
• William J. Tyle, SVP/Financial Principal

• Richard Opalinsky, VP/Principal
• James Robison, Chief Information Officer

BOND ARCHITECTS
200 S CENTRAL AVENUE
SUITE 100
SAINT LOUIS, MO 63105
314-863-4994
Fax: 314-863-4996
www.bondwolfe.com
• Susan Pruchnicki, Principal
• Art Bond, Principal
abond@bondarchitectsinc.com
Description:
Full range of professional design services with expertise in private municipal and institutional sports and recreation facilities.

BOWEN WILLIAMSON ZIMMERMAN INC.
2211 PARMENTER STREET
MIDDLETON, WI 53562
608-831-2900
Fax: 608-831-5800
info@bwzarchitects.com
www.bwzarchitects.com
• Frederick E Zimmerman, Project Director
Description:
Facility engineers.

BRAILSFORD & DUNLAVEY
1140 CONNECTICUT AVENUE, NW
SUITE 400
WASHINGTON, DC 20036
202-289-4455
Fax: 202-289-6461
info@programmanagers.com
• BJ Ruddell, Marketing Director
• Will Mangrum, Senior Vice President
• Brad Noyes, Senior Vice President
• Jeff Turner, Senior Vice President
• Kevin Keegan, Vice President
• Bill Mykins, Vice president
• Alan Resnick, Vice President
• Chris A Dunlavey, President
Year Founded:
1993
Nature of Service:
Facility planning and project management firm to a variety of clients including major and minor league athletic teams, collegiate athletics and recreation, and community recreation. Organization conducts market, financial, and programming analysis, site
Clients Include:
Baltimore Ravens, Ohio Arts and Sports Commission, DC Sport & Entertainment Commission, Duke University, University of Maryland and the Unviersity of Rhode Island.

BRAUN & STEIDL ARCHITECTS INC
1041 W MARKET STREET
AKRON, OH 44313
330-864-7755
Fax: 330-864-3691
www.bsa-net.com
• Charles Schreckenberger, cschreckenberger@bsa-net.com
• Rachel Schwarz, rschwarz@bsa-net.com
• Phillip Steinberg,
• Paula Ryan, Media
• Robert Habel, Vice President
rhabel@bsa-net.com

BRESLIN, RIDYARD, FADERO ARCHITECTS
1226 UNION BOULEVARD
ALLENTOWN, PA 18109
610-437-9626
Fax: 610-437-4769
BRFA@breslinarchitects.com
www.breslinarchitects.com
• Robin W Breslin, President
(610) 437-9626
robinbreslin@breslinarchitects.com
• Robert J. Hayes, Senior Associate
(610) 437-9626

BROSSO, WILHELM & MCWILLIAMS, INC.
1001 CROMWELL BRIDGE ROAD
SUITE 200
BALTIMORE, MD 21286
410-321-6760
Fax: 410-321-6782
• Robert A A. Brosso, President
Description:
Architects/interior designers/consultants of fitness, recreational, wellness and athletic facilities in the U.S., Great Britain and Canada.

BROWNING DAY MULLINS DIERDORF ARCHITECTS
626 N ILLINOIS STREET
INDIANAPOLIS, IN 46204
317-635-5030
Fax: 317-634-5409
info@bdmd.com
www.bdmd.com
• Craig W Mullins, Chairman of the Board
• Uohn JA Dierdorf, Chief Executive Officer
• Jonathan Hess, EVP
• Cynthia Richmond, Senior Marketing Coordinator
Description:
Architectural design and consulting.

BRUNER/COTT & ASSOCIATES INC.
130 PROSPECT STREET
CAMBRIDGE, MA 2139
617-492-8400
Fax: 617-876-4002
info@brunercott.com
www.brunercott.com
• Henry Moss, Prinicipal
• Leland Cott, Founding Principal
• Lynne Brooks, Principal
• Daniel Raih, Principal
• Lawrence Cheng, Associate Principal
• Robert Simmons, Associate Principal
• Simeon Bruner, Founding Principal
Description:
Architecture and interior design of athletic, recreational and multi-purpose spaces, specializing in the renovation and adaptive reuse of older buildings.
Services:
Campus planning, with specialities in Student Amenities: Dormitories, Dining Halls, and Student Center

BRUNGARDT ENTERPRISES, L.L.C.
2195 S TELLURIDE COURT
AURORA, CO 80013
303-537-1285
888-740-2223
Fax: 303-537-1293
info@b-ent.com
www.b-ent.com

• Peter Brungardt, Owner
(303) 537-1285
info@b-ent.com
• Noreen Brungardt, Business Manager
(303) 537-1285
info@b-ent.com
Description:
Computer drafting services, and event layouts.

BSA ARCHITECTS
300 MONTEGOMERY STREET
SUITE 1135
SAN FRANCISCO, CA 94104
415-281-4720
Fax: 415-281-4721
smergy@bsaarchitects.com
www.bsaarchitects.com
• Robert E Allen, Principal
(415) 781-1526
• Michael Pattinson, Int'l Assoc AIA, RIBA, IIDA, BIID Principal
• John Ashworth, Principal
• David D. Ross, Principal
• Sarah Mergy, Senior AssociateDirector of Marketing and Off
• Dillon Parker, Associate
• George Janson, Senior Associate
• Henrik Bull, Principal Emeritus
Year Founded:
1967
Clients:
City, County, State, Federal municipalities, Independent districts, agencies, public and private colleges, universities, private resort, recreation clients.
Nature of Service:
Facility planning and architectural services.

BURBACH AQUATICS - ARCHITECTS & ENGINEERS, INC.
5974 STATE HIGHWAY 80 S
PLATTEVILLE, WI 53818
608-348-3262
Fax: 608-348-4970
baae@centurytel.net
www.burbachaquatics.com
• David Burbach, President
• Roger Schamberger, VP Marketing
Year Founded:
1978
Clients:
Municipal Clients, Park Districts, County Park and Recreation, Local Units of Government.
Nature of Service:
Indoor, outdoor family aquatic centers, technical evualations, feasibility to marketing studies, design of specification construction administration.

BURLEY'S
1500 WESTEC DRIVE
EUGENE, OR 97402
814-262-7313
800-311-5294
Fax: 814-262-7610
www.burley.com
• W Graeme Roustan, Owner
• Robert Heffernan,
Year Founded:
1985
Clients:
Anybody with a dream to own their own ice or inline rink. Domestic and International.
Nature of Service:

Design, manufacture, install and supply ice and inline rink facilities.

BURNHAM REAL ESTATE SERVICES
4435 EASTGATE MALL
SUITE 200
SAN DIEGO, CA 92121
858-452-6500
Fax: 858-452-3206
• Malin Brunham, Chairman
(619) 525-2172
• Stath Karras, President & CEO
(858) 334-4001
Description:
Specializing in projects and construction management for athletic facilities.

BUTLER HEAVY STRUCTURES
HEAVY STRUCTURES
1540 GENESSEE STREET
KANSAS CITY, MO 64102
816-245-6500
Fax: 816-245-6055
heavystructures@bucon.com
www.heavystructures.com
• Mark Cogley, General Management
(816) 245-6777
• Mark Mazzoni, Project Management
(816) 245-6914
• Melessia Jones, Marketing and Website Feedback
(816) 245-6957
• Mike Gravino, Business Development Manager
(727) 934-6805
Description:
General contractor.

C.H. GUERNSEY & CO.
5555 N GRAND BOULEVARD
OKLAHOMA CITY, OK 73112
405-416-8100
Fax: 405-416-8111
www.guernsey.us
• Michael K Moore, President/CEO
• Justin Proctor, Marketing Director
(405) 416-6805
Description:
Architects, engineers, consultants.

CAMBRIDGE SEVEN ASSOCIATES INC.
1050 MASSACHUSETTS AVENUE
CAMBRIDGE, MA 2138
617-492-7000
Fax: 617-492-7007
www.c7a.com
• Peter Kuttner, President
• Dagmar Vonschwerin, Director Marketing
• Ronald Baker, Principal
• Stefanie Greenfield, Principal
• Steven Imrich, Principal
• Patricia Intrieri, Principal
• Gary Johnson, Principal
• Timothy Mansfield, Principal
Description:
Architecture, interiors and graphic design.
Services:
Architectural Design, Urban, Design, Master Planning, Adaptive Reuse/Renovation, Sustainable Design, Feasibility Analysis, Interior Design, programming Exhibit Design, Habitat Design, Graphic Design, Marketing Communications Design, Construction Administration

CARLSON DESIGN/CONSTRUCT CORP.
34 EXECUTIVE PARK
SUITE 250
IRVINE, CA 92614
949-251-0455
Fax: 949-251-0465
www.carlson-dc.com
• Bill Fraser, President
• Kari-ann Godberson, Human Resources Director
• William B. Fraser, PE Chief Executive Officer
• John L. Watts, President
• Tom Ryan, Director of Sales and Marketing
• Sean Suzuki, Director of Operations
• Joe Huebner, Director of Business Development
• Jeanne-Marie Pate, Controller
Service
Provide clients with highest level of services such as consulting, design and construction and offers industry's top skills for the most demanding projects and building programs which includes technologically challenging projects, multi-site rollouts, and projects with aggressive schedules
Clients
Charles Schwab, American Express, Accredited Home Lenders, Washington Mutual, First Tennessee, Mellon Bank One, Bank of America, Bank of New York, Wells Fargo, SAFECO Corp., Dime Savings Bank, Fidelity, State Street, Deutsche Bank, Pershing/DLJ Direct, Citicorp, John Hancock, Boatmen's Bancshares, Inc. Fleet Financial Services

CEI ARCHITECTURE
500 - 1500 W GEORGIA STREET
VANCOUVER, BRITISH COLUMBIA,
CANADA V6G 2Z6
604-687-1898
888-922-2088
Fax: 604-682-5398
tpow@ceiarchitecture.com
www.ceiarchitecture.com
• Mark Hentze, Director Recreation/Culture/Community
mhertze@ceiarchitecture.com
• John Scott, Senior Partner
• Mark Hentze, Partner
• Conrad Boychuk, Senior Director, Recreation and Venue Develop
• Heidi Matthews, Director of Interior Design
• Michael McNaught, Director of Post-Secondary
• Hugh Jansen, Associate, Manager of Operation
• Troy Ransdell, Partner
Service
Provides planning, urban design, architectural and interior design services for an extensive range of individual companies and institutions including hospitals and laboratories.
Clients
Alcan Canada Ltd., BC Hothouse Ltd., B C Rail, BCR Properties, B C Sugar, Beutel Goodman Real Estate, Canada Lands Corporation, Canadian Occidental Petroleum, CB Richard Ellis, CN Real Estate Management, Colliers International, Concert Properties Ltd., Chrysler Canada Ltd., Grosvenor International Ltd., Greyhound Canada Ltd., Intrawest Development Corporation, Metropolitan Life Assurance, Morguard Investments Ltd.,

NISSAN Canada Ltd., Penreal Capital Management Ltd., Pilot Pacific Developments Inc., Progressive Properties, Safeway Canada, Scotiabank, Shell Canada, Slough Estates Canada Ltd., Toronto Dominion Bank, Yaohan USA Corporation, Glen

CHICAGO SCENIC STUDIO
1315 N NORTH BRANCH STREET
CHICAGO, IL 60642
312-274-9900
Fax: 312-274-9901
www.chicagoscenic.com
• Robert F Doepel, President
bdoepel@chicagoscenic.com
• Wayne Sorensen, Chief Financial Officer
• Henry Ng, Controller
• Pete Rahill, Director
• Robert F Doepel, President
• Henry Ng, Comptroller
• Wayne Sorensen, CFO
• Diane Langhorst, Marketing Manager
• Ross Hamilton, Project Manager
• Jean Burch, Project Manger
Sports Service Founded:
1979

CLARK ENTERPRISES
7500 OLD GEORGETOWN ROAD
BETHESDA, MD 20814
301-272-8100
Fax: 301-272-1928
www.clarkus.com
• Alice K. Patterson, Community Relations Officer
• Christie Goldman, Business Development Executive
• Kasey Repass, Office Manager
Service
Offers expertise in the development, financing, construction and/or design-build delivery of major sports facilities from coast to coast; sports facility development professionals highly experienced in preconstruction consultation and construction administration; and unique project delivery methods and project completion guarantees.

THE COLLABORATIVE, INC.,
500 MADISON AVENUE
TOLEDO, OH 43604
419-242-7405
Fax: 419-242-7400
TCI@thecollaborativeinc.com
www.thecollaborativeinc.com
• Michael J. DiNardoi, Managing Partner
(419) 242-7405
mdinardo@thecollaborativeinc.com
• Frank G. Beans, Managing Principal
(419) 242-7405
fbeans@thecollaborativeinc.com
• Ray Micham, Senior Associate
(419) 242-7405
rmicham@thecollaborativeinc.com
• Frank G. Beans, Partner
• Dan Tabor, Architect/Partner
• Mike DiNardo, Architect/Partner
• Ray Micham, Architect/Partner
• Micheal. A Muse, Architect/Partner
• Paul.R Hollenbeck, Architect/Partner Emertius
• Susan Armstrong, Senior Associate
(419) 242-7400
sarmstrong@thecollaborativeinc.com

Service
Provide services in architecture, landscape architecture, planning, interior design, contract furnishings and graphic design such as programming, space planning, zoning process/presentations, site selection and planning and interior architectural detailing
Clients
Adrian College, Adrian, Michigan, University of Akron, Akron, Ohio, Alma College, Alma, Michigan, Ashland University, Ashland, Ohio, Ashland Theological Seminary, Ashland, Ohio, Barton College, Wilson, North Carolina, Bluffton College, Bluffton, Ohio, Bowling Green State University, Bowling Green, Ohio, Centenary College, Hackettstown, New Jersey, Central Ohio Technical College, OSU Newark, Ohio, Columbus Academy, Gahanna, Ohio, Evergreen Schools, Metamora, Ohio, Family Learning Center of NW Ohio, Genoa Schools, Genoa, Ohio, Gesu Parish, Toledo, Ohio, Henry County Board of Co. Commissioners (HOPE School, McClure, Ohio), Leipsic Local Schools,

COMMUNICATION ARTS INCORPORATED
1112 PEARL STREET
BOULDER, CO 80302
303-447-8202
Fax: 303-440-7096
• Daniel Aizemann, Senior Designer
• Richard Foy, Co-Chairman
• Janet A. Martin, President
• Mike Doyle, Vice President/Architect
• Mark Jasin, Senior Designer
Service
Responsible for the development of overall project character as well as planning and retail design for retail environments, adaptive re-use projects and urban spaces and provides strategic services and solutions for internet enabled environments.
Clients
AMC Theaters, Ballys Hotel and Casino, BankBoston, Bass Pro Shops, Ben Carter Properties, CBL & Associates Properties, Centerra Properties, LLC, Century Theaters, Crescent Development, Denver Museum of Natural History, Doubletree Guest Suites, Downtown Denver Partnership, Inc., Famous Players Theaters, Gaylord Entertainment Company, Genesco, Gerald Hines Interests, Horizon Organic Dairy, JFK International Air Terminal LLC, KSL Recreation, L.A. Arena Company, LCOR Incorporated, Madison Square Garden, Ltd, MMI Realty, NASA Human Habitation Module, Port Authorities of New York & New Jersey, Prime Retail, Inc., Prudential Realty Group, Publix, Sa

COOKE DOUGLASS FARR LEMONS/LTD.
3100 N STATE STREET
SUITE 200
JACKSON, MS 39216
601-366-3110
Fax: 601-366-3181
www.cdfl.com
• Robert E. Farr II, Prinicpal/Corporate President
rfarr@cdfl.com
• David A Lemons, Principal
dlemons@cdfl.com
• Jody G. Coleman, Principal
jcoleman@cdfl.com

• Jesse R. Browning, Principal
jbrowning@cdfl.com
• Robert E. Farr, Principal
rfarr@cdfl.com
• David A. Lemons, Principal
dlemons@cdfl.com
• Jody G. Coleman, Principal
jcoleman@cdfl.com
• Ann Somers, Principal
asomers@cdfl.com
• Robert O. Byrd, Principal
• Gene E. Crager, Principal
gcrager@cdfl.com
Service
Provides services on
architecture/engineering, planning, interior
design, design-build management and
facility commissioning. It works
collaboratively to provide innovative
planning, landscape architecture, campus
and urban design solutions, develop ideas,
strategies and concepts on diverse and
challenging sites, offers a complete range of
services for the planning, design and
delivery of interior environments and
specializes in the master planning and
design of sports complexes.

COORE AND CRENSHAW
1800 NUECES STREET
AUSTIN, TX 78701
512-477-5441
Fax: 512-473-2447
www.cooreandcrenshaw.com
• Bill Coore, Partner
• Scott Sayers, Business Manager
sayers@bencrenshaw.com
Services:
Golf Course Architects
Clients:
Lehman Brothers, Dell Computer, Kraft
Foods, Red Herring, McLane Foods,
Motorola, The Security Dealers Association,
EMC Corporation, Tivoli Systems, Adolph
Coors Company, Credit Suisse Bank,
ELoyalty, SMU Athletic Forum,
Southwestern Bell Telephone, Sprint,
PricewaterhouseCoopers, LLP, Paine
Weber, Tenet Healthcare, Nabisco Food.
Sports Service Founded:
1985
Athlete Management Services:
Represents Ben Crenshaw.
Event Management Services:
Golf outings.
Marketing & Consulting Services:
Golf course architectural services, dba
Coore & Crenshaw, Inc.

COUNSILMAN-HUNSAKER
10733 SUNSET OFFICE DRIVE
4TH FLOOR
SAINT LOUIS, MO 63127
314-894-1245
Fax: 314-894-0109
www.counsilmanhunsaker.com
• Scot Hunsaker, President
(314) 894-1245
• Doug Cook, Chairman of the Board
• Darren Bevard, Principal
• Jeff Nodorft, Principal
• Carl Nylander, Principal
• Kevin Post, Principal
• Matt Cappello, Studio Director
Service
Offers an extensive services from existing
facility evaluation to comprehensive concept

development from project visioning through
design, engineering and construction
administration to business management and
aquatic operations.
Clients
Chandler Unified School District, Cheyenne
Mountain High School, Clayton County
Aquatic Center, Cleveland State University,
Delta State University, The City of Dallas,
Great America-Paramount, The City of
Cleburne, Collinsville Area Recreation,
Baylor University, Boston University,
Oklahoma State University, Fort Valley State
University, George Mason University,
Georgia Institute of Technology, Kent State
University, Kenyon College, Massachusetts
Institute of Technology, Middleburry College,
Georgetown Preparatory School, Haslett
Public School District, Hastings Community
Center, Keller Independent School District,
Lakeview High School, New S

CPG ARCHITECTS
ONE DOCK STREET
STAMFORD, CT 6902
203-967-3456
Fax: 203-353-1863
cpgarchitects@hotmail.com
www.cpgarch.com
• Gary Unger, Principal/Founder
gary_unger@cpgarch.com
• Robert Mi Tieni, Principal/President
robert_tieni@cpgarch.com
• Karen Lika, SVP
karen_lika@cpgarch.com
• Karen M. Lika, Principal
• Jenny Paik, Principal
• Carl Mirbach, Creative Director
• Mickey Mallardi, VP-Architecture
mickey_mallardi@cpgarch.com
• James Sackett, VP, Director of Design
Service
Provides unique, future-focused process
and comprehensive array of services such
as creative management solutions as well
as providing design solutions for pre-lease,
architectural and interior planning
Clients
100 Wall Street, NYC, 300 Park Avenue,
NYC, 666 Fifth Avenue, NYC, Amdocs, Ann
Taylor, Bloomberg, Breitling, Chrysler
Building, Citibank, North America, Comedy
Central, Commonfund, Continental Airlines,
Cornell Medical University, Edison Schools,
Ford Motor Company, G.E. Capital,
Greenwich Hospital, Guinness UDV,
Honeywell, IBM, IRS, JP Morgan, Knights of
Columbus, Lincoln Building, Louis Vitton,
Madge Networks, McDonalds, McGraw Hill,
Mitsui, Modern Media, Morgan Stanley,
NBC Olympics, Nine est, Opticare, Paloma
partners, physicians Health Services,
PriceWaterHouseCoopers,, provident Bank,
reader's Digest, Riggs bank, DC, REI
Medical Center,

**CRADDOCK-CUNNINGHAM
ARCHITECTURAL PARTNERS**
10 9TH STREET
LYNCHBURG, VA 24504
434-846-8456
Fax: 434-846-4534
• Hal C. Craddock, Principal
• Lynn Cunningham, Principal
• Tara Cunningham, Marketing Director
• Mark W. Smith, Architect
• Gary Harvey,

• Mark Smith,
• Matt Tyree,
Service
Specializes on master planning and
architectural design for private schools,and
universities, and historical redevelopment
and renovation, with follow-up building
design documents and construction
administration
Clients
Fork Union Military Academy; Estes Athletic
Center, Aquatics Center; Virginia Episcopal
School, Van Avery Athletic Center, Weight
Room, Carrington Tennis Courts, Alumni
Hall, Football Stadium; Averett University
North Campus-Athletics Master

CRP ARCHITECTS, P.C.
100 E SAINT VRAIN STREET
SUITE 300
COLORADO SPRINGS, CO 80903
719-633-5901
Fax: 719-633-5903
www.christiansenreece.com
• Holger Christiansen, Principal Architect
• Leland Reece, Principal Architect
Service
Architectural services

**CSHQA
ARCHITECTS/ENGINEERS/PLANNERS**
250 S 5TH STREET
CW MOORE PLAZA
BOISE, ID 83702
208-343-4635
Fax: 208-343-1858
www.cshqa.com
• Jeffrey A. A. Shneider, President
• Kent A. Hanway, EVP - Board of Directors
• John D. Maulin, Operations VP - Board
Director
• Jeffrey A. A. Shneider, Principal Emeritus
• John D. Maulin, Executive VP - Director
• Craig Slocum, Corporate Secretary -
Board of Directors
• James G. Murray, Principal/Director
• J. Michael Brady, Principal/Director
• Patrizia Morgan Norberg, Principal -
Director
Service
Offers complete in-house design services
specializes in commercial design,
architecture & urban planning, civil,
structural electrical & mechanical
engineering and interior design.
Clients
Boise Airport, Rogue Valley International,
Fresno Yosemite International Airport, Idaho
Air National Guard, CW Moore Plaza, Blue
Cross of Idaho, First National Bank of Idaho,
Farmers and Merchants State Bank, Key
Bank, Spink Butler, Boise Telco Federal
Credit Union, CRI Advantage, KPMG, Stoel
Rives, IPC General Office Complex,
Lewis-Clark State College, BSU Pavilion,
BSU Engineering Technology Complex,
Boise Schools, Nampa Schools, Belgrade
Schools, Lithia Motors, Albertsons,
Safeway, McMillans Corner

**DAHLIN GROUP ARCHITECTS
PLANNERS**
5865 OWENS DRIVE
PLEASANTON, CA 94588
925-251-7200
Fax: 925-251-7201

pleasanton@dahlingroup.com
www.dahlingroup.com
• Doug Dahlin, President/Founder
• Alan J. Burrell, Principal
• Harris P. Pierson, Principal / General Manager
• Mario Aiello, Architect
• Al Burrell, Architect
• Karl Danielson, Architect
• Mark Day, Architect
• Kurt Donnelly, Architect
• Nancy Keenan, Architect
Service
Build and sustain professional design expertise in planning resedential, and community serving architecture.

DAUER HASWELL ARCHITECTS
1748 PLATTE STREET
DENVER, CO 80202
303-458-9600
Fax: 303-458- 9666
• Brad Haswell, RA
• Jim Dauer, partner
Description:
Recreation architects specializing in planning and design of community recreation centers.

DAVIS DESIGN
1221 N ST
SUITE 600
LINCOLN, NE 68508
402-476-9700
Fax: 402-476-9722
www.davisdesign.com
• Matt S Metcalf, Principal
• Mike Wachal, Principal
• Wade Stange, Principal
• Jon Dalton, Principal
• Mike Marsh, Principal
• Ed Bukacek, Senior Associate
• Marilyn Larson, Director of Marketing/Public Relations
(402) 476-9700
Services
Full-service architecture, engineering and interior design firm with experience in the design of stadiums, auditoriums, gymnasiums, swimming facilities, and health, fitness and recreation centers.
Clients
Heritage Park, Husker Auto Group, Electronic Contracting, Inc., Lochland Country Club, Kawasaki Motors Mfg. Corp., West Gate Bank Center, A.G. Edwards & Sons, Inc,, Security Financial Life, National Research Corporation, First National Bank, TierOne Center, Our Savior Lutheran Church, Norfolk Arts Center, First-Plymouth Church, Mid-America Union Conference, Living Water Church, Morrison Cancer Center, Tabtiha LifeQuest Center, Crete Area Medical Center, BryanLGH West Medical Plaza, Sioux Valley Memorial Hospital, Nebraska Orthopaedic & Sports Medicine, SVMH Wellness Center, Ortner Center, Union College, BryanLGH College of Health Sciences, Ha

DES ARCHITECTS/ENGINEERS, INC.
399 BRADFORD STREET
THIRD FLOOR
REDWOOD CITY, CA 94063
650-364-6453
Fax: 650-364-2618

marketing@des-ae.com
www.des-ae.com
• Susan Eschweiler, Principal
seschweiler@des-ae.com
• C. Thomas Gilman, President & Principal
tgilman@des-ae.com
• Craig Ivancovich,
• Tom Gilman, President
• Steve Mincey, Principal/CEO
• Jana Gunsul, Associate Principal
• Melanie Rogers, Associate Principal/Director of Human Resourc
Services
Provides architecture, design and engineering services to corporations, developers, schools, governments and civic organizations through innovative solutions for all types of project.
Clients
BMC (Roche), Genentech Inc, Oral B, Alza Pharmaceuticals, Matrix Pharmaceuticals, Borland (Inprise), Openwave, Hewlett Packard Agilent, Britannia East Grand, PacificShores Center, Moffett Park, Phillips, Verifone, Jefferson Place, Carlmont High Scool, Woodside High School, Sequoia High School, Wilbur Hall, Stern Hall, San Carlos Youth Center, Foster City Government Center, Redwood City Firestation #20, Redwood City Firestation #9, Sequoia Hospital Birthing, Sequoia Hospital Cardiac Cath, Sequoia Hospital Acute Care, 2900 Medical Office Building, Sequoia Hospital Endoscopy, Sequoia House, San Leandro Hospital, Apple Ireland, Claris Software,

DESIGNS IN FITNESS, INC.
1919 N LOOP W
SUITE 435
HOUSTON, TX 77008
910-306-3142
Fax: 713-862-2189
• John Velandra, Personal Trainer

DILULLO ASSOCIATES INC.
16 CRYSTAL STREET
MELROSE, MA 2176
781-662-3498
Fax: 781-662-8389
• Dan Dilullo, contact
Service
Athletic facilities for colleges and high schools

DLR GROUP
6457 FRANCES
SUITE 200
OMAHA, NE 68106
402-393-4100
866-357-8600
Fax: 402-393-8747
www.dlrgroup.com
• Dale Hallock, Principal
• Ken West, Chairman
kwest@dlrgroup.com
• Bryce Pearsall, Principal
• Griff Davenport, Principal
• Jon Petit, Principal
• Griff Davenport, AIA Managing Principal
Service
offers architectural, engineering, and planning services

DLZ
157 EAST MARYLAND STREET
INDIANAPOLIS, IN 46204

317-633-4120
800-336-5352
Fax: 317-633-4177
info@dlz.com
www.dlz.com
• Vikram Rajadhyaksha, Chairman
Service
transportation engineering, architecture, field services, civil engineering, landscape architecture, construction administration, environmental services, and geotechnical engineering
Client
City of Columbus, Department of Public Utilities; U.S. Army Corps of Engineers, Detroit District; Ohio Department of Natural Resources, Department of Engineering; Indiana Department of Natural Resources; U.S. Army Corps of Engineers, Huntington District; Northern Indiana Commuter, Transportation District; City of Cleveland, Department of Port Control; City of Lansing; City of Indianapolis, Department of Capital Asset; Ohio Department of Transportation; Michigan Department of Transportation; Ivy Tech State College; U.S. Postal Service, Facilities Service Office; Lake Michigan College; Indiana Department of Correction; Greater Cleveland Regiona

DON CAREY & ASSOCIATES
9441 NE 16TH STREET
CLYDE HILL, WA 98004
425-454-8166
Fax: 425-462-6188
• Don Carey, Owner
Service
Aquatic design consultants specializing in feasibility studies, permits, funding alternatives and aquatic design

DONALD DEMARS INTERNATIONAL
24201 HIGHLANDER ROAD
WEST HILLS, CA 91307-1245
818-773-6540
Fax: 818-773-8803
• Donald DeMars, Chairman & CEO
• Collin Jones, Controller
• Jay Martinez, Executive Architect
• Dave Hurt, General Manager
Service
Development consulting and architectural/interior design services for sports, fitness, and wellness center developments
Client
Scripps Clinic Integrative Medicine Center Hospital, Braemar Country Club, Pinnacle Fitness, Inc., Georgetown Physical Therapy and Fitness Center, Downtown Athletic Club, The Pomona Healthplex, Manhattan Athletic Club

E.G.A. SITE PLANNING/LANDSCAPE ARCHITECTS
42 MAIN STREET
NYACK, NY 10960
914-358-6444
Fax: 914-358-7403
• Edward Gaudy, Landscape Architect
vega@tco.com
Service
Site planning of athletic fields, playing courts and playgrounds at schools and colleges

ED2 INTERNATIONAL ARCHITECTS/PLANNERS
1426 FILLMORE STREET
SUITE 302
SAN FRANCISCO, CA 94115
415-474-1400
Fax: 415-474-9110
contact2@ed2intl.com
• Frank S Fung, President
Service
planning and design of veterinary medical facilities

EDMOND N. ZISOOK AIA & ASSOCIATES
630 DUNDEE ROAD
SUITE 110
NORTHBROOK, IL 60062
847-564-8333
Fax: 847-564-9989
arenson@sasarch.com
www.sasarch.com
• Edmond N. Zisook, Owner
Service
Fitness and rehabilitation center design and park facilities in the U.S., Canada, U.K. and the Far East

ELLENZWEIG ASSOCIATES, INC.
1280 MASSACHUSETTS AVENUE
CAMBRIDGE, MA 2138
617-491-5575
Fax: 617-868-2318
hunt@ellenzweig.com
www.ellenzweig.com
• Miltos Catmoeris, Principal
catomeris@ellenzweig.com
• Harry Ellenzweig, Principal
harry@ellenzweig.com
• Michael Lauber, Principal
lauber@ellenzweig.com
• Catherine Hunt, Associate Principal and Director of Marketing
hunt@ellenzweig.com
• James Blount, Principal
blount@ellenzweig.com
• Shrine Boulos Anderson, Principal
boulos@ellenzweig.com
• Neil Cahalane, Principal
cahalane@ellenzweig.com
• Steve Mahler, Principal
mahler@ellenzweig.com
• Janet Ross, Principal
ross@ellenzweig.com
Service
Architects for colleges and universities; Master planning, programming, Feasibility study preparation, Architectural design, Laboratory planning and design, Construction administration
Client
Allegheny College, Ariad Pharmaceuticals, Augustana College, Babson College, Blue Cross and Blue Shield of Connecticut, Boston College, Bowdoin College, Brandeis University, Bryn Mawr College, Charitable Leadership Foundation, Charles Stark Draper Laboratory, Childrens Hospital, Childrens Hospital of Philadelphia, Clark University, Connecticut College, Dartmouth College, Dayton International Airport, Dickinson College, Dixie State College, Eisai Research Institute of Boston, EMD Pharmaceuticals, Emory University, Fidelity Corporate Real Estate, Friends of Post Office Square, Hamilton College, Harvard medical School, Harvard University, Hobart
Clients
Johns Hopkins University, Joslin Diabetes Center, Lafayette College, Lawrence University, Lexigen Pharmaceuticals, Loyola University Chicago Stritch School of Medicine, Massachusetts Bay Transporation Authority, Massachusetts Institute of Technology, Memphis Biotech Foundation, Millikin University, Rhodes college, Rowan University, Syracuse University, Tufts University, University of British columbia, University of Chicago, University of Florida, University of Kentucky, University of Massachusetts, University of Miami, University of New England, University of New Hampshire, University of North Carolina Greensboro, University of Notre Dame, Un

ELS ARCHITECTURE AND URBAN DESIGN
2040 ADDISON STREET
BERKELEY, CA 94704
510-549-2929
Fax: 510-843-3304
info@elsarch.com
www.elsarch.com
• Barry Elbasani, Founding Principal
• Carol Shen, Managing Principal
• Bruce Bullman, Principal
• David Fawcett, Principal
• Clarence D. Mamuyac, Jr., Principal
• David Petta, Principal
• Jamie Rusin, Principal
• Kurt Schindler, Principal
• Connie Nitta Curtis, Associate Principal
Service
Architectural Services: Pre-Design Assistance, Capital Campaign Support, Public Process and Facilitation, Site Planning and Programming, Urban Design, Master Planning, Sustainable Design Analysis, LEED Certification, Conceptual Design, Schematic Design, Design Development, Construction Documents, Bidding Assistance, Construction Administration, Post Occupancy Assistance

ERICKSON MCGOVERN
101 E 26TH STREET
SUITE 300
TACOMA, WA 98421
253-531-0206
Fax: 253-531-9197
mail@ericksonmcgovern.com
www.ericksonmcgovern.com
• Jay Peterson, Partner
• Steve Storaasli, Principal
Steve@EricksonMcGovern.com
• Wayne Lerch, Principal
Wayne@EricksonMcGovern.com
• Steve Storaasli, Partner
Service
Architects specializing in educational facilities

EWING COLE CHERRY BROTT
FEDERAL RESERVE BANK BUILDING
100 N 6TH STREET
PHILADELPHIA, PA 19106-1590
215-923-2020
Fax: 215-574-9163
mhenden@ewingcole.com
www.ewingcole.com
• John C. Gerbner, President and COO
(215) 625-4135
• James A Wilson, Managing Principal
jwilson@ewingcole.com
• S. Mark Hebden, President
mhebden@ewingcole.com
• Donald H. Dissinger, Senior Vice President
ddissinger@ewingcole.com
• James A. Wilson, Senior Vice President
jwilson@ewingcole.com
• Jared Loos, Director of Operations
jloos@ewingcole.com
• Robert McConnell, Director of Architecture
• Pradeep Patel, Director of Engineering
• Joseph Kelly, Chief Executive Officer
jkelly@ewingcole.com
Service
Pre-Design Services, Architectural Design, Interior Design, Engineering, Services to Building Owners and Developers, Presentation Service
Client
Atlantic City Racecourse, Atlantic City, NJ; Birmingham Turf Club, Birmingham, AL; Boyd Gaming, Venton, LA; Bucknell University, Lewisburg, PA; Canterbury Downs Shakopee, MN; Churchill Downs, Louisville, KY; The City of Philadelphia, Philadelphia, PA; Clearwater Phillies, Clearwater, FL; Emerald Downs, Auburn, WA; Empire City Trotting Club, Yonkers, NY; Garden State Park, Cherry Hill, NJ; George Mason University, Fairfax, VA; Hamilton College, Clinton, NY; Hollywood Park Racetrack, Los Angeles, CA; Horseshoe International Taipei, Taiwan; Hubbard Enterprises, Ruidosa, NM; LaSalle University, Philadelphia, PA; Lone Star Jockey Club, Grand Prair
Clients
New Jersey Sports and Exhibition Authority, East Rutherford and Atlantic City, NJ; Penn National Racecourse, Grantham, PA; Penn State University, State College, PA; Philadelphia Park, Philadelphia, PA; Philadelphia Phillies, Philadelphia, PA; Remington Park, Oklahoma City, OK; River Downs, Cincinnati, OH; Rosecroft Raceway, Fort Washington, MD; Sam Houston Race Park, Houston, TX; Singapore Turf Club, Kranji, Singapore; United Horseman of Alberta, Calgary, Alberta, Canada; University of Delaware, Newark, DE; University of Indianapolis Indianapolis, IN; University of Pennsylvania, Philadelphia, PA; University of the Sciences Philadelphia, Phila

FANNING/HOWEY ASSOCIATES, INC.
540 EAST MARKET STREET
CELINA, OH 45822
419-586-7771
888-499-2292
Fax: 419-586-2141
www.fhai.com
• Dan H Mader, President/Chief Executive Officer
• Clair E. Howey, Vice-Chairman of the Board
• Randall L Sprunger, AIA, Chief Operating Officer
• Michael E Hall, AIA, Chief Marketing Officer
• Daniel R. Mader, President and Chief Executive Officer
• Michael E. Hall, Vice President and Chief Marketing Officer
• Douglas M. Wickstrom, Secretary/Treasurer and Chief Technology Offi
• Bruce T. Runyon, Chief Operations Officer

- Randall L. Sprunger, Director
- Steve A. Wilczynski, Director
Service
Architects, engineers, consultants specializing in educational facility design

---

FENTRESS ARCHITECTS
421 BROADWAY
DENVER, CO 80203
303-722-5000
Fax: 303-722-5080
studio@fentressbradburn.com
www.fentressbradburn.com
- Jim Bradburn, Architect/Principal
- Agatha Kessler, Chief execuitve officer and Principal
- Karen Gilbert, Director Marketing
- Sue Rossberg, Human Resources Director
jobs@fentressbradburn.com
- Colin Lewis, Chief Financial Officer
- Bob Louden, Principal
- Brian. H. Chaffee, Principal and Director
- Jack Cook, Principal
- Jeff Olson, Principal
- Curt Frentress, President and Principal-in-Charge of Design
Fentress@FentressBradburn.com
Service
Architects specializing in interiors and planning
Client
(Projects) Transportation: Incheon International Airport, Denver International Airport, Seattle-Tacoma International Airport, Raleigh-Durham International Airport, Doha International Airport, Ronstadt Transit Center Civic: Cape Girardeau Federal Courthouse, Oakland Administration Buildings, Clark County Government Center, California Dept of Education HQ, Sacramento City Hall Building, Jefferson County Gov't Center, RTC/RFCD Headquarters, Loveloand Police & Courts Building, Colorado State Capitol Renovations Commercial: Dubai Mixed-Use Towers, Arraya Class A Office Tower, alDiera Tower, 421 Broadway, Norwest Bank Tower, Gulf Canada Resources,
Clients
(Projects) Laboratory: David E Skaggs Federal Center, Natural Resources Building, UCDHSC Research Complex 1&2; Public Assembly: Colorado Convention Center Exp, Palm Springs Convention Center Exp, Vail Conference and Civic Center, Pasadena Conference Center Exp, INVESCO Field at Mile Hi, Santa Fe Civic Center, Eccles Conference, Peery's Theater, Arvada Center Expansion; Education: Tennyson Center for Children, Denver Academy High School, CU Math Bldg & Engineering Library; Hospitality: Tritch Building Renovation, Palmetto Bay Plantation, One Polo Creek, One Wynkoop Plaza, The Watermark

---

FFKR ARCHITECTS
BOGUE BUILDING
730 PACIFIC AVENUE
SALT LAKE CITY, UT 84104
801-521-6186
Fax: 801-539-1916
contactus@ffkr.com
www.ffkr.com
- Richard K. Frerichs, Principal
- Franklin T. Ferguson, Founding Principal
- Kenneth E. Louder, President/Chief Execuitve Officer

- Jeffrey L. Fisher, Principal
- Kenneth Louder, Principal
- James. W. Lewis, Principal
- Mark. R. Wilson, Principal
- Roger P. Jackson, Principal
- J. David Gilis, Principal
- Kevin Mass, Principal
Service
Architectural services include feasibility studies, programming, design-build, conceptual design, architectural design, sustainable design, construction documents, construction administration, and specifications. Interior design services include feasibility studies, programming, space planning, schematic design, design development, construction documents, furnishings, fixtures and equipment, purchasing, construction administration, wayfinding, graphics, and move management
Client
(Projects) Current: Eyring Planetarium, Joseph F. Smith Building BYU, Valley JH Addition/Remodel; Arts and Entertainment: Randall Jones, Abravanal Hall, Sevier Valley Center; College and University: Harold B. Lee Library Expansion, Spori Building Replacement, Sorenson Physical Education Building; Historic and Restoration: Vernal Temple, Joseph Smith Memorial Building, Bogue Supply Building; Hospitality: Aspen Grove Lodge, Orangerie, Casino Arizona at Salt River; Interior Design & Space Planning: Passages, River Rock Casino, Prestige Financial; Laboratories and Technical: Eccles Genetics Building, Moran I, Benson Science Building
Clients
(Projects) Master Planning: Palace Indian Gaming, SUU Master Plan, UVSC West Campus; Office Buildings: Kimball at BYU Idaho, JVWCD, Northwest Pipeline; Parking: River Rock Parking, Jordan Commons, Northwest Pipeline Parking; Religious: Jerusalem Center, John Taylor Building BYU Idaho, Nauvoo Temple; Retail and Commercial: Larry H. Miller Truckland, Megaplex at The Gateway, Jordan Commons; Schools: Viewmont High School, Olympus Junior High, Whittier Elemetary; Sports and Recreation: Cougar Stadium, The Delta Center, Salt Lake Sports, Fairmont

---

FGM ARCHITECTS & ENGINEERS
475 REGENCY PARK
SUITE 200
O'FALLON, IL 62269
618-624-3364
Fax: 618-624-3369
www.fgmarchitects.com
- Jr Ha James, EVP (Past)
- John Ochoa, President/Chief Executive Officer
- Kathleen Miles, Chief Financial Officer
- John Ochoa, President and Chief Executive officer
- Mike Caraker, Chief Information Officer
- Joe Chronister, Director of Higher Education
- John Dzarnowski, Director of Municipal and Recreation
Service
Predesign Consulting, Architectural Planning and Design, Engineering, Interior Architecture
Client

Commercial: Des Plaines Multi-Use, Drake Hotel, General Life Building, Life Insurance Data Processing, Marriott Courtyard Hotels, Meijer Food Stores, Motomart, One Technology Center; K12 Education: Berwyn North SD 98 Prairie Oak Elementary School, Cicero SD 99 Unity Junior High Schook, Cicero SD 99 District Administrict Offices, Frankfort CCSD 157-C Grand Prairie Addition, Grayslake CHSD #127 New High School, Highland CUSD 5 New Middle School, McHenry CHSD 156 East High School Addition & Renovation, McHenry CHSD 156 West High School Addition & Renovation; Higher Education: Kaskaskia College, Olivet Nazarene University Track, SIUC Softball Com
Clients
State/Federal: Bachelor Enlisted Quarters 27 - Historic Rehabilitation, Forrestal Village - Wholehouse Repairs, Ft. Campbell Guest House - new facility, Scott AFB Collocated Club - new facility, Scott AFB TACC Global Decision Center - new facility, United States Postal Service - team contract; Municipal: Addison Village Hall, Huntley Community Center, Kildeer Village Hall, Lake in the Hills Village Hall, New Lenox Village Hall, Warren Town Hall; Public Safety: Addison Fire Station #3, Addison Police Department, Algonquin/Lake in the Hills Fire Headquarters, Algonquin/Lake in the Hills Fire Stations, Arlington Heights Fire Department Headquart

---

FINK ROBERTS & PETRIE
4040 VINCENNES CIRCLE
SUITE 300
INDIANAPOLIS, IN 46268
317-872-8400
800-875-3307
Fax: 317-876-2408
frp@frpinc.com
www.frpinc.com
- Michael C Natali, President, Structural Engineering Department Head
- David Lash, VP, Civil Department Head
- Scott E. Rouse, Vice President, Senior Project Manager
- William G. T. Horton, President, Senior Project Manager
Description:
Specializing in structural engineering for professional, collegiate and recreational sports facilities.

FLAD ARCHITECTS
644 SCIENCE DRIVE
MADISON, WI 53711
608-238-2661
Fax: 608-238-6727
flad@flad.com
www.flad.com
- Laura Stillman, Executive Vice President
- Laura Serebin, Principal
- Rachel Nelan, Principal
- Davis Black, Principal
- Mark Corey, Principal
- Jim Gazvoda, Principal
- Jerry Polly, Principal
- Jeffery Raasch, Principal
Description:
Architects specializing in high technology facilities; structural engineers.
Services:
Interior Design, Landscape, Structural, Master Planning, Sustainable Design

FLEWELLING & MOODY
815 COLORODO BLVD
SUITE 200
LOS ANGELES, CA 90041
626-449-6787
Fax: 323-543-8198
www.flewelling-moody.com
• Scott Gaudineer, President/Principal
• Metthew C. Buchanan, Principal
Services:
Specialize in master planing, new
construction, modernization and facilities
assessment of K-12, community college and
higher education facilities

FLUOR CORPORATION
6700 LAS COLINAS BOULEVARD
IRVING, TX 75039
469-398-7000
Fax: 469-398-7255
www.fluor.com
• Alan L L. Boeckmann, Chairman/Chief
Executive Officer
• Lawrence N. Fisher, Chief Legal
Officer/Secretary
• D. Mi Steuert, SVP/Chief Financial Officer
• Kenneth H. Lockwood, VP, Corporate
Finance & Investor Relations
Services:
Global engineering, construction,
maintenance and diversified services
company
Clients:
KoSa, DSM Elastomers Europe, AECI
Lysine Project, BF Goodrich, Yanpet
Expansion

FOREMAN ARCHITECTS ENGINEERS INC.
525 W NEW CASTLE STREET
PO BOX 189
ZELIENOPLE, PA 16063
724-452-9690
Fax: 724-452-0136
faeinfo@foremangroup.com
www.foremangroup.com
• Phillip G. Foreman, CEO and President
• David E. Foreman, Vice President
Description:
Architects and engineers specializing in
educational facilities.
Services:
Design buildings

FORESITE DESIGN, INC.
3269 COOLIDGE HIGHWAY
BERKLEY, MI 48072
248-547-7757
800-732-0611
Fax: 248-547-0218
info@foresitedesign.com
www.foresitedesign.com
• Bruce C S Lemons, President
• Bruce S. Lemons, President
• Mike Sims, Project Manager
Description:
Landscape architectural/site planning firm
specializing in site evaluation, design,
construction documents and contract
administration of outdoor sports facilities.
Services:
Design services

FOUNTAINHEAD ASSOCIATES
609 DEEP VALLEY DRIVE
SUITE 200
ROLLING HILLS ESTATES, CA 90274

310-378-1410
Fax: 310-378-0719
jerry.papazian@fountainheadassoc.com
www.fountainheadassoc.com
• Jerry Papazian, Managing Director
Description:
Architects and construction managers
specializing in ice skating facilities,
swimming pools and pre-engineered
buildings.
Services:
Assists exisiting business and organizations
develop, implement, manage and sustain
their strategic goals; assists entrepreneurs
in organizing and structuring new business
ventures; provides personal clothing and
mentoring services to executives.

FRIBERG ASSOCIATES INC.
2001 BEACH STREET
SUITE 530
FORT WORTH, TX 76103
817-336-0543
Fax: 817-429-0119
• Emil E Friberg, President
• Larry W. Akers, President/Senior
Mechanical Designer/Project
• Bobby G. Alexander, Vice
President/Secretary
• David W. McDonald, Principal/Electrical
Engineer
• Joshua D. Schmidt, Principal/Mechanical
Engineer
• Will Martin, Plumbing/Fire Protection
Designer
• Emil E. Friberg, Chairman of the Board
Description:
Mechanical, electrical plumbing consultants.
Services:
Offers a range of services that includes
strategic consulting, master planning,
energy studies, systems design,
maintenance analysis, and construction
administration

FTL DESIGN ENGINEERING STUDIO
44 E EAST 32ND STREET
3RD FLOOR
NEW YORK, NY 10016
212-732-4691
Fax: 212-385-1025
www.ftlstudio.com
• Nicholas S Goldsmith, Senior Principal
• Mercedes Gonzalez, CFO
• Ashish Soni, Principal
• Joseph Schedlbauer, Engineering
Principal
Description:
Specializes in lightweight, deployable design
and construction technologies. Offers
consulting and design services.
Services:
Urban iconic, performance building, building
skins, event buildings, and transportation
buildings

GAUDREAU, INC. ARCHITECTS/PLANNERS/ENGINEERS
810 LIGHT STREET
BALTIMORE, MD 21230
410-837-5040
Fax: 410-837-8093
info@gaudreauinc.com
www.gaudreauinc.com
• William A L Gaudreau, President
• David G. Gaudreau, Senior Vice President
• Randal Gaskins, Vice President

Description:
Architecture, planning, engineering for
athletic and recreational facilities ranging
from large college and university complexes
to small corporate executive centers and
community parks
Services:
Comprehensive architectural services,
ranging from site searches, master planning,
strategic planning, programming and design

GEIGER ENGINEERS
2 EXECUTIVE BOULEVARD
SUITE 410
SUFFERN, NY 10901
845-368-3330
Fax: 845-368-3366
dor@geigerengineers.com
www.geigerengineers.com
• David Chen, Principal
• Paul A.Gossen, Principal
• Paul Gossen, Principal
• Mike Liao, Principal
• Stephen P.Emery, Principal
• Timothy D.Mills, Principal
• David M.Campbell, Principal
Nature of Sports Service:
Consulting engineers specializing in sports
structures, long-span roofs, entertainment
events engineering venue evaluations and
rigging.
Other Office:
Geiger Engineers, P.C. Bellingham Office
114 W. Magnolia St. Suite 505 Bellingham
WA 98225 phone: 360-734-7194 fax:
360-734-7399
Services:
Structural design, computer-aided design
and diversified applies science research

GLASS ARCHITECTS
200 E STREET
SUITE 100
SANTA ROSA, CA 95404
707-544-3920
Fax: 707-544-2514
info@glassarchitects.com
www.glassarchitects.com
• Anne Glass, Human Resources Director
aglass@glassarchitects.com
• Eric Glass, Principal
eric@glassarchitects.com
• Charlie Sikes, Associate
csikes@glassarchitects.com
• Jeff Bousfield, Associate
jbousfield@glassarchitects.com
• Dave Zaro, Associate
dzaro@glassarchitects.com
Description:
Architects specializing in community
recreation, sports and aquatic centers

GOODY CLANCY
420 BOYLSTON STREET
BOSTON, MA 02116-3866
617-262-2760
Fax: 617-262-9512
www.goodyclancy.com
• Roger Goldstein, Principal
(617) 850-6537
roger.goldstein@goodyclancy.com
• David Dixon, FAIA, Principle for Planning
& Urban Design
• David Spillane, AICP, RIBA, Principal,
Director of Planning
• Bernard Dooley, AIA, LEED, Director of
Laboratory Planning

Description:
Architecture, planning and urban design firm specializing in academic facilities, campus planning, residential communities and historic preservation

GOSSEN LIVINGSTON ARCHITECTURE
1525 E. DOUGLAS
WICHITA, KS 67211
316-265-9367
Fax: 316-265-5646
• William B Livingston, President/CEO
Description:
Architecture, planning, programming, landscape architecture and interior design for university, college and high school sports facilities
Services:
Provides services in every major architectural field, including discovery/programming, master planning, interior design and landscape architecture

GRAHAM/MEUS, INC. ARCHITECTS
SIX EDGERLY PLACE
BOSTON, MA 2116
617-423-9399
Fax: 617-482-8506
• Daniel L Meus, Principal
• Gary Graham, Principal
• Carolyn Tacelli, Director of Finance
• Melissa Vaillancourt, Director of the Boston Studio
• Linda Tetreault, Project Manager
• Cordelia Dawson, Project Manager/Designer
• Bethany Robertson, Drafting Programs
• Andrew Sikorski, Designer
Year Founded:
1980
Clients:
Institutional, Private Fitness, YMCA, YWCA, Community Fitness, College and University Healthcare.
Nature of Service:
Provide planning, architecture, and interior design services

GREENWAY GROUP, THE
25 TECHNOLOGY PARKWAY SOUTH
SUITE 101
NORCROSS, GA 30092
678-879-0929
800-726-8603
Fax: 678-879-0930
www.greenway.us
• James P Cramer, Principal and Chairman
• Dough Parker, Managing Principal
• Bob Fisher, Principal
• David R. Zimmerman, Consulting Principal
• Lorna Rein, Consulting Principal
• Tonya Smith, Membership Manager and Executive Assistant
• Dave Zimmerman, Consulting Principal
• James P. Cramer, Chairman & Principal
Description:
Natural sport turf specialists; installs and renovates athletic playing fields.
Services:
Consulting and business networking firms for the design and construction industry

GREMMER ASSOCIATES
120 WILSHIRE BOULEVARD NORTH
STEVENS POINT, WI 54481

715-341-4363
Fax: 715-341-1856
www.gremmerassociates.com
• Dave Glodowski, Vice president
Description:
Firm provides transportation engineering, recreational and athletic facility design, municipal engineering, site design, construction services and surveying in the Midwest and West. Specialties include urban and rural highways, bridges, sewage collection
Services:
Transportation design, municipal design, site design, surveying services, construction management, and storm water management

GRILLIAS PIRC ROSIER ALVES
15707 ROCKFIELD BOULEVARD
SUITE 300
IRVINE, CA 92618
949-951-4774
Fax: 949-250-4912
• Peter Grillias, President
Services:
Specializing in planning, architecture, engineering and interior design

GROUNDS MAINTENANCE SERVICES
16982 W. NATIONAL AVE.
NEW BERLIN, WI 53151
262-784-8219
800-227-9381
Fax: 866-236-1546
info@groundsmaintenancewi.com
www.groundsmaintenancewi.com
• Floyd Perry, Marketing Director
Nature of Service
Athletic field risk, injury and prevention consultant and author/lecturer on sports fields, athletic field maintenance, quality supplies and equipment. Instructional groundskeeping books and videos, workshops, retail tools and equipment

HAMMEL, GREEN AND ABRAHAMSON INC.
420 5TH STREET NORTH
SUITE 100
MINNEAPOLIS, MN 55401
612-758-4000
888-442-8255
Fax: 612-758-4199
info@hga.com
www.hga.com
• Daniel Avchen, Chairman/CEO
davchen@hga.com
• Dan Rectenwald, Chief Operating Officer
• Stephen Fiskum, Principal
• Hal Henderson, Principal
• Kent Mainquist, Chief Financial Officer
• Paul Asp, Director of Structural Engineering
• Deb Barnes, Director of Interior Design
Nature of Service
Full service architecture, engineering and planning firm. HGA offers design and engineering expertise for healthcare, corporate, the arts, community and education clients.
Clients
3M, Accenture, ADC Telecommunications, Affinity - Mercy Medical Center, Ag-Chem, Agricultural and Food Sciences Academy, Albermarle County School District, Virginia, All Saints - St. Luke's Hospital, Allina Health System, American Express, American

Medical Systems, American Red Cross, American River College, Andersen Windows Corporation, Andrews University, Anoka Hennepin School District, Anoka Technical Institute, Antioch Public Library, Artspace, Aspen Medical Group, Associated Eye Physicians, Augsburg College, Aurora Health System, Aurora University, Austin Junior College, B.F. Goodrich Aerospace, Baycare Surgery Center, Beaumont Clinic, B

HASTINGS + CHIVETTA ARCHITECTS, INC.
622 EMERSON ROAD
SUITE 200
SAINT LOUIS, MO 63141
314-863-5717
888-659-2724
Fax: 314-863-2823
info@hcarchitects.com
www.hastingschivetta.com
• James R Capps, Principal.
jcapps@hcarchitects.com
• Erik J. Kochner, Principal
ekochner@hcarchitects.com
• James B. Favier, Principal
jfavier@hcarchitects.com
• Christopher Chivetta, President /Principal
cchivetta@hcarchitects.com
• Erik J.Kocher, Design Principal
• James R.Capps, Principal
Nature of Service
Provides a full range of architectural services to institutional, educational, municipal, and corporate clients. Portfolio of experience includes master planning, college and university facilities, community centers, educational, commercial, and sports and recreation facilities.
Clients
MASTER PLANNING (Centre College, Charminade College Preparatory School, Community School of Naples, Fontbonne University, Forsyth School, Hanover College, Lindenwood University, Lutheran North High School, Nebraska College of Technical Agriculture, Pulaski Academy, Rossman School, St. Joseph's Academy, The Bolles School, Union University, University of Tulsa, University of Utah, Villa Duchesne School, Wabash Colege);
COLLEGIATE (Central Missouri State University, Centre College, Fontbonne College, Hanover College, Illinois Wesleyan University, Juniata College, Lindenwood College, Longwood University, Missouri State University, Morehead State
Clients
Private K-12 Projects (Chaminade College Preparatory School, Community School Naples, Community School of Naples, Darlington School, Forsyth School, Girls Preparatory School, St. Joseph's Academy, The McCallie School, The Westminster School, Villa Duchesne School); Public K-12 Projects (Ferguson-Florissant School District, Okemos Public Schools, South Lyon Community Schools; MUNICIPAL (City of Arnold, City of Des Peres, City of Farmington, City of Fort Collins, City of Liberty, City of Mission, City of Richmond Heights, City of St. Peters, City of Thornton, Jewish Community Center, Peoria Park District & OSF Saint Francis Medical Center, St.
Clients
COMMERCIAL/CIVIC (City of Town & Country, Enterprise Rent-A-Car, Federated

Foods, Jefferson Smurfit, Missouri Ahletic Club, National Super Markets, Inc., Roosevelt Federal Savings & Loan, Sachs Properties, St. Louis County, St. Louis County Library

HAYES LARGE ARCHITECTS
LOGAN BOULEVARD & FIFTH AVENUE
SUITE 700
ALTOONA, PA 16602
814-946-0451
888-809-6134
Fax: 814-946-9054
www.hayeslarge.com
• S. Dwight Knouse, AIA, Executive Partner
• Mark Shrift, RSLA, Director of Landscape Architecture
• Randy Hudson, Principal
• Ron Miller, Principal
• W. Joe Mollenauer, Chief Financial Officer
• Bradford J. Furey, Director, Educational Planning Resources
• Mark S. Shrift, Director, Landscape Architecture
• Karl H. Kessler, Director, Electrical Engineering
• Carmen L. Wyckoff, Principal
• Randy Hudson, Director Of Design
Nature of Service
One of America's leading architecture, engineering and planning firms, providing superior client service from six offices in Pennsylvania, Virginia.
Clients
St Louis Cardinals New Ballpark, Comerica Park, Coors Field, The Palace of Auburn Hills, The Coliseum, Edward Jones Dome, Gaylord Entertainment Center, Pro Player Stadium, Raymond James Stadium
Clients
Healthcare: Health Sciences Center Library/Classroom (West Virginia University); Lewistown Hospital (Lewistown, PA); Miners Hospital (Hastings, PA); New Outpatient Center, Atrium and parking Garage Addition (Altoona Hospital, Altoona, PA); Trauma Center (Altoona Hospital)
Clients
Cultural/Civic: (Government) Keystone Building, Department of General Services - Harrisburg, PA; Rachael Carson State Office Building, Harrisburg, PA; (Museum) Baker Mansion, Altoona, PA; The National Civil War Museum, City of Harrisburg - Harrisburg, PA; (Religious) St. John the Evangelist Roman Catholic Church; (Community) Frank J. Paquerilla Conference Center, Johnstown, PA; Mishler Theatre, Altoona, PA; Pennsylvania College of Technology, Community Arts Center - Williamsport, PA; Private Retirement Residence - Central PA; Planning/Studies: DoDea Educational Specifications, US Department of Defense Educational Activity/VA; Loudoun County
Services:
Athletic facility design; synthetic turf; stadium design

HEALTH FITNESS CORPORATION
1700 WEST 82ND STREET
SUITE 200
MINNEAPOLIS, MN 55431
612-831-6830
800-639-7913
Fax: 952-897-5096
info@hfit.com
www.hfit.com

• Gregg V. Lehman, President/Chief Executive Officer
• Paul W. Lotharius, President and Chief Executive Officer
• Mark Totts, Senior Vice President
• Sean McManamy, Senior Vice President
• Brian Harrigan, Vice President
• Kelly Merriman, Vice President
• Tina Loskota, Vice President, Human Resources
• Debra Marshall, Vice President, Marketing
Nature of Service
Consultants/managers specializing in corporate and hospital health and fitness facilities and programs including feasibility studies, facility planning, physical therapy services and ergonomics.
Clients
Waukesha Memorial Hospital, Waukesha, WI; Hewlett-Packard; Health Benefits Wellness and Recognition Services, Texas Instruments, Dallas, TX; Wilton P. Herbert Health and Wellness Center, St. Elizabeth Hospital, Beaumont, TX
Services:
Provider of integrated health and fitness management services for employees and individuals

HEALTH FITNESS DYNAMICS, INC.
1012 N. OCEAN BLVD
SUITE 103
POMPANO BEACH, FL 33062
954-942-0049
Fax: 954-941-0854
hfd@hfdspa.com
www.hfdspa.com
• Judith L Singer, President & Co-Owner
(954) 942-0049
judysinger@hfdspa.com
• Judy A Singer, Founder & Co-Owner
• Patty Monteson, Founder & Co-Owner
• Patricia Monteson, Principal
pattymonteson@hfdspa.com
Nature of Service
Specializing in spa design, planning, and marketing to luxury spa hotels, spa resorts, day spas, and other spa related companies.
Clients
Resorts and Hotels: The Spa at Sawgrass, Alderbrook Resort & Spa,Four Seasons Jackson Hole, Four Seasons New York, Little Dix Bay, Malliouhana, Four Seasons Biltmore Santa Barbara, Ballantyne Resort, Cranwell Resort, Pinehurst Resort, Sandestin Hilton, Mandarin Oriental, Sonesta Key Biscayne, Hotel Cresent Court, Bacara, Royal Sands, Agua at Sanderson, Portofino Bay Hotel, Monterey Plaza Hotel, La Posada de Santa Fe, Silverado Country Club & Resort, The Homestead, Double Tree Islander, Agua at Delano, Wind Spa, The Breakers, Scottsdale Princess, Four Seasons Resort, Hawaii at Hualalai, The Coeur d'Alene, The Salish Lodge, The Disney Institute

HEERY INTERNATIONAL, INC.
999 PEACHTREE STREET NE
ATLANTA, GA 30309-3953
404-881-9880
Fax: 404-946-2398
Corporate@heery.com
www.heery.com
• Jim J. Moynihan, Chairman & CEO
• Bill Heitz, President
• Greg Pierce, Regional Manager

Nature of Service
Architecture, engineering, master planning, design and construction management of sports facilities.
Description:
Architecture, engineering, master planning, design and construction management of sports facilities.
Clients
Architecture: Atlanta Botanical Gardens; Atlanta History Center Museum; Atlanta History Center Parking Deck; Bosch Corporation; Central Michigan University; Citadel; Coca-Cola; Comdisco; Conoco Headquarters, Cumberland County Civic Center; Dare County; Dare County Justice Center; Dekalb County Courthouse; Emory University School of Law; Erie Seawolves Stadium; Franklin Templeton; Georgia Dome; Georgia World Congress Center; Heery D.C. Office; Hotel Thayer; Jacksonville Baptist Hospital; James Madison University; Kennesaw State University; Mayo Clinic; MBNA Multiple Locations; McCoy Stadium; Memorial Mission Parking Deck; Metlife; Missoula Sta
Services:
Architecture, Construction Managemetn, Engineering, Facilities Management, Interior Design, and Program Management

HERBERT LEWIS KRUSE BLUNCK ARCHITECTURE
500 EAST LOCUST
SUITE 300
DES MOINES, IA 50309
515-288-9536
Fax: 515-288-5816
www.hlkb.com
• Kirck V V. Blunk, Principal
• Doug Fey, Senior Architect
• J. Ma Schmidt, Senior Architect
Nature of Service
Offers master planning, architectural design, interior design, and landscape architecture.
Clients
(Parking) : Newton Road Parking + Chilled Water Facility, Center Street Park + Ride, Wells Fargo Financial Parking Facility; (Education) : Visitor Center/Hall of Fame, University of Iowa; Roosevelt Practice Facility, Roosevelt High School; Kimmel Theatre/Youngker Hall, Cornell College; Academic Building, Palmer College of Chiropractic Florida; Mowethy Hall, Cornell College; John Chrystal Center; Grinnell College; Palmer Center for Chiropractic Research, Palmer College of Chiropratic; Palmer Friendship Court, Palmer College of Chiropratic
Clients
(Workplace) : Meredith Corporate Expansion; Coppola Enterprises Office; Landscape Architect's Office; Marakon Associates, New York; Metro Waste Authority; Renaissance Granite, Marble, + Tile; Two River Marketing; Wells Fargo Financial Corporate Expansion; Faegre + Benson Law Office; (Private) Fingerman Residence, Moen Residence, Seely Residence, Rents Loft
Clients
(Renewed) : Glove Factory, Herndon Hall Restoration, Ola Babcock Miller Building, Mowethy Hall, Finkbine Mansion; (Retail) Sticks, M.C, Ginsberg; (Landscape) American College Testing, Grays Lake Pedestrian Bridge, Kautz Plaza, Hilltop

Pedestrian Mall, Drake - West Campus; (In Progress) Blank Honors Center, Melrose Parking Ramp Addition, Papajohn Higher Education Center, ITTC, McLeod, 420 East Locust

HKS INC
1919 MCKINNEY AVENUE
DALLAS, TX 75201
214-969-5599
Fax: 214-969-3397
www.hksinc.com
• H Ralph Hawkins, President/Chief Executive Officer
rhawkins@hksinc.com
• Nunzio M. DeSantis, EVP
ndesantis@hksinc.com
• Ralph Hawkins, Chairman and CEO
Nature of Service
Provides services in architecture, structural engineering, interior design, master planning, project management, architectural programming, multi-media production, graphic design and model services.
Clients
(Aviation) : Dallas/Fort Worth International Airport Terminal D; Dallas/Fort Worth International Airport Terminal B Concourse Addition & Renovation; Phoenix Sky Harbor International Airport Consolidated Rental Car Facility; Orlando International Airport - North Terminal Station BP - S010; Orlando International Airport Airside One FIS Corridor and In-Transit Lounge;
(Commercial) : Hall Office Park, Frisco, TX; Kilroy San Diego Corporate Center; Whole Foods Market; Frost Bank Tower; CNL Center at City Commons; Gallery Place; 3883 Howard Hughes Parkway; Five Houston Center; (Corporate) : Fidelity Investments; Sabre Holdings Headquarters; Nissan Mot
Clients
(Education) : Texas A&M Foundation Jon L. Hagier Center; Southern Methodist University Cox School of Business; University of Kansas Medical Center; Dallas ISD Jesse Owens Memorial Complex; Grand Prairie ISD Gopher-Warrior Bowl; Birdville Independent School District; Garland ISD Special Events Center; (Governmental) : Pinellas County Forensic Science Center; Federal Bureau of Prisons; Henry Wade Juvenile Justice Center; Seminole County Criminal Justice Center; Colorado Department of Corrections San Carlos Special Needs Unit; George H. Mahon Federal Building & Courthouse; Idaho Juvenile Observation and Assessment Center; U.S. Census Headquarters;
Clients
(Graphics) : La Vid, Makara, Aikman's Enzone, HKS Recruitment, Whataburger Field, Miami Children's Hospital, St. Rose Dominican Hospital; (Healthcare) : Emory Crawford Long Hospital, Obici Hospital, M.D. Anderson Cancer Center, Utah Valley Regional Medical Center, Children's Hospital Central California, Abbott Northwestern Heart Hospital, George Washington University Hospital, Clarian West Medical Center, St. Rose Dominican Hospital, Parker Adventist Hospital, Seattle Children's Hospital, Cleveland Clinic Florida Weston Hospital

HNTB CORP
715 KIRK DRIVE
KANSAS CITY, MO 64105
816-472-1201
Fax: 816-472-4516
www.hntb.com
• Ken Graham, CEO
(816) 742-1201
• Mike Handelman, Chief Sales Officer
(816) 472-1201
• Mike Scott, Chief Operating Officer
(816) 472-1201
• Harvey Co Hammond, Executive Chairman
• Paul Yarossi, Executive Vice President
• Ed Mcspedon, Executive Vice President
• Becky Zahner, Chief Planning Officer
(816) 472-1201
Nature of Service
Provides architectural service with clients in the aviation, corporate, education, federal and local government/civic markets. Provides design and project management expertise focused by market and by discipline. Design studios include: Aviation, Civic, Convention Centers, Corporate, Education, Federal, Historic Preservation, Interiors, Parking Facilities, Program Management, Sports Architecture, Structural Engineering, Transportation Architecture.
Clients
(Aviation) : Chicago Midway Airport, Dallas/Forth Worth International Airport Terminal D, T.F. Green Airport, Wilkes-Barre/Scranton International Airport, Kansas City International Airport, Tucson International Airport Terminal Expansion, McGhee Tyson Airport Renovation, Bradley International Airport; (Civic) Union Station; Kansas City Public Library, Central Library; Bartle Hall Convention Center, Boston Convention and Exhibition Center, San Diego Convention Center, Washington D.C. Convention Center Program Management, Rhode Island Convention Center
Clients
(Corporate) : Shook, Hardy & Bacon LLP, Polsinelli Shalton Welte Suelthaus PC, HNTB Headquarters, Kansas City Public Library, Central Library; Sprint ION; (Education) : The Ohio State University Ohio Stadium, University of Southern California Galen Center, Oregon State University Reser Stadium, Purdue University Ross-Ade Stadium, University of Georgia Sanford Stadium, University of Kentucky Commonwealth Stadium, University of Tennessee Aquatics Center, University of Kentucky Basketball Training Facility
Clients
(Federal) : Naval Air Systems Command Headquarters, U.S. Air Force Academy Athletic Complex Expansion, The Mary E. Switzer Memorial Building; (Historic Preservation) : Union Station, Kansas City Public Library, Central Library; (Sports Architecture) INVESCO Field at Mile High; The Ohio State University Ohio Stadium, U.S. Air Force Academy Athletic Complex Expansion, Mid-America Center, Council Bluffs; Fifth Third Field, University of Southern California Galen Center, Oregon State University Reser Stadium, Purdue University Ross-Ade Stadium, University of Georgia Sanford Stadium, University of Kentucky Commonwealth Stadium, University of Tenness

HOLABIRD & ROOT
140 S DEARBORN STREET
SUITE 700
CHICAGO, IL 60603
312-357-1771
Fax: 312-357-1909
holabird@holabird.com
www.holabird.com
• Greg Cook, Principal
gcook@holabird.com
• Jeff Case, Principal
• Jim Miller, Principal
• James Baird, Principal
Description:
Professional architectural design services

INTEGRATED DESIGN SOLUTIONS
425 CASHMAN DRIVE
SUITE 100
CHIPPEWA FALLS, WI 54729
715-723-6500
Fax: 715-723-6523
info@integrateddesign.com
www.integrateddesign.com
• Scott Olson, President
• Stacy Olson, Operations Manager
• Jason Revelle, Buisness Development Manager
• Dave Keys, Industrial Designer
• Bob Fehr, Product Development Engineer
• Katie Remaly, Industrial Designer
• Matt Ludvigson, Graphic Designer
Services:
Industrial designs, Engineering, Graphic Design, Prototyping, Project Management

JOHN M.Y. LEE/MICHAEL TIMCHULA ARCHITECTS
320 W 13TH STREET
NEW YORK, NY 10014-1280
212-929-3131
Fax: 212-463-8964
• John MY Lee,
• Michael Timchula,
Description:
Gymnasium, natatorium and tennis stadium architecture
Description:
Gymnasium, natatorium and tennis stadium architecture.

KIKU OBATA & COMPANY
6161 DELMAR BOULEVARD
SUITE 200
ST LOUIS, MO 63112
314-361-3110
www.kikuobata.com

KINSEY ASSOCIATES
HASTINGS COMMONS BUILDING 2A
486 SCHOOLEYS MOUNTAIN ROAD
SUITE 207
HACKETTSTOWN, NJ 07840
908-850-6488
Fax: 908-788-6788
• John L Jo Belle, President
• Gordon A. Raupp, VP
Sports Service Founded:
1962
Design & Consulting Services:
Recreation Master Plan Planning, Site Studies, Working Drawings and Specifications, Construction Contract Administration, Permitting, and Funding Assistance.

L. ROBERT KIMBALL & ASSOCIATES
615 W HIGHLAND AVENUE
PO BOX 1000
EBENSBURG, PA 15931
814-472-7700
Fax: 814-472-7712
aande@lrkimball.com
• Joel V McCamley, Senior Vice President
• Jeff Kimball, Principal & CEO
• Richard E. Genday, Senior Vice President
• Adam S. Henger, Senior Vice President
• E. Jack Lerch, Senior Vice President
• Rick Taormina, Senior Vice President
• Karen G. Maul, Vice President
Description:
Consulting services for indoor, outdoor and
rooftop tennis facilities for tournaments,
clubs, resort and institutional projects in U.S.
and international markets

LEHMAN-SMITH-MCLEISH PLLC
1212 BANKS NW
WASHINGTON, DC 20007
202-295-4800
Fax: 202-295-4856
info@lsm.com
www.lsm.com
• Debra Lehman-Smith, Partner
• James Black McLeish, III, Partner
Description:
Architectural and interior design services

LMN ARCHITECTS
801 SECOND AVENUE
SUITE 501
SEATTLE, WA 98104
206-682-3460
Fax: 206-343-9388
design@lmnarchitects.com
www.lmnarchitects.com
• Chris Eseman, Partner
• Kristy Kimura, Principal
Nature of Sports Service:
Architectural firm with expertise in the
design of public assembly facilities

**LOCKWOOD, ANDREWS, AND
NEWNAM/LAN**
2925 BRIARPARK DRIVE
SUITE 400
HOUSTON, TX 77042
713-266-6900
Fax: 713-266-2089
info@lan-inc.com
www.lan-inc.com
• Dennis Petersen, President
• Jeremy Nakashima, P.E, Senior Project
Manager
• Daniel B. McCausland, Director of
Program
• Randall C. Hill, Director of Engineering

LOHMANN COMPANIES
18250 BECK ROAD
MARENGO, IL 60152
815-923-3400
Fax: 815-923-3662
design@lohmann.com
www.lohmann.com
• Robert M Lohmann, president and
principal architect
• Todd A. Quitno, Golf Course Architect
Marketing & Consulting Services:
Full-service golf course architectural firm.
Administrates and supervises the complete
golf course construction process

MAHG ARCHITECHTURE
6400 RILEY PARK DRIVE
FORT SMITH, AR 72916
479-782-1051
Fax: 479-782-6019
info@mahgarch.com
www.mahgarch.com
• Hunter Galen D, Partner
Description:
Consultants that specialize in economic
feasibility analyses and market analyses for
recreation and mass spectator facilities

MILTON POWELL & PARTNERS
PO BOX 600984
SUITE 200
DALLAS, TX 75360-0984
214-213-7862
Fax: 214-520-3005
mpowell@mpparchitects.com
www.mpparchitects.com
• Milton Powell, Principal
• Richard C. Robinson, Principal
Description:
Professional services include architectural
design and planning

MITCHEL ABRAMOWITZ, A.I.A.
2526 ROSEWOOD AVENUE
ROSLYN, PA 19001-3012
215-368-9133
Fax: 215-368-8232
faramitch@comcast.net
• Mitchell Abramowitz, President/Owner
Nature of Sports Service:
Architects and designers of ice skating
facilities, swimming pools, and recreational
facilities. Consultants and construction
managers

MURAKAMI/NELSON
100 FILBERT STREET
OAKLAND, CA 94607
510-444-7959
Fax: 510-893-5244
office@murakaminelson.com
www.murakaminelson.com
• Michael Murakami, Principal
• Takane Eshima, Principal Emeritus
• John S. Nelson, Principal
Nature of Service
Architectural, planning, exterior and interior
design for athletic and recreational facilities;
new and remodeling and seismic
strengthening for university, institutional and
private clients.
Clients
City of Alameda, County of Alameda, Bank
of America, Berkeley Unified School District,
Lowell Berry Foundation, Brickyard Cove
Investments, E.D. Bullard Company, C & H
Development Company, California Coastal
Conservancy, California State University,
San Jose; California Department of
Transportation, Contra Costa County, Tom
Dannenberg, Doten Motors, Dinwiddie
Construction, Degenkolb Engineers, Deleuw
Cather, DMJM, Doric Development, City of
Dublin, Duffel Financial & Construction
Company, Duwo Partners, East Bay
Municipal Utility District, East Bay Regional
Park District, East Bay Asian Local
Development Corporation, ED2
International, EDAW,

NBBJ
523 W 6TH STREET
SUITE 300
LOS ANGELES, CA 90014
213-243-3333
Fax: 213-243-3334
losangeles_office@nbbj.com
www.nbbj.com
• Scott Hunter, Principal
(213) 243-3333
• Patrick Winters, Senior Associate
• Robert Mankin, Senior Associate
• Jonathan Ward, Principal
• Paul Becker, Senior Associate
Current Projects:
Milwaukee Brewers, Seattle Mariners,
Cincinnati Bengals, San Francisco 49ers,
LG Twins baseball team in Seoul, Korea,
new arenas for the Los Angeles
Kings/Lakers, Xavier University.
Nature of Sports Service
Architectural design for sports facilities.
Year Founded:
1995

NBBJ SPORTS
2 RECTOR STREET
25 TH FLOOR
NEW YORK, NY 10006
212-924-9000
Fax: 212-924-9292
info@nbbj.com
www.nbbj.com
• Jane Ayers, Principal
(614) 224-7145
sports@nbbj.com

OSBORN ENGINEERING
1300 E 9TH STREET
SUITE 1500
CLEVELAND, OH 44114
216-861-2020
Fax: 216-861-3329
www.osborn-eng.com
• Kurt K. Rim, Chairman
• Eugene P. Baxendale, President
Description:
Planning, design, engineering for new or
renovations, expansions, restorations of
stadiums, arenas, and recreation facilities

PAIGE DESIGN GROUP
5 PEARSE WYND ROAD
BAHAMA, NC 27503
919-620-0300
Fax: 919-620-0091
dpaige@paigedesigngroup.com
www.paigedesigngroup.com
• Don Paige, President and OWNER
dpaige@paigedesigngroup.com
• Tim Murphy, P.E., Associate & Project
Manager
tmurphy@paigedesigngroup.com
• Don Paige, President
dpaige@paigedesigngroup.com
Nature of Sports Service:
Planners, developers, renovators of athletic
facilities including stadiums, arenas, indoor
multi-sport complexes, outdoor fields, park
and recreation facilities; specializes in
synthetic sport surfacing and flooring

PARSONS
401 DIAMOND DRIVE NW
HUNTSVILLE, AL 35806-2192

256-837-5200
Fax: 256-830-0287
www.parsons.com
• Charles L Harrington, Chairman of the
Board & CEO
• Curtis A Bower, Vice Chairman Of The
Board
• William Turner, EVP/Chief Operating
Officer
• Gary Boyd, EVP/Chief Development
Officer
Service
Architecture, Interiors, Construction
Management, Facility Condition
Assessment, Information Technology,
Master Planning, Program and Project
Management

PIPER RUDNICK LLP
2000 AVENUE OF THE STARS
SUITE 400
NORTH TOWER
LOS ANGELES, CA 90067-4704
310-595-3000
Fax: 310-595-3300
info@dlapiper.com
www.dlapiper.com
• Brian C. Lusaght, Partner
• Jannet Abboud, Special Counsel
• Maurad Abida, Practice Group Head
• Therese Zeid, Sr.Consultant
• Norman Abrams, Partner
• Jakub Adam, Partner
• Stephen Abreu, Associate
• Frank Burch, Global Chairman
Nature of Service:
Sports facilities development

RAWHIDE PAVILION & RODEA ARENA
23023 N SCOTTSDALE ROAD
SCOTTSDALE, AZ 85255
480-502-1880
Fax: 480-502-1301
• Trudel St Sandy, Sales/Marketing Director
• Danelle Newton, Event Manager
• Steve Feld, Special Projects Manager
Year Founded:
1970
Seating Capacity:
Pavilion 6,000; Arena 6,800
Track Type:
Dirt track.
Track Size:
1/4 mile

ROSSER
TWO PEACHTREE POINTE
1555 PEACHTREE STREET, NE
SUITE 800
ATLANTA, GA 30309
404-876-3800
Fax: 404-888-6861
www.rosser.com
• Ray Ashe, Project Management Director
Description:
Architectural design for sports facilities

SH GROUP
11 W 42ND STREET
NEW YORK, NY 10036-2300
800-328-1600
800-858-2478
Fax: 212-556-3333
info@syska.com
www.syska.com
• John Magliano, Chairman / Chief
Executive Officer

• Harvery Goldman, President/Chief
Operating Officer
• Robert Dusconi, Chief Financial Officer
• Ann Banning-Wright, Chief Strategy Officer
Services:
Consulting, engineering, technology and
construction services
Clients:
World's leading private and public
corporations, fast-growing and high tech
companies, colleges and universities, real
estate owners and developers, as well as
local, state and federal government
agencies, architects and design
professionals.

SHEN MILSON & WILKE
33 NEW MONTGOMERY STREET
10TH FLOOR
SAN FRANCISCO, CA 94105
415-391-7610
800-221-1444
Fax: 415-391-0171
www.smwinc.com
• Dennis A Paoletti, Principal
• Kevin Eldredge, Associate Principal
Other Office:
5263 South 300 West, Salt Lake City, UT
84107. 801 266-3605; FAX: 801 266-1151
Description:
Professional services include acoustical and
audiovisual consulting

**SINK COMBS DETHLEFS, A
PROFESSIONAL CORPORATION FOR
ARCHITECTURE**
475 LINCOLN STREET
SUITE 100
DENVER, CO 80203
303-308-0200
866-535-5653
Fax: 303-308-0222
marketing@sinkcombs.com
www.sinkcombs.com
• Donald L. Dethlefs, Chief Executive Officer
(303) 308-0200
• B. Stephen King, Project Manager
• Brian Parish, Director of Media
Development
• Jennifer Stephens, Marketing Director
• Jamie Ryan, Director of Accounting and
Human Resource Adm
• Karen Stanzyk, Contract Manager
• April Luxner, Marketing Coordinator
• Kevin Armstrong, Associate
Description:
Sink Combs Dethlefs has had a long
standing reputation for quality design,
creativity, cost effectiveness, innovation,
efficiency and excellence had long
characterized the process and designs of
the firm for more than four decades.

STANMAR INC.
321 COMMONWEALTH ROAD
SUITE 201
WAYLAND, MA 1778
508-310-9922
Fax: 508-310-0479
www.stanmar-inc.com
• Mark Snider, President
sthompson@stanmar-inc.com
Description:
Professional services include architectural
design and construction
Clients:
Tufts University, Philadelphia University,

Nantucket Boys & Girls Club, Eagle Hill
School & more

STANTEC
2335 W HIGHWAY 36
SAINT PAUL, MN 55113
651-636-4724
800-880-4700
Fax: 651-636-1311
www.bonestroo.com
• Sorvala Marvin, President
• Chris Peterson, Human Resources
Director
• David Loskota, Director Marketing
Description:
Architects, engineers and construction
managers specializing in the planning
design and construction administration of ice
arenas and family aquatic centers.

TBSA
27001 US HIGHWAY 19 N
CLEARWATER, FL 33761
727-723-7785
Fax: 727-723-0605
www.funleaguegroup.com
• Terry Killian, Rink Manager
• Kathy Winter, Asst. Skating Director
• Diane Paul, Marketing Director
• Nadine Pearen, Skating Director
Description:
Develops combination ice skating, hockey
and inline skating/hockey facilities.
Services:
Specializing in the ownership and
management of ice sports and family
entertainment centers

THA ARCHITECTS ENGINEERS
817 E KEARSLEY STREET
FLINT, MI 48503
810-767-5600
Fax: 810-767-1650
info@tha-flint.com
www.tha-flint.com
• Jeffrey L. Bennett, Architects Engineer
• Madonna L. Bennett, Project Director
• George S. Anannich, Operations Director
• Donald E. Lee, Project Manager
Services:
Planning Services, Architectural Services,
Interior Design Services, Mechanical
Engineering Services, Electrical Engineering
Services, Structural Engineering Services,
Construction Services, Post Construction
Services

THE DAVIS EXPERIENCE
60 E RIO SALADO PARKWAY
SUITE 200
TEMPE, AZ 85281-9130
480-638-1100
Fax: 602-381-4844
www.thedavisexperience.com
• Michael R Davis, Chief Executive
Officer/Director of Desi
• Lisa Davis, Board Member
ldavis@dfdch.com
• Timothy Sprague, Board Member
• Rory A. Carder, Managing Director,
Principal
(480) 638-1150
• Jamie Moore, Chief Operating Officer
Service
Architecture, Interior Architecture, Space
Planning, Land Planning, Landscape

Architecture, Facilities Management, Graphic Design

THORNTON-TOMASETTI ENGINEERS
51 MADISON AVENUE
NEW YORK, NY 10010-1603
917-661-7800
Fax: 917-661-7801
Careers@TheTTGroup.com
www.thorntontomasetti.com
• Daniel A Cuoco, President/CEO
• Aine M. Brazil, Managing Principal
• Joseph G. Burns, Managing Principal
• Jim C. Kent, Director of Communications
• John Fairbairn, Director of Human Resources
Services:
Provides designs and engineering services for the structural component of major facilities throughout the world.

TVS DESIGN
1230 PEACHTREE STREET NE
2700 PROMENADE TWO
ATLANTA, GA 30309
404-888-6600
Fax: 404-888-6700
www.tvsa.com
• Roger L. Neuenschwander, President
• Marc Hirsch, Marketing Manager
• Kristi Patterson, Information Technology Manager
Services:
International architecture and interior designs services
Clients:
Retail, workplace interiors, hospitality and entertainment markets

U.S. TENNIS COURT & TRACK BUILDERS ASSOCIATION
8480 BALTIMORE
SUITE 307
NATIONAL PIKE
ELLICOT CITY, MD 21043
410-
866-501-2722
Fax: 410-730-8833
info@sportsbuilders.org
www.sportsbuilders.org
• Todd George, Chairman
(813) 645-2315
george@welchtennis.com
• Gordy Pierce, President-Tennis Division
(508) 759-5636
gpierce@tennisandtrack.com
• Sam Fisher, President-Tract Division
(800) 432-3191
sfisher@fishertracks.com
• Alex Levitsky, President-Professional Division
(732) 747-9050
Services:
ASBA is a national organization for builders, designers and suppliers of materials for tennis courts, running tracks, synthetic turf fields, indoor and outdoor synthetic sports surfaces. It is recognized as a centralized source for technical information, including consumer-oriented information.

VALLEY CREST
24151 VENTURA BOULEVARD
CALABASAS, CA 91302
818-223-8500
Fax: 818-223-8142

webmaster@valleycrest.com
www.valleycrest.com
• Burton S. Sperber, Founder / Chief Executive Officer
• Richard A. Sperber, President / CEO
• Po Chen, General Manager
(714) 327-5374
pchen@valleycrest.com
Services:
Sport field consulting, construction and maintenance.

VOA ASSOCIATES INCORPORATED
224 S MICHIGAN AVENUE
SUITE 1400
CHICAGO, IL 60604
312-554-1400
Fax: 312-554-1412
www.voa.com
• Rebel Roberts, PRESIDENT
Services:
Strategy and planning services, architectural design, landscape architecture and comprehensive planning, interior design, graphical services and coputer applications services.
Clients:
Amtrak, Brookfield Zoo, Burlington Northern/Santa Fe Railroad, CB Richard Ellis, Citibank Commercial Development, City of Chicago, Federal Express, Curitiba International Trade Center, Insignia/ESG, Sullivan Building Foundation, Central Florida Communioty Collection, Florida International University, Lawrence University.

WALTER P MOORE
1301 MCKINNEY,
SUITE 1100
HOUSTON, TX 77010
713-630-7300
Fax: 713-630-7396
info@walterpmoore.com
www.walterpmoore.com
• Ray Messer, President / Chairman of the Board
rmesser@walterpmoore.com
• Larry Griffis, Senior Principal & Division President
lgriffis@walterpmoore.com
• Jerry Marcus, Parking Consulting Services Executive Di
jmarcus@walterpmoore.com
• Raymond Messer, President and Chairman of the Board
• Lee Slade, Senior Principal/Executive Director
• Dennis Wittry, Principal/Managing Director
• Dilip Choudhuri, Principal/Executive Director
• Gabriel A. Jimenez, Principal/Managing Director/ Director of Oper
• Charles Penland, Senior Principal/Executive Director
• Doug Coenen, Principal/Managing Directo
Services:
Parking Consulting, Research & Development, Structural Diagnostics, Structural Engineering Services
Clients:
Architects, Colleges and Universities, Corporations, Government Agencies, Hospitals, Institutions, Management Districts, Real Estate Developers, Regional Development Authorities, Tax Increment Reinvestment Zones

WESLEY MEDICAL CENTER
550 N HILLSIDE
WICHITA, KS 67214
316-962-2000
Fax: 316-962-8040
www.wesleymc.com
• Helen Thomas, Director, Marketing and Public Relations
• Mary Singleton, employer relations director
Nature of Service
Health promotion and facility management services.
Services:
Provides a full range of diagnostic and treatment services

WISS, JANNEY, ELSTNER ASSOCIATES, INC./WJE
330 PFINGSTEN ROAD
NORTHBROOK, IL 60062
847-272-7400
Fax: 847-291-9599
info@wje.com
www.wje.com
• William Nugent, President/Senior Principal
wnugent@wje.com
• Gary.J. Klein, Executive Vice president and senior principal
(847) 753-6572
gklein@wje.com
• Brady Thomas, Dir of Corp Ops, Assoc Dir of Proj Ops, Princ
(847) 272-7400
• Calabrese Flora, Associate Principal
(847) 272-7400
fcalabrese@wje.com
• Douglas Crampton, Associate Principal
(847) 272-7400
dcrampton@wje.com
• Timothy Crowe, Associate Principal
(847) 272-7400
tcrowe@wje.com
• Richard Arnold, Associate Principal
(847) 272-7400
rarnold@wje.com
Sports Facility Services Include:
Structural and architectural assessments, repair and rehabilitation design, annual condition surveys; water leakage investigations; concrete deterioration's evaluations, corrosion investigations, seismic analysis and upgrade; testing and instrumentation;

WRIGHTSON, JOHNSON, HADDON & WILLIAMS, INC.
4801 SPRING VALLEY ROAD
SUITE 113
DALLAS, TX 75244
972-934-3700
Fax: 972-934-3720
info@wjhw.com
www.wjhw.com

WSP
512 7TH AVENUE
NEW YORK, NY 10018
212-532-9600
Fax: 212-689-7489
www.wspgroup.com
• Randy Meyers, President and CEO
• Norman D Kurtz, Chairman

Facility Management

ACCESS DATA SUPPORT SERVICES & FACILITY MANAGEMENT GROUP
2425 W LOOP S
SUITE 855
HOUSTON, TX 77027
713-439-0370
800-206-0931
Fax: 713-439-0376
ads@access-data.com
www.access-data.com
• Andrea Renee Logans, President & CEO
• Tom Logans, Support Services VP
• Renee Re Logans, President/Chief Executive Officer
• Tom Logans, Vice President
Nature of Sports Service:
A multi-disciplined, minority-owned service company that provides facility support services, construction management and specialized personnel placement. Organization has years of experience in providing facilities maintenance and management services.

ARAMARK CORPORATION
1101 MARKET STREET
PHILADELPHIA, PA 19107
215-238-3000
800-272-6275
Fax: 215-238-3333
www.aramark.com
• Joseph Neubauer, Chairman
• L Frederick Sutherland, Executive Vice President/Chief Financial Officer
• Cathy Schlosberg, Vice President, Marketing/Education
• David Freireich, Media Relations Coordinator, Sports Entertainment
• Eric Foss, President
Baseball:
MLB; Minor League
College Sponsor:
NCAA; College Bowl
Basketball Sponsor:
NBDL
Football Sponsor:
Indoor League
Hockey Sponsor:
AHL

BARTON MALOW COMPANY
26500 AMERICAN DRIVE
SOUTHFIELD, MI 48034
248-436-5000
Fax: 248-436-5001
info@bartonmalow.com
www.bartonmalow.com
• Ben Maibach, III, President
• Sheryl Mailbach, Chief Marketing Officer & Senior Vice Preside
Description:
Recognized as an innovator of construction and program management, and one of the premier sports builders in the country. Offers comprehensive building services such as general contracting, design/building, construction management and facility management.

BIGELOW COMPANIES, THE
6501 E COMMERCE AVENUE
SUITE 120
KANSAS CITY, MO 64120
816-483-5553
Fax: 816-483-5510
chrisbigelow@bigelowcompanies.com
www.bigelowcompanies.com
• Chris Bigelow, President
(816) 994-3261
chrisbigelow@bigelowcompanies.com
• Lee Roberts, Director of Design
(816) 994-3262
leeroberts@bigelowcompanies.com
• Jason Simpson, Design and Technology Specialist
(816) 994-3268
jasonsimpson@bigelowcompanies.com
• Laurie Roark, Director of Administration
(816) 994-3263
laurieroark@bigelowcompanies.com
Year Founded:
1988
Clients:
Denver Broncos, Kroenke Sports & Entertainment, Quicken Loans Arena, Monumental Sports
Services:
Foodservice design

CENTERPLATE
2187 ATLANTIC ST
STAMFORD, CT 68902
864-598-8600
800-698-6992
Fax: 864-598-8686
info@centerplate.com
www.centerplate.com
• Des Hague, President and Chief Executive Officer
• Kenneth R Frick, VP/Chief Financial Officer
• Steve Trotter, VP, New Business Development
Sports Service Founded:
1973
Description:
The largest hospitality partner to North America's sporting and entertainment venues.
Marketing & Consulting Services:
Food, beverage, merchandise and management provider for sports facilities.

DELOITTE & TOUCHE LLP
100 KIMBALL DRIVE
PARSIPPANY, NJ 07054-2176
973-602-6000
Fax: 973-683-7459
www.deloitte.com
• William G Parrett, Global CEO
• Stewart Rog, Principal
Description:
Management consultants with expertise in all aspects of sports facilities development and operations, including feasibility studies, financing, lease negotiation assistance, premium seating and seat license market analyses, economic impact studies, and ev

FINISH LINE EVENTS
5725-E CONCORD PARKWAY S
CONCORD, NC 28027
704-455-3235
Fax: 704-454-4744
Sports Service Founded:
1960
Nature of Sports Service:
Currently operates at six of the largest sports venues in the United States - Atlanta Motor Speedway, Bristol Motor Speedway, Lowe's Motor Speedway in Charlotte, Texas Motor Speedway in Fort Worth and Infineon Raceway in Sonoma, California.

FIRST AND GOAL, INC.
PO BOX 941176
HOUSTON, TX 77094
713-571-9121
Fax: 206-381-7572
info@teamfirstandgoal.org
www.teamfirstandgoal.org
• Paul G Allen, Chairman
• Jody Patton, Vice Chairman
• Bob Whitsitt, President
• Tyrone Smith, President
Sports Service Founded:
1997
Nature of Sports Service:
Organization founded by Paul G. Allen to manage the development, construction and operation of the Washington State Football/Soccer Stadium and Exhibition Center. Dedicated to working in partnership with the community to build and operate a world-class.

GLOBAL SPECTRUM
3601 SOUTH BROAD STREET
PHILADELPHIA, PA 19148
215-389-9587
Fax: 215-952-5651
tglickman@comcast-spectacor.com
www.global-spectrum.com

HEERY INTERNATIONAL, INC.
999 PEACHTREE STREET NE
ATLANTA, GA 30309-3953
404-881-9880
Fax: 404-892-8479
Corporate@heery.com
www.heery.com
• Jim J. Moynihan, Chairman & CEO
• Bill Heitz, President
• Greg Pierce, Regional Manager
Nature of Service
Architecture, engineering, master planning, design and construction management of sports facilities.
Description:
Architecture, engineering, master planning, design and construction management of sports facilities.
Clients
Architecture: Atlanta Botanical Gardens; Atlanta History Center Museum; Atlanta History Center Parking Deck; Bosch Corporation; Central Michigan University; Citadel; Coca-Cola; Comdisco; Conoco Headquarters, Cumberland County Civic Center; Dare County; Dare County Justice Center; Dekalb County Courthouse; Emory University School of Law; Erie Seawolves Stadium; Franklin Templeton; Georgia Dome; Georgia World Congress Center; Heery D.C. Office; Hotel Thayer; Jacksonville Baptist Hospital; James Madison University; Kennesaw State University; Mayo Clinic; MBNA Multiple Locations; McCoy Stadium; Memorial Mission Parking Deck; Metlife; Missoula Sta
Services:
Architecture, Construction Managemetn, Engineering, Facilities Management, Interior Design, and Program Management

IMS PROPERTIES/INDY MOTOR SPEEDWAY
4790 W 16TH STREET
INDIANAPOLIS, IN 46222
317-492-8500
sales@brickyard.com
www.indianapolismotorspeedway.com

INTERNATIONAL MICRO SYSTEMS, INC.
200 RACOOSIN DRIVE
SUITE 110
ASTON, PA 19014
484-482-1600
800-882-0627
Fax: 484-574-8874
sales-marketing@ims-pos.com
www.ims-pos.com
• Jeff Harvey, Director of Sales
• Rob Rae, Director of Marketing
Nature of Services:
International Micro Systems provides integrated POS (Point of Sales) and venue management solutions with a strong focus on sports arenas, convention centers, amusement facilities, and colleges/universities - products and services include inventory management, food and beverage POS systems, full-scale venue systems planning, installation and support, and pre-paid concession payment systems through ticketing.

JOHN M.Y. LEE/MICHAEL TIMCHULA ARCHITECTS
320 W 13TH STREET
NEW YORK, NY 10014-1280
212-929-3131
Fax: 212-463-8964
www.aecdaily.com
• John MY Lee,
• Michael Timchula,
Description:
Gymnasium, natatorium and tennis stadium architecture
Description:
Gymnasium, natatorium and tennis stadium architecture.

LUNDY'S SPECIAL EVENTS
1385 PRIDEMORE COURT
LEXINGTON, KY 40505
859-255-0717
Fax: 859-253-9790
www.lundyscatering.com
• Abigail Dobson, BOD
• Alissa Tibe, VP
• Jerry Lundergan, Principal Catering Development
Year Founded:
Lundy's: 1965
Event Food Management Services:
National, mobile, full-service special event firm providing corporate hospitality catering, general concessions and facilities management for sports and special events.

MEADOWLANDS/NEW JERSEY SPORTS & EXPOSITION AUTHORITY
50 STATE ROUTE 120
EXECUTIVE OFFICES
E RUTHERFORD, NJ 7073
201-935-8500
Fax: 201-507-8130
www.izodcenter.com
• George R Zottinger, Chairman
• Bruce H Garland, SVP/Racing Operations
• Joseph R Consolazio, SVP/Chief Financial

Officer
• Barbara Lampen, SVP/Strategic Planning/Development
Meadowlands Stadium:
Home field for NY Giants and NY Jets football teams. Robert Castronovo, Exec VP/Gen Mgr; Robert E. Carney, Asst Gen Mgr Ops; William Squires, Dir Stad Ops; Leo Ehrline, Asst Gen Mgr Mktg; 201 935-8500; FAX: 201 460-4294; Gen Mgr FAX: 201 507-8122.
Continental Airlines Arena:
Home field for NY Nets basketball team. Robert Castronovo, Exec VP/Gen Mgr; Robert E. Carney, Asst Gen Mgr Ops; Leo Ehrline, Asst Gen Mgr Mktg; 201 935-8500; FAX: 201 460-4294; Gen Mgr FAX: 201 507-8122.

MORSE DIESEL INTERNATIONAL INC.
148 STATE STREET, 7TH FLOOR
BOSTON, MA 2109
617-725-2788
800-698-4002
Fax: 617-725-4925
• O'Marah Eamon, Business Development Director
• Kevin Collins, Sports Director
• Dave Kersey, Project Executive
Projects Include:
United Center, Fleet Center, Broward County Arena, Tampa Bay Ice Palace, Tampa NFL Stadium, Chicago (AHL) Arena, U. Cal Berkeley Arena, Ohio State Stadium, Philadelphia Eagles Training Center, SF 49ers Stadium, Miami Heat Arena, Pittsburgh Pirates Ballpar
Description:
Premiere Construction Manager, Consultant and Owner's Representative of Major Sports Facility projects. Expertise includes: Site & Foundation, Truss Erection, False-work Framing, Roof/Canopy, Mechanical, Electrical & Plumbing (MEP) Coordination, Precast

PATRON SOLUTIONS, LP
701 LEE ROAD
SUITE 305
WAYNE, PA 19087
610-408-9460
Fax: 610-408-9551
info@patronsolutions.com
www.patronsolutions.com
• Fred Maglione, President/CEO
• Dave Homan, VP/COO
• Christian Varano, New Business Development Director
(610) 854-1104
• Stephen Scalese, Development/Marketing Director
(610) 854-1103
scalese@patronsolutions.com
• Thomas Greco, Call Center Operations Director
tgreco@patronsolutions.com
• Daniel Durso, Finance Director
ddurso@patronsolutions.com
• Dave Homan, Vice President

PRITCHARD INDUSTRIES, INC
4040 DIRECTORS ROW
HOUSTON, TX 77092
713-957-1387
Fax: 713-957-1574
psperduti@pritchardindustries.com
www.pritchardindustries.com

• Peter Sperduti, VP/General Manager
Nature of Sports Service:
Provides industry specific facility services for sports and entertainment complexes including General Cleaning, Intensive Training, Pressure Washing, Quality Control and Recycling.

R.I.C. CORPORATION
6215 CONSTITUTION DRIVE
FORT WAYNE, IN 46804-1517
260-432-0799
Fax: 260-432-9155
sales@riccorp.com
www.riccorp.com
• Rick Kriscka, President
Description:
Developed windows based Facility Management Software system. A completely integrated system with applications for all phases of the operation from initial marketing through to final billing. Each application is licensed separately per user, so you only pa

RODER USA, INC.
1954 N 30TH ROAD
HOLLYWOOD, FL 33021-4401
954-894-6400
Fax: 954-964-1700
www.roderusa.com
• Andrew Soffe, Account Executive (West Coast)
(800) 258-8368
• Keith Krzeminski, Accountt Executive (Northeast)
(540) 992-3377
• Robert Kraak, President
• Russ Sell, Account Executive (Southeast I)

(954) 894-6400
Nature of Sports Service:
Create temporary facilities including; tents, lightweight-construction halls, and steel halls, for golf tournaments, tennis tournaments, etc.

SMG
300 CONSHOHOKEN STATE ROAD
SUITE 450
WEST CONSHOHOKEN, PA 19428
610-729-7900
Fax: 610-729-1590
www.smgworld.com
• Wes Westley, President and CEO
• Maureen Ginty, Executive VP
• John Burns, Executive VP
• Gregg Caren, Sr.VP
Sports Service Founded:
Sports Service Founded: 1977
Event Management Services:
Production and marketing of sporting events.
Marketing & Consulting Services:
Stadiums, arenas, theaters, auditoriums and convention centers under its guidance worldwide. Divisions include SMG Productions, Network International, SMG sports advertising affiliate.

SPEEDWAY MOTORSPORTS, INC.
5555 CONCORD PARKWAY S
CONCORD, NC 28027
704-455-3239
Fax: 704-455-2168
www.speedwaymotorsports.com

- Cary Tharrington, SVP & General Counsel
- Donald Hawk, Chief Racing Development Officer
- Jerry Caldwell, EVP & General Manager

Nature of Sports Services:
A marketer and producer of motorsports entertainment in the United States. The company owns and operates six motorsports facilities including Atlanta Motor Speedway, Bristol (TN), Motor Speedway, Lowe's Motor Speedway, Las Vegas Motor Speedway, Infineon Raceway, and New Hampshire Speedway

---

SPORTSERVICE CORPORATION
FOUNTAIN PLAZA
40 FOUNTAIN PLAZA
BUFFALO, NY 14202
716-858-5000
800-828-7240
800-441-5645
Fax: 716-858-5479
info@delawarenorth.com
www.delawarenorth.com
- Wendy Watkins, Vice President Corporate Communications and Market
- Jeffrey Hess, Director Retail/Marketing Services
- Nancy Parker, President
- Jeremy Jacobs, Chief Executive Officer

Description:
Provides food, beverage and retail services at sports and recreational facilities as well as glittering, upscale, one-of-a-kind events.

VENUEWORKS
4611 MORTENSEN ROAD
SUITE 111
AMES, IA 50014
515-232-5151
888-232-5151
Fax: 515-663-2022
info@venuworks.com
www.venuworks.com
- Steve L Peters, Founder/President
(515) 232-5151
speters@venuworks.com
- Andy Long, Vice President of Events and Entertainment
(515) 232-5151
along@venuworks.com
- Doug Kuhnel, Senior VP Operations
(515) 232-5151
dkuhnel@venuworks.com
- Tammy Roolbeck, Venue Services VP
- Larry Gawronski, Southern Region VP
- Andy Long, National Director Business Development
- Betty Beisker, Human Resources VP
- Joseph Briglia, Vice President of Development
(609) 505-4226
jbriglia@venuworks.com
- Paul Putter, National Director Programming
- Sharon Cummins, National Director of Planning and Development
scummins@venuworks.com

Description:
Provides comprehensive management for arenas, convention centers and theaters, specializing in territory markets. Also provides consulting services for facility planning, feasibility studies and sponsor development.

Managed Facilities Include:
Midwest Wireless Civic Center, Mankato, MN; RiverCenter/Adler Theater, Davenport,

IA; Alerus Center, Grand Forks, ND; U.S. Cellular Center/Paramount Theater, Cedar Rapids, IA; and Brookings Area MultiPlax, SD.

VENUWORKS
4611 MORTENSEN ROAD
SUITE 111
AMES, IA 50014
515-232-5151
Fax: 515-663-2022
info@venuworks.com
www.venuworks.com
- Peters Steve, Founder/President
(515) 232-5151
speters@venuworks.com
- Joseph Briglia, Vice President of Development
(609) 505-4226
jbriglia@venuworks.com
- Andy Long, Vice President of Events and Entertainment
(515) 232-5151
along@venuworks.com
- Sharon Cummins, National Director of Planning and Development
scummins@venuworks.com
- Russell Ferguson, Vice President of Food and Beverage Services
rferguson@venuworks.com
- Doug Kuhnel, Senior Vice President
(515) 232-5151
dkuhnel@venuworks.com

WILLIAM CARUSO & ASSOCIATES, INC.
8055 EAST TUFTS AVENUE
SUITE 1320
DENVER, CO 80237
303-649-1600
Fax: 303-649-1660
wcaruso@wcarusoassoc.com
www.wcarusoassoc.com
- William J Caruso, President
(303) 649-1600
- Stephen K Young, Principal & Director Of Design
(303) 649-1600

Sports Service Founded:
1987

Consulting Services:
Independent consulting firm specializing in the planning and design of food/beverage facilities for the public assembly building industry.

Facility Concession Services

ARAMARK CORPORATION
1101 MARKET STREET
PHILADELPHIA, PA 19107
215-238-3000
800-999-8989
Fax: 215-238-3333
www.aramark.com
- Joseph Neubauer, Chairman
- L Frederick Sutherland, Executive Vice President/Chief Financial Officer
- Cathy Schlosberg, Vice President, Marketing/Education
- David Freireich, Media Relations Coordinator, Sports Entertainment
- Eric Foss, President

Baseball:
MLB; Minor League

College Sponsor:
NCAA; College Bowl
Basketball Sponsor:
NBDL
Football Sponsor:
Indoor League
Hockey Sponsor:
AHL

BIGELOW COMPANIES, THE
6501 E COMMERCE AVENUE
SUITE 120
KANSAS CITY, MO 64120
816-483-5553
Fax: 816-483-5510
chrisbigelow@bigelowcompanies.com
www.bigelowcompanies.com
- Chris Bigelow, President
(816) 994-3261
chrisbigelow@bigelowcompanies.com
- Lee Roberts, Director of Design
(816) 994-3262
leeroberts@bigelowcompanies.com
- Jason Simpson, Design and Technology Specialist
(816) 994-3268
jasonsimpson@bigelowcompanies.com
- Laurie Roark, Director of Administration
(816) 994-3263
laurieroark@bigelowcompanies.com

Year Founded:
1988
Clients:
Denver Broncos, Kroenke Sports & Entertainment, Quicken Loans Arena, Monumental Sports
Services:
Foodservice design

C. CRETORS & CO.
3243 N CALIFORNIA AVENUE
CHICAGO, IL 60618
773-588-1690
800-228-1885
Fax: 773-588-7141
Solesen@Cretors.com
www.cretors.com

CENTERPLATE
2187 ATLANTIC STREET
STAMFORD, CT 6902
800-698-6992
Fax: 864-598-8686
info@centerplate.com
www.centerplate.com
- Des Hague, President and Chief Executive Officer
- Kenneth R Frick, VP/Chief Financial Officer
- Steve Trotter, VP, New Business Development

Sports Service Founded:
1973
Description:
The largest hospitality partner to North America's sporting and entertainment venues.
Marketing & Consulting Services:
Food, beverage, merchandise and management provider for sports facilities.

CENTURY INDUSTRIES, LLC
PO BOX C
SELLERSBURG, IN 47172
812-246-3371
800-248-3371

Fax: 812-246-5446
www.centuryindustries.com
• Michelle McRae, Marketing Director
• Robert Uhl, President
Manufacturer:
Mobile Concessions - Portable Stands,
Seating, Bleachers.
Services:
Vendor Special Event Service, Goldrush
Concession, Kiosk, Tail Cater, P.O.P Cup
Merchandisers, Mobile Kitchens, Ticket
Booths, Special Purpose Trailers, Goldrush,
Mobile Staging, Mobile Bleacher Seating,
Self Service Centers, Drive-Thru Retail
Service Centers, USPS, Expanding Trailers
and Merchandising
Clients:
Sausage Grill, Fried Dough, Elephant Ears,
Route 66 Diner, Cafeteria

CHECKERS DRIVE-IN RESTAURANTS
4300 WEST CYPRESS STREET
SUITE 600
TAMPA, FL 33607
813-283-7000
800-275-3628
Fax: 813-283-7001
www.checkers.com
• Terri Snyder, Executive Vice President and
Chief Marketing
• Adams Noyes, Executive Vice President
Of Operations and Te
• Todd Lindsey, Senior Vice President/
Chief Financial Office
• Enrique Rick Silva, President & CEO
Services:
Official Burger for MLB - Tampa Bay Rays;
Minor League Baseball - Louisville Bats;
University of Florida Gators; Florida State
University Seminoles; University of
Louisville Cardinals.

CONCESSION SOLUTIONS, INC.
16022 26TH AVENUE NE
SHORELINE, WA 98155
206-440-9203
Fax: 206-440-9213
info@concessionsolutions.com
www.concessionsolutions.com
• Theresa Traulsen, President
theresa@concessionsolutions.com
• Bob Traulsen, Vice President
• Hope Kaser, Vice President Operations
• Sandi Burton, Associate
Consulting Services:
Onsite Evaluations; Profitability Analysis;
Product Evaluations; Audit Program; Facility
Design and Systematization; Management
and Staff Training; Request for Proposal
Review and Development; Website Design
and Development; and Concession
Management for

CUSTOM MOBILE FOOD EQUIPMENT
275 SOUTH 2ND ROAD
HAMMONTON, NJ 8037
609-561-6900
800-257-7855
Fax: 609-567-9318
www.customsalesandservice.com
• Cathy Chartier, Contact
(800) 257-7855
lynda.sikora@foodcart.com
Products:
Mobile food equipment - catering trucks,
specialty and general food carts, hot/cold
food equipment.

DAVID & SONS, INC.
PO BOX 7907, 5626 E SHIELDS
FRESNO, CA 93727-7818
209-291-0231
800-876-0231
Fax: 209-291-8239
• Bobby Shehorn, VP Sales
Food Category:
Appetizers and Snacks.

DI/AN CONTROLS, INC.
530 W STREET
BRAINTREE, MA 2184
781-848-1299
Fax: 781-848-1659

EXECUTIVE RESTROOM TRAILERS
1093 A1A BEACH BOULEVARD
SUITE 421
SAINT AUGUSTINE, FL 32080
888-445-4928
888-445-4928
Fax: 904-461-5588
www.exrt.com
• Tim Haszard, President
• Sharon L Haszard, VP
Sports Service Founded:
1971
Event Management Services:
Manufactures and leases upscale restroom
facilities for sporting events; also handles
coordination of portable sanitation for sports
events. Provides services for the Brickyard
400-NASCAR, NFL Quarterback Challenge,
Super Bowl, Family Circle Tennis Tourna

GAME TIME FOOD & BEVERAGE SERVICES, INC.
355 W DUNDEE ROAD
BUFFALO GROVE, IL 60089
847-243-4263
Fax: 847-243-2155
• Blumenthal Steve, Business Development
• Alan Day, Director Operations
Description:
Specializes in minor league facility
concessions.

INTERNATIONAL MICRO SYSTEMS, INC.
200 RACOOSIN DRIVE
SUITE 110
ASTON, PA 19014
484-482-1600
800-882-0627
Fax: 484-574-8874
sales-marketing@ims-pos.com
www.ims-pos.com
• Jeff Harvey, Director of Sales
• Rob Rae, Director of Marketing
Nature of Services:
International Micro Systems provides
integrated POS (Point of Sales) and venue
management solutions with a strong focus
on sports arenas, convention centers,
amusement facilities, and
colleges/universities - products and services
include inventory management, food and
beverage POS systems, full-scale venue
systems planning, installation and support,
and pre-paid concession payment systems
through ticketing.

LEVY RESTAURANTS SPORTS & ENTERTAINMENT
980 NORTH MICHIGAN AVENUE
LEVEL 2
CHICAGO, IL 60611-4501
312-664-8200
Fax: 312-280-2739
www.levyrestaurants.com
• Larry Levy, Chairman/Founder
• John Swanson, SVP Operations
Nature of Sports Service:
Brings restaurant-quality dining from its
base of award-winning restaurants to the
premium food service at 56 sports and
entertainment venues across the country.
Sports Service Founded:
1982

LUNDY'S SPECIAL EVENTS
1385 PRIDEMORE COURT
LEXINGTON, KY 40505
859-255-0717
Fax: 859-253-9790
www.lundyscatering.com
• Abigail Dobson, BOD
• Alissa Tibe, VP
• Jerry Lundergan, Principal Catering
Development
Year Founded:
Lundy's: 1965
Event Food Management Services:
National, mobile, full-service special event
firm providing corporate hospitality catering,
general concessions and facilities
management for sports and special events.

OVATION FOOD SERVICES LP
18228 US HIGWAY 41 N
LUTZ, FL 33549
813-948-6900
Fax: 813-948-6565
www.ovationsfoodservices.com
• Kenneth J Young, President
• Ken Young, President
(813) 948-6900
• Todd Wickner, Founder
• Doug Drewes, Executive Vice President
• Charlie Neary, Executive Vice President
(925) 426-5128
• Mark Healey, Vice President
(617) 733-5505
• Adrienne Hanson, Chief Financial Officer
(813) 948-6900
• Todd Wickner, Founder
Nature of Sports Service:
Organization specializes in concessions,
catering, and other services for arenas,
stadiums, and similar large venues.

PERFECTION EQUIPMENT, INC.
4259 LEE AVENUE
GURNEE, IL 60031
847-244-7200
800-356-6301
Fax: 847-244-7205
www.perfectequip.com
• Sandy Hahn, President
sand@perfectequip.com
• Alan Hale, Operations Manager
alanhale@perfectequip.com
• Sandy Hahn, President
• Alan Hale, Operations Manager/R&D
• Kathy Pino, Sales/Administration
• Robert Barnhisel, Director of Sales and
Installation
• Gene Wood, Purchasing

Description:
Concessions including carbonated beverage dispensing systems; powered condiment dispensing systems; self contained/ sealed system and constant temperature, remote beer system; glycol chillers.

PIONEEER FAMILY BRANDS, INC.
12674 PONY EXPRESS ROAD
SUITE 1
DRAPER, UT 84020
801-523-3850
800-975-4766
Fax: 801-523-3815
sales@pioneerfamilybrands.com
www.tropicalsno.com
• Donald Griffiths, President
(801) 523-3850
donald@pioneerfamilybrands.com
• Steve Griffiths, Assistant Controller
(801) 523-3850
steve@pioneerfamilybrands.com
• David Griffiths, VP Manufacturing/Purchasing
• Debra Didier, Secretary/Treasurer/Chief Financial Offi
Year Founded:
1973
Nature of Service:
Manufacturer, distributor of Tropical Sno Hawaiian Shave Ice products.

SPORTSERVICE CORPORATION
FOUNTAIN PLAZA
40 FOUNTAIN PLAZA
BUFFALO, NY 14202

716-858-5000
800-828-7240
Fax: 716-858-5479
www.delawarenorth.com
• Wendy Watkins, Vice President Corporate Communications and Market
• Jeffrey Hess, Director Retail/Marketing Services
• Nancy Parker, President
• Jeremy Jacobs, Chief Executive Officer
Description:
Provides food, beverage and retail services at sports and recreational facilities as well as glittering, upscale, one-of-a-kind events.

TANGENT ASSOCIATES, INC.
5000 SW 52ND, SUITE 501
FORT LAUDERDALE, FL 33314-5514 Â
954-797-9883
866-287-4736
Fax: 954-797-9887
info@micros.com
www.micros.com
• A.L. Giannopoulos, Executive Chairman
• Peter A. Altabef, President and Chief Executive Officer
• Daniel J. Bell, Senior Vice President, Hotels & Leisure and E
• Don DeMarinis, Vice President, Leisure and Entertainment
• Dan Harley, Vice President, West Major Account Restaurant
• Cynthia A. Russo, Executive Vice President, Chief Financial Off
• James T. Walsh, Chief Information Security Officer

Description:
Provides Point-of-sale and inventory control systems for food and beverage concessions management in the US and Canada. Systems accummulate the volumes of transactions which occur for every event or function at a major stadium and arena.

WILLIAM CARUSO & ASSOCIATES, INC.
8055 EAST TUFTS AVENUE
SUITE 1320
DENVER, CO 80237
303-649-1600
Fax: 303-649-1660
www.wcarusoassoc.com
• William J Caruso, President
(303) 649-1600
• Stephen K Young, Principal & Director Of Design
(303) 649-1600
Sports Service Founded:
1987
Consulting Services:
Independent consulting firm specializing in the planning and design of food/beverage facilities for the public assembly building industry.

8

manufacturers & retailers

Apparel Manufacturers

A-B EMBLEM, 1089
A4, 1089
ABC ACTIVEWEAR LLC, 1090
ACTION SPOT SPORTS, 1216
ADAMS USA, INC., 1093
ALL STAR PRO GOLF, INC., 1095
ALLIAN SNOWBOARDS, 1096
ALPS SPORTSWEAR MFG. COMPANY, INC., 1096
AMF BOWLING WORLDWIDE, 1098
AND 1, 1099
ANTIGUA GROUP, INC., 1099
ANVIL KNITWEAR INC., 1099
ASHWORTH, INC., 1100
ASICS AMERICA CORPORATION, 1100
ATHENA GOLF, 1101
ATHLETIC KNIT, 1101
AUDERO SPORTS SUPPLY, INC., 1101
AUTHENTIC FITNESS CORP., 1102
AVIA AMERICAN SPORTING GOODS, 1102
B' WARMER THERMAL PRODUCTS, 1102
BABY FANATIC, LLC, 1103
BALLGIRL ATHLETIC, 1104
BETHEL INTERNATIONAL, 1106
BIG BOY HEADGEAR, 1106
BIG TIME SPORTS APPAREL, INC., 1106
BLUE FISH, 1108
BLUEFLY, INC., 1220
BOAST, INC., 1108
BODY GLOVE INTERNATIONAL, INC., 1108
BODY WRAPPERS/ANGELO LUZIO, 1109
BOGNER, 1109
BRISTOL ATHLETIC, 1110
BRUTE WRESTLING, 1111
BUFFALO EXPORT, LLC, 1111
BVT PRODUCTS, LLC, 1112
CAMOFACE, 1113
CAMPUS OUTFITTERS, 1113
CASTAWAY COLLECTIBLES, 1114
CENTRALIA KNITTING MILLS, INC., 1115
CEO MANUFACTURERS, 1115
CLUBHOUSEKIT, 1117
CMS SPORTS, 1223
COBBLESTONES ACTIVEWEAR, 1117
COED SPORTSWEAR INC, 1117
COLLEGE CONCEPTS, LLC., 1223
COLLEGIATE LICENSING COMPANY, 778
COLLEGIATE PACIFIC, 1223
COLUMBIA SPORTSWEAR COMPANY, 1118
COMFYFEET, 1118
CROSS CREEK APPAREL, INC., 1121
CROWN PRINCE, INC., 1121
CUSTOM SPORTSWEAR CORP/DBA
    SPORTSWEAR UNLIMITED, 1121
DAEWOO INTERNATIONAL CORPORATION, 1224
DALCO ATHLETIC LETTERING, INC., 1123
DANSKIN, INC., 1123
DC SPORTS, INC., 1224
DEHEN, INC., 1124
DELTA APPAREL COMPANY, 1124
DESCENTE NORTH AMERICA, INC., 1124
DEVENTER'S CHEER & DANCEWEAR
    FACTORY, INC., 1124
DIVOTS SPORTSWEAR COMPANY, INC., 1124
DODGER INDUSTRIES INC., 1125
DUCK HEAD APPAREL COMPANY, 1125
DUNBROOKE, 1125
DYNASTY APPAREL INDUSTRIES, 1126
E.P. PRO, 1127
EARBAGS, 1127
EASTBAY, INC., 1226
EASTERN MOUNTAIN SPORTS, INC., 1226
EIGER SPORTSWEAR, INC., 1128
ELITE SPORTSWEAR, L.P., 1128
ELLESSE U.S.A., INC., 1128
EVERLAST WORLDWIDE, INC., 1130
FERA, 1132
FITNESS TECH INTERNATIONAL, 1133
FRANCO APPAREL GROUP, 1135
FUBU THE COLLECTION, 1135
FUN-TEES, INC., 1135
5TH AND OCEAN CLOTHING, 1089
G GIRL, 1228
G III SPORTS, 1135
GAIAM, 1136
GAME TIME LLC, 1136
GAMETIME PLUSH, 1136

GAMEWEAR, 1136
GARAN, INC., 1136
GEAR FOR SPORTS, 1137
GOTCHA INTERNATIONAL, 1140
GRAVEL GEAR SKATEBOARD CLOTHING, 1140
GTM SPORTSWEAR, 1140
GUESS? INC, 1140
GULBENKIAN SWIM, INC., 1141
HAGGAR CORPORATION, 1141
HANES BRANDS, 1142
HARPER INDUSTRIES INC, 1142
HARTWELL SPORTS, INC., 1143
HASCALL SPORTSWEAR, INC., 1143
HATCHERS MANUFACTURING INC., 1143
HEAD/PENN USA, 1143
HEADMASTER INC, 1143
HELLY HANSEN, (U.S.) INC., 1143
HI STYLE LETTERED SPORTSWEAR
    COMPANY, INC., 1144
HIND, INC., 1144
HOLLOWAY SPORTSWEAR, INC., 1145
HOLOUBEK, INC., 1145
INSPORT INTERNATIONAL, INC., 1148
INVENTION TECHNOLOGIES, 790
IRONMAN PROPERTIES, 1148
JACQUES MORET, 1149
JAMMIN APPAREL, 1149
JANTZEN, INC., 1149
JEFF HAMILTON COLLECTION, 1149
JEM SPORTSWEAR INC., 1149
JH DESIGN GROUP, 1149
K2 INC., 1151
KAEPA USA, INC., 1151
KAMPALA INDUSTRIES, 1151
KAPPA USA, 1151
KEY SPORTZ-WEAR, 1152
KING LOUIE INTERNATIONAL, INC., 1152
L&L GROUP/FOREMOST ATHLETIC APPAREL, 1153
L.A. GEAR, 1153
L.A.T SPORTSWEAR, 1154
LEGEND SPORTS, 1155
LEO'S DANCEWEAR, INC., 1155
LEON LEVIN, 1155
LIEBE ATHLETIC LETTERING, 1155
LILY'S OF BEVERLY HILLS, 1156
LIQUID BLUE, 1156
LITTLE KING MANUFACTURING COMPANY INC, 1156
LOCUST INC., 1157
LONE STAR ATHLETIC DESIGNS, INC., 1157
LOST ARROW CORPORATION, 1157
MARCIA ORIGINALS, 1159
MECA SPORTSWEAR, INC., 1161
MITCHELL & NESS NOSTALGIA COMPANY, 1163
MOPRO, 1164
MOTORSPORTS AUTHENTICS, 1164
MOVING COMFORT, INC., 1165
MTC MARKETING INC, 1165
NATIVE SUN SPORTSWEAR, 1166
NCED SAHARA, 1166
NEUEDGE SPORTSWEAR, 1167
NEW AGENDA BY PERRIN, 1167
NEW BALANCE ATHLETIC SHOE, INC., 1167
NEW ENGLAND CAP CO., 1167
NEWTEX USA, 1168
NIKE GOLF, 1168
NIKE, INC., 1168
NO FEAR, 1169
NORDICA USA, 1169
NORTH FACE, 1169
NUMBERALLS, 1170
NYX GOLF, 1170
O'NEILL, INC., 1170
OCEAN PACIFIC APPAREL CORPORATION, 1170
OLD TIME SPORTS, 1171
OMEGA GEAR INC, 1171
ONFIELD APPAREL, 1171
OT SPORTS, 1172
PEARL IZUMI (USA), 1173
PERFORMANCE SPORTS APPAREL, 1173
PHI-TEN USA INC, 1174
PINE SPORTS, 1174
POLO BY RALPH LAUREN, 1175
POMCHIES LLC, 1175
PONY INTERNATIONAL INC., 1175
PREMIUMWEAR, 1176
PRINCE SPORTS, 1177

PROGEAR, INC., 1178
PSC/ENCORE SELECT INC, 1178
PVH CORP., 1179
QUIKSILVER, 1179
RAMSTAR MILLS, INC., 1180
REEBOK APPAREL GROUP, 1181
REEBOK CANADA INC., 1181
REEBOK INTERNATIONAL LTD.-RETAIL, 1236
RENNOC, 1181
REYN SPOONER INC, 1182
RINGOR, 1182
RIPON ATHLETIC, 1183
ROCKY SHOES & BOOTS, INC., 1183
ROOTS APPAREL, 1183
RUGGERS RUGBY SUPPLY, 1184
RUSSELL ATHLETIC, 1184
SEVEN SONS AND COMPANY INC, 1187
SHYDA'S, 1188
SIDEOUT SPORT, INC., 1188
SIGNATURE DESIGNS, 1188
SMACK APPAREL, 1190
SOFFE COMPANY, INC., 1190
SOLAR TAN THRU SUITS, 1191
SOYAD BROTHERS TEXTILE CORPORATION, 1191
SPEEDLINE ATHLETIC WEAR, INC., 1192
SPORT FACE, 1192
SPORT OBERMEYER, LTD., 1192
SPORTIF U.S.A., 1193
SPORTS-FASHION, 1194
SPRY SPORTS USA, 1195
STAMINA PRODUCTS INC, 1196
SUNDAY PLAYERS, 1197
SURE FOOT CORPORATION, 1198
T3K INC, 1199
TEAM CALIBER, 1199
TEAMLINE, 1200
TEN SECONDS, 1200
TENACIOUS LTD, 1200
TEXTILE REVOLUTION, 1201
TKO SPORTS GROUP, INCORPORATED, 1202
TONIX, 1202
TOP OF THE WORLD CAPS, 1202
TOP-FLITE COMPANY, 1202
TOYQUEST, 1203
TRANS APPAREL, 1203
TROY CORPORATION, 1204
TURFER SPORTSWEAR, 1205
TYCA CORPORATION, 1205
TYR SPORT, INC., 1205
UMBRO U.S.A., 1205
V-FORMATION\THE NEXED LIFE, 1207
VF BRAND SOLUTIONS, 1207
VF CORPORATION, 1208
VITAL/PROMARX, 1208
VITRONIX PROMOTIONAL GROUP, 1208
WARPT INDUSTRIES, INC., 1209
WEEKEND EXERCISE COMPANY, 1209
WINDJAMMER INC., 1210
WINTERLAND PRODUCTIONS, 1210
WOMEN'S GOLF UNLIMITED, INC., 1211
WOOLRICH, INC., 1211
YARRINGTON MILLS CORPORATION, 1212
ZERO GLOVES, 1213
ZORREL INTERNATIONAL, 1213

Archery Manufacturers

BEAR ARCHERY, 1105
BROWNING, 1111
CINCINNATI GAMES, 1116
DARTON ARCHERY, 1224
EASTON TECHNICAL PRODUCTS, 1127
HOYT USA, 1146
SAUNDERS ARCHERY COMPANY, 1186
SPORTS SENSORS INC, 1194
TC SPORTS, 1199

Auto Sports Manufacturers

BUTLER BUILT MOTORSPORTS EQUIPMENT, 1112
PRO SPECIALTIES GROUP, 1177

Badminton Manufacturers

ADA TENNIS, 1093
CINCINNATI GAMES, 1116
CLASSIC SPORT COMPANIES INC, 1116

DUNLOP/MAXFLI/SLAZENGER GROUP
AMERICAS, 1126
FUNLINE MERCHANDISE COMPANY INC, 1135
GENERAL SPORTCRAFT COMPANY, LTD.,
1137
HL BADMINTON, 1144
INNOVA-CHAMPION DISCS INC, 1147
KING COBRA GAMING, 1152
MAXLINE EAGNAS, 1160
TC SPORTS, 1199
YONEX CORPORATION, 1212

Bag Manufacturers

ALGOMA NET COMPANY, 1094
AMF BOWLING WORLDWIDE, 1098
AMINCO INTERNATIONAL (USA)
INCORPORATED, 1098
ARI-MED PHARMACEUTICALS, 1100
BAG BOY COMPANY, 1103
BALAZS, INC., 1103
CLUB GLOVE, 1117
CONCEPT ONE ACCESSORIES, 1119
CREATIONS BY ALAN STUART, 1120
CREATIVE CUSTOM PRODUCTS, 1120
DIVERSA PRODUCTS GROUP, 1124
EASTPAK CORPORATION, 1127
EBONITE INTERNATIONAL, INC., 1127
FISHER ATHLETIC EQUIPMENT, INC., 1133
GERRY COSBY & COMPANY, INC., 1137
GOLD MEDAL RECREATIONAL PRODUCTS,
1138
GTM SPORTSWEAR, 1140
HARDMAN COMPANY, 1142
HARVEST VICTORY LTD, 1143
INNOVO GROUP INC., 1147
IRONMAN PROPERTIES, 1148
ITECH SPORT PRODUCTS, INC., 1149
K2 INC., 1151
KCA ENTERPRISES INC, 791
KING COBRA GAMING, 1152
LACROSSE UNLIMITED, 1154
LEGEND SPORTS, 1155
LOGO CHAIR, INC., 1157
M-F ATHLETIC COMPANY, 1158
MAXLINE EAGNAS, 1160
MELO CO., INC. AND XS BAGGAGE, 1162
MERCURY LUGGAGE MFG. CO., 1162
MOOSE MOUNTAIN SPORTS & GAMES LTD,
1164
NIKE GOLF, 1168
THE ORIGINAL BALL BAG LLC, 1171
PRINCE SPORTS, 1177
RINGOR, 1182
RYNO ATHLETICS, 1184
SEAGULL INTERNATIONAL, INC., 1186
SHERWOOD-DROLET CORPORATION, LTD.,
1188
STADIUM ROLL, 1195
WEST RIDGE DESIGNS, 1210
WOMEN'S GOLF UNLIMITED, INC., 1211

Ball Manufacturers

ADVANTAGE TENNIS SUPPLY, 1094
BADEN SPORTS, INC., 1103
BALLCO PRODUCTS, INC., 1104
C.N. IS BELIEVING, 1112
CLASSIC SPORT COMPANIES INC, 1116
CONTINENTAL SPORTS SUPPLY, INC., 1119
DC SPORTS, INC., 1224
EBONITE INTERNATIONAL, INC., 1127
FITBALL USA, 1133
GAME MASTER ATHLETIC COMPANY, 1136
GEORGI-SPORTS, 1137
HEDSTROM CORPORATION, 1143
JUGS INC/JKP SPORTS, 1151
K2 INC., 1151
KING COBRA GAMING, 1152
MARKWORT SPORTING GOODS COMPANY,
1159
MARTIN SPORTS, INC., 1159
MAXLINE EAGNAS, 1160
MELO CO., INC. AND XS BAGGAGE, 1162
MIKASA SPORTS USA, 1163
MOLTEN USA, INC., 1163
MYLEC, INC., 1166
NIKE GOLF, 1168
PADDLE COMPANY INC, 1172
R.A.M. SPORTS, INC., 1179

RAWLINGS SPORTING GOODS COMPANY
INC., 1180
REEBOK APPAREL GROUP, 1181
REGENT SPORTS CORPORATION, 1181
RICHARDSON SPORTS, INC., 1182
RIPKEN BASEBALL LLC, 1182
SALAUN SPORTS, INC., HENRI, 1185
SELECT SPORT AMERICA, 1187
SHIELD, 1188
SOCCER SPORT SUPPLY CO., INC., 1190
SPORTS TUTOR INC, 1194
SUPERIOR EXERCISE PRODUCTS, 1198
TOP-FLITE COMPANY, 1202
U.S. GAMES, INC., 1205
UMBRO U.S.A., 1205
WEST COAST NETTING, INC., 1209
WILSON SPORTING GOODS COMPANY, 1210
WOMEN'S GOLF UNLIMITED, INC., 1211

Baseball Manufacturers

A-B ASSOCIATES, INC., 1089
A.D. STARR, 1089
ABI TAPE PRODUCTS, 1090
ACADEMY SPORTS TURF, 1090
ADAMS USA, INC., 1093
ADASTRA DESIGNS INC., 1093
ADIRONDACK RUBBER PRODUCTS, 1093
ALCHESTER MILLS COMPANY, INC., 1094
ALGOMA NET COMPANY, 1094
ALL STAR KNITWEAR, INC., 1095
ALL STAR SPORTING GOODS, 1095
ALLESON ATHLETIC, DON, 1096
ALPHA SPORTSWEAR, INC., 1096
ALUMINUM ATHLETIC EQUIPMENT COMPANY
(AAE), 1096
AMAPRO SPORTING GOODS, INC., 1216
AMERICAN ATHLETIC SHOE COMPANY, 1097
AMERICAN NEEDLE & NOVELTY INC., 1098
AMERICAN PLAYGROUND CORPORATION,
1098
ANCHOR INDUSTRIES INC., 1099
APEX ATHLETIC EQUIPMENT INC., 1099
APSCO ENTERPRISES, 1099
ASICS AMERICA CORPORATION, 1100
ATHLETIC TRAINING EQUIPMENT
COMPANY/ATEC, 1101
AUGUSTA SPORTSWEAR, 1101
AUTOMATED BATTING CAGES
CORPORATION, 1102
AWARD DECALS, 1102
BADEN SPORTS, INC., 1103
BALLSTARS, 1104
BASEBALL FIT HITTING & PITCHING
ACADEMY, 1104
BEACON ATHLETICS, 1218
BETLIN INC., 1106
BLAZER MANUFACTURING, INC., 1108
BRONER, INC., 1220
BSN SPORTS, 1111
BUFFALO EXPORT, LLC, 1111
C & H BASEBALL, 1112
C.N. IS BELIEVING, 1112
CANAMER INT'L, LLC, 1113
CANNON SPORTS INC., 1222
CARRON NET COMPANY, INC., 1114
CENTRALIA KNITTING MILLS, INC., 1115
CHAMPION BALL COMPANY, 1115
CINCINNATI GAMES, 1116
CLASSIC SPORT COMPANIES INC, 1116
CLIFF KEEN ATHLETIC INC., 1116
CLUBHOUSEKIT, 1117
COLLEGIATE PACIFIC, 1223
CONVERSE, INC., 1223
COOPERSBURG SPORTS, 1223
COVERMASTER, INC., 1224
CROWN PRINCE, INC., 1121
CUSTOM DECAL & EMBLEMS, INC., 1121
CUSTOM SPORTSWEAR CORP/DBA
SPORTSWEAR UNLIMITED, 1121
CUTTERS GLOVES, 1122
CYRK, INC., 1122
DANDY PRODUCTS, INC., 1123
DC SPORTS, INC., 1224
DEBEER LACROSSE, 1123
DIAMOND SPORTS, 1124
DMI SPORTS INC, 1125
DODD & COMPANY, R.O., 1225
DODGER INDUSTRIES INC., 1125
DORFMAN-PACIFIC COMPANY, INC., 1125

DOUGLAS INDUSTRIES, INC., 1125
DR SPORTS EQUIPMENT, 1125
EASTON SPORTS, INC., 1127
EBBETS FIELD FLANNELS, 1127
EDDY BROS. HAT CO. INC., 1128
EMPIRE SPORTING GOODS MFG. COMPANY,
INC., 1129
EVERLAST WORLDWIDE, INC., 1130
FABRICATION ENTERPRISES, 1131
FIELDMASTER INFIELD GROOMER, 1132
FIRST SERVICE, 1133
FISHER ATHLETIC EQUIPMENT, INC., 1133
FOX RIVER MILLS, INC., 1135
FRANKLIN SPORTS, INC., 1135
FUNLINE MERCHANDISE COMPANY INC, 1135
GAME MASTER ATHLETIC COMPANY, 1136
GARED SPORTS, 1136
GENERAL SPORTCRAFT COMPANY, LTD.,
1137
GERRY COSBY & COMPANY, INC., 1137
GOAL SPORTING GOODS, INC., 1138
GOORIN BROS., INC., 1139
GRANADA PITCHING MACHINES, 1140
GUMRUNNERS, 1141
H E HODGE COMPANY, 1141
HAMMETT COMPANY, J.L., 1142
HANCO-M. HANDELSMAN COMPANY, 1142
HARVEST VICTORY LTD, 1143
HEAD DOWN TRAINERS.COM, 1143
HEAVY HITTER INDUSTRIES, INC., 1143
HI STYLE LETTERED SPORTSWEAR
COMPANY, INC., 1144
HILLERICH & BRADSBY COMPANY, INC., 1144
HOLE IN NONE, INC., 1145
INNOVA-CHAMPION DISCS INC, 1147
INTERNATIONAL SEAWAY TRADING
CORPORATION, 1148
IRON GLOVES INC, 1148
IRWIN SPORTS, 1148
J&B SALES, INC., 1149
JAYPRO SPORTS, LLC, 1149
JKP SPORTS, 1150
JUGS COMPANY, 1151
JUGS INC/JKP SPORTS, 1151
K2 INC., 1151
KEN YOUNG COMPANY, INC., 1152
KRYPTONICS U.S.A., 1153
L&L GROUP/FOREMOST ATHLETIC APPAREL,
1153
LEADER MANUFACTURING COMPANY, INC.,
1154
LETRELL SPORTS, 1155
LJO, INC., 1157
LOGAN INC., 1157
LONE STAR ATHLETIC DESIGNS, INC., 1157
LOUISVILLE SLUGGER, 1157
LOVING ASSOCIATES INC., 1157
MACNEILL ENGINEERING-CHAMPS GOLF
SPIKES, 1158
MAJESTIC ATHLETIC, 1159
MARKWORT SPORTING GOODS COMPANY,
1159
MARTIN SPORTS, INC., 1159
MARTIN STONE QUARRIES, 1160
MARTY GILMAN, INC. DBA GILMAN GEAR, 1160
MECA SPORTSWEAR, INC., 1161
MERRYGARDEN ATHLETIC WEAR, 1162
MINIHANE & ASSOCIATES, 1163
MIRACLE RECREATION EQUIPMENT
COMPANY, 1163
MOOSE MOUNTAIN SPORTS & GAMES LTD,
1164
MOPRO, 1164
MPC PROMOTIONS, 1165
N.J.P. SPORTS, INC., 1166
NATIONAL BATTING CAGES, INC, 1166
NEW ENGLAND CAP CO., 1167
NEW ERA CAP, CO, 1167
NIKE, INC., 1168
NOCONA ATHLETIC GOODS COMPANY, 1169
NOVA SPORTS USA, 1170
NUMBERALLS, 1170
OLD KENTUCKY LEATHERS, 1170
ONFIELD APPAREL, 1171
ONFIELD APPAREL GROUP, LLC HEADWARE
DIVISION, 1171
ORIGINAL MAPLE BAT COMPANY, 1171
PARAMOUNT HEADWEAR, INC., 1172
PARSONS OFFICIALS SUPPLIES, 1172

PARTAC PEAT CORPORATION/BEAM CLAY, 1173
PINCKARD BASEBALL GLOVES, 1174
PINNACLE SPORTS EQUIPMENT INC, 1174
PLASTIMAYD CORPORATION, 1174
POMCHIES LLC, 1175
POWER SOURCE SPORTS INC, 1176
PRO FEET, INC., 1177
PRO PERFORMANCE SPORTS, 1177
PRO-LINE CAP COMPANY, 1177
PROMARX/VITAL, 1178
PUMA NORTH AMERICA, 1178
PUTTERMAN ATHLETICS, 1178
PW ATHLETIC COMPANY, INC., 1179
RAINBOW IMPORTS, 1180
RAWLINGS SPORTING GOODS COMPANY INC., 1180
REEBOK INTERNATIONAL LTD.-RETAIL, 1236
REGENT SPORTS CORPORATION, 1181
RICHARDSON SPORTS, INC., 1182
RIDDELL, INC., 1182
RIPKEN BASEBALL LLC, 1182
ROYAL TEXTILE MILLS, INC., 1184
RUSSELL ATHLETIC, 1184
S.M. ATHLETICS, 1185
SARANAC GLOVE COMPANY, 1185
SAUCONY, 1185
SCHUTT SPORTS INC, 1186
SEAGULL INTERNATIONAL, INC., 1186
SHAMROCK SPORTS BAG COMPANY, 1187
SHOCK DOCTOR INC, 1188
SIPES COMPANY, INC., HOWE K., 1189
SOFFE COMPANY, INC., 1190
SOUTHERN BLEACHER COMPANY, INC., 1191
SOUTHLAND ATHLETIC MANUFACTURING COMPANY, 1191
SPECIALTY NETS, 1192
SPEEDLINE ATHLETIC WEAR, INC., 1192
SPORTCAP, INC., 1193
SPORTDECALS, 1193
SPORTIME, 1193
SPORTLINE INC, 1193
SPORTS BELLE INC., 1193
SPORTS SENSORS INC, 1194
SPORTS SUPPLY GROUP, 1194
SPORTS TUTOR INC, 1194
SPORTS WEST SALES, INC., 1194
SPRI PRODUCTS INC, 1194
STACKHOUSE ATHLETIC EQUIPMENT, INC., 1195
STALKER RADAR, 1196
STALL & DEAN MFG. COMPANY, INC., 1196
STANDARD MERCHANDISING COMPANY, 1196
SUPERIOR EXERCISE PRODUCTS, 1198
SWING AWAY SPORTS PRODUCTS, INC., 1198
T3K INC, 1199
TACKI-MAC GRIPS, INC., 1199
TC SPORTS, 1199
TEAMLINE, 1200
TIDE-RIDER, INC., 1201
TINY TOTS SPORTS, 1201
TOP-COMFO ATHLETIC SOX, INC., 1202
TRENWAY, LLC, 1203
TROPHY GLOVE COMPANY, 1204
TUF-WEAR, 1204
TURFER SPORTSWEAR, 1205
TWIN CITY KNITTING COMPANY, INC., 1205
U.S. GAMES, INC., 1205
ULTRA PLAY SYSTEMS, INC., 1205
UNIQUE SPORTS PRODUCTS, INC., 1206
VARSITY BRANDS, INC., 1207
VICTORY SPORTS NETS, 1208
VIKING TECHNOLOGY INC., 1208
VITRONIX PROMOTIONAL GROUP, 1208
WEST COAST NETTING, INC., 1209
WILSON SPORTING GOODS COMPANY, 1210
WINN, INC., 1210
WITTE GROUP, 1211
WITTEK GOLF SUPPLY COMPANY, 1211
ZERO GLOVES, 1213

Basketball Manufacturers

AALCO MANUFACTURING CO. INC., 1090
ADASTRA DESIGNS INC., 1093
ADP LEMCO, INC., 1093
ALCHESTER MILLS COMPANY, INC., 1094
ALGOMA NET COMPANY, 1094
ALL STAR KNITWEAR, INC., 1095
ALL STAR SPORTING GOODS, 1095

ALPHA SPORTSWEAR, INC., 1096
AMERICAN PLAYGROUND CORPORATION, 1098
AND 1, 1099
AWARD DECALS, 1102
B' WARMER THERMAL PRODUCTS, 1102
BADEN SPORTS, INC., 1103
BALLSTARS, 1104
BANKSHOT SPORTS ORGANIZATION, 1217
BISON, INC., 1107
BSN SPORTS, 1111
CANNON SPORTS INC., 1222
CHAMPION BALL COMPANY, 1115
CLASSIC SPORT COMPANIES INC, 1116
DANDY PRODUCTS, INC., 1123
DC SPORTS, INC., 1224
DOUGLAS INDUSTRIES, INC., 1125
E-Z GARD INDUSTRIES, 1126
ESCALADE SPORTS, 1130
EVERLAST WORLDWIDE, INC., 1130
FILA USA, 1132
FIRST SERVICE, 1133
FISHER ATHLETIC EQUIPMENT, INC., 1133
FRANKLIN SPORTS, INC., 1135
GAME MASTER ATHLETIC COMPANY, 1136
GAME TIME, INC., 1136
GARED SPORTS, 1136
GOALSETTER SYSTEMS, INC., 1138
GUMRUNNERS, 1141
H E HODGE COMPANY, 1141
HAMMETT COMPANY, J.L., 1142
HARVEST VICTORY LTD, 1143
HUFFY SPORTS COMPANY, 1146
HYDRA-RIB, INC., 1146
JAYPRO SPORTS, LLC, 1149
JJ ACCESSORIES, 1150
K2 INC., 1151
KORNEY BOARD AIDS, INC., 1153
LIFETIME, 1156
MARKWORT SPORTING GOODS COMPANY, 1159
MARTY GILMAN, INC. DBA GILMAN GEAR, 1160
MICHAEL JORDAN BRAND/NIKE, 1162
MIKASA SPORTS USA, 1163
MILLERBERND MANUFACTURING COMPANY, 1163
MIRACLE RECREATION EQUIPMENT COMPANY, 1163
MOOSE MOUNTAIN SPORTS & GAMES LTD, 1164
MOPRO, 1164
NUMBERALLS, 1170
THE ORIGINAL BALL BAG LLC, 1171
PERFORMANCE SPORTS SYSTEMS, INC., 1173
PORTER ATHLETIC EQUIPMENT COMPANY, 1175
PRO BOUND SPORTS, 1177
PW ATHLETIC COMPANY, INC., 1179
R.A.M. SPORTS, INC., 1179
RAINBOW IMPORTS, 1180
REGENT SPORTS CORPORATION, 1181
RICHARDSON SPORTS, INC., 1182
ROBBINS SPORTS SURFACES, 1183
SCHELDE NORTH AMERICA, LLC, 1186
SCHUTT SPORTS INC, 1186
SHOCK DOCTOR INC, 1188
SOL-EFFECT ENTERPRISE COMPANY LTD, 1191
SPORTSPLAY EQUIPMENT, INC., 1194
STACKHOUSE ATHLETIC EQUIPMENT, INC., 1195
SUPERIOR EXERCISE PRODUCTS, 1198
SWEDE-O, INC., 1198
TC SPORTS, 1199
TEAMLINE, 1200
TINY TOTS SPORTS, 1201
U.S. GAMES, INC., 1205
ULTRA PLAY SYSTEMS, INC., 1205
VICTORY SPORTS NETS, 1208
WEST COAST NETTING, INC., 1209

Billiards Manufacturers

DMI SPORTS INC, 1125
GLD PRODUCTS, 1138
HALEX, 1142
IMPERIAL INTERNATIONAL, 1147
KING COBRA GAMING, 1152
LION SPORTS INC, 1156

MOOSE MOUNTAIN SPORTS & GAMES LTD, 1164
MURREY INTERNATIONAL, 1165

Boat Manufacturers

ABSOLUTELY NEW, 1090
BOSTON WHALER, INC., 1109
BRUNSWICK CORPORATION, 1111
CANAMER INT'L, LLC, 1113
FROST MOTORSPORTS, LLC, 16
INVENTION TECHNOLOGIES, 790
JOHNSON OUTDOORS, 1150
KOOLATRON, 1153
MERCURY MARINE, 1162
NASH MANUFACTURING INC, 1166
NATIONAL MARINE MANUFACTURERS ASSOCIATION, 64
PELICAN INTERNATIONAL INC, 1173
SEVYLOR USA INC., 1187
SHAW & TENNEY, 1187
WATER SPORTS LLC, 1209

Bowling Manufacturers

ACE MITCHELL BOWLERS MART, 1091
ALL AMERICAN BOWLING PRO SHOP, 1095
AMF BOWLING WORLDWIDE, 1098
BEGNI'RS TO PRO'S, 1218
BOWLERSPARADISE.COM, 1220
BOWLINGSHIRT.COM, 1109
CLASSIC PRODUCTS, 1116
COLUMBIA 300, INC., 1118
EBONITE INTERNATIONAL, INC., 1127
MASTER INDUSTRIES WORLDWIDE, LLC, 1160
MELO CO., INC. AND XS BAGGAGE, 1162
MOOSE MOUNTAIN SPORTS & GAMES LTD, 1164
MURREY INTERNATIONAL, 1165
SATURNIAN 1 INC., 1185
SOYAD BROTHERS TEXTILE CORPORATION, 1191

Boxing Manufacturers

BALAZS, INC., 1103
CLUBHOUSEKIT, 1117
HEAVY HANDS, 1143
IMPACT TRAINING SYSTEMS INC, 1147
MARTY GILMAN, INC. DBA GILMAN GEAR, 1160
OMEGA GEAR INC, 1171
SHOCK DOCTOR INC, 1188
SUPERIOR EXERCISE PRODUCTS, 1198
TKO SPORTS GROUP, INCORPORATED, 1202

Climbing Manufacturers

BLACK DIAMOND EQUIPMENT, LTD., 1107
BOUNTY HUNTER, 1109
BREWER'S LEDGE, INC., 1110
ENTRE-PRISES USA, 1129
FILA USA, 1132
JEEP ELECTRONICS, 1149
LIBERTY MOUNTAIN SPORTS, LLC., 1155

Croquet Manufacturers

CINCINNATI GAMES, 1116
FUNLINE MERCHANDISE COMPANY INC, 1135
KING COBRA GAMING, 1152

Curling Manufacturers

REPUBLIC PACKAGING CORPORATION, 1181
TROPHY GLOVE COMPANY, 1204

Cycling Manufacturers

ABSOLUTELY NEW, 1090
ADVANTAGE SPORTS RACK, 1094
AMERICAN PLAYGROUND CORPORATION, 1098
AMERICAN RECREATION PRODUCTS, INC., 1098
ASA PRODUCTS, INC., 1100
BELL SPORTS INC., 1105
BIKE USA INC., 1106
BION INCORPORATED, 1107
BRUNSWICK BICYCLE DIVISION, 1111
BRUNSWICK CORPORATION, 1111

Eyewear Manufacturers

Facility Manufacturers

Glove Manufacturers

Golf Manufacturers

BOB WARD & SONS, INC., 1220
BOB'S STORES, INC., 1220
BON TON STORES, INC., 1220
BOSCOV'S DEPARTMENT STORES, 1220
BRANCH BROOK COMPANY, 1220
BREEZE SKI RENTAL, 1220
BROOKSTONE COMPANY, 1220
BUILDING #19, 1221
BUNKER JONES GOLF, INC, 1221
BURDINE'S, 1221
BUSYBODY, INC., 1221
BUY.COM SPORTS STORE, 1221
C M T SPECIALTY SPORTS, 1221
CABELA'S, 1221
CAMPING WORLD, 1221
CAMPMOR, INC., 1222
CANAL JEAN CO., 1222
CHAMPS SPORTS, 1222
CHICK'S SPORTING GOODS, INC., 1223
CHRISTY SPORTS/SPORTSTALKER, 1223
CITY SPORTS, 1223
CLARKS COMPANIES NA, 1223
COLOR INC., 1223
CRAZY SHIRTS, 1224
DALEBOOT U.S.A., 1123
DECATHLON USA SPORTS MEGASTORE, 1224
DICK'S SPORTING GOODS INC., 1224
DILLARD DEPARTMENT STORES, 1224
DIXIE SPORTING GOODS, 1224
DOLLAR GENERAL CORPORATION, 1225
DR. JAY'S, 1225
DUCKWALL ALCO STORES, INC., 1225
DUNHAM'S ATHLEISURE CORPORATION, 1225
DUNLAP CO., 1225
E & J LAWRENCE CORP/ JIMMY JAZZ, 1225
EARLY WINTERS, 1225
EASTBAY, INC., 1226
EASTERN MOUNTAIN SPORTS, INC., 1226
EB2B COMMERCE, INC., 1226
ECKERD DRUG, INC., 1226
EDDIE BAUER, INC., 1226
EDWIN WATT'S GOLF SHOP, INC., 1226
EFINGER SPORTING GOODS, 1226
EREHWON MOUNTAIN OUTFITTER, 1226
EXPRESS, 1226
F.A.O. SCHWARZ, 1226
FACTORY 2-U STORES, INC., 1226
FAMILY DOLLAR STORES, 1227
FAMOUS FOOTWEAR, 1227
FANBUZZ.COM, 1227
FANSEDGE.COM, 1227
FEDERATED DEPARTMENT STORES, INC., 1227
THE FEMALE ATHLETE, INC., 1239
FHI, INC./BUSY BODY, 1227
FINGERHUT COMPANIES, INC., 1227
FITNESS COMPANY, 1227
FITNESS SYSTEMS, 1227
FLAGHOUSE, 1227
FLEET FEET, INC., 1228
FOLLETT HIGHER EDUCATION GROUP, 1228
FOOT LOCKER, INC., 1228
FOOTACTION USA, 1228
FRED MEYER STORES, INC., 1228
GADZOOKS, 1228
GALYAN'S TRADING COMPANY, INC., 1228
GANDER MOUNTAIN COMPANY, 1228
GEAR.COM, INC., 1228
GENE TAYLOR'S SPORTSMEN SUPPLY, INC., 1228
GENESCO INC./JOURNEYS, 1229
GIGA, INC., 1229
GOLF MART/WORLDWIDE GOLF/ROGER DUNN GOLF, 1229
GOLF USA, 1229
GOLFERS' WAREHOUSE, INC., 1229
GOLFSMITH INTERNATIONAL, INC., 1229
GREAT OUTDOOR CLOTHING COMPANY, 1229
GREEN TOP SPORTING GOODS CORPORATION, 1229
GYM SOURCE, 1229
HAT WORLD/LIDS CORP., 1229
HEALTH FITNESS CORPORATION, 1230
HERB PHILIPSON'S, 1230
HIBBETT SPORTING GOODS, 1230
HOIGAARD'S INC., 1230
HUDSON TRAIL OUTFITTERS, LTD., 1230
ICONGO.COM, 1214
INTERACTIVECORP/HOME SHOPPING NETWORK, 1230

J. BAKER, INC., 1230
J.C. PENNEY CORPORATION, INC., 1230
JACOBSON STORES, 1230
JOHNNY MAC'S SPORTING GOODS, 1230
JUST FOR FEET, 1230
JUST SPORTS, 1230
JUSTHERSPORTS.COM, 1231
KERR DRUG INC., 1231
KESSLERS SPORT SHOP, INC., 1231
KID'S FOOT LOCKER, 1231
KITTERY TRADING POST, 1231
KLEIN'S ALL SPORT DISTRIBUTORS INC., 1231
KMART CORPORATION, 1231
KOHL'S DEPARTMENT STORES, 1231
L.L. BEAN, 1231
LADY FOOT LOCKER, 1231
LANDS' END, INC., 1154
LANGHORNE SKI & SPORT, 1231
LAS VEGAS GOLF & TENNIS, 1232
LAZARUS, 1232
LEGENDS SPORTING GOODS, 1232
LEVTRAN ENTERPRISES, 1232
LUCY.COM, 1232
MACY'S, CALIFORNIA, 1232
MARK'S OUTDOOR SPORTS, INC, 1232
MARSHALL'S, 1232
MARTIN'S GOLF & TENNIS, INC., 1232
MAURICE SPORTING GOODS, INC., 1232
MAY DEPARTMENT STORES COMPANY, THE, 1232
MC SPORTS, 1232
MCRAE'S, INC., 1233
MEIJER, INC., 1233
MERCHANT OF TENNIS, INC., 1233
MERVYN'S, 1233
MODELL'S SPORTING GOODS, 1233
NATION'S BEST SPORTS, 1233
NEVADA BOB'S INTERNATIONAL, INC., 1233
NEW YORK GOLF CENTER, INC., 1233
NINE WEST GROUP, INC., 1233
NORDICTRACK FITNESS STORES, 1233
NORTH FACE, 1234
ODD JOB TRADING, 1234
ODD LOTS/BIG LOTS, 1234
ORVIS COMPANY, 1234
OUTDOOR WORLD, INC., 1234
OVERTON'S, 1234
PAMIDA, INC., 1234
PARADIES SHOP/PGA TOUR SHOPS, 1234
PARAGON SPORTING GOODS CO. LLC, 1234
PAYLESS SHOESOURCE, INC., 1234
PEEBLES, INC., 1234
PERFORMANCE, INC./PERFORMANCE BICYCLE SHOP, 1234
PETER GLENN SKI & SPORT, 1234
POWERHOUSE GYMS, INTERNATIONAL, 1234
PRICE COSTCO WHOLESALE, 1235
PRO GOLF DISCOUNT, 1235
PRO GOLF OF AMERICA, 1235
PRO IMAGE, 1235
PUSH PEDAL PULL, 1235
QVC NETWORK, 1235
R.H. RENY, 1235
RACK ROOM SHOES, 1235
RAMSEY OUTDOOR STORE, 1235
RECREATIONAL EQUIPMENT, INC./REI, 1235
REDDEN MARINE SUPPLY, INC., 1235
REEBOK INTERNATIONAL LTD.-RETAIL, 1236
RICH'S DEPARTMENT STORES, INC., 1236
ROAD RUNNER SPORTS, 1236
ROCKVILLE WASHINGTON GOLF CENTER, 1236
ROGER DUNN GOLF SHOPS, 1236
RON JON SURF SHOP OF FLORIDA, 1236
SAKS INCORPORATED, 1236
SAM'S CLUB, 1236
SCHEEL'S ALL SPORTS, INC., 1236
SCHOTTENSTEIN DEPARTMENT STORES, 1236
SCHUYLKILL VALLEY SPORTS, 1236
SEARS, ROEBUCK & CO., 1236
SERVICE MERCHANDISE COMPANY, 1236
SHARPER IMAGE, 1237
SHOE CARNIVAL, 1237
SHOE CITY, 1237
SHOE SHOW, INC., 1237
SHOPKO STORES, INC., 1237
SKI MARKET LTD., 1237
SKI MERCHANDISING CORPORATION, 1237
SMITH'S FOOD & DRUG, 1237

SNYDER'S DRUG STORES, INC., 1237
SOCCERMALL.NET, 1190
SPORT CHALET, INC., 1237
SPORTING AUCTION, INC., 1238
SPORTMASTER INTERNATIONAL, 1238
SPORTS AUTHORITY, INC., 1193
SPORTS ENDEAVORS, INC., 1238
SPORTS SPECIALISTS, LTD., 1238
SPORTS WAREHOUSE, INC., 1238
SPORTS, INC., 1238
SPORTSMAN'S GUIDE, 1238
STAGE STORES, INC., 1238
STERNHEIMER BROS/DBA A&N STORES, 1238
SUPER SHOE STORES, 1238
SYMS, 1238
T.J. MAXX, 1239
TEAM ATHLETIC GOODS/TAG, INC., 1239
TGM FITNESS, INC., 1239
TRI-STATE DISTRIBUTOR, 1239
TRIPLE S SPORTING SUPPLIES, INC., 1239
TURNER'S OUTDOORSMAN, 1239
24 HOUR FITNESS CENTERS, 1215
U.S. CAVALRY, INC., 1239
U.S. FACTORY OUTLETS, INC., 1239
UP AGAINST THE WALL, 1240
VALUE CITY DEPARTMENT STORES, 1240
VANS, INC., 1240
VARIETY WHOLESALERS, 1240
VENATOR GROUP, INC., 1240
VIM, 1240
W.H. SMITH, 1240
WAL-MART STORES, INC., 1240
WALGREEN COMPANY, 1240
THE WALKING COMPANY, 1239
WASHINGTON GOLF CENTER, 1240
WAVE RIDING VEHICLES, 1241
WEST MARINE, 1241
WHOLESALE SPORTS OUTDOOR OUTFITTERS, 1241

Roller Hockey Manufacturers

DR SPORTS EQUIPMENT, 1125
RAGE CAGE, 1180

Roller Skating Manufacturers

SHANGHAI WINGO INTERNATIONAL, 1187
SOL-EFFECT ENTERPRISE COMPANY LTD, 1191

Rowing/Crew Manufacturers

BRINE, INC., 1110
CABLEFORM INC., 1113
DURHAM BOAT COMPANY, 1126
HUDSON BOAT WORKS INC., 1146
LITTLE RIVER MARINE COMPANY, 1156
NIELSEN-KELLERMAN, 1168
NIELSEN-KELLERMAN, 1168
PIANTEDOSI OARS, INC., 1174
POCOCK RACING SHELLS, 1175
POWERS EMBROIDERY/ CHENILLE, INC., USA, 1176
SCHOENBROD RACING SHELLS, 1186
SHAW & TENNEY, 1187
VANGUARD SAILBOATS, 1207
VESPOLI USA, INC., 1207

Rugby Manufacturers

ALGOMA NET COMPANY, 1094
ALUMINUM ATHLETIC EQUIPMENT COMPANY (AAE), 1096
BALLSTARS, 1104
BISON, INC., 1107
FUNLINE MERCHANDISE COMPANY INC, 1135
INNOVA-CHAMPION DISCS INC, 1147
MARTY GILMAN, INC. DBA GILMAN GEAR, 1160
MIKASA SPORTS USA, 1163
RUGBY IMPORTS, LTD., 1184
RUGGERS RUGBY SUPPLY, 1184
SPRY SPORTS USA, 1195

Running Apparel/Supplies Manufacturer

BARCO MEDIA, 1104
BION INCORPORATED, 1107
CARDIOSPORT, 1114

Turf Manufacturers

Uniform Manufacturers

Volleyball Manufacturers

Water Ski Manufacturers

BADEN SPORTS, INC., 1103
CONNELLY SKIS, 1119
HEDSTROM CORPORATION, 1143
HO SPORTS INC., 1145
NASH MANUFACTURING INC, 1166
O'BRIEN INTERNATIONAL, 1170
O'NEILL, INC., 1170
ORION ROPEWORKS, 1171
WEST RIDGE DESIGNS, 1210

Water Sports Manufacturers

COMFORT LINE PRODUCTS, 1118
EMPIRE SPORTS/SISCO SPORTS, 1129
FERNO PERFORMANCE POOLS, 1132
FROST MOTORSPORTS, LLC, 16
MIKASA SPORTS USA, 1163
MOREY BODYBOARDS, 1164
NASH MANUFACTURING INC, 1166
OMEGA MARINE PRODUCTS, 1171
ORION ROPEWORKS, 1171
PELICAN INTERNATIONAL INC, 1173
POOLMASTER, INC., 1175
REPUBLIC PACKAGING CORPORATION, 1181
SHAW & TENNEY, 1187
WELLINGTON LEISURE PRODUCTS, 1209

Weightlifting Manufacturers

ABSOLUTE FITNESS, INC,, 1090
CANNON SPORTS INC., 1222
CAP BARBELL, 1113
CERASPORT, 1115
FITNESS EM, LLC, 1133
FITTER INTERNATIONAL INC, 1133
GEAR PRO-TEC, 1137
GRIPWEIGHTS, 1140
HARBINGER, 1142
HEAVY HANDS, 1143
HOIST FITNESS SYSTEMS, 1145
HORIZON FITNESS, 1145
IMPACT TRAINING SYSTEMS INC, 1147
IMPEX INC, 1147
IRON GLOVES INC, 1148
JUMP ROPE TECH INC, 1151
KAMPALA INDUSTRIES, 1151
LION SPORTS INC, 1156
MEDI-DYNE HEALTHCARE PRODUCTS LTD, 1161
OMEGA GEAR INC, 1171
SMC INNOVATIONS, 1190
SPORTLINE INC, 1193
SPORTS SPECIFIC SCIENCES, 1215
SPRI PRODUCTS INC, 1194
STAMINA PRODUCTS INC, 1196
SUPERIOR EXERCISE PRODUCTS, 1198
TKO SPORTS GROUP, INCORPORATED, 1202

TROPHY GLOVE COMPANY, 1204

Windsurfing Equipment Manufacturers

BIC SPORT NORTH AMERICA, 1106
CONCEPT II, INC., 1118
NORTH SPORTS, INC., 1169

Wrestling Manufacturers

ACTION ATHLETIC EQUIPMENT, 1092
ADIDAS WRESTLING, 1093
ALGOMA NET COMPANY, 1094
BRUTE WRESTLING, 1111
CANNON SPORTS INC., 1222
CLUBHOUSEKIT, 1117
E-Z GARD INDUSTRIES, 1126
FISHER ATHLETIC EQUIPMENT, INC., 1133
IMPACT TRAINING SYSTEMS INC, 1147
MATMAN WRESTLING COMPANY, 1160
REPUBLIC PACKAGING CORPORATION, 1181
RESILITE SPORTS PRODUCTS, INC., 1181
SHOCK DOCTOR INC, 1188
SMC INNOVATIONS, 1190
SUPERIOR EXERCISE PRODUCTS, 1198
TC SPORTS, 1199

Equipment & Product Manufacturers

5TH AND OCEAN CLOTHING
160 DELAWARE AVENUE
BUFFALO, NY 14202
716-604-9000
Fax: 716-604-9299
info@5thocean.com
www.5thocean.com
• Alex Leiter, President / Chief Executive
Officer
alex@5thocean.com
• Luis Leiter, Vice President
luisl@5thocean.com
• Ralph Garcia, Chief Operations Officer
ralphg@5thocean.com
Products:
Manufacturers clothing for water sports.

600 RACING, INC.
5245 NC HIGHWAY 49 S
HARRISBURG, NC 28075
704-455-3896
Fax: 704-455-3820
www.uslegendcars.com
• GE Chapman, General Manager
(704) 455-3896
gechapman@uslegendcars.com
• Joe Maylish, 600 West Manager
(702) 643-4386
jmaylish@600racing.com
• James Michael Spink, 600 Kentucky
Manager
(859) 567-4423
jspink@600racing.com
• Kris Perry, Purchasing
(704) 455-3896
kperry@600racing.com
• Haven Kerchner, Communications
Manager/Magazine
(704) 455-3896
hkerchner@600racing.com
• Foxworthy, Parts
(704) 455-1424
jfoxworthy@600racing.com
Nature of Sports Service:
The largest manufacturer of race cars in the
world, and is the exclusive producer of the
Legends Car, Bandolero and Thunder
Roadsters.
Year Founded:
1992

A&H ATHLETIC FLOOR SERVICES, INC.
PO BOX 55502
INDIANAPOLIS, IN 46205
317-598-0159
Fax: 317-845-9139
• Byron Haflich, President/Owner
• James Taylor, Product Manager
Nature of Service:
Sanding & Finishing; Screening &
Recoating; Logos, Lettering, Graphics, &
Emblems; Court Lining; Repair and/or
Replacement; TyKote Dustless Refinishing
System; and Traditional Refinishing System
Year Founded:
1988
Products:
Basic Coatings, Court Clean Maintenance
Systems, Rubbermaid Microfiber Dust
Systems, Ulti Mats Weight Room Flooring,
Humane Rubber Floors, Action Wood Floor
Systems, Action Herculan Synthetic Floors.

A-B ASSOCIATES, INC.
12300 OLD TESSON ROAD
SUITE 300-E
SAINT LOUIS, MO 63128
314-842-1819
800-783-2358
Fax: 314-842-1526
• Rob Amelung, Marketing
Products:
General Sporting Goods.

A-B EMBLEM
291 MERRIMON AVENUE
PO BOX 695
WEAVERVILLE, NC 28787
828-645-3015
800-438-4285
Fax: 800-355-3581
sales@abemblem.com
www.abemblem.com
• Bernie Conrad, President
berniec@abemblem.com
• Andrew Nagle, EVP
andrewn@abemblem.com
• Jackie Reece, Accounting Executive
(888) 438-4024
jackier@abemblem.com
• Leisa Williams, Accounting Executive
Products:
NASA Patches; American Flags; Mouse
Flags; Corporate Use; Scout Patches;
Fotografick Emblems; Soccer Patches; Cap
Collection; Key Fobs; Municipal Emblems;
Youth Patches; Pins & Jewelry; Blazer
Crests; Needlecut Patches; Soccer Pins;
Luggage Tags; Appliques
Clients:
NASA; Boy Scout Troops; and Bowling
Clubs

A-TURF
505 AERO DRIVE
PO BOX 157
CHEEKTOWAGA, NY 14225
716-204-0748
888-777-6910
Fax: 716-204-0189
info@aturf.com
www.aturf.com
• Jim Dobmeier, President & Founder
Products:
Artificial turf for sports facilities.

A.D. STARR
61 S 4TH STREET
PITTSBURGH, PA 15219
412-488-7233
800-487-2448
Fax: 800-487-2448
info@adstarr.com
www.adstarr.com
Products:
Baseballs; Softballs; Batting Helmets;
Uniforms; Catcher's Gear; Women's
Softball; Field Equipment; Umpire Gear; Bas
& Accessories; Pitching Machines; Bats &
Training Aids; Gloves & Mitts; and Safety &
First-aid
Clients:
BPA Baseball; National Club Baseball
Association; USSSA Baseball; Pnoy
Baseball; Dixie Baseball & Softball; Little
League Baseball & Softball; Cal Ripken &
Babe Ruth Baseball; Dizzy Dean Baseball;
American Fastpitch Association; NASI;
USSSA Slow & Fast Pitch; NFHS Baseball
Fast Pitch Softball; American Legion

Baseball; Adult & Federation Leagues;
Palamino Leagues; NSA Slow & Fast Pitch
Softball

A4
6199 MALBURG WAY
VERNON, CA 90058
323-585-0550
888-464-3824
Fax: 323-583-6565
info@a4.com
www.a4.com
• Mark Mertens, Owner
(323) 585-0550
mark@a4.com
• Mike Owings, Vice President Sales
(323) 585-0550
mike@a4.com
Services:
Designing and manufacturing of high quality
athletic gear for onfield and Retail Sales.
Performance gear, PE uniforms, Polos,
Warm-Ups and Bags.
Sports:
Baseball, softball, basketball, football,
soccer, lacrosse, track & field.
Year Founded:
1969
Clients:
6,500 Professional, College & High School
Teams, Chick's, Sports Chalet, M C Sports,
Pomida, 24 Hour Fitness and Hillfits.

AAA FLAG & BANNER
8955 NATIONAL BOULEVARD
LOS ANGELES, CA 90034
310-836-3200
855-218-3300
Fax: 310-836-7253
sales@aaaflag.com
www.aaaflag.com
• Jay Jacoby, Representative
Nature of Services:
AAA Flag & Banner manufacturers and
installs custom displays, banners and flags
for Major Sporting Events and Fortune 500
Companies throughout the United
States-services include concept creation,
banner, sign and flag design, logos and
corporate identity, layout and composition,
marketing materials and event pageantry
consultation.

AACER FLOORING
970 OGDEN ROAD
PO BOX 151
PESHTIGO, WI 54157
715-582-1181
877-582-1181
Fax: 715-582-1182
www.aacerflooring.com
• Kevin Barker, Vice President of Marketing
kbarker@aacerflooring.com
• Nick Larson, MidWestern Regional
Distribution Sales
nickl@aacerflooring.com
• Kelly Kahara, Customer Service Manager
kellyk@aacerflooring.com
• Laurn Fontaine, Customer Service
Representative
laurnf@aacerflooring.com
• Laura Thomson, Human Resource
Manager
laurat@aacerflooring.com
• Koko Thaw, International Sales Manager
kokot@aacerflooring.com
• Jason Nieminksi, Technical Manager

jnieminski@aacerflooring.com
• Kevin Barker, VP of Sales & Marketing
kbarker@aacerflooring.com
Sports Products:
Performance sports flooring systems -
maple & synthetic.

AALCO MANUFACTURING CO. INC.
1650 AVENUE H
SAINT LOUIS, MO 63125
314-544-4300
800-537-1259
Fax: 314-544-2386
www.aalcomfg.com
• Richard Pohrer, President
Products:
Basketball and Volleyball Curtains
Brands:
Basketball: Wall Swing-up: 24WS; Side
Fold: 22 SF; Wall Stationary: 20SW; Series
100 Center Strut; Roll Fold: Series 2000
Solo-Glide; Series 300 Clear View; Series
200 Double Drop Volleyball: Swingline
Ceiling Suspended Volleyball; Spikeline
System; Power Post Gold System: APPS;
Aluminum Standards: PV-35A; Curtains:
Top Roll Divider Curtain: TRU-110; Fold-up
Divider Curtain: VSCM; Slope Fold Divider
Curtain:VSCM-C; Radius Fold-Up Divider
Curtain: VSCM-R; Walk Draw Curtain:WDC

AARDVARK MASCOTS
1199 CHERRYBROOKE COMMONS
SAN LEANDRO, CA 94578
818-508-7900
aardvarkmascots@gmail.com
www.aardvarkmascots.com
• Cindy Maniates, Costume Artist
(818) 508-7900
aardvarkmascots@gmail.com
Products:
Custom made mascot costumes since 1985.

ABC ACTIVEWEAR LLC
16112 NW 13TH AVENUE
SUITE A
MIAMI, FL 33169
305-625-5778
Fax: 305-622-2872
Products:
Activewear; Swimwear

ABC FLAG MANUFACTURING CO.
212 S MAIN STREET
FORT WORTH, TX 76104
817-335-2548
800-288-9625
Fax: 817-877-1610
www.lonestarbannersandflags.com
• Mike Tettleton, President
• Mark Buechele, General Manager
(817) 335-2548
markb@abcflag.com
Products:
Flags, banners (U.S., state, custom, sports).
Distributor and installer of flag poles.

ABI TAPE PRODUCTS
105 WHITTENDALE DRIVE
MOORESTOWN, NJ 8507
856-778-0700
Fax: 888-224-6325
info@abitape.com
www.abitape.com
• Roger S Marcus, Chairman / Chief
Executive Officer

• Richard G Marcus, President / Chief
Operating Officer
• Willaim M Marcus, EVP/Treasurer
• Howard N. Feist III, Chief Financial Officer
/ Finance VP
Products:
Tape Products
Brands:
Ideal Tape Co., Inc.; Transfer Rite; Protect
Rite; Autowrap

ABSOLUTE FITNESS, INC,
149 INTERLOCHEN DRIVE NE
ATLANTA, GA 30342-3711
770-933-8987
Fax: 770-980-9751
• Jeff Kushner, Marketing Director
• Tami Roe, President
Products:
Aquatic Exercise Equipment, Balance
Training Equipment, Barbells,
Cable-Attached Bars, Curling Bars, Olympic
Bars, Power Bars, Specialty Bars, Standard
Weight Bars, Bicycles, Stationary, Body
Composition Analyzers, Skinfold Calipers,
Boxes, Breathing Aids, Conditioning Charts,
Injury Treatment Charts, Nutrition Charts,
Plyometrics Charts, Rehabilitation Charts,
Speed Charts, Strength Charts, Computer
Systems/Software for Athletic Equipment,
Fitness Assessment, and Nutrition,
Conditioning Aids, Conditioning Certification
Programs, Cord Devices, Dumbbells, Power
Hooks, Pro-Style, Educational Books &
Videos, Elevated Shoes, Equipment Storage
Sys

ABSOLUTELY NEW
650 TOWNSEND STREET
SUITE 475
SAN FRANCISCO, CA 94103
415-865-6200
888-946-8368
800-627-5382
Fax: 415-865-6210
• Richard S. Donat, Chief Executive Officer
• Henry Lo, Chief Financial Officer
• Bill Feroe, Executive Vice President
• Steve Lee, Manufacturing Director
Products:
Portable Grills; Trolley; Kitchen Wares;
Grassland Gears; Food Supplements;
Cleaning Materials; Lightings; Christmas
Decorations
Brands:
Porta-Q; Brief Tote, Tuff Tote, Micro Tote,
Shop Tote, Shop Tote Tinted, Travel Tote,
Classic Cart Tote, Click Tote; Roasting
Wand, Shrimp Sheller; Compact Utility
Chair, Garden Tote; First Call; X-Tendo Mitt,
Bucket Wringer, Deco Fresh Brush, Way
Beyond Lint; Solar Camping Light, Areama
Pipe Tool, Candle Cuts; Wonderland Box,
Auto Wreath, Car Get-Ups, Magic Santa
Tracks, Pop-Down Christmas Tree, Magic
Fold Box

ABU GARCIA, INC.
1900 18TH STREET
SPIRIT LAKE, IA 51360
800-228-4272
abugarcia@purefishing.com
www.abu-garcia.com
Products:
Accessories, Baitcast Reels,
Spinning-Spincast Reels, Combos, Clothing
Brands:

Power Handle Accessory, Reel Lube;
Ambassadeur Morrum, Ambassadeur 2005
Low-Profile, Ambassadeur 4007 Low-Profile,
Ambassadeur 5600WS, Ambassadeur D5
Series, Ambassadeur D6 Series,
Ambassadeur C3 Series, Ambassadeur Big
Game Collection, Ambassadeur Trophy
Series, Ambassadeur 1003 Low-Profile,
Ambassadeur B Series, Ambassadeur B
Series; Abumatic 1276, Abumatic
Underspin, Cardinal 500 Series, Cardinal
300 Series, Cardinal 100 Series, Cardinal
170 Saltwater Series, Cardinal 170
Saltwater Series, Cardinal 770 Series,
Cardinal 770 Series; Abumatic Combo,
Agenda Combo, Ambassadeur TGC
Baitcast Combo, Ambassadeur 1003
Low-Profile Combo, Ambassadeur

ACADEMY SPORTS TURF
3740 S JASON STREET
ENGLEWOOD, CO 80110
800-372-6639
Fax: 303-762-8190
steve@academysportsturf.com
www.academysportsturf.com
• Steve Jewell, Marketing
steve@academysportsturf.com
• Paul Kelley, Director
steve@academysportsturf.com
Products:
Turf
Brands:
Academy Sports Turf

ACCELERATED CARE PLUS, LLC
4850 JOULE STREET
SUITE A-1
RENO, NV 89502
775-685-4000
800-350-1100
Fax: 775-685-4013
customersupport@acplus.com
www.acplus.com
• John Beach, Chief Executive Officer
johnbeach@acplus.com
• Chris Castel, President
chriscastel@acplus.com
• Richard Taylor, Chief Operating Officer
richardtaylor@acplus.com
• John Beach, Chief Executive Officer
• Antony Ricketts, Chief Financial Officer
• Debbie Koepsel, Chief Operating Officer
• Richard Taylor, Chief Sales Officer
• Tony Taylor, Chief Marketing Officer
• Curtis Beach, Marketing Director
curtisbeach@acplus.com
• Joe Cummings, Marketing Manager
joecummings@acplus.com
Products:
Electrical Stimulation Products, Ultrasound
Products, Shortwave Diathermy, Infection
Control Supplies, Electrotherapy Supplies
Brands:
OMNISTIM 500A, OMNISTIMr 500B,
OMNISTIM FX2, OMNISTIMr FX2 GOLD,
OMNISTIMr FX2 PRO, OMNISTIM FX2
PRO, OMNISOUND 3000E, OMNISOUND
3000C, SHORTWAVE DIATHERMY
MEGAPULSE II, Delta T Automatic Tissue
Temperature Dose Control, Pulsed
Shortwave Diathermy, GDWP - Germicidal
Disposable Wipe (50/bx), UBF-0406B -
ProBarrier Film (600ft/rl), 20303 - Ultrasound
Probe Sheaths (75/bx), 20325 - Ultrasound
Probe Sheaths (25/bx), 10060-25 - Elastic
Bands (25/bg), SC100 - Megapulse
Applicator Head Cover (100/bx), 3X004 -

Poly Tubing (500ft/rl), ERC2X2, ERC2X4, ERC3X5, ERC4X4, ULTRASOUND GEL

ACCESSORY TIME
3500 SUNSET AVENUE
OCEAN, NJ 7712
732-918-2201
800-826-1355
Fax: 732-918-2203
ikegemal@aol.com
Products:
Watches, Clocks, Watchcases

ACCUFITNESS, LLC
PO BOX 4411
GREENWOOD VILLAGE, CO 80155-4411
303-799-4721
800-866-2727
Fax: 303-799-4778
info@accufitness.com
www.accufitness.com
• Shawn M Gillespie, President
info@accufitness.com
• Carol Fitzgerald, Customer Service
Representative
Products:
Accu-Measure Fitness 3000 Personal Body
Fat Tester, FatTrack Gold Digital Body Fat
Caliper, FatTrack Pro Digital Body Fat
Management System, MYOTape - Body
Tape Measure, HYDRYX - Hardcore
workout towel, Body Tracker - Body
composition tracking software, My Workout
Trainer - Body composition and workout
tracking software, BOA - High speed
professional jump ropes, Bowflex - Heart
rate monitors, Bowflex
Description:
AccuFitness is a worldwide leader in
consumer fitness and body measurement
devices along with other outstanding fitness
products. Likewise we provide industry
leading software packages designed to help
you reach and maintain your fitness goals!
Try My Workout Trainer to accurately track
your workouts, macro-nutrition information,
and body composition measurements &
calculations. If you want to focus solely on
tracking body composition and conditioning
information only - Body tracker software is
the ticket. AccuFitness products are
designed and selected to help you burn
more fat and build cardiovascular strength
during your favorite physical a
Our products are ideal for:
Fitness enthusiasts who want to maximize
fat loss and cardiovascular benefits;
Individuals who are just starting to exercise
or fat burning regimen; Military personnel
maintaining physical readiness; Figure and
Bodybuilding competitors who want to
maintain peak competition form; Those who
want to improve their current health &
fitness status; People who want to monitor
their decrease in body fat and/or increase in
lean muscle mass.
Brands:
Accu-Measure Fitness 3000 Personal Body
Fat Tester, FatTrack GOLD Digital Body Fat
Caliper with MyoTape, Accu-Measure FitKid
Caliper for Children, FatTrack PRO DIGITAL
Body Fat Measurement System, New
MyoTape Body Tape Measure, MyoTape D,
HYDRYX Hard-Core

ACCUSPLIT
3090 INDEPENDENCE DRIVE
SUITE 150
LIVEMORE, CA 94551
925-226-0888
800-965-2008
800-935-1996
Fax: 925-463-0147
sales@accusplit.com
www.accusplit.com
• W. Ron Sutton, Founder
(925) 226-0888
ron@accusplit.com
• Yasuji Kato, Partner
• Yoshiro Hatano, Partner
• W. Ron Sutton, Founder
Products:
Pedometers, Sportswatches-Digital, Timers,
Time-Out Clocks.
Year Founded:
1972
Brands:
AAS420 Steps to Healthy Bones, AAS440
The Step Diet Program, AAS475 Stepping
Out with Stanford, AAS411 Walk Yourself
Thin, AAS416 Walk with Byron Nelson,
AAS480 Tom Lehnan's Family Golf,
AAS413 Walk With Notah, AAS410
Pedometer Walking, Accusplit Eagle,
Accusplit X, Accusplit 10K-A-Day, Accusplit
Healthengine, Accusplit Alliance, Accusplit
Survivor, Accusplit Pro Survivor, Gra Lab.

ACE MITCHELL BOWLERS MART
1946 S ARLINGTON STREET
PO BOX 3168
CUYAHOGA FALLS, OH 44223
330-920-6200
800-321-0309
Fax: 330-785-1060
dbehra@acemitchell.com
www.acemitchell.com
• Dave Grau, Owner
dgrau@acemitchell.com
• Todd Williams, Vice President
(800) 321-0309
twilliams@acemitchell.com
Products:
Bags, Balls, Birthday Party Supplies,
Bowlers Aids and Towels, Bowlers Tape and
Shur Hooks, Gloves and Supports, Grips,
Lane Machines and Parts, Lane Supplies,
Pinsetter Parts, Pro shop supplies, Rental
Shoes/House Balls, Shoes
Brands:
Thunder Alley

ACME WHISTLES/HIATT - THOMPSON CORPORATION
7200 W 66TH STREET
BEDFORD PARK, IL 60638
724-932-2177
Fax: 724-932-2166
sales@combinedsystems.com
www.combinedsystems.com
• Charles Thompson, Director
(708) 496-8595
htsb@sbcglobal.net
• Dawn Thompson, President
(708) 496-8595
Products:
Handcuffs, Chainwork, Transportation
Security, Training Equipment and
Accessories, Legcuffs
Year Founded:
1988

ACO POLYMER PRODUCTS, INC.
12080 RAVENNA ROAD
PO BOX 245
CHARDON, OH 44024
440-285-7000
800-543-4764
Fax: 440-285-7005
info@acousa.com
www.acousa.com
• Josef-Severin Ahlmann, Founder
info@acousa.com
• Hans-Julius Ahlmann, Managing Partner
info@acousa.com
Products:
Drainage Systems for Sports Tracks, Elastic
Railing, Elastic Curb, Sand Traps and Water
Jumps.
Brands:
PowerDrain S100K/S300K, KlassikDrain
K100S/KS100S, FlowDrain FG100/FG200,
Fastform FF300/FF600, SlabDrain,
ChemDrain, Brickslot, Membrane Drain,
MiniKlassik, Cross Sidewalk Drain, Series
600 Catch Basins, Fiberglass Catch Basins,
Sump Boxes, System 1000 Track Trench
Drainage, System 2000 Track Trench
Drainage, System 3000 Track Trench
Drainage, System 4000 Open Trench
Drainage, System 6000 Synthetic Turf
Trench Drainage, System 7000 Sandpit and
Curb System, System 8000 Steeple Chase
Jumps, System 9000 Bleacher System,
HomeDrain, Raindrain, Oil/Water/Sand
Separator, Spill Containment Curbs, AT200
Tunnel, AT500 Tunnel, Amphibian Tunnel
Entrance,

ACOR, INC.
18530 S MILES PARKWAY
CLEVELAND, OH 44128
216-662-4500
800-237-2267
Fax: 216-662-4547
cs@acor.com
www.acor.com
• Greg Alaimo, CP, Co-Owner/Founder
• Jeffrey Alaimo, CPO, Co-Owner/Founder
Products:
Shoes, Orthotic Product Lines, Fabricating
Materials, Accessories, Custom Footwear
Brands:
Spring Street, Activz, Broadway, Comfort
Street, River Walk, Quikfit, QuikFormables,
Sole Defense, KidFits, Rigids, Modification
Components, Top Covers

ACORN PRODUCTS COMPANY, INC.
2 CEDAR STREET
PO BOX 1190
LEWISTON, ME 04240-7874
207-786-3526
800-872-2676
Fax: 800-280-4127
www.acornearth.com
• John Donnelly, President
• David K. Quinn, Founder & Chief
Executive Officer
• John Donnelly, President
Products:
Comfort Footwear Products, Sheepskin
Boots, Sheepskin Slippers and Accessories
Brands:
Toggle Slipper, Highlander, Textured Moc,
Polar Moc, Polar Pair, Summit Slipper,
Slipper Sock, Boiled Wool Moc, Euro Clog,
Euro Closed Clog, Easy Does It, Big Easy,
Big Easy Sheepskin, Dakota Moc, Ultra

Moc, Lifetime Toester, Sheepskin Romeo, Sheepskin Bootie, Sheep-On, Sheepskin Venetian Moc, Sheepskin Woven Moc, Sheepskin Penny Moc, Short Boot, Tall Boot, Felt Dorm Scuff, Felt Dorm Bootie, Cool Down, Chill Out, Unwind, Take Five, Sundal Thong, Sundal Slide, Spa Mule, Knotty Girl, Travel Slipper, Den Slipper, Hampton, Cashmere Ballerina, Cashmere Mule, Cozy Scuff, Ocelot Scuff

ACOUSTICAL INTERIORS
2247 TOMLYN STREET
RICHMOND, VA 23230-3334
804-342-2900
888-765-2900
Fax: 804-342-1107
info@acousticsfirst.com
www.acousticsfirst.com
• Nick Colleran, Principal
Products:
Ceiling Treatments, Wall Treatments, Absorbers: Foam, Glass Fiber, Fabric, Diffusers, Barriers, Industrial, Vibration
Brands:
Cloudscape Hanging Baffles, Cloudscape Banners, FireFlex Baffle, Double Duty Diffuser, Art Diffusors, Respond & Sonora, Quiet Louver, Pyramid Acoustical Foam Panel, Geometrix, Bermuda Triangle Traps, Polyurethane Pyramid, CuttingWedge, Fireproof (Class 1) Wall Panels, Hanging Baffles, Sound Cylinder, Respond & SonoraT Wall Panels & Ceiling Treatment, Sound Channels, Guilford of MainerFR701, Quiet Louver Panels, Cloudscape Ceiling Banners & Baffles, Double Duty Diffuser, Art Diffusors, Pyramidal Diffuser, QuadraPyramid, BlockAid Vinyl Sound Barrier, Foam/Barrier Composites, Blankets & Enclosures

ACT ONE COMMUNICATIONS
314 PASEO TESORO
WALNUT CREEK, CA 92812
909-595-6818
888-228-6631
Fax: 909-595-7388
• Daniel Shih, President
danshih@aol.com
• Christine Lien, Vice President
• Jason Chin, Sales
• Ethan Lin, Marketing Manager
Products:
LED Video Displays and Screens, LED Fascia Displays, LED Architectural Lighting
Brands:
Act One

ACTION ATHLETIC EQUIPMENT
3144 21ST STREET
ZION, IL 60099-1426
847-746-2042
Fax: 847-746-2071
• Tim Higgins, Production Manager
matman@ix.netcom.com
• Joe Higgins, Founder
• Jane Craig, Sales Manager
Products:
General Sports Equipment.

ACTION FLOOR SYSTEMS, LLC
4781 N US HIGHWAY 51
MERCER, WI 54547-9708
715-476-3512
800-746-3512
Fax: 715-476-3585

info@actionfloors.com
www.actionfloors.com
• Gary Stephenson, President
info@actionfloors.com
• Tom Abendroth, Vice President
• Tom Mitchell, General Manager
(410) 838-5318
• Dan Corullo, Secretary
Products:
Premium Sports Floor Systems and Residential Floors
Brands:
ProAction Thrust, ProAction Flex, ChannelFlex Plus, ChannelFlex II, ChannelFlex, ActionThrust I, ActionThrust II, Concorde, Concorde II, Vari-Flex, Vari-Flex Plus Action Interloc I, Action Interloc II, Action Interloc II Plus, Anchored VariFlex, Anchored VariFlex Plus, ActionCush I, ActionCush II, ActionCush II Plus, Anchored ActionCush II, Anchored ActionCush II Plus ActionLoc, ActionFast, ActionFlex, ActionTech I, ActionChannel I, ActionChannel II, Action Fixed-Sleeper, ActionWood, ActionWood Plus, ActionWood Flex, Herculan Synthetic, Action ReFlex, Maple, Cherry, Beech, Birch, Ash

ACTION GRAPHIX
2623 COMMERCE DRIVE
JONESBORO, AR 72401
870-931-7440
800-762-9807
Fax: 870-931-7528
www.actiongraphix.com
• Blant Hurt, President
(870) 931-7440
Products:
Provides graphic images for a variety of sports related accessories.

ACTION IMAGES
33 ALDGATE HIGH STREET
1ST FLOOR, ALDGATE HOUSE
LONDON, ENGLAND EC3N 1DL
-44-7003-5820
www.actionimages.com
• Alan Whiter, Head of Sales/Marketing
alan.whiter@actionimages.com
• Monique Villa, Chairman
• Philip Kelly, Chief Executive
• David Jacobs, Managing Director
Services:
Photography capturing the spirit and passion of sport.
Clients:
FIFA, Coca-Cola, Barclays, Carslberg

ACTION SIGNS AND BILLBOARDS
720 HILLSIDE AVENUE
CHANDLER, MN 56122
507-677-2568
Fax: 507-677-2568
Loren@ActionSignsAndBillboards.com
www.actionsignsandbillboards.com
• Loren Vander Woude, President
loren@frontiernet.net
Products:
Manufacturing of tri-paneled rotating signs, rotating billboards, rotating mobile billboard trucks and trailers

ACTION SPORTS IMAGE
6301 PERFORMANCE DRIVE
CONCORD, NC 28027
704-454-4000
800-952-0708

Fax: 704-454-4030
www.lionelnascarcollectables.com
• Ruth Crowley, President
• Lesa France Kennedy, ISC President
• Marcus Smith, SMI Executive VP, National Sales and Mar
Products:
Produces racing collectibles. Products include a broad range of motorsports-related die-cast car replica collectibles, apparel, souvenirs and other memorabilia.
Brands:
Action Racing Collectables (ARC), the Racing Collectables Club of America (RCCA), Revell Collection, Winner's Circle, and Chase Authentics

ACTION SPORTS SYSTEMS INCORPORATED
617 CARBON CITY ROAD
MORGANTON, NC 28655
828-584-8000
800-631-1091
Fax: 828-584-8440
action_sports@bellsouth.net
www.actionsportsuniforms.com
Description:
Provides support for audio and video systems that record sporting events.

ACTIVE ANKLE SYSTEMS, INC.
233 QUARTERMASTER COURT
JEFFERSONVILLE, IN 47130
812-258-0663
800-800-2896
info@activeankle.com
www.activeankle.com
Products:
General Sports Products for Training & Conditioning, specializing in Ankle Braces.
Brands:
T1 Trainer Ankle Brace, Active Ankle - T2, Active Ankle - CF Pro, Trainer Overhaul Kit, T2 Overhaul Kit, Exercise Pads, EVA Pads, Trainer Strap Kit and T2 Strap Kit.

ACUMEN, INC.
101A EXECUTIVE DRIVE
SUITE 100
STERLING, VA 20166
703-437-7333
Fax: 703-904-0218
Products:
Exercise Accessories, Heart Rate Monitors, Sporting Goods and Sports Equipment.

ACUSHNET COMPANY
333 BRIDGE STREET
FAIRHAVEN, MA 2719
508-979-2000
866-389-2658
Fax: 508-979-3927
ebizhelp@acushnetgolf.com
www.acushnetgolf.com
• Joe Gomes, Director of Communications
Products:
Provides golf products of superior performance and quality.
Brands:
Acushnet Company's primary brands are the Titleist, FootJoy and Cobra. Pinnacle and Scotty Cameron are sub-brands used for specific Titleist products.

AD ART/ELECTRONIC SIGN COMPANY
5 THOMAS MELLON CIRCLE
SUITE 260
SAN FRANCISCO, CA 94134
415-869-6460
Fax: 415-869-6485
www.adart.com
• Bob Kierejczyk, President
• Duane Contento, Senior Vice President
• Jeremy Anderson, Executive Vice President
• Terry Long, Chief Executive Officer

AD MFG. COMPANY
248-44 JERICHO TURNPIKE
BELLEROSE, NY 11001
516-352-6161
800-841-6790
Fax: 516-352-8502
www.adtrophy.com
• Ronald Karmitz, VP
Products:
Trophies, Medals, Ribbons, Plaques, Keychains, Pins, Dog Tags, Gift Items and Mascots.

ADA TENNIS
2925 CHRYSLER ROAD
KANSAS CITY, KS 66115
913-371-2664
800-234-0460
Fax: 913-371-2663
adatennis1@aol.com
• Ray D. Jones, Jr, Owner
• Randy Kempke, Sales Representative
Products:
Tennis, Badmitton, Basketball, Football, and Soccer - Supplies and Equipment.

ADAMS GOLF GP CORPORATION
2801 EAST PLANO PARKWAY
SUITE 572
PLANO, TX 75074
972-673-9000
800-709-6142
Fax: 972-398-8818
• Barney Adams, Chairman of the Board
• John Ward, President
• Russell L. Fleischer, Director
• John M. Gregory, Director
Products:
Golf related products.
Brands:
Air Assault, Assault, VMI, Tight Lies

ADAMS USA, INC.
610 S JEFFERSON AVENUE
COOKEVILLE, TN 38501
931-526-2109
800-251-6857
Fax: 931-526-8357
www.adamsusa.com
• Vaughn Howard, Owner
• Garry McNabb, Stockholder
(931) 526-2109
• Rose Postic, President
Products:
Football helmets, Shoulder pads, Chin straps
Brands:
Adams USA, Trace

ADASTRA DESIGNS INC.
8345 W 16TH AVENUE
LAKEWOOD, CO 80215
303-274-9035
800-638-4667
Fax: 303-274-9038
info@adastran.com
www.adastran.com
Products:
Basketball, Radar Speed Measurement, Music, Interactive Electronic Football, Metaphaser, Sports Score Boards, Custom Products and Electronic Golf Targets.

ADER SPORTING GOODS INC.
10969 SHADY TRAIL
SUITE 105
DALLAS, TX 75220
214-352-7343
800-733-2338
Fax: 214-352-7360
www.aderfitness.com
• Cathay Kang, President
Products:
Exercise Equipment
Brands:
ASI Olympic Plates, ASI Dumbbells, ASI Slectorized Parts, ASI Machine Parts and Lat Pull Down Machines.

ADIDAS WRESTLING
8 CORPORATE BOULEVARD
SINKING SPRING, PA 19608
610-678-4050
800-486-2788
Fax: 887-879-4040
info@brute.com
www.brute.com
• Josiah (J Henson, Founder
• Jeff Bowyer, Co-Founder / National Sales Manager
Products:
Wrestling products and apparel to sporting goods dealers; amateur and professional athletic clubs and teams. Singlets: Phenom 2, Vapor 2, Bionic 2, Freedom 2, Lehigh 2, Solid and Phenom; Earguards: ZerO g Earguard, Quad II Earguard, Shockwave Earguard, Brute ClassiX, LE 03 Earguard, MM3 Earguard and Butt Pad; Kneepads: Sublitek Custom, Adidas, VW01, Equalizer, Youth Predator, Lycra Custom, Nylon Custom and Lyrca Knee Pad; Footwear: Mat Hog, Combat Speed II, adiStar Wrestling, adiStar SL Super Light John Smith Sig., Response Wrestling, A'ttaak, Tyrint II and A'ttaak Womens.
Brands:
Adidas and CCS READY

ADIRONDACK RUBBER PRODUCTS
5633 ROUTE 31
VERONA, NY 13478
315-363-3726
Fax: 315-363-7214
• Debra Parkin, Marketing
• Steven Joanis, Sales
Products:
Baseball/Softball Pitchers Mound Pad; Gymnastics Mats; Non Slip Floors; Interlocking Rubber Mats; Weight Room Flooring; Locker Room Flooring and Tiles; Martial Arts Mats; Indoor Tracks; Weight Room Flooring; Ice Rink Rubber Flooring.

ADOLPH KIEFER & ASSOCIATES
1700 KIEFER DRIVE
ZION, IL 60099
847-872-8866
800-323-4071
Fax: 847-746-8888
info@kiefer.com
www.kiefer.com
• Adolph Kiefer, Founder
(847) 872-8866
• Edita Emini, National Team Sales Manager
Products:
Swimwear, Technical Suits, Goggles, Training, Books & Videos, Swimmer's Gear, Lifeguard Shop, Kiefer Guard, TYR Guard, Speedo Guard, Guard Wear, Guard Gear, Rescue Gear, Lifesaving Equipment, Rescue Training, Kiefer Guard Chairs, Water Safety, AEDs, Kid's Swim Suits, Kid's Kickboards, Kid's Goggles, Pool Games, Learn-To-Swim, Swim Diapers, Ruth Sova Products, Resistance Workout, T & F Books & Videos, T & F Accessories, T & F Suits, Pool Lifts, TYR Triathlete
Brands:
Speedo, TYR, Dolphin Suits, Kiefer suits, Nike, Grab Bag, Workout, Optical, Masks, Finis

ADP LEMCO, INC.
5970 W DANNON WAY
W JORDAN, UT 84081-6203
801-280-4000
800-575-3626
Fax: 801-280-4040
customerservice@adplemco.com
www.adplemco.com
• Mark McCormack, President & Chief Operating Officer
(801) 307-4230
mmccormack@adplemco.com
• David L Hall, Vice President
(801) 280-4000
sales@adplemco.com
• Schyler Sommer, Sales Manager
(807) 307-4230
ssommer@adplemco.com
Products:
Basketball Backstops, Backboard Padding, Portable Backboard, Stationary Backboard, Nets, Breakaway Rims, Goals, Shot Clocks, Gym Divider Curtains, Wall Padding, Scoreboards, Tennis & Volleyball Equipment, and Posts

ADVANCED CUTTING SYSTEMS, INC.
17578 76TH STREET
LIVE OAK, FL 32060
386-330-6889
800-874-8674
Fax: 386-330-6610
beverlyyagins@acsystem.us
www.acsystem.us
• Beverly Yagins, Sales Manager
(800) 874-8674
beverlyyagins@acsystem.us
• Carolyn Miller, Sales & Product Information
info@acsystem.us
Products:
Die Cutter, Steel Rule Dies for Making Lettering & Logos for Uniforms, Computerized Sign Making Equipment.
Year Founded:
2005

ADVANCED DESIGN CONCEPTS
N27 W23655 PAUL ROAD
PEWAUKEE, WI 53072-5793
262-523-1010
Fax: 262-523-1011

• Edward J. Norton, Partner
• Mark O. Schaefer, President & Chief Of Innovation
• Jim Marschalek, Vice President
• Patrick Woodzick, Designer
Services:
Research, design, development, marketing, sourcing of athletic shoes.

ADVANCED EQUIPMENT CORPORATION
2401 W COMMONWEALTH AVENUE
FULLERTON, CA 92833
714-635-5350
Fax: 714-525-6083
www.advancedequipment.com
• Wesley Dickson, Founder / Chief Executive Officer
Products:
Operable walls. Produces manual and electric walls with heights over 40 feet, panel constructions and tracks. Produces Vision, a micro-processor controlled rear projection screen cover which creates a flush wall.
Brands:
Vision

ADVANTAGE SPORTS RACK
2222 QUEEN STREET
BELLINGHAM, WA 98229-4753
360-756-2411
888-722-5240
Fax: 360-756-2414
support@heininger.biz
www.heininger.biz
• Jeffrey V. Heininger, Founder
• Nick Homes, Marketing
Services:
Cycling - Bike Car Racks; Skiing-Alpine - Ski Car Racks.

ADVANTAGE TENNIS SUPPLY
235 ARCADIA STREET
RICHMOND, VA 23225
804-276-0011
800-476-5432
Fax: 804-276-0557
• Toni McDavid, President
• Amy Ward, Manager
Year Founded:
1978.
Brands:
Edwards Sports Products, M Putterman, Igloo Coolers, Penn Tennis Balls, Advantage Tennis Products
Products & Services:
Manufacturer, Distributor of Tennis Court Equipment, Ball Machines, Balls, Divider Nets, Net Center Straps, Net Posts, Nets, Tennis Backdrop Curtains, Windscreens.

AEF EMBLEMS
8770 GUION ROAD
SUITE C
INDIANAPOLIS, IN 46268
317-802-5743
800-983-6662
Fax: 317-802-5750
www.aefemblem.com
• Andrew E. Falender, President
• Phil Stillerman, National Account Manager
Products:
Custom-made Lapel Pins, Commemerorative Coins/Medallions, Trading Pins, Zipper Pulls, Embroidered Patches, PVC Key Tags, Pins.

AEROBICS INC.
34 FAIRFIELD PLACE
WEST CALDWELL, NJ 7006
973-276-9700
Fax: 973-794-6395
www.pacemaster.com
• Gerald J Staub, President
• Thomas N Staub, VP
(973) 276-9700
Products:
Training & Conditioning - Treadmills.
Brands:
Pacemaster

AEROBIE, INC
744 SAN ANTONIO ROAD
SUITE 15
PALO ALTO, CA 94303
650-493-3050
800-999-3565
Fax: 650-493-7050
www.aerobie.com
• Alex Tennant, General Manager
aerobie@aerobie.com
• Charlene Myers, Domestic Customer Service
aerobie@aerobie.com
• Greg Baker, Operations Manager
• Michelle Smith, International Customer Service
aerobie@aerobie.com
• Don Abbott, National Sales Manager
Products:
Flying discs, boomerang, yo-yo, balls
Year Founded:
1984
Brands:
Aerobie, Orbiter, Squidgie, AeroSpin, Skylighter, Epic, SharpShooter, Superdisc

---

AEROMAT
48541 WARM SPRINGS BLVD
SUITE 503
FREMONT, CA 94539
877-278-6158
Fax: 707-221-4040
info@aeromats.com
www.aeromats.com
Products:
Yoga Block, Yoga Wedge, Yoga Mat Carrying Harness, Yoga Straps, Yoga Aeromats, Yoga/Pilates Aeromats, Foam Roller, Pilates/Body Toning Rings, Smooth Surface Aeromat, Dual Surface Aeromat, Aeromat Work-out Mat, Balance Dome, Balance Board, Balance Board with Pad, Balance Disc Cushion, Balance Pad, Fitness Ball, Fitness Ball Kit, Fitness Ball Resistance Kit, Fitness Ball Stacker, De Luxe Figure 8 Tube, Exercise Flex Bar with Tube, Power Flex Bar, APF Aeromat, APL Aeromat, Dual Surface Aeromat, Smooth Surface Aeromat, Workout Mat and more.

AIRCAST, INC.
1430 DECISION STREET
VISTA, CA 92081
760-727-1280
800-336-6569
Fax: 800-936-6569
• Mike S. Zafirovski, Chairman
• Sidney Braginsky, Director
• John Chiminski, Director
• Chinch E. Chu, Director
• Leslie H. Cross, Director
• Julia Kahr, Director
• James R. (Ron) Lawson, Director

Products:
Cryo/Cuff Ankle Sprain Care, Forearm Rotational Brace Arm Immobilizer, AutoChill System with Adjustable Docking Station, Back/Hip/Rib Cryo/Cuff, Calf Cryo/Cuff for Walking Brace Diabetic Replacement, Elbow Cryo/Cuff, Foot Cryo/Cuff FP Walker (foam pneumatic), Hand and Wrist Cryo/Cuff, Hand Bulb with Pressure Gauge Heel Supports, Knee Cryo/Cuff, Knee Immobilizer Leg Brace, Mayo Clinic Elbow Brace Pneumatic Armband, Pneumatic Walker, Diabetic System Pressure Verification Kit, Shoulder Cryo/Cuff, Thigh Cryo/Cuff Tube Assembly
Brands:
AirHeel, AirLift, CryoCuff, Autochill

AJAY SPORTS
37735 ENTERPRISE CT
SUITE 600
FARMINGTON HILLS, MI 48331
248-994-0553
800-776-4653
Fax: 248-489-9334
www.progolfamerica.com
• Thomas W. Itin, Chairman / Chief Executive Officer
• Brian T Donelly, President / Chief Operating Officer
Products:
Golf Clubs - Iron or Wood Sets.
Brands:
Palm Springs Golf, Inc., Prestige Golf Corp., Pro Golf International, Inc., Pro Golf of America, Inc and ProGolf.com, Inc.

ALCHESTER MILLS COMPANY, INC.
1125 WRIGHT AVENUE
CAMDEN, NJ 8103
856-964-9700
Fax: 856-964-9135
• M. Tarnoff, President
Products:
Baseball: Caps, Socks; Basketball: Supporters, Cup Supporters, Gripping Aids, Hats/Caps/Visors, Protective, Socks; Field Hockey: Stick Grips; Football: Knee/Elbow Pads, Socks.

ALDILA
1945 KELLOGG AVE
CARLSBAD, CA 92008
sales@aldila.com
www.aldila.com
• Steve Gandolfo, Customer Service Manager
Products:
Golf Equipment
Brands:
Aldila

ALGOMA NET COMPANY
1525 MUELLER STREET
ALGOMA, WI 54201
920-487-5577
Fax: 920-487-2852
www.algomanet.com
• James L Westrich, VP / General Manager
Products:
Bags and Equipment for Baseball, Basketball, Field Hockey, Football, Gymnastics, Martial Arts, Racquet Sports, Rugby, Soccer, and Field and Track.

ALKAHN LABEL
1430 BROADWAY
7TH FLOOR
NEW YORK, NY 10018
212-768-7700
Fax: 212-768-7794
info@paxar.com
www.alkahn.com
• Max L Kahn, Chairman
• Philip Kahn, President
• Jeff Stern, National Retail Sales Manager
Products:
Variable Data Tickets & Labels, Brand
Promotion & Merchandising Tags, Fabric
Labels & Collections, Brand Protection &
Security, Printers, Accessories, & Supplies,
Monarch Brand Bar Code & RFID Products,
Handheld Labels, Tags, & Attachers

ALKALINE INSTITUTE
915 W FOOTHILL BOULEVARD
SUITE J
CLAREMONT, CA 91711
888-225-6452
www.alkalineinstitute.com

ALL AMERICAN BOWLING PRO SHOP
1148 PULASKI HIGHWAY #152
BEAR, DE 19701
888-626-2695
allamericanbowling@yahoo.com
www.allamericanbowling.com
Products:
AMF Balls, Brunswick Balls, Columbia Balls,
Dexter Mens Shoes, Dynothane Balls,
Ebonite Shirts, Hammer Balls, Linds Mens
Shoes, NXT Ladies Shoes, Roto Grip Balls,
Storm Shirts, Ball Spinners, Brunswick
Shirts, Columbia Shirts, Dynothane ABS
Shoes, Ebonite Bags, Etonic Ladies's
Shoes, K-R Bags, MoRich Balls, NXT Mens
Shoes, Storm Bags, Track Balls, Brunswick
Bags, Columbia Bags, Dexter Ladies Shoes,
Dynothane ABS Shoes LADIES, Ebonite
Balls, Etonic Men's Shoes, Linds Ladies
Shoes, NFL Hand Grip Bags, Nu Line Balls,
Storm Balls, Track Shirts

ALL AMERICAN GOLF SALES, INC.
550 BROOKFOREST AVENUE
SHOREWOOD, IL 60431
815-744-0440
Fax: 815-744-0444
• Edward Rhee, President
Products:
Golf Bags, Drivers/Woods,
Irons/Hybrids/Wedges, Putters, Packaged
Club Sets
Brands:
Pro Fantom, Tour System III, True Flite,
Trueline, Unix

ALL AMERICAN SCOREBOARDS
401 SOUTH MAIN STREET
PO BOX 100
PARDEEVILLE, WI 53954
608-429-2121
800-356-8146
Fax: 877-505-9405
scoreboardsales@everbrite.com
www.allamericanscoreboards.com
• Fred Foster, Sales Service
score@everbrite.com
• Scott Carter, President
• Chris Stark, Sales Manager
score@everbrite.com

Products:
Scoreboards for Football, Baseball,
Basketball, Soccer, Multi-Sport, Hockey and
Racing, Scoretables, Portable, Scoreboard,
Accessories

ALL AMERICAN SPORTS CORP/RIDDELL
ALL AMERICAN
669 SUGAR LANE
ELYRIA, OH 44035
440-366-8225
800-275-5338
Fax: 440-366-6292
help@riddellsports.com
www.riddell.com
• Don Gleisner, President
• Bill Sherman, President / Chief Executive
Officer
Products:
Football: Helments, Helment Accessories,
Shoulder Pads, Footballs & Accessories
Brands:
Maxpror Shockblocker II, Mini Jaw Cutters,
Mox Box Refill, Mox Box Repair Hardware
Kit, Kra-Liter IV Facemasks, Z-Bar Steel
Thick-Coat, Z-Bar Titanium Thin Coat,
Power Varsity Pads, Ultra Varsity Pad,
Evolution Varsity Pads, Air Pac Varsity
Pads, Warrior Varsity/Junior Pads, Warrior II
Youth Pads, X-ForceT Youth Pads, Power
Pad Accessories, Air Pac Pad Accessories

ALL LACROSSE, INC.
147 VALLEY ROAD
MONTCLAIR, NJ 7042
973-509-0303
800-522-7693
Fax: 973-509-1345
www.alllacrosse.com
• Yogi Trivedi, President
Products:
Sticks, Pads, Helmets, Gloves, Accessories,
Shorts and Shirts, Stringing Kits, Stringing
Kits, Lacrosse Cleats & Goals & Nets
Brands:
Brine, DeBeer, STX, Warrior

ALL PRO EXERCISE PRODUCTS, INC.
ALL PRO EXERCISE PRODUCTS INC.
HILLSBOROUGH, NJ 8844
908-281-7100
800-735-9287
Fax: 908-281-5793
support@allproweights.com
www.allproweights.com
• Edie Winston, President
• Scott Winston, President
Brands:
All Pro, Hands Free, Power Walker, Aqua
Power, Thighaciser, Power Stride, Power
Vest, Weight to Jump, Weight-A-Band,
Contour Foam, Weight-A-Toner
Products:
Weight-adjustable exercise & fitness
products including: ankle weights, wrist
weights, vests, belts, thigh weights, upper
arm weights, aquatic ankle weights,
weighted resistance bands, and weighted
jump ropes.

ALL STAR FOWNES
5728 MAJOR BOULEVARD
SUITE 612
ORLANDO, FL 32819
407-351-1611
800-654-5683
Fax: 407-351-1703

• Leslie Armstrong, National Sales Manager
fownes@bellsouth.net
• Robin Morgan, Customer Service / Credit
Manager
fownes@bellsouth.net
• Delila Smalley, Customer Service
Products:
Golf Equipment.
Brands:
Deluxe All Weather, Polartec Winter Pairs,
Shur Soft Crown, Sof-Tac, Super Crown,
SuperTech

ALL STAR INDUSTRIES, INC.
7001-T W 20TH AVENUE
HIALEAH, FL 33014
305-823-4830
800-432-3528
Fax: 305-823-4836
www.asisupplier.com/allstar
• Paul Fields, President
• Clara Zeinfield, VP
Products:
Trophies, Plaques, Medals, Cups & Bowls,
Desk Sets, Specialty Items & name tags
(metal or plastic).

ALL STAR KNITWEAR, INC.
841 E BROADWAY STREET
GRIFFIN, GA 30223
770-227-5016
800-241-0246
Fax: 770-412-6264
www.allstarknit.com
• Robert W. Willis, Sr., President
• Bobby Willis, Jr., Vice President
• Jimmy Willis, Secretary/Treasurer
Products:
Athletic Hosiery, including Football and
Soccer Socks.
Year Founded:
1955
Brands:
All-Star Knitwear

ALL STAR PRO GOLF, INC.
1501 35TH AVENUE WEST
SPENCER, IA 51301-0155
712-262-8891
800-247-4830
Fax: 712-262-8891
www.allstarprogolf.com
• Jay Horton, National Account Manager
• Clark Smith, National Account
Representative
Products:
Golf clubs & accessories

ALL STAR SPORTING GOODS
1 MAIN STREET
PO BOX 1356
SHIRLEY, MA 1464
978-425-6266
800-777-3810
Fax: 978-425-4068
customerservice@all-starsports.com
www.all-starsports.com
• Stanley Jurga, President
(978) 425-6266
jurga@all-starsports.com
• Carol Jurga, Vice President/General
Manager
(978) 425-6266
cjurga@all-starsports.com
• Jeff Johnson, Vice President Sales
(978) 425-6266
jjohnson@all-starsports.com

• Kathie Fontaine, Customer Relation Director
(978) 425-6266
kfontaine@all-starsports.com
Products:
Baseball & Softball: MVP Head Gear, Catcher's Equipment, Umpire's Equipment, Accessories, Baseball Helmets, Women's/Girl's Softball, Gloves & Mitts, Baseballs, Equipment Bags, Cups & Supporters, Bases & Plates. Football: JR.Lite Helmets, Girdles, Shoulder Pads, Hands & Forearm Guards & Accessories.

ALL-SPORT BRUSH LLC
7316 E 38TH STREET
PO BOX 4769
TULSA, OK 74145
918-749-3368
Fax: 918-749-5133
www.causecare.com
• Ed Conn, Chief Executive Officer
(918) 749-3368
• James Evans, Director of Sales/Marketing
(918) 749-3368
Products:
Toothbrushes
Year Founded:
2003

ALLAN ENTERPRISES
7517 N SENECA ROAD
MILWAUKEE, WI 53217
414-352-6152
• Allan Fefer, Owner
Products:
Eyewear
Brands:
All-Guards, Over-Guard, Pro-Guard, Pro-Tector, Sport-Specs, Varsity, Victoria

ALLESON ATHLETIC, DON
2921 BRIGHTON-HENRIETTA TOWN LINE ROAD
ROCHESTER, NY 14623
585-272-0606
800-641-0041
Fax: 800-836-0775
• Todd Levine, VP Marketing / Sales
• Bill Lolas, VP Retail Sales
• Steve Schwarz, VP Manufacturing
• Elena OLiveri, VP Operation
• Steve Schwarz, Head Of Manufacturing Unit
• Yvonne Dailey, Assistant
Products:
Apparel and Uniforms for Baseball/Softball, Football, Basketball, Volleyball, Track and Field, Soccer, Official, Shorts, Field Hockey, Ice HOckey and Cheerleading

ALLIAN SNOWBOARDS
PMB #513 18335 NW W UNION
SUITE C
PORTLAND, OR 97229
mikemiya@alliansnowboards.com
www.alliansnowboards.com
• Mike Miyazawa, President
Products:
Snowboards: Signature Series, Pro Series, Freedom Series, Soft Wear, Tech Points and Line Up
Brands:
Backman 146, Backman154, Backman 157, Backman 160, Stephens 145, Stephens 150, Stephens 155, Stephens 159, Stephens 165, Peter Strom 55, Peter Strom

58, Peter Strom 63, Knock Out 142, Knock Out 153, Knock Out 155, White Out 146, 151, 155, 157, Black OUt 157W, 159, 161, 161W, 163, 165, 167, Freedom Series 136, 142, 146, 136, Freedom Series 150, 155

ALPHA RACQUET SPORTS
7208 MCNEIL DRIVE
207
AUSTIN, TX 78729
512-250-1499
800-922-9024
Fax: 512-279-9454
info@alphatennis.com
www.alphatennis.com
• Mark Gonzalez, Sales Manager
• Greg Gonyea, Customer Sales Manager
Products:
Racquet Sports - Badminton Equipment, Racquet Grips, Racquet String, Racquet Stringing Machines, Tennis Court Equipment.
Brands:
Orbitor, BLU-DC Plus, PIONEER DC, Firecable, Synthetic, Viper, Patriot, GUT200 POLY, COMFORT PLUS, CLAYCOURT PLUS, HARDCOURT SG, GUT 2000, PRODIGY, ELEMENT, ULTRA SPIN SOLID CORE, FIREWEB, FLEXEL, POWERCABLE, POLYCABLE, TOURNABLEND, RAB ENDURA, RAB MONOFLEX, EXCEL I, EXCELL II, AQUAZORB, ALL PLAYER, TRAX, WRAPTOR, IGUANA, GRIP TUBEZ, GRIP BUCKETS, Curved Awl, Scalpel, Digital Calipers, Stringed Cutters, Straight Awl, Alpha RAB, Accuswing, Viper Balance Beam, ALPHA BAll Clip, ALPHA Balancer, ALPHA String Savers, Open Mesh Polypropylene, ALPHA Cap, STRING IT T-Shirt, TOURNAMENT Shuttlecocks, XP-90, XP-80, XP-85

ALPHA SPORTSWEAR, INC.
PO BOX 3652
BLAINE, WA 98231-3652
604-873-2621
866-888-2621
Fax: 604-873-4652
custserv@alphasportswear.com
Products:
Sportswear for Hockey, Basketball, Football, Baseball and Volleyball
Brands:
Superstar Mesh Jersey; Tech Knit Jersey

ALPINA SPORTS CORPORATION
98 ETNA ROAD
LEBANON, NH 3766
603-448-3101
800-425-7462
Fax: 603-448-1586
www.alpinasports.com
• Rolf Schaer, President / Chief Executive Officer
• Steve Kvinlaug, Sales VP
• Gary Fleming, President
Products:
Racing Skis, Boots, Bindings; Sports Skis, Boots, Bindings & Touring Skis, Boots, Bindings, Poles and other kinds of Boots
Brands:
SCL, SK, NNN R3 CLASSIC, NNN NIS CLASSIC, HYPERSONIC C3 CLASSIC COLD, CCS: CARBON CONTROL SKATE, HYPERSONIC C3 MGV, HYPERSONIC C3 CLASSIC WET, NNN NIS SKATE,

HYPERSONIC C3 CLASSIC COLD NIS, HYPERSONIC 3X3 SKATE NIS SC, HYPERSONIC 3X3 SKATE SC, HYPERSONIC 3X3 SKATE NIS R, HYPERSONIC 3X3 SKATE R, HYPERSONIC 3X3 SKATE NIS HP, HYPERSONIC 3X3 SKATE HP, SUPRASONIC SKATE, SUPRASONIC CLASSIC, DIABLO, CRISPI X-R, Rottefella Cobra

ALPS SPORTSWEAR MFG. COMPANY, INC.
15 UNION STREET
LAWRENCE, MA 1840
978-683-2438
800-262-7010
Fax: 978-686-8051
• Marvin Axelrod, President
• David Lane, Merchandising VP
• Jerry Stone, Sales VP
Products:
Ladies Sweater & Shirts, Dream Wear, Men's Sweaters & Shirts, Tees & Hats, Afghans & Mukluk
Brands:
Simple Pleasures, Flirtacious Crew, Crystal Cove Hoodie, Cornucopia Crew, Cornucopia Scarf, Cherry Grove Cardigan, Fox Ridge Vest, Frosty Ridge, Sweet Violet, Jubilee Vee, Holly Hill Vee, Maybell, Kaleidoscope Cardigan, Kaleidoscope Cardigan, Cloud Nine Crew, Tularosa, Apple Valley Vest, Serenade Hoodie #1821, Ariel, Long Haul Vee, Break Away Zip, Crooked Creek, Call of the Road Crew, Moose Trail Crew, Laid Back Henley, Moose River Henley, Laid Back Henley, Moose Ball Cap, Black Label Cap, Aspen Leaf, Shenandoah, Heirloom, Tumbleweed, Eldorado, Holiday Mukluk, Catalina Mukluk, Super Mukluk, Backpacker Mukluk, Sunset Dream Mukluk, Catchin' Som

ALTUS ATHLETIC MFG. COMPANY
709 SOUTH VETERANS DRIVE
PO BOX 736
ALTUS, OK 73521
580-482-0891
800-654-9873
Fax: 580-482-2760
www.altusathletic.com
• John Hetzel, Director Marketing/Product Development
• Bill Goodbread, National Sales Manager
• Felicia Rogers, Customer Service
• Curt Underwood, VP Of Sales
Products:
Belts, Weightlifting Accessories, Gloves, Ankle and Wrist Weights, Hands & Forearm Development, Home Fitness Equipment, Jump Ropes, Combo Packs, Stretching & Toning, Yoga/Pilates, and Fitness Balls

ALUMINUM ATHLETIC EQUIPMENT COMPANY (AAE)
1000 ENTERPRISE DRIVE
ROYERSFORD, PA 19468-1298
610-825-6565
800-523-5471
Fax: 610-825-2378
info@myaaeworld.com
www.aaesports.com
• Timothy W. Driscoll, President / Chief Executive Officer
(610) 825-6565

• Tom Syron, Sales Director
(610) 825-6565
Products:
Accu-Kick Practice Football Goal; Air Horn; Aluminum Pit Cover; Award Stands; Ballstopper System, Football; Ballstopper System, Self-Standing Model; Bell-Lap Counters; Ballstopper System, Ground Sleeve Model; Ballstopper System, Soccer; Benches; Ballstopper System, Multi-Sport; Batons; Bleachers; Batting Tunnels; Bottomboard Cushionong System; Cages; Circles; Combination Football/Soccer Goals, Rollaway; Corner Flags; Crowd Control Fencing; Camera Support Post; Coach's Clipboard; Competition Equipment; Crossbars; Curbing; Canopies; Coach's Lecterns; Cone Makers; Crossbar Lifters; Carts & Carriers; Combination football/Soccer, Goals; Conversion

ALUMINUM SEATING, INC.
555 TENNIS COURT LANE
SAN BERNARDINO, CA 92408
909-884-9449
800-757-7328
Fax: 909-388-2187
sales@aluminumseating.com
www.aluminumseating.com
• Bonnie Gaudesi, Sales Manager
(800) 757-7328
sales@aluminumseating.com
Products:
Aluminum seating products, bleachers, benches, picnic tables, aluminum planks, accessories
Brands:
Aluminum Seating, Inc.
Clients:
Schoools, Municipalities, Little League

ALVARADO MANUFACTURING COMPANY
12660 COLONY STREET
CHINO, CA 91710
909-591-8431
800-423-4143
Fax: 909-628-1403
www.alvaradomfg.com
• Bret Armatas, President
(909) 549-8431
barmatas@alvaradomfg.com
• Brian Dilard, Director of Marketing
(909) 591-8431
Products:
Post and Rail Systems, Eclipse Retractable Belt, Escort Retractable Belt, FP-14 Rope Stanchions, Ultima Retractable Belt, Waist High Turnstiles, Full Height Turnstiles, Optical Turnstiles, Security Gates, 3-arm and 4-arm Turnstiles, self-closing gates, manual swing gates, bumper systems, case guards/posts, Ticket Scanning Turnstiles/Mobile Handheld Scanning, GateLinkT Validation Admission Control Software, Associated Professional Services, Three-Arm and Optical Turnstiles for Patron Counting, GateWatchT Patron Counting Software, ParkWatchT Vehicle Counting System.
Brands:
Supervisor, Defender

AMA GOLF
208 MICHELLE COURT
S SAN FRANCISCO, CA 94080

650-952-2286
800-635-8062
Fax: 650-952-5131
www.amagolf.com
• Ryan Chin, Owner
ryan@amagolf.com
Products:
Manufacturer, Distributor, Importer/Exporter of golf products.

AMERICAN ATHLETIC INC.
200 AMERICAN AVENUE
JEFFERSON, IA 50129
515-386-3125
800-247-3978
Fax: 515-386-4566
www.americanathletic.com
• Mark Shaw, Vice President/General Manager
• Scott Roth, Gymnastics Divisional Director
• Kevin Murphy, Team/Sports Construction Sales
• Les Arp, Engineering/Materials Divisional Director
Products:
Vault, Uneven Bars, Balance Beams, Floor Exercise, Pommel Horse, Rings, Parallel Bars, Horizontal Bar, Accessories, Adapters, Cheer floors, Mats & Pads, Training, Skill Shapes.
Brands:
Infinity ELITE, TAC/10 International LZT, ELITE, CLASSIC

AMERICAN ATHLETIC SHOE COMPANY
15 S STREET
PO BOX 777
WARE, MA 1082
413-967-3511
Fax: 413-967-3585
www.americanathleticshoe.com
• Paul M Opalinski, President
Products:
Figure Skates, Hockey Skates, Rental Skates, Inline Skates & Water Shoes
Brands:
Classic Rentskates, OkeRent Skates, SoftRent Skates, SoftRent Sport Skates, SoftRent Hockey, SoftRent Figure, SoftRent Sport, RentSkate Figure, RentSkate Hockey, OkeRent Figure, OkeRent Hockey, Figure Skates, Beginner Skates, Hockey Skates

AMERICAN CORD & WEBBING COMPANY, INC.
88 CENTURY DRIVE
WOONSOCKET, RI 2895
401-762-5500
Fax: 401-762-5514
www.acw1.com
• Mark Krauss, President
mkrauss@acw1.com
• Dennis Smith, Advertising / Marketing Director
Products:
Webbing, Cord, Plastic Fasteners, Metal Fasteners, Assemies, Buckles
Brands:
Webbing - Comanche, Wave, Custom Logo, Apache, ZZ, Chain, Braid Weave, Flying Saucer; West Havel Plastic Buckles & Fasteners

AMERICAN ELECTRIC LIGHTING
3825 COLUMBUS ROAD SW
BUILDING F
GRANVILLE, OH 43023
770-483-6014
800-754-0463
866-465-6742
Fax: 740-349-4490
customerservice@holophane.com
www.americanelectriclighting.com
Products:
Roadway Luminaries, Decorative Post Top, Security Lighting, Area and Site Lighting, Flood Lighting, Dark to Light Photocontrols, Poles
Brands:
Roadway Lighting Luminaries - DuraStar Series 20, DuraStar Series 30, Wall Pack 882, Roadway-Area-SP2, Roadway-Area-SRP, Roadway-Area-SRX; Decorative Post Top - ConTempo-245, American Revolution 247 Cutoff, American Revolution-247, Cresthill Classic, Cresthill Centennial

AMERICAN FENCERS SUPPLY
1027 TERRA NOVA BOULEVARD
PACIFICA, CA 94044
650-359-7911
Fax: 650-359-7913
www.amfence.com
Products:
Foils, Sabers, Epees, Foil Parts, Saber Parts, Epee Parts, Blades, Jackets, Gloves, Shoes, Stockings, Knickers, Masks and Equipment Bags, Children's Equipment and Clothing, Tools, Shirts and Apparel, Scoring Equipment, Instructors Equipment, Cards & Stickers, Posters & Prints, Videos and DVDs, Starter and Competition Sets, Books, Swords, Broadswords, Daggers, Small, Town and Court Swords, Fencing Weapons modified for theatrical use, Blades, Rapiers, Armour from the Old Met Opera
Brands:
Standard French, Standard Children's French, Leather French, Rubber over Metal French, Standard Belgian, Olympic, Schultz, Visconti, Gerdere, Schermasport, Rambeau, Leon Paul FIE Blade, Leon Paul Blade, Vnti FIE Blade, Leather Thumb Pad, Vniti Guard, German Point Parts, German Guard Socket, Renaissance, Heavy Italian, Florentine, Late Dutch, Medieval Valencia, Zweihander w/parrying hooks, Spanish Fishtail, Claymore

AMERICAN FITNESS EQUIPMENT LLC
412 WASHINGTON STREET
D
NORWELL, MA 02061
781-659-0006
800-244-2856
Fax: 301-770-2104
amfit@gis.net
• Joe Cedrone, Founder/Chief Executive Officer
(781) 659-0006
amfit@gis.net
• Don Cedrone, General Manager
(781) 659-0006
amfit@gis.net
• Mark Cedrone, Warehouse/Service Manager
(781) 659-0006
amfit@gis.net
Products:
Treadmills, Rowers, Bikes, Strength

Training, Free Weights, Benches, Accessories, Multi-Gyms, Ellipticals, Mirrors, Sport Flooring, Mats, Steam Generators, Sauna Rooms and Stoves, Boxing
Brands:
Pace Master, Landice, Blades, Spirit, Nautilus-Schwinn, Keys, Life-Span, Evo, Body Craft, and Fitnet, Sports Art, Kettler, Lamar, Ignite, Monarx, Schwinn Spinners, Water Rower, Body Craft, First Degree Boxing, Everlast, TKO, Century, Balaz

AMERICAN NEEDLE & NOVELTY INC.
1275 BUSCH PARKWAY
BUFFALO GROVE, IL 60089
847-215-0011
800-356-7589
Fax: 847-215-0013
www.americanneedle.com
• Robert Kronenberger, President
ronald@amer-needle.com
• Michael Smucker, Corporate Sales VP
michael@amer-needle.com
• Ronald Kronenberger, Manufacturing VP
• Jason Franklin, Corporate Sales Director
Products:
Embroidered headwear for various sports.
Brands:
CAP B-024, Pose 2, Pose 3

AMERICAN NON-SLIP PRODUCTS
4530-F PATTON DRIVE
EAST ATLANTA, GA 30336
800-221-4329
www.americannonslip.com
Products:
Non Slip Rug Pads, Multi-Purpose Liners, Specific Purpose Liners & Mats, Bath/Kitchen Mats & Liners, Laminate Underlayment
Brands:
Cush-n-Hold, Hold Tight, Miracle Hold Plus, Rug Saver, Slip Not, Sultan, Super Movenot, Wicker Loc, Miracle Hold, Rug Hold Natural, Rug To Rug, Lok Lift, Stay In Place, Patio Pad, Multi-Grip Natural, Cushion-Aire, Double Grip, Rug Preserver, Tiger Grip Blue, Tiger Grip Plus, Cush-N-It Sink Mats, Cush-N-It-Bath Mats, Cush-N-It-Shower Mats, Line It, Super Line It, Line All, Super Line It, Line It

AMERICAN PLAYGROUND CORPORATION
6406 PRODUCTION DRIVE
ANDERSON, IN 46013
765-642-0288
800-541-1602
Fax: 765-649-7162
www.american-playground.com
Products:
Slides, swings, climbers, basketball, soccer, see saws, merry-go-rounds, bike racks, park amenities, bleachers, flags and flag poles
Brands:
Junior Slide, Senior Slide, Straight Slide, Wave Slide, Step Climber, Freedom Climbers, Climbing Ladders, Arched Ladders, Arched Climbers, Friendly Turtles, Critters

AMERICAN RANGE COMPANY
4 VAN AUKER STREET
ROCHESTER, NY 14608
585-328-2480
800-324-9769

Fax: 585-328-2503
www.arcgolf.com
Products:
Golf driving range equipment and services, spare parts for any equipment used in the golf range business
Brands:
ARC-Eliminatore Ball Picker, ARC Glider Nylon Disc Pickers, ARC-Ultra Range Mats, ARC Natural Turf, ARC Trays, SOFTEE Ball Tray, Bell Tee Marker and Tee Receptacle, Circular Marker, Hollow Dimple Tee Marker, Lock Nylon Flag, ARC Solid Polymer Blended Putters, ARC Vision Distance Markers, ARC Range Clubs

AMERICAN RECREATION PRODUCTS, INC.
1224 FERN RIDGE PARKWAY
SAINT LOUIS, MO 63141
314-576-8000
800-325-4121
Fax: 314-576-8072
www.instabed.com
• George J. Grabner Jr, President
• W Le Capps III, CFO
Products:
Subsidiary of Kellwood Company, makes outdoor gear including tents, backpacks, sleeping bags, outdoor clothing, and related camping accessories

AMERICAN SEATING
801 BROADWAY AVE NW
GRAND RAPIDS, MI 49504-4499
616-732-6600
800-748-0268
800-748-0353
Fax: 616-732-6401
info@amseco.com
www.americanseating.com
• Edward Clark, Chief Executive Officer
eclark@americanseating.com
• Owen Fritz, Sales VP
Products:
Public and commercial venue seating
Brands:
Dimension, Omnia by Ares, Spirit, Sports Seating, Stellar, Viva by Sebel, Whirl, Framework Segway, Framework, Accuwerks, Brilliance, Credence, Acton

AMERICAN SOCCER COMPANY, INC.
726 E ANAHEIM STREET
WILMINGTON, CA 90744
800-626-7774
Fax: 800-426-1222
sales@scoresports.com
www.scoresports.com
Products:
Jerseys, shorts, socks, goalkeeper gear, warm-ups, coaches gear, accessories, soccer balls, shin guards, field equipment, bags and referee gear
Brands:
USA #509, Chicago #508, Japan #505, England #535, Brazil #520, Estonia #570, Switzerland #545, Sydney #117A, Milan #155A, Lisbon #115A, Rio #175A, Zurich #120A, Turin # 130A, Edinburgh #153A, Dublin #145A, Vienna # 150A, Striped #810, Solid #800, Flying Feet #825, Ankle Sock #830, GALAPAGOS - #325, MAUI - #330, BORA BORA - #350, TASMANIA PANT - #900A, BAHAMAS SHORT - #903A, BEAR CLAW - #920, FIRE GLOVES - #925, DENALI - #3300, SANTIAGO - #3400,

ATHENS - #163A, LONDON - #167A, PORTFOLIO - #817, COACH/REFEREE BAG - #850, ACCESSORY BAG - #852, SHOE/GLOVE BAG - #853, SPORT BAG - #864, PLAYER BAG - #865, TEAM TRAVEL - #867, SACK PACK - #871, DAY P

AMERICAN WHISTLE CORPORATION
6540 HUNTLEY ROAD
COLUMBUS, OH 43229
614-846-2918
800-876-2918
Fax: 614-846-4821
custserv@americanwhistle.com
www.americanwhistle.com
• Ray Giesse, CEO
Products:
Whistles, Award Whistles, Retail Packages, Lanyards, Safe-T-Tips, Police Accessories
Brands:
American Classic, Patriot Whistle, American Spirit, Safe-T-Tip, Nylon Woven Lanyard, Custom Blister, Snake Chain, Whistle Hook

AMF BOWLING WORLDWIDE
7313 BELL CREEK RD
MECHANICSVILLE, VA 23111
804-730-4000
800-342-5263
Fax: 804-730-1313
benefits@amf.com
www.amf.com
• Fred Hipp, President / Chief Executive Officer
• William McDonnell, Chief Financial Officer
• John Walker, Chief Operating Officer
(804) 730-4301
• David Hankin, Chief Executive Officer
• Farah Boroomand, Chief Financial Officer
• Mark Chamberlain, Chief Operating Officer
Products:
Bowling Centers, Bowling and Billiard Products, Shirts, Ladies Wear, Jackets, Accessories
Brands:
Polo

AMINCO INTERNATIONAL (USA) INCORPORATED
20571 CRESCENT BAY DRIVE
LAKE FOREST, CA 92630-8825
949-457-3261
800-929-4004
Fax: 949-457-3279
www.amincousa.com
• William Wu, President
Products:
Emblematic jewelry, collectible pins, key tags, magnets, zipper pulls, coasters, luggage tags, belt buckles
Brands:
Unforgettaballs, All Star Game, World Series, NHL All-Stars, NBA Championship, Zoo Animals Collection, Wildlife Collection

AMPROS TROPHIES
4830 N FRONT STREET
PHILADELPHIA, PA 19120
215-324-5565
Fax: 215-324-0417
trophywon@aol.com
ampros.com
• Scott Borman, President
Products:
Trophies, Awards - Components, Emblems, Jewelry, Medals, Plaques, Ribbons, Trophies.

ANCHOR INDUSTRIES INC.
1100 BURCH DRIVE
PO BOX 3477
EVANSVILLE, IN 47725
812-867-2421
800-544-4445
Fax: 812-867-1429
corp@anchorinc.com
www.anchorinc.com
• Bill Kinman, International Sales
Representative
(812) 867-4637
bill_kinman@anchorinc.com
• Pete Mogavero, Chairman & President
ext 322
Products:
Tents, Awnings, Pool Covers, Contract
Sewing, Factory Outlet, Field Covers, Circus
Tents, Carnival Ride Tops
Brands:
Clearspan Structures, Camp & Retreat
Tents, Llazar Retractable Awnings, New
Llazar Retractable Awnings

AND 1
101 ENTERPRISE
SUITE 100
ALISO VIEJO, CA 92656
610-249-2255
866-866-1232
customerservice@and1.com
www.and1.com
• Bart Houlahan, President
• Seth Berger, Chief Executive Officer
• James Fox, Chief Financial Officer
• Christina Houlahan, Chief Operating
Officer
Products:
Mens Footwear, Apparel, Kids Footwear,
PreSchool Footwear
Brands:
Lockdown, Grip Mid, Devastate, Phenom,
Fly Mid, In Rande, Tochillin Camput,
Playmaker Low, Haywood, Kids Lockdown,
Kids Grip Mid, Kids Phenom Low, Kids
Desparate, Kids Fly Mid, Diggy Dish Tee,
Diggy Game Tee, Diggy Game Short,
Groupies Tee, Your Girl Tee, Mixtape, Bag
O Chips Pocketed Game Short, Trash 101
Tee, I'm Sorry Tee, Player Original Game
Short, Taste of Defeat Tee, Triple Threat
Tee, Player Practice Fleece Hoody, LTWT,
In Ball We Trust

ANTIGUA GROUP, INC.
16651 N 84TH AVENUE
PEORIA, AZ 85382
623-523-6000
800-528-3133
Fax: 623-523-6016
www.antigua.com
• Ron McPherson, President/CEO
• Jerry K. Whitley, Finance VP
• Joe Blanchette, Information Technology
VP
• Micheal P. Whitley, Director Of Operations
• Penny Larson, Director Of Human
Resources
• Joseph M. Blanchette, VP Of Information
Technology
Products:
Lifestyle apparel, including golf and various
other sports.

ANTIOCH SPORTS
16083 N. 75TH AVENUE
PEORIA, AZ 85382

800-350-7019
Fax: 866-607-9918
• Ryan Coulter, Vice President
(623) 486-7462
Nature of Services:
Product manufacturer of sporting goods.

ANVIL KNITWEAR INC.
NEWTON
CHRIST CHURCH
BARBADOS, 17047
212-476-0300
800-223-0332
Fax: 212-808-4790
www.anvilknitwear.com
• Anthony Corsano, CEO
• Christopher Levesque, Marketing VP
Products:
Long and short sleeve T-shirts, polo shirts,
ringers/baseballs, henleys, athletic shorts,
caps, towels, robes, bags
Brands:
chromaZONE

APEX ATHLETIC EQUIPMENT INC.
160 KIPP AVE
ELMWOOD PARK, NJ 7407
201-475-8282
• Mike Lanzano, General Manager
Products:
Baseball - Bases, Protective-Catcher,
Protective-Umpire; Football - Practice
Equipment; Gymnastics - Mats; Track &
Field/Running - Vaulting Pits or Mattresses;
Wrestling - Mats.

APSCO ENTERPRISES
50TH STREET & FIRST AVENUE
BUILDING 57, 5TH FLOOR
BROOKLYN, NY 11232
718-965-9500
Fax: 718-965-3088
• Philip DiPietro, Owner
• Philip Livoti, President
Products:
Screen Printing, Embroidery, RF Welding,
Graphic Design, Garment Manufacturing

AQUA LEISURE IND., INC.
525 BODWELL STREET EXTENSION
PO BOX 239
AVON, MA 02322-1098
508-587-5400
866-807-3998
Fax: 508-587-5318
customercare@aqualeisure.com
www.aqualeisure.com
• Simon C. Fireman, Chairman
• Steven M. Berenson, President
• Richard Moeller, Sales Asst VP
Products:
Pools, Lounges & Floats, Toys & Games,
Swim & Dive Gear, Sun Protection, Learn to
Swim 1-2-3, Fitness, Winter Fun
Brands:
Simple-Set Pools, SwimSchool, SunSmart,
Dolfino, AquaPools, AquaFitness, Uncle
Bob's, AquaPLAY, AquaSport, AquaPro,
AquaGames, Inflatables

AQUA SPHERE US
2340 COUSTEAU COURT
VISTA, CA 92081
760-597-5082
800-775-3483
Fax: 760-597-4914

support@aqualung.com
www.aquaphereusa.com
• Laguette Olivier, Director Marketing
Products:
Regulators, instrumentation, buoyancy
devices, masks, fins, snorkels, wet suits,
and gear bags
Brands:
Seal Mask, Seal XP, Seal Kid, Kaiman
Goggles, Sphera, Sphera Jr., Zip Fin,
SideDraft Snorkel, Aqua FM Snorkel, Aqua
Skins, Stingray, Wet/Dry Duffel, Anti Fog,
Dry Towel, Kickboard, Protective Case,
Strap, Strap Cover, Aqua Glide Cap, Swim
Glove, Swim Paddles
Swimming Sponsor:
Ford Ironman World Championship

AQUAJOGGER
4660 MAIN STREET
UNIT B270
SPRINGFIELD, OR 97478
541-484-2454
800-922-9544
Fax: 541-484-0501
info@aquajogger.com
www.aquajogger.com
• Steve Bergstrom, Vice President Sales &
Marketing
Nature of Services:
Manufacturer of aquatic exercise equipment.
Brands:
AquaJogger

AQUASPORT CORPORATION
1651 WHITFIELD AVENUE
SARASOTA, FL 34243
941-751-7886
Fax: 941-751-7851
• Dean Samuelson, President

ARBOR
102 WASHINGTON BOULEVARD
VENICE, CA 90292
310-577-1120
Fax: 310-577-1121
www.arborcollective.com
• Bob Carlson, President/Founder
• Greg Bergen, Sales Manager
• Brad Farmer, Marketing Director
Products:
Snowboards, Skateboards, Gears
Brands:
A-Frame, Element, Abacus, Draft, Formula,
Mystic, Crossbow, Roundhouse, Push,
Stance, Basich Series, Mini, Cruiser,
Carver, Hats & Beanies, Men's Tees, Men's
Hoodies, Women's Tees & Hoodies

ARCOA INDUSTRIES
911 S. ANDREASEN DR.
ESCONDIDO, CA 92029
760-599-6915
888-637-1926
Fax: 760-599-6986
info@arcoa.com
www.arcmate.com
• Chet Warfel, Chief Executive Officer
info@arcoa.com
• Marty Ziegenfuss, President
info@arcoa.com
Products:
Labor Saving Devices
Brands:
E-Z Reacher, E-Z Grabber, E-Z Litter Stick

ARI-MED PHARMACEUTICALS
1615 W UNIVERSITY DRIVE
SUITE 135
TEMPE, AZ 85281-3257
480-966-9802
800-527-4923
Fax: 480-966-9806
info@ari-med.com
www.ari-med.com
• Jim Bilas, Director of Marketing
bilas@ari-med.com
Products:
Medical products used for sports training, topical analgesic. Market Flex-All pain releiving gels to the sports medicine marketplace.
Brands:
Flexall 454

ARISTO IMPORT COMPANY, INC.
85 HUNT ROAD
ORANGEBURG, NY 10962
845-359-0720
800-352-6304
Fax: 845-359-0020
aristoinc@aol.com
Products:
Chronographs, Pedometers, Stop Clocks, Stopwatches-Digital, Mechanical, Timers.
Brands:
Apollo, Aristo

ARMOUR GOLF COMPANY
40 KING STREET W
TORONTO, ONTARIO, CANADA M5H 3Y2
416-361-6336
800-723-4653
Fax: 416-785-4276
mail@hilcocc.com
www.tommyarmourgolf.com
• James Salter, Chief Executive Officer
Products:
Golf Apparel, Bags, Balls, Clubs Iron or Wood Sets, Clubs Putters, Clubs Utility, Gloves, Headcovers, Umbrellas.
Brands:
Diamond Scot, Dual Force, Golden Scot, Odyssey, Silver Scot, Soft Scot, Tommy Armour, Tommy Gun, T-Line

ARROYO COMBINATION EXERCISE BIKE
1295 E ATHENS
FRESNO, CA 93720
916-977-0112
Fax: 229-433-0718
• Joe Arroyo, President
Products:
Exercise bicycles.

ARTHRON, INC.
PO BOX 1627
BRENTWOOD, TN 37024
800-758-5633
Fax: 615-371-5405
www.sportsinjuries.com
• Denis Rowe, Director
(615) 377-6595
denisro@comcast.net
• Steven Antonopoulos, Head Athletic Trainer
Products:
Sports Medicine products.
Brands:
Impact Pads, Impact AC Pad, Impact Hip Pad, Impact Quad Pad, Impact Delt Pad, Impact O-S Pad, Impact Clavicle Pad

ARVINMERITOR
2135 W MAPLE ROAD
TROY, MI 48084
248-435-1000
800-535-5560
Fax: 248-435-1393
• Charles G McClure, Chairman, CEO and President
• James Donlon, Senior Vice President and Chief Financial Officer
• Lin Cummins, Senior Vice President and Communications
• Rakesh Sachdev, Senior Vice President/President-Asia & Pacific
• Kevin Nowlan, Vice President and Chief Financial Officer
• Jeffrey A. Craig, Senior Vice President and President, Commerci
• Pedro Ferro, Senior Vice President and President, Aftermar
• Vernon G. Baker II, Senior Vice President and General Counsel
• Barbara G. Novak, Vice President and Corporate Secretary
• Larry E. Ott, Senior Vice President, Human Resources and Co
Products/Services
Manufacturer of automotive/vehicle parts, systems and technologies including: chassis systems; door systems; roof systems, and steel wheels, etc.

ASA PRODUCTS, INC.
532 CORALRIDGE PLACE
CITY OF INDUSTRY, CA 91746
626-855-0900
877-869-6451
Fax: 626-855-0931
sales@mobocruiser.com
www.asaproducts.com
• Melody Hsieh, President/Owner
(626) 855-0900
melody@asaproducts.com
• Jessie Wu, Accounting Manager
jessie@asaproducts.com
• Stephen Collier, Customer Care Specialist
• Harun Riyanto, Executive Administrator
harun@asaproducts.com
Products:
Ultimate Three Wheeled Cruisers: Mobo Shift; Mobo Triton, Mobo Triton pro, Mobo Mobito, Helmets, Combination lock, Bicycle Pump, Pedals, Triton Cruiser Basket, Flashlight, Bottle Holder, Flash Pin and Water Ball.
Year Founded:
1998
Brands:
Mobo

ASCENSION
3526 E FORT LOWELL ROAD
TUCSON, AZ 85716
520-881-3993
800-459-0400
Fax: 520-881-4983
www.wheelchairlift.com
• Megan Ehrnard, Inside Sls Rep
(800) 459-0400
• Timothy C. Mabe, President & CEO
(520) 881-3993
• Andrew Brown, Event Services Manager
Products:
Portable wheelchair lifts for sporting events, vehicle transporting, etc.
Brands:
Ascension

ASERTA SPORTS
1660 MABURY ROAD
SAN JOSE, CA 95133
408-251-PUTT (7888)
• Michael D Bonneau, Founder
• Richard J Selmeier, President & CEO
• Steve Sacks, Vice President Operations
• Steven Gray, National Director Sales
• Richard Parente, Design & Product Development
Products and Services
Aserta Sports, Inc. is in the business of designing, manufacturing and marketing innovative golf products that enhance performance and enjoyment of the game.

ASHAWAY LINE & TWINE MFG. COMPANY
24 LAUREL STREET
ASHAWAY, RI 2804
401-377-2221
800-556-7260
Fax: 401-377-9091
sales@ashawayusa.com
www.ashawayusa.com
• Pamela A. Crandall, Chairperson of the Board
• Kathryn C. Crandall, President
• Steven J. Crandall, VP
Products:
Racquet Sports - Racquet Strings.
Brands:
Crossfire, Dynamite, Flex, Killfire, Microlegend, Powerkill, Powernick, Rally Super-Kill, Super Nick, Super Nick XL, Vantage

ASHWORTH, INC.
5545 FERMI COURT
CARLSBAD, CA 92008-7324
760-438-6610
866-530-8624
Fax: 760-438-6657
• Christa McNamara, Director Public Relations
(760) 918-6466
• Allan Fletcher, Chief Executive Officer
• Greg Slack, Chief Financial Officer/ Treasurer
Products:
Golf Apparel.
Brands:
Ashworht.Corporate, Callaway, The Game

ASICS AMERICA CORPORATION
29 PARKER
SUITE 100
IRVINE, CA 92618
800-678-9435
800-333-8404
Fax: 949-453-0292
consumer@asicsamerica.com
www.asicsamerica.com
• Masaaki Uetsuki, Chmn, CEO, ASICS Tiger
• Kiyomi Wada, Pres / Rep Dir
• Richard Bourne, President
• Motoi Oyama, President & CEO
Products:
Baseball - Shoes; Basketball - Shoes; Warm-Up Suits; Racquet Sports - Apparel, Bags-Equipment, Shoes; Softball - Shoes; Track & Field - Apparel, Bags, Shoes; Training & Conditioning - Cross-training Apparel, Shoes; Volleyball - Shoes; Uniforms; Wrestling; Cheering - Apparels, Footwear, Bag

Brands:
GEL-Lyte, GELS, GT-Intensity

ASTRO TURF MANUFACTURING COMPANY
701 LEANDER DRIVE
LEANDER, TX 78641
706-277-8873
877-723-8873
help@astroturf.com
www.astroturf.com
• Jim Savoca, VP Sales / Marketing
info@astroturf.com
• William La Starks, Manager Golf Products
info@astroturf.com
• Regina Duckett, Administrative Asst
info@astroturf.com
Products:
Synthetic turf products
Brands:
AstroLawnr, AstroPlayr, AstroTurfr, NeXturfr and PureGrassTM

ATHENA GOLF
55706 BRAE BURN
LA QUINTA, CA 92253
760-564-7554
877-328-4362
Fax: 760-771-0321
• Debbie Behlman, Director Marketing
Products:
Women's golf apparel.
Brands:
Athena Golf Apparel

ATHLETIC & PERFORMANCE RIGGING/APR
146 RIVERSIDE DRIVE
TIFFIN, OH 44883-1644
419-443-0500
800-445-1546
Fax: 419-447-5969
www.athleticrigging.net
• Steve Maiberger, VP
Products:
Motorized Netting Systems.

ATHLETIC FIELD SERVICES, INC.
PO BOX 215
GENESEE DEPOT, WI 53127
262-968-9101
Fax: 262-968-9102
www.afstrack.com
• Gwenn Zerull, President
• Bob Zerull, Vice President of Sales & Marketing
• Russell Hansen, Vice President of Production
• Devin Wheat, Project Manager
Products:
Running Track Facilities Surfaces
Brands:
Seal Flex

ATHLETIC KNIT
2 SCARLETT ROAD
TORONTO, ONTARIO, CANADA M6N 4J6
416-766-6151
888-818-5648
Fax: 416-766-7381
www.athleticknit.com
• Bernard Sliwin, President
• David Sliwin, Vice President
(416) 766-6151
david.sliwin@athleticknit.com
• Daniel Sliwin, Vice President

daniel.sliwin@athleticknit.com
• John Larin, Sales Manager
johnl@athleticknit.com
• Aaron Sellon, Sales and Customer Service
aarons@athleticknit.com
• Brian Edwards, Sales and Customer Service
briane@athleticknit.com
• Blair Mcinnins, Sales and Customer Service
blairm@athleticknit.com
• Maria Mcinnins, Sales and Customer Service
Products:
Baseball, Basketball, Football, Hockey, Lacrose and Volleyball Apparel

ATHLETIC TRAINING EQUIPMENT COMPANY/ATEC
655 SPICE ISLAND DRIVE
SPARKS, NV 89431
800-998-2832
800-755-5100
Fax: 800-959-2832
askATEC@wilson.com
www.atecsports.com
• Eugene Grant, President
• Larry Leukhardt, Dir Sls
Products:
Baseball Bags Equipment, Batting Ranges/Indoor/Outdoor, Cages/Backstops, Nets, Pitching Machines; Softball Balls-Molded Urethane, Cages/Backstops, Nets, Pitching Machines, Field Maintenance, Protective Equipment.
Brands:
ATEC, Casey, Hummer, Tuffy, Soft Toss, Hitting Streak, Rookie, Catch Net

ATLANTIC FITNESS PRODUCTS
PO BOX 300
LINTHICUM, MD 21090
410-859-3538
800-445-1855
Fax: 410-859-3907
www.atlantic-fitness.com
• Ronald E. Overby, VP
• Faye Miller, Secretary
• Richard Stone, Sales Manager
Products:
Fitness Equipment.
Brands:
Atlantic

ATOMIC SKI USA
9 COLUMBIA DRIVE
AMHERST, NH 03031
603-880-6143
800-258-5020
Fax: 436-4523900120
info@atomicski.com
www.atomicski.com
• Peter Juric, International Race Director
• Eduardo Guzman, US National Race Director
Products:
Alpine Accessories, Bindings, Boots, Poles, Skis. Nordic Accessories, Mountain Boots, Snowboards, Skis.
Brands:
Atomic, Koflach, Oxygen
Skiing Sponsor:
NYSSRA - New York State Ski Racing Association

ATSKO INC.
2664 RUSSELL S E
ORANGEBURG, SC 29115
803-531-1820
800-845-2728
Fax: 803-531-2139
info@atsko.com
www.atsko.com
• Kurt Besser, President
Kurt@atsko.com
• Kurt Baumgartner, National Sales Manager
Description:
Products to restore performance of outdoor clothes, footwear, and equipment.
Products:
Manufacturer of SNO-SEAL, Sport-Wash, Water-Guard, U-V-Killer, Sensi-Clean, No-O-Dor and other brands to care for clothing, footwear and outdoor gear.
Clients:
Distributors and Retailers of Sporting Goods accessories and equipment.
Brands:
Sno-Seal, Rapid Rod, Sport-Wash, U-V-Killer, U-V Shield, U-V Block, N-O-DOR, Pro-Tech-Skin, Water-Guard

AUDERO SPORTS SUPPLY, INC.
4935 MCCONNELL AVENUE
SUITE 11
LOS ANGELES, CA 90066
310-822-3637
800-443-5037
Fax: 310-822-6308
olympussoc@aol.com
• Jose C. Audero, President
Products:
Soccer equipment and accessories
Brands:
Olympus

AUGUSTA SPORTSWEAR
425 PARK W DRIVE
GROVETOWN, GA 30813
706-860-4633
800-237-6695
Fax: 706-868-5672
sales@augustasportswear.com
www.augustasportswear.com
• Mike Holliman, Vice President Human Resources
• Chad Trollinger, Director Marketing
Products:
Athletic Jerseys, Shorts & Pants, Athletic Fleece, Outerwear, Sport Shirts, Woven Shirts, Corporate Casual, Aprons, Totes, Bags, Headwear and Accessories
Year Founded:
1977
Brands:
Augusta

AUSTIN ATHLETIC COMPANY
1005 E 39TH STREET
SHAWNEE, OK 74804
405-273-8681
800-813-7706
Fax: 405-275-5859
• Orville Austin, Owner
• Craig Ansell, Manager Production
Products:
Shoulder, Hip, Thigh and Knee Pads and accessories and football equipment reconditioning
Brands:
Austin Lok-Cup and Air-Lok shoulder pads,

RC-PRO, RC-P, RC-F, HYL, BSI and SSI hip pads, ATP-R thigh pad, KYL knee pad, A-SYM and A-SYW sideline markers, A-SFW pylons, A-GPR goal post pad, A-GPD deluxe goal post pad, TPZ-8, RRD and STP-8 dummy, SRD-5 CRD-5 and SHD-6 blocking shield

AUTHENTIC FITNESS CORP.
501 7TH AVENUE
NEW YORK, NY 10018
212-287-8250
800-547-8770
Fax: 323-721-3613
• Joseph C. Gromek, President / Chief Executive Officer
• Lawrence Rutkowski, EVP / Chief Financial Officer
• Helen McCluskey, Warnaco Intimate Apparel President
• Frank Tworecke, CFO & Executive Vice President
Products:
Swimwear, fitness apparel and swin accessories
Brands:
Speedo, Ann Cole, Nautica, Sandcastle and Sunset Beach

AUTHENTIC STREET SIGNS
183 MAIN STREET
SAINT PETER, IL 62880
618-349-8878
800-289-4042
Fax: 618-349-6245
www.authenticstreetsigns.com
• Ed Onorato, National Sales Manager
Products:
Authentic street signs, LED night light, Neon signs
Brands:
Chicago Bulls, Denver Broncos, New York Yankees, St. Louis Cardinals, Philadelphia Flyers and Texas Longhorns

AUTOMATED BATTING CAGES CORPORATION
4897 INDIAN SCHOOL ROAD NE
SUITE 150
SALEM, OR 97305
503-304-8899
800-854-3140
Fax: 503-304-1899
parts@jjamusements.com
www.battingcages.com
• Doug Spray, President / Sales Construction
doug@battingcages.com
• Jim Peper, Plant Supervisor
jim@battingcages.com
• Darrin Lenz, Service Manager
Products:
Baseball and softball wheel-style pitching machines, coin/token boxes, conveyor/ball feeding and sorting systems, sign packages, light boxes, control panels, main mast slide collar, complete netting systems, design consultation and more
Brands:
ABC equipments

AVALANCHE SNOWBOARDS INC.
991 TYLER STREET
SUITE 200
BENICIA, CA 94510-2914

707-746-6982
800-541-0218
Fax: 707-746-5769
• Chris Sanders, President
Products:
Snowboards and accessories.
Brands:
MBA, Universal

AVERY SPORTS TURF, INC.
9 RIVERSIDE INDUSTRIAL PARK NE
ROME, GA 30161-8434
706-802-1970
800-765-3034
Fax: 706-802-1737
www.averysportsturf.com
• George Avery, President
Products:
Turf for fairways, target greens, range mats, athletic fields and tennis courts

AVIA AMERICAN SPORTING GOODS
7525 IRVINE CENTER DR
Suite 150
IRVINE, CA 92618
888-855-2842
800-848-8698
service@avia.com
www.avia.com
Products:
Basketball Shoes, Basketball Apparel; Running Shoes; Running Apparel; Women's Fitness Apparel

AWARD DECALS
14802 W 114TH TERRACE
LENEXA, KS 66215
913-677-6681
800-525-9395
Fax: 913-677-4250
order@awarddecals.com
www.awarddecals.com
• Clay Hirner, Partner
• Mallory Hirner, Partner
Products:
Custom decals and signs with mascot or logo, including football helmet decals.

AWARDS ETC.
4333 WELBORN ROAD
BRYAN, TX 77801
979-268-0981
Fax: 979-268-0985
• Robert E. Earle, Owner
Products:
Diploma Plaques, Framing, Laser, Engraving, Plaques, Trophies

B & G EQUIPMENT COMPANY
135 REGION S DRIVE
JACKSON, GA 30233
678-688-5601
800-544-8811
Fax: 678-688-5633
salesdept@bgequip.com
www.bgequip.com
• Bob Mathews, VP Manufacturing
(678) 688-5601
• George Brehm, VP Sales and Marketing
(678) 688-5601
• Lynn Donato, VP Sales - Retail Products
• Cecil Patterson, President, CEO
• Sargent Mark, Senior Vice President of Sales Industrial & J
• Amy Gwara, Pest Control, Industrial & Export Sales Distr

• Heiney Bob, Pest Control Products Sales & Tech Support
Products:
B&G Water Fountain Model WB-45
Brands:
PistrolPro 700 Series, VersaFoamer 4000, Borate 5000 & 5400 Sprayer, 1151-M Mini, 1152-A Hand, Long Reach Granular and 2250 Electric Dust-R, Perimeter Patrol System, 2600 Flex-A-Lite fogger, Robco Perimeter Spray Gun, MultiDose 3000, PestPro2000 Operator, B&G Acid, B&G Chemical Resistant and B&G Industrial Sprayer, Dura Spray, AquaMate, PetWash, PetFood Protectors, Easy Hose, Watering Wand

B&R ERECTORS/BLEACHERS
14200 WASHINGTON STREET
WOODSTOCK, IL 60098
866-253-2247
800-451-0638
Fax: 877-994-1715
bleachers@brbleachers.com
www.brbleachersonline.com
• Roger Be Jr, President
(866) 253-2247
• Terry O'Hagan, Vice President, Operations
(866) 253-2247
tohagan@brbleachers.com
Products:
Seats and Bleachers, including Covers, Mobile Seats, Permanent, Portable and Replacement Seats, as well as Bleacher Repair, Maintenance, Inspection and Consulting
Brands:
BR Bulldog Power System, BR Aisle Way Solutions, BR Rail Systems, BR Closure Systems, BR Surface Components, BR Bleacher R&D Products and BR Bleacher Seating Options

B' WARMER THERMAL PRODUCTS
10828 139TH STREET
EDMONTON, ALBERTA, CANADA T5M 1P7
780-482-6401
888-426-2224
Fax: 780-488-6182
info@bwarmer.com
• Dirk De Man, Chief Financial Officer
• Gordon Red Batty, Equipment Manager
Products:
Hand warmer, mitts and pants that will keep you warm and comfortable
Brands:
B' Warmer Hand Warmer, B' Warmer Hand Dryer, B' Warmer Sideliner Mitts, B' Warmer Tear-Away Pants and B' Warmer Boot Sock

B-BALL LIGHTS
6911 PALMER ROAD
GREENS FORK, IN 47345
800-515-9049
Fax: 765-886-5471
• Bruce Watts, Marketing
Products:
Basketball Facilities; Shot Clocks, Scoreboard Systems; Portable Scoreboards
Brands:
B-Ball Lights

BABOLAT VS NORTH AMERICA, INC.
1775 CHERRY STREET
SUITE 100
LOUISVILLE, CO 80027-3139

720-542-6290
877-316-9435
Fax: 303-444-2088
www.babolat.us
• Jean-Louis Boyre, President
Nature of Service:
Wholesale to dealers
Year Founded:
1999
Products:
Tennis Equipment and Products, Rackets, Strings, Shoes, Bags and Accessories.
Brands:
Babolot

BABY FANATIC, LLC
1901 E FRANKLIN STREET
SUITE 114
RICHMOND, VA 23223
804-644-4707
Fax: 804-644-4709
www.babyfanatic.com
• Tricia Woodson, Chief Executive Officer
(804) 833-3131
Products:
Amusement, decorations, entertainment, toys, embroidered pillow and comforter, shirts and other accessories related to sports teams and events. NCAA, MLB, & NFL-themed baby products.

BACHARACH RASIN SPORTING GOODS, INC.
802 GLEN EAGLES COURT
TOWSON, MD 21204
410-825-6747
800-726-2368
Fax: 410-321-0720
• Chris M. Hutchins, President
Products:
Durable goods, boys clothing & furnishings, apparel & garments, women's apparel, men's clothing & furnishings and sporting goods

BACON & COMPANY
200-208 W SUMMIT HILL
KNOXVILLE, TN 37902
865-523-9181
Fax: 865-546-2212
info@baconco.com
www.baconco.com
Products:
Writing Instruments, Office Essentials, Corporate Events, Employee & Client Rewards, Clothing Accessories
Brands:
Anvil, Ashworth, Augusta, Bic, BlueGeneration, The Brand Book Online, Carhartt, Custom Crest, Cutter & Buck, Gemline, Leeds, Sanford, Port Authority, Vantage, VF Imagewear

BADEN SPORTS, INC.
3401 LIND AVE SW
RENTON, WA 98057
253-925-0500
800-544-2998
Fax: 253-925-0570
info@badensports.com
www.badensports.com
• Michael Shindler, Chief Executive Officer
Products:
Athletic balls for baseball, basketball, football, playgrounds, rugby, soccer, softball, volleyball, water polo, etc. Notebooks, ball bags, soccer socks.

Brands:
Baden Perfection, Baden Lexum, Play ground, Baden Officials

BADGE-A-MINIT LTD.
345 N LEWIS AVENUE
OGLESBY, IL 61348
800-223-4103
800-223-4103
Fax: 815-883-9696
questions@badgeaminit.com
www.badgeaminit.com
• Malcolm Roebuck, Chairman of the Board
• Cindy Kurkowski, President
Products:
Training & Conditioning - Benches, Exercise Boards, Exercise Tables, Leg Elevation Boards, Stall Bars, Incline Boards; Training Room Supplies - Benches, Taping Tables

BAG BOY COMPANY
2701 EMERYWOOD PARKWAY
SUITE 101
RICHMOND, VA 23294
800-955-2269
Fax: 888-822-4269
bagboycs@bagboy.com
www.bagboyllc.com
• David Boardman, President & CEO
Products:
Golf Carts, Golf Bags, Travel Cases and Accessories
Brands:
Bag Boy, AMF, Baby Jogger

BAGGO
600 MID AMERICA BLVD
HOT SPRINGS, AR 71913
501-767-3855
888-323-1813
Fax: 501-767-5173
customerservice@baggo.com
www.baggo.com
• Kirk Conville, President
(888) 323-1813
kirk@baggo.com
Products:
Bag Toss Game; Apparel and Accessories, Bean Bags
Brands:
BAGGO, BAGGO #1, BAGGO #2, BAGGO Build Your Own!, BAGGO Fan, BAGGO Guy, BAGGO Mouth, BAGGO Themed

BAILEY MANUFACTURING COMPANY
PO BOX 130
LODI, OH 44254-0130
800-321-8372
Fax: 800-224-5390
baileytables@gmail.com
www.baileymfg.com
• Larry Strimple, President
Products:
Parallel Bars, Work Tables, Mat Tables, Treatment Tables, Examination Tables, Tilt Tables, Standing Tables, Sports Medicine Tables, Couches/Lounges, Exercise Devices, Weights, Stools, Chairs, Wheelchair Aids, Aids, Posture Mirrors, Training Stairs, Positioning Equipment, Positioning Pillows, Professional Modular Training Room Furniture, Classic Modular Training Room Furniture, Deluxe Taping Table, Whirlpool Tables, Back Extension Treatment Table, Hand Therapy Table & Desk, Economy Electric Hi-Lo Adjustable

Back Treatment Table, Economy Electric Treatment Table, Training Room Furnitures

BALAZS, INC.
625 TODD ROAD
HONEY BROOK, PA 19344
610-433-4515
888-466-6765
Fax: 610-433-4695
info@balazsboxing.com
www.balazsboxing.com
• Brian DeMaris, President
brian@balazsboxing.com
Nature of Service:
Boxing and Fitness Equipment
Products:
Bag Mounts, Bags, Gloves, Protective Gear, Training Accessories, Instructional Videos
Brands:
Balazs, Everlast, Century

BALFOUR CO.
7211 CIRCLE S ROAD
BUILDING A
AUSTIN, TX 78745
877-225-3687
800-225-3687
Fax: 512-443-5213
rings@balfour.com
www.balfour.com
• David G. Fiore, President / Chief Executive Officer
• Sherice P. Bench, Chief Financing Officer
• Parke H. Davis, VP, Retail
Products:
Certificates, medals, rings, high quality jewelry, announcements, and frames for athletics and sporting events.

BALL & HELMET HOLDER, LLC
126 SMITH STREET
DERBY, CT 6418
203-627-6351
• Nicholas Donofrio, Founder
Products:
Ball holder, Helmet holder

BALL DYNAMICS INTERNATIONAL
14215 MEAD STREET
LONGMONT, CO 80504
800-752-2255
800-752-2255
Fax: 877-223-2962
• Joanne Posner-Mayer, Founder
• Cheryl Soleway, Master Trainer
Products:
Balance Tools, Books, DVDs & Videos, Seating, Exercise Mats and Accessories, Exercise Balls, Massage and Sensory Tools, Therapy Mats and Tools, Yoga and Pilates Mats
Brands:
FitBALL, AIREX, Gymnic, ChiBALL

BALLANDRA CORPORATION
3800 BAYVIEW STREET STEVESTON VILLAGE
SUITE 202
RICHMOND, BC, CANADA 90670
604-274-5774
Fax: 604-274-5775
www.balandra.ca
• Caleb Law, President
Products:
Timing Devices - Chronographs, Pedometers, Stopwatches-Digital, Timers

Brands:
Becona, Pateau, Quartz

BALLCO PRODUCTS, INC.
114 W POPLAR AVENUE
SAN MATEO, CA 94402-1152
650-343-2918
Fax: 650-343-0614
• Count Ja Lewenhaupt, President
Products:
Eyewear - Goggles; Racquet Sports - Racquet Strings, Racquet Grips, Tennis Balls, Tennis Racquets; Skiing-Alpine - Bags, Gloves, Poles, Ski Brakes
Brands:
Bota

BALLGIRL ATHLETIC
225 WESTCHESTER AVENUE
PORT CHESTER, NY 10573
877-268-7778
877-268-7778
Fax: 800-385-7804
• Henry Norley, Jr, General Manager
Products:
Sports apparel, team uniforms, jerseys, and bottoms
Brands:
Athena Dazzle Jersey, Excela Short, Game Short, Lightning Rip Away Pant, Lightning Shooting Shirt, Olympia Sleeveless, Competitor Short Sleeve, Medalista 3 Short, Medalista 5 Short, Valda Short Sleeve, Performa Sleeveless

BALLQUBE, INC.
12146 CR 4233 W
CUSHING, TX 75760
903-863-5572
800-543-1470
Fax: 903-863-5571
sales@ballqube.com
www.ballqube.com
• Steve Castleberry, General Manager
Products:
Hat Holder, Baseball Holder, Basketball/Soccer Ball, Bat Rack Holder, Cereal Box Holder, Figure Holder, Grandstand Football Holder, Football Helmet Holder, Golf Ball Holder, Hockey Stick Holder, Hockey Stick Holder, Golf Ball Holder, Jersey Holders, Mini-Helmet Holder, Softball Holder, Three Ball & Three Puck Holders, Team Roster Cabinets, Laser Engraved Team Logo Displays, Card Holders
Brands:
PRO BOX, T-N-T, BallQube, Cap It

BALLSTARS
100 MISSION WOODS DRIVE
NEW CENTURY, KS 66031
913-764-7738
800-237-0653
Fax: 913-254-7803
sales@ballstars.com
www.photoball.com
• Nicole Gresham Perry, Chief Executive Officer
(913) 764-7738
• Marshall Widman, Founder
• Devlan Reeves, Vice President Of Marketing
Description:
Group holds global patents for imprinting photos and logos on balls.sports balls.
Products:

Heat Transfer Systems for imprinting photos, text, logos and other graphics on actual sports balls; Accessories - Baseball Display, Softball Display, Hockey Puck Cube Display/Case, Baseball or Softball Holder, Wire Ornament Hanger, Ornament Tree

BAMBOO & RATTAN WORKS INC.
470 OBERLIN AVENUE S
LAKEWOOD, NJ 8701
732-370-0220
800-422-6266
Fax: 732-905-8386
bambooman1@aol.com
• Arthur Leon Maison, President/Chief Operating Officer
bambooman1@aol.com
• Suzanne M. Maison, Vice President/Marketing Director
Suzbamboo@comcast.net
Services:
Supplier of Manau rattan for martial arts and SCA, whipping poles for greens, fencing materials - custom and stock.
Clients:
Walt Disney, Macy's, Polo Ralph Lauren, African Lion Safari, Six Flags Great Adventure, American National Can, Ball Metal Beverage, Crown Cork and Seal, Henredon Furniture, Ficks Reed, Bauer International, City of Virginia Beach, Cincinnati Zoo, Brooklyn Botanic, Bronx Zoo, Cleveland Botanical, Garden, Como Park Conservatory, Columbia University, Denver Black Arts Festival.
Year Founded:
1880

BANNERMAN LTD.
41 KELFIELD STREET
REXDALE, ONTARIO, CANADA M9W 5A3
416-247-7875
800-665-2696
Fax: 416-247-6540
info@sportsturfmagic.com
www.sportsturfmagic.com
• George Bannerman, Sales
• Ron Bannerman, Sales
Nature of Service:
Equipment for professional turf management.
Year Founded:
1958
Products:
Aeriation equipment, Shaver Mowers, Drag Mats, Seeding Equipment, Lawn Thatchers, Trimmers/Blowers, Turf Comb, Turf Drainer, Top Dressing Equipment, Lawn Bowls Pusher, Greens Thatchers, Rakes, Turf Rollers.

BARCO MEDIA
3059 PREMIERE PARKWAY
DULUTH, GA 30097
678-475-8000
webmaster@barco.com
www.barco.com
• Herman Daems, Chairman
• Eric VanZele, President & CEO
• Filip Pintelon, Chief Operating Officer
• Carl Peeters, Chief Financial Officer
• Jan Van Acoleyen, Chief Human Resources Officer
• Jacques Bertrand, Chief Sales Officer
• Dave Scott, General Manager Defense &

Aerospace Division
• Herman Daems, Chairman
Products:
Visual Displays, Controllers, Graphical Cards, Display Management Service

BARRECRAFTERS
700 BERNARD
GRANBY, CANADA J2G 9H7
800-451-3240
Fax: 800-361-6389
• Mark Snelling, President
• Robert Finnegan, Engineering VP
• Mark Comcowich, National Sales Manager
Products:
Automotive and Rack Accessories, Sport Lockers & Car-Go Boxes, Bike Racks, Hitch Racks
Brands:
Sierra Ski Racks, SB-4 Snowboard Rack, SX-22 Mini-Roof Kit, US-276 - 299 Specialty Hooks, Aerro B-4 & B-6, US-454 Horizontal Ski Kit, SX-53 Sierra Ski Racks, US-243 Factory Mount Snowboard Kit, EL-1 The Elevator, Snap-Around-Mounts, US-207 Mini-Winch Kit, KI-16 Permanent Mounting Gutter, A857 Piranha Upright Bike Rack, US-231 Upright Bike Kit/Locking, US-311 Locking Fork Mount Bike Kit, US-301 Wheel Carrier, A859 Piranha Fork Mount Bike Rack, RP-1 Bike RackPack, A1145 Super Touring, A1166 Super Voyager, A1122 Super Pacer, BSR-1 Hang 2 Bike Storage Rack, A825 Pro Mount Fork Block, APK-400 Pickup Bike Rack, A30503T Hitch N Drive 3-Bike Ball Mo

BASEBALL FIT HITTING & PITCHING ACADEMY
11204 DOVER CT
YUKON, OK 73099
405-373-3253
support@baseballfit.com
www.baseballfit.com
• Steve Zawrotny, Director of Training
(405) 373-3253
steve@baseballfit.com
Products:
Throwing Velocity Booklet, Bat Speed Booklet, Strength & Conditioning Booklet, E-BOOKLETS, Weighted Softballs, BIG Z Bat, Softball Videos, Metal Baseball Bats, Metal Softball Bats, Wood Baseball Bats, Throwing Strikes Booklet, Baseball Videos
Brands:
Baseball Fit, BIG Z

BASIC COATINGS, INC.
1001 BROWN AVENUE
PO BOX 3126
TOLEDO, OH 43607
515-288-0231
800-241-5471
Fax: 800-488-5800
bcinfo@basiccoatings.com
www.basiccoatings.com
• Nels Ingebrigtsen, President
• Mark Vick, Director ofSales
Products:
Water based wood floor coatings, Oil based wood floor coatings, Dustless systems, Maintenance products
Brands:
StreetShoe, Flo-cat, Commercial Catalyzed Sealer, Hydroline Sealer, TyKote, Squeaky, Dustline Dust Mop Treatment, Basic Oil

Modified Urethane MSDS, Heavy Duty
OMU, Amberizer MSDS,

BASS IND INCORPORATED
3485 NE 65TH STREET
MIAMI, FL 33147
305-751-2716
800-346-8575
Fax: 305-756-6165
sales@bassind.com
www.bassind.com
• Robert Baron, President
(305) 751-2716
rmb@bassind.com
• Eric Finnegan, VP
(305) 751-2716
sales@bassind.com
Products:
Theatre Display Systems, Transparency
Showcases, Casino Display Systems, Video
Store Displays, Home Cinema Accessories,
Sports Cinema Seating & Accessories

BASS PRO SHOPS
2500 E KEARNEY
SPRINGFIELD, MO 65898
417-873-5000
800-976-6344
Fax: 417-873-4672
www.basspro.com
• John Morris, Founder
• James Hagale, CEO/President
• Stan Lippelman, Vice President Of
Marketing
• Larry Whitely, Manager Of
Communications and Outdoor Education
• Jenna Kendall, Media Informations
Coordinator
Baseball Sponsor:
MLB St Louis Cardinals
Fishing Sponsor:
National Hunting and Fishing Day.
Brands:
Johnny Morris Signature Series Trigger
Rods, Qualifier XPSTM Trigger R, Tourney
Special Graphite Rods, ExtremeTM XPSTM
Woo Dav, ExtremeTM XPSTM Trigger,
Browning Fishing Citori Trigger Rods,
Browning Fishing SilaFlex Trigger Rods,
Bass Pro Shops Johnny Morris Signature
Series Spinning Rods, Bass Pro Shops Pro
Qualifier XPSTM Spinning, Bass Pro Shops
ExtremeTM XPSTM Spinnin, Bass Pro
Shops ExtremeTM XPSTM Travel, Bass Pro
Shops ExtremeTM XPSTM Woo Dav, Bass
Pro Shops Micro LiteTM Graphite Spinning
Rod, Browning Fishing Citori Spinning Rods,
Browning Fishing SilaFlex Spinning Rods,
Bass Pro Shops Tourney Special Premium
Graphite Casting, Bass P
Products:
Rods, Reels, Combos, Lures, Rainwear &
Footwear, Flies & Kits, Watercraft, Fly
Fishing Apparel, Waders & Accessories,
Sunglasses, Optics, Black Powder, Shooting
Accessories, Decoys & Calls, Treestands,
Hunting Videos & Books, Hunting Clothing,
Hunting Outerwear, Hunting Boots, Tents,
Packs & Bags, Sleeping Bags & Beds, Metal
Detectors, Canoes & Kayaks, Paddles &
Oars, Canoe & Kayak Accessories, GPS
Units, GPS Accessories, Radio &
Accessories, Lanterns, Headlamps,
Spotlights, Flashlights, Dehydrators,
Vacuum Sealers, Kitchen Accesories,
Apparel, Footwear.
Sponsor:
Bass Pro Shops Bassmaster Open

BATTLE CREEK EQUIPMENT COMPANY
702 S REED
PO BOX 629
FREMONT, IN 46737
269-962-6181
800-253-0854
www.battlecreekequipment.com
• David Underhill, President
orders@battlecreekequipment.com
Description:
Maker of hot- and cold-therapy products for
managing pain.
Brands:
Automatic Moist Heat Pads, Joint-specific
Cold Therapy wraps, Microwaveable Moist
Heat wraps, Joint-specific Pain
Management Kits

BAUER NIKE HOCKEY, INC.
150 OCEAN ROAD
GREENLAND, NH 3840
603-430-2111
Fax: 603-430-3010
• Chris Zimmerman, Chief Executive Officer
• Bob Colburn, VP / General Manager
Products:
Ice Hockey - Apparel, Goalie Equipment,
Protective, Skates, Sticks; Ice Skating -
Skates; In-Line Skating - Accessories,
Apparel, Protective, Roller Hockey Skates,
Skates; USA Hockey - Official authentic
competitive apparel provider.
Brands:
Nike N-Dorfin, Tuuk

BAUERFEIND USA INCORPORATED
3005 CHASTAIN MEADOWS PARKWAY
SUITE 700
MARIETTA, GA 30066
770-429-8330
800-423-3405
Fax: 770-429-8477
info@bauerfeindusa.com
www.bauerfeindusa.com
• Bea Bauerfeino, Chief Executive Officer
(770) 429-8330
Products:
Medical equipment and supplies for athletic
applications.

BAUSCH & LOMB
ONE BAUSCH & LOMB PLACE
ROCHESTER, NY 14604-2701
585-338-6000
800-828-1430
Fax: 585-338-6896
www.bausch.com
• Fred Hassan, Chairman
• Brent L. Saunders, President & Chief
Executive Officer
Products:
Eyewear and sunglasses for all uses,
including for athlethes.
Brands:
Ray-Ban, Wayfarer

BD
ONE BECTON DRIVE
FRANKLIN LAKES, NJ 7417
201-847-6800
Fax: 201-847-5741
marilyn_miller@bd.com
www.bd.com
• Edward J. Ludwig, President / Chief
Executive Officer
(201) 847-6800

Products:
Medical Supplies, Devices, Laboratory
Equipment and Diagnostic Products for
competitive athletes and other applications.
Brands:
ABG Syringes, BD Q-SyteT, BD PosiflowT,
Interlinkr System, BD TwinpakT, BD
IntegraT, BD Safety-LokT, BD SafetyGlideT,
BD BBLT CHROMagarT, BD BBLT MI Agar,
BD BBLT Modified mTEC Agar, BD
OptiluxT, BD Auto ISO-FilterT, BD FalconT
6-well Multiwell Plate, BD FalconT HTS
FluoroBlokT, BDT Safety Knife with BD
XstarT BladeT, BD BeaverT, BD XstarT, BD
PocketT, LeVEEN Shunt, BD Insyte-NT
AutoguardT, BD AngiocathT AutoguardT,
BD Autoguard ProT, BD Saf-T-IntimaT, BD
Vacutainerr

BEAR ARCHERY
817 MAXWELL AVENUE
EVANSVILLE, IN 47711
812-467-1200
800-694-9494
Fax: 812-467-1300
bearcustomercare@beararcheryproducts.com
• Jim Allshouse, President
• Jack Bowman, Direcotr Of Business
Development
Products:
Compound Bows, Traditional Bows,
Crossbows

BEARCOM GROUP
4009 DISTRIBUTION DRIVE
BUILDING 200
GARLAND, TX 75041
214-340-8876
800-449-6171
800-252-1691
Fax: 214-340-1738
info@bearcom.com
www.bearcom.com
• Jerry Denham, President/CEO/Founder
• Brest Bisnar, Executive Vice President &
Founder
• John Watson, Chairman

BELL FOUNDRY CO./BFCO FITNESS PRODUCTS
5310 SOUTHERN AVENUE
PO BOX 1070
SOUTHGATE, CA 90280
323-564-5701
Fax: 323-564-9717
info@bfco.com
www.bfco.com
• Cesar Cappellini, President / Chief
Executive Officer
(323) 564-5701
info@bfco.com
• Greg Hach, Marketing Director / Sales
Director
• Edgar Cruz, Aluminum-Marketing Director
ecruz@bfco.com
Products:
Barbells; Weightlifting Equipment and
Accessories.

BELL SPORTS INC.
735 PACESETTER DRIVE
RANTOUL, IL 61866
800-456-2355
800-456-2355
Fax: 800-888-9009
consumersupport@bellsports.com

1105

Products:
Auto Racing and cycling helmets.
Brands:
BSI, CPC, Mongoose, Blackburne, Bellistic, Faction, Metropolis, Citi, Alibi, Trigger, Amigo, Lil' Bell Shell, Boomerang, X-Ray, Influx, Ghisallo, Furio, Sweep R, Sweep XC

BERCO PRODUCTS, INCORPORATED
2437 E. 53RD ST.
LOS ANGELES, CA 90058
323-587-7263
800-858-7444
Fax: 941-927-3699
bercoproducts@sbcglobal.net
• Fred Berger, CEO
Products:
Licensed collegiate bobble head dolls, chain pulls, holiday ornaments, salt & pepper shakers, wind chimes, stepping stones garden stones, and picture frames, including sports related memoribilia.
Brands:
Big Nasty Bobble Head Dolls

BERGAMOT, INCORPORATED
820 WISCONSIN STREET
DELAVAN, WI 53115
262-728-5572 EXT 204
800-922-6733
Fax: 262-728-3750
customerservice@bergamot.net
www.bergamot.net
• Wayne Smith, President
• Craig Halvorsen, Wholesale Sales VP
(262) 728-5572
Products:
Hitch Covers, Logo plates, Travel Mugs, VIP Coffee Mug, S & P Shaker Set, Fluted Shot Glass, Stainless Shot, Square Shot, Key Tags, Hitch Locks, NASCAR Logo Collection, Lapel Pin,Beverage Holders, Belt Buckles, Retro Gas Pump Machine, Reflectors, NFL and MLB Accessories
Brands:
Alfred Hitch Cover, Meridian Metal Works, Logo Plates, Bergamot Buckle and Accessories

BEST PORTABLE FENCE
PO BOX 8434
GOLETA, CA 93118
805-637-6696
866-637-6329
Fax: 805-685-2688
sportfence@yahoo.com
• Donn Zellet, President
• Bill Rozich, VP Marketing
Products:
Manufacturer of foul poles, gates, a full line of picket and lattice fences, and custom tents and canopies

BETHEL INTERNATIONAL
4610 BRAGG BOULEVARD
FAYETTEVILLE, NC 28303
910-868-4554
Fax: 910-868-3658
www.bethelwholesale.com
Products:
Jewelry, apparel, and gifts for the sports industry.
Brands:
Alabama Crimson Tide, Alabama, Arkansas, Auburn, Clemson Tigers, Duke Blue Devils, East Carolina Pirates, Florida Gators, Georgia Bulldogs, Georgia Tech, Kentucky

Wildcats, Louisiana State Tigers, Louisville, Marshall, Maryland, Miami Hurricanes, Michigan Wolverines, Nebraska Cornhuskers, North Carolina Tar Heels, Ohio State Buckeyes, Oklahoma State, Penn State, Oklahoma Sooners, UCLA, Virginia Tech

BETLIN INC.
1445 MARION ROAD
COLUMBUS, OH 43207
614-443-0248
800-923-8546
Fax: 614-443-4658
www.betlin.com
• Robert Archer, President
• Vanda Burdette, External VP
• Pat Silk, Administrative VP
• John Archer, Sales / Marketing VP
Products:
Baseball Uniforms; Basketball Uniforms; Football Uniforms; Warm-Up Suits; Ice Hockey Uniforms; Lacrosse Uniforms; Soccer Uniforms; Softball Uniforms; Track & Field/Running Apparel; Volleyball Uniforms; Wrestling Apparel, Uniforms.
Brands:
Adidas, Mudcats, Wildcats

BIC SPORT NORTH AMERICA
2380 CRANBERRY HIGHWAY
WEST WAREHAM, MA 2576
508-291-2770
Fax: 508-291-2772
• Chris Decerso, Director of Sales and Marketing
(508) 291-2770
chris.decerso@bicworld.com
Products:
Water Sports Equipment: Windsurfing, Surfing, Kayaks, Stand-Up Paddling, Junior Sailboats, Dinghies.
Brands:
Bic, Okespor, Nautix
Year Founded:
1979

BIEBER LIGHTING CORPORATION
970 W MANCHESTER
INGLEWOOD, CA 90301
310-645-6789
800-243-2375
Fax: 310-216-0333
• Joe Fuhrman, Vice President
Products:
Manufacturer of outdoor lighting, poles for tennis courts, parking lots, walkways, and other professional, recreational and commerical applications
Brands:
Bieber Lighting

BIG BOY HEADGEAR
711 E GARDENA BOULEVARD
GARDENA, CA 90248
214-388-2744
866-244-2692
Fax: 310-715-1526
joanne@bigboygear.com
www.bigboygear.com
• Joanne Kim, Co-Owner
Products:
Hats/Headwear, Leather Apparel, Outerwear, Pants/Slacks, Private Label, Sportswear, Printed T-shirts

BIG LEAGUE PROMOTIONS
1974 NW 82 AVENUE
MIAMI, FL 33126
305-640-9606
Fax: 305-640-9845
INFO@RICOINC.COM
Products:
Checkers, Magnetic Darts, Tic Tac Toe, and Chess game sets with sports team logos.
Brands:
Checkers: NFL Checkers, College Rival Checkers, MLB Checkers, Golf and Soccer Checkers; Magnetic Darts: NFL Magnetic Darts, MLB Magnetic Darts, College Magnetic Darts; NFL Tic Tac Toe; Chess: NFL Chess, City Chess, Sport Chess, Theme Chess

BIG TIME SPORTS APPAREL, INC.
3750 W MAIN STREET
NORMAN, OK 73072
405-447-3300
Fax: 405-573-7716
• Tom Lawson, President / Chief Operating Officer
Products:
Athletic Apparel and Collegiate Sportswear - Jerseys, Sweatshirts, Pants, Hats

BIKE USA INC.
2811 BROADHEAD ROAD
BETHLEHEM, PA 18020
610-868-7652
800-225-2453
Fax: 610-868-6335
customerservice@bikeusainc.com
www.bikeusainc.com
• Ssu-Liu Liu, President
• Steve Green, General Manager
• Marc Weiner, Vice President of Sales
(972) 556-1803
marc@bikeusainc.com
Products:
Bikes, Folding Table
Brands:
Bikes: Punisher, Screamin' Eagle, Docksider, Trailblazer, Freestyle BMX, Tomcat BMX, Fold-A-Bike, Scooters, Stabilizer

BILLBOARDS ON WHEELS
2090 FIFTH AVENUE
RONKONKOMA, NY 11779
631-580-7772 EXT 808
Fax: 631-580-3725
mikecutino@aol.com
www.bow1.com
• Michael Cutino, Publisher
Description:
Manufactures outdoor billboards and printing designs for the Tri-State area.

BIODEX MEDICAL SYSTEMS
20 RAMSAY ROAD
SHIRLEY, NY 11967-4704
631-924-9000
800-224-6339
Fax: 631-924-8355
info@biodex.com
www.biodex.com
• James Reiss, President
jreiss@biodex.com
• John Bennett, VP and Chief Financial Officer
info@biodex.com
Products:
Physical Medicine and Rehabilitation

Products; Nuclear Medicine Supplies and Accessories - Dose Calibrators, Lead-Lined Laboratory Furniture Lung Ventilation Systems, PET Positron Emission Tomography Systems, Storage Cabinets, Radiation Shields, Syringe Shields and Vial Shields
Brands:
System 3, Balance System SD, Gait Trainer 2, Atomlab, Pulomonex II Xenon System, Venti-Scan IV Radioaerosol Administration System, Phantom

BIOFREEZE/PERFORMANCE HEALTH PRODUCTS
2230 BOYD ROAD
EXPORT, PA 15632
724-733-9500
800-246-3733
Fax: 724-733-4266
www.biofreeze.com
Products:
Topical pain relieving products in tubes, pump bottles, spray or roll-on
Brands:
Biofreeze

BIOGRIP, INC.
213 LATHROP WAY
SUITE I
SACRAMENTO, CA 95815
916-483-2686
888-590-4747
Fax: 916-483-1654
www.biogrip.com
• Stephen Tamaribuchi, President
• Rebecca Tamaribuchis, Chief Financial Officer
Products:
Fitness, sports medicine, and medical rehabilitation products
Brands:
e3 Fitness Grips, e3 Tricep/Lat, e3 Cable Resist, e3 Elastic Resist, e3 Ski Poles

BIOLIFE, LLC
8163 25TH COURT EAST
SARASOTA, FL 34243
941-360-1300
800-722-7559
Fax: 941-360-1310
customer.care@biolife.com
www.biolife.com
• Douglas Goodman, President
customer.care@biolife.com
• Tim Kelly, VP Sales
tim.kelly@biolife.com
• Andrew McFall, VP Marketing
andrew.mcfall@biolife.com
• Sam Shake, Chief Executive Officer
sam.shake@biolife.com
• Michele Slingluff, Chief Financial Officer
michele.slingluff@biolife.com
• Claudia Masselink, Director of Quality
claudia.masselink@biolife.com
• Kelly Keene, Director of Research & Development
kelly.keene@biolife.com
• Nick Wright, Director Sales
nick.wright@biolife.com
Products:
QR Powder for bleeding control (for Consumers, Medical Professionals), QR Powder for bleeding control (QR Powder for Occupational Health / Worksites, Sports Medicine)
Brands:

UrgentQR, NosebleedQR, SportsQR, KidsQR

BION INCORPORATED
14656 59TH AVENUE
BRITISH COLUMBIA, CANADA V3S 0V7
604-599-8609
Fax: 604-599-8201
bion_inc@yahoo.com
Products:
HRM, Velometer, Cycle Computer, Body Fat Moniftor, Pedometer

BIOSIG INSTRUMENTS, INC.
PO BOX 860
CHAMPLAIN, NY 12919
514-637-0016
800-463-5470
Fax: 514-637-1353
biosig@biosig.net
www.biosiginstruments.com
• Gregory Lekhtman, President
Products:
Insta-Pulse Fitness Heart Rate Monitors, Antense-Fitness Anti-Tension Device, Exerlopers No-Impact Running/Jogging Shoes, Body Trim-Home Exerciser, Insta-Runner Revolutionary Cardio Exerciser, Electronic Gym-Muscle Strength Monitor, Sea Logger-Water Walking System No Impact Exerciser, OEM Custom Designed Fitness Sensors/Electronics and products.
Year Founded:
1975
Clients:
Fitness equipment dealers, schools, universities, museums, exports worldwide.

BISON, INC.
603 L STREET
LINCOLN, NE 68508
800-247-7668
Fax: 800-638-0698
www.bisoninc.com
• Nick Cusick, President
Nature of Service:
Sporting goods manufacturer represented by 1500 dealers across the US
Brands:
Arena, Baseline 180 degrees, CarbonMax, CenterCourt, Centerline, Club Court, Competitor, Court Protector, Dura Steel, DuraSkin, DuraSkin for Soccer, Easy Reach, Easy Store, Easy-Up, Elite, Fail-Safe, FlexCourt, Glass Max, Kids Hoops, Lady CarbonMax, Lifeguard, Magnum, Match Point, PerfectGoal, Perpetual, Playtime, Power Adjust, ProTech, Protector, QwikChange, QwikPrint, Rapid Adjust, ReAction, Ruff Play, Safe Stuff, Sand Bar, Shooting Station, ShootOut, Side Court, Sidecourt, SideLine, Sport Pride, Street Hoops, The Patriot, TimeKeeper, T-Rex, TruFlex, Tuffglass, Ultimate, Ultimate Jr, Weatherbeater, Web Net, Zip Crank
Products:
Manufacturer of goals, gym and field accessories for basketball, volleyball, soccer, football, rugby, lacrosse, field hockey and futsol. Bison has equipment for every level of indoor and outdoor competition and recreation: portable basketball systems, wall mount basketball structures, goal height adjusters; competition, rec and playground basketball goals and backboards; backboard padding;

ball carts; competition, rec and outdoor volleyball systems; player's benches; gymnasium wall padding and scorer's tables; youth goals; portable game bases; tetherball and badminton sets; soccer, fotball, rugby, lacrosse and futsal goals and accessories; sa

BLACK DIAMOND EQUIPMENT, LTD.
2084 E 3900 S
SALT LAKE CITY, UT 84124
801-278-5552
800-775-5552
Fax: 801-278-5544
bdmo@bdel.com
www.bdel.com
• Peter Metcalf, President / Chief Operating Officer
peter@bdel.com
• Colleen Graham, VP Marketing
(801) 365-5522
• Meredith Saarinen, VP Production
Products:
Carabiners/Draws, Protection, Harnesses, BigWall, Belay/Rappel, Helmets, Pads/Bags/Chalk, Rope/Cord/Webbing, Ice Gear, Skis/Bindings, Poles, Backcountry Gear, Gloves/Gaiters, SCARPA Ski Boots, Packs, Trekking Poles, Lightware/Headlamps, Tents/'Mids/Bivys, Clothing, Accessories, Spare Parts, Specials
Brands:
Carabiners/Draws - LiveWire, Dynotron; Protection - Camalots, Camalot C3s, Harnesses - Blizzard, Chaos; Belay/Rappel - ATC-Guide, ATC-XP; Helmets - Tracer, Half Dome; Pads - Mondo II, Drop Zone II; Rope/Cord/Webbing - Rando, Ice Twin; Backcountry Gear - AvaLung II; Glove - Patrol, Patrol Mitt, Prodigy, Kingpin; SCARPA Ski Boots - T1, T2X Men's, T2X Women's; Packs - Predator, Jackal, Revelation; Trekking Poles - Terra CF, Contour; Lightware/Headlamps - Soliras, SpaceShot 2; Tents - Guilding Light, Skylight; Clothing - Alpine Shirt, Alpine Pants, BDYs; Accessories - Microns, JiveWires; Nut Tool; Spare Parts - Rock, Snow

BLADEMASTER
566 RIVERVIEW DRIVE
CHATHAM, ONTARIO, CANADA N7M 5L5
519-352-4550
888-648-7776
Fax: 519-352-7676
blademaster@guspro.com
www.blademaster.ca
• August Sunnen, President
(519) 352-4550
augusts@guspro.com
• Paul Sunnen, Chief Operating Officer
(519) 352-4550
pauls@guspro.com
• Bob Moon, Sales Manager
(519) 352-4550
bobm@guspro.com
• Marcel Michaud, Customer Service Associate
(519) 352-4550
marcelm@guspro.com
Products:
Skate Sharpening Machines (Triples Station, Wheel/Diamonds, Double Station, Sharpening Accessories), Skate Sharpening Machines (Single Station, Service Accessories, Portables,

Holders/Contouring), Boot expander tools and accessories.
Brands:
Blademaster, Lil' Red, Big Red

BLADEZ, INC
20155 ELLIPSE
FOOTHILL RANCH, CA 92610
949-206-0330
888-325-2339
Fax: 949-206-0013
• Stephen Wilkins, President / Chief Operating Officer
• Lenny Vainberg, VP
Products:
Powered Personal Transportation products (Electric Powerboards, Gas Powerboards, Treadmills, Ellipticals, Mobility Vehicles)
Brands:
QCS (Quick Change System, SPS (Smart Power System), GSEV (Electric Vehicle Rated), XTR Comp, XTR Street, XTR SE 450, eLite 300s, eLite 250, XTR-S 450, XTR-Lite 250, XTR-HD 550)

BLAZER MANUFACTURING, INC.
5109 W. 26TH STREET
W INDUSTRIAL SITE
PO BOX 266
COLUMBUS, NE 68601
800-322-2731
Fax: 800-257-4045
info@blazerathletic.com
www.blazerathletic.com
• Gordon Blaser, VP
• Sheila Gottsch, National Sales Manager
Products:
Athletic Equipment (Dryline Marker, Steel High School Vault Std., Steel Adjustable Vault Std., Quick Measure, Alum. SJ. Std. w/Alum., Alum. SJ. Std. w/Round Base, SS Long Jump Tray, Discus Ring, Web Throwing Circles, Shot Put Ring, Hammer Ring, Pole Vault Boxes, Transport Cart; Team Sportswear; Industrial Products
Brands:
Stock Velocity, IO-Skin, 15 & 16, Conquest, 3-Color, Solid, Victory, Triumph, Millenium, Paramax, Duo-MAX Pants, Stock IO-Skin, Ambition, Duo-MAX, 2-Color, Knit Trim Option, All-American, Achiever, Tri-Sleeve, Contender

---

BLUE FISH
5738 SUNSET DRIVE
SUITE 2044
SOUTH MIAMI, FL 33143
305-381-5024
Fax: 786-953-5690
customerservice@bluefishsport.com
www.bluefishsport.com
Products:
Accessories, Tops, Outerwear, Bottoms
Brands:
8203 Spaghetti Top, 6108 BF Jersey Top, 8176 BF Silk Top, 621 Basic Tank, 6142 Surprise Tank, 6138 BF Straps Tank, 8428 Umberella Top, 8170 V Top, 8476 Fit Top, 3/4 Sleeves Top, 8486 Action Top, 8313 T Shirt, 8478 - Justin Top, 6155 - Tic Tac Bra, 8481 Don Top, 8491, Gus Top, 6158 Action Bra, 6156 Tic Tac Top, 8489 Spa Top, 8482 Strong Top, 8484 Sherah Top, 8495 Diamond Top, 8486 Tennis Top, 8497 Silver Top; 8333 Poly Jacket, 8159 Basic Jacket, 8425 Zip Jacket, 8499 Gus Jacket, 8490 Funky Jacket, 8514 Polka Dot Jacket, 8503

Diamond Jacket; 9160 Stud Pant, 9219 Zip Capri, 9249 Tiki Pants, 9289 - Action Pant, 942 - Dual Screen Pant, 841 - Stron

---

BLUE RIDGE MOUNTAIN WOODCRAFTS, INC.
71 MERK DAVIS STREET
PO BOX 566
ELLIJAY, GA 30540
706-276-2222
800-348-0748
Fax: 800-348-9798
sales@blueridgewoodcrafts.com
www.blueridgewoodcrafts.com
• Fred Stahl, Chief Operating Officer
sales@blueridgewoodcrafts.com
Products:
Heavy weight and plastic extrusion columns, wood plaques and accessories, trophy base sets, cup bases, Italian marble and steel rods, figurines and mylars
Brands:
Pro-Wood

BMORE SPORTS
1430 JOH AVENUE
BUILDING M
BALTIMORE, MD 21227
410-247-2345
gandracchio@ptcintl.com
www.bmoresports.com or www.ptcintl.com
• Gianni Andracchio, Account Executive
gandracchio@ptcintl.com
Nature of Services:
Bmore Sports is a manufacturer of a variety of game-day promotional products including sports leather binders and jotters, wood ticket boxes, custom coolers and dog tag collectibles.
Year Founded:
1980

BOAST, INC.
53 W 36TH STREET
SUITE 302
NEW YORK, NY 10018
212-695-6424
800-327-7666
Fax: 561-863-5321
questions@boastusa.com
www.boastusa.com
• Bill St John, President
• Heather Burrows, Credit Manager
Products:
Golf, Tennis, Racquet Sports Apparel and Outerwear.

BOBBY JONES INTERNATIONAL
7406 RT 487 THE MATTERN BLDG
PO BOX 214
MILDRED, PA 18632-9015
585-467-7240
800-767-1260
Fax: 585-467-0854
rochester@hickeyfreeman.com
www.bobbyjones.com
• Carol O'Grady, Director Corporate Tour Sales
Products:
Golf Apparel.

BODY GLOVE INTERNATIONAL, INC.
504 N. BROADWAY
REDONDO BEACH, CA 90277
310-374-3441
Fax: 310-372-7457

---

pr@bodyglove.com
www.bodyglove.com
• Robbie Meistrell, Founder
• Russel Lesser, President
• Celeste Berouty, Sales Director
• Scott Daley, Director Marketing
Products:
Wetsuits, men's apparel, jr. swimwear, technology accessories, personal flotation devices (life vests), snorkeling gear, bags, water sports, sunglasses
Brands:
Vapor, Matrix, Storm Trooper, Stealth Short Zip, Pro 2, Axis, Formula, Arc, Rashguard, Java, Rover, Vibe, Aura

---

BODY SOLID, INC.
1900 S DES PLAINES AVENUE
FOREST PARK, IL 60130
708-427-3555
800-833-1227
Fax: 708-427-3556
sales@bodysolid.com
www.bodysolid.com
• Andy Huck, Eastern Sales Manager
(708) 427-3555
ahuck@bodysolid.com
• Duane Abbott, Western Sales Manager
(708) 427-3555
dabbott@bodysolid.com
• Jeff Estopellan, MidWest Sales Manager
(708) 427-3555
jestopellan@bodysolid.com
Products:
Weightlifting - Benches, Dumbbell Racks, Home Gyms, Power Racks, Lat Machines, Selectorized Single Station Machines for Clubs, Weight Trees.
Brands:
Endurance T3 Treadmill, Endurance Tf3i Treadmill, Endurance T4i Treadmill, Endurance T6iHRC Treadmill, Endurance TF6iHRC Treadmill, Endurance E4 Elliptical, Endurance Cardio E5HRC Elliptical, Endurance Cardio E7 Elliptical, Endurance Cardio E7HRC Elliptical, Endurance B3R Recumbant Bike, Endurance B3U Upright Bike, Body-Solid G1S Home Gym, Body Solid G2B Home Gym, Body-Solid G3S Home Gym, Body Solid G5S Home Gym, Bod-Solid G6B Home Gym, Body-Solid G8I Home Gym, Body-Solid G9S Home Gym, Body-Solid G10B Home Gym, Body-Solid EXM4000S Pro Gym, Body-Solid EXM1500S Home Gym, Body-Solid EXM3000LPS Home Gym, Body-Solid Series

---

BODY WISE INTERNATIONAL
17101 ARMSTRONG AVENUE
SUITE 101
IRVINE, CA 92614
714-505-6121
800-830-9596
Fax: 714-368-1296
services@bodywise.com
www.bodywise.com
• William F Farley, CEO
• Tom Tierney, Founding Chairman
• Debra Meyer, VP Operations
• Kathy Martino, Vice President Community Relations/Consultant
• Leslie Boyd-Bradley, Vice President Business Development
Products:
Sports & dietary supplements.
Brands:
BW365 Shakes, BW365 Lean Support, One

Bite, Right Choice - Am Formula, Right Choice - PM Formula, Beta-C, Essential Calcium, Omega Complete, Cardio-Wise, COmfort Tea, CoQ10, Revitalizing Tea, Glucomine, Male Advantage, MemX2, OptimEyes, Oxy-G2, Super Cell, AG-Immune, NK-Immune, Relief, Aller Wise, Female Advantage Balance, Female Advantage Transitions, Estrenol, Pro Pure, Tiger Vites, Workout Formula, Electro Aloe.

BODY WRAPPERS/ANGELO LUZIO
107 TRUMBULL STREET
ELIZABETH, NJ 07206-2165
908-354-7218
800-323-0786
Fax: 908-354-4023
info@bodywrappers.com
www.bodywrappers.com
• Marie West, President
• Nicholas Karant, Vice President
• Trudy Christ, Marketing Director
Products:
Manufacturer of dance and team dance apparel and distributors of Angelo Luzio dance shops.
Brands:
Body Wrappers, Totalstretch, Princess Aurora, Premiere Collection, Dance Between, totalSTRETCH tights and undergarments

BOELTER BRANDS, LLC
4200 NORTH PORT WASHINGTON RD
GLENDALE, WI 53212
877-233-7287
800-233-7287
Fax: 414-967-4399
sales@boelterbrands.com
www.boelterbrandsproducts.com
Products:
Plastic cups, coasters, glassware, pitchers, buckets.

BOGNER
185 ALLEN BROOK LANE
SUITE 201
WILLISTON, VT 5495
802-861-6900
800-801-0372
Fax: 802-861-6909
www.bogner.com
• Peter Born, President
• Konstantin Brandstetter, Executive Vice President
• Homeira Lane, Bogner Sport Sales & Marketing
• Hannes Bogner, Chief Financial Officer
Products:
Golf - Apparel; Skiing-Alpine - Accessories, Outerwear-Jackets, Vests, Pants; Skiing-Nordic - Accessories, Outerwear-Suits, Tops, Pants.
Nature of Services:
Wholesale sales and marketing of men's and ladies' skiwear and sportswear.

BOSS GRAPHICS, INC.
2668-A HONOLULU AVENUE
MONTROSE, CA 91020
818-248-7066
Fax: 626-398-5123
larry@bossgraphics.com
www.bossgraphics.com
• Larry Lousen, President
Products:
Graphics and Murals for Auditoriums,

Gym/Sport Arenas, Stadiums, Pool Areas, and other Commercial Applications; also Floor Graphics.

BOSS MANUFACTURING COMPANY
221 W FIRST STREET
KEWANEE, IL 61443
309-852-2131
800-447-4581
Fax: 309-852-0848
bossmfg1893@bossgloves.com
• David Hunter, Marketing Director
• Gerry Stockerman, Operations Director
Products:
Gloves, Boots, Protective Wear and Rainwear
Brands:
Boss, Foot Glove, Mesh, Morris Feel, Morris Zip Flap

BOSTON WHALER, INC.
100 WHALER WAY
EDGEWATER, FL 32141
386-428-0057
877-294-5645
Fax: 386-423-8589
www.whaler.com
• John Ward, President
• Tim Schiek, President
Products:
Fiberglass Boats.
Brands:
Sport/Montauk, Dauntless, Ventura, Outrage, Conquest

BOTTELSEN DART COMPANY
945 W MCCOY LANE
SANTA MARIA, CA 93455
805-922-4519
800-537-2164
Fax: 805-922-5961
info@bottelsendarts.com
www.bottelsendarts.com
• Jeff Bryan, Director
Products:
Dart and Related Accessories
Brands:
Megathrust Hammerhead, Buzzbomb, Precision Grip, Precision Grip Hammerhead, G.T., Ohh...Aah!, Mega Thrust, Devastators, Heavy Weights, Tough Koat, Black Knights, Gorilla Grip, 80% Tungsten, Kick Ass Tungsten, Kick Ass Brass, G.T. Stubbies, Buzz BOmbs Tungsten, Buzz Bomb Brass, Skinny's, Skinny's Colors, Gap, Nemesis, Berzerker Brasss, Hammer Head Spinning, Classic G.T. Shafts, New G.T. Shafts, Aluminum Shafts, Nylon, Combo Crackers, Deflectors, Wrenches, O-Rings, Sharpening Stones, Point Protectors, Soft Tip Points, Jug O'Darts, Pro Packs, Quad Cases, Solo Cases, Wedge Cases, Hard Cases, DartBoards, Books, Metallized Polyester Film, Metallize

BOUNTY HUNTER
1465-H HENRY BRENNAN
EL PASO, TX 79936
915-633-8354
800-413-4131
Fax: 915-633-8175
info@frsttx.com
www.detecting.com
Products:
Metal Detector
Brands:
Bounty Hunter Junior, VLF, Gold Digger,

Fast Tracker, Tracker II, Quick Silver, Tracker IV, Lone Star, Quick Draw II, Sharp Shooter II, Land Star, Camo-LS, Land Ranger, Time Ranger.

BOWLINGSHIRT.COM
6262 OLIVE BOULEVARD
SAINT LOUIS, MO 63130
314-426-4886
800-444-1685
Fax: 314-426-1713
www.bowlingshirt.com
• Alan Spetner, Chief Cruisin' Officer
(314) 336-0607
• Helene Spetner, President
(314) 336-0608
• Tim Coggeshall, VP of Sales
(314) 336-0610
Products:
Unisex Bowling Shirts in many styles and colors, Gifts and Accessories
Brands:
Classic Bowlers, Retro Bowlers, Loungemasters, Fifties Bowlers, Swingmasters, The Imperial Line, Slick Daddys

BOYLE & COMPANY, INC.
1803 SALISBURY HIGHWAY
STATESVILLE, NC 28677
704-872-8151
800-438-1061
Fax: 888-867-1337
marketing@johnboyle.com
www.johnboyle.com
• John Bo Bell Jr, Chairman
• Paul B Stelzner, Chief Executive Officer
• Michael B Dorfman, President
• William W White, VP, Sales & Marketing
Products:
Awnings, Banners, Industrial, Marine, Mining, Speacialty, Tents
Brands:
Gulf Stream, Main Street, Pyrotone, Sunbrella, Sunbrella Plus, Sunbrella firesist, Sunbrella firesist plus, Gottschalk Fibers, Signmaster Supreme, Canopy FS, Canopy Plus, Cool Glo, Cool Glo Ultra, BTF-19, Nite Lite, Eradi-Lite, Patio 500, Veranda, Tenara, Star Ultra Dee, Polymatic, Dabond, RIRI Decor, YKK Vislon, YKK Ziplon, YKK Uretex, Zippy Cool Cleaner/Lubricant, Monterey Lateral Arm System, Catalina & Santa Barbara Retractable Systems, Ventura Sun Screen System, Ibiza Retractable Arm System, Robusta Heavy Duty Window System, Siesta Window System, Steel Stitch, Gatorstitch, Armadillo, Stimpson, Fasnap, Dot, Bendarc Bender, Crownarc Crowner

BRAVO SPORTS
12801 CARMENITA ROAD
SANTA FE SPRINGS, CA 90670
562-484-5100
800-234-9737
Fax: 562-484-5183
www.bravosportscorp.com
• Leonardo Pais, Chief Executive Officer
• Cameron Adamson, Chief Financial Officer
• Drew Brassard, Chief Information Officer
Products:
Decks, wheels, components, helmets, longboard skateboards, protective
Brands:
Natural VI, Natural Charcoal VI, Natural Red V2, Natural Blue V2, Standard, Eagle,

Skull-n-Wings, Trucks, ABEC 5 Bearings, Grip Tape, Mounting Bolts, Riser Pads, Transparent Skateboard Helmet, Spiked Helmet, Kore Series Matte Black Helmet, Kore Series Elbow Pads, Kore Series Wrist Guards, Kore Series Knee Pads, Elbow Pads, Wrist Guards, Knee Pads.

BRAZOS SPORTSWEAR
4101 FOUNDERS BOULEVARD
BATAVIA, OH 45103
513-753-3400
Fax: 513-563-6692
Products:
Sports apparel for professional competititon and recreational activities.

BREWER'S LEDGE, INC.
87 YORK AVENUE
RANDOLPH, MA 2368
617-983-5244
800-707-9616
Fax: 781-961-5204
Sales@Treadwall.com
www.brewersledge.com
• Conant Brewer, President
(800) 707-9616
conant@treadwall.com
• Jeff Brewer, Vice President
(800) 707-9616
jeff@treadwall.com
• Howard Richardson, Operations
Products:
Exercise and Fitness Equipment, including Rotating Climbing Walls, Portable Climbing Walls and Rock Climbing Simulators.
Brands:
LedgeWall, WingWall, KidWall, TreadWall, TreadWall Trailers, KidWall Trailers, Climbco
Year Founded:
1990
Description:
Since 1989, Brewer's Ledge has provided over 900 facilities with climbing systems. Brewer's Ledge is a family company offering a full line of fixed, rotating, and portable climbing walls, focusing on kids programs and fitness training. This includes self-installed, textured panels, Treadwall™ and KidWall™ rotating walls, adjustable playground walls, towers, racquetball conversions, custom walls and portable walls. They support customers fully, helping with design, training and equipment needs. Specifications, free quotes and videos are always available.

BRIDGESTONE SPORTS (U.S.A.), INC.
15320 INDUSTRIAL PARK BOULEVARD NE
COVINGTON, GA 30014
770-787-7400
800-358-6319
Fax: 770-786-6416
• Yasuhiko Moteki, President
(822) 558-2235
• Stephen Graham, New Product Manager
• Randy Eaton, Senior Sales Director
Products:
Golf Accessories, Bags, Balls, Clubs-Wood/Iron Sets, Gloves.
Brands:
Precept

BRIGADE QM
1025 COBB INTERNATIONAL DRIVE NW
SUITE 100
KENNESAW, GA 30156-9217
770-428-1234
800-663-7487
Fax: 770-426-7726
brigade@brigadeqm.com
www.brigadeqm.com
• Mitchell L Werbell IV, President
(770) 428-1248
• Mark Smith, Marketing Director
• Geoffrey W. Werbell, Chief Financial Officer
• Mike McCourt, Director Of Merchandising
Products:
Adventure Clothing, Military Field Gear, Bags, Foot, Head & Handwear, Rain Gear, Logo Apparel, Repair Supplies, Survival & First Aid, Vitamins & Body Building Supplements, Eyewear, Books & Manuals, Novelty Items
Brands:
3MT Products, 5.11 Tactical Seriesr, 7.62 Designsr, ACCUSHARPT, Accusplitr, ACRr, ActcelT, Adventure Medical Kits, Adventure ReadyT, Aerko Chemical Defense OC Sprays, Aerobic Oxygen, AimSHOTT, Al Mar KnivesT, All Weather Safety Whistle, Alliance Rubber Company, Alpenr Outdoor, ALTAr Protection Products, Altamar Combat Boots, American Optical, AOSafetyr Products, ASPr, A-TeamT Apparel, ATN Night Vision, Austri-Alpin, AZORAr

BRIGHT SITES, INC
17935 SW LAKE HAVEN DRIVE
LAKE OSWEGO, OR 97035
503-639-0594
800-458-9055
Fax: 503-620-1189
www.brightsights.com
• Marie Mann, President
• Robert Mann, Chief Executive Officer
Products:
Gun Sight Coatings and Application Kit
Brands:
Bright Sights Glow Kit, Bright Sights Kit, Bright Sights High Visibility Coatings, Ghost Glow Luminescent Coatings, Application Kit, Ghost Glow Luminescent Coatings

BRINE, INC.
47 SUMNER STREET
MILFORD, MA 1757
508-478-3250
800-968-7845
Fax: 586-446-1162
www.brine.com
• Sean Fox, President
• Erica Cronan, Senior Media & Communications Manager
(508) 902-2283
Products:
Men's Lacrosse, Women's Lacrosse, Soccer Apparel, Equipment & Accessories, Field Hockey Apparel, Equipment & Accessories
Brands:
Brine, Guru Series, Phenom Series, Prodigy Series

BRISTOL ATHLETIC
700 SHELBY STREET
PO BOX 158
BRISTOL, TN 37620
423-968-4140
800-336-8775

Fax: 423-968-2084
www.bristolproducts.com
• Richard C Horner Jr, President
• Richard Horner, Finance VP
• Chris Horner, Sales VP
• Jan Rainero, Cheerleader Coordinator
Products:
Athletic Socks, Baseball uniforms, Cheerleading uniforms & accessories, Football uniforms, Basketball uniforms, Game Officials uniforms
Brands:
Bristol

BRITTEN-MEDIA
2322 CASS ROAD
TRAVERSE CITY, MI 49684
855-763-8204
800-426-9496
Fax: 231-941-8299
• Tom Britten, President
Auto Sports:
Mazda Raceway Laguna Seca - Preferred Facility Banner and Signage Production and Installation Vendor.

BROOKS
4300 ROOSEVELT WAY NE
SEATTLE, WA 98105
425-488-3131
800-227-6657
Fax: 425-489-1975
www.brooksrunning.com
• James M Weber, President / Chief Executive Officer
• David Bohan, EVP & COO
• Stan Mavis, Senior VP Apparel / Accessories
Products:
Athletic Footwear, Apparel & Accessories.
Brands:
HydroFLX, Diagonal Rollbar, Ethylene Vinyl Acetate, Podular Technology, HydroFlow and Substance 257, Powerpro, Silc, Aireplex and Vapor Dry

BROOKWOOD COMPANIES, INC.
25 W 45TH STREET
11TH FLOOR
NEW YORK, NY 10036
212-551-0100
800-426-5468
Fax: 212-472-0294
webmaster@brookwoodcos.com
www.brookwoodcos.com
• Amber Brookman, President / Chief Executive Officer
Products:
Consumer Fabrics, Industrial/Medical Fabrics, Military Fabrics
Brands:
Cordura, MicroFiber, MicroSupplex, Supplex, Sympatex, Tactel

BROWNELL & CO., INC.
423 E HADDAM-MOODUS ROAD
PO BOX 362
MOODUS, CT 06469-0362
860-873-8625
800-222-4007
Fax: 860-873-1944
www.brownellco.com
• Anthony Ferraz, President
• Cynthia Stakowitz, VP
Products:
Cargo Nets, Posts & Court equipment, Bowstrings, Cordage products for

commercial fishing, Wire & Cable, and Industrial Applications.
Brands:
TS-1, Fast Flight, S4 Thin, D-75, D-75 Thin, Ultra-CAM, Tri-Colors, B50, TCD-150, Diamondback, Excellerant Braided, #5 Polyester Braid, #4 Twisted, #4 Sherwood Forest, Monofilament, CAM EZ and Liquid Lok, String Loop, Brownell Bowstring Server, Brownell Bowstring Jig, Bowstring Video, Wax Stick, 30 DS, 30 DS DT, 40 DS

BROWNING
ONE BROWNING PLACE
MORGAN, UT 84050
801-876-2711
800-333-3288
Fax: 801-876-3331
www.browning.com
• Charles Guevremont, President
• Kraig Walker, Chief Financial Officer / Secretary
• Travis Hall, Senior VP
Products:
Firearms, Apparel, Gun Safes, Gun Cases, Knives, Lights, Accessories, Signature & Gifts, Footwear, Sport Optics
Brands:
T-Bolt, Cynergy, Silver, A-Bolt, Citori, BPS, BAR, Gold, BLR, Centerfire, Buckmark, BT-99

BRUNSWICK BICYCLE DIVISION
4902 HAMMERSLY ROAD
MADISON, WI 53711
847-573-0686
800-626-2811
Fax: 847-573-0602
www.mongoose.com
• George W Buckley, Chairman / Chief Executive Officer
• Dave Duecker, Brand Director
Products:
Bicycles, Protective Gear, BikeBoard, Bike Accessories, Saddles, Electric Scooters, Skateboards, Skateboard Gear
Brands:
Mongoose

BRUNSWICK CORPORATION
1 N FIELD COURT
LAKE FOREST, IL 60045-4811
847-735-4700
Fax: 847-735-4765
services@brunswick.com
www.brunswick.com
• Peter Hamilton, SVP/CFO
• Victoria Reich, VP / President - Brunswick European Grou
• Kathryn Chieger, VP Corporate / Investor Relations
• George W Buckley, Chairman / Chief Executive Officer
Products:
Boats, Marine Engines, Fitness Equipment, Bowling & Billiards Equipment, Brunswick New Technologies
Brands:
Albermatrie, Baja, Bayliner, Boston Whaler, Cabo, Crestliner, HarrisKayot, Hatteras, Lowe, Lund, Maxum, Meridian, Palmetto, Princecraft, Sea Boss, Sea Ray, Sealine, Triton, Trophy, Brunswick CGP, Attwood, Kellogg Marine, Land 'N' Sea, Mercury, MerCruiser, Mariner, Teignbridge, MotorGuide, Cummins-MerCruiser, Mercury Castings, Life Fitness, Hammer Strength,

ParaBody, Brunswick Bowling, Brunswick Billiards, Valley-Dynamo, Navman, Northstar Technologies, IDS/Monolith, MotoTron, MX Marine

---

BRUTE GROUP
8 CORPORATE BOULEVARD
SINKING SPRING, PA 19608
610-678-4050
800-486-2788
Fax: 877-879-4040
info@brute.com
www.brute.com
• John W Purnell, Chief Executive Officer
• Tim Gardner, Sales Manager
Products:
Athletic Goods

BRUTE WRESTLING
8 CORPORATE BOULEVARD
SINKING SPRING, PA 19608
610-678-4050
800-486-2788
Fax: 610-678-4040
info@brute.com
www.brute.com
• Jeff Bowyer, National Sales Manager
• Mary Mallis, Director of Marketing and Communication
(610) 898-1705
Products:
Wrestling Apparel and Accessories
Brands:
Adidas

BSI PRODUCTS
9510 BERGER ROAD
COLUMBIA, MD 21046
410-381-2596
888-381-2596
Fax: 410-995-6268
sales@bsiproducts.com
www.bsiproducts.com
Products:
Motorsports Licensed Products, Collegiate Licensed Products, NFL Licensed Products
Brands:
NASCAR, Nextel, Greg Biffle #16, Kyle Busch #5, Jack Daniels #7, Dale Earnhardt #3, Dale Earnhardt Jr. #8, Carl Edwards #99, Jeff Gordon #24, Kevin Harvick #29, Dale Jarrett #88, Jimmie Johnson #48, Kasey Kahne #9, Matt Kenseth #17, Mark Martin #6, Ryan Newman #12, Elliot Sadler #38, Tony Stewart #20, Brian Vickers #25, Rusty Wallace #2, Checkered, Chevy Racing, Ford Racing, Dodge Racing

---

BSN SPORTS
1901 DIPLOMAT
PO BOX 7726
DALLAS, TX 75209
972-484-9484
800-527-7510
Fax: 800-899-0149
feedbsn@sportsupplygroup.com
www.bsnsports.com
• John Walker, President
(972) 484-9484
• Dave Jones, Marketing Director
Products:
Athletic Goods
Brands:
Multisport Tabletop Electric Scoreboard, Jugs Lite Flite Practice Baseball, FenceMate, MacGregor, Voit, Easton,

Rawlings, Micro-Mesh, GameCraft, Compact, Cramer, Wilson, Penn, PORTaPiT

BSN-JOBST, INC.
5825 CARNEGIE BOULEVARD
CHARLOTTE, NC 28209
704-554-9933
800-537-1063
Fax: 800-835-4325
BSN.Orders@BSNmedical.com
www.jobst-usa.com
• Claus Wiegel, President
• Jake Newman, Marketing Director
(704) 554-9933
jake.newman@bsnmedical.com
Products:
Support Wear, Sensifoot, Medical Legwear, Custom, Compression Bandages, Plastic/Post-Surgical Garments
Brands:
Jobstr

BUCK KNIVES, INC.
660 S LOCHSA STREET
POST FALLS, ID 83854-5200
208-262-0500
800-326-2825
Fax: 208-262-0738
pfstore@buckknives.com
www.buckknives.com
• Charles T Buck, Chairman / Chief Executive Officer
• Charles B Buck, President
• Richard Konopasek, Finance VP / Chief Financial Officer
• C J Buck, CEO
Products:
Knives, Accessories, Apparel
Brands:
Buck Knives

BUFFALO EXPORT, LLC
99 S SPOKANE STREET
SEATTLE, WA 98134
206-682-9900 EXT 206
Fax: 206-682-9907
Larry@BuffaloExportLLC.com
www.buffaloexportllc.com
• Larry Benezra, President / Chief Executive Officer
larry@buffaloexportllc.com
• Adam Benezra, Vice President
Products:
Baseball Caps; General Sports Products - Imprinted Apparel, Sweatclothes.
Description:
Five-generation, family-owned business selling used baseball caps and sports equipment.

BUFFALO TURBINE
180 ZOAR VALLEY ROAD
SPRINGVILLE, NY 14141
716-592-2700
Fax: 716-592-2460
info@buffaloturbine.com
www.buffaloturbine.com
• Jody Smith, Advertising, Marketing
Auto Sports:
Official Debris Blower of the International Hot Rod Association
Description of Company/Product Line:
Debris Blowers, Sprayers, Dusters, Dust Suppression Systems, Top Dressers and the SANDEVIL™ Attachment

---

BUGATTI
100 CONDOR STREET
BOSTON, MA 2128
617-567-7600
800-284-2887
Fax: 617-567-5541
www.bugatti.com

BULOVA WATCH COMPANY
ONE BULOVA AVENUE
WOODSIDE, NY 11377
718-204-3222
800-233-3350
Fax: 718-204-3546
service@bulova.com
www.bulova.com
• Fae Druiz, Vice President
Services:
Manufactures watches featuring the NBA logo on the face of the watch. Bulova has a complete line of NBA sports watches. Logos include all NBA teams

BURTON SNOWBOARDS
80 INDUSTRIAL PARKWAY
BURLINGTON, VT 5401
800-881-3138
Fax: 802-660-3250
info@burton.com
global.burton.com
• Jake Burton, Chief Executive Officer
info@burton.com
• Laurent Potdevin, President / Chief Operating Officer
info@burton.com
• Mike Abbott, Chief Financial Officer
info@burton.com
Products:
Snowboards, Snowboard Apparel, Snowboard Accessories.

BUSHNELL CORPORATION
9200 CODY
OVERLAND PARK, KS 66214-1734
913-752-3400
800-423-3537
Fax: 913-752-3550
www.bolle.com
• Joe Messner, President
• Philip Gyori, VP Marketing / Bushnell
Products:
Eyewear - Sunglasses; Skiing-Alpine - Goggles.
Brands:
Bounce, Demeanor, Heetseeker, J-Walker, Limit, Meanstreak, Meltdown, Mercuria, Pharmium, Sin City, Thunderstruck, Valorium, Vanadium, Zyrium, Canebrake, Chill, Envy, Groove, Mongrel, Morph, Orvet, Piraja, Sidney, Sizzle, Spright, Spry, Swisher, Downdraft, Slipstream, Windshear, Kickback, Kicker, Parole, Supercell, Turbulence, Upshot, Vigilante, Atlantic, Laguna, Santa Marta, Tarpon, Scream, Jinx, Nova, Shark, Zark, Nebula, Simmer, Stoke, Boost, X500, Boost OTG, Bolle 1.0, Bolle 2.0, Shellmet

BUSHNELL SPORT OPTICS
9200 CODY
OVERLAND PARK, KS 66214-1734
913-752-3400
800-423-3537
Fax: 913-752-3550
www.bushnell.com

• Joseph Messner, Chief Executive Officer
• Dave Broadbent, Chief Financial Officer
• Blake Lipham, President & CEO
Products:
Binoculars, Night Vision, Laser Rangefinders, Digital Products, Telescopes, Spotting Scopes, Riflescopes, and Sports Imaging.
Brands:
Bushnell, Browning, and Tasco.

BUTLER BUILT MOTORSPORTS EQUIPMENT
70 PITTS SCHOOL ROAD NW
CONCORD, NC 28027
704-784-1027
800-621-7328
Fax: 704-784-1024
sales@butlerbuilt.net
www.butlerbuilt.net
• Brian Butler, President
sales@butlerbuilt.net
• Jeannie Butler, Secretary Treasury
sales@butlerbuilt.net
• Robert DeRosa, Sales Manager
sales@butlerbuilt.net
• Mark Linkous, Dealer-Wholesale Sales Director
sales@butlerbuilt.net
Products:
Custom Seating, Standard Seating, Accessories, Replacement Covers, Air Management Systems, Aluminum Steering Wheels, Restraint Systems, Technical Assistance, Oil Tanks.

BVT PRODUCTS, LLC
8143 BRUMBY COURT
TRINITY, FL 34655
727-834-8944
Fax: 727-834-8722
vicki@bvtproducts.com
www.bvtproducts.com
• Vicki Forster, President
(727) 834-8944
vicki@bvtproducts.com
Products:
Water Bottle Carriers: The Go Caddy™ and the Golfing Caddy™

C & H BASEBALL
2215 60TH DRIVE E
BRADENTON, FL 34203
941-727-1533
800-248-5192
Fax: 941-727-0588
sales@chbaseball.com
www.chbaseball.com
• Torrey Spears, Operations Manager
• Rob Huff, President
rob@chbaseball.com
• Danielle Huff, Vice President/Owner
danielle@chbaseball.com
• Torrey Spears, Operations Manager
Products:
Batting cages, fielding screens, batting tunnels, windscreen, tarps, wallpadding, bases, and pitching machines.
Year Founded:
1968
Description:
C&H Baseball is the industry leader in supplying field equipment & batting cages for Major League, minor league, colleges and high schools around the nation.
Brands:
Schutt, Spalding, Jugs, Atec, C&H, Wilson

C. CRETORS & CO.
3243 N CALIFORNIA AVENUE
CHICAGO, IL 60618
773-588-1690
800-228-1885
Fax: 773-588-2171
solesen@cretors.com
www.cretors.com
• Gino A Nardulli, Marketing Director
Nature of Service:
Concessions Equipment and Portable Stands.
Products:
Suspended Kettles, Pedestal Poppers, Enclosed Cabinet, Open Cabinet, Giants with Tables, Small Concession Poppers, Cotton Candy, Warmer Cabinets, Hotdog Grills & Bun Warmers, Topping & Dispensing Systems, and Gourmet Retail Equipment

C.N. IS BELIEVING
18 UNION STREET
WOLFEBORO, NH 3894
617-520-4079
Fax: 603-515-1181
www.nitelitesports.com
• Corky Newcomb, Owner/President
• Nolan Antonucci, Marketing & PR Co-ordinator
Products:
Baseball Balls, Metal and Wood Bats, Pitching Machines; Field Hockey Balls; Football Balls; Golf Ball Retrievers, Balls; Ice Hockey Pucks; Lacrosse Balls; Tennis Balls; Rugby Balls; Soccer Balls; Softball Balls, Pitching Machiness, lighted glasses, light sticks

CABANA BANNERS
46946 217TH STREET
BROOKINGS, SD 57006
605-692-4580
800-697-3139
Fax: 605-692-6113
info@cabanabanners.com
www.cabanabanners.com
• Patti Nash, President / Chief Executive Officer
info@cabanabanners.com
• Troy Dubois, Sales/Marketing
info@cabanabanners.com
• Jeff Pitts, Production Manager
info@cabanabanners.com
Products:
Athletic Banners

CABELA'S
ONE CABELA DRIVE
SIDNEY, NE 69160
308-254-6745
800-237-4444
800-237-4444
Fax: 308-254-7345
www.cabelas.com
• Dennis Highby, President / Chief Executive Officer / Di
• Michael Callahan, SVP
• James Cabela, President
• Patrick A. Snyder, Merchandising SVP
• Dave Roehr, Finance VP
• Ralph Castner, VP / Chief Financial Officer
• Steven Krajewski, Real Estate Manager
Products:
Hunting, Fishing and Skiwear

CABLEFORM INC.
8845 THREE NOTCH ROAD
TROY, VA 22974
434-589-8224
Fax: 434-589-3803
sales@cableform.com
www.cableform.com
• Andrew L. Thexton, President
athexton@Cableform.com
Products:
Field Communications Equipment; Battery
Powered Electronic Megaphones.
Brands:
Alert Hailer, Audio Guider, Audio Hailer,
Hailer Alert, Hailer Jr., Little Yeller, Super
Hailer

CALLAWAY GOLF
2180 RUTHERFORD ROAD
CARLSBAD, CA 92008-7328
760-931-1771
800-588-9836
Fax: 760-930-5015
info@callawaygolf.com
www.callawaygolf.com
• George Fellows, President / Chief
Executive Officer
• Oliver S. Brewer III, Chief Executive
Officer, President & Director
Products:
Golf Clubs - Wood/Iron Sets.
Brands:
Big Bertha Metal Woods and Irons, Great
Big Bertha II Titanium Drivers and Fairway
Woods, Big Bertha Steelhead(TM) III
Stainless Steel Drivers and Fairway Woods,
Hawk Eye VFT Tungsten Injected(TM)
Titanium Irons, Big Bertha Stainless Steel
Irons

CAMERA SPORTSEAT, INC.
5517 STATE ROAD
WADSWORTH, OH 44281
330-425-3035
800-649-5261
Fax: 480-990-2088
www.camerasportseat.com
• Hob A. Zabarsky, President
(440) 582-0122
camerasportseat@hotmail.com
• Bill Heideman, Design Engineer
(480) 874-3359
camerasportseat@hotmail.com
Products:
Manufacturer of low profile portable and
permanent camera mounts for TV broadcast
with seated operator which reduces or
eliminates sightline problems for spectators
seated behind cameras.
Year Founded:
1994

CAMOFACE
4275 THUNDERBIRD LANE
CINCINNATI, OH 45246
877-671-2800
www.camoface.com
Services:
Sports team/design face and body painting.

CAMPUS OUTFITTERS
2525 DRANE FIELD RD.
SUITE 11
COLLEGE PARK, MD 20740
888-923-0700
Fax: 301-220-0368
www.rissebrothers.com

Products:
Collegiate Embroidered Sportswear

CANAMER INT'L, LLC
5701 INDUSTRIAL PARK ROAD
WINONA, MN 55987
507-452-1700
800-533-8020
Fax: 507-452-1784
info@canamer.com
www.canamer.com
• Marie Eglinton, Area Sales Representative
ext 104
marier@canamer.com
• Thomas Scott, Sales Manager
ext 105
Products:
Athletic Field Covers, Gym Floor Covers,
Wind Screens, Tennis Courts, Gym
Curtains, Golf Courses and Pond Liners.
Brands:
Polycan™

CANNONDALE BICYCLE CORPORATION
16 TROWBRIDGE ROAD
BETHEL, CT 6801
203-749-7000
800-245-3872
Fax: 203-748-4012
custserv@cannondale.com
www.cannondale.com
• Dan Alloway, Sales and European
Operations VP
custserv@cannondale.com
• Scott Montgomery, Marketing VP
custserv@cannondale.com
Products:
Cycling - Apparel, Bicycles, Bike Bags,
Components, Pumps, Racks, Trailers,
Water Bottles.
Brands:
Coda

CANON U.S.A.
ONE CANON PARK
MELVILLE, NY 11747
631-330-5000
Fax: 516-328-5069
pr@cusa.canon.com
www.usa.canon.com
• Joe Adachi, President & CEO
• Fujio Mitarai, Chairman & CEO
Services:
NFL - Cameras & Equipment, Binoculars;
PGA Tour - Official Copier, Fax,
Multi-Function Printer, Printer, Scanner,
Camera and Binocular of the PGA Tour and
Champions Tour.

CANVAS NURSERY INC
2130-A ANDREA LANE
FORT MYERS, FL 33912
239-433-3335
800-226-3335
Fax: 239-790-2617
canvas@thecanvasnursery.com
www.thecanvasnursery.com
Products:
Handcrafted artificial trees, plants and
foliage in tropical styles using cotton canvas
for interior facilities and stadiums.

CAP BARBELL
3400 ROGERDALE ROAD
HOUSTON, TX 77042

713-977-3090
877-227-0955
Fax: 713-977-3099
CustomerService@capbarbell.com
www.capbarbell.com
Products:
Bar & Handles; Benches & Racks; Free
Weights; Home Gym Accessories;
Additional Manufacturers Parts

CAPITOL PARTITIONS, INC
9199 RED BRANCH ROAD
COLUMBIA, MD 21045
410-740-8870
Fax: 410-740-8865
info@capitolpartitions.com
www.capitolpartitions.com
• James Arnaiz, President
info@capitolpartitions.com
• Patricia Arnaiz, Marketing VP
Products:
Toilet partitions, unit showers, washroom
vanities and related products. Flooring
products and finishes. Cubicles, Modular
Office Furniture, Office Chairs, Office
Partitions

CAPO INC./PANAMA JACK
2 SUNSHINE BOULEVARD
ORMOND BEACH, FL 32174
800-282-7696
Fax: 386-672-8720
www.capo.com
• Jack Hewitt, VP
• Teresa Cox, President
Products:
Sunglasses and visors for athletes and fans
alike.
Brands:
Angler Eyes, Crown, Crystal Vision, Extreme
Optiks, Healthwear, Just Add Kids, Junior
Varsity, Lensis by Polaroid, NASCAR,
Visual

CARAVAN PROTECTIVE CASES
25 HAWTHORNE STREET
ELYRIA, OH 44035
800-477-6780
Fax: 440-366-1809
• Richard Galbraith, President / Sales
(800) 477-6780
• Chuck Patton, Sales / Engineering
(800) 477-6780
Products:
Athletic Cases, Audio Cases, Classical
Instrument Cases, Computer Cases, Drawer
Cases, Lighting Cases, Medical Cases,
Category Cases, Production/Office, Truck
Pack Utility Cases, Video Cases

CARBITE GOLF COMPANY
5816 DRYDEN PLACE
CARLSBAD, CA 92008
760-929-1410
800-272-4325
Fax: 760-929-1360
www.carbitegolf.com
• Chuck Jones, President/Chief Executive
Officer
• Donna Carson, National Sales Manager
• Peter Maglaque, Vice President
• Mike Nelson, Customer Service
Nature of Service:
Manufacturer
Products:
Putters and Wedges - Putterballs

Brands:
Carbite

CARBONMAX SPORTS TECHNOLOGY, INC.
603 L STREET
LINCOLN, NE 68508
800-247-7668
Fax: 800-638-0698
www.carbonmax.com
Products:
Volleyball - Net Systems; Nets, Padding, Posts
Brands:
CarbonMax

CARD EMPORIUM
8028 HIGHWAY 55
GOLDEN VALLEY, MN 55427
763-541-1340
877-709-9585
Fax: 952-417-8146
info@sportbeads.com
www.sportbeads.com
Products:
Collectible cards of sports figures.

CARDIOSPORT
DRAGOON HOUSE, HUSSAR COUR
WATERLOOVILLE, PO7 7SF
-44-225-7388
888-760-3059
Fax: -44-225-7399
• Russell Baier, Vice President
(631) 274-3248
Products:
Heart rate monitors. GO Range, GT Range, Fusion Range, Accessories range. Contour lite chest belt with changeable battery system.
Brands:
Reebok: RS1, RS11, RS111, Cardiosport

CARDS PLUS
PO BOX 131551
STATEN ISLAND, NY 10308
718-966-4250
800-231-9454
Fax: 718-966-4250
cardsplus01@aol.com
www.cardsplus.com
Products:
Collectible cards of sports and other celebrity figures.

CARIBOU MOUNTAINEERING
400 COMMERCE ROAD
ALICE, TX 78332
361-668-3766
800-824-4153
Fax: 361-668-3769
• Richard Current, President
Products:
Camping/Outdoor Products - Accessories, Daypacks, Fanny Packs, Hiking Packs, Luggage, Sleeping Bags.

CARROM COMPANY
218 E DOWLAND STREET
PO BOX 649
LUNDINGTON, MI 49431-2309
231-845-1263
800-223-6047
Fax: 231-843-9276
www.carrom.com

• Terri Dima, Sales/Marketing Coordinator
(231) 845-1263
• Michael McAvay, Sales
(231) 845-1263
• Robert Fortuna, Sales
(231) 845-1263
Products:
Air Powered Hockey, Foosball, Stick Hockey, Basketball
Brands:
Carrom®, Dueke®, Rochelle®

CARRON NET COMPANY, INC.
1623-17TH STREET
PO BOX 177
TWO RIVERS, WI 54241-0177
920-793-2217
800-558-7768
Fax: 920-793-2122
sales@carronnet.com
www.carronnet.com
• Bill Kiel, Jr, President/CEO
Year Founded:
1934.
Products:
Sports nets, Volleyball nets, Basketball nets, Tennis nets & tennis posts, Soccer nets & goal nets, Baseball batting cage nets, Backstop & foul ball nets, Golf nets, Wallyball nets, Nets to enclose athletic courts, Nets to enclose soccer fields, Stadium.

CARTS OF COLORADO, INC.
5420 S QUEBEC
SUITE 204
GREENWOOD VILLAGE, CO 80111
303-329-0101
800-227-8634
Fax: 303-329-6577
www.cartsofcolorado.com
• Dan Gallery, Sales
(800) 227-8634
• Jeff Clark, Parts & Service
Products:
Produce mobile and modular merchandising units used in retailing of food and beverages, hard goods, and various specialty products. Specialize in custom designs, free-standing kiosk units, and modular designs can be disassembled.

CASCO/USA
RR 7 BOX 1972
AUGUSTA, ME 04330
207-623-2918
Fax: 724-746-8500
• Peter J. Tambone, President / Chief Executive Officer
• Barbara Tambone, VP Sales
Products:
Training Room Supplies - Ankle Wraps, Finger Splints, Leg Guards, Rib Guards, Neoprene Supports.
Brands:
Casco, Castiglia

CASSEMCO, INC.
1595 LEMON FARRIS ROAD
COOKEVILLE, TN 38506
931-528-6588
800-844-3626
Fax: 931-528-2290
www.cassemco.com
• Jerry G. Samon, General Manager
(931) 528-6588
jsamon@live.com

• Sam Moody, Director of Operations
(931) 528-6588
• Ernie Julian, Director of Engineering & Q.A.
(931) 528-6588
• Scott Ward, Director of Business Development
(931) 528-6588
• Stuart Norris, Midwest Territory Manager
(931) 528-6588
• Eleanor Hooks, Production Coordinator/Shipping/Rec.
(931) 528-6588
ewhite@cassemco.com
• Mary Smith, Accounting Supervisor/ Office Manager
(931) 528-6588
msmith@cassemco.com
Services:
Foam and soft-goods fabricator offering die cut and profiled products made from all types of foam. Areas of expertise: Die Cutting, Profile Cutting, Sheeting/Convoluting, Contract Sewing, Private Label Packaging, Adhesive Application

CASTAWAY COLLECTIBLES
1480 S HOHOKUM
TEMPE, AZ 85281
602-337-3700
800-952-0708
Fax: 602-337-3790
RCCAInfo@lionelnascar.com
www.lionelnascarcollectables.com
• Howard Hitchcock, Vice President and General Manager
Products:
Produces the most respected racing collectibles in the industry.
Brands:
Action Racing Collectables (ARC), the Racing Collectables Club of America (RCCA), Revell Collection, Winner's Circle, and Chase Authentics

CATEK SNOWBOARD BINDINGS
PO BOX 5111
NEWPORT, RI 2841
401-624-8999
Fax: 401-624-8999
info@catek.com
Products:
Snowboard bindings, parts, accessories and late model parts
Brands:
Coiler, Donek, Madd, Pogo, Prior, Virus

CCM HOCKEY
3400 RAYMOND-LASNIER
MONTREAL, QC, CANADA H4R 3L3
800-451-4600
800-636-5895 (CAN)
Fax: 514-461-8020
ccmhockey.com/en
• Matthew O'Toole, CMO, Head of Global Marketing
• Philippe Dube, President and Chief Executive Officer
• Jamie Coughlin, VP Of Sales
Products:
Ice Hockey - Bags-Equipment, Gloves, Helmets, Masks, Protective, Skates, Uniforms.
Brands:
CCM, JOFA, KOHO, Heaton

CDM SPORT
816 LADERA DRIVE
FORT WORTH, TX 76108
817-448-8908
800-400-7542
Fax: 817-448-8701
steve@cdmsport.com
www.cdmsport.com
• Steve McGee, President
steve@cdmsport.com
• Wren Barnett, Office Manager
wren@cdmsport.com
Products:
Monitored Rehab Systems, Instant Replays, BackSystem, Core Strength Rack, Electro-Therapy
Brands:
Backsystems, Shark, FMS, Pneumex, Stronglite, Flexmonitor, Monitored Rehab Systems, Rehab Education, The Golf Channel, Angler

CELLO PROFESSIONAL PRODUCTS
1354 OLD POST ROAD
HAVRE DE GRACE, MD 21078
800-638-4850
800-638-4850
Fax: 410-939-3028
RBlankenship@carrollco.com
www.cello-online.com
• Thomas Ferraro, Account Manager
(631) 271-8578
• David Hazman, Sales Manager
(800) 638-5990
• Leon Ewell, Sales Manager
(800) 638-5990
• Larry F Nedrow, Executive Vice President
Products:
Floor Care Products, Carpet Care Products, Cleaners/Degreasers, Disinfectants/Restroom, Specialty Products, & Dilution Control
Brands:
Armakote, Commander, Perma-Gloss Plus, 20 Plus, HTF High Traffic Floor Finish, HTF 25 High Traffic Floor Finish, Dimensions, Victory, Paramount, Cellobrate, Oracle, Hi-Production Spray Buff, About Face Spray Buff, Hi-Beam, Dress Up, Silver Streak, Glitz, Cello Seal, Cellothane 25, Clear Concrete Seal, Down & Up, Kleen Strip, Pulverize Dimensions Floor Finish Striper, Mop 'n Strip, Deep Strip, Neutra Strip, Ammoniated Cleaner Striper, On & Off, Floor Care Neutralizer, Carpet Restoration Pre-Spray, Grease-X Traffic Lane Cleaner & Pre-Oil Break, The Natural, Freeze Gum & Candle Wax Remover

CENTAUR FLOOR SYSTEMS, LLC
963 N. SAN MAREAS RD
SANTA BARBARA, CA 93111
805-957-0182
800-536-9007
Fax: 805-957-0125
www.centaurfloors.com
• John Donati, Owner
(800) 536-7007
• Jim Langhorn, Co-Owner
• Terri Cruz, Order Processing
• Peter Hernandez, Bookkeeper
Products:
Flooring - Fitness, Recreational. Flooring Surfaces Include: Rubber, Wood, Multi Sport, Tracks, Specs.
Brands:
Boflex, Rubberflex, Gymlastic Sports Floor,

Sportweave, Bolon
Year Founded:
1997

CENTRALIA KNITTING MILLS, INC.
1002 W MAIN STREET
CENTRALIA, WA 98531
360-736-3994
Fax: 800-723-4317
• Dorothy Thoreson, President
• Ralph E. Thoreson, Vice President
Products:
Letterman Jackets, Corporate Apparel, Embroidery, Sweaters, Chenille, Blankets and Banners
Brands:
Frank Troeh, Octonek, Skookum Sportswear

CENTURY INDUSTRIES, LLC
299 PRATHR STREET
SELLERSBURG, IN 47172
812-246-3371
800-248-3371
Fax: 812-246-5446
www.centuryindustries.com

CENTURY SPORTS, INC.
1995 RUTGERS UNIVERSITY BOULEVARD
PO BOX 2035
LAKEWOOD, NJ 08701-8035
732-905-4422
800-526-7548
Fax: 732-905-7766
www.centurysportsinc.com
• Timothy Fogarty, President
Products:
Eyewear - Protective; Racquet Sports, Badminton Equipment, Gloves, Platform Tennis Equipment, Racquet Grips, Racquet Strings, Racquet Stringing Machines, Shoes, Socks, Squash Equipment, Wilson Tennis Court Equipment
Year Founded:
1972
Brands:
Wilson
Clients:
All tennis end-user facilities in US and around the world.

CEO MANUFACTURERS
1111 BUNKER HILL ROAD
HOUSTON, TX 77055
713-467-6899
800-231-3568
Fax: 713-467-2505
• Carlos Kuri, President
Products:
General Sports Products - Ladies Coordinates & Short Sets.
Brands:
Manufacturer, Custom House

CERASPORT
55 MATHEWS DRIVE
SUITE 220
HILTON HEAD, SC 29926
842-842-2600
888-237-2598
customerservice@ceraproducts.us
www.ceraproductsinc.com
• Charlene Da Riikonen, Founder
(410) 309-1000
• Esko Riikonen, Founder
• Mark Perlotto, Executive Vice President

and General Manager
• Jennifer Rapp, Director of Marketing
(410) 309-1000
Products:
Nutritional supplements and energy drinks.
Brands:
CeraLyte 50, CeraLyte70, CeraLyte 90, CeraLyte 50 Ready-to-drink, CeraLyte Cera Mixed Sampler Pack, Cera Sport Berry Sport Flavor Powder Pouch

CHAMPION BALL COMPANY
3800 DURBIN STREET
IRWINDALE, CA 91706
626-960-2100
888-464-5646
Fax: 626-960-2050
info@championball.com
www.championball.com
• Andrew Barajas, Sales Executive & Trade Show Manager
Products:
Basketballs, Footballs, Volleyballs, Soccer Balls, Playground Balls, Playball, Tether Balls, and Customized Balls
Brands:
Western Star, Mavericks, Outback Steakhouse, Kid Size PVC Soccor, Cheez It, Soccor (Galaxy), Soccor(Otto)

CHAOS SNOWBOARDS
8614 ARGENT STREET
SUITE E
SANTEE, CA 92071
619-258-9911
888-4424-267
Fax: 619-258-1383
www.chaossnowboards.com
• Roselynn Brown, President
• Frank Saputo, Owner
Products:
Snowboarding - Apparel, Bindings, Snowboards.
Brands:
Bratz, Carbon, Dead Knight, Fat Boy, Kaos, Phantom, Poison, Pure Carbon, Snow Goddess, Snow Princess

CHECKERED FLAG SPORTS
545 HOLLIE DRIVE
MARTINSVILLE, VA 24112
276-666-3000
800-278-1940
Fax: 800-240-3382
info@southprintinc.com
www.checkeredflagsports.com
• Debbie Simmons, Customer Service
(276) 666-3000

CHEER KIDS
1315 SUNDAY DRIVE
INDIANAPOLIS, IN 46217-9334
317-780-0609
800-869-0609
800-864-6315
Fax: 317-780-4188
www.cheerkids.com
• Kaitlyn Keller, Contact
• Chuck Pugh, Executive VP Sales & Marketing
(317) 780-0609
• Tina Mollis, Product Manager of Dance
Products:
Cheer Uniforms, Jewelry, and Accessories

CHRISTIAN BROTHERS, INC.
416 PIRKLE FERRY ROAD
BUILDING I
CUMMING, GA 30040
770-619-2855
Fax: 770-619-0123
contact@cbigc.com
www.cbigc.com
• Thomas Slaird, Chief Operating Officer
• Bill Christian, VP
(800) 346-5055
• Daniel Nielsen, President
Products:
Activewear; Ice Hockey Protective, Sticks;
In-Line Hockey Protective, Sticks.

CHUCK ROAST EQUIPMENT, INC.
ODELL HILL ROAD
PO BOX 2080
CONWAY, NH 03818-2080
603-447-5492
800-533-1654
Fax: 603-447-2277
custserv@chuckroast.com
www.chuckroast.com
• Charles Henderson, President
• Laurie Perkins, Marketing
Products:
Cycling Apparel; Skiing-Alpine
Apparel-Outerwear; Skiing-Nordic
Apparel-Outerwear.
Brands:
UNH, New Hampshire, Camp Belknap,
Stonyfield Farm, Maranacook Nordic, Dave
Matthews Band, The HBOMax, NHS,
Calumet, NH Public Radio, Wausau Papers
Safety, Jen's Friends Cancer Foundation

CIMCO REFRIGERATION
65 VILLIERS STREET
TORONTO, CANADA M5A 3S1
416-465-7581
Fax: 416-465-8815
www.cimcorefrigeration.com
• Steve McLeod, President
smcleod@toromont.com
Products:
Refrigeration equipment, such as heat
exchangers and pressure vessels,
packaged refrigeration systems, electrical
control panels and microprocessor control
systems for sports facilities.
Brands:
H.A. Phillips, Alco, Henry, Penn, Hubbell,
Refrigeration Specialties, Honeywell, Lau,
Danfoss, Paragon, Sporlan, Hansen
Technologies

CINCINNATI GAMES
PO BOX 18
KINGS MILLS, OH 45034
513-298-1123
866-574-9330
Products:
Tally Table, Premium Quality Wood Game
Boards, Premium Heavy Duty Bags
Brands:
The Cincinnati Corn Bag Game

CLASSIC MEDALLICS, INC.
520 S FULTON AVENUE
MOUNT VERNON, NY 10550
914-530-6259
800-221-1348
Fax: 800-541-3821
sales@classic-medallics.com
www.classic-medallics.com

• Gerald Singer, President
sales@classic-medallics.com
Year Founded:
1941.
Products:
Medallions Inserts; Medals; Ribbons;
Keyrings with Medals; Pins; Plaques,
Frames, Clocks; Traditional Trophies; Resin
Stoned Trophies; Scholastic Resin Trophies;
Sports & Fireman Trophies; Trophy Cups;
Bowls & Trays; Mugs & Coasters; Corp.
Gifts & Awards; Custom Products.

CLASSIC PRODUCTS
4617 INDUSTRIAL ROAD
FORT WAYNE, IN 46825
260-484-2695
800-444-0123
Fax: 260-483-7421
webmaster@classicproducts.com
www.classicproducts.com
• Robert Gudorf, EVP
webmaster@classicproducts.com
Products:
Bowling supplies

CLASSIC SPORT COMPANIES INC
5151 BANNOCK STREET
SUITE D
DENVER, CO 80216
303-991-8010
800-225-5712
Fax: 720-294-8333
Products:
Table Hockey, Table Soccer, Rod Hockey,
Combo Tables, Billiards, Table Tennis,
Basketball Games, Basketball, Soccer,
Football, Vollyball, Accessories, Goals,
Specialty Balls & Games, Croquet, Bocce,
Horseshoes, Combination Games,
Tetherball

CLEVELAND GOLF COMPANY
5601 SKYLAB ROAD
HUNTINGTON BEACH, CA 92647
714-889-1300
800-999-6263
Fax: 714-889-5890
www.clevelandgolf.com
• Bruno Cercley, Chairman
• Greg Hopkins, President
Products:
Clubs (Woods, Irons, Wedges, Hybrids,
Putters, Women's, Juniors)
Brands:
Woods (Launcher 460 Comp Driver,
Launcher Comp Fairway Woods); Irons (CGI
Black Pearl Irons, CGI Irons); Wedges
(CG11 Wedges, CG11 Black Pearl
Wedges); Hybrids (HALO Hybrid Utility,
LDI); Putters (Design By 1905, Design by
1948); Women's (Launcher Ti460, Launcher
Steel, W-Series Launcher Irons, W-Series
TA6 irons, W-Series CG11, 588W's,
W-Series Halo); Juniors (Gold Model, Silver
Model)

CLIF BAR
1610 5TH STREET
BERKELEY, CA 94710-1715
800-254-3227
800-254-3227
www.clifbar.com
• Gary Erickson, Owner
Nature of Service:
Energy bar maker that uses a healthy
combination of protein, carbohydrates,

vitamins and minerals, that delivers a
moderate, sustained increase in blood sugar
levels, the nutrition for sustained energy that
athletes and other active people need for
peak performance.
Brands:
Clif Bar, Luna Bar, Mojo Bar and Clif Shot.
Cycling Sponsor:
Reach the Beach, Deathride, Seattle to
Portland Bicycle Classic, Hotter-N-Hell 100.
Mountain Biking: WORS MTB Series, 24
Hours of Adrenaline, Niketown Run for the
Parks, Sea Otter Classic, 24 Hours of
Adrenaline at Laguna Seca, Pedro's
Mountain Bike Festival, 24 Hours of
Adrenaline Idyllwild.
Marathons:
LA Marathon, Canyonlands Half Marathon,
Catalina Marathon, John Hancock Sports &
Fitness Expo (Boston Marathon), SLC
Marathon and 5k, Flying Pig Marathon,
Helvatia Half Marathon, Grandma's
Marathon, Seafair Marathon, AFC Half
Marathon, Twin Cities Marathon, Tucson
Marathon, California International Marathon,
Dallas White Rock Marathon.
Triathlons:
Escape from Alcatraz Triathlon, San Diego
International Triathlon, River Cities
Triathlon, Los Angeles Triathlon.

CLIFF KEEN ATHLETIC INC.
4480 VARSITY DRIVE
SUITE B
ANN ARBOR, MI 48108
734-975-8800
800-992-0799
Fax: 800-590-0759
info@cliffkeen.com
www.cliffkeen.com
• James C. Keen, Chief Executive Officer
info@cliffkeen.com
• Thomas P. Keen, President
info@cliffkeen.com
• Barry Bellaire, General Manager
info@cliffkeen.com
• Mary Tolle, Controller
info@cliffkeen.com
• Chad Clark, Vice President/ Sales &
Marketing
• James Ralston, Sales Manager
• Jan Dobbs, Executive Administrator
Description:
Leading manufacturer of wrestling
equipment and officials wear.

CLIMAX MANUFACTURES
3820 OCEANIC DRIVE
SUITE 311
OCEANSIDE, CA 92056
760-722-1455
Fax: 760-967-0554
www.trackertrucks.com
• Larry Balma, Founder
Products:
Tracker Trucks, Accessories, Gear, Decks,
Quads, Books/Mags & Movies Orion Trucks,
Replacement Parts, Hardware
Brands:
Tracker Axis, Tracker Red and White, New
Kevin Staab Purple Signature Tracker,
Slalom Tracker Custom Offset Limited
Edition Racetrack Model, Tracker RT-S &
RT-X Models, Magnesium, New Tracker,
Classic Wing

CLOUDBURST INC.
707 E. HUENEME ROAD
SUITE B
OXNARD, CA 93033
805-986-4125
800-800-5479
Fax: 805-715-0514
info@cloudburst.com
www.cloudburst.com
• Mike Davis, President
mdavis@cloudburst.com
• Steve Wright, President / Public Relations
Sports Dire
Products:
Electric Housewares and Fans (Misting Fan
Kits, Pump Modules, Fixed Lined Systems,
Portable Coolers, Sideline Systems,
Satellite Fans, Misting Nozzles, Mist Rings,
Mist Lines, Water Filtration, Brass Fittings,
Hoses, Water Tanks, Starter Systems &
Kits, Extensions & Hoses, Misting Nozzles,
Compression Fittings, Accessories,
Merchandising Displays)
Brands:
Cloudburst, Mist&Cool

CLUB CAR, INC.
4125 WASHINGTON ROAD
PO BOX 204658
EVANS, GA 30809
706-863-3000
800-258-2227
Fax: 706-863-5808
www.clubcar.com
• Philip Tralies, President / Chief Executive
Officer
• Marc A. Dufour, President & CEO
Products:
Golf Cars, Turf Vehicles
Brands:
Precedent, DS Electric Golf Car-IQ System,
DS Gas Golf Car, Carryall 294, Carryall Turf
1, Carryall Turf 2, Carryall Turf 272, Turf
252, Carryall Turf 6

CLUB GLOVE
17811 JAMESTOWN LANE
HUNTINGTON BEACH, CA 92647
714-843-9288
800-736-4568
info@clubglove.com
www.clubglove.com
• Jim Jamison, Director of Operations
(714) 843-9288
Products:
Golf Bags
Brands:
Elephant Vinyl Cart Bag, Ballistic Nylon Cart
Bag, Hotstepper, Aficionado III

CLUBHOUSEKIT
1545 HIGHWAY 9
TOMS RIVER, NJ 8755
732-240-6900
800-553-4726
Fax: 732-240-3599
www.clubhousekit.com
• Brad Singer, President
(877) 258-2548
Nature of Service:
Full line of amenities for the clubhouse or
lockerroom including industrial strength
cleaning products designed exclusively for
the outdoor sports market.
Products:
Grass & Blood Eliminator, Athletic
Equipment Cleaner, Protective Headgear

Disinfectant, Athletic Equipment Polish,
Claymate Clay Remover, Pro-Detergent with
Color-safe Bleach, Duffel Bag Deodorizer,
Pine Tar, Glove Oil, Rosin Bag, Shoe
Polish, Pine Tar Remover, Hat Cleaner
Brands:
Clubhouse Kit

COBBLESTONES ACTIVEWEAR
7095 W 3500 S
WEST VALLEY CITY, UT 84128
801-250-1865
800-592-7195
Fax: 801-250-6099
CustomerService@cobblestones.com
www.gamegear.com
• Mark Osborn, President
(801) 382-6514
• Clayton Osborn, Marketing, Sales
(801) 382-6564
• Patti Osborn-Bell, Accounting
(801) 382-6513
• Randy Haun, Information System
(801) 250-4500
• Cade Osborn, President
(801) 382-6566
Products:
Activewear for Baseball, Softball,
Basketball, Aerobics / Cheerleader,
Football, Phys Ed/Camp

COBRA PUMA GOLF
1818 ASTON AVENUE
CARLSBAD, CA 92008
800-917-3300
800-843-5464
Fax: 760-929-0374
customerservice@cobragolf.com
www.cobragolf.com
• Robert Dubiel, President
• Mark C. McClure, Chief Executive Officer
& Director
• Jeff Harmet, President
• Robert K. Bruning, Chief Financial Officer
• David A. Schaefer, Senior VP & Chief
Operating Officer
Products:
Drivers, Fairways, Utility Metals Irons
Brands:
Drivers - King Cobra X/Speed, King Cobra
F/Speed, King Cobra M/Speed, King Cobra
M/Speed Seniors', King Cobra M/Speed
Women's, King Cobra 454 COMP, King
Cobra 414 Comp, King Cobra 414 Comp
Tour; Fairways - King Cobra X/Speed, King
Cobra F/Speed, King Cobra M/Speed, King
Cobra M/Speed Seniors', King Cobra
M/Speed Women's, King Cobra COMP
Fairways, Utility Metals - King Cobra Baffler
Men's & Seniors', King Cobra Baffler
Women's; Irons - King Cobra Men's 2300
I/M, King Cobra Men's 3400 I/XH, King
Cobra Senior's 3400 I/XH, King Cobra
Women's 3400 I/XH, King Cobra Men's
3100 I/H, King Cobra Senior's 3100 I/H,
King Cobra Women's 3100 I/H, King Cobr

COED SPORTSWEAR INC
27 PLEASANT STREET
NEWFIELDS, NH 3856
603-772-1990
800-926-6578
Fax: 603-772-0351
donl@coedsportswear.com
www.coedsportswear.com
• Mark Lane, Co-Founder/ President
 ext 106

mark@coedsportswear.com
• Scott MacHardy, Co-founder / VP
(603) 772-1990
• Selim Tobey, Vice President- Sales
selim@coedsportswear.com
Products:
Imprinted T-shirts, sweatshirts, and various
other tops; boxer shorts; athletic shorts and
headwear
Brands:
It's All About, The Power of a Girl, Coed
Naked, Corona, Rebel Flag, Soccer Mom,
Post Card Past, Life's A Bass, Go Figure,
Miller Lite, Miller High Life, Snuggleball,
Definitions, Coots & Biddy's

COLBOND, INC.
PO BOX 1057
ENKA, NC 28728
828-665-5050
800-365-7391
Fax: 828-665-5009
info@colbond-usa.com
www.colbond-usa.com
• Axel Poscher, Vice President
• Tim Woodlee, Sales and Marketing
Manager, NAFTA
(828) 665-5016
• Heather Rohde, Profile Products LLC -
Exclusive Distributor
(847) 215-3454
• Don Brown, Sales, Automotive, Filtration
Colback Support
(828) 665-5075
• Greg Wood, Composites Media, Filtration
Enkamat Spacer M
(828) 665-5084
• Richard Goodrum, Geosynthetics
(828) 665-5023
• Shelia Snyder, Geosynthetics, Roofing
Membrane Reinforcement
(828) 665-5069
shelia.snyder@colbond.com
• Debbie Bailey, Customer Service, Athletic
Fields
(828) 665-5013
Products:
Matrix and nonwoven products
Brands:
Colback Original, Colbonddrain, Easy Tuft,
Enkadrain, Enkadri & Drain, EnkaFusion,
EnkagridGolf Drain, Enkagrid, Enkamat,
Enkamat II, EnkamatPlus, EnkaPath,
Enkaroof Vent, Enkaroof VM,
EnkaShoreline, Enkasonic, EnkaTrap,
Enkaturf Drain, Enkavent, Home Slicker,
MFM, Mortar Break, Mortar Break II, Mortar
Catch

COLEMAN COMPANY INC.
1767 DENVER W BOULEVARD
SUITE 200
GOLDEN, CO 80401
316-832-2700
800-835-3278
Fax: 316-832-3060
newsroom@coleman.com
www.coleman.com
• Gary A. Kiedaisch, President / Chief
Executive Officer
gary@coleman.com
• Nancy Paulson, Global Human Resources
SVP
nancy@coleman.com
• Robert A. Markovitch, President & CEO
Products:
Tents and Shelters, Stoves Lighting,
Inflatables, Sleeping Bags, Sleeping Pads,

Roadtrip Grill, Heaters, Outdoor Fireplaces, Coolers, Gear for Pets, Water Recreation, Mosquito Control, Hot Water Systems, Furniture, Grills & Accessories, Backpacks, Accessories, Storage, Cookware, Emergency Gear, Boats, Outlet Store, Spas, Footwear, Sunglasses, Heating & Cooling, Watches, Cargo Carriers, Exponent, Airpumps, Blankets, Coolers, Airbeds, Cookware, Emergency Gear, Beds & Cots, Inflatable Boats & Kayaks
Brands:
Coleman

COLOR SIGN SERVICE, INC.
11096 61ST STREET NE
PO BOX 124
ALBERTVILLE, MN 55301
763-497-1374
800-497-2141
Fax: 763-497-1375
www.colorsign.com
Products:
Color Sign Systems (Message Centers, Time & Temp, Scoreboards, I.D. Signs, Ground Directional, Signs)

COLORADO DISPLAY SYSTEMS
1551 E 11TH STREET
LOVELAND, CO 80537
970-667-1000
800-299-0111
Fax: 970-667-5876
www.coloradodisplay.com
• Anita Sayed, President / Chief Executive Officer
Commercial Products:
Billboards/Video Display; Marquees; Information Boards; Highway Transportation Signage; Flight Information System

---

COLORADO TIME SYSTEMS
1551 E 11TH STREET
LOVELAND, CO 80537
970-667-1000
800-299-0111
Fax: 970-667-5876
info@coloradotime.com
www.coloradotime.com
• Anita Sayed, President/Chief Executive Officer
Products:
Arena: Full Matrix LED Socreboards; Light-reflective Scoreboards and Products. Ribbon and Fuscia Boards, same for Stadiums and Natatoriums.

COLUMBIA 300, INC.
1813 W 7TH STREET
PO BOX 13430
HOPKINSVILLE, KY 42240
270-881-1300
800-626-8350
Fax: 270-881-1201
www.columbia300.com
• Ronald J. Herrmann, Chief Executive Officer
• Mike Allbritton, President / Chief Operating Officer
• Roger Vessell, Sales VP
• Bob Ried, Vice President
Products:
High Performance Balls; Mid Range Balls; 3-Piece Balls; Polyester Balls; Retired Balls; Houseballs; 1-Ball Bags; 2-Ball Bags; 3-Ball Bags; 4-Ball Bags; 5-Ball Bags; 6-Ball Bags; Cleaners/Polishers; Gloves; Grips; Shoe

Accessories; Tape Products; Columbia 300 Wear; Ball Wear; Active Wear; Towels
Brands:
(High-Performance) Action; Action Packed; Backyard Bully; Big Bully; EPX T1; Full Throttle; (Mid-Performance Balls) Dr.Jekyll; Hyde; Messenger To Low Rg; Messenger Ti Pearl; Overdrive; Panic; Power Drive; Power Drive Sanded; Shock; Super Trooper; U Turn; U Turn; Particle; UTurn Particel Pearl; (3-Piece Balls) Scout; Scout Hi-Flare Particle; Scout Hi-Flare Reactive; Scout Hi-Flare Urethane; Scout Reactive; (Polyester Balls) Blue Dot; White Dots; (Retired Balls) AfterShock; AfterShock Pearlized; Alter Ego; Beast Master; Beast Pearl with MICA; Beast with MICA; Black Knight; Black Knight; Black Shadow; Blue Beast; Blue Knight; Blue Shadow; Boss T

COLUMBIA PARCAR CORP.
1115 COMMERCIAL AVENUE
REEDSBURG, WI 53959
608-524-8888
800-222-4653
Fax: 608-524-8380
info@parcar.com
www.parcar.com
• William R. Sauey, Chairman
• Todd Sauey, President
Products:
Passenger Vehicles
Brands:
Summit; Eagle

COLUMBIA SPORTSWEAR COMPANY
14375 NW SCIENCE PARK DRIVE
PORTLAND, OR 97229-5418
503-985-4000
800-622-6953
Fax: 503-985-5800
www.columbia.com
• Gertrude Boyle, Chairwoman
• Timothy P. Boyle, President & Chief Executive Officer
• Patrick D. Anderson, Chief Operating Officer
Products:
Sportswear
Brands:
Cloud-Bound Jacket; Grangeville Pant; Springbrook Long Sleeve Tee; Skamania Pass; ROC Ball Cap; Delphine Creek Jacket; Sand Creek Pant; Mesa Ridge Lite Long Sleeve Shirt; Tigertooth; Ladies Logo Ball Cap; Switchback Trail Jacket; Challenger II Convertible Pants; Challenger II Shirt; Magneto; ROC Ball Cap; Peak to Creek Shell; Million Mile II Pant; Titanium Diablo Pass; Splendor Peak Shell; Saber XCR; Staubio; Panther Ridge; Boorad; Columbia Logo II Ball Cap; Challenger Tech Organizer; Insulated Products; Tents & Sleeping Bags; Willow Creek; Bugaboo; Omni Released Sheets; Freedom Trail Throws

---

COMFORT LINE PRODUCTS
2717 N TAMIAMI TRAIL
N FORT MYERS, FL 33903
239-997-6366
866-891-5585
888-997-6366
Fax: 239-997-6312
www.clpusa.com
• Richard Doyle, President

Products:
Whirlpools and spa accessories.

COMFORT PRODUCTS, INC.
931 RIVER ROAD
CROYDON, PA 19021
215-781-0300
800-822-7500
Fax: 215-785-5737
info@comfortoandp.com
www.comfortoandp.com
• Harold Bernhardt, President
• Cathy Brown, Customer Service
Products:
Athletic socks, outdoorsmen socks, thermal socks, liner socks, antimicrobial socks, lacrossse socks, logo socks
Brands:
Footwarmer III, ThermaFlex K

COMFYFEET
105 N BROADWAY AVE
PO BOX 352
HARTINGTON, NE 68739
402-999-0371
888-515-6677
Fax: 402-215-0803
www.comfyfeet.biz
Products:
College Slippers; NFL Color Slippers; College Scuff Slippers; College Baby Slippers; College Baby Blanket Set; College Baby Blanket; College Yard Signs; College Hanging Laser Cut Signs; Generic Slippers; Bird Feeders; Bird Houses; Spirit Spirals; Tumblers; Blanket, Throws, and Pillows; Door Mats; Freezer Mugs; Trash Cans; Wall Clocks; Ornaments and Figurines; Snack Helmets; Helmet Piggy Banks; Biederlack; Helmets; Batting Helmets; Banners; Schutt Full Size Replica Helmets
Brands:
Alabama Crimson Tide Original Comfy Feet Slippers; Arizona State Sun Devils Original Comfy Feet Slippers; Arizona Wildcats Original Comfy Feet Slippers; Arkansas Razorbacks Original Comfy Feet Slippers; Auburn Tigers Original Comfy Feet Slippers; Bobby Labonte Original Comfy Feet Slippers; Cincinnati Bearcats Original Comfy Feet Slippers; Clemson Tigers Original Comfy Feet Slippers; Colorado Buffaloes Original Comfy Feet Slippers; Connecticut Huskies Original Comfy Feet Slippers; Duke Blue Devils Original Comfy Feet Slippers; East Carolina Pirates Original Comfy Feet Slippers; Florida Gators Original Comfy Feet Slippers

---

COMMUNITY PROFESSIONAL LOUDSPEAKERS
333 E 5TH STREET
CHESTER, PA 19013-4511
610-876-3400
800-523-4934
Fax: 610-874-0190
info@communitypro.com
www.communitypro.com

CONCEPT II, INC.
105 INDUSTRIAL PARK DRIVE
MORRISVILLE, VT 5661
802-888-7971
800-245-5676
Fax: 802-888-4791
rowing@concept2.com
www.concept2.com

- Richard A. Dreissigacker, President
- Bev Incledon, President

Products:
Indoor Rowers; Oars; DYNO; Slides; Heart Rate Monitors; Clothing

Brands:
(Rower) Model D Indoor Rower; (Oars) Dreissigacker Oars; (DYNO) Dynamic Strength Training; (Slides) TeamBoat Slides; Single Rower Slide; (Clothing) C2 Lightweight Workout T-Shirt; C2 Logo Black T; Women's Tank Top; Men's Tank Top; Performance Shirt; Ladies Scoopneck T

CONCEPT ONE ACCESSORIES
119 W 40TH STREET
NEW YORK, NY 10018
212-868-2590
Fax: 212-868-2595
www.concept1.com
- Sam Hafif, President / Chief Executive Officer
(212) 868-2590
sam@concept1.com
- Harvey Mallis, Sales VP
(212) 868-2590
harvey@concept1.com
- Bernie Hafif, Finance VP / Operations
(212) 868-2590
bernie@concept1.com
- Jason Colin, Director of Communications
(212) 381-3937

Products:
Backpacks; Gloves; Headwear; Umbrellas

Brands:
Akademiks; Blue Marlin; Levi Strauss Signature; Cooperstown Collection; Major League Baseball; Original Penguin; Corona Extra; Sean John; Private Label / C1 Design; U.S. Polo Association; Concept rock (80's Band)

CONCORD INDUSTRIES
19 WILLARD ROAD
NORWALK, CT 6851
203-810-4188
888-441-1603
Fax: 203-286-1188
www.sp-us.com
- Karen Condron, Founder

Products:
Corporate Gifts; Sports Licensed Products; Carriage House Leather; Premium Key Holders; Auto Accessories; Outdoor Licensed Products; Postal Products; Belt Buckles

CONNELLY SKIS
20621 52ND AVENUE W
PO BOX 716
LYNNWOOD, WA 98036
425-775-5416
Fax: 425-778-9590
infobox@connellyskis.com
www.connellyskis.com
- Thomas Stephens, President
tstephens@connellyskis.com
- Gordy Holmes, Marketing VP
(425) 775-5416
- Gordy Holmes, President & CEO

Products:
Water skis, bindings, kneeboards, ropes, vests, gloves, and apparel for the recreation industry.

Brands:
Concept, HC Jumpers, HC Trick, Revolution, Rocket, Silhouette, Team 2,

Proline, Ski Warm

Year Founded:
1965

CONNOR SPORTS FLOORING CORPORATION
1830 HOWARD STREET
SUITE F
ELK GROVE VILLAGE, IL 60007
847-290-9020
800-283-9522
Fax: 847-890-9034
www.connorfloor.com
- Ron Cerny, President
- Doug Grove, National Sales Manager
dgrove@connorfloor.com

Products:
Synthetic Athletic Surfacing, Wood Flooring

Brands:
Duracushion, Grip-Tite, Permalock, Powerstrip, Rezill-CHANNEL

CONROY GLOVES
110 S MARKET STREET
JOHNSTOWN, NY 12095
518-762-9444
Fax: 518-762-0900
- Brian Conroy, President

Products:
Skiing-Alpine - Gloves

CONTINENTAL SPORTS SUPPLY, INC.
3981 S DECATUR STREET
ENGLEWOOD, CO 80110
800-877-5053
Fax: 720-833-0814
info@reuschusa.com
www.reuschusa.com
- David D. Banning, President

Products:
Soccer - Bags-Equipment, Balls-Rubber, Cleats, Corner Flags, Gloves-Goalie, Protective, Shinguards, Socks, Uniforms. Rugby: uniforms, balls, bags. Ski: gloves.

Brands:
Continental, Vici, Reusch

Year Founded:
1980.

CONTOUR SEATS, INC.
6530 CHAPMANS ROAD
ALLENTOWN, PA 18106
610-395-5144
800-247-4509
Fax: 610-398-7099
info@contourseats.com
www.contourseats.com
- Carl A. Gross, President/CEO
c.gross@contourseats.com
- Janine Gross, Officer Manager
j.gross@contourseats.com

Products:
Contour Seats, Stadium Seats, Spectator Seating

COOPER LIGHTING
1121 HIGHWAY 74 S
PEACHTREE CITY, GA 30269
770-486-4680
Fax: 770-486-4318
www.cooperlighting.com
- David Feldman, President
- Terry A Klebe, SVP / Chief Financial Officer
- Donnie Miller, National Account Director
(770) 486-4471

- Wayne Blanton, National Accounts Sales / Marketing Mana
(770) 486-4365

Products:
Incandescent, HID and fluorescent fixtures to architectural, emergency, outdoor and exit lighting

Brands:
Fail-Safe high-abuse, clean room and vandal-resistant lighting. Halo recessed and track lighting. Iris lighting systems. Lumiere outdoor architectural and landscape lighting. McGraw-Edison and Lumark indoor and outdoor HID lighting. Metalux florescent lighting. MWS modular wiring systems. Portfolio architectural recessed lighting. Sure-Lites and AtLite exit and emergency lighting.

COOPSPORT INTERNATIONAL LP
1335 PARK CENTER DRIVE
SUITE B
VISTA, CA 92081
760-727-8697
815-22-515
Fax: 760-727-8699
www.coop.no
- Scott Cooper, Owner / President

Products:
Sporting goods and toys for adult and children such as: CoopSport, CoopKids, CoopHydro, CoopImpulse, CoopSport Pool and Coop Premium

Brands:
Air Rocket, Air Sted, Air Tube, Surfster, Gription Football, WetBall, WetVolley, WetFoot, WetDisk, WetSmash Paddles, Wet Glove, Wet Hoop, Coop Accessories, Hit-A-Way Jr., Tumble Jumbo, Big Time Soccer, First Toss Glove n' Ball, First Pitch Bat n' Ball, First Goal Hockey Set, First Goal Soccer Goal, First Strike Bowling Set, Nuf Nuf, Hydroball Football, HydroBall All Purpose, HydroCatch Game, HydroDisk Flying Disk, HydroGlove Ball Game, HydroSmash Paddled, HydroVolley Volleyball, Zip Stix, SlingBall Tail Ball, Micro Revolution Set, Rookie Hoop, Rookie Football, Rookie Soccer, Rookie Volleyball, Tumble Playball, Revolution Flying Disk, SunSport

CORPORATION FOR LASER OPTICS RESEARCH
47 DURHAM STREET
PORTSMOUTH, NH 3801
603-430-2023
Fax: 603-430-2058
- Masayuki Karakawa, President/Chief Technology Officer
- Robert Zielstorff, Vice President of Finance
- George Naumann, Senior Vice President Operations

Products:
Solid state laser systems for laser video displays.

CORSAIR DISPLAY SYSTEMS, INC.
1236 N. 18TH STREET
SHEBOYGAN, WI 53081-3201
920-457-4851
800-624-2051
Fax: 585-396-5953
sales@corsairdisplay.com
www.vollrath.com

• David W Mansfield, President
sales@corsairdisplay.com
• Nancy Bryan Role, Account Manager
nrole@corsairdisplay.com
Products:
Designing and manufacturing custom and
standard carts, kiosks, inline systems,
merchandisers and pastry cases
Brands:
BBQ Cart NFL Jaguars All Tel Stadium,
Beer Cart MLB Astros, Cleveland Zoo Food
Service, Cocktail Cart Mudhens, Deli Cart
Bilo Center, Kiosk - 8x10 - Red Wings,
Kiosk - St. Petersburg Times, Merchandise
Cart - Beaver Stadium, Retail Merchandise
Box - Cardinal Stadium, Retail Program Cart
- Invesco Field, Locker Box - Pac Bell,
Chesapeake Bay Hyatt, LuLu's Bait Shack,
Lulu's Bait Shack, Murphys Bar and Grill,
12x10 Kiosk Joker's Wild Six Flags, Cold
Beverage Cart - Six Flags, Italian Ice Cart -
Lodge - Jay Vending, Cart - Italian Ice -
Fifties, Gazebo Roseland Waterpark,
Lemonade Cart - Jay Vending, Cold
Beverage Cart - Pepsi - Six Flags, Hot D

COURT COMPANY
5440 S 900 E
MURRAY, UT 84117
801-288-8979
877-273-1172
Fax: 801-266-2949
www.courtcompany.com
• Randy Stafford, Co-Owner/President
thecountco@aol.com
Products:
Racquetball and squash courts along with
other types of athletic court systems.

COURT-1 SPORTS INC.
156 LAWRENCE PAQUETTE
CHAMPLAIN, NY 12919
514-731-3607
800-363-3591
Fax: 514-731-2929
info@court-1.com
www.court-1.com
• Matthew LiLi, President
(514) 731-3607
lili@court-1.com
Products:
Sporting Equipment for Hockey; Tennis;
Soccer Nets & GoalFrames, Marathon &
Gym Mats

COVER SPORTS USA
5000 PASCHALL AVENUE
PHILADELPHIA, PA 19143
215-724-3582
800-445-6680
Fax: 215-724-8706
sales@coversports.com
www.coversports.com
• Ronald Nissenbaum, President
• Victoria Christinzio, Credit Manager
Products:
Field and fence covers and other related
products.
Brands:
FieldSaverT Field Covers, FieldSaverT
Protective Rain Covers, FieldSaverT
Football Sideline Covers, GymGuardT Gym
Floor Covers, SafeFoamT Fence Padding,
Oval Poly Mesh, Soft Knit Mesh,
TempFenceT Pole, 50' Fence Kit, 100'
Fence Kit, 150' Fence Kit, FenceCrownT
Safe, Good-Looking Fence Tops,

FenceMateT Windscreen and Privacy
Screen

**COYLE & GREER AWARDS CANADA
LTD.**
383 SOVEREIGN ROAD
LONDON, ENGLAND N6M 1A3
519-659-5862
800-265-2607
Fax: 519-659-7052
info@talbot-promo.com
www.talbot-promo.com
• Brenda MacDonald, President
• Steve Levschuk, President
Products:
Recognition Awards, Jewelry, Writing
Instruments, Lapel Pins, Medals & Ribbons,
Glassware, Cast Products, Business Gifts &
Wearables, Service & Safety Awards

COYOTE PROMOTIONS
300 NORTHERN BOULEVARD
SUITE 26
GREAT NECK, NY 11021
516-487-5696
800-726-9683
Fax: 516-482-7425
www.coyotepromotions.com
• Marc Simone, Vice President Sales
marc@coyotepromotions.com
Nature of Services:
Adobe Graphics and Design, Inc. are
suppliers of premium and promotional items
to the media industry that includes
custom-imprinted products and sports pins
to both the college and professional sports
market.

CRAMER PRODUCTS, INC.
PO BOX 1001
GARDNER, KS 66030
913-856-7511
800-345-2231
Fax: 913-884-5626
info@cramersportsmed.com
www.cramersportsmed.com
• Tom Rogge, President / Chief Executive
Officer
trogge@cramersportsmed.com
• Matt Conway, Vice President
• Rob Mogolov, Director Of Marketing
Products:
Sports medicine and athletic training room
supplies including tape, athletic trauma kits,
braces & supports and educational
products.
Brands:
CRAMER CO STRETCH NON ADHESIVE
TAPE, SKIN LUBEr LUBRICATING
OINTMENT STICK, CRAMER 1000
ATHLETIC TRAINER'S TAPE, CRAMER
250 ATHLETIC TRAINER'S TAPE,
CRAMER NON-TEAR STRETCH TAPE,
DE-HESIVET TAPE REMOVER SPRAY,
QDAr TAPING BASE, TAPE UNDERWRAP,
AT 2470 SOFT SIDED KIT, AT BACKPACK
DELUXE, AT 1782 / AT 1577 / AT 819 /
SOFT SIDED KITS, AT 273 DELUXE
FANNY PACK, AT 166 FANNY PACK, AT
MESSENGER PACK, ACTIVE ANKLEr
CHAMELEON ANKLE BRACE, ACTIVE
ANKLEr T1, ACTIVE ANKLEr T2, ACTIVE
ANKLEr AS1 ANKLE BRACE, ACTIVE
ANKLEr PRO LACERT ANKLE BRACE,
DELUXE HINGED KNEE BRACE, DELUXE
KNEE STABILIZER, HINGED KNEE

BRACE, PATELLAR SUPPORT, KNEE
SUPPORT, FOOTBALL

CRAN BARRY INC.
3 GRIFFIN WAY
CHELSEA, MA 2150
617-884-6290
800-992-2021
Fax: 617-567-9953
service@cranbarry.com
www.cranbarry.com
• John Vinton, Chief Executive Officer &
President
service@cranbarry.com
Products:
Sports Team Uniforms

CREATIONS BY ALAN STUART
49 W 38 STREET
NEW YORK, NY 10018
212-719-5511
800-866-4424
Fax: 212-719-5267
Products:
Toothbrushes, Collegiates, Bath Supplies &
Bags

CREATIVE AWARDS BY LANE
1713 ELMHURST ROAD
ELK GROVE VILLAGE, IL 60007
847-593-7700
Fax: 847-593-1155
• John P. Erskine, President/CEO
Products:
Trophies/Plaques/Jewelry/Advertising
Special Ties/Engraving/Lasering

CREATIVE CUSTOM PRODUCTS
PO BOX 414
CEDARBURG, WI 53012
800-368-8182
Fax: 262-375-9465
www.creativecustomproducts.com
• John Ochsenwald, Chief Executive Officer
Products:
Athletic training equipment and supplies
Brands:
IC WRAP, I.C. Bags, Tape Tube, CaviCide,
Plastic Ice Bags, Foam Rolls, White

CREATIVE TROPHIES COMPANY
437 AVENUE U
BROOKLYN, NY 11223
718-339-8266
888-807-7835
Fax: 718-998-7082
creativetrophies@aol.com
www.creativetrophies.com
• Joe Minuto, General Manager
(718) 339-8266
creativetrophies@aol.com
Products:
Trophies, Trophy Cups, Plaques, Lucite
Awards, Great Awards, Great Gifts & Desk
Ideas, Promotional Items, Scholastic
Awards, Ribbons, Airflyte & Related
Products
Brands:
American Eagle, Copper Look Figure
Awards, Economical Trophies, Jumbo
Figure Awards, Oscar Like Awards, Resin
Sport Display Dishes, World Series Trophy,
964 SERIES, DA01 SERIES, DA 03
SERIES, DA 04 SERIES, DA 05 SERIES,
DAO6 SERIES, DA 07 SERIES, DA 08
SERIES, Elegant Plaques, Clock Plaques,

Copper Creations, Picture Plaques, A2276, A2966, A3808, A5960, A5968, BC1, BC2, BC6, BC18, BC46, BC850, Walnut Name Block, Walnut Name Block w/ Pen, Wood Pen Box and Pen, Economical Pens, Elite Custom Pens, AP Series Pins, EP Series Pins, Stars & School Pins, NA70G, NA70S

CREATIVE URETHANES
250 INDEPENDENCE DRIVE
WINCHESTER, VA 22602
540-542-6676
888-338-7139
Fax: 540-542-6678
cuinfo@creativeurethanes.com
www.creativeurethanes.com
• Dan Maxwell, Owner
Services:
Reaction Injection Molding, Plastic Pipe - Durothane AR Piping System, Custom Urethane Wheels & Urethane Molding Services
Products:
Urethane wheels and surfaces for rollerskaing and skateboarding.

CROAKIES
88 LIFE LINK WAY
BOZEMAN, MT 59718
307-733-2269
800-443-8620
Fax: 406-587-4303
croakies@croakies.com
www.croakies.com
• John Krisik, President
• John Scott, EVP
jscott@croakies.com
• Fred Bowditch, Manager
• Dinah Delaney, Chief Financial Officer
Products:
Bag Packs, Shovels, Poles, Probes, Accessories, Skis, Bindings, Boots, Clothing and Accessories
Year Founded:
1978

CROSMAN CORPORATION
7629 ROUTES 5 & 20
EAST BLOOMFIELD, NY 14469
418-682-3000
800-724-7486
Fax: 418-682-3343
www.crosman.com
• Ken D'Arcy, President / Chief Executive Officer
• Robert Beckwith, Vice President, Finance
• Steve Upham, Vice President Sales
• Phil Dolci, President & CEO
Products:
Airguns, Rifles, pistols, kits, soft air, ammo/CO2, slingshots & ranges
Brands:
AirSource, Break Barrel, Co2, Pneumatic; 2240, 3576 Revolver, American Classic pump pistol, Auto Air II Red Dot, Repeat Air 1008B CO2 pistol, Repeat Air 1008BRD; 1008 Shooter's Kit, 1008S Air Pistol Kit, 1008S Shooter's Kit, 357 Shooter's Kit, 781 Action Kit, Pumpmaster Starter Kit, Air Mag P50, Pulse R70, Stinger P32, Stinger R34, Stinger R36, Stinger Shotgun, Wingmaster,.177 cal. Hollow Point pellets,.177 cal. Super Match pellets, Model VTS, Model CSS, Model FSS, Large Range, Medium Range, Small Range, Legacy 1000, Legacy Pro Pak

CROSS CREEK APPAREL, INC.
755 LEE STREET
SUITE 1000
ALEXANDER CITY, AL 35011
800-321-1138
• W Ha Spires Jr, President
cc_custservice@russellcorp.com
• John Meis, Sales / Merchandising VP
cc_custservice@russellcorp.com
• Dick Younger, Merchandising General Manager
cc_custservice@russellcorp.com
Products:
General Sports Products - Apparel; Golf - Apparel.
Brands:
Cross Creek

CROSSFIELD PRODUCTS CORPORATION
140 VALLEY ROAD
ROSELLE PARK, NJ 7204
908-245-2800
Fax: 908-245-0659
www.crossfieldproducts.com
• Charles R. Watt, President
• Richard M. Watt, VP
Services:
Flooring for Sports Facilities.
Brands:
Dex-O-Tex Gym-Flor

CROWN INDUSTRIES, INC.
155 N PARK STREET
EAST ORANGE, NJ 7017
973-672-2277
877-747-2457
Fax: 866-200-5546
www.gocrown.com
Products:
Stanchions and Ropes for crowd control, Pipe & Drape, Brass Rails and Brass Fittings, Aluminum Easels, Brass Easels, Bellman's Carts, Luggage Carts, Pedestal Tables, and Folding Table Legs
Brands:
DPendaPull (tm) retractable, King, Crown, Plastic Stanchions, Ropes and Rods, Snap Ends & Wallplates, Signs and sign frames, Tops, Brass Polish, Foot rails, Glassracks, Tubing, Accessories, Ball Fittings, Brackets, Fancy Brackets (animal heads), Finials, Flanges, Flush Fittings, Posts, Bellman's Carts and Luggage Carts, Folding Table Legs Pedestal Tables

CROWN PRINCE, INC.
3670 N 126TH STREET
BROOKFIELD, WI 53005
262-781-7580
800-727-7580
Fax: 800-434-7411
www.greatshirts.com
• Tom Reutman, Chairman
• Scott Roberts, President
• Joe Reutman, VP Sales / Marketing
Products:
Baseball Jerseys; General Sports Products Award and Coaches Jackets, Die Cut Letters-Numerals, Hats/Caps/Visors, Heat Transfers, Sweatclothes, T-shirts, Towels; Golf Shirts.
Brands:
Anvil, Auburn, Cannon, Fruit of the Loom, Hanes, Health Knit, Screen Stars, Signal, Sneakers, Sportowels

CUSHEES, INC.
6590 E ROGERS CIRCLE
BOCA RATON, FL 33487
561-994-3001
800-327-5012
Fax: 561-994-3009
cushees@bellsouth.net
www.cushees.com
• Robert Kenny, President
cushees@bellsouth.net
• Robert F. Kenny, Jr, Assistant Account Manager
• Rose Saul, Controller
Products:
Golf socks, tennis socks, wristbands, headbands, cloth hats, straw hats, sparkle caps, sparkle visors, sequin hats, cowboy hats, gambler hats, fedoras.
Clients:
Golf shops, Tennis shops, sporting goods dealers
Brands:
Solarbloc, Cushees

CUSTOM DECAL & EMBLEMS, INC.
9446 BOND AVENUE
EL CAJON, CA 92021
619-449-5611
800-637-5802
Fax: 619-449-5713
custom@customdecal.com
• Matthew Smoke, President
• Donna Archuletta, Manager
Services:
Helmet Decals for Baseball, Football, Hockey, Motocross
Clients:
High School and College athletics, Surf and Snowboard industries, AMA Supercross and Motocross Teams, No Fear, and DYE Paintball Products

CUSTOM PIN & DESIGN
245 IVANHOE STREET
DENVER, CO 80220-5862
877-307-7467
Fax: 720-524-7376
www.custompin.com
• John Stevenson, Owner
Products:
Lapel Pins. Specializing in custom design. Badges and Buttons

CUSTOM SPORTSWEAR CORP/DBA SPORTSWEAR UNLIMITED
8 ENTERPRISE CT
SEWELL, NJ 8080
856-589-3303
800-697-0330
www.customsportswear.net
• Helen Bowers, General Manager
Products:
Baseball - Socks, Stirrups, Uniforms; Basketball - Uniforms; Bowling - Shirts; Field Hockey - Uniforms; Football - Jerseys; General Sports Bags, Equipment, Screen Printing, T-shirts, Warm-Up Suits; Golf - Apparel; Gymnastics - Apparel; Ice Hockey - Jersey

CUTTER AND BUCK, INC.
701 N 34TH STREET
SUITE 400
SEATTLE, WA 98103
206-622-4191
800-713-7810
Fax: 206-830-6278

help@cutterbuck.com
www.cutterbuck.com
• Douglas G. Southern, Chairman
help@cutterbuck.com
• John T. Wyatt, President / Chief Operating
Officer / Di
help@cutterbuck.com
• Ernie Johnson, SVP / Chief Financial
Officer
Products:
Men and women's shirts, pants, sweaters &
vests, shorts & swimwear, outerwear,
sweaters & vests. Golf Apparels.
Brands:
Annika, Signature, CB ProTec, Super Bowl
XL, Texas Longhorns

CUTTERS GLOVES
110 CHESIRE LANE
SUITE 120
MINNETONKA, MN 55305
602-381-5434
800-233-6956
Fax: 602-381-5658
www.cuttersgloves.com
Products:
Innovator of performance grip material
(football, batting, golf, fitness, racquet,
accessories)

CY YOUNG INDUSTRIES, INC.
16201 W 110TH STREET
LENEXA, KS 66219
913-438-1776
800-729-2610
Fax: 913-888-1774
cyyounginc@aol.com
www.cyyoungind.com
• Carrie Yo Sr, President
cyyounginc@aol.com
Services:
Seat renovations in theatres, auditoriums,
arenas, and stadiums.

CYBEX INTERNATIONAL, INC.
10 TROTTER DRIVE
MEDWAY, MA 2053
508-533-4300
Fax: 508-533-5500
www.cybexintl.com
• John Aglialoro, Chairman
• Arthur W Hicks Jr, President & COO
• Joan Carter, Vice Chairman and Secretary
• John McCarthy, Director
Products:
Training Products, including total body, arc,
recumbent, free weights, treadmills.
Brands:
Trotter, Cybex, Cyclone, Elite

CYGNET TURF & EQUIPMENT
4711 INSLEY ROAD
NORTH BALTIMORE, OH 45872
419-354-1112
888-285-0722
Fax: 419-352-1244
www.cygnetturf.com
• John Noe, Marketing Director
Services:
Stripping old turf and installing new
turf/grass.
Clients:
Cleveland Browns, Cleveland Indians,
Chicago Bears, Toledo Mudhens, New
England Patriots, St. Louis Cardinals.

CYRK, INC.
100 CUMMINGS CENTER
SUITE 250-C
BEVERLY, MA 1915
978-998-7100
800-426-3125
Fax: 978-998-6840
• Jeffrey Werner, Chief Executive Officer
Products:
Athletic Jackets/Parkas, Bags-Equipment,
Hats/Caps/Visors, Screen Printing,
Shoelaces, Shorts, Sweatclothes, Sweaters,
T-shirts, Wristbands/Headbands; Golf
Gloves, Umbrellas; Gymnastics Apparel;
Racquet Sports Apparel, Bags-Equipment;
Skiing-Alpine Gloves
Brands:
Cyrksport, Sondico, Lil Teamwear

D.P.M. ENTERPRISES
128 REGIONAL PARK DRIVE
KINGSPORT, TN 37966
423-349-4129
www.dpmenterprises.net
• Dino Miliotis, Owner
• Pam Peters, VP
Products:
Collectibles - Sports Celebrity Collector
Plates; Signed Sports Art; Signed Sports
Memorabilia; Sports-Related Corporate
Premiums/Gifts.

DA KINE
408 COLUMBIA STREET
HOOD RIVER, OR 97031
541-386-3166
Fax: 541-386-6199
info@dakine.com
www.dakine.com
• Randy Torcom, Snow Team & Marketing
Manager
(541) 386-3166
randyt@dakine.com
Products:
Builds gear for board sport enthusiasts
including bags, snowboarders, surfers,
kiteboarders and windsurfers
Brands:
Leashes: Kanui, Kanui Team, Pro Comp,
Super Lite, Kanui Girls, Longboard; Easy
Clip Leash Release Pin, Surf Packs: Patrol,
Channel, Interval, Point

DACON
3686 SE DIXIE HIGHWAY
STUART, FL 34997
772-288-3111
Fax: 772-288-1893
dacon@daconmfg.com
www.daconmfg.com
• Laurie Cummings, Marketing
Products:
Air Pumps, Flag Markers, Equipment
Hanger, Ball Rack, Bat Cart, Relay Batons

DACOR CORPORATION
1 SELLECK STREET
SHORE POINTE
NORWALK, CT 6855
203-852-7079
Fax: 203-853-2892
dacor@us.head.com
www.divedacor.com
• Carlo Bertozzi, President
• Rob Cairns, Business Development VP
• Matt Mulryan, Sales Manager

Products:
General Sports Products - T-shirts,
Warm-Up Suits, Windbreakers; Water
Sports - Apparel-Fashion, Buoyancy
Compensators, Depth Gauges, Diving
Masks, Fins, Scuba Regulators, Scuba
Valves, Snorkels.

DACOR SPORT
1 SELLECK STREET
SHORE POINTE
NORWALK, CT 6855
203-852-7079
800-323-3483
Fax: 203-853-2892
dacor@us.head.com
www.divedacor.com
• Matt Mulryan, Sales Manager
Products:
Water Recreational Gear Accessories, Fins,
Masks, Snorkels.

DAHLGREN FOOTWEAR INC.
19636 SW 90TH COURT
TUALATIN, OR 97062
503-612-9581
888-870-1156
Fax: 503-885-1821
www.dahlgrenfootwear.com
• Ray Dahlgren, Founder
info@dahlgrenfootwear.com
• Diane Dahlgren, Founder
Products:
Socks for sports.

DAIWA CORPORATION
11137 WARLAND DRIVE
CYPRESS, CA 90630
562-375-6800
800-736-4653
Fax: 800-736-4653
admail@daiwa.com
www.daiwa.com
• Tad Suzuki, President
admail@daiwa.com
• Cynthia Young, VP
admail@daiwa.com
• Terry Pederson, National Sales Manager
admail@daiwa.com
• Taka Inagaki, President
• Tad Kojima, Chairman
Products:
Clothing Accessories, including fighing gear.

DAKTRONICS, INC.
201 DAKTRONICS DRIVE
PO BOX 5128
BROOKINGS, SD 57006-5128
605-692-0200
800-843-5843
Fax: 800-325-8766
www.daktronics.com
• Aelred J Kurtenbach, Chairman
sales@daktronics.com
• Jay Parker, National Sales Manager
• Tom Coughlin, Sales Manager/High
School Sports
• Dean Dodge, Sales Manager/Audio
Division
• Jim Morgan, President & Chief Executive
Officer
sales@daktronics.com
• Philip Pikelny, Vice President & Chief
Marketing Officer
• Frank Kurtenbach, Vice President Sales
sales@daktronics.com
• Bill Retterath, Chief Financial

Officer/Treasurer
sales@daktronics.com
• Mark Steinkamp, Marketing Manager
Nature of Services:
Daktronics is the world's leading designer
and manufacturer of electronic scoreboards
and LED video displays for all levels of
sports.
Customer Demographic:
Thousands of high school and college
facilities, and a majority of professional
sports teams and facilities in the US.
Year Founded:
1968
Products
Large Screen Video Systems, Scoreboards,
Electronic Message Centers, Variable
Message Signs, Display Control Systems,
Sports Sound Systems.
Brands:
ProStar 190 Video Displays, ProAd 190
Digital Advertising Displays, All Sport 190
Scoreboards, OmniSport 190 Timing
Systems, Venus 190 Display Controller.

DALCO ATHLETIC LETTERING, INC.
3719 CAVALIER DRIVE
GARLAND, TX 75042
972-487-1200
800-288-3252
Fax: 972-276-9608
sales@dalcoathletic.com
www.dalcoathletic.com
• Gene Feil, Chief Operating Officer
• Linda Feil, Co-Owner
• Michael D Carter, Sales VP
• Alvion Caywood, Manager
Products:
Official/Umpire Clothing and Accessories,
Athletic Lettering

DALEBOOT U.S.A.
2660 S 300 W
SALT LAKE CITY, UT 84115
801-487-3649
Fax: 801-487-3880
daleboot@dalebootusa.com
www.dalebootusa.com
• Adam Olson, General Manager
(801) 487-3649
daleboot@dalebootusa.com
Products:
Boots, Bags, Caps

DAMASCUS WORLDWIDE, INC.
63 WALES STREET
RUTLAND, VT 5701
805-639-0746
800-451-4167
Fax: 800-305-2417
info@damascusgear.com
www.damascusgear.com
• Lawrence J Welton, President
Products:
Gloves, Tactical Gear, Swat Gear

DANDY PRODUCTS, INC.
PO BOX 1980
WESTERVILLE, OH 43086-1980
740-881-2790
800-591-2284
Fax: 740-881-2791
dlc@dandyproducts.com
www.dandyproducts.com
• Dan Reed, Marketing Officer
Products:
Florr and Wall Padding

Year Founded:
1989
Brands:
Protective Wall Pads

DANSKIN, INC.
1411 BROADWAY
8TH FLOOR
NEW YORK, NY 8810
212-764-4630
877-443-2121
Fax: 212-764-7265
edanskin@danskin.com
www.danskin.com
• Carol J Hochman, President / Chief
Executive Officer
contact_us@danskin.com
• John A Sarto, Chief Financial Officer
contact_us@danskin.com
• Barbara Khouri, President
Products:
Dancewear, Active Wear, Comfortable
clothes

DANT CLAYTON CORPORATION
1500 BERNHEIM LANE
LOUISVILLE, KY 40210-7408
800-626-2177
Fax: 502-637-9983
info@dantclayton.com
www.stadiumbleachers.com

DARBY ATHLETIC HEALTH
300 JERICHO QUADRANGLE
JERICHO, NY 11753
800-247-4768
Fax: 800-430-5612
www.darbymedical.com
Products:
Emergency & First Aid Products, Exam
Room Equipment, Medical Spa Supplies,
Nutritional Products, Orthopedic Products,
Pharmaceuticals, Physical Therapy/
Massage Therapy Aids, Practice Builders,
Sutures, Syringes and Needles, Vitamins
and Supplements, X-Ray Supplies

DART WORLD INC
140 LINWOOD STREET
LYNN, MA 1905
781-581-6035
800-225-2558
Fax: 781-592-8760
info@dartworld.com
www.dartworld.com
• Mark Amirault, Principal
mamirault@dartworld.com
• Brian Dower, National Sales Manager
Products:
Steel/Soft Tips, Flights, Shafts, Cabinets,
Dartboards, Backboards; Indoor and
Outdoor games
Brands:
Dart World; Harrows; Target

DARTFISH USA
6505 SHILOH ROAD
SUITE 110-B
ALPHARETTA, GA 30005
404-685-9505
888-655-3850
Fax: 404-685-9130
usa@dartfish.com
www.dartfish.com
• Victor Bergonzoli, President/CEO
victor.bergonzoli@dartfish.com

• Ron Imbriale, Sales VP
usa@dartfish.com
• Mark Matoza, Golf Director
usa@dartfish.com
Products:
Sports electronics, including software
programs.

DATREK PROFESSIONAL BAG
2701 EMERYWOOD PKWY
SUITE 101
RICHMOND, VA 23294
804-726-1328
800-955-2269
Fax: 888-822-4269
datrekcs@datrek.com
www.datrek.com
• Craig Ramsbottom, President
Products:
Golf Bags and Accessories

DAVID CLARK CO., INC.
360 FRANKLIN STREET
PO BOX 15054
WORCESTER, MA 1604
508-751-5800
800-298-6235
800-900-3434
Fax: 508-753-5827
service@DavidClark.com
www.davidclark.com
• Bob Daigle, Product Manager
(508) 751-5888
bdaigle@davidclark.com
• John Farr, National Sales Manager
• Dennis Buzzell, Market Manager, Aviation
and Airline
(508) 751-5889
DBuzzell@DavidClark.com
• John Tasi, Product Manager,
Government/Military
(508) 751-5886
JTasi@DavidClark.com
• Robert A. Vincent, President
Year Founded:
1935.
Products:
Communication headsets, intercoms,
two-way radios and accessories.

DEBEER LACROSSE
510 MARYVILLE UNIVERSITY DR.
SUITE 110
ST. LOUIS, MO 63141
800-833-3535
• James L Muhlfelder, President / Chief
Executive Officer
• Regy Thorpe, General Manager
Products:
Sticks, Handles, Eyemasks, Gloves,
Equipment Bags, Accesories

DECATUR ELECTRONICS, INC.
3433 EAST WOOD STREET
PHOENIX, AZ 85040
602-428-4315
888-428-4315
Fax: 602-621-4200
www.decaturelectronics.com
• Cody Caldwell, Bids Specialist
Products:
Speed radar for sports applications,
including motorcycles, snowmobiles, boats
and others.
Year Founded:
1955

DECKERS OUTDOOR CORPORATION
250 COROMAR DRIVE
GOLETA, CA 93117
805-967-7611
Fax: 805-967-9722
www.deckers.com
• Angel R Martinez,
CEO/President/Chairman
• Zohar Ziv, Chief Operating Officer
• Thomas A George, Chief Financial Officer
• Graciela Montgomery, Chief Human
Resources Officer
Products:
Sports Sandals and Shoes.

DEHEN, INC.
1040 NE 44TH AVENUE
SUITE 3
PORTLAND, OR 97213
503-222-3871
800-544-8819
Fax: 503-222-2751
www.dehen1920.com
• Jim Artaiz, VP Marketing / Sales
(503) 222-3871
jamesartaiz@dehen.com
• Beezie Lasseigne, Sales
(503) 222-3871
• Gary Hilde, President
 ext 15
• Jim Artaiz, Vice President
Products:
Activewear, Cheerleading Uniforms and
Supplies, Wool and Leather Varsity Jackets,
Custom apparel and outerwear.
Year Founded:
1920

DELTA APPAREL COMPANY
2750 PREMIERE PARKWAY
SUITE 100
DULUTH, GA 30097
678-775-6900
800-285-4456
Fax: 800-588-0199
www.deltaapparel.com
• Robert Humphreys, President / Chief
Executive Officer
• Steve Cochran, President
Products:
Athletic Apparel, Fleecewear.

DELTA GOLF COMPANY
4727 W MONTROSE AVENUE
CHICAGO, IL 60641
773-777-7877
800-909-4653
Fax: 773-777-6543
• Joseph R Morisco, President / Chief
Executive Officer
• Randy Turner, Sls Mgr
Products:
Golf Bags for Clubs, Clubs - Iron or Wood
Sets, Putters, Utility Clubs, Clubheads,
Grips, Shafts.

DESCENTE NORTH AMERICA, INC.
334 MARSHALL WAY N
LAYTON, UT 84041
801-317-0017
800-999-0475
Fax: 801-317-0020
info@descente.com
www.descente.com
• Guy Christie, President
• Johnny Miller, National Sales Manager /
Golf Division

• Curt Geiger, National Sales Manager / Ski
Division
• Nori Higuchi, President
Products:
Team apparel for skiing, cycling, volleyball,
swimming, and speed skating

**DEVENTER'S CHEER & DANCEWEAR
FACTORY, INC.**
105 BASSET HIGHWAY
DOVER, NJ 7801
973-366-7097
Fax: 973-366-7098
• Susan Zakosky, Vice President
(973) 366-7097
Year Founded:
1974
Products:
Dance and activewear.

DEXTER SHOE COMPANY
71 RAILROAD AVE
DEXTER, ME 4930
207-924-7341
Fax: 603-595-2337
www.dextershoe.com
• Jerry Hyde, President
• Theodore Alfond, EVP
• Stephen Tucker, VP Sales / Marketing
• Peter Lunder, Director
Products:
Bowling Shoes and Golf Shoes.

DIADORA AMERICA
2129 67TH AVENUE S
KENT, WA 98032
253-520-8868
800-342-3672
Fax: 253-520-6372
info@gvsamerica.com
www.diadoraamerica.com
• Mauro Visentin, Chief Executive Officer
• Linda Walker, VP Distribution / Customer
Service
• Stephanie Nelson, Director Apparel
Marketing
• William Nutall, President
Products:
Tennis Shoes; Soccer Shoes, Apparel;
Running Shoes-Run/Jog, Shoes-Cross
Training, Sandals.

DIAMOND SPORTS
1880 E. ST. ANDREW PL
SANTA ANA, CA 92705
714-415-7600
Fax: 714-415-7601
www.diamond-sports.com
• Andrea Gordon, President
Products:
Baseballs, softballs, batting gloves, batter's
helmets & accessories, mitts, catcher's gear
& accessories, bags & buckets,
merchandise and apparels. Foot ball
shoulder pads, apparel/accessories. Field
equipment.

DIAMONDBACK BICYCLES
6004 S 190TH STREET
SUITE 101
KENT, WA 98032
253-395-1100
800-776-7641
Fax: 800-851-0807
www.diamondback.com
• Jon Kennedy, Marketing Manager

Products:
Cycling Accessories, Bicycles, BMX, Fitness
Equipment.

DIEBOLD INCORPORATED
5995 MAYFAIR ROAD
N CANTON, OH 44720-8077
330-490-4000
800-999-3600
Fax: 330-490-3794
www.diebold.com
• Kevin J Krakora, Executive VP/CFO
• George S. Mayes, Executive Vice
President and Chief Operating
• Bradley C. Richardson, Executive Vice
President and Chief Financial
• Frank A. Natoli, Executive Vice President
and Chief Innovation
• Henry D.G. W. Wallace, Executive
Chairman of the Board
Sports Related Products:
Kiosks, ATMs, etc. for sports facilities.

DIVERSA PRODUCTS GROUP
1615 W UNIVERSITY DRIVE
SUITE 135
TEMPE, AZ 85281-3257
480-966-9802
800-527-4923
Fax: 480-966-9806
info@bushwalkerbags.com
www.bushwalkerbags.com
• Jim Bilas, Marketing Director
info@bushwalkerbags.com
Products:
Athletic Trainers' Bags, Beltpacks and equip
bags
Brands:
Bushwalker Bags

DIVOTS SPORTSWEAR COMPANY, INC.
5903-A PEACHTREE INDUSTRIAL
BOULEVARD
NORCROSS, GA 30092
770-447-4800
800-847-3467
Fax: 770-448-3244
info@divots.com
www.divots.com
• Bob Friedman, President
info@divots.com
Products:
Golf Apparel
Brands:
Divots
Clients:
Golf Shops

DJ ORTHOPEDICS
1430 DECISION STREET
VISTA, CA 92081
760-727-1280
800-336-6569
Fax: 800-936-6569
officecare@djortho.com
• Chinh E Chu, Chairman of the Board
• Leslie H Cross, President & Chief
Executive Officer
• Vickie L Capps, Finance SVP / Chief
Financial Officer
Products:
Knee Braces, Foot & Ankle Braces, Upper
Extremities & Back Braces

DMI SPORTS INC
1300 VIRGINIA DRIVE
SUITE 401
FORT WASHINGTON, PA 19034
215-283-0153
800-423-3220
Fax: 215-283-9573
www.dmisports.com
• Jeremy Stork,
(215) 283-0153
Products:
Indoor games, featuring complete lines of Billiard, Dart and Table Tennis Equipment, Soccer Tables, Hockey Tables, Garage Door Sports, and Casino

DOCKER'S FOOTWEAR
1415 MURFREESBORO ROAD
SUITE 190
NASHVILLE, TN 37217
800-654-2371
888-324-6189
Fax: 800-654-2371
www.dockersshoes.com
• Hal N. Pennington, Chairman / President / Chief Executive O
• Robert J. Dennis, EVP / Chief Operating Officer
• James C. Estapa, SVP, Genesco Retail
• Jonathan D. Caplan, SVP, Genesco Branded
Products:
Athletic and casual footwear, under a license agreement with Levi Strauss & Co.
Brands:
Dockers

DODGER INDUSTRIES INC.
2705 STULTZ ROAD
PO BOX 711
MARTINSVILLE, VA 24112-07411
800-247-7879
Fax: 276-638-7161
sales@dodgerindustries.com
www.dodgerindustries.com
• Joe Throssel, Vice President
(641) 939-5464
jthrossel@dodgerindustries.com
• Steve Throssel, Chief Executive Officer
(641) 939-2335
sthrossel@dodgerindustries.com
• Clark Lawler, Executive VP
• Mark Adams, Marketing
Products:
Athletic apparel for teams and fans

DOLOMITE AMERICA, INC.
5 COMMERCE AVENUE
WEST LEBANON, NH 3784
800-257-2008
Fax: 203-855-1360
www.dolomiteusa.com
• Erika Smith, Sales / Marketing Director
(800) 257-2008
Products:
A variety of boots, including ski boots.

DORFMAN-PACIFIC COMPANY, INC.
2615 BOEING WAY
STOCKTON, CA 95206
866-304-5468
800-367-3626
Fax: 800-437-4287
custservice@dorfman-pacific.com
www.dorfman-pacific.com
• Doug Highsmith, President / Chief Executive Officer

(209) 982-1400
custservice@dorfman-pacific.com
• John Callanan, VP
Products:
Hats and caps for men, women and children, including those used for a variety of sporting activities.

DOUGLAS INDUSTRIES, INC.
3441 S 11TH AVENUE
ELDRIDGE, IA 52748
800-553-8907
800-553-8907
Fax: 800-443-8907
sales@douglas-sports.com
www.douglas-sports.com
• Brad Fandel, Director of Sales
(800) 553-8907
• Jerry Douglas, CEO & President
jdouglas@douglas-sports.com
Products:
Douglas is a manufacturer of Sport Nets & Equipment for a variety of sports including: Tennis, Baseball, Soccer, Volleyball, Basketball, Hockey, and Golf. Products include: Tennis Nets and Posts, Backdrop Curtains, Gym Dividers, Customer Netting, Protective Padding, Volleyball Posts and Nets, Baseball and Softball Products, Windscreen, and much more.

DR SPORTS EQUIPMENT
5790 PARE
MONTREAL, QUEBEC, CANADA H4P 2M2
514-731-6841
800-567-6777
Fax: 514-342-4059
www.drxsports.com
• Todd Weaving, Sales / Marketing VP
Products:
Hockey, Ski and Baseball Equipment.

DRAPER INC.
411 S PEARL STREET
PO BOX 425
SPICELAND, IN 47385
765-987-7999
800-238-7999
Fax: 765-987-7142
drapercontract@draperinc.com
www.draperinc.com
• Debbie Searcy, Accounts Receivable and Traffic Manager
(765) 856-1224
dsearcy@draperinc.com
• Robert Mathes, AV / Video Market Manager
(765) 987-7999
bmathes@draperinc.com
• Chris Broome, Contract Market Manager
(765) 987-7999
cbroome@draperinc.com
• Neal Turner, Gymnasium Equipment Manager
(800) 238-7999
nturner@draperinc.com
• Lee Denhart, Field Sales Manager
(765) 856-1211
ldenhart@draperinc.com
• Amy Bradway, AV/Video Sales
(765) 856-1252
abradway@draperinc.com
• Steve Cook, National AV Consultant Manager
(765) 987-7999
scook@draperinc.com
• Amy Madden, Sales Support Manager,

Lifts Product Manager
(765) 856-1212
amadden@draperinc.com
Products:
Basketball Backstops, Gym Divider Curtains, Gym Wall Pads, & Volleyball Equipment
Brands:
EZ Fold Backstop
Nature of Service:
Manufacturer of Athletic Equipment.

DRYBRANCH, INC./SPORT DESIGN
1 COMMERCIAL COURT
PLAINVIEW, NY 11803-1600
516-576-7000
800-645-7722
Fax: 516-576-7008
www.drybranch.com
• Arthur Miller, President
Products:
Game Design-Better Quality Adult Games Featuring Chess, Dominoes, Backgammon and More. Sport Design: Smashball & Kadima Racquet Sets. Scatch Reach Volley Toss & Catch Products. Beach and Lawn Games. Soft Smash-Foam Toys and Sports Products.

DUCK HEAD APPAREL COMPANY
1020 BARROW INDUSTRIAL PARKWAY
PO BOX 688
WINDER, GA 30680
770-867-3111
800-933-0680
Fax: 770-307-1800
• Robert Rockey, President
• Billy Mattison, VP Merchandise
• Bill Reese, President
Products:
Men's and boys' casual sportswear products, including shirts, shorts and pants and other apparel and accessory products

DUCK HOUSE INC
4651 STATE STREET
#1 TOPLINE PLAZA
MONTCLAIR, CA 91763
909-628-0720
800-354-3655
Fax: 909-628-0382
sales@duckhouse.com
www.duckhouse.com
• Jeff Sherman, Sales / Marketing EVP
(909) 628-0720
jeff@duckhouse.com
Products:
Freezer Mugs, Glow Mugs, Tumblers, Dinner Sets, Party Packs, Glow Pens, Paper Weights, Placemats, Floor Merchandiser, Availability Charts

DUNBROOKE
4200 LITTLE BLUE PARKWAY
INDEPENDENCE, MO 64057
816-795-7722
800-641-3627
Fax: 816-795-0321
greatservice@dunbrooke.com
www.dunbrooke.com
• Dave Hausen, President
(816) 795-7722
• Jay Jones, Chief Financial Officer
(816) 795-7722
• Bob Pierce, EVP Sales / Marketing
(816) 795-7722

Products:
Athletic Jackets/Parkas; Fashion Jackets & Activewear, Knit Shirts, Woven Shirts, Fleece

---

DUNLOP/MAXFLI/SLAZENGER GROUP AMERICAS
100 MAXFLI DRIVE
WESTMINSTER, SC 29693
864-241-2200
800-768-4727
Fax: 864-647-4087
www.maxfli.com
• David Beanon, Chairman
• Mike Rizzo, President
• Steve Ryan, VP Finance
• Edward Hughes, VP Marketing
Products:
Golf: Bags for Clubs, Luggage, Balls, Clubs-Iron or Wood Sets, Putters, Utility Clubs, Gloves, Hats/Caps, Headcovers, Rainwear. Raquet Sports: Badminton and Tennis equipment, Racquet Grips, Racquet Strings, Shoes

---

DUNN'S
PO BOX 539
SYDNEY, NE 69162
308-233-5862
800-353-8621
Fax: 308-255-2450
www.dunns.com
• Parker Overton, President / Chief Executive Officer
(308) 233-5862
• Larry Carrol, Chief Operating Officer
(308) 233-5862
• Brian Moen, Marketing Director
(308) 233-5862
Products:
Hunting apparel and products, footwear and sporting dog equipment

---

DURHAM BOAT COMPANY
220 NEWMARKET ROAD
ROUTE 108
DURHAM, NH 3824
603-659-7575
Fax: 603-659-2548
cfuerst@durhamboat.com
www.durhamboat.com
• Coleen Fuerst, President
(603) 659-7575
Cfuerst@durhamboat.com
• James Dreher, VP General Manager
Products:
Boat racing equipment and accessories, including Dreher Carbon Sculls, Dreher Carbon Sweeps, Dreher Carbon Footstretchers, Dreher Carbon Riggers, Dreher Carbon Seats, BBG Racing Shells, Racing Shells, Recreational Shells, Travel Accessories, Books, Videos & DVDs, Rowing Clothing, Rigging Accessories, Rowing Electronics, Indoor Rowing Products

---

DYNAFLEX INTERNATIONAL
1144 N GROVE STREET
ANAHEIM, CA 92806
714-630-0909
800-480-8084
Fax: 714-632-5470
• Farren Mataele, Vice President
(714) 630-0909
• Tom Smith, Chief Executive Officer
(714) 630-0909
dynaflexus@aol.com

• Tiffany Ludwig, Sales Manager
(714) 630-0909
Products:
Health and exercise equipment, Dynamax Core Trainer, Yoga Pilates kits, Powerball Blue gyro-hand wrist exerciser, Body Secrets massage rollers, Extreme Grip.
Description:
Unique line of gyro exercisers and many other products to offer on the market today.

DYNAMIC TEAM SPORTS
454 ACORN LANE
DOWNINGTOWN, PA 19335
610-518-3300
800-437-6223
Fax: 610-518-9200
info@dynamicteamsports.com
www.dynamicteamsports.com
• Scott A Samter, President
• Richard Nigro, Sales/Operations Director
(610) 518-3300
sales@dynamicteamsports.com
Products:
Manufactures uniforms for basketball, baseball, softball, soccer, wrestling, lacrosse, field hockey, volleyball, track & field, tennis and cheerleading, football, swimming, ice hockey and rugby.

DYNASTY APPAREL INDUSTRIES
13000 NW 42ND AVENUE
MIAMI, FL 33054
305-685-3490
800-833-8337
Fax: 305-687-1393
hector@dynastyapparel.com
• Ignacio Mendez, President
imendez@dynastyapparel.com
• Armando Mendez, CEO
armendez@dynastyapparel.com
• Lorenzo Mendez, COO
Lorenzo@dynastyapparel.com
• Felix Hernandez, CFO
fhernandez@dynastyapparel.com
• Hector Rodriguez, Executive of Sales and Marketing
Hector@dynastyapparel.com
• Lissette Padron, Marketing Coordinator
Lissette@dynastyapparel.com
• Erica Mendez, Licensing Coordinator
Erica@dynastyapparel.com
Products:
Manufactures sports apparel: T-shirts, pullovers, tank tops; embroidery and screen printing services

---

DYNASTY DESIGNS, LLC
1101 N WARSON ROAD
SAINT LOUIS, MO 63132
314-429-2220
866-892-2225
Fax: 314-429-2234
www.dynastydesigns.com
• Craig Albrecht, CEO
• Ted Albrecht, President & Chief Operations Officer
• Drew Caylor, Vice President
Products:
Collegiate Furniture, Pub Stools, PUb Tables, Gifts, and Holiday Accessories.
Year Founded:
2002

E&D SPECIALTY STANDS INC.
2081 FRANKLIN STREET
PO BOX 700
N COLLINS, NY 14111
800-525-8515
800-525-8515
Fax: 716-337-2903
info@edstands.com
www.edstands.com
• Doug Bigelow, Vice Presidnet
(800) 525-8515
dougb@edstands.com
• Jon Williams, National Sales Manager
(800) 525-8515
Products:
Design, fabrication and installation of bleachers, grandstands, stadium seating and portable seating units (Permanent Beam Design, Angle Frame Design, Portable Bleachers, Seat Boards, Seat Backs, Foot Boards, Riser Boards, Decking Types, VIP Suites & Pressboxes).

E-FORCE
2151 LAS PALMAS DRIVE
SUITE D
CARLSBAD, CA 92011
800-433-6723
Fax: 760-804-0225
warranty@e-force.com
www.e-force.com
• Ron Grimes, President
Products:
Racquetball - Accessories, Bags, Eyewear, Gloves, Racquets, String.

E-Z GARD INDUSTRIES
3405 ANNAPOLIS LANE N
SUITE 200
PLYMOUNTH, MN 55447
800-233-6956
866-253-1314
Fax: 888-446-5999
• Steven J. Washburn, President / Chief Executive Officer
• John McCartan, SVP of Sales
• Jay Turkbas, VP of Marketing and Product Development
Products:
Offers a comprehensive line of innovative performance products, including core protective gear for hockey, football and baseball, lacrosse equipment, and bio-mechanic insoles.

E-Z GO
1451 MARVIN GRIFFIN ROAD
AUGUSTA, GA 30906
706-798-4311
800-241-5855
Fax: 706-771-4609
www.ezgo.com
• Kathleen C Searle, VP Communications
• Kevin Holleran, President
• Jon Phillips, Director International Sales
• Chris Spencer, VP
Products:
Oldest manufacturer of golf cars and utility vehicles, and produces the #1 selling golf car.

E.B. ROTONDI & SONS, INC.
21 MANISON STREET
STONEHAM, MA 02180-3111
781-438-5005
Fax: 781-438-5006
www.ebrotondi.com

• Michael J. Rotondi, Vice President
mjr@ebrotondi.com
• Michael J. Rotondi, Vice President
• Dennis Lawhorne, Project Manager
• Lawrence Schofield, Engineer
• A. Joseph B. Rotondi, President
Nature of Service:
General Contractor Sports Facility
Construction
Year Founded:
1932
Products:
Surfaces Floor and Court Sports Facilities
Brands:
Har Tru Nova

E.P. PRO
8 W 40TH STREET
2ND FLOOR
NEW YORK, NY 10018
855-924-2228
800-926-8010
Fax: 212-302-5982
www.eppro.com
• Larry Mathe, President / Chief Executive
Officer
• Stuart Warshaw, Chief Financial Officer
• Sandy Martinelli, VP Operations
• Rebecca Ryan, VP Sales
Products:
Providing high quality, classic, golf specific
sportswear

E.S. ORIGINALS
450 W 33RD STREET
NEW YORK, NY 10001
212-736-8124
800-677-6557
Fax: 212-736-8366
www.esoriginals.com
• John Otis, Marketing Director
Products:
Manufacturers and importers of fashion
footwears: Athletic Shoes, Canvas
Sneakers, Plush Character Slippers, Quilted
Fabric Slippers, Knit Slippers Socks, Rain
and Snow Boots, Hiker-Style Boots, Clear
Plastic Jelly Shoes, Aqua Socks, Beach
Sandals

EAGLES WINGS
2101 OLD HICKORY TREE ROAD
SAINT CLOUD, FL 34772
407-892-6358
Fax: 407-892-6759
www.eagleswings.com
Products:
Offer a variety of themed ties (Inspirational
ties, Sports ties, Specialty ties, Fashion
Essentials) and men's accessories

EARBAGS
45 KENSICO DRIVE
2ND FLOOR
MOUNT KISCO, NY 10549
914-242-8566
888-327-2241
Fax: 914-242-8567
Julie@sprigsville.com
www.sprigs.com
• Valerie Ciptak, President
val@sprigsville.com
• Dawn Chaskin, VP, Sales & Marketing
dawn@sprigsville.com
Products:
Swedish bandless earmuff for cycling,

riding, and professional athletes in windy or
cold weather.

EARMARK
1125 DIXWELL AVENUE
HAMDEN, CT 06514
203-777-2130
888-327-6275
Fax: 203-777-2886
sales@earmark.com
www.earmark.com
• Andy Cowell, Contact
(203) 777-2130
Founded:
1973
Description:
Earmark designs and manufactures wireless
communication systems.

EARTH & TURF
112 S RAILROAD AVENUE
NEW HOLLAND, PA 17557
717-355-2776
888-693-2638
Fax: 877-243-2442
www.earthandturf.com
• John Bentley, President
Products:
Manufactures Topdressers and Aerators for
the Turgrass Industry.

EASTON SPORTS, INC.
7855 HASKELL AVENUE
SUITE 200
VAN NUYS, CA 91406-1902
800-632-7866
800-632-7866
Fax: 818-782-4407
customerservice@eastonsports.com
www.eastonsports.com
• Jim Easton, Chairman
customerservice@eastonsports.com
• Tony Palma, President
customerservice@eastonsports.com
• Gerry Maurizio, Chief Information Officer
customerservice@eastonsports.com
• Mike Zlatek, VP Bsbl / Softball
Products:
Privately owned manufacturer, marketer,
and distributor of sports equipment.

EASTON TECHNICAL PRODUCTS
5040 HAROLD GATTY DRIVE
SALT LAKE CITY, UT 84116-2897
801-539-1400
Fax: 801-533-9907
techinfo@eastontp.com
www.eastonarchery.com
• Chris Oswald, Director, Marketing & Sales
• Greg Easton, President
Products:
Unparalleled leader in the arrow industry,
delivering the most technologically advanced
arrows and components for target archers
and bowhunters alike.

EASTPAK CORPORATION
PO BOX 1817
APPLETON, WI 54912-1817
800-222-5725
Fax: 920-735-1933
www.eastpak.com
• Gwen Wisler, President / Chief Executive
Officer
• Mark Goldman, Chairman

• Henry Friedman, SVP Sales
• Jim Salzenstein, EVP
Products:
Outdoor Products, Backpacks, Bag.

EASY RACERS
10 HANGAR WAY
WATSONVILLE, CA 95076
831-722-9797
Fax: 831-768-9623
info@easyracers.com
www.easyracers.com
• Denton Worthy Coetzee, Chief Executive
Officer & President
Products:
Industry leader in cutting edge recumbent
bicycle design and manufacture.

EATON GOLF PRIDE
440 MURRAY HILL ROAD
SOUTHERN PINES, NC 28387
910-695-2900
Fax: 910-277-3700
ContactGolfPride@Eaton.com
www.eaton.com
• Jeff Fiorini, General Manager
• Dwight Miles, Director, Sales & Marketing
• Dan Koehler, Global Marketing Manager
• Wright Chandler, Sales Manager
Products:
Leading supplier of grips to the club
manufacturing industry and the top choice
for grip replacement.

EBBETS FIELD FLANNELS
119 S JACKSON STREET
SEATTLE, WA 98104
206-382-7249
888-896-2936
Fax: 206-382-4411
customerservice@ebbets.com
www.ebbets.com
• Jerry Cohen, Founder
(206) 382-7249
jcohen@ebbets.com
Products:
Vintage Baseball Uniforms, Jackets, Jersys,
Ballcaps, Fungo Shirts, T-shirts, Utility
Jersy, Practical Jersy, Gridiron Shirts
Year Founded:
1988

EBONITE INTERNATIONAL, INC.
1813 W 7TH STREET
HOPKINSVILLE, KY 42240
270-881-1200
800-626-8350
Fax: 270-881-1201
www.ebonite.com
• Mike Quitter, VP International
• Carl Rogers, CFO & Treasurer
• Bob Reid, VP, Marketing
• J M. Quitter, VP Sales
Products:
Manufacturer of bowling balls for
professionals and style-concious bowlers. It
also manufactures ball bags and other
accessories.

ECLECTIC PRODUCTS, INC.
101 DIXIE MAE DRIVE
PINEVILLE, LA 71360
318-640-5116
800-349-4667
Fax: 547-746-1983

info@eclecticproducts.com
www.eclecticproducts.com
• Sheila Ecker, Sales Coordinator
• Ken Barton, Vice President, Industrial
Sales and Manufacturing
Description:
Adhesives for the sports and outdoor
markets.
Brands:
Shoe Goo; Sport & Outdoor Goop; Marine
Goop
Clients:
Wal-Mart, Academy Sports, Home Depot,
K-Mart, Dick's Sporting Goods, Bass Pro
Shops

EDDY BROS. HAT CO. INC.
314 E BIDWELL STREET
FOLSOM, CA 95630
916-983-2668
www.eddybros.com
• Jack Eddy, Founder
Products:
Headwear

EIBACH SPRINGS, INC
264 MARIAH CIRCLE
CORONA, CA 92879
951-256-8300
800-507-2338
Fax: 951-256-8333
eibach@eibach.com
Products:
Automotive Suspension Products, as well as
Industrial Springs, Dynaflex Die-Springs and
Seal Components, High Performance Valve
Springs, Children's Play Ground
Components.

EIGER SPORTSWEAR, INC.
4775 S BUTTERFIELD DRIVE
155
TUCSON, AZ 85714
800-527-3757
800-527-3757
Fax: 520-571-0733
• Bruce Caris, Sales Manager
• Wolfgang Weber, Marketing Director
Products:
Custom Apparel, including Soccer Uniforms
(Men's/Women's) Volleyball Uniforms,
Sweatsuits, Bags and Socks.

EKTELON
17110 Marcy Street
LL02
Omaha, NE 68118
402-884-7600
800-283-2635
Fax: 402-884-6286
www.ektelon.com
• Scott Winters, Director
• Jon Panno, Product Manager
Products:
Racquets, Powerpacks, Gloves, Eyeguards,
Footwear, Sportbags, Strings and Grips,
Accessories

ELASCO, INC.
11377 MARKON DRIVE
GARDEN GROVE, CA 92841
714-891-1795
800-827-7887
Fax: 714-895-7031
info@elascourethane.com
www.elascourethane.com

• Henry Larrucea, Partner
info@elascourethane.com
• David Schindler, President
Products:
Electrical, water and pneumatic cable
guards.

ELBY GIFTS
879 INDUSTRIEL
BOIS DES FILION, QUEBEC, CANADA J6Z
4T3
450-965-8288
877-352-9462
Fax: 450-965-8688
info@elbygifts.com
www.elbygifts.com
• Robert Lio, President
(450) 965-8288
robertlio@elbygifts.com
• Sonja Coia, Operating Manager VP
(450) 965-8229
scoia@elbygifts.com
• Jonathan Lio, Sales Coordinator
(450) 965-8242
jonathanlio@elbygifts.com
• Linda Sirois, Customer Service
(450) 965-8222
orders@elbygifts.com
• Barbara Sheppard, Claims Department
(450) 965-8240
claims@elbygifts.com
• Marzieh Tandel, Account Receivables,
Compte Clients
(450) 965-8228
marzieh@elbygifts.com
Products:
Giftware, home d,cor, collectibles, and
licensed products

ELECTRA TARP
2900 PERRY DRIVE SW
CANTON, OH 44706
330-477-7168
800-274-1003
Fax: 330-477-7702
electratarp@sbcglobal.net
www.electratarp.com
• Robert Fulmer, President
• Bitsy Paul, President's Assistant
bitsy@electratarp.com
• Michele Minock, Sales Representative
Products:
All Purpose Tarpaulins & Accessories,
Football Safeline Covers, Anti-Static
Polyethylene, Athletic Covers, Awana Game
Floors, Colorguard Floor, Industrial and
Commercial Tarpaulins, Floor Covers,
Greenhouse Covers, Mobile Storage Racks,
Gym Floor Covers.

**ELECTRO-MECH SCOREBOARD
COMPANY**
72 IINDUSTRIAL BLVD
WRIGHTSVILLE, GA 31096
478-864-3366
800-445-7846
Fax: 478-864-0212
score@electro-mech.com
www.electro-mech.com
• Allen McMichael, President
• Tim Branton, Outside Sales
score@electro-mech.com
• Jim Ledford, National Sales Manager
• Allen McMichael, Internet Sales
• Leslie Lawrence, Inside Sales
Products:
Timing Devices - Scoreboards.

ELITE SPORTSWEAR, L.P.
2136 N 13TH STREET
PO BOX 16400
READING, PA 19612-6400
800-345-4087
Fax: 888-866-9884
info@gkelite.com
• Sallie Weaver, President
• Paul Honig, Finance VP
• Birgitte Sorensen, Marketing Manager
• Kelly McKeown, Executive VP
Products:
GK Competitive Gymnastics Apparel, GK
Workout Gymnastics Apparel, GK
Essentials Apparel, GK Dancewear, GK
Skating Wear, GK Synchro Team Skating
Wear

ELLESSE U.S.A., INC.
3333 NEW HYDE PARK ROAD
SUITE 200
NEW HYDE PARK, NY 11042
516-365-1333
800-ELLESSE
Fax: 516-365-2333
info@ellesse.com
www.ellesse.com
• Stuart Hudson, National Sales Manager
(516) 643-0445
stuartmhudson@aol.com
Products:
Sportswear, Footwear and watches
Year Founded:
1959

EMBROIDERY STORE
3929-A WESTPOINT BOULEVARD
SUITE 100
WINSTON-SALEM, NC 27103
336-765-0910
800-504-9757
Fax: 336-765-0920
info@embstore.com
www.embstore.com
• Bill Fenimore, VP
BFenimore@embstore.com
Products:
Backings and Toppings, Bobbin Cases &
Sewing Hooks, Clearance, Embroidery
Starter Kit, Embroidery Supplies, General
Parts, Gift Card, Hooping Systems, Hoops
and Frames, Logo Builder Software,
Meistergram Designs and Alphabets,
Needles, Scissors and Snips, Stock
Designs, Threads and Bobbins

EMERGENCY MEDICAL SUPPLY
238 SALTWELL ROAD
PO BOX 99
SHEPHERDSVILLE, KY 40165
502-543-2401
Fax: 502-543-5032
• Chip Brake, National Sales Manager
(800) 720-4119
Products:
Clearance Items, Special Items, Airway
Management Items, Apparel, Bags and
Cases, Bandaging, Dressing & Tapes,
Blood Collection, Cold and Hot Packs, Cots,
Defib and Pacing Pads, Diagnostics, ECG
Electrodes, Extrication/Splints, Gloves, Glow
Stick Chemical Lights, Immobilization,
Incident Command/Mass Casualty, Infection
Control, Infusion, Injection, Instruments &
Tools, Monitors & Accessories, Pandemic
Bio Kits, Patient Assesment, Patient Care
Disposable Items, Patient Transport, Sharps

Containers, Stocked Kits, Training Equipment

EMPI, INC.
599 CARDIGAN ROAD
PO BOX 64640
SAINT PAUL, MN 55126-4099
615-415-9000
800-328-2536
Fax: 800-450-3593
support@empi.com
• John Velure, Senior Director of Marketing
• Mark Francois, Director of Corporate Communications
(760) 734-4766
Products:
Transcutaneous Electrical Nerve Stimulation, Interferential Current Pain Management, Clinical Portable Multifunction Electrotherapy System, Neuromuscular Electrical Stimulation, Non-invasive drug delivery system, Non-invasive drug delivery system, Cervical and Lumbar traction, Dynamic Splinting Orthoses, Pelvic Floor Stimulation devices, TENS / NMES electrodes and accessories

EMPIRE SPORTING GOODS MFG. COMPANY, INC.
301 MT PLEASANT AVENUE
NEWARK, NJ 07104-3723
973-497-5600
800-221-3455
Fax: 212-941-7113
www.empiresportinggoods.com
• Charles Rauch, President
Products:
Baseball - Caps, Socks, Stirrups, Uniforms; Basketball - Socks, Uniforms; Boxing - Trunks; Football - Socks, Uniforms; General Sports Products - Athletic Jackets/Parkas, Athletic Supporters, Complete Lettering Department, Referee Uniforms, Warm-Up Suits;

EMPIRE SPORTS/SISCO SPORTS
1639 ABBOT KINNEY BOULEVARD
VENICE, CA 90291
310-450-4114
Fax: 310-301-7962
• Chou Windsor, Owner
• Ray Flores, Product Manager
Products:
1995

ENDLESS POOLS, INC.
1601 DUTTON MILL ROAD
ASTON, PA 19014
610-497-8676
800-910-2714
Fax: 610-497-9328
swim@endlesspools.com
www.endlesspools.com
• James Murdock, Founder/President
swim@endlesspools.com
• Tim Plummer, VP
swim@endlesspools.com
Products:
Workout training pool that uses water-flow resistance in small scale training pools.

ENDURA RUBBER FLOORING
2250 SOUTH TENTH STREET
SAN JOSE, CA 95112
800-669-7010
800-447-8442

Fax: 781-647-4543
info@burkeindustries.com
www.burkeflooring.com
• Dan Kelly, President
• Joseph Balfe, Sales Administration Manager
Products:
Floor tile, stair treads, SRT series spike and skate resistant tile, cove base, stair nosing, accessories, adhesives, maintenance products, and special products.

ENDURANCE NET
PO BOX 127
PO BOX 127
ROEBLING, NJ 8554
609-499-3450
800-808-6387
Fax: 609-499-3520
EnduranceNet@aol.com
www.endurancenetinc.com
• Mike Thompson, Sales Manager
Manufacturer:
Nets - Game Bird Netting, Bird & Wildlife Netting, Barrior Nets for all types of Sports. Fabric Net.

ENELL, INC.
319 SECOND STREET
PO BOX 808
HAVRE, MT 59501
406-265-8250
800-828-7661
Fax: 406-265-5909
info@enell.com
www.enell.com
• Renelle Braaten, Founder and President
(406) 265-8250
renelle.braaten@enell.com
• Mara Bronson, Marketing Director
(406) 265-8250
• Nicole Knowlton, Customer Service
(406) 265-8250
nicole.knowlton@enell.com
Description:
Manufacture, market & distribute high-performance apparel for well-endowed women.
Sports Products Manufactured:
Enell Sports Bra & Enell Lite Bra
Brands:
Enell

ENTRE-PRISES USA
63085 18TH STREET
SUITE 101
BEND, OR 97701
541-388-5463
800-580-5463
Fax: 541-388-3248
Info@epusa.com
www.epusa.com
• Eric Meade, Co-Owner/CEO
• Antoine Richard, CEO / President
Products:
Manufactures, designs, installs and distributes the most diverse line of climbing walls and handholds in the industry.

EPIC METALS
11 TALBOT AVENUE
RANKIN, PA 15104
412-351-3913
877-696-3742
Fax: 412-351-2018
info@epicmetals.com
www.epicmetals.com

• Ed Thomas, General Manager Sales
• Thomas Hartman, Vice President Sales
Products:
Architectural roof and floor deck ceiling systems.

EQUALIZER EXERCISE MACHINES
DEER PARK PO
PO BOX 25105
RED DEER, ALBERTA, CANADA T4R 2M2
403-309-5551
Fax: 403-342-5509
james@equalizerexercise.com
www.equalizerexercise.com
Products:
6000 Series, Home Gym with Gripless, 1000 Series, Single Station, Pec Fly Rear Delt,Leg Curl/ Leg Extension, Free Weights, Half Rack, Pro Power Rack, Flat to Military Bench and Cable Crossover.

EQUIPTO
225 MAIN STREET
TATAMY, PA 18085
610-253-2775
800-323-0801
Fax: 888-859-2121
www.equipto.com
• Tom Matyas, President and Chief Executive Officer
• Joe Gianfalla, Marketing & Sales VP
• Tom Matyas, President and CEO
Products:
Provider of automotive workbench and of complete storage space solutions offering shelving & racks, modular drawer cabinets, mobile aisle systems, mezzanines, workcenters, cabinets and carts

ERIC ARMIN INC./EAI
118 BAUER DRIVE
PO BOX 7046
OAKLAND, NJ 07436-7046
201-891-9466
800-272-0272
Fax: 201-891-5689
info@eaiusa.com
www.eaiusa.com
• Eric Guglberger, President
eguglberger@eaiusa.com
Products:
Calculators, watches, workbooks; vernier probes, manipulatives and EAI science related products; chronographs, stopwatches, timing products and atomic watches.

ERIK SPORTS, INC.
18 INDUSTRIAL AVENUE
MAHWAH, NJ 7430
201-825-2434
800-247-6579
Fax: 201-825-2414
info@eriksports.com
www.eriksports.com
• Michael Messler, President
(800) 247-6579
mmessler@eriksports.com
Products:
Boots, bindings, poles, skis, waxes & accessories and youth equipment; Snowshoe and Snowshoe poles; and Snowboards, bindings, boots and waxes & accessories.

ESCALADE SPORTS
817 MAXWELL AVENUE
EVANSVILLE, IN 47711
812-467-1200
800-467-1421
Fax: 812-467-1245
customerservice@escaladesports.com
www.escaladesports.com
• Bob Keller, President
• Dave Fetherman, Vice President, Sales &
Marketing
• Philip J. Piccolo, Executive VP
• Kirk Williams, VP Of Strategic Analysis &
Development
Products:
Producer of table tennis tables and
accessories; billiards tables; darts,
dartboards, cabinets and accessories;
Aerobic step products; Full line of Archery
Equipment; basketball, volleyball,
badminton, croquet, bocce and soccer
products.
Brands:
Goalrilla, Stiga, Ping-Pong, The Step, USW,
Woodplay, Oasis, Bear Archery, Trophy
Ridge, Musclesmith

ESPORTSMAN.COM
8116 S TRYON STREET
SUITE B3#212
CHARLOTTE, NC 28273
877-343-7767
888-776-7811
Fax: 704-248-8151
• David Singh, Founder

ETCHASOFT, INC.
13400 SUTTON PARK DRIVE S
SUITE 1501
JACKSONVILLE, FL 32224
904-493-0701
Fax: 904-493-0704
info@etchasoft.com
www.etchasoft.com
• Ben Balke, President
Products:
Commercial Product, Commercial Product &
Spin Off company and Beta Product for
commercial use.

ETONIC
350 FIFTH AVENUE
SUITE 6617
NEW YORK, NY 10118
212-273-3301
Fax: 212-273-3345
www.shopetonic.com/
• Tom Elwell, Chief Executive Officer
• Dan Ladd, Global Sales VP
• Karen Pitts, Global Marketing VP
• Dan Werremeyer, President
Products:
Shoes and gloves.

EVAN CORPORATION
22 SW AVENUE
JAMESTOWN, RI 2835
401-423-2230
Fax: 401-423-2785
info@evancorp.com
www.evancorp.com
• David P. Evangelista, President & Chief
Executive Officer
Year Founded:
1995.
Nature of Service:
Provider of rigging and rooftop fall protection

systems for public assembly facilities with
installations in more than 95 facilities
nationwide.

EVENT PROMOTION SUPPLY
11420 E 51ST AVENUE
DENVER, CO 80239
303-371-1717
800-227-0337
Fax: 303-371-9149
allisont@eps-doublet.com
www.eps-doublet.com
• Jon Leasia, President
jleasia@eps-doublet.com
Products:
Banners, Instant Advertising, Flags, Point of
Purchase, Tradeshow Graphics, Display
Frames, Graphic Tents, Event Supplies,
Contestant Number and Bibs, Fences and
Barricades, Fleet and Transit, Traffic and
Safety and Design and Installation.

EVERLAST WORLDWIDE INC
1350 BROADWAY
SUITE 2300
NEW YORK, NY 10018
212-239-0990
Fax: 212-239-4261
info@everlast.com
www.everlast.com
• Adam Geisler, President
Products:
Manufacturer: Boxing - Pro Boxing Gloves,
Training Gloves, Bag Gloves, Evergel Glove
Wraps, Handwrap, Tape, Gauze, Punch
Mitt, Shield, Protector, Boxing Head Gear,
Mouthpiece, Protective Cups, Shoes, Rings,
Punching Bags, Heavy Bags, Speed Bags;
Training & Exercise Equipment.

EVERLAST WORLDWIDE, INC.
1350 BROADWAY
SUITE 2300
NEW YORK, NY 10018
212-239-0990
Fax: 212-239-4261
www.everlast.com
• George Q. Horowitz, Chairman / President
/ Chief Executive O
• Matthew F. Mark, Chief Financial Officer
• Rita Cinque-Kriss, VP / Director
• Wayne Nadorf, Sales Assistant VP /
Director
Products:
Women's activewear, sportswear, swimwear
and coverups and men's activewear,
sportswear and outerwear; line of boxing
related sporting goods such as boxing
gloves, heavy bags, speed bags, boxing
trunks, and miscellaneous gym equipment;
men's, women's and children's apparel,
sleepwear, underwear, hosiery, footwear,
leatherwear, cardiovascular equipment,
eyewear, sports bags, hats and other
accessories.

EVERSAN, INC/UNITEC MFG DIVISION
34 MAIN STREET
WHITESBORO, NY 13492
315-736-3967
800-383-6060
Fax: 315-736-4058
sales@eversan.com
www.eversan.com
• Mustafa Evke, Chief Executive Officer
• Allan Roberts, VP

Products:
Timing Devices - Message Board Systems,
Electronic Scoreboards,
Stopwatches-Digital, Timers, Shot Clocks,
Ski Race Timing.

EVOL SNOWBOARDS
7130 CONVOY COURT
SAN DIEGO, CA 92111
858-874-4970
888-674-7478
Fax: 858-278-3274
• Tony Magnusson, President
• Tony Chen, VP
• Doug Weston, National Sales Manager
Products:
Snowboards, Skateboards, Skateboard
Shoes, Apparel, Wakeboards

EXCALIBUR ELECTRONICS
555 TAXTER ROAD
SUITE 210
ELMSFORD, NY 10523-2336
914-964-5200
800-592-4337
Fax: 914-476-3068
service@excaliburelectronics.com
www.excaliburelectronics.com
• Shane Samole, President
• Mike Catena, EVP
• Andy Stathopolus, Operations VP
• Al Lawrence, Product Development VP
Products:
Sports, Casino & Parlor Games, Chess and
Poker Games.
Brands:
Exploring the Universe, Keepsake Corner,
Master Series

EXCEL VOLLEYBALL PRODUCTS, INC.
15545 COMPUTER LANE
HUNTINGTON BEACH, CA 92649
714-898-7720
800-677-3669
Fax: 714-892-4730
info@excelsportsproducts.com
www.excelsportsproducts.com
• Cherry Blaine, President
• Sharon Shroyer, Marketing Director
Products:
Ankle Protection: ankle braces, Boxes,
Carts, Equipment Storage, Jump-Training
Device, Portable Scoring & Press Tables,
Recreation Swim Equipment

EXCLUSIVELY EXPO, INC.
1225 NAPERVILLE DRIVE
ROMEOVILLE, IL 60446
630-378-4600
Fax: 630-378-4617
Sales@exclusivelyexpo.com
• Jim Buehner, Owner
(630) 378-4600
sales@exclusivelyexpo.com
• Marie Buehner, Marketing Manager
marieb@exclusivelyexpo.com
Products:
Soccer Nets, Volleyball Equipment: Serving
Machines; Net Systems; Padding; Posts;
Volleyballs; Water Polo Equipment

EXECUTIVE DIVERSIONS
1870 COLT ROAD
SUITE 110
MEDIA, PA 19063

610-566-1171
Fax: 610-565-2289
www.edigolfevents.com
• Kevin M. Scanlon, President/CEO
(610) 566-1171
kevin@edigolfevents.com
• Rachel Kane, Development & Marketing Director
(516) 668-2739
Nature of Service:
Manufacturer
Description:
EDI provides sports event management to corporate, charity and private industries. EDI manages up to twenty golf events annually including corporat, charity and Pro-Am golf outings.
Year Founded:
1987
Products:
Cheer Uniforms - Budget to High End, Cheer Apparel, Warm up Jackets and Pants, Dance Team and Dance Recital Costumes.
Brands:
Deventers Cheer, Dancewear Factory.

EXERCYCLE CORPORATION
31 HAYWARD STREET
FRANKLIN, MA 2038
508-528-3100
800-367-6712
Fax: 508-528-8454
www.theracycle.com
• Michael Dugan, President / Chief Executive Officer
• David St. Germain, President
Products:
Stationary Bikes and Exercise Machines for the Physically Challenged

EXERTOOLS
170 EAST MEADOWS
PETALUMA, CA 94952
800-235-1559
Fax: 707-585-8404
customersupport@exertoolsinc.com
www.exertools.com
• Eric Parsells, President
(800) 235-1559
Products:
Exertools manufactures and distributes products to the fitness, therapeutic and rehabilitation markets. Exertools has been a product innovator for years. Products include the industry standard Plyoback rebounder - a market leader in the field of plyometric exercise, DynaDisc balance cushions - a staple in training & conditioning protocols, DynaBoard Balance Boards - used with DynaDiscs to increase the challenge of balance & core training, the Dual Mult-Slant stretching device, and three lines of Medicine Balls designed for a variety of applications. Exertools has expanded their webstore to offer products from other top manufacturers concentra

EXMARK MANUFACTURING
INDUSTRIAL PARK NW
PO BOX 808
BEATRICE, NE 68310-0808
402-223-6300
Fax: 402-223-6384
www.exmark.com
• John Cloutier, Marketing Communications Manager

(402) 223-6308
john.cloutier@exmark.com
• John Swanson, Product Manager
• Daryn Walters, Director of Marketing
• Garry Busboom, Director of Research and Development
• Dave Converse, Director of Engineering
Products:
Mowing systems

EXXEL OUTDOORS
300 AMERICAN BOULEVARD
HALEYVILLE, AL 35565
205-486-5258
Fax: 205-486-9882
www.exxel.com
• Harry Kazazian, CEO
• Armen Kouleyan, President
• Torry H. Upham, VP
Products:
Exporter of high quality camping gear, such as fishing apparel, sleeping bags, hunting apparel, water sports, tents, military apparel

EZ-LINER INDUSTRIES
1920 ALBANY PLACE SE
ORANGE CITY, IA 51041
712-737-4016
800-373-4016
Fax: 712-737-4148
sales@ezliner.com
www.ezliner.com
• Rob Krommendyk, Marketing Manager
Products:
Pavement and field paint striping equipment.
Year Founded:
1965
Description:
EZ-Liner manufactures high-quality striping equipment for rugged use and dependability.

F.I.T. VENTILATION
104 MECO LANE
OAK RIDGE, TN 33760
646-475-2249
Fax: 865-298-0199
www.exai.com
• Eran Shatzman, VP Business Development
• Yosh Sagie, VP Sales
• Gal Moran, Partner and CEO/CFO
gal@exai.com
• Tzvika Agassi, COO
• Shy Rosenzweig, CMO
• Ethan Pogrebizsky, CTO
Products:
Multiple ventilations such as: FIT Fan Models, Single Fan Models, Athletic Model, Wall Mount Model, Misting Option, Compact Model

FABRICATION ENTERPRISES
PO BOX 1500
WHITE PLAINS, NY 10602
914-345-9300
800-431-2830
Fax: 914-345-9800
info@fab-ent.com
www.fab-ent.com
• Elliott Goldberg, President
elliott@Fab-Ent.com
• Andrew Goldberg, Catalog Marketing
andrew@Fab-Ent.com
• Jason Drucker, Sales
jason@Fab-Ent.com

• Linda Goldberg, Director Of Sales
• Andrew Goldberg, Director Of Marketing
Products:
Medical and nutritional products for Physical Therapy, Rehabilitation, Homecare and Sports Medicine

FAIR-PLAY SCOREBOARDS
1700 DELAWARE AVENUE
DES MOINES, IA 50317
515-265-5305
800-247-0265
Fax: 515-265-3364
sales@fair-play.com
www.fair-play.com
• J.M. Allain, President & CEO
• Jeff Reeser, National Sales Manager
Products:
Scoreboards, Control Systems, Sports Message Centers, Accessories, Information Displays, Signage, Scoring & Video Systems
Brands:
Fair-Play and TL Vision

FAIRTRON
26 PEARL STREET
NORWALK, CT 6850
860-269-1578
Fax: 203-852-0836
sales@trans-lux.com
www.trans-lux.com
• Michael R Mulcahy, President/Chief Executive Officer
• Thomas Brandt, EVP / Co-Chief Executive Officer
• Jean-Marc L. D Allain, President & Chief Executive Officer
• Brian Laroche, President, TL Energy
• Karl P. Hirschauer, Vice President
• Thomas F. Mahone, Vice President
• Todd Dupee, Vice President and Controller
• Jay A. Forlenzo, Vice President
• Jane Bauer, Assistant Vice President, Human Resources
Products:
Indoor Programmable LED Signs, Electronic Outdoor Displays, Scoreboards,Electronic Outdoor Displays

FANATICS UNLIMITED
5507 FOXVALE COURT
MIDLOTHIAN, VA 23112
804-739-2392
Fax: 804-601-2820
• Chuck Bajnai, Creator / Executive Manager
Products:
Fun collectibles with sports team and desgins.

FANMATS LLC
3255 SHAWNEE INDUSTRIAL WAY
SUITE 100
SUWANEE, GA 30024
678-730-0600
800-525-5923
Fax: 678-730-0604
sales@FANMATS.com
www.fanmats.com
• Bob Roche, Owner
• GM Onur,
(678) 730-0600
• Iteace Davila, Accounts Receivable
(678) 730-0592

Products:
Tufted floor mats and rugs including athletic mats, entrance mats, area mats, car, truck, tailgate and garage mats
Description;
A licensed MLB, NFL, NBA, NHL and college manufacturer of fangear out of Georgia, developing and making a range of sports licensed mats, mirror covers, fanbrands and official yoga mats.
Teams;
NFL, MLB, NHL, & NBA. Plus 800 College teams as well as Military teams.

FASTECH LABS
1100 OWENDALE
SUITE J
TROY, MI 48083
248-244-9000
800-986-3668
Fax: 248-528-9801
www.fastechlabs.net
• Glenn Cumberland, Founder
(800) 351-3668
fastglenn@aol.com
Products:
Pedorthic Foot Support Products - Arch Cushions & Supports, Foot Orthotics, Heel Supports.

FEDERAL PREMIUM AMMUNITION
900 EHLEN DRIVE
ANOKA, MN 55303-7503
800-379-1732
Fax: 763-323-2506
www.federalpremium.com
• Gerald W. Bersett, President
• Margaret McDonald, VP
Products:
Complete line of shotshell, centerfire, rifle, pistol, slug, buckshot and rimfire ammunition and components

FELDMAR WATCH COMPANY, INC.
9000 W PICO BOULEVARD
LOS ANGELES, CA 90035
310-274-8016
Fax: 310-274-2081
info@feldmarwatch.com
www.feldmarwatch.com
• Sol Meller, President
smeller@feldmarwatch.com
Products:
Watches, Stopwatches, Fine Pens, Accessories

FENWICK GOLF COMPANY
1900 18TH STREET
SPIRIT LAKE, IA 51360
712-336-1520
800-554-4653
Fax: 712-336-5183
Products:
Golf - Graphite Golf Shafts.

FERA
3521 CHALLENGER STREET
TORRANCE, CA 90503
310-370-8538
800-828-3372
Fax: 310-214-3668
info@ferastyle.com
www.ferastyle.com
• Eric Tung, Founder

Products:
Skiing-Alpine - Apparel-Activewear, Outerwear, Sweaters, Base layers.

FERNO PERFORMANCE POOLS
70 WEIL WAY
WILMINGTON, OH 45177
888-206-7802
888-206-7802
Fax: 937-382-0895
www.fernoperformancepools.com
Products:
Commercial and Home Pools, Underwater Treadmills and Water Bike, Pool Accessories and Safety Products, Whirlpool Tanks

FGX DIRECT LLC
500 GEORGE WASHINGTON HIGHWAY
SMITHFIELD, RI 02917
401-231-3800
800-426-6396
crinfo@fgxi.com
gargoyleseyewear.com/
• Don Wanat, President
• Synthia Pope, VP
• Clair Tucker, Advertising Director / Public Relations
Products:
Eyewear - Sunglasses.

FIBERESIN INDUSTRIES, INC.
37031 E WISCONSIN AVENUE
PO BOX 88
OCONOMOWOC, WI 53066-3146
262-567-4427
800-450-0051
Fax: 262-567-4814
info@fiberesin.com
www.fiberesin.com
• Jeff Bahr, Director of Manufacturing
jbahr@fiberesin.com
• Sandy Higgins, Customer Service Manager
(262) 560-4429
shiggins@fiberesin.com
• David Callies, Quality Assurance Manager
dcallies@fiberesin.com
• Jim Schwind, Technical Services Director
(262) 560-4457
jschwind@fiberesin.com
• Lonie Wise, National Sales Manager
(262) 560-4460
lwise@fiberesin.com
• Glenda Kieso, Accounts Payable and Human Resources
(262) 560-4424
gkieso@fiberesin.com
• Jim Lawrence, Controller
jlawrence@fiberesin.com
• Mike MacDougal, President and CEO
(262) 560-4439
mmacdougal@fiberesin.com
Products:
Develops custom solutions for utilizing wood composites, paper, specialty formulated plastics, and resins in laminated products in the athletics facilities and equipment industries.

FIBEROPTIC LIGHTING INC.
950 SE M STREET
GRANTS PASS, OR 97526
541-476-6900
800-543-2533
Fax: 541-476-0796

• Hyla Lipson, President / Chief Executive Officer
• Sam Moon, Sales Consultant
• Carol Porter, Sales Consultant
• John Jones, Structural Consultant
Products:
Custom fiber optic signs and displays

FIELD GENERAL LLC
5662 N. MILLER CIRCLE
STANSBURY PARK, UT 84074
479-872-5388
888-822-3352
Fax: 479-872-5388
info@field-general.com
www.field-general.com
Products:
Baseball and Softball Gloves

FIELD TURF TARKETT
8088 MONTVIEW
MONTREAL, QUEBEC, CANADA H4P 2L7
514-340-9311
800-724-2969
Fax: 514-340-9374
info@fieldturf.com
www.fieldturf.com
• Joe Fields, Chief Executive Officer
• Troy Squires, VP Marketing
(800) 724-2969
• Jim Petrucelli, VP Marketing
(800) 724-2969
• Darren Gill, Director Marketing
(800) 724-2969
dgill@fieldturf.com
Products:
Turf, Hardwood Courts, Running Tracks, PVC Flooring, Tennis Courts.
Year Founded:
1994
Brands:
Field Turf, Prestige, Omnisports, Atlas Resisport, Field Turf Playground, Le Monde

FIELDMASTER INFIELD GROOMER
15551 W 109TH
LENEXA, KS 66219
913-492-7303
800-728-3581
Fax: 913-492-8532
www.fieldmaster.com
• Dan Goldblatt, President
Products:
Grooming system that helps maintain a baseball/softball fields, including level infields.

FILA USA
1 FILA WAY
SPARKS GLENCOE, MD 21152
410-773-3000
800-845-3452
Fax: 410-773-4989
ecommUSA@fila.com
www.fila.com
• Jon Epstein, President
• Young-Chan Cho, Chief Financial Officer
• Lauren Mallon, Global Marketing Manager
• Yoon-Soo Yong, Chairman & CEO
Products:
Basketball Shoes; Golf Apparel, Hats/Caps, Rainwear; Racquet Sports Apparel, Bags, Equipment, Shoes, Socks; Skiing-Alpine Pants, Parkas, Sweaters, Vests, Underclothing; Track & Field/Running Apparel, Shoes; Training & Conditioning Aerobic Shoes; Water Sports

Sponsor:
Tennis Players: James Blake, Anna Chavetadze, Kim Clijsters, Marina Erakovic, Karin Knapp, Svetlana Kuznetsova, Andreas Seppl, and Janko Tipsarevic.

FILIPPI IMPORTERS/ELITE ROWING, INC
233 ASH STREET
WESTON, MA 2493
617-783-8442
Fax: 617-783-8442
info@eliterowing.com
www.eliterowing.com
• Selvig Alex, President
Products:
Provides boats to International rowing teams.

FIRST SERVICE
737 SOUTHPOINT BOULEVARD
SUITE D
PETALUMA, CA 94954
707-781-1960
800-227-1742
Fax: 800-809-9172
www.clubstuff.com
• Dan Goldblatt, President
(800) 227-1742
• Tom Helms, Sales Manager
(800) 227-1742
Products:
Aerobic Flooring, Aerobic Studio Equipment, Court Conversion Systems, Mats, Noise Reduction Systems, Climbing Walls, Locker Room Furnishings, Playground Surfacing, Protective Padding, RCA Rubber Flooring, Seating Solutions, Basketball Equipment, Bleachers, Gym Divider Curtains, Multi-Play Tiles, Player Benches, Protective Floor Covers, Scoreboards, Scorer's Tables & Scorekeepers, Volleyball Equipment, Site Furnishings.
Year Founded:
1974

FISHER ATHLETIC EQUIPMENT, INC.
2060 CAUBLE ROAD
SALISBURY, NC 28147
800-438-6028
800-438-6028
Fax: 800-272-4448
customerservice@fisherathletic.com
• Robert Pritchard, President
(704) 636-5713
bobpritchard@fisherathletic.com
• Brian Pritchard, VP
(704) 636-5713
brianpritchard@fisherathletic.com
• Bill Keeler, Marketing Manager
(704) 636-5713
billkeeler@fisherathletic.com
• Bob Pritchard, President
Products:
Equipments and Accessories for Football, Baseball, Track & Field, Basketball, Soccer; Exercise Mats, Training Equipments, Protective Padding, Gym Dividers, Wind Screen, Rail Padding and Bags

FIT-TRAIL BY SOUTHWOOD CORPORATION
PO BOX 38900
CHARLOTTE, NC 28278
704-588-5000
800-727-6884
Fax: 704-588-5017

vickydwight@southwoodcorp.com
www.fittrail.com
• Vicky Dwight, VP & Account Executive
(704) 588-5000
• Patsi Sheets, Office Manager
(704) 588-5000
Products:
FitTrail outdoor exercise system fitness trail courses (10 or 20-station models)

FITBALL USA
14215 MEAD STREET
LONGMONT, CO 80504
800-752-2255
800-752-2255
Fax: 877-223-2962
• Dale Mayer, Chief Executive Officer
• Gloria Miller, Marketing
Products:
Balance tools, books, DVDs, Videos, Fragrances, Ergonomic Seating, Exercise Mats, Accessories, Body Therapy, Exercise Balls, Massage and Sensory Tools, Therapy Mats, Therapy Tools, Yoga and Pilates Overball and Mats

FITNESS EM, LLC
660 DOUGLAS STREET
UXBRIDGE, MA 01569
508-278-3209
800-704-5561
Fax: 508-278-6145
info@empowerfitness.com
www.fitnessem.com
• Donna Savage, President/Co-Founder
info@fitnessem.com
• Kathy O'Connel Johnson, VP
Sales/Marketing
info@fitnessem.com
Products:
Fitness Equipment
Brands:
Danskin Fitness Accessories, Empower Fitness Equipment

FITNESS FLOORING
6199 NORWALDO AVENUE
INDIANAPOLIS, IN 46220
317-849-6181
800-428-5306
Fax: 317-842-5384
info@fitnessfloors.com
www.exerflex.com
• Mark Center, President / National Sales Manager
mark@exerflex.com
• Dave Osborn, Sales Manager
dave@exerflex.com
Products:
Surfacing for aerobics, basketball, weight rooms. Different products such as Group Exercise, Rubber Flooring, Modular Flooring

FITNESS MASTER INC
11419 MATHIS
#200
DALLAS, TX 75234
214-350-8884
866-434-8639
Fax: 214-350-8876
• Eric R Dick, Manager
info@fitnexonline.com
• Ed Banasky, Vice President
info@fitnexonline.com
• Joe Ramirez, Manager
Products:
Fitness equipment and accessories

FITNESS TECH INTERNATIONAL
40 RONSON DRIVE
UNIT 3
ETOBICOKE, ONTARIO, CANADA M9W 1B3
416-573-0701
800-844-4019
www.thepowersuit.com
• Lebert Veira, CEO and President
Products:
Cross training system

FITTER INTERNATIONAL INC
3050, 2600 PORTLAND STREET SE
CALGARY, ALBERTA, CANADA T2G 4M6
403-243-6830
800-348-8371
Fax: 403-229-1230
orders@fitter1.com
www.fitter1.com
• Louis Stack, President/Founder
(403) 243-6830
louisstack@fitter1.com
Products:
Leading the World to better balance through Retail and WHLS distribution of Exercise balls, balance boards, cobblestone mat, trikke, Boardrock, Bongo board, blideboard, Bosu Ball, Pro Fitter, Indo Board, kid's toys, active sitting.

FLAGS INTERNATIONAL
10845 MCKINLEY HIGHWAY
OSCEOLA, IN 46561
574-674-5125
800-627-3524
Fax: 574-674-5134
info@flagsinternational.com
www.flagsinternational.com
• Cathy M Bolinger, President / Owner
• Michael Shidler, Customer Service Director
info@flagsinternational.com
• David Aker, VP
Products:
Flags, Banners, Custom Designed Flags & Banners, Flagpoles and Flag Items (hats, books, bunting, fans, pulldowns, windsock, arm patches, decals and static clings, lapel pins, stringed flags and fandangles, car window flags, bumper stickers, license plates, keychains, mini-banners, tabletop flags, gravemakers, display cases

FLAMBEAU OUTDOORS
15981 VALPLAST ROAD
MIDDLEFIELD, OH 44062
440-632-1631
800-457-5252
Fax: 440-632-1581
consumer@flambeauoutdoors.com
www.flambeauoutdoors.com
• Jason Sauey, President
Products:
Fishing and hunting gear and accessories.

FLEER/SKYBOX INTERNATIONAL
5909 SEA OTTER PLACE
CARLSBAD, CA 92010-6621
Fax: 760-929-3194
customer_service@upperdeck.com
sports.upperdeck.com
• Roger Grass, President / Chief Executive officer
• Chris Tobias, Chief Financial Officer
• Lloyd Powlak, SVP Marketing / Sales
• Bill Bordegon, VP Marketing / Sales

Products:
Trading Cards

FLEXCO
1401 E 6TH STREET
TUSCUMBIA, AL 35674
800-633-3151
Fax: 800-346-9075
info@flexcofloors.com
www.flexcofloors.com
• Bart Rogers, VP Sales/Marketing
brogers@roppeholdingcompany.com
• Ron Tait, National Sales Manager
rtait@flexcofloors.com
• Norman J. Freebeck, Executive Director of
Manufacturing
njfreebeck@flexcofloors.com
• Jeremy Whipple, Marketing Manager
• Don Blazer, Director of Manufacturing
• Brent Fike, Technical Installation Training
Manager
bfike@flexcofloors.com
• Rex Smallwood, Technical - Quality
Assurance
rsmallwood@flexcofloors.com
• Dale Gross, Director of International Sales
& ESD Product
Products:
Rubber flooring, wall base, stair treads, vinyl
accessories, floor finishing accessories,
vinyl flooring

FLOATING SWIMWEAR INC
1970 S W STREET
WITCHITA, KS 67216-2143
316-942-8899
800-705-1959
Fax: 316-524-0411
www.floatwear.com
• Don Royer, President
Products:
Swimwear, beachwear and protective
playwear

FLOORBOARDZ RUGS
970 CALLE AMANECER
SUITE A
SAN CLEMENTE, CA 92673
949-281-7304
866-585-4886
Fax: 866-680-1061
• Jillian Mintz, Sales Manager
(916) 858-1177
Products:
Tufted and printed rugs in the shape of
surfboards

FLYBAR
PO BOX 563
ELLENVILLE, NY 12428
845-647-8400
800-764-6784
irwin@flybar.com
www.flybar.com
Products:
Pogo Sticks

FN THOMPSON COMPANY
5605 CARNEGIE BOULEVARD
SUITE 200
CHARLOTTE, NC 28209
704-551-2700
Fax: 704-551-2799
www.bekbuildinggroup.com
• Luther P Cochrane, Chairman / Chief
Executive Officer

• Larry M Beasley, President / Chief
Operating Officer
• Trilby Carriker, Chief Financial Officer
• Philip Southerland, President
• Mike Pierle, Executive Vice President
• Trilby Carriker, Chief Administration
Officer/Chief Financial
• Frank Holley, Executive Vice President,
Food & Beverage, L
• Chuck Lewis, General Counsel
• Garland Burton, Director of Diversity and
Community Affairs
• Candace Watson, Human Resources
Director
Services:
Commercial, healthcare, industrial and
institutional construction

FNF ENT/STELLAR TOYS
18308 WARD STREET
FOUNTAIN VALLEY, CA 92708
949-722-8377
877-354-7635
Fax: 714-963-3387
www.flipnflyer.com
• Larry Huset, President
(949) 722-8377
• Debbie Swanson, Director Marketing
(949) 233-7160
Nature of Service:
Manufacturer and Wholesaler Distributor of
Flying Discs
Year Founded:
2002
Products:
Gyroscopic Flying Disc, Flip N Flyer,
Freestyle Spin Sport
Brands:
Flip N Flyer

FNT INDUSTRIES, INC.
1805 PIERCE AVENUE
MARINETTE, WI 54143
715-732-2511
800-338-9860
Fax: 715-732-2574
• Werner Haberl, President
Products:
Netting, twine, rope, cordage, sports nets &
accessories.

FOAMHEADS, LLC
663 S LUCILE STREET
SEATTLE, WA 98108
206-624-5222
Fax: 206-624-5229
info@foamheads.com
www.foamheads.com
• Jeff Richey, Chief Executive Officer
(206) 624-5222
• Jim Bell, Founder
(206) 624-5222
• Kevin Hilisman, Sales Manager
(206) 624-5222
Products:
Foamheads, Action Figures, and 4-in-1
Toppers
Brands:
Foamheads & Actionheads
Clients:
Retailers, stadiums and fan shops

FOCUS GOLF SYSTEMS, INC.
25 DRAPER STREET
GREENVILLE, SC 29611
864-271-0201
800-235-5516

Fax: 864-271-3258
info@focusgroup.com
www.dunlopsportsonline.com
• William Emery, President
info@focusgroup.com
• Brandon Mill, Director
Products:
Golf, Tennis and Sqaush sports equipments
and accessories.

FOGDOG SPORTS
1075 FIRST AVENUE
KING OF PRUSSIA, PA 19406
650-980-2500
800-624-2017
Fax: 610-265-6099
Products:
Sports apparel, accessories and equipment.

FOOTJOY
333 BRIDGE STREET
PO BOX 965
FAIRHAVEN, MA 02719-0965
800-225-8500
800-225-8500
Fax: 508-979-3909
www.footjoy.com
• Jim Connor, President
• John Peal, European Marketing Director
Products:
Golf shoes, gloves, outerwear, socks,
spikeless shoes, belts, hats, and
miscellaneous

FOR BARE FEET INC
1201 SOUTH OHIO STREET
PO BOX 159
MARTINSVILLE, IN 46151
765-349-7474
800-669-0674
Fax: 765-349-7470
fbf@fboriginals.com
www.forbarefeet.com
Products:
Novelty socks, team socks, university socks,
headbands, and wristbands

FOREFRONT GOLF
835 BILL JONES INDUSTRIAL DRIVE
SPRINGFIELD, TN 37172
615-384-1230
800-247-9651
Fax: 615-384-1290
• Stan J Harris, Chief Executive Officer
Products:
Stand bags, Cart bags, Classic, Ladies, and
Customize golf bags.
Brands:
Stand Collection: Alphine, Triad, Trek,
Scout; Cart Collection: Cart Blanche Maxim;
Classic Collection: Destin, Premier,
Signature; Ladies Collection: Lexa,
Platinum, Cloud Nine

FOX 40 INTERNATIONAL INC.
4645 WITMER INDUSTRIAL ESTATE
NIAGARA FALLS, NY 14305-1360
716-298-1129
888-663-6940
Fax: 716-298-1204
foxinfo@fox40world.com
www.fox40world.com
• Ron Foxcroft, Founder/CEO
foxinfo@fox40world.com
• Dave Foxcroft, President & COO

Products:
Fox 40 Whistles (Referee & Coach, Sport & Safety), Lanyards & Flex Coils, Don Cherry Products (Hockey sticks & Mouthguards), Fox 40 Coaching Boards, Fox 40 Marine, Kliptek Intelight, FoxMed, Fox 40 Mouthguards, Protex/PTX/Longdon

FOX RIVER MILLS, INC.
227 POPLAR STREET
PO BOX 298
OSAGE, IA 50461-0298
641-732-3798
800-247-1815
Fax: 641-732-5128
www.foxsox.com
• Jeff Lessard, Executive Vice President
(641) 732-3798
• John Lessard, President
ext 221
Products:
Socks and handwear
Brands:
Fox River Socks & Handwear
Clients:
Sporting Goods and outdoor retailers

FRAMEWORTH SPORTS MARKETING
1198 CALEDONIA ROAD
TORONTO, ONTARIO, CANADA M6A 2W5
416-781-1115
Fax: 416-781-1038
info@frameworth.com
www.frameworth.com
• Brian Ehrenworth, President
• Carmelo Notaro, Retail Store Manager
(416) 781-1115
Products:
NHL, NHL, MLB, NBA, NASCAR, plus golf, soccer and boxing memorabilia and collectibles.

FRANCO APPAREL GROUP
100 W 33RD STREET
SUITE 911
NEW YORK, NY 10001
212-967-7272
Fax: 212-967-7395
info@francoapparel.com
www.francoapparel.com
• Ike Franco, President / Chief Operating Officer
info@francoapparel.com
• Joanne Guglielmo, Chief Financial Officer
• Allen Franco, Sales VP
• Desiree Scialpi, Marketing / Licensing Director
Products:
Childrenwear and sports licensed apparel

FRANKLIN SPORTS, INC.
17 CAMPANELLI PARKWAY
PO BOX 508
STOUGHTON, MA 02072-0508
781-344-1111
800-225-8649
Fax: 781-341-0333
www.franklinsports.com
• Irving Franklin, Chairman/Founder
• Larry Franklin, President / Chief Executive Officer
• Rich Ferenz, Sales VP
Products:
Batting gloves, fielding gloves, fielding/pitching practice, batting practice, balls/accessories, volleyball sets, badminton sets, combination sets, croquet sets, bocce

sets, horseshoe sets, coleman sets, tetherball sets, yard games, accessories, table tennis, darts, table top, ready to go, future champs, MLB, soft sport, learn to play, soccer balls, soccer shinguards, soccer goals & rebounders, accessories, playground balls, basketballs, volleyballs, footballs, and fan products

FREEMAN PRODUCTS, INC.
715 PARK N BOULEVARD
CLARKESTON, GA 30021
404-297-9083
800-537-3362
Fax: 201-475-4818
info@fpworldwide.com
www.freemanproductsworldwide.com
• Vince Cariello, President
• George Ercolino, VP
Products:
Trophies, Awards - Clocks, Components, Engraving Machines, Incentives and Recognition Awards, Medals, Plaques, Ribbons, Trophies.

FREESTYLE USA
47-14 32ND PLACE
LONG ISLAND, NY 11101
805-484-1216
800-874-0907
Fax: 800-776-5997
customerservice@genevawg.com
www.freestyleusa.com
• Jimmy Olmes, President
• Brett Ritter, Brand Manager
• John Katker, National Sales Manager
Products:
Men's and Women's Watches and Accessories with sports logos and designs.

FREMONT DIE CONSUMER PRODUCTS INC
1709A ENDEAVOR DRIVE
WILLIAMSBURG, VA 23185
757-872-6438
800-336-8847
Fax: 757-872-6958
www.fremontdie.com
• James B. Hotze, President
(757) 872-6438
• Sharon Weinberg, Vice President
• Wanda Pullom, General Manager
• Wally Morgan, Operations/EDI/Shipping
• David Hotze, Marketing/Sales
Products:
House flags, steering wheel covers, fuzzy dice, license plate frames, wastebaskets, tire covers, car flags, car socks, mini banners, antenna flags, bike flags, magnets, plastic parking signs, street signs, and stop signs, desk toppers, fight song plaques, wall banners, bar stool covers (top cover with logo), visor organizer, CD/DVD holder, litter bag, tailgate net and tackle buddy/bop bag (inflatable).
Year Founded:
1982

FUBU THE COLLECTION
350 5TH AVENUE
SUITE 6617
NEW YORK, NY 10118
212-273-3300
Fax: 212-273-3333
www.fblegacy.com
• John Daymond, Chief Executive Officer
• Carl Brown, Co-Founder

• Keith Perrin, Co-Founder / VP
• J. Al Martin, VP / Head Designer
Products:
Men's shoes, tuxedos, suits and collectible apparel; Ladies and Children's shoes and apparel and accessories

FULL 90 SPORTS, INC.
10251 VISTA SORRENTO PARKWAY #300
SAN DIEGO, CA 92191
877-438-5590
Fax: 858-777-6592
Questions@Full90.com
www.full90.com
• Jeff Skeen, Founder/Chief Executive Officer
• Dennis Piper, Corporate Affairs VP
• Mark Skeen, Marketing VP
• Tim Killeen, Vice President, Sales
(858) 777-6528
Description:
Manufacturer of state-of-the-art soccer products designed to extend the enjoyment of soccer for players of all ages. Developed unique padded headboard.
Products:
Soccer Headgear
Clients:
Sporting Goods and soccer specialty retailers

FUN & FITNESS LLC
PO BOX 5241
SACRAMENTO, CA 95817
916-599-0490
888-995-4273
Fax: 916-361-5432
playnosweat@aol.com
www.playnosweat.com
Products:
Playground and fitness equipment.

FUN-TEES, INC.
4725 CORPORATE DRIVE NW
SUITE 100
CONCORD, NC 28027
704-788-3003
Fax: 704-795-9300
• Lewis Reid, President
• Mark Weibel, CFO
• Brendi Hensley, Office Manager
Products:
Manufacturer of knitted apparel

FUNLINE MERCHANDISE COMPANY INC
7751 CHERRY AVENUE
FONTANA, CA 92336
909-357-7988
Fax: 626-336-7982
www.musclemachines.com
Products:
Gymnasium apparatus such as trampolines

G III SPORTS
512 SEVENTH AVENUE
NEW YORK, NY 10018
212-403-0500
Fax: 212-403-0551
info@g-iii.com
www.g-iii.com
• Morris Goldfarb, Chief Executive Officer / Chairman
• Jeanette Nostra-Katz, President
• Sammy Aaron, Vice Chairman
• Wayne Miller, Chief Operating Officer
• Neal Nackman, Chief Financial Officer

• Jeffrey Goldfarb, Director of Strategic Planning
Products:
Introduced women's leather outerwear, men's leather apparel, women's textile outerwear and sportswear, men's textile outerwear, and NFL team logo outerwear

G-PUSH SPORT, INC.
277 GLADSTONE AVENUE
ONTARIO, CANADA M6J 3L9
416-532-3870
Fax: 416-530-4826
• Anita Stephan, Communications
Products:
Sports Supplements.

G. LOOMIS INC.
1 HOLLAND DRIVE
IRVINE, CA 92618
877-577-0600
Fax: 360-225-7169
loomis@gloomis.com
www.gloomis.com
• Gary Loomis, Founder
loomis@gloomis.com
• Bruce Holt, Executive Director
loomis@gloomis.com
• Mark Landry, Sales Manager
loomis@gloomis.com
Products:
General Tackle, Fly, Blanks, Clothing, Hats, Collectibles, Travel Gear

GAIAM
833 W S BOULDER ROAD
PO BOX 3095
BOULDER, CO 80307-3095
303-222-3600
877-989-6321
800-254-8464
Fax: 303-222-3700
customerservice@gaiam.com
www.gaiam.com
• Jirka Rysavy, Chairman / Chief Executive Officer
customerservice@gaiam.com
• Lynn Powers, President / Chief Operating Officer
customerservice@gaiam.com
• Janet Mathews, Chief Financial Officer
customerservice@gaiam.com
Products:
Towels, Shower & Bath Filters, Cleaners, Shower Curtains, Bathroom Accesories, Storage & Organization, Laundry, Cleaning Tools, Seventh Generatioh Products, Batteries & Chargers, Energy Efficient Bulbs, Lamps, Light Therapy, Natural Spectrum Bulbs, Heating, Energy Savers, Humidifiers & Dehumidifiers, Fans & Cooling

GAME MASTER ATHLETIC COMPANY
1624 DOLWICK DRIVE
ERLANGER, KY 41018
859-746-9800
800-646-4225
Fax: 859-746-5636
info@gamemasterathletic.com
www.gmasterathletic.com
• Garrett Kamstra, President/CEO
Products:
Softball Pitching Machine, Dual Portable Screen, Synthetic Leather Gloves, Ultimate Bat and Ball, Junior Size College Logo Rubber Footballs, Official Size College Logo Synthetic Leather Autograph Footballs, Mini

Size College Logo Rubber Footballs, Logo Footballs in Blister Packs on Clip Strips, Official Size College Logo Rubber Basketballs, Official Size College Logo Autograph Basketballs, Mini Size College Logo Rubber Basketballs, and more.

GAME TIME LLC
181 BOYD STREET
MONTGOMERY, NY 12549
888-249-9627
cs@genevawg.com
Products:
Watches

GAME TIME, INC.
150 PLAYCORE DRIVE SE
FORT PAYNE, AL 35967
256-845-5610
800-235-2440
800-235-2440
Fax: 256-845-9361
dking@gametime.com
www.gametime.com
• Bob Farnsworth, President
dking@gametime.com
• Tom Norquist, Senior Vice President
dking@gametime.com
• Craig Bierley, GMC Advertising and Sales Promotion Director
Products:
KidTime Slides, WallCan Climbers, Links and Bridges, Panels, Roofs, Swings, Riding, Hands on Playsets, StreetScape, TuffClad, Playground Pets, Benches, Tables, Accessories, FitKid Equipment, Basketball Equipmentss, Baseball Equipment, Soccer Equipment, Volleyball Equipment, Tennis Equipment, Tetherball Equipment, Surfacing, Shade Structures, Spray Parks

GAMETIME PLUSH
9540 PATHWAY STREET
SUITE 101
SANTEE, CA 92071-4178
619-596-6161
888-817-5874
Fax: 619-596-1198
Products:
Officially licensed collegiate fan toys and apparel

GAMEWEAR
79 HUDSON STREET
SECOND FLOOR
HOBOKEN, NJ 7030
973-954-2413
Fax: 973-529-0242
www.gamewear.com
• Frank Cerullo, CEO
• Nick Iovacchini, President
Year Founded:
2003.
Nature of Service:
Products are officially licensed and made from the most iconic element in sports- the ball used in play -so they more closely connect the wearer to their favorite teams and players than any other product.

GARAN, INC.
350 FIFTH AVENUE
NEW YORK, NY 10118
212-563-2000
Fax: 212-971-2250

• Seymour Lichtenstein, Chairman & Chief Executive
• Alexander Sistarenik, Treasurer
• William J Wilson, Finance VP & Chief Financial Officer
• Jerald S Kamiel, President
Products:
Shirts & Blouses, Suits Career, Skirts, Size - Junior, suits, Pants & Trousers, Sportswear, Dresses Casual, Shorts, dresses

GARED SPORTS - SSI VOLLEYBALL
707 N 2ND STREET
SUITE 202
SAINT LOUIS, MO 63102
314-421-0044
800-325-2682
Fax: 314-421-6014
customerservice@garedsports.com
www.garedsports.com
• Dean Baker, Sales / Marketing VP
(314) 421-0044
• Laura St George, National Sales Manager
(314) 421-0044
laura@garedsports.com
• Kevin Needler, Operations Manager
(314) 421-0044
kara@garedsports.com
Products:
Indoor Badminton Systems & Nets, Tether Ball Indoor/Outdoor Sets, Basketball Accessories, Backboards - Glass, Backboards - NOn-Glass, Goals - Breakaway, Goals - Fixed Institutional & Playground, NBA Arena Backboard & Goals, Outdoor, Portables, Residential/Playground Basketball Systems, Scorebooks, Training Aides/Skill Development, 3 POint Wall Mount, 4 Point Wall Mounts, 4 Point Wall Mounts - Side Fold, 4 Point Wall Mounts - Swing Up, Ceiling Suspended Backstops, Electric Adjust-a-Goals, Gym Accessories, Manual Adjust-A-Goals, Wall Padding, Benches, Bike Racks, Bleachers, Official Round Soccer Goals, Official Soccer Goals, Recreational Soccer

GARMONT USA, INC.
170 BOYER CIRCLE
SUITE 20
WILLISTON, VT 5495
802-658-8322
Fax: 802-658-0431
www.garmontusa.com
• John Schweizer, Division Manager / Exel / President
• Bill Hill, Chief Financial Officer
• Gord Bailes, Sales VP
Products:
Footwear, Socks, Winter Gear

GATOR ATHLETIC INC.
1243 IND PARKWAY, IND PARK
PO BOX 1243
CLARKSDALE, MS 38614
662-627-7413
800-572-2470
www.gator-athletics.com
• Billie N Strohm, President
Products:
Football - Jerseys; Softball - Jerseys.

GE LIGHTING SYSTEMS
3010 SPARTANBURG HIGHWAY
EAST FLAT ROCK, NC 28726

800-305-1372
Fax: 800-305-1373
www.ge.com
• Maryrose Sylvester, President / Chief
Executive Officer
Products:
Lighting Fixtures

GE MARQUETTE
3000 N GRANDVIEW BOULEVARD
WAUKAESHA, WI 53188
262-544-3011
800-643-6439
Fax: 262-544-3384
www.gemedicalsystems.com
• David Zachman, National Sales Training &
Marketing Officer
Products:
Training & Conditioning - Stress Testing
Equipment, Treadmills.

GEAR FOR SPORTS
9700 COMMERCE PARKWAY
LENEXA, KS 66219
913-693-3200
800-255-1065
Fax: 913-693-3917
www.gearforsports.com
• Larry Graveel, President / Chief Operating
Officer
• Randy Stabenow, GEAR Manufacturing
VP
Products:
Sportswear, Headwear and Accessories

GEAR PRO-TEC
1901 DIPLOMAT DRIVE
DALLAS, TX 75234
800-859-8625
Fax: 888-858-8337
www.gearprotec.com
• Ed Tobergte, President
• Stanley L. Bryant, President
Year Founded:
1992.
Products:
Z-Cool, Z-Accessories, Z-Cool Youth, X-2
Air, Air-Tech, The Gamer, Youth Pads,
Accessories, Chin Straps.

GENERAL AWARDS, INC.
7715 NW 64TH STREET
MIAMI, FL 33166
305-592-3346
800-327-2846
Fax: 305-592-9304
• Cinthia Waas-Russiyan, President / Owner
• Nicholas Russiyan, Owner
Products:
Awards, Medals, Pins, Ribbons, Color Flex,
Trophy Hardware

GENERAL SPORTCRAFT COMPANY, LTD.
313 WATERLOO VALLEY ROAD
BUDD LAKE, NJ 7828
973-347-3800
800-526-0244
Fax: 973-347-5711
www.sportcraft.com
• Michael J J. Nally, Chief Executive Officer
& President
• Frank Ginolfi, Chief Financial Officer
Products:
Dartboards, Billiard Tables, Table Tennis,
Foosball Tables, Turbo Hockey,

Multi-games Tables, Casino Games,
Volleyball Systems, Combination
Badminton/Volley, Badminton Systems,
Croquet sets, Horseshoes, Bocce,
Tetherball Sets, Monster Games, Bounces
houses, Treadmills

GENERAL SPORTS VENUE ASTROTURF
11550 COMMON OAKS DRIVE
SUITE 206
RALEIGH, NC 27614
919-488-5819
800-723-8873
Fax: 919-488-5802
help@astroturf.com
www.astroturf.com
• Jon L Pritchett, President / Chief Executive
Officer
(919) 488-5800
• Dan Fuhrman, SVP / Chief Finacial Officer
• Jim Petrucelli, Vice President of Business
Development
(919) 488-5800
• Troy Squires, Global Director of Sales and
Marketing
• Vince Yoos, Project Director - Northeast
• Bryan Jones, Project Manager -
Northwest/Southwest
• Mitchell Truban, Project Manager
• Cab Bramlett, Design Engineer
• Robert Staten, Controller
Products:
Synthetic Turf, Fusion Turf, Transition Turf,
Venue Projects.

GEORGI-SPORTS
2191 EMBASSY DRIVE
LANCASTER, PA 17603
717-291-8924
800-338-2527
Fax: 717-291-9188
• George Matthew, President
Products:
Accessories, Field Hockey Balls, Field
Hockey Sticks, Goals and Nets, Protective
Equipment, Referee's Equipment, Stick and
Team Bags, Uniforms

GEORGIA BOOT
39 EAST CANAL STREET
NELSONVILLE, OH 45764
866-442-4908
Fax: 615-790-8005
info@georgiaboot.com
www.georgiaboot.com
• Gerald M Cohn, Chief Executive Officer
info@georgiaboot.com
• Tommy Morrison, President
info@georgiaboot.com
Products:
Outdoor Footwear

GEORGIA MARBLE COMPANY
200 GEORGIA MARBLE LANE
PO BOX 238
TATE, GA 30177
770-735-2611
800-334-0122
Fax: 770-735-2236
www.polycor.com
• Richard Ryan, President
• Brian Mills, VP
• Craig Garland, Sales Manager
• Shari Kort, Advertising Manager
Products:
Granite, Marble, Tiles and Slabs for various
applications, including sports arenas

GERRY COSBY & COMPANY, INC.
11 PENNSYLVANIA PLAZA
NEW YORK, NY 10001
212-563-6464
877-563-6464
Fax: 212-967-0876
gcsmsg@cosbysports.com
www.cosbysports.com
• Michael Cosby, Owner/President
Products:
Professional team bags and equipment; All
equipment bags and football protective
equipment. Professional factory located at
103 Under Mountain Road, Sheffield, MA
01257.
Brands:
Cosby Bags, Mr. Tops Football shoulder
pads, 'The Professionals Choice™'
Clients:
Pro Teams (NY Yankees), College Teams,
High School and Pee Wee Teams, and
individuals

GERSTUNG/GYM-THING, INC.
1400 COPPERMINE TERRACE
BALTIMORE, MD 21209
410-337-7781
800-922-3575
Fax: 410-337-0471
info@gerstung.us
www.gerstung.com
• Siegfried Gerstung, Founder/Owner
(800) 922-3575
• Jeff Tarleton, General Manager
(800) 922-3575
• Fran Ice, Sales Advisor
(800) 922-3575
Products:
Manufacturer of aerobic and dance floors,
weight room flooring, fitness products,
gymnastics equipment.

GETZ CORPORATION
539 WEST WALNUT AVENUE
ORANGE, CA 92868-2232
800-854-7447
Fax: 800-660-6040
www.getzcorp.net
• Micheal Paulsen, President
Year Founded:
1971.
Products:
Score Board, Gameboards, Bullhorns,
Airhorns, Poms, Megaphones, Accessories,
Bags, Puncture Seal, Pine Tar, Water
Bottles, Spirit Items, Miscellaneous

GEXCO ENTERPRISES
PO BOX 6514
NORCO, CA 92860
951-372-4951
800-829-8222
Fax: 800-281-1748
www.gexcoenterprises.com
• Gex Coons, Chief Executive Officer
• Jeff Olsen, President
• Walt Sendziak, Sales Manager
Products:
Ankle Supports, Ball Pressurizers, Elbow
Supports, Gripping Aids, Head Bands, Knee
Supports, Shoe Repair, Shorts, Socks, Sun
Lotion, Wrist Bands; Racquet Sports - Ball
Pick-Up Baskets, Ball Pressurizers, Court
Equipment, Gripping Aids, Racquet Strings

GIACONA CONTAINER
121 INDUSTRIAL AVENUE
NEW ORLEANS, LA 70121
504-835-5465
800-299-4332
Fax: 504-835-5581
giacona@giacona.com
www.giacona.com
• Corrado Giacona, II, President
(504) 835-5465
• Gina Giacona Lynch, Vice President
Products:
Cups, Sculptured Drinkware,
Lanyards/Lasos, Lite-Up Products, Deli
Tubs & Pails, Shots, Insulated Drinkware,
Sipper Bottles, Pubware, Cup Accessories,
CD Music Medallions
Nature of Service:
Manufacturer, Designer and Custom Printer
Brands:
Giacona Container Brand

GILL ATHLETICS
601 MERCURY DRIVE
CHAMPAIGN, IL 61822-9648
212-367-8438
800-367-3090
Fax: 217-367-8440
sales@gillathletics.com
www.gillathletics.com
• Fred Dixon, National Sales Manager
(800) 637-3090
fdixon@gillathletics.com
• David Hodge, President
Products:
Athletic Field Construction Equipment,
Steeple Chase, Track Buring, Cages, Ball
Stop Systems, Goal Posts, Communications
Boxes, Sand Trap Forms, Soccer Goals,
Track & Field/Running Crossbars, Disci,
Hammers, Hurdles, Javelins, Landing Pits,
Shot Puts, Standards, Starting Blocks,
Take-Off Boards, Toe Boards, Vaulting
Boxes, Vaulting Poles; Strength & Training
Equipment.

GIRO SPORT DESIGN
380 ENCINAL STREET
SANTA CRUZ, CA 95060
831-420-4010
800-969-4476
Fax: 831-457-4444
www.giro.com
• Greg Shapleigh, SR. Vice President
• Rob Wesson, R&D Director
Products:
Bicycles, Helmets, Accessories

GLD PRODUCTS
S84W19093 ENTERPRISE DRIVE
MUSKEGO, WI 53150
262-679-8730
800-225-7593
Fax: 262-679-8730
info@gldgames.com
www.gldproducts.com
• Nick Voden, President
Nature of Service:
Wholesale and distributing in the sporting
goods industry.
Year Founded:
1981
Products:
Darts, Billiards, Table Games, Home Casino
Brands:
Fat Cat, Viper

GNC CORPORATION
300 6TH AVENUE
PITTSBURGH, PA 15222
412-288-4600
877-462-4700
Fax: 412-288-8379
www.gnc.com
• Jennifer Brinker, Senior Director of
Advertising
(412) 288-4688
• Mary Breunig, Sales and Promotions
Manager - Midwest
(847) 240-1301
• Mandy Kiggins, Sales and Promotions
Manager - Northeast
(412) 288-2028
• Jim Brooks, Sales and Promotions
Manager - Southern
(727) 572-6338
• Paul Katz, Sales and Promotions Manager
- Western
(949) 458-2700
• John Depcrymski, Advertising/Promotions
Manager
Exercise/Fitness Sponsor:
NPC, Mr. Pittsburgh.

GO FLOW, INC.
2323 CLEAR LAKE CITY BOULEVARD
SUITE 180-232
HOUSTON, TX 77062
281-480-7698
888-463-5699
Fax: 877-849-1406
go4flow@gmail.com
• Monica Barrera, President
Products:
Misting, Heating, Apparel, Bags, Flow
Drinking Device, Air Conditioners

GO FLY A KITE
21749 BAKER PARKWAY
WALNUT, CA 91789
877-875-2557
Products:
Single Line Kites, Diamonds, Dragons,
Flying Wonders, Frameless Flyers, Inflatable
Kites, Interactive Kites, Performance Kites,
Traction Kites, Wind Designs
Brands:
Joel Scholtz, Poldeltas, Superflyers,
Parastunters, Pro Series, Storm Series

GOAL SPORTING GOODS, INC.
37 INDUSTRIAL PARK ROAD
PO BOX 236
ESSEX, CT 6426
860-767-9112
800-334-4625
Fax: 860-767-9121
Goal@GoalSports.com
www.goalsports.com
• Andrew Turek, President
Products:
Soccer - Official Goals / Round, Official
Goals / Square, Official Unpainted Goals,
Recreational Goals, Official Indoor/Outdoor
Goals, Futsal Soccer/Handball Goals,
Patented Telescoping Design, Soccer
League Goals, Transportable/Adjustable
Goals, PowerGoal, Lacrosse, Field Hockey
Goals, Benches and Bleachers.
Year Founded:
1983

GOALSETTER SYSTEMS, INC.
1041 CORDOVA AVE
LYNNVILLE, IA 50153
641-594-4625
800-362-4625
Fax: 641-594-3343
www.goalsetter.com
• Teryl Ver Ploeg, Development & Marketing
• Faye Brand, Sales & Marketing Manager
• Bryan De Jong, Purchasing
• Andy Edwards, Dealer & Inside Sales,
Warranty
• Jennifer Morris, Shipping & Accounting
• Stefanie VanWyk, Graphic Design
• Wayne Woollums, Dealer & Inside Sales,
Scheels Account Manager
Products:
"Made in USA in ground and wall mounted
adjustable height basketball goal systems.
Additional products include: basketball rims,
basketball goals, backboards, wall mounted
basketball goals, basketball pole pads for
6-inch, 5-inch and 4-inch square poles and
other basektball accessories, collegiate
products.
Year Founded:
1991

GOLD CREST ENGRAVING
8847 WILBUR AVENUE
NORTHRIDGE, CA 91324
818-764-3231
888-423-9623
Fax: 818-765-8851
info@goldcrest1.com
www.blazercrests.com
• Bob Harvey, President
• Harvey Parker, Chief Executive Officer
• Steve Parker, EVP
Products:
Trophies, Awards - Bullion Blazer Crests,
Emblems, Jewelry, Plaques, Custom
Trophies.

**GOLD MEDAL RECREATIONAL
PRODUCTS**
20 BLUE MOUNTAIN AVENUE
ANNISTON, AL 36201
800-633-2354
Fax: 256-240-2509
www.gold-medal-rec.com
• Bob Jones, National Sales Manager
Products:
Golf - Indoor safe No Shag Golf Practice
System, Outdoor No Shag Golf Practice
Cage, Safe Stroke-Shaver Practice Net,
Stylish Indoor No Shag Practice Net,
Portable No Shag Indoor/Outdoor Practice
System, Gold Medal Tee Mat, Gold Medal
Commercial Tee Mat, Protective Golf
Netting, Turf Maintenance, Baseball Batting
Cage Nets, Baseball Field fence Screening,
Teammate Patented Baseball/Softball
Pitchback Practice System, Pitchback,
TeamMate Patented Tee Ball Practice Net,
Tennis - Tennis Nets, Tennis Posts, Tennis
Court Divider Netting, Net Court Tennis
Rebound Net, DeLuxe Tennis Rebound Net
and Frame, Volleyball - Invincible
Tournament Volleybal

GOLD'S GYM INTERNATIONAL, INC.
125 E JOHN CARPENTER FWY
SUITE 1300
IRVING, TX 75062

310-392-6004
Fax: 310-396-1065
www.goldsgym.com
• Mike Feinman, COO
• Gene LaMott, President / Chief Executive Officer
• Jim Snow, President
• Randy Schultz, Chief Financial Officer
Products:
Outerwear, Tanks, Pants, Tees, Shorts, Tops, Sports Bag, Fitness Accessories, Books, Caps and Accessories

GOLF & TENNIS HEADWEAR COMPANY
8315 W 20TH AVENUE
HIALEAH, FL 33014
305-558-4310
800-327-4287
Fax: 305-558-2093
• Bernard Maeroff, President/Owner
(305) 558-4310
bmaeroff@triangleheadwear.com
• Jim Miller, Finance Executive
Products:
General Sports Products: Hats, Caps, Visors; Golf: Hats, Caps, Towels & Umbrellas; Racquet Sports: Hats, Caps, Visors.

GOLF DESIGN USA
11591 MARKON DRIVE
GARDEN GROVE, CA 92841
800-854-6148
800-854-6148
Fax: 800-824-0699
mcheek@golfdesignusa.com
www.golfdesignproducts.com
• John R Tate, President
jrtate@golfdesignusa.com
• David Wung, VP Operations
• Jim Tate, VP Advertising
Products:
Ball Mark Repair Tools, golf accessories, custom packaging, putters, bag tags and Point of Purchase displays

GOLF GEAR INTERNATIONAL
5285 INDUSTRIAL DRIVE
HUNTINGTON BEACH, CA 92649
801-364-3885
Fax: 714-899-4284
• Peter H Pocklington, Chairman
• Don Anderson, Chief Executive Officer
• Michael Piraino, President / Chief Operating Officer / Ch
• Chris Holiday, Sales / Marketing SVP

GOLF SOLUTIONS WORLDWIDE
5070 CHANDUS WAY
TOBYHANNA, PA 18466
570-243-8555
855-251-6474
Fax: 570-243-8555
• Frank Kohuth, President
• Barbara Kohuth, VP
Products:
Drivng Range Products: Ball Pickers, Washers & Dispensers, Tees Dividers, Mats & Barrier Netting, Drivers, Balls, Tees & Baskets, Miniature Golf Products: Rubber Putters, Balls & Dispensers, Blacklight Miniature Golf Supplies, Carpet, Obstacles & Other Course Supplies, Carpet, Obstacles & Other Course Supplies, Score Cards, Pencils & Other Supplies, Course Equipment Supplies: Balls, Washers & Custom Tees, Litter Caddies, Flags,

Flagpoles, Pennant Makers, Prefabricated Driving Range Shelters, Paintball Target Range, Soft Swipe Spike Cleaner, Blacklight Miniature Golf Supplies, New Scorecard Stand

GOLF WAREHOUSE
8851 E 34TH STREET N
WICHITA, KS 67226
888-746-7849
888-838-5551
Fax: 316-838-5557
www.tgw.com
• Brian Jones, Manager
Products:
Golf Equipment (Clubs,Bags, Balls), Apparel/Shoes (Men's Apparel, Men'sBusiness Casual, Apres Golf, Women's Apparel, Headwear, Junior Apparel, Rainwear, Mens Shoes, Womens Shoes, Junior Shoes, Shoe Accessories, Lucky Size Sale), Accessories(Gloves, On Course Accessories, Electric/Pull Carts, Learning/Training, Rangefinders, GPS Systems, Travel Covers, Luggage, Sunglasses, Watches, Wood/Iron/Putter Gloves, Health Fitness, Bag Accessories, Shoes Accessories, Club Repair), Multimedia(Books, Videos, DVDs, Software), Home/Gift (Artwork, Home, Accessories, Office, Personal Items, Gift Ideas, Memorabilia, Golf Cards/Gift Wrap, Calendars), Specialty

GOLF-ART.COM, INC.
632 DANBURY ROAD
WILTON, CT 67897
203-438-8989
800-283-3344
Fax: 203-438-8959
www.golf-art.com
• Skip Rooney, Owner/President
(203) 438-8989
skiprooney@mac.com
• Scott Newton, General Manager
(203) 468-8989
• Warren Beardow,
(203) 515-8566
bradbsr@comcast.net
Year Founded:
1986.
Nature of Service:
Classic photos, limited edition lithographs, memorabilia, prints, awards, gifts, decors, originals, golf club decorations, tournament awards, auctions.

GOLFSMITH INTERNATIONAL, INC.
11000 N IH35
SHOWROOM
AUSTIN, TX 78753
512-837-5210
800-925-7709
Fax: 512-837-1245
www.golfgalaxy.com
• James D Thompson, President / Chief Executive Officer
• Virginia Bunte, VP / Chief Financial Officer
• Kiprian Miles, VP / Chief Information Officer
• Ginger Bunte, Chief Financial Officer
• Sue E. Gove, President
Products:
Golf and Tennis accessories, balls, clubs, custom club fitting, gifts, gift cards, gloves, grips, Golf Bags & Travel, Home & Office, Outlet, Personalized Gear, Practice and

Training, Pre-Owned Clubs, Shoes, Teams and Collegiate, Video & Books
Products:
Golf Clubs, Golf Bags, Golf Balls, Golf Gifts, Golf Shoes, Golf Apparel, Accessories, Custom Club Fitting, Gift Cards, Gloves, Grips, Personalized Gear
Brands:
Callaway, TaylorMade, Cleveland, Cobra, Odyssey, Adidas, Maxfli, Ashworth, Adams, Lynx, MacGregor, Nike, Zevo, Snake Eyes, Golfsmith, Killer Bee, GearForGolf, GiftsForGolf

GOLFWORKS
4820 JACKSONTOWN ROAD
PO BOX 3008
NEWARK, OH 43056-3008
740-323-0311
800-800-3290
Fax: 740-323-0311
golfworks@golfworks.com
www.golfworks.com
• Ralph Maltby, Founder
• Mark McCormick, Chief Executive Officer
Products:
Drivers, Iron Sets, Fairways and Hybrids, Wedges, Putters, Full Sets, Golf Balls, Golf Bags, Golf Buddies, Ladies Club & Sets, Left Hand, Junior Gear, Golf shoes, Accessories

GOOD STUFF CORPORATION
47-00 33RD STREET
LONG ISLAND CITY, NY 11101
718-937-3333
888-768-2094
Fax: 718-937-1037
contact@goodstuff.com
www.goodstuff.com
• Josh Parker, Vice President Sales
(719) 937-3333
jparker@goodstuff.com
• Eric Lashin, Sales Manager
(718) 937-3333
Nature of Service:
Wholesale
Year Founded:
1988
Products:
Balls, Baseball Caps, Candy Toys, Everyday Plush, Licensed Plush, Novelties, Novelty Hats, Pillows, Private Label, Sports Sets, Towels
Brands:
MLB, NBA, NFL, NHL, Looney Tunes, Sesame Street, Tootsie Roll, Shrek The Third, Hasbro Brands, Superman, Care Bears, Rock-N-Roll Bands.

GOODE SKI TECHNOLOGIES
2450 WALL AVENUE
OGDEN, UT 84401
801-621-2300
888-464-6633
Fax: 801-621-1434
goode@goode.com
www.goode.com
• David Goode, President
Products:
Water Skis, Water Ski Accessories, PowerShell Boots, Ruber Boots, Snow Skis, Snow Ski Gloves, Close-Outs

GOORIN BROS., INC.
1269 HOWARD STREET
SAN FRANCISCO, CA 94103

800-862-0100
Fax: 415-431-9199
info@goorin.com
www.goorin.com
• Cassel Goorin, Founder
Products:
Unique custom pieces with special
packaging including individual hat boxes,
exclusive satin tip stickers, hard-to-find
fabrics and linings

GOTCHA INTERNATIONAL
15255 ALTON PARKWAY
SUITE 300
IRVINE, CA 92618
949-221-0990
www.gotcha.com
• Michael Tomson, Founder
• Joel Cooper, Founder
Products:
Surf/Sport Shops, junior, girls, footwears,
beach towels, surfboard, wet suit and
accessory products

GOTTA HAVE IT GOLF INC
4231 SW 71ST AVENUE
MIAMI, FL 33155
305-665-7475
888-446-5757
Fax: 305-446-6276
www.gottahaveitgolf.com
Products:
Sports, Entertainment and Historical
collectibles

GRAFALLOY CORPORATION
8275 TOURNAMENT DRIVE
SUITE 200
MEMPHIS, TN 38125
800-355-8783
matt.savard@truetemper.com
www.grafalloy.com
• Graeme Horwood, VP
Products:
Manufacturer of state of the art carbon fiber
wood and iron golf shafts

GRAHAM EMBROIDERY COMPANY
5045 FRANKLIN AVENUE
WACO, TX 76710
888-996-8678
Fax: 888-996-8693
www.grahamembroidery.com
Products:
Embroidery and chenille emblems hand
crafted by artisans for more than 60 years.

GRALAB
900 DIMCO WAY
CENTERVILLE, OH 45458
937-433-7600
800-876-8353
Fax: 937-433-0520
www.gralab.com
• Mike Sieron, President / Chief Executive
Officer
(934) 433-7600
Products:
Ball knobs, push-pull-lift knobs, oval and
tapered knobs, tapered handles, fluted
torque knobs, knurled clamping knobs, three
and four pronged clamping knobs, T-handle
knobs.
Year Founded:
1924

GRAMAN USA, INC.
25 SPECTRUM POINTE
SUITE 403
LAKE FOREST, CA 92630
949-916-3300
800-429-0333
Fax: 949-916-3301
• Ken Chai, President
Products:
Golf Graphite Shafts

GRANADA PITCHING MACHINES
1557 N PENRITH PL
MERIDIAN, ID 83642
800-547-5032
Fax: 208-416-6598
granada@battingpractice.com
www.battingpractice.com
• Norman R. Bruce, President
Products:
Baseball Polyball, Pitching Machines;
Softball Polyball, Pitching Machines,
Electronic instantaneous
mixing/Programmable

GRANDOE CORPORATION
11 GRANDOE LANE
GLOVERSVILLE, NY 12078
518-725-8641
800-472-6363
Fax: 518-773-3388
• Eric Freidman, President
Products:
Gloves for the ski, golf, outdoor and fashion
industries.

GRAPHITE MASTER
3815 MEDFORD STREET
LOS ANGELES, CA 90063
323-261-1107
Fax: 323-261-4813
info@graphitemaster.com
www.graphitemaster.com
• Hank Johns, VP
(323) 261-1107
hjohns@graphitemaster.com
Products:
Fiberglass and composite fabrics for
surfboards, kayaks, boats, marine and sport
applications, industrial, aircraft, prototype,
hobbyists, and more

**GRAVEL GEAR SKATEBOARD
CLOTHING**
PO BOX 60127
SAINT PETERSBURG, FL 33784-0127
727-321-7027
877-752-8344
Fax: 727-321-2124
• Laura Mitchell, Marketing Director
(727) 560-0340
• Marty Martinez, Midwest Sales Manager
(214) 282-5877
dallasmarty@hotmail.com
• Stacey Foster, Art Director
(727) 321-7027
Products:
Full line of skateboarding clothing and
sporting goods accessories.

GREAT AMERICAN PRODUCTS
1661 S SEGUIN AVENUE
NEW BRAUNFELS, TX 78130
830-620-4400
800-341-4436
Fax: 830-620-8430

wally@gap1.com
www.gap1.com
• Roger Tuttle, Sales Representative
(830) 643-8007
rogerk@gap1.com
• Kevin T. Ulbert, VP of Sales
(830) 643-8024
kevin@gap1.com
• Wally Gullick, VP of Licensed Sports
(830) 643-8023
wally@gap1.com
• Ralph Gabriel, Director of Merchandising
(830) 643-8053
ralph@gap1.com
Products:
NFL, NBA, MLB, MLS, NHL licensed
drinkware with dimensional metal logos,
custom manufacturing.

GREENTECH
470 CLUBFIELD DRIVE
ROSWELL, GA 30075
804-363-5048
Fax: 770-587-2445
info@greentechitm.com
www.greentechitm.com
• Christopher P. Scott, Founder
• John Patton, VP
(770) 587-2522
info@greentechitm.com
Brands:
GreenTech Systems
Products:
Natural turf for athletic fields and gold tees.

GRIPWEIGHTS
4889 CULVER ROAD
ROCHESTER, NY 14622
585-314-5161
• Steve Nothnagle, Inventor
(585) 314-5161
Products:
Hand weights

GTM SPORTSWEAR
520 MCCALL ROAD
MANHATTAN, KS 66502
877-558-6510
800-377-8527
Fax: 877-908-7033
Customer_service@igtm.com
• Dave Dreiling, Owner
Customer_service@igtm.com
• Larry Harper, VP of Sales
Products:
Uniforms, warm-ups, performance wear,
t-shirts, shorts, trophies & awards.

GUESS? INC
1444 S ALAMEDA STREET
LOS ANGELES, CA 90021
213-765-3100
800-224-8377
Fax: 213-744-7838
www.guess.com
• Paul Marciano, Co-Founder
• Frederick G. Silny, SVP
Products:
Tees & Tanks, Sweaters, Wraps, Skirts,
Shorts, Capris, Pants, All Jeans, Jackets,
Guess Collection, Guess Swimwear,
accessories, Wedges, Dress, Sandals,
Athletic

GULBENKIAN SWIM, INC.
16 BEAVER BROOK ROAD
DANBURY, CT 6810
203-790-0800
800-431-2586
Fax: 203-791-1449
info@gulbenkianswim.com
www.gulbenkianswim.org
• Edward Gulbenkian, CEO
• Lauren Druckman, Sales Manager
Description:
Manufacture and distribution of cutting edge aquatic products for over 50 years.

GUMRUNNERS
333 WASHINGTON STREET
PO BOX 392
JERSEY CITY, NJ 7302
201-678-9300
Fax: 201-884-1026
info@gumrunners.com
www.gumrunners.com
• Kevin Gass, Co-Founder
kevin@gumrunners.com
• Laurence Molloy, Co-Founder / VP
lmolloy@joltgum.com
Products:
Energy gum and beverages.

GUSTAFSON MANUFACTURING COMPANY
101 44TH STREET
PO BOX 4335
CORPUS CHRISTI, TX 78469
361-882-4025
800-372-4653
Fax: 361-887-7396
gustafsonmfg@earthlink.net
www.lineking.com
• William H. Carney, President
Products:
Athletic field line marker, golf ball retriever

GUTERMAN INTERNATIONAL, INC.
603 PLEASANT STREET
PAXTON, MA 1612
508-852-8206
800-343-6096
Fax: 508-856-0632
www.gutermanintl.com
• Peter S. Guterman, President
Products:
Court Equipment & Ball Throwing Machines, Balls, Racquets, String, & Stringing Machines, Bags, Sports Nutrients, Footwear & Sport Socks, Badminton, Court Equipment, Platform, Squash, Tennis & Racquetball

H E HODGE COMPANY
5971 PARKWAY NORTH BLVD
SUITE 200B
CUMMING, GA 30040
770-205-8312
800-282-2248
Fax: 770-205-8318
www.hehodge.com
• Byron Ebersole, VP Sales
• Eric Bourrie, Sales Representative
• Jody Stage, Accounting Manager
• Ron Saren, Sales Representative
ronsaren@bellsouth.net
• Tucker Green, Project Manager
• Tony Johnson, Project Manager
• Jim Arthurs, President/CEO
Products:
Basketball goals, volleyball equipment,

bleachers, cabinets, lockers, library furniture, office furniture, handicap lifts, computer tables and cafeteria tables

H&B SPECIALIZED PRODUCTS
2629 30TH AVENUE S
MINNEAPOLIS, MN 55406
612-721-5031
800-328-4852
Fax: 952-374-6111
info@hbsponline.com
www.hbsponline.com
• Robert Johnston, President
info@hbsponline.com
• Sherry Ringberg, Chief Finanacial Officer
info@hbsponline.com
• Tom Lerick, General Manager / Construction
info@hbsponline.com
• Stephen Duncan, General Manager, Specialized Products
info@hbsponline.com
Products:
Athletic Equipment, Bleachers, Stadium Seating, Athletic Flooring Systems, Lockers, Athletic & Corridor, Auditorium Seating, Operable Walls, Panel Partitions & Accordion Doors

H & C HEADWARE/KC CAP
17145 MARGAY AVENUE
CARSON, CA 90746
310-324-5263
800-321-9888
Fax: 310-324-8763
www.kccaps.com
• Ken Feldman, Vice President - Sales
Products:
Mfg. Headwear: 6 panel, 5 panel, Beanies Winter Gear: Blankets, scarves Apparel: Polos, aprons

H&H ENTERPRISES
PO BOX 585
GRAND HAVEN, MI 49417
616-846-8972
800-878-7777
Fax: 616-846-1004
www.bleacherpeople.com
• John Heinritz, President
• Dwight Ralya, Operations Manager
• Jim Harding, Sales Manager
• Dan DeVries, Estimating
• Deb Vanderstelt, Administrative Assistant
• Richard Crace, Inspections
• Brad Heinritz, General Manager
Products:
Outdoor aluminum bleachers and grandstands
Brands:
Porter, Gill, Power Max and Pacer

H.H. BROWN SHOE COMPANY
124 W PUTNAM AVENUE
GREENWICH, CT 6830
203-661-2424
888-444-2769
Fax: 203-661-1818
bornservice@hhbrown.com
www.hhbrown.com
• Carmine Iandiorio, General Manager
• Scott Bohling, Chief Financial Officer
• Francis C. Rooney, Jr., Chairman of the Board
Products:
Manufactures and distributes premier work shoes and boots, rugged recreational

footwear and comfort casual shoes for men and women

H.S.T. INC.
8985 CRESTMAR POINT
SAN DIEGO, CA 92121-3222
858-689-0552
800-444-6075
Fax: 858-689-4094
www.hst-inc.com
• Randy M. Beck, Co-Founder / Chief Executive Officer
• Gary D. Beck, Co-Founder / Director
Products:
Golf Shafts, Golf Club Heads, Laser Machined Putter Inserts, Arrows, Speaker Baffles, Bicycle Tubes, Ice Axes, Tie Rods, Industrial Tubes, and more

HAAS-JORDAN COMPANY
1447 SUMMIT STREET
TOLEDO, OH 43604
419-243-2189
800-536-0283
Fax: 419-243-8401
info@haas-jordan.com
www.haas-jordan.com
• Thomas Waltz, President (F.J. Westcott Co.)
• Todd Blackmar, Sales / Marketing Director
• Janet Ritson, Senior Customer Service Representative
• Kelly Mondora, Operations Director
Products:
Golf Ball Retrievers, Umbrellas

HADAR ATHLETIC MFG. COMPANY
1515 N 11TH STREET
PO BOX 218
HUMBOLDT, IA 50548
515-332-5312
888-655-1606
Fax: 515-332-1448
general@hadarathletic.com
www.hadarathletic.com
• Mary Miner, President / Finance Director
(888) 655-1606
mary@hadarathletic.com
• Wayne Miner, General Manager
wayne@hadarathletic.com
Products:
Baseball, Basketball, Football, Rugby, Soccer, Softball, Tract & Field, Volleyball, Wrestling Equipments and Accessories. Gym & Playground Equipment. Matts

HAFER CASE
1018 MULCAHY
ROSENBERG, TX 77471
281-341-5070
800-990-8860
Fax: 281-239-7410
bhafer@hafercase.com
www.hafercase.com
Description:
Design, manufacture and sell ATA re-useable shipping and storage cases.

HAGGAR APPAREL COMPANY
11511 LUNA ROAD
DALLAS, TX 75234
214-352-8481
877-841-2219
Fax: 214-956-0216
www.haggar.com

• Micheal Stitt, CEO
• Frank Bracken, President / Chief
Operating Officer
• Dr. Michelle A. Haggar, MD
Products:
Men's & Women's Casual & Dress Wear

HALEX
45 RANICK ROAD
PO BOX 11357
HAUPPAUGE, NY 11788
631-234-2800
800-645-5190
Fax: 631-234-2948
www.regent-halex.com
Products:
Sporting Good Equipment

HAMILTON ATHLETIC
1605 STANLEY RUSS ROAD
CONWAY, AZ 72034
501-327-0706
Fax: 501-327-0706
www.hamiltonathletic.com
• Bobby Hamilton, Founder
Products:
Pocket Sports Bra

HAMMAKA
PO BOX 837
KAYSVILLE, UT 84037
877-375-4647
877-375-4647
Fax: 877-426-6252
www.hammaka.com
• Braydon Bailey, Chief Executive Officer
Products:
Chairs & Hammocks

HAMMETT COMPANY, J.L.
PO BOX 89057
BRAINTREE, MA 02185-9057
781-848-1000
800-955-2200
Fax: 888-262-1054
• Richmond Y Holden Jr, President
Products:
Arts & Crafts Materials, Teachers Helpers,
Teachers Resources, Bilingual Education
Materials, Children's Books, Classroom
Decor, Game Materials and Accessories,
Learning Toys, Office Supplies, Educational
Music & Video

HANA TIME
226 PUBLIC STREET
PROVIDENCE, RI 2905
800-362-9896
Fax: 401-330-4201
orders@logoart.com
www.logoart.com
Products:
Jewelry, Watch, Clocks & Binoculars

HANCO-M. HANDELSMAN COMPANY
3067 N ELSTON AVENUE
CHICAGO, IL 60618
773-303-1800
800-621-4454
Fax: 773-303-0012
www.hancotee.com
• Ana B. Monzon, Customer Service
(773) 303-1800
• Wilma McDaniel, Customer Service
(773) 303-1800

Products:
Aprons, Bandannas, Baseball Shirts, Bibs,
Bikinis, Blankets, Camouflage Sweat Shirts,
Camouflage T-Shirts, Camouflage Tank,
Caps, Ear Band, Football Shirts, Golf Shirts,
Hav-A-Dannas, Jackets, Jersey, Baseball
Apparel, Pants, Scarf, Scrubs, Shorts,
Smock, Soccer Shirts, Sports Bra, Sports
Shirts, Sweat Pants, Sweat Shirts, Sweat
Bands, Tank Tops, Ties, T-Shirts, Thermal
Underwear, Tote Bags, Towels, Turtleneck,
Underwear, Vests, Visors, Zipper Hoods
Brands:
MLB Apparel, Baseball Caps, NHL Apparel,
NFL Apparel & Caps

HANES
1000 EAST HANES MILL ROAD
WINSTON SALEM, NC 27105
800-503-6702
800-832-0594
contact_us@hanesbrands.com
www.hanes.com
• Rich Noll, Chairman/CEO
• Gerald W Evans, Jr., Chief Operating
Officer
• Richard D Moss, Chief Financial Officer
Products:
Undergarments, Socks, Ladys' Shoes &
Casualwear

HAR-TRU
2200 OLD IVY ROAD
SUITE 100
CHARLOTTESVILLE, VA 22903
877-442-7878
hartru.com
• David Morgen, President
Products:
Tennis Court Products, Tennis Windscreen,
Tennies Nets, Backboard & Rebound Units,
Tennis Ball Machines, Court Accessories,
Sports Nets, Batting Cages/Screens,
Basketball Goal Netting, Indoor and Outdoor
Field Covers, Golf Ball Barrier Netting,
Soccer Goal Netting
Brands:
Royale-Screen, Air Master, Mastershade,
Courtmaster, Tidyfit

HARBINGER
801 CHADBOURNE ROAD
SUITE 103
FAIRFIELD, CA 94534
707-438-7777
800-729-5954
Fax: 800-729-5947
sales@harbingerfitness.com
www.harbingerfitness.com
• David McCrane, President
• Michele Gaedke, Vice President
Product/Marketing
Nature of Service:
Wholesale supplier of fitness accessories.
Year Founded:
1988
Products:
Fitness Accessories & Training Aids
Brands:
Harbinger Fitness

HARBOR SPORTS GEAR
2810 CANON STREET
SAN DIEGO, CA 92106
619-222-5891
Fax: 619-222-5228

---

sales@harborsportsgear.com
www.harborsportsgear.com
• Pete Slaughter,
Products:
Sports & Travel Bags

HARDMAN COMPANY
11/12 TOKENHOUSE YARD
LONDON, ENGLAND EC2R 7AS
20-7929-3399
Fax: 20-7929-3377
hardmanco@aol.com
www.hardmanandco.com
• John Holmes, Chairman
• Roger Hardman, Founder
• Keith Hiscock, Chief Executive Officer
• Steve Clapham, Non-Executive Director
Products:
Athletic Equipment Bags

HARPER INDUSTRIES INC
136 CENTRAL AVENUE
CLARK, NJ 07066
732-815-3200
Fax: 620-896-7129
• Thomas S Friedland, President
• Laura Friedland, VP
Products:
General Sports Products - Shorts,
Sweatclothes, T-shirts, Warm-Up Suits;
Water Sports - Swimming Suits

HARRISON SPORTS, INC.
11247 ILEX AVENUE
PACOIMA, CA 91331
818-834-7600
800-347-4646
Fax: 818-834-7601
info@harrison.com
www.harrison.com
• Michael H Cheng, President
mike@harrison.com
• Eileen S. Lai, VP
eileen@harrison.com
• Chris Elson, Marketing Director
elson@harrison.com
Products:
Golf Shaft & Accessories

HARRISON-HOGE INDUSTRIES, INC.
19 N COLUMBIA STREET
PORT JEFFERSON STATION, NY 11777
631-473-7308
800-748-8066
Fax: 631-473-7398
www.seaeagle.com
• Navneet Syal, Export Manager
navneet@seaeagle.com
Products:
Training & Conditioning Exercise Machines,
Inflatable Boats with Floorboards

HARRISS & COVINGTON INC.
1250 HICKORY CHAPEL ROAD
PO BOX 1909
HIGH POINT, NC 27260
336-882-6811
Fax: 336-889-2412
customerservice@harrissandcov.com
www.harrissandcov.com
• Ned Covington, President/CEO
ncovington@harrissandcov.com
• Darrell Frye, Finance and Administration
VP
dfrye@harrissandcov.com
• Danny McNair, Manufacturing VP

dmcnair@harrissandcov.com
• Edward Harris Covington, President
Products:
Socks

HARTWELL SPORTS, INC.
97 WINFIELD CIRCLE
HARTWELL, GA 30643
706-856-4900
800-849-5555
Fax: 800-849-2121
customerservice@hartwell.com
www.hartwell.com/
• Rick Cesere, Chief Executive Officer
• Ray Titus, President
• Michael Snyder, Sales VP
• Ray Ferrell, VP Of Sales
Products:
Mens apparel, womens apparel, shirts,
outwear, athletic, companion styles, new
styles and closeouts

HARVEST VICTORY LTD
4809 E 49TH STREET
VERNON, CA 90058
323-588-9880
Fax: 323-588-9886
info@harvestvictoryusa.com
www.harvestvictoryusa.com
Products:
Backpack, sport bag, hiking backpack, duffle
bag, school bag, laptop backpack, computer
briefcase, traveling bag, waist bag & fanny
pack

HASCALL SPORTSWEAR, INC.
PO BOX 213
BOSTON, MA 02128-0002
617-567-4160
Fax: 617-567-4195
• Carl R Hascall, President
• Linda Hascall, VP
Products:
General Sports Products - Athletic
Jackets/Parkas

HATCHERS MANUFACTURING INC.
130 CONDOR STREET
E BOSTON, MA 2128
617-568-1262
800-225-6842
Fax: 617-567-9953
• John Vinton, Chief Executive Officer
• Peter Spillane, Production Manager
• Katie Dinsmore, Sales Manager
• Jennifer Clark, Marketing Manager
Products:
General Sports Products Athletic
Jackets/Parkas, Cheerleading Uniforms &
Accessories, Warm-Up Suits

HEAD DOWN TRAINERS.COM
888-422-2768
888-422-2768
Fax: 610-455-0495
www.headdowntrainers.com
• Tom O'Connell, Coach
• Andy Lopez, Head Baseball Coach
Products:
Training glasses

HEAD/PENN USA
306 S 45TH AVENUE
PHOENIX, AZ 85043
602-269-1492
800-289-7366

Fax: 602-484-0533
www.head.com
• Johan Eliasch, Chairman and Chief
Executive Officer, He
headinvestors@aol.com
• Ralf Bernhart, Chief Financial Officer
headinvestors@aol.com
• Klaus Hotter, EVP, Winter Sport Division
headinvestors@aol.com
• Georg Kroell, EVP, Licensing Division
Products:
Tennis, squash and racquetball racquets;
alpine skis and ski boots; snowboarding
boards, bindings and boots; accessories
and apparel; Alpine ski bindings; and Diving
equipment

HEADMASTER INC
3310 S FAIRVIEW STREET
SANTA ANA, CA 92704
714-556-5244
800-241-4442
Fax: 714-556-5243
• Johan Eliasch, Chairman
• Klaus Hotter, Executive Vice President
Products:
Caps, hats, visors, closeout products, bags,
beanies and boxers

HEART RATE, INC.
RATE INC. 1411 E WILSHIRE AVENUE
SANTA ANA, CA 92705
714-850-9716
800-237-2271
Fax: 714-850-9716
www.versaclimber.com
• Richard Charnitski, President
webmaster@heartrateinc.com
• Dan Charnitski, General Manager
webmaster@heartrateinc.com
• Kimberly DuBois, National Sales Manager
webmaster@heartrateinc.com
Brands:
Versaclimber: 108 H, 108 HP, 108 CM, 108
SM, 108 CMA, 108 SMA, 108 LX, 108 LXP,
108 ALX, 108 SRM and ExerVibe, Climber;
VersaPulley: Portable VersaPulley, Wall
Mount VersaPulley and ArmBlaster; 1-2-3
Heart Rate Monitors: Hand-Held, Equipment
Mounted, Wall Mounted and Floor Stand
Products:
Training Equipment

HEARTLINE FITNESS PRODUCTS, INC.
8041 CESSNA AVENUE
SUITE 200
GAITHERSBURG, MD 20879
301-921-0661
800-262-3348
Fax: 301-330-5479
sales@heartlinefitness.com
www.heartlinefitness.com
• Robert F Burgess Jr, President
(301) 921-0661
bob@heartlinefitness.com
• Jason Malecki, Territory Manager, DC/MD
(703) 493-9405
jason@heartlinefitness.com
• Joe Purpura, Territory Manager,
Pennsylvania
(412) 609-6507
joe@heartlinefitness.com
• Doug Meadows, Key Accounts Manager
Products:
CoreRack Training Series, Auxiliary Training
Series, Circuit Training Series, Free Weight
Essentials, Cardiovascular Training Series

HEAVY HANDS
140 FELL COURT
SUITE 120
HAUPPAUGE, NY 11788
631-300-3500
Fax: 631-300-3501
www.heavyhandsfitness.com
• Len Schwartz, Heavyhands Father
Products:
Heavyhands Walking Book / DVD / 2 lb
Combo Special, Heavyhands instructional
DVD, Special: DVD and 2-lb. Combo-Pac
Black Heavyhands, YogaHands Combo
Special, AeroAbs DVD, Heavyhands Walk
Plus DVD #45510, YogaHands DVD and
10-lb. Heavyhands

HEAVY HITTER INDUSTRIES, INC.
PO BOX 2344
VALLEY CENTER, CA 92082
760-749-7833
800-283-1717
Fax: 760-749-7829
info@heavyhitter.com
www.heavyhitter.com
• Margie Nybye, Owner/Vice President
(760) 749-7833
• Lance S Nybye, Marketing Director
info@heavyhitter.com
Products:
Baseball Bats
Year Founded:
1977

HEDMAN MANUFACTURING SOUTH
730 BRANCH DRIVE
ALPHARETTA, GA 30004
770-664-8880
562-921-0404
Fax: 770-664-6885
techsupport@hedman.com
www.hedman.com
• Robert Vandergriff, Chief Executive
Officer/Chairman
• Chris Vandergriff, President

HEDSTROM CORPORATION
3436 N KENNICOTT AVENUE
ARLINGTON HEIGHTS, IL 60004-7801
847-259-4468
800-323-5999
Fax: 847-259-4633
www.hedscape.com
• Michael Johnston, President
• Kenneth J Giacomino, EVP / Chief
Financial Officer
• Susan Meek, Corporate VP
Products:
Basketball - Balls-Vinyl; Football -
Balls-Vinyl; Racquet Sports - Platform
Tennis Equipment; Softball - Balls-Rubber;
Volleyball - Balls-Vinyl. Water Sports -
Personal Flotation; Gym Sets - Balls, Spring
Horses, Trampolines

HELLY HANSEN, (U.S.) INC.
4104 C STREET NE
SUITE 200
AUBURN, WA 98002
866-376-4183
800-435-5901
Fax: 253-852-1481
www.hellyhansen.com
• Ric Long, President
Products:
Men and Women: jackets, pants, thermal,
life base layer, footwear and off hill; Kids:

jackets, pants, suits and accessories;
Accessories: gloves, beanies and bags

HENRY-GRIFFITTS
827 W PRAIRIE AVE.
HAYDEN, ID 83835
208-772-8505
800-446-0036
Fax: 208-772-9632
www.henry-griffitts.com
• Billy McDonald, Board Chairman
• Randy Henry, Founder
• Jim Hofmeister, Chief Executive Officer
• Randall Henry, President
Products:
Model 82 Driver, RDH Fairway Series,
RDH3 irons, GreenBack$ irons, GLII, youth
woods, RHD Wedge Series, Fit2Aim Putter
System, Shafts, Accessories(sun hat, visor,
junior bag, towels, umbrella), golf bags and
travel bags, RDH Deep Fairway Woods,
TS-1 Irons, Evergreen Rescue Woods, RDH
460 Driver.
Nature of Service:
Dynamic Cutoms-Fit Golf Clubs

HENWAY SPORTS & SPECIALTIES, INC.
5693 W HOWARD STREET
NILES, IL 60714
847-588-3500
800-901-0700
Fax: 847-588-1218
• Steve Wilneff, President
• Myron Gruenberg, VP
• Laurence Wilneff, VP
• Evan Alston, Promotions VP
Products:
Corporate and event sales of authentic
sports game items and autographed items

HERE'S FRED GOLF COMPANY, INC.
2205 SAINT JOHNS BLUFF ROAD
JACKSONVILLE, FL 32246-2309
904-645-9790
800-874-7395
Fax: 904-645-9493
info@heresfredgolf.com
www.heresfredgolf.com
• Doughlas Kirchloff, President
(904) 645-9790
dougk@heresfredgolf.com
Products:
Caddy Bibs, Golf Flags, Embroidered
Screen Printing, Headcovers, Tees, Spikes,
Pencils, Golf Towels.

**HI STYLE LETTERED SPORTSWEAR
COMPANY, INC.**
HIGHWAY 65 N
CARROLLTON, MO 64633
660-542-3410
800-821-3610
Fax: 660-542-3467
• Jean Arp, President
• Troy A Howell, VP
Products:
Baseball - Uniforms; Basketball - Uniforms;
Field Hockey - Uniforms; Football -
Uniforms; Soccer - Uniforms; Softball -
Caps, Uniforms; Track & Field/Running -
Apparel-Track & Field; Volleyball - Uniforms

HI-TEC SPORTS USA INC.
4801 STODDARD ROAD
MODESTO, CA 95356

209-545-1111
800-521-1698
Fax: 209-545-2543
retailinfo@hi-tec.com
www.hi-tec.com
• Frank Van Wezel, Chairman / Founder
retailinfo@hi-tec.com
• Paul Brooks, Chief Executive Officer
info@hi-tec.com
Products:
Footwear for Outdoors, Golf, and Court
sport activities

HICKORY BRANDS, INC.
429 27TH STREET NW
PO BOX 429
HICKORY, NC 28601
828-322-2600
800-438-5777
Fax: 800-422-3279
www.hickorybrands.com
• Bob Bell, Chief Executive Officer
• Joseph Nissan, President
• Josh Higgins, Retail Sales Director
Products:
General Sports Products - Athletic Shoe
Cleaners, Waterproofers, Shoelaces,
Leather. Athletic Socks - Over the Calf, Mid
Calf, Anklet, Crew, Quarter, Cushion Sole
Yarns Used Cotton, Acrylic, Nylon,
Performance Fibers

HIGH 5 SPORTSWEAR
18300 CASCADE AVENUE
SUITE 200
SEATTLE, WA 98188
206-574-0123
800-222-4016
Fax: 206-574-0276
customercare@high5sportswear.com
www.high5sportswear.com
• Tom Mercer, Vice President, Sales &
Marketing
tom.mercer@high5sportswear.com
• John Moore, Owner
Products:
Uniforms, Bags, Jerseys, Shorts, and
Warm-Ups.

HIGH END SYSTEMS, INC
2105 GRACY FARMS LANE
AUSTIN, TX 78758
512-836-2242
800-890-8989
Fax: 512-837-5290
jeff.pelzl@barco.com
www.highend.com
• Merritt Belisle, Chairman
• Richard Belliveau, Co-Founder & Chief
Technology Officer
Year Founded:
1986.
Products:
Digital Lighting, Lighting Consoles, and
Automated Luminaires.

HIGH SIERRA SPORT COMPANY
880 CORPORATE WOODS PARKWAY
VERNON HILLS, IL 60061
847-913-1100
800-323-9590
Fax: 800-323-9591
customerservice@highsierrasport.com
www.hssc.com
• Hank Bernbaum, President

Products:
Outdoor Products - Backpacks, Outerwear,
Polar Fleece, Luggage, Duffels.

HILLERICH & BRADSBY COMPANY, INC.
800 W MAIN STREET
LOUISVILLE, KY 40202
877-775-8443
800-282-2287
Fax: 502-585-1179
www.slugger.com
• John A. Hillerich IV, President / Chief
Executive Officer
• Marty Archer, President, Louisville Slugger
Division
• Chuck Schupp, Sales / Promotions
Director, Pro Basebal
• Bill Williams, Public Relations / VP
Products:
Baseball - Bat Racks/Hangers, Bat Tape,
Bat Weights, Bats-Metal, Bats-Wood,
Gloves-Batter, Gloves-Catcher,
Gloves-Fielder, Gloves-First Base, Glove
Oil; Golf - Bags-For Clubs, Clubs-Iron Or
Wood Sets, Clubs-Utility, Headcovers; Ice
Hockey - Sticks;

HIND, INC.
191 SPRING STREET
PO BOX 9191
LEXINGTON, MA 2420
800-365-4933
Fax: 800-797-4248
www.hind.com
• Kenneth L. Minton, President
• Gregory W. Hind, Chairman
• Bruce W. Dixon, Chief Executive Officer
Products:
Cycling - Apparel; General Sports Products -
Bags-Equipment, Silk-screening, Tights,
Training Aids, Warm Global Suits;
Gymnastics - Apparel; Racquet Sports -
Apparel, Bags-Equipment; Track &
Field/Running - Apparel-Run/Jog, Apparel

HINES III
3653 REGENT BOULEVARD
SUITE 405
JACKSONVILLE, FL 32224
904-645-6500
877-645-6501
Fax: 904-645-6655
www.hinesiii.com
• Samuel J. Hines, VP Sales/Marketing
• Judith K. Hines, President
Products:
Benches, Planters and Receptacles for
athletic stadiums and other large facilities.

HIREV
364 WILLIAMSON ROAD
SUITE 301
MOORESVILLE, NC 28117
888-329-4658
Fax: 035-191-0243
www.hirev.com
Products:
Tribute Hoods, Replica Hoods, Computer
Kits, Absorbent Coasters, Computer Mice,
and Computer Mouse Pads with sports
logos and designs.

HL CORPORATION
PO BOX 3327
MANHATTAN BEACH, CA 90266

310-546-3652
800-457-7678
Fax: 310-372-7443
hlcorp7@hotmail.com
www.hlbadminton.com
• Dean Schoppe, President
hlcorp7@hotmail.com
• Dean Schoppe, President
hlcorp7@hotmail.com
Products:
Manufacturer and distributor of badminton
rackets and shuttlecoks.

HO SPORTS INC.
7926 BRACKEN PLACE SE
SNOQUALMIE, WA 98065
425-885-3505
800-938-4646
Fax: 425-867-5327
info@hosports.com
www.hosports.com
• Brian Gardner, VP
Products:
Skiing - Alpine - Snowboards; Water Sports
- Water Skis, Wet Suits; Knee Boards,
Vests, Gloves, Bags and Apparel.

HOCKEY COMPANY
3400 RAYMOND-LASNIER
SAINT-LAURENT, CANADA H4R 3L3
514-461-8000
Fax: 514-937-8276
• Robert A. Desrosiers, Finance and
Administration VP / Chief Fi
Products:
Skates, Sticks, Helmets and protective
equipment products.

HOGGAN HEALTH INDUSTRIES
8020 S 1300 W
PO BOX 488
WEST JORDAN, UT 84088
801-572-6500
800-678-7888
Fax: 801-572-6514
www.hogganhealth.com
• Lynn Hoggan, President
Products:
Training & Conditioning Exercise Machines.

HOIST FITNESS SYSTEMS
11900 COMMUNNITY ROAD
POWAY, CA 92064
858-578-7676
800-548-5438
Fax: 858-578-9558
webprodsupport@hoistfitness.com
www.hoistfitness.com
• Jeffrey Partrick, Chief Executive Officer
• Roger Cloyd, President / Founder
• Rany Webber, VP / Founder
• Mario Lopez, Product Support Manager
(858) 578-7676
mlopez@hoistfitness.com
• Jeremy Miller, International Sales/ Director
of Marketing
(858) 578-7676
jmiller@hoistfitness.com
Products:
Home Gyms, Freeweights, and HD-HS
Series.

HOLE IN NONE, INC.
1247 W WEBB AVENUE
BURLINGTON, NC 27217-1150

336-228-1758
800-444-8933
Fax: 336-228-0703
holeinnone@aol.com
• B. H. Bridgers Jr, President
• W O. Shaw, VP
Products:
Baseball - Socks, Stirrups; Basketball -
Socks; Football - Socks; General Sports
Products - Socks; Golf - Socks; Soccer -
Socks; Softball - Socks, Stirrups; Track &
Field/Running - Socks.

HOLLMAN, INC.
1825 WALNUT HILL LANE
SUITE 110
IRVING, TX 75038
972-815-4000
800-433-3630
Fax: 972-815-2921
www.hollman.com
• Joseph H. Hollman, President
• Vi Ho, Chief Financial Officer
• Sue Hwang, VP Locker Division
• Travis Hollman, VP
travish@hollman.com
Products:
Plastic Laminate and Wood Lockers,
Panelized Racquetball and Squash Courts,
and Athletic Glass Wall Systems.

HOLLOWAY SPORTSWEAR, INC.
2633 CAMPBELL ROAD
PO BOX 4489
SIDNEY, OH 45365
937-497-7575
800-331-5156
Fax: 937-497-8080
sales@hollowayusa.com
www.hollowayusa.com
• Mark S Vondenhuevel, President
Year Founded:
1964.
Products:
Teamwear & Warm-Ups, Sweatshirts,
Pullovers & Windshirts, Canyon Fleece,
Performance Wear/Shirts, Outerwear, Wool
Variety Jackets, Blankets and Bags

HOLMATRO RESCUE EQUIPMENT
505 MCCORMICK DRIVE
GLEN BURNIE, MD 21061
410-768-9662
Fax: 410-768-4878
• William Swayne, President
• Jaap G. Meijer, Chairman

HOLOUBEK, INC.
W238 N1800 ROCKWOOD DRIVE
WAUKESHA, WI 53188-1198
262-547-0500
800-886-4759
Fax: 262-547-6580
• Verne Holoubek, Founder
• Doug Konriff, National Sales Manager
Products:
General Sports Products - Apparel-Screen
Printed, Heat Transfers, Lettering, Transfer
Equipment.

HOOK & HACKLE
607 ANN STREET REAR
HOMESTEAD, PA 15120
412-476-8620
800-552-8342
Fax: 412-476-8639

ron@hookhack.com
www.hookhack.com
Description:
Fly fishing tackle, rod building and fly tying
specialists.

HORIZON FITNESS
1620 LANDMARK DRIVE
COTTAGE GROVE, WI 53527
800-962-3596
www.horizonfitness.com
• Bob Whip, President
• Bill Sotis, Executive Vice President Of
Sales
Products:
Commercial-quality treadmills, ellipticals and
stationary bicycles

HORNER FLOORING COMPANY
23400 HELLMAN DRIVE
PO BOX 380
DOLLAR BAY, MI 49922
906-482-1180
800-380-0119
Fax: 906-482-6115
info@hornerflooring.com
www.hornerflooring.com
• Doug Hamar, President / Chief Executive
Officer
• Mark Young, VP Operations
• Lew Bosco, Director Horner Study Center
Products:
Basketball, Racquetball, Squash, Volleyball
courts and flooring.

HORNUNG'S GOLF PRODUCTS, INC.
815 MORRIS STREET
FOND DU LAC, WI 54935
920-922-2640
800-323-3569
Fax: 920-922-4986
info@hornungs.com
www.hornungs.com
• Robert Hornung, President
(800) 323-3569
bob@hornungs.com
Products:
Golf Course Maintenance. Equipment,
Apparel, Bags-For Clubs, Balls,
Cleats/Spikes, Clubs-Iron Or Wood Sets,
Clubs-Putters, Clubs-Utility, Clubheads,
Club Grips, Club Shafts, Driving Nets/Mats,
Flag Poles, Gloves, Grip Waxes, Hats/Caps,
Headcovers, Mechani

HOT SAUCE HARRYS, INC.
1077 INNOVATION AVENUE
SUITE 109
NORTH PORT, FL 34289
214-902-8552
800-588-8979
Fax: 214-956-9885
info@HotSauceHarrys.com
www.hotsauceharrys.com
• Dianne Harris, Owner/President
• Bob Harris, Vice President
• Lauren Smith, Vice President
Products:
Distributor of Licensed gourmet products for
NCAA, MLB, OCC, Pedregon Racing Team,
Don Garlits, US Duck Stamps
Year Founded:
1995

HOT SOX, INC.
95 MADISON AVENUE
NEW YORK, NY 10016
212-957-2000
Fax: 212-957-1050
inquiries@hotsox.com
www.hotsox.com
• Gary Wolkowitz, President
• Ellie Gordon, Founder / Senior EVP
Products:
Baseball, Basketball, Soccer, Softball, Track
& Field/Running Socks.

HOYT USA
593 NORTH WRIGHT BROTHERS DRIVE
SALT LAKE CITY, UT 84116
801-363-2990
Fax: 801-537-1470
• Randy Walk, President
• Tom Driffill, Human Resource Manager
Products:
Archery - Bows, Accessories
Archery/Bow Hunting Sponsor:
Professional Archers and Bow Hunters;
Team Hoyt and Team Hoyt Recurve.

HT TENNIS
12932 SALEM AVENUE
PO BOX 569
HAGERSTOWN, MD 21741
301-739-3077
800-842-7878
Fax: 301-739-6104
• Richard N Funkhouser Jr, President
(301) 739-3077
Products:
Surfaces and Tennis Court Equipment,
Tennis Nets, Tennis Facility Products

HUBBELL LIGHTING, INC.
701 MILLENIUM BOULEVARD
SUITE L
GREENVILLE, SC 29607
864-678-1000
800-627-3377
Fax: 864-678-1065
info@hubbell.com
www.hubbelllighting.com
• Scott Muse, President
Products:
Boxes and Fittings, Cable/HOse
Management, COmmunication Solutions,
Enclosures, Hazardous Environment,
Industrial Controls, Lighting, Lighting
Controls/Sensors, Telecom and Data,
Testing Equipment, Utility Products and
Tools, Wiring Products and Workstations

HUDSON BOAT WORKS INC.
2519 FANSHAWE PARK ROAD E
LONDON, ON, CANADA N5X 4A1
519-473-9864
Fax: 519-473-2861
hbw@hudsonboatworks.com
www.hudsonboatworks.com
• Jack Coughlan, President/Founder
(519) 473-9864
hbw@hudsonboatworks.com
• Dallas Coughlan, Director
• Hugh Hudson, Sales Manager
(519) 473-9864
hugh@hudsonboatworks.com
• Jeff McIntyre, Sales and Service
(519) 473-9864
hbw@hudsonboatworks.com
• Glen Burston, Operations Manager
(519) 473-9864

glen@hudsonboatworks.com
• Chris McCully, Technical Services
Products:
High Performance Rowing Equipment:
Olympic class racing boats: 1x, 2-, 2x, 4-,
4+, 4x, 8+
Nature of Service:
Customer direct sales, service & delivery; on
site service at select regattas and events

HUFCOR, INC.
2101 KENNEDY ROAD
PO BOX 591
JANESVILLE, WI 53547-0591
608-756-1241
800-542-2371 Ext 214
Fax: 608-758-8253
info@hufcor.com
www.hufcor.com
• Jim Landherr, VP Manufacturing
Products:
Facilities - partial & full height, acoustically
rated operable walls/partitions

HUFFY BICYCLE COMPANY
6551 CENTERVILLE BUSINESS
PARKWAY
CENTERVILLE, OH 45459
937-865-2800
800-872-2453
Fax: 937-865-5470
service@huffy.com
www.huffybikes.com
• John A Muskovich, Chief Executive Officer
/ President
• Nancy A Michaud, Senior VP, General
Counsel - Secretary
• Robert L Diekman, Senior VP, Operations
- Logistics
• Steven D Lipton, Senior VP, Chief
Financial Officer
Products:
Bicycles

HUFFY SPORTS COMPANY
PO BOX 90015
BOWLING GREEN, KY 42103-7932
800-558-5234
Fax: 262-820-6757
service@huffysports.com
www.huffysports.com
• Randy Schickert, President / General
Manager
• Patrick Ehren, VP of Sales and Marketing
Products:
Basketball Systems, Sports balls, Youth
products, Pool Sports, Accessories

HUGGER-MUGGER YOGA PRODUCTS
1190 S PIONEER ROAD
SALT LAKE CITY, UT 84104
801-268-9642
800-473-4888
Fax: 801-268-2629
comments@huggermugger.com
www.huggermugger.com
• Sara Chambers, Founder
• Earl Loveless, Sales Manager
sales@huggermugger.com
Products:
Yoga, Pilates and Meditation Products.

HUMMER TURFGRASS SYSTEMS, INC.
1527 S COLEBROOK ROAD
MANHEIM, PA 17545

717-898-5000
800-872-8873
Fax: 717-898-0770
info@usaturf.com
www.usaturf.com
• Robert Hummer, President
bob@usaturf.com
• Matt Wimer, Director of Field Operations
matt@usaturf.com
Year Founded:
1968.
Products:
Natural grass sports surfaces
Description:
Producing high-quality natural grass playing
surfaces for over 40 years. Specializing in
design, build and construction of first class
athletic fields.

HUNTER MANUFACTURING GROUP INC
201 W LOUDON AVENUE
LEXINGTON, KY 40508
859-254-7573
800-237-1869
Fax: 859-254-7614
• Keith Spaulding, Sales Contact
(800) 237-1869
• Bill Brown, Director of Motorsports
bill.brown@huntermfg.com
• John Miller, Credit Manager
• Bob Johnson, Purchasing Manager
Products:
Bottoms Up Collection, Collector Glasses,
Collector Glasses, Glass Mugs, Stemware,
Coffee Mugs, Specialty Mugs, Sublimated
Coffee Mugs, Ceramic Steins, Stainless
Steel Collection, Collector Plates, Leaded
Crystal, Cooperstown and Heritage Jersey,
Player Products, Game Day Products,
Sporting Goods

HUSSEY SEATING COMPANY
38 DYER STREET EXTENSION
NORTH BERWICK, ME 3906
207-676-2271
800-341-0401
Fax: 207-676-2222
info@husseyseating.com
www.husseyseating.com
• Timothy Hussey, President / Chief
Executive Officer
Thussey@husseyseating.com
• Jack Rogers, Sales VP
jrogers@husseyseating.com
Products:
Auditorium Seating, Stadium Seating,
Telescopic Gym Seats, Telescopic
Platforms

HYDRA-RIB, INC.
PO BOX 90015
BOWLING GREEN, KY 42103-7932
800-558-5234
Fax: 262-820-6757
service@huffysports.com
Products:
Basketball Apparatus

HYDRO SPA
6101 N 45TH STREET
ST PETERSBURG, FL 33714
727-573-9611
877-237-8772
Fax: 727-525-5659
• Tammie Colombotti, National Sales
Coordinator
(727) 573-9611

tammie.colombotti@premiumleisure.com
• Bill Piontek, International Sales
Products:
Luxury Hot Tubs &Personal Hydrotherapy
products, Portable Spas & Backyard Leisure
products

HYP HATS, LTD
10 E 34TH STREET
6TH FLOOR
NEW YORK, NY 10016
212-684-7717
800-331-1181
Fax: 212-684-7589
sales@hyphats.com
• Howard Levy, President
howardl@hyponline.com
• Rob Weingard, Sales VP
• Mike Pascal, Chief Financial Officer and
VP Operations
• Rob Weingard, Accessories Businesses
Products:
Branded & Custom caps, headwear, cold
weather accessories, hair accessories &
hosiery.

ICON HEALTH & FITNESS, INC.
1500 S 1000 W
LOGAN, UT 84321
435-750-5000
866-506-9095
Fax: 435-750-3917
service@iconfitness.com
www.iconfitness.com
• David J Watterson, Chairman / Chief
Executive Officer
• Joseph Brough, Chief Operating Officer
• Fred Beck, Chief Financial Officer
• Matthew N Allen, President / Chief
Merchandising Officer
Products:
Home Fitness Equipment, Accessories,
Spas, Commercial Fitness Gear

IGLOO PRODUCTS CORPORATION
777 IGLOO ROAD
KATY, TX 77494
713-584-6800
800-364-5566
Fax: 713-935-7732
www.igloocoolers.com
• Jim Morley, President
• Eve Heim-Grubb, Marketing Director
Products:
Plastic ice chests and beverage coolers

IMAGE INNOVATIONS INC
432 PARK AVENUE
NEW YORK, NY 10016
518-589-9400
• Michael Preston, Chief Executive Officer /
Director
• Derick Sinclair, Chief Financial Officer /
Director
Services:
Sports-, entertainment- and cause-related
artwork and collectibles

IMPACT TRAINING SYSTEMS INC
8722 LANYARD COURT
RANCHO CUCAMONGA, CA 91730
909-946-1617
877-467-2285
Fax: 909-946-8370
• Richard Pumerantz, President

Products:
Training products

IMPERIAL HEADWEAR, INC.
ONE PARAMOUNT DRIVE
BOURBON, MO 65441
303-597-0206
800-950-1916
Fax: 800-755-5121
www.imperialsports.com
• John Bond, President
• Rick White, President/CEO
Products:
Full service line of men's and ladies
headwear. Custom art, embroidery, sun
protection and technical offering

IMPERIAL INTERNATIONAL
303 PATERSON PLANK ROAD
CARLSTADT, NJ 7072
201-288-9199
800-526-6261
Fax: 201-288-8990
inquiries@imperialusa.com
www.imperialusa.com
Products:
Billiard Tables, Pool Accessories, Furniture,
Cues & Cases

IMPEX INC
2801 S. TOWNE AVE.
POMONA, CA 91766
626-961-8686
800-999-8899
Fax: 626-961-9966
info@impex-fitness.com
www.impex-fitness.com
Products:
Home Fitness equipment

IN GLAS COMPANY
1060 CHERBOURG STREET
SHERBROOKE, QC, CANADA J1K 2N8
819-563-2202
800-563-2202
Fax: 819-566-1846
www.inglasco.com
• Denis Drolet, President / Chief Executive
Officer
• Marc-Andre Watson, Chief Financial
Officer
• Jose Cloutier, Information Technology
Director
Products:
Hockey souvenir pucks, sticks, and other
promotional items

INDUSTRIAL OPPORTUNITIES, INC.
2586 BUSINESS HIGHWAY 19
PO BOX 1649
ANDREWS, NC 28901
828-321-4754
Fax: 828-321-4784
info@elasticproducts.com
www.industrialopportunities.com
• Harry Baughn, Sales / Marketing Director
(828) 321-4754
• Tom O'Brien, President/CEO
ext 211
Products:
suspenders and sewn items
Brands:
Hold-Up Gang

**INFORMATION & DISPLAY SYSTEMS,
INC.**
10275 CENTURION COURT
JACKSONVILLE, FL 32256
904-645-8697
Fax: 904-645-8496
marketing@ids-sports.com
www.ids-sports.com

INLAND ASSOCIATES
18965 W 158TH STREET
OLATHE, KS 66062
913-764-7977
800-888-7800
Fax: 913-764-8721
www.inlandassoc.com
• Peggy Meader, President
Products:
Video displays.

INNOVA-CHAMPION DISCS INC
900 S DUPONT AVE
ONTARIO, CA 91761
909-481-6266
800-408-8449
Fax: 909-481-6263
info@innovadiscs.com
www.innovadiscs.com
Products:
Golf Discs & Accessories

**INNOVATIVE MARKETING
CONSULTANTS**
4282 SHORELINE DRIVE
SPRING PARK, MN 55384
952-252-1254
877-674-8206
Fax: 952-417-8146
info@imcsuccess.com
www.imcsuccess.com
• Shane Erickson, President/Chief Executive
Officer
• Paul Higgins, Operations Manager
• Paul Yahnke, National Sales Manager
• Adam Tschida, Senior Account Executive
adam@imcsuccess.com
• Robert Ed, Marketing Specialist
robert@imcsuccess.com
Nature of Services:
Innovative Marketing Consultants
manufactures on-premise promotional
marketing products for a variety of industries
including Sports Marketing (Sports Beads),
the Retail and Beverage Markets, and
Casinos.

**INNOVATIVE SPORTS
TECHNOLOGIES/IST**
819 18TH STREET
PO BOX 1311
BEDFORD, IN 47421
800-505-2319
Fax: 812-277-0315
Products:
Golf Shafts

INNOVO GROUP INC.
5901 S EASTERN AVENUE
SUITE 1560
COMMERCE, CA 90040
310-786-1789
800-627-2621
Fax: 310-786-1792
• Samuel J Furrow, Chairman of the Board
• Marc Crossman, Interim Chief Executive

Officer / Presid
• Kelly Hoffman, Director
Products:
Private Label and Branded Apparels &
Accessories

INSPORT INTERNATIONAL, INC.
2929 E COMMERCIAL BOULEVARD #205
FORT LAUDERDALE, FL 33308
800-652-5200
• Eric Merk, President
Products:
Cycling, Track & Field/Running, Training &
Conditioning Apparel and Accessories

INSTA GRAPHIC SYSTEMS
13925 E 166TH STREET
CERRITOS, CA 90703
562-404-3000
800-421-6971
Fax: 562-404-3010
sales@instagraph.com
www.instagraph.com
• Janet Wells, President/Chief Executive
Officer
info@instagraph.com
• Larry Johnson, Vice President-Engineering
info@instagraph.com
Nature of Service:
A leader in heat transfer and machine
technology for 48 years designs, develops,
manufactures and sells innovative custom
heat transfers and quality machines
worldwide. Applications in various
industries, including sports apparel and
supplies.
Year Founded:
1959
Products:
Heat seal machines, custom transfers, die
cut letters and numbers

**INSTA-BENCH/CARRY GEAR
SOLUTIONS**
2125 WESTERN AVENUE
SUITE 300
SEATTLE, WA 98121
206-957-6801
Fax: 206-441-4464
info@carrygear.com
www.carrygear.com

INTERKAL INC.
5981 E CORK STREET
KALAMAZOO, MI 49048
269-349-1521
Fax: 269-349-6530
sales@interkal.com
www.interkal.com
• Kevin Hemler, Vice President - Sales and
Marketing
Products:
Gymnasiums, Multipurpose Facilities,
Stadiums & Arenas Seating Systems &
Accessories

**INTERNATIONAL MASCOT
CORPORATION**
125 ROYAL WOODS COURT
SUITE 145
TURKER, GA 30084
770-723-9000
800-834-8588
Fax: 770-723-9007
imcservice@imcmascots.com
www.imcmascots.com

• Jonathan Schloss, Director of US
Operations
jschloss@imcmascots.com
• Joel Leveille, Marketing Director
• David Swangel, Operations Manager
Products:
Costumes, Mascot & Accessories

INTERNATIONAL MICROTECH, INC.
642 ROUTE 109
LINDENHURST, NY 11757
850-897-8666
800-327-1033
Fax: 305-599-0936
• Frank Bianco, President
• J Zabala, Marketing / Sales Manager
Products:
Pet Traning Tools and Gadgets; Pet
Grooming Kit

**INTERNATIONAL SEAWAY TRADING
CORPORATION**
7100 W CAMINO REAL
SUITE 110
BOCA RATON, FL 33433-5510
561-447-4433
Fax: 561-447-4488
seaway222@aol.com
• Larry Satz, SVP
lsatz@aol.com
• Harvey K. Girdy, CEO
• Peter Grzybowski, CFO/VP
Products:
Footware

INTERNATIONAL SPORTS TIMING
3286 KENTLAND COURT SE
GRAND RAPIDS, MI 49548
616-247-1033
800-835-2611
Fax: 616-247-0086
info@istime.com
www.istime.com
• Richard Farnsworth, President
(800) 835-2611
• Jane Farnsworth, Director Marketing
(800) 835-2611
Products:
Scoreboards, Software and Timing Devices
(Swimming & Water Polo).
Year Founded:
1982

IPANEMA WEAR
SAN DIEGO, CA
760-576-6500
Fax: 858-759-5016
• Patricia Martins, Founder, Designer,
President
Products:
Swimming/Diving Apparels

IRA K. MEDALS & AWARDS INC.
4584 AUSTIN BOULEVARD
ISLAND PARK, NY 11558-1695
516-431-2131
Fax: 516-431-2412
• Ira Kartiganer, President
Products:
Trophies, Awards Components, Crests,
Cups, Emblems, Jewelry, Medals, Patches,
Plaques, Ribbons, Trophies.

IRON GLOVES INC
15863 N GREENWAY HAYDEN LOOP
SUITE 117
SCOTTSDALE, AZ 85260
480-905-1109
Fax: 480-905-1112
info@irongloves.com
www.irongloves.com
• Dominick Cirone, President
lsatz@aol.com
Products:
Golf Club Covers, Iron Covers, Putter
Covers, Insulated Water Bottle Holders,
Licensed Beverage holders, Soft Sided
Cooler Bags, Baseball Bat Warmers and
Protectors, complete line of Custom Logo
Neoprene
Nature of Services:
Sporting Goods Designer and Manufacturer
Brands:
Iron Gloves, The Gripp, Gravity Gripp, Putter
Gloves, Therasqueeze, the Bottle Glove,
Tag-A-Longs, Magnacover

IRONMAN PROPERTIES
2701 N ROCKY POINT DRIVE
SUITE 1250
TAMPA, FL 33607
813-868-5940
866-859-3343
Fax: 813-868-5930
bill.potts@ironman.com
www.ironman.com
• Bill Potts, Global Licensing
Services:
Identifies, develops, manufactures and sells
Ironman-Triathlon-branded product.

IRONMAN WETSUITS
3131 WESTERN AVENUE, SUITE 316
SEATTLE, WA 98121
206-632-1994

IRWIN SEATING COMPANY
3251 FRUIT RIDGE AVENUE NW
PO BOX 2429
GRAND RAPIDS, MI 49544
616-574-7400
866-464-7946
Fax: 616-574-7411
sales@irwinseating.com
www.irwinseating.com
• Bruce Cohen, Vice President,
Sales/Marketing
(616) 574-7306
cohenb@irwinseating.com
Products:
Manufacturer of fixed seating and telescopic
bleachers- fixed audience seating for
stadiums and arenas.
Year Founded:
1908

IRWIN SPORTS
43 HANNA AVENUE
TORONTO, ON, CANADA M6K 1X6
800-268-1732
Fax: 800-268-6399
• George Irwin, President
• Greg Anger, Marketing Director
• Dave Callon, Sales Manager
• Susan Pryde, Human Resources Director
Products:
Baseball Bags-Equipment, Balls,
Bats-Metal, Bats-Wood, Batter's Gloves,
Batting Helmets, Catcher's Helmet,
Gloves-Catcher, Gloves-Fielder,

Gloves-First Base, Glove Oil, Masks, Nets, Pine-Tar Cloths, Protective-Catcher, Protective-Umpire, Umpire Indicators

ITECH SPORT PRODUCTS, INC.
18103 TRANSCANADA HIGHWAY
KIRKLAND, QUEBEC, CANADA H9J 3Z4
514-697-9900
• Robin Burns, President
• Dave Smallwood, Director United States
Sales VP
Services:
Manufacturer of Hockey equipment bags, helmets, gloves, sticks, goalie equipment and accessories.

IVANKO BARBELL COMPANY
PO BOX 6224
RENO, NV 89513
775-624-0177
800-759-6399
Fax: 775-624-0188
info@ivanko.com
www.ivanko.com
• Tom I Lincir, President
• Chet Groskreutz, Sales / Marketing VP
Products:
Training and Conditioning Barbells, Dumbells, Free Weights, Olympic plates, Weightlifting bars, Plates, Collars, Benches, and Accessories

J&B SALES, INC.
2307 ROOSEVELT DRIVE
ARLINGTON, TX 76016
817-461-5421
Fax: 817-459-0501
• Jim Reeder, President
Products:
Baseball Bags-Equipment, Bat Tape, Bats-Metal, Gloves-Batter, Gloves-Catcher, Gloves-Fielder, Gloves-First Base, Masks, Protective-Catcher, Shoes-Metal Cleats, Shoes-Rubber Cleats, Socks, Umpire Indicators; Basketball - Backboards, Hoops, Nets, Shoes

JACKSTER COMPANY
670 SURF AVENUE
STRATFORD, CT 6615
203-378-4023
800-225-8370
Fax: 203-378-4605
www.jacksterinc.com
• Jack Kramer, President
Products:
General Sports Products - Athletic Socks, Belts, Gloves, Hats/Caps, Suspenders

JACQUES MORET
1411 BROADWAY
8TH FLOOR
NEW YORK, NY 10018
212-354-2400
800-441-1999
Fax: 212-354-1052
info@moret.com
www.moret.com
• Joseph Harary, President
• Ron Mangini, SVP
• Irwin Luxembourg, Chief Finance Officer
• Gary D Herwitz, EVP
Products:
General sports apparel for athletes and fans.

JAMMIN APPAREL
335 TECHNOLOGY DRIVE
ROCKY MOUNT, VA 24151
540-484-4600
800-852-6646
Fax: 540-484-4601
customercare@jammin.com
www.jammin.com
• Mark Grinde, Partner / Administration
• Brian Grinde, Partner / Production
• Steve Weil, Partner / Sales
Products:
General Sports Products - Accessories, Sport Shirts, Warm Up Suits, Windshirts, Softball Uniforms, Hockey Jerseys, Arctic Fleece, Jackets, Parkas, Swim Parkas, Caps, Bags, and Accessories

JANTZEN, INC.
3000 NW 107TH AVENUE
MIAMI, FL 33172
800-626-0215
www.jantzen.com
• Carl Jantzen, Founder
• John Zehntbauer, Founder
Products:
Swimwear, resortwear, beachwear, accessories and footwear.

JAYPRO SPORTS, LLC
976 HARTFORD TURNPIKE
PO BOX 400
WATERFORD, CT 6385
860-447-3001
800-243-0533
Fax: 860-444-1779
info@jaypro.com
www.jaypro.com
• Robert Ferrara, President
• Bill Wild, CEO
Products:
Archery - Nets, Target Stands; Baseball - Batting Tees, Cages/Backstops, First Base Safety Protectors, Infield Drag Mats, Nets, Pitcher Safety Protectors; Basketball - Backboards, Hoops, Nets, Standards; Facilities - Benches, Divider Nets, Wall Mats

JB SPORTS & HAIRDRESSING
701 BILTMORE STREET
SAN LEANDRO, CA 94577
510-205-3628
Fax: 510-568-3688
www.88288.com
• Rayn Li, Contact
(510) 205-3628
Products:
Manufacturers of skateboard, inline skate, ice skate, roller skates, agressive skates, inline speed skates, kid's skates, scooters, inline hockey skates, skateboard set, high frequency heat transfer paper, skateboard bags, inline skate bag, Mountain Bicycles, Multi-functional Folding Bicycles, and related protective products including helmets, knee and elbow pads, and wrist guards.

JEBCO
125 ADVANCED DRIVE
SPRINGBORO, OH 45066
937-746-2268
800-635-3226
Fax: 800-701-9487
• John Cole, President
Products:
Manufacturer of licensed collectible

Motorsports wall clocks, wall thermometers, desk clocks, custom clocks, custom plaques and awards.

JEEP ELECTRONICS
80-A E JEFRYN BOULEVARD
DEER PARK, NY 11729
631-389-5642
800-357-8785
Fax: 631-242-6177
www.kngamerica.com
• Kash Gobindram, President / Chief Executive Officer
Products:
Novelty and collectible telephones, personal audio electronics, universal remotes, and home decor products.

JEFF HAMILTON COLLECTION
2340 E OLYMPIC BOULEVARD
LOS ANGELES, CA 90021
213-747-1818
Fax: 213-747-4343
jhjackets@aol.com
www.jeffhamilton.com
Products:
Men's and Boy's Collectible Clothing.

JEFFERIES SOCKS
2203 TUCKER STREET
BURLINGTON, NC 27215
336-226-7315
800-334-6831
Fax: 800-727-5502
www.jefferiessocks.com
• Kenneth Hamby, President
Products:
Infants Socks; Boys Socks; Girls Socks; Ladies' socks

JEM SPORTSWEAR INC.
459 PARK AVENUE
SAN FERNANDO, CA 91340
818-365-9361
Fax: 818-361-8055
info@jemsportswear.com
www.jemsportswear.com
• Randi Kagan, VP, Licensing and Marketing
Products:
Golf Apparel; Gymnastics Apparel; Racquet Sports Apparel; Track & Field/Running Apparel-Run/Jog; Water Sports Apparel.

JERSEY NAPS
1954 AIRPORT ROAD
SUITE 207
ATLANTA, GA 30341
678-720-0702
Fax: 678-720-0704
www.JerseyNaps.com
• William Katz, Chief Marketing Officer
Nature of Services:
Jersey Naps are high quality napkins folded into a patented shape that replicates a sports jersey, entertainment character, brand icon or seasonal costume.

JH DESIGN GROUP
940 W WASHINGTON BOULEVARD
LOS ANGELES, CA 90015
213-747-5700
800-353-1010
Fax: 213-747-3648
www.jhdesigngroup.com

• Albert Elkouby, Chief Executive Officer
albert@jhdesigngroup.net
• Jacob Nisim, General Manager
jacob@jhdesigngroup.net
• Vered Nisim, Vice President of Marketing
• Omer Hadad, Sports Division
• Charles Alloun, Controller
Products:
Reversible wool and leather jacket with embroidered logos; Kids twill racing style jacket with embroidered logos; Adults twill racing style jacket with embroidered logos; Leather racing jacket with embroidered logos.

JIFFY LINE STRIPERS
611 KNIGHTSBRIDGE ROAD
PO BOX 35
WAUNAKEE, WI 53597
608-849-4770
800-844-5002
Fax: 608-849-7456
• Peder Bach, President
• Geri Carlson, Vice President
Description:
Manufacturer of line painting equipment for athletic fields; manufacturer of athletic field paints.
Year Founded:
1961

JJ ACCESSORIES
7057 MARCELLE STREET
PARAMOUNT, CA 90723
562-630-6310
Fax: 562-630-6343
sales@jjshoelace.com
www.jjshoelace.com
Products:
Shoelaces; Accessories

JKP SPORTS
11885 SW HERMAN RD.
TUALATIN, OR 97062
503-692-1635
800-547-6843
Fax: 503-691-1100
info@jugssports.com
www.jugssports.com
• Butch Paulson, President
• John Paulson, Service Manager
• Ed Dechenne, Sales Manager
• Curtis Kawasaki, Controller
Products:
Pitching Machines; Protective Screens; Radar Guns; Feeders; Batting Cage Nets; Frames; Baseballs & Softballs; Packages

JOE RAPP, INC.
835 LONGVIEW AVENUE
N WOODMERE, NY 11581
516-792-0230
Fax: 516-792-0131
joerappinc@aol.com
www.therapper.com
• Joe Rapp, President/Owner
joerappinc@aol.com
Nature of Services:
Stadium hand clapper, concession and promotional products.
Year Founded:
1992
Brands:
The Rapper
Description:
Producer of THE RAPPER and THE

RAPPER THUNDERSTIX, two of the best spirit products produced today.

JOFA HOCKEY/THE HOCKEY COMPANY
3400 RAYMOND-LASNIER
SUITE 800
MONTREAL(QUEBEC), CANADA H4R 3L3
514-461-8000
Fax: 514-937-8276
• Robert A. Desrosiers, Finance and Administration VP / Chief Fi
Products:
Skates, Sticks, Helmets and protective equipment products.

JOG-A-LITE, INC.
18 HIGH STREET
PO BOX 149
SILVER LAKE, NH 3875
603-367-4741
800-258-8974
Fax: 603-367-8098
www.jogalite.com
• Barclay Huntington, Founder
• Peter Lang, President
Products:
New Reflective Safety Vest; Reflective Safety Vest; Arm & Leg Bands; Reflective Stick-Ons; Lights & Sound; Pet Savers; Gift Packs; Runner's Log

JOHN R. GREEN COMPANY INC., OLD MASTER PUTTERS
411 W 6TH STREET
COVINGTON, KY 41011
859-431-5568
800-354-9737
Fax: 859-431-0266
www.johnrgreenco.com
• Tom Green, President
Products:
Supplies; Teaching Materials; Furnitures

JOHNSON & JOHNSON CONSUMER PRODUCTS INC.
ONE JOHNSON & JOHNSON PLAZA
NEW BRUNSWICK, NJ 8933
732-524-0400
Fax: 908-874-1123
www.jnj.com
• Mary Sue Coleman, President
• James G. Cullen, Chief Operating Officer
• Alex G. Gorsky, Chairman
Products:
Sports and nutritional supplements.

JOHNSON OUTDOORS
555 MAIN STREET
RACINE, WI 53403
262-631-6600
800-227-6433
Fax: 262-631-6601
corporate@johnsonoutdoors.com
www.johnsonoutdoors.com
• Helen Johnson-Leipold, Chairman / Chief Executive Officer
• Cynthia Georgeson, VP Worldwide Communications
(262) 631-6600
cgeorgeson@johnsonoutdoors.com
• David Johnson, VP Chief Financial Officer
Products:
Outdoor Equipment; Watercraft; Marine Electronics; Diving; JOI Boilerplate.
Nature of Services:
Johnson Outdoors is a global outdoor

recreation company that turns ideas into adventure with innovative, products. The company designs, manufactures and markets a portfolio of consumer-preferred brands across four categories: Watercraft, Marine Electronics, Diving and Outdoor Equipment. Johnson Outdoors' familiar brands include among others: Old Town Canoes and Kayaks; Ocean Kayak and Necky Kayaks; Lendal Paddles; Carlisle and Extrasport Padding Accessories; Minn Kora Motors; Cannon Downriggers; Humminbird Fishfinders; Geonax Chartplotters; SCUBAPRO UWATEC and Seemann Dive Equipment; Silva Compasses; Tech O Digital Instruments; and Eureka Ten

JOHNSON WORLDWIDE ASSOCIATES/CAMPING DIVISION
1326 WILLOW ROAD
STURTEVANT, WI 53177
262-884-1500
Fax: 262-884-1703
www.jwa.com
• Helen Johnson-Leipold, Chairman / Chief Executive Officer
hjohnson@johnsonoutdoors.com
• Terry E. London, Board of Director
Products:
Outdoor Equipment; Watercraft; Motors; Fishing; Diving

JOHNSONITE
16910 MUNN ROAD
CHAGRIN FALLS, OH 44023
440-543-8916
800-899-8916
Fax: 440-543-8920
info@johnsonite.com
www.johnsonite.com
• Laurey Banker, Director of Product Management
Products:
Triumph Skate & Spike-Resistant Tile; Replay Skate & Spike-Resistant Recycled Sports Flooring; Inertia Sport Flooring Tiles

JOSLIN DISPLAYS INC
10 UPTON DRIVE # 8
WILMINGTON, MA 1887
978-284-6660
800-325-1030
Fax: 978-658-4263
sales@joslindisplays.net
www.joslindisplays.net
Products:
Slatwall; Gridwall; Mannequins; Hangers; Showcases; Wall Hardware; Store Supplies; Jewelry Displays; Plexi Displays; Shoe Displays; Wood Fixtures; Packaging; Racks; Signholders

JOY ENTERPRISES/FURY CUTLERY
1862 MLK JR BOULEVARD
PORT COMMERCE CENTER III
WEST PALM BEACH, FL 33404
561-863-3205
800-500-3879
Fax: 561-863-3277
mail@joyenterprises.com
www.joy-247.com
Products:
Folding Knives; Hunting Knives; Collector's Knives

JTD ENTERPRISES INC
4 WALNUT STREET
CHILTON, WI 53014
920-849-2900
888-595-5833
Fax: 586-427-1329
jtdenterprises@frontier.com
www.jtdent.com
Products:
Flagpoles; Search N' Rescue Retrievers

JUGS COMPANY
11885 SW HERMAN RD.
PO BOX 365
TUALATIN, OR 97062
503-692-1635
800-547-6843
Fax: 503-691-1100
info@thejugscompany.com
• Steve Candello, Marketing Director
stevec@jkpsports.com
Products:
Pitching Machines, Accessories, baseballs, softballs, protective screen, nets, batting cage frames, ball feeders, tennis ball, spin tennis machine, spin remote tennis machine, field hockey machine, radar equipment, football passing machine, and soccer machine

JUGS INC/JKP SPORTS
11885 SW HERMAN RD.
PO BOX 365
TUALATIN, OR 97062
503-692-1635
800-547-6843
Fax: 503-691-1100
jugsusa@aol.com
www.jugssports.com
Products:
Pitching Machines; Protective Screens; Radar Guns; Feeders; Batting Cage Nets; Frames; Baseballs & Softballs; Packages

JUMP ROPE TECH INC
PO BOX 5238
WOODBRIDGE, VA 22194
703-580-6302
800-953-5867
Fax: 703-680-2826
Jump4Speed@aol.com
www.jumpropetech.com
• Buddy Lee, President/CEO
• Elvis Malcolm, Technical Advisor
Products:
Patented Swivel Bearing Jump Ropes; Jump Rope Sets; Total Fit Travel Gym; Olympic Kids Gym Sets; Training Aids - Video/Audio; Double Dutch, Beaded and Long Ropes; Toy Ropes with Counter, Music, Lights; Jump Rope Toys - Animal Characters

JUMPSPORT
2055 S 7TH STREET
SUITE A
SAN JOSE, CA 95112
408-213-2551
888-567-5867
Fax: 408-213-2930
www.jumpsport.com
• Mark Publicover, Product Safety Inventor/CEO
(408) 866-3120
Products:
Trampolines; Safety Nets; Rebounders

K-SWISS INC.
31248 OAKCREST DRIVE
WESTLAKE VILLAGE, CA 91361
818-706-5100
800-938-8000
Fax: 818-706-5390
Kscs@k-swiss.com
www.kswiss.com
• Steven Nichols, President/Chairman
Kscs@k-swiss.com
• Preston Davis, VP Sales
Kscs@k-swiss.com
• Tom Harrison, SVP Sales / Georgia
Kscs@k-swiss.com
• George Powlick, VP Finance / Chief Financial Officer
Kscs@k-swiss.com
Products:
Shoes

K2 INC.
4201 6TH AVENUE S
SEATTLE, WA 98108
800-426-1617
info@k2sports.com
www.k2sports.com
• Richard J. Heckmann, Chairman / Chief Executive Officer
• J Wa Merek, EVP / Chief Operating Officer
• John J. Rangel, SVP
• Anthony W. DeRocco, President
Products:
Equipment and supplies for skiing, snowboarding, skating and biking

KAEPA USA, INC.
9050 AUTOBAHN DRIVE
SUITE 500
DALLAS, TX 75237
972-296-7300
800-880-9200
Fax: 972-296-7319
webcontact@kaepa-usa.com
www.kaepa.com
• Russell Shimomura, Product / Creative Director
(972) 296-7300
russells@kaepa-usa.com
• Sharon McCord, Sales Director
(972) 296-7300
sharonm@kaepa-usa.com
• John Atkinson, President
(972) 296-7300
johnat@kaepa-usa.com
Products:
Footwear, Apparel and Accessories for Volleyball, Cheer, Auxiliary Dance and Fitness

KAMPALA INDUSTRIES
19 CUMMINGS ROAD
MONMOUTH JUNCTION, NJ 08852-2915
732-438-9750
877-526-7762
Fax: 732-438-9752
kampalaind@hotmail.com
www.kampala.com.pk
Products:
Gloves, garments and tanned leather

KANGAROO PRODUCTS COMPANY
111 KANGAROO DRIVE
PO BOX 607
COLUMBUS, NC 28722-0607
828-894-8241
800-438-3011

Fax: 828-894-2718
www.kangaroogolf.com
• Michael McCue, President
(828) 894-8241
• Timothy R. Pope, VP New Product Development
(828) 894-8241
• Michael Whitt, Sales Manager
mikewhitt@kangaroogolf.com
Products:
Golf Cart Battery Chargers, Carts-Electric (for walking golfers), Motorized Golf Bag Carriers

KANGOL HEADWEAR, INC.
411 FIFTH AVENUE
SECOND FLOOR
NEW YORK, NY 10016
212-981-9900
800-431-1802
Fax: 212-981-9901
inquiries@kangolheadwearusa.com
www.kangol.com
• David Heys, Chief Executive Officer
Products:
Headwear, Eyewear, Footwear, Bags, Apparel, Wristwear, Accessories

KAPPA USA
350 5TH AVENUE
SUITE 6617
NEW YORK, NY 10118
212-273-3399
Fax: 212-273-3333
info@kappa.com
• Simon Bamber, President
info@kappa.com
• Mike Callahan, Chief Financing Officer / Chief Operatin
info@kappa.com
• Doug Gordon, VP Sales / Marketing
info@kappa.com
• Peter Milone, Director Business Development
Products:
Sports Apparel, Footwear and Accessories

KARHU U.S.A. LIMITED
208 FLYNN AVENUE
STUDIO 3H
BURLINGTON, VT 5401
802-864-4519
888-288-2668
Fax: 800-422-8454
customerservice@kahru.com
www.karhu.com
• Douglas Barbor, President / Chief Executive Officer
customerservice@kahru.com
• David Smallwood, VP Hockey Division
customerservice@kahru.com
• Jacques Lavertue, General Manager / Outdoor Division
customerservice@kahru.com
• Casey Sheahan, VP Marketing Outdoor Division
customerservice@kahru.com
Products:
Hiking - Outdoor Footwear; Ice Hockey - Equipment, Sticks; In-Line Skating - Skates; Skiing-Nordic - Accessories, Bindings, Boots, Skis.

KASCO CORPORATION OF AMERICA
2171 KINGSTON COURT
SUITE H
MARIETTA, GA 30067

770-303-4500
800-431-2560
Fax: 770-303-0044
www.kascogolf.com
• Keiko Morii, Director Of Marketing And
Public Relations
• Yoshihiro Sato, Contact
Products:
Golf Gloves, Clubs, Balls and Bags

KAYSER-ROTH INC.
102 CORPORATE CENTER BOULEVARD
GREENSBORO, NC 27408
800-575-3497
800-327-8769
Fax: 336-854-4352
customerservice@kayser-roth.com
www.kayser-roth.com
• Kevin Toomey, President / Chief Executive
Officer
customerservice@nononsense.com
Products:
Women's athletic undergarments.

KEDS CORPORATION
4200 SOUTH A STREET
RICHMOND, IN 47374
617-824-6000
800-680-0966
Fax: 800-446-1339
customerservice@keds.com
www.keds.com
• Kristin Burrows, President, Keds
• Matthew E Rubel, Chairman of the Board,
President & CEO
Products:
Athletic and casual footwear for children and
adults

KEISER CORPORATION
2470 S CHERRY AVENUE
FRESNO, CA 93706
800-888-7009
Fax: 559-256-8100
info@keiser.com
www.keiser.com
• Dennis L. Keiser, President/Founder
info@keiser.com
• Randy J. Keiser, VP
info@keiser.com
• Tony Peterson, VP International Sales &
Marketing
(425) 402-8509
tonyp@keiser.com
• Anthony A. Peterson, VP
Products:
Training & Conditioning - low-impact
variable resistance exercise machines;
Stretching stations, Indoor Group Cycling
Bikes, Children Play Products

KEN YOUNG COMPANY, INC.
147 HALLS COURT
CAIRO, GA 39828
229-377-9444
800-251-1800
Fax: 229-377-6446
snewmons@kenyoungco.com
www.kenyoungco.com
• Ken Young, Sales
kyoung@kenyoungco.com
• Kim Chelsey, Sales
• LeAnn Maxwell Vickers, Customer Service
Products:
Athletic Apparel

KENYON CONSUMER PRODUCTS, INC.
141 FAIRGROUNDS ROAD
PO BOX 458
W KINGSTON, RI 02892
401-792-3704
800-537-0024
Fax: 401-782-4870
www.kenyonconsumer.com
• Andrew Curtis, President
kcp@kenyonconsumer.com
• Beth Curtis, VP
• David Kenyon, Owner
Products:
Camping accessories, technical thermal
underwear, and fleece and pile garments
and accessories

KENYON INDUSTRIES
25 WEST 45TH STREET
11TH FLOOR
NEW YORK, NY 10036
212-551-0100
Fax: 646-472-0294
www.brookwoodcos.com
• Amber Brookwood, President/CEO
Products:
Performance fabrics specializing in lifestyle
markets, including Activewear, outerwear,
luggage, and specialty bag markets

KEY SPORTZ-WEAR
3301 S GALLOWAY STREET
SUITE 293
PHILADELPHIA, PA 19145
215-339-0605
888-339-0605
Fax: 215-339-8250
liaconijr@aol.com
Products:
Sports apparel.

KEYBEC SUBLIME, INC.
9031 DU PARC
MONTREAL, QC, CANADA H2N 1Z1
514-858-7582
800-516-0396
Fax: 514-858-7597
www.groupetrium.com
• Pierre Bellemarre, Co-founder
• Pierre Gendron, President
Distributor:
Baseball Uniforms; General Sports Products
Athletic Jackets, Headwear; Ice Hockey
Protective, Skates, Socks, Sticks, Sweaters;
Soccer Uniforms.

KEYS FITNESS PRODUCTS
PO BOX 357
HUGHES SPRINGS, TX 75656
888-320-7885
866-962-0173
Fax: 214-340-1768
• Tim Chen, President and Chief Executive
Officer
• Ken Kruebbe, Public Relations Officer
• Kevin Brady, Export Sales Manager
Products:
Treadmills, home gyms, racks, cable
columns, weight storage, benches, ellipticals
and accessory equipment such as weights,
reading racks, medicine balls, bars and
apparel.

KI
1330 BELLEVUE STREET
GREEN BAY, WI 54308

920-468-8100
800-424-2432
Fax: 920-468-0280
salesadvance@ki.com
www.ki.com
• Richard J. Resch, President and Chief
Executive Officer
salesadvance@ki.com
• Mark Olsen, Chief Financial Officer,
Treasurer
salesadvance@ki.com
• Brian Krenke, President
salesadvance@ki.com
• Andy McGregor, Executive Vice President
Products:
AGI Benches, AGI Guest Seating, AGI
Lounge Seating, AGI Multiple Seating, AGI
Occasional Tables, AGI Professional
Seating, Airport Gatehold Seating,
Auditorium/Lecture Hall, Desks -
Accessories, Desks - Adjustable Height,
Desks - Carrels, Desks - Circulation/Library,
Desks - Classroom, Desks - Office, Files,
GS-27F-0513H Household & Quarters
Contract, GS-28F-2002D Special Use
Contract, GS-28F-8022H Office Furniture
Contract, Healthcare Furniture

KIEFER U.S.A.
2910 FALLING WATERS BOULEVARD
LINDENHURST, IL 60046-6799
847-245-8450
800-322-5448
Fax: 847-245-8590
info@kieferusa.com
• Brion Rittenberry, President & CEO
• Dan Kehoe, Vice President, Sales
Year Founded:
1977
Nature of Service:
Sports flooring contractors & distributors
Brands:
Mondo Sports, Connor Sport Surfacing,
PaviGym.

KING COBRA GAMING
4045 NEWBURG ROAD
EASTON, PA 18045
610-762-7335
Fax: 610-614-1066
Products:
Regulation Rubber Quoits, Quoit Slate
Boards, Horseshoes Outfit, Bocce, Darts,
Bar & Shield Darts Kit, Poker Tables,
Blackjack Tables, Roulette / Craps Tables,
Table Game & Accessories (Table Brush,
Cup Holder, Playing Cards, Card Shuffler
and Poker Table Top), Poker Chips,

KING LOUIE INTERNATIONAL, INC.
2700 ROBERTS RD.
BAXTER SPRINGS, KS 66713
620-856-2341
800-521-5212
Fax: 816-765-3228
kloffice@kinglouie.com
www.kinglouie.com
• Robert Palan, President
• Roger P. Carroll, Marketing VP
• Dick McClearen, Manufacturing Executive
• Ruth Ann Shelton, Human Resources
Executive
• Teresa Buchanan, Purchasing Executive
Nature of Sports Services:
Bowling Shirts; Activewear, Athletic
Jackets/Parkas, Fashion Jackets, Fleece,
T-shirts; Golf Apparel; Skiing-Alpine

Outerwear/Jackets-Vests-Pants; Track & Field/Running Apparel-Run/Jog.

KING PAR CORPORATION
G-5140 FLUSHING ROAD
FLUSHING, MI 48433
810-732-2470
888-502-4653
Fax: 810-732-6662
custserv@kingpar.com
• William J. Baird, Chief Executive Officer
• Ryan Coffell, Controller
(810) 410-1840
• L. Toups, Operations Manager
(810) 410-1875
• Doug Hinton, General Sales Manager
(810) 410-1835
Products:
Clubs, bags, balls, tees, accessories, apparel, gloves, hats and shoes for every age group. Types of clubs includes individual woods, fairway woods, hybrids, junior irons.
Brands:
Orlimar, Affinity, InTech.

KITCHENER HOCKEY STICKS LTD.
176 FORFAR AVENUE
KITCHENER, ONTARIO, CANADA N2B 3A1
519-743-9325
888-548-7849
Fax: 519-579-4817
• Sandy Watson, President
(519) 743-9325
• Bob Pastway, General Manager
Products:
Hockey sticks

KOLDER INC
1601 N CLOSNER BOULEVARD
EDINBURG, TX 78541
956-381-9851
877-817-0288
Fax: 956-383-0502
www.kolder.com
• Charlie Meyer, President
(956) 318-9851
• Jody Hancock, Retail Sales Manager
(956) 318-9851
• Brenda Rios, CSR
ext 204
• Vennessa Flores, CSR
ext 250
• Ruby Rivera, CSR
ext 7159
Products:
Licensed & Novelty Items- beverage, bags, computer accessories, glassware, etc.
Teams;
MLB, NHL, NFL, College Teams.

KOOLATRON
27 CATHARINE AVENUE
BRANTFORD ONTARIO, CANADA N3T 1X5
519-756-3950
800-265-8456
Fax: 519-756-3725
service@koolatron.com
www.koolatron.com
• Arun Kulkarni, President
• Carol Murtland, Purchasing Manager
• Gary Sitton, Info Systems Manager
• George Verghese, Operations VP
Products:
Car Accessories, 12V Coolers and

Warmers, 12V Spotlight/Lamps, Auto Fans and Power Inverters, Kitchen Appliances, Total Chef Oven, Robatic Vacuum Cleaner, Wine Cooler and Aerobeds, Toothbrush, sleeping aid and snore stopper and hairbrush, Revolutionary home gym,abdominal exerciser, Yoga Mat, Magnetic Elliptical Trainer, Land Rider Bike and Body Bow, Pet Dish Six Days, Pet Dish, Pet Fountain etc., Mosquito Control, Electronic Pest Control and Ultrasonic Pest Control Products for indoor and outdoor control of pest, mosquitoes, flies etc., Portable Sonar Fish Finder, High Power Dynamo Torch and First Alert Eternal Flashlight

KORNEY BOARD AIDS, INC.
312 HARRISON AVENUE
PO BOX 264
ROXTON, TX 75477
903-346-3269
800-842-7772
Fax: 877-488-3920
sales@kbacoach.com
www.kbacoach.com
• Jeff Reed, President
(800) 842-7772
jcreed65@yahoo.com
Products:
Coaching boards, basketball coaching aids, basketball equipment and training, volleyball coaching and training equipment, coaching and training videos and books for basketball and volleyball, ball racks and ball carriers, gym supplies and equipment
Nature of Service:
Retail & Wholesale
Brands:
Spalding, Korney Boards, Shoot-Away Toss Back, Cramer, Tachikara & Muller

KRUEGER INTERNATIONAL
1330 BELLEVUE STREET
GREEN BAY, WI 54302
920-468-8100
800-424-2432
Fax: 920-468-0280
salesadvance@ki.com
www.ki.com
• Richard J. Resch, President and Chief Executive Officer
salesadvance@ki.com
• Mark Olsen, Chief Financial Officer, Treasurer
salesadvance@ki.com
• Mark Christopher, Sales / Marketing VP
salesadvance@ki.com
Products:
Accessories, Adjustable Worksurfaces, AGI Collections, Auditorium Seating, Classroom furniture, Folding Chairs, Guest Seating, Lecture Hall Furniture, Library Furniture, Lounge Seating, Powered Tables, Public Seating, Residence Hall Furniture, Site Furnishing, Stools, Tables, Healthcare Furniture, Task Seating, Desking, Files and Storage and more.

KRYPTONICS U.S.A.
12801 CARMENITA ROAD
SANTA FE SPRINGS, CA 90670
562-484-5100
800-248-5327
Fax: 562-484-5183
mjoines@bravocorp.com
www.kryptonics.com

• Samuel Kratish, President
• Esther Kratish, Treasurer
Products:
Baseball Caps; Softball Caps.

KTM SPORTMOTORCYCLE USA
1119 MILAN AVENUE
AMHERST, OH 44001
440-985-3553
Fax: 330-645-1586
www.ktmusa.com
• Stefan Pierer, CEO
Description:
KTM Sportmotorcycle is a growing motorcycle company that specializes in dirt bikes. KTM is an international business with numerous locations including several within the United States. KTM has a newly constructed development centre in Mattighofen, Austria that includes an integrated motor sports department in addition to a modern engine factory in Munderfing which has doubled their production capacities in recent years. Thanks to tremendous research and development, competent, highly-motivated staff and innumerable motor sports successes, KTM manufactured approximately 80,400 motorcycles during 2005.

KUNNAN GOLF
470 CLOVERLEAF DRIVE
UNIT B
BALDWIN PARK, CA 91706
626-934-0388
800-399-8599
Fax: 626-934-0377
• Frank Zou, Sales Manager
Description:
Golf - Clubs-Wood/Iron Sets, Individual Woods, Irons.

KWIK GOAL LTD.
140 PACIFIC DRIVE
QUAKERTOWN, PA 18951
215-536-2200
800-531-4252
Fax: 800-778-8869
info@kwikgoal.com
www.kwikgoal.com
Products:
Decks, wheels, components, helmets, Elbow Pads, Wrist Guards and Knee Pads.

L&L GROUP/FOREMOST ATHLETIC APPAREL
1307 E MAPLE ROAD
TROY, MI 48083
248-689-3850
Fax: 248-689-4653
mijgl@llgroup.net
www.llgroup.net
• John G Levy, President/CEO
(248) 689-3850
mijgl@llgroup.net
• Mike Burns, Vice President/Finance
Brands:
Auburn, Augusta, Bike, Crystal Springs, Dunbrooke, Gatorade, Hanes, Lee, New Era
Products:
Sports apparel.

L.A. GEAR
5900 RODEO ROAD
LOS ANGELES, CA 90016-4313

310-822-1995
800-253-7740
Fax: 310-581-7709
www.lagear.com
• William L Benford, President
• David F Gatto, Chairman/CEO
• Bruce Macgregor, SVP Product Marketing
Products:
Basketball - Shoes; Racquet Sports -
Shoes; Training & Conditioning - Aerobic
Shoes, Cross Training Shoes

L.A.T SPORTSWEAR
1200 AIRPORT DRIVE
BALL GROUND, GA 30107
770-479-1877
800-414-5650
Fax: 770-479-4078
www.latsportswear.com
• Isador Mitzner, Chief Executive Officer
• Gina Watson, President / COO / CEO
• Mickie Schneider, EVP / Chief Financial
Officer
• Chuck Phares, Executive VP Of Sales
Products:
General Sports Activewear and T-shirts for
infants, toddlers, youths, ladies, juniors, and
teams

LACROSSE FOOTWEAR, INC.
17634 NE AIRPORT WAY
PORTLAND, OR 97230
503-262-0110
800-323-2668
Fax: 503-262-0115
customerservice@lacrossefootwear.com
www.lacrossefootwear.com
Products:
All Purpose Shoes Leather, Rubber
Footwear, Boots

LACROSSE UNLIMITED
363 NESCONSET HIGWAY
HAUPPAUGE, NY 11788
631-366-5299
800-366-5299
Fax: 631-406-6381
nick@lacrosseunlimited.com
www.lacrosseunltd.com
• Nick Gallagher, Manager
nick@lacrosseunlimited.com
• Sam Desimone, Co-President
Products:
Equipments: Custom Stringing, Custom
Dyed Heads, Unstrung & Factory Sticks,
Handles, Helmets, Gloves, Arm Pads,
Shoulder Pads, Rib Pads, Goalie Pads,
Women's Equipment, Goals & Targets,
Cleats & Footwear, LU Originals Apparel:
Under Armor/Performance Gear, Shorts,
Shirts, Bags, Hats

LAFAYETTE INSTRUMENT COMPANY
3700 SAGAMORE PARKWAY N
PO BOX 5729
LAFAYETTE, IN 47903
765-423-1505
800-428-7545
Fax: 765-423-4111
info@lafayetteinstrument.com
www.lafayetteinstrument.com
• Terry Echard, President / General
Manager
• Chris Fausett, VP/Manager/Sales/Trained
Polygraph Examiner
• Jennifer Rider, Vice President/Chief
Information Officer

• Mike Greene, Operations Manager
• Brent Smitley, Engineering Manager
• Todd Hooker, Traffic Control Manager
• Judy Gledhill, Accounts Receivable
Products:
Instrumentation for Strength Testing, Range
of Motion, Anthropometrics, Sensibilities,
Physiological Measures, Exercise Testing,
Dexterity and Coordination

LAM LIGHTING SYSTEMS
938 S GREEN STREET
TUPELO, MS 38804
714-549-9765
800-234-1890
Fax: 662-680-6619
www.daybrite.com
• Craig Brauks, General Manager
(714) 549-9765
• Bill Busch, Senior Product Manager
• Brandi Sears, Director, Specification
Marketing
(662) 680-6634
Products:
Indoor Lighting for Sports Facilities such as
Curvilinear(Pendant Mount), Wall & Cove,
Asymmetrical, Linear

LAMKIN LEATHER & RUBBER COMPANY
6530 GATEWAY PARK DRIVE
SAN DIEGO, CA 92154
619-661-7090
800-642-7755
Fax: 619-661-0014
info@lamkingrips.com
www.lamkingrips.com
• Bob Lamkin, President / Chief Executive
Officer
• Thomas Lamkin, EVP
• Mike Lamkin, Engineering VP
Products:
Golf Grips

LANDS' END, INC.
1 LANDS' END LANE
DODGEVILLE, WI 53595
608-935-9341
800-356-4444
800-963-4816
Fax: 608-935-4291
www.landsend.com
• Donald R Hughes, Senior VP / Chief
Financial Officer
hughes@landsend.com
• Gary C Comer , Founder
comer@landsend.com
• Mindy C Meads , Merchandising Design
EVP
meads@landsend.com
• Kelly A Ritchie, Senior VP, Employee
Services
ritchie@landsend.com
• Michele Casper, Senior Director of Public
Relations
• Jim Kennedy, Senior Director of Integrated
Marketing
• Adam Weil, Director
• J Henley, Design Director
Products:
Swimwear, Beach Towels & Totes,
Women's Regular: All Styles, Little Black
Suits, Mix & Match Separates, Tankinis &
Bikinis, 1-piece Tanks, Slenderizing Suits,
Swimfinity Suits, Shop by Anxiety Zones,
Shop by Bra Style, Shop by Body Shape,
Mastectomy, Long Torso, Cover-ups,

Women's Plus, Shoes & Sandals, Men's,
Girls', Boys', Outdoor Living

LANDSCAPE STRUCTURES, INC.
601 7TH STREET S
PO BOX 198
DELANO, MN 55328-8605
763-972-5200
888-438-6574
Fax: 763-972-3185
www.playlsi.com
• Barbara King, Co-Founder
• Young Climbers, Manufacturing VP,
Human Resources
Products:
Facilities - Benches, Fitness Trails/Circuits,
Playground Equipment

LANDWAVE PRODUCTS INC
ONE COREWAY DRIVE
PIONEER, OH 43554
419-737-9584
800-922-6956
Fax: 419-737-2130
fun@landwaveproducts.com
www.landwaveproducts.com
• Michael A Nowakowski, Vice President,
Sales & Marketing
(419) 737-9584
mnowakowski@landwaveproducts.com
Products:
Landwave ramp systems and skateboards.

LASER MAGIC
946 CENTURY LANE
APOPKA, FL 32703
407-880-7151
800-771-7151
Fax: 407-880-7150
www.lasermagic.net
Products:
LASER CUT Mirrored License Plates and
other laser cut or engraved products with
sports logos and designs.

LAWRENCE METAL PRODUCTS
260 SPUR DRIVE S
PO BOX 400
BAY SHORE, NY 11706
631-666-0300
800-441-0019
Fax: 631-666-0336
sales@tensator.com
www.tensator.com
• David Lawrence, President
• Betty Castro, Sales / Marketing VP
• Jim Stumpf, Sales Director
Products:
Crowd control and hospitality products,
including Stancions, Post and Ropes,
TensaBarriers, Signage, Barriers, Food
Shields, Sneeze Guards and Railing

LEADER MANUFACTURING COMPANY, INC.
11861 WESTLINE INDUSTRIAL DRIVE
SUITE 100
SAINT LOUIS, MO 63146
314-567-1000
800-325-2666
Fax: 314-567-1006
customerservice@leadermanufacturing.com
www.leadermanufacturing.com
• Marc Tenzer, President
Products:
Baseball - Caps; Softball - Caps

LEADER SPORTS USA/THE HILSINGER COMPANY
33 W BACON STREET
PO BOX 1538
PLAINVILLE, MA 02762-0538
508-699-4406
800-847-2001
Fax: 800-959-4452
kpeever@zleader.com
Products:
Eyewear products such as: Swim Goggles, Water Sports Goggles, Snorkeling, Swim Accessories, Racket Sports, Team Sports

LEADING BRANDS
1500 W GEORGIA
SUITE 1800
VANCOUVER BC, CANADA V6G 2Z6
604-685-5200
866-685-5200
Fax: 604-685-5249
info@LBIX.com
• Ralph McRae, Chairman and Chief Executive Officer
• Dave Read, Executive Vice-President
• Robert Mockford, VP of Operations
• Sinan al Zubaidi, VP of Bottling Operations
• R. Thomas Gaglardi, President, Northland Properties Corporation
• Darryl Eddy, President, Radale Inc.
• James Corbett, President & CEO, Canadian Outback Adventures
• Ralph D. McRae, Chairman and Chief Executive Officer
Brands:
TREK Natural Sports Drink
Nature of Service:
The largest independent, fully integrated premium beverage company in Canada.
NITRO
Energy Drink by Trek

LEE TENNIS PRODUCTS
650 PETER JEFFERSON PARKWAY
SUITE 300 B
CHARLOTTESVILLE, VA 22911
434-295-6167
877-442-7878
Fax: 434-971-6995
• John Welborn, General Manager
(434) 531-9763
• Randy Futty, Sales Engineer
• Ed Montecalvo, Contractor Services
Products:
Facilities - Courts -Tennis; Racquet Sports - Tennis Court Equipment, Tennis Nets/Standards

LEE'S LICENSED ENAMELWARE
2242 HIGHWAY 182
INWOOD, IA 51240
712-753-4403
800-736-6530
Fax: 712-753-4542
Products:
Enamelware kettles for commercial popcorn-making

LEGEND SPORTS
3080 W WILLETLE CIRCLE
W JORDAN, UT 84084
801-964-5600
800-448-4680
Fax: 801-964-5500

LEO'S DANCEWEAR, INC.
1170 TRADEMARK DRIVE
SUITE 112
RENO, NV 89521
773-889-7700
800-736-5367
Fax: 800-736-5330
www.leosdancewear.com
• Glenn Baruck, President
• Barbara Kanies, National Sales Manager
• Sherri Giacone, Marketing / Communications Manager
• Leo Harris, Founder
• Nancy Thomas, Human Resource Manager
Products:
Dance Tights / Liners, Dance Tutus, Nylon Dancewear, Dance Skirts, Performancewear / Dresses, Cotton / Prima-Cotton Dancewear, Performance Spandex Dance, Powerwear, Liturgical Dancewear, Jazz Shoes, Tap Shoes, Ballet / Pointe Shoes, Gymnastic Shoes, Lyrical / Modern Shoes, Shoe Accessories, Performancewear, Kiddazzle, Starlettes, Ballet & Lyrical, Jazz & Taps, Alternatives

LEON LEVIN
CORPORATE PARK DRIVE
SUITE 240
300 OAK STREET
PEMBROKE, MA 02359
212-575-1900
866-937-5366
Fax: 212-944-1482
customerservice@leonlevin.com
www.leonlevin.com
Products:
Sports, golf apparel and casual wear.

LESCO, INC.
650 STEPHENSON HIGHWAY
SUITE 1300
TROY, MI 48083-1110
800-321-5325
800-820-4848
Fax: 800-673-3030
• Jefferey L Rutherford, Chief Execuitve Officer
• Bruce K Thorn, Chief Operating Officer
• Michael Weisbarth, VP / Chief Financial Officer / Treasurer
• Ron E Brown, Branch Manager
• Chris Marsh, Category Manager
Products:
Equipment, Irrigation, Golf Accessories, Turf Grass Seed, Parts, Fertilizers, Pest Control, Merchandise, Combo Products, Control Products

LETRELL SPORTS
3004 INDUSTRIAL PARKWAY W
KNOXVILLE, TN 37921
865-546-8070
800-325-3975
• Dick Jacobstein, Chief Execuitve Officer / Sales Manager
Products:
Athletic Uniforms and Garments for basketball, baseball, and football

LIBERTY MOUNTAIN SPORTS, LLC.
9816 SOUTH JORDAN GATEWAY (500 W)
SANDY, UT 84070
801-307-9200
800-366-2666
Fax: 801-307-9300

sales@libertymtn.com
www.libertymountain.com
• Gary E Heward, President
Products:
Climbing & Mountaineering, Add-on Sales, Soft Goods, Gear Maintenance, First Aid & Personal Care, Camp & Trail Gear, Coghlans, Backpacks, Tents, & Bags, Biking Accessories, Compasses & Instruments, Lights, Knives & Tools, Matches & Fire Starters, Stoves & Lanterns, Food & Cookware, Water Products, Water Sports, Optics, Kids, Books & Maps, Travel, Gifts, Games, & Toys, Emergency Essentials

LIEBE ATHLETIC LETTERING
582 GODDARD AVENUE
CHESTERFIELD, MO 63005-1109
636-530-3700
800-845-4323
Fax: 636-530-3890
info@liebe.com
www.liebe.com
• Robert Liebe, III, President
• Jeanette James, Customer Service Manager
jjames@liebe.com
• Ron Deters, CFO
• Greg Deniszczuk, Marketing Director
• Rob Knoll, Sales/Marketing Manager
Products:
Sewing, Embroidery, Patches, Twill Letters, Vinyl Letters, Finishing, Corporate Apparel

LIFE FITNESS, INC.
5100 N RIVER ROAD
SCHILLER PARK, IL 60176
847-288-3300
800-351-3737
Fax: 800-216-8893
glynis@gibsoncommunications.com
www.lifefitness.com
• John Stransky, President
glynis@gibsoncommunications.com
• Steven Drickey, General Counsel
glynis@gibsoncommunications.com
• Judy L Gustafson, VP Human Resources
glynis@gibsoncommunications.com
• Matthew Johnson, VP Global Strategic Planning & Business
glynis@gibsoncommunications.com
Products:
Treadmills, Elliptical Cross Trainers, Exercise Bikes, Stair Climbers, Home Gms, Free Weight System, Specialized Workout Stations

LIFE PRIORITY, INC.
11184 ANTIOCH RD OULEVARD
#417
OVERLAND PARK, KS 66210
913-438-5433
800-787-5438
Fax: 913-438-5444
www.lifepriority.com
• Greg Pryor, President
gprior@lifepriority.com
• Michelle Pryor, Marketing Director
• Tracey Budz, Public Relations
Products:
Health supplements - Durk Pearson & Sandy Shaw designer foods, creatine, glucosamine

LIFEGEAR INC
9858 BALDWIN PLACE
EL MONTE, CA 91731

626-456-8300
Fax: 626-452-9692
Products:
Fitness equipment and machines.

LIFELINE INTERNATIONAL, INC.
5424 W. ROOSEVELT ROAD
CHICAGO, IL 60644
608-288-9252
800-553-6633
Fax: 312-265-6789
www.lifelineusa.com
• Bobby Hinds, CEO
(800) 553-6633
• Jon Hinds, National Sales Manager
• Joy Hinds, Secretary
• Paul Flowers, President
Products:
Equipments for Sports Training - Core
Strength & Agility, Sports Training - Sports
Specific, Chin Up Devices, Rehab/Fitness
Equipment, Portable Gyms, Resistance
Cables, Jump Ropes, Accessories, Shape
Aerobic Products, Wall Gyms, Balls, Books
and Videos.
Products:
Lifeline's Train Station is a total fitness
rehab center that is quick and convenient
with unlimited exercise possibilities, at a low
cost that is small enough to fit in your back
pocket; The Lifeline USA WHEEL GYM has
been created to maximize the ability of the
wheelchair user to perform an incredible
variety of resistance exercises properly,
conveniently, and independently; Lifeline
USA Kettleballs are effective for fat loss,
strength training, and building muscle -
powerfully train the entire body anytime and
virtually anywhere; Lifeline Portable Gym is
a 2 lb. gym that can tone and shape all the
muscle groups of your body in 1/4 the time
Year Founded:
1973

LIFETIME PRODUCTS, INC.
PO BOX 160010
FREEPORT CENTER BUILDING D-11
CLEARFIELD, UT 84016-0010
801-776-1532
800-242-3865
Fax: 801-776-4397
info@lifetime.com
www.lifetime.com
• Vince Rhoton, Senior Vice President Of
Sales And Marketing
• Richard Hendrickson, President
pmickey@lifetime.com
• Mark Whiting, CFO
• Katie Salter, Communications Manager
Products:
Tables & Chairs, Basketball Equipment,
Outdoor Storage, Recreation

LIGHTNING GOLF DISCS
1402 CORTO
DALLAS, TX 75218
214-328-9017
Fax: 214-328-9088
www.lightninggolfdiscs.com
Products:
Golf Discs, Golf Bags, DB5-Basktet,
Fixtures

LIGHTWEAR
924 KENTUCKY STREET
BELLINGHAM, WA 98225

360-734-8798
800-213-3926
Fax: 360-676-8773
www.lightwear.com
• Jack Hovenier, Founder
Products:
NFL, MLB, NHL, NASCAR, NBA, NCAA
apparel and accessories.

LILY'S OF BEVERLY HILLS
20314 GRAMERCY PLACE
TORRANCE, CA 90501
310-781-2200
Fax: 310-781-2206
www.lbhgroup.com
Products:
Warm-Up Suits, Golf Apparel, Tennis
Apparel

LIND SHOE COMPANY
501 LASER DRIVE
SOMERSET, WI 54025
800-950-4568
800-328-5463
Fax: 715-247-5440
info@linds.com
www.linds.com
• Jeffrey Lind, President
info@linds.com
Products:
Specializes in the importation, selling, and
distribution of a variety of quality bowling
products including rental shoes, resale
shoes, house balls, resale balls, bowling
bags, bowling pins, steel bowling lockers,
and a variety of pro shop accessories.

LINEAR RUBBER PRODUCTS, INC.
5416 46TH STREET
KENOSHA, WI 53144
262-652-3912
800-558-4040
Fax: 262-657-6705
info@rubbermats.com
www.rubbermats.com
• Beth Lane, Sales Director
info@rubbermats.com
Products:
Manufacturer of genuine rubber flooring for
weight rooms and fitness areas to absorb
the impact of free weights, secure exercise
equipment and provide acoustical qualities.
All products are sold at factory-direct pricing.
Brands:
Power Pad Flooring is available in
single-piece mats up to 6' x 16', the largest
in the industry. Gymatts are available in
48-inch x 72-inch sections. Top Mat II
Flooring System comes in black or
color-flecked roll stock, interlocking tiles and
squares.
Year Founded:
1972

LION SPORTS INC
701 KOEHLER AVENUE
SUITE 2
RONKONKOMA, NY 11779
631-580-5010
877-244-5466
Fax: 631-580-7660
www.heavyhandsfitness.com
Products:
Manufacturer of hand weights for exercise
and fitness, weight-loss, sports training,
walkers, and those seeking strength or
endurance training

LIQUID BLUE
ONE CROWNMARK DRIVE
LINCOLN, RI 2865
401-333-6200
866-450-2583
Fax: 401-333-0340
retail@liquidblue.com
www.liquidblue.com
Products:
Manufacturer of T-Shirts, Tie-Dye shirts, and
all kinds of hard to find music and sports
stickers, hats, and collectible memorabilia.

LITHONIA LIGHTING
PO BOX A
CONYERS, GA 30012
770-922-9000
Fax: 770-483-2635
comments@lithonia.com
www.lithonia.com
• Ken Honeycutt, President
comments@lithonia.com
Products:
Manufacturer of lighting equipment for
commercial, industrial, outdoor and
residential applications

LITTLE KING MANUFACTURING COMPANY INC
114 EAST WALNUT
PO BOX 287
ALAMO, TN 38001
731-696-5517
800-530-7024
Fax: 731-696-2289
• Gail Hart, Sales Manager
(731) 696-5517
Year Founded:
1955
Products:
Manufacturer of apparel and childrens sport
wear.
Brands:
Little King

LITTLE MISS TENNIS/T.V. SPORTS
PO BOX 17442
MEMPHIS, TN 38187-0442
901-371-0291
800-388-0291
Fax: 901-371-0293
www.littlemisstennis.com
• Marilyn Kosten, Founder/President
• Herb Kosten, Finance VP
Products:
Manufacturer of tennis player apparel for
boys and girls

LITTLE RIVER MARINE COMPANY
250A SE 10TH AVENUE
GAINESVILLE, FL 32601
352-378-5025
800-247-4591
Fax: 352-378-5025
info@littlerivermarine.com
www.littlerivermarine.com
• Bill Larson, President
info@littlerivermarine.com
• Steve Larson, Marketing VP / Sales
Director
Products:
Manufacturer of hand crafted rowing craft,
rowing shells and rowboats

LJO, INC.
401 HAMBURG TURNPIKE
SUITE 305
WAYNE, NJ 07470-2139
973-956-6990
Fax: 973-956-6991
ljo@ljoinc.com
www.ljoinc.com
• Leif J. Ostberg, Chief Executive Officer
ljo@ljoinc.com
• Louis Destefano, Chief Operating Officer
ljo@ljoinc.com
• Barbara Koetsier, Chief Financial Officer
ljo@ljoinc.com
Services:
Specializes in designing, developing, sampling, sourcing and the manufacturing of high-end branded or designer footwear

LOBSTER SPORTS
7340 FULTON AVENUE
NORTH HOLLYWOOD, CA 91605
818-764-6000
800-210-5992
Fax: 818-764-6061
www.lobstersports.com
• Tony Potter, President
info@lobstersports.com
Products:
Manufacturer of Baseball - Baseball Bucket; Racquet Sports - Tennis Ball Throwing Machines, Tennis Balls, Tennis Racquets; Street Hockey (DEK) - Hockey Bucket.

LOCUST INC.
11-1155 NORTH SERVICE ROAD
W. OAKVILLE, ONTARIO, CANADA L6M 3E3
905-820-0303
800-284-8079
Fax: 905-820-8220
• Michael R Krog, Founder/CEO
(905) 820-0303
• George Azcurra, Sls / Marketing (Canada)
gazcurra@locust.ca
• Luke Deneau, Sales Director / Marketing (Canada)
ldeneau@locust.ca
Products:
Manufacturer and Designer of Soccer Apparel

LOG HOUSE DESIGNS, INC.
HCR-68, BOX 248
CENTER CONWAY, NH 3813
603-694-3300
Fax: 603-694-3374
• Kenyon King, President
• Janice Purslow, VP
Products:
General Sports Products including Bags, Equipment, Apparel and Accessories for Golf, Skiing-Alpine/Nordic.

LOGAN INC.
546 VALLEY ROAD
UPPER MONTCLAIR, NJ 7043
973-509-3190
Fax: 973-509-3191
info@loganandco.com
www.loganandco.com
• Kate Logan, President & CEO
Products:
Bags and Equipment for Baseball, Basketball, Football, Ice Hockey, Skiing-Alpine, Soccer, Softball, Track & Field/Running, Volleyball and Wrestling.

Also Dummies for Blocking, Whirlpool Baths, and Training Room Supplies.

LOGO ART
226 PUBLIC STREET
PROVIDENCE, RI 2905
800-362-9896
800-362-9896
Fax: 401-330-4201
Logoartsales@herffjones.com
www.logoart.com
Products:
Manufacturer of jewelry utilizing logos of colleges, sports teams and corporations

LOGO CHAIR, INC.
117 SE PARKWAY
FRANKLIN, TN 37064
615-261-2100
888-959-3030
Fax: 615-261-9240
• Bill McCauley, Founder
Products:
Manufacturer of high quality sporting goods and tailgating products. Specializing in officially licensed college merchandise.

LOGOART
226 PUBLIC STREET
PROVIDENCE, RI 2905
800-362-9896
Fax: 401-330-4201
orders@logoart.com
www.logoart.com
Products:
Jewelry, Team Logo Watches, Clocks and Binoculars
Brands:
LogoArt, Prospect, TeamTime

LOMMA GOLF
305 CHERRY STREET
SCRANTON, PA 18505
570-346-5555
Fax: 570-346-5580
info@lommagolf.com
www.lommagolf.com
• Gary Knight, Executive VP
• Ralph Lomma, Founder and President
info@lommagolf.com
• Joyce C. Lomma, Esq, Vice President AOO/PR
joylomma@icontech.com
Products:
Pre-fabricated miniature golf courses. Provides design services for both upscale and turnkey solutions for all miniature golfing needs, with waterfalls, caves, ponds, creeks, mountains and more.
Year Founded:
1955

LONE STAR ATHLETIC DESIGNS, INC.
512 W MAIN STREET
PALESTINE, TX 75801
903-729-1643
800-527-2178
Fax: 903-729-4599
www.lonestarathleticsinc.com
• Charles McCullough, President / Sales Director
Products:
Baseball - Caps; General Sports Products - Award Jackets, Embroidery, Heat Transfers, Lettering, Screen Printing, T-shirts.

LORIA AWARDS
1876 CENTRAL PARK AVENUE
YONKERS, NY 10710
914-779-3377
800-540-2927
Fax: 914-779-3587
customerservice@loriaawards.com
www.loriaawards.com
• Roger V. Loria, President
customerservice@loriaawards.com
Products:
Trophies, Awards, Emblems, Medals, Patches, Plaques, Ribbons.

LOST ARROW CORPORATION
259 W SANTA CLARA ST
PO BOX 32050
VENTURA, CA 93001
805-643-8616
800-638-6464
Fax: 805-653-6355
customer_service@patagonia.com
www.patagonia.com
• Michael Crooke, Chief Executive Officer
• Bob Kelleher, Chief Operating Officer
• Perry Klebahn, EVP
• Casey Sheahan, President
• Martha Groszewski, VP/Chief Executive Officer
Products:
Manufacturer of outdoor apparel, rugged clothing and accessories to mountain climbers, skiers, and other extreme sports. Products:Rowing/Crew - Underclothing; Rugby - Jerseys; Skiing-Nordic - Gaiters, Shells, Sweaters, Underclothing; Track & Field/Running - Apparel-Run/Jog.

LOUISVILLE GOLF
2320 WATTERSON TRAIL
LOUISVILLE, KY 40299
800-456-1631
Fax: 502-491-6189
sales@louisvillegolf.com
www.louisvillegolf.com
• Josh Fischer, VP Marketing / Marketing Director
• Larry Fischer, VP, Sales
• Mike Just, President
• Nancy Silk, Office Manager
Products:
A leader in design and production of persimmon wood golf clubs

LOUISVILLE SLUGGER
800 W MAIN STREET
LOUISVILLE, KY 40202
502-585-5226
800-282-2287
Fax: 502-585-1179
www.slugger.com
• John A. Hillerich IV, President / Chief Executive Officer
• Marty Archer, President, Louisville Slugger Division
• John A. Jack Hillerich III, Chairman of the Board
Products:
Baseball, Fastpitch Softball, Slowpitch Softball pitching systems.

LOVING ASSOCIATES INC.
3711 KENNEBEC DRIVE
SUITE 100
EAGAN, MN 55122
952-912-2500
888-796-4997

Fax: 651-379-4082
info@rti-inc.com
www.laloving.com
• Jeffery K Kiesel, President / Chief
Executive Officer
• Darla Czech, Purchasing Director
Products:
Apparel for sports, active and casual wear
for women.

LOWE ALPINE SYSTEMS
ANN STREET
KENDAL, ENGLAND LA9 6AA
44-1539-740840
Fax: 44-1539-726314
www.lowealpine.com
• Ann Ma Tewey, VP, Operations / Finance
lowecs@lowealpine.com
• Jeff Lowe, President
Products:
Technical Outerwear Jackets, Pants, Shirts
& Tees, Pants & Shorts, Baselayer, Clothing
Accessories, Technical Mountain Packs,
Multi-day Packs, Hyperlite Packs, Activist
Packs, Day Packs, Travel Packs, Belt
Packs, Pack Accessories, Military Packs

LOWRANCE ELECTRONICS, INC.
12000 E SKELLY DRIVE
TULSA, OK 74128
918-437-6881
800-628-4487
Fax: 918-234-1705
• Darrell J. Lowrance, President / Chief
Executive Officer / Di
• Mark C. McQuown, VP, Sales
• Bob G. Callaway, VP, Marketing
• Leif C. Ottoson, President
Products:
High-quality sport fishing SONAR and
Global Positioning System (GPS) mapping
instruments

LSI INDUSTRIES
10000 ALLIANCE ROAD
CINCINNATI, OH 45242
513-793-3200
800-436-7800
Fax: 800-373-9998
www.lsi-industries.com
• James Sferra, EVP, Manufacturing /
Secretary / Directo
courtsider@lsi-industries.com
Products:
Sharp cutoff products that provide
environmentally friendly lighting solutions for
the tennis and sports markets

LSI LIGHTING INDUSTRIES
10000 ALLIANCE ROAD
CINCINNATI, OH 45242
513-793-3200
800-794-3448
Fax: 513-984-1335
www.lsi-industries.com
• Robert J. P. Ready, Chairman and Chief
Executive Officer
• David W. McCauley, President, LSI
Graphics Solutions
• Ronald S. Stowell, VP / Chief Financial
Officer / Treasurer
Products:
LSI Lighting Solutions Plus (Accent &
Downlights, Architectural Indoor Lighting,
Architectural Outdoor Lighting, Automotive
Lighting, Courtsider Sports Lighting, Indoor
Lighting, Outdoor Lighting, Petroleum

Lighting, QSR Lighting, Retail National
Accounts Lighting, International Lighting);
LSI Graphic Solutions Plus (Active Digital
Signage, Menu Boards, Floor Graphics,
Fleet Graphics, Kiosks, P.O.P Displays,
Fixtures, Channel Letters, Architectural
Elements, Dimensional Letters, OEM
Products)

LUMASTROBE WARNING LIGHTS
33 GREENWOOD AVENUE
MIDLAND PARK, NJ 7432
201-444-7041
800-775-5862
Fax: 201-445-8575
info@lumastrobe.com
www.lumastrobe.com
• Peter H. Zecher, President
info@lumastrobe.com
• George Shabet, Sales Manager
info@lumastrobe.com
• Jill Opermann, Advertising Director
(201) 444-0600
jill@pmcontrols.com
Products:
Solar and Portable Battery Powered
Warning Lights. Marshalling wands and
flashing warning lights.

LYCIAN STAGE LIGHTING
PO BOX 214
SUGAR LOAF, NY 10981
845-469-2285
Fax: 845-469-5355
slerman@lycian.com
www.lycian.com
• Steve Lerman, Director, Sales and
Marketing
(845) 469-2285
slerman@lycian.com
Products:
Lycian Followspots

LYNX GOLF, INC.
11000 NORTH IH 35
AUSTIN, TX 78753
512-837-4810
800-813-6897
www.golfsmith.com
• Barry King, VP Marketing
comments@golfsmith.com
• Steve Jones, VP, Marketing
Products:
Retailer for golf clubs, accessories, balls,
shoes

M-F ATHLETIC COMPANY
11 AMFLEX DRIVE
CRANSTON, RI 2921
401-942-9363
888-556-7464
Fax: 401-942-7645
mfathletic@mfathletic.com
www.everythingtrackandfield.com
• Bill Falk, Founder
bill.falk@mfathletic.com
• Eric Falk, VP, Administrative
eric.falk@mfathletic.com
• Mark Strawderman, General Manager,
Track & Field Division
Products:
Throwing Equipment, Jumping Equipment,
Shoes & Apparel, Books & Videos, Timing &
Measuring, Tents, Sprints/Hurdles
Equipment, Training Equipment, Meet
Management, In-Ground Equipment

MACGREGOR GOLF COMPANY
11000 NORTH IH 35
AUSTIN, TX 78753
512-837-4810
800-813-6897
Fax: 800-455-1220
www.golfsmith.com
• Barry Schneider, Chairman / Chief
Executive Officer
Products:
Driver, wood, shaft, hybrid, iron, wedge,
putter, and golf accessories

MACHO PRODUCTS, INC.
10045 102ND TERRACE
SEBASTIAN, FL 32958
772-388-9892
800-327-6812
888-388-9892
Fax: 772-388-9859
sales@macho.com
www.macho.com
• Amir Shadab, President / Chief Executive
Officer
• Nancy Grossbart, VP, Marketing
(888) 388-9892
Products:
Sparring Gear such as Universal Face
Shield, Warrior, Dyna, Chest Protectors,
Cloth Guards, XP, Rival, Sewn Vinyl,
Ringstar Shoes & Shins, and XP Cloth
Guards, Belts, Uniforms, Mouth Protectors,
Groin Protectors, Shoes, Chat Kama,
Training Mats, Equipment Bags,
Promotional Items (Headband, Macho Logo
T-Shirts, Macho Towel), TC Training Line,
and Everlast Training Gear

MACKENZIE COMPANY
1066 WEST HASTINGS STREET
SUITE 1240
OCEANIC PLAZA
VANCOUVER, BC, CANADA V6E 3X1
604-685-9227
Fax: 604-685-4060
mackenz@telus.net
www.mackenziecompany.com
• Jim Stewart, Owner
(503) 246-7330
• Daniel Ramsey, Owner
mackenziecompany@yahoo.com
Products:
Golf - Bags, Headcovers, Trophies/Tee
Prizes

**MACNEILL ENGINEERING-CHAMPS
GOLF SPIKES**
140 LOCKE DRIVE
PO BOX 735
MARLBOROUGH, MA 1752
508-481-8830
800-652-4267
Fax: 508-303-4923
www.champspikes.com
• Harris MacNeill, President / Chief
Executive Officer
• Jeffrey Dow, Chief Operating Officer
• Rich Locke, Chief Financial Officer
Products:
Golf: Spikes, ball markers, cleaning tools,
divot tools, shoe trees, wrenches; Football&
Soccer: spikes and wrenches; Baseball:
Cleats; Track: spikes and wrenches

MAGNET SOLUTIONS
5827 LONG
SHAWNEE, KS 66216

913-631-3528
888-875-8768
Fax: 913-631-3528
• Bridget Sossaya, Owner
Products:
Team Schedule Magnets, Promotional
Magnets, Player Card Magnets, Mouse
Pads, Other Promotional Items

MAGNETSTREET
3890 PHEASANT RIDGE DRIVE NE
Suite 190
BLAINE, MN 55449
763-786-9400
800-788-8633
Fax: 763-786-9393
info@magnetstreet.com
www.magnetstreet.com
• Carrie Biddle, Vice President of Sales
Products:
Manufacturer of the highest quality full-color
refrigerator magnets. Creates custom
magnets such as Save the Date magnets,
calendar magnets, wedding magnets or
business card magnets.

MAGNUM FITNESS SYSTEMS
2201 12TH AVENUE
S MILWAUKEE, WI 53172
414-764-4068
800-372-0554
Fax: 414-768-7047
www.magnumfitness.com
• Larry Nelson, VP
Products:
Bikes, steppers, ellipticals, treadmills, upper
body, handles, dumbbells, olympic bars,
olympic plates, and other fitness equipments

MAIN TROPHY SUPPLY COMPANY
1691 W IMPERIAL COURT
MOUNT PROSPECT, IL 60056
847-439-2550
800-323-6054
Fax: 847-439-5199
sales@maintrophysupply.com
www.maintrophy.com
• Dennis Hoggstrom, General Manager
(847) 435-2550
sales@maintrophysupply.com
• Karen Jones, Production Manager
(847) 435-2550
sales@maintrophysupply.com
• Dan Maxinson, Salesperson
(847) 435-2550
sales@maintrophysupply.com
Products:
Metal, Plastics, Plaques, and award covers.

MAJESTIC ATHLETIC WEAR LIMITED
2320 NEWLINS MILLS RD.
EASTON, PA 18045
610-746-6800
866-471-6861
Fax: 610-588-9958
www.majesticathletic.com
• Faust Capobianco, Founder & Chairman
• Rob Brodersen, VP & General Manager
• Jim Pisani, President
Products:
Baseball Jerseys, Uniforms; Basketball
Uniforms; Football Uniforms, Fleece, Shorts;
Softball Uniforms, Licensed Apparel.
Brands:
MLB Authentic Collection, MLB Genuine
Merchandise, Majestic Select, Home Base,
Majestic Threads.

MAJESTIC ATHLETIC WEAR LIMITED
2320 NEWLINS MILL ROAD
EASTON, PA 18045
610-588-0100
888-824-9470
Fax: 610-588-3800
www.majesticathletic.com
• John Wilson, Director Sales
Football:
AFL - Official Replica Jersey Supplier.

MAKOTO USA INC
5689 S OURAY STREET
CENTENNIAL, CO 80015
303-766-3971
Fax: 303-547-3373
info@makoto-usa.com
www.makoto-usa.com
• Dave Shaw, Vice President
Description:
Manufacturer of the Makoto Sports Arena -
used for training cognitive function and
reaction time.

MANCINO MANUFACTURING CO.,INC.
4700 WISSAHICKON AVENUE
BUILDING E SUITE 109
PHILADELPHIA, PA 19144
800-338-6287
800-338-6287
Fax: 800-949-3595
info@mancinomats.com
www.mancinomats.com
• Robert P. Mancino, President
(800) 338-6287
• Wayne L. Agnew, Digital Media Director
(800) 338-6287
Products:
Manufacturer of folding mats, training
shapes, wall padding and custom safety
cushioning.

MARCIA ORIGINALS
20740 PLUMMER STREET
CHATSWORTH, CA 91311-5001
818-993-1003
800-423-5208
Fax: 818-993-1977
• Marcia Grey, Owner
Products:
Golf Apparel; Racquet Sports Apparel;
Track & Field/Running Apparel-Run/Jog.

MARK OF FITNESS INC
850 ROUTE 1 N
NORTH BRUNSWICK, NJ 8902
732-565-0333
800-438-9260
Fax: 732-565-0335
Products:
Manufacturer of precision products
including: blood pressure monitors, pillbox
timer, medical products, heart rate monitors
and other medical instruments.

MARKWORT SPORTING GOODS COMPANY
1101 RESEARCH BOULEVARD
SAINT LOUIS, MO 63132-1711
314-942-1711
800-280-5555
Fax: 314-942-1179
sales@markwort.com
www.markwort.com
• Glenn Markwort, Chief Executive Officer /
VP

(314) 652-8935
• Bob Herman, General Manager
• Jim Tieszen, Advertising Director
Products:
Manufacturer and distributor of sporting
goods equipment and accessories, like
baseballs, softballs, gloves and mitts,
protective equipment, batter's gloves,
uniforms, socks, laces, glove oil and training
accessories.

MARLIN FIREARMS COMPANY
PO BOX 1871
MADISON, NC 27025
203-239-5621
800-544-8892
Fax: 203-234-7991
www.marlinfirearms.com
• Robert W. W. Behn, President
Products:
Manufacturer of firearms.

MARMOT
5789 STATE FARM DRIVE
SUITE 100
ROHNERT PARK, CA 94928
707-544-4590
888-357-3262
Fax: 707-544-1344
www.marmot.com
• Simon Marmot, Director
Products:
Backpacks, Shelter Tents

MARMOT MOUNTAIN LTD.
5789 STATE FARM DRIVE
SUITE 100
ROHNERT PARK, CA 94928
707-544-4590
888-357-3262
Fax: 707-544-1344
info@marmot.com
www.marmot.com
• Stephen Crisafulli, President / Chief
Executive Officer
• Mark Martin, Chief Operating Officer
Products:
Manufacturer of clothing, sportswear, base
layer, gloves, packs, bags, tents and various
accessories.

MARSHALL-BROWNING INTERNATIONAL CORPORATION
353 CHRISTIAN STREET
SUITE 3
OXFORD, CT 6478
203-264-2702
800-336-6756
Fax: 203-264-0543
sales@robictimers.com
www.robictimers.com
Products:
Manufacturer of handheld timers and
stopwatches.

MARTIN SPORTS, INC.
495 INDUSTRIAL ROAD
PO BOX 6532
CARLSTADT, NJ 7072
800-221-1993
Fax: 201-438-7113
orderdesk@martinsports.com
www.martinsports.com
• Don Martin, Principal
Products:
Manufacturer and importer of sports

equipment and apparel, including beach balls, bean bags, bowling equipment, cageballs, coated foam balls, cones, custom balls, flag footballs, girdles, etc.

MARTIN STONE QUARRIES
1355 N READING AVENUE
BECHTELSVILLE, PA 19505
610-367-2011
Fax: 610-367-8613
sales@martinstone.com
www.martinstone.com
• Glenn Martin, President
• Dave Martin, President, Gable
• Rod Martin, VP
Products:
Produces material used for sports fields and other surfaces.

MARTIN-KILPATRICK TABLE TENNIS COMPANY
4482 TECHNOLOGY DRIVE
WILSON, NC 27896
800-334-8315
Fax: 252-291-8203
sales@butterflyna.com
www.butterflyna.com
• Bowie Martin, President
Products:
Provider of table tennis equipment.

MARTY GILMAN, INC. DBA GILMAN GEAR
30 GILMAN ROAD
GILMAN, CT 06336-0097
800-243-0398
Fax: 860-823-1859
sales@gilmangear.com
www.gilmangear.com
• Neil Gilman, President
(860) 383-1980
neil@gilmangear.com
• Shirley Gilman, Chief Executive Officer
• Nadine Parker, Finance Director
accounting@gilmangear.com
• Jon Macrina, Purchasing Manager
purchasing@gilmangear.com
Products:
Manufacturer of football practice equipment and football field equipment. In addition, manufacturer of basketball training equipment, wrestling training equipment and strength and conditioning equipment.
Teams:
All teams in the NFL and CFL. 600 college teams and 7,000 high school teams.

MASTER HOME PRODUCTS
7520 N SAINT LOUIS AVENUE
SKOKIE, IL 60076
888-710-7206
888-710-7206
Fax: 847-674-9400
customerservice@mhpinternational.com
• Michael Friedman, Founder and President
Products:
Imports Portable Massage Tables and Chairs

MASTER INDUSTRIES WORLDWIDE, LLC
1001 S LINWOOD AVE
SANTA ANA, CA 92705
714-361-9767
Fax: 949-660-1678
sales@masterindustries.com
www.masterindustries.com

• Cathy Kay, General Manager/Controller
Products:
Manufacturer of over 100 premium high-performance bowling accessories for serious amateur and professional enthusiasts.

MASTER SPORTS
6206 EASTGATE MALL
SAN DIEGO, CA 92121
www.mastersports.com
• Eric Doden, General Manager
Products:
Products include Machines, Essential Tools, Accessories, Professional Tracking System

MATCH PLAY OF PINEHURST
695 SW BROAD STREET
SOUTHERN PINES, NC 28387
910-692-3741
888-252-4939
Fax: 910-401-1143
• Doug Smith, Founder
Products:
Golf Clubs and Accessories, Bag Tags, Ball Retrievers, Christmas Items, Clothing & Headwear, Club Repair Materials, Divot Repair Tools, Gloves, Golf Bags, Golf Balls, Golf Clubs, Headcovers, Home/Gift Items, Jewelry, Navika Accessories, Night Golf, Novelty Items, Practice Equipment, Purses & Totes, Rain Protection, Shafts, Socks, Spikes, Team Sport Items, Tees, Towels

MATCH POINT
PO BOX 1211
WAUKESHA, WI 53187
262-827-0206
800-670-4964
Fax: 262-827-0771
jhill47733@aol.com
www.match-point.biz
• Jack Hill, President
(262) 827-0206
jhill47733@aol.com
• Peter Adams, President
Products:
Tennis accessories
Clients:
Schools; Tennis Facilities

MATEFLEX-MELE CORPORATION
2007 BEECHGROVE PLACE
UTICA, NY 13501
315-733-1412
800-926-3539
Fax: 315-735-4372
info@mateflex.com
www.mateflex.com
• Gabe Martini, Sales Manager
(315) 733-1412
gmartini@mateflex.com
• Fred Jones, Vice President, Products & Services
(800) 926-3539
• Tony Sardelli, General Manager
(800) 926-3539
• Sandra Radell, Office Manager
(800) 926-3539
• John Gleason, Manager of Field Services
(800) 926-3539
jgleason@mateflex.com
• Kevin Wheelock, Sales Representative
(800) 926-3539
kwheelock@mateflex.com
• Dan Spinella, Sales Representative
(800) 926-3539

Products:
Mat,flex II, Mat,flex III, ProGym, TileFlex, Inline Arena Tile

MATMAN WRESTLING COMPANY
12724 PACIFIC HIGHWAY SW
TACOMA, WA 98499
253-582-5555
800-426-3999
Fax: 253-582-2591
info@matmanwrestling.com
www.matmanwrestling.com
• Warren Deprenger, President
Products:
Uniforms/Singlets, Warmups, Youth, Accessories, Kneepads, Shoes, Ear Guards

MATZIE GOLF COMPANY, INC.
2271 W. MALVERN AVENUE
SUITE 197
FULLERTON, CA 92833
800-783-2255
www.matzie.com
• Fred Matzie, Founder
• Don Gibas, President
Products:
Amazing Assist, Swing Perfecter, E-Z Tempo trainer, Novelty Putters, Training Grips, Long Putters, Logo Putters

MAXIMUS FITNESS PRODUCTS
4752 W MISSION BOULEVARD
SUITE D
MONTCLAIR, CA 91762
909-364-9099
800-634-6294
Fax: 909-364-9033
Products:
Specializes Home, Hotels, YMCA's, Schools Military Resorts, Apartments, Universities, Physical Therapy, Corporate Fitness Recreation Centers, Correctional Facilities, Personal Training Studios, Police & Fire Departments, Rehab Centers & Hospitals Equipment

MAXLINE EAGNAS
18116 S HOBART BOULEVARD
GARDENA, CA 90248
310-523-4641
Fax: 310-523-2851
maxline@eagnas.com
www.eagnas.com
Products:
Portable Electronic, Stringing Machines, Portable Manual, Stringing Machines, Table-top Electronic, Stringing Machines, Table-top Manual, Stringing Machines, Professional Electronic Stringing Machines, Professional Manual, Stringing Machines, Badminton Machines, Stringing Tools, Strings, Grips, Accessories, Bags, Training Devices, Ball Pick Up Devices, Ball Machines

MAXX GROUP
1200 FORUM WAY S
PO BOX 40610
FORT WORTH, TX 76140
817-336-5671
866-362-3904
Fax: 817-551-0698
www.themaxxgroup.com
• Sasha Denman, Licensing Coordinator
(817) 336-5671

Nature of Service:
Manufacturer of Licensed NASCAR Collectibles
Products:
Barstools, Pub Tables, Car Tackers, Signature Tackers, Big GoGriller, Neon Clocks, Night Lights, Plasma Clocks.

MCARTHUR TOWEL AND SPORTS
700 MOORE STREET
PO BOX 448
BARABOO, WI 53913
608-356-8922
800-356-9168
Fax: 608-356-7587
sales@mcarthurtowels.com
www.mcarthur-towels.com
• Vern Fowler, Divisional Sales Manager
(800) 356-9168
Products:
Designs and distributes blank and printed terry products and sports-related gift items under licenses with professional teams in the NFL, NHL, NBA, MBL, NCAA and NASCAR. Also sells blank towels and terry products.
Year Founded:
1885

MCARTHUR TOWELS & SPORTS
700 MOORE STREET
PO BOX 448
BARABOO, WI 53913
608-356-8922
800-356-9168
Fax: 608-356-7587
sales@mcarthurtowels.com
www.mcarthurtowels.com
• Gregg H. McArthur, President
(608) 356-8922
• Neil Mattson, VP, Operations
(800) 356-9168
• Don Carroll, Manager, Athletic Sales
(800) 356-9168
• Kelly Borchert, Manager, Retail Sales
(800) 356-9168
Description:
Brings affordable quality towels to schools, health clubs and retail stores across the U.S. Carries a full line of bath, bench, sweat and workout towels and offers a line of licensed sports products for the NFL, MLB, NHL and NBA. The extensive licensed product line includes beach towels, baby bibs, game day essentials, golf towels and golf accessories that feature professional team logos from acros the nation. The high profile Gatorade Beach Towel, Super Bowl Trophy Towel and the Steelers' Terrible Towel are a few examples of McArthur's many programs.
Year Founded:
1885
Teams:
All NFL, MLB, NHL, NBA and NCAA

MCCARTHY-SORENSEN ATHLETIC, INC.
1700 PIERCE AVENUE
PO BOX 232
MARINETTE, WI 54143
800-521-3153
Fax: 715-735-7193
• Don Sorensen, President
(800) 521-3153
Products:
Manufactures custom jerseys, custom socks, custom football jerseys, custom lacrosse jersey, custom baseball jersey, referee jerseys, cordura garment bags

MCDAVID SPORTS MEDICAL PRODUCTS
10305 ARGONNE DRIVE
WOODBRIDGE, IL 60517
630-783-0600
800-237-8254
Fax: 630-783-1270
• Rey Corpuz, Marketing Director
• Bob McDavid, President
bmcdavid@mcdavidinc.com
Products:
Sports Medicine, Braces, Supports, Athletic Tape, Hot & Cold Therapy, Cups & Supporters, Performance Apparel, Protective Apparel and Hexpad Technology.
Brands:
McDavid, Cowboy Collar, Hexpad Technology.
Clients:
Major Sporting Goods Retailers, Independent Retailers and Team Dealers.

MCNETT CORPORATION
1411 MEADOR AVENUE
BELLINGHAM, WA 98229
360-671-2227
Fax: 360-671-4521
customerservice@mcnett.com
www.mcnett.com
• Duane McNett, President
• Karen Robins, Human Resources Executive
• Liz Mathias, Sales Executive
• Travis Huisman, CFO
Products:
Adhesives & Seam Sealers, Water Repellents, Cleaners & Rejuvenators, Water Treatment, Tape & Patches

MDF INDUSTRIES INC
127 SHELDON DRIVE
UNIT 1
CAMBRIDGE, ONTARIO, CANADA N1R 6T7
800-452-2154
Fax: 519-624-0339
flemgray@sentex.net
• Ted E Gray, President/Owner
• Gerry Blasioll, Operations Officer
Products:
Skate Sharpeners, Boot Maintenance, Sharpeners Supplies and Paint Shakers.

MECA SPORTSWEAR, INC.
1120 TOWNLINE ROAD
TOMAH, WI 54660
651-638-3800
800-729-6322
Fax: 608-374-6405
infoweb@mecasportswear.com
www.mecasportswear.com
• Tom A. Bramwell, President
• Sue Faulkner, Human Resources Executive
• Rick Zimmerman, Sales Executive
• Joe Clary, Purchasing Executive
Products:
School Jacket, Custom Letter Jacket, Award Letters & Patches, Stock Wool Jackets, Stock nylon Jackets, School Apparel, School Accessories, Corporate Items

MEDI-DYNE HEALTHCARE PRODUCTS LTD
1812 INDUSTRIAL BOULEVARD
PO BOX 1649
COLLEYVILLE, TX 76034
817-251-8660
800-810-1740
Fax: 817-488-6616
customersupport@medi-dyne.com
www.medi-dyne.com
• Craig DiGiovanni, Contact
(817) 251-8660
craig@medi-dyne.com
Products:
Tuli's Shock Absorbers for your feet including heel cups, arch supports, insoles and more. StretchRite multipurpose stretching tool. CoreStretch - an effective device for stretching the back, hips. Skin-on-Skin Blister prevention products.
Brands:
Tulis, Skin-On-Skin, ProStretch, StretchRite, CoreStretch.

MEDIC FIRST AID INTERNATIONAL, INC.
1450 WESTEC DRIVE
PO BOX 21738
EUGENE, OR 97402
541-284-3898
800-447-3177
Fax: 541-344-7429
info@medicfirstaid.com
www.hsi.com
• Bill Clendenen, Chief Executive Officer
• Frank Powers, Chief Operating Officer
• Jeff Jackson, Chief Financial Officer and VP of Production
• Steve Barnett, Marketing Director
(541) 344-7099
Description:
MEDIC FIRST AID is the source for your emergency care needs-from CPR, AED, and First Aid Training, to entire AED implementation programs. MEDIC FIRST AID will help you meet federal, state and local regulatory requirements for workplace safety and health.
Nature of Service:
CPR, AED, First Aid Training, Automated External Defibrillator (AED) implementation
Brands:
MEDIC FIRST AID, American Heart Association

MEIER AND FRANK MDSE. COMPANY, INC.
5641 WASHINGTON STREET
DENVER, CO 80216
303-295-1368
800-525-3569
Fax: 303-293-3814
Products:
Direct importers and distributors of wholesale flags of the world, cloisonn pins (hat tacs), pencil sharpeners, custom lapel pins, fire emblems, embroidered patches, custom glassware and promotional mugs. Also importers, manufacturers and distributors of bowling, golf and soccer motif items.

MELEX PRODUCTS INTERNATIONAL, II, INC./DBA MELEX GOLF CARS
3900 BUSINESS HIGHWAY 70 W
CLAYTON, NC 27520

800-334-8665
Fax: 304-748-2700
www.melex.com
• Andrzej Jesionek, Chief Executive Officer
• K. S. Mallory, VP / Chief Financial Officer
• Andy Kielawa, Research / Development Director
Products:
Assembles and sells golf cars and utility vehicles. Also offers a diverse line of utility vehicles for commercial, industrial and personal use.

MELO CO., INC. AND XS BAGGAGE
1848 STATE ROUTE 9J
STUYVESANT, NY 12173
518-732-7791
Fax: 518-684-2688
melobags@att.net
• Jim Melville, President
Products:
Manufacturer of backpacks,duffles/dance bags, messenger bags, shoulder bags, sling bags, small stuff/add-ons, and tote bags.

MEMORY COMPANY
PO BOX 610
PHOENIX CITY, AL 36868
334-448-0708
888-448-1480
Fax: 334-480-0197
info@memorycompany.com
www.memorycompany.com
• Charles Sizemore, CEO
• Randy Brown, President
Products:
Non apparel gifts within college teams, the NFL, MLB, NHL, NASCAR
Year Founded:
1997

MERCURY INTERNATIONAL CORPORATION
19 ALICE AGNEW DRIVE
N ATTLEBORO, MA 2761
508-699-9000
www.mercuryfootwear.com
• Gary Gorsuch, President
• Irving Wiseman, Chairman / Founder
• Howard Wiseman, Chief Executive Officer
• Nicloas De Santis, President
Products:
General Sports Products - Athletic Shoes, Outdoor Casual Shoes, Workboots.

MERCURY LUGGAGE MFG. CO.
4843 VICTOR STREET
PO BOX 47558
JACKSONVILLE, FL 32207
904-733-9595
800-874-1885
Fax: 904-733-9671
www.mercuryluggage.com
Products:
Manufacturer of trunks and footlockers, as well as the largest supplier of luggage and military logo embroidered bags.

MERCURY MARINE
W6250 W PIONEER ROAD
PO BOX 1939
FOND DU LAC, WI 54936-1939
920-929-5040
Fax: 920-929-5893
www.mercurymarine.com

• Patrick Mackey, President
• Coy Sabel, Communications Manager
• Douglas Pietrowski, Finance Director
Products:
A leading manufacturer of marine propulsion systems.

MERRYGARDEN ATHLETIC WEAR
97 WINFIELD CIRCLE
HARTWELL, GA 30643
706-856-4900
800-849-5555
Fax: 800-849-2121
customerservice@hartwell.com
• Burt Severns, VP Sales / Marketing
Products:
Baseball Uniforms; Basketball Uniforms; Jerseys, Shorts, T-shirts; Soccer Jerseys, Uniforms; Softball Uniforms; Track & Field/Running Apparel-Track & Field; Volleyball Uniforms.

METALTEK
455 KITTY HAWK DRIVE
MORRISVILLE, NC 27560
919-544-0344
800-776-6770
Fax: 919-544-1430
metaltek@msn.com
www.playmatetennismachines.com
Products:
Manufacturer of sporting and athletic goods.

METRO SIGNS ADVERTISING, INC.
4608 SCHUFF AVENUE
LOUISVILLE, KY 40213
502-452-2561
800-441-0627
Fax: 502-473-1286
www.1-metro.com
• C.J. Bud Theobald, President
cjt@1-metro.com
• A Kent Brown, VP Operations
(502) 608-9650
• Hank Allgeier, Senior Graphic Tech
(502) 551-3546
hank@1-metro.com
Products:
Banners (Fabric, Vinyl, Mesh), Feather Banners & Harware, Flags, Media Backdrops, 100% Foam Sideline Banner Stands, Collapsible/Expandable Banner/Panel Frames, Retractable Banner Stands.
Nature of Business:
Concept Creation, Design, Large Format Printing, Portable Frame Systems, Custom Metal Fabrication
Brands:
Transframe, AdCades, AdPads
Year Founded:
1984

MEYCO PRODUCTS, INC.
1225 WALT WHITMAN ROAD
MELVILLE, NY 11747
631-421-9800
800-446-3926
Fax: 631-421-8621
sales@meycoproducts.com
www.meycoproducts.com
• David Weissner, President
• John Ciniglio, VP
Products:
Manufacturer of swimming pool covers.

MICHAEL JORDAN BRAND/NIKE
ONE BOWERMAN DRIVE
BEAVERTON, OR 97005
503-671-6453
800-344-6453
Fax: 503-671-6300
www.jordanbrand.com
• Larry Miller, President, The Jordan Brand
• Howard White, VP, The Jordan Brand
Products:
Designs and markets a wide variety of athletic footwear, apparel and related items for competitive and recreational uses.

MICHIGAN LADDER COMPANY
12 E FOREST AVENUE
PO BOX 981307
YPSILANTI, MI 48198
734-482-5946
800-444-6704
Fax: 734-482-8424
www.michiganladder.com
• R. F. Nissly, President
• Tom Harrison, Owner & President
Description:
Racquet Sports - Table Tennis Equipment.

MICROLITE
100 1ST AVENUE WEST
PO BOX 808
OSKALOOSA, IA 52577
641-673-0411
800-825-6020
Fax: 641-673-6360
service@musco.com
www.musco.com
• Heidi Tegtmeier, Partnership Program Manager
Products:
Designs and manufactures lighting control systems for indoor arenas, outdoor stadiums, college facilities, and multi-purpose civic centers.

MIDWEST LETTERING COMPANY
645 BELLEFONTAINE AVENUE
MARION, OH 43302
740-382-1905
800-848-8289
Fax: 740-387-2788
midwestlettering@midohio.twcbc.com
• Richard Vance, President
Products:
Manufactures Sports Lettering Products, including Die Cut Lettering, Heat Transfers, Digi-Cut Names/Numbers, Heat Seal Presses/Supplies, and Screen Printing Equipment & Supplies.

MIDWEST TROPHY MANUFACTURING, INC.
3405 S E 29TH STREET
DEL CITY, OK 73115
405-670-4545
877-686-7464
Fax: 405-672-0964
info@mytrophy.com
www.mwtrophy.com
• David Smith, Founder / Chief Executive Officer
• Roger Mashore, President
Products:
Manufacturer of medals, ribbons, promotional items, apparel, awards, special recognition, banners/certificates and jewelry.

MIKASA SPORTS USA
1821 KETTERING STREET
IRVINE, CA 92614-5617
800-854-6927
Fax: 800-854-6960
info@mikasasports.com
www.mikasasports.com
• Richard McCoy, President
Products:
Manufacturer of basketball, soccer, football, water polo, rugby, tetherballs, kickballs, dodgeballs, and playground balls.

MIKEN SPORTS
131 BISSEN ST
CALEDONIA, MN 55921
877-807-5291
Fax: 507-725-3675
info@mikensports.com
www.mikensports.com
• Jim Hoschert, Business Manager
• Joe Krage, Chief Financial Officer
• Mike Rommes, Sales Manager
mrommes@mikensports.com
Products:
Manufacturer of high-performance softball and baseball bats; fielding gloves; batting gloves; bags and accessories.

MILLER GOLF
835 BILL JONES INDUSTRIAL DRIVE
SPRINGFIELD, TN 37172
615-384-1286
800-343-1000
Fax: 615-384-1290
www.millergolf.com
• Mike Hedge, President
• Max Waits, Chief Operating Officer
Products:
A leading supplier of customized golf accessories and awards, including bag tags, tees, divot tools, ball markers, towels, umbrellas, head-covers, luggage, and tournament prizes and awards.

MILLER SNOWBOARD SPECIALTIES
PO BOX 1510
OREM, UT 84059
801-223-9500
801-223-9500
Fax: 801-223-9105
millerfree@aol.com
• Matthew Miller, Owner
Products:
Snowboards - Releasable Snowboard Binding, Snowboard Retaining Straps, and Ski Bibs.

MILLERBERND MANUFACTURING COMPANY
622 SIXTH STREET S
PO BOX 98
WINSTED, MN 55395
320-485-2111
Fax: 320-485-4420
www.millerberndmfg.com
• David Millerbernd, President
• Dick Clark, Marketing Manager
(320) 485-2111
• Jim Goodwin, Eastern Regional Sales Manager
(802) 362-5346
• Mike Wendolek, Inside & Area Sales, Key Account Manager
(320) 485-2111
• Steve Klobb, Inside Sales, Regional Manager

(320) 485-2111
sklobe@millerberndmfg.com
• Betty Johnson, Inside Sales, Representative Quotations, Cust
(320) 485-2111
bmj@millerberndmfg.com
Products:
Lighting poles & bases, golf carts, floodlighting poles, decorative lighting poles, high mast lighting poles, heavy-duty hinged camera poles and monopole communications towers

MINIHANE & ASSOCIATES
2 WINTER STREET
WALTHAM, MA 2451
781-891-0460
Fax: 781-891-3629
• Robert Minihane, President
Products:
Baseball - Uniforms; Basketball - Goals, Shoes, Uniforms; Football - Helmets, Uniforms; General Sports Products - Hats/Caps, Referee Uniforms, T-shirts (Licensed); Racquet Sports - Shoes; Softball - Uniforms; Track & Field/Running - Apparel-Track & Field

MIRACLE RECREATION EQUIPMENT COMPANY
878 HIGHWAY 60
MONETT, MO 65708
417-235-6917
888-458-2752
Fax: 417-235-3551
play@miraclerec.com
www.miracle-recreation.com
• Mark Burgess, VP, Sales / Marketing
• Dan Guthrie, President
• Don Hemingway, Vice President of Business Development
Products:
KidRox, Webscapes, Mega Towers, Center Stage, City Park Series, Big Timber, Kids Choice, Tots Choice, Toddlers Choice, Outdoor Fitness, Climbers, Decks, Convertibles, Play Panels, Overhead Challenges, Ramps and Bridges, Roofs, Slides, Stairs and Steps, Climbers, KidRox, Overhead Challenges, Slides, Swings, Spring Riders, Sand and Water, Backstop, Basketball, Pool Slides, Water Slides, Benches, Bike Racks, Bleachers, Litter Receptacles, Grills, Tables

MIRACLE-GRIP LETTERING
440 SPEEDWELL AVENUE
MORRIS PLAINS, NJ 7950
973-267-3240
Fax: 973-540-1589
• Lou Culmone, Partner
Products:
Velcro Removable Lettering.

MITCHELL & NESS NOSTALGIA COMPANY
1201 CHESTNUT STREET
PHILADELPHIA, PA 19107
267-273-7622
866-879-6485
Fax: 215-731-0131
www.mitchellandness.com
Products:
Products include authentic vintage jerseys from MLB, the NBA, NFL, and NHL

MITCHELL RUBBER PRODUCTS, INC.
10220 SAN SEVAINE WAY
MIRA LOMA, CA 91752
800-453-7526
Fax: 909-968-2026
sales@mitchellrubber.com
www.mitchellrubber.com
• Jeffrey Mitchell, President
Products:
Heavy Duty Truck Accessories, Safety Surfacing, Weight Room Flooring, and Flooring for Gymnasiums.

MITSUBISHI DIAMOND VISION
530 KEYSTONE DRIVE
WARRENDALE, PA 15086
724-772-2555
Fax: 724-772-2146
DiamondVisionSales@meppi.com
www.diamond-vision.com
• Steve Mathews, VP, Development / Diamond Vision Systems
• Dave Belding, VP, Technical Operations
• Mark Foster, National Sales Manager
• Marian Loveless, Marketing Coordinator
Products:
Provides a variety of screen sizes and resolutions for Stadiums or Outdoor Sports Applications, Arenas or Indoor Sports Applications, Commercial Applications, Transportable, LEDerAD, HDTV.

MITSUSHIBA INTERNATIONAL, INC.
2300 E WALNUT AVENUE
FULLERTON, CA 92831
714-870-1900
800-722-4061
Fax: 714-870-1921
www.mitsushiba.com
Products:
Golf - Graphite Shafts, Golf Clubs, Golf Bags.

MIZOTT
245 N. ERIE ST.
SUITE 1704
TOLEDO, OH 43604
419-537-3401
Fax: 419-536-0008
www.mizott.com
• Stevie D Lott, Founder
• Phyllis Lott, Business Development

MOHAWK INTERNATIONAL LACROSSE
BOX 13
ROOSEVELTOWN, NY 13683
613-936-1175
Fax: 613-936-2283
• Mark Mitchell, President
Products:
Lacrosse: Field Sticks, Goalie Sticks and Clothing, Mini Lacrosse Sticks, Aluminum and Wood Shafts, Ball Caps, Titanium Shafts, NLL Pro Cage
Brands:
The Mission Extreme, The Mission, The Thunder, Lightning

MOLTEN USA, INC.
1170 TRADEMARK DRIVE
SUITE 109
RENO, NV 89521
775-353-4000
800-477-1994
Fax: 775-358-9407

info@moltenusa.com
www.moltenusa.com
• Melissa Dawson, President
Products:
Baseketball, Football, Volleyball
Accessories, Tetherball, Water Polo Ball,
Soccer Accessories, Soccer Match Balls,
Soccer Practice Balls, Soccer Recreational
Balls, Shinguards Award Balls, Bags, Ball
Carts, Marker Cones/Carrier, Miscellaneous,
Protective Gear, Scoreboards

MONDO AMERICA, INC.
2655 FRANCIS HUGHES
LAVAL, QUEBEC, CANADA H7L 3S8
450-967-5800
800-663-8138
Fax: 450-663-7927
mondo@mondousa.com
www.mondousa.com
• Diane Zupicic, Sales Coordinator
dzupicic@mondousa.com
• Bill Mylett, Sales Manager
mondo@mondousa.com
Products:
Healthcare, Education, Fitness &
Recreation, Track & Field, Mondoturf
Systems, Ice Arena surfaces

MONGOOSE ALL-TERRAIN BOARDS
110 E 59TH STREET
SUITE 3201
NEW YORK, NY 10022
212-688-5600
Fax: 212-688-6683
www.flashrollers.com
• Evan Lipstein, President
Products:
Skateboards, Wheel Sets, Helmets, Pads,
T-shirts, and High Performance All-Terrain
Boards and All-Terrain Board Accessories.

MONITOR PREMIUMS
11045 DONNER PASS ROAD
SUITE 2B
TRUCKEE, CA 96161
530-582-5484
866-288-7893
Fax: 530-579-3266
info@monitorpremiums.com
• Drew Tornga, Managing Director
(530) 582.5484
info@monitorpremiums.com
Products:
Flying Disc, Skateboard Grip Tape, Foam
Trucker Hat, Custom BBQ Apron, Poker
Set, Beverage Koozie, Cell Phone Signal
Enhancer, Flashlight Radio, Messenger
Bag, all with sports logos and desgins.

MONOLITHIC DOME INSTITUTE
177 DOME PARK PLACE
ITALY, TX 76651
972-483-7423
Fax: 972-483-6662
email@monolithic.com
www.monolithic.com
• David South, President
Products:
Gymnasiums, Arenas, Sports Halls, Rinks,
Domes & Buildings
Brands:
Monolithic

MONTRAIL, INC.
1414 HARBOUR WAY SOUTH
SUITE 1005
RICHMOND, CA 94804
206-621-9303
855-698-7245
Fax: 206-621-0230
www.montrail.com
• Menno Vanwyk, Chief Executive Officer
• Scott Tucker, SVP, Financial Planning /
Production
• Greg Meyer, Director
Products:
Outdoor Products - Hiking Boots, Running
Shoes, Trail Shoes.

**MOOSE MOUNTAIN SPORTS & GAMES
LTD**
8 WOOD HOLLOW ROAD
SUITE 302
PARSIPPANY, NJ 7054
973-884-8900
888-666-7388
Fax: 973-884-8999
Products:
Manufacturer of electronic toys and games

MOPRO
1024 N COUNTY ROAD W
ODESSA, TX 79763
432-550-2633
866-245-2497
Fax: 432-550-0605
• Reggie Lawrence, Contact
(432) 550-2633
Products:
Leading innovator in hat accessories and
related items to distributors in the
promotional products industry and retailers.

MORETZ SPORTS
514 W 21ST STREET
PO BOX 580
NEWTON, NC 28658
828-464-0751
866-714-8486
Fax: 828-464-8078
www.goldtoe.com
• John Moretz, President / Chief Executive
Officer
(828) 464-0751
• Jeff Wheeler, President, Sales
(828) 464-0751
• Denise Yow, President, Design /
Merchandising
(828) 464-0751
• Paul Delmonico, President
• Dave Johnson, CFO
Products:
Dominant sockwear manufacturer in the
sporting goods trade channel.

MOREY BODYBOARDS
5903 CHRISTIE AVENUE
EMERYVILLE, CA 94608
510-596-4200
888-942-6650
Fax: 510-596-4292
www.moreybodyboards.com
• Greg Lehr, SVP, Manufacturing / Logistics
• Steve Simes, SVP
Products:
Manufacturer of bodyboards, swinfins,
skimboards, gear and surfboards.

MOSLOW & BRO., INC., M.A.
375 NORFOLK AVENUE
BUFFALO, NY 14215
716-896-2950
800-828-7140
Fax: 716-896-2699
sales@moslowbros.com
www.moslowbros.com
• William M. Moslow, President
Products & Services:
Provides products in wood, jade and clear
crystal, acrylic, and marble to the award,
recognition and giftware industries. Also
provides custom product design and
manufacturing, and personalized services
such as drop shipment and custom
packaging.

MOSSBERG & SONS, INC.
7 GRASSO AVENUE
NORTH HAVEN, CT 6473
203-230-5300
800-363-3555
Fax: 203-230-5420
service@mossberg.com
www.mossberg.com
• Alan Iver Mossberg, CEO
• Linda Powell, Director Of Media Relations
• Thomas L. Taylor, VP Of Sales &
Marketing
Products:
Hunting/shooting firearms.

MOTION IMAGING
975 MAIN STREET
FARMINGDALE, NY 11735
516-777-3700
Fax: 516-777-5627
• Robert Thompson, President
• John Conkling, Vice President
Products:
Producer of high quality lenticular posters,
magnets, cups and point of purchase
displays with brilliant 3D imagery.
Year Founded:
1999

MOTORHEAD PRODUCTS
PO BOX 1338
CULLMAN, AL 35056
256-775-6337
866-542-6337
Fax: 256-775-3605
info@motorheadproducts.com
www.motorheadproducts.com
• Mike Rogus, Chief Executive Officer
(256) 775-6337
ceo@motorheadproducts.com
• Jeff Lamote, President
(256) 775-6337
jeff@motorheadproducts.com
Products:
Manufactures fine gift and novelty items
under license from NASCAR, Inc, NASCAR
Racing Teams and Drivers, General Motors
and Dodge Classic Automobiles (Muscle
Cars), Monster Garage, Monster House,
John Deere, NFL, BBQ accessories,
beverage accessories, keychains, leather
accessories and pins
Year Founded:
1999

MOTORSPORTS AUTHENTICS
6301 PERFORMANCE DRIVE
CONCORD, NC 28027

704-454-4000
800-952-0708
RCCAInfo@lionelnascar.com
www.lionelnascarcollectables.com
• Mark Dyer, President/CEO
• Howard Hitchcock, Vice President and General Manager
Products:
Produces racing collectibles with ten years experience in the design, manufacture, and marketing of racing merchandise. Its products include a broad range of motorsports-related die-cast car replica collectibles, apparel, souvenirs and other memorabilia.
Brands:
Action Racing Collectables (ARC), the Racing Collectables Club of America (RCCA), Revell Collection, Winner's Circle, and Chase Authentics

MOTZ GROUP
3607 CHURCH STREET
SUITE 300
CINCINNATI, OH 45244
513-533-6452
800-871-3992
Fax: 513-871-5889
info@themotzgroup.com
www.themotzgroup.com
• Joseph Motz, President/Chief Executive Officer
• Mark Heinlein, Senior Vice President
• John Lill, MCC General Manager
• Zach A. Burns, President
Products:
Designs and constructs quality natural grass adn synthetic turf field systems.
Brands:
Pat®-Moisture Management System for sports fields, 24/7®-Infilled Synthetic Turf, HPG®-Custom Designed Field Systems, TS-II®-Synthetically Stabilized Natural Turf.

MOUNTAIN HARDWEAR
1414 HARBOR WAY S
SUITE 105
RICHMOND, CA 94804
510-558-3000
800-953-8375
877-927-5649
Fax: 510-559-6709
www.mountainhardwear.com
• Topher Gaylord, President
Products:
Manufacturer of men's and women's apparel and outdoor products like outerwear, sleeping bags, tents and other accessories.

MOUNTAIN HIGH HOSIERY, INC.
1791 W DAIRY PLACE
TUCSON, AZ 85705
800-528-5355
• Gerald Birin, Chief Executive Officer
Products:
Manufactures hosiery for men and women.

MOUNTAIN SAFETY RESEARCH
4000 1ST AVENUE S
SEATTLE, WA 98134
205-505-9500
800-531-9531
Fax: 206-682-4184
info@msrgear.com
www.msrgear.com/

• Dave Bartholomew, President / Chief Executive Officer
• Ken Meidell, VP
Products:
Manufacturer of Tents, Stoves & Fuel, Cookware, Hydration, Water Treatment, Packtowl, Snow Equipment, and Poles.

MOUNTED MEMORIES INC
5000 NW 108 AVENUE
SUNRISE, FL 33351
954-742-8544
800-749-7529
Fax: 954-742-7044
www.mountedmemories.com
Products:
An industry leader in sports memorabilia collectibles and acrylic cases. Line of products include baseballs, footballs, basketballs, jerseys and other hand-signed memorabilia.

MOVING COMFORT, INC.
19910 N CREEK PARKWAY
SUITE 200
BOTHELL, WA 98011-8223
800-763-6000
Fax: 425-489-1975
www.movingcomfort.com
• Ellen Wessel, President
Products:
Offers a variety of women's sport bras, sport underwear, shorts, tops, tights and outerwear for running, hiking, walking, weight training, yoga, martial arts, kayaking, skiing and snowshoeing, rock climbing, horseback riding, golf, tennis, basketball, volleyball, soccer, inline skating, etc.

MPC PROMOTIONS
4300 PRODUCE ROAD
LOUISVILLE, KY 40218
502-451-4900
800-331-0989
Fax: 888-451-8475
customerservice@mpcpromotions.com
www.mpcpromotions.com
• Donald V Dobina, President
Products:
Producer of top quality promotional products that can be customized with company logo for promotions, advertising incentives, trade shows, business gifts and employee recognition programs. MPC also designs corporate incentive and licensed apparel programs.

MTC MARKETING INC
1624 WEST CROSBY ROAD
CARROLLTON, TX 75006
972-488-0577
800-295-4995
Fax: 972-488-8595
customerservice@mtcmarketinginc.com
• Odalis Perez, Administrative Assistant
(972) 488-0577
Products:
Manufacturer of Sports Jackets and Caps.

MUELLER SPORTS MEDICINE, INC.
ONE QUENCH DRIVE
PO BOX 99
PRAIRIE DU SAC, WI 53578
608-643-8530
800-356-9522

Fax: 608-643-2568
www.muellersportsmed.com
• Brett Mueller, President
• Curt Mueller, Chief Executive Officer
• Herb Raschka, Senior Vice President
• Rick Olson, National Sporting Goods Sales Manager
• Jeff Mueller, VP
• Jane Volts, National Key Account Rep
Products:
Abrasion Control/Padding, Analgesics, Blood spill/Biohazard Products, Bottles & Bottle Carriers, Braces & Supports, Cleaners/Disinfectants, Cold/Hot Therapy, Grip Enhancers, Mouthguards, Protective Gear, Quench Sports Gum, Sports Accessories, Tapes & Wraps, Trainers Kits
Nature of Service:
Manufacture and distribute complete line of Sports Medicine Products worldwide.
Brands:
No Glare, M-Tape, M-Wrap, Quench, Sport Care, Hg80 (Mueller Mercury), ATF Ankle Brace, and Whizzer

MULTI-AD
1720 W DETWEILLER DRIVE
PEORIA, IL 61615
309-692-1530
800-348-6485
Fax: 309-692-8378
info@multiad.com
www.multi-ad.com
• Brian Jeske, Vice President, Sports Operations
(770) 421-6461
• Joe Dalfonso, Sports Consultant
(800) 348-6485
• Ron Fauss, Sports Consultant
(309) 648-0531
Year Founded:
1945
Sports Service Founded:
1990
Description:
Sports printer specializing in programs, media guides, trading cards, promotional material. Design, mailing and warehouse services offered as well.

MURREY INTERNATIONAL
14150 S FIGUEROA STREET
LOS ANGELES, CA 90061
310-532-6091
800-421-1022
Fax: 310-217-0504
sales@murreybowling.com
www.murreybowling.com
• Patrick Murrey, President
Products:
Bowling Lanes, Seats, Ball Returns, Combo Tables, Food Court Tables, Masking Units, Rack 'N Rolls, Graphics, Pinsetting Machines, Rental Shoes.

MUSCO SPORTS-LIGHTING
100 1ST AVENUE W
PO BOX 808
OSKALOOSA, IA 52577
641-673-0411
800-825-6030
Fax: 641-673-4852
lighting@musco.com
www.musco.com
• Joe Crookham, President
joe.crookham@musco.com
• Jeanie Bieri, Director, Marketing

• Heidi Tegtmeier, Partnership Program Manager
heidi.tegtmeier@musco.com
Products:
Lighting for Sports Fields.

MYLEC, INC.
37 COMMERCIAL DRIVE
WINCHENDON, MA 1475
978-297-0089
Fax: 978-297-1359
berdmann@mylec.com
www.mylec.com
• Ricky Laperriere, President
(978) 297-0089
ricky@mylec.com
• Ken Cashman, Vice President
(978) 297-0089
Products:
Street Hockey - Balls, Goals, Flooring, Protective Equipment, Sticks and Blades.

N CASE IT
19 INDUSTRIAL DRIVE
PACIFIC, MO 63069
636-257-6655
800-536-6655
Fax: 636-257-0531
support@ncaseit.com
www.ati-1.com
• Keith Skubic, Area Sales Representative
(636) 257-6655
keith.skubic@ati-1.com
• Vicki Stone, Area Sales Representative
(636) 257-6655
vicki.stone@ati-1.com
• Thomas C. White, President
• Dave Ambrose, Sales
(636) 257-8929
• Jeff Novak, Outside Sales
(415) 665-6934
jeff.novak@ati-1.com
Products:
Largest stocking distributor/fabricator of thermosets and thermoplastics.

N.J.P. SPORTS, INC.
548 W ARDEN AVENUE
GLENDALE, CA 91203
818-247-3914
800-773-4657
Fax: 818-247-2605
njpsports@earthlink.net
www.njpsports.com
• Norman J. Perry, President
(818) 247-3914
njpsports@earthlink.net
• Regina Perry, VP
(818) 247-3914
njpsports@earthlink.net
Products:
Fabricates and installs windscreens, netting, and other items related to tennis, baseball, and sports. Provides builders with tennis posts, sleeves and other court items.

NASH MANUFACTURING INC
315 W RIPY STREET
PO BOX 11526
FORT WORTH, TX 76110
817-926-5223
800-433-2901
Fax: 817-924-5111
• Russ Miller, President
Products:
Manufactures skateboards, waterboards, bodyboards, waterskiis and wakeboards.

NATARE CORPORATION
5905 W 74TH STREET
INDIANAPOLIS, IN 46278-1786
317-290-8828
800-336-8828
Fax: 317-290-9998
natare@natare.com
www.natare.com
• Michael Walsh, President
(800) 336-8828
• David L. Keim, VP
• Scott C. Calwell, Natare Product Manager
(800) 336-8828
scalwell@natare.com
Products:
Seen as one of the world's most respected manufacturers and suppliers in the pool industry, Natare offers equipment, complete systems, and services for commercial and public swimming pools, water parks, and aquatic facilities. Our products and systems include stainless steel pools and spas, PVC pool membrane lining, pool gutters, filtration systems, bulkheads, and more.

NATIONAL BATTING CAGES, INC
PO BOX 250
FOREST GROVE, OR 97116-0250
800-547-8800
Fax: 503-357-3727
sales@nationalbattingcages.com
www.nationalbattingcages.com
• Fred Schmidtke, President
(503) 357-6615
Products:
Manufacturer of baseball equipment such as Portable Batting Cages, Batting Tunnel Nets, Protective Screens, Batting Tunnel Frames, Pitching Mounds, Windscreen Stadium Netting, Accessories, Pitching Machines, Outdoor Support Frame, and Hitting Cages.

NATIONAL EMBLEM INC
17036 S AVALON BOULEVARD
PO BOX 5325
CARSON, CA 90746-5325
310-515-5055
800-877-6185
Fax: 310-515-5966
bids@nationalemblem.com
www.nationalemblem.com
• David Wilson, Regional Sales Executive
Products:
Manufacturer of custom embroidered emblems, flags, baseball caps, key rings and woven labels for Major League Baseball, National Football League, NBA and NHL.

NATIVE SUN SPORTSWEAR
4590 62ND AVENUE N
PINELLAS PARK, FL 33781
727-528-2111
800-777-5800
Fax: 727-528-8441
info@nativesunsports.com
www.nativesunsports.com
• George A. Mitcheson, President
(727) 528-2111
info@nativesunsports.com
Products:
Caps and Visors, T-Shirts, Lapel Pins, Polos, and Wind Jackets.

NATURAL BALANCE, INC.
3130 N COMMERCE COURT
CASTLE ROCK, CO 80109
800-833-8737
800-624-4260
Fax: 800-661-9890
www.naturalbalance.com
• Mark Owens, Founder
• Caroline Owens, Founder
Products:
Producer of quality herbal and natural products, nutritional supplements for athletes.

NATURAL SPORT
8300 MARYLAND AVENUE
PO BOX 29
SAINT LOUIS, MO 63105
314-854-4000
800-766-6465
Fax: 314-854-2037
www.brownshoecompany.com
• Ronald A. Fromm, Chairman and Chief Executive Officer
(314) 854-4000
• Diane M. Sullivan, President
• Kenneth W. Gilberton, President
• Richard C. Schumacher, VP
Products:
A leading consumer-driven footwear company and a marketer and supplier of branded, private label and licensed footwear to department stores, mass-merchandisers, independent and specialty stores.

NAUTICA INTERNATIONAL
40 W 57TH STREET
NEW YORK, NY 10019
866-376-4184
Fax: 212-887-8136
www.nautica.com
• Zach Augustine, Vice President/Creative Services Director
• Anne Lacombe, Vice President Marketing
Boating/Yachting:
2003 Dennis Conner Stars & Stripes.

NAUTILUS HPS, INC.
17750 SE 6TH WAY
VANCOUVER, WA 98683
360-859-2900
800-782-4799
800-605-3369
Fax: 360-694-7755
sales@nautilus.com
www.nautilusgroup.com
• Gregg Hammann, President and Chief Executive Officer
• Bill Meadowcroft, Chief Financial Officer
• Tim Hawkins, Chief Customer Officer & Chief Marketing
• Darryl Thomas, SVP, Strategic Planning and Internationa
Products:
Provides tools and education necessary to help people achieve a fit and healthy lifestyle. Manufactures and markets a complete line of innovative health and fitness products through direct, commercial, retail, specialty and international channels.

NCED SAHARA
12100 ESTHER LAMA DRIVE
EL PASO, TX 79936
915-833-1145
800-669-5646
Fax: 800-473-4190

• Robert E. Jones, President and Chief Executive Officer
• Ernie Lopez, VP / Chief Operations Officer
• Brian Keiser, Chief Financial Officer
• Steve Wilson, General Manager
Products:
T-Shirts and Sweatshirts, Warm-Ups, Windshirts, Jackets, Caps and Hats, and Bags

NCR
6060 PRIMACY PARKWAY
SUITE 460
MEMPHIS, TN 38119
901-681-2800
800-852-5852
Fax: 901-681-2802
www.counterpointpos.com
• Andee Pure Williamson, Marketing Manager
(901) 681-2800
andee.williamson@radiantsystems.com
• Mike Phelan, Marketing Analyst
(901) 681-2800
• Joanna Cravens, Account Manager
(901) 681-2800
• Beverly Emerson, Account Manager
(901) 681-2800
Products:
CounterPoint Point of sale/inventory management software and accompanying services include CPOnline (integrated Ecommerce package) and CPGateway (2-second card processing)

NDL PRODUCTS, INC.
4031 NE 12 TERRACE
OAKLAND PARK, FL 33334
954-566-0040
800-979-4343
Fax: 954-568-6906
• Joseph Giaquinto, President
(954) 566-0040
Products:
Sports medicine and health care products for the mass-merchant, chain drug and chain food national distribution channels. NDL's collection of brands service specific segments of the sporting goods and health care markets with its sports medicine, protective gear, health supports and magnetic therapy products. NDL also offers private label or house brand programs to major retailers and large wholesalers along with specific OEM programs to outside brands that service the same markets.

NEFF - DEALER DIVISION
645 PINE STREET
PO BOX 218
GREENVILLE, OH 45331
937-548-3194
800-232-6333
Fax: 800-544-9030
www.neffco.com
• Bruce Hines, President
• Micky Sullivan, Athletic Director
Products:
Offers a comprehensive line of awards that includes Plaques, Chenille Letters, Medals, Certificates, Banners, and more, including staff and student apparel, Letter Jackets, and custom scholastic graphics.

NEIL ENTERPRISES
450 E BUNKER COURT
VERNON HILLS, IL 60061

847-549-7627
800-621-5584
Fax: 847-549-0349
info@neilenterprises.com
www.neilenterprises.com
• Neil Fine, President
(847) 549-7627
nfine@neilenterprises.com
• Ted Swiss, Sales Manager
(847) 549-7627
• Micheal Sheck, VP
Products:
Promotional product/photo novelty manufacturer and also a supplier/distributor of Sony Printers and Media. Manufactures a proprietary line of Easy Snapins which can be assembled on the spot. Included are buttons, key tags, mugs, resin sports frames, memory notes, sponsor plaques, water bottles, metal button machines and much more.
Year Founded:
1961

NET RESULTS SPORTS MARKETING/NRSM INC.
3405 OAK STREET
Chicago, IL, 60606
MYRTLE BEACH, SC 29577
843-916-8218
Fax: 843-916-8210
info@netsportsplus.com
www.netsportsplus.com
• Max Davis, President
Nature of Service:
Sports Construction: Includes Paving, Sports Lighting, Sports Fencing, Sport Specific Accessories and Landscaping. Specialize in Tennis Courts, Basketball Courts and Running tracks. Certified Professionals for all applications and projects. Windscreens, Fence Capping, Custom Logos, Sports Netting and Sports Padding for indoor and outdoor applications. Seating (Benches, Custom Sports Seating, Bleachers and Stadium Seating). Also we can supply and install high tech Shade Structures for all types of seating applications. Tennis Accessories: Clay Court Equipment and Supplies, Courts Awning and Cabanas, Nets and Net Posts, and Teaching Equipment.

NEUEDGE SPORTSWEAR
8 CORPORATE BOULEVARD
SINKING SPRING, PA 19068
610-678-4050
800-486-2788
Fax: 610-678-4040
Products:
Manufacturer of uniforms for basketball, soccer, softball and volleyball

NEUMANN & COMPANY, R.
300 OBSERVER HIGHWAY
PO BOX MD
HOBOKEN, NJ 7030
201-659-3400
800-372-4141
Fax: 201-659-6655
• Richard Bernheim, President
Products:
Golf - Leather Grips; Tennis - Leather Grips

NEVCO
301 E HARRIS AVENUE
GREENVILLE, IL 62246-2151

618-664-0360
800-851-4040
Fax: 618-664-0398
sales@nevco.com
www.nevco.com
• Scott Moore, VP Sales & Marketing
• Gary Robert, President and COO
• Paul R. Peterson, Marketing Manager
(800) 851-4040
Products:
Scoreboards for Baseball/Softball, Basketball, Football, Hockey, Soccer, Swimming, Track, Volleyball, Wrestling; Video Displays, Accessories, Signage, Controls, Shot Clocks/Timers

NEVER SUMMER SNOWBOARDS
5077 COLORADO BOULEVARD
DENVER, CO 80216
303-320-1813
Fax: 303-320-0771
info@neversummer.com
www.neversummer.com
• Nick Giancamilli, President
Products:
Snowboards and Clothing

NEW AGENDA BY PERRIN
5320 RUSCHE DRIVE
COMSTOCK PARK, MI 49321
616-785-9091
800-243-6361
Fax: 616-785-9312
canderson@perrinwear.comÿ
www.perrinwear.com
• Todd Dufford, National Sales Manager
(800) 243-6326
Products:
Apparel: Athletic, Children's, Imprinted, Licensed Collegiate apparel, Screen Print and Embroidery.
Year Founded:
1992

NEW BALANCE ATHLETIC SHOE, INC.
BRIGHTON LANDING 20 GUEST STREET
BOSTON, MA 02135-2088
617-783-4000
800-595-9138
Fax: 617-787-9355
info@newbalance.com
www.newbalance.com
• James S. Davis, Chairman and Chief Executive Officer
• Jim Tompkins, President and Chief Operating Officer
Products:
Footwear, Apparel, Accessories and Equipment for all Sports, including Basketball, Outdoor Sports, Hiking, Racquet Sports, Track & Field, Volleyball, Golf, Baseball, Tennis, Football, Training

NEW ENGLAND CAP CO.
756 DERBY AVENUE
SEYMOUR, CT 6483
203-736-6184
Fax: 203-732-5105
www.newenglandcap.com
• Eric Black, Operations Manager
Products:
Clothing, Hats, Caps, Jackets, T-shirts

NEW ERA CAP, CO
160 DELAWARE AVENUE
BUFFALO, NY 14202

716-604-9000
877-NEC-5950
Fax: 716-604-9299
www.neweracap.com
• Gary Matos, Senior Vice President, Marketing
  ext 1169
• John DeWaal, Vice President, Global Marketing
  ext 1137
john.dewaal@neweracap.com
• Jim Wannemacher, Vice President, Advertising
  ext 1286
jim.wannemacher@neweracap.com
• Dana Marciniak, Manager, Corporate Communications
(716) 604-9259
dana.marciniak@neweracap.com
• Katherine Kulczyk, Media Contact
  ext 1463
katherine.kulczyk@neweracap.com
Products:
Manufacturer of sports-licensed headwear.

NEW HERMES INC.
2200 NORTHMONT PARKWAY
DULUTH, GA 30096
770-623-0331
800-543-7637
800-533-7637
Fax: 770-814-7203
www.gravograph.us
• Ben Anderson-Ray, Chief Executive Officer
• Gerard Guyard, Chairman
Products:
Manufacturer of engraving machines, marking equipment, signage and other engraving products.

NEW YORK EMBLEMS & AWARDS, INC.
4644 ELEVENTH STREET
3RD FLOOR
LONG ISLAND CITY, NY 11101
718-786-8852
Fax: 718-786-8857
• David Srebnik, President
Products:
Trophies, Awards - Components, Emblems, Jewelry, Medals, Plaques, Ribbons

NEWSOUTH ATHLETIC COMPANY INC.
301 E MAIN STREET
PO BOX 604
DALLAS, NC 28034
704-922-1557
800-438-9934
Fax: 704-922-5324
• Randy Harris, VP and Chief Operating Officer
Products:
Softball and Baseball Pants, Jerseys and Accessories

NEWTEX USA
8050 VICTOR MENDON ROAD
VICTOR, NY 14564
585-924-9135
800-836-1001
Fax: 585-924-4645
sales@newtex.com
www.newtex.com
• Doug Bailey, President
(716) 909-3477
Products:
Manufacturer of high-tech, heat resistant

products for the industrial and safety markets.

NGI SPORTS
2807 WALKER ROAD
CHATTANOOGA, TN 37421
423-499-5546
800-835-0033
Fax: 423-499-8882
info@ngisports.com
www.ngisports.com
• Rick Burke, Owner/Manager/CEO/COO
• David Burke, East Coast Sales
• Terri West, Office Manager/Sales & Service
• Corey Brisbin, Western States Sales/Technical Manager
Products:
Synthetic Turf Surfaces for Golf, Soccer, Tennis, and Field Sports.
Brands:
Nova Pro Court XP; Nova Pro Bouncer; Nova Pro Clay; Nova Pro Xtreme; Titan Trax Shield

NICKLAUS GOLF EQUIPMENT COMPANY, L.C.
951 US HIGHWAY ONE
SUITE 500
NORTH PALM BEACH, FL 33408
561-691-3434
800-322-1872
Fax: 561-227-0548
contact@nicklausgolf.com
www.nicklaus-golf.com
• Jack Nicklaus, Chairman
• Robert P. Kelly, Chief Executive Officer
• Robert Cook, Chief Financial Officer
• William Henwood, Chief Sales and Marketing Officer
Products:
Golf Clubs

NIELSEN-KELLERMAN
21 CREEK PARKWAY
BOOTHWYN, PA 19061
610-447-1555
800-784-4221
Fax: 610-447-1577
info@nkhome.com
www.nkhome.com
• Richard Kellerman, President
• Katie Gofrey, Kastrel Sales Manager
khorn@nkhome.com
Nature of Service:
Provides electronic equipment for the United States Rowing team.

NIELSEN-KELLERMAN
21 CREEK CIRCLE
BOOTHWYN, PA 19061
610-447-1555
800-784-4221
Fax: 610-447-1577
info@nkhome.com
www.nkhome.com
• Katie Horn, Kastrel Sales Manager
khorn@nkhome.com
• Chris Mesigian, Internal Sales Manager, Rowing
• Michael Naughton, Product Manager
mnaughton@nkhome.com
• Richard Kellerman, President
• Paul Nielsen, VP
• Alix Kocher, Administrator
• Alix James, Marketing

Products:
Rowing/Padding Equipment, Wind/Weather Instruments, Interval Timing Systems, Watches, and other Waterproof Intruments for active lifestyles and technical applications

NIGHT SPORTS
952-935-9140
800-933-7825
Fax: 952-935-9142
info@nightsportsusa.com
www.nightsportsusa.com
• John Gill, President
• David Shirley, European Office
davidshirley@nightsportsuk.com
Products:
Glow in the dark golf/mini putt balls.

NIKE GOLF
ONE BOWERMAN DRIVE
BEAVERTON, OR 97005
503-671-6453
Fax: 503-671-6376
info@nike.com
www.nikegolf.com
• Bob Wood, President
• David Pillsbury, U.S. General Manager
• John Springer, Director, General Operations
Products:
Golf apparel, footwear, headwear, balls, and bags

NIKE, INC.
ONE BOWERMAN DRIVE
BEAVERTON, OR 97005-6453
503-671-6453
800-344-6453
Fax: 503-646-6926
www.nike.com
• Philip H. Knight, Chairman
• Mark Parker, President and Chief Executive Officer
• David Ayre, EVP, Global Human Resources
• Don Blair, EVP/Chief Financial Officer
• Trevor Edwards, President, Nike Brands
• Jeanne P Jackson, President, Product & Merchandising
Products:
Sports footwear, apparel and equipment

NIKON SPORTS & RECREATIONAL OPTICS
1300 WALT WHITMAN ROAD
MELVILLE, NY 11747-3064
631-547-4200
800-645-6678
Fax: 631-547-4025
www.nikonusa.com
• Toshiyuki Masai, Chief Executive Officer & President
• David C. Lee, Senior VP
• Richard LoPinto, Senior VP Of Product
• Joseph Carfora, VP Of Sales
Products:
Photography Equipment, Binoculars, Microscopes, Optical Instruments with special features for use in the sports industry.

NILS, INC.
3550 CADILLAC AVENUE
COSTA MESA, CA 92626

877-412-7467
800-933-6457
Fax: 866-756-4463
info@nils.us
www.nilsskiwear.com
• Lane Fowler, Marketing and Customer Service Manager
• Nils Anderson, Owner & Chief Executive Officer
Products:
Manufacturer and designer of Women's Skiwear and Sportswear.

NIRVE SPORTS
15401 ASSEMBLY LANE
HUNTINGTON BEACH, CA 92649
714-892-5795
888-296-4783
Fax: 714-963-6762
info@nirve.com
www.nirve.com
• Linda Reed, National Sales Manager
(714) 593-8301
Products:
Designer of collectible lifestyle cruiser and chopper bicycles, components, and accessories.

NO FAULT INDUSTRIES
3112 VALLEY CREEK DRIVE
SUITE C
BATON ROUGE, LA 70808
225-215-7760
866-637-7678
Fax: 225-291-3821
info@nofault.com
www.nofault.com
• David Brantley, President and Owner
(225) 215-7760
• Jennifer Smith, Vice President of Sales & Administration
(225) 215-7760
• Jay Ratelle, Vice President of Operations
Products:
Sport and Safety Surface Products, Rubber Mulch, Safety Tile, Sport Floor

NO FEAR
183 MADISON AVE
SUITE 1701
NEW YORK, NY 10016
760-931-9550
877-796-7842
Fax: 760-931-9741
www.nofear.com
• Larry Collette, President
• Anthony Miranda, Sports Marketing
Products:
General Sports Activewear, Athletic Footwear, T-shirts, Eyewear, Watches, Accessories

NOCONA ATHLETIC GOODS COMPANY
2650 SOUTH 46TH STREET
SUITE 105
PHOENIX, AZ 85034
602-381-5434
800-433-0957
Fax: 940-825-4994
info@nokona.com
www.nokona.com
• Robert M. Storey Jr, President
Products:
Baseball - Bases, Batting Helmets, Gloves/Catcher/Fielder/First Base, Protective-Catcher/Umpire; Football - Bags, Equipment, Helmets, Knee/Elbow Pads,

Masks, Shields, Shoulder Pads; Softball - Bases, Gloves-Catcher/Fielder/First Base

NOLIMITZ
1265 NORTH MAIN
WHITE SALMON, WA 98672
509-493-4484 Ext 222
Fax: 509-493-4485
www.nolimitz.com
• Jason Lemieux, Recreational Sales & Marketing
Products:
Windsurfing masts

NORA SYSTEMS, INC.
9 NORTHEASTERN BLVD
SALEM, NH 03079
978-689-1021
800-332-6672
800-332-NORA
Fax: 603-894-6615
www.nora.com/us
• Christine Mousseau, Marketing Specialist
(978) 689-0530
Description:
Durable rubber flooring in a wide range of colors and patterns to create appealing designs. Offering a high degree of slip resistance to ensure safe footing and low maintenance for floors that look as good as they perform.
Year Founded:
1986 (U.S.)
Products:
norament™ grano, norament™ 992
Brands:
norament™, noraplan™

NORDICA USA
VIA FANTE D'ITALIA 56
31040
GIAVERA DEL MONTELLO, TREVISO, ITALY 3784
+39-
800-892-2668
www.nordica.com
• Andy Knittle, President
• Wendy Reger, Marketing Communications Manager
• Kirk Langford, Vice President Sales
• Theresa Powell, Customer Service Manager
Products:
Skiing-Alpine - Accessories, Apparel, Boots, Gloves

NORDICTRACK
1500 S 1000 W
LOGAN, UT 84321
888-308-9616
877-993-7999
Fax: 435-786-3987
service@iconfitness.com
www.nordictrack.com
• Patrick J Hald, President/COO
• Michael Larson, VP, Sales
• Colleen Logan, VP, Marketing
Products:
Treadmills, Ellipticals, Exercise Bikes, Strength Training, Incline Trainers, Skiers, Steppers, Accessories, Men's Apparel, Women's Apparel, Jogging Strollers, Yoga, Relaxation, Pilates, Commercial Grade Equipment

NORSK FITNESS PRODUCTS, INC.
2100 SAINT PATRICK STREET
MONTREAL, QC, CANADA H3K 1B2
514-931-3635
800-667-7510
Fax: 514-932-2779
info@thera-p.com
www.thera-p.com
• Mark Chaimberg, Vice President
info@thera-p.com
• Eric Chaimberg, VP Graphic Design
echaimberg@swingpaints.com
Products:
Manufactures fitness products, including cold and heated compression wraps, and gel packs.
Year founded:
1993.

NORTH FACE
14450 DOOLITTLE DRIVE
SAN LEANDRO, CA 94577
888-863-1968
855-500-8639
Fax: 510-618-3531
tnf_consumerservices@vfc.com
www.thenorthface.com
• Steve Rendle, President
• Dan Templin, Chief Finnacial Officer
• Jody Kalmbach, VP, Marketing
• Dave Sweet, VP, Operations
Products:
Men's apparel, Women's Apparel, Footwear, Tents, Bags, Sleeping Bags, Accessories

NORTH SPORTS, INC.
1 N SHORE DRIVE SE
WHITE SALMON, WA 98672
509-493-4938
Fax: 509-493-4966
www.northsports.com
• David Johnson, President
• Aaron Carpenter, VP
Importer:
Sailboards, Snowboards.

NORTH STAR LIGHTING, INC.
835 INDUSTRIAL DRIVE
ELMHURST, IL 60126
708-681-4330
800-229-4330
Fax: 708-681-4006
www.northstar-lighting.com
• Sobit Inan, President
• Jeffrey Sanders, Marketing Manager
Products:
Sports lighting, Area lighting, Industrial lighting, Floodlighting, Roadway lighting, Commercial lighting, Poles and Accessories, Security Lighting, Tunnel Lighting, Marine & Hazardous lighting

NORTHERN LITES
300 S 86TH AVENUE
WAUSAU, WI 54401
715-848-0490
800-360-5483
Fax: 715-848-0386
www.northernlites.com
• Russell Post, Designer/Founder
• Charles Post, VP
Products:
Snowshoes

NORTHWESTERN GOLF COMPANY
835 N CHURCH COURT
ELMHURST, IL 60126
630-530-1424
800-224-6532
Fax: 630-530-1610
golf.ps@mcimail.com
www.proselectsports.com
• Brian Birkan, VP, Finance
Products:
Golf Bags for Clubs, Clubs-Iron or Wood
Sets, Putters, Utility Clubs, Shafts.

NOVA SPORTS USA
6 INDUSTRIAL ROAD
BUILDING 2
MILFORD, MA 1757
508-473-6540
800-872-6682
Fax: 508-473-4077
bill@novasports.com
www.novasports.com
• Robert Righter, President
• Bill Righter, Chief Financial Officer
• Dave Commito, Operations Director
• Laurie Swanfeldt, Office/Credit Manager
• Jacob Righter, Director of Sales &
Marketing
Products:
Surfacing for Inline Sports, Basketball,
Tennis Courts; Repairs to Surfaces; Tennis
Court Nets and Posts.

NTN COMMUNICATIONS, INC.
2231 RUTHERFORD RD
SUITE 200
CARLSBAD, CA 92008
877-963-9200
800-745-4686
Fax: 760-438-3505
www.buzztime.com
Products:
Sports trivia games.

NUMBERALLS
82 B MCKEE DRIVE
MAHWAH, NJ 7430
201-512-3338
888-788-7133
Fax: 201-512-3240
www.numberalls.com
Products:
Football, Baseball/Softball, Basketball,
Soccer, Volleyball, Classic, Alphabet,
Continental, Champion, Euro, One Color,
Two Color, Mascot Rhinestone, Mascot
Names, Sports Fans, Sports Sheets, Puff
Glitter

NYX GOLF
15936 MIDWAY RD.
ADDISON, TX 75001
972-991-5511
800-505-4699
Fax: 972-385-8607
Sales@nyxgolf.com
www.nyxgolf.com
Products:
NYX Golf Vision System

O'BRIEN INTERNATIONAL
7926 BRACKEN PLACE SE
PO BOX 97087
SNOQUALMIE, WA 98065
425-202-2100
800-662-7436
Fax: 425-831-1052
customerservice@obrien.com
www.obrien.com
Products:
Water Sports - Gloves, Inflatables,
Kneeboards, Personal Flotation, Ropes,
Wakeboards, Water Skis.

O'NEILL, INC.
1071 41ST aVENUE
PO BOX 6300
SANTA CRUZ, CA 95063
866-663-4551
800-538-0764
INFO@ONEILL.COM
www.oneill.com
• Pat O'Neill, President
• Mark Tinkess, Director, Sales
Products:
Jackets, Bags, Full Suits(Cold-Frigid), Full
suits (Warm-Cool), Rash & U.V. Guards,
Spring Suits, Neoprene Tops & Bottoms,
Boardshorts, Thermal Layering, Walkshorts,
Hoods, Knits & Wovens, Gloves, Boots,
Denim, Tees, Footwear

OAKLEY, INC.
ONE ICON
FOOTHILL RANCH, CA 92610
949-951-0991
800-403-7449
Fax: 949-699-3500
customercare@oakley.com
www.oakley.com
• Colin Baden, CEO
Products:
Sunglasses, Wearable Electronics, Apparel,
Watches, Footwear, Bags & Backpacks,
Goggles, Prescription Eyewear, Towels,
Stickers, Posters, Keychains, Lanyards,
Medusa, Umbrellas, Videos

OCEAN HOCKEY SUPPLY COMPANY
197 CHAMBERS BRIDGE ROAD
BRICKTOWN, NJ 08723-3492
732-477-4411
800-631-2159
Fax: 732-477-1167
info@oceanhockey.com
www.oceanhockey.com
• Joan Dwulet, President
Products:
Helmets; Facemasks; Throat & Neck
Guards; Shoulder Pads; Elbow Pads;
Gloves; Jocks; Pants/Girdles; Shin Guards;
Senior Skates; Junior/Youth Skates;
Figure/Recreational Skates; Chest & Arm;
Catch Gloves; Blockers; Goal Pads; Sr
Sticks/Shafts; Intermediate/ Junior/ Youth
Sticks; Goal Sticks; Senior Blades; Junior
Blades; Bags; Performance Wear;
Jerseys/Hose; Apparel; Roller Hockey;
Referee; Gifts/Games; Accessories.

**OCEAN PACIFIC APPAREL
CORPORATION**
3 STUDEBAKER
IRVINE, CA 92618
949-580-1888
Fax: 949-580-1870
www.op.com
• Michael Marcky, VP, Marketing and
Advertising
• Richard A. D. Baker, Chairman
• Jim Jenks, Founder
• Ute Pelzer, Chief Financial Officer

Products:
Product lines: Swimwear & Beachwear,
Coats, Sportswear, Accessories, Outerwear,
Resort Wear, Luggage & Travel Goods,
Jackets, Hair Accessories, Hats & Caps,
Jeans, Dresses Casual, Skirts, Size - Young
Mens, dresses, Headwear, Skiwear, Jog
Suits, Pants & Trousers, T Shirts, Knitwear
& Sweaters, Shorts, Shirts & Blouses,
Athleticwear, Sweaters.

OCEANIC USA
2002 DAVIS STREET
SAN LEANDRO, CA 94577
510-562-0500
800-435-3483
Fax: 510-569-5404
hello@oceanicusa.com
www.oceanicworldwide.com
• Robert Hollis, CEO
• Paul Elsinga, Chief Financial Officer
• Nestor A. Palmero, VP
Products:
Regulators, Computers, Gauges, BCDs,
Masks, Snorkels, Fins, Boots, Gloves,
Hoods, Wetsuits, Bags, Knives, Lights,
Vehicles, Safety Devices, Snorkeling, H2O
Audio.

OCEANTIS SPORTS
12362 BEACH BOULEVARD
SUITE 14D
STANTON, CA 90680
239-217-3150
855-772-6269
Fax: 714-889-7066
• Chuck Flathers, Vice President Of Sales
(360) 808-1861
chuckflathers@oceantis.com
Products:
Wholesaler of bodyboards, skimboards, soft
surfboards and kickboards.

OFF THE WALL PRODUCTS, LLC
PO BOX 1461
SALT LAKE CITY, UT 84110
801-363-7740
877-659-7245
Fax: 801-363-6372
www.multi-barrier.com
• Judd Grayzel, Marketing & Sales Manager
• Marc Christensen, Managing Member
Products:
Specializes in plastic water ballast and
crowd-control barricades, including
construction barricades, roadway
barricades, airport barricades, event
barricade, and military use barricades.

OKLAHOMA LEATHER PRODUCTS, INC.
500 26TH STREET NW
MIAMI, OK 74354
918-542-6651
Fax: 918-542-4340
• Richard Platt, President
Products:
Single Action and Black Powder Holsters,
Cartridge Belts, and Accessories; Tool
Pouches and Holders.

OLD KENTUCKY LEATHERS
125 CALDWELL STREET
AUBURN, KY 42206-0338ÿ
270-542-7107
800-635-0617

Fax: 270-586-4100
www.auburnleather.com
• Lisa Howlett, President
Products:
Leather dyeing and retanning and leather products and accessories for a variety of sports.

OLD TIME SPORTS
10 FANARAS DRIVE
SALISBURY, MA 1952
978-499-1844
888-829-2400
Fax: 978-499-3844
www.oldtimesports.com
Products:
Team Hats, Team Tees, Sweatshirts, Stanley Cap, NHL League, Team Women's Tees, Team Graphics, Garments for Men, Women, and Youth.

OLYMPIA SPORTS
5 BRADLEY DRIVE
WESTBROOK, ME 4092
207-854-2794
Fax: 207-854-4168
www.olympiasports.net
• Dick Coffey, President
• Ed Manganello, Chairman
Products:
Sports equipment, fitness equipment and apparel, athletic footwear, popular sports/leisure wear and accessories.

OLYMPIA SPORTS COMPANY, INC.
500 EXECUTIVE BOULEVARD
ELMSFORD, NY 10523
914-347-4737
800-645-6124
Fax: 914-347-2029
www.olympiagloves.com
• Fred Heumann, Chairman
• Roger Heumann, President
• Paul Janis, Administration
Products:
Manufacturer of quality performance sports gloves.

OLYMPIA TROPHY COMPANY
605 FORREST DRIVE
HAGERSTOWN, MD 21742
301-739-5811
888-448-1305
800-957-6604
Fax: 301-739-8955
olympiatrophy@myactv.net
www.olympiatc.com
• Charles L. Kight, President
Products:
Dash Plaques, Trophies and Awards

OLYMPIC OPTICAL COMPANY
123 EXPLORER STREET
POMONA, CA 91768
909-468-3636
800-423-4277
Fax: 909-468-3640
www.jacksonsafety.com
• Winston Wolfe, President
• Jim McCarty, VP, Sales
• Freida Bushart, National Sales Manager, Key Accounts
• Tom Burns, President & CEO
Products:
Manufacturer of safety eyewear and hearing protection products.

OMEGA GEAR INC
2437 COYLE STREET
BROOKLYN, NY 11235
718-743-7740
866-400-6342
Products:
Kick Shields/Mitts/Pads, Martial Arts Uniforms, Boxing Gloves, Boxing Equipment, Mixed Martial Arts Gloves, Head Guard, Kickboxing Gear, Kickboxing Pants/Shorts, Punching Bags/Balls, and Accessories.

OMEGA MARINE PRODUCTS
18 HALLOCK MEADOW DRIVE
STONY BROOK, NY 11790
631-246-9082
800-966-6342
Fax: 631-246-9084
• Rosemary Gubista, Owner
Products:
Transportation Equipment and Supplies

OMNI BODYWORK
50 O'CONNELL WAY
EAST TAUNTON, MA 2718
508-824-2444
800-448-6664
Fax: 508-822-6030
sales@omnils.com
www.omnils.com
• Richard D Nikolaev, Chairman of the Board
• George B. B. Cipolletti, President & CEO
• David L. LaSalle, Chief Operations Officer
• Edward J. Cheal, Chief Science Officer
• James V. Barrile, Chief Financial Officer
Products:
Designer, manufacturer and distributor of high quality orthotic devices. Also a leader in knee bracing and measurement systems.

ONFIELD APPAREL
8677 LOGO ATHLETIC COURT
INDIANAPOLIS, IN 46219
317-895-7000
Fax: 317-895-7252
• David Baxter, President and Chief Executive Officer
• Edward Ed White, VP, Marketing
Products:
Manufacturer of uniforms, sweatsuits, performance apparel and accessories for professional teams of the NBA, NFL, NHL, and other sports leagues.

ONFIELD APPAREL GROUP, LLC HEADWARE DIVISION
5 INDUSTRIAL DRIVE
MATTAPOISETT, MA 02739-1300
508-758-6101
800-453-3341
Fax: 508-758-3298
• Rick Bednarz, VP, Sales
Products:
Licensed Headwear.

ONPOINT VISUALS
325 POGY PLACE BLDG. B6
FERNANDIAN BEACH, FL 32034
904-206-3299
Fax: 904-491-1286
www.tradeshowsensations.com
• George Nicholas, General Manager
(866) 860-1892
• Bill Anderson, Director Marketing/Business

Development
(866) 860-1892
Nature of Service:
Custom Large Format Graphics/Trade Show Displays
Year Founded:
1892
Products:
Manufacturer of quality, custom large-format graphics such as trade show displays, signage, indoor/outdoor banners on fabric and vinyl substrates, also offer a line of hardware that includes a variety of mounting systems, displays, pop-up tents, and Tension Fabric Structures.
Brands:
onPoint visuals

OOLTEWAH MANUFACTURING COMPANY
5722 MAIN STREET
PO BOX 587
OOLTEWAH, TN 37363
423-238-5388
Fax: 423-238-5387
www.ooltewah.com
• Chuck Daniels, President
Products:
Wholesale distributor of Medical Soft Goods, Bathroom Mats, and other products. Also specializes in Motorcycle Equipment sales, and Web Design.

THE ORIGINAL BALL BAG LLC
125 INDUSTRIAL WAY
COSTA MESA, CA 92627
949-548-2277
Fax: 949-722-1370
sales@ballbag.com
www.ballbag.com
• Doug Rugg, President & CEO
Products:
Official NBA Licensee: NBA Ball Bag, NBA Team logoed BallBags, NBA Jersey Pack, Transporter; BallBags and Packs for all major sports, including baseball, soccer, tennis, football, volleyball, and water polo; a complete line of Golf Bags and accessories with NBA and NBA Team logos.

ORIGINAL MAPLE BAT COMPANY
110 INDUSTRIAL AVE
SUITE 2
CARLETON PLACE, ONTARIO, CANADA
K7C 3T2
613-257-3060
888-726-2287
Fax: 613-257-8577
bats@sambat.com
www.sambat.com
• Sam Holman, Founder
• Arlene Anderson, President
abaca@sambat.com
• Blair Quinn, National Sales Manager
quinnitr@rogers.com
• Lee Carswell, Sales
• Alisa Luoma, Head Office Sales
Products:
Manufacturer of baseball bats.

ORION ROPEWORKS
953 BENTON AVENUE
WINSLOW, ME 4901
888-537-7673
888- 537-7673
Fax: 888-412-7763
sales@orionropeworks.com

• Floyd Kierstead, Vice President Industrial Products
(800) 848-4405
• Floyd Kierstead, Vice President Industrial Products
Products:
Bulk rope for netting applications, dock and anchor lines.

ORLIMAR GOLF COMPANY
G-5140 FLUSHING ROAD
FLUSHING, MI 48433
810-732-0454
888-502-4653
Fax: 810-732-6662
www.orlimar.com
• William J. Baird, Chief Executive Officer
custserv@orlimar.com
• Ryan Coffler, Controller
• L. Toups, Operations Manager
• John Runyon, President
Products:
Golf Clubs - Iron or Wood Sets, Putters.

OSSUR AMERICAS
27412 ALISO VIEJO PARKWAY
ALISO VIEJO, CA 92656
949-382-3883
800-223-6263
Fax: 800-831-3160
ossurusa@ossur.com
www.ossur.com
• Jon Sigurdsson, President/CEO
• Jon Sigurosson, President and Chief Executive Officer
Products:
Knee, Foot & Ankle, Upper Extremity Braces, Suppport & Accessories

OT SPORTS
172 BOONE STREET
BURLINGTON, NC 27215
336-222-8774
800-988-6285
Fax: 336-227-5116
info@otsports.com
www.otsports.com
• Scott Gollnick, VP Sales/Marketing
(336) 222-9774
scott@otsports.com
Products:
Products include: baseball, basketball, football, hockey, socccer and lacrosse jerseys
Year Founded:
1994
Brands:
OT Sports, Brine

OTOMIX ATHLETIC GEAR
7585 COMMERCIAL WAY
SUITE E
HENDERSON, NV 89011
otomix7@aol.com
www.otomix.com
• Mitchell Bobrow, President
• Nancy Barrett, VP, National Sales
otomix3@aol.com
• Belinda Field, International Sales
Products:
General Sports Footwear, Fitness/Street Active Apparel, Training/Martial Arts Accessories, Wrestling Footwear.

PACIFIC CYCLE, LLC
4902 HAMMERSLEY ROAD
MADISON, WI 53711
608-268-2468
800-666-8813
Fax: 608-268-2466
info@pacific-cycle.com
www.pacificcycle.com
• Byron Smith, President / Chief Operating Officer
Products:
Bicycles and accessories for the cyclist.

PACIFIC TRAIL
1700 WESTLAKE AVENUE N
SUITE 200
SEATTLE, WA 98109
206-270-5300
800-622-6953
Fax: 206-270-5301
Info@pacifictrail.com
www.columbia.com
• Gary E Hansen, President
• Todd Gilmer, Marketing Manager
Products:
Casual Outerwear, Active Outerwear and Performance Outerwear. Ski and Snowboard Apparel.

PADDLE COMPANY INC
27 E BROAD STREET
HOPEWELL, NJ 8525
609-466-8000
Fax: 609-466-8834
Products:
Tennis paddles

PADDLE TRAMPS MFG. COMPANY
1317 UNIVERSITY AVENUE
LUBBOCK, TX 79401
806-765-9901
Fax: 806-763-9148
sales@paddletramps.com
www.paddletramps.com
• Thomas Abraham, Owner
Products:
Manufacturer and wholesaler of decorative wood products and paddles custom designed with sports logos and other information.

PAIGE DESIGN GROUP
5 PEARSE WYND ROAD
BAHAMA, NC 27503
919-451-1641
Fax: 919-620-0091
dpaige@paigedesigngroup.com
www.paigedesigngroup.com

PARAGON SPORTS
2300 E WALNUT AVENUE
FULLERTON, CA 92831
714-870-1900
800-722-4061
Fax: 714-870-1921
www.mitsushiba.com
• Richard Tcheng, President
Products:
Golf - Club Components, Shafts.

PARAMOUNT FITNESS CORPORATION
6450 E BANDINI BOULEVARD
LOS ANGELES, CA 90040
323-721-2121
800-721-2121

Fax: 323-724-2000
www.paramountfitness.com
• Steve Rhodes, President
• Jim McIntyre, Vice President of Sales & Marketing
Products:
Training & Conditioning - Benches, Single and Multi Station Exercise Machines.

PARAMOUNT HEADWEAR, INC.
1 PARAMOUNT DRIVE
BOURBON, MO 65441
573-732-4411
800-255-4287
Fax: 573-732-5211
www.paramountapparel.com
• Bruce Levinson, Vice Chairman/Chief Executive Officer
• Steve Lefler, President
• Mark Rubenstein, Chairman & Co-Chief Executive Officer
Products:
Knit Hats and Caps, Screened and Embroidered Tees and Sweats.

PARICON, LLC.
52 PARK STREET
PO BOX 157
SOUTH PARIS, ME 04281
207-743-6896
Fax: 207-743-2530
info@pariconsleds.com
www.pariconsleds.com
• Ted Morton, Partner
ted@pariconsleds.com
• Tom Morton, Partner
tom@pariconsleds.com
Nature of Service:
Wholesales and distributes winter products (Flexible Flyer sleds and snow toys) and summer toss games to major retailers, toy stores, grocery stores, hardware stores, sporting goods stores and webstores.
Products:
Sleds, snowboards, foam sliders, inflatable tubes, wooden toboggans and snow toys
Brands:
Flexible Flyer

PARKER LABORATORIES, INC.
286 ELDRIDGE ROAD
FAIRFIELD, NJ 7004
973-276-9500
800-631-8888
Fax: 973-276-9510
parker@parkerlabs.com
www.parkerlabs.com
• Neal Buchalter, President
• Carol Buchalter, Chairman
• Martin King, Director, International Sales
• Tom Rodenberg, National Sales Manager
• Joan Bartello, Advertising Manager
• Nick Economou, Operations Manager
• Kathleen Tirch, Quality Assurance Manager
• Diane Sharkey, Human Resources Manager
Products:
Manufacturer of electromedical contact media

PARSONS OFFICIALS SUPPLIES
515 W LUNT AVENUE
PO BOX 847
ELGIN, IL 60120

866-664-8840
Fax: 847-352-3375
www.pluspos.com
• Buck Parsons, President
• Sylvia Parsons, Sales Manager
Products:
Baseball, Basketball, & Football coach and Umpire supplies.

PARTAC PEAT CORPORATION/BEAM CLAY
ONE KELSEY PARK
GREAT MEADOWS, NJ 7838
908-637-4191
800-247-2326
Fax: 908-637-8421
sales@partac.com
www.beamclay.com
Products:
Baseball and sports turf surfaces and supplies
Nature of Service:
Manufacturer/Distributor
Brands:
Beam Clay, Partac, All Sports, Fence Guard, Permanent Foul Line

PARTY ANIMAL INC.
909 CROCKER RD.
WESTLAKE, OH 44145
440-471-1030
800-456-0145
Fax: 440-617-9476
sales@partyanimalinc.com
www.partyanimalinc.com
Description:
Manufacturer of high quality flags, banners, & collectible toys licensed for NFL, MLB, NBA, NHL and over 65 colleges.
Products:
Applique & embroidered flags, banners, tall team flags, team decorating strips & Lil' Teammates collectible toys.

PATAGONIA
8550 WHITE FIR STREET
PO BOX 32050
RENO, NV 89523-2050
775-746-6878
800-638-6464
Fax: 775-746-6827
customer_service@patagonia.com
www.patagonia.com
• Ric Hatch, North American Sales Director
• Bill Kulczycki, Sales Director
Products:
Outdoor Sports Apparel.

PAWLING CORPORATION/STANDARD PRODUCTS DIVISION
32 NELSON HILL ROAD
WASSAIC, NY 12592
845-373-9300
800-431-3456
Fax: 845-855-1139
sales@pawling.com
www.pawling.com
• Roger W Smith, Chairman / President
• Rich C Raible, VP / General Manager
Products:
Wall Protection Systems, Entrance Mats & Gratings, Athletic Flooring Systems, Heavy Duty Impact Protection Systems, Parking & Traffic Safety Products, Prespray Watertight Doors and Barriers, Prespray Airtight Doors, etc.

PEARL IZUMI (USA)
1886 PRAIRIE WAY
LOUISVILLE, CO 80027
303-460-8888
800-328-8488
Fax: 303-466-4237
info@pearlizumi.com
www.pearlizumi.com
• Tom Adams, VP, Salels
• Josh Parker, Marketing Coordinator
Products:
Apparel for cycling, general sports, track & field.

PELICAN INTERNATIONAL INC
1000, PLACE PAUL-KANE
LAVAL, QC, CANADA H7C 2T2
450-644-1222
888-669-6960
Fax: 450-664-4522
service@pelicansport.com
www.pelicansport.com
• Christian Elie, President
Products:
Canoes, Kayaks, Pedal Boats, Fishing Boats and Accessories, Toys
Brands:
Pelican

PENN FISHING TACKLE COMPANY
7 SCIENCE COURT
COLUMBIA, SC 29203
215-229-9415
800-892-5444
Fax: 215-223-3017
www.pennreels.com
• Herbert O Henze, President
• Brent Kane, Marketing Director
• Viola Bird, VP
• Bryan Nelson, VP
Products:
Manufacturer of fishing reels, rods, combos, downriggers, hooks, line, accessories, tackle storage, Ltd Ed Prints, Apparel

PENN RACQUET SPORTS
306 S 45TH AVENUE
PHOENIX, AZ 85043
800-289-7366
Fax: 888-329-7366
askus@us.head.com
www.pennracquet.com
• Gregg Weida, President
• Johan Elisch, Chairman
• David Haggerty, President
• Kevin Kempin, VP
Products:
Racquet Sports - Apparel, Bags-Equipment, Racquetball Balls, Racquetball Racquets, Shoes, Tennis Balls.

PEPCO POMS SPORTS
9611 HIGHWAY 60 S
PO BOX 950
WHARTON, TX 77488
979-523-3116
800-527-1150
Fax: 800-762-5532
sales@pepcopoms.com
www.pepcopoms.com
Products:
Producer of cheerleader and promotional pom pons and spirit accessories.

PERFECT CURVE, INC.
200 LINCOLN STREET
5TH FLOOR
BOSTON, MA 2111
617-224-1600
800-244-7733
Fax: 617-224-1601
customerservice@perfectcurve.com
www.perfectcurve.com
• Gregg Myles Levin, President
gregg@perfectcurve.com
• Barry M Levin, Sales VP
• Jason Seavey, Sales Director
• David Carey, Account Executive
Products:
Perfect Curve Cap Curver, Cap Cleaner & Deodorizer, Perfect Curve CapRack, Water & Stain Repellent.

PERFORMANCE SPORTS APPAREL
2201 NORTH FRONT STREET
HARRISBURG, PA 17110
877-263-0350
800-543-8952
Fax: 717-213-6977
info@medalist.com
www.medalist.com
• David Ferguson, President/CEO
(610) 373-5300
dferguson@medalist.com
• Richard Heck, National Sales Manager
Products:
General Sports Products Performance Apparel, including Silk Underwear, Sport Underwear, Thermal Underwear, Turtlenecks.

PERFORMANCE SPORTS SYSTEMS, INC.
9200 E 146TH STREET
SUITE A
NOBLESVILLE, IN 46060
317-774-9840
800-848-8034
Fax: 317-774-9841
info@perfsports.com
www.perfsports.com
• David Byrne, General Manager
Products:
Manufacturer of sporting equipment,

HOGAN COMPANY
3000 NW 107TH AVENUE
MIAMI, FL 33172
305-592-2830
Fax: 305-594-2307
info@pery.com
www.pery.com
Products:
Golf - Apparel, Bags-for Clubs, Bags-Luggage, Balls, Clubs-Iron or Wood Sets, Clubs-Putters, Clubs-Utility, Gloves, Headcovers, Umbrellas.

PETER DAVID INC
10890 THORNMINT ROAD
SUITE A
SAN DIEGO, CA 92127
858-385-2680
800-369-7467
Fax: 858-385-2690
www.peterdavid.com
Products:
Sports collectibles such as lapel pins, earrings, necklaces, key chains, magnets, collector sets

PHI-TEN USA INC
980 KNOX STREET
TORRANCE, CA 90502
310-328-8585
888-774-4836
Fax: 310-328-0716
www.phitenusa.com
• Yoshihiro Hirata, President
• Katashi Santo, Vice President
Products:
Titanium Necklace, Titanium Bracelet,
Titanium Discs, Titanium Tape, Liquid
Titanium, Titanium Wrap, Titanium Waist
Belt, Aqua Titanium Belt, Titanium Insole,
Titanium Support, Moisture Soap, Titanium
Socks, Titanium Shorts, Titanium Compress
Pants, Titanium Shirts

PHILIPS LIGHTING COMPANY
200 FRANKLIN SQUARE DRIVE
PO BOX 6800
SOMERSET, NJ 08875-6800
732-563-3000
800-555-0050
Fax: 732-563-3229
www.lighting.philips.com
• Frans Van Houten, Chairman
• Jim Andrew, Chief Strategy & Innovation
Officer
• Eric Coutinho, Chief Legal Officer
Products:
Manufacturer of lighting for sports Facilities.

PHOENIX VENTURES CORPORATION
777 ALEXANDER ROAD
PRINCETON, NJ 8540
609-734-4999
Fax: 609-734-4994
• Gail C O'Denise, President
Products:
Hunting/Fishing - Equipment; Ice Hockey -
Equipment; Tennis - Equipment.

PHOTO FILE
333 BEDFORD ROAD
SUITE 130
MOUNT KISCO, NY, 10549
914-375-6000
800-346-1678
Fax: 914-375-6009
customerservice@photofile.com
www.photofile.com
Products:
Manufacturer of licensed sports
photography

PIANTEDOSI OARS, INC.
PO BOX 643
W ACTON, MA 1720
978-263-1814
Fax: 978-263-5940
rowalden.com
• Gary G Piantedosi, Partner
Products:
Rowing/Crew - Oars, Shells, Sculls

PINCKARD BASEBALL GLOVES
PO BOX 52026
SALT LAKE CITY, UT 84106
385-232-6460
Fax: 626-683-3103
atozinc@earthlink.net
• Bill Pinckard, Founder
Products:
Baseball and Softball balls and gloves.

PINE SPORTS
208 S MAIN STREET
PO BOX 98
STAR, NC 27356
910-428-2185
800-342-2948
Fax: 910-428-9367
www.pinesports.com
Products:
Provides a variety of products that represent
sports teams and players that includes
NASCAR drivers as part of their product
listings.

PING, INC.
2201 W DESERT COVE
PO BOX 82000
PHOENIX, AZ 85071-2000
800-474-6434
Fax: 602-687-5037
www.ping.com
• John Solheim, Chairman/President
• Mike Trueblood, Chief Financial Officer
• Allan Solheim, EVP
• Stacey Solheim, VP
Products:
Golf Equipment - Metal Woods Setm
Hybrids, Irons, Wedges, Putters, Bags for
Clubs, Accessories.

PINNACLE SPORTS EQUIPMENT INC
3801 VICTORY BOULEVARD
STATEN ISLAND, NY 10314
718-698-0775
Fax: 718-494-1583
info@bamboobat.com
www.bamboobats.net
• Thomas M Verrengia, Chief Executive
Officer / Co-Founder
tverrengia@bamboobat.com
• Hsu Yanshen, President / Founder
yhsu@bamboobat.com
Products:
Manufacturer of Adult BamBooBat, Youth
BamBooBat, Fungo BamBooBat, Softball
BamBooBat, Hardwood Bat, and Equipment
Bag.

PIONEER INDUSTRIES, INC.
171 S NEWMAN STREET
HACKENSACK, NJ 7601
201-933-1900
Fax: 201-933-9580
mdorf@pioneerindustries.com
www.pioneerindustries.com
• Jeffrey Haversat, General Partner
jhaversat@pioneerindustries.com
• Ralph Tarzia, VP Operations
• Mitchel Dorf, President
mdorf@pioneerindustries.com
• Mitchell Dorf, President
• Bill Zerby, Plant Manager
• Gaeton Di Napoli, Controller
Products:
Manufacturer of Hollow Metal Doors,
Frames and Sticks

**PIONEER NEW MEDIA TECHNOLOGIES,
INC.**
1925 E DOMINGUEZ STREET
LONG BEACH, CA 90810
310-952-2000
800-421-1404
Fax: 310-952-2960
www.pioneerelectronics.com

• Michael Townsend, Mobile Entertainment
Marketing VP
• Amy Friend, Public Relations Director
Products:
Plasma, DVD Players & Recorders, A/V
Receivers & Amplifiers, CD & Cassette
Players, Home Theater Systems, Speakers
& Headphones, Turntables, Computer
Drives.

PLASTIMAYD CORPORATION
14151 FIR CITY
OREGON CITY, OR 97045-6806
503-654-8502
800-348-2600
Fax: 503-654-7935
www.plastimayd.com
• Martin Samuelson, President
• Todd Mulvaney, President
• Tim Hartford, Engineer/Technical
• Ron Uenberg, Finance Executive
Products:
Manufacturer of Pool Liners, Safety Covers
and Winter Domes for Swimming Pools.

PLAY VISIONS
19180 144TH AVENUE NE
WOODINVILLE, WA 98072
425-482-2836
800-678-8697
Fax: 425-482-2842
laurab@playvisions.com
www.playvisions.com
• Kiley Rose, Sales Manager
(425) 482-2836
kileyr@playvisions.com
• Mark Chernick, CEO
Products:
Product lines include Horror Balls, Animags,
Stress Balls, Hyperflex, Squishy Stuff,
StuntMaster, Club Earth, Zibbies, Thredz,
OddBall, ZooLights.

PLAYERS GOLF
145 S ORLANDO AVENUE
SUITE 8
MAITLAND, FL 32751
800-550-2223
Fax: 407-677-4878
info@playersgolf.com
www.playersgolf.com
Products:
Golf Equipment: Wood Sets, Irons, Putters,
Utility/Hybrid Clubs, Logo Club Grips, Golf
Bags, Golf Balls, Accessories, Training Aids,
Fitness.

PLAYERS PUBLISHING
7316 ROCHELLE WAY
FAIR OAKS, CA 95628
916-202-9747
800-548-3500
Fax: 916-314-8006
rick@playerspublishing.com
www.playerspublishing.com
Products:
Offers quality artwork of the NBA's top
players.

PLAYFIELD INTERNATIONAL INC.
1220 GREEN ROAD
CHATSWORTH, GA 30705
706-695-4581
800-221-7449
Fax: 706-695-4755
www.playfieldinternational.com

- Steve Linville, President
- Darrel Turner, Chief Operating Officer

Products:
Global supplier of the finest Artificial Turf Surfaces for landscaping, pet areas & kennels, play areas, golf courses, and playing fields.

PLAYOFF CORP.
2300 E RANDOL MILL ROAD
ARLINGTON, TX 76011
817-983-0300
- Larry Blackwell, President
- Stanley St Mayer, Chief Financial Officer
- Steve Peek, Score Entertainment SVP
- Art Young, Managing Director, Donruss Promotions Gr

Products:
Manufacturer of sports trading cards.

POCOCK RACING SHELLS
615 - 80TH STREET SW
EVERETT, WA 98203
425-438-9048
888-762-6251
Fax: 425-438-9043
niki@pocock.com
www.pocock.com
- Bill Tytus, President
bill@pocock.com
- John Tytus, Sales
- Amy Winner, Marketing
- Dave Haworth Jr., Customer Relations

Products:
Manufacturer of Racing Shells/Boats.

POINT BLANK SOLUTIONS
2102 SW 2ND STREET
POMPANO BEACH, FL 33069
954-630-0900
800-413-5155
Fax: 954-630-9225
www.pointblanksolutionsinc.com
- Larry H Ellis, President/CEO
- Michael Foreman, VP, Government and International Sales / Prod
(407) 448 6139
mforeman@pbearmor.com
- Bryant Halstead, Government Sales - Federal and Department of
(954) 629-5920
- Michael Foreman, VP, Government and International Sales / Prod
(407) 448-6139
mforeman@pbearmor.com
- Paul Raspino, Military Sales - U.S. Army and National Guard
(910) 964-6808
praspino@pbsinc.com
- Corey Provenzano, Private Military Contractor Sales, OEM Busine
(754) 581-2758
cprovenzano@pbsinc.com
- Mark T. F. Smith, Vice President, Sales
(859) 620-2344
salesinquiries@pbsinc.com

Products:
Sports medicine, health supports, protective gear and magnetic therapy products.

POLAR ELECTRO INC.
1111 MARCUS AVENUE
SUITE M15
LAKE SUCCESS, NY 11042-1034
800-227-1314
Fax: 516-364-5454

customer.service.usa@polar.com
www.polar.com
- Burt Birnbaum, President
- Herb Baer, President

Products:
Manufacturer of Sports Equipment and Personal Fitness Solution - Heart Rate Monitors, Team System, Precision Performance Software, Accessories.

POLEMAX L.L.C.
8214 WESTCHESTER
SUITE 500
DALLAS, TX 75225
214-692-3532
800-458-0884
Fax: 214-692-3540
- Mac Fuller, Owner

Products:
Padded cover that is placed over poles or ground columns that may include symbols, an advertiser's logo, etc.

POLO BY RALPH LAUREN
625 MADISON AVENUE
11TH FLOOR
NEW YORK, NY 10022
212-318-7000
888-475-7674
Fax: 212-888-5780
www.ralphlauren.com
- Ralph Lauren, Chief Executive Officer
- Roger N Farah, President / Chief Operating Officer
- Tracey Travis, Senior VP and Chief Financial Officer
- Christopher H. Peterson, Chief Financial Officer & Senior VP

Products:
Manufacturer and importer of Polos, Chinos, Denim, Pants, Sweaters, Sweats & Tees, Sport Shirts, including sport apparel.

POMCHIES LLC
4900 E. ARROYO VERDE DRIVE
PARADISE VALLEY, AZ 85253
602-493-1745
888-576-6244
Fax: 602-404-0577
sales@pomchies.com
www.pomchies.com

Products:
Manufacturer of ponytail holders, pomchies, pomsnaps and pomclips for cheerleaders, sports teams, dance, swimming spirit, gymnastic.

PONY INTERNATIONAL INC.
9465 WILSHIRE BOULEVARD
6TH FLOOR
BEVERLY HILLS, CA 90212
866-766-9669
800-826-2205
info@pony.com
www.pony.com
- David Orr, Sales VP
(212) 459-2433

Products:
General Sporting Goods.

POOLMASTER, INC.
770 DEL PASO ROAD
SACRAMENTO, CA 95834-1117
916-567-9800
800-854-1492

Fax: 916-567-9880
www.poolmaster.com
- Lee Tager, President
(916) 567-9800
- Kim Levin, VP Of Sales

Products:
Water Sports Caps, Diving Masks, Goggles, Fins, Personal Flotation, Snorkels, Games for Swimming Pools, Pool & Spa Digital Clock Thermometers

PORSCHE CARS NORTH AMERICA
980 HAMMOND DRIVE
SUITE 1000
ATLANTA, GA 30328
770-290-3500
800-767-7243
Fax: 770-290-3700
www.porsche.com
- Robert Carlson, General Manager/Public Relations
- Tim Mahoney, General Manager/Marketing
- Matthius Muller, President
- Thomas Edig, Deputy Chairman

PORTAFLOOR
939 S 700 W
SALT LAKE CITY, UT 84104
801-972-0260
800-421-8112
801-657-5260
Fax: 801-401-3504
info@portafloor.com
www.portafloor.com
- Jon Isaacs, VP/General Manager
- Ronald N. Cemy, President & CEO

Products:
Grass and Stadium Protection System, Synthetic Surface Covering, Ice Protection Covering, Dirt Covering.

PORTAPIT/CATAPOLE
1901 DIPLOMAT DRIVE
PO Box 7726
DALLAS, TX 75209
800-527-7510
800-899-0149
feedgym@sportsupplygroup.com
www.portapit.com
- Gordon Klunkert, Portapit Advertising
- Robert K Mitchell, Chief Financial Officer
(972) 406-3484
bmitchell@sportsupplygroup.com

Products:
Track & Field - Crossbars, Discs, Hurdles, Landing Pits, Pole Vault Poles, Shots.

PORTER ATHLETIC EQUIPMENT COMPANY
601 MERCURY DRIVE
CHAMPAIGN, IL 61822-9648
217-367-8438
800-637-3090
Fax: 217-367-8440
www.porterathletic.com
- Greg Hege, President
- Edward Schroeder, Product Development VP
- Dan Morgan, Sales / Marketing VP
- David Hodge, President
- Mary Kotelly, Human Resources Executive
- Mike Schendel, Purchasing Executive
- Steve Vogelsang, Chief Marketing Officer

Products:
General Sports Equipment

POWELL GOLF, INC., JOE
1781 BARBER ROAD
SARASOTA, FL 34240
941-377-7742
800-237-4660
Fax: 941-377-7036
joepowellgolf@verizon.net
www.joepowellgolf.com
• John Powell, President
joepowell@acun.com
Products:
Golf - Clubs - Wood/Iron Sets, Putters

POWER SOURCE SPORTS INC
23207 STELLING AVENUE
PORT CHARLOTTE, FL 33980
941-764-9000
Fax: 941-764-0613
Brands:
Power Source
Products:
Sports electronics.

POWERBRANDS LLC
80-A E JEFRYN BOULEVARD
DEER PARK, NY 11729
631-389-5642
800-354-8785
Fax: 631-242-6177
kngny@aol.com
www.kngamerica.com
• Kash Gobindram, President / Chief
Executive Officer
Products:
Phones, clocks, Picture Frames, Lamps, CD
Players, remotes, Headsets, Solar Lanterns,
Radio Coolers, Flashlights, Radios,
Boomboxes, Phonographs, Night Lights

POWERCRANKS
365 PIMLICO DRIVE
WALNUT CREEK, CA 94597
925-480-7697
888-733-2572
Fax: 419-710-8477
customerservice@powercranks.com
www.powercranks.com
• Frank Day, Founder
• Andrew L Weber, Sales / Marketing
Director
• John McKenna, Chief Operating Officer /
Chief Financial Officer
Products:
PowerCranks, PowerCranks xLite,
Stationary Bikes, PowerCranks Training
Tools, PowerCranks Clothing

POWERS COURT/TOA
40 S MAIN STREET
NEW CITY, NY 10956
212-691-3888
800-728-3664
Fax: 212-255-7129
• Mark Sterns, President
Services:
The official U.S. agent for four of the finest
tennis manufacturers from around the globe:
TOA, Kirschbaum, BDE, ISO-Speed. As a
full line distributor we also offer competitive
pricing on all major brands of tennis strings
and accessories, including Wilson, Prince,
Gamma, Tecnifibre and Babolat.

**POWERS EMBROIDERY/ CHENILLE,
INC., USA**
11330 HILLGUARD RD.
DALLAS, TX 75243
214-343-0888
800-227-2040
Fax: 214-349-8884
info@powersembroidery.com
www.chenille.com
• Bob Powers, President / Chief Executive
Officer
• David Gooch, VP
• Jay Powers, Marketing VP
• Ken Gilmer, President
• Theresa Jacks, Human Resources
Executive
• Melissa Dennis, Sales Executive
• Marla Platt, Finance Executive
Products:
Cheerleader Emblems; Awards, Banners,
Chenille Award Emblems, Custom Swiss
Patches, Varsity Jackets.

**PRAIRIE ROSE PERSONALIZED
PRODUCTS**
1941 HIGHWAY 86
MILFORD, IA 51351
712-337-8119
877-337-8119
Fax: 712-337-0184
www.prairierose.com
Products:
Picture Frames with sports logos and
designs.

PRECISE INTERNATIONAL
15 CORPORATE DRIVE
ORANGEBURG, NY 10962
800-267-3577
800-267-3577
Fax: 800-438-5806
www.wengerna.com
• Tom Abbott, Chief Executive Officer
Products:
Manufactures knives, watches, swiss army
fragrance, swiss business tool, knife & swiss
business, tool accessories, watchbands,
tents, backpacks, sleeping bags and air
mattresses, casual travel bags, duffel bags
and travel accessories, computer cases,
leather folios and other business
accessories, corporate gifts.

PRECISION COMPOSITES
19138 WALNUT DRIVE
SUITE 201
ROWLAND HEIGHTS, CA 91748
626-964-4276
800-422-3838
Fax: 626-964-9436
www.precisioncomposites.com
• Peter A'Costa, National Sales Manager
Products:
Offers a complete line of 100% filament
wound graphite golf shafts designed to fit
golfers of all skill levels-from beginner to
professionals.

PRECISION SPORTS
29910 OHANA CIRCLE
LAKE ELSINORE, CA 92532
951-674-1665
800-524-5892
Fax: 951-674-2518
sherri@labeda.com
www.labeda.com

• Sherri Labeda, Corporate Secretary
(951) 674-1665
sherri@labeda.com
• Shelly Labeda, Chief Financial Officer
(951) 674-1665
shelly@labeda.com
• Kevin Labeda, Chemist/Director Of
Operations
kevinl@labeda.com
• Robert Chornomud, National/OEM Sales &
Marketing Manager
Products:
Specializes in high end high rebound
formulas to provide companies the very best
skateboard wheels on the market, from
blank economy wheels, dual durometer
wheels, to super high end four color process
printed wheels.

PRECOR, INC
20031 142ND AVENUE NE
PO BOX 7202
WOODINVILLE, WA 98072-4002
425-486-9292
800-786-8404
Fax: 425-486-3856
commsls@precor.com
www.precor.com
• Robert Baker, President
• Serge Dupuis, Vice President of Finance
• Bill Dixon, Vice President of Operations
• Jim Birrell, Chief Innovation Officer
• Elisa Humphrey, Senior VP of Consumer
Division
Products:
Elliptical Fitness Crosstrainers (EFX),
Treadmills, Cycles, Climbers,
StretchTrainers, Strength Training Systems

PREMIUMWEAR
4375 WILLOW DR.
HAMMEL, MN 55340
952-912-2500
800-488-4800
800-370-8706
Fax: 800-370-8706
sales@riversendtrading.com
www.riversendtrading.com
• Jayme Weber, President Promotional
Products
• Cynthia L Boeddeker, Operations VP
Products:
Sports Apparel and Accessories

PRESS PASS INC
9805 NORTHCROSS CENTER CT.
SUITE H
HUNTERSVILLE, NC 28078
704-942-3060
800-618-0683
Fax: 704-942-3070
www.presspassinc.com
• DJ Kazmiercak, Senior Vice President,
Sales & Marketing
Products:
Collectible trading cards and diecast
vehicles.
Description:
Press Pass, Inc. is a leading designer,
producer, and manufacturer of innovative,
high-quality trading cards and die-cast
collectibles. Press Pass reaches consumers
through multiple channels of distribution
supporting approximately 10,000 retail
outlets.
Brands:
Press Pass, Wheels

PRESTON LEATHER PRODUCTS
44 MITCHELL ROAD
PO BOX 594
IPSWICH, MA 1938
978-356-5701
800-343-8120
Fax: 978-356-9832
www.prestonleather.com
• C.A. Ebinger, General Manager
Products:
Bags, Belts, Dog Collars, Ribbons with
sports logos and designs.

PRIME TIME TOYS
PO BOX 256
POMPTON LAKES, NJ 7442
973-839-5711
Fax: 973-839-5811
pttllc@worldnet.att.net
www.primetimetoys.com
Nature of Service:
Distributor
Year Founded:
1993
Products:
Manufacturers of toys such as Boss Bow,
Rocket Blaster, Sky Diver, Squeeze Blaster,
Target, Lite-Up Sub, Max Liquidator and
Eliminator, Underwater Scramble, Splash
Bombs 4 Pack, Basketball Challenge, and
Glack Blaster.
Brands:
Max Liquidator Splash Bombs

PRINCE SPORTS GROUP, INC.
116 HIGH STREET
HAMPTON HILL, LONDON, ENGLAND
TW121NT
+44-
800-283-6647
Fax: 609-291-5900
• George Napier, Chairman / Chief
Executive Officer
• David Evins, EVP / Chief Financial Officer
• Tom Dye, Operations VP / General
Manager
• Howard Lay, Product Management VP
Products:
Racquet Sports - Apparel,
Bags-Necessities, Racquet Strings,
Racquetball Equipment & Shoes, Shoes,
Rollerblade Skates & Protective Gear,
Squash Racquets, Stringing Machines,
Tennis Racquets, Tennis Ball Machines,
Tennis Shoes

PRO BOUND SPORTS
428 HIGHWAY 40
DORRANCE, KS 67634
785-666-4207
800-525-8580
Fax: 785-666-4410
proboundspts@hbcomm.net
www.proboundsports.com
• Thomas Mahoney, President/Owner
(785) 666-4267
tom.mahoney@proboundsports.com
• Julie Dauber, Sales Representative
(785) 666-4207
Nature of Service:
Manufacturing, sporting goods,
wholesale/retail.
Year Founded:
1993
Products:
Designer and manufacturer of portable
roll-in and stationary basketball goal

supports along with ball returns, ball carts,
bleachers, score tables, and other main line
sporting goods.
Brands:
Ultra-Pro, Pro-Fold II, Pro-Bounder, Hot
Shot, Bull Dog, Score Pro.
Clients:
Colleges, High Schools, YMCA, YWCA,
Recreational Facilities, Residential/Home
Recreation

PRO FEET, INC.
PO BOX 2720
BURLINGTON, NC 27215-2720
336-226-0237
800-334-1101
Fax: 800-811-3338
info@profeet.com
www.profeet.com
• Russell Wilson, CEO
• Callum Brown, Vice President Operations
• Taylor Wilson, Vice President Sales
Year Founded:
1979.
Products:
Socks for Baseball, Basketball, Cycling,
Bowling, Boxing, Curling, Football, Golf,
Gymnastics, Handball, Racquet Sports,
Soccer, Softball, Track & Field, Volleyball,
Wrestling; Universal Tube Socks;
Wristbands/Headbands, Cheerleading.

PRO INNOVATIVE CONCEPTS
3836 E WATKINS STREET
PHOENIX, AZ 85034-7265
602-437-5100
800-858-4121
info@proinnovative.com
www.proinnovative.com
• Mark Scatterday, President
• Andrew Reichlin, Chief Executive Officer
• Bryan Christie, Sales / Marketing Director
info@proinnovative.com
Products:
Benders, Close Outs, Desk & Office
Accessories, Highlighters, Keychains,
Mirrors & Magnifiers, Noisemakers & Music
Related, Pens, Stress Relief, Toys.

PRO KENNEX
1159 MONTEREY PLACE
SUITE A
ENCINITAS, CA 92024-1340
800-778-1755
Fax: 619-635-9205
www.prokennex.com
• Jeff Yao, Chief Executive Officer
• Kevin Gilbert, President
Products:
Manufacturer, distributor and marketer of
various products for tennis, hockey, golf,
racquetball, squash and badminton.

PRO ORTHOPEDIC DEVICES, INC.
2884 E GANLEY ROAD
TUCSON, AZ 85706
520-294-4401
800-523-5611
Fax: 520-294-6116
info@proorthopedic.com
www.proorthopedic.com
• Gerald Detty, President
(800) 323-5611
• Jackie Ingrahm, Team Specialist
(800) 323-5611
jackie@proorthopedic.com
• Gerald Detty, President

• Karl Walton, Finance Executive
• Mark Ellisor, Operations Executive
Products:
Professional Products: Knee Supports,
Patella Stabilizers, Hinged Braces, Thigh
and Groin Supports, Ankle & Calf Supports,
Low Back Supports, Elbow Supports, Wrist
& Shoulder Supports, Training Aids, and
Scuff Pads.

PRO PERFORMANCE SPORTS
12375 WORLD TRADE DRIVE
PO BOX 500127
SAN DIEGO, CA 92128
858-675-3350
877-448-2929
Fax: 858-618-3330
www.properformancesports.com
Products:
Manufacturer, distributor and marketer of
innovative high performance sports products
and trainers.

PRO SELECT SPORTS*USA
19638 EAGLE RIDGE LANE
NORTHRIDGE, CA 91326
877-774-4228
Fax: 866-240-4257
www.proselectsports.com
• Nat C Rosasco, Chairman
• Nat G Rosasco, President
Products:
Bag & Club Sets, Golg Bags, Golf Gear,
Golf Irons & Hybrids, Golf Putters, Golf
Shoes, Golf Wedges, Drivers & Woods

PRO SPECIALTIES GROUP
8221 ARJONS DRIVE
SUITE F
SAN DIEGO, CA 92126
858-541-1100
800-544-564
Fax: 858-268-5801
info@psginc.com
www.psginc.com
• Steven Mendoza, VP, Business
Development
stevenm@psginc.com
• Charles Cooper, Sales Manager
charlesc@psginc.com
• Elizabeth Sanchez, Marketing Manager
info@psginc.com
Products:
Marketers and manufacturers of advertising
specialties and licensed sports products.

PRO STAR SPORTS, INC.
1133 WINCHESTER
KANSAS CITY, MO 64126
816-241-9737
800-821-8482
Fax: 816-241-2459
www.prostarsports.com
Products:
Weight Training Equipment - Racks,
Benches, Olympic Benches

PRO-LINE CAP COMPANY
1332 N MAIN STREET
FORT WORTH, TX 76106
817-246-1978
800-227-2456
Fax: 817-367-1585
charris@prolinecap.com
• Charles Harris, Sales / Marketing VP
(817) 246-1978

charris@prolinecap.com
• Joel Taylor, Sales / Marketing Manager
(817) 246-1978
• Steve Henning, Art Director
(817) 246-1978
• Charles Harris, VP Of Sales & Marketing
charris@prolinecap.com
• Alan Beam, Art Director
Products:
Caps and hats for Baseball, General Sports, Racquet Sports, Softball

PRO-TEC
6550 KATELLA AVE.
CYPRESS, CA 90630
310-318-5897
888-691-8889
Fax: 310-318-8807
www.pro-tec.net
Products:
Offers a wide variety of sports helmets and protection gear.

PROFESSIONAL GYM
805 CHEROKEE
PO BOX 188
MARSHALL, MO 65340
660-886-9628
800-821-7665
Fax: 660-886-3041
• Greg Mach, President
• Dale Thomas, Sales Director
Products:
Training, Conditioning and Physical Fitness Equipment

PROGEAR, INC.
11828 SLATER AVENUE NE
SUITE 150
KIRKLAND, WA 98034
425-814-3900
Fax: 425-814-3902
info@marketsync.com
www.marketsync.com
• Michael Bauer, SVP Marketing/Sales
• Tom Malone, Director
• Bob Wiggins, Director
• Jeremy Whiteley, Founder
• Bill Koszewski, Chief Technology Officer & Interim CEO
Products:
Promotional Products: Apparel & Accessories, Awards & Recognition, bags & Backpacks, Gifts, Golf, Sports & Outdoors

PROMARK 1
6730 N CMINO PDRE ISIDORO
TUCSON, AZ 85718
520-297-2246
aaleamoni@aol.com
• Aran S Aleamoni, President / Chief Executive Officer
Products:
Premium promotional products for golf.

PROMARK EMBLEMS LLC
14052 VALLEY DRIVE
PO BOX 872
LONGMONT, CO 80504
303-926-1328
888-287-0056
Fax: 303-926-1450
www.teampromark.com
Products:
Offers specialty emblems for clubs, organizations or teams.

PROMARX/VITAL
7 NORDEN LANE
HUNTINGTON STATION, NY 11746
631-673-1084
800-777-8482
Fax: 866-326-4478
VitalTeam@Vital-Apparel.com
Products:
Matching Accessories, Sports Themed Apparel, Team Sports Apparel. Matching Accessories include Hair Ribbons, Hair Bows, Hair Scrunchies, Headbands, Knit Hats & Matching Knit Gloves, Mesh Top Socks, Non Terry Socks, Sleeve Holders, Dazzle Tote Bags, Polar Fleece Blankets and Flip Flops

PROMOS - SPORTS & CORPORATE PROMOTIONS LLC
513 W MT PLEASANT AVENUE
SUITE 208
LIVINGSTON, NJ 07039-1721
973-422-0004
800-394-7196
Fax: 973-422-0114
info@PROMOSLLC.com
www.promosllc.com
• Russel Steinberg, President
(973) 422-0004
russel@promosllc.com
Products:
Producers of any promotional item with a logo. Also producers of personalized party favors and gifts like Sweats, Compressed T-shirts, Towels, Hats, Mugs, Candles, Bags, Scrubs, Sport Balls, Mousepads, Blankets, Banners, Posters, Socks, etc.

PROPET USA INC.
2415 W VALLEY HIGHWAY N
AUBURN, WA 98001
253-854-7600
800-877-6738
800-877-6738
Fax: 253-854-7607
customerservice@propetusa.com
www.propetusa.com
• Jack Hawkins, President
• Ali Altaf, EVP
• Rick Wang, Office Manager
Products:
General Sports Products - Walking Shoes

PROTEAM BY HAUSMANN
130 UNION STREET
NORTHVALE, NJ 7647
201-767-0255
888-428-7626
Fax: 201-767-1369
sales@proteamtables.com
www.proteamtables.com
• George Batchelor, Sales / Marketing Director
(201) 767-0255
sales@proteamtables.com
• Joe Patten, National Sales Manager
(201) 767-0255
Products:
Modular Taping Stations, Treatment Tables, Taping Tables, Benches, Lockers, Cabinets, Stools, Weight Racks

PROZRELIEF
115 PERIMETER CENTER PLACE
SUITE 945
ATLANTA, GA 30346

678-990-8002
877-286-7074
Fax: 770-206-2389
Products:
Glucosamine Chondroitin MSM, ProzRelief Joint Formula

PSC/ENCORE SELECT INC
5019 W NASSAU STREET
TAMPA, FL 33607
813-282-7073
800-310-9428
Fax: 813-282-7079
www.encoreselect.com
Products:
Apparel, Autograph Memorabilia, Awards/Trophies, Collectible Wall D,cor, Custom Framing, Display Cases, Game-Used Products, Matted Prints, Stadium Products, and Trading Cards

PUMA NORTH AMERICA
1 CONGRESS ST.
SUITE 110
BOSTON, MA 2114
617-488-2900
Fax: 978-698-1174
info@puma.com
www.puma.com
• Jochen Zeitz, Chairman of the Board/CEO
• Dieter Bock, Chief Financial Officer
• Eric Safin, Classics Category Manager
• Donna Deane, Apparel Category Manager
Products:
Baseball - Shoes-Metal Cleats, Shoes-Rubber Cleats; Basketball - Shoes; Football - Shoes-Cleated; General Sports Products - All-Purpose Shoes, Bags-Equipment, T-shirts; Soccer - Shoes; Softball - Shoes-Metal Cleats, Shoes-Rubber Cleats; Track & Field/Runn

PURE FISHING
7 SCIENCE COURT
COLUMBIA, SC 29203
803-754-7000
800-334-9105
Fax: 712-336-5183
purefishinginquiries@purefishing.com
www.purefishing.com
• Tom Bedell, Owner
Products:
Line, Lures, Reels, Rods, Soft Bait, Terminal Tackle.

PUTT-PUTT GOLF COURSES OF AMERICA, INC.
300 S LIBERTY STREET
SUITE 110
WINSTON-SALEM, NC 27101
336-714-3950
866-788-8788
Fax: 336-714-3955
www.putt-putt.com
• David Callahan, President
• Teresa Greco, Chief Operating Officer
Products:
General Sports Products including Game Rooms and Miniature Golf Courses.

PUTTERMAN ATHLETICS
4834 S OAKLEY PLACE
CHICAGO, IL 60609
773-927-4120
800-621-0146

Fax: 773-650-6046
www.mputterman.com
• Alan Berman, Chief Business
• Edward E Reicin, President
• Benjamin Beiler, President and CEO
Products:
Windscreens, gym floor covers, wall
padding
Description:
90-year old manufacturer of quality sports
equipment.
Brands:
Putterman

IZOD CLUB GOLF & TENNIS
1001 FRONTIER ROAD
BRIDGEWATER, NJ 08807
610-374-4242
800-866-7292
Fax: 610-478-1989
pvh.com
• Mark Webber, Chief Executive Officer
• Robert Rully, Sales VP
• Pam Smith, Marketing / Advertising
Manager
Products:
Golf apparel, hats, caps, visors, socks,
umbrellas, premium knit golf shirts, sweaters
and sweater vests, fleece country club
design sweatshirts, golf windshirts and rain
suits, as well as twill pants and shorts.

PW ATHLETIC COMPANY, INC.
140 N GILBERT ROAD
PO BOX 8760
MESA, AZ 85203-9028
480-962-5289
800-687-5768
Fax: 800-729-2483
info@pwathletic.com
www.pwathletic.com
• Dave Bang, Owner
• Wayne Anderson, Marketing
Products:
Baseball - Cages/Backstops, Dugouts, First
Base Safety Protectors, Foul Line Poles;
Basketball - Backboards, Backstops, Hoops,
Nets, Standards; Bike - Racks; Facilities -
Soccer Field Equipment; Football - Goal
Posts; Racquet Sports - Tennis Court Nets

Q-RAY INC
PO BOX 9
ARLINGTON HEIGHTS, IL 60006
866-5441825
Fax: 847-228-5195
QRay@QRay.com
www.qray.com
Products:
Q-Ray Ionized Bracelets

QUABAUG CORPORATION
DAMON MILL SQUARE
SUITE H3
CONCORD, MA 1742
508-867-7731
Fax: 508-867-4600
sales@vibramusa.com
www.vibram.us
• Robert E Varnum, Chairman
• Michael Gionfriddo, VP
• Tony Post, President & CEO
Products:
General Sports Products - Athletic Footwear

QUANTUM ROCK ENTERPRISES
PO BOX 4032
ROLLING HILLS ESTATES, CA 90274
310-378-2171
Fax: 310-378-9383
QuantumRock@QuantumRock.com
www.quantumrock.com
• Fred Willis, Owner
fredwillis@quantumrock.com
Nature of Services:
Mobile Rock Climbing Walls For Special
Events, Trade Shows, Marketing
Promotions, Corporate Events, Film/TV
Productions.

**QUEST TECHNOLOGIES, A 3M
COMPANY**
1060 CORPORATE CENTER DRIVE
OCONOMOWOC, WI 53066
262-567-9157
800-245-0779
Fax: 262-567-4047
• Melissa Wesemann, Marketing Manager
Products:
Noise Dosimeters, Sound Level Meters, Gas
Detection Monitors, Vibration Monitors,
Indoor Air Quality Monitors, Audiometric
Equipment, Heat Stress & Thermal
Environment Monitors, Applications
Software
Year Founded:
1947

QUIKSILVER
15202 GRAHAM STREET
HUNTINGTON BEACH, CA 92649
714-889-2200
800-435-9917
Fax: 714-889-3700
customerservice@quiksilver.com
www.quiksilverinc.com
• Robert B McKnight Jr, Chairman / Chief
Executive Officer
(714) 889-2200
• Bernard Mariette, President / Director
(714) 889-2200
• Steven L Brink, Chief Financial Officer
(714) 889-2200
• Robert B. McKnight Jr., Executive
Chairman
• Andrew P. Mooney, Chief Executive
Officer & President
Products:
General Sports Apparel

R.A.M. SPORTS, INC.
4640 ADMIRALTY WAY
SUITE 50
MARINA DEL REY
CALIFORNIA, CA 90292
310-496-5728
800-225-5712
Fax: 310-496-5729
• Mike Oister, President
• Matt Torson, Special Accounts Manager
• Mike Gloden, Operations Manager
• Randy Jones, Treasurer
Products:
Balls for volleyball, soccer and football.

R.C.I.
12001 CR 1114
TYLER, TX 75709
903-939-1908
Fax: 903-939-2202
sales@rciracing.com
www.rciracing.com

• Steve Crane, Marketing

R.S. OWENS & CO., INC.
5535 N LYNCH AVENUE
CHICAGO, IL 60630
773-282-6000
800-282-6200
Fax: 773-545-4501
salesinfo@rsowens.com
www.rsowens.com
• Scott Siegel, President
• Dave Kryan, Pubic Relations Manager
• George Sorpremant, Marketing Manager
• Larry Maloney, VP Sales & Marketing
• Jacqueline Duda, Customer Service
Manager
• Lawrence Maloney, VP Of Sales &
Marketing
• Kristen Groote, VP Of Sales & Marketing
Products:
Trophies, Awards, Medals, Plaques,
Ribbons.
Year Founded:
1938

RACEAMERICA, INC.
105 BONVENTURA DRIVE
SAN JOSE, CA 95134
408-988-6188
Fax: 408-988-1603
info@raceamerica.com
www.raceamerica.com
• Phillip Briseno, Sales Manager
• Dennis Laczny, President
• Tina Bozarth, Operations Manager
Nature of Service:
The industry leader in advanced event
critical timing electronics. Designs and
manufactures a complete line of portable
timing systems, software and LED-based
scoreboards and displays for use in both
single and multi-lane snowmobile,
autocross, mud bog, soap boxz derby, ATV,
and drag racing. Also provides a variety of
customized timing solutions for private,
commercial, and industrial applications.
Produces the world's state-of-the-art, fully
wireless drag racing timing system and
continues to innovate with flexibility to match
uniwue customer needs.
Year Founded:
1991
Products:
Timing systems and LED scoreboards for
drag race, autocross, downhill skiing, ATV
and Mudbog racing, soap box derby and
racetracks. track marshalling equipment
including corner safety lights, blag flag
displays and track marshall software. Race
management software, counting displays,
countdown clocks, speed trap, lap timers
and auto timers. Also manufacture custom
timing solutions for a variety of applications.

**RACEBRICKS MEMORABILIA LLC DBA
CLEAR COLLECTIBLES**
21515 ROSCOE BOULEVARD
CANOGA PARK, CA 91304
818-676-1612
877-790-0990
Fax: 818-676-1614
cyracebricks@yahoo.com
• Charles Yacobian, General Manager
(818) 676-1612
cyracebricks@yahoo.com
Year Founded:
2004

1179

Products:
Collegiate logo/image glass and acrylic items.

RACING COMMUNICATIONS
3860 MOON STATION ROAD
KENNESAW, GA 30144
770-429-8783
Fax: 770-429-8835
info@racingcommunications.com
www.racingcommunications.com
• Kraig Pechenino, Marketing Director
Products:
Radio Systems, 2-Way Radios, Headsets, Intercom Systems, Scanners, Racing Helmets, In-Car Accessories

RACING REFLECTIONS INC
556 S MAIN STREET
MARION, VA 24354
276-783-9017
800-883-9017
Fax: 276-783-5939
www.racingreflections.com
• Robert Battaglia, President
Products:
Licensed NASCAR Merchandise

RAE CROWTHER COMPANY
2273 BURKETT DR.
ROCK HILL, SC 29730
800-841-5050
800-841-5050
Fax: 803-366-3633
www.raecrowther.com
• Hans Krause, President
(800) 841-5050
Products:
Football - Dummies, Field Equipment, Shields, Protective Pads, Sleds, Chutes, Running Ropes.
Nature of Service:
Full line of strength equipment for all levels of play.
Brands:
S-Advantage Tackler, S-Advantage Sleds, Attack Sled, Zig-zag Sled, Hit-Tech Station, Classic Two Man Sled, Classic 5 & 7 Man Sled, Classic tackling Sled, Defensive Reaction Machine, Tunch Punch Sled, Cruncher Sled, Run Tunnel, Monster Ropes, Maskill Sled, Parts 2-5-7 sled, parts DFR 1950-2000, Parts DFR 2001-2002, Parts Tackling, Super Chute, Jam Tent, Chutes Stalls, Center Machine, QB Throwing Net, Hanging Net, Tunch Punch Ladder, Pop Up Dummies, Hand Shields, Stand Up Dummies, Step-Overs

RAGE CAGE
357 COUNCIL OAK DRIVE
SEVERN, MD 21144
410-672-0282
Fax: 410-672-0689
info@ragecage.com
www.ragecage.com
• Frank Reeves, President
frank@ragecage.com
Products:
Lacrosse, Hockey Goals, Lacrosse Ground Bracket with hardware, Shot Blocker, ProTraction Feet, Lacrosse Carrying Strap

RAINBOW IMPORTS
421 NE ALDEN AVENUE
BEND, OR 97701

541-389-7129
800-628-7440
Fax: 541-389-7770
Products:
General sporting goods.

RAISINS COMPANY INC.
COSTA MESA, CA 92649
949-493-0651
800-472-4746
Fax: 949-645-0313
• Steve Tully, Raisins Corporate Operations EVP
• Marty Samuels, Sales / National Marketing EVP
Products:
Sports and Team Products: Swimming & Diving

RALEIGH CYCLE
6004 S 190TH STREET
SUITE 101
KENT, WA 98032
253-395-1100
800 222-5527
Fax: 253-872-0257
www.raleighusa.com
• William Austin, President
Products:
Bicycles and cycling accessories

RAMSTAR MILLS, INC.
1107 COMMERICIAL ST.
ATHENS, TX 75751
903-292-1724
800-327-2303
Fax: 903-292-1726
www.ramstaronline.com
• Bob Wielenga, President
(800) 327-2303
• Kenneth Holt, General Manager
(800) 327-2303
Products:
Manufacturer of T-shirts, Tank Tops and Shorts. Also a manufacturer of HydroWick by AmeriTeesr high performance moisture management apparel in short and long sleeve tees, tanks, safety vests and sweatshirts. Made in USA apparel.

RAND INTERNATIONAL
51 EXECUTIVE BOULEVARD
FARMINGDALE, NY 11735
631-249-6000
Fax: 631-249-6015
• Allen Goldmeier, President
• Steven Goldmeier, VP
Products:
Bicycles, Wheel Goods, Bicycle Accessories.

RAPIDRIBBONS
505 S 9TH STREET
PO BOX 222
GOSHEN, IN 46526-3446
800-752-6595
Fax: 800-365-0064
sales@rapidribbons.com
www.rapidribbons.com
• Milton Thomas, Chief Operating Officer
milt.rapidribbons@verizon.net
Products:
Ribbons, Ribbon Logos, Ribbon Tags, Medals, Pins, Certificates, Trophies, Watches, Clothing/Blankets, Gold Awards, Graduation/Honors, Badges/Holders/Tags.

RAPPORT COMPOSITES
8802 BASH STREET
SUITE E
INDIANAPOLIS, IN 46256
866-286-7322
800-783-0196
Fax: 877-783-0196
www.swingscience.net
• Michael Perryman, President
• Connie Nielson, VP Operations
• Caleb Smith, Sales Director
Products:
Supplier of premium golf club components.

RAVENSBURGER FX SCHMID
1 PUZZLE LANE
NEWTON, NH 3858
855-257-1500
800-886-1236
Fax: 603-382-3366
www.ravensburger.com
• Karsten Schmidt, Speaker
• Frank Mallet, Chief Financial Officer / Chief Operatin
Products:
Distributor of children's, adult and family games and puzzles throughout the U.S. and Canada.

RAWLINGS SPORTING GOODS COMPANY INC.
510 MARYVILLE UNIVERSITY DRIVE
SUITE 110
SAINT LOUIS, MO 63141
314-819-2800
800-729-5464
Fax: 314-819-2988
contact@rawlings.com
www.rawlings.com
• Mike Thompson, SVP, Sports Marketing & Bus Development
• David Zumbach, VP Marketing
• Scott Siebers, Product Manager, Baseball
Products:
Baseballs, Custom Bats, MiniBats, Socks, Sport Belts, Shin Guards, Golf Clubs, Golf Balls, Golf Bags, Non-motorized Golf Carts, Golf Club Heads, Leather and Synthetic Golf Gloves.

RAY COOK GOLF COMPANY
2212 GATLIN CREEK ROAD
DRIPPING SPRINGS, TX 78620
512-782-8245
Fax: 817-326-5514
www.raycook.com
• Jack Lynch, Chief Operating Officer
Products:
Golf Clubs and Putters

RAZOR USA LLC
16200-A CARMENTIA ROAD
PO BOX 3610
CERRITOS, CA 90703
562-345-6000
866-467-2967
Fax: 562-345-6087
www.razor.com
• Carlton Calvin, President
• Katherine Mahoney, VP, Marketing
• Katy Fletcher, Brand Manager
Products:
Dirt Bike, Miniature Electric Motorcross Bike, Electric Motorcycle, Electric Scooter

RED LION PRODUCTS
1125 WRIGHT AVENUE
CAMDEN, NJ 8103-1615
856-964-9700
800-526-2363
Fax: 856-964-9135
www.standardmerchandisingco.com/RED-LI
ON-C58.aspx
• Lee Tarnoff, VP
Products:
Baseball, Soccer, Volleyball Socks &
Accessories, Wristbands/Headbands,
Reflective Running Accessories, Training &
Conditioning Tape.

REDLINE PERFORMANCE PRODUCTS, INC.
42670 450TH STREET
PO BOX 399
PERHAM, MN 56573
218-346-7790
Fax: 760-598-0167
www.1redline.com
• Kent H. Harle, Chief Executive Officer /
Founder / Dire
• Mark A. Payne, President / Chief Financial
Officer / Di
• Chris B. Rodewald, Sales / Marketing VP
• Stanley R. Herman, Director
Products:
Designer and manufacturer of snowmobiles.

REEBOK APPAREL GROUP
1895 J W FOSTER BOULEVARD
CANTON, MA 2021
781-401-5000
800-382-3823
Fax: 781-401-7402
www.reebok.com
• Paul Harrington, President / Chief
Executive Officer
• Uli I. Becker, President
• David Baxter, President, Sports Licensed
Division
• John Warren, General Manager, Sports
Licensed Division
• Kenneth Watchmaker, EVP / Chief
Financial Officer
Products:
Manufacturers of sportswear and
accessories. Also sports men's casualwear
and shoes.

REEBOK CANADA INC.
3400 RAYMOND-LASNIER
ST-LAURENT(QUEBEC), CANADA H4R
3L3
514-461-8000
866-870-1743
www.reebok.com
• Paul Harrington, President/CEO
Products:
Sporting apparel, footwear, accessories.

REGENT SPORTS CORPORATION
45 RANICK ROAD
PO BOX 11357
HAUPPAUGE, NY 11788
631-234-2800
800-645-5190
Fax: 631-232-0124
• Harvey Feldman, President
Products:
Sporting goods equipment. Offers products
for outdoor games, baseball gloves and
equipment, basketballs, soccer balls, soccer
equipments and accessories, volleyballs,

table tennis balls, table tennis products and
footballs.

RELIABLE OF MILWAUKEE
6737 W. WASHIONGTON STREET
SUITE 3200
MILWAUKEE, WI 53214
414-272-5084
800-336-6876
Fax: 414-272-6443
www.reliableofmilwaukee.com
• Mark Blutstein, President/CEO
(414) 238-2622
markb@relknit.com
• Janice Betchkal, Chief Financial Officer
(414) 238-2628
Janice@relknit.com
• John Johnson, Chief Operations Officer
(414) 238-2623
johnjohnson@relknit.com
• Kathleen Caylor, EVP Design
(414) 238-2623
kathleenc@relknit.com
• Tanya Thorson, VP Marketing
(414) 238-6359
Tanya@relknit.com
Products:
Headwear, slippers, fashion accessories,
robes, golf accessories or promotional
products, Nitco new and recycled golf balls.
Promotional products distributor.
Year Founded:
1911
Description:
Fifth generation family owned company
headquartered in Milwaukee, producing
brands Muk Luks, Golf Balls Direct and
Nitro, Express Promotions, and Quietwear.
Clients Include:
Kohl's, Walmart, Target, Bon-Ton, Macy's,
JcPenney, QVC, Zulilly, Groupon, DSW,
Dicks Sporting Goods, Cabela's, American
Eagle Outfitters, Urban Outfitters, Dry
Goods, Tilly's, Free People.

RELIABLE RACING SUPPLY, INC.
643 UPPER GLEN STREET
QUEENSBURY, NY 12804
518-793-5677
800-223-4448
Fax: 800-585-4443
customerservice@reliableracing.com
www.reliableracing.com
• John Jacobs, President
(800) 223-4448
john@reliableracing.com
• Kathleen Spear, Vice President
Operations
(800) 223-4448
kathy@reliableracing.com
• Kelli Evans, Creative Desing
(800) 223-4448
kelli@reliableracing.com
Year Founded:
1969.
Nature of Service:
Supplier to ski resorts, golf courses,
recreation facilities and event promoters.
Manufacturer of Break-A-Way® slalom
poles, Porta-flex® - temporary crowd-control
solutions for sports facilities and event
venues. Custom racing bibs, numbers and
banners. US distributor of TAG Heuer and
ALGE sports timing systems and athletic
scoreboards. Full range of golf course and
golf tournament supplies. Direct consumer
source via internet and catalog of ski and

snowboard competition gear and
accessories.

REMINGTON ARMS COMPANY, INC.
870 REMINGTON DRIVE
PO BOX 700
MADISON, NC 27025-0700
800-243-9700
Fax: 336-548-7801
info@remington.com
www.remington.com
• Tommy Millner, President / Chief
Executive Officer
• John Dwyer, Ammunition VP
Products:
Sporting goods products for the hunting and
shooting sports markets, as well as military,
government and law enforcement markets.

RENAISSANCE GOLF DESIGN, INC.
530 E EIGHTH SREET
TRAVERSE CITY, MI 49686
231-941-7499
Fax: 231-941-2114
renaissancegolf@aol.com
www.renaissancegolf.com
• Tom Doak, Principal / Founder
renaissancegolf@aol.com
• Bruce Hepner, VP
renaissancegolf@aol.com
Services:
Golf course design and architecture in the
minimalist style.

RENNOC
645 PINE STREET
GREENVILLE, OH 45331
856-327-5400
800-372-7100
Fax: 800-675-1727
www.rennoc.com
• Richard Conner, Founder / Chief Executive
Officer
• Mike Hess, Co-Chief Executive Officer
Products:
General Sports Products - Manufactures
athletic jackets and warm-up suits

REPUBLIC PACKAGING CORPORATION
9160 S GREEN STREET
CHICAGO, IL 60620
773-233-6530
Fax: 773-233-6005
reppack@repco.com
www.repco.com
• Charles Wood, President / Chief Executive
Officer
reppack@repco.com
• Rose Wood, VP
reppack@repco.com
• Edward Olszewski, Chief Financial Oficer
reppack@repco.com
Services:
Designs, tests, manufactures and delivers
cushion packaging solutions to meet the
unique needs of customers.

RESILITE SPORTS PRODUCTS, INC.
PO BOX 764
SUNBURY, PA 17801
570-473-3529
800-843-6287
800-326-9307
Fax: 570-473-8988
resilite@resilite.com
www.resilite.com

• Paul Gilbert, President
(800) 843-6287
• Jeff Baker, Director of Marketing
Year Founded:
1959.
Nature of Service:
Specializes in customized padding solutions, for post, columns, and other hard-to-cover obstructions. We've solved padding dilemas for thousands of customers!

REVERE PLASTICS, INC.
19 HAMPDEN STREET
BOSTON, MA 2119
617-442-3100
800-226-8374
Fax: 617-442-1152
athleticcovers@revereplastics.com
www.revereplastics.com
• Edward Smith, President
athleticcovers@revereplastics.com
• Tina Walsch, Office Manager
athleticcovers@revereplastics.com
Products:
Produces protective covering for athletic surfaces.

REVGEAR SPORTS CO.
15073 KESWICK STREET
VAN NUYS, CA 91405
818-847-1100
800-767-8288
Fax: 818-781-7833
info@revgear.com
www.revgear.com
• Paul Reavlin, Founder
paulr@revgear.com
Products:
Training tools, aids, apparels, accessories for sparring, boxing and kickboxing, self defense and grappling and aerobic kickboxing such as gloves, shin guards, chest protectors, rib and ab guards, chestguards, groin and abdominal protectors, athletic cup supporters, hand wraps, training aids, mitts and shields, heavy bags, mats and flooring and instructional videaos and DVDs

REYN SPOONER INC
66-1600 LALAMILO ROAD
PO BOX 1509
KAMUELA, HI 96743
808-842-4793
888-289-7396
Fax: 808-847-5296
info@reyns.com
www.reyns.com
• Tim McCullough, President / Chief Executive Officer
info@reyns.com
• Kirk Hubbard, Chief Operating Officer
info@reyns.com
Products:
Manufactures a large and unique selection of authentic Hawaiian aloha shirts printed with Automotive, Major League Baseball and Collegiate Athletics themes.

RHINO SPORTS
15029 N 74TH STREET
SCOTTSDALE, AZ 85260-2406
480-719-8585
800-585-0922
Fax: 480-315-9217
www.rhinocourts.com

• John Shaffer, President
• Jay Abraham, EVP
• Bob Hemming, National Sales Manager
• Joe Kreigbaum, Local Sales/Dealer Support
• Eric Keef, Project Manager
• Ted Waldrup, Dealer, Orange Country
Services:
Rhino Court basketball provides for court flooring and court construction for basketball courts, tennis courts, gym flooring, basketball gym floors and athletic fitness sports.

RHODES WOOD COMPANY, INC.
5909 EVERGREEN BOULEVARD
SAINT LOUIS, MO 63134
314-522-1600
Fax: 314-522-0000
• Marvin Rhodes, President
• Joyce Rhodes, VP
Services:
Trophies, Awards and Components.

RICHARDSON SPORTS, INC.
500 INTERNATIONAL WAY
PO BOX 2440
SPRINGFIELD, OR 97477
541-687-1818
Fax: 541-687-1130
sales@richardsoncap.com
www.richardsoncap.com
• Neil Richardson, President
sales@richardsoncap.com
• Donna Richardson, VP
sales@richardsoncap.com
Products:
Caps, hats, visors

RICO INDUSTRIES/TAG EXPRESS
7000 N AUSTIN AVENUE
NILES, IL 60714
312-427-0313
800-423-5856
Fax: 312-427-1887
info@ricoinc.com
www.ricoinc.com
• Daniel Schack, Contact
info@ricoinc.com
Products:
Licensed MBL, NBA, NFL, NHL, NASCAR and Collegiate Athletics novelty items and accessories for the home, office and car.

RIDDELL ATHLETIC FOOTWEAR
669 SUGAR LANE
ELYRIA, OH 44035
440-366-8225
800-275-5338
Fax: 440-366-6292
www.riddell.com
• Ernie Wood, President
webmaster@riddellfootwear.com
• Ed Travis, SVP
• Chip Walther, Sales VP
• Bill Sherman, President / Chief Executive Officer
Products:
Cleated footwear and other athletic shoes

RIDDELL, INC.
9801 W HIGGINS ROAD
SUITE 800
ROSEMONT, IL 60018
773-794-1994
800-275-5338

Fax: 773-794-6155
help@riddellsports.com
www.riddell.com
• Bill Sherman, President / Chief Executive Officer
Products:
Baseball Batting Helmets, Cycling Helmets, Football Helmets, General Sports Products, Collectibles.

RIEDELL SHOES, INC.
122 CANNON RIVER AVENUE
PO BOX 21
RED WING, MN 55066
651-388-8251
800-698-6893
Fax: 651-385-5500
customerservice@riedellskates.com
www.riedellskates.com
• Bob Riegelman, President / Chief Executive Officer
customerservice@riedellskates.com
• Scott Riegelman, VP
customerservice@riedellskates.com
• Dan Riegelman, Marketing VP
customerservice@riedellskates.com
• Dustin Glebe, Coordinator
customerservice@riedellskates.com
Products:
Ice and roller skates

RIGHT GARD CORPORATION
531 N 4TH STREET
PO BOX 286
DENVER, PA 17517
717-336-2700
800-535-1122
Fax: 717-484-2180
• Richard A. McGrath, President
• Julie Kelly, General Manager
• Stacey Bidges, National Sales Manager
• Richard A. Mc Grath, President
Products:
Soccer shin guards, mouth guards, protective gear, soccer shorts, perfromance wear, sports apparel, accessories

RINGOR
7929 SW BURNS WAY
WILSONVILLE, OR 97070
503-582-9889
800-746-4670
Fax: 503-582-9899
Questions@Ringor.com
www.ringor.com
• Carol Ihlenburg, President
Products:
Baseball & Softball, Non Metal Cleats, Metal Spikes, Athletic Apparel, Turf Shoes/Cross Trainers, Sandals/Shoes Accessories, Bags

RIP FLAG
408 S FEDERAL
MASON CITY, IA 50401
641-423-0044
888-747-3524
Fax: 507-625-5111
customercare@ripflag.com
www.ripflag.com
Products:
Flag, Football, Belts

RIPKEN BASEBALL LLC
1427 CLARKVIEW ROAD
SUITE 100
BALTIMORE, MD 21209

410-823-0808
800-486-0850
Fax: 410-823-0850
www.ripkenbaseball.com
• Cal Ripken, President / Chief Executive Officer
• Bill Ripken, Co-Owner / Executive Vice President
• Karen Desantis, Executive Assistant
• Chris Flannery, Chief Operating Officer
• Brian Thornton, Director of Marketing/Corporate Development
• Jeff Eiseman, Vice President
Products:
Athletic Shorts, Caps, Casual Wear, Children's Apparel, Jackets & Sweatshirts, Jerseys, Mascot Apparel, Novelties, T-shirts, Women's Apparel, Instructional Products, JUGS Equipment like Accessories, Baseballs, Pitching machines, Protective Screens

RIPON ATHLETIC
290 JUNCTION STREET
PO BOX 25
BERLIN, WI 54923
920-361-1500
Fax: 866-997-4766
www.riponathletic.com
• Henry M. Derleth, President
Products:
Athletic Jackets, Athletic Uniforms

RLS LIGHTING, INC.
203 ANSIN BOULEVARD
HALLANDALE, FL 33009
954-458-0345
800-226-1757
Fax: 954-983-3691
info@rlslighting.com
www.rlslighting.com
Products:
Sports Lighting, Street Lighting, Parking Lighting, Area Lighting, Landscape Lighting and Decorative Lighting, Aluminum Park Benches, Bicycle Racks, Mail Boxes, Trash Receptacles & Liners, Street Signs, Sign Lighting

ROBBINS SPORTS SURFACES
4777 EASTERN AVENUE
CINCINNATI, OH 45226
513-871-8889
800-543-1913
Fax: 513-871-7998
info@robbinsfloor.com
www.robbinsfloor.com
• James H. Stoehr, Jr, Owner/Chairman of Board
• Ken Thomas, VP Marketing
(513) 619-5964
• Ken Thomas, Vice President of Marketing
(513) 619-5932
Products:
Maple and synthetic sports flooring

ROBOT FACTORY
3740 INTERPARK DRIVE
COLORADO SPRINGS, CO 80907-5058
719-447-0331
800-717-6268
Fax: 719-447-0332
info@robotfactory.com
www.robotfactory.com
• Skip Engelbrecht, President
• Eileen Engelbrecht, VP

Products:
Robots and robotic devices for education, entertainment, advertising and promotions.
Year Founded:
1966

ROCES USA, INC.
10 TECHNOLOGY DRIVE
UNIT 1B
W LEBANON, NH 3784
603-298-2137
800-770-8750
Fax: 603-298 2139
info@rocesusa.com
www.rocesusa.com
• Dave Smallwood, General Manager
davesmallwood@rocesusa.com
Description:
Inline Skates/Protective Gear, Ice Skates, Quad Skates and Adjustable Ski Boots

ROCKPORT COMPANY
1895 JW FOSTER BOULEVARD
CANTON, MA 2021
781-401-5000
800-828-0545
Fax: 781-401-7402
www.rockport.com
• Paul Fireman, Chairman / Chief Executive Officer
• Jay M. Margolis, President / Chief Operating Officer
• Martin Coles, EVP / President / Chief Operating Office
• Terry R. Pillow, SVP / Chief Executive Officer-Ralph Laur
Products:
Walking shoes

ROCKY SHOES & BOOTS, INC.
39 E CANAL STREET
NELSONVILLE, OH 45764
740-753-1951
866-442-4908
Fax: 740-753-4024
www.rockyboots.com
• Mike Brooks, Chairman of Board / Chief Executive Offi
• David Sharp, President / Chief Operating Officer
• James E. McDonald, EVP / Chief Financial Officer
• David R. Sharp, President
Products:
Premium quality rugged outdoor, occupational, and casual footwear, as well as branded clothing and accessories

ROGERS ATHLETIC COMPANY
3760 W LUDINGTON DRIVE
FARWELL, MI 48622
989-386-2950
800-457-5337
Fax: 888-549-9659
www.rogersathletic.com
Products:
Football practice and field equipments such as sleds, chutes and dummies, strength training equipment, dumbells and weight plates, multi station strength machines.

ROL-DRI, INC.
2048 WIRT ROAD
HOUSTON, TX 77055
Products:
Tennis Court Equipment

ROLLER DERBY SKATE CORPORATION
311 W EDWARDS
PO BOX 249
LITCHFIELD, IL 62056
217-324-3961
Fax: 217-324-2213
info@rollerderbyskates.com
www.rollerderby.com
• Edwin C. Seltzer, President
Products:
Wheeled skates

ROLLERBLADE INC.
VIA FANTE D'ITALIA 56
31040
GIAVERA DEL MONTELLO, ITALY
03784-1673
800-232-7655
www.rollerblade.com
• Nicholas J. Skally, Public Relations and Marketing Manager
nskally@rollerblade.com
• Jeremy Stonier, VP / General Manager
• Stephen Charrier, President
Products:
In-Line Skating Protective Gear, Skates

ROOTS APPAREL
1400 CASTLEFIELD AVENUE
TORONTO, ONTARIO, CANADA M6B 4C4
416-781-3574
866-297-6687
866-297-4327
B2Bsales@roots.com
www.roots.com
• Michael Budman, Co-Founder
• Don Green, Co-Founder
• Robert Sarner, Director Of Communications/Public Affairs
rsarner@roots.com
• Jennifer Cornwell, Marketing Director
Products:
Activewear, Backpacks, Bedding & Bath Linens and Accessories, Belts, Camping Gear and Outdoor Accessories, Casual Bags and Sporting Equipment

ROSSIGNOL SKI COMPANY, INC.
1413 CENTER DRIVE
PO BOX 981060
PARK CITY, UT 84098
371-6762-6025
800-437-6771
Fax: 371-6789-2053
inforossiusa@rossignol.com
www.rossignol.com
• Laurent Boix-Vives, Chairman
• Francois Goulet, President
• Daniel Mornet, VP
• M. Bruno Cercley, President
• Angelo Maina, Director, Racing Department
• Yann Laphin, Communications Director
Products:
Winter Sports Goods like board, binding, boot, pole and clothing

ROYAL PRECISION, INC.
8275 TOURNAMENT DRIVE
#200
MEMPHIS, TN 38125
860-489-9254
800-920-4747
Fax: 860-489-5454
• John C Lauchnor, President / Chief Executive Officer
Sales@RoyalPrecision.com

- Ronald L Chalmers, Manufacturing EVP
- Ray Lucas, SVP Sales / Marketing
- Scott Hennessy, President and CEO
Products:
Component Supply to Golf Club
Manufacturers and Distributors.

ROYAL ROBBINS
1524 PRINCETON AVENUE
MODESTO, CA 95350
209-529-6913
800-587-9044
800-336-8661, CA ONLY
Fax: 209-522-5511
rrmail@royalrobbins.com
www.royalrobbins.com
- Royal Robbins, President / Owner
rrmail@royalrobbins.com
- Dan Costa, Chief Executive Officer
rrmail@royalrobbins.com
Products:
Manufacturer and Distributor of Activewear;
Outdoor Products Apparel.

ROYAL TEXTILE MILLS, INC.
929 FIRETOWER ROAD
PO BOX 159
YANCEYVILLE, NC 27379
800-334-9361
Fax: 800-934-9360
info@dukeathletic-tactical.com
www.dukeathletic-tactical.com
- Mark Atwater, President
Products:
Baseball Protective-Catcher; Basketball
Protective; Football Knee/Elbow Pads;
General Sports Products Athletic Socks,
Athletic Supporters, Support Products-Joint,
T-shirts (Blank), Wristbands/Headbands; Ice
Hockey Protective; Soccer Protective, etc.

ROYCE UNION BICYCLE COMPANY, INC.
6551 CENTERVILLE BUSINESS
PARKWAY
CENTERVILLE, OH 45459
937-865-2800
800-872-2453
Fax: 937-856-5470
service@huffy.com
www.huffy.com
- John A Muskovich, Chief Executive Officer
/ President
customer.service@huffy.com
- Nancy A. Michaud, SVP, General Counsel
/ Secretary
customer.service@huffy.com
- Robert L Diekman, SVP, Operations /
Logistics
customer.service@huffy.com
- Bill D Smith, President andCEO
customer.service@huffy.com
Products:
A diversified sporting goods company,
marketing bicycles and wheeled products.

RPTC, LLC
300 BOSTON POST ROAD
ORANGE, CT 06477-3505
203-795-5696
800-950-5049
Fax: 203-795-9120
rgmtennis@aol.com
www.platformtennis.com
- Christopher Casiraghi, President / Chief
Business
rgmtennis@aol.com
- Chris Casiraghi, President

Products:
Manufactures and Constructs Tennis Courts
and Platform Tennis

RUBATEX CORPORATION
1001 BROAD STREET
BEDFORD, VA 24523
540-587-5870
800-782-2839
Fax: 866-532-4200
www.fostek.com
- Lynn Bakker, Technical Services VP
rubatexsales@rubatex.com
- Roger Schmidt, Manager Marketing /
Technology
(800) 348-3428
- Stephanie Crisara, Sales VP
Products:
Closed cell rubber for use in pads and water
sportswear.

RUBBERMAID INCORPORATED
3124 VALLEY AVENUE
WINCHESTER, VA 22601
540-542-8695
Fax: 540-542-8770
www.rubbermaid.com
- Mark D. Ketchum, Chief Executive Officer
- Hartley Blaha, President, Corporate
Development
- Paul G. Boitmann, President, North
American Sales Operatio
- Gino de Biondi, VP of Marketing
- Steve Pawl, VP of Marketing
Products:
Global marketer of consumer products for
homes, commercial purposes and medical.

RUDIG TROPHIES
580 N 108TH PLACE
PO BOX 26429
WAUWATOSA, WI 53226
414-773-9000
Fax: 414-773-9181
rudigtrophy@sbcglobal.net
www.rudigtrophy.com
- Tom Rudig, President
- Nick Karegeannes, General Manager
Products:
Engravable Trophies, Awards, Components,
Dealer Programs, Emblems, Expert
Engravers, Medals, Plaques, Ribbons,
Signs, Silkscreening.

RUFFOLO ENTERPRISES, INC.
2926 75TH STREET
KENOSHA, WI 53143
262-652-3126
800-877-7025
Fax: 262-652-3188
sales@fktools-us.com
www.fktools-us.com
- Ralph J Ruffolo, President
- Mary Ruffolo, Vice President
sales@fktools-us.com
Products:
Skiing-Alpine - Ski/Snowboard Car Racks;
Skiing-Nordic - Ski Car Racks, FK/SKS Ski
and Snowboard tuning tools, Wax, Irons and
Vises, Diamond Stones.
Year Founded:
1975
Brands:
Ski-Hiker, FK, SKS, DMT

RUGBY IMPORTS, LTD.
885 WARREN AVENUE
E PROVIDENCE, RI 2914
401-438-2727
800-431-4514
Fax: 401-438-8260
gear@rugbyimports.com
www.rugbyimports.com
- Robert J Hoder, President
gear@rugbyimports.com
- Mark Hoder, VP
mark@rugbyimports.com
Products:
Rugby Balls, Jerseys, Shoes/Boots, Shorts,
Socks, Uniforms.

RUGGERS RUGBY SUPPLY
121 UNION STREET
WEST SPRINGFIELD, MA 1089
413-746-9554
877-784-4377
Fax: 413-746-9526
sales@ruggers.com
www.ruggers.com
- Vic Thomas, President
vic@ruggers.com
Products:
Rugby shirts and equipment.

RUSSELL ATHLETIC
PO BOX 90015
BOWLING GREEN, KY 42104
877-879-8410
888-606-5520
Fax: 877-729-4800
www.russellathletic.com
- John F Ward, Chairman / Chief Executive
Officer, Russ
- Calvin Johnston, Chief Executive Officer,
Russell Athleti
- Mike Thorne, President, Russell Athletic
Team and Bik
Products:
Baseball Uniforms; Basketball Uniforms;
Football Uniforms; General Sports Products
Athletic Jackets/Parkas, Sweat Clothes,
Warm-Up Suits; Ice Hockey Uniforms;
Lacrosse Uniforms; Soccer Uniforms;
Softball Uniforms; Track & Field/Running
Apparel

RYKA, INC.
101 ENTERPRISE ROAD
SUITE 100
ALISO VIEJO, CA 92656
978-897-8744
888-295-8864
Fax: 503-525-7953
www.ryka.com
- Lance Rist, President
Products:
Designs, develops and markets leading
performance fitness products including
performance athletic footwear and apparel.

RYNO ATHLETICS
1902 BRANDON DRIVE
TYLER, TX 75703
903-526-4140
888-609-6725
Fax: 800-574-0008
orders@ryno.com
ryno.com
- Brandon Steele, President/Chief Executive
Officer
- Phil Steele, National Sales Manager

Products:
Products include backpacks and garment bags, baseball bags, premium duffels, specialty sport bags, team/travel duffels.
Year Founded:
1996

S'PORTABLE SCOREBOARDS
106 MAX HURT DRIVE
MURRAY, KY 42071
270-759-1600
800-323-7745
Fax: 270-759-4112
www.sportablescoreboards.com
• Michael C. Cowen, Chairman
mikecowen@scoreboard1.com
• Peter Cowen, President / Chief Executive Officer
Products:
Scoreboard Manufacturer, Timing Devices, Numeric Displays.

S.L. OUTERBANKS LLC
1000 EAST HANES MILL RD.
WINSTON-SALEM, NC 27105
800-685-7557
Fax: 800-289-1870
hbi_service@hanesbrands.com
• John Marsh, President
Products:
Manufacturer, Importer, Exporter of Knitted Polo Shirts; Golf Apparel.

S.M. ATHLETICS
10421 LEXINGTON DRIVE
KNOXVILLE, TN 37932
865-966-3434
800-332-3458
Fax: 865-966-3448
sales@smathletics.com
www.smathletics.com
• R. F. Saraceni, President
• John Sewell, VP
Products:
Baseball - Uniforms; Basketball - Uniforms; Football - Uniforms; General Sports Products - Cheerleading, Warm-Up Suits; Ice Hockey - Uniforms; Soccer - Uniforms; Softball - Uniforms; Track & Field/Running; Volleyball - Uniforms.

SACO TECHNOLOGIES INC./SMARTVISION
7809 TRANS CANADA
MONTREAL; QUEBEC, CANADA H4S 1L3
514-745-0310
800-991-7226
Fax: 514-745-0315
www.lsi-industries.com
• Fred Jalbout, President/CEO
Products:
Large video screens for stadiums and other venues.

SAFE-T-GARD CORPORATION
12980 W. CEDAR DRIVE
PO BOX 1468
LAKEWOOD, CO 80228
303-763-8900
800-356-9026
800-382-6789
Fax: 303-763-8071
www.safetgard.com
• Scott Jacobs, President
• Kathy Jensen, Treasurer

Products:
Accessory equipment, ankle protection/stabilizers, bandages, athletic supporters, compression/sliding shorts, hot packs, mouth/nose/shin guards, fans, knee/elbow/forearm/ankle pads & supports, tape underwrap, volleyball padding, whistles, wraps

SAFEGUARD FLOOR SYSTEMS
5617 CROWNDALE DRIVE
PLANO, TX 75093
972-473-6746
Fax: 972-473-6746
• Lisa Willis, President
(972) 473-6746
Products:
Protective floor panel system.

SAFWAY SERVICES, LLC
N19 W24200 RIVERWOOD DRIVE
WAUKESHA, WI 53188
262-523-6500
800-558-4772
Fax: 262-523-9808
www.safway.com
• Jim Walters, Executive Vice President & CFO
• Jerry Johns, EVP / Chief Operating Officer
• Robert Sukalich, VP / Chief Financial Officer
• Jon Weber, VP / Controller
• Bill Hayes, President and CEO
• Chris Wells, Senior Vice President of Acquisitions & Corpo
• Marty McGee, Senior Vice President of Industrial Services
• Dana Valentine, Senior Vice President & Chief Human Resources
• Jon Weber, Vice President & Controller
• Curt Paulsen, VP Human Resources/General Counsel
Products:
Scaffolds and accessories
Year Founded:
1936
Description:
Safway Services rents and sells scaffolding, access equipment, and accessories, and provides labor and service support from project start to finish.

SALAUN SPORTS, INC., HENRI
210 W ROAD
PORTSMOUTH, NH 3801
603-436-0150
800-258-7255
Fax: 603-436-2869
sales@salaunsports.com
www.salaunsports.com
• Henri R Salaun, President
• Pamela Begdan, Manager
Products:
Basketball - Balls-Rubber, Nets; Football - Knee/Elbow Pads; General Sports Products - Athletic Supporters, Ball Inflators, Cones, Markers, Coaches Supplies, Junior and Official Size Goals, Wristbands/Headbands; Racquet Sports, Badminton Equipment, Gloves

SANDSTROM PRODUCTS COMPANY
224 MAIN STREET
PORT BYRON, IL 61275
309-523-2121
800-747-1084
Fax: 309-523-3912

mark@sandstromproducts.com
www.sandstromproducts.com
• Rick J Hartsock, Chairman
(309) 523-2121
• Brian Suhl, VP / Chief Operating Officer
(309) 523-2121
brian@sandstromproducts.com
• Brian Suhl, President
(309) 523-2121
• Mark Lousberg, Director of Sales
• Rick Wahlig, Purchasing Manager
• Dave Steele, Plant Manager
• Russ Burt, Technical Director
• Heather White, Director of Operations
• Linda Hocker, Customer Service
Products:
Solid film lubricants, piston skirt coatings, OEM coatings & product finishes, UV & energy cured coatings, floor coatings & resurfacers.

SARANAC GLOVE COMPANY
999 LOMBARDI AVENUE
GREEN BAY, WI 54304
920-435-3737 EXT 204
800-727-2622
Fax: 920-435-7618
www.saranacglove.com
• John Fabry, President / Chief Executive Officer
• Dan Small, Executive VP Sales / Marketing
• Tina Rooks, Controller
• Judy Lundin, VP Sales Eastern Region
Products:
Sports, winter, motorcycle, industrial/work, home & garden gloves, mechanics, law enforcement gloves and accessories.

SATURNIAN 1 INC.
PO BOX 700538
PLYMOUTH, MI 48170
800-653-2719
Fax: 734-454-6514
info@sat1sport.com
www.sat1sport.com
• Mark Sassak, President
info@sat1sport.com
Products:
Tye dye kites & spinners. Indoor/outdoor games (trapp ball, thumb ball, basketball, beanbag shuffle, hip hopscotch, bat, ball & glove sets, golf, bowling, soft shoes, muckers, toss & target, flyer golf, basketball toss, soccer goal & ball, roll to score, tent & tube EZ twist games. Fun Gripper Balls, Toys and Collegiates.

SAUCONY
4200 SOUTH A STREET
RICHMOND, IN 47374
800-282-6575
Fax: 978-532-6105
customerservice@saucony.com
www.saucony.com
• Richie Woodworth, President
• Charles Gottesman, Vice Chairman / EVP Business Development
• Arthur E Rogers Jr, President Saucony Domestic
• Richie Woodworth, President
• John H. Fisher, Chief Executive Officer/Chairman
• Micheal Umana, Chief Operating Officer/Chief Financial Offic

Products:
Athletic footwear, casual footwear, apparel, and accessories.

SAUNDERS ARCHERY COMPANY
1874 14TH AVENUE
PO BOX 1707
COLUMBUS, NE 68601
402-564-7177
800-228-1408
Fax: 402-564-3260
www.sausa.com
• Gene Saunders, President
• Tom Saunders, Director, Plant 3, Screw Machine Operations
• Charles Saunders, Director, Product Development & Marketing
Products:
Archery equipments and accessories

SAVAGE FITNESS
39 PLEASANT VALLEY ROAD
PO BOX 488
SUTTON, MA 1590
508-865-0097
800-682-8416
Fax: 508-865-1925
• Michael Savage, President
• Donna Savage, VP Marketing
Products:
Treamdill accessories

SCHELDE NORTH AMERICA, LLC
4180 44TH STREET SE
SUITE C
GRAND RAPIDS, MI 49512-4057
616-554-4945
800-823-0182
Fax: 616-554-1623
www.scheldesports.com
• David Noe, Vice President Sales & Marketing
(616) 554-4945
dnoe@scheldesports.com
• David Noe, VP - Sales & Marketing
(616) 554-4945
• Bob Howell, National Sales Manager
(800) 820-7780
• Madelyn Meneghetti, Regional Product Specialist
(616) 554-4945
• John Connors, Service Manager
(616) 554-4945
• Ronna Russell, Regional Sales Manager
(800) 823-0182
• Logsdon, Regional Sales Manager
(800) 823-0182
Products:
Manufacturer of gymnasium equipment: basketball portables, ceiling and wall mounts, volleyball systems, wall pads, scorers tables, etc.

SCHOENBROD RACING SHELLS
596 ELM STREET
BIDDEFORD, ME 4005
207-283-3026
Fax: 207-985-6814
• Charles Dibble, President
Manufacturer & Distributor:
Rowing/Crew - Shells/Sculls.

SCHUESSLER KNITTING MILLS
301 MUNSON AVENUE
MCKEES ROCKS, PA 15136

412-331-6660
800-245-6111
Fax: 412-331-6347
Products:
Knitted Headwear

SCHUTT SPORTS INC
710 S INDUSTRIAL DRIVE
PO BOX 426
LITCHFIELD, IL 62056
217-324-2712
800-426-9784
Fax: 217-324-2732
www.schuttsports.com
• Dave Rossi, VP Marketing
(217) 324-2712
• Robert Erd, Chief Executive Officer
(217) 324-2712
• Kip Meyer, VP and General Manager
• Robert Erb, President and CEO
• Pete Reinke, VP Regional Development
• Mark Watts, Regional Sales Manager
(217) 324-2712
Products:
Baseball Batter's Guards, Catcher's Masks, Helmets; Basketball Backboards, Hoops, Nets, Padding, Rebounders; Football Faceguards, Helmets, Sports Collectibles, Softball Batter's Helmets, Catcher's Helmets. Baseball, Softball, Rec Bases.
Year Founded:
1918

SCHWINN CYCLING & FITNESS
1690 38TH STREET
BOULDER, CO 80301
800-605-3369
800-868-5764
Fax: 303-939-0260
customerservice@schwinnfitness.com
www.schwinn.com
• Jeff Sinclair, Chief Executive Officer
• Pat Warner, Fitness Director
• Charity Emmons, Marketing Manager
Products:
Bikes

SCOTT USA
110 LINDSAY CIRCLE
KETCHUM, ID 83340
208-622-1000
Fax: 208-622-1005
www.scott-sports.com
• Shauna Unser, Sales/Product Manager
• Larry Morton, Winter Sports Vice President/General Manager
• Lance Levy, Sales/Public Relations Coordinator
• Gabe Glosband, Marketing Manager
• Pascal Ducrot, President
Products:
Wintersport - Goggles, Poles, Skis, Protection, Gloves, Apparel, Hats; Motorsport - Goggles, Works system, Goggle Accessories, Replacement Lenses, Grips, Apparel, Sunglasses, Bags & Packs; Bike - Mountain, Road, Junior, Frames, Accessories, Bike wear, Mechanical wear, Eyewear; Paintball - Goggles, Replacement Lenses, Sunglasses, Apparel

SCOTTISH CHRISTMAS
6111 N PERIMETER ROAD
OSCODA, MI 48750
989-739-1600
800-259-6785

Fax: 248-391-5777
www.scottish-christmas.com
• Stan Aldridge, President / Owner
• Kevin Aldridge, Contact
Products:
Licensed Sports Ornaments

SEAGULL INTERNATIONAL, INC.
1220 SPRING GARDEN STREET
PHILADELPHIA, PA 19123
215-922-2100
800-666-9300
Fax: 215-922-0970
info@seagullintl.com
www.seagullintl.com
• Steven A Segal, President
info@seagullintl.com
Products:
Headwear, Bandannas & Headwraps, Tote Bags, Rainwear & Umbrellas, Footwear, Beach & Swim Accessories, Nylon Jackets, Gloves, Custom Designs, Product Display Racks, Souvenirs

SEALFLEX INDUSTRIES, INC.
3303 HARBOR BOULEVARD
SUITE C2
COSTA MESA, CA 92626
714-708-0850
800-651-2098
Fax: 714-708-2711
www.sealflex.com
• Dennis Davis, President
(800) 651-2098
• John Schneider, Vice President
(888) 378-4621
• Joe Luperico, Shipping
(714) 708-0850
• Cindi Miraldi Litecher, National Sales Manager
(623) 376-9231
Nature of Service:
Moisture Mitigation Protecting Flooring Materials
Year Founded:
1985
Products:
Floor Moisture Protection Products, Flooring Adhesives (Moisture resistant) to 8 lbs, 5 year warranty.
Brands:
PH Blocker Primer 100, SL Ultratac 200, SL Ultratac 255, SealFlex Membrane System, MDK Kits.

SEATING SERVICES INCORPORATED
131 AVA DRIVE
HEWITT, TX 76643-2906
254-666-5155
800-433-3116
Fax: 254-666-4472
info@sturdisteel.com
www.sturdisteel.com
• Diane Cooke, President / Chief Executive Officer
(800) 552-9470
• Timothy B Cooke, Sales & Marketing VP
(716) 549-9003
Services:
Seats, Arena & Auditorium, Replacement Seating, Stadium Seating

SEATTLE BIKE SUPPLY
6004 S 190TH STREET
SUITE 202
KENT, WA 98032

425-251-1516
800-283-2453
Fax: 425-251-6041
www.seattlebikesupply.com
• Brent Carlson, Marketing / Sales Director
• Chuck Hooper, President
Products:
Bikes, Bike Parts

SEATTLE SYSTEMS/LENOX HILL BRACE COMPANY
26296 TWELVE TREES LANE NW
POULSBO, WA 98370
360-697-5656
Fax: 360-697-5876
• Anthony Diemont, National Direct Sales Supervisor
(360) 598-8955
• Dave Adams, EVP
(360) 598-8941
• Anna Re Potts, Marketing / Customer Service Director
(360) 598-8990
Products:
Orthotic Bracing, Cold Therapy, Sports Medicine & Artificial Limb Components & Systems

SEAWAY MATS, INC.
252 PARK STREET
MALONE, NY 12953
518-483-2560
800-361-0464
Fax: 518-207-0120
www.quedltd.com
• Gary Madden, Manager
(800) 361-0464
Products:
Gym Mats, Divider Curtains, Goals & Post, Padding, Protective Nets, Sport Nets, Transporters, Wall Pads, Tike Site

SECONDWIND PRODUCTS, INC.
429 27TH STREET NW
HICKORY, NC 28601
828-322-2600
800-438-5777
Fax: 828-328-1700
info@tenseconds.com
www.tenseconds.com
• Steven W Lee, President
• Kevin Hansen, Operations VP / Chief Financial Officer
• Bob Applegate, Marketing VP
• William A Blythe, Research & Development Director
Products:
Insoles, Shoe Care, Cleats/Spikes, Shoe Laces, Custom Laces/Lanyards, Sport Socks

SEIRUS SPORTS ACCESSORIES
13975 DANIELSON STREET
POWAY, CA 92064
858-513-1212
800-447-3787
Fax: 858-513-7878
www.seirus.com
• Mike Carey, President
• Wendy Carey, VP
• Joe Edwards, VP
Products:
Neoprene, Fleece & Weatherproof tri-laminate products

SELECT DISTRIBUTION/VISION STREET WEAR
1763 PLACENTIA AVENUE
COSTA MESA, CA 92627
949-722-8556
800-854-7370
Fax: 949-722-1257
www.selectsk8.com
• Brad Dorfman, Owner
Products:
General Sports Products - Athletic Shoes; Skates; Skateboards; Snowboarding Apparel, Snowboards

SELECT SPORT AMERICA
1015 UNION CENTER DRIVE
SUITE 200
ALPHARETTA, GA 30004
770-751-9930
888-238-3097
Fax: 770-751-9940
info@selectsportamerica.com
www.selectsportamerica.com
• Peter Eigil Nielsen, Chairman
• Soren Nielsen, President
(888) 239-3097
info@selectsportamerica.com
• Peter Knap, CEO in Select Sport A/S
• Finn Martensen, Attorney at law
Nature of Service:
North American Distributor
Year Founded:
1997
Products:
Soccer Balls, Gloves, Shinguards, Club/Camp/Training Apparel & Equipment, Bags
Brands:
Select

SENECA SPORTS INC.
75 FORTUNE BOULEVARD
PO BOX 719
MILDFORD, MA 1757
508-634-3616
800-861-7867
Fax: 508-634-8154
• David L Landay, President
• Carl Fritz, Marketing Manager
• Robert Montolio, Sales Manager / Slumber Bags & Tents
• Kevin Black, Sales Director / Brookfield Division
Products:
Ice Skates; In-Line Skating Accessories, In-Line Skating Protective, In-Line Skating Skates; Skateboarding Protective; Skateboards; Soccer Balls, Soccer Protective; Street Hockey Equipment, Street Hockey Skates: Volleyball Balls

SETCOM CORPORATION
3019 ALVIN DE VANE BOULEVARD
SUITE 560
AUSTIN, TX 78741
650-965-8020
888-673-8266
Fax: 650-965-1193
info@setcomcorp.com
www.setcomcorp.com
• Bob Vo Buelow, Sales / Marketing Director
info@setcomcorp.com
• Donna Gallant, Sales / Marketing Administrator
• Gordon Arnold, Account Executive
• James Roberts, President

Products:
Communication Equipment for firefighters, police motorcycle officers, military, auto racing, entertainment, and public safety and industrial applications

SEVEN SONS AND COMPANY INC
139 INTERSTATE PARK
SPARTANBURG, SC 29303
864-587-5511
800-722-5794
Fax: 864-587-0745
info@sevensons.com
Products:
Sports apparel

SEVYLOR USA INC.
3600 N HYDRAULIC
WINCHITA, KS 67219
320-252-1642
800-835-3278
Fax: 316-832-6201
sevylor@coleman.com
www.sevylor.com
Products:
Kayaks, Canoes, Inflatables and Personal Watercraft

SHAKESPEARE FISHING TACKLE DIVISION
7 SCIENCE COURT
COLUMBIA, SC 29203
800-466-5643
800-334-9105
Fax: 803-786-8902
www.shakespeare-fishing.com
• David Lund, Vice President of Marketing
(803) 754-7000
Products:
Fishing Equipment & Accessories

SHAMROCK SPORTS BAG COMPANY
1000 MERIDIAN STREET
HUNTSVILLE, AL 35807
256-533-0210
800-447-8038
Fax: 256-772-2386
• Tim McCormick, President
Products:
Baseball Bags-Equipment; Basketball Bags-Equipment; Fencing Bags; Football Bags-Equipment; General Sports Products All-Purpose Bags; Golf Bags-Luggage; Ice Hockey Bags-Equipment; Ice Skating Skate Bags; Racquet Sports Bags-Equipment; Soccer Bags-Equipment

SHANGHAI WINGO INTERNATIONAL
NO 1438 SHANXI N ROAD
FORTUNE TIMES BUILDING
UNIT 1507
SHANGHAI, 200060
-86-6231-8482
Fax: -86-6232-0583
www.wingointernational.com
• Chris Young, Director
Products:
Roller Skates and Scooters

SHAW & TENNEY
20 WATER STREET
PO BOX 213
ORONO, ME 4473
207-866-4867
800-240-4867

info@shawandtenney.com
www.shawandtenney.com
• Steven Holt, Owner
• Nancy Forster-Holt, Owner
Products:
Rowing Oars; Specialty and Sculling Oars;
Classic Paddles; For Adirondack Guide
Boats; Marine Hardware; Masts and Spars;
Boat Hooks; Pack Baskets; Canoe Parts &
Accessories; Apparel (Jackets, Hats,
T-shirts); Awards & Gifts (Souvenir and
Trophy Paddles, Souvenir and Trophy
Canoes, Paddle & Canoe Wall Plaque,
Canoe Plaque); Flag Poles and Yardarms

SHER-WOOD HOCKEY INC
2745 RUE DE LA SHERWOOD
SHERBROOKE, QUEBEC, CANADA J1K
1E1
866-563-2205
Fax: 819-821-4848
info@sher-wood.ca
• Bill Clark, President
(502) 588-7303
• Lou Candusso, Director of Operations
(519) 627-2248
• Graham Watson, VP Business
Development / USA Sales Mana
(734) 397-8324
gwlouisville@aol.com
• Dave Timbeck, Import Products Manager
dtimbeck@aol.com
Products:
Ice hockey players and goalies equipment,
bags, apparel and accessories

SHERMAN SPECIALTY COMPANY
300 JERICHO QUADRANGLE
SUITE 240
JERICHO, NY 11753
516-861-6420
800-645-6513
Fax: 516-861-1034
info@ShermanSpecialty.com

**SHERPA INC./DBA MOHN SKI RACK
COMPANY**
6580-B BELLEAU WOOD LANE
SACRAMENTO, CA 95822
916-395-9600
800-543-6646
Fax: 916-395-9625
www.mohnsportracks.com
• Jeff Zimmerman, President / Owner
Products:
Ski, Snowboard, Wakeboard, Skateboard
Racks

**SHERWOOD-DROLET CORPORATION,
LTD.**
2745 SHERWOOD BOULEVARD
QC, CANADA J1K 1E1
819-563-2202
866-563-2202
Fax: 819-821-4848
www.sher-wood.com
• Genevieve Therrien, Marketing Manager
Products:
Players (Player Sticks, Hockey Sticks,
Shafts, Blades, Blades Style, Protective
Equipment, Elbows Pads, Hockey Gloves,
Hockey Pants, Neckguard, Shinguards,
Shoulders Pads); Goalies (Goalie Sticks,
Protective Equipment, Goal Pads, Catch
Mitts, Blockers, Chest & Arm, Goal Pants)

SHIELD MFG, INC.
425 FILLMORE AVENUE
TONAWANDA, NY 14150
716-694-7100
800-828-7669
Fax: 716-694-8652
info@shieldsports.com
www.shieldsports.com
• David Berghash, Chief Executive Officer
dberghash@shieldsports.com
• James Geraci, President
(716) 694-7100
Products:
Team Hockey (Hockey Stick Sizing Chart,
Elementary, Middle School, Senior High
School/Collegiate Indoor, Senior High
School/Collegiate Outdoor); Accessories
(Hockey, Pucks & Balls, General and
Gymnasium).

SHIMANO AMERICAN CORPORATION
ONE HOLLAND DRIVE
IRVINE, CA 92618
949-951-5003
877-577-0600
Fax: 949-768-0920
www.shimano.com
• Yoshizo Shimano, President
• Yozo Shimano, President
Products:
Reels (Conventional Reels, Low Profile
Baitcasting Reels, Round Baitcasting Reels,
Spinning Reels, Saltwater Spinning Reels);
Rods (Freshwater Rods, Muskie Rods,
Salmon/Steelhead Rods, Freshwater
Trolling Rods, Inshore Rods, Butterfly
Jigging, Saltwater Rods, Kingfish Rods)

SHINN FU COMPANY OF AMERICA, INC.
10939 N POMONA AVENUE
KANSAS CITY, MO 64153
816-891-6390
888-332-6419
Fax: 816-891-6599
sfakc@shinnfuamerica.com
www.shinnfuamerica.com
• Joey Su, Executive VP
Products:
Lifting equipment (sevice jacks, jacks
stands, truck jacks, transmission jacks,
engine cranes, end lifts); Collision repair
equipment (porto-power kits, foot and hand
pumps, hydraulic rams, frame straightening
equipment and chainless anchor system)

SHIRTS & SKINS INC
10820 SW TUALATIN SHERWOOD ROAD
TUALATIN, OR 97062
503-646-4263
Fax: 503-646-4261
info@shirtsandskinsinc.com
www.shirtsandskinsinc.com
• Tamer Kiykiuglu, Vice President
(503) 646-4263
Products:
Team Uniforms (Reversible Uniforms -
Reversible Game Jersey, Reversible Game
Short, Reversible Practice Jersey, Practice
Short (non-reversible); Varsity Collection
Uniforms - Varsity Game Jersey, Varsity
Game Short, Varsity LS, Varsity Team
Jacket, Varsity Team Pant), Team Apparel.

SHOCK DOCTOR INC
3405 ANNAPOLIS LANE N
SUITE 200
PLYMOUTH, MN 55447

800-233-6956
866-253-1314
Fax: 888-446-5999
Products:
Lacrosse - Shoulder Pads, Arm Pads,
Gloves, Shorts, Equipment Bag, Backpack,
SlingPack, Impact Shirt, Rib Pads, Slash
Guard, Chin Cup; Baseball -Sliding Shorts,
Insoles; Hockey - Hockey Shorts, Insoles;
Football - Football Chin Cup, Turf Insole

SHYDA'S
1635 S LINCOLN AVENUE
LEBANON, PA 17042
717-274-2551
Fax: 717-274-6702
info@shydas.com
www.shydas.com
• Doris Shyda, Owner
info@shydas.com
• Segmund Sh Jr, President
info@shydas.com
Products:
Line of hunting and shooting clothing
(Hunting - Boots, Down, Fleece,
Hats/Caps/Neck Gaiters/HeadNet,
Jackets/Parkas, Lightweight, Long
Underwear, Pants/Bibs/Coverall, Rain Wear,
Supprescent, Sweaters/Shirts, Upland
Clothing, Vest; Wool -
Pants/Jacket/Shirt/Bib/; Shooting Sports -
Duffles/Backpack, Gloves, Waders/Rubber
Boots, Shirts/Sweaters, Jackets, Vests;
Boots - Boots/Shoes/Chest Waders, Boots,
Waders/Rubber Boots,
Casual/Hunting/Hiker/Snow,
Casual/Hiker/Uniform/Snow/Work,
Laces/Footbeds/Boot Care/Repla,
Hunting/Hikers/Rubber/Snow

SIDEOUT SPORT, INC.
6835 VALJEAN AVENUE
VAN NUYS, CA 91406
818-908-9868
Fax: 818-908-9191
• Robert Margolis, Chairman of the
Board/CEO
• Howard Siegel, President
• Russell Riopelle, Chief Financial Officer
• Sandi Stuart, EVP, Brand Development
Products:
Tank, Hoodie, Tees, Long-sleeve Shirts,
Shirts and Pants, Cargos, Cords, Screen
Tees, Tees and Board Shorts, Skateboard,
Volleyball

SIERRA DESIGNS
2011 CHERRY STREET
SUITE 202
LOUISVILLE, CO 80027
510-450-9555
800-635-0461
Fax: 800-504-2745
www.sierradesigns.com
• Mark Mathews, Director of Sales
• Bob Swanson, Founder
Products:
Tents (Tents, Tarps, Accessories); Sleeping
Bags (Sleeping Bags, Bivies, Accessories)

SIGNATURE DESIGNS
798 RAYS ROAD
SUITE 105C
STONE MOUNTAIN, GA 30083
404-297-0028
866-525-0550
Fax: 706-266-3822

Products:
Full Color Printing for Flyers and Postcards, Posters, Brochures, Business Cards, Presentation Folders, Door Hangers, Rack Cards, CD Inserts Tickets, Print Packages; Apparel Printing for T-shirts and Baby Doll Tees; CD Manufacturing, DVD Manufacturing, Web Design, Cover Design

SIGNCO
5831 NORTH 58th STREET
LINCOLN, NE 68522
402-474-6646
866-848-6646
Fax: 402-474-3212
• Jim Graham, General Manager
(402) 474-6646
Products & Services:
LED Products & Services - LED Scoring Table, Ribbon Board); Rotating/Static Products & Services - Basketball Signs, Baseball Signs, Football Signs; Concourse Renovations - Corporate Sponsor Halo, Wall Mounted Static Light Boxes, Retail Store & Fixtures, Interactive Kiosks, Custom Signs & Marquee, Customize Recognition Wall Customize Recognition Wall/Timeline Wall, Trophy Display Cases; Retail Printing Products & Services - Banners, Vinyl Decals

SILVER KNIGHT SALES & MARKETING
576 GEORGESVILLE ROAD
COLUMBUS, OH 43228
614-274-1141
Fax: 614-274-1284
Products:
Athletic apparel

SIMS SPORTS, INC.
22105 23RD DRIVE, SE
BOTHELL, WA 98021
451-951-2700
Fax: 425-951-2740
www.simsnow.com
• John Textor, Chief Executive Officer
Products:
Snowboards

SIPES COMPANY, INC., HOWE K.
249 E MALLORY AVENUE
MEMPHIS, TN 38109-2598
901-948-0378
800-238-2682
Fax: 901-774-4380
• Howe K Sipes Jr, President
Products:
Athletic apparel - baseball and softball uniforms, satin and wool jackets

SISKIYOU GIFTS
3551 AVION DRIVE
MEDFORD, OR 97504
800-866-7475
Fax: 800-650-9926
CustomerService@siskiyougifts.com
www.siskiyougifts.com
Products:
Belt Buckles, Key Chains, Jewelry and Accessories, Money Clips, Zippos, Beverage Ware, Leather Ware, Gifts, Cell Phone Accessories, MP3 Holders, Toothbrushes, and BBQ Sets.

SKANE LTD.
125 HIGH STREET
FARMINGTON, ME 04938-1929

207-778-9508
800-848-0468
Fax: 207-778-5043
• Leonard J Widen, President
• Kurt J Widen, VP
Products:
Skiing-Alpine - Apparel.

SKB SHOTGUNS
4441 S 134TH STREET
OMAHA, NE 68137-1107
800-752-2767
Fax: 402-330-8040
www.skbshotguns.com
• Robert Johansen, President
Products:
SKB Hunting Shotguns, Accessories/Apparel & Parts/Wood

SKEA, LTD.
41184 HIGHWAY 6
SUITE 240
AVON, CO 81620
970-949-4815
800-338-6303
Fax: 970-949-1592
customersvc@skealimited.com
www.skealimited.com
• Diane J Boyer-Irwin, President
• Jocelyn M Boyer, Owner / Fashion Coordinator
• Georges Boyer, Co Owner
Products:
Skiwear, Outerwear, Shimmies, Accessories

SKECHERS USA
228 MANHATTAN BEACH BOULEVARD
MANHATTAN BEACH, CA 90266
310-318-3100
800-746-3411
Fax: 888-566-5746
info@skechers.com
www.skechers.com
• Robert Greenberg, Chairman / Chief Executive Officer
info@skechers.com
• Michael Greenberg, President / Director
info@skechers.com
• David Weinberg, EVP / Chief Operation Officer
info@skechers.com
• Mark Nason, Merchandising EVP
info@skechers.com
Products:
Footwear for Women, Men & Kids

SKI SKOOT INC
2240 275 COURT
SAMMAMISH, WA 98075
425-557-8985
800-600-6945
Fax: 425-557-8907
www.skiskoot.com
• Dawn Carlton,
(425) 941-3765
Products:
Scooters for Summer and Winter Seasons

SKILLBUILDERS, INC.
1312 W GRANGER
BROKEN ARROW, OK 74012
918-258-9987
800-580-4314
Fax: 918-355-7412
sales@skillbuilder.com
www.skillbuilder.com

• Andi Upson, Office Manager
• Roy Hanks, Sales
roysellssports@gmail.com
• Heidi Robison, Sales
heidisellssports@gmail.com
• Selma Hamlin, IT/Internet Manager
Products:
Batting cages, pitching machines, field turf and equipment, protective screens, windscreen, fence crowns, stance mats, pitching mounds, uniforms, putting greens, flags, cups, golf nets and mats, uniforms.
Founded:
1997

SKIS DYNASTAR INC.
1413 CENTER DRIVE
PO BOX 981060
PARK CITY, UT 84098
435-252-3300
Fax: 435-252-3301
www.dynastar.com
Products:
Ski, Bindings, Ski Boots, Snowboards, Apparel and Accessories

SKYLINE NORTHWEST CORPORATION/DBA BARRACUDA SPORTS PRODUCTS
117 FOOTHILLS ROAD
LAKE OSWEGO, OR 97034
503-697-3225
800-547-8664
FAX: 800-238-4658
Fax: 800-238-4658
skyline@skylinenw.com
• John Runckel, Chief Executive Officer
skyline@skylinenw.com
• Rick Runckel, President
skyline@skylinenw.com
Products:
Ski, Snowboard, Swimwear, Swimming goggles andAccessories for Motorsports, Watersports, Wintersports, Swimwear, googles & fins and eye protection gear

SKYWAY
4451 CATERPILLAR ROAD
REDDING, CA 96003
530-243-5151
800-332-3357
Fax: 530-243-5104
generalinfo@skywaywheels.com
• Kenneth Coster, Chief Executive Officer
ken@skywaywheels.com
• Parrey Cremeans, Sales Deparment
sales@skywaywheels.com
• Ken Coster, Sales Deparment
• Rein Stolz, Engineering Department
• Patrick McEachen, Customer Service
Products:
Different kinds of Wheels such as: BEAD-LOK Wheels, Bicycle Wheels, Caster Wheels, Utility Wheels, Wheelchair Wheels, Standard Hubs, & other wheel accessories

SLAZENGER GOLF PRODUCTS CO
16651 N 84TH AVENUE
PEORIA, AZ 85382
623-523-6000
800-528-3133
• Tony Smith, National Sales Manager -Golf Division
• Dan Moore, National Sales Manager -Corporate Division
• Chris D Daltorio, President and CEO

Products:
Golf Apparel, Balls, Clubs-Wood/Iron Sets, Gloves, Hats/Caps/Visors.

SMACK APPAREL
2310 W STATE STREET
TAMPA, FL 33609
813-250-0627
877-762-2511
Fax: 813-251-4539
www.smackapparel.com
Products:
Designed and Printed high quality sports apparel

SMC INNOVATIONS
103 PARK AVENUE WEST
PO BOX 269
WOODVILLE, WI 54028
715-698-3050
866-450-0200
Fax: 715-698-3061
Products:
High-precision injection molds and plastic parts for sporting goods and other applications.

SMITH SPORT OPTICS, INC.
280 NORTHWOOD WAY
BOX 2999
KETCHUM, ID 83340
208-726-4477
888-206-2995
Fax: 208-726-9584
smith@smithoptics.com
www.smithoptics.com
• Blair Clark, SVP Sales & Marketing
• Ned Post, President
• Ned Post, President
smith@smithoptics.com
Products:
Sunglasses, Snow Goggles, Snow Helmets, Motorsport Goggles, Accessories, Apparel.
Brands:
Smith Optics, Smith Helmets, SunCloud Polarized Optics

SMITH WOOD SPECIALTIES
6150 NW HIGHWAY
CHICAGO, IL 60631
708-209-6401
800-621-6450
Fax: 773-774-1753
jim@smith-wood.com
www.smith-wood.com
• James Smith, President
Products:
Laser and Color Plaques, Rectangular Plaques, State Plaques, Acrylic Awards, Bases and Sets, Certicate and Photo Plaques, Tablets and Trophies

SMITHCO
34 W AVENUE
WAYNE, PA 19087
610-688-4009
800-891-9435
Fax: 610-688-6069
smithco_home@msn.com
www.smithco.com
• Ted Smith, Founder
• Don Smith, President
ds@smithco.com
• Bill Kenney, VP Sales and Marketing
• Scott Taylor, Chief Engineer

Products:
Bunker Rakes, Athletic Field Conditioners, Field Markers, Turf Sweeper, Dedicated Spray Vehicles, Utility Vehicles, Specialized Greens Care Machinery & Other Spayers

SMYTH SYSTEMS, INC.
5 WALNUT GROVE DRIVE
SUITE 100
HORSHAM, PA 19044
888-789-9073
800-462-4372
Fax: 905-763-0527
www.smythsystems.com
• Barry Symons, Chief Executive Officer
Services:
Club Management Software for Country Clubs, Athletic Clus, City Clubs, Golf Coarses, Resorts

SOCCER PAL
1624 CROSBY ROAD
SUITE 124
CARROLLTON, TX 75006
469-574-1300
Fax: 469-574-1350
www.soccerpal.com
• Steve Ferguson, President
• Tina Amason, Marketing / Promotions Director
Products:
Soccer training equipment and accessories.

SOCCER SPORT SUPPLY CO., INC.
1745 FIRST AVENUE
NEW YORK, NY 10128
800-223-1010
Fax: 212-427-8769
soccersport@verizon.net
www.doss-soccer.com
• Hermann Doss, President
(212) 427-6050
• Dorothy Doss, President
• Scott Davidson, Manager
(212) 427-6050
Products:
Everything for soccer: Shoes, Uniforms, Balls, Playground Equipment, Practice Nets, Official Size Nets, Goalie Equipment, Goalie Uniforms, Goalie Gloves, Referee Uniforms, Referee Equipment.

SOCCEREDGE INC
35 MARLBOROUGH STREET
SUITE 7
BOSTON, MA 2116
617-267-0333
Fax: 617-267-0210
mail@socceredge.com
Products:
SoccerEdge Bungee Cord Training Tool

SOCCERMALL.NET
13747 MONTFORT DRIVE
SUITE 300
DALLAS, TX 75240
972-503-5501
866-762-2376
Fax: 972-404-9287
info@soccermall.net
www.soccermall.net

SOCCERPAL
1624 W CROSBY ROAD
SUITE 124
CARROLLTON, TX 75006

469-574-1300
800-676-2237
Fax: 469-574-1350
www.soccerpal.com
Products:
Training devices in Soccer, retail products, player's equipment, coach's equipment

SOF SOLE
9221 GLOBE CENTER DRIVE
MORRISVILLE, NC 27560
919-544-7900
800-446-7587
Fax: 919-314-1960
help@4implus.com
www.sofsole.com
• Todd Vore, President
(919) 544-7900
todd@4implus.com
• Kurt Wineman, Vice President Sales
(919) 544-7900
kurt@4implus.com
• Steve Head, Executive Vice President Sales
(919) 544-7900
steve@4implus.com
• John Andrews, Vice President Marketing
(919) 544-7900
john@4implus.com
Products:
Performance Insoles, Comfort Insoles, Technical Socks, Fashion Accessories, Shoe Care, Traction Devices.
Brands:
Sof Sole®, Yaktrax®, Apar™, Airplus®, Sof Comfort®

SOFFE COMPANY, INC.
ONE SOFFE DRIVE
PO BOX 2507
FAYETTEVILLE, NC 28312
888-257-8673
800-444-0337
Fax: 910-486-9030
www.soffe.com
• Ken Spires, President
• James Soffe, Chief Executive Officer
• Tony Cimaglia, Operations VP
• Dick Soffe, Manufacturing EVP
• Ray Edwards, VP of Strategic
• Evan Gettenberg, Director - Sales Inventory Management
• Greg Roscoe, Midwest Regional Sales Manager
groscoe@mjsoffe.com
• Tim Wann, Southern Regional Sales Manager
twann@mjsoffe.com
Products:
T-shirts, jerseys, shorts, fleece wear

SOFTBALL RAMPAGE
2177 WESTBELT DR.
COLUMBUS, OH 43228
614-629-9934
877-868-8945
Fax: 614-527-8565
service@softballrampage.com
www.softballrampage.com
Nature of Sports Service:
Softball Rampage is the official online retail partner of the National Pro Fastpitch.

SOFTRIDE
4201 MERIDIAN STREET
BELLINGHAM, WA 98226

360-647-7420
888-258-7286
Fax: 360-647-1884
info@softride.com
www.softride.com
• Mike Allsop, Chief Executive Officer
info@softride.com
• Glen Morgan, Business Development VP
info@softride.com
Products:
Bikes, Indoor Cycling Bike, Racks, Towing, Accessories

SOL-EFFECT ENTERPRISE COMPANY LTD
11878 CLARK STREET
ARCADIA, CA 91006
626-599-8277
888-626-2999
Fax: 626-599-9897
sol@soleffect.com
Products:
Balls, Skates, Fitness, Sports Toys, Accessories

SOLAR TAN THRU SUITS
5455 W WATERS AVENUE
SUITE 215
TAMPA, FL 33634-1208
813-886-6800
888-826-8478
Fax: 813-889-9900
sales@solartanthru.com
www.solartanthru.com
• Dale Sanders, President
• Helen Katrnak, VP
Products:
Manufacturers, Distributors, Importers and Exporters of Water Sports Accessories, and Fashion Apparel

SOLE CHOICE, INC.
830 MURRAY STREET
PORTSMOUTH, OH 45662
740-354-2813
800-848-8696
Fax: 740-353-4669
sales@solechoiceinc.com
www.solechoiceinc.com
• Steven Keating, President & Chief Executive Officer
• Bryan Davis, VP Sales
• Beth Minton, Marketing Director
• Michael Keating, Regional Sales Manager
Products:
Blister Pak, Sports Laces, Boot, Work & Military Laces, Hiking & Hunting Laces, Self Shining Liquids, Athletic Creams, Mink Oil and Saddle Soap, Suede & Nubuck Cleaner and Protector, Rain & Stain Repellent, Water Repellent, Silicone Water Repellent, Athletic Shoe Shampoo, Athletic Gel Cleaner, Shoe Deodorizers, Shoe Goo, Boot & Shoe Cleaning Tool
Brands:
MPRO
Year Founded:
1902

SOLE CUSTOM FOOTBEDS
608 CRESCENT CIRCLE
GREAT FALLS, MT 59404
403-204-0907
866-949-7653
Fax: 888-691-0714
sales@yoursole.com
www.yoursole.com

• Mike Baker, President
• Greg Davidson, Web Developer
• Rob Nathan, Product Director
Products:
Heat moldable custom footbeds, performance socks
Nature of Service:
Manufacturer and Distributor of premium custom insoles.
Brands:
SOLE Custom Footbeds, SOLE Performance Socks

SONY COMPUTER ENTERTAINMENT AMERICA, INC.
989 E HILLSDALE BOULEVARD
2ND FLOOR
FOSTER CITY, CA 94404
650-655-8000
800-345-7669
Fax: 650-655-8001
www.us.playstation.com
• Jack Tretton, CEO
Products:
Electronic sports devices.

SONY SPORTS
64-A HALI ROAD
SIE
SIALKOT-4, PAKISTAN 51340
-92-355-6642
Fax: -92-355-4323
info@sony-sports.com
www.sony-sports.com
• M Younus Sony, Chief Executive Officer
info@sony-sports.com
• M Yo Sony, Partner
info@sony-sports.com
• Faisal Yo Sony, Partner
info@sony-sports.com
• M. Younus Sony, Chief Executive
• Yousaf Sony, Director
Products:
Fitness Accessories, Boxing Gloves, Weightlifting Belts, Boxing Accessories, Punching/Boxing Mitts, Sadal/Tool Bags, Motocross Gloves, Sailing Gloves, Cycling Gloves, Weightlifting Gloves, Martial Art Uniforms and track suits, Protection Equipment, Karate Protection Gears

SOUND & VIDEO CREATIONS, INC
2408 FELTS AVE
NASHVILLE, TN 37211
615-460-7330
Fax: 615-460-7331
support@clickeffects.com
www.clickeffects.com
• Ed Filmia, Senior Director
Products:
Click Effects Pro-AV, Click Effects Audio, Click Effects Replay

SOUTHERN BLEACHER COMPANY, INC.
801 FIFTH STREET
PO BOX ONE
GRAHAM, TX 76450
940-549-0733
800-433-0912
Fax: 940-549-1365
www.southernbleacher.com
• Jo Ann Pettus, President
(800) 433-0912
jpettus@southernbleacher.com
• Bill Duckworth, Operations Manager
• Andy Smith, Project Coordinator
• Randy Wray, Installation Manager

• Rusty Hughes, Project Coordinator
• Justin Campbell, Project Coordinator
• Garrett Pettus, VP of Southern Bleacher
(800) 433-0912
gpettus@southernbleacher.com
• Wyatt Pettus, Director Special Events
(800) 433-0912
wpettus@southernbleacher.com
Products:
Stadiums, Grandstands, Decking Systems, Seating Options, Coatings, Bleachers, Press Boxes, High School Facilities
Clients:
School districts and colleges throughout the U.S.
Year Founded:
1946

SOUTHERN UMBRELLA COMPANY, INC./DBA SOUTHERN PLUS
1611 ZION CME CHURCH ROAD
HARTWELL, GA 30643
706-376-5151
800-241-7107
Fax: 706-376-1244
www.southernplus.com
• Grethe Adams, President
• Brannon Craig, National Sales Manager
Products:
Umbrellas, Chairs, Coolers, Blankets, Picnic, Bags, Totes, Fitness, Collections

SOUTHLAND ATHLETIC MANUFACTURING COMPANY
714 E GROVE STREET
PO BOX 280
TERRELL, TX 75160
972-563-3321
800-527-7637
Fax: 972-563-0943
• William C Sturgeon, President
• Armando DeLeon, Plant manager
Products:
Baseball uniforms, Softball uniforms, Basketball uniforms, Track uniforms, Football uniforms

SOYAD BROTHERS TEXTILE CORPORATION
24011 HOOVER ROAD
WARREN, MI 48089
586-755-5700
800-922-9923
Fax: 586-755-3790
www.soyadsocks.com
• Tom Soyad, President
Products:
Sport Socks

SPECIALIZED BICYCLE COMPONENTS, INC.
15130 CONCORD CIRCLE
MORGAN HILL, CA 95037
408-779-6229
877-808-8154
Fax: 408-779-1631
store_customerservice@specialized.com
www.specialized.com
• Mike Sinyard, President / Founder
customerservice@specialized.com
• Michael Haynes, Chief Financial Officer
customerservice@specialized.com
• Bob Margevicius, EVP
customerservice@specialized.com
Products:
Bikes, Equipment

SPECIALTY NETS
535 BRAGATO ROAD
SUITE B
SAN CARLOS, CA 94070
650-591-0505
800-645-6790
Fax: 800-645-6791
info@specialtynets.com
• Victor K. Saiz, General Manager
Nature of Service:
Private labeling - sports and industrial
netting, finished and/or unfinished, knit to
domestic manufactures and importers
specifications - product development
department available.
Year Founded:
1975
Products:
Baseball Nets, Field Hockey Nets, Golf
Driving Nets/Mats, Ice Hockey Nets,
Lacrosse Nets, Racquet Sports Tennis Nets,
Soccer Nets, Softball Nets, Volleyball Nets,
Wind Screens, Bird Protection Nets.
Products also include baseball and
combination baseball/golf batting tunnel
nets.

SPECTRUM CORPORATION
10048 EASTHAVEN BOULEVARD
HOUSTON, TX 77075
713-944-6200
800-392-5050
Fax: 713-944-1290
info@spectrumscoreboards.com
www.spectrumscoreboards.com
• Jim B. Bishop, President
(713) 944-6200
• Gary Liddell, Sales/Marketing VP/Vice
President/Treasurer
(713) 944-62
info@specorp.com
• Tyson Swan, Office Manager
(713) 944-6200
info@specorp.com
• Tim Kyle, Athletic Director
Products:
Scoreboards, Display Solutions, Software
Solutions, Outdoor Message Centers
Nature of Service:
Manufacturer, Sales and Service

SPEED SKATELUBE
5858 ENGINEER DRIVE
HUNTINGTON BEACH, CA 92649
714-898-4377
Fax: 714-891-7467
www.tiodize.com
• Tom Adams, President
(714) 902-0501
tom.adams@tiodize.com
• Wades Friedrichs, Marketing
(714) 902-0507
wade.friedrichs@tiodize.com
• Thomas R. Adams, President
(714) 898-4377
• Wade Friedrichs, Marketing
(714) 898-4377
• Tom Moore, Purchasing
(714) 898-4377
• Gary Wittman, Technical Director
(714) 902-0506
• Rudy Villegas, Material Processing Control
Shipping & Reciev
(714) 902-0510
• Patty Enna, Controller
(714) 898-4377

Products:
Composite Fasteners, Self-Lubricating
Composites, Anodizing, Emissivity, Dry Film
Lubricants, Corrosion Coatings, Sport and
Consumer Products, Racing Products

SPEEDLINE ATHLETIC WEAR, INC.
1804 N HABANA AVENUE
TAMPA, FL 33607
813-876-1375
Fax: 813-873-8714
service@speedlineathletic.com
www.speedlineathletic.com
• Steven Malzone, President
Products:
Baseball Uniforms; Basketball Uniforms;
Football Uniforms; General Sports Products
Athletic Jackets/Parkas, Referee Uniforms,
Warm-Up Suits; Soccer Uniforms; Softball
Uniforms; Track & Field/Running
Apparel-Track & Field; Volleyball Uniforms

SPEEDPLAY, INC.
10151 PACIFIC MESA BOULEVARD
SUITE 107
SAN DIEGO, CA 92121
858-453-4707
800-468-6694
Fax: 858-453-5871
www.speedplay.com
• Richard Bryne, Chief Executive Officer
• Sharon Worman, President
Products:
High-performance pedal systems for
on-road and off-road cyclists

SPIRIT MANUFACTURING
3000 NESTLE ROAD
JONESBORO, AR 72401
870-935-1107
800-258-4555
Fax: 800-935-7611
www.spiritfitness.com
• Roger Hurt, President
Products:
Treadmills, Ellipticals, & Bikes

SPORT CARD CREATIONS INC.
131 S MAIN STREET
NATICK, MA 1760
508-653-1731
Fax: 508-655-7758
ddds11@aol.com
www.sportcardcreations.com
• Denise LePage, President / Chief
Executive Officer
(508) 653-1731
ddds11@aol.com
Products:
Sells sport card displays for sport cards,
collectibles etc.

SPORT COLLECTORS GUILD INC
7310 W ROOSEVELT STREET
SUITE 32
PHOENIX, AZ 85043-2219
623-478-0007
800-950-0320
Fax: 602-233-9490
www.replicastadiums.com
Products:
Unique handicrafted replicas, memorabilia,
and military items

SPORT COURT, INC.
939 S 700 W
SALT LAKE CITY, UT 84104
800-421-8112
Fax: 801-401-3504
www.sportcourt.com
• Ronald N Cerny, President / Chief
Executive Officer
• Ronald Yokubison, VP Finance / Chief
Financial Officer
• Troy Mohr, VP Manufacturing
• Ron Cerny, President
• Andrew Gettig, VP International
• Ryan Burke, International Business
Manager
Products:
Manufacturer of flooring systems, from
outdoor game courts to indoor gymnasiums,
roller hockey rinks to synthetic putting
greens (Tennis-Courts; Racquet Sports;
Flooring; Lighting Systems; Nets)

SPORT FACE
4275 THUNDERBIRD LANE
FAIRFIELD, OH 45014
513-671-2800
877-611-2800
Fax: 513-671-2830
info@sportface.com
www.sportface.com
Products:
Face and body paint in convenient
easy-to-use tubes

SPORT HALEY INC.
4600 E 48TH AVENUE
DENVER, CO 80216
303-320-8800
800-627-9211
800-701-6478
Fax: 303-320-8820
customerservice@sporthaley.com
www.sporthaley.com
• Patrick Hurley, SVP / Chief Financial
Officer
info@SportHaley.com
• Robert Haley, President / Director
• Cathy Blair, President and Creative
Director
• Lisa Langas, National Sales Manager
(303) 320-8815
• Erin Scrimshaw, National Key Accounts
Manager
(303) 946-1254
Products:
Fashion golf apparel and outerwear

SPORT HELMETS, INC.
4635 CROSSROAD PARK DRIVE
LIVERPOOL, NY 13088
315-453-3073
800-537-1702
Fax: 315-453-3762
helmets@cascadehelmets.com
• Stephen Moore, President
• Bill Brine, Founder
Products:
Large manufacturer of lacrosse helmets and
eyemasks, including a water rescue helmet

SPORT OBERMEYER, LTD.
115 AABC
ASPEN, CO 81611
970-925-5060
800-525-4203
Fax: 970-925-9203

custserv@obermeyer.com
www.obermeyer.com
• Klaus Obermeyer, President
(970) 925-5060
lindage@obermeyer.com
• Klaus Obermeyer, Founder and President
(970) 920-6663
lindage@obermeyer.com
• Robert Yturri, Senior VP, Brand Management
Products:
Mens collection, ladies collection, juniors collection and preschool collection of performance clothing.

SPORT PINS INTERNATIONAL, INC.
888 BERRY COURT
UPLAND, CA 91786-8439
909-985-4549
800-949-7467
Fax: 909-982-0912
www.sportpins.com
• Connie Bivens, President
(800) 949-7467
• Jon Bivens, CEO/CFO
(800) 949-7467
jonbivens@sportpins.com
• Jeff Bivens, Director Sales
(800) 949-7467
jeffbivens@sportpins.com
• Maria Bivens, Marketing Manager
• Mike Bivens, Vice President Operations
(800) 949-7467
mbivens@sportpins.com
Nature of Service:
Provider of recognition products to the sports and corporate markets, with special emphasis on the youth and professional soccer markets.
Year Founded:
1980
Products:
Manufacturer of top quality lapel pins, medallions, commemorative coins, embroidered patches, key chains, jewelry and other recognition products, laser engraved glass, wood, and acrylic awards.

SPORTCAP, INC.
3314 INDUSTRY DRIVE
SIGNAL HILL, CA 90755
562-494-8950
877-337-2282
Fax: 562-494-8920
authsportcap@gmail.com
www.authenticsportcap.com
Products:
Baseball Caps/Visors/Hats; General Sports Products Caps/Hats/Visors; Softball Caps

SPORTDECALS
PO BOX 860
SPRING GROVE, IL 60081-0860
815-675-2471
800-435-6110
Fax: 800-557-3322
sports@sportdecals.com
www.sportdecals.com
• Donald Metivier, Founder
Products:
Baseball Helmet Decals; Football Helmet Decals; Athletic Jackets; Cheerleading Supplies; Decals; Die Cut; Letters; Numerals and Illustrations/Calendars; Screen Printing; Sweatclothes; T-shirts; Ice Hockey Helmet Decals; Lacrosse Helmet Decals and Banners

SPORTGRASS, INC.
6718 WHITTIER AVENUE
SUITE 220
MCLEAN, VA 22101
703-288-1800
Fax: 703-288-1873
• William Ward, Chairman
• Brian Wood, General Manager
Services:
Provides construction and installation of SportGrass for athletic field

SPORTIF U.S.A.
1415 GREG STREET
SUITE 101
SPARKS, NV 89431
775-359-6400
800-921-1655
Fax: 775-353-3400
customerservice@sportif.com
www.sportif.com
Products:
Manufacturer of tennis shorts, fishing, nautical and outdoor apparel

SPORTIME
4671 E AIRPORT DRIVE
ONTARIO, CA 91761-7869
909-390-0334
800-472-7790
Fax: 800-497-1444
www.sptdistctr.com
• Troy Niswander, President
• Tanya Purcell, Secretary / Treasurer
• Charlie McWilliams, Wholesale Manager
Products:
Distributor: Sporting goods

SPORTLINE INC
4 EXECUTIVE PLAZA
YONKERS, NY 10701
914-964-5200
800-338-6337
Fax: 914-964-1283
www.sportline.com
• Larry Livingston, Founder
Products:
Manufacturer and distributor of sports timing and fitness products such as stopwatches, pedometers and sport watches

SPORTMASTER
2520 S CAMPBELL STREET
PO BOX 2277
SANDUSKY, OH 44870
419-626-4375
800-395-7325
Fax: 419-626-5477
info@sportmaster.net
www.sportmaster.net
• Jeff Earheart,
info@sportmaster.net
Products:
Sport Surfacing, Traffic Paints, Crack Fillers, Tools/Accessories

SPORTMASTER INC.
521 MADISON AVENUE
COVINGTON, KY 41011
606-431-3555
Fax: 606-431-3556
• Mark Wheatley, President
Products:
Distributor: Logowear

SPORTS ACCESSORIES AMERICA INC.
4935 IRIS STREET
WHEAT RIDGE, CO 80033
303-431-0875
800-321-7245
Fax: 303-431-9873
• Phil Seifert, Chief Executive Officer
Products:
Trophies, Awards Crests, Emblems, Jewelry, Patches

SPORTS AUTHORITY, INC.
1050 W HAMPDEN AVENUE
ENGLEWOOD, CO 80110
303-200-5050
800-589-0483
Fax: 303-863-2240
www.sportsauthority.com
• Doug Morton, Chairman and Chief Executive Officer
• Paul Gaudet, Executive Vice President/Store Operations
• Darrell Webb, Chairman of the Board/Chief Executive Officer
• Thomas Hendrickson, Executive Vice President, Chief Financial Off
• Greg Waters, Executive Vice President/Merchandising
Products:
Sporting goods and information such as apparel, footwear, team sports, golf/racquet, outdoor, action sports, fan shop, games, accessories and women's shop

SPORTS BELLE INC.
6723 PLEASANT RIDGE ROAD
KNOXVILLE, TN 37921
865-938-2063
800-888-2063
Fax: 865-947-4465
www.sportsbelle.com
• Royd Walker, Sales / Marketing Director
Products:
Baseball Jerseys, Uniforms; Basketball Uniforms; Football Uniforms; General Sports Products Apparel

SPORTS COVERAGE
5535 MILITARY PARKWAY
DALLAS, TX 75227
214-381-3096
800-460-8234
Fax: 214-381-4585
www.sportscoverageinc.com
Products:
Shower Curtain, Comforter, Sham, Valance, Drape, Bedskirt, Jersey Sheet Set, Pillow Case, Tail Gate Kit (Apron & Mitt), Apron, Sham Pillow, Box Toss Pillow, Box Floor Pillow, Bath Set

SPORTS HEALTH
865 MUIRFIELD DRIVE
HANOVER PARK, IL 60133
866-323-5465
800-323-1305
Fax: 866-235-1305
info@schoolhealth.com
• John Miller, National Sales Manager
(800) 367-8319
• Gina Streepy, Product Director
(800) 323-1305
gstreepy@schoolhealth.com
• Susan Rogers, President
(800) 323-1305
• Tory L., MA ATC, Associate Athletic Director

• Phil V. MSEd, ATC/L, Assistant Athletic
Director
• Scott O., Assistant Athletic Trainer
• Pat B., Office Assistant
Products:
Asthma and Allergy Products, Diabetic
Products and Syringes, Asthma Treatment
and Response Products, CPR and
Automated External Defibrillators, Fire
Safety, Mobile Communications, Training
Manikins and Resuscitation Devices, First
Aid and Bandages, Furniture and
Equipment, Health Education Resources,
Hot/Cold and Hydro Therapy, Hydration and
Nutrition Products, Infection and Infestation
Control, Paper and Plastic Products,
Pharmacy, Rehab Equipment and Supplies,
Sports Medicine Supplies, Vision and
Hearing products, Vital Statistics and Health
Assessment

SPORTS IMMORTALS MUSEUM
6830 N FEDERAL HIGHWAY
BOCA RATON, FL 33487
561-997-2575
Fax: 561-997-6949
www.sportsimmortals.com
• Jim Platt, Vice President
(561) 997-2575
• Jim Platt, Vice President
(561) 997-2575
Year Founded:
1992.
Description:
Sports Immortals Museum contains over
one million mementos from the world's
greatest athletes.
Sports Products Manufactured or Sold:
Retail store offers a selection of over 20,000
unique sports collectible items for sale.

SPORTS IMPORTS
PO BOX 21040
COLUMBUS, OH 43221
614-771-0246
800-556-3198
Fax: 614-771-0750
info@sportsimports.com
www.sportsimports.com
• Brad Underwood, President
info@sportsimports.com
• Tom Johnson, Athletic Director
Products:
Volleyball, badminton and tennis equipment

SPORTS INC
333 2ND AVENUE N
LEWISTOWN, MT 59457
406-538-3496
Fax: 800-227-7207
Info@hq.sportsinc.com
www.sportsinc.com
Description:
Sporting goods buying group.

SPORTS MEDIA, INC.
520 8TH STREET
QUAD CITIES, IL 61282
309-755-6557
Fax: 801-981-2566
CustomerService@SportsMedia.net
www.sportsmedia.net
• Dan Kosth, Chief Executive Officer
(312) 436-0500
dan@sportsmedia.net
• Scott Posnanski, CIO & CFO

(262) 456-5629
scott@sportsmedia.net
Products:
Sports media stadium concession products
such as CD Cup Lids, 3D Lenticular Cups,
Photo Cups, Plastic Cups, Cup Holders and
Concession Trays
Description:
Sports Marketing Agency

SPORTS POSTER WAREHOUSE
55 QUEEN'S PLATE DRIVE
UNIT 9
TORONTO, ONTARIO, CANADA M9W 6P2
416-696-8353
888-650-3455
Fax: 416-352-5418
info@sportsposterwarehouse.com
www.sportsposterwarehouse.com
• Niel Flagg, President
Products:
sports posters

SPORTS SENSORS INC
11351 EMBASSY DRIVE
PO BOX 46198
CINCINNATI, OH 45420
513-825-5745
888-542-9246
Fax: 513-825-8532
adilz@cinci.rr.com
www.sportssensors.com
• Al Dilz, President
(888) 542-9246
adilz@cinci.rr.com
Year Founded:
1998.
Services:
Affordable, portable supplier radar training
aids and doppler radars for sports
applications.
Products:
Glove radar, swing speed radar, paintball
radarchron, arrowspeed radarchron, swing
speed radar with tempo timer, kickspeed
radar

SPORTS SUPPLY GROUP
1901 DIPLOMAT DRIVE
DALLAS, TX 75234
972-484-9484
800-527-7510
Fax: 972-406-3467
feedgym@sportssupplygroup.com
www.sportssupplygroup.com
• Geoffrey P. Jurick, Chairman / Chief
Financial Officer
feedgym@sportssupplygroup.com
• John P. Walker, President / Director
jwalker@sportssupplygroup.com
• Robert Mitchell, Chief Financial Officer
(972) 406-3484
bmitchell@sportssupplygroup.com
• Michael P. Glassman, Sales / Marketing
VP
mglassman@sportssupplygroup.com
Products:
Recreational equipments, athletic and sports
equipment products

SPORTS TUTOR INC
3300 WINONA AVENUE
BURBANK, CA 91504
818-972-2772
800-448-8867
Fax: 818-972-9651

intl-sales@sportstutor.com
www.sportstutorinc.com
• Thomas Kekalos, Sales Manager
(818) 972-2772
Products:
Sports machines for baseball, volleyball,
soccer and tennis
Year Founded:
1988

SPORTS WEST SALES, INC.
999 OAKCREST AVENUE
BREA, CA 92821
714-671-0895
800-996-2811
Fax: 714-255-0571
normsws@aol.com
• Norm Lamming, President
Products:
Baseball Equipment, Jackets, Socks,
Uniforms, Basketball Equipment, Football
Equipment, Socks, Uniforms, Athletic
Jackets, Nets, Sweatclothes, T-shirts,
Bags-Equipment, Racquet Sports Apparel,
Soccer Bags-Equipment, Balls, Uniforms,
Softball Bags-Equipment

SPORTS-FASHION
5381 RIVERWALK TRAIL
COMMERCE TOWNSHIP, MI 48382
248-310-9462
Fax: 248-366-9779
www.sports-fashion.com
Products:
Fitness and sport wear

SPORTSPLAY EQUIPMENT, INC.
8505 DELMAR BLVD
SUITE G
SAINT LOUIS, MO 63124
314-389-4140
800-727-8180
Fax: 314-389-9034
smeyer@sportsplayinc.com
www.sportsplayinc.com
• Scott Meyer, Director of Marketing
smeyer@sportsplayinc.com
Products:
Basketball backboards and sports
equipment, playground equipment, merry go
rounds, swings, see saws, ADA play
products, spring riders, independent slides,
fitness equipment, and site amenities.
Description:
Known for fun equipment of exceptional
safety and durability since 1996. Offers a full
sports line as well as modern playground
equipment.

SPORTSPRINT
6197 BERMUDA ROAD
SAINT LOUIS, MO 63135
314-521-9000
800-325-4858
Fax: 314-521-0395
www.sportsprint.com
• Ralph Rockamann, Owner / President
ralph@sportsprint.com
• Lance Walker, Sales Manager
• Connie Bailey, Sales Contact
• Tim Bennett, Production Manager

SPRI PRODUCTS INC
1769 NORTHWIND BOULEVARD
LIBERTYVILLE, IL 60048

847-968-7917
800-222-7774
Fax: 847-680-7539
customerservice@spri.com
• Adam Zwyer, Marketing Manager
Products:
SPRI Products, Inc. is the leading manufacturer and distributor of rubberized resistance exercise products for the health and fitness industry and develops a wide range of innovative, affordable fitness tools and supportive educational materials for everyone from the casual exerciser to the professional athlete. Equipment and accessory offerings include those for fitness training for strength, balance, sports conditioning, and many more applications.

SPRINGCO
1450 W 228TH STREET
8
TORRANCE, CA 90501
800-676-7463
888-415-5212
Fax: 805-781-6092
Custserv@vsathletics.com
www.vsathletics.com
• Brian Springer, Owner
brian@vsathletics.com
• Billy Smith, President
rich@vsathletics.com
• Peanut Harms, VP of Marketing/Sales
• Jack Smith, Marketing
• David Ulibarri, Sales, Screening
• Kristin Tumulak, Accounting
Products:
Footwear/Spikes, Apparel/Uniforms, Youth Items, Bags, Repl. Spikes, Misc., Track Equipment, Field Event Equipment, Pole Vault/High Jump, Throwing Equipment, Timing Equipment, Cross Country Equipment, Training Equipment, Books, Videos & Camps

---

SPRINT AQUATICS
ROTHHAMMER INTERNATIONAL INC, DBA SPRINT AQUATICS
PO BOX 3840
SAN LUIS OBISPO, CA 93403
805-541-5330
800-235-2156
Fax: 805-541-5339
info@sprintaquatics.com
www.sprintaquatics.com
• Dianne Rothhammer, President
(805) 541-5330
info@sprintaquatics.com
• Chuck Sheetz, VP
info@sprintaquatics.com
Products:
Aquatic and therapy supplies such as Bags, Balance Boards, Balls, Bells and Bars, Belts, Caps, Children's Therapy, Clothing, Collars and Pillows, Competitive Training, Ear and Nose Protection, Fins, Fitness and Exercise Education, Floatation Devices, Gloves, Goggles, Kickboards, Masks and Snorkels, Personal Care, Pool Equipment, Safety, Shoes, Teaching, Therapy and Exercise Equipment, Therapy Education, Toys and Games, Water Polo, Weights, Whistles and Lanyards

---

SPRY SPORTS USA
842 E 9TH STREET
SUITE 1K
BROOKLYN, NY 11230

718-434-3505
Fax: 718-434-0297
spryusa@sprysports.net
www.sprysports.net
Products:
Sporting products such as Footballs, Volleyballs, Soccer balls, Handballs, Sports wears, Goalkeeper shirts & gloves, knee pad, track suit, soccer uniform, fleece shirts, goal keeper set, shorts and pent, t-shirts, rain coat

---

SPYDER ACTIVE SPORTS
4725 WALNUT STREET
BOULDER, CO 80301
303-544-4000
800-333-0302
Fax: 303-449-1404
spyder-info@spyder.com
www.spyder.com
• David L Jacobs, Founder
spyder-info@spyder.com
• John Walbrecht, VP Sales / Marketing
spyder-info@spyder.com
• Doug Saunders, VP Operations
spyder-info@spyder.com
• Tom McGann, President and Chief Executive Officer
• JJ Collier, VP of Design and Merchandising
• Russ Rowan, Vice President of Sales and Marketing
• Cees De Witte, President, Spyder Europe AG
• Doug Hood, Chief Financial Officer
Products:
Alpine-Skiing, Freeskiing and Outdoor Apparels and Outerwear

SRI SPORTS, INC.
701 LEANDER DRIVE
LEANDER, TX 78641
706-517-5891
800-723-8873
Fax: 512-259-2952
• Thomas DeNova, President
info@srisport.com
• Kevin Swank, Chief Operating Officer / Track / Tennis
• Charles Fleishman, Chief Marketing Officer
• Robert Allison, EVP Special Facilities
Products:
Field, Track, Indoor and Tennis Systems

ST. LOUIS BRAID COMPANY
2035 LUCAS AVENUE
SAINT LOUIS, MO 63103
314-231-0540
800-231-0540
Fax: 314-231-0551
sales@stlouisbraid.com
www.stlouisbraid.com
• Thomas Goltermann, President
sales@stlouisbraid.com
• Chris Goltermann, VP
sales@stlouisbraid.com
Products:
Quality Braided Shoelace, Drawcord, Industrial Braid, Cordage

---

ST. PIERRE MANUFACTURING CORPORATION
317 E MOUNTAIN STREET
WORCESTER, MA 01606
508-853-8010
800-926-2342

Fax: 508-853-3860
info@stpierreusa.com
www.stpierreusa.com
• Edward St. Pierre, Chief Financial Officer
(508) 853-8010
edstpierre@stpierreusa.com
• Peter St. Pierre, Sales
(508) 853-8010
pstpierre@stpierreusa.com
Products:
Made in the USA, Official Forged Pitching Horseshoes
Year Founded:
1920
Brands:
Royal; American; American Presidential; and Wonde

STACKHOUSE ATHLETIC EQUIPMENT, INC.
1450 MCDONALD STREET NE
SALEM, OR 97301
503-363-1840
800-285-3604
Fax: 503-363-0511
sales@stackhouseathletic.com
www.stackhouseathletic.com
• Greg Henshaw, President
greg@stackhouseathletic.com
• Larry D'Amato, Senior Sales/Development Manager
Products:
Athletic Equipments, Discus, Shotputs, Hammers, Starting Blocks, Javelins, High Jump, Pole Vault Misc., Pole Vault Poles, Take Off Boards, Toe Boards Rings, Cages, Measurements, Start Pistols, Surfacing, Batons, Stop Watches, Hurdles
Nature of Service:
Manufacturer and Wholesaler of Team Sports Athletic Goods.
Brands:
Newton, Nordic and Ate

STACKS OF PLAQUES
5019 WEST NASSAU STREET
TAMPA, FL 33607
813-282-7073
Fax: 813-282-7079
mkovel@encoreselect.com
www.stacksofplaques.net
• Lou Scalia, President/Owner

STADIUM ROLL
36250 EASTERDAY WAY
FREMONT, CA 94536-1670
510-792-7655
• Dean Valentine, Owner
Products:
Manufactures security-friendly, alternative carryall for fans to take personal items into stadiums and arenas

---

STAGERIGHT CORP.
495 PIONEER PARKWAY
CLARE, MI 48617
989-386-7393
800-438-4499
Fax: 989-386-3500
info@stageright.com
www.stageright.com
• Sean M Langer, Director Facility Services
info@stageright.com
• O D Rogers, President
info@stageright.com
Products:
Portable staging; portable seating risers;

1195

sound (acoustical) shells and music shells; choral risers and band risers; ADA ramps and infills; fold-and-roll stages; meeting room risers; crowd control barricades; pit fillers and stage extensions; and platforms for outdoor performances

STAHLS
20600 STEPHENS STREET
ST CLAIR SHORES, MI 48080
586-772-5551
800-478-2457
Fax: 586-772-6237
info@stahlsid.com
www.stahlsid.com
• Ted Stahl, Chief Executive Officer
info@stahlsid.com
Year Founded:
1932.
Nature of Service:
Specializes in the development, manufacturing, and distribution of heat printing technologies and equipment. Your source for athletic and personal customization including: pre cut letters and numbers, pre-spaced player names and numbers, CAD-COLOR® Solutions™ digital print media, Hotronix® heat presses, CAD-CUT® heat applied materials by the yard, transfer papers, custom cut applique, computerized cutting systems, and more.

STAIRMASTER HEALTH AND FITNESS PRODUCTS
12421 WILLOWS ROAD NE
SUITE 100
KIRKLAND, WA 98034-8736
425-823-1825
800-635-2936
Fax: 425-821-3794
commericialsales@stairmaster.com
www.stairmaster.com
• Brian Cook, Chief Executive Officer
commericialsales@stairmaster.com
• Tom Bryant, President
Products:
Aerobic Benches, Cardio Equipment, Climbers, Stairclimbers, Step Masters, Steppers

STALKER RADAR
2609 TECHNOLOGY DRIVE
PLANO, TX 75074-7467
972-398-3780
800-782-5537
Fax: 972-398-3781
sales@stalkerradar.com
www.stalkerradar.com
• Alan Mead, Chairman / Chief Executive Officer, Appl
sales@stalkerradar.com
• Stan Partee, President
sales@stalkerradar.com
• George Snarr, Field Sales Representative
Products:
Advanced radar and laser speed measurement equipment for many different customers and applications, including: The Law Enforcement Community, Sports and Testing Applications, O.E.M. Applications
Brands:
Stalker Sports Radar

STALL & DEAN MFG. COMPANY, INC.
120 COMMERCE ROAD
CARLSTADT, NJ 7072

201-729-0333
Fax: 201-729-1222
• CH Dean, Founder
• WT Stall, Founder
Products:
Baseball Uniforms; Hockey Uniforms; Soccer Uniforms; Rugby Jerseys

STAMINA PRODUCTS INC
2040 N ALLIANCE AVENUE
SPRINGFIELD, MO 65803
417-889-7011
800-375-7520
Fax: 417-889-8064
customerservice@staminaproducts.com
www.staminaproducts.com
• Brent Swanson, Vice President of Sales
(417) 889-7011
brents@staminaproducts.com
• Bob McBride, Vice President
(417) 889-7011
bobm@staminaproducts.com
Products:
Fitness Equipments, Apparel and Accessories
Brands:
Stamina, Aero Pilates, Gyrotonic, Avari

STANDARD MERCHANDISING COMPANY
1125 WRIGHT AVENUE
CAMDEN, NJ 08103-1615
856-964-9700
800-526-2363
Fax: 856-964-9135
webmaster@stanmerch.com
www.standardmerchandisingco.com
• Jeff Tarnoff, Owner
thuanbui@gis.net
• Lee Tarnoff, Owner
thuanbui@gis.net
Products:
Socks for Baseball, Soccer, and other sports, Sports accessories

STANLY HEADWEAR
119 W MARION STREET
SHELBY, NC 28150
800-438-1526
Fax: 800-643-8531
• Phillip Johnson, President
• Gay Martin, Sales Coordinator
Products:
Knit Caps, Cloth Caps, Safety Headwear, Straw Hat, Towels, Visors, Hunting and Camo

STARTRAC BY UNISEN, INC.
14410 MYFORD ROAD
IRVINE, CA 92606
714-669-1660
800-228-6635
Fax: 714-508-3303
sales@startrac.com
www.startrac.com
• Keith White, Director
sales@startrac.com
• Steve Nero, President
Products:
Cardio Equipment, Computerized Ellipticals, Computerized Equipment, Computerized Treadmills, Running Simulators, Stairclimbers, Treadmills

STEAMBOAT SKI & BIKE KARE INC.
442 LINCOLN AVENUE
STEAMBOAT SPRINGS, CO 80477

970-879-9144
800-525-5374
Fax: 970-879-9111
info@steamboatskiandbike.com
www.steamboatskiandbike.com
• Harry Martin, Partner
info@steamboatskiandbike.com
• Mike Parra, Partner
info@steamboatskiandbike.com
Products:
Ski and bike equipments, clothing and accessories

STEINER SPORTS MEMORBILIA
145 HUGUENOT STREET
NEW ROCHELLE, NY 10801
914-307-1000
800-759-7267
Fax: 914-632-1102
generalinfo@steinersports.com
www.steinersports.com
• Brandon Steiner, CEO
info@steinersports.com
• Jared Weiss, EVP
info@steinersports.com
• David Fiderer, VP Special Markets
(800) 759-7267
• Scott Rue, VP Operations
info@steinersports.com
Products:
Memorabilia signed by legendary athletes, and current sports figures

STERLING TROPHIES, INC.
373 MAIN ST
BOX 345
CATSKILL, NY 12414
518-943-3707
Fax: 763-576-9156
sterentinc2@aol.com
• John De Giorno, President
sterentinc2@aol.com
Products:
Award Ribbons, Bronze Plaques, Clocks, Desk Sets, Engraved Wall Signs, Flags and Banners, Lead Crystal Awards, Medals and Medallions, NamePlates/Badges, Ribbon Magnets, Sports Magnets, Trophies, Wood Plaques

STICK COMPANY/RPI OF ATLANTA
120 INTERSTATE N PARKWAY E
SUITE 440
ATLANTA, GA 30339-2158
770-850-0750
888-882-0750
Fax: 775-258-2090
www.thestick.com
• Patrick Materna, Vice President Sales/International Markting
Nature of Service:
Manufacturer of The Stick - a self massage tool often seen on TV used by NFL, NBA, MLB, and NHL players.
Year Founded:
1991
Products:
Stick, Stick Systems, Footwheel, TriggerWheel, Little Stick, Posture Curve, Wellness Video, Instructional DVD
Brands:
The Stick, Biostick, Intracell Stick, Posture Curve, FootWheel, TriggerWheel.

STRAUSS SKATES & BICYCLES
1751 E COPE AVENUE
MAPLEWOOD, MN 55109

651-770-1344
888-770-1344
www.straussskatesandbicycles.com
• Donald H. Eyinck, President
Products:
Hockey skates and protective equipment, team uniforms, figure skating clothing, figure skates, in-line skates, letter jackets, lacrosse, broomball, NHL jerseys, factory authorized repair department, bicycles, bicycle repair.
Year Founded:
1887

STRENGTH SYSTEMS, INC.
1344 DANVILLE ST.
SUITE B
KENNER, LA 70062
504-468-9595
800-549-0341
Fax: 504-468-9120
• David Bouza, President
• Kevin Bouza, Marketing / Operations VP
Products:
Shoes, Jump Ropes, Weighted Vests, Weighted Shorts, Training Videos and Manuals, and Chute.

STRENGTH, INC.
164 3RD AVE SOUTH
TWIN FALLS, ID 83301
208-735-8940
800-370-3307
Fax: 208-735-8940
www.strengthequipment.net
• Stephen DeWitt, Owner, Designer, & Builder
Products:
Weight Lifting and Body Building Equipment

STROMGREN SUPPORTS, INC.
600 MAIN ST.
SUITE 201
HAYS, KS 67601
785-625-4674
800-527-1988
Fax: 785-625-9036
www.stromgren.com
• John Flynn, President
• Terry Karlin, VP Team Sales
• Carl Wilhite, VP National Sales Manager
(888) 567-5083
Products:
Compression wear and support products, including football protection, neoprene products, sliding shorts for baseball and softball, ankle and knee support products, exercise clothing, back and wrist support and performance apparel system

STRONG INTERNATIONAL, INC.
13710 FNB PARKWAY
SUITE 400
OMAHA, NE 68154
402-453-4444
800-424-1215
Fax: 402-453-7238
www.strong-cinema.com
• John P. Wilmers, President / Chief Executive Officer
info@strong-cinema.com
• Ray Boegner, SVP
• Pat Moore, VP, Cinema Products
• Gary L. Cavey, President & CEO
Products:
35mm and 70mm film projection, Xenon Consoles and Lamphouses, Film Projection

Systems, Platter Transports, CineNet Automation Systems and Digital Projection Systems

STRONGWALL SYSTEMS INC.
107 CHESTNUT STREET
RIDGEWOOD, NJ 7450
201-445-4633
800-535-0668
Fax: 201-447-2317
info@strongwall.com
www.strongwall.com
• John L. Maggi, National Sales Manager
strongwall@strongwall.com
• George Va Dyk, Sales VP
strongwall@strongwall.com
• Bill Kokoletsos, President
strongwall@strongwall.com
Products:
Sports Surfacing System:
Courts-Racquetball, Courts-Squash, Flooring-Racquetball, Flooring-Anti Slip, Flooring-Squash, Flooring-Gymnasium, Flooring/Multi-Purpose

STURDISTEEL COMPANY
PO BOX 2655
WACO, TX 76702-2655
254-666-5155
800-433-3116
Fax: 254-666-4472
jbledsoe@sturdisteel.com
www.sturdisteel.com
• Johnny Bledsoe, President / Director Marketing
jbledsoe@sturdisteel.com
Services:
Manufactures and designs outdoor stadium seating, bleachers and grandstands

STURM, RUGER & COMPANY, INC.
411 SUNAPEE STREET
NEWPORT, NH 3773
203-259-7843
Fax: 203-256-3367
www.ruger.com
• James E. Service, Chairman
• Stephen L. Sanetti, Vice Chairman, President, Chief Operatin
• Stephen L. M. Sanett, Vice-Chairman, President and Interim Chief Ex
• Christopher Killoy, Vice President of Sales and Marketing
Products:
Golf Club Heads, Hunting/Shooting Firearms

STX INC.
1500 BUSH STREET
BALTIMORE, MD 21230
410-837-2022
800-368-2250
Fax: 410-539-3908
www.stx.com
• Richard Tucker, President
info@stxlacrosse.com
• Jason Goger, President
Products:
Field Hockey Equipment, General Sports Products, Backyard Games, Golf Clubs and Putters, Lacrosse Apparel, Balls, Gloves, Nets, Pockets-Nylon, Sticks, Goalie, Handles, Bags, and Apparel.

STYLE EYES, INC.
824 W 18TH STREET
COSTA MESA, CA 92627
949-548-5355
800-227-6246
Fax: 949-548-5655
info@StyleEyes.com
www.styleeyes.com
• Philip Kahn, President
info@StyleEyes.com
Products:
Sunglasses-Skiing, Sunglasses-Water Sports

SUMMIT - GARDNER & GELDMACHER
960 MAPLEWOOD DRIVE
ITASCA, IL 60143
866-237-0400
Fax: 630-775-0132
info@summitmg.com
www.summitmg.com
• Dan Renz, Chief Executive Officer
chicago@summitmarketing.com
• Mike Harper, President - DC
• Steve Bawden, EVP / General Manager
• Michael Tritt, President - Kansas City
Services:
Provides marketing services such as promotional products, catalog programs, recognition/incentive, sales promotion, direct marketing

SUN MOUNTAIN SPORTS
301 N 1ST STREET W
MISSOULA, MT 59802-3625
406-728-9224
800-227-9224
Fax: 406-728-8998
www.sunmountain.com
• Rick Reimers, Founder
• Ed Kowachek, President
• Blake Ludwig, Chief Financial Officer
Products:
Golf Bags, Outerwear, Carts, Accessories

SUN SHADER INTERNATIONAL, INC./WASHINGTON SQUARE GARDEN, INC
4601 10TH AVENUE N
LAKE WORTH, FL 33463
561-433-9996
wsginc@hotmail.com
• Robert Boswell, President
wsginc@hotmail.com
Products:
Tennis Visors, Golf Visors, Headbands

SUNDAY PLAYERS
1400 BROADWAY
10TH FLOOR
NEW YORK, NY 10018
972-934-6565
Fax: 212-329-3486
info@sundayplayers.net
www.sundayplayers.net
Products:
Performance apparel for athletes: Compression Gear, Pro-Series Compression Gear, Performance Tees, Off-Field Gear

SUNDERLAND OF SCOTLAND
30 WATERWORKS ROAD
GUNTERSVILLE, AL 35976
256-264-0210
800-999-6599

Fax: 256-264-0215
info@sunderlandgolf.com
www.sunderlandgolf.com
• Paul Sunderland, President
info@sunderlandgolf.com
Products:
Golf Apparel

SUNDOG EYEWEAR USA
75 SKYLINE CRES NE
CALGARY, AB, CANADA T2K 5X2
877-205-5722 EXT 3
800-771-4310
Fax: 403-516-3018
Products:
Eyewear, Sunglasses

SUNTEC PAINT, INC.
PO BOX 2278
GAINESVILLE, FL 32602-2278
352-372-3421
800-333-1104
Fax: 352-376-4579
www.suntecpaint.com
• Joseph H. Anderson, President
Products:
Provides athletic field marking paints to
professional, college and high school
athletic stadiums; Coatings for Racquetball
Walls, Field Marking Paint, Gym Floors

SUNTIME/LINKSWALKER
4800 126TH AVENUE N
CLEARWATER, FL 33762
727-572-8443
800-659-2824
Fax: 727-573-4814
info@suntime.com
www.suntime.com
• Janet Lawson, Vendor Support and
Custom Sales Manager
Products:
Supplier and manufacturer of quality sports
related timepieces, specializes in logo 'd
watches and clocks and collegiate products

SUPERIOR EXERCISE PRODUCTS
947 CLOVER STREET
LAKE GENEVA, WI 53147
262-249-8787
Fax: 262-248-9430
www.superiorexerciseproducts.com
Products:
Revolutionary stretching devices

SUPERIOR FLOOR COMPANY, INC.
PO BOX 151
970 OGDEN ROAD
PESHTIGO, WI 54157
715-582-1181
877-582-1181
Fax: 715-582-1182
www.aacerflooring.com
• Michael Kobielak, Chief Operating Officer
mikek@aacerflooring.com
• Kevin Barker, Vice President Of
Sales/Marketing
kbarker@aacerflooring.com
• Kelly Kahara, Customer Service Manager
kellyk@aacerflooring.com
• Nick Larson, MidWestern Regional
Distribution Sales
nickl@aacerflooring.com
• Koko Thaw, International Sales Manager
kokot@aacerflooring.com
• Laurn Fontaine, Customer Service

Representative
laurnf@aacerflooring.com
• Jason Nieminksi, Technical Manager
jnieminski@aacerflooring.com
• Laura Thomson, Human Resource
Manager
laurat@aacerflooring.com
Products:
Indoor Flooring. Sports Flooring

SUPERIOR UNIFORM GROUP INC.
10055 SEMINOLE BOULEVARD
SEMINOLE, FL 33772
727-397-9611
800-727-8643
Fax: 727-393-0238
info@superioruniformgroup.com
www.superioruniformgroup.com
• Alan Schwartz, President
(727) 397-9611
info@superioruniformgroup.com
Products:
Sports uniforms.

SURE FOOT CORPORATION
1401 DYKE AVENUE
GRAND FORKS, ND 58203-2049
701-775-9560
800-722-3668
Fax: 701-775-4867
info@surefoot.net
www.surefoot.net
• Jon Larson, Founder/Partner
info@surefoot.net
• Van Larson, Vice President
info@surefoot.net
• Wayne Waege, General Sales Manager
Products:
Manufacturer, Distributor of specialty
branded outdoor apparel and footwear
accessories

SURFACE AMERICA
PO BOX 157
WILLIAMSVILLE, NY 14231
716-632-8413
800-999-0555
Fax: 716-204-0189
info@surfaceamerica.com
www.surfaceamerica.com
• Jim Dobmeier, President & Founder
(716) 632-8413
• Tom Discipio, Sales
Products:
Manufactures Playground Surfacing,
Gymnasium Flooring, Fitness Flooring,
Specialty Surfacing, Synthetic Grass

SUTTERS MILL SPECIALTIES
921 SOUTH PARK LANE
TEMPE, AZ 85281
602-437-5550
800-824-0594
Fax: 602-437-5551
sales@suttersmill.com
www.suttersmill.com
Products:
Apparel, Beverage, Blankets, College, Desk,
Gifts, Golf, Key Tags, Pen & Writing
Instruments, Seasonal, Tools, Travel,
Wallets and Money Clips, Watches

SWEDE-O, INC.
6459 ASH STREET
NORTH BRANCH, MN 55056

651-674-8301
800-525-9339
Fax: 651-674-8425
• Tom Traver, Vice President
Sales/Marketing
(651) 674-8301
• Michael Kenny, Sales Director
• Dan Kline, Sales Manager
Products:
Swede-O is recognized as a worldwide
leader providing innovative products
designed to prevent or rehabilitate soft
tissue injuries for over 25 years.
Brands:
Swede-o, Thermoskin

SWIM OUTLET
1165 E 230TH STREET
CARSON, CA 90745
310-522-2700
Fax: 310-952-8444
www.swimoutlet.com
• John Wickham, President
• Amber Delecce, Marketing Director
Products:
Swimwear for all swimmers, including
competitive athletes.
Brands:
Jag, Esprit Beach, Daffy Waterwear, Rebel
Beach, Silver Swim, L.E.I., Summer Girl,
Swim Systems, Baja Blue, Sun Blush

SWING AWAY SPORTS PRODUCTS, INC.
4206-A 50TH STREET #7
LUBBOCK, TX 79413
800-999-1968
Fax: 602-801-3300
service@swingaway.com
www.swingaway.com
• John J Flading, President/CEO
• Mark Zender, Sales VP
(360) 825-4299
getgood@swingaway.com
• Trisha Summers, National Sales Support
Manager
(360) 825-4299
getgood@swingaway.com
• John J Flading, President and CEO
(360) 825-4299
getgood@swingaway.com
Products:
Baseball/Softball Pitching/Protection
Screen, Training Aids, Accessories, Upper
Hand Batting Gloves.

SWISS ARMY BRANDS, INC.
1 RESEARCH DRIVE
SHELTON, CT 06484-0874
203-929-6391
800-442-2706
Fax: 203-926-2640
service@trggrp.com
www.victorinox.com
• Rick Taggart, President
• Thomas M Lupinski, SVP / Chief Financial
Officer
info@swissarmy.com
• Cheri McKenzie, SVP / Chief Marketing
Officer
• Pete Mitchell, VP Corporate Markets
Products:
Sunglasses; General Sports Products;
Compasses; Outdoor Products; Knives;
Timing Devices; Watches

SYNTHETIC SURFACES, INC.
PO BOX 241
SCOTCH PLAINS, NJ 07076-0241
908-233-6803
Fax: 908-233-6844
info@nordot.com
www.nordot.com
• Norris Legue, President/Founder
(908) 233-6803
info@nordot.com
Services:
Makers of NORDOT© Adhesives for installing synthetic turf athletic fields and other sport, recreational and aquatic surfaces since 1973.

T.C. THILON USA
1131 BROADWAY STREET
DAYTON, TN 37321-1802
423-775-0792
800-251-1033
Fax: 423-775-5813
www.tencate.com
• Mark Edwards, President
• Ian Petrie, Manager Director
Products:
Artificial Yarn for Sports Fields

T3K INC
6515 CLINTON HIGHWAY
SUITE 207
KNOXVILLE, TN 37912
865-859-9212
www.t3kwear.com
Products:
Apparel that provides flexibility,warmth, and breathe ability to all who work or play in cold weather. It comes as no surprise that snow boarders, skiers, snowmobilers, joggers, skaters, ice climbers, and other outdoor enthusiasts find that T3K is the superior choice for cold weather protection

TABATA USA, INC.
2380 MIRA MAR AVENUE
LONG BEACH, CA 90815
562-498-3708
800-482-2282
Fax: 562-498-0415
info@tusa.com
www.tusa.com
• Eiji Kimura, President
info@tusa.com
Products:
Skiing Goggles; Scuba Equipment; Swimming Goggles

TACHIKARA USA INC.
100 IRELAND DRIVE
MCCARRAN, NV 89434
775-352-3500
800-729-8224
Fax: 775-352-3518
www.tachikara.com
• Dan Burke, President
office@tachikara.com
• Roger Revelle, SVP
Products:
Volleyballs, Soccerballs, Basketballs, Footballs, Playground, Tetherballs, Neo-Glo Balls, Wallyballs, Specialty, Accessories, Ball carts

TACKI-MAC GRIPS, INC.
22000 NORTHPARK DRIVE
KINGWOOD, TX 77339

800-334-7477
www.tackimac.com
Products:
Baseball Metal Bat Grips; Golf Club Grips; Ice Hockey Grips; Racquet Sports Racquet Grips

BIRDAIR, INC.
65 LAWRENCE BELL DRIVE
SUITE 200
AMHERST, NY 14221
716-633-9500
800-622-2246
Fax: 716-633-9850
www.birdair.com
• Yasuyki Kono, President
• David C Capezzuto, Sales VP
Products:
Birdair, Inc. produces lightweight structural support for multi-sports facilities offering unique design and climate controlled interiors creating comfortable environments. These lightweight roof solutions are economical, durable and noncombustible

TANDEM SPORT
440 BAXTER AVENUE
LOUISVILLE, KY 40204
502-582-3530
800-766-1098
Fax: 502-582-1344
www.tandemsport.com
• Anne Brown, President / Owner
(800) 766-1098
anne@tandemsport.com
• Dan Evans, Chief Operating Officer / Owner
(800) 766-1098
dan@tandemsport.com
• Tammy Allgeier, National Sales Manager
(800) 766-1098
• Anne Brown, President/Owner
• Dan Evans, CEO, Owner
dan@tandemsport.com
• Mike Ryan, Owner
• Lindsay Tucker, Sales/Marketing
(800) 766-1098
• Tammy Allgeier, National Sales Manager
• Shelley Benson, Operations Manager
• Heather Isgrigg, Customer Service Manager
Products:
Sports Medicine, Sports Accessories, Tandem Sport Volleyball Equipment, Official Supplies, Cups and Keychains, Tandem Sport Volleyball Apparel, Miller Lite Volleyball Products
Nature of Service:
Distributor and manufacturer of sports medicine and sport accessory
Brands:
Active Ankle, Pro-Tec, Suede-O, Security Equipment, Skids, Tandem Sport
Year Founded:
1989

TANITA CORPORATION OF AMERICA
2625 S CLEARBOOK DRIVE
ARLINGTON HEIGHTS, IL 60005
847-640-9241
800-826-4828
Fax: 847-640-9261
4health@tanita.com
www.tanita.com
• Jeff Kahn, VP Sales
• Keith Erickson, Sales Manager

Products:
Body Composition Monitors for Home Use, InnerScan Monitors, Ironman Monitors, Jenny Craig Scales, Fitness Solution Collections, Scale Plus Body Fat Monitors and with Body Water %, Digital Scales, Digital Lithium Scales, Solar Scales, Analog/Dial Scales, Handheld Health Monitoring Products, Pediatric Scales, Professional Body Composition Analyzer/Scales, Digital Healthcare Scales, Acute and Long-term Care Scales, Veterinary Scales, Food Service/General Purpose Scales, Home Healthcare Products, Mini Scales, Wireless Scales, Segmental Bodyfat Pedometers, Calorie Counting Jumping Rope.
Year Founded:
1946

TASK INDUSTRIES, INC.
PO BOX 420235
PALM COAST, FL 32142
386-246-3439
Fax: 909-629-4967
www.tuffstuff.com
• Sherman Grider, President
• Monica Grider, VP
• Tom Bartsch, Publisher
• Scott Fragale, Editor
• Joe Clemens, Associate Editors
• Steve Madson, Advertising Sales
(800) 726-9966
Products:
Circuit Trainers; Exercisers or Exercise Machines; Free Weight Equipment

TAYLORMADE-ADIDAS GOLF
5545 FERMI COURT
CARLSBAD, CA 92008-7324
760-918-6000
866-530-8624
Fax: 760-918-6008
• Mark King, President / Chief Executive Officer
• Sean Toulon, EVP, Product and Brand Creation
• John Kawaja, EVP, TaylorMade-adidas Golf
• Brad Barnett, SVP, U.S. Operations
Product:
Golf supplies and equipment.

TC SPORTS
7251 FORD HIGHWAY
TECUMSEH, MI 49286
517-451-5221
800-523-1498
Fax: 517-451-8427
www.tc-sports.com
• Jill Felbaum, President
Products:
Athletic Equipment

TEAM CALIBER
4606 ROUSH PLACE
CONCORD, NC 28027
704-720-4800
888-332-9700
Fax: 704-720-4905
www.teamcaliber.com
Products:
Toys; Shirts; T-shirts; Hats; Outerwear

TEAM SHOP PREMIUMS
1140 E WASHINGTON STREET
SUITE 206
PHOENIX, AZ 85034
602-635-6400
800-952-5339
Fax: 602-254-1212
info@hdsideas.com
www.hdsideas.com
• Scott Nash, General Partner
• Bob Nanberg, Managing General Partner
(602) 635-6437
Nature of Services:
Team Shop Premiums produces products
for staff use, game day giveaways as well as
sponsor and sports related gifts.

TEAM SPORTS AMERICA
5790 E SHELBY DRIVE
SUITE 104
MEMPHIS, TN 38141
901-405-8326
888-567-8326
Fax: 901-365-1895
www.teamsportsamerica.com
• David McQuillians, Sales Manager
(901) 365-1779
Products:
Scoreboards: NFL, MLB and Collegiate;
Hammocks; Pool Floats; Welcome Mats
(18x30); Stepping Stones; Standing Stones;
Mini-Standing Stones; Clock Thermometers;
Bird Feeders; Bird Houses; Pin Wheels;
Copper Lanterns, Umbrellas, Area Rugs.

TEAMLINE
989 W SANDY LAKE ROAD
#200
COPPELL, TX 75019
972-471-0200
800-422-577
Fax: 972-471-0300
customerservice@eteamline.com
www.eteamline.com
• Sue Ann Clark, General Manager
saclark@eteamline.com
• Darinda Howeth,
customerservice@eteamline.com
Products:
Team apparel, shoes, equipment, coaches
apparel, outwear, accessories and lettering.
Brands:
Nike, Wilson, Mizuno, Easton, McDavid, and
others
Clients:
Schools and leagues.

TECNICA USA CORPORATION
19 TECHNOLOGY DRIVE
W LEBANON, NH 3784
603-298-8032
800-258-3897
Fax: 603-298-5790
www.tecnicagroup.com
• Gicancarlo Zanatta, President / Tecnica
Group S.P.A.
• John C Stahler, Chief Exeutive Officer /
Tecnical USA
Products:
Ski Boots; Outdoor Footwear; Winter
Footwear; Travel Footwear; Bags; Socks;
Gloves; Apparel; Caps/Hats/Belts

TECNIFIBRE USA
5775 BLUE LAGOON DRIVE
SUITE 110
MIAMI, FL 33126

888-301-7878
Fax: 305-504-8742
info@tecnifibreusa.com
www.tecnifibre.com
• Nicholas Preault, President
(888) 301-7878
• Marco Baron, CEO, North America
(888) 301-7878
mbaron@tecnifibre.com
• Miriam Marquez-Rocha, Office Manager
(888) 301-7878
miriam@tecnifibreusa.com
• Miriam Marquez-Rocha, Office Manager
(786) 380-6353
miriam@tecnifibreusa.com

**TEETER HAND UPS/STL
INTERNATIONAL, INCORPORATED**
9902 162ND STREET
COURT E
PUYALLUP, WA 98375
253-840-5252
800-847-0143
Fax: 253-840-5757
info@teeter-inversion.com
• Roger Teeter, President
rteeter@teeterhangups.com
Products:
Inversion Tables; InversionTable
Accessories

TEN SECONDS
429 27TH STREET NW
HICKORY, NC 28601
828-322-2600
800-438-5777
Fax: 828-328-1700
info@tenseconds.com
www.tenseconds.com
• Rob Bell, CEO
• Josh Higgins, VP of Business
Development
Products:
Insoles; Shoe Care; Cleats/Spikes; Shoe
Laces; Custom Laces/Lanyards; Drymax
Sport Socks

TENACIOUS LTD
123 ONIZUKA STREET
SUITE 207
LOS ANGELES, CA 90012
213-617-0449
Fax: 213-617-1252
mail@tenaciousltd.com
www.tenaciousltd.com
• Michiro Toyoshima, Sales
(213) 617-0449
• Yoshinosuke Kurita, Owner
(213) 617-0449
Products:
Headwear Accessories; Skateboard, surf,
golf

TENNIS MACHINES, INC.
14520 MANCHESTER ROAD
WINCHESTER, MO 63011
636-394-8811
800-572-1055
Fax: 636-394-3271
jhenry@tennismachines.com
www.tennismachines.com
• Jim Henry, President
jhenry@tennismachines.com
Products:
Stringing Machines; Ball Throwing Machines

TENNIS SURFACES COMPANY
7N730 ROUTE 59
BARTLETT, IL 60103
630-213-1163
Fax: 630-213-1164
tennissurfaces@yahoo.com
www.tennissurfaces.com
• Hank Aldrich, President
• Dudley Pankoke, Truck Division President
(630) 561-2982
• Lesley R Aldrich, Secretary / Treasurer
Products:
Flooring & Boards; Installs artificial turf and
dasher boards for indoor soccer fields within
the United States; Installs many types of
surface coatings for tennis courts.
Year Founded:
1968

TERRAMAR SPORTS WORLDWIDE, LTD.
580 WHITE PLAINS ROAD
SUITE 660
PORT CHESTER, NY 10591
914-934-8000
800-468-7455
Fax: 914-937-0600
customerservice@terramarsports.com
www.terramarsports.com
• Ben Lieberman, President
(914) 934-8000
ben@lamour.com
• Russell Pitman, Vice President
Sales/Marketing
(914) 934-8000
rpitman@terramarsports.com
• Marisa Serrao, Vice President, Credit
(914) 934-8000
• Barbara Neves, Customer Service
(914) 934-8000
• Nicole Brickman, Customer Service
(914) 934-8000
• Bruce Schwartz, Vice President Socks
(914) 934-8000
Products:
Sports apparel, including thermal layers,
underwear and accessories
Nature of Service:
Importer
Brands:
Terramar, Thermawool, EC2

TERRAPLAS USA RENTALS, LLC
706 WOODLAWN
SUITE 101
KILGORE, TX 75662
903-983-2111
888-972-6837
Fax: 903-983-2324
www.terraplasusa.com
• Sally Beane, Marketing Director
• Michael Beane, Marketing
• Judy Purvis, Marketing
Services:
Turf Protection

TERVIS TUMBLER COMPANY
201 TRIPLE DIAMOND BOULEVARD
N VENICE, FL 34275
941-966-2114
866-886 2537
Fax: 888-876-6887
customercare@tervis.com
www.tervis.com
• Jennifer Bement, Media Marketing
Manager
(941) 441-3104

Nature of Service:
Crystal clear insulated drinkware, Licensing opportunities available. Customization of tumblers available.
Year Founded:
1946
Products:
Animal & Wildlife Tumblers; Boating & Marine Tumblers; Clear and Colored Tumblers; Collegiate Tumblers; Garden Splendor Tumblers; Glitter Tumblers; Holiday & Celebration Tumblers; Outdoor Sports Tumblers; Personalized Tumblers; Professional & Service Tumblers; Regional Flair Tumblers; Sports & Leisure Tumblers; Water's Edge Tumblers; Lids & Straws; Ice Buckets
Brands:
Tervis Tumbler®

TEVA BRAND
495-A S FAIRVIEW AVENUE
GOLETA, CA 93117
805-967-0961
800-433-2537
Fax: 805-967-9722
hr@deckers.com
www.deckers.com
• Angel R Martinez, CEO, President & Chairman
ext 507
• Zohar Ziv, Chief Operating Officer
• Thomas A George, Chief Financial Officer
• Graciela Montgomery, Chief Human Resource Officer
Products:
Footwear; Apparel & Accessories

TEXACE CORP.
5405 BANDERA ROAD
SUITE 121
SAN ANTONIO, TX 78238
210-227-7551
800-835-8973
Fax: 210-227-4237
• Jim Blugerman, VP Sales / Marketing
Products:
Golf & Fashion Headwear; Premium Signature Cap; Import Base Cap

TEXTILE REVOLUTION
115 PERIMETER CENTER PLACE
SUITE 945
ATLANT, GA 30344
678-990-8002
877-286-7074
Fax: 770-206-2389
Products:
Athletic apparel

TF PUBLISHING
6355 MORENCI TRAIL
INDIANAPOLIS, IN 46268
317-290-1333
888-799-8463
Fax: 317-290-1223
info@tfpublishing.com
www.tfpublishing.com
• Jim Purcell, President
Products:
Sports Calendars

THERMO-SERV/BETRAS
3901 PIPESTONE ROAD
DALLAS, TX 75212

214-631-0307 EXT 7326
800-635-5559
Fax: 214-631-0566
www.thermoserv.com
• Joe Betras, President
(800) 635-5559
Products:
Sport bottles, tumblers, insulated mugs, coffee mugs, clear sports bottles, stainless steel drinkware and novelty items including custom-molded toppers and cappers
Brands:
Spring Summer Deck Tumblers, John Deere, Monster Mug, Collegiate Items, Jumbo Jackets

THOR-LO, INC.
2210 NEWTON DRIVE
STATESVILLE, NC 28677
888-846-7567
www.thorlo.com
• James L. Throneburg, Chief Executive Officer
• Deb An Lazenby, Product Manager
• Jeff Lawson, Director of Marketing
• Rich Burkley, Managing Director
Products:
Athletic Socks

THOUGHT TECHNOLOGY, LTD.
5250 RUE FERRIER
SUITE 812
MONTREAL, QC, CANADA H4P 1L3
514-489-8251
800-361-3651
Fax: 514-489-8255
www.thoughttechnology.com
• Maribel Cunanan, Account Manager - Marketing North America
maribel@thoughttechnology.com
Description:
Manufacturer.

TIDE-RIDER, INC.
987 WAKEFIELD DRIVE
PO BOX 429
OAKDALE, CA 95361-0429
209-848-4420
800-638-8644
Fax: 209-848-4423
info@tideridersports.com
www.tideridersports.com
• James Smith, Owner/President
(209) 848-4420
info@tideridersports.com
• David Smith, Vice President Marketing
(209) 848-4420
info@tideridersports.com
Year Founded:
1950.
Nature of Service:
U.S. Whistle Distributor of Fox 40, Acme, Windsor, and Spalding Electronic; also Lanyards, Carlton Badminton, Lion Table Tennis Equipment, Scoremaster and Mark V Scorebooks.
Products:
Whistles, lanyards, down counters, whistle tip covers, eyeglass guards, clipboards, scorebooks, shuttlecocks, badminton rackets, table tennis balls, table tennis rackets, and table tennis sets
Products:
Whistles, lanyards, down counters, whistle tip covers, eyeglass guards, clipboards, scorebooks, shuttlecocks, badminton rackets, table tennis balls, table tennis

rackets, and table tennis sets
Brands:
Fox 40, Acme, Windsor, Scoremaster, Mark V, Carlton, Lion, Windsor Victor

TIMEX CORPORATION
PO BOX 310
MIDDLEBURY, CT 6762
203-346-5758
800-448-4639
Fax: 203-346-7019
custserv@timex.com
www.timex.com
• Susie Watson, Advertising Director / Public Relations
• Mario Sabatini, Director, Sports Marketing / Sales
• Chris Johnson, Marketing Specialist
• Dan Simoneau, Product Manager, Performance Sports
Products:
Watches, audio, eyewear, thermostats, timer and night lights, weather instruments, pedometers, thermometer, straps, and clock

TINY TOTS SPORTS
7785 SPRING CREEK ROAD
MACUNGIE, PA 18062
610-398-0090
888-299-2880
Fax: 610-398-7831
www.TinyTotSports.com
• John Daddona, Chairman
info@tinytotsports.com
• Dino Daddona, President / Chief Financial Officer
• Jack Da Jr, President, Sales & Marketing
• Alan Lagarde, Executive Producer / VP, Creative Affair
Products:
Sports videos and books

TIREPATCHEZ
4628 WINWARD COVE LANE
WELLINGTON, FL 33467
561-791-8454
877-728-2439
Fax: 561-791-8789
Products:
Tire patches, tire tattoos and tire studs

TITANIUM SPORTS TECHNOLOGIES
1426 E THIRD AVENUE
KENNEWICK, WA 99337
509-586-6117
800-545-2266
Fax: 509-586-2413
tubing@tilite.com
www.titaniumsports.com
• David S. Lippes, President
• Sandra Gladstone, VP Operations
• Mark Westphal, Director Golf Shaft Sales
Products:
Titanium Mountain and Road Bikes; Titanium Golf Shafts

TITLEIST (COBRA/PINNACLE)
333 BRIDGE STREET
FAIRHAVEN, MA 2719
508-979-2000
800-225-8500
Fax: 508-979-3092
ebizhelp@acushnetgolf.com
www.titleist.com
• Walter R. Uihlein, Chairman / Chief Executive Officer

• Gerald M. Bellis, EVP, Sales and Marketing, Titleist
• William C. Burke Sr, SVP, Chief Financial Officer
Products:
Golf balls, clubs, gloves, shoes, cart bags, travel gear, carry bags, headwear, and other golfing equipment and accessories

TKO SPORTS GROUP, INCORPORATED
4660 PINE TIMBERS
SUITE 198
HOUSTON, TX 77041
713-895-9078
866-856-3488
Fax: 713-895-9078
Inquiries@tkosportsgroup.com
www.tko.com
Products:
Sporting goods and boxing and fitness equipment

TM ATHLETICS
9622 40TH AVENUE SW
TACOMA, WA 98499
253-588-3060
Fax: 253-588-3646
tma@tmathletics.com
www.tmathletics.com
• Maurice Thevenoux, President
Products:
Athletic jackets/sweaters/blankets, and cheerleading supplies

TOMCAT USA
5427 N. NATIONAL DR.ÿ
KNOXVILLE, TN 37914
432-694-7070
Fax: 865-673-5818
sales@tomcatusa.com
www.tomcatglobal.com
• John H. James, Chief Executive Officer
• Mitch Clark, President
• Brad Bainhill, Sales Manager
Products:
TOMCAT GLOBAL specializes in the fabrication of aluminum structural components for the entertainmnet and leisure industries, as well as providing related products such as Columbus McKinnon theatrical chain hoists, custom electirc assemblies, lighting products and rigging hardware. TOMCAT USA, TOMCAT Las Vegas, TOMCAT UK, Ltd., TOMCAT Mexico, S.A. de C.V. and Brilliant Stages are subsidiaries of TOMCAT Global Corporation, headquartered in Midland, Texas, USA.

TOMIC GOLF & SKI MFG., INC.
23102 MARIPOSA AVENUE
TORRANCE, CA 90502-2607
310-534-2532
800-678-6642
Fax: 310-539-6010
• Judith Tomic, President
• Jeff Tomic, VP
Products:
Ski poles, paddles ad putter shafts

TOMSED CORPORATION
402 MCKINNEY PARKWAY
LILLINGTON, NC 27546
910-814-3800
800-334-5552
Fax: 910-814-3899

sales@boonedam.us
www.boonedam.us
• Mark Borto, VP, Sales
• Greg Schreiber, National Sales Manager
Products:
Turnstiles, revolving doors, vehicle barriers and entry portals

TONIX CORPORATION
40910 ENCYCLOPEDIA CIRCLE
FREMONT, CA 94538-2470
510-651-8050
800-841-1144
Fax: 510-651-8052
sales@tonixteams.com
www.tonixteams.com
• David T Chen, Owner
sales@tonixteams.com
• Mike Chen, Marketing Director
sales@tonixteams.com
• Chloe Lam, Customer Service Manager
chloe@tonixteams.com
Products:
Team apparel such as sport shirts, warm-up suits, jackets and pullovers
Description:
Supplier of team apparel serving the federal, corporate and athletic industries for over 30 years, Tonix specializes in sports shirts and outerwear.

TOON ART INCORPORATED
581 NORTHLAND BOULEVARD
CINCINNATI, OH 45240
513-851-2357
800-723-2357
Fax: 513-851-2391
www.toonartinc.com
• Greg Akers, President
Products:
Unique, high-value animated products in the sports and entertainment industries

TOP OF THE WORLD CAPS
3001 36TH AVENUE NW
PO BOX 721210
NORMAN, OK 72072
405-360-9856
800-896-8978
Fax: 405-360-0373
info@towcaps.com
www.towcaps.com
• Jasonn Hamby, National Sales Manager
jhamby@towcaps.com
Products:
Sports caps

TOP-COMFO ATHLETIC SOX, INC.
289 GEORGE STREET
LYNCHBURG, VA 24506
804-237-2323
Fax: 804-846-3297
Products:
Athletic Socks

TOP-FLITE COMPANY
425 MEADOW STREET
CHICOPEE, MA 1021
413-536-1200
877-846-9997
Fax: 413-322-2216
www.topflite.com
• Bob Penicka, President/Chief Operating Officer
• Andrew Isaacman, Vice President

• Andrew Kelleher, VP Finance/Administration
Products:
Golf balls

TOPPERSCOT LLC
3600 S. YOSEMITE ST.
SUITE 1000
DENVER, CO 80237
303-936-2444
800-334-2518
Fax: 303-936-2778
www.topperscot.com
Products:
Customized Christmas ornaments and sports ornaments for the NFL, MLB, NHL and NBA.

TOPPS COMPANY, INC.
ONE WHITEHALL STREET
NEW YORK, NY 10004
212-376-0300
Fax: 212-376-0573
www.topps.com
• Arthur T Shorin, Chairman/Chief Executive Officer
• Michael A. Brandstaedter, President/Chief Operating Officer
• Jason K. Thaler, Vice President - Digital
• Douglas P. Kruep, Vice President and General Manager
• Christopher L. Rodman, Vice President and Group Managing Director
• Michael J. Drewniak, VP Manufacturing
Products:
Candies, collectibles, baseball cards and other sports-related trading cards

TORPEDO SPORTS USA, INC.
2401 PGA BOULEVARD
SUITE 190
PALM BEACH GARDENS, FL 33410
561-624-0885
www.torpedosports.com
• Edward Shake, President
• Henry Fong, Chief Executive Officer
• Michael Stanimir, Chief Operating Officer
• Henry Morton, Sales Manager
Products:
Outdoor recreational products for children, such as toboggans, baby sleds, snowboards, skateboards, tricycles and scooters

TOTES ISOTONER, INC.
9655 INTERNATIONAL BOULEVARD
PO BOX 465658
CINCINNATI, OH 45246-5658
513-682-8389
800-762-8712
Fax: 513-682-8606
customerservice@totes.com
www.totes.com
• Douglas Gernert, President / Chief Executive Officer
customerservice@totes.com
• Donna Deye, Chief Financial Officer
customerservice@totes.com
Products:
Umbrellas, gloves, slippers and rubber rainboots

TOWN TALK CAP MFG. COMPANY, INC.
6310 CANE RUN ROAD
LOUISVILLE, KY 40258

502-933-7575
800-626-2220
Fax: 502-933-7599
www.ttcaps.com
• Nancy L. Tanner, Office Manager
• Michial D. Vincent, Plant Manager
• Wayne O. M. Joplin, Sr., Owner and CEO
(502) 933-7575
• Joel S Gary, President
• Rose M. Coomes, Vice President
Products:
Headwear for golf tournaments and
promotions
Year Founded:
1919

TOYQUEST
2228 BARRY AVENUE
PO BOX 71292
CLIVE, IA 50325
310-231-7292
800-434-6178
Fax: 310-231-7565
• Brett Bogar, VP Product Development
Products:
Unique, innovative and quality toys and
sporting goods for children.

TR GEAR/PROTONIC
115 PERIMETER CENTER PLACE
SUITE 945
ATLANTA, GA 30344
678-860-3740
Fax: 770-206-2389
• Michael Smoltz, Chief Operating Officer
(678) 990-8002
Products:
Textile Revolution (by ProTonic) is a new
line of patented athletic performance
apparel focusing on blood flow to muscles,
sweat control, and temperature regulation

TRACE ATHLETIC CORPORATION
SEATTLE, WA 98115
888-662-6330
888-662-6330
Fax: 888-662-5453
www.tr2sports.com
Products:
Elbow and knee/shin guards and sliding
shorts

TRACKER TRUCKS
3820 OCEANIC DRV
SUITE 311
OCEANSIDE, CA 92056
760-722-1455
800-206-5280
Fax: 760-967-0554
www.trackertrucks.com
Products: .
Skateboard trucks

TRACKLITE SYSTEMS
PO BOX 4275
ANDOVER, MA 1810
978-685-9709
800-284-8564
Fax: 978-685-9138
www.tracklite.com
• Arthur H Feinberg,
Products:
Synthetic running tracks

**TRAILER CORPORATION OF AMERICA,
INCORPORATED**
601 S 5TH STREET
EASLEY, SC 29640
864-859-9809
800-448-4841
Fax: 864-859-3000
Products:
Auto Utility Trailers

TRANS APPAREL
5000 S OHIO STREET
MICHIGAN CITY, IN 46360
219-879-7341
800-776-7268
Fax: 219-879-0388
www.hartmarx.com
• Homi B Patel, Chairman/CEO
• Thomas Smith, Assistant VP-General
Services
Products:
Branded tailored clothes, trend-right
sportswear and women's apparel

TRANS-LUX SPORTS
1651 N 1000 W
LOGAN, UT 84321
435-753-2224
800-543-7904
Fax: 435-753-2975
• T. J. Nelligan, Consultant
Products:
Scoreboards, Control Systems, Message
Centers, Accessories, Information Displays,
Signage

TRAVELERS CLUB LUGGAGE
5911 FRESCA DRIVE
LA PALMA, CA 90623
714-523-8808
800-368-2582
Fax: 714-523-0188
info@travelersclub.com
www.travelersclub.com
• Peter Yu, President/CEO
Products:
Luggage, Tote Bags, Garment Bags, Duffel
Bags, Backpack, Accessories, Radio
Collers, Coolers, Specialty Coolers

TREK BICYCLE
801 W MADISON STREET
WATERLOO, WI 53594
920-478-2191
800-473-4743
Fax: 920-478-2774
www.trekbikes.com
• John Burke, President
• Dick Moran, Marketing Director
• John Burke, President
Products:
Manufacturer of bicycles and accessories
sold by specialty retailers

TRENDS INTERNATIONAL
5188 W 74TH STREET
INDIANAPOLIS, IN 46268
317-388-1212
866-406-7771
Fax: 317-388-1414
info@trendsinternational.com
www.trendsinternational.com
• Phil St. Jean, President and CEO
• Jeff Loeser, Vice President Licensing
jloeser@trendsinternational.com

• Michelle Kesler, Director Marketing
mkesler@trendsinternational.com
Products:
Manufacturer of licensed and non-licensed
posters, calendars and doodle activity kits

TRENWAY TEXTILES, LLC.
FORT PAYNE, AL 35968
256-997-1857
800-251-7504
Fax: 800-441-8138
trenway@trenwaytextiles.com
www.trenwaytextiles.com
• Angie Pritchett, Owner, Production
Manager
• Jerome Pritchett, Owner, Accounts
Payable/Receivable
• Lucy Long, Administrative Assistant
• Janie Hyder, Administrative Assistant
Products:
Socks for all sports, accessories (Chin strap
covers, Custom Logo Wristbands,
Headband, Wristbands, Young and Adult
Belt, Hockey Socks.
Year Founded:
1977

TRIMAN TELE-GOAL, INC.
415 S FEDERAL HIGHWAY
PO BOX 247
DANIA BEACH, FL 33004
954-920-2727
800-822-6886
Fax: 954-922-0189
• Brian M Berman, Vice President
texacocb2@bellsouth.net
Products:
Strong, light weight and rust resistant
aluminum goal post assembly, football goal
post pads.
Year Founded:
1969

TRIMOTION
1515 PALISADES DRIVE
SUITE E
PACIFIC PALISADES, CA 900272
310-230-8417
800-874-0035
Fax: 310-230-8418
www.trimotion.com

TRIUS PRODUCTS, LLC.
475 SMITH STREET
MIDDLETOWN, CT 6457
860-632-2020
800-225-9626
Fax: 860-632-1699
• J Ma Thompson, President
Products:
Traps

**TROPAR MANUFACTURING COMPANY,
INC.**
5 VREELAND ROAD
PO BOX 215
FLORHAM PARK, NJ 7932
973-822-2400
Fax: 973-822-2891
tropar@airflyte.com
www.airflyte.com
• Peter V Illaria, President
Products:
Plagues, Wall Clocks, Desk Clocks,
Acrylics, pens, gifts and accessories

TROPHY GLOVE COMPANY
122 WASHINGTON AVENUE
ALBIA, IA 52531
641-932-2183
800-323-2928
Fax: 641-932-7430
trophyglove@hotmail.com
• Patricia Nolan, President
• Charles Nolan, Director
• Mike Nolan, Sales
Products:
Baseball Batter-Gloves, Cycling Gloves, Curling Gloves, Football Gloves, Golf Gloves, Gymnastics Hand Protectors, Racquet Sports Gloves, Softball Gloves-Batter, Training & Conditioning Hand Grips, Weight Lifting Gloves, Alpine-Skiing Gloves, Snowboarding

TROPHY WORLD
6400 NW 77TH COURT
MIAMI, FL 33166
305-592-5850
800-526-8652
Fax: 305-592-5854
• Larry Carvez, President
Products:
Trophies, Awards Desk Sets, Medals, Ribbons

TROPHYLAND USA, INC.
7001 W 20 AVENUE
HIALEAH, FL 33014
305-823-4830
800-327-5820
Fax: 305-823-4836
info@trophyland.com
www.trophyland.com
• Paul Fields, President
• Clara Zeinfeld, VP
Products:
Trophy manufacturer offering wholesale trophies, plaques, desk sets, pens, keychains, ribbons, engraved gifts and awards including corporate awards, athletic, crystal, civic, sports and scholastic awards

TROXEL, LLC
6222 FERRIS SQUARE
SAN DIEGO, CA 92121
858-587-7720
800-288-4280
Fax: 858-587-7733
info@troxelhelmets.com
www.troxelhelmets.com
• Richard Timms, Chairman
• Shay Joaquin, Chief Executive Officer
• Dustin Touchton, Vice President of Marketing
Products:
Provider of ASTM/SEI certified equestrian helmets for competitive, schooling and recreational riding

TROY CORPORATION
2701 N NORMANDY AVENUE
CHICAGO, IL 60707-3605
773-804-9600
800-888-2400
Fax: 773-804-0906
www.troy-corp.com
• Terry Troy, President
Products:
Wholesale manufacturer and distributor of fabrics for the over-the-counter retail market, apparel and craft fabrics for manufacturing, fabric remnants for retail, embroidery and

sewing supplies for the monogramming industry and blank activewear for screen printing and for retail.

TRUE FITNESS TECHNOLOGY
865 HOFF ROAD
SAINT LOUIS, MO 63366
800-426-6570
800-426-6570
Fax: 636-272-7148
www.truefitness.com
• Frank Trulaske, Foudner/CEO
• Scott Euler, VP Sales / Marketing
• Stan Gologader, SVP Operations
• Don Mullen, Hospitality Manager
Products:
Gym equipment like treadmills, elliptical trainers, upright and recumbent bikes, multi-station gyms, and TrueStretch

TRUE TEMPER SPORTS, INC.
8275 TOURNAMENT DRIVE
200
MEMPHIS, TN 38125
901-746-2000
800-355-8783
Fax: 901-746-2160
www.truetemper.com
• Scott Hennessy, President / Chief Executive Officer
• Fred Geyer, Chief Financial Officer
• David Hallford, VP Golf Sales
• Scott Hennessy, President and CEO
• Don Brown, Manager of Product Development
Products:
Golf Shafts

TRUEX GOLF
890 WARRINGTON AVENUE
REDWOOD CITY, CA 94063
650-365-3320
800-348-7839
Fax: 650-365-3017
• Don Fernquest, President
Products:
Golf Clubs-Iron or Wood Sets, Putters, Utility-Clubs, Clubheads.

TRUSCO MFG. COMPANY
545 NW 68TH AVENUE
OCALA, FL 34482-8235
352-237-0311
800-327-8859
Fax: 352-237-0346
contact@truscomfg.com
www.truscomfg.com
• Bruce Harris, VP Marketing
Products:
Pavement Marking Equipment & Athletic Field Liners

TUF-WEAR
1001 INDUSTRIAL AVENUE
NORTH PLATTE, NE 69101
308-532-0187
800-445-5210
Fax: 308-532-9133
www.tufweardirect.com
• John Gaetano, President
(650) 701-1915
• Linda Williams, Sales Manager
(800) 445-5210
Year Founded:
1931.
Products:

Football - Dial-A-Down. Chain Sets, Field Markers Pylons, Officialss Equipment, Kicking Tee's, Sideline Markers.

TUFF TOE
1442 W COLLINS AVENUE
SUITE G
ORANGE, CA 92867-5443
800-888-0802
800-888-0802
Fax: 714-997-9594
www.tufftoesports.com
• Ryan Pribble, President
Products:
Tuff Toe Boot Protection (Work Boots, Motorcycle Booots), Tuff Toe Sports(Tuff Toe Pro, Pre Molded Tuff Toe, Tuff Sleeve), Baseball Cleats with Factory Applied Tuff Toe, Softball Cleats with Factory Applied Tuff Toe

TUFLEX RUBBER PRODUCTS
1401 EAST 6TH STREET
TUSCUMBIA, AL 35674
813-870-0390
800-543-0390
Fax: 813-875-2312
sales@tuflex.com
www.tuflex.com
• Fred Franklin, President
• Jerry Pillard, Sales Manager
Products:
Resilient Rubber Flooring

TUNTURI, INC.
VARUSMESTARINTIE 26
PO BOX 60001
AA ALMERE, THE NETHER FIN-20361
-31-546-0050
Fax: -31-546-0059
info@tunturi.com
www.tunturi.com
• Leo Heikkinen, President
info@tunturi.com
• Karen Dixon, VP General Manager
info@tunturi.com
Products:
Treadmills, Cycle ergometers, Recumbent cycles, Exercise cycles, Crosstrainers, Rowers, Stappers, Bicycles and Bicycle accessories

TURFCO MFG., INC.
1655 101ST AVENUE NE
BLAINE, MN 55449-4420
763-785-1000
800-679-8201
Fax: 763-785-0556
sales@turfco.com
www.turfco.com
• George Kinkead, President
sales@turfco.com
• Scott Kinkead, Vice President
sales@turfco.com
• John Kinkead, Chief Executive Officer
sales@turfco.com
• Bob Brophy, Director of Lawn Care Products
Products:
Equipment for Golf & Sports Turf and Lawn maintenance
Description:
Manufacturer of topdressers, seeders, aerators, spreaders, sprayers, edgers and sod cutters.

TURFER SPORTSWEAR
530 WOOD STREET
SUITE B
BRISTOL, RI 2809
800-222-1312
Fax: 401-253-9875
www.turfer.com
• John St Martin, President
sales@turfer.com
• Christine King, VP Marketing
• Fred Morrison, VP Sales
• Jane Shanley, Sales Director
Products:
Windshirts, Polo, Wovens, Jackets,
Sweaters, Katahdin Tek Fleece and
Accessories

TWIN CITY KNITTING COMPANY, INC.
104 ROCK BARN ROAD NE
CONOVER, NC 28613
828-464-4830
800-438-6884
Fax: 828-465-3209
info@tcksports.com
www.tcksports.com
• Francis B. Davis, President
(828) 464-4830
Products:
Athletic socks, knit hats, wristbands, head
bands, women's lacrosse and volleyball
uniforms, Kelme soccer uniforms, shoes,
balls and bags.
Brands:
Oysox, Racesox, Slog Series, Aware,
Krazisox, TCK Women, Grunge, Ulta
Grunge, Reacs, Blister Register, Chase

TWIN LABORATORIES, INC.
600 E QUALITY DRIVE
AMERICAN FORK, UT 84003-3302
800-645-5626
Fax: 801-763-0700
product@twinlab.com
www.twinlab.com
• Marc Stover, Director Of Marketing
• Niki Simoneaux, Director of Brand
Management
Products:
Nutritional supplements, including a
complete line of vitamins, minerals,
nutraceuticals, herbs and sports nutrition
products

TWINS ENTERPRISES
15 SW PARK
WESTWOOD, MA 02090
800-446-6046
800-446-6046
Fax: 617-585-6231
customorders@47brand.com
www.47brand.com
• Arthur D'Angelo, Owner
info@twinsenterprise.com
• Henry D'Angelo, Owner
info@twinsenterprise.com
• Mark D'Angelo, VP
• David D'Angelo, VP
Products:
Hats, Caps and Visors

TWINS-NY
2171 JERICHO TURNPIKE
SUITE 342
COMMACK, NY 11725-2900
631-858-9184
888-414-4300

Fax: 631-858-9189
rcopp97107@aol.com
Products:
Caps and headwear

TYCA CORPORATION
470 MAIN STREET
CLINTON, MA 1510
978-612-0002
800-522-5387
Fax: 978-612-0003
tyca@tyca.com
www.tyca.com
• Franklin Hardy, President
tyca@tyca.com
• Maryann Castello, Executive Vice
President
• Franklin Hardy, President
Products:
Embossed denim totes, jackets, aprons,
t-shirts and others
Description:
Tyca is a premier manufacturer of
embossed apparel and accessories. USA
and Union-made.

TYR SPORT, INC.
15391 SPRINGDALE STREET
HUNTINGTON BEACH, CA 92649
714-897-0799
800-252-7878
Fax: 714-373-0903
www.tyr.com
• Steve Furniss, EVP
• Hans Fassnacht, VP International
• Carlo Bonza, Manager of TYR's European
distribution
• Jared Berger, Product Manager
• Franck Horter, TYR's European General
Manager
Products:
Water Sports Accessories, Goggles,
Competitive/Performance Swimwear,
Triathlon Apparel and Training Equipment

U.S. GAMES, INC.
1901 DIPLOMAT DRIVE
DALLAS, TX 75234
972-484-3484
bmitchell@sportsupplygroup.com
www.sportsupplygroup.com
• Michael J. Blumenfeld, Chief Executive
Officer
bmitchell@sportsupplygroup.com
• Terrence M. Babilla, EVP, Chief Operating
Officer, General Co
bmitchell@sportsupplygroup.com
• Adam K. Blumenfeld, Chairman and CEO
• Robert Mitchell, Chief Financial Officer
Products:
Archery, baseball, softball, basketball,
camping, football, tennis and other racquet
sports, gymnastics, indoor recration,
physical education, soccer, field and floor
hockey, lacrosse, track and field, volleybal,
weight lifting, fitness equipment and outdoor
playground equipment

**U.S. REPEATING ARMS
COMPANY/WINCHESTER**
275 WINCHESTER AVENUE
MORGAN, UT 84050
801-876-2711
Fax: 801-876-3331
webmaster@winchester-guns.com
www.winchesterguns.com

• Bertrand Devillers, Chief Finanacial Officer
webmaster@winchester-guns.com
• Charles Guevremont, Chief Executive
Officer
webmaster@winchester-guns.com
Products:
Rifles, shotguns, pistols, and accessories,
along with archery and fishing equipment,
knives, flashlights, outdoor apparel,
footwear, and security safes

U.S. TRAFFIC CORPORATION
2906 CORPORATE WAY
PALMETTO, FL 34221
562-923-9600
800-245-7660
Fax: 562-923-7555
www.peektraffic.com
• Timothy O'Leary, President
• Mary Griffin, VP Sales & Marketing
• Luis Lopez, Director of Sales
Products:
Electronic traffic controllers, in-ground
vehicle sensors, traffic conflict monitors,
vehicle and pedestrian signals and power
backup systems, electronic variable
message signs, directional displays and
trailer-mounted arrow panels

U.S.I.A.
1600 RAILROAD AVENUE
PO BOX 1071
ST HELENS, OR 97051
503-366-0212
800-247-8070
Fax: 503-366-0816
www.usia.com
• Lana Johns, Chief Executive Officer
Lana@usia.com
• Kim Johns, President
• Jerry Langan, VP
• Eric Heid, Military Sales & Foreign Military
Sales
Eric@usia.com
Products:
Diving Drysuits, Surface Drysuits,
Thermalwear and accessories

ULTRA PLAY SYSTEMS, INC.
1675 LOCUST STREET
RED BUD, IL 62278
618-282-8200
800-458-5872
Fax: 618-282-8202
customerservice@uplaytoday.com
www.ultraplay.com
• Philip Clemons, Sales Manager
(618) 282-8200
• Linda Nagel, Sales
(618) 282-8200
Products:
Basketball - Backstops; Football and Soccer
- Goal Posts; Racquet Sports - Tennis
Standards; Volleyball - Inserts, Standards
Description:
Manufacturer of outdoor recreational
equipment and site amenities

UMBRO U.S.A.
1936 SE CLATSOP STREET
PORTLAND, OR 97202
503-231-8401
800-762-2376
Fax: 503-897-8403
www.umbro.com
• Dave Wray, Sales Manager

Products:
General Sports Activewear, Soccer Bags, Equipment, Balls, Gloves-Goalie, Nets, Referee Uniforms, Sand Soccer Shoes, Socks, Training Gear, Uniforms

UNDER ARMOUR PERFORMANCE APPAREL
1010 SWAN CREEK DRIVE
CURTIS BAY, MD 21226
410-468-2512
888-727-6687
Fax: 410-439-1292
feedback@underarmour.com
www.underarmour.com
• Kevin Plank, President/Founder
feedback@underarmour.com
• Ryan S. Wood, President, International
feedback@underarmour.com
Products:
Diverse sports apparel for men, women and youth

UNIQUE SPORTS PRODUCTS, INC.
840 MCFARLAND PARKWAY
ALPHARETTA, GA 30004
770-442-1977
800-554-3707
Fax: 770-475-2065
sales@uniquesports.us
• Gene Niksich, President/Owner
gene@uniquesports.us
• Gene Niksich, Owner and President
• Mike Niksich, Vice President
mike@uniquesports.us
• Glinda Powers, Customer Service
glinda@uniquesports.us
• Joe Bertolini, Operations Manager
joe@uniquesports.us
• Kevin Niksich, Vice President
kevin@uniquesports.us
Products:
Baseball Eyeblack, Grips, Practice Aids, Rosin Bags, Tape, Key Chains, Eyeglass Holders, Gripping Aids, Shoelaces, Support Products-Joint, Training Aids, Wristbands/Headbands, Golf Accessories, Hot Glove Baseball Accessories, Tennis Tourna Grip, Tennis Court Equipment, Tennis Strings, Balls and other tennis accessories.
Year Founded:
1972
Clients:
National Chain Stores, Sporting Goods Stores.

UNITED SPORTS TECHNOLOGIES/UST
14950 FAA BOULEVARD
SUITE 200
FT WORTH, TX 76155
817-267-2219
800-621-6728
Fax: 817-283-1722
www.ustmamiya.com
• Gene Simpson, Sales / Marketing VP
• Jamie Pipes, Manager of Product
• Shawn Mullin, Tour Manager
Products:
Graphite golf shaft

UNITED STATES PLAYING CARD COMPANY, THE/WPT
300 GAP WAY
ERLANGER, KY 41018
513-396-5700
800-542-7430

800-543-2273
Fax: 866-781-5866
www.usplayingcard.com
• Scott Madding, Director, Global Casino Sales
(859) 815-7518
scottmadding@usplayingcard.com
• Adam McGregor, Vice President Sales - Asia
(853) 6283-351
Products:
Playing Cards and Poker Chips

UNITED TURF INDUSTRIES
123 N PARKRIDGE
WICHITA, KS 67212
316-945-5996
Fax: 316-266-4295
• Lance Pierce, President
Products:
Carpets and Rugs

UNITED TURF, INC.
120 LEONHAUSER LANE
GRANDY, NC 27939
252-457-0591
800-421-7649
Fax: 252-457-0596
• Keith Hall, President
Products:
Grass, Fungicide/Herbicide, Seed Varieties

UNIVERSAL FABRIC STRUCTURES
3115 STATE R
QUAKERTOWN, PA 18969
215-529-9921
800-634-8368
Fax: 215-529-9936
sales@ufsinc.com
www.ufsinc.com
• Dirk Cos, President
(215) 529-9921
dirk@ufsinc.com
• Kirk Klever, Vice President Sales & Project Management
(800) 634-8368
kirk@ufsinc.com
• Mark Oyer, Business Director
(800) 634-8368
mark@ufsinc.com
• Krista Morris, Customer Service Officer/Sales Assistant
(800) 634-8368
krista@ufsinc.com
• Mike Belisle, Director/ Sports & Recreation
(267) 347-5450
Products:
Manufacturer of custom and pre-engineered fabric structures for use in covering swimming pools, tennis courts, and other sports fields. UFS creates year-round indoor sports facilities at a fraction of the cost of traditional construction and air bubble structures.

UNIVERSAL GYM EQUIPMENT INC.
769 E. MAIN ST.
VERSAILLES, OH 45380
937-526-9544
800-843-3906
Fax: 662-495-2502
• Steve Sadler, President
• Tom Sadler, VP
• Steve Sadler, President
• John Sadler, Vice President
Products:
Computerized and Manual Exercise Bikes,

Selectorized Weight Training Machines, Free Weights, Computerized Rowing Machines, Computerized Stair Machines, Computerized Treadmills

UNIVERSAL NUTRITION
3 TERMINAL ROAD
NEW BRUNSWICK, NJ 8901
732-545-3130
800-872-0101
Fax: 732-509-0458
info@universalnutrition.com
www.universalnutrition.com
• Clyde Rockoff, President
Products:
Sports Nutrition Supplements, Powders, Shirts and Bags

UNIVERSAL SPORTS LIGHTING, INC.
2277 OLD ROUTE 66
PO BOX 486
ATLANTA, IL 61723
217-648-5201
800-933-9741
Fax: 517-439-1194
info@qualite.com
• Chuck Lindstrom, President
Products:
Lighting Fixtures, Mounting Structures, Pole Options

UPPER DECK COMPANY
5909 SEA OTTER PLACE
CARLSBAD, CA 92010-6621
760-929-6500
800-873-7332
Fax: 760-929-6548
www.upperdeck.com
• Richard McWilliam, Chief Executive Officer
customer_service@upperdeck.com
• Mary Province, Chief Financial Officer
customer_service@upperdeck.com
• Bill Dully, Chief Operating Officer
Products:
Sports Cards, Sports Memorabilias, Sports Die-cast Collectibles, Bobble Heads & Figurines, Gift Ideas, Gift Certificates, Display Cases, Poker Chips, Personalized Cards

USAOPOLY
5607 PALMER WAY
CARLSBAD, CA 92010
760-431-5910
888-876-7659
Fax: 760-431-5880
www.usaopoly.com
• Maggie Matthews, Vice President Marketng
(760) 431-5910
• Jeanette Best, Media
(760) 431-5910
• Eric Brendel, Manager Custom Game Development
(760) 431-5910
Products:
Board games and Puzzles

UT GOLF, INC.
4820 JACKSONTOWN ROAD
PO BOX 3008
NEWARK, OH 43056-3008
740-328-4193
800-848-8358
Fax: 800-800-3290

golfworks@golfworks.com
www.golfworks.com
• Dave Stewart, Marketing VP
golfworks@golfworks.com
• Ralph Maltby, Founder
• Britt Lindsey, Vice President Technical
Services
Products:
Heads, Shafts, Grips, Tools

UVEX SPORTS, INC.
110 COMSTOCK PARKWAY
CRANSTON, RI 2921
401-464-8844
888-616-8839
Fax: 401-464-4244
custserv@uvexsports.com
• Carl Helmetag, President
(401) 464-8844
carl@uvexsports.com
• Bruce Campbell, Controller
bruce@uvexsports.com
Products:
Goggles, Winter Helmets, SportGlasses,
Bike Helmets

V-FORMATION\THE NEXED LIFE
99 WOOD AVENUE SOUTH
SUITE 805
ISELIN, NJ 8830
732-321-4040
888-264-5397
Fax: 732-321-4176
www.vformation.com
• Joseph Colonese, President
• Rich Stelnick, Chief Executive Officer
• Theodore Ellenis, Executive VP
• Steve Bogoyevac, General Manager
Products:
Hockey Apparel, Protective Equipment,
Skates, Sticks

VALEO
19275 W CAPITOL DRIVE
SUITE L01
BROOKFIELD, WI 53045
262-314-0070
800-634-2704
Fax: 800-831-9642
valeoinfo@valeoinc.com
www.valeoinc.com
• Chuck Last, National Sales Manager
info@valeoinc.com
Description:
Manufacturer of fitness accessories, lifting
gloves and back support belts.

VALLEY FORGE SPORTS, INC.
533 ABBOTT DRIVE
BROOMALL, PA 19008
610-543-4690
800-220-4834
Fax: 610-328-4582
info@vfgloves.com
• Richard K Greene, President
• John E Csaklos, VP
Products:
Golf Gloves, Putters, Umbrellas, Bags

VANGUARD SAILBOATS
300 HIGHPOINT AVENUE
PORTSMOUTH, RI 2871
401-683-0960
800-966-7245
Fax: 401-683-0990
www.teamvanguard.com

• Chip Johns, President
• Jack McVicker, Manufacturing VP
• Amy Larkin, Mktg Svcs Mgr
• Steve Clark, Chairman
Products:
Boats

VARIFLEX INC.
12801 CARMENITA ROAD
SANTA FE SPRINGS, CA 90670
562-484-5100
800-234-9737
Fax: 562-484-5183
www.bravosportscorp.com
• Leonardo L Pais, Chief Executive Officer
Products:
Skates, Skateboards, Scooters, Body
boards, Safety helmets, Athletic protective
equipment, Trampolines and Recreational
canopies

VARSITY BRANDS, INC.
6745 LENOX CENTER COURT
SUITE 300
MEMPHIS, TN 38115
901-387-4306
Fax: 800-792-4337
nlauchaire@varsityspirit.com
www.varsity.com
• Jeffrey G Webb, Vice Chairman / Chief
Executive Officer
• Leonard Toboroff, VP / Director
• John M Nichols, Senior VP / Chief
Financial Officer
• Sheila Noone, VP, Public Relations
(901) 251-5959
• Marlene Cota, VP, Corporate Alliances
and Business Developm
(901) 387-4306
• Nicole Lauchaire, VP, Corporate Marketing
& Communications
(901) 251-5903
nlauchaire@varsityspirit.com
• Jackie Martin, Content Manager
(901) 251-5899
jackiemartin@varsityspirit.com
Products:
Cheerleading Uniforms, Dance Team
Uniforms

VECTRA FITNESS CORPORATION
7901 S 190TH STREET
KENT, WA 98032
425-291-9550
800-283-2872
Fax: 425-291-9650
info@vectrafitness.com
www.vectrafitness.com
• Doug Maclean, Founder
info@vectrafitness.com
• Bob Rasmussen, Founder
Products:
Weight Machines

VELVETOP PRODUCTS
1455 NEW YORK AVENUE
HUNTINGTON STATION, NY 11746
631-427-5904
Fax: 631-673-3301
info@velvetop.com
www.velvetop.com
• John B Walsh, President
info@velvetop.com
• Linda Walsh, Secretary / Treasurer
info@velvetop.com
Products:
Pavement products, American stone mix for

athletic field surfaces, field marking paints,
tennic court equipment and resurfacing
material.

VENUS SWIMWEAR
11711 MARCO BEACH DRIVE
JACKSONVILLE, FL 32224
800-648-0411
888-782-2224
Fax: 800-648-0411
email@venus.com
• Daryle Scott, President / Chief Executive
Officer
email@venus.com
Products:
Swimwear and Fashion Apparels

VERMONT ORIGINALS
146 INDUSTRIAL PARK DRIVE
SUITE 4
MORRISVILLE, VT 5661
802-888-6400
800-526-3257
Fax: 802-888-3025
www.vermontoriginals.com
• Margaret Krysiak, President
krysiak@vermontoriginals.com
• Annette Gann, Production Manager
annette@vermontoriginals.com
Products:
Hats, Jackets & Vests, Mittens, Scarves,
Head Scarves, Shoulder Wraps, Baby Hats
& Mittens, Team Logowear

VESPOLI USA, INC.
385 CLINTON AVENUE
NEW HAVEN, CT 6513
203-773-0311
Fax: 203-562-1891
www.vespoli.com
• Mike Vespoli, Chief Executive Officer and
Owner
mvespoli@vespoli.com
• Dave Trond, President
dtrond@vespoli.com
• Mike Vespoli, CEO / Owner
mvespoli@vespoli.com
• David Trond, Vice President of Sales
dtrond@vespoli.com
• Walter Torres, Director or Operation
wtorres@vespoli.com
• Fred Aniballi, Business Office
faniballi@vespoli.com
Products:
Rowing/Crew - Oarlocks, Outriggers,
Shells/Sculls, Shoes

VF BRAND SOLUTIONS
545 MARRIOTT DRIVE
PO BOX 140995
NASHVILLE, TN 37214-0995
866-335-1185
800-733-5271
Fax: 800-877-8329
www.vfbrandsolutions.com
• John Mohman, Marketing Services
Manager
• Angie Wilson, Marketing Services
Coordinator
(615) 565-5358
• Scott Roe, Vice President
• Matthew J. Shatock, Director
Products:
Lee Fleece, Lee Casual, Wrangler Hero

VF CORPORATION
105 CORPORATE CENTER BOULEVARD
PO BOX 21488
GREENSBORO, NC 27408
336-424-6000
877-285-4152
Fax: 336-424-7696
www.vfc.com
• Mackey J McDonald, President/CEO
• George N Derhofer, VP / Chairman
• Robert K Shearer, VP, Finance, Chief
Financial Officer
• Eric W C. Wiseman, Chairman, Chief
Executive Officer & President
• Robert K. Shearer, Senior VP & Chief
Financial Officer
• Scott Baxter, VP
Products:
Jeanswear, Global Intimates, Imagewear,
Outdoor, Sportswear

VIBRA-WHIRL & COMPANY
94 MAIN ST
PO BOX 966
PANHANDLE, TX 79068
806-537-3526
800-255-8722
Fax: 806-537-3442
track_sales@vibrawhirl.com
• Lanny Garner, President
• Sheri Urbanczyk, EVP
Products:
Tracks, Turf, Athletic Equipment

VICTORY SPORTS NETS
1805 PIERCE AVENUE
MARINETTE, WI 54143
715-732-2511
800-338-9860
Fax: 715-732-2574
• William Cavill, Sales Manager
Products:
Commercial Fishing Products & Catalog,
Victory Sports Products & Catalog, Craft &
Rosary Twine, Sea King Ultra Fishing Line &
Tip-Up Line, Super Hide Taxidermy Thread,
Custom & Specialty Netting, Seasonal
Specials & Overstock Sales

VIKING ICE, LLC
9450 SW COMMERCE CIRCLE
SUITE 101
WILSONVILLE, OR 97070
503-682-9437
800-698-6036
Fax: 503-682-9098
www.vikingice.com
• Tom Faber, Viking Ice Agent
• Doug McNeill, Viking Ice Agent
Products:
Synthetic Skating Surface

VIKING TECHNOLOGY INC.
2541 STATE ROUTE 250 S.
PO BOX 968
NEW LONDON, OH 44857
419-706-5874
Fax: 419-668-6882
• Leif Ericsson, Owner
lericsson@viking-tech.com
• Cameron Thompson, Founder and
Chairman
(419) 668-8944
Products:
Business Telephone Systems for Sports and
other large facilities.

**VIRCO MANUFACTURING
CORPORATION**
2027 HARPERS WAY
TORRANCE, CA 90501
310-533-0474
800-448-4726
Fax: 800-258-7367
info@virco.com
• Doug Virtue, VP
dougvirtue@virco.com
• Randal Smith, VP Marketing
(800) 448-4726
• Don Curran, Recycling, Resource
Recovery and Grounds
(800) 448-4726
doncurran@virco.com
• Bob Roskos, Corporate Copywriter
(800) 448-4726
Products:
Portable seating and table products for the
public facilities markets

VIRGIL FILMS & ENTERTAINMENT
407 BROOME STREET
#6A
NEW YORK, NY 10013
212-475-2888
646-723-7069
Fax: 212-475-5962
www.virgilfilmsent.com
• Joseph Amodei, President
Joe@virgilfilmsent.com
• Tom O'Hara, CFO
• Kelly O'Brien, Vice President
kelly@virgilfilmsent.com
• James Puleo, Production, Marketing and
Design Manager
James@virgilfilmsent.com
Products:
Various specialty sports DVDs and program
rights.

VISION FITNESS
1600 LANDMARK DRIVE
PO BOX 280
COTTAGE GROVE, WI 53527
920-648-4090
800-335-4348
Fax: 608-839-8994
www.visionfitness.com
• Christa Walter, Retail Brand Manager
(800) 335-4348
• Ron Carringi, General Manager,
Manufacturing Facility
Products:
Treadmills, Elliptical Trainers, Fitness Bikes
and Strength Equipment

VITAL/PROMARX
7 NORDEN LANE
HUNTINGTON STATION, NY 11746
972-874-8653
800-777-8482
Fax: 866-326-4478
VitalTeam@Vital-Apparel.com
www.promarx.com
Products:
Women's Team Sports Apparel, Sports
Themed Apparel and Matching Accessories
in most sports & team colors

VITRONIX PROMOTIONAL GROUP
4680 PARKWAY DRIVE
SUITE 200
MASON, OH 45040
513-398-3695
800 543-4611

Fax: 513-398-7165
customercare@vitronicpromotional.com
www.vitronicpromotional.com
• Steve Hill, General Manager
• Rob Cordes, National Accounts Manager
Products:
Umbrellas, Headwear, Bags & Travel,
Business, Crystal, Promotional, Calendar,
Camouflage, Golf

VOILE MOUNTAIN EQUIPMENT
2636 S 2700 W
SALT LAKE CITY, UT 84119
801-973-8622
800-670-8622
Fax: 801-973-8918
info@voile-usa.com
www.voile-usa.com
• David Grissom, General Manager
Products:
Core telemark and splitboard equipment

VOLKL SPORT AMERICA CORP
290 PLAINFILED ROAD
W LEBANON, NH 3784
603-298-8282
800-264-4579
Fax: 603-298-8754
www.volkl.com
• Christoph Bronder, President & CEO
Products:
Ski Collection, Performance Ski Wear,
Snowboard, Tennis Racquets

VOYAGER EMBLEMS, INC.
PO BOX # 487
LOCKPORT, NY 14095-0487
416-255-3421
800-268-2204
Fax: 416-255-4238
grantr@voyager-emblems.com
www.voyager-emblems.com
• Sally L Grant, President
(800) 268-2204
• Tammy-Lynn Marrelli, Manager Customer
Service
(800) 268-2204
Products:
Baseball - Caps; Trophies/Awards - Crests,
Emblems, Patches; Talc Twill Appliqu,s

VUARNET
3882 DEL AMO BOULEVARD
SUITE 604
TORRANCE, CA 90503
310-793-5180
800-348-0388
Fax: 310-793-5181
sales@vuarnet.com
www.vuarnetusa.com
• Harold Page, President / Chief Executive
Officer
• Angela Torres, Director Business
Operations / Administr
Products:
Eyewear - Sunglasses

WAI LANA YOGA
PO BOX 1369
PO BOX 6146
KAILUA, HI 96734
805-986-3557
800-624-9163
888-924-5262
Fax: 805-986-5447

info@wailana.com
www.wailana.com
• Wai Lana, Owner / Founder
• Wai Lana, Founder and President
• Angie Smith, Press / Media
(805) 986-3557
Products:
Yoga DVDs; Yoga Music; Yoga videos; Gift sets, books, aromatherapy candles, incense, t-shirts, eye pillows, women's clothing, hats, clocks & chimes; Yoga equipments - bolsters, blankets, chairs & cushions, yoga balls, mat bags & carriers, yoga & pilates mats, posture props

WALKER & COMPANY
12007 SUNRISE VALLEY DRIVE
SUITE 400
RESTON, VA 20191
703-648-0900
Fax: 703-648-9344
• Christopher W Walker, Founder / President / Chief Executive Of
• Clark Rheinstein, Chief Financial Officer / Leasing Direct
(703) 648-0900
• Chuck Poulson, Property Management and Construction Dir
• Robin Greenstreet, Property Manager
Services:
Developers of Campus-Style Technology Centers

WALL OF FAME WHOLESALE
1501 ZENITH DRIVE
SIOUX CITY, IA 51103
712-202-0501
Fax: 712-293-1500
• Brad Graff, Contact
(712) 202-0501
Products:
Seller of licensed team logo apparel, merchandise, and collectibles for college and pro sports; Selection of fan apparel, headwear, novelties, gifts, home d,cor, accessories, and memorabilia

WARNER/EXCELLTEK
3875 EMBASSY PARKWAY
FRANKLIN PARK, IL 44333
847-455-6730
800-621-1143
Fax: 330-668-7716
• George Warner, Sr, Founder
Products:
Fine wallcoverings and wallpaper products

WARPT INDUSTRIES, INC.
40960 CALIFORNIA OAKS ROAD
SUITE 178
MURRIETA, CA 92563
909-772-6500
Fax: 909-600-2881
www.warpt.com
• Mike Metzger, Founder
• Eric Verkouteren, Webmaster
(909) 600-2771
• Bob Knight, Hosting Service
Products:
Importer of a freestyle-inspired consumer apparel line that is redefining action sports youth culture; T-shirts, Girly T's, Sweatshirts, Hats, Beanies, Jerseys

WASATCH TOURING
702 E 100 S
SALT LAKE CITY, UT 84102
801-359-9361
Fax: 800-766-9729
www.wasatchtouring.com
• Dwight Butler, Founder
• Charles Butler, Founder
Products:
Sports, skiing, hiking, biking, golf, and fishing equipment; Gift card, packs, clothing, car racks, maps, books, DVDs, and snow shoe

WATER SPORTS LLC
407 N. QUENTIN ROAD
SUITE C
PALATINE, IL 60067-4832
847-701-3018
800-283-1683
Fax: 847-991-7189
sales@StreamMachineStore.com
www.streammachinestore.com
Products:
Sports equipment, toys, media storage, CD/DVD storage cases, TV stand, stream machines, displays and fitness equipments

WAVE INDUSTRIES
1420 FM 1483
YANTIS, TX 75497
903-383-3573
877-484-5462
Fax: 903-383-3582
sales@wavefishing.com
www.wavefishing.com

WEBSTER WATCH CO., ASSOC.
44 E 32ND STREET
7TH FLOOR
NEW YORK, NY 10016
212-889-3560
800-289-8963
Fax: 212-213-2649
www.avalonwatch.com
• Linda Robbins, President
(800) 289-8963
Year Founded:
1927.
Products:
Timing devices, chronographs, digital stopwatches,fashion, sport, novelty, custom imprinted, and contemporary watches
Brands:
Bellagio, Avalon, Meridian, Medana, My Watch, EZC

WEED U.S.A., INC.
5780 HARROW GLEN CT
GALENA, OH 43021
740-548-3881
800-933-3758
Fax: 740-548-3882
info@weedusa.com
www.weedusa.com
• Dennis O'Reilly, VP/ Owner and Operator
Products:
Racquet Sports - Tennis Racquets; Accessories

WEEKEND EXERCISE COMPANY
6017 RANDOLPH STREET
COMMERCE, CA 90040
858-537-5300
800-666-2127
Fax: 858-537-5400

orderinquiries@marika.com
www.marika.com
• Michael Levinson, President
• Arthur Levinson, Chief Executive Officer
• Carrie Henley, Executive VP and General Manager
• Marla Echt, Marketing Director
Products:
Gymnastics and Active Apparel; Swimwear for Water Sports

WELLINGTON LEISURE PRODUCTS
1140 MONTICELLO HIGHWAY
PO BOX 244
MADISON, GA 30650
706-342-1916
800-221-5054
Fax: 706-342-0407
www.wellingtoninc.com
• William Morro, Interim Chief Executive Officer
• Dan Roberts, EVP
• Marc Emmi, Group VP Sporting Goods
• Harold Tamplin, Sales / National Accounts VP1
Products:
Water Sports - Flotation Devices, Water Skis, Water Ski Ropes and Accessories; Manufacturer of consumer and commercial rope and webbing, outdoor cushions, cedar furniture, water sports equipment, Christmas accessories, crafts, and Tink's hunting accessories

WELLS LAMONT SPORTS & SPECIALTIES
6640 W TOUHY AVENUE
NILES, IL 60714
847-647-8200
800-323-2830
Fax: 847-470-1026
www.wellslamont.com
• David W Kennedy, President / Chief Executive Officer
• Tom Palzer, VP / Chief Financial Officer
• Tim Hartigan, SVP / Retail Operations General Manager
• William Trainer, Industrial Marketing and Sales VP
Products:
Manufactures a comprehensive selection of hand protection including cut resistant, heat resistant, general purpose, liquid/chemical resistant, leather gloves and much more

WEST COAST NETTING, INC.
5075 FLIGHTLINE DRIVE
KINGMAN, AZ 86401
928-692-1144
800-854-5741
Fax: 928-692-1501
info@westcoastnetting.com
www.westcoastnetting.com
• Dan Kirkland, President
(928) 692-1144
Dkirkland@westcoastnetting.com
• Jason Joch, Marketing Manager
(928) 692-1144
• Bob Potter, Shop Manager, Production
Bpotter@westcoastnetting.com
• Kim Potter, Purchasing Manager
Products:
Baseball Cages/Backstops, Basketball Nets, Field Hockey Nets, Football Goal Nets, Ice Hockey Stockings, Lacrosse Nets, Racquet Sports Badminton Equipment, Table Tennis Equipment, Tennis Court Nets, Soccer Nets,

Timing Devices, Scoreboards, Volleyball Ball

WEST COAST TURF
42-540 MELANIE PL
PO BOX 4563
PALM DESERT, CA 92211
760-340-7300
888-893-8873
Fax: 760-340-7345
mail@westcoastturf.com
www.westcoastturf.com
• John Foster, President
john.foster@westcoastturf.com
• Joe Foster, VP
joe.foster@westcoastturf.com
• Jeff Cole, Sales VP
jeff.cole@westcoastturf.com
• Danielle Marman, Marketing and PR Director
danielle@westcoastturf.com
Services:
Services such as custom grown sod, world-wide shipping and expert installation of sod, stolons, natural turf

WEST RIDGE DESIGNS
6635 N BALTIMORE AVENUE
241
PORTLAND, OR 97203
503-248-0053
800-548-0053
Fax: 503-274-7685
• Dann Morris, Founder
• Emiko Morris, Founder
Products:
Manufacturing bags and accessories

WESTERN GOLF, INC.
72-105 CORPORATE WAY
PO BOX 970
THOUSAND PALMS, CA 92276
760-343-1050
800-443-4350
Fax: 760-343-2834
info@westerngolf.com
www.westerngolf.com
• Robert Wagner, President
Products:
Golf - Ball Returns, Balls, Clubs-Iron Or Wood Sets, Clubs-Putters/Utility, Course Maintenace Equipment, Driving Range, Nets/Mats, Electric Shoe Cleaner, Flag Poles, Pull Carts, Tees, Ball Washers, Range Ball Pickers, Ball Dispensers.

WHAM-O
5903 CHRISTIE AVENUE
EMERYVILLE, CA 94608
888-942-6650
877-944-7501
Fax: 310-286-2350
www.wham-o.com
• Mojde Esfandiari, President
• Richard Knerr, Founder
Products:
Interactive products for all seasons toys, sporting goods, water and snow tubes, towables, islands and pool products

WIGWAM MILLS, INC.
3402 CROCKER AVENUE
PO BOX 818
SHEBOYGAN, WI 53081-0818
920-783-1000
800-558-7760

Fax: 920-457-5551
socks@wigwam.com
www.wigwam.com
• Robert E Chesebro Jr, President
socks@wigwam.com
• James Einhauser, Sales / Marketing EVP
socks@wigwam.com
• Jay Kroll, Marketing Director
socks@wigwam.com
• Bob Chesebro, President
• Donna Fischer, Marketing Manager
socks@wigwam.com
Products:
Athletic Socks

WILSON SPORTING GOODS COMPANY
8750 W BRYN MAWR AVENUE
CHICAGO, IL 60631
773-714-6400
800-874-5930
Fax: 773-714-4595
www.wilson.com
• Chris Considine, President
(773) 714-6868
askwilson@wilson.com
• Rick Kerpsack, Interactive Marketing Director
(773) 714-6441
• Tim Clarke, Wilson Golf General Manager
Products:
Sports equipment and apparel, Sports equipment and apparel, including tennis, football, major and minor league baseball uniforms

WILSON TROPHY COMPANY OF CALIFORNIA
1724 FRIENZA AVENUE
SACRAMENTO, CA 95815
916-927-9733
800-635-5005
Fax: 916-927-9955
sales@wilsontrophy.com
www.wilsontrophy.com
• Gerald Loomis, President
Gloomis@Wilsontrophy.com
Products:
Sports Memorabilia, Certificates, Custom Apparel, Custom Medals, Custom Patches, Custom Pins, Desksets, Laser Acrylic, Laser Elegance, Little League Baseball, National Accounts, Oval Relief, Plaques, Resins, Ribbons & Chenille Pins, Stock Medals, Time Pieces & Trophies

WINCRAFT INCORPORATED
960 E MARK ST
PO BOX 888
WINONA, MN 55987-0888
800-533-8006
Fax: 507-453-0690
contact@wincraft.com
www.wincraft.com
Description:
Manufacturer of licensed and promotional products. Established in 1961.

WINDJAMMER INC.
525 N MAIN STREET
BANGOR, PA 18013
610-588-0626
800-441-6958
Fax: 610-588-2046
www.windjammerinc.com
• Anthony J Capozzolo, President / Chief Executive Officer
windjammer525@netzero.net

• Joseph H Capozzolo, VP
windjammer@epix.net
• John Cannavo, Public Relations Director
Products:
Sportswear such as Sports Bras, Shorts & Pants; Tees and Tanks; Long Sleeve & Hanley T-Shirts; Golf Shirts; Athletic-Weight Crews, Pants, Jams, Pullover Sweatshirts & Zipper Hooded Jackets; Xtreme T-shirts and Turtle Neck Sweatshirts; Oxford Jackets; Nylon Pullover Jackets & Pants; Satin and Poplin Jackets; and Warm Up Jacket

WINN, INC.
15648 COMPUTER LANE
HUNTINGTON BEACH, CA 92649
714-373-6271
877-854-7601
Fax: 714-379-5463
custsvc@winngrips.com
www.winngrips.com
• Ben Huang, President / Chief Executive Officer
• Mavis Huang, Import VP / Export Manager
• Mike Coelho, National Sales Manager
• Ben Huang, CEO and Founder
• Jeff Shepherd, Marketing Manager
Products:
Different kinds of Grips

WINNERS CIRCLE SPORTS & GIFTS
1480 HOHOKAM DRIVE
TEMPE, AZ 85281
704-454-4176
800-952-0708
Fax: 704-454-4184
RCCAInfo@lionelnascar.com
www.lionelnascarcollectables.com
• Howard Hitchcock, Vice President and General Manager
Products:
Sporting goods and apparel

WINTECH RACING
345 WILSON AVENUE
NORWALK, CT 6854
203-866-7223
Fax: 203-866-7224
info@wintechracing.com
www.wintechracing.com
• Howard Winklevoss, Chairman
• Gheorghe Anghel, Operations Manager
Rowing Sponsor:
Official Launch Supplier of United States Rowing teams.

WINTERLAND PRODUCTIONS
2 BRYANT STREET
SUITE 300
SAN FRANCISCO, CA 94105
415-247-7400
877-687-4277
Fax: 415-247-7407
• Dell Furano, Chief Executive Officer
• Phil Cussen, President / Chief Operating Officer
• Rick Fish, Artist Relations EVP
rfish@signaturesnet.com
• Django Bayless, New Media Technology / Artist Relations
dbayless@signaturesnet.com
Products:
General Sports Products - T-shirts

WISSOTA MANUFACTURING COMPANY
865 HIGHWAY 169 N
PLYMOUTH, MN 55441
763-545-1448
Fax: 763-545-1449
www.wissota.com
• William C Schuessler, President
Products:
Ice Skate Sharpener

WITTE GROUP
925 GOLF VIEW DRIVE
FOND DU LAC, WI 54935
920-923-0211
Fax: 920-923-6092
wittegroup@aol.com
• Jack Witte, President
• Mark Witte, Sales Representative
• Mike Witte, Sales Representative
• Carl Harland, Sales Representative
Products:
Baseball - Bases, Batting Helmets,
Plates-Home, Pitcher, Uniforms; Basketball
- Bags-Equipment, Balls-Other, Nets,
Uniforms; Facilities - Field Marking
Equipment; Field Hockey - Uniforms;
Football - Bags-Equipment, Balls-Other,
Helmets, Masks, Practice Equipment

WITTEK GOLF SUPPLY COMPANY
3865 COMMERCIAL AVENUE
NORTHBROOK, IL 60062
847-943-2399
800-869-1800
Fax: 847-412-9591
info@wittekgolf.com
www.wittekgolf.com
• Mike Hilliard, Vice President
• Tom Illies, Plant Manager, Production and
Quality Control
• Pat Wittek, Secretary / Treasurer
info@wittekgolf.com
• Steve Garske, President
info@wittekgolf.com
• Dan Brown, Sales Manager - Sales,
Marketing and Dealer R
Products:
Driving Range Equipment, Golf Course
Accessories, Display Fixtures & Miniature
Golf Supplies

WITZ® SPORT CASES
11282 PYRITES WAY
GOLD RIVER, CA 95670
916-638-0333
800-499-1568
Fax: 916-638-1250
trent@witzprod.com
www.witzprod.com
• Trent Weitz, President/Shareholder
(800) 499-1568
trent@witzprod.com
• Rob Henby, Vice President
(800) 499-1568
rob@witzprod.com
• Chris Cannon, VP of Sales
(800) 499-1568
chris@witzprod.com
Products:
Compact Cases, Contingency Cases,
Electronics Cases, Eyewear Cases, Utility
Cases, Cell Plate Cases, Passport Cases.
Year Founded:
1989

WOLVERINE WORLD WIDE
9341 COURTLAND DRIVE
HB-242
ROCKFORD, MI 49351
616-866-5500
800-789-8586
Fax: 616-866-5500
www.wolverineworldwide.com
• Timothy J O'Donovan, Chairman of the
Board
• Blake W Krueger, President and Chief
Operating Officer
(616) 866-5570
• Stephen L Gulis Jr, EVP, Chief Financial
Officer, and Treasu
• Blake W. P Krueger, Chairman of the
Board, Chief Executive Office
• R. Paul Guerre, Vice President, General
Counsel and Secretary
• Donald T. Grimes, Senior Vice President,
Chief Financial Office
• Robin J. Kleinjans-McKee, Vice President,
Corporate Planning and Analys
• Pamela L. Linton, Senior Vice President of
Global Human Resourc
• Michael Jeppesen, President, Global
Operations Group
• James D. Zwiers, Senior Vice President
and President, Outdoor
Products:
Athletic Footwear

WOMEN'S GOLF UNLIMITED, INC.
2801 E PLANO PARKWAY
PLANO, TX 75074
973-673-9600
888-894-8465
Fax: 973-227-7018
• Robert L Ross, Chairman / Chief
Executive Officer / Co-
• Richard M Maurer, Secretary /
Co-Managing Partner
• Douglas A Buffington, President / Chief
Operating Officer
Products:
Golf products and accessories

WOMENS GOLFWORKS
PO BOX 3008
NEWARK, OH 43058-3008
740-328-4193
800-848-8358
Fax: 740-323-0311
golfworks@golfworks.com
• Barbara Rathbun, President
Products:
Golf products and accessories such as
heads, shafts, grips & tools

WOODS TO WEDGES, INC.
8230 WEHRLE DRIVE
WILLIAMSVILLE, NY 14221
716-632-3021
Fax: 716-633-2693
• Donna Henrich, President
Products:
Golf Clubs-Iron or Wood Sets, Putters,
Utility and Custom Clubs

WOOLRICH, INC.
2 MILL STREET
WOOLRICH, PA 17779
877-512-7305
800-966-5372
Fax: 570-769-6234
service@woolrich.com
www.woolrich.com

• Richard Insley, Retail and Marketing SVP
• Michael Collin, President
(207) 612-4253
Products:
Athletic clothes and accessories for men,
women and children

WORLD CLASS ATHLETIC SURFACES
817 N BROAD STREET
PO BOX 152
LELAND, MS 38756
662-686-9997
800-748-9649
Fax: 662-686-9977
www.worldclasspaints.com
• David Simmons, President
david@worldclasspaints.com
Year Founded:
1989.
Products:
Full line of athletic field and court
accessories, including high-quality marking
paints, graphic stencils, tennis court coating
materials, and windscreens

WORLD DRYER CORPORATION
5700 MCDERMOTT DRIVE
BERKELEY, IL 60163
708-449-6950
800-323-0701
Fax: 708-449-6958
info@worlddryer.com
www.worlddryer.com
• Tom Vic, President
(708) 949-6950
• Stacey Hefford, Marketing Manager
(708) 949-6950
• Chris Berl, VP of Sales
(708) 949-6950
Products:
Complete line of sanitation products for
sports facilities, including warm air hand
dryers, both push-button and automatic,
automatic soap/lotion/chemical dispensers,
hair dryers and employee sensamatic hand
wash stations.
Description: AIRMAX HAND DRYER
The AirMax high speed hand dryer dries
hands in 15 seconds - half the time of
standard warm-air dryers. Delivering a
high-volume output of 275 CFM. AirMax
operates at the lowest noise level of similar
products. AirMax is available in surface
mount or ADA-compliant recessed models,
both push button and automatic activation.
Cover options include cast iron, stainless
steel and the newly offered colors of
WorldStone, which can also be customized.
Description: MODEL A
The Model A delivers high air velocity to
ensure quick hand drying. Other features
include trouble free operation, high volume
of 200 CFM, a universal type motor (1/10,
7,500 RPM), vandal resistant, and the
renowned Word Dryer durability and
engineering. Automatic dryer shuts off when
hands are removed to conserve energy
costs. Push button models are available.
Recessed models are ADA compliant.
Description: AIRSTYLE
The Airstyle hair dryers are designed for
health clubs, locker rooms and schools.
They are safe, efficient and feature a
high-powered 80-second push button drying
cycle. Available in both surface and recess
mounted, Airstyle hair dryers feature a
swivel nozzle that can be field converted to

the fixed position.
Description: DRY BABY
The DryBaby lines of baby changing stations are durable, easy to clean and built to deliver the World Dryer quality standards. They are designed to be easily maintained while providing a safe changing station. The new vertical changing station provides added space savings. The horizontal ABC-300 HC features plastic laminate inserts to compliment any d,cor.

WORLD FAMOUS TRADING COMPANY LTD.
1478 FAYETTE STREET
EL CAJON, CA 92020
619-448-6563
800-237-0151
800-748-5519
Fax: 619-448-6258
• Terry E Margeson, VP Marketing
Products:
Sporting, Athletic and Recreational Goods and Supplies

WORLD PROMOTIONAL PRODUCTS, INC.
17751 SKY PARK CIRCLE
SUITE F
IRVINE, CA 92614
800-705-7796
Fax: 949-221-0693
• Chris Tyler, Vice President
Description:
World Promotional Products provides logo and imprinted merchandise - services of which include graphic and creative design, screen print and embroidery.
Clients:
World Promotional Products works with many NBA, MLB, NHL and Fortune 500 companies.
Nature of Services:
Trade Shows; Employee Incentives; Events and Meetings; New Product Launches; Brand Marketing Initiatives; Award Programs; Golf and Charity Events.

WORLD SPORTING GOODS, INC.
PO BOX 579
STAPLETON, AL 36578
251-964-7100
800-633-1270
Fax: 251-964-6310
info@worldsportinggoods.com
www.worldsportinggoods.com
• Danny Forrest, Regional Sales Manager
• Mary Forrest, Marketing Director
Products:
Football Dummies, Practice Equipment, Practice Kick Cages, Sleds, Blockers, Barbells, Exercise Machines, Weight Belts

XL VIDEO, INC.
4025 WELCOME ALL ROAD
SUITE 170 BUILDING F
ATLANTA, GA 30349
404-629-3300
Fax: 404-629-3301
www.xlvideo.com
• John Lewis, Account Executive
(770) 795-7576
Products:
Video display systems for trade shows, outdoor events, indoor events, concert touring and television shows

XLM CORPORATION
1639 W SHERIDAN AVENUE
OKLAHOMA CITY, OK 73106
405-239-6141
800-223-3207
Fax: 888-561-6737
• Les Hibdon, Owner
Products:
Cycling Products

YARBOROUGH TIME LTD.
14 CLARKE CIRCLE
BETHEL, CT 6801
203-790-7444
800-431-1582
Fax: 203-778-8717
awardsetc@aol.com
• Martin Steinberg, President
• Rebecca Grinnals, Founder and President
Products:
Clocks, Golf Accessories, Lapel Pins, Medals, Plaques

YARRINGTON MILLS CORPORATION
412 S WARMINSTER ROAD
PO BOX 397
HATBORO, PA 19040
215-674-5125
800-962-3294
Fax: 215-674-0586
Sales@YarringtonMills.com
www.yarringtonmills.com
• James R Yarrington, President / General Manager
• Benjamin S Yarrington, Sales / Marketing Manager
Products:
General Sports Products - Fabrics and Trimmings used to make Award Jackets; Cheerleading Apparel, Uniforms (Team Sports), Warm-Up Suits

YEADON FABRIC STRUCTURES LTD.
KERR INDUSTRIAL PARK
RR 3
GUELPH, ONTARIO, CANADA N1H 6H9
519-821-9301
888-493-2366
888-493-2366
Fax: 519-821-9010
www.yeadondomes.com
• Steve Flanagan, President
• Milosh Nadvornik, President
Products:
Manufacturer and installer of air supported structures for all sports venues

YONEX CORPORATION
20140 S WESTERN AVENUE
TORRANCE, CA 90501
310-793-3800
800-449-6639
Fax: 310-793-3899
support@yonexusa.com
www.yonex.com
• Chitose Renge, EVP Marketing & Sales
• Violet Bernal, Credit
• Jay Tamiya, Customer Service Supervisor
• Minoru Yoneyama, Founding Honorary Chairman
• Ben Yoneyama, President
Products:
Golf Clubs-Iron or Wood Sets; Racquet Sports - Badminton and Tennis Racquets

Z COIL PAIN RELIEF FOOTWEAR
6932 4TH STREET NW
ALBUQUERQUE, NM 87107
505-345-2222
800-268-6239
877-628-1586
Fax: 505-345-2224
painfree@zcoil.com
www.zcoil.com
• Alvaro Gallegos, Chairman of the Board
(505) 838-5750
al@zcoil.com
• Andres A Gallegos, Executive VP
(505) 345-2222
andres@zcoil.com
• Thomas C Clausen, Chief Financial Officer
(505) 345-2222
tom@zcoil.com
• Jean-Paul de Jager, PR & Marketing
(505) 345-2222
jeanpaul@zcoil.com
Products:
Pain-relief shoes

ZAMBONI & COMPANY, INC., FRANK J.
15714 COLORADO AVENUE
PARAMOUNT, CA 90723-4211
562-633-0751
Fax: 562-633-9365
sales@zamboni.com
www.zamboni.com
• Richard Zamboni, President
• Frank J Zamboni, EVP
• Doug Peters, Regional Sales Manager
• Wayne Brewer, Operations Manager
Products:
Ice Rink Resurfacing Machines, Ice Rink Power Edgers, Maintenance Equipment for Astroturf

ZEBCO
6105 E APACHE
TULSA, OK 74115
918-836-5581
800-588-9030
Fax: 918-836-0154
email.zebco@zebco.com
www.zebco.com
• Ed Bedore, Sales VP
contact.zebco@zebco.com
• Steve Self, Regional Sales Manager
contact.zebco@zebco.com
• Ray Moore, Sales Manager
Products:
Fishing Accessories, Electric Motors, Reels, Rods

ZEPHYR GRAF-X INCORPORATED
5443 EARHART ROAD
LOVELAND, CO 80538
970-663-3242
888-282-0994
Fax: 970-663-7695
CustomerService@zhats.com
www.zhats.com
• David Gormley, President
• Wes Gormley, Vice President Product Development
• Jim Seilbach, Chief Financial Officer
Products:
All Headwear/Athletic Hats
Year Founded:
1993

ZEPPELIN PRODUCTS, INCORPORATED
3178 PEMBROKE ROAD
PEMBROKE PARK, FL 33009

954-989-8808
800-270-1477
Fax: 954-989-8578
Info@zeppro.com
www.zeppro.com
Products:
Leather belts, accessories, knives/money clips, sandals and pet products

ZERO GLOVES
605 W STONE AVENUE
PO BOX 500
FAIRFIELD, IA 52256-2223
641-472-3191
800-247-3383
Fax: 641-472-3194
www.zerogloves.com
• Nicole Hunt, Vice President
(800) 247-3383
Products:
Skiing-Alpine Accessories, Face Masks, Glvoes, KnitCaps hats, Skiing-Nordic Gloves, Snowboard Gloves, Prom-Optional Gloves, Youth Ski & Work Gloves, Face Masks, Baseball Caps, Head Bands, Sweatshirts, Tshirts.
Nature of Service:
Sells gloves to retail and manufacturing indutries.
Brands:
Zero Gloves & Mittens, FairField Line, Inc; websites: www.zerogloves.com and www.fairfieldlineinc.com

ZEROFLEX, INC.
3685 QUAIL ROAD NE
SUITE 200
SAUK RAPIDS, MN 56379
320-251-3080
877-251-3080
Fax: 320-654-1505
• James Donaghue, President
• Sean Donaghue, Sales Director
Products:
Outdoor Posts & Boards, Bike Racks, Benches, Picnic Tables

ZORREL INTERNATIONAL
13500 15TH STREET
GRANDVIEW, MO 64030-3082
816-765-5212
800-528-8688
Fax: 816-765-3228
info@zorrel.com
www.zorrel.com
• William Gardiner, VP
Products:
T-shirts

Software Manufacturers

AMERICAN WEIGHT AND MEASURES
16501 ZUMAQUE STREET
PO BOX 227
RANCHO SANTA FE, CA 92067
858-204-9699
800-395-4565
Fax: 858-756-0986
• Kenyon C. Clark, President
• Terry Bagley, Sales Manager
Products:
Cutting edge body composition analyzers
Brands:
Body Comp ScaleTM with Ohms Modulation Logic* Onboard

ARBITRON, INC.
85 BROAD STREET
NEW YORK, NY 10004
410-312-8000
800-864-1224
Fax: 410-312-8607
corporatepressinquiries@nielsen.com
www.nielsen.com
• Amanda Howell, Marketing Services Coordinator
(443) 312-8379
• Trisha Lawson, Sales Assistant
(443) 259-7536
• Mitch Barns, Chief Executive Officer

ATARI INC.
417 5TH AVENUE
FLOOR 7
NEW YORK, NY 10016-2204
212-726-6500
Fax: 212-252-8603
www.atari.com

BOOK4GOLF.COM, INC.
250 FERRAND DRIVE
SUITE 302
TORONTO, ON, CANADA M3C 3G8
416-421-5501
877-662-6654
Fax: 416-429-8457
www.book4golf.com

CONTEMPORARY RESEARCH
4355 EXCEL PKWY
SUITE 600
ADDISON, TX 75001
972-931-2728
888-972-2728
Fax: 972-931-2765
contact@crwww.com
www.contemporaryresearch.com
• Douglas Engstrom, Communications Director
(214) 556-6606
doug@crwww.com
Year Founded:
1993.
Nature of Service:
Designs and creates smart solutions for system integration and HDTV applications.

CRICHLOW DATA SCIENCES
926 E OLEANDER STREET
LAKELAND, FL 33801
863-616-1222
800-678-4535
Fax: 863-616-1219
sales@thegeneralstore.com
www.thegeneralstore.com
• Amanda Rutter, Sales Manager
(800) 678-4535
amanda.rutter@thegeneralstore.com
• Wade Walker, Technical Support Manager
(863) 616-1222
wade@thegeneralstore.com
• Ken Bundy, IT Manager
(863) 616-1222
ken@thegeneralstore.com
Products:
Offers the General Store, an accounting, inventory, POS and management software package for retailers.
Year Founded:
1983

CSI SERVICES/RICS SOFTWARE
4725 MERLE HAY ROAD
SUITE 101
DES MOINES, IA 50322
515-270-8182
800-654-3123
Fax: 515-270-1006
info@ricssoftware.com
• David Becker, Chairman of the Board/CEO
Products:
Developer of RICS. Offers retailers quality computer system.

DARTFISH USA
6505 SHILOH ROAD
SUITE 110-B
ALPHARETTA, GA 30005
404-685-9505
888-655-3850
Fax: 404-685-9130
usa@dartfish.com
www.dartfish.com
• Victor Bergonzoli, President/CEO
victor.bergonzoli@dartfish.com
• Ron Imbriale, Sales VP
usa@dartfish.com
• Mark Matoza, Golf Director
usa@dartfish.com
Products:
Sports electronics, including software programs.

DAXKO
600 UNIVERSITY PARK PLACE
SUITE 500
BIRMINGHAM, AL 35209
205-437-1400
877-729-4786
Fax: 205-437-0225
sales@daxko.com
www.daxko.com
• Tom Patterson, Founder/Chairman
• Anne Randall, Medical Fitness Account Executive
• Barry Thomason, Sales Director
• April Benetallo, Director Marketing/Product Management
• Erie Morring, Medical Fitness Account Executive
Organization
Daxko helps medical fitness centers build healthier communities by driving participation, increasing engagement levels and providing visability into constituents. Only Daxko offers a comprehensive engagement solution consisting of high-quality and customized communication services, best in class consulting and powerful software tools to increase member retention and patient to member conversion. Daxko customers grow 3x faster than centers not partnered with us. Building upon years of knowledge serving 500+ member-based organizations, nobody can touch Daxko's track record for successful project implementation amd amzaing ongoing service.
Sports Organizations served
YMCA's, JCC's, community centers and medical fitness centers.

EA SPORTS
209 REDWOOD SHORES PARKWAY
REDWOOD CITY, CA 94065
650-628-1500
800-959-7331

Fax: 650-628-1323
www.easports.com
• Peter Moore, President EA Sports
• Carolyn Feinstein,
(650) 628-7136
• Brian Movalson, Director of Marketing/EA
Sports
• John Riccitello, CEO
• Frank Gibeau, President of EA Labels
• Chris Erb, Vice President of Brand
Marketing
• David Tinson, Vice President of Corporate
Communications
• Craig Evans, Director of Marketing
• Randy Chase, Senior Product Marketing
Manager
Ice Hockey Sponsor:
NHL
Basketball Sponsor:
NBA, WNBA
College Sponsor:
NCAA Basketball, NCAA Football
Football Sponsor:
NFL

ELITE SPORTS ANALYSIS
59 THE BRIDGES
DALGETY BAY, FIFE, SCOTLAND KY11
9XZ
-44-823-937
sales@elitesportsanalysis.com
www.elitesportsanalysis.com
• David Allan, Sales Manager
dallan@elitesportsanalysis.com
Products:
Computer Systems/Software: Athletic
Training, Computer Systems/Software:
Coaching, Computer Systems/Software:
Conditioning, Computer Systems/Software:
Fitness Assessment, Computer
Systems/Software: Game Statistics,
Computer Systems/Software: Management,
Computer Systems/Software: Recruiting,
Computer Systems/Software: Scouting,
Computer Systems/Software: Strength,
Fitness Performance Testing: Performance
Testing Systems, Mental Training
Equipment, Videotaping Systems: Custom
Camera Systems, Videotaping Systems:
Digital Video Editing Systems, Videotaping
Systems: Video Editing Systems,
Videotaping Systems: Video Recorders

EMS SOFTWARE, LCC
6465 GREENWOOD PLAZA BLVD
SUITE 600
CENTENNIAL, CO 80111
303-771-0110
800-440-3994
Fax: 303-796-7429
sales@emssoftware.com
www.emssoftware.com
• Dean Evans, President
• Craig Halliday, Chief Executive Officer
• Tim Dillon, Vice President, Sales And
Marketing
• Dave Hurley, Executive Sales Director
• Larry Goldman, Director Of Product
Marketing
Year Founded & Description:
Founded in 1986, EMS Software produces a
room and resource scheduling platform
used for sports and meeting venues.

EVENT SOFTWARE
625 N GILBERT ROAD
SUITE 104
GILBERT, AZ 85234
480-517-9990
Fax: 480-517-9994
info@eventsoft.com
www.eventsoft.com

FITNESS VENTURE GROUP
4554 WEST VILLA THERESA DRIVE
GLENDALE, AZ 85308
602-753-5200
Fax: 602-492-9715
www.moreactive.com
• Don Hoskyns, President
• Don Hoskyns, Managing Partner
• John Domrzalski, Designer

ICONGO.COM
888 7TH AVENUE
10TH FLOOR
NEW YORK, NY 10106
312-265-5010
888-342-9457
Fax: 302-295-4801
sales@hybris.com
www.hybris.com
• Irwin Kramer, Chairman/CEO
• Steven Kramer, VP and Chief Technology
Officer
• Joshua Ostrega, VP, Operations
• Robert Rosenbloom, VP, Business
Development
Products:
Developer of e-business systems and
software

INFINITY PRO SPORTS
405 MITCHELL STREET
BRYAN, TX 77801
979-779-5200
Fax: 979-779-3329
info@infinityprosports.com
www.infinityprosports.com
• Joe Scott, Director of Sales
(979) 779-5024
• Susan Cagle, Head of Accounting
• Uri Geva, CEO
Nature of Services:
Infinity Pro Sports provides technologically
advanced web based software and services
to the professional and collegiate sports
industries including creating and developing
web-based solutions, data based marketing
software, online gaming, and real time
streaming for use in the sports industry.

INFUZER.COM, LLC
1300 S GROVE AVENUE
SUITE 204
BARRINGTON, IL 60010
847-898-9194
Fax: 847-277-0805
www.infuzer.com
• John Jocke, General Manager
(847) 898-9194
Description:
Infuzer allows fans to download season
schedules and off field events into an
Outlook, Palm or Lotus Notes calendar and
then will update the calendar entries with
updates, final scores or event time or date
changes.

INTERTICKET, INC.
2 GLENRIDGE DRIVE
BEDFORD, MA 01730
781-275-5724
info@interticket.com
www.interticket.com

MORE ACTIVE
3038 E CACTUS ROAD
PHOENIX, AZ 85032
602-867-1324
Fax: 602-867-3673
www.fitnessventuregroup.com
• Don Hoskyns, President
• Don Hoskyns, Managing Partner
• John Domrzalski, Designer

SNAPSPORTS, INC
2330 CALIFORNIA AVENUE
SALT LAKE CITY, UT 84104
801-746-7555
800-664-3865
Fax: 801-746-7559
info@snapsports.com
www.snapsports.com
• Jorgen Moller, CEO
• Kerry Moller, Chief Operating Officer
• Dan Wollman, Vice President, Sales
• Jeremiah Shapiro, Operations Director
jshapiro@snapsports.com
Description:
The leading manufacturer of suspended
modular indoor & outdoor athletic surfacing
& components. Used for Residential &
Commercial Sports Facilities; as well as
customized sports marketing events.

SOUND & VIDEO CREATIONS, INC
2820 AZALEA PLACE
NASHVILLE, TN 37204
615-460-7330
Fax: 615-460-7331
support@clickeffects.com
www.clickeffects.com
• Ed Filmia, Senior Director
Products:
Click Effects Pro-AV, Click Effects Audio,
Click Effects Replay

SPONSORSHIP PRO+
1954 AIRPORT ROAD
SUITE 207
ATLANTA, GA 30341
678-720-0700
Fax: 678-720-0704
www.sponsorshippro.com
• Tom Stipes, President
Nature of Services:
SponsorshipPRO+ is an easy-to-use and
innovative presentation software tool
designed for the sponsorship industry that
enables sponsorship sellers to identify,
organize, archive and present essential
marketing and media files to clients in a
dynamic format.
Nature of Services:
SponsorshipPRO+ is an easy-to-use and
innovative presentation software tool
designed for the sponsorship industry that
enables sponsorship sellers to identify,
organize, archive and present essential
marketing and media files to clients in a
dynamic format.

SPORTS SPECIFIC SCIENCES
5574 GOLF POINTE DRIVE
SARASOTA, FL 34243
941-351-7780
Fax: 841-240-2117
www.victortraining.com
• Brad Mayer, President
Products:
Software CD-ROM; SPRI Training
Equipment
Brands:
V.I.C.T.O.R.ia Trim & Tone 1.1;
V.I.C.T.O.R.ia Training Pack; Combination
V.I.C.T.O.R.ia Training Pack with
V.I.C.T.O.R.ia Trim & Tone Software;
V.I.C.T.O.R. Men's Fat Burner 1.1;
Combination V.I.C.T.O.R. Training Pack
with V.I.C.T.O.R. Men's Burner Software;
V.I.C.T.O.R. Men's Muscle Builder 1.1;
V.I.C.T.O.R. Golf 1.1; Combination
V.I.C.T.O.R. Training Pack with V.I.C.T.O.R.
Men's Golf Software; V.I.C.T.O.R. Baseball
1.1; Combination V.I.C.T.O.R. Training Pack
with V.I.C.T.O.R. Men's Baseball Software;
V.I.C.T.O.R. Hockey 1.1; Combination
V.I.C.T.O.R. Training Pack with V.I.C.T.O.R.
Hockey Software; V.I.C.T.O.R. Soccer 1.1;
Combination V.I.C.

SPORTS STATS INC.
900 N TUCKER BOULEVARD
SAINT LOUIS, MO 63101
314-340-8000
800-22 STATS
800-227-8287
Fax: 847-583-2600

STORIS MANAGEMENT SYSTEMS
400 VALLEY ROAD
SUITE 302
MT ARLINGTON, NJ 7856
973-601-8200
888-478-6747
Fax: 973-601-0078
www.storis.com
• Donald J Surdoval, CEO/President
• Donald J. Surdoval, President & Chief
Executive Officer
Products:
Management Systems

STRATBRIDGE, INC.
BLANCHARD HOUSE
SUITE 304
249 AYER ROAD
HARVARD, MA 1451
978-772-4647
Fax: 617-977-8630
• Matthew Marolda, Founder/Chief
Executive Officer
• Andrew H. Palmer, Strategy &
Sales/Marketing
• Thomas L. Doorley, III, Strategy &
Growth/Board of Directors
• Anthony J. Marolda, Strategy &
Planning/Board of Directors
• Matthew T. Marolda, CEO and Founder
Nature of Services:
StratBridge provides analytic solutions that
enable professional sports managers to
perform exhaustive diligence research at the
touch of a button - StratBridge.net, a
platform product, is a Web-native system
that seamlessly extracts data from internal
and external sources, regardless of format,
and then visually renders it in
high-resolution plasma displays.

Retailers

24 HOUR FITNESS CENTERS
12647 ACOSTA BOULEVARD
PO BOX 2689
CARLSBAD, CA 92018
925-543-3100
800-224-0240
Fax: 925-543-3200
info@24hourfitness.com
www.24hourfitness.com
• Carl Liebert, III, CEO
info@24hourfitness.com
• Craig Pepin-Donat, Sales and Marketing
EVP
info@24hourfitness.com
Products:
Fitness Accessories, Apparels, Electronics
and Nutritional Products

A&N STORES
6000 RIVER ROAD
SUITE B
RICHMOND, VA 23226
804-226-1324
800-326-1324
Fax: 804-222-4894
info@anstores.com
www.anstores.com
• Mark A Sternheimer, President
(804) 226-1324
info@anstores.com
• Ross Sternheimer, SVP
(804) 226-1324
Products:
Athletic Apparel.

**A-ATHLETIC AND MEDICAL SUPPLY
COMPANY**
406 LINK ROAD
HOUSTON, TX 77009
713-861-4777
800-225-9565
Fax: 713-861-7274
www.a-athletic.com
• Ken Mitschke, Sales Specialist Manager
(713) 861-4777
• Mary Dominguez, Finance/Accounts
Receiveable/Accounts Payable
(713) 861-4777
• Ken Mitschke, Sales Specialist/Manager
• Clarence Mitschke, Shipping and
Receiving
Products:
Athletic, medical and industrial supplies

ABERCROMBIE & FITCH CO.
4 LIMITED PARKWAY E
REYNOLDSBURG, OH 43068
614-577-6500
800-666-2595
Fax: 614-283-6710
www.abercrombie.com
• Mike Jeffries, President / Chief Operating
Officer
(614) 577-6500
Products:
Athletic - Rugged Apparel.

ACADEMY SPORTS & OUTDOORS
565 SOUTH MASON ROAD
#419
KATY, TX 77450
281-646-5200
888-922-2336
Fax: 281-646-5000

academy@academy.com
www.academy.com
• David Gochman, Chairman/CEO
academy@academy.com
• Jim Pierce, EVP / Chief Operating Officer
academy@academy.com
• Robert Frennea, Apparel EVP
academy@academy.com
• AJ Blanchard, Hardgoods EVP
academy@academy.com
Products:
Manufacturer of sporting goods.

ACE HARDWARE
2200 KENSINGTON COURT
OAK BROOK, IL 60523-2100
630-990-6600
866-290-5334
Fax: 630-990-6838
affiliates@acehardware.com
www.acehardware.com
• Ray Griffith, President / Chief Executive
Officer
(630) 990-6635
rgriff@acehardware.com
• Rita Kahle, EVP
(630) 990-2693
kahle@acehardware.com
• Art McGivern, SVP / General Counsel &
Secretary
(630) 990-5975
amcgive@acehardware.com
• J. Thomas Glenn, Chairman of the Board
Regional Member Directo
(630) 990-6646
dmyer@acehardware.com
• Ray A. Griffith, President and CEO
• Rita D. Kahle, Executive Vice President
• Jimmy Alexander, Vice President Human
Resources
• William J. Bauman, Vice President Retail
Support
• Lori L. Bossmann, Vice President
Merchandising, Marketing and A
• Ronald J. Knutson, Vice President Finance
Products:
Equipment and tools for Hardware,
Hand/Power Tools, Electrical, Plumbing,
Lawn and Garden, Cleaning Paint Supplies
and Housewares

ACE MAGNETICS.COM
PO BOX 230670
ENCINITAS, CA 92023
760-479-0202
800-599-9098
Fax: 760-942-0050
info@AceMagnetics.com
www.acemagnetics.com
• J. Robert Miktinj, President
info@AceMagnetics.com
Products:
Magnetic bracelets, copper bracelets,
magnetic jewelry worn by famous golfer Mr.
Arnold Palmer. Home of the lightest weight,
most powerful and waterproof patent
pending 'Rally Band.' AceMagnetics
provides a 60 day money back guarantee
and free magnetic bracelet with any $75
Purchase.

ACTION SPORTS COMPANY
12215 E. SKELLY DR.
TULSA, OK 74128
800-580-0307
Fax: 866-282-2444

sales@actionsportscompany.com
actionsportscompany.com
Description:
Batting Cages, Pitching Machines, Field Turf
and Equipment, Putting Greens, Golf Nets
and Mats, Pool Tables, Saunas and Spas,
Uniforms.
Year Founded:
1998

ACTION SPOT SPORTS
3080 MAIN STREET
BUFFALO, NY 14214
716-833-1787
800-249-1077
Fax: 716-8340-6167
info@actionspotsports.com
www.actionspotsports.com
• Miranda Michael, President
Products:
Custom Athletic Apparel For Professional
NHL Hockey & MLB Baseball Teams.

ADVENTURE 16, INC.
4620 ALVARADO CANYON ROAD
SAN DIEGO, CA 92120
619-283-2362 EXT 100
Fax: 619-283-2362
www.adventure16.com
• John D. D. Mead, President
jdmead@adventure16.com
Products:
Outdoor Outfits such as rain gear, whistle,
water bottle, first aid kit, flashlight, map and
compass, emergency blanket,
matches/match container, extra food, signal
mirror, cord, water purification, candle,
sunscreen, knife

ALLIANCE SPORTS GROUP
3025 N. GREAT SOUTHWEST PARKWAY
GRAND PRAIRIE, TX 75050
972-343-1000
800-255-6061
Fax: 972-343-1190
www.alliancesportsgroup.net
• Glenn Bollinger, Chairman / Chief
Executive Officer
• Bob Bollinger, President / Vice Chairman
Products:
Training & Conditioning - Curl Bars,
Dumbbells, Jogging, Mats, Solar Belt/Shorts
& Wraps, Weight Lifting Belts,
Weights-Legs, Ankle.

ALTREC.COM
725 SW UMATILLA AVENUE
SUITE 1000
REDMOND, OR 97756
541-316-2400
800-369-3949
Fax: 800-783-4217
• Mike Morford, Chief Executive Officer
• Tim Shannon, Operations Director
• Mary Fischer, Controller
Products:
Specializes in active adventure sports,
e-commerce and editorial content covering
11 different categories. Jackets, Fleece,
Shirts, Pants, Shoes, Gloves, Long
Underwear, Hats, Socks, Shoes (such as:
Casual Walking, Running Shoes, Trail
Running Shoes, Hiking Boots, Snow Boots,
Ski Boots, Snowboarding Boots, Kids'
Shoes, Sandals, Water Shoes, Sandals),
Gears (such as: Ski, Snowboard,
Snowshoe, Camp & Hike, Climb, Running,

Paddle, Cycle, Beach, Wakeboarding,
Travel, Pet Gear, Gift Ideas

AMAPRO SPORTING GOODS, INC.
242-A ROUTE 109
FARMINGDALE, NY 11735
631-777-1352
800-426-2776
Fax: 631-777-1353
www.amaprosports.com
• Gary Krupsky, President
Products:
Baseball, Basketball, Softball, Volleyball,
etc- uniforms, jackets, hats & equipment.
Description:
Retail/Wholesale Selling Team Sports
Dealer

AMENIA ARCHERY
5058 NEW YORK 22
AMENIA, NY 12501
845-373-9262
Fax: 845-373-9265
ameniaarchery@yahoo.com
• Anthony Robert, Owner
(845) 373-9262
ameniaarchery@yahoo.com

AMERICAN EAGLE OUTFITTERS
77 HOT METAL STREET
PITTSBURGH, PA 15203
724-776-4857
888-232-4535
Fax: 724-779-5585
custserv@ae.com
www.ae.com
• Roger Markfield, President
• Susan Miller, Merchandising EVP
• Fred Grover, General Merchandise
Manager
• Jenny N, Aerie Accessories Manager
• Laurie Z, Senior PR Manager
• Brandon A., Creative Director
• Paul E., Director of Marketing Stratergies
Products:
Men's and Women's apparel, shoes,
accessories, belts and flip-flops

AMERICAN SPORTING GOODS
COMPANY
2323 MAIN STREET
IRVINE, CA 92614
949-752-6688
800-848-8698
Fax: 949-756-8609
• Margaret Oung, Owner
• Jerry Turner, President
Products:
Outdoor Products - Hiking Boots, Outdoor
Crosstraining; Racquet Sports - Shoes;
Track & Field/Running - Shoes; Training &
Conditioning - Shoes-Aerobic,
Shoes-Crosstraining.

ANACONDA SPORTS
85 KATRINE LANE
LAKE KATRINE, NY 12449
845-336-4024
800-327-0074
Fax: 845-336-4593
• Rob Meyer, Internet Services Director
(203) 926-0249
• Don McGowan, Sales Manager
Products:
Full Line Sporting Goods, apparels and
accessories for baseball, basketball, field

hockey, football, soccer, softball, track and
field, volleyball, wrestling.

ANC SPORTS ENTERPRISES
2 MANHATTANVILLE ROAD
SUITE 402
PURCHASE, NY 10577
914-696-2100
Fax: 914-696-2101
www.ancsports.com
• Jerome Cifarelli, President & Chief
Executive Officer
jcifarelli@ancsports.com
• Daniel Fumai, Executive Vice President,
Finance
dfumai@ancsports.com
• Christopher Mascatello, Executive Vice
President, Technology Sales
cmascatello@ancsports.com
• Mark J. Stross, Chief Technology Officer
mstross@ancsports.com
Services:
Provides a variety of active signage to
sports stadiums, from standard courtside
and field-level rotational signage, to backlit
rotational signage ranging from ribbon to
jumbo sized, and video based LED signage
system. Offers teams, facilities, broadcaste

ANY MOUNTAIN, LTD
71 TAMAL VISTA BOULEVARD
CORTE MADERA, CA 94925
415-927-0170
Fax: 415-927-0170
• Bruno Gotzmer, Area Manager
bgotzmer@ssv.net
• Bruno Gotzmer, RegionalÿManager
• Chi McClean, Sales & Marketing Manager
Products:
Outdoor, ski and snowboard equipment,
apparel and accessories.

ATHLETA, LLC
5900 NORTH MEADOWS DRIVE
GROVE CITY, OH 43123
707-769-2610
877-328-4538
Fax: 707-769-2610
info@athleta.com
www.athleta.gap.com
• Scott Kerslake, President / Chief Executive
Officer
info@athleta.com
• Tami Anderson, Marketing Director
info@athleta.com
Products:
Sports gears, apparrels and accessories for
women.

ATHLETE'S FOOT
3200 WINDY HILL ROAD SE
SUITE 175E
ATLANTA, GA 30339
800-524-6444
888-801-9157
Fax: 770-514-4903
franchise.info@theathletesfoot.com
www.theathletesfoot.com
• Robert J Corliss, President / Chief
Executive Officer
franchiseinfo@theathletesfoot.com
• Don Camacho, Chief Financial Officer
franchiseinfo@theathletesfoot.com
• Robert J. Corliss, CEO
franchiseinfo@theathletesfoot.com
Products:
Athletic footwear

ATHLETIC DEALERS OF AMERICA
5423 VILLAGE DRIVE
ROCKLEDGE, FL 32955-6570
321-254-0091 EXT 304
Fax: 321-242-7419
• Peter Schneider, President
(321) 254-0091
Nature of Service:
Buying Group
Year Founded:
1980.
Products:
Team Athletic Sporting Goods
Brands:
Adams USA, All Star, ATEC Bison, Brine, Champion Sports, Diamond, Easton, Louieville Slugger, JKP/Jugs, Mikasa, Pro Team, Rawlings, Schutt Sports, Spalding, Tachikara, TC Sports, Under Armour, Wilson.

AUBURN LEATHER COMPANY
125 CALDWELL STREET
PO BOX 338
AUBURN, KY 42206-0338
270-542-4116
800-635-0617
Fax: 270-542-7107
Sales1@auburnleather.com
www.auburnleather.com
• Lisa Howlett, President
sales1@auburnleather.com
• Ida Elliott, VP
sales1@auburnleather.com
• Lisa Howlett, President
Products:
Leather Laces, Leather motorcycle saddlebags, Horse Headstalls, Horse Breaststraps, Reins, Training/Misc. Equipment, Trail Tack, Saddle Accessories, Halters and Leads, Arabian Tack, Saddle Bags, Scabbards, Livestock Equipment, Cowboy Up, Leather
Brands:
Lace & Latigo Leather, Rawhide, Skirting Leather, Strap Leather, Latigo Leather, Harness Leather

AUSTAD'S GOLF STORE'S
8851 E 34TH ST N
WICHITA, KS 67226
316-838-5557
800-444-1234
Fax: 316-838-5557
www.austads.com
• Dave Austad, President
customerservice@austads.com
• Pat Penney, VP / Chief Financial Officer
• Tim Madden, Sales Officer
Products:
Golf Clubs, Golf Balls, Golf Shoes, Golf Apparel, Gifts for Golfers, Golf Bags & Transport
Brands:
TAYLORMADE RAC OS 2 IRONS (3-PW) - RH STEEL, CALLAWAY '04 BIG BERTHA IRONS (4-10 W) - RH STEEL, TITLEIST VOKEY BLACK NICKEL WEDGE - RH STEEL, TAYLORMADE R580 XD DRIVER - RH GRAPHITE, CALLAWAY WOMEN'S GAME ENJOYMENT SYSTEM - RH GRAPHITE, TAYLORMADE r7 QUAD 400cc TITANIUM DRIVER - RH GRAPHITE, ODYSSEY WHITE STEEL 2-BALL BLADE PUTTER - RH, ADAMS IDEA A2OS IRON SET (3-4 IW, 5-PW) - RH STEEL, PING G5 460cc TITANIUM DRIVER W/ ALDILA NV65

SHAFT - RH GRAPHITE, CALLAWAY HX TOUR GOLF BALLS, CALLAWAY HX GOLF BALLS, NIKE ONE BLACK GOLF BALL, NIKE MOJO GOLF BALLS 2, PRECEPT PWRDRIVE GOLF BALLS, NIKE ONE PLATINUM GOLF BALL, MAXFLI BLACK MAX GOLF BALLS, TOP

AUSTAD'S GOLF/CATALOG
2801 E 10TH STREET
SIOUX FALLS, SD 57103
316-838-5557
800-444-1234
Fax: 316-838-5557
www.austads.com
• Dave Austad, President
customerservice@austads.com
Products:
Golf Accessories, Golf Apparel, Golf Bags & Transport, Golf Carts, Golf Clubs, Gifts for Golfers, Gift Cards, Golf Gloves, Golf Training Aides, Golf Shoes, Golf Books/Videos
Brands:
ZIVOT STEEL DIVOT TOOL, 6 FOOT POCKET BALL RETRIEVER, TRUNK-IT GOLF GEAR CASE, WIND VENT GOLF UMBRELLA - BLACK/WHITE, GOLFERS WALKING CHAIR, BOXING GLOVE HEADCOVER, FOOTJOY SHOE BAG, NEOPRENE IRON COVERS, ZERO FRICTION GOLF TEE, ARSENAL ULTRALITE STAND BAG, RJ SPORTS WHEELED TRAVEL COVER, SUN MOUNTAIN SPEED CART, RJ SPORTS DELUXE GOLF PULL CART, ARSENAL PREMIUM STAND BAG, SUN MOUNTAIN A-5 STAND BAG, TAYLORMADE TAYLITE 3.5 STAND BAG, TITLEIST X56 3.9 LB STAND BAG, NIKE XTREME SPORT STAND BAG, SUN MOUNTAIN SPEED CART, RJ SPORTS DELUXE GOLF PULL CART, BAG BOY M-310 PULL CART, SUN MOUNTAIN SPEED CART UMBRELLA ATTACHMENT, BAG BOY JUNIOR 3 WHEELED

AUTHENTIC SPORTS INVESTMENTS
28801 US HIGHWAY 19, N
CLEARWATER, FL 33761
727-785-5532
Fax: 727-785-3259
authenticsportsinv@yahoo.com
• Scot Monette, President
• Brad Wells, Executive VP
Description:
Sports Marketing and memorabilia company. Authentic game used and signed memorabilia.
Services Include:
Product Endorsement, Radio/TV Advertisement, Charity/Foundation development, Corporate Player Appearances, Personalized Product Lines, Personal/Client Gifts.

BANKSHOT SPORTS ORGANIZATION
330U N. STONESTREET AVE
SUITE 504
ROCKVILLE, MD 20850
301-309-0260
800-933-0140
Fax: 301-309-0263
bankshotsports@aol.com
www.bankshot.com
• Reeve R. Brenner, Founder/President
bankshotbb@aol.com

• Alan Ray, Technical Director
• Michelle Worthy, Office Manager
Products:
Permanent Courts, Portable Courts, Bankshot On-A-Roll Trailer Stations, Dunkshot Stations, Bankshot Tennis Stations, Bankshot TriúSport Stations, Player Mats
Brands:
Bank-Around-The-Clock, Bankshot Classic, Junior Classic, Shoot-Around, Six-Pack, Three-Pack, Portable Junior Classic, Portable Shoot-Around, Portable Pro-Pack

BASE MOUNTAIN SPORTS
76 AVONDALE LANE
BEAVER CREEK, CO 81620
970-949-4327
877-255-0159
Fax: 970-949-1691
www.basemountainsports.com
• John M Trtanj, President
Products:
Apparel, Ski/Snowboard
Brands:
Arcteryx, Bogner, Descente, Obermeyer, Killy, Icelandic, Marmot, Oakley, Patagonia, Rossignol, Skea, Tommy Bahama, Atomic, Dalbello, Marker, Volkl, Rossignol, Salomon, Tecnica, Marmot, K2, Burton, Dakine, Liberty, Leki, Armada, Oakley, Grandoe, Swany, Maui Jim, Smith

BASEBALLJUNK.COM
2023 S COOPER
ARLINGTON, TX 76010
817-303-6620
800-850-5007
Fax: 206-666-6508
sportjunk@gmail.com
www.baseballjunk.com
• Gary Leland, Owner / President
Products:
Sports apparel, accessories, training aids and equipments
Brands:
DeMarini Diablo 2006 -3, DeMarini Diablo 2005 -5, DeMarini Nitro -3, DeMarini 2006 Vexxum -3, DeMarini 2005 Vexxum -3, DeMarini 2005 Vexxum -5, DeMarini Voodoo, Easton 2005 Stealth Stiff Flex -3, Easton 2006 Havoc -3, Easton 2005 Havoc -3, Easton 2005 Stealth Regular Flex-3, Easton 2006 Stealth Regular Flex-3, Easton 2006 Stealth Stiff Flex-3, Easton Triple 8 - Adult, Easton -3 Triple 7, Louisville Slugger Armor TPX, Louisville Slugger Dynasty Transition -5, Louisville Slugger Dynasty, 2006 Louisville Slugger Air Omaha, 2006 Louisville Slugger Omaha, Miken Freak, Rawlings Liquidmetal Plasma, Worth Asylum -3, Rawlings BGP350 All, Rawlings The

BASS PRO SHOPS
2500 E KEARNEY
SPRINGFIELD, MO 65898
417-873-4383
800-227-7776
Fax: 417-873-4672
www.basspro.com
• John Morris, Founder
• James Hagale, CEO/President
• Stan Lippelman, Vice President Of Marketing
• Larry Whitely, Manager Of Communications and Outdoor Education

• Jenna Kendall, Media Informations Coordinator
Baseball Sponsor:
MLB St Louis Cardinals
Fishing Sponsor:
National Hunting and Fishing Day.
Brands:
Johnny Morris Signature Series Trigger Rods, Qualifier XPSTM Trigger R, Tourney Special Graphite Rods, ExtremeTM XPSTM Woo Dav, ExtremeTM XPSTM Trigger, Browning Fishing Citori Trigger Rods, Browning Fishing SilaFlex Trigger Rods, Bass Pro Shops Johnny Morris Signature Series Spinning Rods, Bass Pro Shops Pro Qualifier XPSTM Spinning, Bass Pro Shops ExtremeTM XPSTM Spinnin, Bass Pro Shops ExtremeTM XPSTM Travel, Bass Pro Shops ExtremeTM XPSTM Woo Dav, Bass Pro Shops Micro LiteTM Graphite Spinning Rod, Browning Fishing Citori Spinning Rods, Browning Fishing SilaFlex Spinning Rods, Bass Pro Shops Tourney Special Premium Graphite Casting, Bass P
Products:
Rods, Reels, Combos, Lures, Rainwear & Footwear, Flies & Kits, Watercraft, Fly Fishing Apparel, Waders & Accessories, Sunglasses, Optics, Black Powder, Shooting Accessories, Decoys & Calls, Treestands, Hunting Videos & Books, Hunting Clothing, Hunting Outerwear, Hunting Boots, Tents, Packs & Bags, Sleeping Bags & Beds, Metal Detectors, Canoes & Kayaks, Paddles & Oars, Canoe & Kayak Accessories, GPS Units, GPS Accessories, Radio & Accessories, Lanterns, Headlamps, Spotlights, Flashlights, Dehydrators, Vacuum Sealers, Kitchen Accesories, Apparel, Footwear.
Sponsor:
Bass Pro Shops Bassmaster Open

BEACON BALLFIELDS
8233 FORSYTHIA ST.
SUITE 120
MIDDLETON, WI 53562
608-824-0068
800-747-5985
Fax: 608-836-0724
info@beaconathletics.com
www.beaconathletics.com
• Jim Myrland, Owner
• Paul Zwaska, Sales Manager
pzwaska@beaconathletics.com
• Benji Brye, Custom Products & Service Specialist
bbrye@beaconathletics.com
• Elizabeth Blum, Custom Products & Service Specialist
eblum@beaconathletics.com
Products:
Field Maintenance & Facilities, Training/Sports Conditioning Equipment, Batting Cages & Accessories, Netting, Windscreen, Padding, Portable Protective Screens & Backstops, Bases, Pitching, Home Plates, Foul Poles, Turf Protection & Practice Mats, Portable Pitching Mounds, Dugouts & Accessories, Football & Soccer Equipment, Golf Equipment & Accessories
Brands:
Beacon Team Cart, SMART HURDLE #3, SMART HURDLE #4, SMART HURDLE #5, SET OF 4 CROOKED STICKS WITH HANDLE, VOICE BLASTER, BEACON INDOOR TENSIONED SOFTBALL BATTING CAGE 55, BEACON INDOOR TENSIONED BASEBALL BATTING CAGE 70, BEACON DOUBLE BATTING CAGE 55 W/POLES, BEACON DOUBLE BATTING CAGE 70 W/POLES, BEACON DOUBLE BATTING CAGE 55 W/O POLES, BEACON DOUBLE BATTING CAGE 70 W/O POLES, BEACON BATTING CAGE 55 SOFT TOSS NET, BEACON BATTING CAGE 70 SOFT TOSS NET, BEACON INDOOR CAGE 55, 4-FRAME FREESTANDING SOFTBALL CAGE, UNPAINTED, BEACON INDOOR CAGE 55, 4-FRAME FREESTANDING SOFTBALL CAGE, POWDER-COAT PAINT, BEACON 5-FRAME FREESTANDING BASEBALL CAGE UNP

BEALLS ENTERPRISES DEPARTMENT STORES
1806 38TH AVENUE E
BRADENTON, FL 34208
941-747-2355
Fax: 941-746-1171
www.beallsinc.com
• Bob Beall, President / Chief Executive Officer
• Jonny Ortiz, Director of EDI/Merchandise Support
Products:
Misses Apparel, Petite Apparel, Positively Plus Apparel, Juniors Apparel, Lingerie, Jewelry & Watches, Sleepwear, Swimwear, Mens Apparel, Big Mens Apparel, Young Mens Apparel, Sleep & Loungewear, Underwear & Socks, Shoes
Brands:
Adidas, Grasshoppers, ParadiseBay, Aerosoles, Keds, Reebok, BayStudio, KSwiss, Roxy, Bongo, LifeStride, Skechers, CBCollections, Naturalizer, Sperry, Columbia, Nike, SunBay, Converse, NineAndCompany, UnionBay, Dockers, ONeill, EasySpirit, Outlooks, EmmaJames, NewYorkLaundry, AlfredDunner, GloriaVanderbilt, Alia, Haggar, NineAndCompany, Izod, Notations, CaribbeanJoe, JHCollectibles, ParadiseBay, CathyDaniels, Koret, SagHarbor, Lee, Levis, LizClaiborne, Jantzen, ParadiseBay, SuitYourself, SunBay

---

BEGNI'RS TO PRO'S
STONERIDGE PLAZA
ROCHESTER, NY 14615
585-663-1020
877-663-1020
Fax: 585-663-0058
service@beginrstopros.com
www.beginrstopros.com
• Brad Buckert, Owner
Products:
Balls, Bags, Shoes, Gloves & Supports, Grips, Cleaners, Polishes, Accessories.

BEI GROUP, INC./BASEBALL EXPRESS, INC.
1003 E NAKOMA
SUITE 104
SAN ANTONIO, TX 78216
210-525-9161
800-937-4824
Fax: 210-344-9080
customer.service@baseballexpress.com
• Fred Lummis, Chairman
• Pat Cowles, President
Products:
Baseball Bats, Baseball Gloves, Baseball Footwear, Baseball Accessories, Baseball Apparel, Baseball Bags, Baseball Caps & Visors, Baseball Training Aids, Baseball Uniforms, Baseballs, Batting Gloves, Batting Helmets, Catcher's Gear, Field Equipment, Gifts & Novelty, Sports Medicine
Brands:
LOUISVILLE 06 EXOGRID -3 BAT, LOUISVILLE 06 DYNASTY ADULT -3 BAT, EASTON 06 STEALTH CNT REG FLEX -3 BAT, EASTON 06 STEALTH CNT STIFF FLEX -3 BAT, LOUISVILLE 06 OMAHA ADULT -3 BAT, DEMARINI 06 VEXXUM ADULT -3 BAT, RAWLINGS 06 LIQUIDMETAL PLASMA -3 BAT, LOUISVILLE 06 AIR OMAHA ADULT -3 BAT, DEMARINI 06 VOODOO BASEBALL -3 BAT, MIZUNO 9SPIKE PRO LIMITED LOW 04 BLK/WHT, NIKE 06 AIR HUARACHE 2K4 BLK/WHT/SIL, NIKE 06 SHOX MONSTER METAL BLK/WHT, MIZUNO 05 CHIPPER 9 SPIKE G3 SPIKE, MIZUNO 9 SPIKE VAPOR MID 04 BLK/SIL, MIZUNO 9 SIKE VAPOR LOW 04 BLK/SIL, ADIDAS 05 EXCELSIOR MID METAL BLK/WHT, ADIDAS 05 EXCELSIOR MID METAL BLK/BLK, ADIDAS 05 EXCELSIOR

BELK STORES SERVICES
2801 W TYVOLA ROAD
PO BOX 1099
CHARLOTTE, NC 28201-1099
704-357-1000
866-235-5443
800-669-6550
Fax: 800-633-8141
belk_customer_care@belk.com
www.belk.com
• John R Belk, President/COO
• Mary R Delk, Merchandising & Marketing President
• Thomas M Belk, Chairman and Chief Executive Officer
• H.W. McKay Belk, President

BELLA BAGNO, INC.
5500 W TOUHY AVENUE
SUITE E
SKOKIE, IL 60077
847-673-7328
Fax: 847-673-7338
customerservice@bellabagno.com
www.bellabagno.com
• Cythia Lazarus, President
customerservice@bellabagno.com
• Cynthia Lazarus, Sales & Marketing Officer
customerservice@bellabagno.com
Products:
Sanitary System
Brands:
Bella Bagno hygoletr Sanitary System

BERNEY-KARP, INCORPORATED
3350 E 26TH STREET
VERNON, CA 90058
323-260-7122
800-237-6395
Fax: 323-260-7245
art@ceramic-source.com
www.ceramic-source.com
• Anna Ramos, VP Sales/Marketing
(323) 260-7122
annar@ceramic-source.com
Products:
Ceramics, Acrylics, Bottles, Stainlesswares, Glasswares
Brands:

60-211RB Pink Ribbon, 60-211RB Yellow Ribbon, 60-211GE Nose Mug, 60-331 Hand Grip Mug, 60-211B Light Bulb, 60-211H Hammer, 60-281TU Thumb, 60-278 VB Vertebrae, 60-211I Hammer, 60-211E Paint Brush, 60-211L Wrench, 60-211F Phone, 60-211SC Spine, 60-211CA Caduceus, 60-211ER Ear, 60-211SP Safety Pin, 60-211CM Computer Mouse, 60-211C Cellular, 60-211CW Cow, 60-211EG Eagle, 60-211HH Horse, 60-211BR Bear, 60-211LN Lion, 60-211EL Elephant, 60-281PT Palm Tree, 60-211G Nose, 60-211PB Dow Paw, 60-512 Gas Pump, 62-713-2, 62-625-2, 62-693-3, 62-811-2, 62-632-2, 62-605-3, 62-652-2, 62-689-2, 62-696, 62-694, 62-694-3, 62-709-3, 62-683, 62-708, 62-612-2, 62-

BEST BIKE BUYS
1150 FOOTHILL BOULEVARD
SUITE J
LA CANADA, CA 91001
626-296-6260
webmaster@bestwebbuys.com
www.bestwebbuys.com
• Steve Loyola, President/CEO/Founder
• Audrey Gubler, VP of Market Research
• Sugi Sorensen, VP of Engineering
• David Werntz, Chief Technology Officer
• Steve Loyola, President/CEO/Founder

BI-MART
1680 W. 18TH
EUGENE, OR 97402
541-342-2687
800-456-0681
Fax: 541-342-4241
comments@bimart.com
www.bimart.com
• Marty W Smith, Chairman & Chief Executive Officer
Products:
Photo Products, Housewares, Sporting Goods, Automotive, Hardware, Health & Beauty Products, Toys, Clothing/Shoes, Beer/Food/Wine, Pharmacy Products, Bed & Bath, Baby Goods, Furnitures, Personal Care Appliances, Watches & Clocks, Weather Instruments, Pet Supplies
Brands:
Abu Garcia, Casio, Century, Davidson Ladder, DeLonghi, Dreamer Design, Eagle Electronics, Haier, More Aire, Nikon, Oregon Scientific, Samsung, Schwinn

BICYCLE EXCHANGE, INC.
2034 EISENHOWER AVENUE
SUITE 250
ALEXANDRIA, VA 22314
703-924-5153
888-424-5387
Fax: 703-548-6980
• Jim Bellas, President

BIG 5 SPORTING GOODS
2525 EL SEGUNDO BOULEVARD
EL SEGUNDO, CA 90245
310-536-0611
Fax: 310-297-7585
info@big5sportinggoods.com
www.big5sportinggoods.com
• Steven G Miller, Chairman / President / Chief Executive O
• Gary S Meade, SVP / Secretary / General Counsel

• Richard A Johnson, Store Operations SVP
• Thomas J Schlauch, SVP - Buying
Products:
Provides a full-line brand name sporting goods products including athletic shoes, apparel, team sports equipment, fitness, camping, hunting, fishing, tennis, golf, snowboarding and in-line skating equipment.
Brands:
Adidas, Oasis, Bauer, Body Gloves, Brooks, Yonex, Browning, Bushnell, Coleman, Wilson, Ultra, Converse, Dunlop, Easton, Edelweiss, Everlast, Fila, Titleist, Speedo, Spalding, Shimano, Saucony, RollerBlade, Head, LouisvilleSlugger, Jansport, Hi-Tec, Reebok, Rawlings, Mizuno, Remington, Lifetime, Nike

BIGG'S HYPER SHOPPES
25 WHITNEY DRIVE
SUITE 122
MILFORD, OH 45150
513-248-9300
Fax: 513-248-9731
www.biggshyper.com
• Pierre A Wevers, President
• Paul McHugh, Divisional Merchandise Manager
• Cindy Oplinger, Divisional Merchandise Manager
Products:
Grocery, Clothing, Durable Goods, Auto/Harware, Electronics, Floral, Garden, Movies, Seasonal, Sporting Goods, Stationery, Toys

BIKE LINE
T 117-119 TURNER LN
TURNER SQUARE SHOPPING CENTER
WEST CHESTER, PA 19380
610-436-8984
800-537-2654
Fax: 610-429-4295
www.bikeline.com
• John W Graves, President / Chief Executive Officer
Products:
Premier chain of bicycles and fitness stores. Offers cycling apparel and accessories. Also promotes and suports many rides and local cycling and fitness events.
Brands:
Trek/Nike, Sugoi, and PearlIzumi

BIKEBOARD COMPANY
PO BOX 8597
NEWPORT BEACH, CA 92658
714-568-1300
Fax: 714-568-1304
www.thebikeboard.com
Products:
Manufacturer of Bikeboards, Accessories and Clothing.
Brands:
BikeBoard

BIRKENSTOCK FOOTPRINT SANDALS INC.
8171 REDWOOD BOULEVARD
PO BOX 6140
NOVATO, CA 94945
415-892-4200
800-867-2475
Fax: 415-899-1324
info@birkenstockusa.com
www.birkenstockusa.com

• Margot Fraser, Founder
• Matt Endriss, President / Chief Executive Officer
• Gene Kunde, Chief Operating Officer
• Patrick Hull, Marketing Senior Director
Products:
Footwear, Socks, Shoes, Sandals, Insoles & Arch Supports and Clogs for women, men and kids
Brands:
Birkenstock, J. Garcia, Heidi Klum

BJ'S WHOLESALE CLUB, INC.
1 MERCER ROAD
PO BOX 9601
NATICK, MA 1760
508-651-7400
Fax: 508-651-6114
• Michael T Wedge, President / Chief Executive Officer
• Herbert J Zarkin, Chairman
• Ronald R Dion, Director
• Bert N Mitchell, Director
Products & Services:
A wholesale club chains. Also a marketer of general products like Apparel, Automotive, Baby's Accessories, Computers & Cameras, Gift Cards, Electronics, Groceries & Gourment Foods, Gas & Propane, Household Basics, Jewelry & Gifts, Pets, Office Supplies, Toys. Business Services include: Healthcare Savings Network, Photo Services, Merchant Payment Processing and Service Agreements-BJ's Protection Plus.
Brands:
For Apparel: Jake & Julia, Generation Me, Lanesboro, Taylor Marcs. For Automotive: Exide, ACDelco. For Baby's Accessories: Eddie Bauer, Munchkin, Nuby. For cameras & computers: Brother, Sharp, BUSlink, Sony, Canon, Konica, Kodak, Nikon,Fuji

BLUE DOLPHIN DISTRIBUTORS
221 BLUE JUNIPER BOULEVARD
VENICE, FL 34292
941-484-2229
866-496-7900
Fax: 941-484-2207
Products:
Sporting Goods products such as New York Yankees Talking Bottle Opener, Alabama Crimson Tide Crimson Bottle Holder, Dallas Cowboys Blue Neoprene Bottle Holder, Oklahoma Sooners Musical Bottle Opener, South Carolina Gamecocks Musical Bottle Opener, Florida Gators Musical Bottle Opener, San Francisco 49ers Black Team Logo Neoprene Bottle Coozie, Georgia Bulldogs Red Bottle Holder W/'G'

BLUE RIBBON BLANKETS
120-B MAST STREET
UNIT B
MORGAN HILL, CA 95037
408-779-1997
800-437-6676
Fax: 408-778-5665
www.royalriders.com
Year Founded:
1977.
Products:
Official Riding Blankets for United States Equestrian Federation.

BLUEFLY, INC.
42 W 39TH STREET
9TH FLOOR
NEW YORK, NY 10018
212-944-8000
877-258-3359
Fax: 212-354-3400
flyrep@bluefly.com
www.bluefly.com
• Alan Kane, Chairman of the Board
• Melissa Payner-Gregor, President / Chief
Executive Officer
• Patrick C Barry, Chief Financial Officer /
Chief Operatin
(212) 944-8000
pat@bluefly.com
• Melissa Payner, President & CEO
Products:
Marketer of brand name designer apparel,
bags, footwear and other general sports
products.
Brands:
Prada, Vera Wang, Nicole Miller, Gucci,
Fendi, Elie Tahari, Giuseppe Zanotti

BOATER'S WORLD
6711 RITZ WAY
BELTSVILLE, MD 20705
877-690-0004
877-999-7489
Fax: 877-552-2244
customerservice@ritzcamera.com
www.boatersworld.com
• Andre Brysha, VP / Chief Marketing Officer
brysha@RitzInteractive.com
Products:
Specializes in fishing tackle, marine
electronics, water sports gear and cruising
equipment for recreational boaters.

BOB WARD & SONS, INC.
3015 PAXSON STREET
MISSOULA, MT 59801
406-728-3220
800-800-5083
Fax: 406-728-5230
www.bobwards.com
• Keith Ward, President
• Chad Ward, Operations VP
• Gary Koprivica, General Manager
• Keith Dustrud, Buyer
Products:
Sporting Goods, Men's & Women's
Clothing, Footwear, Watches, Apparel &
Accessories for Hunting, Fishing and
Camping, Gold Accessories, Outerwear.
Brands:
Alpen, Atlas, Atwater Carey Ltd., Belair,
BenchMade Knives, Black Diamond,
Browning, Brunton, Buck, Caddis,
CamelBak, CarryLite, Citizen, Columbia,
Columbia River Knife and Tool, Dakota
Watch Co., Dan Bailey, Dunham, DUO
Wear, Estwing, Exofficio, Fieldline,
Fishpond, Freestyle, Froghair

BOB'S STORES, INC.
160 CORPORATE COURT
MERIDEN, CT 06450
203-235-5775
866-333-2627
Fax: 203-235-6395
www.bobstores.com
• David Farrell, President / Chief Executive
Officer
• Ava Hill-Gaunt, DMM Kids VP

Products:
Marketer of brand name footwear,
casualwear, workwear, teamwear,
activewear and gift cards.
Brands:
Avia, DVS, Lee, Dickies, Reebok, Element,
Oakley, Split, Nike, Jansport, Hurley,
Dockers, Gandi, Shady, NCAA, Majestic,
Marithe Francois Girbaud, Lee Sports,
Adidas, Mudd

BON TON STORES, INC.
2801 E MARKET STREET
UNIT 25
YORK, PA 17405
717-757-7660
800-233-7626
Fax: 717-751-319
www.bonton.com
• Tim Grumbacher, Chairman of the Board
of Directors
• Byron L Bergren, President / Chief
Executive Officer
• James H Baireuther, Vice Chairman, Chief
Administrative Offi
• James M Zamberlan, EVP, Stores
Products:
Marketer of Ladies', Men's and Kids'
Apparels, Accessories, Fragrances &
Cosmetics, Intimate Apparel, Jewelry,
Shoes
Brands:
Van Heusen, Geoffrey Beene, Angels, Glo,
Levis, Bill Blass, Jeanstar, Goldtoe,
Strivectin, Hylexin, Bali, Playtex,
Maidenform

BOSCOV'S DEPARTMENT STORES
4500 PERKIOMEN AVENUE
READING, PA 19606
610-779-2000
Fax: 610-370-3495
Joanne.Barker@Boscov.com
www.boscovs.com
• Kenneth Lakin, Director of Operations
(610) 779-2000
klakin@boscovs.com
• Burton Krieger, President
• Barry Goodolf, Buyer, Sports
• Albert Boscov, Chairman, Chief Executive
Officer
• Jim Boscov, Vice Chairman of Boscov's
Department Store, L
• Sam Flamholz, Co-President, Boscov's
Department Store, LLC
• Toni Miller, Senior Executive Vice
President, Chief Admini
• Ed McKeaney, Senior Executive Vice
President Merchandising
• Russell C. Diehm, Senior Vice President of
Finance & Chief Acco
• Jon Holmquist, Senior Vice President,
Direct Marketing
Services:
Department store chain.

BOWLERSPARADISE.COM
175 COMMERCE CIRCLE
SUITE A
SACRAMENTO, CA 95815
916-643-9827
888-969-2695
Fax: 916-921-8352
www.bowlersparadise.com
Products:
Bowling Equipment: Balls, Bags, Shoes,
Gloves/Supports, Accessories,

Cleaners/Polishes, Ball Care Products,
Towels, Ball Inserts, Books/Videos, Drilling
Service, Apparel, Gifts/Collectibles
Brands:
AMF, Brunswick, Columbia, Ebonite, Elite,
Hammer, Morich, PBA, Roto Grip, Storm,
Track, NFL Balls, MBL Balls, NCAA Ball, BF
World, Circle, Dexter, Halex, Hammer,
Linds, Master, Turbo, Neo-Tac, Tenth
Frame, Ultimate Bowling

BRANCH BROOK COMPANY
370 ROUTE 36 E
HAZLET, NJ 7730
732-787-6897
Fax: 732-787-0358
customerservice@namcopool.com
• Kevin Ventrice, President
• Raymond Ventrice, VP
Products:
Marketer of Above-Ground Pools, Casual
Furniture, Game Center
Brands:
BBC Billiards, Basketball Battle, Kettler

BREEZE SKI RENTAL
2650 S HAVANA
SUITE 205
AURORA, CO 80014
303-232-7547
888-427-3393
Fax: 303-232-7547
info@SkiRentals.com
www.skirentals.com
• Lewis Sapiro, Owner
• Janet Wrightson, Merchandise Manager
• Leigh Wild, Assistant Merchandise
Manager
Products:
Sports Packages, Boots, Snowboarding,
Snowshoes, Helmets, Skiboards

BRONER, INC.
1750 HARMON ROAD
AUBURN HILLS, MI 48326
800-543-4482
800-521-1318
Fax: 800-276-6375
hats@broner.com
www.broner.com
• David Broner, President
• Robert Broner, VP
Products:
Hats, Caps, Gloves and Accessories
Brands:
Broner

BROOKSTONE COMPANY
ONE INNOVATION WAY
MERRIMACK, NH 3054
866-576-7337
800-846-3000
Fax: 573-581-7361
www.brookstone.com
• Philip W Roizin, Interim President/CEO
• Alexander M Winiecki, Store Operations
EVP
• Gregory B Sweeney, General Manager /
Direct Marketing VP
• M. Ru Woodard, Merchandising VP
Products:
Retailer of consumer products.

BUILDING #19
140 MAIN ST
RTE 18
WEYMOUTH, MA 2043
781-337-1935
800-225-5061
Fax: 781-749-3691
• William Elovitz, President/CEO
(781) 749-6900
• Jerry Ellis, Chairman
• Paul Slovin, Merchant
Products:
Accessories, Basics and Designer Samples, Domestics, Food, Health & Beauty, Party Goods and Trim a Tree, Furniture and Mattresses, Giftware and Books, Handmade Oriental Rugs, Hardware, Housewares, Office Supplies, Electronics and Back to School, Kids', Men's, and Ladies' Clothing, Luggage and Shoes, Machine Made Oriental Rugs and Broadloom, Sporting Goods, Store and Catalog Stocks, Salvage Goods and Special Projects.
Year Founded:
1964

BUNKER JONES GOLF, INC
9792 EDMONDS WAY
SUITE 406
EDMONDS, WA 98020
425-640-0277
Fax: 425-696-0464
Products:
Online retailer of golf products and services.

BURDINE'S
7 WEST SEVENTH STREET
CINCINNATI, OH 45202
305-577-1500
800-289-6229
Fax: 305-577-2234
www.federated-fds.com
• Terry Lundgren, Chairman/President/CEO
• J. Da Scheiner, Stores Vice Chairman / Director
• Terry J. K Lundgren, Chairman, President and Chief Executive Offic
• Jeffrey Gennette, Chief Merchandising Officer
• Julie Greiner, Chief Merchandise Planning Officer
• Karen M. Hoguet, Chief Financial Officer
• Timothy M. Adams, Chief Private Brand Officer
• Peter Sachse, Chief Stores Officer
• Martine Reardon, Chief Marketing Officer
Products:
Bath Towels & Accessories, Beach Towels, Bed in a Bag, Bedding Basics, Bedding Collections, Blankets & Throws, Down Comforters, Featherbeds & Fiberbeds, Mattress Pads, Pillows, Sheets, Slip Covers, Visco Memory Foam, Window Treatments, Housewares, Women's Apparel and Accessories, Men's Apparel, Kids Apparel, Shoes, Beauty Products, Jewelry, Watches
Brands:
Calvin Klein, Charter Club, Court of Versailles, DKNY, Hotel Collection, Lauren Ralph Lauren, Lilly Pulitzer, Missoni, Oscar by Oscar de la Renta, Sigrid Olsen, Tommy Bahama, Tommy Hilfiger, Waterford, Denby, Hotel Collection, Jonathan Adler, Kate Spade, Lauren by Ralph Lauren, Lenox, Michael Aram, Mikasa, Nambe, Noritake

BUSYBODY, INC.
11900 COMMUNITY ROAD
SUITE 100
POWAY, CA 92064
562-818-1543
800-466-3348
Fax: 949-258-5744
info@busybody.com
www.busybody.com
• Brian McDermott, President / Chief Executive Officer
• Kenton Va Harten, Chief Financial Officer
• Keith Lynch, Customer Service Director
(562) 296-1063
Products:
Ellipticals, Treadmills, Exercise Bikes, Steppers, Rowers, Home Gyms, Home Gym Attachments, Freeweight Equipment, Flexibility Equipment, Fitness Accessories

BUY.COM SPORTS STORE
85 ENTERPRISES
SUITE 100
ALISO VIEJO, CA 92656
949-389-2000
Fax: 949-389-2800
www.rakuten.com
• Scott Blum, Founder/Chairman
• Neel Grover, President / Chief Operating Officer
• Robert Price, Chief Financial Officer
• Roger Andelin, Chief Information Officer
Products:
Sports and fitness apparel and footwear, products for team sports, water sports, winter sports, hiking, hunting, fishing, exercise, running, tennis and golf.
Brands:
Adidas, Wenger, Rawlings, Reebok, Magellan

BWM GLOBAL
3740 HAWTHORNE COURT
WAUKEGEN, IL 60087
847-785-1355
800-831-1117
Fax: 847-785-1712
customerrelations@bmwusa.com
www.bwmglobal.com
• Brad Fish, Division President
• Ronald Kruger, Senior VP
Products:
Apparel, Auto Accessories, Name Badges, Plaques, Trophies, Bags & Totes, Balloon Accessories, Business Accessories, Drink ware, Golf Apparel, Golf Equipment, Headwear, Office Accessories, Barbeque Equipment, Beach Umbrellas, Coach, Duffel Bags, Hartmann, Luggage, Passport Wallets, Travel Kits, Writing Instruments
Brands:
Ashworth, Callaway Golf, Coach, Cutter & Buck, Hartmann, Nike, O'Gio, Titleist, Tommy Hilfiger

C M T SPECIALTY SPORTS
199 ZAN ROAD
PO BOX 6427
CHARLOTTESVILLE, VA 22901
434-975-2704
Fax: 434-975-2845
info@downtownathletic.com
www.downtownathletic.com
• Banks Conner, President
• Dave Beeler, Sales Staff
• Robert Bell, Sales Staff

Products:
Hard goods, team uniforms, shoes and cleats, field and gym equipment, awards and promotional items

C4-SPORTS
1137 WOODEDEN DR.
MISSISSAUGA, ON, CANADA L5H 2T7
403-383-1540
800-921-8490
Fax: 410-229-0020
www.c4sports.ca
• Gene Sanders, General Manager
(703) 287-5974

CABELA'S
ONE CABELA DRIVE
SIDNEY, NE 69160
308-254-6745
800-237-4444
800-237-4444
Fax: 308-254-7345
www.cabelas.com
• Dennis Highby, President / Chief Executive Officer / Di
• Michael Callahan, SVP
• James Cabela, President
• Patrick A. Snyder, Merchandising SVP
• Dave Roehr, Finance VP
• Ralph Castner, VP / Chief Financial Officer
• Steven Krajewski, Real Estate Manager
Products:
Hunting, Fishing and Skiwear

CADAC AMERICA
900 MC FARLAND 400 BOULEVARD
ALPHARETTA, GA 30004
770-569-9736
866-641-2291
Fax: 770-751-9458
• Steven Goldstein, President

CAM COMMERCE SOLUTIONS
17075 NEWHOPE STREET
SUITE A
FOUNTAIN VALLEY, CA 92708
714-338-0200
800-726-3282
Fax: 714-241-9893
www.camcommerce.com
• Geoffrey Knapp, Chairman / Chief Executive Officer / Sec
(714) 241-9211
• Paul Ca Jr, Chief Financial Officer / Chief Accounti
• Sherrie Hoffman, Director of Marketing
Products:
Retail STAR Point of Sale POS Software, i.STAR eCommerce Software, Retail ICEr Point of Sale POS Software, CAM32 POS SoftwarE, i.CAM32 eCommerce, MicroBiz Point of Sale POS Software, X-Charger Credit Card Processing Software

CAMPING WORLD
650 THREE SPRINGS ROAD
BOWLING GREEN, KY 42104
270-781-2718
800-626-3636
Fax: 270-796-8991
info@campingworld.com
www.campingworld.com
• Mark T Gilman, President / Chief Executive Officer
• Jim Bullock, VP

Products:
Vehicle & Product Protection, Club & Member Services, Financial Products & Services

CAMPMOR, INC.
400 CORPORATE DRIVE
PO BOX 680
MAHWAH, NJ 7430
201-825-8300
800-525-4784
Fax: 201-236-3601
customer-service@campmor.com
www.campmor.com
• Daniel Jarashow, President
• Frank Kosco, Merchandising VP
• Anna Chirico, Chief Financial Officer
Products:
Bicycles and Accessories, Binoculars, Books, Camp Furniture and Cots, Camp Tools, Car Racks, Climbing Gear, Clothing by Brand, Clothing for Children, Clothing for Men, Clothing for Women, Compasses and Orienteering, DVDs/CDs/Videos, Electronics and Weather Gadgets, First Aid, Food, Footwear, Gear and Clothing Maintenance, Insect Deterrents, Kitchenware, Knives, Lights and Lanterns, Maps, Packs, Paddlesports, Personal Care, Pets, Portable Toilets and Accessories, Rainwear, Sleds and Snow Tubes, Sleeping Gear, Snowsport Accessories Socks, Stoves, Sunglasses and Eyewear Survival, Swimming & Snorkeling, Tents, The Beach Toys, Travel, Ultra
Brands:
Bellwether, Blackburn Products, Cannondale, Diadora, Lone Peak, Pearl Izumi, Planet Bike, Polar, Profile Design, Topeak, Ambler Mountain, Black Dot, Campmor, Cloudvei, Columbia Sportswear, Convert to Columbia, Duofold, Gordini, Hind, Hot Chillys, Isis, Jansport, Manzella, Marmot, Mountain Hardwear, Moving Comfort, Outdoor Research, Prana, Red Ledge, Russell Athletic, Sara's Prints, Seirus, Smartwool, Sorel, Sportif, Spyder, Terramar, The North Face, Thorlo, Trekmor, Turtle Fur, Wigwam

CANAL JEAN CO.
2236 NOSTRAND AVENUE
BROOKLYN, NY 11210
718-421-7590
Fax: 212-353-2601
• Ira Russack, President
• Neal Levitt, Controller
Products:
General Merchandise

CANNON SPORTS INC.
11614 PENDLETON ST
SUN VALLEY, CA 91352
818-683-1000
800-223-0064
Fax: 818-683-1012
www.cannonsports.com
• Jon Warner, President
(800) 223-0064
• Michael Warner, Director of Strategic Operations
(800) 223-0064
• Daniel Perez, Sales Manager
(800) 223-0064
Products:
Athletic Field Paint, Baseball/Softball Equipment, Equipment Storage, Bats, Batter's Gloves, Catchers Equipment,

Pitching Machines, Radar Guns, Base Cover, Umpire Gear, Game Clock. Ankle Braces, Stabilizers, Wraps, Aquatic Therapy Kickboards, Bags, Bandag
Brands:
AAI, BPI, Cliff Keen, Cosom, Cramer, Easton, Harvard, Incrediball, Jaypro, Kettler, Master Lock, Mikasa, Mizuno, Porter, Penn, Rawlings, Seiko, Spalding, Tachikara, Whamo, Wilson
Description:
A one stop shop for your physical education sports equipment needs. Nationwide leader in wholesale sports equipment supplying our nation's publicly funded institutions with the highest quality products, outlasting the competitiors.
Teams:
Dodgers, Lakers, Angels.
Number of Members:
10
Publications:
Cannon Sports Catalog Volume 24

CARHARTT INC.
5750 MERCURY DRIVE
DEARBORN, MI 48126
313-271-8460
800-833-3118
Fax: 313-271-3455
www.carhartt.com
• Gretchen C Valade, Chairman
• Mark Valade, President / Chief Executive Officer
• Peter Krause, Chief Financial Officer
• Andrius Viskantas, Public Relations Manager
Products:
Accessories, Bibs & Coveralls, Flame Resistant, Footwear, Kids & Youth Apparel, Outerwear, Jeans & Work Pants, Shirts, Sweats, Thermal Underwear

CEI
550 PATRICE PLACE
UNIT C
GARDENA, CA 90248
310-630-1690
800-735-0871
Fax: 310-630-1692
feedback@cei-ultrak.com
www.cei-ultrak.com
• Gordon Craig, President
• Merrilee Craig, VP
Products:
Professional Stopwatches, Sport Stopwatches, Seiko Products, Pedometers, Timers, Sport Watches, Multi-Sport Scoreboard, Display Timer, Mechanical stopwatch, Tally Counter
Brands:
Ultrak, Seiko

CENTURY SPORTING GOODS
1000 CENTURY BOULEVARD
MIDWEST CITY, OK 73110
405-732-2226
800-626-2787
Fax: 800-400-5485
customerservice@centurymartialarts.com
www.centurymartialarts.com
• Sarah Fields,
(800) 654-4701
• Dan Bower, President
• Sara Tsoodle, Marketing Director
• Michael Dillard, CEO & Chairman

Products:
Martial Arts Uniform

CHAMPS SPORTS
311 MANATEE AVENUE W
BRADENTON, FL 34205
941-748-0577
800-991-6813
Fax: 941-741-7189
www.champssports.com
• Ronald R Halls, President / Chief Executive Officer
• Marla Anderson, Merchandising EVP
• Nick Grayston, Planning / Allocation SVP
• Rubin Hanan, Marketing VP
Products:
Shoes, Clothing, Fan Gear, Equipment, Accessories
Brands:
Nike, Jordan, adidas, Reebok, Puma, New Balance, K-Swiss, Timberland, Under Armour, Majestic, Mizuno, Spalding, Wilson, Fossil, Ecko, Phat Farm, 3D Sports, ABC Sports, ABI Accessory, Action Images, Active Ankle

CHAPMAN WALTERS INTERCOASTAL GROUP
27671 LA PAZ ROAD
LAGUNA NIGUEL, CA 92677
949-448-9940
800-500-8292
Fax: 949-448-7008
cwicbg@aol.com
• Michael Chapman, President
(949) 448-9940
cwicie@aol.com
• Cindi A Walters, VP
(949) 448-9940
redheaddvr@aol.com
Products:
Snorkeling, Diving and Water Sports Gear and Accessories
Brands:
Body Glove

CHARTER PRODUCTS INC.
111 GATEWAY ROAD
BENSENVILLE, IL 60106-1950
630-616-1927
800-433-9839
Fax: 630-616-0755
www.chartergolf.net
• Thomas A. Krick Sr., President
Products:
Golf Bags for Clubs, Balls, Clubs-Putter, Clubs-Utility, Gloves, Hats/Caps, Headcovers, Socks, Tees

CHICAGO GOLF & SPORTS
4400 118TH AVENUE NORTH
SUITE 104
CLEARWATER, FL 33762
727-571-1556
866-571-1556
Fax: 727-571-1357
golfchicago1@yahoo.com
• Tony Liu, President
• Wei-Ming Liu, VP
Products:
Woods, Irons, Putter, Grips, Shafts, Accessories
Brands:
Chicago Golf, Chicago, Golf Pride, Winn, Grafalloy,

CHICK'S SPORTING GOODS, INC.
1092 NORTHWAY MALL
PITTSBURGH, PA 15237
626-331-8227
877-846-9997
Fax: 626-339-1713
www.dickssportinggoods.com
• James M. Chick, President
• Steve Miller, Chief Financial Officer
• Ed Stack, CEO and Chairman
Products:
Sporting Goods, In-Line Skates, Scooters, Shoes, Ski Hardware, Softwear/Activewear, Team Sports, Tennis and Water Sports

CHRISTY SPORTS/SPORTSTALKER
11005 WEST 8TH
SUITE 102
LAKEWOOD, CO 80215
303-323-6143
888-413-6966
Fax: 303-233-5946
estore@christysports.com
www.christysports.com
• Patrick O'Winter, CEO
• Keith Va Velkinburgh, Director
Products:
Ski Gear, Board Gear, Clothing, Accessories

CITY SPORTS
64 INDUSTRIAL WAY
WILMINGTON, MA 1887
978-988-5100
877-988-2580
Fax: 978-988-5105
www.citysports.com
• Michael R Kennedy, Chief Executive Officer
(978) 988-5100
• Erik Metzdorf, Buyer
(978) 988-5100
Products:
Apparel, Footwear and Sporting Equipment
Brands:
Adidas, Nike, Columbia, Patagonia, Moving Comfore, SportHill, Basics, Puma, Sugoi, Champion, InSport, Helly Hansen, Speedp, Brooks, Reebok, Saucony, Converse, Teva, New Balance, Vans, Timberland, Puma, Merrell, Salomon, Reef, Mizuno, Mission Hockey, RollerBlade, Bell, Jansport, Wilson, Sony, STX, Everlast, Timex, York, Polar, Speedo, Louisville Slugger.

CLARKS COMPANIES NA
156 OAK STREET
NEWTON UPPER FALLS, MA 2464
617-964-1222
800-211-5461
Fax: 617-243-4210
consumer.services@clarksna.com
www.clarks.com
• Robert Infantino, President
• Steve Katsirubas, Business Systems Director
Products:
Footwear
Brands:
Clarks England, Bostonian, Indigo, and Privo

CMS SPORTS
300 S DUNCAN AVENUE
SUITE 218
CLEARWATER, FL 33755

727-441-8450
Fax: 727-441-8439
info@cmssport.com
www.cmssport.com
• Charles Ferrer, President
• John King, Vice President
• Ali Ferrer, Vice President and Treasurer
• Trudy Wise, Manager, Sales and Services

COLLEGE CONCEPTS, LLC.
3350 RIVERWOOD PARKWAY
SUITE 850
ATLANTA, GA 30339
770-859-1420
800-284-4288
Fax: 770-859-1434
webmaster@conceptssport.com
• John C. Staton, President
• Debbie Carlson, EVP
• Rob Manske, Vice President
Products:
Licensed Apparel, Shorts, Sleepwear and T-shirts
Brands:
Concepts Sport

COLLEGIATE PACIFIC
13950 SENLAC DRIVE
PO BOX 7726
DALLAS, TX 75234
972-243-8100
888-566-8966
Fax: 888-455-3551
• Michael J Blumfield, Chairman / Chief Executive Officer
• Adam L Blumfield, President
• William Estill, Chief Financial Officer
• Arthur J Coerver, Chief Operating Officer
Products:
Game Tables, Benches & Bleachers, Scoreboards; Apparel, Equipment and Accessories of Archery, Badminton, Baseball & Softball, Basketball, Boxing, Field Hockey, Football, Gymnastics, Golf, Racquetball, Scoreboard, Soccer, Tennis, Soccer, Tennis, Track, Volleyball, Wallyball, and Outdoor Recreation
Brands:
Adidas, Mark1m Wilson, Spalding, Diamond, Rawlings, Search, Brine.

COLOR INC.
47 OCTOBER HILL ROAD
HOLLISTON, MA 01746
508-474-2900
Fax: 508-474-2800
www.thecolorstores.com
• Tom Emmons, VP
tom@thecolorstores.com
• Al Shemeklis, President
al@thecolorstores.com
• Tom Emmons, Vice President
Products:
Regional Gift Items, Sports Collectibles, Imprinted Sportswear and Apparel

CONAN GOLF
470 CLOVERLEAF DRIVE
UNIT B
BALDWIN PARK, CA 91706
626-934-0388
800-964-4899
Fax: 626-934-0377
www.kunnangolf.com
• Gary Zou, Chief Executive Officer
Products:
Sporting Goods, Gold Equipment

Brands:
Echelon Golf, Kunnan Golf, Tech Edge Golf, Sports Illustrated for Kids Golf

CONVERSE, INC.
ONE HIGH STREET
NORTH ANDOVER, MA 01845-2601
888-792-3307
Fax: 978-983-3503
www.converse.com
• Ellen Garvey, Information Technology Director
• Jerry Lan, Managing Director, Far East Operations
• James Stroesser, VP, Sales
• David M Maddocks, Global Marketing VP
Products:
Apparel, Footwear, Sporting Goods and Equipment
Brands:
Converse, Chuck Taylor, Basketball, Lifestyle, Jack Purcell, Varvatos

COOPERSBURG SPORTS
120 E STATION AVENUE
COOPERSBURG, PA 18036
610-282-1360
800-227-2891
Fax: 610-282-4611
www.coopersburgsports.com
• Scott Pino, President
(610) 282-1360
spino@coopersburgsports.com
• Steve Bishop, National Sales Manager
• Pat O'Connel, ASI & Custom Manager
poconnell@coopersburgsports.com
• Justin Kotarski, Retail Sales
• Debbie Long, Customer Service
• Diane Nace, Artwork/Approvals
• Arthene Derr, Accounts Manager
aderr@coopersburgsports.com
Products:
Manufacturers of licensed sports collectibles.
Brands:
Stackable StarsT

COUCH DISTRIBUTING COMPANY
104 LEE ROAD
PO BOX 50004
WATSONVILLE, CA 95077-5004
831-724-0649
800-542-5555
Fax: 831-724-4293
georgec@couchdistributing.com
www.couchdistributing.com
• Michael Hobby, Vice President - Finance
• Vern Burditt, Vice-President - Administration
• Steve Vargas, Vice President - Sales
• Gary Jensen, Manager - Delivery Operations
• Jim Griffin, Fleet Manager
• George W. Couch III, III, President
• Louie Pieracci, Vice President - General Manager
Auto Sports:
Mazda Raceway Laguna Seca.

COUNTRY CLUB SYSTEMS
500 FAIRPORT ROAD
SUITE 500
FAIRPORT, NY 14450
585-377-6730
800-877-8338
Fax: 585-377-0448
• Don Saleski, President

Products:
General Sports Products - Inventory management systems for the country club and golf industry

COVERMASTER, INC.
100 WESTMORE DRIVE
UNIT 11-D
REXDALE, ON, CANADA M9V 5C3
416-745-1811
800-387-5808
Fax: 416-742-6837
info@covermaster.com
www.covermaster.com
• Robert Curry, President
• Gerald Hackett, Regional Sales Director
• Ken Curry, Regional Sales Director
• Bob Curry, President
• Larry Moreland, Regional Sales Director
Products:
Gym Floor Covers, Handling Systems and Accessories, Divider Curtains, Wall Padding, Gym Floor Covers, On Desk Circles, Batting Practice Turf Protection, Windscreens, Seat Covers, Concert Covers, Rain Covers
Brands:
Ultima 5000, Universal Plus, Reversible 21, Classic 2000, Spartan 1000, CoverMate, CoverClean, PowerMate, Raincover Plus, Raincover Lite, Raincover SuperLite, TarpMate, Tarp Machine

CRAZY SHIRTS
99-969 IWAENA STREET
AIEA, HI 96701-3249
800-486-2720
800-771-2720
Fax: 800-486-1276
www.crazyshirts.com
• Mark Hollander, President / Chief Executive Officer
Products:
T-Shirts; Bottoms, Outerwear, Sportknits, and Tops for Men, Women, and Kids; Accessories, Specialty Dye, Club Card, Gift Certificates

CROWN TROPHY COMPANY
86 NORTH AVENUE
GARWOOD, NJ 7027
908-789-0460
Fax: 908-654-0328
Crown.Trophy@verizon.net
• Dennis Marsh, President
• Leonard Gleckel, Vice President
Products:
Trophies, Medals, Plaques, Ribbons, Resin/Sculptures, Cups, Glass, Desk Accessories, Championship Awards, Clocks, Gavels, Pins, Certificates, Badges, Signage, Banners, Bronze Castings, Embedments, Laminations. Trophy Case, Sport Display Cases, Donor Wall, Seasonal Gifts

CYBERSPORTS, INC.
PO BOX 3216
REDMOND, WA 98073-3216
425-882-8889
800-846-3688
Fax: 425-869-9399

DAEWOO INTERNATIONAL CORPORATION
65 CHALLENGER ROAD
RIDGEFIELD PARK, NJ 07660
201-229-4500
Fax: 822-753-9489
www.daewoo.com
• Michael Tae, Assistant Manager
Products:
Racquet Sports - Apparel; Track & Field/Running - Apparel-Run/Jog; Media & Electronics - Appliances, Robot Related Products, IT Related Products, Telecommunications Equipment and Terminals

DARTON ARCHERY
3540 DARTON ROAD
HALE, MI 48739
989-728-4231
Fax: 989-728-2410
www.dartonarchery.com
• Rex Darton, President
• Ted Harpham, Sales Manager
Products:
Darton Accessories/Clothing, GLC Crossbows, GLC Accessories
Brands:
Darton, Great Lakes, Crossbows

DC SPORTS, INC.
18 HUDSON STREET
MECHANICVILLE, NY 12118
518-665-0370
Fax: 518-665-0378
• Bob Brown, President
Products:
Full team dealer of apparel, bags, shoes, balls, baseball, basketball, soccer
Brands:
Adidas, Nike, Reebok, Russell, Don Alleson, Fruit of the Loom

DECATHLON USA SPORTS MEGASTORE
326 BALLARDVALE STREET
WILMINGTON, MA 1887
978-657-0100
Fax: 978-658-4854
www.decathlon-usa.com
• Matthieu Laclercq, Chief Executive Officer
Products:
Sporting Goods Designer and Retailer
Brands:
Tribord, Quechua, Decathlon Cycle, Kalenji

DIAMOND OIL COMPANY
702 SE RACCOON ST.
DES MOINES, IA 50309
515-244-4271
800-422-7563
Fax: 515-244-4273
info@diamondoilco.com
www.lubricants-oil.com
• Chance Jason, Owner
Services:
Fuel Supplier for Iowa Speedway; Turbo Blue; Brad Penn.

DICK'S SPORTING GOODS INC.
1092 NORTHWAY MALL
PITTSBURGH, PA 15237
412-635-9004
877-846-9997
Fax: 412-635-9429
www.dickssportinggoods.com

• Edward W Stack, Chairman / Chief Executive Officer
• William Colomb, President / Chief Operating Officer / Di
• William Newlin, EVP / Chief Administrative Officer
• Ed Stack, CEO and Chairman
Products:
Sporting Goods
Brands:
Adidas, Bowflex, Callaway Golf, Lifetime Basketball, New Balance, Proform Fitness, Reebok, TaylorMade, Under Armour, Concept Shop, Walter Hagen

DILLARD DEPARTMENT STORES
1600 CANTRELL ROAD
LITTLE ROCK, AR 72201
501-376-5200
800-345-5273
Fax: 501-399-7831
questions@dillards.com
www.dillards.com
• Mike Dillard, EVP / Director
• Drue Corbusier, EVP / Director
• Alex Dillard, President / Director
• James I Freeman, SVP / Chief Financial Officer, Director
Products:
Women's apparel, Men's apparel, Children's apparel, Jewelry & Accessories, Cosmetics, Furniture, Gifts, Housewares
Brands:
Adidas, Adrianna Papell, Alain Weiz, Alex Evenings, Allen by Allen B. Schwartz, Aigle, Antigua, Austin Reed, BCBG Max Azria, Bulova, 6 Degrees, Anne Klein, As U Wish, Avenue of the Stars, B. Darlin, Arthur Court, Artimino, Astor Lane, Atlantis, Barbie, Bernhardt, Brookwood, Gallery, Design, Hooker, Italsofa

DIXIE SPORTING GOODS
2400 WESTWOOD AVENUE
RICHMOND, VA 23230
804-353-4943
800-527-7510
Fax: 703-321-7378
www.bsnsports.com
• Ken Caravati, President
• Michael Caravati, Sales / Marketing VP
Products:
Sport Goods
Brands:
Russell Athletic, Rawlings, Nike, Wilson, Easton, Louisville Slugger, Adams, Champion, Don Alleson, Delong, Cliff Keen, AAI, Bison, Asics, Adidas, Worth, Dudley, Twin City, New Era, Gatorade, Douglas, Holloway, Fisher, Gill

INTERNATIONAL SEEDS, INC.
175 W H STREET
PO BOX 229
HALSEY, OR 97348
541-369-2251
800-445-2251
Fax: 541-369-2640
www.dlfis.com
• Brad Jeffreys, Truf/Forage Sales (541) 369-1837
• Steve Johnson, Research Director (541) 929-3703
• Rick Myers, Director Sales / Marketing (541) 369-1841
• Richard Myers, Vice President, Turf & Retail

(541) 368-184
rickm@dlfis.com
• Roeland Kapsenberg, Vice President, Forage
(541) 369-1840
roelandk@dlfis.com
• Claus Ikjaer, General Manager
(541) 369-1813
clausi@dlfis.com
• Alan Muhl, Finanace / Operations Manager
(541) 369-1816
• Brad Jeffreys, Turf & Forage Sales
(541) 369-1837
bradj@dlfis.com
• Norm Touhy, National Accounts Manager
(303) 347-9245
normt@dlfis.com
• W. Dan Walters, Seed Production Manager
(541) 369-1827
danw@dlfis.com
Products:
Surfaces: Natural Turf, Golf Turf, Seed, Sand - Domestic and International.
Brands:
C.E.O., Cindy, Cobra, Derby Supreme, Eureka, Gator II, Houndog 5, Longfellow, Major League, P.H.D., Pride, R.2, Regal, Sabre II, Top Hat, Viper

DODD & COMPANY, R.O.
2870 MABRY LANE
PO BOX 191107
ATLANTA, GA 30319-2602
404-869-7661
Fax: 404-869-0632
• Zane Dodd, Chief Executive Officer
• Zane Dodd, President
Products:
Baseball - Base Spikes, Bases, Batting Helmets, Faceguards, Caps, Gloves-Batter, Gloves-Catcher/Fielder/First Base, Glove Oil, Jerseys, Masks, Protective-Catcher/Umpire, Uniforms; Basketball - Uniforms; Football - Arm/Hand Pads, Bags, Equipment, Face Prot

DOLLAR GENERAL CORPORATION
100 MISSION RIDGE
GOODLETTSVILLE, TN 37072-0000
615-855-4000
Fax: 615-855-5252
www.dollargeneral.com
• Richard W Dreiling, Chairman / Chief Executive Officer
• David Tehle, Executive Vice President / Chief Financi
• Kathleen Guion, Division President of Store Operations a
• Beryl Buley, Division President of Merchandising, Mar
Products:
Consumable Basics, Refrigerated Items
Brands:
DG Guarantee, Clover Valley

DOVER SADDLERY, INC
PO BOX 1100
LITTLETON, MA 1460
978-952-8062
800-406-8204
Fax: 978-952-6633
www.doversaddlery.com
• Powers David, Founder
• Chesley Chmura, Customer Service Manager

• Patricia Nesto, Buyer
• Laura Derick, Supervisor
• Jim Powers, Founder
Services:
Official mail order catalog company of the United States Equestrian Federation.

DR. JAY'S
7720 KENAMAR COURT
SUITE C
SAN DIEGO, CA 92121-2425
858-634-5595
888-437-5297
Fax: 201-864-1440
service@DrJays.com
www.drjays.com
• Elliott Betesh, President / Apparel
• Raymond Betesh, Buyer / Footwear
Products:
Apparel and Footwear Specialty
Brands:
Adidas, Akademiks, Andrew Stevens, Apple Bottoms, AZZURE, Baby Phat, Basic Essentials, Boutique NYC, Catch A Fire, DKNY Jeans, Ecko Red, Fashion Lab, G-Unit, Girbaud, Graphix Gallery, Guess, Harajuku Lovers, Hustler, JLO, Junk Food, Kenneth Cole, LOT29, New Era, Nike, Pepe Jeans, Prom Shop, Reebok, Request Jeans, Rocawear, Rockers- It's Dangerous, Southpole, T-Star B, The North Face, Timberland, Tommy Girl, Triple 5 Soul, Wanted Shoes, Apple Bottoms,Baby Phat, David & Goliath, Dickies, DKNY Jeans, Dollhouse, Ecko Red, FUBU, Fun Tees, G-Unit, Guess, Hello Kitty, it's happy bunny

DREW PEARSON MARKETING, INC. (DPM)
15006 BELTWAY DRIVE
ADDISON, TX 75001
972-702-8055
800-879-0880
Fax: 972-980-7123
customerservice@drewpearson.com
www.drewpearson.com
• Pearson Drew, Chairman
(952) 939-4900
dpearson@drewpearson.com
Products:
Baseball caps, cold weather headwear and accessories; Silk screening and logo design services

DUCKWALL ALCO STORES, INC.
401 COTTAGE AVENUE
ABILENE, CANADA 67410
785-263-3350
800-976-0542
Fax: 785-263-7531
webmaster@alcostores.com
• Lawrence J Zigerelli, Chief Executive Officer
• James E Schoenbeck, Operations / Advertising SVP
• James E Fennema, Merchandise SVP
• Michael J Gawin, VP / Division Merchandise Manager
Products:
Apparel: Men's, Women's, Kids', Automotive, Candy, Snacks, Food, Crafts, Domestics, Electronics, Video, Audio, Fabrics, Furniture, Gifts, Hardware, Health and Beauty Aids Housewares, Jewelry, Lawn and Garden, Pet Supplies, Seasonal Items, Shoes and Hosiery, Sporting goods, Stationery, Toys

DUNHAM'S ATHLEISURE CORPORATION
5607 NEW KING DRIVE
SUITE #125
TROY, MI 48098
248-674-4991
888-801-9158
Fax: 248-674-4980
www.dunhamssports.com
• Jeff Lynn, President / Chief Executive Officer
• Ken Meehan, EVP / General Merchandise Manager
• Steve Sander, Store Operation EVP
• Marshall Sosne, EVP / Chief Financial Officer
Products:
Sporting Goods
Brands:
Reebok, Adidas, Converse, Nike

DUNLAP CO.
200 BAILEY AVENUE
SUITE 100
FORT WORTH, TX 76107
817-336-4985
Fax: 817-887-1302
• Dale Matthews, SVP / Director, Stores
• Edward Martin, President / Chief Executive Officer
• Reg Martin, Chairman
• Jim Leamy, General Merchandise Manager
Products:
Women's Apparel, Men's Apparel, Children's Apparel, Accessories, Beauty and Fragrance
Brands:
Alfred, Dunner Sag Harbor, Dooney & Bourke, Keds, Van Heusen, Estee Lauder, Bali, Colonial, Candles, Samsonite, Lee Jeans, Gold Toe, Stone, Mountain, Clinique, Haggar, Vanity Fair, Izod, Liz Claiborne, Briggs, Godinger, Cuddlduds, Travel Pro, Dockers, Harve Benard, Wrapper, Lancome, Koret, Fossil, Josephine Chaus, Hanes, Naturalizer, OXO, Malden, Jockey

E & J LAWRENCE CORP/ JIMMY JAZZ
43 HALL STREET
SUITE 7
BROOKLYN, NY 11205
718-596-1414
Fax: 718-596-7288
• Jimmy Khezrie, President / Chief Executive Officer
Products:
Specialty - Apparel/Footwear

EAGLE BUTTON CO.
700-76 BROADWAY
#318
WESTWOOD, NJ 7675
201-652-4063
800-794-6350
Fax: 201-652-2003
info@eaglebutton.com
www.eaglebutton.com
• Arthur Simon, President
Products:
Buttons

EARLY WINTERS
3188 NW ALOCLEK DRIVE
HILLSBSBORO, OR 97124
503-614-4600
877-718-7902
800-458-4438

Fax: 503-614-4601
webrep@nortom.com
www.sahalie.blair.com
Products:
Men's Apparel, Women's Apparel,
Accessories, Shoes, Gift & Gourmet

EASTBAY, INC.
PO BOX 8066
WAUSAU, WI 54402-8066
715-261-9588
800-826-2205
Fax: 715-261-9550
asktheexperts@eastbay.com
www.eastbay.com
• Ken Hicks, Chairman & CEO
• Dowe Tillema, President/CEO
Products:
Athletic apparel, equipment, and footwear.
Brands:
Nike, Reebok, Adidas and New Balance,
Easton, Brute, Phat Farm Baby Phat,
Rocawear

EASTERN MOUNTAIN SPORTS, INC.
1 VOSE FARM ROAD
PETERBOROUGH, NH 3458
603-924-9571
888-463-6367
Fax: 603-924-9138
customerservice@ems.com
www.ems.com
• Will Manzer, President and CEO
Year Founded:
1967
Brands:
Black Diamond, CamelBak Hydration
Systems, Eagle Creek, EMS, Garmin GPS
Units, Gregory Backpacks, Keen Footwear,
Kelty, Leatherman Tools, Marmot, Merrell
Footwear, Mountain Hardwear, MSR
Equipment, Nalgene, Petzl, prAna, Sierra
Designs, SmartWool, Teva Footwear, The
North Face,Thule Racks, Tubbs Snowshoes
Products:
Gear, Clothing

EB2B COMMERCE, INC.
665 BROADWAY
SUITE 301
NEW YORK, NY 10012
212-477-1700
800-828-3932
Fax: 212-477-6207
info@enabletrading.com
www.easylink.com
• Richard S. Cohan, Chief Executive Officer
• Robert Bacchi, Chief Operating Officer
• Alester Spears, Director, Regional Sales
• Stephen Haber, Director, Client Services
Products & Services:
Supplier portal and enablement services,
Business Transaction Outsourcing Services,
and Professional services
Brands:
TradeGateway, TradeEngine

ECKERD DRUG, INC.
6501 LEGACY DRIVE
PLANO, TX 75024
972-431-1000
800-322-1189
Fax: 972-431-1362
www.jcpenney.com
• Myron E Ullman, III, Chairman/CEO
• Jeff Thompson, VP, Marketing
• Joan M. Gallagher, VP, Public Relations

Products & Services:
Apparel, Footwear, and Accessories for
Men, Women and Kids; Shoes; Jewelry;
Bed & Bath; Window Accessories; Home
Furnishings; Eyewear, Portraits, Gift Cards,
Credit Services
Brands:
JCPenney, St. John's Bay, New Balance,
Nike, Reebok, Converse, Adidas, JCP, Flirt

EDDIE BAUER, INC.
PO BOX 7001
GROVEPORT, OH 43125
425-883-2827
800-426-8020
Fax: 425-755-7696
www.eddiebauer.com
• Fabian Mansson, President and Chief
Executive Officer
• Kathy Boyer, SVP and Chief
Merchandising Officer
• Timothy McLaughlin, SVP and Chief
Financial Officer
• John Ball, Division VP, Menswear
Products:
Men and Women's Apparel, Shoes and
Accessories, Gear
Brands:
EddieBauer, Sueded Terry, Simple, Ruston
Fit-Nano-Tex

EDWIN WATT'S GOLF SHOP, INC.
20 HILL AVENUE
FORT WALTON BEACH, FL 32548
850-362-2005
800-443-4167
Fax: 850-244-5217
service_team@wattsgolf.com
www.edwinwatts.com
• Edwin Watts, President
• Ron Watts, EVP
• John Watson, President/CEO, Golf
Operations
• Robert Anthony, VP, Catalog and Online
• Lynda K. Barr, VP, Chief Financial Officer
• Kerry Kabase, VP, Purchasing and
Inventory
• Sven Kessler, VP, Retail Operations
• Robert Anthony, VP, Marketing and
Advertising
• David DeBra, VP, Merchandise Planning
Products:
Golf Clubs, Bags/Shoes Accessories, Golf
Simulators, Golf Balls, Gift Cards, Gloves,
Training Aids, Apparel
Brands:
Callaway, Titleist, Taylormade, Ping, Nike,
Cleveland, Cobra, Mizuno, Macgregor, Ben
Hogan, Footjoy

EFINGER SPORTING GOODS
513 W UNION AVENUE
PO BOX 2003
BOUND BROOK, NJ 08805
732-356-0604
Fax: 732-805-9860
• Thomas Hoey, President
• Murray Greenberg, VP and General
Merchandise Manager
• Patrick Hoey, Store Manager and Buyer
• Evan Greenberg, Vice President
• Joe Collins, Vice President/Sales Manager
jcyank15@aol.com
Products:
Accessories, Apparel, Base/Softball,
Basketball, Football, Soccer, Running,
Wrestling, Field Hockey, Ice Hockey, Golf,

Hunting, Camping, Fishing, Exercise and
Tennis.
Year Founded:
1907

ELAN-MONARK
81-H BRUNSWICK BOULEVARD
DOLLARD DES ORMEAUX, QC, CANADA
H9B 2J5
514-421-7871
Fax: 514-421-7394
• Bob Orbacz, President
• Rick Sceery, VP, Sales and Marketing
Products:
Snow Sport Equipment
Brands:
Elan, Arter, Dalbello

EREHWON MOUNTAIN OUTFITTER
746 W ALGONQUIN ROAD
ARLINGTON HEIGHTS, IL 60005
847-439-1400
www.erehwon.com
• Martin Stilling, Store Manager
Products:
Clothing for Men, Women and Kids;
Footwear; Hats, Gloves & Underwear;
Novelties; Gear for Climbing, Kayaking,
Snowsports; Travel & Luggages
Brands:
Arc'teryx, Icebreaker, Mountain Hardwear,
Terramar, Cloudveil, Kombi, Patagonia, The
North Face, Columbia Sportswear, Marmot,
Smartwool.

EXPRESS
1 LIMITED PARKWAY
COLUMBUS, OH 43230
614-415-4000
800-477-8844
Fax: 614-415-4200
www.express.com
• Ken Stevens, Chief Executive Officer
(614) 415-4000
• Michael J. Wiess, President & Chief
Executive Officer
Products:
Women's Private-Label Apparel and
Accessories; Menswear

F.A.O. SCHWARZ
767 FIFTH AVENUE
SUITE 601
NEW YORK, NY 10153
212-644-9400
800-876-7867
Fax: 212-308-6094
• Barry Erdos, CEO
• David Niggli, EVP, Merchandising
• Lisa Harnisch, Senior Vice President,
General Merchandising
Products:
Easter & Springtime Gifts, Stuffed Animals,
Dolls & Collectible Dolls, Personalized Gifts,
Arts & Crafts, Electronics, Furniture &
Accessories, Sports Equipment &
Accessories.
Brands:
Patrick & Penelope, American Kennel Club,
Madame Alexander, Robert Tonner, Barbie,
Newborn Nursery.

FACTORY 2-U STORES, INC.
15001 FIGUEROA STREET
GARDENA, CA 90248

858-627-1800
Fax: 858-637-4199
www.factory2-u.com
• Norman G. Plotkin, Chief Executive Officer
and Director
• Robert Wr II, Director
Products:
Operates a chain of off-price retail apparel
and housewares stores.

FAMILY DOLLAR STORES
10401 OLD MONROE ROAD
PO BOX 1017
CHARLOTTE, NC 28201-1017
704-847-6961
Fax: 704-847-0189
info@familydollar.com
www.familydollar.com
• Howard R. Levine, Chairman and Chief
Executive Officer
• R. Ja Kelly, Vice Chairman, Chief
Financial Officer a
• Robert George, EVP and Chief
Merchandising Officer
• Charles S. Gibson Jr, EVP, Supply Chain
Products:
Health & Beauty Aids, Automotive, Food &
Candy; Housewares, Pets, Hardware &
Paint, Home Cleaning Aids, Laundry &
Storage, Picture Frames, Ladies, Socks &
Lingerie; Mens, Boys, Girls and Infants
Apparel and Shoes

FAMOUS FOOTWEAR
7010 MINERAL POINT ROAD
MADISON, WI 53717-1701
608-829-3668
888-869-1053
Fax: 608-827-3353
www.famousfootwear.com
• William A. Dandy, SVP, Retail Sales and
Operations
• George Zelinsky, SVP and General
Merchandising Manager
• J. M. Lang, SVP and Chief Financial
Officer
• James M. Roe, SVP, Real Estate
Products:
Name brand shoes
Brands:
Addidas, Aerosoles, Asics, Avia, Brown
Shoe, Buster Brown, Clarks England,
Columbia, Connie, Dr. Scholl's, Eastland,
Eurostep, GBX, Keds, LEI, LifeStride, Luqz,
MUDD, Naturalizer, New Balance, Nike,
Nunn Bush, Reebok, Rocksport, Skechers,
Steve Madden, Timberland, Vans, Westies

FANATICS RETAIL GROUP
5245 COMMONWEALTH AVENUE
JACKSONVILLE, FL 32254
305-348-2000
Fax: 305-348-2963
www.fiusports.com
• Pete Garcia, Athletic Director
(305) 348-0182
pgarcia@fiu.edu
• Alex Duque, Senior Associate AD/CFO
(305) 348-2398
duquea@fiu.edu
• Julie Berg, Senior Associate AD & SWA
(305) 348-2352
bergj@fiu.edu
• Lori-Ann Cox, Senior Associate AD,
Advancement
(305) 348-0372
coxla@fiu.edu

• Heath Glick, Chief of Staff
(305) 348-6711
glickh@fiu.edu
• Lucy Prosper, Assistant Director
HR/Admin Services
(305) 348-2671
lprospe@fiu.edu
• Derrick Mayfield, Assistant AD, Facilities &
Operations
(305) 348-6301
• Pete Garcia, Executive Director, Sports &
Entertainment
(305) 348-0182
pgarcia@fiu.edu
Arena Seating Capacity:
5,000
Stadium Seating Capacity:
Football Track (17,000), Baseball (1500),
Soccer (1,500), Softball (800).

FANBUZZ.COM
10729 BREN ROAD E
MINNETONKA, MN 55343
952-943-6714
Fax: 952-943-6711
www.fanbuzz.com
• J. Da Wible, VP, Operations
• Scott Killian, President
• Mike Grube, Merchandise Manager
• Brian Wright, Marketing Manager
Products:
Sells licensed apparel to sporting goods
industry and customizes individual orders.
Also offers e-commerce solutions to teams,
leagues, colleges via various content
Websites.

FANSEDGE.COM
725 LANDWEHR ROAD
NORTHBROOK, IL 60062
877-965-3955
877-965-3955
Fax: 847-965-2860
www.fansedge.com
• Kevin Bates, Chief Executive Officer
• Brian Neal, Chief Financial Officer and VP,
Business
• Pete Hanna, VP, Operations
• Jeff Basso, VP, Technology
Products:
Apparel, Auto Accessories, Autographed
Memorabilia, Collectibles, Gift Certificates,
Golf Items and Novelties, Hats, Caps,
Visors, Home and Officer, Jewelry,
Watches, Accessories, Tailgating/Stadium
Gear

FEDERATED DEPARTMENT STORES, INC.
7 W SEVENTH STREET
CINCINNATI, OH 45202
513-579-7000
800-261-5385
Fax: 513-579-7555
www.federated-fds.com
• Terry J. Lundgren, Chairman, Chief
Executive Officer, and P
• Karen M. Hoquet, EVP and Chief Financial
Officer
• Thomas G. Gody, Vice Chairman
• Thomas L. Cole, Vice Chairman
Products:
General Goods
Brands:
Bloomingdale's and Macy's

FHI, INC./BUSY BODY
11900 COMMUNITY ROAD
SUITE 100
POWAY, CA 92064
562-818-1543
800-466-3348
Fax: 949-258-5744
info@busybody.com
www.busybody.com
• Brian McDermott, President
• Keith Lynch, Customer Service Director
(562) 296-1063
Products:
Ellipticals, Treadmills, Exercise Bikes,
Steppers, Rowers, Home Gyms, Home Gym
Attachments, Freeweight Equipment,
Flexibility Equipment, Fitness Accessories
Brands:
Life Fitness, Precor, Hoist, Parabody, Vision
Fitness

FINGERHUT COMPANIES, INC.
6250 RIDGEWOOD ROAD
ST CLOUD, MN 56303
952-932-3100
800-208-2500
Fax: 952-936-5441
customerservice@fingerhut.com
www.fingerhut.com
• Theodore Deikel, Chairman and Chief
Executive Officer
• Michael Sherman, General Counsel,
Secretary and SVP, Busi
• John Buck, EVP
• Andy Johnson, SVP, Marketing
Products:
Home Furnishings, Kitchen and Appliances,
Toys and Kids' Stuff, Apparel, Footwear,
Personal Care and Luggage, Sporting
Goods, Video Games & Entertainment
Brands:
Converse, Reebok, Rocawear, Home Deals

FITNESS COMPANY
ISELIN, NJ 08830
732-548-0970
888-353-6754
Fax: 201-626-3173
• Steve Smith, Chief Executive Officer
(732) 548-0970
Products & Services:
Physical Fitness Facilities

FITNESS SYSTEMS
1700 W 82ND STREET
SUITE 200
MINNEAPOLIS, MN 55431
952-897-5275
800-639-7913
Fax: 952-897-5173
info@hfit.com
www.healthfitness.com
• John Hynes, Buyer
• Bill McMann, Buyer
Products & Services:
Health management and Fitness
management

FLAGHOUSE
601 FLAGHOUSE DRIVE
HASBROUCK HEIGHTS, NJ 07604-3116
201-288-7600
800-793-7900
Fax: 800-793-7922
sales@flaghouse.com
www.flaghouse.com

- George Carmel, President
- Keith Gold, Brand Manager

Products:
Sporting Goods, Physical Education, and Recreation.

Year Founded:
1954

FLEET FEET, INC.
406 E MAIN STREET
SUITE 200
CARRBORO, NC 27510
919-942-3102
Fax: 919-932-6176
www.fleetfeetsports.com
- Tom Raynor, Chairman / Chief Executive Officer
- Jeff Phillips, President
- Joey Pointer, Director, Franchise Operations
- Luke Bo Rowe, Vice President

Products:
Footwear, Apparel

Brands:
Saucony, Adidas, Basics, Brooks, Moving Comfort, Mizuno, New Balance, Nike, Insport, Sogoi, Pearl Izumi, Champion, Life is Good, Superfeet, Sporthill

---

FOLLETT HIGHER EDUCATION GROUP
3 WESBROOK CORPORATE CENTER
SUITE 200
WESTCHESTER, IL 60154
630-279-2330
800-365-5388
Fax: 630-279-2569
- Scott Deaton, EVP, Marketing
(630) 279-2330
- Thomas A. Christopher, President
- Jay Amond, SVP, Chief Financial Officer
- Tom C. Christopher, President and Chief Operating Officer
- Steve Pribyl, Executive Vice President of Retail Operations
- Jay Amond, Senior Vice President and Chief Financial Off
- Doug Thompson, Senior Vice President and Chief Information O
- Gary Shapiro, Senior Vice President of Intellectual Propert
- Audrey Southard, Senior Vice President of Human Resources
- Patrick Usher, Senior Vice President of Sales

Products:
Books

FOOT LOCKER, INC.
112 W 34TH STREET
NEW YORK, NY 10120
212-720-3700
800-991-6815
Fax: 212-720-4397
www.footlocker-inc.com
- Lauren Peters, Senior VP Strategic Planning
- John D. Morris, Coordinator Sports Marketing
(212) 720-3901
jmorris@footlocker.com
- Robert McHugh, Chief Financial Officer
(212) 720-3948
- Peter Brown, SVP/CIO/Investor Relations
(212) 720-4254
- Kenneth Hicks, Chairman, President & Chief Executive Officer

Products:
A specialty athletic retailer that operates approximately 3,600 athletic retail stores in 14 countries in North America, Europe and Australia. Operates through its Foot Locker, Lady Foot Locker, Kids Foot Locker and Champs Sports retail stores plus Footaction, Eastboy, Basketball: Women's National Basketball, Association/WNBA, Running: Title - Foot Locker Cross Country Championships

---

FOOTACTION USA
112 W 34TH STREET
NEW YORK, NY 10120
845-727-6500
800-863-8932
Fax: 845-727-6560
www.footaction.com
- Shawn Neville, President
- Keith Daly, SVP, Footaction
- Steven K. Carnley, VP / Regional Sales Manager

Products:
Footwear, Apparel, Accessories, Fan Gear

Brands:
Nike, Adidas, Jordan, Reebok, Timberland

FRED MEYER STORES, INC.
3800 SE 22ND
PORTLAND, OR 97202
503-232-8844
800-576-4377
Fax: 503-797-5609
kroger.investors@kroger.com
www.fredmeyer.com
- Darrell D. Webb, President
- David Deatherage, VP / Chief Financial Officer
- Lynn Gust, President
- Molly Malone, Senior Vice President and Director
- David Deatherage, Senior Vice President and Chief Financial Off
- Robert Clark, Senior Vice President and Director of the Foo
- Jill McIntosh, Vice President of Human Resources
- Kim Swearinger, Director of Customer Communications and Marke
- Rick Heffner, Senior Director of Store Operations

Products:
General Goods

G GIRL
1004 CROCKER STREET
LOS ANGELES, CA 90021
213-748-2462
Fax: 213-748-2402

Products:
Women's Clothing and Cosmetics

GADZOOKS
4121 INTERNATIONAL PARKWAY
CARROLLTON, TX 75007
972-307-5555
800-966-1355
Fax: 972-662-4290
customerservices@forever21.com
www.gadzooks.com
- Paula Y. Masters, President / Chief Merchandise Officer
- James A. Motley, VP / Chief Financial Officer / Secretary
- George S. Sotirin, VP, Store Operations

Products:
Casual tops, Dressy tops, Basics, Sweaters, Outerwear, Pants, Shorts, Skirts, Dresses, Denim, Accessories, Jewelry

---

GALYAN'S TRADING COMPANY, INC.
339 METROPOLIS MILE
PLAINFIELD, IN 46168
317-839-4803
877-846-9997
Fax: 317-532-0253
www.galyans.com
- Robert Mang, Chief Executive Officer / Director
- Edwin J. Holman, Pres / Chief Operating Officer
- C. D. Zoba, EVP / General Counsel / Secretary
- Edward Wozniak, SVP / Chief Financial Officer

Products:
Sporting Goods.

GANDER MOUNTAIN COMPANY
180 E FIFTH STREET
SUITE 1300
ST PAUL, MN 55101
252-355-7600
888-542-6337
Fax: 888-477-4040
www.gandermountain.com
- Mark R. Baker, Chief Executive Officer
- Al Dittrich, Chief Operating Officer
- Gary Hauger, EVP
- Jeff Bergmann, VP, Marketing

Products:
Specialty focus on hunting, fishing, and camping, Apparel, Foorwear

Brands:
Columbia Sportswear, Woolrich, Mossy Oak, Pella, Walls, Carhartt, LaCrosse, Rocky, Vasque, Wrangler

---

GEAR.COM, INC.
6322 S 3000 E
SUITE 100
SALT LAKE CITY, UT 84121
801-947-3100
Fax: 801-944-4629
info@overstock.com
www.gear.com
- Ken Blue, President
- Wayne Wong, Chief Technical Officer
- Dick Holcombe, EVP, Product / Distribution
- Joe Kenny, Chief Financial Officer

Products:
Furniture, Home D,cor, Home Improvement, Housewares, Tools, Jewelry & Watches, Accessories, Recreation & Sport's Collectibles, Sports Gear & Equipment, Audio & Video, Cameras & Optics, Computers & Printers, Home Office Equipment, Telephones, Apparel, Shoes & Access, Books, CDs, Movies & More, Healthcare & Supplies, Gifts & Flowers

Brands:
Dolce & Gabbana, Tahari, Dr Martens, Ralph Lauren, Prada, Betula Birkenstock, Frette, Sony, Movado, Nike

---

GENE TAYLOR'S SPORTSMEN SUPPLY, INC.
201 W TOMICHI
GUNISSON, CO 81230
970-641-1845
www.genetaylors.com

- Duke O. Taylor, President
- Tony S. Taylor, VP, Buyer
- Marshal F. Taylor, VP Buyer
- Gene Taylor, President / Buyer
Products:
Sporting Goods

GENESCO INC./JOURNEYS
GENESCO PARK 1415 MURFREESBORO ROAD
PO BOX 731
NASHVILLE, TN 37202-0731
615-367-7000
Fax: 615-367-8579
www.genesco.com
- Robert J Dennis, President/Chief Executive
- Robert J. Dennis, EVP and Chief Operating Officer
- James S. Gulmi, SVP, Finance and Chief Financial Officer
- James C. Estepa, SVP, Genesco Retail
Products:
Footwear, Headwear and Accessories
Brands:
Journeys, Journeys Kidz, Johnson & Murphy, Underground Station, Hatworld, Lids, Hat Zone, Cap Factory

GIGA, INC.
2448 INDUSTRIAL PARK DRIVE
MACON, GA 31216
478-788-2448
800-388-2448
Fax: 478-788-4108
online@gigainc.com
www.gigainc.com
- Charlton Veazey, Chief Executive Officer
- Walt Miller, Chief Executive Officer and Buyer
Products:
Freedom Boots, Dessert Steel Toe Boots, Clothing
Brands:
Suede/Camouflage Cordura, Steel Toe, Gore-Tex, BDU Camo Scrubs, and Mobility Folders

GNC CORPORATION
300 6TH AVENUE
PITTSBURGH, PA 15222
412-288-4600
877-463-4700
Fax: 412-288-8379
www.gnc.com

GOLF MART/WORLDWIDE GOLF/ROGER DUNN GOLF
1421 VILLAGE WAY
SANTA ANA, CA 92705
714-558-0074
888-216-5252
Fax: 714-543-6622
www.worldwidegolfshops.com
- Craig McCallister, Chief Executive Officer
- Al Morris, General Manager
Products:
Golf Clubs, Golf Bags, Golf Balls, Golf Gifts, Golf Apparel, Training Aids, Books/Videos, Accessories
Brands:
Callaway, Nike, TaylorMade, Ping, Titleist, Cleveland, Adams, Bite, Acer, Bad Boy, Brush Tee, Paragon, Odessey, Carbite, Champ, hiPPO, Golf Pride, Innova, Kodak, Slazenger, Strata

GOLF USA
4405 N HARRISSON ST
SHAWNEE, OK 74804
405-481-7447
800-488-1107
Fax: 405-481-7409
mail@golfusa.com
www.golfusa.com
- Tom Anthony, Chairman/CEO
- Rck Benson, VP, Franchise Sales and Operations
(405) 751-0015
- Bill Overstreet, VP, Marketing, Sales and Promotions
Products:
Golf Clubs, Golf Bags, Golf Balls, Golf Gifts, Golf Shoes, Golf Apparel, Accessories
Brands:
Titleist, TaylorMade, Nike, Cleveland,TourEdge, FootJoy, Cobra, Pinnacle,MacGregor, Adams, TopFlite

GOLFERS' WAREHOUSE, INC.
75 BRAINARD ROAD
HARTFORD, CT 6114
888-216-5252.
Fax: 860-522-5309
www.golferswarehouse.com
- Jameson Lloyd, Director of Instruction
Products:
Retail Golf Equipment, Clubs, Apparel, Bags & Travel Covers, Carts, Golf Shoes, Golf Accessories, Golf Gifts, Gift Cards
Brands:
Taylor Made, Adidas, Titliest, Foot Joy

GOLFSMITH INTERNATIONAL, INC.
11000 N IH35
AUSTIN, TX 78753
512-821-4050
800-813-6897
Fax: 512-837-1245
www.golfsmith.com
- James D Thompson, President / Chief Executive Officer
- Virginia Bunte, VP / Chief Financial Officer
- Kiprian Miles, VP / Chief Information Officer
- Ginger Bunte, Chief Financial Officer
- Sue E. Gove, President
Products:
Golf and Tennis accessories, balls, clubs, custom club fitting, gifts, gift cards, gloves, grips, Golf Bags & Travel, Home & Office, Outlet, Personalized Gear, Practice and Training, Pre-Owned Clubs, Shoes, Teams and Collegiate, Video & Books
Products:
Golf Clubs, Golf Bags, Golf Balls, Golf Gifts, Golf Shoes, Golf Apparel, Accessories, Custom Club Fitting, Gift Cards, Gloves, Grips, Personalized Gear
Brands:
Callaway, TaylorMade, Cleveland, Cobra, Odyssey, Adidas, Maxfli, Ashworth, Adams, Lynx, MacGregor, Nike, Zevo, Snake Eyes, Golfsmith, Killer Bee, GearForGolf, GiftsForGolf

GREAT OUTDOOR CLOTHING COMPANY
341 SKI WAY
SUITE 201
INCLINE VILLAGE, NV 89451
702-832-9100
800-442-5253
Fax: 800-368-6873
www.greatoutdoorclothing.com

- Stephen Meyers, President
Products:
Outerwear, Technical Jackets, Parkas, Vests, pants and Rainwear
Brands:
Black Ice, SnowLion, Teva, Polartec, Caltech, Helly Hansen, Jansport, Merrell, Alpine Designs, Camelbak and Eagle Creek

GREEN TOP SPORTING GOODS CORPORATION
10150 LAKERIDGE PARKWAY
ASHLAND, VA 23005
804-550-2188
Fax: 804-550-2693
info@greentophuntfish.com
www.greentophuntfish.com
- Charles G. Thalhimer Jr, President
Products:
Hunting and Fishing Gear; Clothing, Eyewear, Footwear/Waders, Accessories, Lights, Marine Electronics
Brands:
Duck Commander, Echo, Knight & Hale, Lohman, M.A.D, Penn's Woods, Primos, Quaker Boy

GYM SOURCE
40 E 52ND STREET
NEW YORK, NY 10022
212-688-4222
800-496-768123
Fax: 212-750-2886
sales@gymsource.com
www.gymsource.com
- Richard Miller, President & Chief Executive Officer
Products:
Accessories, Bikes, Ellipticals, Steppers, Treadmills, Free Weights, Home Gym
Brands:
Cybex, Tuff Stuff, True, Universal, Hoist, Pro Spot, Schwinn, Diamond Back

H-E-B
PO BOX 839999
SAN ANTONIO, TX 78283-3999
210-938-8357
800 432-3113
Fax: 210-938-8048
www.heb.com
- Cory Basso, Vice President/Advertising
- Charles Butt, Chairman & CEO

HAT WORLD/LIDS CORP.
7555 WOODLAND DRIVE
INDIANAPOLIS, IN 46278
317-334-9428
888-564-4287
Fax: 317-337-1428
contactus@hatworld.com
www.lids.com
- Kenneth J. Kocher, President
- Glenn Campbell, Chief Operating Officer
- Clyde Roenbeck, VP, Field Operations
Products:
Branded Athletic Headwear, Apparel, Accessories
Brands:
Adidas, Kangol, Majestic, New Era, Nike, Reebok, Top of the World, Twins, Zephy r Graf-x

HEALTH FITNESS CORPORATION
1700 WEST 82ND STREET
Suite 200
MINNEAPOLIS, MN 55431
952-831-6830
800-639-7913
Fax: 952-897-5173
jobs@hfit.com
www.healthfitness.com
• K James Ehlen, CEO
• Paul Lotharius, President and Chief
Executive Officer
• Brian Gagne, Chief Operations Officer
• Dennis Richling, Chief Medical and
Wellness Officer
• Teri Lonergan, Chief Information Officer
• Karen Preusker, Chief Financial Officer
• Mark Totts, Senior Vice President, Product
Development
• Sean McManamy, Senior Vice President,
Corporate Development
Products & Services:
Offers on-site solutions for corporations,
hospitals, communities, and universities in
many delivery modes — face to face,
Web-based, telephone or mail.

HERB PHILIPSON'S
1899 BLACK RIVER BOULEVARD
ROME, NY 13440
315-336-1302
Fax: 315-337-5840
info@herbphilipsons.com
www.herbphilipsons.com
• Gary Philipson, President
Products:
Apparel, Footwear, Sporting Goods
Brands:
Carhartt, Columbia, Lee, Woolrick, Dickies,
Levi's

HIBBETT SPORTING GOODS
2700 MILAN COURT
BIRMINGHAM, AL 35211
205-942-4292
Fax: 205-912-7279
www.hibbett.com
• Michael Newsome, Chairman/Chief
Executive Officer
• Joseph Nissan, President/Chief
Operations Officer
• Gary A. Smith, VP and Chief Financial
Officer
• Jeffry O. Rosenthal, VP Merchandising
• Jeff Rosenthal, President and CEO
Products:
Full Line Sporting Goods
Brands:
New Balance, Easton, Schutt, Fossil,
Adidas, K-Swiss, Mizuno, Louisville Slugger,
Rawlings

HOIGAARD'S INC.
5425 EXCELSIOR BOULEVARD
SAINT LOUIS PARK, MN 55416
952-929-1351
800-266-8157
Fax: 952-929-2669
info@hoigaards.com
www.hoigaards.com
• Mike White, Buyer
• Bob Soash, Buyer
• Rita Lind, Buyer
• Alex Avedikian, Director, Marketing and
Advertising
Products & Services:
Bike Services, Canoe & Kayak Rentals,
In-Line Skate Services, Mounting and Other
Services, Pack Rentals, Toko Thermo Bag,
Snowboard, Tunes

HUDSON TRAIL OUTFITTERS, LTD.
4530 WISCONSON AVE NW
WASHINGTON, DC 20016
202-363-9810
HTO_Customer_Service@hudsontrail.com
• Henry F. Cohan, President
• John Behall, Bike Shop Manager
Products:
Men's and Women's Outerwear, Apparel
and Footwear; Watersports Gear, Fly
Fishing Gear, Climbing Gear, Cycling Gear,
Snowsports Gear, Sleeping Bags, Tents and
Shelters
Brands:
Birkenstock, Havana Joe, CW-X, CamelBak
Logo, Dansko, Ranger

**INTERACTIVECORP/HOME SHOPPING
NETWORK**
1 HSN DRIVE
SAINT PETERSBURG, FL 33729
212-314-7300
800-933-2887
Fax: 212-314-7379
www.hsn.com
• Bob Diener, President, Hotels.com
• David Litman, Chief Executive Officer,
Hotels.com
Products:
Watches, Jewelry, Fashion and
Accessories, Beauty, Health and Fitness
Brands:
Absolute, Andrew Lessman, Carolyn
Strauss, Diane Gilman, Esteban, Euro-Pro,
Gateway, Highgate Manor, Hoover, BFL,
Slinky Brand, Maggie Sweet

J. BAKER, INC.
555 TURNPIKE STREET
CANTON, MA 2021
781-821-2500
800-767-0319
Fax: 781-828-3721
info@CasualMale.com
• Jerry Socol, President and Chief Executive
Officer
• Brian Eddy, Divisional Merchandise
Manager
• Bob Crosby, Buyer
• Mark Fletcher, Buyer
Products:
Shirts, Pants and Jeans, Activewear,
Outerwear, Sweaters and Vests, Suit
Separates, Sportcoats
Brands:
626 Blue, Calvin Klein, Cutter & Buck,
George Foreman, Harbor Bay, Izod, Levi's /
Dockers, Nautica, NFL, Polo Jeans
Company, Polo Ralph Lauren, Reebok

J.C. PENNEY CORPORATION, INC.
6501 LEGACY DRIVE
PO BOX 8178
MANCHESTER, CT 06040-1463
972-431-1000
800-322-1189
Fax: 972-431-1362
www.jcpenney.com
• Myron E. Ullman III, Chairman and Chief
Executive Officer
• Kenneth C. Hicks, President and Chief
Merchandising Office
• Robert B. Cavanaugh, EVP and Chief
Financial Officer
Products:
Women's, Men's and Kid's Apparel and
Sportswear; Jewelry, Window Accessories,
Home Furnishings, Housewares, Gifts and
Registry
Brands:
St. John's Bay, Arizona, Levi's, Dockers,
Delicates, Worthington, a.n.a, Lee

JACOBSON STORES
329 N PARK AVENUE
SUITE 101
WINTER PARK, FL 32789
407-539-2528
• Tammy Giaimo, President
• Beth Aranda, Retail Manager
• Sam June, Creative Director
Products:
Women's Apparel, Women's Shoes and
Handbags, Women's Jewelry and
Accessories, Men's Apparel.
Brands:
Cole Haan, Sandro Moscoloni

JOHNNY MAC'S SPORTING GOODS
10100 WATSON ROAD
SUNSET HILLS, MO 63127
314-966-5444
800-962-8347
Fax: 314-966-6098
www.johnnymacs.com
• Bob McArthur, President & Chief
Executive Officer
• Rick McArthur, Chief Financial Officer
• Bob McArthur, President & CEO
Products:
Sporting Goods, Team Uniforms, Trophies
Brands:
Nike, Under Armour, Rawlings, Easton,
Louisville Slugger, Bauer, Reebok, CCM,
Mizuno, Russell Athletic, Wilson, Worth,
Schutt

JUST FOR FEET
933 MACARTHUR BOULEVARD
MAHWAH, NJ 7430
201-934-2000
Fax: 845-727-6560
www.footstar.com
• Stephen R. Wilson, EVP and Chief
Financial Officer
• Jeffrey A. Gordon, President and Chief
Executive Officer, J
• J. M. Robinson, Chairman / Chief
Executive Officer / Pre
• Joseph C. Caracappa, Chief Information
Officer
Products:
Athletic Footwear
Brands:
New Balance, FootStar

JUST SPORTS
3500 S MERIDIAN
SOUTH HILL MALL
PUYALLUP, WA 98373
253-845-7053
Fax: 818-719-9244
www.justsports.net
• Glen Erikson, President
Products:
Sports Retailer, Shoes, Apparel,
Accessories

JUSTHERSPORTS.COM
6704 FERRIS ST
BELLAIRE, TX 77401
713-661-7272
888-561-3364
Fax: 713-661-7242
info@justhersports.com
www.sportsforher.com
• Mary Stone, Co-Founder
• Howard Stone, Co-Founder
Products:
Sporting goods and accessories for soccer,
softball, basketball, volleyball, cycling,
tennis, golf, lacrosse, field hockey,
swimming, running, gymnastics, and fitness.
Brands:
Wilson, Spalding, Mikasa, STX, Brine,
Champion, Mitre, Tachikara, Penn, Baden,
Zoomers, Worth, Barracuda, InSport,
Babolat, CamelBak, Bellwether, Reusch,
Prince

KERR DRUG INC.
3220 SPRING FOREST ROAD
RALEIGH, NC 27616
919-544-3896
800-494-3053
Fax: 919-544-3796
www.kerrdrug.com
• Anthony Civello, President and Chief
Executive Officer
• Richard D. Johnson, EVP and Chief
Financial Officer
• William B. Baxley, SVP, Merchandising
and Marketing
• Phyllis Patterson,
ppatterson@kerrdrug.com
• Diane Eliezer, Director, Marketing
Products & Services:
Health Store

KESSLERS SPORT SHOP, INC.
930 E MAIN STREET
RICHMOND, IN 47374
765-935-2595
800-527-7510
Fax: 765-935-1866
info@kesslersteamsports.com
www.bsnsports.com
• Robert J. Dickman, President
• Jeff Wise, Sales
Products:
Sporting Goods
Brands:
Nike, Adidas, Converse, Reebok

KID'S FOOT LOCKER
112 W 34TH STREET
NEW YORK, NY 10120
212-720-3700
800-991-6684
Fax: 212-720-4397
• Tim Finn, President and Chief Executive
Officer
• Rubin Hanan, SVP, Retail Brand
Marketing
Products:
Shoes, Clothing, Sports Equipment,
Accessories, Fan Gear for Kids.
Brands:
ABC Sports, All Star, American Spirit,
Baxter, Colorado, Callaway, Champion,
Dickies, Elite Kold, Fubu, Headmaster,
Grabber, Glovemate, Adidas, Reebok, Nike

KITTERY TRADING POST
301 US ROUTE ONE
PO BOX 904
KITTERY, ME 03904
603-334-1157
888-587-6246
888-439-9036
Fax: 207-439-8001
info@kitterytradingpost.com
www.kitterytradingpost.com
• Bob Adams, Facilities Director
• David M. Labbe, Chief Financial Officer
• Kevin F. Adams, Treasurer, Archery and
Shooting Sports A
• Kim C. Adams, President
Products:
Archery, Camping/Hiking, Fishing, Shooting
Sports, Used Guns, Watersports,
Wintersports, Footwear, Men's Clothing
Brands:
Columbia Sportswear Company, Carhartt,
Woolrich, The North Face, Levis, Under
Armour, Exofficio, Mountain Hardwear,
Marmot, Ibex, Patagonia, Advanced
Elements, Ocean Kayak, Old Town, Ranger,
Coleman, Teva, Merrell, Kelty

**KLEIN'S ALL SPORT DISTRIBUTORS
INC.**
14 WETMORE STREET
SUITE 2
NEW YORK MILLS, NY 13417
315-768-8194
Fax: 315-768-1510
• Donald Klein, Chairman
Products:
Sporting and Recreational Goods

KMART CORPORATION
3100 W BIG BEAVER ROAD
TROY, MI 48084
248-463-1000
Fax: 248-463-1454
www.kmart.com
• Aylwin B. Lewis, Chief Executive Officer,
Kmart Retail
• William C. Crowley, EVP and Chief
Financial Officer
• Dene L. Rogers, EVP, Restructuring and
Business Improvem
Products:
Jewelry, Women's and Men's Apparel,
Sports Equipment, Baby's Accessories, and
other name-brand and private-label items.
Brands:
Jaclyn Smith, Thalia Sodi, Route 66, Joe
Boxer, Razor, Schwinn, Martha Stewart

KOHL'S DEPARTMENT STORES
N56 W17000 RIDGEWOOD DRIVE
MENOMONEE FALLS, WI 53051
262-703-7000
855-564-5705
Fax: 262-703-7115
Customer.Service@Kohls.com
www.kohlscorporation.com
• Larry Montgomery, Chairman and Chief
Executive Officer
directors@kohls.com
• Kevin Mansell, President
directors@kohls.com
• Arlene Meier, Chief Operating Officer
directors@kohls.com
• Brian Miller, SVP, Corporate Governance
(262) 703-1723
brian.f.miller@kohls.com
• Steven Burd, Lead Director

directors@kohls.com
• Jen Johnson, Director of Public Relations
(262) 703-5241
jen.johnson@kohls.com
• Molly Verette, Senior Public Relations
Manager
(262) 703-7008
molly.verette@kohls.com
• Kristen Cunningham, Public Relations
Manager
(262) 703-7863
kristen.cunningham@kohls.com
• Tami Kou, Public Relations Manager
(262) 703-7725
tami.kou@kohls.com
Products:
Apparel; Shoes and Accessories for
Women, Children and Men; Home Products
Brands:
Carter'sr, Championr, Columbia Sportswear
Company, Dockers, Haggar, Healthtex,
Jockey, KitchenAid, Krups, Lee, Levi's,
Norton McNaughton, Pfaltzgraff, Playtex,
Reebok, Vanity Fair.

L.L. BEAN
15 CASCO STREET
FREEPORT, ME 04033-0001
207-552-3028
800-559-0747
Fax: 207-552-3080
preferences@llbean.com
www.llbean.com
• Leon A. Gorman, Chairman
• Chris McCormick, President and Chief
Executive Officer
• Mark Fasold, SVP and Chief Financial
Officer
• Leon A. Gorman, Chairman of the Board
• Christopher J. McCormick, President and
CEO
• Bob Peixotto, SVP, Human Resources
Products:
Outerwear, Footwear, Outdoor Gear and
Apparel, Sport Equipment
Brands:
L.L.Bean, Therm-a-Rest, Katahdin, Brown
Bear

LADY FOOT LOCKER
120 W 34TH STREET
NEW YORK, NY 10120
715-261-9709
800-991-6686
Fax: 212-720-4397
www.ladyfootlocker.com
• Nick Grayston, President and Chief
Executive Officer
Products:
Footwear, Sports Apparel, Accessories,
Casualwear and Fan Gear for Women.
Brands:
Ryka, New Balance, Adidas, Converse,
Puma, Champion, Saucony, Reebok,
Concord, All Star, Colorado, Etonic, ESPN,
Ewatch, Franklin, Fox River

LANGHORNE SKI & SPORT
543 LINCOLN HIGHWAY
FAIRLESS HILLS, PA 19030
215-295-4240
800-523-8850
Fax: 215-295-5341
• David M. Constantini, Chief Executive
Officer
• Kathy Constantini, Owner and Buyer

Products:
Offers a full line of downhill and Nordic skis and equipment, snowboards, clothing, skateboards, in-line skates, roof racks, services and various summer sport items.

LAS VEGAS GOLF & TENNIS
4711 DEAN MARTIN DRIVE
LAS VEGAS, NV 89169
702-892-9999
www.lvgolf.com
• Steve Puett, President and Chief Executive Officer
• Ted Kallgren, Chief Operating Officer
• Brian Va Duren, VP, Franchise Sales
Products & Services:
Putters, Golf Balls, Golf and Tennis Bags, Golf Apparel, Golf Gifts, Tennis Racquets, Tennis Apparel, Tennis Accessories, Golf and Tennis Shoes, Wedges, Gloves, Outerwear. Services: Custom Club Fitting, Gift Certificates, Lessons and Swing Analysis
Brands:
Adamsn, Brighton, Adidas, Prince, Spalding, Titleist, Cobra, Ashworth, Cross Creek, Wilson, Ping

LAZARUS
4300 ASHFORD DUNWOODY ROAD
ATLANTA, GA 30346
770-396-2800
800-289-6229
Fax: 770-913-5114
www.macys.com
• Andrew P. Pickman, President and Chief Merchandising Office
• Eric Jimenez, Executive Creative Director
Products:
Private-label Apparel, Cosmetics, Jewelry and Housewares
Brands:
Baby Phat Plus, Sketchers, Calvin Klein

LEGENDS SPORTING GOODS
459 KING STREET
LITTLETON, MA 01460
978-339-5222
Fax: 978-264-2922
kevdogsports@aol.com
• William Kahn, President
• Glenn Ferraro, Owner and VP
Products:
Sporting Goods

LEVTRAN ENTERPRISES
7455 NEW RIDGE ROAD
SUITE N
HANOVER, MD 21076
410-850-5900
Fax: 410-494-8707
www.dtlr.com
• Eric Levin, President
• Tony Trantas, VP
• Rick Levin, ÿCo-Founder and Chief Executive Officer
Products:
Urban apparel, footwear and related accessories.

LUCY.COM
2701 HARBOR BAY PARKWAY
SUITE 300
ALAMEDA, CA 94502
503-228-2142
877-999-5829

Fax: 503-295-2510
www.lucy.com
• Sue Levin, Co-Founder / Chief Executive Officer
• Stephen Hochman, Co-Founder / VP Sales Operations
• Kate Delhagen, VP, Business Development
• Judith Kempe, Director of Design
Products:
E-tailer: Women's sports retail internet site and retail store devoted to merging style with functional sportswear and to meeting the individual needs of active women of all ages, sizes, and fitness levels.

MACY'S
151 W 34TH STREET
NEW YORK, NY 10001
212-695-4400
800-264-0069
Fax: 212-494-1057
www.macys.com
• Terry J. Lundgren, Chairman, President & Chief Executive Officer
Products:
Beauty products, Men's apparel, Women's Apparel, Shoes, Jewelry, Dinnerware, Housewares and Kitchen gadgets, Furniture and Mattresses, Linens, Kitchenware
Brands:
Calvin Klein, Charter Club, Court of Versailles, DKNY, Hotel Collection, Lauren Ralph Lauren, Lilly Pulitzer, Missoni, Oscar by Oscar de la Renta, Sigrid Olsen, Tommy Bahama, Tommy Hilfiger, Waterford

MACY'S, CALIFORNIA
685 MARKET STREET
SAN FRANCISCO, CA 94105
415-397-3333
Fax: 415-296-4126
www.macys.com
• Terry J. Lundgren, Chairman, President & Chief Executive Officer
Products:
Beauty products, Men's apparel, Women's Apparel, Shoes, Jewelry, Dinnerware, Housewares and Kitchen gadgets, Furniture and Mattresses, Linens, Kitchenware
Brands:
Calvin Klein, Charter Club, Court of Versailles, DKNY, Hotel Collection, Lauren Ralph Lauren, Lilly Pulitzer, Missoni, Oscar by Oscar de la Renta, Sigrid Olsen, Tommy Bahama, Tommy Hilfiger, Waterford

MARK'S OUTDOOR SPORTS, INC
1400 MONTGOMERY HIGHWAY
BIRMINGHAM, AL 35216
205-822-2010
877-979-6275
Fax: 205-822-2984
info@marksoutdoors.com
www.marksoutdoors.com
• Mark Whitlock, Owner
(205) 822-2010
Products:
Fishing & Hunting Accessories, Firearms

MARSHALL'S
1 WORCESTER ROAD
FRAMINGHAM, MA 1701
508-872-2684
888-627-7425
Fax: 508-390-2828
www.marshallsonline.com

• Edmond J. English, President, Chief Executive Officer, Dire
• Donald G. Campbell, EVP / Finance / CFO TJX Companies
• Ernie Herrman, EVP / Chief Operating Officer, Marmaxx G
Products:
Apparel & Accessories: Ladies, Men, Teen, Kids; shoes, Housewares

MARTIN'S GOLF & TENNIS, INC.
4010 VENTURE DRIVE
DULUTH, GA 30096
888-200-7428
877-272-6030
Fax: 843-272-4772
customerservice@pgatoursuperstore.com
www.pgatoursuperstore.com
• Martin H. Barrier, President
Products:
Sports Equipment and Apparel for Golf and Tennis.

MAURICE SPORTING GOODS, INC.
1910 TECHNY ROAD
NORTHBROOK, IL 60065
847-715-1500
800-477-3474
Fax: 847-715-1418
www.maurice.net
• Frank Katlin, President
• Bruce Karper, VP / Director Merchandise
Products:
Fishing Tackle, Shooting Sports Accessories, and other Outdoor Sporting and Athletic Goods

MAY DEPARTMENT STORES COMPANY
611 OLIVE STREET
SAINT LOUIS, MO 63101
314-342-6300
Fax: 314-342-3064
www.mayco.com

MAY DEPARTMENT STORES COMPANY, THE
611 OLIVE STREET
SAINT LOUIS, MO 63101
314-342-6300
800-223-7440
Fax: 314-342-3064
www.mayco.com
• Eugene S. Kahn, Chairman / Chief Executive Officer
• John L. Dunham, President / Director
• Thomas D. Fingleton, EVP / Chief Financial Officer
• Jeffrey S. Califano, SVP, Sportwear Product Development
Products:
General Goods

MC SPORTS
3070 SHAFFER SE
GRAND RAPIDS, MI 49512
616-942-2600
800-626-1762
Fax: 616-942-2312
www.mcsports.com
• Bruce Ullery, President / Chief Executive Officer
• Dan Winchester, VP / General Manager
• Joseph Smith, Director of Loss Prevention
(616) 285-1609
• Connie Rush, Director of Human Resources

Products:
Sporting Goods
Brands:
A-Game, A-Tack, A.L.S., B' Warmer, B.S.I. Products, Camelback, Champion Sports, Champro, DAC Technologies, Daisy, Corr, E-Force, Gerber, Halo Sports, Hammer

MCRAE'S, INC.
2801 W TYVOLA ROAD
PO BOX 37201
CHARLOTTE, NC 28217
601-968-6258
866-235-5443
Fax: 601-968-6310
belk_customer_care@belk.com
• Thomas M Belk, Jr, Chairman/CEO
Products:
General Goods

MEGA FITNESS
630 S WICKHAM ROAD, #107
WEST MELBOURNE, FL 32904
321-674-3866
800-925-2772
Fax: 321-694-9914

MEIGRAY GROUP
185 INDUSTRIAL PARKWAY
SUITE C
BRANCHBURG, NJ 8876
908-541-0114
888-463-4472
Fax: 908-541-1123
sales@meigray.com
www.meigray.com
• Barry Meisel, Co-Founder
(908) 541-0114
bmeisel@meigray.com
• Bob Gray, Co-Founder
• Barry Meisel, President
Products:
Jerseys

MEIJER, INC.
2929 WALKER AVENUE, NW
GRAND RAPIDS, MI 49544-9424
616-453-6711
877-363-4537
Fax: 616-791-2572
www.meijer.com
• Larry Zigerelli, SVP, Merchandising
• Paul Boyer, President / Chief Operating Officer
• Doug Meijer, Co-Chairman
• Hendrik G. Meijer, Co-Chairman / Chief Executive Officer
Products:
TVs, VCRs, DVD Players, Audio, Computer Supplies, Photo, Phones, Accessories, Movies, Power Tools, Adhesives, Fasteners, Lighting, Hand Tools, Measurement Tools, Garage, House wares, Kitchenware, Sporting Goods, Toys, Beverages, Specialty Meat and Seafood, Meat and Seafood Sauces, International Cuisine, Gourmet Food Complements, Sweet Delights, Hors d oeuvres

MERCHANT OF TENNIS, INC.
1621 BAYVIEW AVENUE
TORONTO, ON, CANADA M4G 3B5
416-932-2396
888-932-2396
Fax: 416-932-2397

experts@merchantoftennis.com
www.merchantoftennis.com
• Jeff Green, President
• John Ramsbottom, Marketing Manager
Products & Services:
Professional service and the largest selection of racquets, clothing, footwear and accessories.

MERVYN'S
22301 FOOTHILL BOULEVARD
MAILSTOP 2115
HAYWARD, CA 94541
510-727-3000
800-637-8967
Fax: 510-727-2300
• Diane L. Neal, President
• Clay Creasey, Chief Executive Officer
• Maureen W. Kyer, EVP Merchandising
• Lynn Schirmer, EVP / Merchandising Planning
Products:
General Goods

MODELL'S SPORTING GOODS
498 7th AVE
20TH FLOOR
NEW YORK, NY 10018
212-661-4242
800-275-6633
Fax: 212-822-1025
www.modells.com
• William Modell, Chairman
• Mitchell Modell, Chief Financial Officer
• Robert Stevenish, President, Chief Operating Officer
• Lawrence E. Long, Chief Financial Officer
Products:
Sporting Goods, Sporting Apparel, Menswear, Athletic footwear

NATION'S BEST SPORTS
4216 HAHN BOULEVARD
FORT WORTH, TX 76117
817-788-0034
800-379-0155
Fax: 817-788-8542
rmcgill@nbs.com
www.nationsbestsports.com
• Jim Chandley, President
(817) 605-2209
jchandley@nationsbestsports.com
• Angela Mooney, Corporate Secretary
(817) 605-2203
amooney@nationsbestsports.com
• Melissa Offill, Controller
(817) 605-2202
moffill@nationsbestsports.com
• Jim Chandley, President
(817) 605-2209
jchandley@nbs.com
• Bryan Davis, Executive Vice President of Operations
(817) 605-2205
bdavis@nationsbestsports.com
• Steven Baker, Merchandising Vice President
(817) 605-2217
Sbaker@nbs.com
• Dave Nacke, Vice President, Merchandising - Outdoor Divis
(817) 605-2249
dnacke@nbs.com
• Anna VanGoey, Meeting & Exhibit Manager
(817) 605-2214
acorbett@nbs.com

• Julie Cerza, Exhibit Coordinator
(817) 605-2212
jcerza@nbs.com
• Marty Plazo, Divisional Merchandise Manager
(817) 605-2218
mplazo@nbs.com
Products:
National retail buying organization with over 150 members operating more than 1,200 stores

NEVADA BOB'S INTERNATIONAL, INC.
81 BRAINARD ROAD
SUITE 7070
HARTFORD, CT 6114
416-366-2221
800-405-4653
Fax: 416-366-7722
• Kevin R. Baker, President / Chief Executive Officer
(403) 698-8560
• Arnold T. Kondrat, Chairman
(416) 366-2221
• Richard J. Lachcik, Secretary
Products:
Golf Club
Brands:
Adams, Adidas, Armour, Ashworth, Avant, Bag Boy, Bazooka, Ben Hogan, Bennington, Bettinardi, Bite, Bolle, Booklegger, Bushnell, Callaway, Carbite, Cart Caddy, Champ, Cleveland, Club Glove, Cobra, Coppertone, Datrek, Dexter, Dockers, Duck Press, Dunlop, Ecco, Etonic, Fairway, Florsheim, Footjoy, Fore Better Golf, Galaxy Sports, Gean-Edwards, Golden Bear, Golf Achiever, Golf Pride, Great Divide, Greg Norman, GTB, Hi Tec, Hippo, HOG, Izod, Izzo, Kallasy, Sports, Kasco, Kidsklub, La Jolla, Lady Accent, Lady Fairway, Lady Player, Leadbetter, Mac Gregor

NEW YORK GOLF CENTER, INC.
131 W 35TH STREET
NEW YORK, NY 10001
212-564-2255
888-465-7890
Fax: 212-244-6941
contactus@nygolfcenter.com
www.nygolfcenter.com
• Samuel K. Rhee, President
• Jay Shin, Manager Buyer
Products:
Golf Products

NINE WEST GROUP, INC.
1129 WESCHESTER AVENUE
WHITE PLAINS, NY 10604
866-933-9378
800-999-1877
Fax: 914-640-6024
www.ninewest.com
• Rhonda J. Brown, President / Chief Executive Officer
• Wesley R. Card, Chief Financial Officer
Products:
Dress, Sandals, Shoes, Handbags, Jewelry, Wallets, Scarves, Hats
Brands:
Nine West

NORDICTRACK FITNESS STORES
1500 S 1000 W
LOGAN, UT 84321
495-750-5000
877-993-7999

Fax: 435-750-3917
service@iconfitness.com
www.nordictrack.com
• Margie Dupuis, Senior Director,
Merchandise
• Sue Benett, Senior Buyer
Products:
Treadmills, Ellipticals, Exercise Bikes,
Strength Training, Incline Trainers, Skiers,
Steppers, Accessories, Men's Apparel,
Women's Apparel, NordicTrack Yoga Elite
Kit, iFIT Yoga Health Club Kit, NordicTrack
Recovery Premier Kit, Commercial Grade
Equipment
Brands:
NordicTrack

NORTH FACE
14450 DOOLITTLE DRIVE
SAN LEANDRO, CA 94577
855-500-8639
888-863-1968
Fax: 510-618-3531
tnf_consumerservices@vfc.com
www.thenorthface.com
• Michael R Egeck, President
• Dan Templin, Chief Financial Officer
• Jody Kalmbach, VP, Marketing
• Steve Rendle, VP Sales, North America
• Aaron Carpenter, Vice President of
Marketing
Products:
Men's Apparel, Women's Apparel,
Footwear, Accessories, Sleeping Bags,
Bags, Sports Gear

ODD JOB TRADING
200 HELEN STREET
S PLAINFIELD, NJ 07080
908-222-1000
888-262-9464
Fax: 908-222-9756
www.dccreatives.com/amazing/
• Stuart Levy, Chief Financial Officer / Chief
Executiv
Products:
Offers an amazing range of merchandise
such as housewares, electronics, furniture,
fashions, cosmetics, cookware, appliances,
toys and more, including many name
brands.

ODD LOTS/BIG LOTS
300 PHILLIPI ROAD
COLUMBUS, OH 43228-5311
614-278-6800
800-877-1253
Fax: 614-278-6676
talk2us@BigLots.com
www.biglots.com
• Michael J Potter, Chairman / President /
Chief Executive O
• Kent Larsson, EVP, Marketing
• Donald Mierzwa, EVP, Store Operations
• Jeffrey Naylor, SVP / Chief Financial
Officer
• Norman J. Rankin, General Merchandise
Manager
Products:
Consumables, Seasonal Products,
Furniture, Housewares, Toys, Gifts

ORVIS COMPANY
1711 BLUE HILLS DRIVE
ROANOKE, VA 24012
540-345-6789
888-235-9763

Fax: 540-343-7053
customerservice@orvis.com
www.orvis.com
• Leigh Perkins, President / Chief Executive
Officer
• David Perkins, SVP, Retail & Dealer
• Brian Gowan, VP, Finance
• Raymond G. McCready, President
Products:
Fishing Apparel, Line, Lures, Poles, Reels,
Rods, Home Furnishings, Country Gifts

OUTDOOR WORLD, INC.
2720 S RODEO GULCH ROAD
SOQUEL, CA 95073-2026
888-344-9500
888-344-9500
Fax: 831-476-8597
info@theoutdoorworld.com
www.theoutdoorworld.com
• Bob Thomas, Owner
• Chris Thomas, VP, Buyer
Products:
Air Guns Backpacking Batteries Beach &
Swim Bicycle Accessories Boy Scouts
Camping Car Racks Clothing Daypacks
Exercise Equipment Fishing Games &
Sports Hunting, Camouflage Marine
Inflatables Shoes, Boots, Sandals, Cleats
Sleeping Bags, Pads Snowboards & Skis
Sunglasses & Watches Tents & Canopies

OVERTON'S
111 RED BANKS ROAD
PO BOX 8228
GREENVILLE, NC 27858
252-355-7600
800-334-6541
Fax: 252-355-2923
intl@overtons.com
www.overtons.com
• V. Overton, President
• Herman B. Norris, VP
Products:
Sporting Goods

PAMIDA, INC.
8800 F STREET
OMAHA, NE 68127
402-339-2400
Fax: 402-596-7330
www.shopko.com
• Mike Hopkins, President
• Robert Hafner, SVP, Marketing / Business
• Paul Rothamel, SVP, Store Operations
Products:
Sporting Goods

PARADIES SHOP/PGA TOUR SHOPS
2849 PACES FERRY ROAD
OVERLOOK I, SUITE 400
ATLANTA, GA 30339
404-344-7905
Fax: 404-349-3226
www.theparadiesshops.com
• Gregg Paradies, President
• Dick Dickson, Chairman
• James Paradies, Vice Chairman
• Gregg Paradies, President & Chief
Executive Officer
Products:
Apparel, Gifts, Souvenirs, Golf Apparel and
Equipment

PARAGON SPORTING GOODS CO. LLC
867 BROADWAY AT 18TH STREET
SUITE 3N
NEW YORK, NY 10003
212-255-8889
800-961-3030
Fax: 212-929-1831
customerservice@paragonsports.com
www.paragonsports.com
• Jerry Blank, Chief Executive Officer
Products:
Sporting Goods & Sports Apparel

PAYLESS SHOESOURCE, INC.
3231 SE 6TH AVENUE
TOPEKA, CANADA 66607
785-233-5171
877-474-6379
Fax: 785-295-6220
www.payless.com
• Duane L Cantrell, President / Director
(785) 295-2013
duane_cantrell@paylesssshoesource.com
• Ullrich E Porzig, SVP / Chief Financial
Officer / Treasure
• John N Haugh, SVP, Marketing
Products:
Shoes

PEEBLES, INC.
10201 MAIN STREET
HOUSTON, TX 77025
434-447-5200
800-324-3244
Fax: 434-447-5453
• Mike Mooreman, President / Chief
Executive Officer
• E. Lail, SVP / Chief Financial Officer /
Secretar
• Ronnie W Palmore, SVP / Assistant
Secretary
• Marvin H Thomas, Jr., SVP Operations
Products:
General Goods

**PERFORMANCE, INC./PERFORMANCE
BICYCLE SHOP**
PO BOX 2741
CHAPEL HILL, NC 27515
919-933-9113
800-727-2453
Fax: 919-942-5431
www.performancebike.com
• Bob Martin, Chief Executive Officer
Products:
Bicycle & Frames, Men's Clothing, Women's
Clothing, Accessories

PETER GLENN SKI & SPORT
2688 NW 29th TERRACE
OAKLAND PARK, FL 33311
954-484-3606
800-818-0946
Fax: 954-739-5724
questions@peterglenn.com
www.peterglenn.com
• Edward J Hamilton, Chairman
Products:
Ski Equipment and Supplies

POWERHOUSE GYMS, INTERNATIONAL
137 SOUTH MAIN
2ND FLOOR
ADRIAN, MI 49221
517-265-5533
Fax: 248-476-4732

customerservice@powerhousegym.com
www.powerhousegym.com
• William K Dabish, President / Co-Founder
customerservice@powerhousegym.com
Products:
gym licensing

PRICE COSTCO WHOLESALE
999 LAKE DRIVE
ISSAQUAH, WA 98027
425-313-8100
800-955-2292
Fax: 425-313-8114
customerservice@costco.com
www.costco.com
• Richard Galanti, EVP / Chief Financial
Officer
(425) 313-8203
investor@costco.com
• Bob Nelson, VP / Financial Planning &
Investor Relat
(425) 313-8255
investor@costco.com
• Jeff Elliott, Director / Financial Planning &
Investor
(425) 313-8264
investor@costco.com
• Muriel Cooper, Community Relations &
Administration
(425) 313-6182
MCooper@costco.com
Products:
groceries, candy, appliances, television and
media, automotive supplies, tires, toys,
hardware, sporting goods, jewelry, watches,
cameras, books, housewares, apparel,
health and beauty aids, tobacco, furniture,
office supplies and office equipment; special
food packaging, optical laboratories, meat
processing and jewelry distribution

PRO GOLF DISCOUNT
13405 S.E. 30TH STREET
SUITE 1-A
BELLEVUE, WA 98005
425-957-3626
800-394-4653
888-640-4111
Fax: 425-373-3153
service@golfdiscount.com
www.golfdiscount.com
• Randy Silver, President / Buyer
• Perry Ponti, General Manager / Buyer
Products:
golf equipment

PRO GOLF OF AMERICA
23399 COMMERCE DRIVE
SUITE B-1
FARMINGTON HILLS, MI 48335
248-994-0553
800-776-4653
Fax: 248-489-9334
• Brian T Donnelly, President / Chief
Operating Officer
(298) 737-0553
• Kathy Dix, Comptroller
(248) 737-0553
• Jim Rice, VP Franchise Development
(248) 737-0553
• Jeff Griffith, Franchise Sales Director
(248) 737-0553
Products:
golf equipment

PRO IMAGE
250 NORTH RED CLIFFS DR.
SUITE 17
ST. GEORGE, UT 84790
435-674-0128
888-477-6326
Fax: 801-296-1319
www.proimage.net
• Dave Riley, President / Chief Executive
Officer
daver@proimage.net
• Ryan Laws, Chief Operating Officer
ryanl@proimage.net
• Dave Riley, President/CEO
daver@proimage.net
• Ryan Laws, Chief Operating Officer
ryanl@proimage.net
• Bill Townsend, VP / General Merchandise
Manager
billt@proimage.net
• Matt MacKay, National Franchise Manager
Products:
sports fan shop, and one of the greatest
franchising opportunities in the industry

PUSH PEDAL PULL
2306 WEST 41 ST
SIOUX FALLS, SD 57105
605-334-7740
888-861-8978
Fax: 605-336-3328
www.pushpedalpull.com
• Roger D Stewart, President
• Todd Ibis, Chief Operating Officer
• Shelley Kramer, Buyer
Products:
treadmills, ellipticals and climbers, home
gyms, exercise bikes, free weights,
accessories, plate loaded, selectorized,
stretching, single-station gyms

QVC NETWORK
1200 WILSON DRIVE AT STUDIO PARK
WEST CHESTER, PA 19380
484-701-1000
888-345-5788
Fax: 484-701-8170
QVCCares@QVC.com
www.qvc.com
• Douglas Briggs, President
• Darlene Daggett, EVP Apparel
• Gregg Bertoni, Fitness Director, Craftsman
Tools
• Mike George, President and CEO
Products:
accessories and shoes, apparel for men and
women, beauty, jewelry, cooking and dining,
gourmet food, home decor and home
improvement, electronics, sports and
fitness, toys, crafts and leisure

R.H. RENY
731 ROUTE 1
NEWCASTLE, ME 4553
207-563-3177
Fax: 207-563-5681
feedback@renys.com
www.renys.com
• John Reny, President
feedback@renys.com
Products:
all kinds of clothing, outerwear by famous
makers, electronics, housewares, lawn and
garden supplies, sheets and towels

RACK ROOM SHOES
8708 JW CLAY BOULEVARD
CHARLOTTE, NC 28262
704-510-0037
Fax: 704-547-8159
www.rackroomshoes.com
• Bob Hartley, President
• Jan Mauldin, Director of Marketing
Products:
shoes, handbags and accessories, dress,
casual, trends, and athletic wear

RAMSEY OUTDOOR STORE
281 ROUTE 10 EAST
PARAMUS TOWN SQUARE, PO BOX 1689
SUCCASUNNA, NJ 07876
201-261-5000
800-699-5874
Fax: 201-261-2742
customerservice@ramseyoutdoor.com
www.ramseyoutdoor.com
• Stuart Levine, President / Owner
customerservice@ramseyoutdoor.com
Products:
fishing, camping, water sports, climbing,
backpacking, hiking, hunting and the
clothing and footwear

RECREATIONAL EQUIPMENT, INC./REI
6750 S 228TH STREET
KENT, WA 98032
253-891-2500
800-426-4840
Fax: 253-891-2523
ip@rei.com
www.rei.com
• Sally Jewell, President / Chief Executive
Officer
publicaffairs@rei.com
• Brad Brown, VP / Information Services
publicaffairs@rei.com
• Brad Johnson, SVP / Chief Financial
Officer / Corporat
publicaffairs@rei.com
• Sally Jewell, President and Chief
Executive Officer
• Matt Hyde, SVP Merchandising
publicaffairs@rei.com
• Bill Baumann, Vice President of
Information Technology
• Rick Bingle, Vice President of Supply
Chain
• Brad Brown, Vice President of
E-Commerce and Direct Sales
• Michelle Clements, Senior Vice President
of Human Resources
• Michael Collins, Vice President of Public
Affairs
Products:
ice axes and climbing equipment, outdoor
gear and clothing

RECWARE BY ACTIVE.COM, INC.
937 ENTERPRISE DRIVE
SACRAMENTO, CA 95825
916-925-9096
888-732-9273
Fax: 916-925-0649
sales@recware.com
• Duane Harlan, Founder/President
• Cyril Juanitas, VP Sales
sales@recware.com

REDDEN MARINE SUPPLY, INC.
1411 ROEDER AVENUE
BELLINGHAM, WA 98225-2916

360-733-0250
800-426-9284
Fax: 360-733-7180
• Ken Brown, Sportnet Sales
• Alan R Chiabai, President
Products:
Retail And Wholesale Commercial Fishing
Gear Marine Related Products Sports
Netting Construction Netting Gloves
Hydraulics

REEBOK INTERNATIONAL LTD.-RETAIL
1895 JW FOSTER BOULEVARD
CANTON, MA 2021
781-401-5000
888-870-1743
Fax: 781-401-7402
www.reebok.com
• Uli Becker, President
• David Baxter, President, Sports Licensed
Division
• Bill Holmes, Human Resources
• Matt O'Toole, Chief Marketing Officer,
Reebok Brand
• John Warren, General Manager, Sports
Licensed Division

RICH'S DEPARTMENT STORES, INC.
223 PERIMETER CENTER PARKWAY
ATLANTA, GA 30346
770-913-4000
Fax: 770-913-5114
• David L Nichols, President / Chief
Operating Officer
• Karen M Hoguet, SVP / Chief Operating
Officer

ROAD RUNNER SPORTS
5549 COPLEY DRIVE
SAN DIEGO, CA 92111
858-636-7652
800-636-3560
Fax: 858-636-7650
www.roadrunnersports.com
• Dave Jewell, Footwear & Accessories
Director
Products:
shoes, apparel, accessories, nutrition

ROCKVILLE WASHINGTON GOLF CENTER
N89 W16790 APPLETON AVENUE
SUITE 200
MENOMONEE FALLS, WI 53051
262-255-7600
800-967-5342
Fax: 301-948-7052
brian@golftrips.com
www.washingtongolf.com
• Tim Woodruff, Manager
info@washingtongolf.com
Products:
accessories, apparel, bags, balls, belts,
gloves, golf gifts, sandals, polo, outerware,
hats, pants

ROGER DUNN GOLF SHOPS
1421 VILLAGE WAY
SANTA ANA, CA 92705
714-558-0074
888-216-5252
Fax: 714-664-0430
santaana@rdgolf.com
www.worldwidegolfshops.com
• Craig A MaCallister, President
• Steve Carfano, Store Manager

Products:
golf equipment

RON JON SURF SHOP OF FLORIDA
4151 NORTH ATLANTIC AVENUE
COCOA BEACH, FL 32931
321-799-8888
888-757-8737
Fax: 321-799-8805
Info@rjss.com
www.ronjonsurfshop.com
• Ed Moritary, President
• Debbie Harvey, Vice President
Products:
Manufacturer and retailer of surfing apparels
and equipments

RYNO ATHLETICS
316 S. GLENWOOD ST
TYLER, TX 75702
903-526-4140
888-609-6725
Fax: 800-574-0008
orders@ryno.com
www.ryno.com
• Brandon Steele, President/Chief Executive
Officer
• Brandon Steele, President
• Phil Steele, National Sales Manager
Products:
Backpacks and garments bags, baseball
bags, premium duffels, specialty sport bags,
team/travel duffels.
Year Founded:
1996

SAKS INCORPORATED
12 E 49TH STREET
NEW YORK, NY 10017
212-753-4000
Fax: 205-940-4987
www.saksincorporated.com
• Ronald L Frasch, President/Chief
Merchandising Officer
• Stephen I Sadove, Chief Executive Officer
• James A Coggin, President / Chief
Administrative Officer
• Stephen E I. Sadove, Chairman and Chief
Executive Officer
• Ronald L. Frasch, President and Chief
Merchandising Officer
• Douglas Coltharp, EVP / Chief Financial
Officer
Products:
Provides a wide assortment of quality
fashion apparel, shoes, accessories,
cosmetics, and decorative home furnishings

SAM'S CLUB
2101 SE
SIMPLE SAVINGS DRIVE
BENTONVILLE, AR 72716-0745
479-277-7000
888-746-7726
Fax: 479-273-4053
www.samsclub.com
• Brian C Cornell, President / Chief
Executive Officer
• Mark D Goodman, EVP, Membership and
Marketing
• Greg Johnston, EVP, Operations
Products:
Member-only warehouse club that sells
merchandise including appliances and
electronics, office supplies, fresh food,
clothing, optical and pharmacy services,

home furnishings, books, batteries and auto
supplies at very low profit margins

SCHEEL'S ALL SPORTS, INC.
3202 13TH AVENUE S
FARGO, ND 58103-3403
701-232-8903
Fax: 701-298-0706
customerservice@scheelssports.com
www.scheelssports.com
• Steve D Scheel, Chief Executive Officer /
Chairman
• Chris Skalsky, Corporate Clothing Office
Manager
• Dona Ochsner, Store Manager / Partner
• Sherry Senske, Store Manager / Partner
Products:
Retailers of sporting goods and apparel
including bikes, footwear, fitness equipment,
hunting and fishing gear, bike and exercise
machine repairs, raquet stringing, ski
equipment maintenance, warranty repairs
for shotguns, rifles, handguns

SCHOTTENSTEIN DEPARTMENT STORES
1887 PARSONS AVENUE
COLUMBUS, OH 43207-1933
614-443-0171
Fax: 614-478-2253
• Steve Morgan, Board Chairman
• Jay Schottenstein, Chairman, Chief
Executive Officer
• Thomas Ketteler, Chief Operations Officer
Products:
Retailers of clothing goods

SCHUYLKILL VALLEY SPORTS
118 INDUSTRIAL DRIVE
POTTSTOWN, PA 19464
877-711-8100
877-711-8100
Fax: 610-495-8814
customerservice@svsports.com
www.svsports.com
• Jerry Williams, President
(610) 495-8813
• Phil Snyder, Vice President
(610) 495-8813
• Scott Goebel, Vice President
(610) 495-8813
Products:
Retail and wholesale Sporting Goods

SEARS, ROEBUCK & CO.
3333 BEVERLY ROAD
HOFFMAN ESTATES, IL 60179
847-286-2500
800-549-4505
Fax: 847-286-7829
www.sears.com
• Edward S Lampert, Chairman
• Alan J Lacy, Vice Chairman
• Aylwin B Lewis, President / Chief
Executive Officer
Products:
Retailers of tools, lawn and garden, home
electronics, and automotive repair and
maintenance

SERVICE MERCHANDISE COMPANY
PO BOX 810939
SUITE 108
BOCA RATON, FL 33481
561-999-9815
877-643-8165

Fax: 561-999-9817
Info@servicemerchandise.com
www.servicemerchandise.com
• Raymond Zimmerman, Chairman
• Yuyal Moed, Chief Executive Officer
Products:
Retailers of fine jewelry, kitchen and dining, home accents and furniture, watches, electronics, and games and toys

SHARPER IMAGE
1450 BROADWAY
3RD FLOOR
NEW YORK, NY 10018
212-730-0030
877-714-7444
Fax: 212-967-6008
info@sharperimage.com
www.sharperimage.com
• Richard Thalheimer, Chairman / Chief Executive Officer
Richard@sharperimage.com
• Tracey Wan, Vice Chairman / Chief Operating Officer
twan@sharperimage.com
• Bob Thompson, SVP Merchandising
• Craig Traveaux, VP Stores
Products:
retails new, innovative, high-quality proprietary products such as Massage Chairs, Massage & Relaxation, Sound Soothers, Men's Personal Care, Women's Personal Care, Health & Fitness Equipment, Bed & Bath, Electronics & Toys, Personal Care, iPod/MP3, Stereos, DVD, TV & Video, Toys & Games, Robots and Hi-Tech Toys, Cameras & Binoculars, Clocks, Watches, Sports & Recreation, Music CDs, Air Cleaners & Air Purifiers, Office Furnishings, Lamps, Luggage & Travel Accessories, Sports & Recreation, Automotive, Tools & Flashlights, Clocks, Office Electronics, iPod/MP3, MP3 Speakers, ZipConnect, Watches, Safety & Security, Air Cleaners & Air Purifiers, M

SHOE CARNIVAL
7500 E COLUMBIA STREET
EVANSVILLE, IN 47715
812-867-6471
800-430-7463
Fax: 812-867-4261
customerservice@shoecarnival.com
www.shoecarnival.com
• Mark L Lemond, President/Chief Executive Officer
info@shoecarnival.com
• Clifton Sifford, EVP Merchandise Manager
info@shoecarnival.com
• Timothy T Baker, EVP Store Operations
info@shoecarnival.com
• W. Ke Jackson, SVP / Chief Financial Officer / Treasure
info@shoecarnival.com
Products:
family footwear

SHOE CITY
12550 WHITTIER BOULEVARD
SUITE 100
WHITTIER, CA 90602
562-698-2400
Fax: 562-696-6767
info@shoecity.com
www.shoecity.com
• Hau-En Ying, Partner

Products:
athletic shoes for men, women, juniors and infants

SHOE SHOW, INC.
2201 TRINITY CHURCH ROAD
CONCORD, NC 28027
704-782-4143
888-557-4637
Fax: 704-782-3411
www.shoeshow.com
• Robert B Tucker, Owner / President
Products:
boots, shoes, sandals

SHOPKO STORES, INC.
700 PILGRIM WAY
PO BOX 19060
GREEN BAY, WI 54307-9060
920-429-2211
800-791-7333
Fax: 920-429-4799
www.shopko.com
• Jack W Eugster, Acting Chief Executive Officer
OnlineCustomerService@shopko.com
• Brian W Bender, SVP / Chief Financial Officer / Co-Chief
OnlineCustomerService@shopko.com
• L. Te McDonald, SVP Marketing / Communications
• Rodney D Lawrence, SVP Store Marketing
Products:
general merchandise and retail health services; men's, women's, children's and infant's clothing, men's and women's footwear and jewelry and accessories; home furnishings, hardware, domestics, electronics, consumables, health and beauty aids, automotive and toys

SKI MARKET LTD.
161 QUINCY AVE
QUINCY, MA 2169
617-773-3993
888-876-7433
Fax: 781-890-1811
www.countryski.com
• Robert Ferguson, Chairman
• Andrew Ferguson, President
• Jim Isenberg, Marketing Director
Products:
skis, snowboards, bicycles, DVDs, watches, skateboards, kayaks

SKI MERCHANDISING CORPORATION
235 CADWELL DRIVE
PO BOX 3929
SPRINGFIELD, MA 1104
413-739-7331
Fax: 413-731-9335
Tgately@sportsshops.com
www.snowsportsmerchandising.com
• Tom Gately, President
tgately@sportsshops.com
• Tom Gately, President
Tgately@sportsshops.com
• Chuck Camerlin, Vice President
Ccamerlin@sportsshops.com
• Carole Tracy, Executive Assistant
Ctracy@sportsshops.com
Products:
ski, snowboard and other snowsport-related equipment, apparel and accessories

SMACK APPAREL
2310 W STATE STREET
TAMPA, FL 33609
813-250-0627
877-762-2511
Fax: 813-251-4539
www.smackapparel.com

SMITH'S FOOD & DRUG
1550 S REDWOOD ROAD
SALT LAKE CITY, UT 84104
801-974-1400
866-221-4141
Fax: 801-974-1676
kroger.investors@kroger.com
www.smithsfoodanddrug.com
• James Hallsey, President
kroger.investors@kroger.com
• Peter Barth, SVP Human Resources
kroger.investors@kroger.com
• Dave Deatherage, Group VP Chief Financial Officer Fred Me
kroger.investors@kroger.com
Products:
prescription drug plan, health guide

SNYDER'S DRUG STORES, INC.
14525 HIGHWAY 7
MINNETONKA, MN 55345
952-932-5441
888-443-8481
Fax: 952-936-2512
www.snyderdrug.com
• Gordon D Barker, President / Chief Executive Officer
• Williard Wilson, EVP Marketing / Pharmacy
Products:
health care merchandise, as well as beauty care items, general merchandise, and related items and services

SOLAR BLOC HATS
1120 HOLLAND DR
SUITE 9
BOCA RATON, FL 33487-2728
561-994-3001
800-327-5012
Fax: 561-994-3009
cushees@bellsouth.net
www.cushees.com
• Bob Kenny, Founder
cushees@bellsouth.net
Products:
Solarbloc hats and caps, bucket hats, face saver hats, fishing caps and flap caps
Year Founded:
1977
Description:
Solarbloc hats use materials that have been tested to provide sun protection and have been rated atleast 50 upf.
Brands:
Solarbloc; Cushees
Clients:
Golf Shops; Tennis Shops; Beach Shops

SPORT CHALET, INC.
1 SPORT CHALET DRIVE
LA CANADA, CA 91011
818-949-5300
888-801-9162
Fax: 818-790-0087
www.sportchalet.com
• Craig Levra, Chairman/Chief Executive Officer

• Howard Kaminsky, EVP Finance, Chief Financial Officer
• Dennis Trausch, EVP Growth and Development
• Craig Levra, Chairman of the Board, Chief Executive Office
• Tim Anderson, Executive Vice President, Retail Operations,
• Howard Kaminsky, Executive Vice President, Finance, Chief Fina
• Tom Tennyson, Executive Vice President and Chief Merchandis
• Dennis Trausch, Executive Vice President, Growth and Developm
• Brad Morton, Senior Vice President, Sales
• Ted Jackson, Vice President, Information Technology and Ch
Products:
Leading operator of full service specialty sporting goods stores in California, Nevada, Arizona and Utah. Specializes in gear for cold-weather as well as warm weather sports. Stores also sell brand-name shoes, clothes, and equipment.

SPORTING AUCTION, INC.
37 WILTON ROAD
MILFORD, NH 3055
603-732-0031
800-335-4670
Fax: 603-672-3480
support@sportstop.com
www.sportstop.com
• Paul Dell, Chief Executive Officer
paul@sportstop.com
Products:
Specialty sporting goods retailer with a focus for Lacrosse, Snowboarding, Snowshoeing, Field Hockey apparel, equipments, etc.

SPORTMASTER INTERNATIONAL
700 S JOHNSON DRIVE
MCGREGOR, TX 76657
800-999-9764
800-999-9764
Fax: 254-840-8878
• Clay Young, Director of Operations
(254) 840-0494
• Sharon Cid, EVP
(800) 728-6513
Products:
Tennis grips, string, racquets, novelties, racquet stringing and other equipments

SPORTS ENDEAVORS, INC.
431 US HIGHWAY 70A E
HILLSBOROUGH, NC 27278-9912
919-644-6800
Fax: 919-644-6808
custserv@sportsendeavors.com
www.sportsendeavors.com
• Mike Moylan, President, Chief Executive Officer
president.office@sportsendeavors.com
• Brendan Moylan, Chief Operating Officer
custserv@sportsendeavors.com
• Garrett Putman, VP Online Marketing Internet Marketing D
(919) 644-6800
gputman@sportsendeavors.com
• John Crabhill, Online Properties Creative Director
(919) 644-6800
jcrabill@sportsendeavors.com

Products:
Mail order sporting goods & retail soccer supplies.

SPORTS SPECIALISTS, LTD.
590 FISHERS STATION DRIVE
SUITE 110
VICTOR, NY 14564
585-742-1010
Fax: 585-742-2645
www.sportsspecialistsltd.com
• Stephen R Rogers, President, Chief Executive Officer
(585) 742-1010
• Stephen R. Rogers, President & CEO
(585) 742-1010
• Nancy Toscano, Controller
Services:
Retailer-owned marketing, merchandising and purchasing organization currently active in the specialty ski, snowboard, outdoor and casual furniture industries.

SPORTS WAREHOUSE, INC.
PO BOX 2678
OREGON CITY, OR 97045
503-650-4321
Fax: 503-650-1919
Products:
Sells, buys and trades authentic game used uniforms and equipment

SPORTS, INC.
333 SECOND AVENUE N
LEWISTOWN, MT 59457
406-538-3496
Fax: 800-227-7207
Info@hq.sportsinc.com
www.sportsinc.com
• Nancy Wilson, VP
• Dave Salvi, Chief Executive Officer
Services:
National member-owned retail buying syndicate, including member stores from all facets of the sporting goods business.

SPORTSMAN'S GUIDE
411 FARWELL AVENUE
PO BOX 239
SOUTH SAINT PAUL, MN 55075-0239
651-451-3030
888-844-0667
800-882-2962
Fax: 800-333-6933
custserv@sportsmansguide.com
www.sportsmansguide.com
• Gary Olen, Chairman
custserv@sportsmansguide.com
• Greg Binkley, President, Chief Executive Officer
custserv@sportsmansguide.com
• John Casler, EVP Merchandising, Marketing and Creativ
custserv@sportsmansguide.com
• Douglas Johnson, VP Marketing
custserv@sportsmansguide.com
Products:
Catalog and internet company which markets value priced outdoor gear and general merchandise, with a special emphasis on outdoor clothing, equipment and footwear. Products include clothing, footwear, hunting and shooting accessories, camping and outdoor recreation equipment, optics, electronics, personal accessory items and a diverse range of additional offerings.

STAGE STORES, INC.
10201 MAIN STREET
HOUSTON, TX 77025
713-667-5601
800-324-3244
800-743-8730
Fax: 713-660-3330
www.stagestoresinc.com
• Andy Hall, President/CEO
• Michael Glazer, President and Chief Executive Officer
• Steven Lawrence, Chief Merchandising Officer
• Edward Record, Chief Operating Officer
• Oded Shein, Executive Vice President, Chief Financial Off
• Ron Lucas, Executive Vice President, Human Resources
• Steven Hunter, Executive Vice President, Chief Information O
• Richard Stasyszen, Senior Vice President, Finance and Controller
Products:
Brings nationally recognized brand name apparel, accessories, cosmetics and footwear for the entire family to small and mid-size towns and communities. Operates under the Stage, Bealls and Palais Royal and Peebles name.

STERNHEIMER BROS/DBA A&N STORES
6000 RIVER ROAD
SUITE B
RICHMOND, VA 23226
804-226-1325
Fax: 804-222-4894
www.anstores.com
• Mark Sternheimer, President
Products:
Family-owned retail clothing and sportswear store

SUPER SHOE STORES
10365 MOUNT SAVAGE ROAD, NW
CUMBERLAND, MD 21502
301-759-4300
877-704-4106
Fax: 603-386-6126
customercare@supershoes.com
www.supershoes.com
• James Issler, President
Products:
Multi-store footwear retailer. Products include different brands of shoes, boots, accessories, handbags, workwear, and nursing apparel. We carry shoes for every person and every activity; from work boots to hunting boots, sandals to slippers.

SYMS
1 SYMS WAY
SECAUCUS, NJ 7094
201-902-9600
800-322-7967
Fax: 201-902-9874
customerservice@syms.com
www.syms.com
• Sy Syms, Chairman
customerservice@syms.com
• Marcy Syms, Chief Executive Officer
customerservice@syms.com
• Ronald Zindman, EVP, General Merchandise Manager
customerservice@syms.com
• Allen Brailsford, EVP Operations
customerservice@syms.com

Products:
Off-price representative for authentic designer and name brand clothes for men and women.

T.J. MAXX
770 COCHITUATE ROAD
FRAMINGHAM, MA 01701
508-390-1000
800-285-6299
Fax: 508-390-2828
www.tjx.com
• Bernard Cammarata, Chairman
• Carol Meryowitz, President
• Edmond English, VP
• Arnold Barron, Chief Operating Officer
• Carol Meyrowitz, Chief Executive Officer
Products:
The largest off-price retailer. Offers brand-name family apparel, giftware, home fashions, women's shoes, accessories and fine jewelry at prices up to 60% below regular department and specialty store prices.

TEAM ATHLETIC GOODS/TAG, INC.
3 SHARPIE WAY
SHELBYVILLE, TN 37160
615-410-4390
888-796-0734
Fax: 615-410-4388
info@tagsportswear.com
tagsportswear.com
• Philip Rosati, President/Chief Executive Officer
• Darcy Kinder, V.P./Director of Operations
• Robin Catiller, Office Manager/Single Billing
• Tim Loudermilk, Product Manager/Research & Development
• Carrie Bretz, Executive Assistant/Marketing
Year Founded:
1979
Description:
Manufacturer of team sporting goods, equipment and clothing.

TGM FITNESS, INC.
183 S. MAIN ST.
MOUNT CLEMENS, MI 48043
586-775-2760
888-892-784
Fax: 586-741-0052
service@tgmskateboards.com
www.tgmskateboards.com
• Mary Bonten, President, Buyer
• Charles L Bonten, Buyer
Products:
Fitness equipment and apparel

THE FEMALE ATHLETE, INC.
601 PACKARD COURT
SAFETY HARBOR, FL 34695
800-586-7738
Fax: 800-456-1223
• Mary Tenety, Co-Founder, President
mail@sweetandpowerful.com
• Lori Schmid, Co-Founder, VP
Products:
Sportswear and teen clothing store made especially for girls

THE WALKING COMPANY
519 LINCOLN COUNTY PARKWAY
LINCOLNTON, NC 28092

818-709-2200
800-642-9265
Fax: 818-709-2210
www.thewalkingcompany.com
• Greg Milne, Chief Executive Officer
Products:
Provides the most technically-advanced comfort footwear available

TOMMY HILFIGER
601 W 26TH STREET
NEW YORK, NY 10001
212-549-6000
888-866-6948
tommyhelp@tommy.com
www.tommy.com
• Thomas J. Hilfiger, Founder/Principal Designer
• Daniel F. Grieder, CEO
• Ludo Omnisk, Chief Operating Officer
• Avery Baker, Chief Marketing Operator
• Gary Shienbaum, CEO North America
• Tommy Hilfiger, Designer & Visionary
• Quentin Walsh, SVP/Corporate Controller
Description:
Designs, sources and markets men's and women's sportswear.

TOP 100 BASKETBALL RECRUITING SHOWCASE
511 E KING STREET
BOONE, NC 28607
828-264-9547
828-264-9547
Fax: 828-264-0065
www.gamewornuniforms.com
• Wayne Otto, Executive Director
Products:
Team Pins, Balls/Accessories, Misc. Items, Baseball Helmets, Bench Towels, College Items, Football Helmets, Football Jerseys, Compression Shorts, NBA Armbands, NBA Bath Robes, NBA Game Balls, NBA Autographed Game Balls, NBA Game Jerseys, NBA Game Shoes, NBA Game Shorts, NBA Practice Items, NBA Shooting Shirts, NBA Socks, NBA Warm Up Jacket, NBA Warm Up Pants, MLB Baseball Pants, MLB BP Jerseys, MLB Game Bats, MLB Game Jackets, MLB Pull Over Jacket, MLB Game Jerseys, MLB Player Caps, NHL Hockey Gloves, NHL Hockey Jerseys, NHL Hockey Pants, NHL Hockey Skates, NHL Hockey Sticks, Hockey Pucks, Locker Name Plate, Replica Stadiums, Equipment/Travel

TRI-STATE DISTRIBUTOR
1104 PULLMAN ROAD
MOSCOW, ID 83843
208-882-4555
887-878-2835
Fax: 208-882-8427
jpower@t-state.com
www.t-state.com
• L. Connelly, President
Products:
Clothes, shoes and sports equipment.

TRIPLE S SPORTING SUPPLIES, INC.
325 CREEKSIDE DRIVE
AMHERST, NY 14228
716-691-3777
800-942-3777
Fax: 716-691-4305
triple-s@att.com
www.triplessportingsupplies.com

• Dave Sheffield, President
(716) 691-3777
• Gary Sheffield, Vice President
(716) 691-3777
Products:
Fishing Tackle, HUnting Supplies and Footwear
Nature of Service:
Wholesale Distributor Spotring Supplies
Brands:
Purefishing, Zebco, Shakespeare, Doiwa, Shimano, Eagle Claw, Optronics, Wildlife Research Stearns, Hodgman, Minnkota, Normark Challenger, Pradco, Cannon Downriggers Mepps, Mr Twister, Zoom Eyewear and more
Year Founded:
1969

TURNER'S OUTDOORSMAN
11738 SAN MARIN STREET
SUITE A
RANCHO CUCAMONGA, CA 91730
909-923-3009
Fax: 909-923-3022
www.turners.com
• Shirley Andrews, Owner
• Don Small, President / Chief Executive Officer
• Bob Hostetter, Match Director
• Rob Zubak, Director of Sales
robzubak@turners.com
Products:
Spinfisher Metal Series, Cherrywood Rods, Sweep Fire, Pink Fluorocarbon, Hooks, AL391 - Urika Sporting, G22 Semi-Auto.22IR, 870 Special Purpose Shotgun, SIGMA9MM OR 40 S&W, Deckboot and more.

U.S. CAVALRY, INC,
2855 CENTENNIAL AVENUE
RADCLIFF, KY 40160-9000
270-351-1164
800-777-7172
Fax: 270-352-0266
service@uscav.com
www.uscav.com
• Randall Acton, President
Products:
ACU, Bags and Luggage, Clothing, Electronics, Eyewear, Field Equipment, Footwear, Gifts and Novelty, Headwear, Insignia, Knives, Optics, Tools and Watches. Men US Air Force Stealth Pilot Watches, Tactical Full T-Shirt, Waterproof Boots, Desert Mil Spec Boots, Flashlight, Army Combat Uniform (ACU) Shirt, Army Combat Uniform (ACU) Trousers, Com-Tac Headset, 2nd Generation Universal Parka and more.

U.S. FACTORY OUTLETS, INC.
7 PENN PLAZA
NEW YORK, NY 10001
212-563-3650
Fax: 212-967-9872
• Frederic K Raiff, President / Chief Executive Officer
• Frederic K. Raiff, Owner
• Michael Metrose, VP / General Merchandise Manager
Products:
60 percent apparel and 40 percent hard goods and domestics.

UP AGAINST THE WALL
1420 WISCONSIN AVENUE NW
WASHINGTON, DC 20007
202-337-6610
Fax: 202-333-1246
www.upagainstthewall.com
• Charles Rendelman, President
Number/Location of Stores:
16. DC, MD, VA.

VALUE CITY DEPARTMENT STORES
3241 WESTERVILLE ROAD
COLUMBUS, OH 43224
614-471-4722
Fax: 614-478-2253
websupport@vcf.com
www.valuecity.com
• Jay L Schottenstein, Chairman
• John C. Rossler, President / Chief
Executive Officer
• Charles Rath, EVP, Chief Marketing
Officer
Products:
Men's, ladies and kids shoes.

VANS, INC.
6550 KATELLA AVE
CYPRESS, CA
855-909-8267
800-826-7800
Fax: 562-565-8406
vanscustserv@vfc.com
www.vans.com
• Walter E Schoenfeld, Chairman
• Gary H. Schoenfeld, President & Chief
Executive Officer
• Scott J Blechman, VP & Chief Financial
Officer
• Craig E Gosselin, SVP, Secretary &
General Counsel
Products:
CUSTOM SHOES - Full Collection; MENS
SHOES - Classics, Band Classics, Core
Skate, Skate Performance, Sandals;
WOMENS SHOES - Classics, Fashion,
Active, Sandals; BOYS SHOES - Classics,
Band Classics, Core Skate, MISSYS
SHOES - Full Collection; TODDLERS
SHOES - Full Collection; INFANTS SHOES
- Full Collection; MENS APPAREL - Tops,
Tees, Pants; WOMENS APPAREL -
Fashion Tops, Tees, Bottoms and Skirts;
ACCESSORIES - Full Collection.

VARIETY WHOLESALERS
PO BOX 947
HENDERSON, NC 27536
252-430-2600
Fax: 919-790-5349
info@vwstores.com
www.vwstores.com
• Frances Winslow, VP Human Resources
(252) 430-2491
• Art Pope, Vice Chairman, President, and
Chief Fina
apope@vwstores.com
• Frances Winslow, Vice President of
Human Resources
(252) 430-2041
fwinslow@vwstores.com
• Phil Pope Sr., Vice President / Real Estate
(252) 430-2618
ppope@vwstores.com
• Todd Hope, Dispatcher
(252) 430-2196
jhope@vwstores.com
• Terry Ellenwood, Director of

Transportation
(252) 430-2143
terrye@vwstores.com
• Wayne Stainback, Regional Director of
Leasing
(252) 430-2609
wstainback@vwstores.com
• Ken Dickerson, Director of Maintenance
Services
(252) 430-2845
kend@vwstores.com
• Tim Hedgepeth, Inbound Logistics
Manager
(252) 430-2464
thedgepeth@vwstores.com
Products:
Assortment of retail merchandise including
both hardlines (toys, health and beauty aids,
housewares, furniture, sporting goods,
snacks, etc.) and softlines (clothing,
accessories, jewelry, etc.).

VENATOR GROUP, INC.
112 W 34TH STREET
NEW YORK, NY 10120
212-720-3700
800-991-6815
www.footlocker-inc.com
• Matthew D Serra, Chairman of the Board,
President and Chi
• Christopher A. Sinclair, Executive
Chairman of the Board, Scanden
• Purdy Crawford, Corporate Director
• Bruce L. Gi Hartman, Executive Vice
President and Chief Financial
• Lauren B. Peters, Senior Vice President -
Strategic Planning
• John A. Maurer, Vice President, Treasurer
and Investor Relati
Products:
Sports apparel

VIM
164-01 JAMAICA AVENUE
JAMAICA, NY 11432
718-297-3227
888-584-6669
Fax: 718-387-7084
customerservice@vim.com
www.vim.com
• Joseph Joseph, President
• Joseph Renate, Buyer
• Kathy Tema, Buyer
• Vicki Patel, Buyer

W.H. SMITH
3200 WINDY HILL ROAD
1500 W TOWER
ATLANTA, GA 30339
404-952-0705
800-795-0705
Fax: 404-951-1352
www.whsmith.co.uk
• Sara Hinckley, Buyer

WAL-MART STORES, INC.
702 SW 8TH STREET
BENTONVILLE, AR 72716-8611
479-273-4000
800-925-6278
Fax: 479-273-4053
www.walmartstores.com
• Robson S Walton, Chairman
• Lee H. Scott, Jr, President and Chief
Executive Officer
• David D Glass, Executive Committee
Chairman of the Boar

• Eduardo W Castro-Wright, Vice Chairman
• Michael T. Duke, President and Chief
Executive Officer
• M. Susan Chambers, Executive Vice
President, People Division
• Leslie A. Dach, Executive Vice President,
Corporate Affairs
• Brian C. Cornell, Executive VP, President
and CEO, Sam's Club
• Charles M. Holley, Jr., Executive Vice
President and Chief Financial
• Jeffrey J. Gearhart, Executive Vice
President, General Counsel and
Products:
Electronics (MP3 Players, Portable DVD
Players, laptops, cell phones, desktops, and
more); Toys (bikes, scooters chairs & sofas,
play tents & slumber bags, dolls and more);
sports & Fitness (treadmills, home gyms, ab
equipment, ellipticals and more); Apparel
(Women's Piped Stretch Jacket, Faded
Glory - Men's Denim Shirt, accessories and
more); Pharmacy (Blood Pressure Monitors,
Bathroom Safety, Mobility Aids, Contact
Lenses, Exercise Equipment) and more.

WALGREEN COMPANY
200 WILMOT ROAD
DEERFIELD, IL 60015
877-250-5823
800-925-4733
Fax: 847-914-2804
investor.relations@walgreens.com
www.walgreen.com
• Gregory D Wasson, President/CEO
• Jeffrey A. Rein, President and Chief
Operation Officer
• George J Riedl, Marketing EVP
• Trent E Taylor, Chief Information Officer,
EVP
Services:
-Pharmacy Network, Claims Processing,
Implementation and Transition, Formulary
Management, Comprehensive Reporting,
Online Access, Clinical Services,
Advantage90T and Consumer Choice
Pharmacy (CCP). -Dual Verification,
Full-order Imaging, Intercom Plusr and
Pharmacist Supervision. -Respiratory
Services, Home Infusion Therapies and
Home Medical Equipment (HME).
-Cost-containment Solutions, Walgreen
Advantage, Health Management, Benefit
Coordination and Account Management.

WASHINGTON GOLF CENTER
N89 W16790 APPLETON AVENUE
SUITE 200
MENOMONEE FALLS, WI 53051
262-255-7600
800-967-5342
Fax: 301-948-7052
brian@golftrips.com
www.washingtongolf.com
• Chong Su Chay, Chairman
(703) 979-7888
info@washingtongolf.com
• Randy Ramsey, VP
info@washingtongolf.com
Products:
Clubs (Adams 460 Dual, Adams RPM 430Q,
Bridgestone J33R, Callaway Big Bertha 454,
Callaway FT-3 Fusion Drivers, Callaway
Women's X 460 and more); Bags
(Carry/Stand, Cart, Push/Pull Carts, Travel,
Women's bag, Acessories); Shoes (Men's,
Women's, Juniors, Socks, Sandals and
Accessories); Balls (Bridgestone B330,

Bridgestone B330-S, Callaway Big Bertha Balls, Callaway HX Hot Balls, Callaway HX Tour 56 Balls, Callaway HX Tour Balls); Apparel (Men's, Women's, Juniors, Gloves, Accessories and Visors); and Accessories (Golf Gift, Tools, Books/Videos, Practice Aids, Gloves and Golf Grips).

WAVE RIDING VEHICLES
1900 CYPRESS AVENUE
VIRGINIA BEACH, VA 23451
757-422-8823
Fax: 757-428-6328
www.waveridingvehicles.com
• Leslie G Shaw, Jr, President
Products:
Tees (Bond Girl, Electro Tourist, North Shore), hoods (Buckshot, Dali Lama, Formation), mens (Shooter Jacket, Snow Summit, Paolo), chicas (Rastar, Ribbed, Birdie), youth, lids (Cult Flexfit, EOP 2 Flexfit, Low Pro Flexfit) and stuff (3/2 Wetsuit, 4/3 Wetsuit, Non-fade Rack Pads).

WEST MARINE, INC.
PO BOX 50070
WATSONVILLE, CA 95077-0070
831-728-2700
800-262-8464
Fax: 831-761-4421

wmCustomerService@westmarine.com
www.westmarine.com
• Geoff Eisenberg, President/Chief Executive Officer
• Eric Nelson, SVP / Chief Financial Officer
• Geoff Eisenberg, CEO and President
Products:
Anchor & Docking, Boats & Motors, Books & Videos, Cabinet & Deck Hardware, Clothing, Cordage, Electrical, Electronics, Engine Systems, Fasteners, Fishing, Interior, Cabin & Galley, Navigation, Paint & Maintenance, Plumbingm, Safety, Sailboat, Seating & Covers, Trailers & Parts, Ventilation and Watersports.

WHOLESALE SPORTS OUTDOOR OUTFITTERS
25 HERITAGE MEADOWS WAY SE
CALGARY, AB, CANADA T2H 0A7
253-835-4100
800-696-0253
Fax: 403-253-5518
• Norm P. Daniels, Chairman, Pres, Chief Executive Officer
• Phil Pepin, VP / Chief Financial Officer
• Ed Ariniello, VP, Operations
• Ron J. Menconi, VP / Merchandising / Marketing

Services:
Rentals, Bike Services, Tech Services, Guide Services

YORK BARBELL COMPANY
3300 BOARD ROAD
YORK, PA 17406
717-767-6481
800-358-9675
Fax: 717-764-0044
www.yorkbarbell.com
• Tim Bonitz, Marketing and Sales
Products:
Commercial Weight Equipment Quad-Grip Olympic Plates, Solid Rubber Training Bumpers, Olympic Iron Training Plates, Elite Competition Bumper Sets and Plates, USA-Made Elite Competition Olympic Bars, USA-Made Competition/Training Bars, Machine Attachment Bars, PRO-HEX Dumbbells, Rubber Hex Dumbbells, Iron or Rubber Gym-Style Dumbbells, Fixed Curl and Straight Barbells, Neo-Hex Neoprene Fitbells, Vinyl Fitbells and Racks, 2-Sided A-Frame Rack AF-6 (69002), 2-Sided Vertical Dumbbell Rack V-2-8 (69001), 2-Tier Dumbbell Racks with Saddle 2T-SDR-10 (69030), Single-Sided Weight Tree SSWT (69042), 40 lb. Aerobic Weight Set AWS-40 (10164) and 40 lb.

9

events, meetings & trade shows

TBA, 2025
NEBRASKA GOLF SHOW
Omaha, NB
CHi Health Center Omaha
VARSITY COMMUNICATIONS
Phone: 888-367-6420
Fax: 425-412-7082
stephens@varsitycommunications.com
www.varsitycommunications.com

Jan 8 - Jan 12, 2025
CHICAGO BOAT SHOW
Rosemont, IL
Donald E. Stephens Convention &
Conference Center
NATIONAL MARINE MANUFACTURERS
ASSOCIATION
Phone: 312-946-6200
Fax: 312-946-0401
www.nmma.org

Jan 8 - Jan 12, 2025
CHICAGO BOAT, RV & STRICTLY
SAIL SHOW
Rosemont, IL
Donald E Stephens Convention &
Conference Center
NATIONAL MARINE MANUFACTURERS
ASSOCIATION
Phone: 312-946-6200
Fax: 312-946-0401
www.nmma.org

Jan 8 - Jan 12, 2025
NSCAA CONVENTION
Chicago, IL
NATIONAL SOCCER COACHES
ASSOCIATION OF AMERICA
Phone: 816-471-1941
Fax: 816-474-7408
unitedsoccercoaches.org

Jan 10 - Jan 12, 2025
AFCA NATIONAL CONVENTION
Nashville, TN
AMERICAN FOOTBALL COACHES
ASSOCIATION
Phone: 254-754-9900
Fax: 254-754-7373
info@afca.com
www.afca.com

Jan 16 - Jan 19, 2025
SACRAMENTO INTERNATIONAL
SPORTSMEN'S EXPO
Sacramento, CA
Cal Expo, State Fairgrounds
INTERNATIONAL SPORTSMEN'S
EXPOSITIONS
Phone: 800-545-6100
Fax: 360-693-3352
International Ph: 360-693-3700
www.sportsexpos.com

Jan 17 - Jan 19, 2025
GREAT ROCKIES SPORTSHOW
Billings, MT
Metra Park ExpoCenter
GREAT ROCKIES SPORTSHOW
Phone: 406-580-3907
Fax: 406-388-6277
www.greatrockiesshow.com

Jan 17 - Feb 8, 2025
SOUTHWESTERN EXPO AND
LIVESTOCK SHOW
Fort Worth, TX
PROFESSIONAL RODEO COWBOY
ASSOCIATION
Phone: 719-593-8840

webmaster@prorodeo.com
www.prorodeo.com

Jan 17 - Jan 19, 2025
THE FLY FISHING SHOW -
MASSACHUSETTS
Marlborough, MA
Royal Plaza Hotel & Trade Center
FLY FISHING SHOW
Phone: 814-443-3638
Fax: 814-443-3943
info@flyfishingshow.com
www.flyfishingshow.com

Jan 20 - Jan 22, 2025
GOLF BUSINESS CONFERENCE
Orlando, FL
NATIONAL GOLF COURSE OWNERS
ASSOCIATION
Phone: 800-933-4262
Fax: 843-881-9958
ndownie@ngcoa.org
ngcoa.org

Jan 21 - Jan 24, 2025
SHOT SHOW
Las Vegas, NV
Venetian Expo
NATIONAL SHOOTING SPORTS
FOUNDATION
Phone: 203-426-1320
Fax: 203-426-1087
shotshow.com

Jan 22 - Jan 26, 2025
LOUISVILLE BOAT, RV &
SPORTSHOW
Louisville, KY
Kentucky Exposition Center
NATIONAL MARINE MANUFACTURERS
ASSOCIATION
Phone: 312-946-6200
Fax: 312-946-0401
www.nmma.org

Jan 22 - Jan 26, 2025
NEW YORK BOAT SHOW
New York, NY
Jacob Javits Convention Center
NATIONAL MARINE MANUFACTURERS
ASSOCIATION
Phone: 312-946-6200
Fax: 312-946-0401
www.nmma.org

Jan 23 - Jan 26, 2025
CHICAGOLAND FISHING, TRAVEL &
OUTDOOR EXPO
Schaumburg, IL
Schaumburg Convention Center
EASTERN FISHING & OUTDOOR
EXPOSITION
Phone: 603-431-4315
Fax: 603-431-1971
info@sportshows.com
www.sportshows.com

Jan 23 - Jan 26, 2025
MINNEAPOLIS BOAT SHOW
Minneapolis, MN
Minneapolis Convention Center
NATIONAL MARINE MANUFACTURERS
ASSOCIATION
Phone: 312-946-6200
Fax: 312-946-0401
www.nmma.org

Jan 24 - Jan 26, 2025
COLUMBUS GOLF SHOW
Columbus, OH
Ohio Expo Center

NORTH COAST GOLF SHOWS
Phone: 561-320-9782
Fax: 561-320-9783
northcoastgolfandtravelshows.com

Jan 24 - Jan 26, 2025
RED RIVER VALLEY BOAT & MARINE
PRODUCTS SHOW
Fargo, ND
Fargodome
CENAIKO PRODUCTIONS
Phone: 763-755-8111
Fax: 763-755-8124
www.cenaiko.com

Jan 24 - Jan 26, 2025
THE FLY FISHING SHOW - NEW
JERSEY
Edison, NJ
New Jersey Convention & Expo Center
FLY FISHING SHOW
Phone: 814-443-3638
Fax: 814-443-3943
info@flyfishingshow.com
www.flyfishingshow.com

Jan 27 - Jan 30, 2025
INTIX ANNUAL CONFERENCE
New York, NY
New York Hilton Midtown
INTERNATIONAL TICKETING
ASSOCIATION
Phone: 212-629-4036
Fax: 212-629-8532
info@intix.org
intix.org

Jan 29 - Feb 2, 2025
WASHINGTON SPORTSMEN'S SHOW
Puyallup, WA
Washington State Fair Events Center
O'LOUGHLIN TRADE SHOWS
Phone: 503-246-8291
Fax: 503-246-1066
info@otshows.com
www.thesportshows.com

Jan 31 - Feb 2, 2025
PHILADELPHIA GOLF SHOW
Philadelphia, PA
Greater Philadelphia Expo Center
NORTH COAST GOLF SHOWS
Phone: 561-320-9782
Fax: 561-320-9783
northcoastgolfandtravelshows.com

Jan 31 - Feb 2, 2025
ST. LOUIS GOLF EXPO
St. Charles, MO
St. Charles Convention Center
VARSITY COMMUNICATIONS
Phone: 888-367-6420
Fax: 425-412-7082
stephens@varsitycommunications.com
www.varsitycommunications.com

Jan 31 - Feb 2, 2025
THE FLY FISHING SHOW - GEORGIA
Atlanta, GA
Gas South Convention Center
FLY FISHING SHOW
Phone: 814-443-3638
Fax: 814-443-3943
info@flyfishingshow.com
www.flyfishingshow.com

Feb TBA, 2025
INDIANA MOTORCYCLE EXPO
Indianapolis, IN
Indiana State Fairgrounds

RENFRO PRODUCTIONS
Phone: 877-892-1723
Fax: 765-641-7756
info@renfroproductions.com
renfroproductions.com

Feb TBA, 2025
ROCKY MOUNTAIN OUTDOOR SHOW
TBA
WESTERN WINTER SPORTS REP
ASSOCIATION
Phone: 303-532-4002
Fax: 866-929-4572
info@wwsra.com
www.wwsra.com

Feb TBA, 2025
SOARING SOCIETY OF AMERICA
CONVENTION
TBA
SOARING SOCIETY OF AMERICA
Phone: 575-392-1177
Fax: 575-392-8154
www.ssa.org

Feb TBA, 2025
WASHINGTON GOLF SHOW
NORTH COAST GOLF SHOWS
Phone: 561-320-9782
Fax: 561-320-9783
northcoastgolfandtravelshows.com

Feb 3 - Feb 6, 2025
GOLF INDUSTRY SHOW &
EDUCATION CONFERENCE
San Diego, CA
TBA
GOLF COURSE SUPERINTENDENTS
ASSOCIATION OF AMERICA
Phone: 800-472-7878
Fax: 785-832-3643
mbrhelp@gcsaa.org
www.gcsaa.org

Feb 7 - Feb 9, 2025
CINCINNATI GOLF EXPO
Covington, KY
Northern Kentucky Convention Center
HART PRODUCTIONS
Phone: 877-704-8190
Fax: 513-797-1013
hartproductions.com

Feb 7 - Feb 9, 2025
ST. CLOUD SPORTSMEN'S SHOW
St. Cloud, MN
St. Cloud River's Edge
CENAIKO PRODUCTIONS
Phone: 763-755-8111
Fax: 763-755-8124
www.cenaiko.com

Feb 12 - Feb 16, 2025
MIAMI INTERNATIONAL BOAT SHOW
Miami, FL
Miami Marine Stadium Park & Basin
NATIONAL MARINE MANUFACTURERS
ASSOCIATION
Phone: 312-946-6200
Fax: 312-946-0401
www.nmma.org

Feb 12 - Feb 16, 2025
PACIFIC NORTHWEST
SPORTSMEN'S SHOW
Portland, OR
Portland Expo Center
O'LOUGHLIN TRADE SHOWS
Phone: 503-246-8291
Fax: 503-246-1066

info@otshows.com
www.thesportshows.com

Feb 14 - Feb 16, 2025
CLEVELAND GOLF SHOW
Cleveland, OH
I-X Center
NORTH COAST GOLF SHOWS
Phone: 561-320-9782
Fax: 561-320-9783
northcoastgolfandtravelshows.com

Feb 14 - Feb 16, 2025
INDIANAPOLIS BOAT, SPORT &
TRAVEL SHOW
Indianapolis, IN
Indiana State Fairgrounds
RENFRO PRODUCTIONS
Phone: 877-892-1723
Fax: 765-641-7756
info@renfroproductions.com
renfroproductions.com

Feb 14 - Feb 16, 2025
OUTDOOR RECREATION, RV & BOAT
SHOW
Monroeville, PA
Monroeville Convention Center
EXPOSITIONS INC.
Phone: 216-529-1300
Fax: 216-529-0311
chris@expoinc.com
expoinc.com

Feb 18 - Feb 21, 2025
MPRA CONFERENCE & EXPO
Branson, MO
MISSOURI PARK & RECREATION
ASSOCIATION
Phone: 573-636-3828
Fax: 573-635-7988
info@mopark.org
www.mopark.org

Feb 21 - Feb 23, 2025
INDIANA DEER, TURKEY &
WATERFOWL EXPOSITION
Indianapolis, IN
Indiana State Fairgrounds
RENFRO PRODUCTIONS
Phone: 877-892-1723
Fax: 765-641-7756
info@renfroproductions.com
renfroproductions.com

Feb 21 - Feb 23, 2025
PITTSBURGH GOLF AND TRAVEL
SHOW
Monroeville, PA
Monroeville Convention Center
NORTH COAST GOLF SHOWS
Phone: 561-320-9782
Fax: 561-320-9783
northcoastgolfandtravelshows.com

Feb 21 - Feb 23, 2025
THE FLY FISHING SHOW -
COLORADO
Denver, CO
Gaylord Rockies Resort & Convention
Center
FLY FISHING SHOW
Phone: 814-443-3638
Fax: 814-443-3943
info@flyfishingshow.com
www.flyfishingshow.com

Feb 21 - Feb 23, 2025
THE OUTDOOR ADVENTURE SHOW -
TORONTO
Toronto, Canada

The International Centre
NATIONAL EVENT MANAGEMENT INC.
Phone: 800-891-4859
Fax: 905-477-7872
info@nationalevent.com
www.nationalevent.com

Feb 22 - Feb 23, 2025
SALTWATER SPORTSMEN'S SHOW
Portland, OR
Portland Expo Center
O'LOUGHLIN TRADE SHOWS
Phone: 503-246-8291
Fax: 503-246-1066
info@otshows.com
www.thesportshows.com

Feb 23 - Feb 25, 2025
NATIONAL SPORTS FORUM
Boston, MA
NATIONAL SPORTS FORUM
Phone: 800-232-3133
Fax: 619-469-4007
info@sports-forum.com
www.sports-forum.com

Feb 23 - Feb 26, 2025
SOCCEREX USA CONVENTION
Egypt
SOCCEREX
International Ph: +44 208 742 7100
enquiry@soccerex.com
www.soccerex.com

Feb 24 - Feb 26, 2025
LAS VEGAS WORLD AMATEUR
Las Vegas, NV
CASCADIA EVENTS
Phone: 206-659-5703
john@cascadiaevents.com
cascadiaevents.com

Feb 24 - Feb 28, 2025
TRAPS INSTITUTE & EXPO
Allen, TX
TEXAS RECREATION & PARK SOCIETY
Phone: 512-267-5550
Fax: 512-267-5557
traps@traps.org
www.traps.org

Feb 28 - Mar 1, 2025
OTTAWA-GATINEAU GOLF EXPO
Ottawa, Canada
EY Centre
NATIONAL GOLF COURSE OWNERS
ASSOCIATION CANADA
Phone: 866-626-4262
ngcoa@ngcoa.ca
www.ngcoa.ca

Feb 28 - Mar 2, 2025
TAMPA BOAT SHOW
Tampa, FL
Florida State Fairgrounds
TAMPA BAY EXPOS
Phone: 727-893-8523
dlabell@tampabay.com
www.tampabay.com/expos

Feb 28 - Mar 2, 2025
THE FLY FISHING SHOW -
CALIFORNIA
Pleasanton, CA
Alameda County Fairgrounds
FLY FISHING SHOW
Phone: 814-443-3638
Fax: 814-443-3943
info@flyfishingshow.com
www.flyfishingshow.com

Mar TBA, 2025
PORTLAND GOLF SHOW
Portland, OR
Oregon Convention Center
VARSITY COMMUNICATIONS
Phone: 888-367-6420
Fax: 425-412-7082
stephens@varsitycommunications.com
www.varsitycommunications.com

Mar 1 - Mar 2, 2025
THE OUTDOOR ADVENTURE SHOW -
VANCOUVER
Vancouver, Canada
Vancouver Convention Center
NATIONAL EVENT MANAGEMENT INC.
Phone: 800-891-4859
Fax: 905-477-7872
info@nationalevent.com
www.nationalevent.com

Mar TBA, 2025
WORLD FISHING & OUTDOOR
EXPOSITION
Suffern, NY
Rockland Community College Field
House
EASTERN FISHING & OUTDOOR
EXPOSITION
Phone: 603-431-4315
Fax: 603-431-1971
info@sportshows.com
www.sportshows.com

Mar 6 - Mar 9, 2025
ACSM'S HEALTH & FITNESS SUMMIT
& EXPOSITION
Denver, CO
AMERICAN COLLEGE OF SPORTS
MEDICINE
Phone: 317-637-9200
Fax: 317-634-7817
www.ideafit.com

Mar 6 - Mar 9, 2025
CENTRAL OREGON SPORTMEN'S
SHOW
Redmond, OR
Deschutes County Fair & Expo Center
O'LOUGHLIN TRADE SHOWS
Phone: 503-246-8291
Fax: 503-246-1066
info@otshows.com
www.thesportshows.com

Mar 6 - Mar 9, 2025
RED RIVER VALLEY SPORTSMEN'S
SHOW
St. Paul, MN
RiverCenter
CENAIKO PRODUCTIONS
Phone: 763-755-8111
Fax: 763-755-8124
www.cenaiko.com

Mar 7 - Mar 9, 2025
JAPAN GOLF FAIR
Yokohama, Japan
JAPAN GOLF FAIR
International Ph: 011-81-3-3468-4378
International Fax: 011-81-3-3437-8401
info@japangolffair.com
www.japangolffair.com

Mar 7 - Mar 8, 2025
LET'S PLAY HOCKEY EXPO
St. Paul, MN
RiverCentre
LET'S PLAY HOCKEY
Phone: 320-333-3279

letsplay@letsplayhockey.com
www.letsplayhockey.com

Mar 12 - Mar 14, 2025
HFA SHOW
Las Vegas, NV
INTERNATIONAL HEALTH, RACQUET &
SPORTSCLUB ASSOCIATION
Phone: 617-951-0055
info@healthandfitness.org
www.healthandfitness.org

Mar 13 - Mar 16, 2025
SIOUX EMPIRE SPORTSMEN'S
BOAT, CAMPING & VACATIO N
Sioux Falls, SD
Sioux Falls Arena & Convention Center
CENAIKO PRODUCTIONS
Phone: 763-755-8111
Fax: 763-755-8124
www.cenaiko.com

Mar 14 - Mar 15, 2025
GOLF EXPO QUEBEC
Quebec, Canada
Sheraton Laval and Congress Centre
NATIONAL GOLF COURSE OWNERS
ASSOCIATION CANADA
Phone: 866-626-4262
ngcoa@ngcoa.ca
www.ngcoa.ca

Mar 14 - Mar 16, 2025
SALTWATER FISHING EXPO
Edison, NJ
New Jersey Convention & Expo Center
EASTERN FISHING & OUTDOOR
EXPOSITION
Phone: 603-431-4315
Fax: 603-431-1971
info@sportshows.com
www.sportshows.com

5ar 15 - Mar 16, 2025
THE FLY FISHING SHOW -
PENNSYLVANIA
Lancaster, PA
Lancaster County Convention Center
FLY FISHING SHOW
Phone: 814-443-3638
Fax: 814-443-3943
info@flyfishingshow.com
www.flyfishingshow.com

Mar 17 - Mar 18, 2025
BILLIARD & HOME LEISURE EXPO
Las Vegas, NV
Las Vegas Convention Center
BILLIARD CONGRESS OF AMERICA
Phone: 303-243-5070
www.bca-pool.com

Mar 20 - Mar 23, 2025
CALIFORNIA MANIA FITNESS PRO
CONVENTION
California
SCW FITNESS EDUCATION
Phone: 847-562-4020
Fax: 847-562-4080
registration@scwfit.com
scwfit.com

Mar 20 - Mar 23, 2025
SALT LAKE CITY INTERNATIONAL
SPORTSMEN'S EXPO
Salt Lake City, UT
Mountain America Expo Center
INTERNATIONAL SPORTSMEN'S
EXPOSITIONS
Phone: 800-545-6100
Fax: 360-693-3352

International Ph: 360-693-3700
www.sportsexpos.com

Mar 21 - Mar 23, 2025
NORTHEAST FISHING & HUNTING
SHOW
Uncasville, CT
Mohegan Sun
NORTH EAST EXPOS, INC.
Phone: 860-844-8461
kristie@northeastexpos.com
www.northeastexpos.com

Mar 22 - Mar 23, 2025
THE OUTDOOR ADVENTURE SHOW -
MONTREAL
Montreal, Canada
Palais des CongrŠs
NATIONAL EVENT MANAGEMENT INC.
Phone: 800-891-4859
Fax: 905-477-7872
info@nationalevent.com
www.nationalevent.com

Mar 28 - Mar 30, 2025
LOUISIANA SPORTSMAN SHOW &
FESTIVAL
Baton Rouge, LA
LOUISIANA SPORTSMAN SHOW
Phone: 985-758-7217
Fax: 985-758-7000
jackf@lasmag.com
www.louisianasportsmanshow.com

Mar 29 - Mar 30, 2025
THE OUTDOOR ADVENTURE SHOW -
CALGARY
Calgary, Canada
Stampede Park
NATIONAL EVENT MANAGEMENT INC.
Phone: 800-891-4859
Fax: 905-477-7872
info@nationalevent.com
www.nationalevent.com

Apr 1 - Apr 5, 2025
SHAPE AMERICA NATIONAL
CONVENTION & EXPO
Baltimore, MD
SHAPE AMERICA
Phone: 800-213-7193
Fax: 703-476-9527

Apr 3 - Apr 6, 2025
WBCA CONVENTION
Tampa, FL
WOMEN'S BASKETBALL COACHES
ASSOCIATION
Phone: 770-279-8027
Fax: 770-279-8473
membership@wbca.org
www.wbca.org

Apr 9 - Apr 11, 2025
APPA SPRING CONFERENCE
New Orleans, LA
ASSOCIATION OF HIGHER
EDUCATION FACILITIES OFFICERS
Phone: 703-684-1446
Fax: 703-549-2772
www.appa.org

Apr 12 - Apr 13, 2025
HOGEYE MARATHON & RELAYS
Springdale, AR
HOGEYE MARATHON
Phone: 479-445-9251
Fax: 479-575-5778
info@hogeyemarathon.com
www.hogeyemarathon.com

Apr 14 - Apr 17, 2025
SPORTSETA SYMPOSIUM
Portland, OR
SPORTS EVENTS AND TOURISM
ASSOCIATION
Phone: 513-281-3888
Fax: 513-281-1765
info@sportseta.org
www.sportseta.org

Apr 21 - Apr 23, 2025
CAA WORLD CONGRESS OF
SPORTS
Nashville, TN
STREET & SMITH'S SPORTS
BUSINESS JOURNAL
Phone: 704-973-1500
www.sportsbusinessdaily.com

Apr 23 - Apr 26, 2025
NIRSA ANNUAL CONFERENCE &
RECREATIONAL SPORTS EX PO
Kissimmee, FL
NATIONAL INTRAMURAL RECREATION
SPORTS ASSOCIATION
Phone: 541-766-8211
Fax: 541-766-8284
nirsa@nirsa.org
nirsa.net

Apr 25 - Apr 27, 2025
PILATES METHOD ALLIANCE
CONFERENCE
Guangzhou, China
PILATES METHOD ALLIANCE
Phone: 305-573-4946
Fax: 305-573-4461
info@pilatesmethodalliance.org
www.pilatesmethodalliance.org

Apr 27 - Apr 30, 2025
ANA ADVERTISING FINANCIAL
MANAGEMENT CONFERENCE
Carslbad, CA
ASSOCIATION OF NATIONAL
ADVERTISERS
Phone: 212-697-5950
Fax: 212-687-7310
www.ana.net

May 1 - May 4, 2025
FLORIDA MANIA FITNESS PRO
CONVENTION
Orlando, FL
SCW FITNESS EDUCATION
Phone: 847-562-4020
Fax: 847-562-4080
registration@scwfit.com
scwfit.com

May 12 - May 15, 2025
SIBEC EUROPE
Orlando, FL
Caribe Royale Resort
QUESTEX-MCLEAN EVENTS
Phone: 617-219-8300
info@questex.com
hbs.questex.com

May 17 - May 18, 2025
CLEVELAND MARATHON HEALTH &
FITNESS EXPO
Cleveland, OH
CLEVELAND MARATHON
Phone: 800-467-3826
Fax: 216-378-0143
www.clevelandmarathon.com

May 27 - May 30, 2025
NASSM CONFERENCE
San Diego, CA
NORTH AMERICAN SOCIETY FOR
SPORT MANAGEMENT
Phone: 724-482-6277
conference@nassm.org
www.nassm.com

May 31 - June 3, 2025
AEMA CONVENTION
Las Vegas, NV
Planet Hollywood Resort & Casino
ATHLETIC EQUIPMENT MANAGERS
ASSOCIATION
Phone: 217-678-1004
Fax: 217-678-1005
equipmentmanagers.org

Jun 4 - Jun 7, 2025
USA HOCKEY ANNUAL MEETING
Denver, CO
Denver Marriott Tech Center
USA HOCKEY
Phone: 719-576-8724
Fax: 719-538-1160
usah@usahockey.org
www.usahockey.com

Jun 8 - Jun 11, 2025
COSIDA CONVENTION
Orlando, FL
COLLEGE SPORTS INFORMATION
DIRECTORS OF AMERICA
willroleson@cosida.com
www.cosida.com

Jun 8 - Jun 11, 2025
NACDA CONVENTION
Orlando, FL
World Center Marriott Resort
NATIONAL ASSOCIATION OF
COLLEGIATE DIRECTORS OF
ATHLETICS
Phone: 440-892-4000
Fax: 440-892-4007
www.nacda.com

Jun 18 - Jun 20, 2025
MPI WORLD EDUCATION CONGRESS
St. Louis, MO
MEETING PROFESSIONALS
INTERNATIONAL
Phone: 972-702-3000
Fax: 972-702-3065
www.mpiweb.org

Jun 18 - Jun 20, 2025
OUTDOOR RETAILER SHOW
Salt Lake City, UT
Salt Palace Convention Center
EMERALD EXPOSITIONS
Phone: 949-226-5700
info@emeraldexpo.com
www.emeraldexpositions.com

Jul TBA, 2025
SPORTS OFFICIATING SUMMIT
TBA
NATIONAL ASSOCIATION OF SPORTS
OFFICIALS
Phone: 262-632-5448
Fax: 262-632-5460
www.naso.org

Jul 5 - Jul 6, 2025
ICAA CONFERENCE & TRADE SHOW
Anaheim, CA
Anaheim Marriott
INTERNATIONAL COUNCIL ON ACTIVE
AGING

Phone: 604-734-4466
Fax: 604-708-4464
info@icaa.cc
www.icaa.cc

Jul 16 - Jul 19, 2025
NSCA NATIONAL CONFERENCE &
EXHIBITION
Kansas City, MO
NATIONAL STRENGTH &
CONDITIONING ASSOCIATION
Phone: 800-815-6826
Fax: 719-632-6367
conferences@nsca.com
www.nsca.com

Jul 17 - Jul 19, 2025
IDEA WORLD CONVENTION
Sacramento, CA
IDEA HEALTH & FITNESS
ASSOCIATION
Phone: 858-535-8979
Fax: 619-344-0380
contact@ideafit.com
www.ideafit.com

Jul 24 - Jul 27, 2025
ATLANTA MANIA FITNESS PRO
CONVENTION
Atlanta, GA
SCW FITNESS EDUCATION
Phone: 847-562-4020
Fax: 847-562-4080
registration@scwfit.com
scwfit.com

Jul 28 - Jul 31, 2025
IAVM VENUECONNECT ANNUAL
CONFERENCE & TRADE SHOW
New Orleans, LA
INTERNATIONAL ASSOCIATION OF
VENUE MANAGERS
Phone: 972-906-7441
Fax: 972-906-7418
www.iavm.org

Jul 28 - Jul 30, 2025
PGA SHOW
Frisco, TX
PGA FASHION & DEMO EXPERIENCE
Phone: 203-840-5628
Fax: 203-840-9628
inquiry@pga.reedexpo.com
www.pgalasvegas.com

Aug TBA, 2025
ORANGE BOWL FAMILY FUN AND FIT
DAY
Miami, FL
Hard Rock Stadium
CAPITAL ONE ORANGE BOWL
Phone: 305-341-4700
Fax: 305-341-4771
tickets@orangebowl.org
www.orangebowl.org

Aug 8 - Aug 10, 2025
USAG NATIONAL CONGRESS &
TRADE SHOW
New Orleans, LA
Ernest A. Morial Convention Center
USA GYMNASTICS
Phone: 800-345-4719
Fax: 317-237-5069
membership@usagym.org
usagym.org

Aug 15 - Aug 17, 2025
BUCKARAMA
Perry, GA
Georgia National Fairgrounds

GEORGIA WILDLIFE FEDERATION
Phone: 770-787-7887
Fax: 770-787-9229
info@gwf.org
www.gwf.org

Aug 18 - Aug 21, 2025
NATIONAL WELLNESS SUMMIT
Austin, TX
JW Marriott Austin
NATIONAL WELLNESS INSTITUTE
Phone: 715-342-2969
Fax: 715-342-2979
nwc@nationalwellness.org
www.nationalwellness.org

Aug 21 - Aug 24, 2025
DALLAS MANIA FITNESS PRO
CONVENTION
Dallas, TX
SCW FITNESS EDUCATION
Phone: 847-562-4020
Fax: 847-562-4080
registration@scwfit.com
scwfit.com

Aug 28 - Aug 30, 2025
IHRSA FITNESS BRASIL LATIN
AMERICAN CONFERENCE & TRADE
SHOW
Sao Paulo, Brazil
INTERNATIONAL HEALTH, RACQUET &
SPORTSCLUB ASSOCIATION
Phone: 617-951-0055
info@healthandfitness.org
www.healthandfitness.org

Sept TBA, 2025
INDIANAPOLIS FALL BOAT & RV
SHOW
Indianapolis, IN
RENFRO PRODUCTIONS
Phone: 877-892-1723
Fax: 765-641-7756
info@renfroproductions.com
renfroproductions.com

Sept 15 - Sept 18, 2025
AXS DRIVE
Los Angeles, CA
STREET & SMITH'S SPORTS
BUSINESS JOURNAL
Phone: 704-973-1500
www.sportsbusinessdaily.com

Sept 16 - Sept 18, 2025
NRPA CONFERENCE
Orlando, FL
NATIONAL RECREATION & PARK
ASSOCIATION
Phone: 800-626-6772
customerservice@nrpa.org
www.nrpa.org

Sept 18 - Sept 21, 2025
NORWALK BOAT SHOW
Norwalk, CT
Norwalk Cove Marina
NATIONAL MARINE MANUFACTURERS
ASSOCIATION
Phone: 312-946-6200
Fax: 312-946-0401
www.nmma.org

Oct 2 - Oct 5, 2025
MIDWEST MANIA FITNESS PRO
CONVENTION
Chicago, IL
SCW FITNESS EDUCATION
Phone: 847-562-4020
Fax: 847-562-4080

registration@scwfit.com
scwfit.com

Oct 3 - Oct 5, 2025
MEDTRONIC TWIN CITIES
MARATHON
Minneapolis, MN
TWIN CITIES IN MOTION
Phone: 651-289-7700
Fax: 651-289-7720
info@tcmevents.org
www.tcmevents.org

Oct 13 - Oct 16, 2025
TEAMS '25 CONFERENCE & EXPO
Columbus, OH
shapehealthhalf.com

Oct 15 - Oct 17, 2025
2025 CPRA CONFERENCE & TRADE
SHOW
Vail, CO
COLORADO PARKS & RECREATION
ASSOCIATION
Phone: 303-231-0943
Fax: 303-237-9750
cpra@cpra-web.org
www.cpra-web.org

Oct 21 - Oct 24, 2025
ANA MASTERS OF MARKETING
CONFERENCE
Orlando, FL
Rosen Shingle Creek
ASSOCIATION OF NATIONAL
ADVERTISERS
Phone: 212-697-5950
Fax: 212-687-7310
www.ana.net

Oct 28 - Oct 31, 2025
FSB INTERNATIONAL TRADE FAIR
FOR AMENITY AREAS, SPORTS &
POOL FACILITIES
Cologne, Germany
KOELNMESSE
International Ph: +49 1806 603 500
fsb@visitor.koelnmesse.de
www.fsb-cologne.com

Nov 1 - Nov 5, 2025
CSCM NATIONAL CONFERENCE
Detroit, MI
CANADIAN SOCIETY OF CLUB
MANAGERS
Phone: 416-979-0640
Fax: 416-979-1144
national@cscm.org
www.cscm.org

Nov 4, 2025
MFA ANNUAL CONFERENCE
San Diego, CA
San Diego Convention Center
MEDICAL FITNESS ASSOCIATION
Phone: 910-420-8610
www.medicalfitness.org

Nov 5 - Nov 8, 2025
ATHLETIC BUSINESS SHOW
San Diego, CA
San Diego Convention Center
ATHLETIC BUSINESS
Phone: 608-249-0186
www.athleticbusiness.com

Nov 13 - Nov 16, 2025
BOSTON MANIA FITNESS PRO
CONVENTION
Boston, MA

SCW FITNESS EDUCATION
Phone: 847-562-4020
Fax: 847-562-4080
registration@scwfit.com
scwfit.com

Nov 14 - Nov 16, 2025
SNOWBOUND EXPO
Boston, MA
Boston Convention & Exhibition Center
SNOWSPORTS INDUSTRIES AMERICA
Phone: 435-657-5140
Fax: 435-659-3434
info@snowsports.org
snowsports.org

Nov 18 - Nov 20, 2025
GOLF BUSINESS CANADA
CONFERENCE & TRADE SHOW
Niagara Falls, ON, Canada
NATIONAL GOLF COURSE OWNERS
ASSOCIATION CANADA
Phone: 866-626-4262
ngcoa@ngcoa.ca
www.ngcoa.ca

TBA, 2026
CINCINNATI AUTO EXPO
Cincinnati, OH
Duke Energy Convention Center
DUKE ENERGY CONVENTION CENTER
Phone: 513-326-7100
info@cincinnatiautoexpo.com
cincinnatiautoexpo.com

TBA, 2026
DENVER INTERNATIONAL
SPORTSMEN'S EXPO
Denver, CO
Colorado Convention Center
INTERNATIONAL SPORTSMEN'S
EXPOSITIONS
Phone: 800-545-6100
Fax: 360-693-3352
International Ph: 360-693-3700
www.sportsexpos.com

Jan TBA 2026
CINCINNATI TRAVEL, SPORTS &
BOAT SHOW
Cincinnati, OH
Duke Energy Convention Center
HART PRODUCTIONS
Phone: 877-704-8190
Fax: 513-797-1013
hartproductions.com

Jan TBA, 2026
NASHVILLE BOAT SHOW
Nashville, TN
NATIONAL MARINE MANUFACTURERS
ASSOCIATION
Phone: 312-946-6200
Fax: 312-946-0401
www.nmma.org

Jan TBA, 2026
NCAA NATIONAL CONVENTION
TBA
NATIONAL COLLEGIATE ATHLETIC
ASSOCIATION
Phone: 317-917-6222
Fax: 317-917-6888
www.ncaa.org

Jan 7 - Jan 8, 2026
ATA TRADE SHOW
Indianapolis, IN
Indiana Convention Center
ARCHERY TRADE ASSOCIATION
Phone: 507-233-8130

Fax: 507-233-8140
www.archerytrade.org

Jan 8 - Jan 11, 2026
ABCA CONVENTION
Columbus, OH
AMERICAN BASEBALL COACHES
ASSOCIATION
Phone: 336-821-3140
Fax: 336-886-0000
www.abca.org

Jan 18 - Jan 22, 2026
STMA CONFERENCE & EXHIBITION
Fort Worth, TX
Fort Worth Convention Center
SPORTS TURF MANAGERS
ASSOCIATION
Phone: 800-323-3875
Fax: 785-843-2977
stma.org

Feb 6 - Feb 8, 2026
FISHARAMA/TURKEYRAMA
Perry, GA

GEORGIA WILDLIFE FEDERATION
Phone: 770-787-7887
Fax: 770-787-9229
info@gwf.org
www.gwf.org

Feb 20 - Feb 22, 2026
ASBA WINTER MEETING
Costa Rica
AMERICAN SPORTS BUILDERS
ASSOCIATION
Phone: 443-640-1042
info@sportsbuilders.org
www.sportsbuilders.org

Feb 26 - Mar 1, 2026
DC MANIA FITNESS PRO
CONVENTION
Herndon, VA
SCW FITNESS EDUCATION
Phone: 847-562-4020
Fax: 847-562-4080
registration@scwfit.com
scwfit.com

Mar 12 - Mar 15, 2026
TWIF WORLD INDOOR
CHAMPIONSHIP
Chinese Taipei
TUG OF WAR INTERNATIONAL
FEDERATION
International Ph: +31 6 23271158
10cc@hetnet.nl
www.tugofwar-twif.org

Sept 9 - Sept 12, 2026
TWIF WORLD OUTDOOR
CHAMPIONSHIP
Mossel Bay, South Africa
TUG OF WAR INTERNATIONAL
FEDERATION
International Ph: +31 6 23271158
10cc@hetnet.nl
www.tugofwar-twif.org

TBA, 2025
AUTOZONE LIBERTY BOWL
Memphis, TN
Liberty Bowl Memorial Stadium
AUTOZONE LIBERTY BOWL
Phone: 901-795-7700
Fax: 901-795-7826
hgraeter@libertybowl.org
www.libertybowl.org

TBA, 2025
CANADA CUP XCO
TBA
CANADIAN CYCLING ASSOCIATION
Phone: 613-248-1353
Fax: 613-248-9311
general@cyclingcanada.ca
www.cyclingcanada.ca

TBA, 2025
FISU SUMMER WORLD UNIVERSITY
GAMES
TBA
FEDERATION INTERNATIONALE DU
SPORT UNIVERSIADE
International Ph: 41-0-216130810
International Fax: 41-0-216015612
fisu@fisu.net
www.fisu.net

TBA, 2025
GRAND PRIX PHILIPPINES
Philippines, Philippines
INTERNATIONAL FEDERATION OF
BODY BUILDING & FITNESS
contact@ifbb.com
www.ifbb.com

TBA, 2025
MAG CANADIAN GYMNASTIC
CHAMPIONSHIPS
Calgary, AB, Canada
GYMNASTICS CANADA GYMNASTIQUE
Phone: 613-748-5637
Fax: 613-748-5691
info@gymcan.org
www.gymcan.org

TBA, 2025
RG CANADIAN GYMNASTIC
CHAMPIONSHIPS
Calgary, AB, Canada
GYMNASTICS CANADA GYMNASTIQUE
Phone: 613-748-5637
Fax: 613-748-5691
info@gymcan.org
www.gymcan.org

TBA, 2025
SUNSHINE STATE GAMES
TBA
SUNSHINE STATE GAMES
Phone: 850-577-7200
info@playinflorida.com
playinflorida.com

TBA, 2025
TG CANADIAN GYMNASTIC
CHAMPIONSHIPS
Calgary, AB, Canada
GYMNASTICS CANADA GYMNASTIQUE
Phone: 613-748-5637
Fax: 613-748-5691
info@gymcan.org
www.gymcan.org

TBA, 2025
WAG CANADIAN GYMNASTIC
CHAMPIONSHIPS
Calgary, AB, Canada

GYMNASTICS CANADA GYMNASTIQUE
Phone: 613-748-5637
Fax: 613-748-5691
info@gymcan.org
www.gymcan.org

TBA, 2025
YONEX OPEN
USA BADMINTON
Phone: 714-602-1691
ContactUs@usabadminton.org
www.usabadminton.org

Jan TBA, 2025
NCAA DIVISION I FCS
CHAMPIONSHIP
TBA
NATIONAL COLLEGIATE ATHLETIC
ASSOCIATION
Phone: 317-917-6222
Fax: 317-917-6888
www.ncaa.org

Jan TBA, 2025
NEW YORK CITY TRIATHLON
New York, NY
LIFE TIME FITNESS
www.eventsbylifetime.com

Jan TBA, 2025
OPEN 6EM SENS - METROPOLE DE
LYON, FRANCE
Lyon, France
WTA
Phone: 727-895-5000
Fax: 727-894-1982
feedback@wtatennis.com
www.wtatennis.com

Jan 1, 2025
ROSE BOWL GAME
Pasadena, CA
Rose Bowl Stadium
PASADENA TOURNAMENT OF ROSES
ASSOCIATION
Phone: 626-449-4100
www.tournamentofroses.com

Jan 2 - Jan 4 2025
AMATEUR MIXED DOUBLES
Weslaco, TX
NATIONAL SHUFFLEBOARD
ASSOCIATION
www.national-shuffleboard-association.us

Jan 2 - Jan 5, 2025
SENTRY TOURNAMENT OF
CHAMPIONS
Kapalua, HI
Plantation Course at Kapalua
PGA TOUR
Phone: 904-285-3700
www.pgatour.com

Jan 3, 2025
BELK BOWL
Charlotte, NC
Bank of America Stadium
BELK BOWL
Phone: 704-644-4047
Info@CharlotteSports.org
www.belkbowl.com

Jun 4 - Jan 5, 2025
AAU WINTER NATIONALS
Ralston, NE
Ralston Arena
AMATEUR ATHLETIC UNION
Phone: 407-934-7200
Fax: 407-934-7242
www.aausports.org

Jan 6 - Jan 11, 2025
ADELAIDE INTERNATIONAL 1
Adelaide, Australia
WTA
Phone: 727-895-5000
Fax: 727-894-1982
feedback@wtatennis.com
www.wtatennis.com

Jan 6 - Jan 26, 2025
AUSTRALIAN OPEN
Melbourne, Australia
TENNIS AUSTRALIA
International Ph: +61-3-9914-4677
www.tennis.com.au

Jan 6 - Jan 11, 2025
HOBART INTERNATIONAL
Hobart, Australia
WTA
Phone: 727-895-5000
Fax: 727-894-1982
feedback@wtatennis.com
www.wtatennis.com

Jan 7 - Jan 9, 2025
TEXAS OPEN MEN'S & LADIES'
NON-WALKING SINGLES
San Benito, TX
NATIONAL SHUFFLEBOARD
ASSOCIATION
www.national-shuffleboard-association.us

Jan 10, 2025
GOODYEAR COTTON BOWL
CLASSIC
Arlington, TX
AT&T Stadium
GOODYEAR COTTON BOWL CLASSIC
Phone: 817-892-4800
Fax: 817-892-4810
cso@attcottonbowl.com
www.cottonbowl.com

Jan 15 - Jan 20, 2025
EMERALD COAST INLINE
CHALLENGE
Milton, FL
USA ROLLER SPORTS
Phone: 402-483-7551
Fax: 402-483-1465
www.usarollersports.org

Jan 16 - Jan 18, 2025
HERO DUBAI DESERT CLASSIC
Dubai, United Arab Emirates
Emirates Golf Club
PGA EUROPEAN TOUR
International Ph: 44-0-1344-840400
International Fax: 44-0-1344-840500
www.rydercup.com

Jan 16 - Jan 18, 2025
MITSUBISHI ELECTRIC
CHAMPIONSHIP AT HUALALAI
Ka'upulehu-Kona, HI
Hualalai Golf Course
PGA CHAMPIONS TOUR
Phone: 904-285-3700
www.pgatour.com/pgatour-champions

Jan 18 - Jan 19, 2025
AAU WEST COAST FOOTBALL
NATIONAL CHAMPIONSHIPS
Las Vegas, NV
AMATEUR ATHLETIC UNION
Phone: 407-934-7200
Fax: 407-934-7242
www.aausports.org

Jan 23 - Jan 26, 2025
X GAMES ASPEN
Aspen, CO
ESPN
xgames.espn.com/xgames

Jan 27 - Feb 8, 2025
LEXUS PIPE PRO
Oahu, Hawaii
WORLD SURF LEAGUE
International Ph: +1-310-450-1212
www.worldsurfleague.com

Jan 27 - Feb 2, 2025
SENIOR MEN'S NATIONAL
CHAMPIONSHIPS
Duluth, MN
Duluth Entertainment Convention
Center
USA CURLING
Phone: 715-344-1199
Fax: 715-344-2279
www.usacurling.org

Jan 27 - Feb 2, 2025
SENIOR WOMEN'S NATIONAL
CHAMPIONSHIPS
Duluth, MN
Duluth Entertainment Convention
Center
USA CURLING
Phone: 715-344-1199
Fax: 715-344-2279
www.usacurling.org

Jan 27 - Feb 2, 2025
UPPER AUSTRIA LADIES LINZ
Linz, Austria
WTA
Phone: 727-895-5000
Fax: 727-894-1982
feedback@wtatennis.com
www.wtatennis.com

Jan 30 - Feb 2, 2025
AT&T PEBBLE BEACH PRO-AM
Pebble Beach, CA
Pebble Beach Golf Links
PGA TOUR
Phone: 904-285-3700
www.pgatour.com

Jan 30, 2025
EAST WEST SHRINE BOWL
Paradise, NV
Allegiant Stadium
EAST WEST SHRINE GAME
Phone: 813-281-8686
EastWestShrineBowl@shrinenet.org
shrinebowl.com

Jan 30, 2025
NFL PRO BOWL
Orlando, FL
NATIONAL FOOTBALL LEAGUE
Phone: 212-450-2000
www.nfl.com

Jan 30 - Feb 2, 2025
PANAMA CHAMPIONSHIP
Panama City, Panama
Panama Golf Club
PGA KORN FERRY TOUR
Phone: 904-285-3700
Fax: 904-285-7913
www.pgatour.com

Feb TBA, 2025
SWING THOUGHT NATIONAL PRO
SERIES - BENT CREEK
Jax, FL
Bent Creek Golf Club

Feb TBA, 2025
SWING THOUGHT NATIONAL PRO
SERIES - NATIVE OAKS
Valley Center, CA
Native Oaks

Feb TBA, 2025
US OPEN - CLEARWATER
Clearwater, FL
Clearwater Community Sailing Center
US WINDSURFING ASSOCIATION
Phone: 877-386-8708
info@uswindsurfing.org
uswindsurfing.org

Feb TBA, 2025
WOMEN'S WORLD CHAMPIONSHIPS
TBA
AMERICAN BANDY ASSOCIATION
www.usabandy.com

Feb 1, 2025
SENIOR BOWL
Mobile, AL
Ladd-Peebles Stadium
SENIOR BOWL
Phone: 251-438-2276
Fax: 251-432-0409
srbowl@seniorbowl.com
www.seniorbowl.com

Feb 1, 2025
TROPICAL 5K
Miami, FL
LIFE TIME FITNESS
www.eventsbylifetime.com

Feb 2, 2025
COOK OUT CLASH AT BOWMAN
GRAY
Winston-Salem, NC
Bowman Gray Stadium
NASCAR CUP SERIES
www.nascar.com

Feb 2, 2025
MIAMI MARATHON & HALF
Miami, FL
LIFE TIME FITNESS
www.eventsbylifetime.com

Feb 3 - Feb 15, 2025
FIS NORDIC JUNIOR WORLD SKI
CHAMPIONSHIP
Lake Placid, NY
FIS SKIING CHAMPIONSHIPS
International Ph: 44-33-244-6161
International Fax: 44-33-244-6171
mail@fisski.ch
www.fis-ski.com

Feb 3 - Feb 8, 2025
MUBADALA ABU DHABI OPEN
Abu Dhabi, United Arab Emirates
WTA
Phone: 727-895-5000
Fax: 727-894-1982
feedback@wtatennis.com
www.wtatennis.com

Feb 3 - Feb 9, 2025
WASTE MANAGEMENT PHOENIX
OPEN
Scottsdale, AZ

TPC Scottsdale
PGA TOUR
Phone: 904-285-3700
www.pgatour.com

Feb 6 - Feb 8, 2025
COLOMBIA CHAMPIONSHIP
Bogota, Colombia
Country Club de Bogota
PGA KORN FERRY TOUR
Phone: 904-285-3700
Fax: 904-285-7913
www.pgatour.com

Feb 6 - Feb 9, 2025
FOUNDERS CUP
Bradenton, FL
Bradenton Country Club
LPGA TOUR
Phone: 386-274-6200
Fax: 386-274-1099
www.lpga.com

Feb 7 - Feb 9, 2025
USA POND HOCKEY NATIONAL
CHAMPIONSHIPS
Eagle River, WI
Dollar Lake
USA HOCKEY
Phone: 719-576-8724
Fax: 719-538-1160
usah@usahockey.org
www.usahockey.com

Feb 8, 2025
2025 KICK OFF RUN
Westlake, OH
Fleet Feet- Westlake Location
CLEVELAND MARATHON
Phone: 800-467-3826
Fax: 216-378-0143
www.clevelandmarathon.com

Feb 8 - Feb 9, 2025
NATIONAL AGE GROUP LONG
TRACK SPEEDSKATING CHAMP
IONSHIP
Roseville, MN
US SPEEDSKATING
Phone: 801-417-5360
Fax: 801-417-5361
www.usspeedskating.org

Feb 9 - Feb 15, 2025
QATAR TOTALENERGIES OPEN
Doha, Qatar
WTA
Phone: 727-895-5000
Fax: 727-894-1982
feedback@wtatennis.com
www.wtatennis.com

Feb 10 - Feb 16, 2025
CHUBB CLASSIC
Naples, FL
Tiburon Golf Club
PGA CHAMPIONS TOUR
Phone: 904-285-3700
www.pgatour.com/pgatour-champions

Feb 10 - Feb 16, 2025
DELRAY BEACH OPEN
Delray Beach, FL
ATP TOUR 250
www.atptour.com

Feb 10 - Feb 16, 2025
GENESIS INVITATIONAL
Pacific Palisades, CA
Riviera Country Club

PGA TOUR
Phone: 904-285-3700
www.pgatour.com

Feb 13, 2025
BLUEGREEN VACATIONS DUEL
DAYTONA 1&2
Daytona Beach, FL
Daytona International Speedway
NASCAR CUP SERIES
www.nascar.com

Feb 13 - Feb 17, 2025
USA SPIRIT NATIONALS
Anaheim, CA
Anaheim Convention Center
UNITED SPIRIT ASSOCIATION
Phone: 800-533-8022
info@usacamps.com
usa.varsity.com

Feb 14 - Feb 16, 2025
ISI WINTER CLASSIC
St. Peters, MO
City of St. Peters Rec Complex
ICE SKATING INSTITUTE
Phone: 972-735-8800
Fax: 972-735-8815
events@skateisi.org
www.skateisi.org

Feb 14 - Feb 16, 2025
NFAA INDOOR NATIONAL
CHAMPIONSHIPS
Chicago, IL
Navy Pier
NATIONAL FIELD ARCHERY
ASSOCIATION
Phone: 605-260-9279
info@nfaausa.com
www.nfaausa.com

Feb 14 - Feb 23, 2025
SCOTTIES TOURNAMENT OF
HEARTS
Thunder Bay, ON, Canada
Fort William Gardens
CURLING CANADA
Phone: 613-834-2076
Fax: 613-834-0716
championships@curling.ca
www.curling.ca

Feb 14 - Feb 16, 2025
SURF ABU DAHABI PRO
Hudayriyat Island, Abu Dhabi, United
Arab Emerates
WORLD SURF LEAGUE
International Ph: +1-310-450-1212
www.worldsurfleague.com

Feb 14 - Feb 16, 2025
US BIATHLON MASTERS NATIONALS
Brillion, WI
Ariens Nordic Center
UNITED STATES BIATHLON
ASSOCIATION
Phone: 719-632-5551
www.usbiathlon.org

Feb 15 - Feb 16, 2025
AAU 14U INDOOR NATIONAL
CHAMPIONSHIPS
Ypsilanti, MI
Eastern Michigan University
AMATEUR ATHLETIC UNION
Phone: 407-934-7200
Fax: 407-934-7242
www.aausports.org

Feb 15 - Feb 17, 2025
USA COLLEGIATE CHAMPIONSHIPS
Anaheim, CA
Anaheim Convention Center
UNITED SPIRIT ASSOCIATION
Phone: 800-533-8022
info@usacamps.com
usa.varsity.com

Feb 16, 2025
C.R.A.S.H.-B. WORLD INDOOR
ROWING CHAMPIONSHIPS
Boston, MA
Gosman Sports & Convocation Center
CRASH-B SPRINTS
office@crash-b.org
www.crash-b.org

Feb 16 - Feb 22, 2025
CANADIAN UNDER-18 BOYS AND
GIRLS CHAMPIONSHIPS
Saskatoon, SK, Canada
Nutana Curling Club
CURLING CANADA
Phone: 613-834-2076
Fax: 613-834-0716
championships@curling.ca
www.curling.ca

Feb 16, 2025
DAYTONA 500
Daytona Beach, FL
Daytona International Speedway
NASCAR CUP SERIES
www.nascar.com

Feb 16 - Mar 1, 2025
DUBAI DUTY FREE TENNIS
CHAMPIONSHIPS
Dubai, UAE
Dubai Duty Free Tennis Stadium
WTA
Phone: 727-895-5000
Fax: 727-894-1982
feedback@wtatennis.com
www.wtatennis.com

Feb 16, 2025
USA JUNIOR NATIONALS
Anaheim, CA
Anaheim Convention Center
UNITED SPIRIT ASSOCIATION
Phone: 800-533-8022
info@usacamps.com
usa.varsity.com

Feb 17 - Feb 23, 2025
MIXED DOUBLES NATIONAL
CHAMPIONSHIP
Lafayette, CO
Rock Creek Curling
USA CURLING
Phone: 715-344-1199
Fax: 715-344-2279
www.usacurling.org

Feb 17 - Feb 23, 2025
PASCO COUNTY FAIR
CHAMPIONSHIP RODEO
Dade City, FL
PROFESSIONAL RODEO COWBOY
ASSOCIATION
Phone: 719-593-8840
webmaster@prorodeo.com
www.prorodeo.com

Feb 18 - Feb 24, 2025
OMAEZAKI CUP
Omaezaki City, Shizuoka, Japan
Omaezaki Long Beach

INTERNATIONAL WINDSURFING TOUR
internationalwindsurfingtour.com

Feb 19 - Feb 23, 2025
KENYA OPEN
Nairobi, Kenya
Muthaiga Golf Club
PGA EUROPEAN TOUR
International Ph: 44-0-1344-840400
International Fax: 44-0-1344-840500
www.rydercup.com

Feb 19 - Feb 20, 2025
SPEED NATION ALPINE NATIONALS
Val Saint-Come, QC, Canada
CANADA SNOWBOARD
Phone: 778-653-0000
Fax: 604-568-1639
info@canadasnowboard.ca
www.canadasnowboard.ca

Feb 20 - Feb 23, 2025
HONDA LPGA THAILAND
Chonburi, Thailand
Siam Country Club
LPGA TOUR
Phone: 386-274-6200
Fax: 386-274-1099
www.lpga.com

Feb 20 - Feb 23, 2025
HOYT/EASTON PRO/AM
Foley, AL
ARCHERY SHOOTERS ASSOCIATION
Phone: 770-795-0232
Fax: 770-795-0953
info@asaarchery.com
www.asaarchery.com

Feb 21 - Feb 23, 2025
2025 WINTER CUP
Louisville, KY
International Convention Center
USA GYMNASTICS
Phone: 800-345-4719
Fax: 317-237-5069
membership@usagym.org
usagym.org

Feb 22, 2025
2025 ELITE TEAM CUP
Louisville, KY
Freedom Hall
USA GYMNASTICS
Phone: 800-345-4719
Fax: 317-237-5069
membership@usagym.org
usagym.org

Feb 22, 2025
BAYOU CITY CLASSIC
Houston, TX
HOUSTON AREA ROAD RUNNERS
ASSOCIATION
www.bayoucityclassic.org

Feb 22, 2025
MARDI GRAS TOURNAMENT
New Orleans, LA
USA RUGBY
Phone: 303-539-0300
Fax: 303-539-0311
membership@usa.rugby
www.usa.rugby

Feb 23, 2025
AMBETTER HEALTH 400
Hampton, GA
Atlanta Motor Speedway
NASCAR CUP SERIES
www.nascar.com

Feb 23, 2025
NASTIA LIUKIN CUP
Louisville, KY
Freedom Hall
USA GYMNASTICS
Phone: 800-345-4719
Fax: 317-237-5069
membership@usagym.org
usagym.org

Feb 24 - Mar 1, 2025
ABIERTO MEXICANO TELCEL
PRESENTADO POR HSBC
Acapulco, Guerrero
Arena GNP
WTA
Phone: 727-895-5000
Fax: 727-894-1982
feedback@wtatennis.com
www.wtatennis.com

Feb 24 - Feb 26, 2025
AMATEUR MEN'S & LADIES'
DOUBLES
Zephyrhills, FL
NATIONAL SHUFFLEBOARD
ASSOCIATION
www.national-shuffleboard-association.us

Feb 26 - Feb 27, 2025
DUBAI MUSCLE BEACH
Dubai, United Arab Emirates
INTERNATIONAL FEDERATION OF
BODY BUILDING & FITNESS
contact@ifbb.com
www.ifbb.com

Feb 26 - Mar 1, 2025
US SYNCHRONIZED SKATING
CHAMPIONSHIPS
Colorado Springs, CO
U.S. FIGURE SKATING
Phone: 719-635-5200
Fax: 719-635-9548
info@usfigureskating.org
www.usfigureskating.org

Feb 26 - Mar 3, 2025
USA RACQUETBALL NATIONAL HIGH
SCHOOL CHAMPIONSHI PS
Portland, OR
Multnomah Athletic Club
USA RACQUETBALL
Phone: 719-635-5396
Fax: 719-635-0685
jonathan@usaracquetball.com
www.usaracquetball.com

Feb 27 - Mar 2, 2025
ARNOLD ARNOLD SPORTS
FESTIVAL
Columbus, OH
Columbus Convention Center
ARNOLD SPORTS FESTIVAL
Phone: 614-431-2600
Fax: 614-431-3492
www.arnoldsportsfestival.com

Feb 27 - Mar 2, 2025
BASSMASTER ELITE SERIES - LAKE
OKEECHOBEE
Okeechobee, FL
Lake Okeechobee
BASS ANGLERS SPORTSMAN
SOCIETY
Phone: 877-227-7872
bassmaster@emailcustomerservice.com
www.bassmaster.com

Feb 27 - Mar 2, 2025
COGNIZANT CLASSIC
Palm Beach Gardens, FL
PGA National Champion Course
PGA TOUR
Phone: 904-285-3700
www.pgatour.com

Feb 27 - Mar 2, 2025
HSBC WOMEN'S WORLD
CHAMPIONSHIP
Singapore
Sentosa Golf Club
LPGA TOUR
Phone: 386-274-6200
Fax: 386-274-1099
www.lpga.com

Feb 27 - Mar 2, 2025
SOUTH AFRICAN OPEN
Durban, South Africa
Durban Golf Course
PGA EUROPEAN TOUR
International Ph: 44-0-1344-840400
International Fax: 44-0-1344-840500
www.rydercup.com

Feb 28 - Mar 2, 2025
FIRESTONE GRAND PRIX OF ST.
PETERSBURG
St. Petersburg, FL
Streets of St. Petersburg
NTT INDYCAR SERIES
Phone: 317-492-6526
indycar@indycar.com
www.indycar.com

Feb 28, 2025
FITNESS INTERNATIONAL
COMPETITION
Columbus, OH
Columbus Convention Center
ARNOLD SPORTS FESTIVAL
Phone: 614-431-2600
Fax: 614-431-3492
www.arnoldsportsfestival.com

Feb 28 - Mar 9, 2025
MONTANA'S BRIER
Kelowna, BC, Canada
Prospera Place
CURLING CANADA
Phone: 613-834-2076
Fax: 613-834-0716
championships@curling.ca
www.curling.ca

Feb 28 - Mar 2, 2025
US HIGH SCHOOL TEAM
CHAMPIONSHIPS
Philadelphia, PA
Arlen Specter US Squash Center
UNITED STATES SQUASH RACQUETS
ASSOCIATION
Phone: 212-268-4090
Fax: 212-268-4091
tournaments@ussquash.org
www.ussquash.com

Feb 28 - Mar 2, 2025
USA BMX LONE STAR NATIONALS
Houston, TX
RockStar Energy Bike Park
USA BMX
Phone: 480-961-1903
Fax: 480-961-1842
info@usabmx.com
www.usabmx.com

Mar TBA, 2025
NATIONAL COLLEGIATE MIXED
RIFLE FINALS
Lexington, KY
Memorial Coliseum
NATIONAL COLLEGIATE ATHLETIC
ASSOCIATION
Phone: 317-917-6222
Fax: 317-917-6888
www.ncaa.org

Mar TBA, 2025
SWING THOUGHT NATIONAL PRO
SERIES - OKEFENOKEE
Blackshear, GA
Okefenokee Country Club

Mar TBA, 2025
SWING THOUGHT NATIONAL PRO
SERIES - SANCTUARY GO LF CLUB
Waverly, GA
Sanctuary Golf Club

Mar TBA, 2025
USA BROOMBALL NATIONAL
CHAMPIONSHIPS
TBA
USA BROOMBALL
contact@usbabroomball.org
usbabroomball.org

Mar 1, 2025
BIKINI INTERNATIONAL
COMPETITION
Columbus, OH
Columbus Convention Center
ARNOLD SPORTS FESTIVAL
Phone: 614-431-2600
Fax: 614-431-3492
www.arnoldsportsfestival.com

Mar 1, 2025
DISSIDENT ARMS ACTION SHOTGUN
CHAMPIONSHIP
Eagle Lake, TX
US PRACTICAL SHOOTING
ASSOCIATION
Phone: 360-855-2245
Fax: 360-855-0380
office@uspsa.org
www.uspsa.org

Mar 1, 2025
MEN'S PTI 50+
West Chester, PA
AMERICAN PLATFORM TENNIS
ASSOCIATION
Phone: 888-744-9490
apta@platformtennis.org
www.platformtennis.org

Mar 1, 2025
SAN MIGUEL BUZZ MARATHON
San Miguel, CA
Camp Roberts Army National Guard
Reservation
SAN MIGUEL BUZZ MARATHON
Phone: 805-467-3216
Fax: 805-467-3410
www.buzzmarathon.org

Mar 2, 2025
305 HALF MARATHON & 5K
Miami, FL
LIFE TIME FITNESS
www.eventsbylifetime.com

Mar 2, 2025
ARNOLD MASTER'S STRONGMAN
CHAMPIONSHIP
Columbus, OH
AMERICAN STRONGMAN
CORPORATION
Phone: 314-565-5970
americanstrongmancorporation@gmail.co
m
strongmancorporation.com

Mar 2 - Mar 9, 2025
COLOGUARD CLASSIC
Tucson, AZ
La Paloma Country Club
PGA CHAMPIONS TOUR
Phone: 904-285-3700
www.pgatour.com/pgatour-champions

Mar 2, 2025
ECHOPARK AUTOMOTIVE GRAND
PRIX
Austin, TX
Circuit of the Americas
NASCAR CAMPING WORLD TRUCK
SERIES
Phone: 800-630-0535
www.nascar.com

Mar 2, 2025
LEGACY ON ICE
Washington, DC
U.S. FIGURE SKATING
Phone: 719-635-5200
Fax: 719-635-9548
info@usfigureskating.org
www.usfigureskating.org

Mar 3 - Mar 9, 2025
ARNOLD PALMER INVITATIONAL
Bay Hill, FL
Bay Hill Club & Lodge
PGA TOUR
Phone: 904-285-3700
www.pgatour.com

Mar 4, 2025
DAYTONA ATV SUPERCROSS
Daytona, FL
Daytona International Speedway
AMA PRO RACING
Phone: 386-492-1014
Fax: 386-274-2335
communications@amaproracing.com
www.amaproracing.com

Mar 5 - Mar 16, 2025
BNP PARIBAS OPEN
Indian Wells, CA
WTA
Phone: 727-895-5000
Fax: 727-894-1982
feedback@wtatennis.com
www.wtatennis.com

Mar 5 - Mar 9, 2025
THE VEGAS SHOOT
Las Vegas, NV
NATIONAL FIELD ARCHERY
ASSOCIATION
Phone: 605-260-9279
info@nfaausa.com
www.nfaausa.com

Mar 6 - Mar 9, 2025
AMALIE MOTOR OIL NHRA
GATORNATIONALS
Gainesville, FL
Gainesville Raceway

NATIONAL HOT ROD ASSOCIATION
Phone: 626-914-4761
Fax: 626-325-8752
nhra@nhra.com
www.nhra.com

Mar 6 - Mar 8, 2025
APTA MEN'S & WOMEN'S
NATIONALS
Philadelphia, PA
AMERICAN PLATFORM TENNIS
ASSOCIATION
Phone: 888-744-9490
apta@platformtennis.org
www.platformtennis.org

Mar 6 - Mar 9, 2025
ARCADIA ALL-FLORIDA
CHAMPIONSHIP RODEO
Arcadia, FL
PROFESSIONAL RODEO COWBOY
ASSOCIATION
Phone: 719-593-8840
webmaster@prorodeo.com
www.prorodeo.com

Mar 6 - Mar 9, 2025
CSA NATIONAL TEAM
CHAMPIONSHIPS
Philadelphia, PA
Arlen Specter US Squash Center
UNITED STATES SQUASH RACQUETS
ASSOCIATION
Phone: 212-268-4090
Fax: 212-268-4091
tournaments@ussquash.org
www.ussquash.com

Mar 6 - Mar 16, 2025
PARA WORLD CHAMPIONSHIPS
TBA
USA BOBSLED & SKELETON
FEDERATION
Phone: 518-523-1842
Fax: 518-523-9491
www.usabs.com

Mar 6 - Mar 9, 2025
PUERTO RICO OPEN
Rio Grande, Puerto Rico
Grand Reserve Golf Club
PGA TOUR
Phone: 904-285-3700
www.pgatour.com

Mar 6 - Mar 9, 2025
US SQUASH DOUBLES
CHAMPIONSHIPS
Baltimore, MD
Maryland Club
UNITED STATES SQUASH RACQUETS
ASSOCIATION
Phone: 212-268-4090
Fax: 212-268-4091
tournaments@ussquash.org
www.ussquash.com

Mar 7, 2025
RD 2 DECKER TRAINING FACILITY
Fountain, FL
Decker Training Facility
AMA PRO RACING
Phone: 386-492-1014
Fax: 386-274-2335
communications@amaproracing.com
www.amaproracing.com

Mar 7 - Mar 9, 2025
TAMPA BAY OPEN
Tampa Bay, FL

NATIONAL X BALL LEAGUE
info@nxlpaintball.com
nxlpaintball.com

Mar 9 - Mar 10, 2025
AIR NATION FREESTYLE NATIONALS
Barrie, ON, Canada
CANADA SNOWBOARD
Phone: 778-653-0000
Fax: 604-568-1639
info@canadasnowboard.ca
www.canadasnowboard.ca

Mar 9, 2025
SHRINERS CHILDREN'S 500
Avondale, AZ
Phoenix Raceway
NASCAR CUP SERIES
www.nascar.com

Mar 11 - Mar 15, 2025
NCAA DIVISION II MEN/WOMEN'S
SWIMMING & DIVING FINALS
Indianapolis, IN
IU Natatorium (IUPUI)
NATIONAL COLLEGIATE ATHLETIC
ASSOCIATION
Phone: 317-917-6222
Fax: 317-917-6888
www.ncaa.org

Mar 12 - Mar 15, 2025
CCAA MEN'S NATIONAL
BASKETBALL CHAMPIONSHIP
Saint-Laurent, QC, Canada
Vanier College
CANADA BASKETBALL
Phone: 416-614-8037
Fax: 416-614-9570
info@basketball.ca
www.basketball.ca

Mar 12 - Mar 15, 2025
CCAA WOMEN'S NATIONAL
BASKETBALL CHAMPIONSHIP
Fredericton, NB, Canada
The Richard J. Currie Centre
CANADA BASKETBALL
Phone: 416-614-8037
Fax: 416-614-9570
info@basketball.ca
www.basketball.ca

Mar 13 - Mar 15, 2025
NCAA DIVISION II MEN'S/WOMEN'S
TRACK, INDOOR FINALS
Indianapolis, IN
Fall Creek Pavilion, Indiana State
Fairgrounds
NATIONAL COLLEGIATE ATHLETIC
ASSOCIATION
Phone: 317-917-6222
Fax: 317-917-6888
www.ncaa.org

Mar 13 - Mar 14, 2025
THE PLAYERS CHAMPIONSHIP
Ponte Vedra Beach, FL
TPC Sawgrass
PGA TOUR
Phone: 904-285-3700
www.pgatour.com

Mar 14 - Mar 16, 2025
AKC NATIONAL AGILITY
CHAMPIONSHIPS
Tulsa, OK
Built Ford Tough Livestock Complex at
Expo Square
AMERICAN KENNEL CLUB
Phone: 919-233-9767

publiced@akc.org
www.akc.org

Mar 14 - Mar 16, 2025
CANADIAN UNIVERSITY & COLLEGE
CHAMPIONSHIPS
Montreal, QC, Canada
McGill University Athletics and
Recreation
SQUASH CANADA
Phone: 613-228-7724
Fax: 613-228-7232
info@squash.ca
www.squash.ca

Mar 14 - Mar 16, 2025
EASTERN ADULT SECTIONAL
CHAMPIONSHIPS
Indian Trail, NC
U.S. FIGURE SKATING
Phone: 719-635-5200
Fax: 719-635-9548
info@usfigureskating.org
www.usfigureskating.org

Mar 14 - Mar 15, 2025
NCAA DIVISION I MEN'S/WOMEN'S
TRACK, INDOOR FINA LS
Virginia Beach, VA
Virginia Beach Sports Center
NATIONAL COLLEGIATE ATHLETIC
ASSOCIATION
Phone: 317-917-6222
Fax: 317-917-6888
www.ncaa.org

Mar 14 - Mar 15, 2025
NCAA DIVISION II WRESTLING
FINALS
Indianapolis, IN
Corteva Coliseum
NATIONAL COLLEGIATE ATHLETIC
ASSOCIATION
Phone: 317-917-6222
Fax: 317-917-6888
www.ncaa.org

Mar 14 - Mar 15, 2025
NCAA DIVISION III MEN'S
WRESTLING FINALS
Providence, RI
Amica Mutual Pavilion
NATIONAL COLLEGIATE ATHLETIC
ASSOCIATION
Phone: 317-917-6222
Fax: 317-917-6888
www.ncaa.org

Mar 14 - Mar 15, 2025
NCAA DIVISION III MEN'S/WOMEN'S
TRACK, INDOOR FI NALS
Rochester, NY
Golisano Training Center
NATIONAL COLLEGIATE ATHLETIC
ASSOCIATION
Phone: 317-917-6222
Fax: 317-917-6888
www.ncaa.org

Mar 14 - Mar 16, 2025
PACIFIC COAST ADULT SECTIONAL
CHAMPIONSHIPS
Paramount, CA
U.S. FIGURE SKATING
Phone: 719-635-5200
Fax: 719-635-9548
info@usfigureskating.org
www.usfigureskating.org

Mar 14 - Mar 16, 2025
YUENGLING SHAMROCK MARATHON
Virginia Beach, VA
SHAMROCK MARATHON
Phone: 757-412-1056
Fax: 757-412-1058
info@shamrockmarathon.com
www.shamrockmarathon.com

Mar 15 - Mar 25, 2025
MEO RIP CURL PRO PORTUGAL
Supertubos, Peniche, Portugal
WORLD SURF LEAGUE
International Ph: +1-310-450-1212
www.worldsurfleague.com

Mar 16 - Mar 23, 2025
HOAG CLASSIC
Newport Beach, CA
Newport Beach Country Club
PGA CHAMPIONS TOUR
Phone: 904-285-3700
www.pgatour.com/pgatour-champions

Mar 16, 2025
LOS ANGELES MARATHON
Los Angeles, CA
CONQUR ENDURANCE GROUP
Phone: 213-542-3000
info@goconqur.com
goconqur.com

Mar 16 - Mar 21, 2025
MIXED DOUBLES CHAMPIONSHIP
Summerside, PE, Canada
Gerard "Turk" Gallant Arena
CURLING CANADA
Phone: 613-834-2076
Fax: 613-834-0716
championships@curling.ca
www.curling.ca

Mar 16, 2025
PENNZOIL 400
Las Vegas, NV
Las Vegas Motor Speedway
NASCAR CUP SERIES
www.nascar.com

Mar 17 - Mar 23, 2025
VALSPAR CHAMPIONSHIP
Palm Harbor, FL
Innisbrook Resort (Copperhead)
PGA TOUR
Phone: 904-285-3700
www.pgatour.com

Mar 18 - Mar 30, 2025
MIAMI OPEN PRESENTED BY ITAU
Miami, FL
Hard Rock Stadium
WTA
Phone: 727-895-5000
Fax: 727-894-1982
feedback@wtatennis.com
www.wtatennis.com

Mar 19 - Mar 30, 2025
ATP TOUR MASTERS 1000 - MIAMI
OPEN
Miami, FL
ATP TOUR MASTERS 1000
www.atptour.com

Mar 19 - Mar 22, 2025
NCAA DIVISION I WOMEN'S
SWIMMING & DIVING FINALS
Federal Way, WA
Weyerhaeuser King County Aquatics
Center

NATIONAL COLLEGIATE ATHLETIC
ASSOCIATION
Phone: 317-917-6222
Fax: 317-917-6888
www.ncaa.org

Mar 19 - Mar 22, 2025
NCAA DIVISION III MEN'S/WOMEN'S
SWIMMING & DIVIN G FINALS
Greensboro, NC
Greensboro Aquatic Center
NATIONAL COLLEGIATE ATHLETIC
ASSOCIATION
Phone: 317-917-6222
Fax: 317-917-6888
www.ncaa.org

Mar 20, 2025
BIG ISLAND MARATHON
Hilo, HI
BIG ISLAND INTERNATIONAL
MARATHON
Phone: 808-969-7400
www.hilomarathon.org

Mar 20 - Mar 22, 2025
NCAA DIVISION I WRESTLING
FINALS
Philadelphia, PA
Wells Fargo Center
NATIONAL COLLEGIATE ATHLETIC
ASSOCIATION
Phone: 317-917-6222
Fax: 317-917-6888
www.ncaa.org

Mar 20 - Mar 22, 2025
NCAA DIVISION III MEN'S
BASKETBALL FINALS
Fort Wayne, IN
Allen County War Memorial Coliseum
NATIONAL COLLEGIATE ATHLETIC
ASSOCIATION
Phone: 317-917-6222
Fax: 317-917-6888
www.ncaa.org

Mar 20 - Mar 22, 2025
NCAA DIVISION III WOMEN'S
BASKETBALL FINALS
Salem, VA
Cregger Center
NATIONAL COLLEGIATE ATHLETIC
ASSOCIATION
Phone: 317-917-6222
Fax: 317-917-6888
www.ncaa.org

Mar 20 - Mar 23, 2025
PORSCHE SINGAPORE CLASSIC
Singapore
Laguna National Golf Resort Club
PGA EUROPEAN TOUR
International Ph: 44-0-1344-840400
International Fax: 44-0-1344-840500
www.rydercup.com

Mar 21 - Mar 22, 2025
AAU SPRING YOUTH NATIONALS
Kingsport, TN
Tribe Sports Complex
AMATEUR ATHLETIC UNION
Phone: 407-934-7200
Fax: 407-934-7242
www.aausports.org

Mar 21 - Mar 23, 2025
ALL STAR CHAMPIONSHIPS
Los Angeles, CA
UNITED SPIRIT ASSOCIATION
Phone: 800-533-8022

info@usacamps.com
usa.varsity.com

Mar 21 - Mar 23, 2025
COLLEGIATE BMX NATIONAL
CHAMPIONSHIPS
West Monroe, LA
USA CYCLING
Phone: 719-434-4200
Fax: 719-434-4300
help@usacycling.org
www.usacycling.org

Mar 21 - Mar 23, 2025
IWWF WORLD SKI SHOW
CHAMPIONSHIPS
Max Kirwan Lakes Mulwava, Victoria,
Australia
INTERNATIONAL WATERSKI &
WAKEBOARD FEDERATION
info@iwwfed.com
https://iwwf.sport

Mar 21 - Mar 23, 2025
MIDWESTERN ADULT SECTIONAL
CHAMPIONSHIPS
Madison, WI
U.S. FIGURE SKATING
Phone: 719-635-5200
Fax: 719-635-9548
info@usfigureskating.org
www.usfigureskating.org

Mar 21 - Mar 23, 2025
NHRA ARIZONA NATIONALS
Chandler, AZ
Wild Horse Pass Motorsports Park
NATIONAL HOT ROD ASSOCIATION
Phone: 626-914-4761
Fax: 626-325-8752
nhra@nhra.com
www.nhra.com

Mar 21 - Mar 23, 2025
OUTDOORS BASSMASTER CLASSIC
Fort Worth, TX
Lake Ray Roberts
BASS ANGLERS SPORTSMAN
SOCIETY
Phone: 877-227-7872
bassmaster@emailcustomerservice.com
www.bassmaster.com

Mar 21 - Mar 23, 2025
THE THERMAL CLUB INDYCAR
GRAND PRIX
Thermal, CA
NTT INDYCAR SERIES
Phone: 317-492-6526
indycar@indycar.com
www.indycar.com

Mar 21 - Mar 23, 2025
US JUNIOR BRONZE
CHAMPIONSHIPS
Philadelphia, PA
Arlen Specter US Squash Center
UNITED STATES SQUASH RACQUETS
ASSOCIATION
Phone: 212-268-4090
Fax: 212-268-4091
tournaments@ussquash.org
www.ussquash.com

Mar 22, 2025
MARINE CORPS MARATHON
Arlington, VA
MARINE CORPS MARATHON
Phone: 800-786-8762
Fax: 703-784-2265

mcm.info@usmc.mil
www.marinemarathon.com

Mar 22, 2025
NAPA VALLEY TRAIL MARATHON,
HALF MARATHON & 10K
Calistoga, CA
Bothe-Napa State Park
ENVIRO-SPORTS
Phone: 415-868-1829
info@envirosports.com
envirosports.com

Mar 22 - Mar 30, 2025
NEW HOLLAND CANADIAN JUNIOR
MEN'S AND WOMEN'S CURLING
CHAMPIONSHIPS
Summerside, PE, Canada
Gerard "Turk" Gallant Arena
CURLING CANADA
Phone: 613-834-2076
Fax: 613-834-0716
championships@curling.ca
www.curling.ca

Mar 23, 2025
STRAIGHT TALK WIRELESS 400
Homestead, FL
Homestead-Miami Speedway
NASCAR CUP SERIES
www.nascar.com

Mar 23 - Mar 30, 2025
WORLD FIGURE SKATING
CHAMPIONSHIPS
Boston, MA
U.S. FIGURE SKATING
Phone: 719-635-5200
Fax: 719-635-9548
info@usfigureskating.org
www.usfigureskating.org

Mar 24 - Mar 28, 2025
NCAA DIVISION II WOMEN'S
BASKETBALL FINALS
Pittsburgh, PA
UPMC Cooper Fieldhouse
NATIONAL COLLEGIATE ATHLETIC
ASSOCIATION
Phone: 317-917-6222
Fax: 317-917-6888
www.ncaa.org

Mar 24 - Mar 30, 2025
TEXAS CHILDREN'S HOUSTON OPEN
Houston, TX
Memorial Park Golf Course
PGA TOUR
Phone: 904-285-3700
www.pgatour.com

Mar 25 - Mar 29, 2025
NCAA DIVISION II MEN'S
BASKETBALL FINALS
Evansville, IN
Ford Center
NATIONAL COLLEGIATE ATHLETIC
ASSOCIATION
Phone: 317-917-6222
Fax: 317-917-6888
www.ncaa.org

Mar 26 - Mar 29, 2025
CANADIAN YOUTH CHALLENGE
CHAMPIONSHIP
Calgary, AB, Canada
CANADIAN 5 PIN BOWLERS
ASSOCIATION
Phone: 613-744-5090
Fax: 613-744-2217

sheila.c5pba@gmail.com
www.c5pba.ca

Mar 26 - Mar 30, 2025
CLUB NATIONAL CHAMPIONSHIPS
Cedarburg, WI
Milwaukee Curling Club
USA CURLING
Phone: 715-344-1199
Fax: 715-344-2279
www.usacurling.org

Mar 26 - Mar 29, 2025
NCAA DIVISION I MEN'S SWIMMING &
DIVING FINALS
Federal Way, WA
Weyerhaeuser King County Aquatics
Center
NATIONAL COLLEGIATE ATHLETIC
ASSOCIATION
Phone: 317-917-6222
Fax: 317-917-6888
www.ncaa.org

Mar 26 - Mar 29, 2025
US BIATHLON SENIOR NATIONALS
Bozeman, MT
Crosscut Mountain Sports Center
UNITED STATES BIATHLON
ASSOCIATION
Phone: 719-632-5551
www.usbiathlon.org

Mar 27 - Mar 30, 2025
CANADIAN DOUBLES
CHAMPIONSHIP
Toronto, ON, Canada
Granite Club
SQUASH CANADA
Phone: 613-228-7724
Fax: 613-228-7232
info@squash.ca
www.squash.ca

Mar 27 - Mar 30, 2025
HERO INDIAN OPEN
New Dehli, India
DLF G&CC
PGA EUROPEAN TOUR
International Ph: 44-0-1344-840400
International Fax: 44-0-1344-840500
www.rydercup.com

Mar 27 - Mar 30, 2025
LUCAS OIL NHRA
WINTERNATIONALS
Pomona, CA
In-N-Out Burger Pomona Dragstrip
NATIONAL HOT ROD ASSOCIATION
Phone: 626-914-4761
Fax: 626-325-8752
nhra@nhra.com
www.nhra.com

Mar 27, 2025
US BIATHLON COLLEGIATE
NATIONAL CHAMPIONSHIPS
Bozeman, MT
Crosscut Mountain Sports Center
UNITED STATES BIATHLON
ASSOCIATION
Phone: 719-632-5551
www.usbiathlon.org

Mar 27 - Mar 29, 2025
USA RACQUETBALL NATIONAL
INTERCOLLEGIATE CHAMPIO
NSHIPS
Raleigh, NC
North Carolina State Recreation Center

USA RACQUETBALL
Phone: 719-635-5396
Fax: 719-635-0685
jonathan@usaracquetball.com
www.usaracquetball.com

Mar 27 - Apr 6, 2025
YMBL CHAMPIONSHIP RODEO
Beaumont, TX
PROFESSIONAL RODEO COWBOY
ASSOCIATION
Phone: 719-593-8840
webmaster@prorodeo.com
www.prorodeo.com

Mar 28 - Mar 29, 2025
COLLEGIATE CLUB NATIONAL
CHAMPIONSHIPS
Miami, FL
USA TRIATHLON
Phone: 719-955-2807
info@usatriathlon.org
www.usatriathlon.org

Mar 28 - Mar 30, 2025
NATIONAL AGE GROUP SHORT
TRACK SPEEDSKATING CHAM
PIONSHIP
Manmouth Junction, NJ
US SPEEDSKATING
Phone: 801-417-5360
Fax: 801-417-5361
www.usspeedskating.org

Mar 28 - Mar 30, 2025
NCAA DIVISION III WOMEN'S ICE
HOCKEY CHAMPIONSHI PS
River Falls, WI
Hunt Arena
NATIONAL COLLEGIATE ATHLETIC
ASSOCIATION
Phone: 317-917-6222
Fax: 317-917-6888
www.ncaa.org

Mar 28 - Mar 30, 2025
USA BMX CAROLINA NATIONALS
Rock Hill, SC
Rock Hill Super BMX Supercross Track
USA BMX
Phone: 480-961-1903
Fax: 480-961-1842
info@usabmx.com
www.usabmx.com

Mar 28, 2025
WAC ANNUAL GARY "DOC" WELT
MEMORIAL MATCH
Clearwater, FL
US PRACTICAL SHOOTING
ASSOCIATION
Phone: 360-855-2245
Fax: 360-855-0380
office@uspsa.org
www.uspsa.org

Mar 29 - Mar 30, 2025
AAU VOLLEYBALL CLASSIC
Orlando, FL
AMATEUR ATHLETIC UNION
Phone: 407-934-7200
Fax: 407-934-7242
www.aausports.org

Mar 29 - Mar 30, 2025
APTA HUSBAND/WIFE & MIXED
NATIONALS
Franklin Lakes, NJ
AMERICAN PLATFORM TENNIS
ASSOCIATION
Phone: 888-744-9490

apta@platformtennis.org
www.platformtennis.org

Mar 29 - Mar 30, 2025
CLASSIC PHYSIQUE OF AMERICA
Lima, Peru
INTERNATIONAL FEDERATION OF
BODY BUILDING & FITNESS
contact@ifbb.com
www.ifbb.com

Mar 29 - Mar 30, 2025
RD 3 ECHECONNEE MX
Lizella, GA
Echeconnee MX
AMA PRO RACING
Phone: 386-492-1014
Fax: 386-274-2335
communications@amaproracing.com
www.amaproracing.com

Mar 29, 2025
WOMEN'S PTI 50+
Essex, CT
AMERICAN PLATFORM TENNIS
ASSOCIATION
Phone: 888-744-9490
apta@platformtennis.org
www.platformtennis.org

Mar 29 - Apr 6, 2025
WORLD MEN'S CURLING
CHAMPIONSHIP
Moose Jaw, Canada
Moose Jaw Events Centre
CURLING CANADA
Phone: 613-834-2076
Fax: 613-834-0716
championships@curling.ca
www.curling.ca

Mar 29, 2025
YAKIMA RIVER CANYON MARATHON
Selah, WA
Yakima River Canyon Marathon Selah
Civic Center
HARD CORE RUNNER'S CLUB
Phone: 425-226-1518

Mar 31 - Apr 6, 2025
CLUB CAR CHAMPIONSHIP
Savannah, GA
The Landings Club
PGA KORN FERRY TOUR
Phone: 904-285-3700
Fax: 904-285-7913
www.pgatour.com

Mar 31 - Apr 6, 2025
COPA OSTER
Cali, Colombia
WTA
Phone: 727-895-5000
Fax: 727-894-1982
feedback@wtatennis.com
www.wtatennis.com

Mar 31 - Apr 6, 2025
CREDIT ONE CHARLESTON OPEN
Charleston, SC
WTA
Phone: 727-895-5000
Fax: 727-894-1982
feedback@wtatennis.com
www.wtatennis.com

Mar 31 - Apr 6, 2025
VALERO TEXAS OPEN
San Antonio, TX
TPC San Antonio

PGA TOUR
Phone: 904-285-3700
www.pgatour.com

Apr TBA, 2025
BILLIE JEAN KING CUP
TBA
TENNIS CANADA
Phone: 416-665-9777
Fax: 416-665-9017
info@tenniscanada.com
www.tenniscanada.com

Apr TBA, 2025
NORTH POLE MARATHON
Arctic Ocean, NT
Geographic North Pole
POLAR RUNNING ADVENTURES
International Ph: 011 353 91 443 408
International Fax: 011 353 91 443 408
rd@npmarathon.com
www.npmarathon.com

Apr TBA, 2025
ROCKIN K TRAIL MARATHON
Ellsworth, KS
Kanapolis State Park
KANSAS ULTRARUNNERS' SOCIETY
www.ksultrarunners.org

Apr TBA, 2025
TEB BNP PARIBAS TENNIS
CHAMPIONSHIP ISTANBUL
Istanbul, Turkey
WTA
Phone: 727-895-5000
Fax: 727-894-1982
feedback@wtatennis.com
www.wtatennis.com

Apr 1 - Apr 6, 2025
MEGASARAY HOTELS OPEN
Antalya, Turkey
WTA
Phone: 727-895-5000
Fax: 727-894-1982
feedback@wtatennis.com
www.wtatennis.com

Apr 2, 2025
BIG-D TEXAS MARATHON
Dallas, TX
Cotton Bowl, Fair Park
BIG-D TEXAS MARATHON

Apr 2 - Apr 12, 2025
SURF CITY EL SALVADOR PRO
Punta Roca, La Libertad, El Salvador
WORLD SURF LEAGUE
International Ph: +1-310-450-1212
www.worldsurfleague.com

Apr 2 - Apr 5, 2025
US ADULT FIGURE SKATING
CHAMPIONSHIPS
St. Louis Park, MN
U.S. FIGURE SKATING
Phone: 719-635-5200
Fax: 719-635-9548
info@usfigureskating.org
www.usfigureskating.org

Apr 3 - Apr 6, 2025
ADULT MEN'S NATIONAL
CHAMPIONSHIPS
Wesley Chapel, FL
Adventhealth Center Ice
USA HOCKEY
Phone: 719-576-8724
Fax: 719-538-1160

usah@usahockey.org
www.usahockey.com

Apr 4 - Apr 6, 2025
NCAA DIVISION I WOMEN'S
BASKETBALL FINALS
Tampa, FL
Amalie Arena
NATIONAL COLLEGIATE ATHLETIC
ASSOCIATION
Phone: 317-917-6222
Fax: 317-917-6888
www.ncaa.org

Apr 4 - Apr 6, 2025
OPEN WATER NATIONALS &
JUNIORS
Sarasota, FL
USA SWIMMING
Phone: 719-866-3501
info@usaswimming.org
www.usaswimming.org

Apr 4 - Apr 6, 2025
USHA MASTERS SINGLES
INVITATIONAL
TBA
UNITED STATES HANDBALL
ASSOCIATION
Phone: 520-795-0434
Fax: 520-795-0465
handball@ushandball.org
www.ushandball.org

Apr 5, 2025
ANDREW JACKSON MARATHON
Jackson, TN
ANDREW JACKSON MARATHON
steve@gdwm.org
www.facebook.com/RunAJMJackson

Apr 5 - Apr 6, 2025
APTA MEN'S TEAM NATIONALS
Summit, NJ
AMERICAN PLATFORM TENNIS
ASSOCIATION
Phone: 888-744-9490
apta@platformtennis.org
www.platformtennis.org

Apr 5 - Apr 6, 2025
APTA WOMEN'S TEAM NATIONALS
Summit, NJ
AMERICAN PLATFORM TENNIS
ASSOCIATION
Phone: 888-744-9490
apta@platformtennis.org
www.platformtennis.org

Apr 5, 2025
CHARLOTTESVILLE MARATHON
Charlottesville, VA
BAD TO THE BONE
Phone: 434-218-0402
francesca@badtothebone.biz
badtothebone.biz

Apr 5, 2025
COLLEGE 7S NATIONAL
CHAMPIONSHIPS
TBA
USA RUGBY
Phone: 303-539-0300
Fax: 303-539-0311
membership@usa.rugby
www.usa.rugby

Apr 5, 2025
GOLDEN GATE HEADLANDS
MARATHON, HALF MARATHON & 10K
Sausalito, CA

Fort Barry, Golden Gate National
Recreation Area
ENVIRO-SPORTS
Phone: 415-868-1829
info@envirosports.com
envirosports.com

Apr 5 - Apr 7, 2025
NCAA DIVISION I MEN'S
BASKETBALL FINALS
San Antionio, TX
Alamodome
NATIONAL COLLEGIATE ATHLETIC
ASSOCIATION
Phone: 317-917-6222
Fax: 317-917-6888
www.ncaa.org

Apr 6 - Apr 13, 2025
ATP TOUR MASTERS 1000 -
MONTE-CARLO ROLEX MASTERS
Monte Carlo, Monaco
ATP TOUR MASTERS 1000
www.atptour.com

Apr 6, 2025
DELAWARE MARATHON RUNNING
FESTIVAL
Wilmington, DE
Tubman Garrett Riverfront Park
CORRIGAN SPORTS ENTERPRISES
Phone: 410-605-9381
Fax: 410-605-9389
customerservice@corrigansports.com
www.corrigansports.com

Apr 6, 2025
GOODYEAR 400
Darlington, SC
Darlington Raceway
NASCAR CUP SERIES
www.nascar.com

Apr 6, 2025
OHIO RIVER ROAD RUNNERS
MARATHON & HALF MARATHON
Xenia, OH
OHIO RIVER ROAD RUNNERS CLUB
www.orrrc.org

Apr 8 - Apr 12, 2025
STAR NORTH AMERICAN
CHAMPIONSHIP
Pass Christian, MS
Pass Christian Yacht Club
INTERNATIONAL STAR CLASS YACHT
ASSOCIATION
Phone: 619-222-0252
Fax: 619-222-0528
office@starclass.org
www.starclass.org

Apr 10 - Apr 12, 2025
2025 SPEEDO CANADIAN SWIMMING
OPEN
Edmonton, AB, Canada
Edmonton Kinsmen Sports Centre
SWIMMING CANADA
Phone: 613-260-1348
Fax: 613-260-0804
natloffice@swimming.ca
www.swimming.ca

Apr 10 - Apr 13, 2025
ADULT WOMEN'S NATIONAL
CHAMPIONSHIPS
Wesley Chapel, FL
Adventhealth Center Ice
USA HOCKEY
Phone: 719-576-8724
Fax: 719-538-1160

usah@usahockey.org
www.usahockey.com

Apr 10 - Apr 13, 2025
BASSMASTER ELITE SERIES -
PASQUOTANK RIVER
Elizabeth City, NC
Pasquotank River
BASS ANGLERS SPORTSMAN
SOCIETY
Phone: 877-227-7872
bassmaster@emailcustomerservice.com
www.bassmaster.com

Apr 10 - Apr 13, 2025
MASTERS TOURNAMENT
Augusta, GA
Augusta National
Augusta National Golf Club
PGA TOUR
Phone: 904-285-3700
www.pgatour.com

Apr 10 - Apr 12, 2025
NCAA DIVISION I MEN'S ICE HOCKEY
FINALS
St. Louis, MO
Enterprise Center
NATIONAL COLLEGIATE ATHLETIC
ASSOCIATION
Phone: 317-917-6222
Fax: 317-917-6888
www.ncaa.org

Apr 10 - Apr 12, 2025
SPEED NATION SBX NATIONALS
Mont Sainte Anne, QC, Canada
CANADA SNOWBOARD
Phone: 778-653-0000
Fax: 604-568-1639
info@canadasnowboard.ca
www.canadasnowboard.ca

Apr 10 - Apr 16, 2025
TEAM DART CHAMPIONSHIPS
Las Vegas, NV
Westgate Las Vegas Resort & Casino
NATIONAL DART ASSOCIATION
Phone: 800-808-9884
Fax: 708-226-1310
info@ndadarts.com
www.ndadarts.com

Apr 11 - Apr 13, 2025
ACURA GRAND PRIX OF LONG
BEACH
Long Beach, CA
Streets of Long Beach
NTT INDYCAR SERIES
Phone: 317-492-6526
indycar@indycar.com
www.indycar.com

Apr 11 - Apr 13, 2025
CANADIAN JUNIOR CLOSED
CHAMPIONSHIPS
Calgary, AB, Canada
University of Calgary Racquet Centre
SQUASH CANADA
Phone: 613-228-7724
Fax: 613-228-7232
info@squash.ca
www.squash.ca

Apr 11 - Apr 14, 2025
DIVISION I & PARAFENCING
NATIONAL CHAMPIONSHIPS
Los Angeles, CA
USA FENCING
Phone: 719-866-4511
Fax: 719-632-5737

information@usafencing.org
www.usafencing.org

Apr 11 - Apr 13, 2025
NATIONAL COLLEGIATE
TAEKWONDO CHAMPIONSHIPS
Marlborough, MA
NATIONAL COLLEGIATE TAEKWONDO
ASSOCIATION
ncta-usa.com

Apr 11 - Apr 13, 2025
NHRA 4-WIDE NATIONALS
Las Vegas, NV
The Strip at Las Vegas Motor Speedway
NATIONAL HOT ROD ASSOCIATION
Phone: 626-914-4761
Fax: 626-325-8752
nhra@nhra.com
www.nhra.com

Apr 11 - Apr 13, 2025
US MASTERS SQUASH
CHAMPIONSHIPS
Philadelphia, PA
Arlen Specter US Squash Center
UNITED STATES SQUASH RACQUETS
ASSOCIATION
Phone: 212-268-4090
Fax: 212-268-4091
tournaments@ussquash.org
www.ussquash.com

Apr 11 - Apr 13, 2025
US PARENT-CHILD SQUASH
DOUBLES CHAMPIONSHIPS
Philadelphia, PA
Arlen Specter US Squash Center
UNITED STATES SQUASH RACQUETS
ASSOCIATION
Phone: 212-268-4090
Fax: 212-268-4091
tournaments@ussquash.org
www.ussquash.com

Apr 11 - Apr 13, 2025
USA BMX GREAT NORTHWEST
NATIONALS
Redmond, OR
USA BMX
Phone: 480-961-1903
Fax: 480-961-1842
info@usabmx.com
www.usabmx.com

Apr 11 - Apr 13, 2025
USA MASTERS SPRING NATIONAL
CHAMPIONSHIPS
Houston, TX
USA DIVING
Phone: 317-237-5252
Fax: 317-237-5257
Dan.Laak@usadiving.org
www.usadiving.org

Apr 12 - Apr 13, 2025
DAVE FREEMAN JR. SOCIAL OLC
San Diego, CA
San Diego Badminton Club
USA BADMINTON
Phone: 714-602-1691
ContactUs@usabadminton.org
www.usabadminton.org

Apr 12 - Apr 13, 2025
DIAMOND CUP MALTA
Malta
INTERNATIONAL FEDERATION OF
BODY BUILDING & FITNESS
contact@ifbb.com
www.ifbb.com

Apr 12, 2025
HALF MARATHON UNPLUGGED
Burlington, VT
RUN VERMONT
Phone: 802-863-8412
info@runvermont.org
www.runvermont.org

Apr 12 - Apr 13, 2025
MERCOSUR CUP
Porto Alagre, Brazil
INTERNATIONAL FEDERATION OF
BODY BUILDING & FITNESS
contact@ifbb.com
www.ifbb.com

Apr 12, 2025
NIKE HOOP SUMMIT
Portland, OR
Moda Center
USA BASKETBALL
Phone: 719-590-4800
Fax: 719-590-4811
fanmail@usabasketball.com
www.usab.com

Apr 12, 2025
ROMANCING THE ISLAND HALF
MARATHON & 10K
Tiburon, CA
Angel Island State Park
ENVIRO-SPORTS
Phone: 415-868-1829
info@envirosports.com
envirosports.com

Apr 13, 2025
FOOD CITY 500
Bristol, TN
Bristol Motor Speedway
NASCAR CAMPING WORLD TRUCK
SERIES
Phone: 800-630-0535
www.nascar.com

Apr 13, 2025
FUTSAL CANADIAN CHAMPIONSHIP
Regina, SK, Canada
CANADIAN SOCCER ASSOCIATION
Phone: 613-237-7678
Fax: 613-237-1516
info@soccercan.ca
www.canadasoccer.com

Apr 13 - Apr 19, 2025
USA BOXING INTERNATIONAL OPEN
Pueblo, CO
USA BOXING
Phone: 719-866-2323
www.usaboxing.org

Apr 14 - Apr 18, 2025
NGA SPRING MEET
TBA
NATIONAL GREYHOUND
ASSOCIATION
Phone: 785-263-4660
Fax: 785-263-4689
nga@ngagreyhounds.com
www.ngagreyhounds.com

Apr 14 - Apr 20, 2025
OEIRAS LADIES OPEN
Oeiras, Portugal
WTA
Phone: 727-895-5000
Fax: 727-894-1982
feedback@wtatennis.com
www.wtatennis.com

Apr 14 - Apr 21, 2025
PORSCHE TENNIS GRAND PRIX
Stuttgart, Germany
Porsche-Arena
WTA
Phone: 727-895-5000
Fax: 727-894-1982
feedback@wtatennis.com
www.wtatennis.com

Apr 14 - Apr 18, 2025
UNDER 21 GC WORLD
CHAMPIONSHIP
Sarasota, FL
Sarasota Country Croquet Club
US CROQUET ASSOCIATION
usca@msn.com
www.croquetamerica.com

Apr 15 - Apr 20, 2025
RBC HERITAGE
Hilton Head, SC
Harbour Town Golf Links
PGA TOUR
Phone: 904-285-3700
www.pgatour.com

Apr 16 - Apr 19, 2025
LECOM SUNCOAST CLASSIC
Lakewood Ranch, FL
Lakewood National Golf Club
PGA KORN FERRY TOUR
Phone: 904-285-3700
Fax: 904-285-7913
www.pgatour.com

Apr 17 - Apr 19, 2025
NCAA NATIONAL COLLEGIATE
WOMEN'S GYMNASTICS FINA LS
Fort Worth, TX
Dickies Arena
NATIONAL COLLEGIATE ATHLETIC
ASSOCIATION
Phone: 317-917-6222
Fax: 317-917-6888
www.ncaa.org

Apr 17 - Apr 20, 2025
VOLVO CHINA OPEN
Shanghai, China
Shanghai Enhance Anting Golf Course
PGA EUROPEAN TOUR
International Ph: 44-0-1344-840400
International Fax: 44-0-1344-840500
www.rydercup.com

Apr 18, 2025
CLAY SHOOT FOR CONSERVATION
Mansfield, GA
Burge Plantation
GEORGIA WILDLIFE FEDERATION
Phone: 770-787-7887
Fax: 770-787-9229
info@gwf.org
www.gwf.org

Apr 18 - Apr 19, 2025
NCAA NATIONAL COLLEGIATE
MEN'S GYMNASTICS FINALS
Ann Arbor, MI
Crisler Center
NATIONAL COLLEGIATE ATHLETIC
ASSOCIATION
Phone: 317-917-6222
Fax: 317-917-6888
www.ncaa.org

Apr 18 - Apr 28, 2025
RIP CURL PRO BELLS BEACH
Bells Beach, Victoria, Australia

WORLD SURF LEAGUE
International Ph: +1-310-450-1212
www.worldsurfleague.com

Apr 18 - Apr 21, 2025
SIBERIAN POWER SHOW
Krasnoyarsk, Russia
INTERNATIONAL FEDERATION OF
BODY BUILDING & FITNESS
contact@ifbb.com
www.ifbb.com

Apr 18 - Apr 20, 2025
U19 WORLD CHAMPIONSHIP
Czech Republic
INTERNATIONAL KORFBALL
FEDERATION
International Ph: 011-31-343-499655
International Fax: 011-31-343-499650
office@ikf.org
www.ikf.org

Apr 19, 2025
PINE LINE MARATHON
Medford, WI
Medford City Park
PINE LINE TRAIL MARATHON
Phone: 715-748-4729
pinelinemarathon.weebly.com

Apr 21, 2025
BOSTON MARATHON
Boston, MA
BOSTON ATHLETIC ASSOCIATION
Phone: 617-236-1652
Fax: 617-236-4505
info@baa.org
www.baa.org

Apr 21 - Apr 27, 2025
MITSUBISHI ELECTRIC CLASSIC
Duluth, GA
TPC Sugarloaf
PGA CHAMPIONS TOUR
Phone: 904-285-3700
www.pgatour.com/pgatour-champions

Apr 21 - Apr 27, 2025
ZURICH CLASSIC OF NEW ORLEANS
Avondale, LA
TPC Louisiana
PGA TOUR
Phone: 904-285-3700
www.pgatour.com

Apr 22 - May 4, 2025
MUTUA MADRID OPEN
Madrid, Spain
WTA
Phone: 727-895-5000
Fax: 727-894-1982
feedback@wtatennis.com
www.wtatennis.com

Apr 23 - May 4, 2025
ATP TOUR MASTERS 1000 - MUTUA
MADRID OPEN
Madrid, Spain
ATP TOUR MASTERS 1000
www.atptour.com

Apr 23 - Apr 26, 2025
DRAKE RELAYS
Des Moines, IA
Drake Stadium, Drake University
DRAKE RELAYS
Phone: 515-271-2889
Fax: 515-271-4189
www.godrakebulldogs.com

Apr 23 - Apr 26, 2025
INTER PROVINCIAL CHAMPIONSHIP
Saskatoon, SK, Canada
CANADIAN 5 PIN BOWLERS
ASSOCIATION
Phone: 613-744-5090
Fax: 613-744-2217
sheila.c5pba@gmail.com
www.c5pba.ca

Apr 24 - Apr 27, 2025
BASSMASTER ELITE SERIES - LAKE
HARTWELL
Anderson, SC
Lake Hartwell
BASS ANGLERS SPORTSMAN
SOCIETY
Phone: 877-227-7872
bassmaster@emailcustomerservice.com
www.bassmaster.com

Apr 24 - Apr 27, 2025
CHEVRON CHAMPIONSHIP
The Woodlands, TX
The Club At Carlton Woods
LPGA TOUR
Phone: 386-274-6200
Fax: 386-274-1099
www.lpga.com

Apr 24 - Apr 27, 2025
EASTON HOYT PRO/AM
Minden, LA
ARCHERY SHOOTERS ASSOCIATION
Phone: 770-795-0232
Fax: 770-795-0953
info@asaarchery.com
www.asaarchery.com

Apr 24 - Apr 27, 2025
LAND ROVER KENTUCKY
THREE-DAY EVENT
Lexington, KY
Kentucky Horse Park
US EQUESTRIAN FEDERATION
Phone: 859-258-2472
Fax: 859-231-6662
www.usef.org

Apr 24 - Apr 26, 2025
PENN RELAYS
University of Pennsylvania
Franklin Field
UNIVERSITY OF PENNSYLVANIA
Phone: 215-898-6145
pennrela@pobox.upenn.edu
www.thepennrelays.com

Apr 24 - Apr 25, 2025
WALLEYE TOUR-LAKE SHARPE
Pierre, SD
Lake Sharpe
NATIONAL WALLEYE TOUR
Phone: 612-424-0708
Fax: 866-727-2809
outdoorteamworks.com/trail/nwt

Apr 25 - Apr 27, 2025
BALKAN CHAMPIONSHIPS
Niksic, Montenegro
INTERNATIONAL FEDERATION OF
BODY BUILDING & FITNESS
contact@ifbb.com
www.ifbb.com

Apr 25 - Apr 27, 2025
CYCLE NORTH CAROLINA COASTAL
RIDE
Elizabeth City, NC

NORTH CAROLINA AMATEUR SPORTS
Phone: 919-361-1133
Fax: 919-361-2559
ncas@ncsports.org
www.ncsports.org

Apr 25, 2025
EISENHOWER MARATHON
Abilene, TX
Chisholm Trail
EISENHOWER MARATHON
Phone: 785-263-3474
scathey79@yahoo.com
eisenhowermarathon.net

Apr 25 - Apr 27, 2025
NCAA DIVISION III MEN'S
VOLLEYBALL FINALS
Salem, VA
Cregger Center
NATIONAL COLLEGIATE ATHLETIC
ASSOCIATION
Phone: 317-917-6222
Fax: 317-917-6888
www.ncaa.org

Apr 25 - Apr 27, 2025
OKLAHOMA CITY MEMORIAL
MARATHON
Oklahoma City, OK
OKLAHOMA CITY MARATHON
Phone: 405-525-4242
Fax: 405-521-9907
help@okcmarathon.com
www.okcmarathon.com

Apr 25 - Apr 27, 2025
USA BMX GOLDEN STATE
NATIONALS
Bakersfield, CA
Metro BMX
USA BMX
Phone: 480-961-1903
Fax: 480-961-1842
info@usabmx.com
www.usabmx.com

Apr 26, 2025
GO ST. LOUIS MARATHON
St. Louis, MO
SPIRIT OF ST. LOUIS MARATHON
Phone: 314-727-0800
Fax: 314-727-0893
info@gostlouis.org
www.gostlouis.org

Apr 26, 2025
KENTUCKY DERBY FESTIVAL
MARATHON
Louisville, KY
KENTUCKY DERBY FESTIVAL
Phone: 800-928-3378
Fax: 502-589-4674
minimarathon@kdf.org
www.derbyfestivalmarathon.com

Apr 26, 2025
MT. TAM WILD BOAR HALF
MARATHON & 10K
Mill Valley, CA
Mt. Tamalpais State Park
ENVIRO-SPORTS
Phone: 415-868-1829
info@envirosports.com
envirosports.com

Apr 26, 2025
OLATHE KS MARATHON
Olathe, KS
OLATHE CHAMBER OF COMMERCE
Phone: 913-764-1050

Fax: 913-782-4636
marathon@olathe.org
www.olathemarathon.com

Apr 26 - Apr 27, 2025
RD 4 LAKE SUGAR TREE
Axton, VA
Lake Sugar Tree Motorsports Park
AMA PRO RACING
Phone: 386-492-1014
Fax: 386-274-2335
communications@amaproracing.com
www.amaproracing.com

Apr 26, 2025
VENTURA ST
Ventura, CA
Ventura Raceway
AMA PRO RACING
Phone: 386-492-1014
Fax: 386-274-2335
communications@amaproracing.com
www.amaproracing.com

Apr 27, 2025
BIG SUR INTERNATIONAL
MARATHON
Carmel, CA
BIG SUR MARATHON FOUNDATION
Phone: 831-625-6226
Fax: 831-625-2119
info@bsim.org
www.bigsurmarathon.org

Apr 27, 2025
JACK LINK'S 500
Talladega, AL
Talladega Superspeedway
NASCAR CUP SERIES
www.nascar.com

Apr 27, 2025
MAUI MARATHON
Maui, HI
MAUI MARATHON
Phone: 808-222-2484
mauimarathonexpor@gmail.com
www.mauimarathon.com

Apr 27, 2025
MERCY HEALTH GLASS CITY
MARATHON
Toledo, OH
TOLEDO ROAD RUNNERS CLUB
Phone: 419-340-1815
info@glasscitymarathon.org
glasscitymarathon.org

Apr 27, 2025
WHIDBEY ISLAND MARATHON AND
HALF MARATHON
Oak Harbor, WA
WHIDBEY ISLAND MARATHON & HALF
MARATHON
runwhidbey.org

Apr 28 - May 3, 2025
CANADIAN WHEELCHAIR CURLING
CHAMPIONSHIP
Boucherville, QC, Canada
CURLING CANADA
Phone: 613-834-2076
Fax: 613-834-0716
championships@curling.ca
www.curling.ca

Apr 28 - May 3, 2025
CATALONIA OPEN 125
Vic, Spain
WTA
Phone: 727-895-5000

Fax: 727-894-1982
feedback@wtatennis.com
www.wtatennis.com

Apr 28 - May 4, 2025
CJ CUP BYRON NELSON
CHAMPIONSHIP
McKinney, TX
TPC Craig Ranch
PGA TOUR
Phone: 904-285-3700
www.pgatour.com

Apr 28 - May 4, 2025
INSPERITY INVITATIONAL
The Woodlands, TX
The Woodlands Country Club
PGA CHAMPIONS TOUR
Phone: 904-285-3700
www.pgatour.com/pgatour-champions

Apr 28 - May 4, 2025
L'OPEN 35 DE SAINT MALO
Saint Malo, France
WTA
Phone: 727-895-5000
Fax: 727-894-1982
feedback@wtatennis.com
www.wtatennis.com

Apr 30 - May 5, 2025
EUROPEAN CHAMPIONSHIPS
Santa Susana, Spain
INTERNATIONAL FEDERATION OF
BODY BUILDING & FITNESS
contact@ifbb.com
www.ifbb.com

Apr 30 - May 3, 2025
TYR PRO CHAMPIONSHIPS
Fort Lauderdale, FL
USA SWIMMING
Phone: 719-866-3501
info@usaswimming.org
www.usaswimming.org

May TBA, 2025
ARNOLD CLASSIC AFRICA
Johannesburg, South Africa
INTERNATIONAL FEDERATION OF
BODY BUILDING & FITNESS
contact@ifbb.com
www.ifbb.com

May 1 - May 4, 2025
ATLANTIC CITY OPEN
Atlantic City, NJ
NATIONAL X BALL LEAGUE
info@nxlpaintball.com
nxlpaintball.com

May 2 - May 4, 2025
CHILDREN'S OF ALABAMA INDY
GRAND PRIX
Birmingham, AL
Barber Motorsports Park
NTT INDYCAR SERIES
Phone: 317-492-6526
indycar@indycar.com
www.indycar.com

May 2 - May 4, 2025
CINCINNATI FLYING PIG MARATHON
Cincinnati, OH
CINCINNATI FLYING PIG MARATHON
Phone: 513-721-7447
info@flyingpigmarathon.com
flyingpigmarathon.com

May 2 - May 4, 2025
COLLEGIATE ROAD NATIONAL
CHAMPIONSHIPS
Madison, WI
USA CYCLING
Phone: 719-434-4200
Fax: 719-434-4300
help@usacycling.org
www.usacycling.org

May 2 - May 4, 2025
DAVE FREEMAN OPEN
TBA
USA BADMINTON
Phone: 714-602-1691
ContactUs@usabadminton.org
www.usabadminton.org

May 2 - May 4, 2025
FINA DIVING WORLD CUP
Beijing, China
USA DIVING
Phone: 317-237-5252
Fax: 317-237-5257
Dan.Laak@usadiving.org
www.usadiving.org

May 2 - May 4, 2025
LONG ISLAND MARATHON FESTIVAL
East Meadow, NY
LONG ISLAND MARATHON

May 2 - May 4, 2025
NEXTGEN PACIFIC CHAMPIONSHIP
Abbotsford, BC, Canada
Ledgeview Golf Club
ROYAL CANADIAN GOLF
ASSOCIATION
Phone: 905-849-9700
Fax: 905-845-7040
info@golfcanada.ca
www.golfcanada.ca

May 2 - May 4, 2025
NFAA MARKED 3-D NATIONAL
CHAMPIONSHIP
Redding, CA
NATIONAL FIELD ARCHERY
ASSOCIATION
Phone: 605-260-9279
info@nfaausa.com
www.nfaausa.com

May 2, 2025
SHIPROCK MARATHON
Shiprock, NM
FOUR CORNERS FITNESS &
WELLNESS ASSOCIATION
Phone: 435-233-8068
info@shiprockmarathon.com
www.shiprockmarathon.com

May 2 - May 4, 2025
USA BMX DIXIELAND NATIONALS
Powder Springs, GA
USA BMX
Phone: 480-961-1903
Fax: 480-961-1842
info@usabmx.com
www.usabmx.com

May 5 - May 13, 2025
BONSOY GOLD COAST PRO
Gold Coast, Queensland, Australia
WORLD SURF LEAGUE
International Ph: +1-310-450-1212
www.worldsurfleague.com

May 3 - May 4, 2025
FREDERICK RUNNING FESTIVAL
Frederick, MD

Frederick Fair Grounds
CORRIGAN SPORTS ENTERPRISES
Phone: 410-605-9381
Fax: 410-605-9389
customerservice@corrigansports.com
www.corrigansports.com

May 3, 2025
KENTUCKY DERBY
Louisville, KY
Churchill Downs
CHURCHILL DOWNS
Phone: 502-636-4400
customerservice@kyderby.com
www.churchilldowns.com

May 3, 2025
SILVER DOLLAR ST
Chico, CA
Silver Dollar Speedway
AMA PRO RACING
Phone: 386-492-1014
Fax: 386-274-2335
communications@amaproracing.com
www.amaproracing.com

May 4, 2025
AVENUE OF THE GIANTS
MARATHON
Eureka, CA
THE AVE
Phone: 707-822-1861
ctimek@aol.com
www.theave.org

May 4, 2025
COLORADO MARATHON
Fort Collins, CO
COLORADO MARATHON
logan@thecoloradomarathon.com
comarathon.com

May 4, 2025
LINCOLN MARATHON
Lincoln, NE
LINCOLN TRACK CLUB
Phone: 402-435-3504
www.lincolnmarathon.org

May 4, 2025
WURTH 400 PRESENTED BY LIQUI
Fort Worth TX
Texas Motor Speedway
NASCAR CAMPING WORLD TRUCK
SERIES
Phone: 800-630-0535
www.nascar.com

May 5, 2025
WALTER CHILDS MARATHON
Holyoke, MA
Ashley Reservoir @ Elks Lodge
GREATER SPRINGFIELD HARRIERS
Phone: 413-734-0955
marathon@harriers.org
www.harriers.org

May 6 - May 18, 2025
INTERNAZIONALI BNL D'ITALIA
Rome, Italy
WTA
Phone: 727-895-5000
Fax: 727-894-1982
feedback@wtatennis.com
www.wtatennis.com

May 16 - May 18, 2025
USA WATER POLO MEN'S SENIOR
NATIONALS
La Jolla, CA
UCSD Canyonview Recreation Center

USA WATER POLO
Phone: 714-500-5445
Fax: 714-960-2431
www.usawaterpolo.org

May 7 - May 10, 2025
CANADIAN NATIONAL HANDBALL
CHAMPIONSHIPS
Sherwood Park, AB, Canada
Glen Allan Rec Centre
CANADIAN HANDBALL
www.canadianhandball.com

May 7 - May 10, 2025
WCLA NATIONAL CHAMPIONSHIP
Wichita, KS
Stryker Sports Complex
US LACROSSE
Phone: 410-235-6882
Fax: 410-366-6735
membership@usalacrosse.com
www.uslacrosse.org

May 8 - May 11, 2025
BASSMASTER ELITE SERIES - LAKE
FORK
Yantis, TX
Lake Fork
BASS ANGLERS SPORTSMAN
SOCIETY
Phone: 877-227-7872
bassmaster@emailcustomerservice.com
www.bassmaster.com

May 8 - May 10, 2025
NEXTGEN ONTARIO CHAMPIONSHIP
Belleville, ON, Canada
Black Bear Ridge Golf Course
ROYAL CANADIAN GOLF
ASSOCIATION
Phone: 905-849-9700
Fax: 905-845-7040
info@golfcanada.ca
www.golfcanada.ca

May 8 - May 11, 2025
WELLS FARGO CHAMPIONSHIP
Philadelphia, PA
Philadelphia Cricket Club
PGA TOUR
Phone: 904-285-3700
www.pgatour.com

May 9 - May 11, 2025
ELITE BMX NATIONAL
CHAMPIONSHIPS
Tulsa, OK
USA CYCLING
Phone: 719-434-4200
Fax: 719-434-4300
help@usacycling.org
www.usacycling.org

May 9 - May 10, 2025
HERKULES GRAND PRIX
Skopje, North Macedonia
INTERNATIONAL FEDERATION OF
BODY BUILDING & FITNESS
contact@ifbb.com
www.ifbb.com

May 9 - May 11, 2025
NCAA NATIONAL COLLEGIATE
WOMEN'S WATER POLO FINA LS
Indianapolis, IN
NATIONAL COLLEGIATE ATHLETIC
ASSOCIATION
Phone: 317-917-6222
Fax: 317-917-6888
www.ncaa.org

May 9 - May 10, 2025
SONSIO GRAND PRIX
Indianapolis, IN
NTT INDYCAR SERIES
Phone: 317-492-6526
indycar@indycar.com
www.indycar.com

May 10, 2025
AMA PRO HILLCLIMB MINNESOTA
NATIONAL
Red Wing, MN
Indianhead Motorcycle Club
AMA PRO RACING
Phone: 386-492-1014
Fax: 386-274-2335
communications@amaproracing.com
www.amaproracing.com

May 10, 2025
BEACH & BELT WRESTLING
NATIONAL CHAMPIONSHIPS
Carolina Beach, NC
Carolina Beach Boardwalk
USA WRESTLING
Phone: 719-598-8181
Fax: 719-598-9440
www.themat.com

May 10 - May 11, 2025
HARMONY GENEVA MARATHON FOR
UNICEF
Geneva, Switzerland
OC SPORT
www.ocsport.com

May 10, 2025
MUIR WOODS MARATHON, HALF
MARATHON & 7 MILE
Stinson Beach, CA
Stinson Beach Park
ENVIRO-SPORTS
Phone: 415-868-1829
info@envirosports.com
envirosports.com

May 10 - May 11, 2025
RD 5 IRONMAN
Crawfordsville, IN
Ironman Raceway
AMA PRO RACING
Phone: 386-492-1014
Fax: 386-274-2335
communications@amaproracing.com
www.amaproracing.com

May 10 - May 14, 2025
US WOMEN'S AMATEUR FOUR-BALL
Nichols Hills, OK
Oklahoma City Golf & Country Club
U.S. GOLF ASSOCIATION
Phone: 908-234-2300
Fax: 908-234-9687
www.usga.org

May 10 - May 11, 2025
USA ULTIMATE BEACH
CHAMPIONSHIPS
Virginia Beach, VA
USA ULTIMATE
Phone: 800-872-4384
Fax: 719-219-8322
info@usaultimate.org
www.usaultimate.org

May 11, 2025
SUGARLOAF MARATHON & 15K
Carrabassett Valley, ME
SUGARLOAF MARATHON
Phone: 207-237-2000

Fax: 207-237-3768
info@sugarloaf.com
www.sugarloaf.com

May 11, 2025
TRIGIRL SUPER SPRINT TRIATHLON
& DUATHLON
Houston, TX
Alexander Deussen Park
TRIGIRL SPORTS
www.trigirlmultisport.com

May 12 - May 18, 2025
ADVENTHEALTH CHAMPIONSHIP
Kansas City, KS
Blue Hills Country Club
PGA KORN FERRY TOUR
Phone: 904-285-3700
Fax: 904-285-7913
www.pgatour.com

May 12 - May 18, 2025
PGA CHAMPIONSHIP
Charlotte, NC
Quail Hollow Club
PGA TOUR
Phone: 904-285-3700
www.pgatour.com

May 13 - May 25, 2025
INDIANAPOLIS 500
Indianapolis, IN
Indianapolis Motor Speedway
NTT INDYCAR SERIES
Phone: 317-492-6526
indycar@indycar.com
www.indycar.com

May 13 - May 17, 2025
NCAA DIVISION II WOMEN'S GOLF
FINALS
Boulder City, NV
Boulder Creek Golf Club
NATIONAL COLLEGIATE ATHLETIC
ASSOCIATION
Phone: 317-917-6222
Fax: 317-917-6888
www.ncaa.org

May 13 - May 16, 2025
NCAA DIVISION III WOMEN'S GOLF
FINALS
Williamsburg, VA
Kingsmill Resort & Spa
NATIONAL COLLEGIATE ATHLETIC
ASSOCIATION
Phone: 317-917-6222
Fax: 317-917-6888
www.ncaa.org

May 14 - May 19, 2025
REGIONS TRADITION
Birmingham, AL
Greystone Golf & Country Club
PGA CHAMPIONS TOUR
Phone: 904-285-3700
www.pgatour.com/pgatour-champions

May 14 - May 18, 2025
USA RACQUETBALL NATIONAL
INDOOR
Pleasanton, CA
USA RACQUETBALL
Phone: 719-635-5396
Fax: 719-635-0685
jonathan@usaracquetball.com
www.usaracquetball.com

May 15 - May 18, 2025
ROUTE 66 NHRA NATIONALS
Elwood, IL

Route 66 Raceway
NATIONAL HOT ROD ASSOCIATION
Phone: 626-914-4761
Fax: 626-325-8752
nhra@nhra.com
www.nhra.com

May 16 - May 18, 2025
2025 SPEEDO CANADIAN MASTERS
CHAMPIONSHIPS
Saskatoon, SK, Canada
Saskatoon Shaw Centre
SWIMMING CANADA
Phone: 613-260-1348
Fax: 613-260-0804
natloffice@swimming.ca
www.swimming.ca

May 16 - May 18, 2025
ICF CANOE SPRINT WORLD CUP 1
Szeged, Hungary
INTERNATIONAL CANOE FEDERATION
International Ph: 41 (0)21 612 0290
info@canoeicf.com
www.canoeicf.com

May 16 - May 19, 2025
MAY NATIONALS
St. Catherines, ON, Canada
CANADIAN FENCING FEDERATION
Phone: 647-476-2401
Fax: 647-476-2402
cff@fencing.ca
www.fencing.ca

May 16 - May 21, 2025
NCAA DIVISION I WOMEN'S GOLF
FINALS
Carlsbad, CA
Omni La Costa Resort & Spa
NATIONAL COLLEGIATE ATHLETIC
ASSOCIATION
Phone: 317-917-6222
Fax: 317-917-6888
www.ncaa.org

May 17 - May 18, 2025
AMA PRO HILLCLIMB WASHINGTON
NITRO NATIONALS I & II
Sunnyside, WA
Dry Creek ORV
AMA PRO RACING
Phone: 386-492-1014
Fax: 386-274-2335
communications@amaproracing.com
www.amaproracing.com

May 17 - May 18, 2025
CAPITAL CITY MARATHON
Olympia, WA
Sylvester Park
CAPITAL CITY MARATHON
racedirector@ccmaboard.org
www.capitalcitymarathon.org

May 17, 2025
DIAMOND CUP CZECHIA
Czech Republic
INTERNATIONAL FEDERATION OF
BODY BUILDING & FITNESS
contact@ifbb.com
www.ifbb.com

May 17 - May 18, 2025
MED CITY MARATHON
Rochester, MN
MED CITY MARATHON
Phone: 507-254-2703
Fax: 507-288-8058
medcityevents@outlook.com
www.medcitymarathon.com

May 5, 2025
OGDEN MARATHON
Odgen, UT
GOAL FOUNDATION
Phone: 801-399-1773
admin@goalfoundation.com
www.ogdenmarathon.com

May 17, 2025
PREAKNESS STAKES
Baltimore, MD
Pimlico Race Course
PIMLICO RACE COURSE
Phone: 410-542-9400
info@marylandracing.com
www.marylandracing.com

May 17, 2025
TRENT/WALDRON GLACIER HALF
MARATHON
Anchorage, AK
Westchester Lagoon
ANCHORAGE RUNNING CLUB
Phone: 907-258-4964
info@anchoragerunningclub.com
www.anchoragerunningclub.org

May 17 - May 21, 2025
US AMATEUR FOUR-BALL
Westfield, NJ
Echo Lake Country Club
U.S. GOLF ASSOCIATION
Phone: 908-234-2300
Fax: 908-234-9687
www.usga.org

May 17 - May 19, 2025
USA ULTIMATE D-III COLLEGE
CHAMPIONSHIPS
Burlington, WA
USA ULTIMATE
Phone: 800-872-4384
Fax: 719-219-8322
info@usaultimate.org
www.usaultimate.org

May 17 - May 27, 2025
WESTERN AUSTRALIA MARGARET
RIVER PRO
Margaret River, Western Australia
WORLD SURF LEAGUE
International Ph: +1-310-450-1212
www.worldsurfleague.com

May 18, 2025
CARDEROCK RUNNING FESTIVAL
Carderock, MD
MARATHON CHARITY COOPERATION
www.mc-coop.org

May 18, 2025
CHICAGO SPRING HALF MARATHON
& 10K
Chicago, IL
LIFE TIME FITNESS
www.eventsbylifetime.com

May 18 - May 24, 2025
INTERNATIONAUX DE STRASBOURG
Strasbourg, France
WTA
Phone: 727-895-5000
Fax: 727-894-1982
feedback@wtatennis.com
www.wtatennis.com

May 18, 2025
NASCAR ALL-STAR OPEN
North Wilkesboro, NC
North Wilkesboro Speedway

NASCAR CUP SERIES
www.nascar.com

May 18, 2025
NASCAR ALL-STAR RACE
North Wilkesboro, NC
North Wilkesboro Speedway
NASCAR CUP SERIES
www.nascar.com

May 19, 2025
CELLCOM GREEN BAY MARATHON
Green Bay, WI
CELLCOM GREEN BAY MARATHON
Phone: 920-432-6272
info@cellcomgreenbaymarathon.com
www.cellcomgreenbaymarathon.com

May 19 - May 25, 2025
CHARLES SCHWAB CHALLENGE
Fort Worth, TX
Colonial Country Club
PGA TOUR
Phone: 904-285-3700
www.pgatour.com

May 19 - May 24, 2025
GRAND PRIX SON ALTESSE ROYALE
LA PRINCESSE LALLA MERYEM
Rabat, Morocco
WTA
Phone: 727-895-5000
Fax: 727-894-1982
feedback@wtatennis.com
www.wtatennis.com

May 19 - May 23, 2025
NCAA DIVISION II MEN'S GOLF
FINALS
Palm Beach, FL
Pga National Resort
NATIONAL COLLEGIATE ATHLETIC
ASSOCIATION
Phone: 317-917-6222
Fax: 317-917-6888
www.ncaa.org

May 19 - May 26, 2025
NCAA DIVISION III MEN'S/WOMEN'S
TENNIS FINALS
Claremont, CA
Biszant Family Tennis Center
NATIONAL COLLEGIATE ATHLETIC
ASSOCIATION
Phone: 317-917-6222
Fax: 317-917-6888
www.ncaa.org

May 19 - May 26, 2025
PRO ROAD NATIONAL
CHAMPIONSHIPS
Charleston, WV
USA CYCLING
Phone: 719-434-4200
Fax: 719-434-4300
help@usacycling.org
www.usacycling.org

May 19 - Jun 8, 2025
ROLAND GARROS
Paris, France
WTA
Phone: 727-895-5000
Fax: 727-894-1982
feedback@wtatennis.com
www.wtatennis.com

May 19 - May 25, 2025
VISIT KNOXVILLE OPEN
Knoxville, TN

PGA KORN FERRY TOUR
Phone: 904-285-3700
Fax: 904-285-7913
www.pgatour.com

May 20 - May 24, 2025
CANADIAN OPEN CHAMPIONSHIP
Regina, SK, Canada
CANADIAN 5 PIN BOWLERS
ASSOCIATION
Phone: 613-744-5090
Fax: 613-744-2217
sheila.c5pba@gmail.com
www.c5pba.ca

May 20 - May 24, 2025
NCAA DIVISION II MEN'S/WOMEN'S
TENNIS FINALS
Altamonte Springs, FL
Sanlando Park
NATIONAL COLLEGIATE ATHLETIC
ASSOCIATION
Phone: 317-917-6222
Fax: 317-917-6888
www.ncaa.org

May 20 - May 23, 2025
NCAA DIVISION III MEN'S GOLF
FINALS
Penfield, NY
Midvale Country Club
NATIONAL COLLEGIATE ATHLETIC
ASSOCIATION
Phone: 317-917-6222
Fax: 317-917-6888
www.ncaa.org

May 22 - May 25, 2025
ICF CANOE SPRINT WORLD CUP 2
Poznan, Poland
INTERNATIONAL CANOE FEDERATION
International Ph: 41 (0)21 612 0290
info@canoeicf.com
www.canoeicf.com

May 22 - May 25, 2025
ICF PARACANOE WORLD CUP
Poznan, Poland
INTERNATIONAL CANOE FEDERATION
International Ph: 41 (0)21 612 0290
info@canoeicf.com
www.canoeicf.com

May 22 - May 25, 2025
KITCHENAID SENIOR PGA
CHAMPIONSHIP
Frisco, TX
Fields Ranch East
PGA CHAMPIONS TOUR
Phone: 904-285-3700
www.pgatour.com/pgatour-champions

May 22 - May 24, 2025
NCAA DIVISION II MEN'S/WOMEN'S
TRACK, OUTDOOR FINALS
Pueblo, CO
CSU Pueblo ThunderBowl
NATIONAL COLLEGIATE ATHLETIC
ASSOCIATION
Phone: 317-917-6222
Fax: 317-917-6888
www.ncaa.org

May 22 - May 28, 2025
NCAA DIVISION II SOFTBALL FINALS
Chattanooga, TN
Frost Stadium
NATIONAL COLLEGIATE ATHLETIC
ASSOCIATION
Phone: 317-917-6222

Fax: 317-917-6888
www.ncaa.org

May 22 - May 24, 2025
NCAA DIVISION II WOMEN'S
LACROSSE FESTIVAL
Salem, VA
Kerr Stadium
NATIONAL COLLEGIATE ATHLETIC
ASSOCIATION
Phone: 317-917-6222
Fax: 317-917-6888
www.ncaa.org

May 22 - May 25, 2025
NCAA DIVISION III MEN'S/WOMEN'S
TRACK, OUTDOOR F INALS
Geneva, OH
SPIRE Institute
NATIONAL COLLEGIATE ATHLETIC
ASSOCIATION
Phone: 317-917-6222
Fax: 317-917-6888
www.ncaa.org

May 22 - May 23, 2025
WALLEYE TOUR-MISSISSIPPI RIVER
La Crosse, WI
Mississippi River
NATIONAL WALLEYE TOUR
Phone: 612-424-0708
Fax: 866-727-2809
outdoorteamworks.com/trail/nwt

May 23 - May 25, 2025
BUFFALO MARATHON
Buffalo, NY
BUFFALO MARATHON
information@buffalomarathon.com
www.buffalomarathon.com

May 23 - May 25, 2025
MASTERS WATER SKI &
WAKEBOARD TOURNAMENT
Pine Mountain, GA
Callaway Gardens
NAUTIQUE EVENTS
Phone: 407-855-4141
Fax: 407-851-7844
masters@nautique.com
www.masterswaterski.com

May 23 - May 28, 2025
NCAA DIVISION I MEN'S GOLF
FINALS
Carlsbad, CA
Omni La Costa Resort & Spa
NATIONAL COLLEGIATE ATHLETIC
ASSOCIATION
Phone: 317-917-6222
Fax: 317-917-6888
www.ncaa.org

May 23 - May 25, 2025
NCAA DIVISION I WOMEN'S
LACROSSE FINALS
Foxborough, MA
Gillette Stadium
NATIONAL COLLEGIATE ATHLETIC
ASSOCIATION
Phone: 317-917-6222
Fax: 317-917-6888
www.ncaa.org

May 23 - May 25, 2025
NCAA DIVISION III WOMEN'S
LACROSSE FINALS
Salem, VA
Kerr Stadium
NATIONAL COLLEGIATE ATHLETIC
ASSOCIATION

Phone: 317-917-6222
Fax: 317-917-6888
www.ncaa.org

May 23 - May 28, 2025
OPEN NATIONAL CHAMPIONSHIPS
Denver, CO
USA VOLLEYBALL
Phone: 719-228-6800
Fax: 719-228-6899
postmaster@usav.org
usavolleyball.org

May 23 - May 25, 2025
SUMMER SENIOR NATIONAL
CHAMPIONSHIPS
Saskatoon, SK, Canada
DIVING CANADA
Phone: 613-736-5238
Fax: 613-736-0409
cada@diving.ca
www.diving.ca

May 23 - May 26, 2025
USA ULTIMATE D-I COLLEGE
CHAMPIONSHIPS
Burlington, WA
USA ULTIMATE
Phone: 800-872-4384
Fax: 719-219-8322
info@usaultimate.org
www.usaultimate.org

May 24, 2025
BAYSHORE MARATHON
Traverse City, MI
TRAVERSE CITY TRACK CLUB
Phone: 231-941-8118
www.bayshoremarathon.org

May 24 - May 25, 2025
DIAMOND CUP ARMENIA
Yerevan, Armenia
INTERNATIONAL FEDERATION OF
BODY BUILDING & FITNESS
contact@ifbb.com
www.ifbb.com

May 24, 2025
FOX RACEWAY NATIONAL
Pala, CA
Fox Raceway
AMA PRO RACING
Phone: 386-492-1014
Fax: 386-274-2335
communications@amaproracing.com
www.amaproracing.com

May 24 - May 26, 2025
NCAA DIVISION I MEN'S LACROSSE
FINALS
Foxborough, MA
Gillette Stadium
NATIONAL COLLEGIATE ATHLETIC
ASSOCIATION
Phone: 317-917-6222
Fax: 317-917-6888
www.ncaa.org

May 24 - May 25, 2025
RD 6 SUNSET RIDGE MX
Walnut, IL
Sunset Ridge MX
AMA PRO RACING
Phone: 386-492-1014
Fax: 386-274-2335
communications@amaproracing.com
www.amaproracing.com

May 24 - May 25, 2025
US LACROSSE NATIONAL
TOURNAMENT
Amherst, MA
US LACROSSE
Phone: 410-235-6882
Fax: 410-366-6735
membership@usalacrosse.com
www.uslacrosse.org

May 25, 2025
COCA-COLA 600
Concord, NC
Charlotte Motor Speedway
NASCAR CUP SERIES
www.nascar.com

May 25, 2025
COEUR D'ALENE MARATHON
Coeur d'Alene, ID
COEUR D'ALENE MARATHON
runsignup.com/Race/ID/CoeurDAlene/nsp
lit

May 25, 2025
NCAA DIVISION II MEN'S LACROSSE
FINALS
Foxborough, MA
Gillette Stadium
NATIONAL COLLEGIATE ATHLETIC
ASSOCIATION
Phone: 317-917-6222
Fax: 317-917-6888
www.ncaa.org

May 25, 2025
NCAA DIVISION III MEN'S LACROSSE
FINALS
Foxborough, MA
Gillette Stadium
NATIONAL COLLEGIATE ATHLETIC
ASSOCIATION
Phone: 317-917-6222
Fax: 317-917-6888
www.ncaa.org

May 25, 2025
VERMONT CITY MARATHON
Burlington, VT
RUN VERMONT
Phone: 802-863-8412
info@runvermont.org
www.runvermont.org

May 25, 2025
WYOMING MARATHON
Laramie, WY
CHEYENNE TRACK CLUB
Phone: 307-778-7866
Fax: 307-778-7876
mollybeebishop@gmail.com
wyomingmarathonraces.weebly.com

May 26, 2025
BOLDERBOULDER 10K
Boulder, CO
BOLDER BOULDER
Phone: 303-444-7223
www.bolderboulder.com

May 26 - Jun 1, 2025
THE MEMORIAL TOURNAMENT
Dublin, OH
Muirfield Village Golf Club
PGA TOUR
Phone: 904-285-3700
www.pgatour.com

Jun 28 - Jul 2, 2025
MASTERS ROAD NATIONAL
CHAMPIONSHIPS
South East, WI
USA CYCLING
Phone: 719-434-4200
Fax: 719-434-4300
help@usacycling.org
www.usacycling.org

May 28 - Jun 1, 2025
PRINCIPAL CHARITY CLASSIC
Des Moines, IA
Wakonda Club
PGA CHAMPIONS TOUR
Phone: 904-285-3700
www.pgatour.com/pgatour-champions

May 28, 2025
WORLD SPEED SHOOTING
CHAMPIONSHIP
Talladega, AL
US PRACTICAL SHOOTING
ASSOCIATION
Phone: 360-855-2245
Fax: 360-855-0380
office@uspsa.org
www.uspsa.org

May 29 - Jun 6, 2025
NCAA DIVISION I SOFTBALL FINALS
Oklahoma City, OK
Devon Park
NATIONAL COLLEGIATE ATHLETIC
ASSOCIATION
Phone: 317-917-6222
Fax: 317-917-6888
www.ncaa.org

May 29 - Jun 4, 2025
NCAA DIVISION III SOFTBALL FINALS
Bloomington, IL
Inspiration Field
NATIONAL COLLEGIATE ATHLETIC
ASSOCIATION
Phone: 317-917-6222
Fax: 317-917-6888
www.ncaa.org

May 29 - Jun 1, 2025
TRU BALL PRO/AM
London, KY
ARCHERY SHOOTERS ASSOCIATION
Phone: 770-795-0232
Fax: 770-795-0953
info@asaarchery.com
www.asaarchery.com

May 29 - Jun 1, 2025
UNC HEALTH CHAMPIONSHIP
Raleigh, NC
Raleigh Country Club
PGA KORN FERRY TOUR
Phone: 904-285-3700
Fax: 904-285-7913
www.pgatour.com

May 29 - Jun 1, 2025
US WOMEN'S OPEN
Erin, WI
Erin Hills
U.S. GOLF ASSOCIATION
Phone: 908-234-2300
Fax: 908-234-9687
www.usga.org

May 29 - Jun 1, 2025
US WOMEN'S OPEN
Erin Hills, WI
Erin Hills Golf Course

LPGA TOUR
Phone: 386-274-6200
Fax: 386-274-1099
www.lpga.com

May 29 - May 31, 2025
USS CONGRESS
Kearns, UT
US SPEEDSKATING
Phone: 801-417-5360
Fax: 801-417-5361
www.usspeedskating.org

May 30 - Jun 1, 2025
CHEVROLET DETROIT GRAND PRIX
Detroit, MI
Streets of Detroit
NTT INDYCAR SERIES
Phone: 317-492-6526
indycar@indycar.com
www.indycar.com

May 30 - Jun 1, 2025
NCAA DIVISION I ROWING FINALS
West Windsor, NJ
Lake Mercer
NATIONAL COLLEGIATE ATHLETIC
ASSOCIATION
Phone: 317-917-6222
Fax: 317-917-6888
www.ncaa.org

May 30 - Jun 7, 2025
NCAA DIVISION II BASEBALL FINALS
Cary, NC
Usa Baseball National Training Complex
NATIONAL COLLEGIATE ATHLETIC
ASSOCIATION
Phone: 317-917-6222
Fax: 317-917-6888
www.ncaa.org

May 30 - May 31, 2025
NCAA DIVISION II ROWING FINALS
West Windsor, NJ
Lake Mercer
NATIONAL COLLEGIATE ATHLETIC
ASSOCIATION
Phone: 317-917-6222
Fax: 317-917-6888
www.ncaa.org

May 30 - Jun 5, 2025
NCAA DIVISION III BASEBALL FINALS
Eastlake, OH
Classic Park
NATIONAL COLLEGIATE ATHLETIC
ASSOCIATION
Phone: 317-917-6222
Fax: 317-917-6888
www.ncaa.org

May 30 - May 31, 2025
NCAA DIVISION III ROWING FINALS
West Windsor, NJ
Lake Mercer
NATIONAL COLLEGIATE ATHLETIC
ASSOCIATION
Phone: 317-917-6222
Fax: 317-917-6888
www.ncaa.org

May 30 - Jun 1, 2025
NEXTGEN WESTERN
CHAMPIONSHIP
Entwistle, AB, Canada
Trestle Creek Club Resort
ROYAL CANADIAN GOLF
ASSOCIATION
Phone: 905-849-9700
Fax: 905-845-7040

info@golfcanada.ca
www.golfcanada.ca

May 30 - Jun 1, 2025
NHRA NEW ENGLAND NATIONALS
Epping, NH
New England Dragway
NATIONAL HOT ROD ASSOCIATION
Phone: 626-914-4761
Fax: 626-325-8752
nhra@nhra.com
www.nhra.com

May 30 - May 31, 2025
ROMANIAN GRAND PRIX
Bucharest, Romania
INTERNATIONAL FEDERATION OF
BODY BUILDING & FITNESS
contact@ifbb.com
www.ifbb.com

May 31 - Jun 1, 2025
DEADWOOD-MICKELSON TRAIL
MARATHON
Deadwood, SD
DEADWOOD-MICKELSON TRAIL
MARATHON
Phone: 605-390-6137
www.deadwoodmickelsontrailmarathon.com

May 31, 2025
HANGTOWN MOTOCROSS CLASSIC
Rancho Cordova, CA
Prairie City OHV Park
AMA PRO RACING
Phone: 386-492-1014
Fax: 386-274-2335
communications@amaproracing.com
www.amaproracing.com

May 31 - Jun 1, 2025
ROCK 'N' ROLL MARATHON
San Diego, CA
ROCK 'N' ROLL MARATHON SERIES
Phone: 858-450-6510
Fax: 858-450-6905
www.runrocknroll.com

May 31, 2025
SUNBURST MARATHON
South Bend, IN
BEACON HEALTH SYSTEM
Phone: 574-647-1000
sunburst.beaconhealthsystem.org

May 31, 2025
VIRGINIA WINE COUNTRY HALF
MARATHON
Hillsboro, VA
Doukenie Winery
BAD TO THE BONE
Phone: 434-218-0402
francesca@badtothebone.biz
badtothebone.biz

Jun TBA, 2025
LARRY H MILLER UTAH SUMMER
GAMES
Cedar City, UT
Southern Utah University
UTAH SUMMER GAMES
Phone: 435-865-8421
Fax: 435-865-8548
usg@suu.edu
utahsummergames.org

Jun TBA, 2025
SAN JUAN ISLAND MARATHON
Friday Harbor, WA

LAKEDALE RESORT
Phone: 800-617-2267
www.lakedale.com

Jun 1, 2025
AMA PRO HILLCLIMB WHITE ROSE
NATIONAL I
Spring Grove, PA
White Rose Motorcycle Club
AMA PRO RACING
Phone: 386-492-1014
Fax: 386-274-2335
communications@amaproracing.com
www.amaproracing.com

Jun 1, 2025
CASPER WYOMING MARATHON
Casper, WY
CASPER WYOMING MARATHON
Phone: 307-577-4974
www.runwyoming.com

Jun 1, 2025
KONA MARATHON & KONA HALF
MARATHON
Keauhou-Kona, HI
Waikoloa Beach Resort
KONA MARATHON
Phone: 808-967-8285
raceinfo@konamarathon.com
www.konamarathon.com

Jun 1, 2025
NASCAR CUP SERIES AT NASHVILLE
Nashville, TN
Nashville Superspeedway
NASCAR CUP SERIES
www.nascar.com

Jun 1 - Jun 7, 2025
NATIONAL HIGH POWER XTC
CHAMPIONSHIP
Lodi, WI
Winnequah Gun Club
NATIONAL RIFLE ASSOCIATION -
COMPETITIVE SHOOTING DIVISION
Phone: 703-267-1465
competitions.nra.org

Jun 1, 2025
NEWPORT MARATHON
Newport, OR
NEWPORT MARATHON
Phone: 541-265-3446
run@newportmarathon.org
www.newportmarathon.org

Jun 1, 2025
STEAMBOAT MARATHON
Steamboat Springs, CO
STEAMBOAT MARATHON
Phone: 970-879-0880
Fax: 970-879-3550
marathon@steamboatchamber.com
www.steamboatchamber.com

Jun 3 - Jun 6, 2025
CANADIAN UNIVERSITY & COLLEGE
CHAMPIONSHIP
Kamloops, BC, Canada
Rivershore Golf Links
ROYAL CANADIAN GOLF
ASSOCIATION
Phone: 905-849-9700
Fax: 905-845-7040
info@golfcanada.ca
www.golfcanada.ca

Jun 3 - Jun 7, 2025
NATIONAL CHAMPIONSHIPS
Indianapolis, ID

USA SWIMMING
Phone: 719-866-3501
info@usaswimming.org
www.usaswimming.org

Jun 3 - Jun 12, 2025
OUTDOOR NATIONAL
CHAMPIONSHIPS
TBA
USA ROLLER SPORTS
Phone: 402-483-7551
Fax: 402-483-1465
www.usarollersports.org

Jun 4 - Jun 8, 2025
MULTISPORT NATIONAL
CHAMPIONSHIPS FESTIVAL
Omaha, NE
USA TRIATHLON
Phone: 719-955-2807
info@usatriathlon.org
www.usatriathlon.org

Jun 4 - Jun 8, 2025
NATIONAL HIGH POWER MID-RANGE
CHAMPIONSHIP
Arcadia, OK
Oklahoma City Gun Club
NATIONAL RIFLE ASSOCIATION -
COMPETITIVE SHOOTING DIVISION
Phone: 703-267-1465
competitions.nra.org

Jun 4 - Jun 8, 2025
RBC CANADIAN OPEN
Caledon, ON, Canada
ROYAL CANADIAN GOLF
ASSOCIATION
Phone: 905-849-9700
Fax: 905-845-7040
info@golfcanada.ca
www.golfcanada.ca

Jun 5 - Jun 8, 2025
BMW CHARITY PRO-AM
Greer, SC
Thornblade Club
PGA KORN FERRY TOUR
Phone: 904-285-3700
Fax: 904-285-7913
www.pgatour.com

Jun 5 - Jun 8, 2025
CANADA CUP OF DIVING
Gatineau, QC, Canada
DIVING CANADA
Phone: 613-736-5238
Fax: 613-736-0409
cada@diving.ca
www.diving.ca

Jun 5 - Jun 8, 2025
DUTCH OPEN
Cromvoirt, Netherlands
Bernardus Golf
PGA EUROPEAN TOUR
International Ph: 44-0-1344-840400
International Fax: 44-0-1344-840500
www.rydercup.com

Jun 6 - Jun 8, 2025
AMERICAN FAMILY INSURANCE
CHAMPIONSHIP
Madison, WI
University Ridge Golf Club
PGA CHAMPIONS TOUR
Phone: 904-285-3700
www.pgatour.com/pgatour-champions

Jun 6 - Jun 8, 2025
NHRA THUNDER VALLEY NATIONALS
Bristol, TN
Bristol Dragway
NATIONAL HOT ROD ASSOCIATION
Phone: 626-914-4761
Fax: 626-325-8752
nhra@nhra.com
www.nhra.com

Jun 6 - Jun 8, 2025
SHOPRITE LPGA CLASSIC
Galloway, NJ
Seaview, Bay Course
LPGA TOUR
Phone: 386-274-6200
Fax: 386-274-1099
www.lpga.com

Jun 6, 2025
STATE GAMES OF MISSISSIPPI
Meridian, MS
STATE GAMES OF MISSISSIPPI
Phone: 601-482-0205
info@stategamesofms.org
www.stategamesofms.org

Jun 6 - Jun 8, 2025
US OPEN BASKETBALL
CHAMPIONSHIPS EAST
Bermuda Run, NC
USA BASKETBALL
Phone: 719-590-4800
Fax: 719-590-4811
fanmail@usabasketball.com
www.usab.com

Jun 6 - Jun 8, 2025
USA BMX SPRING NATIONALS
Albuquerque, NM
USA BMX
Phone: 480-961-1903
Fax: 480-961-1842
info@usabmx.com
www.usabmx.com

Jun 7 - Jun 8, 2025
DIAMOND CUP HUNGARY & FIT
MODEL AND BIKINI EUROP EAN CUP
Budapest, Hungary
INTERNATIONAL FEDERATION OF
BODY BUILDING & FITNESS
contact@ifbb.com
www.ifbb.com

Jun 7, 2025
SHORT TRACK AT LUCAS OIL
SPEEDWAY
Wheatland, MO
Lucas Oil Speedway
AMA PRO RACING
Phone: 386-492-1014
Fax: 386-274-2335
communications@amaproracing.com
www.amaproracing.com

Jun 8, 2025
AMA PRO HILLCLIMB
FREEMANSBURG NATIONAL I
Freemansburg, PA
Bushkill Valley Motorcycle Club
AMA PRO RACING
Phone: 386-492-1014
Fax: 386-274-2335
communications@amaproracing.com
www.amaproracing.com

Jun 8, 2025
FIREKEEPERS CASINO 400
Brooklyn, MI

Michigan International Speedway
NASCAR CUP SERIES
www.nascar.com

Jun 8, 2025
HATFIELD-MCCOY MARATHON
Williamson, WV
HATFIELD-MCCOY MARATHON
hatfieldmccoymarathontvrrc.com

Jun 9 - Jun 17, 2025
LEXUS TRESTLES PRO
Lower Trestles, San Clemente, CA
WORLD SURF LEAGUE
International Ph: +1-310-450-1212
www.worldsurfleague.com

Jun 9 - Jun 15, 2025
LIBEMA OPEN
S'Hertogenbosch, Netherlands
WTA
Phone: 727-895-5000
Fax: 727-894-1982
feedback@wtatennis.com
www.wtatennis.com

Jun 11 - Jun 15, 2025
EUROPEAN CHAMPIONSHIPS
Viareggio, Italy
Societ... Velica Viareggina
INTERNATIONAL STAR CLASS YACHT
ASSOCIATION
Phone: 619-222-0252
Fax: 619-222-0528
office@starclass.org
www.starclass.org

Jun 11 - Jun 14, 2025
NCAA DIVISION I MEN'S/WOMEN'S
TRACK, OUTDOOR FIN ALS
Eugene, OR
Hayway Field
NATIONAL COLLEGIATE ATHLETIC
ASSOCIATION
Phone: 317-917-6222
Fax: 317-917-6888
www.ncaa.org

Jun 12 - Jun 15, 2025
BASSMASTER ELITE SERIES - LAKE
TENKILLER
Cookson, OK
Lake Tenkiller
BASS ANGLERS SPORTSMAN
SOCIETY
Phone: 877-227-7872
bassmaster@emailcustomerservice.com
www.bassmaster.com

Jun 12 - Jun 15, 2025
MEIJER LPGA CLASSIC FOR SIMPLY
GIVE
Belmont, MI
Blythefield Country Club
LPGA TOUR
Phone: 386-274-6200
Fax: 386-274-1099
www.lpga.com

Jun 12, 2025
NORTH TEXAS OPEN
Waxahachie, TX
US PRACTICAL SHOOTING
ASSOCIATION
Phone: 360-855-2245
Fax: 360-855-0380
office@uspsa.org
www.uspsa.org

Jun 12 - Jun 15, 2025
US OPEN
Oakmont, PA
Oakmont Country Club
U.S. GOLF ASSOCIATION
Phone: 908-234-2300
Fax: 908-234-9687
www.usga.org

Jun 12 - Jun 15, 2025
WESTERN HEMISPHERE
CHAMPIONSHIPS
Gibson Island, MD
Gibson Island Yacht Squadron
INTERNATIONAL STAR CLASS YACHT
ASSOCIATION
Phone: 619-222-0252
Fax: 619-222-0528
office@starclass.org
www.starclass.org

Jun 13 - Jun 21, 2025
2025 FINN WORLD MASTERS
Puntala, Italy
Puntala Camping and Resort
WORLD SAILING
office@sailing.org
www.sailing.org

Jun 13 - Jun 15, 2025
ALABAMA STATE GAMES
Birmingham, AL
ASF FOUNDATION
Phone: 800-467-0422
Fax: 334-280-0988
support@asffoundation.org
www.asffoundation.org

Jun 13 - Jun 15, 2025
CENTRAL AMERICAN
CHAMPIONSHIPS
Guatamala
INTERNATIONAL FEDERATION OF
BODY BUILDING & FITNESS
contact@ifbb.com
www.ifbb.com

Jun 13 - Jun 23, 2025
NCAA DIVISION I BASEBALL FINALS
Omaha, NE
Charles Schwab Field Omaha
NATIONAL COLLEGIATE ATHLETIC
ASSOCIATION
Phone: 317-917-6222
Fax: 317-917-6888
www.ncaa.org

Jun 13 - Jun 15, 2025
NEXTGEN PRAIRIE CHAMPIONSHIP
Warman, SK, Canada
The Legends Golf Club
ROYAL CANADIAN GOLF
ASSOCIATION
Phone: 905-849-9700
Fax: 905-845-7040
info@golfcanada.ca
www.golfcanada.ca

Jun 13 - Jun 15, 2025
USA WATER POLO MASTERS
NATIONAL CHAMPIONSHIPS
Southern California
USA WATER POLO
Phone: 714-500-5445
Fax: 714-960-2431
www.usawaterpolo.org

Jun 13 - Jun 15, 2025
WORLD CHAMPIONSHIPS IN
CHILDREN FITNESS
Cacak, Serbia
INTERNATIONAL FEDERATION OF
BODY BUILDING & FITNESS
contact@ifbb.com
www.ifbb.com

Jun 14 - Jun 15, 2025
BOMMARITO AUTOMOTIVE GROUP
500
Madison, IL
Gateway Motorsports Park
NTT INDYCAR SERIES
Phone: 317-492-6526
indycar@indycar.com
www.indycar.com

Jun 14, 2025
HIGH POINT NATIONAL
Mount Morris, PA
High Point Raceway
AMA PRO RACING
Phone: 386-492-1014
Fax: 386-274-2335
communications@amaproracing.com
www.amaproracing.com

Jun 15, 2025
ESTES PARK MARATHON
Estes Park, CO
Estes Park High School
ESTES PARK MARATHON
Phone: 970-586-8189
belle@epmarathon.org
www.epmarathon.org

Jun 15, 2025
NASCAR CUP SERIES AT MEXICO
CITY
Mexico City, Mexico
Autodromo Hermanos Rodriguez
NASCAR CUP SERIES
www.nascar.com

Jun 16 - Jun 22, 2025
BERLIN TENNIS OPEN
Berlin, Germany
WTA
Phone: 727-895-5000
Fax: 727-894-1982
feedback@wtatennis.com
www.wtatennis.com

Jun 16 - Jun 22, 2025
NOTTINGHAM OPEN
Nottingham, Great Britain
Nottingham Tennis Centre
WTA
Phone: 727-895-5000
Fax: 727-894-1982
feedback@wtatennis.com
www.wtatennis.com

Jun 16 - Jun 22, 2025
ROTHESAY NOTTINGHAM OPEN
Birmingham, Great Britain
WTA
Phone: 727-895-5000
Fax: 727-894-1982
feedback@wtatennis.com
www.wtatennis.com

Jun 16 - Jun 22, 2025
TRAVELERS CHAMPIONSHIP
Cromwell, CT
TPC River Highlands

PGA TOUR
Phone: 904-285-3700
www.pgatour.com

Jun 16 - Jun 21, 2025
USA GYMNASTICS CHAMPIONSHIPS
Providence, RI
Rhode Island Convention Center
USA GYMNASTICS
Phone: 800-345-4719
Fax: 317-237-5069
membership@usagym.org
usagym.org

Jun 18 - Jun 22, 2025
KAULIG COMPANIES CHAMPIONSHIP
Akron, OH
Firestone Country Club
PGA CHAMPIONS TOUR
Phone: 904-285-3700
www.pgatour.com/pgatour-champions

Jun 19 - Jun 21, 2025
GRANDMA'S MARATHON
Duluth, MN
Two Harbors To Duluth
GRANDMA'S MARATHON
Phone: 218-727-0947
grandmas@grandmasmarathon.com
www.grandmasmarathon.com

Jun 19 - Jun 22, 2025
KPMG WOMEN'S PGA
CHAMPIONSHIP
Sammamish, WA
Sahalee Country Club
LPGA TOUR
Phone: 386-274-6200
Fax: 386-274-1099
www.lpga.com

Jun 19 - Jun 22, 2025
US WINGFOIL CHAMPIONSHIP
San Francisco, CA
San Francisco Yacht Club
US SAILING
Phone: 800-877-2451
info@ussailing.org
www.ussailing.org

Jun 19 - Jun 22, 2025
US YOUTH CHAMPIONSHIP
San Francisco, CA
St. Francis Yatch Club
WORLD SAILING
office@sailing.org
www.sailing.org

Jun 19 - Jun 22, 2025
WICHITA OPEN
Wichita, KS
Crestview Country Club
PGA KORN FERRY TOUR
Phone: 904-285-3700
Fax: 904-285-7913
www.pgatour.com

Jun 20 - Jun 22, 2025
MIDWEST OPEN
Cincinnati, OH
NATIONAL X BALL LEAGUE
info@nxlpaintball.com
nxlpaintball.com

Jun 20 - Jun 22, 2025
NHRA VIRGINIA NATIONALS
North Dinwiddie, VA
Virginia Motorsports Park
NATIONAL HOT ROD ASSOCIATION
Phone: 626-914-4761
Fax: 626-325-8752

nhra@nhra.com
www.nhra.com

Jun 20 - Jun 22, 2025
US SINGLEHANDED
CHAMPIONSHIPS
Marion, MA
Tabor Academy
US SAILING
Phone: 800-877-2451
info@ussailing.org
www.ussailing.org

Jun 20 - Jun 22, 2025
X GAMES OSAKA
Osaka, Japan
ESPN
xgames.espn.com/xgames

Jun 20 - Jun 22, 2025
XPEL GRAND PRIX AT ROAD
AMERICA
Elkhart Lake, WI
Road America
NTT INDYCAR SERIES
Phone: 317-492-6526
indycar@indycar.com
www.indycar.com

Jun 21 - Jun 22, 2025
RD 7 BUDDS CREEK
Mechanicsville, MD
Budds Creek Raceway
AMA PRO RACING
Phone: 386-492-1014
Fax: 386-274-2335
communications@amaproracing.com
www.amaproracing.com

Jun 21 - Jun 29, 2025
VIVO RIO PRO
Saquarema, Rio de Janeiro, Brazil
WORLD SURF LEAGUE
International Ph: +1-310-450-1212
www.worldsurfleague.com

Jun 22 - Jun 25, 2025
BAD HOMBURG OPEN
Bad Homburg, Germany
WTA
Phone: 727-895-5000
Fax: 727-894-1982
feedback@wtatennis.com
www.wtatennis.com

Jun 22, 2025
NASCAR CUP SERIES AT POCONO
Long Pond, PA
Pocono Raceway
NASCAR CUP SERIES
www.nascar.com

Jun 23 - Jun 29, 2025
DOW GREAT LAKES BAY
INVITATIONAL
Midland, MI
Midland Country Club
LPGA TOUR
Phone: 386-274-6200
Fax: 386-274-1099
www.lpga.com

Jun 23 - Jun 28, 2025
EASTBOURNE INTERNATIONAL
Eastbourne, Great Britain
WTA
Phone: 727-895-5000
Fax: 727-894-1982
feedback@wtatennis.com
www.wtatennis.com

Jun 25, 2025
SIG SAUER FACTORY GUN
NATIONALS
Marengo, OH
US PRACTICAL SHOOTING
ASSOCIATION
Phone: 360-855-2245
Fax: 360-855-0380
office@uspsa.org
www.uspsa.org

Jun 25 - Jun 29, 2025
USA RACQUETBALL NATIONAL
JUNIOR CHAMPIONSHIPS
Minneapolis, MN
University of Minnesota
USA RACQUETBALL
Phone: 719-635-5396
Fax: 719-635-0685
jonathan@usaracquetball.com
www.usaracquetball.com

Jun 26 - Jun 29, 2025
AAU WEST COAST TRACK & FIELD
NATIONAL CHAMPIONSH IP
Reno, NV
AMATEUR ATHLETIC UNION
Phone: 407-934-7200
Fax: 407-934-7242
www.aausports.org

May 26 - May 29, 2025
ITALIAN OPEN
Rome, Italy
Marco Simone Golf Club
PGA EUROPEAN TOUR
International Ph: 44-0-1344-840400
International Fax: 44-0-1344-840500
www.rydercup.com

Jun 26 - Jun 29, 2025
MATHEWS PRO/AM
Metropolis, IL
ARCHERY SHOOTERS ASSOCIATION
Phone: 770-795-0232
Fax: 770-795-0953
info@asaarchery.com
www.asaarchery.com

Jun 26 - Jun 29, 2025
MEMORIAL HEALTH CHAMPIONSHIP
Springfield, IL
Panther Creek Country Club
PGA KORN FERRY TOUR
Phone: 904-285-3700
Fax: 904-285-7913
www.pgatour.com

Jun 26 - Jun 29, 2025
SUMMIT RACING EQUIPMENT NHRA
NATIONALS
Norwalk, OH
Summit Racing Equipment Motorsports
Park
NATIONAL HOT ROD ASSOCIATION
Phone: 626-914-4761
Fax: 626-325-8752
nhra@nhra.com
www.nhra.com

Jun 26 - Jun 29, 2025
US SENIOR OPEN CHAMPIONSHIP
Colorado Springs, CO
The Broadmoor
PGA CHAMPIONS TOUR
Phone: 904-285-3700
www.pgatour.com/pgatour-champions

Jun 27 - Jun 29, 2025
AAU 10U/4TH - 17U/11TH GRADE
EAST COAST DIV. III
CHAMPIONSHIPS
Hampton, VA
Boo Williams Sportsplex
AMATEUR ATHLETIC UNION
Phone: 407-934-7200
Fax: 407-934-7242
www.aausports.org

Jun 27 - Jun 29, 2025
AAU 11U/5TH GRADE DI & DII WORLD
CHAMPIONSHIPS
Knoxville, TN
Knoxville Convention Center
AMATEUR ATHLETIC UNION
Phone: 407-934-7200
Fax: 407-934-7242
www.aausports.org

Jun 27 - Jun 29, 2025
AAU 17U/11TH GRADE &
SOUTHEAST DIV. III CHAMPION
SHIPS
Hampton,VA
Boo Williams Sportsplex
AMATEUR ATHLETIC UNION
Phone: 407-934-7200
Fax: 407-934-7242
www.aausports.org

Jun 27 - Jun 29, 2025
AAU 8U/2ND GRADE AAU WORLD
CHAMPIONSHIPS
Knoxville, TN
Knoxville Convention Center
AMATEUR ATHLETIC UNION
Phone: 407-934-7200
Fax: 407-934-7242
www.aausports.org

Jun 27 - Jun 30, 2025
CANADIAN ROAD CHAMPIONSHIPS
Saint-Georges, QC, Canada
CANADIAN CYCLING ASSOCIATION
Phone: 613-248-1353
Fax: 613-248-9311
general@cyclingcanada.ca
www.cyclingcanada.ca

Jun 27 - Jun 29, 2025
JUNIOR U.S. OPEN WATER SKI
CHAMPIONSHIPS
Harmony, NC
USA WATER SKI
Phone: 863-324-4341
Fax: 863-325-8259
www.usawaterski.org

Jun 27 - Jun 28, 2025
LIMA HALF-MILE I & II
Lima, OH
Allen County Fairgrounds
AMA PRO RACING
Phone: 386-492-1014
Fax: 386-274-2335
communications@amaproracing.com
www.amaproracing.com

Jun 27 - Jun 29, 2025
US OPEN BASKETBALL
CHAMPIONSHIPS CENTRAL
Kansas City, MO
USA BASKETBALL
Phone: 719-590-4800
Fax: 719-590-4811
fanmail@usabasketball.com
www.usab.com

Jun 27 - Jun 29, 2025
X GAMES SALT LAKE CITY
Salt Lake City, UT
ESPN
xgames.espn.com/xgames

Jun 28 - Jun 29, 2025
AMA PRO HILLCLIMB LLOYDS
PERFORMANCE NITRO NATIO NALS I
& II
Soda Springs, ID
Soda Springs Hillclimb
AMA PRO RACING
Phone: 386-492-1014
Fax: 386-274-2335
communications@amaproracing.com
www.amaproracing.com

Jun 28 - Jul 6, 2025
FIBA BASKETBALL WORLD CUP
Switzerland
USA BASKETBALL
Phone: 719-590-4800
Fax: 719-590-4811
fanmail@usabasketball.com
www.usab.com

Jun 28, 2025
LEADVILLE TRAIL MARATHON &
HEAVY HALF
Leadville, CO
LEADVILLE TRAIL MARATHON
leadville@ltevents.zendesk.com
www.leadvilleraceseries.com

Jun 28, 2025
QUAKER STATE 400 PRESENTED BY
WALMART
Hampton, GA
Atlanta Motor Speedway
NASCAR CUP SERIES
www.nascar.com

Jun 28, 2025
SOUTHWICK NATIONAL
Southwick, MA
The Wick 338
AMA PRO RACING
Phone: 386-492-1014
Fax: 386-274-2335
communications@amaproracing.com
www.amaproracing.com

Jun 28 - Jul 7, 2025
USA FENCING NATIONAL
CHAMPIONSHIPS & JULY CHALLE
NGE (SUMMER NATIONALS)
Milwaukee, WI
USA FENCING
Phone: 719-866-4511
Fax: 719-632-5737
information@usafencing.org
www.usafencing.org

Jun 29 - Jul 5, 2025
AAU TAEKWONDO NATIONAL
CHAMPIONSHIPS
Salt Lake City, UT
Salt Palace Convention Center
AMATEUR ATHLETIC UNION
Phone: 407-934-7200
Fax: 407-934-7242
www.aausports.org

Jun 30 - Jul 7, 2025
AAU JUNIOR NATIONAL VOLLEYBALL
CHAMPIONSHIPS
Orlando, FL
Orange County Convention Center

AMATEUR ATHLETIC UNION
Phone: 407-934-7200
Fax: 407-934-7242
www.aausports.org

Jun 30 - Jul 5, 2025
AAU KARATE NATIONAL
CHAMPIONSHIPS
Ft. Lauderdale, FL
AMATEUR ATHLETIC UNION
Phone: 407-934-7200
Fax: 407-934-7242
www.aausports.org

Jun 30 - Jul 6, 2025
ANNUAL WORLD'S OLDEST
CONTINUOUS RODEO
Prescott, AZ
PROFESSIONAL RODEO COWBOY
ASSOCIATION
Phone: 719-593-8840
webmaster@prorodeo.com
www.prorodeo.com

Jun 30 - Jul 13, 2025
THE CHAMPIONSHIPS
Wimbledon, Great Britain
WTA
Phone: 727-895-5000
Fax: 727-894-1982
feedback@wtatennis.com
www.wtatennis.com

Jun 30 - Jul 13, 2025
WIMBLEDON
London, United Kingdom
THE ALL ENGLAND LAWN TENNIS
CLUB
International Ph: +44 (0)20 89441066
International Fax: +44 (0)20 89478752
www.wimbledon.com

Jul TBA, 2025
JUNEAU MARATHON & HALF
MARATHON
Juneau, AK
JUNEAU TRAIL & ROAD RUNNERS
houstonlaws@yahoo.com
juneauserr.wixsite.com/serr/marathon

Jul TBA, 2025
USA SOFTBALL INTERNATIONAL
CUP
TBA
USA SOFTBALL
www.usasoftball.com

Jul 1 - Jul 4, 2025
HOME OF CHAMPIONS RODEO
Red Lodge, MT
PROFESSIONAL RODEO COWBOY
ASSOCIATION
Phone: 719-593-8840
webmaster@prorodeo.com
www.prorodeo.com

Jul 2 - Jul 6, 2025
BMW INTERNATIONAL OPEN
Munich, Germany
Golf Club Munich Eichenried
PGA EUROPEAN TOUR
International Ph: 44-0-1344-840400
International Fax: 44-0-1344-840500
www.rydercup.com

Jul 2 - Jul 28, 2025
INDOOR NATIONAL CHAMPIONSHIPS
Reno, NV
USA ROLLER SPORTS
Phone: 402-483-7551
Fax: 402-483-1465
www.usarollersports.org

Jul 2 - Jul 6, 2025
JOHN DEERE CLASSIC
Silvis, IL
TPC Deere Run
PGA TOUR
Phone: 904-285-3700
www.pgatour.com

Jul 2 - Jul 6, 2025
NATIONAL HIGH POWER LONG
RANGE CHAMPIONSHIP
Malvern, OH
Alliance Rifle Club
NATIONAL RIFLE ASSOCIATION -
COMPETITIVE SHOOTING DIVISION
Phone: 703-267-1465
competitions.nra.org

Jul 3 - Jul 6, 2025
AAU 14U/8TH GRADE DI & DII WORLD
CHAMPIONSHIPS
Orlando, FL
ESPN Wide World of Sports
AMATEUR ATHLETIC UNION
Phone: 407-934-7200
Fax: 407-934-7242
www.aausports.org

Jul 3 - Jul 5, 2025
AKC RALLY NATIONAL
CHAMPIONSHIP
Gray Summitt, MO
Purina Event Center
AMERICAN KENNEL CLUB
Phone: 919-233-9767
publiced@akc.org
www.akc.org

Jul 3 - Jul 5, 2025
NEXTGEN QUEBEC CHAMPIONSHIP
Manotick, ON, Canada
Rideau View Golf Club
ROYAL CANADIAN GOLF
ASSOCIATION
Phone: 905-849-9700
Fax: 905-845-7040
info@golfcanada.ca
www.golfcanada.ca

Jul 4 - Jul 6, 2025
HONDA INDY 200 AT MID-OHIO
Lexington, OH
Mid-Ohio Sports Car Course
NTT INDYCAR SERIES
Phone: 317-492-6526
indycar@indycar.com
www.indycar.com

Jul 5, 2025
DUQUOIN MILE
Du Quoin, IL
Du Quoin State Fairgrounds
AMA PRO RACING
Phone: 386-492-1014
Fax: 386-274-2335
communications@amaproracing.com
www.amaproracing.com

Jul 5 - Jul 15, 2025
GRAN CANARIA WORLD CUP
Gran Canaria Pozo Izquierdo
INTERNATIONAL WINDSURFING TOUR
internationalwindsurfingtour.com

Jul 5 - Jul 11, 2025
J80 WORLD CHAMPIONSHIP
Nieuwpoort, Belgium
WORLD SAILING
office@sailing.org
www.sailing.org

Jul 5 - Jul 6, 2025
RD 8 TOMAHAWK
Hedgesville, WV
Tomahawk MX Park
AMA PRO RACING
Phone: 386-492-1014
Fax: 386-274-2335
communications@amaproracing.com
www.amaproracing.com

Jul 5 - Jul 27, 2025
TOUR DE FRANCE
Paris, France
AMAURY SPORT ORGANIZATION
International Ph: 33-1-41-33-14-00
contact@aso.fr
www.aso.fr

Jul 6 - Jul 12, 2025
AAU TRACK & FIELD CLUB
CHAMPIONSHIPS
Jacksonville, FL
Hodges Stadium
AMATEUR ATHLETIC UNION
Phone: 407-934-7200
Fax: 407-934-7242
www.aausports.org

Jul 6 - Jul 7, 2025
AKC NATIONAL OBEDIENCE
CHAMPIONSHIP
Gray Summit, MO
Purina Event Center
AMERICAN KENNEL CLUB
Phone: 919-233-9767
publiced@akc.org
www.akc.org

Jul 6 - Jul 10, 2025
NATIONAL PISTOL CHAMPIONSHIPS
Marengo, OH
NATIONAL RIFLE ASSOCIATION -
COMPETITIVE SHOOTING DIVISION
Phone: 703-267-1465
competitions.nra.org

Jul 7 - Jul 10, 2025
AAU 13U/7TH GRADE DI & DII AAU
WORLD CHAMPIONSHI PS
Orlando, FL
ESPN Wide World of Sports
AMATEUR ATHLETIC UNION
Phone: 407-934-7200
Fax: 407-934-7242
www.aausports.org

Jul 7 - Jul 10, 2025
AAU 7U/1ST GRADE AAU WORLD
CHAMPIONSHIPS
Orlando, FL
ESPN Wide World of Sports
AMATEUR ATHLETIC UNION
Phone: 407-934-7200
Fax: 407-934-7242
www.aausports.org

Jul 7 - Jul 13, 2025
DICK'S SPORTING GOODS OPEN
Endicott, NY
En-Joie Golf Club
PGA CHAMPIONS TOUR
Phone: 904-285-3700
www.pgatour.com/pgatour-champions

Jul 7 - Jul 12, 2025
NORDEA OPEN
Bastad, Sweden
WTA
Phone: 727-895-5000
Fax: 727-894-1982

feedback@wtatennis.com
www.wtatennis.com

Jul 7 - Jul 13, 2025
TPC COLORADO CHAMPIONSHIP AT
HERON LAKES
Berthoud, CO
TPC Colorado
PGA KORN FERRY TOUR
Phone: 904-285-3700
Fax: 904-285-7913
www.pgatour.com

Jul 7 - Jul 11, 2025
US JUNIOR WOMEN'S
CHAMPIONSHIP
Macatawa, MI
Macatawa Bay Yacht Club
WORLD SAILING
office@sailing.org
www.sailing.org

Jul 8 - Jul 13, 2025
ICF JUNIOR & U23 CANOE SLALOM
WORLD CHAMPIONSHIP
Foix, France
INTERNATIONAL CANOE FEDERATION
International Ph: 41 (0)21 612 0290
info@canoeicf.com
www.canoeicf.com

Jul 9 - Jul 15, 2025
GIRLS' 16U & 18U GOLD FP
Oklahoma City, OK
USA SOFTBALL
Phone: 405-424-5266
Fax: 405-424-3855
rcress@softball.org
www.usasoftball.com

Jul 10 - Jul 13, 2025
GRANDFATHER MOUNTAIN
HIGHLAND GAMES
Linville, NC
GRANDFATHER MOUNTAIN HIGHLAND
GAMES
Phone: 828-733-1333
Fax: 828-733-0092
admin@gmhg.org
www.gmhg.org

Jul 10 - Jul 12, 2025
ICF WILDWATER CANOEING WORLD
CUP
Banja Luka, Bosnia
INTERNATIONAL CANOE FEDERATION
International Ph: 41 (0)21 612 0290
info@canoeicf.com
www.canoeicf.com

Jul 10 - Jul 13, 2025
THE AMUNDI EVIAN CHAMPIONSHIP
Evian-les-Bains, France
Evian Resort Golf Club
LPGA TOUR
Phone: 386-274-6200
Fax: 386-274-1099
www.lpga.com

Jul 10 - Jul 11, 2025
WALLEYE TOUR-LAKE HURON
Alpena, MI
Lake Huron
NATIONAL WALLEYE TOUR
Phone: 612-424-0708
Fax: 866-727-2809
outdoorteamworks.com/trail/nwt

Jul 11 - Jul 20, 2025
CORONA CERO OPEN J-BAY
Jeffreys Bay, Eastern Cape, South
Africa
WORLD SURF LEAGUE
International Ph: +1-310-450-1212
www.worldsurfleague.com

Jul 11 - Aug 3, 2025
FINA CHAMPIONSHIPS
Singapore
USA DIVING
Phone: 317-237-5252
Fax: 317-237-5257
Dan.Laak@usadiving.org
www.usadiving.org

Jul 11 - Jul 12, 2025
OHIO OPEN MIXED DOUBLES
Lakeside, OH
NATIONAL SHUFFLEBOARD
ASSOCIATION
www.national-shuffleboard-association.us

Jul 11 - Jul 13, 2025
SWISS SENIORS OPEN
Bad Ragaz, Switzerland
PGA EUROPEAN STAYSURE TOUR
International Ph: 44-0-1344-840400
International Fax: 44-0-1344-840500
www.europeantour.com/staysure-tour

Jul 12 - Jul 13, 2025
MR UNIVERSO PARAGUAY
Asuncion, Paraguay
INTERNATIONAL FEDERATION OF
BODY BUILDING & FITNESS
contact@ifbb.com
www.ifbb.com

Jul 12, 2025
SPRING CREEK NATIONAL
Millville, MN
Spring Creek MX Park
AMA PRO RACING
Phone: 386-492-1014
Fax: 386-274-2335
communications@amaproracing.com
www.amaproracing.com

Jul 13 - Jul 20, 2025
THE OPEN CHAMPIONSHIP
Hoylake, Wirral, England
Royal Liverpool
PGA TOUR
Phone: 904-285-3700
www.pgatour.com

Jul 13, 2025
TOYOTA-SAVE MART 350
Sonoma, CA
Sonoma Raceway
NASCAR CUP SERIES
www.nascar.com

Jul 14 - Jul 20, 2025
ENDURANCE MOUNTAIN BIKE
NATIONAL CHAMPIONSHIPS
Roanoke, VA
USA CYCLING
Phone: 719-434-4200
Fax: 719-434-4300
help@usacycling.org
www.usacycling.org

Jul 14 - Jul 16, 2025
OHIO OPEN MEN'S & LADIES'
WALKING & NON-WALKING SINGLES
Lakeside, OH

NATIONAL SHUFFLEBOARD
ASSOCIATION
www.national-shuffleboard-association.us

Jul 14 - Jul 19, 2025
US GIRLS' JUNIOR
Atlanta, GA
Atlanta Athletic Club
U.S. GOLF ASSOCIATION
Phone: 908-234-2300
Fax: 908-234-9687
www.usga.org

Jul 15 - Jul 23, 2025
AAU DIVING NATIONAL
CHAMPIONSHIP
Riverside, CA
Riverside Community College
AMATEUR ATHLETIC UNION
Phone: 407-934-7200
Fax: 407-934-7242
www.aausports.org

Jul 15 - Jul 18, 2025
AAU GIRLS' NATIONAL BEACH
VOLLEYBALL CHAMPIONSHI PS
Hermosa Beach, CA
Hermose Beach Pier
AMATEUR ATHLETIC UNION
Phone: 407-934-7200
Fax: 407-934-7242
www.aausports.org

Jul 15 - Jul 18, 2025
AAU JUNIOR NATIONAL BEACH
VOLLEYBALL CHAMPIONSHI PS
Hermosa Beach, CA
Hermosa Beach Pier
AMATEUR ATHLETIC UNION
Phone: 407-934-7200
Fax: 407-934-7242
www.aausports.org

Jul 15 - Jul 17, 2025
NEXTGEN ATLANTIC CHAMPIONSHIP
Enfield, NS, Canada
Oakfield Golf and Country Club
ROYAL CANADIAN GOLF
ASSOCIATION
Phone: 905-849-9700
Fax: 905-845-7040
info@golfcanada.ca
www.golfcanada.ca

Jul 16, 2025
MULTIGUN NATIONALS
Forest Lake, MN
Forest Lake Sportsmen's Club
US PRACTICAL SHOOTING
ASSOCIATION
Phone: 360-855-2245
Fax: 360-855-0380
office@uspsa.org
www.uspsa.org

Jul 16, 2025
OHIO JUNIOR SINGLES 15 & UNDER
Lakeside, OH
NATIONAL SHUFFLEBOARD
ASSOCIATION
www.national-shuffleboard-association.us

Jul 17 - Jul 20, 2025
MEN'S MAJOR GOLD FP
Oklahoma City, OK
USA SOFTBALL
Phone: 405-424-5266
Fax: 405-424-3855
rcress@softball.org
www.usasoftball.com

Jul 17 - Jul 19, 2025
NARCH FINALS
Irvine, CA
The Rinks, Irvine Inline
NORTH AMERICAN ROLLER HOCKEY
CHAMPIONSHIPS
Phone: 760-889-6909
daryn@narch.com
www.narch.com

Jul 17 - Jul 18, 2025
OHIO OPEN MEN'S & LADIES'
DOUBLES
Lakeside, OH
NATIONAL SHUFFLEBOARD
ASSOCIATION
www.national-shuffleboard-association.us

Jul 17 - Jul 20, 2025
PRICE CUTTER CHARITY
CHAMPIONSHIP
Springfield, MO
Highland Springs Country Club
PGA KORN FERRY TOUR
Phone: 904-285-3700
Fax: 904-285-7913
www.pgatour.com

Jul 17 - Jul 19, 2025
US OPEN - MARTIAL ARTS
CHAMPIONSHIPS
Orlando, FL
USA OPEN KARATE
usopen-karate.com

Jul 18 - Jul 19, 2025
EXTREME EVENTS MINNESOTA
CHAMPIONSHIP RODEO
Waconia, MN
PROFESSIONAL RODEO COWBOY
ASSOCIATION
Phone: 719-593-8840
webmaster@prorodeo.com
www.prorodeo.com

Jul 18 - Jul 20, 2025
NHRA NORTHWEST NATIONALS
Kent, WA
Pacific Raceways
NATIONAL HOT ROD ASSOCIATION
Phone: 626-914-4761
Fax: 626-325-8752
nhra@nhra.com
www.nhra.com

Jul 18 - Jul 20, 2025
ONTARIO HONDA DEALERS INDY
TORONTO
Toronto, Canada
Streets of Toronto
NTT INDYCAR SERIES
Phone: 317-492-6526
indycar@indycar.com
www.indycar.com

Jul 18 - Jul 20, 2025
OUTDOOR FIELD NATIONAL
CHAMPIONSHIPS
Mechanicsburg, PA
NATIONAL FIELD ARCHERY
ASSOCIATION
Phone: 605-260-9279
info@nfaausa.com
www.nfaausa.com

Jul 18, 2025
WISCONSIN STATE WATER SKI
SHOW CHAMPIONSHIPS
Wisconsin Rapids, WI

South Wood County Park, Lake
Wazeecha - Red Beach
WISCONSIN RAPIDS AQUA SKIERS
Phone: 715-323-1577
www.aquaskiers.org

Jul 19 - Jul 20, 2025
RD 9 PLEASURE VALLEY
Seward, PA
Pleasure Valley Raceway
AMA PRO RACING
Phone: 386-492-1014
Fax: 386-274-2335
communications@amaproracing.com
www.amaproracing.com

Jul 19, 2025
SF CLASSIC & UN CHALLENGE
San Francisco, CA
St. Francis Yacht Club
ST. FRANCIS YACHT CLUB
Phone: 415-563-6363
Fax: 415-563-8670
frontdesk@stfyc.com
www.stfyc.com

Jul 19 - Jul 22, 2025
USA WATER POLO NATIONAL
JUNIOR OLYMPICS - SESS 1
Orange County, CA
USA WATER POLO
Phone: 714-500-5445
Fax: 714-960-2431
www.usawaterpolo.org

Jul 19, 2025
WASHOUGAL NATIONAL
Washougal, WA
Washougal MX Park
AMA PRO RACING
Phone: 386-492-1014
Fax: 386-274-2335
communications@amaproracing.com
www.amaproracing.com

Jul 20, 2025
AUTOTRADER ECHOPARK
AUTOMOTIVE 400
Fort Worth, TX
Texas Motor Speedway
NASCAR CUP SERIES
www.nascar.com

Jul 21 - Jul 27, 2025
3M OPEN
Blaine, MN
TPC Twin Cities
PGA TOUR
Phone: 904-285-3700
www.pgatour.com

Jul 21 - Jul 26, 2025
LIVESPORT PRAGUE OPEN
Prague, Czech Republic
WTA
Phone: 727-895-5000
Fax: 727-894-1982
feedback@wtatennis.com
www.wtatennis.com

Jul 21 - Jul 26, 2025
US JUNIOR AMATEUR
Dallas, TX
Trinity Forest Golf Club
U.S. GOLF ASSOCIATION
Phone: 908-234-2300
Fax: 908-234-9687
www.usga.org

Jul 22 - Jul 25, 2025
CANADIAN WOMEN'S AMATEUR
CHAMPIONSHIP
Saint John, NB, Canada
The Riverside Country Club
ROYAL CANADIAN GOLF
ASSOCIATION
Phone: 905-849-9700
Fax: 905-845-7040
info@golfcanada.ca
www.golfcanada.ca

Jul 23 - Aug 2, 2025
AAU JUNIOR OLYMPIC GAMES
Houston, TX
AMATEUR ATHLETIC UNION
Phone: 407-934-7200
Fax: 407-934-7242
www.aausports.org

Jul 23 - Jul 27, 2025
ICF JUNIOR & U23 CANOE SPRINT
WORLD CHAMPIONSHIP
Montemor-o-Velho, Portugal
INTERNATIONAL CANOE FEDERATION
International Ph: 41 (0)21 612 0290
info@canoeicf.com
www.canoeicf.com

Jul 23 - Jul 27, 2025
USA TAEKWONDO NATIONAL
CHAMPIONSHIPS
Ontario, CA
Ontario Convention Center
USA TAEKWONDO
Phone: 719-866-4632
Fax: 719-866-4642
www.usatkd.org

Jul 24 - Jul 27, 2025
NV5 INVITATIONAL
Glenview, IL
The Glen Club
PGA KORN FERRY TOUR
Phone: 904-285-3700
Fax: 904-285-7913
www.pgatour.com

Jul 24 - Jul 27, 2025
TRUST GOLD WOMEN'S SCOTTISH
OPEN
Ayrshire, Scotland
Dundonald Links
LPGA TOUR
Phone: 386-274-6200
Fax: 386-274-1099
www.lpga.com

Jul 24 - Jul 27, 2025
USA WATER POLO NATIONAL
JUNIOR OLYMPICS - SESS 2
Orange County, CA
USA WATER POLO
Phone: 714-500-5445
Fax: 714-960-2431
www.usawaterpolo.org

Jul 24 - Jul 27, 2025
WORLD RECREATIONAL TEAM
CHAMPIONSHIPS
Blaine, MN
NSC Super Rink
ICE SKATING INSTITUTE
Phone: 972-735-8800
Fax: 972-735-8815
events@skateisi.org
www.skateisi.org

Jul 25 - Jul 27, 2025
CANADIAN DOWNHILL MTB
CHAMPIONSHIPS
Sun Peaks, BC, Canada
CANADIAN CYCLING ASSOCIATION
Phone: 613-248-1353
Fax: 613-248-9311
general@cyclingcanada.ca
www.cyclingcanada.ca

Jul 25 - Jul 27, 2025
DENSO NHRA SONOMA NATIONALS
Sonoma, CA
Sonoma Raceway
NATIONAL HOT ROD ASSOCIATION
Phone: 626-914-4761
Fax: 626-325-8752
nhra@nhra.com
www.nhra.com

Jul 25 - Jul 27, 2025
INDYCAR GRAND PRIX OF
MONTEREY
Monterey, CA
WeatherTech Raceway Laguna Seca
NTT INDYCAR SERIES
Phone: 317-492-6526
indycar@indycar.com
www.indycar.com

Jul 25 - Jul 27, 2025
NHRA SONOMA NATIONALS
Sonoma, CA
Sonoma Raceway
NATIONAL HOT ROD ASSOCIATION
Phone: 626-914-4761
Fax: 626-325-8752
nhra@nhra.com
www.nhra.com

Jul 25 - Aug 3, 2025
US DIVING JUNIOR NATIONAL
CHAMPIONSHIPS
Mission Viejo, CA
USA DIVING
Phone: 317-237-5252
Fax: 317-237-5257
Dan.Laak@usadiving.org
www.usadiving.org

Jul 26 - Aug 2, 2025
JUNIOR WATER SKI WORLD
CHAMPIONSHIPS
Calgary, AB, Canada
INTERNATIONAL WATERSKI &
WAKEBOARD FEDERATION
info@iwwfed.com
https://iwwf.sport

Jul 26 - Aug 7, 2025
NATIONAL BANK OPEN
Toronto, Canada
WTA
Phone: 727-895-5000
Fax: 727-894-1982
feedback@wtatennis.com
www.wtatennis.com

Jul 26 - Jul 27, 2025
SAN FRANCISCO MARATHON
San Francisco, CA
SAN FRANCISCO MARATHON
Phone: 888-958-6668
customersupport@thesfmarathon.com
www.thesfmarathon.com

Jun 27 - Jun 29, 2025
AAU 10U/4TH GRADE DI & DII WORLD
CHAMPIONSHIPS
Hampton, VA

Boo Williams Sportsplex
AMATEUR ATHLETIC UNION
Phone: 407-934-7200
Fax: 407-934-7242
www.aausports.org

Jul 27 - Aug 7, 2025
ATP TOUR MASTERS 1000 -
NATIONAL BANK OPEN
Toronto, ON, Canada
ATP TOUR MASTERS 1000
www.atptour.com

Jul 27 - Aug 7, 2025
OMNIUM BANQUE NATIONALE
Montreal, QC, Canada
WTA
Phone: 727-895-5000
Fax: 727-894-1982
feedback@wtatennis.com
www.wtatennis.com

Jul 28 - Jul 31, 2025
CANADIAN MEN'S AMATEUR
CHAMPIONSHIP
Gatineau, QC, Canada
The Royal Ottawa Golf Club
ROYAL CANADIAN GOLF
ASSOCIATION
Phone: 905-849-9700
Fax: 905-845-7040
info@golfcanada.ca
www.golfcanada.ca

July 30 - Aug 2, 2025
AIG WOMEN'S BRITISH OPEN
Royal Porthcawl, Wales
LPGA TOUR
Phone: 386-274-6200
Fax: 386-274-1099
www.lpga.com

Jul 30 - Aug 2, 2025
BAREFOOT NATIONAL
CHAMPIONSHIPS
Auburndale, FL
USA WATER SKI
Phone: 863-324-4341
Fax: 863-325-8259
www.usawaterski.org

Jul 30 - Aug 3, 2025
WYNDHAM CHAMPIONSHIP
Greensboro, NC
Sedgefield Country Club
PGA TOUR
Phone: 904-285-3700
www.pgatour.com

Jul 31 - Aug 3, 2025
DELTA MCKENZIE ASA CLASSIC
Cullman, AL
St. Bernard Abbey
ARCHERY SHOOTERS ASSOCIATION
Phone: 770-795-0232
Fax: 770-795-0953
info@asaarchery.com
www.asaarchery.com

Jul 31 - Aug 3, 2025
MOUNTAIN BIKE NATIONAL
CHAMPIONSHIPS
Big Bear Lake, CA
USA CYCLING
Phone: 719-434-4200
Fax: 719-434-4300
help@usacycling.org
www.usacycling.org

Jul 31 - Aug 3, 2025
USA WATER POLO NATIONAL
JUNIOR OLYMPICS - SESS 3
North Texas
USA WATER POLO
Phone: 714-500-5445
Fax: 714-960-2431
www.usawaterpolo.org

Jul 31 - Aug 3, 2025
UTAH CHAMPIONSHIP
Ogden, UT
Ogden Golf & Country Club
PGA KORN FERRY TOUR
Phone: 904-285-3700
Fax: 904-285-7913
www.pgatour.com

Aug TBA, 2025
AAU JUDO NATIONAL
CHAMPIONSHIP
AMATEUR ATHLETIC UNION
Phone: 407-934-7200
Fax: 407-934-7242
www.aausports.org

Aug TBA, 2025
BLUEGRASS STATE GAMES
Lexington, KY
BLUEGRASS STATE GAMES
Phone: 859-523-0009
info@bgsg.org
www.bgsg.org

Aug TBA, 2025
COLLEGIATE WATER SKI NATIONAL
CHAMPIONSHIPS
TBA
NATIONAL COLLEGIATE WATER SKI
ASSOCIATION
www.ncwsa.com

Aug 1 - Aug 3, 2025
CYCLE NORTH CAROLINA
MOUNTAIN RIDE
Sylva, NC
NORTH CAROLINA AMATEUR SPORTS
Phone: 919-361-1133
Fax: 919-361-2559
ncas@ncsports.org
www.ncsports.org

Aug 1 - Aug 10, 2025
TENERIFE WORLD CUP
El Medano, Tenerife, Canary Islands
INTERNATIONAL WINDSURFING TOUR
internationalwindsurfingtour.com

Aug 2, 2025
AMA PRO HILLCLIMB MOUNT
GARFIELD NATIONAL
Norton Shores, MI
Muskegon Motorcycle Club
AMA PRO RACING
Phone: 386-492-1014
Fax: 386-274-2335
communications@amaproracing.com
www.amaproracing.com

Aug 2, 2025
PARK CITY HALF MARATHON
Park City, UT
UTAH ROAD RUNNERS
pctrailseries.com

Aug 3, 2025
ALCATRAZ SHARKFEST SWIM
San Francisco, CA
Alcatraz Island

ENVIRO-SPORTS
Phone: 415-868-1829
info@envirosports.com
envirosports.com

Aug 4 - Aug 10, 2025
BOEING CLASSIC
Snoqualmie, WA
The Club at Snoqualmie Ridge
PGA CHAMPIONS TOUR
Phone: 904-285-3700
www.pgatour.com/pgatour-champions

Aug 4 - Aug 9, 2025
CANADA BASKETBALL 15U/17U
MEN'S NATIONAL CHAMPIO NSHIPS
TBA
CANADA BASKETBALL
Phone: 416-614-8037
Fax: 416-614-9570
info@basketball.ca
www.basketball.ca

Aug 4 - Aug 9, 2025
CANADA BASKETBALL 15U/17U
WOMEN'S NATIONAL CHAMP
IONSHIPS
TBA
CANADA BASKETBALL
Phone: 416-614-8037
Fax: 416-614-9570
info@basketball.ca
www.basketball.ca

Aug 4 - Aug 5, 2025
JACKPINE GYPSIES ST I & II
Sturgis, SD
Jackpine Gypsies
AMA PRO RACING
Phone: 386-492-1014
Fax: 386-274-2335
communications@amaproracing.com
www.amaproracing.com

Aug 4 - Aug 10, 2025
PINNACLE BANK CHAMPIONSHIP
Omaha, NE
The Club at Indian Creek
PGA KORN FERRY TOUR
Phone: 904-285-3700
Fax: 904-285-7913
www.pgatour.com

Aug 4 - Aug 10, 2025
US WOMEN'S AMATEUR
Bandon, OR
Bandon Dunes Golf Resort
U.S. GOLF ASSOCIATION
Phone: 908-234-2300
Fax: 908-234-9687
www.usga.org

Aug 5 - Aug 9, 2025
GOODE U.S. WATER SKI NATIONAL
CHAMPIONSHIPS
Arvin, CA
USA WATER SKI
Phone: 863-324-4341
Fax: 863-325-8259
www.usawaterski.org

Aug 6 - Aug 8, 2025
CANADIAN WOMEN'S MID-AMATEUR
& SENIOR CHAMPIONSH IP
Lachute, QC, Canada
Club de golf Lachute
ROYAL CANADIAN GOLF
ASSOCIATION
Phone: 905-849-9700
Fax: 905-845-7040

info@golfcanada.ca
www.golfcanada.ca

Aug 6 - Aug 10, 2025
FEDEX ST. JUDE CHAMPIONSHIP
Memphis, TN
TPC Southwind
PGA TOUR
Phone: 904-285-3700
www.pgatour.com

Aug 6 - Aug 10, 2025
MASTERS TRACK NATIONAL
CHAMPIONSHIPS
Colorado Springs, CO
USA CYCLING
Phone: 719-434-4200
Fax: 719-434-4300
help@usacycling.org
www.usacycling.org

Aug 6 - Aug 7, 2025
NATIONAL LEVER ACTION
SILHOUETTE CHAMPIONSHIP
Ridway, PA
Ridway Rifle Club
NATIONAL RIFLE ASSOCIATION -
COMPETITIVE SHOOTING DIVISION
Phone: 703-267-1465
competitions.nra.org

Aug 7 - Aug 10, 2025
2025 US GYMNASTICS
CHAMPIONSHIPS
New Orleans, LA
Smoothie King Center
USA GYMNASTICS
Phone: 800-345-4719
Fax: 317-237-5069
membership@usagym.org
usagym.org

Aug 7 - Aug 18, 2025
ATP TOUR MASTERS 1000 -
CINCINNATI OPEN
Cincinnati, OH
ATP TOUR MASTERS 1000
www.atptour.com

Aug 7 - Aug 10, 2025
BASSMASTER ELITE SERIES - LAKE
ST. CLAIR
Macomb County, MI
Lake St. Clair
BASS ANGLERS SPORTSMAN
SOCIETY
Phone: 877-227-7872
bassmaster@emailcustomerservice.com
www.bassmaster.com

Aug 7 - Aug 18, 2025
CINCINNATI OPEN
Cincinnati, OH
WTA
Phone: 727-895-5000
Fax: 727-894-1982
feedback@wtatennis.com
www.wtatennis.com

Aug 7 - Aug 16, 2025
TAHITI PRO TEAHUPO'O
Teahupo'o, Tahiti
WORLD SURF LEAGUE
International Ph: +1-310-450-1212
www.worldsurfleague.com

Aug 7 - Aug 17, 2025
THE WORLD GAMES
Chengdu, China
THE WORLD GAMES
www.theworldgames.org

Aug 7 0 Aug 8, 2025
WALLEYE TOUR-LAKE ERIE
Bunkirk, NY
Lake Erie
NATIONAL WALLEYE TOUR
Phone: 612-424-0708
Fax: 866-727-2809
outdoorteamworks.com/trail/nwt

Aug 8 - Aug 10, 2025
ELITE & MASTERS CANADIAN
CHAMPIONSHIPS
Victoria, BC, Canada
CANADIAN CYCLING ASSOCIATION
Phone: 613-248-1353
Fax: 613-248-9311
general@cyclingcanada.ca
www.cyclingcanada.ca

Aug 8 - Aug 10, 2025
GRAND PRIX OF PORTLAND
Portland, OR
Portland International Raceway
NTT INDYCAR SERIES
Phone: 317-492-6526
indycar@indycar.com
www.indycar.com

Aug 8, 2025
NATIONAL PISTOL CARTRIDGE
SILHOUETTE CHAMPIONSHI P
Ridway, PA
Ridway Rifle Club
NATIONAL RIFLE ASSOCIATION -
COMPETITIVE SHOOTING DIVISION
Phone: 703-267-1465
competitions.nra.org

Aug 8 - Aug 10, 2025
USA TRIATHLON SPRINT & OLYMPIC
DISTANCE NATIONAL
CHAMPIONSHIPS
Milwaukee, WI
USA TRIATHLON
Phone: 719-955-2807
info@usatriathlon.org
www.usatriathlon.org

Aug 9 - Aug 10, 2025
CANADIAN TRIATHLON
CHAMPIONSHIPS
Kelowna, BC, Canada
TRIATHLON CANADA
Phone: 250-412-1795
Fax: 250-412-1794
info@triathloncanada.com
www.triathloncanada.com

Aug 9, 2025
IRONMAN NATIONAL
Crawfordsville, IN
Ironman Raceway
AMA PRO RACING
Phone: 386-492-1014
Fax: 386-274-2335
communications@amaproracing.com
www.amaproracing.com

Aug 9, 2025
NATIONAL SMALLBORE SILHOUETTE
CHAMPIONSHIP
Ridway, PA
Ridway Rifle Club
NATIONAL RIFLE ASSOCIATION -
COMPETITIVE SHOOTING DIVISION
Phone: 703-267-1465
competitions.nra.org

Aug 9 - Aug 10, 2025
RD 10 BRIARCLIFF MX
Nashport, OH
Briarcliff MX
AMA PRO RACING
Phone: 386-492-1014
Fax: 386-274-2335
communications@amaproracing.com
www.amaproracing.com

Aug 10 - Aug 24, 2025
BASEBALL CANADA CUP
CHAMPIONSHIPS
St. John's, NL, Canada
BASEBALL CANADA
Phone: 613-748-5606
Fax: 613-748-5767
info@baseball.ca
www.baseball.ca

Aug 10, 2025
GO BOWLING AT THE GLEN
Watkins Glen, NY
Watkins Glen International
NASCAR CUP SERIES
www.nascar.com

Aug 10, 2025
STURGIS TT
Sturgis, SD
Streets of Downtown Sturgis
AMA PRO RACING
Phone: 386-492-1014
Fax: 386-274-2335
communications@amaproracing.com
www.amaproracing.com

Aug 11 - Aug 17, 2025
SHAW CHARITY CLASSIC
Calgary, AB
Canyon Meadows Golf & Country Club
PGA CHAMPIONS TOUR
Phone: 904-285-3700
www.pgatour.com/pgatour-champions

Aug 11 - Aug 17, 2025
US AMATEUR
San Francisco, CA
The Olympic Club
U.S. GOLF ASSOCIATION
Phone: 908-234-2300
Fax: 908-234-9687
www.usga.org

Aug 12 - Aug 17, 2025
BMW CHAMPIONSHIP
Owings, MD
Caves Valley Golf Club
PGA TOUR
Phone: 904-285-3700
www.pgatour.com

Aug 12 - Aug 15, 2025
CANADIAN JUNIOR BOYS
CHAMPIONSHIP
Bathurst, NB, Canada
Gowan Brae Golf and Country Club
ROYAL CANADIAN GOLF
ASSOCIATION
Phone: 905-849-9700
Fax: 905-845-7040
info@golfcanada.ca
www.golfcanada.ca

Aug 13 - Aug 16, 2025
CANADIAN JUNIOR GIRLS
CHAMPIONSHIP
Sainte-Marie, QC, Canada
Club de golf Sainte-Marie

ROYAL CANADIAN GOLF
ASSOCIATION
Phone: 905-849-9700
Fax: 905-845-7040
info@golfcanada.ca
www.golfcanada.ca

Aug 14 - Aug 17, 2025
ALBERTSONS BOISE OPEN
Boise, ID
Hillcrest Country Club
PGA KORN FERRY TOUR
Phone: 904-285-3700
Fax: 904-285-7913
www.pgatour.com

Aug 14 - Aug 17, 2025
LUCAS OIL NHRA NATIONALS
Brainerd, MN
Brainerd International Raceway
NATIONAL HOT ROD ASSOCIATION
Phone: 626-914-4761
Fax: 626-325-8752
nhra@nhra.com
www.nhra.com

Aug 14 - Aug 17, 2025
PORTLAND CLASSIC
Portland, OR
Columbia Edgewater Country Club
LPGA TOUR
Phone: 386-274-6200
Fax: 386-274-1099
www.lpga.com

Aug 14 - Aug 17, 2025
US WOMEN'S MATCH RACING
CHAMPIONSHIP
San Francisco, CA
St. Francis Yacht Club
US SAILING
Phone: 800-877-2451
info@ussailing.org
www.ussailing.org

Aug 15 - Aug 22, 2025
NATIONAL BLACK POWDER
CARTRIDGE RIFLE CHAMPIONSH IP
Friendship, IN
NATIONAL RIFLE ASSOCIATION -
COMPETITIVE SHOOTING DIVISION
Phone: 703-267-1465
competitions.nra.org

Aug 16 - Aug 17, 2025
MR AMERICA
Ecuador
INTERNATIONAL FEDERATION OF
BODY BUILDING & FITNESS
contact@ifbb.com
www.ifbb.com

Aug 16, 2025
PEORIA TT
Peoria, IL
Peoria Motorcycle Club
AMA PRO RACING
Phone: 386-492-1014
Fax: 386-274-2335
communications@amaproracing.com
www.amaproracing.com

Aug 16, 2025
UNADILLA NATIONAL
New Berlin, NY
Unadilla MX
AMA PRO RACING
Phone: 386-492-1014
Fax: 386-274-2335
communications@amaproracing.com
www.amaproracing.com

Aug 17, 2025
LAKE TAHOE SHARKFEST SWIM
Incline Village, NV
Sand Harbour State Park
ENVIRO-SPORTS
Phone: 415-868-1829
info@envirosports.com
envirosports.com

Aug 18 - Aug 23, 2025
ABIERTO GNP SEGUROS
Monterrey, Mexico
WTA
Phone: 727-895-5000
Fax: 727-894-1982
feedback@wtatennis.com
www.wtatennis.com

Aug 18 - Aug 24, 2025
THE ALLY CHALLENGE
Grand Blanc, MI
Warwick Hills Golf & Country Club
PGA CHAMPIONS TOUR
Phone: 904-285-3700
www.pgatour.com/pgatour-champions

Aug 18 - Aug 24, 2025
US DRESSAGE FESTIVAL OF
CHAMPIONS
Wayne, IL
HITS Chicago at Lamplight Equestrian
Center
US EQUESTRIAN FEDERATION
Phone: 859-258-2472
Fax: 859-231-6662
www.usef.org

Aug 19 - Aug 22, 2025
CANADIAN MEN'S MID-AMATEUR
CHAMPIONSHIP
North Vancouver, BC, Canada
Seymour Golf and Country Club
ROYAL CANADIAN GOLF
ASSOCIATION
Phone: 905-849-9700
Fax: 905-845-7040
info@golfcanada.ca
www.golfcanada.ca

Aug 20 - Aug 24, 2025
CPKC CANADIAN WOMEN'S OPEN
Mississauga, ON, Canada
Mississauga Golf & Country Club
LPGA TOUR
Phone: 386-274-6200
Fax: 386-274-1099
www.lpga.com

Aug 20 - Aug 24, 2025
ICF CANOE SPRINT WORLD
CHAMPIONSHIPS
Milan, Italy
INTERNATIONAL CANOE FEDERATION
International Ph: 41 (0)21 612 0290
info@canoeicf.com
www.canoeicf.com

Aug 20, 2025
IPSC NATIONALS
Marengo, OH
US PRACTICAL SHOOTING
ASSOCIATION
Phone: 360-855-2245
Fax: 360-855-0380
office@uspsa.org
www.uspsa.org

Aug 20 - Aug 24, 2025
THE TOUR CHAMPIONSHIP
Atlanta, GA

East Lake Golf Club
PGA TOUR
Phone: 904-285-3700
www.pgatour.com

Aug 21 - Aug 24, 2025
BASSMASTER ELITE SERIES -
MISSISSIPPI RIVER
La Crosse, MI
Mississippi River
BASS ANGLERS SPORTSMAN
SOCIETY
Phone: 877-227-7872
bassmaster@emailcustomerservice.com
www.bassmaster.com

Aug 21 - Aug 24, 2025
BETFRED BRITISH MASTERS
Sutton Coldfield, England
The Belfry
PGA EUROPEAN TOUR
International Ph: 44-0-1344-840400
International Fax: 44-0-1344-840500
www.rydercup.com

Aug 21 - Aug 24, 2025
ELITE TRACK NATIONAL
CHAMPIONSHIPS
Colorado Springs, CO
USA CYCLING
Phone: 719-434-4200
Fax: 719-434-4300
help@usacycling.org
www.usacycling.org

Aug 22 - Aug 24, 2025
X GAMES SACRAMENTO
Sacramento, CA
ESPN
xgames.espn.com/xgames

Aug 23, 2025
ANGEL ISLAND HALF MARATHON &
10K
Tiburon, CA
Angel Island State Park
ENVIRO-SPORTS
Phone: 415-868-1829
info@envirosports.com
envirosports.com

Aug 23, 2025
BUDDS CREEK NATIONAL
Mechanicsville, MD
Budds Creek Motocross Park
AMA PRO RACING
Phone: 386-492-1014
Fax: 386-274-2335
communications@amaproracing.com
www.amaproracing.com

Aug 23, 2025
CHICAGO SUPERSPRINT TRIATHLON
Chicago, IL
LIFE TIME FITNESS
www.eventsbylifetime.com

Aug 23, 2025
COKE ZERO SUGAR 400
Daytona Beach, FL
Daytona International Speedway
NASCAR CUP SERIES
www.nascar.com

Aug 23 - Aug 24, 2025
SNAP-ON MILWAUKEE MILE 250
West Allis, WI
Milwaukee Mile
NTT INDYCAR SERIES
Phone: 317-492-6526

indycar@indycar.com
www.indycar.com

Aug 23 - Aug 28, 2025
US SENIOR AMATEUR
San Antonio, TX
Oak Hills Country Club
U.S. GOLF ASSOCIATION
Phone: 908-234-2300
Fax: 908-234-9687
www.usga.org

Aug 24 - Sept 7, 2025
US OPEN
New York, NY
USTA Billie Jean King National Tennis
Center
UNITED STATES TENNIS
ASSOCIATION
Phone: 914-696-7000
www.usta.com

Aug 25 - Sept 7, 2025
2025 US OPEN TENNIS
CHAMPIONSHIPS
Queens, NY
USTA Billie Jean King National Tennis
Center
WTA
Phone: 727-895-5000
Fax: 727-894-1982
feedback@wtatennis.com
www.wtatennis.com

Aug 27 - Sept 4, 2025
LEXUS WSL FINALS FIJI
Cloudbreak, Fiji
WORLD SURF LEAGUE
International Ph: +1-310-450-1212
www.worldsurfleague.com

Aug 27 - Sept 1, 2025
NHRA U.S. NATIONALS
Indianapolis, IN
Lucas Oil Raceway
NATIONAL HOT ROD ASSOCIATION
Phone: 626-914-4761
Fax: 626-325-8752
nhra@nhra.com
www.nhra.com

Aug 28 - Aug 31, 2025
OMEGA EUROPEAN MASTERS
Crans Montana, Switzerland
Cras-sur-Sierre Golf Club
PGA EUROPEAN TOUR
International Ph: 44-0-1344-840400
International Fax: 44-0-1344-840500
www.rydercup.com

Aug 30 - Aug 31, 2025
CANADA CUP DHI
Mount Washington, BC, Canada
CANADIAN CYCLING ASSOCIATION
Phone: 613-248-1353
Fax: 613-248-9311
general@cyclingcanada.ca
www.cyclingcanada.ca

Aug 30 - Aug 31, 2025
MUSIC CITY GRAND PRIX
Nashville, TN
Streets of Nashville
NTT INDYCAR SERIES
Phone: 317-492-6526
indycar@indycar.com
www.indycar.com

Aug 30, 2025
POCATELLO MARATHON
Pocatello, ID

POCATELLO MARATHON
Phone: 208-233-4754
pocatellorun@gmail.com
www.pocatellomarathon.com

Aug 30 - Aug 31, 2025
SPRINGFIELD MILE I & II
Springfield, IL
Illinois State Fairgrounds
AMA PRO RACING
Phone: 386-492-1014
Fax: 386-274-2335
communications@amaproracing.com
www.amaproracing.com

Aug 31, 2025
SOUTHERN 500
Darlington, SC
Darlington Raceway
NASCAR CUP SERIES
www.nascar.com

Sept TBA, 2025
ARNOLD CLASSIC EUROPE
Sevilla, Spain
INTERNATIONAL FEDERATION OF
BODY BUILDING & FITNESS
contact@ifbb.com
www.ifbb.com

Sept TBA, 2025
PREFONTAINE CLASSIC
TBA
OREGON TRACK CLUB
Phone: 541-343-7247
meetingdirector@preclassic.com
www.runnerspace.com/PreClassic

Sept TBA, 2025
USHA NATIONAL THREE-WALL
CHAMPIONSHIPS
TBA
UNITED STATES HANDBALL
ASSOCIATION
Phone: 520-795-0434
Fax: 520-795-0465
handball@ushandball.org
www.ushandball.org

Sept 1, 2025
GOLDEN GATE SHARKFEST SWIM
Sausalito, CA
Under the Golden Gate Bridge
ENVIRO-SPORTS
Phone: 415-868-1829
info@envirosports.com
envirosports.com

Sept 1 - Sept 7, 2025
NORWOOD HILLS COUNTRY CLUB
St. Louis, MO
Norwood Hills Country Club
PGA CHAMPIONS TOUR
Phone: 904-285-3700
www.pgatour.com/pgatour-champions

Sept 4 - Sept 7, 2025
HORIZON IRISH OPEN
Kildare, Ireland
The K Club
PGA EUROPEAN TOUR
International Ph: 44-0-1344-840400
International Fax: 44-0-1344-840500
www.rydercup.com

Sept 4 - Sept 7, 2025
ICF CANOE MARATHON WORLD
CHAMPIONSHIP
Gyor, Hungary
INTERNATIONAL CANOE FEDERATION
International Ph: 41 (0)21 612 0290

info@canoeicf.com
www.canoeicf.com

Spet 4 - Sept 5, 2025
MEN'S SUPER SP
Oklahoma City, OK
USA SOFTBALL
Phone: 405-424-5266
Fax: 405-424-3855
rcress@softball.org
www.usasoftball.com

Sept 4 - Sept 6, 2025
WALLEYE TOUR CHAMPIONSHIP
Marinette, WI
Bay of Green Bay
NATIONAL WALLEYE TOUR
Phone: 612-424-0708
Fax: 866-727-2809
outdoorteamworks.com/trail/nwt

Sept 5 - Sept 7, 2025
NORTH CAROLINA OPEN MEN'S &
LADIES' DOUBLES
Hendersonville, NC
NATIONAL SHUFFLEBOARD
ASSOCIATION
www.national-shuffleboard-association.us

Sept 5 - Sept 7, 2025
WOMEN'S OPEN SP
Oklahoma City, OK
USA SOFTBALL
Phone: 405-424-5266
Fax: 405-424-3855
rcress@softball.org
www.usasoftball.com

Sept 6, 2025
AMA PRO HILLCLIMB KANSAS
NATIONAL
Wathena, KS
Over The Hill Racing
AMA PRO RACING
Phone: 386-492-1014
Fax: 386-274-2335
communications@amaproracing.com
www.amaproracing.com

Sept 7, 2025
ENJOY ILLINOIS 300
Madison, IL
World Wide Technology Raceway
NASCAR CAMPING WORLD TRUCK
SERIES
Phone: 800-630-0535
www.nascar.com

Sept 8 - Sept 14, 2025
JASMIN OPEN TUNISIA
Monastir, Tunisia
WTA
Phone: 727-895-5000
Fax: 727-894-1982
feedback@wtatennis.com
www.wtatennis.com

Sept 8 - Sept 10, 2025
NORTH CAROLINA OPEN MEN'S &
LADIES' SINGLES
Hendersonville, NC
NATIONAL SHUFFLEBOARD
ASSOCIATION
www.national-shuffleboard-association.us

Sept 8 - Sept 14, 2025
SANFORD INTERNATIONAL
Sioux Falls, SD
Minnehaha Country Club

PGA CHAMPIONS TOUR
Phone: 904-285-3700
www.pgatour.com/pgatour-champions

Sept 9 - Sept 12, 2025
CANADIAN MEN'S SENIOR
CHAMPIONSHIP
New Minas, NS, Canada
KenWo Golf Club
ROYAL CANADIAN GOLF
ASSOCIATION
Phone: 905-849-9700
Fax: 905-845-7040
info@golfcanada.ca
www.golfcanada.ca

Sept 10 - Sept 13, 2025
US CHAMPIONSHIP OF CHAMPIONS
Dartmouth, MA
New Bedford Yacht Club
US SAILING
Phone: 800-877-2451
info@ussailing.org
www.ussailing.org

Sept 11 - Sept 14, 2025
BMW PGA CHAMPIONSHIP
Surrey, England
Wentworth Club
PGA EUROPEAN TOUR
International Ph: 44-0-1344-840400
International Fax: 44-0-1344-840500
www.rydercup.com

Sept 11 - Sept 14, 2025
COLLEGIATE TRACK NATIONAL
CHAMPIONSHIPS
Indianapolis, IN
USA CYCLING
Phone: 719-434-4200
Fax: 719-434-4300
help@usacycling.org
www.usacycling.org

Sept 11 - Sept 14, 2025
LONE STAR OPEN
Garland, TX
NATIONAL X BALL LEAGUE
info@nxlpaintball.com
nxlpaintball.com

Sept 11 - Sept 14, 2025
NHRA READING NATIONALS
Mohnton, PA
Maple Grove Raceway
NATIONAL HOT ROD ASSOCIATION
Phone: 626-914-4761
Fax: 626-325-8752
nhra@nhra.com
www.nhra.com

Sept 11 - Sept 13, 2025
NORTH CAROLINA OPEN MIXED
DOUBLES
Hendersonville, NC
NATIONAL SHUFFLEBOARD
ASSOCIATION
www.national-shuffleboard-association.us

Sept 11 - Sept 14, 2025
SIMMONS BANK OPEN FOR THE
SNEDEKER FOUNDATION
College Grove, TN
The Grove
PGA KORN FERRY TOUR
Phone: 904-285-3700
Fax: 904-285-7913
www.pgatour.com

Sept 13 - Sept 14, 2025
AMA PRO HILLCLIMB IDAHO NITRO
NATIONALS I & II
Payette, ID
Idaho Battle of the Bluffs
AMA PRO RACING
Phone: 386-492-1014
Fax: 386-274-2335
communications@amaproracing.com
www.amaproracing.com

Sept 13, 2025
BASS PRO SHOPS NRA NIGHT RACE
Bristol, TN
Bristol Motor Speedway
NASCAR CUP SERIES
www.nascar.com

Sept 13, 2025
LAKE OZARK ST
Eldon, MO
Lake Ozark Speedway
AMA PRO RACING
Phone: 386-492-1014
Fax: 386-274-2335
communications@amaproracing.com
www.amaproracing.com

Sept 13 - Sept 18, 2025
US MID-AMATEUR
Scottsdale, AZ
Troon Country Club
U.S. GOLF ASSOCIATION
Phone: 908-234-2300
Fax: 908-234-9687
www.usga.org

Sept 13 - Sept 18, 2025
US SENIOR WOMEN'S AMATEUR
Hot Springs, VA
The Omni Homestead Resort
U.S. GOLF ASSOCIATION
Phone: 908-234-2300
Fax: 908-234-9687
www.usga.org

Sept 15 - Sept 21, 2025
KOREA OPEN
Seoul, Korea
WTA
Phone: 727-895-5000
Fax: 727-894-1982
feedback@wtatennis.com
www.wtatennis.com

Sept 15 - Sept 21, 2025
NATIONWIDE CHILDREN'S HOSPITAL
CHAMPIONSHIP
Columbus, OH
The OSU Golf Club
PGA KORN FERRY TOUR
Phone: 904-285-3700
Fax: 904-285-7913
www.pgatour.com

Sept 15 - Sept 21, 2025
WALMART NW ARKANSAS
CHAMPIONSHIP
Rogers, AR
Pinnacle Country Club
LPGA TOUR
Phone: 386-274-6200
Fax: 386-274-1099
www.lpga.com

Sept 18 - Sept 20, 2025
AIR FORCE MARATHON
Dayton, OH
Wright-Patterson AFB

USAF MARATHON
Phone: 800-467-1823
Fax: 937-656-1000
usaf.marathon@us.af.mil
www.usafmarathon.com

Sept 18 - Sept 21, 2025
OPEN DE FRANCE
Saint-Nom-la-BretŠche, France
Golf de Saint-Nom-la-BretŠche
PGA EUROPEAN TOUR
International Ph: 44-0-1344-840400
International Fax: 44-0-1344-840500
www.rydercup.com

Sept 19 - Sept 21, 2025
COMMUNITY FIRST FOX CITIES
MARATHON
Appleton, WI
COMMUNITY FIRST FOX CITIES
MARATHON
Phone: 877-230-7223
Fax: 920-830-0921
info@foxcitiesmarathon.org
www.foxcitiesmarathon.org

Sept 19 - Sept 21, 2025
DIAMOND CUP LUXEMBOURG
Luxembourg
INTERNATIONAL FEDERATION OF
BODY BUILDING & FITNESS
contact@ifbb.com
www.ifbb.com

Sept 19 - Sept 21, 2025
OUTDOOR TARGET NATIONAL
CHAMPIONSHIPS
Yankton, SD
NATIONAL FIELD ARCHERY
ASSOCIATION
Phone: 605-260-9279
info@nfaausa.com
www.nfaausa.com

Sept 19 - Sept 21, 2025
PURE INSURANCE CHAMPIONSHIP
Monterey Peninsula, CA
Pebble Beach Golf Links
PGA CHAMPIONS TOUR
Phone: 904-285-3700
www.pgatour.com/pgatour-champions

Sept 20, 2025
AMA PRO HILLCLIMB WHITE ROSE
NATIONAL II
Spring Grove, PA
White Rose Motorcycle Club
AMA PRO RACING
Phone: 386-492-1014
Fax: 386-274-2335
communications@amaproracing.com
www.amaproracing.com

Sept 20 - Sept 27, 2025
MELGES 24 WORLD CHAMPIONSHIP
Trieste, Italy
WORLD SAILING
office@sailing.org
www.sailing.org

Sept 20, 2025
TOP OF UTAH MARATHON
Logan, UT
LOGAN CITY MARATHON
www.logandowntown.org

Sept 20 - Sept 21, 2025
US OPEN WATER SKI RACING
NATIONAL CHAMPIONSHIPS
Havasu Springs, AZ

NATIONAL WATER SKI RACING
ASSOCIATION
www.nwsra.net

Sept 21, 2025
PIKES PEAK MARATHON
Colorado Springs, CO
PIKES PEAK MARATHON
Phone: 719-473-2625
info@pikespeakmarathon.org
www.pikespeakmarathon.org

Sept 21, 2025
SAN DIEGO SHARKFEST SWIM
San Diego, CA
San Diego Harbor
ENVIRO-SPORTS
Phone: 415-868-1829
info@envirosports.com
envirosports.com

Sept 22 - Sept 22, 2025
2025 RYDER CUP
Farmingdale, NY
Bethpage Black
PGA EUROPEAN TOUR
International Ph: 44-0-1344-840400
International Fax: 44-0-1344-840500
www.rydercup.com

Sept 26 - Sept 28, 2025
AAA NHRA MIDWEST NATIONALS
Madison, IL
World Wide Technology Raceway
NATIONAL HOT ROD ASSOCIATION
Phone: 626-914-4761
Fax: 626-325-8752
nhra@nhra.com
www.nhra.com

Sept 26 - Sept 28, 2025
DIAMOND CUP PRAGUE
Prague, Czech Republic
INTERNATIONAL FEDERATION OF
BODY BUILDING & FITNESS
contact@ifbb.com
www.ifbb.com

Sept 26 - Oct 5, 2025
SYLT WORLD CUP
Westerland, Sylt, Germany
INTERNATIONAL WINDSURFING TOUR
internationalwindsurfingtour.com

Sept 26 - Sept 28, 2025
US ADULT SAILING CHAMPIONSHIP
Park City, UT
Park City Sailing Association
US SAILING
Phone: 800-877-2451
info@ussailing.org
www.ussailing.org

Sept 26 - Sept 28, 2025
US PARA SAILING CHAMPIONSHIP
Coronado, CA
Coronado Yacht Club
US SAILING
Phone: 800-877-2451
info@ussailing.org
www.ussailing.org

Sept 26 - Sept 28, 2025
US TEAM RACING CHAMPIONSHIP
Larchmond, NY
Larchmond Yacht Club
US SAILING
Phone: 800-877-2451
info@ussailing.org
www.ussailing.org

Sept 27, 2025
BIG SUR TRAIL MARATHON, HALF
MARATHON & 5 MILE
Big Sur, CA
Andrew Molera State Park
ENVIRO-SPORTS
Phone: 415-868-1829
info@envirosports.com
envirosports.com

Sept 27, 2025
FIRSTENERGY AKRON MARATHON,
HALF MARATHON & TEAM RELAY
Akron, OH
ROAD RUNNER AKRON MARATHON
Phone: 330-434-2786
Fax: 330-434-0738
info@akronmarathon.org
www.akronmarathon.org

Sept 28, 2025
AMA PRO HILLCLIMB
FREEMANSBURG NATIONAL II
Freemansburg, PA
Bushkill Valley Motorcycle Club
AMA PRO RACING
Phone: 386-492-1014
Fax: 386-274-2335
communications@amaproracing.com
www.amaproracing.com

Sept 28, 2025
BOULDERTHON
Boulder, CO
RUN BOULDER EVENTS
Phone: 303-517-7046
www.runboulderevents.com

Sept 28, 2025
HOLLYWOOD CASINO 400
Kansas City, KS
Kansas Speedway
NASCAR CUP SERIES
www.nascar.com

Sept 28, 2025
OMAHA MARATHON
Omaha, NE
OMAHA MARATHON
Phone: 845-247-7275
info@hitsendurance.com
www.omahamarathon.com

Sept 29 - Oct 4, 2025
LOTTE CHAMPIONSHIP
Ewa Beach, Oahu, HI
Hoakalei Country Club
LPGA TOUR
Phone: 386-274-6200
Fax: 386-274-1099
www.lpga.com

Sept 30 - Oct 4, 2025
NRA'S WORLD SHOOTING
CHAMPIONSHIP (WSC)
Edinburgh, IN
Camp Atterbury
NATIONAL RIFLE ASSOCIATION -
COMPETITIVE SHOOTING DIVISION
Phone: 703-267-1465
competitions.nra.org

Oct TBA, 2025
HEARTLAND 100 SPIRIT OF THE
PRAIRIE RACE
Cassoday, KS
TBA
KANSAS ULTRARUNNERS' SOCIETY
www.ksultrarunners.org

Oct TBA, 2025
USA WATER POLO WOMEN'S
SENIOR NATIONALS
TBA
USA WATER POLO
Phone: 714-500-5445
Fax: 714-960-2431
www.usawaterpolo.org

Oct 1 - Oct 12, 2025
ATP TOUR MASTERS 1000 -
SHANGHAI ROLEX MASTERS
Shanghai, China
ATP TOUR MASTERS 1000
www.atptour.com

Oct 1 - Oct 4, 2025
STAR VINTAGE COLD CUP
Gull Lake, MN
Gull Lake Yacht Club
INTERNATIONAL STAR CLASS YACHT
ASSOCIATION
Phone: 619-222-0252
Fax: 619-222-0528
office@starclass.org
www.starclass.org

Oct 1 - Oct 11, 2025
WORLD AMATEUR TEAM
CHAMPIONSHIPS
Singapore
Tanah Merah Country Club
INTERNATIONAL GOLF FEDERATION
International Ph: +41 21 623 12 12
International Fax: +41 +41 216 01 64
info@lgfmail.org
www.igfgolf.org

Oct 3 - Oct 5, 2025
US OFFSHORE CHAMPIONSHIP
Annapolis, MD
US SAILING
Phone: 800-877-2451
info@ussailing.org
www.ussailing.org

Oct 4 - Oct 5, 2025
JETBLUE LONG BEACH MARATHON
& HALF MARATHON
Long Beach, CA
MOTIV RUNNING
lbinfo@motivsports.com
www.motivrunning.com

Oct 4 - Oct 5, 2025
MILWAUKEE LAKEFRONT
MARATHON
Milwaukee, WI
BADGERLAND STRIDERS
Phone: 414-688-7561
milwaukeelakefrontmarathon@gmail.com
www.milwaukeelakefrontmarathon.org

Oct 4, 2025
TOWPATH MARATHON
Boston, OH
Cuyahoga Valley National Park
OHIO CANAL CORRIDOR
Phone: 216-520-1825
Fax: 216-520-1833
www.towpathtrilogy.com

Oct 4 - Oct 9, 2025
US WOMEN'S MID-AMATEUR
Pebble Beach, CA
Monterey Peninsula Country Club
U.S. GOLF ASSOCIATION
Phone: 908-234-2300
Fax: 908-234-9687
www.usga.org

Oct 5, 2025
BANK OF AMERICA ROVAL 400
Concord, NC
Charlotte Motor Speedway
NASCAR CUP SERIES
www.nascar.com

Oct 5 - Oct 10, 2025
CYCLE NORTH CAROLINA
MOUNTAINS TO COAST
Lake Lure to Fort Fisher, NC
NORTH CAROLINA AMATEUR SPORTS
Phone: 919-361-1133
Fax: 919-361-2559
ncas@ncsports.org
www.ncsports.org

Oct 5, 2025
MAINE MARATHON
Portland, ME
THE MAINE MARATHON
Phone: 207-749-9160
racedirector@mainemarathon.com
www.mainemarathon.com

Oct 5, 2025
ST. GEORGE MARATHON
St. George, UT
ST. GEORGE MARATHON
Phone: 435-627-4500
Fax: 435-627-4509
marathon@sgcity.org
www.stgeorgemarathon.com

Oct 6 - Oct 12, 2025
KORN FERRY TOUR CHAMPIONSHIP
French Lick, IN
Pete Dye Course at French Lick Resort
PGA KORN FERRY TOUR
Phone: 904-285-3700
Fax: 904-285-7913
www.pgatour.com

Oct 6 - Oct 12, 2025
SAS CHAMPIONSHIP
Cary, NC
Prestonwood Country Club
PGA CHAMPIONS TOUR
Phone: 904-285-3700
www.pgatour.com/pgatour-champions

Oct 9 - Oct 12, 2025
AAA TEXAS NHRA FALL NATIONALS
Ennis, TX
Texas Motorplex
NATIONAL HOT ROD ASSOCIATION
Phone: 626-914-4761
Fax: 626-325-8752
nhra@nhra.com
www.nhra.com

Oct 9 - Oct 12, 2025
COLLEGIATE MOUNTAIN BIKE
NATIONAL CHAMPIONSHIPS
Grand Junction, CO
USA CYCLING
Phone: 719-434-4200
Fax: 719-434-4300
help@usacycling.org
www.usacycling.org

Oct 9 - Oct 12, 2025
OPEN DE ESPANA
Madrid, Spain
Club de Campo Villa de Madrid
PGA EUROPEAN TOUR
International Ph: 44-0-1344-840400
International Fax: 44-0-1344-840500
www.rydercup.com

Oct 9 - Oct 12, 2025
US MATCH RACING CHAMPIONSHIP
Chicago, IL
Chicago Yacht Club
US SAILING
Phone: 800-877-2451
info@ussailing.org
www.ussailing.org

Oct 10, 2025
CANADIAN CHAMPIONSHIP
TBA, Canada
CANADIAN SOCCER ASSOCIATION
Phone: 613-237-7678
Fax: 613-237-1516
info@soccercan.ca
www.canadasoccer.com

Oct 11 - Oct 12, 2025
ADULT CHAMPIONSHIPS
Denver, CO
South Suburban Sports Complex
ICE SKATING INSTITUTE
Phone: 972-735-8800
Fax: 972-735-8815
events@skateisi.org
www.skateisi.org

Oct 11 - Oct 12, 2025
AMA PRO HILLCLIMB NATIONAL
CHAMPIONSHIP
Oregonia, OH
Dayton Motorcycle Club
AMA PRO RACING
Phone: 386-492-1014
Fax: 386-274-2335
communications@amaproracing.com
www.amaproracing.com

Oct 11 - Oct 12, 2025
CAPE COD MARATHON
Falmouth, MA
CAPE COD MARATHON
Phone: 508-540-6959
Fax: 508-548-0617
info@capecodmarathon.com
www.capecodmarathon.com

Oct 11, 2025
CITY OF TREES MARATHON
Boise, ID
Park Center Park
CITY OF TREES RACING
ASSOCIATION
www.cityoftreesmarathon.org

Oct 11, 2025
EVERSOURCE HARTFORD
MARATHON
Hartford, CT
Bushnell Park
HARTFORD MARATHON FOUNDATION
Phone: 860-652-8866
Fax: 860-652-8145
info@hartfordmarathon.com
www.hartfordmarathon.com

Oct 11 - Oct 13, 2025
US ORIENTEERING NATIONALS
Medfield, MA
Rocky Woods Reservation
US ORIENTEERING
Phone: 215-482-9479
contact@orienteeringusa.org
orienteeringusa.org

Oct 11, 2025
WHISKEY ROW MARATHON
Prescott, AZ

PRESCOTT YMCA
Phone: 928-445-7221
Fax: 928-445-5135
wrm@prescottymca.org
whiskeyrowmarathon.com

Oct 12, 2025
BANK OF AMERICA CHICAGO
MARATHON
Chicago, IL
BANK OF AMERICA CHICAGO
MARATHON
Phone: 312-904-9800
Fax: 312-904-6521
office@chicagomarathon.com
www.chicagomarathon.com

Oct 12, 2025
SOUTH POINT 400
Las Vegas, NV
Las Vegas Motor Speedway
NASCAR CUP SERIES
www.nascar.com

Oct 12, 2025
STEAMTOWN MARATHON
Scranton, PA
STEAMTOWN MARATHON
Phone: 570-342-0427
Fax: 570-342-0422
racecommittee@hotmail.com
www.steamtownmarathon.com

Oct 13 - Oct 24, 2025
ALOHA CLASSIC
Ho'okipa, HI
INTERNATIONAL WINDSURFING TOUR
internationalwindsurfingtour.com

Oct 13 - Oct 19, 2025
DOMINION ENERGY CHARITY
CLASSIC
Richmond, VA
The Country Club of Virginia
PGA CHAMPIONS TOUR
Phone: 904-285-3700
www.pgatour.com/pgatour-champions

Oct 13, 2025
NATIONAL CHAMPIONSHIPS U-15
CUP
Charlottetown, PE, Canada
CANADIAN SOCCER ASSOCIATION
Phone: 613-237-7678
Fax: 613-237-1516
info@soccercan.ca
www.canadasoccer.com

Oct 13, 2025
NATIONAL CHAMPIONSHIPS U-17
CUP
Kamloops, BC, Canada
CANADIAN SOCCER ASSOCIATION
Phone: 613-237-7678
Fax: 613-237-1516
info@soccercan.ca
www.canadasoccer.com

Oct 15, 2025
WORLD TRIATHLON CHAMPIONSHIP
FINALS
Wollongong, Australia
WORLD TRIATHLON
International Ph: +41 21 614 60 30
International Fax: +41 21 614 60 39
www.triathlon.org

Oct 16 - Oct 19, 2025
BMW LADIES CHAMPIONSHIP
TBA, South Korea

LPGA TOUR
Phone: 386-274-6200
Fax: 386-274-1099
www.lpga.com

Oct 17 - Oct 19, 2025
ICF CANOE OCEAN RACING WORLD
CHAMPIONSHIPS
Durban, South Africa
INTERNATIONAL CANOE FEDERATION
International Ph: 41 (0)21 612 0290
info@canoeicf.com
www.canoeicf.com

Oct 18, 2025
BALTIMORE RUNNING FESTIVAL
Baltimore, MD
BALTIMORE MARATHON
Phone: 410-605-9381
Fax: 410-605-9389
customerservice@corrigansports.com
www.thebaltimoremarathon.com

Oct 18, 2025
BROOKINGS MARATHON
Brookings, SD
BROOKINGS MARATHON
run@brookingsmarathon.com
www.brookingsmarathon.com

Oct 18 - Oct 19, 2025
COLUMBUS MARATHON
Columbus, OH
Downtown Columbus
COLUMBUS MARATHON
Phone: 614-421-7866
Fax: 614-263-3518
info@columbusmarathon.com
www.columbusmarathon.com

Oct 19, 2025
CHAMPLAIN ISLANDS MARATHON &
HALF MARATHON
South Hero, VT
Folsom Elementary School
GREEN MOUNTAIN ATHLETIC
ASSOCIATION
info@gmaa.run
gmaa.run

Oct 19, 2025
DES MOINES MARATHON
Des Moines, IA
DES MOINES MARATHON
HEADQUARTERS
Phone: 515-288-2692
Fax: 515-255-9051
info@desmoinesmarathon.com
www.desmoinesmarathon.com

Oct 19, 2025
METRO HEALTH GRAND RAPIDS
MARATHON
Grand Rapids, MI
GRAND RAPIDS MARATHON
Phone: 616-293-3145
rungrmarathon@gmail.com
www.grandrapidsmarathon.com

Oct 19, 2025
MOUNT DESERT ISLAND MARATHON
& HALF MARATHON
Bar Harbor, ME
CROW ATHLETICS
www.crowathletics.com

Oct 20, 2025
FALL CLASSIC HALF MARATHON &
10K
Charlottesville, VA

BAD TO THE BONE
Phone: 434-218-0402
francesca@badtothebone.biz
badtothebone.biz

Oct 20 - Oct 26, 2025
TORAY PAN PACIFIC OPEN
Tokyo, Japan
WTA
Phone: 727-895-5000
Fax: 727-894-1982
feedback@wtatennis.com
www.wtatennis.com

Oct 22, 2025
RACE GUN NATIONALS
Hurricane, UT
US PRACTICAL SHOOTING
ASSOCIATION
Phone: 360-855-2245
Fax: 360-855-0380
office@uspsa.org
www.uspsa.org

Oct 25, 2025
MARATHON 2 MARATHON
Marathon, TX
MARATHON TO MARATHON
www.marathon2marathon.com

Oct 25, 2025
NAPA FALL WINE COUNTRY
MARATHON, HALF MARATHON & 10K
Calistoga, CA
Bothe-Napa State Park
ENVIRO-SPORTS
Phone: 415-868-1829
info@envirosports.com
envirosports.com

Oct 27 - Nov 2, 2025
ATP TOUR MASTERS 1000 - PARIS
ROLEX
Paris, France
ATP TOUR MASTERS 1000
www.atptour.com

Oct 30 - Nov 2, 2025
NHRA NEVADA NATIONALS
Las Vegas, NV
The Strip at Las Vegas Motor Speedway
NATIONAL HOT ROD ASSOCIATION
Phone: 626-914-4761
Fax: 626-325-8752
nhra@nhra.com
www.nhra.com

Oct 31 - Nov 2, 2025
USA BMX FALL NATIONALS
Phoenix, AZ
USA BMX
Phone: 480-961-1903
Fax: 480-961-1842
info@usabmx.com
www.usabmx.com

Nov TBA, 2025
CABLE WAKEBOARD WORLD
CHAMPIONSHIPS
TBA
INTERNATIONAL WATERSKI &
WAKEBOARD FEDERATION
info@iwwfed.com
https://iwwf.sport

Nov TBA, 2025
DAVIS CUP FINAL
INTERNATIONAL TENNIS FEDERATION
International Ph: +44 (0)20 88786464
International Fax: +44 (0)20 88787799
communications@itftennis.com
www.itftennis.com

Nov TBA, 2025
MALIBU INTERNATIONAL HALF
MARATHON & 5K
Malibu, CA
MALIBU INTERNATIONAL MARATHON
Phone: 310-745-8231
www.runmalibu.com

Nov TBA, 2025
TURKEY TROT MIAMI
Miami, FL
LIFE TIME FITNESS
www.eventsbylifetime.com

Nov TBA, 2025
ULTRA RACE OF CHAMPIONS
Blue Ridge Mouuntains, VA
BAD TO THE BONE
Phone: 434-218-0402
francesca@badtothebone.biz
badtothebone.biz

Nov 2, 2025
NASCAR CUP SERIES
CHAMPIONSHIP
Avondale, AZ
Phoenix Raceway
NASCAR CUP SERIES
www.nascar.com

Nov 2, 2025
TCS NEW YORK CITY MARATHON
New York, NY
NEW YORK ROAD RUNNERS
Phone: 855-569-6977
marathonmailer@nyrr.org
www.tcsnycmarathon.org

Nov 3 - Nov 7, 20254
US MULTIHULL CHAMPIONSHIP
Corpus Christi, TX
Corpus Christi Yacht Club
US SAILING
Phone: 800-877-2451
info@ussailing.org
www.ussailing.org

Nov 6 - Nov 9, 2025
ABU DHABI HSBC CHAMPIONSHIP
United Arab Emirates
Yas Links
PGA EUROPEAN TOUR
International Ph: 44-0-1344-840400
International Fax: 44-0-1344-840500
www.rydercup.com

Nov 6 - Nov 9, 2025
TOTO JAPAN CLASSIC
Shiga, Japan
Seta Golf Course
LPGA TOUR
Phone: 386-274-6200
Fax: 386-274-1099
www.lpga.com

Nov 6 - Nov 9, 2025
WORLD WIDE TECHNOLOGY
CHAMPIONSHIP
Mexico
El Cardonal at Diamante
PGA TOUR
Phone: 904-285-3700
www.pgatour.com

Nov 8, 2025
INDIANAPOLIS MARATHON
Indianapolis, IN
INDIANAPOLIS MARATHON CORP
Phone: 317-454-8519

nfo@beyondmonumental.org
www.monumentalmarathon.com

Nov 9, 2025
ATHENS MARATHON
Athens, Greece
ATHENS MARATHON COMMITTEE
Phone: 740-594-3825
Fax: 740-594-2525
athensohiomarathon@gmail.com
www.athensmarathon.com

Nov 9, 2025
MADISON MARATHON FULL & HALF
Madison, WI
MADISON FESTIVALS
Phone: 608-276-9797
Fax: 608-226-9550
events@madisonfestivals.com
www.madisonfestivals.com

Nov 9, 2025
SANTA CLARITA MARATHON
Santa Clarita, CA
SANTA CLARITA MARATHON
Phone: 805-258-3779
bill@elitesportsca.com
santaclaritamarathon.org

Nov 10 - Nov 16, 2025
CHARLES SCHWAB CUP
CHAMPIONSHIP
Phoenix, AZ
Phoenix Country Club
PGA CHAMPIONS TOUR
Phone: 904-285-3700
www.pgatour.com/pgatour-champions

Nov 11 - Nov 23, 2025
NCAA DIVISION I MEN'S/WOMEN'S
TENNIS FINALS
Orlando, FL
USTA National Campus (Collegiate
Center)
NATIONAL COLLEGIATE ATHLETIC
ASSOCIATION
Phone: 317-917-6222
Fax: 317-917-6888
www.ncaa.org

Nov 13 - Nov 16, 2025
DP WORLD TOUR CHAMPIONSHIP
DUBAI
Dubai, United Arab Emirates
Jumeirah Golf Estates
PGA EUROPEAN TOUR
International Ph: 44-0-1344-840400
International Fax: 44-0-1344-840500
www.rydercup.com

Nov 13 - Nov 16, 2025
IN-N-OUT BURGER NHRA FINALS
Pomona, CA
In-N-Out Burger Pomona Dragstrip
NATIONAL HOT ROD ASSOCIATION
Phone: 626-914-4761
Fax: 626-325-8752
nhra@nhra.com
www.nhra.com

Nov 15 - Nov 16, 2025
ISI CALIFORNIA CLASSIC
Vacaville, CA
Vacaville Ice Sports
ICE SKATING INSTITUTE
Phone: 972-735-8800
Fax: 972-735-8815
events@skateisi.org
www.skateisi.org

Nov 15, 2025
RICHMOND MARATHON
Richmond, VA
RICHMOND MARATHON
Phone: 804-285-9495
Fax: 804-285-3132
marathon@sportsbackers.org
www.richmondmarathon.com

Nov 17 - Nov 23, 2025
RSM CLASSIC
Sea Island, GA
Sea Island Golf Club
PGA TOUR
Phone: 904-285-3700
www.pgatour.com

Nov 20 - Nov 23, 2025
CME GROUP TOUR CHAMPIONSHIP
Naples, FL
Tiburon Golf Club
LPGA TOUR
Phone: 386-274-6200
Fax: 386-274-1099
www.lpga.com

Nov 21 - Nov 23, 2025
PHILADELPHIA MARATHON
Philadelphia, PA
PHILADELPHIA MARATHON
Phone: 215-683-2122
Fax: 215-683-2099
info@philadelphiamarathon.com
philadelphiamarathon.com

Nov 22, 2025
NCAA DIVISION I MEN'S CROSS
COUNTRY FINALS
Columbia, MO
Gans Creek Cross Country
NATIONAL COLLEGIATE ATHLETIC
ASSOCIATION
Phone: 317-917-6222
Fax: 317-917-6888
www.ncaa.org

Nov 22, 2025
NCAA DIVISION II MEN'S/WOMEN'S
CROSS COUNTRY FIN ALS
Kenosha, WI
Wayne E Danehl National Cross
Country Course
NATIONAL COLLEGIATE ATHLETIC
ASSOCIATION
Phone: 317-917-6222
Fax: 317-917-6888
www.ncaa.org

Nov 22, 2025
NCAA DIVISION III MEN'S/WOMEN'S
CROSS COUNTRY FI NALS
Spartanburg, Sc
Roger Milliken Center
NATIONAL COLLEGIATE ATHLETIC
ASSOCIATION
Phone: 317-917-6222
Fax: 317-917-6888
www.ncaa.org

Nov 27 - Nov 30, 2025
USA BMX GRANDS RACE OF
CHAMPIONS
Tulsa, OK
USA BMX
Phone: 480-961-1903
Fax: 480-961-1842
info@usabmx.com
www.usabmx.com

Nov 30, 2025
SEATTLE MARATHON & HALF
MARATHON
Seattle, WA
Seattle Center
SEATTLE MARATHON ASSOCIATION
Phone: 206-729-3660
info@seattlemarathon.org
www.seattlemarathon.org

Dec TBA, 2025
AMATEUR MEN'S & LADIES'
NON-WALKING SINGLES
TBA
NATIONAL SHUFFLEBOARD
ASSOCIATION
www.national-shuffleboard-association.us

Dec TBA, 2025
BRISBANE INTERNATIONAL
Brisbane, Australia
WTA
Phone: 727-895-5000
Fax: 727-894-1982
feedback@wtatennis.com
www.wtatennis.com

Dec TBA, 2025
EASYPOST HAWAII BOWL
Honolulu, HI
Aloha Stadium
EASYPOST HAWAII BOWL
www.thehawaiibowl.com

Dec TBA, 2025
FAMOUS IDAHO POTATO BOWL
TBA
FAMOUS IDAHO POTATO BOWL
Phone: 208-424-1011
Fax: 208-424-1121
www.famousidahopotatobowl.com

Dec TBA, 2025
INDEPENDENCE BOWL
TBA
INDEPENDENCE BOWL FOUNDATION
Phone: 318-221-0712
Fax: 318-221-7366
independencebowl.org

Dec TBA, 2025
LENDING TREE BOWL
Mobile, AL
Ladd-Peebles Stadium
LENDING TREE BOWL
Phone: 251-635-0011
contact@mabowl.com
lendingtreebowl.com

Dec TBA, 2025
NEW ORLEANS BOWL
New Orleans, LA
Mercedes-Benz Superdome
NEW ORLEANS BOWL
Phone: 504-525-5678
Fax: 504-529-1622
www.neworleansbowl.org

Dec TBA, 2025
RELIAQUEST BOWL
Tampa, FL
Raymond James Stadium
RELIAQUEST BOWL
Phone: 813-874-2695
Fax: 813-873-1959
www.reliaquestbowl.com

Dec TBA, 2025
SAN FRANCISCO BOWL
Santa Clara, CA

Levi's Stadium
SAN FRANCISCO BOWL GAME
ASSOCIATION

Dec TBA, 2025
TAXSLAYER GATOR BOWL
Jacksonville, FL
Tiaa Bank Field
TAXSLAYER GATOR BOWL
Phone: 904-798-1700
Fax: 904-632-2080
tickets@taxslayerbowl.com
www.taxslayergatorbowl.com

Dec TBA, 2025
TRANSPERFECT MUSIC CITY BOWL
Nashville, TN
Nissan Stadium
TRANSPERFECT MORTGAGE MUSIC
CITY BOWL
Phone: 615-743-3130
tickets@musiccitybowl.com
www.musiccitybowl.com

Dec TBA, 2025
USHA NATIONAL FOUR-WALL
CHAMPIONSHIPS
TBA
UNITED STATES HANDBALL
ASSOCIATION
Phone: 520-795-0434
Fax: 520-795-0465
handball@ushandball.org
www.ushandball.org

Dec TBA, 2025
VALERO ALAMO BOWL
San Antonio, TX
The Alamodome
SAN ANTONIO BOWL ASSOCIATION
Phone: 210-226-2695
Fax: 210-704-6399
info@alamobowl.com
www.alamobowl.com

Dec 2 - Dec 8, 2025
HERO WORLD CHALLENGE
Albany, Bahamas
PGA TOUR
Phone: 904-285-3700
www.pgatour.com

Dec 4 - Dec 6, 2025
NCAA DIVISION III WOMEN'S
SOCCER FINALS
Salem, VA
Kerr Stadium
NATIONAL COLLEGIATE ATHLETIC
ASSOCIATION
Phone: 317-917-6222
Fax: 317-917-6888
www.ncaa.org

Dec 4 - Dec 7, 2025
NCAA DIVISION III WOMEN'S
VOLLEYBALL FINALS
Salem, VA
Cregger Center
NATIONAL COLLEGIATE ATHLETIC
ASSOCIATION
Phone: 317-917-6222
Fax: 317-917-6888
www.ncaa.org

Dec 5 - Dec 7, 2025
NCAA DIVISION III MEN'S SOCCER
FINALS
Salem, VA
Kerr Stadium
NATIONAL COLLEGIATE ATHLETIC
ASSOCIATION

Phone: 317-917-6222
Fax: 317-917-6888
www.ncaa.org

Dec 5 - Dec 7, 2025
NCAA NATIONAL COLLEGIATE
MEN'S WATER POLO FINALS
Stanford, CA
Avery Aquatic Center
NATIONAL COLLEGIATE ATHLETIC
ASSOCIATION
Phone: 317-917-6222
Fax: 317-917-6888
www.ncaa.org

Dec 6, 2025
DEATH VALLEY TRAIL MARATHON &
HALF MARATHON
Death Valley, CA
Titus Canyon
ENVIRO-SPORTS
Phone: 415-868-1829
info@envirosports.com
envirosports.com

Dec 6, 2025
ST. JUDE MEMPHIS MARATHON
Memphis, TN
ST. JUDE MARATHON
Phone: 901-578-1555
Fax: 901-578-6696
marathon@stjude.org
www.stjude.org

Dec 10 - Dec 13, 2025
SPEEDO WINTER JR.
CHAMPIONSHIPS
TBA
USA SWIMMING
Phone: 719-866-3501
info@usaswimming.org
www.usaswimming.org

Dec 11 - Dec 14, 2025
CYCLOCROSS NATIONAL
CHAMPIONSHIPS
Fayetteville, AR
USA CYCLING
Phone: 719-434-4200
Fax: 719-434-4300
help@usacycling.org
www.usacycling.org

Dec 11 - Dec 13, 2025
NCAA DIVISION II MEN'S SOCCER
FINALS
TBA
NATIONAL COLLEGIATE ATHLETIC
ASSOCIATION
Phone: 317-917-6222
Fax: 317-917-6888
www.ncaa.org

Dec 11 - Dec 13, 2025
NCAA DIVISION II WOMEN'S
VOLLEYBALL FINALS
TBA
NATIONAL COLLEGIATE ATHLETIC
ASSOCIATION
Phone: 317-917-6222
Fax: 317-917-6888
www.ncaa.org

Dec 12 - Dec 13, 2025
AKC RACH INVITATIONAL
Orlando, FL
Orange County Convention Center
AMERICAN KENNEL CLUB
Phone: 919-233-9767
publiced@akc.org
www.akc.org

Dec 12 - Dec 14, 2025
BMW DALLAS MARATHON
Dallas, TX
Dallas City Hall Plaza
DWRM
Phone: 214-800-2087
www.rundallas.com

Dec 12 - Dec 15, 2025
NCAA DIVISION I MEN'S SOCCER
FINALS
Cary, NC
WakeMed Soccer Park
NATIONAL COLLEGIATE ATHLETIC
ASSOCIATION
Phone: 317-917-6222
Fax: 317-917-6888
www.ncaa.org

Dec 12 - Dec 20, 2025
YOUTH WORLD CHAMPIONSHIPS
Portugal
WORLD SAILING
office@sailing.org
www.sailing.org

Dec 13 - Dec 14, 2025
AKC OBEDIENCE CLASSIC
Orlando, FL
Orange County Convention Center
AMERICAN KENNEL CLUB
Phone: 919-233-9767
publiced@akc.org
www.akc.org

Dec 13, 2025
HARK THE HERALD ANGELS HALF
MARATHON & 10K
Tiburon, CA
Angel Island State Park
ENVIRO-SPORTS
Phone: 415-868-1829
info@envirosports.com
envirosports.com

Dec 18 - Dec 21, 2025
NCAA DIVISION I WOMEN'S
VOLLEYBALL FINALS
Kansas City, MO
T-Mobile Center
NATIONAL COLLEGIATE ATHLETIC
ASSOCIATION
Phone: 317-917-6222
Fax: 317-917-6888
www.ncaa.org

Dec 20, 2025
NCAA DIVISION II FOOTBALL FINALS
McKinney, TX
McKinney ISD Stadium
NATIONAL COLLEGIATE ATHLETIC
ASSOCIATION
Phone: 317-917-6222
Fax: 317-917-6888
www.ncaa.org

Dec 20 - Dec 21, 2025
PNC CHAMPIONSHIP
Orlando, FL
Ritz-Carlton Golf Club
PGA CHAMPIONS TOUR
Phone: 904-285-3700
www.pgatour.com/pgatour-champions

Dec 31, 2025
FIESTA BOWL
Glendale, AZ
State Farm Stadium
FIESTA BOWL
Phone: 480-350-0900

Fax: 480-350-0915
prdept@fiestabowl.org
www.fiestabowl.org

Dec 31, 2025
TONY THE TIGER SUN BOWL
El Paso, TX
Sun Bowl Stadium
SUN BOWL ASSOCIATION
Phone: 915-533-4416
Fax: 915-533-0661
www.sunbowl.org

TBA, 2026
EASTERN HEMISPHERE
CHAMPIONSHIP
TBA
INTERNATIONAL STAR CLASS YACHT
ASSOCIATION
Phone: 619-222-0252
Fax: 619-222-0528
office@starclass.org
www.starclass.org

TBA, 2026
FIBA AMERICAS U16 CHAMPIONSHIP
FOR MEN
TBA
USA BASKETBALL
Phone: 719-590-4800
Fax: 719-590-4811
fanmail@usabasketball.com
www.usab.com

TBA, 2026
FIBA AMERICAS U16 CHAMPIONSHIP
FOR WOMEN
TBA
USA BASKETBALL
Phone: 719-590-4800
Fax: 719-590-4811
fanmail@usabasketball.com
www.usab.com

TBA, 2026
FIBA U19 WORLD CUP FOR MEN
TBA
USA BASKETBALL
Phone: 719-590-4800
Fax: 719-590-4811
fanmail@usabasketball.com
www.usab.com

TBA, 2026
FIBA U19 WORLD CUP FOR WOMEN
TBA
USA BASKETBALL
Phone: 719-590-4800
Fax: 719-590-4811
fanmail@usabasketball.com
www.usab.com

TBA, 2026
FREESTYLE AERIALS NATIONAL
CHAMPIONSHIPS
TBA
U.S. SKI AND SNOWBOARD
ASSOCIATION
Phone: 435-649-9090
Fax: 435-649-3613
membership@usskiandsnowboard.org
usskiandsnowboard.org

TBA, 2026
FREESTYLE INTERNATIONAL
TBA
U.S. SKI AND SNOWBOARD
ASSOCIATION
Phone: 435-649-9090
Fax: 435-649-3613
membership@usskiandsnowboard.org
usskiandsnowboard.org

TBA, 2026
FRIVOLTEN CUP
Herrljunga, Sweden
GK FRIVOLTEN
frivolten.com

TBA, 2026
STIFEL KILLINGTON CUP
TBA
U.S. SKI AND SNOWBOARD
ASSOCIATION
Phone: 435-649-9090
Fax: 435-649-3613
membership@usskiandsnowboard.org
usskiandsnowboard.org

TBA, 2026
U.S. GRAND PRIX
TBA
U.S. SKI AND SNOWBOARD
ASSOCIATION
Phone: 435-649-9090
Fax: 435-649-3613
membership@usskiandsnowboard.org
usskiandsnowboard.org

Jan TBA, 2026
ASB CLASSIC (M)
Auckland, New Zealand
ATP TOUR 250
www.atptour.com

Jan TBA, 2026
AUSTRALIA OPEN
Melbourne, Australia
ATP TOUR 250
www.atptour.com

Jan TBA, 2026
BALTIMORE BOAT SHOW
Baltimore, MD
Baltimore Convention Center
NATIONAL MARINE MANUFACTURERS
ASSOCIATION
Phone: 312-946-6200
Fax: 312-946-0401
www.nmma.org

Jan TBA, 2026
BOBSLED NORTH AMERICAN CUP
TBA
USA BOBSLED & SKELETON
FEDERATION
Phone: 518-523-1842
Fax: 518-523-9491
www.usabs.com

Jan TBA, 2026
FARMERS INSURANCE OPEN
San Diego, CA
PGA TOUR
Phone: 904-285-3700
www.pgatour.com

Jan TBA 2026
NFAA INDOOR SECTIONAL
CHAMPIONSHIPS
TBA
NATIONAL FIELD ARCHERY
ASSOCIATION
Phone: 605-260-9279
info@nfaausa.com
www.nfaausa.com

Jan TBA, 2026
THE DESERT CLASSIC AC
Rancho Mirage, CA
Mission Hills Country Club
US CROQUET ASSOCIATION
usca@msn.com
www.croquetamerica.com

Jan 6 - Jan 11, 2026
US FIGURE SKATING
CHAMPIONSHIPS
St. Louis, MO
U.S. FIGURE SKATING
Phone: 719-635-5200
Fax: 719-635-9548
info@usfigureskating.org
www.usfigureskating.org

Jan 8 - Jan 10, 2026
CANADIAN JUNIOR LONG TRACK
CHAMPIONSHIPS
Quebec City, QC
SPEED SKATING CANADA
Phone: 613-260-3669
Fax: 613-701-0296
ssc@speedskating.ca
www.speedskating.ca

Jan 9, 2026
CHICK-FIL-A PEACH BOWL
TBA
CHICK-FIL-A PEACH BOWL
Phone: 404-586-8500
Fax: 404-586-8508
tickets@cfabowl.com
www.chick-fil-apeachbowl.com

Jan 10, 2026
NCAA DIVISION III FOOTBALL FINALS
Canton, OH
Tom Benson Hall of Fame Stadium
NATIONAL COLLEGIATE ATHLETIC
ASSOCIATION
Phone: 317-917-6222
Fax: 317-917-6888
www.ncaa.org

Jan 12 - Jan 18, 2026
SONY OPEN IN HAWAII
Honolulu, HI
Waialae Country Club
PGA TOUR
Phone: 904-285-3700
www.pgatour.com

Jan 15 - Jan 18, 2026
WOMEN'S AC WORLD
CHAMPIONSHIP
West Palm, FL
National Croquet Center
US CROQUET ASSOCIATION
usca@msn.com
www.croquetamerica.com

Jan 23 - Jan 25, 2026
CANADIAN MASTERS TEAM
CHAMPIONSHIP
TBA
SQUASH CANADA
Phone: 613-228-7724
Fax: 613-228-7232
info@squash.ca
www.squash.ca

Jan 30 - Feb 1, 2026
SHORT TRACK CANADA CUP 1
TBA
SPEED SKATING CANADA
Phone: 613-260-3669
Fax: 613-701-0296
ssc@speedskating.ca
www.speedskating.ca

Feb TBA, 2026
BOBSLED EUROPEAN CUP
TBA
USA BOBSLED & SKELETON
FEDERATION

Phone: 518-523-1842
Fax: 518-523-9491
www.usabs.com

Feb TBA, 2026
USHA NATIONAL COLLEGIATE
CHAMPIONSHIPS
TBA
UNITED STATES HANDBALL
ASSOCIATION
Phone: 520-795-0434
Fax: 520-795-0465
handball@ushandball.org
www.ushandball.org

Feb 6 - Feb 22, 2026
XXV OLYMPIC WINTER GAMES
Milan-Cortina, Italy
INTERNATIONAL OLYMPIC
COMMITTEE
International Ph: 41-21-621-61-11
International Fax: 41-21-621-62-16
www.olympic.org

Feb 6 - Feb 22, 2026
XXV OLYMPIC WINTER GAMES
Milan, Italy
INTERNATIONAL OLYMPIC
COMMITTEE
International Ph: 41-21-621-61-11
International Fax: 41-21-621-62-16
www.olympic.org

Feb 8, 2026
SUPER BOWL LX
Santa Clara, CA
Levi's Stadium
NATIONAL FOOTBALL LEAGUE
Phone: 212-450-2000
www.nfl.com

Feb 13 - Feb 22, 2026
DELRAY BEACH OPEN
Delray Beach, FL
The Delray Beach Stadium & Tennis
Centre
ATP CHAMPIONS TOUR
www.atptour.com/en

Mar TBA, 2026
NCAA DIVISION III MEN'S ICE
HOCKEY FINALS
TBA
NATIONAL COLLEGIATE ATHLETIC
ASSOCIATION
Phone: 317-917-6222
Fax: 317-917-6888
www.ncaa.org

Mar 6 - Mar 8, 2026
CANADIAN MIXED DOUBLES
CHAMPIONSHIPS
TBA
SQUASH CANADA
Phone: 613-228-7724
Fax: 613-228-7232
info@squash.ca
www.squash.ca

Mar 6 - Mar 8, 2026
LONG TRACK CANADA CUP 2
Calgary, AB, Canada
SPEED SKATING CANADA
Phone: 613-260-3669
Fax: 613-701-0296
ssc@speedskating.ca
www.speedskating.ca

Mar 14 - Mar 22, 2026
WORLD WOMEN'S CURLING
CHAMPIONSHIP
Calgary, AB, Canada
WinSport Event Centre
CURLING CANADA
Phone: 613-834-2076
Fax: 613-834-0716
championships@curling.ca
www.curling.ca

Jun 7, 2025
THUNDER VALLEY NATIONAL
Lakewood, CO
Thunder Valley Motocross Park
AMA PRO RACING
Phone: 386-492-1014
Fax: 386-274-2335
communications@amaproracing.com
www.amaproracing.com

Jun 12 - Jun 14, 2026
CURTIS CUP
Los Angeles, CA
Bel-Air Country Club
U.S. GOLF ASSOCIATION
Phone: 908-234-2300
Fax: 908-234-9687
www.usga.org

Sept 7 - Sept 13, 2026
SOLHEIM CUP
Hertogenbosch, The Netherlands
LPGA TOUR
Phone: 386-274-6200
Fax: 386-274-1099
www.lpga.com

Sept 22 - Sept 27, 2026
PRESIDENT'S CUP
Chicago, IL
Medinah Country Club
PGA TOUR
Phone: 904-285-3700
www.pgatour.com

Sept 25, 2026
AAU STRENGTH SPORTS WORLD
CHAMPIONSHIPS
Laughlin, NV
AMATEUR ATHLETIC UNION
Phone: 407-934-7200
Fax: 407-934-7242
www.aausports.org

Oct 31 - Nov 13, 2026
YOUTH SUMMER OLYMPIC GAMES
Dakar, Senegal
INTERNATIONAL OLYMPIC
COMMITTEE
International Ph: 41-21-621-61-11
International Fax: 41-21-621-62-16
www.olympic.org

Nov 16, 2026
CFL GREY CUP
Calgary, AB, Canada
McMahon Stadium
CANADIAN FOOTBALL LEAGUE
Phone: 416-322-9650
Fax: 416-322-9651
www.cfl.ca

Dec TBA, 2026
ASB CLASSIC
Auckland, New Zealand
WTA
Phone: 727-895-5000

Fax: 727-894-1982
feedback@wtatennis.com
www.wtatennis.com

Jan TBA, 2027
SPECIAL OLYMPICS USA NATIONAL
GAMES
TBA
SPECIAL OLYMPICS
Phone: 202-628-3630
Fax: 202-824-0200
cweir@specialolympics.org
www.specialolympics.org

Jan TBA, 2027
SPECIAL OLYMPICS WORLD
SUMMER GAMES
TBA
SPECIAL OLYMPICS
Phone: 202-628-3630
Fax: 202-824-0200
cweir@specialolympics.org
www.specialolympics.org

Jan TBA, 2028
YOUTH WINTER OLYMPIC GAMES
TBA
INTERNATIONAL OLYMPIC
COMMITTEE
International Ph: 41-21-621-61-11
International Fax: 41-21-621-62-16
www.olympic.org

Jul 14 - Jul 30, 2028
XXXIV OLYMPIC SUMMER GAMES
Los Angeles, CA
INTERNATIONAL OLYMPIC
COMMITTEE
International Ph: 41-21-621-61-11
International Fax: 41-21-621-62-16
www.olympic.org

All Sports

TBA, 2025
FISU SUMMER WORLD UNIVERSITY
GAMES
TBA
FEDERATION INTERNATIONALE DU
SPORT UNIVERSIADE
International Ph: 41-0-216130810
International Fax: 41-0-216015612
fisu@fisu.net
www.fisu.net

Jul 23 - Aug 2, 2025
AAU JUNIOR OLYMPIC GAMES
Houston, TX
AMATEUR ATHLETIC UNION
Phone: 407-934-7200
Fax: 407-934-7242
www.aausports.org

Feb 6 - Feb 22, 2026
XXV OLYMPIC WINTER GAMES
Milan-Cortina, Italy
INTERNATIONAL OLYMPIC
COMMITTEE
International Ph: 41-21-621-61-11
International Fax: 41-21-621-62-16
www.olympic.org

Feb 6 - Feb 22, 2026
XXV OLYMPIC WINTER GAMES
Milan, Italy
INTERNATIONAL OLYMPIC
COMMITTEE
International Ph: 41-21-621-61-11
International Fax: 41-21-621-62-16
www.olympic.org

Oct 31 - Nov 13, 2026
YOUTH SUMMER OLYMPIC GAMES
Dakar, Senegal
INTERNATIONAL OLYMPIC
COMMITTEE
International Ph: 41-21-621-61-11
International Fax: 41-21-621-62-16
www.olympic.org

Jan TBA, 2028
YOUTH WINTER OLYMPIC GAMES
TBA
INTERNATIONAL OLYMPIC
COMMITTEE
International Ph: 41-21-621-61-11
International Fax: 41-21-621-62-16
www.olympic.org

Jul 14 - Jul 30, 2028
XXXIV OLYMPIC SUMMER GAMES
Los Angeles, CA
INTERNATIONAL OLYMPIC
COMMITTEE
International Ph: 41-21-621-61-11
International Fax: 41-21-621-62-16
www.olympic.org

Archery

Feb 14 - Feb 16, 2025
NFAA INDOOR NATIONAL
CHAMPIONSHIPS
Chicago, IL
Navy Pier
NATIONAL FIELD ARCHERY
ASSOCIATION
Phone: 605-260-9279
info@nfaausa.com
www.nfaausa.com

Feb 20 - Feb 23, 2025
HOYT/EASTON PRO/AM
Foley, AL
ARCHERY SHOOTERS ASSOCIATION
Phone: 770-795-0232
Fax: 770-795-0953
info@asaarchery.com
www.asaarchery.com

Mar 5 - Mar 9, 2025
THE VEGAS SHOOT
Las Vegas, NV
NATIONAL FIELD ARCHERY
ASSOCIATION
Phone: 605-260-9279
info@nfaausa.com
www.nfaausa.com

Apr 24 - Apr 27, 2025
EASTON HOYT PRO/AM
Minden, LA
ARCHERY SHOOTERS ASSOCIATION
Phone: 770-795-0232
Fax: 770-795-0953
info@asaarchery.com
www.asaarchery.com

May 2 - May 4, 2025
NFAA MARKED 3-D NATIONAL
CHAMPIONSHIP
Redding, CA
NATIONAL FIELD ARCHERY
ASSOCIATION
Phone: 605-260-9279
info@nfaausa.com
www.nfaausa.com

May 29 - Jun 1, 2025
TRU BALL PRO/AM
London, KY
ARCHERY SHOOTERS ASSOCIATION
Phone: 770-795-0232
Fax: 770-795-0953
info@asaarchery.com
www.asaarchery.com

Jun 26 - Jun 29, 2025
MATHEWS PRO/AM
Metropolis, IL
ARCHERY SHOOTERS ASSOCIATION
Phone: 770-795-0232
Fax: 770-795-0953
info@asaarchery.com
www.asaarchery.com

Jul 18 - Jul 20, 2025
OUTDOOR FIELD NATIONAL
CHAMPIONSHIPS
Mechanicsburg, PA
NATIONAL FIELD ARCHERY
ASSOCIATION
Phone: 605-260-9279
info@nfaausa.com
www.nfaausa.com

Jul 31 - Aug 3, 2025
DELTA MCKENZIE ASA CLASSIC
Cullman, AL
St. Bernard Abbey
ARCHERY SHOOTERS ASSOCIATION
Phone: 770-795-0232
Fax: 770-795-0953
info@asaarchery.com
www.asaarchery.com

Sept 19 - Sept 21, 2025
OUTDOOR TARGET NATIONAL
CHAMPIONSHIPS
Yankton, SD

NATIONAL FIELD ARCHERY
ASSOCIATION
Phone: 605-260-9279
info@nfaausa.com
www.nfaausa.com

Jan TBA 2026
NFAA INDOOR SECTIONAL
CHAMPIONSHIPS
TBA
NATIONAL FIELD ARCHERY
ASSOCIATION
Phone: 605-260-9279
info@nfaausa.com
www.nfaausa.com

Auto Racing

Feb 2, 2025
COOK OUT CLASH AT BOWMAN
GRAY
Winston-Salem, NC
Bowman Gray Stadium
NASCAR CUP SERIES
www.nascar.com

Feb 13, 2025
BLUEGREEN VACATIONS DUEL
DAYTONA 1&2
Daytona Beach, FL
Daytona International Speedway
NASCAR CUP SERIES
www.nascar.com

Feb 16, 2025
DAYTONA 500
Daytona Beach, FL
Daytona International Speedway
NASCAR CUP SERIES
www.nascar.com

Feb 23, 2025
AMBETTER HEALTH 400
Hampton, GA
Atlanta Motor Speedway
NASCAR CUP SERIES
www.nascar.com

Feb 28 - Mar 2, 2025
FIRESTONE GRAND PRIX OF ST.
PETERSBURG
St. Petersburg, FL
Streets of St. Petersburg
NTT INDYCAR SERIES
Phone: 317-492-6526
indycar@indycar.com
www.indycar.com

Mar 2, 2025
ECHOPARK AUTOMOTIVE GRAND
PRIX
Austin, TX
Circuit of the Americas
NASCAR CAMPING WORLD TRUCK
SERIES
Phone: 800-630-0535
www.nascar.com

Mar 6 - Mar 9, 2025
AMALIE MOTOR OIL NHRA
GATORNATIONALS
Gainesville, FL
Gainesville Raceway
NATIONAL HOT ROD ASSOCIATION
Phone: 626-914-4761
Fax: 626-325-8752
nhra@nhra.com
www.nhra.com

Mar 9, 2025
SHRINERS CHILDREN'S 500
Avondale, AZ
Phoenix Raceway
NASCAR CUP SERIES
www.nascar.com

Mar 16, 2025
PENNZOIL 400
Las Vegas, NV
Las Vegas Motor Speedway
NASCAR CUP SERIES
www.nascar.com

Mar 21 - Mar 23, 2025
NHRA ARIZONA NATIONALS
Chandler, AZ
Wild Horse Pass Motorsports Park
NATIONAL HOT ROD ASSOCIATION
Phone: 626-914-4761
Fax: 626-325-8752
nhra@nhra.com
www.nhra.com

Mar 21 - Mar 23, 2025
THE THERMAL CLUB INDYCAR
GRAND PRIX
Thermal, CA
NTT INDYCAR SERIES
Phone: 317-492-6526
indycar@indycar.com
www.indycar.com

Mar 23, 2025
STRAIGHT TALK WIRELESS 400
Homestead, FL
Homestead-Miami Speedway
NASCAR CUP SERIES
www.nascar.com

Mar 27 - Mar 30, 2025
LUCAS OIL NHRA
WINTERNATIONALS
Pomona, CA
In-N-Out Burger Pomona Dragstrip
NATIONAL HOT ROD ASSOCIATION
Phone: 626-914-4761
Fax: 626-325-8752
nhra@nhra.com
www.nhra.com

Apr 6, 2025
GOODYEAR 400
Darlington, SC
Darlington Raceway
NASCAR CUP SERIES
www.nascar.com

Apr 11 - Apr 13, 2025
ACURA GRAND PRIX OF LONG
BEACH
Long Beach, CA
Streets of Long Beach
NTT INDYCAR SERIES
Phone: 317-492-6526
indycar@indycar.com
www.indycar.com

Apr 11 - Apr 13, 2025
NHRA 4-WIDE NATIONALS
Las Vegas, NV
The Strip at Las Vegas Motor Speedway
NATIONAL HOT ROD ASSOCIATION
Phone: 626-914-4761
Fax: 626-325-8752
nhra@nhra.com
www.nhra.com

Apr 13, 2025
FOOD CITY 500
Bristol, TN
Bristol Motor Speedway
NASCAR CAMPING WORLD TRUCK
SERIES
Phone: 800-630-0535
www.nascar.com

Apr 27, 2025
JACK LINK'S 500
Talladega, AL
Talladega Superspeedway
NASCAR CUP SERIES
www.nascar.com

May 2 - May 4, 2025
CHILDREN'S OF ALABAMA INDY
GRAND PRIX
Birmingham, AL
Barber Motorsports Park
NTT INDYCAR SERIES
Phone: 317-492-6526
indycar@indycar.com
www.indycar.com

May 4, 2025
WURTH 400 PRESENTED BY LIQUI
Fort Worth TX
Texas Motor Speedway
NASCAR CAMPING WORLD TRUCK
SERIES
Phone: 800-630-0535
www.nascar.com

May 9 - May 10, 2025
SONSIO GRAND PRIX
Indianapolis, IN
NTT INDYCAR SERIES
Phone: 317-492-6526
indycar@indycar.com
www.indycar.com

May 13 - May 25, 2025
INDIANAPOLIS 500
Indianapolis, IN
Indianapolis Motor Speedway
NTT INDYCAR SERIES
Phone: 317-492-6526
indycar@indycar.com
www.indycar.com

May 15 - May 18, 2025
ROUTE 66 NHRA NATIONALS
Elwood, IL
Route 66 Raceway
NATIONAL HOT ROD ASSOCIATION
Phone: 626-914-4761
Fax: 626-325-8752
nhra@nhra.com
www.nhra.com

May 18, 2025
NASCAR ALL-STAR OPEN
North Wilkesboro, NC
North Wilkesboro Speedway
NASCAR CUP SERIES
www.nascar.com

May 18, 2025
NASCAR ALL-STAR RACE
North Wilkesboro, NC
North Wilkesboro Speedway
NASCAR CUP SERIES
www.nascar.com

May 25, 2025
COCA-COLA 600
Concord, NC
Charlotte Motor Speedway

NASCAR CUP SERIES
www.nascar.com

May 30 - Jun 1, 2025
CHEVROLET DETROIT GRAND PRIX
Detroit, MI
Streets of Detroit
NTT INDYCAR SERIES
Phone: 317-492-6526
indycar@indycar.com
www.indycar.com

May 30 - Jun 1, 2025
NHRA NEW ENGLAND NATIONALS
Epping, NH
New England Dragway
NATIONAL HOT ROD ASSOCIATION
Phone: 626-914-4761
Fax: 626-325-8752
nhra@nhra.com
www.nhra.com

Jun 1, 2025
NASCAR CUP SERIES AT NASHVILLE
Nashville, TN
Nashville Superspeedway
NASCAR CUP SERIES
www.nascar.com

Jun 6 - Jun 8, 2025
NHRA THUNDER VALLEY NATIONALS
Bristol, TN
Bristol Dragway
NATIONAL HOT ROD ASSOCIATION
Phone: 626-914-4761
Fax: 626-325-8752
nhra@nhra.com
www.nhra.com

Jun 8, 2025
FIREKEEPERS CASINO 400
Brooklyn, MI
Michigan International Speedway
NASCAR CUP SERIES
www.nascar.com

Jun 14 - Jun 15, 2025
BOMMARITO AUTOMOTIVE GROUP
500
Madison, IL
Gateway Motorsports Park
NTT INDYCAR SERIES
Phone: 317-492-6526
indycar@indycar.com
www.indycar.com

Jun 15, 2025
NASCAR CUP SERIES AT MEXICO
CITY
Mexico City, Mexico
Autodromo Hermanos Rodriguez
NASCAR CUP SERIES
www.nascar.com

Jun 20 - Jun 22, 2025
NHRA VIRGINIA NATIONALS
North Dinwiddie, VA
Virginia Motorsports Park
NATIONAL HOT ROD ASSOCIATION
Phone: 626-914-4761
Fax: 626-325-8752
nhra@nhra.com
www.nhra.com

Jun 20 - Jun 22, 2025
XPEL GRAND PRIX AT ROAD
AMERICA
Elkhart Lake, WI
Road America
NTT INDYCAR SERIES
Phone: 317-492-6526

indycar@indycar.com
www.indycar.com

Jun 22, 2025
NASCAR CUP SERIES AT POCONO
Long Pond, PA
Pocono Raceway
NASCAR CUP SERIES
www.nascar.com

Jun 26 - Jun 29, 2025
SUMMIT RACING EQUIPMENT NHRA
NATIONALS
Norwalk, OH
Summit Racing Equipment Motorsports
Park
NATIONAL HOT ROD ASSOCIATION
Phone: 626-914-4761
Fax: 626-325-8752
nhra@nhra.com
www.nhra.com

Jun 28, 2025
QUAKER STATE 400 PRESENTED BY
WALMART
Hampton, GA
Atlanta Motor Speedway
NASCAR CUP SERIES
www.nascar.com

Jul 4 - Jul 6, 2025
HONDA INDY 200 AT MID-OHIO
Lexington, OH
Mid-Ohio Sports Car Course
NTT INDYCAR SERIES
Phone: 317-492-6526
indycar@indycar.com
www.indycar.com

Jul 13, 2025
TOYOTA-SAVE MART 350
Sonoma, CA
Sonoma Raceway
NASCAR CUP SERIES
www.nascar.com

Jul 18 - Jul 20, 2025
NHRA NORTHWEST NATIONALS
Kent, WA
Pacific Raceways
NATIONAL HOT ROD ASSOCIATION
Phone: 626-914-4761
Fax: 626-325-8752
nhra@nhra.com
www.nhra.com

Jul 18 - Jul 20, 2025
ONTARIO HONDA DEALERS INDY
TORONTO
Toronto, Canada
Streets of Toronto
NTT INDYCAR SERIES
Phone: 317-492-6526
indycar@indycar.com
www.indycar.com

Jul 20, 2025
AUTOTRADER ECHOPARK
AUTOMOTIVE 400
Fort Worth, TX
Texas Motor Speedway
NASCAR CUP SERIES
www.nascar.com

Jul 25 - Jul 27, 2025
DENSO NHRA SONOMA NATIONALS
Sonoma, CA
Sonoma Raceway
NATIONAL HOT ROD ASSOCIATION
Phone: 626-914-4761
Fax: 626-325-8752

nhra@nhra.com
www.nhra.com

Jul 25 - Jul 27, 2025
INDYCAR GRAND PRIX OF
MONTEREY
Monterey, CA
WeatherTech Raceway Laguna Seca
NTT INDYCAR SERIES
Phone: 317-492-6526
indycar@indycar.com
www.indycar.com

Jul 25 - Jul 27, 2025
NHRA SONOMA NATIONALS
Sonoma, CA
Sonoma Raceway
NATIONAL HOT ROD ASSOCIATION
Phone: 626-914-4761
Fax: 626-325-8752
nhra@nhra.com
www.nhra.com

Aug 8 - Aug 10, 2025
GRAND PRIX OF PORTLAND
Portland, OR
Portland International Raceway
NTT INDYCAR SERIES
Phone: 317-492-6526
indycar@indycar.com
www.indycar.com

Aug 10, 2025
GO BOWLING AT THE GLEN
Watkins Glen, NY
Watkins Glen International
NASCAR CUP SERIES
www.nascar.com

Aug 14 - Aug 17, 2025
LUCAS OIL NHRA NATIONALS
Brainerd, MN
Brainerd International Raceway
NATIONAL HOT ROD ASSOCIATION
Phone: 626-914-4761
Fax: 626-325-8752
nhra@nhra.com
www.nhra.com

Aug 23, 2025
COKE ZERO SUGAR 400
Daytona Beach, FL
Daytona International Speedway
NASCAR CUP SERIES
www.nascar.com

Aug 23 - Aug 24, 2025
SNAP-ON MILWAUKEE MILE 250
West Allis, WI
Milwaukee Mile
NTT INDYCAR SERIES
Phone: 317-492-6526
indycar@indycar.com
www.indycar.com

Aug 27 - Sept 1, 2025
NHRA U.S. NATIONALS
Indianapolis, IN
Lucas Oil Raceway
NATIONAL HOT ROD ASSOCIATION
Phone: 626-914-4761
Fax: 626-325-8752
nhra@nhra.com
www.nhra.com

Aug 30 - Aug 31, 2025
MUSIC CITY GRAND PRIX
Nashville, TN
Streets of Nashville
NTT INDYCAR SERIES
Phone: 317-492-6526

indycar@indycar.com
www.indycar.com

Aug 31, 2025
SOUTHERN 500
Darlington, SC
Darlington Raceway
NASCAR CUP SERIES
www.nascar.com

Sept 7, 2025
ENJOY ILLINOIS 300
Madison, IL
World Wide Technology Raceway
NASCAR CAMPING WORLD TRUCK
SERIES
Phone: 800-630-0535
www.nascar.com

Sept 11 - Sept 14, 2025
NHRA READING NATIONALS
Mohnton, PA
Maple Grove Raceway
NATIONAL HOT ROD ASSOCIATION
Phone: 626-914-4761
Fax: 626-325-8752
nhra@nhra.com
www.nhra.com

Sept 13, 2025
BASS PRO SHOPS NRA NIGHT RACE
Bristol, TN
Bristol Motor Speedway
NASCAR CUP SERIES
www.nascar.com

Sept 26 - Sept 28, 2025
AAA NHRA MIDWEST NATIONALS
Madison, IL
World Wide Technology Raceway
NATIONAL HOT ROD ASSOCIATION
Phone: 626-914-4761
Fax: 626-325-8752
nhra@nhra.com
www.nhra.com

Sept 28, 2025
HOLLYWOOD CASINO 400
Kansas City, KS
Kansas Speedway
NASCAR CUP SERIES
www.nascar.com

Oct 5, 2025
BANK OF AMERICA ROVAL 400
Concord, NC
Charlotte Motor Speedway
NASCAR CUP SERIES
www.nascar.com

Oct 9 - Oct 12, 2025
AAA TEXAS NHRA FALL NATIONALS
Ennis, TX
Texas Motorplex
NATIONAL HOT ROD ASSOCIATION
Phone: 626-914-4761
Fax: 626-325-8752
nhra@nhra.com
www.nhra.com

Oct 12, 2025
SOUTH POINT 400
Las Vegas, NV
Las Vegas Motor Speedway
NASCAR CUP SERIES
www.nascar.com

Oct 30 - Nov 2, 2025
NHRA NEVADA NATIONALS
Las Vegas, NV
The Strip at Las Vegas Motor Speedway

NATIONAL HOT ROD ASSOCIATION
Phone: 626-914-4761
Fax: 626-325-8752
nhra@nhra.com
www.nhra.com

Nov 2, 2025
NASCAR CUP SERIES
CHAMPIONSHIP
Avondale, AZ
Phoenix Raceway
NASCAR CUP SERIES
www.nascar.com

Nov 13 - Nov 16, 2025
IN-N-OUT BURGER NHRA FINALS
Pomona, CA
In-N-Out Burger Pomona Dragstrip
NATIONAL HOT ROD ASSOCIATION
Phone: 626-914-4761
Fax: 626-325-8752
nhra@nhra.com
www.nhra.com

Badminton

TBA, 2025
YONEX OPEN
USA BADMINTON
Phone: 714-602-1691
ContactUs@usabadminton.org
www.usabadminton.org

Apr 12 - Apr 13, 2025
DAVE FREEMAN JR. SOCIAL OLC
San Diego, CA
San Diego Badminton Club
USA BADMINTON
Phone: 714-602-1691
ContactUs@usabadminton.org
www.usabadminton.org

May 2 - May 4, 2025
DAVE FREEMAN OPEN
TBA
USA BADMINTON
Phone: 714-602-1691
ContactUs@usabadminton.org
www.usabadminton.org

Bandy

Feb TBA, 2025
WOMEN'S WORLD CHAMPIONSHIPS
TBA
AMERICAN BANDY ASSOCIATION
www.usabandy.com

Baseball

May 30 - Jun 7, 2025
NCAA DIVISION II BASEBALL FINALS
Cary, NC
Usa Baseball National Training Complex
NATIONAL COLLEGIATE ATHLETIC
ASSOCIATION
Phone: 317-917-6222
Fax: 317-917-6888
www.ncaa.org

May 30 - Jun 5, 2025
NCAA DIVISION III BASEBALL FINALS
Eastlake, OH
Classic Park
NATIONAL COLLEGIATE ATHLETIC
ASSOCIATION
Phone: 317-917-6222

Fax: 317-917-6888
www.ncaa.org

Jun 13 - Jun 23, 2025
NCAA DIVISION I BASEBALL FINALS
Omaha, NE
Charles Schwab Field Omaha
NATIONAL COLLEGIATE ATHLETIC
ASSOCIATION
Phone: 317-917-6222
Fax: 317-917-6888
www.ncaa.org

Aug 10 - Aug 24, 2025
BASEBALL CANADA CUP
CHAMPIONSHIPS
St. John's, NL, Canada
BASEBALL CANADA
Phone: 613-748-5606
Fax: 613-748-5767
info@baseball.ca
www.baseball.ca

Basketball

Mar 12 - Mar 15, 2025
CCAA MEN'S NATIONAL
BASKETBALL CHAMPIONSHIP
Saint-Laurent, QC, Canada
Vanier College
CANADA BASKETBALL
Phone: 416-614-8037
Fax: 416-614-9570
info@basketball.ca
www.basketball.ca

Mar 12 - Mar 15, 2025
CCAA WOMEN'S NATIONAL
BASKETBALL CHAMPIONSHIP
Fredericton, NB, Canada
The Richard J. Currie Centre
CANADA BASKETBALL
Phone: 416-614-8037
Fax: 416-614-9570
info@basketball.ca
www.basketball.ca

Mar 20 - Mar 22, 2025
NCAA DIVISION III MEN'S
BASKETBALL FINALS
Fort Wayne, IN
Allen County War Memorial Coliseum
NATIONAL COLLEGIATE ATHLETIC
ASSOCIATION
Phone: 317-917-6222
Fax: 317-917-6888
www.ncaa.org

Mar 20 - Mar 22, 2025
NCAA DIVISION III WOMEN'S
BASKETBALL FINALS
Salem, VA
Cregger Center
NATIONAL COLLEGIATE ATHLETIC
ASSOCIATION
Phone: 317-917-6222
Fax: 317-917-6888
www.ncaa.org

Mar 24 - Mar 28, 2025
NCAA DIVISION II WOMEN'S
BASKETBALL FINALS
Pittsburgh, PA
UPMC Cooper Fieldhouse
NATIONAL COLLEGIATE ATHLETIC
ASSOCIATION
Phone: 317-917-6222
Fax: 317-917-6888
www.ncaa.org

Mar 25 - Mar 29, 2025
NCAA DIVISION II MEN'S
BASKETBALL FINALS
Evansville, IN
Ford Center
NATIONAL COLLEGIATE ATHLETIC
ASSOCIATION
Phone: 317-917-6222
Fax: 317-917-6888
www.ncaa.org

Apr 4 - Apr 6, 2025
NCAA DIVISION I WOMEN'S
BASKETBALL FINALS
Tampa, FL
Amalie Arena
NATIONAL COLLEGIATE ATHLETIC
ASSOCIATION
Phone: 317-917-6222
Fax: 317-917-6888
www.ncaa.org

Apr 5 - Apr 7, 2025
NCAA DIVISION I MEN'S
BASKETBALL FINALS
San Antionio, TX
Alamodome
NATIONAL COLLEGIATE ATHLETIC
ASSOCIATION
Phone: 317-917-6222
Fax: 317-917-6888
www.ncaa.org

Apr 12, 2025
NIKE HOOP SUMMIT
Portland, OR
Moda Center
USA BASKETBALL
Phone: 719-590-4800
Fax: 719-590-4811
fanmail@usabasketball.com
www.usab.com

Jun 6 - Jun 8, 2025
US OPEN BASKETBALL
CHAMPIONSHIPS EAST
Bermuda Run, NC
USA BASKETBALL
Phone: 719-590-4800
Fax: 719-590-4811
fanmail@usabasketball.com
www.usab.com

Jun 27 - Jun 29, 2025
AAU 10U/4TH - 17U/11TH GRADE
EAST COAST DIV. III
CHAMPIONSHIPS
Hampton, VA
Boo Williams Sportsplex
AMATEUR ATHLETIC UNION
Phone: 407-934-7200
Fax: 407-934-7242
www.aausports.org

Jun 27 - Jun 29, 2025
AAU 11U/5TH GRADE DI & DII WORLD
CHAMPIONSHIPS
Knoxville, TN
Knoxville Convention Center
AMATEUR ATHLETIC UNION
Phone: 407-934-7200
Fax: 407-934-7242
www.aausports.org

Jun 27 - Jun 29, 2025
AAU 17U/11TH GRADE &
SOUTHEAST DIV. III CHAMPION
SHIPS
Hampton,VA
Boo Williams Sportsplex

AMATEUR ATHLETIC UNION
Phone: 407-934-7200
Fax: 407-934-7242
www.aausports.org

Jun 27 - Jun 29, 2025
AAU 8U/2ND GRADE AAU WORLD
CHAMPIONSHIPS
Knoxville, TN
Knoxville Convention Center
AMATEUR ATHLETIC UNION
Phone: 407-934-7200
Fax: 407-934-7242
www.aausports.org

Jun 27 - Jun 29, 2025
US OPEN BASKETBALL
CHAMPIONSHIPS CENTRAL
Kansas City, MO
USA BASKETBALL
Phone: 719-590-4800
Fax: 719-590-4811
fanmail@usabasketball.com
www.usab.com

Jun 28 - Jul 6, 2025
FIBA BASKETBALL WORLD CUP
Switzerland
USA BASKETBALL
Phone: 719-590-4800
Fax: 719-590-4811
fanmail@usabasketball.com
www.usab.com

Jul 3 - Jul 6, 2025
AAU 14U/8TH GRADE DI & DII WORLD
CHAMPIONSHIPS
Orlando, FL
ESPN Wide World of Sports
AMATEUR ATHLETIC UNION
Phone: 407-934-7200
Fax: 407-934-7242
www.aausports.org

Jul 7 - Jul 10, 2025
AAU 13U/7TH GRADE DI & DII AAU
WORLD CHAMPIONSHI PS
Orlando, FL
ESPN Wide World of Sports
AMATEUR ATHLETIC UNION
Phone: 407-934-7200
Fax: 407-934-7242
www.aausports.org

Jul 7 - Jul 10, 2025
AAU 7U/1ST GRADE AAU WORLD
CHAMPIONSHIPS
Orlando, FL
ESPN Wide World of Sports
AMATEUR ATHLETIC UNION
Phone: 407-934-7200
Fax: 407-934-7242
www.aausports.org

Jun 27 - Jun 29, 2025
AAU 10U/4TH GRADE DI & DII WORLD
CHAMPIONSHIPS
Hampton, VA
Boo Williams Sportsplex
AMATEUR ATHLETIC UNION
Phone: 407-934-7200
Fax: 407-934-7242
www.aausports.org

Aug 4 - Aug 9, 2025
CANADA BASKETBALL 15U/17U
MEN'S NATIONAL CHAMPIO NSHIPS
TBA
CANADA BASKETBALL
Phone: 416-614-8037
Fax: 416-614-9570

info@basketball.ca
www.basketball.ca

Aug 4 - Aug 9, 2025
CANADA BASKETBALL 15U/17U
WOMEN'S NATIONAL CHAMP
IONSHIPS
TBA
CANADA BASKETBALL
Phone: 416-614-8037
Fax: 416-614-9570
info@basketball.ca
www.basketball.ca

TBA, 2026
FIBA AMERICAS U16 CHAMPIONSHIP
FOR MEN
TBA
USA BASKETBALL
Phone: 719-590-4800
Fax: 719-590-4811
fanmail@usabasketball.com
www.usab.com

TBA, 2026
FIBA AMERICAS U16 CHAMPIONSHIP
FOR WOMEN
TBA
USA BASKETBALL
Phone: 719-590-4800
Fax: 719-590-4811
fanmail@usabasketball.com
www.usab.com

TBA, 2026
FIBA U19 WORLD CUP FOR MEN
TBA
USA BASKETBALL
Phone: 719-590-4800
Fax: 719-590-4811
fanmail@usabasketball.com
www.usab.com

TBA, 2026
FIBA U19 WORLD CUP FOR WOMEN
TBA
USA BASKETBALL
Phone: 719-590-4800
Fax: 719-590-4811
fanmail@usabasketball.com
www.usab.com

Biathlon

Feb 14 - Feb 16, 2025
US BIATHLON MASTERS NATIONALS
Brillion, WI
Ariens Nordic Center
UNITED STATES BIATHLON
ASSOCIATION
Phone: 719-632-5551
www.usbiathlon.org

Mar 26 - Mar 29, 2025
US BIATHLON SENIOR NATIONALS
Bozeman, MT
Crosscut Mountain Sports Center
UNITED STATES BIATHLON
ASSOCIATION
Phone: 719-632-5551
www.usbiathlon.org

Mar 27, 2025
US BIATHLON COLLEGIATE
NATIONAL CHAMPIONSHIPS
Bozeman, MT
Crosscut Mountain Sports Center
UNITED STATES BIATHLON
ASSOCIATION

Phone: 719-632-5551
www.usbiathlon.org

Bobsledding

Mar 6 - Mar 16, 2025
PARA WORLD CHAMPIONSHIPS
TBA
USA BOBSLED & SKELETON
FEDERATION
Phone: 518-523-1842
Fax: 518-523-9491
www.usabs.com

Jan TBA, 2026
BOBSLED NORTH AMERICAN CUP
TBA
USA BOBSLED & SKELETON
FEDERATION
Phone: 518-523-1842
Fax: 518-523-9491
www.usabs.com

Feb TBA, 2026
BOBSLED EUROPEAN CUP
TBA
USA BOBSLED & SKELETON
FEDERATION
Phone: 518-523-1842
Fax: 518-523-9491
www.usabs.com

Body Building

TBA, 2025
GRAND PRIX PHILIPPINES
Philippines, Philippines
INTERNATIONAL FEDERATION OF
BODY BUILDING & FITNESS
contact@ifbb.com
www.ifbb.com

Jan 18 - Jan 19, 2025
AAU WEST COAST FOOTBALL
NATIONAL CHAMPIONSHIPS
Las Vegas, NV
AMATEUR ATHLETIC UNION
Phone: 407-934-7200
Fax: 407-934-7242
www.aausports.org

Feb 26 - Feb 27, 2025
DUBAI MUSCLE BEACH
Dubai, United Arab Emirates
INTERNATIONAL FEDERATION OF
BODY BUILDING & FITNESS
contact@ifbb.com
www.ifbb.com

Feb 27 - Mar 2, 2025
ARNOLD ARNOLD SPORTS
FESTIVAL
Columbus, OH
Columbus Convention Center
ARNOLD SPORTS FESTIVAL
Phone: 614-431-2600
Fax: 614-431-3492
www.arnoldsportsfestival.com

Feb 28, 2025
FITNESS INTERNATIONAL
COMPETITION
Columbus, OH
Columbus Convention Center
ARNOLD SPORTS FESTIVAL
Phone: 614-431-2600
Fax: 614-431-3492
www.arnoldsportsfestival.com

Mar 1, 2025
BIKINI INTERNATIONAL
COMPETITION
Columbus, OH
Columbus Convention Center
ARNOLD SPORTS FESTIVAL
Phone: 614-431-2600
Fax: 614-431-3492
www.arnoldsportsfestival.com

Mar 29 - Mar 30, 2025
CLASSIC PHYSIQUE OF AMERICA
Lima, Peru
INTERNATIONAL FEDERATION OF
BODY BUILDING & FITNESS
contact@ifbb.com
www.ifbb.com

Apr 12 - Apr 13, 2025
DIAMOND CUP MALTA
Malta
INTERNATIONAL FEDERATION OF
BODY BUILDING & FITNESS
contact@ifbb.com
www.ifbb.com

Apr 12 - Apr 13, 2025
MERCOSUR CUP
Porto Alagre, Brazil
INTERNATIONAL FEDERATION OF
BODY BUILDING & FITNESS
contact@ifbb.com
www.ifbb.com

Apr 18 - Apr 21, 2025
SIBERIAN POWER SHOW
Krasnoyarsk, Russia
INTERNATIONAL FEDERATION OF
BODY BUILDING & FITNESS
contact@ifbb.com
www.ifbb.com

Apr 25 - Apr 27, 2025
BALKAN CHAMPIONSHIPS
Niksic, Montenegro
INTERNATIONAL FEDERATION OF
BODY BUILDING & FITNESS
contact@ifbb.com
www.ifbb.com

Apr 30 - May 5, 2025
EUROPEAN CHAMPIONSHIPS
Santa Susana, Spain
INTERNATIONAL FEDERATION OF
BODY BUILDING & FITNESS
contact@ifbb.com
www.ifbb.com

May TBA, 2025
ARNOLD CLASSIC AFRICA
Johannesburg, South Africa
INTERNATIONAL FEDERATION OF
BODY BUILDING & FITNESS
contact@ifbb.com
www.ifbb.com

May 9 - May 10, 2025
HERKULES GRAND PRIX
Skopje, North Macedonia
INTERNATIONAL FEDERATION OF
BODY BUILDING & FITNESS
contact@ifbb.com
www.ifbb.com

May 17, 2025
DIAMOND CUP CZECHIA
Czech Republic
INTERNATIONAL FEDERATION OF
BODY BUILDING & FITNESS
contact@ifbb.com
www.ifbb.com

May 24 - May 25, 2025
DIAMOND CUP ARMENIA
Yerevan, Armenia
INTERNATIONAL FEDERATION OF
BODY BUILDING & FITNESS
contact@ifbb.com
www.ifbb.com

May 30 - May 31, 2025
ROMANIAN GRAND PRIX
Bucharest, Romania
INTERNATIONAL FEDERATION OF
BODY BUILDING & FITNESS
contact@ifbb.com
www.ifbb.com

Jun 7 - Jun 8, 2025
DIAMOND CUP HUNGARY & FIT
MODEL AND BIKINI EUROP EAN CUP
Budapest, Hungary
INTERNATIONAL FEDERATION OF
BODY BUILDING & FITNESS
contact@ifbb.com
www.ifbb.com

Jun 13 - Jun 15, 2025
CENTRAL AMERICAN
CHAMPIONSHIPS
Guatamala
INTERNATIONAL FEDERATION OF
BODY BUILDING & FITNESS
contact@ifbb.com
www.ifbb.com

Jun 13 - Jun 15, 2025
WORLD CHAMPIONSHIPS IN
CHILDREN FITNESS
Cacak, Serbia
INTERNATIONAL FEDERATION OF
BODY BUILDING & FITNESS
contact@ifbb.com
www.ifbb.com

Jul 12 - Jul 13, 2025
MR UNIVERSO PARAGUAY
Asuncion, Paraguay
INTERNATIONAL FEDERATION OF
BODY BUILDING & FITNESS
contact@ifbb.com
www.ifbb.com

Aug 16 - Aug 17, 2025
MR AMERICA
Ecuador
INTERNATIONAL FEDERATION OF
BODY BUILDING & FITNESS
contact@ifbb.com
www.ifbb.com

Sept TBA, 2025
ARNOLD CLASSIC EUROPE
Sevilla, Spain
INTERNATIONAL FEDERATION OF
BODY BUILDING & FITNESS
contact@ifbb.com
www.ifbb.com

Sept 19 - Sept 21, 2025
DIAMOND CUP LUXEMBOURG
Luxembourg
INTERNATIONAL FEDERATION OF
BODY BUILDING & FITNESS
contact@ifbb.com
www.ifbb.com

Sept 26 - Sept 28, 2025
DIAMOND CUP PRAGUE
Prague, Czech Republic
INTERNATIONAL FEDERATION OF
BODY BUILDING & FITNESS

contact@ifbb.com
www.ifbb.com

Bowling

Mar 26 - Mar 29, 2025
CANADIAN YOUTH CHALLENGE
CHAMPIONSHIP
Calgary, AB, Canada
CANADIAN 5 PIN BOWLERS
ASSOCIATION
Phone: 613-744-5090
Fax: 613-744-2217
sheila.c5pba@gmail.com
www.c5pba.ca

Apr 23 - Apr 26, 2025
INTER PROVINCIAL CHAMPIONSHIP
Saskatoon, SK, Canada
CANADIAN 5 PIN BOWLERS
ASSOCIATION
Phone: 613-744-5090
Fax: 613-744-2217
sheila.c5pba@gmail.com
www.c5pba.ca

May 20 - May 24, 2025
CANADIAN OPEN CHAMPIONSHIP
Regina, SK, Canada
CANADIAN 5 PIN BOWLERS
ASSOCIATION
Phone: 613-744-5090
Fax: 613-744-2217
sheila.c5pba@gmail.com
www.c5pba.ca

Boxing

Jun TBA, 2026
NATIONAL JUNIOR OLYMPICS
TBA
USA BOXING
Phone: 719-866-2323
www.usaboxing.org

Apr 13 - Apr 19, 2025
USA BOXING INTERNATIONAL OPEN
Pueblo, CO
USA BOXING
Phone: 719-866-2323
www.usaboxing.org

Broomball

Mar TBA, 2025
USA BROOMBALL NATIONAL
CHAMPIONSHIPS
TBA
USA BROOMBALL
contact@usbabroomball.org
usbabroomball.org

Canoeing & Kayaking

May 16 - May 18, 2025
ICF CANOE SPRINT WORLD CUP 1
Szeged, Hungary
INTERNATIONAL CANOE FEDERATION
International Ph: 41 (0)21 612 0290
info@canoeicf.com
www.canoeicf.com

May 22 - May 25, 2025
ICF CANOE SPRINT WORLD CUP 2
Poznan, Poland

INTERNATIONAL CANOE FEDERATION
International Ph: 41 (0)21 612 0290
info@canoeicf.com
www.canoeicf.com

May 22 - May 25, 2025
ICF PARACANOE WORLD CUP
Poznan, Poland
INTERNATIONAL CANOE FEDERATION
International Ph: 41 (0)21 612 0290
info@canoeicf.com
www.canoeicf.com

Jul 8 - Jul 13, 2025
ICF JUNIOR & U23 CANOE SLALOM
WORLD CHAMPIONSHIP
Foix, France
INTERNATIONAL CANOE FEDERATION
International Ph: 41 (0)21 612 0290
info@canoeicf.com
www.canoeicf.com

Jul 10 - Jul 12, 2025
ICF WILDWATER CANOEING WORLD
CUP
Banja Luka, Bosnia
INTERNATIONAL CANOE FEDERATION
International Ph: 41 (0)21 612 0290
info@canoeicf.com
www.canoeicf.com

Jul 23 - Jul 27, 2025
ICF JUNIOR & U23 CANOE SPRINT
WORLD CHAMPIONSHIP
Montemor-o-Velho, Portugal
INTERNATIONAL CANOE FEDERATION
International Ph: 41 (0)21 612 0290
info@canoeicf.com
www.canoeicf.com

Aug 20 - Aug 24, 2025
ICF CANOE SPRINT WORLD
CHAMPIONSHIPS
Milan, Italy
INTERNATIONAL CANOE FEDERATION
International Ph: 41 (0)21 612 0290
info@canoeicf.com
www.canoeicf.com

Sept 4 - Sept 7, 2025
ICF CANOE MARATHON WORLD
CHAMPIONSHIP
Gyor, Hungary
INTERNATIONAL CANOE FEDERATION
International Ph: 41 (0)21 612 0290
info@canoeicf.com
www.canoeicf.com

Oct 17 - Oct 19, 2025
ICF CANOE OCEAN RACING WORLD
CHAMPIONSHIPS
Durban, South Africa
INTERNATIONAL CANOE FEDERATION
International Ph: 41 (0)21 612 0290
info@canoeicf.com
www.canoeicf.com

Cheerleading

Feb 13 - Feb 17, 2025
USA SPIRIT NATIONALS
Anaheim, CA
Anaheim Convention Center
UNITED SPIRIT ASSOCIATION
Phone: 800-533-8022
info@usacamps.com
usa.varsity.com

Feb 15 - Feb 17, 2024
USA COLLEGIATE CHAMPIONSHIPS
Anaheim, CA
Anaheim Convention Center
UNITED SPIRIT ASSOCIATION
Phone: 800-533-8022
info@usacamps.com
usa.varsity.com

Feb 16, 2025
USA JUNIOR NATIONALS
Anaheim, CA
Anaheim Convention Center
UNITED SPIRIT ASSOCIATION
Phone: 800-533-8022
info@usacamps.com
usa.varsity.com

Mar 21 - Mar 23, 2025
ALL STAR CHAMPIONSHIPS
Los Angeles, CA
UNITED SPIRIT ASSOCIATION
Phone: 800-533-8022
info@usacamps.com
usa.varsity.com

Jul 15 - Jul 18, 2025
AAU GIRLS' NATIONAL BEACH
VOLLEYBALL CHAMPIONSHI PS
Hermosa Beach, CA
Hermose Beach Pier
AMATEUR ATHLETIC UNION
Phone: 407-934-7200
Fax: 407-934-7242
www.aausports.org

Croquet

Apr 14 - Apr 18, 2025
UNDER 21 GC WORLD
CHAMPIONSHIP
Sarasota, FL
Sarasota Country Croquet Club
US CROQUET ASSOCIATION
usca@msn.com
www.croquetamerica.com

Jan TBA, 2026
THE DESERT CLASSIC AC
Rancho Mirage, CA
Mission Hills Country Club
US CROQUET ASSOCIATION
usca@msn.com
www.croquetamerica.com

Jan 15 - Jan 18, 2026
WOMEN'S AC WORLD
CHAMPIONSHIP
West Palm, FL
National Croquet Center
US CROQUET ASSOCIATION
usca@msn.com
www.croquetamerica.com

Cross Country

Nov 22, 2025
NCAA DIVISION I MEN'S CROSS
COUNTRY FINALS
Columbia, MO
Gans Creek Cross Country
NATIONAL COLLEGIATE ATHLETIC
ASSOCIATION
Phone: 317-917-6222
Fax: 317-917-6888
www.ncaa.org

Nov 22, 2025
NCAA DIVISION II MEN'S/WOMEN'S
CROSS COUNTRY FIN ALS
Kenosha, WI
Wayne E Danehl National Cross
Country Course
NATIONAL COLLEGIATE ATHLETIC
ASSOCIATION
Phone: 317-917-6222
Fax: 317-917-6888
www.ncaa.org

Nov 22, 2025
NCAA DIVISION III MEN'S/WOMEN'S
CROSS COUNTRY FI NALS
Spartanburg, Sc
Roger Milliken Center
NATIONAL COLLEGIATE ATHLETIC
ASSOCIATION
Phone: 317-917-6222
Fax: 317-917-6888
www.ncaa.org

Curling

Jan 27 - Feb 2, 2025
SENIOR MEN'S NATIONAL
CHAMPIONSHIPS
Duluth, MN
Duluth Entertainment Convention
Center
USA CURLING
Phone: 715-344-1199
Fax: 715-344-2279
www.usacurling.org

Jan 27 - Feb 2, 2025
SENIOR WOMEN'S NATIONAL
CHAMPIONSHIPS
Duluth, MN
Duluth Entertainment Convention
Center
USA CURLING
Phone: 715-344-1199
Fax: 715-344-2279
www.usacurling.org

Feb 14 - Feb 23, 2025
SCOTTIES TOURNAMENT OF
HEARTS
Thunder Bay, ON, Canada
Fort William Gardens
CURLING CANADA
Phone: 613-834-2076
Fax: 613-834-0716
championships@curling.ca
www.curling.ca

Feb 16 - Feb 22, 2025
CANADIAN UNDER-18 BOYS AND
GIRLS CHAMPIONSHIPS
Saskatoon, SK, Canada
Nutana Curling Club
CURLING CANADA
Phone: 613-834-2076
Fax: 613-834-0716
championships@curling.ca
www.curling.ca

Feb 17 - Feb 23, 2025
MIXED DOUBLES NATIONAL
CHAMPIONSHIP
Lafayette, CO
Rock Creek Curling
USA CURLING
Phone: 715-344-1199
Fax: 715-344-2279
www.usacurling.org

Feb 28 - Mar 9, 2025
MONTANA'S BRIER
Kelowna, BC, Canada
Prospera Place
CURLING CANADA
Phone: 613-834-2076
Fax: 613-834-0716
championships@curling.ca
www.curling.ca

Mar 16 - Mar 21, 2025
MIXED DOUBLES CHAMPIONSHIP
Summerside, PE, Canada
Gerard "Turk" Gallant Arena
CURLING CANADA
Phone: 613-834-2076
Fax: 613-834-0716
championships@curling.ca
www.curling.ca

Mar 22 - Mar 30, 2025
NEW HOLLAND CANADIAN JUNIOR
MEN'S AND WOMEN'S CURLING
CHAMPIONSHIPS
Summerside, PE, Canada
Gerard "Turk" Gallant Arena
CURLING CANADA
Phone: 613-834-2076
Fax: 613-834-0716
championships@curling.ca
www.curling.ca

Mar 26 - Mar 30, 2025
CLUB NATIONAL CHAMPIONSHIPS
Cedarburg, WI
Milwaukee Curling Club
USA CURLING
Phone: 715-344-1199
Fax: 715-344-2279
www.usacurling.org

Mar 29 - Apr 6, 2025
WORLD MEN'S CURLING
CHAMPIONSHIP
Moose Jaw, Canada
Moose Jaw Events Centre
CURLING CANADA
Phone: 613-834-2076
Fax: 613-834-0716
championships@curling.ca
www.curling.ca

Apr 28 - May 3, 2025
CANADIAN WHEELCHAIR CURLING
CHAMPIONSHIP
Boucherville, QC, Canada
CURLING CANADA
Phone: 613-834-2076
Fax: 613-834-0716
championships@curling.ca
www.curling.ca

Mar 14 - Mar 22, 2026
WORLD WOMEN'S CURLING
CHAMPIONSHIP
Calgary, AB, Canada
WinSport Event Centre
CURLING CANADA
Phone: 613-834-2076
Fax: 613-834-0716
championships@curling.ca
www.curling.ca

Cycling

TBA, 2025
CANADA CUP XCO
TBA

CANADIAN CYCLING ASSOCIATION
Phone: 613-248-1353
Fax: 613-248-9311
general@cyclingcanada.ca
www.cyclingcanada.ca

Feb 28 - Mar 2, 2025
USA BMX LONE STAR NATIONALS
Houston, TX
RockStar Energy Bike Park
USA BMX
Phone: 480-961-1903
Fax: 480-961-1842
info@usabmx.com
www.usabmx.com

Mar 21 - Mar 23, 2025
COLLEGIATE BMX NATIONAL
CHAMPIONSHIPS
West Monroe, LA
USA CYCLING
Phone: 719-434-4200
Fax: 719-434-4300
help@usacycling.org
www.usacycling.org

Mar 28 - Mar 30, 2025
USA BMX CAROLINA NATIONALS
Rock Hill, SC
Rock Hill Super BMX Supercross Track
USA BMX
Phone: 480-961-1903
Fax: 480-961-1842
info@usabmx.com
www.usabmx.com

Apr 11 - Apr 13, 2025
USA BMX GREAT NORTHWEST
NATIONALS
Redmond, OR
USA BMX
Phone: 480-961-1903
Fax: 480-961-1842
info@usabmx.com
www.usabmx.com

Apr 25 - Apr 27, 2025
USA BMX GOLDEN STATE
NATIONALS
Bakersfield, CA
Metro BMX
USA BMX
Phone: 480-961-1903
Fax: 480-961-1842
info@usabmx.com
www.usabmx.com

May 2 - May 4, 2025
COLLEGIATE ROAD NATIONAL
CHAMPIONSHIPS
Madison, WI
USA CYCLING
Phone: 719-434-4200
Fax: 719-434-4300
help@usacycling.org
www.usacycling.org

May 2 - May 4, 2025
USA BMX DIXIELAND NATIONALS
Powder Springs, GA
USA BMX
Phone: 480-961-1903
Fax: 480-961-1842
info@usabmx.com
www.usabmx.com

May 9 - May 11, 2025
ELITE BMX NATIONAL
CHAMPIONSHIPS
Tulsa, OK

USA CYCLING
Phone: 719-434-4200
Fax: 719-434-4300
help@usacycling.org
www.usacycling.org

May 19 - May 26, 2025
PRO ROAD NATIONAL
CHAMPIONSHIPS
Charleston, WV
USA CYCLING
Phone: 719-434-4200
Fax: 719-434-4300
help@usacycling.org
www.usacycling.org

Jun 28 - Jul 2, 2025
MASTERS ROAD NATIONAL
CHAMPIONSHIPS
South East, WI
USA CYCLING
Phone: 719-434-4200
Fax: 719-434-4300
help@usacycling.org
www.usacycling.org

Jun 6 - Jun 8, 2025
USA BMX SPRING NATIONALS
Albuquerque, NM
USA BMX
Phone: 480-961-1903
Fax: 480-961-1842
info@usabmx.com
www.usabmx.com

Jun 27 - Jun 30, 2025
CANADIAN ROAD CHAMPIONSHIPS
Saint-Georges, QC, Canada
CANADIAN CYCLING ASSOCIATION
Phone: 613-248-1353
Fax: 613-248-9311
general@cyclingcanada.ca
www.cyclingcanada.ca

Jul 5 - Jul 27, 2025
TOUR DE FRANCE
Paris, France
AMAURY SPORT ORGANIZATION
International Ph: 33-1-41-33-14-00
contact@aso.fr
www.aso.fr

Jul 14 - Jul 20, 2025
ENDURANCE MOUNTAIN BIKE
NATIONAL CHAMPIONSHIPS
Roanoke, VA
USA CYCLING
Phone: 719-434-4200
Fax: 719-434-4300
help@usacycling.org
www.usacycling.org

Jul 25 - Jul 27, 2025
CANADIAN DOWNHILL MTB
CHAMPIONSHIPS
Sun Peaks, BC, Canada
CANADIAN CYCLING ASSOCIATION
Phone: 613-248-1353
Fax: 613-248-9311
general@cyclingcanada.ca
www.cyclingcanada.ca

Jul 31 - Aug 3, 2025
MOUNTAIN BIKE NATIONAL
CHAMPIONSHIPS
Big Bear Lake, CA
USA CYCLING
Phone: 719-434-4200
Fax: 719-434-4300
help@usacycling.org
www.usacycling.org

Aug 6 - Aug 10, 2025
MASTERS TRACK NATIONAL
CHAMPIONSHIPS
Colorado Springs, CO
USA CYCLING
Phone: 719-434-4200
Fax: 719-434-4300
help@usacycling.org
www.usacycling.org

Aug 8 - Aug 10, 2025
ELITE & MASTERS CANADIAN
CHAMPIONSHIPS
Victoria, BC, Canada
CANADIAN CYCLING ASSOCIATION
Phone: 613-248-1353
Fax: 613-248-9311
general@cyclingcanada.ca
www.cyclingcanada.ca

Aug 21 - Aug 24, 2025
ELITE TRACK NATIONAL
CHAMPIONSHIPS
Colorado Springs, CO
USA CYCLING
Phone: 719-434-4200
Fax: 719-434-4300
help@usacycling.org
www.usacycling.org

Aug 30 - Aug 31, 2025
CANADA CUP DHI
Mount Washington, BC, Canada
CANADIAN CYCLING ASSOCIATION
Phone: 613-248-1353
Fax: 613-248-9311
general@cyclingcanada.ca
www.cyclingcanada.ca

Sept 11 - Sept 14, 2025
COLLEGIATE TRACK NATIONAL
CHAMPIONSHIPS
Indianapolis, IN
USA CYCLING
Phone: 719-434-4200
Fax: 719-434-4300
help@usacycling.org
www.usacycling.org

Oct 9 - Oct 12, 2025
COLLEGIATE MOUNTAIN BIKE
NATIONAL CHAMPIONSHIPS
Grand Junction, CO
USA CYCLING
Phone: 719-434-4200
Fax: 719-434-4300
help@usacycling.org
www.usacycling.org

Oct 31 - Nov 2, 2025
USA BMX FALL NATIONALS
Phoenix, AZ
USA BMX
Phone: 480-961-1903
Fax: 480-961-1842
info@usabmx.com
www.usabmx.com

Nov 27 - Nov 30, 2025
USA BMX GRANDS RACE OF
CHAMPIONS
Tulsa, OK
USA BMX
Phone: 480-961-1903
Fax: 480-961-1842
info@usabmx.com
www.usabmx.com

Dec 11 - Dec 14, 2025
CYCLOCROSS NATIONAL
CHAMPIONSHIPS
Fayetteville, AR
USA CYCLING
Phone: 719-434-4200
Fax: 719-434-4300
help@usacycling.org
www.usacycling.org

Darts

Apr 10 - Apr 16, 2025
TEAM DART CHAMPIONSHIPS
Las Vegas, NV
Westgate Las Vegas Resort & Casino
NATIONAL DART ASSOCIATION
Phone: 800-808-9884
Fax: 708-226-1310
info@ndadarts.com
www.ndadarts.com

Diving

Apr 11 - Apr 13, 2025
USA MASTERS SPRING NATIONAL
CHAMPIONSHIPS
Houston, TX
USA DIVING
Phone: 317-237-5252
Fax: 317-237-5257
Dan.Laak@usadiving.org
www.usadiving.org

May 2 - May 4, 2025
FINA DIVING WORLD CUP
Beijing, China
USA DIVING
Phone: 317-237-5252
Fax: 317-237-5257
Dan.Laak@usadiving.org
www.usadiving.org

May 23 - May 25, 2025
SUMMER SENIOR NATIONAL
CHAMPIONSHIPS
Saskatoon, SK, Canada
DIVING CANADA
Phone: 613-736-5238
Fax: 613-736-0409
cada@diving.ca
www.diving.ca

Jun 5 - Jun 8, 2025
CANADA CUP OF DIVING
Gatineau, QC, Canada
DIVING CANADA
Phone: 613-736-5238
Fax: 613-736-0409
cada@diving.ca
www.diving.ca

Jul 11 - Aug 3, 2025
FINA CHAMPIONSHIPS
Singapore
USA DIVING
Phone: 317-237-5252
Fax: 317-237-5257
Dan.Laak@usadiving.org
www.usadiving.org

Jul 15 - Jul 23, 2025
AAU DIVING NATIONAL
CHAMPIONSHIP
Riverside, CA
Riverside Community College

AMATEUR ATHLETIC UNION
Phone: 407-934-7200
Fax: 407-934-7242
www.aausports.org

Jul 25 - Aug 3, 2025
US DIVING JUNIOR NATIONAL
CHAMPIONSHIPS
Mission Viejo, CA
USA DIVING
Phone: 317-237-5252
Fax: 317-237-5257
Dan.Laak@usadiving.org
www.usadiving.org

Dog Showing

Mar 14 - Mar 16, 2025
AKC NATIONAL AGILITY
CHAMPIONSHIPS
Tulsa, OK
Built Ford Tough Livestock Complex at
Expo Square
AMERICAN KENNEL CLUB
Phone: 919-233-9767
publiced@akc.org
www.akc.org

Jul 3 - Jul 5, 2025
AKC RALLY NATIONAL
CHAMPIONSHIP
Gray Summitt, MO
Purina Event Center
AMERICAN KENNEL CLUB
Phone: 919-233-9767
publiced@akc.org
www.akc.org

Jul 6 - Jul 7, 2025
AKC NATIONAL OBEDIENCE
CHAMPIONSHIP
Gray Summit, MO
Purina Event Center
AMERICAN KENNEL CLUB
Phone: 919-233-9767
publiced@akc.org
www.akc.org

Dec 12 - Dec 13, 2025
AKC RACH INVITATIONAL
Orlando, FL
Orange County Convention Center
AMERICAN KENNEL CLUB
Phone: 919-233-9767
publiced@akc.org
www.akc.org

Dec 13 - Dec 14, 2025
AKC OBEDIENCE CLASSIC
Orlando, FL
Orange County Convention Center
AMERICAN KENNEL CLUB
Phone: 919-233-9767
publiced@akc.org
www.akc.org

Equestrian

Apr 24 - Apr 27, 2025
LAND ROVER KENTUCKY
THREE-DAY EVENT
Lexington, KY
Kentucky Horse Park
US EQUESTRIAN FEDERATION
Phone: 859-258-2472
Fax: 859-231-6662
www.usef.org

Aug 18 - Aug 24, 2025
US DRESSAGE FESTIVAL OF
CHAMPIONS
Wayne, IL
HITS Chicago at Lamplight Equestrian
Center
US EQUESTRIAN FEDERATION
Phone: 859-258-2472
Fax: 859-231-6662
www.usef.org

Fencing

Apr 11 - Apr 14, 2025
DIVISION I & PARAFENCING
NATIONAL CHAMPIONSHIPS
Los Angeles, CA
USA FENCING
Phone: 719-866-4511
Fax: 719-632-5737
information@usafencing.org
www.usafencing.org

May 16 - May 19, 2025
MAY NATIONALS
St. Catherines, ON, Canada
CANADIAN FENCING FEDERATION
Phone: 647-476-2401
Fax: 647-476-2402
cff@fencing.ca
www.fencing.ca

Jun 28 - Jul 7, 2025
USA FENCING NATIONAL
CHAMPIONSHIPS & JULY CHALLE
NGE (SUMMER NATIONALS)
Milwaukee, WI
USA FENCING
Phone: 719-866-4511
Fax: 719-632-5737
information@usafencing.org
www.usafencing.org

Figure Skating

Feb 26 - Mar 1, 2025
US SYNCHRONIZED SKATING
CHAMPIONSHIPS
Colorado Springs, CO
U.S. FIGURE SKATING
Phone: 719-635-5200
Fax: 719-635-9548
info@usfigureskating.org
www.usfigureskating.org

Mar 2, 2025
LEGACY ON ICE
Washington, DC
U.S. FIGURE SKATING
Phone: 719-635-5200
Fax: 719-635-9548
info@usfigureskating.org
www.usfigureskating.org

Mar 14 - Mar 16, 2025
EASTERN ADULT SECTIONAL
CHAMPIONSHIPS
Indian Trail, NC
U.S. FIGURE SKATING
Phone: 719-635-5200
Fax: 719-635-9548
info@usfigureskating.org
www.usfigureskating.org

Mar 14 - Mar 16, 2025
PACIFIC COAST ADULT SECTIONAL
CHAMPIONSHIPS
Paramount, CA
U.S. FIGURE SKATING
Phone: 719-635-5200
Fax: 719-635-9548
info@usfigureskating.org
www.usfigureskating.org

Mar 21 - Mar 23, 2025
MIDWESTERN ADULT SECTIONAL
CHAMPIONSHIPS
Madison, WI
U.S. FIGURE SKATING
Phone: 719-635-5200
Fax: 719-635-9548
info@usfigureskating.org
www.usfigureskating.org

Mar 23 - Mar 30, 2025
WORLD FIGURE SKATING
CHAMPIONSHIPS
Boston, MA
U.S. FIGURE SKATING
Phone: 719-635-5200
Fax: 719-635-9548
info@usfigureskating.org
www.usfigureskating.org

Apr 2 - Apr 5, 2025
US ADULT FIGURE SKATING
CHAMPIONSHIPS
St. Louis Park, MN
U.S. FIGURE SKATING
Phone: 719-635-5200
Fax: 719-635-9548
info@usfigureskating.org
www.usfigureskating.org

Jan 6 - Jan 11, 2026
US FIGURE SKATING
CHAMPIONSHIPS
St. Louis, MO
U.S. FIGURE SKATING
Phone: 719-635-5200
Fax: 719-635-9548
info@usfigureskating.org
www.usfigureskating.org

Fishing

Feb 27 - Mar 2, 2025
BASSMASTER ELITE SERIES - LAKE
OKEECHOBEE
Okeechobee, FL
Lake Okeechobee
BASS ANGLERS SPORTSMAN
SOCIETY
Phone: 877-227-7872
bassmaster@emailcustomerservice.com
www.bassmaster.com

Mar 21 - Mar 23, 2025
OUTDOORS BASSMASTER CLASSIC
Fort Worth, TX
Lake Ray Roberts
BASS ANGLERS SPORTSMAN
SOCIETY
Phone: 877-227-7872
bassmaster@emailcustomerservice.com
www.bassmaster.com

Apr 10 - Apr 13, 2025
BASSMASTER ELITE SERIES -
PASQUOTANK RIVER
Elizabeth City, NC
Pasquotank River

BASS ANGLERS SPORTSMAN
SOCIETY
Phone: 877-227-7872
bassmaster@emailcustomerservice.com
www.bassmaster.com

Apr 24 - Apr 27, 2025
BASSMASTER ELITE SERIES - LAKE
HARTWELL
Anderson, SC
Lake Hartwell
BASS ANGLERS SPORTSMAN
SOCIETY
Phone: 877-227-7872
bassmaster@emailcustomerservice.com
www.bassmaster.com

Apr 24 - Apr 25, 2025
WALLEYE TOUR-LAKE SHARPE
Pierre, SD
Lake Sharpe
NATIONAL WALLEYE TOUR
Phone: 612-424-0708
Fax: 866-727-2809
outdoorteamworks.com/trail/nwt

May 8 - May 11, 2025
BASSMASTER ELITE SERIES - LAKE
FORK
Yantis, TX
Lake Fork
BASS ANGLERS SPORTSMAN
SOCIETY
Phone: 877-227-7872
bassmaster@emailcustomerservice.com
www.bassmaster.com

May 22 - May 23, 2025
WALLEYE TOUR-MISSISSIPPI RIVER
La Crosse, WI
Mississippi River
NATIONAL WALLEYE TOUR
Phone: 612-424-0708
Fax: 866-727-2809
outdoorteamworks.com/trail/nwt

Jun 12 - Jun 15, 2025
BASSMASTER ELITE SERIES - LAKE
TENKILLER
Cookson, OK
Lake Tenkiller
BASS ANGLERS SPORTSMAN
SOCIETY
Phone: 877-227-7872
bassmaster@emailcustomerservice.com
www.bassmaster.com

Jul 10 - Jul 11, 2025
WALLEYE TOUR-LAKE HURON
Alpena, MI
Lake Huron
NATIONAL WALLEYE TOUR
Phone: 612-424-0708
Fax: 866-727-2809
outdoorteamworks.com/trail/nwt

Aug 7 - Aug 10, 2025
BASSMASTER ELITE SERIES - LAKE
ST. CLAIR
Macomb County, MI
Lake St. Clair
BASS ANGLERS SPORTSMAN
SOCIETY
Phone: 877-227-7872
bassmaster@emailcustomerservice.com
www.bassmaster.com

Aug 7 0 Aug 8, 2025
WALLEYE TOUR-LAKE ERIE
Bunkirk, NY
Lake Erie

NATIONAL WALLEYE TOUR
Phone: 612-424-0708
Fax: 866-727-2809
outdoorteamworks.com/trail/nwt

Aug 21 - Aug 24, 2025
BASSMASTER ELITE SERIES -
MISSISSIPPI RIVER
La Crosse, MI
Mississippi River
BASS ANGLERS SPORTSMAN
SOCIETY
Phone: 877-227-7872
bassmaster@emailcustomerservice.com
www.bassmaster.com

Sept 4 - Sept 6, 2025
WALLEYE TOUR CHAMPIONSHIP
Marinette, WI
Bay of Green Bay
NATIONAL WALLEYE TOUR
Phone: 612-424-0708
Fax: 866-727-2809
outdoorteamworks.com/trail/nwt

Football

TBA, 2025
AUTOZONE LIBERTY BOWL
Memphis, TN
Liberty Bowl Memorial Stadium
AUTOZONE LIBERTY BOWL
Phone: 901-795-7700
Fax: 901-795-7826
hgraeter@libertybowl.org
www.libertybowl.org

Jan TBA, 2025
NCAA DIVISION I FCS
CHAMPIONSHIP
TBA
NATIONAL COLLEGIATE ATHLETIC
ASSOCIATION
Phone: 317-917-6222
Fax: 317-917-6888
www.ncaa.org

Jan 1, 2025
ALLSTATE SUGAR BOWL
New Orleans, LA
Mercedes-Benz Superdome
ALLSTATE SUGAR BOWL
Phone: 504-828-2440
Fax: 504-828-2441
info@sugarbowl.org
www.allstatesugarbowl.org

Jan 1, 2025
ROSE BOWL GAME
Pasadena, CA
Rose Bowl Stadium
PASADENA TOURNAMENT OF ROSES
ASSOCIATION
Phone: 626-449-4100
www.tournamentofroses.com

Jan 3, 2025
BELK BOWL
Charlotte, NC
Bank of America Stadium
BELK BOWL
Phone: 704-644-4047
Info@CharlotteSports.org
www.belkbowl.com

Jan 10, 2025
GOODYEAR COTTON BOWL
CLASSIC
Arlington, TX
AT&T Stadium

GOODYEAR COTTON BOWL CLASSIC
Phone: 817-892-4800
Fax: 817-892-4810
cso@attcottonbowl.com
www.cottonbowl.com

Jan 30, 2025
NFL PRO BOWL
Orlando, FL
NATIONAL FOOTBALL LEAGUE
Phone: 212-450-2000
www.nfl.com

Feb 1, 2025
SENIOR BOWL
Mobile, AL
Ladd-Peebles Stadium
SENIOR BOWL
Phone: 251-438-2276
Fax: 251-432-0409
srbowl@seniorbowl.com
www.seniorbowl.com

Dec TBA, 2025
EASYPOST HAWAII BOWL
Honolulu, HI
Aloha Stadium
EASYPOST HAWAII BOWL
www.thehawaiibowl.com

Dec TBA, 2025
FAMOUS IDAHO POTATO BOWL
TBA
FAMOUS IDAHO POTATO BOWL
Phone: 208-424-1011
Fax: 208-424-1121
www.famousidahopotatobowl.com

Dec TBA, 2025
INDEPENDENCE BOWL
TBA
INDEPENDENCE BOWL FOUNDATION
Phone: 318-221-0712
Fax: 318-221-7366
independencebowl.org

Dec TBA, 2025
LENDING TREE BOWL
Mobile, AL
Ladd-Peebles Stadium
LENDING TREE BOWL
Phone: 251-635-0011
contact@mabowl.com
lendingtreebowl.com

Dec TBA, 2025
NEW ORLEANS BOWL
New Orleans, LA
Mercedes-Benz Superdome
NEW ORLEANS BOWL
Phone: 504-525-5678
Fax: 504-529-1622
www.neworleansbowl.org

Dec TBA, 2025
RELIAQUEST BOWL
Tampa, FL
Raymond James Stadium
RELIAQUEST BOWL
Phone: 813-874-2695
Fax: 813-873-1959
www.reliaquestbowl.com

Dec TBA, 2025
SAN FRANCISCO BOWL
Santa Clara, CA
Levi's Stadium
SAN FRANCISCO BOWL GAME
ASSOCIATION

Dec TBA, 2025
TAXSLAYER GATOR BOWL
Jacksonville, FL
Tiaa Bank Field
TAXSLAYER GATOR BOWL
Phone: 904-798-1700
Fax: 904-632-2080
tickets@taxslayerbowl.com
www.taxslayergatorbowl.com

Dec TBA, 2025
TRANSPERFECT MUSIC CITY BOWL
Nashville, TN
Nissan Stadium
TRANSPERFECT MORTGAGE MUSIC
CITY BOWL
Phone: 615-743-3130
tickets@musiccitybowl.com
www.musiccitybowl.com

Dec TBA, 2025
VALERO ALAMO BOWL
San Antonio, TX
The Alamodome
SAN ANTONIO BOWL ASSOCIATION
Phone: 210-226-2695
Fax: 210-704-6399
info@alamobowl.com
www.alamobowl.com

Dec 20, 2025
NCAA DIVISION II FOOTBALL FINALS
McKinney, TX
McKinney ISD Stadium
NATIONAL COLLEGIATE ATHLETIC
ASSOCIATION
Phone: 317-917-6222
Fax: 317-917-6888
www.ncaa.org

Dec 31, 2025
FIESTA BOWL
Glendale, AZ
State Farm Stadium
FIESTA BOWL
Phone: 480-350-0900
Fax: 480-350-0915
prdept@fiestabowl.org
www.fiestabowl.org

Dec 31, 2025
TONY THE TIGER SUN BOWL
El Paso, TX
Sun Bowl Stadium
SUN BOWL ASSOCIATION
Phone: 915-533-4416
Fax: 915-533-0661
www.sunbowl.org

Jan 9, 2026
CHICK-FIL-A PEACH BOWL
TBA
CHICK-FIL-A PEACH BOWL
Phone: 404-586-8500
Fax: 404-586-8508
tickets@cfabowl.com
www.chick-fil-apeachbowl.com

Jan 10, 2026
NCAA DIVISION III FOOTBALL FINALS
Canton, OH
Tom Benson Hall of Fame Stadium
NATIONAL COLLEGIATE ATHLETIC
ASSOCIATION
Phone: 317-917-6222
Fax: 317-917-6888
www.ncaa.org

Feb 8, 2026
SUPER BOWL LX
Santa Clara, CA
Levi's Stadium
NATIONAL FOOTBALL LEAGUE
Phone: 212-450-2000
www.nfl.com

Nov 16, 2026
CFL GREY CUP
Calgary, AB, Canada
McMahon Stadium
CANADIAN FOOTBALL LEAGUE
Phone: 416-322-9650
Fax: 416-322-9651
www.cfl.ca

Frisbee

May 10 - May 11, 2025
USA ULTIMATE BEACH
CHAMPIONSHIPS
Virginia Beach, VA
USA ULTIMATE
Phone: 800-872-4384
Fax: 719-219-8322
info@usaultimate.org
www.usaultimate.org

May 17 - May 19, 2025
USA ULTIMATE D-III COLLEGE
CHAMPIONSHIPS
Burlington, WA
USA ULTIMATE
Phone: 800-872-4384
Fax: 719-219-8322
info@usaultimate.org
www.usaultimate.org

May 23 - May 26, 2025
USA ULTIMATE D-I COLLEGE
CHAMPIONSHIPS
Burlington, WA
USA ULTIMATE
Phone: 800-872-4384
Fax: 719-219-8322
info@usaultimate.org
www.usaultimate.org

State & World Games

TBA, 2025
SUNSHINE STATE GAMES
TBA
SUNSHINE STATE GAMES
Phone: 850-577-7200
info@playinflorida.com
playinflorida.com

Jan 30, 2025
EAST WEST SHRINE BOWL
Paradise, NV
Allegiant Stadium
EAST WEST SHRINE GAME
Phone: 813-281-8686
EastWestShrineBowl@shrinenet.org
shrinebowl.com

Apr 25 - Apr 27, 2025
CYCLE NORTH CAROLINA COASTAL
RIDE
Elizabeth City, NC
NORTH CAROLINA AMATEUR SPORTS
Phone: 919-361-1133
Fax: 919-361-2559
ncas@ncsports.org
www.ncsports.org

Jun TBA, 2025
LARRY H MILLER UTAH SUMMER
GAMES
Cedar City, UT
Southern Utah University
UTAH SUMMER GAMES
Phone: 435-865-8421
Fax: 435-865-8548
usg@suu.edu
utahsummergames.org

Jun 6, 2025
STATE GAMES OF MISSISSIPPI
Meridian, MS
STATE GAMES OF MISSISSIPPI
Phone: 601-482-0205
info@stategamesofms.org
www.stategamesofms.org

Jun 13 - Jun 15, 2025
ALABAMA STATE GAMES
Birmingham, AL
ASF FOUNDATION
Phone: 800-467-0422
Fax: 334-280-0988
support@asffoundation.org
www.asffoundation.org

Aug TBA, 2025
BLUEGRASS STATE GAMES
Lexington, KY
BLUEGRASS STATE GAMES
Phone: 859-523-0009
info@bgsg.org
www.bgsg.org

Aug 1 - Aug 3, 2025
CYCLE NORTH CAROLINA
MOUNTAIN RIDE
Sylva, NC
NORTH CAROLINA AMATEUR SPORTS
Phone: 919-361-1133
Fax: 919-361-2559
ncas@ncsports.org
www.ncsports.org

Oct 5 - Oct 10, 2025
CYCLE NORTH CAROLINA
MOUNTAINS TO COAST
Lake Lure to Fort Fisher, NC
NORTH CAROLINA AMATEUR SPORTS
Phone: 919-361-1133
Fax: 919-361-2559
ncas@ncsports.org
www.ncsports.org

Jan TBA, 2027
SPECIAL OLYMPICS USA NATIONAL
GAMES
TBA
SPECIAL OLYMPICS
Phone: 202-628-3630
Fax: 202-824-0200
cweir@specialolympics.org
www.specialolympics.org

Jan TBA, 2027
SPECIAL OLYMPICS WORLD
SUMMER GAMES
TBA
SPECIAL OLYMPICS
Phone: 202-628-3630
Fax: 202-824-0200
cweir@specialolympics.org
www.specialolympics.org

Golf

Jan 2 - Jan 5, 2025
SENTRY TOURNAMENT OF
CHAMPIONS
Kapalua, HI
Plantation Course at Kapalua
PGA TOUR
Phone: 904-285-3700
www.pgatour.com

Jan 16 - Jan 18, 2025
HERO DUBAI DESERT CLASSIC
Dubai, United Arab Emirates
Emirates Golf Club
PGA EUROPEAN TOUR
International Ph: 44-0-1344-840400
International Fax: 44-0-1344-840500
www.rydercup.com

Jan 16 - Jan 18, 2025
MITSUBISHI ELECTRIC
CHAMPIONSHIP AT HUALALAI
Ka'upulehu-Kona, HI
Hualalai Golf Course
PGA CHAMPIONS TOUR
Phone: 904-285-3700
www.pgatour.com/pgatour-champions

Jan 30 - Feb 2, 2025
AT&T PEBBLE BEACH PRO-AM
Pebble Beach, CA
Pebble Beach Golf Links
PGA TOUR
Phone: 904-285-3700
www.pgatour.com

Jan 30 - Feb 2, 2025
PANAMA CHAMPIONSHIP
Panama City, Panama
Panama Golf Club
PGA KORN FERRY TOUR
Phone: 904-285-3700
Fax: 904-285-7913
www.pgatour.com

Feb TBA, 2025
SWING THOUGHT NATIONAL PRO
SERIES - BENT CREEK
Jax, FL
Bent Creek Golf Club

Feb TBA, 2025
SWING THOUGHT NATIONAL PRO
SERIES - NATIVE OAKS
Valley Center, CA
Native Oaks

Feb 3 - Feb 9, 2025
WASTE MANAGEMENT PHOENIX
OPEN
Scottsdale, AZ
TPC Scottsdale
PGA TOUR
Phone: 904-285-3700
www.pgatour.com

Feb 6 - Feb 8, 2025
COLOMBIA CHAMPIONSHIP
Bogota, Colombia
Country Club de Bogota
PGA KORN FERRY TOUR
Phone: 904-285-3700
Fax: 904-285-7913
www.pgatour.com

Feb 6 - Feb 9, 2025
FOUNDERS CUP
Bradenton, FL

Bradenton Country Club
LPGA TOUR
Phone: 386-274-6200
Fax: 386-274-1099
www.lpga.com

Feb 10 - Feb 16, 2025
CHUBB CLASSIC
Naples, FL
Tiburon Golf Club
PGA CHAMPIONS TOUR
Phone: 904-285-3700
www.pgatour.com/pgatour-champions

Feb 10 - Feb 16, 2025
GENESIS INVITATIONAL
Pacific Palisades, CA
Riviera Country Club
PGA TOUR
Phone: 904-285-3700
www.pgatour.com

Feb 19 - Feb 23, 2025
KENYA OPEN
Nairobi, Kenya
Muthaiga Golf Club
PGA EUROPEAN TOUR
International Ph: 44-0-1344-840400
International Fax: 44-0-1344-840500
www.rydercup.com

Feb 20 - Feb 23, 2025
HONDA LPGA THAILAND
Chonburi, Thailand
Siam Country Club
LPGA TOUR
Phone: 386-274-6200
Fax: 386-274-1099
www.lpga.com

Feb 27 - Mar 2, 2025
COGNIZANT CLASSIC
Palm Beach Gardens, FL
PGA National Champion Course
PGA TOUR
Phone: 904-285-3700
www.pgatour.com

Feb 27 - Mar 2, 2025
HSBC WOMEN'S WORLD
CHAMPIONSHIP
Singapore
Sentosa Golf Club
LPGA TOUR
Phone: 386-274-6200
Fax: 386-274-1099
www.lpga.com

Feb 27 - Mar 2, 2025
SOUTH AFRICAN OPEN
Durban, South Africa
Durban Golf Course
PGA EUROPEAN TOUR
International Ph: 44-0-1344-840400
International Fax: 44-0-1344-840500
www.rydercup.com

Mar TBA, 2025
SWING THOUGHT NATIONAL PRO
SERIES - OKEFENOKEE
Blackshear, GA
Okefenokee Country Club

Mar TBA, 2025
SWING THOUGHT NATIONAL PRO
SERIES - SANCTUARY GO LF CLUB
Waverly, GA
Sanctuary Golf Club

Mar 2 - Mar 9, 2025
COLOGUARD CLASSIC
Tucson, AZ
La Paloma Country Club
PGA CHAMPIONS TOUR
Phone: 904-285-3700
www.pgatour.com/pgatour-champions

Mar 3 - Mar 9, 2025
ARNOLD PALMER INVITATIONAL
Bay Hill, FL
Bay Hill Club & Lodge
PGA TOUR
Phone: 904-285-3700
www.pgatour.com

Mar 6 - Mar 9, 2025
PUERTO RICO OPEN
Rio Grande, Puerto Rico
Grand Reserve Golf Club
PGA TOUR
Phone: 904-285-3700
www.pgatour.com

Mar 13 - Mar 14, 2025
THE PLAYERS CHAMPIONSHIP
Ponte Vedra Beach, FL
TPC Sawgrass
PGA TOUR
Phone: 904-285-3700
www.pgatour.com

Mar 16 - Mar 23, 2025
HOAG CLASSIC
Newport Beach, CA
Newport Beach Country Club
PGA CHAMPIONS TOUR
Phone: 904-285-3700
www.pgatour.com/pgatour-champions

Mar 17 - Mar 23, 2025
VALSPAR CHAMPIONSHIP
Palm Harbor, FL
Innisbrook Resort (Copperhead)
PGA TOUR
Phone: 904-285-3700
www.pgatour.com

Mar 20 - Mar 23, 2025
PORSCHE SINGAPORE CLASSIC
Singapore
Laguna National Golf Resort Club
PGA EUROPEAN TOUR
International Ph: 44-0-1344-840400
International Fax: 44-0-1344-840500
www.rydercup.com

Mar 24 - Mar 30, 2025
TEXAS CHILDREN'S HOUSTON OPEN
Houston, TX
Memorial Park Golf Course
PGA TOUR
Phone: 904-285-3700
www.pgatour.com

Mar 27 - Mar 30, 2025
HERO INDIAN OPEN
New Dehli, India
DLF G&CC
PGA EUROPEAN TOUR
International Ph: 44-0-1344-840400
International Fax: 44-0-1344-840500
www.rydercup.com

Mar 31 - Apr 6, 2025
CLUB CAR CHAMPIONSHIP
Savannah, GA
The Landings Club
PGA KORN FERRY TOUR
Phone: 904-285-3700

Fax: 904-285-7913
www.pgatour.com

Mar 31 - Apr 6, 2025
VALERO TEXAS OPEN
San Antonio, TX
TPC San Antonio
PGA TOUR
Phone: 904-285-3700
www.pgatour.com

Apr 10 - Apr 13, 2025
MASTERS TOURNAMENT
Augusta, GA
Augusta National Golf Club
PGA TOUR
Phone: 904-285-3700
www.pgatour.com

Apr 15 - Apr 20, 2025
RBC HERITAGE
Hilton Head, SC
Harbour Town Golf Links
PGA TOUR
Phone: 904-285-3700
www.pgatour.com

Apr 16 - Apr 19, 2025
LECOM SUNCOAST CLASSIC
Lakewood Ranch, FL
Lakewood National Golf Club
PGA KORN FERRY TOUR
Phone: 904-285-3700
Fax: 904-285-7913
www.pgatour.com

Apr 17 - Apr 20, 2025
VOLVO CHINA OPEN
Shanghai, China
Shanghai Enhance Anting Golf Course
PGA EUROPEAN TOUR
International Ph: 44-0-1344-840400
International Fax: 44-0-1344-840500
www.rydercup.com

Apr 21 - Apr 27, 2025
MITSUBISHI ELECTRIC CLASSIC
Duluth, GA
TPC Sugarloaf
PGA CHAMPIONS TOUR
Phone: 904-285-3700
www.pgatour.com/pgatour-champions

Apr 21 - Apr 27, 2025
ZURICH CLASSIC OF NEW ORLEANS
Avondale, LA
TPC Louisiana
PGA TOUR
Phone: 904-285-3700
www.pgatour.com

Apr 24 - Apr 27, 2025
CHEVRON CHAMPIONSHIP
The Woodlands, TX
The Club At Carlton Woods
LPGA TOUR
Phone: 386-274-6200
Fax: 386-274-1099
www.lpga.com

Apr 28 - May 4, 2025
CJ CUP BYRON NELSON
CHAMPIONSHIP
McKinney, TX
TPC Craig Ranch
PGA TOUR
Phone: 904-285-3700
www.pgatour.com

Apr 28 - May 4, 2025
INSPERITY INVITATIONAL
The Woodlands, TX
The Woodlands Country Club
PGA CHAMPIONS TOUR
Phone: 904-285-3700
www.pgatour.com/pgatour-champions

May 2 - May 4, 2025
NEXTGEN PACIFIC CHAMPIONSHIP
Abbotsford, BC, Canada
Ledgeview Golf Club
ROYAL CANADIAN GOLF
ASSOCIATION
Phone: 905-849-9700
Fax: 905-845-7040
info@golfcanada.ca
www.golfcanada.ca

May 8 - May 10, 2025
NEXTGEN ONTARIO CHAMPIONSHIP
Belleville, ON, Canada
Black Bear Ridge Golf Course
ROYAL CANADIAN GOLF
ASSOCIATION
Phone: 905-849-9700
Fax: 905-845-7040
info@golfcanada.ca
www.golfcanada.ca

May 8 - May 11, 2025
WELLS FARGO CHAMPIONSHIP
Philadelphia, PA
Philadelphia Cricket Club
PGA TOUR
Phone: 904-285-3700
www.pgatour.com

May 10 - May 14, 2025
US WOMEN'S AMATEUR FOUR-BALL
Nichols Hills, OK
Oklahoma City Golf & Country Club
U.S. GOLF ASSOCIATION
Phone: 908-234-2300
Fax: 908-234-9687
www.usga.org

May 12 - May 18, 2025
ADVENTHEALTH CHAMPIONSHIP
Kansas City, KS
Blue Hills Country Club
PGA KORN FERRY TOUR
Phone: 904-285-3700
Fax: 904-285-7913
www.pgatour.com

May 12 - May 18, 2025
PGA CHAMPIONSHIP
Charlotte, NC
Quail Hollow Club
PGA TOUR
Phone: 904-285-3700
www.pgatour.com

May 13 - May 17, 2025
NCAA DIVISION II WOMEN'S GOLF
FINALS
Boulder City, NV
Boulder Creek Golf Club
NATIONAL COLLEGIATE ATHLETIC
ASSOCIATION
Phone: 317-917-6222
Fax: 317-917-6888
www.ncaa.org

May 13 - May 16, 2025
NCAA DIVISION III WOMEN'S GOLF
FINALS
Williamsburg, VA
Kingsmill Resort & Spa

NATIONAL COLLEGIATE ATHLETIC
ASSOCIATION
Phone: 317-917-6222
Fax: 317-917-6888
www.ncaa.org

May 14 - May 19, 2025
REGIONS TRADITION
Birmingham, AL
Greystone Golf & Country Club
PGA CHAMPIONS TOUR
Phone: 904-285-3700
www.pgatour.com/pgatour-champions

May 16 - May 21, 2025
NCAA DIVISION I WOMEN'S GOLF
FINALS
Carlsbad, CA
Omni La Costa Resort & Spa
NATIONAL COLLEGIATE ATHLETIC
ASSOCIATION
Phone: 317-917-6222
Fax: 317-917-6888
www.ncaa.org

May 17 - May 21, 2025
US AMATEUR FOUR-BALL
Westfield, NJ
Echo Lake Country Club
U.S. GOLF ASSOCIATION
Phone: 908-234-2300
Fax: 908-234-9687
www.usga.org

May 19 - May 25, 2025
CHARLES SCHWAB CHALLENGE
Fort Worth, TX
Colonial Country Club
PGA TOUR
Phone: 904-285-3700
www.pgatour.com

May 19 - May 23, 2025
NCAA DIVISION II MEN'S GOLF
FINALS
Palm Beach, FL
Pga National Resort
NATIONAL COLLEGIATE ATHLETIC
ASSOCIATION
Phone: 317-917-6222
Fax: 317-917-6888
www.ncaa.org

May 19 - May 25, 2025
VISIT KNOXVILLE OPEN
Knoxville, TN
PGA KORN FERRY TOUR
Phone: 904-285-3700
Fax: 904-285-7913
www.pgatour.com

May 20 - May 23, 2025
NCAA DIVISION III MEN'S GOLF
FINALS
Penfield, NY
Midvale Country Club
NATIONAL COLLEGIATE ATHLETIC
ASSOCIATION
Phone: 317-917-6222
Fax: 317-917-6888
www.ncaa.org

May 22 - May 25, 2025
KITCHENAID SENIOR PGA
CHAMPIONSHIP
Frisco, TX
Fields Ranch East
PGA CHAMPIONS TOUR
Phone: 904-285-3700
www.pgatour.com/pgatour-champions

May 23 - May 28, 2025
NCAA DIVISION I MEN'S GOLF
FINALS
Carlsbad, CA
Omni La Costa Resort & Spa
NATIONAL COLLEGIATE ATHLETIC
ASSOCIATION
Phone: 317-917-6222
Fax: 317-917-6888
www.ncaa.org

May 26 - Jun 1, 2025
THE MEMORIAL TOURNAMENT
Dublin, OH
Muirfield Village Golf Club
PGA TOUR
Phone: 904-285-3700
www.pgatour.com

May 28 - Jun 1, 2025
PRINCIPAL CHARITY CLASSIC
Des Moines, IA
Wakonda Club
PGA CHAMPIONS TOUR
Phone: 904-285-3700
www.pgatour.com/pgatour-champions

May 29 - Jun 1, 2025
UNC HEALTH CHAMPIONSHIP
Raleigh, NC
Raleigh Country Club
PGA KORN FERRY TOUR
Phone: 904-285-3700
Fax: 904-285-7913
www.pgatour.com

May 29 - Jun 1, 2025
US WOMEN'S OPEN
Erin, WI
Erin Hills
U.S. GOLF ASSOCIATION
Phone: 908-234-2300
Fax: 908-234-9687
www.usga.org

May 29 - Jun 1, 2025
US WOMEN'S OPEN
Erin Hills, WI
Erin Hills Golf Course
LPGA TOUR
Phone: 386-274-6200
Fax: 386-274-1099
www.lpga.com

May 30 - Jun 1, 2025
NEXTGEN WESTERN
CHAMPIONSHIP
Entwistle, AB, Canada
Trestle Creek Club Resort
ROYAL CANADIAN GOLF
ASSOCIATION
Phone: 905-849-9700
Fax: 905-845-7040
info@golfcanada.ca
www.golfcanada.ca

Jun 3 - Jun 6, 2025
CANADIAN UNIVERSITY & COLLEGE
CHAMPIONSHIP
Kamloops, BC, Canada
Rivershore Golf Links
ROYAL CANADIAN GOLF
ASSOCIATION
Phone: 905-849-9700
Fax: 905-845-7040
info@golfcanada.ca
www.golfcanada.ca

Jun 4 - Jun 8, 2025
RBC CANADIAN OPEN
Caledon, ON, Canada
ROYAL CANADIAN GOLF
ASSOCIATION
Phone: 905-849-9700
Fax: 905-845-7040
info@golfcanada.ca
www.golfcanada.ca

Jun 5 - Jun 8, 2025
BMW CHARITY PRO-AM
Greer, SC
Thornblade Club
PGA KORN FERRY TOUR
Phone: 904-285-3700
Fax: 904-285-7913
www.pgatour.com

Jun 5 - Jun 8, 2025
DUTCH OPEN
Cromvoirt, Netherlands
Bernardus Golf
PGA EUROPEAN TOUR
International Ph: 44-0-1344-840400
International Fax: 44-0-1344-840500
www.rydercup.com

Jun 6 - Jun 8, 2025
AMERICAN FAMILY INSURANCE
CHAMPIONSHIP
Madison, WI
University Ridge Golf Club
PGA CHAMPIONS TOUR
Phone: 904-285-3700
www.pgatour.com/pgatour-champions

Jun 6 - Jun 8, 2025
SHOPRITE LPGA CLASSIC
Galloway, NJ
Seaview, Bay Course
LPGA TOUR
Phone: 386-274-6200
Fax: 386-274-1099
www.lpga.com

Jun 12 - Jun 15, 2025
MEIJER LPGA CLASSIC FOR SIMPLY
GIVE
Belmont, MI
Blythefield Country Club
LPGA TOUR
Phone: 386-274-6200
Fax: 386-274-1099
www.lpga.com

Jun 12 - Jun 15, 2025
US OPEN
Oakmont, PA
Oakmont Country Club
U.S. GOLF ASSOCIATION
Phone: 908-234-2300
Fax: 908-234-9687
www.usga.org

Jun 13 - Jun 15, 2025
NEXTGEN PRAIRIE CHAMPIONSHIP
Warman, SK, Canada
The Legends Golf Club
ROYAL CANADIAN GOLF
ASSOCIATION
Phone: 905-849-9700
Fax: 905-845-7040
info@golfcanada.ca
www.golfcanada.ca

Jun 16 - Jun 22, 2025
TRAVELERS CHAMPIONSHIP
Cromwell, CT
TPC River Highlands

PGA TOUR
Phone: 904-285-3700
www.pgatour.com

Jun 18 - Jun 22, 2025
KAULIG COMPANIES CHAMPIONSHIP
Akron, OH
Firestone Country Club
PGA CHAMPIONS TOUR
Phone: 904-285-3700
www.pgatour.com/pgatour-champions

Jun 19 - Jun 22, 2025
KPMG WOMEN'S PGA
CHAMPIONSHIP
Sammamish, WA
Sahalee Country Club
LPGA TOUR
Phone: 386-274-6200
Fax: 386-274-1099
www.lpga.com

Jun 19 - Jun 22, 2025
WICHITA OPEN
Wichita, KS
Crestview Country Club
PGA KORN FERRY TOUR
Phone: 904-285-3700
Fax: 904-285-7913
www.pgatour.com

Jun 23 - Jun 29, 2025
DOW GREAT LAKES BAY
INVITATIONAL
Midland, MI
Midland Country Club
LPGA TOUR
Phone: 386-274-6200
Fax: 386-274-1099
www.lpga.com

Jun 26 - Jun 29, 2025
MEMORIAL HEALTH CHAMPIONSHIP
Springfield, IL
Panther Creek Country Club
PGA KORN FERRY TOUR
Phone: 904-285-3700
Fax: 904-285-7913
www.pgatour.com

Jun 26 - Jun 29, 2025
US SENIOR OPEN CHAMPIONSHIP
Colorado Springs, CO
The Broadmoor
PGA CHAMPIONS TOUR
Phone: 904-285-3700
www.pgatour.com/pgatour-champions

Jul 2 - Jul 6, 2025
BMW INTERNATIONAL OPEN
Munich, Germany
Golf Club München Eichenried
PGA EUROPEAN TOUR
International Ph: 44-0-1344-840400
International Fax: 44-0-1344-840500
www.rydercup.com

Jul 2 - Jul 6, 2025
JOHN DEERE CLASSIC
Silvis, IL
TPC Deere Run
PGA TOUR
Phone: 904-285-3700
www.pgatour.com

Jul 3 - Jul 5, 2025
NEXTGEN QUEBEC CHAMPIONSHIP
Manotick, ON, Canada
Rideau View Golf Club
ROYAL CANADIAN GOLF
ASSOCIATION

Phone: 905-849-9700
Fax: 905-845-7040
info@golfcanada.ca
www.golfcanada.ca

Jul 7 - Jul 13, 2025
DICK'S SPORTING GOODS OPEN
Endicott, NY
En-Joie Golf Club
PGA CHAMPIONS TOUR
Phone: 904-285-3700
www.pgatour.com/pgatour-champions

Jul 7 - Jul 13, 2025
TPC COLORADO CHAMPIONSHIP AT
HERON LAKES
Berthoud, CO
TPC Colorado
PGA KORN FERRY TOUR
Phone: 904-285-3700
Fax: 904-285-7913
www.pgatour.com

Jul 10 - Jul 13, 2025
THE AMUNDI EVIAN CHAMPIONSHIP
Evian-les-Bains, France
Evian Resort Golf Club
LPGA TOUR
Phone: 386-274-6200
Fax: 386-274-1099
www.lpga.com

Jul 11 - Jul 13, 2025
SWISS SENIORS OPEN
Bad Ragaz, Switzerland
PGA EUROPEAN STAYSURE TOUR
International Ph: 44-0-1344-840400
International Fax: 44-0-1344-840500
www.europeantour.com/staysure-tour

Jul 13 - Jul 20, 2025
THE OPEN CHAMPIONSHIP
Hoylake, Wirral, England
Royal Liverpool
PGA TOUR
Phone: 904-285-3700
www.pgatour.com

Jul 14 - Jul 19, 2025
US GIRLS' JUNIOR
Atlanta, GA
Atlanta Athletic Club
U.S. GOLF ASSOCIATION
Phone: 908-234-2300
Fax: 908-234-9687
www.usga.org

Jul 15 - Jul 17, 2025
NEXTGEN ATLANTIC CHAMPIONSHIP
Enfield, NS, Canada
Oakfield Golf and Country Club
ROYAL CANADIAN GOLF
ASSOCIATION
Phone: 905-849-9700
Fax: 905-845-7040
info@golfcanada.ca
www.golfcanada.ca

Jul 17 - Jul 20, 2025
PRICE CUTTER CHARITY
CHAMPIONSHIP
Springfield, MO
Highland Springs Country Club
PGA KORN FERRY TOUR
Phone: 904-285-3700
Fax: 904-285-7913
www.pgatour.com

Jul 21 - Jul 27, 2025
3M OPEN
Blaine, MN

TPC Twin Cities
PGA TOUR
Phone: 904-285-3700
www.pgatour.com

Jul 21 - Jul 26, 2025
US JUNIOR AMATEUR
Dallas, TX
Trinity Forest Golf Club
U.S. GOLF ASSOCIATION
Phone: 908-234-2300
Fax: 908-234-9687
www.usga.org

Jul 22 - Jul 25, 2025
CANADIAN WOMEN'S AMATEUR
CHAMPIONSHIP
Saint John, NB, Canada
The Riverside Country Club
ROYAL CANADIAN GOLF
ASSOCIATION
Phone: 905-849-9700
Fax: 905-845-7040
info@golfcanada.ca
www.golfcanada.ca

Jul 24 - Jul 27, 2025
NV5 INVITATIONAL
Glenview, IL
The Glen Club
PGA KORN FERRY TOUR
Phone: 904-285-3700
Fax: 904-285-7913
www.pgatour.com

Jul 24 - Jul 27, 2025
TRUST GOLD WOMEN'S SCOTTISH
OPEN
Ayrshire, Scotland
Dundonald Links
LPGA TOUR
Phone: 386-274-6200
Fax: 386-274-1099
www.lpga.com

Jul 28 - Jul 31, 2025
CANADIAN MEN'S AMATEUR
CHAMPIONSHIP
Gatineau, QC, Canada
The Royal Ottawa Golf Club
ROYAL CANADIAN GOLF
ASSOCIATION
Phone: 905-849-9700
Fax: 905-845-7040
info@golfcanada.ca
www.golfcanada.ca

Jul 30 - Aug 2, 2025
AIG WOMEN'S BRITISH OPEN
Royal Porthcawl, Wales
LPGA TOUR
Phone: 386-274-6200
Fax: 386-274-1099
www.lpga.com

Jul 30 - Aug 3, 2025
WYNDHAM CHAMPIONSHIP
Greensboro, NC
Sedgefield Country Club
PGA TOUR
Phone: 904-285-3700
www.pgatour.com

Jul 31 - Aug 3, 2025
UTAH CHAMPIONSHIP
Ogden, UT
Ogden Golf & Country Club
PGA KORN FERRY TOUR
Phone: 904-285-3700
Fax: 904-285-7913
www.pgatour.com

Aug 4 - Aug 10, 2025
BOEING CLASSIC
Snoqualmie, WA
The Club at Snoqualmie Ridge
PGA CHAMPIONS TOUR
Phone: 904-285-3700
www.pgatour.com/pgatour-champions

Aug 4 - Aug 10, 2025
PINNACLE BANK CHAMPIONSHIP
Omaha, NE
The Club at Indian Creek
PGA KORN FERRY TOUR
Phone: 904-285-3700
Fax: 904-285-7913
www.pgatour.com

Aug 4 - Aug 10, 2025
US WOMEN'S AMATEUR
Bandon, OR
Bandon Dunes Golf Resort
U.S. GOLF ASSOCIATION
Phone: 908-234-2300
Fax: 908-234-9687
www.usga.org

Aug 6 - Aug 8, 2025
CANADIAN WOMEN'S MID-AMATEUR
& SENIOR CHAMPIONSH IP
Lachute, QC, Canada
Club de golf Lachute
ROYAL CANADIAN GOLF
ASSOCIATION
Phone: 905-849-9700
Fax: 905-845-7040
info@golfcanada.ca
www.golfcanada.ca

Aug 6 - Aug 10, 2025
FEDEX ST. JUDE CHAMPIONSHIP
Memphis, TN
TPC Southwind
PGA TOUR
Phone: 904-285-3700
www.pgatour.com

Aug 11 - Aug 17, 2025
SHAW CHARITY CLASSIC
Calgary, AB
Canyon Meadows Golf & Country Club
PGA CHAMPIONS TOUR
Phone: 904-285-3700
www.pgatour.com/pgatour-champions

Aug 11 - Aug 17, 2025
US AMATEUR
San Francisco, CA
The Olympic Club
U.S. GOLF ASSOCIATION
Phone: 908-234-2300
Fax: 908-234-9687
www.usga.org

Aug 12 - Aug 17, 2025
BMW CHAMPIONSHIP
Owings, MD
Caves Valley Golf Club
PGA TOUR
Phone: 904-285-3700
www.pgatour.com

Aug 12 - Aug 15, 2025
CANADIAN JUNIOR BOYS
CHAMPIONSHIP
Bathurst, NB, Canada
Gowan Brae Golf and Country Club
ROYAL CANADIAN GOLF
ASSOCIATION
Phone: 905-849-9700
Fax: 905-845-7040

info@golfcanada.ca
www.golfcanada.ca

Aug 13 - Aug 16, 2025
CANADIAN JUNIOR GIRLS
CHAMPIONSHIP
Sainte-Marie, QC, Canada
Club de golf Sainte-Marie
ROYAL CANADIAN GOLF
ASSOCIATION
Phone: 905-849-9700
Fax: 905-845-7040
info@golfcanada.ca
www.golfcanada.ca

Aug 14 - Aug 17, 2025
ALBERTSONS BOISE OPEN
Boise, ID
Hillcrest Country Club
PGA KORN FERRY TOUR
Phone: 904-285-3700
Fax: 904-285-7913
www.pgatour.com

Aug 14 - Aug 17, 2025
PORTLAND CLASSIC
Portland, OR
Columbia Edgewater Country Club
LPGA TOUR
Phone: 386-274-6200
Fax: 386-274-1099
www.lpga.com

Aug 18 - Aug 24, 2025
THE ALLY CHALLENGE
Grand Blanc, MI
Warwick Hills Golf & Country Club
PGA CHAMPIONS TOUR
Phone: 904-285-3700
www.pgatour.com/pgatour-champions

Aug 19 - Aug 22, 2025
CANADIAN MEN'S MID-AMATEUR
CHAMPIONSHIP
North Vancouver, BC, Canada
Seymour Golf and Country Club
ROYAL CANADIAN GOLF
ASSOCIATION
Phone: 905-849-9700
Fax: 905-845-7040
info@golfcanada.ca
www.golfcanada.ca

Aug 20 - Aug 24, 2025
CPKC CANADIAN WOMEN'S OPEN
Mississauga, ON, Canada
Mississauga Golf & Country Club
LPGA TOUR
Phone: 386-274-6200
Fax: 386-274-1099
www.lpga.com

Aug 20 - Aug 24, 2025
THE TOUR CHAMPIONSHIP
Atlanta, GA
East Lake Golf Club
PGA TOUR
Phone: 904-285-3700
www.pgatour.com

Aug 21 - Aug 24, 2025
BETFRED BRITISH MASTERS
Sutton Coldfield, England
The Belfry
PGA EUROPEAN TOUR
International Ph: 44-0-1344-840400
International Fax: 44-0-1344-840500
www.rydercup.com

Aug 23 - Aug 28, 2025
US SENIOR AMATEUR
San Antonio, TX
Oak Hills Country Club
U.S. GOLF ASSOCIATION
Phone: 908-234-2300
Fax: 908-234-9687
www.usga.org

Aug 28 - Aug 31, 2025
OMEGA EUROPEAN MASTERS
Crans Montana, Switzerland
Cras-sur-Sierre Golf Club
PGA EUROPEAN TOUR
International Ph: 44-0-1344-840400
International Fax: 44-0-1344-840500
www.rydercup.com

Sept 1 - Sept 7, 2025
NORWOOD HILLS COUNTRY CLUB
St. Louis, MO
Norwood Hills Country Club
PGA CHAMPIONS TOUR
Phone: 904-285-3700
www.pgatour.com/pgatour-champions

Sept 4 - Sept 7, 2025
HORIZON IRISH OPEN
Kildare, Ireland
The K Club
PGA EUROPEAN TOUR
International Ph: 44-0-1344-840400
International Fax: 44-0-1344-840500
www.rydercup.com

Sept 8 - Sept 14, 2025
SANFORD INTERNATIONAL
Sioux Falls, SD
Minnehaha Country Club
PGA CHAMPIONS TOUR
Phone: 904-285-3700
www.pgatour.com/pgatour-champions

Sept 9 - Sept 12, 2025
CANADIAN MEN'S SENIOR
CHAMPIONSHIP
New Minas, NS, Canada
KenWo Golf Club
ROYAL CANADIAN GOLF
ASSOCIATION
Phone: 905-849-9700
Fax: 905-845-7040
info@golfcanada.ca
www.golfcanada.ca

Sept 11 - Sept 14, 2025
BMW PGA CHAMPIONSHIP
Surrey, England
Wentworth Club
PGA EUROPEAN TOUR
International Ph: 44-0-1344-840400
International Fax: 44-0-1344-840500
www.rydercup.com

Sept 11 - Sept 14, 2025
SIMMONS BANK OPEN FOR THE
SNEDEKER FOUNDATION
College Grove, TN
The Grove
PGA KORN FERRY TOUR
Phone: 904-285-3700
Fax: 904-285-7913
www.pgatour.com

Sept 13 - Sept 18, 2025
US MID-AMATEUR
Scottsdale, AZ
Troon Country Club
U.S. GOLF ASSOCIATION
Phone: 908-234-2300

Fax: 908-234-9687
www.usga.org

Sept 13 - Sept 18, 2025
US SENIOR WOMEN'S AMATEUR
Hot Springs, VA
The Omni Homestead Resort
U.S. GOLF ASSOCIATION
Phone: 908-234-2300
Fax: 908-234-9687
www.usga.org

Sept 15 - Sept 21, 2025
NATIONWIDE CHILDREN'S HOSPITAL
CHAMPIONSHIP
Columbus, OH
The OSU Golf Club
PGA KORN FERRY TOUR
Phone: 904-285-3700
Fax: 904-285-7913
www.pgatour.com

Sept 15 - Sept 21, 2025
WALMART NW ARKANSAS
CHAMPIONSHIP
Rogers, AR
Pinnacle Country Club
LPGA TOUR
Phone: 386-274-6200
Fax: 386-274-1099
www.lpga.com

Sept 18 - Sept 21, 2025
OPEN DE FRANCE
Saint-Nom-la-Bretŝche, France
Golf de Saint-Nom-la-Bretŝche
PGA EUROPEAN TOUR
International Ph: 44-0-1344-840400
International Fax: 44-0-1344-840500
www.rydercup.com

Sept 19 - Sept 21, 2025
PURE INSURANCE CHAMPIONSHIP
Monterey Peninsula, CA
Pebble Beach Golf Links
PGA CHAMPIONS TOUR
Phone: 904-285-3700
www.pgatour.com/pgatour-champions

Sept 22 - Sept 22, 2025
2025 RYDER CUP
Farmingdale, NY
Bethpage Black
PGA EUROPEAN TOUR
International Ph: 44-0-1344-840400
International Fax: 44-0-1344-840500
www.rydercup.com

Sept 29 - Oct 4, 2025
LOTTE CHAMPIONSHIP
Ewa Beach, Oahu, HI
Hoakalei Country Club
LPGA TOUR
Phone: 386-274-6200
Fax: 386-274-1099
www.lpga.com

Oct 1 - Oct 11, 2025
WORLD AMATEUR TEAM
CHAMPIONSHIPS
Singapore
Tanah Merah Country Club
INTERNATIONAL GOLF FEDERATION
International Ph: +41 21 623 12 12
International Fax: +41 +41 216 01 64
info@lgfmail.org
www.igfgolf.org

Oct 4 - Oct 9, 2025
US WOMEN'S MID-AMATEUR
Pebble Beach, CA

Monterey Peninsula Country Club
U.S. GOLF ASSOCIATION
Phone: 908-234-2300
Fax: 908-234-9687
www.usga.org

Oct 6 - Oct 12, 2025
KORN FERRY TOUR CHAMPIONSHIP
French Lick, IN
Pete Dye Course at French Lick Resort
PGA KORN FERRY TOUR
Phone: 904-285-3700
Fax: 904-285-7913
www.pgatour.com

Oct 6 - Oct 12, 2025
SAS CHAMPIONSHIP
Cary, NC
Prestonwood Country Club
PGA CHAMPIONS TOUR
Phone: 904-285-3700
www.pgatour.com/pgatour-champions

Oct 9 - Oct 12, 2025
OPEN DE ESPANA
Madrid, Spain
Club de Campo Villa de Madrid
PGA EUROPEAN TOUR
International Ph: 44-0-1344-840400
International Fax: 44-0-1344-840500
www.rydercup.com

Oct 13 - Oct 19, 2025
DOMINION ENERGY CHARITY
CLASSIC
Richmond, VA
The Country Club of Virginia
PGA CHAMPIONS TOUR
Phone: 904-285-3700
www.pgatour.com/pgatour-champions

Oct 16 - Oct 19, 2025
BMW LADIES CHAMPIONSHIP
TBA, South Korea
LPGA TOUR
Phone: 386-274-6200
Fax: 386-274-1099
www.lpga.com

Nov 6 - Nov 9, 2025
ABU DHABI HSBC CHAMPIONSHIP
United Arab Emirates
Yas Links
PGA EUROPEAN TOUR
International Ph: 44-0-1344-840400
International Fax: 44-0-1344-840500
www.rydercup.com

Nov 6 - Nov 9, 2025
TOTO JAPAN CLASSIC
Shiga, Japan
Seta Golf Course
LPGA TOUR
Phone: 386-274-6200
Fax: 386-274-1099
www.lpga.com

Nov 6 - Nov 9, 2025
WORLD WIDE TECHNOLOGY
CHAMPIONSHIP
Mexico
El Cardonal at Diamante
PGA TOUR
Phone: 904-285-3700
www.pgatour.com

Nov 10 - Nov 16, 2025
CHARLES SCHWAB CUP
CHAMPIONSHIP
Phoenix, AZ
Phoenix Country Club

PGA CHAMPIONS TOUR
Phone: 904-285-3700
www.pgatour.com/pgatour-champions

Nov 13 - Nov 16, 2025
DP WORLD TOUR CHAMPIONSHIP
DUBAI
Dubai, United Arab Emirates
Jumeirah Golf Estates
PGA EUROPEAN TOUR
International Ph: 44-0-1344-840400
International Fax: 44-0-1344-840500
www.rydercup.com

Nov 17 - Nov 23, 2025
RSM CLASSIC
Sea Island, GA
Sea Island Golf Club
PGA TOUR
Phone: 904-285-3700
www.pgatour.com

Nov 20 - Nov 23, 2025
CME GROUP TOUR CHAMPIONSHIP
Naples, FL
Tiburon Golf Club
LPGA TOUR
Phone: 386-274-6200
Fax: 386-274-1099
www.lpga.com

Dec 2 - Dec 8, 2025
HERO WORLD CHALLENGE
Albany, Bahamas
PGA TOUR
Phone: 904-285-3700
www.pgatour.com

Dec 20 - Dec 21, 2025
PNC CHAMPIONSHIP
Orlando, FL
Ritz-Carlton Golf Club
PGA CHAMPIONS TOUR
Phone: 904-285-3700
www.pgatour.com/pgatour-champions

Jan TBA, 2026
FARMERS INSURANCE OPEN
San Diego, CA
PGA TOUR
Phone: 904-285-3700
www.pgatour.com

Jan 12 - Jan 18, 2026
SONY OPEN IN HAWAII
Honolulu, HI
Waialae Country Club
PGA TOUR
Phone: 904-285-3700
www.pgatour.com

Jun 12 - Jun 14, 2026
CURTIS CUP
Los Angeles, CA
Bel-Air Country Club
U.S. GOLF ASSOCIATION
Phone: 908-234-2300
Fax: 908-234-9687
www.usga.org

Sept 7 - Sept 13, 2026
SOLHEIM CUP
Hertogenbosch, The Netherlands
LPGA TOUR
Phone: 386-274-6200
Fax: 386-274-1099
www.lpga.com

Sept 22 - Sept 27, 2026
PRESIDENT'S CUP
Chicago, IL

Medinah Country Club
PGA TOUR
Phone: 904-285-3700
www.pgatour.com

Greyhound Racing

Apr 14 - Apr 18, 2025
NGA SPRING MEET
TBA
NATIONAL GREYHOUND
ASSOCIATION
Phone: 785-263-4660
Fax: 785-263-4689
nga@ngagreyhounds.com
www.ngagreyhounds.com

Gymnastics

TBA, 2025
MAG CANADIAN GYMNASTIC
CHAMPIONSHIPS
Calgary, AB, Canada
GYMNASTICS CANADA GYMNASTIQUE
Phone: 613-748-5637
Fax: 613-748-5691
info@gymcan.org
www.gymcan.org

TBA, 2025
RG CANADIAN GYMNASTIC
CHAMPIONSHIPS
Calgary, AB, Canada
GYMNASTICS CANADA GYMNASTIQUE
Phone: 613-748-5637
Fax: 613-748-5691
info@gymcan.org
www.gymcan.org

TBA, 2025
TG CANADIAN GYMNASTIC
CHAMPIONSHIPS
Calgary, AB, Canada
GYMNASTICS CANADA GYMNASTIQUE
Phone: 613-748-5637
Fax: 613-748-5691
info@gymcan.org
www.gymcan.org

TBA, 2025
WAG CANADIAN GYMNASTIC
CHAMPIONSHIPS
Calgary, AB, Canada
GYMNASTICS CANADA GYMNASTIQUE
Phone: 613-748-5637
Fax: 613-748-5691
info@gymcan.org
www.gymcan.org

Feb 21 - Feb 23, 2025
2025 WINTER CUP
Louisville, KY
International Convention Center
USA GYMNASTICS
Phone: 800-345-4719
Fax: 317-237-5069
membership@usagym.org
usagym.org

Feb 22, 2025
2025 ELITE TEAM CUP
Louisville, KY
Freedom Hall
USA GYMNASTICS
Phone: 800-345-4719
Fax: 317-237-5069
membership@usagym.org
usagym.org

Feb 23, 2025
NASTIA LIUKIN CUP
Louisville, KY
Freedom Hall
USA GYMNASTICS
Phone: 800-345-4719
Fax: 317-237-5069
membership@usagym.org
usagym.org

Apr 17 - Apr 19, 2025
NCAA NATIONAL COLLEGIATE
WOMEN'S GYMNASTICS FINA LS
Fort Worth, TX
Dickies Arena
NATIONAL COLLEGIATE ATHLETIC
ASSOCIATION
Phone: 317-917-6222
Fax: 317-917-6888
www.ncaa.org

Apr 18 - Apr 19, 2025
NCAA NATIONAL COLLEGIATE
MEN'S GYMNASTICS FINALS
Ann Arbor, MI
Crisler Center
NATIONAL COLLEGIATE ATHLETIC
ASSOCIATION
Phone: 317-917-6222
Fax: 317-917-6888
www.ncaa.org

Jun 16 - Jun 21, 2025
USA GYMNASTICS CHAMPIONSHIPS
Providence, RI
Rhode Island Convention Center
USA GYMNASTICS
Phone: 800-345-4719
Fax: 317-237-5069
membership@usagym.org
usagym.org

Aug 7 - Aug 10, 2025
2025 US GYMNASTICS
CHAMPIONSHIPS
New Orleans, LA
Smoothie King Center
USA GYMNASTICS
Phone: 800-345-4719
Fax: 317-237-5069
membership@usagym.org
usagym.org

TBA, 2026
FRIVOLTEN CUP
Herrljunga, Sweden
GK FRIVOLTEN
frivolten.com

Handball

Apr 4 - Apr 6, 2025
USHA MASTERS SINGLES
INVITATIONAL
TBA
UNITED STATES HANDBALL
ASSOCIATION
Phone: 520-795-0434
Fax: 520-795-0465
handball@ushandball.org
www.ushandball.org

May 7 - May 10, 2025
CANADIAN NATIONAL HANDBALL
CHAMPIONSHIPS
Sherwood Park, AB, Canada
Glen Allan Rec Centre
CANADIAN HANDBALL
www.canadianhandball.com

Sept TBA, 2025
USHA NATIONAL THREE-WALL
CHAMPIONSHIPS
TBA
UNITED STATES HANDBALL
ASSOCIATION
Phone: 520-795-0434
Fax: 520-795-0465
handball@ushandball.org
www.ushandball.org

Dec TBA, 2025
USHA NATIONAL FOUR-WALL
CHAMPIONSHIPS
TBA
UNITED STATES HANDBALL
ASSOCIATION
Phone: 520-795-0434
Fax: 520-795-0465
handball@ushandball.org
www.ushandball.org

Feb TBA, 2026
USHA NATIONAL COLLEGIATE
CHAMPIONSHIPS
TBA
UNITED STATES HANDBALL
ASSOCIATION
Phone: 520-795-0434
Fax: 520-795-0465
handball@ushandball.org
www.ushandball.org

Horse Racing

May 3, 2025
KENTUCKY DERBY
Louisville, KY
Churchill Downs
CHURCHILL DOWNS
Phone: 502-636-4400
customerservice@kyderby.com
www.churchilldowns.com

May 17, 2025
PREAKNESS STAKES
Baltimore, MD
Pimlico Race Course
PIMLICO RACE COURSE
Phone: 410-542-9400
info@marylandracing.com
www.marylandracing.com

Ice Hockey

Feb 7 - Feb 9, 2025
USA POND HOCKEY NATIONAL
CHAMPIONSHIPS
Eagle River, WI
Dollar Lake
USA HOCKEY
Phone: 719-576-8724
Fax: 719-538-1160
usah@usahockey.org
www.usahockey.com

Mar 28 - Mar 30, 2025
NCAA DIVISION III WOMEN'S ICE
HOCKEY CHAMPIONSHI PS
River Falls, WI
Hunt Arena
NATIONAL COLLEGIATE ATHLETIC
ASSOCIATION
Phone: 317-917-6222
Fax: 317-917-6888
www.ncaa.org

Apr 3 - Apr 6, 2025
ADULT MEN'S NATIONAL
CHAMPIONSHIPS
Wesley Chapel, FL
Adventhealth Center Ice
USA HOCKEY
Phone: 719-576-8724
Fax: 719-538-1160
usah@usahockey.org
www.usahockey.com

Apr 10 - Apr 13, 2025
ADULT WOMEN'S NATIONAL
CHAMPIONSHIPS
Wesley Chapel, FL
Adventhealth Center Ice
USA HOCKEY
Phone: 719-576-8724
Fax: 719-538-1160
usah@usahockey.org
www.usahockey.com

Apr 10 - Apr 12, 2025
NCAA DIVISION I MEN'S ICE HOCKEY
FINALS
St. Louis, MO
Enterprise Center
NATIONAL COLLEGIATE ATHLETIC
ASSOCIATION
Phone: 317-917-6222
Fax: 317-917-6888
www.ncaa.org

Mar TBA, 2026
NCAA DIVISION III MEN'S ICE
HOCKEY FINALS
TBA
NATIONAL COLLEGIATE ATHLETIC
ASSOCIATION
Phone: 317-917-6222
Fax: 317-917-6888
www.ncaa.org

Ice Skating

Feb 14 - Feb 16, 2025
ISI WINTER CLASSIC
St. Peters, MO
City of St. Peters Rec Complex
ICE SKATING INSTITUTE
Phone: 972-735-8800
Fax: 972-735-8815
events@skateisi.org
www.skateisi.org

Jul 24 - Jul 27, 2025
WORLD RECREATIONAL TEAM
CHAMPIONSHIPS
Blaine, MN
NSC Super Rink
ICE SKATING INSTITUTE
Phone: 972-735-8800
Fax: 972-735-8815
events@skateisi.org
www.skateisi.org

Oct 11 - Oct 12, 2025
ADULT CHAMPIONSHIPS
Denver, CO
South Suburban Sports Complex
ICE SKATING INSTITUTE
Phone: 972-735-8800
Fax: 972-735-8815
events@skateisi.org
www.skateisi.org

Nov 15 - Nov 16, 2025
ISI CALIFORNIA CLASSIC
Vacaville, CA

Vacaville Ice Sports
ICE SKATING INSTITUTE
Phone: 972-735-8800
Fax: 972-735-8815
events@skateisi.org
www.skateisi.org

Korfball

Apr 18 - Apr 20, 2025
U19 WORLD CHAMPIONSHIP
Czech Republic
INTERNATIONAL KORFBALL
FEDERATION
International Ph: 011-31-343-499655
International Fax: 011-31-343-499650
office@ikf.org
www.ikf.org

Lacrosse

May 7 - May 10, 2025
WCLA NATIONAL CHAMPIONSHIP
Wichita, KS
Stryker Sports Complex
US LACROSSE
Phone: 410-235-6882
Fax: 410-366-6735
membership@usalacrosse.com
www.uslacrosse.org

May 22 - May 24, 2025
NCAA DIVISION II WOMEN'S
LACROSSE FESTIVAL
Salem, VA
Kerr Stadium
NATIONAL COLLEGIATE ATHLETIC
ASSOCIATION
Phone: 317-917-6222
Fax: 317-917-6888
www.ncaa.org

May 23 - May 25, 2025
NCAA DIVISION I WOMEN'S
LACROSSE FINALS
Foxborough, MA
Gillette Stadium
NATIONAL COLLEGIATE ATHLETIC
ASSOCIATION
Phone: 317-917-6222
Fax: 317-917-6888
www.ncaa.org

May 23 - May 25, 2025
NCAA DIVISION III WOMEN'S
LACROSSE FINALS
Salem, VA
Kerr Stadium
NATIONAL COLLEGIATE ATHLETIC
ASSOCIATION
Phone: 317-917-6222
Fax: 317-917-6888
www.ncaa.org

May 24 - May 26, 2025
NCAA DIVISION I MEN'S LACROSSE
FINALS
Foxborough, MA
Gillette Stadium
NATIONAL COLLEGIATE ATHLETIC
ASSOCIATION
Phone: 317-917-6222
Fax: 317-917-6888
www.ncaa.org

May 24 - May 25, 2025
US LACROSSE NATIONAL
TOURNAMENT
Amherst, MA
US LACROSSE
Phone: 410-235-6882
Fax: 410-366-6735
membership@uslacrosse.com
www.uslacrosse.org

May 25, 2025
NCAA DIVISION II MEN'S LACROSSE
FINALS
Foxborough, MA
Gillette Stadium
NATIONAL COLLEGIATE ATHLETIC
ASSOCIATION
Phone: 317-917-6222
Fax: 317-917-6888
www.ncaa.org

May 25, 2025
NCAA DIVISION III MEN'S LACROSSE
FINALS
Foxborough, MA
Gillette Stadium
NATIONAL COLLEGIATE ATHLETIC
ASSOCIATION
Phone: 317-917-6222
Fax: 317-917-6888
www.ncaa.org

Martial Arts

Jun 30 - Jul 5, 2025
AAU KARATE NATIONAL
CHAMPIONSHIPS
Ft. Lauderdale, FL
AMATEUR ATHLETIC UNION
Phone: 407-934-7200
Fax: 407-934-7242
www.aausports.org

Jul 17 - Jul 19, 2025
US OPEN - MARTIAL ARTS
CHAMPIONSHIPS
Orlando, FL
USA OPEN KARATE
usopen-karate.com

Aug TBA, 2025
AAU JUDO NATIONAL
CHAMPIONSHIP
AMATEUR ATHLETIC UNION
Phone: 407-934-7200
Fax: 407-934-7242
www.aausports.org

Motorcycle Racing

Mar 4, 2025
DAYTONA ATV SUPERCROSS
Daytona, FL
Daytona International Speedway
AMA PRO RACING
Phone: 386-492-1014
Fax: 386-274-2335
communications@amaproracing.com
www.amaproracing.com

Mar 7, 2025
RD 2 DECKER TRAINING FACILITY
Fountain, FL
Decker Training Facility
AMA PRO RACING
Phone: 386-492-1014
Fax: 386-274-2335

communications@amaproracing.com
www.amaproracing.com

Mar 29 - Mar 30, 2025
RD 3 ECHECONNEE MX
Lizella, GA
Echeconnee MX
AMA PRO RACING
Phone: 386-492-1014
Fax: 386-274-2335
communications@amaproracing.com
www.amaproracing.com

Apr 26 - Apr 27, 2025
RD 4 LAKE SUGAR TREE
Axton, VA
Lake Sugar Tree Motorsports Park
AMA PRO RACING
Phone: 386-492-1014
Fax: 386-274-2335
communications@amaproracing.com
www.amaproracing.com

Apr 26, 2025
VENTURA ST
Ventura, CA
Ventura Raceway
AMA PRO RACING
Phone: 386-492-1014
Fax: 386-274-2335
communications@amaproracing.com
www.amaproracing.com

May 3, 2025
SILVER DOLLAR ST
Chico, CA
Silver Dollar Speedway
AMA PRO RACING
Phone: 386-492-1014
Fax: 386-274-2335
communications@amaproracing.com
www.amaproracing.com

May 10, 2025
AMA PRO HILLCLIMB MINNESOTA
NATIONAL
Red Wing, MN
Indianhead Motorcycle Club
AMA PRO RACING
Phone: 386-492-1014
Fax: 386-274-2335
communications@amaproracing.com
www.amaproracing.com

May 10 - May 11, 2025
RD 5 IRONMAN
Crawfordsville, IN
Ironman Raceway
AMA PRO RACING
Phone: 386-492-1014
Fax: 386-274-2335
communications@amaproracing.com
www.amaproracing.com

May 17 - May 18, 2025
AMA PRO HILLCLIMB WASHINGTON
NITRO NATIONALS I & II
Sunnyside, WA
Dry Creek ORV
AMA PRO RACING
Phone: 386-492-1014
Fax: 386-274-2335
communications@amaproracing.com
www.amaproracing.com

May 24, 2025
FOX RACEWAY NATIONAL
Pala, CA
Fox Raceway
AMA PRO RACING
Phone: 386-492-1014

Fax: 386-274-2335
communications@amaproracing.com
www.amaproracing.com

May 24 - May 25, 2025
RD 6 SUNSET RIDGE MX
Walnut, IL
Sunset Ridge MX
AMA PRO RACING
Phone: 386-492-1014
Fax: 386-274-2335
communications@amaproracing.com
www.amaproracing.com

May 31, 2025
HANGTOWN MOTOCROSS CLASSIC
Rancho Cordova, CA
Prairie City OHV Park
AMA PRO RACING
Phone: 386-492-1014
Fax: 386-274-2335
communications@amaproracing.com
www.amaproracing.com

Jun 1, 2025
AMA PRO HILLCLIMB WHITE ROSE
NATIONAL I
Spring Grove, PA
White Rose Motorcycle Club
AMA PRO RACING
Phone: 386-492-1014
Fax: 386-274-2335
communications@amaproracing.com
www.amaproracing.com

Jun 7, 2025
SHORT TRACK AT LUCAS OIL
SPEEDWAY
Wheatland, MO
Lucas Oil Speedway
AMA PRO RACING
Phone: 386-492-1014
Fax: 386-274-2335
communications@amaproracing.com
www.amaproracing.com

Jun 8, 2025
AMA PRO HILLCLIMB
FREEMANSBURG NATIONAL I
Freemansburg, PA
Bushkill Valley Motorcycle Club
AMA PRO RACING
Phone: 386-492-1014
Fax: 386-274-2335
communications@amaproracing.com
www.amaproracing.com

Jun 14, 2025
HIGH POINT NATIONAL
Mount Morris, PA
High Point Raceway
AMA PRO RACING
Phone: 386-492-1014
Fax: 386-274-2335
communications@amaproracing.com
www.amaproracing.com

Jun 21 - Jun 22, 2025
RD 7 BUDDS CREEK
Mechanicsville, MD
Budds Creek Raceway
AMA PRO RACING
Phone: 386-492-1014
Fax: 386-274-2335
communications@amaproracing.com
www.amaproracing.com

Jun 27 - Jun 28, 2025
LIMA HALF-MILE I & II
Lima, OH
Allen County Fairgrounds

AMA PRO RACING
Phone: 386-492-1014
Fax: 386-274-2335
communications@amaproracing.com
www.amaproracing.com

Jun 28 - Jun 29, 2025
AMA PRO HILLCLIMB LLOYDS
PERFORMANCE NITRO NATIO NALS I
& II
Soda Springs, ID
Soda Springs Hillclimb
AMA PRO RACING
Phone: 386-492-1014
Fax: 386-274-2335
communications@amaproracing.com
www.amaproracing.com

Jun 28, 2025
SOUTHWICK NATIONAL
Southwick, MA
The Wick 338
AMA PRO RACING
Phone: 386-492-1014
Fax: 386-274-2335
communications@amaproracing.com
www.amaproracing.com

Jul 5, 2025
DUQUOIN MILE
Du Quoin, IL
Du Quoin State Fairgrounds
AMA PRO RACING
Phone: 386-492-1014
Fax: 386-274-2335
communications@amaproracing.com
www.amaproracing.com

Jul 5 - Jul 6, 2025
RD 8 TOMAHAWK
Hedgesville, WV
Tomahawk MX Park
AMA PRO RACING
Phone: 386-492-1014
Fax: 386-274-2335
communications@amaproracing.com
www.amaproracing.com

Jul 12, 2025
SPRING CREEK NATIONAL
Millville, MN
Spring Creek MX Park
AMA PRO RACING
Phone: 386-492-1014
Fax: 386-274-2335
communications@amaproracing.com
www.amaproracing.com

Jul 19 - Jul 20, 2025
RD 9 PLEASURE VALLEY
Seward, PA
Pleasure Valley Raceway
AMA PRO RACING
Phone: 386-492-1014
Fax: 386-274-2335
communications@amaproracing.com
www.amaproracing.com

Jul 19, 2025
WASHOUGAL NATIONAL
Washougal, WA
Washougal MX Park
AMA PRO RACING
Phone: 386-492-1014
Fax: 386-274-2335
communications@amaproracing.com
www.amaproracing.com

Aug 2, 2025
AMA PRO HILLCLIMB MOUNT
GARFIELD NATIONAL
Norton Shores, MI
Muskegon Motorcycle Club
AMA PRO RACING
Phone: 386-492-1014
Fax: 386-274-2335
communications@amaproracing.com
www.amaproracing.com

Aug 4 - Aug 5, 2025
JACKPINE GYPSIES ST I & II
Sturgis, SD
Jackpine Gypsies
AMA PRO RACING
Phone: 386-492-1014
Fax: 386-274-2335
communications@amaproracing.com
www.amaproracing.com

Aug 9, 2025
IRONMAN NATIONAL
Crawfordsville, IN
Ironman Raceway
AMA PRO RACING
Phone: 386-492-1014
Fax: 386-274-2335
communications@amaproracing.com
www.amaproracing.com

Aug 9 - Aug 10, 2025
RD 10 BRIARCLIFF MX
Nashport, OH
Briarcliff MX
AMA PRO RACING
Phone: 386-492-1014
Fax: 386-274-2335
communications@amaproracing.com
www.amaproracing.com

Aug 10, 2025
STURGIS TT
Sturgis, SD
Streets of Downtown Sturgis
AMA PRO RACING
Phone: 386-492-1014
Fax: 386-274-2335
communications@amaproracing.com
www.amaproracing.com

Aug 16, 2025
PEORIA TT
Peoria, IL
Peoria Motorcycle Club
AMA PRO RACING
Phone: 386-492-1014
Fax: 386-274-2335
communications@amaproracing.com
www.amaproracing.com

Aug 16, 2025
UNADILLA NATIONAL
New Berlin, NY
Unadilla MX
AMA PRO RACING
Phone: 386-492-1014
Fax: 386-274-2335
communications@amaproracing.com
www.amaproracing.com

Aug 23, 2025
BUDDS CREEK NATIONAL
Mechanicsville, MD
Budds Creek Motocross Park
AMA PRO RACING
Phone: 386-492-1014
Fax: 386-274-2335
communications@amaproracing.com
www.amaproracing.com

Aug 30 - Aug 31, 2025
SPRINGFIELD MILE I & II
Springfield, IL
Illinois State Fairgrounds
AMA PRO RACING
Phone: 386-492-1014
Fax: 386-274-2335
communications@amaproracing.com
www.amaproracing.com

Sept 6, 2025
AMA PRO HILLCLIMB KANSAS
NATIONAL
Wathena, KS
Over The Hill Racing
AMA PRO RACING
Phone: 386-492-1014
Fax: 386-274-2335
communications@amaproracing.com
www.amaproracing.com

Sept 13 - Sept 14, 2025
AMA PRO HILLCLIMB IDAHO NITRO
NATIONALS I & II
Payette, ID
Idaho Battle of the Bluffs
AMA PRO RACING
Phone: 386-492-1014
Fax: 386-274-2335
communications@amaproracing.com
www.amaproracing.com

Sept 13, 2025
LAKE OZARK ST
Eldon, MO
Lake Ozark Speedway
AMA PRO RACING
Phone: 386-492-1014
Fax: 386-274-2335
communications@amaproracing.com
www.amaproracing.com

Sept 20, 2025
AMA PRO HILLCLIMB WHITE ROSE
NATIONAL II
Spring Grove, PA
White Rose Motorcycle Club
AMA PRO RACING
Phone: 386-492-1014
Fax: 386-274-2335
communications@amaproracing.com
www.amaproracing.com

Sept 28, 2025
AMA PRO HILLCLIMB
FREEMANSBURG NATIONAL II
Freemansburg, PA
Bushkill Valley Motorcycle Club
AMA PRO RACING
Phone: 386-492-1014
Fax: 386-274-2335
communications@amaproracing.com
www.amaproracing.com

Oct 11 - Oct 12, 2025
AMA PRO HILLCLIMB NATIONAL
CHAMPIONSHIP
Oregonia, OH
Dayton Motorcycle Club
AMA PRO RACING
Phone: 386-492-1014
Fax: 386-274-2335
communications@amaproracing.com
www.amaproracing.com

Jun 7, 2025
THUNDER VALLEY NATIONAL
Lakewood, CO
Thunder Valley Motocross Park

AMA PRO RACING
Phone: 386-492-1014
Fax: 386-274-2335
communications@amaproracing.com
www.amaproracing.com

Orienteering

Oct 11 - Oct 13, 2025
US ORIENTEERING NATIONALS
Medfield, MA
Rocky Woods Reservation
US ORIENTEERING
Phone: 215-482-9479
contact@orienteeringusa.org
orienteeringusa.org

Paintball

Mar 7 - Mar 9, 2025
TAMPA BAY OPEN
Tampa Bay, FL
NATIONAL X BALL LEAGUE
info@nxlpaintball.com
nxlpaintball.com

May 1 - May 4, 2025
ATLANTIC CITY OPEN
Atlantic City, NJ
NATIONAL X BALL LEAGUE
info@nxlpaintball.com
nxlpaintball.com

Jun 20 - Jun 22, 2025
MIDWEST OPEN
Cincinnati, OH
NATIONAL X BALL LEAGUE
info@nxlpaintball.com
nxlpaintball.com

Sept 11 - Sept 14, 2025
LONE STAR OPEN
Garland, TX
NATIONAL X BALL LEAGUE
info@nxlpaintball.com
nxlpaintball.com

Platform Tennis

Mar 1, 2025
MEN'S PTI 50+
West Chester, PA
AMERICAN PLATFORM TENNIS
ASSOCIATION
Phone: 888-744-9490
apta@platformtennis.org
www.platformtennis.org

Mar 6 - Mar 8, 2025
APTA MEN'S & WOMEN'S
NATIONALS
Philadelphia, PA
AMERICAN PLATFORM TENNIS
ASSOCIATION
Phone: 888-744-9490
apta@platformtennis.org
www.platformtennis.org

Mar 29 - Mar 30, 2025
APTA HUSBAND/WIFE & MIXED
NATIONALS
Franklin Lakes, NJ
AMERICAN PLATFORM TENNIS
ASSOCIATION
Phone: 888-744-9490
apta@platformtennis.org
www.platformtennis.org

Mar 29, 2025
WOMEN'S PTI 50+
Essex, CT
AMERICAN PLATFORM TENNIS
ASSOCIATION
Phone: 888-744-9490
apta@platformtennis.org
www.platformtennis.org

Apr 5 - Apr 6, 2025
APTA MEN'S TEAM NATIONALS
Summit, NJ
AMERICAN PLATFORM TENNIS
ASSOCIATION
Phone: 888-744-9490
apta@platformtennis.org
www.platformtennis.org

Apr 5 - Apr 6, 2025
APTA WOMEN'S TEAM NATIONALS
Summit, NJ
AMERICAN PLATFORM TENNIS
ASSOCIATION
Phone: 888-744-9490
apta@platformtennis.org
www.platformtennis.org

Racquetball

Feb 26 - Mar 3, 2025
USA RACQUETBALL NATIONAL HIGH
SCHOOL CHAMPIONSHI PS
Portland, OR
Multnomah Athletic Club
USA RACQUETBALL
Phone: 719-635-5396
Fax: 719-635-0685
jonathan@usaracquetball.com
www.usaracquetball.com

Mar 27 - Mar 29, 2025
USA RACQUETBALL NATIONAL
INTERCOLLEGIATE CHAMPIO
NSHIPS
Raleigh, NC
North Carolina State Recreation Center
USA RACQUETBALL
Phone: 719-635-5396
Fax: 719-635-0685
jonathan@usaracquetball.com
www.usaracquetball.com

May 14 - May 18, 2025
USA RACQUETBALL NATIONAL
INDOOR
Pleasanton, CA
USA RACQUETBALL
Phone: 719-635-5396
Fax: 719-635-0685
jonathan@usaracquetball.com
www.usaracquetball.com

Jun 25 - Jun 29, 2025
USA RACQUETBALL NATIONAL
JUNIOR CHAMPIONSHIPS
Minneapolis, MN
University of Minnesota
USA RACQUETBALL
Phone: 719-635-5396
Fax: 719-635-0685
jonathan@usaracquetball.com
www.usaracquetball.com

Rodeo

Feb 17 - Feb 23, 2025
PASCO COUNTY FAIR
CHAMPIONSHIP RODEO
Dade City, FL
PROFESSIONAL RODEO COWBOY
ASSOCIATION
Phone: 719-593-8840
webmaster@prorodeo.com
www.prorodeo.com

Mar 6 - Mar 9, 2025
ARCADIA ALL-FLORIDA
CHAMPIONSHIP RODEO
Arcadia, FL
PROFESSIONAL RODEO COWBOY
ASSOCIATION
Phone: 719-593-8840
webmaster@prorodeo.com
www.prorodeo.com

Mar 27 - Apr 6, 2025
YMBL CHAMPIONSHIP RODEO
Beaumont, TX
PROFESSIONAL RODEO COWBOY
ASSOCIATION
Phone: 719-593-8840
webmaster@prorodeo.com
www.prorodeo.com

Jun 30 - Jul 6, 2025
ANNUAL WORLD'S OLDEST
CONTINUOUS RODEO
Prescott, AZ
PROFESSIONAL RODEO COWBOY
ASSOCIATION
Phone: 719-593-8840
webmaster@prorodeo.com
www.prorodeo.com

Jul 1 - Jul 4, 2025
HOME OF CHAMPIONS RODEO
Red Lodge, MT
PROFESSIONAL RODEO COWBOY
ASSOCIATION
Phone: 719-593-8840
webmaster@prorodeo.com
www.prorodeo.com

Jul 18 - Jul 19, 2025
EXTREME EVENTS MINNESOTA
CHAMPIONSHIP RODEO
Waconia, MN
PROFESSIONAL RODEO COWBOY
ASSOCIATION
Phone: 719-593-8840
webmaster@prorodeo.com
www.prorodeo.com

Roller Sports

Jan 15 - Jan 20, 2025
EMERALD COAST INLINE
CHALLENGE
Milton, FL
USA ROLLER SPORTS
Phone: 402-483-7551
Fax: 402-483-1465
www.usarollersports.org

Jun 3 - Jun 12, 2025
OUTDOOR NATIONAL
CHAMPIONSHIPS
TBA
USA ROLLER SPORTS
Phone: 402-483-7551

Fax: 402-483-1465
www.usarollersports.org

Jul 2 - Jul 28, 2025
INDOOR NATIONAL CHAMPIONSHIPS
Reno, NV
USA ROLLER SPORTS
Phone: 402-483-7551
Fax: 402-483-1465
www.usarollersports.org

Jul 17 - Jul 19, 2025
NARCH FINALS
Irvine, CA
The Rinks, Irvine Inline
NORTH AMERICAN ROLLER HOCKEY
CHAMPIONSHIPS
Phone: 760-889-6909
daryn@narch.com
www.narch.com

Rowing/Crew

Feb 16, 2025
C.R.A.S.H.-B. WORLD INDOOR
ROWING CHAMPIONSHIPS
Boston, MA
Gosman Sports & Convocation Center
CRASH-B SPRINTS
office@crash-b.org
www.crash-b.org

May 30 - Jun 1, 2025
NCAA DIVISION I ROWING FINALS
West Windsor, NJ
Lake Mercer
NATIONAL COLLEGIATE ATHLETIC
ASSOCIATION
Phone: 317-917-6222
Fax: 317-917-6888
www.ncaa.org

May 30 - May 31, 2025
NCAA DIVISION II ROWING FINALS
West Windsor, NJ
Lake Mercer
NATIONAL COLLEGIATE ATHLETIC
ASSOCIATION
Phone: 317-917-6222
Fax: 317-917-6888
www.ncaa.org

May 30 - May 31, 2025
NCAA DIVISION III ROWING FINALS
West Windsor, NJ
Lake Mercer
NATIONAL COLLEGIATE ATHLETIC
ASSOCIATION
Phone: 317-917-6222
Fax: 317-917-6888
www.ncaa.org

Rugby

Feb 22, 2025
MARDI GRAS TOURNAMENT
New Orleans, LA
USA RUGBY
Phone: 303-539-0300
Fax: 303-539-0311
membership@usa.rugby
www.usa.rugby

Apr 5, 2025
COLLEGE 7S NATIONAL
CHAMPIONSHIPS
TBA

USA RUGBY
Phone: 303-539-0300
Fax: 303-539-0311
membership@usa.rugby
www.usa.rugby

Running

Mar 15, 2025
BEL MONTE ENDURANCE RACES
Blue Ridge Mouuntains, VA
BAD TO THE BONE
Phone: 434-218-0402
francesca@badtothebone.biz
badtothebone.biz

Feb 8, 2025
2025 KICK OFF RUN
Westlake, OH
Fleet Feet- Westlake Location
CLEVELAND MARATHON
Phone: 800-467-3826
Fax: 216-378-0143
www.clevelandmarathon.com

Feb 22, 2025
BAYOU CITY CLASSIC
Houston, TX
HOUSTON AREA ROAD RUNNERS
ASSOCIATION
www.bayoucityclassic.org

Mar 1 - Mar 2, 2025
LITTLE ROCK MARATHON
Little Rock, AR
LITTLE ROCK MARATHON
Phone: 501-371-4639
glamm@littlerock.gov
www.littlerockmarathon.com

Mar 1, 2025
SAN MIGUEL BUZZ MARATHON
San Miguel, CA
Camp Roberts Army National Guard
Reservation
SAN MIGUEL BUZZ MARATHON
Phone: 805-467-3216
Fax: 805-467-3410
www.buzzmarathon.org

Mar 2, 2025
305 HALF MARATHON & 5K
Miami, FL
LIFE TIME FITNESS
www.eventsbylifetime.com

Mar 14 - Mar 16, 2025
YUENGLING SHAMROCK MARATHON
Virginia Beach, VA
SHAMROCK MARATHON
Phone: 757-412-1056
Fax: 757-412-1058
info@shamrockmarathon.com
www.shamrockmarathon.com

Mar 16, 2025
LOS ANGELES MARATHON
Los Angeles, CA
CONQUR ENDURANCE GROUP
Phone: 213-542-3000
info@goconqur.com
goconqur.com

Mar 20, 2025
BIG ISLAND MARATHON
Hilo, HI
BIG ISLAND INTERNATIONAL
MARATHON
Phone: 808-969-7400
www.hilomarathon.org

Mar 22, 2025
MARINE CORPS MARATHON
Arlington, VA
MARINE CORPS MARATHON
Phone: 800-786-8762
Fax: 703-784-2265
mcm.info@usmc.mil
www.marinemarathon.com

Mar 22, 2025
NAPA VALLEY TRAIL MARATHON,
HALF MARATHON & 10K
Calistoga, CA
Bothe-Napa State Park
ENVIRO-SPORTS
Phone: 415-868-1829
info@envirosports.com
envirosports.com

Mar 29, 2025
YAKIMA RIVER CANYON MARATHON
Selah, WA
Yakima River Canyon Marathon Selah
Civic Center
HARD CORE RUNNER'S CLUB
Phone: 425-226-1518

Apr TBA, 2025
NORTH POLE MARATHON
Arctic Ocean, NT
Geographic North Pole
POLAR RUNNING ADVENTURES
International Ph: 011 353 91 443 408
International Fax: 011 353 91 443 408
rd@npmarathon.com
www.npmarathon.com

Apr TBA, 2025
ROCKIN K TRAIL MARATHON
Ellsworth, KS
Kanapolis State Park
KANSAS ULTRARUNNERS' SOCIETY
www.ksultrarunners.org

Apr 2, 2025
BIG-D TEXAS MARATHON
Dallas, TX
Cotton Bowl, Fair Park
BIG-D TEXAS MARATHON

Apr 5, 2025
ANDREW JACKSON MARATHON
Jackson, TN
ANDREW JACKSON MARATHON
steve@gdwm.org
www.facebook.com/RunAJMJackson

Apr 5, 2025
CHARLOTTESVILLE MARATHON
Charlottesville, VA
BAD TO THE BONE
Phone: 434-218-0402
francesca@badtothebone.biz
badtothebone.biz

Apr 5, 2025
GOLDEN GATE HEADLANDS
MARATHON, HALF MARATHON & 10K
Sausalito, CA
Fort Barry, Golden Gate National
Recreation Area
ENVIRO-SPORTS
Phone: 415-868-1829
info@envirosports.com
envirosports.com

Apr 6, 2025
DELAWARE MARATHON RUNNING
FESTIVAL
Wilmington, DE

Tubman Garrett Riverfront Park
CORRIGAN SPORTS ENTERPRISES
Phone: 410-605-9381
Fax: 410-605-9389
customerservice@corrigansports.com
www.corrigansports.com

Apr 6, 2025
OHIO RIVER ROAD RUNNERS
MARATHON & HALF MARATHON
Xenia, OH
OHIO RIVER ROAD RUNNERS CLUB
www.orrrc.org

Apr 12, 2025
HALF MARATHON UNPLUGGED
Burlington, VT
RUN VERMONT
Phone: 802-863-8412
info@runvermont.org
www.runvermont.org

Apr 19, 2025
PINE LINE MARATHON
Medford, WI
Medford City Park
PINE LINE TRAIL MARATHON
Phone: 715-748-4729
pinelinemarathon.weebly.com

Apr 21, 2025
BOSTON MARATHON
Boston, MA
BOSTON ATHLETIC ASSOCIATION
Phone: 617-236-1652
Fax: 617-236-4505
info@baa.org
www.baa.org

Apr 23 - Apr 26, 2025
DRAKE RELAYS
Des Moines, IA
Drake Stadium, Drake University
DRAKE RELAYS
Phone: 515-271-2889
Fax: 515-271-4189
www.godrakebulldogs.com

Apr 24 - Apr 26, 2025
PENN RELAYS
University of Pennsylvania
Franklin Field
UNIVERSITY OF PENNSYLVANIA
Phone: 215-898-6145
pennrela@pobox.upenn.edu
www.thepennrelays.com

Apr 25, 2025
EISENHOWER MARATHON
Abilene, TX
Chisholm Trail
EISENHOWER MARATHON
Phone: 785-263-3474
scathey79@yahoo.com
eisenhowermarathon.net

Apr 25 - Apr 27, 2025
OKLAHOMA CITY MEMORIAL
MARATHON
Oklahoma City, OK
OKLAHOMA CITY MARATHON
Phone: 405-525-4242
Fax: 405-521-9907
help@okcmarathon.com
www.okcmarathon.com

Apr 26, 2025
GO ST. LOUIS MARATHON
St. Louis, MO
SPIRIT OF ST. LOUIS MARATHON
Phone: 314-727-0800

Fax: 314-727-0893
info@gostlouis.org
www.gostlouis.org

Apr 26, 2025
KENTUCKY DERBY FESTIVAL
MARATHON
Louisville, KY
KENTUCKY DERBY FESTIVAL
Phone: 800-928-3378
Fax: 502-589-4674
minimarathon@kdf.org
www.derbyfestivalmarathon.com

Apr 26, 2025
MT. TAM WILD BOAR HALF
MARATHON & 10K
Mill Valley, CA
Mt. Tamalpais State Park
ENVIRO-SPORTS
Phone: 415-868-1829
info@envirosports.com
envirosports.com

Apr 26, 2025
OLATHE KS MARATHON
Olathe, KS
OLATHE CHAMBER OF COMMERCE
Phone: 913-764-1050
Fax: 913-782-4636
marathon@olathe.org
www.olathemarathon.com

Apr 27, 2025
BIG SUR INTERNATIONAL
MARATHON
Carmel, CA
BIG SUR MARATHON FOUNDATION
Phone: 831-625-6226
Fax: 831-625-2119
info@bsim.org
www.bigsurmarathon.org

Apr 27, 2025
MAUI MARATHON
Maui, HI
MAUI MARATHON
Phone: 808-222-2484
mauimarathonexpor@gmail.com
www.mauimarathon.com

Apr 27, 2025
MERCY HEALTH GLASS CITY
MARATHON
Toledo, OH
TOLEDO ROAD RUNNERS CLUB
Phone: 419-340-1815
info@glasscitymarathon.org
glasscitymarathon.org

Apr 27, 2025
WHIDBEY ISLAND MARATHON AND
HALF MARATHON
Oak Harbor, WA
WHIDBEY ISLAND MARATHON & HALF
MARATHON
runwhidbey.org

May 2 - May 4, 2025
CINCINNATI FLYING PIG MARATHON
Cincinnati, OH
CINCINNATI FLYING PIG MARATHON
Phone: 513-721-7447
info@flyingpigmarathon.com
flyingpigmarathon.com

May 2 - May 4, 2025
LONG ISLAND MARATHON FESTIVAL
East Meadow, NY
LONG ISLAND MARATHON

May 2, 2025
SHIPROCK MARATHON
Shiprock, NM
FOUR CORNERS FITNESS &
WELLNESS ASSOCIATION
Phone: 435-233-8068
info@shiprockmarathon.com
www.shiprockmarathon.com

May 3 - May 4, 2025
FREDERICK RUNNING FESTIVAL
Frederick, MD
Frederick Fair Grounds
CORRIGAN SPORTS ENTERPRISES
Phone: 410-605-9381
Fax: 410-605-9389
customerservice@corrigansports.com
www.corrigansports.com

May 4, 2025
AVENUE OF THE GIANTS
MARATHON
Eureka, CA
THE AVE
Phone: 707-822-1861
ctimek@aol.com
www.theave.org

May 4, 2025
COLORADO MARATHON
Fort Collins, CO
COLORADO MARATHON
logan@thecoloradomarathon.com
comarathon.com

May 4, 2025
LINCOLN MARATHON
Lincoln, NE
LINCOLN TRACK CLUB
Phone: 402-435-3504
www.lincolnmarathon.org

May 5, 2025
WALTER CHILDS MARATHON
Holyoke, MA
Ashley Reservoir @ Elks Lodge
GREATER SPRINGFIELD HARRIERS
Phone: 413-734-0955
marathon@harriers.org
www.harriers.org

May 10 - May 11, 2025
HARMONY GENEVA MARATHON FOR
UNICEF
Geneva, Switzerland
OC SPORT
www.ocsport.com

May 10, 2025
MUIR WOODS MARATHON, HALF
MARATHON & 7 MILE
Stinson Beach, CA
Stinson Beach Park
ENVIRO-SPORTS
Phone: 415-868-1829
info@envirosports.com
envirosports.com

May 11, 2025
SUGARLOAF MARATHON & 15K
Carrabassett Valley, ME
SUGARLOAF MARATHON
Phone: 207-237-2000
Fax: 207-237-3768
info@sugarloaf.com
www.sugarloaf.com

May 17 - May 18, 2025
CAPITAL CITY MARATHON
Olympia, WA

Sylvester Park
CAPITAL CITY MARATHON
racedirector@ccmaboard.org
www.capitalcitymarathon.org

May 17 - May 18, 2025
MED CITY MARATHON
Rochester, MN
MED CITY MARATHON
Phone: 507-254-2703
Fax: 507-288-8058
medcityevents@outlook.com
www.medcitymarathon.com

May 5, 2025
OGDEN MARATHON
Odgen, UT
GOAL FOUNDATION
Phone: 801-399-1773
admin@goalfoundation.com
www.ogdenmarathon.com

May 17, 2025
TRENT/WALDRON GLACIER HALF
MARATHON
Anchorage, AK
Westchester Lagoon
ANCHORAGE RUNNING CLUB
Phone: 907-258-4964
info@anchoragerunningclub.org
www.anchoragerunningclub.org

May 18, 2025
CARDEROCK RUNNING FESTIVAL
Carderock, MD
MARATHON CHARITY COOPERATION
www.mc-coop.org

May 18, 2025
CHICAGO SPRING HALF MARATHON
& 10K
Chicago, IL
LIFE TIME FITNESS
www.eventsbylifetime.com

May 19, 2025
CELLCOM GREEN BAY MARATHON
Green Bay, WI
CELLCOM GREEN BAY MARATHON
Phone: 920-432-6272
info@cellcomgreenbaymarathon.com
www.cellcomgreenbaymarathon.com

May 23 - May 25, 2025
BUFFALO MARATHON
Buffalo, NY
BUFFALO MARATHON
information@buffalomarathon.com
www.buffalomarathon.com

May 24, 2025
BAYSHORE MARATHON
Traverse City, MI
TRAVERSE CITY TRACK CLUB
Phone: 231-941-8118
www.bayshoremarathon.org

May 25, 2025
COEUR D'ALENE MARATHON
Coeur d'Alene, ID
COEUR D'ALENE MARATHON
runsignup.com/Race/ID/CoeurDAlene/nsp
lit

May 25, 2025
VERMONT CITY MARATHON
Burlington, VT
RUN VERMONT
Phone: 802-863-8412
info@runvermont.org
www.runvermont.org

May 25, 2025
WYOMING MARATHON
Laramie, WY
CHEYENNE TRACK CLUB
Phone: 307-778-7866
Fax: 307-778-7876
mollybeebishop@gmail.com
wyomingmarathonraces.weebly.com

May 26, 2025
BOLDERBOULDER 10K
Boulder, CO
BOLDER BOULDER
Phone: 303-444-7223
www.bolderboulder.com

May 31 - Jun 1, 2025
DEADWOOD-MICKELSON TRAIL
MARATHON
Deadwood, SD
DEADWOOD-MICKELSON TRAIL
MARATHON
Phone: 605-390-6137
www.deadwoodmickelsontrailmarathon.co
m

May 31 - Jun 1, 2025
ROCK 'N' ROLL MARATHON
San Diego, CA
ROCK 'N' ROLL MARATHON SERIES
Phone: 858-450-6510
Fax: 858-450-6905
www.runrocknroll.com

May 31, 2025
SUNBURST MARATHON
South Bend, IN
BEACON HEALTH SYSTEM
Phone: 574-647-1000
sunburst.beaconhealthsystem.org

May 31, 2025
VIRGINIA WINE COUNTRY HALF
MARATHON
Hillsboro, VA
Doukenie Winery
BAD TO THE BONE
Phone: 434-218-0402
francesca@badtothebone.biz
badtothebone.biz

Jun 1, 2025
CASPER WYOMING MARATHON
Casper, WY
CASPER WYOMING MARATHON
Phone: 307-577-4974
www.runwyoming.com

Jun 1, 2025
KONA MARATHON & KONA HALF
MARATHON
Keauhou-Kona, HI
Waikoloa Beach Resort
KONA MARATHON
Phone: 808-967-8285
raceinfo@konamarathon.com
www.konamarathon.com

Jun 1, 2025
NEWPORT MARATHON
Newport, OR
NEWPORT MARATHON
Phone: 541-265-3446
run@newportmarathon.org
www.newportmarathon.org

Jun TBA, 2025
SAN JUAN ISLAND MARATHON
Friday Harbor, WA

LAKEDALE RESORT
Phone: 800-617-2267
www.lakedale.com

Jun 1, 2025
STEAMBOAT MARATHON
Steamboat Springs, CO
STEAMBOAT MARATHON
Phone: 970-879-0880
Fax: 970-879-3550
marathon@steamboatchamber.com
www.steamboatchamber.com

Jun 8, 2025
HATFIELD-MCCOY MARATHON
Williamson, WV
HATFIELD-MCCOY MARATHON
hatfieldmccoymarathontvrrc.com

Jun 15, 2025
ESTES PARK MARATHON
Estes Park, CO
Estes Park High School
ESTES PARK MARATHON
Phone: 970-586-8189
belle@epmarathon.org
www.epmarathon.org

Jun 19 - Jun 21, 2025
GRANDMA'S MARATHON
Duluth, MN
Two Harbors To Duluth
GRANDMA'S MARATHON
Phone: 218-727-0947
grandmas@grandmasmarathon.com
www.grandmasmarathon.com

Jun 28, 2025
LEADVILLE TRAIL MARATHON &
HEAVY HALF
Leadville, CO
LEADVILLE TRAIL MARATHON
leadville@ltevents.zendesk.com
www.leadvilleraceseries.com

Jul TBA, 2025
JUNEAU MARATHON & HALF
MARATHON
Juneau, AK
JUNEAU TRAIL & ROAD RUNNERS
houstonlaws@yahoo.com
juneauserr.wixsite.com/serr/marathon

Jul 10 - Jul 13, 2025
GRANDFATHER MOUNTAIN
HIGHLAND GAMES
Linville, NC
GRANDFATHER MOUNTAIN HIGHLAND
GAMES
Phone: 828-733-1333
Fax: 828-733-0092
admin@gmhg.org
www.gmhg.org

Jul 26 - Jul 27, 2025
SAN FRANCISCO MARATHON
San Francisco, CA
SAN FRANCISCO MARATHON
Phone: 888-958-6668
customersupport@thesfmarathon.com
www.thesfmarathon.com

Aug 2, 2025
PARK CITY HALF MARATHON
Park City, UT
UTAH ROAD RUNNERS
pctrailseries.com

Aug 23, 2025
ANGEL ISLAND HALF MARATHON &
10K
Tiburon, CA

Angel Island State Park
ENVIRO-SPORTS
Phone: 415-868-1829
info@envirosports.com
envirosports.com

Aug 30, 2025
POCATELLO MARATHON
Pocatello, ID
POCATELLO MARATHON
Phone: 208-233-4754
pocatellorun@gmail.com
www.pocatellomarathon.com

Sept 18 - Sept 20, 2025
AIR FORCE MARATHON
Dayton, OH
Wright-Patterson AFB
USAF MARATHON
Phone: 800-467-1823
Fax: 937-656-1000
usaf.marathon@us.af.mil
www.usafmarathon.com

Sept 19 - Sept 21, 2025
COMMUNITY FIRST FOX CITIES
MARATHON
Appleton, WI
COMMUNITY FIRST FOX CITIES
MARATHON
Phone: 877-230-7223
Fax: 920-830-0921
info@foxcitiesmarathon.org
www.foxcitiesmarathon.org

Sept 20, 2025
TOP OF UTAH MARATHON
Logan, UT
LOGAN CITY MARATHON
www.logandowntown.org

Sept 21, 2025
PIKES PEAK MARATHON
Colorado Springs, CO
PIKES PEAK MARATHON
Phone: 719-473-2625
info@pikespeakmarathon.org
www.pikespeakmarathon.org

Sept 27, 2025
BIG SUR TRAIL MARATHON, HALF
MARATHON & 5 MILE
Big Sur, CA
Andrew Molera State Park
ENVIRO-SPORTS
Phone: 415-868-1829
info@envirosports.com
envirosports.com

Sept 27, 2025
FIRSTENERGY AKRON MARATHON,
HALF MARATHON & TEAM RELAY
Akron, OH
ROAD RUNNER AKRON MARATHON
Phone: 330-434-2786
Fax: 330-434-0738
info@akronmarathon.org
www.akronmarathon.org

Sept 28, 2025
BOULDERTHON
Boulder, CO
RUN BOULDER EVENTS
Phone: 303-517-7046
www.runboulderevents.com

Sept 28, 2025
OMAHA MARATHON
Omaha, NE
OMAHA MARATHON
Phone: 845-247-7275

info@hitsendurance.com
www.omahamarathon.com

Oct TBA, 2025
HEARTLAND 100 SPIRIT OF THE
PRAIRIE RACE
Cassoday, KS
TBA
KANSAS ULTRARUNNERS' SOCIETY
www.ksultrarunners.org

Oct 4 - Oct 5, 2025
JETBLUE LONG BEACH MARATHON
& HALF MARATHON
Long Beach, CA
MOTIV RUNNING
lbinfo@motivsports.com
www.motivrunning.com

Oct 4 - Oct 5, 2025
MILWAUKEE LAKEFRONT
MARATHON
Milwaukee, WI
BADGERLAND STRIDERS
Phone: 414-688-7561
milwaukeelakefrontmarathon@gmail.com
www.milwaukeelakefrontmarathon.org

Oct 4, 2025
TOWPATH MARATHON
Boston, OH
Cuyahoga Valley National Park
OHIO CANAL CORRIDOR
Phone: 216-520-1825
Fax: 216-520-1833
www.towpathtrilogy.com

Oct 5, 2025
MAINE MARATHON
Portland, ME
THE MAINE MARATHON
Phone: 207-749-9160
racedirector@mainemarathon.com
www.mainemarathon.com

Oct 5, 2025
ST. GEORGE MARATHON
St. George, UT
ST. GEORGE MARATHON
Phone: 435-627-4500
Fax: 435-627-4509
marathon@sgcity.org
www.stgeorgemarathon.com

Oct 11 - Oct 12, 2025
CAPE COD MARATHON
Falmouth, MA
CAPE COD MARATHON
Phone: 508-540-6959
Fax: 508-548-0617
info@capecodmarathon.com
www.capecodmarathon.com

Oct 11, 2025
CITY OF TREES MARATHON
Boise, ID
Park Center Park
CITY OF TREES RACING
ASSOCIATION
www.cityoftreesmarathon.org

Oct 11, 2025
EVERSOURCE HARTFORD
MARATHON
Hartford, CT
Bushnell Park
HARTFORD MARATHON FOUNDATION
Phone: 860-652-8866
Fax: 860-652-8145
info@hartfordmarathon.com
www.hartfordmarathon.com

Oct 11, 2025
WHISKEY ROW MARATHON
Prescott, AZ
PRESCOTT YMCA
Phone: 928-445-7221
Fax: 928-445-5135
wrm@prescottymca.org
whiskeyrowmarathon.com

Oct 12, 2025
BANK OF AMERICA CHICAGO
MARATHON
Chicago, IL
BANK OF AMERICA CHICAGO
MARATHON
Phone: 312-904-9800
Fax: 312-904-6521
office@chicagomarathon.com
www.chicagomarathon.com

Oct 12, 2025
STEAMTOWN MARATHON
Scranton, PA
STEAMTOWN MARATHON
Phone: 570-342-0427
Fax: 570-342-0422
racecommittee@hotmail.com
www.steamtownmarathon.com

Oct 18, 2025
BALTIMORE RUNNING FESTIVAL
Baltimore, MD
BALTIMORE MARATHON
Phone: 410-605-9381
Fax: 410-605-9389
customerservice@corrigansports.com
www.thebaltimoremarathon.com

Oct 18, 2025
BROOKINGS MARATHON
Brookings, SD
BROOKINGS MARATHON
run@brookingsmarathon.com
www.brookingsmarathon.com

Oct 18 - Oct 19, 2025
COLUMBUS MARATHON
Columbus, OH
Downtown Columbus
COLUMBUS MARATHON
Phone: 614-421-7866
Fax: 614-263-3518
info@columbusmarathon.com
www.columbusmarathon.com

Oct 19, 2025
CHAMPLAIN ISLANDS MARATHON &
HALF MARATHON
South Hero, VT
Folsom Elementary School
GREEN MOUNTAIN ATHLETIC
ASSOCIATION
info@gmaa.run
gmaa.run

Oct 19, 2025
DES MOINES MARATHON
Des Moines, IA
DES MOINES MARATHON
HEADQUARTERS
Phone: 515-288-2692
Fax: 515-255-9051
info@desmoinesmarathon.com
www.desmoinesmarathon.com

Oct 19, 2025
METRO HEALTH GRAND RAPIDS
MARATHON
Grand Rapids, MI
GRAND RAPIDS MARATHON
Phone: 616-293-3145

rungrmarathon@gmail.com
www.grandrapidsmarathon.com

Oct 19, 2025
MOUNT DESERT ISLAND MARATHON
& HALF MARATHON
Bar Harbor, ME
CROW ATHLETICS
www.crowathletics.com

Oct 20, 2025
FALL CLASSIC HALF MARATHON &
10K
Charlottesville, VA
BAD TO THE BONE
Phone: 434-218-0402
francesca@badtothebone.biz
badtothebone.biz

Oct 25, 2025
MARATHON 2 MARATHON
Marathon, TX
MARATHON TO MARATHON
www.marathon2marathon.com

Oct 25, 2025
NAPA FALL WINE COUNTRY
MARATHON, HALF MARATHON & 10K
Calistoga, CA
Bothe-Napa State Park
ENVIRO-SPORTS
Phone: 415-868-1829
info@envirosports.com
envirosports.com

Nov TBA, 2025
MALIBU INTERNATIONAL HALF
MARATHON & 5K
Malibu, CA
MALIBU INTERNATIONAL MARATHON
Phone: 310-745-8231
www.runmalibu.com

Nov TBA, 2025
TURKEY TROT MIAMI
Miami, FL
LIFE TIME FITNESS
www.eventsbylifetime.com

Nov TBA, 2025
ULTRA RACE OF CHAMPIONS
Blue Ridge Mouuntains, VA
BAD TO THE BONE
Phone: 434-218-0402
francesca@badtothebone.biz
badtothebone.biz

Nov 2, 2025
TCS NEW YORK CITY MARATHON
New York, NY
NEW YORK ROAD RUNNERS
Phone: 855-569-6977
marathonmailer@nyrr.org
www.tcsnycmarathon.org

Nov 8, 2025
INDIANAPOLIS MARATHON
Indianapolis, IN
INDIANAPOLIS MARATHON CORP
Phone: 317-454-8519
nfo@beyondmonumental.org
www.monumentalmarathon.com

Nov 9, 2025
ATHENS MARATHON
Athens, Greece
ATHENS MARATHON COMMITTEE
Phone: 740-594-3825
Fax: 740-594-2525
athensohiomarathon@gmail.com
www.athensmarathon.com

Nov 9, 2025
MADISON MARATHON FULL & HALF
Madison, WI
MADISON FESTIVALS
Phone: 608-276-9797
Fax: 608-226-9550
events@madisonfestivals.com
www.madisonfestivals.com

Nov 9, 2025
SANTA CLARITA MARATHON
Santa Clarita, CA
SANTA CLARITA MARATHON
Phone: 805-258-3779
bill@elitesportsca.com
santaclaritamarathon.org

Nov 15, 2025
RICHMOND MARATHON
Richmond, VA
RICHMOND MARATHON
Phone: 804-285-9495
Fax: 804-285-3132
marathon@sportsbackers.org
www.richmondmarathon.com

Nov 21 - Nov 23, 2025
PHILADELPHIA MARATHON
Philadelphia, PA
PHILADELPHIA MARATHON
Phone: 215-683-2122
Fax: 215-683-2099
info@philadelphiamarathon.com
philadelphiamarathon.com

Nov 30, 2025
SEATTLE MARATHON & HALF
MARATHON
Seattle, WA
Seattle Center
SEATTLE MARATHON ASSOCIATION
Phone: 206-729-3660
info@seattlemarathon.org
www.seattlemarathon.org

Dec 6, 2025
ST. JUDE MEMPHIS MARATHON
Memphis, TN
ST. JUDE MARATHON
Phone: 901-578-1555
Fax: 901-578-6696
marathon@stjude.org
www.stjude.org

Dec 12 - Dec 14, 2025
BMW DALLAS MARATHON
Dallas, TX
Dallas City Hall Plaza
DWRM
Phone: 214-800-2087
www.rundallas.com

Sailing

Apr 8 - Apr 12, 2025
STAR NORTH AMERICAN
CHAMPIONSHIP
Pass Christian, MS
Pass Christian Yacht Club
INTERNATIONAL STAR CLASS YACHT
ASSOCIATION
Phone: 619-222-0252
Fax: 619-222-0528
office@starclass.org
www.starclass.org

Jun 11 - Jun 15, 2025
EUROPEAN CHAMPIONSHIPS
Viareggio, Italy

Societ... Velica Viareggina
INTERNATIONAL STAR CLASS YACHT
ASSOCIATION
Phone: 619-222-0252
Fax: 619-222-0528
office@starclass.org
www.starclass.org

Jun 12 - Jun 15, 2025
WESTERN HEMISPHERE
CHAMPIONSHIPS
Gibson Island, MD
Gibson Island Yacht Squadron
INTERNATIONAL STAR CLASS YACHT
ASSOCIATION
Phone: 619-222-0252
Fax: 619-222-0528
office@starclass.org
www.starclass.org

Jun 13 - Jun 21, 2025
2025 FINN WORLD MASTERS
Puntala, Italy
Puntala Camping and Resort
WORLD SAILING
office@sailing.org
www.sailing.org

Jun 19 - Jun 22, 2025
US WINGFOIL CHAMPIONSHIP
San Francisco, CA
San Francisco Yacht Club
US SAILING
Phone: 800-877-2451
info@ussailing.org
www.ussailing.org

Jun 19 - Jun 22, 2025
US YOUTH CHAMPIONSHIP
San Francisco, CA
St. Francis Yatch Club
WORLD SAILING
office@sailing.org
www.sailing.org

Jun 20 - Jun 22, 2025
US SINGLEHANDED
CHAMPIONSHIPS
Marion, MA
Tabor Academy
US SAILING
Phone: 800-877-2451
info@ussailing.org
www.ussailing.org

Jul 5 - Jul 11, 2025
J80 WORLD CHAMPIONSHIP
Nieuwpoort, Belgium
WORLD SAILING
office@sailing.org
www.sailing.org

Jul 7 - Jul 11, 2025
US JUNIOR WOMEN'S
CHAMPIONSHIP
Macatawa, MI
Macatawa Bay Yacht Club
WORLD SAILING
office@sailing.org
www.sailing.org

Aug 14 - Aug 17, 2025
US WOMEN'S MATCH RACING
CHAMPIONSHIP
San Francisco, CA
St. Francis Yacht Club
US SAILING
Phone: 800-877-2451
info@ussailing.org
www.ussailing.org

Sept 10 - Sept 13, 2025
US CHAMPIONSHIP OF CHAMPIONS
Dartmouth, MA
New Bedford Yacht Club
US SAILING
Phone: 800-877-2451
info@ussailing.org
www.ussailing.org

Sept 20 - Sept 27, 2025
MELGES 24 WORLD CHAMPIONSHIP
Trieste, Italy
WORLD SAILING
office@sailing.org
www.sailing.org

Sept 26 - Sept 28, 2025
US ADULT SAILING CHAMPIONSHIP
Park City, UT
Park City Sailing Association
US SAILING
Phone: 800-877-2451
info@ussailing.org
www.ussailing.org

Sept 26 - Sept 28, 2025
US PARA SAILING CHAMPIONSHIP
Coronado, CA
Coronado Yacht Club
US SAILING
Phone: 800-877-2451
info@ussailing.org
www.ussailing.org

Sept 26 - Sept 28, 2025
US TEAM RACING CHAMPIONSHIP
Larchmond, NY
Larchmond Yacht Club
US SAILING
Phone: 800-877-2451
info@ussailing.org
www.ussailing.org

Oct 1 - Oct 4, 2025
STAR VINTAGE COLD CUP
Gull Lake, MN
Gull Lake Yacht Club
INTERNATIONAL STAR CLASS YACHT
ASSOCIATION
Phone: 619-222-0252
Fax: 619-222-0528
office@starclass.org
www.starclass.org

Oct 3 - Oct 5, 2025
US OFFSHORE CHAMPIONSHIP
Annapolis, MD
US SAILING
Phone: 800-877-2451
info@ussailing.org
www.ussailing.org

Oct 9 - Oct 12, 2025
US MATCH RACING CHAMPIONSHIP
Chicago, IL
Chicago Yacht Club
US SAILING
Phone: 800-877-2451
info@ussailing.org
www.ussailing.org

Nov 3 - Nov 7, 20254
US MULTIHULL CHAMPIONSHIP
Corpus Christi, TX
Corpus Christi Yacht Club
US SAILING
Phone: 800-877-2451
info@ussailing.org
www.ussailing.org

Dec 12 - Dec 20, 2025
YOUTH WORLD CHAMPIONSHIPS
Portugal
WORLD SAILING
office@sailing.org
www.sailing.org

TBA, 2026
EASTERN HEMISPHERE
CHAMPIONSHIP
TBA
INTERNATIONAL STAR CLASS YACHT
ASSOCIATION
Phone: 619-222-0252
Fax: 619-222-0528
office@starclass.org
www.starclass.org

Jan TBA, 2026
BALTIMORE BOAT SHOW
Baltimore, MD
Baltimore Convention Center
NATIONAL MARINE MANUFACTURERS
ASSOCIATION
Phone: 312-946-6200
Fax: 312-946-0401
www.nmma.org

Shooting/Hunting

Mar 1, 2025
DISSIDENT ARMS ACTION SHOTGUN
CHAMPIONSHIP
Eagle Lake, TX
US PRACTICAL SHOOTING
ASSOCIATION
Phone: 360-855-2245
Fax: 360-855-0380
office@uspsa.org
www.uspsa.org

Mar TBA, 2025
NATIONAL COLLEGIATE MIXED
RIFLE FINALS
Lexington, KY
Memorial Coliseum
NATIONAL COLLEGIATE ATHLETIC
ASSOCIATION
Phone: 317-917-6222
Fax: 317-917-6888
www.ncaa.org

Mar 28, 2025
WAC ANNUAL GARY "DOC" WELT
MEMORIAL MATCH
Clearwater, FL
US PRACTICAL SHOOTING
ASSOCIATION
Phone: 360-855-2245
Fax: 360-855-0380
office@uspsa.org
www.uspsa.org

Apr 18, 2025
CLAY SHOOT FOR CONSERVATION
Mansfield, GA
Burge Plantation
GEORGIA WILDLIFE FEDERATION
Phone: 770-787-7887
Fax: 770-787-9229
info@gwf.org
www.gwf.org

May 28, 2025
WORLD SPEED SHOOTING
CHAMPIONSHIP
Talladega, AL
US PRACTICAL SHOOTING
ASSOCIATION

Phone: 360-855-2245
Fax: 360-855-0380
office@uspsa.org
www.uspsa.org

Jun 1 - Jun 7, 2025
NATIONAL HIGH POWER XTC
CHAMPIONSHIP
Lodi, WI
Winnequah Gun Club
NATIONAL RIFLE ASSOCIATION -
COMPETITIVE SHOOTING DIVISION
Phone: 703-267-1465
competitions.nra.org

Jun 4 - Jun 8, 2025
NATIONAL HIGH POWER MID-RANGE
CHAMPIONSHIP
Arcadia, OK
Oklahoma City Gun Club
NATIONAL RIFLE ASSOCIATION -
COMPETITIVE SHOOTING DIVISION
Phone: 703-267-1465
competitions.nra.org

Jun 12, 2025
NORTH TEXAS OPEN
Waxahachie, TX
US PRACTICAL SHOOTING
ASSOCIATION
Phone: 360-855-2245
Fax: 360-855-0380
office@uspsa.org
www.uspsa.org

Jun 25, 2025
SIG SAUER FACTORY GUN
NATIONALS
Marengo, OH
US PRACTICAL SHOOTING
ASSOCIATION
Phone: 360-855-2245
Fax: 360-855-0380
office@uspsa.org
www.uspsa.org

Jul 2 - Jul 6, 2025
NATIONAL HIGH POWER LONG
RANGE CHAMPIONSHIP
Malvern, OH
Alliance Rifle Club
NATIONAL RIFLE ASSOCIATION -
COMPETITIVE SHOOTING DIVISION
Phone: 703-267-1465
competitions.nra.org

Jul 6 - Jul 10, 2025
NATIONAL PISTOL CHAMPIONSHIPS
Marengo, OH
NATIONAL RIFLE ASSOCIATION -
COMPETITIVE SHOOTING DIVISION
Phone: 703-267-1465
competitions.nra.org

Jul 16, 2025
MULTIGUN NATIONALS
Forest Lake, MN
Forest Lake Sportsmen's Club
US PRACTICAL SHOOTING
ASSOCIATION
Phone: 360-855-2245
Fax: 360-855-0380
office@uspsa.org
www.uspsa.org

Aug 6 - Aug 7, 2025
NATIONAL LEVER ACTION
SILHOUETTE CHAMPIONSHIP
Ridway, PA
Ridway Rifle Club

NATIONAL RIFLE ASSOCIATION -
COMPETITIVE SHOOTING DIVISION
Phone: 703-267-1465
competitions.nra.org

Aug 8, 2025
NATIONAL PISTOL CARTRIDGE
SILHOUETTE CHAMPIONSHI P
Ridway, PA
Ridway Rifle Club
NATIONAL RIFLE ASSOCIATION -
COMPETITIVE SHOOTING DIVISION
Phone: 703-267-1465
competitions.nra.org

Aug 9, 2025
NATIONAL SMALLBORE SILHOUETTE
CHAMPIONSHIP
Ridway, PA
Ridway Rifle Club
NATIONAL RIFLE ASSOCIATION -
COMPETITIVE SHOOTING DIVISION
Phone: 703-267-1465
competitions.nra.org

Aug 15 - Aug 22, 2025
NATIONAL BLACK POWDER
CARTRIDGE RIFLE CHAMPIONSH IP
Friendship, IN
NATIONAL RIFLE ASSOCIATION -
COMPETITIVE SHOOTING DIVISION
Phone: 703-267-1465
competitions.nra.org

Aug 20, 2025
IPSC NATIONALS
Marengo, OH
US PRACTICAL SHOOTING
ASSOCIATION
Phone: 360-855-2245
Fax: 360-855-0380
office@uspsa.org
www.uspsa.org

Sept 30 - Oct 4, 2025
NRA'S WORLD SHOOTING
CHAMPIONSHIP (WSC)
Edinburgh, IN
Camp Atterbury
NATIONAL RIFLE ASSOCIATION -
COMPETITIVE SHOOTING DIVISION
Phone: 703-267-1465
competitions.nra.org

Oct 22, 2025
RACE GUN NATIONALS
Hurricane, UT
US PRACTICAL SHOOTING
ASSOCIATION
Phone: 360-855-2245
Fax: 360-855-0380
office@uspsa.org
www.uspsa.org

Shuffleboard

Jan 2 - Jan 4 2025
AMATEUR MIXED DOUBLES
Weslaco, TX
NATIONAL SHUFFLEBOARD
ASSOCIATION
www.national-shuffleboard-association.us

Jan 7 - Jan 9, 2025
TEXAS OPEN MEN'S & LADIES'
NON-WALKING SINGLES
San Benito, TX
NATIONAL SHUFFLEBOARD
ASSOCIATION
www.national-shuffleboard-association.us

Feb 24 - Feb 26, 2025
AMATEUR MEN'S & LADIES'
DOUBLES
Zephyrhills, FL
NATIONAL SHUFFLEBOARD
ASSOCIATION
www.national-shuffleboard-association.us

Jul 11 - Jul 12, 2025
OHIO OPEN MIXED DOUBLES
Lakeside, OH
NATIONAL SHUFFLEBOARD
ASSOCIATION
www.national-shuffleboard-association.us

Jul 14 - Jul 16, 2025
OHIO OPEN MEN'S & LADIES'
WALKING & NON-WALKING SINGLES
Lakeside, OH
NATIONAL SHUFFLEBOARD
ASSOCIATION
www.national-shuffleboard-association.us

Jul 16, 2025
OHIO JUNIOR SINGLES 15 & UNDER
Lakeside, OH
NATIONAL SHUFFLEBOARD
ASSOCIATION
www.national-shuffleboard-association.us

Jul 17 - Jul 18, 2025
OHIO OPEN MEN'S & LADIES'
DOUBLES
Lakeside, OH
NATIONAL SHUFFLEBOARD
ASSOCIATION
www.national-shuffleboard-association.us

Sept 5 - Sept 7, 2025
NORTH CAROLINA OPEN MEN'S &
LADIES' DOUBLES
Hendersonville, NC
NATIONAL SHUFFLEBOARD
ASSOCIATION
www.national-shuffleboard-association.us

Sept 8 - Sept 10, 2025
NORTH CAROLINA OPEN MEN'S &
LADIES' SINGLES
Hendersonville, NC
NATIONAL SHUFFLEBOARD
ASSOCIATION
www.national-shuffleboard-association.us

Sept 11 - Sept 13, 2025
NORTH CAROLINA OPEN MIXED
DOUBLES
Hendersonville, NC
NATIONAL SHUFFLEBOARD
ASSOCIATION
www.national-shuffleboard-association.us

Dec TBA, 2025
AMATEUR MEN'S & LADIES'
NON-WALKING SINGLES
TBA
NATIONAL SHUFFLEBOARD
ASSOCIATION
www.national-shuffleboard-association.us

Skiing

Feb 3 - Feb 15, 2025
FIS NORDIC JUNIOR WORLD SKI
CHAMPIONSHIP
Lake Placid, NY
FIS SKIING CHAMPIONSHIPS
International Ph: 44-33-244-6161
International Fax: 44-33-244-6171

mail@fisski.ch
www.fis-ski.com

TBA, 2026
FREESTYLE AERIALS NATIONAL
CHAMPIONSHIPS
TBA
U.S. SKI AND SNOWBOARD
ASSOCIATION
Phone: 435-649-9090
Fax: 435-649-3613
membership@usskiandsnowboard.org
usskiandsnowboard.org

TBA, 2026
FREESTYLE INTERNATIONAL
TBA
U.S. SKI AND SNOWBOARD
ASSOCIATION
Phone: 435-649-9090
Fax: 435-649-3613
membership@usskiandsnowboard.org
usskiandsnowboard.org

TBA, 2026
STIFEL KILLINGTON CUP
TBA
U.S. SKI AND SNOWBOARD
ASSOCIATION
Phone: 435-649-9090
Fax: 435-649-3613
membership@usskiandsnowboard.org
usskiandsnowboard.org

TBA, 2026
U.S. GRAND PRIX
TBA
U.S. SKI AND SNOWBOARD
ASSOCIATION
Phone: 435-649-9090
Fax: 435-649-3613
membership@usskiandsnowboard.org
usskiandsnowboard.org

Snowboarding

Jan 23 - Jan 26, 2025
X GAMES ASPEN
Aspen, CO
ESPN
xgames.espn.com/xgames

Feb 19 - Feb 20, 2025
SPEED NATION ALPINE NATIONALS
Val Saint-Come, QC, Canada
CANADA SNOWBOARD
Phone: 778-653-0000
Fax: 604-568-1639
info@canadasnowboard.ca
www.canadasnowboard.ca

Mar 9 - Mar 10, 2025
AIR NATION FREESTYLE NATIONALS
Barrie, ON, Canada
CANADA SNOWBOARD
Phone: 778-653-0000
Fax: 604-568-1639
info@canadasnowboard.ca
www.canadasnowboard.ca

Apr 10 - Apr 12, 2025
SPEED NATION SBX NATIONALS
Mont Sainte Anne, QC, Canada
CANADA SNOWBOARD
Phone: 778-653-0000
Fax: 604-568-1639
info@canadasnowboard.ca
www.canadasnowboard.ca

Jun 20 - Jun 22, 2025
X GAMES OSAKA
Osaka, Japan
ESPN
xgames.espn.com/xgames

Jun 27 - Jun 29, 2025
X GAMES SALT LAKE CITY
Salt Lake City, UT
ESPN
xgames.espn.com/xgames

Aug 22 - Aug 24, 2025
X GAMES SACRAMENTO
Sacramento, CA
ESPN
xgames.espn.com/xgames

Soccer

Apr 13, 2025
FUTSAL CANADIAN CHAMPIONSHIP
Regina, SK, Canada
CANADIAN SOCCER ASSOCIATION
Phone: 613-237-7678
Fax: 613-237-1516
info@soccercan.ca
www.canadasoccer.com

Oct 10, 2025
CANADIAN CHAMPIONSHIP
TBA, Canada
CANADIAN SOCCER ASSOCIATION
Phone: 613-237-7678
Fax: 613-237-1516
info@soccercan.ca
www.canadasoccer.com

Oct 13, 2025
NATIONAL CHAMPIONSHIPS U-15
CUP
Charlottetown, PE, Canada
CANADIAN SOCCER ASSOCIATION
Phone: 613-237-7678
Fax: 613-237-1516
info@soccercan.ca
www.canadasoccer.com

Oct 13, 2025
NATIONAL CHAMPIONSHIPS U-17
CUP
Kamloops, BC, Canada
CANADIAN SOCCER ASSOCIATION
Phone: 613-237-7678
Fax: 613-237-1516
info@soccercan.ca
www.canadasoccer.com

Dec 4 - Dec 6, 2025
NCAA DIVISION III WOMEN'S
SOCCER FINALS
Salem, VA
Kerr Stadium
NATIONAL COLLEGIATE ATHLETIC
ASSOCIATION
Phone: 317-917-6222
Fax: 317-917-6888
www.ncaa.org

Dec 5 - Dec 7, 2025
NCAA DIVISION III MEN'S SOCCER
FINALS
Salem, VA
Kerr Stadium
NATIONAL COLLEGIATE ATHLETIC
ASSOCIATION
Phone: 317-917-6222
Fax: 317-917-6888
www.ncaa.org

Dec 11 - Dec 13, 2025
NCAA DIVISION II MEN'S SOCCER
FINALS
TBA
NATIONAL COLLEGIATE ATHLETIC
ASSOCIATION
Phone: 317-917-6222
Fax: 317-917-6888
www.ncaa.org

Dec 12 - Dec 15, 2025
NCAA DIVISION I MEN'S SOCCER
FINALS
Cary, NC
WakeMed Soccer Park
NATIONAL COLLEGIATE ATHLETIC
ASSOCIATION
Phone: 317-917-6222
Fax: 317-917-6888
www.ncaa.org

Softball

May 22 - May 28, 2025
NCAA DIVISION II SOFTBALL FINALS
Chattanooga, TN
Frost Stadium
NATIONAL COLLEGIATE ATHLETIC
ASSOCIATION
Phone: 317-917-6222
Fax: 317-917-6888
www.ncaa.org

May 29 - Jun 6, 2025
NCAA DIVISION I SOFTBALL FINALS
Oklahoma City, OK
Devon Park
NATIONAL COLLEGIATE ATHLETIC
ASSOCIATION
Phone: 317-917-6222
Fax: 317-917-6888
www.ncaa.org

May 29 - Jun 4, 2025
NCAA DIVISION III SOFTBALL FINALS
Bloomington, IL
Inspiration Field
NATIONAL COLLEGIATE ATHLETIC
ASSOCIATION
Phone: 317-917-6222
Fax: 317-917-6888
www.ncaa.org

Jul TBA, 2025
USA SOFTBALL INTERNATIONAL
CUP
TBA
USA SOFTBALL
www.usasoftball.com

Jul 9 - Jul 15, 2025
GIRLS' 16U & 18U GOLD FP
Oklahoma City, OK
USA SOFTBALL
Phone: 405-424-5266
Fax: 405-424-3855
rcress@softball.org
www.usasoftball.com

Jul 17 - Jul 20, 2025
MEN'S MAJOR GOLD FP
Oklahoma City, OK
USA SOFTBALL
Phone: 405-424-5266
Fax: 405-424-3855
rcress@softball.org
www.usasoftball.com

Spet 4 - Sept 5, 2025
MEN'S SUPER SP
Oklahoma City, OK
USA SOFTBALL
Phone: 405-424-5266
Fax: 405-424-3855
rcress@softball.org
www.usasoftball.com

Sept 5 - Sept 7, 2025
WOMEN'S OPEN SP
Oklahoma City, OK
USA SOFTBALL
Phone: 405-424-5266
Fax: 405-424-3855
rcress@softball.org
www.usasoftball.com

Speedskating

Feb 8 - Feb 9, 2025
NATIONAL AGE GROUP LONG
TRACK SPEEDSKATING CHAMP
IONSHIP
Roseville, MN
US SPEEDSKATING
Phone: 801-417-5360
Fax: 801-417-5361
www.usspeedskating.org

Mar 28 - Mar 30, 2025
NATIONAL AGE GROUP SHORT
TRACK SPEEDSKATING CHAM
PIONSHIP
Manmouth Junction, NJ
US SPEEDSKATING
Phone: 801-417-5360
Fax: 801-417-5361
www.usspeedskating.org

May 29 - May 31, 2025
USS CONGRESS
Kearns, UT
US SPEEDSKATING
Phone: 801-417-5360
Fax: 801-417-5361
www.usspeedskating.org

Jan 8 - Jan 10, 2026
CANADIAN JUNIOR LONG TRACK
CHAMPIONSHIPS
Quebec City, QC
SPEED SKATING CANADA
Phone: 613-260-3669
Fax: 613-701-0296
ssc@speedskating.ca
www.speedskating.ca

Jan 30 - Feb 1, 2026
SHORT TRACK CANADA CUP 1
TBA
SPEED SKATING CANADA
Phone: 613-260-3669
Fax: 613-701-0296
ssc@speedskating.ca
www.speedskating.ca

Mar 6 - Mar 8, 2026
LONG TRACK CANADA CUP 2
Calgary, AB, Canada
SPEED SKATING CANADA
Phone: 613-260-3669
Fax: 613-701-0296
ssc@speedskating.ca
www.speedskating.ca

Squash

Feb 28 - Mar 2, 2025
US HIGH SCHOOL TEAM
CHAMPIONSHIPS
Philadelphia, PA
Arlen Specter US Squash Center
UNITED STATES SQUASH RACQUETS
ASSOCIATION
Phone: 212-268-4090
Fax: 212-268-4091
tournaments@ussquash.org
www.ussquash.com

Mar 6 - Mar 9, 2025
CSA NATIONAL TEAM
CHAMPIONSHIPS
Philadelphia, PA
Arlen Specter US Squash Center
UNITED STATES SQUASH RACQUETS
ASSOCIATION
Phone: 212-268-4090
Fax: 212-268-4091
tournaments@ussquash.org
www.ussquash.com

Mar 6 - Mar 9, 2025
US SQUASH DOUBLES
CHAMPIONSHIPS
Baltimore, MD
Maryland Club
UNITED STATES SQUASH RACQUETS
ASSOCIATION
Phone: 212-268-4090
Fax: 212-268-4091
tournaments@ussquash.org
www.ussquash.com

Mar 14 - Mar 16, 2025
CANADIAN UNIVERSITY & COLLEGE
CHAMPIONSHIPS
Montreal, QC, Canada
McGill University Athletics and
Recreation
SQUASH CANADA
Phone: 613-228-7724
Fax: 613-228-7232
info@squash.ca
www.squash.ca

Mar 21 - Mar 23, 2025
US JUNIOR BRONZE
CHAMPIONSHIPS
Philadelphia, PA
Arlen Specter US Squash Center
UNITED STATES SQUASH RACQUETS
ASSOCIATION
Phone: 212-268-4090
Fax: 212-268-4091
tournaments@ussquash.org
www.ussquash.com

Mar 27 - Mar 30, 2025
CANADIAN DOUBLES
CHAMPIONSHIP
Toronto, ON, Canada
Granite Club
SQUASH CANADA
Phone: 613-228-7724
Fax: 613-228-7232
info@squash.ca
www.squash.ca

Apr 11 - Apr 13, 2025
CANADIAN JUNIOR CLOSED
CHAMPIONSHIPS
Calgary, AB, Canada
University of Calgary Racquet Centre

SQUASH CANADA
Phone: 613-228-7724
Fax: 613-228-7232
info@squash.ca
www.squash.ca

Apr 11 - Apr 13, 2025
US MASTERS SQUASH
CHAMPIONSHIPS
Philadelphia, PA
Arlen Specter US Squash Center
UNITED STATES SQUASH RACQUETS
ASSOCIATION
Phone: 212-268-4090
Fax: 212-268-4091
tournaments@ussquash.org
www.ussquash.com

Apr 11 - Apr 13, 2025
US PARENT-CHILD SQUASH
DOUBLES CHAMPIONSHIPS
Philadelphia, PA
Arlen Specter US Squash Center
UNITED STATES SQUASH RACQUETS
ASSOCIATION
Phone: 212-268-4090
Fax: 212-268-4091
tournaments@ussquash.org
www.ussquash.com

Jan 23 - Jan 25, 2026
CANADIAN MASTERS TEAM
CHAMPIONSHIP
TBA
SQUASH CANADA
Phone: 613-228-7724
Fax: 613-228-7232
info@squash.ca
www.squash.ca

Mar 6 - Mar 8, 2026
CANADIAN MIXED DOUBLES
CHAMPIONSHIPS
TBA
SQUASH CANADA
Phone: 613-228-7724
Fax: 613-228-7232
info@squash.ca
www.squash.ca

Surfing

Jan 27 - Feb 8, 2025
LEXUS PIPE PRO
Oahu, Hawaii
WORLD SURF LEAGUE
International Ph: +1-310-450-1212
www.worldsurfleague.com

Feb 14 - Feb 16, 2025
SURF ABU DAHABI PRO
Hudayriyat Island, Abu Dhabi, United
Arab Emerates
WORLD SURF LEAGUE
International Ph: +1-310-450-1212
www.worldsurfleague.com

Mar 15 - Mar 25, 2025
MEO RIP CURL PRO PORTUGAL
Supertubos, Peniche, Portugal
WORLD SURF LEAGUE
International Ph: +1-310-450-1212
www.worldsurfleague.com

Apr 2 - Apr 12, 2025
SURF CITY EL SALVADOR PRO
Punta Roca, La Libertad, El Salvador
WORLD SURF LEAGUE
International Ph: +1-310-450-1212
www.worldsurfleague.com

Apr 18 - Apr 28, 2025
RIP CURL PRO BELLS BEACH
Bells Beach, Victoria, Australia
WORLD SURF LEAGUE
International Ph: +1-310-450-1212
www.worldsurfleague.com

May 5 - May 13, 2025
BONSOY GOLD COAST PRO
Gold Coast, Queensland, Australia
WORLD SURF LEAGUE
International Ph: +1-310-450-1212
www.worldsurfleague.com

May 17 - May 27, 2025
WESTERN AUSTRALIA MARGARET
RIVER PRO
Margaret River, Western Australia
WORLD SURF LEAGUE
International Ph: +1-310-450-1212
www.worldsurfleague.com

Jun 9 - Jun 17, 2025
LEXUS TRESTLES PRO
Lower Trestles, San Clemente, CA
WORLD SURF LEAGUE
International Ph: +1-310-450-1212
www.worldsurfleague.com

Jun 21 - Jun 29, 2025
VIVO RIO PRO
Saquarema, Rio de Janeiro, Brazil
WORLD SURF LEAGUE
International Ph: +1-310-450-1212
www.worldsurfleague.com

Jul 11 - Jul 20, 2025
CORONA CERO OPEN J-BAY
Jeffreys Bay, Eastern Cape, South
Africa
WORLD SURF LEAGUE
International Ph: +1-310-450-1212
www.worldsurfleague.com

Aug 7 - Aug 16, 2025
TAHITI PRO TEAHUPO'O
Teahupo'o, Tahiti
WORLD SURF LEAGUE
International Ph: +1-310-450-1212
www.worldsurfleague.com

Aug 27 - Sept 4, 2025
LEXUS WSL FINALS FIJI
Cloudbreak, Fiji
WORLD SURF LEAGUE
International Ph: +1-310-450-1212
www.worldsurfleague.com

Swimming

Mar 11 - Mar 15, 2025
NCAA DIVISION II MEN/WOMEN'S
SWIMMING & DIVING F INALS
Indianapolis, IN
IU Natatorium (IUPUI)
NATIONAL COLLEGIATE ATHLETIC
ASSOCIATION
Phone: 317-917-6222
Fax: 317-917-6888
www.ncaa.org

Mar 19 - Mar 22, 2025
NCAA DIVISION I WOMEN'S
SWIMMING & DIVING FINALS
Federal Way, WA
Weyerhaeuser King County Aquatics
Center
NATIONAL COLLEGIATE ATHLETIC
ASSOCIATION

Phone: 317-917-6222
Fax: 317-917-6888
www.ncaa.org

Mar 19 - Mar 22, 2025
NCAA DIVISION III MEN'S/WOMEN'S
SWIMMING & DIVIN G FINALS
Greensboro, NC
Greensboro Aquatic Center
NATIONAL COLLEGIATE ATHLETIC
ASSOCIATION
Phone: 317-917-6222
Fax: 317-917-6888
www.ncaa.org

Mar 26 - Mar 29, 2025
NCAA DIVISION I MEN'S SWIMMING &
DIVING FINALS
Federal Way, WA
Weyerhaeuser King County Aquatics
Center
NATIONAL COLLEGIATE ATHLETIC
ASSOCIATION
Phone: 317-917-6222
Fax: 317-917-6888
www.ncaa.org

Apr 4 - Apr 6, 2025
OPEN WATER NATIONALS &
JUNIORS
Sarasota, FL
USA SWIMMING
Phone: 719-866-3501
info@usaswimming.org
www.usaswimming.org

Apr 10 - Apr 12, 2025
2025 SPEEDO CANADIAN SWIMMING
OPEN
Edmonton, AB, Canada
Edmonton Kinsmen Sports Centre
SWIMMING CANADA
Phone: 613-260-1348
Fax: 613-260-0804
natloffice@swimming.ca
www.swimming.ca

Apr 12, 2025
ROMANCING THE ISLAND HALF
MARATHON & 10K
Tiburon, CA
Angel Island State Park
ENVIRO-SPORTS
Phone: 415-868-1829
info@envirosports.com
envirosports.com

Apr 30 - May 3, 2025
TYR PRO CHAMPIONSHIPS
Fort Lauderdale, FL
USA SWIMMING
Phone: 719-866-3501
info@usaswimming.org
www.usaswimming.org

May 16 - May 18, 2025
2025 SPEEDO CANADIAN MASTERS
CHAMPIONSHIPS
Saskatoon, SK, Canada
Saskatoon Shaw Centre
SWIMMING CANADA
Phone: 613-260-1348
Fax: 613-260-0804
natloffice@swimming.ca
www.swimming.ca

Jun 3 - Jun 7, 2025
NATIONAL CHAMPIONSHIPS
Indianapolis, ID
USA SWIMMING
Phone: 719-866-3501

info@usaswimming.org
www.usaswimming.org

Aug 3, 2025
ALCATRAZ SHARKFEST SWIM
San Francisco, CA
Alcatraz Island
ENVIRO-SPORTS
Phone: 415-868-1829
info@envirosports.com
envirosports.com

Aug 17, 2025
LAKE TAHOE SHARKFEST SWIM
Incline Village, NV
Sand Harbour State Park
ENVIRO-SPORTS
Phone: 415-868-1829
info@envirosports.com
envirosports.com

Sept 1, 2025
GOLDEN GATE SHARKFEST SWIM
Sausalito, CA
Under the Golden Gate Bridge
ENVIRO-SPORTS
Phone: 415-868-1829
info@envirosports.com
envirosports.com

Sept 21, 2025
SAN DIEGO SHARKFEST SWIM
San Diego, CA
San Diego Harbor
ENVIRO-SPORTS
Phone: 415-868-1829
info@envirosports.com
envirosports.com

Dec 10 - Dec 13, 2025
SPEEDO WINTER JR.
CHAMPIONSHIPS
TBA
USA SWIMMING
Phone: 719-866-3501
info@usaswimming.org
www.usaswimming.org

Dec 13, 2025
HARK THE HERALD ANGELS HALF
MARATHON & 10K
Tiburon, CA
Angel Island State Park
ENVIRO-SPORTS
Phone: 415-868-1829
info@envirosports.com
envirosports.com

Taekwondo

Apr 11 - Apr 13, 2025
NATIONAL COLLEGIATE
TAEKWONDO CHAMPIONSHIPS
Marlborough, MA
NATIONAL COLLEGIATE TAEKWONDO
ASSOCIATION
ncta-usa.com

Jun 29 - Jul 5, 2025
AAU TAEKWONDO NATIONAL
CHAMPIONSHIPS
Salt Lake City, UT
Salt Palace Convention Center
AMATEUR ATHLETIC UNION
Phone: 407-934-7200
Fax: 407-934-7242
www.aausports.org

Jul 23 - Jul 27, 2025
USA TAEKWONDO NATIONAL
CHAMPIONSHIPS
Ontario, CA
Ontario Convention Center
USA TAEKWONDO
Phone: 719-866-4632
Fax: 719-866-4642
www.usatkd.org

Tennis

Jan TBA, 2025
OPEN 6EM SENS - METROPOLE DE
LYON, FRANCE
Lyon, France
WTA
Phone: 727-895-5000
Fax: 727-894-1982
feedback@wtatennis.com
www.wtatennis.com

Jan 6 - Jan 11, 2025
ADELAIDE INTERNATIONAL 1
Adelaide, Australia
WTA
Phone: 727-895-5000
Fax: 727-894-1982
feedback@wtatennis.com
www.wtatennis.com

Jan 6 - Jan 26, 2025
AUSTRALIAN OPEN
Melbourne, Australia
TENNIS AUSTRALIA
International Ph: +61-3-9914-4677
www.tennis.com.au

Jan 6 - Jan 11, 2025
HOBART INTERNATIONAL
Hobart, Australia
WTA
Phone: 727-895-5000
Fax: 727-894-1982
feedback@wtatennis.com
www.wtatennis.com

Jan 27 - Feb 2, 2025
UPPER AUSTRIA LADIES LINZ
Linz, Austria
WTA
Phone: 727-895-5000
Fax: 727-894-1982
feedback@wtatennis.com
www.wtatennis.com

Feb 3 - Feb 8, 2025
MUBADALA ABU DHABI OPEN
Abu Dhabi, United Arab Emirates
WTA
Phone: 727-895-5000
Fax: 727-894-1982
feedback@wtatennis.com
www.wtatennis.com

Feb 9 - Feb 15, 2025
QATAR TOTALENERGIES OPEN
Doha, Qatar
WTA
Phone: 727-895-5000
Fax: 727-894-1982
feedback@wtatennis.com
www.wtatennis.com

Feb 10 - Feb 16, 2025
DELRAY BEACH OPEN
Delray Beach, FL
ATP TOUR 250
www.atptour.com

Feb 16 - Mar 1, 2025
DUBAI DUTY FREE TENNIS
CHAMPIONSHIPS
Dubai, UAE
Dubai Duty Free Tennis Stadium
WTA
Phone: 727-895-5000
Fax: 727-894-1982
feedback@wtatennis.com
www.wtatennis.com

Feb 24 - Mar 1, 2025
ABIERTO MEXICANO TELCEL
PRESENTADO POR HSBC
Acapulco, Guerrero
Arena GNP
WTA
Phone: 727-895-5000
Fax: 727-894-1982
feedback@wtatennis.com
www.wtatennis.com

Mar 5 - Mar 16, 2025
BNP PARIBAS OPEN
Indian Wells, CA
WTA
Phone: 727-895-5000
Fax: 727-894-1982
feedback@wtatennis.com
www.wtatennis.com

Mar 18 - Mar 30, 2025
MIAMI OPEN PRESENTED BY ITAU
Miami, FL
Hard Rock Stadium
WTA
Phone: 727-895-5000
Fax: 727-894-1982
feedback@wtatennis.com
www.wtatennis.com

Mar 19 - Mar 30, 2025
ATP TOUR MASTERS 1000 - MIAMI
OPEN
Miami, FL
ATP TOUR MASTERS 1000
www.atptour.com

Mar 31 - Apr 6, 2025
COPA OSTER
Cali, Colombia
WTA
Phone: 727-895-5000
Fax: 727-894-1982
feedback@wtatennis.com
www.wtatennis.com

Mar 31 - Apr 6, 2025
CREDIT ONE CHARLESTON OPEN
Charleston, SC
WTA
Phone: 727-895-5000
Fax: 727-894-1982
feedback@wtatennis.com
www.wtatennis.com

Apr TBA, 2025
BILLIE JEAN KING CUP
TBA
TENNIS CANADA
Phone: 416-665-9777
Fax: 416-665-9017
info@tenniscanada.com
www.tenniscanada.com

Apr 1 - Apr 6, 2025
MEGASARAY HOTELS OPEN
Antalya, Turkey
WTA
Phone: 727-895-5000

Fax: 727-894-1982
feedback@wtatennis.com
www.wtatennis.com

Apr TBA, 2025
TEB BNP PARIBAS TENNIS
CHAMPIONSHIP ISTANBUL
Istanbul, Turkey
WTA
Phone: 727-895-5000
Fax: 727-894-1982
feedback@wtatennis.com
www.wtatennis.com

Apr 6 - Apr 13, 2025
ATP TOUR MASTERS 1000 -
MONTE-CARLO ROLEX MASTERS
Monte Carlo, Monaco
ATP TOUR MASTERS 1000
www.atptour.com

Apr 14 - Apr 20, 2025
OEIRAS LADIES OPEN
Oeiras, Portugal
WTA
Phone: 727-895-5000
Fax: 727-894-1982
feedback@wtatennis.com
www.wtatennis.com

Apr 14 - Apr 21, 2025
PORSCHE TENNIS GRAND PRIX
Stuttgart, Germany
Porsche-Arena
WTA
Phone: 727-895-5000
Fax: 727-894-1982
feedback@wtatennis.com
www.wtatennis.com

Apr 22 - May 4, 2025
MUTUA MADRID OPEN
Madrid, Spain
WTA
Phone: 727-895-5000
Fax: 727-894-1982
feedback@wtatennis.com
www.wtatennis.com

Apr 23 - May 4, 2025
ATP TOUR MASTERS 1000 - MUTUA
MADRID OPEN
Madrid, Spain
ATP TOUR MASTERS 1000
www.atptour.com

Apr 28 - May 3, 2025
CATALONIA OPEN 125
Vic, Spain
WTA
Phone: 727-895-5000
Fax: 727-894-1982
feedback@wtatennis.com
www.wtatennis.com

Apr 28 - May 4, 2025
L'OPEN 35 DE SAINT MALO
Saint Malo, France
WTA
Phone: 727-895-5000
Fax: 727-894-1982
feedback@wtatennis.com
www.wtatennis.com

May 6 - May 18, 2025
INTERNAZIONALI BNL D'ITALIA
Rome, Italy
WTA
Phone: 727-895-5000
Fax: 727-894-1982
feedback@wtatennis.com
www.wtatennis.com

May 18 - May 24, 2025
INTERNATIONAUX DE STRASBOURG
Strasbourg, France
WTA
Phone: 727-895-5000
Fax: 727-894-1982
feedback@wtatennis.com
www.wtatennis.com

May 19 - May 24, 2025
GRAND PRIX SON ALTESSE ROYALE
LA PRINCESSE LALLA MERYEM
Rabat, Morocco
WTA
Phone: 727-895-5000
Fax: 727-894-1982
feedback@wtatennis.com
www.wtatennis.com

May 19 - May 26, 2025
NCAA DIVISION III MEN'S/WOMEN'S
TENNIS FINALS
Claremont, CA
Biszant Family Tennis Center
NATIONAL COLLEGIATE ATHLETIC
ASSOCIATION
Phone: 317-917-6222
Fax: 317-917-6888
www.ncaa.org

May 19 - Jun 8, 2025
ROLAND GARROS
Paris, France
WTA
Phone: 727-895-5000
Fax: 727-894-1982
feedback@wtatennis.com
www.wtatennis.com

May 20 - May 24, 2025
NCAA DIVISION II MEN'S/WOMEN'S
TENNIS FINALS
Altamonte Springs, FL
Sanlando Park
NATIONAL COLLEGIATE ATHLETIC
ASSOCIATION
Phone: 317-917-6222
Fax: 317-917-6888
www.ncaa.org

Jun 9 - Jun 15, 2025
LIBEMA OPEN
S'Hertogenbosch, Netherlands
WTA
Phone: 727-895-5000
Fax: 727-894-1982
feedback@wtatennis.com
www.wtatennis.com

Jun 16 - Jun 22, 2025
BERLIN TENNIS OPEN
Berlin, Germany
WTA
Phone: 727-895-5000
Fax: 727-894-1982
feedback@wtatennis.com
www.wtatennis.com

Jun 16 - Jun 22, 2025
NOTTINGHAM OPEN
Nottingham, Great Britain
Nottingham Tennis Centre
WTA
Phone: 727-895-5000
Fax: 727-894-1982
feedback@wtatennis.com
www.wtatennis.com

Jun 16 - Jun 22, 2025
ROTHESAY NOTTINGHAM OPEN
Birmingham, Great Britain
WTA
Phone: 727-895-5000
Fax: 727-894-1982
feedback@wtatennis.com
www.wtatennis.com

Jun 22 - Jun 25, 2025
BAD HOMBURG OPEN
Bad Homburg, Germany
WTA
Phone: 727-895-5000
Fax: 727-894-1982
feedback@wtatennis.com
www.wtatennis.com

Jun 23 - Jun 28, 2025
EASTBOURNE INTERNATIONAL
Eastbourne, Great Britain
WTA
Phone: 727-895-5000
Fax: 727-894-1982
feedback@wtatennis.com
www.wtatennis.com

Jun 30 - Jul 13, 2025
THE CHAMPIONSHIPS
Wimbledon, Great Britain
WTA
Phone: 727-895-5000
Fax: 727-894-1982
feedback@wtatennis.com
www.wtatennis.com

Jun 30 - Jul 13, 2025
WIMBLEDON
London, United Kingdom
THE ALL ENGLAND LAWN TENNIS
CLUB
International Ph: +44 (0)20 89441066
International Fax: +44 (0)20 89478752
www.wimbledon.com

Jul 7 - Jul 12, 2025
NORDEA OPEN
Bastad, Sweden
WTA
Phone: 727-895-5000
Fax: 727-894-1982
feedback@wtatennis.com
www.wtatennis.com

Jul 21 - Jul 26, 2025
LIVESPORT PRAGUE OPEN
Prague, Czech Republic
WTA
Phone: 727-895-5000
Fax: 727-894-1982
feedback@wtatennis.com
www.wtatennis.com

Jul 26 - Aug 7, 2025
NATIONAL BANK OPEN
Toronto, Canada
WTA
Phone: 727-895-5000
Fax: 727-894-1982
feedback@wtatennis.com
www.wtatennis.com

Jul 27 - Aug 7, 2025
ATP TOUR MASTERS 1000 -
NATIONAL BANK OPEN
Toronto, ON, Canada
ATP TOUR MASTERS 1000
www.atptour.com

Jul 27 - Aug 7, 2025
OMNIUM BANQUE NATIONALE
Montreal, QC, Canada
WTA
Phone: 727-895-5000
Fax: 727-894-1982
feedback@wtatennis.com
www.wtatennis.com

Aug 7 - Aug 18, 2025
ATP TOUR MASTERS 1000 -
CINCINNATI OPEN
Cincinnati, OH
ATP TOUR MASTERS 1000
www.atptour.com

Aug 7 - Aug 18, 2025
CINCINNATI OPEN
Cincinnati, OH
WTA
Phone: 727-895-5000
Fax: 727-894-1982
feedback@wtatennis.com
www.wtatennis.com

Aug 18 - Aug 23, 2025
ABIERTO GNP SEGUROS
Monterrey, Mexico
WTA
Phone: 727-895-5000
Fax: 727-894-1982
feedback@wtatennis.com
www.wtatennis.com

Aug 24 - Sept 7, 2025
US OPEN
New York, NY
USTA Billie Jean King National Tennis
Center
UNITED STATES TENNIS
ASSOCIATION
Phone: 914-696-7000
www.usta.com

Aug 25 - Sept 7, 2025
2025 US OPEN TENNIS
CHAMPIONSHIPS
Queens, NY
USTA Billie Jean King National Tennis
Center
WTA
Phone: 727-895-5000
Fax: 727-894-1982
feedback@wtatennis.com
www.wtatennis.com

Sept 8 - Sept 14, 2025
JASMIN OPEN TUNISIA
Monastir, Tunisia
WTA
Phone: 727-895-5000
Fax: 727-894-1982
feedback@wtatennis.com
www.wtatennis.com

Sept 15 - Sept 21, 2025
KOREA OPEN
Seoul, Korea
WTA
Phone: 727-895-5000
Fax: 727-894-1982
feedback@wtatennis.com
www.wtatennis.com

Oct 1 - Oct 12, 2025
ATP TOUR MASTERS 1000 -
SHANGHAI ROLEX MASTERS
Shanghai, China
ATP TOUR MASTERS 1000
www.atptour.com

Oct 20 - Oct 26, 2025
TORAY PAN PACIFIC OPEN
Tokyo, Japan
WTA
Phone: 727-895-5000
Fax: 727-894-1982
feedback@wtatennis.com
www.wtatennis.com

Oct 27 - Nov 2, 2025
ATP TOUR MASTERS 1000 - PARIS
ROLEX
Paris, France
ATP TOUR MASTERS 1000
www.atptour.com

Nov TBA, 2025
DAVIS CUP FINAL
INTERNATIONAL TENNIS FEDERATION
International Ph: +44 (0)20 88786464
International Fax: +44 (0)20 88787799
communications@itftennis.com
www.itftennis.com

Nov 11 - Nov 23, 2025
NCAA DIVISION I MEN'S/WOMEN'S
TENNIS FINALS
Orlando, FL
USTA National Campus (Collegiate
Center)
NATIONAL COLLEGIATE ATHLETIC
ASSOCIATION
Phone: 317-917-6222
Fax: 317-917-6888
www.ncaa.org

Dec TBA, 2025
BRISBANE INTERNATIONAL
Brisbane, Australia
WTA
Phone: 727-895-5000
Fax: 727-894-1982
feedback@wtatennis.com
www.wtatennis.com

Jan TBA, 2026
ASB CLASSIC (M)
Auckland, New Zealand
ATP TOUR 250
www.atptour.com

Jan TBA, 2026
AUSTRALIA OPEN
Melbourne, Australia
ATP TOUR 250
www.atptour.com

Feb 13 - Feb 22, 2026
DELRAY BEACH OPEN
Delray Beach, FL
The Delray Beach Stadium & Tennis
Centre
ATP CHAMPIONS TOUR
www.atptour.com/en

Dec TBA, 2026
ASB CLASSIC
Auckland, New Zealand
WTA
Phone: 727-895-5000
Fax: 727-894-1982
feedback@wtatennis.com
www.wtatennis.com

Track & Field

Mar 13 - Mar 15, 2025
NCAA DIVISION II MEN'S/WOMEN'S
TRACK, INDOOR FIN ALS
Indianapolis, IN
Fall Creek Pavilion, Indiana State
Fairgrounds
NATIONAL COLLEGIATE ATHLETIC
ASSOCIATION
Phone: 317-917-6222
Fax: 317-917-6888
www.ncaa.org

Mar 14 - Mar 15, 2025
NCAA DIVISION I MEN'S/WOMEN'S
TRACK, INDOOR FINA LS
Virginia Beach, VA
Virginia Beach Sports Center
NATIONAL COLLEGIATE ATHLETIC
ASSOCIATION
Phone: 317-917-6222
Fax: 317-917-6888
www.ncaa.org

Mar 14 - Mar 15, 2025
NCAA DIVISION III MEN'S/WOMEN'S
TRACK, INDOOR FI NALS
Rochester, NY
Golisano Training Center
NATIONAL COLLEGIATE ATHLETIC
ASSOCIATION
Phone: 317-917-6222
Fax: 317-917-6888
www.ncaa.org

May 22 - May 24, 2025
NCAA DIVISION II MEN'S/WOMEN'S
TRACK, OUTDOOR FI NALS
Pueblo, CO
CSU Pueblo ThunderBowl
NATIONAL COLLEGIATE ATHLETIC
ASSOCIATION
Phone: 317-917-6222
Fax: 317-917-6888
www.ncaa.org

May 22 - May 25, 2025
NCAA DIVISION III MEN'S/WOMEN'S
TRACK, OUTDOOR F INALS
Geneva, OH
SPIRE Institute
NATIONAL COLLEGIATE ATHLETIC
ASSOCIATION
Phone: 317-917-6222
Fax: 317-917-6888
www.ncaa.org

Jun 11 - Jun 14, 2025
NCAA DIVISION I MEN'S/WOMEN'S
TRACK, OUTDOOR FIN ALS
Eugene, OR
Hayway Field
NATIONAL COLLEGIATE ATHLETIC
ASSOCIATION
Phone: 317-917-6222
Fax: 317-917-6888
www.ncaa.org

Jun 26 - Jun 29, 2025
AAU WEST COAST TRACK & FIELD
NATIONAL CHAMPIONSH IP
Reno, NV
AMATEUR ATHLETIC UNION
Phone: 407-934-7200
Fax: 407-934-7242
www.aausports.org

Jul 6 - Jul 12, 2025
AAU TRACK & FIELD CLUB
CHAMPIONSHIPS
Jacksonville, FL
Hodges Stadium
AMATEUR ATHLETIC UNION
Phone: 407-934-7200
Fax: 407-934-7242
www.aausports.org

Sept TBA, 2025
PREFONTAINE CLASSIC
TBA
OREGON TRACK CLUB
Phone: 541-343-7247
meetingdirector@preclassic.com
www.runnerspace.com/PreClassic

Triathlon

Jan TBA, 2025
NEW YORK CITY TRIATHLON
New York, NY
LIFE TIME FITNESS
www.eventsbylifetime.com

Feb 1, 2025
TROPICAL 5K
Miami, FL
LIFE TIME FITNESS
www.eventsbylifetime.com

Feb 2, 2025
MIAMI MARATHON & HALF
Miami, FL
LIFE TIME FITNESS
www.eventsbylifetime.com

Mar 28 - Mar 29, 2025
COLLEGIATE CLUB NATIONAL
CHAMPIONSHIPS
Miami, FL
USA TRIATHLON
Phone: 719-955-2807
info@usatriathlon.org
www.usatriathlon.org

May 11, 2025
TRIGIRL SUPER SPRINT TRIATHLON
& DUATHLON
Houston, TX
Alexander Deussen Park
TRIGIRL SPORTS
www.trigirlmultisport.com

Jun 4 - Jun 8, 2025
MULTISPORT NATIONAL
CHAMPIONSHIPS FESTIVAL
Omaha, NE
USA TRIATHLON
Phone: 719-955-2807
info@usatriathlon.org
www.usatriathlon.org

Aug 8 - Aug 10, 2025
USA TRIATHLON SPRINT & OLYMPIC
DISTANCE NATIONAL
CHAMPIONSHIPS
Milwaukee, WI
USA TRIATHLON
Phone: 719-955-2807
info@usatriathlon.org
www.usatriathlon.org

Aug 9 - Aug 10, 2025
CANADIAN TRIATHLON
CHAMPIONSHIPS
Kelowna, BC, Canada

TRIATHLON CANADA
Phone: 250-412-1795
Fax: 250-412-1794
info@triathloncanada.com
www.triathloncanada.com

Aug 23, 2025
CHICAGO SUPERSPRINT TRIATHLON
Chicago, IL
LIFE TIME FITNESS
www.eventsbylifetime.com

Oct 15, 2025
WORLD TRIATHLON CHAMPIONSHIP
FINALS
Wollongong, Australia
WORLD TRIATHLON
International Ph: +41 21 614 60 30
International Fax: +41 21 614 60 39
www.triathlon.org

Dec 6, 2025
DEATH VALLEY TRAIL MARATHON &
HALF MARATHON
Death Valley, CA
Titus Canyon
ENVIRO-SPORTS
Phone: 415-868-1829
info@envirosports.com
envirosports.com

Volleyball

Feb 15 - Feb 16, 2025
AAU 14U INDOOR NATIONAL
CHAMPIONSHIPS
Ypsilanti, MI
Eastern Michigan University
AMATEUR ATHLETIC UNION
Phone: 407-934-7200
Fax: 407-934-7242
www.aausports.org

Mar 29 - Mar 30, 2025
AAU VOLLEYBALL CLASSIC
Orlando, FL
AMATEUR ATHLETIC UNION
Phone: 407-934-7200
Fax: 407-934-7242
www.aausports.org

Apr 25 - Apr 27, 2025
NCAA DIVISION III MEN'S
VOLLEYBALL FINALS
Salem, VA
Cregger Center
NATIONAL COLLEGIATE ATHLETIC
ASSOCIATION
Phone: 317-917-6222
Fax: 317-917-6888
www.ncaa.org

May 23 - May 28, 2025
OPEN NATIONAL CHAMPIONSHIPS
Denver, CO
USA VOLLEYBALL
Phone: 719-228-6800
Fax: 719-228-6899
postmaster@usav.org
usavolleyball.org

Jun 30 - Jul 7, 2025
AAU JUNIOR NATIONAL VOLLEYBALL
CHAMPIONSHIPS
Orlando, FL
Orange County Convention Center
AMATEUR ATHLETIC UNION
Phone: 407-934-7200
Fax: 407-934-7242
www.aausports.org

Jul 15 - Jul 18, 2025
AAU JUNIOR NATIONAL BEACH
VOLLEYBALL CHAMPIONSHI PS
Hermosa Beach, CA
Hermosa Beach Pier
AMATEUR ATHLETIC UNION
Phone: 407-934-7200
Fax: 407-934-7242
www.aausports.org

Dec 4 - Dec 7, 2025
NCAA DIVISION III WOMEN'S
VOLLEYBALL FINALS
Salem, VA
Cregger Center
NATIONAL COLLEGIATE ATHLETIC
ASSOCIATION
Phone: 317-917-6222
Fax: 317-917-6888
www.ncaa.org

Dec 11 - Dec 13, 2025
NCAA DIVISION II WOMEN'S
VOLLEYBALL FINALS
TBA
NATIONAL COLLEGIATE ATHLETIC
ASSOCIATION
Phone: 317-917-6222
Fax: 317-917-6888
www.ncaa.org

Dec 18 - Dec 21, 2025
NCAA DIVISION I WOMEN'S
VOLLEYBALL FINALS
Kansas City, MO
T-Mobile Center
NATIONAL COLLEGIATE ATHLETIC
ASSOCIATION
Phone: 317-917-6222
Fax: 317-917-6888
www.ncaa.org

Water Polo

May 16 - May 18, 2025
USA WATER POLO MEN'S SENIOR
NATIONALS
La Jolla, CA
UCSD Canyonview Recreation Center
USA WATER POLO
Phone: 714-500-5445
Fax: 714-960-2431
www.usawaterpolo.org

May 9 - May 11, 2025
NCAA NATIONAL COLLEGIATE
WOMEN'S WATER POLO FINA LS
Indianapolis, IN
NATIONAL COLLEGIATE ATHLETIC
ASSOCIATION
Phone: 317-917-6222
Fax: 317-917-6888
www.ncaa.org

Jun 13 - Jun 15, 2025
USA WATER POLO MASTERS
NATIONAL CHAMPIONSHIPS
Southern California
USA WATER POLO
Phone: 714-500-5445
Fax: 714-960-2431
www.usawaterpolo.org

Jul 19 - Jul 22, 2025
USA WATER POLO NATIONAL
JUNIOR OLYMPICS - SESS 1
Orange County, CA
USA WATER POLO
Phone: 714-500-5445

Fax: 714-960-2431
www.usawaterpolo.org

Jul 24 - Jul 27, 2025
USA WATER POLO NATIONAL
JUNIOR OLYMPICS - SESS 2
Orange County, CA
USA WATER POLO
Phone: 714-500-5445
Fax: 714-960-2431
www.usawaterpolo.org

Jul 31 - Aug 3, 2025
USA WATER POLO NATIONAL
JUNIOR OLYMPICS - SESS 3
North Texas
USA WATER POLO
Phone: 714-500-5445
Fax: 714-960-2431
www.usawaterpolo.org

Oct TBA, 2025
USA WATER POLO WOMEN'S
SENIOR NATIONALS
TBA
USA WATER POLO
Phone: 714-500-5445
Fax: 714-960-2431
www.usawaterpolo.org

Dec 5 - Dec 7, 2025
NCAA NATIONAL COLLEGIATE
MEN'S WATER POLO FINALS
Stanford, CA
Avery Aquatic Center
NATIONAL COLLEGIATE ATHLETIC
ASSOCIATION
Phone: 317-917-6222
Fax: 317-917-6888
www.ncaa.org

Water Skiing

Mar 21 - Mar 23, 2025
IWWF WORLD SKI SHOW
CHAMPIONSHIPS
Max Kirwan Lakes Mulwava, Victoria,
Australia
INTERNATIONAL WATERSKI &
WAKEBOARD FEDERATION
info@iwwfed.com
https://iwwf.sport

May 23 - May 25, 2025
MASTERS WATER SKI &
WAKEBOARD TOURNAMENT
Pine Mountain, GA
Callaway Gardens
NAUTIQUE EVENTS
Phone: 407-855-4141
Fax: 407-851-7844
masters@nautique.com
www.masterswaterski.com

Jun 27 - Jun 29, 2025
JUNIOR U.S. OPEN WATER SKI
CHAMPIONSHIPS
Harmony, NC
USA WATER SKI
Phone: 863-324-4341
Fax: 863-325-8259
www.usawaterski.org

Jul 18, 2025
WISCONSIN STATE WATER SKI
SHOW CHAMPIONSHIPS
Wisconsin Rapids, WI
South Wood County Park, Lake
Wazeecha - Red Beach

WISCONSIN RAPIDS AQUA SKIERS
Phone: 715-323-1577
www.aquaskiers.org

Jul 26 - Aug 2, 2025
JUNIOR WATER SKI WORLD
CHAMPIONSHIPS
Calgary, AB, Canada
INTERNATIONAL WATERSKI &
WAKEBOARD FEDERATION
info@iwwfed.com
https://iwwf.sport

Jul 30 - Aug 2, 2025
BAREFOOT NATIONAL
CHAMPIONSHIPS
Auburndale, FL
USA WATER SKI
Phone: 863-324-4341
Fax: 863-325-8259
www.usawaterski.org

Aug TBA, 2025
COLLEGIATE WATER SKI NATIONAL
CHAMPIONSHIPS
TBA
NATIONAL COLLEGIATE WATER SKI
ASSOCIATION
www.ncwsa.com

Aug 5 - Aug 9, 2025
GOODE U.S. WATER SKI NATIONAL
CHAMPIONSHIPS
Arvin, CA
USA WATER SKI
Phone: 863-324-4341
Fax: 863-325-8259
www.usawaterski.org

Aug 7 - Aug 17, 2025
THE WORLD GAMES
Chengdu, China
THE WORLD GAMES
www.theworldgames.org

Sept 20 - Sept 21, 2025
US OPEN WATER SKI RACING
NATIONAL CHAMPIONSHIPS
Havasu Springs, AZ
NATIONAL WATER SKI RACING
ASSOCIATION
www.nwsra.net

Nov TBA, 2025
CABLE WAKEBOARD WORLD
CHAMPIONSHIPS
TBA
INTERNATIONAL WATERSKI &
WAKEBOARD FEDERATION
info@iwwfed.com
https://iwwf.sport

Weightlifting

Mar 2, 2025
ARNOLD MASTER'S STRONGMAN
CHAMPIONSHIP
Columbus, OH
AMERICAN STRONGMAN
CORPORATION
Phone: 314-565-5970
americanstrongmancorporation@gmail.com
strongmancorporation.com

Sept 25, 2026
AAU STRENGTH SPORTS WORLD
CHAMPIONSHIPS
Laughlin, NV

AMATEUR ATHLETIC UNION
Phone: 407-934-7200
Fax: 407-934-7242
www.aausports.org

Windsurfing

Feb TBA, 2025
US OPEN - CLEARWATER
Clearwater, FL
Clearwater Community Sailing Center
US WINDSURFING ASSOCIATION
Phone: 877-386-8708
info@uswindsurfing.org
uswindsurfing.org

Feb 18 - Feb 24, 2025
OMAEZAKI CUP
Omaezaki City, Shizuoka, Japan
Omaezaki Long Beach
INTERNATIONAL WINDSURFING TOUR
internationalwindsurfingtour.com

Jul 5 - Jul 15, 2025
GRAN CANARIA WORLD CUP
Gran Canaria Pozo Izquierdo
INTERNATIONAL WINDSURFING TOUR
internationalwindsurfingtour.com

Jul 19, 2025
SF CLASSIC & UN CHALLENGE
San Francisco, CA
St. Francis Yacht Club
ST. FRANCIS YACHT CLUB
Phone: 415-563-6363
Fax: 415-563-8670
frontdesk@stfyc.com
www.stfyc.com

Aug 1 - Aug 10, 2025
TENERIFE WORLD CUP
El Medano, Tenerife, Canary Islands
INTERNATIONAL WINDSURFING TOUR
internationalwindsurfingtour.com

Sept 26 - Oct 5, 2025
SYLT WORLD CUP
Westerland, Sylt, Germany
INTERNATIONAL WINDSURFING TOUR
internationalwindsurfingtour.com

Oct 13 - Oct 24, 2025
ALOHA CLASSIC
Ho'okipa, HI
INTERNATIONAL WINDSURFING TOUR
internationalwindsurfingtour.com

Wrestling

Jun 4 - Jan 5, 2025
AAU WINTER NATIONALS
Ralston,NE
Ralston Arena
AMATEUR ATHLETIC UNION
Phone: 407-934-7200
Fax: 407-934-7242
www.aausports.org

Mar 14 - Mar 15, 2025
NCAA DIVISION II WRESTLING
FINALS
Indianapolis, IN
Corteva Coliseum
NATIONAL COLLEGIATE ATHLETIC
ASSOCIATION
Phone: 317-917-6222
Fax: 317-917-6888
www.ncaa.org

Mar 14 - Mar 15, 2025
NCAA DIVISION III MEN'S
WRESTLING FINALS
Providence, RI
Amica Mutual Pavilion
NATIONAL COLLEGIATE ATHLETIC
ASSOCIATION
Phone: 317-917-6222
Fax: 317-917-6888
www.ncaa.org

Mar 20 - Mar 22, 2025
NCAA DIVISION I WRESTLING
FINALS
Philadelphia, PA
Wells Fargo Center
NATIONAL COLLEGIATE ATHLETIC
ASSOCIATION
Phone: 317-917-6222
Fax: 317-917-6888
www.ncaa.org

Mar 21 - Mar 22, 2025
AAU SPRING YOUTH NATIONALS
Kingsport, TN
Tribe Sports Complex
AMATEUR ATHLETIC UNION
Phone: 407-934-7200
Fax: 407-934-7242
www.aausports.org

May 10, 2025
BEACH & BELT WRESTLING
NATIONAL CHAMPIONSHIPS
Carolina Beach, NC
Carolina Beach Boardwalk
USA WRESTLING
Phone: 719-598-8181
Fax: 719-598-9440
www.themat.com

10
indexes

A

A A. Brosso, Robert President
BROSSO, WILHELM & MCWILLIAMS, INC.,
1051

A L Gaudreau, William President
GAUDREAU, INC.
ARCHITECTS/PLANNERS/ENGINEERS, 1057

A Paniagua Jr., Ralph President & CEO
R. PANIAGUA, INC., 804

A'Costa, Peter National Sales Manager
PRECISION COMPOSITES, 1176

A., Brandon Creative Director
AMERICAN EAGLE OUTFITTERS, 1216

A. A Castiglia, Dennis Partner, Investment
Management
LUMSDEN & MCCORMICK, LLP, 841

A. A Davis, Jeremy Associate Attorney
COHN, WILLIAM A., 873

A. A Durost, Richard Executive Director
MAINE PRINCIPAL'S ASSOCIATION, 200

A. A. Kanai, Mark Member
KANAI, MARK A., 887

A. A. Shneider, Jeffrey Principal Emeritus
CSHQA
ARCHITECTS/ENGINEERS/PLANNERS, 1053

A. A. Zinn, Harry Attorney
BATE, PETERSON, DEACON, ZINN & YOUNG,
LLP, 864

A. Beesley III, Wilford Lawyer
PRINCE YEATES, 900

A. D. Baker, Richard Chairman
OCEAN PACIFIC APPAREL CORPORATION,
1170

A. De Francis, Joseph VP - Treasurer
TRIPLE CROWN PRODUCTIONS, 815

A. E. Barbour, John CEO & Chairman of the
Board
GURWIN, DAVID A., 836

A. H. Murray, Vincent Attorney
MURRAY & MURRAY, 897

A. Hillerich IV, John President / Chief Executive
Officer
LOUISVILLE SLUGGER, 1144, 1157

A. Jack Hillerich III, John Chairman of the Board
LOUISVILLE SLUGGER, 1157

A. Krick Sr., Thomas President
CHARTER PRODUCTS INC., 1222

A. M Bevan, Lee Local Office Administrator
DAVIS & KUELTHAU, S.C., 875

A. Mc Grath, Richard President
RIGHT GARD CORPORATION, 1182

A. Murray Jr, Vincent Founding Member
MURRAY & MURRAY, 897

A. P. Salminen, Judith Director of Human
Resources
FOSTER, SWIFT, COLLINS & SMITH, P.C.,
880

A. R Lombardi, Robert Execuitve Director
PENNSYLVANIA INTERSCHOLASTIC
ATHLETIC ASSOCIATION, 202

A. R. Arestides, Alexander Associate
WATTS, STEVEN R., 914

A. Sims Jr, James President/Principal
SIMS JAMES A., 855

A. Van Deuren, Richard Chairman
REINHART, BOERNER, VAN DEUREN S.C.,
902

A. Van Wert, Ronald Member
ETTER, MCMAHON, LAMBERSON & CLARY,
P.C.A., 879

A. W. Walden, James Founder
WALDON, GROUP THE, 859

A. W. Whitman, Robert Chairman
FRANKLIN COVEY, 783

A.Gossen, Paul Principal
GEIGER ENGINEERS, 1057

Aaberg, Brad Officials Coordinator
NORTH COUNTRY REGION/USA
VOLLEYBALL, 212

Aagaard, Claus Chief Financial Officer
MARS NORTH AMERICA, 729

Aamodt, Dave General Manager
KIT, 620

Aamodt, Jason Assistant Dean of Online Legal
Education
THE UNIVERSITY OF TULSA COLLEGE OF
LAW, 911

Aamodt, Norman President/Chief Executive
Officer
EVENT STRATEGY GROUP, 782

Aanenson, Bill General Sales Manager
KOMO 1000 AM RADIO, 625

Aanenson, Steve President
OLD DUTCH FOODS, 731

Aanonsen, Aaron Senior Associate Director of
Athletics
LAKELAND COLLEGE ATHLETICS, 390

Aaron, Arnold Assistant Football Coach
NJCAA REGION VI WOMEN'S, 287

Aaron, Candice Chair
LANCE ARMSTRONG FOUNDATION, 192

Aaron, Cheryl Director of Athletics
WENTWORTH INSTITUTE OF TECHNOLOGY
ATHLETICS(WIT), 405

Aaron, Matthew President & CEO
SPECIAL OLYMPICS PENNSYLVANIA, 197

Aaron, Rick Sports Director
KSTU-TV, 695

Aaron, Sammy Vice Chairman
G III SPORTS, 1135

Aaron, Thomas Chair/Director
WEBBER INTERNATIONAL UNIVERSITY, 437

Aarons, Jared Sports Anchor
KGAN-TV, 690

Abaray, Christyn Director of Athletics
LAWRENCE UNIVERSITY ATHLETICS, 390

Abarca, Carlos Lawyer
SCHUTTS & BOWEN, 905

Abare, Terri Partner
LAMPLEY, NATHANIEL, 889

Abare, TerriReyering Partner
LAMPLEY, NATHANIEL, 889

Abascal, Manuel Partner
SAUER, RUSSELL F., 904

Abatemarco, Tracy Partner
WILSON, ELSER, MOSKOWITZ ET AL, 916

Abbinanti, Sandy Commissioner/CEO
GREAT LAKES REGION/USA VOLLEYBALL,
211

Abbot, Jeff Executive Director
TENNESSEE PGA SECTIONAL OFFICE, 108

Abbott, C. Owner & Governor
ONTARIO HOCKEY LEAGUE, 134

Abbott, Carter WG Committee Chair
US LACROSSE, 141

Abbott, Chad Program Director
KFXN-AM, 618

Abbott, Darren President
AMERICAN HOCKEY LEAGUE/AHL, 128

Abbott, Don National Sales Manager
AEROBIE, INC, 551, 1094

Abbott, Duane Western Sales Manager
BODY SOLID, INC., 1108

Abbott, Eddie Operations Manager
VIKING HALL CIVIC CENTER, 1016

Abbott, Gary Special Projects/Communications
Director
USA WRESTLING, 213

Abbott, Jim Director of Athletics
OKLAHOMA CITY UNIVERSITY ATHLETICS,
318

Abbott, Kevin Partner
REED SMITH, 901

Abbott, Kevin Operations Manager
VAN ANDEL ARENA, 1015

Abbott, Mark President & Deputy Commissioner
MAJOR LEAGUE SOCCER, 157

Abbott, Michael Partner
ADKINS, M. DOUGLAS, 861

Abbott, Mike Chief Financial Officer
BURTON SNOWBOARDS, 1112

Abbott, Neil Founder/Partner
ABBOTT MANAGEMENT GROUP, 823

Abbott, Scott Executive Director
SACRAMENTO RUNNING ASSOCIATION, 149

Abbott, Tom Chief Executive Officer
PRECISE INTERNATIONAL, 1176

Abboud, Jannet Special Counsel
PIPER RUDNICK LLP, 1062

Abdo, Amy Director
FENNEMORE CRAIG, A PROFESSIONAL
CORPORATION, 879

Abdou, Mark Head General Counsel
PARK LANE - INVESTMENT BANKING
SERVICES, 769

Abdourazakou, Yann Assistant Professor
CANISIUS COLLEGE - SCHOOL OF
EDUCATION & HUMAN SERVICES, 412

Abdur-Rahim, Shareef President
NATIONAL BASKETBALL ASSOCIATION
DEVELOPMENT LEAGUE, 58

Abdur-Rahkman, Dawud Coordinator of Diversity
MUHLENBERG COLLEGE ATHLETICS, 394

Abdur-Rahman, Kevin Director of Athletics
CITY COLLEGE OF NEW YORK ATHLETICS,
380

Abeel, Timothy Partner
RAWLE LAW OFFICES, 901

Abeita, April Licensing Administrator
NEW MEXICO RACING COMMISSION, 81

Abel, Bill Contact
INDY PRO 2000, 22

Abel, Cabrelle Associate, Seattle
PRESTON, GATES & ELLIS, 900

Abel, Jim Chairman
HAYMARKET PARK, 970

Abel, Liz Assistant Athletic Director/Sports Infor
JON M. HUNTSMAN CENTER, 977

Abeles, Dan Member
ECKERT SEAMANS, 877

Abeles, Jerrold Partner
MCSHERRY, WILLIAM J., 843

Abell, Gene Sports Editor
LEXINGTON HERALD-LEADER, 502

Abello, Paola Associate
GREENBERG TRAURIG, LLP, 882

Abendroth, Thomas Partner
SCHIFF HARDIN LLP, 853

Abendroth, Tom Vice President
ACTION FLOOR SYSTEMS, LLC, 1092

Abercrombie, W. Attorney
MCKENZIE, W. SHELBY, 894

Aberg, Cissy Sports Marketing Manager
PLANO CONVENTION & VISITORS BUREAU,
243

Abernathy, Joe Vice President, Stadium
Operations
BUSCH STADIUM, 953

Abernethy, Ted Undergraduate Program
Coordinator
ST. THOMAS UNIVERSITY, 434

Abes, Alan Partner
COMODECA, JAMES A., 873

Abes, Edward Partner
ABES & BAUMANN, 861

Abhraham, David VP
GAGLIARDI INSURANCE SERVICES, 768

Abida, Maurad Practice Group Head
PIPER RUDNICK LLP, 1062

Abney, Jordan Executive Director
BC SCHOOL SPORTS, 199

Abney, Robertha Associate Professor
SLIPPERY ROCK UNIVERSITY, 432

Abode, Joe PPA Commisioner
PROFESSIONAL PUTTERS ASSOCIATION,
109

Aboid, Joe PPA Commissioner
PROFESSIONAL PUTTERS ASSOCIATION,
109

Abott, Jim Speaker
NATIONWIDE SPEAKERS BUREAU, 845

Abraham, Dennis Director, Pro Scouting
NATIONAL FOOTBALL LEAGUE/NFL, 95

Abraham, Dirk News/Sports Director
KDOM-FM, 616

Abraham, Jay EVP
RHINO SPORTS, 1182

Abraham, Lynne Partner
EGAN, ROBERT T., 878

Abraham, Magid President/Chief Executive
Officer/Co-Fou
COMSCORE MEDIA METRIX, 779

Abraham, Nathan Assistant Director of Turf &
Grounds
CARTER FINLEY STADIUM, 955

Abraham, Scott Sports Anchor
KHAS-TV, 690

Abraham, Thomas Owner
PADDLE TRAMPS MFG. COMPANY, 1172

Abraham, Trisonya Director of Basketball
SPORTS MANAGEMENT WORLDWIDE, 810

Abramowitz, Mitchell President/Owner
MITCHEL ABRAMOWITZ, A.I.A., 1061

Abramowski, Tammy Traffic Director
WQSN AM 1660, 662

Abrams, Cassandra Asst. Athletic Dir., Academic Support Se
BETHUNE-COOKMAN UNIVERSITY ATHLETICS, 325

Abrams, David Executive Director/Sports Financing
FLORIDA ATLANTIC UNIVERSITY COLLEGE OF BUSINESS, 418

Abrams, Harvey President
INTERNATIONAL INSTITUTE FOR SPORT HISTORY, 253

Abrams, John Facilities/Operations Manager
PETERSEN EVENTS CENTER, 992

Abrams, Kevin SVP, Football Operations
NATIONAL FOOTBALL LEAGUE/NFL, 96

Abrams, Nicola Vice President
HARNESS HORSE YOUTH FOUNDATION, 75

Abrams, Norman Partner
PIPER RUDNICK LLP, 1062

Abramson, Bill Sports Editor
ENTERPRISE, 487

Abramson, Mike Assistant General Manager
EASTERN LEAGUE, 38

Abramson, Paul Vice President of National Accounts
PROFESSIONAL SPORTS PUBLICATIONS, 577

Abreu, Edson Girls Academy Director
WOMEN'S PREMIER SOCCER LEAGUE, 169

Abreu, Stephen Associate
PIPER RUDNICK LLP, 1062

Abreu De Campos, Maira Head Coach
WOMEN'S PREMIER SOCCER LEAGUE, 169

Abromaitis, Jim Director of Athletics
ALBERTUS MAGNUS COLLEGE ATHLETICS, 376

Abruzzo, Joe Head Athletic Trainer
STATEN ISLAND ATHLETICS, COLLEGE OF (CSI), 402

Abts, Patrick VP, Marketing
AMERICAN LEAGUE OF PROFESSIONAL BASEBALL CLUBS, THE, 30

Accardi, Jonathan Assistant Athletics Director
KEUKA COLLEGE ATHLETICS, 389

Acee, Kevin Sports Reporter
SAN DIEGO UNION-TRIBUNE, 528

Acevedo, Ramon Past President
WORLD BOXING ORGANIZATION, 67

Aceves, William Law Professor/Director, International Le
CALIFORNIA WESTERN SCHOOL OF LAW, 871

Achenbach, James Associate Editor
GOLFWEEK, 562

Achey, Jeff Managing Editor
CLIMBING, 555

Achilles, Jennifer Associate
REED SMITH LLP, 901

Ackelson, Mike Anchor
WFMJ-TV, 702

Acker, Ann Partner
CHAPMAN & CUTLER, 872

Acker, Beth Execuitve Assistant
PROTECT MANAGEMENT CORP., 850

Acker, Brian Sports Information Director
ROCKFORD COLLEGE ATHLETICS, 398

Acker, Joe Director of Athletic Media Relations
LAWRENCE UNIVERSITY ATHLETICS, 390

Ackerman, Robert Faculty Athletics Representative
WAYNE STATE UNIVERSITY, 436

Ackerman, Val Commissioner
BIG EAST CONFERENCE, 283, 292

Ackerman, Wystan Partner
DANIELS, ERIC D., 875

Ackermann, Kristina Associate Editor
TRANSWORLD BUSINESS, 553, 589

Ackley, Brek Director, College Scouting
NATIONAL FOOTBALL LEAGUE/NFL, 94

Acklin, Kevin President, Business Operations
NATIONAL HOCKEY LEAGUE/NHL, 125

Acklin, Russell Sport Information Director
FISK UNIVERSITY ATHLETICS, 384

Ackourey, Peter Shareholder
BUCHANAN INGERSOLL ROONEY PC, 869

Acock, Dakota Head Coach
WOMEN'S PREMIER SOCCER LEAGUE, 167

Acoleyen, Jan Chief Human Resources Officer
BARCO MEDIA, 1104

Acosta, Janis Partner
MCCAREINS, R. MARK, 893

Acosta, Rafael Chief Executive
WOIZ-AM, 660

Acosta, Tina International Travel Consultant
ANTHONY TRAVEL, INC., 925

Acosta, Tony Sports Copy Editor
RECORD (CA), 523

Acquarulo, JoAnn Assistant Athletic Director for Operatio
TRINITY COLLEGE ATHLETICS, 403

Acton, Randall President
U.S. CAVALRY, INC,, 1239

Adachi, Joe President & CEO
CANON U.S.A., 1113

Adachi, Themy Director of Athletics
MILLS COLLEGE ATHLETICS, 393

Adair, Will Associate Commissioner
PENNSYLVANIA STATE ATHLETIC CONFERENCE, 303

Adam, Barnes Associate AD/CFO, Business Operations
WISCONSIN ATHLETICS, UNIVERSITY OF, 349

Adam, Jakub Partner
PIPER RUDNICK LLP, 1062

Adama, James Partner
ADKINS, M. DOUGLAS, 861

Adamany, Katherine Associate
JOHNSON & BELL, 886

Adamle, Mark President, Sales
INTERSPORT, INC., 600

Adams, Alan Contributing Writer
RINKSIDE, 578

Adams, Alfred Lawyer
WOMBLE, CARLYLE, SANDRIDGE & RICE, PLLC, 916

Adams, Allen President
UNITED STATES YOUTH VOLLEYBALL LEAGUE, 179

Adams, Alvan VP Facility Manager
US AIRWAYS CENTER, 1014

Adams, Barney Chairman of the Board
ADAMS GOLF GP CORPORATION, 1093

Adams, Benjamin Member
DANIELS, ERIC D., 875

Adams, Bob Facilities Director
KITTERY TRADING POST, 1231

Adams, Brett Director of Athletics
STEVENSON UNIVERSITY, 402, 1031

Adams, Bruce Partner
RICE & RICE, 852

Adams, Charlie Sports Director
WSBT-TV, 709

Adams, Craig Vice President of Game Day Operations
DEVAULT MEMORIAL STADIUM, 961

Adams, Dan Advertising Vice President
TUCSON CITIZEN, 542

Adams, Darrel News Director
WBBH - NBC 2, 699

Adams, Dave EVP
SEATTLE SYSTEMS/LENOX HILL BRACE COMPANY, 1187

Adams, Don Chief Executive Officer
SAIL CANADA, 181

Adams, Emily Administrative Assistant Sr.
IDAHO, UNIVERSITY OF, 420

Adams, Gardner General Manager
WIKC-AM, 650

Adams, Gary Lawyer
PELLETTIERI RABSTEIN AND ALTMAN, 899

Adams, Gerald Co-Founder and group Director
VISION SPORTS & ENTERTAINMENT PARTNERS, 816

Adams, Gray Attorney
PELLETTIERI RABSTEIN AND ALTMAN, 899

Adams, Greg Partner
SMITH, PAYTON, 907

Adams, Greg Partner
TARSHES, DAVID C., 910

Adams, Gregory Chair & CEO
KAISER FOUNDATION HEALTH PLAN, 729

Adams, Gregory Associate
FENNEMORE CRAIG, A PROFESSIONAL CORPORATION, 879

Adams, Grethe President
SOUTHERN UMBRELLA COMPANY, INC./DBA SOUTHERN PLUS, 1191

Adams, Hank Chief Executive Officer
SPORTVISION, 602

Adams, Jackie Director, Marketing Promotions
TURNER SPORTS, INC., 677

Adams, Jameson Associate Athletic Director
ST. EDWARDS UNIVERSITY ATHLETICS, 371

Adams, Jamie Assistant Athletic Director, Marketing &
UNIVERSITY OF NORTH TEXAS-COLISEUM, 1013

Adams, Jason Assistant General Manager/Ticketing
FLORIDA STATE LEAGUE, 39

Adams, Jean Lawyer
WOMBLE, CARLYLE, SANDRIDGE & RICE, PLLC, 916

Adams, Jennifer Associate
ECKERT SEAMANS, 877

Adams, Jennifer Partner
GOLDSMITH, JAMES A., 882

Adams, Jessica Vice President, Operations
EAST COAST HOCKEY LEAGUE/ECHL, 130

Adams, Joe Sports Director
WOPP-AM, 660

Adams, John Director, University Marketing
JOHN F. SAVAGE HALL, 500, 976

Adams, John Counsel
SCHIFF HARDIN LLP, 853

Adams, Josh Sports Producer
WNCN-TV, 579, 707

Adams, K.S. Founder, Owner, Chairman of the Board, P
LP FIELD, 984

Adams, Katrina Vice President
INTERNATIONAL TENNIS FEDERATION, 174

Adams, Kenneth Co-Chair
NATIONAL FOOTBALL LEAGUE/NFL, 96

Adams, Kevin Treasurer, Archery and Shooting Sports A
KITTERY TRADING POST, 1231

Adams, Kevyn General Manager
NATIONAL HOCKEY LEAGUE/NHL, 123

Adams, Kim President
KITTERY TRADING POST, 1231

Adams, Lynne Attorney
OSBORN MALEDON, P.A., 898

Adams, Mark Marketing
DODGER INDUSTRIES INC., 1125

Adams, Mary Lawyer
WOMBLE, CARLYLE, SANDRIDGE & RICE, PLLC, 916

Adams, Michael UGA President
SANFORD STADIUM, 1001

Adams, Michelle Law Professor
BERSHAD, LAWRENCE, 866

Adams, Mike Treasurer
SNOWSPORTS INDUSTRIES AMERICA, 153

Adams, Nathan Overnight DJ/Sports Anchor
WBXX-FM, 640

Adams, Nick Chief Marketing Officer
USA/BMX, THE AMERICAN BICYCLE ASSOCIATION, 71

Adams, Payton Coordinator of Athletic Operations
WILLIAM R. JOHNSON COLISEUM, 1019

Adams, Peg Treasurer
GEORGIA AAU ASSOCIATION, 214

Adams, Peter President
MATCH POINT, 1160

Adams, Reid Lawyer
WOMBLE, CARLYLE, SANDRIDGE & RICE, PLLC, 916

Adams, Robert
WILSON, ELSER, MOSKOWITZ ET AL, 916

Adams, Russell Sports Writer
WALL STREET JOURNAL, 545

Adams, Sam Owner & Chief Executive Officer
INDOOR FOOTBALL LEAGUE, 94, 526, 614, 689

Adams, Sarah Senior Associate AD/SWA
WICHITA STATE UNIVERSITY ATHLETICS, 349

Adams, Sherry Corporate Partnerships/Hospitality Spons
HOMESTEAD MIAMI SPEEDWAY, 757

Adams, Steve Associate AD, Internal Operations
WAKE FOREST BASEBALL PARK, 644, 1017

SAN FRANCISCO ATHLETICS, UNIVERSITY OF, 343

Allonardo, Jenna Head Athletic Trainer
GWYNEDD MERCY COLLEGE ATHLETICS, 386

Alloun, Charles Controller
JH DESIGN GROUP, 1149

Alloway, Dan Sales and European Operations VP
CANNONDALE BICYCLE CORPORATION, 1113

Allred, Darin Sports Editor
GAINESVILLE DAILY REGISTER, 490

Allred, David Executive Director
USL LEAGUE TWO, 164

Allred, Ed Owner
LOS ALAMITOS RACE COURSE, 1041

Allred, Jay Publisher
TRIAD GOLF TODAY, 589

Allshouse, Jim President
BEAR ARCHERY, 1105

Allsop, Mike Chief Executive Officer
SOFTRIDE, 1190

Allspach, Steven Sports Writer / Columnist
SIOUX CITY JOURNAL, 531

Allstetter, Robert Sports Deputy Editor
DETROIT NEWS, 483

Allvin, Patrik General Manager
NATIONAL HOCKEY LEAGUE/NHL, 126

Almada, Gabriel President
WOMEN'S PREMIER SOCCER LEAGUE, 166

Almanza, Steven Production Manager
JOHN THURMAN FIELD, 977

Almasi, George Sports Editor
TIMES RECORD, 539

Almendarez, Chris General Manager
PACIFIC COAST LEAGUE OF PROFESSIONAL BASEBALL CLUBS, 49

Almlie, Mary Business Manager
PHILIP B. ELFSTROM STADIUM, 992

Almond, Elliott Sports Reporter
SAN JOSE MERCURY NEWS, 528

Almoney, Kyle Women's Swimming Head Coach
MILLERVILLE UNIVERSITY, 427

Almonrode, Sharon Senior Litigation Attorney/Partner
SULLIVAN, WARD, BOME, TYLER & ASHER, P.C., 909

Alnutt, Mark Athletic Director
SUNY BUFFALO, 345

Aloi, Joanne General Manager
WENE, 645

Alonge, Shauna Partner
SOOY, KATHLEEN T., 907

Alonzo, Adam Assistant Director - Facility & Game Ope
STRAHAN COLISEUM, 1006

Alonzo, Rick Sports Reporter (Timberwolves)
SAINT PAUL PIONEER PRESS, 527

Alp, Paul Counsel
SOOY, KATHLEEN T., 907

Alperin, Howard Attorney/Partner
BLECHER & COLLINS, 867

Alpern, Dave President
NASCAR XFINITY SERIES, 23, 24

Alpers, Laurie Director of administration and finance
GENERAL SPORTS TURF SYSTEMS, 835

Alpert, Ryan Deputy AD/COO
TENNESSEE KNOXVILLE ATHLETICS, UNIVERSITY OF, 346

Alsafeer, Saif Head Coach
USL LEAGUE TWO, 162

Alsandor, Butch Sports Anchor
KHOU-TV, 690

Alsberg, Bill Associate VP
ARANDA GROUP, 824

Alsop, Tom Founder/Chief Executive Officer
AMERICAN SINGLES GOLF ASSOCIATION, 99

Alspach, Pam Chief Financial Officer
TOLEDO MUD HENS, 1010

Alstadt, Lynn Shareholder
BUCHANAN INGERSOLL ROONEY PC, 869

Alstine, Tim Director of Athletics
CARDINAL STRITCH UNIVERSITY ATHLETICS, 310, 974

Alston, Alex Director of Sales & Marketing
JACKSONVILLE VETERANS MEMORIAL ARENA, 975

Alston, Craig Head Coach
WOMEN'S PREMIER SOCCER LEAGUE, 165

Alston, Evan Promotions VP
HENWAY SPORTS & SPECIALTIES, INC., 1144

Alston, Ken Interim Athletics Director
SAINT XAVIER UNIVERSITY ATHLETICS, 319

Alston, Malachi Associate
TAULBEE, GEORGE M., 911

Alstott, Ken CEO
COW PALACE, 960

Altabef, Peter President and Chief Executive Officer
TANGENT ASSOCIATES, INC., 1068

Altaf, Ali EVP
PROPET USA INC., 1178

Altemus, David Honorary President
SOUTHERN TEXAS PGA SECTIONAL, 108

Alten, John Partner
GOLDSMITH, JAMES A., 882

Alter, Adam Sports Reporter
KSNT-TV, 695

Alter, Larry Information Director
MID-STATES FOOTBALL ASSOCIATION, 284

Alter, Michael Principal Owner
WOMEN'S NATIONAL BASKETBALL ASSOCIATION, 60

Altes, Scott Director
FENNEMORE CRAIG, A PROFESSIONAL CORPORATION, 879

Althaus, Bill Sports Writer
EXAMINER, 487

Altherton, Sue Vice President of Sales and Marketing
PEORIA AREA CONVENTION & VISITORS BUREAU, 243

Altier, Jeff Director of Athletics
STETSON UNIVERSITY ATHLETICS, 345

Altieri, Joe Assistant Director
NEW YORK STATE PUBLIC HS ATHLETIC ASSOCIATION, 201

Altieri, Michael Senior VP, Marketing, Communications & C
NATIONAL HOCKEY LEAGUE/NHL, 124

Altman, Koby President, Basketball Operations
NATIONAL BASKETBALL ASSOCIATION DEVELOPMENT LEAGUE, 56, 58

Altman, Peggy Visitor & Partner Services Coordinator
LAKE COUNTY, ILLINOIS - CONVENTION & VISITORS BUREAU, 238

Altschuler, Judy President
WOMEN'S SOUTHERN CALIFORNIA GOLF ASSOCIATION, 118

Alumbaugh, Jeremy Chair
USL CHAMPIONSHIP, 159

Alvarez, Barry Director of Athletics
WISCONSIN-MADISON FIELDHOUSE, 954, 980, 1019

Alvarez, Mike Assistant Athletic Director
RUTGERS UNIVERSITY-NEWARK ATHLETICS, 399

Alvarez, Niki Women's Swimming/Women's Cross Country H
LYNN UNIVERSITY, 424

Alves, Catherine Senior Associate Athletic Director
JOHN JAY COLLEGE OF CRIMINAL JUSTICE ATHLETICS, 388

Alves, Jordan Sports Information Director
CAMPBELLSVILLE UNIVERSITY ATHLETICS, 310

Alves, Merritt Membership Coordinator
ASSOCIATION OF MARINA INDUSTRIES, 63

Alvidrez, Tina Advertising Director
COFFEYVILLE JOURNAL, 471

Alvstad, Stephen Counsel
BEAUTYMAN ASSOCIATES, P.C., 865

Alway, Sally Head Athletic Trainer
CALIFORNIA INSTITUTE OF TECHNOLOGY ATHLETICS, 379

Alzate, Xavier Men's Athletic Trainer
YESHIVA UNIVERSITY ATHLETICS, 408

Amack, Kate Vice Chair
NATIONAL SENIOR GAMES ASSOCIATION, 223

Amaker, Tami Special Program Director
BOOMER ESIASON FOUNDATION, 191

Amar, Christopher Associate
BUCHANAN INGERSOLL ROONEY PC, 869

Amaral, Russ VP, Facilities & Event Services
CHASE FIELD BALL PARK, 957

Amaro, Matthew Associate
BARTH, BERUS & CALDERON, LLP, 864

Amasay, Tal Assistant Professor, Coordinator, Physic
BARRY UNIVERSITY, 410

Amason, Tina Marketing / Promotions Director
SOCCER PAL, 1190

Amato, Tony Home Clubhouse/Equipment Manager
AMERICAN LEAGUE OF PROFESSIONAL BASEBALL CLUBS, THE, 29

Amblo, Don VP , Operations
AMERICAN LEISURE CORPORATION, 1049

Ambriz, Mike Executive Vice President
LONG DRIVERS OF AMERICA, 103

Ambrose, Carlie Manager, Sales and Contract
EQUIBASE COMPANY, 928

Ambrose, Chace Sports Reporter/Photographer
WGXA-TV, 703

Ambrose, Christopher Attorney
AMBROSE LAW GROUP, LLP, 862

Ambrose, Dan Assistant Athletic Director
CATHOLIC UNIVERSITY OF AMERICA ATHLETICS (CUA), 380

Ambrose, Dave Sales
N CASE IT, 1166

Ambrose, David Attorney
AMBROSE LAW GROUP, LLP, 862

Ambrose, Dillon Associate
DAVIS & KUELTHAU, S.C., 875

Ambrose, Heather Associate
IBACH, JOHN R., 885

Ambrose, Lennie Sports Anchor
KXLF-TV, 698

Ambrosie, Randy Commissioner
CANADIAN FOOTBALL LEAGUE/CFL, 92

Ambrosius, Greg Editor
FANTASY SPORTS, 559

Ambrozik, Steve President
WOMEN'S PREMIER SOCCER LEAGUE, 165

Amburgey, Tricia Senior Director Sponsorship Sales
CHURCHILL DOWNS, 1036

Ameault, Tim President/Chief Executive Officer
MOUNTAINEER CASINO, RACE TRACK & RESORT, 1041

Amelung, Rob Marketing
A-B ASSOCIATES, INC., 1089

Americus, Bruce Shareholder
BUCHANAN INGERSOLL ROONEY PC, 869

Amernick, Burton Partner
DURANTE, CHARLES J., 877

Ames, Bob Senior Vice President, Chief Finanical O
AMERICAN LEAGUE OF PROFESSIONAL BASEBALL CLUBS, THE, 29

Ames, Brad President
PRIORITY SPORTS & ENTERTAINMENT, 848, 849

Ames, Craig Executive Director
NEBRASKA GOLF ASSOCIATION, 113

Ames, Larry Sports Editor
VENTURA COUNTY STAR, 544

Ames, Robert Chief Financial Officer
ED SMITH STADIUM/SPORTS COMPLEX, 963

Ames, Scott Interim Athletic Director
WESTERN CONNECTICUT STATE UNIVERSITY ATHLETICS, 405, 989

Ames, Scott Of Counsel
FENNEMORE CRAIG, A PROFESSIONAL CORPORATION, 879

Ames, Whitney Associate AD & SWA
MARYLAND-BALTIMORE COUNTY ATHLETICS, UNIVERSITY OF, 336

Amey, Andy Sports Reporter
TRIBUNE-STAR, 541

Amhaus, Craig Business Development Manager
DOVER INTERNATIONAL SPEEDWAY, 1024

Amicone, Marc General Manager
PACIFIC COAST LEAGUE OF PROFESSIONAL BASEBALL CLUBS, 49, 1003

Amigone, Nick First Vice President
BUFFALO DISTRICT GOLF ASSOCIATION, 110

Anderson, Phyllis National Sales Manager
HARTFORD SPORTS COMMISSION, GREATER (CONVENTION & VISITORS BUREAU, 0

Anderson, Ray Assistant Athletic Director
BARCLAY COLLEGE ATHLETICS, 351

Anderson, Raymond Partner
VORYS, SATER, SEYMOUR & PEASE, 884, 913

Anderson, Richard Chairman
ATLANTA SPORTS COUNCIL, 227

Anderson, Rick Program Director
WILD-AM, 650

Anderson, Robert Director
FENNEMORE CRAIG, A PROFESSIONAL CORPORATION, 879

Anderson, Robin Executive Director
MASON CITY CONVENTION & VISITOR BUREAU, 240

Anderson, Rod Partner
HOLLAND & KNIGHT, 884

Anderson, Ron Director of Financial Aid
ASBURY COLLEGE ATHLETICS, 307

Anderson, S. Executive Director
MCKENNA, LONG & ALDRIDGE, LLP, 894

Anderson, Sandra Finance Director
IOWA HS ATHLETIC ASSOCIATION, 200

Anderson, Sandra Partner
VORYS, SATER, SEYMOUR & PEASE, 913

Anderson, Scott General Manager
KSKI-FM, 529, 629

Anderson, Scyld Attorney
ISAAC, BRANT, LEDMAN & TEETOR, 885

Anderson, Shawn Product Supervisor
EXIBITION PARK - LETHBRIDGE, 1037

Anderson, Shelly Reporter
PITTSBURGH POST-GAZETTE, 520

Anderson, Shrine Principal
ELLENZWEIG ASSOCIATES, INC., 1055

Anderson, Stanice Owner
ANDERSON & TUCKER, 862

Anderson, Steve EVP, News, Talent, and Content Operation
ESPN TELEVISION, 604, 609, 674

Anderson, Tami Marketing Director
ATHLETA, LLC, 1216

Anderson, Tim Executive Vice President, Retail Operati
SPORT CHALET, INC., 1237

Anderson, Todd Director of Communications
UNIVERSITY OF NORTH CAROLINA PEMBROKE ATHLETICS(UNCP), 366

Anderson, Tom Director Of Athletics
NJCAA REGION IX WOMEN'S, 259, 287, 1032

Anderson, Wally Vice President of Baseball Operations
PECOS LEAGUE (INDEPENDENT LEAGUE), 49

Anderson, Wayne Marketing
PW ATHLETIC COMPANY, INC., 1179

Anderson, Wes Sports Director
WGRE-FM, 648

Anderson, Wesley Health Care Attourney
REINHART, BOERNER, VAN DEUREN S.C., 902

Anderson, Woody Sports Reporter (College)
HARTFORD COURANT, 492

Anderson, Zellina Ticket Office Manager
WJ HALE STADIUM, 1019

Anderson-Ray, Ben Chief Executive Officer
NEW HERMES INC., 1168

Ando, Bill Senior Editor
SOUTHERN BOATING MAGAZINE, 569, 582

Andorka, Frank Managing Editor
GOLFDOM, 562

Andracchi, Frank Chairman
SPECIAL OLYMPICS MARYLAND, 195

Andracchio, Gianni Account Executive
BMORE SPORTS, 1108

Andrade, Frank Publisher
LA OFERTA NEWSPAPER, 500

Andrade, Lydia Faculty Athletic Representative
UNIVERSITY OF THE INCARNATE WORD ATHLETICS, 360

Andrade-Morioka, Angie President/Regional Commissioner
MOKU O KEAWE REGIONAL COMMISSIONER/USA VOLLEYBALL, 212

Andrassy, AJ National Sports Forum (NSF) Competition
OHIO UNIVERSITY, 430

Andre, Scott Sports Lawyer
LAURIA TOKUNGA GATES & LINN, LLP, 889

Andreadis, Petro Club Director
WOMEN'S PREMIER SOCCER LEAGUE, 169

Andreeta, Mike Director of Competiton
PLACERVILLE SPEEDWAY, 1030

Andrejko, J.P. Assistant Director of Intercollegiate At
KING'S COLLEGE ATHLETICS, 389

Andreoff, Christopher Member
JAFFE, RAITT, HEUER & WEISS, PC, 886

Andreoli, Ron Simulcast Coordinator
LES BOIS PARK, 1041

Andreozzi, Mark Fitness Coordinator, Club Sports Directo
ROGER WILLIAMS UNIVERSITY ATHLETICS, 399

Andreson, Barry Maintenance Mechanic II
NJCAA REGION III MEN'S, 286

Andreson, Charlotte ASSISTANT TO THE PRESIDENT AND CEO
RENO-SPARKS CONVENTION AUTHORITY, 244

Andreson, Stephen President, S.H.A. Enterprises
NEWPORT SPORTS MUSEUM, 257

Andretti, Michael CEO/Chair
INDYCAR, 21, 22

Andrew, Aguilar Assistant General Manager
SMITH-WILLIS STADIUM, 1003

Andrew, Jim Chief Strategy & Innovation Officer
PHILIPS LIGHTING COMPANY, 731, 1174

Andrew, Marcia Partner
TAFT, STETTINIUS & HOLLISTER, 857

Andrew, Mary Chair/Commissioner
FLORIDA REGIONAL COMMISSIONER/USA VOLLEYBALL, 211

Andrew, Michael Chairman
KPMG CONVENTION, SPORTS & ENTERTAINMENT PRACTICE, 758

Andrew, Troy Executive Director/CEO
WASHINGTON STATE GOLF ASSOCIATION, 117

Andrew An Rodrigues, M. President
ARCHITECTS DELAWIE WILKES RODRIGUES BARKER, 1049

Andrews, Art News Director
WPEN-AM, 661

Andrews, Brad Senior Director, Hockey & Business Opera
AMERICAN HOCKEY LEAGUE/AHL, 128

Andrews, Carley Partner
PRESTON, GATES & ELLIS, 900

Andrews, Damon Sports Director
KTLA-TV, 680, 695

Andrews, David Chairman, Board of Governors
AMERICAN HOCKEY LEAGUE/AHL, 126

Andrews, David Attorney
HERSHNER, HUNTER, ANDREWS, NEILL & SMITH L,L,P., 883

Andrews, Don President
QUICK TICK INTERNATIONAL, INC., 932

Andrews, Greg VP of Business Operations
GLOBAL SPORTS PRODUCTIONS, 594

Andrews, Jerald President/Executive Director
MISSOURI SPORTS HALL OF FAME, 255

Andrews, Jim Senior Vice President, Content Strategy
IEG, LLC, 565, 788

Andrews, John Vice President Marketing
SOF SOLE, 1190

Andrews, Johnny Vice President/General Manager
WWL, 671

Andrews, Kelly Senior Associate AD/SWA
TOLEDO ATHLETICS, UNIVERSITY OF, 347

Andrews, Ken Executive Director
MIDDLE ATLANTIC STATES COLLEGIATE ATHLETIC CORPORATION, 299

Andrews, Lisa Assistant President
QUICK TICK INTERNATIONAL, INC., 932

Andrews, Michelle Orthopaedic Surgeon
CINCINNATI SPORTSMEDICINE & ORTHOPAEDIC CENTER, 919

Andrews, Phil Chief Executive Officer/General Secretar
USA WEIGHTLIFTING, 213, 590

Andrews, Scott President
EL MIRAGE DRY LAKE, 1033

Andrews, Shirley Owner
TURNER'S OUTDOORSMAN, 1239

Andrews, Skip Program Director
WHAN-AM, 648

Andrews, Thomas Shareholder
JOHNSON & BELL, 886

Andriatch, Mike Sports Information Director
SPECIAL OLYMPICS STADIUM, 1004

Andriola, James Partner
REED SMITH LLP, 901

Andrus, James Partner
PRESTON, GATES & ELLIS, 900

Andrus, Jim Assoc. Commissioner Business/Finance
MOUNTAIN WEST CONFERENCE, 300

Andrusyszyn, Adam Assistant Director, Facilities & Ops.
COLLEGE OF WILLIAM & MARY, 958

Anesh, Mark Partner
WILSON, ELSER, MOSKOWITZ ET AL, 916

Anez, Scott Sports Director
WDBO-AM, 642

Anfang, Jill Assistant Director
ROSEVILLE PARKS AND RECREATION, 245

Angarola, Joann Shareholder
JOHNSON & BELL, 886

Angel, Margaret Shareholder
BUCHANAN INGERSOLL ROONEY PC, 869

Angel, Rex President
LYNCHBURG CITY STADIUM, 984

Angel, Seth EVP & General Manager
ROYAL PURPLE RACEWAY, 1032

Angelico, Paul Secretary-Treasurer
COLORADO HS ACTIVITIES ASSOCIATION, 199

Angelillo, Greg Sports Reporter
WZBN-TV, 713

Angeline, Dave News Director
WJVS-FM, 653

Angelis, Theodore Partner
PRESTON, GATES & ELLIS, 900

Angell, Bill Supritenent
NEBRASKA STATE FAIR, 1042

Angelo, Arlene Partner
WEBB, WILLIAM Y., 914

Angelo, Dan Sports Editor
SANDUSKY REGISTER, 529

Angelos, Craig Deputy Director of Athletics
TEMPLE UNIVERSITY ATHLETICS, 335, 345, 996

Angelos, John Chair & Managing Partner
AMERICAN LEAGUE OF PROFESSIONAL BASEBALL CLUBS, THE, 29

Angelos, Peter Chief Executive Officer
ED SMITH STADIUM/SPORTS COMPLEX, 963

Anger, Greg Marketing Director
IRWIN SPORTS, 1148

Anger, Kimberly Advertising Director
LODI NEWS-SENTINEL, 503

Anghel, Gheorghe Operations Manager
WINTECH RACING, 1210

Angilly, Paul Sports Editor
BRISTOL PRESS, 466

Angioli, Carmine Sports Editor
STATEN ISLAND ADVANCE, 535

Angle, Martin Non-Executive Chairman
N.E.C. ARENA BIRMINGHAM, 988

Anglin, Ruth Fair Activities Manager
YAKIMA VALLEY SUNDOME, 1021

Angott, Chris Secretary
GOLF ASSOCIATION OF MICHIGAN, 111

Angotti, Vince Sports Management Program Coordinator
TOWSON STATE UNIVERSITY, 435

Angulo, Oscar Sports Producer
WFTS-TV, 679, 702

Angus, Nancy Executive Director
MARIO LEMIEUX FOUNDATION, 192

Angyan, James Paralegal
MILLER CANFIELD SPORTS, 844

Anholt, Peter General Manager
WESTERN HOCKEY LEAGUE, 138

Aniballi, Fred Business Office
VESPOLI USA, INC., 1207

Ankenbrand, Larry Professor
EASTERN ILLINOIS UNIVERSITY, 417

Barnes, Kiki Athletic Director
DILLARD UNIVERSITY ATHLETICS, 312

Barnes, Mike Sports Director/Anchor
KVUE-TV, 697

Barnes, Peggy Dept. Chair/PE Associate
Professor
NEWBERRY COLLEGE, 428

Barnes, Rebecca Live Interviews
WRJW-AM, 664

Barnes, Scott Director of Intercollegiate Athletics
OREGON STATE UNIVERSITY ATHLETICS,
341

Barnes, Stu Ownership Partner/Head Coach
WESTERN HOCKEY LEAGUE, 139

Barnes, Susan Social Marketing/Social Media
Manager
ONEWORLD COMMUNICATIONS, 799

Barnes, Tracey President
BLIMP WORKS, INC., 776

Barnes, Tracy President/Designer
BLIMP WORKS, INC., 776

Barnett, Brad SVP, U.S. Operations
TAYLORMADE-ADIDAS GOLF, 1199

Barnett, Geoff Marketplace Advertising
CALIFORNIA CITYSPORTS/EVENT DIVISION,
751

Barnett, Jennifer Vice President of Convention
Development
LOUISVILLE CONVENTION & VISITORS
BUREAU, 239

Barnett, Josh Sports Editor
PHILADELPHIA DAILY NEWS, 519

Barnett, Kate Asst. Commissioner For
Championships
OHIO VALLEY CONFERENCE, 302

Barnett, Loreen First Vice President
INTERNATIONAL TRIATHLON UNION, 178

Barnett, Matt EVP
SPORTS MARKETING & ENTERTAINMENT,
INC, 810

Barnett, Melissa Senior Vice President, Network
Business
HBO SPORTS, 676

Barnett, Ruth Promotions Manager
KGAN-TV, 690

Barnett, Stan Program Director
WNES-AM, 658

Barnett, Steve Marketing Director
MEDIC FIRST AID INTERNATIONAL, INC.,
1161

Barnett, Wren Office Manager
CDM SPORT, 1115

Barney, Alfred Athletic Director
NJCAA REGION XVII WOMEN'S, 289

Barney, Danielle Associate Director of Athletics
LOCK HAVEN UNIVERSITY ATHLETICS
(LHU), 362

Barney, Jo Executive Director
WOMEN'S PREMIER SOCCER LEAGUE, 169

Barney, Justin Sports Editor
ST. AUGUSTINE RECORD, 533

Barney, Kevin Vice President & General Manager
MAJOR LEAGUE LACROSSE, 141

Barney, Rob Sports Director
KNEB-FM, 624

Barney, Samantha Marketing & Promotions
Manager
CAROLINA LEAGUE, 37

Barnhart, Ashley Junior Tournament Coordinator
COLORADO GOLF ASSOCIATION, 110

Barnhart, Eric General Manager
OKLAHOMA MEMORIAL STADIUM, 990

Barnhart, Mitch Director of Athletics
KENTUCKY, UNIVERSITY OF, 334, 422, 959,
986

Barnhill, Rob Director of Athletics
CONCORDIA UNIVERSITY (WI) ATHLETICS
(CUW), 381

Barnhill, Robert Athletic Director
ILLINIBADGER FOOTBALL CONFERENCE,
297

Barnhisel, Robert Director of Sales and
Installation
PERFECTION EQUIPMENT, INC., 1067

Barnhouse, Wendell Senior Reporter
FORT WORTH STAR-TELEGRAM, 489

Barnidge, Dennis Sports Editor
JEFFERSON COUNTY JOURNAL, 498

Barnidge, Noell Sports Reporter
SAVANNAH MORNING NEWS, 529

Barns, Mitch Chief Executive Officer
ARBITRON, INC., 1213

Baron, John Partner in Charge
TAULBEE, GEORGE M., 911

Baron, Marco CEO, North America
TECNIFIBRE USA, 1200

Baron, Robert President
BASS IND INCORPORATED, 1105

Baroncelli, Craig Publisher
ATHLETICS ADMINISTRATION, 550

Barr, Brian Shareholder
LEVIN, PAPANTONIO, THOMAS, MITCHELL,
ECHSNER & PROCTOR, P.A., 890

Barr, Carol Associate Department Head
WONG, GLENN M., 916

Barr, Darin Senior Associate
BALLARD KING & ASSOCIATES, 1050

Barr, Emily President
WLS-TV, 706

Barr, Jason Associate
REED SMITH LLP, 901

Barr, John Director
CALIFORNIA THOROUGHBRED BREEDERS
ASSOCIATION, 74

Barr, Josh High School Sports Reporter
WASHINGTON POST, 91, 545

Barr, Karen Technical Manager
TBO (WFLA) NEWS CHANNEL 8, 698

Barr, Lynda VP, Chief Financial Officer
EDWIN WATT'S GOLF SHOP, INC., 1226

Barr, Nick Vice President, Corporate Partnerships
EAST COAST HOCKEY LEAGUE/ECHL, 130

Barr, Ron CEO
SPORTS OVERNIGHT AMERICA WEEKEND,
602, 609, 610

Barr, Sara Marketing Director
IOWA STATE CENTER, 973

Barra, Mary Chair and CEO
GENERAL MOTORS, 728

Barracato, Denee Deputy AD, Operations &
Capital Projects
NORTHWESTERN UNIVERSITY ATHLETICS,
340

Barran, Rishi Sports Anchor
WTVH-TV, 711

Barren, Brian President, Business Operations
AMERICAN LEAGUE OF PROFESSIONAL
BASEBALL CLUBS, THE, 29

Barren, Mike Assistant Commissioner
KENTUCKY HS ATHLETIC ASSOCIATION, 200

Barrer, Joe Head Coach
NATIONAL BASKETBALL ASSOCIATION
DEVELOPMENT LEAGUE, 59

Barrera, Brenda Editor
CHICAGO'S AMATEUR ATHLETE, 554

Barrera, Monica President
GO FLOW, INC., 1138

Barrett, Bill Director Marketing/Booking
US BANK ARENA, 1014

Barrett, Bruce Vice-President
INTERNATIONAL HANDGUN METALLIC
SILHOUETTE ASSOCIATION, 150

Barrett, Chuck Executive Producer/Host
SPORTS RAP, 606

Barrett, Connell Senior Editor
GOLF MAGAZINE, 561

Barrett, Dan Associate Regional Vice President
INTERNATIONAL SPORTS PROPERTIES,
INC., 789

Barrett, Jeff Chief Executive Officer
AMERICAN HOCKEY LEAGUE/AHL, 129

Barrett, Nancy VP, National Sales
OTOMIX, 1172

Barrett, Paul Sports Editor
DETROIT FREE PRESS, 483

Barrett, Richard Sales Director
BADGER STATE GAMES, 250, 260

Barrett, Rowan General Manager/Executive VP,
Senior Men
CANADA BASKETBALL, 53

Barrett, Scott Sports Editor
NEWPORT DAILY NEWS, 511

Barrett, Ted Vice President
MAJOR LEAGUE BASEBALL UMPIRES
ASSOCIATION, 27

Barrett, Tim Senior Associate Director of Athletics
CASTLETON STATE UNIVERSITY
ATHLETICS, 380

Barrett, William Staff
MAUPIN, TAYLOR, P.A., 842

Barrett, William Partner
BARRETT, WILLIAM A., 863

Barrette, Craig Chief Communications Officer
USA/BMX, THE AMERICAN BICYCLE
ASSOCIATION, 71

Barrick, Steve Associate AD/Director of Facilities
BELMONT UNIVERSITY ATHLETICS, 325

Barrickman, Bob Sports Director
WBVP-AM, 640

Barrientos, Edard President & CEO
GEORGE WASHINGTON UNIVERSITY - THE
GW SCHOOL OF BUSINESS, 419

Barrier, Martin President
MARTIN'S GOLF & TENNIS, INC., 1232

Barrile, James Chief Financial Officer
OMNI BODYWORK, 1171

Barringer, Scott Head Athletic Trainer
AMERICAN LEAGUE OF PROFESSIONAL
BASEBALL CLUBS, THE, 29

Barrington, Deborah Senior Sports Assignment
Editor
USA TODAY, 543

Barrio, Brian Director of Athletics
MARYLAND-BALTIMORE COUNTY
ATHLETICS, UNIVERSITY OF, 336

Barrios, George CFO
WORLD WRESTLING ENTERTAINMENT, 181

Barron, Allen Affiliated Partner
STRATEGIC RESOURCES, 749

Barron, Arnold Chief Operating Officer
T.J. MAXX, 1239

Barron, David Sports Reporter
HOUSTON CHRONICLE, 495

Barron, Wendy Assistant Dean, Financial Aid
TAGGART, WALTER J., 858

Barror, Sean Partner
BENNETT GLOBAL MARKETING GROUP, 775

Barroso, Chris Director of Athletic
Communications
SAINT ANSELM COLLEGE ATHLETICS, 369

Barrouquere, Peter Sports Writer
TIMES-PICAYUNE, 540

Barrow, Bill Executive Director
DELAWARE STATE GOLF ASSOCIATION, 110

Barrow, Joe Vice Chairman
NATIONAL GOLF FOUNDATION, 104

Barry, Amy Sports Information Director
SUFFOLK UNIVERSITY ATHLETICS, 402

Barry, Bob Sports Director
KFOR-TV, 690

Barry, Brent General Manager
NATIONAL BASKETBALL ASSOCIATION
DEVELOPMENT LEAGUE, 58

Barry, Britt Sports Turf Manager
FIFTH THIRD FIELD, 965

Barry, Chris Head Athletic Trainer
MASSACHUSETTS MARITIME ACADEMY
ATHLETICS (MMA), 393

Barry, David Director of Tickets and Finance
CALIFORNIA LEAGUE (A-LEVEL), 36, 259, 970

Barry, Erin Hospitality Manager
CHICAGOLAND SPEEDWAY, 1023

Barry, Jack Sports Director
WDUX-FM, 643, 644

Barry, Jay Sports Director
KGMM ""THE GAME"" 1280 SPORTS, 619

Barry, John Sports Writer
JANESVILLE GAZETTE, 497

Barry, John Chief Financial Officer
KENYON & KENYON (DC OFFICE), 888

Barry, Mark Marketing Senior Vice President
HCC SPECIALTY UNDERWRITERS, INC, 756

Barry, Mike Associate Athletic Director
WAYNE STATE COLLEGE, 374, 1017

Barry, Patrick Chief Financial Officer / Chief
Operatin
BLUEFLY, INC., 1220

Barry, Rick Sports Columnist
SAN FRANCISCO EXAMINER, 528

Barry, Sue Advertising Vice President
PRESS-ENTERPRISE (CA), 522

Barry, Van Executive Director
USTA TEXAS, 176

Bell, Cindy EVP Meeting Services
PGI, INC., 801

Bell, Daniel Game Presentation Manager
AMERICAN HOCKEY LEAGUE/AHL, 128

Bell, Daniel Senior Vice President, Hotels &
Leisure
TANGENT ASSOCIATES, INC., 1068

Bell, David Head Coach
AMERICAN HOCKEY LEAGUE/AHL, 126

Bell, Dee Marketing Manager
ANTHONY TRAVEL, INC., 925

Bell, Dwight President
USA LUGE, 142, 209

Bell, Gregg Sports Senior Writer
SACRAMENTO BEE, 526

Bell, Hilton Managing Partner
MILLING BENSON WOODWARD, L.L.P., 896

Bell, James Audit Committee
JPMORGAN CHASE BANK, N.A., 768

Bell, Jan Director
ST. THOMAS UNIVERSITY, 434

Bell, Jarrett Professional Football Reporter
USA TODAY, 543

Bell, Jaymie Chief Marketing Officer
JACKSON WALKER LLP, 839

Bell, Jennifer Associate Athletic Director
ANDERSON UNIVERSITY ATHLETICS, 346,
351

Bell, Jim Founder
FOAMHEADS, LLC, 1009, 1134

Bell, John VP / Shareholder
JOHNSON & BELL, 886

Bell, John. Vice President
JOHNSON & BELL, 886

Bell, Marty Vice President of Intercollegiate Athlet
QUINCY UNIVERSITY ATHLETICS, 368

Bell, Michael Partner
DURANTE, CHARLES J., 877

Bell, Monroe Asst. Sports Information Director
POINT UNIVERSITY ATHLETICS, 319

Bell, Nicholas Attorney
MEYER, UNKOVIC & SCOTT, LLP, 895

Bell, Paul Dean and Vice Provost for Instruction
OKLAHOMA, UNIVERSITY OF, 430

Bell, Rob CEO
TEN SECONDS, 1200

Bell, Robert Sales Staff
C M T SPECIALTY SPORTS, 1221

Bell, Samuel Treasurer
NATIONAL CLUB ASSOCIATION, 222

Bell, Sue Business Manager & Membership
Director
CONNECTICUT PGA SECTIONAL OFFICE,
105

Bell, Susan Promotions Manager
WCBI-TV, 700

Bell, Terry Co-Founder
AMERICAN POOLPLAYERS ASSOCIATION,
INC., 61

Bellaire, Barry General Manager
CLIFF KEEN ATHLETIC INC., 1116

Bellairs, Bart Athletics Director
STRAWBERRY STADIUM, 1006

Bellairs, Bart Athletics Director
UNIVERSITY CENTER, 1012

Bellamy, Rhonda News Director
WAAV-AM, 635

Bellamy, Ron Sports Editor
REGISTER-GUARD, 524

Bellan, Brigitte GM, International
STUBHUB, 932

Bellantoni, Cassandra Executive Producer and
Creative Director
MEDIA VISTA PRODUCTIONS, 600, 843

Bellas, Chrisanne Host
HOCKEY HOTLINE, 683

Bellas, Jim President
BICYCLE EXCHANGE, INC., 1219

Belle, Tom President, CEO
GAGE MARKETING GROUP, 784

Belleman, Ben Director Of Member Services &
Compliance
NATIONAL CHRISTIAN COLLEGE ATHLETIC
ASSOCIATION/NCCAA, 285

Bellemarre, Pierre Co-founder
KEYBEC SUBLIME, INC., 1152

Belli, Dave Assistant Sports Editor
ALAMEDA JOURNAL, 459

Bellia, Patricia Faculty Athletics Representative
JOYCE ATHLETIC & CONVOCATION
CENTER, 978

Bellis, Gerald EVP, Sales and Marketing, Titleist
TITLEIST (COBRA/PINNACLE), 1201

Bellis, Jennifer Sports Reporter
SAN ANTONIO EXPRESS-NEWS, 528

Bellis-Jones, Hugh Executive Director
AMERICAN HANOVERIAN SOCIETY, 73

Bellissima, Vincent Advertising Manager
RING, 578

Belliveau, Richard Co-Founder & Chief
Technology Officer
HIGH END SYSTEMS, INC, 1144

Belmont, Dan President, Sports
MARKETING ARM, 794, 795, 841, 842

Belmont, Daniel President
MILLSPORT, LLC, 795

Belmonte, Mike General Manager
ILLINOIS OFF TRACK BETTING, 1040

Belskus, Jeff EVP
INDIANAPOLIS MOTOR SPEEDWAY
CORPORATION, 1026

Belsky, Gary Editor
ESPN THE MAGAZINE, 558

Belt, Mimi Vice President
TELEMUNDO, 677

Beltran, John Sports Director
KPRB-FM, 626

Beltran, Tony General Manager
USL CHAMPIONSHIP, 160

Beltz, Robert Member
RIDENOUR, HIERDON, HARPER &
KELHOFFER P.L.L.C., 902

Belz, Colleen Director of Development
TAGGART, WALTER J., 858

Belza, Rob Vice President, Corporate
Partnerships
AMERICAN HOCKEY LEAGUE/AHL, 129

Bembry, Jerry Senior Writer
ESPN THE MAGAZINE, 558

Bement, Jennifer Media Marketing Manager
TERVIS TUMBLER COMPANY, 1200

Bemis, Michelle Vice President Events &
Business Develop
TIGER WOODS FOUNDATION, 193

Ben Namer Kevehazi, Ilana Assistnat to the ED
MACCABI WORLD UNION, 221

BenDor, Liron Vice President of Marketing
OVERLAND PARK CONVENTION & VISITORS
BUREAU, 243, 263

Benavides, Allan General Manager
NORTHWEST BASEBALL LEAGUE, 47, 993

Benavidez, Julie Event Manager
ROSE BOWL STADIUM, 999

Bench, Sherice Chief Financing Officer
BALFOUR CO., 1103

Bendelow, Edward Managing Partner
BENDELOW LAW FIRM, 865

Bender, Brian SVP / Chief Financial Officer /
Co-Chief
SHOPKO STORES, INC., 1237

Bender, Dick Sports Director
WRLS-FM, 664

Bender, Edward Lawyer
WOOD & LAMPING LLP, 916

Bender, Nathan Director, Soccer
WOMEN'S PREMIER SOCCER LEAGUE, 166

Bender, Nick Director of Athletic Training Services
COE COLLEGE ATHLETICS, 381

Bender, Rich Executive Director
USA WRESTLING, 181, 213

Bender, Susan Membership
GATEWAY PGA SECTIONAL OFFICE, 105

Bendix, Peter President, Baseball Operations
NATIONAL LEAGUE OF PROFESSIONAL
BASEBALL CLUBS, THE, 31

Bendure, P. Partner
CONNER & WINTERS, P.L.L.C., 874

Benedek, Karl Editor
OREGON CYCLING MAGAZINE, 574

Benedetto, Jim CTO and Co-founder
GRAVITY TELEVISION & SPORTS
MARKETING, 599, 786

Benedick, John Associate Director of Athletics
MASSACHUSETTS INSTITUTE OF
TECHNOLOGY (MIT), 392

Benedict, Darcy General Manager
WRCU-FM, 663

Benedict, David Director of Athletics
CONNECTICUT ATHLETICS, UNIVERSITY OF,
327, 949, 968, 1004

Benedict, Michael Assistant Coach
NORTH AMERICAN HOCKEY LEAGUE, 132

Benefield, Greg General Manager
WSSO-AM, 667

Beneke, Cortlund Operations Manager
DURHAM BULLS ATHLETIC PARK, 963

Benetallo, April Director Marketing/Product
Management
DAXKO, 1213

Benett, Sue Senior Buyer
NORDICTRACK FITNESS STORES, 1233

Benevento, Don Sports Reporter
COURIER-POST, 474

Benezra, Adam Vice President
BUFFALO EXPORT, LLC, 1111

Benezra, Larry President / Chief Executive Officer
BUFFALO EXPORT, LLC, 1111

Benford, William President
L.A. GEAR, 1153

Bengtson, Russ Editor-in-Chief
SLAM, 581

Bengttson, Bob Finance Director
BATTLE CREEK SPORTS PROMOTION, 228

Benham, Terry Owner & President
IMPACT MANAGEMENT GROUP, INC., 789

Beniash, Michael Sports Editor
CALEDONIAN RECORD, 467

Benitez, Ken News Director
WFPR-AM, 646

Benjamin, Alex SVPof Finance & Operations
JHG TOWNSEND, 790, 821

Benjamin, Carrie Event Manager
SAN JOSE SPORTS AUTHORITY, 245

Benjamin, Peter Athletic Trainer
MADONNA UNIVERSITY ATHLETICS, 315

Benjamin, Steve Executive VP
SPL INTEGRATED SOLUTIONS, 822

Benjamin F. Payton, Dr. President
TUSKEGEE UNIVERSITY, 1011

Benke, Michael Director of Facilities & Operations
LEWIS-CLARK STATE COLLEGE ATHLETICS,
315

Benko, Jared Director of Athletics
GEORGIA SOUTHERN UNIVERSITY
ATHLETICS, 331

Benner, Jack Promotions Manager
KTBB-AM, 629

Bennett, Aaron Sports Reporter
WCIA-TV, 700

Bennett, Andy Head Coach
WOMEN'S PREMIER SOCCER LEAGUE, 166

Bennett, Anthony Director of Athletics
FAYETTEVILLE STATE UNIVERSITY (FSU)
ATHLETICS, 358

Bennett, Chuck President IMG Golf ,
Tennis,Fashion and
IMG LOS ANGELES/IMG X SPORTS, 17, 838

Bennett, Clarence President
MASSACHUSETTS GOLF ASSOCIATION, 112

Bennett, Clay Chair
NATIONAL BASKETBALL ASSOCIATION/NBA,
57

Bennett, Clayton Vice Chair
NATIONAL FOOTBALL FOUNDATION AND
COLLEGE HALL OF FAME, INC., THE, 252,
256

Bennett, Craig Director of Sports Medicine
UNIVERSITY OF PUGET SOUND, 397

Bennett, Dan General Manager
KTCK/THE TICKET, 629

Bennett, Derrick Chairman
PANAMA CITY BEACH CHAMBER OF
COMMERCE, 243

Bennett, Dusty Executive AD, Admin. & Capital
Projects
TENNESSEE STATE UNIVERSITY
ATHLETICS, 346

Bennett, Ed SVP/Chief Administrative Officer
NASCAR, 17, 686

Bennett, Jack Advertising Manager
CLEVELAND DAILY BANNER, 471

Bennett, Jamie Registrar
POTOMAC VALLEY AAU ASSOCIATION, 215

Bennett, Jay Sports Reporter
PARKERSBURG NEWS, 518

Berkner, Sandra Treasurer
UNITED STATES CORPORATE ATHLETICS
ASSOCIATION, 225
Berl, Chris VP of Sales
WORLD DRYER CORPORATION, 1211
Berlamino, Betty Vice President
WPIX-TV, 708
Berland, Leslie EVP & Chief Marketing Officer
VERIZON COMMUNICATIONS, 734
Berlet, Bruce Sports Writer (Golf)
HARTFORD COURANT, 492
Berlin, Andrew Owner & Chairman
MIDWEST LEAGUE, 45, 1005
Berlin, Michael Shareholder
GREENBERG TRAURIG, LLP, 882
Berlin, Peter Sports Editor
INTERNATIONAL HERALD TRIBUNE, 497
Berlin, Ryan Director of Operations
AMERICAN POWER BOAT ASSOCIATION, 63
Berlin, Steve Chief Financial Officer
PETRY TELEVISION, 677
Berlinger, Ellen Tournament Coordinator
PHILADELPHIA PGA SECTIONAL OFFICE,
107
Berlo, Josh Athletic Director
MINNESOTA-DULUTH ATHLETICS,
UNIVERSITY OF (UMD), 328, 364
Berman, Alan Chief Business
PUTTERMAN ATHLETICS, 1178
Berman, Brian Vice President
TRIMAN TELE-GOAL, INC., 1203
Berman, Chris Host
NFL PRIMETIME, 682, 683, 684
Berman, Doug Chairman
U.S. ARMY ALL-AMERICAN BOWL, 203
Berman, Howard Partner
BERMAN, HOWARD E., 865
Berman, Jessica Commissioner
NATIONAL WOMEN'S SOCCER LEAGUE, 158
Berman, Len Sports Director
WNBC-TV, 707
Berman, Mark Sports Director
KRIV-TV, 525, 694
Berman, Mark Partner
CONNER & WINTERS, P.L.L.C., 874
Berman, Samantha Senior Editor
SKI MAGAZINE, 580
Bermudez, John Executive Director
CINDRICH & COMPANY, 872
Berna, Jason Assistant Athletic Director
UNIVERSITY OF DUBUQUE ATHLETICS, 383
Bernabe, Sam President/General Manager
PACIFIC COAST LEAGUE OF
PROFESSIONAL BASEBALL CLUBS, 48, 953,
1002
Bernal, Kathy Asst. Athletic Director
NJCAA REGION XXIV MEN'S, 290
Bernal, Violet Credit
YONEX CORPORATION, 1212
Bernard, Bryce Faculty Athletics Representative
CORBAN UNIVERSITY ATHLETICS, 311
Bernard, Gary Chief Executive Officer
CANADIAN PROFESSIONAL GOLFERS'
ASSOCIATION, 100
Bernard, Jay Program Director
KIKR-AM, 620
Bernard, Mark President, Hockey
Operations/General Man
AMERICAN HOCKEY LEAGUE/AHL, 128
Bernard, Mary Chair
STATE OF RHODE ISLAND DEPARTMENT OF
BUSINESS REGULATION, 82
Bernard, Pamela VP/General Counsel
BERNARD, PAMELA J., 865
Bernard, Pamela Vice President and General
Counsel
DUKE LEGAL COUNSEL, 877
Bernard, Randy Chief Executive Officer
RFDTV, 686
Bernard, William Partner
BERNARD, WILLIAM DAVID, 865
Bernardi, Rob Director of Athletics
MANNING FIELD AT JOHN L. GUIDRY
STADIUM, 985
Bernardo, Meg ASP North America General
Manager
WORLD SURF LEAGUE, 172
Bernasconi, Luca President & CEO
ROLEX WATCH USA, 732

Bernat, Bonny Sports/Event Sales Manager
VISIT WINSTON-SALEM, 250
Bernatow, Andy Sports Information Director
MOUNT MARTY COLLEGE ATHLETICS, 317
Bernbaum, Hank President
HIGH SIERRA SPORT COMPANY, 1144
Berner, Fred Publisher
ANTIGO DAILY JOURNAL, 461
Berney, Larry Chief Operating Officer
DON JAGODA ASSOCIATES, INC., 780
Bernhardt, Harold President
COMFORT PRODUCTS, INC., 1118
Bernhardt, Steve Chief Baseball Officer
BASEBALL FACTORY, 26
Bernhart, Ralf Chief Financial Officer
HEAD/PENN USA, 1143
Bernheim, Richard President
NEUMANN & COMPANY, R., 1167
Bernick, Jeffrey Member
RIDENOUR, HIERDON, HARPER &
KELHOFFER P.L.L.C., 902
Bernick, Sarah Administrative Coordinator
HAMPTON ROADS CHAMBER OF
COMMERCE, 235
Bernier, Hugo General Manager, Business
Operations
QUEBEC MARITIMES MAJOR JUNIOR
HOCKEY LEAGUE, 135
Bernier, Kristy Director
ALASKA STATE FAIR, 260
Berninger, Jack Sports Editor
RICHMOND TIMES-DISPATCH, 525
Berninger, Paul Partner
WOOD & LAMPING LLP, 916
Bernon, Bernadette Consulting Editor
BOAT U.S. MAGAZINE, 553
Bernos, Adam Sports Sales Manager
ALPHARETTA CONVENTION & VISITORS
BUREAU, 227
Bernreuter, Hugh Assistant Sports Editor
SAGINAW NEWS, 526
Bernstein, Bruce Coordinating Producer
ESPN, 683
Bernstein, David News Director
WPRO-AM, 662
Bernstein, Jeffrey Athletic Director of Sports
Information
NEW YORK UNIVERSITY ATHLETICS(NYU),
395
Bernstein, Michael Sports Agent
PRO FOOTBALL MANAGEMENT, 849
Bernstein, Randy President & CEO
PREMIER PARTNERSHIPS, 802
Bernstein, Rick Sports Director
REAL SPORTS WITH BRYANT GUMBEL, 682,
684, 685
Bernstein, William Partner
MANATT, PHELPS & PHILLIPS, LLP, 892
Bernthal, Matthew Dept. Associate Professor
SOUTH CAROLINA, UNIVERSITY OF, 432
Berouty, Celeste Sales Director
BODY GLOVE INTERNATIONAL, INC., 1108
Berres, Mike Sports Writer
READING EAGLE, 523
Berret, Thomas Attorney
MEYER, UNKOVIC & SCOTT, LLP, 895
Berrian, Frank Community Relations & Game
Presentation
AMERICAN HOCKEY LEAGUE/AHL, 127
Berringer, John Partner
REED SMITH LLP, 901
Berry, Andrew General Manager/Executive VP,
Football O
NATIONAL FOOTBALL LEAGUE/NFL, 94
Berry, Carder VP, Corporate Partnerships
EAST COAST HOCKEY LEAGUE/ECHL, 129
Berry, David Sports Reporter
BEAUMONT ENTERPRISE, 464
Berry, Edward Tech
SOUTH ALABAMA SPEEDWAY, 1033
Berry, Greg Sports Director
KIMT-TV, 691
Berry, Jack Secretary/Treasurer
GOLF WRITERS ASSOCIATION OF AMERICA,
102
Berry, Jim Sports Director
WBFS-TV, 700
Berry, Matt VP, Player Acquisition
NATIONAL FOOTBALL LEAGUE/NFL, 96

Berry, Michael President
NATIONAL SKI AREAS ASSOCIATION, 152
Berry, Mike Director of Sports Medicine
UNIVERSITY OF MISSOURI-ST. LOUIS
ATHLETICS(UMSL), 373
Berry, Patricia Attorney
BATE, PETERSON, DEACON, ZINN & YOUNG,
LLP, 864
Berry, Peter Advertising Director
POCONO RECORD, 520
Berry, Rick General Manager
PIONEER BASEBALL LEAGUE, 50, 952
Berry, Robert Professor Emeritus
BERRY, ROBERT C., 866
Berry, Sara Director of Partnerships and
Marketing
MAJOR LEAGUE LACROSSE, 141
Berry, Scott Assistant Athletic Director
MAYVILLE STATE UNIVERSITY ATHLETICS,
316
Berry, Tom Sports Columnist
HIGH POINT ENTERPRISE, 494
Berryhill, Damon Manager
PACIFIC COAST LEAGUE OF
PROFESSIONAL BASEBALL CLUBS, 49, 983
Bersch, Jeff Sports Editor
WINONA DAILY NEWS, 547
Bersett, Gerald President
FEDERAL PREMIUM AMMUNITION, 1132
Bershad, Lawrence Law Professor
BERSHAD, LAWRENCE, 866
Berson, David EVP, CBS Sports/President, CBS
College S
CBS SPORTS, 673
Berst, David Chief of Staff Division I
NATIONAL COLLEGIATE ATHLETIC
ASSOCIATION/NCAA, 285
Bertagna, Joe Executive Director
AMERICAN HOCKEY COACHES
ASSOCIATION/AHCA, 122
Bertino, Joe Executive Director
WESTERN NEW YORK PGA SECTION
OFFICE, 108
Bertka, Todd Vice President, Sales
GREENVILLE CONVENTION & VISITORS
BUREAU, 235
Bertke, Susan Senior Administrative Assistant
DAYTON ATHLETICS, UNIVERSITY OF, 328
Bertman, Skip Athletic Director
TIGER STADIUM, 1010
Bertolini, Joe Operations Manager
UNIQUE SPORTS PRODUCTS, INC., 1206
Bertoni, Al Concessions Manager
LEE CIVIC CENTER, 982
Bertoni, Gregg Fitness Director, Craftsman Tools
QVC NETWORK, 1235
Bertozzi, Carlo President
DACOR CORPORATION, 1122
Bertram, David VP National Priorities
HOST MANAGED EVENTS, 788
Bertram, Steve Sports Director
WHBN-AM, 649
Bertrand, Jacques Chief Sales Officer
BARCO MEDIA, 1104
Bertrand, Peter Shareholder
LAMPART, ABE, 888
Bertuzzi, Lawrence Partner
BERTUZZI, LAWRENCE, 866
Berube, Gilles Operational Director
QUEBEC MARITIMES MAJOR JUNIOR
HOCKEY LEAGUE, 135
Berube, Sis Classified Manager
NAPLES DAILY NEWS, 510
Berus, Joy Partner
BARTH, BERUS & CALDERON, LLP, 864
Berzonsky, Angela Executive Business Officer
USL CHAMPIONSHIP, 159
Bes, Jeff Head Coach/Director, Hockey
Operations
SOUTHERN PROFESSIONAL HOCKEY
LEAGUE, 136
Besbris, Dan Director of Broadcasting and Media
Relat
SAM LYNN BALLPARK, 1000
Beseda, Jim Sports Reporter
OREGONIAN, 516
Beshoff, Ray Owner/Chair
USL CHAMPIONSHIP, 160

Blythe, Donovan Director
BLYTHE, DONOVAN A., 827

Blythe, William Research & Development Director
SECONDWIND PRODUCTS, INC., 1187

Bo Bell Jr, John Chairman
BOYLE & COMPANY, INC., 1109

Boal, Frank Sports Director
WDAF-TV, 701

Board, Fred Advertising Director
REDLANDS DAILY FACTS, 524

Board, Marquita General Manager
WOMEN'S FOOTBALL ALLIANCE / WFA, 97

Board, Mike General Manager
NATIONAL LACROSSE LEAGUE, 142

Boardman, David President & CEO
BAG BOY COMPANY, 1103

Boardman, Joseph President/Chief Executive
Officer
AMTRAK, 925

Boath, Kimberley Director Advertising
RECORD-JOURNAL, 524

Boatman, Jacquie Director of Community &
Media Relations
NATIONAL PRO FASTPITCH, 171

Boatman-Roush, Lori Sports Editor
TIMES GAZETTE, 539

Boatright, Darron Director of Athletics
WICHITA STATE UNIVERSITY ATHLETICS,
349, 956

Boatright, Douglas
ISAAC, BRANT, LEDMAN & TEETOR, 885

Boatwright, Marc Seior Vice President
ADOLFSON & PERTSON, INC., 1048

Boaz, Jon Advertising Manager
KBTX-TV, 688

Boaz, Keith Sr. Assoc. AD, Athletics &
Entertainment
MISSOURI STATE ATHLETICS, 337, 969, 993

Bob, Heiney Pest Control Products Sales & Tech
Suppo
B & G EQUIPMENT COMPANY, 1102

Bob, Severs President
ONTARIO HOCKEY LEAGUE, 134

Bobe, Steve Secretary, Dixie Section PGA
DIXIE PGA SECTIONAL OFFICE, 105

Boberg, James Advertising Manager
FORUM, 489

Bobert, Sarah Executive Associate AD, Internal
Operati
MARQUETTE UNIVERSITY ATHLETICS, 336

Bobinski, Mike Director of Athletics
XAVIER UNIVERSITY, 342, 438

Boblink, David Chief Financial Officer
INTERSPORT, INC., 600

Bobrow, Mitchell President
OTOMIX, 1172

Bocaccio, Gerard Senior Vice President,
Advertising Sales
FX NETWORKS, LLC, 675

Bochnak, John Senior VP, Finance &
Administration
ALABAMA SPORTS FOUNDATION, 227

Bock, Dieter Chief Financial Officer
PUMA NORTH AMERICA, 1178

Bockelman, Pete Director of Operations &
Sponsorships
DISSON SKATING, 780

Bodammer, Jared Associate Athletic Director
BRIAR CLIFF UNIVERSITY ATHLETICS, 309

Bodani, Frank Sports Reporter
YORK DAILY RECORD/YORK SUNDAY
NEWS, 548

Bodden, Heather Operations Manager
CANADIAN PROFESSIONAL GOLFERS'
ASSOCIATION, 100

Boddicker, Daniel President
BODDICKER SPORTS MANAGEMENT, 827

Bode, Bruce Executive Director
UNITED STATES ADULT SOCCER
ASSOCIATION, 156

Bodenahmer, John Publisher & Editor
PACIFIC NORTHWEST GOLFER, 575

Bodenheimer, George President
ESPN CLASSIC SPORTS NETWORK, 674

Bodenheimer, George President
OUTSIDE THE LINES, 680

Bodenschatz, Mark Associate Athletic Director,
Facilities
BRYCE JORDAN CENTER, 949, 953

Bodenstadt, Jamie President
KANSAS SPEEDWAY, 1025, 1026

Bodenstadt, Sue Treasure
KANSAS SPEEDWAY, 1026

Bodensteiner, Jill Athletic Director
ST. JOSEPH'S UNIVERSITY ATHLETICS, 345,
874, 978

Bodkins, Carrie Senior Associate Athletic Director
ALDERSON-BROADDUS UNIVERSITY
ATHLETICS, 350

Bodley, Hal Professional Baseball Columnist
USA TODAY, 543

Bodley, Linda VP
DEKAI ENTERPRISES, 831

Bodo, Peter Senior Editor
TENNIS, 588

Boeck, Greg Sports Reporter
USA TODAY, 543

Boeddeker, Cynthia Operations VP
PREMIUMWEAR, 1176

Boedeker, Adam Sports Reporter
DENTON RECORD-CHRONICLE, 482

Boeger, Chad General Manager/Program Director
SPORTS RADIO 810/WHB-AM, 634

Boegner, Ray SVP
STRONG INTERNATIONAL, INC., 1197

Boehm, Cyndi MIS Manager/Editor
NSGA BUYING GUIDE, 596

Boehm, Steven Attorney/Partner
BOEHM, STEVE B., 867

Boehm, Todd Comptroller
OHIO HS ATHLETIC ASSOCIATION, 201

Boehm, Tom Administration and Finance EVP
RCA GROUP EVENT MARKETING +
MANAGEMENT, 805

Boehmer, Greg Simulcast Manager
ROSECROFT RACEWAY, 1043

Boehmke, Reghan Head Athletic Trainer
FRANCIS MARION UNIVERSITY ATHLETICS
(FMU), 359

Boele, Michael 3rd Vice President
COLLEGE ATHLETIC BUSINESS
MANAGEMENT ASSOCIATION/CABMA, 283,
373

Boenau, Rob Marketing Director
WUAB-TV, 711

Boer, James Sports Information Director
EASTERN MENNONITE UNIVERSITY (EMU)
ATHLETICS, 383

Boer, Ralf-Reinhard Partner
FOLEY & LARDNER, 880

Boerigter, Bob Athletic Director
RICKENBRODE STADIUM, 997

Boese, James General Manager
HARRINGTON RACEWAY & CASINO, 1039

Boese, Jim Director Simulcast/Publicity
HARRINGTON RACEWAY & CASINO, 1039

Boesel, Terry Director of Athletics
CHAPMAN UNIVERSITY ATHLETICS, 380

Boessneck, Kirsten Coordinator
PALMETTO REGIONAL COMMISSIONER/USA
VOLLEYBALL, 212

Boettcher, Jim Director of Operations-Levy
Restaurants
LAMBEAU FIELD, 981

Boettcher, Shelley Operations Manager
ROCHESTER AMATEUR SPORTS
COMMISSION, 244

Boey, Kris Associate Athletics Director
OHIO WESLEYAN UNIVERSITY ATHLETICS,
396

Boff, Vic Founder
ASSOCIATION OF OLDETIME BARBELL &
STRONGMEN (AOBS), 83

Boffey, Adam Sports Editor
SUMMIT DAILY NEWS, 536

Bogaczyk, Jeff News Director
WAVL-AM, 637

Bogan, Mike Sports Editor
HURON DAILY TRIBUNE, 495

Bogar, Brett VP Product Development
TOYQUEST, 1203

Bogdan, Elise VP/Client Services Director
NEWMAN COMMUNICATIONS, 798

Bogden, Randy Advisory Board Chairman
MONTANA EXPOPARK, 987

Bogert, Jon Editor
SPORTING GOODS INTELLIGENCE, 584

Boggan, Daniel Chief Operations Officer
NATIONAL COLLEGIATE ATHLETIC
ASSOCIATION/NCAA, 285

Boggie, Tom Assistant Sports Editor
DAILY GAZETTE (NY), 476

Boggs, Jamie Senior Associate Athletics Director,
Com
GEORGIA STATE UNIVERSITY, 331, 419

Boggs, Thomas Chairman/Partner
PATTON BOGGS, 899

Boghossian, Christopher Sports Source Editor
CHICAGO TRIBUNE SPORTS, 713

Bogl, Helen CFO
GRAND RIVER RACEWAY (GRR), 1039

Bogner, Hannes Chief Financial Officer
BOGNER, 1109

Bogoyevac, Steve General Manager
V-FORMATION\THE NEXED LIFE, 1207

Bogucki, Peter Publisher
NEW ENGLAND WINDSURFING JOURNAL,
573

Boguniecki, Eric Assistant Coach
AMERICAN HOCKEY LEAGUE/AHL, 127

Bogus, Justin Men's & Women's Soccer Head
Coach
NJCAA REGION I WOMEN'S, 286

Bohach, Arlene General Manager
WLOH-AM, 656

Bohan, David EVP & COO
BROOKS, 1110

Bohannan, Larry Sports Reporter
DESERT SUN, 483

Bohinski, Martin CFO
HDS PROMOTIONAL MARKETING, 787

Bohl, Allan Adjunct Sports Management
FLAGLER COLLEGE, 417

Bohl, Craig Executive Director
AMERICAN FOOTBALL COACHES
ASSOCIATION, 87

Bohl, Perry Secretary/Treasurer
NORTH DAKOTA GOLF ASSOCIATION, 114

Bohling, Scott Chief Financial Officer
H.H. BROWN SHOE COMPANY, 1141

Bohman, Barry Board of Governor/Owner
NORTH AMERICAN HOCKEY LEAGUE, 133

Bohman, Brenda Board of Governor/Owner
NORTH AMERICAN HOCKEY LEAGUE, 133

Bohn, Mike Director of Athletics
SOUTHERN CALIFORNIA ATHLETICS,
UNIVERSITY OF, 344, 989

Bohnen, Thomas Member
ROSENTHAL, ROBERT E., 903

Bohnenkamp, John Sports Editor
HAWK EYE, 492

Boies, David Director, Operations
QUEBEC MARITIMES MAJOR JUNIOR
HOCKEY LEAGUE, 135

Boileau, Bob President
PIKES PEAK INTERNATIONAL RACEWAY,
1030

Boillat, Matthew Head Athletic Trainer
MASSACHUSETTS COLLEGE OF LIBERAL
ARTS ATHLETICS(MCLA), 392

Boitmann, Paul President, North American Sales
Operatio
RUBBERMAID INCORPORATED, 1184

Boitz, David General Manager
NORTH AMERICAN HOCKEY LEAGUE, 133

Boix-Vives, Laurent Chairman
ROSSIGNOL SKI COMPANY, INC., 1183

Boje, Cathy Vice President/Operations
WEST GLEN COMMUNICATIONS, INC., 603

Boje, Jeff Co-Owner
ST. LOUIS CARDINALS HALL OF FAME
MUSEUM, 65, 258

Bokelman, R.J. Director of Facilities Operations
BRAMLAGE COLISEUM, 950, 951

Boken, Paul Executive Managing Director
VAINISI, JEROME R., 913

Bokosky, Mike Assistant Athletics Director
CHAPMAN UNIVERSITY ATHLETICS, 380

Boland, Ryan Sports Editor
FULTON SUN, 490

Bolas, Rich Sports Editor
DAILY NEWS SUN, 478

Bolch, Ben College Sports Staff Writer
LOS ANGELES TIMES, 503

Bold, Tom Sr. Associate Director of Athletics, Fac
BROWN STADIUM, 952

Borg, Kevin Owner
ONTARIO HOCKEY LEAGUE, 133, 963
Borges, Lisa Executive Director
DOUG FLUTIE FOUNDATION FOR AUTISM, 191
Borghetti, Peter Attorney
MEYER, UNKOVIC & SCOTT, LLP, 895
Borgonzi, Mike General Manager
NATIONAL FOOTBALL LEAGUE/NFL, 96
Boring, Rick Senior Systems Consultant
CCI SOLUTIONS, 820
Borkowski, Shek Head Coach
USL LEAGUE TWO, 163
Borkowski, Tyler Assistant General Manager
FRONTIER LEAGUE, 41
Borland, Mary Assistant AD for Academic Services/SWA
STRAWBERRY STADIUM, 1006
Borland, Matt Crew Chief
NASCAR CUP SERIES, 23
Borland, Will Tickets & Ops Coordinator
ALABAMA SPORTS FOUNDATION, 227
Borland, Winston President & Chief Executive Officer
MEDICAL CENTER ARLINGTON, 921
Borman, Matt Senior Associate AD/Executive Director
WEST VIRGINIA UNIVERSITY/WVU COLISEUM, 1018
Borman, Scott President
AMPROS TROPHIES, 1098
Born, David Guest Service Director
SAVVIS CENTER, 1001
Born, Mike Director of NBA Scouting
KAUFFMAN SPORTS MANAGEMENT GROUP, 840
Born, Peter President
BOGNER, 1109
Bornstein, Steve Media EVP
BERTHELSEN, RICHARD, 826
Boroomand, Farah Chief Financial Officer
AMF BOWLING WORLDWIDE, 1098
Borrego, Heather Director, Operations
WOMEN'S PREMIER SOCCER LEAGUE, 166
Borrego, Rene President/CEO
NATIONAL BASKETBALL ASSOCIATION DEVELOPMENT LEAGUE, 59
Borrelli, Tom Sports Writer
BUFFALO NEWS, 467
Borreson, Candy Marketing SVP
KEYSTONE MARKETING, INC., 792
Borrie, Stuart Director of Operations
BADMINTON WORLD FEDERATION, 25
Borris, Jeff General Counsel
BEVERLY HILLS SPORTS COUNCIL, 826, 866
Borst, Nichole Head Athletic Trainer
MONTANA STATE UNIVERSITY-NORTHERN ATHLETICS, 317
Borsuk, Marie Business Manager
WORLD KARTING ASSOCIATION, 19
Borthwick, Alastair Chief Financial Officer
BANK OF AMERICA CORPORATION, 725
Bortner, Jan Assistant Athletic Director
BEAVER STADIUM, 949
Borto, Mark VP, Sales
TOMSED CORPORATION, 1202
Borton, John Editor
WOLVERINE, 593
Bortscheller, Sara Athletic Trainer
MOUNT MARTY COLLEGE ATHLETICS, 317
Bos, Matt Sports Information Director
NORTHWESTERN COLLEGE (IA) ATHLETICS, 317
Bosalavage, Wendy President
AMERICAN LEISURE CORPORATION, 1049
Bosch, Joseph Executive Vice President/Chief HR Office
DIRECTV, INC., 686
Bosch, Manel CEO Worldwide Operations
INTERPERFORMANCES, INC., 839
Bosco, Lew Director Horner Study Center
HORNER FLOORING COMPANY, 1145
Bosco, Mary Partner
PATTON BOGGS, 899
Boscolo, Benjamin Attorney
CHASEN & BOSCOLO CHARTERED, 872
Boscov, Albert Chairman, Chief Executive Officer
BOSCOV'S DEPARTMENT STORES, 1220

Boscov, Jim Vice Chairman of Boscov's Department Sto
BOSCOV'S DEPARTMENT STORES, 1220
Bosh, Jon Head Athletics Trainer
WHITWORTH COLLEGE ATHLETICS, 406
Boshers, Connie Director of Administration
NASHVILLE SUPERSPEEDWAY, 1029
Bosiwick, Larry General Manager/Owner
WRMS-FM, 664
Boskey, Craig Senior VP Finance
NATIONAL MARINE MANUFACTURERS ASSOCIATION, 64
Bossard, Roger Head Groundskeeper
AMERICAN LEAGUE OF PROFESSIONAL BASEBALL CLUBS, THE, 29
Bossell, Candace Head Coach, Women's Lacrosse
MCCARTHY STADIUM, 985
Bossmann, Lori Vice President Merchandising, Marketing
ACE HARDWARE, 1215
Bosso, Sarah Assistant General Manager
CALIFORNIA LEAGUE (A-LEVEL), 36, 970
Bostian, Kevin Director of Athletics
NORTHWESTERN STATE UNIVERSITY OF LOUISIANA ATHLETICS, 340
Bostic, Kyle Sports Editor
NEW YORK DAILY CHALLENGE, 510
Bostic, Renee Director of Athletics
MEDGAR EVERS COLLEGE ATHLETICS (MEC), 393
Bostock, Roy Co-Owner
SOUTH ATLANTIC LEAGUE (A LEVEL), 51
Boston, Wallace President & Chief Executive Officer
AMERICAN MILITARY UNIVERSITY, 409
Bostwick, Kyle Vice President
NEW YORK-PENNSYLVANIA LEAGUE, 47, 1016
Boswell, Jackie Assistant Athletics Director
STEVENSON UNIVERSITY, 402
Boswell, Robert President
SUN SHADER INTERNATIONAL, INC./WASHINGTON SQUARE GARDEN, INC., 1197
Botelho, Dave Head Athletic Trainer
NORWICH UNIVERSITY ATHLETICS, 396
Botkin, Brad Sports Writer
TIMES-STANDARD, 540
Bott, Jason Producer
PRIME TIME PADRES, 680, 682, 685
Bottelo, Nancy President/CEO
SPECIAL OLYMPICS HAWAII, 194
Botterill, Kevin Executive Director
WOMEN'S PREMIER SOCCER LEAGUE, 167
Bottke, Warren President
SOUTH FLORIDA PGA, 115
Botts, Jeff Program Director
KANE-AM, 613
Bouchard, Gilles Head Coach
QUEBEC MARITIMES MAJOR JUNIOR HOCKEY LEAGUE, 136
Bouchard, Joel Head Coach
AMERICAN HOCKEY LEAGUE/AHL, 128
Bouchard-Hall, Derek President/Chief Operating Officer
USA CYCLING, 71, 208
Boucher, Mathieu Director, Performance Development
CYCLING CANADA, 70
Boucher, Robert Dean of Human Kinetics
WINDSOR, UNIVERSITY OF, 438
Bouchez, Richard Promotions Manager
KOAA-TV, 692
Bouck, Craig President, CEO
BARKER RINKER SEACAT ARCHITECTURE, 1050
Bouclet, Philippe Vice President
WORLD ARCHERY FEDERATION, 15
Bouda, Michael Manager
JEDC SPORTS AND ENTERTAINMENT DIVISION/JACKSONVILLE FLORIDA, 237
Boudreau, Ben Head Coach
ONTARIO HOCKEY LEAGUE, 134
Boudreau, Monica Account Manager
RIDEAU CARLETON RACEWAY, 1043
Boudreaux, Robert Executive Vice President
UNITED STATES SPECIALTY SPORTS ASSOCATION, 170

Boudriex, Sou Advertising Sales
WBUK-FM, 639
Bough, Deborah Computer & Information Systems Manager
GREATER LANSING CONVENTION & VISITORS BUREAU, 235
Boughton, Debra Executive Associate Athletic Director
MARSHALL UNIVERSITY ATHLETICS, 336
Bouko, Darren Manager Business Development
HOCKEY HALL OF FAME AND MUSEUM, 252
Boulay, Pat President
SHOOTING FEDERATION OF CANADA, 150
Boulerice, Pierre Vice President
RESEAU DU SPORTETUDIANT DU QUEBEC, 203
Boulton, Frank Principal Owner
ATLANTIC LEAGUE, 35, 948, 949
Bouma, Glenn Athletics Director
DORDT COLLEGE ATHLETICS, 312
Bounds, Martin VP Business Development
STREET & SMITH'S SPORTSBUSINESS JOURNAL, 587
Bounsall, Phil Treasurer
SPECIAL OLYMPICS INDIANA, 195
Bourg, Michelle Co-Editor & Features Writer
WINGFOOT, 592
Bourgeois, Beth Director, Communications
U.S. OLYMPIC COMMITTEE BROADCASTING DIVISION, 603
Bourgeois, Pat President/CEO
SPECIAL OLYMPICS LOUISIANA, 195
Bourgerie, Alexia Principal
STEIN, SPERLING, BENNETT, DE JONG, DRISCOLL & GREENFEIG, P.C., 908
Bouris, Greg Director Communications
MAJOR LEAGUE BASEBALL PLAYERS ASSOCIATION, 842
Bourke, Kevin Chief Creations Officer
IOWA GAMES, 262
Bourne, David Special Reports Editor
SPORTS BUSINESS JOURNAL, 584
Bourne, Jeff Director of Athletics
JAMES MADISON UNIVERSITY ATHLETICS, 333
Bourne, Jenny Faculty Athletic Representative
CARLETON COLLEGE ATHLETICS, 379
Bourne, Richard President
ASICS AMERICA CORPORATION, 1100
Bourque, Peter Assistant Athletic Director
CATAWBA COLLEGE ATHLETICS, 354
Bourquin, Bruce Sports Reporter
SIERRA VISTA HERALD, 531
Bourrie, Eric Sales Representative
H E HODGE COMPANY, 1141
Bousfield, Jeff Associate
GLASS ARCHITECTS, 1057
Bouska, Dan Equipment Manager
UNITED STATES HOCKEY LEAGUE, 138
Boutcher, David Chair of Business & Finance Department
REED SMITH, 901
Boutillier, Carol Office Administrator
LAYMAN, MICHAEL L., 889
Boutin, Stephen Founder
BOUTIN, DENTINO, GIBSON, DI GUISTO, HODELL, INC., 867
Bouvier, Arthur Director of Stadium Operations
G. RICHARD PFITZNER STADIUM, 967
Bouyea, Brien Communications coordinator
NATIONAL MUSEUM OF RACING HALL OF FAME, 256
Bouza, David President
STRENGTH SYSTEMS, INC., 1197
Bouza, Kevin Marketing / Operations VP
STRENGTH SYSTEMS, INC., 1197
Bouzidi, Karim Executive Director
INTERNATIONAL BOXING ASSOCIATION (AIBA), 67
Bove, Jeffrey Partner
DURANTE, CHARLES J., 877
Bovee, Jerry Deputy AD, External Affairs
UTAH STATE UNIVERSITY ATHLETICS, 348, 961
Bowden, Paul Associate AD, Student-Athlete Support Se
HOWARD UNIVERSITY ATHLETICS, 332
Bowditch, Fred Manager
CROAKIES, 1121

Bozeka, George President
PROFESSIONAL FOOTBALL RESEARCHERS ASSOCIATION, 89

Bozic, Petar Head Coach
NATIONAL BASKETBALL ASSOCIATION DEVELOPMENT LEAGUE, 58

Bozich, Mike Ass. Director of Operations
HAZEL PARK HARNESS RACEWAY (HPHR), 1039

Bozich, Richard Sports Columnist
COURIER-JOURNAL, 474

Bozzuto, Barbara Partner
LOWENSTEIN EVENT MARKETING GROUP, 793

Bozzuto, Bob Field Manager
FRONTIER LEAGUE, 41

Braaten, Renelle Founder and President
ENELL, INC., 1129

Brabury, Kevin Sr. VP , Player Relations
BDA SPORTS MANAGEMENT, 826

Braccini, Rosanna Director of Special Projects and Publica
HAMPTON CLASSIC HORSE SHOW, 75

Brace, Paul Partner
BERTUZZI, LAWRENCE, 866

Brace, Rick Vice President
CTV TELEVISION NETWORK LTD., 598

Bracken, Adam Assistant Athletic Director
ASHLAND UNIVERSITY ATHLETICS, 351

Bracken, Frank President / Chief Operating Officer
HAGGAR CORPORATION, 1141

Bracken, Sherri Regional Director of Administration
BINGHAM MCCUTCHEN LLP, 866

Brackin, Dennis Sports Team Leader
STAR TRIBUNE, 534

Bradburn, Jim Architect/Principal
FENTRESS ARCHITECTS, 1056

Bradbury, Jonathan Director of Athletics
MARYGROVE COLLEGE ATHLETICS, 336

Bradbury, Kevin Player Representation VP
BDA SPORTS MANAGEMENT, 826

Braden, Tracey Senior Women's Administrator
WESTMINSTER COLLEGE (MO) ATHLETICS, 406

Bradford, Cindy Office Manager
INTERNATIONAL MOTOR SPORTS HALL OF FAME, 253

Bradford, Demp VP of Operations
GREENSBORO SPORTS COMMISSION, 235

Bradford, Donna Director Operations
RED MILE, THE, 1043

Bradford, Hugh Director, Coaching
WOMEN'S PREMIER SOCCER LEAGUE, 166

Bradford, John Head Coach & Sporting Director
USL LEAGUE TWO, 161, 163

Bradford, Katie Chairman
INDUSTRIAL FABRICS ASSOCIATION INTERNATIONAL, 220

Bradford, Keith Sports Editor
CALGARY HERALD, 467

Bradford, Neil National Director of Coaching
SOCCER ASSOCIATION FOR YOUTH, 267

Bradford, William President/CEO
ADOLFSON & PERTSON, INC., 1048

Bradlet-Doppes, Peg Vice Chancellor for Athletics and Recrea
DENVER, UNIVERSITY OF, 416

Bradley, Ann Associate University Counsel
DUKE LEGAL COUNSEL, 877

Bradley, Ann Partner
DUANE MORRIS LLP, 877

Bradley, Barry Managing partner
BRADLEY & GMELICH, 867

Bradley, Brock Head Equipment Manager
UNITED STATES HOCKEY LEAGUE, 138

Bradley, Gary Partner
BRADLEY & GMELICH, 867

Bradley, Jeff Senior Writer
ESPN THE MAGAZINE, 558

Bradley, Joe Producer
THE JOHN CORBY SHOW, 607

Bradley, John Special Contributor
SPORTS ILLUSTRATED, 585

Bradley, Kay Athletic Administrative Assistant
PERKINS STADIUM, 992

Bradley, Kirby Senior Producer
REAL SPORTS WITH BRYANT GUMBEL, 685

Bradley, Lindy Partner
BRADLEY & GMELICH, 867

Bradley, Michael Treasurer
U.S. LIFESAVING ASSOCIATION, 173

Bradley, Scott Senior Advisor to the General Manager
NATIONAL HOCKEY LEAGUE/NHL, 123, 655, 662

Bradley, Shawn VP/Chief Operating Officer
BONHAM GROUP, INC., 776

Bradley, Steve Sports Assistant Editor
DEMOCRAT AND CHRONICLE, 482

Bradley, Tom Box Office Manager
USF SUN DOME, 487, 756, 1014

Bradley, Tracy Executive Director
ORIENTEERING CANADA, 206

Bradley, Valerie Communications Manager
MACON-BIBB COUNTY CONVENTION AND VISITORS BUREAU, 240

Bradshaw, Ali Director,Ticket Sales
HOMESTEAD-MIAMI SPEEDWAY, LLC, 1025

Bradshaw, Bill Interim Director of Athletics
MCCARTHY STADIUM, 985

Bradshaw, Gayle Executive Vice President, Rules & Compet
ATP WORLD TOUR, 174

Bradway, Amy AV/Video Sales
DRAPER INC., 1125

Bradwisch, Todd Torch Run Liaison
SPECIAL OLYMPICS SOUTH DAKOTA, 197

Brady, Charles Sports Editor
MONETT TIMES, 508

Brady, Chris Staff Writer
STANDARD-JOURNAL, 534

Brady, Erik Sports Features Reporter
USA TODAY, 543

Brady, J. Principal/Director
CSHQA ARCHITECTS/ENGINEERS/PLANNERS, 1053

Brady, Joe Associate Athletic Director
CLARK UNIVERSITY ATHLETICS, 380

Brady, Kevin Export Sales Manager
KEYS FITNESS PRODUCTS, 945, 1152

Brady, Rick Sports & Training Coordinator
SPECIAL OLYMPICS MICHIGAN, 195

Braff, Lee Editor
HEARTLAND BOATING, 563

Bragg, Beth Sports Editor
ANCHORAGE DAILY NEWS, 460

Braginsky, Sidney Director
AIRCAST, INC., 1094

Braig, Robin President
DAYTONA INTERNATIONAL SPEEDWAY, 1024

Brailsford, Allen EVP Operations
SYMS, 1238

Braithwaite, Marcel Senior VP, Business Operations
AMERICAN LEAGUE OF PROFESSIONAL BASEBALL CLUBS, THE, 30

Brake, Chip National Sales Manager
EMERGENCY MEDICAL SUPPLY, 1128

Bram, Jim President
NATIONAL ASSOCIATION OF UNDERWATER INSTRUCTORS, 222

Bramble, Todd Deputy AD, Intercollegiate Sports
GEORGE MASON UNIVERSITY ATHLETICS, 331

Bramer, Jenny Executive Associate AD/SWA
SAN DIEGO STATE UNIVERSITY ATHLETICS, 343

Bramlett, Cab Design Engineer
GENERAL SPORTS VENUE ASTROTURF, 1137

Bramlett, Dale HESRM Senior Secretary
MISSISSIPPI, UNIVERSITY OF, 427

Bramucci, Lino Vice President Sales
LE RESEAU DES SPORTS (RSD) INC., 698

Bramwell, Tom President
MECA SPORTSWEAR, INC., 1161

Branch, Andrea Executive Assistant
UNIVERSITY OF NORTH CAROLINA PEMBROKE ATHLETICS(UNCP), 366

Branch, Barclay Vice President, Hockey Operations
ONTARIO HOCKEY LEAGUE, 133

Branch, Dallas Sport Management Program Coordinator
WEST VIRGINIA UNIVERSITY, 437

Branch, John Associate Athletics Director, External A
WILLIAM R. JOHNSON COLISEUM, 511, 971, 1019

Branch, Tonia Publisher & Editor
MICHIGAN LINKS, 570

Branch, Trisha Ticket Manager
ARMED FORCES BOWL, 89

Branchaud, Mike Manager - National Teams/Canadian Champi
SOFTBALL CANADA, 170

Brand, Elton General Manager
NATIONAL BASKETBALL ASSOCIATION/NBA, 57

Brand, Faye Sales & Marketing Manager
GOALSETTER SYSTEMS, INC., 1138

Brand, Matt Senior VP, Corporate Partnerships
AMERICAN LEAGUE OF PROFESSIONAL BASEBALL CLUBS, THE, 30

Brand, Scott President
FEDERAL PROSPECTS HOCKEY LEAGUE (FPHL), 131

Brand, Stan Vice President
ISOTOPES PARK, 972, 974

Brandel, Norma President & Executive Director
AMERICAN AUTO RACING WRITERS AND BROADCASTERS ASSOCIATION, 15

Brandenburg, Tricia Deputy Director of Athletics/SWA
TOWSON STATE UNIVERSITY ATHLETICS, 347

Brandes, Steve President
NATIONAL BASKETBALL ASSOCIATION DEVELOPMENT LEAGUE, 60

Brandl, Tara Advertising Manager
MARSHALL INDEPENDENT, 505

Brandon, Russ Business Development/Marketing VP
RALPH WILSON STADIUM, 995

Brandon, Steve Sports Editor
PORTLAND TRIBUNE, 521

Brandstaedter, Michael President/Chief Operating Officer
TOPPS COMPANY, INC., 1202

Brandstatter, Jim Sports
WJR-AM, 652

Brandstetter, Konstantin Executive Vice President
BOGNER, 1109

Brandt, Andy Head Coach/General Manager
UNITED STATES HOCKEY LEAGUE, 137

Brandt, Thomas EVP / Co-Chief Executive Officer
FAIRTRON, 1131

Branecky, Paul Vice President, Marketing & Communicatio
AMERICAN HOCKEY LEAGUE/AHL, 127

Brannan, Mark Sports Reporter
WPAX-AM, 660

Brannberg, Joe Project Manager
CCI SOLUTIONS, 820

Brannen, Connie Operations Manager
EQUIBASE COMPANY, 928

Branner, Wade Associate AD, Athletic Communications
VIRGINIA MILITARY INSTITUTE ATHLETICS, 348

Brannon, Britni Assistant Athletic Director
CENTRAL OKLAHOMA ATHLETICS, UNIVERSITY OF, 354

Brannon, Ed Sports Editor
DERRICK, 482

Branon, Lisa Athletic Trianer
PAINE COLLEGE, 367

Branson, Bix Vice President
FRONTIER LEAGUE, 40

Branson, Paulette Executive Director
BLACK WOMEN IN SPORT FOUNDATION, 218

Brant, Doug President
BETA DESIGN GROUP, INC., 1050

Brant, Joel Attorney
KATZ, TELLER, BRANT & HILD, 887

Brant, Joseph Of Counsel
KATZ, TELLER, BRANT & HILD, 887

Brant, Robert Attorney
KATZ, TELLER, BRANT & HILD, 887

Brant, Ryan Sports Director
WKEF-TV, 705

Brown, Vanessa Managing Director
NEW ENGLAND SPORTS NETWORK/NSEN, 676

Brown, William Chair & Chief Executive Officer
3M, 725

Brown, Yolanda Assistant Athletic Director
TOUGALOO COLLEGE ATHLETICS, 322

Brown, Zak CEO
FORMULA 1, 20, 791

Brown-Lemm, Ginger Communications Director
WOMEN'S GOLF COACHES ASSOCIATION, 118

Browne, Chris General Manager
COMMUNITYAMERICA BALLPARK, 959

Browne, Joe EVP Communications
NATIONAL FOOTBALL LEAGUE, 844

Browne, Michael Editor
DIRT RAG, 556

Brownell, Greg Sports Editor
POST-STAR, 521

Brownell, Rick Associate Director of Athletics
ARCADIA UNIVERSITY ATHLETICS
DEPARTMENT-GLENSIDE, 377

Browning, Chris President
DARLINGTON RACEWAY, 1024

Browning, Jesse Principal
COOKE DOUGLASS FARR LEMONS/LTD., 1052

Browning, Joe Senior Associate AD,
Communications
NORTH CAROLINA WILMINGTON
ATHLETICS, UNIVERSITY OF, 339

Browning, Steve Director of Athletics
WILKINS STADIUM, 1018

Brownlee, Don Executive Director
KANSAS RACING AND GAMING
COMMISSION, 80

Brownlee, Rick Executive Director
MANITOBA SPORTS HALL OF FAME &
MUSEUM INC., 255

Brownlow, Kathy Manager of Operations
NATIONAL ASSOCIATION OF UNDERWATER
INSTRUCTORS, 222

Brownrout, Todd Advertising Senior VP
LOS ANGELES TIMES, 503

Brownstein, Glenn Sports Assistant Editor
COURIER-JOURNAL, 474

Broy, Tom President
INDEPENDENT BOATBUILDERS INC., 63

Broyles, Beverly Executive Director
ROCKFORD AREA CONVENTION & VISITORS
BUREAU, 244

Broyles, Tim General Manager
INDYCAR, 22

Brubacher, Don Director of Athletics
HILLSDALE COLLEGE ATHLETICS, 360

Brubaker, Andy Director of Development
NJCAA REGION XVII MEN'S, 289

Bruce, Harris CEO
U.S. TAEKWONDO UNION, 143

Bruce, Keith Chief Marketing Officer
SPORTSMARK MANAGEMENT GROUP, 762

Bruce, Kenny President
NATIONAL MOTORSPORTS PRESS
ASSOCIATION, 256

Bruce, Norman President
GRANADA PITCHING MACHINES, 1140

Bruce, Peter Of Counsel
DAVIS & KUELTHAU, S.C., 875

Bruce, Randy Sports Assistant Editor
COMMERCIAL APPEAL, 472

Bruce, Sam Assistant Editor
LIVING ABOARD MAGAZINE, 568

Bruce, Sheila Vice President, Sales
FOX SPORTS NETWORKS/FOX SPORTS
NET, 675

Bruce, Steve Director of Athletics
INDIANA UNIVERSITY SOUTH BEND
ATHLETICS, 314

Bruce, Thomas Director Legal Information
Institute
BRIGGS, BUCK, 868

Bruchey, Bob Director of Community Affairs
SOUTH ATLANTIC LEAGUE (A LEVEL), 51

Bruckner, Wally Sports Reporter
WRC-TV, 708

Brudenell, Mike Sports Staff Writer
DETROIT FREE PRESS, 483

Bruder, Kevin Chief Executive Officer
EAST COAST HOCKEY LEAGUE/ECHL, 130

Bruebaker, Bruce Director, Human Resource
SUNLAND PARK RACETRACK & CASINO, 1044

Brueggeman, Steve Chief Financial Officer
WESTERN GOLF ASSOCIATION, EVANS
SCHOLARS FOUNDATION, 118

Brueggemann, Chuck Athletic Director
MCKENDREE UNIVERSITY ATHLETICS, 363

Bruelisauer, Jolanda Assistant To President
FEDERATION INTERNATIONALE DE SKI
(FIS), 203

Bruenjes, Don Head Athletic Trainer
CONCORDIA COLLEGE (MN) ATHLETICS, 381

Bruffett, Darryl Sports Director
KBTX-TV, 688

Bruggeman, Jared Director of Athletics
MISSOURI SOUTHERN STATE UNIVERSITY
ATHLETICS, 364

Bruggen, Kim CEO
TRIATHLON CANADA, 178

Bruggen, Mikeee Director of Sports Medicine
CARSON-NEWMAN COLLEGE ATHLETICS, 353

Bruggenthies, George General
Manager/President
ROAD AMERICA, 1031

Brugger, Jenny Officer Coordinator
WORLD ARCHERY FEDERATION, 15

Bruha, Brian Director of Athletic Facilities
LAKE FOREST COLLEGE ATHLETICS, 390

Brukoff, William Senior Shareholder
ROLAND, LENORA, R., 903

Brule, David Executive Committee
U.S. NATIONAL SKI HALL OF FAME &
MUSEUM, 259

Brulport, Lisa Executive Assistant
USA CRICKET ASSOCIATION, 69

Brumage, Glenn Vice President
INTERNATIONAL ASSOCIATION OF
SKATEBOARD COMPANIES, 151

Brumfield, Dennis Treasurer
U.S. YOUTH SOCCER ASSOCIATION, 267

Brumfield, Victoria Executive Director
KORFF ENTERPRISES, 758

Brummel, Steve Associate Athletic Director
Facilities
WESTERN WASHINGTON UNIVERSITY
ATHLETICS (WWU), 375

Brummell, Sharon Exec. Senior Associate Ad,
Business & Fi
GEORGETOWN UNIVERSITY ATHLETICS, 331

Brummer, Terry Chief Operating Officer
STINSON MORRISON HECKER LLP, 908

Brundage, Dale Manager
INTERNATIONAL LEAGUE, 42

Brunelle, Aimee Athletic Trainer
NJCAA REGION III MEN'S, 286

Bruner, Simeon Founding Principal
BRUNER/COTT & ASSOCIATES INC., 1051

Bruneteau, Matt Associate Head Coach
UNITED STATES HOCKEY LEAGUE, 137

Bruneteau, Nick Head Coach
NORTH AMERICAN HOCKEY LEAGUE, 133

Brunette, Andrew Head Coach
NATIONAL HOCKEY LEAGUE/NHL, 125

Brunetti, John Chairman
HIALEAH PARK RACING & CASINO, 1040

Brunetz, Courtney Marketing Director
TENNESSEE SECONDARY SCHOOL
ATHLETIC ASSOCIATION, 202

Brunfelt, Mitch Secretary
U.S. HOCKEY HALL OF FAME, 259

Brungardt, Noreen Business Manager
BRUNGARDT ENTERPRISES, L.L.C., 1051

Brungardt, Peter Owner
BRUNGARDT ENTERPRISES, L.L.C., 1051

Brunham, Malin Chairman
BURNHAM REAL ESTATE SERVICES, 1051

Bruni, Robert Vice President Sales
PROJECT SPORTS MARKETING, 803

Bruning, Robert Chief Financial Officer
COBRA PUMA GOLF, 1117

Bruning, Steve Director of Athletics
CAPITAL UNIVERSITY ATHLETICS, 379

Brunk, David Commissioner
PEACH BELT ATHLETIC CONFERENCE, 303

Brunker, Maria Registrar/Treasurer
PACIFIC SOUTHWEST ASSOCIATION, 215

Brunker, Michael Governor
PACIFIC SOUTHWEST ASSOCIATION, 215

Brunner, Debbie Advertising Manager
POST-JOURNAL, 521

Brunner, Jim Sports Director
WGOM-AM, 648

Bruno, Anthony Senior VP & Yankee Global
Enterprises CF
AMERICAN LEAGUE OF PROFESSIONAL
BASEBALL CLUBS, THE, 30

Bruno, Christopher Partner/Attorney
BRUNO, CHRISTOPHER J., 869

Bruno, Howard General Manager
FREEHOLD RACEWAY, 1038

Bruno, James VP/Shareholder
BUTZEL LONG, A PROFESSIONAL
CORPORATION, 870

Bruno, Joseph Managing Partner
BRUNO, CHRISTOPHER J., 869

Bruno, Tony Host - Morning Show
WPEN-AM, 610, 661

Bruns, Bob Associate Director
METHODIST COLLEGE PROFESSIONAL
GOLF MANAGEMENT PROGRAM, 103

Brunsdon, Melanie Assistant Director of Athletics
BELLARMINE UNIVERSITY ATHLETICS, 352

Brunson, Burlie President and Chief Operating
Officer De
GEORGE WASHINGTON UNIVERSITY - THE
GW SCHOOL OF BUSINESS, 419

Brunson, Dennis Sports Editor
ITEM, 497

Brunson, Lori Vice President of Finance
ATLANTIC LEAGUE, 35

Brunswick, Tim Vice President, Baseball &
Business Oper
ISOTOPES PARK, 27, 41, 972, 974

Brusati, Jeff Director
SPORTING GOODS AGENTS ASSOCIATION, 224

Bruser, Diane Assistant Director
MISSISSIPPI HS ACTIVITIES ASSOCIATION, 200

Brush, Craig President & Arena CEO
EAST COAST HOCKEY LEAGUE/ECHL, 129

Brush, Richard Dean
JOHNSON & WALES UNIVERSITY
SPORTS/ENTERTAINMENT & EVENT
MANAGEMEN, 422

Brutsche, Dominique Assistant
BECHTA, JACK D./JB SPORTS, 826

Bruuns, Clark Marketing/Promotions Manager
RED MC EWEN BASEBALL FIELD, 996

Bruxvoort, Kent President
DIXIE YOUTH BASEBALL, 26

Bryan, Charity VP Research
NATIONAL ASSOCIATION FOR GIRLS AND
WOMEN IN SPORT, 221

Bryan, Harry Sports Editor
COURIER-JOURNAL, 474

Bryan, Jeff Director
BOTTELSEN DART COMPANY, 1109

Bryan, Royce Athletic Director
BARCLAY COLLEGE ATHLETICS, 351

Bryan, Tanya CEO & Founder
WOMEN'S FOOTBALL ALLIANCE / WFA, 97

Bryan-Labega, Jacinth Second Vice President
WORLD BOXING ORGANIZATION, 67

Bryant, BJ Secretary
BADGER REGIONAL VOLLEYBALL
ASSOCIATION/USA VOLLEYBALL, 210

Bryant, Barbara Chief Marketing Officer
TAULBEE, GEORGE M., 911

Bryant, Billy Sports Executive Editor
HUNTSVILLE TIMES, 495

Bryant, Brandi Associate AD, Student-Athlete
Services
STEPHEN F. AUSTIN STATE UNIVERSITY
ATHLETICS, 345

Bryant, Cedric Chief Science Officer
AMERICAN COUNCIL ON EXERCISE, 83

Bryant, Clint Director of Athletics
AUGUSTA STATE UNIVERSITY ATHLETICS, 351

Bryant, Cynthia Director
CALEXPO, 1023

Bryant, Geoff President
UNITED STATES GOLF TEACHERS
FEDERATION, 118
Bryant, Jennifer Editor
USDF CONNECTION, 590
Bryant, John Commissioner
PUGET SOUND REGIONAL
COMMISSIONER/USA VOLLEYBALL, 212
Bryant, Karen Chief Administrative Officer
WOMEN'S NATIONAL BASKETBALL
ASSOCIATION, 60
Bryant, Keith Chief Executive Officer
USA JUDO, 209
Bryant, Larry Governor
ARKANSAS AAU ASSOCIATION, 213
Bryant, Leroy Sports Editor
INDIANA HERALD, 496
Bryant, Mark Director of Multimedia Development
BIG SOUTH CONFERENCE, 292
Bryant, Philip Commissioner
GULF COAST REGIONAL
COMMISSIONER/USA VOLLEYBALL, 211
Bryant, Richard President
INDIANA FOOTBALL HALL OF FAME, 253
Bryant, Rick VP
SUNFLOWER STATE GAMES, 264
Bryant, Rusty Executive Director & General
Manager
USL LEAGUE TWO, 163
Bryant, Sam Vice President
UNITED STATES GOLF TEACHERS
FEDERATION, 118
Bryant, Stanley President
GEAR PRO-TEC, 1137
Bryant, Steve President, Majority Owner
CAROLINA LEAGUE, 36, 37, 806
Bryant, Tom President
STAIRMASTER HEALTH AND FITNESS
PRODUCTS, 1196
Bryce, Charles Sports Editor
SAN ANGELO STANDARD TIMES, 527
Bryce, Lisa Business Manager
KGSO 1410 SPORTS RADIO, 605
Brye, Benji Custom Products & Service Specialist
BEACON ATHLETICS, 1218
Brylin, Sergei Assistant Coach
NATIONAL HOCKEY LEAGUE/NHL, 125
Brylinsky, Jody Dept. Professor
WESTERN MICHIGAN UNIVERSITY, 437
Bryne, Richard Chief Executive Officer
SPEEDPLAY, INC., 1192
Brysha, Andre VP / Chief Marketing Officer
BOATER'S WORLD, 1220
Brzeski, Lisa Executive Assistant, Revenue
NATIONAL LEAGUE OF PROFESSIONAL
BASEBALL CLUBS, THE, 32
Brzezinski, Rob Executive VP, Football
Operations
NATIONAL FOOTBALL LEAGUE/NFL, 95
Brzóstowski, Sammy Ticket Office Manager
VETERANS MEMORIAL STADIUM (CEDAR
RAPIDS), 1016
Bubach, Brian Associate Director
NORTH DAKOTA HS ACTIVITIES
ASSOCIATION, 201
Bubb, Paul Administration - Associate AD -
External
ROY STEWART STADIUM, 995, 999
Bubb, Sean Executive Director
WOMEN'S PREMIER SOCCER LEAGUE, 166
Buccelli, Tod Marketing/Promotion Director
WIAT - CBS 42, 704
Bucci, Dan General Manager
LINCOLN PARK, 1046
Bucci, Steve Sports Reporter
KYW-TV, 698
Bucciarelli, Brain Vice President
ASSOCIATION OF LUXURY SUITE
DIRECTORS, 218
Buccilli, Tony Director of Team Operations
NATIONAL PRO FASTPITCH, 171
Buchalter, Carol Chairman
PARKER LABORATORIES, INC., 1172
Buchalter, Neal President
PARKER LABORATORIES, INC., 1172
Buchan, Jim Sports Editor
WALLA WALLA UNION-BULLETIN, 545

Buchan, Mary Assoc. Athletics Director/Fiscal
Operati
WAYNE STATE UNIVERSITY, 436
Buchan, Ryan Sports Editor
DODGE CITY DAILY GLOBE, 484
Buchan, Stephem Associate Program Director /
Adjunct Pro
LONG BEACH STATE UNIVERSITY, 423
Buchanan, Chad General Manager
NATIONAL BASKETBALL ASSOCIATION/NBA,
57
Buchanan, Eugene Publisher
PADDLER, 575
Buchanan, Ginger Promotions Director
KBEE-FM, 613
Buchanan, Kathy Director Of Computer Services
U.S. PROFESSIONAL TENNIS ASSOCIATION,
175
Buchanan, Megan Associate Athletic Director
SKIDMORE COLLEGE ATHLETICS, 400
Buchanan, Matthew Principal
FLEWELLING & MOODY, 1057
Buchanan, Michael Sports Anchor
WTRP-AM, 669
Buchanan, Mike News Director
KBIZ-AM, 614
Buchanan, Rusty
FLORIDA'S SPACE COAST OFFICE OF
TOURISM, 234
Buchanan, Sally Program Director
WPRZ-AM, 662
Buchanan, Sharon National Sales Manager
WMAQ TV CHICAGO, 706
Buchanan, Teresa Purchasing Executive
KING LOUIE INTERNATIONAL, INC., 1152
Buchanan, Thomas President
BAKER, DAVID L., 863
Buchanan, Zack Sports Editor
DAILY NEWS (WA), 478
Buche, Time President and CEO
MOTORCYCLE SAFETY FOUNDATION, 144
Bucher, Christine Senior Editor
BICYCLING, 552
Bucher, Ric Senior Writer
ESPN THE MAGAZINE, 558
Buchko, Garth President and Chief Executive
Officer
THE WINNIPEG BLUE BOMBERS, 1009
Buchman, Bruce Treasurer
SUN COUNTRY AMATEUR GOLF
ASSOCIATION, 116
Buchner, Mary Assistant To The VP For Athletics
COKER COLLEGE ATHLETICS, 355
Bucholz, Seymour Of Counsel
GARVEY, SCHUBERT & BARER, 881
Buck, C CEO
BUCK KNIVES, INC., 1111
Buck, Chad Interim Vice President, Business
Operati
AMERICAN HOCKEY LEAGUE/AHL, 128
Buck, Charles President
BUCK KNIVES, INC., 1111
Buck, Charles Chairman / Chief Executive Officer
BUCK KNIVES, INC., 1111
Buck, David Assistant Athletic Director
UNIVERSITY OF FINDLAY (UF) ATHLETICS,
358
Buck, Fred Partner
RAWLE LAW OFFICES, 901
Buck, John EVP
FINGERHUT COMPANIES, INC., 1227
Buck, Kelcey Sports Information Director
WASHINGTON UNIVERSITY ATHLETICS, 405
Buck, Michele President & CEO
THE HERSHEY CO., 733
Buck, Ray Sports Columnist
FORT WORTH STAR-TELEGRAM, 489
Buck, Rogers General Manager
HUNTSVILLE STARS, 972
Buckert, Brad Owner
BEGNI'RS TO PRO'S, 1218
Buckingham, Bill Director Of Member Services
U.S. SQUASH, 171
Buckingham, Jackie Chief Executive Officer
SYNCHRO CANADA, 173
Buckle, Alan Deputy Chairman
KPMG CONVENTION, SPORTS &
ENTERTAINMENT PRACTICE, 758

Buckles, Nick Group Chief Executive
WACKENHUT SPORTS SECURITY, 766
Buckley, Bredan Booking & Scheduling Director
VALUE CITY ARENA/JEROME
SCHOTTENSTEIN CENTER, 1015
Buckley, Clint Sports Reporter
TYLER MORNING TELEGRAPH, 542
Buckley, Donald EVP, Program Marketing, Digital
Services
SHOWTIME SPORTS, 678
Buckley, George Chairman / Chief Executive
Officer
BRUNSWICK CORPORATION, 1111
Buckley, Mike Goaltending Coach
NATIONAL HOCKEY LEAGUE/NHL, 124
Buckley, Nick General Sports
BATTLE CREEK ENQUIRER, 463
Buckley, Sheila Publisher
SPORTS ILLUSTRATED, 585
Buckley, Steve Sports Columnist
BOSTON HERALD, 466
Buckley, Tim Sports Writer
DESERET MORNING NEWS, 483
Bucklin-Webber, Shari Men's and Women's
Tennis Head Coach
MILLERVILLE UNIVERSITY, 427
Buckman, Franki Vice President
FIREBIRD INTERNATIONAL RACEWAY, 1025
Buckner, Jack CEO
BRITISH TRIATHLON ASSOCIATION, 178
Buckner, Wanda Advertising Manager
SAMPSON INDEPENDENT, 527
Buczkowski, Michael Vice President/General
Manager
INTERNATIONAL LEAGUE, 42, 958
Budd, Sarah Director, Ticket Operations &
Community
NEW YORK-PENNSYLVANIA LEAGUE, 47,
948
Budd, TJ Sports Information Director
PALM BEACH ATLANTIC UNIVERSITY
ATHLETICS(PBA), 367
Buddie, Mike Director of Athletics
U.S. MILITARY ACADEMY ATHLETICS, 347
Budenholzer, Mike Head Coach
NATIONAL BASKETBALL ASSOCIATION/NBA,
57
Budig, Dr. Co-Owner
JOSEPH P. RILEY PARK, 978
Budine, Marc Interactive/Online Sales Manager
SPORTS TALK/THE TICKET, 606
Budman, Michael Co-Founder
ROOTS APPAREL, 1183
Budz, Tracey Public Relations
LIFE PRIORITY, INC., 1155
Buechele, Mark General Manager
ABC FLAG MANUFACTURING CO., 1090
Buehler, Gary Treasurer
NATIONAL HORSESHOE PITCHERS
ASSOCIATION, 139
Buehler, Jana Academic Learning Specialist
WAGNER FIELD/KSU, 1017
Buehner, Jim Owner
EXCLUSIVELY EXPO, INC., 1130
Buehner, Marie Marketing Manager
EXCLUSIVELY EXPO, INC., 1130
Buelow, Bob Sales / Marketing Director
SETCOM CORPORATION, 1187
Buendorf, Larry Chief Security Officer
HAMAKAWA, CURT L., 837
Bueno, Luis Sports Columnist
PRESS-ENTERPRISE (CA), 522
Buerger, Mark Communications Director
SPECIAL OLYMPICS KENTUCKY, 195
Buetel, Barry Sports Director
WTEV-TV, 710
Buether, Eric Shareholder
DALTON, MICHAEL, 875
Buffett, Warren Chief Executive Officer
BERKSHIRE HATHAWAY, INC., 726
Buffington, Douglas President / Chief Operating
Officer
WOMEN'S GOLF UNLIMITED, INC., 1211
Buford, Durrell Associate Superintendent,
Athletics Grou
VAUGHT-HEMINGWAY
STADIUM/HOLLINGSWORTH FIELD, 1015

Byrne, Aidan Head Coach
USL LEAGUE TWO, 161

Byrne, Colin Chief Executive Officer, Weber Shandwick
WEBER SHANDWICK WORLDWIDE, 816

Byrne, Dave Sports Reporter
SUNDAY NEWS, 536

Byrne, David General Manager
PERFORMANCE SPORTS SYSTEMS, INC., 1173

Byrne, Greg Director, Athletics
ALABAMA ATHLETICS, UNIVERSITY OF, 324, 970, 986

Byrne, John Associate Athletics Director
MORAVIAN COLLEGE ATHLETICS, 394, 748

Byrne, Patrick Director of Sales and Marketing
LIBERTY BOWL MEMORIAL STADIUM, 983

Byrne, Peter Sports Anchor
WSBT-TV, 709

Byrne, Ted Operations Manager
CHARLESTON SPORTS RADIO, 605

Byrnes, Austin Sports Information Director
SAINT MARTIN'S COLLEGE ATHLETICS, 369

Byrnes, Daniel Director, Sports Facilities & Recreation
WORTHEN ARENA (WR), 1020

Byrnes, Jenna Senior Vice President
PACIFIC COAST LEAGUE OF PROFESSIONAL BASEBALL CLUBS, 49

Byrnes, Josh Sr. Vice President, Baseball Operations
DODGER STADIUM, 962

Byrnes, Kevin Vice President Advertising Sales
GOLF CHANNEL, THE, 599, 687

Byrnes, Michael President/General Manager
PACIFIC COAST LEAGUE OF PROFESSIONAL BASEBALL CLUBS, 49

Byron, Francis General Counsel
METROPOLITAN AMATEUR GOLF ASSOCIATION, 113

Bytheway, Sam General Manager
USL LEAGUE TWO, 161

Bytomski, Jeff First Vice President
AMERICAN OSTEOPATHIC ACADEMY OF SPORTS MEDICINE, 83

C

C C Alkire, John Chief Executive Officer
BIG FRESNO FAIR (BFF), 1036

C Comer , Gary Founder
LANDS' END, INC., 1154

C Horner Jr, Richard President
BRISTOL ATHLETIC, 1110

C Meads , Mindy Merchandising Design EVP
LANDS' END, INC., 1154

C S Lemons, Bruce President
FORESITE DESIGN, INC., 1057

C Ver. Halen, Peter Of Counsel
SOROY, H. MICHAEL, 907

C. Burke Sr, William SVP, Chief Financial Officer
TITLEIST (COBRA/PINNACLE), 1201

C. C. Katz, Hardy Manager
SHOWPROCO, LLC, 761

C. G. Karsner, Colleen Attorney
KARSNER & MEEHAN P.C., 887

C. Hinkle II, Lawrence President
BLACK ENTERTAINMENT & SPORTS LAWYERS ASSOCIATION INC, 218

C. Jack Miller, W. Vice Chair
SHIRK STADIUM, 1002

C. Liebmann III, Herbect Partner
LIEBMANN, CONWAY, OLEJNICZAK & JERRY, 891

C. M. Beams, Christian Associate
STINSON MORRISON HECKER LLP, 908

C. M. Leite, Eduardo Chairman of execuitve board
BAKER & MCKENZIE, 863

C. P. Abeles, Daniel Member
ECKERT SEAMANS, 877

C. Pecor Jr., Raymond President
VERMONT LAKE MONSTERS, 1016

C. Poston III, Carl Agent
PROFESSIONAL SPORTS PLANNING, 850

C. Powers Jr, William President
WORLEY, JAMES G., 917

C. R. Conte, Nicholas Chairman of the Board
CARDWELL, VICTOR, 871

C. Sutton Jr., Ben President
INTERNATIONAL SPORTS PROPERTIES, INC., 789

CTA, Jay President and CEO
ANAHEIM/ORANGE COUNTY VISITOR & CONVENTION BUREAU, 227

Ca Mayo Jr, J. Partner
CONNELL, MARY ANN, 874

Caballero, Lenny Event Facilities Director
CIVIC CENTER COMPLEX, 958

Cabela, James President
CABELA'S, 1112, 1221

Cabell, Terry Sports Writer
MICHIGAN CHRONICLE, 507

Cable, Bob Associate Athletic Director
FAIRMONT STATE UNIVERSITY ATHLETICS, 358

Cable, Jason Director of Athletics
ALABAMA STATE UNIVERSITY ATHLETICS, 324

Cable, Shawn Chief Financial Officer
ANDRE AGASSI FOUNDATION FOR EDUCATION, 191

Caboni, Timothy Vice Chancellor forPublic Affairs
POTTORFF, JAMES P. JR., 900

Cabot, Mary Sports Reporter (Football)
PLAIN DEALER, 520

Cabott, Christopher Associate Attorney
ZANE MANAGEMENT, INC., 860

Cabrera, Christy High School Sports Writer
SOUTH FLORIDA SUN-SENTINEL, 532

Cabrera, Rick Sports Director
KVIA-TV, 696

Cacioppo, Jenny EVP/Managing Director
FRANKEL SPORTS GROUP, 755

Caddigan, Michelle Associate Athletic Director, Internal Op
WINGATE UNIVERSITY ATHLETICS, 375

Caddy, Kai Video Marketing Coordinator
UNIVERSITY OF CENTRAL ARKANSAS ATHLETICS, 354

Cade, Tom Senior Director of Communications & Mark
WASHINGTON STATE GOLF ASSOCIATION, 117

Cafardo, Nicholas Sports Reporter
BOSTON GLOBE, 465

Caffin, Michael Managing Editor
FACILITIES & EVENT MANAGEMENT MAGAZINE, 558

Caflisch, Robert Lawyer
CAFLISCH, ROBERT J., 827

Cagle, Susan Head of Accounting
INFINITY PRO SPORTS, 1214

Cahalane, Neil Principal
ELLENZWEIG ASSOCIATES, INC., 1055

Cahall, Diane Advertising Manager
DELAWARE STATE NEWS, 482

Cahan, Adam SVP of Mobile and Emerging Products
YAHOO! SPORTS, 715

Cahill, Alison Athletic Facilities Director
NORTHWESTERN COLLEGE (IA) ATHLETICS, 317

Cahill, Megan Director, Public Relations & Digital Med
AMERICAN HOCKEY LEAGUE/AHL, 128

Cahoon, Diane Director of Ticket Operations
RICHMOND INTERNATIONAL RACEWAY, 1031

Caillier, Bil Chairperson
PUGET SOUND REGIONAL COMMISSIONER/USA VOLLEYBALL, 212

Cain, Farrin 1ST Lt Governor
ARKANSAS AAU ASSOCIATION, 213

Cain, Sandra Executive Assistant to the President
NJCAA REGION XXI WOMEN'S, 290

Cain, Tina Business Compliance Manager
NATIONAL WHEELCHAIR BASKETBALL ASSOCIATION, 55

Caine, Paul Chief Executive Officer and Director
WESTWOODONE, 604

Cains, Isis Advertising Manager
NEWS-DISPATCH, 512

Cains, Rick Advertising Director
POST-TRIBUNE (IN), 521

Cairns, Laurie Director of Finance
CANADIAN PARALYMPIC COMMITTEE, 193

Cairns, Mike Sports Reporter
WKYC-TV, 706

Cairns, Rob Business Development VP
DACOR CORPORATION, 1122

Caithness, Kate President
WORLD CURLING FEDERATION, 70, 205

Calabrese, Amy Deputy AD/SWA
LOUISVILLE ATHLETICS, UNIVERSITY OF, 335

Calabro, Dave Sports Director
WTHR-TV, 678, 710

Calado, Manuel News Director
WJFD-FM, INC., 652

Calcara, Vincent Associate
QUATRINI, JAY, 850

Calcara, Vincenza Associate
QUATRINI, JAY, 850

Calcasola, Craig VP/Director of Events
UNITED SPORTS ASSOCIATES/USA, 815

Calder, Tom Director of Athletics & Recreation
HOMEWOOD FIELD, 971

Calderon, David Partner
BARTH, BERUS & CALDERON, LLP, 864

Caldwell, Cody Bids Specialist
DECATUR ELECTRONICS, INC., 1123

Caldwell, Dave Sports Reporter
NEW YORK TIMES, 511

Caldwell, David Promotions Manager
KTXS-TV, 696

Caldwell, Jerry EVP & General Manager
SPEEDWAY MOTORSPORTS, INC., 18, 1023, 1065

Caldwell, Kirk Partner
ASHFORD & WRISTON, 862

Caldwell, Matthew President & CEO
NATIONAL HOCKEY LEAGUE/NHL, 124

Caldwell, Paul Physician
ORTHOPAEDIC RESEARCH OF VIRGINIA, 922

Caldwell, Richard Partner Litigation
ANDREWS KURTH LLP, 862

Caldwell, Ron Sports Editor
DE SOTO TIMES TODAY, 482

Caley, Len Treasurer
NORTHERN NEVADA GOLF ASSOCIATION, 114

Calfapietra, Joe Field Manager
FRONTIER LEAGUE, 41

Calhoun, Anthony Anchor
SPORTS LOCKER, 681

Calhoun, Belinda Vice President
WOMEN'S PROFESSIONAL BILLIARD ASSOCIATION, 62

Calhoun, Grace Vice President, Atheltics & Recreation
JOHN BROWN UNIVERSITY ATHLETICS, 314

Calhoun, M. Director of Athletics and Recreation
FRANKLIN FIELD, 966

Cali, Jeff Sports Editor
ADA EVENING NEWS, 459

Caliendo, Mark Secretary
WESTERN PENNSYLVANIA GOLF ASSOCIATION, 117

Califano, Jeffrey SVP, Sportwear Product Development
MAY DEPARTMENT STORES COMPANY, THE, 1232

Calkins, Geoff Sports Columnist
COMMERCIAL APPEAL, 472

Calkins, Jeff General Manager
BLUE CROSS ARENA, 950

Calkins, Keith Host
FOX SPORTS XTRA, 679

Call, Andy Sports Reporter
REPOSITORY, 524

Call, Bob General Manager
KKFN, 621

Call, Jeff Sports Writer
DESERET MORNING NEWS, 483

Callaghan, B.J. Head Coach
MAJOR LEAGUE SOCCER, 158

Callaghan, Tyler Assistant Director
ALBERTA SCHOOLS' ATHLETIC ASSOCIATION, 199

Callahan, Amanda Assistant Athletic Director
ROGER WILLIAMS UNIVERSITY ATHLETICS, 399

Callahan, Brian Head Coach
NATIONAL FOOTBALL LEAGUE/NFL, 96

Cardwell, Derek Host
LET'S TALK RACING, 605

Cardwell, Victor Principal
CARDWELL, VICTOR, 871

Care, James Promotions Producer
WHOI-TV, 704

Caren, Gregg Sr.VP
SMG, 761, 1065

Carey, Chet Assistant General Manager/Sales
Marketin
SMITH-WILLS STADIUM, 1003

Carey, David Account Executive
PERFECT CURVE, INC., 1173

Carey, Don Owner
DON CAREY & ASSOCIATES, 1054

Carey, Harveycutter Director of Civic Facilities
SALEM CIVIC CENTER, 1000

Carey, Jack Sports Writer
USA TODAY, 543

Carey, Len Senior Vice President/Facilities
PAXRACING, 1042

Carey, Michael President
SPORTS PERSONALITIES, INC., 856

Carey, Mike President
SEIRUS SPORTS ACCESSORIES, 1187

Carey, Tim President
CHICAGOLAND SPEEDWAY, 1023

Carey, Tim President & General Manager
HAWTHORNE RACE COURSE, 1039

Carey, Wayne Vice President
DELAWARE STATE GOLF ASSOCIATION, 110

Carey, Wendy VP
SEIRUS SPORTS ACCESSORIES, 1187

Carfagna, Peter Chairman, Secretary/Treasurer
CLASSIC PARK, 958

Carfano, Steve Store Manager
ROGER DUNN GOLF SHOPS, 1236

Carfora, Joseph VP Of Sales
NIKON SPORTS & RECREATIONAL OPTICS,
1168

Cargnan, Travis Athletic Director
MAINE AT MACHIAS ATHLETICS,
UNIVERSITY OF, 315

Carideo, Chris Assistant Athletic Director
WIDENER UNIVERSITY ATHLETICS, 406

Cariello, Vince President
FREEMAN PRODUCTS, INC., 1135

Carifo, Edward Sports Editor
MARSHALL NEWS MESSENGER, 505

Caris, Bruce Sales Manager
EIGER SPORTSWEAR, INC., 1128

Carkner, Matt Head Coach & General Manager
EAST COAST HOCKEY LEAGUE/ECHL, 127,
130

Carl, Peggy Director of Athletics & Recreation
SALEM STATE COLLEGE ATHLETICS, 399

Carle, Jack Sports Editor
SENTINEL-TRIBUNE, 530

Carley, Cole President/CEO
FARGO-MOORHEAD CONVENTION &
VISITOR BUREAU, 233

Carlile, Rob Sports Director
WZCT-AM, 672

Carlin, Dan Vice President, Programming &
Research
FOX SPORTS NETWORKS/FOX SPORTS
NET, 675

Carlin, Linda Treasurer
SISKAYOU MOTOR SPEEDWAY, 1033

Carlin, Rob Sports Anchor
WVTM-TV, 712

Carlin, Trevor Founder
INDYCAR, 21, 22

Carling, Scott Advertising Manager
EQUESTRIAN, 74, 557

Carlisle, Chris Senior Vice President, Marketing
FX NETWORKS, LLC, 675

Carlisle, Doug News Director
WMFD-AM, 656

Carlisle, Jim Sports Writer
VENTURA COUNTY STAR, 544

Carlisle, Rick Head Coach
NATIONAL BASKETBALL ASSOCIATION/NBA,
57

Carlo, Louis Director, Operations
NORTHVILLE DOWNS, 1042

Carlo, Theresa CFO
WHEELSTV, 678

Carlock, Lisa Finance & Operations Director
USA BOBSLED & SKELETON, 65, 208

Carlomagno, Matthew Vice President, Human
Resources
INTERNATIONAL SPORTS PROPERTIES,
INC., 789

Carloni, Ben General Manager
NATIONAL BASKETBALL ASSOCIATION
DEVELOPMENT LEAGUE, 59

Carlsen, Tony Secretary/Treasurer
CANADIAN SOCIETY FOR PSYCHOMOTOR
LEARNING & SPORT PSYCHOLOGY, 218

Carlson, Andrew Head Athletic Trainer
JUDSON UNIVERSITY, 314

Carlson, Bob President/Founder
ARBOR, 513, 1099

Carlson, Brent Marketing / Sales Director
SEATTLE BIKE SUPPLY, 1186

Carlson, Charle Sports Editor
RENO GAZETTE-JOURNAL, 524

Carlson, Cheryl Director of Finance and Human
Resources
MIDWEST LEAGUE, 45, 1005

Carlson, Cort Executive Director
AURORA AREA CONVENTION & VISITORS
BUREAU, 228

Carlson, Debbie EVP
COLLEGE CONCEPTS, LLC., 1223

Carlson, Donald Attorney
CRIVELLO, CARLSON, MENTKOWSKI S.C.,
875

Carlson, Geri Vice President
JIFFY LINE STRIPERS, 1150

Carlson, Jenni Sports Columnist
OKLAHOMAN, 515

Carlson, Jennie Executive Vice President
YMCA USA, 85

Carlson, Jill Sports Anchor
WFLD-TV, 702

Carlson, Linda Classified Manager
DAILY SENTINEL (NY), 480

Carlson, Mark Head Coach
UNITED STATES HOCKEY LEAGUE, 137

Carlson, Matt President & Chief Executive Officer
NATIONAL SPORTING GOODS ASSOCIATION
(NSGA), 224, 285, 797

Carlson, Paula Chair, Presidents Council
IOWA INTERCOLLEGIATE ATHLETIC
CONFERENCE, 297

Carlson, Peter Promotions Manager
WCIA-TV, 700

Carlson, Richard Founder
AMERICAN WHEELCHAIR BOWLING
ASSOCIATION, 65

Carlson, Richard Attorney
HUNEGS, STONE, LENEAVE, KYAS &
THORNTON, P.A., 884

Carlson, Robert General Manager/Public
Relations
PORSCHE CARS NORTH AMERICA, 1175

Carlson, Tammy Director, Sales & Operations
UNITED STATES HOCKEY LEAGUE, 137

Carlson, W. Executive Vice President, Operations
DISH NETWORK, 686

Carlson, Zac Operations Coordinator
ROCHESTER AMATEUR SPORTS
COMMISSION, 244

Carlsson, Bo Scientific Committee
EUROPEAN ASSOCIATION FOR SPORT
MANAGEMENT, THE, 219

Carlton, Chuck Sports Reporter
DALLAS MORNING NEWS, 481

Carlton, Dawn
SKI SKOOT INC, 1189

Carlton, Dean President
BALLOON FEDERATION OF AMERICA, 13

Carlton, Jeff Sports Reporter
GREENSBORO NEWS & RECORD, 491

Carlton, Kristen Editor
PRICE MEDIA, 577

Carlton, M. Head Athletic Trainer
HANOVER COLLEGE ATHLETICS, 386

Carlton, Michelle Commissioner
KEYSTONE REGIONAL COMMISSIONER/USA
VOLLEYBALL, 211

Carlucci, Carl Chief Financial Officer/President
RED MC EWEN BASEBALL FIELD, 996

Carmack, Bryan Executive Board
WESTERN COLORADO DRAGWAY, 1035

Carmack, Lesa Booking Coordinator
ARKANSAS STATE UNIVERSITY
CONVOCATION CENTER, 947

Carmann, Kami Sports Reporter
WTVF-TV, 711

Carmel, George President
FLAGHOUSE, 1227

Carmichael, Don General Manager
WBAY - WBAY-TV 2, 699

Carmichael, Jason Director of Athletics
CALIFORNIA STATE UNIVERSITY-EAST BAY
ATHLETICS, 353

Carmichael, Kim Chief Of Staff
TEXAS UNIVERSITY INTERSCHOLASTIC
LEAGUE, 202

Carmichael, Rob Head Athletic Trainer
CULVER-STOCKTON COLLEGE ATHLETICS,
311

Carmody, Stephen Attorney
BRUNINI, GRANTHAM GROWE & HEWES,
P.L.L.C, 868

Carnahan, Scott Athletic Director
LINFIELD COLLEGE ATHLETICS, 390

Carnathan, Edward Sports Sales
LAS CRUCES CONVENTION & VISITORS
BUREAU, 238

Carneiro, Yolanda VP,Sales Development
CAREY WORLDWIDE CHAUFFERED
SERVICES, 925

Carnell, Bradley Head Coach
MAJOR LEAGUE SOCCER, 158

Carnell, Doug EVP of Operations
SPL INTEGRATED SOLUTIONS, 822

Carnes, Jenny Associate Executive Director,
Business D
SAN ANTONIO SPORTS, 245

Carnevali, Michael Personal Trainer
FITNESS PERFORMANCE CENTERS, 833

Carney, Bob Associate Athletic Director, Facilities
BRONCO STADIUM, 952

Carney, Gerard Attorney/Partner
CARNEY & TROUPE, 871

Carney, Joseph General Manager
SEABROOK PARK, 1047

Carney, Mike Executive VP, Business Operations
NATIONAL LEAGUE OF PROFESSIONAL
BASEBALL CLUBS, THE, 32

Carney, Patrick Partner
SKODA, MINOTTI & CO., 907

Carney, Wayne Executive Director
SOUTH DAKOTA HS ACTIVITIES
ASSOCIATION, 202

Carney, William President
GUSTAFSON MANUFACTURING COMPANY,
1141

Carney-DeBoard, Nan Director of Athletics
DENISON UNIVERSITY(DU)ATHLETICS, 382

Carnley, Steven VP / Regional Sales Manager
FOOTACTION USA, 1228

Carnochan, Jessica Marketing Manager
CLINTON RACEWAY, 1037

Carns, John Senior Associate AD, Compliance
LOUISVILLE ATHLETICS, UNIVERSITY OF,
335

Caro, Peter General Counsel
MASSACHUSETTS GOLF ASSOCIATION, 112

Carolis, Bob Deputy AD
SANTA CLARA UNIVERSITY ATHLETICS, 343

Caroll, Sarah Executive Assistant
NORFOLK CONVENTION & VISITORS
BUREAU, 242

Carollo, Bill Coordinator of Football Officials
COLLEGE CONFERENCE OF ILLINOIS AND
WISCONSIN, 221, 292, 294

Carollo, Keri Senior Woman Administrator
UNIVERSITY OF WISCONSIN-WHITEWATER,
408

Carollo, William Coordinator of Officials
MISSOURI VALLEY FOOTBALL
CONFERENCE, 88

Caron, Darryl Publisher
ADIRONDACK SPORTS & FITNESS, 548

Caron, Mona Editor
ADIRONDACK SPORTS & FITNESS, 548

Caron, Tom Host
FRONT ROW, 683

Carp, Steve Reporter
LAS VEGAS REVIEW-JOURNAL, 501

Cesare, Denise Program Assistant
HASKELL INDIAN NATIONS UNIVERSITY
ATHLETICS, 313

Cesarek, Bobbie President
NATIONAL ASSOCIATION OF COLLEGIATE
GYMNASTICS COACHES - WOMEN, 120

Cesaretti, Jeff Stadium Co-ordinator
SCOTTSDALE STADIUM, 1001

Cesarone, Nando President, U.S. Operations
UNITED PARCEL SERVICE OF AMERICA,
INC./UPS, 734

Cesere, Rick Chief Executive Officer
HARTWELL SPORTS, INC., 1143

Cesmat, Brad Sports Reporter
KTVK-TV, 696

Cessar, Scott Attorney in Charge
ECKERT SEAMANS, 877

Cessna, Jay President/Sports Director
WBFD-AM, 637, 638

Cessna, Robert Sports Editor
BRYAN-COLLEGE STATION EAGLE, 467

Cetak, Brian Treasurer
SPECIAL OLYMPICS WYOMING, 198

Cetta, Mike Director, Scouting Research
NATIONAL FOOTBALL LEAGUE/NFL, 94

Ch Le Vine, D. Financial Services Director
SENIOR MANAGEMENT GROUP, 853

Chabot, Frederic Goaltending Coach
NATIONAL HOCKEY LEAGUE/NHL, 124

Chad, Huss Groundskeeper
PHOENIX MUNICIPAL STADIUM, 993

Chadick, Terri Of counsel
CONNER & WINTERS, P.L.L.C., 874

Chadiha, Jeffri Senior Writer
SPORTS ILLUSTRATED, 585

Chadwick, Joanna Sports Reporter
WICHITA EAGLE, 547

Chadwick, Wayne Assistant Athletic Director
BEMIDJI STATE UNIVERSITY ATHLETICS,
352

Chafe, Patricia Chief Sport Development Officer
SKATE CANADA, 86

Chaffee, Brian. Principal and Director
FENTRESS ARCHITECTS, 1056

Chaffin, Dale Treasurer
SPECIAL OLYMPICS KANSAS, 195

Chaffin, David Asst. Commissioner for
Technology & Conf
WESTERN ATHLETIC CONFERENCE, 307

Chaffin, Eric Associate Director, Game
Operations & Fa
VANDERBILT STADIUM, 1015

Chafin, Kathy Advertising Manager
LOGAN BANNER, 503

Chagnon, Jamie Athletic Communications
Director
VASSAR COLLEGE ATHLETICS, 404

Chai, Ken President
GRAMAN USA, INC., 1140

Chaimberg, Eric VP Graphic Design
NORSK FITNESS PRODUCTS, INC., 1169

Chaimberg, Mark Vice President
NORSK FITNESS PRODUCTS, INC., 1169

Chaimovitch, Jason VP, Communications
AMERICAN HOCKEY LEAGUE/AHL, 126

Chakraborty, Tony Editor
PANASTADIA INTERNATIONAL, 575

Chalifoux, Mark Sports Reporter
COMMUNITY JOURNAL-CLERMONT, 472

Chalip, Laurence Sport Management Program
Coordinator
TEXAS AT AUSTIN, UNIVERSITY OF, 434

Chalmers, Ronald Manufacturing EVP
ROYAL PRECISION, INC., 1183

Chalton, John Vice President, Finance
FOX SPORTS NETWORKS/FOX SPORTS
NET, 675

Chamberlain, Lew CEO/Managing Partner
MIDWEST LEAGUE, 45

Chamberlain, Mark Chief Operating Officer
AMF BOWLING WORLDWIDE, 1098

Chamberlain, Michael Sr. Assoc. AD,
Compliance & Student-Athl
LAFAYETTE COLLEGE ATHLETICS, 334

Chamberlain, Peggy News Director
WFYY-FM, 647

Chamberlain, Richard Senior Staff Writer
AMERICAN QUARTER HORSE RACING
JOURNAL, 549

Chamberlain, Sandra Vice President
AMERICAN CUESPORTS ALLIANCE, 61

Chamberland, Mathieu Chief Operating Officer
CANADA SOCCER, 154

Chamberlin, Carolyn President/CEO
SPECIAL OLYMPICS NEBRASKA, 196

Chamberlin, Dawn Associate Athletic Director
SALISBURY UNIVERSITY ATHLETICS, 400

Chamberlin, Lew CEO
FIFTH THIRD BALLPARK, 965

Chambers, Bill General Manager
THE SHOW PLACE ARENA & PRINCE
GEORGE'S EQUESTRIAN CENTER, 1044

Chambers, Bradley President
MEDSTAR UNION MEMORIAL SPORTS
MEDICINE, 921

Chambers, Carolyn Chief Executive Officer
KEZI-TV, 689

Chambers, Greg Marketing Services Director
SPORTS PLUS, 762

Chambers, James Head Coach
USL CHAMPIONSHIP, 159

Chambers, Jeffrey Assistant Athletic Director
MINNESOTA STATE UNVERSITY - MANKATO
ATHLETICS (MSUM), 364

Chambers, Lisa News Director
WGRE-FM, 648

Chambers, M. Executive Vice President, People
Divisio
WAL-MART STORES, INC., 1240

Chambers, Mike Sports Writer
DENVER POST, 482

Chambers, Miles Equipment Manager
ROY STEWART STADIUM, 999

Chambers, Sandra Assistant Athletic Director
SUL ROSS STATE UNIVERSITY ATHLETICS,
403

Chambers, Sara Founder
HUGGER-MUGGER YOGA PRODUCTS, 1146

Chambers, Scott President
KEZI-TV, 647, 689

Chambers, Seymour Chief Judicial Officer
HUGHES STADIUM (MD), 972

Chambers, Thea Marketing Director
EL PASO COUNTY COLISEUM, 964

Chambers, Tim Sports Writer
ELIZABETHTON STAR, 486

Chamblin, Keith Chief Operating Officer
NATIONAL THOROUGHBRED RACING, 76

Chamness, Lisa Director
FREEDOM HALL CIVIC CENTER, 967

Champagne, Gayle Past President
AMERICAN JUNIOR GOLF ASSOCIATION, 99

Champagne, Lance Head Athletic Trainer
LOUISIANA STATE UNIVERSITY
(SHREVEPORT) ATHLETICS, 315

Champlin, Dave Director of Corporate
Partnerships
BIG SKY CONFERENCE, 292

Chan, Michael Head Athletic Trainer
WAYNE STATE UNIVERSITY ATHLETICS, 374

Chan, Ray VP, Information Technology
NATIONAL LEAGUE OF PROFESSIONAL
BASEBALL CLUBS, THE, 32

Chan, Scott Stadium Manager
ALOHA STADIUM, 946

Chan, Sharon Finance Manager
BADMINTON WORLD FEDERATION, 25

Chance, Jennifer VP of Finance & Administration
JACKSON CONVENTION & VISITORS
BUREAU, 236

Chancellor, David Sports Anchor/Reporter
WOAI-TV, 707

Chancey, Scott Sports Editor
INDEX-JOURNAL, 496

Chandler, Carleton Secretary/Treasurer
MARSHFIELD FAIR, 1041

Chandler, Evelyn President
NATIONAL ASSOCIATION OF WOMEN'S
GYMNASTICS JUDGES, 120

Chandler, Greg Publicist
MICHIGAN INTERCOLLEGIATE ATHLETIC
ASSOCIATION, 298, 700

Chandler, Holly Admissions Incharge
BEULAH PARK, 1036

Chandler, John Athletic Director
COE COLLEGE ATHLETICS, 381

Chandler, Kim Director of Athletics
MACALESTER COLLEGE ATHLETICS, 391

Chandler, T. Chairman
MARSHALL UNIVERSITY, 425

Chandler, Travis Assistant Athletic Director
CHARLESTON ATHLETICS, UNIVERSITY OF,
354

Chandler, Tye Sports Editor
ENNIS DAILY NEWS, 486

Chandler, Wright Sales Manager
EATON GOLF PRIDE, 1127

Chandley, Jim President
NATION'S BEST SPORTS, 1233

Chaney, Elizabeth Director of Member Services
NATIONAL ASSOCIATION OF SPORTS
COMMISSIONS, 796

Chang, Naomi Athletic Trainer
BARUCH COLLEGE ATHLETICS, 377

Channer, Vicki Administrative Assistant
NJCAA REGION XXIV MEN'S, 290

Chao, John Editor
AMERICAN WINDSURFER, 550

Chapdelaine, Chris Director, Operations
WOMEN'S PREMIER SOCCER LEAGUE, 169

Chapin, Josh Sports Editor
PALLADIUM-ITEM, 513, 517

Chaplin, Paul President
AMERICAN WATER SKI EDUCATIONAL
FOUNDATION/WATER SKI HALL OF FAME/,
251

Chaplin, Scott General Counsel/Secretary/Senior
Vp
STANLEY & ASSOCIATES, 856

Chapman, Allen Director
LADD PEEBLES STADIUM, 980

Chapman, Briana GM Championship Travel
THS COMPANY, 927

Chapman, Cory General Manager
BRYCE JORDAN CENTER, 953

Chapman, Craig Event Coordinator
RELIANT ASTRODOME, 996

Chapman, Dave IT Director
RALEIGH CONVENTION AND CONFERENCE
CENTER COMPLEX, 995

Chapman, GE General Manager
600 RACING, INC., 19, 1089

Chapman, John Sports Anchor
WOWT-TV, 707

Chapman, Joy General Manager
KXCA-AM, 632

Chapman, Karl Finance Manager
SAN ANTONIO SPORTS, 245

Chapman, Micah Sports Information Director
ROBERTS WESLEYAN COLLEGE
ATHLETICS, 319

Chapman, Michael President
CHAPMAN WALTERS INTERCOASTAL
GROUP, 1222

Chapman, Neil Senior Vice President
EXXON MOBIL CORPORATION, 727

Chapman, Ralph President
SOUTHERN ILLINOIS GOLF ASSOCIATION,
115

Chapman, Randi Director Client Services
PROFILES SPORTS, INC., 850

Chapman, Rich Director
CENTRAL NEW YORK PGA SECTIONAL
OFFICE, 105

Chapman, Scott Founder/CEO
POSITIVE COACHING ALLIANCE
(WASHINGTON, DC), 0

Chapman, Steve Executive VP/Chief Revenue &
Marketing O
NATIONAL HOCKEY LEAGUE/NHL, 125

Chapman, Sue Assistant Commissioner
MASSACHUSETTS STATE COLLEGE
ATHLETIC CONFERENCE, 298

Chapman, Will Local Sales Manager
WIP SPORTSRADIO 610, 651

Chappell, Henry Managing Director
PITCH PR, 801

Chappell, Mike Sports Reporter
INDIANAPOLIS STAR, 496

Chappell, Whit Director of Athletic Development
VALDOSTA STATE UNIVERSITY
ATHLETICS(VSU), 374

Chappin, Gina Director of Media, Rose Bowl
Game
ROSE BOWL, 92

Charapp, David Partner
DUANE MORRIS LLP, 877

Charbonneau, Johanne Vice President/CFO
CANADIAN BROADCASTING
CORPORATION/CBC, 673
Chardis, Phil Sports Reporter
JOURNAL INQUIRER, 498
Charisse, Sahar News Director
WBYT-FM, 640
Charland, Tonya Assistant Commissioner,
Compliance/Senio
GREAT LAKES VALLEY CONFERENCE, 296
Charles, Mickey CEO/President
THE SPORTS NETWORK, 687
Charles, Ron COO
LAUREL PARK, 1041
Charles, Roxanne General Manager
WDSM-AM, 643
Charles, Terry Manager, Public Relations
UNITED STATES HOCKEY LEAGUE, 137
Charmes, Nathan President
GATEWAY PGA SECTIONAL OFFICE, 105
Charnitski, Dan General Manager
HEART RATE, INC., 1143
Charnitski, Richard President
HEART RATE, INC., 1143
Charpentier, Sebastien Assistant General
Manager & Head Scout
QUEBEC MARITIMES MAJOR JUNIOR
HOCKEY LEAGUE, 136
Charrier, Stephen President
ROLLERBLADE INC., 1183
Charters, Tom President & CEO
HAMBLETONIAN SOCIETY, 75
Chartier, Cathy Contact
CUSTOM MOBILE FOOD EQUIPMENT, 1067
Chasanoff, Tommmy Sports Information Director
CUMBERLAND COLLEGE ATHLETICS, 311
Chasanoff, Tommy Sports Information Director
SAVANNAH COLLEGE OF ART & DESIGN
ATHLETICS, 400
Chase, Adam President
AMERICAN TRAIL RUNNING ASSOCIATION,
148
Chase, Art Athletic Director
CITADEL ATHLETICS, THE, 327
Chase, Christy Convention Sales Manager
MANHATTAN AREA SPORTS COMMISSION
(CONVENTION AND VISITORS BUREAU), 240
Chase, Cole Vice President, Vocational
Rehabilitatio
NOBIS WORKS CENTER, 192
Chase, Dave General Manager
FRONTIER LEAGUE, 41
Chase, Denny Sports Editor
TRAVERSE CITY RECORD-EAGLE, 541
Chase, Jim Operations Director
THE ACCESS FUND, 69
Chase, Larry Sport Management Program
Coordinator
TOMPKINS CORTLAND COMMUNITY
COLLEGE, 435
Chase, Nicole Manager of Athletic Facilities
DAVENPORT UNIVERSITY ATHLETICS, 312
Chase, Randy Senior Product Marketing Manager
EA SPORTS, 1213
Chase, Ricky Program Director
KHKC-FM, 619
Chase, Scott Program Director
WDAE-AM 620, 642
Chasen, Barry Attorney
CHASEN & BOSCOLO CHARTERED, 872
Chasen, Barry Attorney
CHASEN & BOSCOLO CHARTERED, 872
Chaskin, Dawn VP, Sales & Marketing
EARBAGS, 1127
Chass, Murray Sports Columnist
NEW YORK TIMES, 511
Chasteen, Tim Production Manager/Producer
AM 850 THE BUZZ SPORTS RADIO, 611
Chau, Arasi Head Coach
WOMEN'S FOOTBALL ALLIANCE / WFA, 98
Chaulk, Colin Head Coach
AMERICAN HOCKEY LEAGUE/AHL, 126
Chaves, Carlos President
USL LEAGUE TWO, 164
Chavez, Brian President
NATIONAL WHEELCHAIR SOFTBALL
ASSOCIATION, 170
Chavez, David President, CEO
PROSPORTS MVP, 803

Chavez, Debbie Director of Financial Reporting
FOX SPORTS PRIME TICKET, 675
Chavez, James President & CEO
CLARKSVILLE MONTGOMERY COUNTY
CONVENTION & VISITORS BUREAU, 230
Chavez, Joel Director of Stadium Operations
SOUTH ATLANTIC LEAGUE (A LEVEL), 51
Chavez, Norma Administrative Assistant to CVB
MIDLAND CHAMBER CONVENTION &
VISITORS BUREAU, 241
Chavez, Patricia Customer Service
GAGLIARDI INSURANCE SERVICES, 768
Chavez, Zack Sports Information Coordinator
LUBBOCK CHRISTIAN UNIVERSITY
ATHLETICS, 315
Chay, Chong Chairman
WASHINGTON GOLF CENTER, 1240
Chea, Albert Secretary
AMERICAN AMATEUR KARATE
FEDERATION, 142
Cheal, Edward Chief Science Officer
OMNI BODYWORK, 1171
Cheaney, Willis General Manager
BUTLER BOWL, 953
Cheek, Jimmy Chancellor
LEADBETTER, RONALD C., 889
Cheek, Jimmy Chancellor
MCINNIS, MALCOLM C., 894
Cheek, Patricia Advertising Manager
MIDDLESBORO DAILY NEWS, 507
Chehansky, Alex Managing Director, Business
Development
VANTAGE SPORTS MANAGEMENT, 859
Chelladurai, Packianathan Professor
OHIO STATE UNIVERSITY, 430
Chelsey, Kim Sales
KEN YOUNG COMPANY, INC., 1152
Chen, David Principal
GEIGER ENGINEERS, 1057
Chen, David Owner
TONIX, 1202
Chen, Li Dept. Chairperson
DELAWARE STATE UNIVERSITY, 415
Chen, Mike Marketing Director
TONIX, 1202
Chen, Po General Manager
VALLEY CREST, 1063
Chen, Steve Director of New Media
BIG WEST CONFERENCE, 292
Chen, Tim President and Chief Executive Officer
KEYS FITNESS PRODUCTS, 1152
Chen, Tony VP
EVOL SNOWBOARDS, 1130
Chenault, Venida University President
HASKELL INDIAN NATIONS UNIVERSITY
ATHLETICS, 313
Chenes, Chris Media/Production Manager
JOSEPH L. BRUNO STADIUM, 977
Cheney, Bob Interim Operations Director
RESER STADIUM, 996
Cheney, John Deputy Athletic Director
NORTHERN ILLINOIS UNIVERSITY
ATHLETICS, 340, 959
Cheney, Mike General Manager
KBND-AM, 614
Cheng, Kelly Finance Director
TIGER WOODS FOUNDATION, 193
Cheng, Lawrence Associate Principal
BRUNER/COTT & ASSOCIATES INC., 1051
Cheng, Michael President
HARRISON SPORTS, INC., 1142
Cheng, Stephanie Vice President, Marketing
Services
PREMIER PARTNERSHIPS, 802
Chenier, Adelle Event Manager
DC SPORTS & ENTERTAINMENT
COMMISSION, 232
Chepulis, Brian Assoc. AD, Facilities &
Operations
AMERICAN UNIVERSITY ATHLETICS, 324
Cherblanc, Joyce Operations Manager
SOUTH CENTRAL PGA SECTIONAL OFFICE,
108
Chere, Richard Sports Reporter (Hockey)
STAR-LEDGER, 535
Cherner, Reid Sports Senior Editor
USA TODAY, 543
Chernesky, Joshua Associate
WATTS, STEVEN R., 914

Chernesky, Richard Managing Partner
WATTS, STEVEN R., 872, 914
Chernick, Mark CEO
PLAY VISIONS, 1174
Cherniske, Nick Stadium Operations Manager
CHENEY STADIUM, 957
Chernoff, Mike General Manager
AMERICAN LEAGUE OF PROFESSIONAL
BASEBALL CLUBS, THE, 29
Cherrington, Kent Sports Information Director
PLYMOUTH STATE UNIVERSITY ATHLETICS,
397
Cherry, Brice Sports Columnist
WACO TRIBUNE-HERALD, 545
Cherry, Don Senior Contributing Editor
RINKSIDE, 578
Cherry, Jessica Senior Women Administrator
YORK COLLEGE (CUNY) ATHLETICS, 408
Cherundolo, Steve Head Coach
MAJOR LEAGUE SOCCER, 158
Cherwa, John Deputy Editor
LOS ANGELES TIMES, 503
Chesebro, Bob President
WIGWAM MILLS, INC., 1210
Chesick, Carlin Associate Commissioner
PENNSYLVANIA STATE ATHLETIC
CONFERENCE, 303
Chesla, Pam Membership Chair
ANCHORAGE WOMEN'S GOLF
ASSOCIATION, 109
Chesler, Barbara Senior Associate Athletics
Director for
INGALLS RINK, 973
Chesney, Lauren Director, Community Relations
SMOKIES PARK, 1003
Chesney, Rob Associate Director of Athletics
MONTCLAIR STATE UNIVERSITY
ATHLETICS, 394
Chesser, Andrew General Manager
MIDWEST LEAGUE, 45
Chessick, Judy Associate
SULLIVAN FIRM, LTD., THE, 909
Chesteen, Gloria Advertising Manager
UNION CITY DAILY MESSENGER, 542
Chetan, Daniela Vice President
STRATEGIC RESOURCES, 749
Cheung, Erika Sr. Associate Athletics Director
APPALACHIAN STATE UNIVERSITY
ATHLETICS, 324
Chevat, Caroline Manager, Brand Content &
Communications
SPECIAL OLYMPICS INTERNATIONAL, 193
Cheveldayoff, Kevin Executive VP & General
Manager
NATIONAL HOCKEY LEAGUE/NHL, 126
Cheverie, Leah Secretary
HARNESS HORSE YOUTH FOUNDATION, 75
Cheynet, Jerry Coordinator, Operations
CASSELL COLISEUM, 956
Chi, Victor Sports Reporter
SAN JOSE MERCURY NEWS, 528
Chiabai, Alan President
REDDEN MARINE SUPPLY, INC., 1235
Chiarucci, Mark Director Corporate Sponsorships
Regional
NAIA, 572
Chiccitt, Kelly VP of Marketing
HDS PROMOTIONAL MARKETING, 787
Chick, James President
CHICK'S SPORTING GOODS, INC., 1223
Chickering, Sammi Sports Information Director
ANNA MARIA COLLEGE
ATHLETICS-PAXTON, 376
Chieger, Kathryn VP Corporate / Investor
Relations
BRUNSWICK CORPORATION, 1111
Chighizola, Kristen Outdoor Sports Coordinator
BATON ROUGE AREA SPORTS
FOUNDATION, 228
Child, Martha Managing Officer
MAJOR LEAGUE BASEBALL PLAYERS
ASSOCIATION, 842
Childers, John VP / Shareholder
JOHNSON & BELL, 886
Childers, Troy Director Circulation
ATHLON SPORTS COMMUNICATIONS, 550
Childress, Bernard Executive Director
TENNESSEE SECONDARY SCHOOL
ATHLETIC ASSOCIATION, 202

Childress, Deirdre Sports Deputy Editor
PHILADELPHIA INQUIRER, 519

Childress, Richard Chairman/CEO
NASCAR XFINITY SERIES, 23, 24

Childs, Henry Communications & Membership
Coordinator
OREGON GOLF ASSOCIATION, 114

Chiles, Adrian Chief Presenter
ITV SPORT, 600

Chiles, Sandra Senior Vice President & GM,
Affiliate Sa
HBO SPORTS, 676

Chilton, Grahame CEO
INDYCAR, 21, 22

Chiminski, John Director
AIRCAST, INC., 1094

Chin, Deborah Associate Vice President, Director
of At
NEW HAVEN, UNIVERSITY OF, 428

Chin, Jason Sales
ACT ONE COMMUNICATIONS, 1092

Chin, Ken Vice President, Events
ATLANTA SPORTS COUNCIL, 227

Chin, Ryan Owner
AMA GOLF, 1097

Chin-Farrell, Shawn Director of Athletics
CAL STATE NORTHRIDGE ATHLETICS, 326

Chinen, Richard President
ROSE BOWL HALL OF FAME, 258

Ching, Calvin Sr. Manager, Stadium Events &
Operations
ANGELS STADIUM OF ANAHEIM, 946

Chinn, Jason Vice President
PROTECT MANAGEMENT CORP., 850

Chiodo, Andy Goaltending Coach
NATIONAL HOCKEY LEAGUE/NHL, 125

Chiodo, Wade President, Head Scout & Dir.,
Player Per
NORTH AMERICAN HOCKEY LEAGUE, 133

Chipman, Mark Executive Chair
NATIONAL HOCKEY LEAGUE/NHL, 126, 954

Chipman, Mike General Partner
NATIONAL LEAGUE OF PROFESSIONAL
BASEBALL CLUBS, THE, 31

Chipps, Lisa Associate Athletic Director/SWA
CREIGHTON UNIVERSITY ATHLETICS, 328

Chipps, William Senior Editor
IEG SPONSORSHIP REPORT, 565

Chirico, Anna Chief Financial Officer
CAMPMOR, INC., 1222

Chismar, Michael Senior Associate AD
SUN DEVIL STADIUM, 1006

Chitwood, Joie President/Chief Operations
Officer IMS
INDIANAPOLIS MOTOR SPEEDWAY
CORPORATION, 757, 1026

Chivetta, Christopher President /Principal
HASTINGS + CHIVETTA ARCHITECTS, INC.,
1058

Chizer, DeJuena Associate Athletics
Director/SWA
JOHN O'QUINN FIELD AT ROBERTSON
STADIUM, 977

Chlad, Pam Head Athletic Trainer
URSINUS COLLEGE ATHLETICS(UC), 404

Chmura, Chesley Customer Service Manager
DOVER SADDLERY, INC, 1225

Chmura, Matt Sports Information Director
WIDENER UNIVERSITY ATHLETICS, 406

Cho, Cheryl Director of Footwear
TALON GROUP INTERNATIONAL
D/B/A/MANAGEMENT RECRUITERS OF
MERCER I, 749

Cho, Gordon Secretary
HAWAII STATE GOLF ASSOCIATION, 111

Cho, Young-Chan Chief Financial Officer
FILA USA, 1132

Choate, Abram Assistant Director of Athletics,
Sports
BROWNWOOD COLISEUM, 952

Choate, David Vice President & COO
CONVENTURES, INC., 753

Choate, Trish Sports Editor
ABILENE REPORTER NEWS, 459

Chodos, Leigh Business Technology
Development Director
BENNETT GLOBAL MARKETING GROUP, 775

Choi, Paul Assistant Professor of Recreation
MISSOURI WESTERN STATE COLLEGE, 427

Chomet, Charles Attorney
KELMAN, LORIA, WILL HARVEY &
THOMPSON, 840

Chong, Sonney Director
CALIFORNIA EXPOSITION & STATE FAIR,
1023, 1036

Choquette, Matt Director of Athletic
Communications
DREW UNIVERSITY(DU) ATHLETICS, 383

Chorman, Vicki Associate Director
VALUE CITY ARENA/JEROME
SCHOTTENSTEIN CENTER, 1001

Chornomud, Robert National/OEM Sales &
Marketing Manager
PRECISION SPORTS, 1176

Choti, Joe Chief Technology Officer
TICKETS.COM, 933

Chotivkova, Jana VP, Finance
MIDWEST LEAGUE, 45

Choudhuri, Dilip Principal/Executive Director
WALTER P MOORE, 1063

Choue, Chungwon President
WORLD TAEKWONDO FEDERATION (WTF),
144

Chrampanis, Rich Sports Director
WPDE-TV, 707

Chrestman, Angie Associate Director, Career
Center
MISSISSIPPI STATE UNIVERSITY/GOLF
MANAGEMENT PROGRAM, 103

Chris, Phillips
MONTGOMERY MOTORSPORTS PARK
(MMP), 1029

Chrisom, Kathleen Vice President, Sales &
Marketing
CONVENTURES, INC., 753

Christ, Trudy Marketing Director
BODY WRAPPERS/ANGELO LUZIO, 1109

Christensen, Brian General Manager
KWDM-FM, 631

Christensen, Casey VP, Ticket Sales
EAST COAST HOCKEY LEAGUE/ECHL, 130

Christensen, Charlene Director of Services
VALDOSTA-LOWNDES COUNTY
CONFERENCE CENTER & TOURISM
AUTHORITY/CVB, 248, 249

Christensen, Colleen Project Manager
GAGE MARKETING GROUP, 784

Christensen, Dawn Director of Communications
LAS VEGAS CONVENTION & VISITOR'S
AUTHORITY, 982

Christensen, Kenneth Lawyer
RAWLINGS, WILLIAM R., 901

Christensen, Marc Managing Member
OFF THE WALL PRODUCTS, LLC, 1170

Christensen, Melissa Assistant Athletic Director,
External Op
DONALD E. YOUNG FITNESS CENTER, 962

Christensen, Michelle Marketing Director
WLOW-FM, 656

Christensen, Rick Associate AD, Admin. &
Compliance
DUQUESNE UNIVERSITY ATHLETICS, 329

Christensen, Tom Assistant Sports Editor
SOUTH FLORIDA SUN-SENTINEL, 112, 199,
532

Christensen, Troy Executive Director
IOWA PGA SECTIONAL OFFICE, 106

Christenson, Cheri Director of Professional
Development
NATIONAL INTRAMURAL RECREATIONAL
SPORTS ASSOCIATION/NIRSA, 222

Christenson, Pat President
LAS VEGAS EVENTS, 238

Christian, Bill VP
CHRISTIAN BROTHERS, INC., 1116

Christian, Judy Advertising Manager
WATERTOWN DAILY TIMES, 546

Christian, Tiffany Assistant Athletics Director,
Compliance
WILLIAM & MARY HALL, 1018

Christiansen, Holger Principal Architect
CRP ARCHITECTS, P.C., 1053

Christiansen, Lucas General Manager
USL LEAGUE TWO, 164

Christianson, Mike Sports Editor
ELKO DAILY FREE PRESS, 486

Christiarnsen, Paul Director of Event Services
SPOKANE REGIONAL SPORTS
COMMISSION, 246

Christie, Andrew Executive Director, Player
Development
NATIONAL LEAGUE OF PROFESSIONAL
BASEBALL CLUBS, THE, 32

Christie, Bryan Sales / Marketing Director
PRO INNOVATIVE CONCEPTS, 946, 1177

Christie, Doug Head Coach
NATIONAL BASKETBALL ASSOCIATION/NBA,
58

Christie, Guy President
DESCENTE NORTH AMERICA, INC., 1124

Christie, Mike Assistant Commissioner
USA SOUTH CONFERENCE, 297, 306

Christie, Shannon Region Services Administrator
NORTHERN CALIFORNIA REGIONAL
COMMISSIONER/USA VOLLEYBALL, 212

Christine, Bill Sports Writer (Horse Racing)
LOS ANGELES TIMES, 503

Christine, Ed Sports Editor
TRIBUNE, SCRANTON TIMES, 540, 541

Christinzio, Victoria Credit Manager
COVER SPORTS USA, 1120

Christman, Will Head Athletic Trainer
WOFFORD COLLEGE ATHLETICS, 376

Christner, Mike Assistant Athletic Director
WILLIAM PENN UNIVERSITY ATHLETICS, 323

Christopher, Dean Chief Financial officer
FAMILIE, 832

Christopher, Greg Director of Athletics
XAVIER UNIVERSITY ATHLETICS, 350

Christopher, Jimmy News Director
KTBK-FM, 629

Christopher, Mark Sales / Marketing VP
KRUEGER INTERNATIONAL, 1153

Christopher, Marv Athletic Director
CALIFORNIA MARITIME ACADEMY
ATHLETICS, 309

Christopher, Mary Retail Advertising Manager
SLIDELL SENTRY-NEWS, 531

Christopher, Morgan Director of Sales
LACKAWANNA COUNTY CONVENTION &
VISITORS BUREAU, 238

Christopher, Paul Manager
LADD PEEBLES STADIUM, 980

Christopher, Thomas President
FOLLETT HIGHER EDUCATION GROUP, 1228

Christopher, Tom President and Chief Operating
Officer
FOLLETT HIGHER EDUCATION GROUP, 1228

Christopherson, Brett Sports Reporter
POST-CRESCENT, 521

Christy, Betsy Director Of Accounting
DAN MARINO FOUNDATION, 191

Christy, Dick Athletics Director
UNIVERSITY OF NORTH CAROLINA
PEMBROKE ATHLETICS(UNCP), 366

Christy, Larry Sports Director
WMTR-FM, 658

Chritton, Charles VP/Shareholder
WENDEL, CHRITTON, PARKS, AND DEBARI
CHARTERED, 915

Chrnelich, Ben Coach & Sporting Director
WOMEN'S PREMIER SOCCER LEAGUE, 168

Chrockrom, Charles Chairman
BIRMINGHAM RACING COMMISSION, 119

Chronister, Joe Director of Higher Education
FGM ARCHITECTS & ENGINEERS, 1056

Chu, Chinch Director
AIRCAST, INC., 1094

Chu, Chinh Chairman of the Board
DJ ORTHOPEDICS, 1124

Chue, Jessica Associate
ANDREWS KURTH LLP, 862

Chugg, Kelsey Membership Director
UTAH GOLF ASSOCIATION, 116

Chuks, Jennifer Assistant Athletic Administrator
WILLIAMS COLLEGE ATHLETICS, 1019

Chumbley, Brent Men's & Women's Cross
Country/Track & Fi
RADFORD UNIVERSTIY, 431

Chun, Christopher Executive Director
HAWAII HS ATHLETIC ASSOCIATION, 199

Chun, Kyra Executive Secretary
ALOHA PGA SECTIONAL OFFICE, 105

Chun, Liz Sports Director
KGMV-TV, 690

Clark, Steve Chairman
VANGUARD SAILBOATS, 517, 754, 1207

Clark, Sue General Manager
TEAMLINE, 1200

Clark, Tania Station Manager
WYYZ-AM, 672

Clark, Tim President, Emirates Airline
THE EMIRATES GROUP, 733

Clark, Todd Communicators Director
WISCONSIN INTERSCHOLASTIC ATHLETIC
ASSOCIATION, 203

Clark, Tom Commissioner
PROFESSIONAL BOWLERS ASSOCIATION,
66

Clark, Tommy Senior Vice President
TREATY OAK BANK, 770

Clark, Tony Executive Director
MAJOR LEAGUE BASEBALL PLAYERS
ASSOCIATION, 27

Clark, Walter Faculty Athletics Representative
UC RIVERSIDE ATHLETICS, 373

Clarke, Amy Gift Shop Manager
GRAND RIVER RACEWAY (GRR), 1039

Clarke, Bill Director
LISTON B. RAMSEY REGIONAL ACTIVITY
CENTER, 983

Clarke, Bob Director General Manager
WRUF, 665

Clarke, Brian Associate
ANDREWS KURTH LLP, 862

Clarke, David Editor-in-Chief
GOLF MAGAZINE, 561

Clarke, Evelyne President
WERA MOTORCYCLE ROADRACING, 144

Clarke, Gerry Sports Marketing
WBIG-AM, 639

Clarke, Jayne Vice President
KANSAS WOMEN'S GOLF ASSOCIATION, 112

Clarke, Joe Communications Coordinator
USA DIVING, 208

Clarke, John Managing Editor
GOLFER, 562

Clarke, Karey Box Office Manager
WOLSTEIN CENTER, 1020

Clarke, Keia CEO
WOMEN'S NATIONAL BASKETBALL
ASSOCIATION, 60

Clarke, Pat Sports Director
WESH-TV, 702

Clarke, Renee Facilities Operations Coordinator
SWARTHMORE COLLEGE ATHLETICS, 403

Clarke, Ted General Manager
GRAND RIVER RACEWAY (GRR), 1039

Clarke, Tim Wilson Golf General Manager
WILSON SPORTING GOODS COMPANY, 1210

Clarkson, James Head Coach
USL LEAGUE TWO, 161

Clarkson, Priscilla Editorial Board Member
INTERNATIONAL JOURNAL OF SPORT
NUTRITION, 566

Clary, Joe Purchasing Executive
MECA SPORTSWEAR, INC., 1161

Clary, John Contact
SPORTS MEDIA ENTERPRISES, 762

Clary, Kevin Second Vice President
RHODE ISLAND GOLF ASSOCIATION, 115

Clary, Mike Director of Athletics
RHODES COLLEGE ATHLETICS, 398

Clary, Raymond Member
ETTER, MCMAHON, LAMBERSON & CLARY,
P.C.A., 879

Clasen, Jon Compliance Director
HOPE INTERNATIONAL UNIVERSITY
ATHLETICS, 313

Clausen, Randy Sports Director
KLGR-FM, 622

Clausen, Thomas Chief Financial Officer
Z COIL PAIN RELIEF FOOTWEAR, 1212

Claussen, Cathryn Associate Professor
WASHINGTON STATE UNIVERSITY, 436

Claussen, Connie Athletic Director Emeritus
NEBRASKA AT OMAHA ATHLETICS,
UNIVERSITY OF, 365

Claussen, Drew Sports Reporter
ALBERT LEA TRIBUNE, 459

Clawson, Chris Secretary/Treasurer
THE SPORTS & FITNESS INDUSTRY
ASSOCIATION (SFIA), 813

Clay, Andy Sports Copy Editor
FORT WORTH STAR-TELEGRAM, 489

Clay, Bobby Senior Editor
SPORTS ILLUSTRATED, 585

Clay, Jack Advertising Director
TIMES-REPORTER, 540

Clay, James President
IMSA MICHELIN PILOT CHALLENGE, 20

Clay, John Sports Columnist
LEXINGTON HERALD-LEADER, 502

Clay, Les News Director
KOZB-FM, 626

Clay, Nikki Advertising Director
DAILY INDEPENDENT, 477

Clay, Tyler Facilities Manager
HEC EDMUNDSON PAVILION, 970

Clayborne, Courtney Attorney (Past)
CLAYBORNE, COURTNEY, 873

Claybourn, David Sports Editor
GREENVILLE HERALD BANNER, 491

Claybrook, Jennifer Athletic Director
LA GRANGE COLLEGE ATHLETICS, 389

Claybrook, Leslie Assistant Commissioner
Championships
SOUTHEASTERN CONFERENCE/SEC, 304

Claymore, Jay Sports Anchor
KINI-FM, 620

Clayton, Anne General Manager
PEORIA CIVIC CENTER, 991

Clayton, Carolyn Team Member
CHARLES SCHWAB & CO., 768

Clayton, Heather Chief Financial Officer
NATIONAL HOCKEY LEAGUE/NHL, 126

Clayton, Joseph President/Chief Executive
Officer
DISH NETWORK, 686

Clayton, Kelli Director of Operations
METROPOLITAN PROFESSIONAL GOLFERS
ASSOCIATION, 106

Clayton, Laura Assistant Athletic Director
UNIVERSITY OF WEST GEORGIA
DEPARTMENT OF INTERCOLLEGIATE
ATHLETIC, 372

Claywell, Josh Sports Writer
NEWS-ENTERPRISE, 512

Cleanthes, Jeff Assistant Athletic Director
RHODES COLLEGE ATHLETICS, 398

Clearkin, Kim Director of National Championships
U.S. SQUASH, 171

Cleary, Brian Program Director
WWFG-FM, 671

Cleary, Jadine Domestic Technical Director
SYNCHRO CANADA, 173

Cleary, Joey Professional Scout
NATIONAL FOOTBALL LEAGUE/NFL, 94

Cleary, Kevin General Manager
NATIONAL DIRECTORY OF COLLEGE
ATHLETICS ONLINE & APP, 595

Cleary, Michael Executive Editor
ATHLETICS ADMINISTRATION, 550

Cleary, Sean Women's Track and Cross Country
WEST VIRGINIA UNIVERSITY, 437

Cleary, Valerie Athletics Director
WILLAMETTE UNIVERSITY ATHLETICS, 406

Cleaveland, Roger Sports Reporter
WATERBURY REPUBLICAN-AMERICAN, 545

Cleek, Ryan Assistant Editor
MOUNTAIN BIKE ACTION, 571

Clegg, Monty Associate Manager of Events
ARMED FORCES BOWL, 89

Clemens, Joe Associate Editors
TASK INDUSTRIES, INC., 1199

Clement, Annie Sport Management
Coordinator/Professor
BARRY UNIVERSITY, 410

Clement, Dallas Executive Vice President/Chief
Financial
AUTOTRADER.COM, INC, 673

Clement, George General Manager
WCCP, 640

Clements, Barry Deputy AD/Capital Projects
SOUTH FLORIDA ATHLETICS, UNIVERSITY
OF, 344, 996, 1014

Clements, Chris Chief Financial Officer
NATIONAL FOOTBALL LEAGUE/NFL, 95

Clements, Ed Sports Director
KLBJ-AM, 622

Clements, Jeremy Co-Owner
NASCAR XFINITY SERIES, 24

Clements, Ken Retail Advertising Manager
POST REGISTER, 521

Clements, Mark Director for Internal Operations
NORTHWEST MISSOURI STATE
UNIVERSITY(NWMSU), 366

Clements, Michelle Senior Vice President of
Human Resources
RECREATIONAL EQUIPMENT, INC./REI, 1235

Clements, Miles Partner
FRILOT, PARTRIDGE, KOHNKE &
CLEMENTS, L.C., 881

Clements, Tony Co-Owner
NASCAR XFINITY SERIES, 24

Clemons, Deborah Director of Community Affairs
RICHMOND INTERNATIONAL RACEWAY,
1031

Clemons, Michael General Manager
CANADIAN FOOTBALL LEAGUE/CFL, 93

Clemons, Philip Sales Manager
ULTRA PLAY SYSTEMS, INC., 1205

Clendaniel, Allen President
USTA PACIFIC NORTHWEST, 176

Clendenen, Bill Chief Executive Officer
MEDIC FIRST AID INTERNATIONAL, INC.,
1161

Clenney, Ralph Advertising Manager
WKJQ-FM 97.3, 653

Clenney, Steve Program Director
WKJQ-FM 97.3, 653

Clennon, Marian Director
RIVERSIDE ARENA, 997

Clermont, Chantal Director Of Finance
CANADIAN GYMNASTICS FEDERATION, 120

Cleveland, Rick Sports Columnist
CLARION-LEDGER, 471

Cleves, Randy Vice President, Communications
AMERICAN HOCKEY LEAGUE/AHL, 127

Clibanoff, Jim President
JAMES CLIBANOFF BASKETBALL SERVICES,
840

Cliburn, Stan Manager
ATLANTIC LEAGUE, 35

Click, Paul Sports Editor
MOHAVE VALLEY DAILY NEWS, 508

Cliffel, Susan Partner
WOOD & LAMPING LLP, 916

Clifford, Andrew Marketing Art Director
LINKS MAGAZINE-THE BEST OF GOLF, 568

Clifford, Annmarie Ticket Sales Manager
LAKEWOOD BLUECLAWS, 981

Clifford, Bob Athletic Director
NEW MEXICO HIGHLANDS
UNIVERSITY(NMHU), 365

Clifford, Jon Sports Editor
DAILY NEWS (CA), 478

Clifford, Peter President
NATIONAL HOT ROD ASSOCIATION, 17

Clifford, Shane Goalie Coach
UNITED STATES HOCKEY LEAGUE, 137

Clifton, Cody Sports Information Director
VIRGINIA WESLEYAN COLLEGE
ATHLETICS(VWC), 404

Clifton, Sue Editor-in-Chief
SKYDIVING, 581

Climaco, John Founder
LEFKOWITZ, PAUL, 890

Climbers, Young Manufacturing VP , Human
Resources
LANDSCAPE STRUCTURES, INC., 1154

Climer, David Sports Columnist
TENNESSEAN, 538

Clinard, Brian Sports Information Director
SPALDING UNIVERSITY ATHLETICS, 321

Clinard, Keith Attorney
CLINARD, KEITH ASHFORD, 873

Cline, Cliff News Director
KXDL-FM, 632

Cline, Jim Sports Reporter
WGGB-TV, 703

Cline, Russ President
RCA GROUP EVENT MARKETING +
MANAGEMENT, 805

Cline, Steve Pitching Coach
ARIZONA LEAGUE (ROOKIE), 34

Clingan, Cindy Advertising Manager
MORNING SUN (KS), 509

Clinkscales, Cliff Head Coach
NATIONAL BASKETBALL LEAGUE OF
CANADA, 58

Cohen, Bruce Vice President, Sales/Marketing
IRWIN SEATING COMPANY, 1148

Cohen, Bryan Special Projects Coordinator
HAMPTON CLASSIC HORSE SHOW, 75

Cohen, Cheryl Vice President/Executive Producer
PLATINUM ENTERTAINMENT PARTNERS II, 601

Cohen, Cindy Associate Athletic Director
WILLIAM PATERSON UNIVERSITY OF NEW JERSEY ATHLETICS, 407

Cohen, Doug Assistant General Manager
BETHPAGE BALLPARK, 949

Cohen, Evan Program Director
WTLX-FM, 668

Cohen, Ilene Athletic Director
NJCAA REGION XIX WOMEN'S, 289

Cohen, Irwin Commissioner
NEW ENGLAND INTERCOLLEGIATE AMATEUR ATHLETIC ASSOCIATION, 286

Cohen, Jack Publisher
COLLEGE & PRO FOOTBALL NEWSWEEKLY, 533, 555

Cohen, Jeff Director of Merchandising
NEW YORK-PENNSYLVANIA LEAGUE, 46, 982

Cohen, Jennifer Director of Athletics
WASHINGTON ATHLETICS, UNIVERSITY OF, 348, 970

Cohen, Jerry Founder
EBBETS FIELD FLANNELS, 1017, 1127

Cohen, Jim EVP,Mergers and Acquisition
CONSOLIDATED GRAPHICS, 779

Cohen, John Athletics Director
AUBURN UNIVERSITY ATHLETICS, 229, 325

Cohen, Joshua Manager
BARRETT SPORTS GROUP, 774

Cohen, Kathryn General Manager
FOX SPORTS PRIME TICKET, 675

Cohen, Ken Editor
GOLF TRAVELER, 562

Cohen, Kenneth Partner
RAGSDALE, RICHARD A., 900

Cohen, Kevin Sports Director
WCOS, 641

Cohen, Laura Web Editor
GATOR BAIT, 560

Cohen, Lee Head Athletic Trainer
SPECIAL OLYMPICS STADIUM, 1004

Cohen, Louis Partner
PIPER MARBURY RUDNICK & WOLFE, 899

Cohen, Mark Partner
MARGOLIS EDELSTEIN, 892

Cohen, Marty General Manager/Editor
GATOR BAIT, 560

Cohen, Mitch Strategic Execution Leader
PRICEWATERHOUSECOOPERS, 760

Cohen, Neil Managing Editor
SPORTS ILLUSTRATED FOR KIDS, 585

Cohen, Rachel Sports Reporter
DALLAS MORNING NEWS, 481

Cohen, Renee Marketing Manager
PAC-10 PROPERTIES, 799

Cohen, Richard President
WALDON, GROUP THE, 859

Cohen, Robert Partner
COHEN, ROBERT M., 873

Cohen, Robert Founder
COHEN, ROBERT M., 873

Cohen, Rod Sports Producer
KTTV-TV, 688, 695

Cohen, Sanford Host
LET'S TALK SPORTS, 605

Cohen, Steve Vice President
NEW YORK-PENNSYLVANIA LEAGUE, 46

Cohen, Steven Owner, Chair & CEO
NATIONAL LEAGUE OF PROFESSIONAL BASEBALL CLUBS, THE, 32

Cohen, Steven Director, Medical Services
NATIONAL LEAGUE OF PROFESSIONAL BASEBALL CLUBS, THE, 32

Cohen, Tim Treasurer
CALIFORNIA THOROUGHBRED BREEDERS ASSOCIATION, 74

Cohen, Walter Attorney
OBERMAYER, REBMANN, MAXWELL & HIPPEL, LLP, 898

Cohn, Bob Sports Writer
WASHINGTON TIMES, 545

Cohn, David Director Of Member Services & Communicat
WISCONSIN STATE GOLF ASSOCIATION, 117

Cohn, Gerald Chief Executive Officer
GEORGIA BOOT, 1137

Cohn, Justin Sports Reporter
JOURNAL GAZETTE, 498

Cohn, Linda Anchor
ESPN, 683

Cohn, Lowell Sports Reporter
PRESS DEMOCRAT, 522

Cohn, William Principal Attorney
COHN, WILLIAM A., 873

Coia, Sonja Operating Manager VP
ELBY GIFTS, 1128

Coiner, Skip Art Director
SAND SPORTS, 579

Coito, Wayne Multimedia Specialist
PACIFIC WEST CONFERENCE, 302

Colarossi, Robert Publisher
USA GYMNASTICS, 590

Colbert, Cary Sup. Of Ops & Sales Fulfillment
NEW MEXICO BOWL, 91

Colbert, Dan Director, College Scouting
NATIONAL FOOTBALL LEAGUE/NFL, 96

Colbert, Kelly Assistant Athletic Director
STATE UNIVERSITY OF NEW YORK INSTITUTE OF TECHNOLOGY ATHLETICS(SU, 402

Colbert, Kevin General Manager
HEINZ FIELD, 970

Colboch, Craig General Manager
WIBW AM 580 RADIO, 650

Colbrese, Mike Executive Director
WASHINGTON INTERSCHOLASTIC ACTIVITIES ASSOCIATION, 202

Colburn, Bob VP / General Manager
BAUER NIKE HOCKEY, INC., 1105

Colburn, David Provost & Vice President Academic Affair
FLORIDA, UNIVERSITY OF, 418

Colby, Joan Editor/Advertising Manager
ILLINOIS RACING NEWS, 565

Colby, Susan VP Guest Services
NEW HAMPSHIRE MOTOR SPEEDWAY, 1030

Cole, Bill College Sports Reporter
WINSTON-SALEM JOURNAL, 547

Cole, Carleton Sports Producer
KHOU-TV, 690

Cole, Cheryl Senior Woman Administrator
STATE UNIVERSITY OF NEW YORK COLLEGE AT PLATTSBURGH ATHLETICS(SUN, 402

Cole, Darlene Venue Manager
VIKING HALL CIVIC CENTER, 1016

Cole, Dayton University Attorney
COLE, DAYTON T., 873

Cole, Jack Director of Athletics
MESSIAH COLLEGE ATHLETICS, 393, 426

Cole, Jason Sports Writer
MIAMI HERALD, 506

Cole, Jeff Sales VP
WEST COAST TURF, 1210

Cole, Jim Director of Athletics
MERCER UNIVERSITY ATHLETICS, 336

Cole, John President
JEBCO, 1149

Cole, Justin General Manager
TEXAS BASEBALL LEAGUE, 53

Cole, Kelly Head Coach, Women's Basketball
MATTHEWS ARENA, 985

Cole, Kim Assistant Director
NEW JERSEY STATE INTERSCHOLASTIC ATHLETIC ASSOCIATION, 201

Cole, Lady President
ALLEN UNIVERSITY ATHLETICS, 307

Cole, Ozzie Racing Secretary
ROCKINGHAM PARK, 1043

Cole, Pam Administrative Assistant
WILLIAM R. JOHNSON COLISEUM, 1019

Cole, Ray President
WOI-TV, 707

Cole, Rick Director of Athletics
HOFSTRA UNIVERSITY ATHLETICS, 332

Cole, Rod Director for Athletic Performance
TARLETON STATE UNIVERSITY ATHLETICS, 372

Cole, Roz President
PPI MARKETING, 848

Cole, Steve Associate Athletics Director, Internal A
WILLIAM & MARY HALL, 1017, 1018

Cole, Thomas Vice Chairman
FEDERATED DEPARTMENT STORES, INC., 1227

Coleman, Andrew Assistant Professor
LIBERTY UNIVERSITY, 423

Coleman, Bill Owner/News Director
KOKB-AM, 625

Coleman, Chris Chair
DES MOINES AREA SPORTS COMMISSION, 232

Coleman, Dennis Partner
COLEMAN, DENNIS M., 829

Coleman, Derek Sports Reporter
STAR-DEMOCRAT, 534

Coleman, Fred President
USA BADMINTON, 25

Coleman, Greg President
EASTERN LEAGUE, 38, 976

Coleman, Jasmonn Associate Athletic Director for Developm
RICHMOND ATHLETICS, UNIVERSITY OF, 342

Coleman, Jennifer Associate Athletic Director, Facilities
CHICAGO ATHLETICS, UNIVERSITY OF, 380

Coleman, Jerry Host
PADRES MAGAZINE, 680

Coleman, Jody Principal
COOKE DOUGLASS FARR LEMONS/LTD., 1052

Coleman, Kristal Athletic Business Coordinator
LE MOYNE-OWEN COLLEGE ATHLETICS (LOC), 361

Coleman, Margo Executive Director
MISSISSIPPI GOLF ASSOCIATION, 113

Coleman, Mary President
JOHNSON & JOHNSON CONSUMER PRODUCTS INC., 1150

Coleman, Rick Sports Anchor/Reporter
KWWL-TV, 697

Coleman, Robert Executive Director of Athletics
WHITTIER COLLEGE ATHLETICS, 406

Coleman, Selina Senior Associate
BURGOYNE, ROBERT A., 870

Coleman, Steve Assistant Coach
WOMEN'S PREMIER SOCCER LEAGUE, 169

Coleman, Susie President
SUNFLOWER STATE GAMES, 264

Coleman, Terri Advertising Manager
DAILY DUNKLIN DEMOCRAT, 476

Coleman, Trey Treasurer
AMERICAN WHITEWATER, 63

Coleman, Will senior Event Manager-Zoom Motorsports
ALABAMA SPORTS FOUNDATION, 227

Colen, Gary President of Agency
ALLOY MEDIA & MARKETING, 772

Coler, Trudy Communications Director
NATIONAL INSTITUTE FOR FITNESS AND SPORT, 84

Coles, Andre Head Coach
INDOOR FOOTBALL LEAGUE, 93

Coles, Jon Associate Athletic Director
FERRIS STATE UNIVERSITY (FSU) ATHLETICS, 358

Coles, Martin EVP / President / Chief Operating Office
ROCKPORT COMPANY, 1183

Coles, Phillip Vice President
WORLD TAEKWONDO FEDERATION (WTF), 144

Colgan, Chris President
EXCLUSIVE SPORTS MARKETING, INC., 782

Colglazier, Kelsey Director of Sports Marketing and Public
TUSCALOOSA CONVENTION & VISITORS BUREAU, 248

Colin, Jason Director of Communications
CONCEPT ONE ACCESSORIES, 1119

Colin, Michele Head Risk Management
ASSURED GUARANTY CORPORATION, 767

Colino, Jon Head Coach
USL LEAGUE TWO, 162

Coppola, Rich Sports Director
WTIC-TV, 710

Copps, Kenny Ticket Manager
ANDY KERR STADIUM, 946

Coppus, Troy Instructor
EVANSVILLE, UNIVERSITY OF, 417

Corales, Alan General Manager
WKVM-AM, 654

Corbet, Peter Co-Chief Executive Officer
TEAMWORKS CENTERS, 1008

Corbett, Bruce Attorney
CORBETT & STEELMAN, 874

Corbett, Christi Promotion Manager
KDLH-TV, 689

Corbett, David Founder and Senior Consultant
NEW DIRECTIONS, 926

Corbett, James President & CEO, Canadian
Outback Advent
LEADING BRANDS, 549, 1155

Corbett, John Chief Executive Officer
SPECIAL OLYMPICS WEST VIRGINIA, 197

Corbett, Neil Sports Editor
CITIZENS' VOICE, 470

Corbin, Dan General Manager
RIVERFRONT STADIUM, 997

Corbin, Herbert Founding Partner
KCSA PUBLIC RELATIONS WORLDWIDE, 791

Corbin, Jeffrey Managing Partner/Chief Executive
Officer
KCSA PUBLIC RELATIONS WORLDWIDE, 791

Corbin, Laura Chairwoman, Publicity Manager
SPARTANBURG CONVENTION & VISITORS
BUREAU, 246

Corbusier, Drue EVP / Director
DILLARD DEPARTMENT STORES, 1224

Corby, John Host
THE JOHN CORBY SHOW, 607

Corcoran, Chris Vice President/Affiliate
Management
WESTWOODONE, 604

Corcoran, Chuck Entertainment VP
GEM GROUP, 835

Corcoran, Jack Sports Reporter
TALLAHASSEE DEMOCRAT, 537

Corcoran, Nicole Deputy Athletics Dir. for Sports
Admin./
KANSAS UNIVERSITY ATHLETICS, 334

Cordaro, John Assistant Executive Director for
Ticketi
INDEPENDENCE STADIUM, 973

Cordaro, Martie President
USL LEAGUE ONE, 49, 161, 999

Cordasco, Nicholas Talent representation
PRINCE MARKETING GROUP, 802, 848

Cordell, Bethany Associate AD, Annual Giving &
Fan Develo
MONTANA STATE UNIVERSITY ATHLETICS,
338

Cordell, Carten Sports Editor
ROSWELL NEIGHBOR, 526

Cordell, De Sales and Marketing VP / ACC
Properties
RAYCOM SPORTS, 805

Cordell, Leigha Event Sales Coordinator
LAWRENCE JOEL VETERANS MEMORIAL
COLISEUM, 982

Cordell, Martha Assistant Dean for Student
Compliance an
THE UNIVERSITY OF TULSA COLLEGE OF
LAW, 911

Cordella, Rick Senior VP & General Manager,
Digital Med
ROTOWORLD, 713

Cordero, Dave Director of Communications
WORLD GOLF VILLAGE, 119

Cordes, Rob National Accounts Manager
VITRONIX PROMOTIONAL GROUP, 1208

Cordick, Denis VP, Marketing
AMJ CAMPBELL, 924

Cordill, Brian Director of Event Operations
BRAMLAGE COLISEUM, 951

Cordingley, Troy Head Coach
NATIONAL LACROSSE LEAGUE, 142

Cordischi, Scott Sports Director
WPRO, 661

Cordova, Art Director, Accounting & Finance
HOMESTEAD-MIAMI SPEEDWAY, LLC, 1025

Core-Drevecky, Leslie President, PGA
COLORADO SECTION PGA, 100

Corelis, Jim AVP, Applications
STATS LLC, 929

Corey, Bill Sports Editor
PROVIDENCE JOURNAL, 523

Corey, Mark Principal
FLAD ARCHITECTS, 1056

Corey, Mike Chief Steward
REMINGTON PARK, 1043

Corey, Steven Attorney
BLANC, DAVID, 867

Corhern, Thomas Sports Writer
HERALD-CITIZEN, 493

Corino, Mark President elect, 1st VP
EASTERN ASSOCIATION OF ROWING
COLLEGES, 147

Corino, Mark Director of Athletics
CALDWELL UNIVERSITY ATHLETICS, 352

Corkran, Steve Sports Reporter (NFL)
CONTRA COSTA TIMES, 473

Corl, Chris General Manager
U.S. CELLULAR CENTER, 1011

Corley, Kelly Vice President Finance
LANCE ARMSTRONG FOUNDATION, 192

Corley, Scott Director of Athletics
BELMONT UNIVERSITY ATHLETICS, 325

Corliss, Robert President / Chief Executive
Officer
ATHLETE'S FOOT, 1216

Corliss, Robert CEO
ATHLETE'S FOOT, 1216

Cormier, Gilles Executive Director & Corporate
Sales
QUEBEC MARITIMES MAJOR JUNIOR
HOCKEY LEAGUE, 135

Cormier, Mary 1st Vice President
NEW HAMPSHIRE WOMEN'S GOLF
ASSOCIATION, 114

Corn, Mike Assistant Director
U.S. TRACK & FIELD AND CROSS COUNTRY
COACHES ASSOCIATION, 177

Cornacchione, Matt Director of Athletic Facilities
NYACK COLLEGE ATHLETICS, 367

Cornelis, Thom Sports Director
KWQC-TV, 697

Cornelison, Edna Promoter
NEA SPEEDWAY, 1030

Cornelison, Hugh Promoter
NEA SPEEDWAY, 1030

Cornelius, Judy Promotions Manager
WHNT-TV, 704

Cornelius, Steve Sports Editor
COMMONWEALTH-JOURNAL, 472

Cornell, Brian Chair & CEO
TARGET STORES, 733

Cornell, Brian President / Chief Executive Officer
SAM'S CLUB, 1236

Cornell, Brian Executive VP, President and CEO,
Sam's C
WAL-MART STORES, INC., 1240

Cornell, Kyle Chief Operating Officer
WOMEN'S PREMIER SOCCER LEAGUE, 161,
166

Cornell, Robert Director
STARR RINK, 1005

Cornetta, Louise Senior Coordinating Producer
WEEKEND GAMENIGHT, 609, 610

Cornilles, Robert Founder/CEO
GAME FACE, INC., 747

Cornish, Brett Marketing/Sales Director
I WIRELESS CENTER, 973

Cornwall, Danielle Assistant Director Of
Educational Progra
JACKIE ROBINSON FOUNDATION, 191

Cornwall, Josh Sports Information Director
GORDON COLLEGE ATHLETICS, 385

Cornwell, Bill News Director
WKEE-FM, 653

Cornwell, Brittany Graduate Assistant, Events
and Conferenc
ROSE BASKETBALL ARENA, 979, 998

Cornwell, Jennifer Marketing Director
ROOTS APPAREL, 1183

Cornwell, Lisa Weekend Sports Anchor/Reporter
WCPO-TV, 701

Cornwell, Scott Director Of Operations
UNIVERSITY HALL, 991, 1012

Cornwell, Steve Executive Vice President
Operations
HOST COMMUNICATIONS, INC., 788

Cornwell, Tanya Ticket Manager
ROBINS CENTER, 998

Coro, Paul Sports/NBA Reporter
ARIZONA REPUBLIC, 461

Corpos, Mike Sports Writer
DAILY REPUBLIC, 479

Corpuz, Rey Marketing Director
MCDAVID, 1161

Corr, David EVP / Executive Creative Director
PUBLICIS NEW YORK, 804

Corrada, Santiago President/Chief Executive
Officer
TAMPA CONVENTION & VISITORS BUREAU,
247

Corrao, Robert Chairman/Chief Executive Officer
SPORTS IMPACT, INC., 578, 856

Corredor, Nestor Manager
ARIZONA LEAGUE (ROOKIE), 34

Corrigan, Boo Director of Athletics
NORTH CAROLINA STATE UNIVERSITY
ATHLETICS, 339, 957, 986

Corrigan, Leo Treasurer
TRANS-MISSISSIPPI GOLF ASSOCIATION,
116

Corriveau, Dave Sports Reporter
VALLEY NEWS, 543

Corry, Stacey Director of Athletic Communications
STATE UNIVERSITY OF NEW YORK
COLLEGE AT BROCKPORT ATHLETICS
(SUNY, 401

Corsano, Anthony CEO
ANVIL KNITWEAR INC., 1099

Corsi, Fred Operations VP
SAVVIS CENTER, 1001

Corso, Cliff Managing Director
MBIA INSURANCE CORPORATION, 768

Corsoe, Frank Sports Editor
BLADE, 465

Corullo, Dan Secretary
ACTION FLOOR SYSTEMS, LLC, 1092

Corum, Debbie Athletic Director
SOUTHERN UTAH UNIVERSITY ATHLETICS,
345

Corvini, Margaret Sports Editor
NEWSDAY, 513

Corvino, John VP, General Counsel
AMERICAN LEAGUE OF PROFESSIONAL
BASEBALL CLUBS, THE, 29

Corvino, Maria Assistant Director of Athletics,
Ticket
HOFSTRA UNIVERSITY STADIUM & ARENA,
971

Corvino, Rich Executive Director
USL LEAGUE TWO, 162

Corwin, Dean News Director
WICK-AM, 650

Cory, Rose General Manager
HARA ARENA, 969

Coryell, Don Director of Athletics
TEXAS STATE UNIVERSITY ATHLETICS, 346,
1006

Cos, Dirk President
UNIVERSAL FABRIC STRUCTURES, 1206

Cosby, Chip Sports Reporter
LEXINGTON HERALD-LEADER, 502

Cosby, Chris Advertising Manager
DIRT RAG, 556

Cosby, Michael Owner/President
GERRY COSBY & COMPANY, INC., 1137

Cosden, Darrell Academics/Athletics Liaison
JUDSON UNIVERSITY, 314

Cosentino, Micheal VP, Ticket Sales
NATIONAL LEAGUE OF PROFESSIONAL
BASEBALL CLUBS, THE, 32

Cosentino, Mike Senior VP, Sales, Service &
Business Int
NATIONAL HOCKEY LEAGUE/NHL, 125

Cosgrove, Delos President & Chief Executive
Officer
CLEVELAND CLINIC, 920

Cosgrove, Jim Executive Director
U.S. YOUTH SOCCER ASSOCIATION, 267

Cosgrove, Richard Chief Executive Partner
CHAPMAN & CUTLER, 872

Cosgrove-Labrecque, Ellen Sports Associate
Editor
SPORTS ILLUSTRATED FOR KIDS, 585

Coslik, Tony Assignment Editor
WIGG-AM, 650

Deloatche, Darren Founder
ASCENSION ENTERPRISES INC., 825

Delong, John Sports Reporter
WINSTON-SALEM JOURNAL, 547

Delorenzo, Ron President
FREEDOM SPORTS NETWORK/DELCOM
MARKETING GROUP, 599

Deluca, Ted Sports Director
WHEN, 649

Deluge, Kathy Comptroller
HAZEL PARK HARNESS RACEWAY (HPHR),
1039

Delvalle, Sarvelio Sports Editor
EL NUEVO PATRIA, 486

Delvicio, Chris Program Director
WCHC-FM, 641

Delzeit, Greg Athletic Director
NJCAA REGION VI WOMEN'S, 287

Demaison, Francois-Xavier Technical Chief
FORMULA 1, 20

Demak, Richard Chief of Reporters & Senior
Editor
SPORTS ILLUSTRATED, 585

Demant, Tim Director of Athletics
WHITWORTH COLLEGE ATHLETICS, 406

Demaris, Seann Sports Sales & Services
AMES AREA SPORTS COMMISSION, 227

Demartini, John President/Chief Executive Officer
STANDOUT SPORTS & EVENTS, 763

Demasio, Nunyo
SPORTS ILLUSTRATED, 585

Dembinski, Dan District Registrar
CONNECTICUT AAU ASSOCIATION, 214

Dembo, Mark Senior Vice President/Marketing
WEST GLEN COMMUNICATIONS, INC., 603

Demchak, William Chairman, President and CEO
PNC FINANCIAL SERVICES, 731

Deme, Mike Editor
ADVENTURE CYCLIST, 549

Demere, Charles President
STADE CANAC, 1005

Demers, Charles President
FRONTIER LEAGUE, 41

Demers, Ruth Executive Director
ROME SPORTS HALL OF FAME & MUSEUM,
258

Demick, Jim Executive Director
FLORIDA STATE GOLF ASSOCIATION, 111

Demitchev, Igor Founder & Chair
CANADIAN SOCCER LEAGUE, 157

Demko, Rob Director of Finance
MIDWEST LEAGUE, 45

Demling, Jody Sports Reporter
COURIER-JOURNAL, 474

Demo, Brad Executive Director
MIDWEST PGA SECTIONAL OFFICE, 106

Demoff, Kevin President
NATIONAL FOOTBALL LEAGUE/NFL, 95

Demola, Julia Merchandise & Community
Relations Coordi
SOUTHERN PROFESSIONAL HOCKEY
LEAGUE, 136

Dempsey, Ellen Director of Athletics
HIRAM COLLEGE ATHLETICS, 387

Dempsey, Kristin Director of ASG Fulfillment
AMATEUR SPORTS GROUP, INC., 824

Dempsey, Lynne Acting Director of Athletics
BRANDEIS UNIVERSITY ATHLETICS, 378

Demyan, David Director of Sports & Competition
SPECIAL OLYMPICS NEBRASKA, 196

DenBeste, Bill Co-Owner
NASCAR XFINITY SERIES, 24

DenBeste, Lori Co-Owner
NASCAR XFINITY SERIES, 24

Denbo, Katie Assistant Editor
FORE, 560

Deneau, Luke Sales Director / Marketing
(Canada)
LOCUST INC., 1157

Denesen, Kevin President
USA BROOMBALL, 67

Denesha, Kathy Editor
TROTTINGBRED, 589

Denham, Jerry President/CEO/Founder
BEARCOM GROUP, 1105

Denham, Marla Coordinator of Basketball,
Volleyball Of
BIG SKY CONFERENCE, 292

Denhart, Lee Field Sales Manager
DRAPER INC., 1125

Denholm, Jack Director of Athletics
BUENA VISTA UNIVERSITY ATHLETICS, 378

Denicola, Lisa Head Athletic Trainer
BRANDEIS UNIVERSITY ATHLETICS, 378

Denise, Layton CEO, COO
SOARING SOCIETY OF AMERICA, 13

Denison, Shelley Secretary/Treasurer
U.S. POWERLIFTING ASSOCIATION, 180

Denison, Steve President
U.S. POWERLIFTING ASSOCIATION, 180

Deniszczuk, Greg Marketing Director
LIEBE ATHLETIC LETTERING, 1155

Denk, Susan Sports Reporter
HAWK EYE, 492

Denlinger, Tom Vice President
SOUTH ATLANTIC LEAGUE (A LEVEL), 51,
981

Denman, Sasha Licensing Coordinator
MAXX GROUP, 1160

Dennehy, Mike Chairperson
SPECIAL OLYMPICS NEW HAMPSHIRE, 196

Dennett, Todd Director Mutuels
WICHITA GREYHOUND PARK, 1048

Denney, Jon President & Chief Development
Officer
U.S. OLYMPIC AND PARALYMPIC
FOUNDATION, 206

Dennis, Adam President & Director, Hockey
Operations
ONTARIO HOCKEY LEAGUE, 134

Dennis, Alfton Operations Director
TARGET FIELD, 1007

Dennis, Craig Advertising Director
UNION, 542

Dennis, Melissa Sales Executive
POWERS EMBROIDERY/ CHENILLE, INC.,
USA, 1176

Dennis, Robert EVP and Chief Operating Officer
GENESCO INC./JOURNEYS, 1125, 1229

Dennis, Robert President/Chief Executive
GENESCO INC./JOURNEYS, 1229

Dennison, Maria President Corporate Office (New
York)
CHASE AMERICA, 747, 828

Denny, Matt General Manager
USL LEAGUE ONE, 161

Denny, Roger Executive Senior Associate Dir. of
Athle
ILLINOIS ATHLETICS, UNIVERSITY OF, 332

Deno, Linda Associate Director of Athletics
SAINT JOSEPH'S COLLEGE ATHLETICS, 369

Denomme, Jeff President/Chief Operating
Officer/Treasu
HOCKEY HALL OF FAME AND MUSEUM, 252

Densa, Steve Executive Director, Communications
ISOTOPES PARK, 972, 974

Densevich, Amy Associate AD, Academic
Services
KENT STATE UNIVERSITY ATHLETICS, 334

Densmore, Michaela Research and Information
Coordinator
FLORIDA STATE UNIVERSITY, 418

Denson, Donna Advertising Manager
SOUTHEAST MISSOURIAN, 532

Dent, Steve Sports Director
KTVM-TV, 696

Dente, Jim Sports Editor
NEW JERSEY HERALD, 510

Dentino, William Principal
BOUTIN, DENTINO, GIBSON, DI GUISTO,
HODELL, INC., 867

Denton, Neal Sports Reporter
BAXTER BULLETIN, 463

Denton, Sandy President
DECATUR AREA CONVENTION & VISITORS
BUREAU, 232

Denucci, Ken News Director
WAQE-FM, 636

Denys, Alec VP High Performance
FEDERATION OF CANADIAN ARCHERS, 14

Denzel, Kyle General Manager
SCOTT STADIUM, 1001

Deol, Manav General Counsel
MAJOR LEAGUE SOCCER, 158

Depcrymski, John Advertising/Promotions
Manager
GNC CORPORATION, 1138

Deprenger, Warren President
MATMAN WRESTLING COMPANY, 1160

Depta, Linda Advertising Director
KALAMAZOO GAZETTE, 499

Derby, Toni-Ann Sr. Associate Director, Athletics
AUSTIN PEAY STATE UNIVERSITY
ATHLETICS, 325

Derda, Bob General Manager
A.J. PALUMBO CENTER, 945

Derhofer, George VP / Chairman
VF CORPORATION, 1208

Derick, Laura Supervisor
DOVER SADDLERY, INC, 1225

Derigan, Tammy Senior Dir of Cultural and
Consumer insi
JAVELIN, 757

Derlago, Mark Assistant Coach
WESTERN HOCKEY LEAGUE, 138

Derleth, Henry President
RIPON ATHLETIC, 1183

Dermenstein, Cindy Convention Services
Coordinator
BLACKHAM COLISEUM, 950

Dermidoff, Evan Athletics Academic Adviser
OAKLAND UNIVERSITY ATHLETICS(OU), 367

Dermody, Rob Director of Ticket Operations
FRONTIER FIELD, 967

Dermutz, Peter Chief Technology Officer
RAPIDTRON, 822

Derr, Arthene Accounts Manager
COOPERSBURG SPORTS, 1223

Derr, Cathy Senior Manager, Arena Events
RUPP ARENA, 999

Derr, Debra President
MASON CITY CONVENTION & VISITOR
BUREAU, 240

Derrick, Curt Assistant General Manager, Director
of T
COLONIAL LIFE ARENA, 958

Derrick, Shannon Public Relations Director
PORTLAND SPEEDWAY, 1031

Dershowitz, Rana VP-Legal and Business Affairs
JEANNIE BAUMGARTNER, 886

Dery, Matt Sports Director
WDFN - 1130 AM THE FAN, 642

Derzes, Pete Senior VP University
Marketing/Program
ESPN REGIONAL TELEVISION, 599

DesLauriers, Kevin Assistant Director of
Athletics, Operati
MOLLOY COLLEGE ATHLETICS, 356, 365

Desalvo, Steve Vice President
SOUTHERN LEAGUE OF PROFESSIONAL
BASEBALL CLUBS, 52

Desantis, Karen Executive Assistant
RIPKEN BASEBALL LLC, 1182

Deschamps, Jeff President
IZAAK WALTON LEAGUE OF AMERICA, 87

Deschamps, Roger Vice President
JUDO CANADA, 143

Desclos, Gena Vice President, Post Production
HBO SPORTS, 676

Deshazier, John Sports Columnist
TIMES-PICAYUNE, 540

Deshields, Delino Manager
SOUTHERN LEAGUE OF PROFESSIONAL
BASEBALL CLUBS, 52

Desimone, Sam Co-President
LACROSSE UNLIMITED, 1154

Desir, Patrick Manager of Facilities Operations
LAWRENCE A. WIEN STADIUM, 962, 982

Desir, Rob Sports Reporter
KTVI-TV, 696

Desjardins, Willie General Manager & Head
Coach
WESTERN HOCKEY LEAGUE, 138

Deskins, Jason Co-General Manager/VP, Hockey
Operations
UNITED STATES HOCKEY LEAGUE, 138

Deslauriers, Lisa Chairman
HAMPTON CLASSIC HORSE SHOW, 75

Desmarteau, Tim Assistant Athletic Director
WEBBER INTERNATIONAL UNIVERSITY
ATHLETICS, 323

Desmond, David Sales Director, Digital Media &
Entertai
PGA TOUR, 105, 108

Desmond, Laura CEO
STARCOM MEDIAVEST GROUP, 811

Dicasmirro, Nate Assistant Coach
AMERICAN HOCKEY LEAGUE/AHL, 127

Dicato, Amy Office Manager
NATIONAL WRESTLING COACHES
ASSOCIATION, 180

Dicera, Domenic Executive Director
ILLINOIS RACING BOARD, 79

Dicesare, Bob Sports Columnist
BUFFALO NEWS, 467

Dichiera, Lisa Director of Advocacy
LANDMARK SPORT GROUP, 840

Dick, Eric Manager
FITNESS MASTER INC, 1133

Dick, Nicky Director Age-Group Team
BRITISH TRIATHLON ASSOCIATION, 178

Dickens, Bill Executive Director
IOWA GOLF ASSOCIATION, 112

Dickens, Emily Secretary
BLACK ENTERTAINMENT & SPORTS
LAWYERS ASSOCIATION INC, 218

Dickensheets, John Sports Director
WBES-AM, 638

Dickenson, Dave General Manager & Head
Coach
CANADIAN FOOTBALL LEAGUE/CFL, 92

Dickerman, Shawn Promotion Director
WGEM-TV, 703

Dickerson, Dave VP/Chief Financial Officer
NATIONAL FOOTBALL LEAGUE/NFL, 94

Dickerson, Jeff Co-Owner
NASCAR CUP SERIES, 23

Dickerson, Ken Director of Maintenance Services
VARIETY WHOLESALERS, 779, 1240

Dickerson, Peggy Sales Director
SALEM CIVIC CENTER, 1000

Dickey, Charlotte Editor
CONQUISTADOR, 556

Dickey, Daryl Athletic Director
UNIVERSITY OF WEST GEORGIA
DEPARTMENT OF INTERCOLLEGIATE
ATHLETIC, 372

Dickey, Jeramiah Director of Athletics
BOISE STATE UNIVERSITY ATHLETICS, 325

Dickey, Walter Deputy Athletic Director
WISCONSIN-MADISON FIELDHOUSE, 1019

Dickinson, Elaine Managing Editor
BOAT U.S. MAGAZINE, 553

Dickinson, Roger Publisher
INDIANA BASKETBALL HISTORY, 565

Dickman, Catheryn Director of Wellness
Programs
EARLHAM COLLEGE (EC) ATHLETICS, 383

Dickman, Robert President
KESSLERS SPORT SHOP, INC., 1231

Dickman, Tom Director of Athletics
HOOD COLLEGE ATHLETICS, 387

Dicks, Rob Director of Athletic Training
LA GRANGE COLLEGE ATHLETICS, 389

Dickson, Andrew Assistant Athletic Director
BRESCIA COLLEGE ATHLETICS, 309

Dickson, Darnell Sports Editor
DAILY HERALD (UT), 477

Dickson, Dick Chairman
PARADIES SHOP/PGA TOUR SHOPS, 1234

Dickson, Rick Director of Athletics
TULSA ATHLETICS, UNIVERSITY OF, 347,
1011

Dickson, Scott Director of Event Services and
Security
VALUE CITY ARENA/JEROME
SCHOTTENSTEIN CENTER, 1001

Dickson, Stacey President
LAKE LANIER CVB, 238

Dickson, Tim Executive Associate AD,
Development
PACIFIC ATHLETICS, UNIVERSITY OF THE,
341

Dickson, Wesley Founder / Chief Executive
Officer
ADVANCED EQUIPMENT CORPORATION,
1094

Dicomo, Phillip Partner
HAILE, SHAW & PFAFFENBERGER, P.A., 882

Dicter, Heather Assistant Professor
ITHACA COLLEGE, 421

Dicun, Ignacio Head Coach
USL LEAGUE TWO, 162

Dicuollo, John Advertising Director
CLIMBING, 555

Dideriksen, Duayne General Manager
LES BOIS PARK, 1041

Didier, Debra Secretary/Treasurer/Chief Financial
Offi
PIONEEER FAMILY BRANDS, INC., 1068

Didio, Larry Assistant Operations Manager
GLENS FALLS CIVIC CENTER, 968

Dieckhaus, Chris News/Promotions Director
KWMO-AM, 632

Diegelman, Matt Athletic Facilities Coordinator
HILBERT COLLEGE ATHLETICS, 387

Diehl, Toni Stadium Supervisor
VA MEMORIAL STADIUM, 1015

Diehm, Russell Senior Vice President of Finance
& Chief
BOSCOV'S DEPARTMENT STORES, 1220

Diekman, Robert SVP, Operations / Logistics
ROYCE UNION BICYCLE COMPANY, INC.,
1146, 1184

Dielen, Tom Secretary General/Executive Director
WORLD ARCHERY FEDERATION, 15

Diemont, Anthony National Direct Sales
Supervisor
SEATTLE SYSTEMS/LENOX HILL BRACE
COMPANY, 1187

Diener, Bob President, Hotels.com
INTERACTIVECORP/HOME SHOPPING
NETWORK, 1230

Diercks, Kelly Associate Athletic Director
AUGSBURG COLLEGE ATHLETICS, 377

Diercks, Walter Esquire
RUBIN, ERIC M., 903

Dierdorf, Uohn Chief Executive Officer
BROWNING DAY MULLINS DIERDORF
ARCHITECTS, 1051

Dieringer, Kathy Secretary/Treasurer
NATIONAL ATHLETIC TRAINERS'
ASSOCIATION, 84

Dierks, Zach Producer, writer and editor
COSTANTE GROUP SPORTS & EVENT
MARKETING, LLC, 753

Diese, Herve Head Coach
USL CHAMPIONSHIP, 160

Diestler, Crystal Administrative Assistant
JAMESTOWN CIVIC CENTER, 975

Dietrich, Aaron Sports Director
KNOE-TV, 692

Dietrich, John Executive Vice President & CFO
FEDEX CORPORATION, 728

Dietrich, Steve General Manager
NATIONAL LACROSSE LEAGUE, 142

Dietrich, Wendy Athletic Trainer
EAST STROUDSBURG UNIVERSITY (ESU) OF
PENNSYLVANIA ATHLETICS, 357

Dietz, Beth National Events Manager
POP WARNER LITTLE SCHOLARS, 89

Dietz, Diane Chief communications officer
BIG TEN ATHLETIC CONFERENCE, 826

Dietz, Jerry Program Director
KOAK-AM, 615, 625

Dietz, Phil Sports Director
KOHI-AM, 625

Dietzen, Nick MSGA Commmunications Director
MONTANA STATE GOLF ASSOCIATION, 113

Diffley, John Deputy AD/COO
ST. JOHN'S UNIVERSITY ATHLETICS, 345

Difilippo, James Contact
DIFILIPPO, JAMES, 876

Digges, Charlie Secretary/Treasurer
MISSOURI GOLF ASSOCIATION, 113

Diggs, Tony Manager
PIONEER BASEBALL LEAGUE, 50

Dighton, Trevor Chief Financial Officer
WACKENHUT SPORTS SECURITY, 766

Digianfilippo, Denise Dean of Academic Affairs
NJCAA REGION I MEN'S, 286

Dijkema, Jan President
INTERNATIONAL SKATING UNION (ISU), 86,
205

Dikmen, F. Publisher
GREAT LAKES BOATING MAGAZINE, 563

Dilard, Brian Director of Marketing
ALVARADO MANUFACTURING COMPANY,
1097

Dilbeck, Kathy Scheduling Coordinator
ISLAND GROVE REGIONAL PARK (IGRP),
1040

Dilbeck, Steve Sports Columnist
DAILY NEWS (CA), 478

Diles, Dave Athletic Director
CAMERON HALL, 954

Dilger, Mardi Board Chair
INTERNATIONAL TICKETING ASSOCIATION
(INTIX), THE, 931

Diliberto, Matt Partner
NASCAR CUP SERIES, 23

Dill, Jason Sports Reporter
BRADENTON HERALD, 466

Dill, Linda Advertising Director
SAND SPORTS, 579

Dill, Meredith Head Athletic Trainer
MISSOURI BAPTIST COLLEGE ATHLETICS,
316

Dill, Tracy Director of Athletics
BEMIDJI STATE UNIVERSITY ATHLETICS,
123, 352

Dillabaugh, Kim Goaltending Coach
NATIONAL HOCKEY LEAGUE/NHL, 125

Dillard, Alex President / Director
DILLARD DEPARTMENT STORES, 1224

Dillard, Floyd Promoter
THUNDER VALLEY RACEWAY, 1034

Dillard, Michael CEO & Chairman
CENTURY SPORTING GOODS, 1222

Dillard, Mike EVP / Director
DILLARD DEPARTMENT STORES, 1224

Dillard, Paul National Commander
AMERICAN LEGION BASEBALL, 25

Dillard, Tommy Sports Editor
MURRAY LEDGER AND TIMES, 509

Dillard, Vance Program Director
WVRY-FM, 670

Dille, Penny Advertising Director
LONGMONT DAILY TIMES-CALL, 503

Diller, Susan Membership Director
USA CYCLING NEWSLETTER, 590

Dilley, Jeff Chief Financial Officer
GOLF CHANNEL, THE, 599, 687

Dillhyon, Mike Executive Director
NATIONAL ASSOCIATION OF POLICE
ATHLETIC/ACTIVITES LEAGUES (NATL P,
221

Dillman, Lisa Sports Reporter (Tennis)
LOS ANGELES TIMES, 503

Dillon, Dan Promotions Director
KMOV-TV, 692

Dillon, Jarrod President, Business Operations
MAJOR LEAGUE SOCCER, 158

Dillon, Mike Chief Financial Officer
NATIONAL HOCKEY LEAGUE/NHL, 125, 851

Dillon, Pat Director of Corporate Partnerships
EVERETT MEMORIAL STADIUM, 964

Dillon, Tim Vice President, Sales And Marketing
EMS SOFTWARE, LCC, 1214

Dillon, Travis SVP, Marketing
AMERICAN LEAGUE OF PROFESSIONAL
BASEBALL CLUBS, THE, 30

Dillow, Lindsey Accounting Assistant
INDEPENDENT BOATBUILDERS INC., 63

Dilullo, Dan contact
DILULLO ASSOCIATES INC., 1054

Dilz, Al President
SPORTS SENSORS INC, 1194

Dima, Terri Sales/Marketing Coordinator
CARROM COMPANY, 1114

Dimaio, Rob General Manager
AMERICAN HOCKEY LEAGUE/AHL, 128

Dimeo, John General Manager
KELA, 616

Dimitrov, Kiril General Manager
CANADIAN SOCCER LEAGUE, 157

Dimmick, Mike Weekend Sports Anchor
WEEK-TV, 702

Dimon, Jamie Chairman/Executive Committee
JPMORGAN CHASE BANK, N.A., 728, 768

Dimond, Mike President Emeritus/Treasurer
AMERICAN AMATEUR BASEBALL
CONGRESS, 25

Dimperio, Leda Systems Administrator
BIRMINGHAM RACING COMMISSION, 79

Dinardo, Dominick Sports Editor
MEADVILLE TRIBUNE, 506

Dinauer, Jake Head Athletic Trainer
CARTHAGE COLLEGE ATHLETICS, 379

Dineen, Gord Assistant Coach
AMERICAN HOCKEY LEAGUE/AHL, 128

Dineen, Kevin Head Coach
AMERICAN HOCKEY LEAGUE/AHL, 129

Doyle, Judy Advertising Manager
POLO PLAYERS EDITION, 576

Doyle, Justin Director of Business Development
OHIO STATE UNIVERSITY, 430, 1001

Doyle, Kevin President, Sales & Distributor
Operation
MILLERCOORS, 730

Doyle, Matt Sports Writer
TULSA WORLD, 542

Doyle, Michael President, Business Operations
NATIONAL HOCKEY LEAGUE/NHL, 126

Doyle, Mike Vice President/Architect
COMMUNICATION ARTS INCORPORATED,
1052

Doyle, Patrick Executive Vice President/Chief
Financial
DIRECTV, INC., 686

Doyle, Paul Sports Reporter (Baseball)
HARTFORD COURANT, 492

Doyle, Richard President
COMFORT LINE PRODUCTS, 1118

Dozier, Missye Sports Director
MISSISSIPPI, STATE GAMES OF, 263

Dozier, Tom Sports Editor
PROGRESS-INDEX, 523

Drachkovitch, Rasha Founder
44 BLUE PRODUCTIONS, INC., 597

Draft, Howard Executive Chairman
DRAFTWORLDWIDE, 781

Dragan, Stephanie Assistant Athletics Director
FRANKLIN PIERCE UNIVERSITY ATHLETICS,
359

Drager, Ron President & Chief Executive Officer
ARCA RACING SERIES, 16

Dragone, Christopher Director
NATIONAL MUSEUM OF RACING HALL OF
FAME, 256

Draine, Michael Sports Agent
INTRASPORT MANAGEMENT GROUP, 839

Drake, Alan News/Sports Director
WIRY-AM, 651

Drake, Ducky News Director ; Sports Director
WIRY-AM, 651

Drapcho, Gary Sports Director
WSEE-TV, 709

Drape, Joe Sports Reporter
NEW YORK TIMES, 511

Draper, Kris Director, Amateur Scouting
NATIONAL HOCKEY LEAGUE/NHL, 124

Draper, Laurie Member Services & Program
Director
ROCKY MOUNTAIN PGA SECTIONAL
OFFICE, 107

Drass, Mike Executive Director of Athletics
WESLEY COLLEGE ATHLETICS, 405

Drayer, Matt General Manager
RUSSELL E. DIETHRICK JR. PARK, 1000

Drayer, Matthew General Manager
NEW YORK-PENNSYLVANIA LEAGUE, 47

Dreher, James VP General Manager
DURHAM BOAT COMPANY, 1126

Dreher, Josh Head Athletic Trainer
ADAMS STATE UNIVERSITY ATHLETICS, 350

Dreiling, Dave Owner
GTM SPORTSWEAR, 1140

Dreiling, Richard Chairman / Chief Executive
Officer
DOLLAR GENERAL CORPORATION, 1225

Dreissigacker, Richard President
CONCEPT II, INC., 1118

Dreistadt, Michele Director of Intramurals
MOUNT ST. MARY COLLEGE ATHLETICS,
394

Dressel, Jim Editor
BOWLERS JOURNAL INTERNATIONAL, 553

Dreves, Mike Interim Department Chair
GROVE CITY COLLEGE ATHLETICS, 386

Drew, Chelsea Legal Assistant
BECKER, WILLIAM F.X., 865

Drew, Homer Associate Director of Athletics
VALPARAISO UNIVERSITY, 436

Drew, Jay Sports Reporter
SALT LAKE TRIBUNE, 527

Drew, Loyda Project Manager
MOBIVITY, 758, 795

Drew, Pearson Chairman
DREW PEARSON MARKETING, INC. (DPM), 0

Drew, Tyson Associate AD, Facility
Operations/Event
WAR MEMORIAL STADIUM (WY), 1017

Drewes, Doug Executive Vice President
OVATION FOOD SERVICES LP, 1067

Drewniak, Michael VP Manufacturing
TOPPS COMPANY, INC., 1202

Drews, David EVP/Chief Financial Officer
GEORGE P. JOHNSON COMPANY, 784

Drickey, Steven General Counsel
LIFE FITNESS, INC., 1155

Drie-Andrzjewski, Linda Director of Athletics
WILMINGTON UNIVERSITY ATHLETICS
(DELAWARE), 375

Driedger, Andrea Vice President, Finance &
Admin.
CANADA BASKETBALL, 53

Driessen, Christine EVP & CFO
OUTSIDE THE LINES, 674, 680

Driffill, Tom Human Resource Manager
HOYT USA, 1146

Driggers, Justin Sports Writer
MORNING NEWS (SC), 497, 508

Drigotas, John Group Sales Director
TOP OF THE THIRD, 1010

Drikos, Peter Assistant Coach
EAST COAST HOCKEY LEAGUE/ECHL, 130

Drimmer, Lillian Associate Professor of
Management
TIFFIN UNIVERSITY, 435

Drinen, Doug Football Operations
SPORTS REFERENCE, THE, 929

Dring, Scott Executive Director
DUBLIN CONVENTION & VISITOR BUREAU,
233

Drinkill, Dave General Manager
ONTARIO HOCKEY LEAGUE, 134

Driscoll, David Principal
STEIN, SPERLING, BENNETT, DE JONG,
DRISCOLL & GREENFEIG, P.C., 908

Driscoll, Dennis Director of Athletic
Communications
MARIAN COLLEGE OF FOND DU LAC
ATHLETICS, 392

Driscoll, Dill Founder
IGNITION, INC., 788

Driscoll, Elaine Director of Communications
MASSACHUSETTS GAMING COMMISSION,
80

Driscoll, Jenny Assistant Editor
SKATING, 580

Driscoll, Lori Advertising Director
TIMES HERALD (MI), 539

Driscoll, Mark Founder
IGNITION, INC., 788

Driscoll, Mike Treasurer-South West Region
U.S. HANDBALL ASSOCIATION, 121

Driscoll, Robert Athletic Director/Vice President
PROVIDENCE COLLEGE ATHLETICS, 342

Driscoll, Sean Director, Ticket Sales & Services
EAST COAST HOCKEY LEAGUE/ECHL, 129

Driscoll, Susan Founder
IGNITION, INC., 788

Driscoll, Terry Athletics Director
WILLIAM & MARY HALL, 958, 1017, 1018

Driscoll, Timothy President / Chief Executive
Officer
ALUMINUM ATHLETIC EQUIPMENT
COMPANY (AAE), 1096

Driskell, Lavon Athletic Director
BLUE MOUNTAIN COLLEGE ATHLETICS, 309

Driskill, Dustin Director of Sports Medicine
LUBBOCK CHRISTIAN UNIVERSITY
ATHLETICS, 315

Driver, Brian Program Director
WNKT-FM, 658

Driver, Kristi Sports Manager
NORTH CAROLINA SPORTS DEVELOPMENT
OFFICE, 242

Driver, Spruell Academic Affairs and Student
Success (Ch
MIZELL, CATHERINE, 896

Droddy, J.D. League Adjudicator
PECOS LEAGUE, 49, 50

Droge, Brandon Sports Information Director
AVILA UNIVERSITY ATHLETICS, 308

Drohan, Kate 2nd VP
NATIONAL FASTPITCH COACHES
ASSOCIATION/NFCA, 169

Drolet, Denis President / Chief Executive Officer
IN GLAS COMPANY, 1147

Drucker, Jason Sales
FABRICATION ENTERPRISES, 1131

Druckman, Lauren Sales Manager
GULBENKIAN SWIM, INC., 1141

Druenen, Sid Director, Sporting Development
USL LEAGUE TWO, 162

Druiz, Fae Vice President
BULOVA WATCH COMPANY, 1112

Drummey, Maureen Sports Assistant Editor
SKI MAGAZINE, 580

Drummond, Troy Associate Director of Athletics,
Operati
BROWNWOOD COLISEUM, 952

Drury, Chris President & General Manager
NATIONAL HOCKEY LEAGUE/NHL, 125

Dryden, Deidra Associate Athletic Director
SOUTHERN VIRGINIA UNIVERSITY
ATHLETICS, 401

DuBoi, Cari Secretary
NATIONAL ASSOCIATION OF COLLEGIATE
GYMNASTICS COACHES - WOMEN, 120

DuBois, Brent Athletic Trainer
UNITED STATES HOCKEY LEAGUE, 137

DuBois, David President/CEO
FORT WORTH CONVENTION & VISITORS
BUREAU, 234

DuBois, Kimberly National Sales Manager
HEART RATE, INC., 1143

DuBois, Patric Deputy Athletic Director
NORTHWESTERN STATE UNIVERSITY OF
LOUISIANA ATHLETICS, 340

DuBrueler, Justin Sr.Director Accounting
RICHMOND INTERNATIONAL RACEWAY,
1031

DuBuis, Carolyn Human Resources Director
BETA DESIGN GROUP, INC., 1050

DuPree, David Sports Reporter
USA TODAY, 543

DuPuis, Carol Director of Sales and Marketing
SEAGATE CENTRE, 1002

DuPuy, Robert President/Chief Operating Officer
MAJOR LEAGUE BASEBALL PROPERTIES,
892

DuTeau, Randy Event Manager
AUGUSTA SPORTS COUNCIL, GREATER, 228

DuVivier, Lynne President
CREATIVE FACTOR, INC., 753

Duarte, Miguel Chief of Staff
AMERICAN LEAGUE OF PROFESSIONAL
BASEBALL CLUBS, THE, 30

Dubas, Kyle President, Hockey Operations &
General M
NATIONAL HOCKEY LEAGUE/NHL, 125

Dubb, Michael Principal
AQUEDUCT, 1042

Dube, Philippe President and Chief Executive
Officer
CCM HOCKEY, 1114

Dubicki, Stan Goaltending Coach
AMERICAN HOCKEY LEAGUE/AHL, 127

Dubiel, Robert President
COBRA PUMA GOLF, 1117

Dubin, Dave Circulation Director
ATHLETIC MANAGEMENT, 550

Dubin, Stephen Partner
YEE & DUBIN LLP, 860

Dubois, Troy Sales/Marketing
CABANA BANNERS, 1112

Dubose, Antoinette 1st Lt. Governor/Office
Manager
MARYLAND AAU ASSOCIATION, 214

Dubow, Brad General Manager
KROD, 627

Dubra, Charles Interim Director of Athletics
HUSTON-TILLOTSON COLLEGE ATHLETICS,
314

Dubrasich, Paul Senior Counsel
CAMPBELL, ROBERT G., 871

Ducey, Marjie State College Sports Writer
OMAHA WORLD-HERALD, 516

Ducharme, Edward Sports Agent
PROFESSIONAL SPORTS MANAGEMENT
GROUP, 850

Ducharme, Mark Sports Reporter
ENTERPRISE, 487

Ducharme, Patrick Sports Agent
PROFESSIONAL SPORTS MANAGEMENT GROUP, 850
Duchesneau, Jerome General Manager
FRONTIER LEAGUE, 41
Duchossois, Richard Chairman
ARLINGTON INTERNATIONAL, 1035
Duckett, Regina Administrative Asst
ASTRO TURF MANUFACTURING COMPANY, 1101
Duckler, Ray Sports Columnist
CONCORD MONITOR, 473
Duckworth, Bill Operations Manager
SOUTHERN BLEACHER COMPANY, INC., 1191
Duckworth, Paul Program/News Director
KOMO 1000 AM RADIO, 625
Duckworth, Ryan National Conferences/Events
RILEY, WILLIAM T., 852
Ducrot, Pascal President
SCOTT USA, 1186
Duda, Doug Sports Director
KICS-AM, 620
Duda, Jacqueline Customer Service Manager
OWENS & CO., INC., 1179
Dudley, Jeff Marketing Manager
WMAZ-TV, 706
Dudley, Rick President/Chief Executive Officer
OCTAGON ATHLETE REPRESENTATION (ATTORNEYS), 799, 833, 845, 898
Dudrick, Darian Sports Editor
PLAINSMAN, 520
Dudzik, Ken Marketing Director
KMTV-TV, 692
Due, Chris Director of Athletic Communication
LUBBOCK CHRISTIAN UNIVERSITY ATHLETICS, 315
Dueck, Noreen Program Director
SPORTS LINE LIVE, 681
Duecker, Dave Brand Director
BRUNSWICK BICYCLE DIVISION, 1111
Duellman, Christine News Director
WRFW-FM, 664
Duenkel, Bob Executive Director/Curator
INTERNATIONAL SWIMMING HALL OF FAME, 254
Duerr, Chris Sports Director
KHQA-TV, 690
Duey, Duane Certified Athletic Trainer
LINFIELD COLLEGE ATHLETICS, 390
Dufek, Joe Sports Anchor
KDLH-TV, 689
Duff, Chris General Manager/Vice President
NORTHWEST BASEBALL LEAGUE, 48, 948
Duff, Dale Program Director/WZON
AM 620 WZON THE SPORTS ZONE, 611
Duff, Gill President / Chief Executive Officer
PUBLICIS NEW YORK, 804
Duff, Sean Sports Editor
COLORADOAN, 471
Duffin, Larry Director
LAVELL EDWARDS STADIUM, 982
Dufford, Todd National Sales Manager
NEW AGENDA BY PERRIN, 1167
Duffy, A.J. Head Athletic Trainer
WIDENER UNIVERSITY ATHLETICS, 406
Duffy, Amy Chief of Staff
SOUTH CAROLINA PARKS, RECREATION & TOURISM, 232, 246, 264
Duffy, Bill President/Chief Executive Officer
BDA SPORTS MANAGEMENT, 826
Duffy, Bill Chairman and CEO
BDA SPORTS MANAGEMENT, 826
Duffy, Brian Sports Anchor/Reporter
WOIO-TV, 707
Duffy, Clayton Sports Director
WLFI-TV, 706
Duffy, Dan Executive Director
OREGON, STATE GAMES OF, 263
Duffy, Danielle Head Athletic Trainer
ARCADIA UNIVERSITY ATHLETICS DEPARTMENT-GLENSIDE, 377
Duffy, Edward Chief Executive Officer
CHICAGOLAND SPEEDWAY, 1023
Duffy, Judy Tee Off Time Editor
NEBRASKA WOMEN'S AMATEUR GOLF ASSOCIATION, 113
Duffy, Kathy Marketing Director
NEW MEXICO STATE FAIR, 1042

Duffy, Kerry President/Chief Executive Officer
OREGON, STATE GAMES OF, 263
Duffy, Matt Handicap Services Manager
NORTHERN OHIO GOLF ASSOCIATION, 104
Duffy, Michael Athletic Director
ADRIAN COLLEGE ATHLETICS-ADRIAN, 376
Duffy, Randee Senior Associate AD, NCAA Eligibility
OHIO UNIVERSITY ATHLETICS, 340
Duffy, Timothy Member
BURELSON, PATE & GIBSON, L.L.P., 869
Dufoe, William Partner
WRIGHT, DOUGLAS A., 917
Dufour, Marc President & CEO
CLUB CAR, INC., 1117
Dufresne, Chris Sports Reporter
LOS ANGELES TIMES, 503
Dugan, Brad Senior Director, Ticketing & Public Even
NATIONAL FOOTBALL LEAGUE/NFL, 96
Dugan, Chris Sports Editor
OBSERVER-REPORTER, 515
Dugan, Dick Security Manager
TARGET FIELD, 1007
Dugan, Erin Assoc Director Media Relations & Externa
MID-AMERICAN ATHLETIC CONFERENCE, 299
Dugan, Michael President / Chief Executive Officer
EXERCYCLE CORPORATION, 1131
Duggan, Dan Chair & CEO
USL LEAGUE TWO, 162
Duggan, John First Vice President
WORLD BOXING ORGANIZATION, 67
Duggan, Mary Manager
CANADIAN SOCIETY FOR EXERCISE PHYSIOLOGY, 83
Dugger, Barclay Coordinator of Athletic Training Service
SPRINGFIELD COLLEGE ATHLETICS, 371
Dugger, Jason Sports Copy Editor
DALLAS MORNING NEWS, 481
Dugger, Keith Head Athletic Trainer
NATIONAL LEAGUE OF PROFESSIONAL BASEBALL CLUBS, THE, 31
Dugre, Claude Vice President Operations
LE RESEAU DES SPORTS (RSD) INC., 698
Duhon, Felicia Controller
LAFAYETTE CONVENTION & VISITORS BUREAU, 238
Duke, Michael President and Chief Executive Officer
WAL-MART STORES, INC., 1240
Duke, Oak Advertising Manager
WELLSVILLE DAILY REPORTER, 546
Duke, Stephanie Associate Athletic Director
CALIFORNIA STATE POLY UNIVERSITY ATHLETICS, 353
Duke, Tom Account Executive
WBET-AM, 638
Dukelow, Rick Sales Representative
GAGLIARDI INSURANCE SERVICES, 768
Dukes, Al Sports Director
WZTM, 672
Dukes, Carl Host
SPORTSBEAT, 606
Dukes, Charlene President
NJCAA REGION XX MEN'S, 289
Dulaney, Brett Executive Director
ST. PETERSBERG BOWL, 92
Dully, Bill Chief Operating Officer
UPPER DECK COMPANY, 1206
Dulude, Meggan Associate Director of Athletics
ST. MICHAEL'S COLLEGE ATHLETICS(SMC), 371
Dumas, Clyde Director
LADD PEEBLES STADIUM, 980
Dunaway, Jim Sports Director
WVTM-TV, 712
Dunaway, Vic Senior Editor
FLORIDA SPORTSMAN, 559
Dunbar, J.L Program Director
WNLS, 634, 658
Dunbar, Kit Sales manager of sports commission
ST. PETERSBURG/CLEARWATER SPORTS COMMISSION, 247

Dunbar, Kris Athletic Director
LAKE SUPERIOR STATE UNIVERSITY ATHLETICS (LSSU), 361
Dunbar, Lisa Director, Marketing & Communications
SPECIAL OLYMPICS CANADA, 194
Dunbar, Loraine Athletics Operations Coordinator
BENEDICT COLLEGE ATHLETICS, 352
Duncalfe, Michael Contact
INDY PRO 2000, 22
Duncan, Alan Business Litigation
SMITH MOORE LEATHERWOOD, LLP, 855
Duncan, Claudia Dept. Chairperson
BARTON COLLEGE, 411
Duncan, Curtis News Director
KLOE-AM, 622
Duncan, Heather Secretary
GATOR BOWL, 90
Duncan, Jeff Sports Columnist (NFL)
TIMES-PICAYUNE, 540
Duncan, Mike Sr. Associate Athletic Director, Facilit
AUTZEN STADIUM, 615, 947
Duncan, Neal Sponsorship Sales Manager
POLK COUNTY SPORTS MARKETING, 244
Duncan, Scott Marketing And Sales Leader
PRICEWATERHOUSECOOPERS, 760
Duncan, Sean Sports Editor
TIMES-MAIL, 540
Duncan, Shelley Manager
NORTHWEST BASEBALL LEAGUE, 47
Duncan, Stephen General Manager, Specialized Products
H&B SPECIALIZED PRODUCTS, 1141
Duncan, Tim Director of Athletics
CLAYTON COLLEGE & STATE UNIVERSITY ATHLETICS, 338, 355
Duncker, C. Secretary
TRIPLE CROWN PRODUCTIONS, 815
Dundon, Tom Owner & Governor
NATIONAL HOCKEY LEAGUE/NHL, 123
Dunham, John President / Director
MAY DEPARTMENT STORES COMPANY, THE, 1232
Dunham, Jon Advertising Director
STATESVILLE RECORD & LANDMARK, 535
Dunivant, Todd Vice President & General Manager
USL CHAMPIONSHIP, 160
Dunk, Alico Assistant Athletic Director - Academics
ELIZABETH CITY STATE UNIVERSITY (ECSU) ATHLETICS, 357
Dunkley, Eugene Biology Department Chair and Associate P
GREENVILLE COLLEGE, 419
Dunlap, Jeff Director of Operations
CARTER FINLEY STADIUM, 955
Dunlap, Jim Editor-in-Chief
CRITTENDEN GOLF, 556
Dunlap, John Assistant Athletic Director
WARNER UNIVERSITY ATHLETICS, 323, 705
Dunlap, John Partner
GOWEN, GEORGE W., 882
Dunlap, Keith Sports Reporter
OAKLAND PRESS, 515
Dunlap, Meghann Project Manager
TEAM MARKETING REPORT, 588
Dunlavey, Chris President
BRAILSFORD & DUNLAVEY, 1050
Dunleavy, Kevin Sports Editor
FAIRFAX JOURNAL, 488
Dunleavy, Mike General Manager
NATIONAL BASKETBALL ASSOCIATION/NBA, 56
Dunlop, Rob General Manager
KOMO 1000 AM RADIO, 625
Dunmyer, Stephany Assistant Director of Athletics
VIRGINIA WESLEYAN COLLEGE ATHLETICS(VWC), 404
Dunn, Andrew Athletic Trainer
CHEYNEY UNIVERSITY ATHLETICS, 49, 50, 354
Dunn, Andy President
CALIFORNIA LEAGUE (A-LEVEL), 36
Dunn, Billy Manager
REYNOLDS COLISEUM, 996
Dunn, Craig Sports Editor
LOGAN DAILY NEWS, 503

Farrell, Kenny Senior VP, Marketing & Analytics
NATIONAL LEAGUE OF PROFESSIONAL
BASEBALL CLUBS, THE, 31
Farrell, Kristine Director of Sports Medicine
MIDAMERICA NAZARENE UNIVERSITY
ATHLETICS, 316
Farrell, Matt Chief Marketing Officer
USA SWIMMING, 209
Farrell, Mickey Dir. of Operations
RAYMOND JAMES STADIUM, 247, 995
Farrell, Pat Head Coach, Men's Soccer
MCCARTHY STADIUM, 985
Farrell, Perry Sports Reporter
DETROIT FREE PRESS, 483
Farrell, Ryan Marketing Coordinator
NATIONAL FEDERATION OF PROFESSIONAL
TRAINERS, 222
Farrell, Thomas Owner
WOMEN'S FOOTBALL ALLIANCE / WFA, 98
Farrell, Timothy Assistant Commissioner
EMPIRE 8, 295
Farrell, William Partner/Attorney
FINKELMEIER LAW FIRM, 880
Farris, Marjorie Member
STITES & HARBISON, 857
Farris, Ryan President
CONSOLIDATED GRAPHICS, 779
Farris, Sandra Event Coordinator/Accounting
UTC MCKENZIE ARENA, 1015
Farry, Anthony Head Coach, Men's National
Program
FIELD HOCKEY CANADA, 121
Farwell, Russ Vice President, Hockey Operations
WESTERN HOCKEY LEAGUE, 139
Fasel, Ren, President
INTERNATIONAL ICE HOCKEY FEDERATION
(IIHF), 204
Fasol, Bruce Sports Director
WFRX-AM, 642, 646
Fasold, Mark SVP and Chief Financial Officer
L.L. BEAN, 1231
Fass, Jonathan Sports Director
WGHT-AM, 648
Fassnacht, Hans VP International
TYR SPORT, INC., 1205
Fassnacht, Micheal President
DRAFTWORLDWIDE, 781
Fasulo, Robert Director , Corporate
Development-Interna
PARK LANE - INVESTMENT BANKING
SERVICES, 769
Fasy, Bill EVP/Chief Operating Officer
DELAWARE PARK RACETRACK & SLOTS,
1037
Faticoni, Tony Deputy Director of Athletics
PFEIFFER UNIVERSITY ATHLETICS, 368
Fatta, Robert Director, Ticket Operations
EAST COAST HOCKEY LEAGUE/ECHL, 129
Fatzinger, Curt PAC/Intramural Director
PIONEER FIELD, 993
Fauber, Gary Sports Assistant Editor
REGISTER-HERALD, 524
Faucett, Michael Assistant Athletic Director
BENEDICTINE COLLEGE ATHLETICS, 308
Faught, Phil Athletic Trainer/Strength Coach
UNITED STATES HOCKEY LEAGUE, 137
Faulk, Marshall Founder
MARSHALL FAULK FOUNDATION, 192
Faulkner, Barry Sports Writer
NEWPORT BEACH COSTA MESA DAILY
PILOT, 511
Faulkner, Colin Executive VP & Chief Commercial
Officer
NATIONAL LEAGUE OF PROFESSIONAL
BASEBALL CLUBS, THE, 31
Faulkner, Dillon Communications Manager
CHICK-FIL-A PEACH BOWL, 90
Faulkner, Doug Athletic Director; Associate
Professor o
GREENVILLE COLLEGE, 419
Faulkner, Jaime President, Business Operations
NATIONAL HOCKEY LEAGUE/NHL, 124
Faulkner, Sue Human Resources Executive
MECA SPORTSWEAR, INC., 1161
Faulstick, Don Director of Athletics
AMHERST COLLEGE ATHLETICS-AMHERST,
376
Fause, Kenneth Principal/VP
SMITH, FAUSE, MCDONALD, INC., 822

Fausett, Chris VP/Manager/Sales/Trained
Polygraph Exami
LAFAYETTE INSTRUMENT COMPANY, 1154
Fauss, Ron Sports Consultant
MULTI-AD, 1165
Fausti, Michele Assistant to CEO
HDS PROMOTIONAL MARKETING, 787
Fautas, Jason Assistant Athletic Director
WALSH UNIVERSITY ATHLETICS, 323
Faux, Ian VP/Chief Operating Officer
SUPERSTAR MANAGEMENT, INC., 857
Favier, James Principal
HASTINGS + CHIVETTA ARCHITECTS, INC.,
1058
Favier, Matthew Director
AUSTRALIAN SPORTS COMMISSION, 260
Favila, David Sports Editor
VALLEY MORNING STAR, 543
Favilla, David General Manager
WKWZ-FM, 654
Fawcett, Dave Sports Editor
POTOMAC NEWS, 505, 522
Fawcett, David Principal
ELS ARCHITECTURE AND URBAN DESIGN,
1055
Fawcett, Karen Athletics Secretary
CAMPBELLSVILLE UNIVERSITY ATHLETICS,
310
Fawcett, Laura Editor
SKATING, 580
Fawcett, Rae Sr.VP, Organisational Development
and Hu
CAREY WORLDWIDE CHAUFFERED
SERVICES, 925
Fay, David Sports Reporter (Hockey)
WASHINGTON TIMES, 545
Fay, Jillian Communications Manager
MAJOR LEAGUE LACROSSE, 141
Fay, John Sports Reporter
CINCINNATI ENQUIRER, 470
Fay, Ted Chair/Director
SUNY, STATE UNIVERSITY OF NEW
YORK-CORTLAND, 434
Faye, Wood President
METRAPARK, 1041
Fayfield, Bradford Publisher
FREESKIER, 560
Fazio, Alice Director of Athletics
NEW JERSEY CITY UNIVERSITY (NJCU), 395
Fazio, Mike Asst. General Manager & Dir., Player
Dev
UNITED STATES HOCKEY LEAGUE, 137
Fazio, Rosemary Partner
ASHFORD & WRISTON, 862
Fazzone, Anthony Attorney
FAZZONE & BAILLIE, 833
Feasel, Gregory President & COO
NATIONAL LEAGUE OF PROFESSIONAL
BASEBALL CLUBS, THE, 31
Feaster, Dan Secretary
FEDERATION OF PETANQUE USA, 145
Feather, Dave Assistant General Manager
SOUTHERN PROFESSIONAL HOCKEY
LEAGUE, 136
Feaver, Chris Sports Editor
ITHACA JOURNAL, 497
Feazell, Trey Senior Vice President and General
Manage
PHILIPS ARENA, 993
Febles, Carlos Manager
CAROLINA LEAGUE, 37
Febus, Jeff Sports Information Coordinator
CALVIN COLLEGE ATHLETICS, 379
Fechtig, Mary President/CEO
JHG TOWNSEND, 790, 821
Fedko, John Sports Director
WPXI-TV, 708
Fee, Frank Advertising Manager/Sports Director
KROX-AM, 628
Feeley, Ted Media Relations Director
BIRMINGHAM BOWL, 89
Feeney-Caito, Kay Promotions Director
WTLC-FM, 668
Feenick, John Director
CASTLETON STATE COLLEGE, 412
Fees, Brian Sports Editor
DAILY REVIEW (PA), 479
Fefer, Allan Owner
ALLAN ENTERPRISES, 1096

Fegley, Lisa Assistant General Manager
FRONTIER LEAGUE, 41, 998
Fehlmann, Gayle CFO
SPECIAL OLYMPICS MASSACHUSETTS, 195
Fehn, Bruce Treasurer
SCOTT, DAVID R., 905
Fehr, Bob Product Development Engineer
INTEGRATED DESIGN SOLUTIONS, 1060
Fehr, Donald Executive Director
WEINER, MICHAEL, 842, 915
Fehr, Fred Sports Editor
SHAWNEE NEWS-STAR, 530
Fehrenbach, Leslie Secretary
SCOTT, DAVID R., 905
Feigin, Peter President
NATIONAL BASKETBALL ASSOCIATION/NBA,
57
Feil, Gene Chief Operating Officer
DALCO ATHLETIC LETTERING, INC., 1123
Feil, Linda Co-Owner
DALCO ATHLETIC LETTERING, INC., 1123
Feiler, Jeff Assistant Director of Athletics
ALBRIGHT COLLEGE ATHLETICS-READING,
376
Feilke, Kelly Executive Director
USA CYCLING, 208
Fein, Alan Shareholder
STEARNS WEAVER MILLER, 908
Fein, Jason Director of Athletics
DREW UNIVERSITY(DU) ATHLETICS, 383
Fein, Robert Vice President
WESH-TV, 702
Feinberg, Arthur
TRACKLITE SYSTEMS, 1203
Feinberg, Teddy Sports Editor
LAS CRUCES SUN-NEWS, 501
Feiner, Andrew Partner
ANDREWS KURTH LLP, 862
Feinglass, Evan Associate Director of Athletics,
Facilit
GEORGE J. SHERMAN FAMILY-SPORTS
COMPLEX, 968
Feinman, Mike COO
GOLD'S GYM INTERNATIONAL, INC., 1138
Feinstein, Carolyn
EA SPORTS, 1213
Feinstein, Dan Asst. General Manager, Major
League
AMERICAN LEAGUE OF PROFESSIONAL
BASEBALL CLUBS, THE, 30
Feinstein, Sara Marketing Director
MACCABI USA/SPORTS FOR ISRAEL, 221
Feit, Noah Sports Editor
AIKEN STANDARD, 459
Feiti, Steve Sports Editor
COURIER NEWS, 474
Feitl, Steve Sports Editor
ASBURY PARK PRESS, 461
Felbaum, Jill President
TC SPORTS, 1199
Feld, Joel VP of Programming/Executive Producer
NEW ENGLAND SPORTS NETWORK/NESN,
676
Feld, Kenneth Chairman/Chief Executive Officer
FELD ENTERTAINMENT, 755
Feld, Steve Special Projects Manager
RAWHIDE PAVILION & RODEA ARENA, 1062
Felder, Ken Advertising Manager
KMPH-TV, 692
Felder, Mark Executive Director
OKLAHOMA GOLF ASSOCIATION, 114
Feldkamp, Sarah Director, Finance
AMERICAN LEAGUE OF PROFESSIONAL
BASEBALL CLUBS, THE, 30
Feldman, Barry Vice President Research
AMERICAN URBAN RADIO NETWORKS, 604
Feldman, Bruce Senior Writer
ESPN THE MAGAZINE, 558
Feldman, Dave Sports Director
WTTG-TV, 680, 710
Feldman, David President
COOPER LIGHTING, 1119
Feldman, Douglas Attorney
LINDNER & MARSACK, S.C., 891
Feldman, Harvey President
REGENT SPORTS CORPORATION, 1181
Feldman, Josh Director of Communications
CMC-NORTHEAST STADIUM, 958

Feldman, Ken Vice President - Sales
H&C HEADWARE/KC CAP, 1141

Feldman, Nancy Head Coach, Women's Soccer
NICKERSON FIELD, 989

Feldmeier, John Director Product Development
MYTEAM.COM, 713

Feliciano, Arnold Sports Editor
GAINESVILLE SUN, 490

Felix, Jerry Chief Financial Officer
ACTION SPORTS MEDIA, 771

Fellenz, Hillary Marketing
LUCKY'S CARD ROOM, 1046

Feller, Lucas Assistant
Commissioner/Administration &
ATLANTIC 10 CONFERENCE, 291

Feller, Paul President/Chief Executive Officer
PRO SPORTS & ENTERTAINMENT, 760

Felli, Gilbert Executive Director, Olympic Games
INTERNATIONAL OLYMPIC COMMITTEE
(IOC), 206

Felling, Gene Executive Director
US CELLULAR CENTER, 1014

Fellinger, Lewis Registrar
LAKE ERIE AAU ASSOCIATION, 214

Fellingham, Rich President/CEO
SPECIAL OLYMPICS IOWA, 195

Fellows, George President / Chief Executive
Officer
CALLAWAY GOLF, 1113

Felsher, Louise SVP Event Marketing
WILKINSON GROUP, 817

Felt, Bryan Director of Athletics
SETON HALL UNIVERSITY ATHLETICS, 343

Felt, Pat Financial Assistnat
BRENAU UNIVERSITY ATHLETICS, 309

Felton, Claude Senior Associate Athletic Director
- Spo
SANFORD STADIUM, 1001

Felton, Renee Head, Communications
USA BASKETBALL, 55, 208

Felts, Clayton Director of Athletic Communication
SEWANEE, UNIVERSITY OF THE SOUTH
ATHLETICS, 400

Fenech, Craig President
SPARTA GROUP MEDIA/COACHES, INC., 855

Feneque, Jason Senior Director of Sales &
Marketing
YANKEES ENTERTAINMENT & SPORTS
NETWORK/YES, 678

Fenimore, Bill VP
EMBROIDERY STORE, 1128

Fenley, Matt Associate Athletics Director,
Compliance
WILLIAM R. JOHNSON COLISEUM, 1019

Fenley, Mike Program Director
WMFR-AM, 656

Fennell, Greg Sports Reporter
VALLEY NEWS, 543

Fennell, James Director
COLLEGE OF IDAHO, 414

Fennelly, Martin Sports Columnist
TAMPA TRIBUNE, 537

Fennema, James Merchandise SVP
DUCKWALL ALCO STORES, INC., 1225

Fennern, Nikki Athletic Director
SAINT MARY'S UNIVERSITY (MN)
ATHLETICS, 399

Fensin, Lee Sports Editor
FREEMAN, 489

Fenske, Doug Manager, Racing
HORSE RACING ALBERTA, 79

Fenster, Darren Manager
SOUTH ATLANTIC LEAGUE (A LEVEL), 51

Fenstermacher, Kevin Assistant Commissioner /
Director of Com
PRESIDENTS' ATHLETIC CONFERENCE, 303

Fenstermaker, Ross General Manager
AMERICAN LEAGUE OF PROFESSIONAL
BASEBALL CLUBS, THE, 30

Fenton, Bob President
CANADIAN BLIND SPORTS ASSOCIATION,
193

Fenton, Jim Sports Writer
ENTERPRISE, 487

Fenton, William General Manager
WVCH-AM, 670

Fentress, Aaron Sports Writer
OREGONIAN, 516

Feo, Toni Ass.Director of Finance and HR
SEBRING INTERNATIONAL RACEWAY, 1032

Ferderer, Todd Director, Finance
PREMIER PARTNERSHIPS, 802

Ferenz, Michelle Associate Athletic Director
WHITMAN COLLEGE ATHLETICS, 406

Ferenz, Rich Sales VP
FRANKLIN SPORTS, INC., 1135

Ferguson, Andrew President
SKI MARKET LTD., 1237

Ferguson, David President/CEO
PERFORMANCE SPORTS APPAREL, 619,
1173

Ferguson, Don Head Coach, Women's Volleyball
O'NEILL CENTER, 989

Ferguson, Franklin Founding Principal
FFKR ARCHITECTS, 1056

Ferguson, James Attorney
SPAIN & GILLON, LLC, 855

Ferguson, John General Manager
AMERICAN HOCKEY LEAGUE/AHL, 129, 542

Ferguson, Kimberly Director of Operations
MARYLAND STATE GOLF ASSOCIATION, 112

Ferguson, Lora Head Athletic Trainer
EASTERN NEW MEXICO UNIVERSITY
(ENMU) ATHLETICS, 357

Ferguson, Margot Marketing Specialist
UAA SPORTS ARENA, 1012

Ferguson, Matt Vice President of Ticket Sales
SIOUX FALLS STADIUM, 1003

Ferguson, Michael Partner
FERGUSON, BRIG GEN/USA RET., MICHAEL
L., 880

Ferguson, Rhonda Administrative Assistant to the
AD
JAYNE STADIUM, 945, 975

Ferguson, Richard Sports Director
KXOX-FM, 633

Ferguson, Robert Tournament Chairman
WESTCHESTER GOLF ASSOCIATION, 117

Ferguson, Robert Chairman
SKI MARKET LTD., 1237

Ferguson, Russell Vice President of Food and
Beverage Serv
VENUWORKS, 1066

Ferguson, Sam Director of Athletics
MCMURRY UNIVERSITY ATHLETICS, 393

Ferguson, Steve President
SOCCER PAL, 1190

Ferguson, Trent Director, Sales
EAST COAST HOCKEY LEAGUE/ECHL, 129

Ferman, Gary Managing Editor
FLORIDA TENNIS, 560

Fermin, Felix Manager
MEXICAN LEAGUE A.C., 43

Fern, Janet Senior Vice President/General
Manager
COMCAST SPORTSNET BAY AREA, 674

Fernald, Lucinda Executive Director
GARVEY, SCHUBERT & BARER, 881

Fernandes, Doug Sports Writer
SARASOTA HERALD-TRIBUNE, 529

Fernandez, Alberto Majority Owner
NORTH AMERICAN HOCKEY LEAGUE, 133

Fernandez, Alfonso Station Manager
WREV-AM, 664

Fernandez, Andre High School Sports Writer
MIAMI HERALD, 506

Fernandez, Arturo Associate
STEARNS WEAVER MILLER, 908

Fernandez, Bernard Sports Writer
PHILADELPHIA DAILY NEWS, 519

Fernandez, Jordie Head Coach
NATIONAL BASKETBALL ASSOCIATION/NBA,
56

Fernandez, Joseph Sports Director
KERO-TV, 689

Fernandez, Kim Principal
ALBANESE/BROOKS/ASSOCIATES P.C., 1049

Fernandez, Raul Vice Chairman
VERIZON CENTER, 1015

Fernandez, Rolando VP, International Scouting &
Development
NATIONAL LEAGUE OF PROFESSIONAL
BASEBALL CLUBS, THE, 31

Fernandez, Rudy Program Director
THE POWER PLAY, 608

Fernandez, Sam Senior Vice President and
General Counse

FERNANDEZ, SANTIAGO/SENIOR
VP/GENERAL COUNSEL LOS ANGELES
DODGERS, 880

Fernchick, Larry Marketing Director
WTXF-TV, 711

Fernquest, Don President
TRUEX GOLF, 1204

Feroe, Bill Executive Vice President
ABSOLUTELY NEW, 1090

Ferran, Rene Sports Writer
TRI-CITY HERALD, 541

Ferrante, Billy Vice President/Marketing/Events
NEW ORLEANS SPORTS FOUNDATION,
GREATER, 242

Ferranti, Kim Treasurer
ALBANESE/BROOKS/ASSOCIATES P.C., 1049

Ferrantie, Bill Executive Director
SUGAR BOWL, 92

Ferrara, Danielle Senior Woman Administrator
WENTWORTH INSTITUTE OF TECHNOLOGY
ATHLETICS(WIT), 405

Ferrara, Joe Director, Soccer Operations
USL LEAGUE TWO, 164

Ferrara, Michael President
IMPORT DRAG RACING CIRCUIT, 17

Ferrara, Robert President
JAYPRO SPORTS, LLC, 1149

Ferrari, Paolo President and CEO, Bridgestone
Americas
BRIDGESTONE AMERICAS, 726

Ferraro, Carlos President Unisource Global
Solutions
THE SPORTS & FITNESS INDUSTRY
ASSOCIATION (SFIA), 813

Ferraro, Clayton Sports Director
WINK-TV, 704

Ferraro, Glenn Owner and VP
LEGENDS SPORTING GOODS, 1232

Ferraro, James Attorney/Share Holder
THE FERRARO LAW FIRM, 911

Ferraro, Joe Sports Editor
WEST HAWAII TODAY, 546

Ferraro, John COO
ERNST & YOUNG, 768

Ferraro, Thomas Account Manager
CELLO PROFESSIONAL PRODUCTS, 1115

Ferraz, Anthony President
BROWNELL & CO., INC., 1110

Ferre, Loren Director of Athletics
WASHBURN UNIVERSITY OF TOPEKA
ATHLETICS, 374, 982, 1020

Ferreira, Raquel EVP & Assistant General
Manager
AMERICAN LEAGUE OF PROFESSIONAL
BASEBALL CLUBS, THE, 29, 965

Ferrell, Ray VP Of Sales
HARTWELL SPORTS, INC., 1143

Ferrell, Scott Gary Player Design President
GARY PLAYER GROUP, INC, 538, 834

Ferrentino, Mike Editor
BIKE, 552

Ferrer, Ali Vice President and Treasurer
CMS SPORTS, 1223

Ferrer, Charles President
CMS SPORTS, 1223

Ferriani, Ivo President
INTERNATIONAL BOBSLEIGH & SKELETON
FEDERATION, 204

Ferrin, Mike Sports Producer
WGN-AM, 648

Ferris, Chris Executive Sr. Assoc. AD, External
Affair
COLORADO STATE UNIVERSITY ATHLETICS,
327

Ferris, Mike Sales Representative
LA CROSSE CENTER, 980

Ferro, Pedro Senior Vice President and President,
Aft
ARVINMERITOR, 1100

Ferruzzi, Marco Sporting Director
USL CHAMPIONSHIP, 160

Ferry, Danny President of Basketball Operations
and G
PHILIPS ARENA, 993

Ferry, Rick Co-Director of Athletics
ALBRIGHT COLLEGE ATHLETICS-READING,
376

Fertig, Jennifer VP of Finance & Operations
FRONTIER LEAGUE, 41, 1021

Fried, Barry Director of Athletics
VITERBO ATHLETICS UNIVERSITY, 322

Fried, Gil Professor/Chair
NEW HAVEN, UNIVERSITY OF, 428

Fried, Jeffrey President
FRIED & COMPANY, P.C., 834

Fried, Kenny Executive Vice President
BROTMAN WINTER FRIED
COMMUNICATIONS, INC., 751

Friedberg, James
ISRAEL, FRIEDBERG & KORBATOV L.L.P.,
886

Friedland, Laura VP
HARPER INDUSTRIES INC, 1142

Friedland, Lloyd Attorney
LIBRETT, FRIEDLAND & LIEBERMAN, 847,
890

Friedland, Robert Head Coach
USL LEAGUE TWO, 162

Friedland, Thomas President
HARPER INDUSTRIES INC, 1142

Friedlander, Andy Sports Reporter
FORT WORTH STAR-TELEGRAM, 489

Friedlander, Brett Contributing Writer
RINKSIDE, 578

Friedlander, Joshua Chief Human Resources
Officer
SAUER, RUSSELL F., 904

Friedman, Andrew President, Baseball
Operations
NATIONAL LEAGUE OF PROFESSIONAL
BASEBALL CLUBS, THE, 31

Friedman, Bob President
DIVOTS SPORTSWEAR COMPANY, INC.,
1124

Friedman, Brian EVP & COO
NATIONAL FOOTBALL LEAGUE/NFL, 96

Friedman, Dick Senior Editor
SPORTS ILLUSTRATED, 585

Friedman, Gary Director of Athletics
REDBIRD ARENA, 996

Friedman, Henry SVP Sales
EASTPAK CORPORATION, 1127

Friedman, Michael Founder and President
MASTER HOME PRODUCTS, 1160

Friedman, Mike Sports Director
KFDM-TV, 689

Friedman, Tedd Attorney
KATZ, TELLER, BRANT & HILD, 887

Friedman, Vicki Sports Writer
VIRGINIAN-PILOT, 544

Friedrich, Joe Coordinator of Sports Medicine
GEORGIAN COURT COLLEGE ATHLETICS,
359

Friedrichs, Wade Marketing
SPEED SKATELUBE, 1192

Friedrichs, Wades Marketing
SPEED SKATELUBE, 1192

Friedson, Richard Treasurer
MULTICULTURAL GOLF ASSOCIATION OF
AMERICA, 104

Friello, Mike Governor
ADIRONDACK AAU ASSOCIATION, 213

Friend, Amy Public Relations Director
PIONEER NEW MEDIA TECHNOLOGIES,
INC., 1174

Friend, John Athletics Consultant
PURDUE UNIVERSITY CALUMET ATHLETICS,
319

Friend, Rob CEO
CANADIAN PREMIER LEAGUE, 156

Friend, Tom Senior Writer
ESPN THE MAGAZINE, 558

Fries, Jared Assoc. AD, Student-Athlete High
Performa
CAMPBELL UNIVERSITY ATHLETICS, 326

Friesen, Rudy GM
EXIBITION PARK - LETHBRIDGE, 1037

Friesen, Stewart Co-Owner
NASCAR GANDER OUTDOORS TRUCK
SERIES, 23

Frieze, Irene Professor
HOLMES, RICH, 884

Friisdahl, Michael President & CEO, Maple Leaf
Sports & Ent
SCOTIABANK ARENA, 950, 1001

Frijia, Mark General Manager
NATIONAL BASKETBALL LEAGUE OF
CANADA, 58

Frijia, Vito Owner
NATIONAL BASKETBALL LEAGUE OF
CANADA, 58

Frimmel, Gabe Advertising Manager
PAINTBALL MAGAZINE, 548, 575

Frisbee, Shane Marketing Committee Chair
JACKSONVILLE AND THE BEACHES
CONVENTION AND VISITORS BUREAU, 236

Frisbey, Jinni Senior Associate AD/SWA
SOUTH ALABAMA ATHLETICS, UNIVERSITY
OF, 344

Frisch, Diane General Manager
ESPN 1490 THE FAN, 612

Frisk, Robert Assistant Managing Editor/Sports
DAILY HERALD (IL), 476

Fritz, Bob Manager
PECOS LEAGUE, 49

Fritz, Carl Marketing Manager
SENECA SPORTS INC., 1187

Fritz, Douglas President
RICHMOND INTERNATIONAL RACEWAY,
1031

Fritz, Owen Sales VP
AMERICAN SEATING, 1098

Fritz, Richard Director of Events
STABLER ARENA, 1005

Fritz, Robbie Director of Instruction, PGA Certified
METHODIST COLLEGE PROFESSIONAL
GOLF MANAGEMENT PROGRAM, 103

Fritz, Ron Sports Editor
SUN (MD), 463, 512, 536

Fritz, Steve Athletic Director
ST. THOMAS UNIVERSITY ATHLETICS, 401

Fritze, Greg Vice President
KANSAS SPEEDWAY, 1026

Frizzel, Ron General Manager
WVMJ-FM, 670

Froehle, Paul VP, Ticket Operations
AMERICAN LEAGUE OF PROFESSIONAL
BASEBALL CLUBS, THE, 30

Froehlich, Bob Owner & Board of Directors
MIDWEST LEAGUE, 45

Froehlich, Cheryl Owner & Board of Directors
MIDWEST LEAGUE, 45

Froehlich, Ron President
INTERNATIONAL WORLD GAMES
ASSOCIATION/IWGA, 262

Froelich, Cezar Partner
SHEFSKY, LLOYD E., 905

Froendt, Bruce Commissioner
NATIONAL WHEELCHAIR SOFTBALL
ASSOCIATION, 170

Froggatt, Matthew Chief development Officer
TNS SPORT - NORTH AMERICA, 814

Fromer, Todd Managing Partner/Investor
Relations
KCSA PUBLIC RELATIONS WORLDWIDE, 791

Fromm, Ronald Chairman and Chief Executive
Officer
NATURAL SPORT, 1166

Frommeyer, Tim Executive Vice President &
Chief Financi
NATIONWIDE FINANCIAL SERVICES, 730

Frood, Brett Commissioner
NATIONAL LACROSSE LEAGUE, 142

Frosch, Melanie Vice President, Sports and
Competition
SPECIAL OLYMPICS SOUTH DAKOTA, 197

Frost, Allen Mizzou Sports Park Facils. Mgr. -
Memori
FAUROT FIELD AT MEMORIAL STADIUM, 965

Frost, Andy Vice President
ST. LOUIS DISTRICT GOLF ASSOCIATION,
116

Frost, Brad Head Coach, Women's Hockey
MARIUCCI ARENA, 985

Frost, Mike General Manager
GREENSBORO COLISEUM COMPLEX, 969

Frost, Ray Assistant Manager for Operations
JS DORTON ARENA, 978

Frost, Rufus Managing Director
AURA360 VENTURES, 774

Frost, Ryan Assistant Athletic Director
SPRING ARBOR COLLEGE ATHLETICS, 321

Frost, Shelley President & CEO
PACIFIC COLISEUM, 990

Frost, Steve Sports Information Coordinator
SIMON FRASER UNIVERSITY ATHLETICS,
370

Frost, Timothy President
FROST MOTORSPORTS, LLC, 16

Frostner, Manfred Contact
THINK TANK COMMUNICATIONS, 764

Frostrom, Karen Partner
THORSNES, BARTOLOTTA & MCGUIRE, 912

Frugoli, William Auditor
MARSHFIELD FAIR, 1041

Fry, Chris Managing Director of Corporate
CANADIAN PROFESSIONAL GOLFERS'
ASSOCIATION, 100

Fry, Doug President
WISCONSIN STATE GOLF ASSOCIATION,
117

Fry, Helen Business Operations Director
WORLD SAILING, 205

Fry, Kindra Director of Sales-Sports &
Conventions
BRYAN-COLLEGE STATION CONVENTION &
VISITORS BUREAU, SPORTS DEPT, 260

Fry, Mike Maintenance Manager
MEMPHIS MOTORSPORTS PARK (MMP),
1028

Fry, Pat Technical Chief
FORMULA 1, 19

Frye, Darrell Finance and Administration VP
HARRISS & COVINGTON INC., 1142

Frye, Jay President
INDYCAR, 22

Frye, Whitney Associate Commissioner
NORTH CAROLINA HS ATHLETIC
ASSOCIATION, 201

Fryer, Steve Sports Reporter
ORANGE COUNTY REGISTER, 516

Fryling, Mike General Manager
TED CONSTANT CONVOCATION CENTER,
1008

Fryman, Travis Team Manager
NEW YORK-PENNSYLVANIA LEAGUE, 47

Frysinger, Brittany Director, Operations
WOMEN'S PREMIER SOCCER LEAGUE, 167

Fucci, Jeanmarie Director of Marketing
FOX SPORTS OHIO, 675

Fuchs, Aaron Operating Manager
WRXX-FM, 665

Fuchs, Christian Co-Founder
WOMEN'S PREMIER SOCCER LEAGUE, 167

Fuchs, Jesse Sports Reporter
WEST CENTRAL TRIBUNE, 546

Fuchs, Lars Secretary
NATIONAL OPERATING COMMITTEE ON
STANDARDS FOR ATHLETIC EQUIPMENT, 84

Fuchs, Raluca Co-Founder
WOMEN'S PREMIER SOCCER LEAGUE, 167

Fucile, Matt Stadium Operations Director
RALEY FIELD, 995

Fuehring, Alan Broadcaster/Media Relations
Manager
EAST COAST HOCKEY LEAGUE/ECHL, 127,
129

Fuentes, Alejandro EVP/General Manager
EL COMANDANTE RACE TRACK, 1037

Fuentes, Ralph Editor
LOWRIDER BICYCLE, 569

Fuerst, Coleen President
DURHAM BOAT COMPANY, 1126

Fuest, Fredrick President, International Division
ACTIVE INTERNATIONAL, 766

Fuez, Richard General Manager
NATIONAL WOMEN'S SOCCER LEAGUE, 158

Fugazy, John VP
SPORTS ADVERTISING NETWORK, INC., 810

Fugler, Jon Founder
RECRUIT-ME, 930

Fuhler, Justin Athletic Director
MACMURRAY COLLEGE ATHLETICS, 391

Fuhr, Joe Faculty
WIDENER UNIVERSITY SPORT
MANAGEMENT, 860

Fuhrman, Dan SVP / Chief Finacial Officer
GENERAL SPORTS VENUE ASTROTURF,
1137

Fuhrman, Joe Vice President
BIEBER LIGHTING CORPORATION, 1106

Fuhro, Brian Esquire
FUHRO, HANLEY & BEUKAS, 834

Fujiwara, Lance Associate AD, Sports Medicine
VIRGINIA MILITARY INSTITUTE ATHLETICS,
348

Garbett, Mike Sports Copy Editor
TAMPA TRIBUNE, 537

Garcia, Al Vice President of Operations
HOMESTEAD-MIAMI SPEEDWAY, LLC, 1025

Garcia, Albert VP/Operations
HOMESTEAD-MIAMI SPEEDWAY, LLC, 1025

Garcia, Arthur Sports Writer (College)
FORT WORTH STAR-TELEGRAM, 489

Garcia, Danny Director Tournament Operations
RICHLIN GROUP, 760

Garcia, Debbie Executive Senior Associate
AD/SWA
TEXAS AT ARLINGTON ATHLETICS,
UNIVERSITY OF, 346

Garcia, Dinora Executive Assistant
SOUTH PADRE ISLAND CONVENTION &
VISITORS BUREAU, 246

Garcia, Gary SVP, Business Development,
Tickets
NATIONAL FOOTBALL LEAGUE/NFL, 95

Garcia, Irma Director of Athletics
ST. FRANCIS COLLEGE ATHLETICS (SFC),
371

Garcia, Jaime Athletic Trainer
EAST COAST HOCKEY LEAGUE/ECHL, 129

Garcia, Jose President
MEXICAN LEAGUE A.C., 43

Garcia, Kim Director of Events
DISCOVER ORANGE BOWL, 91

Garcia, Marta Sports Editor
MUNDO HISPANICO, 509

Garcia, Patricia Sports Editor
MINIONDAS, 507

Garcia, Paul Sports Anchor/Reporter
WKOW-TV, 705

Garcia, Pete Executive Director, Sports &
Entertainme
FANATICS RETAIL GROUP, 1227

Garcia, Ralph Chief Operations Officer
5TH AND OCEAN CLOTHING, 1089

Garcia, Rick Sports Director
KTTV-TV, 688, 695

Garcia, Roberto WPSL Head Coach
WOMEN'S PREMIER SOCCER LEAGUE, 166

Garcia, Stephen Sports Reporter
ALICE ECHO NEWS, 460

Gard, Jeff Head Men's Basketball Coach
PIONEER FIELD, 993

Garden, Noah Deputy Commissioner, Business &
Media
NATIONAL LEAGUE OF PROFESSIONAL
BASEBALL CLUBS, THE, 31

Gardener, Laura General Manager
THOROUGHBRED CLUB OF AMERICA, 77

Gardiner, Andy Sports Writer
USA TODAY, 543

Gardiner, William VP
ZORREL INTERNATIONAL, 1213

Gardner, Billy Manager
INTERNATIONAL LEAGUE, 43

Gardner, Bob Executive Director
NATIONAL FEDERATION OF STATE HIGH
SCHOOL ASSOCIATIONS, 198

Gardner, Brian VP
HO SPORTS INC., 96, 1145

Gardner, Carrie Associate Director of Athletics
CHRISTOPHER NEWPORT UNIVERSITY
ATHLETICS, 380

Gardner, Chene Chief Financial Officer
SPORTSNUTS, INC., 714

Gardner, Cheryl Athletic Department Secretary
LOCK HAVEN UNIVERSITY ATHLETICS
(LHU), 362

Gardner, Chris Marketing Director
WPRO, 661

Gardner, Dallas Board Chairman
NATIONAL HOT ROD ASSOCIATION, 1029

Gardner, Eric General Manager of Operations
CAROLINA LEAGUE, 37

Gardner, Megan Marketing Opportunities
BLALOCK COMPANY, JANE, 750

Gardner, P. Owner
KGPQ-FM, 619

Gardner, Paul Sports Reporter
NEW YORK SUN, 511

Gardner, Scott President
INTERNATIONAL HOT ROD ASSOCIATION,
17

Gardner, Susan Counsel
ARNET, WILLIAM F., 862

Gardner, Tanner Senior Associate AD/COO
RICE UNIVERSITY ATHLETICS, 342

Gardner, Tim Sales Manager
BRUTE GROUP, 704, 1111

Gardula, Peter Senior Associate Director of
Athletics
ASSUMPTION COLLEGE ATHLETICS, 351

Garey, Rix Advertising Manager
KFDM-TV, 689

Garfield, Dana Director of Athletics
MITCHELL COLLEGE ATHLETICS, 394

Garfield, Frederick Partner
SPAIN & GILLON, LLC, 855

Garfield, Jay Head Athletic Trainer
NOTRE DAME COLLEGE ATHLETICS, 367

Garfinkel, Tom Vice Chair/President/CEO
NATIONAL FOOTBALL LEAGUE/NFL, 95, 1007

Gargalianos, Peter Director, Field Operations
TRAKUS, INC., 930

Gargan, Daniel Managing Director
WOMEN'S PREMIER SOCCER LEAGUE, 167

Gargano, Jeri VP,Managing Director
ASAP SPORTS, 819

Gargiulo, Tina Event Marketing Director
NATIONAL MEDIA GROUP, INC., 796

Garibaldi, Antoine President
GOLDMAN, LEE, 882

Garin, Michael VP, Hospitality
CANTERBURY PARK, 1036

Garland, Bruce SVP/Racing Operations
MEADOWLANDS/NEW JERSEY SPORTS &
EXPOSITION AUTHORITY, 1065

Garland, Chad Assistant Director, Events and
Conferenc
ROSE BASKETBALL ARENA, 979, 998

Garland, Craig Sales Manager
GEORGIA MARBLE COMPANY, 1137

Garley, Rosemary Manager
NEW MEXICO RACING COMMISSION, 81

Garlits, Don Chief Executive Officer
DON GARLITS MUSEUM OF DRAG RACING
AND INTERNATIONAL DRAG RACING H, 252

Garlock, Pete Director Of Sales
ELGIN AREA CONVENTION & VISITORS
BUREAU, 228, 233

Garman, Mike Head Coach & General Manager
UNITED STATES HOCKEY LEAGUE, 137

Garner, Andrew Sports Editor
ANDALUSIA STAR NEWS, 460

Garner, Chad Sports Editor
SENTINEL AND ENTERPRISE, 530

Garner, Darrin Manager
ARIZONA LEAGUE (ROOKIE), 34

Garner, David Chairman
NJCAA REGION XXIII WOMEN'S, 290

Garner, Gary Advertising Manager
TEMPLE DAILY TELEGRAM, 538

Garner, Jeff President
USL CHAMPIONSHIP, 160

Garner, Lanny President
VIBRA-WHIRL & COMPANY, 1208

Garner, Mitchell President
ROAD RUNNERS CLUB OF AMERICA, 149

Garner, Sean Strength & Conditioning Coach
EAST COAST HOCKEY LEAGUE/ECHL, 130

Garnes, Michael President
NEXT LEVEL EXECUTIVE SEARCH, 748

Garnes, Michael Founder/President
NEXT LEVEL SPORTS, INC., 798

Garnhum, Shawnna Sales
SAINT JOHN DESTINATION MANAGEMENT
INC, 245

Garofalo, Robb Sports Information Director
PRESENTATION COLLEGE ATHLETICS, 319,
708

Garrard, Michael Sports Information
OREGON INSTITUTE OF TECHNOLOGY
ATHLETICS, 318

Garraway, Jay Finance/Administration Director
MOBILE BAY CONVENTION & VISITORS
BUREAU, 241

Garretson, Jeff General Manager
YAKIMA COUNTY STADIUM, 1020

Garrett, Brad Assistant Executive Director
OREGON SCHOOL ACTIVITIES
ASSOCIATION, 201

Garrett, Daniel Assistant Director of
Intercollegiate At
CALIFORNIA STATE UNIVERSITY-LOS
ANGELES ATHLETICS, 353

Garrett, Dr. Senior Associate AD/Sport Admin.
and Sup
RICE STADIUM, 996

Garrett, Greg Sports Host
WSHW-FM, 666

Garrett, Jim Advertising Manager
LAWTON CONSTITUTION, 230, 502

Garrett, Kevin Director of Athletics
CONCORD UNIVERSITY ATHLETICS, 355

Garrett, Mary Director Marketing/Communications
NORFOLK CONVENTION & VISITORS
BUREAU, 242

Garrett, Matt Sport Management Coordinator
LORAS COLLEGE, 423

Garrett, Norb Editorial Director
TENNIS, 588

Garrett, Salina Financial Analyst
KNOXVILLE CIVIC AUDITORIUM/COLISEUM,
980

Garrett, Scott Sr. Associateathletic Director,
External
BILL SNYDER FAMILY STADIUM, 550, 950

Garrett, Todd Director of Athletics
MIDAMERICA NAZARENE UNIVERSITY
ATHLETICS, 316

Garrettt, Scott President, Advertising Sales
ATHLON SPORTS COMMUNICATIONS, 550

Garrick, Kelly Director of Sports and Competition
SPECIAL OLYMPICS SOUTH CAROLINA, 197

Garriett, Robbie Coordinator of Administrative
Services
QUEENS UNIVERSITY OF CHARLOTTE, 368

Garrigan, Mike anchor
WIFR-TV, 704

Garrigus, R.L. News Director
KICE-AM, 620

Garrioch, Bruce Contributing Writer
RINKSIDE, 578

Garrison, Carri Association Director
WESTERN WINTER SPORTS
REPRESENTATIVES ASSOCIATION, 226

Garrison, David Chairman/Chief Executive Officer
VERESTAR, 687

Garrison, Jay Sports Director
WHBU-AM, 649

Garrison, Laurie Copy Editor, Sports Business
Awards Coor
SPORTS BUSINESS RESOURCE GUIDE &
FACT BOOK, 596

Garrison, Rose Event Manager
BRAGG MEMORIAL STADIUM, 951

Garrison, Tim Head Coach, Gymnastics
MEMORIAL COLISEUM, 986

Garrison, Webster Manager
ARIZONA LEAGUE (ROOKIE), 34

Garrity, Kevin Sports Anchor
SPORTS ON 1, 685

Garrity, Tom President/CEO
SIOUX FALLS STADIUM, 1003

Garry, Julie First Vice Chair
SNOWSPORTS INDUSTRIES AMERICA, 153

Garshow, James Sports Director
KUPI-AM, 631

Garske, Steve President
WITTEK GOLF SUPPLY COMPANY, 1211

Garst, Sally Special Events
PENSACOLA SPORTS ASSOCIATION, 243

Garten, Beth Director, Operations
WOMEN'S PREMIER SOCCER LEAGUE, 165

Gartenfeld, Mark
NATIONAL SENIOR ASSOCIATION, 104

Gartenmayer, Charles Athletic Director
BENEDICTINE COLLEGE ATHLETICS, 308

Gartland, Thomas President ,North America
AVIS RENT A CAR SYSTEM, 925

Gartner, Michael Chairman
PACIFIC COAST LEAGUE OF
PROFESSIONAL BASEBALL CLUBS, 48, 1002

Garven, Rich Sports Reporter
TELEGRAM & GAZETTE, 537

Garvey, Edward Shareholder/Founder
GARVEY & STODDARD, 881

Garvey, Ellen Information Technology Director
CONVERSE, INC., 1223

Geiser, Jayson Sports Anchor/Reporter
WPBN-TV, 706, 707

Geiser, Jeff Athletic Director
GREYHOUND STADIUM, 969

Geisler, Adam President
EVERLAST WORLDWIDE INC, 1130

Geisler, Connie President
AMERICAN VAULTING ASSOCIATION, 74

Geisler, Melissa Sports Editor
TRIBUNE (CA), 541

Geist, Alan Athletic Director
CEDARVILLE UNIVERSITY ATHLETICS, 310

Geist, Dave Program Director
KOWB-AM, 626

Gejdosova, Maria Vice President, Finance &
Acquisitions
CURTIS MANAGEMENT GROUP, 829, 830

Gelan, Simon Senior VP, Operations
NATIONAL FOOTBALL LEAGUE/NFL, 94

Gelder, Roger Chief Operating Officer
KZMQ-AM, 633

Gelestor, Judy Advertising Manager
HERALD-STAR, 494

Geletka, John Sports Agent
PRO SPORT MANAGEMENT, INC., 849

Geleynse, Jesse Sports Editor
LE MARS DAILY SENTINEL, 502

Gelfond, Gordon Partner
MARGOLIS EDELSTEIN, 892

Gelfond, Richard Director of Operations
SPECIAL OLYMPICS NEW JERSEY, 196

Geller, Eric Sports Director
KMVT-TV, 692

Geller, Mitch Chief Technical Officer
DIVING PLONGEON CANADA, 72

Geller, Nancie PRESIDENT
BELMONT PARK, 1036

Gellert, Ryan Treasurer
THE ACCESS FUND, 69

Genday, Richard Senior Vice President
L. ROBERT KIMBALL & ASSOCIATES, 1061

Gendler, Beth VP Sales
ALABAMA GULF COAST CONVENTION &
VISITORS BUREAU, 226

Gendron, Pierre President
KEYBEC SUBLIME, INC., 1152

Gennarelli, Bob Senior Associate
Commissioner/COO
MID-AMERICAN ATHLETIC CONFERENCE,
299

Gennette, Jeffrey Chief Merchandising Officer
BURDINE'S, 1221

Gensiak, Rich Program Director
WMUH-FM, 658

Genske, Gregory
LEGACY SPORTS GROUP, 841

Genter, Jill Promotion Manager
WKOW-TV, 705

Genthner, Jeffrey General Manager
P.A.S.S. SPORTS, 601

Gentile, Andrew General Manager
DELAWARE PARK RACETRACK & SLOTS,
1037

Gentile, David Founder/Chairman
EXHIBIT ENTERPRISES, 782

Gentile, Derek President/Chief Executive Officer
EXHIBIT ENTERPRISES, 782

Gentile, Ian Vice President, Hockey Operations
UNITED STATES HOCKEY LEAGUE, 136

Gentile, Rick Senior Associate Commissioner
(Men's Bas
COLLEGIATE COMMISSIONER'S
ASSOCIATION, 283

Gentry, Brad Marketing Director
SHOW ME CENTER, 1002

Gentry, Gayle Accounting Manager
KNOLOGY PARK, 980

Gentry, Jim Sports Editor
DAILY REFLECTOR, 479

Gentry, Marie Director of Sponsor Services
GRAYSON STADIUM, 968

Gentry, Mike Associate Director of Athletics for
Athl
LANE STADIUM/WORSHAM FIELD, 981

Gentry, Tim Editor
WOMEN'S PRO RODEO NEWS, 593

Gentry, Vickie Dept. Chairperson
NORTHWESTERN STATE UNIVERSITY OF
LOUISIANA, 429

Gentzkow, Marci Senior Director,
Communications & Market
TIGER WOODS FOUNDATION, 193

Genung, Jack Sports Editor
HOME NEWS TRIBUNE, 494

Genuser, Taylor Head Coach
INDOOR FOOTBALL LEAGUE, 93

Genzler, Dan Sports Information Director
SIOUX FALLS ATHLETICS, UNIVERSITY OF,
370

Geocaris, Kerry Co-Founder & Executive Director
WOMEN'S PREMIER SOCCER LEAGUE, 167

Geoffery, Ginger Sports Anchor
WKBW-TV, 705

Geoffroy, Gregory President
BLACKWELDER, MURRAY, 827

Geoghan, Robert President/Chief Executive
Officer/Founde
SPORTS AMERICA, INC., 762

Geoghegan, Steve Sports Writer
HOUR, 495

Georgatos, Dennis Sports Reporter
SAN JOSE MERCURY NEWS, 528

George, Brandon Sports Reporter
DALLAS MORNING NEWS, 481

George, Dave Sports Columnist
PALM BEACH POST, 517

George, Eric Deputy AD/CFO
MISSISSIPPI STATE UNIVERSITY
ATHLETICS, 337

George, Jason Executive VP/Assistant GM
TEXAS BASEBALL LEAGUE, 53

George, Kevin Sports Assistant Editor
STAR-DEMOCRAT, 534

George, Kyle Executive Associate AD, External
Ops.
TROY UNIVERSITY ATHLETICS, 347

George, Laura National Sales Manager
GARED SPORTS, 1136

George, Michelle Dan Certification Manager
U.S. TAEKWONDO UNION, 143

George, Mike President and CEO
QVC NETWORK, 1235

George, Rick Athletic Director
COLORADO ATHLETICS, UNIVERSITY OF,
327, 959, 966

George, Robert EVP and Chief Merchandising
Officer
FAMILY DOLLAR STORES, 1227

George, Steve Athletic Director
SHIRK STADIUM, 1002

George, Sue Secretary to Executive Associate AD
PETERSON EVENTS CENTER, 992

George, Thomas Sports Columnist
DENVER POST, 482

George, Thomas Chief Financial Officer
TEVA BRAND, 1124, 1201

George, Todd Chairman
U.S. TENNIS COURT & TRACK BUILDERS
ASSOCIATION, 1063

Georges, Francine Human Resources Generalist,
Athletics
YALE BOWL, 973, 1021

Georgeson, Cynthia VP Worldwide
Communications
JOHNSON OUTDOORS, 1150

Georgie, Trevor President
QUEBEC MARITIMES MAJOR JUNIOR
HOCKEY LEAGUE, 135

Geppert, William Senior Vice President
COX CABLE - SAN DIEGO, 674

Gera, Holly Director of Athletics
MONTCLAIR STATE UNIVERSITY
ATHLETICS, 394

Gerace, Sam Advertising Manager
WTRS-FM, 669

Geraci, James President
SHIELD, 1188

Geracie, Bud Sports Executive Editor
SAN JOSE MERCURY NEWS, 528

Geraghty, Timothy Attorney
CLARK, CAROL, 873

Geragotelis, Brittany Associate Editor
AMERICAN CHEERLEADER, 549

Geratowski, MK Director of Compliance
RANDOLPH-MACON COLLEGE ATHLETICS,
397

Gerber, Chad Program Director
WAVT-FM, 637

Gerber, Chuck Executive VP/General Manager
ESPN REGIONAL TELEVISION, 599

Gerber, Errol Director Sales
WGN-9 CHICAGO'S CW, 703

Gerber, R. Sports Editor
COURIER-NEWS, 474

Gerber, R.J. Sports Editor
NAPERVILLE SUN, 464, 509

Gerbner, John President and COO
EWING COLE CHERRY BROTT, 1055

Gerbo, Geno General Manager
INDOOR FOOTBALL LEAGUE, 93

Gerbrandt, Larry Analyst
MEDIA SPORTS BUSINESS, 569

Gerdes, Dan Health Human Performance
Professor
CENTRAL MISSOURI STATE UNIVERSITY,
413

Gerding, Kelli Project Coordinator
MARYLAND SPORTS, 240

Gerencir, Shannon Assistant Athletic Director
WEST VIRGINIA STATE COLLEGE
ATHLETICS (WVSU), 375

Gerend, Jim President and CEO
NORTHWESTERN MUTUAL LIFE, 731

Gergen, Joe Sports Columnist
NEWSDAY, 513

Gerhardson, Jessica Operations Manager
BASSFORD, LOCKHART, TRUESDELL &
BRIGGS, P.A., 864

Gerhardt, Clark Secretary
AMERICAN ALPINE CLUB, 68

Gerhart, Mitch Sports Director
WEEU-AM, 644

Gerik-Fordyce, Melanie Sports Assistant Editor
PALM BEACH POST, 517

Gerke, Kevin Sports Producer
WSB-TV, 709

Gerken, Matthew Head Athletic Trainer
SOUTHERN MAINE ATHLETICS, UNIVERSITY
OF, 400

Gerlach, Lance General Manager
FOLSOM FIELD, 966

Gerlach, Tara Head Athletic Trainer
RIO GRANDE ATHLETICS, UNIVERSITY OF,
319

Gerlinger, Ken Assistant Commissioner for
Communication
PEACH BELT ATHLETIC CONFERENCE, 303

Germain, Ariel Director of Marketing and Special
Events
C.E. GAINES CENTER, 953

Germain, Bob Owner
NASCAR CUP SERIES, 23

Germain, Brent Sports Editor
DAILY COMET, 475

Germain, David President
EXERCYCLE CORPORATION, 1131

German, Lorie Advertising Manager
TRENTONIAN, 541

German, Robert Managing Shareholder
SHERRARD, GERMAN & KELLY, 906

Germelmann, Claas Treasurer
EUROPEAN ASSOCIATION FOR SPORT
MANAGEMENT, THE, 219

Gernert, Douglas President / Chief Executive
Officer
TOTES ISOTONER, INC., 1202

Gerow, Sezy Marketing Director
KTZN-AM, 630

Gerrety, Chad Associate AD, External Affairs
WESTERN CAROLINA UNIVERSITY
ATHLETICS, 349

Gerrity, Brian Deputy AD/Executive Director, MAF
MERCER UNIVERSITY ATHLETICS, 336

Gerrity, Dave Associate AD
LOYOLA UNIVERSITY MARYLAND
ATHLETICS, 335

Gerrity, Mike Head Coach
NATIONAL BASKETBALL ASSOCIATION
DEVELOPMENT LEAGUE, 58

Gerry, E. President
HARNESS RACING MUSEUM & HALL OF
FAME, THE, 252

Gerschwer, David Executive VP
PSP SPORTS MARKETING, 804

Gershon, Michael Associate Head Coach
UNITED STATES HOCKEY LEAGUE, 137

Giesler, Mary Special Counsel
AMERICAN LEAGUE OF PROFESSIONAL
BASEBALL CLUBS, THE, 30

Giesse, Ray CEO
AMERICAN WHISTLE CORPORATION, 1098

Gifford, Debra General Manager
WQEL-FM, 662

Gifford, Jim Program Director
WSJM-AM, 666

Gifford, Matt VP/General Manager
TEXAS BASEBALL LEAGUE, 32, 53

Gifford, Mike Advertising Manager
SEMINOLE PRODUCER, 530

Giglia, Charles Director of Sport Sales
BUFFALO NIAGARA SPORTS COMMISSION,
229

Giglio, Jennifer Senior VP, Chief
Communications Officer
NATIONAL LEAGUE OF PROFESSIONAL
BASEBALL CLUBS, 32

Giguiere, Terry Dept. Coordinator
CITADEL, THE, 413

Gil, Noryoli Operations
WORLD BOXING ASSOCIATION, 67

Gilbert, Brad Athletic Trainer
DAKOTA STATE UNIVERSITY ATHLETICS,
311

Gilbert, Carol Executive Vice President, Programs
& Mar
AMERICAN MILITARY UNIVERSITY, 409

Gilbert, Dan Chair
AMERICAN HOCKEY LEAGUE/AHL, 56, 127,
731

Gilbert, David President & CEO
GREATER CLEVELAND SPORTS
COMMISSION, 231, 234

Gilbert, Jack Past President
NORTHERN NEVADA GOLF ASSOCIATION,
114

Gilbert, Jamie Executive Director, Coaching
WOMEN'S PREMIER SOCCER LEAGUE, 166

Gilbert, Jennifer Associate Athletic Director/SWA
MIAMI UNIVERSITY ATHLETICS, 337

Gilbert, Jon Director of Athletics
EAST CAROLINA UNIVERSITY ATHLETICS,
329

Gilbert, Karen Director Marketing
FENTRESS ARCHITECTS, 1056

Gilbert, Kevin President
PRO KENNEX, 1177

Gilbert, Lori Sports Columnist
RECORD (CA), 523

Gilbert, Lucia Provost
LEVY, HERMAN M., 890

Gilbert, Marie Associate A.D./Chief Financial
Officer
THOMAS ASSEMBLY CENTER, 976, 1009

Gilbert, Nick Assistant Coordinator
NATIONAL SPORTS FORUM, 797

Gilbert, Paul President
RESILITE SPORTS PRODUCTS, INC., 1181

Gilbert, Pete Sports Reporter
WBAL-TV, 699

Gilbert, Skip CEO
US YOUTH SOCCER, 155, 156

Gilberti, Andrew Ticket Sales Manager
LAKEWOOD BLUECLAWS, 981

Gilberton, Kenneth President
NATURAL SPORT, 1166

Gilbert, Ingrid Online Marketing Coordinator
FARMINGTON CONVENTION & VISITORS
BUREAU, 233

Gilbin, David Chair
BOSTON CONVENTION & VISITORS
BUREAU/SPORTS MARKETING DIVISION,
GR, 229

Gilboe, Mike Head Athletic Trainer
LAKE FOREST COLLEGE ATHLETICS, 390

Gilbride, Kevin Publisher
GOLF COURSE NEWS, 561

Gilbride, Paul President
EXHIBITION PARK, 1037

Giles, Brian Manager, Facilities
TD PLACE, 1008

Giles, Carmen Director of Event Services
SIOUX FALLS ARENA, 1003

Giles, Lisa Promotion Manager
KPSI-AM, 202, 626

Giles, Rick Founder/President
GAZELLE GROUP, 784

Giles, Ryan Promotions
1500 ESPN SPORTSTALK, 605

Gilhooly, Trina Housing Director
NORTH AMERICAN HOCKEY LEAGUE, 132

Gilis, J. Principal
FFKR ARCHITECTS, 1056

Gilkey, Christopher Tournament Director
SOUTH FLORIDA PGA, 115

Gill, Chelsea Director of Development
SPECIAL OLYMPICS NEW HAMPSHIRE, 196

Gill, Chris Coach
NATIONAL LACROSSE LEAGUE, 142

Gill, Chuck President
U.S. PROFESSIONAL TENNIS ASSOCIATION,
175

Gill, Darren Director Marketing
FIELD TURF TARKETT, 1132

Gill, Evelyn Vice-President
U.S. YOUTH SOCCER ASSOCIATION, 267

Gill, John President
NIGHT SPORTS, 1168

Gill, Keith Director of Athletics
ROBINS STADIUM, 998

Gill, Michele President
NEBRASKA WOMEN'S AMATEUR GOLF
ASSOCIATION, 113

Gill, Roger Sports Director
WTGG-FM, 668

Gill, Tracy Assistant Athletic Director
CONCORD UNIVERSITY ATHLETICS, 355

Gillard, Carol Vice President
KANSAS CITY GOLF ASSOCIATION, 112

Gillen, Jim Associate Athletic Director
METROPOLITAN STATE UNIVERSITY OF
DENVER ATHLETICS, 363

Gillen, Lolly President
SQUASH CANADA, 171

Gillen, Michael Tax Accounting Director
DUANE MORRIS LLP, 877

Gillentine, Andy Chair/Director
MIAMI, UNIVERSITY OF, 426

Gillenwater, Chad Vice Chairman
SPL INTEGRATED SOLUTIONS, 822

Gillespie, Aaron Sports Information Director
MENLO COLLEGE ATHLETICS, 316

Gillespie, Bob Golf Columnist
STATE, 535

Gillespie, Bree Chair
USA FIELD HOCKEY, 208

Gillespie, Daniel Sponsorship & Member Benefits
Manager
USA CYCLING, 71

Gillespie, Dave Director of Athletics
MIDLAND UNIVERSITY, 316

Gillespie, Ellis Player Relations VP
PRO-REP, INC., 803

Gillespie, Jeff Sports Editor
ROCKDALE CITIZEN, 525

Gillespie, Larissa Associate Director of Athletics
WIDENER UNIVERSITY ATHLETICS, 406

Gillespie, Mary Director of Athletics
BROWN COUNTY VETERANS MEMORIAL
ARENA, 55, 952

Gillespie, Matthew Assistant Executive Director
TENNESSEE SECONDARY SCHOOL
ATHLETIC ASSOCIATION, 202

Gillespie, Rory Editor
AMERICAN BOWLER, 549

Gillespie, Russell Classified Director
INTELLIGENCER JOURNAL, 496

Gillespie, Shawn President
ACCUFITNESS, LLC, 1091

Gillespie, Steve General Manager, Operations
BLOODHORSE MAGAZINE, 74

Gilliam, Chris Sports Editor
BANNER-NEWS, 463

Gilliam, Dyanne Managing Editor
RACER, 577

Gilliland, Bret Deputy Commissioner
MOUNTAIN WEST CONFERENCE, 300

Gilliland, David Co-Owner
NASCAR GANDER OUTDOORS TRUCK
SERIES, 19, 23

Gilliland, Lew Sports Editor
TIMES JOURNAL, 539

Gillin, Doug Director of Athletics
APPALACHIAN STATE UNIVERSITY
ATHLETICS, 324

Gillingham, Terry General Manager
WIMZ-FM, 651

Gillis, David Advertising Director
VICKSBURG POST, 544

Gillis, H. Managing Partner
THOMAS, MEANS & GILLIS, P.C., 912

Gillis, Michael Agent
M.D. GILLIS & ASSOCIATES LTD., 841

Gillis, Sandra Advertising Director
ISLAND PACKET, 497

Gillispie, Mick Director, Broadcasting
SMOKIES PARK, 1003

Gillman, Brian EMS Coordinator
INTERNATIONAL POLICE MOUNTAIN BIKE
ASSOCIATION (IPMBA), 70

Gillman, Stewart Program Chair
ST. LEO UNIVERSITY, 433

Gillot, Sebastien Head of Communications
UNION CYCLISTE INTERNATIONALE (UCI),
71

Gills, Mike President/General Manager Canucks
ORCA BAY SPORTS & ENTERTAINMENT, 223

Gilman, C. President & Principal
DES ARCHITECTS/ENGINEERS, INC., 1054

Gilman, Laurence Sr. VP & Governor
AMERICAN HOCKEY LEAGUE/AHL, 129

Gilman, Mark President / Chief Executive Officer
CAMPING WORLD, 1221

Gilman, Neil President
MARTY GILMAN, INC. DBA GILMAN GEAR,
1160

Gilman, Shirley Chief Executive Officer
MARTY GILMAN, INC. DBA GILMAN GEAR,
1160

Gilman, Tom President
DES ARCHITECTS/ENGINEERS, INC., 1054

Gilmer, Bill News Director
WPHM-AM, 639, 661

Gilmer, Ken President
POWERS EMBROIDERY/ CHENILLE, INC.,
USA, 1176

Gilmer, Todd Marketing Manager
PACIFIC TRAIL, 1172

Gilmore, Brandon Media & Communications
Coordinator
NATIONAL CHRISTIAN COLLEGE ATHLETIC
ASSOCIATION/NCCAA, 285

Gilmore, Chris Director of Athletics
DANIEL WEBSTER COLLEGE ATHLETICS
(DWC), 382

Gilmore, Dan Athletic Director
ROWAN UNIVERSITY ATHLETICS, 399

Gilmore, Don Assistant Director, Sports
Information
MASTER'S COLLEGE ATHLETICS, THE, 316

Gilmore, Jay Sports Reporter/Anchor
WPTV-TV, 708

Gilmore, Jon Secretary
SIKESTON JAYCEE BOOTHEEL RODEO
ARENA, 1044

Gilmore, Louis Director of Business Developmetn
RICHMOND INTERNATIONAL RACEWAY,
1031

Gilmore, Steward Director
SOUTHERN ILLINOIS GOLF ASSOCIATION,
115

Gilner, Brian Operations Manager
BB&T CENTER, 949

Gilroy, Maureen Marketing Director
IEG SPONSORSHIP SOURCEBOOK, 595

Gilson, Rick Vice-Presdient
ALBERTA SCHOOLS' ATHLETIC
ASSOCIATION, 199

Gilson, Todd Secretary/Treasurer
ASSOCIATION FOR APPLIED SPORT
PSYCHOLOGY/AAASP, 217

Gilula, Jonathan EVP & COO
AMERICAN LEAGUE OF PROFESSIONAL
BASEBALL CLUBS, THE, 29

Gimblette, Peter Marketing Manager
WOFX-AM, 659

Gimelstob, Justin Player Representative
ATP WORLD TOUR, 174

Gines, D. Vice President of Intercollegiate Athlet
TEXAS A&M UNIVERSITY-KINGSVILLE
ATHLETICS, 372

Glennie, Gordon Assistant General Manager
NATIONAL PRO FASTPITCH, 171

Glennon, Billy Group CEO
VISION SPORTS & ENTERTAINMENT
PARTNERS, 816

Glennon, John Chief Information Officer
MASSACHUSETTS STATE RACING
COMMISSION, 80, 119

Glennon, John Sports Reporter
TENNESSEAN, 538

Gleockler, Kyle Manager, Ticketing and
Merchandise
FLORIDA STATE LEAGUE, 40

Glesinger, Mike Sports Director
KCOW-AM, 612, 615

Glez, Myriam High Performance Director & CEO
USA SYNCHRO, 173, 209

Glick, Gareth Head Coach
USL LEAGUE TWO, 161

Glick, Heath Senior Associate Athletic
Director/COO
FLORIDA INTERNATIONAL UNIVERSITY
ATHLETICS, 330, 1227

Glick, Shav Sports Writer (Motor Sports)
LOS ANGELES TIMES, 503

Glickman, Michael Event Marketing President
INTERFERENCE, 789

Glickman, Ronald Sports Agent
CENTURY CITY SPORTS &
ENTERTAINMENT, 828

Glickman, Todd Vice President
GLOBAL SPECTRUM, 756, 820

Glier, Ray Sports Writer
NEW YORK TIMES, 511

Glincher, Andrew Office Managing Partner
NIXON, PEABODY, 897

Gliner, Steve Chief Operating Officer
FLORIDA STATE LEAGUE, 39

Glinski, Andrea Promotions Director
WGR 55 SPORTS RADIO, 648

Glinton, Gavin Head Coach
USL CHAMPIONSHIP, 160

Glisson, Mike Stadium Operations Manager
TURNER FIELD, 1011

Gloden, Mike Operations Manager
R.A.M. SPORTS, INC., 1179

Glodowski, Dave Vice president
GREMMER ASSOCIATES, 1058

Glon, Tim Sports Information Director
OHIO NORTHERN UNIVERSITY
ATHLETICS(ONU), 396

Glosband, Gabe Marketing Manager
SCOTT USA, 1186

Glovaski, Matt Director of Athletics
IONA COLLEGE ATHLETICS, 333

Glover, Andrew Sports Information Director
WILEY COLLEGE ATHLETICS, 323

Glover, Joe Director of Athletics
INDIANA UNIVERSITY SOUTHEAST
ATHLETICS, 297, 314

Glover, Kevin VP
PAIGE & RICE, 846

Glover, Larry Athletics Director
FISK UNIVERSITY ATHLETICS, 384

Glover, Lynn 1st Vice President
LADIES BIRMINGHAM GOLF ASSOCIATION,
112

Glover, Paul Sports Editor
BATESVILLE GUARD, 463

Glover, Richard Managing Editor
HORSEMAN'S JOURNAL, 564

Glover, Walter Interim Chief Financial Officer
HAMAKAWA, CURT L., 837

Glowacki, Autumn Coordinator of Operations,
Events and Fa
CHARLES E. SMITH CENTER, 956

Glower, Walt Treasurer
STATE GAMES OF AMERICA, 264

Glozek, John President
INTERNATIONAL NETWORK OF GOLF, 103

Glozek, John Publisher
LONG ISLAND GOLFER MAGAZINE, 569

Glueck, Milton Account Manager
KLUP-AM, 623

Gmelich, Thomas Attorney/Partner
BRADLEY & GMELICH, 867

Gmitter, Janine Head Athletic Trainer
HUSSON UNIVERSITY ATHLETICS, 388

Gnan, Pete Director of Athletics
CONCORDIA UNIVERSITY CHICAGO
ATHLETICS (CU), 381

Gnodtke, Doug Executive Associate AD/Chief of
Staff
MICHIGAN ATHLETICS, UNIVERSITY OF, 337

Gnuse, Holly Administrative Assistant
MASTER'S COLLEGE ATHLETICS, THE, 316

Goatley, James President
SPORTS TURF MANAGERS ASSOCIATION,
225

Gobar, Alfred President and Chairman
ALFRED GOBAR ASSOCIATES, 1049

Gober, Gary Principal Attorney/Founder
GOBER LAW FIRM, 882

Gober, Michelle Associate Director of Athletics
KUTZTOWN UNIVERSITY ATHLETICS (KU
ATHLETICS), 361

Gobiel, Eric Associate Director of Athletics
NICHOLS COLLEGE ATHLETICS, 395

Gobindram, Kash President / Chief Executive
Officer
POWERBRANDS LLC, 1149, 1176

Goble, Ed Executive Sr. Associate AD, Facilities
DARRELL K ROYAL - TEXAS MEMORIAL
STADIUM, 960

Goch, Ron Assoc. AD, External Ops.
WEBER STATE UNIVERSITY ATHLETICS,
349, 961

Gochenour, Mike Advertising Manager
PROGRESS-INDEX, 523

Gochman, David Chairman/CEO
ACADEMY SPORTS & OUTDOORS, 1215

Godberson, Kari-ann Human Resources Director
CARLSON DESIGN/CONSTRUCT CORP.,
1052

Goddard, Jim EVP/General Manager
HP PAVILION AT SAN JOSE, 971

Goddard, Joann Staff Writer
SOUNDINGS:TRADE ONLY, 582

Goddard, Lee Sports Reporter
CORPUS CHRISTI CALLER-TIMES, 473

Goddard, Tamara Director Strategic Alliance
PIER 39 MARKET DEVELOPMENT, 759

Goddard, Timothy Attorney
HASLER, FONFARA AND MAXWELL, LLP, 883

Godding, Jesse Athletic Director
SOUTHWESTERN ASSEMBLIES OF GOD
UNIVERSITY ATHLETICS, 320

Godfread, Jon Secretary
SPECIAL OLYMPICS NORTH DAKOTA, 196

Godfrey, Ed Sports Writer
OKLAHOMAN, 515

Godleski, Christine Chief Operating Officer
ACKERMAN, VALERIE B., 861

Godsey, Billi Assoc. Commissioner of Operations
NEW YORK COLLEGIATE ATHLETIC
CONFERENCE, 301

Godwin, Raef Director, Sales & Marketing
Operations
PGA TOUR, 108

Gody, Thomas Vice Chairman
FEDERATED DEPARTMENT STORES, INC.,
1227

Goe, Ken Sports Reporter
OREGONIAN, 516

Goebel, Scott Vice President
SCHUYLKILL VALLEY SPORTS, 1236

Goehring, Ruth Associate Athletic Director/Events
& Fac
ROBINS CENTER, 998

Goering, Jeff Chief Financial Officer
NATIONAL FOOTBALL LEAGUE/NFL, 94

Goethel, Tom Assistant General Manager
FRONTIER LEAGUE, 41

Goetz, Beth Deputy AD/SWA/COO
IOWA ATHLETICS, UNIVERSITY OF, 333, 985,
1004, 1019

Goetz, Dan Advertising Director
DAILY GAZETTE (IL), 476

Goetz, Robert Sports Editor
PRESS REPUBLICAN, 522

Goetz, Tom Sports Editor
DAILY LEADER (MS), 477

Goetze-Ackerman, Vicki Player
Director-President (LGPA)
SYMETRA TOUR, 103, 109

Goff, Alfreeda Sr. Assoc. Commissioner/Chief
Staff
HORIZON LEAGUE, 297

Goff, Corey Director of Athletics
MUHLENBERG COLLEGE ATHLETICS, 394

Goff, Mike Manager
ARIZONA LEAGUE (ROOKIE), 34

Goff, Ryan Interim Sports Information Director
LEWIS & CLARK COLLEGE ATHLETICS (L &
C), 390

Goff, Travis Director of Athletics
KANSAS UNIVERSITY ATHLETICS, 334

Goforth, Mike Associate Director of Athletics for
Spor
LANE STADIUM/WORSHAM FIELD, 981

Gofrey, Katie Kastrel Sales Manager
NIELSEN-KELLERMAN, 1168

Goger, Jason President
STX INC., 1197

Gohl, Pam Associate Athletic Director
SIOUX FALLS ATHLETICS, UNIVERSITY OF,
370

Goicouria, Luis Vice President, Digital Media
Business D
PGA TOUR, 108

Goings, Gregory Sports Information Director
BOWIE STATE UNIVERSITY ATHLETICS, 352

Goings, Linda Advertising Director
PALM BEACH DAILY NEWS, 517

Goins, Rich Sports Director
KRFX-FM, 627

Gold, Adam Host
THE ADAM GOLD SHOW, 607

Gold, Alan Editor
CUTTING HORSE CHATTER, 556

Gold, Eli Host
NASCAR LIVE, 609

Gold, Evan Assistant General Manager & Dir.,
Legal
NATIONAL HOCKEY LEAGUE/NHL, 123

Gold, Keith Brand Manager
FLAGHOUSE, 1227

Gold, Kevin Administrative Chair
GOLD, KEVIN M.UIRE, 1227

Gold, Steve Director of Field Operations
CAROLINA LEAGUE, 37, 978

Golda, Gene Associate Producer
HIGH SCHOOL WEEKLY, 683

Goldammer, Mike Executive Director
USTA NORTHERN, 176

Goldbeck, Will Sports Reporter
SOUTH COUNTY NEWS, 531

Goldberg, Adam President & Governor
EAST COAST HOCKEY LEAGUE/ECHL, 130

Goldberg, Andrew Director Of Marketing
FABRICATION ENTERPRISES, 32, 1131

Goldberg, Bernard Correspondent
REAL SPORTS WITH BRYANT GUMBEL, 685

Goldberg, Carole Vice Chancellor
JASPER, PATRICIA M., 886

Goldberg, David EVP, Corporate Development
SPORTVISION, 602

Goldberg, Elliott President
FABRICATION ENTERPRISES, 1131

Goldberg, Hank Reporter
NFL 2NIGHT, 684

Goldberg, Jeff Sports Columnist/Reporter
HARTFORD COURANT, 492

Goldberg, Linda Director Of Sales
FABRICATION ENTERPRISES, 1131

Goldberg, Mark Publisher
TRAINING AND CONDITIONING, 550, 555, 589

Goldberg, Michael Chief Executive Officer
NATIONAL MEDIA GROUP, INC., 796

Goldberg, Stan Sports Editor
FREDERICK NEWS-POST, 489

Goldberg, Steve Sports Producer
WBBM-TV, 699

Goldblatt, Dan President
FIRST SERVICE, 1132, 1133

Goldbloom, Jonathan Chair
HOCKEY CANADA, 122

Golden, Andrew Advertising Manager
SPEEDHORSE-THE RACING REPORT, 583

Golden, Brian Sports Writer
ANTELOPE VALLEY PRESS, 460

Golden, Connie Publisher
SPEEDHORSE-THE RACING REPORT, 583

Goodmon, James Vice President, CBC New Media Group
CAPITOL SPORTS NETWORK, 604, 685

Goodmon, Michael Vice President, Real Estate
CAPITOL SPORTS NETWORK, 685

Goodner, Donna Administrative Coordinator
ST. EDWARDS UNIVERSITY, 433

Goodolf, Barry Buyer, Sports
BOSCOV'S DEPARTMENT STORES, 1220

Goodrich, Andrew Vice President & Director of Athletics
GARDNER-WEBB UNIVERSITY ATHLETICS, 330

Goodrich, Brenda General Manager
KKML-AM, 621

Goodrum, Richard Geosynthetics
COLBOND, INC., 1117

Goodson, Michael Chief Investment Officer
WOLF GROUP-NY, 817

Goodspeed, Gail Treasurer
NATIONAL ASSOCIATION OF COLLEGIATE GYMNASTICS COACHES - WOMEN, 120

Goodwin, Brian Technical Director
AMERICAN BOAT & YACHT COUNCIL, 63, 181

Goodwin, Charles Head Athletic Trainer
OTTERBEIN UNIVERSITY ATHLETICS, 396

Goodwin, Elizabeth Museum Services Director
VIRGINIA SPORTS HALL OF FAME & MUSEUM, 259

Goodwin, Jim Eastern Regional Sales Manager
MILLERBERND MANUFACTURING COMPANY, 1163

Goodwin, Jimmy Promoter
FLOMATON SPEEDWAY, 1025

Goodwin, Kevin Sports Editor
PRESS DISPATCH-TRIBUNE, 522

Goodwin, Lee Sports Editor
RECORD-HERALD, 524

Goodwin, Pete Copy Editor
BOSTON GLOBE, 465

Goodwin, Steven 2nd Vice President
DISABLED SPORTS USA, 193

Googins, Scott Baseball Head Coach
XAVIER UNIVERSITY, 438

Goold, Derrick Sports Reporter
SAINT LOUIS POST-DISPATCH, 527

Goonetilleke, Harendra Operations Director
USL LEAGUE TWO, 163

Goor, Joe Sports Director
KVTK-AM, 631

Goorin, Cassel Founder
GOORIN BROS., INC., 1139

Goossens, Thijs Deputy AD, Internal Operations/CFO
MONTANA STATE UNIVERSITY ATHLETICS, 338

Goralski, Keith Senior Producer
COUNTDOWN TO KICKOFF, 608

Gorbman, Randy News Director
WHTK-AM, 650

Gorchov, Andy Events Director
INVESCO FIELD AT MILE HIGH STADIUM, 973

Gorden, Ginger Chief Financial Officer
CSMG INTERNATIONAL, LTD, 779

Gorder, Joe President/Chief Executive Officer
VALERO TEXAS OPEN, 116

Gordon, Amanda Sports Marketing & CommunicationsManage
LAFAYETTE-WEST LAFAYETTE CONVENTION & VISITORS BUREAU, 238

Gordon, Andrea President
DIAMOND SPORTS, 1124

Gordon, Anita Aid To Athletic Director
HILLSDALE COLLEGE ATHLETICS, 360

Gordon, Ben Assistant Coach
UNITED STATES HOCKEY LEAGUE, 138

Gordon, Britany Events and communications coordinator
CANADIAN LACROSSE ASSOCIATION, 141

Gordon, Chris Program Director
TEAM 1200 SPORTS RADIO, 635

Gordon, Denny Event Specialist
AMATEUR SPORTS GROUP, INC., 824

Gordon, Doug VP Sales / Marketing
KAPPA USA, 1151

Gordon, Ellie Founder / Senior EVP
HOT SOX, INC., 1146

Gordon, Gilbert Partner
MARKS, MARKS & KAPLAN, 893

Gordon, Grant Sports Editor
SIGNAL, 490, 531

Gordon, Jaime Director of Athletics
MOREHEAD STATE UNIVERSITY ATHLETICS, 338

Gordon, Janice Publisher
MARINA DOCK AGE, 552, 569

Gordon, Jeff Founder
JEFF GORDON FOUNDATION, 192

Gordon, Jeffrey President and Chief Executive Officer, J
JUST FOR FEET, 1230

Gordon, Judith Marketing director
LAMPART, ABE, 888

Gordon, Judy Senior Woman Administrator
WILLAMETTE UNIVERSITY ATHLETICS, 406

Gordon, Ken Sports Reporter
COLUMBUS DISPATCH, 472

Gordon, Kevin Director
CROWE & DUNLEVY, 830

Gordon, Kim PSA Director/Sports
KKNN-FM, 621

Gordon, Lee Associate Sports Editor
CHICAGO TRIBUNE, 470

Gordon, Scott Assistant Executive Director
GEORGIA PGA SECTIONAL OFFICE, 105

Gore, Steve Sports Editor
WFNR, 646

Gore, Tom Owner
PALACE SPORTS & ENTERTAINMENT, INC., 224, 846

Goreham, Betsy Advertising Director
SCOTTSDALE TRIBUNE, 529

Goren, Ed Vice Chairman
FOX SPORTS NETWORKS/FOX SPORTS NET, 675

Gores, Tom Owner & CEO
NATIONAL BASKETBALL ASSOCIATION/NBA, 56

Gorgemans, Anne Publisher
INTERNATIONAL HANDBOOK FOR THE SPORTING GOODS INDUSTRY, 595

Goricki, Dave Sports Reporter
DETROIT NEWS, 483

Gorman, Bill Associate Director of Athletics
WENTWORTH INSTITUTE OF TECHNOLOGY ATHLETICS(WIT), 405

Gorman, Brian Sports Reporter
HERALD-SUN, 494

Gorman, Doug Sports Editor
NEWS DAILY, 511, 512

Gorman, Leon Chairman of the Board
L.L. BEAN, 1231

Gorman, Stan Honorary President
CENTRAL NEW YORK PGA SECTIONAL OFFICE, 105

Gormley, Chuck Sports Reporter
COURIER-POST, 474

Gormley, David President
ZEPHYR GRAF-X INCORPORATED, 1212

Gormley, Wes Vice President Product Development
ZEPHYR GRAF-X INCORPORATED, 1212

Gormon, Michelle Sports Editor
TIPTON COUNTY TRIBUNE, 540

Gornick, Gregory Athletic Communications Coordinator
CHESTNUT HILL COLLEGE ATHLETICS, 354

Gorrasi, Mike Executive Vice President
CALIFORNIA LEAGUE (A-LEVEL), 36, 977

Gorretta, Lisa Vice President
UNITED STATES DRESSAGE FOUNDATION, 77

Gorse, Keith Clinical Coordinator
DUQUESNE UNIVERSITY, 416

Gorsky, Alex Chairman
JOHNSON & JOHNSON CONSUMER PRODUCTS INC., 1150

Gorsuch, Gary President
MERCURY INTERNATIONAL CORPORATION, 1162

Gortmaker, Jeff Director of Operations
SIOUX FALLS ARENA, 1003

Gortman, Travis Director of Group Sales
SOUTH ATLANTIC LEAGUE (A LEVEL), 51

Gorton, Jeff Executive VP, Hockey Operations
NATIONAL HOCKEY LEAGUE/NHL, 124

Gortsema, Tim President
AMERICAN HOCKEY LEAGUE/AHL, 127

Gorum, Kim Sports Editor
WACO TRIBUNE-HERALD, 545

Goslin, Craig President & Managing Partner
ONTARIO HOCKEY LEAGUE, 134

Gosper, Brett Chief Executive Officer
WORLD RUGBY, 148

Goss, Dick Sports Editor
HERALD-NEWS, 493

Goss, Fred Secretary
INDIANA FOOTBALL HALL OF FAME, 253

Goss, Josh Owner & Goalkeeper Coach
WOMEN'S PREMIER SOCCER LEAGUE, 167

Gossage, Eddit President/General Manager
TEXAS MOTOR SPEEDWAY/TMS, 1034

Gosse, Tonya Finance
ROAD AMERICA, 1031

Gosselin, Craig SVP, Secretary & General Counsel
VANS, INC., 1240

Gosselin, Mario Owner
NASCAR XFINITY SERIES, 24

Gosselin, Rick Sports Columnist
DALLAS MORNING NEWS, 481

Gossen, Paul Principal
GEIGER ENGINEERS, 1057

Gossett, Jill General Manager
WSFN-AM SPORTS RADIO, 666

Gossow, Joachim Chief Executive Officer
INTERNATIONAL WORLD GAMES ASSOCIATION/IWGA, 262

Gotham, Rich President, Basketball Operations
NATIONAL BASKETBALL ASSOCIATION/NBA, 56

Gotkin, Brandon Assistant Coach
UNITED STATES HOCKEY LEAGUE, 138

Gott, Kevin President
ADOLFSON & PERTSON, INC., 1048

Gottesman, Charles Vice Chairman / EVP Business Development
SAUCONY, 1185

Gottlieb, Doug Host
GAMENIGHT, 609

Gottlieb, Alan Chief Operating Officer, Lerner Sports
NATIONAL LEAGUE OF PROFESSIONAL BASEBALL CLUBS, THE, 32

Gottlieb, Doug Host
ESPN RADIO - SUNDAY GAMENIGHT, 608

Gottlieb, Justin Director Of Communications & PR
INTERBIKE, 757

Gottlieb, Richard President
SPORTS MARKET PLACE DIRECTORY, 596

Gottlieb, Ryan Sr. Associate AD/Revenue Generating Offi
COLORADO ATHLETICS, UNIVERSITY OF, 327

Gottsch, Gatsby EVP, Finance
RFDTV, 686

Gottsch, JJ Chief Operating Officer
DELL DIAMOND, 961

Gottsch, Patrick Founder/President
RFDTV, 686

Gottsch, Raquel EVP, Corporate Communications
RFDTV, 686

Gottsch, Sheila National Sales Manager
BLAZER MANUFACTURING, INC., 1108

Gottsegen, Francie President
USL LEAGUE ONE, 159, 161

Gottsegen, Steve Weekend Sports Anchor
KMGH-TV, 692

Gotwals, Ed Sports Editor
PUBLIC OPINION, 523

Gotzmer, Bruno RegionalManager
ANY MOUNTAIN, LTD, 1216

Goudeau, Jonathan Secretary
BILLIARD CONGRESS OF AMERICA, 62

Goudeseune, Scott President & CEO
AMERICAN COUNCIL ON EXERCISE, 83

Goudie, Mark President & Chief Executive Officer
CANADIAN FOOTBALL LEAGUE/CFL, 93

Goudreau, Trace Director of Sales & Marketing
WISCONSIN CENTER DISTRICT, 1019

Goudy, Roger President
AMATEUR ATHLETIC UNION OF THE UNITED STATES, INC./AAU, 142, 213

Grant, Anthony Director of Athletics
METROPOLITAN STATE UNIVERSITY OF
DENVER ATHLETICS, 363
Grant, Bob Director of Athletics
WRIGHT STATE UNIVERSITY ATHLETICS,
350
Grant, Brett General Manager
KSHP-AM, 629
Grant, Byron General Manager
GOLF SCORECARDS, INC, 785, 820
Grant, Chris Sports Editor
IMPERIAL VALLEY PRESS, 496
Grant, Christine Athletic Administration
IOWA, UNIVERSITY OF, 421
Grant, Cory Secretary
WHEELCHAIR & AMBULATORY SPORTS, 198
Grant, Cynthia President
GOLF SCORECARDS, INC, 785, 820
Grant, David President
GRANT ASSOCIATES, 747, 786, 816, 836
Grant, Eugene President
ATHLETIC TRAINING EQUIPMENT
COMPANY/ATEC, 1101
Grant, Evan Sports Reporter (Baseball)
DALLAS MORNING NEWS, 481
Grant, Garry Head Athletic Trainer
UNIVERSITY OF WISCONSIN - EAU CLAIRE
BLUGOLD ATHLETICS, 407
Grant, Heather Director of Clinical Athletic
Training
BRIDGEWATER COLLEGE ATHLETICS, 378
Grant, Jason Head Coach
WOMEN'S FOOTBALL ALLIANCE / WFA, 97
Grant, Jim Head Athletic Trainer
ST. JOHN FISHER COLLEGE ATHLETICS
(SJFC), 401
Grant, Joe Sports Editor
PORTLAND PRESS HERALD, MAINE SUNDAY
TELEGRAM, 521
Grant, Sabrina Director of Athletics
WILLIAM PATERSON UNIVERSITY OF NEW
JERSEY ATHLETICS, 407
Grant, Sally President
VOYAGER CUSTOM PRODUCTS, 1208
Grant, Thomas Sports Senior Reporter
TIMES AND DEMOCRAT, 539
Grant, Todd President/Executive Director
NATIONAL BICYCLE DEALERS
ASSOCIATION, 70
Grantham, Lance Assistant AD/Ticket Operations
WILLIAMS-BRICE STADIUM, 1019
Grass, John Head Coach, Football
BURGESS-SNOW FIELD AT JSU STADIUM,
953
Grass, Peter Vice President
GOLF COURSE SUPERINTENDENTS
ASSOCIATION OF AMERICA/GCSAA, 102
Grass, Roger President / Chief Executive officer
FLEER/SKYBOX INTERNATIONAL, 1133
Grassl, Herb Publisher
DESERT BOWLER, 556
Grasso, Michael Associate Director of Athletics
MOLLOY COLLEGE ATHLETICS, 365
Grattan, Mike Director, Scouting/Assistant Coach
NORTH AMERICAN HOCKEY LEAGUE, 132
Grau, Dave Owner
ACE MITCHELL BOWLERS MART, 1091
Graupe, Jeff VP & Asst. GM, Player Acquisition &
Stra
NATIONAL LEAGUE OF PROFESSIONAL
BASEBALL CLUBS, THE, 31
Gravalos, Tom Vice-Chairman
MOTORSPORTS MUSEUM AND HALL OF
FAME OF AMERICA, 255
Graveel, Larry President / Chief Operating Officer
GEAR FOR SPORTS, 1137
Gravelle, Jimena Events Manager
BADMINTON CANADA, 24
Gravelle, Steve Sports Editor
IOWA CITY GAZETTE, 490, 497
Graven, Jenn Director of Marketing and
Promotions
SOUTHWEST MINNESOTA STATE
UNIVERSITY ATHLETICS, 371
Graveoey, Nick Program Director
WIRQ-FM, 651
Graves, Andrea Advertising Manager
CHILLICOTHE CONSTITUTION-TRIBUNE, 470

Graves, Cindy Director of Administration
WINSTEAD ATTORNEYS, 916
Graves, Gary Sports Reporter
USA TODAY, 543
Graves, Greg Mutuel Manager
FAIRMOUNT PARK RACETRACK, 1038
Graves, Jennifer News Director
WLS-TV CHANNEL 7 ABC (CHICAGO), 706
Graves, John President / Chief Executive Officer
BIKE LINE, 1219
Graves, Justin Sports Editor
CULLMAN TIMES, 474
Graves, Karen Assistant Athletic Director
CONCORDIA UNIVERSITY (MI) ATHLETICS,
311
Graves, Steve Head Athletic Trainer
CLAREMONT-MUDD-SCRIPPS COLLEGES
ATHLETICS, 380
Gravino, Mike Business Development Manager
BUTLER HEAVY STRUCTURES, 1051
Gray, Bob Co-Founder
MEIGRAY GROUP, 1233
Gray, Dave Director, Coaching
WOMEN'S PREMIER SOCCER LEAGUE, 165
Gray, Della Operations Director
ELITE INTERNATIONAL SPORTS
MARKETING, INC., 781
Gray, Eric Afternoon Producer
TICKET760 KTKR, 635
Gray, Gary Director of Athletics
UNIVERSITY OF ALASKA FAIRBANKS
ATHLETICS, 373
Gray, Jeff General Manager
BOWEN FIELD, 951
Gray, Jen Director of Operations
USA RUGBY, 148
Gray, Jeremy Sports/News Director
WHCC-FM, 649
Gray, Jerry Associate Dean
RICHARDSON, DEAN, 902
Gray, Joel Advertising Manager
CHARLES CITY PRESS, 469
Gray, Johnny Co-Owner
ARCA MENARDS SERIES EAST, 19, 575
Gray, Josh General Manager
WOMEN'S PREMIER SOCCER LEAGUE, 164
Gray, Kami Deputy AD, Internal Operations/SWA
ST. MARY'S COLLEGE ATHLETICS, 345
Gray, Mathew Associate
ANDREWS KURTH LLP, 862
Gray, Matt Applications Engineer
INNOVATIVE ELECTRONIC DESIGNS, INC.,
821
Gray, Mickey President
SOUTHERN PROFESSIONAL HOCKEY
LEAGUE, 136
Gray, Nancy Legal Recruiting Manager
WEIL, GOTSHAL & MANGES, 914
Gray, Rob Sports Writer (High School)
DES MOINES REGISTER, 483
Gray, Roger Program Director
KTBB-AM, 616, 629
Gray, Simon Associate Vice President for
Athletics
NIAGARA UNIVERSITY ATHLETICS, 339
Gray, Steven National Director Sales
ASERTA SPORTS, 1100
Gray, Tanya Director of Events Services
RUSHMORE PLAZA CIVIC CENTER, 999
Gray, Ted President/Owner
MDF INDUSTRIES INC, 1161
Gray E. Little, Bernadette University Chancellor
POTTORFF, JAMES P. JR., 900
Gray-little, Bernadette University chancellor
MCCLOUD, BARBARA, 894
Graybeal, Jerry Assoc. AD, Development
WEBER STATE UNIVERSITY ATHLETICS, 349
Grayer, Dee Football Commissioner
AMERICAN YOUTH FOOTBALL, 88
Grayson, Jeff Sports Director
KMSP-TV, 692
Grayson, Mike Sports Director
KCFV-FM, 614
Grayston, Nick President and Chief Executive
Officer
LADY FOOT LOCKER, 1222, 1231
Grayzel, Judd Marketing & Sales Manager
OFF THE WALL PRODUCTS, LLC, 1170

Grealish, Tom President
MARIO LEMIEUX FOUNDATION, 192
Grecinger, Brandon Athletic Trainer
NORTH AMERICAN HOCKEY LEAGUE, 133
Greco, Michael Sports Editor
NORWALK REFLECTOR, 515
Greco, Phil President
ODEUM EXPO CENTER, 990
Greco, Piero Goaltending Coach
NATIONAL HOCKEY LEAGUE/NHL, 125
Greco, Teresa Chief Operating Officer
PUTT-PUTT GOLF COURSES OF AMERICA,
INC., 1178
Greco, Thomas Call Center Operations Director
PATRON SOLUTIONS, LP, 1065
Greco-Walker, Alica Associate Athletic Director,
Events & Op
BOB CARPENTER CENTER, 950
Greeberg, Steve Managing Editor
SPORTING NEWS, 584
Greehan, Mike Secretary
NATIONAL BICYCLE DEALERS
ASSOCIATION, 70
Greeley, Steve Owner
KJJJ-FM, 621
Green, A.C. Founder/President
A.C. GREEN YOUTH FOUNDATION, 191
Green, Al Head Athletic Trainer
FLORIDA SOUTHERN COLLEGE ATHLETICS
(FSC), 358
Green, Andrew Technical Chief
FORMULA 1, 20, 232
Green, Angela VIP Services Manager & Group
Sales
JAX EVENTS PRESENTED BY SMG, 975
Green, Barry Evp Sales
ACTIVE INTERNATIONAL, 766
Green, Brienne Sports Editor
ARTESIA DAILY PRESS, 461
Green, Buddy Sports Editor
VALLEY MORNING STAR, 543
Green, Carlton Producer
SPORTS TALK, 610
Green, Carrie Business Manager
FRONTIER LEAGUE, 41
Green, Cassie Sales & Social Media Manager
VISIT BINGHAMTON, 249
Green, Charmelle Deputy AD, Internal Operations
& COO
UTAH ATHLETICS, UNIVERSITY OF, 348, 949
Green, Chris Ass. Executive
Director-Communications
NATIONAL ASSOCIATION OF COLLEGIATE
MARKETING ADMINISTRATORS/NACMA, 284,
354
Green, Dave General Manager
WHBQ SPORTS 56, 649
Green, Deb Advertising Manager
MARSHALL NEWS MESSENGER, 505
Green, Don Co-Founder
ROOTS APPAREL, 1183
Green, Elizabeth Executive Assistant to the
President
ELSWIT, LAWRENCE S., 878
Green, Ernie Sports Editor
TONAWANDA NEWS, 541
Green, Gary Chief Executive Officer
PACIFIC COAST LEAGUE OF
PROFESSIONAL BASEBALL CLUBS, 49, 999
Green, Greg News Director/Sports Director
WKZS-FM, 655
Green, Gregory President
THE NATIONAL BOWLING ASSOCIATION,
INC, 66
Green, Janet Administrative Associate
BAYLOR UNIVERSITY, 411
Green, Jason General Manager
RICHARD M BORCHARD REGIONAL
FAIRGROUNDS/SPECTRA, 997
Green, Jeff President
MERCHANT OF TENNIS, INC., 1233
Green, Jeffrey Senior Producer
DYNOCOMM SPORTS TV, 598
Green, Jerry Secretary
MASSACHUSETTS GOLF ASSOCIATION, 112
Green, Jim Assistant General Manager
BRIDGESTONE ARENA, 952
Green, Joanne Sports Information Director
HUNTINGTON UNIVERSITY ATHLETICS, 314

Green, Johnny Sports Editor
TEXARKANA GAZETTE, 538
Green, Lorna Director, Operations
LEAGUE OF AMERICAN BICYCLISTS, 71
Green, Matt Athletic Director
LINCOLN MEMORIAL UNIVERSITY
ATHLETICS (LMU), 362
Green, Melanie Director of Business Development
& Marke
BAKER & DANIELS, 863
Green, Mike Assoc. Director
JACK TRICE STADIUM, 974
Green, Mona Executive Assistant
PICO RIVERA SPORTS ARENA, 993
Green, Nancy Administrative Assistant
TACOMA DOME, 1007
Green, Peter Maintenance Office Manager
JS DORTON ARENA, 978
Green, Rick General Manager
SPORTS RADIO 1260-AM WNDE, 634
Green, Ron Sports Writer
CHARLOTTE OBSERVER, 469
Green, Sahron Vice President, Finance &
Administration
CLARKSVILLE MONTGOMERY COUNTY
CONVENTION & VISITORS BUREAU, 230
Green, Scott Chief Administrative Officer
QUINN, JAMES W., 900
Green, Shawn Assistant Director of Athletics
SOUTHERN NEW HAMPSHIRE UNIVERSITY
ATHLETICS, 370
Green, Shirley Interim VP Student Affairs
NJCAA REGION I MEN'S, 286
Green, Steve General Manager
BIKE USA INC., 1018, 1106
Green, Sue Secretary
CALIFORNIA THOROUGHBRED BREEDERS
ASSOCIATION, 74
Green, Susan Executive
WOMEN'S PREMIER SOCCER LEAGUE, 164
Green, Tamera Vice President
GMR MARKETING, 756
Green, Ted Sports Writer
KTLA-TV, 680, 695
Green, Terri Director Of Membership
ARKANSAS STATE GOLF ASSOCIATION, 110
Green, Thomas Partner
ADAMSKI MOROSKI MADDEN & GREEN LLP,
861
Green, Tom President
JOHN R. GREEN COMPANY INC., OLD
MASTER PUTTERS, 1150
Green, Tracy Office Manager
KVON-AM, 631
Green, Travis Head Coach
NATIONAL HOCKEY LEAGUE/NHL, 125
Green, Tucker Project Manager
H E HODGE COMPANY, 1141
Green, Wade Head Athletic Trainer
HARDIN-SIMMONS UNIVERSITY ATHLETICS,
387
Green, Willie Head Coach
NATIONAL BASKETBALL ASSOCIATION/NBA,
57
Greenbaum, Jeffrey Partner in Advertising,
Marketing
FRANKFURT, KURNIT, KLEIN & SELZ, P.C.,
881
Greenberg, Ben Sports Information Director
JOHN E. TUCKER COLISEUM, 976
Greenberg, Bernie Sales
SPORTS NETWORK, THE, 687, 714
Greenberg, Brett Assistant General Manager,
Strategy & An
NATIONAL BASKETBALL ASSOCIATION/NBA,
58
Greenberg, Chuck CEO, General Partner
TEXAS BASEBALL LEAGUE, 37, 53, 192, 801,
962, 1009
Greenberg, Evan Vice President
EFINGER SPORTING GOODS, 1226
Greenberg, George EVP Programming &
Production
FOX SPORTS NETWORKS/FOX SPORTS
NET, 675
Greenberg, Jay Contributing Writer
RINKSIDE, 510, 578
Greenberg, Jeff Sports Producer
WRC-TV, 708

Greenberg, Jon President
AMERICAN HOCKEY LEAGUE/AHL, 128
Greenberg, Mel Sports Reporter
PHILADELPHIA INQUIRER, 519
Greenberg, Michael President / Director
SKECHERS USA, 1189
Greenberg, Mike Sports Host
KMVP-AM, 609, 624
Greenberg, Murray VP and General Merchandise
Manager
EFINGER SPORTING GOODS, 1226
Greenberg, Peter President
PETER GREENBERG & ASSOCIATES, 846
Greenberg, Robert Chairman / Chief Executive
Officer
SKECHERS USA, 1189
Greenblatt, Sherwin President
BOSE CORPORATION, 819
Greenburg, Bob Sports Director
WPIC-AM, 661
Greenburg, Chuck Chairman and Managing
Partner
NEW YORK-PENNSYLVANIA LEAGUE, 47
Greenburg, Ross Executive Producer
REAL SPORTS WITH BRYANT GUMBEL, 682,
685
Greene, Allen Senior Deputy AD, External
Relations
MISSISSIPPI ATHLETICS, UNIVERSITY OF,
337
Greene, Brandon General Manager
SOUTH ATLANTIC LEAGUE (A LEVEL), 51,
981
Greene, Chris Sports Editor
FACTS, 488
Greene, Dana Sports Reporter
KTVX-TV, 696
Greene, Dennis President of Business Operations
FEDEXFIELD, 965
Greene, Garrett Media Relations Manager &
Broadcaster
SOUTHERN LEAGUE OF PROFESSIONAL
BASEBALL CLUBS, 52
Greene, Herbert Executive Director
COLUMBUS, GA SPORTS & EVENTS
COUNCIL, 231
Greene, James Director of Championships
BIG EAST CONFERENCE, 292
Greene, Jason Director of Athletic Communication
SETON HILL UNIVERSITY ATHLETICS, 320
Greene, Joe President & COO
UNITED STATES HOCKEY LEAGUE, 138
Greene, Joey Vice President of Operations
ROAD ATLANTA, 1032
Greene, John Marketing Director
KUTV-TV, 696
Greene, Kemberly Assistant AD, Community
Relations & Dev.
SOUTH CAROLINA STATE UNIVERSITY
ATHLETICS, 344
Greene, Kendra Deputy AD, Internal Affairs/SWA
NORTH CAROLINA CENTRAL UNIVERSITY
ATHLETICS, 339
Greene, Kevin President, General Manager
PIONEER BASEBALL LEAGUE, 50
Greene, LaToya Associate Director of Athletics
MOUNT OLIVE COLLEGE ATHLETICS, 365
Greene, Leon Undergraduate Coordinator
KANSAS UNIVERSITY, 422
Greene, Mike Operations Manager
LAFAYETTE INSTRUMENT COMPANY, 1154
Greene, Richard President
VALLEY FORGE SPORTS, INC., 1207
Greene, Tiffany Sports Reporter
WTOC-TV, 710
Greene, Tom Director Stadium Operations
SEC TAYLOR STADIUM, 1002
Greener, Geoffrey Chief Risk Officer
BANK OF AMERICA CORPORATION, 725
Greenfield, Michele Vice President Of Outreach,
Marketing& I
WOMEN'S METROPOLITAN GOLF
ASSOCIATION, 117
Greenfield, Stefanie Principal
CAMBRIDGE SEVEN ASSOCIATES INC., 1051
Greening, Mary Contact
AON ENTERTAINMENT, 767
Greenleaf, Brandi Executive Director
MARSHALL FAULK FOUNDATION, 192

Greenleaf, Jared Sports Editor
CHEBOYGAN DAILY TRIBUNE, 469
Greenman, Larry President
NORTHERN NEVADA GOLF ASSOCIATION,
114
Greenslit, Dave Sports Editor
TELEGRAM & GAZETTE, 537
Greenspan, Bud President
CAPPY PRODUCTIONS INC., 598
Greenspan, Rick Director of Athletics
RICE STADIUM, 996
Greenspun, Scott Co-Founder/Principal
ECLIPSE SPORTS MANAGEMENT, 831
Greenstein, Teddy Sports Reporter
CHICAGO TRIBUNE, 470
Greenstreet, Robin Property Manager
WALKER & COMPANY, 1209
Greenwald, Jeffery Manager
BAKER, DAVID L., 863
Greenway, Robert SVP
Production/Programming/Ops
GOLF CHANNEL, THE, 599, 687
Greenwell, James Executive Senior Associate
Athletics Dir
GEORGIA STATE UNIVERSITY, 419
Greenwood, Alan Sports Editor
TELEGRAPH (NH), 537
Greenwood, Ben Sponsorship Sales
WORLD SPORTS & MARKETING, 180
Greenwood, Giles Golf Tourism Development
Director
INTERNATIONAL ASSOCIATION OF GOLF
TOUR OPERATORS, 102
Greenwood, Pat Sports Director
WPMI - NBC 15, 708
Greer, Bill NAIA COP Representative
APPALACHIAN ATHLETIC CONFERENCE, 291
Greer, Carrie Office Manager
MOUNTAIN BIKE ACTION, 571
Greer, Charvi Deputy AD/COO
TULANE UNIVERSITY ATHLETICS, 347
Greer, Jarvis Sports Director
WMC-TV, 706
Greer, Otis Director of Community Affairs
CALIFORNIA SPEEDWAY, 1022
Greeson, Jay Sports Editor
CHATTANOOGA TIMES FREE PRESS, 469
Greff, Steve Sports Editor
CORVALLIS GAZETTE-TIMES, 473
Gregg, Brad Operations Director
COLONIAL ATHLETIC ASSOCIATION, 294
Gregg, Matt Assistant Athletic Director
WARNER PACIFIC COLLEGE ATHLETICS,
323
Gregg, Melanie Secretary Communications
CANADIAN SOCIETY FOR PSYCHOMOTOR
LEARNING & SPORT PSYCHOLOGY, 218
Greggs, Kevin VP, Communications
NATIONAL LEAGUE OF PROFESSIONAL
BASEBALL CLUBS, THE, 32
Gregor, Chris Associate Athletic Director
SAINT MARTIN'S COLLEGE ATHLETICS, 369
Gregorchik, Karen Assistant General Manager
CAMBRIA COUNTY WAR MEMORIAL, 954
Gregory, Ardie Vice President/GM, WRAL-FM
CAPITOL SPORTS NETWORK, 685
Gregory, Ashley Group Tours & Meeting Manager
LAFAYETTE-WEST LAFAYETTE
CONVENTION & VISITORS BUREAU, 238
Gregory, Dan Director of Stadium Operations
BALLPARK AT HARBOR YARD, 948
Gregory, Debbie Senior Associate AD, Business
Affairs
SAINT PETER'S UNIVERSITY ATHLETICS,
343
Gregory, Joe General Manager
INTERNATIONAL LEAGUE, 42, 969
Gregory, John Director
ADAMS GOLF GP CORPORATION, 1093
Gregory, Jon Assistant Director of Athletics,
Facilit
HOMEWOOD FIELD, 971
Gregory, Josh Mens's Golf Head Coach
AUGUSTA STATE UNIVERSITY ATHLETICS,
351
Gregory, Keith Member
KEITH O. GREGORY, 888
Gregory, Kevin Director, Marketing
HOMESTEAD-MIAMI SPEEDWAY, LLC, 1025

Guersch, Mike Sports Deputy Editor
SAN JOSE MERCURY NEWS, 528

Guertin, Steve Sports Editor
BENICIA HERALD, 464

Guess, Adam CFO
AMERICAN FOOTBALL COACHES
ASSOCIATION, 87

Guest, Liam General Manager
USL LEAGUE TWO, 163

Guest, Tom Advertising Manager
PRINCETON DAILY CLARION, 523

Guevara, Keith Chairman, Director, President and
Chief
NEIGHBORHOOD BOX OFFICE, 931

Guevara, Tony President
OREGON SCHOOL ACTIVITIES
ASSOCIATION, 201

Guevremont, Charles Chief Executive Officer
U.S. REPEATING ARMS
COMPANY/WINCHESTER, 1111, 1205

Gugerty, Cathy General Manager
WDEF, 701

Guglberger, Eric President
ERIC ARMIN INC./EAI, 1129

Guglielmetti, Petra Asociate Fashion Editor
FOOTWEAR PLUS, 560

Guglielmo, Joanne Chief Financial Officer
FRANCO APPAREL GROUP, 1135

Guglielmo, Mark Senior VP, Ballpark Operations
NATIONAL LEAGUE OF PROFESSIONAL
BASEBALL CLUBS, THE, 32

Guglielmucci, Nicole Director of
Marketing/Events
DOUG FLUTIE FOUNDATION FOR AUTISM,
191

Guglieri, Ann-Marie Deputy AD
YALE UNIVERSITY ATHLETICS, 350

Gugliucci, Steve Director of Marketing, Ticket
Operations
COWBOY STADIUM, 960

Guhl, Jon Executive Director
MIDDLE ATLANTIC PGA, 106

Guiberson, Ann Executive Director
COLORADO WOMEN'S GOLF ASSOCIATION,
110

Guicheteau, Megan Head Athletic Trainer
COLLEGE OF NEW JERSEY ATHLETICS
(TCNJ), 381

Guidera, Tim Sports Writer
SAVANNAH MORNING NEWS, 529

Guidi, Gene Sports Reporter
DETROIT FREE PRESS, 483

Guido, Al President, Business Operations
NATIONAL FOOTBALL LEAGUE/NFL, 96

Guido, Anthony Managing Editor
SOCCER JR., 582

Guidry, Al Sports Editor
NATCHITOCHES TIMES, 480, 510

Guilarte, Miguel Sports Editor
EL TIEMPO LATINO, 486

Guild, Ron Sports Writer
CENTRAL NEWS/JOURNAL/STAR WAVE, 468

Guilfoil, Marc Executive Director
KENTUCKY HORSE RACING COMMISSION,
80

Guillen, Patrick Director of Athletics
UNIVERSITY OF HAWAII AT HILO (UHH)
ATHLETIC, 360

Guillory, Don Executive Director
RAPIDES PARISH COLISEUM, 995

Guimento, DJ Assistant Athletic Director, Facility
Op
BRONCO STADIUM, 952

Guiness, Ted Sports Editor
KCRH-FM, 615

Guingona, Dave Sports Producer
KRON-TV, 694

Guinness, Chris President-Octagon Television
OCTAGON ATHLETE REPRESENTATION
(AGENTS), 845

Guion, Kathleen Division President of Store
Operations a
DOLLAR GENERAL CORPORATION, 1225

Guiremand, Steve Sports Reporter
LAS VEGAS SUN, 501

Guiry, Philip Assistant General Manager
SAM LYNN BALLPARK, 1000

Guise, Scott Director of Athletic Communications
YORK COLLEGE (PENNSYLVANIA)
ATHLETICS, 408

Guissinger, Lynn Chief Financial Officer/Legal
CATALYST COMMUNICATION, 777

Guistina, Joe Associate Athletic Director of
Communica
LYCOMING COLLEGE ATHLETICS, 391

Gulas, Ike Attorney
GULAS LAW FIRM, P.C., 882

Gulbenkian, Edward CEO
GULBENKIAN SWIM, INC., 1141

Gulden, Bjorn Chief Executive Officer & Global
Brands
ADIDAS AMERICA, 725

Gulik, Glenn Director, Information Services and
Techn
CANADIAN CURLING ASSOCIATION, 69

Gulino, Matt Director, Ticket Sales & Operations
RICHMOND COUNTY BANK BALLPARK, 997

Gullberg, Ron Sports Editor
STAR-TRIBUNE, 535

Gullett, Wes Director of Sports Information
GREENSBORO COLLEGE ATHLETICS, 386

Gulley, Michael Associate Director
MALIVAI WASHINGTON KIDS FOUNDATION,
192

Gullick, John Chair
CANADIAN SAFE BOATING COUNCIL, 63

Gullick, Wally VP of Licensed Sports
GREAT AMERICAN PRODUCTS, 1140

Gullum, Frank VP Sales
SONOMA RACEWAY, 1033

Gully, Clay Vice President, Marketing
SOUTHERN PROFESSIONAL HOCKEY
LEAGUE, 136

Gulmi, James SVP, Finance and Chief Financial
Officer
GENESCO INC./JOURNEYS, 1229

Gulutzan, Glen Assistant Coach
NATIONAL HOCKEY LEAGUE/NHL, 124

Gulyas, Greg Sports Director
KMLB, 623

Gulyas, Sharon General Manager
ASSINIBOIA DOWNS, 1035

Gumbach, Chris Honorary President
ILLINOIS PGA SECTIONAL OFFICE, 106

Gumbart, Ted Commissioner
ATLANTIC SUN CONFERENCE, 291

Gumbel, Bryant Host
REAL SPORTS WITH BRYANT GUMBEL, 685

Gumienny, Frank Senior VP & COO
NATIONAL FOOTBALL LEAGUE/NFL, 96

Gund, Gordon Chief Executive Officer
QUICKEN LOANS ARENA, 994

Gundaker, Brandy Marketing Incharge
WATKINS GLEN INTERNATIONAL, 1035

Gundaker, Kevin Contact
WATKINS GLEN INTERNATIONAL, 1035

Gundaker, Tammy Contact Person
WATKINS GLEN INTERNATIONAL, 1035

Gundling, Andrew Sports Director
WJPZ-FM, 652

Gundolff, Rene, Membership Manager
USA RACQUETBALL, 146

Gundrum, Mark VP, Business Development &
Corporate Par
ARCA RACING SERIES, 16

Gunn, Jon Managing Editor
NASCAR ILLUSTRATED, 572

Gunn, Michael Vice President Sales
BIRMINGHAM, GREATER CONVENTION &
VISITORS BUREAU, 228, 260

Gunn, Rachel Department Assistant
WELSH RYAN ARENA, 1018

Gunning, Mary Director of Athletics and
Recreation
MARYWOOD UNIVERSITY ATHLETICS, 392

Gunnoe, Charles Provost & Dean of Faculty
AQUINAS COLLEGE SPORTS MANAGEMENT
PROGRAM, 409

Gunsul, Jana Associate Principal
DES ARCHITECTS/ENGINEERS, INC., 1054

Gunter, Jeff News Director
WIMA-AM, 639, 651

Gunter, Kelley Coordinator of Athletic Operations
LYNCHBURG COLLEGE ATHLETICS, 391

Gunter, Michael Lawyer
WOMBLE, CARLYLE, SANDRIDGE & RICE,
PLLC, 916

Gunther, Aaron Head Athletic Trainer
PACIFIC LUTHERAN UNIVERSITY
ATHLETICS, 396

Gunther, John Sports Editor
WORLD, 548

Gunty, Murry Co-Owner/Governor
UNITED STATES HOCKEY LEAGUE, 138

Guppy, John Founder/President
GILT EDGE SOCCER MARKETING, LLC, 785

Gupta, Suresh Owner
USL LEAGUE TWO, 162

Gura, Joe Governor
LAKE ERIE AAU ASSOCIATION, 214

Gurganious, Kyle Director of Athletic
Communications
MARYMOUNT UNIVERSITY, 392

Gurgiolo, Glenn President
FOX SPORTS DIRECT, 686

Gurian, Erica Client Services
ARANDA GROUP, 824

Guridy, Mickey Senior Associate AD, Internal
Operations
LIBERTY UNIVERSITY ATHLETICS, 334, 1016,
1019

Gurka, Mykhailo General Manager
CANADIAN SOCCER LEAGUE, 157

Gurley, Alfred Promoter
TALLADEGA SHORT TRACK, 1033

Gurnett, Terry Associate Director of Advancement
UNIVERSITY OF ROCHESTER ATHLETICS,
398

Gurney, Bill Director
GOLF BUSINESS, 560

Gurney, Ursula Deputy Director of Athletics/SWA
MISSOURI-KANSAS CITY ATHLETICS,
UNIVERSITY OF, 337

Gurskis, John Assistant Coach
EAST COAST HOCKEY LEAGUE/ECHL, 131

Gurwin, David Entertainment Chair/Media Law
Group/Tech
GURWIN, DAVID A., 836

Gusick, Phyllis Vice President Of Competitions
WOMEN'S METROPOLITAN GOLF
ASSOCIATION, 117

Gusky, Alan Controller
FAGUE, TERENCE L., 879

Gust, Lynn President
FRED MEYER STORES, INC., 1228

Gust, Tina Vice President, Business Development
ISOTOPES PARK, 972, 974

Gustafson, Eric Head Athletic Trainer
CHOWAN COLLEGE ATHLETICS, 354

Gustafson, John Contributing Writer
ESPN THE MAGAZINE, 13, 558

Gustafson, Jon President/SVP/Governor
AMERICAN HOCKEY LEAGUE/AHL, 128

Gustafson, Judy VP Human Resources
LIFE FITNESS, INC., 1155

Gustafson, Kevin Chief Executive Officer
SKYQUEST CHARTERS, 926

Gustafson, Kyle Assistant Coach
WESTERN HOCKEY LEAGUE, 138

Gustafson, Mark Deputy Counsel
DUKE LEGAL COUNSEL, 877

Gustafson, Staci Deputy AD
SANTA CLARA UNIVERSITY ATHLETICS, 343

Gustavson, David Associate Athletic Director
LOUISIANA STATE UNIVERSITY
(SHREVEPORT) ATHLETICS, 315

Gustek, Greg Director
HESTAND STADIUM FAIRGROUNDS, 970,
1040

Guster, Joe Sports Information Director
UNITED STATES MERCHANT MARINE
ACADEMY ATHLETICS, 404

Gustin, Sarah Associate Athletics Director for
Complia
MARYMOUNT UNIVERSITY, 392

Gustkey, Noah Assistant AD, Facilities
FRANKLIN FIELD, 966

Gutekunst, Brian General Manager
NATIONAL FOOTBALL LEAGUE/NFL, 95

Gutelius, Carl Corporate Secretary
NEW YORK-PENNSYLVANIA LEAGUE (A
LEVEL), 46

Guterman, Peter President
GUTERMAN INTERNATIONAL, INC., 1141

Gutgsell, Kurt Sports Director
WAXL-FM, 637

Gutheil, Laurie Women's Head Coach
WOMEN'S PREMIER SOCCER LEAGUE, 168

Guthmiller, Jarod Head Athletic Trainer
DAKOTA WESLEYAN UNIVERSITY
ATHLETICS, 311

Guthrie, Blake VP Operations
MIAMI BEACH BOWL, 91

Guthrie, Charles Director Of Athletics
SAN FRANCISCO STATE UNIVERSITY
ATHLETICS, 369

Guthrie, Dan President
MIRACLE RECREATION EQUIPMENT
COMPANY, 1163

Guthrie, Doug Professor/ Dean GS School of
Business
GEORGE WASHINGTON UNIVERSITY - THE
GW SCHOOL OF BUSINESS, 419

Guthrie, Kim Senior Vice President of Radio
COX MEDIA GROUP, 604

Guthrie, Sharon Dept. Chairperson
LONG BEACH STATE UNIVERSITY, 423

Guthrie, Wendy Interim Commissioner
NORTHWEST CONFERENCE, 302

Guthro, Dave Sports Anchor/Reporter
WMTW-TV, 707

Gutierez, Carl News Director
WIUS-AM, 651

Gutierrez, Derek Past President
SUN COUNTRY PGA SECTIONAL OFFICE,
108

Gutierrez, Dominic Director, Marketing
ONTARIO HOCKEY LEAGUE, 134

Gutierrez, Donatian Managing Director
MEXICAN LEAGUE A.C., 43

Gutierrez, Orlando Marketing Director & Media
LOS ALAMITOS RACE COURSE, 1041

Gutierrez, Paul Sports Writer (Soccer)
LOS ANGELES TIMES, 503

Gutman, Raila Marketing Manager
CORUS RADIO, 604

Gutschmidt, Donna Technical Writer
BALDWIN-WALLACE COLLEGE - LOU
HIGGINS CENTER, 410

Guttenplan, Dan Sports Editor
DAILY NEWS OF NEWBURYPORT, 478

Gutterman, Alan VP, Marketing
BETFAIR HOLLYWOOD PARK, 1036

Guy, Cathy Owner
INDOOR FOOTBALL LEAGUE, 94

Guy, Jeremy Communications Director
MID-AMERICAN ATHLETIC CONFERENCE,
299

Guy, Kevin Team President/Head Coach
INDOOR FOOTBALL LEAGUE, 93

Guy, Rob CEO
ATHLETICS CANADA, 177

Guy, Sharon Advertising Director
DAILY REPUBLIC, 479

Guyard, Gerard Chairman
NEW HERMES INC., 1168

Guyer, Shelly Vice President Competitions
CONNECTICUT STATE GOLF ASSOCIATION,
110

Guzda, Brad Goaltender Coach
WESTERN HOCKEY LEAGUE, 139

Guzdzial, Ann Chief Program Officer
SPECIAL OLYMPICS MICHIGAN, 195

Guzman, Eduardo US National Race Director
ATOMIC SKI USA, 1101

Guzman, Julian Sporting Director
USL CHAMPIONSHIP, 158, 160

Guzman, Oscar Sports News Anchor
WSNS-TV, 709

Guzzardo, BJ Assistant Executive Director
LOUISIANA HS ATHLETIC ASSOCIATION, 200

Gwaltney, Kathryn Executive Director, Operations
NATIONAL CENTER FOR SPORTS SAFETY,
266

Gwaltney-Harris, Robin Administrative Assistant
ST. PETERSBURG/CLEARWATER SPORTS
COMMISSION, 247

Gwara, Amy Pest Control, Industrial & Export
Sales
B & G EQUIPMENT COMPANY, 1102

Gwinn, Robert Of Counsel
GWINN & ROBY, 836

Gwynn, Michael Vice President of Sales &
Marketing
INTERNATIONAL LEAGUE, 43

Gyori, Philip VP Marketing / Bushnell
BUSHNELL CORPORATION, 1112

H

H Brown Jr, Bernard Chief Executive Officer
BERNIER, CARR & ASSOCIATES, 1050

H Mow Jr, Robert Partner
HUGHES & LUCE, 884

H. Bridgers Jr, B President
HOLE IN NONE, INC., 1145

H. L. Hughes, Hillary Owner
GARVEY, SCHUBERT & BARER, 881

H. Tilelli Jr., John Vice Chair
WIDENER UNIVERSITY SPORT
MANAGEMENT, 860

Ha Spires Jr, W President
CROSS CREEK APPAREL, INC., 1121

Haag, Anthony Marketing Manager
LAKE COUNTY, ILLINOIS - CONVENTION &
VISITORS BUREAU, 238

Haag, Erik Executive Vice President
NEW YORK-PENNSYLVANIA LEAGUE, 47

Haas, Elizabeth Senior VP/General Counsel
NATIONAL LEAGUE OF PROFESSIONAL
BASEBALL CLUBS, THE, 32

Haas, Gene Co-Owner
NASCAR XFINITY SERIES, 20, 23, 24

Haas, Katie VP, Ballpark Operations
NATIONAL LEAGUE OF PROFESSIONAL
BASEBALL CLUBS, THE, 32

Haas, Michael Girls Sporting Director
WOMEN'S PREMIER SOCCER LEAGUE, 165

Haas, Rick SNTV North America Editor
ASSOCIATED PRESS, 462

Haas, Ryan General Manager
TEXAS MOTORPLEX, 1034

Haas, Sarah Vice President
SOUTHERN ILLINOIS GOLF ASSOCIATION,
115

Haase, William Senior Vice President
NATIONAL BASEBALL HALL OF FAME AND
MUSEUM, 255

Habbena, Colette Administrative Assistant
HURON ARENA, 973

Habecker, Jimmy Sports Information Director
KEUKA COLLEGE ATHLETICS, 389

Habeeb, Kellie Editor
USA ROLLER SPORTS MAGAZINE, 590

Habel, Doug Executive Director
KANSAS CITY GOLF ASSOCIATION, 112

Habel, George Vice President
INTERNATIONAL LEAGUE, 42, 685

Habel, George Vice President Radio
Networks/Sports/99.
CAPITOL BROADCASTING COMPANY, 604

Habel, Robert Vice President
BRAUN & STEIDL ARCHITECTS INC, 1050

Haber, Brett Sports Director
WUSA-TV, 711

Haber, Stephen Director, Client Services
EB2B COMMERCE, INC., 1226

Haberl, Werner President
FNT INDUSTRIES, INC., 1134

Haberman, Guy Sports Director
KFSR-FM, 618

Habershaw, Ed Sports Information Director
SALVE REGINA UNIVERSITY ATHLETICS, 400

Haberstro, Philip Executive Director
WELLNESS INSTITUTE OF GREATER
BUFFALO, 85

Habgood, Doug Senior VP Golf division
ALABAMA SPORTS FOUNDATION, 227

Habjan, Ed President
TRI-STATE PGA SECTIONAL OFFICE, 108

Hach, Greg Marketing Director / Sales Director
BELL FOUNDRY CO./BFCO FITNESS
PRODUCTS, 1105

Hack, Damon Sports Reporter
NEW YORK TIMES, 511

Hackenberg, Dave Sports Reporter
BLADE, 465

Hackett, Amy Director of Athletics
UNIVERSITY OF PUGET SOUND, 397

Hackett, Chris President
WOMEN'S PREMIER SOCCER LEAGUE, 166

Hackett, David Partner Chicago
BAKER & MCKENZIE, 863

Hackett, Dr. Faculty Athletic Representative
CAL STATE NORTHRIDGE ATHLETICS, 326

Hackett, Gerald Regional Sales Director
COVERMASTER, INC., 1224

Hackett, Karen Chief Executive Officer
AMERICAN ACADEMY OF ORTHOPAEDIC
SURGEONS, 918

Hackett, Keith Director of Athletics
UNIVERSITY OF ALASKA ANCHORAGE
ATHLETICS, 350

Hackford, Rick Head Athletic Trainer
WESTMINSTER COLLEGE (UT) ATHLETICS,
375

Hackman, Sally Faculty Athletics Representative
CENTRAL METHODIST COLLEGE
ATHLETICS, 310

Hackney, Hugh Shareholder
GREENBERG TRAURIG, LLP, 882

Hadad, Omer Sports Division
JH DESIGN GROUP, 1149

Hadden, Jennifer Executive Producer
YAHOO! SPORTS RADIO, 604

Haddon, Bill Founder / Managing Principal
WRIGHTSON, JOHNSON, HADDON &
WILLIAMS, INC., 823

Haddon, William Co-Founder/Managing Principal
WRIGHTSON, JOHNSON, HADDON &
WILLIAMS, INC., 823

Hadgitorov, Assen VP Europe
WORLD ARMWRESTLING FEDERATION, 15

Hadl, John Associate Athletic
Director/Development
UNIVERSITY OF KANSAS, 1013

Hadley, Edward Lawyer
NORTH, PURSELL, RAMOS & JAMESON,
PLC, 897

Hadszicki-Ryno, Lolly Secretary/Treasurer
KITE TRADE ASSOCIATION INTERNATIONAL,
140

Hadubiak, Conrad President
WATER POLO CANADA, 179

Haduca, Marcie Associate Director of Athletics
HOLY NAMES COLLEGE ATHLETICS, 360

Haefner, Dick News Director
WJR-AM, 652

Haegele, John Chief Operating Officer
DORNA USA, LLC, 781

Haen, Mary Marketing & Promotions
ROAD AMERICA, 1031

Haen, Mary Marketing
ROAD AMERICA, 1031

Haenke, Greg Vice President
EDGE SPORTS INTERNATIONAL, INC., 832

Haensel, Mike News Director
WJDK-FM, 652

Haeringer, Stephan Executive Vice Chairman
UBS FINANCIAL SERVICES, 764

Haff, Gregory President
NATIONAL STRENGTH AND CONDITIONING
ASSOCIATION, 85

Haffener-Salmond, Loida Director of Events
LLOYD NOBLE CENTER, 983

Haffey, Kenneth Partner
SKODA, MINOTTI & CO., 907

Hafif, Bernie Finance VP / Operations
CONCEPT ONE ACCESSORIES, 1119

Hafif, Sam President / Chief Executive Officer
CONCEPT ONE ACCESSORIES, 1119

Hafizov, Rinat Associate
ANDREWS KURTH LLP, 862

Hafley, Kimberly Director of Marketing &
Recruitment
FOSTER, SWIFT, COLLINS & SMITH, P.C.,
880

Hafley, W. General Manager
WWKC-FM, 671

Haflich, Byron President/Owner
A&H ATHLETIC FLOOR SERVICES, INC., 1089

Hafling, Chris Associate AD, Operations & Event
Managem
NORTHERN KENTUCKY UNIVERSITY
ATHLETICS, 340

Hafling, Jeff General Manager
INTERNATIONAL LEAGUE, 42

Hammeke, Curtis Athletic Director
FORT HAYS STATE UNIVERSITY ATHLETICS (FHSU), 358

Hammel, Bruce Sports Copy Editor
SAN JOSE MERCURY NEWS, 528

Hammel, Dave Principal
BARKER RINKER SEACAT ARCHITECTURE, 1050

Hammel, Steve Vice President/GM, WRAL-TV
CAPITOL SPORTS NETWORK, 685

Hammel, Teri Director of Sales & Finance
DECATUR AREA CONVENTION & VISITORS BUREAU, 232

Hammer, Alison Assistant Director of Athletics, Sports
UNIVERSITY OF DISTRICT OF COLUMBIA ATHLETICS, 356

Hammer, Bonnie Chairman
USA NETWORK, 677

Hammer, Dick Sports Director
WEST-AM, 645

Hammer, Kelly Program Director
KBER-FM, 613

Hammer, Lee Program Director
KNBR RADIO, 624

Hammer, Matt Athletic Director/Men's Basketball Coach
NJCAA REGION IX MEN'S, 287

Hammerstrom, Art Account Executive
MURPHY & ORR EXHIBITS, 796

Hammes, Dan Deputy Commissioner
IOWA INTERCOLLEGIATE ATHLETIC CONFERENCE, 297

Hammill, Ryan Sports Reporter
ORANGE COUNTY REGISTER, 516

Hammock, David General Manager
KMUN-FM, 624

Hammock, Robby Manager
SOUTHERN LEAGUE OF PROFESSIONAL BASEBALL CLUBS, 52

Hammock, Will Sports Editor
GWINNETT DAILY POST, 492

Hammon, Becky Head Coach
WOMEN'S NATIONAL BASKETBALL ASSOCIATION, 60

Hammond, Curt Vice President
PACIFIC NORTHWEST SKI ASSOCIATION, 152

Hammond, Emmett Vice President/Secretary/Treasurer
PACIFIC COAST LEAGUE OF PROFESSIONAL BASEBALL CLUBS, 48

Hammond, Eric Sports Copy Editor
BISMARCK TRIBUNE, 465

Hammond, Evan Editorial Director
BLOODHORSE MAGAZINE, 74

Hammond, Harvey Executive Chairman
HNTB CORP., 1060

Hammond, Jeff Athletics Director
PETE TAYLOR BASEBALL PARK, 992

Hammond, John General Manager
KAUFFMAN SPORTS MANAGEMENT GROUP, 840

Hammond, Jonathan Chief Executive Officer & Head Coach
WOMEN'S PREMIER SOCCER LEAGUE, 167

Hammond, Matt Sports Editor
BELLEFONTAINE EXAMINER, 464

Hammond, Paul Assistant Athletic Director/Facilities O
JAMES A. RHODES ARENA, 975

Hammond, Phyllis VP Public Relations
DALLAS CONVENTION & VISITORS BUREAU, 231

Hammond, Robert Sports Editor
LARAMIE DAILY BOOMERANG, 501

Hammond, Seth Vice President
WESTERN RACING ASSOCIATION, 19

Hammond, Tiffany Head Athletic Trainer
INDIANA UNIVERSITY SOUTHEAST ATHLETICS, 314

Hammond, Troy President
NORTH CENTRAL COLLEGE ATHLETICS, 395

Hammons, Randy Sports Editor
LAUREL LEADER-CALL, 502

Hamp, Sheila Principal Owner/Chair
NATIONAL FOOTBALL LEAGUE/NFL, 95

Hampel, Phil Independent Director
UNITED STATES SOO BAHK DO FEDERATION, 143

Hampson, Joe VP Sports & Community Outreach
SPECIAL OLYMPICS WASHINGTON, 197

Hampton, Alvin Sales/Marketing Director
LOUISVILLE METRO HALL, 984

Hampton, Danny News Director
KXKX-FM, 629, 632

Hampton, Herlecia General Manager
GREENETRACK INC., 1046

Hampton, Michael Executive Director
NATIONAL SPORTING CLAYS ASSOCIATION (NSCA), 150

Hampton, Nate Assistant Director
MICHIGAN HS ATHLETIC ASSOCIATION, 200

Hampton, Rickey Sports Columnist
FLINT JOURNAL, 488

Hampton, Rusty Sports Editor
CLARION-LEDGER, 471

Hampton, Stephanie Director of Operations
NATIONAL MOBILE TELEVISION PRODUCTIONS, INC., 601

Hamre, John 2nd Vice President
NATIONAL WHEELCHAIR SOFTBALL ASSOCIATION, 170

Hamrick, Kyle Producer and Video Specialist
COSTANTE GROUP SPORTS & EVENT MARKETING, LLC, 753

Hamrick, Liz Event Coordinator
PENSACOLA SPORTS ASSOCIATION, 243

Hamrick, Mike Dept. Chairperson
MEMPHIS, UNIVERSITY OF, 425, 954, 976

Hamzy, Donnia Office Manager
LIME ROCK PARK, 1027

Han, Bernie EVP/Chief Operating Officer
DISH NETWORK, 686

Han, JH Vice Chairman & CEO
SAMSUNG ELECTRONICS NA, 732

Han, Jong-Hee President & CEO
SAMSUNG ELECTRONICS NA, 732

Hana, James Sports Director
WRDL-FM, 663

Hanagriff, Charles Sports Director
WIBR, 650

Hanan, Rubin SVP, Retail Brand Marketing
KID'S FOOT LOCKER, 1222, 1231

Hanberry, Dwayne Sports Information Director
SOUTHERN COLLEGIATE ATHLETIC CONFERENCE, 304

Hancock, Jayne President/CEO
JHG TOWNSEND, 790

Hancock, Jennifer Editor
AMERICAN QUARTER HORSE RACING JOURNAL, 549

Hancock, Jeremy Head Athletic Trainer
ASHLAND UNIVERSITY ATHLETICS, 351

Hancock, Jody Retail Sales Manager
KOLDER INC, 1153

Hancock, Katrina Sports Anchor
WDIV-TV, 701

Hancock, Mike Vice President, Business Development
NOBIS WORKS CENTER, 192

Hancocks, Matthew Group Director
VISION SPORTS & ENTERTAINMENT PARTNERS, 816

Hand, Cory Girls Director of Coaching
WOMEN'S PREMIER SOCCER LEAGUE, 169

Hand, Deanna Associate Director of Athletics
HOUGHTON COLLEGE ATHLETICS, 388

Handel, Jeremy Senior Manager, Public Affairs
LAS VEGAS CONVENTION & VISITOR'S AUTHORITY, 982

Handel, Ray Promotions Director
WKXW-FM, 654

Handel, Ted Senior Counsel
CAMPBELL, ROBERT G., 871

Handelman, Mike Chief Sales Officer
HNTB CORP, 1060

Handerland, Karina Senior Associate AD
PORTLAND ATHLETICS, UNIVERSITY OF, 341

Handley, Brian Sports Assistant Editor
DETROIT NEWS, 483

Handy, Alan Track Manager
PLACERVILLE SPEEDWAY, 1030

Handy, Sherry Program Director
WWAG-FM, 670

Hanefeld, Bill Sports Information Director
BLUFFTON UNIVERSITY ATHLETICS, 378

Hanes, Jason Sports Information Director
REINHARDT UNIVERSITY ATHLETICS, 319

Hanes-Romano, Katie Head Athletic Trainer
JOHNSON C. SMITH UNIVERSITY ATHLETICS, 361

Hanessian, Jack General Manager
BELTERRA PARK, 1036

Haney, Dave Sports Director
WKDE-FM, 653

Haney, Jeff Sports Columnist
LAS VEGAS SUN, 501

Haney, Kelley Assistant Director Of Athletics
VIRGINIA HS LEAGUE, 202

Hanish, Jan Assistant Vice President for Administrat
UNI-DOME, 1012

Hankin, David Chief Executive Officer
AMF BOWLING WORLDWIDE, 1098

Hankin, Ira Production Director
SPORTS BYLINE USA, 602

Hankin, Steve Chief Executive Officer
SENTIENT, 926

Hankins, Dewayne President, Business Operations
NATIONAL BASKETBALL ASSOCIATION/NBA, 58

Hankins, Dona Sports Night Editor
ST. PETERSBURG TIMES, 533

Hankins, Jamie 2nd Vice President
WALKING HORSE TRAINER'S ASSOCIATION, 78

Hankins, Kim First Vice President
HARNESS HORSEMEN INTERNATIONAL, 75

Hankins, Patsy Women's Chairman
INTERNATIONAL GOLF FEDERATION, 102

Hankins, Tom Head Coach
NATIONAL BASKETBALL ASSOCIATION DEVELOPMENT LEAGUE, 59

Hankle, James
SHERRARD, GERMAN & KELLY, 906

Hankosky, Scott Chief Executive Officer
HEALTHANDWELLNESSJOBS.COM, 747

Hanks, Fiona Head Athletic Trainer
UNIVERSITY OF FINDLAY (UF) ATHLETICS, 358

Hanks, Roy Sales
SKILLBUILDERS, INC., 1189

Hanks, Sheryll Associate Director For Compliance
EAST TENNESSEE STATE UNIVERSITY ATHLETICS, 329

Hanley, Bill President
TEXAS GOLF ASSOCIATION, 116

Hanley, Brian Sports Writer (Hockey)
CHICAGO SUN-TIMES, 469

Hanline, Brian Sr. VP Anf Chief Medical Officer
NATIONAL COLLEGIATE ATHLETIC ASSOCIATION/NCAA, 285

Hanlon, Pat Senior VP, Communications
NATIONAL FOOTBALL LEAGUE/NFL, 96

Hanna, Al Sports Director
KCMC, 615

Hanna, Gary Head Athletic Trainer
EDINBORO UNIVERSITY OF PENNSYLVANIA ATHLETICS, 357

Hanna, John Advertising Manager/Publisher
NET NEWS, 175, 573

Hanna, Mike Director of Athletics
HOBART COLLEGE ATHLETICS, 387

Hanna, Pete VP, Operations
FANSEDGE.COM, 1227

Hannah, Chris Director of Facilities and Game Ops.
BOBCAT STADIUM TEXAS STATE, 951

Hanneke, Dan Executive Director
LAS VEGAS BOWL, 91

Hannell, Nancy Advertising Director
DAVIS ENTERPRISE, 481

Hanners, Chris Owner
VA MEMORIAL STADIUM, 1015

Hannes, Ted Vice President/Fundraising Chair
DWARF ATHLETIC ASSOCIATION OF AMERICA, 219

Hannes, V. Sports Host
WMAQ-TV, 706

Hannon, Bob Sports Director
WYTV-TV, 712

Harkins, Mindy Marketing
COLORADO NATIONAL SPEEDWAY, 1023
Harlan, Duane Founder/President
RECWARE BY ACTIVE.COM, INC., 1235
Harlan, Mark Athletics Director
UTAH ATHLETICS, UNIVERSITY OF, 348,
1014
Harlan, Sophie Director, Football Operations
NATIONAL FOOTBALL LEAGUE/NFL, 95
Harland, Carl Sales Representative
WITTE GROUP, 1211
Harland, Jim President
UTAH GOLF ASSOCIATION, 116
Harle, Kent Chief Executive Officer / Founder /
Dire
REDLINE PERFORMANCE PRODUCTS, INC.,
1181
Harlen, T.R Sports Editor
CHESTERTON TRIBUNE, 469
Harley, Dan Vice President, West Major Account
Resta
TANGENT ASSOCIATES, INC., 1068
Harley, Khai Executive VP, Football
Administration
NATIONAL FOOTBALL LEAGUE/NFL, 96
Harley, Scott Head Athletic Trainer
MARYVILLE UNIVERSITY ATHLETICS, 363
Harlfinger, Richard Vice President
MARSHFIELD FAIR, 1041
Harlon, Andre Head Coach
WOMEN'S FOOTBALL ALLIANCE / WFA, 97
Harlow, Jeff Tour Director
NGA HOOTERS PRO GOLF TOUR, 104
Harlow, Matt Director, Hockey Operations
AMERICAN HOCKEY LEAGUE/AHL, 127
Harlow, Sherman Head Coach
WOMEN'S FOOTBALL ALLIANCE / WFA, 98
Harman, Dan Opertaing Manager
GATEWAY MOTORSPORTS PARK, 1025
Harman, Mark Director Of Education
UNITED STATES GOLF TEACHERS
FEDERATION, 118
Harman, Susan Sports Reporter
IOWA CITY PRESS-CITIZEN, 497
Harmet, Jeff President
COBRA PUMA GOLF, 1117
Harmon, Bob President, MCC, CTC
HARMON TRAVEL SERVICE, 926
Harmon, Dana Director of Athletics
WORCESTER POLYTECHNIC INSTITUTE
ATHLETICS, 408
Harmon, Dave Coordinating Producer
INSIDE THE NFL, 684
Harmon, David Group Dept Manager
HARMON TRAVEL SERVICE, 926
Harmon, Dawn Media Director
WOLVERINE-HOOSIER ATHLETIC
CONFERENCE, 307
Harmon, Eleanor Co-Founder
HARMON TRAVEL SERVICE, 926
Harmon, Mark Weekend Sports Anchor
WGCL-TV, 703
Harmon, Mike Owner
NASCAR XFINITY SERIES, 24
Harmony, Robin Head Coach, Women's
Basketball
MONTAGNE CENTER, 987
Harmount, Lynn Treasurer
MISSISSIPPI WOMEN'S GOLF ASSOCIATION,
113
Harms, Danny Graphic Design & Web Manager
BLOOMINGTON-NORMAL AREA SPORTS
COMMISSION, 229
Harms, Janet Advertising Manager
BEATRICE DAILY SUN, 464
Harms, Karen Administrative Assistant
SHOW ME STATE GAMES, 263
Harms, Monica Principal
STEIN, SPERLING, BENNETT, DE JONG,
DRISCOLL & GREENFEIG, P.C., 908
Harms, Peanut VP of Marketing/Sales
SPRINGCO, 1195
Harms, Ted President
CANADIAN CUE SPORTS ASSOCIATION, 62
Harn, Tim Treasurer
MIDWEST RUGBY FOOTBALL UNION, 147
Harnden, Greg Athletic Director
HARDING UNIVERSITY ATHLETICS, 359

Harner, Billy Director of Communications
KEYSPAN PARK, 979
Harnett, Joel Publisher
SPORTS ARIZONA MAGAZINE, 584
Harnisch, Lisa Senior Vice President, General
Merchandi
F.A.O. SCHWARZ, 1226
Harnum, Don Athletic Director
RIDER UNIVERSITY ATHLETICS, 342
Haroutunian, Kenji Vice President
THE ACCESS FUND, 69
Harp, Dennis Director Of Athletic Advancement
NJCAA REGION VI MEN'S, 287
Harp, Joanna Publisher
AMERICAN CHEERLEADER, 549
Harper, Brian Corporate Sales Senior Manager
DAYTONA INTERNATIONAL SPEEDWAY,
1024
Harper, Dave Director of Athletics
DUQUESNE UNIVERSITY ATHLETICS, 329
Harper, Erick Director of Athletics
NEVADA AT LAS VEGAS ATHLETICS,
UNIVERSITY OF, 338
Harper, Joe President & GM
DEL MAR THOROUGHBRED CLUB, 1037
Harper, Joe President/General Manager
DEL MAR THOROUGHBRED CLUB, 1037
Harper, John Commissioner
NEW ENGLAND FOOTBALL CONFERENCE,
300
Harper, Jonathan Commissioner
LITTLE EAST CONFERENCE, 297
Harper, Justin Sports Editor
NORMAN TRANSCRIPT, 514
Harper, Larry VP of Sales
GTM SPORTSWEAR, 1140
Harper, Mike President - DC
SUMMIT - GARDNER & GELDMACHER, 1197
Harper, Paul Promotions Assistant Director
WCPO-TV, 701
Harpham, Ted Sales Manager
DARTON ARCHERY, 1224
Harpole, Devin Program Director
KTMT-AM, 630
Harral, Paul Editorial Director
STAR-TELEGRAM (FORT WORTH), 535
Harrell, Frank Special Assistant to the Director of
Ath
TENNESSEE TECH UNIVERSITY ATHLETICS,
346, 1011
Harrell, Leon Stadium Operations
FLORIDA STATE LEAGUE, 39
Harrell, Roger Associate Publisher
SKATEBOARDER MAGAZINE, 580
Harrell, Steve Administration - Associate AD -
Complian
ROY STEWART STADIUM, 995, 999
Harrelson, Bud Owner
ATLANTIC LEAGUE, 35
Harrier, Anna Events Director
FREEMAN COLISEUM, 967
Harriford, Kim Assistant to the Athletic Director
KENTUCKY STATE UNIVERSITY ATHLETICS,
361
Harrigan, Brian Vice President
HEALTH FITNESS CORPORATION, 1059
Harrigan, Luke Assistant Athletic Director
ALDERSON-BROADDUS UNIVERSITY
ATHLETICS, 350
Harrigan, Rich Co-Owner & Head Coach
WOMEN'S FOOTBALL ALLIANCE / WFA, 99
Harriger, Ginny Advertising Director
PUBLIC OPINION, 523
Harriman, Sue Assistant Athletic Director
BATES COLLEGE ATHLETICS, 377
Harrington, Annie Secretary
AMERICAN MOUNTAIN GUIDES
ASSOCIATION, 68
Harrington, Bill Senior Associate Director of
Athletics
JOHNS HOPKINS UNIVERSITY ATHLETICS,
388
Harrington, Charles Chairman of the Board &
CEO
PARSONS, 1061
Harrington, Gayla Administration
WOMEN'S FOOTBALL ALLIANCE / WFA, 98

Harrington, Joe General Manager
NEW YORK-PENNSYLVANIA LEAGUE, 46,
500, 981
Harrington, Kevin Chief Executive
BOSTON HANNAH INTERNATIONAL, 553
Harrington, Michael Director of Athletics
FARMINGDALE STATE UNIVERSITY (FSU)
ATHLETICS, 384
Harrington, Mike Sports Writer
BUFFALO NEWS, 467
Harrington, Paul President/CEO
REEBOK CANADA INC., 1181
Harrington, Rod Chief Administrative Officer
SAUER, RUSSELL F., 904
Harrington, Scott Technical Specialist, University
Events
ROSE BASKETBALL ARENA, 979, 998
Harrington, Theresa Executive Director
CLARKSVILLE MONTGOMERY COUNTY
CONVENTION & VISITORS BUREAU, 230
Harrington, Tim CEO
DUFFY JENNINGS COMMUNICATIONS, 781
Harris, Alan Counsel
HARRIS, ALAN E., 883
Harris, Belinda Librarian
ROANOKE TIMES, 525
Harris, Bob Vice President
HOT SAUCE HARRYS, INC., 1145
Harris, Brent Director of Sports Information
WABASH COLLEGE ATHLETICS, 404
Harris, Brian Events Director
THE SPORTS AND ENTERTAINMENT
COMPANY LLC, 603
Harris, Bruce VP Marketing
TRUSCO MFG. COMPANY, 1204
Harris, Charles VP Of Sales & Marketing
PRO-LINE CAP COMPANY, 1177
Harris, Cindi Accounting Manager
CARDWELL, VICTOR, 871
Harris, Cindy Senior Associate Athletics
Director/Comp
REDBIRD ARENA, 996
Harris, Clay Deputy Director of Athletics, Revenue
Ge
LOUISIANA AT MONROE ATHLETICS,
UNIVERSITY OF, 335
Harris, D'Ree Business Manager
SPORTS TALK 790 THE ZONE (ATLANTA),
635
Harris, David Director of Athletics
NORTHERN IOWA ATHLETICS, UNIVERSITY
OF, 340, 654, 973, 974
Harris, Desi Marketing Director
ILLINOIS BUREAU OF TOURISM & FILM, 236
Harris, Dianne Owner/President
HOT SAUCE HARRYS, INC., 1145
Harris, Don Sports Anchor
WOAI-TV, 474, 707
Harris, Doug President
WOMEN'S PREMIER SOCCER LEAGUE, 168,
481
Harris, Ed Athletic Director
KIMBROUGH MEMORIAL STADIUM, 223, 979
Harris, Gabriel General Manager
NATIONAL BASKETBALL ASSOCIATION
DEVELOPMENT LEAGUE, 60
Harris, Gladstone Sports Information Director
BLOOMFIELD COLLEGE ATHLETICS, 352
Harris, Greg Owner
SOUTHERN PROFESSIONAL HOCKEY
LEAGUE, 136
Harris, Harry Medical Director
MARYLAND THOROUGHBRED HORSEMEN'S
ASSOCIATION, 76
Harris, James President
WIDENER UNIVERSITY SPORT
MANAGEMENT, 860
Harris, Jerry Attorney
HARBOUR, SMITH, HARRIS & MERRITT, 883
Harris, Jim Chief Financial officer
MAZDA RACEWAY LAGUNA SECA, 1028
Harris, Joan Advertising Director
RECORD (NY), 523
Harris, Joey President
CANADIAN LACROSSE ASSOCIATION, 141
Harris, John Owner/President
VISION SPORTS, INC., 53, 654, 661, 931
Harris, Jonathan Chief of staff
SAPIR, EDDIE L., THE HONORABLE, 904

Harris, Josh Co-Managing Partner, Vice Chair & Alt. G
NATIONAL HOCKEY LEAGUE/NHL, 57, 96, 125

Harris, Kylie Girls Director & Goalkeeping Director
WOMEN'S PREMIER SOCCER LEAGUE, 169

Harris, Leo Founder
LEO'S DANCEWEAR, INC., 1155

Harris, Louise Chief Global Strategist
RUDER/FINN SPORTS, INC., 806

Harris, Mary General Manager/Advertising Director
KQWC-AM, 627

Harris, Matt Vice President - Global Marketing
UNGERBOECK SYSTEMS, INC., 225

Harris, Michael CEO, President
MARKETING DRIVE WORLDWIDE, 794

Harris, Michelle Advertising Director
COURIER, 473

Harris, Mike Consultant Account Manager
BASSMASTERS, THE, 70, 525, 537, 545, 576, 597

Harris, Moira Editor
HORSE ILLUSTRATED, 564

Harris, Nessie Associate Commissioner
SOUTH CAROLINA HIGH SCHOOL LEAGUE, 202

Harris, Nicole President
ANCHORAGE WOMEN'S GOLF ASSOCIATION, 109

Harris, Noel Assistant Sports Editor
MODESTO BEE, 508

Harris, Patsy Producer
SPORTS SUNDAY, 681

Harris, Randy VP and Chief Operating Officer
NEWSOUTH ATHLETIC COMPANY INC., 1168

Harris, Ray President
EAST COAST HOCKEY LEAGUE/ECHL, 129

Harris, Robert Fitness Center Director
LEHMAN COLLEGE ATHLETICS, 390

Harris, Robin Executive Director
IVY LEAGUE GROUP, 297

Harris, Ryan Assistant Editor
WESTERN GUIDE TO SNOWMOBILING, 571, 581, 592

Harris, Scott Assistant Sports Information Director
HAMPDEN-SYDNEY COLLEGE (HSC) ATHLETICS, 29, 386

Harris, Shannon Sports & Special Events Coordinator
NORTH LITTLE ROCK VISITORS BUREAU, 242

Harris, Stan Chief Executive Officer
FOREFRONT GOLF, 1134

Harris, Steve Promotions Manager
KOVR-TV, 693

Harris, Terrance Sports Writer
HOUSTON CHRONICLE, 495

Harris, Terry Sports Director
WWEL-FM, 671

Harris, Tim President, Business Operations
NATIONAL BASKETBALL ASSOCIATION/NBA, 57

Harris, Tom Executive VP/Chief Financial Officer
NATIONAL LEAGUE OF PROFESSIONAL BASEBALL CLUBS, THE, 31, 70, 498

Harris, Will Sports Writer
DAILY ADVANCE, 475

Harris, William President
JOE L. REED ACADOME, 976

Harrison, Allan News/Programming Director
WEMJ-AM, 645

Harrison, Andrew Head Coach
SOUTHERN PROFESSIONAL HOCKEY LEAGUE, 136

Harrison, Brad Web Content Manager
ATLANTA MOTOR SPEEDWAY, 951, 1022

Harrison, C. Associate Professor
DEVOS SPORT BUSINESS MANAGEMENT, 416

Harrison, Gerald Director of Athletics
AUSTIN PEAY STATE UNIVERSITY ATHLETICS, 325

Harrison, James General Manager
KTON-AM, 630

Harrison, Jamey Deputy Director/Marketing
TEXAS UNIVERSITY INTERSCHOLASTIC LEAGUE, 202

Harrison, Jeanne Membership Coordinator
WORLD KARTING ASSOCIATION, 19

Harrison, Jeff Sports Editor
DAILY JEFFERSONIAN, 477

Harrison, Jennifer Director of Sports Information
TENNESSEE WESLEYAN COLLEGE ATHLETICS, 321

Harrison, Jeremy Sports technical director
DWARF ATHLETIC ASSOCIATION OF AMERICA, 219

Harrison, Karen Director Of Health & Athletic Developmen
INTERNATIONAL JUNIOR GOLF ACADEMY, 102

Harrison, L. Partner
RUBIN, MICHAEL D., 903

Harrison, Mark Executive Director
NORTHERN TEXAS PGA SECTIONAL OFFICE, 107

Harrison, Mary Senior Director, Handicapping
TEXAS GOLF ASSOCIATION, 116

Harrison, Nico General Manager/President, Basketball Op
NATIONAL BASKETBALL ASSOCIATION/NBA, 56

Harrison, Phil Marketing Manager
SYDNEY MOTORSPORT PARK, 1033

Harrison, Randy Sports Editor
ALBUQUERQUE JOURNAL, 459

Harrison, Ryan Director, Marketing & Corporate Sales
FEDERAL PROSPECTS HOCKEY LEAGUE (FPHL), 131

Harrison, Shawn Sports Editor
HERALD JOURNAL, 493

Harrison, Steve Head Coach
FEDERAL PROSPECTS HOCKEY LEAGUE (FPHL), 131

Harrison, Todd Program Chair, Sport Management Dept.
ST. JOHN FISHER COLLEGE, 433

Harrison, Tom Owner & President
MICHIGAN LADDER COMPANY, 1151, 1162

Harrison, Wayde Development Director
ACME MASCOTS, INC., 771

Harrison, Zac Sports Information Coordinator
LYNDON STATE COLLEGE ATHLETICS, 391

Harrison-Dyer, Stephanie Assistant Athletic Director
ALBANY STATE COLLEGE ATHLETICS, 350

Harriss, Matt Director, Football Administration
NATIONAL FOOTBALL LEAGUE/NFL, 94

Harrity, Dana President
NEW HAMPSHIRE WOMEN'S GOLF ASSOCIATION, 114

Harrity, Mike Director of Athletics & Recreation
DARTMOUTH COLLEGE ATHLETICS, 328

Harrop, Jeff President
CANADIAN PREMIER LEAGUE, 156

Harry, Jack Sports Director
KSHB-TV, 694

Harshbarger, Ted Associate Athletic Director
PERU STATE COLLEGE ATHLETICS, 318

Harshman, Shannon Membership Director
WOMEN'S OCEAN RACING SAILING ASSOCIATION, 64

Hart, Alta Assistant to the Director of Athletics
KUTZTOWN UNIVERSITY ATHLETICS (KU ATHLETICS), 361

Hart, Amy Associate Professor, Sports & Exercise S
COLUMBUS STATE COMMUNITY COLLEGE, 414

Hart, Brad Associate Director/Sports
NATIONAL PAL COPSNKIDS CRONICLES, 572

Hart, Brett President
UNITED CONTINENTAL HOLDINGS, 734

Hart, Britton Secretary-Treasurer
KANSAS STATE HS ACTIVITIES ASSOCIATION, 200

Hart, Curt Assistant Athletics Director
DAKOTA WESLEYAN UNIVERSITY ATHLETICS, 311

Hart, Dan Director, Media Relations
NATIONAL LEAGUE OF PROFESSIONAL BASEBALL CLUBS, THE, 32

Hart, Dana President
WOMEN'S BASKETBALL HALL OF FAME, 259

Hart, Dave Director of Athletics
NEYLAND STADIUM, 989

Hart, Eric President & CEO
RAYMOND JAMES STADIUM, 247, 995

Hart, Erick Director of Athletics
STATE UNIVERSITY OF NEW YORK COLLEGE AT BROCKPORT ATHLETICS (SUNY, 401

Hart, Gail Sales Manager
LITTLE KING MANUFACTURING COMPANY INC, 1156

Hart, Gleen Senior Associate AD, Student-Athlete Dev
GEORGIA SOUTHERN UNIVERSITY ATHLETICS, 331

Hart, Jackie Director, Mutuels
RETAMA PARK, 1043

Hart, Jeff Sports Director
WDUN-AM, 643

Hart, Joe President
MIDWEST LEAGUE, 45, 468, 1005

Hart, Johnny Promotions Manager
WLQM-FM, 656

Hart, Jon Athletic Director
DAKOTA WESLEYAN UNIVERSITY ATHLETICS, 311

Hart, Ken Sports Editor
VALLEJO TIMES-HERALD, 543

Hart, Loren Program Director
KRFO-FM, 627

Hart, Nick Head Athletic Trainer
UNITED STATES HOCKEY LEAGUE, 137

Hart, Nicole Finance
MARYLAND MILLION, 76

Hart, Rick Director of Intercollegiate Athletics
TENNESSEE-CHATTANOOGA, UNIVERSITY OF, 344, 371, 434, 987

Hart, Sean Boys Director
USL LEAGUE TWO, 164

Hart, Stephen Sports Columnist
STATEN ISLAND ADVANCE, 535

Harten, Kenton Chief Financial Officer
BUSYBODY, INC., 1221

Harter, Jill Director of Athletics
ST. LOUIS COLLEGE OF PHARMACY ATHLETICS, 321

Hartford, Tim Engineer/Technical
PLASTIMAYD CORPORATION, 1174

Hartigan, Jon Chief Financial Officer
GAYLORD SPORTS MANAGEMENT, 834

Hartigan, Tim SVP / Retail Operations General Manager
WELLS LAMONT SPORTS & SPECIALTIES, 1209

Hartl, Renae Athletic Director
LUTHER COLLEGE ATHLETICS, 390

Hartley, Bob President
RACK ROOM SHOES, 1235

Hartley, Brad General Manager
KNWD-FM, 625

Hartley, Gary Executive Vice President, Graphics
FOX SPORTS NETWORKS/FOX SPORTS NET, 675

Hartley, Gregg VP
THE SPORTS & FITNESS INDUSTRY ASSOCIATION (SFIA), 813

Hartley, Laura BoatHouse Event Manager
STATE OF KANSAS SPORTS HALL OF FAME, 258

Hartman, Bernard VP
HAZEL PARK HARNESS RACEWAY (HPHR), 1039

Hartman, Chris Assistant Athletic Director
HAMLINE UNIVERSITY ATHLETICS, 386

Hartman, Josh Director of sales and marketing
GENERAL SPORTS TURF SYSTEMS, 835

Hartman, Lee Advertising Manager
FORT BEND HERALD & TEAXS COASTER, 488

Hartman, Steve Sports Reporter
KCBS-TV, 688

Hartman, Thomas Vice President Sales
EPIC METALS, 1129

Hartmann, Cindy Deputy AD, Administration
FLORIDA STATE UNIVERSITY ATHLETICS, 330

Hartmann, Ken Senior Director Of Rules & Competition
GOLF ASSOCIATION OF MICHIGAN, 111

Haynes, Michael Chief Financial Officer
SPECIALIZED BICYCLE COMPONENTS, INC., 1191

Haynes, Roger Director of Athletics
MONMOUTH COLLEGE ATHLETICS, 394

Haynes, Sheila President
MISSISSIPPI WOMEN'S GOLF ASSOCIATION, 113

Hays, Kim Advertising Director
WINCHESTER SUN, 547

Hays, Sharon Office Manager
FOUR STATES FAIR & RODEO, 1038

Hayward, Len Sports Editor
MIDLAND REPORTER-TELEGRAM, 507

Hayward, Wally Chief Executive Officer
RELAY SPORTS AND ENTERTAINMENT MARKETING, 805

Haywood, Jerry Faculty Athletic Representative
FORT VALLEY STATE UNIVERSITY ATHLETICS (FVSU), 359

Hazel, Donna Managing Editor
BOWLING WORLD, 553

Hazeltine, Rick Sports Assistant Editor
DAILY NEWS (CA), 478

Hazelton, Rich Editor
48 DEGREES NORTH, 548

Hazen, Mike Executive VP/General Manager
NATIONAL LEAGUE OF PROFESSIONAL BASEBALL CLUBS, THE, 31, 965

Hazlett, Carl Attorney/Partner
HAZLETT, WILKES & BAYHAM, 883

Hazman, David Sales Manager
CELLO PROFESSIONAL PRODUCTS, 1115

Heacock, Jeff Director, Hockey Operations
FEDERAL PROSPECTS HOCKEY LEAGUE (FPHL), 131

Heacock, Lesa Advertising Manager
KENTON TIMES, 499

Head, Albon Managing Partner
JACKSON WALKER LLP, 839

Head, Daniel Athletic Director
NJCAA REGION XXII WOMEN'S, 290

Head, Jerad Team Manager
NEW YORK-PENNSYLVANIA LEAGUE, 46

Head, Stacy President
SAPIR, EDDIE L., THE HONORABLE, 904

Head, Steve Executive Vice President Sales
SOF SOLE, 1190

Headley, Richard Sports Editor
HOLDREGE DAILY CITIZEN, 494

Headrick, Melba Advertising Manager
KSMO-AM, 629

Healey, Mark Vice President
OVATION FOOD SERVICES LP, 1067

Health, Mary Chief Marketing Officer
INTERNATIONAL TENNIS HALL OF FAME AND MUSEUM, 254

Healy, Doug COO & CFO
NATIONAL LEAGUE OF PROFESSIONAL BASEBALL CLUBS, THE, 31

Healy, Francis Host
HALLS OF FAME, 683

Healy, Jim Treasurer
CONNECTICUT STATE GOLF ASSOCIATION, 110

Healy, Jon Vice President, Ticket Operations
LELACHEUR PARK, 982

Healy, Mike EVP, Venue Operations & Guest Experience
AMERICAN LEAGUE OF PROFESSIONAL BASEBALL CLUBS, THE, 30

Healy, Norleen Secretary
NJCAA REGION IX MEN'S, 287

Healy, Paul Attorney
HEALY, PAUL J., 837

Heaney, Kevin Executive Director
SOUTHERN CALIFORNIA GOLF ASSOCIATION, 115

Heaps, Jay President/General Manager
USL CHAMPIONSHIP, 159

Heard, Chris Head Athletic Trainer
MONTANA TECH ATHLETICS, 317

Hearns, Greg Senior Systems Consultant
CCI SOLUTIONS, 820

Hearst, Denise Publisher
ARABIAN HORSE WORLD, 550

Hearty, Kitty Editor-in-Chief
SHOW CIRCUIT MAGAZINE, 580

Heasley, Erik General Manager
AMERICAN HOCKEY LEAGUE/AHL, 129

Heasley, Kristi Advertising Account Executive
BLOODHORSE MAGAZINE, 74

Heaston, Sally Advertising Manager
NORTHWEST-SIGNAL, 514

Heath, Chuck First Vice President
WISCONSIN STATE GOLF ASSOCIATION, 117

Heath, Don Sports Writer
SAVANNAH MORNING NEWS, 529

Heath, Martin President/Treasurer/Men's
COLLEGE SQUASH ASSOCIATION/MENS & WOMEN'S INTERCOLLEGIATE COMPETI, 171

Heath, Steve Sports Information Director
ANDERSON UNIVERSITY ATHLETICS-ANDERSON, 376

Heath, Susan Associate Athletic Director
WESTMINSTER COLLEGE (UT) ATHLETICS, 375

Heath, Will Sports Editor
TALLADEGA DAILY HOME, 537

Heathcock, Jamie Program Director
WABO-AM, 636

Heaton, Rebecca Editor
ROCKY MOUNTAIN SPORTS, 556, 578

Heavner, Jim President
VILCOM, 603

Hebden, S. President
EWING COLE CHERRY BROTT, 1055

Hebel, Tom Promotions Manager
WLS-TV, 706

Heberger, David Sports Information Director
JUNIATA COLLEGE ATHLETICS, 389

Hebert, Eddie Dept. Head/Associate Professor
SOUTHEASTERN LOUISIANA UNIVERSITY, 432

Heck, Carl Senior Associate AD, Capital/Events/Faci
PENN STATE UNIVERSITY ATHLETICS, 341

Heck, John Interim Head Athletic Trainer
CONNECTICUT COLLEGE ATHLETICS, 382

Heck, Jon Director of Athletic Operations
RICHARD STOCKTON COLLEGE OF NJ ATHLETICS, 398

Heck, Kim CEO
SPORTS TURF MANAGERS ASSOCIATION, 225

Heck, Richard National Sales Manager
PERFORMANCE SPORTS APPAREL, 1173

Heck, William Sports Agent
PROREPS AGENCY, INC./SPORTS STAR, 850

Hecker, Jeff VP, Ticket Operations
NATIONAL FOOTBALL LEAGUE/NFL, 96

Hecker, Jennifer Operations Director
LUXECONCIERGE, 926

Heckert, Linda Chairman
ROCKFORD AREA CONVENTION & VISITORS BUREAU, 244

Heckman, Rod Sports Reporter
TIMES NEWS, 539

Heckmann, Richard Chairman / Chief Executive Officer
K2 INC., 1151

Hecquet, Beth Meetings & Events Director
NATIONAL ASSOCIATION OF SPORTS COMMISSIONS, 796

Hecquet, Mark Governor
OHIO AAU ASSOCIATION, 215

Hedes, Ed Managing Sports Editor
TIMES NEWS, 539

Hedge, Mike President
MILLER GOLF, 1163

Hedgepeth, Tim Inbound Logistics Manager
VARIETY WHOLESALERS, 1240

Hedges, Rolland Agent
FIDELIS COUNSEL ASSOCIATES, 880

Hedlund, Chris General Manager
NORTH AMERICAN HOCKEY LEAGUE, 133

Hedman, Dan Sports Reporter
WILX-TV, 704

Hedrick, Cara Marketing and Sales Manager
BIG SANDY SUPERSTORE ARENA, 949

Hedrick, Dave President
WGAD-AM, 647

Hedrick, Jeff Sr.Director of Operations
RICHMOND INTERNATIONAL RACEWAY, 1031

Hedrick, Tracy Promotions Director
VALUE CITY ARENA/JEROME SCHOTTENSTEIN CENTER, 1015

Hedrick, Tyler Sports Reporter
KCEN-TV, 688

Hee, Miles Director of Athletics
WESTERN STATE COLLEGE ATHLETICS (WSC), 375

Heeke, Dave Vice President/Director of Athletics
ARIZONA ATHLETICS, UNIVERSITY OF, 324

Heeren, Dave Sports Reporter
SOUTH FLORIDA SUN-SENTINEL, 532

Heeren, Lois Head Coach, Women's Basketball
MITCHELL HALL GYMNASIUM, 987

Heerji, Asif Sports Editor
WREK-FM, 663

Heeter, Judy Business Affairs and Licensing Director
WEINER, MICHAEL, 842, 915

Heffelfinger, Matt Director of Athletic Communications
ELIZABETHTOWN COLLEGE ATHLETICS, 383

Hefferman, Jim Wrestling Head Coach
ILLINOIS AT URBANA-CHAMPAIGN, UNIVERSITY OF, 420

Heffernan, Glenn President & Commissioner
UNITED STATES HOCKEY LEAGUE, 136

Heffernan, Robert
BURLEY'S, 1051

Heffernan, Sean Chief Financial Officer
CANADA SOCCER, 154

Hefflinger, Bruce Sports Editor
CRESCENT-NEWS, 474

Heffner, Rick Senior Director of Store Operations
FRED MEYER STORES, INC., 1228

Hefford, Stacey Marketing Manager
WORLD DRYER CORPORATION, 1211

Heflin, Jud Director of Planning and Logistics
COWBOYS STADIUM, 960

Hegans, Derrick Managing Director
SHROPSHIRE, KENNETH L., 906

Hege, Greg President
PORTER ATHLETIC EQUIPMENT COMPANY, 1175

Hegenauer, Kent Senior Associate Athletic Director/Direc
PETE TAYLOR BASEBALL PARK, 992

Heggem, Heath Sports Director
KRTV-TV, 694

Hegger, Keith Chief Financial Officer
NATIONAL HOCKEY LEAGUE/NHL, 125

Hegmann, Jessica Senior Associate Commissioner
METRO ATLANTIC ATHLETIC CONFERENCE, 298

Hegmann-Wary, Samantha Associate Athletic Director, Compliance/
MAINE ATHLETICS, UNIVERSITY OF, 335

Hegstrom, Anthony Sr. Director, Game Night Operations & Me
UNITED STATES HOCKEY LEAGUE, 137

Heher, Melissa Marketing VP
PLB SPORTS, 801

Heid, Eric Military Sales & Foreign Military Sales
U.S.I.A., 1205

Heideman, Bill Design Engineer
CAMERA SPORTSEAT, INC., 1113

Heidesch, Becky Founder & Chief Executive Officer
WSS EXECUTIVE SEARCH, 593, 817

Heidrich, Ryan Marketing Department
NATIONAL SPORTS FORUM, 797

Heidtke, Jon Vice President/General Manager
FOX SPORTS NET SOUTHWEST, 91, 599

Heien, Laura Tournament Operations & Communications M
DELAWARE STATE GOLF ASSOCIATION, 110

Heier, Greg Director of Athletics
PRESENTATION COLLEGE ATHLETICS, 319

Heika, Mike Sports Reporter
DALLAS MORNING NEWS, 481

Heiken, Bobby Associate Athletic Director
SOUTHERN OREGON UNIVERSITY ATHLETICS, 320

Heikkinen, Leo President
TUNTURI, INC., 1204

Heilala, Pat Treasurer
LADIES BIRMINGHAM GOLF ASSOCIATION, 112

Hendrick, Steve Chief Operating Officer
ORTHOCAROLINA, 922
Hendricks, Daniel President
UNITED FOUNDATION FOR DISABLED
ARCHERS, 15
Hendricks, Glenn VP Business
Development/Licensing
SLOANE VISION UNLIMITED, 808
Hendricks, Jeff Executive Director DACVB
DECATUR AREA CONVENTION & VISITORS
BUREAU, 232
Hendricks, Jim Associate Publisher
TRAILER BOATS, 589
Hendricks, Kate Deputy Counsel for Duke
University
DUKE LEGAL COUNSEL, 877
Hendricks, Keith Attorney
STOREY, MOYES, 909
Hendrickson, Amy Vice President/Affiliate
Sales/Marketing
OUTDOOR CHANNEL, 698
Hendrickson, Darby Assistant Coach
NATIONAL HOCKEY LEAGUE/NHL, 125
Hendrickson, Ed VP
PEREY TURNSTILES, INC, 932
Hendrickson, Haynes President, Turnkey
Intelligence
TURNKEY SPORTS & ENTERTAINMENT, 749,
815
Hendrickson, Jeff Sports Editor
DESERT SUN, 483
Hendrickson, Richard President
LIFETIME, 1156
Hendrickson, Scott Advertising Director
SPORTS ILLUSTRATED FOR KIDS, 585
Hendrickson, Thomas Executive Vice President,
Chief Financia
SPORTS AUTHORITY, INC., 1193
Hendrix, Keith Director for Championships
ATLANTIC SUN CONFERENCE, 291
Hendrix, Rashidi General Manager
WOMEN'S FOOTBALL ALLIANCE / WFA, 99
Hendrix, Rob Program Director
WJEL-FM, 652
Hendrix, Robert Executive Director
DOTHAN AREA CONVENTION & VISITORS
BUREAU, 233
Hendry, Alan Sports Writer
ANTELOPE VALLEY PRESS, 460
Hendryx, Travis Sports Information Coordinator
SUL ROSS STATE UNIVERSITY ATHLETICS,
403
Henery, Mike News Director
KBST-AM, 614
Henger, Adam Senior Vice President
L. ROBERT KIMBALL & ASSOCIATES, 1061
Henke, Les Advertising Manager
KRSY-AM, 628
Henkel, Lindsay Senior VP, Business
Development
AMERICAN LEAGUE OF PROFESSIONAL
BASEBALL CLUBS, THE, 29
Henkelman, Amy Acting Director of Athletics
DOMINICAN UNIVERSITY OF CALIFORNIA
ATHLETICS, 356
Henkin, Gary President
WTS INTERNATIONAL, 818
Henley, Carrie Executive VP and General
Manager
WEEKEND EXERCISE COMPANY, 1209
Henley, Gary Sports Writer
DAILY ASTORIAN, 475
Henley, J Design Director
LANDS' END, INC., 1154
Henn, Daniel General Manager
WEDM-FM, 644
Hennecy, Bill Track Manager
MYRTLE BEACH SPEEDWAY(MBS), 1029
Hennelly, Chris Associate AD, Student-Athlete
Health
GEORGE WASHINGTON UNIVERSITY
ATHLETICS, 331
Hennen, Margaret Office & Communication
Director
HELENA AREA CHAMBER OF COMMERCE,
970
Hennes, Ty Assistant Coach
NATIONAL HOCKEY LEAGUE/NHL, 125

Hennessey, Rod Treasurer
YOUTH BOWL CANADA, 65, 66
Hennessy, Scott President and CEO
TRUE TEMPER SPORTS, INC., 1183, 1204
Hennessy, Terry CEO
SENIOR SOFTBALL-USA, 170
Hennessy, Mary President and CEO
INDUSTRIAL FABRICS ASSOCIATION
INTERNATIONAL, 220
Henniger, Rai Senior Vice President Marketing &
Promot
SKY SOX STADIUM, 1003
Henning, Kent President
THE MIDWEST COLLEGIATE CONFERENCE,
306
Henning, Lynn Sports Reporter
DETROIT NEWS, 483
Henning, Steve Art Director
PRO-LINE CAP COMPANY, 1177
Henrich, Donna President
WOODS TO WEDGES, INC., 1211
Henry, Brian Director of Athletic Communications
UNIVERSITY OF WEST FLORIDA ATHLETICS
(UWF), 374
Henry, Daniel Lawyer & Partner
VILLARINI & HENRY, 913
Henry, Don Marketing Director
CALEXPO, 1023
Henry, Ian Director, Public & Media Relations
WESTERN HOCKEY LEAGUE, 139
Henry, James Governor
GEORGIA AAU ASSOCIATION, 214
Henry, Jennifer Chief Financial Officer
MARKETING ARM, 794
Henry, Jessica Support Staff - Administrative
Assistant
STRAHAN COLISEUM, 1006
Henry, Jim President
TENNIS MACHINES, INC., 498, 509, 1200
Henry, John Owner
NASCAR CUP SERIES, 23, 676
Henry, John Principal Owner
AMERICAN LEAGUE OF PROFESSIONAL
BASEBALL CLUBS, THE, 23, 29
Henry, Patricia Sr. Associate Director of Athletics
HARVARD UNIVERSITY - BRIGHT ARENA,
969
Henry, Randall President
HENRY-GRIFFITTS, 1144
Henry, Randy Founder
HENRY-GRIFFITTS, 1144
Henry, Rick Sports Director
WIS-TV, 704
Henry, Sean Chief Executive Officer
NATIONAL HOCKEY LEAGUE/NHL, 125
Henry, Whitney Marketing & Sales Coordinator
USF SUN DOME, 1014
Hensey, Thomas Head of USA Operations
RHINO SPORTS MARKETING, 805
Henshaw, Greg President
STACKHOUSE ATHLETIC EQUIPMENT, INC.,
1195
Hensler, Rick Promotions Director
ST. AUGUSTINE, PONTE VEDRA & THE
BEACHES VISITORS & CONVENTION BU, 246
Hensley, Andrew Assistant Director of Facilities
CONVOCATION CENTER: EMU, 959
Hensley, Brendi Office Manager
FUN-TEES, INC., 1135
Hensley, Roger Sports Deputy Editor
SAINT LOUIS POST-DISPATCH, 527
Henson, Geoff Sports Information Director
OLIVET COLLEGE ATHLETICS, 396
Henson, Josiah Founder
ADIDAS WRESTLING, 1093
Henson, Rob Booking Manager
TACOMA DOME, 1007
Henson, Steve Sports Writer
LOS ANGELES TIMES, 503
Hentze, Mark Partner
CEI ARCHITECTURE, 1052
Henwood, William Chief Sales and Marketing
Officer
NICKLAUS GOLF EQUIPMENT COMPANY,
L.C., 1168
Henze, Herbert President
PENN FISHING TACKLE COMPANY, 1173
Heon, Corey President
NORTH AMERICAN HOCKEY LEAGUE, 132

Hepfinger, Briana Sports Information Director
ST. LOUIS COLLEGE OF PHARMACY
ATHLETICS, 321
Hepner, Bruce VP
RENAISSANCE GOLF DESIGN, INC., 1181
Hepola, Cory Sports Director
WENY-TV, 702
Heppel, Jennifer Commissioner
PATRIOT LEAGUE, 303
Herald, Bill Sports Columnist
SARASOTA HERALD-TRIBUNE, 529
Herauf, Brad Head Coach
WESTERN HOCKEY LEAGUE, 139
Herbers, Jason Director of Intercollegiate
Athletics
MINNESOTA-MORRIS ATHLETICS,
UNIVERSITY OF (UMM), 394
Herbert, Kim Editor
HORSE, 564
Herbert, Luke Assistant Athletic Director for
Communic
CROWN COLLEGE ATHLETICS, 311
Herbster, Carol Executive Assistant
RUSSELL ATHLETIC BOWL, 92
Herbster, David Athletics Director
DAKOTADOME, 960
Herendeen, Steve Sports Reporter
TRI-VALLEY HERALD, 515, 541
Herget, Joe Executive Director
U.S. BICYCLING HALL OF FAME, 259
Hering, Martin Founder/President
ENTRY MEDIA, INC., 781
Hering, Thom Chief Operating Officer
PROFESSIONAL SPORTS PUBLICATIONS,
577
Herington, Ashley News Director
WQKE-FM, 662
Herlan, Richard Chief Financial Officer
JACKSON WALKER LLP, 839
Herman, Bob General Manager
MARKWORT SPORTING GOODS COMPANY,
1159
Herman, Brian Sports Editor
VALLEY INDEPENDENT, 543
Herman, Cory CEO
NORTH AMERICAN HOCKEY LEAGUE, 132
Herman, Deb Executive Assistant And Business
Manager
PATRIOT LEAGUE, 303
Herman, Geoff Coordinating Producer
ESPN, 683
Herman, Howard Sports Columnist
BERKSHIRE EAGLE, 464
Herman, Maury Founder
HERMAN, HERMAN, KATZ & COTLAR, L.L.P.,
883
Herman, Russ Founder
HERMAN, HERMAN, KATZ & COTLAR, L.L.P.,
883
Herman, Stanley Director
REDLINE PERFORMANCE PRODUCTS, INC.,
1181
Herman, Stephen. Attorney
HERMAN, HERMAN, KATZ & COTLAR, L.L.P.,
883
Hermann, Mike Director of Athletics
KANSAS WESLEYAN UNIVERSITY
ATHLETICS, 314
Hermez, Carl Team Manager
IMSA MICHELIN PILOT CHALLENGE, 20
Herms, Larry Senior Director, Media Relations
NATIONAL LEAGUE OF PROFESSIONAL
BASEBALL CLUBS, THE, 31
Hernandez, Eric VP, Finance
NATIONAL LEAGUE OF PROFESSIONAL
BASEBALL CLUBS, THE, 31
Hernandez, Felix CFO
DYNASTY APPAREL INDUSTRIES, 1126
Hernandez, Joe Associate Athletics Director for
Sports
WORTHEN ARENA (WR), 1020
Hernandez, Juan Head Coach
WOMEN'S PREMIER SOCCER LEAGUE, 165
Hernandez, Louis Advertising Sales Director
KUVN-TV, 696
Hernandez, Manolo Sports Editor
EL NUEVO HERALD, 486

Hopper, Randy General Manager
WMBE-AM AND WCLB, 656
Hopson, Jay Head Coach, Football
M.M. ROBERTS STADIUM, 984
Hopwood, Jeremy Creative Director
IN STORE SPORTS NETWORK, 676
Hoquet, Karen EVP and Chief Financial Officer
FEDERATED DEPARTMENT STORES, INC.,
1227
Horak, Rob Secretary
WESTERN NEW YORK PGA SECTION
OFFICE, 108
Horan, Craig Managing Editor
GOLFWEEK, 562
Horan, Tim Managing Editor
GREYHOUND REVIEW, 563
Horan, Tom Vice President/Sports Marketing
WLW, 656
Horcoff, Shawn General Manager
AMERICAN HOCKEY LEAGUE/AHL, 127
Horejs, Sean Weekend Sports Anchor
KRIS-TV, 694
Horitz, Joe General Manager
NATIONAL FOOTBALL LEAGUE/NFL, 95
Horlock, Phil President nad CEO
BLUE BIRD CORPORATION, 925
Horn, Andy Director of Operations
USA TABLE TENNIS, 173, 210
Horn, Brad Communications Manager
INDIANAPOLIS RACEWAY PARK, 1026
Horn, Christian Assistant Coach
EAST COAST HOCKEY LEAGUE/ECHL, 130
Horn, Erin Director Communications-Membership
KENTUCKY GOLF ASSOCIATION, 112
Horn, Jason Director of Athletics and Recreation
XAVIER UNIVERSITY OF LOUISIANA
ATHLETICS, 324
Horn, Jennifer Marketing Vice President
SPORTS CORNER, 685
Horn, Judy Deputy AD, Internal Ops. & Risk
Mangemen
SOUTH CAROLINA ATHLETICS, UNIVERSITY
OF, 344
Horn, Katie Kastrel Sales Manager
NIELSEN-KELLERMAN, 1168
Horn, Kevin News Director
KCOW-AM, 612, 615
Horn, Michael President
SPORTS CORNER, 685
Horn, Randall President/CEO
COLONIAL LIFE & ACCIDENT INSURANCE
COMPANY, 779
Horn, Rick Advertising Manager
WELLINGTON DAILY NEWS, 546
Horn, Tara Contact person
CROFT CLASSIC & HISTORIC
MOTORSPORTS LTD (CCHM), 1024
Horn, Thelma Associate Editor/Social Psychology
JOURNAL OF APPLIED SPORT
PSYCHOLOGY, 566
Hornak, James Dept. Chairman
CENTRAL MICHIGAN UNIVERSITY, 413
Hornbacher, Rebecca Women's Soccer Coach
IOWA STATE UNIVERSITY ATHLETICS, 973
Hornbeck, Jack President
HAMPTON ROADS SPORTS COMMISSION,
235
Hornbeck, John President/CEO
HAMPTON ROADS CHAMBER OF
COMMERCE, 235
Hornburg, Will Director of Sales & Promotions
ARKANSAS STATE FAIR, 947
Hornby, John Chief Operating Officer
N.E.C. ARENA BIRMINGHAM, 988
Horne, Erik Sports Editor
DAILY ARDMOREITE, 475
Horne, Gail Administrator
HEAD, ALBON O., 839, 883
Horne, Lewis Secretary
AMERICAN JUNIOR GOLF ASSOCIATION, 99
Horner, Adam Director, Ballpark Operations
CANAL PARK, 954
Horner, Chris Sales VP
BRISTOL ATHLETIC, 1110
Horner, Christian Team Chief
FORMULA 1, 20
Horner, H.B. Chairman
WOODBINE ENTERTAINMENT GROUP, 78

Horner, Richard Finance VP
BRISTOL ATHLETIC, 1110
Horner, Robyn Assistant Athletic Director
PFEIFFER UNIVERSITY ATHLETICS, 368
Hornstein, Robert Attorney
BREAUX, PAUL P., 868
Hornung, Robert President
HORNUNG'S GOLF PRODUCTS, INC., 1145
Hornyak, Ron Mutuels Manager
RACEWAY PARK, 1043
Horodyski, MaryBeth Vice President
NATIONAL ATHLETIC TRAINERS'
ASSOCIATION, 84
Horoitz, Judith Associate Professor, Associate
Vice Pres
MEDAILLE COLLEGE, 425
Horovitz, Bruce Advertising Reporter
USA TODAY, 543
Horowitz, George Chairman / President / Chief
Executive O
EVERLAST WORLDWIDE, INC., 1130
Horowitz, Justin Senior Director, Amateur
Scouting
NATIONAL LEAGUE OF PROFESSIONAL
BASEBALL CLUBS, THE, 32
Horowitz, Nancy President -Elect
USTA FLORIDA, 175
Horrigan, Joe Vice President and Chief Financial
Offic
PRO FOOTBALL HALL OF FAME, 257
Horrocks, Tom Marketing Communications
Manager
SNOCOUNTRY MOUNTAIN REPORTS, 634
Horrow, Rick Counsel
SQUIRE, SANDERS & DEMPSEY, LLP, 787,
837, 908
Horsley, Paul Operations Superintendent
MACKEY ARENA, 985
Horsman, Dave Senior Director, Ballpark
Operations
TARGET FIELD, 1007
Horst, Jon General Manager
NATIONAL BASKETBALL ASSOCIATION/NBA,
57
Horter, Franck TYR's European General Manager
TYR SPORT, INC., 1205
Horton, Brad Senior Associate AD,
Student-Athlete Dev
GEORGIA STATE UNIVERSITY ATHLETICS,
331
Horton, Frank Past President
WASHINGTON STATE GOLF ASSOCIATION,
117
Horton, Jay National Account Manager
ALL STAR PRO GOLF, INC., 1095
Horton, Josh Director of Sports Information
UNIVERSITY OF PITTSBURGH AT
BRADFORD ATHLETICS, 397
Horton, Lisa Co-Head Coach
WOMEN'S FOOTBALL ALLIANCE / WFA, 98
Horvath, Michael Strategic Alliances/Board of
Directors
STRATBRIDGE, INC., 812, 929
Horvath, Nick Sports Editor
PATRIOT-NEWS, 518
Horvath, Rich Stadium Manager
POINT STADIUM, 994
Horvath, Robert Chief Financial Officer
GOLDSMITH, JAMES A., 882
Horwood, Graeme VP
GRAFALLOY CORPORATION, 1140
Hoschert, Jim Business Manager
MIKEN SPORTS, 1163
Hosey, Janice Executive assistant
TAMPA SPORTS AUTHORITY, 247
Hoskins, Simon Chief Operating Officer
U.S. FIELD HOCKEY ASSOCIATION, 121
Hoskinson, Heidi Conference Registrar
KANSAS COLLEGIATE ATHLETIC
CONFERENCE, 297
Hoskyns, Don Managing Partner
MORE ACTIVE, 1214
Hosokawa, Noritada Chairman/President
NIPPON TELEVISION NETWORK
CORPORATION, 676
Hostetler, Mike Sports Anchor
WGAL-TV, 703
Hostetter, Bob Match Director
TURNER'S OUTDOORSMAN, 1239

Hotter, Klaus EVP, Winter Sport Division
HEAD/PENN USA, 1143
Hotz, Ross Treasurer
MOTORSPORTS MUSEUM AND HALL OF
FAME OF AMERICA, 255
Hotze, David Marketing/Sales
FREMONT DIE CONSUMER PRODUCTS INC,
1135
Hotze, James President
FREMONT DIE CONSUMER PRODUCTS INC,
1135
Houck, Clarence Athletic Director
MORRIS COLLEGE ATHLETICS, 317
Houck, John Manager, Cowboy Athletic Facilities
BOONE PICKENS STADIUM, 951
Houde, John Vice President New Media
GOLF CHANNEL, THE, 599, 687
Houde, Matthew Associate AD, Communications
NORTHEASTERN UNIVERSITY ATHLETICS,
340
Houlahan, Bart President
AND 1, 1099
Houlahan, Christina Chief Operating Officer
AND 1, 1099
Houle, J-F Assistant Coach
AMERICAN HOCKEY LEAGUE/AHL, 126
House, Emmett Grounds Supervisor
ANDY KERR STADIUM, 946
House, Larry Asst Commissioner
Championships/Business
MID-AMERICA INTERCOLLEGIATE
ATHLETICS ASSOCIATION, 298
House, Mike Promotions Director
WTVT-TV, 711
Householder, Mark President
ATHLETES IN ACTION, 218
Houser, Russell Assistant Director of Athletics
WOOSTER ATHLETICS, THE COLLEGE OF,
408
Houslet, Travis Sports Editor
PORTAGE DAILY REGISTER, 521
Housley, Arik Owner & General Manager
WOMEN'S PREMIER SOCCER LEAGUE, 167
Housley, Phil Assistant Head Coach
NATIONAL HOCKEY LEAGUE/NHL, 125
Houston, Allan General Manager
NATIONAL BASKETBALL ASSOCIATION
DEVELOPMENT LEAGUE, 60
Houston, Andree Assistant AD For Compliance
AUBURN UNIVERSITY AT MONTGOMERY
ATHLETICS, 307
Houston, Carolyn
SPORTS MARKETING SURVEYS USA, 811
Houston, Dot Associate Athletic Director for
Administ
MASSACHUSETTS COLLEGE OF LIBERAL
ARTS ATHLETICS(MCLA), 392
Houston-Wilson, Cathy Associate Department
Chairperson
THE COLLEGE AT BROCKPORT STATE
UNIVERSITY OF NEW YORK, 435
Houten, Frans Chairman
PHILIPS LIGHTING COMPANY, 1174
Houtman, Jan Administrative Assistant
RUTGERS, 431
Hovda, Lynn Chief Veterinarian
MINNESOTA RACING COMMISSION, 80
Hove, Aaron Sports Agent
SCRIMMAGE LINE SPORTS, 853
Hovenier, Jack Founder
LIGHTWEAR, 1156
Hover, Craig Marketing/Public Relations Director
I-70 SPEEDWAY, 1026
Hover, Erich Ticket Sales Director/Operations
ROSENBLATT STADIUM, 999
Hovey, Sue Senior Deputy Editor
ESPN THE MAGAZINE, 558
Hovis, Scott Executive Director
MISSOURI GOLF ASSOCIATION, 113
Hovland, James Lawyer
ROLLINS, RON, 903
Howald, Jeana Assistant Director of Athletics
MOUNT VERNON NAZARENE UNIVERSITY
ATHLETICS, 317
Howard, Adam Editor
BACK COUNTRY MAGAZINE, 551
Howard, Antony Director of Coaching, Boys
U15-19
USL LEAGUE TWO, 161

Howard, Barry Secretary
SOUTH CENTRAL PGA SECTIONAL OFFICE, 108

Howard, Bea Ticket Office
VOLCANOES STADIUM, 1016

Howard, Berg Director, Public Relations and Marketing
MARDI GRAS CASINO, 1046

Howard, Brett Room Manager
BEST BET, 1045

Howard, Bruce Director of Pulications and Communicatio
NFHS NEWS, 256, 573

Howard, Cassandra Administrative Director
GEORGE WASHINGTON UNIVERSITY - THE GW SCHOOL OF BUSINESS, 419

Howard, Chip Executive Associate AD, Internal Affairs
FLORIDA ATHLETICS, UNIVERSITY OF, 330

Howard, Chris Associate Athletics Director
UNIVERSITY OF KANSAS, 1013

Howard, Chuck Sports Director
WCNC-TV, 701

Howard, Crystal Director
BLOOMINGTON-NORMAL AREA SPORTS COMMISSION, 229

Howard, Cynthia Director, Digital Sales
PGA TOUR, 108

Howard, Dale Director of Athletics
WALSH UNIVERSITY ATHLETICS, 323

Howard, Dennis Professor
OREGON, UNIVERSITY OF/ WARSAW SPORTS MARKETING CENTER, 430

Howard, Derrick Executive Director
FREEMAN COLISEUM, 967

Howard, Drew Associate Athletic Director
FLORIDA SOUTHERN COLLEGE ATHLETICS (FSC), 358

Howard, George Promoter
HUNTSVILLE DRAGWAY, 1026

Howard, Hugh Director of Sports Information
WOOSTER ATHLETICS, THE COLLEGE OF, 408

Howard, Ian President
BRITISH TRIATHLON ASSOCIATION, 178

Howard, Jake Associate Editor
SURFER, 587

Howard, Jay Contact
INDY PRO 2000, 22, 630, 659

Howard, Jeffrey Publisher
WALKING HORSE REPORT, 591

Howard, Jerry Senior Account Executive
VOLCANOES STADIUM, 1016

Howard, Jim
MONTGOMERY MOTORSPORTS PARK (MMP), 1029

Howard, John Track Manager
LASSITER MOUNTAIN DRAGWAY, 690, 1027

Howard, Johnette Contributing Writer
GOLF FOR WOMEN, 513, 561

Howard, Justin Program Director
WILLTIME MOTORSPORTS, 608

Howard, Landon Executive Director
ROANOKE VALLEY CONVENTION & VISITORS BUREAU, 244

Howard, Lois Secretary
MANITOBA SPORTS HALL OF FAME & MUSEUM INC., 255

Howard, Mark Sr. Associate AD, Operations
EASTERN KENTUCKY UNIVERSITY ATHLETICS, 329, 711

Howard, Matt Advertising
LASSITER MOUNTAIN DRAGWAY, 1027

Howard, Mike General Manager
EVANGELINE DOWNS, 1037

Howard, Robert Secretary
BELLEVUE UNIVERSITY, 411

Howard, Shanice Event Manager
ALBANY CIVIC CENTER, 945

Howard, Steve Head Coach/General Manager
NORTH AMERICAN HOCKEY LEAGUE, 132

Howard, Tanisha Sports/Entertainment Management
FRIED & COMPANY, P.C., 834

Howard, Terry Vice President/Chief Technology Officer
SUN LIFE STADIUM, 1007

Howard, Vaughn Owner
ADAMS USA, INC., 1093

Howard, Willie Sports Reporter
PALM BEACH POST, 517

Howard-Cooper, Scott Sports Senior Writer
SACRAMENTO BEE, 526

Howarth, Kim Partner
BLACKBOURN, LISLE W., 866

Howat, Amy Advertising Director
HERALD-DISPATCH, 493

Howd, Lynne Director, Handicapping
TENNESSEE GOLF ASSOCIATION/TGA, 116

Howdeshell, Matt Sr Associate AD, Administration & Capita
NORTHERN ARIZONA UNIVERSITY ATHLETICS, 340

Howe, Dean Sports Columnist
FLINT JOURNAL, 488

Howe, James Associate
BLACKBOURN, LISLE W., 866

Howell, Amanda Marketing Services Coordinator
ARBITRON, INC., 1213

Howell, Betsey Executive Director
CENTRAL PENNSYLVANIA/PENN STATE COUNTRY CVB, 230

Howell, Bob National Sales Manager
SCHELDE NORTH AMERICA, LLC, 1186

Howell, Brian Sports Editor
LONGMONT DAILY TIMES-CALL, 503

Howell, David Sports Information Director
CABRINI COLLEGE ATHLETICS, 379

Howell, Ellen Advertising Manager
NEWPORT DAILY EXPRESS, 511

Howell, Greg Director Of Member Services & Junior Gol
NEW HAMPSHIRE GOLF ASSOCIATION, 114

Howell, Jeff Program Director
KGHL-AM, 619

Howell, Kenneth Director of Athletics
WEST VIRGINIA UNIVERSITY INSTITUTE OF TECHNOLOGY ATHLETICS (WVU), 323

Howell, Lloyd Executive Director
NFL PLAYERS ASSOCIATION, 88

Howell, Richard Sports Agent
RICHARD HOWELL SPORTS MANAGEMENT, INC., 852

Howell, Ron Sports Writer
SWEETWATER REPORTER, 536

Howell, Scott Sports Editor
LODI NEWS-SENTINEL, 503

Howell, Toby Program Director
SPORTS RADIO 1510 KGA, 634

Howell, Troy VP
HI STYLE LETTERED SPORTSWEAR COMPANY, INC., 1144

Howell-Williams, Elisha Senior Associate AD, Business & Human Re
GEORGIA STATE UNIVERSITY ATHLETICS, 331

Howes, Terri Senior Associate AD/Sports Administratio
WEST VIRGINIA UNIVERSITY/WVU COLISEUM, 1018

Howeth, Darinda
TEAMLINE, 1200

Howey, Clair Vice-Chairman of the Board
FANNING/HOWEY ASSOCIATES, INC., 1055

Howieson, Shelley Manager of Facilities
SIMON FRASER UNIVERSITY ATHLETICS, 370

Howland, Raymond Managing Editor-Special Reports
JOYCE JULIUS AND ASSOCIATES, INC., 790

Howle, Anna Assistant Athletics Director
OKLAHOMA BAPTIST UNIVERSITY ATHLETICS, 367

Howlett, Jeff General Manager
WHTK-AM, 650

Howlett, Lisa President
AUBURN LEATHER COMPANY, 1170, 1217

Howser, Colin Sports Editor
IDAHO PRESS-TRIBUNE, 464, 495

Howson, D. President & CEO
AMERICAN HOCKEY LEAGUE/AHL, 126

Hoxie, Hal President
MIDLANDS COLLEGIATE ATHLETIC CONFERENCE, 299

Hoy, April Associate Athletics Director
AZUSA PACIFIC UNIVERSITY ATHLETICS, 308

Hoy, Matt Senior Vice President, Operations
TARGET FIELD, 1007

Hoy, Tim Executive Officer
SFX SPORTS GROUP, INC., 854

Hoye, Cindy Executive Director
INDIANA STATE FAIR/FAIRGROUNDS, 1040

Hoye, Daniel Of Counsel
MCKENNA, LONG & ALDRIDGE, LLP, 894

Hoye, William Associate Dean, Admissions and Financial
WEISTART, JOHN C., 915

Hoyer, Jed President, Baseball Operations
NATIONAL LEAGUE OF PROFESSIONAL BASEBALL CLUBS, THE, 31

Hoyes, Len Sports Reporter
FLINT JOURNAL, 488

Hoyle, Mike Operations Manager/Program Director
WGNC, 648

Hoyles, Christine Asst. Commissioner Championships/Admin.
PACIFIC-10 CONFERENCE, 303

Hoynes, Paul Sports Reporter
PLAIN DEALER, 520

Hoyt, Jason Account Executive
ALFOND ARENA, 946

Hoyt, Ray Sr. VP
TULSA SPORTS COMMISSION, 248

Hoyt, Seth Publisher (PGA Tour Partners)
NORTH AMERICAN MEDIA GROUP, INC., 576, 601

Hozak, Sue Associate Athletic Director
SAINT VINCENT COLLEGE ATHLETICS, 399

Hrabi, Ward Vice President of Officials
CANADIAN TEAM HANDBALL FEDERATION, 121

Hradek, E.J. Senior Writer
ESPN THE MAGAZINE, 558

Hreshko, Frank Managing Partner
HRESHKO CONSULTING GROUP, 747

Hrichak, Phil Sports Editor
WINSTON-SALEM JOURNAL, 547

Hrobsky, Donna Box Office Manager
US CELLULAR ARENA, 1014

Hromadka, Clayton Director of Business Development & Tourn
SOUTHERN TEXAS PGA SECTIONAL, 108

Hrubetz, JC General Manager
FREEMAN COLISEUM, 967

Hruby, Gary Secretary
KANSAS CITY GOLF ASSOCIATION, 112

Hruska, Ed Executive Director
ROCHESTER AMATEUR SPORTS COMMISSION, 244

Hruza, Jeff Sports Clerk
SAINT PAUL PIONEER PRESS, 527

Hsieh, Melody President/Owner
ASA PRODUCTS, INC., 1100

Hsu, William Attorney/Partner
BLECHER & COLLINS, 867

Huang, Ben CEO and Founder
WINN, INC., 1210

Huang, Mavis Import VP / Export Manager
WINN, INC., 1210

Huang, Mimi Associate Director of Admissions
BERSHAD, LAWRENCE, 866

Huang, Steven Sports Copy Editor
CHICAGO TRIBUNE, 470

Hubart, Sarah Managing Editor
NIRSA JOURNAL, 574

Hubbard, Bill Chairman
HCC SPECIALTY UNDERWRITERS, INC, 756

Hubbard, Chess Web Designer
DIRECTION, 780

Hubbard, Chinyere Vice President, Communications and Marke
DC SPORTS & ENTERTAINMENT COMMISSION, 232

Hubbard, Fletcher General Manager
WLLL-AM, 655

Hubbard, John Chairman
INDEPENDENCE STADIUM, 91, 973

Hubbard, Kirk Chief Operating Officer
REYN SPOONER INC, 1182

Hubbard, Nathan Chief Executive Officer of Ticketing
TICKETMASTER, 814, 933

Hubbard, R. Owner
RUIDOSO DOWNS RACE TRACK CASINO, 1043

Hubbard, Savanah Traffic Director
WLLL-AM, 655

Hubbard, Stan Chair & CEO
NORTH AMERICAN HOCKEY LEAGUE, 133

Hubbard, Susan Director of Booking and Administration
ROY WILKINS AUDITORIUM, 999

Hubbard, Tom Editor
SOUNDINGS:TRADE ONLY, 582

Hubbard, Tyler Senior Director, Ticket Operations
NATIONAL LEAGUE OF PROFESSIONAL BASEBALL CLUBS, THE, 32

Hubbart, Larry Co-Founder
AMERICAN POOLPLAYERS ASSOCIATION, INC., 61

Hubble, Craig Vice President
NORTH AMERICAN BOXING FEDERATION, 67

Huber, Chip Director of Athletics
CORNERSTONE COLLEGE ATHLETICS, 311

Huber, Debbie Chairperson
SPECIAL OLYMPICS WYOMING, 198

Huber, Dick Vice-President
SPECIAL OLYMPICS DELAWARE, 194

Huber, Larry Executive Director
MANITOBA HORSE RACING COMMISSION, 80

Huber, Megan Business Manager
NEBRASKA SCHOOL ACTIVITIES ASSOCIATION, 201

Huber, Mic Assistant Sports Editor
SARASOTA HERALD-TRIBUNE, 529

Huberman, Mitch SVP, Fox Sports Enterprises/Pac-10 Prope
PAC-10 PROPERTIES, 799

Hubert, Erin EVP
ROSE QUARTER BOX OFFICE, 634, 999

Hubert, Mick Broadcast Announcer
GATOR IMG SPORTS NETWORK, 605

Hubert, Sarah Editor
RECREATIONAL SPORTS DIRECTORY, 596

Hubsch, Andy Vice President of Finance
FOX SPORTS PRIME TICKET, 675

Hubschman, Francoise President
MD STADIUM AUTHORITY, 843

Huck, Andy Eastern Sales Manager
BODY SOLID, INC., 1108

Huckaby, Ken Manager
MIDWEST LEAGUE, 45

Huckstep, M. Chairman/Executive Committee
ADAMS & REESE, 861

Huda, Jess Assistant Director of Athletics
CABRINI COLLEGE ATHLETICS, 379

Hudgins, Richard Advertising Manager
SADDLE HORSE REPORT, 579

Hudgins, Richard Advertising Manager
VOICE OF THE TENNESSEE WALKING HORSE MAGAZINE, 591

Hudnall, Hugh Director of Marketing/Advertising/Market
TRIBUNE-DEMOCRAT, 541

Hudson, Andrea Volleyball Head Coach
LEE UNIVERSITY ATHLETICS, 361

Hudson, Arlene Advertising Manager
SANTA CRUZ SENTINEL, 529

Hudson, Becky Secretary/Treasurer
ARIZONA REGIONAL COMMISSIONER/USA VOLLEYBALL, 210

Hudson, Ben Publisher
SOUTHWEST HORSE TRACK, 583

Hudson, Bob Sports Editor
SPECTRUM, 533

Hudson, Carolyn Recording Secretary
MARYLAND STATE GOLF ASSOCIATION - WOMEN'S DIVISION, 112

Hudson, Clarence Executive Director
IOWA GAMES, 262

Hudson, Emanuel Track & Field/Football/Tennis, Attorney
HS INTERNATIONAL, 837

Hudson, Gene Advertising Manager
DAILY SOUTHERNER, 480

Hudson, Hugh Sales Manager
HUDSON BOAT WORKS INC., 1146

Hudson, Joe General Manager
CALIFORNIA LEAGUE (A-LEVEL), 36

Hudson, Karen Vice Chairman
SPECIAL OLYMPICS NEW MEXICO, 196

Hudson, Kathleen Controller
FRONTIER LEAGUE, 41

Hudson, Katy Coord Financial Services
BAKER, DAVID L., 863

Hudson, Lise Director of Sales
THE ZONE SPORTS RADIO 1300 AM, 635

Hudson, Mark President
OKLAHOMA SECONDARY SCHOOL ACTIVITIES ASSOCIATION, 201

Hudson, Mike General Manager
KWIK, 632

Hudson, Randy Director Of Design
HAYES LARGE ARCHITECTS, 1059

Hudson, Stuart National Sales Manager
ELLESSE U.S.A., INC., 1128

Hudson, Thomas Publisher
FOOTWEAR PLUS, 560

Hudson, Tom Sports Director
KREM-TV, 694

Hudspeth, Brian Director, College Scouting
NATIONAL FOOTBALL LEAGUE/NFL, 95

Hue, Laura Associate AD, Compliance
INDIANA UNIVERSITY-PURDUE UNIVERSITY INDIANAPOLIS, 333

Huebel, Kerri Assistant Athletic Director
MARIAN COLLEGE OF FOND DU LAC ATHLETICS, 392

Huebner, Brett Associate Director of Athletics / CFO
RED MC EWEN BASEBALL FIELD, 996

Huebner, Joe Director of Business Development
CARLSON DESIGN/CONSTRUCT CORP., 1052

Huebner, Vic Treasurer
U.S. CURLING ASSOCIATION, 69

Huelfing, Tim General Manager
WYXY-FM, 672

Hueregue, Paul Design Director
SQUASH MAGAZINE, 586

Huerta, Terry Human Resource & Payroll Manager
SEAGATE CENTRE, 1002

Huey, J.D. Vice President/General Manager
WIAT - CBS 42, 704

Huff, Bill Sports Director
WBAG-AM, 637

Huff, Cliff Senior Associate Athletics Director
CLARK ATLANTA UNIVERSITY ATHLETICS, 355

Huff, Danielle Vice President/Owner
C & H BASEBALL, 1112

Huff, Kyle Head Athletic Trainer
HUNTINGDON COLLEGE ATHLETICS, 388

Huff, Laura Director of Marketing
LISTON B. RAMSEY REGIONAL ACTIVITY CENTER, 983

Huff, Megan Sports Sales Manager
SOUTH BEND/MISHAWAKA CONVENTION & VISITORS BUREAU, 264

Huff, Rob President
C & H BASEBALL, 1112

Huff, Samantha Program & Planning Manager
GOLF COURSE BUILDERS ASSOCIATION OF AMERICA, 101

Huff, Stephanie Hr and Contract Services Manager
SPOKANE VETERANS MEMORIAL ARENA, 1004

Huffman, Aaron Athletic Director
WEST LIBERTY UNIVERSITY ATHLETICS, 374

Huffman, Kris Assistant Athletics Director
DE PAUW UNIVERSITY ATHLETICS, 382

Huffman, Rick Director of Sales & Marketing
SIOUX FALLS ARENA, 1003

Huftalen, Steve AVP of Corporate Development & Special E
SPECIAL OLYMPICS MASSACHUSETTS, 195

Hugdahl, Geroge Secretary
US LACROSSE, 141

Huge, Thom News Director
KZMQ-AM, 633

Hugelmeyer, Frank President
OUTDOOR INDUSTRY ASSOCIATION, 224

Huggins, Billy Vice President
WPDE-TV, 707

Huggins, Jeff Senior Vice President
YESAWICH, PEPPERDINE, BROWNE & RUSSELL, 818

Huggins, Malcolm Assistant Director of Athletics
STATE UNIVERSITY OF NEW YORK COLLEGE AT OSWEGO(SUNY), 402

Hugh, Leslie Parks/Recreation Director
LAKEVIEW ARENA, 981

Hughes, Brian News Director
WARM-AM, 605, 637

Hughes, Dan News Director
WPCD-FM, 661

Hughes, David Sports Reporter
TRIBUNE-STAR, 541

Hughes, Donald Senior VP / Chief Financial Officer
LANDS' END, INC., 1154

Hughes, Edward VP Marketing
DUNLOP/MAXFLI/SLAZENGER GROUP AMERICAS, 1126

Hughes, Ellen Ticket Manager
SUN BOWL, 92

Hughes, Francine EVP & General Manager, Stadium Operation
NATIONAL FOOTBALL LEAGUE/NFL, 96

Hughes, G. President
CAROLINAS GOLF ASSOCIATION, 110

Hughes, Jack Executive Director
GAINESVILLE SPORTS COMMISSION, 234

Hughes, Jami Assistant Athletic Director-Daily Operat
HOLY FAMILY COLLEGE ATHLETICS, 360

Hughes, Janine Managing Editor
GOLF FOR WOMEN, 561

Hughes, Jerry Athletics Director
CENTRAL MISSOURI STATE UNIVERSITY ATHLETICS, 354, 1016

Hughes, Joe Sports Director
KIVI-TV, 691

Hughes, John Commissioner/Executive Director
WESTERN EMPIRE, 212

Hughes, John Sports Information Director
LA GRANGE COLLEGE ATHLETICS, 389, 592

Hughes, Kent General Manager
NATIONAL HOCKEY LEAGUE/NHL, 124

Hughes, Kevin President
NORTHEASTERN NEW YORK PGA SECTIONAL OFFICE, 107

Hughes, Kit Associate VP, Intercollegiate Athletics
HOLY CROSS ATHLETICS, COLLEGE OF THE, 332

Hughes, Lee Sports Director
KMA-AM, 623

Hughes, Lindsey Assistant Athletic Director
COLUMBIA COLLEGE OF S. CAROLINA ATHLETICS, 311

Hughes, Lisa Vice President, Human Resources & Admini
NOBIS WORKS CENTER, 192

Hughes, Mark Senior Vice President/Assistant General
NATIONAL BASKETBALL ASSOCIATION/NBA, 57

Hughes, Merrill Treasurer
UNITED STATES BILLIARD ASSOCIATION, 62

Hughes, Michael Chief Executive Officer
NATIONAL GOLF COURSE OWNERS ASSOCIATION, 104

Hughes, Michelle Promotions Manager
KKTV-TV, 691

Hughes, Paul Attorney
PIERCE & HUGHES P.C., 899

Hughes, Paul Lawyer
TALLEY, ANTHONY, HUGHES & KNIGHT L.L.C., 910

Hughes, Rob Sports Reporter
INTERNATIONAL HERALD TRIBUNE, 497

Hughes, Rusty Project Coordinator
SOUTHERN BLEACHER COMPANY, INC., 1191

Hughes, Scott Project Manager
COMPASS COLLECTIVE, 752

Hughes, Theresa Racing Secretary
LUCKY'S CARD ROOM, 1046

Hughes, Tim Director of Facilities
VICTORY FIELD, 1016

Hughes, Tom Vice President
HOPE-BECKHAM, INC., 787

J

Jackson, Mark Director of Athletics
VILLANOVA UNIVERSITY ATHLETICS, 244, 348

Jackson, Michael Graduate Program Dir. in Sport Admin.
TEMPLE UNIVERSITY, 434

Jackson, Michelle Partner
MCKENNA, LONG & ALDRIDGE, LLP, 894

Jackson, Paula Chief of Staff/Interim Director of Athle
HAMPTON UNIVERSITY ATHLETICS, 331

Jackson, Robert Editor-at-Large
SLAM, 581

Jackson, Roger Principal
FFKR ARCHITECTS, 1056

Jackson, Shebeney Owner
UNITED STATES WOMEN'S FOOTBALL LEAGUE, 96

Jackson, Sonia Promotions Director
KHYL-FM, 620

Jackson, Stu Associate Commissioner
COLLEGIATE COMMISSIONER'S ASSOCIATION, 283

Jackson, Ted Vice President, Information Technology a
SPORT CHALET, INC., 1237

Jackson, Terilyn Director of Equity and Inclusion
CONCORDIA UNIVERSITY IRVINE ATHLETICS, 356

Jackson, Tim General Manager
DELL DIAMOND, 961

Jackson, Tom General Manager
SPORTS TALK, 593, 610

Jackson, Tracy President & Chief Executive Officer
COLLEGE PROSPECTS OF AMERICA, 930

Jackson, W. SVP / Chief Financial Officer / Treasure
SHOE CARNIVAL, 1237

Jaclin, Gregg Partner
ANSLOW, RICHARD I., 824

Jacob, Daniel Assistant Coach
AMERICAN HOCKEY LEAGUE/AHL, 127, 128

Jacob, Lisa Senior Manager, Las Vegas News Bureau
LAS VEGAS CONVENTION & VISITOR'S AUTHORITY, 982

Jacob, Richard Sport Management Program Coordinator
MEDAILLE COLLEGE, 425

Jacober, Ron Sports Director
KMOX, 606, 624

Jacobs, Bic Program Director
XTRA SPORTS RADIO 1150 AM, 673

Jacobs, Charlie Chief Executive Officer & Alternate Gove
NATIONAL HOCKEY LEAGUE/NHL, 123

Jacobs, Curt Advertising Manager
MADISON COURIER, 504

Jacobs, David Managing Director
ACTION IMAGES, 1092

Jacobs, David Founder
SPYDER ACTIVE SPORTS, 1195

Jacobs, Doug Deputy Sports Editor
TAMPA TRIBUNE, 537

Jacobs, Gary Owner
CALIFORNIA LEAGUE (A-LEVEL), 36, 980

Jacobs, Jay Executive Associate AD, External Affairs
FLORIDA ATHLETICS, UNIVERSITY OF, 330, 949

Jacobs, Jeff Sports Columnist
HARTFORD COURANT, 492

Jacobs, Jeremy Owner & Governor; Chair, NHL Board of Go
NATIONAL HOCKEY LEAGUE/NHL, 123

Jacobs, Jeremy Chief Executive Officer
SPORTSERVICE CORPORATION, 1066, 1068

Jacobs, John Owner
WDUN-AM, 643

Jacobs, John President
RELIABLE RACING SUPPLY, INC., 1181

Jacobs, Kiki Associate Director of Athletics
SPRINGFIELD COLLEGE ATHLETICS, 371

Jacobs, Martin General Counsel
PIMLICO RACE COURSE, 1042

Jacobs, Mary Head Athletic Trainer
INDIANA WESLEYAN UNIVERSITY ATHLETICS, 314

Jacobs, Melissa Producer
ESPN THE MAGAZINE, 608

Jacobs, Mike General Manager
MAJOR LEAGUE SOCCER, 158, 644

Jacobs, Norman Publisher
FOOTBALL DIGEST, 551, 560

Jacobs, Robert Executive Director/Chief Executive Offic
SLAM DUNK TO THE BEACH, 808

Jacobs, Scott President
SAFE-T-GARD CORPORATION, 1003, 1185

Jacobsen, Cyrille Head of Marketing
UNION CYCLISTE INTERNATIONALE (UCI), 71

Jacobsen, Laura Associate Director, Academic and Career
UNIVERSITY OF KANSAS, 1013

Jacobsen, Lynn Sports Reporter
TULSA WORLD, 542

Jacobsen, Peter President & Chief Executive Officer
PETER JACOBSEN PRODUCTIONS, 759

Jacobson, Aileen Advertising Writer
NEWSDAY, 513

Jacobson, David Marketing Communications Manager
POSITIVE COACHING ALLIANCE, 267

Jacobson, Gary Sports Editor
DALLAS MORNING NEWS, 481

Jacobson, Jane Secretary Treasurer
NATIONAL DEAF WOMEN'S BOWLING ASSOCIATION, 66

Jacobson, Jared Owner/Governor
WESTERN HOCKEY LEAGUE, 138

Jacobson, Shari Director Of Membership & Club Relations
WASHINGTON STATE GOLF ASSOCIATION, 117

Jacobson, Willis Sports Writer
ROBESONIAN, 525

Jacobstein, Dick Chief Exceuitve Officer / Sales Manager
LETRELL SPORTS, 1155

Jacoby, Jay Representative
AAA FLAG & BANNER, 771, 1089

Jacox, Russell IT Manager
FAGUE, TERENCE L., 879

Jacque, Alan President
THREE COUNTY FAIR, 1045

Jacquemin, Marc Operations Director/Tournament Coordinat
SOCCER MARKETING & PROMOTIONS, INC., 761

Jacques, Marcel Senior Developer
IVRNET, 713

Jacques, Mike Sports Director
WSAW-TV, 709

Jacques, Triplett General Manager
CORPUS CHRISTI GREYHOUND RACE TRACK, 1045

Jaecks, Steve Athletic Director
NJCAA REGION VII WOMEN'S, 288

Jaffe, Ira Senior Vice President, Account Services
EVENTNET USA, 782

Jaffe, J. Principal Consultant
ACENTECH INC., 819

Jager, Jean-Paul PR & Marketing
Z COIL PAIN RELIEF FOOTWEAR, 1212

Jager, Tim Athletic Director
MORNINGSIDE COLLEGE ATHLETICS, 317

Jagger, Sheila Senior Vice President
TREATY OAK BANK, 770

Jagla, Peter Vice President, Marketing
HOCKEY HALL OF FAME AND MUSEUM, 252

Jagoditz, Joe General Manager
CINCINNATI GARDENS, 957

Jagolinzer, David Attorney/ Shareholder
THE FERRARO LAW FIRM, 911

Jahn, Dan VP, Brand Promotions
LEADDOG MARKETING GROUP, 793

Jahn, T.J. Vice President of Ticket Sales
NEW YORK-PENNSYLVANIA LEAGUE, 47

Jahner, Rod Vice President
SPORTS GROUP INTERNATIONAL, 748

Jahnke, Steve Sports Director
KCOP-TV, 688

Jahrling, Megan Associate AD, External Relations
DUQUESNE UNIVERSITY ATHLETICS, 329

Jaklin, Ben Tournament Operations Associate
INTERNATIONAL JUNIOR GOLF TOUR/IJGT, 102

Jakob, Mike Chief Operating Officer
SPORTVISION, 602

Jakubowski, Shawn Sports Information Director
BEREA COLLEGE ATHLETICS, 308

Jalbert, Jay Vice President Production Services
JALBERT PRODUCTIONS, INC., 600

Jalbert, Joe President
JALBERT PRODUCTIONS, INC., 600

Jalbout, Fred President/CEO
SACO TECHNOLOGIES INC./SMARTVISION, 1185

Jalcovik, Mark President, Business Operations/Owner
UNITED STATES HOCKEY LEAGUE, 138

Jalil, Abdul President/Chief Executive Officer
SUPERSTAR MANAGEMENT, INC., 857

Jallen, Tim Director of Field & Stadium Operations
NEWMAN OUTDOOR FIELD, 989

James, Alix Marketing
NIELSEN-KELLERMAN, 1168

James, Ben News Director
KCFV-FM, 614

James, Bill Director Triathlon England
BRITISH TRIATHLON ASSOCIATION, 178

James, Blake Director of Athletics
BOSTON COLLEGE ATHLETICS, 325, 875

James, Brant Sports Writer
ST. PETERSBURG TIMES, 533

James, Carney President
SEABROOK PARK, 1047

James, Derek Sports Editor
STANDARD DEMOCRAT, 534

James, Dolan Executive Chairman
MADISON SQUARE GARDEN, 985

James, Jamal Lead Athletic Trainer
PARK UNIVERSITY PIRATE ATHLETICS, 318

James, Jeanette Customer Service Manager
LIEBE ATHLETIC LETTERING, 1155

James, John Chief Executive Officer
TOMCAT USA, 1202

James, Jr EVP (Past)
FGM ARCHITECTS & ENGINEERS, 1056

James, Kathryn Managing Director, National Exhibition C
N.E.C. ARENA BIRMINGHAM, 988

James, Keith President
JACK ROUSE ASSOCIATES, 790

James, Kitty Editor
SANTANA, 579

James, Marty Sports Editor
NAPA VALLEY REGISTER, 509

James, Mike Program Director
WONN-AM, 660

James, Richard Editor
SPORTSCAR, 586

James, Ron Head Coach
INDOOR FOOTBALL LEAGUE, 93, 639

James, Samantha Head Athletic Trainer
DOMINICAN COLLEGE (DC) ATHLETICS, 356

Jameson, Michael Lawyer
NORTH, PURSELL, RAMOS & JAMESON, PLC, 897

Jamieson, Lynn Editor
RECREATIONAL SPORTS JOURNAL, 578

Jamieson, Patty Dept. Coordinator
COLUMBUS STATE UNIVERSITY, 414

Jamison, Ed VP/General Manager
ARLINGTON INTERNATIONAL, 1035

Jamison, Greg Chair
SAN JOSE SPORTS AUTHORITY, 245

Jamison, Jim Director of Operations
CLUB GLOVE, 1117

Jamison, Mike Executive Director
INTERNATIONAL NETWORK OF GOLF, 103

Jamison, Renee Director Of Administration & Olympic Rel
U.S. SPORTS ACROBATICS/USSA, 120

Jamros, Brian Director of Athletics
CONCORDIA UNIVERSITY (OR) ATHLETICS, 356

Janchick, Michael Race Secretary
NORTHVILLE DOWNS, 1042

Jane, Rollinson President and CEO
THE ROWERS' CODE, 813

Johnson, Mike Sports Producer
WLS-TV, 706

Johnson, Monica Box Office Manager
CANTON MEMORIAL CIVIC CENTER, 955

Johnson, Neal President/CEO
SPECIAL OLYMPICS NEW YORK, 196

Johnson, North General Manager
INTERNATIONAL LEAGUE, 42

Johnson, Pamela Sales Director
LEE ISLAND COAST VISITOR &
CONVENTION BUREAU, 239

Johnson, Paul Promotions Manager
KMVT-TV, 108, 692

Johnson, Paula Secretary
YWCA USA, 85

Johnson, Phillip President
STANLY HEADWEAR, 1196

Johnson, Porscha Manager Of Corporate Sale
JOLIET COMMUNITY BASEBALL &
ENTERTAINMENT LLC, 43

Johnson, Rich Chief Editorial Officer
SPORTS PAGES, 585

Johnson, Richard Director of Athletics
WOFFORD COLLEGE ATHLETICS, 376

Johnson, Richard Store Operations SVP
BIG 5 SPORTING GOODS, 1219

Johnson, Richard EVP and Chief Financial
Officer
KERR DRUG INC., 1231

Johnson, Rob Chief Executive Officer
BILLIARD CONGRESS OF AMERICA, 62

Johnson, Robert Chair
NATIONAL FOOTBALL LEAGUE/NFL, 96

Johnson, Robert Professor/Department Head
GREENVILLE COLLEGE, 419

Johnson, Rodney Sports Information Director
EASTERN INTERCOLLEGIATE ATHLETIC
CONFERENCE, 295

Johnson, Ron Manager
INTERNATIONAL LEAGUE, 42

Johnson, Ryan Assistant Director, Player
Development
NATIONAL HOCKEY LEAGUE/NHL, 126

Johnson, Sally Executive Director
NATIONAL COUNCIL OF YOUTH SPORTS,
267

Johnson, Scott Deputy Director
GREENSBORO COLISEUM COMPLEX, 643,
969

Johnson, Sean Director of Athletics
UNIVERSITY OF JAMESTOWN ATHLETICS,
322

Johnson, Sheila Secretary
U.S. GOLF ASSOCIATION/USGA, 109

Johnson, Sheila Vice Chairman
VERIZON CENTER, 1015

Johnson, Sherree Accountant
UNITED MARINE MANUFACTURERS
ASSOCIATION, 64

Johnson, Stephanie Assistant Stadium
Co-ordinator
SCOTTSDALE STADIUM, 1001

Johnson, Steve Research Director
DLF INTERNATIONAL SEEDS, 590, 1224

Johnson, Stuart News/Sports Director
KAAN-FM, 612

Johnson, Suzy Membership Services
UNITED STATES GOLF TEACHERS
FEDERATION, 118

Johnson, Swen Sports Director
KSJS-FM, 629

Johnson, Tammy Customer Service/Ticketing
Manager
GRAND PRIX ASSOCIATION OF LONG
BEACH, 16

Johnson, Tank Sports Editor
OAK RIDGER, 515

Johnson, Teresa Director of Communications and
Public Re
ARCHERY TRADE ASSOCIATION, 14

Johnson, Terry Executive Director
BLUEGRASS STATE GAMES, 81, 260

Johnson, Theodore Partner
BLACKBOURN, LISLE W., 866

Johnson, Todd Executive Director
GREATER CINCINNATI GOLF ASSOCIATION,
111

Johnson, Tom Athletic Director
SPORTS IMPORTS, 1194

Johnson, Toni Advertising Director
JACKSONVILLE DAILY PROGRESS, 497

Johnson, Tony Project Manager
H E HODGE COMPANY, 1141

Johnson, Travis Sports Reporter
EVENING SUN (PA), 487

Johnson, Trisha Editorial Coordinator
BARREL HORSE NEWS, 551

Johnson, Troy Sports Reporter
TELEGRAPH HERALD, 538

Johnson, Tucker President and CEO
UNITED STATES EQUESTRIAN TEAM
FOUNDATION, 78

Johnson, Wally Director of Athletic Media
Relations
ST. LAWRENCE UNIVERSITY ATHLETICS,
401

Johnson, Wayne Owner
KRDZ-AM, 547, 618, 627

Johnson, William President / Shareholder
JOHNSON & BELL, 886

Johnson-Leipold, Helen Chairman / Chief
Executive Officer
JOHNSON WORLDWIDE
ASSOCIATES/CAMPING DIVISION, 1150

Johnson-Lynch, Christy President
AMERICAN VOLLEYBALL COACHES
ASSOCIATION, 178

Johnson-McKewan, Karen Partner
ORRICK, HERRINGTON & SUTCLIFFE LLP,
898

Johnston, Alastair Co-Chief Executive Officer
SCHOEPPLER, KURT J., 853

Johnston, Calvin Chief Executive Officer, Russell
Athleti
RUSSELL ATHLETIC, 1184

Johnston, Dan Associate Athletic Director,
Development
UNIVERSITY OF NORTH TEXAS-COLISEUM,
1013

Johnston, Duke President
MAYWOOD PARK, 1041

Johnston, Edward General Counsel
MIDDLE ATLANTIC GOLF ASSOCIATION, 113

Johnston, Greg EVP, Operations
SAM'S CLUB, 961, 1236

Johnston, Jim Head Athletic Trainer
HIRAM COLLEGE ATHLETICS, 70, 387

Johnston, Joey Sports Writer
TAMPA TRIBUNE, 537

Johnston, Mary Assistant Director of Athletics
FRANKLIN COLLEGE ATHLETICS (FC), 385

Johnston, Michael President
HEDSTROM CORPORATION, 1143

Johnston, Mike President, General Manager &
Head Coach
WESTERN HOCKEY LEAGUE, 138

Johnston, Natasha Executive Director
RINGETTE CANADA, 146

Johnston, Nick Sports Writer
GADSDEN TIMES, 490

Johnston, Robert President
H&B SPECIALIZED PRODUCTS, 1141

Johnston, Ron Sports Editor
MARIETTA TIMES, 505

Johnston, Scott Sports Assistant Editor
BUFFALO NEWS, 467

Johnston, Steve President
IRONMAN PROPERTIES, 178

Johnston, Susan Marketing Director
WNYY, 192, 659

Johnston, Tom COO
AMERICAN LEISURE CORPORATION, 484,
1049

Johnston, Zachary Sports Information Director
CONCORDIA UNIVERSITY (MI) ATHLETICS,
311

Joliffs, Charles Contact
GEORGE RAY'S DRAGSTRIP, 1025

Jolley, Frank Sports Editor
DAILY COMMERCIAL, 476

Jolly, Molly Senior VP, Finance & Administration
AMERICAN LEAGUE OF PROFESSIONAL
BASEBALL CLUBS, THE, 30

Jolly, Tom Sports Editor
NEW YORK TIMES, 511

Jonasson, Jon Assistant Coach
NORTH AMERICAN HOCKEY LEAGUE, 132

Jones, Alan Executive Editor
BOATING WORLD, 553

Jones, Allison Director Of Event Services
LAKELAND CENTER, THE, 981

Jones, Amy Convention & Event Sales Manager
FORT SMITH CONVENTION & VISITORS
BUREAU, 234

Jones, Andy Director of Hospitality
YAKIMA COUNTY STADIUM, 1020

Jones, Ann Advertising Manager
WSYL-AM, 667

Jones, Anna-Marie VP Grants/Programs
LA84 FOUNDATION, 220

Jones, Ben Sports Editor
ROCKY MOUNT TELEGRAM, 526

Jones, Berniece Dept. Chairperson/Associate
Professor
NEBRASKA WESLEYAN UNIVERSITY, 428

Jones, Bill Athletic Marketing Manager
SKIDMORE COLLEGE ATHLETICS, 400

Jones, Billy Vice President
KITE TRADE ASSOCIATION INTERNATIONAL,
140

Jones, Blake Managing Partner
SHEUERMANN & JONES, 906

Jones, Bob National Sales Manager
GOLD MEDAL RECREATIONAL PRODUCTS,
1138

Jones, Bobbi Marketing
SOUTHLAND PARK, 1047

Jones, Bobby Manager
PACIFIC COAST LEAGUE OF
PROFESSIONAL BASEBALL CLUBS, 49

Jones, Brad Athletic Director
BRIGHAM YOUNG UNIVERSITY-HAWAII
ATHLETICS, 352

Jones, Brent Director of Athletics
TROY UNIVERSITY ATHLETICS, 347, 816

Jones, Brian Manager
GOLF WAREHOUSE, 1139

Jones, Bryan Project Manager -
Northwest/Southwest
GENERAL SPORTS VENUE ASTROTURF,
1137

Jones, Butch Head Coach, Football
NEYLAND STADIUM, 989

Jones, Buzz Sports Director
KDWN, 616

Jones, C General Manager
KRMD-AM, 627

Jones, Charlotte Executive VP/Chief Brand
Officer
NATIONAL FOOTBALL LEAGUE/NFL, 94

Jones, Cheryl Director/Off Track Wagering/OTBs
PORTLAND MEADOWS, 1042

Jones, Chris General Manager & Head Coach
CANADIAN FOOTBALL LEAGUE/CFL, 93, 980,
1020

Jones, Chuck President/Chief Executive Officer
CARBITE GOLF COMPANY, 512, 1113

Jones, Cindy Scorekeeping
PLACERVILLE SPEEDWAY, 1030

Jones, Collin Controller
DONALD DEMARS INTERNATIONAL, 1054

Jones, D.J. Sports Director
WCGQ-FM, 641

Jones, Dana Director of finance and
administration
WISCONSIN CONVENTION & VISITORS
BUREAU, 250

Jones, Dave Marketing Director
BSN SPORTS, 1111

Jones, David General Manager
MOBILE GREYHOUND PARK, 1047

Jones, Deborah Assistant Athletic Director
MILES COLLEGE ATHLETICS, 364

Jones, Drew Head Coach
NATIONAL BASKETBALL ASSOCIATION
DEVELOPMENT LEAGUE, 59

Jones, Earl Advertising Director
SUFFOLK NEWS-HERALD, 536

Jones, Eric Marketing/Sales Director
RELIANT ASTRODOME, 996

Jones, Floyd Sport Mgmt. Undergraduate
Coordinator
WEST VIRGINIA UNIVERSITY, 437

Jones, Fred Vice President, Products & Services
MATEFLEX-MELE CORPORATION, 1160

Jones, Glenn Racing Secy
SEABROOK PARK, 1047

Jones, Grahame Sports Reporter (Soccer)
LOS ANGELES TIMES, 503

Jones, Greg Senior Editor
BLUE WATER SAILING, 552

Jones, Harvey VP/Genral Manager
ORCA BAY SPORTS & ENTERTAINMENT, 223

Jones, Heather Head Athletic Trainer
NEW ENGLAND COLLEGE ATHLETICS, 395

Jones, J Commissioner/CEO
DIXIE BOYS & MAJORS BASEBALL, 265

Jones, James General Manager & President of
Basketbal
NATIONAL BASKETBALL ASSOCIATION/NBA,
57

Jones, Jay Chief Financial Officer
DUNBROOKE, 1125

Jones, Jeff Executive Senior Associate AD,
Internal
SOUTHERN ILLINOIS UNIVERSITY
ATHLETICS, 344

Jones, Jenna Athletics Program Coordinator
LA GRANGE COLLEGE ATHLETICS, 389

Jones, Jennifer Sr. Associate AD, Academics &
Student De
BRADLEY UNIVERSITY ATHLETICS, 325, 669

Jones, Jeremy Associate AD,
Compliance/Student Service
NORTHWESTERN OKLAHOMA STATE
UNIVERSITY ATHLETICS, 340

Jones, Jerry Executive VP, Sales & Marketing
NATIONAL FOOTBALL LEAGUE/NFL, 94

Jones, Jerry Owner/President/General Manager
NATIONAL FOOTBALL LEAGUE/NFL, 94

Jones, Jim Assistant General Manager
SOUTH ATLANTIC LEAGUE (A LEVEL), 51,
1005

Jones, John Structural Consultant
FIBEROPTIC LIGHTING INC., 386, 615, 1132

Jones, Karen Production Manager
MAIN TROPHY SUPPLY COMPANY, 1159

Jones, Kathy Administrative Assistant
BUNTING, ELIZABETH C., 869

Jones, Keith President, Hockey Operations &
Alternate
NATIONAL HOCKEY LEAGUE/NHL, 125

Jones, Kelly Sports Writer
MODESTO BEE, 508

Jones, Kelth Mutuel Manager
PORTLAND MEADOWS, 1042

Jones, Kevin Assistant AD, Athletic Training
GARDNER-WEBB UNIVERSITY ATHLETICS,
323, 330

Jones, Kira Marketing and Communications
Associate
INTERNATIONAL JUNIOR GOLF TOUR/IJGT,
102

Jones, Kirk Head Athletic Trainer
POMONA-PITZER COLLEGES ATHLETICS,
397

Jones, LaShaunta Sports Information Director
CENTRAL STATE UNIVERSITY ATHLETICS,
310

Jones, Lenette Assistnat Athletic Director
HENDERSON STATE UNIVERSITY (HSU)
ATHLETICS, 360

Jones, Lindsay President
PRO FOOTBALL WRITERS OF AMERICA, 89

Jones, Margaret Athletics Compliance
Coordinator
BENEDICT COLLEGE ATHLETICS, 352

Jones, Marge Advertising Manager
MCCURTAIN DAILY GAZETTE, 506

Jones, Marie Attorney-at-Law
MEYER, DARRAGH, BUCKLER, BEBENEK &
ECK, PLLC, 895

Jones, Mark Chief Executive
BARC LIMITED, 603, 766, 1022

Jones, Matthew Assistant Director of Athletics
BENEDICTINE UNIVERSITY ATHLETICS, 378

Jones, Melessia Marketing and Website
Feedback
BUTLER HEAVY STRUCTURES, 1051

Jones, Mike Athletic Director
MISSISSIPPI COLLEGE ATHLETICS (MC),
364, 473, 489, 538

Jones, Nate Associate Sports Information Director
STATE UNIVERSITY OF NEW YORK

COLLEGE AT ONEONTA ATHLETICS(SUNY),
402

Jones, Pam Sales Administrative
RELIANT ASTRODOME COMPLEX, 996

Jones, Philip President & CEO
DALLAS CONVENTION & VISITORS BUREAU,
231

Jones, Phillip Advertising Manager
VALLEY TIMES-NEWS, 544

Jones, Randy Treasurer
R.A.M. SPORTS, INC., 351, 536, 1179

Jones, Ray Owner
ADA TENNIS, 1093

Jones, Rich News Director
WTKG-AM, 668

Jones, Robert President and Chief Executive
Officer
NCED SAHARA, 1166

Jones, Robin Program Director
WDZN-FM, 644

Jones, Rock Vice President
NORTH COAST ATHLETIC CONFERENCE,
301

Jones, Rocky Director Finance
I WIRELESS CENTER, 973

Jones, Roxanne Senior Editor
ESPN THE MAGAZINE, 558

Jones, Roy Executive Vice President
QUICKEN LOANS ARENA, 994

Jones, Ryan Editor-in-Chief
SLAM, 581

Jones, Sandy Commissioner & CEO
DIXIE BOYS BASEBALL, 26

Jones, Scott Station Director
WSDM-FM/WBOW-AM ESPN SPORTS RADIO,
665

Jones, Sean President
WOMEN'S PREMIER SOCCER LEAGUE, 164

Jones, Seth Senior Associate Editor
GOLF COURSE MANAGEMENT, 561

Jones, Shawn Director of Athletics
HENDERSON STATE UNIVERSITY (HSU)
ATHLETICS, 360

Jones, Stephen COO/Director, Player Personnel
NATIONAL FOOTBALL LEAGUE/NFL, 94

Jones, Steve VP, Marketing
LYNX GOLF, INC., 467, 1029, 1158

Jones, Tamica Director of Intercollegiate Athletics
UC RIVERSIDE ATHLETICS, 373

Jones, Terry Vice President of Baseball
Operations
REYNOLDS SPORTS MANAGEMENT, 851

Jones, Tina Director of Corporate & Group
Tourism
TUSCALOOSA CONVENTION & VISITORS
BUREAU, 248

Jones, Todd Sports Columnist
COLUMBUS DISPATCH, 472

Jones, Tom Thruxton Facilities Supervisor
BARC LIMITED, 533, 1022

Jones, Troy Assistant Athletics Director,
Operations
TARLETON STATE UNIVERSITY ATHLETICS,
372

Jones, Ty Executive Director
IDAHO HS ACTIVITIES ASSOCIATION, 199

Jones, Val News Director
WAZZ-AM, 637

Jones, Vicki Executive Assistant to Athletic
Director
WAGNER FIELD/KSU, 1017

Jones, Warren Attorney
EBERLE, BERLIN, KADING, TURNBOW &
MCKLVEEN, 877

Jones, Wiley Interim Athletic Director
JACK SPINKS STADIUM, 974

Jong, Bryan Purchasing
GOALSETTER SYSTEMS, INC., 1138

Joos, Nick Senior Associate AD, Communications
IOWA STATE UNIVERSITY ATHLETICS, 333,
965

Jordan, Andrea Assistant Dean of Administration
and Fin
UNITED STATES SPORTS ACADEMY, 435,
590

Jordan, Barbara Color Analyst
NATIONAL PRO FASTPITCH, 170

Jordan, Dave Sports Editor
BRUNSWICK NEWS, 467

Jordan, Glenn Sports Reporter
PORTLAND PRESS HERALD, MAINE SUNDAY
TELEGRAM, 521

Jordan, Gregory Global Managing Partner
REED SMITH LLP, 901

Jordan, James Sports Writer
DAILY ARDMOREITE, 475

Jordan, John Sports Information Director
FLAGLER COLLEGE ATHLETICS, 295, 358

Jordan, Linda Executive Director
YUMA CONVENTION & VISITORS BUREAU,
251

Jordan, Michael Alternate Governor
NATIONAL BASKETBALL ASSOCIATION/NBA,
56, 991

Jordan, Rob Advertisin Sales/Sports Director
WJJC-AM, 652

Jordan, Ted Vice President
WBZ-AM, 640

Jordan, Terri Chief Clerk
ILLINOIS STATE UNIVERSITY, 421

Jordan, Tom Managing Director
MBIA INSURANCE CORPORATION, 589, 768

Jorden, Jim Vice President/Producers
NFL FILMS, 601

Jorden, Ken VP
INDIANA FOOTBALL HALL OF FAME, 253

Jordheim, Vione Senior Administrative Assistant
ALERUS CENTER, 945

Jorge, Karina Assistant Director of Athletics
CITY COLLEGE OF NEW YORK ATHLETICS,
380

Jorgensen, Casey General Counsel
USA HOCKEY, 123

Jorgensen, Chris Senior Associate AD,
Operations
IOWA STATE UNIVERSITY ATHLETICS, 333,
973, 974

Jorgensen, Coralee Executive Director, First Tee
of South D
SOUTH DAKOTA GOLF ASSOCIATION, 115

Jorgensen, Josh Senior Associate Athletic
Director
UNIVERSITY OF NEBRASKA-KEARNEY
ATHLETICS (UNK), 365, 963

Jorgensen, Loren Sports Writer
DESERET MORNING NEWS, 483

Jorgensen, Steve Guest Services Manager
DENVER COLISEUM, 961

Jorgensen, Susanne Chief Financial Officer
WACKENHUT SPORTS SECURITY, 766

Jorgenson, Todd Sports Editor
DENTON RECORD-CHRONICLE, 482

Jorn, Liz Faculty Athletic Representative
TRUMAN STATE UNIVERSITY ATHLETICS,
373

Joseph, Dave Sports Columnist
SOUTH FLORIDA SUN-SENTINEL, 532

Joseph, Dwayne Directer, Pro Personnel
NATIONAL FOOTBALL LEAGUE/NFL, 95

Joseph, Joseph President
VIM, 1240

Joseph, Machli Deputy Director of Athletics
BARUCH COLLEGE ATHLETICS, 377

Joseph B. Rotondi, A. President
E.B. ROTONDI & SONS, INC., 1126

Joseph R. Mattioli, Dr Chief Executive
Officer/Chairman
POCONO RACEWAY, 1031

Josetti, Danielle Exec. Associate AD,
Compliance, Marketin
MARQUETTE UNIVERSITY ATHLETICS, 336

Josey, Mac Vice President & General Manager
DARLINGTON RACEWAY, 1024

Josh, Olerud President & General Manager
INTERNATIONAL LEAGUE, 43

Josh, Robertson Asst. GM/Director,
Stadium/Baseball Oper
LAWRENCE-DUMONT STADIUM, 982

Joshi, Amit Vice President
CRICKET CANADA, 69

Josker, Jay Sport Services Manager
BUFFALO NIAGARA SPORTS COMMISSION,
229

Jost, Kristy News Director
WHHS-FM, 649

Jost, Monte Advertising Manager
LE MARS DAILY SENTINEL, 502

Keating, Sonja SVP, General Counsel
UNITED STATES EQUESTRIAN
FEDERATION, 78

Keating, Steven President & Chief Executive
Officer
SOLE CHOICE, INC., 1191

Keaton, Lottie Treasurer
ARKANSAS AAU ASSOCIATION, 213

Keck, Al Sports Director
WFTS-TV, 679, 702

Keddie, Alex Senior Associate AD/Compliance
EAST CAROLINA UNIVERSITY ATHLETICS,
329

Kee, Ed Cabinet Secretary of Agriculture
STATE OF DELAWARE, DEPARTMENT OF
AGRICULTURE, 81

Keech, Michael Sports Assistant Editor
VIRGINIAN-PILOT, 544

Keef, Eric Project Manager
RHINO SPORTS, 1182

Keefe, Brian Head Coach
NATIONAL BASKETBALL ASSOCIATION/NBA,
58

Keefe, Rob Head Coach/President, Football
Operation
INDOOR FOOTBALL LEAGUE, 93

Keefe, Sheldon Head Coach
NATIONAL HOCKEY LEAGUE/NHL, 125

Keefer, Kip Executive Secretary
BIRMINGHAM RACING COMMISSION, 79, 119

Keefer, Todd Vice President
SOUTHERN CALIFORNIA PGA SECTIONAL
OFFICE, 108

Keegan, Kevin Vice President
BRAILSFORD & DUNLAVEY, 1050

Keegan, Sharyn Production Manager
ATHLETIC GUIDE PUBLISHING, 594

Keegan, Tom Publisher/Editor
ATHLETIC GUIDE PUBLISHING, 594

Keehn, Sandy Operations Director
SPORT MANAGEMENT RESEARCH
INSTITUTE, 809

Keel, Greg Assistant AD, External Relations
SOUTH ALABAMA ATHLETICS, UNIVERSITY
OF, 344

Keelan, Edward VP
ROCKINGHAM PARK, 1043

Keelan, Edward President
SEABROOK PARK, 1047

Keeler, Bill Marketing Manager
FISHER ATHLETIC EQUIPMENT, INC., 1133

Keeley, Michael Broadcasting & Media Relations
NORTH AMERICAN HOCKEY LEAGUE, 132

Keeling, Chuck General Manager
SANDOWN PARK, 1038, 1043

Keels, Gary Sports Reporter
WAYCROSS JOURNAL-HERALD, 546

Keen, Dawn VP, Corporate Partnerships
NATIONAL BASKETBALL ASSOCIATION/NBA,
56

Keen, James Chief Executive Officer
CLIFF KEEN ATHLETIC INC., 1116

Keen, Laureen
GEIGER & KEEN LLP, 882

Keen, Thomas President
CLIFF KEEN ATHLETIC INC., 1116

Keenan, Derek General Manager & Co-Head
Coach
NATIONAL LACROSSE LEAGUE, 142

Keenan, Nancy Architect
DAHLIN GROUP ARCHITECTS PLANNERS,
1053

Keenan, Sandy Deputy Sports Editor
NEW YORK TIMES, 511

Keene, Kathy Sr. Associate Commissioner / COO
SUN BELT CONFERENCE, 305

Keene, Kelly Director of Research & Development
BIOLIFE, LLC, 1107

Keener, Stephen President & CEO
LITTLE LEAGUE BASEBALL AND SOFTBALL,
27

Keeney, Mike Head Athletic Trainer
SUSQUEHANNA UNIVERSITY ATHLETICS,
403

Keeping, Eric Social Media Coordinator
CANADIAN SPORTING GOODS
ASSOCIATION, 219

Keeping, Troy President and GM
SOUTHLAND PARK, 1047

Keeton, Hugh Sports Reporter
WAAY-TV, 698

Kehner, Kevin Attorney
OBERMAYER, REBMANN, MAXWELL &
HIPPEL, LLP, 898

Kehoe, Dan Vice President, Sales
KIEFER U.S.A., 1152

Kehoe, Joe Past President
IOWA GOLF ASSOCIATION, 112

Kehres, Larry Director of Athletics
UNIVERSITY OF MOUNT UNION ATHLETICS,
404

Keidel, Kenneth Advertising Manager
EAGLES DIGEST, 557

Keifer, Tom Executive Director
TAYLOR, TODD, 858

Keiffer, Larry Publication Manager
FLORIDA GREEN, 559

Keil, Alex Sports Information Director
ILLINOIS COLLEGE ATHLETICS, 388

Keilitz, Craig Executive Director
AMERICAN BASEBALL COACHES
ASSOCIATION, 25

Keim, David VP
NATARE CORPORATION, 1166

Kein, Chris Athletic Director
UNITY COLLEGE ATHLETICS, 322

Keiser, Brian Chief Financial Officer
NCED SAHARA, 1166

Keiser, Dennis President/Founder
KEISER CORPORATION, 1152

Keiser, Ingrid General Counsel, Secretary, &
Executive
CLUBCORP, 100

Keiser, Randy VP
KEISER CORPORATION, 1152

Keisser, Bob Sports Columnist
PRESS-TELEGRAM, 665

Keister, Josh Associate Athletic Director
GOSHEN COLLEGE ATHLETICS, 313

Keister, Shaun Vice Chancellor
TOOMEY FIELD, 1010

Keister, Tripp Manager
ARIZONA FALL LEAGUE (ROOKIE), 34

Keitel, Bill VP
U.S. WINDSURFING, 180

Keith, Bill General Manager
WSDP-FM, 665

Keith, Collen Senior Director of Business Affairs
NATIONAL SENIOR GAMES ASSOCIATION,
223

Keith, Jamie Vice President and General Counsel
BERNARD, PAMELA J., 865

Keith, Maark Senior Director of Development
GRAND CANYON STATE GAMES, 262

Keith, Perry Baseball Head Coach
NJCAA REGION II WOMEN'S, 286

Keith, Phil Athletic Trainer
CORNERSTONE COLLEGE ATHLETICS, 311

Keith, Ted Sports Reporter
SPORTS ILLUSTRATED FOR KIDS, 585

Kejci, Bill Athletic Director
NJCAA REGION XI WOMEN'S, 288

Kekalos, Thomas Sales Manager
SPORTS TUTOR INC, 1194

Kekaula, Robert Sports Anchor
KITV-TV, 691

Kelchner, Bill Publisher
SOCCER JR., 582

Keleta, Habtom Sports Information Director
DILLARD UNIVERSITY ATHLETICS, 312

Kellas, Casey Sports Writer
OBSERVER (OR), 515

Kelleher, Andrew VP Finance/Administration
TOP-FLITE COMPANY, 1202

Kelleher, Bob Chief Operating Officer
LOST ARROW CORPORATION, 1157

Kelleher, Pat Executive Director
USA HOCKEY, 123

Keller, Ben News Director
KKRF-FM, 621

Keller, Bob President
ESCALADE SPORTS, 1130

Keller, D'Ann Senior Associate AD,
Administration/SWA
SUNY BUFFALO, 345

Keller, Dennison Sports Reporter
WKRC-TV, 705

Keller, Frank Founder/CEO
ALPHA & OMEGA MOUNTED SECURITY
PATROL, 765

Keller, Gary Co-Owner
NASCAR XFINITY SERIES, 24

Keller, Joanne Registered Investment Assistant
ARANDA GROUP, 824

Keller, Josh Associate AD, Development
PORTLAND STATE UNIVERSITY ATHLETICS,
342

Keller, Kaitlyn Contact
CHEER KIDS, 1115

Keller, Mark Sports Editor
MORNING HERALD, 477, 508

Keller, Matt Director of Sports Medicine
FRANKLIN & MARSHALL COLLEGE
ATHLETICS (FMC), 385

Keller, Patricia Director of Prospect Research
JOHN F. SAVAGE HALL, 976

Keller, Robert Secretary General
INTERNATIONAL POWERLIFTING
FEDERATION, 180

Keller, Scott Head Athletic Trainer
ROSE-HULMAN INSTITUTE OF
TECHNOLOGY, 399

Kellerman, Richard President
NIELSEN-KELLERMAN, 1168

Kellermann, Chris Director of Corporate
Partnerships
FRONTIER LEAGUE, 40

Kelley, Alex Associate AD, Revenue Generation &
Engag
FLORIDA INTERNATIONAL UNIVERSITY
ATHLETICS, 330

Kelley, Brian Member
KELLEY, MCELWEE & SCHMIDT, P.A., 888

Kelley, Bryan Advertising Director
YORK DAILY RECORD/YORK SUNDAY
NEWS, 548

Kelley, Creigh President
BKB LTD., 775

Kelley, Dale Director of Athletics
BETHEL COLLEGE (TN) ATHLETICS, 308

Kelley, Hagan Associate Editor
SURFING, 587

Kelley, Kathleen Accounting Manager
HARMON TRAVEL SERVICE, 926

Kelley, Larry President
NEW ENGLAND PGA SECTIONAL OFFICE,
107

Kelley, Michele Special Events Coordinator
QUALCOMM STADIUM, 994

Kelley, Paul Director
NEW HAMPSHIRE RACING AND
CHARITABLE GAMING COMMISSION, 81, 119

Kelley, Paul Director
ACADEMY SPORTS TURF, 1090

Kelley, Rusty Managing Partner
HEIDRICK & STRUGGLES, 787

Kelley, Steve Sports Columnist
SEATTLE TIMES, 103, 530

Kelley, Thomas Director of Athletics
FRAMINGHAM STATE UNIVERSITY
ATHLETICS, 385

Kelliher, Marsha Dean of School Management &
Business
ST. EDWARDS UNIVERSITY, 433

Kellogg, Derek Head Coach, Men's Basketball
MULLINS CENTER, 988

Kellogg, Mike General Manager
1510 THE ZONE, 611

Kellogg, William President
USTA SOUTHERN CALIFORNIA, 176

Kellough, Aaron Director of Communications
COLORADO GOLF ASSOCIATION, 110

Kellum, Sharon President
LADIES BIRMINGHAM GOLF ASSOCIATION,
112

Kelly, Ann VP/Marketing & Strategic Planning
MEDIAMARK RESEARCH INC./MRI, 795

Kelly, Brendan Owner
MAJOR LEAGUE LACROSSE, 45, 141

Kelly, Brian News Director
KTRS-AM, 630

Kelly, Caryn Client Services Manager
TD BANKNORTH GARDEN, 1008

Kelly, Chris Assistant Coach
NATIONAL HOCKEY LEAGUE/NHL, 123

Kelly, Claudia Membership Director
NATIONAL INTERCOLLEGIATE RODEO ASSOCIATION (NIRA), 146
Kelly, Dan President
ENDURA RUBBER FLOORING, 1129
Kelly, Doug Media Services
FOSTERS FARM BOWL, 90
Kelly, Frank President
USTA TEXAS, 176
Kelly, Godwin Sports Editor (Motor Sports)
DAYTONA BEACH NEWS-JOURNAL, 481
Kelly, Grant Director of Development
JOHNS HOPKINS UNIVERSITY ATHLETICS, 388
Kelly, Jason Sports Reporter
SOUTH BEND TRIBUNE, 531
Kelly, Jennifer Executive Director
WOLSTEIN CENTER, 1020
Kelly, Jill Co-Founder
HUNTER'S HOPE FOUNDATION, 191
Kelly, Jim Co-Founder
HUNTER'S HOPE FOUNDATION, 191
Kelly, Joe Vice President of Facilities
RENO-SPARKS CONVENTION AUTHORITY, 107, 244
Kelly, John Publisher
NORTH AMERICAN PYLON, 571, 574
Kelly, John Publisher & Editor
MOTORACING, 571
Kelly, Joseph Chief Executive Officer
EWING COLE CHERRY BROTT, 1055
Kelly, Julie General Manager
RIGHT GARD CORPORATION, 1182
Kelly, Katie Association Manager
SAIL AMERICA, 64, 149
Kelly, Keenan Assistant Coach
NORTH AMERICAN HOCKEY LEAGUE, 132
Kelly, Kerry Ass. To Partner
16W MARKETING, LLC, 770
Kelly, Kevin Director, College Scouting
NATIONAL FOOTBALL LEAGUE/NFL, 95
Kelly, Maisha Director of Athletics
DREXEL UNIVERSITY ATHLETICS, 329
Kelly, Matt Sr. Associate AD, Student-Athlete Suppor
MURRAY STATE UNIVERSITY ATHLETICS, 338, 995, 999
Kelly, Michael Vice President of Athletics
SOUTH FLORIDA ATHLETICS, UNIVERSITY OF, 344, 686
Kelly, Mike Assistant to the Athletic Director
DAYTON ATHLETICS, UNIVERSITY OF, 134, 328, 516
Kelly, Omar Sports Reporter
SOUTH FLORIDA SUN-SENTINEL, 532
Kelly, Pam Assistant Raceway Manager
WESTERN FAIR ENTERTAINMENT CENTRE, 1045
Kelly, Patricia Advertising Manager
MOTORACING, 571
Kelly, Patricia Business Manager
NORTH AMERICAN PYLON, 574
Kelly, Philip Chief Executive
ACTION IMAGES, 1092
Kelly, R. Vice Chairman, Chief Financial Officer a
FAMILY DOLLAR STORES, 1227
Kelly, Rita
SHERRARD, GERMAN & KELLY, 906
Kelly, Robert Chief Executive Officer
NICKLAUS GOLF EQUIPMENT COMPANY, L.C., 1168
Kelly, Rose Assistant Director of Athletics
PHILADELPHIA UNIVERSITY ATHLETICS, 368
Kelly, Ryan Deputy Athletic Director
LONG ISLAND UNIVERSITY BROOKLYN ATHLETICS, 335
Kelly, Sandra Sports Editor
MOSCOW-PULLMAN DAILY NEWS, 509
Kelly, Sloane Director of Interactive strartegy
BFG COMMUNICATIONS, 775
Kelly, Suzanne News Director
WXBD-AM, 671
Kelly, Tim VP Sales
BIOLIFE, LLC, 1107
Kelly, Todd Sports Director
KTVK-TV, 696
Kelly, Tom Advertising Director
WINONA DAILY NEWS, 547

Kelly, Wendy Dircetor of Community Outreach and Partn
SPECIAL OLYMPICS UTAH, 197
Kelm, Candice Sports Information Specialist
NJCAA REGION V WOMEN'S, 287
Kelso, Laura Advertising Manager
KFYN-AM, 618
Kelso, Theresa Office Manager
SPORTHILL MARKETING, 761
Kelton, Aaron Interim Athletic Director
SHORTER UNIVERSITY ATHLETICS, 369
Kemezis, Jon Vice President of Finance
MAJOR LEAGUE LACROSSE, 141
Kemmy, David Director of Athletics
ROGER WILLIAMS UNIVERSITY ATHLETICS, 399
Kemna, Betty Assistant Athletic Director
LINCOLN UNIVERSITY (MISSOURI) ATHLETICS, 362
Kemp, Chuck General Manager
US BANK ARENA, 1014
Kemp, Thomas General Counsel
LONG DRIVERS OF AMERICA, 103
Kemp, Timothy VP, Marketing
NATIONAL FOOTBALL LEAGUE/NFL, 96
Kempczinski, Chris President & CEO
MCDONALD'S CORPORATION, 729
Kempe, Judith Director of Design
LUCY.COM, 1232
Kemper, Scott Partner/Creative
ASA PRODUCTIONS, 597
Kempf, Cheri President/Commissioner
NATIONAL PRO FASTPITCH, 170
Kempf, Gary Athletic Director
STERLING COLLEGE ATHLETICS, 321
Kempf, Penny Associate Athletic Director
ROWAN UNIVERSITY ATHLETICS, 399
Kempin, Kevin VP
PENN RACQUET SPORTS, 1173
Kempke, Randy Sales Representative
ADA TENNIS, 1093
Kempken, Tina Events/Programs Director
FOREVER YOUNG FOUNDATION, 191
Kemple, Chris General Manager
CAROLINA LEAGUE, 37
Ken, Ungar President
U/S SPORTS ADVISORS, 859
Ken, Young President
ISOTOPES PARK, 974
Kendall, Barbara Vice President
INTERNATIONAL SURFING ASSOCIATION, 172
Kendall, Curt Director of Athletics
BRIDGEWATER COLLEGE ATHLETICS, 302, 378
Kendall, David Partner
WILLIAMS & CONNOLLY, 860
Kendall, Gary Manager
EASTERN LEAGUE, 38
Kendall, Jenna Media Informations Coordinator
BASS PRO SHOPS, 1105, 1217
Kendall, Lisa VP Business Partnerships
JHG TOWNSEND, 790, 821
Kendall, Mitchell Associate Commissioner/Finance
ATLANTIC 10 CONFERENCE, 291
Kendra, Tom Sports Editor
MUSKEGON CHRONICLE, 509
Kendrick, Brandon Assistant Director of Facilities
DONALD L. TUCKER CIVIC CENTER, 962
Kendrick, Graham Director, Media & Public Relations
WESTERN HOCKEY LEAGUE, 138
Kendrick, Ken Managing General Partner
NATIONAL LEAGUE OF PROFESSIONAL BASEBALL CLUBS, THE, 31, 957
Kendrick, Kevin Senior Associate AD, Compliance
FLORIDA INTERNATIONAL UNIVERSITY ATHLETICS, 330
Kendrick, Pam Vice President & General Manager
MEMPHIS MOTORSPORTS PARK (MMP), 1028
Kendrick, Scott Sports Editor
NEWS-HERALD (WILLOUGHBY), 488, 513
Kenefick, Dean Senior Associate AD, Communications
VILLANOVA UNIVERSITY ATHLETICS, 348

Kenger, John Assistant Athletic Director
MIDWAY UNIVERSITY ATHLETICS, 316
Kengerski, Ed Sports Director
WWMT-TV, 712
Kenley, Caroline Secretary
ALASKA STATE FAIR, 260
Kennaugh, Claudia Assistant Director
MILLER & ASSOCIATES, CATHERINE, 758
Kennedy, Becky Chief Financial Officer
SPECIAL OLYMPICS COLORADO, 194
Kennedy, Bob Sports Editor
STAMFORD ADVOCATE, 534
Kennedy, Brendan Director of Sports Information
MOUNT ST. VINCENT ATHLETICS, COLLEGE OF, 394
Kennedy, Brian President/CEO
EL PASO COUNTY COLISEUM, 595, 964
Kennedy, Chris Senior Deputy AD
DUKE UNIVERSITY ATHLETICS, 329
Kennedy, Darryl Manager
ARIZONA LEAGUE (ROOKIE), 35
Kennedy, David President / Chief Executive Officer
WELLS LAMONT SPORTS & SPECIALTIES, 1209
Kennedy, Dinah Secretary
MISSISSIPPI WOMEN'S GOLF ASSOCIATION, 113
Kennedy, Elizabeth Office Administrator
NIXON, PEABODY, 897
Kennedy, Garland Sports Editor
DAILY SITKA SENTINEL, 480
Kennedy, Jay President
MIDWEST PGA SECTIONAL OFFICE, 106
Kennedy, Jim Senior Director of Integrated Marketing
LANDS' END, INC., 1154
Kennedy, Jodee Administrative Assistant
ATLANTA DRAGWAY, 1022
Kennedy, Jon Marketing Manager
DIAMONDBACK BICYCLES, 1124
Kennedy, Kevin Vice President Public Relations
PCGCAMPBELL, 783, 800
Kennedy, Laing Director of Athletics
KENT STATE UNIVERSITY ATHLETICS, 979
Kennedy, Lesa ISC President
ACTION SPORTS IMAGE, 1092
Kennedy, Michael Chief Executive Officer
CITY SPORTS, 1223
Kennedy, Michelle President, COO, & Alternate Governor
NATIONAL HOCKEY LEAGUE/NHL, 125
Kennedy, Mike Sports Reporter (Local)
LOS ANGELES TIMES, 503
Kennedy, Pat Associate Athletic Director
CASE WESTERN RESERVE UNIVERSITY ATHLETICS, 38, 379
Kennedy, Randy Sports Editor
PRESS-REGISTER, 522
Kennedy, Rich Director of Handicapping & Membership Se
NEW JERSEY STATE GOLF ASSOCIATION, 114
Kennedy, Rusty Athletic Director
MIDWAY UNIVERSITY ATHLETICS, 316
Kennedy, Sam President & CEO
AMERICAN LEAGUE OF PROFESSIONAL BASEBALL CLUBS, THE, 29, 783, 965
Kennedy, Tommy Director of Administration
ALABAMA SPORTS FESTIVAL, 260
Kennedy, Will Sports Reporter
WAFF-TV, 698
Kennell, Scott Athletic Director
MADONNA UNIVERSITY ATHLETICS, 315
Kenner, Nolan General Manager
WKEQ, 653
Kenneth E. Peacock, Dr. The Chancellor
COLE, DAYTON T., 873
Kenney, Bill VP Sales and Marketing
SMITHCO, 1190
Kenney, Crane President, Business Operations
NATIONAL LEAGUE OF PROFESSIONAL BASEBALL CLUBS, THE, 31
Kenney, Crane SVP/General Counsel & Secretary
SENNET, CHARLES J., 854
Kenney, Keith Director of Wellness & Recreation
STATE UNIVERSITY OF NEW YORK AT NEW PALTZ ATHLETICS(SUNY), 401

Executive Index

Kuhnel, Doug Senior Vice President
VENUWORKS, 1066

Kuhns, Mike Sports Editor
POCONO RECORD, 520

Kukla, Ryan Director of Ticket Operations
SCHAUMBURG BOOMERS STADIUM, 1001

Kuklinski, Dan Director of Athletic
Communications
CARDINAL STRITCH UNIVERSITY
ATHLETICS, 310

Kulczycki, Bill Sales Director
PATAGONIA, 1173

Kulczyk, Katherine Media Contact
NEW ERA CAP, CO, 1167

Kulesza, J. Vice-President
NJCAA REGION XXI WOMEN'S, 290

Kulfan, Ted Sports Reporter
DETROIT NEWS, 483

Kulina, Robert VP/General Manager
MONMOUTH PARK, 1041

Kulish, Rob Director of Athletic Communications
RUTGERS UNIVERSITY-NEWARK
ATHLETICS, 399

Kulkarni, Arun President
KOOLATRON, 1153

Kull, Ed Director of Intercollegiate Athletics
FORDHAM UNIVERSITY ATHLETICS, 330

Kull, Scott Deputy AD, External Operations
UTAH ATHLETICS, UNIVERSITY OF, 348

Kulland, Jake Sports Director
KNDK-FM, 624

Kullenberg, David Tournmant Official, PGA
CAROLINAS PGA SECTION, 105

Kulp, Kevin President
EASTERN LEAGUE, 38

Kumar, Emma Associate Director of Athletics
BALL STATE UNIVERSITY ATHLETICS, 325

Kumar, Rajni Manager
FAIRMOUNT PARK RACETRACK, 1038

Kummer, Andrew Senior Director, Coaching -
Girls
WOMEN'S PREMIER SOCCER LEAGUE, 165

Kump, Joan Promotions Director
WJPZ-FM, 652

Kunde, Gene Chief Operating Officer
BIRKENSTOCK FOOTPRINT SANDALS INC.,
1219

Kuntz, Daniel Athletic Director
CALIFORNIA LUTHERAN UNIVERSITY
ATHLETICS / CLU SPORTS, 379

Kuntz, Will General Manager
MAJOR LEAGUE SOCCER, 158

Kunz, Mark Sports Director
WBKB-TV, 700

Kupec, Matt Interim Athletic Director
SOUTHERN ILLINOIS UNIVERSITY
ATHLETICS, 344

Kupelian, Peter Lawyer
KUPELIAN, ORMOND & MAGY, 888

Kupen, Marcel President
MARCEL V. KUPER, CPA/PFS, CFE, 768

Kuper, Melissa Assistant GM
ROGER DEAN STADIUM, 998

Kuperstein, Adam Sports Anchor/Reporter
WTVJ-TV, 711

Kupper, Mike Senior Assistant Sports Editor
LOS ANGELES TIMES, 503

Kupperman, Louis Partner
OBERMAYER, REBMANN, MAXWELL &
HIPPEL, LLP, 898

Kuppig, Vince Sports Editor
HASTINGS TRIBUNE, 492

Kura, Michael
POITINGER REDMOND LYONS KURA &
WALKER, 847

Kuri, Carlos President
CEO MANUFACTURERS, 1115

Kurita, Yoshinosuke Owner
TENACIOUS LTD, 1200

Kurkjian, Adam Sports Writer
DAILY NEWS TRANSCRIPT, 478

Kurkowski, Cindy President
BADGE-A-MINIT LTD., 1103

Kurkowski, Sue Director, Facility Operations
STATE UNIVERSITY OF NEW YORK, 1006

Kurn, Werner Secretary
DIVING EQUIPMENT & MARKETING
ASSOCIATION, 72

Kurpius, David Associate Vice Chancellor for
Enrollment
TIGER STADIUM, 1010

Kurtenbach, Aelred Chairman
DAKTRONICS, INC., 1122

Kurtenbach, Frank Vice President Sales
DAKTRONICS, INC., 1122

Kurtin, Anthony Associate Director of Athletics
ST. FRANCIS COLLEGE ATHLETICS (SFC),
371

Kurtz, Amanda Senior Associate AD/SWA
PEPPERDINE UNIVERSITY ATHLETICS, 341

Kurtz, Glory Editor
WOMEN'S PRO RODEO NEWS, 551, 577, 593

Kurtz, Jason Sports Director
WZVN-TV, 713

Kurtz, Jesse Weekend Sports Anchor
KKTV-TV, 691

Kurtz, Nolan Executive Director/Practice
Operations
BUCHANAN INGERSOLL ROONEY PC, 836,
869

Kurtz, Norman Chairman
WSP, 1063

Kurtzner, Bob Strength & Conditioning
Coordinator
SOUTHERN VERMONT COLLEGE
ATHLETICS, 400

Kurvers, Peter Honorary President
MINNESOTA PGA SECTIONAL OFFICE, 106

Kurvers, Tom Assistant General Manager
NATIONAL HOCKEY LEAGUE/NHL, 124

Kurz, Jason Sports Director
WZVN-TV, 713

Kush, Ken Sports Editor/Writer
YORK NEWS-TIMES, 548

Kushner, Jeff Marketing Director
ABSOLUTE FITNESS, INC., 1090

Kushner, Scott Chief Operating Officer
IN STORE SPORTS NETWORK, 676

Kusinski, Peggy Sports Reporter
WMAQ-TV, 706

Kusinuk, Michael Sports Marketing Director
LEHIGH VALLEY SPORTS COMMISSION, 239

Kutches, Alex Secretary
THE ACCESS FUND, 69

Kutler, Ken Intercollegiate Athletics Director
ITHACA COLLEGE ATHLETICS, 974

Kuttner, Peter President
CAMBRIDGE SEVEN ASSOCIATES INC., 1051

Kuwada, Robert Sports Reporter (UCLA)
ORANGE COUNTY REGISTER, 516

Kuykendall, Charles SVP/Principal
BMK ARCHITECTS, 1050

Kuykendall, Steve Crew Chief
NASCAR GANDER OUTDOORS TRUCK
SERIES, 23

Kuzca, Kathy Circulation
AROUND THE RINGS, 604

Kuzmick, Thomas Partner
RAWLE LAW OFFICES, 901

Kuznar, Christine Senior Associate AD,
Academics/SWA
INDIANA UNIVERSITY-PURDUE UNIVERSITY
FORT WAYNE, 333

Kvas, William Attorney
HUNEGS, STONE, LENEAVE, KYAS &
THORNTON, P.A., 884

Kvederis, Brad Sports Writer
VALLEJO TIMES-HERALD, 543

Kvinlaug, Steve Sales VP
ALPINA SPORTS CORPORATION, 1096

Kwapis, John Chief Operating Officer
BLUE BIRD CORPORATION, 925

Kwasney, Ben Sports Copy Editor
VENTURA COUNTY STAR, 544

Kwon, Sungwon President & CEO
KIA CANADA, 729

Kyer, Maureen EVP Merchandising
MERVYN'S, 1233

Kyle, Tim Athletic Director
SPECTRUM CORPORATION, 1192

Kyler, Jake Copy Editor
STREET & SMITH'S SPORTSBUSINESS
JOURNAL, 587

Kyler, Jodi VP of Marketing and Communications
SPOKANE REGIONAL SPORTS
COMMISSION, 246

Kyles, Charles Member
STUART LAW FIRM, P.L.L.C, 909

Kyrias, Alex Director, Communications & Sales
NORTH AMERICAN HOCKEY LEAGUE, 131

Kysela, Chris Sales
M.B.I. PRODUCTS CO., INC., 821

L

L Gulis Jr, Stephen EVP, Chief Financial Officer,
and Treasu
WOLVERINE WORLD WIDE, 1211

L J. Harper, Scott Attorney
BROWN, HALL, SHORE & MCKINLEY LLP,
868

L Jo Belle, John President
KINSEY ASSOCIATES, 1060

L L. Boeckmann, Alan Chairman/Chief Executive
Officer
FLUOR CORPORATION, 1057

L Werbell IV, Mitchell President
BRIGADE QM, 1110

L. A. Sellers, Jeffery Attorney
STOREY, MOYES, 909

L. D Allain, Jean-Marc President & Chief
Executive Officer
FAIRTRON, 1131

L. Gi Hartman, Bruce Executive Vice President
and Chief Finan
VENATOR GROUP, INC., 1240

L. Howson Jr, Arthur Shareholder
CLARDY, DON S., 872

L. Jo Katz, Brian President
PINNACLE ENTERPRISES, INC., 847

L. M. Layman, Michael Attorney
LAYMAN, MICHAEL L., 889

L. M. Sanett, Stephen Vice-Chairman, President
and Interim Chi
STURM, RUGER & COMPANY, INC., 1197

L. Tanner Jr, James Partner
WILLIAMS & CONNOLLY, 860

LaBarbera, Mark Director of Athletics
VALPARAISO UNIVERSITY, 348, 436

LaBelle, Kurt Sports Anchor
KHQA-TV, 690

LaBianco, Jaime Executive Secretary
WILLIAM & MARY HALL, 1017, 1018

LaBoy, Drew Director of Ticket Sales/Operations
ATLANTIC LEAGUE, 35, 948

LaBrake, Randy Associate Director of Athletics
ST. LAWRENCE UNIVERSITY ATHLETICS,
401

LaBrie, Brad Sports Editor
PENINSULA DAILY NEWS, 519

LaBroad, Michael Chief Marketing Officer
RFDTV, 686

LaChica, Angela Vice President
SAN DIEGO HALL OF CHAMPIONS SPORTS
MUSEUM, THE, 258

LaComfora, Peggy Promotions Manager
KYTV-TV, 698

LaCroix, Norman Chief Financial Officer
QUINN, JAMES W., 900

LaFleur, Matt Head Coach
NATIONAL FOOTBALL LEAGUE/NFL, 95

LaFollette, Drew Director of Promotions &
Marketing
MIDWEST LEAGUE, 45

LaForest, Leonardo President
MARSHFIELD FAIR, 1041

LaFoy, Cheryl Director of Event Operations
BOBBY DODD STADIUM AT HISTORIC
GRANT FIELD, 950

LaGamma, Sean Managing Director
TIMELINE VIDEO, 603

LaGesse, Bobby Sports Editor
DAILY TRIBUNE (IA), 480

LaJeunesse, Teri Sports Information Director
EAST CENTRAL UNIVERSITY ATHLETICS,
357

LaMarche, Blair Athletic Trainer
EAST COAST HOCKEY LEAGUE/ECHL, 129

LaMendola, T.J. Senior VP & Chief Financial
Officer
NATIONAL HOCKEY LEAGUE/NHL, 124

LaMere, Lydia Associate Head Athletic Trainer
MOUNT MERCY COLLEGE ATHLETICS, 317

LaMonica, Mark Sports Writer
NEWSDAY, 513

Lambdin, Dolly President
SHAPE AMERICA SOCIETY OF HEALTH AND PHYSICAL EDUCATORS, 224

Lamberson, Stephen Member
ETTER, MCMAHON, LAMBERSON & CLARY, P.C.A., 879

Lambert, Dan Assistant Coach
NATIONAL HOCKEY LEAGUE/NHL, 123

Lambert, Dana Sports Information Liaison
SOUTHWEST ATHLETICS, COLLEGE OF THE, 320

Lambert, Karen Classified Manager
LONGMONT DAILY TIMES-CALL, 503

Lambert, Nicole Sr. Assoc. AD/SWA
BRYANT UNIVERSITY ATHLETICS, 326

Lambert, Paul Sports Reporter
POST REGISTER, 521

Lambert, Ryan Assistant Executive Director
INDIANA GOLF ASSOCIATION, 106, 111

Lamberth, Mark Chair
ASSOCIATION OF RACING COMMISSIONERS INTERNATIONAL, 81, 119

Lamberti, Jeff Commissioner
IOWA RACING & GAMING COMMISSION, 79

Lamberton, Jack President
USA DEAF SPORTS FEDERATION, 198

Lamboni, Pat Head Athletic Trainer
SALISBURY UNIVERSITY ATHLETICS, 400

Lambrecht, Keith Director, Sport Management Program
LOYOLA UNIVERSITY CHICAGO, 424

Lamkin, Bob President / Chief Executive Officer
LAMKIN LEATHER & RUBBER COMPANY, 1154

Lamkin, Mike Engineering VP
LAMKIN LEATHER & RUBBER COMPANY, 1154

Lamkin, Thomas EVP
LAMKIN LEATHER & RUBBER COMPANY, 1154

Lamming, Norm President
SPORTS WEST SALES, INC., 1194

Lamontagne, Debby Controller
FLORIDA STATE GOLF ASSOCIATION, 111

Lamontagne, Mike President and Chair
SPECIAL OLYMPICS CANADA, 194

Lamoriello, Chris General Manager
AMERICAN HOCKEY LEAGUE/AHL, 127

Lamoriello, Lou President, General Manager & Alternate G
NATIONAL HOCKEY LEAGUE/NHL, 125

Lamote, Jeff President
MOTORHEAD PRODUCTS, 1164

Lamountain, Jason Senior Methodologist
TAYLOR RESEARCH & CONSULTING GROUP, INC., 813

Lamoureux, Danny Director, Championship Services
CANADIAN CURLING ASSOCIATION, 69

Lampe, Chris Chief Operating Officer
SAN JOSE MUNICIPAL STADIUM, 1001

Lampe, Jeff Sports Reporter
JOURNAL STAR, 498

Lampen, Barbara SVP/Strategic Planning/Development
MEADOWLANDS/NEW JERSEY SPORTS & EXPOSITION AUTHORITY, 1065

Lamper, Laurie Promotions Director
WBZ-AM, 640

Lampert, Edward Chairman
SEARS, ROEBUCK & CO., 1236

Lamping, Mark President
NATIONAL FOOTBALL LEAGUE/NFL, 95

Lampman, Peter President
COMMONWEALTH GAMES OF VIRGINIA, 249, 261

Lampman, Renne HR
PALM BEACH KENNEL CLUB, 1047

Lampros, Nick Member
LAMPROS & ROBERTS CONSULTING, 840

Lan, Jerry Managing Director, Far East Operations
CONVERSE, INC., 1223

Lana, Wai Founder and President
WAI LANA YOGA, 1208

Lanagan, Justin Superintendent
YACK ARENA, 1020

Lancaster, Dave Sports Director
KBCR-FM, 613

Lancaster, James Owner & Head Coach
WOMEN'S FOOTBALL ALLIANCE / WFA, 99

Lance, Tony Associate Editor
TENNIS, 588

Lance, Wilson Program Director
KILI-FM, 620

Land, Marilyn Advertising Manager
RUSHVILLE REPUBLICAN, 526

Land, Matt Athletic Director
TRINE UNIVERSITY ATHLETICS, 322

Land, Victory Contact
MACON COUNTY GREYHOUND PARK, INC., 1046

Landa, Terri Advertising Manager
KANE COUNTY CHRONICLE, 499

Landay, David President
SENECA SPORTS INC., 1187

Landers, Bobbi League Administrator
APPALACHIAN LEAGUE (ADVANCED ROOKIE), 33

Landers, Jim Sports Director
KEWI-AM, 617

Landers, Lee President (Appalachian League)
BURKE FIELD, 33, 953

Landers, Rhonda Chief Financial Officer
MUSEUM OF YACHTING, 255

Landes, Kurt President & General Manager
INTERNATIONAL LEAGUE, 42

Landesberg, Dave Director of Licensing
SLOANE VISION UNLIMITED, 808

Landgraf, John President/General Manager
FX NETWORKS, LLC, 675

Landgraf, Thomas Director, Administration and Operations,
FOLEY & LARDNER, 880

Landherr, Jim VP Manufacturing
HUFCOR, INC., 1146

Landis, Chuck Sports Reporter
CHRONICLE-TRIBUNE, 470

Landon, Eric Head Coach
USL LEAGUE TWO, 163

Landphere, Ken Director
OCTAGON FOOTBALL, 845

Landreman, Jamie Club Owner & Head Coach
WOMEN'S PREMIER SOCCER LEAGUE, 166

Landreth, Jack Program Director
KSFN-AM, 628

Landrum, Rick Vice President
ATHLETIC RESOURCE MANAGEMENT, INC., 825

Landry, Chris Sports Editor
DAILY IBERIAN, 477

Landry, Jacques High Performance Director/Head Coach
CYCLING CANADA, 70

Landry, Mark Sales Manager
G. LOOMIS INC., 1136

Landry, Victor Director of Event Services
THE CROWN COMPLEX, 1009

Landsberg, Marc Global President
FRANKEL SPORTS GROUP, 755

Landsverk, Rocky Editorial Director
TUFF STUFF PUBLICATIONS, 589

Lane, Beth Sales Director
LINEAR RUBBER PRODUCTS, INC., 1156

Lane, Brad Programming
1500 ESPN SPORTSTALK, 605

Lane, Cedric Head Coach
WOMEN'S FOOTBALL ALLIANCE / WFA, 97

Lane, David Merchandising VP
ALPS SPORTSWEAR MFG. COMPANY, INC., 33, 1096

Lane, Debbie Treasurer
WOMEN'S GOLF ASSOCIATION OF BALTIMORE, 118

Lane, Dwight Station Manager
107.9 THE BULL, 611

Lane, Homeira Bogner Sport Sales & Marketing
BOGNER, 1109

Lane, Illana Dean, School of Education, Associate Pro
MEDAILLE COLLEGE, 425

Lane, Laura-Ann Senior Women's Administrator
GWYNEDD MERCY COLLEGE ATHLETICS, 386

Lane, Maria National Sales Manager
PHOENIX CONVENTION & VISITORS BUREAU, GREATER, 243

Lane, Mark Co-Founder/ President
COED SPORTSWEAR INC, 1117

Lane, Michael Managing Editor
TEAM MARKETING REPORT, 588

Lane, Phil Producer
GV SPORTS, 680

Lane, Scott President
MIDWEST LEAGUE, 45

Lane, Steven Owner
NASCAR GANDER OUTDOORS TRUCK SERIES, 23

Lane, Steven. Attorney
HERMAN, HERMAN, KATZ & COTLAR, L.L.P., 883

Laney, Jay Chief Operating Officer
MID-SOUTH SPORTS MANAGEMENT, 843

Lang, Andrew Sports Reporter
BELLINGHAM HERALD, 464

Lang, Bob Director of Mutuels
ILLINOIS RACING BOARD, 79

Lang, David CPA
USA KARATE FEDERATION, 143

Lang, Doug Program Director
KPUG-AM, 626

Lang, Gregory Assistant Sports Editor
BOSTON GLOBE, 465

Lang, J. SVP and Chief Financial Officer
FAMOUS FOOTWEAR, 1227

Lang, Joseph Senior Associate Director of Athletics
UNIVERSITY OF DISTRICT OF COLUMBIA ATHLETICS, 356

Lang, Mitch Head Athletic Trainer
UNIVERSITY OF JAMESTOWN ATHLETICS, 322

Lang, Morgan Hampton Roads Sports Commission
HAMPTON ROADS SPORTS COMMISSION, 235

Lang, Peter President
JOG-A-LITE, INC., 1150

Lang, Scott Attorney
LANG, XIFARAS & BULLARD, 889

Lang, Thomas Vice President
MOAG & COMPANY, 769

Langan, Bryan Athletic Trainer
MACMURRAY COLLEGE ATHLETICS, 391

Langan, Jerry VP
U.S.I.A., 1205

Langas, Lisa National Sales Manager
SPORT HALEY INC., 1192

Langdon, Trajan General Manager
NATIONAL BASKETBALL ASSOCIATION DEVELOPMENT LEAGUE, 56, 58

Lange, Cassidy President
NORTH AMERICAN HOCKEY LEAGUE, 132

Langenbrunner, Jamie Assistant General Manager, Player Person
NATIONAL HOCKEY LEAGUE/NHL, 123

Langenderfer, Kate Director, Storytelling, Production, & Om
EAST COAST HOCKEY LEAGUE/ECHL, 130

Langer, Scott Head Coach & General Manager
NORTH AMERICAN HOCKEY LEAGUE, 132

Langer, Sean Director Facility Services
STAGERIGHT CORP., 1195

Langford, Celia Director of Community Relations
FRONTIER LEAGUE, 40

Langford, Kirk Vice President Sales
NORDICA USA, 1169

Langford, Vince Sports Copy Editor
FORT WORTH STAR-TELEGRAM, 489

Langhorn, Jim Co-Owner
CENTAUR FLOOR SYSTEMS, LLC, 1115

Langhorst, Diane Marketing Manager
CHICAGO SCENIC STUDIO, 1052

Langley, Kyle Chief Research Officer
BFG COMMUNICATIONS, 775

Langlois, Ed MBA Program Director
PALM BEACH ATLANTIC UNIVERSITY, 431

Langlois, Joel President
DELTAPLEX ENTERTAINMENT & EXPO CENTER, 961

Langlois, Susan
SPRINGFIELD COLLEGE, 433

Langmyer, Tom VP/General Manager
KMOX, 624

Lango, Chris Sports Writer
KCRA-TV, 688

Lastra, Bill President
PLATINUM ENTERTAINMENT PARTNERS II, 601

Lastringer, Joe President/Sports & News Director
WFIS-AM, 646

Latch, Jarod Sports Reporter
WSOC-TV, 709

Latham, Charlotte Concessions Supervisor
BOUTWELL MUNICIPAL AUDITORIUM, 951

Latham, Dan General Manager
WCHO-AM, 641

Latham, Krista Sports Reporter
DETROIT FREE PRESS, 483

Latham, Nicholas Associate AD, Operations
HOWARD UNIVERSITY ATHLETICS, 332

Lathey, Daniel Associate Athletic Director
TEXAS A&M INTERNATIONAL UNIVERSITY ATHLETICS, 372

Lathrop, Happ Executive Director
SOUTH CAROLINA GOLF ASSOCIATION, 115

Latimer, Clay Sports Reporter
ROCKY MOUNTAIN NEWS, 526

Latino, Heather Associate
PAOLI & SHEA, P.C., 846

Latkovski, Brennan Co-Owner
ZOOPERSTARS!, 775, 818

Latkovski, Dominic Owner
BIRDZERK!, 775

Latora, Andy Sports Copy Editor
JOURNAL STAR, 498

Latzer, Jon General Sales Manager
WIP SPORTSRADIO 610, 651

Lau, Phillip Art Director
BOSTON HANNAH INTERNATIONAL, 553

Laub, JR Assistant General Manager
FLORIDA STATE LEAGUE, 39

Laubach, Edward Sports Editor
EXPRESS-TIMES, 488

Laube, Heidi Head Athletic Trainer
WALDORF COLLEGE ATHLETICS, 323

Lauber, Michael Principal
ELLENZWEIG ASSOCIATES, INC., 1055

Laubscher, Brian Sports Information Director
WASHINGTON AND LEE UNIVERSITY ATHLETICS, 405

Lauchaire, Nicole VP, Corporate Marketing & Communications
VARSITY BRANDS, INC., 1207

Lauchnor, John President / Chief Executive Officer
ROYAL PRECISION, INC., 1183

Laudano, Eric Senior Associate AD, High Performance
ST. JOSEPH'S UNIVERSITY ATHLETICS, 345

Lauder, Sue Director of Athletics
FITCHBURG STATE COLLEGE (FSC) ATHLETICS, 385

Lauderdale, Darrel Governor
SOUTHEASTERN AAU ASSOCIATION, 216

Lauderdale, Tim Associate AD, Internal Operations
NORTHWESTERN OKLAHOMA STATE UNIVERSITY ATHLETICS, 340

Lauer, Harvey President
AMERICAN SPORTS DATA, INC., 773

Laufenberg, Babe Sports Anchor
KTVT-TV, 682, 696

Laughlin, Arthur General Manager
PALM BEACH KENNEL CLUB, 1047

Laughlin, Roy General Manager
XTRA SPORTS RADIO 1150 AM, 633, 673

Laughren, Christine Manager of Marketing & Communications
YPSILANTI AREA CONVENTION AND VISITORS BUREAU, 250

Laundner, David Government Affairs DVP
MASON CITY CONVENTION & VISITOR BUREAU, 240

Launius, Jeff General Manager
MYLAN WORLD TEAM TENNIS, 177

Laur, Bernie Online Sales
1500 ESPN SPORTSTALK, 605

Laura, Mark General Manager
WSHR-FM, 666

Lauren, Ralph Chief Executive Officer
POLO BY RALPH LAUREN, 1175

Laurenzano, Carol Stadium Operations Director
YANKEE STADIUM, 1021

Lauria, Anthony Lawyer
LAURIA TOKUNGA GATES & LINN, LLP, 889

Laurita, Brandi Director of Athletics
UNIVERSITY OF FINDLAY (UF) ATHLETICS, 358

Lauscha, Dennis President
NATIONAL FOOTBALL LEAGUE/NFL, 57, 58, 96

Lauzon, Nicole Membership Coordinator
EVENT SERVICE PROFESSIONALS ASSOCIATION, 219

Lavallee-Smotherman, Jordan General Manager/Head Coach
EAST COAST HOCKEY LEAGUE/ECHL, 131

Laven, Pete President/General Manager
FRONTIER LEAGUE, 41, 966, 967, 1001

Laverentz, Rusty Womens Basketball Head Coach
NJCAA REGION II WOMEN'S, 286

Lavertue, Jacques General Manager / Outdoor Division
KARHU U.S.A. LIMITED, 1151

Laviano, Don Producer
SUNDAY SPORTS REPLAY, 682

Lavigne, Lauren Assistant Athletic Director
PLYMOUTH STATE UNIVERSITY ATHLETICS, 397

Laviolette, Peter Head Coach
NATIONAL HOCKEY LEAGUE/NHL, 125

Lavone, Randy President/General Manager
APPALACHIAN LEAGUE, 33

Law, Caleb President
BALLANDRA CORPORATION, 1103

Law, Doug Sports Reporter
SIDNEY SUN TELEGRAPH, 531

Law, Jason Weekend Sports Anchor/Reporter
WDEF-TV, 701

Lawhorne, Dennis Project Manager
E.B. ROTONDI & SONS, INC., 1126

Lawing, Chelsea Assistant Athletic Trainer
MARS HILL UNIVERSITY ATHLETICS, 363

Lawing, Todd Associate Athletics Director
SHUFORD GYM/STADIUM, 1002

Lawler, Clark Executive VP
DODGER INDUSTRIES INC., 1125

Lawler, Micky President
WOMEN'S TENNIS ASSOCIATION TOUR, 176

Lawler, Nicole Director of TourismMarketing & Developm
SOUTH BEND/MISHAWAKA CONVENTION & VISITORS BUREAU, 264

Lawler, Suzanne News/Sports Anchor/Reporter
WMAZ-TV, 706

Lawler, Whitney Sports Information Director
REGIS UNIVERSITY ATHLETICS, 368

Lawler, Will Deputy AD, Legal & Regulatory Affairs
GEORGIA ATHLETICS, UNIVERSITY OF, 331

Lawlor, Anita Chief Operating Officer
INTERNATIONAL HEALTH, RACQUET & SPORTSCLUB ASSOCIATION (IHRSA), 0

Lawlor, Margie Controller
CHICAGO DISTRICT GOLF ASSOCIATION, 110

Lawn, John President & CEO
AMERICAN HOCKEY LEAGUE/AHL, 127

Lawrence, Al Product Development VP
EXCALIBUR ELECTRONICS, 1130

Lawrence, Allen Vice President/Assistant GM
CAROLINA LEAGUE, 37

Lawrence, Andy Head Athletic Trainer
ALBION COLLEGE ATHLETICS-ALBION, 376

Lawrence, Brad Group Sales
SONOMA RACEWAY, 1033

Lawrence, Brent Chief Executive Officer/Managing Attorne
BUSINESS LAW VENTURES, 870

Lawrence, Chris VP, Tickets & Premium
NATIONAL FOOTBALL LEAGUE/NFL, 29, 96, 1020

Lawrence, David President
LAWRENCE METAL PRODUCTS, 1154

Lawrence, Frank President, Basketball Operations
NATIONAL BASKETBALL ASSOCIATION/NBA, 57

Lawrence, Fred President
U.S. COLLEGIATE SPORTS COUNCIL, 290

Lawrence, Jim Controller
FIBERESIN INDUSTRIES, INC., 1132

Lawrence, Leslie Inside Sales
ELECTRO-MECH SCOREBOARD COMPANY, 1128

Lawrence, Mickey President
IMAGE IMPACT, 757

Lawrence, Reggie Contact
MOPRO, 1164

Lawrence, Rodney SVP Store Marketing
SHOPKO STORES, INC., 1237

Lawrence, Steven Chief Merchandising Officer
STAGE STORES, INC., 1238

Lawrence, Terri Director Library & Information Resources
WINSTEAD ATTORNEYS, 916

Lawrence, Wendy President/Women's
COLLEGE SQUASH ASSOCIATION/MENS & WOMEN'S INTERCOLLEGIATE COMPETI, 171

Lawrenson, Scott Assistant AD, Sports Medicine
LIBERTY UNIVERSITY ATHLETICS, 334

Laws, P. Promotion Director
KTVB-TV, 695

Laws, Ryan Chief Operating Officer
PRO IMAGE, 1235

Lawson, Angela Athletic Coordinator
TEXAS COLLEGE ATHLETICS, 322

Lawson, Brian Sports Director
WWUP-TV, 712

Lawson, Cody Maintenance Crew Chief
CASPER EVENTS CENTER, 955

Lawson, Daniel Executive Committee Member
MEYER, DARRAGH, BUCKLER, BEBENEK & ECK, PLLC, 895

Lawson, James Chief Executive Officer
WOODBINE ENTERTAINMENT GROUP, 78

Lawson, Janet Vendor Support and Custom Sales Manager
SUNTIME/LINKSWALKER, 1198

Lawson, Jeff Director of Marketing
THOR-LO, INC., 1201

Lawson, Joleen Director
BILLIARD AND BOWLING INSTITUTE OF AMERICA, 61, 65

Lawson, Josh Tickets and Merchandise
APPALACHIAN LEAGUE, 33

Lawson, Kerry GM
LES BOIS PARK, 1041

Lawson, Stephanie Publisher
PENNSYLVANIA EQUESTRIAN, 576

Lawson, Tom President / Chief Operating Officer
BIG TIME SPORTS APPAREL, INC., 1106

Lawson, Trisha Sales Assistant
ARBITRON, INC., 1213

Lawther, Josh General Manager
FLORIDA STATE LEAGUE, 39

Lawton, Holly Deputy Sports Editor
KANSAS CITY STAR, 499

Lawton, Logan Collegiate Sports Director
TEXAS FOOTBALL, 588

Lax, Emil Lawyer
SEGAL & LAX, 905

Lax, Skip Assistant Commissioner
SOUTH CAROLINA HIGH SCHOOL LEAGUE, 202

Lay, Howard Product Management VP
PRINCE SPORTS, 1177

Lay, Philip Head of UK Operations
RHINO SPORTS MARKETING, 805

Lay, Rob President
NATIONAL LITTLE BRITCHES RODEO ASSOCIATION, 267

Layhew, Vicki Sales & Marketing Manager
KANKAKEE COUNTY CONVENTION & VISITORS BUREAU, 237

Layman, Andrew Assistant General Manager
CAROLINA LEAGUE, 37

Layman, Michael Attorney/CPA
LAYMAN, MICHAEL L., 889

Layton, Denise Managing Editor
SOARING, 581

Layton, Jason Deputy Director of Athletics
MIAMI ATHLETICS, UNIVERSITY OF, 336

Layton, Jim General Manager
NATIONAL TRAIL RACEWAY, 1029

Lazaro, Patrick Interim Head Athletic Trainer
CALIFORNIA STATE UNIVERSITY-EAST BAY ATHLETICS, 353

Leivermann, Corey Associate Head Coach
UNITED STATES HOCKEY LEAGUE, 137
Leiweke, Tim Chair & CEO, OVG360
CANADA LIFE PLACE, 954
Lekhtman, Gregory President
BIOSIG INSTRUMENTS, INC., 1107
Leland, Carl Vice President
NATIONAL ASSOCIATION OF COLLEGIATE
GYMNASTICS COACHES - WOMEN, 120
Leland, Gary Owner / President
BASEBALLJUNK.COM, 1217
Leloudis, George Executive Director
CARDWELL, VICTOR, 871
Lemak, Lawrence Founder
NATIONAL CENTER FOR SPORTS SAFETY,
921
Lemak, Matthew Chairman
NATIONAL CENTER FOR SPORTS SAFETY,
266
Lemak, Matthew Chief Executive Officer
LEMAK SPORTS MEDICINE &
ORTHOPEDICS, 920
Lemay, Christina Associate Director
ESPN TELEVISION, 674
Lembo, Elaine Managing Editor
CRUISING WORLD, 556
Lemerand, Eric IRM Operations Manager
ELLIS PARK, 1037
Lemieux, Jason Recreational Sales & Marketing
NOLIMITZ, 1169
Lemieux, Mario Minority Owner
NATIONAL HOCKEY LEAGUE/NHL, 125, 192
Lemm, Erica Senior Woman Administrator
YESHIVA UNIVERSITY ATHLETICS, 408
Lemon, Brian VP, Lacrosse Operations
NATIONAL LACROSSE LEAGUE, 142
Lemon, Chet Director
FLORIDA AAU ASSOCIATION, 214
Lemon, Jennifer Advertising Director
PRESS-TELEGRAM, 523
Lemon, John Director, System Implementation
and Cus
TICKET TO GO, LLC, 933
Lemond, Mark President/Chief Executive Officer
SHOE CARNIVAL, 1237
Lemons, Bruce President
FORESITE DESIGN, INC., 1057
Lemons, David Principal
COOKE DOUGLASS FARR LEMONS/LTD.,
1052
Lemons, David Principal
COOKE DOUGLASS FARR LEMONS/LTD.,
1052
Lemox, Cheryl Senior Vice President, Marketing
& Promo
INTEGRATED SPORTS MARKETING, 678
Lempke, Roger VP
NEBRASKA SPORTS COUNCIL, 263
Len, Robert Partner
WOLF GROUP-NY, 817
Lenarz, Josh Assistant Athletics Director
TRINITY CHRISTIAN COLLEGE ATHLETICS,
322
Lenfest, Richard Athletics Director
WESTFIELD STATE COLLEGE ATHLETICS
(WSC), 405
Lengerich, Ryan Director of Sports Information
MOUNT ST. JOSEPH ATHLETICS, COLLEGE
OF, 394
Lenggenhager, Marilyn Treasurer
ARKANSAS WOMEN'S GOLF ASSOCIATION,
110
Lenich, Mike Treasurer
U.S. HOCKEY HALL OF FAME, 259
Lennon, Dale Director of Athletics
SAINT MARY ATHLETICS, UNIVERSITY OF,
319
Lennon, Dave Sports Reporter (Yankees)
NEWSDAY, 513
Lennon, Elizabeth Sports Life coach
PATTERSON SPORTS VENTURES, 800
Lennox, Dave President/CEO
SPECIAL OLYMPICS WASHINGTON, 197
Lennox, William University President
SAINT LEO UNIVERSITY, 369
Lenstrom, Jay Chief Marketing Officer
GMR MARKETING, 756
Lenth, Teri Corporate Sponsorships Director
BIG TEN ATHLETIC CONFERENCE, 292

Lentz, Ben Director, Ticket Operations
NATIONAL FOOTBALL LEAGUE/NFL, 96
Lentz, Heather Promotions Director
KSDR-AM, 628
Lentz, Mike Senior Director, Ticket Operations
AMERICAN LEAGUE OF PROFESSIONAL
BASEBALL CLUBS, THE, 30
Lenz, Darrin Service Manager
AUTOMATED BATTING CAGES
CORPORATION, 1102
Lenz, John Sports Editor
DAILY STAR, 480
Lenz, Mark Group SVP/Chief Financial Officer
SHOR, ALAN P., 906
Lenz, Melanie Chief Planning & Development
Officer
AMERICAN LEAGUE OF PROFESSIONAL
BASEBALL CLUBS, THE, 30
Leo, Don Sports Director
WJOX-AM SPORTS RADIO, 652
Leon, Lee Director of Athletics
ABILENE CHRISTIAN UNIVERSITY
ATHLETICS, 337, 350, 1013
Leon, Rene Program Director
KZNM-FM, 633
Leon, Rennie Director of Marketing Development
SMOKIES PARK, 1003
Leonard, Amy Director of Development for
Athletics
CALIFORNIA BAPTIST UNIVERSITY
ATHLETICS, 309
Leonard, Bruce Classified Manager
STANDARD-SPEAKER, 534
Leonard, John Executive Director
AMERICAN SWIMMING COACHES
ASSOCIATION, 172
Leonard, Kelly General Manager
KRAN, 627
Leonard, Leanne Secretary
WOMEN'S METROPOLITAN GOLF
ASSOCIATION, 117
Leonard, Ran Chairman
OKLAHOMA HORSE RACING COMMISSION,
81
Leonard, Scott CEO
A.D.D. MARKETING AND ADVERTISING, 771
Leonard, Sean Svp/CFO
AMBAC ASSURANCE CORPORATION, 767
Leonard, Tod Sports Reporter
SAN DIEGO UNION-TRIBUNE, 528
Leonardi, Dave Publisher
SKIER NEWS, 581
Leone, Charles Operations Division Manager
ORLANDO CITRUS BOWL, 990
Leone, Mike Head Coach & General Manager
UNITED STATES HOCKEY LEAGUE, 137
Leonis, Ted Founder/Chairman/Majoriy
Owner/CEO
VERIZON CENTER, 1015
Leonsis, Ted Founder, Chair, Principal Partner &
CEO
NATIONAL HOCKEY LEAGUE/NHL, 58, 126
Lepine, Gilles Director, Performance and Team
Support
BRITISH COLUMBIA ATHLETICS,
UNIVERSITY OF, 309
Lepkowski, Craig Secretary
INTERNATIONAL POLICE MOUNTAIN BIKE
ASSOCIATION (IPMBA), 70
Lepore, Marianne Office Administrator
GARDEN EMPIRE VOLLEYBALL
ASSOCIATION, 211
Lepping, Rich Chairman of the Board
U.S. CURLING ASSOCIATION, 69
Lerch, E. Senior Vice President
L. ROBERT KIMBALL & ASSOCIATES, 1061
Lerch, Wayne Principal
ERICKSON MCGOVERN, 1055
Lerette, Lindsay Sales and Marketing Manager
KELLOGG ARENA, 246, 978
Lerick, Tom General Manager / Construction
H&B SPECIALIZED PRODUCTS, 1141
Lerman, Steve Director, Sales and Marketing
LYCIAN STAGE LIGHTING, 1158
Lermond, David Deputy Executive Secretary
VIRGINIA RACING COMMISSION, 82
Lerner, Mark Principal Owner
NATIONAL LEAGUE OF PROFESSIONAL
BASEBALL CLUBS, THE, 32

Lerner, Stephen Partner
SQUIRE, SANDERS & DEMPSEY, LLP, 908
Lerner, Theodore Managing Principal Owner
NATIONALS PARK, 988
Les, Wally GHIN Regional Manager-SE Florida
FLORIDA STATE GOLF ASSOCIATION, 111
Lesako, Mark Head Athletic Trainer
WASHINGTON & JEFFERSON COLLEGE
ATHLETICS (W&J), 405
Lesane, Jamaal COO, Madison Square Garden
Sports
NATIONAL BASKETBALL ASSOCIATION/NBA,
57
Lesar, Al Sports Assistant Editor
SOUTH BEND TRIBUNE, 531
Leschper, Lee Advertising Manager
JUNEAU EMPIRE, 499
Lese, Jon Treasurer
FAIRFIELD COUNTY SPORTS COMMISSION,
233
Lesene, Troy Head Coach
MAJOR LEAGUE SOCCER, 157
Lesher, Wayne President
AMERICAN RACING DRIVERS CLUB
INC./ARDC, 15
Leske, Lucy Vice-Chairman
NJCAA REGION XXI MEN'S, 289
Lesley, Campbell Publicity Director
WHEELING ISLAND GAMING, INC., 1047
Leslie, Chad General Manager
WESTERN HOCKEY LEAGUE, 139
Leslie, Jack Chairman
WEBER SHANDWICK WORLDWIDE, 816
Lesmerises, Doug Sports Reporter
NEWS JOURNAL (DE), 512
Lesniak, Raymond Senior Partner/Corporate Law
Department
WEINER LESNIAK LLP, 859
Lesnick, David Sports Editor
DAILY INTER LAKE, 477
Lesnik, Josh President
KEMPERLESNIK, 103
Lessard, Jeff Executive Vice President
FOX RIVER MILLS, INC., 1135
Lessard, John President
FOX RIVER MILLS, INC., 1135
Lesser, Jonathan Sports Associate Editor
T & L GOLF, 587
Lesser, Russel President
BODY GLOVE INTERNATIONAL, INC., 1108
Lessinger, Claire Sales/Events Manager
TAMPA BAY SPORTS COMMISSION, 247
Lessiter, Frank Editor
AMERICAN FARRIERS JOURNAL, 549
Lessiter, Mike President
AMERICAN FARRIERS JOURNAL, 549
Lester, Jason Event Manager
US CELLULAR CENTER, 1014
Lester, Kerril Sports Editor
DAILY TIMES (OK), 480
Lester, Mike Director of Compliance
SAINT MARY'S UNIVERSITY (MN)
ATHLETICS, 399
Lester, Pamela President
LESTER SPORTS & ENTERTAINMENT, 793
Lester, Robin Treasurer
SOUTHERN ILLINOIS GOLF ASSOCIATION,
115
Lester, Sean Deputy AD, Administration
KANSAS UNIVERSITY ATHLETICS, 334
Lester, William Executive Director
METROPOLITAN SPORTS FACILITIES
COMMISSION, 240
Letang, Alan Head Coach
ONTARIO HOCKEY LEAGUE, 134
Letcher, Mark President - EWIOA Officials
Association
EASTERN INTERCOLLEGIATE WRESTLING
ASSOCIATION, 180
Letellier, Joe Executive Director
MASHANTUCKET PEQUOT TRIBAL NATION'S
ATHLETIC COMMISSION, 240
Letizia, Mike Head Coach
NORTH AMERICAN HOCKEY LEAGUE, 132
Letourneau, Richard President & Governor
QUEBEC MARITIMES MAJOR JUNIOR
HOCKEY LEAGUE, 135
Letsinger, Ed Managing Editor
HOMETOWN GOLF, 563

Letson, Wayne Facility Engineer
USF SUN DOME, 756, 1014

Lett, Frank Associate Executive Director/Sports
KINGSPORT CONVENTION & VISITORS BUREAU, 237

Letterman, David Co-Owner
INDYCAR, 18, 22

Lettre, Scott Director of Sales
PIONEER BASEBALL LEAGUE, 50, 956

Letuligasenoa, Nona Assistant Athletic Director, Communicati
UNIVERSITY OF ALASKA FAIRBANKS ATHLETICS, 373

Letzler, Jon President & CEO Augusta Sportswear Group
THE SPORTS & FITNESS INDUSTRY ASSOCIATION (SFIA), 813

Leube, Steve Executive Director
USTA NORTHERN CALIFORNIA, 176

Leukhardt, Larry Dir Sls
ATHLETIC TRAINING EQUIPMENT COMPANY/ATEC, 1101

Leung, Linden Finance & Operations Director
VOLLEYBALL CANADA, 179

Leutholtz, Brain Graduate Program Director
BAYLOR UNIVERSITY, 411

Lev, Mark Co-Managing Director
FENWAY SPORTS GROUP, 783

Lev, Michael Sports Reporter
ORANGE COUNTY REGISTER, 516

Levac, Lynn Administrative Assistant
LAURENTIAN UNIVERSITY, 422

Levak, Larry Advertising Manager
CHARLESTON GAZETTE, 469

Levanda, Eric Associate Athletic Director
HUNTINGDON COLLEGE ATHLETICS, 388

Levandoski, Brian NCRC Arena Manager
CAMBRIA COUNTY WAR MEMORIAL, 954

Leveille, Joel Marketing Director
INTERNATIONAL MASCOT CORPORATION, 1148

Levendusky, Roger News Director
WDOR-FM, 643

Levengood, Barney Executive Director
LUCAS OIL STADIUM, 984

Levesque, Christopher Marketing VP
ANVIL KNITWEAR INC., 1099

Levesque, John Sports Columnist
SEATTLE POST-INTELLIGENCER, 529

Levesque, Julie Senior Associate AD/SWA
TEXAS AT EL PASO ATHLETICS, UNIVERSITY OF, 346

Levesque, Lucas Assistant Director of Athletics
MAINE AT FORT KENT ATHLETICS, UNIVERSITY OF, 315

Levesque, Paul Executive VP, Talent, Live Events & Crea
WORLD WRESTLING ENTERTAINMENT, 181

Levesque, Sarah Associate Athletic Director
BEMIDJI STATE UNIVERSITY ATHLETICS, 352

Levey, Jon Senior Editor
TENNIS, 588

Levi, David Dean
WEISTART, JOHN C., 915

Levick, Cheryl Director of Athletics
GEORGIA STATE UNIVERSITY, 419

Levien, Jason Co-Chair & Chief Executive Officer
MAJOR LEAGUE SOCCER, 157

Levin, Adam Sports Information Director
BRANDEIS UNIVERSITY ATHLETICS, 378

Levin, Alan Principal Owner
NEW YORK-PENNSYLVANIA LEAGUE, 47, 1005

Levin, Andrew EVP and Chief Legal Officer
SFX/CLEAR CHANNEL COMMUNICATIONS, 807

Levin, Barry Sales VP
PERFECT CURVE, INC., 1173

Levin, Brian Field Manager
NATIONAL PRO FASTPITCH, 171

Levin, Don Chair & Governor
AMERICAN HOCKEY LEAGUE/AHL, 127

Levin, Ed Publicity Director
DAD VAIL REGATTA, 147

Levin, Eric President
LEVTRAN ENTERPRISES, 1232

Levin, Gregg President
PERFECT CURVE, INC., 1173

Levin, Kim VP Of Sales
POOLMASTER, INC., 1175

Levin, Rick Co-Founder and Chief Executive Officer
LEVTRAN ENTERPRISES, 1232

Levin, Sue Co-Founder / Chief Executive Officer
LUCY.COM, 1232

Levine, Brian Vice President of Corporate Relationship
NEW YORK-PENNSYLVANIA LEAGUE, 47, 997

Levine, David President
PROMARK TELEVISION, 601

Levine, Deborah Vice President
SPORTS PROFILES, 585

Levine, Drew President Security Services
WACKENHUT SPORTS SECURITY, 766

Levine, Ed President
INTERNATIONAL BOXING ORGANIZATION, 67

Levine, Heather Partner
FOSTER, DON, 880

Levine, Howard Chairman and Chief Executive Officer
FAMILY DOLLAR STORES, 1227

Levine, Jay General Manager
KZEP SPORTS RADIO, 633

Levine, Jeremy Vice President
INTERNATIONAL BOXING ORGANIZATION, 67

Levine, Joel Counsel
MCBRIDE, B. GARY, 893

Levine, Jordan Associate Director of Athletics
MERCY COLLEGE ATHLETICS, 363

Levine, Lisa President
CHICAGO SPORTS PROFILE, 554

Levine, Lisa President
SPORTS PROFILES, 585

Levine, Michael President
DORNA USA, LLC, 781

Levine, Pamela EVP, Marketing
HBO SPORTS, 676

Levine, Patricia Executive Administrator
INTERPERFORMANCES, INC., 839

Levine, Randy President
AMERICAN LEAGUE OF PROFESSIONAL BASEBALL CLUBS, THE, 30, 1021

Levine, Shana Director of Athletics
LEWIS & CLARK COLLEGE ATHLETICS (L & C), 390

Levine, Stuart President / Owner
RAMSEY OUTDOOR STORE, 1235

Levine, Todd VP Marketing / Sales
ALLESON ATHLETIC, DON, 1096

Levine, Zach Creative Director
PROJECT SPORTS MARKETING, 803

Levins, Matt Sports Reporter
HAWK EYE, 492

Levinson, Arthur Chief Executive Officer
WEEKEND EXERCISE COMPANY, 1209

Levinson, Bruce Vice Chairman/Chief Executive Officer
PARAMOUNT HEADWEAR, INC., 1172

Levinson, Michael President
WEEKEND EXERCISE COMPANY, 1209

Levinthal, Keith Director of Athletics
MANHATTANVILLE COLLEGE ATHLETICS, 391

Levit, Janet Dean
THE UNIVERSITY OF TULSA COLLEGE OF LAW, 911

Levitsky, Alex President-Professional Division
U.S. TENNIS COURT & TRACK BUILDERS ASSOCIATION, 1063

Levitt, Chris Vice President
DETLEF SCHREMPF FOUNDATION, 191

Levitt, Neal Controller
CANAL JEAN CO., 1222

Levitt, Steven President
THE Q SCORES COMPANY, 813

Levoy, Jamie Executive Director
WOMEN'S PREMIER SOCCER LEAGUE, 165

Levra, Craig Chairman of the Board, Chief Executive O
SPORT CHALET, INC., 1237

Levschuk, Steve President
COYLE & GREER AWARDS CANADA LTD., 1120

Levy, Alan Attorney
LINDNER & MARSACK, S.C., 891

Levy, Bill Director of Ticket Operations
FLORIDA STATE LEAGUE, 39

Levy, Charles Attorney
CASTILLO, ANGEL, 871

Levy, David President
TURNER SPORTS, 715

Levy, Evan Senior Event Manager/Talent Producer
GLOBAL SPORTS & ENTERTAINMENT, 198, 785

Levy, Howard President
HYP HATS, LTD, 1147

Levy, Jay Coordinating Producer
ESPN, 682, 683

Levy, John Chairman of the Board
THE SCORE TELEVISION NETWORK, 677

Levy, John President/CEO
L&L GROUP/FOREMOST ATHLETIC APPAREL, 1153

Levy, Lance Sales/Public Relations Coordinator
SCOTT USA, 1186

Levy, Larry Chairman/Founder
LEVY RESTAURANTS SPORTS & ENTERTAINMENT, 1067

Levy, Leonard President
SPORTSWORLD CONSULTANTS, 856

Levy, Matt Director of Sports Information
DELAWARE VALLEY COLLEGE(DVC) ATHLETICS, 382

Levy, Michael Founder/President/Chied Executive Office
SPORTSLINE USA, INC./CBS.SPORTSLINE.COM, 929

Levy, Paul Vice President
PGA OF AMERICA/PROFESSIONAL GOLFERS' ASSOCIATION OF AMERICA, 105

Levy, Richard Team Doctor
NATIONAL PRO FASTPITCH, 171

Levy, Richard Chief Business Development Officer
INTERNATIONAL CREATIVE MANAGEMENT, INC., 839

Levy, Robert Chief Business
ATLANTIC CITY RACE COURSE, 1035

Levy, Steve Anchor
ESPN, 683

Levy, Stuart Chief Financial Officer / Chief Executiv
ODD JOB TRADING, 1234

Lew, Susan Head Athletic Trainer
UNIVERSITY OF WISCONSIN - STOUT ATHLETICS (UW-STOUT), 407

Lewandowski, John Senior Associate AD, Communications
LOUISIANA AT MONROE ATHLETICS, UNIVERSITY OF, 335

Lewandowski, Randy General Manager
INTERNATIONAL LEAGUE, 42, 1016

Lewczyk, Henry Vice President Marketing/Research
STRIKE TEN ENTERTAINMENT, INC., 812

Lewellen, Shelly Sports Reporter
TUCSON CITIZEN, 542

Lewellyn, Mark Sales and Marketing Director
INNOVATIVE ELECTRONIC DESIGNS, INC., 821

Lewenhaupt, Count President
BALLCO PRODUCTS, INC., 1104

Lewin, Harris Vice Chancellor
TOOMEY FIELD, 1010

Lewis, AJ Box Office Manager
WHITTEMORE CENTER ARENA, 1018

Lewis, Aylwin Chief Executive Officer, Kmart Retail
KMART CORPORATION, 1231

Lewis, Aylwin President / Chief Executive Officer
SEARS, ROEBUCK & CO., 1236

Lewis, Barry Sports Writer
TULSA WORLD, 542

Lewis, Brad Director, Racing
FINGER LAKES GAMING & RACETRACK, 1038

Lewis, Brian Sports Reporter
NEW YORK POST, 510

Lewis, Chad Associate AD, Development
BRIGHAM YOUNG UNIVERSITY ATHLETICS, 325

MacDonald, Stew President & Chief Revenue Officer
NATIONAL HOCKEY LEAGUE/NHL, 124

MacDougal, Mike President and CEO
FIBERESIN INDUSTRIES, INC., 1132

MacDougall, Gardiner Head Coach
QUEBEC MARITIMES MAJOR JUNIOR HOCKEY LEAGUE, 135

MacDougall, Taylor General Manager, Hockey Operations
QUEBEC MARITIMES MAJOR JUNIOR HOCKEY LEAGUE, 135

MacFarland, Chris General Manager
NATIONAL HOCKEY LEAGUE/NHL, 124

MacGregor, Cameron Tournament Director
NORTHERN CALIFORNIA SECTIONAL OFFICE, 107

MacGregor, Ian President
CROQUET CANADA, 69

MacHardy, Scott Co-founder / VP
COED SPORTSWEAR INC, 1117

MacInnis, Marty Executive VP/CFO
COTTON BOWL CLASSIC, 90

MacIntyre, Drew Developmental Goaltending Coach
AMERICAN HOCKEY LEAGUE/AHL, 128

MacKay, Matt National Franchise Manager
PRO IMAGE, 1235

MacKeigan, Richard General Manager
VAN ANDEL ARENA, 1015

MacKenzie, Ken Head Coach & Assistant General Manager
ONTARIO HOCKEY LEAGUE, 135

MacKinnon, Dan Senior VP & Assistant General Manager
NATIONAL HOCKEY LEAGUE/NHL, 125

MacLachlan, Don Executive Vice President of Administrati
LP FIELD, 984

MacLean, Cail Assistant Coach
NATIONAL HOCKEY LEAGUE/NHL, 123

MacLellan, Brian President, Hockey Operations & General M
NATIONAL HOCKEY LEAGUE/NHL, 126

MacLeod, Brian Director
INTERNATIONAL BLIND GOLF ASSOCIATION, 102

MacLeod, Bruce Sports Columnist
MACOMB DAILY, 504

MacLeod, Judy Commissioner
CONFERENCE USA, 295

MacMahon, Tim Sports Reporter
DALLAS MORNING NEWS, 481

MacNeill, Brandon Deputy AD/Chief Revenue Officer
DENVER ATHLETICS, UNIVERSITY OF, 328

MacNeill, Harris President / Chief Executive Officer
MACNEILL ENGINEERING-CHAMPS GOLF SPIKES, 1158

MacPhail, Andy President
CITIZENS BANK PARK, 957

MacPherson, Aimee Director, Soccer Operations
WOMEN'S PREMIER SOCCER LEAGUE, 167

Macapugay, Anthony Manager of Athletic Communications
ST. JOSEPH'S COLLEGE (NY) ATHLETICS, 401

Macaulay, Colin Sports Producer
WCAU-TV, 700

Maccholz, Mike Associate Athletic Director
MISSOURI VALLEY COLLEGE ATHLETICS, 316

Macdonald, James Professor
MACDONALD, JAMES, 891

Mace, Corey Head Coach & Defensive Coordinator
CANADIAN FOOTBALL LEAGUE/CFL, 93

Mace, Gregg Sports Director
WHTM-TV, 704

Macgregor, Bruce SVP Product Marketing
L.A. GEAR, 1153

Mach, Greg President
PROFESSIONAL GYM, 1178

Machado, Colleen Advertising Manager
KINGMAN DAILY MINER, 500

Machado, Emily Director of Sports Information
LASELL COLLEGE ATHLETICS, 390

Machado, Manny Sports Director
KIEM-TV, 691

Macheen, Bernie President
FLORIDA, UNIVERSITY OF, 418

Machen, Bob President
US AIRWAYS CENTER, 1014

Machen, James President
BERNARD, PAMELA J., 865

Machi, Mario Director of Handicapping
GOLF ASSOCIATION OF PHILADELPHIA, 111

Macias, Sabrina Director, Brand & Consumer Marketing Com
NASCAR, 686

Maciaszek, Marty Communications Director
NATIONAL SPORTING GOODS ASSOCIATION, 285

Maciejewski, Sue HRM
TAMPA SPORTS AUTHORITY, 247

Maciocia, Danny General Manager
CANADIAN FOOTBALL LEAGUE/CFL, 93

Mack, Art Sports Director
KRIS-TV, 688, 694

Mack, Brian Program Director
KOOC-FM, 626

Mack, Ed Vice President - HWS Beverage
CALIFORNIA LEAGUE (A-LEVEL), 36, 977

Mack, John Ford Family Director of Athletics
PRINCETON UNIVERSITY ATHLETICS, 342

Mack, Marta Chair/Director
CLAFLIN UNIVERSITY, 413

Mack, Tim Weekend Sports Anchor
WRGB-TV, 708

Mackall, Dave Sports Reporter
PITTSBURGH TRIBUNE-REVIEW, 520

Mackay, Ally General Manager & Chief Soccer Officer
MAJOR LEAGUE SOCCER, 157

Mackay, Barry Owner
BMK SPORTS, 751

Mackay, Greg Director of Public Facilities
KNOXVILLE CIVIC AUDITORIUM/COLISEUM, 980

Mackenroth, Kellie Marketing & Circulation Manager
SOUTHERN BOATING MAGAZINE, 569, 582

Mackensen, Sebastian President & CEO
BMW OF NORTH AMERICA, LLC, 726

Mackenzie, Leslie Publisher
SPORTS MARKET PLACE DIRECTORY, 596

Mackenzie, Paige LPGA Player Director
LADIES PROFESSIONAL GOLF ASSOCIATION/LPGA, 103

Mackenzie, Scott Academy Director
USL LEAGUE TWO, 160, 164

Mackey, Brian President
MACKEY MARKETING GROUP, INC., 794

Mackey, Kimberly Office Administrator
VIRGINIA RACING COMMISSION, 82

Mackey, Marcia Sport Management Program Director
CENTRAL MICHIGAN UNIVERSITY, 413

Mackey, Patrick President
MERCURY MARINE, 1162

Mackey, Rich Marketing/Sales
MONROE COUNTY SPORTS COMMISSION, 241

Mackie, Leila Comm & Player Development
PHILADELPHIA PGA SECTIONAL OFFICE, 107

Mackin, Brian Director of Athletics
NORTH CAROLINA GREENSBORO ATHLETICS, UNIVERSITY OF, 339

Mackin, Todd President, Spire Holdings
EAST COAST HOCKEY LEAGUE/ECHL, 129, 130

Mackinnon, Dan General Manager
AMERICAN HOCKEY LEAGUE/AHL, 129

Mackinnon, Kyle Director, Pro Scouting
NATIONAL HOCKEY LEAGUE/NHL, 124

Maclean, A.J. Assistant Coach
AMERICAN HOCKEY LEAGUE/AHL, 128

Maclean, Doug Founder
VECTRA FITNESS CORPORATION, 1207

Maclean, Gordon Secretary
U.S. CURLING ASSOCIATION, 69

Maclean, John Associate Coach
NATIONAL HOCKEY LEAGUE/NHL, 125

Maclean, Tom General Sales Manager
P.A.S.S. SPORTS, 601

Maclellan, Dan President
OPENSEATS, INC., 932

Maclin, Elizabeth Executive Vice President
TROUT UNLIMITED, 87

Macready, Melanie Account Executive
CENTER CITY FILM & VIDEO, 598

Macrina, David Human Studies Professor
UNIVERSITY OF ALABAMA - COLLEGE OF EDUCATION/ HUMAN ENVIRONMENTAL, 435

Macrina, Jon Purchasing Manager
MARTY GILMAN, INC. DBA GILMAN GEAR, 1160

Macur, Juliet Sports Reporter
NEW YORK TIMES, 511

Macy-Baker, Lisa Compliance Officer
LINFIELD COLLEGE ATHLETICS, 390

Madden, Amy Sales Support Manager, Lifts Product Man
DRAPER INC., 1125

Madden, Gary Manager
SEAWAY MATS, INC., 1187

Madden, John President
MIDDLE ATLANTIC PGA, 75, 106

Madden, Larry Chief Financial officer
ROSE BOWL STADIUM, 999

Madden, Lee Sr. Director of Administrative Services
NATIONAL STRENGTH AND CONDITIONING ASSOCIATION, 921

Madden, Mark Host
THE MARK MADDEN SHOW, 607

Madden, Midge Administrative Assistant
HOPE INTERNATIONAL UNIVERSITY ATHLETICS, 313

Madden, Steve Editor-in-Chief
BICYCLING, 552

Madden, Thomas Chairman & Chief Executive Officer
TRANSMEDIA GROUP, 603

Madden, Thomas Partner
ADAMSKI MOROSKI MADDEN & GREEN LLP, 861

Madden, Tim Sales Officer
AUSTAD'S GOLF STORE'S, 1217

Madden, Warren Business and Finance VP
BLACKWELDER, MURRAY, 827

Madding, Scott Director, Global Casino Sales
UNITED STATES PLAYING CARD COMPANY, THE/WPT, 1206

Maddocks, David Global Marketing VP
CONVERSE, INC., 1223

Maddoni, Gaston Head Coach
USL CHAMPIONSHIP, 159

Maddox, Artis Assistant Athletic Director
FLORIDA MEMORIAL UNIVERSITY ATHLETICS, 312

Maddox, Rick Director of Food and Beverage
EVERETT MEMORIAL STADIUM, 964

Mader, Dan President/Chief Executive Officer
FANNING/HOWEY ASSOCIATES, INC., 1055

Mader, Daniel President and Chief Executive Officer
FANNING/HOWEY ASSOCIATES, INC., 1055

Maderer, Jason Volusia County Sports Marketing Manager
KLXS-FM, 623

Madgiak, Jennifer Associate Athletic Director
PURDUE UNIVERSITY CALUMET ATHLETICS, 319

Madia, Matthew Head Athletic Trainer
STATE UNIVERSITY OF NEW YORK INSTITUTE OF TECHNOLOGY ATHLETICS(SU, 402

Madigan, Andrew Operations Director
THE SPORTS AND ENTERTAINMENT COMPANY LLC, 603

Madigan, Jim Director of Athletics and Recreation
NORTHEASTERN UNIVERSITY ATHLETICS, 340, 985

Madison, Dale Chairperson
RIVERSIDE ARENA, 997

Madison, Jacque Director of Club Services
KANSAS CITY GOLF ASSOCIATION, 112

Madkour, Abraham Executive Editor
STREET & SMITH'S SPORTSBUSINESS JOURNAL, 584, 586, 587

Madorin, Debbie Publisher & Editor
NATIONAL HAWKEYE RACING NEWS, 572

Madrigal, Rachelle Director of Sales and General Manager
FLORIDA STATE LEAGUE, 39
Madsen, Gary Operations Manager
DAKOTADOME, 960
Madsen, Kent Assistant Athletic Director
WHEATON COLLEGE (IL) ATHLETICS, 406
Madsen, Lisa Commissioner
HEART OF AMERICA REGIONAL COMMISSIONER/USA VOLLEYBALL, 211
Madsen, Susie Visitor and Group Tour Information
HESTAND STADIUM FAIRGROUNDS, 970, 1040
Madson, Steve Advertising Sales
TASK INDUSTRIES, INC., 1199
Maduro, Victor Board Member
WORLD POOL BILLIARD ASSOCIATION, 62
Mae, Hazel Anchor
NESN SPORTSDESK: THE WEEKEND EDITION, 684
Maeroff, Bernard President/Owner
GOLF & TENNIS HEADWEAR COMPANY, 1139
Maes, Chuck Senior Associate AD, Facilities & Events
MONTANA ATHLETICS, UNIVERSITY OF, 337
Maffey, Hugh News Director
WHAI-FM/WPVQ, 648
Magan, Thomas Managing Partner
WILLIAMS, BRIAN P., 915
Magana, Cheryl Sales Representative
ILLINOIS RACING NEWS, 565
Maged, Danielle Global Head of Partnership
STUBHUB, 932
Magenhofer, Karl News Director
WHBG-AM, 649
Maggard, Bryan Vice President for Intercollegiate Athle
LOUISIANA AT LAFAYETTE ATHLETICS, UNIVERSITY OF, 335
Maggard, Dave Athletic Director
JOHN O'QUINN FIELD AT ROBERTSON STADIUM, 977
Maggi, John National Sales Manager
STRONGWALL SYSTEMS INC., 1197
Maggi, Osvaldo President
INTERNATIONAL RACQUETBALL FEDERATION (IRF), 145
Maggiacomo, Thoams Chairman
SPECIAL OLYMPICS RHODE ISLAND, 197
Maggio, T. Program Director
WTGG-FM, 668
Magid, Rich Chief Financial Officer
SPORTVISION, 602
Magie, Susie Advertising Manager
JACKSONVILLE PATRIOT, 497
Maglaque, Peter Vice President
CARBITE GOLF COMPANY, 1113
Magliano, John Chairman / Chief Executive Officer
SH GROUP, 1062
Maglio, Donna Advertising Manager
LA PORTE HERALD-ARGUS, 500
Magliocchetti, Jennifer Assistant Director of Ticket Operations
FLORIDA STATE LEAGUE, 40, 968
Maglione, Fred President/CEO
PATRON SOLUTIONS, LP, 1065
Maglione, Julio President
FEDERATION INTERNATIONALE DE NATATION (FINA), 72, 204
Magnante, Rick Manager
CALIFORNIA LEAGUE (A-LEVEL), 36
Magnuson, Jackie Event Marketing Manager
U.S. SPORTS ACROBATICS/USSA, 120
Magnusson, Tony President
EVOL SNOWBOARDS, 1130
Magoffin, Brian Director of Sports Communications
SPRINGFIELD COLLEGE ATHLETICS, 371
Magoni, Ed Editor
INSIDE INDIANA, 565
Magrath, Bill Media Relations Manager
STREET & SMITH'S SPORTSBUSINESS DAILY, 586
Magrisso, Jason Sports Director
KSCU-FM, 628

Maguire, Diane PGA Golf Management Assistant
FERRIS STATE UNIVERSITY/PROFESSIONAL GOLF MANAGEMENT PROGRAM, 101
Maguire, Erin Athletics Operations Manager
SCRANTON ATHLETICS, UNIVERSITY OF, 400
Maguire, Ryan Programming/Promotions Director
WQSN AM 1660, 662
Maguire, Sean Director of communications and marketing
OKLAHOMA CITY ALL SPORTS ASSOCIATION, 242
Mah, Richard Principal
HUNT, ORTMANN, PALFFY & ROSSELL, INC., 885
Mahaffey, Steve Associate Athletics Director
ANGELO STATE UNIVERSITY ATHLETICS, 351
Mahagan, Mark Advertising Director
DAILY NEWS (KY), 478
Mahal, Chris Account Executive
TOTAL SPORTS ENTERTAINMENT, 814
Mahalic, Drew Chief Executive Officer
OREGON SPORTS AUTHORITY, 242
Maharaj, Sudarshan Goaltending Coach
NATIONAL HOCKEY LEAGUE/NHL, 123
Maher, Bill Director of Athletics
CANISIUS COLLEGE ATHLETICS, 326, 412
Maher, Christopher VP/Boston Garden Dev
TD BANKNORTH GARDEN, 1008
Maher, Jeremiah Assistant Athletics Director, Ticket Sal
CARRIER DOME, 955
Maher, Kevin Sports Director
WTVH-TV, 711
Maher, Tom Executive Director, Marketing
GEORGE P. JOHNSON COMPANY, 753, 784
Mahfouz, Sharif Global Tax Director
WOLF GROUP-NY, 817
Mahler, Don Sports Editor
VALLEY NEWS, 543
Mahler, Jonathan Sports Columnist
NEW YORK SUN, 511
Mahler, Steve Principal
ELLENZWEIG ASSOCIATES, INC., 1055
Mahncke, Kelly Assistant Executive Director, Finance
USA HOCKEY, 123
Mahon, James Director Marketing/Communications
AKRON SUMMIT CONVENTION & VISITORS BUREAU, 226
Mahone, Glenn Partner
MAHONE, GLENN R., 892
Mahone, Thomas Vice President
FAIRTRON, 1131
Mahoney, Beth Administrative Assistant to the Director
SILVIO O. CONTE FORUM, 1002
Mahoney, Buck Sports Editor
KEARNEY HUB, 499
Mahoney, Courtney President, Operations
AMERICAN HOCKEY LEAGUE/AHL, 127
Mahoney, Dan Faculty Athletic Representative
CULVER-STOCKTON COLLEGE ATHLETICS, 311
Mahoney, Duffy Chief of Sport Performance
USA TRACK & FIELD, 210
Mahoney, Gary President
DELAWARE STATE GOLF ASSOCIATION, 110
Mahoney, Gerrie Senior Associate AD
HARVARD UNIVERSITY ATHLETICS, 332
Mahoney, Katherine VP, Marketing
RAZOR USA LLC, 1180
Mahoney, Kevin General Manager
NEW YORK-PENNSYLVANIA LEAGUE, 46, 979
Mahoney, Lauren Manager, Sales and Corporate Partnership
FLORIDA STATE LEAGUE, 40
Mahoney, Mark Advertising Services Manager
ENTERPRISE, 487
Mahoney, Rachael Territory Manager
WESTERN WINTER SPORTS REPRESENTATIVES ASSOCIATION, 226
Mahoney, Thomas President/Owner
PRO BOUND SPORTS, 1177
Mahoney, Tim General Manager/Marketing
PORSCHE CARS NORTH AMERICA, 1175

Mahood, Harry Head Coach/General Manager
NORTH AMERICAN HOCKEY LEAGUE, 132
Maibach, Ben President
BARTON MALOW COMPANY, 1064
Maiberger, Steve VP
ATHLETIC & PERFORMANCE RIGGING/APR, 1101
Mail, Steven President
WOMEN'S PREMIER SOCCER LEAGUE, 166
Mailbach, Sheryl Chief Marketing Officer & Senior Vice Pr
BARTON MALOW COMPANY, 1064
Mailer, Allison Executive Director
BRITISH COLUMBIA SPORTS HALL OF FAME MUSEUM, 251
Mailhot, Sue Regional Commissioner
GREAT PLAINS REGIONAL VOLLEYBALL ASSOCIATION, 211
Maina, Angelo Director, Racing Department
ROSSIGNOL SKI COMPANY, INC., 1183
Maines, Bill Owner
EASTERN LEAGUE, 38
Maines, David Board of Directors
EASTERN LEAGUE, 38
Maino, John Sports Talk Show
WNFL 1140-AM, 658
Mainquist, Kent Chief Financial Officer
HAMMEL, GREEN AND ABRAHAMSON INC., 1058
Mains, Harold President
APPALACHIAN LEAGUE, 33
Mains, Mike General Manager
APPALACHIAN LEAGUE, 33
Mair, Adam Director, Player Development
NATIONAL HOCKEY LEAGUE/NHL, 123
Mairs, Donna National Sales Manager
SPORTS TALK/THE TICKET, 606
Maisel, Ivan Sports Senior Writer
ESPN THE MAGAZINE, 558
Maison, Arthur President/Chief Operating Officer
BAMBOO & RATTAN WORKS INC., 1104
Maison, Suzanne Vice President/Marketing Director
BAMBOO & RATTAN WORKS INC., 1104
Maites, Alan President
RADIAN 1, 805
Maitre, Chris Deputy AD, Internal Operations
TULANE UNIVERSITY ATHLETICS, 347
Maizes, Michael Senior Vice President/In-House Counsel
SFM ENTERTAINMENT, 602
Majeske, Jeff Sports Editor
SPRINGFIELD NEWS-LEADER, 533
Majka, Matt Chief Executive Officer
NATIONAL HOCKEY LEAGUE/NHL, 124
Major, David Account Services
PROMARK ADVERTISING, INC., 803
Major, Jean Chief Executive Officer
ALCOHOL AND GAMING COMMISSION OF ONTARIO, 79
Majors, Andrew Sports Editor
PARIS DAILY BEACON NEWS, 518
Majorwitz, Mary Client Relations Coordinator
RELIANT ASTRODOME, 996
Makara, Juliette President
UNITED STATES HOCKEY LEAGUE, 137
Maki, Rudy Executive Committee
U.S. NATIONAL SKI HALL OF FAME & MUSEUM, 259
Maki, Steve Director of Facilities/Engineering
HUMBERT HUMPHREY METRODOME, 972
Makofski, Dawn Assistant Athletic Director
MONTEVALLO ATHLETICS, UNIVERSITY OF (UM), 365
Makohus, Kraig Chief Executive Officer
SPECIAL OLYMPICS OHIO, 196
Malach, Mike Sr. Associate AD for Finance/Operations
CONVOCATION CENTER: EMU, 959
Malaguti, Sean Office Manager
SNOCOUNTRY MOUNTAIN REPORTS, 634
Maland, Justin Associate Athletic Director, Facilities
DONALD W. REYNOLDS RAZORBACK STADIUM, 962
Malasarn, Ruem Assistant Athletics Director
CALIFORNIA STATE POLY UNIVERSITY ATHLETICS, 353

Malawsky, Curt General Manager & Head Coach
NATIONAL LACROSSE LEAGUE, 142

Malay, Kathy Principal Secretary, Facilities
BERRY EVENTS CENTER, 949

Malby, Jeff Sports Information Director
ROCKY MOUNTAIN COLLEGE ATHLETICS, 319

Malchow, Steve Sr. Assoc. AD/Communications
JACK TRICE STADIUM, 974

Malcolm, Elvis Technical Advisor
JUMP ROPE TECH INC, 1151

Maldonado, Monica Director of Special Events
PICO RIVERA SPORTS ARENA, 993

Maleady, Anne President
AMERICAN CANOE ASSOCIATION, 67

Malecek, Dave Head Coach, Wrestling
MITCHELL HALL GYMNASIUM, 987

Malecki, Jason Territory Manager, DC/MD
HEARTLINE FITNESS PRODUCTS, INC., 1143

Maledon, William Lawyer
OSBORN MALEDON, P.A., 898

Malekoff, Robert Sport Studies Coordinator
GUILFORD COLLEGE, 420

Malen, Don Director
CONNECTICUT PGA SECTIONAL OFFICE, 105

Malenfant, Mark VP Sales
NEW TIER COMMUNICATIONS, 797, 821

Maletz, Jon Sports Editor
BOZEMAN DAILY CHRONICLE, 466

Malick, Mark Chairperson
SPECIAL OLYMPICS KANSAS, 195

Malik, Steve Chair & Owner
USL LEAGUE TWO, 161, 163

Malin, John Athletic Director
BLACKBURN COLLEGE ATHLETICS, 378

Malinowski, John Honorary President
MIDDLE ATLANTIC PGA, 106

Maliske, Brian General Manager
RUSHMORE PLAZA CIVIC CENTER, 999

Malkin, Scott Co-Owner & Governor
AMERICAN HOCKEY LEAGUE/AHL, 125, 127

Mallardi, Mickey VP-Architecture
CPG ARCHITECTS, 1053

Mallery, Jerry Registrar
ADIRONDACK AAU ASSOCIATION, 213

Mallet, Frank Chief Financial Officer / Chief Operatin
RAVENSBURGER FX SCHMID, 1180

Mallet, Kristan Assistant Director of Athletics
NICHOLS COLLEGE ATHLETICS, 395

Mallette, Carl Head Coach
QUEBEC MARITIMES MAJOR JUNIOR HOCKEY LEAGUE, 136

Mallette, Pope Partner
CONNELL, MARY ANN, 874

Malley, Steve (212)515-1000
ESPN THE MAGAZINE, 558

Mallicone, Wes Director of Sports Medicine
SHIPPENSBURG UNIVERSITY OF PENNSYLVANIA ATHLETICS, 369

Malliet, Steve President, General Manager
FRONTIER LEAGUE, 41

Mallin, Edward President
INFOUSA, 789

Mallin, Joshua Partner
WEG & MEYERS, 859

Mallis, Harvey Sales VP
CONCEPT ONE ACCESSORIES, 1119

Mallis, Mary Director of Marketing and Communication
BRUTE WRESTLING, 1111

Mallon, Lauren Global Marketing Manager
FILA USA, 1132

Mallon, Todd CFO
ADVOCARE INTERNATIONAL, 725

Mallory, Deborah Associate Athletic Director, Compliance
VIRGINIA STATE UNIVERSITY ATHLETICS(VSU), 374

Mallory, Geoffery Men's Basketball Head Coach
KNOXVILLE COLLEGE ATHLETICS, 389

Mallory, K. VP / Chief Financial Officer
MELEX PRODUCTS INTERNATIONAL, II, INC./DBA MELEX GOLF CARS, 1161

Mallory, Ken Administrator, Baseball Operations
AMERICAN LEAGUE OF PROFESSIONAL BASEBALL CLUBS, THE, 30

Mallory, Rob Director of Athletics
KENTUCKY WESLEYAN COLLEGE ATHLETICS, 361

Malloy, Dorothy VP/General Counsel
MALLOY, DOROTHY A., 892

Malloy, Nicole Director of Athletics for Internal Opera
MARYWOOD UNIVERSITY ATHLETICS, 392

Malloy, Randy News Director
WWCD-FM, 670

Malmberg, Mary Director of Sports Tourism
CEDAR RAPIDS TOURISM OFFICE, 229

Malone, Brad Interim Head Coach
ONTARIO HOCKEY LEAGUE, 134

Malone, Deanna News Director
WRNL-AM, 664

Malone, Mark Reporter
ESPN, 683

Malone, Matt Sports Information Director
VALDOSTA STATE UNIVERSITY ATHLETICS(VSU), 374

Malone, Michael Head Coach
NATIONAL BASKETBALL ASSOCIATION/NBA, 56

Malone, Molly Senior Vice President and Director
FRED MEYER STORES, INC., 1228

Malone, Sharon Operations Manager
WSEW-FM, 666

Malone, Tom Director
PROGEAR, INC., 1178

Maloney, Brian General Manager
AM 850 THE BUZZ SPORTS RADIO, 611

Maloney, Don President, Hockey Operations
NATIONAL HOCKEY LEAGUE/NHL, 123

Maloney, Jay Promotions Manager
KMGH-TV, 692

Maloney, Larry VP Sales & Marketing
OWENS & CO., INC., 1179

Maloney, Lawrence VP Of Sales & Marketing
OWENS & CO., INC., 1179

Maloney, Mark Sports Reporter
LEXINGTON HERALD-LEADER, 502

Maloney, Ray Sports Editor
DEVILS LAKE DAILY JOURNAL, 484

Malonis, Karen Sports Managing Editor
GREAT LAKES BOATING MAGAZINE, 563

Maloughney, Teri Director, Sales & Marketing
ADVENTURE CYCLING ASSOCIATION, 70

Mals, Jason Director, Communications
EAST COAST HOCKEY LEAGUE/ECHL, 131

Maltby, Ralph Founder
UT GOLF, INC., 1139, 1206

Maluso, Tony Sports
ADVERTISER-TRIBUNE, 459

Malveaux, Greg Personal assistant
SAPIR, EDDIE L., THE HONORABLE, 904

Malychenkov, Andrei Head Coach
CANADIAN SOCCER LEAGUE, 157

Malynchenkov, Andrei Head Coach
CANADIAN SOCCER LEAGUE, 157

Malzone, Steven President
SPEEDLINE ATHLETIC WEAR, INC., 1192

Mamuyac, Clarence Principal
ELS ARCHITECTURE AND URBAN DESIGN, 1055

Man, Dirk Chief Financial Officer
B' WARMER THERMAL PRODUCTS, 1102

Manahan, Kevin Sports Reporter
STAR-LEDGER, 535

Manak, Pat Sr. Associate Executive Director
NATIONAL ASSOCIATION OF COLLEGIATE MARKETING ADMINISTRATORS/NACMA, 283, 284

Manak, Pat Senior Associate Executive Director
NATIONAL ASSOCIATION OF COLLEGIATE DIRECTORS OF ATHLETICS/NACDA, 284

Mancheck, Hunter Sports Director
KVCU-AM, 631

Mancini, Carol Publisher
CALIFORNIA BOWLING NEWS, 554

Mancini, Marie Head Athletic Trainer
SWARTHMORE COLLEGE ATHLETICS, 403

Mancini, Mike Director of Athletics for Communications
OBERLIN COLLEGE ATHLETICS, 396

Mancino, Robert President
MANCINO MANUFACTURING CO.,INC., 1159

Manck, Josh Assistant AD For Communications
TEXAS A&M UNIVERSITY-COMMERCE ATHLETICS, 372

Mancone, John Chief Public Protection Inspector
STATE OF RHODE ISLAND DEPARTMENT OF BUSINESS REGULATION, 82

Mancuso, Bob Chairman
GREATER OMAHA SPORTS COMMITTEE, 235

Mandalinski, Sarah Marketing Director
US CELLULAR CENTER, 1014

Mandel, Eric Sports Reporter
DAILY BREEZE, 475

Mandel, Irwin SVP, Financial & Legal
MANDEL, IRWIN,, 892

Mandelaro, James Sports Writer
DEMOCRAT AND CHRONICLE, 482

Mandell, Bruce Owner/Chair
USL CHAMPIONSHIP, 159

Mandery, Sharon Event Services Director
PERSHING CENTER, 992

Mandeville, Karen Administrative Assistant
WEST VIRGINIA INTERCOLLEGIATE ATHLETIC CONFERENCE, 306

Mandeville, Lou Sports Director
WOON-AM, 660

Mandraccia, Jenna Attoney
ELY, BETTINI, ULMAN & ROSENBLATT, 878

Mandrick, Fred Owner/Founder
A.V. CONCEPTS, 819

Manemek, Craig Associate
LICARI & WALSH, L.L.C., 891

Maner, Sue Executive Vice President
SPECIAL OLYMPICS SOUTH CAROLINA, 197

Maneri, Lauren Program Specialist
SPECIAL OLYMPICS NEW YORK, 196

Manetta, Edward Commissioner
NEW YORK COLLEGIATE ATHLETIC CONFERENCE, 301

Maney, Tom Senior Vice President Advertising Sales
FOX SPORTS NETWORKS/FOX SPORTS NET, 675

Manfred, Rob Executive Vice President, Economics & Le
KAUFFMAN STADIUM, 27, 29, 31, 978

Manfred, Robert Baseball Commisioner
AMERICAN LEAGUE OF PROFESSIONAL BASEBALL CLUBS, THE, 29

Mang, Robert Chief Executive Officer / Director
GALYAN'S TRADING COMPANY, INC., 1228

Mangan, Chris Sports Editor
CAPITAL JOURNAL, 468

Mangan, John Program Director
KVTI-FM, 631

Mangan, Tony News Director
KLXS-FM, 623

Manganello, Ed Chairman
OLYMPIA SPORTS, 1171

Mangano, Edward Ex Officio
NASSAU COUNTY SPORTS COMMISSION, 241

Mangano, Mary Membership Coordinator
ICE SKATING INSTITUTE, 86

Mangas, Mike Sports Director
KRCR-TV, 694

Mange, Tela Vice President Communications
SPECIAL OLYMPICS TEXAS, 197

Mangels, Tonya Marketing/Sales Director
KAUFFMAN STADIUM, 978

Manget, Daniel Sports Information Director
MILLIGAN COLLEGE ATHLETICS, 316

Mangini, Ron SVP
JACQUES MORET, 1149

Mangione, Fred Chief Operating Officer
BARCLAYS CENTER, 948

Manglesdorf, Liz ISI National Skating Programs Coordinato
ICE SKATING INSTITUTE, 86

Mango, James Chief Operating Officer
PIMLICO RACE COURSE, 1042

Mangrum, Will Senior Vice President
BRAILSFORD & DUNLAVEY, 1050

Mangum, A. Editor
WESTERN HORSEMAN, 592

Manheimer, Micki Sports Information Associate
WHITTIER FIELD, 1018

Manhertz, Joe Director of Athletics
ST. BONAVENTURE UNIVERSITY
ATHLETICS, 345
Manhing, Don President
NJCAA REGION IV WOMEN'S, 287
Manhufe, Paul Advertising Manager
SIERRA VISTA HERALD, 531
Maniates, Cindy Costume Artist
AARDVARK MASCOTS, 1090
Manickam, Shanta Manager of Marketing and
Digital Service
AMERICAN URBAN RADIO NETWORKS, 604
Manion, Kirt Sports Editor
NEBRASKA CITY NEWS-PRESS, 510
Manion, Laura Business Development
GROUP II COMMUNICATIONS, 836
Mankin, Robert Senior Associate
NBBJ, 1061
Manley, Dirk Director, New Business
Development
EAST COAST HOCKEY LEAGUE/ECHL, 129
Manley, Greg Vice President
PACIFIC NORTHWEST PGA SECTIONAL
OFFICE, 107
Manley, Len Sales
KART MARKETING INTERNATIONAL, INC,
567, 791
Mann, Aaron Communications and Media
USA CANOE/KAYAK, 68, 208
Mann, Brian Athletics Director
WILLIAM & MARY ATHLETICS, COLLEGE OF,
349
Mann, Harold News/Sports Director
KLVI-AM 560, 623
Mann, Jennifer Reporter -Advertising, Marketing,
Public
KANSAS CITY STAR, 499
Mann, Marie President
BRIGHT SITES, INC, 1110
Mann, Michael Sales Manager
CHET COPPOCK, 608
Mann, Mitch Associate AD, External Operations
FALCON STADIUM, 964
Mann, Randy Vice President for Athletics
MARY HARDIN-BAYLOR ATHLETICS(UMHB),
392
Mann, Robert Chief Executive Officer
BRIGHT SITES, INC, 1110
Mann, Troy Head Coach
ONTARIO HOCKEY LEAGUE, 134
Manning, Archie Chairman
NATIONAL FOOTBALL FOUNDATION AND
COLLEGE HALL OF FAME, INC., THE, 252,
256
Manning, D. Marketing Director
CELEBRITY SUPPLIERS OF LAS VEGAS, 828
Manning, Jeff Advertising Reporter
OREGONIAN, 516
Manning, Jonathan Sports Editor
SOUTHWEST DAILY NEWS, 532
Manning, Joshua Editor
FLORIDA HORSEMEN, 559
Manning, Julie Deputy Athletics Director/SWA
MINNESOTA ATHLETICS, UNIVERSITY OF,
337
Manning, Lisa Senior VP, Marketing
NATIONAL FOOTBALL LEAGUE/NFL, 94
Manning, Marcus Director of Athletics
MARYVILLE UNIVERSITY ATHLETICS, 363
Manning, Michael Partner
STINSON MORRISON HECKER LLP, 908
Manning, Michelle Senior Woman Administrator
ITHACA COLLEGE ATHLETICS, 388
Manning, Steven Partner
MANNING, MARDER, KASS, ELLROD, &
RAMIREZ, 892
Manning, Tom Director, Marketing/Sales/Public
Relatio
PRAIRIE MEADOWS RACETRACK AND
CASINO, INC, 1043
Mannino, Brian Director of Baseball Operations
VA MEMORIAL STADIUM, 1015
Mannion, Dennis President & CEO
PALACE OF AUBURN HILLS, THE, 224, 846,
991
Mannix, Dan President/CEO
LEADDOG MARKETING GROUP, 793
Manns, Kevin Director of Athletics for Media
Relation

WINSTON-SALEM STATE UNIVERSITY
ATHLETICS, 375
Mano, Barry Publisher
REFEREE MAGAZINE, 221, 578
Manoloff, Dennis Sports Writer
PLAIN DEALER, 520
Manos, Mike Program Director
KADA-AM, 612
Mansell, John Senior Analyst/Consultant
KAGAN WORLD MEDIA, 569, 791
Mansell, Kevin President
KOHL'S DEPARTMENT STORES, 1231
Mansfield, Christina Vice President Human
Resources
GARDA WORLD, 766
Mansfield, David President
CORSAIR DISPLAY SYSTEMS, INC., 1119
Mansfield, Eileen Managing Editor
POWER & MOTORYACHT, 576
Mansfield, Gregg Editor
POWERBOAT, 576
Mansfield, Jim Executive Director
MUNCIE SPORTS COMMISSION INC, 241
Mansfield, Timothy Principal
CAMBRIDGE SEVEN ASSOCIATES INC., 1051
Manske, Rob Vice President
COLLEGE CONCEPTS, LLC., 1223
Mansolino, Tony Hitting Coach
EASTERN LEAGUE, 37
Manson, Dan Treasurer
MONROE COUNTY SPORTS COMMISSION,
241
Manson, Dave Assistant Coach
AMERICAN HOCKEY LEAGUE/AHL, 126
Mansson, Fabian President and Chief Executive
Officer
EDDIE BAUER, INC., 1226
Mansueto, Joe Owner/Chairman
MAJOR LEAGUE SOCCER, 157
Mansur, Linda Editor/Publisher
REVENUES FROM SPORTS VENUES, 596
Mansusi, Thomas General Sales Manager
WFAN SPORTS RADIO, 645
Manthei, Farrah Deputy AD/SWA/COO
ILLINOIS AT CHICAGO ATHLETICS,
UNVIERSITY OF, 332
Mantz, Sheila Advertising Manager
VICKSBURG POST, 544
Manuel, John Co-Editor in Chief
BASEBALL AMERICA, 551
Manuel, Ryan VP - Baseball Operations
CAROLINA LEAGUE, 37
Manuel, Warde Director of Athletics
MICHIGAN ATHLETICS, UNIVERSITY OF, 337,
987
Manzano, Rinny Vice President
STELLARTV-SPORTS, 602
Manzello, Nick Sports Columnist
TELEGRAM & GAZETTE, 537
Manzer, Will President and CEO
EASTERN MOUNTAIN SPORTS, INC., 1226
Manzi, John Director, Public Relations
MONTICELLO RACEWAY, 1041
Manzione, AmySue Operations Coordinator
GEORGE M. STEINBRENNER FIELD, 968
Manzo, Barbara Vice president
USTA FLORIDA, 175
Mapes, Cliff Executive Director, Business
Operations
WESTERN HOCKEY LEAGUE, 139
Maple, Shea Assistant Athletic Director, External
Af
WINTHROP UNIVERSITY ATHLETICS, 349
Maples, Steve Executive Director
VON BRAUN CENTER, 1017
Maquire, Mick Assistant Athletic Director
CLARKSON UNIVERSITY ATHLETICS, 381
Mara, Chris Senior VP, Player Personnel
NATIONAL FOOTBALL LEAGUE/NFL, 96
Mara, Dan Internal Operations
CENTRAL ATLANTIC COLLEGIATE
CONFERENCE, 293
Mara, John President/CEO
NATIONAL FOOTBALL LEAGUE/NFL, 96
Marano, Brandon General Manager
LAKEWOOD BLUECLAWS, 981
Marca, Gian-Michele Partner
COOLEY, GODWARD, LLP, 874

Marcel, Andre Program Director
WDKX-FM, 643
Marcelo, Cassandra Marketing and Box Office
Coordinator
U.S. CELLULAR CENTER, 1011
March, Cody Director of Operations
COLUMBIA EMPIRE REGIONAL
COMMISSIONER/USA VOLLEYBALL, 211
March, Jason Head Coach
NATIONAL BASKETBALL ASSOCIATION
DEVELOPMENT LEAGUE, 59
Marchese, Denise Associate Director of
Athletics/SWA
HARTFORD ATHLETICS, UNIVERSITY OF,
331
Marchetti, Beth Director of Development
DUPAGE CONVENTION & VISITORS
BUREAU, 233
Marchiano, Sal Weeknight Sports Anchor
WPIX-TV, 708
Marchwinski, Laurie Director of Basketball
Operations
INTERNATIONAL SWIMMING HALL OF FAME,
254
Marchyshyn, Pam Managing Editor
DRAG REVIEW, 557
Marciani, Lou Dept. School Director
SOUTHERN MISSISSIPPI, UNIVERSITY OF,
433
Marciano, Marco Goaltending Coach
AMERICAN HOCKEY LEAGUE/AHL, 127
Marciano, Paul Co-Founder
GUESS? INC, 1140
Marcinek, Arlene Secretary
LAKE COUNTY FAIR, 1041
Marcinek, Frank Assistant Director of Athletics
SUSQUEHANNA UNIVERSITY ATHLETICS,
403
Marciniak, Dana Manager, Corporate
Communications
NEW ERA CAP, CO, 1167
Marcinkoski, Tim Sports Copy Editor
DETROIT FREE PRESS, 483
Marcky, Michael VP, Marketing and Advertising
OCEAN PACIFIC APPAREL CORPORATION,
1170
Marco, Donna Advertising Reporter
WASHINGTON TIMES, 545
Marco, Paul Director, Coaching
WOMEN'S PREMIER SOCCER LEAGUE, 165
Marcotte, Greg Director of Finance and HR
SEBRING INTERNATIONAL RACEWAY, 1032
Marcoux, Tara Advertising Manager
MARSHFIELD NEWS-HERALD, 505
Marculescu, Cornel Executive Director
FEDERATION INTERNATIONALE DE
NATATION (FINA), 72, 204
Marcum, Bill Advertising Manager
EAST OREGONIAN, 485
Marcum, Bryan President
INTERNATIONAL BOWHUNTING
ORGANIZATION, 14
Marcus, Jerry Parking Consulting Services
Executive Di
WALTER P MOORE, 1063
Marcus, John Vice President
NJCAA REGION XXI WOMEN'S, 290
Marcus, Richard President / Chief Operating
Officer
ABI TAPE PRODUCTS, 1090
Marcus, Roger Chairman / Chief Executive Officer
ABI TAPE PRODUCTS, 1090
Marcus, Steven Sports Reporter
NEWSDAY, 513
Marcus, Willaim EVP/Treasurer
ABI TAPE PRODUCTS, 1090
Marden, Andrew Weekend Sports Anchor
KBCI-TV, 688
Marek, Dave Senior Vice President, Marketing
ATLANTIC LEAGUE, 35
Marenghi, Julio President
WSBK-TV, 709
Maresh, Carl Department Head/Professor
CONNECTICUT, UNIVERSITY OF, 414
Marfise, Larry Athletic Director
TAMPA ATHLETICS, UNIVERSITY OF, 372
Marful, Allysea Head Coach
WOMEN'S FOOTBALL ALLIANCE / WFA, 97

Marg, Jake Assistant Athletic Director
UNIVERSITY OF WEST FLORIDA ATHLETICS
(UWF), 374

Margaret, Zayti Executive Manager
NORTHVILLE DOWNS, 1042

Margeson, Terry VP Marketing
WORLD FAMOUS TRADING COMPANY LTD.,
1212

Margevicius, Bob EVP
SPECIALIZED BICYCLE COMPONENTS, INC.,
1191

Margolis, Alan Partner
MARGOLIS EDELSTEIN, 892

Margolis, Jay President / Chief Operating Officer
ROCKPORT COMPANY, 1183

Margolis, Lenn Director of Sports Information
LEHMAN COLLEGE ATHLETICS, 390

Margolis, Robert Chairman of the Board/CEO
SIDEOUT SPORT, INC., 1188

Margulies, Alex Director of Broadcasting
JOHN THURMAN FIELD, 977

Marhanka, Brett Athletics Communications
Director
WHEATON COLLEGE (IL) ATHLETICS, 406

Marhefka, Tom Owner
KUKU-AM, 631

Marhevko, Thomas Senior VP
NATIONAL MARINE MANUFACTURERS
ASSOCIATION, 64

Mari, Luis Technical Supervisor
WOIZ-AM, 660

Mariani, Mark Sales/Marketing President
SPORTSLINE USA,
INC./CBS.SPORTSLINE.COM, 929

Mariano, Anthony Director of Athletics
NORWICH UNIVERSITY ATHLETICS, 396

Mariash, Julie Coordinating Producer
ESPN, 683

Maric, Novi CEO
WOMEN'S PREMIER SOCCER LEAGUE, 166

Marie, Bridgette Program Director
WLLL-AM, 655

Marie, Dale Owner, General Manager
KGBR-FM, 618

Marier, Delaney Technical Director
WOMEN'S PREMIER SOCCER LEAGUE, 168

Mariette, Bernard President / Director
QUIKSILVER, 1179

Marin, Angela Assistant Athletic Director
TEXAS AT DALLAS ATHLETICS, UNIVERSITY
OF, 403

Marinak, Chris Chief Operations & Strategy
Officer
NATIONAL LEAGUE OF PROFESSIONAL
BASEBALL CLUBS, THE, 31

Marinelli, Joseph Chair
DESTINATION MARKETING ASSOCIATION
INTERNATIONAL, 219

Mariner, Jonathan Executive Vice President and
Chief Finan
KAUFFMAN STADIUM, 892, 978

Marines, Amanda Front Office Manager
NORTH AMERICAN HOCKEY LEAGUE, 132

Marinho, Raquel President
CANADIAN TEAM HANDBALL FEDERATION,
121

Marino, Claire Co-Founder/Treasurer
DAN MARINO FOUNDATION, 191

Marino, Dan Co-Founder/Chairman
DAN MARINO FOUNDATION, 191

Marino, Wayne Head of Human Kinetics
WINDSOR, UNIVERSITY OF, 438

Mariolle, Elaine Public Affairs
PERIMETER BICYCLING ASSOCIATION OF
AMERICA, INC., 70

Marion, Michael General Manager
ALLTEL ARENA, 946

Marion, Paul President
TIFFIN UNIVERSITY, 435

Mariscal, Ricky Program Director
KWTS-FM, 632

Marix, Amy Associate Director - Federal Aid &
Schol
TIGER STADIUM, 1010

Mark, Dennis Director, Creative Services
FRONTIER LEAGUE, 41

Mark, Matthew Chief Financial Officer
EVERLAST WORLDWIDE, INC., 1130

Mark, Sargent Senior Vice President of Sales
Industria
B & G EQUIPMENT COMPANY, 1102

Mark, Steve Sports Anchor
KPRC-TV, 693

Mark, Tom Sports Editor
TIFTON GAZETTE, 538

Marketti, James Promotion Vice President
WFLD-TV, 702

Markey, Edward Communications VP
QUICKEN LOANS ARENA, 994

Markey, Gareth Vice President, Facilities
LELACHEUR PARK, 982

Markey, Matt Outdoors Editor
BLADE, 465

Markfield, Roger President
AMERICAN EAGLE OUTFITTERS, 1216

Markham, Lisa Senior Vice President
MILLSPORT, LLC, 795

Markiewicz, Todd Director of Sales
WBNS AM/FM - 1460 ESPN COLUMBUS &
97.1 THE FAN, 639

Markionni, Robert Executive Director
CHICAGO DISTRICT GOLFER, 110, 554

Markland, Lisa Assistant Director of Training
CENTER FOR THE STUDY OF SPORT IN
SOCIETY, 219

Markley, Jodi Senior Vice President, International
Pro
ESPN TELEVISION, 674

Markley, Scott Senior Associate AD,
Communications
UC LOS ANGELES ATHLETICS, 347

Markovitch, Robert President & CEO
COLEMAN COMPANY INC., 1117

Markowski, Tom Sports Reporter
DETROIT NEWS, 483

Marks, Al Sports Director
KTVH-TV, 696

Marks, Alan Sports Director
KTVH-TV, 696

Marks, Andy Sports Editor
CITRUS COUNTY CHRONICLE, 471

Marks, Errol CEO/Editor/Host
WORLD WIDE SPORTS RADIO NETWORK,
593

Marks, Ian Sports Information Director
MESA STATE COLLEGE ATHLETICS(MSC),
363

Marks, Jeff Senior Marketing Executive
SPORTS BUSINESS GROUP, 802, 810

Marks, Jesse Deputy AD, Development
NORTHWESTERN UNIVERSITY ATHLETICS,
340

Marks, Mellissa Promotion Director
WEHT-TV, 702

Marks, Sean Alternative Governor, General
Manager
NATIONAL BASKETBALL ASSOCIATION/NBA,
56

Marks, Spencer Partner
MARKS, MARKS & KAPLAN, 893

Marks-Peltz, Jeremy Sports Director
WVUM-FM, 670

Markuson, Chad Deputy Athletic Director
MINNESOTA STATE UNIVERSITY -
MOORHEAD ATHLETICS (MSUM), 364

Markwort, Glenn Chief Executive Officer / VP
MARKWORT SPORTING GOODS COMPANY,
1159

Marleau, Giff Program Director
SPOKANE HOOPFEST, 55

Marlin, Dana Publisher
HOOK, 563

Marlin, Todd General Manager
CAMPANELLI STADIUM, 954

Marlock, Scott Sports Anchor / Reporter
WXXA-TV, 712

Marlow, Mike Vice President for Intercollegiate
Athle
NORTHERN ARIZONA UNIVERSITY
ATHLETICS, 340

Marman, Danielle Marketing and PR Director
WEST COAST TURF, 1210

Marmion, Dave Executive Sr. Associate Athletic
Directo
DARRELL K ROYAL - TEXAS MEMORIAL
STADIUM, 960

Marmol, Oliver Manager
FLORIDA STATE LEAGUE, 40

Marmot, Simon Director
MARMOT, 1159

Marolda, Anthony Strategy & Planning/Board of
Directors
STRATBRIDGE, INC., 812, 929, 1215

Marolda, Matthew Founder/Chief Executive
Officer
STRATBRIDGE, INC., 812, 929, 1215

Marolda, Matthew CEO and Founder
STRATBRIDGE, INC., 1215

Maroney, Troy Sports Editor
BROOKINGS REGISTER, 466

Marquardt, Matt Assistant Coach
WESTERN HOCKEY LEAGUE, 139

Marquez, Paty Project Architect
ALBANESE/BROOKS/ASSOCIATES P.C., 1049

Marquez, Sally Executive Director
NEW MEXICO ACTIVITIES ASSOCIATION,
201

Marquez-Rocha, Miriam Office Manager
TECNIFIBRE USA, 1200

Marquis, Trent Chairman
YAKIMA VALLEY SUNDOME, 1021

Marr, Greg Editor-in-Chief
SILENT SPORTS, 580

Marran, Dave Sports Editor
KENOSHA NEWS, 499

Marrapese-Burrell, Nancy Sports Reporter
BOSTON GLOBE, 465

Marrelli, Tammy-Lynn Manager Customer
Service
VOYAGER CUSTOM PRODUCTS, 1208

Marrello, John General Manager
USL LEAGUE TWO, 164

Marrero, Eli Manager
FLORIDA STATE LEAGUE, 39

Marrochello, Drew Director of Athletics
BOSTON UNIVERSITY ATHLETICS, 325, 989

Marrone, Phillip Member
MARRONE, ROBINSON, FREDERICK &
FOSTER, 893

Mars, Jacqueline Vice Chairman
NATIONAL SPORTING LIBRARY, THE, 256

Mars-Proietti, Laura Editorial Director
SPORTS MARKET PLACE DIRECTORY, 596

Marsack, Gary Attorney
LINDNER & MARSACK, S.C., 891

Marschalek, Jim Vice President
ADVANCED DESIGN CONCEPTS, 1093

Marsee, Mike Sports Writer
ADVOCATE-MESSENGER, 459

Marsh, Chris Category Manager
LESCO, INC., 15, 1155

Marsh, Dave Athletic Director
NORTHWOOD UNIVERSITY, 366

Marsh, David VP
PELTON MARSH KINSELLA, 822

Marsh, Dennis President
CROWN TROPHY COMPANY, 1224

Marsh, Jim Advertising Manager
CANOE & KAYAK MAGAZINE, 554

Marsh, John President
S.L. OUTERBANKS LLC, 1185

Marsh, Mike Principal
DAVIS DESIGN, 1054

Marshall, Bryan Director for Sports Information
MILLIKIN UNIVERSITY ATHLETICS, 393

Marshall, Chris Director, Corporate Sales &
Partnerships
PIONEER BASEBALL LEAGUE, 50, 950

Marshall, Clint News Director
WDPN-AM, 643

Marshall, Darlene Executive Director of
Elementary Educati
TRINITY MOTHER FRANCES ROSE
STADIUM, 1011

Marshall, Debra Vice President, Marketing
HEALTH FITNESS CORPORATION, 1059

Marshall, Douglas Attorney
KAY & MERKLE, 887

Marshall, Eugene Director of Athletics
BINGHAMTON UNIVERSITY, 325

Marshall, Ian Vice President
CONNECTICUT PGA SECTIONAL OFFICE,
105

Marshall, Jim Vice President
WYOMING STATE GOLF ASSOCIATION, 118

Martinez, Marino Sports Editor
DIARIO LAS AMERICAS, 484

Martinez, Marty Midwest Sales Manager
GRAVEL GEAR SKATEBOARD CLOTHING, 1140

Martinez, Nate Sports Director
KWCR-FM, 631

Martinez, Ramon Sporting Director
WOMEN'S PREMIER SOCCER LEAGUE, 166

Martinez, Raul Sports Director
KVIA-TV, 696

Martinez, Tim Assistant Sports Editor
COLUMBIAN, 472

Martinez, Tony Vice Pesident
NORTHERN TEXAS PGA SECTIONAL OFFICE, 107

Martinez, Will Pro Scouting Coordinator
NATIONAL FOOTBALL LEAGUE/NFL, 96

Martini, Gabe Sales Manager
MATEFLEX-MELE CORPORATION, 1160

Martino, Bob Chair & Owner
USL LEAGUE ONE, 160

Martino, Kathy Vice President Community Relations/Consu
BODY WISE INTERNATIONAL, 1108

Martino, Mike Tournament Director
SOUTHWEST PGA SECTIONAL OFFICE, 108

Martino, Tom President
BOWLING PROPRIETORS' ASSOCIATION OF AMERICA, 65

Martinov, William Director of Athletics
LONG ISLAND UNIVERSITY BROOKLYN ATHLETICS, 335

Martins, Alex CEO/Alternate Governor
EAST COAST HOCKEY LEAGUE/ECHL, 57, 130

Martins, Ilidio Sports Editor
LUSO AMERICANO, 504

Martins, Patricia Founder, Designer, President
IPANEMA WEAR, 1148

Martins, Rose Administrative Assistant to the Vice Dea
BERSHAD, LAWRENCE, 866

Martinson, Barbara Advertising Manager
KNEB-FM, 624

Marton, Florin Athletic Director
SALEM INTERNATIONAL UNIVERSITY ATHLETICS, 369

Martz, Jim Editor
FLORIDA TENNIS, 560

Marum, Morgan Director, Corportate & Media Relations
SPOKANE HOOPFEST, 55

Marvez, Alex Sports Writer
SOUTH FLORIDA SUN-SENTINEL, 532

Marvin, Alexander Promoter
DALLAS COUNTY DRAGWAY, 1024

Marvin, Meg Assistant to CEO
INTERNATIONAL SWIMMING HALL OF FAME, 254

Marvin, Pete Security Director
HAZEL PARK HARNESS RACEWAY (HPHR), 1039

Marvin, Sorvala President
STANTEC, 1062

Marx, Linda Classified Manager
MADISON PRESS, 504

Mas, John Vice President Marketing
KING PANIAGUA, 567

Mas, Jorge Managing Owner
MAJOR LEAGUE SOCCER, 157

Mas, Miguel 1st Vice President
HANDBALL, INTERNATIONAL FEDERATION, 121

Masai, Toshiyuki Chief Executive Officer & President
NIKON SPORTS & RECREATIONAL OPTICS, 1168

Masayda, Samantha Sports Information Director
ALBERTUS MAGNUS COLLEGE ATHLETICS, 376

Mascari, Michelle Creative Director
ECA WORLD FITNESS ALLIANCE, 84

Mascaro, Juan Athletic Director
BREVARD COLLEGE ATHLETICS, 309

Mascatello, Christopher Executive Vice President, Technology Sal
ANC SPORTS ENTERPRISES, 1216

Mascatello, John President SFX Golf
SFX SPORTS GROUP, 854

Mascherano, Javier Head Coach
MAJOR LEAGUE SOCCER, 157

Masco, Vincent Associate Director of Athletics
DREW UNIVERSITY(DU) ATHLETICS, 383

Mascoll, Emerson Governor
CANADA'S SPORTS HALL OF FAME, 251

Mascorella, Randy Executive Director
SPECIAL OLYMPICS NEW MEXICO, 196

Maser, Adam Sports Information Director
HASTINGS COLLEGE ATHLETICS, 313

Masewicz, Bob Owner, Chief Consultant
TOTAL SPORTS ENTERTAINMENT, 814

Masewicz, Robert Founder/Owner
TOTAL SPORTS ENTERTAINMENT, 814

Mashore, Roger President
MIDWEST TROPHY MANUFACTURING, INC., 1162

Masin, Herman Editor
SCHOLASTIC COACH & ATHLETIC DIRECTOR MAGAZINE, 579

Maskrey, Fritz Sr. Director of Corporate Sales & Market
CALIFORNIA SPEEDWAY, 1022

Maslowsky, Jerry Vice President of Marketing & Brand Deve
THE WINNIPEG BLUE BOMBERS, 1009

Mason, Amy Director of Ticket Services, Director, C
PHILIP B. ELFSTROM STADIUM, 992

Mason, Angela President
WOMEN'S FOOTBALL ALLIANCE / WFA, 97

Mason, Brandon
SPORTS MARKETING SURVEYS USA, 811

Mason, Charles Executive Editor
SAIL MAGAZINE, 579

Mason, Charlie President/Managing Principal
MASON & MADISON, 758

Mason, Dale International Tax Director and Chief Ope
WOLF GROUP-NY, 817

Mason, Dan General Manager
INTERNATIONAL LEAGUE, 43, 967

Mason, Francine Vice President Communcations
GREATER FORT LAUDERDALE CONVENTION & VISITORS BUREAU, 234

Mason, Jordan Sports Director
KOBI-TV, 693

Mason, Mark Manager
ATLANTIC LEAGUE, 35

Mason, Marty Pitching Coach
INTERNATIONAL LEAGUE, 43

Mason, Mike Senior Vice President/Chief Financial Of
SPECIAL OLYMPICS CONNECTICUT, 194

Mason, Peter Partner-In-Charge
FULBRIGHT & JAWORSKI .L.L.P., 881

Mason, Robert Commissioner
INTERNATIONAL SPORT KARATE ASSOCIATION, 143

Mason, Suzy Sr. Associate Director of Athletics, Fac
HI CORBETT FIELD, 970

Mason, Tim Program Manager
BSKYB, 611

Mason, Vic Publishing Director
BEULAH PARK, 1036

Masosko, Ron Director of Athletics
SCHREINER UNIVERSITY ATHLETICS, 320

Masquelier, Michel President IMG Media
IMG LOS ANGELES/IMG X SPORTS, 838

Masrani, Bharat Chief Executive Officer, TD Bank Group
TD CANADA TRUST, 733

Mass, Kevin Principal
FFKR ARCHITECTS, 1056

Massa, Laurie Director of Athletics
JOHN CARROLL UNIVERSITY ATHLETICS, 388

Massa, Mike Sports News Editor
SAN FRANCISCO CHRONICLE, 528

Massa, Patrick Dept. Chairperson/Professor
YORK COLLEGE OF PENNSYLVANIA, 439

Massarelli, John Manager, Director of Baseball Operations
COMMUNITYAMERICA BALLPARK, 959

Massaro, Chris Director of Athletics
MIDDLE TENNESSEE ATHLETICS, 337, 977

Massaroni, John Co-Owner, General Counsel, Agent
NATIONAL SPORTS MANAGEMENT INC., 845

Masselink, Claudia Director of Quality
BIOLIFE, LLC, 1107

Massengale, Alan Sports Anchor
KCAL-TV, 688

Massengale, John Sports Studies Director
NEVADA, LAS VEGAS, UNIVERSITY OF, 428

Massengill, Shari Assistant General Manager
INTERNATIONAL LEAGUE, 42

Massey, Sarah Marketing & Events Director
FIELD HOCKEY, FEDERATION INTERNATIONALE DE HOCKEY (FIH), 0

Massey, Terry Columnist
SUN NEWS, 536

Massie, Jim Sports Reporter
COLUMBUS DISPATCH, 472

Massoels, Bill Athletic Director
SAINT JOSEPH'S COLLEGE ATHLETICS, 369

Massoglia, Mark Sports Editor
DAILY TRIBUNE (WI), 480

Masson, Will President
NEW ENGLAND SPORTS REPRESENTATIVES, 152

Massoni, John Executive VP Operations & Partner
DORNA USA, LLC, 781

Mast, Greg Sports Editor
OTTAWA HERALD, 517

Mastel, Jill Event Manager
ROY WILKINS AUDITORIUM, 999

Masteller, Scott Program Director
KESN-FM, 617

Master, John EVP, Chief Legal & Strategy Officer/Alt.
NATIONAL HOCKEY LEAGUE/NHL, 125

Master, Kathy Advertising Coordinator
LEADER-TIMES, 502

Master, Stephen Vice President, Operations Manager Niels
NIELSEN SPORTS, 798

Masteralexis, Lisa Chair/Director
MASSACHUSETTS AMHERST, UNIVERSITY OF, 425

Masteralexis, Lisa Department Head
WONG, GLENN M., 916

Masters, Eris Database manager
ST. AUGUSTINE, PONTE VEDRA & THE BEACHES VISITORS & CONVENTION BU, 246

Masters, Paula President / Chief Merchandise Officer
GADZOOKS, 1228

Mastervick, Greg Treasurer
CANADIAN BROOMBALL FEDERATION, 67

Mastro, Don EVP, Sales
SPL INTEGRATED SOLUTIONS, 822

Mastrobuoni, Lauren Head Athletic Trainer
BLOOMFIELD COLLEGE ATHLETICS, 352

Mastroeni, Pablo Head Coach
MAJOR LEAGUE SOCCER, 158

Mastronardi, Ben Tournament Director
CENTRAL NEW YORK PGA SECTIONAL OFFICE, 105

Mastronardi, Corinne President
PRO-REP, INC., 803

Masur, Andy Sports Reporter
WGN-AM, 648

Mata, Ray Events & Production Manager
YAKIMA VALLEY SUNDOME, 1021

Mataele, Farren Vice President
DYNAFLEX INTERNATIONAL, 1126

Matalka, Jutta Director of Tourism & Amarillo Film Comm
AMARILLO CONVENTION & VISITOR COUNCIL, 227

Matarazzo, Nick Sr. VP/Director Group Publisher Automoti
HACHETTE FILIPACCHI MEDIA, 563

Matarese, Elizabeth Secretary
NATIONAL AERONAUTIC ASSOCIATION, 13

Matchett, Ben Assistant Athletic Director
CALGARY ATHLETICS, UNIVERSITY OF, 309

Matchett, Rick President
NORTH AMERICAN HOCKEY LEAGUE, 133

Mate, Edward Executive Director
COLORADO GOLF ASSOCIATION, 110

Mauro, Robert Managing Partner
MEYER, UNKOVIC & SCOTT, LLP, 895

Mavis, Stan Senior VP Apparel / Accessories
BROOKS, 1110

Mavrikes, George Sports Agent
BUSINESS ARENA, INC., 827

Mawicke, Megan Sports Reporter
WBBM-TV, 699

Max, Doug Snr. Assoc. Athl. Dir. for Facilities &
MOBY ARENA, 972, 987

Max, Mike Sports Reporter
WCCO-TV, 606, 640, 700

Maxam, Dan Assistant Athletics Director, Facilities
WILLIAMS STADIUM, 1016, 1019

Maxey, Cullen Executive VP, Business Ops/Chief
Revenue
NATIONAL LEAGUE OF PROFESSIONAL
BASEBALL CLUBS, THE, 31

Maxey, David Partner
SPAIN & GILLON, LLC, 855

Maxinson, Dan Salesperson
MAIN TROPHY SUPPLY COMPANY, 1159

Maxse, Joe Sports Writer
PLAIN DEALER, 520

Maxson, Chip General Manager
PACIFIC COAST LEAGUE OF
PROFESSIONAL BASEBALL CLUBS, 49

Maxwell, Becky Advertising Manager
DAILY IOWEGIAN, 477

Maxwell, Bob Assistant Athletic Director for
Facility
STATE UNIVERSITY OF NEW YORK, 1006

Maxwell, Dan Owner
CREATIVE URETHANES, 1121

Maxwell, Karen Classified Manager
MADISON DAILY LEADER, 504

Maxwell, Kevin General Manager
AMERICAN HOCKEY LEAGUE/AHL, 128

Maxwell, Michael Attorney
HASLER, FONFARA AND MAXWELL, LLP, 883

May, Andrew Sports Editor
MCKINNEY COURIER-GAZETTE, 506

May, Chris Director of Athletics
SAINT LOUIS UNIVERSITY ATHLETICS, 343,
949

May, Jeff Director of Athletics
LANDER UNIVERSITY ATHLETICS, 361

May, Mike Director of Communications & DTMBA
SPORTING GOODS MANUFACTURERS
ASSOCIATION, 224

May, Rick Program Director
KWTX THE TICKER 1460AM, 632

May, Ricky Sales/Marketing VP
LAS VEGAS MOTOR SPEEDWAY/LVMS, 1027

May, Tim Sports Reporter
COLUMBUS DISPATCH, 472

May, Tom Advertising Manager
CHRONICLE (WA), 470

May, Velma News Director
WUNR-AM, 669

Maybell, Bob Facilities Manager
THUNDERHILL RACEWAY PARK, 1034

Maye, Willie Sports Director
WILD-AM, 650

Mayer, Brad President
SPORTS SPECIFIC SCIENCES, 1215

Mayer, Dale Chief Executive Officer
FITBALL USA, 1133

Mayer, Ira Publisher
EPM LICENSING LETTER SOURCEBOOK,
THE, 557, 594

Mayer, Mercedes Sports Reporter
FORT WORTH STAR-TELEGRAM, 489

Mayer, Mika Partner
MORRISON & FOERSTER LLP, 896

Mayer, Mitch Advertising Manager
NEW JERSEY HERALD, 510

Mayer, Sally Sr. Manager
NEW MEXICO STATE FAIR, 964, 1042

Mayer, Sean Sports Editor
JOURNAL NEWS, 498

Mayer, Stanley Chief Financial Officer
PLAYOFF CORP., 1175

Mayers, Ronnie Director of Athletics
DELTA STATE UNIVERSITY (DSU)
ATHLETICS, 356

Mayes, Eric Secretary
INTERNATIONAL FEDERATION OF
AMERICAN FOOTBALL, 88

Mayes, George Executive Vice President and
Chief Opera
DIEBOLD INCORPORATED, 1124

Mayfield, Derrick Assistant AD, Facilities &
Operations
FANATICS RETAIL GROUP, 1227

Mayfield, Donny Athletic Director
TENNESSEE WESLEYAN COLLEGE
ATHLETICS, 321

Mayforth, Tyler Communications assistant
U.S. TRACK & FIELD AND CROSS COUNTRY
COACHES ASSOCIATION, 177

Maygurov, Victor First Vice President
INTERNATIONAL BIATHLON UNION (IBU), 61,
204

Mayhew, Lori Softball Head Coach
WESTERN NEW ENGLAND COLLEGE, 405,
437

Mayle, Michael Chief Technical Officer
TURNKEY SPORTS & ENTERTAINMENT, 749,
815

Maylish, Joe 600 West Manager
600 RACING, INC., 1089

Maynard, Melanie Social, Military, Education,
Religious,
NEBRASKA DIVISION OF TRAVEL AND
TOURISM, 241

Maynard, William Secretary/Treasurer
GOLF COURSE SUPERINTENDENTS
ASSOCIATION OF AMERICA/GCSAA, 102

Mayne, Brad President and CEO
INTERNATIONAL ASSOCIATION OF VENUE
MANAGERS/IAVM, 220

Mayne, Kenny Anchor
ESPN, 683

Maynor, Michelle Business Manager
CAPITOL SPEEDWAY, 1023

Maynulet, Javier Chief Financial Officer
TELEMUNDO, 677

Mayo, Dave Sports Writer
GRAND RAPIDS PRESS, 491

Mayo, Jamaal Director of Athletics
HARRIS-STOWE STATE COLLEGE
ATHLETICS, 313

Mayo, Mike CFO
SPECIAL OLYMPICS NORTHERN
CALIFORNIA, 196

Mayo, Shaun Chief People Officer
NATIONAL FOOTBALL LEAGUE/NFL, 94

Mayor, V Director, Marketing & Communications
SPORTING GOODS MANUFACTURERS
ASSOCIATION, 224

Mays, Lowry Chairman of the Board
SFX/CLEAR CHANNEL COMMUNICATIONS,
807

Mays, Mark Chairman
CLEAR CHANNEL ENTERTAINMENT, INC.,
687

Mays, Mark Chief Executive Officer
SFX/CLEAR CHANNEL COMMUNICATIONS,
807

Mays, Randall Vice Chairman
CLEAR CHANNEL ENTERTAINMENT, INC.,
687

Mays, Randall President and Chief Financial
Officer
SFX/CLEAR CHANNEL COMMUNICATIONS,
807

Mays, Randall President/Chief Financial Officer
CLEAR CHANNEL ENTERTAINMENT, INC.,
829

Mayse, Gary Executive Vice President, General
Manage
MIDWEST LEAGUE, 45

Mazek, Michael Editor
BOWLING CENTER MANAGEMENT, 553

Mazek, Mike Editor
BOWLING CENTER MANAGEMENT, 553

Mazza, Jillian Sponsorship Coordinator
CHRISTL ARENA, 957

Mazzante, Lou Managing Editor
BIKE, 552

Mazzei, Diane Board Chair
NORTHERN CALIFORNIA REGIONAL
COMMISSIONER/USA VOLLEYBALL, 212

Mazzella, Rocco Stadium Services Manager
ARROWHEAD STADIUM, 947

Mazzeo, Krista General Manager
WYBF-FM, 672

Mazzoni, Gale Marketing
MAZZ MARKETING, INC., 795

Mazzoni, Mark Project Management
BUTLER HEAVY STRUCTURES, 1051

Mazzoni, Trish President/CEO
SPECIAL OLYMPICS KENTUCKY, 195

Mazzoni, Wayne President
MAZZ MARKETING, INC., 795

Mazzotta, Donald Attorney
MAZZOTTA LAW OFFICES, 893

Mazzulla, Joe Head Coach
NATIONAL BASKETBALL ASSOCIATION/NBA,
56

McAdoo, Marilyn General Office Support
KANKAKEE COUNTY CONVENTION &
VISITORS BUREAU, 237

McAfee, Kate Associate Athletic Director for Event
Ma
WHITTEMORE CENTER ARENA, 122, 1018

McAfee, Mike Executive Director
BLOOMINGTON CONVENTION & VISITORS
BUREAU, 229

McAfee, Roger Director for Sports Media
Relations
UNIVERSITY OF WISCONSIN-PARKSIDE
ATHLETICS (UW-P), 375

McAffe, Mike Director Joplin Convention/Visotrs
Burea
JOPLIN CONVENTION & VISITORS BUREAU
AND SPORTS AUTHORITY, 237

McAffee, Brooke Vice President & Chief Financial
Officer
U.S. SKI AND SNOWBOARD ASSOCIATION
(USSA), 153, 154, 207

McAlear, Matt Brand CEO
DODGE, 727

McAleenan, Gregory VP for Institutional
Advancement
AQUINAS COLLEGE SPORTS MANAGEMENT
PROGRAM, 409

McAlister, James Attorney
DEUTCH, ALLAN H, 876

McAllister, Bryon Sports Information Contact
CAZENOVIA COLLEGE ATHLETICS, 380

McAllister, Mac Sports Producer/Photographer
WEAR-TV, 701

McAllister, R. News Director
KWTO-FM, 632

McAlpine, Jim Chief Financial Officer
SANTA ANITA PARK, 1044

McAndrew, Marty finance
SOLDIER FIELD, 1004

McAneny, Mike Director of Tournaments & Media
Relation
NEW JERSEY STATE GOLF ASSOCIATION,
114

McAninch, Jay President and CEO
ARCHERY TRADE ASSOCIATION, 14

McArdle, Amy Director of Accounting and Finance
JERRY UHT PARK, 976

McArdle, Rich Radio Network Sales Manager
CHIEFS RADIO NETWORK, 605

McArthur, Bob President & CEO
JOHNNY MAC'S SPORTING GOODS, 1230

McArthur, Gregg President
MCARTHUR TOWELS & SPORTS, 1161

McArthur, Rick Chief Financial Officer
JOHNNY MAC'S SPORTING GOODS, 1230

McAtee, Mike Interim Executive Director
USA BOXING, 67, 208

McAteer, Carol Executive Assistant to the
General Manag
ROGER DEAN STADIUM, 998

McAuley, Sheehan Program Director
FUTURE FOR KIDS, 834

McAuliff, Curtis Director of Athletic Training
OKLAHOMA CHRISTIAN UNVERSITY
ATHLETICS, 367

McAvay, Michael Sales
CARROM COMPANY, 1114

McBeain, Brandon Chief Operating Officer
NATIONAL WHEELCHAIR BASKETBALL
ASSOCIATION, 55

McBee, Billy President
TRANS-MISSISSIPPI GOLF ASSOCIATION,
116

McBratney, Dana Sports Editor
MAUI NEWS, 505

McDermid, Riley Editor
WINGFOOT, 592

McDermond, Kevin Public Relations Director
SENIOR BOWL, 92

McDermot, Deb President
KRON-TV, 694

McDermott, Brian President
FHI, INC./BUSY BODY, 1221, 1227

McDermott, Cathy Assistant Director of Athletics
for Deve
SAN FRANCISCO STATE UNIVERSITY
ATHLETICS, 369

McDermott, Erin Director of Athletics
CHICAGO ATHLETICS, UNIVERSITY OF, 332,
380

McDermott, Greg Commissioner
WV RACING COMMISSION, 82

McDermott, Jack Sports Writer
PLAIN DEALER, 520

McDermott, Joan Director of Athletics
SAN FRANCISCO ATHLETICS, UNIVERSITY
OF, 343

McDermott, John Sports Reporter
NEWS-REVIEW, 513

McDermott, Joseph Executive Director
NEBRASKA STATE FAIR, 1042

McDermott, Josh Sports Information Director
SOUTHERN OREGON UNIVERSITY
ATHLETICS, 320

McDermott, Marissa Attorney
EFRON, MORTON L., 878

McDermott, Mark Sports Writer
SACRAMENTO BEE, 526

McDermott, Paula Marketing Director
WPVI-TV, 708

McDermott, Sean Head Coach
NATIONAL FOOTBALL LEAGUE/NFL, 94

McDermott, Stephen Chief Financial Officer/Chief
Operations
GUNSTER, YOAKLEY & STEWART, P.C., 836

McDermott, Tim President
MAJOR LEAGUE SOCCER, 126, 158

McDermott, Tom Sports Information Consultant
DAEMEN COLLEGE ATHLETICS, 356

McDevitt, Jack General Manager
WBCK - BATTLE CREEK, 638

McDiffett, Tim Senior Associate Director of
Athletics
UNIVERSITY OF ALASKA ANCHORAGE
ATHLETICS, 350, 1012

McDole, Stew Associate Athletic Director
GRACELAND UNIVERSITY ATHLETICS, 313

McDonald, Allison Internal Operations
CENTRAL ATLANTIC COLLEGIATE
CONFERENCE, 293

McDonald, Billy Board Chairman
HENRY-GRIFFITTS, 1144

McDonald, Brad President
TRANSWORLD BUSINESS, 589

McDonald, Bruce Founding Partner
MCDONALD, FLEMING, MOORHEAD &
FERGUSON, GREEN & SMITH, 894

McDonald, Bryan National Director
U.S. WINDSURFING, 180

McDonald, Cameron Board Member
DELAWARE STATE GOLF ASSOCIATION, 110

McDonald, Cary Dept. Head
ILLINOIS AT URBANA-CHAMPAIGN,
UNIVERSITY OF, 420

McDonald, Chris Director of Operations
EASTERN LEAGUE, 38

McDonald, David Principal/Electrical Engineer
FRIBERG ASSOCIATES INC., 1057

McDonald, Dennis Director of Athletics
EVANGEL UNIVERSITY ATHLETICS, 312

McDonald, Diane Accountant
PIMA COUNTY FAIR, 1042

McDonald, Gene Attorney
MCDONALD, SNYDER & WILLIAMS P.C., 894

McDonald, Jack Director of Athletics
NEW ENGLAND ATHLETICS, UNIVERSITY
OF, 395

McDonald, James EVP / Chief Financial Officer
ROCKY SHOES & BOOTS, INC., 1183

McDonald, Jeremy Facilities General Manager
HOFHEINZ PAVILION, 970

McDonald, John General Manager
KGFW-AM, 618

McDonald, Kevin Assistant General Manager
AMERICAN HOCKEY LEAGUE/AHL, 88, 90,
127

McDonald, Korey Executive Vice President
UNITED STATES HOCKEY LEAGUE, 137

McDonald, L. SVP Marketing / Communications
SHOPKO STORES, INC., 1237

McDonald, Laura Assistant Professor/Exercise &
SportsSc
EVANSVILLE, UNIVERSITY OF, 417

McDonald, Mackey President/CEO
VF CORPORATION, 1208

McDonald, Margaret VP
FEDERAL PREMIUM AMMUNITION, 1132

McDonald, Peter Principal/Founder/President
SMITH, FAUSE, MCDONALD, INC., 822

McDonald, Phil Sports Director
WSJM-AM, 666

McDonald, Robert President
AMERICAN BLIND BOWLING ASSOCIATION,
65

McDonald, Scott Sports Writer
BAXTER BULLETIN, 463

McDonald, Sylvia Sports Director
WGCL-TV, 703

McDonald, Todd Vice President, Sales & Strategy
AMERICAN HOCKEY LEAGUE/AHL, 128

McDonell, Pat Editor
WESTERN OUTDOOR NEWS, 592

McDonell, Terry Managing Editor
SPORTS ILLUSTRATED, 585

McDoniel, George Senior Dir., Corporate
Partnerships Sale
AMERICAN LEAGUE OF PROFESSIONAL
BASEBALL CLUBS, THE, 29

McDonnal, Michael Sports Director
KONA-AM, 626

McDonnell, Erin Associate Athletics Director for
Facilit
ST JOHN'S UNIVERSITY, 1005

McDonnell, Matt Executive Director
MISSISSIPPI COAST COLISEUM AND
CONVENTION CENTER, 987

McDonnell, Pat Editorial Director
WESTERN OUTDOORS, 592

McDonnell, William Chief Financial Officer
AMF BOWLING WORLDWIDE, 1098

McDonough, Dan Assistant GM/Sales
FLORIDA STATE LEAGUE, 39

McDonough, Jason Director, Ticketing &
Premium Seating
NATIONAL FOOTBALL LEAGUE/NFL, 95

McDonough, Lorraine Office Adminstrator
NIXON, PEABODY, 897

McDonough, Patrick Chief Financial Officer
NATIONAL BASKETBALL ASSOCIATION/NBA,
57

McDowell, Chad Athletic Director
LOUISIANA STATE UNIVERSITY
(SHREVEPORT) ATHLETICS, 315

McDowell, Eric Sports Information Director
UNION COLLEGE (NY) ATHLETICS, 404

McDowell, Jack Manager
ARIZONA LEAGUE (ROOKIE), 34

McDuffee, Ben News Director
WVAC-FM, 670

McDuffie, Rich Director Athletics
LANTZ ARENA, 981

McEacharn, Joe President
EASTERN LEAGUE (AA LEVEL), 37

McEachen, Patrick Customer Service
SKYWAY, 1189

McEachern, Lon Partner
CALAMARI VIDEO, 598

McElhinney, Curtis Director, Goaltending
Development & Scou
NATIONAL HOCKEY LEAGUE/NHL, 126

McElroy, Clint Program Director
WTCR-AM, 668

McElroy, Jesse Stage Manager
BOUTWELL MUNICIPAL AUDITORIUM, 951

McElroy, Lee Athletic Director
RENSSELAER POLYTECHNIC INSTITUTE
ATHLETICS, 398

McElvania, Kent Associate Athletic Director
UPPER IOWA UNIVERSITY ATHLETICS(UIU),
373

McElveen-Hunter, Bonnie Chairman
AMERICAN RED CROSS NATIONAL
HEADQUARTERS, 217

McElwain, Jim Head Coach
HUGHES STADIUM (CO), 972

McElwee, Therese Member
KELLEY, MCELWEE & SCHMIDT, P.A., 888

McErlean, Chris VP Racing Operations
MEADOWLANDS RACING &
ENTERTAINMENT, 1046

McErlean, Christopher VP
ROSECROFT RACEWAY, 1043

McEver, John Publisher
WATER SKI, 553, 591

McEvoy, Bob Director of Athletics
METHODIST COLLEGE ATHLETICS, 393

McEvoy, Cheryl Operations Manager
SQUASH CANADA, 171

McEvoy, Marty Managing Director
SPORTSEARCH, INC., 748

McEvoy, Neil Vice President, Football Operations
CANADIAN FOOTBALL LEAGUE/CFL, 92

McEvoy, Steve Marketing Director
KERO-TV, 689

McEwan, Taras Head Coach
WESTERN HOCKEY LEAGUE, 139

McEwen, Ray Assistant Director/Facilities
SANFORD STADIUM, 1001

McFadden, Michael Treasurer
NEW JERSEY STATE GOLF ASSOCIATION,
114

McFadden, Susan Advertising Manager
DAILY SITKA SENTINEL, 480

McFall, Andrew VP Marketing
BIOLIFE, LLC, 1107

McFarland, Caden Sports Director
KRBC-TV, 694

McFarland, Cary Account Executive
SCARBOROUGH SPORTS MARKETING, 807

McFarland, Cayden Sports Anchor
KJRH-TV, 691

McFarland, Karen Treasurer
USTA FLORIDA, 175

McFarland, Michael Director of Athletics
BLOOMSBURG UNIVERSITY ATHLETICS, 352

McFarland, Ozzie Director of Athletics
CHOWAN COLLEGE ATHLETICS, 354

McFarland, Paul Head Coach
WESTERN HOCKEY LEAGUE, 138

McFarland, Rebekah Head Athletic Trainer
UNION UNIVERSITY ATHLETICS, 373

McFarland, Stan President
CONNECTICUT STATE GOLF ASSOCIATION,
110

McFarlane, Chris Deputy AD, External Relations
& Business
CENTRAL FLORIDA ATHLETICS, 326

McFarlane, Stephen Of Counsel
BLACK, WILLIAM D., LAW OFFICES OF, 866

McFarling, Aaron Sports Columnist
ROANOKE TIMES, 525

McFeeley, Paige Assistant Director of Athletic
Communica
UNIVERSITY OF PUGET SOUND, 397

McGOLDRICK, DAVID Member
MORTON & MCGOLDRICK, P.S., 897

McGann, Todd Deputy Athletic Director
EASTERN WASHINGTON UNIVERSITY
ATHLETICS, 329

McGann, Tom President and Chief Executive
Officer
SPYDER ACTIVE SPORTS, 1195

McGarity, Greg Director of Athletics
SANFORD STADIUM, 1001

McGarry, Michael Sports Writer
PRESS OF ATLANTIC CITY, 522

McGarvey, Jason Editor
OUTDOOR AMERICA MAGAZINE, 574

McGarvey, Michael VP Marketing
ENTER SPORTS MANAGEMENT, 832

McGauchie, Blair General Manager
TD STATION, 1008

McGaughey, Bill Chairman
MEMPHIS & SHELBY COUNTY SPORTS
AUTHORITY, 240

McGearty, Larry Chief Creative Strategists
BFG COMMUNICATIONS, 775

McGee, Diane East Coast Sales Manager
SPECIAL EVENTS MAGAZINE, 583

McGee, Marty Senior Vice President of Industrial Serv
SAFWAY SERVICES, LLC, 1185

McGee, Michael Professor, Program Chair
LENOIR-RHYNE COLLEGE, 361, 423

McGee, Pat Sports Director
KTHN-FM, 614, 630

McGee, Shawn VP/Sales and Marketing
HOMESTEAD-MIAMI SPEEDWAY, LLC, 1025

McGee, Steve President
CDM SPORT, 1115

McGhee, Jenny Assoc. Commissioner, External Relations
SOUTHLAND CONFERENCE, 305

McGillis, Bill Exec. Director of Athletics
SAN DIEGO ATHLETICS, UNIVERSITY OF, 343, 984, 996

McGillis, Jeff Chief Operating Officer
WESTERN HOCKEY LEAGUE, 138

McGillivray, David Race Director
BOSTON ATHLETIC ASSOCIATION, 148

McGillivray, Pamela Shareholder
GARVEY & STODDARD, 881

McGinley, Michael Chief Operating Officer
DEMAYO, LAW OFFICES OF MICHAEL L.L.P., 876

McGinnis, Anna News Director
WOHS, 648, 659

McGinnis, Tom Senior Associate AD/CFO
WILLIAMS ARENA, 1019

McGivern, Art SVP / General Counsel & Secretary
ACE HARDWARE, 1215

McGivern, Gene Sports Information Director
ST. THOMAS UNIVERSITY ATHLETICS, 401

McGiveron, Brian Vice President
OVER-THE-LINE PLAYERS ASSOCIATION, 170

McGlade, Bernadette Commissioner
ATLANTIC 10 CONFERENCE, 291

McGlaughlin, Allen General Manager
KQLL - AM, 627

McGlone, Colleen President
SSLASPA DBA SPORT & RECREATION LAW ASSOCIATION, 225

McGlynn, Denis President/Chief Executive Officer
DOVER INTERNATIONAL SPEEDWAY, 1024

McGlynn, Denis president and CEO of Dover Motorsports
GATEWAY MOTORSPORTS PARK, 1025

McGonagle, George President
APPALACHIAN LEAGUE, 33, 951

McGough, Aaron Head Coach
WOMEN'S PREMIER SOCCER LEAGUE, 168

McGovern, Gail President/CEO
AMERICAN RED CROSS NATIONAL HEADQUARTERS, 217

McGovern, Jeremy Executive Editor/Publisher
AMERICAN FARRIERS JOURNAL, 549

McGovney, Carol Sales Support Manager
SOURCE INTERLINK MEDIA, 582

McGowan, Bob Chairman/Professor
CENTRAL WASHINGTON UNIVERSITY, 413

McGowan, Brad Assistant Athletic Director for Developm
PROVOST UMPHREY STADIUM, 994

McGowan, Diane Director
NEW JERSEY AAU ASSOCIATION, 215

McGowan, Don Sales Manager
ANACONDA SPORTS, 1216

McGowan, Mike General Manager
WGAD, 647

McGowan, Pat Program Director
WGCM-AM, 647

McGowan, R President
LONG ISLAND CVB & SPORTS COMMISSION, 239

McGowan, Rick Sports Reporter
NEWPORT DAILY NEWS, 511

McGowan, Willie HPER Instructor
ALCORN STATE UNIVERSITY, 409

McGrady, Paul Associate Director of Athletics
SOUTHERN NAZARENE UNIVERSITY ATHLETICS, 370

McGrail, Jack Executive Director
OREGON RACING COMMISSION, 81

McGrail, Sean President
NEW ENGLAND SPORTS NETWORK/NESN, 676

McGrann, Jason Sports Editor
DAILY IOWEGIAN, 477

McGrath, Daniel Vice President
CAPITOL SPORTS NETWORK, 685

McGrath, Jim Acting Secretary
U.S. WINDSURFING, 180

McGrath, Joan Office Administration
ARIZONA FALL LEAGUE (ROOKIE LEVEL), 34

McGrath, John Sports Columnist
NEWS TRIBUNE, 512

McGrath, Richard President
RIGHT GARD CORPORATION, 1182

McGrath, Terri Manager
SENIOR MANAGEMENT GROUP, 853

McGraw, Margaret Assistant Athletic Director
OUACHITA BAPTIST UNIVERSITY ATHLETICS, 367

McGregor, Adam Vice President Sales - Asia
UNITED STATES PLAYING CARD COMPANY, THE/WPT, 1206

McGregor, Andy Executive Vice President
KI, 1152

McGregor, Kate Director of Sales & Marketing
SOLDIER FIELD, 1004

McGrew, Ray Advertising Manager
OLNEY DAILY MAIL, 516

McGrew, Ron Director of Athletic Facilities
CALIFORNIA UNIVERSITY OF PENNSYLVANIA ATHLETICS, 353

McGroarty, Jim General Manager
UNITED STATES HOCKEY LEAGUE, 137

McGrory, Jeanine Senior VP, Finance
NATIONAL HOCKEY LEAGUE/NHL, 125

McGuffin, Kurt Director of Athletics
MISSOURI WESTERN STATE COLLEGE ATHLETICS (MWSU), 346, 364

McGuffin, Seth
SELBY STADIUM, 1002

McGuinness, Lori Assistant Director of Athletics, Complia
FELICIAN COLLEGE ATHLETICS, 358

McGuinness, Scott Director of Athletics
WASHINGTON & JEFFERSON COLLEGE ATHLETICS (W&J), 405

McGuinty, Ryan Assistant Commissioner for Media Relat
MID-EASTERN ATHLETIC CONFERENCE, 299

McGuire, Bill Managing Partner
MAJOR LEAGUE SOCCER, 158

McGuire, Charlie Director of Sports Information
DICKINSON COLLEGE(DC) ATHLETICS, 383

McGuire, Chaz Host
THE POWER PLAY, 608

McGuire, Duncan President
USA CYCLING, 72

McGuire, John Partner
THORSNES, BARTOLOTTA & MCGUIRE, 912

McGuire, John Founding Partner
THORSNES, BARTOLOTTA & MCGUIRE, 912

McGuire, Kennard Executive Vice President, Sports
CSMG INTERNATIONAL, LTD, 779

McGuire, Kevin Director Marketing
PROFILES SPORTS, INC., 850

McGuire, Randy Head Athletic Trainer
GEORGETOWN COLLEGE ATHLETICS, 261, 313

McGuirk, Lisa Director of Athletics
GANNON UNIVERSITY ATHLETICS (GU), 359

McGuirk, Terry Chair
NATIONAL LEAGUE OF PROFESSIONAL BASEBALL CLUBS, THE, 31

McGurk, Tom Sports Reporter
PHILADELPHIA INQUIRER, 519

McHale, John Executive Vice President, Administration
KAUFFMAN STADIUM, 978

McHale, Kevin Basketball Operations VP
TARGET CENTER, 1007

McHargue, Steven Chief Information Officer
JACKSON WALKER LLP, 839

McHatten, Tyson Senior Associate AD, External Ops./Commu
MAINE ATHLETICS, UNIVERSITY OF, 335

McHorney, Mark Director of Athletics
BENEDICTINE UNIVERSITY ATHLETICS, 378

McHugh, Craig Sports Editor
STATE, 535

McHugh, Eric Sports Writer
PATRIOT LEDGER, 518

McHugh, Joe Advertising Staff
SAXTON COMMUNICATIONS INC., 558, 806

McHugh, Kevin Director of Athletics
BATES COLLEGE ATHLETICS, 377, 967

McHugh, Liam Sports Director
WTHI-TV, 710

McHugh, Paul Divisional Merchandise Manager
BIGG'S HYPER SHOPPES, 1219

McHugh, Robert Chief Financial Officer
FOOT LOCKER, INC., 1228

McHugh, Yvonne Director of Marketing and Communications
SCARBOROUGH SPORTS MARKETING, 807

McIlroy, Gareth Managing Partner
HEIDRICK & STRUGGLES, 787

McIlvain, Jim Editor
MOUNTAIN BIKE ACTION, 571

McIlvane, Matt Head Coach
AMERICAN HOCKEY LEAGUE/AHL, 128

McInerney, John Director, Consumer Affairs
RUDER/FINN SPORTS, INC., 806

McInerney, Ryan Chief Executive Officer
VISA USA, 734

McInnis, Kyle 1st Vice-Chairman
INDEPENDENCE STADIUM, 91, 973

McInnis, Malcolm Staff
MCINNIS, MALCOLM C., 894

McIntire, Danny President
LEMOORE RACEWAY, 1027

McIntosh, Chuck Director of Athletics
WISCONSIN ATHLETICS, UNIVERSITY OF, 349

McIntosh, Duncan Publisher
SEA MAGAZINE, 553, 569, 580

McIntosh, Jill Vice President of Human Resources
FRED MEYER STORES, INC., 1228

McIntosh, Matthew Chair/Director
SHEPHERD UNIVERSITY, 432

McIntyre, Frank Sports Agent
AKIN & RANDOLPH AGENCY, 824

McIntyre, Jeff Sales and Service
HUDSON BOAT WORKS INC., 539, 1146

McIntyre, Jessica Director of Internal Affairs
LEE UNIVERSITY ATHLETICS, 361

McIntyre, Jim Vice President of Sales & Marketing
PARAMOUNT FITNESS CORPORATION, 662, 1172

McIntyre, Kevin Director of Operations
LLOYD NOBLE CENTER, 983

McIntyre, Martin Advertising Manager
WTCQ-FM, 667

McIntyre, Reggie Associate AD, External Relations
LOUISIANA TECH UNIVERSITY ATHLETICS, 335

McIver, Dan Deputy AD
NORTHERN KENTUCKY UNIVERSITY ATHLETICS, 340

McIver, Scott Head Athletic Trainer
MANHATTANVILLE COLLEGE ATHLETICS, 391

McJunkin, John Managing Partner
PIPER MARBURY RUDNICK & WOLFE, 899

McKane, Dan Executive Director
MINNESOTA INTERCOLLEGIATE ATHLETIC CONFERENCE, 300

McKavitt, Tom Assoc. AD, Facilities & Maintenance
NAVY-MARINE CORPS MEMORIAL STADIUM, 988

McKay, Andy Vice President & Assistant General Manag
AMERICAN LEAGUE OF PROFESSIONAL BASEBALL CLUBS, THE, 30

McKay, John Executive Director, Security
NATIONAL LEAGUE OF PROFESSIONAL BASEBALL CLUBS, THE, 32

McKay, Ray Fair Director
MARSHFIELD FAIR, 1041

McKay, Rich Chief Executive Officer
NATIONAL FOOTBALL LEAGUE/NFL, 94

McKeaney, Ed Senior Executive Vice President Merchand
BOSCOV'S DEPARTMENT STORES, 1220

Meleney, Margaret Chief Financial Officer
CLUB MANAGERS ASSOCIATION OF
AMERICA, 219

Melewski, Steve Sports Director
WBAL RADIO, 637

Melhorn, Mark Sports Assistant Editor
PRESS OF ATLANTIC CITY, 522

Meli, Larry President
NATIONAL BASKETBALL ASSOCIATION
DEVELOPMENT LEAGUE, 59

Melia, Andrew Sports Director
KLOE-AM, 622

Melia, Erica Senior VP of Accounts Management
ALLOY MARKETING & PROMOTION, 772

Melkonian, Lois Host
SPORTS ZOO, 606

Mell, Randall Sports Columnist
SOUTH FLORIDA SUN-SENTINEL, 532

Mell, Randy Sports Writer (Golf)
SOUTH FLORIDA SUN-SENTINEL, 532

Meller, Sol President
FELDMAR WATCH COMPANY, INC., 1132

Mellinger, Howard Publisher
MID-STATES RACING NEWS, 570

Mellinger, Sam Sports Writer
KANSAS CITY STAR, 499

Mellman, Gerald Sports Editor
INTERMOUNTAIN JEWISH NEWS, 497

Mello, Rick Deputy Athletics Director
RICE UNIVERSITY ATHLETICS, 342, 996

Mellor, John President/Chief Executive Officer
WORK IN SPORTS, 749

Mellor, Kyle Account Executive
INTEGRATED SPORTS MARKETING, 678

Mellott, Dennis President/General Manager
MICHIGAN RADIO NETWORK, 606

Melrose, Andrew VP, Partnership Marketing
CHUKCHANSI PARK, 957

Melton, Bill Commissioner
KENTUCKY INTERCOLLEGIATE ATHLETIC
CONFERENCE, 297

Melton, Esther General Manager
KWRD-AM, 632

Melton, Jane Program Implementation
UNITED MARINE MANUFACTURERS
ASSOCIATION, 64

Melton, Ron Eligibility Chairman
SOUTHERN STATES ATHLETIC
CONFERENCE, 305

Melton, Ronald Faculty Athletics Representative
BREWTON PARKER COLLEGE ATHLETICS,
220, 309

Melton, Tim Weekend Sports Anchor
KTRK-TV, 679, 695

Melville, Jim President
MELO CO., INC. AND XS BAGGAGE, 1162

Melville, Kelly Head Athletic Trainer
CURRY COLLEGE ATHLETICS, 382

Melvin, Brian General Manager
NATIONAL LEAGUE OF PROFESSIONAL
BASEBALL CLUBS, THE, 32

Melvin, Richard Sports Editor
CLEVELAND DAILY BANNER, 471

Memkeen, Kate Director, Operations
NORTH AMERICAN HOCKEY LEAGUE, 133

Menachem, Jesse Executive Director
MASSACHUSETTS GOLF ASSOCIATION, 112

Menahem, Morgan Managing Director
360 MANAGEMENT, LLC, 770

Menconi, Ron VP / Merchandising / Marketing
WHOLESALE SPORTS OUTDOOR
OUTFITTERS, 1241

Mendel, Ronald Chair of Human
Performance/Sport Busines
UNIVERSITY OF MOUNT UNION ATHLETICS,
436

Mendelson, Cara Sales & Marketing Coordinator
UNITED STATES HOCKEY LEAGUE, 137

Mendelson, Littler Chair
SPECIAL OLYMPICS NEVADA, 196

Mendesh, John Secretary
WESTERN GOLF ASSOCIATION/EVANS
SCHOLARS FOUNDATION, 117

Mendesh, John Secretary
WESTERN GOLF ASSOCIATION, EVANS
SCHOLARS FOUNDATION, 118

Mendez, Adolfo Managing Editor
BOAT & MOTOR DEALER, 552

Mendez, Armando CEO
DYNASTY APPAREL INDUSTRIES, 1126

Mendez, Carlos Sports Reporter
FORT WORTH STAR-TELEGRAM, 489

Mendez, Erica Licensing Coordinator
DYNASTY APPAREL INDUSTRIES, 1126

Mendez, Ignacio President
DYNASTY APPAREL INDUSTRIES, 1126

Mendez, Lorenzo COO
DYNASTY APPAREL INDUSTRIES, 1126

Mendez, Tony Station Manager
WPMZ-AM, 661

Mendoroz, Randy President
AQUATIC DESIGN GROUP, INC., 1049

Mendoza, Carole Promotion Manager
KCUB-AM, 615

Mendoza, Gilberto Executive Vice President
WORLD BOXING ASSOCIATION, 67

Mendoza, Jeanna Director of Events
U.S. TAEKWONDO UNION, 143

Mendoza, Luis Head Coach
USL LEAGUE TWO, 164

Mendoza, Steven VP, Business Development
PRO SPECIALTIES GROUP, 1177

Mendrick, Michael Executive Director
PROFESSIONAL SNOWSPORTS
INSTRUCTORS OF AMERICA - EASTERN, 153

Meneely, Jane Managing Editor
CHESAPEAKE BAY MAGAZINE, 554

Meneghetti, Madelyn Regional Product Specialist
SCHELDE NORTH AMERICA, LLC, 1186

Menio, Staphanie Deputy AD
NORTH CAROLINA STATE UNIVERSITY
ATHLETICS, 339

Menning, Rick Sports Editor
CORAL SPRINGS-PARKLAND FORUM, 473

Mensheha, Mark Assistant Managing Editor
STREET & SMITH'S SPORTSBUSINESS
JOURNAL, 587

Mentgen, Barbara Director of Operations
JOHNSON CITY CONVENTION & VISITORS
BUREAU, 237

Mentone, Mark Sports Information Director
FELICIAN COLLEGE ATHLETICS, 358

Mentz, Joe Operations & Tournament Director
CONNECTICUT PGA SECTIONAL OFFICE,
105

Menzer, Eric President
ATLANTIC LEAGUE, 35

Menzer, Rod Chair
USA ARCHERY, 207

Menzies, Hue Executive Director
WOMEN'S PREMIER SOCCER LEAGUE, 166

Menzies, John Sports Editor
STEPHENVILLE EMPIRE-TRIBUNE, 535

Menzies, Marvin Head Coach, Men's Basketball
PAN AMERICAN CENTER, 991

Meoli, Marc General Manager
WOMEN'S PREMIER SOCCER LEAGUE, 167

Meranto, Tom Advertising Manager
TONAWANDA NEWS, 541

Mercer, John Dept. Chairperson
NEVADA, LAS VEGAS, UNIVERSITY OF, 428

Mercer, Rob Advertising Director
SPRINGFIELD NEWS-SUN, 533

Mercer, Tenisha Advertising Reporter
DETROIT NEWS, 483

Mercer, Tom Vice President, Sales & Marketing
HIGH 5 SPORTSWEAR, 1144

Merchant, Bruce Program/Sports Director
KEZM-AM, 617

Merchant, Fazal Senior Vice President/Treasurer
DIRECTV, INC., 686

Merchant, Megan Senior Woman Administrator
OLIVET COLLEGE ATHLETICS, 396

Merchant, Todd Sports Writer
DAILY PROGRESS, 479

Mercurio, Mario Associate AD, Basketball Admin.
XAVIER UNIVERSITY ATHLETICS, 350

Mercurio, Tony Sports Director
WGH-AM THE SCORE, 647

Merdanov, Berdi Coach
USL LEAGUE TWO, 163

Meredith, Lee Vice President
WAFF-TV, 698

Meredith, Rick Advertising Manager
TEXARKANA GAZETTE, 538

Merek, J EVP / Chief Operating Officer
K2 INC., 1151

Merendino, Joe Supervisor of Baseball Officials
WEST VIRGINIA INTERCOLLEGIATE
ATHLETIC CONFERENCE, 306

Mergenthaler, Mike Vice President
HELENA AREA CHAMBER OF COMMERCE,
970

Mergy, Sarah Senior AssociateDirector of
Marketing an
BSA ARCHITECTS, 1051

Meriwether, Denise Promotions Coordinator
WVEE-FM, 670

Merk, Eric President
INSPORT INTERNATIONAL, INC., 1148

Merkin, Randy Executive Producer
YAHOO! SPORTS RADIO, 604

Merkle, John Attorney
KAY & MERKLE, 887

Merkle, Lauren Sport Sciences Assistant
Professor
WINGATE UNIVERSITY, 438

Merkowitz, Mary Director of Library Services
CHERNESKY, RICHARD, 872

Merola, Matt President
MATTGO ENTERPRISES, INC., 842

Merrell, Amy Chief Operating Officer
JACK ROUSE ASSOCIATES, 790

Merrell, Gary Advertising Vice President
COLUMBUS DISPATCH, 472

Merriam, Roger Sports Editor
WATERTOWN PUBLIC OPINION, 546

Merrill, Elizabeth Sports Reporter
OMAHA WORLD-HERALD, 516

Merrill, Emily League Administrator
ATLANTIC LEAGUE OF PROFESSIONAL
BASEBALL, THE, 35

Merrill, Jeff Director of Compliance
LEES-MCRAE COLLEGE ATHLETICS, 361

Merrill, Joanne Athletic Director
RIVIER UNIVERSITY ATHLETICS, 398

Merrill, Miriam Associate Director of Athletics
HAMILTON COLLEGE ATHLETICS, 386

Merriman, James Head Coach
CANADIAN PREMIER LEAGUE, 156

Merriman, Kelly Vice President
HEALTH FITNESS CORPORATION, 1059

Merriman, Peter Financial Officer
DANIELS, ERIC D., 875

Merritt, Brenda General Manager
1390AM AND 97.1FM THE POINT, 611

Merritt, Edward Attorney
HARBOUR, SMITH, HARRIS & MERRITT, 883

Merritt, Trent General Manager
USF SUN DOME, 1014

Merrow, Bob Head Athletic Trainer
KEENE STATE COLLEGE ATHLETICS, 389

Merry, Glenn Chief Executive Officer
USROWING, 147

Merry, Tim Vice President
MIDDLE ATLANTIC GOLF ASSOCIATION, 113

Merry, Wade Executive Director
SOUTH DAKOTA GOLF ASSOCIATION, 115

Merryman, Tim Executive Producer
TICKET760 KTKR, 635

Mertens, Jerome President
BERTHELSEN, RICHARD, 826

Mertens, Mark Owner
A4, 1089

Mertz, Adam Sports Editor
CAPITAL TIMES, 468

Mertz, Carie General Manager
WORW-FM, 660

Mertz, Dolores Commissioner
IOWA RACING & GAMING COMMISSION, 79

Mertz, Tim Director of Recreational Sports
MASSACHUSETTS INSTITUTE OF
TECHNOLOGY (MIT), 392

Meruelo, Alex Majority Owner, Chair & Governor
NATIONAL HOCKEY LEAGUE/NHL, 123

Mervis, Gary Secretary
MONROE COUNTY SPORTS COMMISSION,
241

Mervis, Gregg VP/COO
AKRON SUMMIT CONVENTION & VISITORS
BUREAU, 226

Meryowitz, Carol President
T.J. MAXX, 1239

Merz, Erin Sports Information Director
GREAT LAKES VALLEY CONFERENCE, 296

Mescall, Greg Director Of Communications
AMERICAN WATER POLO COACHES
ASSOCIATION, 179

Mesecher, Robb Advertising Manager
MOUNTAIN BIKE ACTION, 571

Mesereau, Thomas Attorney
COLLINS, MESEREAU, REDDOCK & YU, LLP,
873

Meseroll, Bob Sports Editor
MISSOULIAN, 507

Meserve, Robert President
DISABLED SPORTS USA, 193

Mesigian, Chris Internal Sales Manager, Rowing
NIELSEN-KELLERMAN, 1168

Mesker, Bobby Director of Athletics
SUL ROSS STATE UNIVERSITY ATHLETICS,
403

Messemer, Melissa General Manager
WOMEN'S FOOTBALL ALLIANCE / WFA, 98

Messenger, Steve Assistant AD, Operations &
Events
DOYT PERRY FIELD STADIUM, 962

Messer, Jeff Assistant Professor
SLIPPERY ROCK UNIVERSITY, 432

Messer, Ray President / Chairman of the Board
WALTER P MOORE, 1063

Messer, Raymond President and Chairman of the
Board
WALTER P MOORE, 1063

Messerlie, Doug Founder
RMI/ATLANTA, 852

Messerly, April Assistant Athletic Director for
Faciliti
WEST VIRGINIA UNIVERSITY/WVU
COLISEUM, 988, 1018

Messerschmidt, Rick Secretary/Treasurer
DES MOINES AREA SPORTS COMMISSION,
232

Messier, Francois Vice President Programming
LE RESEAU DES SPORTS (RSD) INC., 698

Messler, Michael President
ERIK SPORTS, INC., 1129

Messmer, Wayne Senior EVP
AMERICAN HOCKEY LEAGUE/AHL, 127

Messner, Joe President
BUSHNELL CORPORATION, 1112

Messner, Joseph Chief Executive Officer
BUSHNELL SPORT OPTICS, 1112

Metcalf, Matt Principal
DAVIS DESIGN, 1054

Metcalf, Peter President / Chief Operating Officer
BLACK DIAMOND EQUIPMENT, LTD., 1107

Metcalf, Steve Deputy Athletic Director
WHITTEMORE CENTER ARENA, 1018

Metcalfe, Scott Sports Director
CJCL, 612

Metchori, Rodger Sales Director
ACTIVE ALERT, 819

Metheney, Doug News Director
WTIV-AM, 668

Metivier, Donald Founder
SPORTDECALS, 1193

Metress, Dip Men's Basketball Head Coach
AUGUSTA STATE UNIVERSITY ATHLETICS,
351

Metrose, Michael VP / General Merchandise
Manager
U.S. FACTORY OUTLETS, INC., 1239

Mettlen, Sara Sports Editor
LEAVENWORTH TIMES, 502

Metz, Carol Promotion Manager
WBTM-AM, 639

Metzdorf, Erik Buyer
CITY SPORTS, 1223

Metzen, Ryan Sports Editor
WELLINGTON DAILY NEWS, 546

Metzen, Tom 1st Vice President
HORSEMEN'S BENEVOLENT AND
PROTECTIVE ASSOCIATION, 76

Metzger, Dan President
THOROUGHBRED OWNERS AND BREEDERS
ASSOCIATION, 77

Metzger, Mike Founder
WARPT INDUSTRIES, INC., 1209

Metzger, Pat Sports Director
KTIK SPORTS RADIO 1350, 630

Metzker, J. Sports Director
KTVN-TV, 696

Meus, Daniel Principal
GRAHAM/MEUS, INC. ARCHITECTS, 1058

Mevorach, Josh Community Relations Manager
KEYSPAN PARK, 979

Mewhirter, Jack President
HALO BRANDED SOLUTIONS, 786

Meyer, Charlie President
KOLDER INC, 970, 1153

Meyer, Chuck Program Director
THE ZONE SPORTS RADIO 1300 AM, 635

Meyer, Dan Senior Associate AD, Resource
Developmen
BOWLING GREEN STATE UNIVERSITY
ATHLETICS, 325

Meyer, Debra VP Operations
BODY WISE INTERNATIONAL, 1108

Meyer, Greg Director
MONTRAIL, INC., 1164

Meyer, JOhn Vice Chancellor
TOOMEY FIELD, 1010

Meyer, Jim Co-Owner
INDYCAR, 22

Meyer, John Sports Writer
DENVER POST, 482

Meyer, Kip VP and General Manager
SCHUTT SPORTS INC, 1186

Meyer, Linda VP of Finance
EXCLUSIVE SPORTS MARKETING, INC., 782

Meyer, Mark Sports Editor
LANSING STATE JOURNAL, 229, 501

Meyer, Martin Partner
ARCHITECHNICS INC., 1049

Meyer, Michael Director
TRIBLER, ORPETT & CRONE, 912

Meyer, Nancy Director of Athletics, Internal
Operatio
CALVIN COLLEGE ATHLETICS, 379

Meyer, Nathalie Secretary
AQUINAS COLLEGE SPORTS MANAGEMENT
PROGRAM, 409

Meyer, Paul Sports Writer
PITTSBURGH POST-GAZETTE, 520

Meyer, Pete Director of Athletics
FLORIDA SOUTHERN COLLEGE ATHLETICS
(FSC), 358

Meyer, Rob Internet Services Director
ANACONDA SPORTS, 1216

Meyer, Scott Director of Marketing
SPORTSPLAY EQUIPMENT, INC., 1194

Meyer, Tex General Manager
WVGM-AM, 670

Meyer, Tonda Advertising Manager
INDEPENDENT RECORD, 496

Meyer, Urban Head Coach, Football
OHIO STADIUM, 990

Meyers, Bob Executive Vice President/President
Media
PLAYBOY ENTERTAINMENT GROUP, 847

Meyers, Buddy Vice Chair
AMERICAN HOCKEY LEAGUE/AHL, 127

Meyers, Charlie Outdoors Editor
DENVER POST, 482

Meyers, D Chairman
CROWE & DUNLEVY, 830

Meyers, John Physician
ORTHOPAEDIC RESEARCH OF VIRGINIA,
922

Meyers, Kate Contributing Writer
GOLF FOR WOMEN, 561

Meyers, Mark Director of Communications
PICO RIVERA SPORTS ARENA, 993

Meyers, Randy President and CEO
WSP, 1063

Meyers, Rob Associate AD, Business
STEPHEN F. AUSTIN STATE UNIVERSITY
ATHLETICS, 345, 1019

Meyers, Stephen President
GREAT OUTDOOR CLOTHING COMPANY,
1229

Meyerson, Adam Regional Sales Director
HACHETTE FILIPACCHI MEDIA, 563

Meyocks, Terrence President/Chief Operating
Officer
AQUEDUCT, 1042

Meyoucks, Terrence President/Chief Operating
Officer
BELMONT PARK, 1036

Meyrowitz, Carol Chief Executive Officer
T.J. MAXX, 1239

Mezzanotte, Thomas Executive Director
RHODE ISLAND INTERSCHOLASTIC
LEAGUE, INC., 202

Mezzatesta, Jeffrey Publisher
MARINER, 569

Miazga, Mike Editor
VOLLEYBALL MAGAZINE, 591

Micale, John Vice President, Sports Production
HBO SPORTS, 676

Micco, Jerry Assistant Managing Editor/Sports
PITTSBURGH POST-GAZETTE, 520

Miceli, Janice VP
16W MARKETING, LLC, 770

Michael, Bill Football Coach
UNIVERSITY OF NORTH TEXAS-COLISEUM,
1013

Michael, Kevin Senior Editor
WAKE BOARDING MAGAZINE, 591

Michael, Mike Program Director
WHBU 1240, 649

Michael, Miranda President
ACTION SPOT SPORTS, 1216

Michael, Sandra Assistant Vice President of
Athletics
HOLY FAMILY COLLEGE ATHLETICS, 360,
420

Michael, Tom Athletic Director
EASTERN ILLINOIS UNIVERSITY ATHLETICS,
329, 989

Michael, Vollmer Vice Chair
CANADIAN SAFE BOATING COUNCIL, 63

Michaelian, Jim President/CEO
GRAND PRIX ASSOCIATION OF LONG
BEACH, 16

Michaelis, Marcelo President, Labatt Canada
BUDWEISER CANADA, 726

Michaelis, Vicki (703)570-8777
USA TODAY, 543

Michaels, Andrea President of Extraordinary
Events
EXTRAORDINARY EVENTS, 754

Michaels, Bob Sports Director
WELM-AM, 644

Michaels, Brendan Operations Manager
WKAN AM 1320, 653

Michaels, Carrie Associate Director of Athletics
SHIPPENSBURG UNIVERSITY OF
PENNSYLVANIA ATHLETICS, 369

Michaels, Chad Sports Director
WDOR-FM, 643

Michaels, Dan Program Director
WBIZ-AM SPORTS RADIO, 639

Michaels, Elaine President
SAN DIEGO COUNTY WOMEN'S GOLF
ASSOCIATION, 115

Michaels, Jeff Director of Athletics
SHIPPENSBURG UNIVERSITY OF
PENNSYLVANIA ATHLETICS, 369

Michaels, Jon EVP Operations
EXTRAORDINARY EVENTS, 754

Michaels, Scott General Manager
PETERSEN EVENTS CENTER, 992

Michalec, Matt Director of Sports
Communications
NORFOLK STATE UNIVERSITY
ATHLETICS(NSU), 366

Michalik, Bettiann Sports Information Director
FITCHBURG STATE COLLEGE (FSC)
ATHLETICS, 385

Micham, Ray Architect/Partner
THE COLLABORATIVE, INC.,, 1052

Michaud, Marcel Customer Service Associate
BLADEMASTER, 1107

Michaud, Nancy Senior VP, General Counsel -
Secretary
HUFFY BICYCLE COMPANY, 1146

Michaud, Nancy SVP, General Counsel /
Secretary
ROYCE UNION BICYCLE COMPANY, INC.,
1184

Michaux, Scott Sports Columnist
AUGUSTA CHRONICLE, 462

Michele, Dennis President
AMERICAN VOLKSSPORT
ASSOCIATION/AVA, 217

Micheletto, John Head Coach, Ice Hockey
MULLINS CENTER, 988

Michelle A. Haggar, Dr. MD
HAGGAR CORPORATION, 1141

Michelotti, Brian Assistant Director
MONTANA HS ASSOCIATION, 201

Michiaels, Jeramy Associate Director of Broadcasting
NCAA, 601

Michlig, Keith Assistant Athletic Director for Sports I
GEORGIA SOUTHWESTERN STATE UNIVERSITY ATHLETICS, 359

Middlebrook, Chris President
USA BANDY, 25

Middleburg, Ira Managing Partner
MIDDLEBERG RIDDLE GROUP, 895

Middleton, Donnie Sports Director
KMEM-FM, 623

Middleton, John Managing Partner & CEO
NATIONAL LEAGUE OF PROFESSIONAL BASEBALL CLUBS, THE, 32

Middleton, Kisha Athletic Business Manager
LINCOLN UNIVERSITY ATHLETICS, 362

Middleton, Michelle Administrative and Finance
EXPLORE FAIRBANKS, 233

Middleton, Rand Sports Reporter
WEST CENTRAL TRIBUNE, 546

Midgley, Jim Head Coach
QUEBEC MARITIMES MAJOR JUNIOR HOCKEY LEAGUE, 135

Midkiff, Patty Controller
NATIONAL SPORTS AGENCY, 844

Midland, Greg Associate Editor
GOLF MAGAZINE, 561

Miebach, Michael CEO
MASTERCARD, 729

Miech, Rob Sports Reporter
LAS VEGAS SUN, 501

Miedema, Laurence Sports Reporter
SAN JOSE MERCURY NEWS, 528

Mientkiewicz, Doug Manager
SOUTHERN LEAGUE OF PROFESSIONAL BASEBALL CLUBS, 52, 983

Miers, Don Florida Operations Director
JOKER MARCHANT STADIUM, 977

Mierzwa, Donald EVP, Store Operations
ODD LOTS/BIG LOTS, 1234

Mietus, Jeff President
WESTERN NEW YORK PGA SECTION OFFICE, 108

Migala, Dan Executive Editor
TEAM MARKETING REPORT, 571, 588

Migala, Katie Customer Service
MIGALA REPORT, 571

Miglia, Dave Operations Manager
CARSON EVENTS INTERNATIONAL, INC., 752

Migliano, Kristen Director of Athletics
LYNN UNIVERSITY, 424

Migra, Bob Sports Writer
PLAIN DEALER, 520

Miguel-Minford, Dawne Advertising Manager
MAUI NEWS, 505

Mike, Vickee Advertising Manager
EVENING TIMES (PA), 487

Mike, Woleben President
PHILIP B. ELFSTROM STADIUM, 992

Mikel, Seth Assitant Athletics Director for Communic
TAYLOR UNIVERSITY ATHLETICS, 321

Mikells, Kathryn Senior Vice President & Chief Financial
EXXON MOBIL CORPORATION, 727

Mikesch, Pat Head Coach
EAST COAST HOCKEY LEAGUE/ECHL, 130

Miketinac, Chuck Host
MAXIMUM SPORTS, 680

Mikkelson, Chastity Secretary
JAMESTOWN CIVIC CENTER, 975

Mikkelson, Ryan Sports Information Director
UNIVERSITY OF JAMESTOWN ATHLETICS, 322

Miklasz, Bernie Sports Columnist
SAINT LOUIS POST-DISPATCH, 527

Mikler, Kip Editor
VELO NEWS, 591

Mikoshiba, Toshiaki Chairman & CEO, American Honda Motor Co.
AMERICAN HONDA MOTOR CO., 725

Miktinj, J. President
ACE MAGNETICS.COM, 1215

Mikulik, Joe Manager
TEXAS BASEBALL LEAGUE, 53

Miladi, Alex Refree Director
UNITED STATES SOO BAHK DO FEDERATION, 143

Milam, Brian Sports Director
WYMT-TV, 712

Milani, Jerry Assoc. Commissioner Media Relations
NEW YORK COLLEGIATE ATHLETIC CONFERENCE, 301

Milani, Mo Treasurer
GREENSBORO SPORTS COMMISSION, 235

Milanovich, Jasmina Corporate Secretary & Director
ALCOHOL AND GAMING COMMISSION OF ONTARIO, 79

Milanovich, Scott Head Coach & Offensive Coordinator
CANADIAN FOOTBALL LEAGUE/CFL, 93

Milby, Caitlyn General Manager
NATIONAL WOMEN'S SOCCER LEAGUE, 159

Miles, Brent President
NORTHWEST BASEBALL LEAGUE, 36, 48, 983, 1010

Miles, David Assistant Director- Booking
LAVELL EDWARDS STADIUM, 982

Miles, Dwight Director, Sales & Marketing
EATON GOLF PRIDE, 1127

Miles, Gary Sports Deputy Editor
PHILADELPHIA INQUIRER, 519

Miles, Kathleen Chief Financial Officer
FGM ARCHITECTS & ENGINEERS, 1056

Miles, Kiprian VP / Chief Information Officer
GOLFSMITH INTERNATIONAL, INC., 1139, 1229

Miles, Mark CEO
INDYCAR, 22

Miles, Mark President
WESTERN HOCKEY LEAGUE, 139

Miles, Patrick Advertising Manager
REFEREE MAGAZINE, 578

Miles-Ralston, Cathy Editor
CHICAGO DISTRICT GOLFER, 554

Miley, Josh Head Athletic Trainer
HANNIBAL-LA GRANGE COLLEGE ATHLETICS, 313

Milholm, Joelle Sports Reporter
LODI NEWS-SENTINEL, 503

Milian, Jorge Sports Reporter
PALM BEACH POST, 517

Milios, Andrew VP, Ticket Sales
CHUKCHANSI PARK, 957

Miliotis, Dino Owner
D.P.M. ENTERPRISES, 1122

Miliotto, Sal Vice President, Sales
UNITED STATES HOCKEY LEAGUE, 137

Milkman, Velvet Administration - Senior Woman Administra
ROY STEWART STADIUM, 999

Mill, Brandon Director
FOCUS GOLF SYSTEMS, INC., 1134

Millar, Alan VP, Hockey Operations & General Manager
WESTERN HOCKEY LEAGUE, 139

Millar, Matt Goaltending Development Coach
AMERICAN HOCKEY LEAGUE/AHL, 128

Millar, T.J. Associate Coach
WESTERN HOCKEY LEAGUE, 139

Millen, Corey Head Coach
NORTH AMERICAN HOCKEY LEAGUE, 133

Millen, Michael Secretary
VIRGINIA STATE GOLF ASSOCIATION, 116

Millen, Pat President, Chief Executive Officer
INTEGRITY SPORTS MARKETING, MEDIA & MANAGEMENT, 789

Millen, Rod President/Chief Executive Officer
RHYS MILLEN RACING, 18

Miller, Abby Senior Director, Ticket Operations
NATIONAL FOOTBALL LEAGUE/NFL, 94

Miller, Alex National Competition Director
SPORTSCAR VINTAGE RACING ASSOCIATION, 18

Miller, Alison Chief Development Officer
SPECIAL OLYMPICS MICHIGAN, 195

Miller, Allyn President
FLAIR COMMUNICATIONS, 783

Miller, Amy Corporate Press Contact
PRIORITY HEALTH, 71

Miller, Andre Head Coach
NATIONAL BASKETBALL ASSOCIATION DEVELOPMENT LEAGUE, 59

Miller, Aon President
TENNESSEE GOLF ASSOCIATION/TGA, 116

Miller, Arthur President
DRYBRANCH, INC./SPORT DESIGN, 1125

Miller, B.J. Assistant General Manager
PIONEER BASEBALL LEAGUE, 50

Miller, Becky Promotions Director
KWNB-TV, 697

Miller, Beth Sr. Associate Athletic Director/Senior W
KENAN MEMORIAL STADIUM, 979

Miller, Bethany Director of Athletics
BIOLA UNIVERSITY ATHLETICS, 308

Miller, Bill Director of Athletics
TEXAS LUTHERAN UNIVERSITY ATHLETICS, 27, 403

Miller, Bob Sports Editor
TYRONE DAILY HERALD, 542

Miller, Brian SVP, Corporate Governance
KOHL'S DEPARTMENT STORES, 387, 393, 1231

Miller, Brooks Assistant Athletic Director
TRINE UNIVERSITY ATHLETICS, 322

Miller, Bryce Executive Sports Editor
DES MOINES REGISTER, 483

Miller, Buddy Advertising Manager
WAGT-TV, 699

Miller, Carolyn Sales & Product Information
ADVANCED CUTTING SYSTEMS, INC., 1093

Miller, Casey Membership Manager
U.S. TAEKWONDO UNION, 143

Miller, Catherine Owner & Director
MILLER & ASSOCIATES, CATHERINE, 758

Miller, Chance Senior Deputy AD
SOUTH CAROLINA ATHLETICS, UNIVERSITY OF, 327, 344

Miller, Charlie Managing Editor
ATHLON SPORTS COMMUNICATIONS, 550

Miller, Chris Head Athletic Trainer
LINDSEY WILSON COLLEGE ATHLETICS, 97, 115, 315, 534, 646, 702

Miller, Curt Head Coach
WOMEN'S NATIONAL BASKETBALL ASSOCIATION, 60

Miller, Dan Executive Director
KIIN-TV, 243, 689, 691

Miller, Danny Associate Director of Athletics
AVERETT UNIVERSITY ATHLETICS (AU), 377

Miller, David President
INTEGRATED SPORTS MARKETING, 373, 678

Miller, Dennis Sports Editor (Local)
TRI-VALLEY HERALD, 541

Miller, Donnie National Account Director
COOPER LIGHTING, 1119

Miller, Doug Vice President
MIAMI VALLEY GOLF ASSOCIATION, 113

Miller, Eric Communications Director
AMARILLO CONVENTION & VISITOR COUNCIL, 227

Miller, Faye Secretary
ATLANTIC FITNESS PRODUCTS, 1101

Miller, Forrest Sports Writer
SOUTH BEND TRIBUNE, 531

Miller, Gail Owner
PACIFIC COAST LEAGUE OF PROFESSIONAL BASEBALL CLUBS, 49

Miller, Garry Assistant Athletic Trainer
BALDWIN-WALLACE COLLEGE ATHLETICS, 377

Miller, Geoffrey Director of Athletics
GOUCHER COLLEGE ATHLETICS, 385

Miller, Gina Sports Reporter
WFAA-TV, 702

Miller, Gloria Marketing
FITBALL USA, 1133

Miller, Grace Associate AD, Academics/SWA
LIPSCOMB UNIVERSITY ATHLETICS, 334

Miller, Gregory President
AMERICAN HIKING SOCIETY, 68

Miller, Hannah Sports Information Director
MOUNT VERNON NAZARENE UNIVERSITY ATHLETICS, 317

Miller, J
MILLER, J. BRUCE, 844

Miller, Jacob Director Of Rules & Competition
UTAH GOLF ASSOCIATION, 116

Monfrey, Pat Publisher
HEALTH & FITNESS MAGAZINE, 563

Mong, Harry Regional Sports Director
SPECIAL OLYMPICS NEVADA, 196

Mongell, Mike President
GEORGIA PGA SECTIONAL OFFICE, 105

Mongello, Kara Office Administrator
AMERICAN HORSE COUNCIL, 73

Moniaci, Steve Director of Athletics
HOUSTON BAPTIST UNIVERSITY
ATHLETICS, 314

Moninghoff, Mick Sports Director
WQAD-TV, 708

Monke, Dustin Sports Editor
DICKINSON PRESS, 484

Monken, Jeff Head Coach, Football
MICHIE STADIUM, 986

Monkiewicz, Diane Interim Assistant Director of
Athletics
MANSFIELD UNIVERSITY ATHLETICS, 363

Monkres, Kim Assistant Director
UTAH HIGH SCHOOL ACTIVITIES
ASSOCIATION, 202

Monnin, Mary Sports Writer
BUFFALO NEWS, 467

Monopli, Joy Advertising Director
NEWS & ADVANCE, 511

Monroe, Mark Sports Writer
BLADE, 465

Monroe, Melanie Head Athletic Trainer
TRINITY CHRISTIAN COLLEGE ATHLETICS,
322

Monroe, Mike NBA Sports Writer
SAN ANTONIO EXPRESS-NEWS, 528

Monsky, Robin President
ROUND ROBIN SPORTS, 806

Monson, Doug Director of Athletic
Communications
STONEHILL COLLEGE ATHLETICS, 372

Monson, Gordon Sports Columnist
SALT LAKE TRIBUNE, 527

Monson, Lisa Chief Human Resources Officer
NATIONAL HOCKEY LEAGUE/NHL, 123

Montagna, Deanna Director Of Office Operations
& Students
ALASKA SCHOOL ACTIVITIES ASSOCIATION,
199

Montague, Jeff Undergraduate Coordinator/Asst.
Dean
TEMPLE UNIVERSITY, 434

Montague, Krista Athletic Director
MONTANA STATE UNIVERSITY BILLINGS
ATHLETICS, 365

Montana, Todd Assistant Director of Athletics
LASELL COLLEGE ATHLETICS, 390

Montanez, Roberto President
PARACHUTE INDUSTRY ASSOCIATION, 13

Montecalvo, Ed Contractor Services
LEE TENNIS PRODUCTS, 1155

Montes, Cesar Director, Coaching
USL LEAGUE TWO, 162

Montesi, Robert Marketing Director
WFSB-TV, 702

Monteson, Patricia Principal
HEALTH FITNESS DYNAMICS, INC., 1059

Monteson, Patty Founder & Co-Owner
HEALTH FITNESS DYNAMICS, INC., 1059

Montez, Mario Sports Director
KUVN-TV, 696

Montgomery, Annalece Marketing Coordinator
USA WATER POLO, INC., 213

Montgomery, Daron Director of Athletics
SAINT ANSELM COLLEGE ATHLETICS, 369

Montgomery, David General Partner
FLORIDA STATE LEAGUE, 39, 957

Montgomery, Eric Director of Sports info. /
Marketing
HEART OF AMERICA ATHLETIC
CONFERENCE, 297, 507

Montgomery, Gary Host
SPORTS PAGE, 681

Montgomery, Graciela Chief Human Resource
Officer
TEVA BRAND, 1124, 1201

Montgomery, Janet Associate Athletic Director
WEST ALABAMA ATHLETICS, UNIVERSITY
OF, 374

Montgomery, Jim Head Coach
NATIONAL HOCKEY LEAGUE/NHL, 123, 125

Montgomery, Kevin HPER Instructor
ALCORN STATE UNIVERSITY, 409

Montgomery, Kyle Head Athletic Trainer
NJCAA REGION VI WOMEN'S, 287

Montgomery, Larry Chairman and Chief
Executive Officer
KOHL'S DEPARTMENT STORES, 1231

Montgomery, Mike Sports Director
WSAL-AM, 665

Montgomery, Paige Circulation Director
STREET & SMITH'S SPORTSBUSINESS
JOURNAL, 587

Montgomery, Scott Marketing VP
CANNONDALE BICYCLE CORPORATION,
1113

Montgomery, Steve Marketing Sales Manager
RUSHMORE PLAZA CIVIC CENTER, 999

Montigny, Michael Treasurer
RHODE ISLAND GOLF ASSOCIATION, 115

Montinieri, Josh Executive Director, Tickets
EASTERN LEAGUE, 38

Montmollin, Phil Public Relations
HOMESTEAD MOTORSPORTS COMPLEX,
1025

Montolio, Robert Sales Manager / Slumber Bags
& Tents
SENECA SPORTS INC., 1187

Montoya, Dave Mutuel Manager
PUEBLO GREYHOUND PARK, 1047

Montoya, Jorge Advertising Manager
KTXS-TV, 696

Montri, Ron Sports Editor
MONROE EVENING NEWS, 508

Monty, Mark Director of Athletics Department
LAWRENCE A. WIEN STADIUM, 982

Monzon, Ana Customer Service
HANCO-M. HANDELSMAN COMPANY, 1142

Moody, Darrell Sports Reporter
NEVADA APPEAL, 510

Moody, Jen Owner
WOMEN'S FOOTBALL ALLIANCE / WFA, 99

Moody, Keegan Ticket Operations
CAROLINA LEAGUE, 37

Moody, Roger Deputy Director Sports
BSKYB, 611

Moody, Sam Director of Operations
CASSEMCO, INC., 1114

Moody, Walt Sports Editor
CENTRE DAILY TIMES, 469

Moon, Bob Sales Manager
BLADEMASTER, 1107

Moon, Danielle Sales & Marketing Coordinator
MINNEAPOLIS METRO NORTH CONVENTION
& VISITORS BUREAU, 241

Moon, Ingrid President/Chief Executive Officer
PACIFIC SPORTFEST, 759

Moon, Je Of Counsel
GARVEY, SCHUBERT & BARER, 881

Moon, Jordan Associate Editor
SPORT JOURNAL, 583

Moon, Josh Director of Athletics
NORTHERN STATE UNIVERSITY(NSU), 349,
366

Moon, Leroy Advertising Manager
WSMG-AM, 666

Moon, Sam Sales Consultant
FIBEROPTIC LIGHTING INC., 1132

Mooney, Andrew Chief Executive Officer &
President
QUIKSILVER, 1179

Mooney, Angela Corporate Secretary
NATION'S BEST SPORTS, 1233

Mooney, Erin Director of Communications
NATIONAL SPORTS FORUM, 797

Mooney, Jeff Owner
CALIFORNIA LEAGUE (A-LEVEL), 36

Mooney, John President, Racing Services
LAUREL PARK, 1041

Mooney, Kevin News Director
KNEB-FM, 624

Mooney, Laura Director of Athletics
MASSACHUSETTS COLLEGE OF LIBERAL
ARTS ATHLETICS(MCLA), 392

Mooney, Mike Director of Athletics
STATE UNIVERSITY OF NEW YORK
COLLEGE AT GENESEO ATHLETICS (SUNY),
402

Mooney, Pat Volleyball Head Coach
NJCAA REGION I WOMEN'S, 286

Mooney, Starr Promoter
BATESVILLE MOTOR SPEEDWAY, 1022

Mooney, Tim Associate AD for External
Operations
IDAHO, UNIVERSITY OF, 332, 420

Mooneyham, Mike Sports Columnist
POST AND COURIER, 521

Mooradian, Jody Senior Associate Athletics
Director - SW
SILVIO O. CONTE FORUM, 400, 1002

Moore, A.A. Assistant Sports Information Director
GULF SOUTH CONFERENCE, 296

Moore, Alice Director of Human Resources
DAN MARINO FOUNDATION, 191

Moore, Austin Sports Assistant Editor
TALLADEGA DAILY HOME, 537

Moore, Ben Pitching Coach
FRONTIER LEAGUE, 41

Moore, Bill Manager
PECOS LEAGUE, 49, 114

Moore, Billy Track Suprintendent
MARTINSVILLE SPEEDWAY, 1028

Moore, Bob Director for Kinesiology, Sport And
Recr
HARDIN-SIMMONS UNIVERSITY, 420

Moore, Brian Director of Marketing
FINGER LAKES GAMING & RACETRACK,
1038

Moore, Butch The Dispatch Printing Company
GREATER COLUMBUS SPORTS
COMMISSION, 234

Moore, Carlitta Director of Sports Medicine
FAYETTEVILLE STATE UNIVERSITY (FSU)
ATHLETICS, 358

Moore, Carrie Director of Physical Education
MASSACHUSETTS INSTITUTE OF
TECHNOLOGY (MIT), 392

Moore, Casey Head Coach
WOMEN'S PREMIER SOCCER LEAGUE, 163,
168

Moore, Charles Executive Director
WYOMING PARI-MUTUEL COMMISSION, 82

Moore, Colin Executive Editor
OUTDOOR LIFE, 574

Moore, Dan National Sales Manager -Corporate
Divisi
SLAZENGER GOLF PRODUCTS CO, 1189

Moore, Danta Match Secretary
WESTERN SUBURBS RUGBY FOOTBALL
CLUB, 148

Moore, Darin Head Athletic Trainer
MISSOURI SOUTHERN STATE UNIVERSITY
ATHLETICS, 364

Moore, Donald President/General Manager
SOUTH ATLANTIC LEAGUE (A LEVEL), 51

Moore, Doug Advertising Manager
PORTERVILLE RECORDER, 82, 521

Moore, Eric Managing Editor
ONNIDAN GROUP, THE, 929

Moore, Erika Executive Assistant / Director of
Specia
REYNOLDS SPORTS MANAGEMENT, 851

Moore, Gary Promoter
MOBILE DRAGWAY, 1029

Moore, Greg Under-17 Team Head Coach
UNITED STATES HOCKEY LEAGUE, 138

Moore, Gregory Commissioner
SOUTHERN INTERCOLLEGIATE ATHLETIC
CONFERENCE, 304

Moore, Hayley VP, Hockey Operations
AMERICAN HOCKEY LEAGUE/AHL, 126

Moore, Jamie Chief Operating Officer
THE DAVIS EXPERIENCE, 1062

Moore, Jim Sports Columnist
SEATTLE POST-INTELLIGENCER, 529

Moore, Jo-Anne Director
WATER SKI & WAKEBOARD CANADA, 180

Moore, Joe Host
NASCAR TODAY, 609

Moore, John Associate Athletic Director
WESTMONT COLLEGE ATHLETICS, 323,
1144

Moore, Kellen Head Coach
NATIONAL FOOTBALL LEAGUE/NFL, 96

Moore, Kirsten Associate Athletic Director
WESTMONT COLLEGE ATHLETICS, 323

Moore, Kris Advertising Manager
KBST-AM, 614

Mrozek, Donald Chairman
HINSHAW & CULBERSON LLP, 837
Mrozek, Donald Chairman
VAINISI, JEROME R., 837, 913
Mucher, Jason Director of Compliance and Communication
HOUGHTON COLLEGE ATHLETICS, 388
Muchmore, Clyde Chairman Appellate Practice
CROWE & DUNLEVY, 830
Mudd, Michael Director of Athletics
WORCESTER STATE UNIVERSITY ATHLETICS, 408
Mudd, Ray Events Manager
THUNDERHILL RACEWAY PARK, 1034
Muder, Craig Directoro of Communications
NATIONAL BASEBALL HALL OF FAME AND MUSEUM, 255
Mueller, Blaine Head Coach
NATIONAL BASKETBALL ASSOCIATION DEVELOPMENT LEAGUE, 59
Mueller, Brett President
MUELLER SPORTS MEDICINE, INC., 1165
Mueller, Curt Chief Executive Officer
MUELLER SPORTS MEDICINE, INC., 1165
Mueller, Doris Chairman
GREATER AUSTIN SPORTS ASSOCIATION, 234
Mueller, E.C. Racetrack Manager
PORTLAND INTERNATIONAL RACEWAY, 1031
Mueller, Ed Sales
WMBE-AM AND WCLB, 656
Mueller, Frederick Sport Administration Professor
NORTH CAROLINA, UNIVERSITY OF, 429
Mueller, Jeannette Chief Financial Officer
RELAY SPORTS AND ENTERTAINMENT MARKETING, 805
Mueller, Jeff VP
MUELLER SPORTS MEDICINE, INC., 1165
Mueller, Matt Director, Coaching & Competition
WOMEN'S PREMIER SOCCER LEAGUE, 167
Mueller, Tim General Manager
SOUTH ATLANTIC LEAGUE (A LEVEL), 52, 947
Mueller, Tino Technical Director
WOMEN'S PREMIER SOCCER LEAGUE, 164, 168
Mugford, Angus President
ASSOCIATION FOR APPLIED SPORT PSYCHOLOGY/AAASP, 217
Muhl, Alan Finanace / Operations Manager
DLF INTERNATIONAL SEEDS, 1224
Muhlfelder, James President / Chief Executive Officer
DEBEER LACROSSE, 1123
Muhlhauser, Mark COO/Deputy Director of Athletics & Exter
ILLINOIS STATE UNIVERSITY ATHLETICS, 332
Muir, Bernard Director of Athletics
STANFORD UNIVERSITY ATHLETICS, 345
Muir, Norman Associate Professor, and Dean, Undergrad
MEDAILLE COLLEGE, 425
Mukhamedolla, Agzamov VP Asia
WORLD ARMWRESTLING FEDERATION, 15
Mulay, Rene Editor
EMPLOYEE SERVICES MANAGEMENT, 557
Mulcahy, Charles Partner
WYNN & WYNN, P.C., 917
Mulcahy, Michael President/Chief Executive Officer
FAIRTRON, 1131
Mulcahy, Robert Athletic Director
LOUIS BROWN ALTHETIC CENTER, 984
Mulch, Lori Assistant General Manager
KANSAS STATE FAIR (KSF), 1040
Muldoon, Barb Treasurer
NEBRASKA WOMEN'S AMATEUR GOLF ASSOCIATION, 113
Muldoon, James Asst. Commissioner of Public Relations
PACIFIC-10 CONFERENCE, 303
Muldoon, Liz Second VP
QUINTE EX FALL FAIR, 1043
Muldoon, Mike Sports Writer
EAGLE-TRIBUNE, 485
Mule, Marty Sports Writer
TIMES-PICAYUNE, 540

Mulhausen, Dan VP, Business Operations & Marketing Comm
WESTERN HOCKEY LEAGUE, 139
Mulhern, Tom Sports Reporter
WISCONSIN STATE JOURNAL, 547
Mulholland, Thad Partner
ENG & WOODS, 879
Mullany, Joe President
DMC ORTHOPAEDICS & SPORTS MEDICINE, 920
Mullen, Bryan Sports Writer
TENNESSEAN, 538
Mullen, Don Hospitality Manager
TRUE FITNESS TECHNOLOGY, 1204
Mullen, Jim Assistant Director of Athletics
ASSUMPTION COLLEGE ATHLETICS, 351
Mullen, Mike Athletics Senior Editor/Sports Director
WBUK-FM, 639
Mullen, Scott Executive Director
I WIRELESS CENTER, 973
Mullens, Rob Athletic Director
OREGON ATHLETICS, UNIVERSITY OF, 341, 947, 985
Muller, Angela Associate Director Of Athletics
CONCORDIA UNIVERSITY (NE) ATHLETICS, 311
Muller, Jim Associate Director
WAGNER FIELD/KSU, 951, 1017
Muller, Joe Athletic Director
CENTRAL OKLAHOMA ATHLETICS, UNIVERSITY OF, 354
Muller, Kira Director of Advertising Sales
LACROSSE MAGAZINE, 568
Muller, Matthius President
PORSCHE CARS NORTH AMERICA, 1175
Muller, Todd Club Coordinator
USA CYCLING, 72
Mullholland, Chris Producer
FIRST 4 SPORTS - SATURDAY, 679
Mulligan, Mike Sports Columnist
CHICAGO SUN-TIMES, 469
Mulliken, Ron Advertising Director
GOLF MAGAZINE, 561
Mullikin, Jeff Assistant Athletic Director
TOCCOA FALLS COLLEGE ATHLETICS, 372
Mullin, Jennifer Marketing & Public Relations Assistant
NORFOLK CONVENTION & VISITORS BUREAU, 242
Mullin, Jim Vice President
INTERNATIONAL FEDERATION OF AMERICAN FOOTBALL, 88
Mullin, Mark Director of Athletics
MISSOURI-ROLLA ATHLETICS, UNIVERSITY OF (UMR), 364
Mullin, Michelle Sales Vice President
METRO SPORTS NY, 570
Mullin, Paul Sponsorship Services Manager
NEW YORK-PENNSYLVANIA LEAGUE, 46, 964
Mullin, Shawn Tour Manager
UNITED SPORTS TECHNOLOGIES/UST, 1206
Mullins, Carl Publisher
QUARTER HORSE NEWS, 76, 551, 577
Mullins, Craig Chairman of the Board
BROWNING DAY MULLINS DIERDORF ARCHITECTS, 1051
Mullins, Dave Account Executive
GMR MARKETING, 756
Mullins, Jim Assistant Director of Athletics
UMASS DARTMOUTH ATHLETIC DEPARTMENT, 392
Mullins, Steve Director of Athletics
ARKANSAS TECH UNIVERSITY ATHLETICS, 351, 953, 976
Mullins, Susan Vice President
WYTI-AM/FM, 672
Mullins, Tabatha Executive Director
PRINCE WILLIAM COUNTY/MANASSAS CONVENTION & VISITORS BUREAU, 244
Mullison, Dave Manager Marketing/Communications
ATLANTA MOTOR SPEEDWAY, 1022
Mullon, Bill Director of Sports Marketing
WQAM 560 SPORTS RADIO, 662
Mulloy, Mark Sports Information/Media Relations
MID-SOUTH CONFERENCE, 299

Mulock, Micah Sports Information Director
LIFE PACIFIC COLLEGE ATHLETICS, 362
Mulrenin, Patrick Director
ACKERMAN, VALERIE B., 861
Mulrooney, Pat Program Director/Sports
WRTK, 665
Mulroy, Paola VP Finance
SOCCER MARKETING & PROMOTIONS, INC., 761
Mulroy, Thomas Founder/President
SOCCER MARKETING & PROMOTIONS, INC., 761
Mulryan, Matt Sales Manager
DACOR SPORT, 1122
Multer, Mark Sports Editor
WAUSAU DAILY HERALD, 546
Mulvaney, Todd President
PLASTIMAYD CORPORATION, 1174
Mulvenna, Mary Chief of Staff/Senior Associate Athletic
DREXEL UNIVERSITY ATHLETICS, 329
Munday, Trevor Managing Director
DESTINET LIMITED, 931
Mundell, Don Head Athletic Trainer
WESTERN STATE COLLEGE ATHLETICS (WSC), 375
Mundle, Michelle Athletic Department Secretary
HANNIBAL-LA GRANGE COLLEGE ATHLETICS, 313
Mundy, Megan Athletic Business and Operations Coordin
KING'S COLLEGE ATHLETICS, 389
Mungham, Tom Chief Operating Officer
ALCOHOL AND GAMING COMMISSION OF ONTARIO, 79
Mungo, Leonard Regional Field Director
MUNGO AND ASSOCIATES, P.C., 897
Munjoy, Ken Advertising Director
DAILY JOURNAL (IL), 477
Munk, Josh Associate Director of Football Operation
BIG TEN ATHLETIC CONFERENCE, 292
Munn, Scott Sports Assistant Editor
OKLAHOMAN, 515
Munoz, Carlos Sports Reporter
KTMD-TV, 695
Munoz, Daniel Editor
LA PRENSA SAN DIEGO, 500
Munoz, Jose President & CEO, Hyundai Motor North Ame
HYUNDAI MOTOR AMERICA, 728
Munoz, SJ Sports Editor/Writer
YORK NEWS-TIMES, 548
Munroe, Mark Commissioner
OHIO STATE RACING COMMISSION, 81
Munroe, Morgan Compliance Officer
ALBERTA SCHOOLS' ATHLETIC ASSOCIATION, 199
Munroe, Tim VP Business Development
CONE COMMUNICATIONS, 752
Munsell, Joe General Manager
KXMO-FM, 633
Munson, Larry Sports Host
WSB-AM, 665
Munson, William Operations VP
RALPH WILSON STADIUM, 995
Munt, Glada Director of Intercollegiate Athletics
SOUTHWESTERN UNIVERSITY ATHLETICS, 401
Murakami, Michael Principal
MURAKAMI/NELSON, 1061
Murase, Etsuko Chief Financial Officer/Chief Operations
BOOMER ESIASON FOUNDATION, 191
Murat, Caroline Finance Manager
WORLD ARCHERY FEDERATION, 15
Murchie, Amanda Assistant Athletics Director, Business O
WESTERN CAROLINA UNIVERSITY ATHLETICS, 349
Murdoch, James Chariman/Chief Executive Officer
STAR GROUP LIMITED, 687
Murdoch, Paul President
U.S. HANG GLIDING AND PARAGLIDING ASSOCIATION, 14
Murdock, Allison Deputy Managing Partner
STINSON MORRISON HECKER LLP, 908

Murdock, James Founder/President
ENDLESS POOLS, INC., 1129

Murdock, Justin Sports Writer
ENQUIRER-JOURNAL, 487

Murdock, Mark Sports Editor
THE STAR, 538

Murdy, Wayne Chair
DENVER, UNIVERSITY OF, 416

Murillo, Ken Team Owner
IMSA MICHELIN PILOT CHALLENGE, 20

Murnane, Jim Associate Athletic Director
UTICA COLLEGE ATHLETICS(UC), 404

Muroski, Liz Director of Media and Promotions
CAROLINAS PGA SECTION, 105

Murphy, Brad Executive Director
ADAMS CENTER, 945

Murphy, Brian Head Athletic Trainer
LA SIERRA UNIVERSITY ATHLETICS, 122,
314, 534

Murphy, Brian Publisher/Editor
SPORTS MARKETING LETTER COMPANY,
585

Murphy, Brian
BRIAN J. MURPHY CONSULTANT, 776

Murphy, Chad Executive Director
UNITED STATES BOWLING CONGRESS, 66

Murphy, Chetara Assistant Director of Athletics
MEDGAR EVERS COLLEGE ATHLETICS
(MEC), 393

Murphy, Chris President
NATIONAL BASKETBALL ASSOCIATION
DEVELOPMENT LEAGUE, 59, 649

Murphy, Dan Sports Director
WTEN-TV, 710

Murphy, Daniel Chairman
GATOR BOWL, 90

Murphy, Dawn Finance and Administrative
Director
EXPLORE FAIRBANKS, 233

Murphy, Dennis President/Commissioner
NATIONAL JUNIOR BASKETBALL, 54

Murphy, Diana Vice President
U.S. GOLF ASSOCIATION/USGA, 109

Murphy, Eric Weekend Sports Anchor
WOI-TV, 707

Murphy, Erich Sports Editor
DAILY LEADER (IL), 477

Murphy, Gord Associate Head Coach
AMERICAN HOCKEY LEAGUE/AHL, 127

Murphy, Jack Head Coach, Men's Basketball
J. LAWRENCE WALKUP SKYDOME, 974

Murphy, James President/General Manager
ATLANTIC CITY RACE COURSE, 1035

Murphy, Jason Facilities Director
UNIVERSITY OF WISCONSIN-LA CROSSE,
407, 987

Murphy, Jerome Sports Reporter
ARGUS-PRESS, 461

Murphy, Jim Sports Editor
JUICE SOUND, SURF SKATE MAGAZINE, 567

Murphy, Joe Sports Writer
EAGLE-TRIBUNE, 485

Murphy, John Assistant Sports Information
Director
MAYVILLE STATE UNIVERSITY ATHLETICS,
316, 705, 1049

Murphy, John SVP/Controller/Chief Accounting
Officer
DIRECTV, INC., 686

Murphy, Karen Chief Financial Officer
NATIONAL FOOTBALL LEAGUE/NFL, 94

Murphy, Katie Sales & Event Coordinator
UNITED STATES HOCKEY LEAGUE, 137

Murphy, Keith Sports Director
WHO-TV, 704

Murphy, Kelly Host Appearances
YAHOO! SPORTS RADIO, 604

Murphy, Kevin Team/Sports Construction Sales
AMERICAN ATHLETIC INC., 141, 1097

Murphy, Leslie Executive Director
NATIONAL DART ASSOCIATION, 72

Murphy, Logan Assistant Coach
NORTH AMERICAN HOCKEY LEAGUE, 132

Murphy, Malia Head Athletic Trainer
BLACKBURN COLLEGE ATHLETICS, 378

Murphy, Mark President/CEO
NATIONAL FOOTBALL LEAGUE/NFL, 95, 466

Murphy, Mark President
LAMBEAU FIELD, 981

Murphy, Matt Manager of Athletic Operations
NOTRE DAME COLLEGE ATHLETICS, 367,
608

Murphy, Matthew Editor
WOODENBOAT, 593

Murphy, Megan Event and Group Manager
SAM LYNN BALLPARK, 1000

Murphy, Michael Editor
BALLOON LIFE, 551

Murphy, Mike Sports Host
WJPF-AM, 652

Murphy, Nancy Vice President Sales
LAS VEGAS CONVENTION & VISITORS
AUTHORITY, 116, 238

Murphy, Nicola Director Marketing, Athlete &
Property M
OCTAGON ATHLETES & PERSONALITIES
DIVISION, 845

Murphy, Pat General Manager
NATIONAL LEAGUE OF PROFESSIONAL
BASEBALL CLUBS, THE, 32

Murphy, Patrick President, Business Operations
NATIONAL HOCKEY LEAGUE/NHL, 105, 123,
851

Murphy, Paul Associate Director of Athletics
GWYNEDD MERCY COLLEGE ATHLETICS,
386

Murphy, R. Vice President Network Operations
GOLF CHANNEL, THE, 599, 687

Murphy, Ric President/Chief Executive Officer
USADATA.COM, 816

Murphy, Rick General Manager
JOSEPH L. BRUNO STADIUM, 977

Murphy, Rita Vice Chairman of Captains Charities
CLASSIC PARK, 958

Murphy, Robert President
MIDWEST LEAGUE, 45, 965

Murphy, Sean Assistant Managing Editor - Sports
VICKSBURG POST, 54, 544

Murphy, Steve President
ALOHA PGA SECTIONAL OFFICE, 105

Murphy, Tim P.E., Associate & Project Manager
PAIGE DESIGN GROUP, 556, 754, 1061

Murphy, Tom General Manager
GEORGE J. SHERMAN FAMILY-SPORTS
COMPLEX, 968

Murphy, Traci Associate Athletic Director
CANISIUS COLLEGE - SCHOOL OF
EDUCATION & HUMAN SERVICES, 412

Murpy, John Manager/Curator
SPORTS IMMORTALS, 258

Murraine, Clair Sports Reporter
TALLAHASSEE DEMOCRAT, 537

Murray, Annette Public Information Director
NJCAA REGION IX MEN'S, 287

Murray, Ben Creative Specialist
SOUTH BEND/MISHAWAKA CONVENTION &
VISITORS BUREAU, 264

Murray, Bill Director of Fun
JOSEPH P. RILEY PARK, 978

Murray, Bruce VP Standardbred Racing
MOHAWK RACETRACK, 1041

Murray, Carol Executive Assistant to the
President
NJCAA REGION XV WOMEN'S, 289

Murray, Chris Sports Editor
PHILADELPHIA TRIBUNE, 519

Murray, James Principal/Director
CSHQA
ARCHITECTS/ENGINEERS/PLANNERS, 1053

Murray, Jane Director of Services
THOROUGHBRED RACING ASSOCIATIONS,
77

Murray, John Attorney
LINDNER & MARSACK, S.C., 891

Murray, Kristen Incoming Vice Chair
US LACROSSE, 141

Murray, LaKitha Senior Associate Director of
Athletics
COLLEGE OF NEW JERSEY ATHLETICS
(TCNJ), 381

Murray, Lisa Executive Vice President & Chief
Marketi
OCTAGON SPORTS, 799, 833, 845

Murray, Marty General Manager/Head Coach
WESTERN HOCKEY LEAGUE, 138

Murray, Melanie Advertising Manager
VALLEY NEWS DISPATCH, 544

Murray, Mike President/General Manager
SOUTHERN PROFESSIONAL HOCKEY
LEAGUE, 127, 136

Murray, Natalie Vice President, Regional Sales
Manager
FOX SPORTS NETWORKS/FOX SPORTS
NET, 675

Murray, Neil News Director
WGMA-AM, 648

Murray, Patrick News Director
WZLX-FM, 672

Murray, Rob Head Coach/Director, Hockey
Operations
EAST COAST HOCKEY LEAGUE/ECHL, 130

Murray, Scott Goaltending Coach
NATIONAL HOCKEY LEAGUE/NHL, 126, 697

Murray, Sherrie Administrative Assistant & Office
Manage
CHARLES M. MURPHY ATHLETIC CENTER,
956

Murray, Steve Commissioner
PENNSYLVANIA STATE ATHLETIC
CONFERENCE, 303

Murray, Tim Director of Athletics
MARIST COLLEGE ATHLETICS, 336

Murray-MacDonell, Sandra Executive Director
CANADIAN COLLEGIATE ATHLETIC
ASSOCIATION, 283

Murrell, Tony Controller
METROPOLITAN PROFESSIONAL GOLFERS
ASSOCIATION, 106

Murrey, Bob President, Owner
USA COACHES CLINICS, INC., 816

Murrey, Daniel Chief Executive Officer
ORTHOCAROLINA, 922

Murrey, Patrick President
MURREY INTERNATIONAL, 1165

Murrietta, Jeannette Booking Manager
DENVER COLISEUM, 961

Murry, Saye Advertising Manager
OWENSBORO MESSENGER-INQUIRER, 517

Murstein, Andrew Co-Owner
NASCAR CUP SERIES, 23

Murtha, Francis President
PROFESSIONAL SPORTS CONSULTANTS,
INC., 850

Murtha, Matthew VP, Stadium/Structures
PROFESSIONAL SPORTS CONSULTANTS,
INC., 850

Murtland, Carol Purchasing Manager
KOOLATRON, 1153

Murton, Luke Director, Player Development
NATIONAL LEAGUE OF PROFESSIONAL
BASEBALL CLUBS, THE, 32

Murumets, Kelly President & Chief Executive
Officer
TENNIS CANADA, 174

Murzynski, Terrence Owner
SPORTSVISIONS, 762

Musa, Scott Athletic Communications Director
SHENANDOAH UNIVERSITY ATHLETICS, 400

Musallam, Husain Vice President
FEDERATION INTERNATIONALE DE
NATATION (FINA), 72, 204

Muscari, David Vice President
WFAA-TV, 702

Muscutt, Scott General Manager
NORTH AMERICAN HOCKEY LEAGUE, 133

Muse, Bill Athletic Director
NJCAA REGION II WOMEN'S, 286

Muse, Micheal. Architect/Partner
THE COLLABORATIVE, INC.,, 1052

Muse, Scott President
HUBBELL LIGHTING, INC., 1146

Musgjerd, Jean Women's Athletic Director
NJCAA REGION XIII WOMEN'S, 288

Musgrave, Chuck Principal, CFO
BARKER RINKER SEACAT ARCHITECTURE,
1050

Musgrove, Peter Facilities/Operations Manager
GREAT CANADIAN GAMING CORPORATION,
1039

Mushel, Jessica Assistant Director of Athletics
MOUNT ST. MARY COLLEGE ATHLETICS,
394

Mushinski, Ian Head Athletic Trainer
WINSTON-SALEM STATE UNIVERSITY
ATHLETICS, 375

Mushnick, Phil Sports Columnist
NEW YORK POST, 510
Music, Lyn Facilities/Events Management Director
SUN DEVIL STADIUM, 1006
Musick, Ashley Head Athletic Trainer
CALIFORNIA STATE
UNIVERSITY-DOMINGUEZ HILLS ATHLETICS,
353
Musil, Matt Sports Reporter
KHOU-TV, 690
Muskewitz, Al Golf and JSU Teams Writer
ANNISTON STAR, 460
Muskovich, John Chief Executive Officer /
President
ROYCE UNION BICYCLE COMPANY, INC.,
1146, 1184
Mussellam, Geoff Communications Manager
HASTINGS RACECOURSE, 1039
Musselman, Gary Executive Director
KANSAS STATE HS ACTIVITIES
ASSOCIATION, 198, 200
Musselwhite, Susan Assistant Athletic Director
MISSISSIPPI COLLEGE ATHLETICS (MC), 364
Musso, Mark President/CEO
SPECIAL OLYMPICS MISSOURI, 195
Musson, Renne Associate Director
STEPHEN C O'CONNELL CENTER, 1006
Must, Gary General Manager
DELAWARE COUNTY FAIR, 1037
Muston, Jen Assistant Director of Athletics
YORK COLLEGE (PENNSYLVANIA)
ATHLETICS, 408
Mutti, Raj Marketing Manager
HASTINGS RACECOURSE, 1039
Muus, Charlie Director of Maintenance &
Operations
RALPH ENGELSTAD ARENA, 995
Muzzi, Luiz EVP, Soccer Operations/GM
MAJOR LEAGUE SOCCER, 158
Myatt, Michael Director of Corporate Relations
INTERNATIONAL GAME FISH ASSOCIATION,
87
Mycoskie, Chris Sports Director
KTVE-TV, 696
Mydra, Jonny President
EAST COAST HOCKEY LEAGUE/ECHL, 129
Myer, Brad Sports Director
WNSV-FM, 659
Myer, Marissa Chief Executive Officer, President,
Dire
YAHOO! SPORTS, 715
Myer, Mike Executive Editor
INTELLIGENCER, 496
Myers, Andre Aquatics Director
UNIVERSITY OF DISTRICT OF COLUMBIA
ATHLETICS, 356
Myers, Chad Vice President/Treasurer
MIDWEST PGA SECTIONAL OFFICE, 106
Myers, Charlene Domestic Customer Service
AEROBIE, INC, 1094
Myers, Chris Sports Information Director
WHEELING JESUIT UNIVERSITY ATHLETICS
(WJU), 375
Myers, Darren Exec. Vice-Pres. & CFO
CANADIAN TIRE, 726
Myers, Deana Analyst
MEDIA SPORTS BUSINESS, 569
Myers, Gene Sports Editor
DETROIT FREE PRESS, 483
Myers, Gerald Director of Athletics
JONES SBC STADIUM, 977
Myers, Harriette Treasurer
MISSOURI WOMEN'S GOLF ASSOCIATION,
113
Myers, Harry News Director
WBAG-AM, 637
Myers, Julie Director of Communications
U.S. PROFESSIONAL TENNIS ASSOCIATION,
175
Myers, Mary Assistant Executive Director
SSLASPA DBA SPORT & RECREATION LAW
ASSOCIATION, 225
Myers, Nancy Ticket Assistant
MINNESOTA STATE HS LEAGUE, 200
Myers, Richard Vice President, Turf & Retail
DLF INTERNATIONAL SEEDS, 1224
Myers, Rick Director Sales / Marketing
DLF INTERNATIONAL SEEDS, 459, 1224

Myers, Robert Dept. Dean
PALM BEACH ATLANTIC UNIVERSITY, 431
Myers, Rod Host
SPORTS CORNER, 685
Myers, Ron Director of Florida Operations
FLORIDA STATE LEAGUE, 39, 40
Myers, Tom Associate Athletic Director/Facilities
WEEDE ARENA, 955, 1017
Myerson, Bob President
K & S PROMOTIONS, 791
Myerson, Joe Senior Editor
OFFSHORE, 574
Myford, Greg Associate Athletic Director of
Business
BEAVER STADIUM, 949
Myhre, Rich Sports Reporter
HERALD (WA), 493
Mykins, Bill Vice president
BRAILSFORD & DUNLAVEY, 1050
Myler, Cameron Associate
FRANKFURT, KURNIT, KLEIN & SELZ, P.C.,
881
Myles, Richard HPER Instructor
ALCORN STATE UNIVERSITY, 409
Mylett, Bill Sales Manager
MONDO AMERICA, INC., 1164
Mylor, Pam Service Coordinator
KENTUCKY SPEEDWAY, 1027
Mylor, Terry Operations
SAN JOSE MUNICIPAL STADIUM, 1001
Mylowe, Douglas VP & Chief Financial Officer
NATIONAL LEAGUE OF PROFESSIONAL
BASEBALL CLUBS, THE, 31
Mylymok, Clint Head Coach/General Manager
NORTH AMERICAN HOCKEY LEAGUE, 133
Myrland, Jim Owner
BEACON ATHLETICS, 1218
Myrold, Chris Director
BURWASH INTERNATIONAL, PETER, 751
Myron, Dennis Ticket Operations Director
ST JOHN'S UNIVERSITY, 1005

N

N, Jenny Aerie Accessories Manager
AMERICAN EAGLE OUTFITTERS, 1216
N Funkhouser Jr, Richard President
HT TENNIS, 1146
N. Feist III, Howard Chief Financial Officer /
Finance VP
ABI TAPE PRODUCTS, 1090
N. H. Boeder, Jeremy Attorney
TRIBLER, ORPETT & CRONE, 912
N. N Mertz, Melissa Associate Executive Director
PENNSYLVANIA INTERSCHOLASTIC
ATHLETIC ASSOCIATION, 202
N. W. Adams, Diana President and Chief
Executive Officer
AMBAC ASSURANCE CORPORATION, 767
N/A, Derrick Editor
SPORTS EYE, 533
Naamani, Jadd Program Director
WMLN-FM, 657
Naatz, Duey Athletic Director
UNIVERSITY OF WISCONSIN - STOUT
ATHLETICS (UW-STOUT), 407
Nabozny, Heather Head Groundskeeper
COMERICA PARK, 959
Nace, Diane Artwork/Approvals
COOPERSBURG SPORTS, 1223
Nace, Kelly Event Director
TAP, LLC, 62
Nacewicz, Steve President
CENTRAL NEW YORK PGA SECTIONAL
OFFICE, 105
Nachand, Jean Vice President, Competition
WOMEN'S TENNIS ASSOCIATION TOUR, 176
Nachbaur, Don Head Coach
WESTERN HOCKEY LEAGUE, 139
Nacke, Dave Vice President, Merchandising -
Outdoor
NATION'S BEST SPORTS, 1233
Nackman, Neal Chief Financial Officer
G III SPORTS, 1135
Naddelman, Rob President
BASEBALL FACTORY, 26
Nadeau, Brad Director of Athletic
Communications

MIDDLEBURY COLLEGE ATHLETICS (MCA),
393
Nadeau, Donny Sports Information Director
SAINT MARY'S UNIVERSITY (MN)
ATHLETICS, 399
Nadel, Roger VP/General Manager
KMPC-AM, 624
Nadella, Satya Chief Executive Officer
MICROSOFT CORPORATION, 730
Nader, Tom Sports Editor
RECORD-COURIER, 475, 524
Nading, Lance President
U.S. JUDO, INC/USA JUDO, 143
Nadolski, Jaynee Asst.
Commissioner/Championships Info
BIG SKY CONFERENCE, 292
Nadorf, Wayne Sales Assistant VP / Director
EVERLAST WORLDWIDE, INC., 1130
Nadvornik, Milosh President
YEADON FABRIC STRUCTURES LTD., 1212
Nafe, Rick Operations/Facilities VP
TROPICANA FIELD, 1011
Naff, Abe Director of Athletics
FERRUM COLLEGE ATHLETICS, 384
Nagao, Danielle Vice President of Financial
Operations
TICKETS.COM, 933
Nagel, Linda Sales
ULTRA PLAY SYSTEMS, INC., 1205
Nagel, Mark Chairman
SAN JOSE STATE UNIVERSITY, 419, 432
Naggar, Sara Communications Director
BIG EAST CONFERENCE, 292
Nagle, Andrew EVP
A-B EMBLEM, 1089
Nagle, Kevin Managing Partner
USL CHAMPIONSHIP, 160
Nagle, Patrick Executive Director
ALLSTATE ARENA, 946
Nagy, Chris Sports Editor
NEWS-ITEM, 513
Nahas, Jim VP / Assistant General Manager
SEC TAYLOR STADIUM, 1002
Nahas, Sean Head Coach
NATIONAL WOMEN'S SOCCER LEAGUE, 159
Nahigian, Matt Program Director
WAIT-AM, 604, 610, 636
Nahon, Paul General Manager
MYLAN WORLD TEAM TENNIS, 177
Naidoo, Urvasi CEO
NETBALL ASSOCIATIONS, INTERNATIONAL
FEDERATION OF, 144
Naidu, Dan Director of Coaching, Girls
WOMEN'S PREMIER SOCCER LEAGUE, 169
Naifeh, Larry Executive Associate AD
OKLAHOMA ATHLETICS, UNIVERSITY OF,
341
Naik, Sudhir Deputy Director
NEW HAMPSHIRE RACING AND
CHARITABLE GAMING COMMISSION, 81, 119
Najjar, Sinan Coordinator, Sales And Partnerships
NATIONAL BASKETBALL LEAGUE OF
CANADA, 58
Nakaahiki, Nina Secretary
SPECIAL OLYMPICS HAWAII, 194
Nakama, Wes High School Sports Reporter
HONOLULU ADVERTISER, 494
Nakashima, Jeremy Senior Project Manager
LOCKWOOD, ANDREWS, AND
NEWNAM/LAN, 1061
Nalchajian-Cohen, Debbie
Communications/Media Relations
BIG FRESNO FAIR (BFF), 1036
Namm, Keith Sports Reporter
POST AND COURIER, 521
Nanberg, Bob Managing General Partner
TEAM SHOP PREMIUMS, 1200
Nance, Carolyn HPER Complex Facilities
Manager
GOLDEN LION STADIUM, 968
Nance, Frederick Managing Partner
SQUIRE, SANDERS & DEMPSEY, LLP, 908
Nance, Jack Executive Director
CAROLINAS GOLF ASSOCIATION, 110
Nance, Martin Executive VP/Chief Marketing
Officer
NATIONAL FOOTBALL LEAGUE/NFL, 95

Nance, Stanford Senior Associate Director of Athletics
EMERSON COLLEGE ATHLETICS, 384

Nancy, Wilfried Head Coach
MAJOR LEAGUE SOCCER, 157

Nangle, Shelly Executive VP & COO
SPECIAL OLYMPICS NEW YORK, 196

Nanney, David Head Groundskeeper
JOE O'BRIEN FIELD, 976

Nanninga, Brett Associate Director
IOWA HS ATHLETIC ASSOCIATION, 200

Napier, Claude President/CEO
MILWAUKEE MILE, 1029

Napier, George Chairman / Chief Executive Officer
PRINCE SPORTS, 1177

Napoli, Gaeton Controller
PIONEER INDUSTRIES, INC., 1174

Napoli, Joe President/CEO
EAST COAST HOCKEY LEAGUE/ECHL, 43, 130, 1010

Napolillo, Steve Senior Executive Associate AD, External
PROVIDENCE COLLEGE ATHLETICS, 342

Napolitano, Val President & CEO, Petry Television
PETRY TELEVISION, 677

Napper, Marshall Shareholder
SHOTWELLE, BROWN & SPERRY, 906

Narayan, Ash Treasurer
SPORTS LAWYERS ASSOCIATION, 224

Narayanan, Raj General Manager/Director of Sales
CALIFORNIA LEAGUE (A-LEVEL), 36

Nardella, Bob Assistant Coach
AMERICAN HOCKEY LEAGUE/AHL, 127

Narducci, Marc Sports Reporter
PHILADELPHIA INQUIRER, 519

Nardulli, Gino Marketing Director
C. CRETORS & CO., 1112

Narracci, Michael Senior Coordinating Director
NEW ENGLAND SPORTS NETWORK/NESN, 676

Nash, Eric Executive Director
INTERNATIONAL SPORTS HALL OF FAME AND OLYMPIC MUSEUM, 254

Nash, Jeff President
TREATY OAK BANK, 770

Nash, Linda Assistant Athletic Director
AQUINAS COLLEGE ATHLETICS, 307

Nash, Marc Promotions Manager
WGXA-TV, 703

Nash, Michael President
SPECIAL OLYMPICS DELAWARE, 194

Nash, Myranda Associate Athletics Director
WINONA STATE UNIVERSITY ATHLETICS, 375

Nash, Patti President / Chief Executive Officer
CABANA BANNERS, 1112

Nash, Robert Treasurer
ARABIAN HORSE ASSOCIATION, 74

Nash, Scott General Partner
TEAM SHOP PREMIUMS, 787, 1200

Nason, Mark Merchandising EVP
SKECHERS USA, 1189

Nass, Mike Secretary
CHICAGO DISTRICT GOLF ASSOCIATION, 110

Nasser, Mark Director of Broadcasting
ROSENBLATT STADIUM, 999

Nassetta, Christopher President and CEO
HILTON HOTELS, 728

Natal, Angel Senior Sales Manager
ST. PETERSBURG/CLEARWATER SPORTS COMMISSION, 247

Natali, Michael President, Structural Engineering Depart
FINK ROBERTS & PETRIE, 1056

Natalie, Williams General Manager
WOMEN'S NATIONAL BASKETBALL ASSOCIATION, 60

Nathan, Greg Senior Vice President
NATIONAL GOLF FOUNDATION, 104

Nathan, Kevin Sports Anchor
WVIT-TV, 682, 711

Nathan, Rob Product Director
SOLE CUSTOM FOOTBEDS, 1191

Nathan, Terry President
MUSEUM OF YACHTING, 255

Nathanson, Ken Partner
SHERMAN & NATHANSON, A PROFESSIONAL CORPORATION, 906

Nation, Fred EVP/Corporate Communications
INDIANAPOLIS MOTOR SPEEDWAY CORPORATION, 1026

Natkin, Eric Sports Director
KRCR-TV, 694

Natoli, Frank Executive Vice President and Chief Innov
DIEBOLD INCORPORATED, 1124

Natvig, Paula Head Athletic Trainer
MACALESTER COLLEGE ATHLETICS, 391

Nau, Brad Executive Producer
COMCAST SPORTSNET BAY AREA, 674

Nau, Terry Sports Editor
CALL, 468

Naughton, John High School/Prep Sports Chief
DES MOINES REGISTER, 483

Naughton, Michael Product Manager
NIELSEN-KELLERMAN, 1168

Naumann, George Senior Vice President Operations
CORPORATION FOR LASER OPTICS RESEARCH, 1119

Naumovich, Jim Commissioner
GREAT LAKES VALLEY CONFERENCE, 296

Nava, Miguel Director of Latin Operations
SROBA & ASSOCIATES, 763

Navarro, Manny Sports Writer
MIAMI HERALD, 506

Navarro, Robert President/CEO
HERITAGE CORRIDOR CONVENTION & VISITORS BUREAU, 236

Navarro, Yolanda Program Director
KRAN, 627

Navy, Brian National Sales Manager
WIP SPORTSRADIO 610, 651

Nay, Dave Sports Editor
PALISADIAN, 517

Naylor, Alicia Assistant to the VP of Athletics & Recre
HARTFORD ATHLETICS, UNIVERSITY OF, 331

Naylor, Jeffrey SVP / Chief Financial Officer
ODD LOTS/BIG LOTS, 1234

Naylor, Jim Promoter
VENTURA RACEWAY, 1035

Naylor-Johnson, Darrell Faculty Athletics Representative
SAVANNAH COLLEGE OF ART & DESIGN ATHLETICS, 400

Nazzaro, Jay Chief Financial Officer
NEW YORK-PENNSYLVANIA LEAGUE, 47

Neace, John Chair & CEO
USL CHAMPIONSHIP, 159

Neal, Bobby Vice-Chairman
NJCAA REGION V MEN'S, 287

Neal, Brian Chief Financial Officer and VP, Business
FANSEDGE.COM, 1227

Neal, David EVP, NBC Olympics/Executive Producer, NB
NBC SPORTS DIVISION, 506, 676

Neal, Diane President
MERVYN'S, 1233

Neal, Don Food & Beverage Coordinator
ROYAL PURPLE RACEWAY, 1032

Neal, Jay Sports Editor
JACKSONVILLE DAILY PROGRESS, 497

Neal, Michael Sports Information Director
BLACKBURN COLLEGE ATHLETICS, 378

Neal, Mike Founder and Chief Scientist
NETWORK FOUNDATON TECHNOLOGIES (NFT), 797

Neal, Stephen Chairman
COOLEY, GODWARD, LLP, 874

Neale, JoAnn President & Chief Administrative Officer
MAJOR LEAGUE SOCCER, 157

Nealy, Wren Vice President
INTERNATIONAL POLICE MOUNTAIN BIKE ASSOCIATION (IPMBA), 70

Neander, Erik President, Baseball Operations
AMERICAN LEAGUE OF PROFESSIONAL BASEBALL CLUBS, THE, 30

Near, Dan Commissioner
WESTERN HOCKEY LEAGUE, 138

Neary, Charlie Executive Vice President
OVATION FOOD SERVICES LP, 1067

Nease, Gary News/Sports Director
WPIG-FM, 649, 661

Nechemias, Stephen Partner
TAFT, STETTINIUS & HOLLISTER, 857

Neck, Mike Sports Director
KAPB-FM, 613

Nedrow, Larry Executive Vice President
CELLO PROFESSIONAL PRODUCTS, 1115

Needels, Chris Executive Director
PARACHUTIST, 575

Needhan, Dick Editor
SKIING HERITAGE, 581

Needler, Kevin Operations Manager
GARED SPORTS, 1136

Neels, Tim Commissioner
GATEWAY REGIONAL COMMISSIONER/USA VOLLEYBALL, 211

Neely, Cam President & Alternate Governor
NATIONAL HOCKEY LEAGUE/NHL, 123

Neely, Kelly Senior Director of Handicapping & Course
OREGON GOLF ASSOCIATION, 114

Neely, Mark Head Athletic Trainer
MONTREAT COLLEGE ATHLETICS, 317

Neely, Richard President
AMERICAN AMATEUR BASEBALL CONGRESS, 25

Neely, Sarah Director of Public Relations & Administr
NATIONAL INTERCOLLEGIATE RODEO ASSOCIATION (NIRA), 146

Neely, Wade Assistant Athletic Director
MARTIN METHODIST COLLEGE ATHLETICS, 316

Neese, Jim Rider Development
COMPETITION PARK MOTOCROSS, 1024

Neese, John Director of Athletics
HARDIN-SIMMONS UNIVERSITY ATHLETICS, 387

Neff, Bob Executive Creative Director
RADIAN 1, 805

Neff, Brenda Account Specialist
UNI-DOME, 1012

Neff, Graham Director of Athletics
CLEMSON UNIVERSITY ATHLETICS, 327, 958, 966, 977

Negandhi, Kevin Sports Anchor
WWSB-TV, 712

Neglia, Gianleonardo Sporting Director
USL CHAMPIONSHIP, 159

Negoro, Yasuchika Chairman
JAPANESE BASEBALL HALL OF FAME AND MUSEUM, 254

Negre, Leandro President
FIELD HOCKEY, FEDERATION INTERNATIONALE DE HOCKEY (FIH), 0

Negrete, Tom Assistant Managing Ed., Sports and Busin
SACRAMENTO BEE, 526

Nehr, George Promotions Director
WTNY-AM, 668

Neidert, Tanya Assistant Executive Director
WOMEN'S PREMIER SOCCER LEAGUE, 168

Neidig, Chase Director of Athletic Broadcasting
BLUEFIELD COLLEGE ATHLETICS, 309, 352

Neidre, Peter Director of Coach and Athlete Developmen
CANOEKAYAK CANADA, 68

Neilson, David Commissioner
MICHIGAN INTERCOLLEGIATE ATHLETIC ASSOCIATION, 298

Neilson, Robbie Head Coach
WOMEN'S PREMIER SOCCER LEAGUE, 160, 169

Neistadt, Leslie Managing Editor
JOURNAL OF ATHLETIC TRAINING, 566

Neitzey, J. Executive Director
PRINCE GEORGE'S COUNTY CONFERENCE & VISITORS BUREAU, INC., 244

Neklawy, Hassan Chair, Lincolnshire Marriott Resort
LAKE COUNTY, ILLINOIS - CONVENTION & VISITORS BUREAU, 238

Nekoloff, JJ Commissioner
OLD DOMINION ATHLETIC CONFERENCE, 302

Outlaw, Mike Managing Director
PRO ATHLETES OUTREACH, 224
Ovalle, Adolfo Technical Director, Coach &
Founder
WOMEN'S PREMIER SOCCER LEAGUE, 167
Ovenden, Mark Sports Director
KDLT-TV, 689
Over, Stephen Executive Director
SKI PATROL, 580
Overbeck, Dan President, Assistant Rules Official
ROCHESTER DISTRICT GOLF ASSOCIATION,
115
Overbeeke, Len Operations Manager
ENMAX CENTRE, 964
Overbey, Rhonda Advertising Manager
LOG CABIN DEMOCRAT, 503
Overby, Ronald VP
ATLANTIC FITNESS PRODUCTS, 1101
Overfelt, William General Manager
FRESNO CONVENTION & ENTERTAINMENT
CENTER, 967
Overholt, Alison General Editor
ESPN THE MAGAZINE, 558
Overlan, Mary Director, Finance
NEW ENGLAND SPORTS NETWORK/NESN,
676
Overlan, Matt Chief Financial/Chief Operations
Officer
HCC SPECIALTY UNDERWRITERS, INC, 756
Overman, Jason Advertising Manager
HARRISON DAILY TIMES, 492
Overstreet, Bill VP, Marketing, Sales and
Promotions
GOLF USA, 1229
Overton, Milton Director of Athletics
KENNESAW STATE UNIVERSITY ATHLETICS,
334, 951
Overton, Parker President / Chief Executive
Officer
DUNN'S, 1126
Overton, V. President
OVERTON'S, 1234
Ovies, Joe Producer
THE ADAM GOLD SHOW, 607
Owen, Bill President and CEO
RUPP ARENA, 999
Owen, Mark Compliance Officer
ALBERTSON COLLEGE OF IDAHO
ATHLETICS, 307
Owen, Robert Partner
BURGOYNE, ROBERT A., 870
Owen, Spike Manager
SOUTH ATLANTIC LEAGUE (A LEVEL), 51
Owens, Billy Asst. General Manager/Dir. of Player
Per
AMERICAN LEAGUE OF PROFESSIONAL
BASEBALL CLUBS, THE, 30
Owens, Brigman Attorney
OWENS, BRIGMAN, 846
Owens, Caroline Founder
NATURAL BALANCE, INC., 1166
Owens, Dale Senior Vice President, Corporate
Sales
INTERNATIONAL LEAGUE, 42, 984
Owens, Dan Events
SOUTHWESTERN INTERNATIONAL
RACEWAY, 1033
Owens, Jeff Program/Sports Director
WEIU-FM, 644
Owens, Joe Senior Associate AD, Performance
Enhance
DAYTON ATHLETICS, UNIVERSITY OF, 328
Owens, John Sports Director
KKTV-TV, 691
Owens, Lewis Governor
INDIANA AAU ASSOCIATION, 214
Owens, Lindsey Associate Athletic Dir. for
External Ops
SOUTHEASTERN LOUISIANA UNIVERSITY
ATHLETICS, 344
Owens, Lynn Dept. Coordinator
MONTANA STATE UNIVERSITY-BOZEMAN,
428
Owens, Mark Founder
NATURAL BALANCE, INC., 1166
Owens, Scott Interim Chair of Health, Exercise
Scienc
MISSISSIPPI, UNIVERSITY OF, 427

Owens, Sean Director of Ticket Sales &
Hospitality
KNIGHTS STADIUM, 979
Owens, Stephen General Counsel
ARNET, WILLIAM F., 862
Owens, Terry Director of Sports Information
BELOIT COLLEGE ATHLETICS, 377
Owens, Tim Chief Executive Officer/Event
Producer
EVENTS PROMOTIONS USA, 754
Owings, Mike Vice President Sales
A4, 1089
Ownens, Tara Director of Athletics
MARYLAND EASTERN SHORE ATHLETICS,
UNIVERSITY OF, 336
Oxby, Murray Director Communications
ASSANTE SPORTS MANAGEMENT GROUP,
825
Oxley, Brad Promoter
COSTA MESA SPEEDWAY, 1024
Oxley, Chris General Manager
ROSE QUARTER BOX OFFICE, 999
Oxnard, Whitney VIP Services Coordinator
JACKSONVILLE VETERANS MEMORIAL
ARENA, 975
Oyama, Motoi President & CEO
ASICS AMERICA CORPORATION, 226, 1100
Oyer, Mark Business Director
UNIVERSAL FABRIC STRUCTURES, 1206
Ozbun, Jim Chairman of the Commission
NORTH DAKOTA RACING COMMISSION, 81
Ozer, Mark Founder, Chairman
GLOBAL SPORTS CONNEXION, 930
Ozer, Ronald Attoney
ELY, BETTINI, ULMAN & ROSENBLATT, 878

P

P Adams Jr, Charles Managing Partner
ADAMS & REESE, 861
P. DG Baldwin, William Partner
LAMPLEY, NATHANIEL, 889
P. E. Nolan, Lawrence Chair
THOMAS M. COOLEY LAW SCHOOL, 911
P. J. Bohnen, Thomas Associate
ROSENTHAL, ROBERT E., 903
P. J. Bulinski, Gregory Chief Executive Officer
BASSFORD, LOCKHART, TRUESDELL &
BRIGGS, P.A., 864
P. Lopez III, Patricio Attorney
LOPEZ, PAT P., 891
P. M. Smith, Bruce Dean
ROSS, STEPHEN F., 903
P.Emery, Stephen Principal
GEIGER ENGINEERS, 1057
Paasschen, Mark Weekend Sports Anchor
KXII-TV, 698
Pabst, Augie Contact
INDY PRO 2000, 22
Pace, Bobby Racing Secretary
FAIRMOUNT PARK RACETRACK, 1038
Pace, Joe CEO & Director, Hockey Operations
FEDERAL PROSPECTS HOCKEY LEAGUE
(FPHL), 131
Pacheco, Nayeli Executive Administrative
Assistant & Hos
ROYAL PURPLE RACEWAY, 1032
Pacheco, Richard Senior Vice President
GALAVISION, 676
Pachter, Jason Head Athletic Trainer
STATE UNIVERSITY OF NEW YORK
COLLEGE AT PLATTSBURGH
ATHLETICS(SUN, 402
Pacifico, Sabrina Publicity Coordinator
WPHL-TV, 708
Pacini, Quinn General Manager
BOBCAT STADIUM (MSU), 951
Pack, Chance Vice Chairman
BILLIARD CONGRESS OF AMERICA, 62
Pack, Eric Sports Editor
ORANGE COUNTY REGISTER, 516
Packer, Lauren Associate Director of Athletics
MERCYHURST UNIVERSITY ATHLETICS, 363
Packett, John Sports Reporter
RICHMOND TIMES-DISPATCH, 525
Paczak, Susan Esquire
ABES & BAUMANN, 861
Paddock, Scott President
CHICAGOLAND SPEEDWAY, 1023

Pade, Timothy Publisher
COLORADO GOLF MAGAZINE, 556
Padecky, Bob Sports Reporter
PRESS DEMOCRAT, 522
Paden, Janet Chief Financial & Human Resources
Office
U.S. FIELD HOCKEY ASSOCIATION, 121
Padfield, Joel General Manager
FRONTIER LEAGUE, 40, 951
Padgett, Beverly Director of Circulation
STREET & SMITH'S SPORTSBUSINESS
DAILY, 586
Padilla, Josi Sports Director
WONQ-AM, 660
Padjen, Alan Track Manager
SILVER DOLLAR SPEEDWAY, 1032
Padjen, John Sullivan
PLACERVILLE SPEEDWAY, 1030
Padover, Dan General Manager
WOMEN'S NATIONAL BASKETBALL
ASSOCIATION, 60
Padron, Lissette Marketing Coordinator
DYNASTY APPAREL INDUSTRIES, 1126
Padula, Joe Promoter
THUNDER VALLEY SPEEDWAY, 1034
Padula, John First Vice President
USA TRACK & FIELD - NEW YORK, 178
Padula, Morgan General Manager
THUNDER VALLEY SPEEDWAY, 1034
Pagan, Joe Station Manager
WLEY-AM, 655
Pagano, Chuck EVP & CTO
OUTSIDE THE LINES, 680
Page, Andrew Manager, Coach Development
ATHLETICS CANADA, 177
Page, Carter Senior Director Of Rules &
Competitions
WEST VIRGINIA GOLF ASSOCIATION, 117
Page, Dennis Publisher
SLAM, 581
Page, Douglas Sports Information Director
SALEM INTERNATIONAL UNIVERSITY
ATHLETICS, 369
Page, Harold President / Chief Executive Officer
VUARNET, 1208
Page, Harry Sports Reporter
SAN ANTONIO EXPRESS-NEWS, 528
Page, John President, Wells Fargo Complex
WELLS FARGO CENTER, 820, 1018
Page, Ken Executive Director
VERMONT PRINCIPALS' ASSOCIATION, 202
Page, Kerry Associate Director, Facilities & Sports
VAUGHT-HEMINGWAY
STADIUM/HOLLINGSWORTH FIELD, 1015
Page, Kirk SCJGA Director of Competitions
SOUTH CAROLINA GOLF ASSOCIATION, 115
Page, Rodney Sports Writer
ST. PETERSBURG TIMES, 533
Page, Steve Sports Editor
REPORTER-TIMES, 524
Pagliocca, Jeff General Manager
WOMEN'S NATIONAL BASKETBALL
ASSOCIATION, 60
Pagon, Marshall Chairman of the Board
U.S. SQUASH, 171
Pahigian, Cary General Manager
WGAN, 647
Pahl, David Senior Vice President/General
Counsel
ESPN TELEVISION, 674
Paiement, Criag Assistant Professor and Chair
Graduate P
ITHACA COLLEGE, 421
Paige, Don President
PAIGE DESIGN GROUP, 1061
Paige, Peter Publisher
TOUCHLINE-EASTERN PENNSYLVANIA, 588
Paige, Tony President/Chief Executive Officer
PAIGE & RICE, 846
Paige, Woody Sports Columnist
DENVER POST, 482
Paik, Jenny Principal
CPG ARCHITECTS, 1053
Paim, Eduardo Sports Director
KIGS-AM, 620
Paine, Neil User Affairs Coordinator
SPORTS REFERENCE, THE, 929
Painter, Bill Vice-Chairman
NJCAA REGION X MEN'S, 288

Pechenino, Kraig Marketing Director
RACING COMMUNICATIONS, 1180
Peck, Arnie Sales Manager
WDLB, 643
Peck, Darren President
SPORTS OVERNIGHT AMERICA WEEKEND,
602, 609, 610
Peck, David President
COMPASS COLLECTIVE, 752
Peck, Dennis Sports Editor
OREGONIAN, 516
Peck, Kyle Sports Division
SUPERSTAR MANAGEMENT, INC., 857
Peck, Mike VP, Marketing, Content & Operations
AMERICAN HOCKEY LEAGUE/AHL, 128
Peck, Ryan Deputy AD, External Operations
NORTH TEXAS ATHLETICS, UNIVERSITY OF,
339
Peck, Terri Marketing Director
KVVU-TV, 697
Pecor, Ray Principal Owner/President
NEW YORK-PENNSYLVANIA LEAGUE, 47
Pecora, Pat Athletic Director
UNIVERSITY OF PITTSBURGH AT
JOHNSTOWN ATHLETICS, 368
Peden, Harry President
FAIRFIELD COUNTY SPORTS COMMISSION,
233
Peden, Jimmy Commissioner
PALMETTO REGIONAL COMMISSIONER/USA
VOLLEYBALL, 212
Pederson, Steve Athletic Director
PETERSON EVENTS CENTER, 992
Pederson, Terry National Sales Manager
DAIWA CORPORATION, 1122
Pedley, Jim Sports Writer
KANSAS CITY STAR, 499
Pedrin, Alonzo Principal
ALFRED GOBAR ASSOCIATES, 1049
Pedrique, Al Manager
EASTERN LEAGUE, 39
Pedulla, Tom Sports Reporter
USA TODAY, 543
Peech, Brian Editor-in-Chief
SKATEBOARDER MAGAZINE, 580
Peed, Steve Director of Athletics
MAINE MARITIME ACADEMY
ATHLETICS(MMA), 391
Peek, Barry Member
MEYER, SUOZZI, ENGLISH & KLEIN, 895
Peek, Steve Score Entertainment SVP
PLAYOFF CORP., 1175
Peeler, Mark Vice President for Intercollegiate
Athle
ERSKINE COLLEGE ATHLETICS, 357
Peeples, Jim Director of Athletics
PIEDMONT COLLEGE ATHLETICS, 397
Peery, Camp President & COO
USL LEAGUE ONE, 161
Peeters, Carl Chief Financial Officer
BARCO MEDIA, 1104
Peetoom, Kelly Vice President Sales
OVERLAND PARK CONVENTION & VISITORS
BUREAU, 243, 263
Peevy, DeWayne Director of Athletics
DEPAUL UNIVERSITY ATHLETICS, 328
Peffer, Matthew Attorney
CHASEN & BOSCOLO CHARTERED, 872
Pegoraro, Ann Director and Associate Professor
LAURENTIAN UNIVERSITY, 422
Pegula, Kim Co-Owner
AMERICAN HOCKEY LEAGUE/AHL, 94, 123,
128
Pegula, Terrence Owner & President
AMERICAN HOCKEY LEAGUE/AHL, 128
Pegula, Terry Owner
NATIONAL LACROSSE LEAGUE, 94, 123, 142
Peitersen, Wade Head Athletic Trainer
UNIVERSITY OF WISCONSIN - OSHKOSH
TITANS, 407
Peixoto, Dave Commissioner
NEW ENGLAND REGIONAL
COMMISSIONER/USA VOLLEYBALL, 212
Peixotto, Bob SVP, Human Resources
L.L. BEAN, 1231
Pekarske, Meg Shareholder
REINHART, BOERNER, VAN DEUREN S.C.,
902

Peladeau, Pierre Owner
CANADIAN FOOTBALL LEAGUE/CFL, 93
Pelfrey, Dennis Field Manager
FRONTIER LEAGUE, 40
Pelfrey, Ray Owner/Chief Executive Officer
PROFESSIONAL KICKING SERVICES, INC.,
849
Pelfrey, Rob President
PROFESSIONAL KICKING SERVICES, INC.,
849
Pelinka, Rob VP, Basketball Operations &
General Mana
NATIONAL BASKETBALL ASSOCIATION/NBA,
57
Pellegrini, James Shareholder
REINHART, BOERNER, VAN DEUREN S.C.,
902
Pellegrom, Jeff Chief Financial Officer &
Executive VP
NATIONAL HOCKEY LEAGUE/NHL, 124
Pellerin, Charles President
QUEBEC MARITIMES MAJOR JUNIOR
HOCKEY LEAGUE, 136
Pelletier, David President
PROMONDE, 803
Pelliccia, Michael Athletics Physical Education
Director
NJCAA REGION XV MEN'S, 289
Pellin-Scott, Roxanna (214)977-8961
DALLAS MORNING NEWS, 481
Pelote, Willie Director
CALIFORNIA EXPOSITION & STATE FAIR,
1023, 1036
Pelster, Sarah Associate Athletic Director
SHENANDOAH UNIVERSITY ATHLETICS, 400
Peltoma, Ryan Assistant General Manager
NORTH AMERICAN HOCKEY LEAGUE, 133
Peltz, Barbara Advertising Manager
BOWLING CENTER MANAGEMENT, 553
Peluso, Nick Senior Vice President Radio
Operations
COX MEDIA GROUP, 604
Pelzer, Ute Chief Financial Officer
OCEAN PACIFIC APPAREL CORPORATION,
1170
Pemble, Mat Head of Information And
Communications T
INTERNATIONAL TENNIS FEDERATION, 174
Pena, Carlos VP, Racing Operations
EL COMANDANTE RACE TRACK, 1037
Penberthy, DaWayne Assistant Director Of Golf
INTERNATIONAL JUNIOR GOLF ACADEMY,
102
Pence, Carol Employment Service Consultant
NORTHERN CALIFORNIA SECTIONAL
OFFICE, 107
Pendergraft, Jennifer General Manager
CALIFORNIA LEAGUE (A-LEVEL), 36
Pendergrass, Ben Vice President, Government
Affairs
AMERICAN HORSE COUNCIL, 73
Pendery, Kim MLB/Rays/Auto Racing/Colleges
TAMPA TRIBUNE, 537
Pendleton, Brian Executive Director
USA KARATE FEDERATION, 143
Pendleton, Larry President/CEO
SUNSHINE STATE GAMES, 233, 264
Penegar, Jim Circulation General Manager
STREET & SMITH'S SPORTS GEAR, 587
Penegor, Todd President & Chief Executive
Officer
PAPA JOHN'S INTERNATIONAL, 731
Penicka, Bob President/Chief Operating Officer
TOP-FLITE COMPANY, 1202
Penland, Charles Senior Principal/Executive
Director
WALTER P MOORE, 1063
Pennello, Joan Senior Vice President, Operations
WOMEN'S TENNIS ASSOCIATION TOUR, 176
Penner, Bob Equipment Manager
DICKINSON COLLEGE(DC) ATHLETICS, 383
Penner, Greg Owner & CEO
NATIONAL FOOTBALL LEAGUE/NFL, 94
Penner, Mike Executive Associate AD, Internal
Operati
OHIO STATE UNIVERSITY ATHLETICS, 340
Pennetti, Mike Sports Team Leader
TAMPA TRIBUNE, 537

Penney, Pat VP / Chief Financial Officer
AUSTAD'S GOLF STORE'S, 1217
Penningroth, Ailey Senior Vice President and
Chief Marketin
PHILIPS ARENA, 993
Pennington, Bill (212)556-7371
NEW YORK TIMES, 511
Pennington, Cyndee General Manager
PENSACOLA BAY CENTER, 991
Pennington, Hal Chairman / President / Chief
Executive O
DOCKER'S FOOTWEAR, 1125
Pennington, Jerry Corporate Account Executive
MEMPHIS MOTORSPORTS PARK (MMP),
1028
Penny, Francis Marketing Manager/Publicist
FRASER DOWNS, 1038
Penny, Josh Head Athletic Trainer
UNIVERSITY OF NORTH ALABAMA
ATHLETICS(UNA), 366
Penny, Steve President/CEO
U.S. SPORTS ACROBATICS/USSA, 120
Penny, Steven President
USA GYMNASTICS, 590
Penrod, Ann Classified Manager
WACO TRIBUNE-HERALD, 545
Penrod, Barbara Advertising Manager
HOLDREGE DAILY CITIZEN, 494
Pens, Charles CEO/President/General Manager
FEDERAL PROSPECTS HOCKEY LEAGUE
(FPHL), 131
Pens, Charlie General Manager
FEDERAL PROSPECTS HOCKEY LEAGUE
(FPHL), 131
Penske, Roger Founder/Chair
NASCAR XFINITY SERIES, 22, 23, 24
Pentico, Derrick Event Manager
NASHVILLE MUNICIPAL AUDITORIUM, 988
Pentima, Matt Director of Ticket & Baseball
Operations
EASTERN LEAGUE, 39, 1000
Pentz, Jamie Publisher
SKIING, 581
Peoples, Daryl President
IBF/USBA, 66
Peoples, Kim Marketing Director
WKMG-TV, 705
Pepe, Anthony Director of Marketing
1510 THE ZONE, 611
Pepe, Christopher Western Operations VP
PREMIER PARTNERSHIPS, 802
Peper, Jim Plant Supervisor
AUTOMATED BATTING CAGES
CORPORATION, 1102
Pepin, Phil VP / Chief Financial Officer
WHOLESALE SPORTS OUTDOOR
OUTFITTERS, 1241
Pepin, William President
WWLP-TV, 712
Pepin-Donat, Craig Sales and Marketing EVP
24 HOUR FITNESS CENTERS, 1215
Peppas, Josh Sports Information Director
UNIVERSITY OF THE OZARKS ATHLETICS,
396
Pepperman, Donald Attorney/Partner
BLECHER & COLLINS, 867
Peppler, Mike Head Athletic Trainer
GREENVILLE COLLEGE ATHLETICS, 386
Pequeno, Joe Sports Producer/Reporter/Anchor
KPNX-TV, 693
Pera, Robert Owner/Chair
NATIONAL BASKETBALL ASSOCIATION/NBA,
57
Peraza, Katty Design
EXCLUSIVE SPORTS MARKETING, INC., 782
Percarpio, David Group Sales Manager
NEW YORK-PENNSYLVANIA LEAGUE, 47
Perdue, Mark Athletic Director
ASBURY COLLEGE ATHLETICS, 288, 307
Perdue, Reuben Sports Director
WWKC-FM, 639, 671
Peregoy, Robert Advertising Manager
OUTSIDE PITCH, 575
Pereira, Christine Assistant AD, Compliance
LA SALLE UNIVERSITY ATHLETICS, 334
Pereira, Ed Promotion Manager
WNBH-AM, 658
Pereira, Les President
TRIATHLON CANADA, 178

Pfaff, Christopher CEO
IMSA WEATHERTECH SPORTSCAR
CHAMPIONSHIP, 21

Pfaff, Michael President, General Manager
BETHPAGE BALLPARK, 949

Pfaff, Mike President and General Manager
ATLANTIC LEAGUE, 35

Pfaffenberger, William Lawyer
HAILE, SHAW & PFAFFENBERGER, P.A., 882

Pfaffl, John Assistant Director of Athletics
CARDINAL STRITCH UNIVERSITY
ATHLETICS, 310

Pfander, Jim General Manager/COO
EASTERN LEAGUE, 37, 954

Pfannenstein, Dave Executive Director
VERMONT GOLF ASSOCIATION, 116

Pfannenstein, Shari Website/Communications
VERMONT GOLF ASSOCIATION, 116

Pfefer, Mark Director Of Business Development
DAN MARINO FOUNDATION, 191

Pfeifer, Eric Executive Director
GEORGIA STATE GAMES COMMISSION, 143,
261

Pfeiffer, Katie Program Director
KURE-FM, 631

Pfeninger, Christa Women's Softball Head Coach
NJCAA REGION I WOMEN'S, 286

Pfiffner, Matt Sports Editor
CRESTON NEWS-ADVERTISER, 474

Pfuller, Thomas Vice President, Marketing
INTERNATIONAL BIATHLON UNION (IBU), 61,
204

PhD., Scott President
TAYLOR RESEARCH & CONSULTING
GROUP, INC., 813

Phan, Khuong Sports Writer
CITRUS COUNTY CHRONICLE, 471

Phan, Monty Advertising Reporter
NEWSDAY, 513

Phaneuf, Wayne Executive Editor
UNION-NEWS, SUNDAY REPUBLICAN, 543

Phares, Chuck Executive VP Of Sales
L.A.T SPORTSWEAR, 1154

Phegley, Lance Editor
TEXAS RUNNER & TRIATHLETE, 565, 588

Phelan, Mike Marketing Analyst
NCR, 1167

Phelps, Digger Analyst
COLLEGE GAMEDAY, 608

Phelps, Gene Sports Editor
NORTHEAST MISSISSIPPI DAILY JOURNAL,
514

Phelps, Jake Editor
THRASHER SKATEBOARD MAGAZINE, 588

Phelps, Steve Chief Marketing Officer
NASCAR, 686

Phelps, Steven Director of Sports Information
BUENA VISTA UNIVERSITY ATHLETICS, 378

Phelps, Todd Deputy Director of Athletics
NORTH DAKOTA STATE UNIVERSITY
(NDSU), 366

Phil, Ruffin Owner
WICHITA GREYHOUND PARK, 1048

Philbeck, Jason Sports Marketing Manager
RALEIGH CONVENTION & VISITORS
BUREAU (GREATER), 244

Philippon, Marc Managing Partner
THE STEADMAN CLINIC, 924

Philipson, Gary President
HERB PHILIPSON'S, 1230

Phillips, Al Co-Owner
JOSEPH P. RILEY PARK, 978

Phillips, Ashley Sr. Account Executive
TR HUGHES BALLPARK, 991, 1010

Phillips, Benny Sports Editor
HIGH POINT ENTERPRISE, 494

Phillips, Buzz Director of Athletics Emeritus
HUNTINGDON COLLEGE ATHLETICS, 388

Phillips, Chuck Vice President
FLORIDA STATE GOLF ASSOCIATION, 111

Phillips, Danny Commissioner
DIZZY DEAN BASEBALL, 27

Phillips, Esther Promotions Manager
KTVE-TV, 696

Phillips, Gary Executive Director
GEORGIA HS ASSOCIATION, 199

Phillips, J. Sports Announcer
WRGS-AM, 664

Phillips, Jan News Director
KYCX-FM, 633

Phillips, Jared Assistant Athletic Director
GUSTAVUS ADOLPHUS COLLEGE
ATHLETICS, 386

Phillips, Jason Advertising Director
SAN FRANCISCO EXAMINER, 528

Phillips, Jay Sports Director
WRGS-AM, 664

Phillips, Jeff President
FLEET FEET, INC., 1228

Phillips, Jennifer Associate AD,
Compliance/SWA
JAMES MADISON UNIVERSITY ATHLETICS,
333

Phillips, Jim President
NATIONAL ASSOCIATION OF ACADEMIC
ADVISORS FOR ATHLETICS/N4A, 284, 1000,
1018

Phillips, John Director of Athletics
EMBRY-RIDDLE AERONAUTICAL
UNIVERSITY ATHLETICS - (FL), 312, 357

Phillips, Jon Director International Sales
E-Z GO, 1126

Phillips, Julie Athletic Trainer
NJCAA REGION XII MEN'S, 288, 1033

Phillips, Justin Director of
Tournaments/Operations
MICHIGAN PGA SECTIONAL OFFICE, 106

Phillips, Les Contact
BUTTONWILLOW RACEWAY PARK, 1023

Phillips, Lynn Chief Administrative Officer &
General M
WOMEN'S FOOTBALL ALLIANCE / WFA, 98,
1033

Phillips, Matt Senior Editor
MOUNTAIN BIKE, 571

Phillips, Michael Shareholder
PHILLIPS & AKERS PC, 676, 899

Phillips, Mike Sports Reporter
MIAMI HERALD, 506

Phillips, Pam Senior Women's Administrator
STILLMAN COLLEGE ATHLETICS, 372

Phillips, Paul Assistant Athletic Director
CLARK UNIVERSITY ATHLETICS, 380

Phillips, Rick Operations Director
CLARDY, DON S., 872

Phillips, Robert President
PHILLIPS MARKETING, 801

Phillips, Scott Sports Editor
AMERICUS TIMES-RECORDER, 460

Phillips, Skin Editor-in-Chief
TRANSWORLD SKATEBOARDING, 589

Phillips, Teresa Athletics Director
HOWARD C. GENTRY COMPLEX, 971

Phillips, Teresa Director of Athletics
WJ HALE STADIUM, 1019

Phillips, Terri VP, Business Operations/Dir.,
Game Night
UNITED STATES HOCKEY LEAGUE, 137

Phillips, Thomas Managing Director
MILLER CANFIELD SPORTS, 844

Phillips, Tina Assistant Athletic Director
UNIVERSITY OF PITTSBURGH AT
BRADFORD ATHLETICS, 397

Phillips, Tom Finance Manager
RICHMOND COUNTY BANK BALLPARK, 997

Phillips, Troy Sports Writer
FORT WORTH STAR-TELEGRAM, 489

Phillips, Wayne Sports Editor
GREENEVILLE SUN, 491

Phillips, Wes Sports Copy Editor
TAMPA TRIBUNE, 537

Phillips, Winfred VP for Research & Dean of the
Graduate S
FLORIDA, UNIVERSITY OF, 418

Phipps, Dean Dir. Marketing Development &
Corp. Partn
ALASKA STATE FAIR, 260

Phipps, Jason Director of Online Media
FX NETWORKS, LLC, 675

Phipps, Ogden Honorary Chairman
JOCKEY CLUB, 76

Phyfe, Gaelen Managing Editor
OFFSHORE, 574

Piacentini, Tyler Assistant Coach
SOUTHERN PROFESSIONAL HOCKEY
LEAGUE, 136

Piantedosi, Gary Partner
PIANTEDOSI OARS, INC., 1174

Piasecki, Marl Lawyer
PIASECKI, MARK J., 899

Piazza, Mark Senior VP, Sports Team Operations
NATIONAL HOCKEY LEAGUE/NHL, 125

Picard, Olivier Managing Director
QUEBEC MARITIMES MAJOR JUNIOR
HOCKEY LEAGUE, 135

Picciotto, Phil Founder & President
OCTAGON MARKETING NORTH AMERICA,
799

Picciotto, Phil Founder & President
OCTAGON SPORTS, 799, 845

Picciotto, Phil President, Athletes & Personalities
OCTAGON ATHLETE REPRESENTATION
(ATTORNEYS), 833, 898

Piccirillo, Rick Owner
ARCTIC SPORTS, 825

Piccolo, Philip Executive VP
ESCALADE SPORTS, 1130

Pickel, Nathan Head Athletic Trainer
BARTON COLLEGE ATHLETICS, 351

Pickens, Ernest Station Manager
KTKC-FM, 630

Pickens, H. Publisher
GOLFER, 562

Pickens, John Assistant Athletic Director
BACONE COLLEGE ATHLETICS, 308

Pickerill, Ken Eligibility Chair/FAR
KENTUCKY INTERCOLLEGIATE ATHLETIC
CONFERENCE, 297

Pickerill, Roy Sports Information Director
KENTUCKY WESLEYAN COLLEGE
ATHLETICS, 361

Pickett, Al Producer
SPORTSLINE, 606

Pickett, Donn Partner
BINGHAM MCCUTCHEN LLP, 866

Pickett, Harry Sports Deputy Editor
CHARLOTTE OBSERVER, 469

Pickford, Sarah Global Development Manager
NETBALL ASSOCIATIONS, INTERNATIONAL
FEDERATION OF, 144

Pickle, P. Editor
NCAA NEWS, 573

Picklesimer, Tyler Assistant Racing Secretary
TURFWAY PARK, 1045

Pickman, Andrew President and Chief
Merchandising Office
LAZARUS, 1232

Pickron-Davis, Marcine Chief Community
Engagement and Diversity
WIDENER UNIVERSITY SPORT
MANAGEMENT, 860

Picollo, J.J. Executive Vice President & General
Manag
AMERICAN LEAGUE OF PROFESSIONAL
BASEBALL CLUBS, THE, 30

Picone, Gary Athletic Director
LEWIS-CLARK STATE COLLEGE ATHLETICS,
315

Picozzi, Bob News Anchor
COLLEGE FOOTBALL CENTER, 608

Pidto, Bill Anchor
ESPN, 683

Pieart, Nicki Assistant Director of Athletics
AURORA UNIVERSITY ATHLETICS (AU), 377

Piepenkotter, Julie Research Senior Vice
President
FX NETWORKS, LLC, 675

Piepkorn, David Commissioner
NORTH DAKOTA RACING COMMISSION, 81

Pier, Chris Operations Director for Compliance
LAKE FOREST COLLEGE ATHLETICS, 390

Pier, Dave Chief Marketing Officer
WESTERN HOCKEY LEAGUE, 139

Pieracci, Louie Vice President - General Manager
COUCH DISTRIBUTING COMPANY, 1223

Pierce, Antonio Head Coach
NATIONAL FOOTBALL LEAGUE/NFL, 95

Pierce, Bob EVP Sales / Marketing
DUNBROOKE, 996, 1125

Pierce, Brendan Director, Ticket Sales & Service
NATIONAL FOOTBALL LEAGUE/NFL, 94

Pierce, Buck Head Coach
CANADIAN FOOTBALL LEAGUE/CFL, 92

Pierce, Christina Advertising Director
NEWS-STAR, 513

Pierce, Christy Advertising Manager
DAILY AMERICAN REPUBLIC, 475

Pierce, David Program Director
KLRM-FM, 622

Pierce, Gina Director, Game Entertainment
DR. PEPPER BALLPARK, 962

Pierce, Gordy President-Tennis Division
U.S. TENNIS COURT & TRACK BUILDERS
ASSOCIATION, 1063

Pierce, Greg Regional Manager
HEERY INTERNATIONAL, INC., 1059, 1064

Pierce, Jack Track and Field Manager
SPORTS MANAGEMENT AND MARKETING,
INC., 856

Pierce, Jim EVP / Chief Operating Officer
ACADEMY SPORTS & OUTDOORS, 1215

Pierce, Kristyn Director, Baseball Administration
NATIONAL LEAGUE OF PROFESSIONAL
BASEBALL CLUBS, THE, 31

Pierce, Lance President
UNITED TURF INDUSTRIES, 658, 1206

Pierce, Larry Marketing Manager
WABI-AM, 635

Pierce, Luke Head Coach
WESTERN HOCKEY LEAGUE, 138

Pierce, Michael Attorney
PIERCE & HUGHES P.C., 899

Pierce, Philip Director of Athletic Development
MARY WASHINGTON UNIVERSITY
ATHLETICS, 392

Piercy, Jennifer Director of the Pulp and Paper
Foundatio
NORTH CAROLINA STATE UNIVERSITY, 429

Piercy, Kevin Promoter
HICKORY MOTOR SPEEDWAY, 1025

Piercy, Kyle Sports Information Director
INDIANAPOLIS ATHLETICS, UNIVERSITY OF,
360

Pierer, Stefan CEO
KTM SPORTMOTORCYCLE USA, 1153

Pierle, Mike Executive Vice President
FN THOMPSON COMPANY, 1134

Pierre, Al Sports Editor
COURIER-OBSERVER, 474

Pierre, Edward Chief Financial Officer
ST. PIERRE MANUFACTURING
CORPORATION, 1195

Pierre, Peter Sales
ST. PIERRE MANUFACTURING
CORPORATION, 1195

Pierson, Harris Principal / General Manager
DAHLIN GROUP ARCHITECTS PLANNERS,
1053

Pierson, Neil Sports Editor
PENINSULA GATEWAY/GATEWAY PLUS, 519

Piester, John Executive Vice President
IGNITION, INC., 788

Pietrafesa, Dan Sports Editor
POUGHKEEPSIE JOURNAL, 522

Pietrok, Mark Head Athletic Trainer
LEWIS & CLARK COLLEGE ATHLETICS (L &
C), 390

Pietrowiak, Katie Director, Tickets/Merchandise
POHLMAN FIELD, 993

Pietrowski, Douglas Finance Director
MERCURY MARINE, 1162

Piette, Ed Vice President/General Manager
KSTP - KSTP 5/ABC, 695

Pifer, Kyle Deputy Athletics Director/COO
WESTERN CAROLINA UNIVERSITY
ATHLETICS, 349

Pifer, Mark Sports Editor
VIRGINIAN REVIEW, 544

Pigge, Joyce Eligibility Chair
MIDLANDS COLLEGIATE ATHLETIC
CONFERENCE, 297, 299

Pignanelli, D'Arcy President/Chief Executive
Officer
SPECIAL OLYMPICS UTAH, 197

Pike, Doug Sports Writer
HOUSTON CHRONICLE, 495

Pike, Eric Athletic Trainer
NORTH AMERICAN HOCKEY LEAGUE, 133

Pike, Lee General Manager, Gaucho Sports
Propertie
HARDER STADIUM, 969

Pikelny, Philip Vice President & Chief Marketing
Officer
DAKTRONICS, INC., 1122

Pikus, Bill Sports Anchor
KMBC-TV, 691

Pilacek, Jason Administrative Assistant
THOMAS PILACEK & ASSOCIATES, 912

Pilacek, Thomas Lawyer
THOMAS PILACEK & ASSOCIATES, 912

Pilger, Hal Sports Writer
STATE JOURNAL-REGISTER, 535

Pill, Taylor Sports Information Director
MARANATHA BAPTIST UNIVERSITY, 391

Pillar, John President
PHILADELPHIA PGA SECTIONAL OFFICE,
107

Pillard, Jerry Sales Manager
TUFLEX RUBBER PRODUCTS, 1204

Pillari, Stephanie Assistant Sports Information
Director
NEW JERSEY INSTITUTE OF
TECHNOLOGY(NJIT), 395

Pilli, Dominick President and Chief Contract
Advisor
SPORTS MANAGEMENT GROUP
WORLDWIDE, INC./SMGW, 856

Pilling, Peter Director of Intercollegiate Athletics
COLUMBIA UNIVERSITY ATHLETICS, 327

Pillow, Terry SVP / Chief Executive Officer-Ralph
Laur
ROCKPORT COMPANY, 1183

Pillsbury, David U.S. General Manager
NIKE GOLF, 1168

Pilon, Chris VP Administration
CANADIAN BROOMBALL FEDERATION, 67

Pilson, Neal President
PILSON COMMUNICATIONS, INC., 822

Pilz, Brad President
PROMARK ADVERTISING, INC., 803

Pim, Dr. 3D Coach
PATTERSON SPORTS VENTURES, 800

Pincince, Thomas Director of Athletics
CENTRAL CONNECTICUT STATE
ATHLETICS, 326

Pinckard, Bill Founder
PINCKARD BASEBALL GLOVES, 1174

Pinckney, Charles Faculty Athletic
Representative
LIVINGSTONE COLLEGE ATHLETICS, 362

Pinckney, Roger (817)390-7760
FORT WORTH STAR-TELEGRAM, 489

Pincock, Don President
MANITOBA SPORTS HALL OF FAME &
MUSEUM INC., 255

Pine, Gary Director of Athletics
AZUSA PACIFIC UNIVERSITY ATHLETICS,
308

Pine, Melissa Vice President, Tournament
Director
WOMEN'S TENNIS ASSOCIATION TOUR, 176

Pine, Nathan Director of Athletics
U.S. AIR FORCE ACADEMY ATHLETICS, 347

Pine, Sheri Sports Information Director
GOLDEN STATE ATHLETIC CONFERENCE,
296

Pinella, Bill Sports Assistant Editor
PRESS DEMOCRAT, 522

Pingalore, David Sports Anchor/Reporter
WKMG-TV, 705

Pinkela, Eric Sports Copy Editor
SAN JOSE MERCURY NEWS, 528

Pinkerton, Stanley VP/Chief Financial Officer
EL COMANDANTE RACE TRACK, 1037

Pinkham, Jeff Sports Editor
POST REGISTER, 521

Pinkney, Rick President
CANADIAN ARMWRESTLING FEDERATION,
15

Pinkus, Craig Partner/Co-Chair of the Intellectual
Pro
BOSE MCKINNEY & EVANS LLP, 867

Pino, Kathy Sales/Administration
PERFECTION EQUIPMENT, INC., 1067

Pino, Scott President
COOPERSBURG SPORTS, 1223

Pinske, Marlys President
HARNESS HORSE YOUTH FOUNDATION, 75

Pinsky, Michael Vice President
HOLMES, RICH, 884

Pinson, Clyde Advertising Director
EAGLE-TIMES, 485

Pinson, Mark Sports Editor
HIGHLANDS TODAY, 494

Pinson, Sherry Director of Communications
TURFWAY PARK, 1045

Pintelon, Filip Chief Operating Officer
BARCO MEDIA, 1104

Pintens, Craig Athletic Director
LOYOLA MARYMOUNT UNIVERSITY, 335

Pinto, Francisco Sports Anchor
KMEX-TV, 692

Pinto, Mike Chief Operating Officer
FRONTIER LEAGUE, 41

Pinton, Rachel Director of Sports Information
RAMAPO COLLEGE OF NEW JERSEY
ATHLETICS, 397

Piontek, Bill International Sales
HYDRO SPA, 1146

Pipal, Frank President
FEDERATION OF PETANQUE USA, 145

Pipal, Rob VP, Competitive League
WOMEN'S PREMIER SOCCER LEAGUE, 167

Piper, Deb Sports Director
WPNE-TV, 704, 706, 708

Piper, Dennis Corporate Affairs VP
FULL 90 SPORTS, INC., 1135

Piper, Michael Associate AD, Sports Performance
CENTRAL CONNECTICUT STATE
ATHLETICS, 326

Pipes, Jamie Manager of Product
UNITED SPORTS TECHNOLOGIES/UST, 1206

Pippenger, Julie COO
ANDRE AGASSI FOUNDATION FOR
EDUCATION, 191

Pippenger, Kathy Advertising Manager
CLAY CENTER DISPATCH, 471

Piquard, Scott Director of Event Operations
US CELLULAR CENTER, 1014

Piraino, Michael President / Chief Operating
Officer / Ch
GOLF GEAR INTERNATIONAL, 1139

Pirallo, Luis Program Director
WAEL-AM, 636

Pirmann, Ben Head Coach
USL CHAMPIONSHIP, 159

Pirrello, Mark Director of Merchandise/Box Office
Manag
JERRY UHT PARK, 976

Pirrello, Mike Assistant GM/Sales
EASTERN LEAGUE, 38

Pirzadeh, Olie President
IMAGE IMPACT, 757

Pirzer, Christian CEO Marketing AG
FEDERATION INTERNATIONALE DE SKI
(FIS), 203

Pisani, Jim President
MAJESTIC ATHLETIC, 1159

Pisani, Matteo IT Manager
WORLD ARCHERY FEDERATION, 15

Pisarcik, Joe President/CEO
NATIONAL FOOTBALL LEAGUE ALUMNI, 192

Pitarresi, John Sports Writer
OBSERVER-DISPATCH, 515

Pitcher, Red General Manager
WJBC, 651

Pitchford, Mark Administrative and Legal Practice
Partne
COOLEY, GODWARD, LLP, 874

Piter, Jason Chair
GREATER DENTON SPORTS COMMISSION,
234

Pitkanen, Eric Head Athletic Trainer
PACIFIC UNIVERSITY ATHLETICS, 397

Pitman, Deena Assistant Executive Director
STATE OF INDIANA HORSE RACING
COMMISSION, 82

Pitman, Russell Vice President Sales/Marketing
TERRAMAR SPORTS WORLDWIDE, LTD.,
1200

Pitoniak, Scott Sports Writer
DEMOCRAT AND CHRONICLE, 482

Pitt, Erica Head Athletic Trainer
UNIVERSITY OF PIKEVILLE ATHLETICS, 322

Pitt, Layne Sports Information Director
UNIVERSITY OF WISCONSIN - STOUT
ATHLETICS (UW-STOUT), 407

Pitt, Timothy Editorial Director
SPORTS ILLUSTRATED FOR KIDS, 585

Pitterman, Adam Director of Athletic
Communications

Purdum, David Sports Editor
SLIDELL SENTRY-NEWS, 531
Purdy, Jamie Assistant Director of Athletics
PIEDMONT COLLEGE ATHLETICS, 397
Purdy, Mark Sports Columnist
SAN JOSE MERCURY NEWS, 528
Purdy, Patience Director of Community Relations
SAMUEL J. PLUMERI FIELD AT MERCER
COUNTY WATERFRONT PARK, 1000
Puri, Ashwin Senior Associate AD/COO
VILLANOVA UNIVERSITY ATHLETICS, 348
Purinton, Jeff Vice Chancellor for Intercollegiate
Athl
ARKANSAS STATE UNIVERSITY ATHLETICS,
325
Purks, Scott Sports Writer
ST. PETERSBURG TIMES, 533
Purnell, Jamie Associate Director of
Athletics/SWA
CALIFORNIA STATE
UNIVERSITY-DOMINGUEZ HILLS ATHLETICS,
353
Purnell, John Chief Executive Officer
BRUTE GROUP, 1111
Purpur, Ray Deputy AD
STANFORD UNIVERSITY ATHLETICS, 345
Purpura, Joe Territory Manager, Pennsylvania
HEARTLINE FITNESS PRODUCTS, INC., 1143
Purpura, Vinney Vice President
PIONEER BASEBALL LEAGUE (ADVANCED
ROOKIE LEVEL), 50
Pursell, Kris Director or Event Operations
PALM BEACH COUNTY SPORTS
COMMISSION, INC., 243
Pursell, Ronald Lawyer
NORTH, PURSELL, RAMOS & JAMESON,
PLC, 897
Purslow, Janice VP
LOG HOUSE DESIGNS, INC., 1157
Purtell, Ryan Director, Coaching
WOMEN'S PREMIER SOCCER LEAGUE, 166
Purtill, Jim Football Coach
SAINT NORBERT COLLEGE ATHLETICS, 399
Purvis, Judy Marketing
TERRAPLAS USA RENTALS, LLC, 1200
Puscavage, Carl Marketing Sales Manager
LACKAWANNA COUNTY CONVENTION &
VISITORS BUREAU, 238
Puskar, Jay Weekend Sports Anchor
WICU-TV, 704
Putman, Garrett VP Online Marketing Internet
Marketing D
SPORTS ENDEAVORS, INC., 1238
Putnam, Bob Sports Writer
ST. PETERSBURG TIMES, 533
Putnam, Lou Vice President
UNITED STATES CORPORATE ATHLETICS
ASSOCIATION, 225
Putney, Kelly Management Committee Member
BASSFORD, LOCKHART, TRUESDELL &
BRIGGS, P.A., 864
Putter, Paul National Director Programming
VENUEWORKS, 1066
Putzel, Michelle Administrative
Assistant,Coordinator
U.S. HOCKEY HALL OF FAME, 259
Pyfrom, Shamika Associate AD, Athletics
Development
NORTH CAROLINA A&T STATE UNIVERSITY
ATHLETICS, 339
Pyle, Jeff Director, Hockey Operations
EAST COAST HOCKEY LEAGUE/ECHL, 129
Pyle, Tim Sports Reporter
COLUMBIAN, 472
Pyle, Trevor Sports Reporter
SKAGIT VALLEY HERALD, 531
Pym, David Managing Director
CANADIAN SNOWSPORTS ASSOCIATION,
151
Pyne, George President IMG Sports &
Entertainment
IMG LOS ANGELES/IMG X SPORTS, 838

Q

Quade, Bruce Chairman
MARYLAND RACING COMMISSION, 80
Quade, Mike Manager
INTERNATIONAL LEAGUE, 43

Quagliariello, Ed Head of New York Sales
DIALGLOBAL, INC., 604
Quagliata, Erica Account Executive
SILVERMAN MEDIA & MARKETING GROUP,
808
Quaife, Steve Advertising Manager
DAILY NEWS (WA), 478
Qualls, Kent Director, Minor League Operations
AMERICAN LEAGUE OF PROFESSIONAL
BASEBALL CLUBS, THE, 29
Quan, Rick Sports Anchor
KPIX-TV, 693
Quandt, Dan Executive Director
AMARILLO CONVENTION & VISITOR
COUNCIL, 227
Quarles, Shelton Director, Football Operations
NATIONAL FOOTBALL LEAGUE/NFL, 96
Quatraro, Matt Manager
ARIZONA FALL LEAGUE (ROOKIE), 34
Quatrocky, Sara Associate Athletics Director
LYNN UNIVERSITY ATHLETICS, 362
Quattlebaum, Gus VP, Scouting Development &
Integration
AMERICAN LEAGUE OF PROFESSIONAL
BASEBALL CLUBS, THE, 29
Quattlebaum, Julien Vice President
FOX SPORTS PRIME TICKET, 675
Quattrone, Joel Senior Associate Athletics
Director
DICKINSON COLLEGE(DC) ATHLETICS, 383
Quave, Betty Secretary
SOUTH CAROLINA AAU ASSOCIATION, 216
Qubti, Ziad College Scouting Coordinator
NATIONAL FOOTBALL LEAGUE/NFL, 96
Queally, Alicia Deputy AD/SWA
STETSON UNIVERSITY ATHLETICS, 345
Quebedeaux, Chris Sports Editor
CROWLEY POST-SIGNAL, 474
Queen, Debbie Secretary
COLORADO HILL CLIMB ASSOCIATION, 83
Queen, Marty Sports Editor
MCDOWELL NEWS, 506
Queeney, Tim Editor
OCEAN NAVIGATOR, 574
Queensland, Randy Vice-Chairperson
RIVERSIDE ARENA, 997
Quel, Casey Advertising Director
GARDEN ISLAND, 490
Queliz, Kelvin Director of Sports Information
TEXAS A&M UNIVERSITY-KINGSVILLE
ATHLETICS, 372
Quesada, Raul Vice President, Marketing
Communications
FOX SPORTS NETWORKS/FOX SPORTS
NET, 675
Quesnel, Donita Promotions Director
KOTV-TV, 693
Questa, Barb Deputy Director of Athletics/SWA
ST. BONAVENTURE UNIVERSITY
ATHLETICS, 345
Quevedo, Juan Director Market Intelligence
IMAGES USA, 788
Quezada, Edgar General Manager
WOMEN'S PREMIER SOCCER LEAGUE, 168
Quick, Glenn Associate Athletics Director -
Academic
UNIVERSITY OF KANSAS, 1013
Quick, Jason Sports Reporter
OREGONIAN, 516
Quick, Mike Host
HIGH SCHOOL WEEKLY, 683
Quick, Scott General Manager
BRAINARD INTERNATIONAL RACEWAY, 1023
Quick, Vic Sports Director
KTVZ-TV, 696
Quigley, Carl Assistant Athletic Director
ST. FRANCIS COLLEGE ATHLETICS (SFC),
371
Quigley, Rich Manager
PETRY MEDIA, 677
Quill, Eric Head Coach
MAJOR LEAGUE SOCCER, 157
Quilley, Jason Executive VP, Finance & CFO
NATIONAL HOCKEY LEAGUE/NHL, 124
Quincey, James CEO
COCA-COLA COMPANY, 727
Quinlan, Jimmy Associate General Manager &
Co-Head Coac
NATIONAL LACROSSE LEAGUE, 142

Quinlan, Keith Secretary, Racing
SANDOWN PARK, 1038, 1043
Quinlan, Mike President
SUN COUNTRY AMATEUR GOLF
ASSOCIATION, 116
Quinlan, Steve Editor
TRAILER BOATS, 589
Quinlan, Tom Sports Editor
DAILY HERALD (IL), 476
Quinlin, Kelly Head Athletic Trainer
NORTHWEST MISSOURI STATE
UNIVERSITY(NWMSU), 366
Quinn, Blair National Sales Manager
ORIGINAL MAPLE BAT COMPANY, 1171
Quinn, Bruce President
SOUTH ATLANTIC LEAGUE (A LEVEL), 51,
988
Quinn, Dan Head Coach
NATIONAL FOOTBALL LEAGUE/NFL, 96
Quinn, David Founder & Chief Executive Officer
ACORN PRODUCTS COMPANY, INC., 1091
Quinn, Dick Sports Information Director
WILLIAMS COLLEGE ATHLETICS, 407
Quinn, Elise Board Secretary
PUGET SOUND REGIONAL
COMMISSIONER/USA VOLLEYBALL, 212
Quinn, Erin Director of Athletics
MIDDLEBURY COLLEGE ATHLETICS (MCA),
393
Quinn, James Senior Partner
QUINN, JAMES W., 900
Quinn, Janice Senior Associate Director of
Athletics
NEW YORK UNIVERSITY ATHLETICS(NYU),
395
Quinn, John Sports Deputy Editor
PHILADELPHIA INQUIRER, 519
Quinn, Kevin President
SOFTBALL CANADA, 170
Quinn, Lauren Park Supervisor
LINCOLN PARK, 1046
Quinn, Nick Sports Director
WMLN-FM, 657
Quinn, Noelle Head Coach
WOMEN'S NATIONAL BASKETBALL
ASSOCIATION, 61
Quinn, Pat Deputy Athletics Director, Operations
EMENS AUDITORIUM, 114, 964
Quinn, Rob General Manager
KYBG-AM SPORTS RADIO, 633
Quinn, Tim President
SOUTHERN NEVADA GOLF ASSOCIATION,
116
Quinney, Nekisha Assistant Athletic Director
SKIDMORE COLLEGE ATHLETICS, 400
Quinnon, Larry Co-Counsel
US LACROSSE, 141
Quinonez, Erving Billing Director
WOIZ-AM, 660
Quinonez, Manuel Program Director
WOIZ-AM, 660
Quintana, Cris Senior Director, Broadcasting
AMERICAN LEAGUE OF PROFESSIONAL
BASEBALL CLUBS, THE, 29
Quintana, Steve Assistant Managing
Editor/Sports, Online
SAN ANTONIO EXPRESS-NEWS, 528
Quirk, David Director of Development
OKLAHOMA, UNIVERSITY OF, 430
Quirk, Jennifer Senior Associatte Athletic
Director, Com
FAIRLEIGH DICKINSON UNIVERSITY
ATHLETICS, 330
Quirk, Joseph Vice President
AMERICAN JUNIOR GOLF ASSOCIATION, 99
Quirk, Sean Head Coach
MAJOR LEAGUE LACROSSE, 141
Quist, Phyllis Secretary
NATIONAL HORSESHOE PITCHERS
ASSOCIATION, 139
Quitney, Randy Sports Director
KDJS-AM, 616
Quitno, Todd Golf Course Architect
LOHMANN COMPANIES, 1061
Quitter, J VP Sales
EBONITE INTERNATIONAL, INC., 1127
Quitter, Mike VP International
EBONITE INTERNATIONAL, INC., 1127

Rauscher, Nathan Assistant Director of Athletics
MOUNT ST. VINCENT ATHLETICS, COLLEGE OF, 394

Rautio, Trudy EVP and Chief Financial Officer
CARLSON TRAVEL NETWORK, 925

Ravech, Karl Anchor
ESPN, 682, 683

Ravelo, Vania Media Manager
MEXICAN LEAGUE A.C., 43

Raven, Greg Technical Support &Webmaster
U.S. RACQUET STRINGERS ASSOCIATION, 175

Ravencraft, Michele Senior Director of Events
NATIONAL THOROUGHBRED RACING, 76

Rawak, Chrissi Dir. of Intercollegiate Athletics & Rec.
DELAWARE ATHLETICS, UNIVERSITY OF, 328

Rawitzer, Kasey Account Executive
LAKE ELSINORE STORM, 980

Rawlings, Andy Executive VP/COO
LEARFIELD SPORTS, 600

Rawlings, Guy Sports Anchor
WTVJ-TV, 682, 711

Rawlings, John Senior Vice President/Editorial Director
SPORTING NEWS, 584

Rawlings, William Lawyer
RAWLINGS, WILLIAM R., 901

Ray, Alan Technical Director
BANKSHOT SPORTS ORGANIZATION, 1217

Ray, Allan Technical
US CELLULAR ARENA, 1014

Ray, David Wrestling Head Coach
SOUTHERN ILLINOIS UNIVERSITY AT EDWARDSVILLE, 432, 566

Ray, Eric Operations Manager
KFNZ, 618

Ray, Kevin Sports Director
KMVP-AM, 624

Ray, Laura Senior Women Administrator
RIVIER UNIVERSITY ATHLETICS, 398

Ray, Logan Director Of Championship Operations
LOUISIANA GOLF ASSOCIATION, 103

Ray, Margie Treasurer
EVERGREEN REGIONAL COMMISSIONER/USA VOLLEYBALL, 211

Ray, Mike Executive Director
SOUTHERN TEXAS PGA SECTIONAL, 108

Ray, Patricia Chief Operating Officer
CANADIAN CURLING ASSOCIATION, 69

Ray, Quinton Head Coach
WOMEN'S FOOTBALL ALLIANCE / WFA, 97

Ray, Radio Sports Director
KGAL-AM, 618

Ray, Rich Sports Director
KHUB-AM, 618, 619

Ray, Ricky Senior Associate AD, External Operations
WILLIAM & MARY ATHLETICS, COLLEGE OF, 349

Ray, Rob News Director
WCDO-AM, 640

Ray, Sara Assoc. AD, Academic Services
UNIVERSITY OF WYOMING ARENA-AUDITORIUM, 1013

Ray, Tarlin Director ,Entrepenuer in Residence
PARK LANE - INVESTMENT BANKING SERVICES, 769

Ray, Tim General Manager
PIONEER BASEBALL LEAGUE, 50

Raya, Al Coordinator of Women's Basketball Offici
COLLEGE CONFERENCE OF ILLINOIS AND WISCONSIN, 294

Raybern, Jennifer Head Athletic Trainer
OTTAWA UNIVERSITY ATHLETICS, 318

Rayburn, Jimmy Chief Operating Officer
RAYCOM SPORTS, 600, 805

Rayburn, Sonya Sales & Community Affairs Director
SENIOR BOWL, 92

Rayfield, Marc Vice President/General Manager
WIP SPORTSRADIO 610, 651

Raymond, Eric Goaltending Coach
AMERICAN HOCKEY LEAGUE/AHL, 124, 127

Raymond, Steve Program Director
WZXL-FM, 673

Rayne, Todd Faculty Athletics Representative
HAMILTON COLLEGE ATHLETICS, 386

Rayner, Jay Technical Director
WOMEN'S PREMIER SOCCER LEAGUE, 165

Raynor, Mike Supervisor of Officials
NATIONAL PRO FASTPITCH, 170

Raynor, Tom Chairman / Chief Executive Officer
FLEET FEET, INC., 1228

Raythatha, Ashish Principal
TRITON SPORTS ASSOCIATES, 764

Raz, Michael Advertising Director
REGISTER-GUARD, 524

Razak, Brian Head Athletic Trainer
NEW ENGLAND ATHLETICS, UNIVERSITY OF, 395

Razzano, Andrew Team Physician
NATIONAL LEAGUE OF PROFESSIONAL BASEBALL CLUBS, THE, 31

Rea, Dan SVP/General Manager
INTERNATIONAL LEAGUE, 43, 985

Read, Bryan Sports Director
BROWNSVILLE HERALD, 466

Read, Dave Executive Vice-President
LEADING BRANDS, 1155

Read, Jeremy Advertising Manager
ST. ALBANS MESSENGER, 533

Read, Kirk General Manager
TBO (WFLA) NEWS CHANNEL 8, 698

Read, Kristian Sports Director
KECI-TV, 689

Read, Tim VP , Operations & Collective Bargain
DEL MAR THOROUGHBRED CLUB, 1037

Reade, Ian Director of Athletics
ALBERTA ATHLETICS, UNIVERSITY OF, 307

Readenour, Dustin President
NATIONAL VENTURING DIVISION, BOY SCOUTS OF AMERICA, 267

Reader, Bill Sports Assistant Editor
SEATTLE TIMES, 530

Ready, Danielle Secretary
NJCAA REGION XXIII WOMEN'S, 290

Ready, George Vice President
AMERICAN PAINT HORSE ASSOCIATION, 73

Ready, Keith Sports Director
WBRY-AM, 639

Reagins, Tony Chief Baseball Development Officer
NATIONAL LEAGUE OF PROFESSIONAL BASEBALL CLUBS, THE, 31

Reale, John Partner
DREW, ECKL & FARNHAM, LLP, 876

Reardon, Adam Sports Director
WMOP-AM, 657

Reardon, Jim President
ONE-ON-ONE SPORTS CONSULTANTS, 822

Reardon, Martine Chief Marketing Officer
BURDINE'S, 1221

Reardon, Thomas Esquire
HARBOUR, SMITH, HARRIS & MERRITT, 883

Reasoner, David Vice President
NEW JERSEY PGA SECTION, 107

Reasoner, Scott General Manager
PIONEER BASEBALL LEAGUE, 50, 956

Reasso, Bob Vice President for Athletics
PFEIFFER UNIVERSITY ATHLETICS, 368

Reasy, Justin Tournament Assistant
GOLF ASSOCIATION OF PHILADELPHIA, 111

Reaume, Josh Owner
NASCAR GANDER OUTDOORS TRUCK SERIES, 24

Reaves, Tammy Classified Manager
FLINT JOURNAL, 488

Reavlin, Paul Founder
REVGEAR SPORTS CO., 1182

Rebecca, Accounting - Administration
KAY RODGERS PARK, 978, 1040

Rebel, Nancy Director of Content Development
SPORT INFORMATION RESOURCE CENTER/SIRC, 258

Rebholz, Josh Senior Associate AD, External Relations
UC LOS ANGELES ATHLETICS, 347

Rebholz, Ryan Sports Information Director
INDIANA UNIVERSITY OF PENNSYLVANIA ATHLETICS, 360

Rebney, Bjorn Chief Executive Officer
SPIKE TV, 677

Rebolledo, Kevyn Crew Chief
NASCAR XFINITY SERIES, 24

Rebowe, Tim Head Coach, Football
MANNING FIELD AT JOHN L. GUIDRY STADIUM, 985

Rebstock, Dave Sports Information Director
MORNINGSIDE COLLEGE ATHLETICS, 317

Record, Edward Chief Operating Officer
STAGE STORES, INC., 1238

Record, Melvyn VP Marketing
SONOMA RACEWAY, 1028, 1033

Rectenwald, Dan Chief Operating Officer
HAMMEL, GREEN AND ABRAHAMSON INC., 1058

Rector, Mel President
ST. LOUIS DISTRICT GOLF ASSOCIATION, 116

Redd, Bob Sports Information Director
BLUEFIELD COLLEGE ATHLETICS, 309, 352

Redd, James Athletic Director
RICKENBRODE STADUIM, 997

Redden, Trent General Manager
NATIONAL BASKETBALL ASSOCIATION/NBA, 57

Reddick, Britney Asst. Commissioner For New Media
SOUTHERN INTERCOLLEGIATE ATHLETIC CONFERENCE, 304

Reddig, Fred Director of Facilities
FORD FIELD, 966

Redding, Rob Director for Sports Medicine
HENDERSON STATE UNIVERSITY (HSU) ATHLETICS, 288, 360

Reddish, Bill News Director
WICO-AM, 650

Reddy, Vikash Program Director
WFRD-FM, 646

Redinger, Dale Advertising Manager
RACING WHEELS, 577

Redman, Allen Chief Financial Officer
SPORTS PROFILES, 585

Redman, Austin Ticket Operations Manager
TRI-CITIES STADIUM, 1010

Redman, Jody Associate Director
MINNESOTA STATE HS LEAGUE, 200

Redmond, Charles
SPRINGFIELD COLLEGE, 433

Redmond, James
POITINGER REDMOND LYONS KURA & WALKER, 847

Redmond, Jeffrey Partner, Director, and Senior Consultant
NEW DIRECTIONS, 926

Redmond, Jill Assistant Commissioner/Compliance & Gove
ATLANTIC 10 CONFERENCE, 291

Redmond, Mark President & Chief Executive Officer
SIRIUS XM RADIO INC., 611

Redstone, Shari Vice Chairman
CBS SPORTS, 673

Redstone, Summer Executive Chairman
CBS SPORTS, 673

Redwine, Larry Chief Executive Officer
CONTINENTAL AMATEUR BASEBALL ASSOCIATION, 26

Redwine, Thomas Lawyer
REDWINE, THOMAS R., 901

Reece, Beasley Sports Director
KYW-TV, 698

Reece, Jackie Accounting Executive
A-B EMBLEM, 1089

Reece, Leland Principal Architect
CRP ARCHITECTS, P.C., 1053

Reece, Shannon COMMUNITY STATE COORDINATOR
SPECIAL OLYMPICS IDAHO, 194

Reed, Andy Sports Editor
LEBANON DEMOCRAT, 502

Reed, Cecil Program Director
WBCV-AM, 638

Reed, Clifford VP/Chief Financial Officer
TURFWAY PARK, 1045

Reed, Cory Director Series/Sanctioning
DIRTCAR RACING, 16

Reed, Dan Marketing Officer
DANDY PRODUCTS, INC., 1123

Reed, Dave General Manager
KDAK-AM, 615

Reed, David Sports Director ; Anchor
KXII-TV, 579, 698

Reed, Don Sports Editor
NEWS DEMOCRAT JOURNAL, 512
Reed, Donald Athletic Director
PRAIRIE VIEW A&M UNIVERSITY
ATHLETICS, 342, 527
Reed, Ed Sports Editor
NEWS-PRESS (FL), 513
Reed, Greg General Manager
WQAM 560 SPORTS RADIO, 566, 567, 662
Reed, Hunter General Manager
SOUTHERN LEAGUE OF PROFESSIONAL
BASEBALL CLUBS, 33, 52
Reed, Janice Executive Support Assistant
FLORIDA STATE UNIVERSITY, 418
Reed, Jeff President
KORNEY BOARD AIDS, INC., 497, 1153
Reed, Jerry Sports Editor
SARASOTA HERALD-TRIBUNE, 529
Reed, Joyce Vice President
KWTV-TV, 697
Reed, Kari Business Operations Manager
EAST COAST HOCKEY LEAGUE/ECHL, 129
Reed, Kevin VP
DAVIS & WILKERSON, 875
Reed, Lee Director of Athletics
GEORGETOWN UNIVERSITY ATHLETICS,
331
Reed, Linda National Sales Manager
NIRVE SPORTS, 1169
Reed, Mary Associate Editor
CALIFORNIA DIVING NEWS, 554
Reed, Rachel Display Advertising Manager
FULTON SUN, 490
Reed, Randal Executive Director
MIDDLE ATLANTIC GOLF ASSOCIATION, 113
Reed, Richard President
MISSISSIPPI GOLF ASSOCIATION, 113
Reed, Rusty National Sponsorship Director
CAMELLIA BOWL, 90
Reed, Steve Senior Associate Director
SUPERIOR DOME, 1007
Reed, Susan Editor
GOLF FOR WOMEN, 561
Reed, Twiggs Athletic Director
CENTRAL CHRISTIAN COLLEGE, 310
Reed, Wimp Technical Support
BATESVILLE MOTOR SPEEDWAY, 1022
Reed-Francois, Desiree Director of Athletics
MISSOURI ATHLETICS, UNIVERSITY OF, 337
Reeder, Ann General Manager/President
THUNDER RIDGE RACING AND
ENTERTAINMENT COMPLEX, 1045
Reeder, Henry President/Principal
ARCHITECTURAL RESOURCES CAMBRIDGE
INC., 1049
Reeder, Jim President
J&B SALES, INC., 1149
Reeder, Jonathan Exec. Assoc. Athletics
Director/CFO
APPALACHIAN STATE UNIVERSITY
ATHLETICS, 324
Reeder, Kassidy Administrative Assistant
OZARK CIVIC CENTER, 990
Reeds, Kevin Chief Dvelopment Officer
SPECIAL OLYMPICS NEVADA, 196
Reedy, Jim Local News Reporter
ROANOKE TIMES, 525
Reedy, Joe Sports Reporter
CINCINNATI ENQUIRER, 470
Rees, Gareth Chairman
BRITISH COLUMBIA SPORTS HALL OF FAME
MUSEUM, 251
Rees, Gary Vice President (District 1)
WASHINGTON STATE GOLF ASSOCIATION,
117
Rees, Jennie Sports Writer
COURIER-JOURNAL, 474
Rees, Tom Vice President/Director of Advertising
ST. LOUIS POST-DISPATCH, 533
Reese, Bill President
DUCK HEAD APPAREL COMPANY, 1125
Reese, Chris Associate Athletic Director
CEDARVILLE UNIVERSITY ATHLETICS, 310
Reese, Jennifer Chief Operating Officer
ACTION SPORTS INTERNATIONAL, 771
Reese, Kirk Secretary
NATIONAL CLUB ASSOCIATION, 222
Reese, Tim Manager
THOMPSON-BOLING ARENA, 1009

Reeser, Jeff National Sales Manager
FAIR-PLAY SCOREBOARDS, 1131
Reeser, Todd Director of Athletics
COLUMBUS STATE UNIVERSITY ATHLETICS
(CSU), 355
Reesing, Brad Sports Editor
MCCURTAIN DAILY GAZETTE, 506
Reeve, Cheryl Head Coach & President,
Basketball Opera
WOMEN'S NATIONAL BASKETBALL
ASSOCIATION, 60
Reeve, Seth Stadium Operations Manager
MIDWEST LEAGUE, 45
Reeves, Brandon Director, Stadium Operations
MCCORMICK FIELD, 985
Reeves, Dan Editor
ACTION PURSUIT GAMES, 548
Reeves, Devlan Vice President Of Marketing
BALLSTARS, 1104
Reeves, Dick Program Director
WACK 1420-AM HOMETOWN SPORTS, 636
Reeves, Frank President
RAGE CAGE, 1180
Reeves, Glenn Sports Editor
SAN MATEO COUNTY TIMES, 529
Reeves, Jim Sports Columnist
FORT WORTH STAR-TELEGRAM, 489
Reeves, Lehel President/Head Of Business
Development
WHEELSTV, 678
Reeves, Lindsay Director of Athletics
NORTH GEORGIA COLLEGE & STATE
UNIVERSITY ATHLETICS, 366
Reeves, Scott Sport Performance Director
PROVOST UMPHREY STADIUM, 994
Reeves, Suzanne Director of Business Operations
FLORIDA STATE LEAGUE, 39
Reeves, Tom Director of Game Operations
EAST-WEST SHRINE GAME, 90
Reeves-Maybin, Jalen President
NFL PLAYERS ASSOCIATION, 88
Refermat, Jason Director Of Markering
LAKELAND CENTER, THE, 981
Regalado, Sara Marketing Director
KXPS-AM, 633
Regan, Maura Executive Vice President
LICENSING INDUSTRY MERCHANDISERS'
ASSOCIATION, 221
Regan, Michael President
BRONSKILL & CO., 819
Regan, Phil Pitching Coach
TRADITION FIELD SPORTS COMPLEX, 1010
Regan, Thomas Dept. Chairperson
SOUTH CAROLINA, UNIVERSITY OF, 432
Reger, Wendy Marketing Communications
Manager
NORDICA USA, 1169
Reggiani, Andrea Communications
FERRARI CHALLENGE NORTH AMERICA, 19
Reggiani, Ryan Deputy AD, External Operations
ST. MARY'S COLLEGE ATHLETICS, 345, 953
Regina, Bob Director
ESPN CLASSIC SPORTS NETWORK, 674
Regis, Ross Founder/President
SEARCH SYNERGY INC., 748
Regnier, Joni Advertising Manager
NEWTON KANSAN, 514
Regnier, Tom Advertising Manager
DAILY COURIER (AZ), 476
Reh, Kyle Director, Business Operations
INTERNATIONAL LEAGUE, 42
Rehbaum, Kara Assistant Athletics Director
HILBERT COLLEGE ATHLETICS, 387
Rehder, Tim Senior VP Program Operations
SPECIAL OLYMPICS KANSAS, 195
Rehlander, Jodi Head Coach & Defensive
Coordinator
WOMEN'S FOOTBALL ALLIANCE / WFA, 98
Reich, Leonard Sports Information Director
CAPITAL UNIVERSITY, 404, 412
Reich, Robert Vice President
AMERICAN WATER SKI EDUCATIONAL
FOUNDATION/WATER SKI HALL OF FAME/,
251
Reich, Victoria VP / President - Brunswick
European Grou
BRUNSWICK CORPORATION, 1111
Reichel, Rick Treasurer
HERITAGE CLASSIC FOUNDATION, 756

Reichelt, Dave Sports Director
KPVI-TV, 694
Reichley, Rob Executive Producer
RAYCOM SPORTS, 805
Reichlin, Andrew Chief Executive Officer
PRO INNOVATIVE CONCEPTS, 1177
Reicin, Edward President
PUTTERMAN ATHLETICS, 1178
Reid, Alistair Director
INTERNATIONAL BLIND GOLF ASSOCIATION,
102
Reid, Andy Head Coach
NATIONAL FOOTBALL LEAGUE/NFL, 95
Reid, Ashley Assistant Athletic Director for
Inclusio
WOOSTER ATHLETICS, THE COLLEGE OF,
408
Reid, Bob VP, Marketing
EBONITE INTERNATIONAL, INC., 1127
Reid, Chris Vice President
BURWASH INTERNATIONAL, PETER, 751
Reid, Heather Sales & Stakes Manager
STANDARDBRED CANADA, 77
Reid, James Interim Director of Athletics
ANGELO STATE UNIVERSITY ATHLETICS,
351, 966
Reid, Jared President
EAST COAST HOCKEY LEAGUE/ECHL, 130
Reid, John Sports Columnist
TIMES-PICAYUNE, 540
Reid, John President
JTR PRODUCTIONS, 791
Reid, Jonathan Operations Director
AMATEUR SPORTS GROUP, INC., 824
Reid, Levan Sports Anchor (Weekend)
WUSA-TV, 711
Reid, Lewis President
FUN-TEES, INC., 1135
Reid, Neal Editor
PRORODEO SPORTS NEWS, 577
Reid, Sarah Director of Sports Marketing
GEORGE FOX UNIVERSITY ATHLETICS
(GFU), 385
Reid, Scott Sports Reporter
ORANGE COUNTY REGISTER, 516
Reid, Shawn Member
NEVADA GAMING CONTROL BOARD, 81
Reid, Wendy Sports Information Director
OLIVET NAZARENE UNIVERSITY ATHLETICS,
318
Reider, Bruce Editor
THE AMERICAN JOURNAL OF SPORTS
MEDICINE, 588
Reider, Ryan Program Director
KDSJ-AM, 616
Reidy, Francis Director of Athletics
SAINT LEO UNIVERSITY, 369
Reierson, Brad Sports Director
KAPP-TV, 687
Reifert, Scott Senior VP, Communications
AMERICAN LEAGUE OF PROFESSIONAL
BASEBALL CLUBS, THE, 29
Reiff, Jonna Executive Director
ASHEVILLE CONVENTION & VISITORS
BUREAU, 227
Reiff, Ralph Sr. Associate AD, Student-Athlete
Health
BUTLER UNIVERSITY ATHLETICS, 326
Reigeluth, Bob Sports Reporter
NEWS-TIMES, 513
Reightler, Barroe Director of Publications
MARYLAND MILLION, 76
Reiland, Mark 2nd Vice President
USA WRESTLING, 213
Reilly, Bryan Photo Editor
PHOTO FILE, 801
Reilly, Gail President
SOUTH JERSEY GOLF ASSOCIATION, 115
Reilly, Josh Director of Athletic Communications
MERCYHURST UNIVERSITY ATHLETICS, 363
Reilly, Marianne Director of Intercollegiate
Athletics
MANHATTAN COLLEGE ATHLETICS, 336
Reilly, Meredith Specialist, PR
SOOY, KATHLEEN T., 907
Reilly, Paul Chairman/Interim President, EMEA
KORN/FERRY INTERNATIONAL, 748
Reilly, Robert Chief Financial Officer
PNC FINANCIAL SERVICES, 731

BRADLEY UNIVERSITY ATHLETICS, 325, 639, 966

Reynolds, Christopher EVP & Chief Strategy Officer
TOYOTA MOTOR SALES, U.S.A., 734

Reynolds, Craig President & CEO
CANADIAN FOOTBALL LEAGUE/CFL, 93

Reynolds, Dave Sports Reporter
JOURNAL STAR, 498

Reynolds, Gary Member
BANSHEE MUSIC, 756, 774

Reynolds, Jake President
NATIONAL HOCKEY LEAGUE/NHL, 125

Reynolds, Jamie Director of Athletics
MARYMOUNT UNIVERSITY, 392, 629

Reynolds, John News Director
KLIF-FM, 622

Reynolds, Larry President/CEO
REYNOLDS SPORTS MANAGEMENT, 851

Reynolds, Mary General Manager/VP Sales & Marketing
NORTH STAR BROADCASTING, 606

Reynolds, Ned Sports Director
KYTV-TV, 698

Reynolds, Tucker Executive Director
WOMEN'S PREMIER SOCCER LEAGUE, 165

Reynolds, Vivian Group Sales
MOBILE GREYHOUND PARK, 1047

Rezachek, Bree Director, Team Operations
WOMEN'S PREMIER SOCCER LEAGUE, 167

Rezendes, Dan Director of Fitness
BRIDGEWATER STATE COLLEGE ATHLETICS, 378

Rhamstine, John Director
SCOPE ARENA, 1001

Rhea, Talisa General Manager
WOMEN'S NATIONAL BASKETBALL ASSOCIATION, 61

Rheaume, Tom Head Athletic Trainer
SAINT SCHOLASTICA ATHLETICS, COLLEGE OF, 399

Rhee, Edward President
ALL AMERICAN GOLF SALES, INC., 1095

Rhee, Samuel President
NEW YORK GOLF CENTER, INC., 1233

Rheims, Derrick Sports Director
WDKD-AM, 643

Rheinstein, Clark Chief Financial Officer / Leasing Direct
WALKER & COMPANY, 1209

Rheney, Clarke President
SOUTHERN GOLF ASSOCIATION, 115

Rhine, Randy President
CHADRON STATE COLLEGE ATHLETICS, 354

Rhinehart, Richard Director of Communications
WORLD T.E.A.M. SPORTS, 226

Rhoades, Cher Advertising Manager
NEWS-RECORD, 513

Rhoades, Mack VP & Director of Intercollegiate Athleti
BAYLOR UNIVERSITY ATHLETICS, 325, 965

Rhoden, Brad Treasurer
SUNFLOWER STATE GAMES, 264

Rhoden, William Sports Columnist
NEW YORK TIMES, 511

Rhodes, DeRetta Executive VP & Chief Culture Officer
NATIONAL LEAGUE OF PROFESSIONAL BASEBALL CLUBS, THE, 31

Rhodes, Dusty President
CONVENTURES, INC., 753

Rhodes, Eva Staff
BAYLOR UNIVERSITY, 411

Rhodes, Frank Associate Director of Broadcasting
NCAA, 601

Rhodes, Jenny General Manager
WQTM, 663

Rhodes, John President & COO
CONTINENTAL AMATEUR BASEBALL ASSOCIATION, 26

Rhodes, Joyce VP
RHODES WOOD COMPANY, INC., 1182

Rhodes, Lauren Senior Associate AD, Student-Athlete Per
PENN STATE UNIVERSITY ATHLETICS, 43, 341

Rhodes, Marvin President
RHODES WOOD COMPANY, INC., 1182

Rhodes, Seth Director of Promotions & In-Game Enterta
INTERNATIONAL LEAGUE, 42

Rhodes, Steve President
PARAMOUNT FITNESS CORPORATION, 1172

Rhodes, Valerie Commodore
WOMEN'S OCEAN RACING SAILING ASSOCIATION, 64

Rhodis, Craig Technical Director
WOMEN'S PREMIER SOCCER LEAGUE, 165

Rhone, Molly President
NETBALL ASSOCIATIONS, INTERNATIONAL FEDERATION OF, 144

Rhoton, Vince Senior Vice President Of Sales And Marke
LIFETIME, 1156

Rhymer, Sarah Box Office Manager
VIKING HALL CIVIC CENTER, 1016

Rhymes, William VP, Player Development
NATIONAL LEAGUE OF PROFESSIONAL BASEBALL CLUBS, THE, 31

Rhyne, Robert Treasurer
USA WATER SKI, 179

Rhyns, Cherise Player Relations Director
PAIGE & RICE, 846

Riba, George Sports Director
WFAA-TV, 702

Riber, Burch President
RIBER SPORTS MARKETING GROUP, 760

Riber, Burch Founder
RIBER SPORTS MARKETING GROUP, 760

Riber, Sam President
RIBER SPORTS MARKETING GROUP, 760

Ricard, Ginette SC Field Representative
SULKY TROIS RIVIERES, 1044

Ricci, Nicolas Senior Vice President, Sales & Marketing
HACHETTE FILIPACCHI MEDIA, 563

Riccitello, John CEO
EA SPORTS, 1213

Ricciuti, Phillip Attorney
FAZZONE & BAILLIE, 833

Rice, Bruce Attorney
RICE & RICE, 852

Rice, Cathy General Manager
SOUTH BOSTON SPEEDWAY, 1033

Rice, Chris President
NASCAR XFINITY SERIES, 24

Rice, Diane Associate Editor
APPALOOSA JOURNAL, 550

Rice, Jeff Sports Reporter
CENTRE DAILY TIMES, 469

Rice, Jim VP Franchise Development
PRO GOLF OF AMERICA, 491, 1235

Rice, Joe Publisher
GOLF BUSINESS, 560

Rice, Jordan Athletic Trainer
NJCAA REGION IX WOMEN'S, 287

Rice, Laurie Director, Finance
NATIONAL FOOTBALL LEAGUE/NFL, 94

Rice, Lisa General Manager
WMJK-FM, 657

Rice, Nathan Associate Athletics Director, Advancemen
CAMPBELL UNIVERSITY ATHLETICS, 326

Rice, Norm Treasurer
SPORTSPLEX OPERATORS AND DEVELOPERS ASSOCIATION/SODA, 225

Rice, Priscilla Director
BUCKS COUNTY COMMUNITY COLLEGE - DEPT OF HEALTH, PE & NURSING, 411

Rice, Rodney Chief Financial Officer/Partner
PAIGE & RICE, 846

Rice-Smith, Valerie Head Athletic Trainer
DELAWARE VALLEY COLLEGE(DVC) ATHLETICS, 382

Rich, Allison Director of Athletics
NEW HAMPSHIRE ATHLETICS, UNIVERSITY OF, 338

Rich, Charles Sports Reporter
GLENDALE NEWS-PRESS, 490

Rich, David Advertising Manager
WFIS-AM, 646

Rich, Melinda President, Rich Entertainment Group
INTERNATIONAL LEAGUE, 42

Rich, Rikki Assistant Athletic Director of Communica

NORTH CAROLINA WESLEYAN COLLEGE ATHLETICS, 395

Rich, Robert Owner/President
INTERNATIONAL LEAGUE, 42

Rich, Steve VP Operations
UTAH SPORTS COMMISSION, 248

Richard, Antoine CEO / President
ENTRE-PRISES USA, 1129

Richard, Mark Director of Athletics
MONTEVALLO ATHLETICS, UNIVERSITY OF (UM), 365

Richard, Melissa Controller
WQSN AM 1660, 662

Richards, Andy Sports Director
WTCH-AM, 131, 667

Richards, Craig Program Director
WZBB-FM, 672

Richards, Ed Sports Reporter
DAILY PRESS (VA), 478

Richards, Huw Sports Reporter
INTERNATIONAL HERALD TRIBUNE, 497

Richards, Mellisa Marketing Director
WSPD, 667

Richards, Nathan Assoc. AD, Facilities/Events
CHARLESTON SOUTHERN UNIVERSITY ATHLETICS, 326

Richards, Phil Sports Reporter
INDIANAPOLIS STAR, 496

Richards, Sheri Vice President, Cloent Relations
CORPORATE SPORTS MARKETING GROUP/ATLANTA OFFICE, 779

Richards, William President
NJCAA REGION XV WOMEN'S, 289

Richardson, Anwar Sports Reporter
TAMPA TRIBUNE, 537

Richardson, Barbara Executive Vice President
AMTRAK, 925

Richardson, Bill Manager
TEXAS BASEBALL LEAGUE, 53

Richardson, Bradley Executive Vice President and Chief Finan
DIEBOLD INCORPORATED, 1124

Richardson, Cindy Secretary
UNITED STATES CORPORATE ATHLETICS ASSOCIATION, 225

Richardson, Connie Associate Athletic Director
OTTERBEIN UNIVERSITY ATHLETICS, 396

Richardson, Cynthia President
ARABIAN HORSE ASSOCIATION, 74

Richardson, David Chief Executive Officer
INTERNATIONAL CRICKET COUNCIL, 69

Richardson, Dean Professor
RICHARDSON, DEAN, 902

Richardson, Dona Head Athletic Trainer
LAKELAND COLLEGE ATHLETICS, 390

Richardson, Donna VP
RICHARDSON SPORTS, INC., 1182

Richardson, Drew President & CEO
PROFESSIONAL ASSOCIATION OF DIVING INSTRUCTORS (PADI), 149

Richardson, Harold Executive Director
EAST-WEST SHRINE GAME, 90

Richardson, Howard Operations
BREWER'S LEDGE, INC., 1110

Richardson, Jerry Owner, Founder
BANK OF AMERICA STADIUM, 89, 948

Richardson, Kate Assistant
SKI MAGAZINE, 580

Richardson, Kim Sports Editor
VILLAGER, 544

Richardson, Merrill Director of Facilities Administration
RUPP ARENA, 999

Richardson, Neil President
RICHARDSON SPORTS, INC., 1182

Richardson, Paul SVP Human Resources
ESPN TELEVISION, 674

Richardson, Robin Treasurer
FIELD HOCKEY CANADA, 121

Richardson, Russ Director of Athletics
MONTANA WESTERN ATHLETICS, THE UNIVERSITY OF, 317

Richardson, Shandel Sports Reporter
SOUTH FLORIDA SUN-SENTINEL, 532

Richardson, Steve Executive Director
FOOTBALL WRITERS ASSOCIATION OF AMERICA, 88

Robbins, Royal President / Owner
ROYAL ROBBINS, 1184
Robbins, Shawn Producer/Director
ROBBINS MEDIA, 602
Robbins, Tom EVP, Racing & Industry Realtions
DEL MAR THOROUGHBRED CLUB, 1037
Robbs, Harrison Manager of Event Operations
INTERNATIONAL SURFING ASSOCIATION,
172
Roberson, Corey General Manager & Head
Coach
INDOOR FOOTBALL LEAGUE, 93
Roberson, Doug Sports Editor
DAILY PRESS (VA), 478
Roberson, Mo Interim Director of Athletics
CONCORDIA UNIVERSITY IRVINE
ATHLETICS, 356
Roberson, Pat VP/Chief Media Strategist
TAYLOR WEST ADVERTISING, 764
Roberston, Todd President
GULF STATES PGA SECTIONAL OFFICE, 105
Robert, Anthony Owner
AMENIA ARCHERY, 1216
Robert, Brown Manager, Stadium Operations
RICHMOND COUNTY BANK BALLPARK, 997
Robert, Debbie Administrative Assistant
WELSH RYAN ARENA, 1018
Robert, Gary President and COO
NEVCO, 1167
Robert, Smith Member
SMITH & SMITH ATTORNEYS AT LAW, 907
Robert, Teaff Principal
THOMAS & TEAFF, 911
Robert, Timothy Chief Science Officer
AEGIS SCIENCES CORPORATION, 918
Robertello, Steve Associate A.d
BULLDOGS STADIUM, 953
Roberts, Aaron Program Director
WGMN-AM, 648
Roberts, Allan VP
EVERSAN, INC, 1130
Roberts, Andrew Senior Associate AD, Finance
MEMPHIS ATHLETICS, UNIVERSITY OF, 336
Roberts, Barry President/CEO
UPSTARES MEDIA, 816
Roberts, Beth EVP, Business Affairs, NBC
Universal Cab
USA NETWORK, 677
Roberts, Bill Advertising Manager
WHAN-AM, 648
Roberts, Bob Sports Reporter
PLAIN DEALER, 520
Roberts, Bonnie Assistant General
Manager/Hillcats
LYNCHBURG CITY STADIUM, 984
Roberts, Brian Chair & CEO
COMCAST CORPORATION, 727
Roberts, Caitlin Sports Information Director
CURRY COLLEGE ATHLETICS, 382
Roberts, Catherine Promotion Director
WBLK-FM, 639
Roberts, Chris Director of Operations
GREAT CANADIAN GAMING CORPORATION,
1039
Roberts, Dan EVP
WELLINGTON LEISURE PRODUCTS, 1209
Roberts, David COO
SPORT INFORMATION RESOURCE
CENTER/SIRC, 258, 596
Roberts, Deana Business Manager
FRONTIER LEAGUE, 41
Roberts, Don Chairman
PROFESSIONAL PADDLESPORTS
ASSOCIATION, 140
Roberts, Gary Law Program Director
TULANE LAW SCHOOL, 435
Roberts, George Advertising Manager
WAYY-AM, 637
Roberts, J. Managing Partner
HINSHAW & CULBERTSON, 837
Roberts, Jack Executive Producer
SPORTS CORNER, 685
Roberts, James President
SETCOM CORPORATION, 1187
Roberts, Jason General Manager/Program
Director/Sports
WSKW, 666
Roberts, Jay General Manager
CONSOL ENERGY CENTER, 959

Roberts, Jill CFO
EAST COAST HOCKEY LEAGUE/ECHL, 130
Roberts, Joe Public Relations/Broadcaster
EAST COAST HOCKEY LEAGUE/ECHL, 130
Roberts, John Executive Director
MICHIGAN HS ATHLETIC ASSOCIATION, 200
Roberts, John Assistant Director, Booking and
Scheduli
TACO BELL ARENA, 1007
Roberts, Julie Secretary
MIDWEST PGA SECTIONAL OFFICE, 106
Roberts, Karl Operations Manager
USL LEAGUE TWO, 162
Roberts, Kenneth Sports Reporter
SAINT LOUIS POST-DISPATCH, 527
Roberts, Kevin Managing Editor
SPORTBUSINESS GROUP, 584
Roberts, Lee Director of Design
BIGELOW COMPANIES, THE, 1064, 1066
Roberts, Marie Advertising Manager
FLORIDA GREEN, 559
Roberts, Matt Director of Athletics
COLLEGE OF CHARLESTON ATHLETICS, 327
Roberts, Melanie Fitness Center Director
NATIONAL INSTITUTE FOR FITNESS AND
SPORT, 84
Roberts, Mitch Sports Director
KVBC-TV, 696
Roberts, Nathan Chief Marketing Officer
AMERICAN HOCKEY LEAGUE/AHL, 128
Roberts, Neil Head Coach, Men's Soccer
NICKERSON FIELD, 989
Roberts, Patrick Publisher
GOLFDOM, 562
Roberts, Paul Sports Talk Show Host
WEEU-AM, 625, 644
Roberts, Rachel Editor
PARKS & RECREATION, 575
Roberts, Rebel PRESIDENT
VOA ASSOCIATES INCORPORATED, 1063
Roberts, Renae Classified Manager
CHARLESTON GAZETTE, 469
Roberts, Ronnie General Manager
CAROLINA LEAGUE, 37
Roberts, Scott President
CROWN PRINCE, INC., 1121
Roberts, Sean Head Athletic Trainer
BUFFALO STATE COLLEGE ATHLETICS, 378
Roberts, Simon Team Chief
FORMULA 1, 20
Roberts, Steve EVP/Business Development
SPORTVISION, 602
Roberts, Thomas General Manager
HARRAH'S LOUISIANA DOWNS, 1039
Roberts, Tim Vice President/Sports News Director
SPORTS NEWSATELLITE, 602, 668, 686
Roberts, Valeria Advertising Manager
JACKSON COUNTY FLORIDAN, 497
Roberts, Vern Executive Director
U.S. HANDBALL ASSOCIATION, 121
Roberts, Veronica General Manager
TALK 1450 WMIQ RADIO, 635
Robertshaw, Elizabeth President
INTERCOLLEGIATE WOMEN'S LACROSSE
COACHES ASSOCIATION, 141
Robertshaw, Liz Head Coach, Women's Lacrosse
NICKERSON FIELD, 989
Robertson, Barbara Director of Finance
CALIFORNIA POLICE ACTIVITIES LEAGUE,
265
Robertson, Bethany Drafting Programs
GRAHAM/MEUS, INC. ARCHITECTS, 1058
Robertson, Brad Advertising Vice President
DES MOINES REGISTER, 483
Robertson, Carter President and CEO
CITYSEATS.COM, 931
Robertson, Dale Sports Columnist
HOUSTON CHRONICLE, 495
Robertson, Dennis Vice Chair
CHAMPAIGN COUNTY CONVENTION &
VISITORS BUREAU, 230
Robertson, Gordon Director, Mutuels
FAIR GROUNDS CORPORATION, 1038
Robertson, Jacob Executive Coordinator
KANSAS CITY SPORTS COMMISSION AND
FOUNDATION, 237
Robertson, Jen Head Athletic Trainer
ST. MARY'S COLLEGE OF MARYLAND
ATHLETICS, 401

Robertson, John General Manager
CHARLESTON CIVIC CENTER, 957
Robertson, Julie Marketing SVP
FELD ENTERTAINMENT, 755
Robertson, Linda Sports Columnist
MIAMI HERALD, 506
Robertson, Molly Assistant to
Commissioner/Championships
OLD DOMINION ATHLETIC CONFERENCE,
302
Robertson, Randall President / Chief Executive
Officer
R.B. ROBERTSON & COMPANY, 804
Robertson, Sheila Editor
COACHES REPORT, 555
Robertson, Walt VP of Sales
KEENELAND ASSOCIATION, INC, 1040
Robichaux, Craig Lawyer/Member
TALLEY, ANTHONY, HUGHES & KNIGHT
L.L.C., 910
Robie, Anne Director , Human resources
STUBHUB, 932
Robillard, Jeff Manager of Marketing and
Communications
HORSE RACING ALBERTA, 79
Robillard, Yvonne Advertising Manager
DAILY MINING GAZETTE, 478
Robilotti, JG Sr. VP , Client Services
LEADDOG MARKETING GROUP, 793
Robin, Lucas Director of Sports Management
Program
COLUMBIA UNIVERSITY, 414
Robins, Jason Chief Executive Officer &
Co-Founder
DRAFTKINGS, INC., 727
Robins, Karen Human Resources Executive
MCNETT CORPORATION, 1161
Robinson, Andrew Vice President
MILLSPORT, LLC, 795
Robinson, Ashley Vice President & Director of
Athletics
JACKSON STATE UNIVERSITY ATHLETICS,
333
Robinson, Barb Assistant to the Commissioner
APPALACHIAN ATHLETIC CONFERENCE, 291
Robinson, Brad Producer
THE KEVIN WHEELER SHOW, 610
Robinson, Brady Executive Director
THE ACCESS FUND, 69
Robinson, Chris Director of Athletics
ARKANSAS PINE BLUFF ATHLETICS,
UNIVERSITY OF, 324
Robinson, Craig Executive Director
NATIONAL ASSOCIATION OF BASKETBALL
COACHES, 54
Robinson, Dave Sports Deputy Managing Editor
DETROIT FREE PRESS, 483
Robinson, David Vice Chairman
WESTERN GOLF ASSOCIATION/EVANS
SCHOLARS FOUNDATION, 117
Robinson, David Vice Chairman
WESTERN GOLF ASSOCIATION, EVANS
SCHOLARS FOUNDATION, 118
Robinson, Dwight Sports Agent
BEST IN SPORTS, 826
Robinson, Ella Racing Secretary
HUMBOLDT COUNTY FAIR ASSN, 1040
Robinson, Eric Sports Editor
HENDERSON DAILY DISPATCH, 492
Robinson, Frank Executive Vice President of
Baseball Dev
KAUFFMAN STADIUM, 978
Robinson, Fred Sports Reporter
TIMES-PICAYUNE, 540
Robinson, Gary Executive Sports Editor
COMMERCIAL APPEAL, 472
Robinson, George Sports Reporter
LEAF-CHRONICLE, 502
Robinson, Gerry Owner/Chairman
CINCINNATI GARDENS, 957
Robinson, J. Chairman / Chief Executive Officer /
Pre
JUST FOR FEET, 1230
Robinson, Jay Co-Owner
NASCAR CUP SERIES, 23
Robinson, Jesse Director of Athletics
Communications
SAINT SCHOLASTICA ATHLETICS, COLLEGE
OF, 399

Robinson, Jill Executive VP/Chief Financial
Officer
NATIONAL LEAGUE OF PROFESSIONAL
BASEBALL CLUBS, THE, 31
Robinson, John Deputy Athletics Director
JOHN O'QUINN FIELD AT ROBERTSON
STADIUM, 977
Robinson, Kent Sports Director
WLGC, 655
Robinson, Laura Senior Major Gift Officer
JOHN F. SAVAGE HALL, 976
Robinson, Len Advertising Manager
WPAX-AM, 660
Robinson, Lybrant Co-Owner
WOMEN'S FOOTBALL ALLIANCE / WFA, 99
Robinson, Lynne Director of Athletics
MOUNT ST. MARY'S UNIVERSITY
ATHLETICS, 338
Robinson, Maggie Executive Director
JOHN LYNCH FOUNDATION, 192
Robinson, Mary Human Resources Director
DUANE MORRIS LLP, 877
Robinson, Matthew Director
UNIVERSITY OF DELAWARE, 435
Robinson, Michelle Head Coach
WOMEN'S FOOTBALL ALLIANCE / WFA, 98
Robinson, Mike Director of Community & Fan
Development
EASTERN LEAGUE, 38
Robinson, Patrick President
WESTERN SUBURBS RUGBY FOOTBALL
CLUB, 148
Robinson, Pete President/CEO
CINCINNATI GARDENS, 957
Robinson, Rachel Founder
JACKIE ROBINSON FOUNDATION, 191
Robinson, Richard Associate Dean for
Administration and Fi
BRIGGS, BUCK, 868
Robinson, Richard Principal
MILTON POWELL & PARTNERS, 1061
Robinson, Ryan Executive Associate
AD/Revenue Generatio
EAST CAROLINA UNIVERSITY ATHLETICS,
329
Robinson, Sharon CFO
RALEIGH CYCLE, 760, 851
Robinson, Stephen Sports Anchor ; Reporter
WXVT-TV, 712
Robinson, Stuart Director of Athletics
STATE UNIVERSITY OF NEW YORK AT NEW
PALTZ ATHLETICS(SUNY), 401
Robinson, Terry Women's Basketball Head
Coach
NJCAA REGION I WOMEN'S, 286
Robinson, Thomas Sports Columnist
VIRGINIAN-PILOT, 544
Robinson, Tim Sports Editor
LIVINGSTON COUNTY DAILY PRESS &
ARGUS, 503
Robinson, Todd Assistant Coach
UNITED STATES HOCKEY LEAGUE, 137
Robison, Heidi Sales
SKILLBUILDERS, INC., 1189
Robison, James Chief Information Officer
BMK ARCHITECTS, 1050
Robison, Pam Administrative Assistant
NATIONAL CUTTING HORSE ASSOCIATION,
76
Robitaille, Deb Softball Head Coach
SOUTHERN NEW HAMPSHIRE UNIVERSITY,
433
Robitaille, Louis Head Coach
QUEBEC MARITIMES MAJOR JUNIOR
HOCKEY LEAGUE, 135
Robitaille, Mike Host
HOCKEY HOTLINE, 683
Robotham, Melanie Assistant Commissioner
LONE STAR CONFERENCE, 298
Robson, Charlie Executive Director
METROPOLITAN PROFESSIONAL GOLFERS
ASSOCIATION, 106
Robson, David Office Manager
MILLER CANFIELD SPORTS, 844
Robustelli, Jim President
ROBUSTELLI SPORTS MARKETING, 806
Robustelli, Richard Chairman/President
ROBUSTELLI SPORTS MARKETING, 806

Roby, Peter Athletic Director
PARSONS FIELD/FRIEDMAN DIAMOND, 985,
991
Roby, Robert Managing Partner
GWINN & ROBY, 836
Roche, Beth Client Services Specialist
COSTANTE GROUP SPORTS & EVENT
MARKETING, LLC, 753
Roche, Bob Owner
FANMATS LLC, 1131
Roche, Dan Sports Reporter
WBZ-TV, 700
Roche, Michelle Classified Manager
SAILING WORLD, 579
Roche, Rachel Sports Information Director
REDLANDS ATHLETICS, UNIVERSITY OF,
398
Rochelle, Kate Classified Manager
BUCKS COUNTY COURIER TIMES, 467
Rochester, Geof Senior Vice President, Marketing
SHOWTIME SPORTS, 678
Rochlitz, Kevin Chief Sales Officer
NATIONAL FOOTBALL LEAGUE/NFL, 94
Rochon, Thomas President
WOLOHAN, JOHN T., 916
Rock, Agnes Director of Finance
SEAGATE CENTRE, 1002
Rock, Brad Sports Columnist
DESERET MORNING NEWS, 483
Rock, Don Director of Stadium Grounds
NEW YORK-PENNSYLVANIA LEAGUE, 46,
963
Rock, George Advertising Manager
PRESS REPUBLICAN, 522
Rock, Sean Sports Writer
MALVERN DAILY RECORD, 505
Rockamann, Ralph Owner / President
SPORTSPRINT, 1194
Rockefeller, Mark Board Chairman/CEO
PROPERTYPORT, 803
Rocker, Tommy Program Director
KKNN-FM, 621
Rockey, Robert President
DUCK HEAD APPAREL COMPANY, 1125
Rockoff, Clyde President
UNIVERSAL NUTRITION, 1206
Rockwell, David News Director
WTZN-AM, 669
Rodd, Donald Professor Exercise
SportScience/Physica
EVANSVILLE, UNIVERSITY OF, 417
Rodd, Linda Of Counsel
MEYER, SUOZZI, ENGLISH & KLEIN, 895
Roddick, Daniel Director
MATTEL SPORTS PROMOTION
DEPARTMENT, 795
Roddie, Robert Girls Director, Coaching &
Director, Ope
WOMEN'S PREMIER SOCCER LEAGUE, 167
Rodenberg, Tom National Sales Manager
PARKER LABORATORIES, INC., 1172
Rodenburg, John Publisher
T & L GOLF, 587
Roderick, Lindsay Head Athletic Trainer
JOHN JAY COLLEGE OF CRIMINAL JUSTICE
ATHLETICS, 388
Rodewald, Chris Sales / Marketing VP
REDLINE PERFORMANCE PRODUCTS, INC.,
1181
Rodgers, Casey Chief Financial Officer
NATIONAL HOCKEY LEAGUE/NHL, 126
Rodgers, Charles Owner
WEPG-AM, 645
Rodgers, Dan Promoter
COMPETITION PARK MOTOCROSS, 1024
Rodgers, Janet President/CEO
ALPHARETTA CONVENTION & VISITORS
BUREAU, 227
Rodgers, Jill Fair Activities Assistant
YAKIMA VALLEY SUNDOME, 1021
Rodgers, John Sports Editor
PASADENA/SAN GABRIEL VALLEY
JOURNAL-NEWS, 518
Rodgers, Stephen Chief Executive Officer
PETER ROGERES, INC LTD, 601
Rodgers, Tammy News Director
KBEE-FM, 613
Rodgers, Travis Producer
THE JIM ROME SHOW, 610

Rodgers, Will News Director
WEPG-AM, 645
Rodman, Bill Executive Producer
GAMEDAY, 609
Rodman, Christopher Vice President and Group
Managing Direct
TOPPS COMPANY, INC., 1202
Rodowicz, Fran Regional Vice President
LIACOURAS CENTER, 983
Rodrigo, Alex SVP & General Manager
NATIONAL BASKETBALL ASSOCIATION/NBA,
58
Rodrigue, Sylvain Goaltending Coach
AMERICAN HOCKEY LEAGUE/AHL, 126
Rodrigues, M. Principal
ARCHITECTS DELAWIE WILKES RODRIGUES
BARKER, 1049
Rodrigues, Steve Secretary
U.S. HANG GLIDING AND PARAGLIDING
ASSOCIATION, 14
Rodriguez, Bert Maintenance Manager
PIMA COUNTY FAIR, 1042
Rodriguez, Hector Executive of Sales and
Marketing
DYNASTY APPAREL INDUSTRIES, 1126
Rodriguez, Jeison Senior Art Director
SPIKE/DDB PRODUCTIONS, 809
Rodriguez, Jessica Executive Vice President of
Program Sche
GALAVISION, 676
Rodriguez, Johnny Manager
NEW YORK-PENNSYLVANIA LEAGUE, 47
Rodriguez, Jorge Sports Director
KWEX-TV, 697
Rodriguez, Juan Manager
MEXICAN LEAGUE A.C., 44, 532
Rodriguez, Justin Sports Reporter
TIMES HERALD RECORD, 539
Rodriguez, Luis President/General Manager
WOIZ-AM, 660
Rodriguez, Mike VP, Ticket Operations
PACIFIC COAST LEAGUE OF
PROFESSIONAL BASEBALL CLUBS, 48
Rodriguez, Nathalie Chief Executive Officer
FEDERATION INTERNATIONALE D'ESCRIME
(FIE), 85, 204
Rodriguez, Raul Executive President
MEXICAN LEAGUE A.C., 44
Rodriguez, Robert Equity and Managing Partner
MILLER, KAGAN RODRIGUEZ AND SILVER,
P.A., 895
Rodriguez, Sam Sports Editor
DAILY JEFFERSON COUNTY UNION, 477
Rodriguez, Sophie Office Coordinator
NJCAA REGION I WOMEN'S, 286
Rodriguez, Stephen Chairman
NATIONAL SENIOR GAMES ASSOCIATION,
223
Rodriguez, Stephen Vice President
SUNSHINE STATE GAMES, 264
Rodriguez, Steven Vice President
FLORIDA SPORTS FOUNDATION, 233
Roe, James SVP, Real Estate
FAMOUS FOOTWEAR, 1227
Roe, Scott Vice President
VF BRAND SOLUTIONS, 1207
Roe, Stephanie Director of Administration
BIG SOUTH CONFERENCE, 292
Roe, Tami President
ABSOLUTE FITNESS, INC., 1090
Roe, Tim Sports Editor
REPORTER, 524
Roebuck, Malcolm Chairman of the Board
BADGE-A-MINIT LTD., 1103
Roeder, Jesse Sports Turf Manager
VETERANS MEMORIAL STADIUM (CEDAR
RAPIDS), 1016
Roedl, Eric Deputy Athletic Director
OREGON ATHLETICS, UNIVERSITY OF, 341
Roegiers, Kelcey Senior Associate AD/SWA
GEORGIA STATE UNIVERSITY ATHLETICS,
331
Roehr, Dave Finance VP
CABELA'S, 1112, 1221
Roel, Gustave President/Executive Director
RESEAU DU SPORTETUDIANT DU QUEBEC,
203
Roenbeck, Clyde VP, Field Operations
HAT WORLD/LIDS CORP., 1229

Rosenzweig, Shy CMO
F.I.T. VENTILATION, 1131

Roser, Jerit Sports Writer
NEWS-STAR, 513

Rosetta-Smith, Leslie Promotions Director
WQXI-AM, 663

Rosiek, Cari Associate AD, Student-Athlete
Enhancemen
COASTAL CAROLINA UNIVERSITY
ATHLETICS, 327

Rosiere, Kevin Graduate Asst Sports Informations
Golf H
WILLIAM CAREY COLLEGE ATHLETICS, 323

Roski, Edward Owner
NATIONAL HOCKEY LEAGUE/NHL, 124

Roskos, Bob Corporate Copywriter
VIRCO MANUFACTURING CORPORATION,
1208

Rosner, Arthur Office Managing Partner
NIXON, PEABODY, 897

Rosner, Ron Sports Editor
DAILY FREEMAN, 476

Roso, Rick Press, PR & Editorial Director
LIME ROCK PARK, 1027

Ross, Betsy President
GAME DAY COMMUNICATIONS, 784

Ross, Brenda Classified Manager
HUNTINGTON HERALD-PRESS, 495

Ross, Bryan Senior Director, Ballpark Operations
AMERICAN LEAGUE OF PROFESSIONAL
BASEBALL CLUBS, THE, 30

Ross, David Principal
BSA ARCHITECTS, 1051

Ross, Dean Sports Director
WKXQ-FM, 654

Ross, JJ Urban Representative
MANITOBA HS ATHLETIC ASSOCIATION, 200

Ross, Jamie Interim Director of Athletics
CROWN COLLEGE ATHLETICS, 311

Ross, Janet Principal
ELLENZWEIG ASSOCIATES, INC., 1055

Ross, Jason Sports Director
KHTK 1140 SPORTS RADIO, 619

Ross, Jim Secretary
CAROLINA REGIONAL VOLLEYBALL
ASSOCIATION/USA VOLLEYBALL, 210

Ross, Jonathan Partner
BRADLEY & GMELICH, 867

Ross, Katherine Co-Founder and Creative
Director
GLOBAL REACH SPORTS, 713

Ross, Kelly Editor
WISCONSIN SOCCER POST, 592

Ross, Maggie Administration Manager
NETBALL ASSOCIATIONS, INTERNATIONAL
FEDERATION OF, 144

Ross, Martin Sports Director
KCFW-TV, 688

Ross, Nicole Athletic Trainer
VITERBO ATHLETICS UNIVERSITY, 322

Ross, Patrick Director of Media Relations
MIDDLE ATLANTIC STATES COLLEGIATE
ATHLETIC CORPORATION, 299

Ross, Robert Chairman / Chief Executive Officer /
Co-
WOMEN'S GOLF UNLIMITED, INC., 1211

Ross, Ruby General Sales Manager
CBS PHILLY - SPORTSRADIO 94WIP, 605

Ross, Stephen Chair & Managing General Partner
NATIONAL FOOTBALL LEAGUE/NFL, 95, 1007

Ross, Stephen Professor
ROSS, STEPHEN F., 903

Ross, Tom President
BUNTING, ELIZABETH C., 869

Rossberg, Sue Human Resources Director
FENTRESS ARCHITECTS, 1056

Rossetti, Dan Senior Vice President/Turnkey
Search
TURNKEY SPORTS & ENTERTAINMENT, 749

Rossi, Cathy Deputy Athletics Director
WISCONSIN MILWAUKEE ATHLETICS,
UNIVERSITY OF, 349, 998

Rossi, Dave VP Marketing
SCHUTT SPORTS INC, 1186

Rossi, Jack Chairman
WV RACING COMMISSION, 82

Rossi, John Executive assistant dean
ROSS, STEPHEN F., 903

Rossi, Mark Sales/Marketing VP
DOVER INTERNATIONAL SPEEDWAY, 1024

Rossi, Mary Office Manager
THOMPSON SPEEDWAY MOTORSPORTS
PARK, 1034

Rossi, Reagan Director of Athletics
ALBERTSON COLLEGE OF IDAHO
ATHLETICS, 295, 307

Rossi, Rob Sports Information Director
EASTERN NAZARENE COLLEGE(ENC)
ATHLETICS, 383

Rossi, Silas Vice President
AMERICAN MOUNTAIN GUIDES
ASSOCIATION, 68

Rossini, Graham Vice President for University
Athletics
ARIZONA STATE UNIVERSITY ATHLETICS,
324

Rossiter, Jay Executive Vice President, Platforms
YAHOO! SPORTS, 715

Rossler, John President / Chief Executive Officer
VALUE CITY DEPARTMENT STORES, 1240

Rossman, Michael President & Chief Executive
Officer
NEW TIER COMMUNICATIONS, 797, 821

Rossman, Mike Sports Director
WRCT-FM, 663

Rossman, Robert Professor/Dean
ILLINOIS STATE UNIVERSITY, 421

Rossman, Scott Sports Director
WJHG-TV, 705

Rosson, Judy Advertising Manager
TEXAS THOROUGHBRED, 588

Rossow, Jim Sports Editor
NEWS-GAZETTE, 513

Roswell, Jessica Assistant Athletic Director for
Marketin
PACIFIC LUTHERAN UNIVERSITY
ATHLETICS, 396

Rote, Rock Sports Director
WDJT-TV, 701

Rotert, Terry Arena Activities Director/Arena
Manager
HURON ARENA, 973

Roth, Bill Promoter
MOBILE INTERNATIONAL SPEEDWAY, 1029

Roth, Chris Sports Director
WBAY-TV, 699

Roth, David Executive Director
USL LEAGUE TWO, 162

Roth, Ellen President
U.S. DEAF SKI & SNOWBOARD
ASSOCIATION, 153

Roth, Garrett Head Coach & General Manager
NORTH AMERICAN HOCKEY LEAGUE, 133

Roth, Jeff
PRIORITY SPORTS & ENTERTAINMENT, 848,
849

Roth, Leo Sports Columnist
DEMOCRAT AND CHRONICLE, 482

Roth, Merianne Vice President Marketing &
Communication
FORT WORTH CONVENTION & VISITORS
BUREAU, 234

Roth, Scott Gymnastics Divisional Director
AMERICAN ATHLETIC INC., 1097

Rothamel, Paul SVP, Store Operations
PAMIDA, INC., 1234

Rothenberg, Alan Chairman
PREMIER PARTNERSHIPS, 802

Rothenberg, Alan Chairman
PREMIER PARTNERSHIPS, 802

Rothermel, Will Associate Athletic Director
ITHACA COLLEGE ATHLETICS, 388

Rothhammer, Dianne President
SPRINT AQUATICS, 1195

Rothman, Evan Executive Editor
GOLF MAGAZINE, 561

Rothman, Jennifer Sales Manager
LONG ISLAND CVB & SPORTS COMMISSION,
239

Rothman, Richard Founder
ROTHMAN INSTITUTE, 922

Rothrock, Ben Assistant General Manager of
Operations
DIAMOND FIELD, 961

Rothschild, Philip Director
SOUTHWEST MISSOURI STATE
UNIVERSITY, 433

Rothstein, Michael Sports Writer
JOURNAL GAZETTE, 498

Rotondi, Michael Vice President
E.B. ROTONDI & SONS, INC., 1126

Rottenberg, Paul Chair
DES MOINES AREA SPORTS COMMISSION,
232

Rotter, Merton Lawyer
WARSHAFSKY LAW FIRM, 914

Rottier, Bart Executive Director
DIXIE PGA SECTIONAL OFFICE, 105

Rouge, Jean General Secretary
INTERNATIONAL JUDO FEDERATION, 204

Roughton, Keith Senior Associate AD, NCAA
Compliance
GEORGIA SOUTHERN UNIVERSITY
ATHLETICS, 331

Roundtree, Jim CFO
FIRST PLUS SPORTS MARKETING, 783

Rountree, Mark Sports Editor
ENID NEWS AND EAGLE, 486

Rourke, Jonathan Owner
CHAMPIONSHIP SPORTS GROUP, 752

Rouse, Jack Chief Executive Officer
JACK ROUSE ASSOCIATES, 790

Rouse, Scott Vice President, Senior Project
Manager
FINK ROBERTS & PETRIE, 1056

Roussel, David Director of Athletics
THOMAS COLLEGE ATHLETICS, 403

Rousso, Doug CTO/CIO
CBS SPORTS, 673

Rousso, Nick Sports Editor
SEATTLE POST-INTELLIGENCER, 529

Roustan, W Owner
BURLEY'S, 1051

Roux, Antoine CEO, Internet Operations
M-NET TELEVISION, 678

Roux, Dennis News Director
KRJB-FM, 627

Roux, Jon Director
WESTERN PENNSYLVANIA ASSOCIATION,
216

Roux, Valerie S&E General Manager
HOFHEINZ PAVILION, 970

Rovine, David Director, Marketing
GULFSTREAM RACING & CASINO PARK,
1039

Rowan, Jennifer Publisher
SKI AREA MANAGEMENT, 580

Rowan, Olivia Associate Publisher
SKI AREA MANAGEMENT, 580

Rowan, Pat Sports Director
KDIN-TV, 689

Rowan, Russ Vice President of Sales and
Marketing
SPYDER ACTIVE SPORTS, 1195

Rowat, Bill Director
CROQUET CANADA, 69

Rowdon, Andy Deputy AD, External Operations
EASTERN MICHIGAN UNIVERSITY
ATHLETICS, 329

Rowe, Chase Manager of Athletic Facilities
LA ROCHE COLLEGE ATHLETICS (LRC), 389

Rowe, David Co-Owner & Managing Partner
NORTH AMERICAN HOCKEY LEAGUE, 133

Rowe, Denis Director
ARTHRON, INC., 1100

Rowe, Doug Advertising Director
SANFORD HERALD, 529

Rowe, Howard Senior Editor
AMERICAN TURF MONTHLY, 549

Rowe, Kermit Sports Editor
SPRINGFIELD NEWS-SUN, 533

Rowe, Luke Vice President
FLEET FEET, INC., 1228

Rowe, Marty General Manager
KOHI-AM, 625

Rowe, Ray Facility Manager
ROBERTS STADIUM (IA), 997

Rowe, Robert Executive Vice President
IRWIN BROH RESEARCH, 790

Rowek, Joseph Vice President
CONWAY, MICHAEL W., 829

Rowlett, Jim Marketing Director
NATIONAL STREET ROD ASSOCIATION, 18

Rowley, David News Director
WDOE-AM/FM, 643

Schachter, Sam Marketing Director Special Events
NATIONAL HOLE-IN-ONE ASSOCIATION, 104

Schack, Daniel Contact
RICO INDUSTRIES/TAG EXPRESS, 1182

Schack, Jarrett Group Sales & Operations Coordinator
YOGI BERRA STADIUM, 1021

Schackow, Brian VP, Finance
MIDWEST LEAGUE, 45

Schaefer, Chris Assistant Athletic Director for Annual G
RICHMOND ATHLETICS, UNIVERSITY OF, 342

Schaefer, Darien Executive Director
BADGER STATE GAMES, 250, 260

Schaefer, David Managing Partner/Co-Chair
REICH, ROBERT S., 902

Schaefer, David Senior VP & Chief Operating Officer
COBRA PUMA GOLF, 1117

Schaefer, Mark President & Chief Of Innovation
ADVANCED DESIGN CONCEPTS, 1093

Schaefer, Paul Editor
NASCAR MAGAZINE, 572

Schaefer, Richard Chief Executive Officer
GOLDEN BOY PROMOTIONS, 785

Schaeffer, Michael Sports Assistant Editor
PHILADELPHIA INQUIRER, 519

Schaeffer, Paul Vice Chairman/CEO
MANDALAY ENTERTAINMENT COMPANY, 794

Schaeffer, Rick Host
SPORTS LINE LIVE, 681

Schaeffer, Warren Manager
SOUTH ATLANTIC LEAGUE (A LEVEL), 50

Schaer, Rolf President / Chief Executive Officer
ALPINA SPORTS CORPORATION, 1096

Schafer, Amy Director of Athletics
THIEL COLLEGE ATHLETICS, 403

Schafer, Cory President
INTERNATIONAL SPORT KARATE ASSOCIATION, 143

Schafer, Patrick Assistant Coach
NORTH AMERICAN HOCKEY LEAGUE, 133

Schafer, Steve Sports Information Director
WAYNE STATE COLLEGE, 1017

Schaffel, Martin Executive Chairman
SPL INTEGRATED SOLUTIONS, 822

Schaffer, Jeff Sports Director
WBKB-TV, 700

Schaffer, Mike Sports Director
WSDP-FM, 519, 665

Schaffer, Peter Sports Agent
ALL PRO SPORTS & ENTERTAINMENT, 824

Schak, Jennifer Marketing/Special Events Coordinator
BLOOMINGTON CONVENTION & VISITORS BUREAU, 229

Schaly, Joe Assistant Director of Athletics
THIEL COLLEGE ATHLETICS, 403

Schamberger, Roger VP Marketing
BURBACH AQUATICS - ARCHITECTS & ENGINEERS, INC., 1051

Schanen, William Publiser/Editor
SAILING MAGAZINE, 579

Schanke, Adam Sports Marketing Manager
FOX CITIES CONVENTION AND VISITORS BUREAU, 234

Schanowski, Mark Sports Reporter
WMAQ-TV, 706

Schanwald, Steve Senior Vice President of Operations
UNITED CENTER, 1012

Scharf, Charles President & CEO
WELLS FARGO & CO, 735

Scharf, Howard Assistant General Manager
INTERNATIONAL LEAGUE, 42

Scharf, Richard President/CEO
DENVER METRO CONVENTION & VISITORS BUREAU, 232

Scharlau, Charles Attorney
CONNER & WINTERS, P.L.L.C., 874

Scharlau, Greg Partner
CONNER & WINTERS, P.L.L.C., 874

Scharr, Jack Chairman International Advisory Board
AMERICAN SPORT ART MUSEUM AND ARCHIVES (ASAMA), 251

Schatzman, John Lawyer
WARSHAFSKY LAW FIRM, 914

Schauer, Steve Director, Communications
NORTHERN COLLEGIATE HOCKEY ASSOCIATION, 122

Schauer, Steven Director of Athletic Communications
CONCORDIA UNIVERSITY (WI) ATHLETICS (CUW), 381

Scheaffer, Danny Manager
APPALACHIAN LEAGUE, 33

Schechter, Sid Chief Operating Officer
NATIONAL MEDIA GROUP, INC., 796

Schedlbauer, Joseph Engineering Principal
FTL DESIGN ENGINEERING STUDIO, 1057

Scheel, Steve Chief Executive Officer / Chairman
SCHEEL'S ALL SPORTS, INC., 1236

Scheele, Edward Director
GREYHOUND HALL OF FAME, 252

Scheeler, Ken Maintainace Supritendent
SHASTA DISTRICT FAIR, 1032

Scheepstra, Dennis Track manager
SOUTHWESTERN INTERNATIONAL RACEWAY, 1033

Scheets, Bryan Sports Director
WIUS-AM, 651

Scheibe, Bill Sports Writer
HERALD-NEWS, 493

Scheibler, Kevin GM
SPORTS PROMOTION - BATTLE CREEK, MICHIGAN, 228, 246

Scheibler, Kevin General Manager
KELLOGG ARENA, 246, 978

Scheibly, Rob General Manager
WLGC, 655

Scheide, Lee Sports Reporter (Minors)
SAN ANTONIO EXPRESS-NEWS, 528

Scheinberg, David President/Chief Executive Officer
PCGCAMPBELL, 800

Scheiner, Alec President
FIRST ENERGY STADIUM, 965

Scheiner, J. Stores Vice Chairman / Director
BURDINE'S, 1221

Schelde, Mark Founder/President
GRAVITY TELEVISION & SPORTS MARKETING, 786

Schellhardt, Marshall Stadium Operations Manager
ONEOK FIELD, 990

Schemm, Adam Senior Associate AD, External Relations
WISCONSIN MILWAUKEE ATHLETICS, UNIVERSITY OF, 349

Schemmel, Justin Deputy AD, Internal Operations
NORTHERN IOWA ATHLETICS, UNIVERSITY OF, 340

Schendel, Mike Purchasing Executive
PORTER ATHLETIC EQUIPMENT COMPANY, 1175

Schenk, Jennifer Chief Counsel & Chief Compliance Officer
ORTHOCAROLINA, 922

Schenk, Nancy President Elect
BOWLING PROPRIETORS' ASSOCIATION OF AMERICA, 65

Schenkel, Greg Vice Chairman
STATE OF INDIANA HORSE RACING COMMISSION, 82

Schenone, Dean Vice President
ALAMEDA COUNTY FAIRGROUNDS, 1035

Schepanovich, Branny Lawyer
BALTIMORE, BRYON, 863

Schepel, Bill Athletics Director
TRINITY CHRISTIAN COLLEGE ATHLETICS, 322

Schepker, Steve Tournament Assistant
DIXIE PGA SECTIONAL OFFICE, 105

Scher, George Chief Operations Officer
WORLDWIDE TICKET CRAFT, 933

Scherf, Christopher Executive Vice President
THOROUGHBRED RACING ASSOCIATIONS, 77

Schermerhorn, Dave Assistant General Manager
NEW YORK-PENNSYLVANIA LEAGUE, 46, 1009

Schermerhorn, Jan 2nd Vice President
SUN COUNTRY AMATEUR GOLF ASSOCIATION, 116

Schermick, Casey Sports Information Director
MANHATTANVILLE COLLEGE ATHLETICS, 391

Scherr, Jim Chief Executive Officer
HAMAKAWA, CURT L., 837

Scherting, Mike Assistant Sports Editor
BILLINGS GAZETTE, 465

Scheuermann, Arthel Partner
SHEUERMANN & JONES, 906

Scheumann, David President
KEYSTONE MARKETING, INC., 792

Scheuring, Paul News Director
WKBK-AM, 653

Schiavone, Tony Sports Reporter
WSB-AM, 647, 665

Schiavoni, Teddy Chairman
NATIONAL SKI & SNOWBOARD RETAILERS ASSOCIATION, 152

Schick, Bob Advertising Sales
WJR-AM, 652

Schick, Matt Sports Director
KWNB-TV, 689, 697

Schickendantz, Mark Head Team Physician
AMERICAN LEAGUE OF PROFESSIONAL BASEBALL CLUBS, THE, 29

Schickert, Randy President / General Manager
HUFFY SPORTS COMPANY, 1146

Schiek, Tim President
BOSTON WHALER, INC., 1109

Schierfelbein, Joseph Executive Sports Editor
ADVOCATE, 459

Schiffman, Roger Managing Editor
GOLF DIGEST, 561

Schild, John Assistant Athletic Director
CULVER-STOCKTON COLLEGE ATHLETICS, 311

Schildgen, Robert Managing Director
SIERRA MAGAZINE, 580

Schiller, Derek President/CEO
NATIONAL LEAGUE OF PROFESSIONAL BASEBALL CLUBS, THE, 31

Schiller, Harvey President
USA TEAM HANDBALL, 210

Schilling, Blake General Manager
CANTON MEMORIAL CIVIC CENTER, 955

Schilling, Charlie Assistant General Manager
PINNACLE BANK ARENA, 993

Schimmel, Ed Coordinating Producer
ESPN, 682, 683

Schimmel, Lori Director of Compliance
THIEL COLLEGE ATHLETICS, 403

Schimmel, Megan Treasurer
DWARF ATHLETIC ASSOCIATION OF AMERICA, 219

Schimmelpfenning, Jeff Commissioner
CHICAGOLAND COLLEGIATE ATHLETIC CONFERENCE, 294

Schimmoeller, Kim Associate Athletics Director
BLUFFTON UNIVERSITY ATHLETICS, 378

Schindler, David President
ELASCO, INC., 1128

Schindler, Kurt Principal
ELS ARCHITECTURE AND URBAN DESIGN, 1055

Schirmer, Bob Associate Athletic Director, Finance
BRIGHAM YOUNG UNIVERSITY ATHLETICS, 325

Schirmer, Lynn EVP / Merchandising Planning
MERVYN'S, 1233

Schlatter, Terry Treasurer
NATIONAL OPERATING COMMITTEE ON STANDARDS FOR ATHLETIC EQUIPMENT, 84

Schlauch, Thomas SVP - Buying
BIG 5 SPORTING GOODS, 1219

Schlee, Sandy EVP
LEIGH STOWELL & COMPANY, 793

Schleiden, Keith Managing Editor
PRO FOOTBALL WEEKLY, 577

Schlein, Mark Vice President of Accounting/Finance
MIDWEST LEAGUE, 45

Schlender, Laurie Assistant General Manager
PACIFIC COAST LEAGUE OF PROFESSIONAL BASEBALL CLUBS, 49, 999

Schlereth, Mark Host
HILL & SCHLERETH, 609

Schlesinger, Rick President, Business
Operations
NATIONAL LEAGUE OF PROFESSIONAL
BASEBALL CLUBS, THE, 32

Schlesinger, Sally Executive Vice President
CHICAGO SOUTHLAND CONVENTION &
VISITORS BUREAU, 230

Schlichting, Warren Senior Vice President, Ad
Sales
DISH NETWORK, 686

Schlick, Dave LT.Governor
CENTRAL CALIFORNIA AAU ASSOCIATION,
213

Schlickmann, Paul Director of Athletics
FAIRFIELD UNIVERSITY ATHLETICS, 330

Schliesmann, Barry EVP Interactive Technology
SPORTVISION, 602

Schline, Mike General Manager
PACIFIC COAST LEAGUE OF
PROFESSIONAL BASEBALL CLUBS, 49

Schlissel, Mark President
YOST ICE ARENA, 960, 1021

Schloessman, Kathryn President
LOS ANGELES SPORTS & ENTERTAINMENT
COMMISSION, 239

Schloffman, John Director, Ticket Operations
AMERICAN HOCKEY LEAGUE/AHL, 128

Schlosberg, Cathy Vice President,
Marketing/Education
ARAMARK CORPORATION, 773, 1064, 1066

Schlosberg, Hilton Chairman and CEO
MONSTER BEVERAGE CORPORATION, 730

Schloss, Jonathan Director of US Operations
INTERNATIONAL MASCOT CORPORATION,
1148

Schlosser, Andy General Manager
WOMEN'S PREMIER SOCCER LEAGUE, 169

Schlosser, Bob Associate Director of Athletics
ELIZABETHTOWN COLLEGE ATHLETICS, 383

Schlosser, Chris Head Groundskeeper
SEC TAYLOR STADIUM, 1002

Schlough, Bill Senior VP/Chief Information Officer
NATIONAL LEAGUE OF PROFESSIONAL
BASEBALL CLUBS, THE, 32

Schluter, Becky Administrative Assistant to the
Associat
IWIRELESS CENTER, 974

Schluter, Bradley Technical Director
WOMEN'S PREMIER SOCCER LEAGUE, 166

Schmerbauch, Ann Head Athletic Trainer
FONTBONNE UNIVERSITY ATHLETICS, 385

Schmetzer, Brian Head Coach
MAJOR LEAGUE SOCCER, 158

Schmid, Fredi Director General
INTERNATIONAL SKATING UNION (ISU), 171,
205

Schmid, Ivonne Assistant to Executive Director
INTERNATIONAL SWIMMING HALL OF FAME,
254

Schmid, Kurt Sporting Director
MAJOR LEAGUE SOCCER, 158

Schmid, Lori Co-Founder, VP
THE FEMALE ATHLETE, INC., 1239

Schmid, Ron Executive Director
CAROLINAS PGA SECTION, 105

Schmidt, Barbara Executive VP & Director
AMERICAN HANOVERIAN SOCIETY, 73

Schmidt, Bill Senior Vice President & General
Manager
NATIONAL LEAGUE OF PROFESSIONAL
BASEBALL CLUBS, THE, 31

Schmidt, Gina Coordinator
BEULAH PARK, 1036

Schmidt, J. Senior Architect
HERBERT LEWIS KRUSE BLUNCK
ARCHITECTURE, 1059

Schmidt, Joshua Principal/Mechanical Engineer
FRIBERG ASSOCIATES INC., 1057

Schmidt, Karsten Speaker
RAVENSBURGER FX SCHMID, 1180

Schmidt, Keith Sports Editor
WEST BEND DAILY NEWS, 546

Schmidt, Kyle Sports Information Director
INDIANA WESLEYAN UNIVERSITY
ATHLETICS, 299, 314

Schmidt, Lee President
AMERICAN SOCIETY OF GOLF COURSE
ARCHITECTS, 100

Schmidt, Lisa Promotions Manager
KVII-TV, 697

Schmidt, Matt Executive Director
NEW HAMPSHIRE GOLF ASSOCIATION, 114

Schmidt, Paul Member
KELLEY, MCELWEE & SCHMIDT, P.A., 888

Schmidt, Roger Manager Marketing / Technology
RUBATEX CORPORATION, 1184

Schmidt, Sam Co-Owner
INDYCAR, 22

Schmidt, Scot Co-Founder/Athlete Relations VP
GO WITH A PRO, INC., 926

Schmidt, Scott Director
CORN PALACE, 960

Schmidt, Teri CVB Executive Director
SIOUX FALLS CONVENTION & VISITORS
BUREAU, 245

Schmidtke, Fred President
NATIONAL BATTING CAGES, INC, 1166

Schmiechen, Tim Director of Athletics
BELOIT COLLEGE ATHLETICS, 377

Schmieder, John President
MARICOPA COUNTY SPORTS COMMISSION,
240

Schmieder, Jon Executive Director
USA/BMX, THE AMERICAN BICYCLE
ASSOCIATION, 71

Schmies, Holly Director of Athletic Training
Education
UNIVERSITY OF WISCONSIN - STEVENS
POINT ATHLETICS (UW-STEVENS POI, 407

Schmit, Joe Sports Director
KSTP - KSTP 5/ABC, 695

Schmitt, Karl SVP Corporate Communications
CHURCHILL DOWNS, 1036

Schmitz, Brian Sports Columnist
ORLANDO SENTINEL, 516

Schmitz, Robert Chairman
OHIO STATE RACING COMMISSION, 81

Schmuecker, Rick Sports Information Director
DOANE COLLEGE ATHLETICS, 312

Schmutz, James Executive Director
AMERICAN SPORT EDUCATION
PROGRAM/ASEP, 217

Schmutz, Jim President/CEO
SPECIAL OLYMPICS MARYLAND, 195

Schnabel, Mark Sports Editor
NEWTON KANSAN, 514

Schnacke, Ken President, General Manager
INTERNATIONAL LEAGUE, 42, 972

Schnall, Rick Co-Chair & Governor
NATIONAL BASKETBALL ASSOCIATION/NBA,
56

Schnatz, Kristofer Athletic Director
INDIANA UNIVERSITY NORTHWEST
ATHLETICS, 314

Schnatz, Pete Sports Writer
PHILADELPHIA INQUIRER, 519

Schnebly, Jim Assistant Editor
SKI PATROL, 580

Schneck, B.J. Sports Information Director
GREENVILLE COLLEGE ATHLETICS, 386

Schneekloth, Aaron Head Coach
AMERICAN HOCKEY LEAGUE/AHL, 127

Schneider, Barry Chairman / Chief Executive
Officer
MACGREGOR GOLF COMPANY, 1158

Schneider, Bill Promoter
JULESBURG DRAGSTRIP, 1026

Schneider, David Sales Manager
US CELLULAR ARENA, 106, 483, 1014

Schneider, Jess Manager, Umpire Operations
PROFESSIONAL BASEBALL UMPIRE
CORPORATION, 28

Schneider, Jochen Head of Sport
MAJOR LEAGUE SOCCER, 158

Schneider, John Vice President
SEALFLEX INDUSTRIES, INC., 96, 1186

Schneider, Mickie EVP / Chief Financial Officer
L.A.T SPORTSWEAR, 1154

Schneider, Nate Director of Partner Services
BB&T BALLPARK AT HISTORIC BOWMAN
FIELD, 948

Schneider, Paul Chairman of the Commission
IDAHO STATE POLICE, 79

Schneider, Peter President
ATHLETIC DEALERS OF AMERICA, 1217

Schneider, Roz Principal
BARKER RINKER SEACAT ARCHITECTURE,
1050

Schneider, Scott Chief Digital Officer
RUDER/FINN SPORTS, INC., 806

Schneider, Steve Athletic Director
PERU STATE COLLEGE ATHLETICS, 318, 698

Schneider, Suzy Administrative Assistant
NORTHERN CALIFORNIA SECTIONAL
OFFICE, 107

Schneider, Timothy Publisher
SPORTSTRAVEL MAGAZINE, 586

Schneiderer, Larry Director of Athletic Operations
DENISON UNIVERSITY(DU)ATHLETICS, 382

Schneider, Matthew Managing Director
GARVEY, SCHUBERT & BARER, 881

Schnelle, Lock Head Athletic Trainer
SOUTHWESTERN COLLEGE ATHLETICS, 320

Schnepf, Kevin Sports Editor
FORUM, 489

Schnitzer, Beth Vice President Strategic Alliance
PIER 39 MARKET DEVELOPMENT, 759

Schnitzer, Jenny Executive Director & Chief
Operating Off
USTA EASTERN, 175

Schnurbusch, Jim Contact
HUGHES SPORTS MARKETING, 788

Schoaf, Mike Director Media & Communications
ILLINOIS PGA SECTIONAL OFFICE, 106

Schoeb, Brent Chief Revenue/Marketing Officer
NATIONAL FOOTBALL LEAGUE/NFL, 96

Schoellkopf, Rosemary Editor
BULLPEN, 554

Schoen, Bill Publisher
CALIFORNIA HOCKEY & SKATING, 554

Schoen, Joe SVP/General Manager
NATIONAL FOOTBALL LEAGUE/NFL, 96

Schoen, Todd Senior Vice President Affiliate
FX NETWORKS, LLC, 675

Schoenadal, Tracy VP
TNS SPORT - NORTH AMERICA, 814

Schoenadel, Tracy Director, Center for Sports
Research
MASSACHUSETTS AMHERST, UNIVERSITY
OF, 425

Schoenbeck, James Operations / Advertising
SVP
DUCKWALL ALCO STORES, INC., 1225

Schoenbeck, Roger Vice President/Treasurer
VERMONT GOLF ASSOCIATION, 116

Schoenfeld, Gary President & Chief Executive
Officer
VANS, INC., 1240

Schoenfeld, Walter Chairman
VANS, INC., 1240

Schoeni, K. Partner
SCHOENI, K. ROGER, 904

Schoenike, Scott President
SOUTHERN PROFESSIONAL HOCKEY
LEAGUE, 136

Schoening, Bill General Manager
WFNZ-AM 610 SPORTS RADIO, 646

Schoenly, Karla Head Athletic Trainer
FROSTBURG STATE UNIVERSITY
ATHLETICS (FSU), 385

Schoenrock, Ashley Assistant General Manager
LEWIS AND CLARK PARK, 982

Schoenstein, Eric President
OREGON GOLF ASSOCIATION, 114

Schoenthaler, Todd Sports News Assistant
OKLAHOMAN, 515

Schoenwetter, Phil Head Athletic Trainer
MCPHERSON COLLEGE ATHLETICS, 316

Schoessel, Scott Sales VP/New Business
Development
GIGUNDA GROUP, 785

Schofield, Lawrence Engineer
E.B. ROTONDI & SONS, INC., 1126

Schoh, Eric Director of Athletics
WINONA STATE UNIVERSITY ATHLETICS,
375

Scholl, Bill Director of Athletics
MARQUETTE UNIVERSITY ATHLETICS, 336

Scholleart, Laurie Art Director
PRICE MEDIA, 577

Scholten, Bill President
SOUTH DAKOTA GOLF ASSOCIATION, 115

SOUTHWESTERN UNIVERSITY ATHLETICS, 401

Schwab, Jay Sports Editor
KANE COUNTY CHRONICLE, 499

Schwaiger, Gabi Vice Commodore
WOMEN'S OCEAN RACING SAILING ASSOCIATION, 64

Schwan, Axel President
TIM HORTONS, 733

Schwanke, Kelly Manager
BANSHEE MUSIC, 774

Schwartz, Alan President
SUPERIOR UNIFORM GROUP INC., 862, 1198

Schwartz, Andrew Senior Associate Director of Athletics
NEW JERSEY INSTITUTE OF TECHNOLOGY(NJIT), 395

Schwartz, Bruce Vice President Socks
TERRAMAR SPORTS WORLDWIDE, LTD., 1200

Schwartz, Dave Sports Director
KTAL-TV, 695

Schwartz, David Chief Operations Officer/Chief Technolog
SEATS 3D, 807, 932

Schwartz, Gil EVP/Chief Communications Officer
CBS SPORTS, 673

Schwartz, H. Publisher
HORSE OF DELAWARE VALLEY, 564

Schwartz, Howard Founder and CEO
HDS PROMOTIONAL MARKETING, 787

Schwartz, Jackie Manager marketing & Promotions
HOCKEY HALL OF FAME AND MUSEUM, 252

Schwartz, James Security Director
NAPLES-FORT MYERS GREYHOUND TRACK, 1047

Schwartz, Jennifer Assistant Director
NEBRASKA SCHOOL ACTIVITIES ASSOCIATION, 201

Schwartz, Jon Sports Information Director
CASE WESTERN RESERVE UNIVERSITY ATHLETICS, 101, 379, 686

Schwartz, Kyle Assistant Commissioner for Strategic Com
OHIO VALLEY CONFERENCE, 302

Schwartz, Len Heavyhands Father
HEAVY HANDS, 1143

Schwartz, Leonard Partner
RAGSDALE, RICHARD A., 900

Schwartz, Leonard Lawyer
ROLAND, LENORA, R., 903

Schwartz, Lois Publisher/Photo Ed/Event Sales
CITY SPORTS MAGAZINE, 555

Schwartz, Louis President/Founder
AMERICAN SPORTSCASTERS ASSOCIATION, INC., 217

Schwartz, Paul Sports Reporter
NEW YORK POST, 510

Schwartz, Phyllis President
KNSD-TV, 692

Schwartz, Rebecca Marketing & Entertainment Manager
KEYSPAN PARK, 979

Schwartz, Rod Advertising Manager
KHTR-FM, 619

Schwartz, Roger Associate
WEISS, STEPHEN L., 915

Schwartz, Steven Lawyer
ROLAND, LENORA, R., 903

Schwartz, Susan Director of Athletic Ticketing
UNLV TICKETS, 1013

Schwarz, David Vice President, Communications
SPIKE TV, 677

Schwarz, Paul News Director
KMRS-AM, 624

Schwarz, Rachel
BRAUN & STEIDL ARCHITECTS INC, 1050

Schwarz, Sandro Head Coach
MAJOR LEAGUE SOCCER, 158

Schwarz, Steve Head Of Manufacturing Unit
ALLESON ATHLETIC, DON, 1096

Schweickert, Jim Director of Facilities and Operations
HIRAM COLLEGE ATHLETICS, 387

Schweigardt, Andrew Director of Industry Relations and Devel
THOROUGHBRED OWNERS AND BREEDERS ASSOCIATION, 77

Schweigert, Keith Sports Writer
LANCASTER NEW ERA, 501

Schweiter, Lauren Game Operations
MILITARY BOWL, 91

Schweitzer, Jon Senior VP/General Manager
WTMJ, 668

Schweitzer, Kasey Event Presentation
COSTANTE GROUP SPORTS & EVENT MARKETING, LLC, 753

Schweitzer, Scott Owner
BAKERSFIELD SPEEDWAY, 1022

Schweizer, John Division Manager / Exel / President
GARMONT USA, INC., 1136

Schweizer, Lynn Senior Associate Director of Athletics
DENISON UNIVERSITY(DU)ATHLETICS, 382

Schwepker, Steve Sports Information Director
POINT UNIVERSITY ATHLETICS, 319

Schweppe, Lauren Associate Producer
MOTOR RACING NETWORK/MRN, 604, 634

Schwieterman, Jaclyn Head Athletic Trainer
MARIETTA COLLEGE ATHLETICS, 392

Schwind, Jim Technical Services Director
FIBERESIN INDUSTRIES, INC., 1132

Scialabba, Mark VP, Player Personnel/Assistant General M
NATIONAL LEAGUE OF PROFESSIONAL BASEBALL CLUBS, THE, 32

Scialpi, Desiree Marketing / Licensing Director
FRANCO APPAREL GROUP, 1135

Sciarra, Adrian Director
LANDMARK SPORT GROUP, 840

Sciarrino, Tom Director of Stadium Operations
INTERNATIONAL LEAGUE, 42, 958

Scislo, Brian Senior Associate AD, Administration
TULSA ATHLETICS, UNIVERSITY OF, 347

Scissons, Michael Business Manager
WESTERN HOCKEY LEAGUE, 139

Sclafani, Steve Founder & Chief Executive Officer
BASEBALL FACTORY, 26

Scodellaro, John Chief Financial Officer
PCGCAMPBELL, 800

Scohy, Jeff Secretary
MIAMI VALLEY GOLF ASSOCIATION, 113

Scoles, Jon Executive Director
WOMEN'S PREMIER SOCCER LEAGUE, 166

Scollard, Jim Governor
MONTANA AAU ASSOCIATION, 215

Scollin, Priscilla Marketing Manager & Registration
WORLD SPORTS & MARKETING, 180

Scopel, Doug VP, Operations
PACIFIC COAST LEAGUE OF PROFESSIONAL BASEBALL CLUBS, 48

Scott, Adam Assistant Director
MISSISSIPPI STATE UNIVERSITY/GOLF MANAGEMENT PROGRAM, 103

Scott, Amy Director Ticket Operations
COTTON BOWL CLASSIC, 90

Scott, Andrea Head Athletic Trainer
MINNESOTA STATE UNIVERSITY - MOORHEAD ATHLETICS (MSUM), 364, 661

Scott, Bill President
SUMMIT POINT MOTORSPORTS PARK, 649, 1033

Scott, Brad Executive Director
WEIL, GOTSHAL & MANGES, 900, 914

Scott, Buddy Program Director
KHMX-FM, 611, 619

Scott, Casey Exec. Associate AD, Internal Ops. & Even
KANSAS STATE UNIVERSITY ATHLETICS, 333, 951

Scott, Cheryl Business Manager
LONE STAR CONFERENCE, 298

Scott, Christopher Founder
GREENTECH, 1140

Scott, Cindy Assistant Athletic Director
BENTLEY UNIVERSITY ATHLETICS, 352

Scott, Dalila EVP & Chief Diversity Officer
COMCAST CORPORATION, 727

Scott, Damon Program Director
WSRW-FM, 667

Scott, Daryle President / Chief Executive Officer
VENUS SWIMWEAR, 1207

Scott, Dave General Manager Defense & Aerospace Divi
BARCO MEDIA, 374, 1104

Scott, David Sports Columnist
CHARLOTTE OBSERVER, 225, 469

Scott, Derek Associate AD, Internal Operations
JACKSON STATE UNIVERSITY ATHLETICS, 333

Scott, Edward Deputy AD
VIRGINIA ATHLETICS, UNIVERSITY OF, 348

Scott, Eric News Director
WKXW-FM, 654

Scott, Ernest Head Coach
NATIONAL BASKETBALL ASSOCIATION DEVELOPMENT LEAGUE, 59

Scott, Frank Program Director
WQLA-FM, 662

Scott, Gary General Manager
WEAI-FM, 644

Scott, Jeff Promoter
MARBURY DIRT TRACK & KART SHOP, 1028

Scott, Joe Director of Sales
INFINITY PRO SPORTS, 1214

Scott, John Chief Executive Officer
SPORTAMERICA, 810

Scott, John EVP
CROAKIES, 1052, 1121

Scott, Josh Secretary
NATIONAL INTERSCHOLASTIC ATHLETIC ADMINISTRATORS ASSOCIATION/NIAA, 203

Scott, Justin Assistant Athletic Director
ARCADIA UNIVERSITY ATHLETICS DEPARTMENT-GLENSIDE, 377

Scott, Kelly Box Officer Manager
FLORIDA STATE LEAGUE, 39

Scott, Kenzie Account Manager
RIDEAU CARLETON RACEWAY, 1043

Scott, Lee President and Chief Executive Officer
WAL-MART STORES, INC., 1240

Scott, Lori Veterinarian Member
COLORADO RACING COMMISSION, 79

Scott, Marcus Box Office Manager
VAN ANDEL ARENA, 1015

Scott, Merle Player Representative
BDA SPORTS MANAGEMENT, 826

Scott, Mickey Secretary
TOLEDO DISTRICT GOLF ASSOCIATION, 116

Scott, Mike Chief Operating Officer
HNTB CORP, 1060

Scott, Peter Attorney
BENDELOW LAW FIRM, 865

Scott, Reed Attorney
BROWN, HALL, SHORE & MCKINLEY LLP, 868

Scott, Reggie President
PROFESSIONAL FOOTBALL ATHLETIC TRAINERS SOCIETY, 89

Scott, Rick Chief Executive Officer
SPORTS PAGES, 585

Scott, Rob Executive Director
USTA INTERMOUNTAIN, 175

Scott, Robb Advertising Manager
LEAF-CHRONICLE, 502

Scott, Robert Chairman
NATIONAL SHOOTING SPORTS FOUNDATION, 150

Scott, Robert Adelphi University President
ADELPHI UNIVERSITY - RUTH S. AMMON SCHOOL OF EDUCATION, 409

Scott, Schoenike Executive Director
US CELLULAR CENTER, 1014

Scott, Steve President
WEEDE ARENA, 1017

Scott, Stewart Host
MONDAY NIGHT COUNTDOWN, 684

Scott, Thomas Sales Manager
CANAMER INT'L, LLC, 1113

Scott, Timothy Sports Writer
VALLEJO TIMES-HERALD, 543

Scott, Tom Promotion Manager
WBYL-FM, 640

Scott, Tommy President/Managing Partner
NORTH AMERICAN HOCKEY LEAGUE, 133

Scott, Trayvean Vice President, Intercollegiate Athletic
GRAMBLING STATE UNIVERSITY ATHLETICS, 331

Scott, Troy VP, Ballpark Operations & Security
AMERICAN LEAGUE OF PROFESSIONAL BASEBALL CLUBS, THE, 29, 232

executive index

Speight, Joel Deputy Executive Director
TEXAS RACING COMMISSION, 82
Spelius, George President Emeritus
MIDWEST LEAGUE (A LEVEL), 44
Speltz, Bill Sports Reporter
TELEGRAPH HERALD, 538
Speltz, Tim General Manager
AMERICAN HOCKEY LEAGUE/AHL, 127
Spence, Evelyn Articles Editor
SKIING, 581
Spence, Michael Facility Director
SUN BOWL, 1006
Spence, Mike Director of Special Facilities
Managemen
UTEP SPECIAL EVENTS, 1006, 1015
Spence, Tariq Sports Director
WDKX-FM, 643
Spence, Tim Sports Director
KKFN, 621
Spencer, Angie Classified Manager
PARAGOULD DAILY PRESS, 518
Spencer, Arik Secretary/Treasurer
PRAIRIE ROSE STATE GAMES, 263
Spencer, Beau Sports Director
WLMD-FM, 655
Spencer, Chris VP
E-Z GO, 1126
Spencer, Clark Sports Reporter
MIAMI HERALD, 506
Spencer, Cole Executive Director, Player
Personnel
NATIONAL FOOTBALL LEAGUE/NFL, 94
Spencer, H. Publisher
HEARTLAND BOATING, 563
Spencer, Jackie Director of Marketing
WSCR THE SCORE SPORTSRADIO 670, 665
Spencer, Jamie Head Golf Coach
LYCOMING COLLEGE ATHLETICS, 124, 391
Spencer, Jon Sports Columnist
NEWS JOURNAL (OH), 512
Spencer, Joyce 1st Vice President
AMERICAN BLIND BOWLING ASSOCIATION,
65
Spencer, Kara Front Desk
KENTUCKY SPEEDWAY, 1027
Spencer, Kelly Marketing/Communications
Manager
GRAND RIVER RACEWAY (GRR), 1039
Spencer, Leslie Executive Director
CINCINNATI SPORTS CORPORATION,
GREATER, 230
Spencer, Luke Head Coach
USL CHAMPIONSHIP, 159
Spencer, Natanee Business Manager
BIG SKY CONFERENCE, 292
Spencer, Parke President
CIVIC ENTERTAINMENT GROUP, 752
Spencer, Tracy Athletic Ticket Manager
SAN JOSE STATE UNIVERSITY, 432
Spengler, Chris Director of Advancement
Relations
JOHN F. SAVAGE HALL, 976
Spentzos, George Executive Advisory Board
DENVER, UNIVERSITY OF, 416
Speraw, John Head Coach, Men's Volleyball
PAULEY PAVILION, 991
Sperber, Bryan President
PHOENIX INTERNATIONAL RACEWAY, 1030
Sperber, Burton Founder / Chief Executive Officer
VALLEY CREST, 1063
Sperber, Richard President / CEO
VALLEY CREST, 1063
Sperduti, Peter VP/General Manager
PRITCHARD INDUSTRIES, INC, 1065
Spetner, Alan Chief Cruisin' Officer
BOWLINGSHIRT.COM, 1109
Spetner, Helene President
BOWLINGSHIRT.COM, 1109
Spevak, Shon Executive Senior Associate AD,
Revenue G
SOUTHERN UTAH UNIVERSITY ATHLETICS,
345
Spicer, Chuck Falcon Sports Properties General
Manager
DOYT PERRY FIELD STADIUM, 962
Spicer, Tom Director of Athletics
MESA STATE COLLEGE ATHLETICS(MSC),
363

Spiegel, David Director of Athletic
Communications
PACE UNIVERSITY ATHLETICS, 367
Spiegler, Julie Program Manager
U.S. HANG GLIDING AND PARAGLIDING
ASSOCIATION, 14
Spielbauer, Brian Athletics Director
CENTRAL METHODIST COLLEGE
ATHLETICS, 310
Spielman, Chris Host, The Big Show
SPORTS RADIO 97.1 THE FAN, 634
Spielman, Rachel Global Head of Corporate
Communications
RUDER/FINN SPORTS, INC., 806
Spier, James Executive Director
NATIONAL SCHOLASTIC ATHLETICS
FOUNDATION, INC., 797
Spiess, Tom Chief Financial Officer
AMERICAN ASSOCIATION OF SNOWBOARD
INSTRUCTORS, 154
Spigelmyer, BJ Sports Information Director
DE SALES UNIVERSITY ATHLETICS, 382
Spigone, Rob DCU Event Specialist
AMATEUR SPORTS GROUP, INC., 824
Spillane, David AICP, RIBA, Principal, Director of
Plann
GOODY CLANCY, 1057
Spillane, Jay Attorney/Partner
FOX & SPILLANE, LLP, 881
Spillane, Peter Production Manager
HATCHERS MANUFACTURING INC., 1143
Spillman, Mike President
CAROLINA REGIONAL VOLLEYBALL
ASSOCIATION/USA VOLLEYBALL, 210
Spina, Pete Publisher
SPORTING NEWS, 584
Spina, Peter Vice President/Publisher
SPORTING NEWS, 584
Spindler, Blake Director of Athletic Training
Services
PRESENTATION COLLEGE ATHLETICS, 319
Spindler, Richard Publisher
LATITUDE 38, 568
Spinella, Dan Sales Representative
MATEFLEX-MELE CORPORATION, 1160
Spingola, Paul Promotions Director
WTNH-TV, 710
Spink, James 600 Kentucky Manager
600 RACING, INC., 1089
Spinosa, Charles Group Director
VISION SPORTS & ENTERTAINMENT
PARTNERS, 816
Spiotti, Lou Executive Director of Athletics
ROCHESTER INSTITUTE OF TECHNOLOGY
ATHLETICS, 398
Spires, Ken President
SOFFE COMPANY, INC., 1190
Spiros, Lindsay Sales & Marketing Manager
MINNEAPOLIS METRO NORTH CONVENTION
& VISITORS BUREAU, 241
Spitger, Ken General Manager
WHTK, 650
Spitz, Eric Program Director
WFAN SPORTS RADIO, 645
Spitz, Robert Attorney
SPITZ, ROBERT J., 855
Spitzer, Ken General Manager
WRSN-FM, 665
Spivak, Robert Chairman
MACCABI USA/SPORTS FOR ISRAEL, 221
Splaine, David SVP Sales
TD BANKNORTH GARDEN, 1008
Spoelstra, Erik Head Coach
NATIONAL BASKETBALL ASSOCIATION/NBA,
57
Spoelstra, Jon President
MANDALAY ENTERTAINMENT COMPANY,
794
Sponzo, Kevin Senior Associate AD, Facilities &
Operat
SETON HALL UNIVERSITY ATHLETICS, 343
Spoon, Doug Sports Editor
SAN GABRIEL VALLEY DAILY TRIBUNE, 528
Spooner, Bill President
USA ROLLER SPORTS, 209
Spooner, Bridget Head Athletic Trainer
ELIZABETHTOWN COLLEGE ATHLETICS, 383
Spooner, Pat Secretary
NEW HAMPSHIRE GOLF ASSOCIATION, 114

Spott, Steve Assistant Coach
NATIONAL HOCKEY LEAGUE/NHL, 124
Spragg, Aaron Sports Director
WHIZ-TV, 703
Sprague, Carol Senior Associate Athletic Director
PETERSON EVENTS CENTER, 992
Sprague, Chris Assistant to the President
INTERNATIONAL LEAGUE (AAA LEVEL), 41
Sprague, Derek President
PGA OF AMERICA/PROFESSIONAL
GOLFERS' ASSOCIATION OF AMERICA, 105
Sprague, Ed Director, Player Development
AMERICAN LEAGUE OF PROFESSIONAL
BASEBALL CLUBS, THE, 30
Sprague, Mary Associate Athletic Director
PRINCIPIA COLLEGE ATHLETICS, 397
Sprague, Matt Sports Editor
BERKSHIRE EAGLE, 464
Sprague, Richard Chief Inspector
THOMPSON SPEEDWAY MOTORSPORTS
PARK, 1034
Sprague, Thomas Executive Director
BUFFALO DISTRICT GOLF ASSOCIATION,
110
Sprague, Timothy Board Member
THE DAVIS EXPERIENCE, 1062
Sprangler, Natalie Head Athletic Trainer
MILLS COLLEGE ATHLETICS, 393
Spratt, Gerry Sports Editor
SANTA BARBARA NEWS-PRESS, 529
Spray, Doug President / Sales Construction
AUTOMATED BATTING CAGES
CORPORATION, 1102
Spriggs, Katie Associate Athletic Director
ALBERTA ATHLETICS, UNIVERSITY OF, 307
Spring, Tony President & CEO
MACY'S, 729
Springer, Bill Senior Editor
SAIL MAGAZINE, 579
Springer, Brian Owner
SPRINGCO, 1195
Springer, Doug President & Governor
ONTARIO HOCKEY LEAGUE, 134
Springer, Grant
STAMBAUGH STADIUM, 1005
Springer, John Director, General Operations
NIKE GOLF, 1168
Springer, Shira Sports Reporter
BOSTON GLOBE, 465
Springs, Andre Men's Golf Coach
LIVINGSTONE COLLEGE, 362, 423
Sprinkle, Joey Sports Editor
ARKANSAS CITY TRAVELER, 461
Sproat, Scott President, Business
Operations/Co-Owner
EAST COAST HOCKEY LEAGUE/ECHL, 129
Sprout, Greg Sports Senior Editor
WISCONSIN STATE JOURNAL, 547
Sprout, Nancy Assistant Athletic Director for
Business
WESTERN HALL, 1018
Sprouy, Nancy Asst. Director Of Athletics,
Business Op
IWIRELESS CENTER, 974
Sprunger, Chris VP, Ticket Operations & Strategy
NATIONAL FOOTBALL LEAGUE/NFL, 48, 96
Sprunger, Randall Chief Operating Officer
FANNING/HOWEY ASSOCIATES, INC., 1055
Sprunger, Randall Director
FANNING/HOWEY ASSOCIATES, INC., 1055
Spugnardi, John Sports Information Director
BELLARMINE UNIVERSITY ATHLETICS, 352
Spurney, Peter President
SPURNEY ASSOCIATES, PETER, 763
Spytek, John General Manager
NATIONAL FOOTBALL LEAGUE/NFL, 95
Squeri, Stephen Chairman & CEO
AMERICAN EXPRESS COMPANY, 725
Squires, Dutch Vice President
AMERICAN POWER BOAT ASSOCIATION, 63
Squires, Joe Director of Athletic Events
WALDORF COLLEGE ATHLETICS, 323
Squires, Troy Global Director of Sales and
Marketing
GENERAL SPORTS VENUE ASTROTURF,
1132, 1137
Sr, Carrie President
CY YOUNG INDUSTRIES, INC., 1122

Stewart, Marissa Athletic Trainer
CLARKE UNIVERSITY ATHLETICS, 310

Stewart, Mark Chairman, CEO and President
GOODYEAR TIRE & RUBBER CO., THE, 728

Stewart, Michael Promotions Director
KPRC-TV, 693

Stewart, Nate Director of Athletics
EASTERN UNIVERSITY(EU) ATHLETICS, 383

Stewart, Patrick Sports Information Director
ADRIAN COLLEGE ATHLETICS-ADRIAN, 376

Stewart, Patty Director of Human Resources
(Dallas)
WINSTEAD ATTORNEYS, 916

Stewart, R. Athletic Director
CARL WOOTEN STADIUM, 955

Stewart, Randall Director of Athletic
Communications
NEWBERRY COLLEGE ATHLETICS(NCAA),
365

Stewart, Renee Lawyer
NORTH, PURSELL, RAMOS & JAMESON,
PLC, 897

Stewart, Richard Chief Operating & Financial
Officer
AMERICAN ACADEMY OF ORTHOPAEDIC
SURGEONS, 918

Stewart, Roger President
PUSH PEDAL PULL, 1235

Stewart, Taylor Associate AD, External
Relations/Chief o
GRAMBLING STATE UNIVERSITY
ATHLETICS, 331

Stewart, Todd Director of Athletics
WESTERN KENTUCKY UNIVERSITY
ATHLETICS, 349, 962, 984

Stewart, Tony Co-Owner
NASCAR CUP SERIES, 23

Stewart, Wayne Athletic Director
OKLAHOMA PANHANDLE STATE
UNIVERSITY ATHLETICS(OPSU), 367

Stice, Todd Director Of Rules & Competitions
KANSAS CITY GOLF ASSOCIATION, 112

Stich, Jennifer Event Booking Manager
HSBC ARENA, 972

Stick, Tony Treasurer
BILLIARD CONGRESS OF AMERICA, 62

Stickel, Brian General Manager, Promoter
KNOXVILLE RACEWAY, 1027

Stickel, Jamie Advertising Director
YAKIMA HERALD-REPUBLIC, 548

Stickney, Hank Chief Executive Officer
MANDALAY ENTERTAINMENT COMPANY,
794

Stickney, Ken Managing Director
MANDALAY ENTERTAINMENT COMPANY,
794

Stickney, William Sports Reporter
HOUSTON CHRONICLE, 495

Stieber, Christopher Account Executive
RIPKEN STADIUM, 997

Stieger, Jerry Sports Management Program
Coordinator
VALPARAISO UNIVERSITY, 436

Stienstra, Tom Sports Reporter
SAN FRANCISCO CHRONICLE, 528

Stiepock, Chris Vice President
ESPN X GAMES, 261

Stier, William Director: Athletic Admin/Sport Mgmt
& Co
SUNY, STATE UNIVERSITY OF NEW
YORK-BROCKPORT, 434

Stiff, Julyn Director of Guest Services
CHICAGOLAND SPEEDWAY, 1023

Stigliano, Ann Secretary
RED RIVER ATHLETIC CONFERENCE, 303

Stigliano, Tony Commissioner
RED RIVER ATHLETIC CONFERENCE, 303

Stiglich, Joe Sports Staff Writer
CONTRA COSTA TIMES, 473

Stiglitz, Jan Law Professor/Co-Director,
Innocence Pro
CALIFORNIA WESTERN SCHOOL OF LAW,
871

Stiles, Bill Director of Athletics
ALVERNIA UNIVERSITY
ATHLETICS-READING, 376

Stiles, Mike News Director
WBET-AM, 638

Still, Paul Advertising Manager
INDEX-JOURNAL, 496

Stillerman, Phil National Account Manager
AEF EMBLEMS, 1094

Stilling, Martin Store Manager
EREHWON MOUNTAIN OUTFITTER, 1226

Stillitano, Charlie Chief Executive Officer
CHAMPIONS WORLD, 777

Stillman, Cory Head Choach
ONTARIO HOCKEY LEAGUE, 134

Stillman, Kevin Attorney
CHASEN & BOSCOLO CHARTERED, 872

Stillman, Laura Executive Vice President
FLAD ARCHITECTS, 1056

Stillman, Tom Chairman/Governor
NATIONAL HOCKEY LEAGUE/NHL, 125

Stills, Sonja Associate Commissioner for
Administratio
MID-EASTERN ATHLETIC CONFERENCE, 299

Stillson, Luke Director of Sports Information
MCDANIEL COLLEGE ATHLETICS, 393

Stilp, Ben Controller
PICO RIVERA SPORTS ARENA, 993

Stilwel, Jennifer Chief Marketing Officer
GREENVILLE CONVENTION & VISITORS
BUREAU, 235

Stilwell, Christoper Facility and Operations
manager
NATIONAL TRAIL RACEWAY, 1029

Stimac, Vicci Senior Woman Administrator
UNIVERSITY OF WISCONSIN - OSHKOSH
TITANS, 407

Stimpert, Daniel Attorney
STIMPERT & FORD, LLP, 908

Stine, Greg President
NEBRASKA GOLF ASSOCIATION, 113

Stine, Justin Director
OVERLAND PARK CONVENTION & VISITORS
BUREAU, 243, 263

Stine, Tom Editor
PGA TOUR PARTNERS, 576

Stinger, Julie Office Manager
LEWIS AND CLARK PARK, 982

Stinson, Chuck Sports Reporter
WLBT-TV, 706

Stinson, Geoff ASG Digital Event Specialist
AMATEUR SPORTS GROUP, INC., 824

Stinson, Harry Associate Athletic Director
CENTRAL STATE UNIVERSITY ATHLETICS,
310

Stinson, James Head Coach Men's Basketbal
LIVINGSTONE COLLEGE, 423

Stinson, Patrick Publisher
EMPLOYEE SERVICES MANAGEMENT, 557

Stinson, Shawn Director Communications
SALT LAKE CONVENTION & VISITORS
BUREAU, 245

Stinson, Tom Assistant Managing Editor
STREET & SMITH'S SPORTSBUSINESS
JOURNAL, 587

Stinson, Tonya Executive Director
FARMINGTON CONVENTION & VISITORS
BUREAU, 233

Stipes, Tom President
SPONSORSHIP PRO+, 1214

Stitt, Erin Sports Editor
BEACH REPORTER, 463

Stitt, Micheal CEO
HAGGAR CORPORATION, 1141

Stitt, Mike Vice President
INTERNATIONAL BOWHUNTING
ORGANIZATION, 14

Stiver, Ron Vice-Chair
SPECIAL OLYMPICS INDIANA, 195

Stockbridge, Travis General Manager
NATIONAL BASKETBALL ASSOCIATION
DEVELOPMENT LEAGUE, 59

Stockdale, Dave Sports Copy Editor
DES MOINES REGISTER, 483

Stocker, Scott Sports Reporter
ROCKY MOUNTAIN NEWS, 526

Stockerman, Gerry Operations Director
BOSS MANUFACTURING COMPANY, 1109

Stockman, Casey Advertising Manager
SALAMANCA PRESS, 527

Stockman, Gary CEO
PORTER NOVELLI, 801

Stocks, Melanie Director
BRICK BREEDEN FIELDHOUSE, 951, 952

Stockton, Henderson Member
STOCKTON & HING, P.A., 909

Stockton, Riley Executive Director
SPOKANE HOOPFEST, 55

Stockwell, Benjamin Director of Athletic
Communications
CASTLETON STATE UNIVERSITY
ATHLETICS, 380

Stockwell, Caren Corporate Secretary &
Executive Assistan
STANDARDBRED CANADA, 77

Stoda, Greg Sports Columnist
PALM BEACH POST, 517

Stoddard, Jodi President
NATIONAL LITTLE BRITCHES RODEO
ASSOCIATION, 146

Stoddard, Zane Vice President
NASCAR, 686

Stoebling, Ann Head Athletic Trainer
NEW JERSEY CITY UNIVERSITY (NJCU), 395

Stoeckel-Whaylen, Brooke Director/Meetings &
Events
MINNEAPOLIS METRO NORTH CONVENTION
& VISITORS BUREAU, 241

Stoecklein, Denny General Manager
KANSAS STATE FAIR (KSF), 1040

Stoehr, James Owner/Chairman of Board
ROBBINS SPORTS SURFACES, 1183

Stoen, Ellen Assistant Professor of Health and
Physic
LUTHER COLLEGE, 424

Stoetzer, Pat Sports Reporter
CARROLL COUNTY TIMES, 468

Stoffel, Mark Senior Director Operations
XCEL ENERGY CENTER, 999, 1020

Stohrer, Bob President
CLEAR CHANNEL ENTERTAINMENT, INC.,
687

Stokes, Jay Chairman
UNITED STATES PARACHUTE
ASSOCIATION, 14

Stokold, Jill Promotions Director
WJBO-AM, 651

Stolfa, Jeremy Assistant Athletic Director,
Facilities
BOBCAT STADIUM TEXAS STATE, 951

Stoller, Joann Senior Director of Sports
SPECIAL OLYMPICS OREGON, 196

Stoltenberg, Chase Assistant Athletics Trainer
TEXAS A&M UNIVERSITY-COMMERCE
ATHLETICS, 372

Stoltenberg, Ryan Manager of Stadium
Operations
INTERNATIONAL LEAGUE, 42

Stoltz, Rob General Manager/Volume Services
KAUFFMAN STADIUM, 978

Stolz, Rein Engineering Department
SKYWAY, 1189

Stolz, Shane Sports Information Director
WILLIAMS BAPTIST COLLEGE ATHLETICS,
323

Stone, Barbara Executive Administrative Assistant
JOHN O'QUINN FIELD AT ROBERTSON
STADIUM, 977

Stone, Carolyn Director of Athletics
PALM BEACH ATLANTIC UNIVERSITY
ATHLETICS(PBA), 367

Stone, Chase VP, Eastern Sales
CALIFONE INTERNATIONAL, INC., 820

Stone, Chris President
GREENVILLE CONVENTION & VISITORS
BUREAU, 235

Stone, Cynthia Facilities/Operations Assistant
KENT STATE UNIVERSITY ATHLETICS, 979

Stone, Danny Head Coach
USL CHAMPIONSHIP, 160

Stone, Everett President
ELS MANAGEMENT INC., 832

Stone, Harlan Principal
VELOCITY SPORTS & ENTERTAINMENT, 816

Stone, Howard Co-Founder
JUSTHERSPORTS.COM, 1231

Stone, Jamey Advertising Director
TRANSWORLD SKATEBOARDING, 589

Stone, Jeff Head Athletic Trainer
SUFFOLK UNIVERSITY ATHLETICS, 349, 402

Stone, Jerry Sales VP
ALPS SPORTSWEAR MFG. COMPANY, INC.,
294, 1096

executive index

Strickland, Scott Director of Stadium Operations
DURHAM BULLS ATHLETIC PARK, 963
Strickland, William Executive Editor
BICYCLING, 552
Strickland, William Managing Partner
MCGUIREWOODS, 894
Stricklin, Scott Director of Athletics
MISSISSIPPI STATE UNIVERSITY, 330, 427,
960, 963
Striker, Rob General Manager
THE GAME 730 AM/WVFN, 635
Strimple, Larry President
BAILEY MANUFACTURING COMPANY, 1103
Stringer, Amanda Group Sales/Ticket Marketing
Director
SMITH-WILLIS STADIUM, 1003
Stringer, Jo Athletic Director
NJCAA REGION XVI MEN'S, 289
Stringer, Michael Asst General Manager/Food &
Beverage Man
DAYTONA BEACH KENNEL CLUB, 1046
Stringer, Ralph President / Chief Executive
Officer
NEOSTAR SPORTS AND ENTERTAINMENT,
845
Strittmatter, Charles Treasurer
NATIONAL STEEPLECHASE ASSOCIATION,
76
Strittmatter, Scott Director of Student Life
INDIANA UNIVERSITY SOUTH BEND
ATHLETICS, 314
Strittmatter, Skip Executive Director
DUPAGE CONVENTION & VISITORS
BUREAU, 233
Strobel, Greg 1st Vice president
USA WRESTLING, 180, 213
Stroble, Erin Associate Athletic Director
URSINUS COLLEGE ATHLETICS(UC), 404
Strockbine, Dick Athletics Director
UNIVERSITY OF DALLAS ATHLETICS (UD),
382
Strode, Dale Sports Editor
ASPEN TIMES, 462
Stroesser, James VP, Sales
CONVERSE, INC., 1223
Stroh, Bryan Vice President and General Counsel
PNC PARK, 993
Strohm, Billie President
GATOR ATHLETIC INC., 1136
Strollo, Ron Exec. Director of Intercollegiate
Athlet
YOUNGSTOWN STATE UNIVERSITY
ATHLETICS, 350, 949
Strom, Lisa Assistant Coach Representative
WOMEN'S GOLF COACHES ASSOCIATION,
118
Strom, Mike Sports Reporter
TIMES-PICAYUNE, 540
Stroman, Marie Coordinator of MAC 100
MIDDLE ATLANTIC STATES COLLEGIATE
ATHLETIC CORPORATION, 299
Stromme, Karen Associate Athletic Director
MINNESOTA-DULUTH ATHLETICS,
UNIVERSITY OF (UMD), 364
Stronach, Frank Chairman
REMINGTON PARK, 1043
Strong, Chris Business Development Director
THE SPORTS & FITNESS INDUSTRY
ASSOCIATION (SFIA), 813
Strong, Dana Sports Writer
LEWISTON MORNING TRIBUNE, 502
Strong, Jeff President
SOUTHERN TEXAS PGA SECTIONAL, 108
Strong, Patrick Associate
CAMPBELL, JOHN RUSSELL (RUSS), 0
Stross, Mark Chief Technology Officer
ANC SPORTS ENTERPRISES, 1216
Stroth, Andrew Executive Vice President, Talent
Marketi
CSMG INTERNATIONAL, LTD, 779
Stroud, Frankie Dept. Receptionist/Senior
Secretary
TENNESSEE, KNOXVILLE, UNIVERSITY OF,
434
Stroud, Jeff General Manager
COWBOYS STADIUM, 960
Stroud, Joe President
SOUTHERN PROFESSIONAL HOCKEY
LEAGUE, 136

Stroud, Rick Sports Writer
ST. PETERSBURG TIMES, 533
Stroud, Steve Deputy Athletic Dir./Chief Dev. &
Revenu
NEW ORLEANS ATHLETICS, UNIVERSITY
OF, 338
Stroup, Ben Sports Editor
DELAWARE GAZETTE, 482
Strout, Dawn Strength & Conditioning Coordinator
COLBY COLLEGE ATHLETICS, 381
Strout, Will Advertising Manager
DAILY ITEM (PA), 477
Strubbe, Jeanne Classified Manager
JACKSONVILLE JOURNAL-COURIER, 497
Strubel, Michael Sports Sales
VISIT EAU CLAIRE, 249
Struch, Dave Head Coach
WESTERN HOCKEY LEAGUE, 139
Struder, Quintan Owner, Director
SOUTHERN LEAGUE OF PROFESSIONAL
BASEBALL CLUBS, 52
Strunk, Amy Owner & Co-Chair
NATIONAL FOOTBALL LEAGUE/NFL, 96
Strus, Helen VP, Stadium/Arena Event Marketing
GIANTS STADIUM, 1039
Strutner, Matt Director, Corporate Ticket
Development
SMOKIES PARK, 1003
Struzyk, Mike Controller
FINGER LAKES GAMING & RACETRACK,
1038
Stryken, Richard Director
ALASKA STATE FAIR, 260
Strykowski, Joseph First Vice President
NEW YORK STATE GOLF ASSOCIATION, 114
Stuart, Andy General Manager
WSPD, 667
Stuart, Brandi Executive Senior Associate
AD/SWA
TEXAS TECH UNIVERSITY ATHLETICS, 346
Stuart, Catherine Member
STUART LAW FIRM, P.L.L.C, 909
Stuart, Chris Principal , Sports Licensing &
Estates
PARK LANE - INVESTMENT BANKING
SERVICES, 769
Stuart, Dan Director of Sponsorship Development
& CI
KENTUCKY SPEEDWAY, 1027
Stuart, Jacquie Ticket Operations Manager
CALIFORNIA LEAGUE (A-LEVEL), 36
Stuart, James Member
STUART LAW FIRM, P.L.L.C, 909
Stuart, Michael Co-Director
MAYO CLINIC SPORTS MEDICINE, 921
Stuart, Sandi EVP, Brand Development
SIDEOUT SPORT, INC., 1188
Stuart, Tex Director
GOWDY PRINTCRAFT PRESS, 562
Stuart, Tim Senior Associate AD
YOUNGSTOWN STATE UNIVERSITY
ATHLETICS, 350, 949
Stubblefield, Jeff Treasurer
KEYSTONE REGIONAL COMMISSIONER/USA
VOLLEYBALL, 211
Stubblefield, Kellyann Director of Athletics
COLUMBIA COLLEGE OF S. CAROLINA
ATHLETICS, 311
Stubbs, Charles President & CEO
PRIMEDIA, 760
Stubbs, Charles President/CEO
PRIMEDIA, 760
Stubbs, Greg Director of Operations
SULLIVAN ARENA, 1006
Stuchal, Dan Chief Communications Officer
NATIONAL HOCKEY LEAGUE/NHL, 124
Stuck, Dan Manager, Wellness & Team Affairs
AMERICAN HOCKEY LEAGUE/AHL, 127
Stuckey, Dennis Sports Director
WPHM-AM, 639, 661
Stuckey, Gail Stadium Operations Director
INVESCO FIELD AT MILE HIGH STADIUM, 973
Stuckey, Jason Attorney
GULAS LAW FIRM, P.C., 882
Stuckey, Justin Men's and Women's Head Coach
WITTENBERG UNIVERSITY, 438
Stuckey, Sheryl Paralegal
BOUTIN, DENTINO, GIBSON, DI GUISTO,
HODELL, INC., 867

Stuckly, Derrick Sports Editor
BROWNWOOD BULLETIN, 467
Stucky, Amy Associate Athletics Director
TAYLOR UNIVERSITY ATHLETICS, 321
Studstill, Cole Program Director
WIVQ-FM, 651
Stukenborg, Phil Sports Writer
COMMERCIAL APPEAL, 472
Stukes, Bill Associate Athletics Director
WHEATON COLLEGE (IL) ATHLETICS, 406
Stull, Rob Managing Director
USA PENTATHLON, 145, 207
Stultz, Thomas Senior Vice President/Managing
Director
HOST COMMUNICATIONS, INC., 788
Stultz, Thomas Senior Vice President/Managing
Director
HOST MANAGED EVENTS, 788
Stumpf, Jim Sales Director
LAWRENCE METAL PRODUCTS, 1154
Stuparyk, Melanie Managing Editor
METRO SPORTS NY, 570
Stupples, Karen LPGA Player Director
LADIES PROFESSIONAL GOLF
ASSOCIATION/LPGA, 103
Sturbin, John Auto Racing Staff Writer
FORT WORTH STAR-TELEGRAM, 489
Sturgeon, Jeremy Stadium Operations
TEXAS BASEBALL LEAGUE, 53
Sturgeon, Tracy Senior Manager, Administration
FOOTBALL CANADA, 88
Sturgeon, William President
SOUTHLAND ATHLETIC MANUFACTURING
COMPANY, 1191
Sturm, Marco Head Coach
AMERICAN HOCKEY LEAGUE/AHL, 128
Sturm, Paul Sports Editor
CHILLICOTHE CONSTITUTION-TRIBUNE, 470
Sturner, Benjamin Marketing Director
BENNETT GLOBAL MARKETING GROUP, 775
Sturt, Adam Operations Manager
DELTAPLEX ENTERTAINMENT & EXPO
CENTER, 961
Sturtevant, C. Editor
HAND GLIDING & PARA GLIDING MAGAZINE,
563
Stutler, Maurine Classified Manager
TAYLOR DAILY PRESS, 537
Stutz, Ken Sports Copy Editor
SAN JOSE MERCURY NEWS, 528
Stutz, Logan General Manager & Head Coach
NATIONAL BASKETBALL LEAGUE OF
CANADA, 58
Stuver, Doug VP, Finance
NATIONAL FOOTBALL LEAGUE/NFL, 96
Styers, Doug President
WESTERN COLORADO DRAGWAY, 1035
Styles, Patty Promoter
CENTERVILLE DRAGWAY PARK INC, 1023
Styles, Wayne President
CENTERVILLE DRAGWAY PARK INC, 1023
Styres, Curt Owner/General Manager
NATIONAL LACROSSE LEAGUE, 142
Stys, David SVP, Product Development
TURNKEY SPORTS & ENTERTAINMENT, 815
Styskal, Jennifer Editorial Director
WALKING HORSE REPORT, 591
Su, Joey Executive VP
SHINN FU COMPANY OF AMERICA, INC.,
1188
Suan, Marty Director Of Programs
ASSOCIATION OF VOLLEYBALL
PROFESSIONALS/AVP, 178
Suarez, Alex Producer
SUNDAY SPORTS FINAL, 682
Suber, Elke Chairperson
BLACK ENTERTAINMENT & SPORTS
LAWYERS ASSOCIATION INC, 218
Subero, Carlos Manager
ARIZONA FALL LEAGUE (ROOKIE), 34
Subido, Cindy SVP
JHG TOWNSEND, 790, 821
Subramaniam, Mohan Director, Coaching & High
Performance
USA BADMINTON, 25
Subramaniam, Raj President and COO
FEDEX CORPORATION, 728
Subsara, Peter Director of Promotions
SOUTH ATLANTIC LEAGUE (A LEVEL), 51

Sylvester, Maryrose President / Chief Executive Officer
GE LIGHTING SYSTEMS, 1136
Sylvester, Treasa Finance Director
KELLOGG ARENA, 978
Sylvia, Vin Sports Editor
UNION LEADER, 542
Symes, Dominic Partner/Creative Director
NUVISIONS, 798
Symes, Merle Leader
WALDON, GROUP THE, 859
Symons, Barry Chief Executive Officer
SMYTH SYSTEMS, INC., 1190
Symons, Jerry Sports Director
WEAI-FM, 644
Syms, Marcy Chief Executive Officer
SYMS, 1238
Syms, Sy Chairman
SYMS, 1238
Synovitz, Linda Graduate Coordinator
SOUTHEASTERN LOUISIANA UNIVERSITY, 432
Synowka, David Chairman/Program Head Sports Management
ROBERT MORRIS UNIVERSITY, 431
Sypher, Mike Sports Editor
CHRONICLE (CT), 470
Syreini, Cathy Advertising Manager
DAILY GLOBE (MI), 476
Syron, Tom Sales Director
ALUMINUM ATHLETIC EQUIPMENT COMPANY (AAE), 1096
Szafnauer, Otmar Team Chief
FORMULA 1, 20
Szarka, Ken Performance Coach
NATIONAL LACROSSE LEAGUE, 142
Szarowicz, Hilarie Marketing Manager
VAN ANDEL ARENA, 1015
Szott, David Director, Player Development
NATIONAL FOOTBALL LEAGUE/NFL, 96
Szul, Michael Senior Associate AD/Business Operations
WEST VIRGINIA UNIVERSITY/WVU COLISEUM, 1018
Szymanski, David Faculty Athletics Representative
MYRL H. SHOEMAKER CENTER, 988
Szymkoiwak, Mary Communications/Group Tour Specialist
DUBLIN CONVENTION & VISITOR BUREAU, 233

T

T, Phillips Director
FIRST PLUS SPORTS MARKETING, 783
T Akre jr, Charles Treasurer
NATIONAL SPORTING LIBRARY, THE, 256
T. A. Egan, Robert. Partner
EGAN, ROBERT T., 878
T. F. Smith, Mark Vice President, Sales
POINT BLANK SOLUTIONS, 1175
T. Riley Jr, William Managing Principal
RILEY, WILLIAM T., 852
T. Wyrick III, Samuel Lawyer
WYRICK, ROBBINS, YATES & PONTON, L.L.P., 917
True, Jeff Director, Marketing
LOS ALAMITOS RACE COURSE, 1041
Taaffe, Paul Chairman & Chief Executive Officer
HILL AND KNOWLTON PUBLIC RELATIONS, 787
Tabano, L. Producer
SPORTS PAGE, 685
Tabassi, Mahmoud Treasurer
AMERICAN AMATEUR KARATE FEDERATION, 142
Tabert, Eileen National VP, Admin. & Management
AMERICAN YOUTH SOCCER ORGANIZATION, 265
Tabler, Biggs President
GOLF MARKETING BY BIGGS, 599
Tabor, Dan Architect/Partner
THE COLLABORATIVE, INC.,, 1052
Tacelli, Carolyn Director of Finance
GRAHAM/MEUS, INC. ARCHITECTS, 1058
Tackett, Gary Advertising Director
CORVALLIS GAZETTE-TIMES, 473

Tackett, Julian Commissioner
KENTUCKY HS ATHLETIC ASSOCIATION, 200
Tackett, Shawn Head Athletic Trainer
LYON COLLEGE ATHLETICS, 315
Tad, Brown CEO
NATIONAL HOCKEY LEAGUE/NHL, 125
Tae, Michael Assistant Manager
DAEWOO INTERNATIONAL CORPORATION, 1224
Taffer, Jon Owner
SPIKE TV, 677
Taffin, Remi Technical Chief
FORMULA 1, 19
Tafrow, Chris General Manager
SOUTH ATLANTIC LEAGUE (A LEVEL), 51
Taft, Larry Sports Editor
TENNESSEAN, 538
Tager, Lee President
POOLMASTER, INC., 1175
Taggart, Rick President
SWISS ARMY BRANDS, INC., 1198
Tagilabue, Paul Consultant
NFL BUSINESS VENTURES, 798
Tagliaferri, John Director of Athletic Media Relations
CALDWELL UNIVERSITY ATHLETICS, 352
Tagliarino, David Deputy Athletics Director, External
HOUSTON ATHLETICS, UNIVERSITY OF, 332
Taglieri, Paul Executive Director
FLORIDA STATE LEAGUE, 39, 40, 1010
Tague, Rick President
BERNIER, CARR & ASSOCIATES, 1050
Tague, Rick President
BERNIER, CARR & ASSOCIATES, 1050
Tague, Trish Marketing Director
KWQC -TV6, 697
Tagyer, Jason News Director
WRCT-FM, 663
Tahsler, Steve Commissioner
FRONTIER LEAGUE OF PROFESSIONAL BASEBALL/INDEPENDENT LEAGUE, 40
Taila, Ray Head Coach
WOMEN'S PREMIER SOCCER LEAGUE, 168
Tainsh, Alex Marketing & Promotions Manager
AT&T FIELD, 947
Tait, Ron National Sales Manager
FLEXCO, 1134
Taitano, Haley Assoc. AD, External Relations & Sr. Wome
TURPIN STADIUM, 994, 1011
Takata, George Sports Anchor
KGPE-TV, 690
Takizawa, Kazuhiro President & CEO, Honda Motor Co.
AMERICAN HONDA MOTOR CO., 725
Talal, Sheikh World Bowling President
WORLD BOWLING, 66
Talalay, Sarah Sports Business Writer
SOUTH FLORIDA SUN-SENTINEL, 532
Talarico, Tom Sports Editor
WATERBURY REPUBLICAN-AMERICAN, 545
Talarico, Wendy Communications Manager
FAIRPLEX, 1025, 1038
Talavinia, Phil Athletics Director
BLUFFTON UNIVERSITY ATHLETICS, 378
Talbert, Britt Corporate Sales Manager
NORTHWEST BASEBALL LEAGUE, 47
Talbert, Terrie Department Manager
VIKING HALL CIVIC CENTER, 1016
Talboom, Lindsey Communications & Public Relations Coordi
SOUTH BEND/MISHAWAKA CONVENTION & VISITORS BUREAU, 264
Talbot, Bruce Head Coach/General Manager, Youth Dir. o
USL LEAGUE TWO, 162
Talbot, Josh Sports Editor
ATHOL DAILY NEWS, 462
Talbott, Greg Director of Broadcast/ Media Relations
TR HUGHES BALLPARK, 1010
Talbut, Greg Business Manager
SHOW ME CENTER, 1002
Talent, Kristen Sports Reporter
WAFF-TV, 698
Taliaferro, Judi Convention Services/National Accounts
HOUSTON SPORTS DIVISION/GREATER

HOUSTON CONVENTION & VISITORS BUR, 236
Taliaferro, Tricia Executive Director
USL LEAGUE TWO, 164
Tallas, Robb Goaltending Coach
NATIONAL HOCKEY LEAGUE/NHL, 124
Talley, Kevin Promotions Director
WSMI-AM, 666
Talley, Mike Facilities and Event Management
LINDSEY WILSON COLLEGE ATHLETICS, 315
Tallon, Mireille Program Coordinator
ITTF NORTH AMERICA, 173
Tam, Martin Treasurer
BADMINTON CANADA, 24
Tamajka, Angela Marketing Manager
TACOMA DOME, 1007
Tamaribuchi, Stephen President
BIOGRIP, INC., 1107
Tamaribuchis, Rebecca Chief Financial Officer
BIOGRIP, INC., 1107
Tambellini, Jeff Director, Player Development
NATIONAL HOCKEY LEAGUE/NHL, 125
Tambellini, Marla Interim Executive Director
ASHEVILLE CONVENTION & VISITORS BUREAU, 227
Tambone, Barbara VP Sales
CASCO/USA, 1114
Tambone, Peter President / Chief Executive Officer
CASCO/USA, 1114
Tamburro, Joe Program Director
WDAS-AM, 642
Tamburro, Mike Vice Chairman
INTERNATIONAL LEAGUE, 43
Tamiya, Jay Customer Service Supervisor
YONEX CORPORATION, 1212
Tammer, Erik Owner
USL LEAGUE TWO, 162
Tamplin, Harold Sales / National Accounts VP1
WELLINGTON LEISURE PRODUCTS, 1209
Tamraz, Cathy Chairman/Chief Executive Officer
SPORTSWIRE/BUSINESS WIRE, 714
Tamura, Mike President
JUDO CANADA, 143
Tanaka, Dwight Director, Operations
GRAND PRIX ASSOCIATION OF LONG BEACH, 16
Tandel, Marzieh Account Receivables, Compte Clients
ELBY GIFTS, 1128
Tanenbaum, Joe Director, Communications
GULFSTREAM RACING & CASINO PARK, 1039
Tangquist, Jason Assistant Athletic Director
MINNESOTA-CROOKSTON ATHLETICS, UNIVERSITY OF (UMC), 364
Tanguay, Alexa Assistant Coach
NATIONAL HOCKEY LEAGUE/NHL, 124
Tanguay, Alexandre Co-Owner & Governor
QUEBEC MARITIMES MAJOR JUNIOR HOCKEY LEAGUE, 135
Tanner, Ernst Sporting Director
MAJOR LEAGUE SOCCER, 158
Tanner, Hugh Chairman
LITTLE LEAGUE BASEBALL AND SOFTBALL, 27
Tanner, Mike Executive Vice President
U.S. TROTTING ASSOCIATION, 77
Tanner, Nancy Office Manager
TOWN TALK CAP MFG. COMPANY, INC., 1202
Tanner, Nikki Group Sales Director
FAIRMOUNT PARK RACETRACK, 1038
Tanner, Ray Athletics Director
SOUTH CAROLINA ATHLETICS, UNIVERSITY OF, 344, 1019
Tanner, Sterling President/Executive Director
FOREVER YOUNG FOUNDATION, 191
Tanney, Matt Director of Athletics
WESTERN HALL, 974, 1018
Tansey, David Advertising Manager
WATERLOO-CEDAR FALLS COURIER, 545
Tanton, Bill Senior Associate Editor
LACROSSE MAGAZINE, 568
Taormina, Rick Senior Vice President
L. ROBERT KIMBALL & ASSOCIATES, 1061
Tappa, Steve Sports Reporter
DISPATCH (IL), 484

executive index

Wallace, Kendal Assistant Athletic Director
LA GRANGE COLLEGE ATHLETICS, 389

Wallace, Kendra Director of Sports and Training
SPECIAL OLYMPICS WEST VIRGINIA, 197

Wallace, Lloyd Sports Editor
LUDINGTON DAILY NEWS, 504

Wallace, Lowell Account Director, Strategy
RADIAN 1, 805

Wallace, Michael Marketing Manager
SCHOLASTIC COACH & ATHLETIC
DIRECTOR MAGAZINE, 579

Wallace, Nancy Promoter
FAIRBANKS RACING LIONS, 1025

Wallace, Peter Director of Ticketing
DURHAM BULLS ATHLETIC PARK, 963

Wallace, Phillip Athletic Director
MILES COLLEGE ATHLETICS, 364

Wallace, Richard Advertising Manager
VALLEY NEWS, 543

Wallace, Rick Advertising Director
HERALD JOURNAL, 493

Wallace, Robert Faculty Athletics Representative
MCMURRY UNIVERSITY ATHLETICS, 393

Wallace, Roger Sports Director
KXAM-TV, 697

Wallace, Wayne Treasurer
WOMEN'S OCEAN RACING SAILING
ASSOCIATION, 64

Wallace, Wes Promoter
FAIRBANKS RACING LIONS, 1025

Wallace-Hetzel, Circe Sports Agent
IMS SPORTS, 838

Wallach, George President
WALLACH ENTERTAINMENT, 603, 859

Wallack, Roy Outdoor Editor
SPORTS EDGE MAGAZINE, 585

Wallens, David Editor
GRASSROOTS MOTORSPORTS, 562

Waller, Al Commissioner/Secretary/Treasurer
MIDLANDS COLLEGIATE ATHLETIC
CONFERENCE, 299

Waller, Kristin Associate AD of Student-Athlete
Services
KANSAS STATE UNIVERSITY ATHLETICS,
333

Wallgren, Jackie Associate Athletic Director
UNIVERSITY OF SOUTHERN COLORADO
ATHLETICS, 324, 370

Wallin, Fred Host
SPORTS BIZ, 609

Wallin, Jon Sports Information Director
MARY HARDIN-BAYLOR ATHLETICS(UMHB),
392

Wallin, Terrence Head Coach & General Manager
EAST COAST HOCKEY LEAGUE/ECHL, 130

Wallington, Mark Media Relations
LAS VEGAS BOWL, 91

Wallis, Gabriel Sports Information
Director/Webmaster
MID-CENTRAL COLLEGE CONFERENCE, 299

Walljasper, Joe Sports Editor
COLUMBIA DAILY TRIBUNE, 471

Walls, Caroline Event Coordinator
TEXAS UNIVERSITY INTERSCHOLASTIC
LEAGUE, 202

Walls, Jeremy Chief Operating Officer
NATIONAL FOOTBALL LEAGUE/NFL, 94, 1007

Walls, Rick Vice President
INTERNATIONAL SPORTS HERITAGE
ASSOCIATION, 254

Walls, Robert Executive Vice President/General
Counsel
CLEAR CHANNEL ENTERTAINMENT, INC.,
687

Walrath, Gary Chief Executive Officer
STATS LLC, 687, 714, 929

Walsch, Tina Office Manager
REVERE PLASTICS, INC., 1182

Walseth, Natalie Assistant Athletic Director for
New Medi
ST. OLAF COLLEGE ATHLETICS, 401

Walsh, Bob President/Chief Executive Officer
WALSH ENTERPRISES , BOB, 765

Walsh, Brad Facility Manager
ODEUM EXPO CENTER, 990

Walsh, Brian Partner
WEBB, WILLIAM Y., 914

Walsh, Carrie Interim Chief Executive Officer
SUBWAY RESTAURANTS, 733

Walsh, Connor Manager, Programs & Events
SPOKANE HOOPFEST, 55

Walsh, Darrell Associate Athletic Director
UNIVERSITY OF CENTRAL ARKANSAS
ATHLETICS, 354

Walsh, David Deputy Athletic Director
ROBINS STADIUM, 998

Walsh, Donnie President of Basketball Operations
KAUFFMAN SPORTS MANAGEMENT GROUP,
840

Walsh, Geoff Handicapper
WESTERN AUSTRALIA BLIND GOLF
ASSOCIATION, 118

Walsh, James Chief Information Security Officer
TANGENT ASSOCIATES, INC., 1068

Walsh, Joe Senior VP, People & Culture
NATIONAL LEAGUE OF PROFESSIONAL
BASEBALL CLUBS, THE, 31

Walsh, John Managing Editor
GOLF COURSE NEWS, 561

Walsh, John President
VELVETOP PRODUCTS, 1207

Walsh, Kevin Director of Events
SOLDIER FIELD, 1004

Walsh, Lana Administrative Assistant
ITHACA COLLEGE, 421

Walsh, Larry Snowsports Reporter
PITTSBURGH POST-GAZETTE, 520

Walsh, Lenore Director of Athletics
STATE UNIVERSITY OF NEW YORK
COLLEGE AT OLD WESTBURY
ATHLETICS(SU, 402

Walsh, Linda Secretary / Treasurer
VELVETOP PRODUCTS, 1207

Walsh, Maggie Associate Vice President,
Marketing
AECOM, 1048

Walsh, Marty Executive Director
NATIONAL HOCKEY LEAGUE PLAYERS'
ASSOCIATION/NHLPA, 122

Walsh, Michael President
NATARE CORPORATION, 1166

Walsh, Michelle Director of Athletics
VASSAR COLLEGE ATHLETICS, 404

Walsh, Quentin SVP/Corporate Controller
TOMMY HILFIGER, 1239

Walsh, Sharon Advertising Manager
SKI AREA MANAGEMENT, 580

Walsh, Todd Sports Director
KDKB-FM, 616

Walsh, William Director
ARIZONA DEPARTMENT OF RACING, 227

Walsh, Wendy Assistant Athletic Director
WORCESTER POLYTECHNIC INSTITUTE
ATHLETICS, 408

Walter, Andy Sports Editor
DELAWARE STATE NEWS, 482

Walter, Christa Retail Brand Manager
VISION FITNESS, 1208

Walter, Gerri Marketing & Communications
Director
SPECIAL OLYMPICS RHODE ISLAND, 197

Walter, Greg Assistant Commissioner for
Institutional
MISSOURI VALLEY CONFERENCE, 88, 300,
1022

Walter, Kristy Director of Athletics
LASELL COLLEGE ATHLETICS, 390

Walter, Mark Chair/Owner
NATIONAL LEAGUE OF PROFESSIONAL
BASEBALL CLUBS, THE, 31

Walter, Olivia Director of Broadcast Services
ATLANTIC SUN CONFERENCE, 291

Walter, Terry Sports Director
KCOB-AM, 615

Walter, Zach Assistant General Manager
SAN JOSE MUNICIPAL STADIUM, 1001

Walters, Allen Publisher
AVID GOLFER MAGAZINE, 551

Walters, Brodie Senior Director of Museum
Operations
WORLD GOLF VILLAGE, 119

Walters, Chris Program Director
KWFS-FM, 631

Walters, Cindi VP
CHAPMAN WALTERS INTERCOASTAL
GROUP, 1222

Walters, Daryn Director of Marketing
EXMARK MANUFACTURING, 1131

Walters, Dave Sports Inforamtion Director
GUILFORD COLLEGE ATHLETICS, 386

Walters, Fred Publisher
LIVING ABOARD MAGAZINE, 568

Walters, Gary Athletic Director
JADWIN GYMNASIUM, 975

Walters, Greg Head Coach
ONTARIO HOCKEY LEAGUE, 135

Walters, Greg Global COO
BAKER & MCKENZIE, 863

Walters, Jamie Executive Vice President, Sales
CLUBCORP, 100

Walters, Jim Executive Vice President & CFO
SAFWAY SERVICES, LLC, 1185

Walters, Joey Deputy Executive Director
ARKANSAS ACTIVITIES ASSOCIATION, 199

Walters, John Sports Director
WOI-TV, 707

Walters, Kyle General Manager
CANADIAN FOOTBALL LEAGUE/CFL, 93

Walters, Mitch Assistant Athletics Director
CUMBERLAND UNIVERSITY ATHLETICS, 311

Walters, Nick Head Coach
NORTH AMERICAN HOCKEY LEAGUE, 132

Walters, Rex Men's Baskebtall Head Coach
SAN FRANCISCO, UNIVERSITY OF, 432

Walters, Roger Commissioner
NATIONAL INTERCOLLEGIATE RODEO
ASSOCIATION (NIRA), 146

Walters, W. Seed Production Manager
DLF INTERNATIONAL SEEDS, 1224

Walther, Chip Sales VP
RIDDELL ATHLETIC FOOTWEAR, 1182

Walther, Jim Chair
ALBUQUERQUE SPORTS COUNCIL, 227

Walton, Craig Advertising Manager
WQKT-FM, 654, 662

Walton, Glenn Vice President
NEW HAMPSHIRE GOLF ASSOCIATION, 114

Walton, Karl Finance Executive
PRO ORTHOPEDIC DEVICES, INC., 1177

Walton, Peter President/Chief Executive Officer
INTERNATIONAL ASSOCIATION OF GOLF
TOUR OPERATORS, 102

Walton, Robson Chairman
WAL-MART STORES, INC., 1240

Walton, Ron General Manager
WFNR, 646

Walton, Tim Founder
INTEGRITY SPORTS PLAYER
MANAGEMENT, 838

Walts, Cory Fitness Center Director
HAVERFORD COLLEGE ATHLETICS, 387

Waltz, Aaron PGA Golf Management Director
FERRIS STATE UNIVERSITY/PROFESSIONAL
GOLF MANAGEMENT PROGRAM, 101

Waltz, Thomas President (F.J. Westcott Co.)
HAAS-JORDAN COMPANY, 1141

Waluszko, Laura News Director
WZVN-FM, 673

Walz, Bob Chief Operating Officer
FLAIR COMMUNICATIONS, 783

Walz, Gregor Director of Athletic Communications
UNIVERSITY OF PUGET SOUND, 397

Walz, Liz Executive Editor
BOATING INDUSTRY, 553

Walz, Ryan Physical Education/Religion
SIMMONS FIELD, 1002

Wampler, Karen Public Relations Director
HARA ARENA, 969

Wampler, Kimberly Event Coordinator
HARA ARENA, 969

Wan, Karen Manager, Financial Services
CANADIAN CURLING ASSOCIATION, 69

Wan, Tracey Vice Chairman / Chief Operating
Officer
SHARPER IMAGE, 1237

Wanat, Don President
FGX DIRECT LLC., 1132

Wandell, Chris Director, Business Development
PGA TOUR, 108

Wandishin, Michael Racing Secretary
ROSECROFT RACEWAY, 1043

Wandling, Gene EVP/Chief Financial Officer
LICENSING RESOURCE GROUP, INC., 793

Wang, Liwei Honorary Vice President
WORLD POOL BILLIARD ASSOCIATION, 62

Wang, Phil Senior Associate AD, External Affairs
UC IRVINE ATHLETICS, 347

executive index

Williams, Faith Administrative Partner
BRICKER & ECKLER, 868

Williams, Flo Manager of Facilities & Grounds
ALEX BOX STADIUM, 945

Williams, Francine Managing Partner
NATIONAL PRO FASTPITCH, 171

Williams, Gary Director of Athletics & Recreation
WITTENBERG UNIVERSITY ATHLETICS, 408, 657

Williams, George President
UNITED STATES DRESSAGE FOUNDATION, 77

Williams, George Athletic Director
ST. AUGUSTINE'S UNIVERSITY ATHLETICS, 371

Williams, Gloria Advertising Manager
CULPEPER STAR-EXPONENT, 474

Williams, Grant First Vice President
NATIONAL BASKETBALL PLAYERS ASSOCIATION/NBPA, 54

Williams, Gregg Treasurer
OVER-THE-LINE PLAYERS ASSOCIATION, 170

Williams, H. Director of Athletics
CALIFORNIA MEMORIAL STADIUM, 954

Williams, Henry Sr.Director of Facility Operations
MARTINSVILLE SPEEDWAY, 1028

Williams, Jack Senior Vice President
EXXON MOBIL CORPORATION, 727

Williams, James Sports Editor
TEXARKANA GAZETTE, 538

Williams, Jason Associate Athletic Dir., Comms. & Brandi
CAMPBELL UNIVERSITY ATHLETICS, 326

Williams, Jeff Director of Athletics
EAST CENTRAL UNIVERSITY ATHLETICS, 357, 588

Williams, Jennifer College Sports Reporter
DAILY PRESS (VA), 478

Williams, Jerry President
SCHUYLKILL VALLEY SPORTS, 1236

Williams, Jim Athletic Trainer
NJCAA REGION XIII WOMEN'S, 288

Williams, Joe Sports Reporter
ORLANDO SENTINEL, 516

Williams, John CenterLines Editor
NATIONAL CENTER FOR BICYCLING & WALKING (NCBW), 70

Williams, John General Manager
WSRN-FM, 667

Williams, Jolisa Sports Information Director
SHAW UNIVERSITY ATHLETICS, 369

Williams, Jon National Sales Manager
E&D SPECIALTY STANDS INC., 1126

Williams, Joseph Chair
NATIONAL LEAGUE OF PROFESSIONAL BASEBALL CLUBS, THE, 31

Williams, Justin Director of Ticket Operations
NEW YORK-PENNSYLVANIA LEAGUE, 46, 1004

Williams, Karen Executive Vice President
GREATER LOUISVILLE CONVENTION & VISITORS BUREAU, 235

Williams, Keith Sales Manager
WTLX-FM, 668

Williams, Ken President
DIALGLOBAL, INC., 220, 604

Williams, Kevin Treasurer
WOMEN'S GOLF COACHES ASSOCIATION, 118

Williams, Kimberly CFO
NFL BUSINESS VENTURES, 798

Williams, Kirk VP Of Strategic Analysis & Development
ESCALADE SPORTS, 1130

Williams, Larry Chief Operating Officer
RAPIDTRON, 237, 822

Williams, Lavon Chairman/Associate Professor
GUILFORD COLLEGE, 420

Williams, Leisa Accounting Executive
A-B EMBLEM, 1089

Williams, Lesa Assistant General Manager
RICHMOND COLISEUM, 997

Williams, Linda Sales Manager
TUF-WEAR, 342, 1204

Williams, Lisa Vice President
GEORGIA HS ASSOCIATION, 199

Williams, Lori Deputy Athletics Director, Leadership &

LOUISIANA AT MONROE ATHLETICS, UNIVERSITY OF, 335

Williams, LuWanna Associate Director of Athletics
FORT VALLEY STATE UNIVERSITY ATHLETICS (FVSU), 359

Williams, Luther President
TUSKEGEE UNIVERSITY, 1011

Williams, Marcus Vice President
STRATEGIC RESOURCES, 749

Williams, Marianne National Sales Manager/Special Events
970 WATH, 605

Williams, Marilyn Founder
WOMEN'S FOOTBALL ALLIANCE / WFA, 97

Williams, Matt Executive Director
GEORGIA STATE GOLF ASSOCIATION, 101

Williams, McK Associate Athletic Director
RUTGERS ATHLETIC CENTER, 1000

Williams, Michael Partner
FRANKFURT, KURNIT, KLEIN & SELZ, P.C., 881

Williams, Mitchell Sports Director
WDAM-TV, 701

Williams, Mori President
APPALACHIAN LEAGUE, 33

Williams, Nancy Managing Partner
PERKINS COIE LAW FIRM, 899

Williams, Neil Professor/Chair
EASTERN CONNECTICUT STATE UNIVERSITY, 417

Williams, Nicholas Athletics Communications Director
ROGER WILLIAMS UNIVERSITY ATHLETICS, 399

Williams, Nicole Director of Finance
USF SUN DOME, 1014

Williams, Preston CEO
GWINNETT SPORTS COMMISSION, 235

Williams, Ragan Event Director/State Games
NORTH CAROLINA AMATEUR SPORTS, 242

Williams, Ray Director of Sports Facilities
ERIE INSURANCE ARENA, 964

Williams, Richard Director of Athletics
ALBANY STATE COLLEGE ATHLETICS, 350

Williams, Richie Head Coach
USL LEAGUE ONE, 161

Williams, Rob Vice President
U.S. LIFESAVING ASSOCIATION, 173

Williams, Robert Director
USGA MUSEUM AND LIBRARY, 259

Williams, Robert Partner-International Tax Dept
NORONHA-ADVOGADOS CONSULTING, 897

Williams, Robin Management Committee Member
BASSFORD, LOCKHART, TRUESDELL & BRIGGS, P.A., 864

Williams, Rodney Assistant Director of Sports
SPECIAL OLYMPICS DC, 194

Williams, Roger Drag Racing Director
SACRAMENTO RACEWAY PARK (DRAGSTRIP/MX), 1032

Williams, Rosemary Director of Racing
MOUNTAINEER CASINO, RACE TRACK & RESORT, 1041

Williams, Ryan Sports Director
YAHOO! SPORTS RADIO, 604

Williams, Ryun Head Coach, Women's Basketball
MOBY ARENA, 987

Williams, Sam President
ATLANTA SPORTS COUNCIL, 227

Williams, Sandye Director of Marketing and Development
SPECIAL OLYMPICS SOUTH CAROLINA, 197

Williams, Scott Sports Reporter
STEVENS POINT JOURNAL, 535

Williams, Shane President/Chief Executive Officer
FELLOWSHIP OF CHRISTIAN ATHLETES, 220

Williams, Sharon Executive Associate
PROVOST UMPHREY STADIUM, 994

Williams, Stephen Sports Information Director
COLUMBUS STATE UNIVERSITY ATHLETICS (CSU), 355

Williams, Steve Senior Director, Player Personnel
NATIONAL LEAGUE OF PROFESSIONAL BASEBALL CLUBS, THE, 32, 589

Williams, Susan Secretary
PALM BEACH ATLANTIC UNIVERSITY, 236, 431

Williams, Tad Marketing Director
SPONSORWISE, 634, 761

Williams, Thom Station and General Sales Manager
970 WATH, 605

Williams, Todd Vice President
ACE MITCHELL BOWLERS MART, 1091

Williams, Travis President
NATIONAL LEAGUE OF PROFESSIONAL BASEBALL CLUBS, THE, 32

Williams, Yolanda CFO
YOUTH DEVELOPMENT/A DIVISION OF THE NATIONAL ALLIANCE FOR YOUTH S, 266

Williams-Eggen, Carey Media Relations/Web Site Director
MASSACHUSETTS STATE COLLEGE ATHLETIC CONFERENCE, 298

Williamson, Andee Marketing Manager
NCR, 1167

Williamson, Bill Advertising Director
NORTH COUNTY TIMES, 514

Williamson, Cliff Director of Health & Regulatory Affairs
AMERICAN HORSE COUNCIL, 73

Williamson, Connie Advertising Manager
KPIC-TV, 693

Williamson, Jane Secretary and Hospitality
GEORGIA AAU ASSOCIATION, 214

Williamson, Jared Associate Athletic Director - Chicago
ROBERT MORRIS COLLEGE (IL) ATHLETICS, 319

Williamson, Kenny Chairman
SPECIAL OLYMPICS MISSISSIPPI, 195

Williamson, Mark Manager Of Marketing Operations
SPORTSEARCH, INC., 748

Williamson, Marty General Manager/Head Coach
ONTARIO HOCKEY LEAGUE, 133

Williamson, Norby Managing Editor
BASEBALL TONIGHT, 682

Williamson, Percy Director
DAYTONA BEACH LEISURE SERVICES, 961

Williamson, Stan Director of Athletics
WEST ALABAMA ATHLETICS, UNIVERSITY OF, 374

Williamson, Steve Athletic Director
IOWA WESLEYAN COLLEGE ATHLETICS, 388

Williard, Dewey Finance Director
LAWRENCE JOEL VETERANS MEMORIAL COLISEUM, 982

Williford, Glynn Account Executive / Sponsor Relations
MEMPHIS MOTORSPORTS PARK (MMP), 1028

Williford, Sherry Executive Producer
SPORTS TALK, 606

Willig, Petra Track Sales Manager
LIME ROCK PARK, 1027

Willingham, Gayle President
NATIONAL DEAF WOMEN'S BOWLING ASSOCIATION, 66

Willingham, Janet Recruiting Department Administrator
SPORTS DISPLAY, 810

Willis, Bob Deputy AD, Community & Diversity
DENVER ATHLETICS, UNIVERSITY OF, 328, 526

Willis, Bobby Vice President
ALL STAR KNITWEAR, INC., 1095

Willis, Dartis President & CEO
NATIONAL BASKETBALL LEAGUE OF CANADA, 58

Willis, Fred Owner
QUANTUM ROCK ENTERPRISES, 1179

Willis, George Sports Columnist
NEW YORK POST, 510

Willis, James Sports Reporter
TRIBUNE-STAR, 541

Willis, Jimmy Secretary/Treasurer
ALL STAR KNITWEAR, INC., 1095

Willis, Ken Sports Columnist
DAYTONA BEACH NEWS-JOURNAL, 481

Willis, Kevin Sports Director
WSFN-AM, 666

Willis, Lenny Director of Facilities
MEMORIAL STADIUM (ILLINOIS), 986

Willis, Lisa President
SAFEGUARD FLOOR SYSTEMS, 1185

Executive Index

Wines, April Associate AD/SWA
HIGH POINT UNIVERSITY ATHLETICS, 332

Winfield, Mickey Sports Director
KBIM-TV, 688

Winfrey, Chris Chairman and CEO
CHARTER COMMUNICATIONS, 727

Wingard, Adrien Events & Promotion Coordinator
ADAMS CENTER, 945

Wingate, Suzanne Coordinator
SUNY, STATE UNIVERSITY OF NEW
YORK-CORTLAND, 434

Wingen, Corey Head Athletic Trainer
VIRGINIA WESLEYAN COLLEGE
ATHLETICS(VWC), 404

Wingo, Barbara Associate Vice President and
Deputy Gene
BERNARD, PAMELA J., 865

Wingo, Trey Host
NFL 2NIGHT, 683, 684

Winiecki, Alexander Store Operations EVP
BROOKSTONE COMPANY, 1220

Winkel, Vicki VP of Business Development
FRONTIER LEAGUE, 41

Winkeler, Les Sports Editor
SOUTHERN ILLINOISAN, 532

Winkelfoos, Natalie Director of Athletics
OBERLIN COLLEGE ATHLETICS, 396

Winkler, Bill Chief Financial Officer/Chief
Operating
ACKERMAN MCQUEEN ADVERTISING, 1048

Winkler, Matt Associate Dean of MPS Sports
Industry Ma
GEORGETOWN UNIVERSITY, 419

Winklevoss, Howard Chairman
WINTECH RACING, 1210

Winmill, Candace Executive Administrative
Assistant
UTAH VALLEY CONVENTION & VISITORS
BUREAU, 248

Winn, Kevin Director of Umpires
AMERICAN ASSOCIATION OF INDEPENDENT
PROFESSIONAL BASEBALL, 33

Winn, Luke General Manager
NATIONAL BASKETBALL ASSOCIATION
DEVELOPMENT LEAGUE, 59

Winn, Mike Associate Athletics Director
PACE UNIVERSITY ATHLETICS, 367

Winner, Amy Marketing
POCOCK RACING SHELLS, 1175

Winner, Reggie Managing Editor
CALIFORNIA HOCKEY & SKATING, 554

Winnicker, Alex Interim Director of Athletics
ST. JOSEPH'S COLLEGE (NY) ATHLETICS,
401

Winske, Thomas Baseball Coach
SAINT NORBERT COLLEGE ATHLETICS, 399

Winslow, Adam EVP & Chief Marketing Officer
EAST COAST HOCKEY LEAGUE/ECHL, 129

Winslow, Frances Vice President of Human
Resources
VARIETY WHOLESALERS, 1240

Winslow, Warren Second Vice President
NEW YORK STATE GOLF ASSOCIATION, 114

Winstanley, John General Manager
ONTARIO HOCKEY LEAGUE, 134

Winstead, Ken Senior Associate AD,
Development
OHIO UNIVERSITY ATHLETICS, 340

Winstead, Perry Chief Financial Officer
LIBERTY BOWL MEMORIAL STADIUM, 983

Winstead, Richard Vice President
CENTRAL NEW YORK PGA SECTIONAL
OFFICE, 105

Winston, Chris Pro General Manager Director
KZEP SPORTS RADIO, 633

Winston, Edie President
ALL PRO EXERCISE PRODUCTS, INC., 1095

Winston, Matt Assistant Director, College
Scouting
NATIONAL FOOTBALL LEAGUE/NFL, 95

Winston, Scott President
ALL PRO EXERCISE PRODUCTS, INC., 1095

Winter, Kathy Asst. Skating Director
TBSA, 1062

Winter, Nick Engineering Executive
KLAY, 622

Winter, Ronald Dept. Associate Professor
WESTERN MICHIGAN UNIVERSITY, 437

Winter, Steve President/Chief Operating Officer
BROTMAN WINTER FRIED
COMMUNICATIONS, INC., 751

Winters, Melanie Associate Editor
SOUNDINGS:TRADE ONLY, 582

Winters, Patrick Senior Associate
NBBJ, 1061

Winters, Scott Director
EKTELON, 1128

Winters, Thomas Commissioner
OHIO STATE RACING COMMISSION, 81

Winters, Tom Chairman
FLORIDA STATE LEAGUE, 39, 1004

Winters, Tony General Manager
MABEE CENTER ARENA, 984

Winterton, Scott Athletic Relations
SOUTHERN VIRGINIA UNIVERSITY
ATHLETICS, 401

Winther, Hakon Founder
PLAYER HISTORY.COM, 929

Winzenread, Steve Sports Editor
INDEPENDENT TRIBUNE, 496

Wire, Adam Sports Editor
CHRONICLE-TRIBUNE, 470

Wirkus, Shari News Director
KSDR-AM, 628

Wirnsberger, Dan President - EIWA Coaches
Association
EASTERN INTERCOLLEGIATE WRESTLING
ASSOCIATION, 180

Wirski, Jim Advertising Manager
TIMES-HERALD, 540

Wirth, Marcus Assistant Athletics Director
UNIVERSITY OF CALIFORNIA SANTA CRUZ
ATHLETICS, 309, 379

Wirth, Michael Chairman and CEO
CHEVRON CORPORATION, 727

Wirtz, Danny Chair & CEO
NATIONAL HOCKEY LEAGUE/NHL, 124

Wirz, Bob Founder/President
WIRZ & ASSOCIATES, 765

Wise, Jacob Director of Media/Broadcasting
ROCKFORD AVIATORS, 998

Wise, James Chief Financial Officer/Treasurer
VERNON DOWNS, 1045

Wise, Jeff Sales
KESSLERS SPORT SHOP, INC., 1231

Wise, Lonie National Sales Manager
FIBERESIN INDUSTRIES, INC., 1132

Wise, Mark CEO
WOMEN'S PREMIER SOCCER LEAGUE, 165

Wise, Robby Director of Sports Medicine
WINGATE UNIVERSITY ATHLETICS, 375

Wise, Tim Associate Athletic Director
MILLSAPS COLLEGE ATHLETICS (MCA), 393

Wise, Trudy Manager, Sales and Services
CMS SPORTS, 1223

Wiseman, Howard Chief Executive Officer
MERCURY INTERNATIONAL CORPORATION,
1162

Wiseman, Irving Chairman / Founder
MERCURY INTERNATIONAL CORPORATION,
1162

Wiseman, Kevin Sports Editor
ATHENS MESSENGER, 462

Wisener, Bob Sports Editor
SENTINEL-RECORD, 530

Wiser, Elliott General Manager
SPORTS CONNECTION, 685

Wish, Sheri Chief Revenue Officer
ROSE BOWL, 92

Wisler, Gwen President / Chief Executive Officer
EASTPAK CORPORATION, 1127

Wisniewski, Robert Athletic Director
NJCAA REGION XIX MEN'S, 288

Wisniewski, Robert Of Counsel
BLACK, WILLIAM D., LAW OFFICES OF, 866

Wissing, Diane Assistant Compliance Officer
UNIVERSITY OF HAWAII AT HILO (UHH)
ATHLETIC, 360

Wissing, Erin Sr. Assoc. AD/Director of Athletics
Deve
FURMAN UNIVERSITY ATHLETICS, 330

Wissing, Jake Co-Sports Information Director
UNIVERSITY OF WISCONSIN - RIVER FALLS
ATHLETICS (UW-RIVER FALLS), 407

Wissmiller, Brock Assistant Athletic Director
UPPER IOWA UNIVERSITY ATHLETICS(UIU);
373

Wistrcill, Tom Director of Athletics
JAMES A. RHODES ARENA, 975

Witcher, Debra Owner
KACQ-FM, 612

Witcher, Ronald General Manager
KCYL-AM, 615

Witcher, Ronnie General Manager
KACQ-FM, 612

Withelder, Geno Vice President
SOUTHERN NEVADA GOLF ASSOCIATION,
116

Withers, Bud Sports Reporter
SEATTLE TIMES, 530

Witherspoon, Larry Chief Executive Officer
TICKETS.COM, 933

Witlin, Barry President
WITLIN PROFESSIONAL MANAGEMENT, 860

Witosky, Tom Sports Writer (Football)
DES MOINES REGISTER, 483

Witte, Cees President, Spyder Europe AG
SPYDER ACTIVE SPORTS, 1195

Witte, Eileen Vice President
WOMEN'S GOLF ASSOCIATION OF
BALTIMORE, 118

Witte, Jack President
WITTE GROUP, 1211

Witte, Kate Senior Woman Administrator
OHIO NORTHERN UNIVERSITY
ATHLETICS(ONU), 396

Witte, Mark Sales Representative
WITTE GROUP, 1211

Witte, Mike Sales Representative
WITTE GROUP, 755, 1211

Witte, Randy Publisher
WESTERN HORSEMAN, 592

Wittek, Pat Secretary / Treasurer
WITTEK GOLF SUPPLY COMPANY, 1211

Wittenberg, Curtis Assistant Athletic Director for
Operatio
FINLANDIA UNIVERSITY (FU) ATHLETICS,
384

Wittenwyler, Grant Golf Director
ALL PRO SPORTS & ENTERTAINMENT, 824

Wittman, Gary Technical Director
SPEED SKATELUBE, 1192

Wittmer, Rod Vice-President
KANSAS STATE HS ACTIVITIES
ASSOCIATION, 200

Wittner, J.R. Sports Editor
MISSISSIPPI PRESS, 507

Wittrock, Tony Sales Director
STANLEY COVELESKI REGIONAL STADIUM,
1005

Wittry, Dennis Principal/Managing Director
WALTER P MOORE, 1063

Wittwer, Tony SVP / Chief Marketing Officer
AMERICAN SPECIALTY INSURANCE & RISK
SERVICES, INC., 773

Witz, Elise News Director
WSBU-FM, 665

Witz, Jennifer Chief Executive Officer
SIRIUS XM RADIO, 732

Witzel, Joss Director Of Operations
HDS PROMOTIONAL MARKETING, 787

Wixey, Bill Sports Anchor
KCPQ-TV, 688

Wlezien, Chris Interim Director of Compliance
IWIRELESS CENTER, 974

Wnek, Bill Associate AD, Compliance
LOYOLA UNIVERSITY MARYLAND
ATHLETICS, 335

Wochnick, Megan Sports Reporter
OLYMPIAN, 516

Wodarczyk, Mark News Director
KDUZ-AM, 616

Wodlinger, Kevin Marketing Manager
KKNN-FM, 621

Wodraska, Lya Sports Writer
SALT LAKE TRIBUNE, 527

Woebkenberg, Thomas Lawyer
WOOD & LAMPING LLP, 916

Wofford, Henry Sports Director
WZZM-TV, 713

Wofford, Jon Sports Director
KLKN-TV, 691

Wofford, Peter Editor
ARIZONA, THE STATE OF GOLF, 550

Wogan, Jim Sports Director
WATE - 6 WATE, 699

JUNEAU CONVENTION & VISITORS BUREAU, 237
JUNEAU EMPIRE, 499
KBYR - TALK 700, 614
KENAI RIVER BROWN BEARS, 132
KETCHIKAN DAILY NEWS, 500
KJNO-AM, 621
KTUU-TV, 695
KTZN-AM, 630
MITCHELL RACEWAY, 1029
MUSHING MAGAZINE, 572
SPECIAL OLYMPICS ALASKA, 194
SULLIVAN ARENA, 1006
TWIN CITY RACEWAY, 1035
UAA SPORTS ARENA, 1012
UNIVERSITY OF ALASKA ANCHORAGE ATHLETICS, 350
UNIVERSITY OF ALASKA FAIRBANKS ATHLETICS, 373
UNIVESRITY OF ALASKA FAIRBANKS ATHLETICS, 373
UNVIERSITY OF ALASKA ANCHORAGE ATHLETICS, 350
VISIT ANCHORAGE, 249

ARIZONA

A.V. CONCEPTS, 819
AEROBICS AND FITNESS ASSOCIATION OF AMERICA, 82
ALBANESE/BROOKS/ASSOCIATES P.C., 1049
ANTIGUA GROUP, INC., 1099
ANTIOCH SPORTS, 1099
ARI-MED PHARMACEUTICALS, 1100
ARIZONA ANGELS, 34
ARIZONA ATHLETICS, 34
ARIZONA ATHLETICS, UNIVERSITY OF, 324
ARIZONA BREWERS, 34
ARIZONA CARDINALS, 94
ARIZONA CUBS, 34
ARIZONA DAILY STAR, 461
ARIZONA DAILY SUN, 461
ARIZONA DEPARTMENT OF RACING, 79, 119, 227
ARIZONA DIAMONDBACKS, 31, 34
ARIZONA DODGERS, 34
ARIZONA EXPOSITION & STATE FAIR, 1035
ARIZONA FALL LEAGUE (ROOKIE LEVEL), 34
ARIZONA FALL LEAGUE (ROOKIE), 34
ARIZONA GIANTS, 34
ARIZONA GOLF ASSOCIATION, 109
ARIZONA INDIANS, 34
ARIZONA INTERSCHOLASTIC ASSOCIATION, 199
ARIZONA LEAGUE (ROOKIE), 34, 35
ARIZONA MARINERS, 34
ARIZONA PADRES, 34
ARIZONA RANGERS, 35
ARIZONA RATTLERS, 93
ARIZONA REDS, 35
ARIZONA REGIONAL COMMISSIONER/USA VOLLEYBALL, 210
ARIZONA REPUBLIC, 461
ARIZONA ROYALS, 35
ARIZONA STADIUM, 947
ARIZONA STATE UNIVERSITY, 410
ARIZONA STATE UNIVERSITY ATHLETICS, 324
ARIZONA WHITE SOX, 35
ARIZONA WOMEN'S GOLF ASSOCIATION, 109
ARIZONA, THE STATE OF GOLF, 550
ASCENSION, 1100
ASSOCIATION OF GOLF MERCHANDISERS, 100
ASSOCIATION OF PROFESSIONAL BALL PLAYERS OF AMERICA, 26
BISBEE DAILY REVIEW, 465
BLACK, WILLIAM D., LAW OFFICES OF, 866
BLADES ON ICE, 552
CACTUS BOWL, 90
CANTOR, DAVID MICHAEL P.C., LAW OFFICES OF, 871
CANYON SPEEDWAY, 1023
CASA GRANDE DISPATCH, 468
CASTAWAY COLLECTIBLES, 1114
CHASE FIELD BALL PARK, 957
CLARKE, ALLEN R., 828
COLLEGIATE BASEBALL, 555
CORE DIGITAL, 598
COX SPORTS/CHANNEL 9, 687
DAILY COURIER (AZ), 476

DAILY DISPATCH, 476
DAILY NEWS SUN, 478
THE DAVIS EXPERIENCE, 1062
DECATUR ELECTRONICS, INC., 1123
DEGREES IN SPORTS, 594
DESERT BOWLER, 556
DEWALD, SCOTT D., 876
DIVERSA PRODUCTS GROUP, 1124
EAGLE INTERNATIONAL TENTS & AIR DOMES, 754
EAST VALLEY TRIBUNE, 485
EIGER SPORTSWEAR, INC., 1128
ELY, BETTINI, ULMAN & ROSENBLATT, 878
ESPN 1490 THE FAN, 612
EVENT SOFTWARE, 1214
FC ARIZONA, 166
FC TUCSON, 166
FENNEMORE CRAIG, A PROFESSIONAL CORPORATION, 879
FIESTA BOWL, 90
FIREBIRD INTERNATIONAL RACEWAY, 1025
FITNESS VENTURE GROUP, 1214
FLAGSTAFF CONVENTION AND VISITORS BUREAU, 261
FOREVER YOUNG FOUNDATION, 191
FOX SPORTS NET ARIZONA, 674
FREEDOM PRO BASEBALL LEAGUE, 40
FUTURE FOR KIDS, 834
GAYLORD SPORTS MANAGEMENT, 834
GLENDALE DESERT DOGS, 34
GLOBAL SPORTS MARKETING & EVENTS, 835
GOLF CLEARING HOUSE/NATIONAL GOLF SALES REPRESENTATIVES ASSOCIATION (NGSA), 101
GOLFUTURES, INC., 786
GRAND CANYON STATE GAMES, 262
GRAND CANYON UNIVERSITY ATHLETICS, 331
HAMILTON ATHLETIC, 1142
HARNESS TRACKS OF AMERICA, 75
HAZLETT, WILKES & BAYHAM, 883
HDS PROMOTIONAL MARKETING, 787
HEAD/PENN USA, 1143
HI CORBETT FIELD, 970
HINSHAW & CULBERSON LLP, 837
HOHOKAM STADIUM, 971
INDOOR FOOTBALL LEAGUE, 93, 94
INTERCOLLEGIATE TENNIS ASSOCIATION, 174
IRON GLOVES INC, 1148
J LAWRENCE WALK-UP SKYDOME, 974
J. LAWRENCE WALKUP SKYDOME, 974
KCUB-AM, 615
KDKB-FM, 616
KDRX-TV, 689
KDUS-AM 1060 SPORTS, 616
KELLEY, MCELWEE & SCHMIDT, P.A., 888
KINGMAN DAILY MINER, 500
KJJJ-FM, 621
KMVP 860 AM SPORTS RADIO, 624
KMVP-AM, 624
KNXV-TV, 692
KOY-AM, 626
KPNX-TV, 693
KTVK-TV, 696
KURT WARNER FIRST THING'S FIRST FOUNDATION, 192
KVOA-TV, 697
LET'S TALK SPORTS, 605
LEWIS AND ROCA LLP, 890
LOPEZ, PAT P., 891
LUBIN & ENOCH, P.C., 891
MANAGEMENT ONE, 842
MANZANITA SPEEDWAY, 1028
MARATHON, 794
MARICOPA COUNTY SPORTS COMMISSION, 240
MARISCAL, WEEKS, MCINTYRE & FRIELANDER, P.A., 893
MARYVALE BASEBALL PARK, 985
MCKALE MEMORIAL CENTER, 986
MESA CONVENTION & VISITORS BUREAU, 240
MESA SOLAR SOX, 34
METROPOLITAN TUCSON CONVENTION & VISITORS BUREAU, 241
MOBIVITY, 758, 795
MOHAVE VALLEY DAILY NEWS, 508
MORE ACTIVE, 1214
MOUNTAIN HIGH HOSIERY, INC., 1165
NATIONAL ACADEMY OF SPORTS MEDICINE, 84, 921

NATIONAL HIGH SCHOOL BASEBALL COACHES ASSOCIATION, 28, 267
NATIONAL SPORTS MANAGEMENT INC., 845
NEW TIER COMMUNICATIONS, 797, 821
NJCAA REGION I MEN'S, 286
NJCAA REGION I WOMEN'S, 286
NOCONA ATHLETIC GOODS COMPANY, 1169
NORTHERN ARIZONA UNIVERSITY ATHLETICS, 340
NORTHERN ARIZONA WRANGLERS, 93
OSBORN MALEDON, P.A., 898
OVATION ENTERTAINMENT, 758
PARACHUTE INDUSTRY ASSOCIATION, 13
PATTERSON SPORTS VENTURES, 800
PENN RACQUET SPORTS, 1173
PEORIA DIAMOND CLUB, 28
PEORIA JAVELINAS, 34
PEORIA SPORTS COMPLEX, 991
PERIMETER BICYCLING ASSOCIATION OF AMERICA, INC., 70
PHOENIX CONVENTION & VISITORS BUREAU, GREATER, 243
PHOENIX GREYHOUND PARK, 1047
PHOENIX INTERNATIONAL RACEWAY, 1030
PHOENIX MERCURY, 61
PHOENIX MUNICIPAL STADIUM, 993
PHOENIX ORTHOPEDIC GROUP, 922
PHOENIX RISING FC, 160
PHOENIX SUNS, 57
PIMA COUNTY FAIR, 1042
PING, INC., 1174
POMCHIES LLC, 1175
POSITION SPORTS MARKETING, 848
PRO INNOVATIVE CONCEPTS, 1177
PRO ORTHOPEDIC DEVICES, INC., 1177
PRO SPORT MANAGEMENT, 849
PRO SPORT MANAGEMENT, INC., 849
PROMARK 1, 1178
PROMOTION EVENT & HOSPITALITY EXCHANGE, 803
PW ATHLETIC COMPANY, INC., 1179
RAWHIDE PAVILION & RODEA ARENA, 1062
RHINO SPORTS, 1182
RIDENOUR, HIERDON, HARPER & KELHOFFER P.L.L.C., 902
SALT RIVER RAFTERS, 34
SC DEL SOL, 168
SCOTTSDALE SCORPIONS, 34
SCOTTSDALE STADIUM, 1001
SCOTTSDALE TRIBUNE, 529
SIERRA VISTA HERALD, 531
SLAZENGER GOLF PRODUCTS CO, 1189
SOCIETY FOR AMERICAN BASEBALL RESEARCH, 28
SOUTHWEST PGA SECTIONAL OFFICE, 108
SOUTHWESTERN INTERNATIONAL RACEWAY, 1033
SPECIAL OLYMPICS ARIZONA, 194
SPORT COLLECTORS GUILD INC, 1192
SPORT SEARCH.MVP GROUP, 748
SPORTS 'N SPOKES MAGAZINE, 584
SPORTS ARIZONA MAGAZINE, 584
SPORTS DESTINATION NETWORK, INC., 927
SPORTS GUIDES, LLC, 748
SPORTS NIGHT, 606, 681
SPORTSEARCH, INC., 748
STINSON MORRISON HECKER LLP, 908
STOCKTON & HING, P.A., 909
STOREY, MOYES, 909
STRATEGIC INSIGHT, LLC, 812
SUN DEVIL STADIUM, 1006
SURPRISE SAGUAROS, 34
SUTTERS MILL SPECIALTIES, 1198
SWIMMING WORLD & JUNIOR SWIMMER, 587
TEAM SHOP PREMIUMS, 1200
THUNDER RACEWAY, INC., 1034
THUNDERBIRDS, THE, 248
TODAY'S NEWS HERALD, 541
TUCSON CITIZEN, 542
TUCSON ELECTRIC PARK, 1011
TUCSON FC, 161
TUCSON GREYHOUND PARK, INC., 1047
TUCSON RACEWAY PARK, 1034
TUCSON ROADRUNNERS, 129
TUCSON SAGUAROS, 50
TUCSON SUGAR SKULLS, 94
TURF PARADISE, 1045
U.S. HANDBALL ASSOCIATION, 121
UNIVERSITY OF PHOENIX STADIUM, 1013
UPDIKE, THEODORE R., 859

COLORADO

CALIFORNIA

CONNECTICUT

DELAWARE

DISTRICT OF COLUMBIA

GERMANY

GEORGIA

HOLLAND

HUNGARY

HAWAII

ITALY

IDAHO

ILLINOIS

SPORTS PROFILES, 585, 811
SPORTS TRAVELER, 586
SPORTSCORP LTD., 811
SPORTVISION, 602
SPRI PRODUCTS INC, 1194
SPRINGFIELD JR. BLUES, 133
ST. FRANCIS ATHLETICS, UNIVERSITY OF, 321
STAR-COURIER, 534
STARCOM MEDIAVEST GROUP, 811
STATE JOURNAL-REGISTER, 535
STATS, 714
STATS LLC, 929
STOP SPORTS INJURIES, 923
SULLIVAN FIRM, LTD., THE, 909
SUMMIT - GARDNER & GELDMACHER, 1197
TANITA CORPORATION OF AMERICA, 1199
TEAM MARKETING REPORT, 588
TELEGRAPH (IL), 537
TENNIS SURFACES COMPANY, 1200
THIES, DAVID, 911
TICKET RESERVE, THE, 933
TIMES-COURIER, 540
TONY BRUNO SHOW, 610
TOURISM BUREAU ILLINOISOUTH, 248
TRI CITY SPEEDWAY, 1034
TRIBLER, ORPETT & CRONE, 912
TRINITY CHRISTIAN COLLEGE ATHLETICS, 322
TROY CORPORATION, 1204
361o EXPERIENTIAL, 770
U.S. SOCCER, 207
U.S. SOCCER FEDERATION, 155
ULTRA PLAY SYSTEMS, INC., 1205
UNITED CENTER, 1012
UNITED CONTINENTAL HOLDINGS, 734
UNITED MIDGET AUTO RACING
    ASSOCIATION/UMRA, 18
UNITED STATES ADULT SOCCER
    ASSOCIATION, 156
UNIVERSAL SPORTS ASSOCIATES, INC., 859
UNIVERSAL SPORTS LIGHTING, INC., 1206
UNIVERSITY OF ST. FRANCIS ATHLETICS, 321
US CELLULAR FIELD, 1014
VAINISI, JEROME R., 913
VERMILION COUNTY BOBCATS, 136
VOA ASSOCIATES INCORPORATED, 1063
WAIK-AM, 636
WAIT-AM, 636
WALGREEN COMPANY, 1240
WALS-FM, 636
WALTER AND CONNIE PAYTON FOUNDATION,
    193
WARNER/EXCELLTEK, 1209
WATER SPORTS LLC, 1209
WBBM-TV, 699
WBIG-AM, 639
WCFN-TV, 700
WCIA-TV, 700
WDDD-AM, 642
WDDD-FM, 642
WEAI-FM, 644
WEEK-TV, 702
WEIU-FM, 644
WELLS FARGO INSURANCE INC., 770
WELLS LAMONT SPORTS & SPECIALTIES,
    1209
WELSH RYAN ARENA, 1018
WESTERN GOLF ASSOCIATION, EVANS
    SCHOLARS FOUNDATION, 118
WESTERN GOLF ASSOCIATION/EVANS
    SCHOLARS FOUNDATION, 117
WESTERN HALL, 1018
WESTERN ILLINOIS UNIVERSITY, 437
WESTERN ILLINOIS UNIVERSITY ATHLETICS,
    349
WFLD TV CHANNEL 32 CHICAGO/FOX, 702
WFLD-TV, 702
WFMB-AM SPORTS RADIO 1450, 646
WFRX-AM, 646
WGBK-FM, 647
WGCY-FM, 647
WGEM-TV, 703
WGN-9 CHICAGO'S CW, 703
WGN-AM, 648
WHEATON COLLEGE (IL) ATHLETICS, 406
WHOI-TV, 704
WIFR-TV, 704
WILSON SPORTING GOODS COMPANY, 1210
WINDY CITY BULLS, 60
WINDY CITY SPORTS, 592, 817
WINDY CITY THUNDERBOLTS, 41

WISS, JANNEY, ELSTNER ASSOCIATES,
    INC./WJE, 1063
WITTEK GOLF SUPPLY COMPANY, 1211
WIVQ-FM, 651
WJBC, 651
WJCI-AM, 651
WJDK-FM, 652
WJPF-AM, 652
WKAN AM 1320, 653
WKAN-AM, 653
WKRV-FM, 654
WKXQ-FM, 654
WLKL-FM, 655
WLMD-FM, 655
WLS-TV, 706
WLS-TV CHANNEL 7 ABC (CHICAGO), 706
WMAQ TV CHICAGO, 706
WMAQ-TV, 706
WMMC-FM, 657
WMOI-FM, 657
WNOI-FM, 659
WNSV-FM, 659
WOLFE LAW, P.C., 916
WOODFIELD CHICAGO NORTHWEST
    CONVENTION BUREAU, 250
WORLD DRYER CORPORATION, 1211
WPCD-FM, 661
WPMB-AM, 661
WPXN-FM, 662
WQAD-TV, 708
WRAM-AM, 663
WRIGLEY FIELD, 1020
WRMS-FM, 664
WRRG-FM, 664
WRSE-FM, 665
WRXX-FM, 665
WSCR THE SCORE SPORTSRADIO 670, 665
WSIL-TV, 709
WSMI-AM, 666
WSNS-TV, 709
WSQR-AM, 667
WTAD-AM, 667
WTVO-TV, 711
WUSI-FM, 670
WZZT-FM, 673
YMCA USA, 85
ZURICH AMERICAN INSURANCE CO., 735

INDIANA

A&H ATHLETIC FLOOR SERVICES, INC., 1089
ACTIVE ANKLE SYSTEMS, INC., 1092
AEF EMBLEMS, 1094
ALLEN COUNTY WAR MEMORIAL COLISEUM,
    946
AMERICAN COLLEGE OF SPORTS MEDICINE,
    83, 918
AMERICAN LEGION BASEBALL, 25
AMERICAN PLAYGROUND CORPORATION,
    1098
AMERICAN SPECIALTY, 773
AMERICAN SPECIALTY INSURANCE & RISK
    SERVICES, INC., 773
ANCHOR INDUSTRIES INC., 1099
ANDERSON UNIVERSITY ATHLETICS, 351, 376
ANDERSON UNIVERSITY
    ATHLETICS-ANDERSON, 376
ANDRETTI AUTOSPORT, 20, 21, 22
ANDRETTI STEINBRENNER RACING, 21
ARROW MCLAREN SP, 22
ASA PRODUCTIONS, 597
ASSEMBLY HALL, 947
ASSOCIATION FOR APPLIED SPORT
    PSYCHOLOGY/AAASP, 217
B-BALL LIGHTS, 1102
BAKER & DANIELS, 863
BALL STATE UNIVERSITY, 410
BALL STATE UNIVERSITY ATHLETICS, 325
BANNER-GRAPHIC, 463
BATTLE CREEK EQUIPMENT COMPANY, 1105
BEAR ARCHERY, 1105
BETHEL COLLEGE ATHLETICS, 378
BOSE MCKINNEY & EVANS LLP, 867
BOSSE FIELD, 951
BRAZIL TIMES, 466
BROWNING DAY MULLINS DIERDORF
    ARCHITECTS, 1051
BUTLER BOWL, 953
BUTLER UNIVERSITY ATHLETICS, 326
CALL-LEADER, 468

CALUMET COLLEGE OF ST. JOSEPH
    ATHLETICS, 310
CENTURY INDUSTRIES, LLC, 1066, 1115
CHEER KIDS, 1115
CHESTERTON TRIBUNE, 469
CHRONICLE-TRIBUNE, 470
CLASSIC PRODUCTS, 1116
CMG WORLDWIDE, 829
COLLEGE FOOTBALL HALL OF FAME, 252
CONBOY, MELISSA L., 874
CONNERSVILLE NEWS-EXAMINER, 473
CONQUEST RACING, 20
COURIER-TIMES, 474
CURTIS MANAGEMENT GROUP, 830
DE PAUW UNIVERSITY ATHLETICS, 382
DECATUR DAILY DEMOCRAT, 482
DLZ, 1054
DON MCBRIDE STADIUM, 962
DRAPER INC., 1125
EARLHAM COLLEGE (EC) ATHLETICS, 383
EARLHAM COLLEGE ATHLETICS, 383
ED CARPENTER RACING, 22
EFRON, MORTON L., 878
ELKHART TRUTH, 486
EMENS AUDITORIUM, 964
EMERICK, WILLIAM E., 878
ESCALADE SPORTS, 1130
EVANSVILLE ATHLETICS, UNIVERSITY OF, 329
EVANSVILLE COURIER & PRESS, 487
EVANSVILLE OTTERS, 40
EVANSVILLE THUNDERBOLTS, 136
EVANSVILLE, UNIVERSITY OF, 417
FC PRIDE, 166
FC SPIRIT, 166
FILLENWARTH DENNERLINE GROTH & TOWE,
    880
FINK ROBERTS & PETRIE, 1056
FIRST JOB IN SPORTS, 930
FITNESS FLOORING, 1133
FLAGS INTERNATIONAL, 1133
FOR BARE FEET INC, 1134
FORT WAYNE KOMETS, 129
FORT WAYNE MAD ANTS, 59
FORT WAYNE TINCAPS, 45
FOX 59 OVERTIME, 679
FRANKLIN COLLEGE ATHLETICS, 385
FRANKLIN COLLEGE ATHLETICS (FC), 385
GAINBRIDGE FIELDHOUSE, 967
GALYAN'S TRADING COMPANY, INC., 1228
GARY SOUTH SHORE RAILCATS, 967
GOSHEN COLLEGE ATHLETICS, 313
GRACE COLLEGE ATHLETICS, 313
GRAND SLAM III, 836
GREAT LAKES VALLEY CONFERENCE, 296
GREENSBURG DAILY NEWS, 491
HANOVER COLLEGE ATHLETICS, 386
HARNESS HORSE YOUTH FOUNDATION, 75
HAT WORLD/LIDS CORP., 1229
HERALD-BULLETIN, 493
HERALD-TIMES, 494
HINKLE FIELDHOUSE, 970
HOOSIER PARK, 1040
HOOSIER REGION COMMISSIONER/USA
    VOLLEYBALL, 211
HORIZON LEAGUE, 297
HULMAN CENTER, 972
HUNTER & SPORT HORSE, 564
HUNTINGTON HERALD-PRESS, 495
HUNTINGTON UNIVERSITY ATHLETICS, 314
IMS PROPERTIES/INDY MOTOR SPEEDWAY,
    757, 1065
INDIANA AAU ASSOCIATION, 214
INDIANA BASKETBALL HALL OF FAME, 253
INDIANA BASKETBALL HISTORY, 565
INDIANA FEVER, 60
INDIANA FOOTBALL HALL OF FAME, 253
INDIANA GOLF ASSOCIATION, 111
INDIANA HERALD, 496
INDIANA HS ATHLETIC ASSOCIATION, 200
INDIANA INSTITUTE OF TECHNOLOGY
    ATHLETICS, 314
INDIANA PACERS, 57
INDIANA PGA, 106
INDIANA SPORTS CORPORATION, 236
INDIANA SPORTS TALK, 609
INDIANA STATE FAIR/FAIRGROUNDS, 1040
INDIANA STATE UNIVERSITY, 421
INDIANA STATE UNIVERSITY ATHLETICS, 332
INDIANA UNIVERSITY, 421
INDIANA UNIVERSITY ATHLETICS, 333

ISRAEL

JAPAN

KANSAS

KOREA

KANSAS

KENTUCKY

LIECHTENSTEIN

LOUISIANA

MASSACHUSETTS

MICHIGAN

TGM FITNESS, INC., 1239
THA ARCHITECTS ENGINEERS, 1062
THOMAS M. COOLEY LAW SCHOOL, 911
THREE RIVERS COMMERCIAL-NEWS, 538
TIMES HERALD (MI), 539
TRAVERSE CITY BEACH BUMS, 41
TRAVERSE CITY RECORD-EAGLE, 541
TROY TIMES, 541
U.S. NATIONAL SKI HALL OF FAME & MUSEUM, 259
U.S. OLYMPIC TRAINING SITE, 206
UNITED STATES OLYMPIC EDUCATION CENTER, 226
US NATIONAL TEAM DEVELOPMENT PROGRAM (USNTDP), 138
USA HOCKEY ARENA, 1014
VAN ANDEL ARENA, 1015
VNEA, 62
WALKER ARENA, 1017
WARREN WEEKLY, 545
WAYNE STATE UNIVERSITY, 436
WAYNE STATE UNIVERSITY ATHLETICS, 374
WBCK - BATTLE CREEK, 638
WBCK-AM, 638
WBET-AM, 638
WBFH RADIO, 608
WBFN-AM, 638
WBKB-TV, 700
WBTI-FM, 639
WBXX-FM, 640
WCCW-AM, 640
WDFN, 642
WDFN - 1130 AM THE FAN, 642
WDIV-TV, 701
WDOW-AM, 643
WEST MICHIGAN WHITECAPS, 45
WESTERN MICHIGAN UNIVERSITY, 437
WESTERN MICHIGAN UNIVERSITY ATHLETICS, 349
WFAT-FM, 645
WFDF 910AM RADIO, 645
WHTC-AM, 650
WIBM-AM, 650
WILX-TV, 704
WINGS EVENT CENTER, 1019
WJBK-TV, 705
WJR-AM, 652
WKNW-AM, 654
WKZO-AM, 654
WLHT-FM, 655
WMHW-FM, 657
WMJZ-FM, 657
WMLM-AM, 657
WMPX-WMRX AM AND FM, 657
WMRX-FM, 657
WNEM-TV, 707
WOES-FM, 659
WOLVERINE, 593
WOLVERINE WORLD WIDE, 1211
WOLVERINE-HOOSIER ATHLETIC CONFERENCE, 307
WORW-FM, 660
WPBN-TV, 707
WPHM-AM, 661
WQBX-FM, 662
WQSN AM 1660, 662
WRCC-FM, 663
WRKR-FM, 664
WSDP-FM, 665
WSFN-AM SPORTS RADIO, 666
WSHN-AM, 666
WSJM-AM, 666
WSMK-FM, 666
WTKG-AM, 668
WTOM-TV, 710
WVAC-FM, 670
WWMT-TV, 712
WWTV-TV, 712
WWUP-TV, 712
WXDX-AM, 671
WXYT-AM, 672
WZZM-TV, 713
YACK ARENA, 1020
YOST ICE ARENA, 1021
YPSILANTI AREA CONVENTION AND VISITORS BUREAU, 250

MINNESOTA

ACTION SIGNS AND BILLBOARDS, 1092

ADOLFSON & PERTSON, INC., 1048
AECOM, 1048
ALBERT LEA CITY ARENA, 945
ALBERT LEA TRIBUNE, 459
ARCHERY TRADE ASSOCIATION, 14
AUGSBURG COLLEGE ATHLETICS, 377
AUSTIN BRUINS, 132
AUSTIN DAILY HERALD, 462
BASSFORD, LOCKHART, TRUESDELL & BRIGGS, P.A., 864
BASSMASTERS, THE, 597
BEMIDJI STATE UNIVERSITY, 411
BEMIDJI STATE UNIVERSITY ATHLETICS, 352
BLOOMINGTON CONVENTION & VISITORS BUREAU, 229
BOATING INDUSTRY, 553
BRAINARD INTERNATIONAL RACEWAY, 1023
BRAINERD DAILY DISPATCH, 466
BURICH ARENA, 953
CANAMER INT'L, LLC, 1113
CANTERBURY PARK, 1036
CARD EMPORIUM, 1114
CARLETON COLLEGE ATHLETICS, 379
CARLSON TRAVEL NETWORK, 925
COLOR SIGN SERVICE, INC., 1118
CONCORDIA COLLEGE (MN) ATHLETICS, 381
CROOKSTON DAILY TIMES, 474
CROWN COLLEGE ATHLETICS, 311
CUTTERS GLOVES, 1122
DULUTH NEWS-TRIBUNE, 484
E-Z GARD INDUSTRIES, 1126
EMPI, INC., 1129
FANBUZZ.COM, 1227
FARIBAULT DAILY NEWS, 488
FEDERAL PREMIUM AMMUNITION, 1132
FINGERHUT COMPANIES, INC., 1227
FITNESS SYSTEMS, 1227
FOX SPORTS NET NORTH, 675
FREE PRESS, 489
FRONT RUNNER, 755
GAGE MARKETING GROUP, 784
GANDER MOUNTAIN COMPANY, 1228
GUSTAVUS ADOLPHUS COLLEGE ATHLETICS, 386
H&B SPECIALIZED PRODUCTS, 1141
HAMLINE UNIVERSITY ATHLETICS, 386
HAMMEL, GREEN AND ABRAHAMSON INC., 1058
HEALTH FITNESS CORPORATION, 1059, 1230
HIBBING DAILY TRIBUNE, 494
HITCHCOCK LAW FIRM, 884
HOIGAARD'S INC., 1230
HUMBERT HUMPHREY METRODOME, 972
HUNEGS, STONE, LENEAVE, KYAS & THORNTON, P.A., 884
INDUSTRIAL FABRICS ASSOCIATION INTERNATIONAL, 220
INNOVATIVE MARKETING CONSULTANTS, 789, 1147
INTERNATIONAL SLED DOG RACING ASSOCIATION, 153
JDC MOTORSPORTS, 21
JDC-MILLER MOTORSPORTS, 21
JOE FABER FIELD, 976
JOY ATHLETIC, 167
KARE-TV, 687
KBUN-AM, 614
KBUN-AM SPORTS RADIO, 614
KCCW-TV, 688
KDJS-AM, 616
KDLH-TV, 689
KDOM-AM, 616
KDOM-FM, 616
KDUZ-AM, 616
KDWA-AM, 616
KDXL-FM, 616
KFAN SPORTS RADIO, 617
KFML-FM, 617
KFXN-AM, 618
KGHS-AM, 619
KKIN-AM, 621
KKRC-FM, 621
KLCI-FM, 622
KLGR-FM, 622
KLTF-AM, 623
KLZZ-FM, 623
KMFY-FM, 623
KMRS-AM, 624
KMSP-TV, 692
KNUTE NELSON MEMORIAL FIELD, 980

KQAD-AM, 626
KQAL-FM, 626
KRFO-FM, 627
KRJB-FM, 627
KROX-AM, 628
KSDM-FM, 628
KSTP - KSTP 5/ABC, 695
KTTC-TV, 695
KWNO-FM, 632
KXDL-FM, 632
KYMN-AM, 633
LANDSCAPE STRUCTURES, INC., 1154
LETS PLAY HOCKEY, 568
LETS PLAY SOFTBALL, 568
LOVING ASSOCIATES INC., 1157
MACALESTER COLLEGE ATHLETICS, 391
MAGNETSTREET, 1159
MANITOU FC, 167
MANKATO UNITED SOCCER CLUB, 167
MAPLEBROOK FURY, 167
MARIUCCI ARENA, 985
MARSHALL INDEPENDENT, 505
MARSHALL RADIO, 634
MARTIN LUTHER COLLEGE ATHLETICS, 315
MAYO CLINIC SPORTS MEDICINE, 921
METROPOLITAN SPORTS FACILITIES COMMISSION, 240
MIKEN SPORTS, 1163
MILLERBERND MANUFACTURING COMPANY, 1163
MINNEAPOLIS CONVENTION & VISITORS ASSOCIATION, GREATER, 241
MINNEAPOLIS METRO NORTH CONVENTION & VISITORS BUREAU, 241
MINNEAPOLIS STAR TRIBUNE, 507
MINNESOTA AAU ASSOCIATION, 214
MINNESOTA ATHLETICS, UNIVERSITY OF, 337
MINNESOTA DUTCH LIONS FC, 167
MINNESOTA GOLF ASSOCIATION, 113
MINNESOTA GOLFER, 571
MINNESOTA HOCKEY JOURNAL, 571
MINNESOTA INTERCOLLEGIATE ATHLETIC CONFERENCE, 300
MINNESOTA LYNX, 60
MINNESOTA MINX, 98
MINNESOTA PGA SECTIONAL OFFICE, 106
MINNESOTA RACING COMMISSION, 80
MINNESOTA STATE HS LEAGUE, 200
MINNESOTA STATE UNIVERSITY - MOORHEAD ATHLETICS, 364
MINNESOTA STATE UNIVERSITY-MANKATO, 427
MINNESOTA STATE UNVERSITY - MANKATO ATHLETICS, 364
MINNESOTA STATE UNVERSITY - MANKATO ATHLETICS (MSUM), 364
MINNESOTA THUNDER, 167
MINNESOTA TIMBERWOLVES, 57
MINNESOTA TWINS, 30
MINNESOTA UNITED FC, 158
MINNESOTA VIKINGS, 95
MINNESOTA VIXEN, 98
MINNESOTA WILD, 124
MINNESOTA WILDERNESS, 133
MINNESOTA, UNIVERSITY OF, 427
MINNESOTA-CROOKSTON ATHLETICS, UNIVERSITY OF, 364
MINNESOTA-CROOKSTON ATHLETICS, UNIVERSITY OF (UMC), 364
MINNESOTA-DULUTH ATHLETICS, UNIVERSITY OF, 364
MINNESOTA-DULUTH ATHLETICS, UNIVERSITY OF (UMD), 364
MINNESOTA-MORRIS ATHLETICS, UNIVERSITY OF, 394
MINNESOTA-MORRIS ATHLETICS, UNIVERSITY OF (UMM), 394
NATIONAL ASSOCIATION OF WOMEN'S GYMNASTICS JUDGES, 120
NJCAA REGION XIII MEN'S, 288
NJCAA REGION XIII WOMEN'S, 288
NORTH AMERICAN MEDIA GROUP, INC., 601
NORTH COUNTRY REGION/USA VOLLEYBALL, 212
NORTHERN COLLEGIATE HOCKEY ASSOCIATION, 122
NORTHERN SUN INTERCOLLEGIATE CONFERENCE, 301
NORTHWESTERN COLLEGE (MN) ATHLETICS, 317

MISSISSIPPI

MISSOURI

NEW MEXICO

ALBUQUERQUE ISOTOPES, 48
ALBUQUERQUE JOURNAL, 459
ALBUQUERQUE SPORTS COUNCIL, 227
AMERICAN AMATEUR BASEBALL CONGRESS, 25
ARTESIA DAILY PRESS, 461
DAILY TIMES (NM), 480
THE DOWNS RACETRACK & CASINO AT ALBUQUERQUE, 1044
DUKE CITY GLADIATORS, 93
EASTERN NEW MEXICO UNIVERSITY (ENMU) ATHLETICS, 357
EASTERN NEW MEXICO UNIVERSITY ATHLETICS, 357
EXPO NEW MEXICO, 964
FARMINGTON CONVENTION & VISITORS BUREAU, 233
GALLUP INDEPENDENT, 490
GREYHOUND STADIUM, 969
HOBBS DAILY NEWS-SUN, 494
ISOTOPES PARK, 974
KBIM-TV, 688
KCHS-AM, 614
KCLV-AM, 615
KNML - ALBUQUERQUE, 625
KOAT-TV, 693
KOCT-TV, 693
KOVT-TV, 693
KRQE-TV, 694
KRSY-AM, 628
KSSR-AM, 629
KSVP-AM, 629
KZNM-FM, 633
LAS CRUCES CONVENTION & VISITORS BUREAU, 238
LAS CRUCES SUN-NEWS, 501
LAS CRUCES VAQUEROS, 49
LAS VEGAS DAILY OPTIC, 501
LOS ALAMOS MONITOR, 503
MATHEWSON, ALFRED D., 893
NEW MEXICAN, 510
NEW MEXICO AAU ASSOCIATION, 215
NEW MEXICO ACTIVITIES ASSOCIATION, 201
NEW MEXICO BANITAS, 98
NEW MEXICO BOWL, 91
NEW MEXICO GAMES, 263
NEW MEXICO HIGHLANDS UNIVERSITY ATHLETICS, 365
NEW MEXICO HIGHLANDS UNIVERSITY(NMHU), 365
NEW MEXICO ICE WOLVES, 133
NEW MEXICO RACING COMMISSION, 81
NEW MEXICO STATE FAIR, 1042
NEW MEXICO STATE UNIVERSITY ATHLETICS, 338
NEW MEXICO UNITED, 160
NEW MEXICO UNITED U23, 163
NEW MEXICO, UNIVERSITY OF, 338
OUTSIDE MAGAZINE, 575
PAN AMERICAN CENTER, 991
PECOS LEAGUE, 49, 50
ROSWELL INVADERS, 49
RUIDOSO DOWNS RACE TRACK CASINO, 1043
SANTA FE FUEGO, 49
SANTA FE NEW MEXICAN, 529
SILVER CITY DAILY PRESS & INDEPENDENT, 531
SOARING, 581
SOARING SOCIETY OF AMERICA, 13
SOUTHWEST ATHLETICS, COLLEGE OF THE, 320
SPECIAL OLYMPICS NEW MEXICO, 196
SUN COUNTRY AMATEUR GOLF ASSOCIATION, 116
SUN COUNTRY PGA SECTIONAL OFFICE, 108
SUNLAND PARK RACETRACK & CASINO, 1044
UNIVERSITY ARENA, 1012
UNIVERSITY STADIUM, 1013
UNM ARENA, 1013
USA DEAF SPORTS FEDERATION, 198
WHITE SAND PUPFISH, 50
Z COIL PAIN RELIEF FOOTWEAR, 1212

NEW YORK

A-TURF, 1089
ABC SPORTS, INC., 673
ABEL BANNISON BUTZ, 1048
ACKERMAN, VALERIE B., 861
ACME MASCOTS, INC., 771

ACTION SPORTS ADVENTURE, 597
ACTION SPOT SPORTS, 1216
ACTIVE INTERNATIONAL, 766
AD MFG. COMPANY, 1093
ADELPHI UNIVERSITY - RUTH S. AMMON SCHOOL OF EDUCATION, 409
ADELPHI UNIVERSITY ATHLETICS, 350
ADIRONDACK AAU ASSOCIATION, 213
ADIRONDACK DAILY ENTERPRISE, 459
ADIRONDACK RUBBER PRODUCTS, 1093
ADIRONDACK SPORTS & FITNESS, 548
ADIRONDACK THUNDER, 129
ADLER & BLASS, 861
ALAN TAYLOR COMMUNICATIONS, INC., 772
ALFRED STATE COLLEGE- SUNY COLLEGE OF TECHNOLOGY, 409
ALFRED UNIVERSITY ATHLETICS, 376
ALFRED UNIVERSITY ATHLETICS-ALFRED, 376
ALKAHN LABEL, 1095
ALL-CITY SPORTS MARKETING, 772
ALLESON ATHLETIC, DON, 1096
ALSTRAR INC. SPORTS & ENTERTAINMENT, 824
AM NEW YORK, 460
AMAPRO SPORTING GOODS, INC., 1216
AMBAC ASSURANCE CORPORATION, 767
AMENIA ARCHERY, 1216
AMERICAN CHEERLEADER, 549
AMERICAN EXPRESS COMPANY, 725
AMERICAN FOOTBALL ASSOCIATION, 87
AMERICAN LEISURE CORPORATION, 1049
AMERICAN MARKETING AND MOTORSPORTS GROUP, 750
AMERICAN RANGE COMPANY, 1098
AMERICAN SPORTSCASTERS ASSOCIATION, INC., 217
AMERICAN TURF MONTHLY, 549
AMERICAN URBAN RADIO NETWORKS, 604
ANACONDA SPORTS, 1216
ANC SPORTS ENTERPRISES, 1216
ANDREWS KURTH LLP, 862
ANDY KERR STADIUM, 946
ANHEUSER-BUSCH INBEV, 725
ANN LIGUORI PRODUCTIONS, INC., 673
AOL SPORTS, 597
APSCO ENTERPRISES, 1099
AQUEDUCT, 1042
ARBITRON, INC., 773, 1213
ARISTO IMPORT COMPANY, INC., 1100
ARTHUR ASHE LEARNING CENTER, 191
ARTHUR ASHE STADIUM, 947
ASAP SPORTS, 819
ASSOCIATED PRESS, 462
ASSOCIATION OF OLDETIME BARBELL & STRONGMEN (AOBS), 83
ASSURED GUARANTY CORPORATION, 767
ATARI INC., 1213
ATHLETIC MANAGEMENT, 550
AUBURN DOUBLEDAYS, 46
AUTHENTIC FITNESS CORP., 1102
BAKER ATHLETICS COMPLEX, 948
BALLGIRL ATHLETIC, 1104
BARCLAYS CENTER, 948
BARD COLLEGE ATHLETICS, 377
BARUCH COLLEGE ATHLETICS, 377
BASEBALL ASSISTANCE TEAM, 26
BASKETBALL CITY, 948
BATAVIA MUCKDOGS, 46
BAUSCH & LOMB, 1105
BC UNITED, 165
BEGNI'RS TO PRO'S, 1218
BENJAMIN, GLEN, 826
BERMAN, HOWARD E., 865
BERNIER, CARR & ASSOCIATES, 1050
BERTHELSEN, RICHARD, 826
BESSEMER TRUST, 767
BETHPAGE BALLPARK, 949
BGA NEW MEDIA, 775
BIG BOARD SPORTS, 679
BIG EAST CONFERENCE, 292
BILLBOARDS ON WHEELS, 1106
BINGHAMTON BLACK BEARS, 131
BINGHAMTON METS, 38
BINGHAMTON UNIVERSITY, 325
BINGHAMTON UNIVERSITY ATHLETICS, 325
BIODEX MEDICAL SYSTEMS, 1106
BIOSIG INSTRUMENTS, INC., 1107
BIRDAIR, INC., 1199
BLACK ATHLETE SPORTS NETWORK, 552

BLACK ENTERTAINMENT & SPORTS LAWYERS ASSOCIATION INC, 218
BLACKMAN & RABER, LTD., 827
BLUE CROSS ARENA, 950
BLUEFLY, INC., 1220
BOAST, INC., 1108
BOB COSTAS NOW, 682
BOMBO SPORTS & ENTERTAINMENT, 597
BOOMER ESIASON FOUNDATION, 191
BOSTON HANNAH INTERNATIONAL, 553
BRIGGS, BUCK, 868
BROOKLYN CITY FC, 165
BROOKLYN COLLEGE OF THE CITY UNIVERSITY OF NEW YORK, 411
BROOKLYN CYCLONES, 46
BROOKLYN NETS, 56
BROOKWOOD COMPANIES, INC., 1110
BROOME COUNTY VETERANS MEMORIAL ARENA, 952
BUFFALO BANDITS, 142
BUFFALO BILLS, 94
BUFFALO BISONS, 42
BUFFALO DISTRICT GOLF ASSOCIATION, 110
BUFFALO NEWS, 467
BUFFALO NIAGARA SPORTS COMMISSION, 229
BUFFALO SABRES, 123
BUFFALO STATE COLLEGE ATHLETICS, 378
BUFFALO TURBINE, 1111
BULOVA WATCH COMPANY, 1112
BWD GROUP LLC, 767
CADWALADER, WICKERSHAM & TAFT, 751
CANAAN PUBLIC RELATIONS, 777
CANAL JEAN CO., 1222
CANISIUS COLLEGE - SCHOOL OF EDUCATION & HUMAN SERVICES, 412
CANISIUS COLLEGE ATHLETICS, 326
CANON U.S.A., 1113
CAPPY PRODUCTIONS INC., 598
CARAT NORTH AMERICA, 777
CARDS PLUS, 1114
CARRIER DOME, 955
CASTLEREAGH, INC., 828
CATHOLIC YOUTH ORGANIZATION (CYO), 265
CATSKILL FLY FISHING CENTER & MUSEUM, 87, 252
CAZENOVIA COLLEGE, 412
CAZENOVIA COLLEGE ATHLETICS, 380
CBS SPORTS, 673
CBS SPORTS COLLEGE NETWORK, 598
CENERGY SPORTS & ENTERTAINMENT, 777
CENTRAL NEW YORK PGA SECTIONAL OFFICE, 105
CHASE AMERICA, 828
CHASEAMERICA, INC., 747
CHRISTL ARENA, 957
CITI FIELD, 957
CITIGROUP, INC., 727
CITIZEN, 470
CITY COLLEGE OF NEW YORK ATHLETICS, 380
CITY UNIVERSITY OF NEW YORK/CUNY ATHLETIC CONFERENCE, 294
CIVIC ENTERTAINMENT GROUP, 752
CLARKSON UNIVERSITY ATHLETICS, 381
CLARKSTOWN SOCCER CLUB, 165
CLASSIC MEDALLICS, INC., 1116
CLAYTON, LORINZO, 829
CMI, 778
COACHING MANAGEMENT, 555
COCA-COCA FIELD, 958
COHN & WOLFE, 778
COLGATE UNIVERSITY ATHLETICS, 327
COLLEGE & PRO FOOTBALL NEWSWEEKLY, 555
THE COLLEGE AT BROCKPORT STATE UNIVERSITY OF NEW YORK, 435
COLLEGE OF SAINT ROSE ATHLETICS, 369
COLLEGE OF SAINT ROSE, ALBANY- SCHOOL OF BUSINESS, 414
COLONY SPORTS, 598
COLUMBIA UNIVERSITY, 414
COLUMBIA UNIVERSITY ATHLETICS, 327
COMSCORE MEDIA METRIX, 779
CONCEPT ONE ACCESSORIES, 1119
CONCORDIA COLLEGE (NY) ATHLETICS, 356
CONROY GLOVES, 1119
CONSOLIDATED MANAGEMENT GROUP, INC., 829
CORNELL SPORTS MARKETING, 779

WORLD T.E.A.M. SPORTS, 226
WORLD WIDE SPORTS RADIO NETWORK, 593
WORLDWIDE SPORTS MANAGEMENT, 860
WPDM-AM/WSNN-FM, 661
WPIG-FM, 661
WPIX-TV, 708
WQKE-FM, 662
WRCU-FM, 663
WRGB-TV, 708
WRHU-FM, 664
WRNN-TV, 709
WRUC-FM, 665
WSBU-FM, 665
WSHR-FM, 666
WSLJ-FM, 666
WSLL-FM, 666
WSLO-FM, 666
WSP, 1063
WTEN NEWS 10/ABC, 710
WTEN-TV, 710
WTNY-AM, 668
WTSX-FM, 669
WTVH-TV, 711
WUNDERMAN, 818
WUSB-FM, 670
WXLU-FM, 671
WXXA-TV, 712
WYSL-AM, 672
WZMR-FM, 672
XA, THE EXPERIENTIAL AGENCY, 818
YANKEE STADIUM, 1021
YANKEES ENTERTAINMENT & SPORTS
    NETWORK/YES, 678
YESHIVA UNIVERSITY ATHLETICS, 408
YONKERS RACEWAY, 1045
YORK COLLEGE (CUNY) ATHLETICS, 408

NORTH CAROLINA

A-B EMBLEM, 1089
ACC PROPERTIES, 771
ACTION SPORTS IMAGE, 1092
ACTION SPORTS SYSTEMS INCORPORATED,
    1092
THE ADAM GOLD SHOW, 607
AM 850 THE BUZZ SPORTS RADIO, 611
AM RACING, 23
AMATEUR SPORTS TRAVEL GROUP, INC, 924
AMERICAN ASSOCIATION OF INDEPENDENT
    PROFESSIONAL BASEBALL, 33
AMERICAN BASEBALL COACHES
    ASSOCIATION, 25
AMERICAN SINGLES GOLF ASSOCIATION, 99
AMERICAN WHITEWATER, 63
ANDREA KIRBY COACHES, INC., 747
APPALACHIAN ATHLETIC CONFERENCE, 291
APPALACHIAN STATE UNIVERSITY, 409
APPALACHIAN STATE UNIVERSITY
    ATHLETICS, 324
ARCA MENARDS SERIES EAST, 19
ARCA MENARDS SERIES WEST, 19
ASHEVILLE CHAMBER OF COMMERCE, 227
ASHEVILLE CITIZEN-TIMES, 461
ASHEVILLE CITY SC, 161
ASHEVILLE CONVENTION & VISITORS
    BUREAU, 227
ASHEVILLE TOURISTS, 50
ATLANTIC COAST CONFERENCE, 291
B.J. MCLEOD MOTORSPORTS, 22, 23, 24
BANK OF AMERICA CORPORATION, 725
BANK OF AMERICA STADIUM, 948
BARBER-SCOTIA COLLEGE, 308
BARTON COLLEGE, 411
BARTON COLLEGE ATHLETICS, 351
BASEBALL AMERICA, 551
BASKETBALL TIMES, 551
BB&T BALLPARK, 948
BELK BOWL, CHARLOTTE SPORTS
    FOUNDATION, 89
BELK STORES SERVICES, 1218
BERNARD, WILLIAM DAVID, 865
BETHEL INTERNATIONAL, 1106
BIG SOUTH CONFERENCE, 292
BLIMP WORKS, INC., 776
BOJANGLES' COLISEUM, 951
BOYLE & COMPANY, INC., 1109
BREVARD COLLEGE ATHLETICS, 309
BSN-JOBST, INC., 1111
BUNTING, ELIZABETH C., 869
BURLINGTON ATHLETIC STADIUM, 953

BURLINGTON ROYALS, 33
BUTLER BUILT MOTORSPORTS EQUIPMENT,
    1112
C.E. GAINES CENTER, 953
CAMPBELL UNIVERSITY - COLLEGE OF ARTS
    & SCIENCES, 412
CAMPBELL UNIVERSITY ATHLETICS, 326
CAPITOL BROADCASTING COMPANY, 604
CAPITOL SPORTS NETWORK, 685
CAROLINA HURRICANES, 123
CAROLINA LEAGUE, 37
CAROLINA LEAGUE (A-LEVEL), 36
CAROLINA MUDCATS, 37
CAROLINA PANTHERS, 94
CAROLINA PHOENIX, 97
CAROLINA REGIONAL VOLLEYBALL
    ASSOCIATION/USA VOLLEYBALL, 210
CAROLINA SPORTS FRIDAY, 679
CAROLINA THUNDERBIRDS, 131
CAROLINAS GOLF ASSOCIATION, 110
CAROLINAS PGA SECTION, 105
CAROLINAS-VIRGINIA ATHLETICS
    CONFERENCE, 293
CARTER FINLEY STADIUM, 955
CATAWBA COLLEGE ATHLETICS, 354
CHAPEL HILL NEWS, 469
CHARLOTTE CHECKERS, 127
CHARLOTTE EAGLES, 161, 165
CHARLOTTE HORNETS, 56
CHARLOTTE HOUNDS, 141
CHARLOTTE INDEPENDENCE, 159
CHARLOTTE KNIGHTS, 42
CHARLOTTE MOTOR SPEEDWAY, 1023
CHARLOTTE OBSERVER, 469
CHARLOTTE REGIONAL SPORTS
    COMMISSION, 230
CHIP GANASSI RACING, 22
CHOWAN COLLEGE ATHLETICS, 354
CHOWAN UNIVERSITY, 413
CLINARD, KEITH ASHFORD, 873
CMC-NORTHEAST STADIUM, 958
COLBOND, INC., 1117
COLE, DAYTON T., 873
COMPETITION PARK MOTOCROSS, 1024
CRAVEN, JAMES B., III, 830
THE CROWN COMPLEX, 1009
DAILY ADVANCE, 475
DAILY REFLECTOR, 479
DAILY SOUTHERNER, 480
DAVIDSON COLLEGE ATHLETICS, 328
DEAN E. SMITH CENTER, 961
DEMAYO, LAW OFFICES OF MICHAEL L.L.P.,
    876
DGR-CROSLEY, 19, 23
DUKE LEGAL COUNSEL, 877
DUKE UNIVERSITY ATHLETICS, 329
DURHAM BULLS, 42
DURHAM BULLS ATHLETIC PARK, 963
DURHAM CONVENTION & VISITORS BUREAU,
    233
EAST CAROLINA UNIVERSITY - DEPARTMENT
    OF KINESIOLOGY, 416
EAST CAROLINA UNIVERSITY ATHLETICS, 329
EASTERN BASKETBALL, 557
EASTERN INTERCOLLEGIATE ATHLETIC
    CONFERENCE, 295
EATON GOLF PRIDE, 1127
ELIZABETH CITY STATE UNIVERSITY (ECSU)
    ATHLETICS, 357
ELIZABETH CITY STATE UNIVERSITY
    ATHLETICS, 357
ELON UNIVERSITY, 417
ELON UNIVERSITY ATHLETICS, 329
EMBROIDERY STORE, 1128
ENQUIRER-JOURNAL, 487
ENSIGN, 557
ESPN REGIONAL TELEVISION, 599
ESPORTSMAN.COM, 1130
FAMILY DOLLAR STORES, 1227
FAST TRACK RACING, 16
FAYETTEVILLE MARKSMEN, 136
FAYETTEVILLE OBSERVER, 488
FAYETTEVILLE STATE UNIVERSITY (FSU)
    ATHLETICS, 358
FAYETTEVILLE STATE UNIVERSITY
    ATHLETICS, 358
FINISH LINE EVENTS, 1064
FISHER ATHLETIC EQUIPMENT, INC., 1133
FIT-TRAIL BY SOUTHWOOD CORPORATION,
    1133

FLEET FEET, INC., 1228
FN THOMPSON COMPANY, 1134
THE FOX 8 10:00 PM WEEKEND NEWS, 682
FRONT ROW MOTORSPORTS, 23
FUN-TEES, INC., 1135
GARDNER-WEBB UNIVERSITY, 418
GARDNER-WEBB UNIVERSITY ATHLETICS, 330
GASTON GAZETTE, 490
GE LIGHTING SYSTEMS, 1136
GENERAL SPORTS VENUE ASTROTURF, 1137
GERMAIN RACING, 23
GMS RACING, 19, 23, 24
GREENSBORO COLISEUM COMPLEX, 969
GREENSBORO COLLEGE, 419
GREENSBORO COLLEGE ATHLETICS, 386
GREENSBORO GRASSHOPPERS, 51
GREENSBORO NEWS & RECORD, 491
GREENSBORO SPORTS COMMISSION, 235
GREENSBORO SWARM, 59
GROUP FIVE SALES, EVENT & SPORTS
    MARKETING, 756
GUILFORD COLLEGE, 420
GUILFORD COLLEGE ATHLETICS, 386
HAAS, 20
HANES, 1142
HANES BRANDS, 1142
HARRISS & COVINGTON INC., 1142
HATTORI RACING ENTERPRISES, 23
HENDERSON DAILY DISPATCH, 492
HENDRICK MOTORSPORTS, 23
HERALD-SUN, 494
HICKORY BRANDS, INC., 1144
HICKORY CRAWDADS, 51
HICKORY DAILY RECORD, 494
HICKORY MOTOR SPEEDWAY, 1025
HIGH POINT ENTERPRISE, 494
HIGH POINT UNIVERSITY - EARL N. PHILLIPS
    SCHOOL OF BUSINESS, 420
HIGH POINT UNIVERSITY ATHLETICS, 332
HIREV, 1144
HOLE IN NONE, INC., 1145
IMAGE MARKETING, 788
IMG MOTORSPORTS (NC), 17
INDEPENDENT TRIBUNE, 496
INDUSTRIAL OPPORTUNITIES, INC., 1147
INDYCAR, 22
INTEGRITY SPORTS MARKETING, MEDIA &
    MANAGEMENT, 789
INTERNATIONAL SPORTS PROPERTIES, INC.,
    789
JACKSONVILLE-ONSLOW COUNTY SPORTS
    COMMISSION, 237
JEFF GORDON FOUNDATION, 192
JEFFERIES SOCKS, 1149
JENNIFER JO COBB RACING, 23
JERNIGAN LAW FIRM, 886
JIMMY MEANS RACING, 24
JOE GIBBS RACING, 23, 24
JOHNSON C. SMITH UNIVERSITY ATHLETICS,
    361
JORDAN ANDERSON RACING, 23
JOSEPH ATHLETIC MANAGEMENT, 840
JR MOTORSPORTS, 24
JS DORTON ARENA, 978
KANGAROO PRODUCTS COMPANY, 1151
KANNAPOLIS INTIMIDATORS, 51
KAULIG RACING, 24
KAYSER-ROTH INC., 1152
KEITH O. GREGORY, 888
KENAN MEMORIAL STADIUM, 979
KERR DRUG INC., 1231
KEYSTONE MARKETING, INC., 792
KIDD BREWER STADIUM, 979
THE KING PARTNERSHIP, 813
KYLE BUSCH MOTORSPORTS, 23
L.P. FRANS STADIUM, 980
LATE MODEL DIGEST, 568
LAWRENCE JOEL VETERANS MEMORIAL
    COLISEUM, 982
LEAVINE FAMILY RACING, 23
LEES-MCRAE COLLEGE ATHLETICS, 361
LEES-MCRAE COLLEGE- WILLIAMS PHYSICAL
    EDUCATION CENTER, 423
LEGION STADIUM COMPLEX, 982
LENOIR-RHYNE COLLEGE, 423
LENOIR-RHYNE UNIVERSITY ATHLETICS, 361
LISTON B. RAMSEY REGIONAL ACTIVITY
    CENTER, 983
LIVINGSTONE COLLEGE, 423
LIVINGSTONE COLLEGE ATHLETICS, 362

OKLAHOMA

WAYC-FM, 637
WAYNESBURG COLLEGE ATHLETICS, 405
WAYZ-FM, 637
WBAX-AM, 638
WBFD-AM, 638
WBGG-AM, 638
WBPZ-AM, 639
WBUT-AM, 639
WBVP-AM, 640
WBYL-FM, 640
WBZD-FM, 640
WCAU-TV, 700
WCBG-AM, 640
WCLH-FM, 641
WCYJ-FM, 642
WDAS-AM, 642
WEBB, WILLIAM Y., 914
WEDO-AM, 644
WEEO-AM, 644
WEEU-AM, 644
WEEX-AM, 644
WEJL-AM, 644
WELLS FARGO CENTER, 1018
WEST CHESTER UNITED SC, 164
WEST CHESTER UNIVERSITY, 437
WEST CHESTER UNIVERSITY ATHLETICS, 374
WEST CHESTER UNIVERSITY ATHLETICS(WCU), 374
WEST-AM, 645
WESTERN PENNSYLVANIA GOLF ASSOCIATION, 117
WESTMINSTER COLLEGE (PA) ATHLETICS, 406
WESTMINSTER COLLEGE (PA) ATHLETICS (WC), 406
WFMZ-TV, 702
WFRM-AM, 646
WFSE-FM, 646
WFYY-FM, 647
WGAL-TV, 703
WGET, 647
WGLU-FM, 648
WHHS-FM, 649
WHKS-FM, 649
WHOL-AM, 650
WHTM-TV, 704
WICK-AM, 650
WICU-TV, 704
WIDENER UNIVERSITY, 438
WIDENER UNIVERSITY ATHLETICS, 406
WIDENER UNIVERSITY SPORT MANAGEMENT, 860
WILKES-BARRE/SCRANTON PENGUINS, 129
WILLIAMSPORT CROSSCUTTERS, 47
WILLIAMSPORT SUN-GAZETTE, 547
WILQ-FM, 651
WILT-AM, 651
WINDJAMMER INC., 1210
WIP SPORTSRADIO 610, 651
WJUN-AM, 652
WLBR-AM, 655
WLER-FM, 655
WMBA 1460, 656
WMCE-FM, 656
WMKX-FM, 657
WMSS-FM, 657
WMUH-FM, 658
WNPV-AM, 659
WOMEN'S GOLF ASSOCIATION OF WESTERN PENNSYLVANIA, 117
WOOLRICH, INC., 1211
WOYL-AM, 660
WPEN-AM, 661
WPHL-TV, 708
WPIC-AM, 661
WPPA-AM, 661
WPVI-TV, 708
WPXI-TV, 708
WQIC-FM, 662
WRCT-FM, 663
WRSC, 665
WSEE-TV, 709
WSRN-FM, 667
WTIV-AM, 668
WTKT-AM, 668
WTPA-FM, 669
WTRN-AM, 669
WTXF-TV, 711
WTZN-AM, 669
WVBU-FM, 670

WVCH-AM, 670
WVMW-FM, 670
WWLU-FM, 671
WYBF-FM, 672
WYLN-TV, 712
WZZE-FM, 673
YARRINGTON MILLS CORPORATION, 1212
YORK BARBELL COMPANY, 1241
YORK COLLEGE (PENNSYLVANIA) ATHLETICS, 408
YORK COLLEGE OF PENNSYLVANIA, 439
YORK DAILY RECORD/YORK SUNDAY NEWS, 548
YORK DISPATCH, 548
YORK REVOLUTION, 35
ZANE MANAGEMENT, INC., 860

RHODE ISLAND

AMERICAN BOAT BUILDERS & REPAIRERS ASSOCIATION, 63
AMERICAN CORD & WEBBING COMPANY, INC., 1097
ASHAWAY LINE & TWINE MFG. COMPANY, 1100
ASSOCIATION OF MARINA INDUSTRIES, 63
BLUE WATER SAILING, 552
BROWN STADIUM, 952
BROWN UNIVERSITY ATHLETICS, 326
BRYANT UNIVERSITY ATHLETICS, 326
CALL, 468
CATEK SNOWBOARD BINDINGS, 1114
CRUISING WORLD, 556
EVAN CORPORATION, 1130
EVAN FALL PROTECTION SYSTEMS, INC., 1130
FGX DIRECT LLC, 1132
FGX DIRECT LLC., 1132
HANA TIME, 1142
INSTITUTE FOR INTERNATIONAL SPORT, 220
INTERNATIONAL TENNIS HALL OF FAME AND MUSEUM, 254
JOHNSON & WALES UNIVERSITY SPORTS ENT. / EVENT MANAGEMENT, 422
JOHNSON & WALES UNIVERSITY SPORTS/ENTERTAINMENT & EVENT MANAGEMENT PROGRAM, 422
KENYON CONSUMER PRODUCTS, INC., 1152
LEDBETTER, BEVERLY E., 890
LINCOLN PARK, 1046
LIQUID BLUE, 1156
LOGO ART, 1157
LOGOART, 1157
M-F ATHLETIC COMPANY, 1158
MCCOY STADIUM, 985
MUSEUM OF YACHTING, 255
NEW ENGLAND AAU ASSOCIATION, 215
NEWPORT DAILY NEWS, 511
PAWTUCKET RED SOX, 43
PERFORMANCE RESEARCH, 800
PROVIDENCE BRUINS, 128
PROVIDENCE COLLEGE ATHLETICS, 342
PROVIDENCE JOURNAL, 523
RHODE ISLAND ATHLETICS, UNIVERSITY OF, 342
RHODE ISLAND COLLEGE ATHLETICS, 398
RHODE ISLAND GOLF ASSOCIATION, 115
RHODE ISLAND INTERSCHOLASTIC LEAGUE, INC., 202
ROGER WILLIAMS UNIVERSITY ATHLETICS, 399
RUGBY IMPORTS, LTD., 1184
RYAN CENTER, 1000
SAIL AMERICA, 64, 149
SAILING WORLD, 579
SALVE REGINA UNIVERSITY ATHLETICS, 400
SPECIAL OLYMPICS RHODE ISLAND, 197
STATE OF RHODE ISLAND DEPARTMENT OF BUSINESS REGULATION, 82
TURFER SPORTSWEAR, 1205
US SAILING, 149, 207
UVEX SPORTS, INC., 1207
VANGUARD SAILBOATS, 1207
WCTK-FM, 642
WNBH-AM, 658
WOON-AM, 660
WPMZ-AM, 661
WPRI-TV, 708
WPRO, 661
WPRO-AM, 662

SCOTLAND

ELITE SPORTS ANALYSIS, 1214

SOUTH AFRICA

M-NET TELEVISION, 678

SPAIN

BARCELONA MUSEUM AND SPORTS STUDY CENTER, 251
INTERNATIONAL FEDERATION OF BODYBUILDING AND FITNESS, 84
WORLD KARATE FEDERATION, 144

SWEDEN

ORIENTEERING FEDERATION, INTERNATIONAL, 145

SWITZERLAND

FEDERATION EQUESTRE INTERNATIONALE, 75
FEDERATION EQUESTRE INTERNATIONALE (FEI), 203
FEDERATION INTERNATIONALE DE VOLLEYBALL (FIVB), 178
HANDBALL, INTERNATIONAL FEDERATION, 121
INTERNATIONAL CANOE FEDERATION (ICF), 68
INTERNATIONAL COMMITTEE OF SPORTS FOR THE DEAF, 193
INTERNATIONAL GOLF FEDERATION, 102
INTERNATIONAL GYMNASTICS FEDERATION (FIG), 120
INTERNATIONAL HANDBOOK FOR THE SPORTING GOODS INDUSTRY, 595
INTERNATIONAL ICE HOCKEY FEDERATION (IIHF), 122
INTERNATIONAL MASTERS GAMES ASSOCIATION, 262
INTERNATIONAL SKATING UNION (ISU) (ICE SKATING), 171
INTERNATIONAL WATER SKI & WAKEBOARD FEDERATION, 179
MOTORCYCLISTE, FEDERATION INTERNATIONALE, 144
OLYMPIC MUSEUM, LIBRARY AND STUDIES CENTRE, 257
UNION CYCLISTE INTERNATIONALE (UCI), 71
UNITED WORLD WRESTLING, 180
WORLD BASEBALL SOFTBALL CONFEDERATION, 29, 170, 205

SINGAPORE

FOX SPORTS ASIA, 674

SOUTH CAROLINA

AIKEN STANDARD, 459
ALLEN UNIVERSITY ATHLETICS, 307
AMERICAN SPORTS DATA, INC., 773
ANDERSON INDEPENDENT-MAIL, 460
ATSKO INC., 1101
BEAR FOOT SPORTS, 750
BENEDICT COLLEGE ATHLETICS, 352
BFG COMMUNICATIONS, 775
BLUFFTON RUSH SC, 165
BON SECOURS WELLNESS ARENA, 951
CAPITAL CITY STADIUM, 955
CDM ENTERPRISES, INC., 777
CERASPORT, 1115
CHARLESTON BATTERY, 159
CHARLESTON METRO SPORTS COUNCIL, 230
CHARLESTON RIVERDOGS, 51
CHARLESTON SOUTHERN UNIVERSITY ATHLETICS, 326
CHARLESTON SPORTS RADIO, 605
CHARLOTTE INDEPENDENCE 2, 162
CITADEL ATHLETICS, THE, 327
CITADEL, THE, 413
CITY OF GREENVILLE - SPECIAL EVENTS, 230
CIVIC CENTER OF ANDERSON, 958
CLAFLIN UNIVERSITY, 413

CLAFLIN UNIVERSITY ATHLETICS, 355
CLARDY, DON S., 872
CLEMSON MEMORIAL STADIUM, 958
CLEMSON UNIVERSITY ATHLETICS, 327
COASTAL CAROLINA UNIVERSITY ATHLETICS, 327
COKER COLLEGE ATHLETICS, 355
COLLEGE OF CHARLESTON ATHLETICS, 327
COLONIAL LIFE & ACCIDENT INSURANCE COMPANY, 779
COLONIAL LIFE ARENA, 958
COLUMBIA COLLEGE OF S. CAROLINA ATHLETICS, 311
COLUMBIA FIREFLIES, 51
COLUMBIA REGIONAL SPORTS COUNCIL, 231
CONTINENTAL AMATEUR BASEBALL ASSOCIATION, 26
CORE AUTOSPORT, 21
DARLINGTON RACEWAY, 1024
DIVISION OF BUSINESS & COMMUNITY DEVELOPMENT/SOUTH CAROLINA, 232
DUNLOP/MAXFLI/SLAZENGER GROUP AMERICAS, 1126
ERSKINE COLLEGE ATHLETICS, 357
ERSKINE COLLEGE- DEPT OF HEALTH, PE, SPORTS MANAGEMENT, 417
FLORENCE CIVIC CENTER, 966
FOCUS GOLF SYSTEMS, INC., 1134
FRANCIS MARION UNIVERSITY ATHLETICS, 359
FRANCIS MARION UNIVERSITY ATHLETICS (FMU), 359
FRANK HOWARD FIELD AT MEMORIAL STADIUM, 966
FURMAN UNIVERSITY ATHLETICS, 330
GOLF BUSINESS, 560
GREENVILLE CONVENTION & VISITORS BUREAU, 235
GREENVILLE DRIVE, 51
GREENVILLE NEWS, 491
GREENVILLE SWAMP RABBITS, 129
GREENVILLE TRIUMPH, 160
HERALD-JOURNAL, 493
HERITAGE CLASSIC FOUNDATION, 756
HOLLER, J. EDWARD, 884
HUBBELL LIGHTING, INC., 1146
INDEX-JOURNAL, 496
INTERNATIONAL JUNIOR GOLF ACADEMY, 102
INTERNATIONAL JUNIOR GOLF TOUR/IJGT, 102
ISLAND PACKET, 497
ITEM, 497
JACKSON DAWSON MOTOR SPORTS, 790
JD MOTORSPORTS, 24
JOHNSON HAGOOD STADIUM, 977
JOSEPH P. RILEY, JR PARK, 978
KNIGHTS STADIUM, 979
LANDER UNIVERSITY ATHLETICS, 361
THE LEGENDARY DARLINGTON, 1034
LIMESTONE COLLEGE ATHLETICS, 362
LIMESTONE COLLEGE ATHLETICS (LC), 362
LIMESTONE COLLEGE- SPORT MANAGEMENT, 423
LINKS MAGAZINE-THE BEST OF GOLF, 568
MCCULLOCH, JOSEPH M. JR., 894
MORNING NEWS (SC), 508
MORRIS COLLEGE ATHLETICS, 317
MYRTLE BEACH PELICANS, 37
MYRTLE BEACH SPEEDWAY(MBS), 1029
NATIONAL CHRISTIAN COLLEGE ATHLETIC ASSOCIATION/NCCAA, 285
NATIONAL GOLF COURSE OWNERS ASSOCIATION, 104
NATIONAL MOTORSPORTS PRESS ASSOCIATION, 256
NET RESULTS SPORTS MARKETING/NRSM INC., 1167
NEWBERRY COLLEGE, 428
NEWBERRY COLLEGE ATHLETICS, 365
NEWBERRY COLLEGE ATHLETICS(NCAA), 365
NGA HOOTERS PRO GOLF TOUR, 104
NJCAA REGION X MEN'S, 288
NORTH CHARLESTON COLISEUM, 989
PALMETTO REGIONAL COMMISSIONER/USA VOLLEYBALL, 212
PENN FISHING TACKLE COMPANY, 1173
POST AND COURIER, 521
PRESBYTERIAN COLLEGE ATHLETICS, 368
PROFESSIONAL TENNIS REGISTRY, 174
PURE FISHING, 1178

RAE CROWTHER COMPANY, 1180
ROCK HILL/YORK COUNTY CONVENTION & VISITORS BUREAU, 244
SADLER & COMPANY, INC., 769, 806
SADLER AND COMPANY INC, 769
SC UNITED BANTAMS, 163
SEEKINGS, MICHAEL, 905
SEVEN SONS AND COMPANY INC, 1187
SHAKESPEARE FISHING TACKLE DIVISION, 1187
SILVERMAN SPORTS CONSULTANTS, 808
SODA CITY FC, 168
SOUTH ATLANTIC CONFERENCE, 304
SOUTH CAROLINA AAU ASSOCIATION, 216
SOUTH CAROLINA ATHLETICS, UNIVERSITY OF, 344
SOUTH CAROLINA GOLF ASSOCIATION, 115
SOUTH CAROLINA HIGH SCHOOL LEAGUE, 202
SOUTH CAROLINA PARKS, RECREATION & TOURISM, 246, 264
SOUTH CAROLINA SCORPIONS, 96
SOUTH CAROLINA STATE UNIVERSITY, 1004
SOUTH CAROLINA STATE UNIVERSITY ATHLETICS, 344
SOUTH CAROLINA STINGRAYS, 130
SOUTH CAROLINA, UNIVERSITY OF, 432
SOUTH CAROLINA-SPARTANBURG ATHLETICS, UNIVERSITY OF, 370
SOUTHERN CONFERENCE, THE, 304
SOUTHERN WESLEYAN UNIVERSITY ATHLETICS, 371
SPARTANBURG CONVENTION & VISITORS BUREAU, 246
SPARTANBURG HERALD-JOURNAL, 533
SPECIAL OLYMPICS SOUTH CAROLINA, 197
SPORTS TALK, 606, 610
STATE, 535
SUMMERVILLE SPEEDWAY, 1033
SUN NEWS, 536
TAP, LLC, 62
TEAM SPARTANBURG, 246
TENNIS INDUSTRY ASSOCIATION, 174
THOMSON, WILLIAM R., 858
TICKETRETURN.COM FIELD, 1009
TIMES AND DEMOCRAT, 539
TRAILER CORPORATION OF AMERICA, INCORPORATED, 1203
UNION DAILY TIMES, 542
VOORHEES COLLEGE ATHLETICS, 323
WCCP, 640
WCIV-TV, 700
WCOS, 641
WCSC-TV, 701
WDKD-AM, 643
WDOG-FM, 643
WFGN-AM, 646
WFIS-AM, 646
WHEELIN' SPORTSMAN, 592
WILLIAMS-BRICE STADIUM, 1019
WINTHROP UNIVERSITY, 438
WINTHROP UNIVERSITY ATHLETICS, 349
WIQB-AM, 651
WIS-TV, 704
WKCL-FM, 653
WLOW-FM, 656
WLSC-AM, 656
WNKT-FM, 658
WOFFORD COLLEGE ATHLETICS, 376
WOIC-AM, 660
WOLO-TV, 707
WORD, 660
WORD-AM, 660
WORG-FM, 660
WPCH-AM, 661
WPDE-TV, 707
WSPA-TV, 709

SOUTH DAKOTA

ABERDEEN AMERICAN NEWS, 459
ABERDEEN WINGS, 132
ARGUS LEADER, 461
AUSTAD'S GOLF/CATALOG, 1217
BLACK HILLS PIONEER, 465
BLACK HILLS UNIVERSITY ATHLETICS, 308
BROOKINGS REGISTER, 466
CABANA BANNERS, 1112
CAPITAL JOURNAL, 468
CLAYBORNE, COURTNEY, 873

CORN PALACE, 960
DAKOTA STATE UNIVERSITY ATHLETICS, 311
DAKOTA WESLEYAN UNIVERSITY, 415
DAKOTA WESLEYAN UNIVERSITY ATHLETICS, 311
DAKOTADOME, 960
DAKTRONICS, INC., 1122
DONALD E. YOUNG FITNESS CENTER, 962
HURON ARENA, 973
KAUR-FM, 613
KBFS-AM, 613
KBHU-FM, 613
KCFS-FM, 614
KDLT-TV, 689
KDSJ-AM, 616
KELO-AM, 616
KEVN-TV, 689
KFCR-AM, 617
KILI-FM, 620
KINI-FM, 620
KLXS-FM, 623
KORN-AM, 626
KPRY-TV, 694
KSDR-AM, 628
KSFY-TV, 694
KVHT-FM, 631
KVTK-AM, 631
KWSN-AM, 632
KZMX-AM, 633
MADISON DAILY LEADER, 504
MOUNT MARTY COLLEGE ATHLETICS, 317
NATIONAL FIELD ARCHERY ASSOCIATION, 14
NORTH CENTRAL INTERCOLLEGIATE ATHLETIC CONFERENCE, 301
NORTHERN STATE UNIVERSITY ATHLETICS, 366
NORTHERN STATE UNIVERSITY(NSU), 366
PLAINSMAN, 520
PRESENTATION COLLEGE ATHLETICS, 319
PUSH PEDAL PULL, 1235
RAPID CITY JOURNAL, 523
RAPID CITY RUSH, 130
RUSHMORE PLAZA CIVIC CENTER, 999
SIOUX FALLS ARENA, 1003
SIOUX FALLS ATHLETICS, UNIVERSITY OF, 370
SIOUX FALLS CITY FC, 168
SIOUX FALLS CONVENTION & VISITORS BUREAU, 245
SIOUX FALLS SKYFORCE, 59
SIOUX FALLS SNOW LEOPARDS, 98
SIOUX FALLS STADIUM, 1003
SIOUX FALLS STAMPEDE, 137
SIOUX FALLS STORM, 93
SONIFI SOLUTIONS, 602
SOUTH DAKOTA AAU ASSOCIATION, 216
SOUTH DAKOTA GOLF ASSOCIATION, 115
SOUTH DAKOTA HS ACTIVITIES ASSOCIATION, 202
SOUTH DAKOTA SCHOOL OF MINES & TECHNOLOGY ATHLETICS, 344
SOUTH DAKOTA STATE UNIVERSITY ATHLETICS, 370
SPECIAL OLYMPICS SOUTH DAKOTA, 197
STANLEY J MARSHALL HPER CENTER, 1005
WATERTOWN PUBLIC OPINION, 546
YANKTON DAILY PRESS & DAKOTAN, 548

TENNESSEE

ACTION SPORTS MEDIA, 771
ADAMS USA, INC., 1093
AEGIS SCIENCES CORPORATION, 918
AMERICA OUTDOORS/AO, 217, 924
AMERICAN ARMSPORT ASSOCIATION, 15
ARTHRON, INC., 1100
AT&T FIELD, 947
ATHLETIC RESOURCE MANAGEMENT, INC., 825
ATHLON SPORTS COMMUNICATIONS, 550
AUSTIN PEAY STATE UNIVERSITY ATHLETICS, 325
AUTOZONE, 612
AUTOZONE PARK, 947
BACON & COMPANY, 1103
THE BALLPARK AT JACKSON, 1009
BEHIND THE WHEEL, 551
BELMONT UNIVERSITY ATHLETICS, 325
BELMONT UNIVERSITY SPORT MANAGEMENT PROGRAM, 411

WRCB-TV, 708
WREG-TV, 708
WRGS-AM, 664
WSMG-AM, 666
WSMV-TV, 709
WTPR-AM, 669
WTVC-TV, 710
WTVF-TV, 711
WTXM-FM, 669
WTZX-AM, 669
WUCZ-FM, 669
WVLT-TV, 711
WVLZ-AM, 670
WVRY-FM, 670
WWTN-FM, 671

TEXAS

A-ATHLETIC AND MEDICAL SUPPLY
    COMPANY, 1215
A.J. FOYT RACING, 22
AAI SPORTS INC. & AAI INTERNATIONAL, INC.,
    771, 823
ABC FLAG MANUFACTURING CO., 1090
ABILENE CHRISTIAN UNIVERSITY ATHLETICS,
    350
ABILENE CIVIC CENTER, 945
ABILENE REPORTER NEWS, 459
ABRAHAM, WATKINS, NICHOLS, SORRELS,
    MATTHEWS & FRIEND, 861
ACADEMY SPORTS & OUTDOORS, 1215
ACCESS DATA SUPPORT SERVICES &
    FACILITY MANAGEMENT GROUP, 1064
ACTION INK, INC., 771
ADAMS GOLF GP CORPORATION, 1093
ADER SPORTING GOODS INC., 1093
ADKINS, M. DOUGLAS, 861
ADVANTAGE MARKETING GROUP, INC., 749
ADVOCARE INTERNATIONAL, 725
AHFC ROYALS, 161
AHFC ROYALS WPSL, 164
AL G. LANGFORD CHAPARRAL CENTER, 945
ALAMO BOWL, 89
ALAMODOME SAN ANTONIO, 945
ALICE ECHO NEWS, 460
ALLEN AMERICANS, 129
ALLIANCE SPORTS GROUP, 1216
ALPHA & OMEGA MOUNTED SECURITY
    PATROL, 765
ALPHA RACQUET SPORTS, 1096
ALPINE COWBOYS, 49
AMARILLO CIVIC CENTER COMPLEX, 946
AMARILLO CONVENTION & VISITOR COUNCIL,
    227
AMARILLO GLOBE-NEWS, 460
AMARILLO WRANGLERS, 132
AMERICAN AIRLINES, 725
AMERICAN AIRLINES CENTER, 946
AMERICAN FOOTBALL COACHES
    ASSOCIATION, 87
AMERICAN MINIATURE HORSE ASSOCIATION,
    73
AMERICAN PAINT HORSE ASSOCIATION, 73
AMERICAN QUARTER HORSE ASSOCIATION,
    74
AMERICAN QUARTER HORSE RACING
    JOURNAL, 549
AMERICAN SOUTHWEST CONFERENCE, 291
AMERICAN VOLKSSPORT ASSOCIATION/AVA,
    217
AMON G. CARTER STADIUM, 946
ANGELO STATE UNIVERSITY ATHLETICS, 351
ANTHONY TRAVEL, INC., 925
ARLINGTON CONVENTION & VISITORS
    BUREAU, 227
ARLINGTON IMPACT, 97
ARMED FORCES BOWL, 89
ASCENSION ENTERPRISES INC., 825
ASTRO TURF MANUFACTURING COMPANY,
    1101
AT&T CENTER, 947
AT&T INC., 725
ATHENS DAILY REVIEW, 462
AUSTIN AMERICAN-STATESMAN, 462
AUSTIN FC, 157
AUSTIN OUTLAWS, 97
AUSTIN RISE FC, 165
AUSTIN SPORTS MEDICINE, 919
AUSTIN SPURS, 58
AWARDS ETC., 1102

BALFOUR CO., 1103
BALLQUBE, INC., 1104
BARREL HORSE NEWS, 551
BASEBALLJUNK.COM, 1217
BASEBALLVIDEOS.COM, 597
BAY CITY TRIBUNE, 463
BAYLOR UNIVERSITY, 411
BAYLOR UNIVERSITY ATHLETICS, 325
BAYTOWN SUN, 463
BEARCOM GROUP, 1105
BEAUMONT CONVENTION & VISITORS
    BUREAU, 228
BEAUMONT ENTERPRISE, 464
BEI GROUP, INC./BASEBALL EXPRESS, INC.,
    1218
BERNARD G. JOHNSON COLISEUM, 949
BIG 12 CONFERENCE, 291
BILLIARD AND BOWLING INSTITUTE OF
    AMERICA, 61, 65
BLACK TENNIS MAGAZINE, 552
BLAIR, ROBERT W., 866
BOBCAT STADIUM TEXAS STATE, 951
BODDICKER SPORTS MANAGEMENT, 827
BORGER NEWS-HERALD, 465
BOUNTY HUNTER, 1109
BOWLING PROPRIETORS' ASSOCIATION OF
    AMERICA, 65
BRAZOS VALLEY CAVALRY FC, 161
BRENHAM BANNER-PRESS, 466
BROWNSVILLE HERALD, 466
BROWNWOOD BULLETIN, 467
BROWNWOOD COLISEUM, 952
BRYAN-COLLEGE STATION CONVENTION &
    VISITORS BUREAU, SPORTS DEPT., 260
BRYAN-COLLEGE STATION EAGLE, 467
BSN SPORTS, 1111
BURELSON, PATE & GIBSON, L.L.P., 869
BURWASH INTERNATIONAL, PETER, 751
CAP BARBELL, 1113
CARIBOU MOUNTAINEERING, 1114
THE CARRELL CLINIC, 923
CDM SPORT, 1115
CELEBRITY MARKETING GROUP, 828
CEO MANUFACTURERS, 1115
CERTIFIED ATHLETE, 930
CHALLENGE RED DEVILS, 165
CHRISTENSEN STADIUM, 957
CIVIC CENTER COMPLEX, 958
CLEAR CHANNEL ENTERTAINMENT, INC., 687,
    829
CLEBURNE TIMES-REVIEW, 471
CLUBCORP, 100
COHEN STADIUM, 958
COLLEGIATE PACIFIC, 1223
CONBOY, JOSEPH B., 874
CONCORDIA UNIVERSITY AT AUSTIN
    ATHLETICS, 381
CONFERENCE USA, 295
CONROE COURIER, 473
CONSOLIDATED GRAPHICS, 779
CONTEMPORARY RESEARCH, 1213
COORE AND CRENSHAW, 1053
COPELAND COMPANY, INC., HAL, 779
CORPUS CHRISTI CALLER-TIMES, 473
CORPUS CHRISTI CONVENTION & VISTORS
    BUREAU, 231
CORPUS CHRISTI FC, 162
CORPUS CHRISTI GREYHOUND RACE TRACK,
    1045
CORPUS CHRISTI HOOKS, 53
CORPUS CHRISTI ICERAYS, 132
CORSICANA DAILY SUN, 473
COTTON BOWL CLASSIC, 90
COTTON BOWL/FAIR PARK, 960
COWBOYS STADIUM, 960
COWTOWN COLISEUM, 960
CUTTING HORSE CHATTER, 556
DALCO ATHLETIC LETTERING, INC., 1123
DALLAS ATHLETICS, UNIVERSITY OF, 382
DALLAS BAPTIST UNIVERSITY, 415
DALLAS BAPTIST UNIVERSITY ATHLETICS, 356
DALLAS CHARGE, 171
DALLAS CONVENTION & VISITORS BUREAU,
    231
DALLAS CONVENTION CENTER, 231
DALLAS COWBOYS, 94
DALLAS MAVERICKS, 56
DALLAS MORNING NEWS, 481
DALLAS STARS, 124
DALLAS WINGS, 60

DALTON, MICHAEL, 875
DARRELL K ROYAL - TEXAS MEMORIAL
    STADIUM, 960
DAVIS & WILKERSON, 875
DEFORCE RACING, 22
DELL DIAMOND, 961
DELL TECHNOLOGIES, 727
DELMAR STADIUM COMPLEX, 961
DENTON RECORD-CHRONICLE, 482
DESIGNS IN FITNESS, INC., 1054
DIXIE YOUTH BASEBALL, 26, 265
DKSC BADTOP, 166
DR. PEPPER BALLPARK, 962
DUNLAP CO., 1225
EASTMAN & BEAUDINE, INC., 747
ECKERD DRUG, INC., 1226
ED & RAE SCHOLLMAIER ARENA, 963
EL HISPANO NEWS, 486
EL INFORMADOR HISPANO, 486
EL NUEVO HERALDO BROWNSVILLE, 486
EL PASO CHIHUAHUAS, 48
EL PASO COUNTY COLISEUM, 964
EL PASO LOCOMOTIVE FC, 159
EL PASO RHINOS, 132
EL PASO SURF, 166
EL PASO TIMES, 486
ENNIS DAILY NEWS, 486
EXTRA POINTS, 679
EXXON MOBIL CORPORATION, 727
FACTS, 488
FAIR PARK COLISEUM, 964
FC DALLAS, 157, 166
FERRELL CENTER, 965
FIRST AMERICAN BANK BALLPARK, 965
FIRST AND GOAL, INC., 1064
FITNESS MASTER INC, 1133
FLUOR CORPORATION, 1057
FLY, WILLIAM L., 880
FONDREN ORTHOPEDIC GROUP, 920
FORT BEND HERALD & TEAXS COASTER, 488
FORT WORTH CONVENTION & VISITORS
    BUREAU, 234
FORT WORTH STAR-TELEGRAM, 489
FOSTER FIELD, 966
FOX SPORTS DIRECT, 686
FOX SPORTS NET SOUTHWEST, 599
FOX SPORTS SUNDAY, 679
FOX SPORTS XTRA, 679
FRANK ERWIN CENTER, 966
FRAZIER & FRAZIER, 834
FREEMAN COLISEUM, 967
FRIBERG ASSOCIATES INC., 1057
FRISCO FIGHTERS, 93
FRISCO ROUGHRIDERS, 53
GADZOOKS, 1228
GAINESVILLE DAILY REGISTER, 490
GALVESTON COUNTY DAILY NEWS, 490
GEAR PRO-TEC, 1137
GENESCO SPORTS ENTERPRISES, INC., 784
GLOBAL PRODUCTIONS, 785
GO FLOW, INC., 1138
GOLD'S GYM INTERNATIONAL, INC., 1138
GOLFSMITH INTERNATIONAL, INC., 1139, 1229
GRAHAM EMBROIDERY COMPANY, 1140
GRAND SLAM SPORTS MARKETING, 786
GREAT AMERICAN PRODUCTS, 1140
GREATER AUSTIN SPORTS ASSOCIATION, 234
GREATER DENTON SPORTS COMMISSION,
    234
GREENVILLE HERALD BANNER, 491
GULF AAU ASSOCIATION, 214
GUSTAFSON MANUFACTURING COMPANY,
    1141
GWINN & ROBY, 836
H-E-B, 1229
HAFER CASE, 1141
HAGGAR APPAREL COMPANY, 1141
HAGGAR CORPORATION, 1141
HAMBRIC SPORTS MANAGEMENT, 837
HARBOUR, SMITH, HARRIS & MERRITT, 883
HARDIN-SIMMONS UNIVERSITY, 420
HARDIN-SIMMONS UNIVERSITY ATHLETICS,
    387
HEAD, ALBON O., JR., 883
HEALTH & FITNESS MAGAZINE, 563
HEALTHANDWELLNESSJOBS.COM, 747
HEART OF DALLAS BOWL, 91
HENDERSON DAILY NEWS, 493
HERALD DEMOCRAT, 493
HICKS, JERRY, 884

U.S. VIRGIN ISLANDS

UNITED ARAB EMIRATES

UTAH

VERMONT

VIRGINIA

WEST VIRGINIA

WISCONSIN

WYOMING

Titles from Grey House

Visit www.GreyHouse.com for Product Information, Table of Contents, and Sample Pages.

Opinions Throughout History

Opinions Throughout History: Church & State
Opinions Throughout History: Conspiracy Theories
Opinions Throughout History: The Death Penalty
Opinions Throughout History: Diseases & Epidemics
Opinions Throughout History: Domestic Terrorism
Opinions Throughout History: Drug Use & Abuse
Opinions Throughout History: The Environment
Opinions Throughout History: Free Speech & Censorship
Opinions Throughout History: Gender: Roles & Rights
Opinions Throughout History: Globalization
Opinions Throughout History: Guns in America
Opinions Throughout History: Immigration
Opinions Throughout History: Law Enforcement in America
Opinions Throughout History: Mental Health
Opinions Throughout History: Nat'l Security vs. Civil & Privacy Rights
Opinions Throughout History: Presidential Authority
Opinions Throughout History: Refugees & Asylum Seekers
Opinions Throughout History: Robotics & Artificial Intelligence
Opinions Throughout History: Social Media Issues
Opinions Throughout History: The Supreme Court
Opinions Throughout History: Truth & Lies in the Media
Opinions Throughout History: Voters' Rights
Opinions Throughout History: War & the Military
Opinions Throughout History: Workers Rights & Wages

General Reference

American Environmental Leaders
Constitutional Amendments
Encyclopedia of African-American Writing
Encyclopedia of Invasions & Conquests
Encyclopedia of Prisoners of War & Internment
Encyclopedia of the Continental Congresses
Encyclopedia of the United States Cabinet
Encyclopedia of War Journalism
The Environmental Debate
Financial Literacy Starter Kit
From Suffrage to the Senate
The Gun Debate: Gun Rights & Gun Control in the U.S.
Historical Warrior Peoples & Modern Fighting Groups
Human Rights and the United States
Political Corruption in America
Privacy Rights in the Digital Age
The Religious Right and American Politics
Speakers of the House of Representatives, 1789-2021
US Land & Natural Resources Policy
The Value of a Dollar 1600-1865 Colonial to Civil War
The Value of a Dollar 1860-2024

This is Who We Were

This is Who We Were: Colonial America (1492-1775)
This is Who We Were: Civil War & Reconstruction
This is Who We Were: 1880-1899
This is Who We Were: In the 1900s
This is Who We Were: In the 1910s
This is Who We Were: In the 1920s
This is Who We Were: A Companion to the 1940 Census
This is Who We Were: In the 1940s (1940-1949)
This is Who We Were: In the 1950s
This is Who We Were: In the 1960s
This is Who We Were: In the 1970s

This is Who We Were: In the 1980s
This is Who We Were: In the 1990s
This is Who We Were: In the 2000s
This is Who We Were: In the 2010s

Working Americans

Working Americans—Vol. 1: The Working Class
Working Americans—Vol. 2: The Middle Class
Working Americans—Vol. 3: The Upper Class
Working Americans—Vol. 4: Children
Working Americans—Vol. 5: At War
Working Americans—Vol. 6: Working Women
Working Americans—Vol. 7: Social Movements
Working Americans—Vol. 8: Immigrants
Working Americans—Vol. 9: Revolutionary War to the Civil War
Working Americans—Vol. 10: Sports & Recreation
Working Americans—Vol. 11: Inventors & Entrepreneurs
Working Americans—Vol. 12: Our History through Music
Working Americans—Vol. 13: Education & Educators
Working Americans—Vol. 14: African Americans
Working Americans—Vol. 15: Politics & Politicians
Working Americans—Vol. 16: Farming & Ranching
Working Americans—Vol. 17: Teens in America
Working Americans—Vol. 18: Health Care Workers
Working Americans—Vol. 19: The Performing Arts

Grey House Health & Wellness Guides

Addiction Handbook & Resource Guide
Adolescent Mental Health Handbook & Resource Guide
The Autism Spectrum Handbook & Resource Guide
Autoimmune Disorders Handbook & Resource Guide
Cardiovascular Disease Handbook & Resource Guide
Chronic Pain Handbook & Resource Guide
Dementia Handbook & Resource Guide
Depression Handbook & Resource Guide
Diabetes Handbook & Resource Guide
Nutrition, Obesity & Eating Disorders Handbook & Resource Guide

Consumer Health

Complete Mental Health Resource Guide
Complete Resource Guide for Pediatric Disorders
Complete Resource Guide for People with Chronic Illness
Complete Resource Guide for People with Disabilities
Older Americans Information Resource
Parenting: Styles & Strategies
Teens: Growing Up, Skills & Strategies

Business Information

Business Information Resources
Complete Broadcasting Industry Guide: TV, Radio, Cable & Streaming
Directory of Mail Order Catalogs
Environmental Resource Handbook
Food & Beverage Market Place
The Grey House Guide to Homeland Security Resources
The Grey House Performing Arts Industry Guide
Guide to Healthcare Group Purchasing Organizations
Guide to U.S. HMOs and PPOs
Guide to Venture Capital & Private Equity Firms
Hudson's Washington News Media Contacts Guide
New York State Directory
Sports Market Place

Grey House Publishing | Salem Press | H.W. Wilson | 4919 Route 22, PO Box 56, Amenia NY 12501-0056

 Grey House Publishing

Grey House Imprints

Visit www.GreyHouse.com for Product Information, Table of Contents, and Sample Pages.

 Grey House Publishing

Grey House Titles, continued

Education
Complete Learning Disabilities Resource Guide
Digital Literacy: Skills & Strategies
Educators Resource Guide
Special Education: Policy & Curriculum Development

Statistics & Demographics
America's Top-Rated Cities
America's Top-Rated Smaller Cities
The Comparative Guide to American Suburbs
Profiles of America
Profiles of California
Profiles of Florida
Profiles of Illinois
Profiles of Indiana
Profiles of Massachusetts
Profiles of Michigan
Profiles of New Jersey
Profiles of New York
Profiles of North Carolina & South Carolina
Profiles of Ohio
Profiles of Pennsylvania
Profiles of Texas
Profiles of Virginia
Profiles of Wisconsin

Canadian Resources
Associations Canada
Canadian Almanac & Directory
Canadian Environmental Resource Guide
Canadian Parliamentary Guide
Canadian Venture Capital & Private Equity Firms
Canadian Who's Who
Cannabis Canada
Careers & Employment Canada
Financial Post: Directory of Directors
Financial Services Canada
FP Bonds: Corporate
FP Bonds: Government
FP Equities: Preferreds & Derivatives
FP Survey: Industrials
FP Survey: Mines & Energy
FP Survey: Predecessor & Defunct
Health Guide Canada
Libraries Canada
Major Canadian Cities: 50 Cities Compared, Ranked & Profiled

Weiss Financial Ratings
Financial Literacy Basics
Financial Literacy: How to Become an Investor
Financial Literacy: Planning for the Future
Weiss Ratings Consumer Guides
Weiss Ratings Guide to Banks
Weiss Ratings Guide to Credit Unions
Weiss Ratings Guide to Health Insurers
Weiss Ratings Guide to Life & Annuity Insurers
Weiss Ratings Guide to Property & Casualty Insurers
Weiss Ratings Investment Research Guide to Bond & Money Market
    Mutual Funds
Weiss Ratings Investment Research Guide to Exchange-Traded Funds
Weiss Ratings Investment Research Guide to Stock Mutual Funds
Weiss Ratings Investment Research Guide to Stocks

BOOKS IN PRINT®

Books in Print Series
American Book Publishing Record® Annual
American Book Publishing Record® Monthly
Books In Print®
Books In Print® Supplement
Books Out Loud™
Bowker's Complete Video Directory™
Children's Books In Print®
El-Hi Textbooks & Serials In Print®
Forthcoming Books®
Law Books & Serials In Print™
Medical & Health Care Books In Print™
Publishers, Distributors & Wholesalers of the US™
Subject Guide to Books In Print®
Subject Guide to Children's Books In Print®

Grey House Publishing | Salem Press | H.W. Wilson | 4919 Route 22, PO Box 56, Amenia NY 12501-0056

Titles from Salem Press

Visit www.SalemPress.com for Product Information, Table of Contents, and Sample Pages.

LITERATURE

Critical Insights: Authors

Louisa May Alcott
Sherman Alexie
Dante Alighieri
Isabel Allende
Maya Angelou
Isaac Asimov
Margaret Atwood
Jane Austen
James Baldwin
Saul Bellow
Roberto Bolano
Ray Bradbury
The Brontë Sisters
Gwendolyn Brooks
Albert Camus
Raymond Carver
Willa Cather
Geoffrey Chaucer
John Cheever
Joseph Conrad
Charles Dickens
Emily Dickinson
Frederick Douglass
T. S. Eliot
George Eliot
Harlan Ellison
Ralph Waldo Emerson
Louise Erdrich
William Faulkner
F. Scott Fitzgerald
Gustave Flaubert
Horton Foote
Benjamin Franklin
Robert Frost
Neil Gaiman
Gabriel Garcia Marquez
Thomas Hardy
Nathaniel Hawthorne
Robert A. Heinlein
Lillian Hellman
Ernest Hemingway
Langston Hughes
Zora Neale Hurston
Henry James
Thomas Jefferson
James Joyce
Jamaica Kincaid
Stephen King
Martin Luther King, Jr.
Barbara Kingsolver
Abraham Lincoln
C.S. Lewis
Mario Vargas Llosa
Jack London
James McBride
Cormac McCarthy
Herman Melville
Arthur Miller
Toni Morrison
Alice Munro
Tim O'Brien

Flannery O'Connor
Eugene O'Neill
George Orwell
Sylvia Plath
Edgar Allan Poe
Philip Roth
Salman Rushdie
J.D. Salinger
Mary Shelley
John Steinbeck
Amy Tan
Leo Tolstoy
Mark Twain
John Updike
Kurt Vonnegut
Alice Walker
David Foster Wallace
Edith Wharton
Walt Whitman
Oscar Wilde
Tennessee Williams
Virginia Woolf
Richard Wright
Malcolm X

Critical Insights: Works

Absalom, Absalom!
Adventures of Huckleberry Finn
The Adventures of Tom Sawyer
Aeneid
All Quiet on the Western Front
All the Pretty Horses
Animal Farm
Anna Karenina
The Awakening
The Bell Jar
Beloved
Billy Budd, Sailor
The Book Thief
Brave New World
The Canterbury Tales
Catch-22
The Catcher in the Rye
The Color Purple
Crime and Punishment
The Crucible
Death of a Salesman
The Diary of a Young Girl
Dracula
Fahrenheit 451
Frankenstein; or, The Modern Prometheus
The Grapes of Wrath
Great Expectations
The Great Gatsby
Hamlet
The Handmaid's Tale
Harry Potter Series
Heart of Darkness
The Hobbit
The House on Mango Street
How the Garcia Girls Lost Their Accents
The Hunger Games Trilogy
I Know Why the Caged Bird Sings

In Cold Blood
The Inferno
Invisible Man
Jane Eyre
The Joy Luck Club
Julius Caesar
King Lear
The Kite Runner
Life of Pi
Little Women
Lolita
Lord of the Flies
The Lord of the Rings
Macbeth
The Merchant of Venice
The Metamorphosis
Midnight's Children
A Midsummer Night's Dream
Moby-Dick
Mrs. Dalloway
Nineteen Eighty-Four
The Odyssey
Of Mice and Men
The Old Man and the Sea
On the Road
One Flew Over the Cuckoo's Nest
One Hundred Years of Solitude
Othello
The Outsiders
Paradise Lost
The Pearl
The Plague
The Poetry of Baudelaire
The Poetry of Edgar Allan Poe
A Portrait of the Artist as a Young Man
Pride and Prejudice
A Raisin in the Sun
The Red Badge of Courage
Romeo and Juliet
The Scarlet Letter
Sense and Sensibility
Short Fiction of Flannery O'Connor
Slaughterhouse-Five
The Sound and the Fury
A Streetcar Named Desire
The Sun Also Rises
A Tale of Two Cities
The Tales of Edgar Allan Poe
Their Eyes Were Watching God
Things Fall Apart
To Kill a Mockingbird
Twelfth Night, or What You Will
Twelve Years a Slave
War and Peace
The Woman Warrior

Critical Insights: Themes

The American Comic Book
American Creative Non-Fiction
The American Dream
American Multicultural Identity
American Road Literature
American Short Story

Grey House Publishing | Salem Press | H.W. Wilson | 4919 Route 22, PO Box 56, Amenia NY 12501-0056

SALEM PRESS

Titles from Salem Press

Visit www.SalemPress.com for Product Information, Table of Contents, and Sample Pages.

SALEM PRESS

American Sports Fiction
The American Thriller
American Writers in Exile
Censored & Banned Literature
Civil Rights Literature, Past & Present
Coming of Age
Conspiracies
Contemporary Canadian Fiction
Contemporary Immigrant Short Fiction
Contemporary Latin American Fiction
Contemporary Speculative Fiction
Crime and Detective Fiction
Crisis of Faith
Cultural Encounters
Dystopia
Family
The Fantastic
Feminism Flash Fiction
Gender, Sex and Sexuality
Going Into the Woods
Good & Evil
The Graphic Novel
Greed
Harlem Renaissance
The Hero's Quest
Historical Fiction
Holocaust Literature
The Immigrant Experience
Inequality
LGBTQ Literature
Literature in Times of Crisis
Literature of Protest
Love
Magical Realism
Midwestern Literature
Modern Japanese Literature
Nature & the Environment
Paranoia, Fear & Alienation
Patriotism
Political Fiction
Postcolonial Literature
Power & Corruption
Pulp Fiction of the '20s and '30s
Rebellion
Russia's Golden Age
Satire
The Slave Narrative
Social Justice and American Literature
Southern Gothic Literature
Southwestern Literature
The Supernatural
Survival
Technology & Humanity
Truth & Lies
Violence in Literature
Virginia Woolf & 20th Century Women Writers
War

Critical Insights: Film

Bonnie & Clyde
Casablanca
Alfred Hitchcock
Stanley Kubrick

Critical Approaches to Literature

Critical Approaches to Literature: Feminist
Critical Approaches to Literature: Moral
Critical Approaches to Literature: Multicultural
Critical Approaches to Literature: Psychological

Literary Classics

Recommended Reading: 600 Classics Reviewed

Novels into Film

Novels into Film: Adaptations & Interpretation
Novels into Film: Adaptations & Interpretation, Volume 2

Critical Surveys of Literature

Critical Survey of American Literature
Critical Survey of Drama
Critical Survey of Long Fiction
Critical Survey of Mystery and Detective Fiction
Critical Survey of Poetry
Critical Survey of Poetry: Contemporary Poets
Critical Survey of Science Fiction & Fantasy Literature
Critical Survey of Shakespeare's Plays
Critical Survey of Shakespeare's Sonnets
Critical Survey of Short Fiction
Critical Survey of World Literature
Critical Survey of Young Adult Literature

Critical Surveys of Graphic Novels

Heroes & Superheroes
History, Theme, and Technique
Independents & Underground Classics
Manga

Critical Surveys of Mythology & Folklore

Creation Myths
Deadly Battles & Warring Enemies
Gods & Goddesses
Heroes and Heroines
Love, Sexuality, and Desire
World Mythology

Cyclopedia of Literary Characters & Places

Cyclopedia of Literary Characters
Cyclopedia of Literary Places

Introduction to Literary Context

American Poetry of the 20th Century
American Post-Modernist Novels
American Short Fiction
English Literature
Plays
World Literature

Magill's Literary Annual

Magill's Literary Annual, 2024
Magill's Literary Annual, 2023
Magill's Literary Annual, 2022
Magill's Literary Annual, 2021
Magill's Literary Annual (Backlist Issues 2020-1977)

Titles from Salem Press

Visit www.SalemPress.com for Product Information, Table of Contents, and Sample Pages.

Grey House Publishing | Salem Press | H.W. Wilson | 4919 Route 22, PO Box 56, Amenia NY 12501-0056

Titles from Salem Press

Visit www.SalemPress.com for Product Information, Table of Contents, and Sample Pages.

Great Lives from History

Great Athletes
Great Athletes of the Twenty-First Century
Great Lives from History: The 17th Century
Great Lives from History: The 18th Century
Great Lives from History: The 19th Century
Great Lives from History: The 20th Century
Great Lives from History: The 21st Century, 2000-2017
Great Lives from History: African Americans
Great Lives from History: The Ancient World
Great Lives from History: American Heroes
Great Lives from History: American Women
Great Lives from History: Asian and Pacific Islander Americans
Great Lives from History: Autocrats & Dictators
Great Lives from History: The Incredibly Wealthy
Great Lives from History: Inventors & Inventions
Great Lives from History: Jewish Americans
Great Lives from History: Latinos
Great Lives from History: LGBTQ+
Great Lives from History: The Middle Ages
Great Lives from History: The Renaissance & Early Modern Era
Great Lives from History: Scientists and Science

History & Government

American First Ladies
American Presidents
The 50 States
The Ancient World: Extraordinary People in Extraordinary Societies
The Bill of Rights
The Criminal Justice System
The U.S. Supreme Court

Innovators

Computer Technology Innovators
Fashion Innovators
Human Rights Innovators
Internet Innovators
Music Innovators
Musicians and Composers of the 20th Century
World Political Innovators

SOCIAL SCIENCES

Civil Rights Movements: Past & Present
Countries, Peoples and Cultures
Countries: Their Wars & Conflicts: A World Survey
Education Today: Issues, Policies & Practices
Encyclopedia of American Immigration
Ethics: Questions & Morality of Human Actions
Issues in U.S. Immigration
Principles of Sociology: Group Relationships & Behavior
Principles of Sociology: Personal Relationships & Behavior
Principles of Sociology: Societal Issues & Behavior
Racial & Ethnic Relations in America
Weapons, Warfare & Military Technology
World Geography

HEALTH

Addictions, Substance Abuse & Alcoholism
Adolescent Health & Wellness
Aging
Cancer
Community & Family Health Issues
Integrative, Alternative & Complementary Medicine
Genetics and Inherited Conditions
Infectious Diseases and Conditions
Magill's Medical Guide
Men's Health
Nutrition
Parenting: Styles & Strategies
Psychology & Behavioral Health
Teens: Growing Up, Skills & Strategies
Women's Health

Principles of Health

Principles of Health: Allergies & Immune Disorders
Principles of Health: Anxiety & Stress
Principles of Health: Depression
Principles of Health: Diabetes
Principles of Health: Hypertension
Principles of Health: Nursing
Principles of Health: Obesity
Principles of Health: Occupational Therapy & Physical Therapy
Principles of Health: Pain Management
Principles of Health: Prescription Drug Abuse

SCIENCE

Ancient Creatures
Applied Science
Applied Science: Engineering & Mathematics
Applied Science: Science & Medicine
Applied Science: Technology
Biomes and Ecosystems
Digital Literacy: Skills & Strategies
Earth Science: Earth Materials and Resources
Earth Science: Earth's Surface and History
Earth Science: Earth's Weather, Water and Atmosphere
Earth Science: Physics and Chemistry of the Earth
Encyclopedia of Climate Change
Encyclopedia of Energy
Encyclopedia of Environmental Issues
Encyclopedia of Global Resources
Encyclopedia of Mathematics and Society
Forensic Science
Notable Natural Disasters
The Solar System
USA in Space

Grey House Publishing | Salem Press | H.W. Wilson | 4919 Route 22, PO Box 56, Amenia NY 12501-0056

Titles from Salem Press

Visit www.SalemPress.com for Product Information, Table of Contents, and Sample Pages.

Principles of Science

Principles of Aeronautics
Principles of Anatomy
Principles of Architecture
Principles of Astronomy
Principles of Behavioral Science
Principles of Biology
Principles of Biotechnology
Principles of Botany
Principles of Chemistry
Principles of Climatology
Principles of Computer-aided Design
Principles of Computer Science
Principles of Cybersecurity
Principles of Digital Arts & Multimedia
Principles of Ecology
Principles of Energy
Principles of Fire Science
Principles of Forestry & Conservation
Principles of Geology
Principles of Information Technology
Principles of Marine Science
Principles of Mass Communications
Principles of Mathematics
Principles of Mechanics
Principles of Microbiology
Principles of Modern Agriculture
Principles of Pharmacology
Principles of Physical Science
Principles of Physics
Principles of Probability & Statistics
Principles of Programming & Coding
Principles of Robotics & Artificial Intelligence
Principles of Scientific Research
Principles of Sports Medicine & Exercise Science
Principles of Sustainability
Principles of Zoology

CAREERS

Careers: Paths to Entrepreneurship
Careers in Archaeology & Museum Services
Careers in Artificial Intelligence
Careers in the Arts: Fine, Performing & Visual
Careers in the Automotive Industry
Careers in Biology
Careers in Biotechnology
Careers in Building Construction
Careers in Business
Careers in Chemistry
Careers in Communications & Media
Careers in Cybersecurity
Careers in Education & Training
Careers in Engineering
Careers in Environment & Conservation
Careers in Financial Services
Careers in Fish & Wildlife
Careers in Forensic Science
Careers in Gaming
Careers in Green Energy
Careers in Healthcare

Careers in Heavy Equipment Operation, Maintenance & Repair
Careers in Hospitality & Tourism
Careers in Human Services
Careers in Illustration & Animation
Careers in Information Technology
Careers in Intelligence & National Security
Careers in Law, Criminal Justice & Emergency Services
Careers in the Music Industry
Careers in Manufacturing & Production
Careers in Medical Technology
Careers in Nursing
Careers in Physics
Careers in Protective Services
Careers in Psychology & Behavioral Health
Careers in Public Administration
Careers in Sales, Insurance & Real Estate
Careers in Science & Engineering
Careers in Social Media
Careers in Sports & Fitness
Careers in Sports Medicine & Training
Careers in Technical Services & Equipment Repair
Careers in Transportation
Careers in Writing & Editing
Careers Outdoors
Careers Overseas
Careers Working with Infants & Children
Careers Working with Animals

BUSINESS

Principles of Business: Accounting
Principles of Business: Economics
Principles of Business: Entrepreneurship
Principles of Business: Finance
Principles of Business: Globalization
Principles of Business: Leadership
Principles of Business: Management
Principles of Business: Marketing

Titles from H.W. Wilson

Visit www.HWWilsonInPrint.com for Product Information, Table of Contents, and Sample Pages.

The Reference Shelf
Affordable Housing
Aging in America
Alternative Facts, Post-Truth and the Information War
The American Dream
Artificial Intelligence
Book Bans & Censorship
The Business of Food
Campaign Trends & Election Law
College Sports
Democracy Evolving
The Digital Age
Embracing New Paradigms in Education
Food Insecurity & Hunger in the United States
Future of U.S. Economic Relations: Mexico, Cuba, & Venezuela
Gene Editing & Genetic Engineering
Global Climate Change
Guns in America
Hacktivism
Hate Crimes
Immigration
Income Inequality
Internet Abuses & Privacy Rights
Internet Law
LGBTQ in the 21st Century
Marijuana Reform
Mental Health Awareness
Money in Politics
National Debate Topic 2014/2015: The Ocean
National Debate Topic 2015/2016: Surveillance
National Debate Topic 2016/2017: US/China Relations
National Debate Topic 2017/2018: Education Reform
National Debate Topic 2018/2019: Immigration
National Debate Topic 2019/2021: Arms Sales
National Debate Topic 2020/2021: Criminal Justice Reform
National Debate Topic 2021/2022: Water Resources
National Debate Topic 2022/2023: Emerging Technologies &
    International Security
National Debate Topic 2023/2024: Economic Inequality
National Debate Topic 2024/2025: Intellectual Property Rights
New Developments in Artificial Intelligence
New Frontiers in Space
Policing in 2020
Pollution
Prescription Drug Abuse
Propaganda and Misinformation
Racial Tension in a Postracial Age
Reality Television
Renewable Energy
Representative American Speeches, Annual Editions
Reproductive Rights
Rethinking Work
Revisiting Gender
Russia & Ukraine
The South China Sea Conflict
Sports in America
The Supreme Court
The Transformation of American Cities
The Two Koreas
UFOs
Vaccinations
Voting Rights
Whistleblowers

Core Collections
Children's Core Collection
Fiction Core Collection
Graphic Novels Core Collection
Middle & Junior High School Core
Public Library Core Collection: Nonfiction
Senior High Core Collection
Young Adult Fiction Core Collection

Current Biography
Current Biography Cumulative Index 1946-2021
Current Biography Monthly Magazine
Current Biography Yearbook

Readers' Guide to Periodical Literature
Abridged Readers' Guide to Periodical Literature
Readers' Guide to Periodical Literature

Indexes
Index to Legal Periodicals & Books
Short Story Index
Book Review Digest

Sears List
Sears List of Subject Headings
Sears List of Subject Headings, Online Database
Sears: Lista de Encabezamientos de Materia

History
American Game Changers: Invention, Innovation & Transformation
American Reformers
Speeches of the American Presidents

Facts About Series
Facts About the 20th Century
Facts About American Immigration
Facts About China
Facts About the Presidents
Facts About the World's Languages

Nobel Prize Winners
Nobel Prize Winners: 1901-1986
Nobel Prize Winners: 1987-1991
Nobel Prize Winners: 1992-1996
Nobel Prize Winners: 1997-2001
Nobel Prize Winners: 2002-2018

Famous First Facts
Famous First Facts
Famous First Facts About American Politics
Famous First Facts About Sports
Famous First Facts About the Environment
Famous First Facts: International Edition

American Book of Days
The American Book of Days
The International Book of Days

Grey House Publishing | Salem Press | H.W. Wilson | 4919 Route 22, PO Box 56, Amenia NY 12501-0056